University Textbook Series

November, 1992

Especially Designed for Collateral Reading

HARRY W. JONES
Directing Editor
Professor of Law, Columbia University

ADMINISTRATIVE LAW AND PROCESS, Second Edition (1992)
Richard J. Pierce, Jr., Professor of Law, Columbia University.
Sidney A. Shapiro, Professor of Law, University of Kansas.
Paul R. Verkuil, President and Professor of Law, College of William and Mary.

ADMIRALTY, Second Edition (1975)
Grant Gilmore, Professor of Law, Yale University.
Charles L. Black, Jr., Professor of Law, Yale University.

AGENCY (1975)
W. Edward Sell, Dean of the School of Law, University of Pittsburgh.

ANTITRUST LAW, PRINCIPLES OF (1993)
Stephen F. Ross, Professor of Law, University of Illinois.

BANKRUPTCY, THE ELEMENTS OF (1992)
Douglas G. Baird, Professor of Law, University of Chicago.

BUSINESS ORGANIZATION AND FINANCE, Fourth Edition (1990)
William A. Klein, Professor of Law, University of California, Los Angeles.
John C. Coffee, Jr., Professor of Law, Columbia University.

CIVIL PROCEDURE, BASIC, Second Edition (1979)
Milton D. Green, Professor of Law Emeritus, University of California, Hastings
College of the Law.

COMMERCIAL TRANSACTIONS, INTRODUCTION TO (1977)
Hon. Robert Braucher, Associate Justice, Supreme Judicial Court of Massachusetts.
Robert A. Riegert, Professor of Law, Cumberland School of Law.

**CONFLICT OF LAWS, COMMENTARY ON THE, Third Edition (1986) with 1991
Supplement**
Russell J. Weintraub, Professor of Law, University of Texas.

CONSTITUTIONAL LAW, AMERICAN, Second Edition (A TREATISE ON) (1988)
Laurence H. Tribe, Professor of Law, Harvard University.

CONTRACT LAW, THE CAPABILITY PROBLEM IN (1978)
Richard Danzig.

CONTRACTS, CONCEPTS AND CASE ANALYSIS IN THE LAW OF (1990)
Marvin A. Chirelstein, Professor of Law, Columbia University.

CORPORATE TAXATION, FEDERAL, Second Edition (1990)
Howard E. Abrams, Professor of Law, Emory University.
Richard L. Doernberg, Professor of Law, Emory University.

CORPORATIONS, Second Edition (1971)
Norman D. Lattin, Professor of Law, University of California, Hastings College of
the Law.

CORPORATIONS IN PERSPECTIVE (1976)
Alfred F. Conard, Professor of Law, University of Michigan.

CRIMINAL LAW, Third Edition (1982)
Rollin M. Perkins, Professor of Law, University of California, Hastings College of the Law.
Ronald N. Boyce, Professor of Law, University of Utah College of Law.

CRIMINAL PROCEDURE, Third Edition (1993)
Charles H. Whitebread, II, Professor of Law, University of Southern California.
Christopher Slobogin, Professor of Law, University of Florida.

ESTATES IN LAND & FUTURE INTERESTS, PREFACE TO, Second Edition (1984)
Thomas F. Bergin, Professor of Law, University of Virginia.
Paul G. Haskell, Professor of Law, University of North Carolina.

EVIDENCE: COMMON SENSE AND COMMON LAW (1947)
John M. Maguire, Professor of Law, Harvard University.

JURISPRUDENCE: MEN AND IDEAS OF THE LAW (1953)
The late Edwin W. Patterson, Cardozo Professor of Jurisprudence, Columbia University.

LABOR RELATIONS The Basic Processes, Law and Practice (1988)
Julius G. Getman, Professor of Law, University of Texas.
Bertrand E. Pogrebin, Member, New York State Bar.

LEGAL CAPITAL, Third Edition (1990)
Bayless Manning.

LEGAL RESEARCH ILLUSTRATED, Fifth Edition with 1990 Assignments Supplement
J. Myron Jacobstein, Professor of Law, Emeritus, Stanford University.
Roy M. Mersky, Professor of Law, Director of Research, University of Texas.

LEGAL RESEARCH, FUNDAMENTALS OF, Fifth Edition with 1990 Assignments Supplement
J. Myron Jacobstein, Professor of Law, Emeritus, Stanford University.
Roy M. Mersky, Professor of Law, Director of Research, University of Texas.

PROCEDURE, THE STRUCTURE OF (1979)
Robert M. Cover, Professor of Law, Yale University.
Owen M. Fiss, Professor of Law, Yale University.

PROPERTY, PRINCIPLES OF THE LAW OF, Third Edition (1989)
John E. Cribbet, Dean, Chancellor, Professor of Law Emeritus, University of Illinois.
Corwin W. Johnson, Professor of Law Emeritus, University of Texas.

TAX, FEDERAL INCOME, Second Edition (1992)
Douglas A. Kahn, Professor of Law, University of Michigan.

TAXATION OF S CORPORATIONS, FEDERAL INCOME (1992)
John K. McNulty, Professor of Law, University of California, Berkeley

TAXATION, FEDERAL INCOME, Sixth Edition (1991)
Marvin A. Chirelstein, Professor of Law, Columbia University.

TAXATION, PARTNERSHIP INCOME (1991)
Alan Gunn, Professor of Law, University of Notre Dame.

TORTS, Second Edition (1980)
Clarence Morris, Professor of Law, University of Pennsylvania.
C. Robert Morris, Professor of Law, University of Minnesota.

WILLS AND TRUSTS, THE PLANNING AND DRAFTING OF, Third Edition (1991)
Thomas L. Shaffer, Professor of Law, University of Notre Dame.
Carol Ann Mooney, Associate Professor of Law, University of Notre Dame.

WILLS, TRUSTS AND ADMINISTRATION, PREFACE TO (1987)
Paul G. Haskell, Professor of Law, University of North Carolina.

CRIMINAL PROCEDURE

AN ANALYSIS

OF

CASES AND CONCEPTS

THIRD EDITION

By

CHARLES H. WHITEBREAD
The George T. Pfleger Professor of Law, University of
Southern California Law Center

CHRISTOPHER SLOBOGIN
Professor of Law, University of Florida

Westbury, New York
THE FOUNDATION PRESS, INC.
1993

615 Merrick Ave.
Westbury, N.Y. 11590

Library of Congress Cataloging-in-Publication Data
Whitebread, Charles H.
  Criminal procedure : an analysis of cases and concepts / by
Charles H. Whitebread, Christopher Slobogin. — 3rd ed.
     p.   cm. — (University textbook series)
  Includes bibliographical references and indexes.
  ISBN 0–88277–993–1
  1. Criminal procedure—United States. I. Slobogin, Christopher,
1951–   . II. Title. III. Series.
KF9619.W47 1992
347.73'05—dc20
[347.3075]   92–31412

W. & S. Crim.Proc. 3rd Ed. UTS

For my father
Dr. Joseph B. Whitebread

For my parents
Peter M. and Becky P. Slobogin

*

PREFACE

This third edition of *Criminal Procedure* represents a complete reworking of the second edition (published in 1986). With minor exceptions, the chapter headings remain the same. But the content of each chapter is not only updated through the 1991–92 term of the Supreme Court, but also significantly revamped, resulting in what we hope is an even more sophisticated and useful product. With the exception of sentencing, every major area of "criminal procedure," from the investigative phase through habeas corpus, is covered.

As with the second edition, the principal goal of this effort has been to provide an analytical framework in the areas addressed. While restating the law and describing how and why it developed is certainly important, this book goes beyond these objectives by giving the reader a step-by-step methodology for evaluating the subject matter. Thus, the reader with a "problem" concerning search and seizure, interrogation, double jeopardy or effective assistance of counsel should be able to use this book to identify the crucial issues and discover the relevant caselaw and policy arguments. For those who need a quick rebriefing, both the numbered conclusion section at the end of each chapter and the relevant portion of the table of contents should serve as a reminder of the relevant principles.

Our belief is that this book is considerably richer than a canned "outline," yet at the same time does not drown the reader in detail concerning lower court cases or minor nuances in the law. For those wishing to delve further into a given subject, an updated bibliography is provided at the end of each chapter. As with the second edition, this edition will be supplemented on an annual basis, after the completion of the Supreme Court's term.

Of course, a work of this magnitude rests on the labor of many besides the two of us. In an area of the law which changes so rapidly, we counted heavily on the aid of numerous students. For their work on the third edition, we would like to recognize Russell Beyer, Jennifer Cates, Rob Feldman, Michael Rainerman, Mitchell

S. Ritchie, Dani D. Smith, and Frederick R. Wallstead, all students at the University of Florida College of Law during the 1991–92 school year.

CHARLES H. WHITEBREAD
George T. Pfleger Professor of Law
University of Southern California
Law Center

CHRISTOPHER SLOBOGIN
Professor of Law
University of Florida
College of Law

July, 1992

SUMMARY OF CONTENTS

TABLE OF CONTENTS

ix

TABLE OF CONTENTS

PART B. THE FIFTH AMENDMENT'S PRIVILEGE AGAINST SELF–INCRIMINATION

PART C. IDENTIFICATION PROCEDURES

PART H. THE RELATIONSHIP BETWEEN THE FEDERAL AND STATE COURTS

TABLE OF CONTENTS

CRIMINAL PROCEDURE

AN ANALYSIS

OF

CASES AND CONCEPTS

*

Chapter One

INTRODUCTION: THE STUDY OF CRIMINAL PROCEDURE

1.01 The Warren Court, Incorporation, and the Federalization of Criminal Procedure

As late as 1960, the study of criminal procedure was a fledgling discipline. Few law schools offered courses on the subject.[1] The relevant decisions of the United States Supreme Court focused on confessions and certain narrow problems connected with the conduct of trial. The task of monitoring the criminal process was in large part left up to the states, which varied widely in their approach.

The last several decades have witnessed an enormous increase in the amount of litigation concerning the procedural rights of the criminally accused. This upsurge has been the direct result of Supreme Court activism. In the early and mid-1960's, the Court began fashioning a wide variety of rules designed to provide those enmeshed in the criminal justice system with adequate protection from overreaching by the state. In 1961, for example, it decided *Mapp v. Ohio*,[2] which held that any evidence seized in violation of the defendant's Fourth Amendment rights must be excluded from state as well as federal prosecutions. Two years later, the Court established a right to counsel for the indigent accused in all state felony prosecutions.[3] And in 1966, it enunciated the now well-known *Miranda* warnings as a constitutional prerequisite to the admissibility of any statement produced during custodial police interrogation.[4]

At least part of this judicial awakening was triggered by the Supreme Court's growing appreciation of the position occupied by the "underprivileged" of society—minority groups, the poor and the young. In decisions such as *Brown v. Board of Education*,[5] the Warren Court, so called after the appointment of Earl Warren as Chief Justice in 1953, attempted to break down some of the social barriers that operated to exclude these groups from mainstream society. It is no coincidence that the Court's rising interest in the procedural rights of the criminally accused—a group which is disproportionately composed of the minorities, the poor and the young—followed hard on its important civil rights decisions.

1. See A. Goldstein, Reflections on Two Models: Inquisitorial Themes in Criminal Procedure, 26 Stan.L.Rev. 1009 (1974).

2. 367 U.S. 643, 81 S.Ct. 1684 (1961).

3. *Gideon v. Wainwright*, 372 U.S. 335, 83 S.Ct. 792 (1963).

4. *Miranda v. Arizona*, 384 U.S. 436, 86 S.Ct. 1602 (1966).

5. 347 U.S. 483, 74 S.Ct. 686 (1954).

The Warren Court's activism focused primarily on the pretrial stages of the criminal process. Legal scholars had for some years been suggesting that the trial itself played a relatively minor role in the criminal justice system.[6] The majority of cases never reach open court; they are settled through the plea bargaining process. Moreover, even if the accused pleads not guilty, the integrity of the resulting trial can still be tainted by police misconduct—an illegal search, a coerced confession or an inappropriately suggestive lineup. The Warren Court, sensitive to these concerns, shifted its attention to those stages of the criminal process where the exercise of police and prosecutorial discretion is most evident. *Mapp* and *Miranda* illustrate its attitude toward police investigation; it also sought to regulate other key elements of the pretrial process, from the preliminary hearing [7] and pretrial identification procedures [8] to plea taking itself.[9]

In order to ensure a uniform system of justice nationwide, the Warren Court made avid use of the incorporation concept previous decisions had developed as a means of determining which Bill of Rights guarantees were so fundamental that, as a matter of due process, they applied to the states under the Fourteenth Amendment, as well as to the federal government.[10] Earlier decisions had refused to apply the Fifth Amendment's provision for indictment by grand jury to the states[11] and suggested that the Eighth Amendment's prohibition against excessive bail was inapplicable to the states as well.[12] But, during the Warren Court's tenure, virtually every other Bill of Rights guarantee pertaining to the criminal process was found necessary to due process of law and was thus imposed on the states through incorporation into the Fourteenth Amendment. The following list outlines by amendment the relevant Warren Court decisions applying federal constitutional principles to the states:

6. See, e.g., A. Goldstein, "The State and the Accused: Balance of Advantage in Criminal Procedure," 69 Yale L.J. 1149 (1960).

7. *Coleman v. Alabama*, 399 U.S. 1, 90 S.Ct. 1999 (1970) (right to counsel at preliminary hearing).

8. *United States v. Wade*, 388 U.S. 218, 87 S.Ct. 1926 (1967) (right to counsel at lineups); *Stovall v. Denno*, 388 U.S. 293, 87 S.Ct. 1967 (1967) (prohibiting unnecessarily suggestive identification procedures).

9. *McCarthy v. United States*, 394 U.S. 459, 89 S.Ct. 1166 (1969); *Boykin v. Alabama*, 395 U.S. 238, 89 S.Ct. 1709 (1969) (requiring intelligent and voluntary pleas).

10. See generally, *Palko v. Connecticut*, 302 U.S. 319, 58 S.Ct. 149 (1937) (describing circumstances under which a Bill of Rights guarantee is "selectively incorporated" by the Fourteenth Amendment's prohibition on state laws that violate due process).

11. *Hurtado v. California*, 110 U.S. 516, 4 S.Ct. 111 (1884) (holding that an indictment by a grand jury is not necessary to due process of law under the Fourteenth Amendment).

12. In *Stack v. Boyle*, 342 U.S. 1, 72 S.Ct. 1 (1951) the Court explained the meaning of the Eighth Amendment's bar against "excessive bail" without according it full constitutional status under the Fourteenth Amendment.

(1) Fourth Amendment: the exclusionary remedy—*Mapp v. Ohio* (1961); [13]

(2) Fifth Amendment: the privilege against self-incrimination—*Malloy v. Hogan* [14] (1964); the ban against double jeopardy—*Benton v. Maryland* [15] (1969); the reasonable doubt standard of proof—*In re Winship* [16] (1970);

(3) Sixth Amendment: the right to speedy trial—*Klopfer v. North Carolina* [17] (1967); the right to jury trial—*Duncan v. Louisiana* [18] (1968); the right to appointed counsel—*Gideon v. Wainwright* [19] (1963); the right to confront and cross-examine witnesses—*Pointer v. Texas* [20] (1965); the right to compulsory process for obtaining witnesses—*Washington v. Texas* [21] (1967);

(4) Eighth Amendment: the ban against cruel and unusual punishment—*Robinson v. California* [22] (1962).

It is probable that many state courts resented this sudden upheaval in criminal procedure. In any event, the Warren Court felt that state court judges could not be counted upon to support enthusiastically its departures from tradition. Accordingly, in conjunction with its expansion of substantive constitutional causes of action, the Court opened wide the door to the federal court system through a series of cases redefining the scope of the writ of habeas corpus.[23] The increased availability of the writ, which under common law was designed to challenge the legality of detention by the government, handed to state prisoners a new method of attacking state judicial decisions on federal constitutional matters.

1.02   The Post-Warren Court: Four Themes

The Warren era, then, saw a dramatic expansion of the state defendant's federally protected constitutional rights and an equally dramatic widening of access to the federal courts as a means of vindicating those rights. With President Nixon's four appointments (Chief Justice Burger in 1969, Blackmun in 1970, Powell and Rehnquist in 1972), the Court's orientation in both of these

---

13. The Fourth Amendment was actually applied to the states in Wolf v. Colorado, 338 U.S. 25, 69 S.Ct. 1359 (1949), but *Mapp* was needed to give *Wolf* teeth. See § 2.02.

14. 378 U.S. 1, 84 S.Ct. 1489 (1964).

15. 395 U.S. 784, 89 S.Ct. 2056 (1969).

16. 397 U.S. 358, 90 S.Ct. 1068 (1970).

17. 386 U.S. 213, 87 S.Ct. 988 (1967).

18. 391 U.S. 145, 88 S.Ct. 1444 (1968).

19. 372 U.S. 335, 83 S.Ct. 792 (1963).

20. 380 U.S. 400, 85 S.Ct. 1065 (1965).

21. 388 U.S. 14, 87 S.Ct. 1920 (1967).

22. 370 U.S. 660, 82 S.Ct. 1417 (1962).

23. *Brown v. Allen,* 344 U.S. 443, 73 S.Ct. 397 (1953); *Fay v. Noia,* 372 U.S. 391, 83 S.Ct. 822 (1963); *Townsend v. Sain,* 372 U.S. 293, 83 S.Ct. 745 (1963), discussed in § 33.02.

areas began to shift noticeably, a shift which continued after Justice Rehnquist took over the Chief Justice position in 1987. In analyzing the criminal procedure decisions of the post-Warren Court four themes seem to emerge as central.

The first theme is the "post-Warren Court's" [24] belief that the ultimate mission of the criminal justice system is to convict the guilty and let the innocent go free. The Warren Court tried to encourage respect for individual rights in the aggregate. In so doing, it often required the release of a factually guilty defendant in order to ensure an appropriate process. While some decisions of the post-Warren Court have produced the same result, it is clear that since the early 1970's the Court has been far more impressed than its predecessor with the importance of the defendant's guilt. Its decisions suggest that the rights enumerated in the Constitution are not all entitled to the same degree of judicial protection, but instead should be valued according to their impact on the adequacy of the guilt determining process.

In evolving this hierarchy among the provisions of the Bill of Rights, the Court has placed the Fourth Amendment's ban on unreasonable searches and seizures at the bottom. Suppose an individual is found in possession of a gram of cocaine. Whether the search that produced the cocaine is unlawful is irrelevant to the issue of the defendant's guilt. Yet if this evidence is excluded because the search *is* illegal then conviction for possession of the drug will be all but impossible. For this reason, application of the exclusionary rule to Fourth Amendment violations has received less than enthusiastic support from the post-Warren Court.

The most prominent illustration of the lowly position the Amendment occupies in the hierarchy of rights is the Court's ruling that one who is not aware of his prerogatives under the Fourth Amendment can still "voluntarily" waive them; [25] such is not the case with other rights. [26] The Court has also singled out Fourth Amendment claims by holding that they are not justiciable in federal habeas proceedings if they were fairly adjudicated by the state courts; [27] to date it has not extended this holding to other guarantees found in the Bill of Rights.

---

24. The use of the terms "Warren Court" and "post-Warren Court" is not meant to imply that the same justices always voted as a bloc on the decisions discussed nor is it meant to suggest that those forming the majority of these decisions hold identical views. The terms are merely shorthand labels designed to symbolize the dichotomy between the Supreme Court's decisions in the past several decades.

25. *Schneckloth v. Bustamonte,* 412 U.S. 218, 93 S.Ct. 2041 (1973).

26. See *Miranda v. Arizona,* 384 U.S. 436, 86 S.Ct. 1602 (1966) (Fifth Amendment waiver must be voluntary and intelligent); *Johnson v. Zerbst,* 304 U.S. 458, 58 S.Ct. 1019 (1938) (waiver of all fundamental rights must be knowing and intelligent).

27. *Stone v. Powell,* 428 U.S. 465, 96 S.Ct. 3037 (1976).

4

The right not to incriminate oneself, which derives from the Fifth Amendment, is more closely bound up with the truth-finding mission at trial. If a confession is extracted by methods that would make anyone say anything, the confession cannot be considered reliable. But while the post-Warren Court is not at all reticent about barring the courtroom use of statements produced in this manner,[28] it appears to be extremely hostile toward the *Miranda* rule, which can operate to exclude statements which are not directly "coerced." Thus, for example, the Court has permitted the use of a confession obtained in violation of *Miranda* for impeachment purposes, if the confession is shown to have been uncoerced.[29] It has also held that evidence obtained in violation of *Miranda* is still admissible in the prosecution's case-in-chief if the questioning was necessitated by an objective threat to the safety of the public or the arresting officer.[30]

A similar tension is evidenced in the Court's decisions regarding the Fifth Amendment's ban on trying an individual twice for the same offense—the double jeopardy clause. More recent Court decisions have shifted the emphasis away from the Warren Court's concern over the deleterious impact of two separate proceedings on the defendant's well-being toward whether the reason for aborting the first trial is bottomed on a decision that the defendant is not guilty.[31] If no acquittal occurs at the first proceeding, the post-Warren majority sees little sense in barring a second trial.

On the other hand, the current Court has been relatively zealous in scrutinizing such Sixth Amendment rights as the right to counsel at trial and the right to public jury trial, because these guarantees are viewed as essential to an accurate determination of guilt. The Court has staunchly supported the right to trial counsel as the key to ensuring a balance of power between the state and the accused, at least when confinement results,[32] and has bolstered the right to counsel on appeal.[33] Several decisions have also emphasized that the criminal trial is to be held in open court barring exceptional circumstances.[34] Less forcefully, the Court has maintained the jury's historic function as a buffer between the

28. See, e.g., *Mincey v. Arizona*, 437 U.S. 385, 98 S.Ct. 2408 (1978).

29. *Harris v. New York*, 401 U.S. 222, 91 S.Ct. 643 (1971).

30. *New York v. Quarles*, 467 U.S. 649, 104 S.Ct. 2626 (1984).

31. *Burks v. United States*, 437 U.S. 1, 98 S.Ct. 2141 (1978); *United States v. Scott*, 437 U.S. 82, 98 S.Ct. 2187 (1978), discussed in § 30.03.

32. See *Argersinger v. Hamlin*, 407 U.S. 25, 92 S.Ct. 2006 (1972) (right to counsel in misdemeanor cases).

33. *Evitts v. Lucey*, 469 U.S. 387, 105 S.Ct. 830 (1985) (failure to meet filing deadline for appeal is ineffective assistance).

34. *Richmond Newspapers, Inc. v. Virginia*, 448 U.S. 555, 100 S.Ct. 2814 (1980); *Press-Enterprise Co. v. Superior Court*, 464 U.S. 501, 104 S.Ct. 819 (1984), discussed in § 27.06.

state and the criminal defendant.[35]   The focus on the trial as the central battleground between the accused and the government represents a substantial departure from the Warren Court's emphasis.

A second noticeable trait exhibited by the Court since 1970 is its devotion to "totality of the circumstances" analysis as distinct from a rule-oriented approach to criminal procedure.   The Warren Court appeared to prefer the adoption of specific rules to guide law enforcement officers, as well as the courts which evaluate their behavior.[36]   The post-Warren Court, on the other hand, has, with a few exceptions,[37] opted for a case-by-case approach which makes the precedential value of any one decision suspect.[38]   Depending upon one's perspective, this tendency can be praised because it gives police and courts more flexibility in evaluating the propriety of particular acts and omissions, or criticized because it encourages standardless police conduct and judicial review.   In practical terms, the end result of totality of the circumstances analysis has been a relaxation of constitutional restrictions on law enforcement.[39]

A third related theme running through the Court's decisions since the early 1970's is its greater faith in the integrity of the police and other officials who administer the criminal justice system.   Whereas the Warren Court saw a need for strict judicial scrutiny of the law enforcement process, the post-Warren Court tends to give government officials wider latitude.   Thus, it has frequently been willing to assume that police investigating crime will act in good faith,[40] and has likewise assumed that magis-

---

35.   *Ballew v. Georgia,* 435 U.S. 223, 98 S.Ct. 1029 (1978) (five member jury unconstitutional); *Burch v. Louisiana,* 441 U.S. 130, 99 S.Ct. 1623 (1979) (nonunanimous vote by six member jury unconstitutional); *Taylor v. Louisiana,* 419 U.S. 522, 95 S.Ct. 692 (1975) (cross-representative jury pool required).   But see, *Williams v. Florida,* 399 U.S. 78, 90 S.Ct. 1893 (1970) (six member jury constitutional); *Johnson v. Louisiana,* 406 U.S. 356, 92 S.Ct. 1620 (1972) (9–3 verdict constitutional).

36.   See e.g., *Miranda v. Arizona,* 384 U.S. 436, 86 S.Ct. 1602 (1966) (requiring specific warnings before custodial interrogation); *Chimel v. California,* 395 U.S. 752, 89 S.Ct. 2034 (1969) (adopting "armspan" rule for scope of search incident).

37.   See *United States v. Robinson,* 414 U.S. 218, 94 S.Ct. 467 (1973) (permitting search incident to arrest for all crimes); *New York v. Belton,* 453 U.S. 454, 101 S.Ct. 2860 (1981) (permitting search of car's interior when occupant arrested).

38.   See generally, § 16.03 on Court's emasculation of *Miranda* rule; *Illinois v. Gates,* 462 U.S. 213, 103 S.Ct. 2317 (1983) (definition of probable cause); *Rawlings v. Kentucky,* 448 U.S. 98, 100 S.Ct. 2556 (1980) (Fourth Amendment standing analysis); *Manson v. Brathwaite,* 432 U.S. 98, 97 S.Ct. 2243 (1977) (admissibility of lineup identifications).

39.   See cases cited supra note 38. Even those post-Warren Court decisions which adopt the rule-oriented approach fashioned prosecution-oriented rules, however.   See note 37 supra.

40.   See e.g., *Nix v. Williams,* 467 U.S. 431, 104 S.Ct. 2501 (1984) (police will not knowingly violate Constitution merely because they think sought-after evidence will be discovered in any event); *Segura v. United States,* 468 U.S. 796, 104 S.Ct. 3380 (1984) (police

trates [41] and prosecutors [42] can be trusted to protect the rights of criminal defendants. It has also granted state correctional officials broad authority in supervising those confined in jail or prison.[43]

The fourth theme underlying many recent Court decisions is a corollary of the third; the Court believes that state judges can be entrusted to enforce federal constitutional rights, with the caveat that when those rights impinge directly upon the question of guilt there should be no obstacle to seeking collateral relief in federal court.[44] Thus, it has prohibited federal habeas courts from announcing "new rules"—that is, rules that are not "dictated" by precedent—unless the habeas claim is one that questions the jurisdictional basis or the accuracy of the state court conviction.[45] And, as noted earlier, when the claim involves the Fourth Amendment, even well-accepted law cannot be applied by habeas courts when the petitioner has received a full and fair opportunity to raise the claim in state court.[46] The Court has also substantially narrowed the Warren Court's decisions governing the ability of those who fail to assert their constitutional claims in state court to assert them for the first time in federal court.[47] Finally, it has repeatedly emphasized and diligently applied the statutory requirement that state court determinations of factual issues relating to federal constitutional claims be accorded a "presumption of correctness."[48] As a result of this "New Federalism," state court decisions are much less likely to be reviewed by the federal courts than in the Warren Court era.

As the substantive and procedural avenues of relief under the federal constitution have been narrowed by the post-Warren Court, two interesting counter-developments have occurred. First,

---

will not illegally enter premises to secure evidence pending arrival of a warrant); *New York v. Quarles,* 467 U.S. 649, 104 S.Ct. 2626 (1984) (police will not take advantage of public safety exception to *Miranda* to obtain incriminating statements).

41. *United States v. Leon,* 468 U.S. 897, 104 S.Ct. 3405 (1984) (magistrates will not rubber stamp warrant requests).

42. *Wayte v. United States,* 470 U.S. 598, 105 S.Ct. 1524 (1985) (minimizing need for judicial supervision of charging process); *United States v. Ash,* 413 U.S. 300, 93 S.Ct. 2568 (1973) (prosecutor can be counted upon to treat defendant fairly at photo identification in absence of defendant's counsel); *United States v. Bagley,* 473 U.S. 667, 105 S.Ct. 3375 (1985) (prosecutor can be trusted to dis-

close to defense counsel information which might be exculpatory).

43. *Block v. Rutherford,* 468 U.S. 576, 104 S.Ct. 3227 (1984); *Hudson v. Palmer,* 468 U.S. 517, 104 S.Ct. 3194 (1984); *Bell v. Wolfish,* 441 U.S. 520, 99 S.Ct. 1861 (1979), discussed in § 20.04.

44. *Jackson v. Virginia,* 443 U.S. 307, 99 S.Ct. 2781 (1979); *Murray v. Carrier,* 477 U.S. 478, 106 S.Ct. 2639 (1986).

45. *Teague v. Lane,* 489 U.S. 288, 109 S.Ct. 1060 (1989).

46. *Stone v. Powell,* 428 U.S. 465, 96 S.Ct. 3037 (1976).

47. See generally, § 33.03(c).

48. *Wainwright v. Witt,* 469 U.S. 412, 105 S.Ct. 844 (1985); *Marshall v. Lonberger,* 459 U.S. 422, 103 S.Ct. 843 (1983).

some state courts have found Supreme Court precedent inapplicable in their jurisdictions by interpreting *state* constitutional provisions to provide more protection for criminal defendants. Between 1970 and 1986, over 150 state court decisions repudiated Supreme Court criminal procedure rulings on independent state grounds.[49] At the same time, some federal courts, also apparently unsympathetic to the higher court's goals, resorted to their "supervisory" authority over the federal system as a means of redressing what they perceived as inappropriate, albeit "constitutional," actions in federal court. For instance, in *United States v. Payner*,[50] a federal district court suppressed evidence despite the defendant's inability to challenge its admission under the Court's standing cases, on the ground that the government had "affirmatively counsel[led] its agents that the Fourth Amendment standing limitation permits them to purposefully conduct an unconstitutional search and seizure of one individual in order to obtain evidence against third parties." In *United States v. Hasting*,[51] the Seventh Circuit admitted that a Fifth Amendment error committed by the prosecutor during closing argument was "harmless" under the Court's harmless error doctrine, but nonetheless reversed the conviction in an attempt to penalize the prosecutor's office for committing the error in case after case.

The Supreme Court has responded to both developments. In reaction to the rebellion at the state court level, it held, in *Michigan v. Long*,[52] that a state court decision relying on state constitutional provisions may nonetheless be subject to federal review unless the decision clearly indicates that it is based *solely* on state law. *Long* has meant that some ambiguously reasoned state court rulings have been considered and overturned by the Supreme Court. But it has not stifled state court activism; its "plain statement" requirement is easily met, thus permitting a competent state court to insulate from federal review any decisions that meet the federal minimum and are truly based on independent state grounds.[53] The Court has been more successful in curtailing the activism of lower federal courts. For example, in *Hasting*, described above, it reinstated the conviction and held that local disciplinary action, not reversal, is the correct sanction for repeated prosecutorial error that is deemed harmless.[54] In *Payner*, also noted above, it disapproved the district court's use of its supervisory power to accomplish something (i.e., suppression)

49. Collins & Galie, "The Methodology of State Court Decisions," Nat'l L.J., Sept. 29, 1986, at S–9.

50. 434 F.Supp. 113 (N.D.Ohio 1977).

51. 660 F.2d 301 (7th Cir.1981).

52. 463 U.S. 1032, 103 S.Ct. 3469 (1983).

53. See Chapter Thirty-Four for examples of state court decisions repudiating Supreme Court standards.

54. 461 U.S. 499, 103 S.Ct. 1974 (1983).

the defendant had no constitutional authority to request.[55] Thus, the current Court appears committed not only to restricting defendants' rights, but also to ensuring, to the limits of its authority, that state and federal courts do not evade those restrictions.[56]

The foregoing is not meant to imply that the post-Warren Court's philosophy has in all respects been diametrically opposed to that of the Warren Court; many Supreme Court decisions since 1970 have reaffirmed the new law announced in the 1960's.[57] The point is that the post-Warren Court is more cautious in asserting the interests of the individual over those of the state in its monitoring of the criminal justice system.

1.03 The Crime Control and Due Process Models of Criminal Procedure

The difference in emphasis between the Warren and post-Warren Courts suggests the diverging approaches that can be taken toward the central problem encountered in the study of criminal procedure: how best to protect the rights and interests of the criminally accused without at the same time unduly inhibiting law enforcement. It is interesting to view the dichotomy between the two Courts against the backdrop of Herbert Packer's study of the criminal process in his book *The Limits of the Criminal Sanction.*[58]

Packer posits two opposing trends in the administration of criminal justice, the Crime Control Model and the Due Process Model. He is careful to point out that neither model necessarily represents the "ideal." Rather each model offers advantages of its own and compromise between the two may often offer the best resolution, depending upon the issue at stake.

The Crime Control Model places a premium on efficiency and quick adjudication. The goal is to convey the guilty as rapidly as possible toward a conviction at trial or, better yet, a guilty plea, while ferreting out those who are unlikely to be offenders. Inherent in this model is what Packer calls the "presumption of guilt"—that the person who enters the system is probably *factual-*

---

55. 447 U.S. 727, 100 S.Ct. 2439 (1980).

56. The Court has also emphasized the obvious point that federal habeas courts have no supervisory power over state agencies. *Smith v. Phillips,* 455 U.S. 209, 102 S.Ct. 940 (1982) (federal courts hearing state habeas claims "may intervene only to correct wrongs of constitutional dimension," even when failing to intervene would permit prosecutorial misbehavior to "reign unchecked.").

57. Compare *Hayes v. Florida,* 470 U.S. 811, 105 S.Ct. 1643 (1985) with *Davis v. Mississippi,* 394 U.S. 721, 89 S.Ct. 1394 (1969) (stationhouse detention for fingerprinting on less than probable cause unconstitutional); *Moore v. Illinois,* 434 U.S. 220, 98 S.Ct. 458 (1977) with *United States v. Wade,* 388 U.S. 218, 87 S.Ct. 1926 (1967) (right to counsel at lineups conducted after initial appearance or indictment).

58. Packer, H.L. *The Limits of the Criminal Sanction,* ch. 8.

ly guilty. To ensure that these guilty parties are brought to justice, any limitations placed on law enforcement officials should be motivated solely out of a desire to promote the reliability of the outcome; purely "technical" controls on police behavior are unnecessary and inimical to this model of the criminal process.

The Due Process Model likewise stresses reliability in the accumulation and presentation of evidence but, given the "gross deprivation of liberty" resulting from conviction, mandates a higher degree of accuracy than the Crime Control Model. It assumes that, as Packer describes it:

> People are notoriously poor observers of disturbing events . . . confessions and admissions by persons in police custody may be induced by physical or psychological coercion so that the police end up hearing what the suspect thinks they want to hear rather than the truth; witnesses may be animated by a bias or interest that no one would trouble to discover except one specially charged with protecting the interests of the accused (as the police are not).[59]

Thus, those administering the criminal process should be as certain as possible that the information used to convict an individual is accurate.

Beyond this heightened emphasis on reliability is a more global concern that the integrity of the criminal justice system, and therefore the integrity of society as a whole, be preserved. Thus, advocates of the Due Process Model are more willing to hinder the efficiency of the system through prophylactic rules designed to remind law enforcement officials of their duty toward the criminally accused. They are less concerned with letting off the factually guilty if, due to a failure on the part of the state to follow these rules, *legal* guilt has not been established.

Packer hypothesizes that the means of implementing these two models are decidedly different:

> Because the Crime Control Model is basically an affirmative model, emphasizing at every turn the existence and exercise of official power, its validating authority is ultimately legislative. . . . Because the Due Process Model is basically a negative model, asserting limits on the nature of official power and on the modes of its exercise, its validating authority is judicial and requires an appeal to supra-legislative law, the law of the Constitution.[60]

This hypothesis is especially interesting given the post-Warren Court's arguably greater deference to the legislative process.[61]

59. Id. at 163.

60. Id. at 173.

61. Compare *Miranda v. Arizona,* 384 U.S. 436, 86 S.Ct. 1602 (1966) (establishing detailed protections during in-

In any event, it should be evident that each of Packer's models has its appealing aspects. Choosing between the two, or arriving at some middle ground, is not an easy task, regardless of whether the judiciary or the legislature makes the ultimate decision.

Dispassionate discussion about the "rights" of criminal defendants is further hindered by the emotionally-charged nature of the subject. Opinions as to what to do with the "criminal element" can vary with the type of crime, the possible outcomes, and the experiences of the opinion-giver himself. One might prefer the full panoply of constitutional safeguards in cases involving minor crimes such as gambling or vagrancy, but tend to opt for the less technical "crime control" approach where a crime of violence is concerned.[62] Conversely, one could reasonably favor greater protections for those individuals most likely to receive the most significant sanctions and be willing to permit relaxed procedures when the consequences of mistake are not significant.[63] Regardless of the crime involved, the student who has been "busted" understandably may take a different view of the process than the student who has just been robbed of his prize record collection. There is no easy way to control for the impact of such personal biases, whether the debate takes place in the classroom, the legislature or the Supreme Court. But it is essential to be aware of the fact that they play a crucial role in the evolution of public policy.

The student of criminal procedure should also be aware of the relatively hidden world of discretion in the criminal process. The police, the prosecutor and the courts all have varying degrees of power to "push" a case or to drop it altogether, depending upon what stage the case has reached. Their decisions can have as much significance for the accused as any opinion delivered by the Supreme Court. A police officer may decide not to report a first offender, a prosecutor may refuse to accept a plea, a judge may divert a case out of the criminal system at a preliminary hearing. Existing statutory and case law may exert little or no influence

terrogation) with *Missouri v. Hunter,* 459 U.S. 359, 103 S.Ct. 673 (1983) (legislative intent determinative as to whether two offenses are the "same offense" for purposes of deciding whether multiple punishment is permissible under double jeopardy clause) and Chief Justice Burger's dissent in *Bivens v. Six Unknown Named Agents,* 403 U.S. 388, 91 S.Ct. 1999 (1971) (arguing that legislative sanctions should replace the Fourth Amendment exclusionary rule).

62. See Wilkey, "The Exclusionary Rule: Why Suppress Valid Evidence?"

62 Judicature 214 (1978) (arguing that the rule should at least be eliminated with respect to serious crimes).

63. This apparently was the premise of the juvenile court movement in its early years, when procedural protections afforded juveniles were minimal given the belief that the consequences of a delinquency adjudication were principally "therapeutic." See M. Paulsen & C. Whitebread, Juvenile Law and Procedure, ch. 1 (1974).

over such decisions. Yet they are a part of the everyday workings of our criminal justice system.

1.04 The Stages of the Criminal Process

This book cannot hope to convey all of the nuances underlying the everyday operations of the criminal process, especially given the wide variations from state to state. Nonetheless, the following outline of what could be called the "Ordinary Model" of the process may prove useful to the student as a preface to the rest of this book.

A typical case normally begins either with a complaint by a private citizen, or when police directly observe what looks like criminal activity. In the former instance, police usually have time to investigate the complaint through questioning of witnesses and examination of physical evidence. If they decide they have enough evidence to establish "probable cause" [64] that a particular individual committed the crime, they will often approach a magistrate and swear out an arrest warrant on the suspected culprit (as well as, perhaps, a search warrant authorizing search of his home). When police observe crime, on the other hand, there is normally no time to secure a warrant. In such cases, if the police have probable cause to believe the individual has committed or is committing a crime, they may arrest him without a warrant; if they do not have probable cause, they may still be able to question him and, if probable cause then develops, arrest him.

During arrest the police may conduct a search of the individual and begin to question him concerning the alleged offense. Soon after arrest, the arrestee is taken to the stationhouse for "booking," which usually involves being fingerprinted and photographed. At this point, when minor charges are involved, the police may release the arrestee on "stationhouse bail." For serious charges, the person usually remains in custody and a more formal interrogation may take place; additionally, the arrestee may be required to participate in a lineup or submit to scientific tests (such as blood tests) if they were not administered in the field, and further searches may also occur.

Fairly soon after arrest and booking (usually within 48 hours) comes the initial appearance in front of a judicial officer (sometimes called an "arraignment on the warrant"). Here the arrestee is informed of the charge (usually written up by the police or prosecutor in the form of a "complaint"), and of his rights to counsel and to remain silent. In many states, if the charges are minor, the magistrate may proceed to try the case at this time as well. In felony cases, if there is no arrest warrant, the magistrate

---

64. This term, explicated in § 3.03, is found in the Fourth Amendment.

must determine, either at the initial appearance or at a proceeding soon thereafter, whether there is probable cause to detain the individual.[65] If probable cause is found, or there is an arrest warrant, a decision is then made as to whether the arrestee can be released on personal recognizance, subjected to bail conditions, or detained preventively.[66]

In the meantime, the prosecutor formalizes the charges against the arrestee, now more appropriately called the defendant. In some states, the prosecutor need merely file an "information" describing the charges. In other states and the federal system, he must go to a grand jury to obtain an "indictment" stating the charges. In the former jurisdictions, he is usually required to make out a prima facie case on the charges in the information during a preliminary hearing in front of a magistrate. In the latter jurisdictions, he may have to go through the preliminary hearing before he can get to the grand jury.

The Constitution allows the defendant to *demand* counsel only at certain isolated "stages" of the pretrial process such as interrogation or a lineup identification.[67] But in practice counsel is often appointed as early as the initial appearance. Once appointed, counsel can make several different types of pretrial motions, seeking dismissal of the case, change of venue, suppression of illegally obtained evidence, discovery of evidence, or the implementation of a statutory "speedy trial" right. Many of these motions cannot be made after trial or judgment. Defense counsel may also enter into negotiations with the prosecutor with a view to having his client plead guilty in exchange for a reduction in charges or a lenient sentence recommendation.

Sometime before trial, the defendant is brought before the court that will try him. With misdemeanants, as already noted, this is often the initial appearance. With more serious charges, a separate stage, called the "arraignment on the information" (or indictment) occurs, at which the court informs the defendant of his charges and asks him how he pleads. There are three pleas: not guilty, guilty and nolo contendere. If either of the latter two pleas are entered, the court conducts a hearing to ensure the plea is voluntarily and intelligently entered and to discover the terms of any plea agreement that has been reached. Roughly 90 percent of all cases which are not dismissed previously by the police or the prosecutor are adjudicated via plea.

If the defendant pleads not guilty, the case is set for trial. In most cases, the defendant is entitled to a jury, which consists of twelve people in federal court and varies from six to twelve in

65. The Supreme Court so held in *Gerstein v. Pugh,* 420 U.S. 103, 95 S.Ct. 854 (1975).

66. See § 20.03.

67. See § 31.03.

state courts. In jury cases, voir dire of the jury panel is conducted, during which counsel for both sides, using peremptory and "for cause" challenges,[68] attempt to obtain a jury to their liking. Most states also require that notice of an alibi or insanity defense be made prior to or at this time.

At trial, the prosecution bears the burden of proving each element of the crime beyond a reasonable doubt.[69] After the presentation of evidence, with the defendant's case following the state's case, a verdict is reached and sentence imposed. In jury trials, the judge normally imposes sentence after a separate hearing, although some states permit sentencing by the trial jury.

An appeal may be automatic or discretionary, depending upon the level of the original trial court and the type of crime (misdemeanor or felony) involved. For instance, many states provide for automatic appeal from courts "not of record" to a higher court at which a record of the proceedings is kept (and at which the charges will usually be adjudicated *de novo*), but make further appeal to the state supreme court or intermediate appellate court discretionary with that court. An appeal must usually be taken within a specified time limit. If the defendant does appeal, the bail question may again arise. At any time after conviction, the defendant may also "collaterally" attack the verdict through a writ of habeas corpus.

A major variation on the Ordinary Model described above occurs when the grand jury indictment *precedes* arrest. In these cases, typically involving political corruption or organized crime, the grand jury functions not as a check on charge selection but as an investigatory body. When arrest is predicated on an indictment, there is normally no need for a preliminary hearing other than an initial appearance to set bail, advise the defendant of his rights and appoint counsel, if necessary. No probable cause determination is necessary since the grand jury has already found it exists.

1.05 A Brief Outline of the Book

This book is devoted to examining the legal doctrines which govern the operation of the system described above. The first half of the book (Parts A through D) discusses the constraints the Constitution places on law enforcement officials in their effort to investigate crime. Specifically, it looks at the legal rules governing search and seizure (Part A), state compulsion of self-incriminating information (Part B), identification procedures (Part

---

68. Each side receives a limited number of peremptory challenges permitting automatic removal of prospective jurors and an unlimited number of for cause challenges requiring the challenging party to prove potential prejudice toward it. See § 27.04(a).

69. *In re Winship,* 397 U.S. 358, 90 S.Ct. 1068 (1970).

C), and police attempts to lure—or perhaps "entrap"—individuals into committing crime (Part D). The second half of the book (Parts E through H) examines the adversary system, including the formal stages of the pretrial process (Part E), trial and appeals (Part F), the role of defense counsel during these stages (Part G), and federal habeas review of state court decisions (Part H). In addition to the habeas issue, the last Part covers a second subject having to do with the relationship between the federal and state criminal justice systems—the recent tendency of state courts, discussed above, to ignore Supreme Court pronouncements and relying on their own constitutions to enforce stricter controls on law enforcement officials.

BIBLIOGRAPHY

Allen, Francis. The Judicial Quest for Penal Justice: The Warren Court and Criminal Cases. 1975 Ill.L.F. 518.

Arenella, Peter. Rethinking the Functions of Criminal Procedure: The Warren and Burger Courts' Competing Ideologies. 72 Geo.L.J. 185 (1984).

Bradley, Craig. Criminal Procedure in the Rehnquist Court: Has the Rehnquisition Begun? 62 Ind.L.J. 273 (1987).

Feeley, Malcolm M. Two Models of the Criminal Justice System: An Organizational Perspective. 7 Law and Society Review 407 (1973).

Israel, Jerold H. Criminal Procedure, the Burger Court and the Legacy of the Warren Court. 75 Mich.L.Rev. 1320 (1977).

Kamisar, Yale. The Warren Court (Was It Really So Defense-Minded?), The Burger Court (Is It Really So Prosecution-Oriented?) and Police Investigatory Practices. In: The Burger Court: The Counter-Revolution That Wasn't (V. Blasi ed. 1983).

Kurland, Philip B. Politics, the Constitution and the Warren Court. Chicago: Univ. of Chicago Press (1970).

Packer, Herbert. The Limits of the Criminal Sanction, Chap. 8. Stanford: Stanford University Press, 1968.

Pye, Kenneth. The Warren Court and Criminal Procedure. 67 Mich.L.Rev. 249 (1968).

Saltzberg, Stephen A. Foreword: The Flow and Ebb of Constitutional Criminal Procedure in the Warren and Burger Courts, 69 Geo.L.J. 151 (1980).

Whitebread, Charles. The Burger Court's Counter-Revolution in Criminal Procedure: The Recent Criminal Decisions of the United States Supreme Court. 24 Washburn L.J. 41 (1985).

Part A

THE FOURTH AMENDMENT: SEARCH AND SEIZURE LAW

The Fourth Amendment guarantees the "right of the people to be secure in their persons, houses, papers, and effects, against unreasonable searches and seizures. . . ." It also states that "no warrants shall issue, but upon probable cause, supported by oath or affirmation, and particularly describing the place to be searched, and the persons or things to be seized." The first part of the Amendment confers upon the citizenry protection against intrusion into their privacy. Under no circumstances will a governmental search or seizure of one's person or possessions be condoned if it is "unreasonable." The second section of the Amendment provides that warrants authorizing searches or seizures meet certain requirements before they can be regarded as valid. By implication, an invalid warrant will not support a search. The language of the Amendment does not require that every search be authorized by a warrant; indeed, as noted in the following chapters,[1] there has been considerable debate over whether the Amendment even expresses a *preference* for warrants.

The following chapters describe how the Supreme Court and the lower courts have grappled with the language of the Fourth Amendment. Chapter Two examines the exclusionary rule and other remedies available for violations of the Amendment's guarantees. Chapter Three discusses the law of arrest and related seizures of the person. Chapters Four through Fourteen cover the jurisprudence of searches. Chapter Four explores the definition of "search" for purposes of the Fourth Amendment, Chapter Five describes the components of a valid warrant and the probable cause concept, and the bulk of the remaining chapters deal with exceptions to the warrant and probable cause requirements. Chapter Fourteen discusses the special search context of electronic surveillance.

1. See in particular § 4.05(a).

Chapter Two

THE EXCLUSIONARY EVIDENCE RULE AND OTHER REMEDIES FOR CONSTITUTIONAL VIOLATIONS

2.01 Introduction

The exclusionary evidence rule is the result of an effort on the part of the judiciary to ensure that constitutional limitations on law enforcement are safeguarded. Simply stated, the rule prohibits the use of evidence or testimony obtained by government officials through means violative of the Constitution. In the Fourth Amendment context, the rationale for the rule is that government officials, and in particular, the police, will be deterred from using illegal means to obtain evidence if such evidence may not be employed to support a conviction. A further rationale for the rule—which in recent Supreme Court decisions has received more lipservice than actual support—is found in the sentiment that the judiciary should not be a partner to or otherwise sanction the lawlessness of a coordinate branch of government.

For these reasons, evidence obtained through an unlawful search of one's house, or an illegal arrest, even if highly probative, will be suppressed. For much the same reasons, the courts also often exclude evidence obtained in contravention of the Fifth Amendment's prohibition against compelled self-incrimination or evidence procured in violation of the Sixth Amendment's admonition that counsel be provided the accused at particular stages of the criminal process. Though the rule is thus useful in protecting a number of constitutional rights, this chapter will focus on the development of the rule in the Fourth Amendment context. Later chapters will make note of the rule's applicability to Fifth and Sixth Amendment issues.[1]

This chapter also examines the civil and criminal alternatives to the exclusionary rule. Here again, the discussion will proceed primarily from the Fourth Amendment perspective, although it should be remembered that these remedies for constitutional violations can apply when other types of claims are made as well.

2.02 History of the Rule: From *Weeks* to *Mapp* to *Ker*

Though certain early decisions are said to contain embryonic statements of the exclusionary rule,[2] its first clear espousal is found in the landmark case, *Weeks v. United States*.[3] In that case,

1. See in particular, §§ 16.05, 17.05.

2. E.g., *Boyd v. United States*, 116 U.S. 616, 6 S.Ct. 524 (1886).

3. 232 U.S. 383, 34 S.Ct. 341 (1914).

the Supreme Court held that articles seized through an unlawful search and seizure of petitioner's home by federal officials should have been returned to him upon demand, and, further, that their use as evidence against the petitioner in a criminal trial constituted prejudicial error. Justice Day, writing for a unanimous Court, stated the reason for excluding such illegally obtained evidence:

> To sanction such proceedings would be to affirm by judicial decision a manifest neglect if not an open defiance of the prohibitions of the Constitution, intended for the protection of the people against such unauthorized action.

Such strong language seemed to indicate the constitutional necessity of the exclusionary rule. Indeed, in *Silverthorne Lumber Co. v. United States,*[4] Justice Holmes stated that without the exclusionary rule to suppress evidence obtained by means of an unconstitutional search and seizure, "the Fourth Amendment [is reduced] to a form of words." Yet, when the Fourth Amendment ban was first applied to the states under the Fourteenth Amendment's Due Process clause in *Wolf v. Colorado,*[5] the Court refused to go so far as to say that the exclusionary rule was also constitutionally mandated to enforce that ban in state cases.

The Court's reasoning in *Wolf* is epitomized by the following passage:

> Granting that in practice the exclusion of evidence may be an effective way of deterring unreasonable searches, it is not for this Court to condemn as falling below the minimal standards assured by the Due Process Clause a State's reliance upon other methods which, if consistently enforced, would be equally effective. . . . We cannot brush aside the experience of States which deem the incidence of such conduct by the police too slight to call for a deterrent remedy not by way of disciplinary measures but by overriding the relevant rules of evidence.

Thus, the Court left it for the states to decide how to safeguard the Fourth Amendment's guarantees.

At the time *Wolf* was decided, eighteen states had adopted some form of the exclusionary rule. By 1960, eleven years later, eight more states had adopted the rule,[6] suggesting that, as far as a majority of states were concerned, there was no other effective remedy. Not surprisingly, the Court was called upon to overrule *Wolf* on more than one occasion. At first it was unwilling to consider the issue.[7] In *Rochin v. California,*[8] it did hold, three

---

4. 251 U.S. 385, 40 S.Ct. 182 (1920).

5. 338 U.S. 25, 69 S.Ct. 1359 (1949).

6. See Appendix in *Elkins v. United States,* 364 U.S. 206, 80 S.Ct. 1437 (1960).

7. See, e.g., *Irvine v. California,* 347 U.S. 128, 74 S.Ct. 381 (1954); *Frank v. Maryland,* 359 U.S. 360, 79 S.Ct. 804 (1959).

8. 342 U.S. 165, 72 S.Ct. 205 (1952).

years after *Wolf*, that if a search or seizure conducted by state police "shocked the conscience," then exclusion is mandated as a matter of due process. In *Rochin*, the Court found that police use of an emetic to force the defendant to disgorge swallowed drugs was sufficiently repugnant to merit application of the exclusionary rule despite *Wolf*.[9] And, in *Elkins v. United States*,[10] it rejected the "silver platter" doctrine, which permitted *federal* use of evidence illegally obtained by state officials. It was not until 1961, however, in the case of *Mapp v. Ohio*,[11] that the Supreme Court finally agreed to undertake a full-fledged reconsideration of *Wolf*.

In *Mapp*, the Court decided, 5–4, to make the exclusionary rule binding on the states. The Court took a pragmatic approach to the question by recognizing that "the factual considerations supporting the failure of the *Wolf* Court to include the *Weeks* exclusionary rule . . . could not . . . now be deemed controlling." While the *Wolf* Court had felt that remedies other than exclusion might be applied to Fourth Amendment violations, the *Mapp* Court concluded that "other remedies have been worthless and futile," and viewed the exclusionary rule as necessary to the existence of the Fourth Amendment guarantee. As stated for the Court by Justice Clark:

> [T]he admission of the constitutional right by *Wolf* could not consistently tolerate denial of its most important constitutional privilege, namely, the exclusion of the evidence which an accused had been forced to give by reason of the unlawful seizure. To hold otherwise is to grant the right but in reality to withhold its privilege and enjoyment.

Justice Clark recognized, using Justice Cardozo's famous words, that under the rule "[t]he criminal is to go free because the constable has blundered."[12] But he gave a second reason for the exclusionary rule—"the imperative of judicial integrity."

> The criminal goes free, if he must, but it is the law that sets him free. Nothing can destroy a government more quickly than its failure to observe its own law, or worse, its disregard of the charter of its own existence.[13]

9. However, it refused to apply the "due process exclusionary rule" to a month-long illegal wiretap, *Irvine v. California*, 347 U.S. 128, 74 S.Ct. 381 (1954), or extraction of blood from an unconscious person. *Breithaupt v. Abram*, 352 U.S. 432, 77 S.Ct. 408 (1957).

10. 364 U.S. 206, 80 S.Ct. 1437 (1960).

11. 367 U.S. 643, 81 S.Ct. 1684 (1961).

12. *People v. Defore*, 242 N.Y. 13, 150 N.E. 585 (1926), cert. den. 270 U.S. 657, 46 S.Ct. 353 (1926).

13. See also, *Elkins v. United States*, 364 U.S. 206, 80 S.Ct. 1437 (1960).

Thus, both deterrence of police misconduct and maintaining judicial "clean hands" justified applying the exclusionary rule to the states.

The final touch in terms of "constitutionalizing" the exclusionary rule came in *Ker v. California.*[14] While *Wolf* had spoken of applying only "the core of the Fourth Amendment" to the states, *Mapp* declared that state and federal officers were bound by "the same fundamental criteria," leaving some doubt as to whether all standards based on the Fourth Amendment applied to the states. In *Ker,* the Court was presented with the question of whether state laws relating to arrests and searches had been supplanted by federal standards. The Court emphasized that the Supreme Court had no "supervisory authority over state courts . . ., and, consequently, [*Mapp*] implied no *total* obliteration of state laws relating to arrests and searches in favor of federal law." However, the Court went on to hold that, while the states still had the general power to determine what constituted a reasonable search, seizure, or arrest, this finding of reasonableness could be "respected only insofar as consistent with federal constitutional guarantees." Thus, any time a claim of unconstitutional search and seizure or arrest is advanced as a defense to a criminal action in a state court, that court must apply federal standards to the lawfulness or reasonableness of the action in question, unless the state standard is *more* restrictive than the federal standard.[15] In light of this result, *Ker* is often said to be the culmination of the "federalization" of the exclusionary rule. It is important to recognize, however, that when the rule violated is not of constitutional dimension (but is imposed on the federal courts via the supervisory power or is a state rule), *Mapp* does not mandate exclusion.[16]

2.03 The Scope of the Exclusionary Rule

Mapp established that illegally obtained evidence must be excluded at trial in both federal and state prosecutions. But, beginning in the 1970's, the Court has made clear that the Fourth Amendment exclusionary rule does not operate in most settings outside of trial, and has slowly constricted its operation at trial as well. The premise of this retrenchment is that the primary, if not the only, purpose of the exclusionary rule is to deter illegal police behavior; thus, the rule should not apply when it is unlikely to deter, given the cost associated with its application (i.e., benefitting guilty persons). Moreover, the Court has stressed that the

---

14. 374 U.S. 23, 83 S.Ct. 1623 (1963).

15. Several state courts have announced rules more restrictive than the federal standard based on their interpretation of state law. See § 34.02(c).

16. See, e.g., *Cady v. Dombrowski,* 413 U.S. 433, 93 S.Ct. 2523 (1973), where the Court strongly implied that rules governing the listing of items in a post-search inventory are a matter of state law.

rule is "a judicially-created remedy designed to safeguard Fourth Amendment rights generally through its deterrent effect, rather than a personal constitutional right of the party aggrieved." [17] In effect, this means that, on the issue of the rule's scope, the language and history of the Fourth Amendment are not dispositive; rather, the breadth of the rule is entirely up to the Court.

(a) Criminal Proceedings Other Than Trial. After *Mapp* and *Ker*, courts were asked to apply the exclusionary rule in a variety of proceedings other than trial. The Supreme Court's first decision on this issue was *United States v. Calandra*,[18] where both the primacy of the deterrence objective and the prophylactic nature of the rule were clearly established. In *Calandra*, the Court decided that a witness summoned to appear and testify before a grand jury could not refuse to answer questions merely because they were based on evidence obtained from an unlawful search and seizure. In outlining the reasons for the Court's decision, Justice Powell first noted that

> [d]espite its broad deterrent purpose, the exclusionary rule has never been interpreted to proscribe the use of illegally seized evidence in all proceedings or against all persons. As with any remedial device, the application of the rule has been restricted to those areas where its remedial objectives are thought most efficaciously served.

With this statement, Justice Powell opened the door for the following "balancing" test for when to use the exclusionary rule:

> In deciding whether to extend the exclusionary rule to grand jury proceedings, we must weigh the potential injury to the historical role and functions of the grand jury against the potential benefits of the rule as applied in this context.

The Court concluded that "extension of the exclusionary rule would seriously impede the grand jury" in its investigatory function, whereas "[a]ny incremental deterrent effect which might be achieved by extending the rule to grand jury proceedings is uncertain at best," particularly since illegally seized evidence would still be barred at trial.

Calandra makes sense if the person who is seeking to exclude evidence at the grand jury proceeding is later indicted. But if, as was true in *Calandra,* the person seeking exclusion is a witness, rather than the putative defendant, *Calandra* means that the police action will never be challenged in a criminal proceeding, since the defendant, under the rules of standing, cannot challenge a violation of someone else's privacy rights.[19] *Calandra* thus

---

17. *United States v. Calandra,* 414 U.S. 338, 94 S.Ct. 613 (1974).

18. Id.

19. See § 4.04.

sends the wrong message to police who are conducting searches and seizures of people unlikely to be indicted, but who are somehow relevant to an investigation.

In *Stone v. Powell*,[20] the Court relied heavily on *Calandra's* balancing analysis in rejecting application of the exclusionary rule in habeas corpus proceedings. The Court held, 6–3, that where the state has provided an opportunity for the "full and fair litigation" of a Fourth Amendment claim,[21] a state prisoner may not be granted federal habeas relief on that claim regardless of its merit. Justice Powell, again writing the Court's decision, stated that the "deflection of truthfinding" inherent in the use of the exclusionary rule outweighed any deterrent force that use of the rule might have in a federal habeas corpus proceeding—a proceeding which takes place well after the initial criminal trial and therefore is unlikely to be of concern to police when deciding whether to make a search or arrest. The Court glossed over the possibility that lack of federal review would reduce the rule's deterrent effect on state officers and state courts.

Lower courts have for the most part adopted the Supreme Court's perspective on the exclusionary rule, accepting deterrence as the rule's objective and avoiding a detailed analysis of how that objective might be undermined by failing to apply the rule. For instance, even before *Calandra,* courts were holding that the rule should not be applied to sentencing proceedings [22] or parole revocation proceedings [23] because police know that, even if the rule is not applicable at these proceedings, it will be applicable at the predicate criminal trial. Although this assumption is true as a general matter, it fails to recognize that under some circumstances a search or seizure may be carried out solely with an intent to affect sentencing or parole. Moreover, in the parole setting, the police know there is often no predicate criminal trial; parole may be revoked solely on the basis of evidence adduced at the parole hearing.[24]

(b) Non–Criminal Proceedings. Four years after *Mapp,* the Warren Court was asked to decide, in *One 1958 Plymouth Sedan v. Pennsylvania*,[25] whether the exclusionary rule applies in a civil proceeding seeking the forfeiture of an automobile that had been used in the illegal transportation of liquor. The Court answered

20. 428 U.S. 465, 96 S.Ct. 3037 (1976).

21. See § 33.02(b) for a detailed discussion of the full and fair litigation issue.

22. *United States v. Schipani,* 315 F.Supp. 253 (E.D.N.Y.1970), aff'd 435 F.2d 26 (2d Cir.1970), cert. denied 401 U.S. 983, 91 S.Ct. 1198 (1971). For a later decision, see *United States v. McCrory,* 930 F.2d 63 (D.C.Cir.1991).

23. *United States ex rel. Sperling v. Fitzpatrick,* 426 F.2d 1161 (2d Cir.1970).

24. See generally, *State v. Shirley,* 117 Ariz. 105, 570 P.2d 1278 (1977).

25. 380 U.S. 693, 85 S.Ct. 1246 (1965).

in the affirmative when, as here, there "is nothing even remotely criminal in possessing an automobile" and the nature of the proceeding would subject the person to significant penalties (here deprivation of a $1000 automobile). On the other hand, suggested the Court, when the individual subject to a forfeiture proceeding seeks to exclude contraband or other items which are illegal to possess, the result might be different.[26] In such cases, permitting exclusion would be tantamount to returning the items to the owner, which "would clearly . . . frustrate . . . the express public policy against the possession of such objects."

If the evidence sought to be excluded in a forfeiture proceeding is a *fruit* of a crime, such as gambling proceeds, the analysis is less clear. One might argue that, under *Plymouth Sedan,* the rule should apply since possession of such money may not be a crime and, in any event, deprivation of it might work a substantial hardship. In this context, however, the Court has moved away from *Plymouth Sedan's* focus on the type of penalty that might be imposed in the civil proceeding and relied instead on the *Calandra* balancing test. In *United States v. Janis,*[27] Janis successfully excluded cash and wagering records at his trial on illegal gambling charges and then moved to exclude them again in a subsequent civil action brought by the Internal Revenue Service. Despite evidence that the police officer involved in the illegal search routinely notified the IRS when he uncovered major gambling operations, the Court concluded that the gain in deterrence from suppression in an IRS proceeding would be negligible, since the civil proceeding "falls outside the offending officer's zone of primary interest."

This type of reasoning might also support foregoing application of the exclusionary rule in other civil proceedings that are subsidiary to criminal prosecutions investigated by the police.[28] But where the civil proceeding is the principal focus of the investigating agent, then the lower courts have applied the exclusionary rule. Thus, for instance, the rule has been applied in juvenile delinquency proceedings [29] and certain types of administrative proceedings.[30]

26. Cf. *United States v. Jeffers,* 342 U.S. 48, 72 S.Ct. 93 (1951) (government may refuse to return unlawfully seized narcotics); *Trupiano v. United States,* 334 U.S. 699, 68 S.Ct. 1229 (1948) (government may refuse to return unregistered still and mash).

27. 428 U.S. 433, 96 S.Ct. 3021 (1976).

28. E.g., addict commitment proceedings that take place after criminal conviction for drug use. Cf. *People v.*

Moore, 69 Cal.2d 674, 72 Cal.Rptr. 800, 446 P.2d 800 (1968).

29. *State in Interest of T.L.O.,* 94 N.J. 331, 463 A.2d 934 (1983), rev'd on other grounds *New Jersey v. T.L.O.,* 469 U.S. 325, 105 S.Ct. 733 (1985).

30. *Donovan v. Sarasota Concrete Co.,* 693 F.2d 1061 (11th Cir.1982) (OSHA proceedings, but adopting a good faith exception as well); *Midwest Growers Cooperative Corp. v. Kirkemo,* 533 F.2d 455 (9th Cir.1976) (ICC); *Knoll*

As sensible as this "zone of primary interest" analysis might seem from the deterrence perspective, the Supreme Court has been unwilling to apply it in at least one case. In *Immigration and Naturalization Service v. Lopez-Mendoza,*[31] the Court, relying on the more general balancing test adopted in *Calandra*, held that the rule need not apply in civil deportation hearings even though these proceedings are the principal "zone of interest" of INS officers. Looking first at the social benefits derived from applying the rule in such proceedings, the Court concluded that any deterrent value would be slight. Justice O'Connor's majority opinion pointed out, for instance, that since most illegal aliens agree to voluntary deportation without a formal hearing, INS officers know a Fourth Amendment challenge is rare and are therefore unlikely to be concerned about having evidence excluded. Moreover, the INS has its own comprehensive scheme for regulating detentions and searches and providing remedies for violations of the regulations. Among the social costs of imposing the rule, on the other hand, are the release of illegal aliens in this country and a "severe" burden on the INS' "deliberately simple deportation hearing system, streamlined to permit the quick resolution of very large numbers of deportation actions." The Court concluded that the balancing test made exclusion of illegally obtained evidence unnecessary in such a system.

Missing from all of these decisions is any serious effort to assess the value of the second benefit which the *Mapp* Court felt would derive from the exclusionary rule—the preservation of judicial integrity. The Court's analysis of the exclusionary rule in contexts outside the initial criminal trial has focused almost entirely on weighing the deterrent effect of the rule against the cost to society of losing the probative value of the evidence.

(c) The Reasonable "Good Faith" Exception. The Court's willingness to balance the social costs and benefits of the exclusionary rule has also been manifested in cases involving the rule's application at the criminal adjudication itself. Specifically, the Court has slowly, though inexorably, moved toward the position that when an illegal search or seizure is committed by police who are "reasonably" not aware they are violating Fourth Amendment principles, the exclusionary rule can have no deterrent effect and therefore, in light of the "enormous cost" associated with exclusion, should not operate to exclude evidence at trial. In decisions adopting this approach, the majority has again either ignored the precept that the judicial system should not be a party to police illegality, or argued that judicial integrity is not implicated be-

Associates, Inc. v. FTC, 397 F.2d 530 (7th Cir.1968) (FTC).   **31.** 468 U.S. 1032, 104 S.Ct. 3479 (1984).

cause the violation has already occurred by the time the evidence is used in court.

(1) Early manifestations. One of the first Supreme Court decisions recognizing the so-called "good faith" concept was *United States v. Peltier,*[32] a 1975 decision which declined to apply retroactively the Court's decision in *Almeida-Sanchez v. United States* (holding unconstitutional random stops by roving border patrols).[33] Noting that immigration officers operating such patrols *before* the *Almeida-Sanchez* decision could not have known their actions were illegal, the Court reasoned "[i]f the purpose of the exclusionary rule is to deter unlawful police conduct, then evidence obtained from a search should be suppressed only if it can be said that the law enforcement officer had knowledge, or may properly be charged with knowledge, that the search was unconstitutional under the Fourth Amendment."[34]

Just one year after *Peltier,* Justice White, in a dissenting opinion to *Stone v. Powell,*[35] advocated extending *Peltier's* reasoning beyond cases involving the retroactivity issue. Specifically, he argued that the exclusionary rule "should be substantially modified so as to prevent its application in those many circumstances where the evidence at issue was seized by an officer acting in the good-faith belief that his conduct comported with existing law and having reasonable grounds for this belief." After cataloging several situations in which he thought an officer might justifiably, although mistakenly, believe he had probable cause to arrest or search, Justice White continued:

> In these situations, and perhaps many others, excluding the evidence will not further the ends of the exclusionary rule in any appreciable way; for it is painfully apparent that in each of them the officer is acting as a reasonable officer would and should act in similar circumstances. Excluding the evidence can in no way affect his future conduct unless it is to make him less willing to do his duty. It is true that in such cases the courts have ultimately determined that in their view the officer was mistaken; but it is also true that in making constitutional judgments under the general language used in some parts of our Constitution, including the Fourth Amendment, there is much room for disagreement among judges each of whom is convinced that both he and his colleagues are reasonable men.

32. 422 U.S. 531, 95 S.Ct. 2313 (1975).

33. See § 13.05(b).

34. For further discussion of retroactivity doctrine, see § 29.07.

35. 428 U.S. 465, 96 S.Ct. 3037 (1976).

Although no member of the Court joined Justice White's opinion in *Powell, Michigan v. DeFillippo,*[36] decided three years later, made it clear that a majority of the Court was at least sympathetic with his views.[37] DeFillippo was arrested by Detroit police for violating a city "Stop and Identify" ordinance. The ordinance provided that a police officer may stop and question an individual if the officer has reasonable cause to believe that the individual's behavior warrants further investigation for criminal activity. A 1976 amendment to the ordinance provided that it is unlawful for any person stopped under the section to refuse to identify himself and produce evidence of his identity. The Michigan courts held that the ordinance was unconstitutionally vague and that, because it was the basis for DeFillippo's arrest, both the arrest and subsequent search were invalid. The Supreme Court reversed, holding that "[a] prudent officer, in the course of determining whether respondent had committed an offense under all the circumstances shown by this record, should not have been required to anticipate that a court would later hold the ordinance unconstitutional." In terms echoing its *Calandra* balancing analysis,[38] the Court noted that excluding the evidence under such circumstances would be unlikely to deter police. However, the Court refused to cast its holding broadly, noting that the case did not involve a statute authorizing unconstitutional *searches or seizures.*[39]

Despite the narrow scope of its holding, *DeFillippo* illustrated the Court's continued interest in the good faith notion. For several years the Court continued to flirt with the idea. In 1980 it denied *certiorari* on a decision which had adopted a good faith exception to the exclusionary rule.[40] In 1983, the Court asked the parties in *Illinois v. Gates*[41] to argue the validity of the exception even though the state had not asserted good faith as a defense in the lower courts. Then, at least in part because the issue had not

36. 443 U.S. 31, 99 S.Ct. 2627 (1979).

37. See also, *United States v. Caceres,* 440 U.S. 741, 99 S.Ct. 1465 (1979). Respondent had challenged evidence obtained during an Internal Revenue Service monitoring to which he had consented, on the grounds that the I.R.S. had not complied with its own regulations governing such monitoring. The Court refused, 7–2, to adopt a rigid exclusionary rule in situations where the agency action demonstrates a reasonable, good faith attempt to comply with its regulations. Here the Court found there had been such a good faith effort.

It should be noted, however, that *Caceres* did not involve a Fourth Amendment violation (the respondent had consented to the monitoring), but merely a violation of internal agency guidelines. While respondent (and Justice Marshall in dissent) argued that this oversight implicated a constitutional *due process* interest, the majority refused to so find.

38. See § 2.03(a).

39. Eventually, the Court did away with this limitation. See, *Illinois v. Krull,* 480 U.S. 340, 107 S.Ct. 1160 (1987), discussed in § 2.03(c)(4).

40. *United States v. Williams,* 622 F.2d 830 (5th Cir.1980), cert. denied 449 U.S. 1127, 101 S.Ct. 946 (1981).

41. 462 U.S. 213, 103 S.Ct. 2317 (1983).

been argued below, the Court, "with apologies to all," decided *Gates* on other grounds.

(2) Warrant-based searches. One year later, in the companion cases of *United States v. Leon* [42] and *Massachusetts v. Sheppard*,[43] the Court finally did address the appropriateness of the exception, at least as it applied to searches conducted pursuant to a warrant. In *Leon*, it held, by a 6–3 margin, that evidence may be used in the prosecution's case-in-chief when obtained by police acting on authority of a warrant subsequently found to be unsupported by probable cause, provided that they had an objective good faith belief the warrant was valid and that the warrant was issued by a "neutral and detached" magistrate. In *Sheppard*, it concluded, again 6–3, that evidence obtained pursuant to a warrant for which there is probable cause but which is defective on its face is also admissible in the prosecution's case-in-chief, at least when the officer executing the warrant is the one who requested it. Both decisions mark a major change in the Court's stance on the exclusionary rule.

Not surprisingly, given his vigorous advocacy of the good faith exception over the previous decade, Justice White was chosen to write the majority opinion for both decisions. He began by asserting, as the Court had in several past cases, that the exclusionary rule is not constitutionally required but rather is a judicially created remedy which may be modified when its social costs outweigh its benefits. In the specific context of searches conducted pursuant to a warrant, Justice White perceived few benefits to weigh against the cost of excluding relevant evidence of criminal activity. Imposing the exclusionary rule in such a situation could have virtually no deterrent effect on the police, he argued, because the judicial officer makes the decision to arrest or search. Nor, in White's opinion, would it act as a significant deterrent on judges and magistrates.

> [W]e cannot conclude that admitting evidence obtained pursuant to a warrant while at the same time declaring that the warrant was somehow defective will in any way reduce judicial officers' professional incentives to comply with the Fourth Amendment, encourage them to repeat their mistakes, or lead to the granting of all colorable warrant requests.

Thus, "when an officer acting with objective good faith has obtained a search warrant and acted within its scope" there is no point in imposing the exclusionary rule if the warrant happens to be invalid.

Justice White emphasized that the good faith test he announced is an objective one. From this, he derived several limita-

42. 468 U.S. 897, 104 S.Ct. 3405 (1984).   **43.** 468 U.S. 981, 104 S.Ct. 3424 (1984).

tions. If the affidavit supporting the warrant is "so lacking in indicia of probable cause as to render official belief in its existence entirely unreasonable" [44] or if the warrant is "so facially deficient—i.e., in failing to particularize the place to be searched or things to be seized—that the executing officers cannot reasonably presume it to be valid," [45] then the exception does not apply. Moreover, regardless of good faith, suppression will still occur when the magistrate is misled by information in the affidavit that the affiant knew was false,[46] or when the magistrate "wholly abandon[s] his judicial role" in issuing the warrant.[47]

Justice White's opinion relies heavily on several questionable assumptions about police and judicial behavior. For instance, commentators have long expressed fear that a good faith exception will encourage "shopping" for magistrates willing to act as "rubber-stamps" for police who will now realize that most illicit actions, once judicially authorized, no longer lead to exclusion. Although Justice White recognized the possibility of compliant or incompetent magistrates, he stated, despite evidence to the contrary,[48] that "we are not convinced that this is a problem of major proportions." He also may have been unduly sanguine about the willingness of even those magistrates who are competent to scrutinize warrant applications, now that a good faith exception exists. As Justice Brennan argued in dissent,

> [c]reation of this new exception for good faith reliance upon a warrant implicitly tells magistrates that they need not take much care in reviewing warrant applications, since their mistakes will from now on have virtually no consequence: If their decision to issue a warrant is correct, the evidence will be admitted; if their decision was incorrect but [not "entirely unreasonable" and] the police rely in good faith on the warrant, the evidence will also be admitted. Inevitably, the care

---

44. See, e.g. *United States v. Hove,* 848 F.2d 137 (9th Cir.1988); (obviously deficient affidavit cannot be cured by affiant's later testimony); *United States v. Huggins,* 733 F.Supp. 445 (D.C.1990) (belief that probable cause existed unreasonable where no way for magistrate to determine whether information in affidavit stale).

45. See, e.g., *United States v. Leary,* 846 F.2d 592 (10th Cir.1988) (warrant so factually overbroad in description of items to be seized that agents could not reasonably rely on it).

46. See, e.g., *United States v. Baxter,* 889 F.2d 731 (6th Cir.1989) (exception does not apply where affidavit contained knowing misstatement as to nature of informant).

47. *Lo–Ji v. State of New York,* 442 U.S. 319, 99 S.Ct. 2319 (1979) (discussed in § 5.02).

48. See Van Duizend, Sutton and Cater, The Search Warrant Process: Preconceptions, Perceptions and Practices 32 (National Center for State Courts) (study of seven cities finding that "judge shopping" often occurs). See also, 2 W. LaFave, Search and Seizure § 4.1 (1978); Kamisar, "Does (Did) (Should) the Exclusionary Rule Rest on a 'Principled Basis' Rather than an 'Empirical Proposition'?," 16 Creighton L.Rev. 565, 569–71 (1983); Schroeder, "Deterring Fourth Amendment Violations: Alternatives to the Exclusionary Rule," 69 Geo.L.J. 1361, 1412 (1981).

and attention devoted to such an inconsequential chore will dwindle.

Similarly, Justice Brennan argued that police training programs will deemphasize Fourth Amendment jurisprudence as a result of *Leon* and *Sheppard.* Although the majority opinion asserted that the reasonableness standard would forestall such a development,[49] it is not unrealistic to predict that some officers will now merely be taught to recognize when, to use the majority's language, it is "*entirely* unreasonable" to believe probable cause exists. In all other cases, suggested Justice Brennan, police will be told simply to make sure the warrant has been signed, because "there will no longer be any incentive to err on the side of constitutional behavior."

Two additional concerns about the good faith exception which are given similarly short shrift by the majority opinion have to do with its effect on appellate review. First, as with other "totality of the circumstances" tests, the good faith exception might cause considerable judicial confusion. In response to this concern, Justice White simply stated that the exception, "turning as it does on objective reasonableness, should not be difficult to apply in practice." But the decision as to what is "entirely unreasonable" is sure to vary across jurisdictions depending upon a particular court's views on the costs of the exclusionary rule. Indeed, a survey of lower court cases between 1984 and 1990 found considerable conceptual confusion about the good faith exception and many examples of its "misapplication," in large part because the exception "introduces new uncertainty about when the [exclusionary] rule will apply, producing an excess of discretionary leeway." [50]

Secondly, the good faith exception might remove incentive to develop or clarify substantive Fourth Amendment law, since the courts can avoid such decisions, which are often difficult, simply by holding the officer acted in reasonable good faith reliance on a warrant. This latter point is illustrated by both *Leon* and *Sheppard.* In *Leon,* the warrant application was based in part on information supplied by a confidential informant of unproven reliability who came to police over five months before the application was submitted. Although the police independently investigat-

---

49. The Court quoted Professor Israel to the effect that "the possibility that illegally obtained evidence may be admitted in borderline cases is unlikely to encourage police instructors to pay less attention to the Fourth Amendment" nor should it "encourage officers to pay less attention to what they are taught, as the requirement that the officer act in 'good faith' is inconsistent with closing one's mind to the possibility of illegality." Israel, "Criminal Procedure, the Burger Court and the Legacy of the Warren Court," 75 Mich.L. Rev. 1319, 1412–13 (1977).

50. Esseks, "Errors in Good Faith: The *Leon* Exception Six Years Later," 89 Mich.L.Rev. 625 (1990).

ed this information, both the district court and the court of appeals concluded that the additional data failed to corroborate the details of the tip in the manner required under the Court's decisions in *Aguilar v. Texas*[51] and *Spinelli v. United States.*[52] However, as Justice Stevens pointed out in his dissent to *Leon*, the Court's subsequent decision in *Illinois v. Gates*[53] had modified the *Aguilar-Spinelli* test to the point where the tip might have been sufficient to issue the warrant.[54] Because the majority found that the officer in *Leon* acted in good faith, it neglected to decide whether the warrant was in fact valid under *Gates,* and thus failed to clarify this point.

Similarly, *Sheppard* conceivably could have been decided on substantive grounds rather than as a "good faith" case. In *Sheppard,* the Massachusetts Supreme Court had excluded certain evidence connecting the defendant to a murder because the search which produced it had been conducted pursuant to a warrant which, on its face, authorized only a search for controlled substances, and which thus violated the "particularity" requirement of the Fourth Amendment.[55] The Supreme Court, relying on the newly created good faith exception, reversed this decision because the officer who conducted the search had drafted an affidavit which in fact set out sufficient facts to establish probable cause with respect to the seized items; the reason the warrant had not listed those items is because at the time the warrant was issued the issuing judge had only been able to find a warrant form for controlled substances and had neglected to replace the references to controlled substances with the appropriate evidentiary descriptions. As Justice Stevens pointed out, the same reasoning could have supported a holding that the particularity clause of the Fourth Amendment was not violated in the first place, since "the judge who issued the warrant, the police officers who executed it, and the reviewing courts all were able to ascertain the precise scope of the authorization provided by the court" by consulting the attached affidavit. Regardless of the validity of Justice Stevens' analysis, the point is that the majority failed even to consider it because the good faith analysis made such consideration unnecessary.

(3) Warrantless searches. Obviously, a number of empirical issues are raised by *Leon* and *Sheppard* regarding the impact of the good faith exception on police, magistrates and the courts. In a concurring opinion, Justice Blackmun indicated that he, at least, would reconsider the decision "[i]f it should emerge from experi-

---

51. 378 U.S. 108, 84 S.Ct. 1509 (1964).

52. 393 U.S. 410, 89 S.Ct. 584 (1969).

53. 462 U.S. 213, 103 S.Ct. 2317 (1983).

54. See § 5.03(b) for a discussion of the *Aguilar-Spinelli* rules and *Gates'* modification of them.

55. See § 5.04 for a discussion of the particularity requirement.

ence that, contrary to our expectations, the good faith exception to the exclusionary rule results in a material change in police compliance with the Fourth Amendment." There are vague indications that other members of the majority feel similarly.[56] However, there is a greater possibility that, rather than retreating from the good faith exception as adopted in *Leon* and *Sheppard,* the Court will expand on the idea and apply it to any case, including those involving warrantless searches and seizures, in which the officer reasonably believed he acted constitutionally. Relevant to this point, it is noteworthy that, in *Leon,* Justice White quoted liberally from *Peltier* and his dissent in *Powell* to the effect that a search conducted in reasonable good faith should not trigger the exclusionary sanction. His subsequent statement that this precept was "particularly true" in situations such as those involved in *Leon* suggests that it might also be "true," as far as the majority is concerned, in cases which do not involve warrants.

At least one federal court of appeals has adopted a broad good faith exception,[57] and several state legislatures have followed suit.[58] A good faith exception to exclusion of evidence illegally obtained via a warrantless search or seizure suffers from the same defects as the *Leon* exception: Fourth Amendment jurisprudence becomes secondary to what a "reasonable officer" would believe, thus encouraging police nonchalance toward the law and retarding its development. In addition, of course, the broader good faith exception does not offer whatever protection against abuse that review by a judicial officer provides.

Nonetheless, it cannot be denied that exclusion under all circumstances (such as on the facts of *Sheppard*) seems silly. Sometimes the substantive law can be modified to take into account a minor divergence from the traditional rule (as might have been the case with the particularity requirement at issue in *Sheppard*). But, if not, something short of a full-blown good faith exception to the exclusionary rule may be appropriate. Perhaps a *de minimis* violation or "clerical error" exception should be recognized.[59]

56. In *Immigration & Naturalization Service v. Lopez-Mendoza,* supra note 31, Justices O'Connor, Blackmun, Powell and Rehnquist joined in that part of the opinion which, in the context of holding the exclusionary rule need not apply in civil deportation proceedings, stated: "Our conclusions concerning the exclusionary rule's value [in deportation proceedings] might change, if there developed good reason to believe that Fourth Amendment violations by INS officers were widespread." The opinion then cited Blackmun's concurring opinion in *Leon.*

Presumably, Justices Brennan, Marshall, and Stevens, all of whom dissented in *Lopez-Mendoza,* would agree with this statement.

57. *United States v. Williams,* 622 F.2d 830 (5th Cir.1980).

58. Ariz.Rev.Stat. § 12–3925; Colo. Rev.Stat.1973, 16–3–308.

59. See *United States v. Gordon,* 901 F.2d 48 (5th Cir.1990) (good faith exception applies when warrant invalid because of incorrect street address, since executing officer was also the affiant and had recently viewed the location).

(4) Statute–based searches. Like *DeFillippo, Illinois v. Krull,*[60] involved police activity pursuant to a law subsequently found unconstitutional. However, *Krull* differed from *DeFillippo* in one respect. Whereas the ordinance in *DeFillippo* had unconstitutionally criminalized innocent behavior, the statute in *Krull* was found to authorize unconstitutional *searches.* As pointed out earlier, the *DeFillippo* majority had carefully avoided applying its holding to the latter type of statute, noting that several previous Court decisions had excluded evidence seized pursuant to such laws after they were found unconstitutional.[61] The five-member majority in *Krull* saw no difference between the two types of enactments, however. Instead, it found that the situation in *Krull* was analogous to the situation in *Leon,* with the sole difference that the police were relying on a decision of the *legislature* rather than a magistrate. And just as the *Leon* Court had felt that the threat of exclusion was not necessary to ensure carefulness on the part of the magistrate, the Court in *Krull* asserted that a legislature was unlikely to pass unconstitutional statutes merely because the exclusionary remedy was unavailable to defendants searched under such laws. However, analogous to its holding in *Leon* permitting exclusion of evidence when the warrant issued by the magistrate is entirely unreasonable on its face, the Court stated that in the statutory search context exclusion would be appropriate when the legislature "wholly abandon[s] its responsibility to enact constitutional laws."

In dissent, Justice O'Connor, joined by Justices Brennan, Marshall and Stevens, argued that the analogy to *Leon* was inapposite. Legislation affects many more individuals than a single warrant and is more likely to be the product of political pressure. Thus, O'Connor suggested, the need for deterrence is heightened. Yet without the exclusionary remedy, individual litigants are unlikely to challenge legislation (although, as the majority pointed out, injunctive and declaratory relief is still available). O'Connor also noted the difficulty of defining "good faith" in the statutory context. Whereas *Leon* merely requires proof of a facially valid warrant in order to trigger the good faith exception of that case, the rule in *Krull* requires courts "to determine at what point a reasonable officer should be held to know that a statute has, under evolving legal rules, become 'clearly' unconstitutional." [62]

An analogous exception has developed in determining the appropriate sanction under the federal electronic surveillance statute. See § 14.03(g)(2), (3).

60. 480 U.S. 340, 107 S.Ct. 1160 (1987).

61. See, e.g., *Torres v. Puerto Rico,* 442 U.S. 465, 99 S.Ct. 2425 (1979); *Al-*

meida–Sanchez v. United States, 413 U.S. 266, 93 S.Ct. 2535 (1973); *Berger v. New York,* 388 U.S. 41, 87 S.Ct. 1873 (1967).

62. As Justice O'Connor pointed out, the constitutionality of the statute at issue in *Krull* was still unclear six years after the search in that case.

(d) Impeachment Evidence. Unless one of the good faith exceptions is met, evidence obtained through an illegal search and seizure is excludable from the prosecution's case-in-chief. However, if the prosecution seeks to use the evidence to impeach the defendant once he takes the stand, then exclusion is unlikely. Again, the Court has reasoned that excluding the evidence from the prosecution's case-in-chief has sufficient deterrent effect. Rebuttal of testimony from persons other than the defendant, however, may not rely on evidence obtained through an illegal search and seizure.

(1) Against the defendant. The Court first considered use of such evidence as an impeachment device in *Agnello v. United States*,[63] decided in 1925. There the Court held that illegally seized evidence may not be relied upon in federal cases for any purpose. Almost thirty years later, in *Walder v. United States*,[64] the Court permitted a limited exception to this rule, where the defendant in effect waives his Fourth Amendment protection by testifying on direct examination to matters going beyond the elements of the charge against him. In such cases, the Court held, the prosecution may rebut the tangential assertions with illegally obtained evidence. In *Walder,* involving a narcotics charge, the Court approved prosecution use of heroin illegally seized two years earlier to impeach statements the defendant made on direct to the effect that he had *never* purchased, sold or possessed narcotics. But the Court emphasized that the defendant must be "free to deny all the elements of the [current] case against him."

The next time the Court considered the impeachment issue, some twenty-five years later, it overruled *Agnello* (without mentioning the case) and ignored the limitations imposed in *Walder.* Building on its earlier decision permitting impeachment with evidence seized in violation of the Fifth Amendment,[65] the Court's decision in *United States v. Havens*[66] authorized use of illegally seized items to contradict statements about the crime charged as well as testimony on collateral matters. In a 5–4 opinion, the Court, through Justice White, reasoned that exclusion in such cases would only minimally deter police misconduct, and at the same time encourage perjury by the defendant.

Concern about perjury also led the *Havens* Court to permit impeachment of statements first made on *cross*-examination. Because of "the importance of arriving at the truth in criminal trials, as well as the defendant's obligation to speak the truth in response to proper questions," there is "no difference of constitu-

---

63. 269 U.S. 20, 46 S.Ct. 4 (1925).

64. 347 U.S. 62, 74 S.Ct. 354 (1954).

65. *Harris v. New York,* 401 U.S. 222, 91 S.Ct. 643 (1971), discussed in detail in § 16.05(b)(1).

66. 446 U.S. 620, 100 S.Ct. 1912 (1980).

tional magnitude between the defendant's statements on direct examination and his answers to questions put to him on cross-examination that are plainly within the scope of the defendant's direct examination." The test of admissibility should be whether the questions on cross "would have been suggested to a reasonably competent cross-examiner" by direct testimony.

The Court found this test met in *Havens*. The defendant took the stand after one McLeroth testified that Havens had cut swatches out of his T-shirt and used them to sew pockets in McLeroth's undershirt for the purpose of carrying cocaine. On direct, Havens denied that he had engaged in any activity like that described by McLeroth, but made no mention of the T-shirt. On cross-examination, in response to questions, Havens more specifically denied having anything "to do with the sewing of the cotton swatches to make pockets on that T-shirt," and answered "Not to my knowledge" when asked if he had a T-shirt with missing patches in his luggage at the time he was arrested. In rebuttal, the government introduced a T-shirt, from which material had been cut, that had been found in Havens luggage after an illegal search. The Court found nothing improper in this action, noting that the trial judge instructed the jury to consider the impeachment evidence only on the issue of credibility.

Even if the Court is right that exclusion of such evidence is unlikely to deter illegal searches, *Havens* is sure to discourage some defendants from taking the stand, in derogation of their right to testify.[67] Defendants must now take into consideration that anything they say on direct examination, even if it merely involves denying the charge, might be impeached with illegally obtained evidence. And even if they avoid saying something rebuttable during direct, they may nonetheless be forced to do so during cross, since, as Justice Brennan pointed out in dissent, "even the moderately talented prosecutor [can] work in . . . evidence on cross-examination." *Walder's* waiver approach has been significantly undermined, if not rejected completely. *Havens'* ultimate impact on the accuracy of the fact-finding process is harder to gauge.

(2) Against other witnesses. While there are few restrictions on using illegally obtained evidence to impeach the defendant, the state is prohibited from impeaching a witness *other* than the defendant with such evidence. In *James v. Illinois*,[68] the Court decided, 5–4, that such a rule is necessary, despite its possible impact on truthfinding, for three reasons. First, while a perjury prosecution is unlikely to be a significant concern for a defendant

67. The Court recognized this right in *Rock v. Arkansas*, 479 U.S. 1079, 107 S.Ct. 1276 (1987), discussed in § 28.07(a).

68. 493 U.S. 307, 110 S.Ct. 648 (1990).

already facing possible conviction and sentence, it is likely to deter outright falsification by other witnesses; accordingly, the additional incentive to tell the truth provided by impeachment with illegally obtained evidence is not as great.   Second, a rule permitting such impeachment would chill the defendant's willingness to put on witnesses, thus detracting from, rather than enhancing, the truthseeking function of trial.   Third, such a rule would give even more incentive to the police to violate the Fourth Amendment, since they would know that even though such a violation would mean exclusion from the prosecution's case-in-chief, it would permit impeachment not only of the defendant but of the defendant's witnesses.

The dissent, written by Justice Kennedy, labelled as speculative or unrealistic the assumptions made by the majority.   Kennedy indicated he might be willing to distinguish between treatment of defendants and other witnesses to the extent of banning illegal evidence impeachment of cross-examination statements made by the latter (a rule *Havens* rejected as to statements by the defendant).   But he characterized the majority's holding as "a wooden rule immunizing . . . defense testimony from rebuttal, without regard to knowledge that the testimony introduced at the behest of the defendant is false or perjured."

2.04   The "Fruit of the Poisonous Tree" Doctrine

(a) **Rationale.**   Unlike the doctrines previously discussed, the "fruit of the poisonous tree" doctrine tends to expand rather than restrict the use of the exclusionary rule.   Suppose that certain evidence is excluded because it was procured through unconstitutional means.   Suppose further that this evidence, though excluded, leads the police to the discovery of other evidence which is procured through *lawful* means.   Should this derivatively acquired evidence be admissible?   The "fruit of the poisonous tree" doctrine is intended to answer this question.   In broad form, the rule states that evidence derived from information acquired by police officials through unlawful means is not admissible in a criminal prosecution.   As such, it represents an extension of the exclusionary rule.

The doctrine is usually said to have originated in *Silverthorne Lumber Co. v. United States.*[69]   In that case, the defendant company was convicted on contempt charges for failing to produce documents the existence of which the government discovered through an illegal search.   The Supreme Court, speaking through Justice Holmes, reversed the conviction, 7–2, holding that "[t]he essence of a provision forbidding the acquisition of evidence in a certain way is that not merely evidence so acquired shall not be

---

69.   251 U.S. 385, 40 S.Ct. 182 (1920).

used before the Court but that it shall not be used at all." To hold otherwise, reasoned Holmes, "reduces the Fourth Amendment to a form of words." The Court reaffirmed this notion in *Nardone v. United States,*[70] but recognized that merely establishing a logical connection between an illegality and the procurement of evidence should not automatically lead to exclusion. In doing so, the Court, through Justice Frankfurter, developed the colorful lexicon that today is associated with derivative evidence analysis. Frankfurter stated that it should be left to the discretion of "experienced trial judges" whether "a substantial portion of the case against [the accused] was a fruit of the poisonous tree." In some cases, "sophisticated argument may prove a causal link obtained through [illegality] and the Government's proof. As a matter of good sense, however, such a connection may have become so attenuated as to dissipate the taint."

In determining when "fruit" of police illegality is nonetheless admissible, three related doctrines have been developed by the courts: the attenuation doctrine (so-called as a result of Frankfurter's usage of that term in *Nardone*), the independent source doctrine, and the inevitable discovery doctrine. Here these doctrines will be examined primarily through cases in which the initial illegality was a violation of the Fourth Amendment. However, as subsequent discussion shows,[71] the triggering violation may be of other constitutional provisions as well. As one might expect, in light of the Court's recent pronouncements concerning the exclusionary rule, the modern rationale for all three doctrines is that fruit of an illegality should be excluded only when the deterrence objective of the rule would be meaningfully furthered.

(b) The Attenuation Exception. Twenty-five years after *Nardone,* Justice Brennan, in the case of *Wong Sun v. United States,*[72] reframed Frankfurter's "attenuation" idea as an analysis of whether the derivative evidence "has been come at by exploitation of [the initial] illegality or instead by means sufficiently distinguishable to be purged of the primary taint." [73] Using this test, the Court excluded various admissions and confessions by one defendant because they were acquired immediately following his unlawful arrest, as well as narcotics obtained from another person because their whereabouts were discovered solely as a result of the defendant's declarations. However, the Court felt that the statement of a second defendant, voluntarily made when he returned to the stationhouse on his own initiative several days after he was released on his own recognizance, could not be said to have been

---

70. 308 U.S. 338, 60 S.Ct. 266 (1939).

71. See § 2.04(c). See also, § 16.05(c) (confession as poisonous tree) and § 17.05 (identification as poisonous tree).

72. 371 U.S. 471, 83 S.Ct. 407 (1963).

73. This phrase was taken from Maguire, Evidence of Guilt 221 (1959).

obtained by exploitation of the illegally acquired information. Even though he too was located as a result of an unlawful arrest, the relation between the arrest and the defendant's voluntary statement "had 'become so attenuated as to dissipate the taint.'"

The attenuation doctrine has since been applied in a number of Supreme Court cases. Considered first are the cases, like *Wong Sun*, in which the "fruit" is a confession. Then we examine those cases in which other types of fruit are involved.

(1) Confessions as fruit. *Wong Sun* made clear that the overriding issue in deciding whether the taint of an illegality has been dissipated is whether the resulting confession is "an act of free will." In *Brown v. Illinois*,[74] the Court catalogued several factors courts should consider in deciding whether a confession is an act of free will rather than tainted by previous illegality: (1) whether *Miranda* warnings [75] were given prior to any confession or admission; (2) the "temporal proximity" of the illegal police conduct and the verbal statements; (3) the presence of intervening circumstances or events; and (4) the "purpose and flagrancy of the official misconduct."

Several cases flesh out these factors. In *Dunaway v. New York*,[76] police brought the defendant to the stationhouse for an interrogation even though they had no probable cause to arrest him. After being given *Miranda* warnings, Dunaway confessed to a robbery-murder. Justice Brennan, writing for the majority, first found that a detention merely for custodial interrogation "intrudes so severely on interests protected by the Fourth Amendment as necessarily to trigger the traditional safeguards against illegal arrest." He then stated that the confession deriving from this illegal detention should have been suppressed despite the police's compliance with *Miranda*. Citing *Brown*, he noted that the confession had followed so closely upon the detention and the police's conduct had so clearly violated Fourth Amendment policies that the confession could not be separated from the initial illegality. To hold otherwise would allow " 'law enforcement officers to violate the Fourth Amendment with impunity, safe in the knowledge that they could wash their hands in the "procedural safeguards" of the Fifth.' "

Similarly, in *Taylor v. Alabama*,[77] the Court held that even though: (1) the defendant had been given *Miranda* warnings three times between the illegal arrest and his confession; (2) six hours had elapsed between the arrest and the confession; and (3) the

74. 422 U.S. 590, 95 S.Ct. 2254 (1975).

75. See § 16.02(d) for a discussion of the warning requirement announced in *Miranda v. Arizona*, 384 U.S. 436, 86 S.Ct. 1602 (1966).

76. 442 U.S. 200, 99 S.Ct. 2248 (1979).

77. 457 U.S. 687, 102 S.Ct. 2664 (1982).

defendant was permitted to see two friends before the confession, there were insufficient intervening events to attenuate the taint of the arrest. In contrast, in *Rawlings v. Kentucky,*[78] even though the incriminating statements were made a mere 45 minutes after the illegal arrest, they were admissible because (1) the defendant received *Miranda* warnings just prior to making the statements; (2) the defendant was in a house, in a "congenial atmosphere" with several companions present, when he made the statements; (3) the statements were spontaneous rather than a response to direct questioning; (4) the police's violation of the Fourth Amendment was not flagrant but rather apparently was a good faith mistake; and (5) the defendant did not argue his admission was involuntary.[79]

These cases suggest that the most important factors of the four listed in *Brown* are the last two: intervening events and the flagrancy of police conduct. As *Dunaway* recognized, if giving *Miranda* warnings were considered significant, police could too easily immunize their conduct. And as *Taylor* shows, a long lapse of time should not necessarily attenuate the taint; otherwise, police would be encouraged to hold those they have illegally arrested for long periods before questioning, which would only exacerbate the illegality. On the other hand, as *Rawlings* illustrates, the overall spontaneity of the statement and the good faith of the police can play an important role in determining whether the exclusionary rule applies. Recognizing these as factors to be considered in deciding whether exclusion should occur does not create as much of an incentive for police to abuse Fourth Amendment guarantees.

The Court was unwilling to consider even these factors in *New York v. Harris,*[80] however. There the police, acting without a warrant, arrested the defendant in his home several days after developing probable cause. They obtained incriminating statements from him both while he was still inside his home and after he had been taken to the stationhouse. The Supreme Court assumed with the lower courts that the arrest violated *Payton v. New York,*[81] which requires an arrest warrant for non-exigent home arrests. It further agreed with the lower courts that the statements made *in* the home should be excluded as fruit of the *Payton* violation. But while the lower appellate courts held that

---

78. 448 U.S. 98, 100 S.Ct. 2556 (1980).

79. For further contrast, compare these cases to *Oregon v. Elstad,* 470 U.S. 298, 105 S.Ct. 1285 (1985), which held that a confession given after *Miranda* warnings is never tainted by an earlier illegally obtained *confession* unless the earlier confession was the result of

"physical violence or other deliberate means calculated to break the suspect's will." See § 16.05(e)(1).

80. 495 U.S. 14, 110 S.Ct. 1640 (1990).

81. 445 U.S. 573, 100 S.Ct. 1371 (1980), discussed in § 3.04(b).

Brown's attenuation analysis also required exclusion of the stationhouse statement, the Supreme Court held, 5–4, that *Brown* was not even applicable.

Crucial to the Court's opinion, which was written by Justice White, was that a violation of *Payton* does not prevent the government from maintaining custody of an arrested defendant; the Fourth Amendment is implicated by a *Payton* violation because the police failed to get a warrant, not because they lacked probable cause to arrest. Thus, unlike in *Brown, Dunaway,* or *Taylor*— where the defendant's presence in the stationhouse was illegal because the police lacked probable cause—the stationhouse statement in *Harris* was not the product of an ongoing illegality. According to the majority, only statements made in the home are fruit of the illegality against which *Payton* was meant to protect.

As Justice Marshall, joined by Justices Brennan, Blackmun and Stevens, pointed out in dissent, this latter fact should be irrelevant to attenuation analysis. First, as contemplated by the attenuation cases, there is a clear connection between a *Payton* violation and out-of-home statements. The suspect who has been arrested in and removed from his home and family "is likely to be so frightened and rattled that he will say something incriminating. These effects, of course, extend far beyond the moment the physical occupation of the home ends." Second, Marshall argued, the majority's rule would encourage flagrant violations of *Payton* by officers who have probable cause to arrest but who want more information from the defendant and hope that a sudden warrantless home arrest will allow them to obtain it.

(2) Other types of fruit. As the preceding discussion suggests, most of the cases in which the attenuation doctrine has surfaced have involved analysis of when a confession obtained as a result of a Fourth Amendment violation is admissible. Occasionally, however, the fruit of an illegal seizure will be something else, such as identification of a person or another search. In such cases, the last three of *Brown's* factors are still relevant (*Miranda* warnings, of course, are relevant only to confessions). For instance, whether an identification during a properly conducted lineup should be admissible despite the fact it resulted from an illegal arrest depends upon intervening events (such as whether the defendant was taken before a magistrate), the voluntariness of the defendant's participation in the lineup, and the flagrancy of the arrest.[82] A similar analysis may also lead to admission of evidence found after an illegal stop if it is shown that the person stopped

---

82. See, e.g., *Johnson v. Louisiana,* 406 U.S. 356, 92 S.Ct. 1620 (1972) (where the Court held that a lineup identification need not be excluded despite an illegal arrest because the detention was under the authority of the magistrate's commitment); see also, *United States v. Crews,* 445 U.S. 463, 100 S.Ct. 1244 (1980), discussed in § 17.05.

"voluntarily" consented to the search,[83] although here one must carefully analyze both the voluntariness and flagrancy issues.

In *United States v. Ceccolini*,[84] the Court used *Brown's* analysis in deciding whether a *witness* discovered as the result of an illegal search was inadmissible fruit. In *Ceccolini*, the Fourth Amendment violation occurred when a police officer stopped to talk to his friend Hennessey at work, in the defendant's shop. In the course of their conversation, the officer peeked into a package and saw money and gambling slips. He found out from Hennessey that the package belonged to her boss and reported the incident to local detectives. They alerted the FBI, which the year before had been conducting an investigation of gambling operations in the area, including surveillance of the defendant's shop. Four months after the illegal search of the package, the FBI conducted an interview with Hennessey, and a year and a half after the search her testimony in front of a grand jury and a later trial helped convict the defendant on perjury charges.

In upholding use of Hennessey's testimony, the Court, per Justice Rehnquist, noted the "length of the road" between the search and the testimony, the fact that the witness testified of her own free will, and the absence of evidence that the search's objective was obtaining a witness against Ceccolini. The latter finding may be the most important, assuming the ultimate goal is assuring that the deterrent effect of the exclusionary rule is not undermined. While it may be true, as the Court asserted in *Ceccolini*, that witnesses "can, and often do, come forward and offer evidence entirely of their own volition" (thus giving rise to an analogy to the Court's result in *Wong Sun*), a per se rule that witnesses should not ever be considered "fruit" (which Chief Justice Burger urged in a concurring opinion) would open the door to illegal searches designed to find them.[85]

(c) The Independent Source Doctrine. Both *Silverthorne* and *Nardone* recognized that when the government can establish that evidence was obtained from a source independent of the illegal action, exclusion should not result. In such cases, there is no taint to attenuate. Thus, for instance, in *Segura v. United States*,[86] the Court held that evidence found in an apartment pursuant to a valid search warrant is admissible even if the police illegally entered the apartment prior to obtaining the warrant, so long as the warrant is based on information wholly unconnected with the initial entry and known to the police before the entry.

83. See *State v. Fortier*, 113 Ariz. 332, 553 P.2d 1206 (1976).

84. 435 U.S. 268, 98 S.Ct. 1054 (1978).

85. Another rationale for the result in *Ceccolini*, suggested by Justice Marshall in dissent, is that, in light of the ongoing FBI investigation, the government inevitably would have discovered Hennessey. See § 2.04(c).

86. 468 U.S. 796, 104 S.Ct. 3380 (1984).

The illegal entry in *Segura* took place after Segura was arrested in the lobby of his apartment building. Upon taking him back to his apartment, the police found defendant Colon, arrested him as well, and took both into custody. Agents then secured the apartment for nineteen hours pending arrival of a warrant based on information developed before their entry.

The Court, in an opinion by Chief Justice Burger, assumed that the post-arrest entry was illegal, and declared that any evidence found as a direct result of that entry was inadmissible. But it emphasized the independent basis of the warrant, and thus concluded that evidence discovered pursuant to its execution was admissible. The defendant's argument that, "but for" the initial entry, Colon could have destroyed the evidence and thus prevented its discovery was dismissed by Burger as "pure speculation." "Even more important," stated Burger, "we decline to extend the exclusionary rule . . . to further 'protect' criminal activity." To the contention of the four dissenters that its holding would encourage illegal entries to "secure" the premises pending a warrant, the majority stated "[w]e are unwilling to believe that officers will routinely and purposely violate the law as a matter of course."

Because *Segura* emphasizes that only that evidence found pursuant to a warrant based on independently obtained information is admissible, the dissent's concern about encouraging illegal entries seems exaggerated.[87] *Segura* left intact a disincentive to enter illegally because, under that decision, the police knew that anything they discovered during the illegal entry would be inadmissible, including items which they could have legally seized pursuant to a warrant. That is no longer the case, however, since *Murray v. United States,*[88] in which the Court held that evidence discovered during the initial illegal entry *is* admissible if it is also discovered during a later search pursuant to a warrant that is based on information obtained wholly independently of the initial entry. In *Murray,* the police suspected that the defendants were storing marijuana in a warehouse, but instead of seeking a warrant before searching the building, they went in without one, apparently believing that evidence would be destroyed or co-participants would escape if they did not do so. The search revealed numerous bales of marijuana, but no people. At this point the police successfully applied for a search warrant, based on an affidavit which did not mention the discovered bales nor the

---

87. As for the defendant's argument that evidence might have been destroyed but for the "illegal" entry, to the extent evidence destruction is a probable consequence of an arrest, the police may be authorized to make a warrantless entry to prevent it, thus removing the initial illegality. See § 6.04(b)(2).

88. 487 U.S. 533, 108 S.Ct. 2529 (1988).

prior entry. On the basis of the warrant, they "rediscovered" the marijuana. The Supreme Court assumed without deciding that the initial entry was unlawful because, contrary to what the police allegedly thought, exigent circumstances had not existed. It went on to hold, however, that if the police could show they had probable cause sufficient for a warrant even had they not entered the warehouse, then the bales would be admissible because the second discovery would be based on an independent, untainted source.[89]

Unlike *Segura, Murray* encourages the police to enter illegally; once they think they have probable cause, they have nothing to lose if they enter without a warrant.[90] Justice Scalia, in his opinion for the Court, asserted that when the police who enter illegally subsequently attempt to get a warrant, they must meet the "onerous burden of convincing a trial court that no information gained from the illegal entry affected the law enforcement officers' decision to seek a warrant or the magistrate's decision to grant it." But, as Justice Marshall pointed out in dissent, police who are willing to manipulate the facts can easily meet this second burden. Moreover, regardless of the perjury problem, *Murray* is questionable because it clearly encourages warrantless searches of houses when the police believe they have probable cause. The decision to intrude should not be left up to the police unless emergency circumstances dictate it.[91] Thus, the government should not be able to rely upon an "independent source" analysis to immunize from exclusion evidence found during an illegal entry.

An analogous practice engaged in by many lower courts—approving warrants based in part on tainted evidence so long as the untainted evidence supports a probable cause determination—is also suspect.[92] This approach encourages police to supplement borderline warrant applications with illegally obtained information. At the least, this use of the independent source doctrine should be permitted only when the tainted evidence constitutes an insignificant proportion of the basis for the warrant.[93]

(d) The Inevitable Discovery Exception. The inevitable discovery doctrine is closely related to the independent source idea (indeed some courts call it the "hypothetical independent source" rule). As described by most courts, if it can be proven that the derivative information *would have been* discovered by the police regardless of their unconstitutional acts, the evidence will be

---

89. The case was remanded for a determination by the district court on this issue.

90. See Stuntz, Warrants and Fourth Amendment Remedies, 77 Va.L.Rev. 881, 933–34 (1991).

91. See generally, discussion of the warrant requirement in § 4.05(a).

92. See, e.g., *James v. United States,* 418 F.2d 1150 (D.C.Cir.1969).

93. See, e.g., *United States v. Langley,* 466 F.2d 27 (6th Cir.1972).

admissible. Since many courts have required a fairly high degree of proof in this regard, this exception is known as the "inevitable discovery" limitation. By the time the Supreme Court finally endorsed the inevitable discovery doctrine in *Nix v. Williams*,[94] every federal circuit had already adopted it.[95]

The illegality in *Williams* involved the Sixth Amendment right to counsel rather than the Fourth Amendment. The fruit in this case—the body of a young girl allegedly killed by the defendant—was found as a result of questioning the defendant about the body's location in the absence of counsel and in violation of an express promise not to do so.[96] However, the state was also able to show that, at the time the body was found, a volunteer search party organized by the police was two-and-one-half miles away from the culvert in which the body lay and would have searched the area within the next several hours. The Iowa Supreme Court affirmed use of the illegally obtained evidence because "(1) the police did not act in bad faith for the purpose of hastening discovery of the evidence in question, and (2) . . . the evidence in question would have been discovered by lawful means." [97]

In subsequent habeas proceedings, the Eighth Circuit accepted the Iowa court's two-prong test, which represented the typical formulation of the inevitable discovery doctrine at the time, but decided that the state produced insufficient evidence of good faith. The Supreme Court, in a 7–2 decision by Chief Justice Burger, reversed the Eighth Circuit and upheld the result of the Iowa court, on the ground that the motivation of the offending officer is irrelevant to inevitable discovery analysis. Burger reached this conclusion by analogizing to the independent source test.[98] As with the operation of that test, admitting evidence that would have been found in any event "ensures that the prosecution is not put in a worse position simply because of some earlier police error or misconduct." Requiring a good faith showing would violate this notion by placing "courts in the position of withholding from juries relevant and undoubted truth that would have been available to police absent any lawful activity."

Burger is correct that, when discovery of the evidence was clearly inevitable, a good faith prerequisite would put police in a worse position than if there had been no police misconduct. But this conclusion should not govern the scope of the exclusionary rule. If it did, police would have no disincentive to engage in illegality when they believe that they already have a legal source

94. 467 U.S. 431, 104 S.Ct. 2501 (1984).

95. See cases cited at 467 U.S. 431 n. 2, 104 S.Ct. 2501 n. 2.

96. See *Brewer v. Williams*, 430 U.S. 387, 97 S.Ct. 1232 (1977), discussed in § 16.04.

97. *Iowa v. Williams*, 285 N.W.2d 248 (Iowa 1979).

98. See § 2.04(c).

for the evidence or that one will develop shortly. The result could be that, in cases like *Murray* (discussed in connection with the independent source doctrine), they will be able to justify an illegal warrantless search on the theory that they would have eventually obtained the evidence through a lawful warrant-based search. As one court put it, this type of inevitable discovery argument "would tend in actual practice to emasculate the search warrant requirement of the Fourth Amendment." [99] In response to this type of argument, Burger unrealistically asserted that police officers will "rarely, if ever, be in a position to calculate whether the evidence sought would inevitably be discovered," and that, even if they were, they "will try to avoid engaging in any questionable practice."

The Court's position in *Williams* might be more tenable if it had required the state to show that the discovery of the evidence through legal means was truly inevitable had the illegality not intervened. But the *Williams* Court held that proof of inevitability may be by a preponderance of the evidence, over the objection of the dissenters, Brennan and Marshall, who argued for a clear and convincing standard of proof. The elasticity of the majority's standard creates significant potential for speculative conclusions about what the police might have been able to accomplish, at the least increasing the possibility of hindsight justification and at worst encouraging police to take illegal shortcuts in the belief that legal investigatory methods can be imagined by the time of the suppression hearing. To avoid these problems, the inevitable discovery doctrine should apply only when the government can show, as it did in *Williams,* that (1) a legal investigation (2) conducted by officers other than those who committed the illegality (3) was ongoing at the time of the illegality.[1]

2.05 Should the Rule Be Abolished?: Other Remedies for Constitutional Violations

Despite the Supreme Court's recent inroads, the exclusionary rule still operates to exclude most illegally obtained evidence from

99. *United States v. Griffin,* 502 F.2d 959 (6th Cir.1974). But see, *United States v. Hidalgo,* 747 F.Supp. 818 (D.Mass.1990), where the Court refused to suppress evidence procured in violation of the warrant and knock-and-announce requirements because evidence would inevitably have been found pursuant to a valid search warrant which was being obtained at the time of the entry.

1. See, e.g., *United States v. Rullo,* 748 F.Supp. 36 (D.Mass.1990) (inevitable discovery doctrine does not permit admission of gun discovered by police as a result of involuntary statements made by defendant after his arrest, since the officers who directed the "inevitable" search for the gun were the same officers who were involved in beating the defendant and hearing him disclose location of weapon). But see, *United States v. Rodriguez,* 750 F.Supp 1272 (W.D.N.C.1990) (crack cocaine illegally found in defendant's pocket admissible because officer would inevitably have searched her person after discovering handgun in car and drugs in purse).

the guilt adjudication stage. Many critics have argued that this last vestige of *Mapp* should be eradicated as well.[2] The two principal arguments in favor of eliminating the rule entirely are that it does not deter police misconduct and that it allows a significant number of guilty persons to go free. Scholars have attempted to collect evidence on both these points, with mixed results.

Research on the deterrent effect of the rule is inconclusive. Professor Davies, after reviewing the methodological difficulties associated with testing the deterrence hypothesis, concluded:

> "When all factors are considered, there is virtually no likelihood that the Court is going to receive any 'relevant statistics' which objectively measure the 'practical efficacy' of the exclusionary rule. . . . Whichever side is required to prove the effect of the rule loses."[3]

In light of this empirical failure, commonsense must guide one's conclusions with respect to the deterrent effect of the rule. It is often pointed out that individual police officers are not directly affected by the exclusion of evidence they obtained illegally, because the exclusion takes place long after the search which produced the evidence.[4] Yet lessons are undoubtedly learned every time an officer testifies at a suppression hearing. More importantly, the exclusion of evidence does have a *systemic* effect. There is clear evidence that, since *Mapp*, prosecutors and police chiefs, fearful of losing cases on technicalities, have initiated programs designed to teach the individual officer relevant Fourth Amendment law.[5] Training classes and detailed search and seizure manuals are the surest legacy of the exclusionary rule. Given this fact, it would seem the rule has had a positive impact on police behavior.

As to the exclusionary rule's "costs," the word so often used by the Supreme Court in describing the convictions lost due to application of the rule, the available evidence suggests that only a small percentage of cases in which charges are brought are actually dismissed on Fourth Amendment grounds. For instance, Professor Nardulli examined the court records of 7,500 felony cases

---

2. See Wilkey, "Why Suppress Valid Evidence," 62 Judicature 214 (1978); Posner, "Excessive Sanctions for Governmental Misconduct in Criminal Cases," 57 Wash.L.Rev. 635 (1982).

3. Davies, "On the Limitations of Empirical Evaluations of the Exclusionary Rule: A Critique of the Spiotto Research and United States v. Calandra," 69 Nw.L.Rev. 740, 763–64 (1974).

4. See Wilkey, supra note 2, at 226–27; Chief Justice Burger's dissent in *Bivens v. Six Unknown Named Agents of Federal Bureau of Narcotics*, 403 U.S. 388, 416, 91 S.Ct. 1999, 2015 (1971).

5. Canon, "Is the Exclusionary Rule in Failing Health: Some New Data and a Plea Against a Precipitous Conclusion," 62 Ky.L.J. 681, 715 (1971); Kamisar, "Does (Did) (Should) the Exclusionary Rule Rest on a 'Principled Basis' Rather Than an 'Empirical Proposition'?", 16 Creighton 565, 590–1 (1983).

closed in 1979–80, and found that only 40 (or roughly one-half of one percent) ended in nonconvictions following a defendant's motion to suppress evidence seized illegally by police.[6] Similar figures are reported in most other studies.[7] Inserting this information into the equation favored by the current Court, the continued viability of the exclusionary rule is dependent upon how one balances the societal interest in increasing the proportion of those convicted by a figure somewhat under one percent against the value to society of ensuring that the police are informed of the privacy interests protected by the Fourth Amendment.

Of course, it can be argued that even if one values assuring Fourth Amendment protection over convicting a small group of defendants, the exclusionary rule is not the only method of guaranteeing this protection. There are various other remedies for unconstitutional police conduct: civil suits seeking monetary and injunctive relief, criminal actions, and even non-judicial remedial measures. These devices will now be examined, with particular attention paid to each remedy's effectiveness as an alternative to the exclusionary rule. Again, the focus will be on how these alternative sanctions might ensure that the *police* abide by the *Fourth Amendment.* At several points, however, the impact of these remedies on other officials involved in the legal system, and on the enforcement of other constitutional rights, will be noted.

(a) Damages. The elements of a damage action for a violation of the constitution depend upon whether the civil defendant represents federal or state law enforcement and whether the defendant is an individual officer or a governmental entity. On the whole, the differences between state and federal causes of action are minimal, but there are enough variations to warrant separate treatment. The differences between suits aimed at individuals and those aimed at governments are significant, particularly in terms of defenses.

(1) Federal officers: Bivens actions. Until 1971, it was not clear that federal officers could be sued for failing to abide by the strictures of the Fourth Amendment. However, in *Bivens v. Six Unknown Named Agents,*[8] the Court created an implied private

---

6. Nardulli, "The Societal Cost of the Exclusionary Rule: An Empirical Assessment," 1983 Amer.Bar Found.J. 585 (1983).

7. Less than .7% of 2,804 defendants handled during a two-month period in 1978 by U.S. Attorneys' offices won suppression motions and eluded conviction. Impact of the Exclusionary Rule on Federal Criminal Prosecutions (Report of the Comptroller General, April 19, 1979). Less than .8% of all felony

complaints in California during 1976–79 were rejected primarily for search and seizure problems. National Institute of Justice, The Effects of the Exclusionary Rule: A Study in California (1982). See also, Davies, "A Hard Look at What We Know (and Still Need to Learn) About the 'Costs' of the Exclusionary Rule: The NIJ Study and Other Studies of 'Lost' Arrests," 1983 Amer.Bar Found.J. 611 (1983).

8. 403 U.S. 388, 91 S.Ct. 1999 (1971).

cause of action under the Fourth Amendment and permitted suit against federal officers who, without a warrant, had manacled, searched and arrested the plaintiff and ransacked his apartment. There are two essential elements in a *Bivens* action. First, the government official must have been acting "under color of authority." This is generally given a broad interpretation—an act is said to be within the scope of an official's authority if such act is "within the outer perimeter of [his] line of duty." [9] Second, the official must have deprived the individual of his constitutional rights under the Fourth Amendment or some other constitutional provision.[10]

After proving these two elements, a plaintiff has sustained his burden of persuasion. However, government officials may still have an immunity defense. Some government officials may be able to claim absolute immunity, while virtually all other officials, including the police, are entitled to qualified immunity, colloquially known as a "good faith defense." In *Butz v. Economou*,[11] the Court identified several factors which should be considered in deciding whether a particular official should be afforded only qualified rather than absolute immunity: (1) the need to assure that the individual can perform his functions without harassment or intimidation; (2) the presence of safeguards that reduce the need for private damages actions as a means of controlling unconstitutional conduct; (3) insulation from political influence; (4) the importance of precedent set by the individual; (5) the adversary nature of the process used by the individual in making decisions; and (6) the correctability of error on appeal. In light of these factors, the Court has concluded that "qualified immunity represents the norm." [12] Thus, while federal judges [13] and prosecutors,[14] and officials who perform similar functions, enjoy absolute immunity, federal agency heads[15] presidential aides [16] and, most importantly for present purposes, the police,[17] have been extended only qualified immunity.

9. *Barr v. Matteo*, 360 U.S. 564, 575, 79 S.Ct. 1335, 1341 (1959).

10. Since *Bivens*, other constitutional torts have been recognized. See, e.g., *Davis v. Passman*, 442 U.S. 228, 99 S.Ct. 2264 (1979) (Fifth Amendment remedy available for federal sex discrimination); *Carlson v. Green*, 446 U.S. 14, 100 S.Ct. 1468 (1980) (claim of incompetent care of federal prisoner recognized under Eighth Amendment); *Sonntag v. Dooley*, 650 F.2d 904 (7th Cir.1981) (*Bivens* remedy under Fifth Amendment for coerced resignation from civil service position).

11. 438 U.S. 478, 98 S.Ct. 2894 (1978).

12. *Harlow v. Fitzgerald*, 457 U.S. 800, 102 S.Ct. 2727 (1982).

13. *Bradley v. Fisher*, 80 U.S. (13 Wall.) 335 (1872).

14. *Yaselli v. Goff*, 275 U.S. 503, 48 S.Ct. 155 (1927), affirming 12 F.2d 396 (2d Cir. 1926). But see infra note 38.

15. *Butz v. Economou*, supra note 11.

16. *Harlow v. Fitzgerald*, supra note 12.

17. *Bivens v. Six Unknown Named Agents of Federal Bureau of Narcotics*, 456 F.2d 1339 (2d Cir.1972).

Even qualified immunity provides significant protection, however. According to the Court's decision in *Harlow v. Fitzgerald*,[18] an official protected by qualified immunity may not be held personally liable for an official action if the action meets the test of "objective legal reasonableness" in light of legal rules that were "clearly established" at the time the act occurred. If there is no clearly established rule governing the official's act, or if there is such a rule, but the act, while in violation of the rule, was based on a reasonable interpretation of it, then no liability attaches. This formulation, stated the Court, should "permit the resolution of many insubstantial claims on summary judgment."

In *Anderson v. Creighton*[19] the Court affirmed that *Harlow's* test applies to searches by police officers as well as actions by other government agents. In dissent, Justice Stevens argued that police should be more vulnerable to suit given the degree of discretion already afforded them by the "reasonableness" standard provided in the Fourth Amendment; he also noted the relatively minor interference litigation causes police who, unlike many other government officials, already spend considerable time testifying in court. But the majority refused to create different types of qualified immunity. Thus, the Court held, if the police activity as alleged by the plaintiff are actions that a reasonable police officer could have believed lawful, the suit may be dismissed on a motion for summary judgment prior to discovery. It also emphasized that the subjective beliefs of the officer are "irrelevant" to the immunity issue, thus making clear that a police officer could escape liability for actions he knows are in violation of the Fourth Amendment because they were "objectively" legally reasonable.[20]

(2) Federal government: FTCA. Bivens explicitly left to Congress whether the federal government could be held liable for the "constitutional" torts of its officers, because "the federal purse was involved." At the time of *Bivens*, the Federal Tort Claims Act provided that a prima facie case against the government existed if the plaintiff could prove:

> (1) damage to or loss of property, or death or bodily injury, which was

> (2) caused by a negligent or wrongful act

> (3) committed by a federal employee acting within the scope of employment

18. Harlow v. Fitzgerald, 457 U.S. 800, 102 S.Ct. 2727 (1982).

19. 483 U.S. 635, 107 S.Ct. 3034 (1987).

20. Compare this result to that reached under the good faith exception to the exclusionary rule, discussed in § 2.03(c)(2).

(4) in a state where the act committed would lead to legal liability for a private person.[21]

Although these elements would seem to encompass suits claiming police misconduct, the Act specifically barred recovery for a number of intentional torts which might normally form the basis for such suits, including false arrest, false imprisonment, abuse of process, assault, battery, and malicious prosecution. The Act also extended immunity to acts committed by a government employee in the exercise of his discretion, "whether or not the discretion involved be abused."

After *Bivens,* however, the Act was amended to make it applicable "to acts or omissions of investigative or law enforcement officers of the United States Government" on any claim arising out of such torts.[22] The term "law enforcement officers" was defined to include any officer "who is empowered by law to execute searches, to seize evidence, or to make arrests for violations of Federal law." The intent of the provision, according to the Senate report, is "to deprive the federal Government of the defense of sovereign immunity in cases . . . [involving] the same kind of conduct that is alleged to have occurred in *Bivens* and for which that case imposes liability upon the individual Government officials involved."[23] It is not clear whether this language means that the good faith defense recognized in *Bivens* is available to the government under the FTCA as well.[24]

Given the government's financial resources, an FTCA action is now clearly superior to a *Bivens* suit, even if good faith is a defense in the former cause of action. The Supreme Court has held that the amendments to the FTCA were not meant to render *Bivens* obsolete, however; both causes of action may be brought simultaneously.[25] Thus the plaintiff whose constitutional rights have been violated by a federal police officer in bad faith can be assured of monetary compensation at the same time he can exact direct "revenge" against the official to the extent the official can afford it.

(3) State officers: § 1983. At one time, suits against state officers (or state governmental entities) were rare because of official (and governmental) immunity. Today over thirty states have waived immunity either partially or wholly, thus making

21. 28 U.S.C.A. § 1346(b); see also, 28 U.S.C.A. §§ 1291, 1346(c), 1402(b), 1504, 2110, 2401(b), 2402, 2411(b), 2412(c), 2671–2680.

22. 28 U.S.C.A. § 2680(h).

23. Sen.Rep. No. 93–588, 93d Cong., 2d Sess., 1974 U.S.Code Cong. and Ad. News 2789, 2791 (1974).

24. See *Norton v. United States,* 581 F.2d 390 (4th Cir.1978), cert. denied 439 U.S. 1003, 99 S.Ct. 613 (1978) (defense available). But see *Owen v. City of Independence,* infra note 45, which held that municipalities do not have a good faith defense in § 1983 actions.

25. *Carlson v. Green,* 446 U.S. 14, 100 S.Ct. 1468 (1980).

suits based on state tort law feasible.[26] Even so, when the suit is against a municipality or county, or one of its officers (as opposed to a state-run institution or its employees), the most popular cause of action for damages arising out of non-federal conduct is provided by 42 U.S.C.A. § 1983, because it permits suit in federal court and significantly abrogates immunity protection for municipalities and similar governmental units regardless of state law on the subject.

Section 1983 provides that any "person" who "under color of" state law deprives another of "any rights, privileges, or immunities secured by the Constitution and laws shall be liable in an action at law, suit in equity, or other proper proceeding for redress." This provision, enacted as part of the Ku Klux Klan Act of 1871, was disinterred as a possible cause of action for police misconduct in *Monroe v. Pape*,[27] decided the same year as *Mapp*, and like that case, involving an illegal search and arrest.

The elements of a cause of action under § 1983, as laid out by the Supreme Court in *Pape* and summarized in *Parratt v. Taylor*,[28] are similar to those required for a *Bivens* suit. First, the conduct complained of must be committed by a person acting "under color of state law." Generally, as under *Bivens*, this term is construed broadly so as to include any actions of a law enforcement officer committed within the scope of his employment. Second, the conduct must have deprived the complainant of rights, privileges, or immunities secured by the Constitution or the laws of the United States.

Parratt had suggested that the deprivation required for a § 1983 violation need not be intentional: "[S]imply because a wrong was negligently as opposed to intentionally committed [does] not foreclose the possibility that such action could be brought under § 1983." However, in *Daniels v. Williams*,[29] the Court explicitly overruled *Parratt* to the extent it held that negligent actions by state officials can lead to recovery under § 1983. The *Daniels* Court pointed out that no previous Court decision had permitted recovery under § 1983 for negligent conduct. It found this fact to be with good reason:

> [L]ack of due care suggests no more than a failure to measure up to the conduct of a reasonable man. To hold that injury caused by such conduct is a deprivation within the meaning of the Fourteenth Amendment would trivialize the centuries-old principle of due process of law.

26. Mayhew, "The Abrogation of Sovereign Immunity in Mississippi: The Legislative Problem," 3 Miss.Coll.L. Rev. 209, 220–23 (1983).

27. 365 U.S. 167, 81 S.Ct. 473 (1961).

28. 451 U.S. 527, 101 S.Ct. 1908 (1981).

29. 474 U.S. 327, 106 S.Ct. 662 (1986).

Moreover, as with a *Bivens* suit, state and local police sued under § 1983 are entitled to qualified immunity protecting them from liability for actions which are reasonable in light of clearly established legal standards.[30] Of particular relevance here is *Malley v. Briggs*,[31] which held that a warrant authorizing an officer's actions does not automatically make them reasonable. There, an officer being sued for wrongfully searching the plaintiff's home claimed that because he believed in good faith that information he provided a magistrate established probable cause and because the magistrate subsequently signed a warrant based on that information, he should be immune from suit under § 1983. But the Court held he would not have a defense if "a reasonably well-trained officer in petitioner's position would have known that his affidavit failed to establish probable cause and that he should not have applied for the warrant." The theoretical fact that no judge should issue a warrant when probable cause is absent did not persuade the Court that a judicially authorized warrant should immunize an officer, since "ours is not an ideal system, and it is possible that a magistrate, working under docket pressures, will fail to perform as a magistrate should." Thus, to minimize this possibility, officers should be exposed to liability for unreasonable warrant requests. The Court went on to hold that the reasonableness test in this context was the equivalent of the test established by the Court in *United States v. Leon* [32] for deciding whether a search based on a warrant is valid despite the absence of probable cause.

The Court has also addressed the liability of other officials under § 1983. As at the federal level, while judges are immune from § 1983 damage suits,[33] most executive branch state and local officials—police chiefs, governors, and agency heads—can be sued individually under the statute.[34] They too have a good faith defense, however, the scope of which varies depending "upon the scope of discretion and responsibilities of the office and all the circumstances as they reasonably appeared at the time of the

---

30. The qualified immunity defense in § 1983 actions was first recognized in *Pierson v. Ray*, 386 U.S. 547, 87 S.Ct. 1213 (1967). It would appear that the Court's holding in *Anderson v. Creighton*, supra note 19, is applicable here as well.

31. 475 U.S. 335, 106 S.Ct. 1092 (1986).

32. See § 2.03(c)(2).

33. In *Stump v. Sparkman*, 435 U.S. 349, 98 S.Ct. 1099 (1978), the Court upheld the absolute immunity of a state court judge even when he takes actions in excess of his authority, or acts mali-

ciously or corruptly, so long as he has jurisdiction over the subject matter and the acts he takes in regard to it can be characterized as "judicial." However, when the § 1983 suit is for injunctive relief, judicial immunity is not absolute. See *Pulliam v. Allen*, 466 U.S. 522, 104 S.Ct. 1970 (1984).

34. *Scheuer v. Rhodes*, 416 U.S. 232, 94 S.Ct. 1683 (1974) (state governors); *Procunier v. Navarette*, 434 U.S. 555, 98 S.Ct. 855 (1978) (state prison officials); *Wood v. Strickland*, 420 U.S. 308, 95 S.Ct. 992 (1975) (school board members).

action on which liability is sought to be based." [35]   Thus, for instance, while prosecutors are generally absolutely immune from liability under § 1983,[36] one court has held a prosecutor liable for false statements made on the stand in response to a judicial inquiry as to whether there were any government informants among the witnesses called by the prosecutor.[37]   Similarly, the Supreme Court has held that a prosecutor's actions *outside* the courtroom may be afforded only qualified immunity.[38]

(4) State governmental units: § 1983.   In *Pape*, the Court held that the city of Chicago could not be held liable under § 1983 because Congress did not consider municipal corporations to be "persons" within the ambit of the section.   But in *Monell v. Department of Social Services of New York,*[39] the Court overruled *Pape* insofar as it held that local governments are wholly immune from suit under § 1983.   Rather, it permitted liability when the constitutional violation is sanctioned by official municipal policy or custom.   This latter stipulation represented a compromise between making municipalities liable under a *respondeat superior* theory (which holds employers responsible for *all* acts of their employees within the scope of employment) and according them absolute immunity.   It should be noted that suits against the *federal* government under the Federal Tort Claims Act need not allege or prove that official policy was being implemented at the time of the alleged official misconduct.   This difference results entirely from the Court's reading of the legislative history associated with the two statutes at issue.

Monell included within its definition of "policy and custom" "custom [which] has not received formal approval through the body's official decisionmaking channels."   This language suggests that unwritten, informal practice can form the basis for liability. The question then becomes how one establishes evidence of such a practice.   In *Oklahoma City v. Tuttle,*[40] the Court found improper an instruction allowing the jury to infer a municipal policy of "inadequate training" from a single incident of "unusually excessive force" which resulted in serious injury.   *Tuttle* seemed to suggest that an official act or failure to act not specifically

35.   *Scheuer v. Rhodes,* 416 U.S. 232, 94 S.Ct. 1683 (1974).   In *Gomez v. Toledo,* 446 U.S. 635, 100 S.Ct. 1920 (1980), the Court held that the defendant-official bears the burden of alleging and proving good faith.

36.   *Imbler v. Pachtman,* 424 U.S. 409, 96 S.Ct. 984 (1976).

37.   *Briggs v. Goodwin,* 569 F.2d 10 (D.C.Cir.1977), cert denied 437 U.S. 904, 98 S.Ct. 3089 (1978).   But see *Taylor v. Kavanagh,* 640 F.2d 450 (2d Cir.1981) (prosecutor not liable for making false

statements during course of plea bargaining).

38.   *Burns v. Reed,* 500 U.S. ___, 111 S.Ct. 1934 (1991) (prosecutor has only qualified immunity in a § 1983 action alleging he gave unconstitutional advice to police officers).

39.   436 U.S. 658, 98 S.Ct. 2018 (1978).

40.   471 U.S. 808, 105 S.Ct. 2427 (1985).

authorized in writing by the appropriate body must cause more than an isolated occurrence in order to meet the policy or custom stipulation of *Monell.* Then, in *Pembaur v. Cincinnati,*[41] the Court held that an isolated incident *was* actionable under § 1983 when police, acting under instructions from the county prosecutor to "go and get" the petitioner, chopped down the petitioner's door after he had refused them entrance on the ground they had no warrant. Although no similar incident by local police was proven, the Court's plurality opinion, written by Justice Brennan, distinguished *Tuttle* on the ground that the injury in the latter case was not committed *"pursuant"* to municipal policy. In *Pembaur,* on the other hand, the police acted under the orders of the prosecutor. Brennan concluded that so long as the official making the decision has authority to establish final policy on the action in question,[42] a single decision by that official, like a single legislative act by the municipality's legislative body, can form the basis for liability.

Two justices joined Justice Brennan's opinion and a fourth, Justice Stevens, concurred in the judgment on the ground that, under his interpretation of § 1983, municipalities should be liable on a *respondeat superior* theory. Two other justices, White and O'Connor, joined the result but wrote separate opinions to emphasize that, at the time the prosecutor gave his instruction, the type of act he authorized (a warrantless entrance in the absence of exigent circumstances to effect an arrest of an individual who did not own the premises) had not yet explicitly been held unconstitutional.[43] According to White and O'Connor, had a court decision or a statute made clear the action was impermissible, then a decision by the prosecutor in violation of the legal rule could not be said to be an execution of county policy. Thus, the stance of the current Court appears to be that a single unwritten decision by a municipal official who has authority to make such a decision can form the basis for municipal liability, but only if it does not run counter to established judicial or legislative rulings.

In many cases, the question is not whether an official custom or policy exists, but whether an official custom or policy can be said to have caused a deprivation of constitutional rights. In connection with suits over police conduct, the most common allegation in this vein, illustrated by *Tuttle,* is that the municipality's "policy" of failing to train its police to carry out particular types

---

41. 475 U.S. 469, 106 S.Ct. 1292 (1986).

42. Under Ohio law, the prosecutor is specifically authorized to give instructions to police "in matters connected with their official duties." Ohio Rev. Code Ann. § 390.90 (1979).

43. *Steagald v. United States,* 451 U.S. 204, 101 S.Ct. 1642 (1981), so held, four years after the incident at issue in *Pembaur* took place. See § 3.04(c).

of duties has lead to such a deprivation. In *City of Canton v. Harris*,[44] the Supreme Court explicitly held, 6–3, that a failure to train claim may be the basis for § 1983 liability, but only where such a claim "amounts to deliberate indifference to the rights of persons with whom the police come into contact." Moreover, held the Court, a training program is not to be found inadequate merely because "an otherwise sound program has occasionally been negligently administered" or because an injury could have been avoided had an officer received better training. Finally, "for liability to attach . . . the identified deficiency in a city's training program must be closely related to the ultimate injury." According to the Court, adopting lesser standards of fault and causation would open municipalities to "unprecedented liability" because "[i]n virtually every instance where a person has had his or her constitutional rights violated by a city employee, a § 1983 plaintiff will be able to point to something the city 'could have done' to prevent the unfortunate incident."

In a footnote, the Court provided illustrations of the rare situations where liability might be imposed under its "deliberate indifference" standard:

> For example, city policy makers know to a moral certainty that their police officers will be required to arrest fleeing felons. . . . Thus, the need to train officers in the constitutional limitations on the use of deadly force . . . can be said to be 'so obvious,' that failure to do so could properly be characterized as 'deliberate indifference' to constitutional rights. It could also be that the police, in exercising their discretion, so often violate constitutional rights that the need for further training must have been plainly obvious to the city policy makers, who, nevertheless, are 'deliberately indifferent' to the need.

The standard adopted in *Harris* ensures that municipalities will not be liable under § 1983 for injuries stemming from most nonroutine violations of the constitution by their police, at least under a failure to train theory.

A Supreme Court decision which more clearly enhances the ability of the plaintiff to gain recovery from a municipality is *Owen v. City of Independence*,[45] which held that municipalities do not enjoy good faith immunity from liability. *Owen* found that the common law did not recognize immunity for municipalities and that the policies supporting good faith immunity for individuals—the injustice of subjecting an official acting in good faith to liability and the danger that the threat of such liability would deter the official's willingness to execute his office effectively—are

44. 489 U.S. 378, 109 S.Ct. 1197 (1989).

45. 445 U.S. 622, 100 S.Ct. 1398 (1980).

"less compelling, if not wholly inapplicable, when the liability of the municipal entity is at issue." However, municipalities are not liable for punitive damages.[46]

Although municipalities may be sued under § 1983 with the limitations described above, states, and state officials acting in their official capacities, may not be. In *Will v. Michigan Dept. of State Police*,[47] the Supreme Court held, 5–4, that a state is not a "person" under § 1983 and thus cannot be subject to a suit bringing such a claim. The Court pointed out that a "principal purpose" behind § 1983 was to provide a federal forum for civil rights claims, yet the Eleventh Amendment forbids suits in federal court against a *state* unless the state has waived immunity; thus, concluded the majority, "we cannot accept petitioner's argument that Congress intended nevertheless to create a cause of action against States to be brought in state courts, which are precisely the courts Congress sought to allow civil rights claimants to avoid through § 1983." [48] The Court held further that, because "a suit against a state official in his or her official capacity is not a suit against the official but rather is a suit against the official's office," filing against a state official rather than the state itself does not avoid the statutory bar. As Justice Brennan pointed out in dissent, the import of the Court's decision is to prohibit § 1983 suits against a state even if the state is willing to consent to such suits through abrogation of sovereign immunity.

(5) Summary. As the foregoing suggests, damages actions should not be thought of as a substitute for the exclusionary rule. First, each remedy serves a purpose the other does not. A suit for damages does not enable the judiciary to overcome the "tainting effect" that comes from using illegally obtained evidence in a court of law; the exclusionary rule cannot financially compensate victims for their injuries and provides no remedy at all for the innocent victim. Second, although both share the goal of deterring police misconduct, they diverge markedly in their impact on police behavior. A damages action, if successful, has the advantage of making the offending officer, rather than the prosecutor, "pay" for the violation. But because it is such a rare occurrence, it is much less likely than the exclusionary rule to actually shape police conduct. A damages suit is not feasible when damages are

46. *Newport v. Fact Concerts, Inc.,* 453 U.S. 247, 101 S.Ct. 2748 (1981).

47. 491 U.S. 58, 109 S.Ct. 2304 (1989).

48. The Eleventh Amendment literally forbids suit in federal court by the citizen of one state against another state. But the Court has held that the Amendment bars all nonconsensual suits against a state in federal court,

Edelman v. Jordan, 415 U.S. 651, 94 S.Ct. 1347 (1974), and that *Monell* did not abrogate that immunity. *Quern v. Jordan,* 440 U.S. 332, 99 S.Ct. 1139 (1979). Of course, these decisions came well after passage of § 1983, which makes the majority's characterization of congressional intent somewhat disingenuous.

negligible, as is the case with many Fourth Amendment (and other constitutional) violations,[49] and the victim poor, as are most persons investigated by the police. Even if damages are sizeable, a civil suit is unlikely to be attractive; since constitutional violations will often be the result of idiosyncratic misconduct rather than government policy, the (often judgment proof) officer will usually be the only legitimate defendant, at least in state litigation. Moreover, most individuals with possible damages claims will be charged with a criminal offense; because they will be incarcerated or feel estopped by some notion of "unclean hands" they will seldom bring a civil suit. Finally, even if suit is brought, the police know that good faith is a defense in any suit against an individual.

In contrast, the exclusionary rule operates in every case of illegality and is not dependent upon the status of the victim or the good faith of the police (except in those situations identified earlier).[50] Thus, as between the two remedies, the exclusionary rule is significantly more likely to be applied, a fact which both the police and their superiors surely know. Most importantly, whereas the exclusionary rule has clearly had an impact on police training, the threat of civil suit alone is unlikely to exert pressure on police departments to prevent any but the most egregious actions on the part of their employees. Indeed, because under § 1983 damages against a municipality or state are possible only if a government policy or custom is violated, that statute provides some incentive for state governmental units to *avoid* promulgating rules regulating police conduct and training. If substantive Fourth Amendment law is to be more than "a form of words," something more than monetary compensation is necessary.

(b) Injunctive Relief. For some time, injunctions against governmental officials were difficult to obtain because of sovereign immunity. As early as 1939, however, the Supreme Court recognized that unconstitutional acts by a state official could be enjoined under § 1983,[51] and ten years later it permitted injunctions

49. The Court has held that, to recover damages under § 1983, "actual injury" must be proven. *Carey v. Piphus*, 435 U.S. 247, 98 S.Ct. 1042 (1978). See also, *Memphis School Dist. v. Stachura*, 477 U.S. 299, 106 S.Ct. 2537 (1986) (damages based on abstract value of constitutional rights not awardable under § 1983). The FTCA stipulates that liability will lie only when a private individual could recover under state law (which often severely limits recovery for "mental distress" and will usually also limit compensation to "actual" damages). Additional-

ly, of course, punitive damages cannot be obtained from the government under either § 1983 or the FTCA, *Newport v. Fact Concerts, Inc.*, supra note 46; 28 U.S.C.A. § 2674, and are not likely to be obtainable from individual officers.

50. See § 2.03(c).

51. *Hague v. C.I.O.*, 307 U.S. 496, 59 S.Ct. 954 (1939). In *Pulliam v. Allen*, 466 U.S. 522, 104 S.Ct. 1970 (1984), the Court, based on its reading of legislative history, held that judges are not immune from prospective relief sought under § 1983.

against federal officials for such acts.[52] Traditionally, a court order enjoining particular conduct has only been available if there is no remedy at law, such as a damages action. In seeking to enjoin police actions, this requirement has usually meant that the plaintiff must prove that repeated violations have occurred and that further violations are imminent and cannot otherwise be stopped. Often, some showing of bad faith on the part of the police is also imposed. *Lankford v. Gelston* [53] illustrates these points. There, the police had, on 300 occasions over 19 days, conducted warrantless searches of the appellant's and other persons' homes, relying on uninvestigated and anonymous tips about the location of certain criminal suspects. The Fourth Circuit granted injunctive relief, focusing on the number of illegalities involved, the flagrancy of the misconduct, and the police officers' probable inability to satisfy any damage claim. The court also pointed out that since the proponents for relief were not being criminally prosecuted, the exclusionary rule would not deter the continued unconstitutional conduct of the police.

The Supreme Court has been cautious about granting injunctive relief. In *Rizzo v. Goode,*[54] for instance, the Court emphasized that unless illegal action is (1) the product of deliberate action giving rise to a persistent pattern of police violation, or (2) the result of official policy, harm is not imminent and equitable relief should not be granted by the federal courts. In *Rizzo,* the district court found that some Philadelphia police officers had engaged in misconduct against minority and other citizens, but that no policy on the part of the police department directed or encouraged such action. However, it also found that the city's procedures for handling citizen complaints discouraged the filing of complaints and minimized the consequences of police misconduct. The court thus ordered the city to develop a program for acting on citizen complaints. The Supreme Court refused to uphold the order, stating that a "*failure* to act in the face of a statistical pattern is distinguishable from . . . active conduct." It also emphasized that federal courts should be extremely reticent about interfering with the internal affairs of a state agency.

The Court made the same points in *Los Angeles v. Lyons.*[55] There the plaintiff alleged that he had been rendered unconscious and suffered damage to his larynx when police officers stopped him for a traffic violation and applied a "chokehold" to his neck. He also alleged that the Los Angeles police routinely apply such chokeholds in situations where they are not threatened by the use of deadly force. The Court held, in a 5–4 decision authored by

52. *Larson v. Domestic & Foreign Commerce Corp.,* 337 U.S. 682, 69 S.Ct. 1457 (1949).

53. 364 F.2d 197 (4th Cir.1966).

54. 423 U.S. 362, 96 S.Ct. 598 (1976).

55. 461 U.S. 95, 103 S.Ct. 1660 (1983).

Justice White, that these allegations "fall[ ] far short of the allegations that would be necessary to establish a case or controversy between these parties" for an injunction action. In order to meet this requirement, the Court explained, the defendant "would have had not only to allege that he would have another encounter with the police but also to make the 'incredible' assertion either, (1) that all police officers in Los Angeles *always* choke any citizen with whom they happen to have an encounter, whether for purposes of arrest, issuing a citation or for questioning, or, (2) that the city ordered or authorized police officers to act in such a manner." White also asserted that the plaintiff's proposed relief, which included a training program as well as an injunction against use of chokeholds in other than life-threatening situations, would entail "massive structural" changes that a federal court should generally be reluctant to order.

Clearly equitable relief is not a substitute for the exclusionary rule. Most obviously, an injunction is prospective in nature and thus cannot rectify past wrongs. Theoretically, injunctions could be a useful mechanism for bringing about systemic change. But, as *Rizzo* and *Lyons* demonstrate, even relatively flexible court orders that allow the state agency to devise and carry out its own programs will not be countenanced by the Supreme Court. This "hands-off" attitude toward police departments, combined with the rigorous pleading requirements imposed by the Court's cases, mean that injunctive actions are unlikely to be effective in controlling the police.

(c) Criminal Remedies. At the *state* level, most jurisdictions provide criminal sanctions for illegal police conduct, including false arrest and trespass. Due to a large number of common law limitations on these actions, however, state prosecution for illegal police conduct is rare. In general, most states require criminal intent as an element of the crime, making subjective *good faith alone* a complete defense to a criminal charge such as trespass or breach of the peace.[56]

As a supplement to state criminal remedies for police misconduct, 18 U.S.C.A. § 242 imposes a federal penalty on anyone who, under color of state law, willfully deprives a person of his constitutional rights.[57] As one might suppose from this language, this

---

56. See *Henderson v. State* 95 Ga. App. 830, 99 S.E.2d 270 (1957) (in criminal prosecution for false arrest defendant must have criminal intent); *White v. Mississippi Power & Light Co.*, 196 So.2d 343 (Miss.1967) (criminal trespass to property must be accompanied by breach of peace). See also 75 Am.Jur. 2d Trespass, § 86 (1974).

57. The statute reads:

Whoever, under color of any law, statute, ordinance, regulation, or custom, willfully subjects any inhabitant of any State, Territory, or District to the deprivation of any rights, privileges, or immunities secured or protected by the Constitution or laws of the United States, or to different punishments, pains, or penalties, on account of such inhabitant being an alien, or by rea-

criminal action is similar to the civil action under § 1983. Indeed the elements for a cause of action under § 242 and § 1983 are essentially the same. However, because § 242 is a criminal statute, it is construed strictly. In *Screws v. United States*,[58] the Supreme Court, while upholding § 242 against an attack that it was void for vagueness, interpreted the statutory requirement of willful violation to mean that the defendant must have had or been motivated by a specific intent to deprive a person of his constitutional rights.

This narrow construction of the statute, together with the natural reticence of prosecutors to bring actions against the police, has rendered § 242 an ineffective deterrent to police misconduct. Although there have been a handful of cases brought under this provision and some convictions, this sanction has normally been applied only to the most outrageous kinds of police misconduct, usually involving brutality,[59] and thus is unlikely to apply in relatively nonviolent Fourth Amendment cases.

At the *federal* level, criminal sanctions for police misconduct are also relatively impotent. The criminal actions covered include unlawful search and seizure,[60] malicious procurement of a warrant, and exceeding the authority of a warrant.[61] Yet few cases have applied these provisions, graphically underscoring the fact that these federal criminal statutes serve as little deterrent to police misconduct.

Some mention should also be made of the long-standing suggestion that judges should use their contempt power to discipline offending officers. This remedy would be available at both the state and federal levels. The first formulation of this proposal is in the third edition of Wigmore's *Evidence:* [62]

> The natural way to do justice here would be to enforce the healthy principle of the Fourth Amendment directly, i.e., by sending for the high-handed, overzealous marshal who had searched without a warrant, imposing a thirty-day imprisonment for his contempt of the Constitution, and then proceeding to affirm the sentence of the convicted criminal.

son of his color, or race, than are prescribed for the punishment of citizens, shall be fined not more than $1,000 or imprisoned not more than one year, or both; and if death results shall be subject to imprisonment for any term of years or for life.

58. 325 U.S. 91, 65 S.Ct. 1031 (1945).

59. See, e.g., *Miller v. United States*, 404 F.2d 611 (5th Cir.1968), cert. denied 394 U.S. 963, 89 S.Ct. 1314 (1969) (defendant bitten by dog acting at police direction); *Williams v. United States*, 341 U.S. 97, 71 S.Ct. 576 (1951) (defendant "beaten, threatened and unmercifully punished for several hours until he confessed"); *Lynch v. United States*, 189 F.2d 476 (5th Cir.1951), cert. denied 342 U.S. 831, 72 S.Ct. 50 (1951) (police assault, battery and torture of black defendants).

60. 18 U.S.C.A. § 2236.

61. 18 U.S.C.A. §§ 2234, 2235.

62. 8 J. Wigmore, Evidence § 2184 (3d ed. 1940).

More recent formulations of the suggestion also can be found.[63] However, the drawbacks of this sanction are obvious. Because judges are probably institutionally incapable of discovering on their own initiative instances of police misconduct, the contempt sanction would only be applied when the given facts in an adversary proceeding clearly indicate unlawful police action. Moreover, since the proposed "contempt of the Constitution" is an indirect criminal contempt, the accused police officer might have a right to a separate jury trial,[64] a burden the exclusionary rule does not require.

On the whole, though the exclusionary rule and criminal remedies are imposed for essentially the same reasons in the police misconduct area—i.e., to deter such conduct and to "purge" the legal system of its effect—the criminal remedy is shackled with substantive and procedural limitations which make its use ineffective as a method of shaping police behavior. The exclusionary rule, on the other hand, does not require proof of criminal intent and operates automatically[65] in the sense that it does not require a completely separate proceeding. In addition, unlike criminal remedies, its invocation is not controlled by the state but can occur at the behest of the aggrieved party.

(d) Non-Judicial Remedies. In addition to the traditional civil and criminal modes of relief, there are certain remedies for police misconduct that operate outside the judicial system. As such, they carry none of the stigma or force of law associated with the legal forms of redress. Rather, their efficacy stems from the force of public and peer disapprobation which usually manifests itself in some form of political or economic pressure.

(1) Internal review. One such non-judicial form of relief is a police department's internal review of its own misconduct. Every major police department has formal machinery for processing citizen complaints. There is much to be said for this form of police discipline, at least in the abstract. Internal review is potentially the most efficient method of regulating the conduct of peace officers because organizational superiors are in control of both the procedure and substance of the review. A punishment carried out by an insider for a violation of a regulation promulgated by an insider is likely to be accepted by both the miscreant officer and the department as a whole.[66]

Unfortunately, in practice, such machinery has proven ineffective. First, many complaints are never heard. For obvious

---

63. See, e.g., Blumrosen, Contempt of Court and Unlawful Police Action, 11 Rutgers L.Rev. 526 (1957).

64. See § 27.02(c).

65. The defendant, of course, must raise the defense of unconstitutional misconduct.

66. See generally Amsterdam, "Perspectives on the Fourth Amendment," 58 Minn.L.Rev. 349 (1974).

reasons, the police do not encourage initiation of internal review procedures; indeed, there is evidence suggesting that potential allegations of police misconduct are withheld because of fear of retaliation.[67] Moreover, in some instances, complex procedural formalities operate as a disincentive to the filing of grievances.[68]

Second, internal review often produces inadequate discipline. For example, a review of 126 discipline cases—involving 234 officers—processed by Detroit's internal review board "led to the conclusion that even when serious misconduct was found, departmental sanctions were mild, often inconsistent, and that there appeared to be 'little likelihood the Department will impose *meaningful* discipline when a citizen complains genuinely.'"[69]

Third, even if all citizen complaints are properly processed and the misbehaving officers are appropriately disciplined, internal review is not likely to reach the more subtle privacy violations that the Fourth Amendment is meant to protect, either because citizens do not complain about them or because police departments may not see them as important and therefore not regulate against them. Quite naturally, both citizens and police, lacking the perspective of the courts, may not put as great a premium on privacy.

(2) Civilian review boards. Dissatisfaction with both internal and judicial processing of police misconduct complaints prompted a few cities to experiment with another remedy for such misconduct—civilian review boards.[70] These boards, sitting independently of the police structure, adjudicate the merits of citizen grievances, either dismissing them as groundless or recommending that departmental superiors discipline the miscreant officer. Such external review is designed to project an appearance of fairness unattainable by internal mechanisms. At the same time, the civilian review boards can pass judgment on discourteous or harassing police practices which do not constitute judicially remediable wrongs but which nevertheless annoy the complainant and intensify community hostility toward the police.

Yet civilian review boards have been a failure, in large part due to vigorous opposition by the police themselves. Officers express concern over civilian ignorance of police procedures, the

67. See J. Lohman and G. Misner, The Police and the Community: The Dynamics of Their Relationship in a Changing Society, Vol. II, at 174 (1966).

68. See Commission on Civil Rights Report: Justice 82–83, 108 (1961).

69. Littlejohn, "The Civilian Police Commission: A Deterrent of Police Misconduct," 59 Det.J.Urb.L.Rev. 5, 45 (1981) (emphasis in original). This article advocates a civilian review board (see below), but notes that there "re-mains a great reluctance among police officials to punish 'one of our own' when a citizen complains, [a phenomenon which] will not be changed through self-induced reforms or by the external review of complaints."

70. See Commission on Civil Rights Report: Justice 83–84 (1961). Civilian review boards have operated at one time or another in Philadelphia, New York, Washington, and Rochester.

adverse effect on morale, the intrusion into their work, and the informal nature of the review process.[71]　In practice, the review boards have been relatively powerless in the face of police disenchantment, lack of political support, and weak authorizing legislation which, as described above, leaves the ultimate authority to discipline officers up to the department itself; accordingly, many of them have been abolished.[72]

(3) Ombudsman.　A third remedial system which, like the civilian review board, operates outside the judicial and internal police spheres, is the Scandinavian ombudsman system.　The ombudsman is, most simply, an external critic of administration.[73] His goal is improvement of administration rather than punishment of administrators or redress of individual grievances.　Thus, instead of conducting formal hearings associated with adjudicating individual complaints, he relies primarily on his own investigations to collect information.　To facilitate his inquiries, he may request an explanation from appropriate officials, examine departmental files, or call witnesses and conduct a hearing.　On the basis of his findings, he may recommend corrective measures to the department, although he cannot compel an official to do anything.　In essence, unlike the exclusionary rule, the focus of an ombudsman's evaluation is not the guilt of a particular policeman, but the policies and procedures by which police superiors have assessed citizens' allegations of guilt.　For this reason, any deterrent effect is extremely indirect.

(4) Quasi-judicial review.　While these non-judicial forms of relief for police misconduct are potentially efficacious, those that have been tried have not provided an adequate alternative to the exclusionary rule.　One reason for this is that these forms of relief *are* non-judicial and, as such, do not carry the force of law.

Two other proposals rely partially on judicial enforcement.　A variation on the ombudsman approach would allow the ombudsman to authorize the appointment of private counsel at public expense to sue the offending official or officials, whenever he found probable cause to believe that a constitutional or other legal violation had occurred.[74]　The proposal would also make recovery against the government possible, if a violation is found to have occurred but the offending official acted in good faith or is unknown.　This proposal corrects the basic deficiency of the

71. Note, "The Administration of Complaints Against the Police," 77 Harv.L.Rev. 499, 518 (1963); *Lohman & Misner,* supra note 67, generally and at 68.

72. For a description of the failed New York and Philadelphia boards, see *Littlejohn,* supra note 69, at 15–23.

73. The following description of the ombudsman's powers is taken from Gwyn, Transferring the Ombudsman, in Ombudsmen for American Government? 37 (1968).

74. Davidow, "Criminal Procedure Ombudsman Revisited," 73 J.Crim.L. & Criminol. 939 (1982).

Scandanavian approach by allowing individualized accountability. Its principal drawback is that, like damages actions generally, it is unlikely to have a significant deterrent effect.

Finally, Chief Justice Burger, in *Bivens,* suggested that a quasi-judicial body be established to allow recovery of damages against the government.[75] Under Burger's plan, if damages are awarded, the record of the condemned conduct would become part of the relevant officer's files. He would also allow appellate judicial review of decisions made by the tribunal. To date, no jurisdiction has adopted such a system.

2.06 Conclusion

The exclusionary evidence rule operates to bar evidence that was unconstitutionally obtained. Originally created to protect the integrity of the judicial process and deter illegal police conduct, more recent Court decisions have made clear that deterrence is the dominant objective of the rule. The following can be said about its scope in the Fourth Amendment context.

(1) While the exclusionary rule clearly applies at trial, its use has been ruled inappropriate at grand jury, habeas corpus, sentencing, and parole revocation proceedings, as well as at civil forfeiture and civil deportation proceedings, on the ground that holding otherwise would have little deterrent effect on police and prevent access to probative information.

(2) The rule has also been held inapplicable at *trial* when the illegally procured evidence (a) was obtained pursuant to an invalid warrant, so long as the warrant was issued by a neutral and detached magistrate and police reasonably believed it to be valid; (b) was obtained pursuant to a law subsequently found unconstitutional, so long as the law does not represent a total abandonment of the legislature's responsibility to enact constitutional laws; (c) is used solely for the purpose of impeaching the defendant on issues raised during direct examination.

(3) On the other hand, the "fruit of the poisonous tree" doctrine extends application of the rule to exclude *legally* obtained evidence which appears to have been discovered as a result of evidence that was procured in violation of the Fourth Amendment. This doctrine operates unless the government can show (a) that the connection between the illegally obtained evidence and the evidence derived from it is so attenuated that the derivative evidence is not tainted with the illegality of the original evidence; (b) that in fact the proffered evidence was obtained from a source independent of the illegally obtained evidence; or (c) that the

---

75. *Bivens v. Six Unknown Named Agents of Federal Bureau of Narcotics,* 403 U.S. 388, 422, 91 S.Ct. 1999, 2018 (1971) (Burger, C.J., dissenting).

derivative evidence would have been discovered even had the illegally obtained evidence never been procured.

(4) The primary means of seeking damages for the misconduct of federal law enforcement officials are a *Bivens* action, which permits suit against the individual official for actions depriving the plaintiff of constitutional rights, and a claim under the Federal Tort Claims Act, which permits suit against the federal government under similar circumstances. Individual federal officers may assert a good faith defense; it is not clear whether the federal government may do so. The primary method of seeking monetary compensation for the misconduct of local officials is a suit under 42 U.S.C.A. § 1983, which permits recovery against both the individual officer and the relevant government unit when the officer acts under color of state law to deprive the plaintiff of constitutional rights. However, only municipalities and other local government units and their officials may be sued under § 1983; states and state officials who are acting in their official capacity are immune from such suits. Moreover, as is true at the federal level, individual officers at the local level may assert a good faith defense. Local governments do not have such a defense, but they may be found liable only if the act of their employee is authorized by official policy or custom.

(5) Other methods of controlling police misconduct include injunctive relief for repeated misconduct, criminal sanctions for willful trespass, breach of the peace or assault and battery, and non-judicial remedies such as internal review boards, civilian review boards, and ombudsmen.

Despite periodic criticism of the exclusionary evidence rule and despite the existence of several "alternative" remedies for unconstitutional police conduct, the rule remains one of the fundamental institutions of the American criminal law system. Only the exclusionary rule can serve the dual purpose of deterring police misconduct and maintaining the judiciary's "clean hands" when the government seeks to employ unconstitutionally obtained evidence to attach criminal stigma. Civil, criminal, and non-judicial remedies can supplement the rule's deterrent impact but are either too cumbersome or too indirect in their effect to act as a complete substitute for it.

BIBLIOGRAPHY

Amsterdam, Anthony G. Perspectives on the Fourth Amendment. 58 Minn.L.Rev. 349 (1974).

Canon, Bradley. The Exclusionary Rule: Have Critics Proven that it Doesn't Deter Police? 62 Judicature 398 (1979).

Casper, J., K. Benedict, & J.L. Perry. The Tort Remedy in Search and Seizure Cases: A Case Study in Jury Decisionmaking. 13 Law and Social Inquiry 279 (1988).

Dripps, Donald. Living with *Leon*. 95 Yale L.J. 906 (1986).

Dworkin, Roger B. Fact Style Adjudication and the Fourth Amendment: The Limits of Lawyering. 48 Ind.L.J. 329 (1973).

Forbes, Jessica. The Inevitable Discovery Doctrine, Primary Evidence, and the Emasculation of the Fourth Amendment. 55 Fordham L.Rev. 1221 (1987).

Geller, William. Enforcing the Fourth Amendment: The Exclusionary Rule and its Alternatives. 1975 Wash.U.L.Q. 621 (1975).

Ingber, Stanley. Defending the Citadel: The Dangerous Attack of "Reasonable Good Faith." 36 Vand.L.Rev. 1511 (1983).

Kamisar, Yale. Does (Did) (Should) the Exclusionary Rule Rest on a "Principled Basis" Rather Than an "Empirical Proposition"? 16 Creighton L.Rev. 565, 590–1 (1983).

La Fave, Wayne. Controlling Discretion by Administrative Regulations: The Use, Misuse, and Nonuse of Police Rules and Policies in Fourth Amendment Adjudication. 89 Mich.L.Rev. 442 (1990).

Morris, Arval. The Exclusionary Rule, Deterrence and Posner's Economic Analysis of Law. 57 Wash.L.Rev. 647 (1982).

Nardulli, Vincent. The Societal Costs of the Exclusionary Rule Revisited. 1987 Ill.L.Rev. 223.

Traynor, Roger J. Mapp v. Ohio at Large in the Fifty States. 1962 Duke Law Journal 319 (1962).

Weinreb, Lloyd L. Generalities of the Fourth Amendment. 42 U.Chi.L.Rev. 47 (1974).

Wilkey, Malcolm Richard. A Call for Alternatives to the Exclusionary Rule: Let Congress and the Trial Courts Speak. 62 Judicature 351 (1979).

Yarbrough, Tinsley E. The Flexible Exclusionary Rule and the Crime Rate. 6 Am.J.Crim.L. 1 (1978).

Chapter Three

THE LAW OF ARREST

3.01 Introduction

The law of arrest is primarily important in constitutional terms because of its effect on the legality of a search. An unconstitutional or otherwise illegal arrest in itself has little significance in the prosecution of a given case. Of course, it is true, as Justice Powell has said, that

> a search may cause only an annoyance and temporary inconvenience to the law-abiding citizen, assuming more serious dimensions only when it turns up evidence of criminality. An arrest, however, is a serious personal intrusion regardless of whether the person seized is guilty or innocent.[1]

Nevertheless, aside from the possibility of a civil action in particularly egregious cases, the remedy for an illegal arrest is simply the release from detention. Moreover, even in cases in which probable cause is lacking at the time of an arrest, the subsequent development of probable cause justifies a re-arrest. And the Court has firmly established that an "illegal arrest does not void a subsequent prosecution."[2] That is, the defendant cannot escape prosecution or avoid being present in court simply because his initial arrest was illegal.[3] This is so even when the arrest consists of "kidnapping" the defendant from a foreign country over that country's protest.[4]

On the other hand, the legality of an arrest is often of crucial importance in determining the admissibility of evidence. As noted in the last chapter, it is well established that evidence seized pursuant to an unlawful arrest, and other evidence (e.g. confessions, identifications) which results from such an arrest, may constitute "fruit of the poisonous tree" and is generally subject to suppression under the exclusionary rule.[5] It is not surprising, therefore, that the bulk of arrest cases which have reached the Supreme Court arise from efforts by a convicted defendant to have his arrest declared unconstitutional in order to effect the suppression of damaging evidence. Like other aspects of Fourth Amend-

1. *United States v. Watson,* 423 U.S. 411, 428, 96 S.Ct. 820, 830 (1976) (Powell, J., concurring).

2. *Gerstein v. Pugh,* 420 U.S. 103, 95 S.Ct. 854 (1975).

3. *Frisbie v. Collins,* 342 U.S. 519, 72 S.Ct. 509 (1952).

4. *United States v. Alvarez–Machain,* 504 U.S. ___, 112 S.Ct. 857 (1992); *Ker v. Illinois,* 119 U.S. 436, 7 S.Ct. 225 (1886). Note, that in cases where the arrest involves "outrageous" conduct by government officials, conviction may be barred. *Hampton v. United States,* 425 U.S. 484, 96 S.Ct. 1646 (1976) (Powell, J., concurring), discussed in § 19.02(c).

5. See § 2.04(a).

ment jurisprudence, the development of the law of arrest is due in large measure to the development of the exclusionary rule and its application to the states in *Mapp v. Ohio.*[6]

With these points in mind, we can address the following components of the law of arrest: (1) the definition of arrest; (2) the level of suspicion (probable cause) necessary to justify an arrest; (3) the arrest warrant requirement; and (4) arrest procedure.

3.02 The Definition of Arrest

Distinguishing between an arrest and lesser types of detentions is important, because only arrests require probable cause. Early decisions of the Court suggested that an arrest occurred any time police restricted a person's movement. For instance, in *Henry v. United States,*[7] the Court found that an arrest occurred when police stopped a car whose occupants were suspected of transferring stolen liquor. According to the Court, "[w]hen the officers interrupted the two men and restricted their liberty of movement, the arrest, for purposes of this case, was complete." Since the police did not have probable cause at that moment, their action was unconstitutional.

But nine years later, the Court made clear that something more than a restriction in movement is required for an arrest. In *Terry v. Ohio,*[8] an officer observed three men behaving in a manner which suggested they were planning a store robbery. He approached the men and asked what they were doing. When they failed to respond adequately, he grabbed each one of the suspects and patted down their outer clothing. In the process, he found two weapons. Clearly, the suspects' freedom was restricted at the moment the officer was frisking them. But had the Court considered this procedure an "arrest," it would have been unconstitutional, because the officer concededly lacked probable cause at that time. Instead, the Court distinguished between arrests—which "eventuate in a trip to the station house and prosecution for crime"—and lesser seizures, which can occur "whenever a police officer accosts an individual and restrains his freedom to walk away."[9] For the type of "stop-and-frisk" action involved in *Terry,* the officer needed only "reasonable suspicion" that criminal activity was afoot, a lower level of suspicion than probable cause.[10]

6. 367 U.S. 643, 81 S.Ct. 1684 (1961), discussed in § 2.02.

7. 361 U.S. 98, 80 S.Ct. 168 (1959).

8. 392 U.S. 1, 88 S.Ct. 1868 (1968).

9. For further discussion of what constitutes a seizure, see § 11.02.

10. Although *Terry* focused on the constitutionality of the frisk rather than of the stop, later cases applied the reasonable suspicion concept to the latter as well as the former. For further discussion of the reasonable suspicion concept, see § 11.03(a).

Since *Terry* the Court has had many occasions to distinguish between arrests, which require probable cause, and lesser detentions, which do not require as much justification. These cases can be categorized in terms of whether they deal with encounters in the stationhouse, in the field, at the border, in the home, and at the behest of a grand jury.

(a) Detentions in the Stationhouse or Its Equivalent. In *Davis v. Mississippi*,[11] some 24 black youths, including Davis, were taken into custody for the purpose of fingerprinting during a rape investigation in which the only lead was the victim's broad description of her assailant as a black youth. Probable cause was clearly lacking for the detentions, yet Davis was twice held overnight and interrogated. On the basis of fingerprint evidence and damaging admissions made during the interrogations, he was convicted and sentenced to death. The Supreme Court reversed, finding that the length of the stationhouse detention, coupled with the interrogation, was too instrusive to be undertaken without probable cause.

Because the evidence available to police at the time Davis was detained had been so minimal, *Davis* left open the possibility that investigative stationhouse detentions of potential criminal defendants were permissible if police have reasonable suspicion of their involvement in crime. But in *Dunaway v. New York*,[12] the Court settled that stationhouse questioning of a suspect normally requires probable cause. In *Dunaway*, police officers took the defendant into custody in the course of investigating an attempted robbery and felony murder, gave him *Miranda* warnings, and subjected him to questioning, all without probable cause. In reversing Dunaway's conviction, the Supreme Court avoided the precise issue of whether the detention was an "arrest," but made clear that a detention for custodial interrogation requires probable cause. The majority found *Terry* inapplicable because the stop and frisk implicates only a "limited violation of individual privacy" while advancing substantial "interests in both crime prevention and detection and in the police officer's safety." The intrusive stationhouse encounter of the type involved in *Dunaway*, on the other hand, does little to prevent incipient criminal activity in the field.

In *Florida v. Royer*,[13] the Court indicated that a nonconsensual investigative detention *outside* the stationhouse can, under circumstances resembling a stationhouse encounter, require probable cause. In *Royer*, airport police stopped the defendant, suspect-

11. 394 U.S. 721, 89 S.Ct. 1394 (1969).

12. 442 U.S. 200, 99 S.Ct. 2248 (1979).

13. 460 U.S. 491, 103 S.Ct. 1319 (1983).

ed of carrying narcotics, and asked him to accompany them to a room in the airport approximately forty feet away. Royer followed them to what one of the detectives later described as "a large storage closet," containing a small desk and two chairs. The detectives then retrieved two pieces of Royer's luggage without his consent. Upon request, Royer produced a key and unlocked one of the suitcases, in which marijuana was found, and consented to the agents prying open the second piece of luggage, which also contained marijuana. He was then placed under arrest. The Court held that the detention in the "storage closet" prior to the opening of the luggage—an encounter which lasted fifteen minutes—constituted an "arrest" as well. As Justice White stated for the Court: "What had begun as a consensual inquiry in a public place had escalated into an investigatory procedure in a police interrogation room, where the police, unsatisfied with previous explanations, sought to confirm their suspicions." The Court found the officers' conduct "more intrusive than necessary to effectuate an investigative detention otherwise authorized by the *Terry* line of cases," and, as discussed in more detail later in this chapter,[14] found that probable cause had not existed at the time of the detention. Therefore, the evidence found in the luggage was inadmissible.

Not all nonconsensual detentions at the stationhouse or its equivalent require probable cause, however. As discussed below, such detentions at the *border* are justifiable on reasonable suspicion. The Court has also intimated that detentions at the stationhouse for purposes other than holding a person on charges or for interrogation may not rise to the level of an arrest. In *Davis,* for instance, the Court called "arguable" the proposition "that, because of the unique nature of the fingerprinting process, [detentions for the sole purpose of obtaining fingerprints] might, under narrowly defined circumstances, be found to comply with the Fourth Amendment even though there is no probable cause in the traditional sense." Similarly, in *Hayes v. Florida,*[15] while the Court held impermissible a stationhouse fingerprinting because, as in *Davis,* the police had forcibly taken the suspect to the station without probable cause to arrest, the majority also recognized, with apparent approval, that several states had established procedures for *judicial authorization* of fingerprinting on less than probable cause.

Finally, of course, if the "detention" is consensual, then the police cannot be said to have arrested the person. Thus, the Supreme Court's *Miranda* decisions have consistently held that a person questioned at the police station is not in "custody" (and

14. See § 3.03(b)(3).   **15.** 470 U.S. 811, 105 S.Ct. 1643 (1985).

thus not under arrest) when *he* initiates a stationhouse encounter.[16]

(b) Detentions in the Field. While police questioning of a suspect in the stationhouse or its equivalent will normally require probable cause, such questioning conducted on the "street" will usually only require reasonable suspicion, as *Terry* held. However, *Terry* also held that the stop it authorized must be "brief," implying that a prolonged encounter would require probable cause. In *Royer* the Court explicitly stated that "an investigative detention [in the field] must be temporary and last no longer than is necessary to effectuate the purpose of the stop." Thus, at some point in time detentions in the field automatically become arrests. The American Law Institute Code of Pre-Arraignment Procedure provides that a stop lasting over twenty minutes is not appropriate on less than probable cause.[17] In *United States v. Place,*[18] decided the same year as *Royer,* the Court seemed willing to consider this rule-oriented approach when it found that a 90–minute airport detention of luggage while awaiting a trained narcotics dog was "alone" sufficient to render the seizure impermissible under *Terry.*

But the Court ultimately refused to put a precise durational limit on stops. In *United States v. Sharpe,*[19] it stated:

> While it is clear that 'the brevity of the invasion of the individual's Fourth Amendment interests is an important factor in determining whether the seizure is so minimally intrusive as to be justifiable on reasonable suspicion' [citing *Place*], we have emphasized the need to consider the law enforcement purposes to be served by the stop as well as the time reasonably needed to effectuate these purposes. . . . Much as a 'bright line' rule would be desirable in evaluating whether an investigative detention is unreasonable, common sense and ordinary human experience must govern over rigid criteria.

In *Sharpe* itself, the Court sanctioned a twenty minute detention of respondent Savage and his pickup truck on less than probable cause. For fifteen minutes of this period, Savage was held by State Trooper Thrasher pending arrival of Drug Enforcement Administration agent Cooke, who had become separated from Thrasher when he stopped Savage's accomplices and Thrasher had continued in pursuit of Savage. The final five minutes involved Cooke's investigation of Savage's documents and the truck itself, resulting in the discovery of what turned out to be marijuana and Savage's arrest.

---

16. See § 16.03(a)(3).

17. ALI, Model Code of Pre-Arraignment Procedure 110.2(1) (1975).

18. 462 U.S. 696, 103 S.Ct. 2637 (1983).

19. 470 U.S. 675, 105 S.Ct. 1568 (1985).

The Fourth Circuit held that the length of Savage's detention transformed it into a *de facto* arrest, which was invalid because neither Cooke nor Thrasher had possessed probable cause to believe the truck contained drugs at the time it was stopped. The Court's majority opinion, authored by Chief Justice Burger, concluded that the seizure was merely a *Terry* stop. It was not an arrest because the police had not unnecessarily delayed Savage's detention; rather, they had conducted the investigation "in a diligent and reasonable manner." Cooke had attempted to raise Thrasher on the radio once the two had become separated and had arrived at the scene as soon as he could arrange for two other officers to detain the persons he had stopped. The state trooper's failure to conduct the search himself was justified because he had joined the pursuit late and thus "could not be certain that he was aware of all the facts that had aroused Cooke's suspicions," and because "as a highway patrolman, he lacked Cooke's training and experience in dealing with narcotics investigation." Burger contrasted the police behavior here with that in *Place,* where the Court had noted that the government agents had been remiss in not assuring the narcotic dog's presence at the time the luggage arrived in the airport.

Justice Marshall concurred in the result, concluding that the prolonged detention was Savage's fault: he should have pulled over when his accomplices were stopped by Cooke, but instead he continued to drive, necessitating Cooke's separation from the state trooper.[20] But both Justice Marshall and Justice Brennan, who dissented, rightfully pointed out that the due diligence of the police should be irrelevant to whether a field detention is an arrest. When the defendant does not contribute to the delay, no amount of honest effort by the police should convert an arrest into something less.

Marshall also argued that the due diligence test will " 'inevitably produce friction and resentment [among the police], for there are bound to be inconsistent and confusing decisions." Justice Brennan illustrated this last point by noting that the police in *Sharpe* could have been considerably more "diligent:" he suggested that a simultaneous stop of Savage and his accomplices should have been possible, that in any event Thrasher should have been able to conduct a competent investigation without Cooke, and that if he couldn't, *Cooke,* not Thrasher, should have followed Savage. He also pointed out that prior to the initial stop Cooke had had ample time to summon other DEA agents, who were "swarming throughout the immediate area," but that communications snafus had prevented his reaching them. Both Marshall and Brennan

---

20. The majority indicated that its holding would be the same whether or not Savage had tried to elude the police.

contended that the majority opinion would lessen pressure on the police to correct such problems and, more generally, to "structure their *Terry* encounters so as to confirm or dispel the officer's reasonable suspicion in a brief time."

Whether or not this latter observation is true, *Sharpe* does mean that determining whether prolonged detentions in the field are arrests will require careful case by case assessment of the extent to which the police attempt to minimize the duration of the detention.

(c) **Detentions at the Border.** The normal Fourth Amendment requirements are relaxed at the border, on the theory that the government's interest in protecting the integrity of the country's boundaries is paramount.[21] Relying heavily on this rationale, the Supreme Court, in *United States v. Montoya de Hernandez*,[22] granted the government broad authority to detain, on less than probable cause, individuals crossing the border. In *Montoya de Hernandez*, border officials had a reasonable suspicion that the defendant had ingested "balloons" containing drugs in an attempt to smuggle then into the country. After the defendant refused to undergo an x-ray examination, the police detained her incommunicado for 16 *hours* in an effort to produce the evidence via the "calls of nature." When this proved unsuccessful, due to what the court of appeals described as "heroic efforts" by the defendant, they obtained a warrant authorizing a search of her alimentary canal, which produced 88 balloons of cocaine.

Six members of the Court sanctioned the delay on the ground that the length and discomfort of the defendant's detention "resulted solely from the method by which she chose to smuggle illicit drugs into this country." To them, the only alternative to the officers' action was to allow the defendant to pass into the interior, which could not be countenanced in light of the officers' reasonable suspicion and the government's strong interest in protecting its borders. Justice Stevens agreed with the result, but on the ground—reminiscent of the holding in *Sharpe*—that the officers' attempt to minimize the delay by offering an x-ray examination had been rejected by the defendant.

Justice Brennan, joined by Justice Marshall, cogently argued that the detention in this case—"indefinite confinement in a squalid back room cut off from the outside world, the absence of basic amenities that would have been provided to even the vilest of hardened criminals, repeated strip-searches"—was tantamount to an arrest and should have been based on probable cause. Lacking probable cause the officers should either have allowed the defendant to enter the country *or* turned her away. Addressing

21. See § 13.05.　　　　　**22.** 473 U.S. 531, 105 S.Ct. 3304 (1985).

Justice Stevens' rationale, Brennan pointed out that an x-ray examination can have damaging effects and involves bodily intrusion; thus, it should be undertaken nonconsensually only if judicially authorized.[23]

While the majority stressed that the Fourth Amendment offers less protection at the border, it is not a foregone conclusion that a similar situation *inside* the border would require the Court to reach a different conclusion than the one it reached in *Montoya de Hernandez*, given the majority's preoccupation with the fact that the defendant was "responsible" for her lengthy detention. Even if limited to border situations, the holding is wrong, because it permits prolonged custodial detentions on less than probable cause. If probable cause is not to be required in border cases, the better approach would be to give the person suspected of being a drug smuggler the option of leaving the country or submitting to an x-ray, dog sniff, or other search device, assuming appropriate judicial authorization can be obtained. Moreover, if one of the latter options is chosen, police should implement it as soon as possible. This would appear to be the message of *Place*, which sanctioned failure of the police to have dogs at the ready.

(d) Detentions in the Home. Nonconsensual confrontation in the home may or may not rise to the level of an arrest, depending upon its purpose. In *Beckwith v. United States*,[24] for instance, the Court found routine questioning by several IRS agents in the defendant's living room noncustodial. In contrast is *Rawlings v. Kentucky*,[25] in which police executing an arrest warrant in the home of the person named in the warrant failed to find the named person but did discover evidence of drug possession as well as a number of occupants. Some of the officers detained the individuals in the house for 45 minutes while others went to obtain a search warrant for the house. The Supreme Court treated this detention as if it were an arrest and found it impermissible because probable cause with respect to the detained individuals was not shown to exist.

However, in *Michigan v. Summers*[26] the Court held that an individual may be detained during a search of his residence if the police arrive with a valid *search* warrant, even though probable cause to arrest him does not exist. A primary reason the Court gave for this result was that such a detention occurs on private property; detention in the home, the Court concluded, is neither as inconvenient nor as stigmatizing as detention elsewhere. A

23. See § 13.05(b) for further discussion of this issue.

24. 425 U.S. 341, 96 S.Ct. 1612 (1976), discussed in § 16.03(a)(2).

25. 448 U.S. 98, 100 S.Ct. 2556 (1980).

26. 452 U.S. 692, 101 S.Ct. 2587 (1981). See also § 5.05(c).

second rationale for the Court's decision was that a search warrant clearly indicates that there is probable cause to believe criminal activity has occurred or is occurring on the premises searched, thus implying that people on those premises may be involved in criminal activity. Given this reasoning, *Summers* is strictly limited to cases in which the detaining officers possess a valid search warrant based on probable cause to believe there is evidence of crime on the premises. When, as in *Rawlings,* they possess only an arrest warrant, they presumably may not detain individuals in the home who are not listed in the warrant unless probable cause to arrest develops as they legitimately execute the warrant.[27]

(e) Grand Jury Subpoenas. In the course of performing its investigative function, the grand jury may demand the appearance of witnesses and potential defendants through use of the subpoena *ad testificandum.*[28] The Supreme Court has indicated that such detentions may occur on less than probable cause and, indeed, on virtually no suspicion, for two reasons.[29] First, requiring a showing of probable cause would complicate the legitimate investigative objectives of the grand jury, which has traditionally possessed wide-ranging powers. More importantly, because a subpoena can be contested in court, is just as often served on concededly innocent persons as those suspected of crime, and does not require immediate compliance, this method of effecting an investigative detention is not considered as abrupt, demeaning, stigmatizing, or inconvenient as typical methods used by the police.[30]

(f) Summary. Determining whether a given detention is an arrest can often be a difficult endeavor. On the one hand, it seems apparent that seizures accompanied by handcuffing, drawn guns, or words to the effect that one is under arrest qualify as an "arrest" and thus require probable cause. On the other, brief questioning on the street will generally not rise to the level of an arrest. In analyzing the nature of those nonconsensual detentions lying in between, the key factors to consider are the purpose (e.g., questioning v. fingerprinting), manner (police detentions v. grand jury subpoenas), location (stationhouse confrontations v. seizures in the "field" or at the border), and duration of the detention. Also relevant, at least at the border, is the extent to which the defendant frustrates police efforts to minimize the intrusiveness of

27. See § 6.04(b).

28. See generally, § 23.05(a).

29. See, *United States v. Dionisio,* 410 U.S. 1, 93 S.Ct. 764 (1973) (grand jury subpoena for purpose of obtaining voice exemplar not a seizure or a violation of the Fifth Amendment); *United States v. Mara,* 410 U.S. 19, 93 S.Ct. 774 (1973) (grand jury subpoena of person's handwriting not a seizure or a violation of the Fifth Amendment).

30. Note that the grand jury cannot compel testimony from the subpoenaed witness. However, *non*-testimonial evidence, such as handwriting and voice exemplars, may be compelled. See § 23.05(a)(2).

the detention. None of these factors alone are determinative; the test is the familiar "totality of the circumstances" standard. Of course, regardless of what type of detention is involved, if the police have probable cause, the "arrest" issue is mooted.

3.03 The Probable Cause Requirement for Arrests

In *Beck v. Ohio*,[31] the Supreme Court declared that police have probable cause to make an arrest when "the facts and circumstances within their knowledge and of which they [have] reasonably trustworthy information [are] sufficient to warrant a prudent man in believing that the [suspect] had committed or was committing an offense." As this language suggests, probable cause is an objective standard; a subjective test, as the *Beck* Court pointed out, would mean that arrests could take place "in the discretion of the police." The Supreme Court has also stated, not particularly helpfully, that the probable cause standard falls somewhere between a "mere suspicion" and the no-reasonable-doubt showing imposed at trial.[32] As the name implies, probable cause may necessitate a more probable than not showing,[33] though many federal judges appear to think that the term refers to a level of certainty somewhat lower than that.[34] Defining such a fact-specific concept is obviously difficult. The discussion below will focus on the categories of information the courts have indicated can form the basis for probable cause to arrest.

(a) Secondhand Sources. *Beck* required that probable cause arise from "reasonably trustworthy information" that is "within [the officer's] knowledge." The Court has also established, however, that the arresting officer need not have personal, direct knowledge of the facts and circumstances which establish probable cause.[35] The three most common secondhand sources of information are "informants" who receive some specific benefit (often money) for providing information to the police, victims and other eyewitnesses, and other police.

(1) Informants. Police rely heavily on information from people who are acquainted with criminals or who may be criminals

---

31. 379 U.S. 89, 85 S.Ct. 223 (1964).

32. *Brinegar v. United States,* 338 U.S. 160, 69 S.Ct. 1302 (1949).

33. See, e.g., *Mallory v. United States,* 354 U.S. 449, 77 S.Ct. 1356 (1957) (arrest of three black men with access to a basement where rape by a masked black man occurred was illegal, because police may not "arrest, as it were, at large . . . in order to determine whom they should charge before a committing magistrate on 'probable cause.' ").

34. See McCauliff, "Burdens of Proof: Degrees of Belief, Quanta of Evidence, Or Constitutional Guarantees?," 35 Vand.L.Rev. 1293, 1325 (1983) (when asked to quantify the degree of certainty represented by the phrase "probable cause," 166 federal judges gave, as an average response, 45.78%).

35. *Jones v. United States,* 362 U.S. 257, 80 S.Ct. 725 (1960).

themselves. The usual issue in cases involving such informants is not whether their information, if believed, establishes probable cause, but the predicate issue of whether their information is accurate. Informants might give police distorted reports for a host of reasons, including a wish to curry favor with those who might charge them, a desire to exact revenge against a criminal colleague, or simply because they are liars. Some rules are necessary for assessing the credibility of their information, to reduce the chance that arrests will be conducted merely on the say-so of such an informer. A second reason for putting strictures on informant tips is to better enable magistrates and reviewing courts to determine when an "informant" has been concocted by police to cover the fact that their information has actually been acquired illegally.[36]

The Warren Court attempted to standardize analysis of informant credibility in *Aguilar v. Texas*,[37] where it held that an affidavit based on a tip from an informer must state: (1) sufficient underlying circumstances to demonstrate how the informant reached his conclusion, and (2) sufficient underlying circumstances establishing the reliability of the informant. The first, basis-of-knowledge prong attempts to discern whether the informant personally observed the reported criminal activity, or instead heard about it from other sources. If the latter, the information might be viewed more skeptically. The second, "veracity" prong directly attempts to evaluate whether the informant is lying or distorting the truth.

In *Spinelli v. United States*,[38] the Court elaborated on the first prong by concluding that insufficient detail as to the informant's basis of knowledge can be overcome if "the tip describe[s] the accused's criminal activity in sufficient detail that the magistrate knows that he is relying on something more substantial than a casual rumor . . . or an accusation based merely on an individual's general reputation." And in *United States v. Harris*,[39] a plurality of the Court held that a failure to meet the second "veracity" prong was not fatal if the informant's statements were a declaration against penal interest.

The *Aguilar–Spinelli* test, as *Aguilar's* two-prong formulation came to be called, was modified even more substantially in *Illinois v. Gates*,[40] where the Court formally eschewed a requirement that both prongs be met. Rather, the credibility of an informant's

---

36. For allegations that this occurs despite current rules, see Bradley, "*Murray v. United States:* The Bell Tolls for the Search Warrant Requirement," 64 Ind.L.J. 907 (1989).

37. 378 U.S. 108, 84 S.Ct. 1509 (1964).

38. 393 U.S. 410, 89 S.Ct. 584 (1969).

39. 403 U.S. 573, 91 S.Ct. 2075 (1971).

40. 462 U.S. 213, 103 S.Ct. 2317 (1983).

information must be based on the "totality of the circumstances." Thus, while the basis-of-knowledge and veracity ideas are "highly relevant," "a deficiency in one may be compensated for . . . by a strong showing as to the other."

The above cases all involved searches and thus are discussed in more detail elsewhere in this book.[41] The focus here is their relevance to the probable cause determination in the arrest context. The leading case on this issue, *Draper v. United States*,[42] preceded *Aguilar* but is still informative. In *Draper*, an informant who had provided reliable information in the past, advised police officers that the defendant was selling drugs, that he had gone to Chicago to secure a new supply and that he would be returning on a train carrying a tan bag that would contain the purchased drugs. Further, the informant described what Draper would be wearing and said that he would "walk real fast". The officers observed a man fitting the description emerge from the train carrying a tan zipper bag and walking very quickly. They arrested Draper without a warrant, searched him, and found drugs. The Supreme Court, in upholding Draper's conviction, said the informant's tip, coupled with the corroboration of the information from the observation of the officers themselves, sufficed to establish probable cause to arrest.

In the language of *Jones v. United States*,[43] *Draper* established that so long as the informant's tip "is reasonably corroborated by other matters within the officer's knowledge," the tip can be considered credible for consideration on the probable cause issue. Yet, as Justice Douglas, the lone dissenter, pointed out, a troubling aspect of *Draper* is the fact that the police observed nothing incriminating about Draper's actions before arresting him; the Court in effect held that because the informant had given an accurate description of Draper, the police were also justified in believing the informant's account of his criminal activity. Neither information as to how the informant knew about that activity (as required by *Aguilar*) or descriptive detail about the activity (as later permitted by *Spinelli*) was required.

Justice White, in a concurring opinion in *Gates,* explained how the Court in *Draper* should have analyzed the basis-of-knowledge prong to reach the result in that case: because the informant could predict two days in advance what Draper would be wearing, Draper must have "planned in advance to wear these specific clothes so that an accomplice could identify him," giving rise to a "clear inference . . . that the informant was either involved in the criminal scheme himself or that he otherwise had access to reliable, inside information." Unfortunately, instead of adopting

41. See § 5.03(b).

42. 358 U.S. 307, 79 S.Ct. 329 (1959).

43. 362 U.S. 257, 80 S.Ct. 725 (1960).

this interpretation of *Draper*, the majority in *Gates* reaffirmed the *Draper* majority's suggestion that the basis of knowledge about criminal activity need not be shown at all, and that informant veracity can be established through police corroboration of innocent information contained in the informant's tip, at least when the innocent information is detailed, as was the case in *Draper*. *Gates* also suggested that even the absence of corroboration would not be fatal, if the informant's reputation for veracity was well-known: if "a particular informant is known for the unusual reliability of his predictions of certain types of criminal activities in a locality, his failure, in a particular case, to thoroughly set forth the basis of his knowledge surely should not serve as an absolute bar to a finding of probable cause based on his tip." [44]

Based on the foregoing, factors to consider in determining whether an informant's information may form the basis for a probable cause determination include whether: (1) the informant gives a description of how he found out about the criminal activity; (2) the informant gives a detailed description of that activity; (3) there is evidence that the informant has been reliable in the past; (4) the informant predicts activity on the part of the suspect which is corroborated by the police; and (5) the informant implicates himself in the criminal activity. After *Gates*, no particular combination of these factors is required; a strong showing with respect to (1) or (3), for instance, might be sufficient.

An example of an arrest case in which this relatively relaxed test is *not* met is provided by *Beck*, decided well before *Gates* but reaffirmed by that case. There the informant merely stated that the suspect was engaged in gambling, with no detail as to time and place. This statement, even when combined with the officer's knowledge of Beck's prior gambling record, was insufficient; to hold otherwise, concluded the Court, would permit the state to arrest anyone with a prior record.

(2) Victims and eyewitnesses. When the informant is a "respectable citizen" who has been a victim or otherwise an eyewitness to crime, the two prongs of *Aguilar–Spinelli,* while theoretically still relevant, are usually not applied with much rigor. In *Jaben v. United States,* [45] the Supreme Court held that "whereas some supporting information concerning the credibility of informants in narcotics cases or other common garden varieties of crime may be required, such information is not so necessary in the

---

44. An example of such a case might be *McCray v. Illinois,* 386 U.S. 300, 87 S.Ct. 1056 (1967), where the police informant had provided information on fifteen or sixteen previous occasions, which led to numerous arrests and convictions. Of course, there is much to be said, contrary to the rule in *Gates,* for the position that past accuracy should not be *dispositive* of the accuracy issue in a subsequent case. See § 5.03(b)(3).

45. 381 U.S. 214, 85 S.Ct. 1365 (1965).

context of the case before us [where third parties provided information about the defendant's financial situation in a tax evasion case]." Similarly, in *Chambers v. Maroney*,[46] which did involve "garden-variety crime," the Court upheld an arrest for robbery of a service station for which probable cause was established through a report from two teenagers who happened to be in the vicinity. *Chambers* recognizes that, with the typical eyewitness, the first-hand basis of the informant's knowledge is evident and there is usually no motive to fabricate information.

Of course, as always, the information provided by such individuals, even if believed, must still establish probable cause to arrest. In *Chambers*, the teenagers told police investigating the robbery that a blue compact station wagon containing four men, one with a green sweater, had been circling in the vicinity of the gas station and later sped away from it. When the service station attendant verified that one of the two men who robbed the station had been wearing a green sweater, and that the other had been wearing a trench coat, "the police had ample cause to stop [within two miles of the station] a light blue compact station wagon carrying four men and to arrest the occupants, one of whom was wearing a green sweater and one of whom had a trench coat with him in the car."

(3) Other police. When a police officer is the informant, the veracity inquiry is even further relaxed; indeed, in *United States v. Ventresca*,[47] the Supreme Court stated that "[o]bservations of fellow officers of the Government engaged in a common investigation are plainly a reliable basis for a warrant applied for by one of their number." Yet, again, those observations must amount to probable cause, or an arrest based on them will be invalid. Thus, in *Whiteley v. Warden*,[48] an arrest based on a radio bulletin from a sheriff in another jurisdiction advising that a warrant had been issued there for the suspect's arrest was held invalid, because the warrant affidavit failed to state any basis for the probable cause finding.

However, the *Whiteley* Court also stated that, had the warrant from the other jurisdiction been valid, the arrest would have been constitutional. *Whiteley* thus approves the common police practice of making arrests based on reports from other officers, whether or not information in the report was obtained firsthand, provided that it establishes probable cause. If the police bulletin is not based on probable cause, then an arrest founded on it is improper, regardless of how reasonable the arresting officer's belief in the report's validity may be. This rule deters the police from immu-

---

46. 399 U.S. 42, 90 S.Ct. 1975 (1970). **48.** 401 U.S. 560, 91 S.Ct. 1031 (1971).
47. 380 U.S. 102, 85 S.Ct. 741 (1965).

nizing misconduct through reliance on other officers to conduct the actual arrest.

(b) First-hand Knowledge.   When the arresting officer is also the "informant" then the key issue in most Supreme Court decisions has not been the accuracy or truthfulness of his observations but whether, based on what the officer knew, probable cause existed.   A few recurring situations in which this issue has been raised are explored below.

(1) Post-detention information.   A key tenet of arrest law is that probable cause must be established by evidence obtained independently of the arrest.   In *Sibron v. New York*,[49] the Supreme Court stated: "It is axiomatic that an incident search may not precede an arrest and serve as part of its justification."   This language should not be construed to prevent seizure of evidence before an arrest for which probable cause already exists becomes "official";[50] it is merely meant to deter police from illegally seizing and searching people solely for the purpose of establishing probable cause to arrest.

On the other hand, it is generally well-established that evidence noticed or seized during a legal encounter which has not yet reached the level of an "arrest" may properly be used to establish probable cause.   The clearest example of this rule is the situation where, upon "reasonable suspicion," a police officer stops a suspect, receives an inadequate explanation for his "suspicious" behavior, and discovers incriminating evidence during the course of a protective frisk.   Already noted was *Terry v. Ohio*,[51] the primary "stop and frisk" case, in which furtive conduct by three men alerted an experienced police officer that a robbery might be imminent.   The officer approached the men and asked them what they were doing.   They merely "mumbled something," whereupon the officer frisked them and discovered weapons.   The defendant was then arrested, charged with carrying a concealed weapon, and convicted.   The Supreme Court affirmed, holding that, if a protective frisk is justified and a weapon is discovered, probable cause to arrest may be established.[52]

Similarly, if in the course of the temporary detention, the suspect fails adequately to account for his suspicious actions, or if he affirmatively discloses incriminating evidence or makes incriminating statements, probable cause to arrest may be established.[53] Further, while the Supreme Court has suggested that the fact of

49.   392 U.S. 40, 88 S.Ct. 1889 (1968).

50.   See § 6.03.

51.   392 U.S. 1, 88 S.Ct. 1868 (1968).

52.   For further explication of this aspect of stop and frisk law, see § 11.06(c).

53.   See *Cook,* Constitutional Rights of the Accused: Pre-trial Rights 130–31 (1972).

flight alone does not create probable cause,[54] it noted in *Sibron* that flight can also be an important factor in the probable cause determination. Lower courts have also held that an attempt to conceal from police view a highly suspicious object may give rise to probable cause.[55]

(2) Proximity to criminal suspects. In *United States v. Di Re,*[56] government investigators justified their arrest of Di Re from the front passenger seat of a car on the ground that, at the time of his arrest, there were two other men in the car, both of whom were validly arrested for engaging in a transaction involving counterfeit ration coupons. The Court held that the police lacked probable cause to arrest Di Re, concluding that the circumstances were not such that a person in Di Re's position would necessarily know about or be involved in the illegal transaction. The Court noted that the transaction was not "secretive," but carried out in "broad daylight, in plain sight of passers-by, in a public street of a large city," and that "the alleged substantive crime [was] one which does not necessarily involve any act visibly criminal." If Di Re had seen the passing of coupons, "it would not follow that he knew they were ration coupons, and if he saw that they were ration coupons, it would not follow that he would know them to be counterfeit" (a fact apparently proven at trial by expert testimony). Thus, Di Re's proximity to criminal activity did not establish probable cause.

This principle has been reiterated by the Court on several occasions. In *Johnson v. United States,*[57] decided during the same term as *Di Re,* police were informed that some persons of unknown identity were smoking opium in a hotel room. From outside the room, the officers could smell burning opium. They entered the room, announced that all of its occupants were under arrest, and proceeded to search the premises.[58] Opium was discovered and introduced into evidence at trial. The Supreme Court reversed the convictions, holding that the officers had probable cause to believe that a crime had been committed but that they lacked sufficient information to determine which of the occupants had committed it. Consequently the arrests—and the search incident thereto—were illegal.

The *Johnson* analysis should be read in light of the Supreme Court's later holding in *Ker v. California,*[59] which indicated that

---

54. *Wong Sun v. United States,* 371 U.S. 471, 83 S.Ct. 407 (1963).

55. *People v. Howell,* 394 Mich. 445, 231 N.W.2d 650 (1975).

56. 332 U.S. 581, 68 S.Ct. 222 (1948).

57. 333 U.S. 10, 68 S.Ct. 367 (1948).

58. The search in *Johnson* incident to the arrest was conducted long before

the Court's opinion in *Chimel v. California,* 395 U.S. 752, 89 S.Ct. 2034 (1969), in which the permissible scope of searches incident was severely restricted to the area within the arrestee's reach. See § 6.04(a).

59. 374 U.S. 23, 83 S.Ct. 1623 (1963).

under somewhat different circumstances probable cause might be more readily found. Armed with both their own visual observations and an informant's tip that George Ker had engaged in the purchase and sale of marijuana, police officers entered Ker's apartment. Inside were Ker and his wife. Upon spotting a brickshaped package of marijuana in the kitchen, they arrested both persons. The Supreme Court upheld both arrests, stating with respect to Mrs. Ker:

> Even assuming that her presence in a small room with the contraband in a prominent position on the kitchen sink would not alone establish a reasonable ground for the officers' belief that she was in joint possession with her husband, that fact was accompanied by the officers' information that Ker had been using his apartment as a base of operations for his narcotics activities. Therefore, we cannot say that at the time of her arrest there were not sufficient grounds for a reasonable belief that Diane Ker . . . was committing the offense of possession of marijuana in the presence of the officers.

A more recent Supreme Court case which helps define the extent to which police may infer probable cause from the defendant's presence at the scene of criminal activity is *Ybarra v. Illinois*.[60] In *Ybarra* police procured a valid search warrant authorizing both the search of a tavern believed to be a center of drug transactions and the search of the tavern's bartender. When executing the warrant, the police searched the dozen or so patrons of the tavern, including the petitioner, Ybarra. The Court held, 6–3 that the warrant did not give the officers authority "to invade the constitutional protections possessed individually by the tavern's customers." While the case thus dealt with the validity of a search, it contains language which is applicable to arrests:

> [A] person's mere propinquity to others independently suspected of criminal activity does not, without more, give rise to probable cause to search that person. Where the standard is probable cause, a search or *seizure of a person* must be supported by probable cause particularized with respect to that person. This requirement cannot be undercut or avoided by simply pointing to the fact that coincidentally there exists probable cause to search or seize another or to search the premises where the person may happen to be. [emphasis added]

Justice Stewart, writing for the majority, rejected the state's contention that when the police have a "reasonable belief" that individuals on "compact" premises "are connected with" drug trafficking and "may be concealing or carrying away the contraband," there is no bar to a search or seizure of those individuals.

---

60.   444 U.S. 85, 100 S.Ct. 338 (1979).

Citing *Di Re*, he emphasized that probable cause is necessary before such a search or seizure can take place, except when, as set out in *Terry*, there is a particularized fear that an individual is armed and dangerous. He noted that police could point to no specific fact that would have justified such a suspicion in Ybarra's case.

(3) Investigative profiles. A recent development in law enforcement has been the use of so-called "profiles," designed to take advantage of statistical or experiential information suggesting the common characteristics of certain types of criminal actors (e.g., hihijackers, drug couriers). Several Supreme Court cases involve the use of such profiles.

In *Reid v. Georgia*,[61] for instance, the court of appeals held that a narcotics agent had reasonable grounds to stop two individuals because they met the following elements of an informal "drug courier profile:" (1) the petitioner had arrived from Fort Lauderdale, a principal place of origin for cocaine; (2) he arrived early in the morning, when law enforcement activity is diminished; (3) he and his companion appeared to be trying to conceal the fact that they were travelling together, and (4) they apparently had no luggage other than their shoulder bags. The Supreme Court concluded there were no grounds for a stop, much less an arrest, on these facts: only the third observation specifically related to the individuals concerned and this, in itself, was insufficient to give rise to a reasonable suspicion that the individuals were carrying drugs.

In *Florida v. Royer*,[62] the police detained an individual in a small airport room because he fit the following elements of a drug courier profile: he was carrying American Tourister luggage which appeared to be heavy; was young and casually dressed; appeared nervous and evasive; paid for his ticket with cash; did not write his full name and address on his luggage identification tickets; and was departing from Miami, a major import center for illicit drugs and was destined for New York, a major drug distribution center. Further, the police determined that the name on the ticket was not Royer's. After finding that the detention constituted an arrest, the Court held that these factors did not constitute probable cause. "We cannot . . . agree that every nervous young man paying cash for a ticket to New York City under an assumed name and carrying two heavy American Tourister bags may be arrested and held to answer for a serious felony charge." However, the Court did hold that there were sufficient grounds in this case to stop the defendant.

61. 448 U.S. 438, 100 S.Ct. 2752 (1980).   **62.** 460 U.S. 491, 103 S.Ct. 1319 (1983).

The Court came to a similar conclusion in *United States v. Sokolow*,[63] again involving a seizure in an airport. There, at the time the defendant was stopped, his behavior "had all the classic aspects of a drug courier," according to an agent. More specifically, at the time of the stop, "the agents knew, *inter alia*, that (1) he paid $2,100 for two airplane tickets from a roll of $20 bills; (2) he traveled under a name that did not match the name under which his telephone number was listed; (3) his original destination was Miami, a source city for illicit drugs; (4) he stayed in Miami for only 48 hours, even though a round-trip flight from Honolulu to Miami takes 20 hours; (5) he appeared nervous during his trip; and (6) he checked none of his luggage. The Court found this information sufficient for a stop, but not an arrest.

The profiles at issue in these and other cases [64] barely deserve the name, given their transparently post hoc nature. As Justice Marshall pointed out in his dissent in *Sokolow*, the elements of particular drug courier profiles have been manipulated from case to case, apparently to justify seizures after the fact.[65] Probably wisely, therefore, the Court's penchant in "profile cases" seems to be to look at the underlying factual basis of the detention without squarely addressing the usefulness of the profiles, *qua* profiles, in determining reasonable suspicion or probable cause. Even in *Sokolow*, the case in which it came closest to explicitly authorizing their use, the Court was equivocal, merely stating that "the fact that these factors may be set forth in a 'profile' does not somehow detract from their evidentiary significance as seen by a trained agent."

On the other hand, a seizure based on a profile should not automatically be rejected, if two conditions are met: (1) the profile is empirically proven to produce a constitutionally adequate success rate (say, a 50% success rate to justify an arrest, or a 30% success rate to justify a *Terry* stop); and (2) it is filed with the court beforehand so as to prevent the post hoc manipulation of which Marshall complained. The mere fact that a profile allows police to base a detention on group data, rather than "particularized suspicion," should not defeat its use in the investigative context, where, as the Court has stated many times, probabilities are the issue.[66] The main reason profiles are unlikely to become

---

63. 490 U.S. 1, 109 S.Ct. 1581 (1989).

64. See, e.g., *United States v. Mendenhall*, 446 U.S. 544, 100 S.Ct. 1870 (1980); *Florida v. Rodriguez*, 469 U.S. 1, 105 S.Ct. 308 (1984).

65. Marshall listed a number of seemingly contradictory factors that have been deemed important elements of various "profiles": person deplaned first, deplaned last, deplaned in the middle; one-way ticket, round trip ticket; non-stop flight, changed planes; no luggage, gym bag, new suitcases; traveling alone, traveling with companion; acted nervously, acted too calmly.

66. For a more detailed investigation of the attack against profiles, see Slobogin, "The World Without a Fourth Amendment," 39 U.C.L.A.L.Rev. 1, 380–85 (1991).

the norm is the difficulty of arriving at a list of traits (at least with respect to drug couriers) that will lead to an empirically verifiable level of certainty sufficient to meet the dictates of probable cause or reasonable suspicion.

(c) Mistake.　Once the objective facts known to the police establish probable cause, whether they come from informants or firsthand information, it is immaterial that some or all of those facts later turn out to be false,[67] so long as the officer reasonably believed them to be true at the time of arrest.[68]　The one exception to this rule would appear to be when the false information relied upon is from another police officer who knows the information to be false.　Without such an exception, the rationale for the decision in *Whiteley,* discussed above,[69] would be completely undermined.

Another species of mistake is when the police have probable cause to arrest one person but, as a result of reasonable mistake, arrest another.　In such circumstances, the arrest is valid for purposes of determining the admissibility of any evidence thereby discovered.　This scenario describes the facts of *Hill v. California,*[70] where the police, having probable cause to arrest Hill, went to his apartment and knocked; the person who answered the door, one Miller, fit Hill's description and was arrested.　Although at this point Miller provided identification showing he was not Hill, the Court noted that "aliases and false identifications are not uncommon" and that Miller had denied knowledge of firearms in the apartment although a pistol and loaded ammunition clip were in plain view in the room.　Thus, the police could reasonably have believed Miller was Hill and anything seized pursuant to a search incident to the arrest was admissible against Hill.[71]　The Court emphasized that "sufficient probability, not certainty, is the touchstone of reasonableness under the Fourth Amendment and on the record before us the officers' mistake was understandable and the arrest a reasonable response to the situation facing them at the time."

3.04　The Arrest Warrant Requirement

The Fourth Amendment states that arrest warrants may only issue upon a showing of probable cause and must state with particularity the person to be seized.　The question addressed here

67.　*Henry v. United States,* 361 U.S. 98, 80 S.Ct. 168 (1959).　See also, *United States v. Garofalo,* 496 F.2d 510 (8th Cir.1974), cert. denied 419 U.S. 860, 95 S.Ct. 109 (1974).

68.　Id.　See also, discussion of *Franks v. Delaware,* 438 U.S. 154, 98 S.Ct. 2674 (1978), in § 5.03(d).

69.　See § 3.03(a)(3).

70.　401 U.S. 797, 91 S.Ct. 1106 (1971).

71.　Note that one could also conclude that Hill lacked standing to challenge Miller's arrest.　See § 4.04.

is when such a warrant is required.[72]   Under the common law rule, if the arresting officer had probable cause to believe that: (1) a person was committing or had committed a felony, or (2) a person was committing a misdemeanor involving a breach of the peace in the officer's presence, then an arrest warrant was not required. Thus, the only situation in which an arrest warrant was necessary was for arrest on a misdemeanor charge committed outside the officer's presence or not involving a breach of the peace.[73] The reasoning behind this rule was described by the Supreme Court in *Carroll v. United States:* [74]

> The reason for arrest for misdemeanors without warrant at common law was to promptly suppress breaches of the peace . . . while the reason for arrest without a warrant on a reliable report of a felony was because the public safety and the due apprehension of criminals charged with heinous offenses required that such arrests should be made at once without warrant.

As discussed below, since *Carroll* the Court has explicitly upheld the common law rule, except with respect to arrests in the suspect's home and arrests in the homes of third parties. Note, however, that when an arrest is *not* authorized by a warrant, the police must obtain a judicial determination, within a short time of the arrest, that it was based on probable cause.[75]

   (a) Public Arrests. *United States v. Watson* [76] was the first case in which the Court squarely upheld, as a matter of constitutional law, the common law rule permitting warrantless arrest in public even when there is time to obtain a warrant. The Court expressed confidence in the ability of police officers to make determinations of probable cause and stated: "we decline to transform [a] judicial preference [for arrest warrants] into a constitutional rule when the judgment of the Nation and Congress has for so long been to authorize warrantless public arrests on probable cause." Since most public arrests are made under exigent circumstances, a different decision in *Watson* would have affected only a small number of people. Nonetheless, the fact that non-exigent warrantless arrests were allowed under common law does not

---

72. Other issues associated with the warrant process are dealt with in Chapter 5, dealing with search warrants, since they tend to be identical to those raised with respect to arrests.

73. Most jurisdictions have modified the misdemeanor arrest rule to permit warrantless arrests for *any* misdemeanor occurring in the officer's presence. The ALI's Model Code of Pre–Arraignment Procedure also permits, at § 120.1, a warrantless arrest for a mis-

demeanor "when the officer has reasonable cause to believe that the misdemeanant will not be apprehended or may cause injury to himself, to others, or to property, unless immediately arrested."

74.   267 U.S. 132, 45 S.Ct. 280 (1925).

75.   *Gerstein v. Pugh,* 420 U.S. 103, 95 S.Ct. 854 (1975), discussed in § 20.02.

76.   423 U.S. 411, 96 S.Ct. 820 (1976).

provide a persuasive reason for foregoing judicial authorization when there is time to seek it.

The Court has also held that a warrant is not required to make an arrest on the "curtilage" of one's home. In *United States v. Santana*,[77] the police, with cause to arrest Santana, arrived at her house to find her standing in her front doorway. When she saw the officers approaching, she retreated into the vestibule and closed the door behind her. The officers followed her inside and there effected her arrest without a warrant. The Supreme Court affirmed the validity of the arrest procedure. When Santana stood in the doorway, the Court explained, "[s]he was not in an area where she had any expectation of privacy" and her arrest at that point would therefore have been permissible under a *Watson* public-arrest analysis. When she retreated into her house, she created exigent circumstances necessitating warrantless entry.[78]

(b) Arrests in the Home. For some time, the Court also seemed willing to permit warrantless arrests that *commence* inside the home. As already noted, at common law, it was well-settled that a warrantless entry to effect a felony arrest in a private home constituted a reasonable exercise of the police power, regardless of the existence of exigent circumstances. The validity of such a procedure was accepted *sub rosa* by the Supreme Court in a number of its early decisions.[79] It was not until *Payton v. New York*,[80] however, that the Court addressed directly the issue of warrantless home arrests. Despite the implications of its earlier decisions, the Court in *Payton* held, 6–3, that the Fourth Amendment prohibits a warrantless, nonconsensual entry into a suspect's home to make an arrest, unless exigent circumstances are present.

The Supreme Court's majority opinion, written by Justice Stevens, emphasized that "physical entry of the home is the chief evil against which the wording of the Fourth Amendment is directed." He also noted that the Court had long established that a *search* of a home requires a warrant unless there are exigent circumstances.[81] To the dissenters' argument that a search is more intrusive than an arrest Stevens rightly responded that "any differences in the intrusiveness of entries to search and entries to arrest are merely ones of degree rather than kind," especially since a search may occur in the course of attempting to apprehend the subject of an arrest warrant.[82] Stevens also pointed out that, in comparison to the warrantless public arrest rule, the warrantless home arrest rule advanced by the dissent was not as widely

---

77. 427 U.S. 38, 96 S.Ct. 2406 (1976).

78. For further discussion of the exigency issue, see § 3.04(d).

79. See, e.g., *Trupiano v. United States*, 334 U.S. 699, 68 S.Ct. 1229 (1948).

80. 445 U.S. 573, 100 S.Ct. 1371 (1980).

81. See § 4.03(a).

82. See § 6.04(b) & (c).

supported. Although admitting that a large number of states followed the latter rule, he detected a trend toward the majority's position, noting that five of the seven federal circuit courts of appeal that had considered the question had found warrantless home arrests unconstitutional, as had ten state courts (although two state courts had found to the contrary).

The Court also concluded that the only probable cause showing that need be made to support an arrest warrant is that connecting the suspect with criminal activity. Although arguing for warrantless arrests, Justice White's dissent contended that probable cause to believe the suspect was in his home should be established as well. The majority countered that "[i]f there is sufficient evidence of a citizen's participation in a felony to persuade a judicial officer that his arrest is justified, it is constitutionally responsible to require him to open his doors to the officers of the law."

(c) Arrests in Third Party Homes. When the police obtain an arrest warrant, but seek to execute it in the home of someone other than the person named in the warrant, different considerations come into play. As Justice Marshall pointed out in the majority opinion in *Steagald v. United States,*[83] while an arrest warrant may protect the suspect "from an unreasonable seizure, it [does] absolutely nothing to protect [a third party's] privacy interest in being free from an unreasonable invasion and search of his home." Thus, held the *Steagald* Court, in such situations the police must not only obtain an arrest warrant but also a search warrant, based upon a probable cause finding that the suspect is located in the third party's home.

The government in *Steagald* had contended that requiring a search warrant in such cases would unduly hamper law enforcement because the inherent mobility of the suspect might require several trips to the magistrate as the suspect moved from place to place. Marshall gave three reasons why the majority's rule would not "significantly impede effective law enforcement efforts." First, under *Payton,* an arrest warrant *is* sufficient authority to enter the suspect's *own* home. Secondly, under *Watson,* police can always arrest a suspect in public, and thus can wait to apprehend him as he leaves the dwelling. Finally, as with arrests in the defendant's own home, a warrant is not required to enter a house when exigent circumstances make obtaining one unfeasible.

As in *Payton,* Justices Rehnquist and White dissented, criticizing the Court's opinion primarily on practical grounds. They felt that, after the Court's ruling, police, magistrates and trial judges "will, in their various capacities, have to weigh the time during

83. 451 U.S. 204, 101 S.Ct. 1642 (1981).

which a suspect for whom there is an outstanding arrest warrant has been in the building, whether the dwelling is the suspect's home, how long he has lived there, whether he is likely to leave immediately, and a number of related and equally imponderable questions." While the dissenters are probably more realistic in their assessment of the impact of *Steagald* on law enforcement, the majority's concern that a contrary result would create significant potential for abuse is also well founded. As Justice Marshall pointed out, under such a ruling, the police, "[a]rmed solely with an arrest warrant for a single person, . . . could search all the homes of that individual's friends and acquaintances."

(d) Hot Pursuit: The Exception to the Warrant Requirement. Both *Payton* and *Steagald* indicated that "exigent circumstances" would justify warrantless entry to effect an arrest. The principal cases cited in support of this proposition were *Warden v. Hayden* [84] and *United States v. Santana.* [85] Both of these cases upheld warrantless home arrests relying on what has come to be known as the "hot pursuit" doctrine.

Under the hot pursuit doctrine, first announced in *Hayden,* if police have probable cause to believe a criminal suspect they are pursuing has fled into a dwelling, they may make a warrantless entry of that dwelling for the purpose of arresting him. In *Hayden,* police were informed that the defendant had robbed a taxi company at gunpoint and had been followed to a particular house. Within five minutes of the defendant's entry into the house, the police had arrived at the home, gained entrance, and arrested the defendant. The Court upheld the arrest of the defendant because the "Fourth Amendment does not require police officers to delay in the course of an investigation if to do so would gravely endanger their lives or the lives of others."

A slightly different emergency rationale led to the Court's decision to uphold the warrantless home arrest in *Santana.* In *Santana,* it will be remembered, the police, with probable cause to arrest the defendant, followed her inside her house after spotting her in her vestibule. To have required a warrant in this situation, the Court felt, would have permitted her almost certain escape. Thus, the Court has recognized both imminent danger to others and imminent escape of the suspect as exigencies permitting warrantless entry.

A third type of exigency which might justify such entries is when evidence would otherwise be destroyed. In *Minnesota v. Olson,* [86] the Court noted with approval the lower court's conclusion that "a warrantless intrusion may be justified by hot pursuit

84. 387 U.S. 294, 87 S.Ct. 1642 (1967).

85. 427 U.S. 38, 96 S.Ct. 2406 (1976).

86. 495 U.S. 91, 110 S.Ct. 1684 (1990).

of a fleeing felon, or *imminent destruction of evidence, . . .* or the need to prevent a suspect's escape, or the risk of danger to the police or to other persons inside or outside the dwelling."[87]   Although dictum, this language seems a sensible delineation of the exigency concept.[88]   Thus, it seems likely that police may make a warrantless home arrest not only of suspects who are dangerous or escape risks, but also of those who might otherwise destroy evidence.

Unfortunately, in a case decided after *Payton* and *Steagald,* the Court has also held that a fourth factor—the gravity of the offense charged—is relevant in determining when exigent circumstances exist.   In *Welsh v. Wisconsin,*[89] police had probable cause to believe the defendant was driving while intoxicated based on a witness' account that the defendant had been driving erratically, crashed his car, and acted bizarrely upon leaving his immobilized vehicle.   Ascertaining the defendant's address from the registration left in the car, police proceeded to his home, arrested him and took a blood sample later used against him, all without a warrant. The Court, in a 7–2 decision, held the arrest invalid, because under Wisconsin law the defendant was guilty only of a civil traffic offense.   Justice Brennan's majority opinion quoted Justice Jackson in *McDonald v. United States*[90] to justify its position: "When an officer undertakes to act as his own magistrate, he ought to be in a position to justify it by pointing to some real immediate and serious consequences if he postponed action to get a warrant."   To the state's argument that exigency existed because evidence of the defendant's blood level needed to be preserved, the Court merely observed that when the offense is a noncriminal "minor" one, "a warrantless home arrest cannot be upheld simply because evidence of the petitioner's blood-alcohol level might have dissipated while the police obtained a warrant."

What the Court seems to be saying in *Welsh* is that when a "nondangerous" offense is involved, it will be almost impossible to prove exigency.   Yet the nature of the offense being investigated is not necessarily relevant to whether there is time to obtain a warrant.   If there is true exigency (for instance, where the misdemeanant is about to escape, harm someone, or destroy crucial evidence), the fact that the offense allegedly committed is "minor" should not prevent arrest.   A separate problem with *Welsh* is defining when an offense is so trivial that a warrantless home arrest for it is not permitted.   For instance, the crime involved in

87. *State v. Olson,* 436 N.W.2d 92 (Minn.1989) (emphasis added).

88. For further treatment of the exigency idea, in the context of warrantless entries to *search,* see §§ 6.04(b) & (c), 8.03, and 9.02(a).

89. 466 U.S. 740, 104 S.Ct. 2091 (1984).

90. 335 U.S. 451, 69 S.Ct. 191 (1948).

Welsh—driving while intoxicated—is considered quite serious in many states; presumably in these states warrantless home arrests would be permitted.   In short, the fact that a crime is minor should not, by itself, prohibit warrantless actions.

At the same time, merely because an offense is serious should not authorize the police to proceed without a warrant.   Unfortunately, many lower courts have suggested otherwise, following the lead of the D.C. Circuit Court of Appeals in *Dorman v. United States*.[91] *Dorman* identified seven factors that might permit warrantless entry: (1) the offense under investigation is grave; (2) the suspect is reasonably believed to be armed; (3) the police have a high degree of probable cause for the arrest; (4) there is an especially strong reason to believe that the suspect is on the premises; (5) it is likely that the suspect will escape if not quickly apprehended; (6) the entry may be made peaceably; and (7) the entry is during the day.   Factor (5) is a legitimate exigency that permits a warrantless entry, and factor (2) could be.   The heightened probable cause findings required by factors (3) and (4) are perhaps justifiable given the absence of judicial intervention.   But factor (1), either by itself or in combination, should not be relevant unless the nature of the offense somehow suggests imminent danger to others.   Merely because the alleged offense is murder should not mean the warrant requirement may be dispensed with.   Indeed, in such a situation judicial authorization is even more important, as the police naturally tend to become most zealous when serious offenses are involved.

The last two factors listed by the *Dorman* court, (6) and (7), are an admirable attempt to limit the intrusiveness of a warrantless entry.   But if probable cause and true exigency are present, then the fact that a warrantless entry may have to be somewhat unruly or occur at night should not prevent it.   Despite these observations, the lower courts continue to apply the *Dorman* factors, giving them different weights and applying them in different combinations depending upon the circumstances.[92]

3.05   Executing an Arrest

Four issues arise in connection with executing an arrest: (1) what time constraints does an arrest warrant place on the executing officer?; (2) when are the police required to knock and announce their presence when they make a home arrest?; (3) when may police use deadly force to effect an arrest?; and (4) to what

91.   435 F.2d 385 (D.C.Cir.1970).

92.   See, e.g., *United States v. Reed,* 572 F.2d 412 (2d Cir.1978); *State v. Gregory,* 331 N.W.2d 140 (Iowa 1983), cert. denied 464 U.S. 833, 104 S.Ct. 115 (1983); *People v. Abney,* 81 Ill.2d 159, 41 Ill.Dec. 45, 407 N.E.2d 543 (1980).   For an example of a warrantless entry case which does not rely on *Dorman,* see *United States v. Forker,* 928 F.2d 365 (11th Cir.1991).

extent may the police search individuals whom they arrest, or search and detain those whom they discover in the course of making the arrest? The first topic is covered in this book's discussion of search warrants, since the issues are similar.[93] The second topic, although also an issue that arises in the search context, is discussed here, since most of the Court's decisions on the subject have been arrest cases. The third topic is obviously relevant only to arrest procedure and will be examined in the second subsection below. The final issue is best dealt with in the context of the search incident to arrest exception.[94]

(a) The Method of Entry. In English law—a source to which the Supreme Court regularly refers in arrest entry cases—police were entitled to break into a house to effect an arrest after stating their authority and their purpose for demanding admission.[95] In this country, the notice requirement was further relaxed in the existence of exigent circumstances very early on in *Read v. Case.*[96] Since then, the standards for arrest entries have generally been set out in legislation. The federal statute, 18 U.S.C.A. § 3109, provides that an officer "may break open any outer or inner door or window of a house . . . to execute a search warrant, if, after notice of his authority and purpose, he is refused admittance." This statute has been held to govern arrests, as well as searches, both with and without a warrant.[97] The American Law Institute in its Model Code of Pre-Arraignment Procedure has promulgated a similar rule, which adds that an arrest entry without a prior demand is justified if the making of the demand would allow the arrestee to escape, subject the officer or another to harm, or permit the destruction of evidence or the damage or loss of property.[98]

The reasons for requiring notice in most cases are several: (1) needless property destruction will be avoided; (2) needless violence by surprised or fearful occupants will be prevented; and (3) the dignity and privacy of the occupants will be respected. At the same time, some sort of exigency exception is necessary to prevent against the same dangers (harm, escape or evidence destruction) that permit conducting an arrest without a warrant.[99]

93. See § 5.05(a).

94. See § 6.04.

95. Semayne's Case, 50 Co.Rep. 91a, 11 E.R.C. 629, 77 Eng.Repr. 194 (K.B.1603), is the oft-cited authority for this proposition. "In all cases where the King is party," the Court declared, at 195, "the sheriff (if the doors be not open) may break the party's house, either to arrest him, or to do other execution of the K[ing]'s process, if otherwise he cannot enter. But before he breaks it, he ought to signify the cause of his coming, and to make request to open doors . . .."

96. 4 Conn. 166 (1822).

97. See, e.g., *Miller v. United States,* 357 U.S. 301, 78 S.Ct. 1190 (1958).

98. ALI, A Model Code of Pre-Arraignment Procedure § 120.6(1) and (2) (Official Draft 1975).

99. See § 3.04(d).

The Supreme Court has apparently held that, under the Fourth Amendment, the police are normally required to knock and announce their presence, but it has also broadly defined the exigent circumstances that justify dispensing with these requirements. In *Ker v. California*,[1] the police failed to announce their presence when they entered the Kers' apartment, instead entering quietly with a passkey obtained from the apartment manager. The Supreme Court barely upheld their action, 5–4, with Justice Harlan joining the result on the ground that state search and seizure rules should not be governed by Fourth Amendment standards but by the more flexible due process clause. The four remaining members of the majority approved the entry because: (1) the police believed the Kers were in possession of narcotics, "which could be quickly and easily destroyed," and (2) Mr. Ker's "furtive conduct . . . before the arrest was ground for the belief that he might well have been expecting the police."

The majority's finding of exigency in *Ker* is somewhat stretched, since the "furtive conduct" alluded to by the Court consisted of a U-turn executed by Mr. Ker while the police were following his car. Although this maneuver resulted in the police losing track of him after a drug transaction, it is not clear Ker knew of the police's presence. It also meant that—as a result of efforts to relocate Mr. Ker through his automobile license—a considerable period of time elapsed before the entry into the apartment, during which the evidence could easily have been destroyed had Ker decided to do so. Further, dispensing with the notice requirement anytime possession of drugs is the offense and the suspect "might well suspect" their discovery would emasculate the knock and announce requirement. In dissent, Justice Brennan offered a set of rules that more sensibly balance the interests involved:

> [T]he Fourth Amendment is violated by an unannounced police intrusion into a private home, with or without an arrest warrant, except (1) where the persons within already know of the officers' authority and purpose, or (2) where the officers are justified in the belief that persons within are in imminent peril of bodily harm, or (3) where those within, made aware of the presence of someone outside (because, for example, there has been a knock at the door), are then engaged in activity which justifies the officers in the belief that an escape or the destruction of evidence is being attempted.

An alternative might be to permit unannounced entry when a magistrate finds a probability that notice will lead to destruction of evidence or escape (as is authorized by "no-knock" legislation in some states).[2]

---

1. 374 U.S. 23, 83 S.Ct. 1623 (1963).

2. For a defense of the "no-knock" statute, see Sonnenreich & Ebner, "No–

Although *Ker* remains the only Supreme Court case to address constitutional aspects of the method of entry issue, a few other Court cases construe the federal statute, § 3109, doing so quite strictly. In *Miller v. United States*,[3] a District of Columbia police officer, accompanied by a federal narcotics agent, arrived at Miller's apartment at 3:45 a.m. without a warrant, for the purpose of arresting Miller for narcotics offenses. One of the officers knocked on the apartment door. Miller asked who it was, and the officers identified themselves simply as "police." Then Miller opened the door slightly—the door was secured by a chain—and inquired as to the officers' purpose. Without waiting for a response, Miller attempted to close the door. Before it could be shut, however, the officers reached inside, tore away the chain, entered the apartment and arrested Miller. While inside, the officers also seized several bills of incriminating marked currency.

The Supreme Court reversed Miller's conviction, holding that the method of entry failed to comport with § 3109. The officers, the Court felt, never adequately announced their purpose prior to the forcible entry, and Miller's attempt to close the door on them was an ambiguous act which could not conclusively reflect an understanding that they had arrived to arrest him.

In *Sabbath v. United States*,[4] the Court focused on the meaning of "break open an outer or inner door or window" in § 3109. In *Sabbath* federal customs officers enlisted the aid of one Jones, who they had caught trying to smuggle cocaine into the country, to apprehend "Johnny," the intended recipient of the drug. Jones agreed to deliver the cocaine while the police watched. Shortly after Jones entered "Johnny's" apartment, the officers knocked. Receiving no response, they entered through the unlocked door with guns drawn. Sabbath, the occupant of the apartment, was arrested, and a subsequent search resulted in the seizure of a quantity of cocaine. The Supreme Court reversed Sabbath's conviction, rejecting the court of appeal's judgment that the officers did not "break open" the door within the meaning of § 3109 and thereby trigger the identification and announcement requirements. Rather, it concluded: "An unannounced intrusion into a dwelling—what § 3109 basically proscribes—is no less an unannounced intrusion whether officers break down a door, force open a chain lock on a partially open door, open a locked door by use of a passkey, or, as here, open a closed but unlocked door." The Court was careful to note, however, that entries obtained by ruse or deception do not constitute a "breaking" within the meaning of § 3109; otherwise, a good deal of undercover work by police would be in violation of federal law.

Knock and Nonsense: An Alleged Constitutional Problem," 44 St. Johns L.Rev. 626 (1970).

3. 357 U.S. 301, 78 S.Ct. 1190 (1958).

4. 391 U.S. 585, 88 S.Ct. 1755 (1968).

(b) The Use of Deadly Force. Virtually every state has a statute or, at the least, a police regulation specifying the circumstances in which violence or the threat of violence may be used to apprehend an arrestee. The statute promulgated by the American Law Institute in its Model Code of Pre-Arraignment Procedure is exemplary. Section 120.7 provides that an officer "may use such force as is reasonably necessary to effect the arrest, to enter premises to effect the arrest, or to prevent the escape from custody of an arrested person." *Deadly* force is authorized when the arrest is for a felony, the use of such force "creates no substantial risk to innocent persons," and the officer "reasonably believes" that the felony involved the use or threat of use of deadly force or there is "substantial risk" that the arrestee will cause other deaths or serious bodily harm if deadly force is not employed.[5]

In *Tennessee v. Garner*,[6] the Supreme Court held that the Model Code's approach to the use of deadly force, or one essentially like it, is required by the Fourth Amendment. *Garner* declared unconstitutional a Tennessee statute which permitted an officer who has given notice of an intent to arrest a criminal suspect to "use all the necessary means to effect the arrest" if the suspect flees or forcibly resists. Construing "all necessary means" to include deadly force, the Court held that, under the Fourth Amendment's reasonableness requirement, such means cannot be used to effect an arrest unless (1) it is necessary to prevent escape and (2) the officer has probable cause to believe the suspect poses a significant threat of death or serious physical injury to the officer or others. The Court also agreed with the court of appeals ruling that because the officer in *Garner* had been "reasonably sure" the suspect was unarmed, young and of slight build, he acted unreasonably in shooting (and killing) the suspect as he fled over a fence at night in the backyard of a house he was suspected of burglarizing. Justice O'Connor's dissent, joined by Chief Justice Burger and Justice Rehnquist, argued that statutes like the one struck down by the majority "assist the police in apprehending suspected perpetrators of serious crimes and provide notice that a lawful police order to stop and submit to arrest may not be ignored with impunity."

The Court later held, in *Graham v. Connor*,[7] that all claims of excessive force—whether deadly or not, and whether involving arrest or some other type of seizure—are governed by the Fourth Amendment reasonableness requirement. This inquiry, stated the Court, requires looking into a number of factors, including: (1) the severity of the crime; (2) whether the suspect poses an immediate

---

5. American Law Institute, A Model Code of Pre-Arraignment Procedure § 120.7 (Official Draft 1975).

6. 471 U.S. 1, 105 S.Ct. 1694 (1985).

7. 490 U.S. 386, 109 S.Ct. 1865 (1989).

threat; and (3) whether he is actively resisting arrest or attempting to evade arrest by flight. Moreover, it "must embody allowance for the fact that police officers are often forced to make split-second judgments—in circumstances that are tense, uncertain, and rapidly evolving—about the amount of force that is necessary in a particular situation." Finally, as with all other Fourth Amendment inquiries, it is objective, "without regard to [the officers'] underlying intent or motivation." Because both *Garner* and *Graham* involved damages claims, still unclear is whether, if excessive force is used, exclusion of any evidence thereby obtained is admissible in evidence. Arguably, the deterrent effect of damages, unlike in other contexts,[8] is sufficient here to obviate the need for the exclusionary rule.

3.06 Conclusion

The following comments summarize the law of arrest:

(1) An illegal arrest or detention standing alone has little if any impact on the subsequent prosecution. The citizen's remedy for an illegal arrest is a separate civil suit for damages. However, tangible evidence sought to be introduced as incident to a lawful arrest and other types of evidence (confessions, lineup identifications) which are "fruit" of an unlawful arrest will often be suppressed.

(2) An "arrest," at a minimum, is some type of restriction of an individual's liberty by the police. Clearly, any action by the police that makes it impossible for an individual to leave and which makes use of the formal trappings of police detention (e.g., handcuffs, full body searches, or forced movement to the stationhouse or other "private" area for interrogation) constitutes an arrest. Whether other seizures are "arrests" depends upon the purpose, manner, location and duration of the detention. If the police detention is an arrest or its equivalent, it must be based on probable cause; for other seizures, police need at most possess only a reasonable suspicion of criminal intent, as contemplated under *Terry v. Ohio.*

(3) Probable cause to arrest is an objectively-defined standard, which focuses on whether there are reasonable grounds to believe the suspect has committed an offense. If the factual basis for the probable cause determination is hearsay, highly relevant is the two-prong test of *Aguilar* —that is, (a) whether sufficient facts are available to inform a magistrate of how the informant reached his conclusions, and (b) whether sufficient indicia of the informant's reliability exist. But a deficiency in one prong may be compensated for by a strong showing with respect to the other prong; the ultimate test is whether, under the totality of the circumstances,

8. See § 2.05(a)(5).

probable cause exists. When the arresting officer's own observations are the basis for arrest, only indicia of criminality noted independently of the arrest (but including evidence obtained as the result of a legitimate patdown based on reasonable suspicion) may be relied upon to develop probable cause. Moreover, mere failure to identify oneself or distance oneself from criminal suspects is, by itself, not sufficient to constitute probable cause.

(4) An arrest warrant is not required to effect an arrest in public when the arresting officer has probable cause to believe that a felony has been or is being committed by the arrestee or that a misdemeanor is being committed by the arrestee in his presence. However, a warrant is required to make an arrest inside a private dwelling, unless exigent circumstances are present. Moreover, police must obtain a *search* warrant before they may enter the house of a third party to effect a non-exigent arrest.

(5) Generally, under common law, police must knock and announce their purpose before entering to make an arrest, though these requirements may be dispensed with if by following them the suspect might escape, harm someone or destroy evidence. The Supreme Court has indicated an exigent circumstances exception is constitutional; however, it has also indicated that it will interpret strictly the federal statute pertaining to arrest procedure.

(6) The use of deadly force is permitted in making an arrest only if necessary to prevent both escape and the use of deadly force by the suspect.

BIBLIOGRAPHY

Black, D.J. Social Organization of Arrest. 23 Stan.L.Rev. 1087 (1971).

Cantrell, C.L. Reasonable Cause in Warrantless Arrests: An Analysis of Some Selected Factors. 6 Am.J. of Crim.L. 267 (1978).

Cerruti, Eugene. The Demise of the *Aguilar-Spinelli* Rule: A Case of Faulty Reception. 61 Den.L.J. 431 (1984).

Cloud, Morgan. Search and Seizure by the Numbers: The Drug Courier Profile and Judicial Review of Investigative Formulas. 65 B.U.L.Rev. 843 (1985).

Dix, George. Means of Executing Searches and Seizures as Fourth Amendment Issues. 67 Minn.L.Rev. 89 (1982).

Groot, Roger D. Arrests in Private Dwellings. 67 Va.L.Rev. 275 (1981).

Harbaugh, Faust. "Knock on Any Door"—Home Arrests After Payton and Steagald. 86 Dick.L.Rev. 191 (1982).

Karsch, Mitchell. Excessive Force and the Fourth Amendment: When Does Seizure End? 58 Fordham L.Rev. 823 (1990).

LaFave, Wayne. Seizures Typology: Classifying Detentions of the Person to Resolve Warrant, Grounds, and Search Issues. Univ.Mich.J.L.Ref. 417 (1984).

———. Probable Cause from Informants: The Effects of Murphy's Law on Fourth Amendment Adjudication. 1977 U.Ill.L.F. 1 (1977).

Schroeder, William. Factoring the Seriousness of the Offense into Fourth Amendment Equations—Warrantless Entries into Premises: The Legacy of *Welsh v. Wisconsin*. 38 U.Kan.L.Rev. 439 (1990).

Williamson, Richard A. The Dimensions of Seizure: The Concepts of "Stop" and "Arrest". 43 Ohio St.L.J. 771 (1982).

Chapter Four

INTRODUCTION TO THE LAW OF SEARCHES: A FRAMEWORK FOR ANALYZING WHEN "SEARCHES" OCCUR AND WHEN THEY ARE REASONABLE

4.01 Introduction

This chapter attempts to make some sense out of search and seizure law apart from the law of arrest and other detentions. In other words, this chapter is concerned with searches, and with seizures of evidence. The bare words of the Fourth Amendment require only that such searches and seizures be reasonable and that, if and when a warrant is issued, it must be based on "probable cause," "supported by oath or affirmation," and particularly describe what is to be searched or seized. Over the years, the Supreme Court has added several layers of interpretation to this basic text. Without a framework for analyzing these decisions, one may quickly become lost in a maze of cases which seem neither consistent nor comprehensible.

This analysis can be divided into two stages. The first stage involves defining the types of activity that trigger the protections of the Fourth Amendment. On the assumption the Fourth Amendment is implicated, the second stage concerns the nature of the protection to be afforded. This chapter takes a comprehensive look at Stage I of the analysis. In addition, it provides a brief overview of Stage II, to assist in understanding the scope of the "Fourth Amendment's protections. These protections—the warrant requirement and the specific situations in which it may be ignored—will then be discussed in the chapters to follow.

In answering the question posed in Stage I—i.e., when is the Fourth Amendment implicated by the evidence-gathering activity in question?—three elements must be considered: whether the intrusion is the product of governmental action, whether it breaches society's "reasonable expectations of privacy," and whether it breaches the "legitimate expectations of privacy" of the individual intruded upon. The Fourth Amendment is not implicated unless each of these elements is present.

4.02 Defining Governmental Conduct

The Fourth Amendment's proscription against illegal searches and seizures, like other Bill of Rights guarantees,[1] has been

---

1. See generally, *Adamson v. California*, 332 U.S. 46, 67 S.Ct. 1672 (1947).

judicially construed to apply only to governmental conduct. Thus, when a *private* individual illegally acquires evidence which the government later seeks to use in a criminal prosecution, there is no Fourth Amendment violation upon which to support a motion for exclusion of the evidence.

The inapplicability of the Fourth Amendment to searches by private individuals was first recognized by the Supreme Court in *Burdeau v. McDowell.*[2] In that case, certain private individuals, at the instigation of McDowell's former employer, illegally entered and searched McDowell's business office and seized certain papers. These papers were later turned over to Burdeau, a Special Assistant to the Attorney General of the United States, who intended to use them as evidence in a criminal prosecution against McDowell for fraudulent use of the mails. McDowell sought a court order for the return of the papers so that they could not be used against him. The district court granted his petition. The Supreme Court reversed, reasoning as follows:

> The Fourth Amendment gives protection against unlawful searches and seizures, and as shown in the previous cases, its protection applies to governmental action. Its origin and history clearly show that it was intended as a restraint upon the activities of sovereign authority, and was not intended to be a limitation upon other than governmental agencies; . . .

The holding and rationale found in *Burdeau* have retained their validity through the years. In *Coolidge v. New Hampshire,*[3] the Supreme Court stated that if a private citizen "wholly on [his] own initiative" turns over certain articles to the police for use in a criminal investigation, "[t]here can be no doubt under existing law that the articles would later [be] admissible in evidence." And in *Walter v. United States,*[4] decided in 1980, the Court held that "a wrongful search and seizure conducted by a private party does not violate the Fourth Amendment and . . . does not deprive the government of the right to use evidence that it has acquired [from the third party] lawfully."[5]

In ascertaining whether governmental conduct has occurred, three questions commonly reoccur: (1) who is a government official?; (2) when is a private citizen, to use *Coolidge's* words, not acting "wholly on his own initiative," but rather at the behest of a government official?; and (3) once it is established that an action is purely private, what subsequent governmental action does the

2. 256 U.S. 465, 41 S.Ct. 574 (1921).

3. 403 U.S. 443, 91 S.Ct. 2022 (1971).

4. 447 U.S. 649, 100 S.Ct. 2395 (1980).

5. See also, *State v. Oldaker,* 304 S.E.2d 843 (W.Va.1983) (search by land-lord not subject to Fourth Amendment); *Comm. v. Goldhammer,* 469 A.2d 601 (Pa.1983) (evidence procured by witness and attorney not subject to Fourth Amendment).

private search authorize? A fourth, related issue is when, if ever, actions by a *foreign* government implicate the Fourth Amendment.

(a) Government Officials. Clearly the actions of police officers employed by an American governmental entity are covered by the Fourth Amendment. However, the police represent only a small portion of those government officials whose primary or secondary task is enforcement of criminal and other laws. The Supreme Court has indicated that, even if their actions rarely or never result in criminal prosecution, the Fourth Amendment governs the actions of these other law enforcement officials as well, albeit often with less rigor than the police.[6] Thus, in *Camara v. Municipal Court*,[7] the Court held that searches by regulatory officials conducting safety and health inspections are subject to Fourth Amendment requirements. Since these searches can involve significant intrusions, it would be "anamolous to say that the individual and his private property are fully protected by the Fourth Amendment only when the individual is suspected of criminal behavior." The Court has explicitly extended this rationale to many other types of government inspectors.[8] Similarly, the Court has held that government agencies pursuing *internal*, work-related investigations of their employees must abide by the constitution.[9]

Public school teachers are also included within the rubric of government actors for purposes of the Fourth Amendment. Although some lower courts had held that teachers act *in loco parentis,* and thus that their searches of children should be no more restricted than those conducted by parents,[10] the Supreme Court, in *New Jersey v. T.L.O.*,[11] rejected this position, stating that "[t]oday's public school officials do not merely exercise authority voluntarily conferred on them by individual parents; rather, they act in furtherance of publicly mandated educational and disciplinary policies." Moreover, pointed out the Court, it had already found teachers answerable under both the Fifth Amendment [12] and the due process clause.[13]

6. Thus, in virtually all the cases discussed below, the Court, after finding that the Fourth Amendment applied, relaxed the probable cause requirement, and in most it eliminated the warrant requirement as well. See generally, Chapter Thirteen.

7. 387 U.S. 523, 87 S.Ct. 1727 (1967).

8. See, e.g., *Michigan v. Tyler,* 436 U.S. 499, 98 S.Ct. 1942 (1978) (fire inspectors); *Marshall v. Barlow's, Inc.,* 436 U.S. 307, 98 S.Ct. 1816 (1978) (OSHA inspectors); *Donovan v. Dewey,* 452 U.S. 594, 101 S.Ct. 2534 (1981) (federal mine inspectors).

9. *O'Connor v. Ortega,* 480 U.S. 709, 107 S.Ct. 1492 (1987).

10. See, e.g., *R.C.M. v. State,* 660 S.W.2d 552 (Tex.App.1983).

11. 469 U.S. 325, 105 S.Ct. 733 (1985).

12. *Tinker v. Des Moines Independent Community School District,* 393 U.S. 503, 89 S.Ct. 733 (1969).

13. *Goss v. Lopez,* 419 U.S. 565, 95 S.Ct. 729 (1975).

A more difficult question is whether the Fourth Amendment governs the actions of persons who the government does not employ or influence in any other direct manner, but who conduct law enforcement-type searches and seizures on a routine basis as part of their job. Most courts have held that such individuals need not abide by constitutional strictures, whether they be store detectives,[14] security guards,[15] or insurance inspectors.[16] However, some have argued that, where the primary purpose of the privately paid personnel is to supplant the public police, then the Fourth Amendment should apply.[17]

(b) Government Agents. A purely private person may nonetheless become a "government official" for purposes of the Fourth Amendment if he acts at the behest of a bona fide official, as defined above. As *Coolidge* put it, "[t]he test . . . is whether [the private citizen] in light of all the circumstances of the case, must be regarded as having acted as an 'instrument' or agent of the state." Thus, where government officials actively join in the private search,[18] or instruct the private individual to conduct it,[19] there is sufficient state action. Analogously, the Supreme Court has indicated that when alcohol and drug tests carried out by a private employer are mandated or strongly encouraged by government regulations, the Fourth Amendment applies.[20]

On the other hand, where a government official does not "direct" the private action, but merely provides information that leads to it, courts often reach a different result. In *United States v. Lamar*,[21] a police officer notified an airline employee that he was interested in a certain unclaimed bag, believing it to belong to a person suspected of various narcotics violations. In the presence of the officer, the employee searched the bag for identification and

14. *Gillett v. State*, 588 S.W.2d 361 (Tex.Crim.App.1979); *People v. Horman*, 22 N.Y.2d 378, 292 N.Y.S.2d 874, 239 N.E.2d 625 (1968), cert. denied 393 U.S. 1057, 89 S.Ct. 698 (1969).

15. *Stanfield v. State*, 666 P.2d 1294 (Okl.Crim.1983); *People v. Trimarco*, 41 Misc.2d 775, 245 N.Y.S.2d 795 (1963).

16. *Lester v. State*, 145 Ga.App. 847, 244 S.E.2d 880 (1978); *State v. Hughes*, 8 Ariz.App. 366, 446 P.2d 472 (1968), cert. denied 395 U.S. 940, 89 S.Ct. 2010 (1969).

17. See, e.g., *People v. Mangiefico*, 25 Cal.App.3d 1041, 102 Cal.Rptr. 449 (1972); Comment, 38 U.Chi.L.Rev. 555, 581–82 (1971) (arguing an analogy to *Marsh v. Alabama*, 326 U.S. 501, 66 S.Ct. 276 (1946), which held that the actions of a private company in running its own town are subject to the same constraints as the government of a public town).

18. See, e.g., *State v. Cox*, 100 N.M. 667, 674 P.2d 1127 (App.1983); *Corngold v. United States*, 367 F.2d 1 (9th Cir.1966).

19. See, e.g., *Machlan v. State*, 248 Ind. 218, 225 N.E.2d 762 (1967).

20. *Skinner v. Railway Labor Executives' Ass'n*, 489 U.S. 602, 109 S.Ct. 1402 (1989). Although the Court noted that the regulations in *Skinner* left some testing to the discretion of the private railway, it pointed out that the law strongly encouraged and endorsed the tests and conferred upon the Federal Railway Administration the right to certain samples.

21. 545 F.2d 488 (5th Cir.1977), cert. denied 430 U.S. 959, 97 S.Ct. 1609 (1977).

found what he and the police officer suspected was heroin. Despite the officer's involvement in the search, the court found the Fourth Amendment not implicated because the officer had neither requested nor physically participated in the search, and the employee "was acting in the usual and ordinary course of his customary duties when he searched the bag for identification and address purposes." [22] Similarly, in *People v. Boettner*,[23] the court upheld a search by a private university official based on information supplied by the police, emphasizing that the private search had been conducted without the knowledge of the police, who had been proceeding with their own investigation.

The results in the latter two cases are suspect because they encourage the police to use private parties as a means of evading Fourth Amendment requirements. Arguably, they run counter to the Supreme Court's decision in *Elkins v. United States*,[24] which held, before *Mapp v. Ohio* [25] applied the exclusionary rule to the states, that the federal exclusionary rule should apply to evidence obtained in a search by state police when the federal and state police had a general understanding that the evidence would be used in federal prosecutions.

(c) What a Private Search Authorizes. A third area of concern is when the government does not direct the private search but later seeks to benefit from it. The Supreme Court's approach has been to leave unregulated those government searches that do not exceed the scope of the private search but to prohibit a government search not meeting Fourth Amendment standards if it extends beyond the private search. Thus, in *Walter v. United States*,[26] the Court invalidated a conviction which was based on the warrantless viewing of obscene films by the FBI, even though the packages containing the films had been opened by private parties and the markings on the cannisters revealed that they contained obscene material. Since the private parties had not actually viewed the films, the FBI agents were constitutionally prohibited from viewing them without a warrant. However, the Court also accepted the notion that a government search which is not "a significant expansion of the search which had been previously conducted" is not violative of the Fourth Amendment.

In *United States v. Jacobsen*,[27] a majority of the Court explicitly affirmed this latter rule. In *Jacobsen*, two Federal Express employees opened a package which had been damaged by a forklift

---

22. See also, *United States v. Morgan*, 744 F.2d 1215 (6th Cir.1984) (same holding on similar facts).

23. 80 Misc.2d 3, 362 N.Y.S.2d 365 (1974).

24. 364 U.S. 206, 80 S.Ct. 1437 (1960), discussed in § 2.02.

25. 367 U.S. 643, 81 S.Ct. 1684 (1961).

26. 447 U.S. 649, 100 S.Ct. 2395 (1980).

27. 466 U.S. 109, 104 S.Ct. 1652 (1984).

and found five or six pieces of crumpled newspaper covering a tube about 10 inches long. They cut open the tube and discovered a series of four zip-lock plastic bags which contained white powder. After notifying the Drug Enforcement Administration of their find, they placed the bags back in the tube, and the tube and newspapers back in the box. Justice Stevens, writing for a six-member majority, sanctioned the subsequent warrantless search by a DEA official because his removal of the tube from the box and removal of the plastic bags from the tube "enabled the agent to learn nothing that had not previously been learned during the private search."

Carried to its logical extreme, this language would severely detract from the warrant requirement. Information about criminal evidence which the police do not directly acquire themselves always comes from private parties. Thus, under a loose interpretation of *Jacobsen,* police could conduct warrantless searches any time a private party has already done so and told the police about his discovery. In an attempt to avoid this result, the majority placed several limitations on its holding. It emphasized that the Federal Express employees had only recently examined the package, that they had invited the federal agent to view its contents, and that the agents had already learned a great deal about the contents of the package from the employees, "all of which was consistent with what they could see." Most importantly, the agent who searched the package had "a virtual certainty that nothing else of significance [other than the contraband] was in the package and that a manual inspection of the tube and its contents would not tell him anything more than he already had been told." Even with these restrictions, as Justice White pointed out in a separate opinion, it would be difficult to distinguish this case from "one in which the private party knew to a certainty that a container *concealed* contraband and nothing else as a result of conversations with its owner." Moreover, there is nothing in the majority opinion explicitly limiting its holding to searches of containers.[28] The better approach, as Justice White suggested, is to permit warrantless searches only of those items the police find in plain view as a result of the private party's search.[29]

(d) Searches in Foreign Countries. It is well-established that a search of an American citizen conducted in a foreign country by foreign police does not implicate the Fourth Amendment, even if the search is at the behest of, or based upon

---

28. Indeed, the majority pointed out that "warrantless searches of [letters and other sealed packages] are presumptively unreasonable," yet went on to conclude that they too could be searched under the circumstances present in *Jacobsen.*

29. Note that where a private party has legitimate access to the searched area, the issue in *Jacobsen* could be mooted by obtaining that person's consent. See § 12.04.

information provided by, American authorities.[30] This stance is generally justified on the ground that foreign police cannot be expected to know or abide by American law, nor will they be deterred by American sanctions. But if the United States government is *heavily* involved in the search, it would seem that, for reasons similar to those given above, the fact that it takes place outside American borders should not render the constitution ineffective.

If the target of the foreign search is an alien, it may be that even a search conducted solely by American officers will not trigger Fourth Amendment protection, unless the foreign resident has a "substantial connection with our country." This was the holding of the Supreme Court, in *United States v. Verdugo–Urquidez*,[31] where DEA agents, assisted by Mexican authorities, conducted warrantless searches of two residences of a Mexican citizen who had been turned over to United States authorities two days earlier. Since, according to the Court, the defendant's sole connection with the United States was his detention, and this was not a "voluntary attachment," the defendant was not one of the "people" protected by the Fourth Amendment, a word which "refers to a class of persons who are part of a national community or who have otherwise developed sufficient connection with this community to be considered part of that community." The reach of *Verdugo–Urquidez* is unclear, however, since two members of the six-member majority emphasized that, even had the searchers wanted to comply with American law, there was no reasonable way they could have done so, given the absence of magistrates in the locality and the fact that American magistrates lacked jurisdiction. Under circumstances in which the functional equivalent of Fourth Amendment protections could be achieved, a different result might be reached by the Court.

4.03 Defining "Search" and "Seizure"

Not every attempt by government officials to obtain evidence is regulated by the language of the Fourth Amendment. Unless the investigative action involves a "search" or "seizure", as those terms are defined by the Court, the Fourth Amendment is not implicated. One might define a "search" as a layperson would, to mean any action by government officials which involves looking for evidence of a violation of the law. By the same token, a "seizure" of something would mean an assertion of control over it for the purpose of using it in evidence. In defining the scope of the Fourth Amendment, however, the Supreme Court has chosen not to follow the semantic route. Instead, other considerations,

---

30. *United States v. Rose*, 570 F.2d 1358 (9th Cir.1978).

31. 494 U.S. 259, 110 S.Ct. 1056 (1990).

primarily relating to privacy and a perceived need for fewer strictures on the police, have come into play.

Originally under the Court's cases, a "search" occurred solely when there was a physical intrusion into one of the "constitutionally protected areas" set out in the Fourth Amendment: persons, houses, papers and effects.[32] Thus, whereas police entry into a home (or the functional equivalent thereof) [33] was clearly a search, use of an electronic device to overhear conversations in the home was not, if it did not result in a trespass on private property.[34] Then, in *Katz v. United States*,[35] the Court, in an opinion by Justice Stewart, rejected the trespass approach to Fourth Amendment protection as both over- and under-inclusive:

> [T]he Fourth Amendment protects people, not places. What a person knowingly exposes to the public, even in his own home or office, is not a subject of Fourth Amendment protections. . . . But what he seeks to preserve as private, even in an area accessible to the public, may be constitutionally protected.

Applying this "exposure-to-the public" idea to the facts of *Katz,* the Court held that words spoken in a public telephone booth overheard on an electronic eavesdropping device were constitutionally protected even though the wording of the Fourth Amendment does not encompass phone booths and no trespass of private property had occurred. According to the Court, "a person who occupies [a phone booth], shuts the door behind him, and pays the toll that permits him to place a call is surely entitled to assume that the words he utters into the mouthpiece will not be broadcast to the world."

Still another way of defining "search," one which the Court increasingly relies upon, was provided in Justice Harlan's concurring opinion in *Katz.* While Harlan agreed with the majority that the Fourth Amendment protects "people," he also felt that it was hard to talk about the scope of that protection without referring to a place. Thus he suggested that the focus of the Amendment should be whether one's subjective and reasonable expectations of privacy in the place searched have been infringed by a police action. In a later decision, he wisely discarded the subjective component of his formulation, noting that if a person's beliefs about the privacy afforded him in a given place were relevant, the scope of the Fourth Amendment could be manipulated by the

32. *Silverman v. United States,* 365 U.S. 505, 81 S.Ct. 679 (1961).

33. See, e.g., *Stoner v. California,* 376 U.S. 483, 84 S.Ct. 889 (1964) (hotel room protected); *Amos v. United States,* 255 U.S. 313, 41 S.Ct. 266 (1921) (stores protected).

34. *Olmstead v. United States,* 277 U.S. 438, 48 S.Ct. 564 (1928) (tapping of telephone wires outside suspects' premises not a search).

35. 389 U.S. 347, 88 S.Ct. 507 (1967).

government, since it would depend upon what people are used to, not what they should be entitled to expect.[36] The expectation of privacy test, when relied upon by the Court, is now solely objective.

Both the public-exposure and the reasonable expectation of privacy doctrines have been relied upon in analyzing seizures as well as searches of evidence. For instance, as developed below,[37] the Court has applied the public exposure doctrine in addressing the propriety of seizing voice and handwriting exemplars. In most cases concerning whether a seizure has occurred, however, the Court has focused on whether the government action deprives the individual of a "possessory interest" in the item.[38]

The following discussion fleshes out the Supreme Court's interpretation of these various definitions of the Fourth Amendment's scope in a number of contexts.

(a) Undercover and "Institutional" Agents. Under the old trespass doctrine, the Court decided several cases involving the use of undercover agents. In each, the issue was whether the defendant consented to the action taken by the agent; if so, then no trespass occurred and the Fourth Amendment was not implicated. Thus, in *Gouled v. United States*,[39] the Court found unreasonable an undercover agent's search of the defendant's desk; although the defendant had invited the agent into his office, he had not "consented" to him rummaging through his papers. By the same token, in *Lewis v. United States*,[40] the Court found the Fourth Amendment did not apply to an undercover agent's entry into a home for the purpose of completing a drug transaction, when the owner had invited him there over the phone.

The Court's analysis did not change when the police were after private conversations rather than a tangible object. The same term as *Lewis*, the Court held in *Hoffa v. United States*[41] that the Fourth Amendment does not prevent using agents to eavesdrop, so long as the defendant is aware they are listening. Although the conversation "seized" in *Hoffa* took place in the defendant's private suite, a "constitutionally protected area," the agent—a union official who spent considerable time with Hoffa—"was not a surreptitious eavesdropper," but someone who "was in the suite by invitation, and every conversation which he heard was either directed to him or knowingly carried on in his presence."

36. *United States v. White*, 401 U.S. 745, 91 S.Ct. 1122 (1971) (Harlan, J., dissenting).

37. See § 4.03(b).

38. See, e.g., *Hale v. Henkel*, 201 U.S. 43, 26 S.Ct. 370 (1906) (defining seizure as "a forcible dispossession of the owner.").

39. 255 U.S. 298, 41 S.Ct. 261 (1921).

40. 385 U.S. 206, 87 S.Ct. 424 (1966).

41. 385 U.S. 293, 87 S.Ct. 408 (1966).

A harder question under the trespass doctrine was whether the undercover agent could wear an electronic eavesdropping device. As Justice Burton pointed out in his dissent to *On Lee v. United States*,[42] the addition of a concealed recorder "amount[s] to [the agent] surreptitiously bringing [the police] with him." Yet the five-member majority in *On Lee* held that because the defendant invited the agent who was "bugged" into his laundry and voluntarily conversed with him, no search occurred. The listening device merely improved the accuracy of the government's evidence. In a case involving substantially similar facts, *Lopez v. United States*,[43] the Court later affirmed *On Lee*, 6–3, again on the ground that no trespass occurred. Both of these decisions came before *Hoffa*, making the conclusion in that case inevitable.

But soon after *Hoffa*, the Court's decision in *Katz* repudiated the trespass doctrine. Under either the "public exposure" or "reasonable expectation of privacy" analysis announced in that case, the argument for characterizing at least some types of undercover activity as searches becomes stronger. In particular, *Hoffa* (where the agent was the defendant's compatriot) and *On Lee* (where the agent was a former employee) are suspect. Private conversations are not "knowingly exposed to the public," and it should be reasonable to expect that one's acquaintances, conferred with in private, are not government informers. The argument for applying the Fourth Amendment in *Lewis* is weaker, since the agent there was a stranger to the defendant, and the intrusion was limited to that necessary to complete a drug sale, but even in that case the defendant was not knowingly exposing the privacy of his home to the public at large.

Nonetheless, on two occasions,[44] the post-*Katz* Court has reaffirmed *On Lee*, the trespass case with the furthest reach, thus implicitly confirming the other cases as well. More understandably, it has also held, in *Maryland v. Macon*,[45] that an undercover agent's entry of an adult bookstore during regular store hours and his examination of materials offered for sale there was not a "search," nor was his purchase of allegedly obscene publications a "seizure," given the public, consensual nature of the transactions involved. As a result of these decisions, most undercover activity is unregulated under the Fourth Amendment.

Even more questionable than its reaffirmance of the trespass cases are the Court's post-*Katz* cases permitting state use of everyday institutions as "undercover" agents. In *United States v.*

42. 343 U.S. 747, 72 S.Ct. 967 (1952).

43. 373 U.S. 427, 83 S.Ct. 1381 (1963).

44. *United States v. Caceres*, 440 U.S. 741, 99 S.Ct. 1465 (1979); *United States v. White*, 401 U.S. 745, 91 S.Ct. 1122 (1971) (plurality opinion).

45. 472 U.S. 463, 105 S.Ct. 2778 (1985).

Miller,[46] the Court held that a subpoena of records containing financial information voluntarily surrendered to a bank is not a search for Fourth Amendment purposes. The Court relied heavily on its undercover cases for the proposition that a "depositor takes the risk, in revealing his affairs to another, that the information will be conveyed by that person to the government." Similarly, in *Smith v. Maryland,*[47] the Court held that a person does not have a reasonable expectation of privacy in the identity of phone numbers he calls, because he knows or should know that these numbers are recorded as a matter of routine by the phone company. The voluntary "assumption of risk" rationale, however plausible it may be in the undercover agent cases, seems completely unrealistic in *Miller* and *Smith,* given the modern-day necessity of using the banking and telephone systems.

(b) Physical Characteristics. A second category of cases in which the Court has found that the Fourth Amendment is not implicated involves the "seizure" of a person's physical attributes. In *United States v. Dionisio,*[48] a grand jury subpoenaed about twenty persons, including Dionisio, to give voice examplars for identification purposes. The Court, relying on *Katz's* public exposure doctrine, dismissed Dionisio's Fourth Amendment claim, stating:

> [t]he physical characteristics of a person's voice, its tone and manner, as opposed to the content of a specific conversation, are constantly exposed to the public. Like a man's facial characteristics, or handwriting, his voice is repeatedly produced for others to hear. No person can have a reasonable expectation that others will not know the sound of his voice, any more than he can reasonably expect that his face will be a mystery to the world.

Not surprisingly, given the above language, in *United States v. Mara,*[49] a companion case to *Dionisio*, the Court reached the same conclusion with respect to a person's handwriting. Presumably, any physical characteristic that is discernable by mere observation could be included among those things a person holds out to the public.[50]

46. 425 U.S. 435, 96 S.Ct. 1619 (1976).

47. 442 U.S. 735, 99 S.Ct. 2577 (1979).

48. 410 U.S. 1, 93 S.Ct. 764 (1973).

49. 410 U.S. 19, 93 S.Ct. 774 (1973).

50. Cf. *Davis v. Mississippi*, 394 U.S. 721, 89 S.Ct. 1394 (1969) (discussion of Fourth Amendment implications of fingerprinting). In *Cupp v. Murphy*, 412 U.S. 291, 93 S.Ct. 2000 (1973), respondent was held to have a Fourth Amendment right to privacy with respect to the scrapings from his fingernails, because "the search . . . went beyond mere 'physical characteristics . . . constantly exposed to the public.'" The characteristics of the scrapings could not have been obtained by mere observation.

It should be noted, however, that the seizure of the *person* necessary to obtain evidence of physical characteristics may have to meet certain Fourth Amendment requirements. *Dionisio* and *Mara* both held that the investigative traditions of the grand jury and the minimal intrusion associated with a grand jury subpoena allow relaxation of normal Fourth Amendment restrictions even in this respect.[51] But if the detention involves a forcible police seizure from the home, a warrant may be required, even if the sole purpose for the detention is to obtain evidence of physical characteristics.[52]

(c) **Open Fields and Curtilage.** While the home and private office are protected by the Fourth Amendment, areas adjacent to these localities may not be. In the pre-*Katz* case of *Hester v. United States*,[53] the Court upheld a warrantless search conducted by officers who were admittedly trespassing on the defendant's land, on the ground that the property searched was not "curtilage" immediately surrounding the defendant's home, but rather part of the "open fields." In *Oliver v. United States*,[54] decided after *Katz*, the Court reaffirmed the open fields doctrine in two cases involving entry onto private property which was fenced in and marked by "No Trespassing" signs. Justice Powell, writing for a 6–3 majority, held that landowners do not possess a legitimate expectation of privacy in fields which are far removed from the landowner's home and "curtilage," even if efforts have been made to maintain some degree of isolation. According to Powell:

> [O]pen fields do not provide the setting for those intimate activities that the Amendment is intended to shelter from government interference or surveillance. There is no societal interest in protecting the privacy of those activities, such as the cultivation of crops, that occur in open fields. Moreover, as a practical matter these lands usually are accessible to the public and the police in ways that a home, office or commercial structure would not be. It is not generally true that fences or no trespassing signs effectively bar the public from viewing open fields in rural areas.

Oliver involved land far removed from the defendant's home. *Dow Chemical Co. v. United States*[55] and *California v. Ciraolo*[56] concerned searches of property adjacent to the defendants' premises. Yet the Court, in both cases by a majority of one, found that aerial surveillance of this property did not violate legitimate expectations of privacy. In *Dow Chemical*, the Environmental

51. See § 3.02(e).

52. See *Hayes v. Florida*, 470 U.S. 811, 105 S.Ct. 1643 (1985), discussed in § 3.02(d).

53. 265 U.S. 57, 44 S.Ct. 445 (1924).

54. 466 U.S. 170, 104 S.Ct. 1735 (1984).

55. 476 U.S. 227, 106 S.Ct. 1819 (1986).

56. 476 U.S. 207, 106 S.Ct. 1809 (1986).

Protection Agency hired a commercial aerial photographer, using highly sophisticated equipment, to photograph the defendant's plant from the air after being refused an on-site inspection. While recognizing that the area photographed did not fall squarely within the "open fields" doctrine, Chief Justice Burger, writing for the Court, found that it did not constitute "curtilage" either, apparently on the grounds of size (the plant consisted of 2,000 acres). Yet, as Justice Powell, the author of *Oliver*, pointed out in dissent, the area was immediately adjacent to the plant, and well defined by fences and an elaborate security system designed to discourage competitors from discovering trade secrets. Perhaps realizing that a direct analogy to *Oliver* was not apposite, Burger also sought to justify the decision by pointing out that the aerial photography had not involved a physical intrusion, and that while it permitted better viewing of the premises than the naked eye, it did not reveal identifiable human faces, secret documents or any interior that implicated privacy interests. Finally, he pointed out that commercial enterprises had traditionally been accorded less privacy protection.[57]

In *Ciraolo,* the aerial photography occurred after police received an anonymous phone tip that the defendant had marijuana in his back yard and found themselves unable to see it because of two high fences. The plane flew roughly 1,000 feet above the yard and a photograph was taken. In finding that this flight did not constitute a search, Chief Justice Burger conceded that the area under surveillance was "curtilage" and thus normally should be accorded Fourth Amendment protection. But, as he had in *Dow Chemical*, he found relevant the manner in which the surveillance was conducted. He pointed out that the police observation took place within public navigable airspace and that anyone casually flying over the property could have spotted the marijuana with the naked eye.

Similar in vein to *Ciraolo* and *Dow Chemical* is *Florida v. Riley*,[58] which involved police use of a helicopter hovering at 400 feet to discover marijuana in a backyard greenhouse. In an opinion by Justice White, four members of the Court held that this flight did not constitute a search. White offered three reasons for the decision. First, helicopter flights at this height do not violate Federal Aviation Administration regulations (which limit flights by fixed wing aircraft to 500 feet but permit helicopter flights at any altitude "if operation is conducted without hazard to persons or property on the surface.") Second, there was "nothing in the

---

57. See § 4.03(g). See also, *Air Pollution Variance Bd. v. Western Alfalfa Corp.*, 416 U.S. 861, 94 S.Ct. 2114 (1974) (Fourth Amendment not implicated by outdoor pollution test conducted on "open fields" belonging to defendant company).

58. 488 U.S. 445, 109 S.Ct. 693 (1989).

record or before us to suggest that helicopters flying at 400 feet are sufficiently rare in this country" to justify the defendant's claim of a reasonable expectation of privacy. Third, the helicopter did not interfere with the defendant's "normal use" of the greenhouse or reveal "intimate details connected with the use of the home or curtilage." Justice O'Connor joined the plurality because she believed that public use of airspace at 400 feet and above is "considerable". But she emphasized that public use of airspace below that altitude "may be sufficiently rare that police surveillance from such altitudes would violate reasonable expectations of privacy, despite compliance with FAA air safety regulations." Thus, a majority of the Court might be willing to limit warrantless overflights to the 400 foot region.

Although, after *Ciraolo* and *Riley,* aerial surveillance of the home's curtilage is largely ungoverned by the Fourth Amendment, *physical* intrusion into the curtilage remains a search. One year after *Ciraolo,* the Court established criteria for determining when an area is within the curtilage of the home, rather than in the open fields. In *United States v. Dunn,*[59] the Court held that curtilage questions "should be resolved with particular reference to four factors:"

> the proximity of the area claimed to be curtilage to the home, whether the area is included within an enclosure surrounding the home, the nature of the uses to which the area is put, and the steps taken by the resident to protect the area from observation by people passing by.

In *Dunn,* police entered the defendant's property without a warrant, climbed over several fences, and peered inside his barn, discovering evidence of drug production; they subsequently obtained a warrant to enter the barn and seized drug laboratory equipment and chemicals. The Court found that the initial viewing of the barn was valid because, under the four factor test set out above, the barn was not on the defendant's curtilage. The barn was 60 yards from the home, 50 yards outside the fence enclosing the home, used to produce drugs rather than to house "intimate activities of the home," and surrounded only by low fences designed to corral livestock rather than prevent persons from viewing the barn. The majority emphasized that, even if the defendant did possess an expectation of privacy in the contents of the barn, so that a warrant was required to enter it, the police could validly view the contents from the "open fields" outside the barn.

As Justice Brennan pointed out in dissent, the defendant had locked the entrance to his driveway off the main road, erected a

---

59. 480 U.S. 294, 107 S.Ct. 1134 (1987).

wooden fence around the barn, and covered the barn's open end with a locked gate and fish netting which made it impossible to see inside the barn without standing immediately next to it. The consequence of the majority's decision is to require owners to take extraordinary measures to protect the privacy of the land around their buildings if they want to avoid unrestrained police surveillance.

The "flyover" cases (*Dow Chemical, Ciraolo, Riley*) and *Dunn* seriously erode Fourth Amendment protections. All of these decisions justify deliberate warrantless, suspicionless police searches by engaging in the fiction that the public could just as easily have viewed the searched areas through casual observance. In fact, it is unlikely, and the defendants in these cases undoubtedly thought it unlikely, that a member of the public would go to the trouble the police did to view the defendants' premises. These cases stretch to the breaking point the pronouncement in *Katz* that Fourth Amendment protection does not extend to what a person "knowingly exposes to the public".

(d) Containers. Very often evidence of criminal activity is not found in plain view, but rather within a container of some sort. The Court has clearly established that if the object is "abandoned" then no Fourth Amendment right attaches. Under the old trespass doctrine, for instance, the Court indicated that property left by the owner in a hotel waste basket just before checking out could be seized and searched without implicating the Fourth Amendment.[60] In *California v. Greenwood*,[61] the Court reinvigorated this property-based holding by concluding that no legitimate expectation of privacy exists in garbage left in opaque bags outside the curtilage of the home. The Court reasoned that it is "common knowledge that plastic garbage bags left on or at the side of a public street are readily accessible to animals, children, scavengers, snoops, and other members of the public." Furthermore, one should know that once garbage is conveyed to a third party, it can easily be made accessible to the police. As Justice Brennan pointed out in dissent, trash contains information about one's intimate private thoughts and actions; the mere possibility that others might rifle through it should not authorize *police* to do so without probable cause or a warrant. That the defendant left his garbage at curbside with the express purpose of conveying it to the city garbage collector should also be irrelevant to Fourth Amendment analysis; such an argument, noted Brennan, would eliminate Fourth Amendment protection of mail surrendered to a mailman as well. Although garbage left *on* the curtilage might be treated differently, that result is unlikely,

60. *Abel v. United States,* 362 U.S. 217, 80 S.Ct. 683 (1960).

61. 486 U.S. 35, 108 S.Ct. 1625 (1988).

given the majority's reliance on the owner's "intent-to-convey" as support for its holding, language which is reminiscent of *Miller's* reasoning allowing unregulated searches of bank records.

Where the abandonment notion cannot easily be applied to the "container," however, the post-*Katz* Court is much more likely to find a search and seizure has occurred. The Court has made clear, for instance, that searches of the interiors of cars must abide by constitutional mandates,[62] and suggested that, under some circumstances, even car *exteriors* are covered by the Fourth Amendment.[63] And in *United States v. Chadwick*,[64] the Court forcefully supported the idea that other containers have Fourth Amendment protection. Indeed, the *Chadwick* Court held that, in contrast to what is normally required for cars,[65] a warrant is necessary to search a locked footlocker seized in public; according to the Court, because a footlocker is likely to contain personal effects and is not subject to the type of public regulation a car is, it deserves a greater privacy expectation. In *Arkansas v. Sanders*,[66] the Court added that suitcases too are "inevitably associated with the expectation of privacy." [67] Furthermore, according to *Sanders*, the only non-abandoned containers which do not enjoy Fourth Amendment protection are those which somehow "reveal the nature of their contents," such as a transparent vial or a gun case.

A more subtle case in this regard is *Lo–Ji Sales, Inc. v. New York*,[68] in which local government officials, entering after hours, seized books and films off the shelves of an "adult" book store without paying for them and examined them there despite the fact that they were packaged and not to be opened in the store. Although the Court would later hold that an undercover agent does not engage in a search or seizure when he buys material as a

---

62. See, e.g., *United States v. Ross,* 456 U.S. 798, 102 S.Ct. 2157 (1982). However, in *New York v. Class,* 475 U.S. 106, 106 S.Ct. 960 (1986), the Court held that entry into a car to discover its Vehicle Identification Number is not a search, in light of government regulations requiring it to be in plain view, a holding which erroneously allows the public nature of the information sought to justify a search of private property for it.

63. Although a plurality of the Court in *Cardwell v. Lewis,* 417 U.S. 583, 94 S.Ct. 2464 (1974), stated that "we fail to comprehend what expectation of privacy was infringed" by an examination of the exterior of a car parked in a public parking lot and taking paint scrapings, it also emphasized

that probable cause to search the car's exterior existed, thus suggesting that the Fourth Amendment is implicated in such situations.

64. 433 U.S. 1, 97 S.Ct. 2476 (1977).

65. See § 7.02.

66. 442 U.S. 753, 99 S.Ct. 2586 (1979).

67. Although *Sanders'* holding that a warrant is required to search a suitcase seized from a car has been overruled, *California v. Acevedo,* 500 U.S. ___, 111 S.Ct. 1982 (1991), the aspect of *Sanders* discussed in the text remains intact.

68. 442 U.S. 319, 99 S.Ct. 2319 (1979).

customer would,[69] here the police were not acting like the ordinary customer. Thus, a search and seizure occurred.

What the Court appears to be saying in *Chadwick, Sanders* and *Lo-Ji* is that only that portion of a container which the public would normally view is denied Fourth Amendment protection. As Justice Stevens eloquently put it in *United States v. Ross,*[70] "just as the most frail cottage in the kingdom is absolutely entitled to the same guarantees of privacy as the most majestic mansion, so also may a traveler who carries a toothbrush and a few articles of clothing in a paper bag or a knotted scarf claim an equal right to conceal his possessions from official inspection as the sophisticated executive with the locked attaché case."

(e) **Controlled Delivery.** There is one situation where a container which is neither abandoned nor reveals the nature of its contents may be opened without implicating the Fourth Amendment. This occurs in the so-called "controlled delivery" cases, whereby a container is lawfully intercepted and searched, found to contain contraband, repackaged, and then delivered to the addressee. The addressee is then eventually arrested for possession of the contraband. For instance, in *Illinois v. Andreas,*[71] during a routine inspection at an international airport, customs agents opened a metal container which housed a wooden table, inside of which they found drugs. They resealed the container and delivered it to the defendant's apartment. Thirty to forty-five minutes later, the defendant came out of the apartment with the container, at which point the container was reopened and he was arrested.

The Court in *Andreas* found that, on these facts, the Fourth Amendment was not implicated. According to the Court, "[n]o protected privacy interest remains in contraband in a container once government officers lawfully have opened that container and identified its contents as illegal." The fact that the container was resealed "does not operate to revive or restore the lawfully invaded rights." Thus, held the Court, so long as there is "a substantial likelihood that the contents of the container [remain the same] during the gap in surveillance," no search occurs when the container is reopened after the controlled delivery. In *Andreas,* the Court found that such a likelihood existed.

(f) **Enhancement Devices.** A particularly problematic area of Fourth Amendment jurisprudence involves the use of devices, ranging from flashlights to satellite photography, designed to enhance the police's ability to discern criminal activity or evidence

---

69. See *Maryland v. Macon,* 472 U.S. 463, 105 S.Ct. 2778 (1985), discussed in § 4.03(a).

70. 456 U.S. 798, 102 S.Ct. 2157 (1982).

71. 463 U.S. 765, 103 S.Ct. 3319 (1983).

of crime. What should society's "reasonable expectations" be with respect to use of such devices? The Supreme Court has sent mixed signals on this issue.

(1) Monitoring public activities. One way of answering the question in the above paragraph is to limit unregulated use of enhancement devices to situations where they will reveal only that information which is already voluntarily exposed to the public. This appeared to be the underlying rationale of two Court cases dealing with police use of "beepers" to determine the defendant's whereabouts. In the first case, *United States v. Knotts,*[72] federal agents obtained permission to place a beeper in a five gallon container of chloroform, which was subsequently picked up by one Petschen. Although the agents followed Petschen's car, they eventually lost sight of it and were able to track it to the defendant's cabin only with the aid of the beeper. The Court upheld this aspect of the police activity in *Knotts,* concluding that "[a] person travelling in an automobile on public thoroughfares has no reasonable expectation of privacy in his movements from one place to another," and that the fact that a beeper, rather than visual surveillance, was used in this case to track those movements "does not alter the situation." The Court stretched this notion a bit further in *United States v. Karo,*[73] where the beeper was used not only to track a container to a particular house, but also to track its departure from that house and its arrival at a public warehouse. The Court found that no search occurred here either,[74] despite the fact that, in this case, the beeper was used to discover information that would have been difficult to obtain from a public vantage point, i.e., the removal of the container from the house and its re-location in the warehouse. But a solid majority of the Court agreed, in both *Knotts* and *Karo,* that when a beeper is used to detect the movement of something once it is *inside* a house, then the Fourth Amendment is implicated.

(2) Discovering only evidence of crime. While the public exposure rationale might explain the beeper cases, it does not explain many of the Court's other decisions regarding enhancement devices. Some of these decisions are based on the plausible idea that when the enhancement device is capable of detecting only evidence of criminal activity, its use does not violate any *reasonable* expectation of privacy even if the activity is hidden from public view. For instance, the Supreme Court appears to have held, in

72. 460 U.S. 276, 103 S.Ct. 1081 (1983).

73. 468 U.S. 705, 104 S.Ct. 3296 (1984).

74. The Court also held that installation of the beeper in the defendant's container was not a "seizure"; to the dissent's argument that the installation was an assertion of control over the defendant's property, the Court responded that no possessory interest of the defendant's was compromised.

United States v. Place,[75] that the sniffing of luggage by a drug-detecting dog does not amount to a search because the dog sniff does not involve opening the searched container, nor does it "expose noncontraband items that otherwise would remain hidden from public view," but instead is limited to discovering the presence or absence of narcotics. This same reasoning would support a dog sniff of a person, although *Place* did not involve such a situation. Similarly, in *United States v. Jacobsen,*[76] the Court found that a field test designed to discover only whether the substance tested is cocaine is neither a search nor a seizure. As Justice Stevens put it, "Congress has decided . . . to treat the interest in 'privately' possessing cocaine as illegitimate; thus governmental conduct that can reveal whether a substance is cocaine, and no other arguably 'private' fact, compromises no legitimate privacy interest."

Although devices that detect only illegal activity may not intrude upon any legitimate privacy interest, analysis of their use must be contextual. For instance, *Place's* assumption that dog sniffs do not intrude upon expectations of privacy is fanciful; especially if the sniff is of a person, an insult to dignity is likely. Justice Stevens' rule in *Jacobsen* must be carefully followed or else, as Justice Brennan pointed out in dissent, it could be read to "allow . . . law enforcement officers free rein in utilizing a potentially broad range of surveillance techniques that reveal only whether or not contraband is present in a particular location," including the home. Use of such techniques, which might reveal *movements* of the contraband (as well as the person carrying it), should be governed by the Fourth Amendment, as *Knotts* and *Karo* seem to recognize.

(3) Other enhanced searches and seizures. Finally, the Court has found some enhanced searches to be outside the purview of the Fourth Amendment even when they meet neither of the two rationales advanced above (that is, they discover legitimate, as well as illegitimate, activity not meant to be exposed to the public). For instance, in *Texas v. Brown,*[77] the Court held that use of a flashlight to expose darkened areas inside a car was not a search under the Fourth Amendment. Although the specific result in *Brown* might be justifiable on the *Knotts–Karo* ground that the flashlight merely exposed what would have been easily visible by day, when a flashlight is used to reveal activity in other, more private areas (e.g., a home or apartment), then these deci-

---

75. 462 U.S. 696, 103 S.Ct. 2637 (1983). The holding discussed is arguably dictum, because the Court had already held that the detention of the luggage in *Place* was invalid given its duration. See § 3.02(b).

76. 466 U.S. 109, 104 S.Ct. 1652 (1984).

77. 460 U.S. 730, 103 S.Ct. 1535 (1983).

sions would suggest that the Fourth Amendment should apply.[78] The same type of analysis should govern use of binoculars or telescopes: spying on people in public areas with these devices may not violate *Knotts* and *Karo,* but looking in private homes with them clearly does. Unfortunately, some lower courts do not appear to recognize this distinction.[79]

While the Supreme Court has not gone as far as these lower courts, it clearly went beyond the *Knott-Karo* and *Jacobsen* rationales, as well as *Brown,* in *Dow Chemical Company v. United States.*[80] There it held that use of sophisticated aerial photography equipment, permitting identification as small as ½ inch in diameter from pictures taken from a plane, does not implicate the Constitution when used to survey quasi-public areas. The Court distinguished the camera, which it termed "a conventional, albeit precise, commercial camera commonly used in map-making," from "unique" sensory devices that can penetrate walls and record conversations or pictures taken from satellites. Here because the photographs, although "undoubtedly" giving more detail than a naked eye view, did not reveal "intimate details" but rather only the outline of Dow Chemical's plant buildings, no Fourth Amendment interest was implicated. Even taking into account the majority's further statement that a different result might be reached as to "an area immediately adjacent to a private home, where privacy interests are most heightened," this holding is suspect. As Justice Powell pointed out in dissent, the pictures could easily be magnified by the government to reveal greater detail. More importantly, Powell noted, under the Court's apparent analysis, "privacy rights would be seriously at risk as technological advances become generally disseminated and available in our society." The scope of the Fourth Amendment cannot depend upon the extent to which use of a given observation device has become "common" if a modicum of privacy from governmental surveillance is to be maintained.

(g) Government Monitored Institutions. One final area in which the Court has utilized the public exposure doctrine involves intrusions which take place as part of a pervasive governmental regulatory scheme. In these cases, according to the Court, privacy

78. But see *United States v. Dunn,* 480 U.S. 294, 107 S.Ct. 1134 (1987) ("the officers' use of the beam of a flashlight, directed through the essentially open front of respondent's barn, did not transform their observations into an unreasonable search within the meaning of the Fourth Amendment.").

79. See, e.g., *People v. Arno,* 90 Cal. App.3d 505, 153 Cal.Rptr. 624 (1979) (use of binoculars to view eighth floor office to observe pornographic materials not a search since viewable by naked eye from a better vantage point); *Commonwealth v. Williams,* 262 Pa.Super. 508, 396 A.2d 1286 (1978) (use of binoculars to see into home not a search because suspect could have closed curtains), rev'd in part, 494 Pa. 496, 431 A.2d 964 (1981).

80. 476 U.S. 227, 106 S.Ct. 1819 (1986).

interests are minimal because a person should know his personal effects will be exposed to government agents, if not the public at large. Thus, one has a limited expectation of privacy at the international border.[81] Similarly, while the Court has generally accorded businesses the same protection as residences because, as it stated in *See v. Seattle*,[82] "[t]he businessman, like the occupant of a residence, has a constitutional right to go about his business free from unreasonable official entries upon his private commercial property," it has recognized an exception for pervasively regulated industry. For example, in *United States v. Biswell*,[83] it permitted a federal agent's warrantless, "spot" inspection of a licensed gun dealer's storeroom, in part because "a dealer [who] chooses to engage in this pervasively regulated business and to accept a federal license, . . . does so with the knowledge that his business records, firearms and ammunition will be subject to effective inspection." In other words, a person selling firearms has no justifiable expectation his goods will be immune from exposure to government monitoring.[84]

Another decision along these lines is *Hudson v. Palmer*,[85] which held that a prisoner has no reasonable expectation of privacy in his prison cell and thus cannot claim a Fourth Amendment violation when his personal effects are confiscated or destroyed by prison authorities. Quoting from *Lanza v. New York*,[86] the Court concluded that, a prison "shares none of the attributes of privacy of a home, an automobile, an office or a hotel room," and that the need for institutional security outweighs this almost nonexistent expectation of privacy. Therefore, the prisoner's sole remedies against harassment or destruction of his property come from the Eighth Amendment's protection against "cruel and unusual punishment" and state tort and common-law provisions.

The Court resisted applying this analysis to schools, however. In *New Jersey v. T.L.O.*,[87] the state argued that because schoolchildren are subject to pervasive disciplinary supervision and because they have no need to bring personal property to school, they have no legitimate expectation of privacy on school grounds. In rejecting these arguments, the Court specifically distinguished *Hudson* from the situation before it: whereas security needs dictate the abrogation of privacy rights in prisons, discipline problems in

81. See § 13.05.

82. 387 U.S. 541, 87 S.Ct. 1737 (1967).

83. 406 U.S. 311, 92 S.Ct. 1593 (1972).

84. The Court has never explicitly held that such inspections are not searches. But it places very few restrictions on them. See § 13.03(a).

85. 468 U.S. 517, 104 S.Ct. 3194 (1984).

86. 370 U.S. 139, 82 S.Ct. 1218 (1962).

87. 469 U.S. 325, 105 S.Ct. 733 (1985).

the schools are "not so dire that students in the schools may claim no legitimate expectations of privacy." And students may, for perfectly sound reasons, bring highly personal items to school. However, the Court avoided the question whether a schoolchild has a legitimate expectation of privacy in school property, such as lockers and desks, in which he keeps personal items. Because this property is owned by the school, and may often be subject to periodic inspection, the Court may find a significantly reduced expectation of privacy in these areas.[88]

(h) An Alternative Definition. The question of when police have conducted a "search" for purposes of the Fourth Amendment is an important one since it determines whether the reasonableness and warrant requirements of that constitutional provision need be met. Ultimately, the issue involves defining the type of society in which we wish to live.[89] Some of the Court's decisions— *Hoffa, Miller, Ciraolo* and *Dow Chemical,* for instance—are questionable because of the degree of discretion they give law enforcement officers to pry into the personal lives of citizens without obtaining a warrant or possessing even an articulable suspicion that criminal activity is afoot. Obviously, some police actions are not as intrusive as others. For instance, the aerial surveillance of factory grounds for technical information in *Dow Chemical* and the trespass on farmland in *Oliver* are not nearly as intrusive as the eavesdropping that took place in *Katz* or an entry into a home to look for personal effects. But this conclusion merely recognizes that the extent to which privacy is implicated may depend upon the nature of: (1) the place intruded upon (a home v. open fields); (2) the intrusion itself (e.g., a physical invasion of space v. aerial surveillance); and (3) the object of the intrusion (e.g., conversations v. crops).[90] It does not necessarily suggest that less intrusive actions such as those in *Dow Chemical, Oliver* and similar Court cases should go unregulated.

An alternative to the Court's "all-or-nothing" approach would be to construe the scope of the Fourth Amendment broadly—by, for instance, defining searches and seizures to encompass any action that meets the lay definition of those words—but to gauge the degree of Fourth Amendment protection by the level of intrusion involved in the action. Thus, while a search of a home for

88. Compare *Zamora v. Pomeroy,* 639 F.2d 662 (10th Cir.1981) ("Inasmuch as the school had assumed joint control of the locker it cannot be successfully maintained that the school did not have a right to inspect it."), with *State v. Engerud,* 94 N.J. 331, 463 A.2d 934 (1983) ("For the four years of high school, the school locker is a home away from home. In it the student stores the kind of personal 'effects' protected by the Fourth Amendment").

89. See generally Amsterdam, "Perspectives on the Fourth Amendment," 58 Minn.L.Rev. 349 (1974).

90. See Wilkins, "Defining the 'Reasonable Expectation of Privacy:' An Emerging Tripartite Analysis," 40 Vand.L.Rev. 1077 (1987).

120

personal effects would require a warrant based on probable cause, a search of open fields for marijuana crops would require only a minimal level of suspicion. This "sliding scale" approach would subject to regulation a vastly greater number of police activities. But the cost to law enforcement, a factor which often seems to drive the Supreme Court's decisions in this area, would probably not be significantly greater; under this alternative approach, the results in many of the cases discussed above would have been the same, given the degree of suspicion possessed at the time of the search or seizure and the level of intrusion involved. The difference would be the absence of precedents telling the police that, for a wide variety of actions that most people would call a search or seizure, they need not worry about the Fourth Amendment at all.

4.04 Standing

Not every individual who is subjected to a "search," as defined above, has standing to contest the action. The Supreme Court has indicated that, as in other constitutional contexts,[91] the Fourth Amendment right cannot be asserted vicariously. That is, a right to exclude evidence that is illegally obtained does not automatically vest in the person against whom it is used, even when that person can prove that the purpose of the search was to gather evidence against him. Rather, under current law, that right may be asserted only by those individuals whose privacy is directly violated by the government action.[92] Although the Supreme Court did not arrive at this conceptualization of standing until 1978, its previous cases are illuminating and will be discussed prior to describing current standing rules.

(a) **Property-Based Standing.** Originally, as with the definition of "search," the courts did not use privacy language in grappling with the standing issue, but rather focused on property concepts. Only if one had a *possessory interest* in either the thing seized or the place searched was one able to assert a Fourth Amendment claim. Derived from the common law rules of trespass to real property, the requirement barred all but a very narrow class of persons from invoking the exclusionary rule.

91. See, e.g., *Warth v. Seldin,* 422 U.S. 490, 95 S.Ct. 2197 (1975) ("the [party] generally must assert his own legal rights and interests and cannot rest his claim to relief on the legal rights or interests of third parties."); *Couch v. United States,* 409 U.S. 322, 93 S.Ct. 611 (1973) (privilege against self-incrimination a personal right).

92. Thus, in *United States v. Payner,* 447 U.S. 727, 100 S.Ct. 2439 (1980), the defendant was unable to contest admission of records concerning his financial affairs despite the fact that they were obtained when government agents burglarized a third party's hotel room. The Supreme Court upheld this result even though, according to the lower court, "the Government [had] affirmatively counsel[led] its agents that the Fourth Amendment standing limitation permits them to purposefully conduct an unconstitutional search and seizure of one individual in order to obtain evidence against third parties."

Among those who had standing under the old rubric were owners, lessees or licensees, persons with "dominion," occupants in a boarding house and guests in a hotel. House guests, business invitees, and employees, though legitimately on the premises, had no standing.[93]

(b) The *Jones* Criteria. In *Jones v. United States*,[94] the Supreme Court significantly reoriented standing law. Jones had been denied standing in the lower courts because he could claim no possessory interest in the place searched; the apartment in which both he and the drugs he was charged with possessing were found belonged to a friend, who had left for two weeks and given Jones a key and permission to stay there. In reversing the lower courts, the Court, through Justice Frankfurter, declared: "[I]t is unnecessary and ill-advised to import into the law surrounding the constitutional right to be free from unreasonable searches and seizures subtle distinctions, developed and refined by the common law in evolving the body of private property law." To replace the property-based rules, the Court developed two independent tests.

Frankfurter first addressed what he labeled a "dilemma" for the defendant charged with a possessory offense. For such a defendant, standing under the old approach would require the defendant to assert that which convicts him on the merits—namely, possession of the item seized. To avoid this dilemma, the Court held that defendants charged with possessory offenses have *automatic* standing. In addition to the avoidance of self-incrimination rationale, Frankfurter gave a second reason for an automatic standing rule:

> [T]o hold that petitioner's failure to acknowledge interest in the narcotics or the premises prevented his attack upon the search, would be to permit the Government to have the advantage of contradictory positions as a basis for conviction. Petitioner's conviction flows from his possession of the narcotics at the time of the search. Yet the fruits of that search, upon which the conviction depends, were admitted into evidence on the ground that petitioner did not have possession of the narcotics at that time. . . . It is not consonant with the amenities, to put it mildly, of the administration of criminal justice to sanction such squarely contradictory assertions of power by the Government.

The Court's second, independent basis for finding that Jones had standing to challenge the search in his case was more obviously a rejection of property-based standing. Reasoning that constitutional safeguards should not depend upon such "gossamer

---

93. See summary of case law in *Jones v. United States,* 362 U.S. 257, 80 S.Ct. 725 (1960).

94. 362 U.S. 257, 80 S.Ct. 725 (1960).

distinctions" as those between "lessee," "licensee," "invitee," "guest," and "owner," the Court held that "anyone legitimately on premises where a search occurs may challenge its legality by way of a motion to suppress, when its fruits are proposed to be used against him." Frankfurter made no effort to link this new test to any theoretical approach to the Fourth Amendment, however.

(c) Legitimate Expectations of Privacy Analysis. Seven years after *Jones,* the Court decided *Katz v. United States,*[95] the rationale of which eventually lead to elimination of both of *Jones'* standing criteria. Although *Katz,* as discussed earlier in this chapter,[96] focused on the definition of "search" rather than the standing question, the reasonable expectation of privacy language found in Justice Harlan's concurring opinion soon found its way into the Court's standing decisions; indeed, in two cases decided within two years of *Katz,* the Court relied exclusively on expectation of privacy analysis and virtually ignored *Jones.*[97] Finally, in *Rakas v. Illinois,*[98] the Court explicitly recognized the connection between search and standing analysis. That is, the Court held that standing should depend on whether the police action sought to be challenged is a search (i.e., a violation of legitimate expectations of privacy) *with respect to the person challenging the intrusion.*

Rakas also used the expectation of privacy notion to justify rejection of *Jones'* legitimate presence test. Justice Rehnquist, who wrote the majority opinion in *Rakas,* concluded that, now that privacy interests are the focal point of standing analysis, the presence test creates "too broad a gauge for measurement of Fourth Amendment rights." Although the Court reaffirmed the result in *Jones,* it chose to read that case as standing for the "unremarkable proposition that a person can have a legally sufficient interest in a place other than his own home." Applying these ideas to the facts in *Rakas,* the Court held that the defendants there did not have standing to contest the search of a car merely because they were passengers in it at the time. Nor did the fact that the driver of the car was the ex-wife of one of the defendants impress the Court. Rehnquist noted that the defendants did not claim a possessory interest in the items seized—a sawed-off rifle and some shells—and could not assert "any legitimate expectation of privacy in the glove compartment or area

95. 389 U.S. 347, 88 S.Ct. 507 (1967).

96. See § 4.02.

97. See, e.g., *Mancusi v. DeForte,* 392 U.S. 364, 88 S.Ct. 2120 (1968) (finding a union official had standing to contest documents taken from his office not because he was legitimately present but because a "reasonable expectation of

freedom from governmental intrusion."); *Alderman v. United States,* 394 U.S. 165, 89 S.Ct. 961 (1969) (homeowner has standing to contest eavesdropping in house whether or not present during eavesdrop). Both of these cases are discussed further below.

98. 439 U.S. 128, 99 S.Ct. 421 (1978).

under the seat of the car" where these items were found. "Like the trunk of an automobile, these are areas in which a passenger *qua* passenger simply would not normally have a legitimate expectation of privacy."

Rakas left unclear whether, had the defendants claimed a possessory interest in the items seized, they would have had standing to contest the search by virtue of that fact alone. Two years later, in *Rawlings v. Kentucky*,[99] the Court answered this question in the negative. The Court's version of the facts in *Rawlings* was as follows: just prior to police entering the dwelling in which Rawlings and Cox were guests, Rawlings dumped drugs into Cox's purse, despite Cox's protestations. When the police ordered Cox to empty her purse onto a table, Rawlings, with some hesitation, claimed they were his. The Court rejected Rawlings' claim that he should have standing to challenge the legality of this incident because of his possessory interest in the drugs, noting that he had no "right to exclude other persons" from the purse, and never had access to it prior to putting the drugs there. Further, the "precipitous nature" of his "bailment" to Cox "hardly supports a reasonable inference that petitioner took normal precautions to maintain his privacy." Finally, Rehnquist pointed out that, at the suppression hearing, Rawlings admitted to having no subjective expectation of privacy in the purse. Although thus suggesting a number of possible bases for standing under expectation of privacy analysis, *Rawlings* clearly established that possession of the seized item, by itself, is not one of them.

In *United States v. Salvucci*,[1] a companion case to *Rawlings*, the Court partially relied on this latter notion in abolishing the other doctrine announced in *Jones*, automatic standing. By the time of *Salvucci*, the self-incrimination dilemma that Frankfurter had relied upon as justification for automatic standing had been eliminated by the Court's decision in *Simmons v. United States*,[2] which held that pretrial suppression hearing testimony is inadmissible on the issue of guilt. *Rakas* and *Rawlings* provided an additional reason for discarding the rule. As Justice Rehnquist stated for the Court in *Salvucci*, "[w]e simply decline to use possession of a seized good as a substitute for a factual finding that the owner of the good had a legitimate expectation of privacy in the area searched." Given this conclusion, Rehnquist also felt able to ignore Frankfurter's second rationale for automatic standing—the vice of prosecutorial contradiction: it is now possible, he concluded, for the prosecutor to assert, without contradiction, that the defendant does not have standing (i.e., a legitimate expectation

---

99. 448 U.S. 98, 100 S.Ct. 2556 (1980).

1. 448 U.S. 83, 100 S.Ct. 2547 (1980).

2. 390 U.S. 377, 88 S.Ct. 967 (1968), discussed in § 15.02(c).

of privacy in the place searched) and contend at trial that the defendant owns the property seized.[3]

(d) Current Standing Rules. With the endorsement in *Rakas* of the expectation of privacy approach to standing, the Court has moved toward a totality of the circumstances analysis. *Rakas* and *Rawlings* indicate that factors such as the individual's interest in the property searched, his interest in the property seized, and his presence in the area searched have been downgraded from dispositive rules to mere factors to be considered in the aggregate. Yet these factors remain relevant to standing analysis. From a reading of the Court's cases, there seem to be four situations in which a defendant may establish a legitimate expectation of privacy sufficient to permit challenge of a search or seizure.[4]

(1) The right to exclude others. Most prominently, the defendant who can show he has the "right to exclude others" from the searched property will often have the capacity to contest the search. The Court used this language in both *Rakas* and *Rawlings* when describing its standing analysis. Clearly, as Justice Rehnquist recognized in *Rakas,* if one owns the area searched, one will generally possess a right to exclude others.[5] In *Alderman v. United States,*[6] a case decided before *Rakas* but affirmed by that decision, the Court held that a person not only has standing to contest conversations in his home that take place while he is present, but also conversations that take place when he is not there. This holding is consistent with the notion advanced in *Rakas* that expectations of privacy are not always associated with physical presence. Clearly, a homeowner should not have to be at home in order to enjoy a right to exclude unwanted eavesdroppers or intruders from the premises.

The right to exclude may also be asserted by non-owners. In *Rakas,* for instance, the Court stated that both the defendant in *Katz,* who "occupied a phone booth and closed the door," and the defendant in *Jones,* who had "complete dominion and control" over the searched premises by virtue of his possession of the

---

3. This latter reasoning is somewhat disingenuous, however, since at least some bases for standing may depend in part upon a property interest in the item seized. See § 4.04(d)(2) & (3).

4. Theoretically, one should distinguish between standing to contest searches and standing to contest seizures. In *Salvucci,* the Court noted that while a possessory interest in the item seized was insufficient for the former, it "may be sufficient in some circumstances to entitle a defendant to seek the return of the seized property if the seizure, as opposed to the search, was illegal." However, such standing will usually be superfluous and, if not, will rarely be useful. See Slobogin, "Capacity to Contest a Search and Seizure: The Passing of Old Rules and Some Suggestions for New Ones," 18 Am.Crim.L.Rev. 387, 413–16 (1981).

5. The one exception might be if ownership is in title only, such as in the case of a landlord's ownership of rented property.

6. 394 U.S. 165, 89 S.Ct. 961 (1969).

absent owner's key, could "exclude all others" and thus had standing. Another pre-*Rakas* holding that was reaffirmed by that case was *Mancusi v. DeForte*,[7] in which the Court granted standing to a union official to contest the seizure of documents from a one-room office he shared with other officials. The reasoning underlying the result in that case, as described by Justice White, seems consistent with a right to exclude rationale:

> DeForte would have been entitled to expect that he would not be disturbed except by personal or business invitees, and that records would not be taken except with his permission or that of his union superiors. It seems to us that the situation was not fundamentally changed because DeForte shared an office with other union officers. DeForte still could reasonably have expected that only those persons and their personal or business guests would enter the office, and that records would not be touched except with their permission or that of union higher-ups.

Although further elaboration of the right to exclude is needed, one way of thinking about its scope might be to analogize it to the capacity to consent to a search. As developed elsewhere in this book,[8] non-owners as well as owners may consent to search of property so long as they have sufficient control over that property. If an individual can be said to possess such control for purposes of consent, he should also have a right to exclude. "After all, these rights are but converse aspects of the same phenomenon—the effort to regulate one's privacy."[9]

(2) Continuing access plus possessory interest. Another pre-*Rakas* case suggests a second basis upon which a non-owner can obtain standing. In *United States v. Jeffers*,[10] the Court granted standing to a defendant who not only did not own the searched apartment, but lacked the "complete dominion" and control possessed by Katz and Jones, and shared by DeForte. Although Jeffers did have a key to the apartment, and could use it "at will," it was rented and occupied by his aunts and he did not live there. Thus, he did not have the right to exclude others from the apartment (nor a right to consent to its search). But he did have continuing access to the apartment; additionally, he claimed a possessory interest in the seized contraband. These two elements together are apparently sufficient to gain standing; according to the *Rakas* Court, "[s]tanding in *Jeffers* was based on Jeffers's possessory interest in both the premises searched and the property seized."[11] This variety of standing, like the right to exclude, does

---

7. 392 U.S. 364, 88 S.Ct. 2120 (1968).

8. See § 12.04.

9. *Slobogin,* supra note 4, at 401–02.

10. 342 U.S. 48, 72 S.Ct. 93 (1951).

11. Note also that *Rawlings* spoke of the degree of "previous access" to the searched area.

not require that the defendant be present during the search; neither Jeffers nor his aunts were in the apartment when the contraband was found.

(3) Legitimate presence plus possessory interest. Legitimate presence on the premises may remain a third way to establish standing, *if* it is combined with a possessory interest in the item seized. Although *Rakas* rejected as overbroad the legitimate presence test, Rehnquist noted that this conclusion "is not to say that [visitors in a house] could not contest the lawfulness of the seizure of evidence of the search if their *own* property were seized during the search."

The Court was later confronted with a version of this scenario in *Minnesota v. Olson.*[12] In contrast to Jones, Olson had slept in the apartment searched for only one night and was never left alone there. In contrast to Jeffers, he was never given a key. Despite these minimal contacts with the apartment, seven members of the Court held that the defendant had standing to contest the fact that the police did not have a warrant when they arrested him there.[13] Justice White, writing for the Court, rejected the state's argument that because the host had ultimate authority to admit and exclude visitors, a guest should lack standing. "If the untrammeled power to admit and exclude were essential to Fourth Amendment protection, an adult daughter temporarily living in the home of her parents would have no legitimate expectation of privacy because her right to admit or exclude would be subject to her parents' veto." While the "item" seized in *Olson* was the person of the defendant, the legitimate presence-possessory interest test probably also applies, as *Rakas* suggested, when the casual visitor's personal effects are seized: in *Olson,* the Court stated that an overnight guest "seeks shelter in another's home precisely because it provides him with privacy, a place where he and his *possessions* will not be disturbed by anyone but his host and those his host allows inside."

Whether this latter rule also applies to other areas such as cars is not clear. Broadly construed, the legitimate presence-possessory interest rule would have conferred standing in *Rakas* had the defendants simply asserted ownership over the seized items. Yet the Court's conclusion that those defendants, as passengers, had no legitimate expectation of privacy in the glove compartment, under the seat or in the trunk suggests a more niggardly application of standing analysis. Perhaps the Court's general derogation of privacy interests in the automobile, dis-

12. 495 U.S. 91, 110 S.Ct. 1684 (1990).

13. Note that a person always has standing to contest his arrest. Here the defendant was contesting the warrantless *entry* to make the arrest.

cussed elsewhere in this book,[14] will be used to justify a distinction between homes and cars when analyzing standing to contest a search. However, as six members of the Court pointed out in *Rakas,* a passenger's ability to contest the *seizure* of the car should not be diminished simply because he does not own it and is not driving it. Thus, if items belonging to a passenger are taken from the trunk after an illegal stop, the passenger should be able to exclude the evidence as fruit of the illegality.[15]

(4) Bailment. A fourth situation in which one may be able to claim standing is suggested by the facts in *Rawlings.* While the Court found that Rawlings' "bailment" of his drugs to Cox had been too "precipitous" to create an expectation of privacy, its focus on the bailment issue implies that, were one to make a valid bailment, a legitimate expectation of privacy might be established. To reason otherwise would be tantamount to saying that no one who shared his property with someone else can challenge a search of that property. On the other hand, the Court's holding in *United States v. Miller,*[16] that a person who voluntarily surrenders information to a bank lacks standing to contest a subpoena for records containing that information, casts some doubt on this conclusion.

(5) Subjective expectations of privacy. A final factor which should *not* play a role in the standing inquiry, but which unfortunately was given some credence by the Court in *Rawlings,* is the defendant's own perception of his privacy interests. If, in future cases, the Court explicitly adopts a subjective standard in assessing one's legitimate expectation of privacy, it could seriously derogate the Fourth Amendment right. As Professor Amsterdam pointed out in 1974:

> An actual, subjective expectation of privacy . . . can neither add to, nor can its absence detract from, an individual's claim to fourth amendment protection. If it could, the government could diminish each person's subjective expectation of privacy merely by announcing half-hourly on television that 1984 was being advanced by a decade and that we were all forthwith being placed under comprehensive electronic surveillance.[17]

4.05 Determining Whether a Search or Seizure Is Reasonable

If it is determined that a given search or seizure does not implicate the Fourth Amendment, either because no governmental

---

14. See § 7.02.

15. The one exception to this rule would be when the passenger is not "legitimately" present, as when the car is stolen. See, *State v. Bottelson,* 102 Idaho 90, 625 P.2d 1093 (1981).

16. 425 U.S. 435, 96 S.Ct. 1619 (1976), discussed in § 4.03(a).

17. Amsterdam, "Perspectives on the Fourth Amendment," 58 Minn.L. Rev. 349, 384 (1974).

conduct occurred, no "search" occurred, or the defendant's legitimate expectations of privacy were not infringed, then the evidence so procured is admissible in subsequent prosecution. If it is determined that a Fourth Amendment right does exist, the next step is to determine whether the government's conduct was reasonable. This stage requires determining whether a valid warrant has been issued, and, if not, whether the criteria for one of the exceptions to the warrant requirement have been met. These aspects of Fourth Amendment analysis are the subject of the next ten chapters. For purposes of overview, however, this section will briefly describe the structure of the Fourth Amendment, in the process explaining the organization of these chapters.

(a) **The Warrant Requirement.** Looking closely at the Fourth Amendment, one notices that the first clause bars unreasonable searches and seizures, while the second clause requires that warrants be based on probable cause and meet certain other requirements. The Amendment is silent as to how the "Reasonableness Clause" and the "Warrant Clause" interact with one another, nor is it clear which clause should be considered the most important. As detailed elsewhere in this book,[18] in the arrest context the manner in which the Supreme Court has interpreted the relationship between the two clauses is fairly straightforward. For other searches and seizures, the Court's jurisprudence has been somewhat more difficult to pin down.

Two competing approaches can be discerned in the Court's cases. The first assumes that the Warrant Clause is the predominate clause in the Fourth Amendment, thus establishing a presumption in favor of warrants for any given search. On this view, searches and seizures that are not based on a valid warrant are unreasonable unless the state can produce a very good justification (usually based on exigent circumstances) as to why obtaining such a warrant was not feasible. This perspective was most forcefully presented by Justice Stewart, who, in *Katz v. United States*,[19] stated that a warrant is required before every search or seizure, "subject only to a few specifically established and well-delineated exceptions." Since *Katz*, this phrase has been repeated in Court opinions many times.[20]

However, there is a competing perspective on the Fourth Amendment which, in practice if not in theory, seems to have gained the ascendancy. As summarized by the Court in *Terry v. Ohio*,[21] a case decided one year after *Katz*, "the central inquiry

---

18. See § 3.04 (warrants only required for non-exigent home arrests).

19. 389 U.S. 347, 88 S.Ct. 507 (1967).

20. See, e.g., *United States v. Ross*, 456 U.S. 798, 102 S.Ct. 2157 (1982). Recently, the phraseology has sometimes varied. See, e.g., *Illinois v. Rodriguez*, 497 U.S. 177, 110 S.Ct. 2793 (1990) (speaking of the "ordinary requirement of a warrant").

21. 392 U.S. 1, 88 S.Ct. 1868 (1968).

under the Fourth Amendment [is] the reasonableness in all the circumstances of the particular governmental invasion of a citizen's personal security." As construed by some members of the Court, in particular Chief Justice Rehnquist,[22] this approach treats the Reasonableness Clause as the most important command in the Fourth Amendment and the absence of a warrant as merely one factor among many to consider in evaluating the "reasonableness" of a search. On this view, the Warrant Clause was not included in the amendment to create a presumption in favor of warrants, but to describe the elements of a valid warrant (e.g., the probable cause, particularity, and oath requirements), should the state decide to seek one.

There is considerable historical support for this second version of the Fourth Amendment. Research indicates that, in drafting the amendment, the Framers' *sole* concern was avoiding a repetition of the British colonial practice of issuing so-called "general warrants," or warrants which were based on a "bare suspicion" and authorized fishing expeditions for evidence inside the home.[23] A second possible reason for preferring the "totality of the circumstances" analysis demanded by a "reasonableness" test is that it results in a more fine-tuned assessment of the competing values at stake. On the other hand, for those interested in controlling the police through relatively precise rules that eliminate much of their discretion, the *Katz* approach is more appealing.[24]

Both approaches have been adopted in Supreme Court opinions.[25] As noted, the Supreme Court continues to pay lipservice to the primacy of the Warrant Clause, and occasionally it strongly endorses that view. For instance, in *Mincey v. Arizona*,[26] it refused to adopt a "murder scene exception" to the warrant requirement under an Arizona statute which permitted "reasonable" searches of homes without a warrant. Quoting Justice Stewart's language from *Katz*, it unanimously held (in an opinion by Stewart) that the "seriousness of the offense" was not, by itself, a

22. See, e.g., Rehnquist's dissenting opinion in *Michigan v. Clifford*, 464 U.S. 287, 104 S.Ct. 641 (1984) ("In my view, the utility of requiring a magistrate to evaluate the grounds for a search following a fire is so limited that the incidental protection of an individual's privacy interests simply does not justify imposing a warrant requirement.").

23. T. Taylor, Two Studies in Constitutional Interpretation 24–41 (1969).

24. On the general desirability of rules versus case-by-case analysis when it comes to controlling the police, see LaFave, "The Fourth Amendment in an Imperfect World: On Drawing 'Bright Lines' and 'Good Faith.'" 43 Pitt.L. Rev. 307 (1982).

25. For an early pair of cases in which these contrasting viewpoints were adopted, see *Johnson v. United States*, 333 U.S. 10, 68 S.Ct. 367 (1948) (apparently asserting the primacy of the Warrant Clause) and *United States v. Rabinowitz*, 339 U.S. 56, 70 S.Ct. 430 (1950) (adopting a totality of the circumstances analysis).

26. 437 U.S. 385, 98 S.Ct. 2408 (1978). Reaffirmed in *Thompson v. Louisiana*, 469 U.S. 17, 105 S.Ct. 409 (1984).

sufficient "exigency" to justify a warrantless search. Nonetheless, what may have been true at the time *Katz* was decided can no longer be seriously contended: the situations in which the Court has permitted warrantless searches are neither few in number nor "well-delineated." Rather, as Professor Bradley noted in 1985 (before many current exceptions came into being),[27] the various exceptions number well over twenty and become murkier as time goes on.

In order to facilitate analysis of Fourth Amendment cases, some reduction and categorization of the exceptions is important. Doing so in the broadest fashion possible, one might organize the caselaw described in the next ten chapters around four types of exceptions: (1) exceptions based on a perception that exigent circumstances make obtaining a warrant impossible or impractical (e.g., the "hot pursuit" exception);[28] (2) exceptions resting on a finding that the police action does not impinge upon a substantial privacy interest (e.g., the "heavily regulated industry" exception);[29] (3) situations involving "special needs" of law enforcement (a phrase coined by the Supreme Court) where warrants might frustrate legitimate purposes of the government other than crime control (e.g., the public school search exception);[30] and (4) situations where warrants are considered unnecessary because other devices already curb police discretion (e.g., the inventory search exception).[31] As described in detail below, this book uses a more specific categorization, based more directly on language from the Supreme Court's cases.

(b) The Probable Cause Requirement. The debate over the reach of the Warrant Clause concerns the procedural issue of when police should be forced to seek before-the-fact review. A separate issue is a substantive one: what level of certainty must the police have before they conduct a search, whether or not it is authorized by a warrant? The only level of certainty mentioned in the Fourth Amendment is probable cause, a standard which connotes something akin to a more-likely-than-not finding.[32] However, a number of Supreme Court decisions have recognized that some searches are "reasonable" even if carried out on less than probable cause. Thus, in attempting to develop a framework for analyzing Fourth Amendment cases, one must look not only at exceptions to the warrant requirement, but also exceptions to the probable cause requirement.

27. Bradley, "Two Models of the Fourth Amendment," 83 Mich.L.Rev. 1468, 1473, 1479 (1985).

28. See Chapter Eight.

29. See § 13.03(a).

30. See § 13.08.

31. See § 13.07.

32. See § 5.03(a).

Of course, if a search requires a warrant, it must be based on probable cause, given the language of the Fourth Amendment. If a search does not require a warrant, then several factors have been considered by the Court in determining whether a level of suspicion lower than probable cause is permissible: (1) the intrusiveness of the search; (2) the nature of the harm being investigated; (3) the difficulty of detecting the harm if probable cause is required; and (4) the extent to which a probable cause requirement would disrupt smooth government functioning. For instance, in permitting suspicionless alcohol and drug testing of railway workers, the Court has asserted that such testing is less intrusive and less violative of expectations of privacy than many other types of searches, that the harm caused by drug- and alcohol-impaired railway workers is substantial, that such impairment would be difficult to detect if individualized suspicion were required, and that developing such suspicion would distract railway employers from their other, primary tasks.[33] The Court has relied on one or more of these four factors in every case in which it has permitted a search on less than probable cause.[34]

With these points in mind, we can look at how the remainder of Part A's treatment of the Fourth Amendment is organized.

(c) Adequacy of the Warrant. Again, once it is established that the Fourth Amendment is implicated by a particular action, the next question is whether a valid warrant justified that action. To be valid, a warrant must meet several requirements. The most important of these are that the warrant:

(1) be issued by a neutral and detached decisionmaker;

(2) be based on probable cause that the items sought are in the place to be searched;

(3) describe with particularity the place to be searched and the items to be seized; and

(4) be executed within a reasonable period of time.

These and other aspects of the search warrant are discussed in Chapter Five. Chapter Fourteen discusses search warrants in the special context of electronic surveillance.

(d) Exceptions to the Warrant and Probable Cause Requirements. If a warrant is obtained, but is invalid, or if no warrant was ever obtained, evidence seized by government officials is still admissible if discovered:

(1) "incident" to a lawful arrest (see Chapter Six);

(2) in a movable vehicle in circumstances giving rise to the so-called "automobile exception;" (see Chapter Seven);

---

33. See, *Skinner v. Railway Labor Executives' Association,* 489 U.S. 602, 109 S.Ct. 1402 (1989), discussed in § 13.09(b).

34. See, Slobogin, "The World Without a Fourth Amendment," 39 U.C.L.A. 1 (1991), for elaboration of the points in this and the preceding subsection.

(3) while police are in "hot pursuit" of a suspected felon (see Chapter Eight);

(4) in an "evanescent" or "endangered" state (see Chapter Nine);

(5) in "plain view" from a lawful vantage point (see Chapter Ten);

(6) during a "frisk" after a valid stop (see Chapter Eleven);

(7) in the course of a search authorized by a voluntary consent (see Chapter Twelve);

(8) in the course of inspections or searches conducted for certain "regulatory" purposes (see Chapter Thirteen).

The first five doctrines listed above all require probable cause either to arrest or to search or seize, and thus can be viewed as exceptions to the warrant requirement alone. The sixth and seventh doctrines are exceptions to both the warrant and probable cause requirements. Finally, regulatory inspections (as opposed to searches and seizures conducted primarily to garner evidence of criminal activity) are placed in a special category because there are so many variations, although most also involve situations where neither a warrant nor probable cause is required.

The parameters of these exceptions are not always clear and occasionally overlap. But their organization in the manner described above should facilitate working through the large number of Supreme Court holdings concerning the Fourth Amendment. With respect to each exception, it is useful to ask three questions: (1) what is its rationale?; (2) when is it triggered?; and (3) what is the scope of the search and seizure it authorizes? Chapters Six through Thirteen provide the answers to these questions.

(e) Burdens and Standards of Proof. Whether a "search" occurred, the defendant has standing, a warrant was valid, or one of the exceptions applies is usually decided at a "suppression hearing" prior to trial. In practice, the burden and standard of proof at this proceeding are often not enunciated. In part this may be because the parties do not perceive these matters to be an issue. In part, it derives from the fact that the law on proof matters is not very clear.

In the few cases in which it has addressed the issue, the Supreme Court has indicated that the burden can vary between the defense and the prosecution, depending on the question involved. In *Bumper v. North Carolina*,[35] it appeared to hold that the prosecution bears the burden of proving the voluntariness of a consent. This holding might be said to follow from the Court's earlier decision that the government bears the burden of proving the voluntariness of a confession.[36] In *Florida v.*

---

35. 391 U.S. 543, 88 S.Ct. 1788 (1968).

36. *Miranda v. Arizona*, 384 U.S. 436, 86 S.Ct. 1602 (1966).

Riley,[37] on the other hand, five members of the Court asserted that the burden of proving a government action is a search should be on the defendant. Despite the contrast with *Bumper*, this decision makes some sense, since the defendant has the best access to information concerning expectations of privacy.

The Court has been silent with respect to the burden on other issues. Because the standing issue is similar to the search issue, the burden on the former point should probably be on the defendant.[38] In contrast, when the issue is whether probable cause existed, or a search was otherwise reasonable, the government is in the best position to prove the relevant facts, and should probably bear the burden. However, the lower courts' approach to this matter is not quite so simple.[39]

Whatever party bears the burden of proof, it appears that proof by a preponderance of the evidence level is sufficient. This would seem to follow from the Court's willingness to impose this standard in the confessions context.[40] If the Court is willing to use the civil standard to resolve the admissibility of a confession, which can occasionally be unreliable, then it probably would be willing to apply the same standard in judging the admissibility of tangible evidence, which is always reliable.

4.06 Conclusion

On the following page is a flow chart representing schematically the analysis of Fourth Amendment cases set forth in this chapter. The chart divides the analysis into two "Stages". Stage I asks whether the Fourth Amendment is implicated. Stage II asks whether, if the Amendment is implicated, the search or seizure was reasonable.

This chapter focused on Stage I, which deals with the scope of the Fourth Amendment right. An individual can claim Fourth Amendment protection only when "governmental conduct" infringes upon society's "reasonable expectations of privacy," and further infringes upon the individual's "legitimate expectations of privacy," concepts which can be summarized as follows:

(1) Governmental conduct includes conduct by any public official, including law enforcement officials, fire, health and safety inspectors, and public school teachers. It also includes conduct by

---

37. 488 U.S. 445, 109 S.Ct. 693 (1989).

38. Cf. *Jones v. United States*, 362 U.S. 257, 80 S.Ct. 725 (1960) (holding it "entirely proper" to place the burden on the defendant on the standing issue).

39. See, e.g., *United States v. Longmire*, 761 F.2d 411 (7th Cir.1985) (burden on defendant if search with a war-

rant, on state if not, on ground that in the former case the state has already made out a prima facie case that search is reasonable). See also, *State v. Vrtiska*, 225 Neb. 454, 406 N.W.2d 114 (1987).

40. See discussion of *Lego v. Twomey*, 404 U.S. 477, 92 S.Ct. 619 (1972), discussed in § 16.06(b).

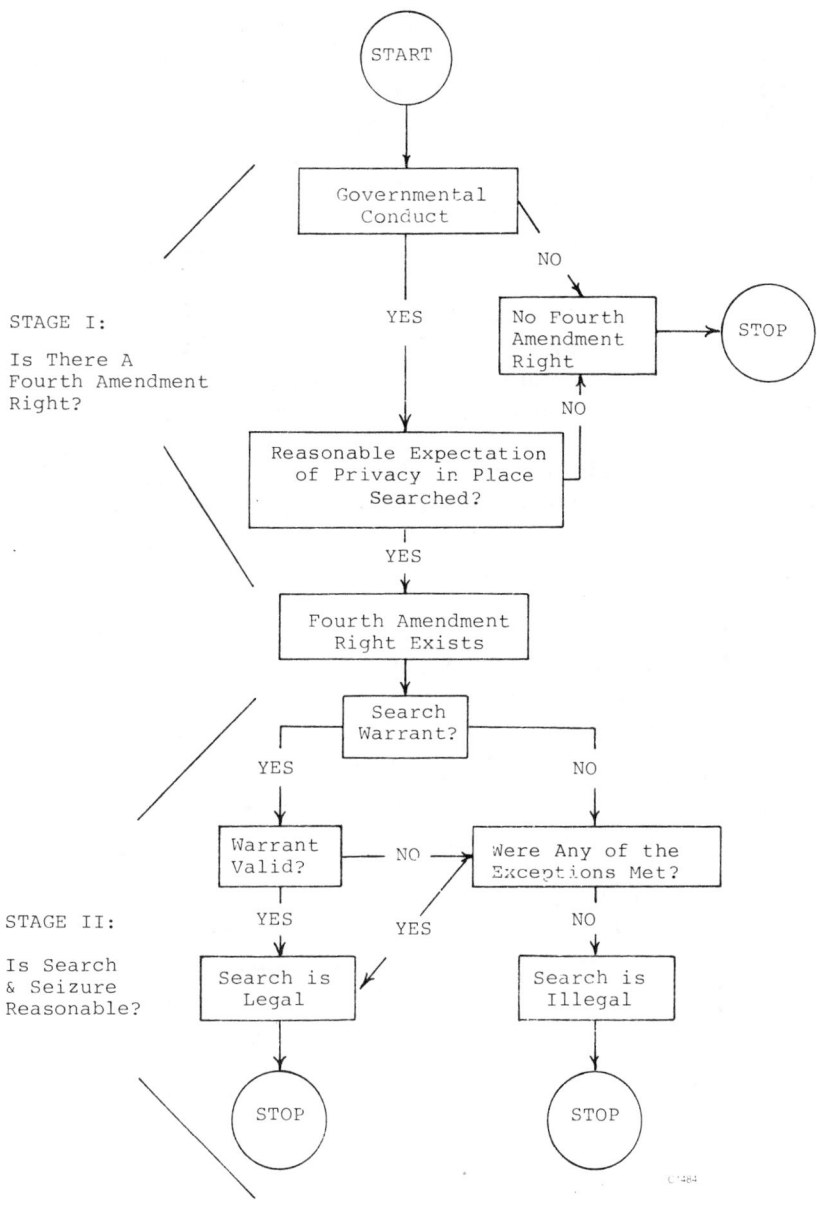

private persons acting as agents of these officials. Searches by private individuals who are not acting as agents of government officials do not implicate the Fourth Amendment; nor is the Amendment implicated by searches by governmental officials that essentially duplicate a previous independent search by a private individual, at least when the latter search reveals nothing of privacy significance other than contraband.

(2) Generally, one has a reasonable expectation of privacy in one's home, one's vehicles, one's personal effects, and one's person, meaning that the Fourth Amendment is implicated by governmental intrusions into these areas. However, one does not have a reasonable expectation of privacy in what one exposes to the public, whether the exposure occurs in the home or elsewhere. In such situations, governmental intrusion is not a "search" for purposes of the Fourth Amendment. Relying on this rationale the Supreme Court has held that a search does not occur if government agents acquire information about an individual in any of the following ways: (a) from persons or institutions to whom the individual has voluntarily revealed information; (b) from observation of the individual's physical characteristics and abilities; (c) from physical intrusion into the "open fields;" (d) from flying over either open fields or curtilage; (e) from containers which are "abandoned" (including garbage bags left at curbside) or reveal the nature of their contents; (f) from devices which make it easier to perceive what the individual has already exposed to the public (e.g., beepers, flashlights, aerial mapmaking cameras) or which enable perception of what is not exposed to the public in a nonintrusive fashion that detects only incriminating evidence (e.g., field tests for drugs, dog searches); (g) in the course of conducting an inspection of a jail cell.

(3) Even if a "search" has occurred, the person seeking the protection of the Fourth Amendment must show that *his* legitimate expectations of privacy were violated by the governmental conduct before he may contest the search. He can do this by showing: (a) the area searched was one from which he had the right to exclude others; or (b) continuing access to the place searched and a possessory interest in the item seized; and perhaps also by showing either (c) legitimate presence in the place searched and a possessory interest in the item seized; or (d) a valid bailment of the item seized to a person whose legitimate expectations of privacy were violated by the search for the item.

BIBLIOGRAPHY

Amsterdam, Anthony G. Perspectives on the Fourth Amendment. 58 Minn.L.Rev. 349 (1974).

Bradley, Craig. Two Models of the Fourth Amendment. 83 Mich.L.Rev. 1468 (1985).

Junker, John. The Structure of the Fourth Amendment: The Scope of the Protection. 79 J.Crim.Law & Criminol. 1105 (1989).

Katz, Lewis. In Search of a Fourth Amendment for the Twenty-First Century. 65 Indiana L.Rev. 549 (1990).

Loewy, Arnold H. The Fourth Amendment as a Device for Protecting the Innocent. 81 Mich.L.Rev. 1229 (1983).

Moylan, Charles E. Jr. Fourth Amendment Inapplicable vs. Fourth Amendment Satisfied: The Neglected Threshold of "So What?" 1977 S.Ill.U.L.J. 75 (1977).

Power, Robert. Technology and the Fourth Amendment: A Proposed Formulation for Visual Searches. 80 J.Crim.Law & Criminol. 1 (1989).

Slobogin, Christopher. Capacity to Contest a Search and Seizure: The Passing of Old Rules and Some Suggestions for New Ones, 18 Am.Crim.L.Rev. 387 (1981).

_____. The World Without a Fourth Amendment. 39 U.C.L.A. L.Rev. 1 (1991).

Wasserstrom, S. The Incredible Shrinking Fourth Amendment. 21 Am.Crim.L.Rev. 257 (1984).

_____. The Court's Turn Toward a General Reasonableness Interpretation of the Fourth Amendment. 27 Am.Crim.L.Rev. 119 (1989).

White, Welsh S. and Greenspan, Robert S. Standing to Object to Search and Seizure. 118 Pa.L.Rev. 333 (1970).

Chapter Five

THE SEARCH WARRANT

5.01 Introduction

Whether or not the Fourth Amendment states a preference for warrants,[1] the rationale for such a preference is clear. As Justice Jackson stated in *Johnson v. United States:*[2]

> The point of the Fourth Amendment . . . is not that it denies law enforcement the support of the usual inferences reasonable men draw from evidence. Its protection consists in requiring that those inferences be drawn by a neutral and detached magistrate instead of being judged by the officer engaged in the often competitive enterprise of ferreting out crime.

The assumption underlying this statement is that the interposition of a magistrate in the investigative decisionmaking process improves that process. While this premise can be questioned, it is probably sound. A study conducted by the National Center for State Courts found that magisterial review of warrant applications is often "perfunctory" (seldom lasting longer than five minutes), and rarely results in denial of an application.[3] At the same time, the study found that searches based on warrants are only occasionally found to be illegal,[4] and that the requirement that police obtain approval of their actions increases their "standard of care" because they, and the prosecutors advising them, know that a third party will be judging their decision to search.[5] According to the study, although the warrant requirement is perceived as "burdensome, time-consuming, intimidating, frustrating, and confusing" by the police, it seldom, if ever, results in the loss of "good cases."[6] Moreover, the advent of "telephonic warrants" and other time-saving devices can potentially improve the efficiency of the warrant process enormously.[7]

The language of the Fourth Amendment requires that a warrant be founded on "probable cause supported by oath or affirmation," and that it describe "with particularity the place to be searched and the things to be seized." As noted above, accord-

---

1. See § 4.05(a).

2. 333 U.S. 10, 68 S.Ct. 367 (1948).

3. See Van Duizend, Sutton & Cater, The Search Warrant Process: Preconceptions, Perceptions, and Practices 31 (National Center for State Courts, undated).

4. The reversal rate appears to be less than 5%. Id. at 56.

5. Id. at 148–49.

6. Id. at 149, 96.

7. See Fed.R.Crim.P. 41(c)(2), permitting the police to call a magistrate and, based on recitation of the facts known to them, receive a judicial ruling over the phone, all of which is recorded and later transcribed.

ing to the Supreme Court, the Fourth Amendment also requires that the warrant be issued by a neutral and detached decisionmaker. Additional requirements, not clearly of constitutional stature, have been placed on the execution of warrants by statute or judicial decision. All of these issues are addressed in this chapter.

5.02 The Neutral and Detached Decisionmaker

Because the primary purpose of the warrant requirement is to force the probable cause determination to be made by someone removed from the pressures of criminal investigation, the Supreme Court has taken pains to assure the decisionmaker is independent from law enforcement activities. Thus, in *Coolidge v. New Hampshire,*[8] search warrants issued by the state attorney general were declared invalid, even though he was authorized by state law to issue them. The Court concluded that the attorney general was not a "neutral and detached magistrate," especially since he was also the chief prosecutor in the case.

Although *Coolidge* left open the possibility that a prosecutor not involved in the case could constitutionally approve a warrant, the Court suggested otherwise in *United States v. United States Dist. Court.*[9] At issue there was the President's power, acting through the Attorney General, to authorize electronic surveillance in internal security matters without prior judicial approval. The Court found the surveillances unlawful, again emphasizing the need for a neutral and detached magistrate. Justice Powell wrote:

> The Fourth Amendment does not contemplate the executive officers of Government as neutral and detached magistrates. Their duty and responsibility is to enforce the laws, to investigate and to prosecute. . . . [T]hose charged with this investigative and prosecutorial duty should not be the sole judges of when to utilize constitutionally sensitive means in pursuing their tasks. The historical judgment, which the Fourth Amendment accepts, is that unreviewed executive discretion may yield too readily to pressures to obtain incriminating evidence and overlook potential invasions of privacy and protected speech.

In some cases, even a magistrate may not be sufficiently neutral. In *Lo-Ji Sales, Inc. v. New York,*[10] the magistrate issued a search warrant for two specific "obscene" items, but also included in the warrant an authorization to seize any other items which he himself might find obscene upon examination at the searched premises. He then accompanied the police to the premises, decided which items beyond the two named in the warrant were to be

---

8. 403 U.S. 443, 91 S.Ct. 2022 (1971).   **10.** 442 U.S. 319, 99 S.Ct. 2319
9. 407 U.S. 297, 92 S.Ct. 2125 (1972).   (1979).

seized, and added each to the initial warrant. The Supreme Court unanimously refused to accept the state's argument that the presence and participation of the magistrate in the search ensured that no items would be seized without probable cause. The Court found that the magistrate had failed to manifest the detached neutrality demanded of a judicial officer by the Fourth Amendment when he "conducted a generalized search under authority of an invalid warrant; he was not acting as a judicial officer but as an adjunct law-enforcement officer". The Court also found an infirmity in the fact that, upon finding a particular item obscene, the magistrate ordered the police to seize all "similar" items and allowed them to add the titles of the items they seized to the warrant. *Lo-Ji* demonstrates that a judicial officer, even if initially "independent" of the law enforcement process, can lose that independence through his own actions. It also stands for the proposition that the authority to decide probable cause cannot be delegated to police officers.

The Supreme Court has also recognized that a magistrate's objectivity may be compromised by pressure from something other than a desire to "ferret out crime." In *Connally v. Georgia*,[11] the Court was confronted with a statute which provided that unsalaried justices of the peace were to receive five dollars for each warrant issued but nothing if they reviewed an application and denied it. Finding that this statute subjected suspects to "judicial action by an officer of a court who has 'a direct, personal, substantial, pecuniary interest' in his conclusion to issue or to deny the warrant," a unanimous Court found that it violated the Fourth Amendment.

If the necessary neutrality is present, warrants may be issued by someone who is not a judicial officer, at least in some circumstances. In *Shadwick v. Tampa*,[12] the Court held that clerks of the Tampa municipal court were qualified as "neutral and detached" magistrates for the purpose of issuing arrest warrants for violations of city ordinances, because they were appointed from a classified civil service list, under the supervision of the municipal court judge, and removed from the prosecutor and police. The Court noted that nonlawyers not only have been acting as magistrates for years but have also been assumed to be competent to make decisions as members of grand juries and juries. It could also be pointed out that the police are considered capable of determining probable cause in the many situations where a warrantless search may be conducted. The key inquiry should be whether the third party decisionmaker has sufficient objectivity to

11. 429 U.S. 245, 97 S.Ct. 546 (1977).   12. 407 U.S. 345, 92 S.Ct. 2119 (1972).

make a better decision than the law enforcement officers on the "frontlines."

5.03 The Probable Cause Determination

Assuming the person making the probable cause determination is sufficiently divorced from law enforcement activity, the next question is whether the warrant issued was supported by probable cause. This section explores the meaning the Supreme Court has given this elusive term, the procedure for determining whether it exists, and ways of attacking that determination.

It is important to note that the probable cause concept is also extremely important in connection with many of the *exceptions* to the search warrant requirement, because they often require probable cause as a predicate, in addition to some type of exigent circumstances.[13] Thus, although the discussion below focuses on cases involving search warrants, it is relevant to several subsequent chapters in this book.

(a) A General Definition. The Supreme Court has explained that probable cause to search exists when the facts and circumstances in a given situation are sufficient to warrant a person of reasonable caution to believe that seizable objects are located at the place to be searched.[14] This language makes clear that probable cause is objectively defined, and not dependent upon the subjective views of the searching officer or authorizing magistrate. The degree of certainty required lies somewhere between "reasonable suspicion," the quantum of certainty required to justify a "stop and frisk,"[15] and "beyond a reasonable doubt," the standard of proof in a criminal trial. Literally interpreted, the term seems to require a more likely than not showing that the evidence sought will be found. Whether this is indeed the standard is open to question. The American Law Institute's formulation uses the term "reasonable cause" rather than probable cause, apparently to avoid the implication that a standard of "more probable than not" is required.[16]

Perhaps more importantly, the Supreme Court has made clear that probable cause is a flexibly defined concept. In *United States v. Ventresca,*[17] FBI agents observed repeated deliveries of loads of sugar in 60-pound bags, smelled the odor of fermenting mash, and heard sounds similar to that of a motor or a pump coming from

---

13. E.g., the "automobile exception" (Chapter Seven) and the "plain view" exception (Chapter Ten). Other exceptions require probable cause to arrest, e.g., the "search incident" exception (Chapter Six) and the "hot pursuit" exception (Chapter Eight).

14. *Brinegar v. United States,* 338 U.S. 160, 69 S.Ct. 1302 (1949).

15. See § 11.03(a) for a discussion of the reasonable suspicion standard.

16. ALI, Model Code of Pre-Arraignment Procedure § 220.1(5) (1975).

17. 380 U.S. 102, 85 S.Ct. 741 (1965).

the direction of Ventresca's house. In concluding that the agents' affidavit, stating these facts amply established probable cause to support the issuance of the warrant, the Court held that affidavits should be tested in "a commonsense and realistic fashion," and reviewing courts should "not invalidate the warrant by interpreting the affidavit in a hypertechnical, rather than a commonsense, manner." The Court has vigorously reaffirmed *Ventresca* in more recent decisions to be discussed below.

The Court has also emphasized, somewhat inconsistently, that the probable cause standard usually represents the same general "level of certainty" regardless of the type of search contemplated. For example, in *New York v. P.J. Video*,[18] it held that searches for material which may be protected by the First Amendment need not be justified by any greater level of suspicion than searches seeking other types of evidence.[19] Occasionally, however, the Court has defined probable cause to mean a level of certainty below the more-likely-than not standard. In particular, some of its regulatory decisions, while requiring warrants based on "probable cause," actually permit inspections based on a very low probability that evidence of illegal activity will be found.[20]

"Probable cause" is required to justify an arrest as well as a search and much of what is said in this book concerning probable cause in the former context is relevant here as well.[21] However, it should be clear that probable cause for a search does not automatically support an arrest, nor does a valid arrest warrant automatically support a search. Thus, for example, in order to obtain a search warrant, police need not allege that the place to be searched is controlled by a person connected with a crime (though this, of course, will frequently be the case). Conversely, the fact that a person believed to have committed a crime is in a certain location does not necessarily justify a search of every inch of that location. In short, a search is founded upon differing probabilities than an arrest.[22]

(b) Hearsay Information: Criteria for Use. Several Supreme Court cases have held that, as Federal Rule of Criminal Procedure 41(c) provides: "The finding of probable cause may be based upon hearsay evidence in whole or in part." Because the probable cause finding is based on probabilities, it may rely on evidence that would not be admissible at trial. However, as the

18. 475 U.S. 868, 106 S.Ct. 1610 (1986).

19. However, the Court has also indicated that when a seizure may act as a "prior restraint," an adversary proceeding must precede the seizure. *Marcus v. Search Warrants*, 367 U.S. 717, 81 S.Ct. 1708 (1961), discussed in § 5.06(b).

20. See, e.g., *Camara v. Municipal Court*, 387 U.S. 523, 87 S.Ct. 1727 (1967), discussed in § 13.02.

21. See § 3.03.

22. See Imwinkelreid, et al. Criminal Evidence 216, n. 14 (1976).

Court stated in *Jones v. United States*,[23] there should be a "substantial basis for crediting the hearsay" before it forms the predicate for a probable cause determination. When the hearsay upon which the affiant-officer relies is from another police officer, or from a "respectable citizen" who has been the victim of a crime or witnessed it, the Court has been relatively relaxed about evaluating its basis.[24] But when the hearsay comes from "informants"— that is, people whose motivation to inform is money, or a reduction in charges or some other direct benefit from the police—the Court has been much more careful about gauging reliability.

The two leading cases in this regard during the Warren Court years were *Aguilar v. Texas*[25] and *Spinelli v. United States*.[26] In *Aguilar,* a search warrant had issued upon an affidavit from two police officers who swore only that they had "received reliable information from a credible person and do believe" that narcotics were being illegally stored on the described premises. The Court held the affidavit inadequate for two reasons: (1) The affidavit did not state sufficient underlying circumstances to permit a neutral and detached magistrate to understand how the informant reached his conclusion; and (2) the affidavit did not state sufficient underlying circumstances establishing the reliability or credibility of the informant. According to the Court, both the "basis-of-knowledge" prong and the "veracity" prong of this test had to be met to support a warrant's issuance.

In *Spinelli*, the Court reaffirmed *Aguilar's* two-prong test. There, a search warrant was issued on the basis of an FBI agent's affidavit alleging: (1) that an informant had told the agent that Spinelli was taking bets over two telephone numbers; (2) that FBI surveillance had independently resulted in knowledge that Spinelli had gone to the apartment where these two phones were located four times in a five-day period; and (3) that Spinelli was a known gambler and an associate of gamblers. The Court found this affidavit insufficient as well, because it failed to set forth the "underlying circumstances" describing how the informant obtained his information and did not contain reasons for the FBI agent's belief that the informant was reliable.[27] The information that Spinelli was a known gambler was viewed as irrelevant, by itself, on the issue of the informant's credibility.

The two-prong *Aguilar-Spinelli* test remained the law for over a decade. But in *Illinois v. Gates*,[28] a five-member majority explicitly "abandoned" the *Aguilar-Spinelli* rules and "reaf-

23. 362 U.S. 257, 80 S.Ct. 725 (1960).

24. See §§ 3.03(a)(2) & (3), for a discussion of this issue, in the context of probable cause to arrest.

25. 378 U.S. 108, 84 S.Ct. 1509 (1964).

26. 393 U.S. 410, 89 S.Ct. 584 (1969).

27. Indeed, there was some indication the "informant" was an illegal wiretap of Spinelli's phone.

28. 462 U.S. 213, 103 S.Ct. 2317 (1983).

firm[ed] the totality of the circumstances analysis that traditionally has informed probable cause determinations." The search warrant issued in *Gates* was based on an anonymous handwritten letter sent to the Bloomingdale, Illinois police department. It charged that the defendants, Lance and Susan Gates, were involved in ferrying drugs from Florida to Illinois and that they had over $100,000 worth of drugs in their home. The letter also specified that the Gates were about to receive a new drug shipment. According to the letter, Sue Gates would drive to Florida to pick up the drugs on May 3rd, leave the car at West Palm Beach and fly back; Lance Gates would then fly down to drive the car back. The police verified that an L. Gates did in fact fly to Florida on May 5th; they also observed him rendezvous with a woman staying in a room registered to Susan Gates, and leave with her the next morning driving in the direction of Illinois. The warrant was issued on the basis of this information, and the subsequent search of the Gates' car and home after they arrived in Chicago uncovered several hundred pounds of marijuana, weapons and other contraband.

In invalidating the warrant and the search based on it, the Illinois Supreme Court evaluated the probable cause determination in light of each of the *Aguilar-Spinelli* test.[29] It concluded that the "veracity" prong of the test was not satisfied because, "[t]here was simply no basis [for] conclud[ing] that the anonymous person [who wrote the letter to the Bloomingdale police department] was credible." In addition, according to the court, the letter gave no indication of the basis for the writer's knowledge of the defendants' activities. The United States Supreme Court, in an opinion by Justice Rehnquist, found the Illinois court's treatment of the warrant in *Gates* hypertechnical. While affirming that an informant's "veracity" and "basis of knowledge" are highly relevant to the probable cause determination, the Court did not view these elements as separate and independent requirements to be rigidly interpreted in every case. Rather, "they should be understood simply as closely intertwined issues that may usefully illuminate the commonsense, practical question whether there is 'probable cause.'" Thus, the Court concluded, "a deficiency in one may be compensated for, in determining the overall reliability of a tip, by a strong showing as to the other, or by some other indicia of reliability." Applying this "commonsense" approach to the *Gates* facts, the Court reversed the Illinois Supreme Court. It held that the letter alone would not have furnished probable cause but that once most of its contents were corroborated by the police, a warrant could validly be issued.

29. *People v. Gates*, 85 Ill.2d 376, 53 Ill.Dec. 218, 423 N.E.2d 887 (1981).

The majority opinion in *Gates* reiterated at several points the need to avoid burdening the probable cause determination with "legal technicalities" or one "neat set of rules." But several lower court decisions after *Gates* suggested that while the decision had refocused the analysis of probable cause, it would have little impact on individual cases.[30] Perhaps aware of this tendency, the Supreme Court subsequently warned against dismissing *Gates* as a mere "refinement." In summarily reversing *Massachusetts v. Upton*,[31] a decision in which the Massachusetts Supreme Judicial Court stated that *Gates* did not mark a "significant change in the appropriate Fourth Amendment treatment of applications for search warrants,"[32] the Supreme Court insisted that *Gates* was not meant merely as a qualification of the two-pronged test, but rather sought to reject the test as "hypertechnical."

There follows an attempt to parse out the factors that are relevant to evaluating hearsay information after *Gates*. Because *Gates* and *Upton* have emphasized that "a deficiency in one [factor] may be compensated for . . . by a strong showing as to the other, or by some other indicia of reliability," any one of these factors, by itself, may be sufficient to establish that a tip is reliable enough to be used in evaluating whether probable cause exists.[33]

(1) Basis of knowledge. As established in *Aguilar*, a good description of how the informant came to know about the alleged criminal activity is an important element in assessing credibility. If the informant persuasively shows that he was personally involved in the criminal transaction or otherwise observed it first-hand, his credibility will be viewed as relatively high. For instance, the affidavit which the Court upheld in *Jones v. United States*,[34] stated, among other things,[35] that the informant had "on many occasions . . . gone to [the suspects'] apartment and purchased narcotic drugs from the [suspects]," a statement which was bolstered by the affiant's own statement that he knew the informant to be a drug user and had seen needle marks on his arm. On the other hand, if the informant's allegations appear to be based on gossip, or do not have an identified basis, their credibility is questionable. As the Court's decisions indicate, the tips in *Agui-*

---

30. See *Whisman v. Commonwealth*, 667 S.W.2d 394 (Ky.App.1984); *State v. Ricci*, 472 A.2d 291 (R.I.1984); *State v. Yananokwiak*, 65 N.C.App. 513, 309 S.E.2d 560 (1983). But see *United States v. Mendoza*, 722 F.2d 96 (5th Cir. 1983).

31. 466 U.S. 727, 104 S.Ct. 2085 (1984).

32. *Commonwealth v. Upton*, 390 Mass. 562, 458 N.E.2d 717 (1983).

33. Note, however, that even if a tip is considered reliable, the information it provides may not establish probable cause. See, e.g., § 3.03(a)(2).

34. 362 U.S. 257, 80 S.Ct. 725 (1960).

35. The affidavit also stated that the informant's information had been corroborated "by other sources of information" and that the informant had given reliable information in the past.

lar and *Spinelli,* and the anonymous letter in *Gates,* were completely lacking on this score.

(2) Detailed description of activity. In *Spinelli,* the Court announced an alternative method of conforming to the "basis-of-knowledge" prong. As Justice Harlan stated for the Court, "[i]n the absence of a statement detailing the manner in which the information was gathered, it is especially important that the tip describe the accused's criminal activity in sufficient detail that the magistrate may know that he is relying on something more substantial than a casual rumor . . . or an accusation based merely on an individual's general reputation." In *Spinelli,* this test was not met because the only facts supplied—that Spinelli was using two specified phones and that these phones were being used in gambling operations—"could easily have been obtained from an offhand remark heard at a neighborhood bar." A case in which suitable detail was provided, according to Harlan, was *Draper v. United States,*[36] in which the informant alleged that Draper would arrive on a particular train from Chicago on one of two specified mornings, wear particular clothes and be carrying a briefcase.

In a concurring opinion in *Gates,* Justice White suggested that the anonymous letter in that case provided detail on a par with the informant's information in *Draper.* According to White, given the amount of detail about the suspects' travel plans in the letter, "the magistrate could reasonably have inferred, as he apparently did, that the informant, . . . obtained his information in a reliable way." Of course, as Justice Stevens pointed out in his dissent in *Gates,* "each year dozens of perfectly innocent people fly to Florida, meet a waiting spouse, and drive off together in the family car." But the point of *Spinelli* is that when, as in both *Draper* and *Gates,* the informant states he knows or can predict *intimate* things about the suspect, the probability that he has reliable "inside" information about the suspect's criminal activity is greater. A rich description of the suspect's home can be obtained from many sources and usually does not connote any knowledge about his crime; a point-by-point recitation of travel plans is likely to be available only to a few, and thus suggests the close relationship necessary to find out about criminal activity as well.

Spinelli also made clear, however, that no amount of detail is, by itself, enough; as noted above, it also required some showing of veracity on the part of the informant. Detailed information is not particularly helpful in this regard, since an informant can "fabricate in fine detail as easily as with rough brush strokes."[37] Yet

36. 358 U.S. 307, 79 S.Ct. 329 (1959).   **37.** *Stanley v. State,* 19 Md.App. 507, 313 A.2d 847 (1974).

the Court seemed to disregard this admonition in *Gates.* Justice Rehnquist stated that "even if we entertain some doubt as to an informant's motives, his explicit and detailed description of alleged wrongdoing, along with a statement that the event was observed firsthand, entitles his tip to greater weight than might otherwise be the case." If this statement is taken seriously, detailed allegations by informants would have to be treated with the same generosity as those made by police officers or "respectable" citizens.

(3) Past reliability. The primary way of meeting the "veracity" prong of the *Aguilar–Spinelli* test was to establish that the informant had given reliable information in the past. Perhaps the strongest example of this sort, from the Court's cases, is *McCray v. Illinois,*[38] where the informant had provided information on fifteen or sixteen previous occasions, many of which resulted in arrests and convictions.[39] But the Court has also sanctioned boilerplate statements to the effect that the informant "has given reliable information in the past," albeit with the additional requirement that there should be some other indicia of reliability as well.[40]

In *Gates,* consistent with its totality of the circumstances ruling, the Court suggested that sufficient allegations of veracity may, by themselves, meet the standard announced in that case. As an example of how a deficiency in the basis-of-knowledge prong could be compensated for, Justice Rehnquist stated: if "a particular informant is known for the unusual reliability of his predictions of certain types of criminal activities in a locality, his failure, in a particular case, to thoroughly set forth the basis of his knowledge surely should not serve as an absolute bar to a finding of probable cause based on his tip." But this statement should be read narrowly. As Justice White stated in his concurrence, even *police officers* who are known to be honest should have to provide some basis for their belief that evidence is located in a particular area.

(4) Corroboration by police. An informant's veracity can also be supported by police corroboration of his statements. In both *Draper* and *Gates,* for instance, the Court emphasized that the police observed events that fit the information given by the informant.[41] Of course, to be useful to a magistrate making the

---

38. 386 U.S. 300, 87 S.Ct. 1056 (1967).

39. Although information that results merely in arrest, as opposed to conviction, is not necessarily reliable, the recency of the arrest (and thus the likelihood the charge has not yet been adjudicated) should be taken into account.

40. In *Jones v. United States,* 362 U.S. 257, 80 S.Ct. 725 (1960), the affidavit included the boilerplate about informant reliability but added that the informant's information had been corroborated by "other sources of information."

41. For further description of *Draper,* see § 3.03(a)(1).

probable cause determination, this corroboration should occur before a warrant is sought by the police. Thus, the fact that the police in *Gates* eventually found drugs in the suspects' basement, as predicted by the anonymous letter, was irrelevant, since the discovery came after the warrant was issued.

Apparently it is not fatal if, during their attempts to corroborate the informant's information, police find some of it to be in error. In his dissent in *Gates,* Justice Stevens pointed out that the anonymous letter had been incorrect with respect to what he termed a "material" fact (that Lance Gates would drive the car back to Illinois *alone*). Justice Rehnquist discarded this mistake as unimportant, on the ground that "[w]e have never required that informants used by the police be infallible, and can see no reason to impose such a requirement in this case." [42] It also appears, once again, that boilerplate language to the effect that corroboration has taken place may be sufficient if other factors are present as well.[43]

(5) Other indicia of reliability. In holding that "other indicia of reliability" besides the basis-of-knowledge and veracity prongs should be considered in evaluating the credibility of tips, *Gates* cited *United States v. Harris.*[44] That decision, handed down two years after *Spinelli,* advanced two additional ways of supporting an informant's allegations, in a melange of opinions which showed a Court already somewhat dissatisfied with the *Aguilar–Spinelli* formulation. In *Harris,* the affidavit stated that the affiant had viewed the informant and judged him to be "prudent;" that the informant had purchased illegal whiskey from the suspect; and that the suspect had a reputation for trafficking in whiskey. A divided Court reversed the lower court's determination that the affidavit was insufficient under *Aguilar's* veracity prong. Four justices reached this result because they were willing to permit both police knowledge of the suspect's reputation and the informant's declaration against penal interest to bolster his credibility. Justice Stewart was willing to subscribe only to the first rationale, while Justice White would only sign on to the second. The four dissenters criticized both methods of judging reliability.

Chief Justice Burger's opinion for the Court acknowledged that, in *Spinelli,* the Court had called the assertion that the suspect was known to the affiant as a gambler "bald and unilluminating" and had concluded that it was entitled to "no weight." But he felt that a suspect's reputation was a "practical

---

42. While Rehnquist is correct that courts do not require informants to be infallible, the cases that stand for this proposition have involved discovery of the error *after* the search or seizure took place. See § 5.03(d).

43. See *Jones,* supra note 40.

44. 403 U.S. 573, 91 S.Ct. 2075 (1971).

consideration of everyday life" that should be considered in assessing reliability, and thus rejected *Spinelli's* indication to the contrary. With respect to declarations against interest, Burger asserted that "[p]eople do not lightly admit a crime and place critical evidence in the hands of the police in the form of their own admissions." Thus, such declarations "carry their own indicia of credibility—sufficient at least to support a finding of probable cause to search."

While the reputation of the suspect may bolster the informant's allegations to the extent they are consistent with that reputation, a conclusory statement in this regard is not particularly helpful to a magistrate because it does not tell him whether the reputation is deserved. At best, unless the reputation evidence is supported factually, it is useful only as support for an *officer's* probable cause determination in those situations where he is allowed to proceed without a warrant. And, as Justice Harlan pointed out in his dissenting opinion, declarations against interest in the informant context should be taken with a grain of salt, since the informant may be anonymous, or may have already received or be expecting to receive assurances that his indiscretions will not be prosecuted. Yet *Gates* apparently allows both conclusory statements about reputation and declarations against interest to be considered in the magistrate's totality of the circumstances analysis.

(c) Oath or Affirmation. Typically, the application for a warrant must describe the place to be searched, the property to be seized, the person having the property (if it is to be taken from his control), and the underlying crime. Other facts necessary to support a probable cause determination may be included in affidavits attached to the application or provided in statements taken before the magistrate. Given the explicit language of the Fourth Amendment, all of these documents (i.e., the application for a warrant and any accompanying documentation or statements) must be "affirmed" or sworn to by the officer making the application, usually in writing. If oral testimony is given, it too must be given under oath. For example, the federal rules provide that "[b]efore ruling on a request for a warrant the federal magistrate or state judge may require the affiant to appear personally and may examine under oath the affiant and any witness he may produce," provided the proceeding is recorded and made part of the affidavit.[45] Neither the oath nor the testimony need be made in the magistrate's presence, at least when pursuant to rules governing the issuance of telephonic warrants.[46]

---

45. Fed.R.Crim.P. 41(c).

46. See *United States v. Turner,* 558 F.2d 46 (2d Cir.1977) (finding that magistrate's approval, over the phone, of warrant requested by officer in the field who swears to sufficient facts complies with oath or affirmation clause).

(d) Challenging the Probable Cause Determination; The Informant Privilege. A frequent issue in suppression hearings is whether the magistrate, or the police officer in cases where no warrant was necessary, had probable cause to act. In cases where there is a warrant, this challenge usually must be based entirely on information provided in the warrant application and supporting affidavits. As the Supreme Court stated in *Whiteley v. Warden*,[47] "an otherwise insufficient affidavit cannot be rehabilitated by testimony concerning information possessed by the affiant when he sought the warrant but not disclosed to the issuing magistrate." A contrary ruling, reasoned the Court, would "render the warrant requirement of the Fourth Amendment meaningless."

Occasionally, however, the defendant will want to challenge the accuracy of the statements made by the affiant or the affiant's informants. To do so requires going behind the warrant application and supporting documentation. Under the Supreme Court's cases, such challenges will rarely be successful. First, the Court seems to have held, and rightly so, that even if information underlying a probable cause determination turns out to be false, the warrant, or the warrantless search, is not defective if the information was such that a "prudent reasonable person" could rely on it and the officer honestly relied on it.[48] Second, even if the information was unreasonably relied upon, the defendant's ability to prove this fact at a hearing, and to have the tainted search declared invalid, has been severely circumscribed by the Court's decision in *Franks v. Delaware.*[49]

In *Franks,* the defendant sought a hearing to challenge a statement in the warrant affidavit to the effect that one of his co-workers had implicated him in criminal activity. In view of the defendant's proffer of testimony from the co-worker that such statements were never made, the Supreme Court was willing to grant a hearing. But in doing so, it required prospective challengers to meet three conditions before a hearing could take place, and also announced several government-oriented rules concerning the hearing itself, the combined effect of which is to ensure that most defendants will find it difficult to successfully mount such challenges.

First, the allegation that the information was false must be more than conclusory and must be supported by more than a desire to cross-examine. Specifically, the defendant must: (1) allege that statements were made deliberately or with reckless

---

47. 401 U.S. 560, 91 S.Ct. 1031 (1971).

48. *Henry v. United States,* 361 U.S. 98, 80 S.Ct. 168 (1959). The exception to this rule is when the information is provided by another police officer who knows or has reason to believe it is false. See infra note 53.

49. 438 U.S. 154, 98 S.Ct. 2674 (1978).

disregard for the truth; (2) specifically point out the portion of the warrant that is claimed to be false; (3) accompany this proffer with a statement of supporting reasons; and (4) furnish affidavits of sworn or otherwise reliable statements of witnesses concerning the statements, or explain the absence of such witnesses. Allegations of negligent or innocent mistake are insufficient.

Secondly, the defendant is permitted to challenge only information supplied by affiants (i.e., police officers). With this limitation, the Court meant to implement the so-called "informant's privilege," which keeps the identity of police informants confidential in order to maintain their usefulness and prevent reprisals against them (and thus encourages others to inform as well).[50] In *McCray v. Illinois*,[51] the Court had already held that, despite the accused's right of confrontation under the Sixth Amendment, a defendant's motion to subpoena an informant for trial may be denied whenever the trial judge feels that the informant's testimony would not contradict other evidence before the court.[52] This wide-ranging discretion granted the trial judge in *McCray* was reinforced at the pretrial stage by the holding in *Franks*, which not only immunizes from pretrial attack the veracity of an informant, but also makes very difficult any challenge of a police officer's statement about what the informant said.[53]

As a third condition, the defendant must show that, assuming the challenged information is indeed false and thus must be deleted, the remainder of the information in the warrant application would not support a probable cause finding. Only if the rest of the evidence is insufficient for this purpose is the defendant entitled to a hearing under *Franks*.

If the defendant is successful in making the showing required to earn a hearing, he must still establish at that hearing, by a preponderance of the evidence, that the false statement was made by the affiant deliberately, or with reckless disregard for the truth. He must also demonstrate that the false statement was necessary to the showing of probable cause in the warrant. If the defendant can make this showing, the search warrant is voided, and the fruits of the search are excluded in the same manner as if the defect appeared on the face of the warrant.

Franks can be criticized on a number of levels. First, its ban on challenging informant tips is an overly broad attempt to

50. See 8 J. Wigmore, Evidence § 2374 (1961).

51. 386 U.S. 300, 87 S.Ct. 1056 (1967).

52. See § 28.04(a).

53. However, *Franks* suggested that, when the informant is another officer, police cannot "insulate one officer's deliberate misstatement merely by relaying it through an officer-affiant personally ignorant of its falsity." See § 3.03(c).

protect the informant privilege, particularly in light of the recognized tendency on the part of the police to commit perjury.[54] As several lower courts have held, an informant can be interviewed *in camera* by the judge,[55] thus protecting against disclosure of his identity while at the same time permitting some assessment of a defendant's claims of falsehood. Second, *Franks'* requirement that the defendant allege and prove the affiant was reckless with respect to the truth disregards the Fourth Amendment's requirement that officers be "reasonable," a requirement which suggests that only negligence need be shown. Third, once the defendant shows a statement to be false, the burden of showing recklessness or negligence, as the case may be, should be on the officer, in line with the normal burden allocation in civil cases on the issue of a party's mental state (which only the party can truly know). Finally, *Franks'* "independent source" rule—that a warrant based on false statements will be allowed to stand if probable cause still exists upon removal of the tainted information—is suspect, to the extent it encourages officers to fabricate intentionally in cases where there is significant evidence against the defendant.[56]

5.04 The Particularity Requirement

The Fourth Amendment requires that warrants state with "particularity the place to searched and the things to be seized." The original purpose of this clause was to prevent the practice, common during colonial times, of relying on "general warrants" to search for "evidence of treason" and similarly broadly phrased objectives.[57] When a warrant specifies the place to be searched and things to be seized, it limits the scope of the search. Additionally, an application which is particular as to these facts is more likely to be founded on a thorough investigation, and thus more likely to establish probable cause, which of course is required for any warrant to issue. The discussion below looks at both aspects of the particularity rule, in terms of their effect on the content of the warrant and the way in which the warrant is executed.

(a) Place to Be Searched. The warrant need not state with precision the place to be searched. It "is enough if the description is such that the officer with a search warrant can, with reasonable effort, ascertain and identify the place intended."[58] Occasionally, the warrant description will be mistaken. In *Maryland v. Garri-*

---

54. See, e.g., Younger, "The Perjury Routine," The Nation, May 8, 1967.

55. See, e.g., *People v. Brown,* 207 Cal.App.3d 1541, 256 Cal.Rptr. 11 (4th Dist.1989).

56. See also, in this regard, § 2.04(c), discussing the independent source doctrine and the exclusionary rule.

57. See T. Taylor, Two Studies in Constitutional Interpretation 23–50 (1969).

58. *Steele v. United States,* 267 U.S. 498, 45 S.Ct. 414 (1925).

son,[59] the Supreme Court held that whether a mistake as to the place to be searched renders the warrant invalid depends upon the extent to which it was possible for an officer, acting reasonably, to discover a mistake either at the time the warrant was sought or at the time it was executed.

In *Garrison*, police officers sought and obtained a warrant to search the person of one Lawrence McWebb and "the premises known as 2036 Park Avenue third floor apartment," alleging that McWebb's apartment occupied the entire third floor of his apartment building. Actually, there were two apartments on the third floor, one belonging to Garrison, a fact the police claimed they did not discover until they had begun searching Garrison's apartment and found contraband. The Court, in a 6–3 opinion authored by Justice Stevens, found that neither the warrant nor its execution violated the particularity requirement and that the contraband was admissible.

Stevens first found that the warrant was valid when it was issued, despite the mistake as to the configuration of the third floor.

> Just as the discovery of contraband cannot validate a warrant invalid when issued, so is it equally clear that the discovery of facts demonstrating that a valid warrant was unnecessarily broad does not retroactively invalidate the warrant. The validity of the warrant must be assessed on the basis of the information that the officers disclosed, or had a duty to discover and to disclose, to the magistrate.

Stevens noted that the informant who had provided police with information about McWebb had not mentioned a second apartment on McWebb's floor and that police inquiries at the local utility company had left the impression that the third floor had only one apartment. Finding that the officers had been sufficiently diligent in their attempts to ascertain who lived on the third floor prior to seeking the warrant, the Court held that the warrant was valid when issued.

Stevens then considered whether, once the officers were in the process of executing the warrant, they should have had reason to know that there were two apartments on the floor, only one of which could be validly searched on authority of the warrant they possessed. Again, Stevens found that "[t]he objective facts available to the officers at the time suggested no distinction between McWebb's apartment and the third-floor premises." The dissent, authored by Justice Blackmun, was particularly disturbed by this finding. Blackmun noted that, upon arriving at the building to execute the warrant, the officers discovered that there were seven

---

59. 480 U.S. 79, 107 S.Ct. 1013 (1987).

mailboxes to the three-floor apartment building. Once on the third floor, they encountered Garrison at the door of his apartment in his pajamas but never asked him where he lived or what he was doing on the third floor. Finally, as part of a preliminary sweep of the third floor, they found that the floor was divided into two virtually identical living areas, each with a bathroom, a kitchen, a living room, and a bedroom. As Blackmun concluded, "it is difficult to imagine that, in the initial security sweep, a reasonable officer would not have discerned that two apartments were on the third floor, realized his mistake, and then confined the ensuing search to McWebb's residence."

While it may be necessary to give police some leeway in their efforts to describe and find premises to be searched given the occasional difficulty of the enterprise, *Garrison's* treatment of the facts is troubling. As Justice Blackmun demonstrates, the actions of the police in that case once they arrived at the apartment building at best constituted willful blindness of the "objective" facts. Yet the majority found them to be reasonable.

(b) Things to Be Seized. The magistrate should ensure that the warrant is as specific as possible in identifying the items to be seized. A good example of a case where this admonition was not followed is *Lo–Ji Sales, Inc. v. New York,*[60] which concerned a warrant that authorized search of an adult book store not only to seize two specified films, but also to seize any items which the issuing magistrate might find "obscene" when he examined them at the store. A unanimous Court found that this warrant failed to "particularly describe . . . the things to be seized." In addition to surrendering his neutrality by going into the field, the magistrate had issued a warrant "reminiscent of the general warrants" meant to be prohibited by the Fourth Amendment.

In contrast, in *Andresen v. Maryland,*[61] the Court upheld a warrant which authorized seizure of a long list of specified documents, but ended with the phrase "together with other fruits, instrumentalities and evidence of crime at this [time] unknown." After construing this phrase to refer to the crime under investigation and noting that the crime was a complex one which "could be proved only by piecing together may bits of evidence," the Court upheld the warrant. The Court seemed impressed by the fact that the investigating agents had included in the warrant application all the evidence then thought to be on the premises searched.

With respect to executing a warrant, the rule at one time, as stated in *Marron v. United States,*[62] was that only those items

60. 442 U.S. 319, 99 S.Ct. 2319 (1979).

61. 427 U.S. 463, 96 S.Ct. 2737 (1976).

62. 275 U.S. 192, 48 S.Ct. 74 (1927).

listed in the warrant could be seized; according to the Court, "[t]he requirement that warrants shall particularly describe the things to be seized makes general searches under them impossible and prevents the seizure of one thing under a warrant describing another." In *Marron*, for example, the Court found that a search warrant describing intoxicating liquors and articles for their manufacture did not authorize the seizure of a ledger and bills of account found in a search of the premises specified in the warrant.

In *Coolidge v. New Hampshire*,[63] however, the Court carved out a significant exception to the *Marron* rule: whenever police executing a valid warrant "inadvertently" find in "plain view" evidence of criminal activity which is "immediately apparent" as such, they may seize that evidence even if it is not listed in the warrant. Under such circumstances, stated the Court, "[a]s against the minor peril to Fourth Amendment protections, there is a major gain in effective law enforcement." Requiring the police to refrain from seizing such evidence and to seek another warrant based on what they have seen would not provide any appreciable protection of privacy, and might result in the loss of the evidence prior to execution of the second warrant.

As developed elsewhere in this book,[64] the "plain view" exception to the warrant requirement has been expanded substantially since *Coolidge*. Evidence need no longer be "immediately apparent" as such; rather the police need merely have probable cause to believe that what they see in plain view is evidence of crime.[65] Further, the "inadvertence" requirement has been eliminated, on the ground that even if police do not include in the warrant application all of the items that they suspect are on the premises to be searched, they have at least established probable cause to believe some evidence of criminal activity is there, and thus sufficient protection against arbitrary entries has been afforded.[66]

Nonetheless, the rule announced in *Marron* retains considerable force. First, the nature of the items listed in the warrant may prevent a legitimate "plain view seizure" in many instances. As stated by the Court in *Harris v. United States*,[67] "the same meticulous investigation which would be appropriate in a search for two small canceled checks could not be considered reasonable where agents are seeking a stolen automobile or an illegal still." When the warrant lists a 12-gauge shotgun as the item to be seized, the police may not look in a cookie jar or a desk drawer. Moreover, items which do not, by their appearance, provide probable cause

---

63. 403 U.S. 443, 91 S.Ct. 2022 (1971).

64. See Chapter Ten.

65. *Texas v. Brown*, 460 U.S. 730, 103 S.Ct. 1535 (1983), discussed in § 10.03.

66. *Horton v. California*, 496 U.S. 128, 110 S.Ct. 2301 (1990), discussed and criticized in § 10.04.

67. 331 U.S. 145, 67 S.Ct. 1098 (1947).

may not be seized.   An example of this situation is provided in *Stanley v. Georgia*,[68] in which agents executing a warrant authorizing a search for gambling paraphernalia found some film cannisters, viewed the contents, and then seized them as pornographic. In *Coolidge*, the Court endorsed Justice Stewart's concurring opinion in *Stanley* arguing that, before viewing the films, the agents could not have known their contents "by mere inspection" and thus violated the Fourth Amendment by viewing and seizing them.[69]

5.05   Execution of the Warrant

Four major issues arise with respect to executing a search warrant: (1) when may a warrant be executed?; (2) must officers executing a warrant knock and announce their presence?; (3) what authority beyond that provided in the warrant do police have to search or seize persons or evidence found during its execution?; and (4) what requirements are imposed on officers after they have seized the evidence?   These issues are discussed here.

(a) **Time Limitations.**   Service of the warrant should take place promptly so that the conditions underlying the probable cause determination do not dissipate.   In some circumstances, delay may void the warrant.   Two such situations would be if the language of the warrant itself commands that the search be conducted within a certain time, or if the underlying statute contains a time limit that will result in void service if it is exceeded.   The federal rules, for instance, provide that the warrant must command the officer to search within a specified period of time not to exceed ten days.[70]   Construing a predecessor to this rule in *Sgro v. United States*,[71] the Supreme Court found invalid a search of a hotel room for illegal intoxicants pursuant to a warrant affidavit which alleged a purchase of beer there three weeks earlier.   *Sgro* also suggests that the Fourth Amendment itself prohibits undue delay in the absence of time constraints imposed by statute or warrant.

It is common to restrict service of warrants (both for arrests and searches) to the daytime unless nocturnal execution is specifically authorized.   Federal Rule 41(c) requires daytime execution unless the issuing authority, by provision in the warrant and for

68.   394 U.S. 557, 89 S.Ct. 1243 (1969).

69.   However, *if* probable cause exists, a "search" of an item in plain view is permitted to determine if the item is indeed evidence of crime.   *Arizona v. Hicks*, 480 U.S. 321, 107 S.Ct. 1149 (1987), discussed in § 10.03.

70.   Fed.R.Crim.P. 41(c).

71.   287 U.S. 206, 53 S.Ct. 138 (1932). See also, *State v. Burgos*, 7 Conn.App. 265, 508 A.2d 795 (1986) (search warrant executed within 10-day statutory limit may still violate constitutional reasonableness requirement).

reasonable cause shown, authorizes execution at other times.[72] Some Supreme Court members have expressed the opinion that, given its intrusive nature, a nighttime search should only be permitted upon a showing of higher-than-normal probable cause.[73]

(b) Announcement of Presence. At common law, officers executing a warrant were required to knock and announce their presence prior to executing a warrant, in order to avoid the unnecessary violence or property destruction that might result from a surprise entry. However, the Supreme Court has recognized a significant exception to this rule, holding in *Ker v. California* [74] that officers may dispense with the knock and announce requirement when they have reason to believe evidence may be destroyed, or a suspect may escape. Many states now permit officers to forego announcing their presence when a magistrate has found probable cause for doing so.[75]

Ker and other issues associated with the knock and announce rule are discussed in detail in this book's treatment of arrest procedure.[76] The only issue not replicated in arrest cases is whether surreptitious entry is permitted to install a listening device on a suspect's premises. In *Dalia v. United States,* [77] the Supreme Court held that such entry is not banned by the Fourth Amendment, so long as it is authorized by statute and is conducted in a reasonable manner (e.g., no property is destroyed). If these requirements are met, the entry does not even need to be authorized by a magistrate (although the magistrate must still issue a warrant based on probable cause to believe installation of the device is warranted).[78]

(c) Seizures Not Authorized by the Warrant. This chapter has already discussed those situations in which searches and seizures of places and items not particularly described in the warrant may be carried out.[79] Generally, any items found in plain view during a search of those areas indicated in the search warrant may be seized, even if they are not listed in the warrant, so long as there is probable cause to believe they are evidence of criminal activity. Yet to be addressed is the extent to which the police may detain or search *persons* found on the premises which are the subject of the warrant.

---

72. The term "daytime" is used in this rule to mean the hours from 6:00 a.m. to 10:00 p.m. Fed.R.Crim.P. 41(h).

73. See opinion of Justice Marshall, joined by Justices Douglas and Brennan, in *Gooding v. United States*, 416 U.S. 430, 94 S.Ct. 1780 (1974). The majority found that the federal statute at issue in *Gooding* did not require such a showing.

74. 374 U.S. 23, 83 S.Ct. 1623 (1963).

75. For an example of such a "no-knock" statute, see McKinney's N.Y. Crim.Proc.Law § 690.35(3)(b).

76. See § 3.05(a).

77. 441 U.S. 238, 99 S.Ct. 1682 (1979).

78. See § 14.03(e)(1).

79. See § 5.04.

In *Michigan v. Summers,*[80] the Supreme Court held that "a warrant to search for contraband founded on probable cause implicitly carries with it the limited authority to detain the occupants of the premises while a proper search is conducted." In *Summers,* Detroit police with a warrant to search Summers' house for narcotics stopped him as he was walking down his steps. They asked Summers to help them get in the house and then detained him while they searched the premises. During the search, the police discovered narcotics and arrested Summers. They then conducted a search incident to the arrest and found heroin in Summers' coat.

Writing for the majority, Justice Stevens admitted that the detention of Summers during the search of the house was a seizure within the meaning of the Fourth Amendment, and that the officers had not had probable cause to arrest Summers prior to the search. However, he also pointed out that "some seizures significantly less intrusive than an arrest have withstood scrutiny under the reasonableness standard embodied in the Fourth Amendment." Here Stevens was referring to *Terry v. Ohio,*[81] and its progeny, cases which held that a lesser "reasonable suspicion" standard is sufficient to authorize a brief stop and a limited frisk for weapons.[82]

In determining whether Summers' detention was similarly "reasonable," Stevens analyzed both the character of the official intrusion and its justification. "Of prime importance" in assessing the intrusion was the fact that the police had a search warrant for Summers' house. The brief detention, according to the Court, was "surely less intrusive" than the substantial invasion of privacy involved in the search of the house. "Indeed, we may safely assume that most citizens—unless they intend flight to avoid arrest—would elect to remain in order to observe the search of their possessions." In addition, such a detention is not likely to be exploited or prolonged by police because the information the police seek will normally be obtained from the search, not the detention. Nor is detention in one's own home likely to involve inconvenience or public stigma.

In assessing the justification for the detention, the Court found several factors important. First, it found a legitimate law enforcement interest in preventing flight if incriminating evidence is found. Second, detention minimized harm to police and to the occupants. Third, the "orderly completion of the search" may be facilitated if the occupants are present. The Court also pointed out that the existence of a search warrant provides an objective

80. 452 U.S. 692, 101 S.Ct. 2587 (1981).

81. 392 U.S. 1, 88 S.Ct. 1868 (1968).

82. See § 11.01.

justification for the detention, since it indicates that "a judicial officer has determined that police have probable cause to believe that someone in the home is committing a crime."

Given its rationale, *Summers* probably only permits detention of non-arrestable "occupants" who either live in the searched premises or house their belongings there.[83] If the occupants of searched premises do not fit either of these two categories, then usually they may leave the premises at the time police arrive.[84] However, the police may be able to subject them to further inconvenience under limited circumstances. This possibility is suggested by the holding of *Ybarra v. Illinois*,[85] in which police executing a search warrant authorizing a search of a tavern and its bartender also conducted a patdown of the tavern's patrons and a subsequent full search of Ybarra. The Court, in a 6–3 decision written by Justice Stewart, not only prohibited full searches in such a situation, but also rejected the state's argument that a more limited "frisk" should have been permitted under *Terry's* "stop-and-frisk" rule. Although the tavern was a "compact" area known to be a center for drug trafficking, the Court held that the state failed to provide any articulable suspicion that Ybarra, as a patron at the tavern, was a threat to the officers. Conversely, however, *Ybarra* suggests that if such suspicion does exist, then occupants of premises who cannot be detained under *Summers* may nonetheless be detained long enough to conduct a frisk.[86]

(d) Inventory of Seized Evidence. Statutes commonly require that an inventory be prepared of all property taken during the search, and that a copy be given to someone on the searched premises, and a copy be attached to the return of the warrant. Federal Rule 41(d) is a typical provision. It requires that the inventory be made in the presence of both the applicant for the warrant and the person from whose possession or premises the property was taken, or in the presence of at least one credible person if one of the first two individuals is not present. This type of provision is meant to protect against police theft and assure the person searched that his property is accounted for. However, in *Cady v. Dombrowski*,[87] the Supreme Court strongly suggested that failure to comply with a state requirement for submitting an

---

83. Moreover, it may be limited to search warrants authorizing searches for instrumentalities of crime, as opposed to searches for "mere evidence." See § 5.06(a).

84. This conclusion is supported by the Court's decision in *Rawlings v. Kentucky,* 448 U.S. 98, 100 S.Ct. 2556 (1980), in which the Court assumed that detention of houseguests by police executing

an arrest warrant for the owner was illegal.

85. 444 U.S. 85, 100 S.Ct. 338 (1979).

86. *Ybarra* is discussed further in § 11.04 in the context of adequate grounds for a frisk.

87. 413 U.S. 433, 93 S.Ct. 2523 (1973).

inventory to the court raised only a question of state law. Thus, the Fourth Amendment probably does not require an inventory.

5.06 When a Warrant Is Insufficient

Although a warrant is typically viewed as the preeminent protection afforded by the Fourth Amendment, in some situations it may be inadequate. This section explores those situations.

(a) The "Mere Evidence" Rule. At one time, warrants were insufficient to authorize searches for "mere evidence." In the 1921 decision of *Gouled v. United States,*[88] the Court held that only contraband, the fruits of crime, or the instrumentalities of crime could be seized under a warrant. Other types of evidence were viewed as so private that they were not seizable by any means, or were seizable only through a subpoena, which could be challenged through an adversary proceeding.[89] Thus, while a warrant could authorize searches for drugs, gambling proceeds, murder weapons, lottery tickets, and the like, a warrant was insufficient authority to gain entry into the home to search for most private documents and many types of circumstantial evidence.

In *Warden v. Hayden,*[90] the Court rejected *Gouled* to the extent it prevented seizure of "non-testimonial" evidence (as opposed to "testimonial," or documentary, evidence). There, the Court permitted the *warrantless* seizure of clothing subsequently shown to have been worn in a robbery that was not a fruit or instrumentality of the crime, or contraband; clearly, the Court felt that the clothing could have been seized with a warrant as well. The majority noted that the Fourth Amendment's language did not make a distinction between different types of evidence and that "[privacy] is disturbed no more by a search directed to a purely evidentiary object than it is by a search directed to an instrumentality, fruit, or contraband." However, *Hayden* reserved the question of whether documents which are mere evidence could be seized with a warrant, out of concern not so much for Fourth Amendment values, but for reasons connected with the Fifth Amendment, which protects against compelled disclosure of "communicative" or "testimonial" evidence which is self-incriminating.[91]

---

88. 255 U.S. 298, 41 S.Ct. 261 (1921).

89. Note that, while a subpoena is less intrusive, in that the search for subpoenaed items is carried out by the owner rather than the police, and can be challenged in court, a subpoena issued by a grand jury need not be based on probable cause, but rather may be based on "tips" and "rumors." *United States v. Dionisio,* 410 U.S. 1, 93 S.Ct. 764 (1973), discussed in § 23.05(a).

90. 387 U.S. 294, 87 S.Ct. 1642 (1967).

91. See § 15.04.

Then, in *Andresen v. Maryland,*[92] the Court significantly reduced this last impediment to seizure of "mere evidence" by pointing out that, even though documents are communicative, their seizure pursuant to a warrant does not "compel" self-incrimination: such a seizure compels the possessor neither to create the document nor produce it.[93] While this reasoning, followed to its logical conclusion, removes Fourth Amendment protection from all documents, *Andresen* involved business papers, not personal papers. Other Court decisions suggest that some private papers, such as a diary, may be afforded special protection;[94] at least one justice has argued that the Fourth Amendment prohibits the seizure of this type of documentary evidence.[95]

Theoretically, the mere evidence doctrine could focus not just on the types of documents being seized, but also on whom they are being seized from. In *Zurcher v. Stanford Daily,*[96] the police searched a newspaper office pursuant to a warrant, hoping to find photographs of a demonstration which had resulted in injury to several police officers. Justice Stevens, in his dissent in *Zurcher,* argued for the proposition that, when the premises of innocent third parties (such as the newspaper) are involved, warrants are inadequate authorization for searches for "mere evidence," unless it can be shown that the third party will destroy or remove the evidence if afforded a pre-search hearing. According to Stevens, "[m]ere possession of documentary evidence . . . is much less likely to demonstrate that the custodian is guilty of any wrongdoing or that he will not honor a subpoena or informal request to produce it." But the *Zurcher* majority rejected this view, primarily because it is often difficult, especially at the early stage of an investigation, to determine who is "innocent" and who is likely to destroy or remove evidence.

There is at least one instance in which a search for mere evidence is more circumscribed than other searches. In *Michigan v. Summers,*[97] the Court was unwilling to extend its holding—permitting detention of occupants of a home being searched pursuant to a search warrant—to searches solely for "mere evidence." Apparently, the Court felt that failing to recognize this exception would make much more likely the detention of persons who had no connection with criminal acitivity. This possibility is illustrated by the facts of *Zurcher.* To construe *Summers* as a basis for

92. 427 U.S. 463, 96 S.Ct. 2737 (1976).

93. On the other hand, when the document is seized via subpoena, there is compulsion to produce the document. For a discussion of the Fifth Amendment consequences of document production, see § 15.06.

94. *Fisher v. United States,* 425 U.S. 391, 96 S.Ct. 1569 (1976).

95. *Couch v. United States,* 409 U.S. 322, 93 S.Ct. 611 (1973) (Marshall, J., dissenting).

96. 436 U.S. 547, 98 S.Ct. 1970 (1978).

97. 452 U.S. 692, 101 S.Ct. 2587 (1981), discussed in § 5.05(c).

detaining the occupants of the newspaper office merely on the basis of the warrant in that case seems farfetched, in light of their tenuous connection with the criminal activity in question.

(b) First Amendment Material. A subtext in *Zurcher* was the fact that the search involved intrusion onto premises typically associated with the First Amendment's guarantees of free speech and press. In addition to rejecting the Fourth Amendment claim summarized above, the *Zurcher* majority also refused to accept the contention that the First Amendment requires protections in this situation beyond those provided by a search warrant. But it did emphasize the need for courts to "apply the warrant requirement with particular exactitude when First Amendment interests would be endangered by the search." By this it meant not that a "higher standard" of probable cause should apply,[98] but that the government should avoid using warrants to effect a prior restraint on the material in question (by, for instance, preventing its dissemination). Moreover, Congress has directed that subpoenas should be the preferred method of seeking information from newspapers and others engaged in First Amendment activities.[99]

In other contexts as well, the interests underlying the First Amendment have led to greater protections under the Fourth. Thus, in obscenity cases, when the government wants to seize large quantities of books or other materials, the Supreme Court has required a pre-search adversarial hearing in order to avoid the "danger of abridgement of the right of the public in a free society to unobstructed circulation of nonobscene books."[1] However, when a small number of copies, or a single item, are sought, the typical warrant procedure suffices, so long as a judicial proceeding takes place promptly after the seizure.[2]

(c) Bodily Intrusions. The Supreme Court has also indicated that certain types of investigative intrusions into the body are not permissible simply on the authority of a warrant. In *Rochin v. California*,[3] the Court held, under the Due Process Clause, that using an emetic to induce vomiting of drugs is never permissible. And while other, narrowly limited types of bodily intrusions have been permitted *without* a warrant when there is no time to obtain one,[4] in *Winston v. Lee*,[5] the Court suggested that, when there is no emergen-

---

98. In *New York v. P.J. Video, Inc.,* 475 U.S. 868, 106 S.Ct. 1610 (1986), briefly discussed in § 5.03(a), the Court overturned a lower court ruling that seizures of publications and films require a different showing of probable cause than in the normal case.

99. Privacy Protection Act, 42 U.S. C.A. § 2000D. See also, 28 C.F.R. § 59.

1. *Quantity of Copies of Books v. Kansas,* 378 U.S. 205, 84 S.Ct. 1723 (1964).

2. *Heller v. New York,* 413 U.S. 483, 93 S.Ct. 2789 (1973).

3. 342 U.S. 165, 72 S.Ct. 205 (1952).

4. See, e.g., *Schmerber v. California,* 384 U.S. 757, 86 S.Ct. 1826 (1966) (warrantless blood test), discussed in § 9.02.

5. 470 U.S. 753, 105 S.Ct. 1611 (1985).

cy, an adversarial hearing is required prior to such intrusions, at which a much heavier burden will be placed on the government than is usually the case.

In *Lee,* the government sought to have a bullet surgically removed from the defendant's collarbone. The Court not only required a warrant prior to such an intrusion, but also listed three other factors that should be considered before investigative surgery is authorized: (1) the extent to which the procedure threatens the safety or health of the individual; (2) the extent to which the intrusion impinges upon the individual's "dignitary interests in personal privacy and bodily integrity;" and (3) the extent to which prohibiting the intrusion would affect the "community's interest in fairly and accurately determining guilt or innocence." In applying these factors in *Lee,* Justice Brennan's opinion for the Court was very sensitive to the individual interests at stake. Confronted with a dispute as to how hazardous the procedure would be—with one witness indicating that considerable probing of muscle tissue might be necessary and could take as long as two and one-half hours, and another calling the surgery "minor"— Brennan upheld the court of appeals finding that the procedure might be medically risky. The Court also found that the defendant's dignitary interests would be harmed, primarily because the surgery would require use of anesthesia, which would render the defendant unconscious. Finally, the Court questioned the probative value of the bullet, given possible corrosion while in the shoulder, the difficulty with firearm identification generally, and the substantiality of the rest of the state's evidence. Although only six members of the Court joined Brennan's opinion, the Court was unanimous in finding the surgery proposed in *Lee* impermissible.

The Court did not specifically consider the procedural requirements for authorizing surgery, but did cite *United States v. Crowder,*[6] in which the D.C. Circuit Court of Appeals afforded the defendant an adversary hearing and immediate appellate review of a decision to permit surgery. At least one other court has overturned a conviction based on surgically seized evidence because the defendant had not been given such a hearing.[7]

5.07 Conclusion

The warrant requirement is designed to implement the Fourth Amendment's prohibition against unreasonable searches and seizures by requiring that whenever feasible a neutral and

---

6. 543 F.2d 312 (D.C.Cir.1976), cert. denied 429 U.S. 1062, 97 S.Ct. 788 (1977).

7. *State v. Overstreet,* 551 S.W.2d 621 (Mo.1977).

detached magistrate determine whether a search is justified. The following elements are necessary for issuance of a valid warrant.

(1) The person issuing the warrant must be "neutral and detached" in the sense that he should not be involved in either the investigation or prosecution of crime. He should refrain from becoming involved in any search he authorizes and from delegating his authority to law enforcement officers. In cases involving minor crimes, persons who are not judicial officers may be competent to issue warrants.

(2) The official should issue a search warrant only if he finds, based on facts provided in an affidavit or oral testimony sworn by the complaining officer, probable cause to believe that there is evidence of crime in the place to be searched. Relevant to this determination is whether there is evidence suggesting (a) that the informant—whether a police officer or a third party—is reliable (e.g., because of reliable information provided in the past, police corroboration of some details, or a declaration against interest), and (b) that the stated basis for the informant's belief is credible (e.g., there are sufficient facts or descriptive detail to believe the informant observed what is described rather than merely repeated rumor). In deciding whether probable cause exists, a deficiency in one of these two areas may be compensated for by a strong showing in the other, so that probable cause ultimately depends upon a flexible evaluation of the totality of the circumstances.

(3) Subsequent evaluation of the probable cause determination usually focuses entirely on the warrant application and accompanying documents. However, if the defendant can make a substantial preliminary showing that: (a) the affiant-officer (as opposed to an informant); (b) recklessly or intentionally; (c) made false statements; (d) that were necessary to the probable cause finding, he may obtain a hearing, which will result in invalidation of the warrant if he can show these elements by a preponderance of the evidence.

(4) A warrant must state with particularity the place to be searched. However, a mistake as to the location of the place searched does not invalidate the warrant if it is based on information police obtain after a reasonably diligent investigation and if the objective facts confronting the police executing the warrant do not make clear that a mistake has been made. A warrant must also state with particularity the items to be seized. However, unlisted items discovered while conducting the search authorized by the warrant are still admissible if found in plain view and probable cause exists to believe they are evidence of criminal activity.

(5) A warrant should be executed within the time prescribed by warrant, statute or rule, and, in any event, must be executed

before probable cause dissipates. In executing the warrant, officers are generally required to knock and announce their presence, unless they reasonably believe a suspect will escape or evidence will be destroyed. While police are executing a warrant to search a home, they may detain its occupants, at least when the evidence named in the warrant is contraband, and may frisk those who are reasonably suspected to be dangerous. An inventory is usually mandated by statute, but is not a constitutional requirement.

(6) When the government seeks large quantities of materials associated with First Amendment protection or evidence that necessitates a serious bodily intrusion, a pre-search adversarial hearing may be required in addition to or in lieu of a warrant.

BIBLIOGRAPHY

Bacigal, Ronald. Dodging a Bullet, But Opening Old Wounds in Fourth Amendment Jurisprudence. 16 Seton Hall L.Rev. 597 (1986).

Goldstein, Abraham. The Search Warrant, The Magistrate, and Judicial Review. 62 N.Y.U.L.Rev. 1173 (1987).

Grano, Joseph D. Probable Cause and Common Sense: A Reply to the Critics of Illinois v. Gates. 17 Mich.J.L.Ref. 465 (1984).

———. Rethinking the Warrant Requirement. 19 Amer.Crim.L. Rev. 603 (1982).

Herman, Lawrence. Warrants for Arrest or Search: Impeaching the Allegations of a Facially Sufficient Affidavit. 36 Ohio St. L.J. 721 (1975).

Kamisar, Yale. *Gates,* "Probable Cause," "Good Faith," and Beyond. 69 Iowa L.Rev. 551 (1984).

LaFave, Wayne R. Probable Cause from Informants: The Effects of Murphy's Law on Fourth Amendment Adjudication. 1977 U.Ill.L.F. 1 (1977).

Moylan, Charles E., Jr. Illinois v. Gates: What It Did and Did Not Do. 20 Crim.L.Bull. 93 (1984).

Project on Law Enforcement Policy and Rulemaking. Search Warrant Execution. Tempe, Arizona: The Project, 1974. (Model Rules for Law Enforcement Series).

Stuntz, William. Warrants and Fourth Amendment Remedies, 77 Va.L.Rev. 881 (1991).

Teeter, Dwight L., Jr. and Singer, Griffin S. Search Warrants in Newsrooms: Some Aspects of the Impact of Zurcher v. The Stanford Daily. 67 Kent.L.J. 847 (1978–79).

Chapter Six

SEARCH INCIDENT TO A LAWFUL ARREST

6.01 Introduction

Suppose a person who has been arrested suddenly reaches into his coat pocket. Clearly, refraining from searching the suspect's pockets and seizing whatever they may contain until a search warrant is obtained could result in grave danger to the police or perhaps the destruction of crucial contraband. The search incident to a lawful arrest exception to the warrant requirement seeks to protect against these twin dangers. As the Court stated in *Chimel v. California*,[1] a search incident to arrest is permitted "to remove any weapons that the [arrestee] might seek to use in order to resist arrest or effect his escape" and to "seize any evidence on the arrestee's person in order to prevent its concealment or destruction."

Among all of the exceptions to the warrant requirement, the search incident doctrine is the oldest. In *Weeks v. United States*,[2] the Supreme Court noted that this exception has "always (been) recognized under English and American law." Three issues arise under search incident doctrine: (1) what types of arrests justify a search incident? (2) when must searches be undertaken? and (3) what is the permissible scope of these searches?

6.02 Arrests Which Justify a Search

The most basic principle of search incident law is that the warrantless search is justified only if the arrest is lawful. When the arrest is not valid, the search is not valid.[3] A separate inquiry is whether the search incident doctrine permits searches when the underlying arrest is for a crime that is unlikely to involve dangerous weapons or contraband. In other words, when the rationale for the exception (protection of police and prevention of evidence destruction) is unlikely to apply, does the exception still operate?

In two controversial cases, the Supreme Court has answered this question in the affirmative. In *United States v. Robinson*,[4] an officer arrested the defendant for driving with a revoked license and then searched him; in the defendant's coat pocket, he found a package, in which he discovered heroin. The court of appeals held the evidence inadmissible, on the ground that the crime of driving

---

1. 295 U.S. 752, 89 S.Ct. 2034 (1969).
2. 232 U.S. 383, 34 S.Ct. 341 (1914).
3. *Draper v. United States*, 358 U.S. 307, 79 S.Ct. 329 (1959). The various criteria for determining the legality of an arrest are discussed in Chapter Three.

4. 414 U.S. 218, 94 S.Ct. 467 (1973).

with a revoked license is not associated with any "fruits" or "instrumentalities;" thus, concluded the court, while a limited patdown of the arrestee's outer clothing for weapons was permissible under *Terry v. Ohio,*[5] a full search of the person arrested for such a crime was not necessary. The Supreme Court, in a 6–3 opinion written by Justice Rehnquist, reversed the lower court, holding that, under the Reasonableness Clause of the Fourth Amendment, *all* lawful custodial arrests justify a full search of the person without a warrant. Similarly, in a companion case to *Robinson, Gustafson v. Florida,*[6] the Court found no error when police searched the defendant—and opened a cigarette box found as a result—after his arrest for failure to have his driver's license in his possession.

The Court offered two primary reasons for these decisions. First, when police decide to take someone into custody, a mere patdown for weapons is insufficient protection. According to Rehnquist, "[i]t is scarcely open to doubt that the danger to an officer is far greater in the case of the extended exposure which follows the taking of a suspect into custody and transporting him to the police station than in the case of the relatively fleeting contact resulting from the typical *Terry*-stop." Second, the Court felt it important to adopt a "bright-line" rule which could be easily followed by police making arrests in the field. As Rehnquist stated the matter, "[a] police officer's determination as to how and where to search the person of a suspect whom he has arrested is necessarily a quick *ad hoc* judgment which the Fourth Amendment does not require to be broken down in each instance into an analysis of each step in the search." Thus, the legitimacy of a search incident should not depend upon "what a court may later decide was the probability in a particular arrest situation that weapons or evidence would in fact be found upon the person of the suspect."

Given the first rationale, the one limitation on the *Robinson–Gustafson* holdings is that the initial arrest result in the person being taken into custody, or at least be for a crime which authorizes custodial arrest. It should also be noted that the Constitution may limit the types of crimes subject to such arrests. In a concurring opinion in *Gustafson,* Justice Stewart wrote that the defendant there might have prevailed had he asserted that his custodial arrest "for a minor traffic offense violated his rights under the Fourth and Fourteenth Amendments."[7] Subject to these considerations, a search is permitted incident to any arrest.

---

5.   392 U.S. 1, 88 S.Ct. 1868 (1968), discussed in § 11.01.

6.   414 U.S. 260, 94 S.Ct. 488 (1973).

7.   Note, however, that even in the case of crimes not permitting a custodi-

al arrest, the police can order a person out of the car, see *Pennsylvania v. Mimms,* 434 U.S. 106, 98 S.Ct. 330 (1977), discussed in § 11.03(b)(2), and can conduct a *Terry* patdown.

The *Robinson-Gustafson* holdings have stimulated a reaction among state legislatures and courts. Several legislatures have reduced certain violations of their traffic codes to infraction status, thus preventing operation of the search incident doctrine, which requires a custodial arrest.[8] In other states, the highest state court has interpreted the state constitution to require more than the federal constitutional minimum.[9] In support of *Robinson,* it can be argued that the Court's rule-oriented decision will relieve the police from engaging in an uncertain calculus each time they want to perform a search incident to arrest. On the other hand, had *Robinson* forbade full searches absent probable cause in the limited context of arrests for minor traffic violations, it would have better implemented the rationale behind the search incident exception and still adopted a relatively precise rule.

6.03   The Timing of the Search

A fundamental tenet of search incident doctrine is that probable cause to make the arrest must precede the warrantless search.[10] The exception will not permit officers to conduct a "fishing expedition;" that is, a random warrantless search in the hope that contraband or some other unlawful item is found that will support an arrest. The central idea is that the arrest justifies the warrantless search, not the reverse. However, so long as probable cause to arrest precedes the search, a formal "arrest" is not required to justify the search.[11]

Equally important to search incident doctrine is the requirement that the warrantless arrest take place *soon* after there is probable cause to arrest. As Justice Black, speaking for a unanimous Court, noted in *Preston v. United States,*[12] the "justifications [for the search incident] rule are absent where a search is remote in time or place from the arrest." Thus, in *Preston,* a warrantless search of a car towed to a garage after its occupants were arrested and taken to jail was not a valid search incident: neither destruction of evidence nor harm to the officers could have occurred at that time. The Court came to the same conclusion in *Chambers v. Maroney,*[13] involving similar facts. And in *United States v. Chadwick,*[14] a search of a footlocker more than an hour after the defendant's arrest and after agents had gained exclusive control of it was found invalid.

One limited exception to the "contemporaneousness" element of search incident doctrine may have been announced in *United*

---

8. See, e.g., Or.Rev.Stat. § 133.045.

9. See *People v. Marsh,* 20 N.Y.2d 98, 281 N.Y.S.2d 789, 228 N.E.2d 783 (1967).

10. *Sibron v. New York,* 392 U.S. 40, 88 S.Ct. 1889 (1968).

11. *Rawlings v. Kentucky,* 448 U.S. 98, 100 S.Ct. 2556 (1980).

12. 376 U.S. 364, 84 S.Ct. 881 (1964).

13. 399 U.S. 42, 90 S.Ct. 1975 (1970).

14. 433 U.S. 1, 97 S.Ct. 2476 (1977).

States v. Edwards.[15] There the Court, in a 5–4 decision, approved the warrantless seizure and search of an arrestee's clothing ten hours after his arrest, while he was in jail. In the course of its opinion, the Court made the broad statement that "searches and seizures that could be made on the spot at the time of arrest may legally be conducted later when the accused arrives at the place of detention." But the Court also pointed out that taking Edwards' clothes at the time of arrest would have been impracticable, as it "was late at night[,] no substitute clothing was then available for Edwards to wear, and it would certainly have been unreasonable for the police to have stripped respondent of his clothing and left him exposed in his cell throughout the night." Noteworthy also is the fact that, while Edwards apparently was not aware of the clothing's evidentiary value, had he become so he could have easily destroyed it. *Edwards* should be narrowly construed to permit a later search incident only when an immediate search is virtually impossible and exigency still exists at the time of the later search.[16] A different rule would stretch search incident doctrine well beyond its twin rationales of protecting officers and evidence from harm.

It should also be noted, however, that other exceptions to the warrant and probable cause requirements might permit warrantless searches well after arrest. For instance, in *Chambers v. Maroney,* mentioned above, the Court found that, while not justified under search incident doctrine, the later warrantless search of the car was permissible under the "automobile exception" to the warrant requirement.[17] And, since *Edwards,* the Court has firmly held that routine "inventory" searches of cars, and of personal effects of arrestees detained in jail, are permissible in the absence of any suspicion.[18]

6.04   The Scope of a Search Incident

Originally, the scope of a search conducted contemporaneous with a lawful arrest was quite broad, permitting not just search of the arrestee but also of any nearby area that he "possessed," including areas not proximate to his person. The Supreme Court then adopted a rule which limited the search to the area within

15. 415 U.S. 800, 94 S.Ct. 1234 (1974).

16. The Court also emphasized that the police had probable cause to believe the clothing had evidentiary value, thus perhaps adding a third limitation on the *Edwards* exception to the contemporaneousness rule.

17. The *Chambers* rationale requires that the police have probable cause to

search the car, not just probable cause to arrest. See § 7.03(c)(3).

18. See *South Dakota v. Opperman,* 428 U.S. 364, 96 S.Ct. 3092 (1976) (cars); *Illinois v. Lafayette,* 462 U.S. 640, 103 S.Ct. 2605 (1983) (effects), discussed in § 13.07. However, these cases prohibit use of the inventory as a "pretext concealing investigatory motives," and thus would have been to no avail in *Edwards.*

reach of the defendant. However, this so-called "armspan rule" has since been significantly modified in several situations.

(a) The Armspan Rule. In *United States v. Rabinowitz,*[19] the police, armed with a valid arrest warrant, arrested the defendant for forgery and then conducted a warrantless search of his one-room business, including the desk, safe, and file cabinets. Five members of the Court, evaluating the search under the totality of the circumstances, held that the search was reasonable. They gave a number of reasons, including the room's quasi-public nature and the fact that it "was small and under the immediate and complete control of respondent." But, as Justice Frankfurter pointed out in dissent, the agents had plenty of time to obtain a search warrant (they not only were able to obtain an arrest warrant, but also arranged to bring two forgery experts with them). Thus, the majority's disposition of the case encouraged unnecessary evasion of the particularity requirement and other guarantees afforded by a search warrant.

Almost twenty years later, in *Chimel v. California,*[20] the Court voted, 7–2, to overturn *Rabinowitz.* While the search in *Chimel* involved a three-bedroom home rather than a one-room business, the majority pointed out that *Rabinowitz* had come to stand for the broad proposition that "a warrantless search 'incident to a lawful arrest' may generally extend to the area that is considered to be in the 'possession' or under the 'control' of the person arrested." As *Rabinowitz* demonstrated, this vague standard gave police "the opportunity to engage in searches not justified by probable cause, by the simple expedient of arranging to arrest suspects at home rather than elsewhere." To replace the case-by-case "reasonableness" analysis endorsed in *Rabinowitz,* Justice Stewart, who wrote the Court's opinion, devised the "armspan" rule. As before, the arresting officer may search the arrestee's person to discover and remove weapons and to seize evidence. But beyond this, a search incident is limited to the area "within [the] immediate control" of the arrestee—that is, "the area from within which he might have obtained either a weapon or something that could have been used as evidence against him."

Although *Chimel* was an attempt to clarify the scope of a search incident, the armspan rule itself is subject to several interpretations. Does it, for instance, permit searches of opaque effects (e.g., wallets and purses) found on the arrested person, or closed containers (e.g., suitcases) near his person at the time of the arrest? Given the facts and results of *Robinson* and *Gustafson,* discussed earlier,[21] it appears that the arresting officer may look

---

19. 339 U.S. 56, 70 S.Ct. 430 (1950).   **21.** See § 6.02.

20. 395 U.S. 752, 89 S.Ct. 2034 (1969).

into any containers found on the arrestee, even though, as the dissent in *Robinson* pointed out, it is impossible for the arrestee to obtain a weapon from the container once it is in the possession of the officer. As for searches of containers proximate to the arrestee, the Court has not clearly spoken on the issue. In *United States v. Chadwick*,[22] it will be remembered, the Court prohibited a *later* warrantless search of a footlocker found in the arrestee's possession. But it was unclear as to whether a search incident at the time of arrest was permissible. One justice (Brennan) argued that an immediate search would not have been justified, since the footlocker was not within the "immediate control" of the arrestees, while two dissenting justices (Blackmun and Rehnquist) argued the opposite.

The armspan rule should be interpreted with the twin rationales of search incident doctrine in mind, as many lower courts appear to do. Thus, for instance, a search of an arrestee's backpack after she was arrested was found to violate search incident doctrine because agents were in possession of it when it was searched and were in no danger of harm.[23] Similarly, a search of a light fixture which turned up a cache of marijuana was held illegal because the fixture was outside the defendant's reach at the time of arrest.[24] In contrast, when the defendant, after his arrest, went to a locker to retrieve a bag, the police were authorized to conduct a warrantless search of it, because the defendant had extended the area of his immediate control by going to the locker.[25]

The Supreme Court has indicated that this "extension of control" rationale also allows *entries* into the home, if the arrestee chooses to go there after the arrest. In *Washington v. Chrisman*,[26] an officer stopped a student on suspicion of drinking underage, an action which the Court termed an "arrest." The officer asked the student for his identification and followed him to his room when he went to get it. While there, the officer saw in plain view marijuana and drug paraphernalia. In upholding the subsequent seizure of this evidence, the Court disagreed with the lower court's finding that no danger to either the officer or evidence was apparent on these facts; relying on *Robinson*, the Court stated that "[e]very arrest must be presumed to present a risk of danger to the arresting officer. . . . Moreover, the possibility that an arrested person will attempt to escape if not properly supervised is obvious." Thus, the Court held, "it is not unreasonable, under the

22. 433 U.S. 1, 97 S.Ct. 2476 (1977), discussed further in § 7.02.

23. *United States v. Robertson*, 833 F.2d 777 (9th Cir.1987).

24. *State v. Rhodes*, 80 N.M. 729, 460 P.2d 259 (App.1969).

25. *Parker v. Swenson*, 332 F.Supp. 1225 (E.D.Mo.1971), aff'd 459 F.2d 164 (8th Cir.1972), cert. denied 409 U.S. 1126, 93 S.Ct. 943 (1973).

26. 455 U.S. 1, 102 S.Ct. 812 (1982).

Fourth Amendment for an officer, as a matter of routine, to monitor the movements of an arrested person, as his judgment dictates, following the arrest." [27]

(b) Confederates and Destructible Evidence. All of the cases discussed above focus on the danger that the *arrestee* poses for the police. As Justice White pointed out in his dissent in *Chimel,* the arrestee is not the only legitimate focus of the police when making an arrest: "there must always be a strong possibility that confederates of the arrested man will in the meanwhile remove the items for which the police have probable cause to search." This concern over confederates, either as destroyers of evidence or as independent threats to the police, has led to significant modifications of the armspan rule, as the following discussion bears out.

(1) Searches for confederates. In *Maryland v. Buie,*[28] the Court expanded the scope of a search incident in two ways. First, apparently for reasons similar to those used to justify the armspan rule, it held that the police may, incident to a home arrest, look in areas immediately adjoining the place of arrest for other persons who might attack the police, without having probable cause or even the lesser level of "reasonable suspicion." [29] Second, *Buie* held that if, at any moment up to the time the arrest is completed and the police depart, the police have reasonable suspicion that *other* areas of the premises harbor an individual who poses a danger to them, they may undertake a "protective sweep," limited to "a cursory visual inspection of those places in which a person might be hiding." In reaching the latter holding, the Court concluded that, in contrast to the type of search at issue in *Chimel,* such sweeps only minimally invade the arrestee's privacy. It analogized the protective sweep to the protective field patdown authorized in *Terry v. Ohio,*[30] and the limited "armspan" car search permitted by *Michigan v. Long,*[31] both of which are permissible based on a reasonable suspicion that the police or others are in danger.

In dissent, Justice Brennan, joined by Justice Marshall, argued that, despite the majority's efforts at limiting its scope, the protective sweep authorized by *Buie* far exceeded in intrusiveness the police actions permitted by *Terry* and *Long:*

> A protective sweep would bring within police purview virtually all personal possessions within the house not hidden from

27. On remand, the Washington Supreme Court held that, under the state constitution, the evidence should be suppressed. *State v. Chrisman,* 100 Wn.2d 814, 676 P.2d 419 (1984).

28. 494 U.S. 325, 110 S.Ct. 1093 (1990).

29. The reasonable suspicion standard is discussed in § 11.03(a).

30. 392 U.S. 1, 88 S.Ct. 1868 (1968), discussed in § 11.01.

31. 463 U.S. 1032, 103 S.Ct. 3469 (1983), discussed in § 11.05.

view in a small enclosed space. Police officers searching for potential ambushers might enter every room including basements and attics; open up closets, lockers, chests, wardrobes, and cars; and peer under beds and behind furniture. The officers will view letters, documents and personal effects that are on tables or desks or are visible inside open drawers; books, records, tapes, and pictures on shelves; and clothing, medicines, toiletries and other paraphernalia not carefully stored in dresser drawers or bathroom cupboards.

Thus, according to the dissent, protective sweeps should be permitted only if police have probable cause to believe they may otherwise be attacked.

Contrary to the dissent's suggestion, the protective sweep authorized by the Court is not as thoroughgoing as the warrantless searches authorized by *Rabinowitz,* and probable cause probably should not be required. But even the majority's reasonable suspicion standard requires an "articulable" suspicion that confederates are on the premises. On remand from the Supreme Court, the Maryland Court of Appeals erroneously found that this standard was met in *Buie.*[32] Although Buie was known to have an accomplice, the police had not seen the latter during three days of surveillance of Buie's house. More importantly, the sweep took place *after* Buie had been arrested, handcuffed and taken outside. On these facts, the sweep (which turned up a red running suit in the basement) seems gratuitous.[33] Another lower court decision which reached a similarly questionable result is *United States v. Bennett,*[34] in which the court permitted a warrantless search of luggage despite the fact that the defendants were handcuffed and placed against the wall at the time, because the officers feared that "someone else" would enter the room and obtain a weapon from the luggage in an effort to free the arrestees.[35]

A separate question is whether persons who are found on the premises in the course of an arrest or a search incident may be searched or arrested (assuming there is no warrant authorizing such actions). In *Ybarra v. Illinois,*[36] the Supreme Court held that mere proximity to a suspect is not a sufficient basis for an arrest or a full search, even if the premises are "compact." However,

32. *Buie v. State,* 320 Md. 696, 580 A.2d 167 (1990).

33. Compare *United States v. Holzman,* 871 F.2d 1496 (9th Cir.1989) (sweep not permissible upon officers' mere suspicion that accomplices may have been in hotel rooms or in general vicinity); *United States v. Baker,* 577 F.2d 1147 (4th Cir.1978) (sweep permissible when police knew that a confederate of the arrestees had been seen with one of the arrestees the day before and was probably armed).

34. 908 F.2d 189 (7th Cir.1990).

35. Compare *United States v. Satterfield,* 743 F.2d 827 (11th Cir.1984) (danger from unknown accomplices insufficient to justify search of house for shotgun after all occupants had been taken into custody).

36. 444 U.S. 85, 100 S.Ct. 338 (1979).

consonant with the *Terry* stop-and-frisk doctrine, *Ybarra* permitted a patdown of other persons on the premises if there is an articulable suspicion of danger.[37]

(2) Searches for evidence. Closely related to the fear that accomplices are on the premises is the concern, expressed by Justice White in *Chimel,* that these accomplices, or someone else sympathetic to the defendant, will destroy probative evidence once they know he has been discovered and arrested. To date, the Supreme Court has not clearly addressed this concern. A number of Supreme Court decisions prohibited searches of a home, after an arrest made outside it, where there was no indication that evidence was being destroyed,[38] but only one decision explicitly deals with a government claim that a warrantless post-arrest search was needed to prevent evidence destruction, and that decision is difficult to interpret. In *Vale v. Louisiana,*[39] police had two warrants permitting arrest of the defendant for bond violations. While conducting surveillance of a house to see if the defendant lived there, they saw him come out and make what appeared to be a drug sale. They arrested him outside the house, but then searched the premises, apparently because two relatives of the defendant had arrived in the meantime and could have destroyed any narcotics inside.

The state claimed, and the Louisiana Supreme Court agreed, that the search was justified by exigent circumstances, but the Supreme Court reversed. In the course of its opinion, it stated: "We decline to hold that an arrest on the street can provide its own 'exigent circumstance' so as to justify a warrantless search of the arrestee's house." However, this broad conclusion, which would seem to prohibit post-arrest searches for evidence without judicial authorization, must be read in conjunction with the Court's further statement that there was "no reason, so far as anything before us appears, to suppose that it was impracticable for [the officers] to obtain a search warrant as well." Apparently, the Court believed, as it had in *Chimel,* that the police were using the arrest warrants and surveillance as a pretext to gain warrantless entry into the home. The Court also seemed to think the relatives were not a threat to the evidence, as it stated "the goods ultimately seized were not in the process of destruction."

Whatever the reach of *Vale,* lower courts have routinely permitted warrantless searches of homes for evidence after an arrest, some requiring a probable cause belief, some only a reasonable suspicion, that the evidence is on the premises and will have

---

37. See § 3.03(b)(2) for further discussion of this point.

38. See *Shipley v. California,* 395 U.S. 818, 89 S.Ct. 2053 (1969); *McDonald v. United States,* 335 U.S. 451, 69 S.Ct. 191 (1948) (warrant needed, as no "property in the process of destruction" or "likely to be destroyed.").

39. 399 U.S. 30, 90 S.Ct. 1969 (1970).

disappeared by the time a warrant is obtained.[40]   In this situation, in contrast to the protective sweep, probable cause should be required, since evidentiary searches are more intrusive. So limited, this policy seems sensible so long as, in conformance with what appeared to be the *ratio decidendi* of *Vale,* the police are not permitted to use it as a pretext to make warrantless searches of homes, but rather only become aware of the evidence's existence at the time of the arrest. This latter condition is necessary to avoid undoing what *Chimel* set out to do when it overturned *Rabinowitz.*

(3) *An alternative: securing the premises.* Another way of dealing with the "destructible evidence" problem is to secure the premises in which, or next to which, the arrestee is found, pending the procural of a search warrant. This practice would ensure that no evidence is destroyed, at least after a "sweep" of the premises ensures that no confederates are already there. Such a "seizure" of the home is arguably preferable to the search contemplated in *Vale,* since it is the less intrusive warrantless procedure. And it is often as feasible as a search, at least for smaller premises which can be secured with one or two officers.

In *Segura v. United States,*[41] the Court held, 5–4, "that where officers, having probable cause, enter premises . . ., arrest the occupants . . . and take them into custody and, for no more than the period here involved [i.e., 19 hours], secure the premises from within to preserve the status quo while others, in good faith, are in the process of obtaining a warrant, they do not violate the Fourth Amendment's proscription against unreasonable seizures." Whether one agrees with *Segura* may depend on a number of factors. In particular, if there are other occupants of the premises (besides those who have been arrested and taken into custody), a prolonged seizure may not be appropriate. But if, under the lower court cases described above, their presence authorizes an immediate warrantless search of the house, these other occupants might welcome the seizure option.

(c) **Search Incident Doctrine and Cars.** There is at least one circumstance in which the police may rely on the search incident doctrine to justify searching an area beyond either the initial *or* "extended" control of the arrestee or his accomplices. In *New York v. Belton,*[42] the Supreme Court held, 6–3, that the search of a car and the contents of containers inside it is permissible even if the car's occupants have been removed from the car, so long as

---

40. See, e.g., *United States v. Hoyos,* 892 F.2d 1387 (9th Cir.1989) (reasonable suspicion); *United States v. Rubin,* 474 F.2d 262 (3d Cir.1973), cert. denied 414 U.S. 833, 94 S.Ct. 173 (1973) (probable cause).

41. 468 U.S. 796, 104 S.Ct. 3380 (1984), discussed further in § 2.04(c).

42. 453 U.S. 454, 101 S.Ct. 2860 (1981).

the occupants have been lawfully arrested and the search is contemporaneous with the arrest. Belton and three companions were stopped by a New York officer for speeding. Upon coming to the car door, the officer noticed the odor of marijuana emanating from the car, as well as other evidence of marijuana use. He directed the men out of the car and placed them under arrest for unlawful possession of marijuana. After searching each one of the arrestees, he searched the passenger compartment of the car, including the pockets of a leather jacket belonging to Belton. Inside one of the pockets he discovered cocaine.

The Appellate Division of the New York Supreme Court overturned Belton's subsequent conviction for possession of the cocaine on the ground that a "warrantless search of the zippered pockets of an unaccessible jacket may not be upheld as a search incident to a lawful arrest where there is no longer any danger that the arrestee or a confederate might gain access to the article." The Court's decision to reinstate Belton's conviction, written by Justice Stewart, seemed to be based entirely on the perception that the armspan rule had been difficult to apply in cases involving automobiles. Thus, stated Stewart, the time had come to enunciate a " 'single, familiar standard' " for the benefit of courts and police alike. With no further discussion, Stewart concluded:

> Our reading of the cases suggests the generalization that articles inside the relatively narrow compass of the passenger compartment of an automobile are in fact generally, even if not inevitably, within 'the area into which an arrestee might reach in order to gain a weapon or evidentiary item' . . . Accordingly, we hold that when a policeman has made a lawful custodial arrest of the occupant of an automobile, he may, as a contemporaneous incident of that arrest, search the passenger compartment of that automobile."

The Court also sanctioned the search of any containers in the passenger compartment, "for if the passenger compartment is within reach of the arrestee, so also will containers in it be within his reach."

After *Belton,* it appears that once a lawful arrest has been made of a car's occupants, police may conduct a warrantless search of any part of the car's interior, as well as packages, clothing and other containers in it, so long as the search is contemporaneous with the arrest. Only the trunk, and other areas that are relatively inaccessible to the car's passengers (such as the area behind the dashboard), cannot be searched as a search incident. Further, this rule applies regardless of whether the occupants of the car outnumber the police (as was true in *Belton*), and regardless of whether they are anywhere near the car at the time of the search.[43] As the dissenters in *Belton* pointed out, the decision "adopts a fiction—that the interior of a car is *always* within the immediate control of an arrestee who has recently been in the car." As a result, *Belton* permits the police to conduct searches of a private area, supposedly protected by the Fourth Amendment,[44] without any articulable suspicion that evidence will be found. While limited to custodial arrests, it also encourages the police to arrest car occupants for minor "custodial" crimes whenever they want to search the car. *Belton* represents a "bright-line" rule that strays too far from its premises.

6.05 Conclusion

Searches incident to arrest, traditionally conducted to prevent harm to the police and destruction of evidence, may be conducted without a warrant under the following circumstances:

(1) The arrest must be lawful and result in custodial detention, or at least be for a crime which authorizes such detention.

(2) The search must take place soon after probable cause to arrest exists; it may not take place prior to that time.

(3) The police must limit themselves to (a) searching the person arrested and any containers thereby discovered; (b) searching the immediate area within the arrestee's control, meaning that area within the armspan of the defendant and, in the case of cars, the entire interior of the car; (c) conducting a "protective sweep" of the area adjoining the arrest; and (d) conducting a sweep of any other area within the premises which they reasonably suspect might harbor persons who could endanger them. Additionally, the lower courts have allowed the police to (e) search the arrestee's premises (when he is arrested on or near them), if they have a reasonable belief that evidence is in imminent danger of disappearing.

BIBLIOGRAPHY

Aaronson, David E., and Rangeley, Wallace. A Reconsideration of the Fourth Amendment's Doctrine of Search Incident to Arrest. 64 Geo.L.J. 53 (1975).

Dressler, Joshua. A Lesson in Incaution, Overwork and Fatigue: The Judicial Miscraftmanship of Segura v. United States. 26 Wm. & Mary L.Rev. 375 (1985).

Hancock, Catherine. State Court Activism and Searches Incident to Arrest. 68 Va.L.Rev. 1085 (1982).

43. However, if the arrest takes place in the home, the fact that a car is nearby does not justify its search without a warrant. *Commonwealth v. Santiago*, 410 Mass. 737, 575 N.E.2d 350 (1991).

44. See § 4.03(d).

Kelder, Gary and Alan J. Statman. The Protective Sweep Doctrine: Recurring Questions Regarding the Propriety of Searches Conducted Contemporaneously With An Arrest On Or Near Private Premises. 30 Syracuse L.Rev. 973 (1979).

LaFave, Wayne R. "Case-by-Case Adjudication" Versus "Standardized Procedures": The Robinson Dilemma. 1974 Sup.Ct. Rev. 172 (1974).

——. The Fourth Amendment in an Imperfect World: On Drawing "Bright Lines" and "Good Faith." 43 U.Pitt.L.Rev. 307 (1982).

Rudstein, David S. The Search of an Automobile Incident to An Arrest: An Analysis of New York v. Belton. 67 Marq.L.Rev. 205 (1984).

Salken, Barbara. Balancing Exigency and Privacy in Warrantless Searches to Prevent Destruction of Evidence: The Need for a Rule. 39 Hastings L.J. 283 (1988).

White, James B. The Fourth Amendment as a Way of Talking About People: A Study of Robinson and Matlock. 1974 Sup. Ct.Rev. 165 (1974).

Chapter Seven

THE "AUTOMOBILE EXCEPTION"

7.01 Introduction

In *Carroll v. United States*,[1] the Supreme Court laid down a set of principles governing searches of movable vehicles which has since been labelled the "automobile exception" to the warrant requirement. Specifically, *Carroll* held that a warrantless search of an automobile is permitted when: (1) there is probable cause to believe the vehicle contains evidence of crime; and (2) the police did not have time to obtain a search warrant prior to the search. Both of these elements were met in *Carroll*. There, agents stopped a person they knew had previously engaged in selling bootleg whiskey while he was driving what appeared to be a heavily-laden car, along a road known for its bootleg traffic. A search behind the car's upholstery produced 68 bottles of illicit liquor. The officers had not arrested the driver prior to the search (apparently because his crime was a misdemeanor that was not committed in their presence),[2] and thus search incident doctrine was irrelevant.[3] But the Supreme Court sanctioned the search on the ground that the officers came upon the defendant unexpectedly, had full probable cause to believe his car contained evidence, and would have lost the evidence had they allowed the defendant to go on his way while they sought a warrant.

Unfortunately, lawyers and judges who have taken the words "automobile exception" literally have created considerable confusion about the parameters of the *Carroll* decision and its progeny. The exception is neither limited to automobile searches, nor does it cover all searches of automobiles. On the one hand, the exception may be applicable to searches of airplanes, boats, and other modes of transportation. In *United States v. Lee*,[4] for instance, the Court applied *Carroll* in upholding the warrantless search of a boat. Conversely, it should not be assumed that the automobile exception is relevant in every search and seizure case which involves an automobile or other movable vehicle. Many warrantless searches of movable vehicles are properly analyzed only in terms of other exceptions to the Fourth Amendment's warrant requirement. For instance, the Court has explicitly rejected use of the *Carroll* doctrine in analyzing searches of cars crossing the international border.[5] Likewise, a search of all or

1. 267 U.S. 132, 45 S.Ct. 280 (1925).

2. Such arrests required a warrant under the common-law. See § 3.04.

3. *Carroll* was decided well before *Chimel v. California*, 395 U.S. 752, 89 S.Ct. 2034 (1969), and thus searches incident to arrest for cars were as wide-ranging in scope as they are today under *New York v. Belton*, 453 U.S. 454, 101 S.Ct. 2860 (1981), which did away with *Chimel's* armspan rule in the car arrest context. See §§ 6.04(a) and (c).

4. 274 U.S. 559, 47 S.Ct. 746 (1927).

5. See § 13.05(a).

part of an automobile may be justified independently of the automobile exception if conducted incident to a lawful arrest,[6] in performing a stop and frisk of a car's occupants,[7] under the authority of the plain view doctrine,[8] while inventorying a car,[9] or upon the consent of a car's occupant.[10] Other constitutional searches of automobiles may not involve the Fourth Amendment at all.[11]

This chapter will focus on the automobile exception doctrine as set forth in *Carroll* and explicated in later cases. Other exceptions to the warrant requirement which may have an impact on searches of movable vehicles are discussed elsewhere.

7.02 The Rationale for the Exception

There are two justifications for permitting the police to conduct warrantless searches of cars, boats and similar vehicles when they have probable cause to do so. The first is the inherent mobility of such conveyances. *Carroll*'s most important contribution to analysis of Fourth Amendment cases is its differentiation between fixed and movable premises:

> The guaranty of freedom from unreasonable searches and seizures by the Fourth Amendment has been construed, practically since the beginning of the Government, as recognizing a necessary difference between a search of a store, dwelling house or other structure in respect of which a proper official warrant readily may be obtained, and a search of a ship, motor boat, wagon or automobile, for contraband goods, where it is not practicable to secure a warrant because the vehicle can be quickly moved out of the locality or jurisdiction in which the warrant must be sought.

The second rationale for the automobile exception is the public character of movable vehicles, in particular the automobile. The principal case supporting this point, ironically, did not involve a search of a vehicle. In *United States v. Chadwick*,[12] federal agents with probable cause to believe that the defendants' footlocker contained marijuana arrested the defendants and seized their footlocker at a train station. An hour and a half later they searched the footlocker without the defendants' consent or a

---

6. See *New York v. Belton*, 453 U.S. 454, 101 S.Ct. 2860 (1981), discussed in § 6.04(c).

7. *Adams v. Williams*, 407 U.S. 143, 92 S.Ct. 1921 (1972), discussed in § 11.03.

8. *Harris v. United States*, 390 U.S. 234, 88 S.Ct. 992 (1968) (per curiam).

9. *South Dakota v. Opperman*, 428 U.S. 364, 96 S.Ct. 3092 (1976), discussed in § 13.07(a).

10. *Schneckloth v. Bustamonte*, 412 U.S. 218, 93 S.Ct. 2041 (1973), discussed in § 12.04.

11. *New York v. Class*, 475 U.S. 106, 106 S.Ct. 960 (1986), discussed in § 4.03(d).

12. 433 U.S. 1, 97 S.Ct. 2476 (1977).

warrant. The government attempted to justify this search primarily by relying on an analogy to the automobile exception: since the police had probable cause to search the footlocker and the footlocker was inherently mobile, the police should not have been required to seek a warrant before searching it. The Court admitted the police had probable cause. But it noted that once the police had seized the footlocker, exigent circumstances no longer existed. More significantly, the Court concluded that a search of a footlocker involves considerably different privacy considerations than does a search of a car.

The Court pointed out that cars are associated with a diminished privacy interest because: (1) automobiles function on the public thoroughfares; (2) they are subject to state registration and licensing requirements; (3) other aspects of automobile operation are strictly regulated; (4) periodic inspections are commonly mandated; and (5) automobiles may be impounded by police for public safety reasons. Footlockers, on the other hand, are not as heavily regulated or monitored by the state, and the expectation of privacy with respect to such repositories of personal belongings is greater than the privacy associated with a car. Therefore, concluded the Court, the automobile exception should not apply to searches of such items, despite their inherent mobility.[13]

Thus, after *Chadwick*, the automobile exception is based on the twin premises that cars, and other vehicles such as boats and planes, are: (1) easily moved out of the jurisdiction and (2) associated with a lesser expectation of privacy than are other movable items. The first rationale makes some sense, although it can be questioned. Cars are *not* mobile once police have stopped them. If a house which is suspected of containing destructible evidence can be secured pending a warrant,[14] a car could be seized while police obtain judicial authorization to search it. But the Court, not without some reason, has been unwilling to require police to resort to this sometimes dangerous practice.[15]

The second rationale is much less supportable. The reasons the Court gave in *Chadwick* for distinguishing the privacy interest associated with cars from that associated with other effects do not explain why the areas in which evidence is usually found (e.g., glove compartments, trunks and so on) are less protected than other private areas which house personal property. More importantly, even if the car and its interior do have a diminished aura of privacy, this fact should not be relevant to whether a warrant is

---

13. The Court would later hold, however, that these items *lose* their heightened privacy protection when they are put in a car, *California v. Acevedo*, 500 U.S. ___, 111 S.Ct. 1982 (1991), discussed in § 7.04.

14. See § 6.04(b)(3).

15. See *Chambers v. Maroney*, 399 U.S. 42, 90 S.Ct. 1975 (1970), discussed in § 7.03(b)(2).

required, assuming judicial decisionmaking is to be preferred over decisionmaking of officers in the field.   Only the presence of exigent circumstances should permit dispensing with a warrant.

7.03   Elements of the Exception

Given the rationales for the automobile exception, three elements must be met before it applies.   First, the area searched must be one that is both inherently mobile and associated with a lessened expectation of privacy.   Second, police must have probable cause to search the vehicle.   Third, exigent circumstances must exist.   These elements are explored below.

(a) **Vehicles Covered.**   As noted, searches of cars, boats and planes are covered by the exception, although if a vehicle of this type is clearly not mobile, then the exception would presumably not apply.   In *California v. Carney,*[16] the Court was confronted with a hybrid situation: a warrantless search of a "mini" mobile home parked in a parking lot.   While recognizing that the vehicle had "many of the attributes of a home," the six-member majority concluded that this type of mobile home is more like a car than a house.   According to the Court, the test of whether a "vehicle" is one or the other should be whether the setting of the vehicle "objectively indicates that the vehicle is being used for transportation."   Factors relevant to this determination are the vehicle's location, whether it is readily mobile or stationary (e.g., elevated on blocks), whether it is licensed, whether it is connected to utilities, and whether it has convenient access to the road.   In dissent, Justice Stevens, making reference to *Chadwick,* argued that one has a *greater* expectation of privacy in vehicles such as the one at issue in *Carney* than in one's footlocker; he compared the mini-home to a hotel room or a hunting and fishing cabin.   As he rightly pointed out, "searches of places that regularly accommodate a wide range of private human activity are fundamentally different from searches of automobiles which primarily serve a public transportation function."

The debate in *Carney* about whether the privacy associated with a mobile home makes it more like a car or a house seems beside the point; even if the majority had adopted Justice Stevens' position, it still could have upheld a warrantless search if exigent circumstances existed.[17]   In other words, the focus in *Carney* should have been on whether the police had time to obtain a

16. 471 U.S. 386, 105 S.Ct. 2066 (1985).

17. There was no analysis of this issue in the majority opinion. The dissent stated that since curtains covered the windshield of the motor home, it "offered no indication of any imminent departure."   On the other hand, the home was parked in a public lot, and the person from whom the police obtained probable cause (a client of the defendant) might have alerted the occupant had police gone to get a warrant.

warrant before searching the vehicle, the same question that would arise in a search of a house. Unfortunately, the Court's attempt to distinguish cars from footlockers in *Chadwick* has led it down a blind alley.

(b) Probable Cause. *Carroll* warned that "where seizure is impossible except without warrant, the seizing officer acts unlawfully and at his peril unless he can show the court probable cause." Probable cause to search has been defined elsewhere.[18] The important point here is that, while probable cause to arrest and probable cause to search often co-exist, they are not congruent. Thus, in *Carroll,* the police could not arrest the defendant, but still had probable cause to search the car. In contrast the police may have sufficient grounds for arrest, but not for a search. In *Preston v. United States,*[19] the police arrested the occupants of a car for vagrancy. The Court held that this arrest did not, by itself, give police probable cause to search the car's glove compartment and trunk (in which guns and burglary tools were found).[20]

There is one situation where a warrantless, exigent search of an automobile does not require probable cause to believe evidence of crime is in the car. In *New York v. Class,*[21] the Court held, 5–4, that when the focus of the search is an automobile's Vehicle Identification Number (VIN), the car may be entered even when the police lack probable cause to believe the car is stolen and have no other reason for observing the VIN, so long as a valid stop for a traffic violation or some other offense has taken place. The Court based this holding both on the lessened expectation of privacy associated with the VIN (which federal regulations require to be visible to someone outside the car) and the minimal intrusiveness of a search designed merely to obtain a VIN. This conclusion can be challenged. As the lower court in *Class* observed in explaining its decision to exclude a gun found by police during the VIN search, "[t]he fact that certain information must be kept, or that it may be of a public nature, does not automatically sanction police intrusion into private space in order to obtain it."

(c) Exigency. *Carroll* emphasized that exigency should be narrowly defined, stating that "[i]n cases where the securing of a warrant is reasonably practicable, it must be used." In discussing the nature of the exigency exception in automobile exception cases, it is useful to distinguish between exigency measured "backward" from the time the car is discovered or stopped and exigency measured "forward" from that time.[22] The first type of exigency

---

18. See § 5.03.

19. 376 U.S. 364, 84 S.Ct. 881 (1964).

20. Note further that, although modern search incident doctrine would probably have permitted search of the glove compartment in *Preston,* it would

not have authorized the search of the trunk. See § 6.04(c).

21. 475 U.S. 106, 106 S.Ct. 960 (1986).

22. See Moylan, "The Automobile Exception: What It Is and What It Is

has to do with whether a warrant could have been obtained between the development of probable cause and the discovery of the car. The second concerns whether events after the latter occurrence justified foregoing a warrant.

(1) Measuring exigency "backward". Often, as in *Carroll*, probable cause develops at the same time the car is sighted, thus leaving no time to obtain a warrant prior to its discovery. At other times, probable cause may exist some time before the car is encountered, but police justifiably act without a warrant because they reasonably believe the car may disappear if they don't. In *Husty v. United States*,[23] for instance, a police officer, acting on an informant's tip, found contraband whiskey in Husty's unattended car. To the contention that the officer had time to get a warrant, the Court responded: "[The officer] could not know when Husty would come to the car or how soon it would be removed." A slightly different variant of this scenario occurred in *Chambers v. Maroney*,[24] where a description of a car involved in a recently completed robbery went out over police radio, and the car was stopped soon thereafter.

In some cases, however, exigency measured "backward" does not exist. In *Coolidge v. New Hampshire*,[25] for instance, the Court found that the automobile exception did not justify the warrantless seizure and search of two cars located on the defendant's property because the police had had probable cause to search the cars for two-and-a-half weeks prior to the search. When the search warrant police had procured turned out to be invalid,[26] they could not, according to four members of the Court, fall back on the automobile exception, since exigency measured backward from the time the cars were "discovered" did not exist. The Court probably should have made a similar finding in *Cardwell v. Lewis*.[27] There the police, after developing probable cause to believe the defendant had committed murder and that his car was used in the crime, called the defendant to the station for questioning. After arresting him there, they seized his car from a public parking lot, and then searched it, all without a warrant. While there was some indication that the defendant's wife could have driven the car away after his arrest, the police had plenty of time to obtain a warrant before the arrest. Yet four members of the Court upheld the search; they avoided the exigency issue almost entirely, instead resting the decision on the seemingly irrelevant ground that, unlike in *Coolidge*, the car had been located on public property.

Not—A Rationale in Search of a Clearer Label," 27 Mercer L.Rev. 987 (1976).

23. 282 U.S. 694, 51 S.Ct. 240 (1931).

24. 399 U.S. 42, 90 S.Ct. 1975 (1970).

25. 403 U.S. 443, 91 S.Ct. 2022 (1971).

26. See § 5.02.

27. 417 U.S. 583, 94 S.Ct. 2464 (1974).

(2) Measuring exigency "forward". In analyzing the exigency issue, *Carroll* focused solely on the time period between the development of probable cause and the stopping of the car. In *Husty,* however, the Court noted that exigent circumstances do not necessarily disappear once the car is stopped and under the officer's control: "In such circumstances we do not think the officers should be required to speculate upon the chances of successfully carrying out the search, after the delay and withdrawal from the scene of one or more officers which would have been necessary to procure a warrant." *Husty's* suggestion—that securing a car pending a warrant is not required by the Fourth Amendment—was turned into a holding in *Chambers v. Maroney.*[28] There, the Court held that, where probable cause and exigency, measured backward, exist, the police may either seize the car "for whatever period is necessary to obtain a warrant for the search" or search it "immediately without a warrant." The Court, through Justice White, continued:

> Arguably, because of the preference for a magistrate's judgment, only the immobilization of the car should be permitted until a search warrant is obtained; arguably, only the "lesser" intrusion is permissible until the magistrate authorizes the "greater." But which is the "greater" and which the "lesser" intrusion is itself a debatable question and the answer may depend on a variety of circumstances. For constitutional purposes, we see no difference. . . .

Justice Harlan argued in dissent that the majority's ambivalence about which option is the most intrusive was disingenuous. While seizure of a car is inconvenient, a search is much more invasive of privacy and possessory interests and can result in putting the car's occupants in jail. And in those cases where an occupant, "having nothing to hide and lacking concern for privacy of the automobile may feel a seizure does constitute a greater imposition than a search, the device of consent is readily available." These points seem valid. But they do not necessarily provide a convincing case against the result in *Chambers.* When a car is stopped at night, or the occupants outnumber the officers, both of which were true in *Chambers,* a prolonged wait while one officer goes to get a warrant might not be the most "practicable" solution. An immediate search seems justifiable in these circumstances, and in many others.[29] Again, as in *Carney,* both the

---

28. 399 U.S. 42, 90 S.Ct. 1975 (1970).

29. For instance, when only one officer makes the stop, when the magistrate is far away, or when the occupants of the car seem violent. See also, *Colorado v. Bannister,* 449 U.S. 1, 101 S.Ct. 42 (1980), where a unanimous Court held that when probable cause to search develops after a car is stopped for a traffic violation, "it would be especially unreasonable to require a detour to a magistrate before the unanticipated evidence could be lawfully seized."

majority and dissenting opinions in *Chambers* were distracted by the intrusiveness question, when the focus should have been the existence of exigent circumstances.

(3) The continuing exigency rule. A second, and much more questionable, holding in *Chambers* was its announcement of a "continuing exigency" rule: if the elements of the automobile exception are met at the time the car is discovered—that is, if there is probable cause and exigent circumstances as measured "backward" in time—police may forego both securing the car *and* an immediate search, and instead bring the car in from the field and conduct a warrantless search at the stationhouse. As later described by the Court,[30] "the actual search of the automobile in *Chambers* was made at the police station many hours after the car had been stopped on the highway, when the car was no longer movable, any 'exigent circumstances' had passed, and, for all the record shows, there was a magistrate easily available." Yet, noting only that the requirements of the automobile exception had been met in the field, the *Chambers* Court sanctioned the later search.

There is no apparent justification for this holding. For reasons already discussed, *Chambers'* focus on the relative intrusiveness of a seizure versus a search is arguably irrelevant. But even if it is not, and even if one decides that the seizure involved in taking the car to the station is less intrusive than an immediate search, this second holding in *Chambers* permits not just the seizure, but a subsequent *search* without a warrant. An alternative way of rationalizing *Chambers'* continuing exigency rule might be to point to the fact, noted earlier, that the arrest of the car's occupants took place late at night under dangerous circumstances. Thus, one might argue that the warrantless stationhouse search was a permissible way of protecting the officers. But this gloss on *Chambers* was eliminated as a possibility in *Texas v. White,* [31] where the Court reaffirmed the continuing exigency rule despite the absence of such dangerous circumstances. In any event, neither explanation for *Chambers* is supportable, because there is *no* exigency once the car is taken to the station and its occupants arrested.[32]

Chambers was not clear as to whether exigency measured "forward" from the discovery of the car exists forever. Later cases indicated that a warrantless search conducted under the continuing exigency rule cannot be unreasonably delayed. In

---

30. *Coolidge v. New Hampshire,* 403 U.S. 443, 91 S.Ct. 2022 (1971).

31. 423 U.S. 67, 96 S.Ct. 304 (1975).

32. It should be noted, however, that even if *Chambers* had been decided correctly, the type of search conducted there would have been authorized under the Court's inventory cases, had the car been subject to lawful impoundment after arrest of its occupants. See § 13.07(a).

particular, in *United States v. Johns,*[33] the Court held that a search under *Chambers* may not be postponed for so long that it "adversely affect[s] a privacy [or] possessory interest."[34]   However, it appears that a long hiatus between the original stop and the later search will often be found reasonable.   In *Johns,* the Court held that a three-day delay was permissible, in part because the owners, who had been arrested, had made no claim for the property in the interim.

7.04   Scope of the Search

Once the requirements of the automobile exception are met, police can obviously seize whatever they find in plain view.   But what about items that are not immediately visible?   Suppose, for instance, that the police have probable cause to believe that a car contains contraband and that they lawfully stop it.   If they find a footlocker in the car, may they conduct a warrantless search of *it* as well, or does *United States v. Chadwick,* discussed above, forbid such a search?   The Supreme Court has wrestled with this question in several cases, only recently making clear that *Carroll* always "trumps" *Chadwick*: that is, once containers are placed in a car, they lose the relatively greater protection they usually possess and are treated like other areas within the car.

For some time, it appeared the Court would hold to the opposite result.   In *Arkansas v. Sanders,*[35] the Court concluded that a warrantless search of a suitcase for which the police have probable cause is not permissible merely because police wait until it is put in a car before they search it.   Rather, as in *Chadwick,* the police must secure the luggage and obtain a warrant for its search.   And in *Robbins v. California,*[36] the Court held, 6–3, that even containers that are discovered for the first time during a car search must be seized pending procural of a warrant, rather than subjected to a warrantless search at the time of discovery.   In *Robbins,* the police stopped the defendant's car because it had been weaving erratically.   When Robbins opened the car door, they smelled marijuana smoke.   They asked him out of the car, patted him down, found marijuana and related paraphernalia, and then searched the passenger compartment and luggage compartments.   In the latter area they found two packages wrapped in green opaque plastic, which turned out to contain marijuana.   Justice Stewart stated that, under these circumstances, only a

33. 469 U.S. 478, 105 S.Ct. 881 (1985).

34. Additionally, the author of *Chambers,* Justice White, later stated in *Coolidge* that *Chambers* "contemplated some expedition in completing the [stationhouse] searches so that automobiles

could be released and returned to their owners."

35. 442 U.S. 753, 99 S.Ct. 2586 (1979).

36. 453 U.S. 420, 101 S.Ct. 2841 (1981).

container which "somehow reveals the nature of its contents" (such as a glass vial or a gun case) may be searched without a warrant. Search of any other container, including the green plastic in which the marijuana was found, must be preceded by a warrant, since "[w]hat one person may put into a suitcase, another may put into a paper bag." [37]

Despite the size of the majority in *Robbins,* it was clear that the three dissenters were not alone in feeling uncomfortable with the result. In particular, Justice Powell—who wrote a tortured concurring opinion explaining why he would apply the majority's ruling to the type of package in *Robbins,* which had been "neatly wrapped," but not to other, less private receptacles, such as "a cigar box or a Dixie cup"—and Chief Justice Burger, who did not join in the majority opinion but merely entered a separate concurrence, seemed ambivalent about the decision. When the author of *Robbins,* Justice Stewart, was replaced by Justice O'Connor, the stage was set for a repudiation of *Robbins.*

One year later, the Court handed down *United States v. Ross,*[38] which overturned *Robbins* and which backed away from much of the reasoning in *Sanders.* *Ross* held that once the requirements of the automobile exception are met, the police have authority to conduct a warrantless search "that is as thorough as a magistrate could authorize in a warrant." The only limitations on the scope of the search are "defined by the object of the search and the places in which there is probable cause to believe that it may be found." Thus, the Court explained, police cannot conduct a warrantless search of a suitcase in a car when they are looking for illegal aliens. Conversely, however, if the police are looking for contraband, they may constitutionally search any area of the car in which the contraband might be contained, including luggage and other receptacles. In *Ross* itself, the Court upheld the warrantless search of a paper bag found in a car trunk after police, with probable cause to believe the trunk contained heroin, stopped the car, searched its interior, and then searched its trunk.

The Court's opinion, written by Justice Stevens, justified its aboutface in *Ross* by carefully examining *Carroll* and its progeny. It noted, for instance, that the whiskey discovered in *Carroll* had not been in plain view, but rather had been found only after an officer opened the rumble seat and tore open its upholstery. Similarly, some of the whiskey used against the defendants in

---

37. Note that, in the same Term, Justice Stewart also authored *New York v. Belton,* 453 U.S. 454, 101 S.Ct. 2860 (1981), which permitted warrantless searches of any containers found in a car contemporaneous with an arrest of its occupants, a decision which reduces substantially the protection afforded cars (although it would not have permitted the search of the luggage compartment in *Robbins*). See § 6.04(c).

38. 456 U.S. 798, 102 S.Ct. 2157 (1982).

Husty was found in "whiskey bags" which could have contained other goods. After looking at other Court decisions, Stevens concluded:

> [T]he decision in *Carroll* was based on the Court's appraisal of practical considerations viewed in the perspective of history. It is therefore significant that the practical consequences of the *Carroll* decision would be largely nullified if the permissible scope of a warrantless search of an automobile did not include containers and packages found inside the vehicle. Contraband goods rarely are strewn across the trunk or floor of a car; since by their very nature such goods must be withheld from public view, they rarely can be placed in an automobile unless they are enclosed within some form of container.

Thus, containers found in a car are subject to no greater protection than the car itself.[39]

Ross explicitly refused to reconsider *Sanders,* thus leaving intact the rule that if probable cause to search a container exists *before* it is placed in a car, the police may not conduct a warrantless search of it. In *California v. Acevedo,*[40] the Court, by a 6–3 margin, took the last step toward removing warrant protection for searches of automobiles by overruling *Sanders.* Justice Blackmun, who wrote the Court's opinion, argued that *Sanders* provided only minimal protection of privacy in any event, quoting from his dissent in that case: "Since the police, by hypothesis, have probable cause to seize the property, we can assume that a warrant will be routinely forthcoming in the overwhelming majority of cases." He also noted that the warrantless search permitted in *Carroll* (which, it will be remembered, involved slashing the upholstery) was more intrusive than many container searches. Finally, Blackmun asserted that the "anomaly" created by the different treatment of containers in *Ross* and *Sanders* had confused and inconvenienced police and should be eliminated.

Assuming the requisite exigency "backwards" in time, police may now conduct a warrantless search of any container they have probable cause to search once it is placed in a car. However, the majority in *Acevedo* emphasized that police may not search the rest of the car unless they have probable cause to search that area as well. Moreover, as Justice Stevens pointed out in dissent, an "anomaly" still exists after *Acevedo:* a container carried in the street is still protected by the warrant requirement, yet loses that protection as soon as it is put in a car. Recognizing this fact,

---

39. The Court later made clear, in *United States v. Johns,* 469 U.S. 478, 105 S.Ct. 881 (1985), that any containers searchable under *Ross* are also searchable at a later point in time under the "continuing exigency" rule. See § 7.03(c)(3).

40. 500 U.S. ___, 111 S.Ct. 1982 (1991).

Justice Scalia wrote a concurring opinion in *Acevedo* arguing that, in line with his perception of the common law, only searches of containers inside a private building should require a warrant. A consistent approach which makes more sense conceptually is to require warrants for all container searches. Once the container is seized, whether from a car or the street, there is no exigency and thus time to obtain a warrant. If Justice Blackmun is right that warrants will routinely be forthcoming in such cases, then the police are caused no inconvenience short of that justified by a preference for judicial, rather than police, determinations of probable cause.

7.05 Conclusion

The basic tenets of the automobile exception can be summarized as follows:

(1) The area searched must be a movable vehicle associated with a lessened expectation of privacy; that is, a vehicle whose setting objectively indicates that it is being used for transportation.

(2) There must be probable cause to believe the vehicle contains evidence of crime.

(3) There must be exigent circumstances justifying a warrantless search of the vehicle, meaning that the time between the development of probable cause and the discovery or stopping of the vehicle was insufficient to procure a warrant.

(4) If these elements are met, any area of the car or any container therein for which probable cause exists may be searched immediately, or at some later time, provided any delay which occurs does not unreasonably interfere with privacy or possessory interests.

BIBLIOGRAPHY

Gardner, Martin R. Searches and Seizures of Automobiles and Their Contents: Fourth Amendment Considerations in a Post-*Ross* World. 62 Neb.L.Rev. 1 (1983).

Katz, Lewis R. *United States v. Ross*: Evolving Standards for Warrantless Searches. 74 J.Crim.L. & Criminol. 172 (1983).

Moylan, C.E., Jr. The Automobile Exception: What It Is and What It Is Not—A Rationale in Search of a Clearer Label. 27 Mercer L.Rev. 987 (1976).

Warrantless Searches and Seizures of Automobiles [comment]. 87 Harv.L.Rev. 835 (1974).

Wilson, Vivian D. The Warrantless Automobile Search: Exception Without Justification. 32 Hast.L.J. 127 (1980).

Chapter Eight

HOT PURSUIT

8.01 Introduction

As discussed earlier in this book,[1] police are allowed to enter premises to make an arrest, without an arrest warrant, when they are in "hot pursuit" of a person they believe to have committed a crime. This chapter will look at the closely related issue of when police are permitted to enter premises to conduct a *search*, without a *search* warrant, while trying to find a suspect they are pursuing. The Supreme Court first explicitly recognized the hot pursuit exception to the search warrant requirement in *Warden v. Hayden*.[2] There, the police were summoned by taxi drivers who reported that their taxi company had been robbed and that they had followed the suspect to a particular house. The police were shown the house and were admitted by the wife of the defendant, who was upstairs feigning sleep. In the course of searching for the defendant they found clothing in a washing machine and under a mattress and a shotgun and a pistol in a bathroom. The clothing and weapons were later used in evidence against the defendant.

The Court, in an opinion by Justice Brennan, noted that this situation was not covered by search incident doctrine. That doctrine only permits a search *after* a person is seized pursuant to an arrest.[3] Here the evidence was found before and contemporaneously with the arrest, which occurred an entire floor away. Nevertheless, a unanimous Court found both the warrantless entry and the subsequent search "reasonable," because the "exigencies of the situation made that course imperative." As Brennan stated for the Court, the officers "acted reasonably when they entered the house," because "[t]he Fourth Amendment does not require police officers to delay in the course of an investigation if to do so would gravely endanger their lives or the lives of others." With respect to the search, "[s]peed here was essential, and only a thorough search of the house for persons and weapons could have insured that Hayden was the only man present and that the police had control of all weapons which could be used against them or to effect an escape."

The paradigmatic case of a hot pursuit search is clear. The police either witness or receive a "hot tip" on a felony and chase

1. See § 3.04(d).

2. 387 U.S. 294, 87 S.Ct. 1642 (1967). Only Justice Fortas, in a concurring opinion, actually used the term "hot pursuit". The term was first used by the Court in *Johnson v. United States*, 333 U.S. 10, 68 S.Ct. 367 (1948).

3. See § 6.03.

the alleged felon, who flees to shelter. They apprehend him there after a search that additionally happens to turn up evidence that is used at trial. The rapidity with which all of this occurs argues for dispensing with a warrant. But hot pursuit doctrine is more complicated than this typical scenario suggests. Several aspects require more development: (1) when hot pursuit justifies entry; (2) the definition of hot pursuit; and (3) the scope of a search while in pursuit.

8.02   When Hot Pursuit Justifies Entry

Not every hot pursuit of a suspect permits warrantless entry. The courts have imposed at least four limitations on hot pursuit doctrine which significantly circumscribe the extent to which a police chase can end up in the home.

(a) Probable Cause as to Crime and Location. Warrantless entry may not occur under the hot pursuit doctrine unless police have probable cause to believe that the person they are chasing has committed a crime and is on the premises entered. Although *Hayden* did not explicitly require a probable cause showing of these facts, probable cause was clearly present there, and other Supreme Court cases have established that an entry of the home must normally be preceded by a probable cause showing.[4] Of course, as *Hayden* demonstrates, neither the crime nor the suspect's entry into the home need be observed by the police. Rather, probable cause can come from third parties.[5]

(b) Probable Cause as to Exigency. In addition to having probable cause to believe a suspect is on the premises, the police should also have reason to believe that the suspect will escape or that some further harm will occur unless the warrantless entry occurs immediately. As one court put it, "[a] hot pursuit, by itself, creates no necessity for dispensing with a warrant."[6] Hot pursuit may explain why police have not obtained a warrant up to the time they arrive at the suspect's house. But warrantless entry at that point should not be automatic. Rather, as summarized by the court in *United States v. George*,[7] a warrant should still be obtained unless "the arresting officers reasonably believe [: (1)] that the suspects either know or will learn at any moment that they are in immediate danger of apprehension;" (2) that the "evidence is being currently removed or destroyed and it is impractical to advert the situation without immediately arresting the suspects or seizing the evidence;" or (3) that "a suspect is currently endangering the lives of themselves or others."

4. See *Payton v. New York*, 445 U.S. 573, 100 S.Ct. 1371 (1980); *Carroll v. United States*, 267 U.S. 132, 45 S.Ct. 280 (1925).

5. See § 5.03(b).

6. *State v. Wren*, 115 Idaho 618, 768 P.2d 1351 (1989).

7. 883 F.2d 1407 (9th Cir.1989).

Again, *Hayden* did not directly address this point, although the Court did emphasize the possibility of danger to the police and others; *Hayden* may suggest that, when pursuit is particularly "hot," additional exigency (such as escape or harm to others) will always be present. In any event, other Supreme Court cases have seemed to require proof of one of these emergency conditions before allowing police to proceed without a warrant,[8] and several lower courts besides *George* have explicitly come to this conclusion.[9] Whether the existence of such an exigency must be shown at the probable cause level, or whether a lesser showing is permitted, is not normally addressed by the courts. Since the issue is whether the home and similar premises may be entered, probable cause would seem to be the appropriate standard.

(c) Lawful Starting Point. A third limitation on the hot pursuit doctrine is that the police start the pursuit from a legitimate place. In *Hayden,* this limitation was not an issue, since the police obviously began their pursuit of the suspect from a public area. But, as developed elsewhere in this book,[10] police may not initiate a search on *private* property unless they are already lawfully there. For instance, an officer who does not know about criminal activity until he has trespassed on private property and looked in the window does not have legitimate grounds for invoking the hot pursuit exception to justify a subsequent entry. By the same token, if the police are legitimately on the premises when they begin their pursuit, then a warrant is not required (assuming the other elements of the hot pursuit doctrine are met). Thus, in *Mincey v. Arizona,*[11] the Court stated, in dictum, that police may make a "prompt warrantless search" of the scene of a homicide for the victim or the killer after they have lawfully entered the premises upon reports of a death.

In *United States v. Santana,*[12] the Court was confronted with a hybrid situation: the police started their pursuit on public property based on what they saw taking place on private property. In *Santana,* police had probable cause to believe Santana had marked money in her possession used to make a heroin buy. When they arrived at her house, she was standing in the doorway of the house

---

8. See, e.g., *Johnson v. United States,* 333 U.S. 10, 68 S.Ct. 367 (1948) (no sufficient reason for dispensing with a warrant where there was no risk of imminent harm to any person, no evidence was being destroyed or likely to be destroyed, and the suspect was not likely to flee while the police obtained a warrant); *United States v. Jeffers,* 342 U.S. 48, 72 S.Ct. 93 (1951) (invalidating warrantless entry, noting that "[t]here was no question of violence, no moveable vehicle was involved, nor was there an arrest or imminent destruction, removal, or concealment of the property intended to be seized.").

9. See *Jeffcoat v. Hinson,* 851 F.2d 356 (4th Cir.1988); *State v. Storvick,* 423 N.W.2d 398 (Minn.App.1988), rev'd in part, 428 N.W.2d 55 (Minn.1988).

10. See § 10.02.

11. 437 U.S. 385, 98 S.Ct. 2408 (1978).

12. 427 U.S. 38, 96 S.Ct. 2406 (1976).

with a brown paper bag in her hand. As the officers approached, Santana retreated into the vestibule, where she was arrested and the bag, containing narcotics, was searched. Justice Rehnquist, writing an opinion for four members of the Court,[13] held that Santana was in a "public" place for purposes of the Fourth Amendment since "[s]he was not in an area where she had any expectation of privacy," and thus the arrest and search were legitimate. Although the search in *Santana* was closer to a search incident than a hot pursuit search, the case apparently established that police may pursue from a public vantage point a suspect they first see on private property.

(d) Type of Crime. A final prerequisite of the hot pursuit doctrine is that the person chased be suspected of a law violation that is "serious." While this designation clearly includes felonies, and perhaps most misdemeanors, if the person pursued is suspected only of a minor infraction of the law, *Hayden* does not apply. In *Welsh v. Wisconsin*,[14] the police: (1) found a car abandoned in a ditch; (2) learned from a bystander that the driver had appeared to be drunk; (3) found the petitioner's address on the car's registration; and (4) entered the petitioner's home to make a warrantless arrest. Writing for six members of the Court, Justice Brennan found this action unconstitutional, despite the state's argument that an immediate entry was necessary to obtain evidence of the petitioner's blood-alcohol level. The Court held that warrantless entry, "the chief evil against which the wording of the Fourth Amendment is directed," is not permitted unless the state can point to "some real immediate and serious consequences if [the officer] postponed action to get a warrant." The "best indication" of how serious the state's interest was in this case was the fact that Wisconsin classified the petitioner's offense "as a noncriminal, civil forfeiture offense for which no imprisonment is possible." Given this minor penalty, concluded the Court, "a warrantless home arrest cannot be upheld simply because evidence of the petitioner's blood-alcohol level might have dissipated while the police obtained a warrant."

While, as a theoretical matter, it may make sense to prohibit warrantless entries when an offense is truly minor, the holding in *Welsh* does not follow. The civil scheme adopted by Wisconsin, requiring revocation of a drunk driver's license and civil fines, reflected a strong interest in deterring drunken driving. Nonetheless, under *Welsh*, until the state begins imprisoning such drivers, or at least begins prosecuting them as criminal, it may be prevented from obtaining probative evidence in cases where the driver

---

13. Justice White concurred on the ground that entry to make an arrest never requires a warrant, a position which was rejected four years later in

Payton v. New York, 445 U.S. 573, 100 S.Ct. 1371 (1980).

14. 466 U.S. 740, 104 S.Ct. 2091 (1984).

reaches home before the officer does, an occurrence that is apparently fairly frequent.[15]   Beyond this, there are good reasons for not basing the scope of the warrant requirement on the nature of the offense, discussed in detail elsewhere in this book.[16]

8.03   The Definition of "Hot Pursuit"

Suppose the police develop probable cause that a person is engaged in selling narcotics out of his home and, instead of seeking a warrant, stake out the house for several hours to see if the suspect is there.   Suddenly the door opens, and the suspect comes out, sees one of the officers, and retreats into the living room.   Would a warrantless entry be permitted out of fear that the suspect, now alerted to the officers' presence, will try to destroy the narcotics?   The answer should be no, even assuming the police are not responsible for the exigency.[17]   Unless the police are in *hot* pursuit of a suspect at the time they arrive at the home, a warrantless entry should not be permitted, even when the police can show that an exigency—such as imminent destruction of evidence—existed.   Otherwise, the police could engage in warrantless entries in situations where they had plenty of time to procure a warrant.   Put another way, analogous to the analysis under the automobile exception,[18] exigency in hot pursuit cases should be shown to exist both forward (in terms of destruction of evidence, etc.) and backward (in terms of pursuit) from the time the police trace the suspect to the premises.   While the Supreme Court, to date, has for the most part rigidly construed the pursuit notion, many lower courts have been less careful.

(a) **Supreme Court Cases.**   The pursuit in *Hayden* was clearly "hot."   The police answered the taxi driver's radio call "in less than five minutes" and proceeded directly to the house in which the suspect was located.   In *Santana* too, there was exigency, although perhaps of an "illegitimate" type.   There, the state sought to justify the lack of a warrant on the ground that they had just arrested an accomplice of Santana's a block and a half from her house and "word would have been back within a matter of seconds or minutes."   No member of the Court disputed this contention.   But, as Justice Brennan pointed out in dissent, "[t]he exigency that justified the entry and arrest was solely a product of police conduct."   Had police made the arrest of the accomplice at some later point in time, which they easily could have done, no

---

15. See, e.g., *State v. Griffith*, 61 Wash.App. 35, 808 P.2d 1171 (1991); *Hamrick v. State*, 198 Ga.App. 124, 401 S.E.2d 25 (1990); *City of Wenatchee v. Durham*, 43 Wash.App. 547, 718 P.2d 819 (1986).

16. See § 3.04(d).

17. But cf. *United States v. Shye*, 492 F.2d 886 (6th Cir.1974) (warrantless entry permitted when door opened after one-hour stakeout).

18. See § 7.03(c).

exigency would have arisen. Echoing the Court's search incident cases,[19] Brennan stated: "[w]hen an arrest is so timed that it is no more than an attempt to circumvent the warrant requirement, I would hold the subsequent arrest or search unlawful."

Whatever the right outcome in *Santana,* it seems clear that exigency existed in *Welsh,* where police proceeded from the scene of the drunk driving violation to the defendant's house in a matter of minutes. Yet Justice Brennan found the state's "claim of hot pursuit . . . unconvincing because there was no immediate or continuous pursuit of the petitioner from the scene of the crime." While the "immediate and continuous" language well summarizes the hot pursuit notion, Brennan's inexplicable application of it in *Welsh* would also require a different holding in *Hayden,* a decision which Brennan also authored. The Court's crabbed treatment of the exigency issue in *Welsh* should be read in light of the fact that it was ultimately unnecessary to the decision, since the Court held that, when entry to obtain evidence of a minor violation is involved, a warrant is required regardless of exigency.

In contrast to *Hayden* and *Santana* are decisions in which the Court has found the trail too cold to justify a warrantless entry. In *Mincey v. Arizona,*[20] for instance, police first removed the defendant and the body of the victim from an apartment, and then returned to spend four days searching the premises. Two to three hundred items were inventoried, but no warrant was ever obtained. The state sought to justify the search on a so-called "murder scene" exception to the warrant requirement. Justice Stewart, writing for the majority, firmly rejected such an exception, stating that a warrantless search must be "strictly circumscribed by the exigencies which justify its initiation." He noted that by the time this search had begun, the police had already checked the apartment for other victims or suspects, thus eliminating any emergency. Similarly, in *Thompson v. Louisiana,*[21] a unanimous Court refused to sanction a two-hour search of a murder scene by homicide squad members 35 minutes after the premises were secured by the police. The state pointed out that the duration of the search in this case was substantially shorter than that which occurred in *Mincey* and occurred on the same day as the murder. But the Court noted that "nothing in *Mincey* turned on the length of time taken in the search or the date on which it was conducted." Because the homicide squad had entered the premises "at a later time" to conduct a separate search, a warrant was required. Although neither *Mincey* nor *Thompson* were explicitly hot pursuit cases, they both indicate that the Court

---

19.　See § 6.04(a).

20.　437 U.S. 385, 98 S.Ct. 2408 (1978).

21.　469 U.S. 17, 105 S.Ct. 409 (1984).

believes the justification for a warrantless entry must be exigency. In neither case was there a "pursuit" which justified foregoing a warrant.

(b) Lower Court Cases. In seeking further clarification of the term "hot pursuit," one must turn to lower court decisions. Many have sanctioned warrantless entries after pursuits of somewhat longer duration than those involved in *Hayden* and *Santana*. Of course, to use *Welsh's* language, if the pursuit is "immediate and continuous," the fact that it is prolonged is not necessarily fatal. For instance, in *United States v. Holland,*[22] police began their pursuit of a suspected bank robber by following footprints made in the snow to a spot from which it appeared (based on analysis of impressions made in the snow) a car with two passengers had recently been driven. The pursuers obtained the name of the car's driver from the residents of a nearby house, located the driver, and obtained from him the name of his passenger (the eventual defendant). The officers then went to the home of the defendant, were admitted by one of the occupants and found the defendant hiding upstairs. Time in pursuit was approximately 30 minutes, but, as the court stated, "the fact that there were three houses involved in this chain of circumstances and, hence, a somewhat longer pursuit, neither breaks the chain nor alters the concept of hot pursuit."

In *United States v. Scott,*[23] four black males armed with a sawed-off shotgun and revolvers robbed a bank. A witness gave a general description of the getaway car along with part of the license number. When that vehicle was found abandoned, the police determined that the suspects had switched cars. They then followed a trail of tire marks produced by high acceleration to a parking lot of an apartment complex, where they found a car fitting the description of eye-witnesses who had observed the speeding car. By questioning the resident manager the police found out which apartments were occupied by black males. A search narrowed down the possible apartments to one; scuffling was heard inside, the police entered, made arrests, and seized evidence. Here entry and seizure took place 1 hour and 45 minutes after commission of the crime. The court nonetheless found sufficiently exigent circumstances, stating that "had the officers delayed their entry to apartment 7 to secure a search warrant for that apartment, the suspects might well have escaped or concealed evidence, and the risks of armed confrontation would have been increased."

22. 511 F.2d 38 (6th Cir.1975), cert. denied 421 U.S. 1001, 95 S.Ct. 2401 (1975).

23. 520 F.2d 697 (9th Cir.1975), cert. denied 423 U.S. 1056, 96 S.Ct. 788 (1976).

More questionable are those cases which allow a warrantless pursuit that is neither immediate or continuous. A notable example of this tendency is *Dorman v. United States,*[24] which in effect endorsed a "warm pursuit" doctrine. There, four men had held up a clothing store at gunpoint. In the ensuing investigation the police discovered Dorman's pants (discarded by Dorman after putting on a new suit), in which they found copies of his monthly probation report identifying him and his place of residence. Since it was late at night, and a magistrate was difficult to find, the police made a warrantless entry into Dorman's residence, four hours after the commission of the crime. In upholding the entry, which did not produce Dorman but did result in the discovery of evidence behind a sofa, the District of Columbia Circuit Court of Appeals admitted that hot pursuit was not proven on these facts. Nonetheless, it found that the police had an "urgent need" to forego obtaining a warrant. It listed six conditions which might lead to a finding of "urgent need:" (1) the offense is a grave one, particularly one of violence; (2) the suspect is reasonably believed to be armed; (3) there is clear evidentiary support for a showing of probable cause; (4) there is strong reason to believe the suspect is on the premises entered; (5) there is a strong likelihood of escape if the suspect is not immediately apprehended; and (6) police entry is peaceable. The court focused on the facts that Dorman had been armed and abused his victims, the delay was not the fault of the police, and the entry was peaceable (Dorman's mother had let the police in). It also discussed magistrate availability and the preference for daytime entries as separate, somewhat offsetting, issues bearing on the reasonableness of the police's failure to obtain a warrant.

Dorman appears to expand the emergency concept considerably. Only the fifth factor listed above is directly related to exigency concerns and, as the court admitted, this factor did not weigh heavily in the court's analysis given the four-hour hiatus between the crime and the entry. Yet *Dorman's* factors have been widely cited.[25] One explanation for the popularity of *Dorman's* warm pursuit doctrine is that "pursuit" cases are concerned initially with the efficacy of obtaining an arrest warrant rather than a search warrant. Some courts might believe that a warrantless entry should be easier to justify when it is designed merely to apprehend a fleeing suspect, because the privacy intrusion is less. But, as the facts of *Dorman* illustrate, in relaxing the prerequisites for a warrantless arrest,[26] the courts are in effect expanding the scope of warrantless searches as well, and they should therefore proceed with greater caution.

24. 435 F.2d 385 (D.C.Cir.1970) (en banc).

25. See, e.g., *United States v. Kulcsar,* 586 F.2d 1283 (8th Cir.1978); *Unit-* ed *States v. Campbell,* 581 F.2d 22 (2d Cir.1978).

26. See § 3.04(d) for criticism of this tendency.

8.04 Scope of the Search

The scope of a hot pursuit search is wide-ranging. As the *Hayden* Court stated: "The permissible scope of search must, at the least, be as broad as may reasonably be necessary to prevent the dangers that the suspect at large in the house may resist or escape." Thus, police may search any location which might hide the suspect or suspected accomplices, as well as any area which might contain weapons. In *Dorman,* for instance, police did not exceed their authority by looking in the closet and behind the sofa (although the court suggested that "rummaging through drawers" may have been inappropriate). Moreover, any evidence discovered in "plain view" while looking for the suspect or weapons is admissible as well.[27] In *Hayden* the Court held that clothing found in a washing machine was admissible because the officer who found it could have been looking for weapons.

There are two limitations on the hot pursuit search, however. First, the search, in the words of the *Hayden* Court, must be "prior to or immediately contemporaneous with" the arrest of the suspect; once the suspect is found, the scope of the search is determined by search incident to arrest doctrine, which adequately provides for police protection.[28] Of course, if more than one suspect is involved, police may look for all of them.[29] If no suspect is found, however, the police must leave the premises; *Mincey* and *Thompson* hold that further scouring of the dwelling is not permissible.

The second limitation on the scope of a hot pursuit search is based on the protection rationale of the doctrine. Officers may search *only* where the suspect or weapons might reasonably be found. Thus, looking in jars and jewelry boxes will normally be inappropriate. Following this reasoning, if the suspect is not believed to be armed and there is no reason to believe weapons are in the house, then a hot pursuit search should be limited to those areas where a *person* could be located. Of course, after *Welsh,* the hot pursuit doctrine may not apply to nondangerous crimes in any event.

8.05 Conclusion

The hot pursuit doctrine permits warrantless entries of premises when suspects have fled there. The principal components of the doctrine are as follows:

(1) Before entering the premises, the police must have probable cause to believe: (a) that the person they are pursuing has

---

27. See § 10.02.

28. See § 6.04. However, *Hayden* indicated that for officers who are not aware of the arrest, hot pursuit doctrine applies.

29. See also *Simpson v. State,* 486 S.W.2d 807 (Tex.Crim.App.1972) (police could search throughout house for wanted individual after occupants had scattered upon police's arrival).

committed a crime which is not "minor"; and (b) that the person is on the premises they wish to enter. In addition, they should at least have reason to believe: (c) that the suspect will escape or harm someone, or evidence will be destroyed or lost, unless a warrantless entry is made. The observations informing these beliefs must be lawfully acquired; that is, they must come from third parties or police observation from a lawful vantage point.

(2) The pursuit must be immediate and continuous from the time of the crime or the time the suspect is spotted outside the premises, and should not be extremely prolonged; in other words, if the police can reasonably procure a warrant before they arrive at the premises, they should do so.

BIBLIOGRAPHY

Donnino, William C., and Anthony J. Girese. Exigent Circumstances for a Warrantless Home Arrest. 45 Albany L.Rev. 90 (1980).

Evans, Jeffrey L. Constitutional Restraints on Residential Warrantless Arrest Entries: More Protection for Privacy Interests in the Home. 10 Amer.J.Crim.L. 1 (1982).

Project on Law Enforcement Policy and Rulemaking. Warrantless Searches of Persons and Places: Model Rules. Washington, D.C.: Police Foundation, 1974. Rule 401 and commentary.

Salken, Barbara. Balancing Exigency and Privacy in Warrantless Searches to Prevent Destruction of Evidence: The Need for a Rule. 39 Hastings L.J. 283 (1988).

Williamson, R. The Supreme Court, Warrantless Searches, and Exigent Circumstances. 31 Okla.L.Rev. 110 (1978).

Chapter Nine

EVANESCENT EVIDENCE AND ENDANGERED PERSONS

9.01 Introduction

The previous three chapters—discussing the search incident, automobile and hot pursuit exceptions to the warrant requirement—cover most situations in which an emergency search is legitimately conducted by police investigating street crime.[1] But there remain some situations in which the criteria for these exceptions are not met, yet exigency seems to justify a full warrantless search by the police. In the types of searches discussed in this chapter, the primary objective of the police is either to obtain evidence or prevent harm. These searches thus diverge from the search incident and hot pursuit scenarios, where the originating motivation for the police action is apprehension of a suspect. And while the primary objective in the automobile exception cases is evidence, the cases discussed here differ because the exigent circumstances come from the evidence itself, not from the fact it is in a movable vehicle.

Unlike the other exceptions described in this book, the Supreme Court has not attached a label to these types of cases; here the terms used will be the "evanescent evidence" and the "endangered persons" exceptions. The caselaw suggests that if the police have reason to believe either that something of evidentiary significance is about to disappear or that a person is in imminent danger of serious harm, they may engage in a search necessary to prevent the threat, even when apprehension of a suspect or search of a mobile vehicle is not involved. The various cases endorsing this notion will be discussed here within the framework provided by the language of the Fourth Amendment, beginning with searches of persons, the issue on which the Supreme Court has focused most of its attention, and then continuing with searches of houses, papers and effects.

9.02 Persons

The classic example of "evanescent," or vanishing, evidence is alcohol in the blood. The first Supreme Court case upholding a warrantless intrusion into a person's body to obtain such evidence was *Breithaupt v. Abram.*[2] There, police took an injured and unconscious individual to a hospital where a routine blood test

1. As to situations in which "frisks," as opposed to searches, are justified, see Chapter Eleven. As to emergency searches in the regulatory context, see Chapter Thirteen.

2. 352 U.S. 432, 77 S.Ct. 408 (1957).

disclosed that he had been drinking. The defendant argued that this procedure violated *Rochin v. California,*[3] where the Court had found that forcible use of a stomach pump to obtain evidence violated the Due Process Clause because it "shocked the conscience." But the majority in *Breithaupt* distinguished *Rochin* by concluding that the blood test procedure used in the former case "would not be considered offensive even by the most delicate," because it had "become routine in our everyday life." The three dissenters, Chief Justice Warren and Justices Black and Douglas, argued that neither the nature of the procedure, nor whether it was "forcibly" administered, should be relevant to due process analysis. Rather, "due process means at least that law-enforcement officers in their efforts to obtain evidence from persons suspected of crime must stop short of bruising the body, breaking skin, puncturing tissue or extracting body fluids, whether they contemplate doing it by force or by stealth."

The majority in *Breithaupt* was careful to note "that the indiscriminate taking of blood under different conditions or by those not competent to do so," might amount to "brutality" under the *Rochin* rule. Moreover, because it was decided under the Due Process Clause, *Breithaupt* did not directly address whether, or when, a warrant was required prior to a bodily intrusion. In *Schmerber v. California,*[4] the Supreme Court developed both of these points in the course of upholding a warrantless blood test. The majority opinion, authored by Justice Brennan, first found that the Fourth Amendment was clearly meant to protect the dignity and privacy interests implicated by body searches. Second, it agreed with *Breithaupt* that such searches could be conducted without a warrant, provided that: (1) there is no time to obtain one; (2) there is a "clear indication" that the search will result in the desired evidence; and (3) the search is conducted in a "reasonable manner."

(a) The Exigency Requirement. Because a body search is particularly intrusive, the *Schmerber* Court authorized warrantless action only when "there [is] no time to seek out a magistrate and secure a warrant." The Court refused to resort to search incident doctrine, even though the defendant had been arrested at the time of the search. That doctrine requires only a valid arrest, not a showing that evidence is about to be destroyed, on the theory that protecting police or evidence from the arrestee is a paramount concern overriding the interest in ensuring that police are relatively certain their search will produce something.[5] According to the Court:

3. 342 U.S. 165, 72 S.Ct. 205 (1952).   **5.** See § 6.01.

4. 384 U.S. 757, 86 S.Ct. 1826 (1966).

Whatever the validity of these considerations in general, they have little applicability with respect to searches involving intrusions beyond the body's surface. The interests in human dignity and privacy which the Fourth Amendment protects forbid any such intrusions on the mere chance that desired evidence might be obtained. In the absence of a clear indication that in fact such evidence will be found, these fundamental human interests require law officers to suffer the risk that such evidence may disappear unless there is an immediate search.

Thus, an arrest by itself does not permit a warrantless bodily intrusion; there must be good reason to believe "an immediate search" will produce evidence.

A different type of body search confronted the Court in *Cupp v. Murphy.*[6] There, the defendant, after officially being informed of his wife's death by strangulation, volunteered to come to the police station for questioning. Soon after his arrival, the police noticed a spot on the defendant's finger and asked him if they could take a sample of scrapings from under his fingernails. He refused and began rubbing his hands behind his back and placing them in his pockets. At this point, the police forcibly, and without a warrant, removed some of the matter under his nails. As in *Schmerber,* the Court reasoned that although the search incident doctrine might not apply (there being no arrest), the police had probable cause to believe that "highly evanescent evidence" was in the process of being destroyed and acted reasonably in preventing its destruction.

(b) **The Clear Indication Standard.** As the passage quoted above indicates, *Schmerber* required that, in addition to exigency, there must be a "clear indication" that an immediate search will produce evidence before a warrantless body search may occur. The *Schmerber* Court seemed to link its "clear indication" language with probable cause, at least for the blood test at issue in that case; the Court noted that the discovery of a near-empty whiskey bottle in the glove compartment of the defendant's car, his "glassy appearance," and the odor of liquor on his breath had given the police probable cause to believe there would be alcohol in his blood. *Murphy* as well noted that the police had probable cause to believe probative evidence was being destroyed.

However, in *United States v. Montoya de Hernandez,*[7] the Court equated the clear indication phraseology with the lesser "reasonable suspicion" standard, at least when police want to determine whether an alien is smuggling drugs across the border

---

6. 412 U.S. 291, 93 S.Ct. 2000 (1973).   7. 469 U.S. 1204, 105 S.Ct. 1164 (1985).

in her alimentary canal.[8] The Court did not authorize any particular type of body search in that case, focusing instead on the constitutionality of a 16–hour detention designed to produce the drugs through the "call of nature."[9] It also declined to consider "what level of suspicion, if any, is required for nonroutine border searches such as strip, body cavity, or involuntary x-ray searches." But the Court emphasized that "not only is the expectation of privacy less at the border than in the interior, but the Fourth Amendment balance between the interests of the Government and the privacy right of the individual is struck much more favorably to the Government at the border."[10] Moreover, in a concurring opinion, Justice Stevens argued that the defendant's refusal to undergo an x-ray test legitimated the detention. In short, the overall tone of the majority and concurring opinions in *Montoya de Hernandez* suggests that some forms of bodily intrusions will be allowed at the border on less than probable cause.[11]

The lower courts have permitted body searches at the border on less than probable cause for some time, relying on the rationale expressed in *Montoya de Hernandez.*[12] Some lower courts have also authorized a lesser showing for investigative body searches at other locales, at least for the least intrusive procedures (such as blood and urine tests).[13]

(c) The Reasonable Manner Requirement. With respect to the conduct of the search, the Court looked at several factors in upholding the blood test in *Schmerber.* First, the test was an effective means of determining blood alcohol levels. Second, it involved "virtually no risk, trauma, or pain." And finally, it was conducted in a hospital environment, by a trained physician and in accordance with medical practices, thus minimizing any negative effects. These three requirements state the minimum limitations on performance of emergency bodily intrusions.[14]

In both *Schmerber* and *Murphy,* there are additional intimations that, to be reasonable, a warrantless search of the body must be the least intrusive method available to the police. In *Schmerber,* the Court noted that the defendant there was "not one of the

---

8. On the difference between probable cause and "reasonable suspicion," see § 11.03(a).

9. See § 3.02(c) for analysis of this aspect of the case.

10. See § 13.05 for further discussion of border searches.

11. The Supreme Court has also authorized *suspicionless* blood tests, urinalysis and breathalyzer tests designed to detect drug and alcohol use when the results will not be used for criminal prosecution. See § 13.09(b).

12. See, e.g., *United States v. Couch,* 688 F.2d 599 (9th Cir.1982).

13. See, e.g., *Ewing v. State,* 160 Ind. App. 138, 310 N.E.2d 571 (1974) (warrantless taking of urine sample proper). See also, *United States ex rel. Guy v. McCauley,* 385 F.Supp. 193 (E.D.Wis. 1974) (search of vagina invalid, not because no probable cause, but because not conducted "by skilled medical technicians.").

14. Procedures for conducting nonexigent searches of the body are discussed in § 5.06(c)

few who on grounds of fear, concern for health, or religious scruple might prefer some other means of testing, such as the 'breathalyzer' test petitioner refused," although it went on to state that "[w]e need not decide whether such wishes would have to be respected." In *Murphy,* the Court stressed that the police action was not a full search of the person. But in *Montoya de Hernandez,* the Court, quoting from cases involving other types of searches and seizures, emphasized that "[t]he fact that the protection of the public might, in the abstract, have been accomplished by 'less intrusive' means does not, in itself, render the search unreasonable." [15] Further, "[a]uthorities must be allowed 'to graduate their response to the demands of any particular situation.' " [16] Whatever the validity of this point of view in the context of other types of searches, it is not appropriate where bodily intrusions are involved. In *Montoya de Hernandez,* for instance, when the defendant had not "produced" the suspected evidence after 16 hours of detention, the government resorted to an involuntary rectal examination, despite the availability of an x-ray. The Supreme Court did not consider the viability of either alternative, but had it done so, it should have required that the government use the less intrusive method of discovering the drugs given the dignity interests involved.

9.03 Houses, Papers and Effects

Most warrantless searches for evidence in homes and other areas are governed by either the search incident, hot pursuit or automobile exceptions.[17] Occasionally, however, police may have reason to believe that evidence in a house or container will disappear, even though no suspect or vehicle is involved. In *United States v. Chadwick,*[18] for instance, the Supreme Court required a warrant prior to a non-exigent search of a footlocker, but noted that a warrant would not be required where officers have "reason to believe that the footlocker contained explosives or other inherently dangerous items, or that it contained evidence which would lose its value unless the footlocker were opened at once." The *Chadwick* dissenters added that where an immediate search would "facilitate the apprehension of confederates or the termination of continuing criminal activity," a warrantless action might be permitted.

As *Chadwick's* reference to "dangerous items" suggests, protection of the public may also justify a warrantless search. For

---

15. See *United States v. Sharpe,* 470 U.S. 675, 105 S.Ct. 1568 (1985), discussed in § 3.02(b) (field detention of person).

16. Quoting *United States v. Place,* 462 U.S. 696, 103 S.Ct. 2637 (1983), discussed in § 11.02(b) (detention of luggage).

17. See §§ 6.04; 8.04; § 7.01.

18. 433 U.S. 1, 97 S.Ct. 2476 (1977), discussed in § 7.02.

instance, in *Mincey v. Arizona*,[19] the Supreme Court quoted favorably a lower court opinion which stated that "[t]he need to protect or preserve life or avoid serious injury is justification for what would be otherwise illegal absent an exigency or emergency."[20] This language can apply in a number of contexts. For instance, in *State v. McCleary*,[21] the Arizona Supreme Court upheld a warrantless search for bound and gagged robbery victims. In *United States v. Brock*,[22] the Ninth Circuit sanctioned a warrantless search of a motor home to avoid a possible explosion caused by chemicals used in making methamphetamine. The American Law Institute's Code of Pre–Arraignment Procedure probably provides an accurate summary of the law. It allows warrantless entries upon reasonable cause to believe that the premises contain: (1) individuals in imminent danger of death or serious bodily harm; (2) things imminently likely to burn, explode, or otherwise cause death, serious bodily harm, or substantial destruction of property; and (3) things subject to seizure . . . which will cause or be used to cause death or serious bodily harm if their seizure is delayed."[23]

The common thread joining all of these warrantless searches is that the nature of the evidence being sought, or the danger involved, creates a "compelling urgency" to act immediately. If the warrant requirement is to retain some viability, this justification should be interpreted narrowly. Thus, in *Mincey,* the Court emphasized that where there is neither an arrest or a pursuit, and there is "no danger to life or limb," a warrantless search is not permitted, regardless of the seriousness the crime being investigated. As is true with body searches, a warrantless search of other areas for evanescent evidence (or endangered individuals) should: (1) be based on probable cause to believe that an immediate search is necessary to obtain the the evidence or avert the harm; (2) offer an effective means of preventing the threat; (3) be limited in scope to the purpose of the search; and (4) be reasonably conducted.

Another limitation on searches of houses and effects that has been imposed by some lower courts, analogous to that found in search incident and hot pursuit jurisprudence,[24] is that the compelling urgency not be created by the police. Thus, for instance, in *United States v. Curran*,[25] the Ninth Circuit invalidated a warrantless entry when it occurred after agents knocked on the door of a house they knew to contain marijuana. As the court put it, "the officers consciously established the condition which the government now points to as an exigent circumstance." Some

19. 437 U.S. 385, 98 S.Ct. 2408 (1978).

20. *Wayne v. United States,* 318 F.2d 205 (D.C.Cir.1963).

21. 116 Ariz. 244, 568 P.2d 1142 (1977).

22. 667 F.2d 1311 (9th Cir.1982).

23. ALI, Model Code of Pre–Arraignment § 260.5.

24. See § 6.04(b)(2); § 8.03.

25. 498 F.2d 30 (9th Cir.1974).

courts have called this latter limitation a "good faith" requirement. According to *United States v. Allard*,[26] "[g]ood faith means
not acting with the intent improperly to circumvent the warrant
requirement by purposefully precipitating a situation, 'through
illegal conduct,' in which the destruction of evidence or contraband is likely."

9.04　Conclusion

In circumstances where the search incident, hot pursuit, and
automobile exceptions do not apply, the "evanescent evidence"
and "endangered person" exceptions to the warrant requirement
permit searches of persons, houses, papers and effects when:

(1) There is reason to believe (which in most cases should
mean probable cause to believe) that an immediate search is
necessary to prevent the disappearance of evidence or serious
harm to a person, and the exigency is not police-created.

(2) The search is otherwise reasonable. In the case of bodily
intrusions, this requirement means, at the least: (a) that the
procedure used is effective at obtaining the sought-after evidence;
(b) that it does not involve a significant amount of pain or trauma;
and (c) that the medical procedures followed are appropriate and
necessary. Analogous requirements presumably apply to searches
of houses, papers and effects. Assuming these requirements are
met, it is doubtful that the search must be the least intrusive
means of obtaining the evidence.

BIBLIOGRAPHY

Mascolo, Edward. The Emergency Doctrine Exception to the
　　Warrant Requirement Under the Fourth Amendment. 22
　　Buffalo L.Rev. 419 (1973).

Salken, Barbara. Balancing Exigency and Privacy in Warrantless
　　Searches to Prevent Destruction of Evidence: The Need for a
　　Rule. 39 Hastings L.J. 283 (1988).

Sarnacki, David. Analyzing the Reasonableness of Bodily Intru-
　　sions [Note]. 68 Marq.L.Rev. 130 (1984).

Strossen, Nadine. The Fourth Amendment in the Balance: Accu-
　　rately Setting the Scales Through the Least Intrusive Alterna-
　　tive Analysis. 63 N.Y.U.L.Rev. 1173 (1988).

26.　634 F.2d 1182 (9th Cir.1980).

Chapter Ten

PLAIN VIEW

10.01 Introduction

The so-called "plain view" exception to the warrant requirement was birthed in *Coolidge v. New Hampshire.*[1] The central
issue in *Coolidge* was whether the police could seize and then
search cars belonging to Coolidge without a warrant (the warrant
the police possessed being invalid). The state argued that even
though the warrant was deficient, evidence procured from one of
the cars should still be admissible, because the car was in "plain
view" from both the public street and from inside the house where
Coolidge was arrested. A plurality of the Court, in an opinion by
Justice Stewart, rejected this claim, noting that, "in the vast
majority of cases, *any* evidence seized by police will be in plain
view, at least at the moment of seizure." Thus, the mere fact that
the police could see the car from the public street did not give
them authority to search it. However, the Court went on to hold
that, if the police are already lawfully *in* an area such as a house
or car, evidence which is "immediately apparent as such" and
which is discovered "inadvertently" may be *seized.* When a
search is already underway, seizure of evidence in plain view
works no additional intrusion. "As against the minor peril to
Fourth Amendment protections, there is a major gain in effective
law enforcement."

From the foregoing, it should be clear that the plain view
doctrine enunciated in *Coolidge* is designed to permit warrantless
seizures, as opposed to searches. The doctrine can be more precisely stated as follows: police may seize items without a warrant
authorizing such seizure if (1) their intrusion into the area in
which the evidence is located is lawful; (2) the items are "immediately apparent" as evidence of criminal activity; and (3) the
discovery of the evidence is "inadvertent." As the following
discussion makes clear, the *Coolidge* plurality's holding on the
first element seems to have withstood the test of time, while the
second and third elements of the rule have been modified significantly.

10.02 Prior Valid Intrusion

In *Coolidge,* the Court stated:

[P]lain view *alone* is never enough to justify the warrantless
seizure of evidence. This is simply a corollary of the familiar
principle . . . that no amount of probable cause can justify a

1. 403 U.S. 443, 91 S.Ct. 2022 (1971).

209

warrantless search or seizure absent "exigent circumstances." Incontrovertible testimony of the senses that an incriminating object is on premises belonging to a criminal suspect may establish the fullest possible measure of probable cause. But even where the object is contraband, this Court has repeatedly stated and enforced the basic rule that the police may not enter and make a warrantless seizure.

This passage from *Coolidge* distinguishes between plain view seizures from public places and plain view seizures from private premises. If a police officer sees marijuana on a public sidewalk, he may surely seize it without a warrant. In this situation, as discussed elsewhere in this book,[2] no search occurs. But suppose, instead, that the officer is walking on the public sidewalk and sees the marijuana inside one's home or car, through a window? In this situation, despite the existence of probable cause, the plain view doctrine would not permit intrusion into the house or vehicle to seize the evidence; such action would constitute a "search" which must be authorized in some other way.[3]

Of course, authorization to enter premises might derive from a number of sources, including search and arrest warrants, other exceptions to the warrant requirement, and legitimate non-investigative operations of government agencies. Once this authorization exists, the plain view doctrine is often unnecessary. Illustrative is *Colorado v. Bannister,*[4] in which a police officer approached a stopped vehicle in order to issue a traffic citation. Standing by the front door of the car, the officer happened to see, in "plain view," chrome lug nuts which matched a police radio description of some of those recently stolen in the vicinity, and observed also that the occupants of the car met the radio description of those suspected of the crime. The Supreme Court's per curiam decision upheld the officer's seizure of the lug nuts and other evidence, not on plain view grounds, but under the "automobile exception" announced in *Carroll v. United States,*[5] which permits warrantless searches of cars, and seizures and search of items therein, when there is probable cause to believe the car contains the items and some sort of exigency exists. The probable cause came from sighting the subjects matching the radio description, and the inherent mobility of the car provided the exigency. The Court rightly concluded that the automobile exception authorized both

2. See § 4.03.

3. If, on the other hand, the marijuana were seen inside a *container* on the sidewalk, a seizure could take place, as the Fourth Amendment does not protect a container that somehow "reveals the nature of its contents." *Arkansas*

v. Sanders, 442 U.S. 753, 99 S.Ct. 2586 (1979).

4. 449 U.S. 1, 101 S.Ct. 42 (1980).

5. 267 U.S. 132, 45 S.Ct. 280 (1925), discussed in § 7.01.

the intrusion *and* the seizure of the lug nuts; the plain view doctrine was not applicable.

In other situations, on the other hand, the plain view doctrine may come into play because the original authorization does not clearly permit seizure of the items in question. For instance, as discussed in connection with the particularity requirement,[6] when the police have a valid warrant to search a house, they may seize not only items in the warrant but also evidence that is not listed, if it is found in plain view in an area the warrant allows them to search. Similarly, evidence found by the police in hot pursuit of a suspect may be seized even though it is not a weapon that the suspect could use to escape or harm the officers.[7] And, as discussed in a later chapter,[8] police may seize evidence found during a lawful consent search even if it is not the evidence the police or the consentor contemplated when the consent was given. Other plain view seizures have been upheld when executed by government officers who were: (1) accompanying an arrestee to his room;[9] (2) investigating a fire in a home;[10] (3) conducting an inventory search of a car;[11] (4) searching for a Vehicle Identification Number;[12] and (5) in a car rolling up a window to protect it against the rain.[13]

The scenarios in which the plain view doctrine could operate are as numerous as the situations in which police may validly intrude upon private premises. The important point to remember is that the doctrine does not justify the predicate intrusion.

10.03 Items Which May Be Seized

The *Coolidge* plurality opinion made two important statements about the type of evidence which may be seized under the plain view doctrine. First, it reiterated the Supreme Court's rejection, six years earlier in *Warden v. Hayden,*[14] of the so-called "mere evidence" rule. This rule had required the government to obtain a subpoena, challengeable through judicial process, whenever it sought evidence other than contraband, an instrumentality or crime, or a fruit of crime; reliance on a warrant or a warrant exception to obtain such evidence was impermissible. The rationale for this rule grew from a concern that private papers and the

---

6. See § 5.04.

7. *Warden v. Hayden,* 387 U.S. 294, 87 S.Ct. 1642 (1967), discussed in § 8.04.

8. See § 12.03.

9. *Washington v. Chrisman,* 455 U.S. 1, 102 S.Ct. 812 (1982), discussed in § 6.04(a).

10. *Michigan v. Tyler,* 436 U.S. 499, 98 S.Ct. 1942 (1978), discussed in § 13.04.

11. *South Dakota v. Opperman,* 428 U.S. 364, 96 S.Ct. 3092 (1976), discussed in § 13.07(a).

12. *New York v. Class,* 475 U.S. 106, 106 S.Ct. 960 (1986), discussed in § 7.03(b).

13. *Harris v. United States,* 390 U.S. 234, 88 S.Ct. 992 (1968) (per curiam).

14. 387 U.S. 294, 87 S.Ct. 1642 (1967).

like should receive special protection.[15] In *Hayden,* however, the Court noted that the Fourth Amendment's language did not make a distinction between "mere evidence" and other types of evidence, and concluded that "[privacy] is disturbed no more by a search directed to a purely evidentiary object than it is by a search directed to an instrumentality, fruit, or contraband." Thus, "[a] magistrate can intervene in both situations."

But while the *Coolidge* Court did not depart from *Hayden's* teaching that "mere evidence" may be seized without resorting to a subpoena, it also wanted to ensure that the plain view doctrine it announced would not encourage the type of behavior associated with the infamous "general warrants" of colonial times, which had authorized seizure of any object the executing officers thought relevant. Thus, the plurality required that items seized as evidence of criminal activity must be "immediately apparent as such." As Justice Stewart explained, "the 'plain view' doctrine may not be used to extend a general exploratory search from one object to another until something incriminating at last emerges." Here he cited *Stanley v. Georgia,*[16] in which the three justices who reached the Fourth Amendment issue found that the warrantless seizure of film cannisters, which later proved to contain obscene films, was not permissible even though the cannisters had been in plain view, because their contents had not been.

However, in *Texas v. Brown,*[17] the Court made clear that the police need not be *certain* that the item seized is evidence of criminal activity. In *Brown,* a police officer stopped the defendant's car at a routine driver's license checkpoint late at night. As Brown reached across the passenger seat to open the glove compartment and look for his license, the officer observed him drop an opaque green party balloon, knotted at the opening, into the passenger's seat. Upon seeing the balloon, the officer shifted his position to obtain a view of the glove compartment. He noticed, with the help of a flashlight, that it contained several small plastic vials, quantities of loose white powder, and an open bag of party balloons. The officer eventually seized the green balloon, which later proved to contain heroin.

The Texas Court of Criminal Appeals, in reversing Brown's conviction, held that in order for the plain view doctrine to apply, the officer had to know that "incriminatory evidence was before him when he seized the balloon." A unanimous Supreme Court reversed, holding that *Coolidge* had not required such a high degree of certainty as to the nature of the seized item; to the

15. See, e.g., *Gouled v. United States,* 255 U.S. 298, 41 S.Ct. 261 (1921), discussed in § 5.06(a).

16. 394 U.S. 557, 89 S.Ct. 1243 (1969).

17. 460 U.S. 730, 103 S.Ct. 1535 (1983).

extent the phrase "immediately apparent" connoted otherwise, it "was very likely an unhappy choice of words." Instead, concluded the Court, all that is required to meet this criterion of the plain view doctrine is probable cause. Here, the officer knew from previous narcotics arrests and discussions with other officers that balloons tied in the manner Brown's balloon was tied frequently contained narcotics. "The fact that [the officer] could not see through the opaque fabric of the balloon is all but irrelevant; the distinctive character of the balloon itself spoke volumes as to its contents—particularly to the trained eye of the officer."

Although the Court's equation of the "immediately apparent as such" language in *Coolidge* with probable cause seems sensible, the fact that the Court felt the need to reach this question on the facts in *Brown* is somewhat troubling. All three of the opinions in *Brown* assumed that the plain view doctrine authorized the officer's intrusion into the car to obtain the balloon. But, as pointed out earlier in this chapter,[18] the plain view doctrine traditionally has authorized only seizure, once there has been a valid intrusion.[19] It is highly likely that the officer's reach into the car and the ensuing search of the balloon in *Brown* was justified under the automobile exception to the warrant requirement,[20] given the Court's finding that probable cause existed. But recognition of this fact should have obviated the discussion of the plain view doctrine.

While *Brown* held that police need only probable cause in order to meet the second element of the plain view exception, *Arizona v. Hicks*[21] established that a *lesser* degree of suspicion is insufficient to meet this element. In *Hicks,* an officer validly in an apartment for the purpose of investigating a shooting incident spotted two sets of expensive stereo components which he suspected were stolen. In order to check their serial numbers, he moved some of the components. The state conceded that at the time the officer moved the components he had only a reasonable suspicion that the equipment was stolen.

The Supreme Court held, 6–3, in an opinion by Justice Scalia, that the officer's moving of the components was a "search" of the equipment that required probable cause. The officer's act was a search because it involved an invasion of the defendant's privacy beyond that authorized by the initial intrusion to investigate the shooting. It required probable cause because to hold otherwise would "cut the 'plain view' doctrine loose from its theoretical and

18. See § 10.02.

19. Since *Brown*, however, the Court has also held that a warrantless *inspection* of an item police have probable cause to believe is evidence of crime is justified as well. *Arizona v. Hicks*, 480

U.S. 321, 107 S.Ct. 1149 (1987), discussed below.

20. See Chapter Seven.

21. 480 U.S. 321, 107 S.Ct. 1149 (1987).

practical moorings." While efficiency concerns permit warrant-less plain view seizures, "[n]o reason is apparent why an object should routinely be seizable on lesser grounds, during an unrelat-ed search and seizure, than would have been needed to obtain a warrant for that same object if it had been known to be on the premises." To the dissent's argument that the officer's search in this case was merely "cursory" and therefore should be justified if based on reasonable suspicion, Scalia stated: "[w]e are unwilling to send police and judges into a new thicket of Fourth Amendment law, to seek a creature of uncertain description that is neither a plain-view inspection nor yet a 'full-blown search'".

Note that *Hicks* allows, for the first time, warrantless "plain view searches" as well as warrantless seizures, so long as there is probable cause. That is, if police validly on premises develop probable cause to believe an item is evidence of criminal activity, they may not only seize that item without a warrant, but conduct a warrantless "search" of it as well. In most instances, such a preliminary inspection is preferable because it will help avoid unnecessary seizures. In others, however, it might tend to expand the scope of the plain view doctrine, which has traditionally authorized only seizures. Just as the Court has held that the "automobile exception" permits a warrantless search of all con-tainers within the automobile which police have probable cause to believe contain evidence of crime,[22] *Hicks* may be construed to allow warrantless searches of all containers in a house which police have probable cause to believe contain such evidence.

Although the name of the plain view doctrine obviously focus-es on what police discern visually, there is no reason, in theory,[23] to limit the doctrine's reach to such cases. If police are validly on premises and smell an odor or feel an object that gives them probable cause to believe an item is evidence of criminal activity, they should be able to seize it without a warrant as well.[24] Similarly, whatever "items" police "plainly hear" from a lawful listening point is also admissible. This situation most commonly arises during properly authorized electronic surveillance, when police hear conversation about an offense or offenses which were not the original reason for the interception described in the surveillance warrant. Under Title III of the Omnibus Crime Control and Safe Streets Act of 1968, this information may be used in court if specific procedures are followed.[25]

---

22. See § 7.04.

23. But see, Comment, "The Case Against a Plain Feel Exception to the Warrant Requirement," 54 Chi.L.Rev. 683 (1987) (giving practical reasons for limiting the plain view doctrine to visi-ble items).

24. Cf. *United States v. Place*, 462 U.S. 696, 103 S.Ct. 2637 (1983) (dictum holding that dog sniff of luggage lawful-ly detained is not a "search").

25. 18 U.S.C.A. § 2517(5), discussed in § 14.03(c)(3).

10.04   Inadvertence and Pretextual Searches

A third requirement of the plain view doctrine announced by the *Coolidge* plurality, now eliminated, was that the discovery of the evidence must be inadvertent. This requirement was thought to flow from the general proposition that, when there is no exigency, a warrant must be obtained. As Justice Stewart stated in *Coolidge:*

> The rationale of the [plain view] exception to the warrant requirement . . . is that a plain view seizure not turn an initially valid (and therefore limited) search into a "general" one, wh[ere] the inconvenience of procuring a warrant to cover an inadvertent discovery is great. But where the discovery is anticipated, where the police know in advance the location of the evidence and intend to seize it, the situation is altogether different. The requirement of a warrant imposes no inconvenience in a legal system that regards warrantless searches as "*per se* unreasonable" in the absence of "exigent circumstances."

Thus, according to the *Coolidge* plurality, evidence that is "immediately apparent as such" and seized after a valid intrusion was still inadmissible if police anticipated its discovery and did not obtain a warrant authorizing a search for it.

The problem that arose as a result of the inadvertence requirement was determining precisely when a discovery was "inadvertent" for purposes of the plain view exception. Most courts allowed the exception to apply so long as the police did not have, prior to the search, probable cause to believe the evidence was on the premises; any lesser degree of suspicion that the evidence was there did not bar a finding of inadvertence.[26] This position reflects the reality that if the police do not have probable cause, they cannot obtain a warrant for the desired item even if they want to. On the other hand, such a stance might encourage an officer, acting on a mere "hunch" that evidence of criminal activity can be found on certain premises, to "create" a trivial purpose for entering the premises (e.g., a residential safety inspection or a traffic stop), hoping that in the ensuing search he will come across the evidence he really wants, without having to develop probable cause or seek a warrant.[27] In order to discourage such pretextual searches, one might advocate that *any* specific pre-search suspicion that evidence is on the premises should invalidate its seizure,

26. See, e.g., *United States v. Hare,* 589 F.2d 1291 (6th Cir.1979); *United States v. Hillstrom,* 533 F.2d 209 (5th Cir.1976), cert. denied 429 U.S. 1038, 97 S.Ct. 734 (1977); *United States v. Medows,* 540 F.Supp. 490 (S.D.N.Y. 1982).

27. See, e.g., *United States v. Smith,* 799 F.2d 704 (11th Cir.1986), in which a valid arrest for "weaving" from one lane to another was determined to be pretextual and the subsequent seizure of narcotics from the car illegal.

unless the police obtain a warrant for that evidence or give a reasonable, non-pretextual explanation of why they did not obtain such a warrant.[28] A "non-pretextual explanation" would consist of proof that the officer's action was of a type *routinely* taken, as a matter of departmental policy, under the circumstances in question.[29]

In *Horton v. California*,[30] the Supreme Court mooted the debate over whether inadvertence should be equated with a lack of probable cause by eliminating the inadvertence requirement altogether. The majority opinion, by Justice Stevens, noted that this requirement only attracted a plurality of the Court in *Coolidge* and in any event was unnecessary to that decision. It then concluded that, contrary to Justice Stewart's statements in *Coolidge*, the inadvertence requirement was not needed to protect against general warrants. In doing so, the Court also seemed to dismiss the concern over pretextual searches described above:

> [E]venhanded law enforcement is best achieved by the application of objective standards of conduct, rather than standards that depend upon the subjective state of mind of the officer. The fact that an officer is interested in an item of evidence and fully expects to find it in the course of a search should not invalidate its seizure if the search is confined in area and duration by the terms of the warrant or a valid exception to the warrant requirement. . . . [I]f he or she has a valid warrant to search for one item and merely a suspicion concerning the second, whether or not it amounts to probable cause, we fail to see why that suspicion should immunize the second item from seizure if it is found during a lawful search for the first.

Stevens used the facts in *Horton* to illustrate the conclusion that the inadvertence requirement is unnecessary to protect against illegitimate intrusions. After investigating a robbery, an officer filed an application for a warrant which referred to police reports describing both the proceeds of the robbery and the weapons used. However, the warrant actually issued authorized a search only for the proceeds, including three specifically described rings. During the subsequent search, the officer did not find the

---

28. See Note, "The Pretext Problem Revisited: A Doctrinal Exploration of Bad Faith in Search and Seizure Cases," 70 Boston Univ.L.Rev. 111 (1990).

29. Compare *United States v. Cardona–Rivera*, 904 F.2d 1149 (7th Cir. 1990) (officers' testimony that car later found to contain drugs was stopped for a traffic violation "not worthy of belief," since officers were not traffic police and did not have traffic books), with *State v. Bolton*, 111 N.M. 28, 801 P.2d 98 (1990) (stated purpose of police roadblock to detect license violations not a pretext to enforce immigration or drug laws even though Border Patrol officers were also present and police asked to search all vehicles referred to secondary checkpoint).

30. 496 U.S. 128, 110 S.Ct. 2301 (1990).

rings but did find the weapons. He later admitted that when he entered the house he had been interested in finding not just the rings but other evidence connected with the robbery. According to the majority, despite the lack of inadvertence, no privacy interests would be vindicated by excluding the weapons. In conducting the search, the officer did not go beyond the boundaries prescribed by the warrant. "Indeed, if the three rings and other items named in the warrant had been found at the outset—or if petitioner had them in his possession and had responded to the warrant by producing them immediately—no search for weapons could have taken place."

Justice Brennan's dissent, joined by Justice Marshall, claimed that since the facts of *Horton* did not involve an obviously pretextual search its holding did not authorize such searches. Unfortunately, such a view is not easily squared with the majority's language emphasizing the objective nature of the Fourth Amendment inquiry and the legitimacy of any search authorized by the Court's current rules. Other cases reflect a similar stance. Of particular interest here, in *United States v. Villamonte–Marquez*,[31] the Court refused to consider the defendant's pretext argument, on the ground that the officers' actions should be judged solely according to whether they met objective Fourth Amendment requirements.[32]

10.05 Conclusion

The principles relevant to plain view analysis can be summarized as follows:

(1) A prior valid intrusion is required, based on a warrant, an exception to the warrant requirement, or some other circumstance (such as a lawful inspection).

(2) Items not contemplated by the initial authorization may nonetheless be seized (or searched) without a warrant, so long as—by look, feel, smell or sound—they give police probable cause to believe they are evidence of criminal activity.

BIBLIOGRAPHY

Burkoff, John M. Rejoinder: Truth, Justice, and the American Way—or Professor Haddad's "Hard Choices." 18 U.Mich.L. Ref. 695 (1985).

31. 462 U.S. 579, 103 S.Ct. 2573 (1983), discussed in § 13.06(d).

32. See also, *Scott v. United States,* 436 U.S. 128, 98 S.Ct. 1717 (1978) and *Maryland v. Macon,* 472 U.S. 463, 105 S.Ct. 2778 (1985), which also appear to hold that, whatever might have been the case in the past, Fourth Amendment analysis is now "wholly objective."

Butterfoss, Edwin. Solving the Pretext Puzzle: The Importance of Ulterior Motives and Fabrications in the Supreme Court's Fourth Amendment Pretext Doctrine. 79 Ken.L.Rev. 1 (1991).

Haddad, James B. Pretextual Fourth Amendment Activity: Another Viewpoint. 18 Mich.J.L.Ref. 639 (1985).

Moylan, Charles E., Jr. Plain View Doctrine: Unexpected Child of the Great "Search Incident" Geography Battle. 26 Mercer L.Rev. 1047 (1975).

Wallin, Howard. The Uncertain Scope of the Plain View Doctrine. 16 Balt.L.Rev. 266 (1987).

Chapter Eleven

STOP AND FRISK

11.01 Introduction

In *Terry v. Ohio*,[1] the Supreme Court recognized for the first time that a search or seizure might be constitutional on less than probable cause. Specifically, *Terry* held that a frisk, or patdown of outer clothing, is authorized when the police have "reasonable suspicion," a lesser level of certainty than probable cause. It also strongly suggested that the predicate "stop," or temporary detention, is also permissible on reasonable suspicion. The "stop and frisk" doctrine thus announced represents an exception to both the warrant and probable cause requirements.

Long before *Terry,* legislatures had authorized stops and frisks on less than probable cause. For instance, as early as 1942, several states had adopted the Uniform Arrest Act,[2] which empowered an officer to stop a person in public based upon "reasonable ground to suspect" that the person "is committing, has committed, or is about to commit a crime," and then search him "for a dangerous weapon" if the officer has "reasonable ground to believe that he is in danger."[3] By 1967, the stop and frisk concept had been endorsed by both the American Law Institute,[4] the President's Commission on Law Enforcement and Administration of Justice,[5] and several lower courts.[6]

Thus, when the Supreme Court decided *Terry* in 1968, it was not working on a blank slate. In *Terry*, a detective of 30 years' experience noticed Terry and a companion hovering about a street corner for an extended length of time. He observed them pace alternately along an identical route, pause to stare in the same store window some 24 times and confer on the corner immediately thereafter. A third man appeared to join in one of these conferences, left swiftly, and was followed and rejoined a few minutes later by the other two. Suspecting that the men were contemplating a daylight robbery, the detective approached the men, identi-

1. 392 U.S. 1, 88 S.Ct. 1868 (1968).

2. Interstate Commission on Crime, The Handbook on Interstate Crime Control 86–89 (1942).

3. See, e.g., Del.Code tit. 11, §§ 1901–12 (1953); N.H.Rev.Stat.Ann. 594:1–25 (1955).

4. ALI, Model Code of Pre–Arraignment Procedure § 2.02 (Tent.Draft No. 1, 1966). The ALI eventually adopted a modified version of this draft, printed in § 11.07.

5. President's Commission on Law Enforcement and Administration of Justice, The Challenge of Crime in a Free Society 95 (1967).

6. *State v. Williams,* 97 N.J.Super. 573, 235 A.2d 684 (1967), cert. denied 397 U.S. 1069, 90 S.Ct. 1510 (1970); *People v. Rivera,* 14 N.Y.2d 441, 252 N.Y.S.2d 458, 201 N.E.2d 32 (1964), cert. denied 379 U.S. 978, 85 S.Ct. 679 (1965).

fied himself as a policeman, and asked their names. When they mumbled a response, the officer, fearing they were armed, spun Terry around and patted down his outer clothing. He felt and subsequently removed a revolver from Terry's overcoat pocket, and charged him with carrying a concealed weapon.

In upholding this action, Chief Justice Warren, who wrote the opinion for the Court, stated:

> We merely hold that where a police officer observes unusual conduct which leads him reasonably to conclude in light of his experience that criminal activity may be afoot and that the persons with whom he is dealing may be armed and presently dangerous, where in the course of investigating this behavior he identifies himself as a policeman and makes reasonable inquiries, and where nothing in the initial stages of the encounter serves to dispel his reasonable fear for his own or others' safety, he is entitled for the protection of himself and others in the area to conduct a carefully limited search of the outer clothing of such persons in an attempt to discover weapons which might be used to assault him. Such a search is a reasonable search under the Fourth Amendment, and any weapons seized may properly be introduced in evidence against the person from whom they were taken.

While the Court explicitly purported to "decide nothing today concerning the constitutional propriety of an investigative 'seizure' upon less than probable cause for purposes of 'detention' and/or interrogation," it shortly followed this disavowal with the declaration that "a police officer may in appropriate circumstances and in an appropriate manner approach a person for purposes of investigating possibly criminal behavior even though there is no probable cause to make an arrest."

The Court's rationale for approving stops and frisks on reasonable suspicion rather than probable cause came from the Reasonableness Clause of the Fourth Amendment. According to the Court, this clause requires an analysis of whether a given police action "was justified at its inception" and "was reasonably related in scope to the circumstances which justified the interference in the first place." The Court felt that the strong state interest in preventing criminal activity, combined with the relatively minor intrusion associated with a stop (as opposed to an arrest) and a frisk (as opposed to a full search), justified such actions on a lesser showing of suspicion than probable cause.

The *Terry* Court could have analyzed the constitutionality of stops and frisks in at least two other ways. It could have ruled that an investigative stop is not a "seizure" and that a frisk is not a "search," thus eliminating any Fourth Amendment regulation of these actions. But this approach would have immunized a vast segment of police conduct from constitutional challenge. Alternatively, after holding, as it did, that a seizure and search were involved, it could have adhered to the traditional "probable cause" language, but held that this standard varies depending upon the circumstances. This was the approach the Court adopted for administrative searches in *Camara v. Municipal Court,*[7] decided a year earlier. There, the Court held that residential health and safety inspections require "probable cause", but also made clear that, given the "valid public interest" and "limited invasion" involved, the term in this context did not require *any* level of suspicion with respect to a particular house, but only a showing that the area as a whole required inspection. This "sliding scale" definition of probable cause has been criticized as well, as likely to convert the Fourth Amendment "into one immense Rohrshach blot."[8] As subsequent discussion will show, however, other than substituting the reasonable suspicion label, *Terry's* holding is very similar to this approach.[9] Indeed, the Court's application of *Terry* in later cases suggests that, without admitting to doing so, the Court has endorsed a sliding scale perspective on the Fourth Amendment when less intrusive seizures and searches are involved.

Terry raises four distinct issues: (1) the definition of "stop," which also requires defining the word "seizure" for Fourth Amendment purposes; (2) the justification for a stop and lesser seizures; (3) the justification for a frisk; and (4) the scope of the frisk. This chapter examines how the Supreme Court and the lower courts have addressed these issues, and then provides the American Law Institute's version of the stop and frisk rule, as an example of a comprehensive effort to deal with this difficult area.

11.02 Defining "Seizures" and "Stops"

(a) Of the Person. Until *Terry,* the Supreme Court's cases suggested that the only seizure of the person governed by the Fourth Amendment was an arrest. Once *Terry* recognized that the Reasonableness Clause applies to detentions short of arrest, it became important to discern the dividing line between arrests and other seizures; while arrests must be based on probable cause, stops and other seizures may be based on a lower level of certainty. As discussed in detail in this book's treatment of arrests,[10] distinguishing between an arrest and an investigative stop depends upon a number of factors, including the purpose of the detention (e.g., fingerprinting versus interrogation), its location

7. 387 U.S. 523, 87 S.Ct. 1727 (1967), discussed in § 13.02.

8. Amsterdam, "Perspectives on the Fourth Amendment," 58 Minn.L.Rev. 349 (1974).

9. See Slobogin, "The World Without a Fourth Amendment," 39 U.C.L.A. 1, 39–43 (1991).

10. See § 3.02.

(e.g., the field versus the stationhouse), and, probably most importantly, its duration (e.g., a temporary confrontation versus a custodial detention). The Supreme Court has been unwilling to set a precise time limit on stops, but has indicated that a twenty-minute detention is a *Terry* stop, not an arrest, so long as the police exercise "diligence" in expediting the detention, and are not unreasonable in failing to recognize or to pursue less intrusive alternatives.[11]

The focus here will be on the other end of the spectrum: when has a "seizure" of the person occurred so as to implicate the Fourth Amendment and the *Terry* balancing analysis? In *Terry*, the Court stated that "whenever a police officer accosts an individual and restrains his freedom to walk away, he has 'seized' that person." It also stated, however, that "not all personal intercourse between policemen and citizens involves 'seizures' of persons. Only when the officer, by means of force or show of authority, has in some way restrained the liberty of a citizen may we conclude that a seizure has occurred." The Supreme Court has since narrowed the definition of "seizure" even further, holding, in *California v. Hodari D.*,[12] that while restraint is a necessary condition for a seizure, it is not necessarily sufficient. Rather the question is a more complex one that is very fact specific. Thus, a close look at the cases is necessary.

In *United States v. Mendenhall*,[13] a twenty-two-year-old black woman was confronted in the Detroit airport by two plain-clothes DEA officials who identified themselves and asked her for her ticket and identification. After returning her ticket and license, the agents asked her why her ticket was not in her name and, when she became incoherent, asked her to accompany them to a private room in the airport. Two members of the Court, Justices Stewart and Rehnquist, felt that this confrontation was not a seizure and that therefore the agents did not need to meet the reasonable suspicion standard set forth in *Terry*. They stated that the test for determining when someone was "seized" under the Fourth Amendment should be when "a reasonable person would have believed that he was not free to leave," and suggested several factors which might be considered in determining whether this test was met: "[T]he threatening presence of several officers, the display of a weapon by an officer, some physical touching of the person of the citizen, or the use of language or tone of voice indicating that compliance with the officers' request might be compelled." None of the other members of the Court directly

---

11. *United States v. Sharpe,* 470 U.S. 675, 105 S.Ct. 1568 (1985), discussed in § 3.02(b).

12. 499 U.S. ___, 111 S.Ct. 1547 (1991).

13. 446 U.S. 544, 100 S.Ct. 1870 (1980).

addressed the seizure issue, however, in large part because it was not addressed by the lower courts. Thus, *Mendenhall* did not provide a clear message as to what constitutes a seizure.

In *Florida v. Royer*,[14] the Court was more explicit on the issue. *Royer* involved facts virtually identical to *Mendenhall* with one exception: the officers did not return Royer's ticket or driver's license. The Court held, 5–4, that under these circumstances, and when the officers did not indicate in any way that Royer was "free to depart," a Fourth Amendment seizure had taken place.

The Court has indicated that no seizure takes place, however, when police merely question an individual for a few moments, at least if the questioning occurs at his place of work. In *Immigration & Naturalization Service v. Delgado*,[15] the INS obtained two warrants authorizing a "survey" of the work force at a factory in southern California to determine whether any illegal aliens were present. The warrants were based on a probable cause showing that numerous illegal aliens were employed at the factory, but did not name any specific individuals. In executing the survey, several agents positioned themselves near the buildings' exits, while other agents dispersed throughout the factory questioning most, but not all, of the employees at their work stations. The agents displayed badges, carried walkie-talkies, and were armed, although no weapons were drawn. Employees were asked from one to three questions relating to their citizenship; if they gave credible answers, the questioning ended. Respondent Delgado and the three other respondents were all questioned in this manner and, after answering apparently satisfactorily, were left alone.

Justice Rehnquist, writing for a six-member majority, noted that in *Royer* the Court had implicitly permitted both questioning relating to one's identity and a request for identification; neither, by itself, constituted a Fourth Amendment seizure. He also pointed out that in *Brown v. Texas*,[16] in which the Court found a seizure did occur when police stopped and questioned the defendant, the officers had physically restrained the defendant after he refused to give his identity. Here, however, the respondents were questioned at their place of work and not physically detained. Only "if the person refuses to answer and the police take additional steps—such as those taken in *Brown*—to obtain an answer, . . . [does] the Fourth Amendment impose some minimal level of objective justification to validate the detention or seizure."

Justice Rehnquist also rejected the respondents' argument that the stationing of agents at the doors of the factory constituted

14. 460 U.S. 491, 103 S.Ct. 1319 (1983).

15. 466 U.S. 210, 104 S.Ct. 1758 (1984).

16. 443 U.S. 47, 99 S.Ct. 2637 (1979).

a seizure. He pointed out that the employees' freedom was already somewhat restricted by the demands of their workplace and that the surveys did not prevent the employees from pursuing their ordinary business. He went on to conclude that had the questioning taken place at the exits, it would have been no more a seizure than what occurred inside the factory. "[T]he mere possibility that [the employees] would be questioned if they sought to leave the buildings should not have resulted in any reasonable apprehension by any of them that they would be seized or detained in any meaningful way."

The Court reaffirmed *Delgado* and favorably cited Stewart's opinion in *Mendenhall* in another airport stop case, *Florida v. Rodriguez.*[17] There the Court held that a seizure did not occur when a plain-clothes officer approached the defendant in a public airport, showed his badge, obtained agreement from the defendant to talk, and requested him to move approximately 15 feet to where his companions were standing with another police officer. The Court termed these events "clearly the sort of consensual encounter that implicates no Fourth Amendment interest."

A unanimous Court also found no seizure in *Michigan v. Chesternut,*[18] where the defendant started running upon spying a police patrol car and the officers in the car accelerated to catch up with him "to see where he was going." The Court noted that the police did not activate a siren or flashers, command the defendant to halt, display any weapons, or operate the car so as to block the defendant's course. While admitting that operating a police car parallel to a running pedestrian could be "somewhat intimidating" it found that this action was not so intimidating that, under *Mendenhall's* test, the defendant could reasonably have believed that he was not free to disregard the police presence. The Court noted that a different situation might be presented if the officers had been on foot and visibly chased the defendant.

Yet, three terms later, the Court decided that even this latter situation does not result in a seizure for purposes of the fourth amendment. In *California v. Hodari D.,*[19] police in an unmarked vehicle came upon four or five youths huddled around a red car. When the youths saw the officers' vehicle they took flight, and the red car left at high speed. An officer gave chase to one of the youths, who tossed away crack cocaine just before being tackled. The defendant argued that at the time of the chase he had been "seized," and that the cocaine was inadmissible because the officers lacked reasonable suspicion at that point. In a 7–2 decision authored by Justice Scalia, the Court held that a mere show of

17. 469 U.S. 1, 105 S.Ct. 308 (1984).

18. 486 U.S. 567, 108 S.Ct. 1975 (1988).

19. 499 U.S. ___, 111 S.Ct. 1547 (1991).

authority, absent physical contact or submission to that authority, is not a seizure as that word is commonly understood, and is therefore not a seizure under the Fourth Amendment. Scalia also contended that this ruling would not encourage improper police behavior, "[s]ince policemen do not command 'Stop!' expecting to be ignored, or give chase hoping to be outrun . . ." The dissent, by Justice Stevens, argued that the attempted detention in this case presented a situation in which "a reasonable person would not feel free to leave." But the majority, as noted earlier, countered that this language, from *Mendenhall,* merely stated a necessary, rather than a sufficient, condition for a seizure.

The Court continued its movement away from *Mendenhall's* definition of seizure in *Florida v. Bostick.*[20] There, pursuant to a routine policy designed to detect drug trafficking, two police officers, one of them armed, boarded a bus and surveyed the passengers. Without any articulable suspicion, they asked to examine the defendant's ticket and identification, and then asked to search his luggage, advising him of his right to refuse consent. The Florida Supreme Court held that at this point the defendant was seized for purposes of the Fourth Amendment, and that the drugs found in his luggage were thus inadmissable. The Supreme Court decided, 6–3, that this holding was not necessarily correct. The Florida court had accepted the defendant's argument that with officers blocking his way to the exit he was not free to leave and that, in any event, leaving the bus was not feasible since the bus was about to depart. But the Supreme Court, in an opinion by Justice O'Connor, held that whether someone in the defendant's position felt free to leave was not the dispositive issue. O'Connor pointed out that the defendant would not have felt free to leave even if the police had not been there, given the imminent departure of the bus. His sense of constraint, according to O'Connor, "was the natural result of his decision to take the bus; it says nothing about whether or not the police conduct at issue was coercive."

Quoting from *Chesternut,* O'Connor stated that the proper test for determining whether a seizure took place was whether "a reasonable person . . . was not at liberty to ignore the police presence and go about his business." The case was remanded to the Florida Supreme Court to determine whether this was the case. However, the Court cautioned the state court that mere questioning by the police should not lead to a finding of coercion, relying in particular on *Delgado.* The police conduct must "have communicated to a reasonable person that the person was not free to decline the officers' requests or otherwise terminate the encoun-

20. 501 U.S. ___, 111 S.Ct. 2382 (1991).

ter." The Court also rejected the defendant's argument that he must have been seized because no reasonable person would freely consent to a search of luggage which he knows contains drugs. This argument was unpersuasive, stated O'Connor, because "the 'reasonable person' test presupposes an innocent person."

In dissent, Justice Marshall, joined by Justices Blackmun and Stevens, did not object to the majority's definition of seizure. Rather he focused on the fact that the officers never apprised the defendant of his right to refuse to answer questions, and argued that, under the circumstances, a reasonable person would have felt compelled to cooperate with the police. He also distinguished *Bostick* from *Delgado*, where workers wishing to avoid confrontation with government officials were free to walk around or even leave the factory, and would not have abandoned their personal belongings or been stranded in an unknown environment had they exercised the latter option.

While the Court's definition of seizure is acceptable, its application of that definition tortures the spirit of the Fourth Amendment, which is designed to regulate coercive government intrusions into privacy and autonomy. People who are questioned by armed police at their place of work (as in *Delgado*), asked to accompany a police officer elsewhere (as in *Mendenhall* and *Rodriguez*), chased by the police (as in *Chesternut* and *Hodari*), or confronted by armed officers in the cramped confines of a bus (as in *Bostick*) are unlikely to feel they are free to go about their business, especially if they are not told they may do so. At the same time, assuming that all of these cases involved seizures, applying *Terry's* balancing approach might produce the same result in at least some of them. For instance, in *Delgado*, the "warrant" obtained by the police was based on probable cause to believe there was a significant percentage of illegal aliens employed in the surveyed factory.[21] In *Rodriguez*, the seizure did not occur until after the defendant and his two companions acted furtively upon sighting plain-clothes officers, one told the other to "Get out of here," and the defendant made a half-hearted running effort. And in *Hodari*, the flight from the police, although something an innocent person might do, nonetheless gave police ample reason to believe some sort of investigation was called for. In contrast, the complete lack of suspicion in *Bostick*[22] should prevent any intrusion that would be unwanted by a reasonable person. The level of suspicion necessary before a seizure short of arrest may take place is addressed further in the next section.

21. For additional discussion of this "generalized" type of suspicion, see § 11.03(c)(3).

22. One court noted that in a sweep of 100 buses (potentially involving four to five thousand people), only seven arrests resulted. *United States v. Flowers*, 912 F.2d 707 (4th Cir.1990), cert. denied ___ U.S. ___, 111 S.Ct. 2895 (1991).

(b) Of Effects. While *Terry* and its progeny have focused on seizures of the person, a few cases have also addressed the validity of seizures of effects on less than probable cause. As with seizures of the person, both ends of the spectrum must be examined. On the one hand, probable cause is required for any seizure of personal property which, because of its owner's proximity to it, or desire to retain it, amounts to an arrest of the owner. Thus, in *United States v. Place*,[23] a 90–minute detention of the defendant's luggage at the airport to arrange for a dog sniff was held unconstitutional because of its duration, and "the failure of the agents to accurately inform respondent of the place to which they were transporting his luggage, of the length of time he might be dispossessed, and of what arrangements would be made for return of the luggage if the investigation dispelled the suspicion." This language suggests, conversely, that if luggage can be detained without interrupting a person's travel plans or other liberty interests, a seizure of luggage on less than probable cause would be permissible. Indeed, *Place* also stated that, under the *Terry* balancing test, "some brief detentions of personal effects may be so minimally intrusive of Fourth Amendment interests that strong countervailing governmental interests will justify a seizure based only on specific articulable facts that the property contains contraband or evidence of a crime."

Furthermore, consistent with the Court's cases concerning detentions of persons, at the far end of the spectrum there are some situations in which restraints on effects do not even amount to a seizure. For instance, in *United States v. Van Leeuwen*,[24] the police, contacted by a suspicious postal clerk, asked postal officials to hold two packages of coins for 29 hours while they investigated the situation and obtained a search warrant. Although a unanimous Court noted that the suspicious circumstances "certainly justified detention, without a warrant, while an investigation was made," it went on to hold that no suspicion was even necessary, since "[n]o interest protected by the Fourth Amendment was invaded by forwarding the packages the following day rather than the day when they were deposited." The warrantless police action did not invade either the defendant's privacy interest in the content of the packages or any possessory interest.

11.03 Permissible Grounds for Seizures and Stops

Generally, as *Terry* provided, a seizure is not permitted unless police possess at least a reasonable suspicion that criminal activity is afoot. But since *Terry*, the Court has sanctioned some types of seizures on less than reasonable suspicion, and has made it clear

23. 462 U.S. 696, 103 S.Ct. 2637 (1983).

24. 397 U.S. 249, 90 S.Ct. 1029 (1970).

that *Terry's* standard is not to be rigidly applied. In the discussion which follows, the Court's decisions applying the reasonable suspicion standard will be treated chronologically, in order to gain an historical perspective on the Court's evolving (and occasionally vacillating) approach. A separate discussion will focus on the sources of information upon which police may rely in deciding whether reasonable suspicion exists and the types of crimes which justify a stop.

(a) The Reasonable Suspicion Standard. In *Terry,* the Court defined reasonable suspicion as "specific and articulable facts" that lead the officer to believe "criminal activity is afoot." Such suspicion may not be based upon an "inchoate or unparticularized suspicion or 'hunch,'" but must be grounded on facts which, in light of the officer's experience, support "specific reasonable inferences" that justify the intrusion. The level of suspicion contemplated by this language is clearly something less than probable cause, although how much less has not been spelled out by the Court.[25] The Court's cases suggest that the level will vary, depending upon the level of intrusion on the one hand and the importance of the state's interest on the other.

Thus, in *Sibron v. New York,*[26] a companion case to *Terry,* the Court held that the "mere act of talking to a number of known addicts" and reaching into a pocket does not produce a reasonable inference that criminal activity is afoot sufficient to justify an officer's search of the pocket. In contrast, in *Peters v. New York,*[27] another companion case to *Terry,* the Court found that an off-duty officer had sufficient grounds for a stop and a patdown of two individuals when he saw them tiptoe down a hallway and run when they saw him. According to the Court, "deliberate furtive actions and flight at the approach of strangers or law officers are strong indicia of *mens rea.*"

The first major post-*Terry* decision to deal comprehensively with the reasonable suspicion standard was *United States v. Brignoni-Ponce.*[28] Like many other cases concerning the definition of reasonable suspicion, *Brignoni-Ponce* involved enforcement of the immigration laws, in this case by roving car patrols operating on roads near the border. Although the federal statute was unclear on their authority, in practice these patrols made random stops of cars in an effort to detect the entry of illegal aliens. One of these patrols stopped Brignoni-Ponce's car; after questioning

---

25. A survey of federal judges indicated that, on average, they would attribute a 31% level of certainty to a finding of reasonable suspicion (compared to 46% for probable cause). McCauliff, "Burdens of Proof: Degrees of Belief, Quanta of Evidence, or Constitutional Guarantee?" 35 Vand.L.Rev. 1293, 1325 (1982).

26. 392 U.S. 40, 88 S.Ct. 1889 (1968).

27. 392 U.S. 40, 88 S.Ct. 1912 (1968).

28. 422 U.S. 873, 95 S.Ct. 2574 (1975).

revealed that his two passengers had entered the country illegally, he was arrested and later convicted for transporting illegal aliens.

The government contended that, given the proportions of the immigration problem, it should be able to stop any persons near the border for "limited" questioning about their immigration status. The Supreme Court disagreed in a unanimous opinion, holding that, except at the border or its functional equivalents,[29] border patrol officers are prohibited from stopping vehicles unless they know of specific articulable facts, together with rational inferences from those facts, that a particular vehicle contains illegal aliens. Noting that the sole justification border patrol officers gave for the stop of Brignoni-Ponce was that he and his companions had appeared to be of Mexican ancestry, the Court reversed his conviction. The Court listed a number of factors the patrol could consider in deciding whether reasonable suspicion existed: the characteristics of the area where the vehicle is found and its proximity to the border, information about recent illegal border crossings in the area, the driver's behavior, aspects of the vehicle itself, *and* the appearance of the automobile's occupants. But it emphasized that the latter factor by itself could not justify a stop: "[t]he likelihood that any given person of Mexican ancestry is an alien is high enough to make Mexican appearance a relevant factor, but standing alone it does not justify stopping all Mexican-Americans to ask if they are aliens."

In *Delaware v. Prouse*,[30] the Court held inadmissible marijuana found by a police officer on the floor of a car he had stopped in order to check the driver's license and car registration. The officer's actions in stopping the car were prompted neither by his observance of a traffic or equipment violation nor by any suspicious behavior by any of the car's occupants. In finding this seizure violative of the Fourth Amendment, the Court stated that such "discretionary spot checks" were no less offensive than the roving border patrol stops it had earlier found impermissible in *Brignoni-Ponce*. Thus, an officer may stop an automobile to undertake a license check only when he holds an "articulable and reasonable suspicion that a motorist is unlicensed or that an automobile is not registered, or that either the vehicle or an occupant is otherwise subject to seizure for violation of law."

The same term it decided *Prouse*, the Court invalidated the seizure in *Brown v. Texas*.[31] In *Brown*, two police officers were cruising in a patrol car when they observed Brown and another man walking away from one another in an alley. Officer Venegas

---

29. At these locations, the Court has held a citizen has no reasonable expectation of privacy and is not entitled to the usual Fourth Amendment protection. See § 13.05(a).

30. 440 U.S. 648, 99 S.Ct. 1391 (1979).

31. 443 U.S. 47, 99 S.Ct. 2637 (1979).

later testified that both officers had believed their arrival either broke up or prevented a meeting between the two. Venegas got out of the patrol car and asked Brown to identify himself and explain his presence there; the other individual was not detained. Brown refused to identify himself and asserted that the officers had no right to stop him. Venegas replied that Brown was in a "high drug problem area;" the other officer then frisked Brown, but found nothing. Brown was arrested and later convicted under a Texas statute which makes it a criminal act for a person to refuse to give his name and address to an officer "who has lawfully stopped him and requested the information."

The Supreme Court concluded that reasonable suspicion did not exist on these facts. The sole justification the officers gave for the stop was that the situation "looked suspicious and we had never seen that subject in that area before." Although the area in which Brown was stopped did have a high incidence of drug traffic, the officers did not claim any specific misconduct on the part of Brown, nor did they believe he was armed. Reminiscent of its holding in *Sibron,* the Court stated:

> There is no indication in the record that it was unusual for people to be in the alley. The fact that the appellant was in a neighborhood frequented by drug users, standing alone, is not a basis for concluding that the appellant himself was engaged in criminal conduct. In short, the appellant's activity was no different from the activity of other pedestrians in that neighborhood.

Although the Court did not invalidate the statute under which Brown was arrested and convicted, it did hold that stops pursuant to it must be based on reasonable suspicion that the person stopped "was engaged or had engaged in criminal conduct."

But the Court seemed to retreat from this strong statement in *United States v. Mendenhall.*[32] In that case, it will be remembered, narcotics agents stopped the defendant as she got off an airplane in Detroit. The officers decided to stop the defendant because she fit a so-called "drug courier profile," an informal compilation of characteristics considered typical of individuals carrying illicit drugs.[33] Specifically, the agents relied upon the facts that the defendant arrived from Los Angeles (regarded as frequent source of drugs), that she was the last person to leave the plane, that she appeared to be very nervous, that she "scanned" the area as she left the plane, that she did not claim any luggage, and that she went to the desk of another airline than the one on which she arrived, apparently for the purpose of leaving Detroit.

32. 446 U.S. 544, 100 S.Ct. 1870 (1980).

33. See § 3.03(b)(3) for a discussion of investigative profiles.

At least three members of the Court,[34] felt the stop was reasonable, emphasizing that the difficulty in detecting the transportation of drugs had prompted the training of special drug enforcement agents who are "able to perceive and articulate meaning in given conduct which would be wholly innocent to the untrained observer." The four dissenters, on the other hand, felt that none of the defendant's actions noticed by the police were unusual, but were "rather the kind of behavior that could reasonably be expected of anyone changing planes in an airport terminal." They labeled the officers' suspicion a "hunch" rather than one based on "specific reasonable inferences."

In sharp contrast to *Mendenhall* is *Reid v. Georgia,*[35] another airport stop case decided the same term. In *Reid,* the entire Court indicated that reasonable suspicion of criminal activity does *not* exist when a person (1) gets off a plane from Ft. Lauderdale (a supposed drug source) at a time in the morning when law enforcement activity is minimal; (2) has no luggage other than a shoulder bag; (3) apparently makes efforts to conceal he is travelling with someone else; and (4) occasionally looks back at that person. The per curiam opinion stated that with the exception of the last factor, these "circumstances describe a very large category of presumably innocent travellers, who would be subject to virtually random seizures were the Court to conclude that as little foundation as there was in this case could justify a seizure."

Certainly, much, if not all, of Mendenhall's behavior was "innocent" as well; at least some members of the Court seemed to be sending mixed signals. A third airport stop case, *Florida v. Royer,*[36] did not provide much further clarification. The principal focus of the decision was on other issues, including, as previously described, when a Fourth Amendment seizure occurs. Moreover, there were four separate opinions in *Royer.* But it appears that eight members of the *Royer* Court sanctioned the initial encounter in that case between the defendant and two drug enforcement agents, based on the following factors: (1) the defendant's American Tourister luggage, which appeared to be heavy; (2) his youth and casual dress; (3) his pale and nervous appearance; (4) his use of cash to pay for his ticket; (5) his failure to give full identifying information on his luggage tags, and (6) his arrival from a known drug import center (Miami) and expected departure from a known distribution center (New York). Justice Brennan was the only member who explicitly dissented on this point, stating that the agents' observations, "considered individually or collectively, . . . are perfectly consistent with innocent behavior and cannot possi-

---

34. As noted in § 11.03, two members of the Court concluded that no seizure occurred, and thus did not reach the reasonable suspicion issue.

35. 448 U.S. 438, 100 S.Ct. 2752 (1980).

36. 460 U.S. 491, 103 S.Ct. 1319 (1983).

bly give rise to any inference supporting a reasonable suspicion of activity."[37]

The emerging majority stance toward *Terry* analysis appears to be premised on a healthy respect for the deductive processes of trained officers, once they have diligently accumulated as much information about the suspect's behavior as they can. The language of Chief Justice Burger in *United States v. Cortez*,[38] handed down a year after *Mendenhall* and *Reid,* captures the approach. The assessment of a police action under *Terry,* stated Burger, should be based on "the whole picture." It should take into account "all of the circumstances," including observations, information from police reports, and "consideration of the modes or patterns of operation of certain kinds of lawbreakers." And, most importantly, this information should be viewed from the perspective "of those versed in the field of law enforcement," not "in terms of library analysis by scholars." Finally, as have several Court opinions, *Cortez* reminds courts that the trained officer may often be able to deduce more from given facts than the untrained layperson.

(b) Seizures on Less Than Reasonable Suspicion. In several instances, the Court has upheld a seizure on less than reasonable suspicion, using *Terry's* balancing test. In each of these decisions, the Court found the individual's interests minimal, the state's interests significant, and the procedure chosen by the state to achieve its objectives reasonable.

(1) Roadblocks. In *United States v. Martinez–Fuerte,*[39] the Court held for the first time that a Fourth Amendment seizure may be permitted on virtually no suspicion. Border officials had established fixed checkpoints some distance from the border but along major arteries leading directly from it. Drivers were stopped initially to allow inquiries to be made, and then referred to a secondary inspection point if officials thought it necessary to check documents. The initial stop consisted either of a "wave-through" or a stop of a few seconds, while the secondary inspection lasted, on average, about five minutes and consisted primarily of a document check. The Supreme Court, in an opinion by Justice Powell, held that both of these stops were seizures under the Fourth Amendment. It also admitted that the initial stop could not be based on reasonable suspicion, "because the flow of traffic tends to be too heavy to allow the particularized study of a

---

37. See also, *United States v. Sokolow,* 490 U.S. 1, 109 S.Ct. 1581 (1989) (reasonable suspicion exists when a person buys two roundtrip tickets from Honolulu to Miami, with a return time 48 hours after arrival in Miami, pays for the tickets with $2,100 in cash from a roll of what appeared to be $4,000, and gives the ticket agent a false phone number.

38. 449 U.S. 411, 101 S.Ct. 690 (1981).

39. 428 U.S. 543, 96 S.Ct. 3074 (1976).

given car that would enable it to be identified as a possible carrier of illegal aliens," and that the secondary referral might be based on race alone, a practice found impermissible in *Brignoni–Ponce*. Yet the Court upheld both seizures by a vote of 7–2.

The Court found that the state and individual interests involved here were different from those implicated in the typical stop and frisk situation. On the state side of the ledger was the "substantial" nature of the illegal immigration problem and the difficulty of detecting and deterring it in the absence of the government's action. These factors were arguably present in *Brignoni–Ponce* as well. But, in contrast to that case, because officials other than officers in the field established the location of the checkpoint and their decision could easily be reviewed, the government's program was more reasonable. With respect to the individual interests, Powell concluded that a fixed checkpoint, again in contrast to the roving patrols at issue in *Brignoni–Ponce*, both minimized "potential interference with legitimate traffic" and provided "visible manifestations" of the field officers' authority.

The Court has applied the reasoning of *Martinez–Fuerte* to both license and sobriety checkpoints. In *Delaware v. Prouse*,[40] it suggested in dictum that, while the random license check in that case was unconstitutional, "spot checks that involve less intrusion or that do not involve the unconstrained exercise of discretion," such as the "questioning of all oncoming traffic at roadblock-type stops," might be permissible. And in *Michigan Dept. of State Police v. Sitz*,[41] the Court relied heavily on *Martinez–Fuerte* in authorizing a roadblock which briefly stops every driver to ascertain whether he is drunk. The "magnitude of the drunk driving crisis," combined with minimal intrusion occasioned by such a roadblock, justified its use, concluded the Court.

While nothing in the Fourth Amendment prohibits a seizure on less than reasonable suspicion, the Reasonableness Clause presumably requires *some* non-trivial showing of suspicion whenever there is a seizure. Arguably, a sufficient showing was made in *Martinez–Fuerte*, where the government provided statistics indicating that, at one of the roadblocks at issue, 20% of those referred to the secondary inspection point were illegal aliens. In *Sitz*, however, only 1.6% (2 out of 126) of the drivers stopped turned out to be drunk. Moreover, as Justice Stevens pointed out in his *Sitz* dissent, the roadblock in *Sitz* should have required *more* justification than did the roadblocks in *Martinez–Fuerte*. The roadblocks in the latter case were permanent, thus reducing surprise to motorists and eliminating low-level discretion as to the

40. 440 U.S. 648, 99 S.Ct. 1391 (1979).   **41.** 496 U.S. 444, 110 S.Ct. 2481 (1990).

checkpoint's location.   In *Sitz,* on the other hand, officers in the field were authorized to set up temporary checkpoints at a wide range of locations under guidelines established by the state.   The document check procedures at the secondary checkpoint in *Marti-nez–Fuerte* were also more standardized that the inquiry process at the sobriety checkpoint in *Sitz,* where, as Stevens noted, "[a] ruddy complexion, an unbuttoned shirt, bloodshot eyes or a speech impediment may suffice to prolong the detention."   Finally, drunken driving is far less difficult to detect than illegal immigration. Stevens pointed out that a roadblock program in Maryland similar to that involved in *Sitz* had netted only 143 arrests in 41,000 stops and had failed to reduce alcohol-related fatalities.   He also noted that traditional patrols resulted in far more arrests.   Distinguishing *Martinez–Fuerte* from *Sitz* on this point, he stated:

> Common sense . . . suggests that immigration checkpoints are more necessary than sobriety checkpoints; there is no reason why smuggling illegal aliens should impair a motorist's driving ability, but if intoxication did not noticeably affect driving ability it would not be unlawful.   Drunk driving, unlike smuggling, may thus be detected absent any checkpoints.   A program that produces thousands of otherwise impossible arrests is not a relevant precedent for a program that produces only a handful of arrests which would be more easily obtained without resort to suspicionless seizures of hundreds of innocent citizens.

(2) Seizures of car occupants.   In *Pennsylvania v. Mimms,*[42] decided a year after *Martinez–Fuerte,* the Court again dispensed with *Terry's* requirement that suspicion be based on "specific and articulable facts" in a situation where the government's interests were perceived to be much stronger than the individual's.   In *Mimms,* two officers stopped a car for driving with expired license plates.   One of the officers asked the driver to step out of the car. The Pennsylvania Supreme Court held that this act was a "seizure" and that it was unlawful because the officer could not point to objective facts supporting a suspicion of criminal activity or danger.   The Supreme Court agreed that a seizure occurred and that no individualized suspicion existed, but found the seizure reasonable, in a per curiam opinion.

The Court pointed out that, once a car has been stopped, the added intrusion associated with requesting the driver to alight is *de minimis.*   The driver "is being asked to expose very little more of his person than is already exposed," and the restriction of the driver's liberty will occur whether he stays inside or comes outside the car.   At the same time, according to the Court, a police officer takes an "inordinate risk" when he approaches a person seated in

---

42.   434 U.S. 106, 98 S.Ct. 330 (1977).

an automobile, even when the only offense suspected is a traffic violation and the driver has done nothing to make the officer feel uneasy.[43]   Thus, such seizures are legitimate, provided they occur after a lawful stop for some violation of the law.

(3) Regulatory "inspections".   A third situation encompassing a wide variety of seizures on less than reasonable suspicion occurs in connection with inspections for non-criminal activity.   For instance, using reasoning similar to that relied upon in *Martinez–Fuerte* and *Mimms,* the Supreme Court has ruled that when the government can show that significant harm may result from substance abuse, the difficulty of otherwise detecting or deterring that harm permits the seizure necessary to administer urinalysis, breathalyzer, and blood tests (as well as the tests themselves), without any showing of individualized suspicion.   These and other seizures designed to effect a regulatory purpose are discussed in this book's treatment of regulatory inspections.[44]

(c) **Permissible Sources of Information.**   Most of the time, as in *Terry* itself, reasonable suspicion develops as a result of direct police observation of ongoing events.   But, as with probable cause, reasonable suspicion may be based on information provided by third parties.   Where probable cause is concerned, the police must have fairly substantial grounds for crediting the hearsay information, particularly when it is from an informant.[45]   When reasonable suspicion is the standard, however, the *"Aquilar–Spinelli"* requirements that the informant's basis-of-knowledge and reliability be established, already modified for probable cause determinations by modern Court decisions,[46] have been relaxed even further.

(1) Informants.   In *Adams v. Williams,*[47] a police officer confronted and then frisked a person on the basis of a tip from an informant.   The Court held that because the informant was known to the officer and had provided information in the past, had come forward "personally to give information that was immediately verifiable at the scene," and was "subject to immediate arrest for making a false complaint" had the tip proven incorrect, there was "enough indicia of reliability to justify [the] stop."   These facts provide no information as to how the informant came by her

---

43. To this claim, the three dissenters responded that the available data, as well as some police manuals, suggest that harm is more likely when a car occupant gets out of the car than when he stays inside. But in *United States v. Hensley,* 469 U.S. 221, 105 S.Ct. 675 (1985), the Court held that it was "well within the permissible range" of police behavior to ask the driver *and* the passenger to alight from the car.

44. See § 13.12 and Chapter Thirteen generally.

45. See § 5.03(b).

46. See *Illinois v. Gates,* 462 U.S. 213, 103 S.Ct. 2317 (1983), discussed in § 5.03(b) (*Aguilar–Spinelli* two-prong test rejected in favor a totality of the circumstances approach).

47. 407 U.S. 143, 92 S.Ct. 1921 (1972).

information, and very little information about her reliability, particularly since it is unlikely people are aware they can be arrested for making a false complaint. But at least the presence of the informant at the scene of the stop provided some incentive to be truthful.

In contrast, in *Alabama v. White,*[48] the police acted on an anonymous tip that a certain female person would leave a certain room in a particular apartment complex, get into a brown Plymouth station wagon with a broken right taillight, and drive toward Dobey's Hotel while in possession of an ounce of cocaine inside a brown attache case. Police proceeded to the designated apartment complex, spotted the Plymouth as described, and shortly thereafter observed the defendant, without a briefcase, leave the indicated apartment and get in the car. They then followed her as she took the most direct route to Dobey's Hotel. They stopped her just short of the hotel, obtained consent to search her vehicle, and found cocaine in a brown briefcase. The Court found, 6–3, that although the information possessed by the police prior to the stop did not rise to the level of probable cause, it was sufficient to give them reasonable suspicion. Justice White, writing for the Court, was particularly impressed with the fact that the caller accurately *predicted* what the defendant would do, because this demonstrated inside information rather than information that could easily be obtained by any casual observer. Although calling it a "close case," White felt that this fact, plus the other corroboration by the police, was sufficient to justify a stop.

As Justice Stevens, joined by Justices Brennan and Marshall, noted in dissent:

> Anybody with enough knowledge about a given person to make her the target of a prank, or to harbor a grudge against her, will certainly be able to formulate a tip about her like the one predicting Vanessa White's excursion. In addition, under the Court's holding, every citizen is subject to being seized and questioned by any officer who is prepared to testify that the warrantless stop was based on an anonymous tip predicting whatever conduct the officer just observed.

The better approach in such cases is to require informant information to meet the same credibility test that is required for probable cause findings. While the police need only reasonable suspicion in stop cases, that suspicion should be based on facts as credible as the facts relied upon in making probable cause determinations.

(2) Police flyers. The Court *has* analogized to probable cause analysis where the "informant" is another police officer or department. In *United States v. Hensley,*[49] the Court unanimously held

---

48. 496 U.S. 325, 110 S.Ct. 2412 (1990).   **49.** 469 U.S. 221, 105 S.Ct. 675 (1985).

that police are entitled to rely on notices and "wanted flyers" from other jurisdictions in stopping individuals, so long as the jurisdiction which issued the flyer had specific and articulable facts to suspect the individual of past or present criminal activity at the time the flyer was issued and the stop is not significantly more intrusive than would have been permitted the issuing department. This holding follows the rule established in *Whiteley v. Warden,*[50] which permitted arrests based on radio bulletins so long as the source of the bulletin had probable cause to arrest.

(3) Profiles and plans. In a number of the Court's cases, the police have relied on so-called "drug-courier profiles" in determining who to stop.[51] As discussed in more detail in connection with arrests,[52] the Court has been cautious about authorizing use of such profiles, instead requiring an independent assessment of the facts to determine whether probable cause or reasonable suspicion exists. A second type of "generalized," as opposed to "individualized," method of showing adequate suspicion is through an investigative "plan." This technique was approved in the regulatory inspection case of *Camara v. Municipal Court,*[53] in which the Court allowed health and safety inspections of residences under an administrative plan based on the age of the houses and other "neutral" factors, instead of requiring individualized suspicion with respect to each house. A similar type of "plan" was relied upon by border officials in *I.N.S. v. Delgado,*[54] in which a warrant was obtained based on a showing that numerous illegal aliens were employed at a particular factory, without naming any specific individuals. Although the Court did not directly address its validity, such a "general" warrant might permit some types of seizures, if a statistical correlation between the factors in the plan and the alleged activity (e.g., employment of illegal immigrants) exist. This conclusion would seem to follow from the Court's attempts in *Martinez–Fuerte* and *Sitz* to evaluate the "effectiveness" of roadblocks using statistical information.

(d) Types of Crimes. In *Sibron v. New York,*[55] the Court suggested that a stop merely to obtain evidence of narcotics possession was never permissible. Such a rule arguably makes sense under the *Terry* balancing test, since where there is no imminent danger to the officer or the public, the intrusion associated with a stop may not be justifiable. In contrast, in *Adams v. Williams,*[56] a stop and frisk to obtain narcotics and a *gun* was

50. 401 U.S. 560, 91 S.Ct. 1031 (1971), discussed in § 3.03(a)(3).

51. See, e.g., *Florida v. Royer,* 460 U.S. 491, 103 S.Ct. 1319 (1983); *United States v. Sokolow,* 490 U.S. 1, 109 S.Ct. 1581 (1989).

52. See § 3.03(b)(3).

53. 387 U.S. 523, 87 S.Ct. 1727 (1967), discussed in § 13.02.

54. 466 U.S. 210, 104 S.Ct. 1758 (1984).

55. 392 U.S. 40, 88 S.Ct. 1889 (1968).

56. 407 U.S. 143, 92 S.Ct. 1921 (1972).

permitted, even though the officer acted on a tip that was relatively unreliable and there was no indication the gun was unlicensed. The nature of the criminal situation being investigated may have made the difference in *Adams*.

Since these cases, the Court has permitted stops for a number of lesser crimes.[57] However, there may be one situation in which a stop for a minor crime requires more than reasonable suspicion. In *United States v. Hensley*,[58] as a predicate to allowing stops based on "wanted flyers," the Court had to decide whether stops based on a reasonable suspicion of past criminal activity was permissible. All of the Court's opinions up to *Hensley* had involved stops based on suspicion of imminent or ongoing crime. In *Hensley,* on the other hand, the police stopped the defendant 12 days after the commission of the aggravated robbery of which he was suspected. The Court found that requiring probable cause in such situations "would not only hinder the investigation, but might also enable the suspect to flee in the interim and to remain at large." Thus, reasonable suspicion was sufficient. But the Court also recognized that allowing stops based on a mere suspicion of past crime might allow officers more discretion than a rule limiting stops to present criminal activity. Thus, it left open the possibility that stops on a reasonable suspicion of past criminal activity might be impermissible if the crime is minor.

11.04 Permissible Grounds for a Frisk

A valid stop does not automatically justify a frisk. *Terry* permitted a frisk only when the officer has, in addition to the suspicion necessary to justify a stop, a reasonable suspicion that the person stopped is "armed and dangerous." This rule follows from the *Terry* balancing test: each intrusion by the government must be justified by a legitimate objective.

Terry's holding also suggested that, before a frisk takes place, the officer must "identif[y] himself as a policeman and make[ ] reasonable inquiries." As the Court later recognized in *Adams v. Williams*,[59] however, the exigencies of the situation often do not permit such niceties. In *Adams,* the officer, acting on a tip that a person seated in a nearby car was carrying narcotics and a gun at his waist, approached the person and asked him to open the door. When the defendant rolled down the window instead, the officer reached into the car and removed a revolver from his waistband. Although the officer's question was the only exchange between the officer and the defendant, the Court found the officer's seizure of

---

57. See, e.g., *United States v. Brignoni–Ponce,* 422 U.S. 873, 95 S.Ct. 2574 (1975) (stops for violations of immigration laws).

58. 469 U.S. 221, 105 S.Ct. 675 (1985).

59. 407 U.S. 143, 92 S.Ct. 1921 (1972).

the weapon reasonable in light of the defendant's apparent unwillingness to cooperate.

A few other Court cases flesh out the types of situations where a frisk may be justified. In *Terry* itself, the officer's observations of the defendants' actions, plus their furtive, "mumbling" behavior once he had accosted them, permitted a frisk. Similarly, in *Pennsylvania v. Mimms,*[60] the Court approved a frisk when the officer observed a large bulge under the sports jacket of a driver who had just been asked to get out of his car. On the other hand, in *Ybarra v. Illinois,*[61] the Court held that the police did not have sufficient grounds for a frisk. There, police executing a warrant for search of a tavern and its bartender frisked each of the twelve patrons after announcing they were going to conduct "a cursory search for weapons." One officer felt what he described as a "cigarette pack with objects in it" on Ybarra, and later returned to remove it from his person. The Court refused to uphold this action, despite the state's and the dissent's contention that the tavern was a "compact, dimly lit" area which needed to be "frozen" to prepare for the search. As Justice Stewart stated for the Court, "[t]he 'narrow scope' of the *Terry* exception does not permit a frisk for weapons on less than reasonable belief or suspicion directed at the person to be frisked, even though that person happens to be on premises where an authorized narcotics search is taking place."

Ybarra also emphasized that the frisk must be directed at discovering weapons, not evidence. The government had argued that its interest in controlling the sale of hard drugs and the ease with which such drugs can be concealed also justified the frisk in that case. But the Court concluded that the *Terry* doctrine should not be expanded from a device for protecting the police to an "aid [to] the evidence-gathering function of the search warrant."

11.05 The Scope of a Frisk

Once a frisk is justified, *Terry* allows the officer to undertake "a carefully limited search of the outer clothing . . . in an attempt to discover weapons which might be used to assault him." In *Sibron v. New York,*[62] one of *Terry's* companion cases, the Court suggested that reaching into a person's pocket went beyond the scope of this patdown when the officer makes "no attempt at an initial limited exploration for arms." But in *Adams,* the Court upheld the officer's reaching into the defendant's waistband, when he had information that a gun was there and the defendant appeared to be uncooperative, again illustrating the proposition that the nature of the danger defines the scope of the intrusion.

60. 434 U.S. 106, 98 S.Ct. 330 (1977).   **62.** 392 U.S. 40, 88 S.Ct. 1889 (1968).
61. 444 U.S. 85, 100 S.Ct. 338 (1979).

Of course, if the officer feels a weapon-like object, he may seize the item to protect himself.[63]

Additionally, analogous to the armspan rule in the search incident context,[64] the police may search any area from which the person stopped might be able to obtain a weapon. This was the holding of *Michigan v. Long*,[65] where two officers on evening patrol stopped to investigate a car which they had observed driving erratically and which had ended up in a ditch. They met the defendant, the only occupant of the car, at the rear of the vehicle and noted that he appeared to be intoxicated. When asked for his license and registration, the defendant returned to the car and the officers followed; while doing so they saw a hunting knife on the floorboard of the car. After patting down the defendant and finding no weapons, one of the officers shined his flashlight into the car and saw something protruding from the armrest under the frontseat. Lifting the armrest revealed an open leather pouch which the officer "determined" to contain marijuana.

Although the defendant had not been arrested for any crime at the time of the search, the Court disagreed with the Michigan Supreme Court's holding that the search of the passenger compartment was invalid. Instead, the Court emphasized that *Terry* did not restrict the "frisk" for weapons to the person but rather permitted a protective search of any area which might contain a weapon posing danger to the police. Here, the Court concluded, the observance of the hunting knife, the intoxicated state of the defendant, and the fact that the encounter took place at night in an isolated rural area gave the police specific and articulable facts which, taken together with the rational inferences from those facts, reasonably warranted the search. The Court noted that the search had been limited to "those areas to which Long would generally have immediate control, and that could contain a weapon."

While the Court's extension of *Terry* is an appropriate means of protecting the police, its application of this concept to the facts of *Long* is questionable, given the location of the pouch and the fact that Long was in the control of the officers at the time of the search. To the suggestion that the officers could have moved the defendant further from the car if they were worried about his use of a weapon in the car, the Court stated that police are not required to "adopt alternate means to insure their safety in order to avoid the intrusion involved in a *Terry* encounter," a statement which does not explain why the police are allowed to go *beyond* the intrusion associated with a *Terry* encounter when it is not neces-

63. *Pennsylvania v. Mimms*, 434 U.S. 106, 98 S.Ct. 330 (1977) (permitting a seizure of a gun felt through sports jacket).

64. See § 6.04(a).

65. 463 U.S. 1032, 103 S.Ct. 3469 (1983).

sary. *Long* should be read in light of the long list of Supreme Court decisions minimizing Fourth Amendment protection of automobiles.[66]

As a limitation on *Long* and other Court decisions construing *Terry,* one might argue that, because the goal of a frisk is to prevent harm, only *weapons* discovered as a result of a frisk should be admissible in evidence. *Terry* itself spoke only of admitting weapons discovered in the course of a lawful frisk. Excluding other types of evidence would deter the police from engaging in fishing expeditions in situations where they know they are not in danger but the objective facts provide "reasonable suspicion" that a person is armed and dangerous. On the other hand, assuming such facts exist, the police should not be deterred from protecting themselves. In any event, the Court in *Long* specifically held that "[i]f, while conducting a legitimate *Terry* search . . . the officer should, as here, discover contraband other than weapons, he clearly cannot be required to ignore the contraband, and the Fourth Amendment does not require its suppression in such circumstances." Probably behind the Court's statement is the belief that a clearly guilty person should not go free when his objectively-defined rights have not been violated.[67]

11.06 Stop and Frisk in the Lower Courts

A look at lower court decisions will help flesh out the standards set by *Terry* and later decisions. The discussion of these cases is organized under the same four headings used in the last section.

(a) **Defining Seizures and Stops.** In determining whether a confrontation is a seizure, the lower courts have focused on the degree of coercion present. Two cases are representative. In *State v. Tsukiyama,*[68] the Hawaii Supreme Court found that no seizure occurred when a policeman asked Tsukiyama a number of questions, including his name, after Tsukiyama had requested a flashlight from the officer to use in fixing his automobile. Unlike the defendant in *Brown v. Texas,*[69] the defendant here initiated the conversation; furthermore, the court specifically found no element of command, force or coercion, and no physical restraint.

66. See, e.g., *New York v. Belton,* 453 U.S. 454, 101 S.Ct. 2860 (1981), discussed in § 6.04(d); *California v. Acevedo,* 500 U.S. ___, 111 S.Ct. 1982 (1991), discussed in § 7.04; *South Dakota v. Opperman,* 428 U.S. 364, 96 S.Ct. 3092 (1976), discussed in § 13.07(a).

67. Cf. § 11.04 (discussing the Court's resistance to pretextual search arguments).

68. 56 Hawaii 8, 525 P.2d 1099 (1974).

69. 443 U.S. 47, 99 S.Ct. 2637 (1979), discussed in § 9.02.

In a more recent case, *Login v. State*,[70] a detective approached the defendant as he was walking in the Miami airport and displayed his badge and identification. He stated: "I am a narcotics officer with the sheriff's office and I would like to talk to you; do you have a minute?" The defendant replied, "Yes." At that moment, the officer noticed cocaine residue around the defendant's nostrils, which observation eventually led to the defendant's arrest. The Florida District Court of Appeal held that no Fourth Amendment seizure had taken place at the time the cocaine was observed. The court recognized the practical advantage of a rule holding that a stop occurs as soon as police initially approach the individual, identify themselves and begin to question him. But it rejected a per se rule, based on the following reasoning:

> [A]pplication of such a rule would cover a multitude of police-citizen street encounters which in no way approach a police seizure of the person, such as police questioning of a probable witness to a crime or police inquiries directed to a stranded motorist in need of assistance. To label all police encounters with the public as seizures when accompanied by questioning, no matter how cordial, would tremendously impede the police in the effective performance of both their criminal investigation and community assistance functions. . . .

The court noted that it would not hesitate to find a seizure when police use language which "in tone and content bespeak an order to stop, particularly when employed during a fast moving criminal investigation on the street." Unfortunately, these types of subtle factors may be difficult to convey to a court. But the lower courts consistently hold that no seizure occurs when an officer merely confronts a citizen and asks questions.[71]

Toward the other end of the seizure spectrum, the courts have had to interpret the Supreme Court's ruling that the permissible duration of a stop is dependent upon the reasonableness of the officer's attempts to reduce delay.[72] In *Courson v. McMillian*,[73] for example, the court held in the context of a damages action that a deputy did not violate clearly established law when he stopped the occupants of a car on a suspicion that they were involved in growing marijuana, and then held them at gunpoint for 30 minutes, most of which was spent awaiting assistance. The Court pointed out that, even though the officer lacked probable cause for

70. 394 So.2d 183 (Fla. 3d D.C.A.1981).

71. See, e.g., *State v. Davis*, 543 So. 2d 375 (Fla. 3d D.C.A.1989) (no seizure when uniformed officer inquires if he might speak with bicyclist and bicyclist stops); *People v. King*, 72 Cal.App.3d 346, 139 Cal.Rptr. 926 (1977) (no seizure when officer overtakes a pedestrian and asks him to halt).

72. *United States v. Sharpe*, 470 U.S. 675, 105 S.Ct. 1568 (1985), discussed in § 3.02(b).

73. 939 F.2d 1479 (11th Cir.1991).

an arrest, the deputy was alone late at night at a vacant construction site, the occupants of the car appeared uncooperative and one of them was abusive; thus, the court granted summary judgment against the plaintiffs.

(b) Permissible Grounds for Seizures and Stops. Many lower courts require rather specific facts linking the individual to criminal activity before they are willing to find an investigatory stop valid. For example, the Michigan Supreme Court, in *People v. Parisi,*[74] found the police unjustified in stopping an automobile based upon: (1) the officer's concern that the occupants were "sleeping or ill;" (2) the fact that the car was traveling more slowly than the posted speed; and (3) the youthful appearance of the occupants, noting that there was no minimum speed and the local curfew did not apply to cars. The court in *United States v. Bell*[75] found inadequate cause for an investigatory stop of a van on suspicion of criminal drug-related activity where: (1) the van, which had out-of-state license plates, was traveling eastward (away from California) on an interstate highway; and (2) the van was driven by a youthful driver. An investigative stop was also held unreasonable in *State v. Saia,*[76] where officers observed a woman leave a known drug outlet and saw her reach twice inside her waistband while apparently aware of police surveillance.

Other decisions in which courts have found suspicion to be short of the threshold level justifying detention are *State v. Kupihea*[77] and *United States v. Brown.*[78] In *Kupihea*, police stopped two individuals in an automobile who had looked back at the police and then crouched down. In *Brown*, the defendants were stopped because they paid for airline tickets in cash, came from West Palm Beach, and looked at the police. In short, as the court in *State v. Key*[79] stated: where the "conduct of the defendant [is] just as consistent with innocent as with illicit behavior," reasonable suspicion does not exist.

Other cases have found adequate cause for an investigative stop when the defendant's conduct is less than innocent. For instance, in *State v. Purnell,*[80] the police were justified in stopping a defendant who was seen looking into every business at 2:00 a.m. when all the stores were closed, and who walked away hurriedly when the police car approached. Also found permissible was a stop of four large tractor-trailers on a highway in a coastal area where drug smuggling often took place, after the trucks had left a deep-water docking facility at a time of night when no commercial

74. 393 Mich. 31, 222 N.W.2d 757 (1974).

75. 383 F.Supp. 1298 (Neb.1974).

76. 302 So.2d 869 (La.1974), cert. denied 420 U.S. 1008, 95 S.Ct. 1454 (1975).

77. 59 Hawaii 386, 581 P.2d 765 (1978).

78. 731 F.2d 1491 (11th Cir.1984).

79. 375 So.2d 1354 (La.1979).

80. 621 S.W.2d 277 (Mo.1981).

activity occurred there and the weather was such that no boats were available for transporting goods.[81]   Much more questionable is the decision, by a divided Supreme Court of Indiana, upholding a police stop of a car driven by a single black male based upon knowledge: (1) that two black men, one armed with a sawed-off shotgun, had robbed a motel several miles away; (2) that they were believed to be traveling in the general direction of the police officers; and (3) that they might reasonably be passing the officer's position about that time.[82]

Some cases have also considered the usefulness of informants in making the reasonable suspicion determination.   For instance, in *Commonwealth v. Anderson,*[83] the police received an anonymous tip scrawled upon a newspaper that had been thrown into a toll booth from a passing bus.   The tip stated that police would find an armed and dangerous drug courier on a particular bus, and included a description of the supposed drug courier.   The court held that the tip had the requisite indicia of reliability to support a stop of an individual who matched the description and who got off the indicated bus, walked quickly through the bus terminal while glancing back at the police several times, and made a gesture to get rid of a bag in his possession when he came face to face with two other officers.

(c) Permissible Grounds for a Frisk.   Many lower courts have conscientiously applied the requirement that police have articulable grounds for believing a stopped individual is armed and dangerous before they undertake a frisk.   In *United States v. Johnson,*[84] for instance, the Tenth Circuit found the police justified in stopping a car for having a noisy muffler, but held illegal a frisk of a passenger in the car when both the driver and his wife were very cooperative but the passenger could not produce identification.   Similarly, in *People v. Superior Court of Los Angeles County,*[85] police stopped an automobile that was being driven at night without lights.   The driver could produce no identification, license or registration and was therefore arrested pursuant to state law. The driver was then frisked, although the officer conducting the search admitted having no fear for his safety.   In holding the search unlawful, the California Supreme Court concluded that a patdown search in the context of a detention for a traffic violation must be supported by specific facts or circumstances that could give rise to a reasonable belief that a weapon is concealed on the motorist.   The minor infractions involved in this case, by them-

81.   *United States v. Ogden,* 703 F.2d 629 (1st Cir.1983).

82.   *Williams v. State,* 261 Ind. 547, 307 N.E.2d 457 (1974).

83.   366 Mass. 394, 318 N.E.2d 834 (1974).

84.   463 F.2d 70 (10th Cir.1972).

85.   7 Cal.3d 186, 101 Cal.Rptr. 837, 496 P.2d 1205 (1972).

selves, were not sufficient, to support such a belief. Although the U.S. Supreme Court has since held that a *full* search is permitted incident to a custodial arrest,[86] a few lower courts continue to invalidate frisks incident to non-custodial traffic arrests unless there is articulable suspicion.[87]

Unfortunately, unlike the *Johnson* and *Superior Court* decisions, some lower court opinions have handled the power to frisk and the authority to stop as aspects of a single question. One result of this analytical impurity is that the case law reflects a substantial correlation between the adequacy of the grounds for an investigative stop and the likelihood that a frisk will be found permissible; the more convincing the justification for investigation, the more willing the courts have been to find that a protective search is warranted. It is possible, however, to parse from the decisions a number of discrete factors which have consistently been found relevant to a judgment by police that an individual may be armed and presently dangerous and thus worthy of a frisk after the initial stop.

The specific criminal activity which the police suspect may be afoot is always a relevant and often a dispositive consideration in the determination of the reasonableness of a frisk. If a crime of violence or serious property theft is suspected, it is rare that a court will fail to find reasonable grounds to conclude that the suspect may be armed and presently dangerous.[88] If, on the other hand, the suspected criminal activity merely involves violation of minor crimes such as shoplifting, then, as the decision in *Superior Court* illustrates, independent grounds are often required to support a finding of danger.[89] Narcotics cases are harder to categorize. When the offense involves *sales* of significant amounts of narcotics, a frisk is often automatically allowed,[90] whereas when the offense concerns narcotics possession, other factors, such as the dangerous location and time of the stop, must usually be articulated.[91]

86. *United States v. Robinson*, 414 U.S. 218, 94 S.Ct. 467 (1973), discussed in § 6.02. The California Supreme Court, however, has rejected this stance, based on an interpretation of the state constitution. *People v. Brisendine*, 13 Cal.3d 528, 119 Cal.Rptr. 315, 531 P.2d 1099 (1975).

87. *United States v. Wanless*, 882 F.2d 1459 (9th Cir.1989).

88. *Wright v. State*, 88 Nev. 460, 499 P.2d 1216 (1972) (frisk allowed when stopped for driving with stolen license plates). But see *Commonwealth v. Pegram*, 450 Pa. 590, 301 A.2d 695 (1973) (frisk of suspected burglar not permitted).

89. *United States v. Santillanes*, 848 F.2d 1103 (10th Cir.1988) (violation of pretrial conditions; defendant had just passed through airport magnetometer); *Whitten v. United States*, 396 A.2d 208 (D.C.App.1978) (shoplifting); *People v. Sherman*, 197 Colo. 442, 593 P.2d 971 (1979) (drinking underage).

90. *People v. Finn*, 73 Misc.2d 266, 340 N.Y.S.2d 807 (Crim.Ct.N.Y.1973) ("It is generally known by the police and others that those who traffic in large quantities of narcotics are often armed.")

91. *Commonwealth v. Patterson*, 405 Pa.Super. 17, 591 A.2d 1075 (1991).

Although the mere knowledge of a prior conviction record standing alone has been found insufficient to establish probable cause or to provide a foundation for reasonable suspicion,[92] such information is often accorded substantial weight when considered in conjunction with other factors. A particularly serious criminal reputation may alone be found an adequate cause for fear. The Second Circuit, in *United States v. Santana*,[93] declared that it is reasonable to assume that a suspect on the "top 100 narcotics violators" list of the New York police department would be armed or otherwise violent. Similarly, if, as in *Adams v. Williams*,[94] an informant has specifically warned that an individual is armed, and if that information is not completely without "indicia of reliability," such information alone will ordinarily be found to justify a frisk during an investigative stop.[95]

Courts often recite, but rarely rely strongly upon, the physical appearance of a suspect in supporting a police frisk. Youthfulness, long hair, and dishevelled clothing are thus largely discounted in the calculus of reasonable suspicion, though they are treated as touching the margins of relevance.[96] Substantial weight, however, is given to any visual clues indicating the presence of a weapon; one major motif of the "stop and frisk" case law, illustrated by *Pennsylvania v. Mimms*,[97] is the recurrent "suspicious bulge" noticed in the pocket of a suspect.[98]

Although the validity of such decisions is suspect after *Ybarra v. Illinois*,[99] many opinions have treated association with arrested individuals as dispositive of the "armed and presently dangerous" question. Illustrative is *United States v. Berryhill*,[1] where the court wrote that:

> [a]ll companions of the arrestee within the immediate vicinity, capable of accomplishing a harmful assault on the officer, are constitutionally subjected to the cursory 'pat-down' reasonably necessary to give assurance that they are unarmed.

Similar in tone is *United States v. Bonds*,[2] where the court stated that a frisk may be permitted whenever the officer reasonably believes himself in danger, "whether he is investigating the individual or not."[3]

---

92. See, e.g., *United States v. Cupps,* 503 F.2d 277 (6th Cir.1974).

93. 485 F.2d 365 (2d Cir.1973), cert. denied 415 U.S. 931, 94 S.Ct. 1444 (1974).

94. 407 U.S. 143, 92 S.Ct. 1921 (1972), discussed in § 11.04.

95. See, e.g., *United States v. Poms,* 484 F.2d 919 (4th Cir.1973).

96. See, e.g., *State v. Hennecke,* 78 Wash.2d 147, 470 P.2d 176 (1970).

97. 434 U.S. 106, 98 S.Ct. 330 (1977), discussed in § 11.04.

98. See, e.g., *United States v. Peep,* 490 F.2d 903 (8th Cir.1974).

99. 444 U.S. 85, 100 S.Ct. 338 (1979), discussed in § 9.05.

1. 445 F.2d 1189 (9th Cir.1971).

2. 829 F.2d 1072 (11th Cir.1987).

3. See also, *People v. Evans,* 22 Ill. App.3d 733, 317 N.E.2d 734 (1974); but see *United States v. Tharpe,* 526 F.2d

Finally, although the Supreme Court in *Sibron v. New York*,[4] did not consider the act of reaching into a pocket sufficiently suspicious to warrant a frisk, the lower courts have consistently given considerable weight to any suggestive movements by suspects. Two Delaware Supreme Court decisions, *State v. Wausnock*,[5] where the movement suggested the concealment of something under the driver's seat, and *Nash v. State*,[6] where the suspect reached for a small tin box resembling a pistol container, provide representative examples.

(d) The Scope of a Frisk. While the lower courts have generally limited frisks to a patdown unless the officer's information suggests immediate, more intrusive action is necessary,[7] in other respects the scope of a frisk has been expanded considerably beyond that contemplated by *Terry*. Long before *Michigan v. Long*,[8] lower courts had included within the scope of a permissible frisk searches of a shoulderbag;[9] of the area under the suspect's car seat after he appeared to hide something there;[10] of the front seat and floor of a car by flashlight when the officer knew that the driver carried a concealed weapon;[11] of a glove compartment within the reach of a suspect;[12] of a limited area within the passenger compartment of a car though the suspects were then outside the car;[13] of the suspect's coat after he had removed it;[14] and of a bag on the floor of an automobile and a few feet away from the suspect.[15]

Some lower courts have maintained a strict definition of what may be considered a weapon in the context of a protective frisk. The Supreme Court of California, in *People v. Collins*,[16] held that, absent unusual circumstances, feeling a soft object during a patdown does not warrant retrieving the object from the suspect's pocket. Likewise, in *United States v. Del Toro*,[17] the Second Circuit found as a matter of law that a ten dollar bill, folded 2″ by ³⁄₄″ and containing cocaine, could not reasonably have seemed to be a weapon when felt in a suit pocket, and therefore was illegally

326 (5th Cir.1976) (broad rule of *Berryhill* inconsistent with Supreme Court decisions).

4. 392 U.S. 40, 88 S.Ct. 1889 (1968), discussed in § 11.03(a).

5. 303 A.2d 636 (Del.1973).

6. 295 A.2d 715 (Del.1972).

7. *United States v. Santillanes*, 848 F.2d 1103 (10th Cir.1988); *Gray v. Alaska*, 798 P.2d 346 (Alaska App.1990).

8. 463 U.S. 1032, 103 S.Ct. 3469 (1983), discussed in § 11.05.

9. *United States v. Poms*, 484 F.2d 919 (4th Cir.1973).

10. *State v. Wausnock*, 303 A.2d 636 (Del.1973).

11. *State v. Howard*, 7 Wash.App. 668, 502 P.2d 1043 (1972).

12. *State v. Zantua*, 8 Wash.App. 47, 504 P.2d 313 (1972).

13. *United States v. Thomas*, 314 A.2d 464 (D.C.App.1974).

14. *Modesto v. State*, 258 A.2d 287 (Del.Super.1969).

15. *Williams v. State*, 19 Md.App. 204, 310 A.2d 593 (1973).

16. 1 Cal.3d 658, 83 Cal.Rptr. 179, 463 P.2d 403 (1970).

17. 464 F.2d 520 (2d Cir.1972).

seized. However, the "weapon-like object" limitation to the permissible scope of a frisk has been substantially diluted by other courts through imaginative definition of what reasonably might be considered a weapon. Courts have condoned the seizure of a marijuana cigarette which the searching officer pulled from a pocket at the same time as a lipstick container which the officer believed to be a 12-gauge shotgun shell; [18] of a cigarette lighter containing hashish because it could be used in a doubled up fist, or thrown, or used to burn the officer; [19] of a large envelope containing lottery slips on the theory that it could have hidden a thin knife or blade; [20] and of a bag of marijuana cigarettes which came out of a pocket along with a long-stemmed smoking pipe which the officer believed to be a knife.[21]

Once an object that may pose a threat to the officer is discovered and in his possession, it would seem that the protective function of a search during an investigative stop has been accomplished and further investigation of the object is not necessary. In *Jackson v. Alaska*,[22] the court prohibited searches of small containers, such as wallets, absent articulable reasons for believing it may contain an "atypical weapon." But in Taylor v. Superior Court,[23] the court found the further examination of a cigarette lighter in police possession to be reasonable because it might have concealed dangerous razor blades. In *Nash v. State,*[24] the opening of a box already seized was held to be reasonable. Such cases, though not uncommon, appear to be deviations from, rather than elaborations of, the underlying rationale of the *Terry* decision.

11.07   The American Law Institute Formulation

The American Law Institute, in § 110.2 of its Model Code of Pre-Arraignment Procedure (1975), provides one of the more well thought-out formulations of the stop and frisk procedure. In its commentary on that section, the ALI explains the purpose and justification for both the procedure and the explicit authorizing provision:

> The purpose of this Section is to authorize a brief period of on-the-spot detention in circumstances where there does not exist reasonable cause [the phrase the ALI uses in place of probable cause] to believe that the person to be detained is guilty of crime. Such an authority seems essential to the control of crime in an urban, mobile and anonymous environ-

---

18. *People v. Atmore,* 13 Cal.App.3d 244, 91 Cal.Rptr. 311 (2d Dist.1970).

19. *Taylor v. Superior Court,* 275 Cal.App.2d 146, 79 Cal.Rptr. 677 (4th Dist.1969).

20. *State v. Campbell,* 53 N.J. 230, 250 A.2d 1 (1969).

21. *People v. Watson,* 12 Cal.App.3d 130, 90 Cal.Rptr. 483 (3d Dist.1970).

22. 791 P.2d 1023 (Alaska App. 1990).

23. 275 Cal.App.2d 146, 79 Cal.Rptr. 677 (4th Dist.1969).

24. 295 A.2d 715 (Del.1972).

ment. Only by providing for this authority explicitly is it possible to confine its exercise even approximately to those situations of genuine urgency which best justify it.[25]

The complete text of that section reads as follows:

(1) *Cases in Which Stop is Authorized.* A law enforcement officer, lawfully present in any place, may, in the following circumstances, order a person to remain in the officer's presence near such place for such period as is reasonably necessary for the accomplishment of the purposes authorized in the Subsection, but in no case for more than twenty minutes:

(a) *Persons in suspicious circumstances relating to certain misdemeanors and felonies.*

(i) Such person is observed in circumstances such that the officer reasonably suspects that he has just committed, is committing, or is about to commit a misdemeanor or felony, involving danger of forcible injury to persons or of appropriation of or damage to property, and

(ii) such action is reasonably necessary to obtain or verify the identification of such person, to obtain or verify an account of such person's presence or conduct, or to determine whether to arrest such persons.

(b) *Witnesses near scene of certain misdemeanors and felonies.*

(i) The officer has reasonable cause to believe that a misdemeanor or felony, involving danger of forcible injury to persons or of appropriation of or danger to property, has just been committed near the place where he finds such person, and

(ii) the officer has reasonable cause to believe that such person has knowledge of material aid in the investigation of such crime, and

(iii) such action is reasonably necessary to obtain or verify the identification of such person, or to obtain an account of such crime.

(c) *Suspects sought for certain previously committed felonies.*

(i) The officer has reasonable cause to believe that a felony involving danger of forcible injury to

---

25. *ALI*, Model Code of Pre-Arraignment Procedure, at 269 (1975).

persons or of appropriation of or damage to property has been committed, and

(ii) he reasonably suspects such person may have committed it, and

(iii) such action is reasonably necessary to obtain or verify the identification of such person for the purpose of determining whether to arrest him for such felony.

(2) *Stopping of Vehicles at Roadblock.* A law enforcement officer may, if

(a) he has reasonable cause to believe that a felony has been committed; and

(b) stopping all or most automobiles, trucks, buses or other such motor vehicles moving in a particular direction or directions is reasonably necessary to permit a search for the perpetrator or victim of such felony in view of the seriousness and special circumstances of such felony, order the drivers of such vehicles to stop, and may search such vehicles to the extent necessary to accomplish such purpose. Such actions shall be accomplished as promptly as possible under the circumstances.

(3) *Use of Force.* In order to exercise the authority conferred in Subsections (1) and (2) of this Section, a law enforcement officer may use such force, other than deadly force, as is reasonably necessary to stop any person or vehicle or to cause any person to remain in the officer's presence.

(4) *Frisk for Dangerous Weapons.* A law enforcement officer who has stopped any person pursuant to this Section may, if the officer reasonably believes that his safety or the safety of others then present so requires, search for any dangerous weapon by an external patting of such person's outer clothing. If in the course of such search he feels an object which he reasonably believes to be a dangerous weapon, he may take such action as is necessary to examine such object.

(5) *Questioning of Suspects.*

(a) *Warnings.* If a law enforcement officer stops any person who he suspects or has reasonable cause to suspect may have committed a crime, the officer shall warn such person as promptly as is reasonable under the circumstances, and in any case before engaging in any sustained questioning

(i) that such person is not obliged to say anything, and anything he says may be used in evidence against him,

(ii) that within twenty minutes he will be released unless he is arrested,

(iii) that if he is arrested he will be taken to a police station where he may promptly communicate by telephone with counsel, relatives or friends, and

(iv) that he will not be questioned unless he wishes, and that if he wishes to consult a lawyer or have a lawyer present during questioning, he will not be questioned at this time, and that after being taken to the stationhouse a lawyer will be furnished him prior to questioning if he is unable to obtain one.

(b) *Limitations on Questioning.* No law enforcement officer shall question a person detained pursuant to the authority in this Section who he suspects or has reasonable cause to suspect may have committed a crime, if such person has indicated in any manner that he does not wish to be questioned, or that he wishes to consult counsel before submitting to any questioning.

(6) *Action to Be Taken After Period of Stop.* Unless an officer acting hereunder arrests a person during the time he is authorized by Subsections (1) and (2) of this Section to require such person to remain in his presence, he shall, at the end of such time, inform such person that he is free to go.

(7) *Records Relating to Persons Stopped.* In accordance with regulations to be issued pursuant to Section 10.3, a law enforcement officer, who has ordered any person to remain in his presence pursuant to this Section, shall with reasonable promptness thereafter make a record of the circumstances and purposes of the stop.

11.08　Conclusion

Based on the Supreme Court's decisions and the lower courts' interpretation of those decisions, the following general principles about the stop and frisk doctrine can be stated:

(1) A police-citizen encounter is not governed by the Fourth Amendment unless it is considered a "seizure." Factors to consider in deciding whether a "seizure" has taken place include: (a) the duration of the detention; (b) whether police actions were threatening; (c) whether the person detained was physically touched by the police; (d) whether the detention took place in a enclosed area as opposed to an area open to public view; and, most importantly, (e) whether the police action would have communicated to a

reasonable, innocent person that the person was not free to decline police requests or otherwise terminate the encounter.

(2) A person may be seized on less than probable cause to arrest only if the seizing officer (a) observes the person engage in unusual conduct leading to a reasonable suspicion that criminal activity has occurred, is occurring or is about to occur and can point to specific and articulable facts to warrant the suspicion; (b) receives information from an informant having some indicia of reliability (but not necessarily that required for probable cause) from which such a suspicion to be drawn; or (c) receives a communication from another police department that the person is believed to have engaged in criminal activity, which belief is based on specific and articulable facts. Exceptions to this rule include stops at a fixed traffic or sobriety checkpoint, and requests to disembark from a car following a legal stop.

(3) If a stop is authorized by reasonable suspicion or a lesser level of suspicion, reasonable inquiries designed to test the suspicion should generally be made. If the officer reasonably believes after these inquiries or for other reasons that the person may be armed and presently dangerous, he may also frisk the person. Factors determining the reasonableness of the frisk may include the type of criminal activity that is thought to be afoot, the person's reputation for dangerousness, visual clues as to the presence of a weapon, and suggestive movements by the suspect. Mere proximity to wanted persons is an insufficient ground for a frisk.

(4) If a frisk is authorized, it may include not only a patdown of the person's outer clothing but also a search of the area immediately surrounding the person when there is a reasonable fear that it might contain an instrument of assault. Weapon-like objects may be removed, although whether containers so removed may be searched further without a warrant is unclear.

BIBLIOGRAPHY

American Law Institute. A Model Code of Pre-Arraignment Procedure. Philadelphia: American Law Institute, 1975. 110.2 commentary, pp. 262–303.

Bogomolny, R.L. Street Patrol: The Decision to Stop a Citizen. 12 Crim.L.Bull. 544 (1976).

Butterfoss, Edwin. Bright Line Seizures: The Need for Clarity in Determining When Fourth Amendment Activity Begins. 79 J.Crim.L. & C. 437 (1988).

Cook, J.G. The Art of Frisking. 40 Fordham L.Rev. 789 (1972).

Dix, George, Non–Arrest Investigatory Detentions in Search and Seizure Law. 1985 Duke L.J. 849.

Greenberg, Peter S. Drug Courier Profiles, Mendenhall and Reid: Analyzing Police Intrusions on Less Than Probable Cause. 19 Amer.Crim.L.Rev. 49 (1981).

LaFave, Wayne R. "Street Encounters" and the Constitution: *Terry, Sibron, Peters,* and Beyond. 67 Mich.L.Rev. 40 (1968).

_____. Seizures Typology: Classifying Detentions of the Person to Resolve Warrant, Grounds, and Search Issues. 17 Univ.Mich. J.L.Ref. 417 (1984).

Maclin, Tracey. The Decline of the Right of Locomotion: The Fourth Amendment on the Streets. 75 Cornell L.Rev. 1258 (1990).

Misner, Robert L. The New Attempt Law: Unsuspected Threat to the Fourth Amendment. 33 Stan.L.Rev. 201 (1981).

Project on Law Enforcement. Policy and Rulemaking. Stop and Frisk. Washington, D.C.: Police Foundation, 1974.

Reich, Charles A. Police Questioning of Law Abiding Citizens. 75 Yale L.J. 1161 (1966).

Van Cleave, Rachel. Michigan v. Chesternut and Investigatory Pursuits: Is There No End to the War Between the Constitution and Common Sense? 40 Hastings L.J. 203 (1988).

Williamson, Richard. The Dimensions of Seizure: The Concepts of "Stop" and "Arrest". 43 Ohio St.L.Rev. (1982).

Chapter Twelve

CONSENT SEARCHES

12.01 Introduction

As early as 1921, the Supreme Court recognized that a valid consent waives the warrant and probable cause protections afforded by the Fourth Amendment.[1] The theory behind this rule is that once a person consents to a search of a given area she surrenders her expectation of privacy in that area. Thus, a valid consent eliminates both the warrant and suspicion requirements for searches.

This chapter discusses the elements of a valid consent given to an *identified* police officer. In a number of cases, the Supreme Court has sometimes used the language of consent in analyzing encounters with undercover agents, typically holding that the Fourth Amendment does not regulate such activity when its target voluntarily deals with the agent.[2] These cases are distinguishable from those discussed here for two reasons. First, despite the Court's characterization of undercover encounters as consensual, these cases have nothing to do with consent as that concept is normally understood, since the nature of what is being agreed to is never made clear to the "consentor." Second, the central issue in the undercover cases is whether or not the Fourth Amendment should apply at all; thus, they are treated in the portion of this book dealing with that question.[3] Consent given to an identified officer, on the other hand, may obviate the need for a warrant or probable cause, but only if other Fourth Amendment requirements are met. In particular, determining whether a consent is valid under the Fourth Amendment requires close attention to: (1) whether the consent is voluntary; (2) whether the search conforms to the consent given; and (3) whether the consentor had authority to give consent to the area searched.

12.02 The Voluntariness Requirement

Obviously, if the police search an area over the owner's objection, then the owner has not surrendered her expectation of privacy. In *Schneckloth v. Bustamonte*,[4] the Supreme Court held that "the Fourth and Fourteenth Amendments require that a

---

1. *Amos v. United States*, 255 U.S. 313, 41 S.Ct. 266 (1921).

2. See e.g., *On Lee v. United States*, 343 U.S. 747, 72 S.Ct. 967 (1952) (no search, since agent entered defendant's laundry with defendant's "consent"); *Gouled v. United States*, 255 U.S. 298, 41 S.Ct. 261 (1921) (search, because defendant only "consented" to agent entering home, not rummaging through drawers).

3. See § 4.03(a).

4. 412 U.S. 218, 93 S.Ct. 2041 (1973).

consent not be coerced, by explicit or implicit means, by implied threat or covert force." *Schneckloth* went on to define voluntariness in terms of the same "totality of the circumstances" analysis that the Court had already adopted in confession cases.[5] According to the Court, by looking at the "surrounding circumstances" of the consent, including the impact of "subtly coercive police questions" and the "possibly vulnerable subjective state of the person who consents," invalid searches can "be filtered out without undermining the continuing validity of consent searches." The following discussion looks at various circumstances that might affect this analysis.

(a) **Knowledge of the Right.** In *Johnson v. Zerbst*,[6] the Supreme Court held that, at least when constitutional rights are involved, a waiver "is ordinarily an intentional relinquishment or abandonment of a known right or privilege." Thus, for instance, the Court has held that a person in custody must be told she has a right to remain silent and a right to have an attorney present during questioning, or any statement she makes will be the product of an invalid waiver.[7] This warning is meant to inform the person of her rights under the Fifth and Sixth Amendments. One of the more controversial issues in the consent search area is whether the prosecution must show that the defendant knew of her right to refuse consent. Must a consent to search be "knowing and intelligent," or is "voluntariness" the sole standard? Even if voluntariness is the standard, does it make any sense to say that a consent is voluntary when the person giving that consent was unaware of her right to refuse?

Early decisions of the Court suggested it might adopt a voluntary and intelligent standard. In *Johnson v. United States*,[8] for instance, the Court held a consent invalid because it "was granted in submission to authority rather than as an understanding and intentional waiver of a constitutional right." But in *Schneckloth* the Court held that knowledge of the right to refuse consent is only one of the circumstances to be considered in the totality of the circumstances analysis. The Court gave three reasons for holding that "the prosecution is not required to demonstrate such knowledge as a prerequisite to establishing a voluntary consent." First, the need to show the consenting party was aware of her rights would "create serious doubt whether consent searches could continue to be conducted" in light of the difficulty of proving such awareness. Second, trying to eradicate this difficulty by imposing a requirement on the police to warn prospective targets of their

---

5. See § 16.02(a).

6. 304 U.S. 458, 58 S.Ct. 1019 (1938).

7. *Miranda v. Arizona*, 384 U.S. 436, 86 S.Ct. 1602 (1966). See also, *United States v. Wade*, 388 U.S. 218, 87 S.Ct.

1926 (1967) (counsel at pretrial lineups); *Patton v. United States*, 281 U.S. 276, 50 S.Ct. 253 (1930) (jury trial).

8. 333 U.S. 10, 68 S.Ct. 367 (1948).

right, as the Court had done in the confession context with its warnings requirement in *Miranda v. Arizona,*[9] "would be thoroughly impractical." Consent searches:

> normally occur on the highway, or in a person's home or office, and under informal and unstructured conditions. The circumstances that prompt the initial request to search may develop quickly or be a logical extension of investigative police questioning. The police may seek to investigate further suspicious circumstances or to follow up leads developed in questioning persons at the scene of a crime. These situations are a far cry form the structured atmosphere of a trial where, assisted by counsel if he chooses, a defendant is informed of his trial rights . . . And, while surely a closer question, these situations are still immeasurably far removed from "custodial interrogation" where, in *Miranda v. Arizona,* we found that the Constitution required certain now familiar warnings as a prerequisite to police interrogation.

As a third reason for not requiring knowledge of the right to refuse consent, the Court stated that the *Zerbst* standard for waiver applies only "to those rights guaranteed to a criminal defendant to insure . . . a fair criminal trial," and thus does not extend to the protections of the Fourth Amendment, which "are of a wholly different order, and have nothing whatever to do with promoting the fair ascertainment of truth at a criminal trial."

Schneckloth's distinction between Fourth Amendment protections and other rights accorded defendants is unpersuasive. A simple warning can easily be given in the former context, as the experience of the F.B.I. and the Bureau of Narcotics and Dangerous Drugs bears out.[10] The Court's real concern appears to be that probative evidence may not be discovered if suspects know of their right to refuse consent. But an analogous concern exists in the interrogation setting. Indeed, it may well be that both the Fifth Amendment's right to remain silent and the Sixth Amendment's right to counsel are more likely to impede conviction of a guilty person than is the Fourth Amendment's prohibition of unreasonable searches.[11] More importantly, the Court's willingness to treat the privacy interests protected by the Fourth Amendment as inferior to the interests protected by the Fifth and Sixth Amendments is suspect as a matter of constitutional interpretation, since

9. 384 U.S. 436, 86 S.Ct. 1602 (1966), discussed in § 16.02(d).

10. See commentary to ALI Model Code of Pre–Arraignment § 240.2(2), at 532–37.

11. For instance, research described in § 16.02(d)(2) suggests that *Miranda* may lower the conviction rate by as much as 2%, whereas the analogous impact of the exclusionary rule may be closer to 1%. See § 2.05.

neither the language nor the history of the Bill of Rights suggests any such hierarchy.[12]

It should be re-emphasized that, even after *Schneckloth*, the subject's knowledge of her right to refuse consent remains a crucial factor to be considered in determining the validity of a consent. Thus, in *United States v. Mendenhall,* [13] the Supreme Court judged "highly relevant" the fact that the defendant had twice been told of her right to refuse consent, and found the defendant's acquiescence to the search of her handbag and person voluntary. Conversely, in *Rosenthall v. Henderson,* [14] a lower court case decided before *Schneckloth*, the failure to give such a warning was found relevant to a finding of involuntariness.

(b) Custody. *Schneckloth* suggested, in dictum, that an arrested person may be under more duress than one who is not, and thus more likely to feel coerced into consenting. This observation, combined with the admission in *Schneckloth* that, however "impractical" they are otherwise, warnings are possible in the "structured" setting following a custodial arrest, suggested that the Court might find that an unwarned person who has been arrested cannot give a valid consent. But three years later, in *United States v. Watson,* [15] the Court found valid the consent of a person who was arrested on a public street and then asked if his car could be searched. The police did tell the individual that anything they found could be used against him, but did not state that he had a right to refuse consent. And in a pre-*Schneckloth* case, *Davis v. United States,* [16] the Court found that the agreement of a filling station owner, after an initial objection, to unlock a room and allow police to search for rationing coupons was a valid consent, even though he was under arrest at the time and not warned. In the words of Justice Douglas:

> The public character of the property, the fact that the demand was made during business hours at the place of business where the coupons were required to be kept, the existence of the right to inspect, the nature of the request, the fact that the initial refusal to turn the coupons over was soon followed by acquiescence in the demand—these circumstances all support the conclusion of the District Court.

These cases present an interesting contrast to *Miranda* and its progeny, which rely on the assumption that arrest is "inherently coercive" and require warnings about the right to remain silent to

12. See Weinreb, "Generalities of the Fourth Amendment," 42 U.Chi.L. Rev. 47 (1974).

13. 446 U.S. 544, 100 S.Ct. 1870 (1980).

14. 389 F.2d 514 (6th Cir.1968).

15. 423 U.S. 411, 96 S.Ct. 820 (1976).

16. 328 U.S. 582, 66 S.Ct. 1256 (1946).

counteract this coercive atmosphere.[17] The two lines of cases seem inconsistent. But one might try to reconcile them by noting that *Miranda* itself recognized that unwarned statements might not be involuntary "in traditional terms." Moreover, as already noted, the Court is much more willing to favor the state when the Fourth Amendment right is involved.

(c) **Force, Show of Force and Threats.** As noted above, *Schneckloth* concluded that a consent is not valid if "coerced, by explicit or implicit means, by implied threat or covert force." *Schneckloth* itself did not provide much of an indication how the Court would construe this language in hard cases, since there the consent was clearly voluntary. In that case, one police officer lawfully stopped a car with six occupants. To his request to search the car, the brother of the absent owner of the car responded "Sure, go ahead" and even assisted the police in opening the glove compartment and trunk. The consentor apparently had nothing to hide, since the car was not his and the evidence subsequently found was used against another occupant of the car.

In earlier cases, the Court seemed willing to construe "coercion" quite broadly. In *Amos v. United States,*[18] for instance, two government agents went to the defendant's home, identified themselves to his wife, and told her they had come to search the premises "for violations of the revenue laws." Recounting nothing but these facts, the Court found her consent to their subsequent search involuntary, stating simply that "under the implied coercion here presented, no such waiver was intended or effected."

Similarly, in *Johnson v. United States,*[19] the Court held that coercion exists when the police, lacking the requisite warrant or suspicion, announce they are going to search. A somewhat more subtle situation was presented in *Bumper v. North Carolina,*[20] where the Supreme Court found invalid the consent of the defendant's grandmother, a 66 year-old black widow, to a search of her house after four white police officers appeared at her door and announced they had a search warrant. The primary ground for the Court's conclusion was that the officers' "show of authority" coerced the consent. As Justice Stewart stated for the Court, "[w]hen a law enforcement officer claims authority to search a home under a warrant, he announces in effect that the occupant has no right to resist the search. The situation is instinct with coercion." On the other hand, in *Coolidge v. New Hampshire,*[21] where the police came to the defendant's house merely to ask his

17. See § 16.02(d)(1).

18. 255 U.S. 313, 41 S.Ct. 266 (1921).

19. 333 U.S. 10, 68 S.Ct. 367 (1948).

20. 391 U.S. 543, 88 S.Ct. 1788 (1968).

21. 403 U.S. 443, 91 S.Ct. 2022 (1971).

wife questions and she volunteered to procure items that they wanted, no coercion was involved.

United States v. Mendenhall [22] is a more recent example of how the Court has applied the totality of the circumstances analysis to situations where no direct force or threat is involved. In *Mendenhall*, officers of the Drug Enforcement Administration posted at the Detroit airport to check for signs of narcotics trafficking observed several aspects of the defendant's conduct that suggested to them she might be carrying narcotics. They approached her, identified themselves, and asked her to produce identification and her plane ticket. After examining both, the agents questioned her as to why the ticket was in another name, to which she responded that she "just felt like using that name." Their suspicions were further aroused when she told them that she had been in California only two days, and they were strengthened again when she began shaking and became somewhat incoherent after one agent told her that he was a federal narcotics agent. Asked to accompany the agents for further questioning to the DEA office located elsewhere in the airport, Mendenhall walked with them to the office. There she was asked if she would allow them to search her person and handbag. Although she was told that she could decline, she agreed. A search of the handbag yielded another ticket in a third name. A female police officer, assigned to search Mendenhall further, again asked if she consented. Although Mendenhall stated she had a plane to catch, she agreed to the search. After partially disrobing, she handed over two packages of heroin to the policewoman.

The Court examined both the "consent" to accompany the officers to the DEA office and the consent to the searches conducted there. As to the voluntariness of the first "consent," the Court noted that Mendenhall was not *told* that she had to go to the office but rather was simply *asked* if she would accompany the officers. "There were neither threats nor any show of force." The Court also pointed out that the initial questioning by the narcotics agents had been brief. The Court dismissed Mendenhall's argument that, as a 22 year old black female who had not graduated from high school, she felt unusually threatened by the officers, who were white males. "While these factors were not irrelevant . . . neither were they decisive, and the totality of the evidence in this case was plainly adequate to support the District Court's finding that the respondent voluntarily consented to accompany the officers to the DEA office." Turning to an analysis of the consent to have her handbag and her person searched, the Court was most impressed with the fact that the agents twice told

22. 446 U.S. 544, 100 S.Ct. 1870 (1980).

Mendenhall she was free to decline to consent to those searches. As noted earlier, the Court termed this fact "highly relevant" to its conclusion that the consents were voluntary. It also refused to view Mendenhall's statement that she had a plane to catch as evidence of resistance to the body search, but rather agreed with the District Court that this statement could be seen simply as an expression that the search be conducted quickly.

Mendenhall suggests that, in determining whether a consent is voluntary, the Court is reluctant to consider subtly coercive factors that may play on the individual who is confronted by government officials or to attribute importance to *non*verbal responses, such as "shaking" or incoherence, which may indicate some degree of intimidation. As the four dissenters in *Mendenhall* pointed out: "On the record before us, the Court's conclusion can only be based on the notion that consent can be assumed from the absence of proof that a suspect resisted police authority."

The lower courts have, not surprisingly, dealt with a number of situations involving subtle and not so subtle forms of coercion. Representative is *United States v. Whitlock*, [23] in which the defendant was approached at gun point, handcuffed and escorted to his apartment where he was surrounded by five drug enforcement agents. The federal District Court found that, given these circumstances of "surprise, confusion and fright," the consent was involuntary.[24] However, on substantially similar facts, the Virginia Supreme Court found consent voluntary.[25] The crucial distinction appeared to be that in this case the defendant had been told he had the right to refuse.

The lower courts have also invalidated consents that are the product of verbal threats. In *Jones v. Unknown Agents of the Federal Election Commission*, [26] the defendant's consent was found involuntary because an FEC official had threatened him with 10 years in jail, a $10,000 fine, and the possibility of losing his house if he did not turn over incriminating evidence. In *Lightford v. State*, [27] the suggestion by one of several officers detaining the defendant that they kick in the defendant's door if he did not produce the key to it was found unconstitutionally coercive.

(d) Personal Characteristics. *Schneckloth* noted that, in determining the validity of a consent, the "traditional definition of voluntariness we accept today has always taken into account evidence of minimal schooling [and] low intelligence." The Court

---

23. 418 F.Supp. 138 (E.D.Mich.1976), aff'd 556 F.2d 583 (6th Cir.1977).

24. See also, *Rodriquez v. State*, 262 Ark. 659, 559 S.W.2d 925 (1978) (consent invalid when defendant surrounded by police officers).

25. *Lowe v. Commonwealth*, 218 Va. 670, 239 S.E.2d 112 (1977), cert. denied 435 U.S. 930, 98 S.Ct. 1502 (1978).

26. 613 F.2d 864 (D.C.Cir.1979), cert. denied 444 U.S. 1074, 100 S.Ct. 1019 (1980).

27. 90 Nev. 136, 520 P.2d 955 (1974).

also mentioned age as a consideration in totality of the circumstances analysis. Lower courts have also considered these factors important,[28] and have indicated that factors such as illiteracy,[29] substance abuse,[30] emotional state,[31] and difficulty with the English language[32] are pertinent as well. Presumably, the same variables found relevant in confessions cases will be relevant here.[33] Evaluation of these types of factors can be extremely problematic, given the spectrum of dysfunction possible. *Mendenhall,* seems to indicate that, as far as the Court is concerned, these factors must have a significant effect on the defendant's ability to consent voluntarily before they will result in a finding that waiver was invalid.

A separate issue is whether a waiver that is subsequently established to be involuntary due to some dysfunction is nonetheless valid if the police could not have recognized the problem under the circumstances. One might conclude that if a personal trait renders consent truly involuntary, then the fact that the police could not reasonably have discerned its effect should be irrelevant.[34] In such an instance, the person has not actually surrendered any expectation of privacy. But, as discussed below, the Supreme Court has found third party consents valid even when the third party does not have actual authority to consent, so long as it reasonably *appears* the third party has authority.[35] And, in the confession context, the Court has held that the confession of a mentally ill individual is "voluntary" so long as police do not recognize and exploit the illness in their attempts to obtain information.[36] These decisions flow from the premise that the Constitution is meant to impose constraints on the police, not protect individual rights in situations where the police could not have been deterred by a constitutional ruling.

12.03   The Scope of a Consent Search

The scope of a search conducted pursuant to a consent is governed by the nature of the consent. If a person consents to a search of area X but specifically denies access to area Y, the police may not search, without more, area Y. On the other hand, *any* articles within area X may be examined, if it is "objectively

28. See, e.g., *United States v. Mayes,* 552 F.2d 729 (6th Cir.1977) (age and immaturity).

29. *Suggars v. State,* 520 S.W.2d 364 (Tenn.Crim.App.1974).

30. *United States v. Leland,* 376 F.Supp. 1193 (D.Del.1974).

31. *People v. Gonzalez,* 39 N.Y.2d 122, 383 N.Y.S.2d 215, 347 N.E.2d 575 (1976).

32. *United States v. Wai Lau,* 215 F.Supp. 684 (S.D.N.Y.1963).

33. See § 16.02(a)(2).

34. See, e.g., *United States v. Elrod,* 441 F.2d 353 (5th Cir.1971).

35. See *Illinois v. Rodriguez,* 497 U.S. 177, 110 S.Ct. 2793 (1990), discussed in § 12.04.

36. *Colorado v. Connelly,* 479 U.S. 157, 107 S.Ct. 515 (1986).

reasonable" for the officer to believe that the scope of the person's consent permits him to do so. This was the holding of *Florida v. Jimeno*,[37] which involved a search of a folded, brown paper bag on the floorboard of a car after the driver had told police they could search the car. Although the driver later contended that he had meant to consent only to a search of the visible interior of the vehicle, and not closed containers within it, the Supreme Court pointed out that the consent came after the officer had informed the defendant that he believed the defendant was carrying narcotics. Under these circumstances, the Court concluded, 7–2, that the officer was reasonable in assuming that the consent authorized search of any items within the car that might contain drugs. The Court distinguished this situation from one in which the defendant consents to search of a trunk, where the police find a locked briefcase and pry it open. In the latter instance, the Court stated, "[i]t is very likely unreasonable" to believe the person consented to search of the briefcase (apparently even if the person knew the police were looking for drugs).[38]

If the officer in *Jimeno* had obtained consent based on a representation that he wanted to look for weapons, and he instead found drugs in an area where weapons would not normally be placed, a different result might be reached. In *State v. Gonzales*,[39] for instance, the Court held that a person's consent to search his residence for stolen jewelry, radios, and equipment did not contemplate a search which turned up marijuana in a paper bag. On the other hand, if a consent search is limited to intrusion into those areas that a reasonable person would assume is covered by the consent, then the mere fact that the police find items other than those contemplated by the police or the consentor usually should not render the search illegal. More questionably, given its cases in analogous contexts, the Supreme Court is likely to subscribe to this position even if the police act pretextually—that is, even if they ask for consent to search for item X when in fact they wish to obtain item Y and then discover Y.[40]

A second issue regarding the scope of a consent search is whether it can be modified after consent is given. The American Law Institute's Model Code of Pre–Arraignment Procedure would permit the withdrawal or limitation of consent at any time prior

---

37. 500 U.S. ___, 111 S.Ct. 1801 (1991).

38. Compare *United States v. Pena*, 920 F.2d 1509 (10th Cir.1990) (consent to search for drugs in car authorized tapping of external fender and probing of rear door panel after officer observed loose, crooked and missing screws); *United States v. Lechuga*, 925 F.2d 1035 (7th Cir.1991) (consent to search for drugs in apartment authorized search of suitcase in closet).

39. 46 Wash.App. 388, 731 P.2d 1101 (1986).

40. See discussion of pretextual searches in § 10.04.

to the completion of the search.[41] Although noting that caselaw on the issue is scanty and divided, the Reporters for the Code felt that the reasoning behind the decisions permitting withdrawal of a waiver to police questioning [42] supported a similar rule in the consent search context. The analogy to confessions seems appropriate in light of *Schneckloth's* use of the voluntariness standard employed in confession cases.

Some courts have also recognized what could be called "constructive withdrawal." For instance, in *State v. Brochu*,[43] the Maine Supreme Court held that a defendant's consent to search of his house for evidence concerning his wife's murder did not survive his subsequent arrest for that crime; the court noted that when he consented the defendant was still in the role of a husband assisting the police in investigating his wife's death, not a suspect. Accordingly, a second search the day following his arrest was not authorized by the consent.

The Supreme Court has at least obliquely accepted the idea of constructive withdrawal. In *Thompson v. Louisiana*,[44] Mrs. Thompson called her daughter to tell her that Mr. Thompson was dead and that she had swallowed some pills but no longer wanted to commit suicide. The daughter summoned police to the defendant's home, let them in, and showed them the location of Mrs. Thompson and her husband. Some 35 minutes after deputies had transported the defendant to the hospital, two members of the homicide squad arrived to conduct a follow-up investigation, which they termed a "general exploratory search for evidence of crime." During this second entry, the police found evidence that helped prove Mrs. Thompson had killed her husband. While the Court sanctioned the initial entry on a combination emergency/consent ground, it invalidated the subsequent search, which had not been authorized by a warrant. The Court stated that the defendant's "call for help can hardly be seen as an invitation to the general public that would have converted her home into the sort of public place for which no warrant to search would be necessary."

12.04. Third Party Consent

In most of the consent search cases which have reached the Supreme Court, the consent to search was not given by the person against whom the evidence was used. In *Schneckloth*, the car search which produced evidence against the defendant was authorized by another passenger, whose absent brother owned the car. In *Coolidge v. New Hampshire*,[45] consent was given by the wife of

---

41. ALI Model Code of Pre–Arraignment Procedure § 240.3(3) (1975).

42. See cases discussed in § 16.03(e).

43. 237 A.2d 418 (Me.1967).

44. 469 U.S. 17, 105 S.Ct. 409 (1984).

45. 403 U.S. 443, 91 S.Ct. 2022 (1971).

the defendant. And, although the consent in *Bumper v. North Carolina* [46] was ultimately found invalid on involuntariness grounds, the Court never questioned the authority of the defendant's grandmother to consent to a search of her house.

These decisions flow from the Court's view of the scope of the Fourth Amendment. Originally, that scope was defined by property concepts. Thus, if a person owned or had a significant possessory interest in the area in question, she could consent to its search. Although the majority opinion in *Katz v. United States* [47] later rejected a property-based understanding of the Fourth Amendment, stating that the Amendment "protects people, not places," Justice Harlan's concurring opinion in that case, which averred that discussion about Fourth Amendment protection usually requires reference to a place, has dominated subsequent Court decisionmaking.[48] The Court's post-*Katz* focus on "reasonable expectations of privacy" in the area searched has meant that when a place is shared by more than one person, more than one person may consent to its search. Thus, once again, the Fourth Amendment is treated differently than the right to remain silent or the right to counsel, neither of which can be waived by a third party.[49]

The earlier, property-based rationale for this view is reflected in several cases pre-dating *Katz*. For instance, in *Chapman v. United States*,[50] the Court held invalid a consent by a landlord of a tenant's home, despite the state's claim that a landlord has authority to view premises which are being "wasted and used for criminal purposes." The Court was unable to find any state or common law "holding that a landlord, in the absence of an express covenant so permitting, has a right forcibly to enter the demised premises without the consent of the tenant 'to view waste.' " And in *Stoner v. California*,[51] consent by a hotel clerk of a room in the hotel was found insufficient because a guest can surrender his Fourth Amendment right only "directly or through an agent" and there was nothing in the record to indicate that "the night clerk had been authorized by the petitioner to permit the police to search the petitioner's room."

After *Katz*, the Court's cases began analyzing third party consent cases in terms of reasonable expectations concerning the searched area. For example, in *Frazier v. Cupp*,[52] the Court upheld a consent by the defendant's cousin to search a duffel bag

---

46. 391 U.S. 543, 88 S.Ct. 1788 (1968).

47. 389 U.S. 347, 88 S.Ct. 507 (1967).

48. See § 4.03 for further discussion of this development.

49. See § 15.05 (right to remain silent); § 31.04 (right to counsel).

50. 365 U.S. 610, 81 S.Ct. 776 (1961).

51. 376 U.S. 483, 84 S.Ct. 889 (1964).

52. 394 U.S. 731, 89 S.Ct. 1420 (1969).

which both of them used and which had been left in the cousin's house, because the defendant had "assumed the risk that [the cousin] would allow someone else to look inside." It was in *United States v. Matlock,*[53] however, that the Court first firmly discarded a property-based view of third party consents in favor of a analysis which asked whether the third party possesses "common authority or other sufficient relationship to the premises or property or effects sought to be inspected." In a footnote the Court explained:

> Common authority, is of course, not to be implied from the mere property interest a third party has in the property. The authority which justifies the third-party consent does not rest upon the law of property, with its attendant historical and legal refinements, but rests rather on mutual use of the property by persons generally having joint access or control for most purposes, so that it is reasonable to recognize that any of the coinhabitants has the right to permit the inspection in his own right and that the others have assumed the risk that one of their number might permit the common area to be searched.

The Court's application of this language to the facts of *Matlock* is instructive. There, the defendant was arrested in the front yard of a house in which he lived with several others. Instead of asking the defendant if they could search his room, the police proceeded to the house, where they were admitted by a Mrs. Graff, one of the other tenants. Although she later denied that she acted voluntarily, Mrs. Graff then consented to a search of the house, including the bedroom which she said she shared with the defendant. There, in a closet on the floor, the police found incriminating evidence in a diaper bag. The Court assumed Mrs. Graff's consent was voluntary and found it sufficient authorization for the search, because she had "common authority" over the searched area. The Court did not consider whether she had common authority over the diaper bag, presumably because, as it had stated in response to the defendant's argument in *Frazier* that his cousin had access to only part of the duffel bag, "[w]e will not . . . engage in such metaphysical subtleties." Based on the Court's treatment of the facts in *Matlock,* it appears that if the state can establish that the third party shares an area with another more or less equally,[54] that party's consent authorizes a search of the entire area regardless of the other person's proximity

---

53. 415 U.S. 164, 94 S.Ct. 988 (1974).

54. Note that when the third party's authority over a place is clearly inferior, as in *Chapman* and *Stoner,* then the consent is not valid. The same should hold true of an area within premises that is clearly within the exclusive control of the defendant. See, e.g., *United States v. Heisman,* 503 F.2d 1284 (8th Cir.1974) (consent by one tenant not valid as to another tenant's room).

to, agreement with, or relationship with the third party.[55] Thus, the common authority test, to the extent it differs from the property-agency theory earlier endorsed by the Court, probably broadens the scope of third party consent.

The Court's finding in *Matlock* that Mrs. Graff possessed actual authority over the bedroom meant that the Court did not reach the government's further contention in that case, that a third party consent should be deemed valid whenever the searching officers reasonably believe that the party has such authority, whether or not it actually exists. When given the opportunity to consider this so-called "apparent authority" doctrine, in *Illinois v. Rodriguez,*[56] six members of the Court voted to adopt it. In *Rodriguez,* police obtained evidence used to convict the defendant after his ex-girlfriend let them into his apartment with her key. Prior to the search she referred to the premises as "our" apartment and said she had clothes and furniture there. In fact, however, she had moved out of the apartment almost a month earlier, taking with her most of her belongings; since that time she had visited Rodriguez infrequently, never invited her friends there, and never went there herself when he was not at home. On these facts, both the lower courts and the Supreme Court held that she had no actual authority to consent to a search of the apartment. But the Court then held that this conclusion did not necessarily invalidate the search.

According to Justice Scalia, who wrote the Court's opinion, the question to be addressed in such cases is whether the facts available to the officer warranted "a man of reasonable caution in the belief that the consenting party had authority over the premises." This rule is justified, he asserted, because the Fourth Amendment does not require that factual determinations made by magistrates or police be correct, but only that they be reasonable. However, Scalia also cautioned that "[e]ven when the invitation is accompanied by an explicit assertion that the person lives there, the surrounding circumstances could conceivably be such that a reasonable person would doubt its truth and not act upon it without further inquiry." The case was remanded for consideration in light of these points.[57]

As Justice Marshall pointed out in dissent, third party consent searches are usually not conducted in exigent circumstances.

---

55. Some courts appear to stretch even this broad rule a bit far. See, e.g., *United States v. Clutter,* 914 F.2d 775 (6th Cir.1990) (children 12 and 14 years of age could consent to search of bedroom occupied by their mother and her male companion since they "were routinely left in exclusive control of the house.")

56. 497 U.S. 177, 110 S.Ct. 2793 (1990).

57. Compare *State v. Penn,* 61 Ohio St.3d 720, 576 N.E.2d 790 (1991) (police would not reasonably believe pharmacist had authority to consent to search of pharmacy when they were "on notice" that he had terminated his employment there four days earlier).

Thus, when the police fail to get a warrant, instead relying on the consent of a third party who may not have authority to consent, the police, rather than the defendant, should "accept the risk of error." Marshall's critique of the apparent authority doctrine might arguably be extended more generally to the entire notion of third party consent, which allows the police to conduct non-exigent warrantless and suspicionless searches over the objection, actual or implied, of the person whose privacy they seek to invade. To the extent such an objection is designed purely to protect against discovery of incriminating evidence, it should be inoperative.[58] But given the difficulty of ascertaining whether this is the case, and the fact that the third party will often be unaware of, or unsympathetic to, other privacy interests that will be infringed by the search, the third party consent notion can be viewed as an inappropriate diminishment of Fourth Amendment protection.

12.05 Conclusion

The principal tenets of the consent search exception to the warrant requirement can be described as follows:

(1) In order for a consent to be valid it must be voluntary under the totality of the circumstances test developed in confessions cases. In determining whether a consent is voluntary, one of the factors that may be considered is whether the consentor knew of his right to refuse the search, but failure of the police to apprise the consentor of this right is not an automatic grounds for exclusion of the evidence. Other factors which might impinge upon the voluntariness decision are (a) whether the consentor was in custody at the time of consent; (b) the extent to which police used force, shows of force or threats to obtain the consent; (c) whether police claimed to have authority to conduct a search; and (d) the extent to which the consentor, due to personal characteristics, finds it particularly difficult to resist police suggestions.

(2) The scope of a consent search can be limited by the consentor to specific areas or types of items. Theoretically, at least, the consent search may be terminated at any time by the consentor. In either case, however, the nature of the consent is governed by what an "objectively reasonable" police officer would believe under the circumstances, not by the subjective beliefs of the consentor or the officer.

(3) In general, the consent of a person who shares authority over an area more or less equally with an absent or nonconsenting party will authorize a search of that area and seizure of property within it, assuming the consent of the third party is voluntary.

---

58. Cf. *United States v. Jacobsen,* 466 U.S. 109, 104 S.Ct. 1652 (1984), discussed in § 4.03(f)(2) (use of drug field test not a search because only contraband is examined).

Also valid is a voluntary consent by anyone whom the police reasonably believe possess such actual authority.

BIBLIOGRAPHY

Coombs, Mary. Shared Privacy and the Fourth Amendment, or the Rights of Relationships. 75 Calif.L.Rev. 1593 (1987).

Deschene, Robert. The Problem of Third-Party Consent in Fourth Amendment Searches: Toward a "Conservative" Reading of the Matlock Decision. 42 Maine L.Rev. 159 (1990).

Gardner, Martin. Consent as a Bar to Fourth Amendment Scope: A Critique of a Common Theory. 71 J.Crim.L. and Criminol. 443 (1980).

Goldberger, Peter. Consent, Expectations of Privacy, and the Meaning of "Searches" in the Fourth Amendment. 75 J.Crim.L. and Criminology 319 (1984).

Schneckloth v. Bustamonte: The Question of Noncustodial and Custodial Consent Searches [Comment]. 66 J.Crim.L. and Criminology 286 (1975).

Stuntz, William. Waiving Rights in Criminal Procedure. 75 Va. L.Rev. 761 (1989).

Wefing, John B. and John G. Miles, Jr. Consent Searches and the Fourth Amendment: Voluntariness and Third-Party Problems. 5 Seton Hall L.Rev. 211 (1974).

Weinreb, Lloyd L. Generalities of the Fourth Amendment. 42 U.Chi.L.Rev. 47 (1974).

Chapter Thirteen

REGULATORY INSPECTIONS AND SEARCHES

13.01 Introduction

In addition to their efforts at investigating and solving "street crime," federal and state governments have attempted to curtail various other types of conduct considered to be against the public interest. In order to do so, they have devised a vast array of "administrative" schemes designed to monitor the activities of their constituents, ranging from highway license checks and safety inspections of residential and commercial buildings to border patrols and school disciplinary rules. Although differentiating precisely between regulatory searches and other searches is difficult, the former actions share two features: (1) their predominant objective is to procure evidence for "administrative" purposes that at most can result in a misdemeanor conviction (although sometimes evidence of serious crime is discovered in plain view during such searches); and (2) they are usually conducted by officials other than the police.

The Supreme Court has recognized that many of these regulatory efforts can result in significant intrusions on personal privacy or autonomy, and thus has usually held that they implicate the Fourth Amendment. At the same time, the Court has been willing to relax the typical warrant and probable cause requirements in virtually all of the regulatory situations it has confronted. In doing so, the Court has relied on a balancing analysis first developed in *Camara v. Municipal Court*.[1] In that case, dealing with residential health and safety inspections, the Court concluded that "there can be no ready test for determining reasonableness other than by balancing the need to search against the invasion which the search entails." Since *Camara*, the Court has used the balancing test not only in analyzing regulatory searches but also in analyzing police searches, beginning with its decision in *Terry v. Ohio*,[2] a year after *Camara*.

In applying the *Camara* invasion-versus-need balancing test to regulatory inspections, the Court has looked at several factors. On the individual side of the balance, the Court has emphasized the lesser intrusion involved when the government's motivation is regulatory rather than investigative. On the government side, it has pointed to one or more of the following factors: (1) the difficulty of detecting the harm caused by regulatory violations if

---

1. 387 U.S. 523, 87 S.Ct. 1727 (1967). 2. 392 U.S. 1, 88 S.Ct. 1868 (1968), discussed in Chapter Eleven.

a warrant and probable cause are required; (2) the likelihood that regulatory officials will experience difficulty mastering the warrant procedure and the "niceties" of probable cause; and (3) the disruption a warrant and probable cause requirement will cause to the smooth operation of the government. Application of these factors has always led to a modification of the probable cause standard, and often resulted in the elimination of a warrant requirement. Indeed, in its most recent regulatory inspection cases, the Court has begun referring to situations in which one or more of these criteria are met as "exceptional circumstances in which special needs, beyond the normal needs for law enforcement, make the warrant and probable cause requirement impracticable." [3] This chapter looks at a wide array of "special needs" situations, including residential, business and fire inspections, border searches, airport and traffic screenings, inventory searches, school and workplace searches, and searches of probationer's homes.

13.02 Inspections of Homes

(a) **Health and Safety Inspections.** One of the first types of administrative searches addressed by the Supreme Court concerned health and safety inspections of residential buildings. For some time, the Court refused to apply Fourth Amendment strictures to such inspections. In *Frank v. Maryland,*[4] for instance, it upheld the constitutionality of a statute punishing property holders for refusing to cooperate with a warrantless inspection. Because a safety inspection does not ask the property owner to open his doors to a search for "evidence of criminal action," it "touch[es] at most upon the periphery of the important interests safeguarded by the Fourteenth Amendment's protection against official intrusion." In 1967, however, the Court overruled *Frank* in *Camara v. Municipal Court.*[5] Noting that most regulatory violations *can* result in criminal penalties, and that a warrantless search gives the occupant inadequate proof of the inspector's authority to conduct the search, the Court, in an opinion by Justice White, held that nonconsensual administrative searches of private residences constitute a "significant intrusion upon the interests protected by the Fourth Amendment" and thus are unreasonable without a warrant.

At the same time, the majority significantly modified the basis for obtaining a warrant in the administrative search context. Rather than requiring that the magistrate find probable cause with respect to each building inspected, the Court found sufficient

---

3. As Justice Blackmun first put it in his concurring opinion in *New Jersey v. T.L.O.,* 469 U.S. 325, 105 S.Ct. 733 (1985), discussed in § 13.08.

4. 359 U.S. 360, 79 S.Ct. 804 (1959).

5. 387 U.S. 523, 87 S.Ct. 1727 (1967).

a "probable cause" finding that the area, "as a whole," needed inspection, based on such factors as the age of the buildings, the passage of time, and other conditions. This type of probable cause is not "individualized," nor does it resemble the more-likely-than-not finding to which traditional probable cause has often been analogized.[6] But Justice White gave three reasons for adopting it when the search is a residential health or safety inspection:

> First, such programs have a long history of judicial and public acceptance. Second, the public interest demands that all dangerous conditions be prevented or abated, yet it is doubtful that any other canvassing technique would achieve acceptable results. . . . Finally, because the inspections are neither personal in nature nor aimed at the discovery of evidence of crime, they involve a relatively limited invasion of the urban citizen's privacy.

These reasons all make sense. While the dissent in *Frank* spoke of "acquiescence" to, rather than acceptance of, these inspection programs, it is not farfetched to conclude that, on the whole, the public welcomes government efforts to make their homes safer, and that this attitude lessens the sense of intrusion associated with such searches. The Court is also correct in asserting that the types of problems these inspections are designed to correct—faulty wiring, ventilation, plumbing and other unsafe or unhealthy conditions—would be very difficult to detect (or would lead to an unacceptable increase in undercover activity and similar efforts) if probable cause were required. And an inspection is a relatively limited invasion, in the sense that it does not involve rummaging through personal belongings or the stigmatization associated with a criminal investigation. Taken together, these reasons support the idea that such inspections may be authorized based on the type of low-level, "generalized" suspicion described by the majority.

The three-member dissent did not disagree with these findings. Rather, it inveighed against *Camara's* warrant requirement, arguing that it would result in the advent of "boxcar warrants . . . identical as to every dwelling in the area, save the street number itself . . . printed up in pads of a thousand or more . . . and issued by magistrates in broadcast fashion as a matter of course." But because most residents consent to such inspections,[7] warrants will seldom be necessary. If a refusal does occur, a resident is unlikely to be able to hide any unsafe conditions by

6. See § 5.03.

7. In his dissenting opinion in *Camara*, Justice Clark noted that in one voluntary inspection program initiated in Oregon the consent rate was 5 out of 6, a fact which he used to support his argument that warrants would have to be obtained in an inordinate number of cases, but which can also support the conclusion that most people welcome such inspections.

the time a warrant is obtained; further, if the condition is corrected, the government's objective will have been achieved in any event. A more telling criticism of *Camara* is that it did not require the inspecting agency, when conducting the initial warrantless inquiry, to give the resident notice regarding its intention and the right to refuse consent. Without such notice, the resident is more likely to succumb to the implicit "claim of authority" that any inspector carries with him.[8]

It should also be noted that there are some situations when even the watered-down warrant requirement of *Camara* is inapplicable, because the inspection must take place immediately. Usually, residential inspections do not involve an emergency, because, as noted above, if the violation is corrected before the inspectors arrive, the government's objective is achieved. However, occasionally exigency does exist. The Supreme Court has permitted warrantless entries in cases involving unwholesome food,[9] compulsory small pox vaccination,[10] and health quarantines.[11] Elimination of a warrant requirement does not, of course, eliminate the need to show some level of suspicion that the entry is necessary to avert the perceived harm.

(b) Welfare Inspections. In *Wyman v. James,*[12] the Supreme Court upheld a New York law that permitted caseworkers to make warrantless visits to the homes of welfare beneficiaries, the consequence of which could be the termination of benefits. Compared to health and safety inspections, such visits are arguably less "accepted," more "invasive," and not as indispensable to the government's aim of detecting welfare fraud. Yet the Supreme Court did not rely on the *Camara* factors in analyzing the statute. Rather it declared that welfare visitations are not searches under the Fourth Amendment, primarily because they cannot result in criminal sanctions. This reasoning, which was also the basis of *Franks,* had been squarely rejected in *Camara.* At the least, such visitations should require administrative warrants in all non-exigent situations, based on neutral factors that correlate with violation of welfare rules. Given the intrusion involved, one could even make a case for requiring normal warrants, based on the usual individualized probable cause. A countervailing factor in

---

8. The Court has held that warning a person of his right to refuse consent is not required. *Schneckloth v. Bustamonte,* 412 U.S. 218, 93 S.Ct. 2041 (1973), discussed in § 12.02(a). But the primary reason for that holding was the often unstructured setting of a field search. In the regulatory context, this rationale does not apply.

9. *North American Cold Storage Co. v. Chicago,* 211 U.S. 306, 29 S.Ct. 101 (1908).

10. *Jacobsen v. Commonwealth of Massachusetts,* 197 U.S. 11, 25 S.Ct. 358 (1905).

11. *Compagnie Francaise de Navigation a Vapeur v. Louisiana State Board of Health,* 186 U.S. 380, 22 S.Ct. 811 (1902).

12. 400 U.S. 309, 91 S.Ct. 381 (1971).

this regard is that, if invasiveness is judged from the perspective of the children who are often protected by welfare legislation,[13] such visits might be welcomed as readily as the health and safety inspections at issue in *Camara*.

13.03 Inspections of Businesses

See v. Seattle,[14] a companion case to *Camara*, involved a city-wide inspection of businesses for violations of the fire code. The Court, again through Justice White, concluded that "[t]he businessman, like the occupant of a residence, has a constitutional right to go about his business free from unreasonable official entries upon his private commercial property." Thus, *Camara*-type warrant and probable cause requirements were held to apply to the type of inspections at issue in *See*. The Court seemed determined to ensure that "the decision to enter and inspect will not be the product of the unreviewed discretion of the enforcement officer in the field." Within five years of *See*, however, the Court had created an exception to this rule which has since come to be called the "closely regulated business" exception to the warrant requirement. The scope of this exception has become so broad that it appears to apply to all but a few types of business inspections, without regard to their invasiveness or the difficulty of otherwise detecting statutory violations, the types of factors considered important in *Camara*.

(a) The Closely Regulated Business Doctrine. The first decision tempering *See* was *Colonnade Catering Corp. v. United States*.[15] In a brief opinion, the Court approved a federal statute criminalizing refusal to allow warrantless entry of liquor stores by government inspectors, who in this case were attempting to discover if liquor bottles had been refilled illegally. Two years later came *United States v. Biswell*,[16] which upheld a warrantless entrance of a gun store to inspect documents and check whether any unlicensed guns were on the premises. Justice White, who wrote the Court's opinion in *Biswell*, distinguished his opinion in *See* by noting that the conditions sought to be discovered in the latter case were relatively difficult to conceal or to correct in a short time; requiring a warrant after refusal would thus not frustrate the regulatory purpose. Effective implementation of the Gun Control Act, on the other hand, required "unannounced, even frequent inspections." Of course, a *Camara*-type warrant issued *ex parte* would permit such surprise inspections. Moreover, the

13. See Burt, "Forcing Protection on Children and Their Parents: The Impact of Wyman v. James," 69 Mich.L. Rev. 1259 (1971).

14. 387 U.S. 541, 87 S.Ct. 1737 (1967).

15. 397 U.S. 72, 90 S.Ct. 774 (1970).

16. 406 U.S. 311, 92 S.Ct. 1593 (1972).

Court's approach in *Colonnade* and *Biswell* ignored *See's* conclusions about the importance of protecting business privacy from the unmonitored discretion of field officers. On the first point, the *Biswell* Court apparently felt that requiring a warrant in each instance would be inefficient, perhaps having in mind the *Camara* dissent's lamentation about "boxcar warrants." As to the second objection, the *Biswell* majority concluded: "When a dealer chooses to engage in this pervasively regulated business and to accept a federal license, he does so with the knowledge that his business records, firearms and ammunition will be subject to effective inspection." The Court did state, however, that "unauthorized force" cannot be used to gain entrance, apparently meaning to prohibit unnecessarily rough entry.

Biswell's "pervasively" or "closely" regulated business exception to the warrant requirement appeared to consist of two elements: (1) the violations sought to be discovered must be of the type that are easily hidden—as opposed to easily correctable—thus allowing the business owner to frustrate government policy if the usual process of seeking consent and obtaining a warrant or subpoena upon refusal were followed; (2) the industry in question must be pervasively regulated so that an owner is put on notice as to the types of surprise inspections to which he will be subjected. In *Marshall v. Barlow's, Inc.,*[17] however, the Court indicated that merely satisfying these two requirements might not be enough. There, the Secretary of Labor argued that inspections under the Occupational Health and Safety Act met both conditions; the safety violations targeted under the Act could be subject to "speedy alteration and disguise" and the regulations under the Act specified in detail the types of things that would be inspected. But the Court held otherwise, in an opinion remarkable for its opaqueness.

The Court glossed over the government's "speedy alteration" argument, merely asserting that most business owners would consent to OSHA inspections. Apparently the Court had in mind, as it had in *Camara* and *See,* that in most instances the government objective of achieving a safe workplace would be achieved even if the officials had to seek a warrant after being refused entry, either because the deficiencies would be corrected before their return or violations subjected to "alterations" or "disguise" could be discerned by the inspectors. As to the government's argument that the Act provided precise inspection guidelines, the Court simply stated that *Barlow's* did not involve a "closely regulated industry," since OSHA applied to a wide range of businesses, not all of which were associated with the long tradition

17. 436 U.S. 307, 98 S.Ct. 1816
(1978).

of extensive regulation experienced by the liquor and gun industries at issue in *Colonnade* and *Biswell*. Apparently the reasoning here was that the "implied consent" rationale of *Biswell* would be meaningless if it applied to virtually any type of business. In any event, the Court went on to hold that, to make a nonconsensual entry under OSHA, the government must obtain a *Camara*–type warrant based on a showing that the inspection is part of a general enforcement plan based on neutral criteria such as number of employees and accident experience.

In its next business inspection case, *Donovan v. Dewey*,[18] the Court further modified the "closely regulated industry" exception, in the course of concluding that warrantless inspections of coal mines under the Federal Mine Safety and Health Act were permissible. First, its holding made clear that, contrary to the Court's implication in *Barlow's* (as well as in *Colonnade* and *Biswell*), an industry need not have experienced a long tradition of regulation to be "closely regulated;" as Justice Stewart pointed out in dissent, the coal mining industry had been extensively monitored for less than two decades when *Dewey* came to the Court. The duration of regulation is only one factor to consider, concluded the majority; the key threshold issue is the comprehensiveness of regulatory scheme. However, the Court also held that a finding that an industry is pervasively regulated is not enough to justify warrantless business inspections. Three criteria additional must be met: (1) the government must have a "substantial" interest in the activity being regulated; (2) warrantless searches must be necessary to the effective enforcement of the law, as in *Biswell;* and (3) the inspection program must provide "a constitutionally adequate substitute for a warrant." The Court found that all three criteria were met in *Dewey*. With respect to the all-important third criterion, the Court noted that the Act required inspection of "*all* mines," defined the frequency of inspection, provided precise standards "with which a mine operator is required to comply," and established "a specific mechanism for accommodating any special privacy concerns that a specific mine operator might have" by allowing the owner to refuse entry and force the government to seek an injunction in federal court.

The OSHA inspection at issue in *Barlow's* had provided the same sort of protections (including, in practice, the refusal-and-injunction process). But the majority in *Dewey* explained that the Federal Mine Safety Act applied to a specific industry "with a notorious history of serious accidents and unhealthful conditions," whereas the statute in *Barlow's* would have permitted indiscriminate inspections of many businesses with no history of safety

18. 452 U.S. 594, 101 S.Ct. 2534 (1981).

violations. In any event, it would appear that the injunction process mandated by the Federal Mine Safety Act provides as much protection as does a warrant (at least to refusing owners). Indeed, given this latter aspect of *Dewey,* the decision called into doubt the broad scope of *Biswell's* ruling allowing "unannounced" nonconsensual inspections.

But the Court's next business inspection decision, *New York v. Burger,*[19] reinvigorated that ruling. The junkyard industry at issue in that case did not have a "notorious history" of violations, nor did the statute regulating it provide any type of judicial procedure. But the inspection process was upheld nonetheless by a vote of 6–3. The statute involved in *Burger* allowed warrantless, surprise inspections of junkyards and "vehicle dismantlers" for the purpose of checking whether they are licensed as required by the statute and, if so, whether their records are in order and any vehicles or parts on the premises were stolen. Unlike the Federal Mine Safety Act at issue in *Dewey,* the statute did not purport to regulate the condition of the premises, the method of operation, or the equipment utilized. But the Court, finding the registration and record-keeping aspects of the statute "extensive" (and relying as well on the "history of regulation of *related* industries"), held that the New York junkyard industry is "closely regulated." The Court went on to reiterate that, even if an industry is closely regulated, the statute regulating the industry must meet the three criteria established in *Dewey* in order to satisfy the Fourth Amendment. But Justice Blackmun, writing for the Court, quickly found that the New York law met all three criteria. First, the state has a "substantial interest" in regulating the vehicle dismantling industry because this industry is closely associated with motor vehicle theft, a significant problem in New York. Second, the statute serves this interest effectively; its surprise inspection provision is "crucial" if stolen vehicles and parts are to be detected. Third, the statute provides a constitutionally "adequate substitute for a warrant" by informing operators of junkyards that inspections will be made on a regular basis and by limiting the inspection to regular business hours and to vehicles and parts subject to its record-keeping requirements.

As Justice Brennan argued in dissent, "if New York City's administrative scheme renders the vehicle-dismantling business closely regulated, few businesses will escape such a finding." And even if the junkyard industry is heavily regulated, the New York statute did not meet *Dewey's* criteria. In particular, it provided no standard to guide inspectors and no injunction process: government officials are allowed to search any junkyard without any

19. 482 U.S. 691, 107 S.Ct. 2636 (1987).

justification any time they are open. Brennan also cautioned that the administrative scheme was merely a pretext for allowing police to uncover evidence of crime without obtaining a warrant. He noted that the statute specifically authorized police to conduct such inspections.

(b) An Alternative to the Court's Approach. Brennan's warning in *Burger* that the "implications of the Court's decision, if realized, will virtually eliminate Fourth Amendment protection of commercial entities in the context of administrative searches," is not far off the mark. As indicated in *Dewey*, inspectors may have to obtain some sort of judicial authorization to override a refusal when doing so will not frustrate the objective of the inspection process.[20] That case, as well as *Barlow's* and *Camara*, involved safety and health inspections where, as already noted, the delay occasioned by seeking such authorization after a refusal will often lead to correction of the deficiencies the government wants corrected. However, if the statutory scheme is aimed at a discreet industry (rather than at all businesses, as in *Barlow's*), and if obtaining judicial authorization will give the business owner time to hide or destroy evidence of a regulatory violation (a situation illustrated by *Colonnade, Biswell,* and *Burger*), then an immediate, warrantless entry is apparently permitted, so long as "unauthorized force" is not used.

Ironically, these latter searches are probably most likely to be perceived as invasive by those affected. Contrary to the Court's insinuation in *Biswell*, one does not "consent" to surprise searches merely because one enters a "closely regulated industry" (indeed, as in *Burger*, the regulation may *follow* entry into the industry). The invasiveness of the inspection should be measured in less fictional ways. In this regard, it is worthwhile noting that, whereas any business inspection will probably cause inconvenience and disruption, the types of safety and hazard inspections at issue in *Barlow's* and *Dewey*, like the home inspections in *Camara*, at least bring some benefit to the workers (who occupy the space inspected). The inspections in *Colonnade, Biswell,* and *Burger*, on the other hand, lack any clear advantage for the owner and thus are likely to be seen as more intrusive.

In short, the Court's cases appear to permit the most invasive business inspections without any showing of suspicion, at the discretion of officers in the field. The alternative would be to require these officials to obtain warrants, prior to attempting entry, based on the types of neutral factors sanctioned in *Camara*,

---

20. Cf. *Donovan v. Lone Steer, Inc.,* 464 U.S. 408, 104 S.Ct. 769 (1984) (approving a subpoena duces tecum against a company employee because (a) it does not contemplate nonconsensual entry and (b) no penalty may be imposed for failure to comply with the subpoena until the employer has the opportunity to question, in open court, its reasonableness).

See, and *Barlow's.*   It is unlikely this requirement would lead to the "boxcar warrants" of which the *Camara* dissenters complained, in that the number of businesses subjected to "preemptive" searches is far fewer than the number of residences inspected each year.   A more serious objection to this alternative approach is that it may not provide any additional protection, given the low level of "probable cause" that it permits.   But, in *See* and other cases,[21] the Court itself has recognized that the regulatory inspection process can be abused unless it is monitored, and schemes like those at issue in *Burger,* where the police are often involved, are likely to encourage such abuse if not subjected to some outside scrutiny.[22]

(c) **Non–Regulatory Searches.**   When a business search is not conducted pursuant to an inspection scheme, but rather for some other purpose, then the usual Fourth Amendment protections apply.   This is true even when the purpose of a search is something other than criminal investigation.   For instance, in *G.M. Leasing Corp. v. United States,*[23] the Supreme Court held that a warrant, based on the "usual" quantum of probable cause, is required before agents from the Internal Revenue Service may enter business premises to seize assets to satisfy tax assessments.[24]

13.04   Fire Inspections

In *Michigan v. Tyler,*[25] the Court approved a warrantless search and seizure of burned premises the night of the fire and another seizure the next morning while the cause of the fire was still undetermined.   However, it held unconstitutional a warrantless search weeks later that produced further evidence on which to ground prosecution of the defendant property owner for arson.   It concluded that once the exigency produced by the fire (including the need to determine its cause after it is extinguished) is ended, the police and fire marshal must secure an administrative warrant to conduct further searches.   Moreover, the more permissive *Camara/See* standards for determining probable cause were found

---

21.   In *Barlow's* it stated that "[t]he authority to make warrantless searches devolves almost unbridled discretion upon executive and administrative officers."   In a much earlier decision, it also noted the possibility that inspectors may serve as a "front" for the police.   *Abel v. United States,* 362 U.S. 217, 80 S.Ct. 683 (1960).

22.   See, e.g., *Turner v. Dammon,* 848 F.2d 440 (4th Cir.1988) (civil suit alleging police made a disproportionate number of "bar checks"); *People v. Tillery,* 211 Cal.App.3d 1569, 260 Cal.Rptr. 320 (1989) (finding inadmissible marijuana plants discovered by police of-

ficers executing an administrative building-inspection warrant over the occupant's resistance).

23.   429 U.S. 338, 97 S.Ct. 619 (1977).

24.   The Court also permitted a warrantless seizure of the corporation's cars, despite the absence of exigency, because they were on the public streets and thus "seizable by levy without an intrusion into privacy."   This aspect of *G.M. Leasing* is more questionable.   See § 7.03(c) on the automobile exception.

25.   436 U.S. 499, 98 S.Ct. 1942 (1978).

to require tightening in *Tyler,* because a fire scene presents a different situation than a routine inspection. A fire search is necessarily responsive to an individualized event, rather than to a random inspection pattern. For this reason, the Court concluded, a more particularized inquiry may be necessary to justify the warrant to search a fire scene than for a normal business investigation. The Court listed several factors to consider in this determination, including: (1) the number of prior entries, (2) the scope of the search, (3) the time of day when it is proposed to be made, (4) the time lapse since the fire, (5) the continued use of the building, and (6) the owner's efforts to secure the building against intruders.

In *Michigan v. Clifford,*[26] the Court partially reaffirmed *Tyler* but also appeared to reject at least some of its reasoning. *Clifford* involved an inspection of burned premises five hours after the extinction of the blaze during which evidence of arson was discovered, and a continued search for further evidence of arson. The entire Court agreed that the second phase of the search required a conventional warrant, since the government admitted it was part of a criminal investigation. But only four members of the Court agreed that the first search required a *Camara*-type search warrant. Four other justices felt that no warrant was needed to support this search, on the ground that it was a continuation of the original entry to extinguish the blaze. Justice Stevens, the swing vote, reasoned that a *Camara* warrant would provide no real protection in such cases. He concluded that instead "the home owner is entitled to reasonable advance notice that officers are going to enter his premises for the purposes of ascertaining the cause of the fire." After *Clifford* then, it appears any inspection conducted within a reasonable time after the fire must be preceded by notice but need not be authorized by a warrant of any type. After such time, the modified administrative warrant described in *Tyler* is required, unless suspicion develops as to a criminal motive, in which case, a traditional warrant must be sought to continue the search.

These rules seem needlessly complicated. An immediate warrantless post-fire search is justified by the indisputable facts that a fire has occurred and that determining its origins is an important task which requires quick entry of the premises. If further entries are necessary to determine the fire's origins, a requirement that a magistrate make a probable cause finding to that effect would prevent arbitrary decisions by fire officials and not be unduly burdensome. Trying to distinguish between routine post-five inspections and situations where inspectors develop a "suspi-

---

26. 464 U.S. 287, 104 S.Ct. 641 (1984).

cion" that arson has occurred is likely to create considerable confusion as to when an ongoing investigation must stop to obtain a conventional warrant.

13.05 Border Inspections

Unfortunately, the heavy volume of litigation on the subject leaves the impression that "border searches" constitute a separate exception to the warrant requirement. It is true, as developed below, that at the border itself the authority of the United States to exclude illegal aliens and contraband from the country can be exercised through the mechanism of warrantless inspections and searches. But searches and seizures conducted *near* the border are treated no differently than searches and seizures conducted elsewhere in the country. The Supreme Court's "border search" decisions rely on traditional analysis, in particular the automobile exception to the warrant requirement and the "stop and frisk" doctrine. Thus, for instance, in *Almeida–Sanchez v. United States* [27] and *United States v. Ortiz,*[28] the Court reaffirmed that the elements of the automobile exception, including probable cause, must be met before a car found on the highway may be searched, even when the search takes place near the border.[29] In *United States v. Brignoni–Ponce,*[30] it made clear that the fact that a car is stopped near the border does not eliminate the reasonable suspicion requirement for brief investigative detentions.[31] And the analysis in *United States v. Martinez–Fuerte* [32] used to justify warrantless and suspicionless illegal immigrant checkpoints has since been applied to other types of checkpoints having nothing to do with illegal immigration and border searches and seizures.[33]

These cases are thus more relevant to other search and seizure issues. Here the focus will be on the government's authority *at* the border to conduct searches and seizures as a way of regulating who and what enters the country. The rules discussed here also apply at "functional equivalents" of the border, including "an established station near the border, at a point marking the confluence of two or more roads that extend from the border," [34] and international airports.[35]

27. 413 U.S. 266, 93 S.Ct. 2535 (1973).

28. 422 U.S. 891, 95 S.Ct. 2585 (1975).

29. For a description of the automobile exception, see Chapter Seven.

30. 422 U.S. 873, 95 S.Ct. 2574 (1975).

31. For discussion of stop jurisprudence, see § 11.03.

32. 428 U.S. 543, 96 S.Ct. 3074 (1976).

33. See *Michigan Dept. of State Police v. Sitz,* 496 U.S. 444, 110 S.Ct. 2481 (1990), discussed in § 11.03(b)(1).

34. *Almeida–Sanchez v. United States,* 413 U.S. 266, 93 S.Ct. 2535 (1973).

35. See *Illinois v. Andreas,* 463 U.S. 765, 103 S.Ct. 3319 (1983), discussed in § 4.03(e).

(a) **Routine Searches.** In *Carroll v. United States,*[36] the Supreme Court stated that "national self-protection" permits the government to require "one entering the country to identify himself as entitled to come in, and his belongings as effects which may be lawfully brought in." Sixty years later, in *United States v. Montoya de Hernandez,*[37] the Court put the matter more explicitly: "Routine searches of the persons and effects of entrants [at the border] are not subject to any requirement of reasonable suspicion, probable cause, or warrant." The Court gave two justifications for this stance. First, one's expectation of privacy [is] less at the border than in the interior," and second, the Fourth Amendment balance between the interests of the government and the individual "is struck much more favorably to the Government at the border." These rationales reflect the *Camara* balancing analysis: the invasiveness of routine searches at the border is said to be minimal because people expect and understand the need for such searches, and the significant government interest in monitoring what enters the country could not be effectively protected unless such routine searches are permitted. Thus, neither a warrant or any individualized suspicion need be shown before a frisk of one's person or a search of one's effects by border authorities.

(b) **Nonroutine Searches.** Whatever the validity of this reasoning when a "routine" search is conducted at the border, it is considerably harder to swallow when the government engages in more intrusive searches and prolonged seizures. Yet the courts are willing to relax Fourth Amendment protections in these situations as well. In *Montoya de Hernandez,* the Supreme Court permitted a 16–hour detention at the border based on reasonable suspicion,[38] despite conceding that the seizure "undoubtedly exceeds any other detention we have approved under reasonable suspicion." There, at least, the defendant was in part at fault for the length of the detention, since she refused an x-ray examination to determine whether she was carrying "drug balloons" in her alimentary canal. Lower courts, however, have permitted rectal examinations and other body cavity searches on less than probable cause, regardless of the defendant's expressed wishes.[39] Strip searches have also been permitted on reasonable suspicion.[40]

---

36. 267 U.S. 132, 45 S.Ct. 280 (1925).

37. 473 U.S. 531, 105 S.Ct. 3304 (1985).

38. The reasonable suspicion stemmed from the following facts: (1) the defendant had made eight recent trips from South America to either Miami or Los Angeles; (2) this trip was from Bogota, Columbia, a "source city" for drugs; and (3) the defendant had no

appointments with vendors, no order forms, and no hotel reservations, despite claiming that she was in Los Angeles to buy goods for her husband's store.

39. See, e.g., *United States v. Carpenter,* 496 F.2d 855 (9th Cir.1974).

40. *United States v. Guadalupe–Garza,* 421 F.2d 876 (9th Cir.1970).

(c) **International Mail.** Federal law authorizes inspection of international mail whenever there is "reasonable cause to suspect" that the mail contains illegally imported merchandise.[41] Neither a warrant nor probable cause is required. However, the implementing regulations do prohibit reading correspondence without a warrant.

In *United States v. Ramsey,*[42] customs officials opened incoming international mail because they knew that the envelopes were from Thailand, often a source of illegal drugs, and because they had observed the envelopes were bulky and heavier than normal airmail letters. The Supreme Court held that these facts gave the inspectors reasonable cause to suspect, within the statutory framework. It also held that the Fourth Amendment did not prohibit the actions taken by the inspectors, despite the absence of a warrant and probable cause, because the search was the equivalent of one conducted at the border, where the sovereign's right to control what enters the country prevails. Justice Rehnquist, writing for the majority, reasoned that because INS agents may search the citizen's person without a warrant as he crosses the border and seize and inspect the contents of any envelope he may have in his possession, there is no persuasive reason to require more in order to inspect a letter arriving through the mail. The Court left open, however, whether a warrant is required before an official may *read* written material in letters. Given current regulations, and First as well as Fourth Amendment concerns, such a result seems likely.

13.06   Checkpoints

Checkpoints are useful as a means of investigating a large number of people in an efficient manner; typically, only a small portion of those stopped are likely to be in violation of the law. The border searches just discussed are one example. Inside the country, checkpoints are also common. The Supreme Court has addressed the constitutionality of checkpoints used on the highways to detect illegal immigration, drunk driving, and violation of licensing laws, and on the waterways to check for proper documentation. These cases are discussed here, along with lower court decisions on checkpoints situated at airports to discover weapons.

(a) **Illegal Immigrants.** *United States v. Martinez–Fuerte*[43] was the Court's first and most elaborate treatment of checkpoints. The Immigration and Naturalization Service had established several roadblocks near the Mexican border in an effort to detect and deter the flow of illegal immigrants attempting to get inside the

---

41. 19 U.S.C.A. § 482.

42. 431 U.S. 606, 97 S.Ct. 1972 (1977).

43. 428 U.S. 543, 96 S.Ct. 3074 (1976).

country using major arteries. Although the Court recognized that stops made at these roadblocks were neither authorized by warrant nor based on individualized suspicion, it found them constitutional using the *Camara–Terry* balancing test. To the respondents' contention that a *Camara* –type warrant should be required for such roadblocks, the Court responded: (1) that "[t]he degree of intrusion upon privacy that may be occasioned by a search of a house hardly can be compared with the minor interference with privacy resulting from the mere stop for questioning as to residence;" (2) that the notice provided by such a warrant was unnecessary, given the "visible manifestations" of the officers' authority at a checkpoint; (3) that, given its fixed nature, the validity of the checkpoint could easily be reviewed after a challenged stop; and perhaps most importantly, (4) that the location of the roadblock was not established by officers in the field "but by officials responsible for making overall decisions." Suspicionless stops were permissible because: (1) again, the intrusion was minimal, especially since motorists knew where the checkpoint was and could avoid it if they wanted to; (2) the traffic flow was too heavy to allow particularized study of vehicles; (3) a suspicion requirement "would neutralize the deterrent which fixed checkpoints present to well-disguised smuggling operations."

In permitting suspicionless housing inspections, *Camara* had emphasized not only their minimal invasiveness, but also the difficulty of otherwise detecting illegal activity. Yet the majority in *Martinez–Fuerte* refused to address the defendants' contention that other, less intrusive ways of detecting illegal aliens were available. Moreover, it rejected a particularized suspicion requirement not only for the initial stop at the roadblock, but also for the referral of motorists to a secondary inspection area, where a more prolonged perusal of documents took place. At this point, arguably, the seizure became more closely analogous to a *Terry* stop and should have required some degree of suspicion. Yet the Court explicitly rejected a reasonable suspicion requirement, and indicated that Mexican ancestry alone might form the basis for such action. Further, although the data provided by the government indicated that roughly 20% of those referred to the secondary area were found to be illegal aliens, a figure which might justify such an intrusion, the Court did not appear to put much weight on this fact, thus suggesting that such roadblocks are permissible regardless of their "success rate."

(b) Sobriety Checkpoints. The Court's neglect of the less-intrusive-alternative and effectiveness issues reoccurred in *Michigan Dept. of State Police v. Sitz,*[44] which upheld warrantless,

44. 496 U.S. 444, 110 S.Ct. 2481 (1990).

suspicionless roadblocks designed to detect drunk driving. To the dissent's argument that patrols designed to single out erratic drivers were a less intrusive, more effective means of detecting drunken driving than are roadblocks, Chief Justice Rehnquist responded that, even if this were so, "the choice among . . . reasonable alternatives remains with the governmental officials who have a unique understanding of, and a responsibility for, limited public resources, including a finite number of police officers." The dangerous breadth of this remark was exacerbated by the Court's cavalier assessment of the roadblock's success rate, which was only 1.6% (2 out of 126 drivers). Although this measure of effectiveness did not compare to the 20% rate shown by the government in *Martinez–Fuerte*,[45] the Court was satisfied that there was not "a complete absence of empirical data." Rehnquist concluded that the "magnitude of the drunk driving problem" justified the minimal intrusion occasioned by the brief seizure at the roadblock (which, on average, lasted 25 seconds).

A further deficiency of the police procedure in *Sitz* was that, in contrast to *Martinez–Fuerte*, the location of the roadblock was chosen by officers in the field. While the Court did not specifically address the warrant issue, it did note that the officers were operating under guidelines established by the state and stopped every car that came to the roadblock, two factors which diminished their discretion to some extent. Nonetheless, the holding in *Sitz* is particularly troublesome because, unlike most of the cases discussed in this chapter, it involved an investigation into serious criminal activity by the police, the situation most likely to result in arbitrary behavior by the government.[46]

(c) **License and Safety Checks.** In *Delaware v. Prouse*,[47] decided after *Martinez–Fuerte* and before *Sitz*, the Supreme Court held that the police may not randomly stop drivers as a means of checking licenses. In doing so, it engaged in the least-restrictive-alternative analysis eschewed in these other roadblock cases. While recognizing the government's substantial need to ensure that drivers have licenses and are driving safe cars, the Court concluded that random stops are unlikely to detect either type of violation. Limiting license checks to those stopped for committing a traffic violation is "much more likely to uncover an unlicensed driver," and vehicle registration can be checked by observing the license plates without any stop at all. Likewise, safety violations can often be observed without a stop and, in any event, can be detected by an "annual safety inspection" scheme. Balanced

---

45. Rehnquist concluded otherwise, erroneously comparing the rate in *Sitz* to the fact that only .12% of those stopped at the *initial* roadblock in *Martinez–Fuerte* were illegal aliens.

46. *Sitz* is discussed further in § 11.03(b)(1), in the context of police investigative stops.

47. 440 U.S. 648, 99 S.Ct. 1391 (1979).

against the weak government interest in suspicionless stops was the individual's interest in avoiding the anxiety, interference, and inconvenience of a stop. Thus, absent at least a reasonable suspicion that traffic laws are being violated, such stops may not take place.

However, the Court went on to state that "this holding does not preclude the State of Delaware or other States from developing methods for spot checks that involve less intrusion or that do not involve the unconstrained exercises of discretion." Thus, for example, "[q]uestioning of all oncoming traffic at roadblock-type stops is one possible alternative." In a concurring opinion, Justice Blackmun correctly noted that any pre-specified pattern of stops (e.g., every tenth vehicle) would meet the majority's objective of limiting officers' discretion. The Court also stressed that its ruling was not intended to "cast doubt on the permissibility of roadblock truck weigh stations and inspection checkpoints, at which some vehicles may be subject to further detention for safety and regulatory inspection than are others." While *Prouse* thus reached a result similar to the holdings in *Sitz* and *Martinez–Fuerte,* it is more easily justified, because its implicit contention that checkpoints are necessary to achieve the government's objectives is more realistic.

Assuming such roadblocks are constitutional, a separate issue that has arisen in the lower courts is whether a motorist's attempt to evade the roadblock authorizes chase. In *Martinez–Fuerte,* the Court had suggested that one reason a fixed checkpoint is constitutional is that it does not take motorists "by surprise" and can be avoided. But some courts have nonetheless held that turning around prior to a license check roadblock provides reasonable suspicion of involvement in some sort of illegality.[48] Others have held to the contrary, emphasizing that the mere act of avoiding contact with the police should not create an articulable suspicion of criminal activity.[49]

(d) Boat Inspections. Boats on inland waterways could be analogized to cars using public thoroughfares. But the Supreme Court feels a better analogy is with border searches, at least when the waterways have ready access to the sea. In *United States v. Villamonte-Marquez,*[50] customs officials boarded the defendants' boat to inspect their papers pursuant to 19 U.S.C.A. § 1581(a), which authorizes officers to board any vessel at any time and at any place in the United States to examine the vessel's manifest and other documents. While examining a document, the officer

48. *Coffman v. Arkansas,* 26 Ark. App. 45, 759 S.W.2d 573 (1988).

49. *Utah v. Talbot,* 792 P.2d 489 (Utah App.1990).

50. 462 U.S. 579, 103 S.Ct. 2573 (1983).

smelled what he thought to be burning marijuana and, looking through an open hatch, saw burlap-wrapped bales that proved to be marijuana. Although recognizing that the customs officer had had no reason to believe, before he boarded the boat, that it contained contraband, the Supreme Court distinguished this case from *Prouse* by noting that such boardings are essential to ensure enforcement of the complex documentation requirements for boats, "particularly in waters where the need to deter or apprehend drug smugglers is great". According to the Court, "fixed checkpoints" are an impractical means of achieving the document-inspection objective on waterways that have access to the sea. Thus, so long as the detention is "brief" and limited to inspecting documents, a suspicionless boarding of a boat by customs officials is constitutional and any evidence in plain view is admissible.

(e) **Airport Screenings.** The first case to consider the constitutionality of airport screening procedures was *United States v. Lopez.*[51] The procedure considered there consisted of four stages: (1) identification of a person as one who fit a "behavioral profile" of a plane hijacker; (2) who would then be required to pass through a magnetometer; (3) which, if triggered, would be followed by an interview; and, (4) if suspicion were not thereby eliminated, a frisk of the person and a search of his luggage. The *Lopez* Court purported to apply the *Terry* criteria,[52] finding that if a person progressed through the first three stages, there was reasonable suspicion to frisk the individual and search the luggage.[53] Most other courts, relying instead on the *Camara–Terry* balancing test, permit frisks on little or no suspicion, given "the enormous consequences" which may flow from a hijacking and the fact that persons can choose not to fly if they wish to avoid the intrusion.[54] The most balanced approach would be to subject all passengers to the relatively uninvasive magnetometer procedure and all luggage to an x-ray; those who are thereby suspected of carrying something dangerous might then be subject to a frisk of their person and a search of their luggage.

13.07　Inventories

(a) **Of Vehicles.** Car inventories occur after a car has been impounded for a traffic or parking violation, or because its occupants have been arrested or abandoned it. Assuming probable cause to search does not exist at the time of impoundment, warrantless inventories of cars cannot be justified under the

---

51. 328 F.Supp. 1077 (E.D.N.Y.1971).

52. See § 11.03(a).

53. The data showed that a person who went through the first three stages was found to be carrying a weapon six percent of the time.

54. *United States v. Lindsey,* 451 F.2d 701 (3d Cir.1971), cert. denied 405 U.S. 995, 92 S.Ct. 1270 (1972). See also, *United States v. Skipwith,* 482 F.2d 1272 (5th Cir.1973); *People v. Hyde,* 12 Cal.3d 158, 115 Cal.Rptr. 358, 524 P.2d 830 (1974).

automobile exception.   Nor would that exception apply if probable cause subsequently developed because, say, police see evidence of criminal activity through the car window; once impounded the car will not leave the impoundment lot until the owner collects it, and thus no exigency exists.[55]   In *South Dakota v. Opperman,*[56] however-er, the Supreme Court held that warrantless inventories are permissible on *regulatory* grounds.   In *Opperman,* the police impounded the defendant's locked, unoccupied automobile after issuing two parking tickets warning that the car was parked illegally in a restricted zone.   At the impound lot, an officer observed through the car's windows a watch and other items of personal property.   At his direction, the car was unlocked and the contents of the car inventoried.   In the glove compartment police found a bag of marijuana.   The Court upheld the search, concluding that inventory searches are permissible, provided they are: (1) pursuant to a lawful impoundment; (2) of a routine nature "essentially like that followed throughout the country;" and (3) not a mere "pretext concealing an investigatory police motive."

The Court offered three justifications for an inventory: avoiding harm to the police, avoiding false claims of theft, and preventing vandalism of property.   None of these justifications seem persuasive.   If an explosive or some other harmful device is in the car and for some reason hasn't already been triggered, opening the car doors and compartments would often *increase* the risk to the police.   If a person is willing to make a claim of theft by the police, then he will probably also be willing to claim (just as persuasively) that police falsified any inventory tending to disprove that claim.   And vandalism can be prevented by putting the car in a secure impound lot or, if one is not available, contacting the owner and asking if he wants the contents of his car secured (in *Opperman,* the Court merely noted that the owner "was not present to make other arrangements for the safekeeping of his belongings").   At bottom, the problem with inventory searches is the ease with which they can be used to evade the warrant and probable cause requirements any time a car may be lawfully impounded.   Only if the inventory search is strictly limited can the "pretextual" actions prohibited by the Court actually be avoided.

Instead, the Court has not only affirmed *Opperman* but significantly expanded its scope.   In *Colorado v. Bertine,*[57] for instance, the Court opted for a crime control resolution of several issues not explicitly addressed in *Opperman.*   First, it made clear that containers found in the course of an inventory search may be

---

55. See § 7.03 for discussion of the elements of the automobile exception.

56. 428 U.S. 364, 96 S.Ct. 3092 (1976).

57. 479 U.S. 367, 107 S.Ct. 738 (1987).

searched, so long as such a search is authorized by departmental inventory regulations.[58] It rejected the Colorado Supreme Court's finding that such searches violated the Court's "container cases" requiring a warrant prior to the search of an opaque container,[59] on the ground that these cases involved investigations of criminal conduct whereas inventory searches do not. Second, it refused to alter the inventory search rule when a secure impound facility is available. As Chief Justice Rehnquist stated for the Court, "the security of the storage facility does not completely eliminate the need for inventorying; the police may still wish to protect themselves or the owners of the lot against false claims of theft or dangerous instrumentalities." Finally, the Court was unwilling to adopt as a constitutional ruling a requirement that police allow owners of cars about to be impounded an opportunity to make alternate arrangements, stating that "[t]he reasonableness of any particular governmental activity does not necessarily or invariably turn on the existence of alternative 'less intrusive' means."

Although *Opperman* and *Bertine* at least suggest that an inventory search is limited to those areas where valuables might normally be kept, the Court has also indicated that under certain circumstances police may search other areas of the car as well. In *Michigan v. Thomas,*[60] the car in which Thomas was a passenger was stopped for a traffic violation committed by its 14 year-old driver. The driver was issued a citation for driving without a licence; Thomas was arrested for possession of open intoxicants in a motor vehicle. The car was then impounded and, pursuant to departmental policy, was inventoried prior to towing. The arresting officer found two bags of marijuana in the unlocked glove compartment. A second officer then searched the car more thoroughly, including under the front seat, inside the locked trunk, and under the dashboard. In the air vents located under the dashboard, he found a loaded .38 revolver.

The Michigan state appellate court reversed Thomas' subsequent conviction for possession of a concealed weapon on the ground that an inventory inspection, while permissible under *Opperman,* should not include searches of air ducts, which are neither customary places for the storage of valuables nor in plain view. Although discovery of the marijuana gave rise to probable

---

58. In *Florida v. Wells,* 495 U.S. 1, 110 S.Ct. 1632 (1990), the Court held unconstitutional an inventory search of a container when no such regulations existed. However, the Court indicated that virtually any regulations that *are* promulgated would pass constitutional muster. In dictum, it stated that such regulations would be adequate if they mandated that all containers be opened, that no containers be opened, or that the police officer in his discretion determine which containers should be opened based on "the nature of the search and characteristics of the container itself."

59. See § 7.04.

60. 458 U.S. 259, 102 S.Ct. 3079 (1982).

cause, the police should then have sought a warrant, since the car was securely immobilized. The Supreme Court's per curiam opinion reversed, concluding that once discovery of the marijuana gave the police probable cause to believe further contraband was in the car, exigent circumstances were not required to authorize a warrantless search. By analogy to *Chambers v. Maroney,*[61] which authorized stationhouse searches of cars that could have been searched in the field under the "automobile exception," the police were permitted to conduct a thorough warrantless search of the car any time after the marijuana was discovered.

In *Florida v. Meyers,*[62] the Court relied on the *Chambers* analogy again in the course of extending the scope of the inventory search even further. In *Meyers,* police arrested the defendant and conducted a search of his car that the lower state court characterized "as an incident thereto and for inventory purposes." A second search some eight hours later after the car was in the impound lot was also lawful, according to the Court, because, as in *Thomas,* the *Chambers* rationale applied. In effect, then, an inventory search for valuables may take place well after the original impoundment, despite the seeming inconsistency between this rule and the supposed purpose of inventories, to wit, protecting against theft of valuables or danger to police.

After the Court's car inventory decisions, police departments have every incentive to promulgate car impoundment policies that are as broad as possible. Once a car is lawfully impounded, police may inventory any "accessible" items in it without a warrant, so long as the scope of the inventory is authorized by departmental procedures. If police discover evidence giving rise to probable cause, they may conduct an even more intrusive search, again without a warrant. Furthermore, the inventory may take place well after impoundment, so long as it was authorized at the time of the impoundment. The only limitations on the initial inventory, aside from those police departments gratuitously place on themselves, are that the police may not intrude into areas where valuables are not normally kept and that, as required in *Opperman,* the inventory not be a pretext for an investigative search. Given recent Court decisions in other areas,[63] this second limitation may also be moot, so long as the requirements of the inventory search exception are met.

(b) Of Persons. The effects of a person subjected to a lawful custodial arrest are subject to an inventory search as well. In *Illinois v. Lafayette,*[64] the defendant was arrested for disturbing

61. 399 U.S. 42, 90 S.Ct. 1975 (1970), discussed § 7.03(c)(2).

62. 466 U.S. 380, 104 S.Ct. 1852 (1984).

63. See § 10.04.

64. 462 U.S. 640, 103 S.Ct. 2605 (1983).

the peace and taken to the police station where, in the process of booking him, police removed the contents of a shoulder bag and found amphetamine pills. The Illinois appellate court affirmed the trial court's suppression of the pills on the grounds that no warrant had been obtained and that the search could not be justified as an inventory search or a search incident to a lawful arrest. The Supreme Court unanimously reversed, citing *Opperman* in holding that "[t]he justification for such searches does not rest on probable cause and hence the absence of a warrant is immaterial to the reasonableness of the search." According to the Court, protection of a suspect's property, deterrence of false claims of theft against the police, security, and identification of the suspect all provide valid reasons for permitting examination of an arrested suspect and his personal effects, so long as it is part of a routine police procedure. As it had in *Opperman,* the Court refused to require police to set aside for safekeeping items that did not appear to be evidence of criminal activity or usable as weapons. "Even if less intrusive means existed of protecting some particular type of property, it would be unreasonable to expect police officers in the everyday course of business to make fine and subtle distinctions in deciding which containers or items may be searched and which must be sealed as a unit."

13.08 School Disciplinary Searches

In *New Jersey v. T.L.O.,*[65] a school teacher discovered the 14 year old respondent smoking cigarettes in a school lavatory in violation of school rules. When questioned about the smoking incident by the Vice Principal, the respondent denied she had been smoking or had ever smoked. The Vice Principal looked through her purse, found a pack of cigarettes and noticed a package of rolling papers. He then searched the purse more carefully and found several incriminating items, including some marijuana and two letters implicating the respondent in marijuana dealing. Upon appeal from a delinquency conviction in juvenile court, the New Jersey Supreme Court ordered the suppression of the evidence.

The Supreme Court reversed in a decision written by Justice White. It first held, unanimously, that public school officials are government officials for purposes of the Fourth Amendment[66] and that schoolchildren are entitled to some protection under the Amendment because they have a legitimate expectation that school officials will not intrude unreasonably upon their privacy.[67] However, six members of the Court refused to apply the warrant

65. 469 U.S. 325, 105 S.Ct. 733 (1985).

66. See § 4.02(a) for further discussion of this issue.

67. See § 4.03(g) for further discussion of this issue.

or probable cause requirements to the school search situation involved in *T.L.O.* A warrant requirement "would unduly interfere with the maintenance of the swift and informal disciplinary procedures needed in the schools." And a high suspicion requirement would be unduly burdensome in light of "the substantial need of teachers and administrators for freedom to maintain order in the schools," and the necessity of their learning "the niceties of probable cause."

Justice Blackmun's concurring opinion is also important, because it introduced the "special needs" label that would become popular in future Court cases. As he put it, "[o]nly in those exceptional circumstances in which special needs, beyond the normal need for law enforcement, make the warrant and probable-cause requirement impracticable, is a court entitled to substitute its balancing of interests for that of the Framers." Blackmun found that such an "exceptional circumstance" existed here, because of the government's "heightened obligation to safeguard students whom it compels to attend school" and the inefficiency of meeting that obligation if the investigation necessary to meet the probable cause standard were required.

In place of the warrant and probable cause requirements, the Court substituted the "reasonableness" analysis, first developed in *Camara* and *Terry*. That analysis, according to the majority, "involves a twofold inquiry: first, one must consider 'whether the . . . action was justified at its inception; second, one must determine whether the search as actually conducted 'was reasonably related in scope to the circumstances which justified the interference in the first place.' " The Court felt an added advantage of this test was that it would relieve school officials from "schooling themselves in the niceties of probable cause."

Applying this test to the facts, Justice White found that the report from the teacher about the smoking in the lavatory gave the Vice Principal sufficient suspicion that the purse contained cigarettes, and that the discovery of rolling papers gave him reason to suspect that marijuana was in the purse. This in turn allowed a search of all the purse's contents. When the Vice Principal found an index card containing a list of "people who owe me money" as well as drug paraphenalia, the inference that respondent was dealing in drugs was strong enough to permit reading the letters he had discovered.

The principal thrust of Justice Brennan's dissent was that, for the first time, the Court had authorized a full search in the absence of probable cause despite the conclusion that reasonable expectations of privacy existed. Although the Vice Principal probably had probable cause to search the purse for cigarettes—a reliable informant had told him he had just seen the respondent smoking—he did not, according to Brennan, have probable cause to continue the search of the purse after finding the rolling papers: "Just as a police officer could not obtain a warrant to search a home based solely on his claim that he had seen a package of cigarette papers in that home, Mr. Choplick was not entitled to search possibly the most private possession of T.L.O. based on the mere presence of a package of cigarette papers."

As Justice Brennan pointed out, *Terry* and *Camara* do not support the majority's position in *T.L.O.*, at least in any direct sense. *Terry's* holding recognizing the lesser "reasonable suspicion" standard involved a frisk. And *Camara* and its progeny also involved relatively unintrusive searches, together with a showing that a significant government objective would be difficult to achieve if a full quantum of probable cause were required. *T.L.O.*, on the other hand, involved a full search of personal effects on less than probable cause in a situation where a probable cause requirement would not render the government's objective impossible.

One might justify *T.L.O.* on the ground that it, like *Camara*, applies only to "administrative" searches. The initial search in *T.L.O.* was for evidence of a disciplinary infraction, not a crime, and the majority indicated that its holding did not necessarily apply to searches by the police or by school officials acting at the behest of the police. But even if the Court adheres to this limitation, its ruling is hard to sustain. A search of a purse is equally intrusive whether the wrong being investigated is administratively or criminally defined. And the assertion that lay investigators would be burdened by the police model is suspect as well. As Justice Brennan noted, if the police can fathom probable cause, so can school administrators, especially now that the Court has rejected a rule-bound approach to the issue.[68] Further, if resorting to a judicial warrant procedure for disciplinary infractions is overly cumbersome, some sort of in-house pre-search review could replace it for all non-exigent searches.[69] Similar points can be made in connection with the Court's other "special needs" cases, discussed in subsequent sections.

13.09　Workplace Investigations

(a) **Routine Investigations.** Similar in tone to *T.L.O.* is *O'Connor v. Ortega*,[70] which held that neither a warrant nor probable cause is required to justify a search of a government employee's office, at least when the search is not a criminal investigation but rather "a noninvestigatory work-related intru-

---

68. See *Illinois v. Gates*, 462 U.S. 213, 103 S.Ct. 2317 (1983), discussed in § 5.03(b).

69. See Slobogin, "A World Without the Fourth Amendment," 39 U.C.L.A. 1, 34–36 (1991).

70. 480 U.S. 709, 107 S.Ct. 1492 (1987).

sion or an investigatory search for evidence of suspected work-related employee misfeasance".[71]   As in *T.L.O.*, the validity of such searches is to be measured by the general standard of "reasonableness."   Again, a majority [72] of the Court was willing to discard the warrant requirement because of the perceived hardship it would impose on those conducting the search (in this case, employers).   And, as in *T.L.O.*, the Court saw no reason to impose a probable cause standard on work-related investigations when the primary purpose is not criminal investigation but the smooth functioning of the institution.   According to Justice O'Connor, "[t]he delay in correcting the employee misconduct caused by the need for probable cause rather than reasonable suspicion will be translated into tangible and often irreparable damage to the agency's work, and ultimately to the public interest."   Moreover, analogous to its reasoning in *T.L.O.*, the Court felt that employers should not be expected to school themselves in the "niceties" of probable cause determinations.   Balanced against these government interests was what Justice O'Connor termed the "relatively limited invasion" of the work-related search: the employee "may avoid exposing personal belongings at work by simply leaving them at home."

Justice Blackmun, who had concurred in *T.L.O.*, dissented in *Ortega*, joined by three other justices.   While he had been willing to recognize a "special need" for relaxed Fourth Amendment requirements in the school context, he found no such special need in *Ortega*.   The search involved in the case was of the entire contents of a doctor's office desk and files.   The search took place while the doctor was on administrative leave and not permitted to enter the hospital.   Thus, Dr. Ortega's employers could have obtained a warrant based on probable cause "[w]ithout sacrificing their ultimate goal of maintaining an effective institution. . . ."   Furthermore, seeking a warrant would have forced the employers "to articulate their exact reasons for the search and to specify the items in Dr. Ortega's office they sought, which would have prevented the general rummaging through the doctor's office, desk, and file cabinets" that occurred in the case.   Although the dissent could envisage routine situations in which a warrant should not be

---

71. The Court stated: "we do not address the appropriate standard when an employee is being investigated for criminal misconduct or breaches of other nonwork-related statutory or regulatory standards."

72. Justice Scalia refused to join language in the Court's four-member plurality opinion stating that expectations of privacy in the office should be

determined on a case-by-case basis rather than assumed.   But he agreed with the plurality that, in his words, "government searches to retrieve work-related materials or to investigate violations of workplace rules—searches of the sort that are regarded as reasonable and normal in the private-employer context—do not violate the Fourth Amendment."

required prior to a work-related investigation, it found the Court's formulation too sweeping.

(b) Testing for Drug and Alcohol Use. The Court has been willing to relax Fourth Amendment strictures even further when the employer "search" consists of a test to determine whether the employee is using drugs or alcohol. In *Skinner v. Railway Labor Executives' Association* [73] and *National Treasury Employees Union v. Von Raab* [74] the Court upheld regulations which permit such tests, not only without a warrant or probable cause, but also in the absence of any individualized suspicion. In *Skinner,* the Court considered regulations promulgated by the Federal Railroad Administration (FRA) which require drug and alcohol testing of *any* employee who is involved in an accident or who is suspected of having violated certain rules (such as failing to heed a signal). *Von Raab* concerned an employee drug test program administered by the Customs Service which permits testing of *anyone* who applies for or seeks promotion to a customs job connected with one of three functions—interdicting drugs, use of arms, or access to classified material. Under either program, if an employee tests positive, dismissal may result. [75]

Justice Kennedy, who wrote the majority opinion in both cases, began each by analyzing whether the types of tests used were "searches" under the Fourth Amendment. Because the FRA regulations focus on investigations of accidents and rules violations, they rely primarily on blood and breath tests (which are best at discerning very recent drug and alcohol use), and reserve urinalysis as a backup procedure. In contrast, because the Customs Service regulations aim at screening job and promotion applicants who will be notified of the test, they authorize only urinalysis, which can detect substances in the blood stream that were ingested 60 days or more before the test. The Court found that all three types of tests are searches when administered by the government or a government agent. [76] Blood and breath tests violate "bodily integrity", and urinalysis may reveal private facts about persons other than their drug or alcohol usage, in addition to requiring a significant invasion of privacy if implemented properly. [77] However, the majority was unwilling to hold that the

---

73. 489 U.S. 602, 109 S.Ct. 1402 (1989).

74. 489 U.S. 656, 109 S.Ct. 1384 (1989).

75. While approving both these programs the Court, as it had in *Ortega,* reserved the question as to whether they would be allowed if the test results were routinely used for law enforcement rather than the avowed regulatory purposes.

76. Under the FRA regulations, the railroads administer the tests and private hospitals analyze the test product. But the Court found sufficient government involvement to implicate the Fourth Amendment. See § 4.02(b).

77. Under the Customs Service regulations, monitors are to accompany the subject to the bathroom and listen for the "usual sounds of urination."

nature of these intrusions justified imposing the warrant or probable cause requirements, or even a requirement of reasonable suspicion.[78] Once again, it relied on *T.L.O.'s* "special need" rubric in deciding to forego these traditional Fourth Amendment protections.

As to the warrant requirement, analogous to its decisions in *T.L.O.* and *Ortega* the Court found that mandating a warrant before testing would frustrate the smooth operation of the testing programs. Additionally, Kennedy concluded that the specificity of the regulations obviated the need for a magistrate. In *Skinner,* for instance, he stated that "in light of the standardized nature of the tests and the minimal discretion vested in those charged with administering the program, there are virtually no facts for a neutral magistrate to evaluate." Similarly, in *Von Raab,* Kennedy concluded that because the testing is automatic for anyone who applies for a job, the Service does not exercise any discretion in deciding who to test; "there are simply 'no special facts for a neutral magistrate to evaluate.' "

In holding that individualized suspicion was also unnecessary under the regulations at issue, the Court found that the employees' interest in avoiding suspicionless invasions of privacy was outweighed by the government's interest in blanket testing. On the employee's side of the balance, both *Skinner* and *Von Raab* emphasized *Ortega's* conclusion that an individual's privacy right is often significantly diminished by the demands of the workplace. In *Von Raab,* for instance, Kennedy stated that the " 'operational realities of the workplace' may render entirely reasonable certain work-related intrusions by supervisors and co-workers that might be viewed as unreasonable in other contexts." Customs employees who are involved in drug interdiction or carry firearms should expect that information about their fitness will be elicited.[79] Similarly, in *Skinner,* the Court stated that railway workers cannot expect as much privacy at work as they enjoy at home because they are aware that their employer may subject them to various

---

78. A further indication of the Court's belief that testing is a minimal intrusion came in *Consolidated Railway Corp. v. Railway Labor Executives' Ass'n,* 491 U.S. 299, 109 S.Ct. 2477 (1989), a labor case decided the same term as *Skinner* and *Von Raab.* There, the Court held that private railroad and airline companies may unilaterally require random drug and alcohol tests under existing labor contracts because such a requirement is only a "minor change" in the existing relationship between employers and employees.

79. With respect to the third group covered by the Services' testing program—those who sought jobs permitting access to classified materials—the Court remanded for a determination as to whether the specific job categories that the regulations included within this group—among them, for instance, baggage clerk, animal caretaker, and electric equipment repairer—in fact had such access. It suggested however, that, in theory, this group of people could be subjected to suspicionless testing as well.

examinations to determine their ability to operate the railways safely.

Ranged against this diminished privacy interest, stated Kennedy, are "compelling" governmental interests. One such interest, which the Court found to be present in both cases, is preventing impairment of employees with important responsibilities. Without suspicionless testing, Kennedy asserted, employees will know that use of psychoactive substances might go undetected and thus may be more likely to engage in such use, with possibly serious consequences. In the railway industry lives might be lost; with customs agents the "national interest in self protection could be irreparably damaged if those charged with safeguarding it were, because of their own drug use, unsympathetic to their mission of interdicting narcotics" or impaired while using their weapons. In *Skinner,* the Court identified, in addition to the deterrence rationale, a second reason for supporting suspicionless testing: the railways' interest in obtaining information about the causes of major accidents and taking appropriate steps to counteract them.

It was this second rationale that prompted Justice Stevens to join the majority in *Skinner.* In a concurring opinion, he cogently explained why the deterrence rationale was unsatisfactory:

> Most people—and I would think most railroad employees as well—do not go to work with the expectation that they may be involved in a major accident, particularly one causing such catastrophic results as loss of life or the release of hazardous material requiring an evacuation. Moreover, even if they are conscious of the possibilities that such an accident might be a contributing factor, if the risk of serious personal injury does not deter their use of these substances, it seems highly unlikely that the additional threat of loss of employment would have any effect on their behavior.

Only Justices Marshall and Brennan dissented in *Skinner.* In *Von Raab,* they were joined by Justices Scalia and Stevens. Scalia's dissent provides persuasive reasons for distinguishing the two cases:

> I joined the Court's opinion [in *Skinner*] because the demonstrated frequency of drug and alcohol use by the targeted class of employees, and the demonstrated connection between such use and grave harm, rendered the search a reasonable means of protecting society. I decline to join the Court's opinion in the present case because neither frequency of use nor connection to harm is demonstrated or even likely. In my view the Customs Service rules are a kind of immolation of privacy and human dignity in symbolic opposition to drug use.

Scalia pointed to statistics that showed the rarity of drug use among customs agents compared to high usage of drugs and alcohol among railway workers. He also found it implausible that customs officers in charge of drug interdiction will be less "sympathetic" to this mission if they use drugs, "any more than police officers who exceed the speed limit in their private cars are appreciably less sympathetic to their mission of enforcing the traffic laws." Similarly, he did not believe that a drug testing program would be more effective at reducing such usage among those officers who carry firearms than the fear of being impaired when confronted by danger.

Today, drug testing by the government is widespread. Lower court cases have considered the legality of programs which permit warrantless, suspicionless testing of teachers, police, utility workers, horse jockeys and several other groups.[80] After *Skinner* and *Von Raab,* the constitutionality of such programs will depend in large part on three factors: (1) the extent to which the type of employee to be tested is subject to privacy intrusions as a routine aspect of the job; (2) the extent to which the job involves potential harm to the public or is otherwise deemed "sensitive"; and (3) the extent to which drug or alcohol use can be deterred by a testing program.

13.10 Probation Supervision

The same term that *Ortega* was decided, the Court recognized still another "special need" situation in which the warrant and probable cause requirements may be relaxed. In *Griffin v. Wisconsin,*[81] the Court upheld a warrantless search of a probationer's home under a Wisconsin statute authorizing such searches whenever a probation officer has "reasonable grounds" to believe the home contains items unauthorized by the probation order. The 5–4 decision, written by Justice Scalia, found that, in light of the rehabilitative and preventive goals of probation, probation supervision "is a 'special need' of the State permitting a degree of impingement upon privacy that would not be constitutional if applied to the public at large."

According to Scalia, a warrant requirement would interfere with the probation officer's ability to respond quickly to evidence of misconduct and thus reduce the rehabilitative and deterrent effects of supervision. Moreover, the need for the independent review of a magistrate is reduced when a probation officer—who is

---

80. See e.g. *Policemen's Benevolent Ass'n. of New Jersey v. Washington Township,* 850 F.2d 133 (3d Cir.1988), cert. denied 490 U.S. 1004, 109 S.Ct. 1637 (1989) (police). See generally, Bookspan, "Jar Wars: Employee Drug Testing, The Constitution, and the American Drug Problem," 26 Am.Crim. L.Rev. 359 (1988).

81. 483 U.S. 868, 107 S.Ct. 3164 (1987).

"supposed to have in mind the welfare of the probationer"—rather than a police officer is making the decision to search. The probable cause requirement would also make searches more difficult and thus again "reduce the deterrent effect of the supervisory arrangement". Additionally, the greater degree of reliability required by the probable cause standard might prevent intervention at the first sign of trouble, before a probationer does damage to himself or society.

Griffin does not make clear what standard should govern searches of probationers' homes. The basis of the search in *Griffin* was apparently a tip from an unidentified police officer that Griffin "had or might have guns"; no basis for the tip was provided. The four dissenters, while disagreeing among themselves as to the proper standard to be applied in probation supervision cases, agreed that this information did not even amount to reasonable suspicion. Three of the dissenters also failed to see how eliminating the neutral review of a magistrate lent itself to the rehabilitation of the probationer or preserved the probation relationship, and believed that the probation officers in this case could have obtained a warrant, since two or three hours elapsed from the time of the tip to the search.

13.11 Conclusion

The Supreme Court has addressed the Fourth Amendment implications of a number of so-called "administrative" or "regulatory" search situations. Its pronouncements are summarized below.

(1) Nonconsensual health and safety inspections of residences, and of most businesses, are permissible only if authorized by a *"Camara* warrant." The warrant need not be based on probable cause to believe that the particular residence or business is in violation of health and safety laws, but may instead be issued if there is probable cause to believe a general inspection plan is necessary to enforce those laws. The schedule of inspections should be based on "neutral" criteria (e.g., geographic area to be inspected in the case of residence inspections, number of employees in the case of business inspections) that inhibit arbitrary intrusions.

(2) Inspections of "closely regulated" businesses do not require a warrant nor, apparently, even *Camara*-type suspicion, if: (a) the government has a substantial interest in regulating the business; (b) surprise inspections are required to implement the interest effectively; and (c) the statute provides an adequate substitute for a warrant. Where violations of the regulations are easily hidden, this latter requirement may be met if the time, place and scope limitations of the inspection are spelled out in the statute. In

other cases, the government may, in addition, have to seek an injunction to enter if the owner refuses. In any case, "unauthorized force" may not be used to gain entry.

(3) Searches of a building conducted during and immediately after a fire may be made without a warrant. Once exigent circumstances are no longer present, however, the owner is entitled either to notice of the government's intention to inspect the scene or a "*Camara* warrant." If the inspection evolves into a search for evidence of crime, a warrant meeting all the requirements of a typical criminal search warrant must authorize it.

(4) Routine stops and searches at the border do not implicate the Fourth Amendment, as persons crossing the border have no reasonable expectation that their possessions will be immune from government scrutiny. International mail may be searched without a warrant or probable cause (although *reading* mail may require a warrant). Prolonged detention or nonroutine searches at the border require at least reasonable suspicion but may not require probable cause, at least when necessitated by the detained person's refusal to contemplate less intrusive alternatives.

(5) The Supreme Court has approved checkpoints to detect illegal immigration, drunken driving, automobile licenses and registration violations, and violations of boating rules on waterways connected to the sea. Lower courts have approved airport checkpoints to detect hijackers and other dangerous individuals. Generally, no individualized suspicion is required at any of these checkpoints, so long as the intrusion is minimal and there is some attempt to minimize discretion (by having higher authorities establish the checkpoint, or by checking those who pass through according to a pre-specified pattern).

(6) An inventory of a car which has been impounded or of the personal effects of an individual who has been lawfully arrested does not require a warrant so long as conducted pursuant to police department regulations. A car inventory must be limited to a search of places in which valuables might reasonably be kept (which includes glove compartments and trunks). If the inventory reveals items giving rise to probable cause to believe that contraband or other illegal items are somewhere in the car, a warrantless search of other parts of the car may be conducted at that time or at a later time.

(7) Searches of public schoolchildren's personal effects for evidence of disciplinary infractions are governed by the Fourth Amendment. However, neither a warrant nor probable cause are required to conduct such searches; rather, the validity of the search depends upon its "reasonableness"—the reasonableness of the initial intrusion and the reasonableness of the search's scope in light of the surrounding circumstances.

(8) Searches of government employees' offices are governed by the Fourth Amendment, but neither a warrant nor probable cause is required to conduct such searches if they are work-related rather than criminal investigations; as with public school searches, the governing test is "reasonableness." A warrantless test of employees for drug or alcohol use is reasonable, even if not based on individualized suspicion, if the government employer's interest in detecting such use is "compelling" enough to outweigh the employees' privacy interest.

(9) Searches of probationers' homes do not require either a warrant or probable cause.

The Court's recent regulatory search cases (e.g., *Burger, T.L.O., Ortega, Griffin*) have created a "second class" Fourth Amendment right, applicable when the government can justify its desire to intrude on some ground other than a need for evidence of criminal law violations. In effect, this second class right provides very little protection. It recognizes neither a warrant requirement nor a probable cause requirement. Government officials need only act "reasonably," which will often be the case if they can merely articulate statute- or regulation-based justification for the search. Depending upon the government's willingness and ability to create "administrative" rationales for its searches, this second class right could supercede in significance the original Fourth Amendment right.

BIBLIOGRAPHY

Bookspan, Phyllis. Jar Wars: Employee Drug Testing, The Constitution, and the American Drug Problem. 26 Am.Crim.L. Rev. 359 (1988).

Buss, William G. The Fourth Amendment and Searches of Students in Public Schools. 59 Iowa L.Rev. 739 (1974).

Christenson, Steven. Colorado v. Bertine Opens the Inventory Search to Containers. 73 Iowa L.Rev. 771 (1988).

Cotton, William T. and Lisa Anne Haage. Students and the Fourth Amendment: The Torturable Class. 16 U.C. Davis L. Rev. 709 (1983).

Greenberg, Peter S. The Balance of Interests Theory and the Fourth Amendment: A Selective Analysis of Supreme Court Action Since *Camara* and *See.* 61 Cal.L.Rev. 1011 (1973).

Mandell, Leonard B. and Richardson, L. Anita. Lengthy Detentions and Invasive Searches at the Border: In Search of a Magistrate. 28 Ariz.L.Rev. 331 (1986).

McManis, Charles R. and Barbara M. McManis. Structuring Administrative Inspections: Is There Any Warrant for a Search Warrant? 26 Am.U.L.Rev. 942 (1977).

Moylan, Charles E., Jr.   Inventory Search of an Automobile: A Willing Suspension of Disbelief.   5 Univ.Balt.L.Rev. 203 (1976).

Plass, Stephen.   A Comprehensive Assessment of Employment Drug Testing: Legal Battles Over Delicate Interests.   27 San Diego L.Rev. 29 (1990).

Rosenweig, Paul.   Functional Equivalents of the Border, Sovereignty, and the Fourth Amendment.   52 Univ. Chicago L.Rev. 1119 (1985).

Rothstein, Mark A.   OSHA Inspections after Marshall v. Barlow's, Inc. 1979 Duke L.J. 63 (1979).

Stack, Rebecca.   Airport Drug Searches: Giving Content to the Concept of Free and Voluntary Consent.   77 Va.L.Rev. 183 (1991).

Strossen, Nadine.   Michigan Department of Police v. Sitz: A Roadblock to Meaningful Judicial Enforcement of Constitutional Rights.   42 Hastings L.J. 285 (1991).

Yurow, Lois.   Alternative Challenges to Drug Testing of Government Employees: Options After *Von Raab* and *Skinner.*   58 Geo.Wash.L.Rev. 148 (1989).

Chapter Fourteen

ELECTRONIC SURVEILLANCE

14.01 Introduction

Electronic surveillance encompasses a wide variety of techniques which make use of electronic equipment to eavesdrop or spy on the activities of others. These techniques include wiretapping (the interception of telephone calls by physical penetration of the wire circuitry), "bugging" (listening to conversations over a transmitting device installed either on premises or on individuals), electronic tracking (through use of "beepers") and video surveillance (watching activities through a camera). More sophisticated techniques are being developed at a rapid pace.[1] All of this technology permits surveillance, without detection, of private conversations and actions.

When used by the government, electronic surveillance creates a particularly dramatic threat to the privacy of individual citizens. Yet the legal system has been slow to respond to this unique type of "search and seizure." While law enforcement agencies began using some electronic techniques as early as the 1920's,[2] the first comprehensive effort toward regulating their use did not occur until the late 1960's. And recent developments suggest that scientific advancement and law enforcement ingenuity will continue to outpace judicial and legislative monitoring.

This chapter explores early treatment of electronic surveillance by the courts and legislatures and then examines in detail Title III of the Omnibus Crime Control and Safe Streets Act,[3] which was passed by Congress in 1968 and presently governs both federal and state practice with respect to electronic eavesdropping. It concludes with a brief look at efforts to regulate tracking devices and video surveillance.

14.02 Regulation Prior to Title III

(a) **The Trespass Doctrine.** The first case involving electronic surveillance to reach the Supreme Court was *Olmstead v. United States*.[4] There, federal agents had set up a tap of the telephone wires outside the defendants' premises, without a war-

---

1. "Heat sensors" permitting "viewing" through walls, infrared night photography and sonic enhancement devices which permit listening through walls and or over long distances without the necessity of a "bug" are all possibilities. See, generally, Katz, "In Search of a Fourth Amendment for the Twenty-First Century," 65 Ind.L.Rev. 549 (1990).

2. See *Olmstead v. United States*, 277 U.S. 438, 48 S.Ct. 564 (1928).

3. 18 U.S.C.A. §§ 2510–2520.

4. 277 U.S. 438, 48 S.Ct. 564 (1928).

rant. Over strong dissents by Justice Brandeis and Justice Holmes, the Court held that since the tap was not a "trespass" on the defendants' property and did not seize tangible "things" protected by the language of the Fourth Amendment, no search or seizure occurred. Although it eventually discarded the notion that conversations were not "things" for Fourth Amendment purposes, for the next forty years the Court continued to analyze electronic surveillance cases in terms of whether the surveillance worked a trespass. Thus, in *Goldman v. United States,*[5] the Court held that the use of a detectaphone placed against an office wall in order to hear private conversations in the office next door did not violate the Fourth Amendment because there was no physical trespass in connection with the relevant interception. Conversely, in *Silverman v. United States,*[6] eavesdrop evidence was excluded because it was obtained through use of a "spike mike" inserted under the baseboard of a wall until it made contact with a heating duct running throughout Silverman's house.

Even when the surveillance involved a physical invasion of property by a government agent, the Court refused to apply the Fourth Amendment if there was "consent." Thus, in *On Lee v. United States,*[7] the Court upheld, 5–4, use of a "body bug" concealed on an ex-employee of the defendant who entered the defendant's laundry without objection and engaged him in conversation. Neither the argument that the government's actions were fraudulent or the contention that the body bug allowed another agent, outside the laundry, to listen to the defendant swayed the Court; these facts did not convert the action into a trespass. Similarly, in *Lopez v. United States,*[8] the Court sanctioned use of a recording device on a government agent, because "the device was used only to obtain the most reliable evidence possible of a conversation in which the Government's own agent was a participant" and "was not planted by means of an unlawful physical invasion of petitioner's premises."

(b) The Federal Communications Act. While the Court was reluctant to regulate electronic surveillance, Congress, six years after *Olmstead,* did undertake that task in cases involving federal agents. In § 605 of the Federal Communications Act of 1934, Congress provided that "no person not being authorized by the sender shall intercept any communication and divulge or publish the existence, contents, purport, effect or meaning of such intercepted communications to any person." As with the trespass doctrine, if a party to the conversation allowed the eavesdropping, the Act was not triggered.[9] But nonconsensual wiretapping was

---

5. 316 U.S. 129, 62 S.Ct. 993 (1942).

6. 365 U.S. 505, 81 S.Ct. 679 (1961).

7. 343 U.S. 747, 72 S.Ct. 967 (1952).

8. 373 U.S. 427, 83 S.Ct. 1381 (1963).

9. *Rathbun v. United States,* 355 U.S. 107, 78 S.Ct. 161 (1957).

curtailed significantly under § 605. In *Nardone v. United States*,[10] the Supreme Court held that, in federal cases, § 605 required exclusion of all evidence obtained from a surreptitious interstate wiretap; to hold otherwise, explained the Court, would be to allow an unauthorized person to "divulge" the contents of the message.[11] The Court later held that this rule applied to *intra*state taps as well,[12] and also to evidence procured by state officers that was later used in federal court.[13]

However, all of these cases preceded *Mapp v. Ohio*,[14] and made clear that the Act did not mandate exclusion in state cases.[15] It was not until 1968, seven years after *Mapp*, that violations of the Act were found to require exclusion in state prosecutions.[16] Moreover, § 605 applied only to tapping of phone, telegraph or radiotelegraph lines. It did not cover use of the more sophisticated devices that did not involve tapping. Finally, the Act did nothing to prevent private eavesdropping, while at the same time prohibiting entirely nonconsensual electronic surveillance by government officials. Developments in Fourth Amendment jurisprudence and, eventually, the passage of Title III, would make the Federal Communications Act of tangential relevance to regulation of eavesdropping law.[17]

(c) *Katz* and Expectation of Privacy Analysis. In 1967, the Supreme Court decided the seminal case of *Katz v. United States*.[18] There, government agents attached an electronic listening and recording device to the outside of a booth known to be used by the defendant for phone conversations. Although no physical trespass of the booth occurred (and in any event the booth was not the defendant's property), the Court excluded the conversations thereby obtained, in the process overturning *Olmstead* and rejecting the trespass doctrine. Because the government action "violated the privacy upon which Katz justifiably relied while using the telephone booth," the Fourth Amendment was implicated and the agents should have obtained a warrant. Justice Harlan's concurring language referring to "reasonable expecta-

---

10. 302 U.S. 379, 58 S.Ct. 275 (1937).

11. Two years later, the Court held in the same case that "fruit" of the wiretap could not be used in federal court. *Nardone v. United States*, 308 U.S. 338, 60 S.Ct. 266 (1939), discussed in § 2.04(a).

12. *Weiss v. United States*, 308 U.S. 321, 60 S.Ct. 269 (1939).

13. *Benanti v. United States*, 355 U.S. 96, 78 S.Ct. 155 (1957).

14. 367 U.S. 643, 81 S.Ct. 1684 (1961).

15. The Court explicitly so held in *Schwartz v. Texas*, 344 U.S. 199, 73 S.Ct. 232 (1952).

16. *Lee v. Florida*, 392 U.S. 378, 88 S.Ct. 2096 (1968).

17. With the enactment of Title III, Congress amended § 605 to limit its coverage solely to interception of radio communications, which Title III does not cover. Act of June 19, 1968, Pub.L. No. 90–351, § 803, 82 Stat. 212.

18. 389 U.S. 347, 88 S.Ct. 507 (1967).

tions of privacy" soon became the theoretical basis of Fourth Amendment protection.[19]

However, the post-*Katz* Court has refused to back away from the holdings in *On Lee* and *Lopez* involving "consensual" eavesdropping. In *United States v. White*,[20] a plurality of the Court upheld the result in those cases despite *Katz'* rejection of the trespass rationale. Noting that one assumes the risk that one's acquaintances will be government agents, the majority stated "it is only speculation to assert that the defendant's utterances would be substantially different or his sense of security any less if he also thought it possible that the suspected colleague is wired for sound." In dissent, Justice Harlan argued otherwise: "Were third-party bugging a prevalent practice, it might well smother that spontaneity—reflected in frivolous, impetuous, sacrilegious, and defiant discourse—that liberates daily life." Thus, the Fourth Amendment should protect "the expectation of the ordinary citizen, who has never engaged in illegal conduct in his life, that he may carry on his private discourse freely, openly, and spontaneously without measuring his every word against the connotations it might carry when instantaneously heard by others unknown to him and unfamiliar with his situation or analyzed in a cold, formal record played days, months, or years after the conversation." As developed elsewhere in this book,[21] the deeper problem with *White* lies in the failure of either the majority or the dissent to recognize that even undercover activity that is not electronically assisted violates normal expectations of privacy.

(d) The Fourth Amendment Warrant Requirement. If a particular type of electronic eavesdropping does implicate the Fourth Amendment, one must determine the kind of protection thereby afforded. The same term as *Katz*, the Supreme Court decided *Berger v. New York*,[22] which, for the first time, addressed the precise application of the Fourth Amendment to electronic surveillance cases.

At issue in *Berger* was a New York eavesdropping statute which permitted an eavesdrop order to be issued by a detached magistrate if a specified state law enforcement officer stated that there was reasonable ground to believe that evidence of a crime could thus be obtained. Since this was the only requirement for an order to issue, the Supreme Court determined that the statute was deficient on its face in six specific areas: (1) it failed to require a showing of probable cause that a particular offense had been or was being committed; (2) it did not require a particularized

---

19. See § 4.03 for further discussion of *Katz*.

20. 401 U.S. 745, 91 S.Ct. 1122 (1971). *White* was affirmed by a majority of the Court in *United States v.*

Caceres, 440 U.S. 741, 99 S.Ct. 1465 (1979).

21. See § 4.03(a).

22. 388 U.S. 41, 87 S.Ct. 1873 (1967).

description of the communications, conversations or discussions that were to be seized; (3) it provided for the grant of a two-month period eavesdrop that could and often did lead to a series of intrusions, searches and seizures pursuant to a single showing of probable cause whereby all conversations were seized, not just incriminating ones; (4) the statute failed to provide for a termination date on the eavesdrop once the conversation sought was seized; (5) it provided no requirement for notice, as do conventional warrants, but rather permitted uncontested entry without any showing of exigency; and (6) it failed to require return on the warrant, thus making judicial supervision of the eavesdropping difficult.

In short, *Berger* notified the states that statutes authorizing eavesdropping under court order would, at the least, have to comply with traditional Fourth Amendment search warrant requirements.[23] The precise reach of *Berger* is discussed in more detail in the discussion of Title III, which was enacted one year after *Berger* and which, to a substantial extent, preempted state statutes regulating electronic eavesdropping.

14.03 Federal Eavesdropping Law: Title III

In apparent response to the legal uncertainties in electronic surveillance and wiretapping, and spurred on by the *Berger* and *Katz* decisions, Congress passed Title III of the Omnibus Crime Control and Safe Streets Act of 1968.[24] The law is particularly important because it preempts state law pertaining to eavesdropping.[25] Pursuant to § 2516(2) of Title III, a state court judge may grant an eavesdropping order only if the entire application process is in conformity with Title III as well as with the applicable state statute.[26] If a state statute does not conform to Title III with regard to the procedures for obtaining a valid wiretap order, the order will be unlawful even though authorized by state law. As evidenced by the legislative history, however, Congress clearly intended that the states could enact more restrictive electronic surveillance statutes or construe existing statutes narrowly to protect privacy more fully than Title III.[27]

In 1986, Congress enacted the Electronic Communications Privacy Act,[28] which significantly amended Title III in several

---

23. See Chapter Five for a description of these requirements.

24. 18 U.S.C.A. §§ 2510–20 (originally enacted as Act of June 19, 1968, Pub. L. No. 90–351, § 802, 82 Stat. 212). The textual references throughout the rest of this chapter refer to Title III.

25. 18 U.S.C.A. § 2516(2), cf. *United States v. Tortorello,* 480 F.2d 764 (2d

Cir.1973), cert. denied 414 U.S. 866, 94 S.Ct. 63 (1973).

26. 18 U.S.C.A. § 2516(2).

27. S.Rep. No. 1097, 90th Cong., 2d Sess. (1968), U.S.Code Cong.Adm.News 2177, 2187.

28. Pub.L. No. 99–508 (1986).

ways. A summary of Title III, as amended, and the decisions by the Supreme Court relevant to it follow.

(a) **The Scope of Title III.** Title III prohibits the "interception" of "wire, oral or electronic communications," unless such interception is authorized by the statute. As originally enacted, Title III protected only wire communications and oral communications. In 1986, responding to the explosion of telecommunication and computer technologies, Congress added "electronic communications" as a protected category.[29] The 1986 amendments also make clear that Title III protects *private* wire and electronic communications;[30] the previous version had referred exclusively to wire communications "operated by any person engaged as a common carrier." Finally, the amendments extend protection to electronic storage and processing of information.[31] To the extent such storage or processing is under the auspices of a third party computer operator, the amendments thus provide protection the Fourth Amendment may not.[32]

(1) Types of communications protected. The three types of communications covered by Title III are precisely defined. Wire communication is defined as:

"any aural transfer made in whole or in part through the use of facilities for the transmission of communications by the aid of wire, cable, or other like connection . . . [that affects interstate commerce] . . . such term includes any electronic storage of such communication but such term does not include the radio portion of a cordless telephone communication that is transmitted between the cordless telephone handset and the base unit.[33]

The cordless phone exception was adopted in 1986 on the dubious ground that communications "on some cordless telephones can be intercepted easily with readily available technologies, such as an AM radio."[34] Ease of detection should not determine whether one loses an expectation of privacy as to one's phone calls. Nonetheless, several courts have accepted this ground as a basis for exempting cordless phones from Fourth Amendment, as well as statutory, protection.[35]

29. 18 U.S.C.A. § 2511(2)(a)(ii).

30. See 5 U.S.Code Congressional and Administrative News 3559 (99th Cong.2d Sess.1986) [hereafter referred to as 5 U.S.Code News].

31. 18 U.S.C.A. § 2701 et seq.

32. Cf. *United States v. Miller,* 425 U.S. 435, 96 S.Ct. 1619 (1976), discussed in § 4.03(a). However, the amendments do not require a "Title III" warrant, but only a regular warrant for

access to information that is in storage less than 180 days, and only a subpoena for access to information in storage over 180 days. 18 U.S.C.A. § 2703.

33. Id. § 2510(1).

34. 5 U.S.Code News, supra note 30, at 3566.

35. *State v. Howard,* 235 Kan. 236, 679 P.2d 197 (1984); *Dorsey v. State,* 402 So.2d 1178 (Fla.1981).

Oral communication is defined as "any oral communication uttered by a person exhibiting an expectation that such communication is not subject to interception under circumstances justifying such expectation, but such term does not include any electronic communication."[36] The 1968 legislative history suggests that this language would not cover conversations in certain quasi-public areas, such as a jail cell or "open fields."[37] Admittedly, the Supreme Court has found the Fourth Amendment inapplicable to searches for *effects* in these areas.[38] But the reasoning in these cases does not necessarily apply to "searches" for conversations which the parties expect to be private.

Electronic communication means

> any transfer of signs, signals, writing, images, sounds, data, or intelligence of any nature transmitted in whole or in part by wire, radio, electromagnetic, photoelectronic, or photooptical systems that affects interstate or foreign commerce but does not include (A) [the radio portion of cordless phones]; (B) any wire or oral communication; (C) any communication made through a tone-only paging device; (D) any communication from a tracking device. . . .[39]

In general, according to the legislative history of the 1986 amendment to Title III, "a communication is an electronic communication protected by the federal wiretap law if it is not carried by sound waves and cannot fairly be characterized as containing the human voice."[40] The term is meant to cover electronic mail, computer-to-computer communications, microwave transmissions, and cellular telephones, among other modern communication techniques. Tone-only paging devices were excluded by analogy to "pen registers" which, for reasons discussed below,[41] are exempted from coverage. Tracking devices are handled under separate provisions.[42] The distinction between electronic communications and other types of communications is important in several respects; most significantly, as discussed below, violation of the rules relating to the former type of communication does not require suppression of illegally obtained evidence.

(2) *The definition of "interception".* Interception is defined as "the aural or other acquisition of the contents of any wire, electronic, or oral communication through the use of any electronic, mechanical, or other device."[43] Telephone and telegraph

---

36. 18 U.S.C.A. § 2510(2).

37. S.Rep. No. 1097, 90th Cong.2d Sess. 89–90 (1968).

38. *Oliver v. United States*, 466 U.S. 170, 104 S.Ct. 1735 (1984) (open fields); discussed in § 4.03(c); *Hudson v. Palmer*, 468 U.S. 517, 104 S.Ct. 3194 (1984), discussed in § 4.03(g).

39. Id. § 2510(12).

40. 5 U.S.Code News, supra note 30, at 3568, 3562–64.

41. See § 14.03(a)(2).

42. See § 14.04.

43. 18 U.S.C.A. § 2510(4).

equipment used in the ordinary course of business and hearing aids are not considered a "device" under the statute.[44] Moreover, using a device which does not intercept the "contents" of a communication, as defined by the Act, does not violate Title III. Contents for purposes of the Act "includes any information concerning the identity of the parties to such communication or the existence, substance, purport, or meaning of that communication."[45] In *United States v. New York Telephone Co.,*[46] the Supreme Court held that a "pen register," which merely records numbers dialed on a telephone without overhearing verbal communications, does not fall within this definition. Thus after *New York Telephone,* the government could obtain pen register information simply by seeking a typical warrant rather than the more protective warrant required by Title III.

Two years later, in *Smith v. Maryland,*[47] the Court eliminated even this requirement by finding that use of pen registers does not constitute a "search" within the meaning of the Fourth Amendment. The Court reasoned that there is no reasonable expectation of privacy in numbers dialed because (1) individuals assume the risk of disclosure when they voluntarily convey such information to the phone company; and (2) the phone company, in its daily operations, regularly records numbers dialed. However, in 1986, Congress provided that before information from a pen register may be obtained by police, they must obtain a court order finding the information "relevant" to an ongoing criminal investigation.[48]

(b) Authorized Interceptions. As should be clear from the above, Title III is meant to regulate interception of almost all varieties of communication. However, there are several exceptions to its ban on interception of wire, oral or electronic transmissions. First, analogous to Fourth Amendment jurisprudence, a party to a communication or a person authorized by one of the parties to the communication may intercept the communication.[49] Second, for obvious reasons, the Act permits interception of electronic communication made through an "electronic communication system that is configured so that such electronic communication is readily accessible to the general public" and of radio communications meant to be heard by the public.[50] Third, quality control checks by common carriers and government agencies are allowed for that specific purpose.[51] Fourth, interceptions neces-

---

44. Id. § 2510(5).

45. Id. § 2510(8).

46. 434 U.S. 159, 98 S.Ct. 364 (1977).

47. 442 U.S. 735, 99 S.Ct. 2577 (1979).

48. 18 U.S.C.A. § 3121 et seq. The court need not make an independent investigation of the facts, however; its

function is to certify the completeness of the application. Id. § 3123(a).

49. Id. § 2511(2)(c), (d). "Retroactive" consent is not permitted, however. Sen.Rep., supra note 37, at 94.

50. Id. § 2511(2)(g).

51. Id. § 2511(2)(a)(i), (b). This exception permits interceptions to procure

sary to protect the national security are permitted,[52] although the Supreme Court has interpreted this exception narrowly. In *United States v. United States District Court,*[53] the Court held (1) that the national security exception did not purport to eliminate the necessity of a court order for federal investigations of "internal security matters" which are not linked to foreign powers and (2) that, in any event, the Fourth Amendment would not allow this practice.[54] A fifth exception is permitted in certain emergency situations involving "immediate danger of death or serious physical injury to any person," and "conspiratorial activities threatening the national security interest or . . . characteristic of organized crime."[55] Application for a court order approving the emergency interception must be made within 48 hours, however.

Finally, of course, interceptions may be made if authorized by a proper court order.[56] As detailed below, Title III sets out specific rules governing the application for the eavesdrop order, its content, and procedures for performing an interception pursuant to the order. It also provides specific remedies, including suppression of illegally seized evidence and civil and criminal penalties, if its provisions are violated.

(c) Application for an Order. The application for a Title III warrant must meet several requirements,[57] many of which go beyond that required for the typical warrant application. The application must provide: (1) the identity of the investigative officer making the application and of the officer authorizing the application; (2) "a full and complete statement of the facts and circumstances relied upon by the applicant to justify his belief that an order should be issued," including "details as to the particular offense;" (3) "a particular description of the nature and location of the facilities from which or the place where the communication is to be intercepted," "a particular description of the type of communications sought to be intercepted;" and "the identity of the person, if known, committing the offense and whose communications are to be intercepted;" (4) a "full and complete statement as to whether or not other investigative procedures have been tried and failed or why they reasonably appear to be unlikely to succeed if tried or to be too dangerous;" (5) "a statement of the period of time for which the interception is

evidence of wire fraud, even if they last several weeks, in an effort to identify all the perpetrators. *United States v. Harvey,* 540 F.2d 1345 (8th Cir.1976).

52. Id. § 2511(2)(e), (f).

53. 407 U.S. 297, 92 S.Ct. 2125 (1972).

54. The Court also held, however, that it might be permissible to relax some of Title III's requirements when

domestic activities directly implicate national security. Electronic surveillance of *foreign* intelligence information is now regulated by the Foreign Intelligence Surveillance Act of 1978, 50 U.S. C.A. § 1801 et seq.

55. 18 U.S.C.A. § 2518(7).

56. Id. § 2511(a)(ii).

57. These are set out in 18 U.S.C.A. § 2518(1).

required to be maintained," including, if necessary, "a particular description of facts establishing probable cause to believe that additional communications of the same type will occur" after "the described type of communication has been first obtained;" (6) "a full and complete statement of the facts concerning all previous applications . . . involving any of the same persons, facilities or places specified in the application, and the action taken by the judge on each such application;" and (7) where an extension of an order is at issue, "a statement setting forth the results thus far obtained from the interception, or a reasonable explanation of the failure to obtain such results." These seven elements are discussed below, with the focus on their relationship to Fourth Amendment law.

(1) Identity of the applicant. The original Act required that an application for an order be authorized by the Attorney General, or any Assistant Attorney General specifically designated by the Attorney General. The 1986 amendments allow any acting Assistant Attorney General and any Deputy Assistant Attorney General (Criminal Division) to sign applications to intercept wire and oral communications [58] and "any attorney for the Government" to authorize applications for interception of electronic communications.[59] Only the attorneys authorizing wire and oral communications need be specially designated by the Attorney General. Thus, the number of federal officials who can authorize surveillance applications has been expanded by the 1986 amendments and the number of attorneys who can authorize surveillance applications for electronic communications is vastly greater than the number who can authorize applications for wire and oral communications. (On the state level, officials holding positions analogous to those federal officials described above may authorize applications.[60])

In *United States v. Giordano*,[61] the Supreme Court strictly construed the 1968 Act's provisions concerning authorization of applications. It held that the Attorney General or his special designee must sign each application because Congress intended that responsibility for the proper use of surveillance be placed on an official responsive to the political process. This interpretation of congressional intent no longer seems accurate now that lower level attorneys have been authorized to sign applications. For the same reason, the issue resolved in the government's favor in *United States v. Chavez* [62]—whether an application is valid when it is actually authorized by the Attorney General but is erroneously

58. Id. § 2516(1).

59. Id. § 2516(3).

60. See, e.g. *State v. Farha*, 218 Kan. 394, 544 P.2d 341 (1975), cert. denied 426 U.S. 949, 96 S.Ct. 3170 (1976).

61. 416 U.S. 505, 94 S.Ct. 1820 (1974).

62. 416 U.S. 562, 94 S.Ct. 1849 (1974).

asserted to be authorized by an assistant Attorney General—is now mooted by the 1986 amendments.

(2) Details of the offense. As originally enacted, Title III specified that electronic surveillance may be used only to investigate certain types of crimes. Under the 1986 amendments, however, the list of federal crimes which can trigger interception of wire and oral communications was expanded to include virtually any felony; [63] when electronic communications are to be intercepted, the amendments specifically allowed application concerning "any Federal felony." [64] State statutes may authorize court orders to obtain evidence regarding "murder, kidnapping, gambling, robbery, bribery, extortion, or dealing in [drugs], or other crime dangerous to life, limb, or property, and punishable by imprisonment for more than one year . . . or any conspiracy to commit any of the foregoing offenses." [65] So long as one of these crimes is alleged in the application, this component of Title III is met.

(3) Particularity requirements. The provisions of Title III which mandate descriptions of what is to be "seized," and where and whom it is to be seized from, may be constitutionally required by *Berger v. New York,* [66] which held that merely naming the person whose communications are to be overheard or recorded violates the particularity requirement of the Fourth Amendment.[67] The *Berger* Court reasoned that "the need for particularity . . . is especially great in the case of eavesdropping [because it] involves an intrusion on privacy that is broad in scope." But while lower courts generally require an indication in the application of the the identity of the target and the facility to be tapped,[68] most have not required, beyond a description of the offense being investigated, a precise delineation of the "type of communications sought to be intercepted," on the ground that such a requirement would be very difficult to meet.[69]

Whether the lower courts' approach conforms with *Berger* has not yet been ruled on by the Court. But the Supreme Court has held that investigating agents need not list the identity of *everyone* they believe might be overheard, thus suggesting that they need not predict all types of conversations which they will uncover. In

---

63. 18 U.S.C.A. § 2516(1).

64. Id. § 2516(3).

65. Id. § 2516(2).

66. 388 U.S. 41, 87 S.Ct. 1873 (1967), discussed in § 14.02(d).

67. For a discussion of this requirement, see § 5.04.

68. Where "roving taps" are necessary because it is not known where the subject will make the designated communication or the subject is shown to be deliberately changing locations to avoid tapping, the 1986 amendments allow specification of a limited geographic area, the number of phones to be intercepted and the time in which the interception is to be accomplished. Id. § 2518(11). See also, 5 U.S.Code News, supra note 30, at 3586.

69. See, e.g., *United States v. Fino,* 478 F.2d 35 (2d Cir.1973).

United States v. Kahn,[70] the government intercepted conversations between the defendant and his wife, as well as between his wife and other gamblers, pursuant to a warrant which named the defendant but not his wife. The court of appeals suppressed all of these conversations, including the defendant's, reasoning that the government should have discovered the wife's involvement in the defendant's gambling operations prior to the search and included her name on the application. But the Supreme Court reversed, holding that "Title III requires the naming of a person in the application or interception order only when the law enforcement authorities have probable cause to believe that that individual is 'committing the offense' for which the wiretap is sought." Pre-application investigation of all possible suspects is not required. This holding is analogous to the Court's later ruling in *Horton v. California,*[71] which eliminated the inadvertence requirement in plain view cases on the ground that, if probable cause exists to obtain a warrant, other evidence discovered in plain view in the course of executing the warrant is admissible even if police suspected it might be discovered. The difference where eavesdropping is concerned is that considerable additional private material will almost always be "discovered" when an unnamed third party is involved. The Court felt, however, that the "minimization" requirement, discussed below,[72] would reduce unnecessary privacy invasions.[73]

(4) The last resort requirement. In *Giordano,* the Supreme Court stated that the provision in Title III requiring a showing that other investigative procedures have failed is designed to ensure that electronic eavesdropping is not "routinely employed as the initial step in criminal investigation." Language in *Kahn* also endorses this notion. But the lower courts have not construed the provision literally, instead permitting electronic surveillance when other methods might be considered dangerous or more difficult.[74] The Supreme Court itself has generally looked with disfavor on least drastic means analysis in the investigative context,[75] although it has yet to speak directly on the issue when electronic surveillance is concerned.

(5) Durational elements. Discussed here are the last three elements of the application process, all of which relate to the

70. 415 U.S. 143, 94 S.Ct. 977 (1974).

71. 496 U.S. 128, 110 S.Ct. 2301 (1990), discussed in § 9.04.

72. See § 14.03(e)(2).

73. The Court has also held that, if the police fail to list a person for whom they *do* have probable cause, this error is harmless, because the listing requirement does not play a "substantive role" in the regulatory scheme. *United States v. Donovan,* 429 U.S. 413, 97 S.Ct. 658 (1977), discussed further in § 14.03(g)(1).

74. See J. Carr, The Law of Electronic Surveillance 179 (1977).

75. See, e.g., discussion of checkpoints in § 13.06.

duration of an interception. Not only must investigators indicate the amount of time they need to complete the interception (which in any event may not exceed 30 days per order),[76] but they must also explain why the interception should not be "automatically terminated when the described type of communication has been first obtained." Of course, the significance of this latter requirement is diminished by the lower courts' previously discussed disinclination to require any specificity with respect to type of communication sought to be intercepted. The investigators must also describe any previous applications for the same persons or places, again a provision designed to sensitize the judge to any overly intrusive or prolonged surveillance. As this provision only requires disclosure of past interceptions of previously *named* targets, the holding in *Kahn* (which does not require listing all possible targets in an application) assumes greater significance.[77] Finally, any attempt to continue interception beyond the statutory 30–day period requires a second application, including an explanation of why the first interception failed.

Relevant to interpretation of all of these provisions is the Supreme Court's opinion in *Berger*. There the Court seemed particularly concerned about the duration of the typical eavesdrop. In finding the New York statute unconstitutional, it stressed that the law permitted an extension of an order "without a showing of present probable cause for the continuance of the eavesdrop," and placed "no termination date on the eavesdrop once the conversation sought is seized." Title III, at least on its face, seems to avoid both of these problems. But the Court also emphasized that the 60–day surveillance in *Berger* was "the equivalent of a series of intrusions, searches, and seizures pursuant to a single showing of probable cause." Title III appears to run afoul of this language, since only one showing of probable cause need be made every 30 days. *Berger* would seem to require that continuous applications be made, and orders issued, on a much more frequent basis.

The lower courts have not adopted this interpretation of *Berger*, however. Instead, they have permitted, based on a single application, wiretaps which last several days and involve many different conversations.[78] Whether this position is supportable depends upon the nature of the surveillance. As Justice Harlan argued in his *Berger* dissent, a prolonged electronic eavesdrop can be seen as a single search, during which particularly described conversations may be seized. If one is to adopt this stance, however, it becomes important to be specific with respect to the

---

76. 18 U.S.C.A. § 2518(5).

77. As does the holding in *Donovan*, described supra note 73, which does not penalize the government for failure to list even those targets for whom the government has probable cause.

78. See, e.g., *Hanger v. United States*, 398 F.2d 91 (8th Cir.1968).

types of conversations sought to be seized, a requirement which, as noted above, the lower courts have been reluctant to impose. Additionally, serious effort must be made to minimize interception of conversations that are irrelevant to the investigation,[79] which can be aided by requiring periodic reports to the court,[80] as authorized under Title III.

(d) The Wiretap Order. The judge must make several findings before a Title III warrant may be issued,[81] and include within the order certain provisions.[82] The findings he must make are four in number: (1) a probable cause belief that an enumerated offense has been, is being, or will be committed; (2) a probable cause belief that particular communications concerning that offense will be obtained through the proposed interception; (3) a belief that "normal investigative procedures have been tried and failed or reasonably appear to be unlikely to succeed if tried or to be too dangerous;" and (4) a probable cause belief that the facilities to be subject to surveillance are connected with the offense or the person named. In *Berger,* the majority suggested that the probable cause required for electronic surveillance is higher than normal. As stated by Justice Stewart, "[o]nly the most precise and rigorous standard of probable cause should justify an intrusion of this sort." But the lower courts have not so held in interpreting Title III.[83]

If the judge decides the order should issue, the order must: (1) identify "the person, if known, whose communications are to be intercepted;" (2) identify "the nature and location of the communications facilities as to which, or the place where, authority to intercept is granted;" (3) describe "the type of communications sought to be intercepted, and a statement of the particular offense to which it relates;" (4) identify the person authorizing the application and the agency performing the interception; (5) provide "that the authorization to intercept shall be executed as soon as practicable;" (6) specify "the period of time during which such interception is authorized," and "whether or not the interception shall automatically terminate when the described communication has been first obtained;" (7) provide that the interception "be conducted in such a way as to minimize the interception of communications not otherwise subject to interception;" and (8) at the discretion of the court, "require reports to be made to the judge who issued the order showing what progress has been made toward achievement of the authorized objective and the need for continued interception." The order must also, in cases where so

---

79. See § 14.03(e)(2).

80. See § 14.03(f).

81. These are described in 18 U.S.C.A. § 2518(3).

82. Id. § 2518(4) and (5).

83. *United States v. Falcone,* 505 F.2d 478 (3d Cir.1974).

requested by the applicant, order relevant common carriers, land-lords, and similar agencies or individuals to cooperate with the investigation.

As the provisions of the order track very closely the elements of the application, the comments made earlier with respect to the application process are equally applicable here. In particular, it should be noted that since the government is not required to list in the application those individuals for whom it does not have proba-ble cause, the order need not list these individuals either. To hold otherwise, reasoned the Court in *Kahn,* would require the judge to conduct his own investigation of nonlisted parties.

(e) Executing the Order. Execution of a Title III warrant is governed by several rules. First, Title III provides that all inter-ceptions "shall, if possible, be recorded on tape or wire or other comparable device . . . in such way as will protect the recording from editing or other alterations." [84] This provision helps ensure accuracy by making the evidence procured through electronic surveillance as "tangible" as the evidence obtained in a more typical search. Second, as noted above, the Title III order places several limitations on execution of the interception. Most impor-tant are the commands concerning durational limits, periodic reports, and the minimization requirement.

This latter issue requires elaboration. In addition, two other execution issues—the amendment process which is required when evidence of other crimes is obtained and the propriety of covert entry to plant an eavesdropping device—will be explored in some detail, in the order in which they are likely to occur during an interception.

(1) Covert entry. Occasionally, agents must enter private property to install, and remove, the eavesdropping device. Title III is silent as to the circumstances under which this type of action may take place. In *Dalia v. United States,*[85] the Supreme Court held that such entries are reasonable under the Fourth Amend-ment and permitted under Title III as well, so long as no property is damaged and the entry is otherwise conducted reasonably. More questionably, five members of the Court held that the covert entry need not be authorized by the court but can be carried out at the discretion of the officers. The majority, via Justice Powell, found nothing in the language of the Fourth Amendment regulat-ing the method by which a search is carried out and called the imposition of such a requirement in the electronic surveillance context "an empty formalism," given the obvious necessity of covert entry in some cases. As two of the dissenters pointed out, however, a court can meaningfully regulate such entries by requir-

---

84. 18 U.S.C.A. 2518(8)(a).

85. 441 U.S. 238, 99 S.Ct. 1682 (1979).

ing proof that they are necessary and limiting the extent of intrusion they entail.

(2) The minimization requirement. In *Berger,* the Supreme Court stressed that one unconstitutional aspect of the statute under consideration there was that it allowed seizure of "the conversations of any and all persons coming into the area covered by the device . . . indiscriminately and without regard to their connection to the crime under investigation." Title III seeks to avoid this problem by providing that the interception "be conducted in such a way as to minimize the interception of communications not otherwise subject to interception."

Scott v. United States [86] illustrates the difficulty of implementing this provision. In *Scott,* the officers admitted to having made no efforts to minimize the intrusion into defendant's privacy. For a month, with only one short exception, virtually every call made on the phone was intercepted, although only 40% were pertinent (narcotics related) calls. However, apparently no patterns developed that indicated to listening agents that nonpertinent matters were being intercepted and that the remainder of the conversation would be nonpertinent as well. The Supreme Court, speaking through Justice Rehnquist, held that, in analyzing whether minimization has occurred, courts should take into account: (1) the percentage of nonpertinent calls, (2) the length of the calls, (3) the ambiguity of the language used, (4) the type of use to which the telephone is normally put, (5) the scope of the investigation, (6) whether the calls involve one or more of the co-conspirators and (7) at what point during the authorized period the interception was made (with less minimization required at the outset as officers establish the pattern of calls). In *Scott* itself, no violation of the minimization rule was found, despite the officers' admitted bad faith, because the 60% of the calls which were not pertinent were either "very short," "ambiguous in nature," or "one-time conversations" which did not fit any known pattern.

The majority also held that the investigators' subjective attitude toward minimization was irrelevant to the analysis. This holding, which replicates the Court's objective approach in other Fourth Amendment situations,[87] tells officers to err on the side of interception, since plausible explanations for a failure to minimize can often be made. It also undercuts the Court's ruling in *Kahn* (which, it will be remembered, had relied on the minimization requirement in permitting a failure to list in the application all possible parties whose conversations would be intercepted), and undermines as well the rationale for allowing thirty-day surveillance based on one showing of probable cause.

86. 436 U.S. 128, 98 S.Ct. 1717 (1978). **87.** See § 10.04.

(3) Amendments. If officers overhear conversations about offenses not named in the warrant, they may, in circumstances analogous to those found in plain view cases,[88] "seize" these conversations as well. However, Title III requires that, to be admissible in criminal proceedings, these communications must be forwarded to the court "as soon as practicable" and the court must find that "the contents were otherwise intercepted in accordance with the provisions of this chapter."[89] This would appear to mean, for instance, that if the communications were overheard during a period when the minimization requirement should have applied, they may not be used in court.[90]

(f) Post-Interception Procedures. Once an interception has been completed, two important steps must be taken. First, sealing provisions protect against the editing or alteration of recorded interceptions and the destruction, editing, or alteration of eavesdrop orders or applications.[91] If these provisions are not followed, and a "satisfactory explanation" is not provided, exclusion of the evidence must result.[92] Second, within 90 days of the termination of the order, the issuing judge must have an inventory served on the persons named in the order or application.[93] The inventory must give notice of the entry of the order or application, the disposition of the application, and information as to whether there was an interception. Here too exclusion is mandated if the inventory does not reach the relevant parties within 10 days of trial or other proceeding.[94] This inventory provision also allows the judge to give discretionary notice to other parties to the intercepted communications if the judge concludes that such notice would be in the "interests of justice."[95]

In *United States v. Donovan,*[96] the Court held that, as an aid to the inventory process, the government has a duty to classify all persons whose conversations have been intercepted and to transmit this information to the judge. If instead, as in *Donovan,* the government merely supplies the judge with a list of all identifiable persons whose conversations were intercepted that list must at least be complete. Although the inadvertent failure to include the names of two "non-target" persons on the list was held to be "harmless" in *Donovan,* when names are deliberately withheld or prejudice to the defendant results from the exclusion, the Court suggested a different result might be reached.

---

88. See § 10.04.

89. 18 U.S.C.A. § 2517(5).

90. See Sen.Rep., supra note 37, at 100.

91. Id. § 2518(8)(a)–(b).

92. Id.

93. Id. § 2518(8)(d).

94. Id. § 2518(9).

95. Id. § 2518(8)(d).

96. 429 U.S. 413, 97 S.Ct. 658 (1977).

An individual who suspects that the government will use or is using information obtained or derived from an illegal wiretap, but who does not receive notice under the statute, may force the prosecution to affirm or deny the existence of the surveillance.[97] This provision is designed to assist the defendant who otherwise would have a difficult time proving surveillance took place. However, at least one court has held that the allegation of surveillance must be supported by specific facts.[98]

(g) The Suppression Remedy. Of course, any communications seized in violation of the Fourth Amendment must be suppressed unless an exception to the Fourth Amendment exclusionary principle, such as the good faith rule announced in *United States v. Leon,*[99] applies. Thus, in light of *Berger,* for example, evidence obtained pursuant to a Title III warrant that fails to provide any description of what is being seized, or that does not indicate the duration of the order, should be excluded, barring the unlikely finding that police were reasonable in believing the warrant to be valid.

Title III also contains its own exclusionary rules, which have independent effect. Already noted are the provisions requiring exclusion when: (1) communications not related to the offense being investigated are intercepted and are not disclosed to the judge "as soon as practicable;" (2) intercepted communications are not sealed and no satisfactory explanation is given for the oversight; and (3) the inventory is not provided to parties named in the order or application at least 10 days before trial or other proceeding. Title III also has a general exclusion provision which requires suppression when: (4) "the communication was unlawfully intercepted;" (5) "the order of authorization or approval under which it was intercepted is insufficient on its face;" or (6) "the interception was not made in conformity with the order of authorization or approval." [1]

(1) General scope. The relative scope of these rules and the Fourth Amendment exclusionary rule is clear in some cases. Title III's rules provide protection beyond that afforded by the Fourth Amendment in at least two ways: they apply to private, as well as government, interceptions,[2] and to all hearings, not just trial.[3] At

---

97. Id. § 3504(a).

98. Matter of Grand Jury, 529 F.2d 543 (3d Cir.1976), cert. denied 425 U.S. 992, 96 S.Ct. 2203 (1976).

99. 468 U.S. 897, 104 S.Ct. 3405 (1984), discussed in § 2.03(c)(2).

1. 18 U.S.C.A. § 2518(10)(a).

2. 5 U.S.Code News, supra note 30, at 3559. Compare § 4.02.

3. 18 U.S.C.A. § 2518(10)(a). Compare § 2.03(a) and (b). But see, *Gelbard v. United States,* 408 U.S. 41, 92 S.Ct. 2357 (1972) (where Justice White joined the plurality ruling that Title III required suppression of illegally obtained evidence at a grand jury proceeding only because no warrant had been obtained; where there is a warrant "the deterrent value of excluding the evidence will be marginal at best.")

the same time, unlike the Fourth Amendment rule, these exclusionary provisions apply only to interceptions of wire and oral communications, not to interceptions of electronic communications. The legislative history to the 1986 amendments offers no rationale for this difference in treatment, merely stating that the position was adopted "as a result of discussions with the Justice Department." [4] Thus, outside any protection afforded by the Fourth Amendment, the civil and criminal remedies described in the next section are the sole remedies afforded those whose electronic communications have been illegally intercepted.

More complicated is the comparison of Title III and Fourth Amendment exclusionary rules on the trial admissibility of wire and oral communications illegally obtained by the state. The effect of Title III's rules in this respect are limited by the "central rule" test, a good faith exception, and standing requirements.

(2) The "central role" test. Because Title III's substantive rules are so complex, the Supreme Court has been cautious about giving full sway to its general exclusionary remedies. Instead, as the Court stated in *United States v. Giordano,*[5] suppression is required only when the statutory provision which has been violated "was intended to play a central role in the statutory scheme."

This idea has been applied in several cases. In *Giordano,* the Court held that the pre–1986 requirement that all applications be authorized by the Attorney General or his designee did play a central role in the statutory scheme, because it was "reasonable to believe that such a precondition would inevitably foreclose resort to wiretapping in various situations where investigative personnel would otherwise seek intercept authority from the court and the court would very likely authorize its use." In *United States v. Chavez,*[6] on the other hand, the provision requiring accurate identification of the authorizing official was viewed as not "substantive" enough to require suppression upon violation (although the dissent pointed out that this provision played the important role of holding the authorizing official accountable for his actions). In *United States v. Donovan,*[7] the Court came to a similar conclusion regarding the provision requiring identification in the application and order of all parties for whom the government has probable cause. So long as at least one such party is identified in the order, it is "sufficient on its face," according to the Court, and thus suppression is not required under the "fifth" exclusionary rule described above even if other parties are left out. This conclusion is debatable; as the dissenters pointed out, the listing provision arguably does play a "central role" in the statutory

---

4. 5 U.S.Code News, supra note 30, at 3577.

5. 416 U.S. 505, 94 S.Ct. 1820 (1974).

6. 416 U.S. 562, 94 S.Ct. 1849 (1974).

7. 429 U.S. 413, 97 S.Ct. 658 (1977).

scheme, since both the provision requiring notification of previous applications and the requirement for inventory notice only operate with respect to parties *named* in the application.

Donovan also held that suppression is not required by a failure to send a post-surveillance inventory to persons whose communications have been intercepted but who were not named in the application or order. This holding is probably correct as a matter of statutory interpretation, since none of the general exclusionary rules (numbers four through six above) deals with post-interception matters, and the specific rule dealing with inventories (number three) only requires exclusion when the inventory is denied to a person named in the order or application. Whether failure to provide a discretionary inventory should result in exclusion as a *Fourth Amendment* matter is not as clear; *Donovan* left open the possibility that a deliberate, prejudicial action might require suppression.

The Court has not applied the central role test to other aspects of Title III, but some predictions about likely outcomes can be made, based on analogous Fourth Amendment provisions. Presumably, the probable cause requirements with respect to the offense, the communications sought, and the parties to be intercepted play a central role in Title III's statutory scheme, given their congruence with Fourth Amendment principles. Similarly, violation of the 30–day limitation on a single warrant is likely to require exclusion, given the Court's concern in *Berger* over the length of the interception in that case.

With less confidence, one can predict that the minimization requirement will be viewed as central, because it provides the only concrete means of avoiding a "general" search during the time period authorized by the order. Although *Scott v. United States* [8] suggested as much, it also stated, in dictum, that had the minimization requirement been violated in that case, only the improperly intercepted conversations would have to be suppressed. If the Court adheres to this rule, the minimization provision will be emasculated. Officers will know that even if they intercept every call and make no effort to minimize, they will still be able to introduce conversations relevant to the offense named in the warrant.

The "centrality" of Title III's provision mandating a finding that other investigative methods have been tried is even more difficult to predict. On the one hand, Title III's intent is to reserve electronic surveillance as a back-up investigative tool. On the other, as indicated in the discussion of the last resort requirement, the lower courts have not adhered rigidly to this requirement and the Supreme Court has rejected less intrusive means

---

8.   436 U.S. 128, 98 S.Ct. 1717 (1978).

analysis in other search contexts. As it has with the minimization requirement, the Court will probably give lipservice to the provision, but make clear that the government's burden in meeting it is not particularly heavy.

(3) The good faith exception. Even if exclusion is mandated under Title III, the government may be able to take advantage of a good faith exception analogous to that which exists in Fourth Amendment cases. In *United States v. Ojeda Rios,*[9] the Court considered Title III's requirement that the government seal tapes immediately after the expiration of the surveillance order or provide a "satisfactory explanation" for failing to do so, one of the provisions that requires exclusion for violation of its terms. Relying on this provision, the district court in *Ojeda Rios* excluded evidence obtained from two wiretaps because of long delays (82 and 118 days, respectively) between the termination of the orders for each tap and sealing of the tapes, a decision which the Second Circuit affirmed.

The Supreme Court agreed with the lower courts that the government must provide a satisfactory explanation not only for a failure to seal the tapes but also for any delay in sealing. It also rejected the government's argument that a "satisfactory explanation" includes a showing that the tapes had not been altered during the delay, for "even if we were confident that tampering could always be easily detected, . . . it is obvious that Congress had another view when it imposed the sealing safeguard." But six members of the Court nonetheless voted to remand the case for a determination as to whether the prosecutor reasonably believed that when a tap is one of many in the same investigation, as was true of both wiretaps at issue in *Ojeda Rios,* the tapes for the wiretap do not need to be sealed until the entire investigation is terminated. The relevant caselaw appeared to permit a delay in sealing the tapes in such cases only when subsequent court orders are continuous extensions of the first order; in *Ojeda Rios,* there was a gap between the surveillance periods authorized by the first orders and the orders authorizing the taps in question. But, according to the Court, "[t]he government is not required to prove that a particular understanding of the law is correct but rather only that its interpretation was objectively reasonable at the time." The result in *Ojeda Rios* permits a type of good faith defense akin to that recognized in *United States v. Leon.*[10]

(4) Standing. Under the Fourth Amendment, only those persons who can show that a search infringed upon their "legitimate

9. 495 U.S. 257, 110 S.Ct. 1845 (1990).

10. 468 U.S. 897, 104 S.Ct. 3405 (1984), discussed in § 2.03(c)(2).

expectations of privacy" may challenge the search.[11] In *Alderman v. United States*,[12] the Supreme Court held that this test gives Fourth Amendment standing to the parties to an intercepted conversation, as well as to the owners of premises on which an intercepted conversation took place, whether or not they were present at the time. Under Title III, any "aggrieved person" may move to suppress oral or wire communications, a term which is defined as one "who was a party to any intercepted . . . communication or a person against whom the interception was directed."[13] In contrast to Fourth Amendment doctrine, this definition would appear to deny Title III standing to a homeowner not involved in the conversation, and at the same time confer such standing on any "target" of an interception, even if that person's "legitimate expectations of privacy" are not infringed by the interception.

The contradictions between Fourth Amendment and Title III standing are apparently resolved in the legislative history to Title III, which indicates that the phrase "aggrieved person" is to be construed "in accordance with existent standing rules."[14] *Alderman* itself noted this language, and concluded that Title III was intended "to reflect existing law," not "extend" the exclusionary rule to all targets of an interception. Presumably, this also means that, to the extent Title III's language denies standing to persons whose premises are used for conversations to which they are not a party, it is overridden by *Alderman.*

Alderman also held that a defendant should receive *all* surveillance records as to which he has standing, not just those considered relevant by the judge exercising *in camera* review. The Court reasoned that a judge might not be able to ascertain the relevance of every communication: "An apparently innocent phrase, a chance remark, a reference to what appears to be a neutral person or event, the identity of a caller or the individual on the other end of a telephone, or even the manner of speaking or using words may have special significance to one who knows the more intimate facts of an accused's life." The Court also held, however, that the court could order the defendant and his counsel to avoid unwarranted disclosures that might harm innocent third parties. Additionally, in *Taglianetti v. United States*,[15] it concluded that the defendant is not entitled to examine surveillance records for which he does not have standing, on the ground that the judge can be trusted to identify the defendant's voice.

(h) Criminal and Civil Remedies. In addition to the exclusionary remedy, the Act provides for criminal and civil remedies

11. See § 4.04(c).

12. 394 U.S. 165, 89 S.Ct. 961 (1969).

13. 18 U.S.C.A. § 2518(11).

14. Sen.Rep., supra note 37, at 106.

15. 394 U.S. 316, 89 S.Ct. 1099 (1969).

similar to those available for typical Fourth Amendment violations.[16] "Intentional" violations of the Act are punishable as
criminal offenses and carry penalties of a fine of not more than
$10,000, or imprisonment for not more than five years, or both.[17]
Additionally, any person whose wire, oral or electronic communications are intercepted, disclosed, or used in violation of Title III
has a civil cause of action for damages under Title III against the
transgressor.[18] Recovery may include actual damages, punitive
damages, and reasonable attorney's fees and litigation expenses.
The actual damages provision establishes minimum liquidated
damages of $100 for each day of violation or $1,000, whichever is
higher.[19] In both criminal and civil cases, good faith is a defense.[20]

14.04   Tracking Devices

A relatively new electronic investigative device is the
"beeper," which emits muted signals that can be picked up by a
transmitter geared to the appropriate frequency. The use of
beepers is not seriously regulated by Title III,[21] yet their existence
creates special problems which should probably be legislatively
redressed. The Supreme Court has addressed the use of beepers
in two decisions.

In *United States v. Knotts,*[22] federal agents placed a beeper in
a container of chloroform housed in a store, with the consent of
the storeowner. The container was subsequently picked up by a
person named Petschen, who put it in his car. Although the
police saw Petschen take the can, they lost visual track of him
sometime after he left the store. Relying on the beeper, police
traced Petschen's car to defendant's cabin. After visual surveillance of the cabin, they were able to obtain a search warrant and
search the cabin, which was found to contain a drug laboratory.
Although the police had not obtained a warrant before placing the
beeper in the chloroform can, the Supreme Court held that use of
the beeper to locate evidence later used against the defendant was
permissible. Because Petschen's car travelled public thoroughfares, no expectation of privacy was violated when police relied on
the beeper rather than eyesight to track the car.

The decision in *Knotts* is a variant of the "untrustworthy ear"
doctrine discussed earlier.[23] Like the defendants who "voluntari-

---

16. See § 2.05.

17. 18 U.S.C.A. § 2511.

18. Id. § 2520.

19. Id. § 2520(a).

20. Id. § 2511(4)(a).

21. 18 U.S.C.A. § 3117(a) simply
provides: "[I]f a court is empowered to
issue a warrant or other order for the
installation of a mobile tracking device,
such order may authorize the use of
that device within the jurisdiction of
the court, and outside the jurisdiction if
the device is installed in that jurisdiction."

22. 460 U.S. 276, 103 S.Ct. 1081
(1983).

23. See § 14.02(a).

ly" talked to government agents wearing concealed body bugs, Petschen had knowingly exposed his car to the public when he used public roads. The beeper merely assisted police in keeping track of him while he was on those public roads.

A more difficult case is *United States v. Karo*.[24] There, agents once again placed a beeper in a can, this time containing ether, with the owner's consent. They saw Karo pick up the can from the owner and, using visual and beeper surveillance, followed the can to his house. Up until this point, the case paralleled *Knotts*. But then, undetected by police visually, the can was moved to other locations on four occasions. Had it not been for the beeper, police would not have discovered any of these transfers, except the last one, when they used visual as well as beeper surveillance to follow a truck containing the ether from a warehouse to a residence in Taos.

Seven members of the Court held that the police should have obtained a warrant before placing the beeper in the can because the beeper allowed the covert monitoring of the can inside the Taos residence. As the Court stated: "Had a DEA agent thought it useful to enter the Taos residence to verify that the ether was actually in the house and had he done so surreptitiously and without a warrant, there is little doubt that he would have engaged in an unreasonable search within the meaning of the Fourth Amendment." This was not an "untrustworthy ear" situation, since the beeper was not "invited," but rather entered surreptitiously.

The Court was willing, however, to tailor the warrant requirement to meet the specific needs of beeper tracking. The government had contended that requiring judicial authorization of beeper installations would render beepers useless: the particularity requirement of the warrant clause mandates a description of the location of any evidence to be seized,[25] but the whole point of the beeper is to ascertain that location. Although the Court declined to eliminate the warrant requirement altogether in beeper cases, it took the government's observations into account in holding that to obtain a warrant for purposes of beeper installation the government need merely show: (1) the object into which the beeper is to be placed; (2) the circumstances that led the police to want to install the beeper; and (3) the length of time for which beeper surveillance is requested. It also expressly left open the question of whether mere reasonable suspicion of criminal activity would be sufficient to issue a warrant.

More questionably, the Court ultimately allowed the admission of the evidence found in the Taos house. It noted that even

24. 468 U.S. 705, 104 S.Ct. 3296   **25.** See § 5.04.
(1984).

without the knowledge gained from the beeper that the ether was actually located in the Taos house and remained there, police had probable cause to believe they knew its location; they had used *visual* (as well as beeper) surveillance to trace the truck from its penultimate resting place to the Taos residence and, additionally, had observed a window open in the house despite the fact it was cold, indicating, in the opinion of the police, that the occupants wanted to avoid suffocation from the ether. But counting the police surveillance of the truck from the warehouse to Taos as one of the legitimate factors to be considered in determining whether there was probable cause for the search warrant, is not justified by *Knotts,* because in the latter case the police did not rely on the beeper to "search" any private dwelling prior to the car's arrival at its ultimate destination. In *Karo,* on the other hand, had the beeper not existed, the police would not have known that the car was in the warehouse or that it had left there. As Justice Stevens stated, "[b]ecause the beeper enabled the agents to learn the location of property otherwise concealed from public view, it infringed a privacy interest protected by the Fourth Amendment." While people might be expected to know their travels on the public roads are subject to scrutiny, they do not expect their premises to be monitored continuously by outsiders and should be protected from unchecked government attempts to do so.

14.05   Video Surveillance

Probably the most invasive type of electronic surveillance in use today is video surveillance, the installation of cameras which not only allow police to hear what is said on private premises but also, of course, permit observation of what occupants of the premises are doing. Nothing more dramatically conjures up the image of an "Orwellian society" than a surreptitiously planted government "eye" in one's living room.

Legislation purporting to regulate such surveillance was introduced during the 1984 session of Congress (and subsequent sessions) but has not passed.[26] The proposal, intended as an amendment to Title III, would have treated video surveillance no differently from other types of electronic surveillance, with two exceptions. First, it would have added a provision making bad faith failure to minimize irrelevant interceptions automatic grounds for exclusion. Second, it sought to limit surveillance to ten days per warrant, as opposed to the thirty-day term permitted for electronic eavesdropping. As suggested below, considerably more regulation seems necessary in this area.

26. H.R. 6343, 98th Cong., 2d Sess. (1984).

326

One of the more interesting video surveillance cases is *United States v. Torres*.[27] There, the FBI obtained judicial authorization to install cameras in "safehouses" used by four members of FALN, a Puerto Rico separatist group, thought to be making explosives for terrorist purposes. The district court held the videotapes thus obtained inadmissible in the absence of any statutory basis for the authorizing order. The Seventh Circuit reversed, holding that although Title III did not cover video surveillance, its provisions could be applied by analogy. In its opinion, the FBI's warrant met the particularity, least restrictive means and minimization requirements in that statute. Two features of the case particularly impressed the Seventh Circuit. First, it felt that no other investigative alternatives to video surveillance existed. The terrorists were allegedly aware that the "safe houses" in which they assembled bombs might be bugged and thus played the radio loudly and spoke in code; furthermore, as the FBI pointed out, the act of making bombs is largely a silent affair. Second, the "safehouses" in which the bombs were assembled were more like businesses than homes and thus were associated with a lesser expectation of privacy.[28]

The willingness of the Seventh Circuit and other courts[29] to apply Title III guidelines to video surveillance is unfortunate. Even Title III's restrictions are not stringent enough for monitoring investigative use of cameras. If video surveillance is to be permitted, several rules should be followed at a *minimum*. First, because the intrusion they seek is so significant, the police should have to show more than ordinary probable cause, perhaps rising to the preponderance level required in civil trials. Second, particularity requirement should be heightened as well; only those rooms in which essential elements of the crime are to take place should be observed. In *Torres*, the FBI planted bugs and cameras in every room of the "safehouses." If evidence of bombmaking was all that was being sought, this arrangement was not necessary. Third, because minimization is particularly difficult to enforce where cameras are involved, a stringent prohibition against bad faith viewing of activities which are innocent or which do not involve the suspects, as in the proposed federal statute, is appropriate. Given the invasion of privacy involved, perhaps even negligent failures to minimize should result in exclusion. One appropriate minimization method, approved by the district court in *Application of Order Authorizing Interception*,[30] is prohibition of video surveillance until audio surveillance indicates criminal activity is taking place.

27. 751 F.2d 875 (7th Cir.1984).

28. See § 13.03(b).

29. See, e.g., *United States v. Cuevas–Sanchez*, 821 F.2d 248 (5th Cir.

1987); *Ricks v. State*, 70 Md.App. 287, 520 A.2d 1136 (1987).

30. 513 F.Supp. 421 (D.Mass.1980).

Fourth, a warrant should not be issued unless no other method, including eavesdropping, can accomplish the investigative objective. In *Torres,* for instance, there may have been probable cause sufficient to obtain a search warrant authorizing entry of the safehouses while the bombs were being made. This alternative may not have produced as much evidence as video surveillance but may still have been preferable to it. In *People v. Teicher,*[31] on the other hand, there probably was no alternative to installing a camera focused on the dental chair of a dentist suspected of sexually abusing his patients. Before applying for the warrant granted in that case, police had questioned the defendant about one of the complaints of sexual abuse, had equipped two of the female complainants with hidden recorders and transmitters in an attempt to elicit admissions from the defendant, and had tapped the telephone of a complainant who had received repeated calls from the defendant, all to no avail. Furthermore, stated the court, "the use of a police decoy without the protection of visual surveillance would not have produced the needed evidence in this case, since the decoy, of necessity, would have been heavily sedated and might not have been able to relate what transpired."

The federal proposal's provision shortening the duration of video surveillance under each warrant is also a worthwhile idea. The time of surveillance per warrant should be less than ten days, however. If evidence of criminal activity sufficient to make a case is not obtained within a very short time—perhaps even within a single day—police should have to justify further surveillance. Finally, at least one court has rightly held that, in contrast to the rule for other types of surveillance, warrantless video surveillance should be prohibited even when one of those surveilled consents to it.[32] The assumption that a person assumes the risk that government will seize everything another person hears, which is questionable enough, should not be extended to permit government observation of everything another person sees. Moreover, of course, what a video camera "observes" may be quite different from what a government agent might see.

If video surveillance is to be authorized, legislation akin to Title III but which takes into account the particularly intrusive nature of visual observation is necessary. Without tight legislation, a good case can be made for prohibiting such surveillance altogether.

---

31. 52 N.Y.2d 638, 439 N.Y.S.2d 846, 422 N.E.2d 506 (1981).

32. *People v. Henderson,* 220 Cal. App.3d 1632, 270 Cal.Rptr. 248 (1990).

14.06 Conclusion

This chapter has examined the most prominent forms of electronic surveillance. There follow some general points that can be made about this problematic type of search and seizure.

(1) Electronic surveillance infringes upon the privacy interests protected by the Fourth Amendment only when it intrudes upon one's reasonable expectation of privacy. The Supreme Court has held that one does not possess such an expectation when voluntarily conversing with another (the "untrustworthy ear" exception). Similarly, the Supreme Court has held that when one travels in public, one cannot reasonably expect protection from visual surveillance. Hence, government's use of electronic devices to enhance its ability to conduct surveillance in these situations is not governed by the Fourth Amendment.

(2) Similarly, one only has standing to contest government surveillance when one's privacy interests are infringed. Thus, in the eavesdropping context, a person may contest an electronic search only of his own conversation or when the conversation takes place on his property. It may be that, by analogy, one may only contest electronic tracking or visual surveillance if the tracking or visual surveillance is of oneself or intrudes into one's property.

(3) Electronic surveillance at both the federal and state level is governed by Title III of the Omnibus Crime Control and Safe Streets Act of 1968, as amended by the Electronic Communications Privacy Act of 1986, or provisions substantially similar to it. The Act requires that all nonconsensual surveillance for the purpose of investigating domestic crime must take place pursuant to a warrant and establishes a detailed regulatory scheme for implementing this objective. However, while the Act provides for criminal penalties for intentional violation of its provisions, it provides a suppression remedy only in the case of illegally intercepted "wire" and "oral" communications, not in the case of illegally intercepted "electronic" communications. Moreover, the Supreme Court has held that even in the former instance, only violation of provisions which play a "central role" in the regulatory scheme will lead to suppression of evidence discovered as a result of the violation. The provisions most likely to be considered "central" include the following: (a) applications for warrants must be authorized by certain designated federal attorneys or, at the state level, their equivalent; (b) warrants must be based on findings of probable cause to believe that (i) an individual is involved in criminal activity, (ii) the communications to be intercepted concern this criminal activity, and (iii) the facilities to be tapped are being used in connection with the criminal activity; (c) during execution of the warrant, attempts must be made to minimize the

interception of irrelevant conversation if objectively possible; (d) warrants are limited to 30 days in duration.

(4) Police do not need a warrant to authorize use of an electronic beeper to monitor travel in public. When a beeper is used to locate evidence or a person in a private dwelling, however, a warrant is required for its installation. This warrant may issue if police adequately describe (a) the object into which the beeper is to be placed; (b) the circumstances that suggest the beeper will provide evidence of crime; and (c) the length of time for which the beeper is requested. The court has not settled whether police need to show probable cause to believe the beeper will provide evidence of criminal activity or whether reasonable suspicion is sufficient to obtain such a warrant.

(5) Video surveillance should require a warrant. The requirements for the warrant and its execution should be much more stringent than those required for electronic eavesdropping.

BIBLIOGRAPHY

Carr, J. The Law of Electronic Surveillance (1977).

Dash, Samuel, Katz—Variations on a Theme By Berger. 17 Cath. L.Rev. 296 (1968).

Fishman, Clifford S. Electronic Tracking Devices and the Fourth Amendment: Knotts, Karo, and the Questions Still Unanswered. 34 Cath.L.Rev. 277 (1985).

———. The "Minimization" Requirement in Electronic Surveillance. 28 Am.U.L.Rev. 315 (1979).

———. The Interception of Communications Without a Court Order: Title III, Consent, and the Expectation of Privacy. 51 St. John's L.Rev. 41 (1976).

Hodges, David P. Electronic Visual Surveillance and the Fourth Amendment: The Arrival of Big Brother? 3 Hastings Const. L.Q. 261 (1976).

Goldsmith, Michael. The Supreme Court and Title III: Rewriting the Law of Electronic Surveillance. 74 J.Crim.L. & C. 1 (1983).

Greenawalt, Kenneth. The Consent Problem in Wiretapping and Eavesdropping. 68 Colum.L.Rev. 189 (1968).

Katsenmeier, Robert, Deborah Leavy and David Beier. Communications Privacy: A Legislative Perspective. 1989 Wisc.L.Rev. 715 (1989).

Katz, Lewis. In Search of a Fourth Amendment for the Twenty-First Century. 65 Ind.L.J. 549 (1990).

LaDue, John. Electronic Surveillance and Conversations in Plain View. 65 Notre Dame L.Rev. 490 (1990).

Landever, Arthur R. Electronic Surveillance, Computers, and the Fourth Amendment—The New Telecommunications Environment Calls for Reexamination of the Doctrine. 15 U.Tol.L. Rev. (1984).

Pulaski, Charles. Authorizing Wiretap Applications Under Title III: Another Dissent to Giordano and Chavez. 123 U.Pa.L. Rev. 750 (1977).

Report of the U.S. National Commission for the Review of Federal and State Laws Relating to Wiretapping and Electronic Surveillance. Washington, D.C.: The Commission (1976).

Schmidt, Pamela. The Suppression Sanction in the Federal Electronics Surveillance Statute. 62 Wash.U.L.Q. 707 (1985).

Schwartz, H. The Legitimation of Electronic Eavesdropping: The Politics of "Law and Order." 67 Mich.L.Rev. 455 (1969).

Steinberg, David. Making Sense of Sense-Enhanced Searches. 74 Minn.L.Rev. 563 (1990).

Part B

THE FIFTH AMENDMENT'S PRIVILEGE AGAINST SELF-INCRIMINATION

The portion of the Fifth Amendment which governs the content of the next two chapters guarantees that "no person shall be compelled in any criminal case to be a witness against himself . . . .." This language, applied to the states in *Malloy v. Hogan*,[1] has not been interpreted literally. Rather the Supreme Court has sought to balance the values underlying the privilege against the needs of an efficient system of criminal justice. According to *Malloy*, the objectives sought to be implemented by the privilege are manifold: the prevention of abuse of citizens by government officials, the protection of privacy, the fear that coerced statements will be unreliable, "our unwillingness to subject those suspected of crime to the cruel trilemma of self-accusation, perjury or contempt," the "preference for an accusatorial rather than an inquisitorial system of criminal justice," and "our sense of fair play which dictates 'a fair state-individual balance . . . by requiring the government in its contest with the individual to shoulder the entire load. . . .' " Particularly important is the idea that ours is an accusatorial system, in which the government is required to obtain evidence of guilt by its own labors, rather than from the accused through inquisitional practices. Thus, when the government confronts a person with the "cruel trilemma of self-accusation, perjury or contempt" of which *Malloy* speaks, the protections of the Fifth Amendment are usually implicated. However, occasionally a fair state-individual balance will permit the government to force an individual to make such a choice.

Chapter Fifteen explores the complex elements constituting the constitutional right which has become known as the "privilege against self-incrimination." Chapter Sixteen then applies these principles to one of the most heavily litigated, and after the Supreme Court's decision in *Miranda v. Arizona*,[2] also one of the best-known areas of constitutional criminal procedure—the law of confessions.

1. 378 U.S. 1, 84 S.Ct. 1489 (1964).   2. 384 U.S. 436, 86 S.Ct. 1602 (1966).

Chapter Fifteen

OVERVIEW OF THE PRIVILEGE AGAINST
SELF–INCRIMINATION

15.01 Introduction

One way of attempting to understand the privilege against self-incrimination is by breaking its language down into component parts. Literally, it states that no person (1) shall be compelled; (2) in any criminal case; (3) to be a witness; (4) against himself. First, the privilege is not triggered unless there is *compulsion* to talk; of course, as with all of the other criminal process rights, this compulsion must come from the state. Second, the compulsion must lead to the revelation of *incriminating* material, material that will help lead to criminal punishment. Third, state compulsion of incriminating material may nonetheless be permissible if it does not require a person to be a "witness"—that is, provide *testimonial*, as opposed to "non-communicative," evidence. And only the person who is compelled may assert the privilege; to implicate the Fifth Amendment, the compelled evidence must be *self*-incriminating. The first four sections of this chapter look at these components of the privilege against self-incrimination. The final section applies them to a particularly complex area of Fifth Amendment jurisprudence: use of the subpoena *duces tecum.*

15.02 Compulsion

As Chief Justice Burger wrote in *United States v. Washington,*[1] "absent some officially coerced self-accusation, the Fifth Amendment privilege is not violated by even the most damning admissions." Another way the Court has characterized this issue, as Justice Powell recognized in *Garner v. United States,*[2] is in terms of "waiver." That is, the Court has attempted to determine whether the failure to assert the privilege against self-incrimination is "voluntary and intelligent."

For some time, it appeared that the only type of compulsion or involuntary waiver that would implicate the Fifth Amendment was that resulting from "legal" process, such as a contempt citation, a criminal penalty or some other type of sanction imposed by statute or a court. But the Court eventually recognized that unconstitutional compulsion can result from other types of pressure, in particular pressure exerted by the police. As the Court stated, in the landmark case of *Miranda v. Arizona,*[3] unless the

---

1. 431 U.S. 181, 97 S.Ct. 1814 (1977).   **3.** 384 U.S. 436, 86 S.Ct. 1602 (1966).
2. 424 U.S. 648, 96 S.Ct. 1178 (1976).   In the much earlier case of *Bram v.*

333

Fifth Amendment applied during interrogation, "all the careful safeguards erected around the giving of testimony, whether by an accused or a witness, would become empty formalities in a procedure where the most compelling possible evidence of guilt, a confession, would have already been obtained at the unsupervised pleasure of the police." Thus, compulsion implicating the Fifth Amendment can occur in both formal and informal settings. Here the discussion will be organized under three broad categories: compulsion during questioning, statutory compulsion, and compulsion by threat of noncriminal sanctions.

(a) During Questioning. Governmental questioning comes in many forms. For the purpose of defining compulsion under the Fifth Amendment, the Court has distinguished between custodial interrogation, cross-examination during trial, and questioning of grand jury witnesses.

(1) Defendants in custody. In *Miranda,* the Supreme Court held that "custodial interrogation" is "inherently coercive." Thus, unless special precautions are taken, statements made during such interrogation are unconstitutionally compelled. The Court held that the coercive nature of an interrogation setting can be ameliorated only if two steps take place: (1) the suspect is told he has a right to remain silent, that anything he says may be used against him, and that he has a right to an attorney during interrogation, at state expense if necessary; and (2) the suspect "voluntarily and intelligently" waives his right to remain silent and his right to an attorney. *Miranda* and police interrogation are discussed in detail in the next chapter;[4] the brief description here is useful for comparison purposes.

(2) Trial witnesses. In contrast to its holding in *Miranda,* the Supreme Court has repeatedly held that a witness at trial is not entitled to warnings, nor to an assessment of whether any subsequent testimony is a voluntary and intelligent waiver of his right to remain silent (rather, the mere act of speaking is seen as a valid waiver). As Justice Frankfurter stated in *United States v. Monia,*[5] "if [a witness] desires the protection of the privilege, he must claim it or he will not be considered to have been 'compelled' within the meaning of the Amendment."[6]

A witness in the trial setting does not necessarily *feel* less "compelled" to talk than the suspect subjected to interrogation. But there are good reasons for the Court's different treatment of

United States, 168 U.S. 532, 18 S.Ct. 183 (1897), the Court also seemed to hold that police interrogation implicated the Fifth Amendment, but *Bram* was ignored until *Miranda.* See § 16.02(d).

4. See, in particular, §§ 16.03(c)(d) & (e).

5. 317 U.S. 424, 63 S.Ct. 409 (1943) (Frankfurter, J., dissenting).

6. See also, *United States v. Kordel,* 397 U.S. 1, 90 S.Ct. 763 (1970); *United States ex rel. Vajtauer v. Commissioner of Immigration,* 273 U.S. 103, 47 S.Ct. 302 (1927).

the compulsion/waiver concept in these two situations. First, the physical setting of the government-citizen encounter is different. It seems fair to assume that questioning conducted at a public proceeding with a judge is less coercive than interrogation at the stationhouse. At the same time, the trial witness, having had time to prepare for trial, is much more likely to know about and understand his right to remain silent than is the suspect who has just been arrested. Of course, if the witness is the defendant, he will also have counsel to make sure his statements are not coerced and are the product of an intelligent waiver. Second, at least when the witness is not a defendant or putative defendant, the government's attitude is not aggressively adversarial or prosecutorial, but rather inquisitive. This attitude is not only likely to diminish coercion, but also means that putting the onus on the government to assure that any waiver is "intelligent" makes less sense. Because "only the witness knows whether the apparently innocent disclosure sought may incriminate him,"[7] the witness should bear the burden of asserting the privilege.

(3) Grand jury witnesses. A grand jury proceeding falls in between custodial interrogation and trial questioning. On the one hand, its objective is primarily investigative and some of the witnesses questioned may be suspects or putative defendants; moreover, the proceedings are secret,[8] and counsel is usually not permitted in the grand jury room.[9] On the other, the proceeding is conducted in front of members of the public, usually numbering over ten,[10] is monitored by the court (although a judge is not present),[11] and does not take the questioned individual by "surprise" in the same way custodial interrogation after arrest does. Responding to this hybrid situation in three separate cases, the Supreme Court has declined to hold that grand jury witnesses are entitled to *Miranda* warnings prior to their testimony, but has also held that any subsequent use of grand jury testimony requires the state to show that the statements represented a voluntary and intelligent waiver of the Fifth Amendment.

In *United States v. Mandujano,*[12] the respondent was charged with perjury for admittedly false statements he made while testifying before a grand jury. He successfully moved in the lower court to suppress the false statements because he was a putative defendant and had not received the *Miranda* warnings prior to testifying. The Supreme Court reversed, holding that failure of the state to provide *Miranda* warnings at a grand jury hearing is no basis for the suppression of false statements in a subsequent

---

7. *Garner v. United States,* 424 U.S. 648, 96 S.Ct. 1178 (1976).

8. See § 23.03.

9. See § 23.04(c).

10. See § 23.02(b).

11. See § 23.05(d).

12. 425 U.S. 564, 96 S.Ct. 1768 (1976).

perjury proceeding. Similarly, in *United States v. Wong*,[13] the Court rejected petitioner's claim to the *Miranda* warnings in the perjury context. It stated that whether or not the average witness might be entitled to the warnings, no witness was permitted to lie; therefore, the absence of the warnings could not bar the perjury prosecution. Because *Mandujano* and *Wong* considered perjury hearings, however, they were not entirely determinative of what warnings would be required as a prerequisite to the admissibility of a putative defendant's statements in the more typical case.

United States v. Washington[14] involved such a case. The respondent was a putative defendant who, before testifying in front of a grand jury, had been warned of his right to remain silent and of the admissibility of his statements in future criminal proceedings; he had not, however, been told his testimony could lead to indictment. The Supreme Court held that the warnings given to the respondent before his testimony were sufficient to remove any possibility of compulsion. Chief Justice Burger wrote for the majority: "[I]t seems self-evident that one who is told he is free to refuse to answer questions is in a curious posture to later complain that his answers were compelled." Thus, warning a grand jury witness that he is a "target" of the investigation is not necessary under the Fifth Amendment. The Court also stopped short of holding that the grand jury setting is inherently coercive, suggesting that even the abbreviated warning given in *Washington* may not be required.[15] However, the Court did at least consider whether a voluntary and intelligent waiver occurred, which is more than has been required in the trial context. Moreover, because they are so easily given, most jurisdictions provide the *Miranda* warnings prior to grand jury testimony of putative defendants and many also give the "target warning" to putative defendants.[16]

(4) The fair examination rule. If a witness at either a trial or a grand jury proceeding testifies and provides incriminating information, the government is permitted to compel answers to questions asking for explication of that information, apparently on a waiver theory. This rule is most broadly interpreted when the witness is a defendant at trial. In *Brown v. United States*,[17] the petitioner testified at a denaturalization proceeding that she had not engaged in communist activities for the ten years prior to her

13. 431 U.S. 174, 97 S.Ct. 1823 (1977).

14. 431 U.S. 181, 97 S.Ct. 1814 (1977).

15. Note also that in *Minnesota v. Murphy*, 465 U.S. 420, 104 S.Ct. 1136 (1984), the Court held that a probationer questioned by his probation officer is not entitled to *Miranda* warnings, in part because this setting was "less intimidating" than the grand jury setting, where the Court had "never held that [the warnings] must be given."

16. See, e.g., *State v. Cook*, 11 Ohio App.3d 237, 464 N.E.2d 577 (1983); Idaho Code § 19–1121; South Dakota Laws § 23–A–5–12.

17. 356 U.S. 148, 78 S.Ct. 622 (1958).

application for citizenship. On cross-examination, she claimed the Fifth Amendment privilege when asked whether she was presently a member of the Communist Party. The Supreme Court affirmed her contempt conviction for refusing to answer. Justice Frankfurter, writing for the Court, stated that holding otherwise would be "a positive invitation to mutilate the truth." According to the Court, testifying defendants may be cross-examined, provided that the questions are directed to the purpose of impeaching their credibility or to the substance of their testimony on direct examination.

Some courts have construed *Brown* broadly to stand for the proposition that when the accused testifies concerning the offense for which he is on trial, he forfeits the privilege as to all facts relevant to that offense, even if they were not mentioned on direct.[18] Others apparently permit cross-examination to the extent permitted by the normal rules relating to the scope of cross-examination,[19] which in some jurisdictions allow questioning on any subject about which the subject has knowledge.[20] Although a fair state-individual balance would seem to support the general holding in *Brown*, the cross-examination allowed should be limited to whatever is necessary to test the truth of the statements made on direct. Allowing cross-examination beyond this point unfairly tips the state-individual balance or, if one prefers waiver language, works an involuntary "waiver" of the Fifth Amendment.

When the person testifying is not the accused, the courts have been more careful about limiting cross-examination. In *Rogers v. United States*,[21] the petitioner appeared before a grand jury and testified concerning her relationship with the Communist Party. She admitted, without asserting a Fifth Amendment objection, that she had at one time possessed Party documents. She then refused to divulge to whom she had given the documents, relying on her Fifth Amendment privilege. The Supreme Court, affirming her contempt conviction for refusing to answer, held that a witness' admission of an incriminating fact constitutes a waiver of Fifth Amendment protection with respect to the details surrounding that admission. Justice Vinson, writing for the majority, reasoned that extending Fifth Amendment protection to the details associated with an admission that had already been made would allow the witness to pick and choose those details she would admit, resulting in distortion of the testimony. The Court viewed the witness' incriminating admission as a waiver because, by making the admission, she had voluntarily subjected herself to the

---

18. McCormick, Evidence § 132, at 323–24. See also *Johnson v. United States,* 318 U.S. 189, 63 S.Ct. 549 (1943).

19. See *People v. Perez,* 65 Cal.2d 615, 55 Cal.Rptr. 909, 422 P.2d 597 (1967), writ dism'd 395 U.S. 208, 89 S.Ct. 1767 (1969).

20. McCormick, Evidence § 21, at 51.

21. 340 U.S. 367, 71 S.Ct. 438 (1951).

criminal sanction resulting from the admission. The increased possibility that criminal sanctions would be imposed due to the forced admission of details was not considered important, in light of the need for reliable testimony. The Court did recognize the abuses this exception might permit, however, and held that details may not be compelled if they present a " 'real danger' of further incrimination."

Early applications of the *Rogers* holding in federal courts had rather harsh effects on witnesses. *Rogers* was interpreted to prevent only compelled admissions of new crimes not divulged in prior testimony.[22] More recent cases have demonstrated greater sensitivity to the possibility of incrimination by compelled admission of details; thus, while questions about other parties (such as those in *Rogers* itself) must be answered,[23] most courts now will not allow the compulsion of any self-incriminating details that "might provide a link not already provided." [24]

(5) The continuing waiver theory. Normally, if a witness does waive the Fifth Amendment by testifying, that waiver is applicable only throughout that proceeding. However, some courts have held that, under certain circumstances, a waiver at a grand jury proceeding also operates at trial. For instance, in *Ellis v. United States*,[25] the court ruled that a grand jury witness who voluntarily makes incriminating statements may not invoke the privilege for the same statements at a criminal trial following the grand jury's indictment of other persons, primarily because the government already has access to the grand jury testimony and thus the compelled trial testimony poses little or no danger of eliciting additional incriminating material. Other courts have adopted this "continuing waiver" theory, but, as in *Ellis*, do not apply it to criminal defendants.[26] Another useful limitation of the continuing waiver rule would be to prohibit its operation unless the grand jury witness is given warnings apprising him of the consequences of a decision to testify.

(b) Statutory Compulsion. Many federal and state statutes require citizens to create documents, or answer questions posed on a document, that may prove self-incriminating. As with compulsion of witnesses, the Supreme Court's analysis of this type of compulsion has focused on the setting in which the information is given and the purpose behind the government's request for infor-

---

22. See National Lawyers Guild, Representation of Witnesses before Federal Grand Juries § 13.7(b) (1976).

23. Id.

24. *Shendal v. United States*, 312 F.2d 564 (9th Cir.1963); see Note, 92 Harv.L.Rev. 1752, 1754–60 (1979).

25. 416 F.2d 791 (D.C.Cir.1969).

26. *Salim v. United States*, 480 A.2d 710 (D.C.App.1984); see also *United States v. Miller*, 904 F.2d 65 (D.C.Cir. 1990). The theory is not applied to defendants out of fear that this will "chill" their right to testify. See § 15.02(c).

mation. As a general rule, the Court has held that, like the trial witness, the person subject to statutory compulsion loses the privilege if he does not assert it by refusing to answer. However, the Court has also identified situations in which the statutory compulsion is more "adversarial," and the privilege accordingly provides more comprehensive protection. Finally, a third series of cases hold that where the statute requires disclosure of "public" information for legitimate, non-criminal purposes, the Fifth Amendment provides no protection at all.

(1) Innocently-posed questions. In *United States v. Sullivan,*[27] the Court upheld the defendant's conviction for failure to file an income tax return. The defendant argued that submission of the return would have been self-incriminating, but the Court concluded that the privilege entitled the taxpayer, at most, to refrain from answering specific questions that might tend to incriminate him. As to what information the taxpayer could have withheld, the Court's only statement, in dictum, was that "[i]t would be an extreme if not an extravagant application of the Fifth Amendment to say that it authorized a man to refuse to state the amount of his income because it had been made in crime."

Fifty years later, the Court explicated this holding in *Garner v. United States,*[28] where the defendant was convicted of conspiring to fix sporting events, based in part upon admissions contained in his tax form. As in *Sullivan,* the defendant argued that not submitting the form would have led to a conviction, but added that returning an incomplete form would result in punishment under a federal statute criminalizing the filing of incomplete returns. A unanimous Court, noting that prosecution for a good faith assertion of the privilege is not permitted under the latter statute, refused to find that use of the tax statements violated the Fifth Amendment. As with the trial witness, a person who answers an innocently posed question on the tax form cannot be said to have been "compelled" by the state to answer. Indeed, "a taxpayer, who can complete his return at leisure and with legal assistance, is even less subject to . . . psychological pressures . . . than a witness who has been called to testify in judicial proceedings." On the other hand, the Court confirmed that a taxpayer may assert the privilege with impunity with respect to specific incriminating items on the form at the time it is prepared.[29]

---

27. 274 U.S. 259, 47 S.Ct. 607 (1927).

28. 424 U.S. 648, 96 S.Ct. 1178 (1976).

29. The majority opinion, joined by seven members of the Court, concluded by stating that the Fifth Amendment claim must be *valid,* not just in good faith. But, as the two concurring members pointed out, 26 U.S.C.A. § 7203 provides that the failure to provide information on the return must be "willful," and the government conceded that a defendant cannot properly be convicted for an erroneous claim of privilege asserted in good faith.

The *Sullivan–Garner* approach to statutory compulsion would seem to apply to many situations in which the government asks citizens for information via registration forms, welfare applications, professional license applications and the like.[30] Unless the privilege is asserted at the time the forms are filled out, the privilege is lost, since the questions posed are not adversarial, and thus not instinct with coercion.

(2) The suspect class exception. When, in contrast to the situation in *Sullivan* and *Garner,* the statutory request is not "innocently posed" but rather prosecutorial in nature, the privilege not only permits a refusal to answer specific questions but also a refusal to file the forms in the first instance. The leading case in this regard is *Albertson v. Subversive Activities Control Board,*[31] which involved a statute requiring communists to register with the government. The petitioners, who were communists, claimed this provision violated their right against self-incrimination, given the fact that mere association with the Communist Party could lead to criminal charges. In agreeing with this argument and reversing their convictions for failing to register, the Court rejected the government's contention that, in light of *Sullivan,* the petitioners were only permitted by the Fifth Amendment to refrain from answering specific questions on the Communist registration form. Justice Brennan, writing for the majority, observed:

> In *Sullivan* the questions in the income tax return were neutral on their face and directed at the public at large, but here they are directed at a highly selective group inherently suspect of criminal activities. Petitioners' claims are not asserted in an essentially noncriminal and regulatory area of inquiry, but against an inquiry in an area permeated with criminal statutes, where response to any of the form's questions in context might involve the petitioners in the admission of a crucial element of a crime.

Cases applying *Albertson* have focused on the extent to which the statutory purpose requires revelation of obviously incriminating information from "a highly selective group inherently suspect of criminal activities." In *Marchetti v. United States,*[32] the Court held that registration and occupational tax laws which applied only to gamblers violated the Fifth Amendment rights of those who were required to register. These statutes had the "direct and unmistakable consequence of incriminating" the respondents because wagering is "permeated with criminal statutes" and gamblers are "inherently suspect of criminal activities." Thus

---

30. But see *Selective Service System v. Minnesota Public Interest Research Group,* 468 U.S. 841, 104 S.Ct. 3348 (1984), discussed in § 15.02(b)(2).

31. 382 U.S. 70, 86 S.Ct. 194 (1965).

32. 390 U.S. 39, 88 S.Ct. 697 (1968).

Marchetti's conviction for a failure to file the required forms was reversed. The Court applied a similar analysis to two companion cases, *Haynes v. United States,*[33] which involved a statute requiring registration of firearms possessed by those who had violated other provisions of the National Firearms Act, and *Grosso v. United States,*[34] dealing with a statute providing for registration of those who paid excise taxes on wagering. In *Leary v. United States,*[35] decided a year later, the Court voided the self-reporting provisions of the Marijuana Tax Act, which required informing authorities of drug possession for tax purposes, relying heavily on the fact that such reporting necessarily involved an admission of conduct which was a crime under state law.

In all of these cases, the Court recognized that by filing an incomplete form, or explicitly invoking their Fifth Amendment privilege on the form itself (as required in *Sullivan* and *Garner*), the petitioners would incriminate themselves by informing the government that they were involved in illegal activities. As the Court stated in *Grosso,* a "statutory system . . . utilized to pierce the anonymity of citizens engaged in criminal activity, is invalid." Even a grant of immunity as to prosecutorial use of the identification was seen as insufficient protection by the Court. In *Albertson,* for instance, the Court expressed its concern that, once possessed of the individual's identity, the government could use it to acquire other incriminating information that would be hard to trace back to the registration form, and thus evade the immunity grant.[36]

At times, it can be difficult to determine when *Albertson* rather than *Garner* should apply. *Selective Service System v. Minnesota Public Interest Research Group,*[37] involved a federal statutory scheme that required male college students to show they had registered for the draft before they could receive federal financial assistance and allowed late registration for those who had not registered when they were supposed to. Although students who took advantage of the late registration option would expose themselves to criminal prosecution under the Selective Service Act, a majority of the Court upheld the statute, and the use of any incriminating responses discovered on the registration forms. At the same time, citing *Garner,* the Court strongly

33. 390 U.S. 85, 88 S.Ct. 722 (1968).

34. 390 U.S. 62, 88 S.Ct. 709 (1968).

35. 395 U.S. 6, 89 S.Ct. 1532 (1969).

36. Of course, total (or "transactional") immunity from prosecution would solve this problem, but the Court has been unwilling to read an immunity provision into legislation, see *Marchetti v. United States,* 390 U.S. 39, 88 S.Ct.

697 (1968), and in other settings has held that the Fifth Amendment requires only use and derivative use immunity. *Kastigar v. United States,* 406 U.S. 441, 92 S.Ct. 1653 (1972), discussed in § 15.03(c)(1).

37. 468 U.S. 841, 104 S.Ct. 3348 (1984).

implied that students could exercise their Fifth Amendment right when registering, and that the government could not compel their answers at that point without immunization. The problem with this holding, as Justice Marshall pointed out in dissent, is that, unlike the tax laws at issue in *Garner,* the late registration provision in this case was aimed at an inherently suspect group, "the 674,000 existing nonregistrants." And, as in the *Albertson* line of cases, the scope of the immunity available was unclear. Thus, allowing assertion of the privilege on the registration form would provide insufficient protection to these people, since it would still permit the government to discover the identity of the nonregistrants and, armed with that information, make its case against them.

(3) The "regulatory purpose" doctrine. A final series of cases which further complicates the analysis of statutory compulsion stands for the proposition that when a statutory reporting requirement is essential to a public, regulatory scheme, rather than designed to obtain private information (as in *Garner*) or evidence of criminal activity (as in *Albertson*), it does not implicate the Fifth Amendment at all, even when it happens to compel incriminating disclosures. The Court's first case in this regard was *Shapiro v. United States,*[38] which upheld the conviction of a business owner based in part on information found in records he was required to keep and produce for the government under the Emergency Price Control Act. In *Grosso,* the Court later described the rationale for *Shapiro* as follows:

> [F]irst the purposes of the United States' inquiry must be essentially regulatory; second, information is to be obtained by requiring the preservation of records of a kind which the regulated party has customarily kept; and third, the records themselves must have assumed "public aspects" which render them at least analogous to public documents.

The first requirement distinguished *Shapiro* from the *Albertson* line of cases, which were aimed at discovering evidence of criminal activity rather than regulating a non-criminal enterprise. The latter two requirements differentiated *Shapiro* from cases like *Sullivan* and *Garner,* since tax forms are not routinely kept records nor are they public in nature.

However, in *California v. Byers,*[39] a plurality of the Court significantly modified this characterization of the regulatory purpose doctrine, shedding any requirement that the incriminating information be found in routinely kept records. The defendant in *Byers* left the scene of a traffic accident without reporting his name and was charged with unsafe passing and failure to stop and

38.   335 U.S. 1, 68 S.Ct. 1375 (1948).   **39.**   402 U.S. 424, 91 S.Ct. 1535 (1971).

identify himself. He demurred to the second charge, claiming that California's reporting requirement under its hit-and-run statute violated his privilege against self-incrimination. Chief Justice Burger's opinion reasoned that where there is a "strong polic[y] in favor of disclosure," such as here, the defendant must demonstrate "substantial hazards of self-incrimination." Applying the *Albertson* criteria, he found that the disclosure requirement under the hit-and-run statute did "not entail the kind of substantial risk of self-incrimination involved in *Marchetti, Grosso,* and *Haynes.*" The vehicle code's requirements were directed at the public at large rather than an inherently suspect group, and the reporting provision was motivated by a non-criminal purpose, "to promote the satisfaction of civil liabilities arising from automobile accidents."

Burger seems clearly wrong in his assertion that the vehicle code's requirements were directed at the public at large. As the four dissenters pointed out, the statute is directed at a more select group, namely drivers involved in accidents causing property damage, and clearly requires them to surrender their "anonymity," a concern in *Albertson.* At the same time, the statute in *Byers* does seem different from the statutes involved in the *Albertson* line of cases in that, as in *Shapiro,* the group it focused on was not "inherently suspect" of criminal activity; many drivers involved in accidents are not chargeable criminally. Justice Harlan's concurring opinion offers a better rationale for the decision. He concluded, contrary to the plurality, that the risk of incrimination in *Byers* was "real." But, he argued that, balancing the state's interest against the individual's, the "assertedly non-criminal governmental purpose in securing information, the necessity for self-reporting as a means of securing the information, and the nature of the disclosures required" meant Byers could not assert the privilege in this situation. As Harlan pointed out:

> Byers having once focused attention on himself as an accident-participant, the State must still bear the burden of making the main evidentiary case [under the vehicle code]. To characterize this burden as a merely ritualistic confirmation of the "conviction" secured through compliance with the reporting requirement in issue would be a gross distortion of reality; on the other hand, that characterization of the evidentiary burden remaining on the [government] after compliance with the regulatory scheme involved in *Marchetti* and *Grosso* seems proper.

Harlan's rationale seems to be the one preferred by the Court in later cases. In *Garner,* in distinguishing the hit-and-run statute in *Byers* from the income tax laws involved in that case, the Court emphasized that *Byers* only involved questions about name and address and that the various opinions in that case had "suggested that the privilege might be claimed appropriately against other questions." *Byers,* continued the *Garner* Court, thus holds "only that requiring certain basic disclosures fundamental to a neutral reporting scheme does not violate the privilege."[40] Similarly, in *Baltimore City Department of Social Services v. Bouknight,*[41] while the Court held that the privilege does not prevent the government from compelling a woman to produce her child in custody proceedings given the regulatory purpose of those proceedings, it cautioned that if the state subsequently sought to use the act of production (or lack thereof) against the mother in a criminal prosecution, the Fifth Amendment might be implicated.[42]

Most lower court decisions seem to apply *Byers* consistently with this approach. For instance, in *United States v. San Juan,*[43] the court upheld against a Fifth Amendment challenge the provisions of the Bank Secrecy Act that require disclosure of amounts in excess of $5,000 transported across United States borders. The court found that the government had a clear and continuing interest in controlling international transactions, that the provisions were neutral on their face, in that they apply to all international travelers, and that they do not require admissions of criminal activity (although disclosure may lead to inquiry). In contrast, in *Bionic Auto Parts & Sales, Inc. v. Fahner,*[44] the court struck down statutory requirements that auto parts dealers record and report altered serial numbers, given "the degree to which the information request in and of itself is incriminatory and the degree to which those required to keep the records are suspected of criminal activity." The statute at issue imposed absolute criminal liability for possession or sale of parts with altered serial numbers.

One might analyze the cases adopting the public records exception to the privilege in terms of waiver; that is, one could say that organizations or persons who choose to operate in certain highly regulated activities automatically forego Fifth Amendment protection of certain information. But it makes more sense to say that these cases rest on a conclusion that, in light of the strong public interest involved, a "fair state-individual balance" means

---

40. Indeed, the disclosures in *Byers* could be seen as nontestimonial. See § 15.04.

41. 493 U.S. 549, 110 S.Ct. 900 (1990).

42. The Court also sought to explain *Bouknight* by analogy to its collective entity cases, which hold that a subpoena may compel information that is held in a "representative" capacity. See § 15.06. Here, the Court asserted, the child was held in such a capacity by the mother, who had reacquired custody, after an initial determination of unfitness, on condition that she meet several requirements, including cooperating with the social services department.

43. 405 F.Supp. 686 (D.Vt.1975), rev'd on other grounds 545 F.2d 314 (2d Cir.1976).

44. 721 F.2d 1072 (7th Cir.1983).

there is no right to waive. The key question addressed in these cases appears to be "whether a particular reporting requirement is designed to facilitate the government's legitimate needs for regulatory information rather than undercut the adversary system by covertly aiding the investigation and prosecution of crime." [45]

(c) Compulsion Through Non-Criminal Sanctions. In the cases discussed above, state compulsion is implemented through the threat of criminal contempt citation or some other criminal punishment. A final group of cases dealing with compulsion focuses on the extent to which exercise of the Fifth Amendment right is "chilled" by state actions which do not involve direct use of criminal sanctions. The first case explicitly examining this problem was *Griffin v. California*,[46] in which the Court held that a prosecutor's reference to the defendant's failure to testify, designed to convince the jury to draw an adverse inference therefrom, was reversible error. The Court held that "the imposition of any sanction which makes assertion of the Fifth Amendment 'costly' is constitutionally impermissible compulsion." Here, the types of comments made by the prosecutor could inhibit exercise of the defendant's Fifth Amendment right to refrain from testifying, a corollary of the right to remain silent.[47]

The Court has since held that, under limited circumstances, the judge,[48] and even the prosecutor,[49] may make reference to a non-testifying defendant's silence. But *Griffin's* basic premise— that the state should not be able to inhibit free exercise of the right to remain silent in any way—is reflected in several other cases. In *Garrity v. New Jersey*,[50] for instance, police officers summoned during an investigation of police corruption were informed that they would be discharged if they refused to answer questions. The Court held that such compulsion violated their rights and required reversal of convictions based on their testimony. In *Simmons v. United States*,[51] the Court held that the defendant's pretrial testimony at a hearing to determine the validity of a search and seizure could not be used against him at trial on the question of guilt, concluding that forcing a choice

---

45. Mosteller, "Simplifying Subpoena Law: Taking the Fifth Amendment Seriously," 73 Va.L.Rev. 1, 67 (1987).

46. 380 U.S. 609, 85 S.Ct. 1229 (1965).

47. See § 28.03(c)(1).

48. In *Lakeside v. Oregon*, 435 U.S. 333, 98 S.Ct. 1091 (1978), the Court rejected the defendant's argument that an instruction telling the jury to disregard the defendant's muteness would serve to call attention to his choice to remain silent, reasoning that "[i]t would be strange indeed to conclude that this cautionary instruction violates the very constitutional provision it is intended to protect."

49. Prosecutorial comment is permitted if the reference constitutes a "fair response" to defense allegations that the prosecution had denied the defendant the opportunity to explain his case. *United States v. Robinson*, 485 U.S. 25, 108 S.Ct. 864 (1988).

50. 385 U.S. 493, 87 S.Ct. 616 (1967).

51. 390 U.S. 377, 88 S.Ct. 967 (1968).

between one's Fourth and Fifth Amendment rights was "intolerable." In *Lefkowitz v. Turley,*[52] the Court invalidated a New York statute requiring public contractors either to waive immunity or to suffer forfeiture of existing and future state contracts for the next five years. And in *Lefkowitz v. Cunningham,*[53] it held unconstitutional a statute which provided that an officer of a political party must either answer questions posed by the grand jury or be immediately disqualified from holding any other party or public office for a period of five years.

It should be noted that, in some situations, the "Hobson's choice" confronting the defendant may not involve the Fifth Amendment, despite first appearances. This was the case in *South Dakota v. Neville,*[54] involving a statute which required a driver stopped for drunken driving either to take a blood-alcohol test or suffer revocation of his driver's license. The Supreme Court upheld the admission of the defendant's refusal to take the test, in part because "the state did not directly compel respondent to refuse the test, for it gave him the choice of submitting to the test or refusing." More importantly, this choice did not include sacrificing the privilege against self-incrimination as one option because, concluded the Court, the results of a blood-alcohol test are "nontestimonial."[55]

15.03 Incrimination

The Fifth Amendment prohibits the state from compelling information only if it might be used in a "criminal proceeding." As the Court stated in *Lefkowitz v. Turley,*[56] the privilege not only permits an individual to remain silent at grand jury and trial proceedings in which he is a criminal defendant, but also to refuse "to answer official questions put to him in any . . . proceeding, civil or criminal, formal or informal, where the answers might incriminate him in *future* criminal proceedings."[57] By the same token, if an individual subjected to questioning can be assured that the information will not be used in a "criminal" proceeding, he has no right to remain silent. Such assurance may derive from: (1) the nature of the information requested (e.g., its irrelevance to any criminal matter); (2) a grant of immunity protecting against its future use; or (3) some other guarantee that the

52. 414 U.S. 70, 94 S.Ct. 316 (1973).

53. 431 U.S. 801, 97 S.Ct. 2132 (1977).

54. 459 U.S. 553, 103 S.Ct. 916 (1983).

55. See § 15.04 for further discussion of the testimonial/nontestimonial distinction.

56. 414 U.S. 70, 94 S.Ct. 316 (1973).

57. Emphasis added. In addition to this "witness privilege," so-called because it permits persons who are asked questions to remain silent, courts sometimes speak of a "defendant's privilege," which permits the defendant in criminal proceedings to exclude compelled statements already made. The Fifth Amendment exclusionary rule is discussed in § 16.05.

information cannot be used to prosecute for a given crime (e.g., expiration of the relevant statute of limitations). The definition of "criminal proceeding," and these related aspects of the incrimination concept are taken up here.

(a) The Definition of Criminal Proceeding. In deciding whether a proceeding is "criminal" for purposes of the privilege, courts look principally at whether "punitive" sanctions could be imposed at the proceeding in question, not at the label—i.e., "civil" or "criminal"—traditionally affixed to the proceeding. Trials which may result in incarceration are generally the best example of criminal proceedings. But the *purpose* of the sanction, not whether it results in loss of liberty, is the important variable. Thus, proceedings that require the convicted defendant to pay fines or forfeit property as "punishment" rather than for compensatory reasons may be characterized as "criminal," [58] whereas, as developed below, proceedings which can result in prolonged confinement meant to be rehabilitative rather than punitive may be termed "civil" for Fifth Amendment purposes.

For some time, it appeared that loss of liberty was more than a secondary factor in Fifth Amendment analysis. In *In re Gault*,[59] the Court justified its holding that the privilege may be raised at all stages of a juvenile delinquency proceeding with the following words: "our Constitution guarantees that no person shall be 'compelled' to be a witness against himself when he is threatened with deprivation of his liberty." The Court found that the state's designation of delinquency proceedings as "civil" in nature was irrelevant; what was important in determining the availability of the privilege is "the nature of the statement or admission and the exposure which it invites." Justice Fortas, who wrote the majority opinion, concentrated on the fact that in over half the states children adjudicated delinquent could be housed with adults and that in every state children over a certain age could be transferred to adult court jurisdiction for trial, thereby creating exposure to imprisonment.

However, in *Minnesota v. Murphy*,[60] the Court stated in a footnote that if questions put to a probationer were relevant only to his probationary status and "posed no realistic threat of incrimination in a separate criminal proceeding" (e.g., questions about residence), then the probationer could not refuse to answer them. The Court further stated that the probationer could even be forced to answer questions about *crimes* he may have committed (and the answers used at a revocation proceeding), so long as the state is prevented from using these disclosures in separate criminal pro-

---

58. See, e.g., *United States v. United States Coin & Currency*, 401 U.S. 715, 91 S.Ct. 1041 (1971); *Boyd v. United States*, 116 U.S. 616, 6 S.Ct. 524 (1886).

59. 387 U.S. 1, 87 S.Ct. 1428 (1967).

60. 465 U.S. 420, 104 S.Ct. 1136 (1984).

ceedings. Since a probation revocation proceeding can obviously result in a loss at liberty, *Gault's* language was called into question.

Finally, in *Allen v. Illinois*,[61] the Court settled that *Gault's* deprivation of liberty criterion "is plainly not good law" and that the extent to which a given proceeding is punitive in nature is the sole factor to be considered in determining the applicability of the privilege. *Allen* involved application of the Fifth Amendment to psychiatric evaluations and adjudicatory proceedings under the Illinois Sexually Dangerous Persons Act. The Act permits the prosecutor to initiate "civil" proceedings designed to commit an individual who has been found beyond a reasonable doubt to have committed at least one criminal sexual offense and to be "sexually dangerous." Justice Rehnquist, writing the 5–4 opinion, focused entirely on the purpose of the Act, as construed by the Illinois Supreme Court. He noted that the Act created a statutory obligation to provide care and treatment for those adjudicated sexually dangerous and that release was required if the "patient was found to be no longer dangerous." Thus, the Court concluded, the "Act does not appear to promote either of 'the traditional aims of punishment—retribution or deterrence.' " The fact that the Act provided the individual subjected to commitment proceedings with procedural rights akin to those accorded the criminal defendant was deemed irrelevant. Nor was the fact that the petitioner had been confined in a psychiatric unit located at the state's maximum security prison material. The Court did note, however, that had the petitioner shown that the confinement of sexually dangerous individuals "imposes on them a regimen which is essentially identical to that imposed upon felons with no need for psychiatric care, this might well be a different case."

The Court's decision in *Allen* is insensitive to the reality of the commitment system. As Justice Stevens noted in dissent, the maximum penalty for the petitioner's crime was less than a year's imprisonment and a $500 fine, yet under authority of the Illinois act he had been committed for five years at the time of the Court's decision. While loss of liberty should perhaps not be the dispositive factor in determining the applicability of the Fifth Amendment, a statute which permits indeterminate confinement in the equivalent of prison, should not, regardless of its purpose, be designated "civil" in nature. Even analyzing the statute in the Court's terms, the result in *Allen* seems misguided. The principal goal of the Illinois statute, as indicated by its release provisions, is not treatment but incapacitation, a primary goal of punishment, and one which is closely related to retribution where individuals

61. 478 U.S. 364, 106 S.Ct. 2988 (1986).

thought to be "sexually dangerous" are concerned. Yet *Allen* now permits the states to compel individuals charged with sexual offenses to submit to psychiatric evaluations and answer questions, upon penalty of contempt, that will assist the state in committing them indefinitely under such statutes, so long as any disclosures made are not used to convict the individual in separate criminal proceedings.

Presumably, after *Allen,* there is no Fifth Amendment privilege in civil commitment proceedings either.[62] While *Gault's* holding that the privilege applies to juvenile delinquency proceedings is still good law, its application to other juvenile court matters (such as Children in Need of Supervision cases) is doubtful, given the rehabilitative goals of these proceedings. The Court has also indicated that child custody proceedings, in which the goal of the state is to remove a child from the mother's custody, are not "criminal" for purposes of the Fifth Amendment.[63]

Even proceedings which are directly associated with the criminal process are not necessarily "criminal" proceedings for purposes of the Fifth Amendment. As noted earlier, in *Murphy* the Court explicitly stated that a probation revocation hearing is not a "criminal proceeding" and that "a State may validly insist on answers to even incriminating questions and hence sensibly administer its probation system, as long as it recognizes that the required answers may not be used in a criminal proceeding and thus eliminates the threat of incrimination." In the same vein, in *Estelle v. Smith,*[64] the Supreme Court held that the state may compel answers from the defendant during a pretrial psychiatric evaluation to determine his competency to stand trial, so long as the information obtained is used for its "avowed purpose"—as evidence at a proceeding to determine competency. Under such circumstances, the pretrial competency proceeding is not "criminal" for purposes of the Fifth Amendment.

Smith also held, however, that a capital sentencing proceeding *is* a "criminal proceeding;" thus, on the facts of that case, the privilege was violated when competency results were used at capital sentencing without obtaining a valid waiver. According to the seven member majority, "[g]iven the gravity of the decision to be made at the penalty phase" of a capital sentencing proceeding, there is "no basis to distinguish between the guilt and penalty

---

62. The court has already indicated as much by summarily affirming *French v. Blackburn,* 428 F.Supp. 1351 (M.D.N.C.1977), which held that the Fifth Amendment does not apply in civil commitment proceedings.

63. *Baltimore City Department of Social Services v. Bouknight,* 493 U.S. 549, 110 S.Ct. 900 (1990) (state may compel mother to produce her child at custody hearings in juvenile court, although state use of act of production in subsequent criminal proceedings might be prohibited).

64. 451 U.S. 454, 101 S.Ct. 1866 (1981).

phases . . . so far as the protection of the Fifth Amendment privilege is concerned." The Court concluded that when the defendant "neither initiates a psychiatric evaluation nor attempts to introduce any psychiatric evidence, [he] may not be compelled to respond to a psychiatrist if his statements can be used against him at a capital sentencing proceeding." The Court also implied, however, that if the defendant does initiate the evaluation, or the evaluation is requested by the prosecution in a case where the defense has indicated it will introduce psychiatric testimony at sentencing, then the defendant cannot assert the Fifth Amendment with impunity. In these two situations, the Court appears willing to hold that the defendant has "waived" the privilege.

The application of the Fifth Amendment to non-capital sentencing proceedings is not clear. The majority in *Smith* noted that "we do not hold that the same Fifth Amendment concerns are necessarily presented by all types of interviews and examinations that might be ordered or relied upon to inform a sentencing determination." Of course, if the information sought can be used in a future prosecution against the defendant, he need not provide it.[65] But, following the "limited-use" approach of *Murphy* and *Smith,* the question remains whether the state may compel statements about an offense for which the defendant has just been convicted, if it uses them only at his sentencing proceeding.

Under the Court's cases, the answer could go either way. *Murphy's* holding that the privilege is unavailable at probation revocation proceedings suggests the privilege is not available at sentencing either, since revocation hearings are in a sense merely delayed sentencing proceedings. *Allen's* holding is also significant, since the Sexually Dangerous Persons Act at issue in that case was in effect a dispositional "sentencing" mechanism for persons convicted of sexual offenses.[66] On the other hand, as *Smith* recognized, statements made at or prior to a sentencing proceeding can lead to significant enhancement of a person's sentence on grounds that are more directly "punitive" than those underlying a probation revocation or a sexual offender disposition. At least one court has recognized as much, holding that a witness testifying at her co-defendant's trial may assert the privilege with respect to the crime for which she has just been convicted, when the trial court has indicated it would consider any additional

---

65. *Roberts v. United States,* 445 U.S. 552, 100 S.Ct. 1358 (1980).

66. See also, *Reina v. United States,* 364 U.S. 507, 81 S.Ct. 260 (1960) ("The ordinary rule is that once a person is convicted of a crime, he no longer has the privilege against self-incrimination as he can no longer be incriminated by his testimony about the crime."). Some courts have held that, if there is a possibility of a new trial after an appeal, this ordinary rule does not apply. McCormick, Evidence § 121.

statements made by her in reaching a conclusion as to her sentence.[67]

(b) The Link-in-the-Chain Rule. Only if information is usable in a "criminal proceeding," as defined above, may it be withheld under the Fifth Amendment. A witness cannot invoke the privilege merely to avoid a non-criminal sanction or revelation of information which tends to "disgrace him or bring him into disrepute." [68] On the other hand, any information which might be used at a criminal proceeding need not be disclosed. In *Hoffman v. United States*,[69] the Supreme Court held that a witness may refuse to answer any question the response to which might "furnish a link in the chain of evidence needed to prosecute."

The *Hoffman* language has been given broad construction. In *Hoffman* itself, the Court overruled the lower court's holding that there was "no real danger of incrimination" from questions about a grand jury witness' current occupation and contacts with a person who was a fugitive witness. Since the grand jury investigation was about racketeering, the Court noted, answers to the first question might have revealed information relating to violations of various gambling laws, and answers to the second question might have disclosed information about the witness' attempt to hide the fugitive. Similarly, in *Simpson v. United States*,[70] the Court summarily reversed a lower court decision upholding a contempt of Congress conviction of a witness who had refused to divulge to the House UnAmerican Activities Committee his address, present occupation, where he had attended school, and whether he had ever been in the armed services.

Hoffman also set out the procedure for asserting the privilege and determining the validity of the assertion. A witness intending to refuse to answer a question because of possible self-incrimination must inform the court that his refusal is based on his Fifth Amendment privilege. Unexplained silence may result in a valid contempt citation. However, the witness may not be required to assert that the response is actually incriminating or to prove the possibility of incrimination; *Hoffman* held that either burden would force the witness to surrender the very protection the Fifth Amendment provides. If the prosecutor does not believe

67. *Mills v. United States*, 281 F.2d 736 (4th Cir.1960). See also, *Smith v. State*, 283 Md. 187, 388 A.2d 539 (1978), cert. denied 439 U.S. 1130, 99 S.Ct. 1050 (1979); McCormick, Evidence (2d Ed. 1972), at 257.

68. *Brown v. Walker*, 161 U.S. 591, 16 S.Ct. 644 (1896). See also *Ullmann v. United States*, 350 U.S. 422, 76 S.Ct. 497 (1956) (holding that a person may not refuse to acknowledge membership in the Communist party to avoid subsidiary repercussions such as "loss of job, expulsion from labor unions, state registration and investigation statutes, passport eligibility, and general public opprobrium.")

69. 341 U.S. 479, 71 S.Ct. 814 (1951).

70. 355 U.S. 7, 78 S.Ct. 14 (1957) (per curiam), reversing *Wollam v. United States*, 244 F.2d 212 (9th Cir.1957).

that a witness's assertion of the Fifth Amendment is justified, he may object. The prosecutor then bears the burden of proving to the court that the witness's claim is unfounded. To sustain an assertion of the Fifth Amendment privilege, *Hoffman* stated, "it need only be evident from the implications of the question, in the setting in which it is asked, that a responsive answer . . . might be dangerous because injurious disclosure could result." In adjudicating the validity of the claim, the judge "must be governed as much by his personal perception of the peculiarities of the case as by the facts actually in evidence." To overrule a witness's Fifth Amendment claim, the judge must be "*perfectly clear* . . . that the witness is mistaken, and that the answer(s) cannot possibly have such tendency to incriminate." Further, the witness has a right to present evidence demonstrating the validity of his Fifth Amendment claim.

Overall, in any "criminal proceeding," or when one is in the offing, the evidentiary burden established in *Hoffman* to protect a witness's Fifth Amendment claim is virtually insurmountable. Generally, prosecutors who object to an individual's assertion of the right to silence cannot meet this burden, and instead confer immunity or attempt to establish the point with other evidence.

(c) Immunity. Persons may not claim a Fifth Amendment right to be free from compelled self-incrimination if their testimony has been rendered nonincriminating by a governmental grant of immunity. Immunity statutes developed out of the state's need to compel from witnesses testimony which will facilitate prosecution of other individuals considered more important. They have been attacked on the ground that, while preventing prosecution of the witness based on his immunized statements, they do not protect against the opprobrium, civil liability and danger from third parties which may result from the disclosure of criminal acts. Yet the courts have uniformly rejected such challenges on the ground that a grant of immunity need merely provide protection congruent with the privilege, which only prevents compelled *incrimination.*[71]

(1) Types of Immunity. Immunity exists in two forms, "use and derivative use" immunity, and "transactional" immunity. The former forbids the admission of any testimony that is specifically immunized, and any evidence derived therefrom. In contrast, transactional immunity protects the individual from prosecution for *any* activity mentioned in the immunized testimony. Thus, witnesses given transactional immunity may testify about matters far beyond the subject of the questions asked in order to "bathe" themselves in immunity. To limit such unjustified bene-

---

71. See, e.g., *Ullmann v. United States*, 350 U.S. 422, 76 S.Ct. 497 (1956);   *Patrick v. United States*, 524 F.2d 1109 (7th Cir.1975).

fits most jurisdictions now utilize use and derivative use immunity. New York, which has transactional immunity, immunizes only answers which are responsive to the questions asked.[72]

The Supreme Court first approved the concept of statutory immunity in *Counselman v. Hitchcock.*[73] In early cases, *Counselman* was interpreted to require transactional immunity because, at the end of that opinion, the Court stated that a valid immunity grant "must afford absolute immunity against future prosecution for the offense to which the question relates." [74] But in *Murphy v. Waterfront Commission,*[75] the Court seemed willing to recognize use and derivative use immunity as constitutionally adequate. In that case, the Court held that, in order to ensure the full protection guaranteed by the Fifth Amendment, testimony obtained pursuant to a grant of immunity by a state must also be excluded from federal prosecutions, and vice versa.[76] In doing so, it spoke only of use and derivative use immunity, not immunity from prosecution for the crime in question. Finally, in *Kastigar v. United States,*[77] the Court explicitly approved use and derivative use immunity. Reasoning that the Fifth Amendment does not protect against prosecution, which is the effect of transactional immunity, but only against incrimination resulting from compelled disclosure, the Court concluded that use and derivative use immunity is "coextensive with the scope of the privilege against self-incrimination."

The dissent's major objection to this ruling was its perception that prosecutors would be able to disguise when evidence in a subsequent prosecution is derived from leads developed from the immunized testimony. The majority responded by referring to the heavy burden the government must bear in showing the subsequent prosecution is based on an independent source. This burden "imposes on the prosecution the affirmative duty to prove that the evidence it proposes to use is derived from a legitimate source wholly independent of the compelled testimony." Since it can often be difficult to meet this burden, it is common for prosecutors to deliver sealed files to the court containing the evidence they have secured against the immunized witness, before the witness testifies.

(2) Use of immunized testimony to impeach. In *New Jersey v. Portash,*[78] the Court relied on its reasoning in *Kastigar* in prohibiting the use of immunized testimony even for impeachment pur-

72. N.Y.—McKinney's Crim.Proc. Law § 190.40(2)(b) (1984–85).

73. 142 U.S. 547, 12 S.Ct. 195 (1892).

74. Imwinkelreid, et al., Criminal Evidence (1979), at 304.

75. 378 U.S. 52, 84 S.Ct. 1594 (1964).

76. *Murphy* also supports the proposition that immunity extends to other state prosecutions as well.

77. 406 U.S. 441, 92 S.Ct. 1653 (1972).

78. 440 U.S. 450, 99 S.Ct. 1292 (1979).

poses. In *Portash*, the respondent, who had testified before a grand jury pursuant to an immunity grant, was indicted for official misconduct and extortion. At Portash's trial, the judge ruled that the immunized grand jury testimony would be admissible for the purpose of exposing inconsistencies in the respondent's trial testimony. As a consequence of the judge's ruling, Portash did not testify at his trial. Affirming the reversal of the respondent's conviction, the Supreme Court held that immunized testimony "is the essence of coerced testimony." Thus, the admission of immunized testimony in a criminal proceeding to impeach the defendant's testimony at trial is a violation of his Fifth Amendment right.

The majority opinion in *Portash* reserved a possible exception to its decision in the case of perjury trials. In *United States v. Apfelbaum*,[79] the Court explicitly held that not only alleged false statements, but also any other statements made during immunized testimony that are relevant to whether the alleged false statements are in fact perjured, are admissible at a subsequent perjury trial in the prosecution's case-in-chief. Writing for a unanimous Court, Justice Rehnquist pointed out that while the Fifth Amendment guarantees protection against self-incrimination, it has never been held by the Court to protect "false swearing." Because the immunity statute in question likewise provided protection against self-incrimination with regard to immunized true statements, but not from prosecution for making false statements, its protection, concluded Rehnquist, was co-extensive with the Fifth Amendment. In short, any immunized statements, whether true or untrue, can be used in a trial for making false statements.

(3) The effect on testimony in later proceedings. A separate immunity issue the Court has confronted is the extent to which an immunity grant permits the individual who has been immunized to refuse to testify in *later* proceedings. In *Pillsbury Co. v. Conboy*,[80] Conboy had been granted use immunity on testimony before a federal grand jury. In a subsequent civil antitrust suit, the plaintiff sought Conboy's deposition. At the deposition, Conboy was asked the same questions he had been asked at the grand jury proceeding and then was read the answers he gave at that proceeding in an effort to determine whether he had "so testified." He refused to answer, asserting his privilege against self-incrimination. The trial court held Conboy in contempt, apparently in the belief that the grant of immunity protected against prosecution use of any of Conboy's disclosures. But Conboy argued that even if no new information came from his being asked to adopt his

---

79. 445 U.S. 115, 100 S.Ct. 948 (1980).

80. 459 U.S. 248, 103 S.Ct. 608 (1983).

answers to the grand jury, he was at risk because other parties in the suit had the right to cross-examine him. Thus, they might demand information that would not be seen as derivative of the immunized testimony. The Supreme Court agreed, holding that unless the government expressly grants a new assurance of immunity at the civil trial, no contempt citation may be issued for refusal to repeat answers previously immunized in the criminal setting.

(4) The procedure for granting immunity. In *Conboy,* the Court stated that the authority for granting immunity rests with the executive branch. Generally, to the extent courts are involved at all in immunity procedure,[81] they merely ensure that the relevant statutory procedures are followed. Under the federal statute,[82] the court must issue an order if the request for immunity is approved by the Attorney General, the Deputy Attorney General or a designated Assistant Attorney General, and the attorney making the request states that the "testimony or other information [sought from the witness] may be necessary to the public interest" and is not likely to be disclosed by the witness voluntarily. As indicated earlier, if a properly immunized witness refuses to testify under such an order, he may be held in contempt, even if he fears retaliation for his testimony or some other non-criminal liability.

(d) Other Means of Avoiding Incrimination. The privilege may not be invoked with respect to the facts of an offense for which the statute of limitations has run, the person has been finally sentenced,[83] or the person has been pardoned. In none of these cases can compulsion of admissions result in a criminal penalty. The government bears the burden of demonstrating that the relevant event has occurred.[84] Until the government makes this showing, the witness may validly refuse to answer questions under the Fifth Amendment.

15.04 The "Testimonial Evidence" Requirement

Unless the compulsion of incriminating information requires a person to be a "witness" against himself, the Fifth Amendment is not implicated. The Supreme Court has relied on this language in concluding that only "testimony" or "communication" is protected by the Fifth Amendment. As Justice Holmes stated in *Holt v. United States,*[85] "the prohibition of compelling a man in a

81. Although many jurisdictions require a court order, in virtually all jurisdictions prosecutors can avoid even this minimal limitation through an informal promise of non-prosecution, a practice which accomplishes the same objective as immunization, but can be seen as an exercise of the prosecutorial prerogative. See § 21.01.

82. 18 U.S.C.A. § 6003.

83. See supra note 66.

84. McCormick, Evidence § 139.

85. 218 U.S. 245, 31 S.Ct. 2 (1910).

criminal court to be witness against himself is a prohibition of the use of physical or moral compulsion to extort communications from him, not an exclusion of his body as evidence when it may be material." To hold otherwise, Holmes asserted, "would forbid a jury to look at a prisoner and compare his features with a photograph in proof." The modern formulation of this idea was stated by Justice Brennan in *Schmerber v. California:* [86] "We hold that the privilege protects an accused only from being compelled to testify against himself, or otherwise provide the State with evidence of a testimonial or communicative nature."

Relying on this testimonial/nontestimonial distinction, the Court has permitted the government to force the accused to don clothing in order to facilitate identification (in *Holt*), submit to the extraction of blood (in *Schmerber*), participate in a line-up,[87] produce a writing exemplar,[88] and produce a voice exemplar.[89] It has also stated in dictum that the Fifth Amendment "offers no protection against compulsion to submit to fingerprinting, photography, or measurements, . . . to appear in court, to stand, to assume a stance, to walk, or to make a particular gesture." [90]

However, the Court has also noted that not all "physical" or "real" evidence obtained from a person is necessarily noncommunicative. In *Schmerber,* the forcible extraction of blood in that case was permissible not only because it did not involve "the cruel, simple expedient of compelling [evidence] from [the accused's] own mouth," but also because "his participation, except as a donor, was irrelevant to the results of the test, which depend on chemical analysis and on that alone." On the other hand, suggested the Court, physical evidence from a lie detector test might be testimonial: "To compel a person to submit to testing in which an effort will be made to determine his guilt or innocence on the basis of physiological responses, whether willed or not, is to evoke the spirit and history of the Fifth Amendment."

Two other Court cases shed further light on the testimonial evidence requirement. In *California v. Byers* [91] a plurality of the Court held that statutory provisions requiring accident-involved drivers to stop and leave their names "does not provide the State with 'evidence of a testimonial or communicative nature.' " Chief Justice Burger reasoned that stopping is no more testimonial than standing in a lineup and that giving one's name "is an essentially

---

86. 384 U.S. 757, 86 S.Ct. 1826 (1966).

87. *United States v. Wade,* 388 U.S. 218, 87 S.Ct. 1926 (1967).

88. *Gilbert v. California,* 388 U.S. 263, 87 S.Ct. 1951 (1967); *United States v. Mara,* 410 U.S. 19, 93 S.Ct. 774 (1973).

89. *United States v. Dionisio,* 410 U.S. 1, 93 S.Ct. 764 (1973).

90. *United States v. Wade,* 388 U.S. 218, 87 S.Ct. 1926 (1967).

91. 402 U.S. 424, 91 S.Ct. 1535 (1971).

neutral act." This analysis has been rejected by several commentators, who believe that the statute compels drivers to admit participation in criminal acts [92] and to surrender the anonymity [93] that protects them from criminal prosecution. In this regard, the statute in *Byers* is like the statutes at issue in the line of cases beginning with *Albertson v. Subversive Activities Control Board*,[94] which also sought identifying information in connection with a specific crime. Arguably, even giving fingerprints under such circumstances would be "testimonial."

The Court looked more closely at the circumstances under which verbal responses may be nontestimonial in *Pennsylvania v. Muniz*.[95] There the state introduced the defendant's somewhat slurred and unresponsive answers to a series of booking questions about his height, weight and so on in an effort to prove him guilty of drunken driving. The Court held unanimously that, under *Schmerber* and *Holt*, the "physical inability to articulate words in a clear manner" was not testimonial evidence and could be used against the defendant. However, the Court split on the admissibility of the defendant's answers to one of the questions asked, specifically, "Do you know what the date was of your sixth birthday?" The defendant's first response to this question was inaudible; when asked again he replied, "I don't know." Five members of the Court agreed that asking the sixth birthday question, at least when no *Miranda* warnings have been given, subjected the defendant to the cruel trilemma of choosing between truth, falsity or silence. As Justice Brennan put it for the majority:

> By hypothesis, the inherently coercive environment created by the custodial interrogation precluded the option of remaining silent. Muniz was left with the choice of incriminating himself by admitting that he did not then know the date of his sixth birthday, or answering untruthfully by reporting a date that he did not then believe to be accurate (an incorrect guess would be incriminating as well as untruthful).

Since the *content* as well as the delivery of the answer to the birthday question was incriminating and went beyond mere identification, it was testimonial.[96] In dissenting to this part of the Court's opinion, Chief Justice Rehnquist, joined by Justices White,

---

92. Note, 26 Ark.L.Rev. 81, 84–85 (1972).

93. The Supreme Court, 1970 Term, 85 Harv.L.Rev. 3, 269 (1971).

94. 382 U.S. 70, 86 S.Ct. 194 (1965), discussed in § 15.02(b)(2).

95. 496 U.S. 582, 110 S.Ct. 2638 (1990).

96. The Court avoided deciding whether two other questions—asking the defendant to count while performing a "walk-the-line" test and during a "one leg stand" test—were testimonial. But the four dissenters indicated they were willing to hold that neither these "statements" nor the "*Byers*-type" responses to the booking questions were testimonial.

Blackmun and Stevens, contended that "[i]f the police may require Muniz to use his body in order to demonstrate the level of his physical coordination, there is no reason why they should not be able to require him to speak or write in order to determine his mental coordination."

15.05   The Personal Basis of the Right

The Fifth Amendment's prescription that "no person" shall be compelled to be a witness "against himself" has been construed literally by the Court. Thus, the only person who can prevent revelation of incriminating, testimonial information is the person being compelled, not some third party. As the Supreme Court stated in *Couch v. United States:* [97] "The Constitution explicitly prohibits compelling an accused to bear witness 'against himself': it necessarily does not proscribe incriminating statements elicited from another. Compulsion upon the person asserting it is an important element of the privilege."

In *Couch* itself the Court found that a sole proprietor could not rely on the Fifth Amendment to prevent production of papers possessed by her tax accountant. The accountant, not the defendant, was "the only one compelled to do anything." And because the accountant made no claim that the records would incriminate him, the Fifth Amendment was not implicated. Although recognizing that the defendant was the owner of the papers, the Court stated that "possession [not ownership] bears the closest relationship to the personal compulsion forbidden by the Fifth Amendment." In *Fisher v. United States* [98] the Court explained further that "[w]e cannot cut the Fifth Amendment completely loose from the moorings of its language and make it serve as a general protector of privacy—a word not mentioned in its text and a concept directly addressed in the Fourth Amendment."

However, the Court has recognized two exceptions to the general rule that only the person against whom the compulsion is directed may assert the privilege. In *Couch,* the Court noted that "situations may well arise where constructive possession is so clear or the relinquishment of possession is so temporary and insignificant as to leave the personal compulsions upon the accused substantially intact," a statement reiterated in *Fisher.* The lower courts have construed this idea very restrictively,[99] as indeed they should if the locus of compulsion is the key issue. The second exception to the personalized compulsion idea comes from *Fisher.* When documents are transferred to an attorney "for the purpose of obtaining legal advice," then the attorney may assert

97. 409 U.S. 322, 93 S.Ct. 611 (1973).

98. 425 U.S. 391, 96 S.Ct. 1569 (1976).

99. See *Matter of Grand Jury Empanelled February 14, 1978,* 597 F.2d 851 (3d Cir.1979).

the Fifth Amendment claim for the client's protection. This exception is not based on the Fifth Amendment, however. Rather, it is founded on a desire to implement the purpose underlying the attorney-client privilege—that of encouraging the uninhibited exchange of information between attorneys and their clients.

It should be noted that the personalized compulsion concept applies in the interrogation context as well. Of course, a person cannot prevent another from voluntarily waiving his Fifth Amendment right merely because the waiver will provide the state with evidence against him. More dramatically, the *Couch* rationale means that even an *involuntary,* coerced statement may be used against someone else without violating the Fifth Amendment.[1]

15.06 The Fifth Amendment and Subpoenas

This section examines the complicated set of rules dealing with the extent to which the privilege against self-incrimination may be used to prevent the government from obtaining evidence via a subpoena *duces tecum* or similar compulsory process. The previous section has already noted that only the person against whom the subpoena is directed, usually the "custodian" of the records, may assert the privilege. As it turns out, in most cases even the custodian is afforded very little protection by the Amendment.

(a) Boyd and the "Zone of Privacy." For a time, beginning in 1886, it appeared that the Fifth Amendment would provide very wide-ranging protection against document subpoenas. In that year, the Supreme Court decided *Boyd v. United States,*[2] which relied on both the Fourth and Fifth Amendments in holding unconstitutional a court order requiring an importing firm to produce an invoice concerning items it allegedly had imported illegally. The Court pointed to the common law prohibition against forcing documentary evidence "out of the owner's custody by process,"[3] and averred that compulsory production of books and papers, even when sought to obtain evidence of a serious crime, is "contrary to the principles of free government." With respect to the Fifth Amendment in particular, the Court concluded that just as the Fifth Amendment prohibited "compulsory discovery by extorting the party's oath," so it prohibited discovery by "compelling the production of his private books and papers." *Boyd* thus appeared to hold that government could never use a subpoena to force an individual to turn over papers, whether

---

1. See § 16.05(a).

2. 116 U.S. 616, 6 S.Ct. 524 (1886).

3. The Court relied primarily on *Entick v. Carrington,* 19 Howell, St.Tr. 1029 (1765).

private or business, given their association with the individual's personal sphere of privacy.[4]

(b) The Collective Entity Doctrine. In 1906, the Court significantly eroded the "zone of privacy" created by *Boyd* by removing Fifth Amendment protection of most business papers. In *Hale v. Henkel,*[5] the Court upheld a subpoena of corporate records against a Fifth Amendment challenge on the ground that a corporation is a fictional entity (and thus not a "person" to which the Fifth Amendment refers), and because, as a "creature of the state," it is entitled to less protection from the government than is the individual. In *United States v. White,*[6] the Court extended this exception to unincorporated organizations, in this case a labor union. As in *Henkel,* the Court held that whenever an organization takes on an impersonal quality rather than embodying "the purely private or personal interests of its constituents," Fifth Amendment protection is not available to the organization. It also emphasized "the inherent and necessary power of the federal and state governments to enforce their laws" against business organizations, which would be stymied if a Fifth Amendment challenge were sustained. This same reasoning led the Court to hold, in *Bellis v. United States,*[7] that a partnership with an "established institutional identity" is not protected by the privilege.

Bellis suggested that the only organizations which might assert the privilege are "small family partnerships" and sole proprietorships (of any size). Why these business organizations should be exempted from the collective entity exception to the privilege is not entirely clear. Except in a technical legal sense, their business records are no more "personal" than the records of corporations, and the organizations themselves are just as subject to the state's regulatory interests as other business entities.[8]

(c) The Rejection of a Privacy Basis for the Amendment. The next major change in Fifth Amendment jurisprudence relating to subpoenas occurred in *Fisher v. United States.*[9] There, the Court upheld a subpoena of documents prepared by the defendant's accountant that were in the possession of the defendant's

---

4. Although *Boyd* concluded that a subpoena could be used to obtain contraband or a fruit or instrumentality of crime, this issue rarely arises, since a search warrant is the preferred method of obtaining readily destructible evidence, the existence of which is uncertain.

5. 201 U.S. 43, 26 S.Ct. 370 (1906).

6. 322 U.S. 694, 64 S.Ct. 1248 (1944).

7. 417 U.S. 85, 94 S.Ct. 2179 (1974).

8. Note that under the Court's "regulatory purpose" cases, see § 15.02(b)(3), even "personal" organizations can be compelled to produce records that are regularly kept as part of a neutral reporting scheme. However, in the context at issue here, the government has usually already focused on the business as a defendant, and the contention that the compulsion has a "non-criminal" purpose will be weak.

9. 425 U.S. 391, 96 S.Ct. 1569 (1976).

attorney. Although the papers at issue were business records, the collective entity doctrine did not apply, since the defendant was a sole proprietor. And, as noted earlier,[10] *Fisher* was willing to recognize an exception to the personalized compulsion rule when a client seeks to prevent surrender of documents he gives to his attorney for the purpose of seeking legal advice; thus, the client had standing to assert the privilege despite the fact the documents were not in his possession. But the Court went on to hold that, in this case, the client had no privilege to assert. In doing so, it modified even further the scope of *Boyd* by rejecting its conceptual basis and indicating that "private," as well as business, papers are entitled to considerably less protection than the latter decision had indicated.

Boyd had focused on the privacy interest in papers afforded by the Fourth and Fifth Amendments. *Fisher* separated the Fourth and Fifth Amendment issues and held that, while the Fourth Amendment does protect privacy, the Fifth Amendment does not. Rather it protects only against compulsion of incriminating, testimonial information. On this assumption, concluded Justice White for the Court, the Fifth Amendment generally does not prevent use of subpoenas as a means of obtaining documents, because subpoenas usually compel nothing of incriminating value.

In reaching this latter conclusion, White first noted that a subpoena clearly does not compel *creation* of the documents; thus, the privilege cannot be asserted with respect to their contents. In his concurring opinion, Justice Brennan argued that if the Fifth Amendment prohibits "compelling one to disclose the contents of one's mind," it must also prohibit "compelling the disclosure of the contents of that scrap of paper [on which] persons would, at their peril, record their thoughts and the events of their lives." But the fact remains that, unlike compulsion of verbal testimony, a document has already been created at the time of the compulsion. As Justice O'Connor latter stated in *United States v. Doe*[11] (which permitted a subpoena of the *defendant's* business records from the *defendant's* possession) this fact suggests that "the Fifth Amendment provides absolutely no protection for the contents of private papers of any kind."[12] Although this statement may prove to be an exaggeration,[13] the Court's reasoning in *Fisher* and *Doe* supports her conclusion.

10. See § 15.05.

11. 465 U.S. 605, 104 S.Ct. 1237 (1984).

12. The *Fourth* Amendment might provide some protection, however. First, the typical subpoena requires a showing of relevance. See 23.05(a)(1). Second, a subpoena for a very private document such as a diary might require

a showing of probable cause. See § 5.06(a).

13. The majority in *Fisher* noted that the case did not raise the "special problems of privacy which might be presented by subpoena of a personal diary" or direct compulsion of other "private papers."

As *Fisher* noted, however, a subpoena does compel the act of *producing* the documents, an act which will occasionally have incriminating aspects. Specifically, White pointed out, incriminating evidence will be compelled by a subpoena if the government needs to use the act of producing the records to prove, in a prosecution against the custodian: (1) that they existed; (2) that the custodian possessed or controlled the documents; or (3) that they are authentic. In the normal case, proof of existence, possession, or authentication are not important. For instance, in *Fisher,* the Court held that it was a "foregone conclusion" both that the tax documents existed and that either the defendant or an agent possessed them; these "admissions" inherent in the act of producing the documents added "little or nothing to the sum total of the Government's information." Likewise, because the documents were authored by the accountant, the act of production by itself did not, and could not, authenticate their source or accuracy.

In some cases, however, such admissions are not "foregone conclusions." For instance, if the mere existence of a particular item proves the crime being investigated,[14] or if the document cannot be authenticated on its face or by testimony of a noncustodian, the fact that a particular person produced it can be very useful to the prosecution's case against that person. In such situations, suggested *Fisher,* the prosecution must either forego use of a subpoena or grant use and derivative use immunity as to the act of production. To obtain such immunity, the prosecution should have to show that it can prove existence, possession or authentication in some other way (otherwise, there is no need for the documents, since they would not be admissible). In some cases, such as, for instance, a subpoena for contraband, records of illegal activities, or private records accessed by only one person, such proof may be impossible.[15] Thus, the Fifth Amendment may still prevent use of a subpoena to obtain records under limited circumstances.[16]

Although there are intimations in *Fisher* that the act of production may at times not be "testimonial," this issue was not emphasized in later cases. It would seem that the implied assertion in the act of production—that the documents exist or are authentic—are "testimony" in the sense required by the Fifth Amendment. To be distinguished from the act of production, however, is the act of facilitating production by another party,

---

14. See *United States v. (Under Seal),* 745 F.2d 834 (4th Cir.1984) (subpoena for records of purchases and sales of controlled substances).

15. See generally, Mosteller, "Simplifying Subpoena Law: Taking the Fifth Amendment Seriously," 73 Va.L. Rev. 1, 40–49 (1987).

16. Note that, in some of these situations, use of a search warrant to obtain records which the prosecution has probable cause to believe exist in a certain location may be possible. *Andresen v. Maryland,* 427 U.S. 463, 96 S.Ct. 2737 (1976). A search warrant does not "compel" an act of production.

which may often not be testimonial. In *Doe v. United States* [17] (not to be confused with *United States v. Doe,* discussed above), the Court held that forcing the defendant to sign a blanket consent form authorizing disclosure of records related to his bank accounts, but not requiring him to indicate the location or number of any account, did not "explicitly or implicitly, relate a factual assertion or disclose information." At most it required the *banks* to declare that certain records of the defendant's were in their possession. Thus, the government was not forcing the defendant to be a "witness" against himself.

(d) Custodians of Impersonal Records. Prior to *Fisher,* the Court had repeatedly held that the custodian of records owned by collective entities could not resist a subpoena even if the records would clearly incriminate him as well. [18] These decisions made sense given the prevailing theory that the Fifth Amendment protected personal records, not impersonal ones. But after *Fisher's* replacement of the privacy theory with one focusing on compulsion, the stage seemed to be set for holding that custodians of records held by collective entities could resist a subpoena if the act of production thereby compelled would tend to incriminate them and immunity were not granted.

However, in *Braswell v. United States,* [19] the Court decided to adhere to its earlier collective entity cases in situations where a custodian asserts the privilege on personal grounds. Although recognizing that *Fisher* and *Doe* had "embarked upon a new course of Fifth Amendment analysis," Chief Justice Rehnquist, who wrote the Court's 5–4 opinion, reasoned that the collective entity cases were not obsolete because "the custodian of corporate or entity records holds those documents in a representative rather than a personal capacity," and agents who accept custody of such documents accept the same responsibility to permit inspection as the entity is required by law to assume. As the Court had in *Henkel,* he also stressed that recognizing a privilege in this setting would hinder the government's efforts to prosecute white collar crime. The defendant had offered two solutions to this latter problem: allowing the corporation to choose an alternative custodian who would not be incriminated by the act of production or granting immunity for that act. But Rehnquist rejected both proposals. The alternative custodian solution does not work if, as is often the case, the subpoenaed custodian is the only person who knows the location of the records: unless he is willing to give the alternate self-incriminating information, the custodian cannot tell

17. 487 U.S. 201, 108 S.Ct. 2341 (1988).

18. *Wilson v. United States,* 221 U.S. 361, 31 S.Ct. 538 (1911). See also, *Bellis* and *White* supra notes 6 and 7.

19. 487 U.S. 99, 108 S.Ct. 2284 (1988).

the alternate where the records are, thus inhibiting the production of the records. And an immunity grant would make any derivative use of the act of production impossible, which could have "serious consequences," given the heavy burden the government must meet in showing the independent source of its evidence.[20]

Rehnquist did state that the government "may make no evidentiary use of the 'individual act' against the individual." Thus, "in a criminal prosecution against the custodian, the Government may not introduce into evidence before the jury the fact that the subpoena was served upon and the corporation's documents were delivered by one particular individual, the custodian." Instead, the government should be limited to showing that the entity had produced the records and were authentic, and let the jury draw its own conclusions about what the custodian knew. Rehnquist also left open the question of "whether the agency rationale supports compelling a custodian to produce corporate records when the custodian is able to establish, by showing for example that he is the sole employee and officer of the corporation, that the jury would inevitably conclude that he produced the records." The importance of this last caveat was diminished by the failure of the Court to make such a finding in *Braswell,* despite the fact that the custodian there was the only shareholder in one of the two corporations involved, and the only person with any authority over either corporations' business affairs.

Left intact by *Braswell* was the Court's earlier decision in *Curcio v. United States.*[21] That case held that, in a prosecution against the collective entity, a custodian could be forced to produce records, and to testify as to their authenticity (something implicit in the act of production in any event), but could not be compelled to give further oral testimony incriminating himself. Further, of course, if the subpoenaed records truly are personal, rather than organizational, the privilege may be asserted even by an employee of a collective entity. Thus, for instance, whereas desk calendars—provided by the corporation, used for scheduling corporate business, and accessible to secretaries and other employees—are probably not privileged, pocket calendars owned by the witness, containing personal as well as corporate entries, and not accessible to others may be privileged.[22] Again, however, all that is protected is the act of production to the extent it is incriminating, not the contents of the record.

20. See § 15.03(c)(1).

21. 354 U.S. 118, 77 S.Ct. 1145 (1957).

22. See *Grand Jury Subpoena Duces Tecum Dates April 23, 1981,* 657 F.2d 5 (2d Cir.1981).

15.07   Conclusion

The Fifth Amendment privilege against self-incrimination precludes state compulsion of incriminating, testimonial statements from the person whom the state seeks to compel. The four components of this rule are summarized below, with a separate synopsis of the privilege's application to disclosures pursuant to subpoena.

(1) *Compulsion.* The extent to which failure to assert the right to remain silent will be viewed as the product of compulsion rather than a valid waiver depends primarily upon: (a) the setting of the state's attempt to get information, and (b) the extent to which the government's purpose is to elicit self-incriminating information. Thus, in the custodial interrogation setting, the suspect must be told of his right to remain silent and the government must show that any subsequent statements were voluntarily and intelligently made. In the trial setting, neither the warnings or proof of waiver is necessary, while in the grand jury setting it appears that only proof of a valid waiver is required. Similarly, a statute which has as its primary purpose the disclosure of incriminating information from an inherently suspect group violates the Fifth Amendment, while a statute which has as its primary purpose the implementation of a non-criminal, regulatory reporting scheme does not. A statute, such as the Internal Revenue Act, which falls somewhere in between is valid, but sanctions cannot be imposed on a person who refuses, in good faith, to report specific information thought to be incriminating. Exercise of the right to remain silent might be unconstitutionally inhibited not only by imposition of criminal or contempt sanctions for not talking, but also by noncriminal sanctions such as, for instance, conditioning continuance in a job on disclosure of incriminating statements.

(2) *Incrimination.* The privilege may only be asserted to prevent compulsion of information that will be usable in a criminal proceeding. A criminal proceeding is one that may result in criminal punishment, which, in addition to criminal trials, includes juvenile delinquency proceedings, grand jury proceedings, and capital sentencing hearings, but does not include commitment proceedings, child custody proceedings, and other proceedings the purpose of which is primarily rehabilitative or regulatory. Disclosures may also be compelled at a criminal proceeding if immunity is granted, which requires, at the least, that the government guarantee it will not use the disclosures, or evidence derived therefrom, in subsequent proceedings (unless these proceedings are aimed at proving the immunized person committed perjury during the earlier proceeding).

(3) *Testimonial evidence.* The privilege applies only to information which is testimonial in nature, which means that it com-

municates something beyond the physical characteristics of a person, the identity of a person, or his appearance in certain clothing.

(4) *Personalized compulsion.* A person's Fifth Amendment privilege is not violated by compulsion against another unless the compulsion seeks documents from the person's attorney, given to that attorney for the purpose of obtaining legal advice, or unless the person has only temporarily surrendered the items compelled and still constructively possesses them.

(5) *Subpoenas.* A subpoena for documents compels only the production of the documents, not their creation, and thus is not subject to quashing through assertion of the privilege unless the act of production provides evidence of existence, possession or authentication that is not a foregone conclusion. When the subpoena is for documents owned by a collective entity, such as a corporation or sizeable partnership, then the privilege may not be asserted even when the act of production might incriminate the custodian. However, at any subsequent trial of the custodian, the act of production may not be directly linked with him.

BIBLIOGRAPHY

Alito, Samuel. Documents and the Privilege Against Self-Incrimination. 48 U.Pitt.L.Rev. 27 (1986).

Arenella, Peter. Schmerber and the Privilege Against Self-Incrimination: A Reappraisal. 20 Am.Crim.L.Rev. 31 (1982).

Ayer, Donald B. The Fifth Amendment and the Inference From Silence: Griffin v. California After Fifteen Years. 78 Mich.L. Rev. 841 (1980).

Bauer, W.J. Reflections on the Role of Statutory Immunity in the Criminal Justice System. 67 J.Crim.L. 143 (1976).

——. Formalism, Legal Realism and the Constitutionally Protected Privacy under the Fourth and Fifth Amendments. 90 Harv.L.Rev. 945 (1977).

Dolinko, David. Is There A Rationale for the Privilege Against Self-Incrimination? 33 U.C.L.A. L.Rev. 1063 (1986).

Gerstein, Robert S. The Demise of Boyd: Self-Incrimination and Private Papers in the Burger Court. 27 U.C.L.A.L.Rev. 343 (1979).

Geyh, Charles. The Testimonial Component of the Right Against Self-Incrimination. 36 Cath.U.L.Rev. 611 (1987).

Heidt, Robert H. The Fifth Amendment Privilege and Documents: Cutting Fisher's Tangled Line. 49 Miss.L.Rev. 439 (1984).

Mosteller, Robert. Simplifying Subpoena Law: Taking the Fifth Amendment Seriously. 73 Va.L.Rev. 1 (1987).

Newman, M.F. The Suspect and the Grand Jury: A Need for Constitutional Protection. 11 U.Rich.L.Rev. 1 (1976).

Ritchie, L.J. Compulsion that Violates the Fifth Amendment. 61 Minn.L.Rev. 303 (1977).

____. The Scope of Testimonial Immunity under the Fifth Amendment. 6 Loy.U.L.Rev. 350 (1973).

Saltzburg, Stephen. The Required Records Doctrine: Its Lessons for the Privilege Against Self-Incrimination. 53 U.Chi.L.Rev. 6 (1986).

Slobogin, Christopher. Estelle v. Smith: The Constitutional Contours of the Forensic Evaluation. 31 Emory L.J. 71 (1982).

Strachan, Kristine. Self-Incrimination, Immunity, and Watergate. 56 Tex.L.Rev. 791 (1978).

Chapter Sixteen

CONFESSIONS

16.01 Introduction

Confessions have long been recognized as an essential and accepted part of law enforcement. They not only provide direct evidence against the accused, but also provide leads to additional evidence against him or his colleagues in crime, at the same time they may clear the name of other individuals. The principal question with respect to attempts at obtaining confessions is not whether they should be allowed but how they should be regulated.

Today, as a result of *Miranda v. Arizona,*[1] most litigation about confessions centers on the applicability of the Fifth Amendment. But until 1966, when *Miranda* was decided, the courts relied on other mechanisms for determining the validity of confessions. Under the common law, the principal focus was the evidentiary one of whether the confession was reliable, a finding which was most likely when the statement was perceived to be "voluntary" rather than the product of promises or torture.[2] In 1936, the Supreme Court gave the "voluntariness" test constitutional stature, under the Due Process Clause.[3] For the next twenty-eight years, the due process standard held sway. Then, for a short time beginning in 1964, it appeared the Court might treat the admissibility of confessions primarily as a matter of when questioning in the absence of an attorney violates the accused's Sixth Amendment right to counsel.[4] But, two years later, the Court decided *Miranda,* which made the Fifth Amendment "the pervasive perspective for evaluating statements of the accused."[5] Since *Miranda,* the requirement that persons subjected to custodial interrogation be told of their right to remain silent has been the predominant focus of the Court. The due process and right to counsel approaches remain important in various settings, however; indeed, both have been rejuvenated in more recent years.

This chapter begins by detailing the development of the Court's confessions jurisprudence, from the due process test through *Miranda.* It then looks closely at the various elements of *Miranda* and the right to counsel approach. It ends with a

1. 384 U.S. 436, 86 S.Ct. 1602 (1966).

2. *The King v. Warickshall,* 168 Eng.Rep. 234, L. Leach Cr. Cases 263 (K.B.1783).

3. *Brown v. Mississippi,* 297 U.S. 278, 56 S.Ct. 461 (1936). In one early case, *Bram v. United States,* 168 U.S. 532, 18 S.Ct. 183 (1897), the Court ex-

cluded a confession on Fifth Amendment grounds, but this case remained dormant until *Miranda.*

4. *Massiah v. United States,* 377 U.S. 201, 84 S.Ct. 1199 (1964).

5. J. Cook, Constitutional Rights of the Accused: Pretrial Rights 305 (1974).

discussion of the exclusionary rule as it applies to confessions and evidence derived therefrom, and of the procedure for determining the admissibility and credibility of confessions.

16.02 Approaches to Regulating the Interrogation Process

The Supreme Court's efforts at regulating the process of obtaining confessions has vacillated between a desire to protect against police misconduct which might lead to an unwilling confession and a belief that all reliable confessions should be admitted into evidence. While these objectives are not necessarily contradictory, a broad definition of misconduct could exclude many confessions that are clearly reliable; at the same time, permitting use of all reliable confessions might sanction a wide range of unpleasant, degrading or painful police practices which pressure or trick persons into giving confessions they do not really "want" to give. Each of the approaches described below reflects this tension.

(a) The Due Process "Voluntariness" Test. At the time of *Brown v. Mississippi,*[6] the first Supreme Court case involving a state confession, neither the Fifth or Sixth Amendment had been applied to the states. The Court analyzed the case under the Due Process Clause. The facts in *Brown* presented an extreme situation which the Court could not ignore. Police officers used hanging, severe whippings, and other brutal methods to extort the signatures of three black defendants to confessions which had been dictated by the police in a murder case. Convictions were obtained on the basis of these confessions alone. The Court, expressing great dissatisfaction with the police conduct involved, found the convictions void for want of the essential elements of due process.

After *Brown,* the Court decided roughly 35 confessions cases relying solely on the due process approach.[7] In *Fikes v. Alabama,*[8] the Court reviewed a number of its decisions since *Brown* and summarized the standard applied in these cases as whether the "totality of the circumstances that preceded the confessions" deprived the defendant of his "power of resistance." Applying this standard requires a fact specific case-by-case analysis. But the factors that the courts have identified in assessing the voluntariness of a confession can be broken down into two broad categories: the police conduct involved and the characteristics of the accused.

(1) Police conduct. The most obviously unacceptable type of police conduct is the use of physical brutality to coerce a confes-

---

6. 297 U.S. 278, 56 S.Ct. 461 (1936).   **8.** 352 U.S. 191, 77 S.Ct. 281 (1957).

7. B. George, Constitutional Limitations on Evidence in Criminal Cases 260–61 (1973).

sion, such as occurred in *Brown*. As stated by Justice Douglas in *Williams v. United States,*[9] confessions obtained through the use of physical brutality and torture "cannot be admissible under any concept of due process." In the years immediately following *Brown,* physical mistreatment of suspects and the threat of violence were predominant concerns of the Court.[10]

As time went on, however, the Court began to confront cases involving more subtle police conduct. In *Rogers v. Richmond,*[11] the defendant confessed after the police told him they were going to take his wife into custody. In *Lynumn v. Illinois,*[12] the defendant made incriminating statements after being told that cooperation would lead to leniency, but that failure to cooperate could result in loss of welfare payments and the custody of her children. Both confessions were found to be coerced. A modern case involving perhaps even subtler coercion by government agents is *Arizona v. Fulminante.*[13] Fulminante was suspected of molesting and killing his 11 year-old stepdaughter. Incarcerated in prison for another crime, he was approached by one Sarivola, a fellow inmate who was a paid informant for the FBI but who posed as an organized crime figure. Sarivola raised the subject of the stepdaughter's death with Fulminante on several occasions, but the defendant at first denied any participation. The FBI instructed Sarivola to find out more. Eventually, Sarivola told Fulminante that he knew other inmates were giving Fulminante "tough treatment" because of the rumor that he was a child-murderer and that he, Sarivola, could protect him, but only if Fulminante disclosed what he knew. Calling it a "close question," Justice White, joined by four other members of the Court, concluded that Fulminante's subsequent statement to Sarivola was coerced by a "credible threat." According to the majority, "it was fear of physical violence, absent protection from his friend (and Government agent) Sarivola, which motivated Fulminante to confess."[14]

Fulminante can also be seen as an example of the "false friend" technique confronted in earlier cases. A classic example of this type of case came in *Spano v. New York,*[15] in which detectives brought in a young police officer, a close friend of the accused, to question him. The officer stated that if he did not get a statement from the accused his job was in jeopardy, and that the loss of job would be disastrous to his wife and children, all of

---

9. 341 U.S. 97, 71 S.Ct. 576 (1951).

10. See, e.g., *Chambers v. Florida,* 309 U.S. 227, 60 S.Ct. 472 (1940); *Ward v. Texas,* 316 U.S. 547, 62 S.Ct. 1139 (1942).

11. 365 U.S. 534, 81 S.Ct. 735 (1961).

12. 372 U.S. 528, 83 S.Ct. 917 (1963).

13. 499 U.S. ——, 111 S.Ct. 1246 (1991).

14. The Court also noted that Fulminante was of slight build and had not adapted well to the stress of prison life on previous occasions.

15. 360 U.S. 315, 79 S.Ct. 1202 (1959).

which was fabricated. The Court considered the falsely aroused sympathy of the accused as one of the factors in the totality of the circumstances, and concluded that the will of the accused had been overborne. Similarly, in *Leyra v. Denno*,[16] a state-employed psychiatrist was introduced to the accused as a "doctor" brought to give him medical relief from a painful sinus. By subtle and suggestive questioning the psychiatrist induced the accused to admit his guilt. The Court found the suspect's ability to resist interrogation had been broken by the arts of the psychiatrist, and held the use of confessions extracted in this manner inconsistent with due process.

While use of the "false friend" technique may often be unconstitutional, mere misrepresentation does not necessarily violate due process. In *Frazier v. Cupp*,[17] for instance, the police falsely told the defendant that his co-defendant had already confessed. The Court found this fabrication "relevant," but "insufficient in our view to make this otherwise voluntary confession inadmissible."

The extent to which the accused is isolated from family, friends, or counsel is also frequently cited as a factor bearing upon the voluntariness determination.[18] In *Fikes v. Alabama*,[19] for example, the fact that the accused had been questioned far from his home, and had seen no one other than his accusers for over a week before confessing, was weighed heavily by the Court in holding his confession inadmissible. A similar crucial inquiry into the validity of police conduct is whether an accused is provided with basic amenities, such as food or cigarettes, during an extended interrogation. Many of the interrogations found to be improper by the Court in its due process days involved a denial of these amenities.[20] In *Crooker v. California*,[21] however, the accused was questioned only intermittently, was given milk and a sandwich shortly after his arrest, and was provided with coffee and permitted to smoke whenever he wished, factors which led the Supreme Court to find that his confession was voluntary.

Still another factor the Court has looked at in deciding voluntariness is the length of the interrogation.[22] In *Ashcraft v. Tennessee*[23] relays of police questioned the suspect continuously for

16. 347 U.S. 556, 74 S.Ct. 716 (1954).

17. 394 U.S. 731, 89 S.Ct. 1420 (1969).

18. See *Darwin v. Connecticut*, 391 U.S. 346, 88 S.Ct. 1488 (1968), for a discussion of cases.

19. 352 U.S. 191, 77 S.Ct. 281 (1957).

20. See, e.g., *Payne v. Arkansas*, 356 U.S. 560, 78 S.Ct. 844 (1958) (two sandwiches in 40 hours).

21. 357 U.S. 433, 78 S.Ct. 1287 (1958). *Crooker* was expressly overruled in *Miranda v. Arizona*, 384 U.S. 436, 86 S.Ct. 1602 (1966).

22. See *Davis v. North Carolina*, 384 U.S. 737, 86 S.Ct. 1761 (1966) for citations to cases.

23. 322 U.S. 143, 64 S.Ct. 921 (1944).

thirty-six hours without allowing him rest or sleep. The confession ultimately obtained was ruled inadmissible. A similar ruling was made in *Chambers v. Florida*,[24] where the suspects had steadfastly refused to confess through five days of interrogation, only to break down after an all-night examination on the fifth day. The timing of the interrogation is also important. In *Spano*, for instance, the Court noted that the questioning occurred after indictment, which the Court felt showed "the undeviating intent of the officers to extract a confession." According to the Court, "when such intent is shown, this Court has held this confession obtained must be examined with the most careful scrutiny."

Finally, even prior to *Miranda*, police failure to apprise the accused of his right to remain silent, or his rights respecting counsel, was a significant factor in judging the voluntariness of his statements. In *Davis v. North Carolina*,[25] for instance, the Court noted that "the fact that Davis was never effectively advised of his rights gives added weight to the other circumstances described [in the opinion] which made his confessions involuntary." Several due process decisions overturning confessions also relied in part on the fact that the accused was prevented from consulting with his attorney after asking to see him.[26] However, in *Moran v. Burbine*,[27] decided after *Miranda*, the Court held that deliberately lying to the defendant's attorney in order to keep him from being present during interrogation does not violate due process when the defendant has been told of his right to counsel and does *not* ask to see him. In this instance, no compulsion occurs.

(2) Characteristics of the accused. The second broad category of factors to be weighed in the "totality of the circumstances" relates to the special characteristics of the accused. If the case is close, obvious disabilities on the part of the accused tip the balance in favor of the defendant. Thus, for instance, in *Haley v. Ohio*,[28] the Court reversed the conviction of a fifteen year-old boy who had confessed after a night-long interrogation. Justice Douglas wrote: "Mature men possibly might stand the ordeal from midnight to 5 a.m. But we cannot believe that a lad of tender years is a match for the police in such a contest." The Court has also considered the level of intelligence and education of the accused in determining the voluntariness of a confession. In *Davis v. North Carolina*,[29] the confession of a borderline retarded individual with a third or fourth grade education was found invalid; in contrast, in

24. 309 U.S. 227, 60 S.Ct. 472 (1940).

25. 384 U.S. 737, 86 S.Ct. 1761 (1966). See, also *Haynes v. Washington*, 373 U.S. 503, 83 S.Ct. 1336 (1963); *Culombe v. Connecticut*, 367 U.S. 568, 81 S.Ct. 1860 (1961); *Turner v. Pennsylvania*, 338 U.S. 62, 69 S.Ct. 1352 (1949).

26. See, *George*, supra note 7, at 260–61.

27. 475 U.S. 412, 106 S.Ct. 1135 (1986) discussed further in § 16.03(d)(2).

28. 332 U.S. 596, 68 S.Ct. 302 (1948).

29. 384 U.S. 737, 86 S.Ct. 1761 (1966).

finding the statements in *Crooker v. California*[30] voluntary, the Court considered extremely important the fact that the accused was 31 years-old and a college graduate who had attended law school for one year and studied criminal law. Similarly, any evidence of mental illness will weigh heavily in the totality of the circumstances analysis. In *Blackburn v. Alabama*,[31] the Court found involuntary a confession by an accused with a lengthy history of mental problems who might have been "insane" at the time of the interrogation.

Physical fatigue or pain that could impair the accused mentally have also been considered important. In *Ashcraft v. Tennessee*,[32] the fatigue brought on by 36 hours of continuous questioning was the major reason for excluding the confession in that case. In *Beecher v. Alabama*,[33] a confession was found to be the product of "gross coercion" when it was made to a hospital doctor one hour after arrest, while the accused was in extreme pain from a gunshot wound and was under the influence of morphine. A post-*Miranda* case arriving at a similar result was *Mincey v. Arizona*,[34] which involved questioning of an accused who was in the hospital for treatment of a gunshot wound, had received some drugs (albeit none which impaired his ability to remain alert), and was in "unbearable" pain. In finding the accused's incriminating admissions involuntary, the Court noted that the questioning had taken place over a four-hour period (punctuated by treatment and occasional losses of consciousness), and had continued despite Mincey's physical helplessness, his often incoherent answers, and his entreaties that the questioning be postponed until the next day or until his attorney could be present.

In none of these cases were the characteristics of the accused alone enough to support a finding of involuntariness. Some evidence of abusive police conduct was also necessary. In *Colorado v. Connelly*,[35] the Court made explicit that, unless the state somehow takes advantage of the disabilities of an accused, no constitutional violation has taken place. In *Connelly*, the defendant appeared at a police stationhouse and stated that he wanted to talk about a murder he had committed. He was given the *Miranda* warnings, but continued to talk about the murder and showed police the supposed location of the crime. It later developed that the defendant may have been mentally ill at the time of his incriminating statements and actions; at a preliminary hearing, a psychiatrist testified that Connelly had approached the police because he

30. 357 U.S. 433, 78 S.Ct. 1287 (1958).

31. 361 U.S. 199, 80 S.Ct. 274 (1960).

32. 322 U.S. 143, 64 S.Ct. 921 (1944).

33. 408 U.S. 234, 92 S.Ct. 2282 (1972).

34. 437 U.S. 385, 98 S.Ct. 2408 (1978).

35. 479 U.S. 157, 107 S.Ct. 515 (1986).

thought he had been commanded to do so by the "voice of God." The Supreme Court held that, even assuming this testimony to be correct, neither the Due Process Clause nor the Fifth Amendment was violated, since no action by the police "coerced" the defendant into waiving his rights. While the fact of his mental illness might have affected the *reliability* of Connelly's statements and thus their admissibility under local evidence rules, the Constitution did not require exclusion on involuntariness grounds.

While the Court's conclusion that some sort of state action is required in order to find that a confession is "coerced" is consistent with the usual treatment of criminal process rights,[36] it is not obvious that Connelly's post-warning confession should have been admissible. Subsequent discussion will make clear that determining when police have exploited weaknesses of the accused is extremely difficult.[37] As Justice Stevens stated in a separate opinion, once a defendant like Connelly is in a "custodial relationship" with the police, questioning takes on a "presumptively coercive character." Moreover, as Justice Brennan's dissent noted, even if confessions which are not "caused" by the police are never involuntary under the Constitution, their reliability, a matter traditionally subsumed in the voluntariness inquiry, should still be a matter of constitutional concern because the state is relying on them in its courts of law. *Connelly* appears to hold, however, that the Constitution does not address the reliability issue independently of the voluntariness issue.

(3) Analysis of the "voluntariness" test. The major problem with the voluntariness test is a practical one: it gives neither the police or the courts much guidance. As the preceding discussion illustrates, a host of factors can be relevant in the "totality of the circumstances;" rarely does one factor predominate. The difficulty of applying the test is exacerbated by the murkiness of its rationale. Although the common law voluntariness test was bottomed on a concern about reliability, the due process voluntariness test, as applied by the Court, slowly changed the focus to police behavior. Indeed, by 1961, Justice Frankfurter's opinion in *Rogers v. Richmond,*[38] went so far as to say that involuntary confessions are excluded "not because such confessions are unlikely to be true but because the methods used to extract them offend an underlying principle in the enforcement of our criminal law: that ours is an accusatorial and not an inquisitorial system—a system in which the State must establish guilt by evidence independently and freely secured and may not by coercion prove its charge against an accused out of his own mouth."[39] While deter-

---

36. See, e.g., § 4.02, discussing the scope of Fourth Amendment.

37. See, e.g., §§ 16.03(b)(d).

38. 365 U.S. 534, 81 S.Ct. 735 (1961).

39. Ironically, the Court's move away from reliability as the touchstone

mining the reliability of a confession is no easy task, evaluating whether it is "coerced" is even more difficult, given the unlimited ways in which police conduct and individual characteristics might interact, and the metaphysical nature of the inquiry into whether that interaction results in the accused's "will" being "overborne" or merely exercised.

The practical and conceptual difficulties with the voluntariness test helped smooth the way for more prophylactic approaches—that is, approaches which set out straightforward, if somewhat rigid, rules for the police to follow when they want to interrogate a suspect. As discussed below, the Supreme Court has, since *Brown* and the initial due process cases, endorsed three different prophylactic approaches, ending with *Miranda*. But the advent of these more rule-oriented tests has not spelled the end of due process analysis, as indicated by the number of post-*Miranda* decisions described above in which the Court resorted to this analysis (e.g., *Fulminante, Burbine, Mincey* and *Connelly*).

Due process precedents remain important for a number of reasons. First, there are points in the criminal process at which *Miranda* and the other prophylactic approaches may not apply (e.g., grand jury proceedings,[40] or pre-custodial questioning) and thus the voluntariness test may come into play. For instance, *Fulminante* represents a case in which the *Miranda* and right to counsel approaches were inapposite (because the defendant was not in "custody" and had not been indicted for the charge in question [41]), but a colorable claim of involuntariness remained. Second, the post-*Miranda* Court has indicated that, for purposes of determining whether a confession may be used for impeachment purposes or whether it taints any "fruits" it helps police obtain, the appropriate standard is whether the confession was "coerced" in the due process sense, not whether it was obtained in violation of *Miranda*.[42] In *Mincey*, for example, due process analysis was important because the prosecution, which implicitly conceded that the statements at issue in that case were obtained in violation of *Miranda*, sought to use them for impeachment purposes rather than in its case-in-chief. Third, and perhaps most importantly, under all the prophylactic approaches, waiver is still possible. This means that, when a person does decide to talk, a determination of whether the statements were "voluntarily" made may become the primary issue.[43] In both *Burbine* and *Connelly*, for example, the defendants received warnings as required by *Miran-*

of due process analysis also made possible its decision in *Connelly*, which in essence holds that the Constitution does not have anything to say about *un*reliable confessions that are not coerced by the police.

40. See § 15.02(a)(3).

41. See §§ 16.03(a)(5) & 16.04(a).

42. See § 16.05(b) & (c).

43. See §§ 16.03(d) and 16.04(c).

da; the question was whether their subsequent statements were voluntary. In short, the analysis of confessions that was refined during the "due process period" remains a significant facet of confessions jurisprudence.

(b) The McNabb–Mallory Rule. At the same time the voluntariness test was being applied to confessions used in state courts, the Supreme Court began developing, at the federal level only, a different approach to the regulation of interrogation. In 1944, it decided *McNabb v. United States*,[44] which involved confessions of several individuals suspected of murdering a federal revenue agent. The Court found it unnecessary to address the constitutionality of the police conduct, relying instead on its "supervisory authority" over the administration of criminal justice in the federal courts. Pointing to a number of federal statutes calling for prompt arraignment of arrested persons, the Court held that confessions obtained during an unnecessary delay between the time of arrest and arraignment should be excluded. Although the statutes did not specifically call for exclusion of confessions made during this period, "to permit such evidence to be made the basis of conviction in the federal courts would stultify the policy which Congress has enacted into law."

Because the Court's opinion in *McNabb* also spent considerable effort analyzing the voluntariness of the confessions in that case, it was not clear how important the decision was. But five years later, the Court restated that "a confession is inadmissible if made during illegal detention due to failure promptly to carry a prisoner before a committing magistrate."[45] And in 1957, in *Mallory v. United States*,[46] a unanimous Court held that Federal Rule of Criminal Procedure 5(a), enacted in 1946 to replace the prompt arraignment statutes at issue in *McNabb,* prohibits delay that would "give opportunity for the extraction of a confession."

On its face, *Mallory* appeared to prohibit *any* interrogation, other than that necessary for booking purposes, between the time of arrest and arraignment (at which point a lawyer was usually appointed). However, *Mallory* did not overturn an earlier post-*McNabb* decision in which the Court had admitted a confession made immediately after arrest,[47] and lower courts had excused delay that was not the fault of the police.[48] In any event, in 1968, as part of an unsuccessful attempt to "repeal" *Miranda,* Congress successfully "repealed" the *McNabb–Mallory* rule, which, unlike *Miranda,* was not based on the Constitution. The new statute

44. 318 U.S. 332, 63 S.Ct. 608 (1943).

45. *Uphsaw v. United States,* 335 U.S. 410, 69 S.Ct. 170 (1948).

46. 354 U.S. 449, 77 S.Ct. 1356 (1957).

47. *United States v. Mitchell,* 322 U.S. 65, 64 S.Ct. 896 (1944).

48. *Williams v. United States,* 273 F.2d 781 (9th Cir.1959); *Proctor v. United States,* 338 F.2d 533 (D.C.Cir.1964).

provides that no confession shall be excluded "solely because of delay" if it was obtained within six hours of arrest, and permits extension of the six-hour period when the location of the magistrate makes it necessary. After that period, delay is one of the factors to be considered in deciding whether the confession is voluntary.[49] Of course, this statute eliminates the *McNabb–Mallory* doctrine only to the extent it does not violate *Miranda* or other constitutional rules.

The *McNabb–Mallory* rule provided more "guidance" to the police and the courts than the voluntariness test, but guidance apparently neither wanted. While it reduced the opportunity of the police to coerce confessions, it also reduced significantly their ability to use any *voluntary* statements made after arrest. The Court has never considered adopting a similar rule as a matter of constitutional law.

(c) Massiah and Escobedo: The Right to Counsel Approach. The first constitutionally-based deviation from the due process approach was predictable. In its due process cases, two factors which the Court often mentioned as tending to make a confession "involuntary" were the formal charging of the suspect and police efforts to prevent access to an attorney. For instance, as noted earlier, in *Spano v. New York*,[50] the Court considered significant the fact that Spano had been indicted, because that event meant the police had clearly focused their attention on him; the majority also noted that Spano had asked for his attorney. Four members of the Court who concurred in finding Spano's confession invalid argued that it was inadmissible solely on the ground that, just as an accused is accorded trial counsel, an indicted individual should be afforded counsel during post-charge interrogation.

In *Massiah v. United States*,[51] a six-member majority finally held that the Sixth Amendment guarantee of "the assistance of counsel" in all "criminal prosecutions" is violated when government agents "deliberately elicit" statements from an indicted person in the absence of counsel. In *Massiah,* the accused, who had been indicted for violating federal narcotics laws, was released on bail. A friend of his allowed the government to install a radio transmitter in his car, and then invited Massiah to enter the car and discuss the pending case. Massiah made incriminating statements that were overheard by the police. The dissent noted that no coercion was present on these facts, and that Massiah's access to counsel was not infringed in any way, nor was counsel's ability

49. 18 U.S.C.A. § 3501(c)(a); § 3501(b).

50. 360 U.S. 315, 79 S.Ct. 1202 (1959).

51. 377 U.S. 201, 84 S.Ct. 1199 (1964).

to prepare for trial impaired by the police action. But Justice Stewart wrote for the majority that if the right to counsel is "to have any efficacy it must apply to indirect and surreptitious interrogations as well as those conducted in the jailhouse." According to Stewart, "Massiah was more seriously imposed upon . . . because he did not even know that he was under interrogation by a government agent."

Massiah was a significant step away from the case-by-case voluntariness analysis; it provided a relatively precise rule by which the admissibility of confessions could be determined.[52] Yet, as one commentator writes: "The lower courts . . . generally construed *Massiah* as narrowly as possible."[53] When the "interrogation" in *Massiah* took place, the defendant had already been indicted and had retained an attorney. Thus, courts could find that *Massiah* does not apply at any time before indictment or the retention or appointment of counsel. Moreover, given the facts of that case, they could limit its application to confrontations initiated by the police that involved trickery. In any event, *Massiah* lay dormant at the Supreme Court level for another thirteen years, perhaps because *Miranda* and the Fifth Amendment occupied the Court's attention. These latter developments will be discussed after looking at *Miranda* and its progeny.[54]

An offshoot of *Massiah* which is important primarily as the most significant precursor to *Miranda* was decided five weeks later. In *Escobedo v. Illinois,*[55] Escobedo was arrested for murder, questioned, and then released the same day, after his lawyer obtained a writ of *habeas corpus.* Ten days later an alleged accomplice implicated Escobedo and he was rearrested. On route to the station he was advised of his accomplice's accusation. His request to consult with his attorney was denied, as were several requests of counsel to consult with Escobedo. The two were kept apart until Escobedo, after four hours of questioning, made a damaging statement. He was convicted of murder, based in part on the statement, and the Supreme Court of Illinois affirmed.

Justice Goldberg stated the Supreme Court's holding as follows:

> We hold . . . that where, as here, the investigation is no longer a general inquiry into an unsolved crime but has begun to focus on a particular suspect, the suspect has been taken into police custody, the police carry out a process of interrogations that lends itself to eliciting incriminating statements, the suspect has requested and been denied an opportunity to

52. The *Massiah* doctrine was made binding on the states under the Fourteenth Amendment in *McLeod v. Ohio,* 381 U.S. 356, 85 S.Ct. 1556 (1965) (per curiam).

53. Cook, supra note 5, at 299.

54. See § 16.04.

55. 378 U.S. 478, 84 S.Ct. 1758 (1964).

consult with his lawyer, and the police have not effectively warned him of his absolute constitutional right to remain silent, the accused has been denied "the Assistance of Counsel" in violation of the Sixth Amendment . . . and that no statement elicited by the police during the interrogation may be used against him at a criminal trial.

To the five-member majority, the fact that the interrogation was conducted before the accused was formally indicted, as was the case in *Massiah,* made no difference. The investigation had begun to focus on the accused, so the purpose of the interrogation was to induce him to confess. The opinion reviewed various decisions in which the "guiding hand of counsel" was thought to be essential, and concluded that Escobedo's need for a lawyer's help at this stage was no less critical. Justice Goldberg wrote that "no system of criminal justice can, or should, survive if it comes to depend for its continued effectiveness on the citizens' abdication through unawareness of their constitutional rights."

Unlike *Massiah, Escobedo* did not provide much guidance to the courts or the police. *Escobedo* held that once an individual is the focus of investigation by the police, he may not be denied access to his attorney—if he has one *and* if he asks for him. But it did not define precisely when a suspect becomes "the accused." More importantly, the decision did not state what rights accrue to a person who does not have, and cannot afford, an attorney, or to a person who has an attorney but does not ask to see him. In *Miranda,* the Court took a significant step toward resolving those questions, effectively limiting the *Escobedo* holding to its facts.[56]

(d) Miranda and Fifth Amendment Analysis. In 1964, the Supreme Court decided *Malloy v. Hogan,*[57] which held that the Fifth Amendment applied to the states. In doing so, it announced that "today the admissibility of a confession in a state criminal prosecution is tested by the same standard applied in federal prosecution since 1897." In that year, the Court had decided *Bram v. United States,*[58] which had relied on the privilege against self-incrimination in evaluating the admissibility of a confession in federal court. But no other case prior to *Malloy* had done so; rather, the voluntariness standard had dominated analysis of confessions. Even *Massiah* and *Escobedo,* decided after *Malloy,* did not pick up on its message. Two terms later, however, the Court firmly shoved aside both due process analysis and the *Massiah* approach. In *Miranda v. Arizona,*[59] Chief Justice Warren, for a five-member majority, announced the following rule:

56. See *Kirby v. Illinois,* 406 U.S. 682, 92 S.Ct. 1877 (1972).

57. 378 U.S. 1, 84 S.Ct. 1489 (1964).

58. 168 U.S. 532, 18 S.Ct. 183 (1897).

59. 384 U.S. 436, 86 S.Ct. 1602 (1966).

> [T]he prosecution may not use statements, whether exculpatory or inculpatory, stemming from custodial interrogation of the defendant unless it demonstrates the use of procedural safeguards effective to secure the privilege against self-incrimination.

With these words, *Miranda* established the Fifth Amendment as the basis for ruling on the admissibility of a confession.

(1) The holding. The most important aspects of the *Miranda* decision [60] are the set of warnings it requires to be given, and the valid waiver it mandates before a confession by an accused can be considered admissible. Under *Miranda,* a person subjected to a custodial interrogation must be warned that he has a right to remain silent, that any statement he does make may be used in evidence against him, and that he has the right to the presence of an attorney, either retained or appointed, before and during questioning. A defendant may waive these rights, but only if the waiver is made voluntarily, knowingly, and intelligently will it render subsequent confessions admissible.

The procedural safeguards announced in *Miranda* are required "unless other fully effective means are devised to inform accused persons of their right of silence and to assure a continuous opportunity to exercise it." The Court recognized that Congress and state legislatures might be able to devise effective alternatives which would protect the rights of the individual and promote effective law enforcement. In the absence of a fully effective legislative or judicial equivalent, however, the proper warnings must be given and a valid waiver must be found before any statement may be admitted.

The opinion explains further that if, at any stage of the interrogation, an accused indicates that he wishes to speak with a lawyer, there can be no more questioning. Similarly, if the accused indicates in any other way that he does not wish to be interrogated, the police may not question him. Even if he has answered some questions or volunteered some statements, he may refuse to answer further questions until he sees an attorney and thereafter consents to be questioned. The decision is unclear about the limits of interrogation when counsel is present, although the Court suggests in a footnote that when an individual indicates a desire to remain silent, there may be circumstances in which further questioning will be permitted if counsel is present.

---

60. *Miranda* actually combined consideration of four cases: *State v. Miranda,* 98 Ariz. 18, 401 P.2d 721 (1965); *People v. Vignera,* 15 N.Y.2d 970, 259 N.Y.S.2d 857, 207 N.E.2d 527 (1965); *Westover v. United States,* 342 F.2d 684 (9th Cir.1965); *People v. Stewart,* 62 Cal.2d 571, 43 Cal.Rptr. 201, 400 P.2d 97 (1965).

The Court based its opinion in large part on its view of the interrogation process in practice. Relying on what it called "police manuals and texts,"[61] the majority described certain procedures that it felt were standard in all police interrogations. Among them were isolation of the suspect to deprive him of outside support and lengthy interrogation sessions. When these fail, the Court stated, various deceptive tactics are often employed to confuse or threaten the suspect. To counteract use of these practices, the warnings and the right to presence of counsel was necessary.

(2) Research on Miranda. Several empirical studies have attempted to assess the impact of *Miranda* and to check the validity of the Court's assumptions regarding the reality of police interrogation. One of the best known studies, conducted in New Haven,[62] found the interrogation process to be somewhat different from that pictured by the majority. First, the study found that only rarely were any directly coercive methods used to secure a confession. And it suggested that if custody and confrontation with police exert a more subtle pressure to confess, the warnings do not appear to alleviate that pressure in most cases because few warned suspects refrained from talking or asked for counsel. This second finding supports Justice White's statement in dissent that *Miranda* is based on an inconsistency: if custodial interrogation is so "inherently coercive" that due process analysis is insufficient, "how can the court ever accept [the accused's] negative answer to the question of whether he wants to consult his retained counsel or counsel whom the court will appoint?" Tempering the findings of the New Haven study, however, was the fact that, largely because *Miranda* had just been decided, the police seldom gave the full warnings in the interrogations studied. Other studies, apparently conducted in jurisdictions experiencing better compliance with *Miranda,* found a significant (10 to 20%) drop in confessions after *Miranda* went into effect.[63] These findings suggest the warnings did have some impact.

The results of the New Haven study were more obviously at variance with some of the views expressed by the dissenters in *Miranda.* One argument the dissenters made against the majori-

61. E.g., F. Inbau & J. Reid, Criminal Interrogation and Confessions (1962). The Court also quoted extensively from the Wickersham Report of 1931, IV National Comm'n on Law Observance and Enforcement, Report on Lawlessness in Law Enforcement, and from the 1961 U.S. Commission on Civil Rights Report.

62. Wald, et al., "Interrogations in New Haven: The Impact of *Miranda,*"

76 Yale L.J. 1519 (1967). One of the authors participated in this study while a student at Yale Law School.

63. See Seeburger & Wettick, "*Miranda* in Pittsburgh: A Statistical Study," 29 U.Pitt.L.Rev. 1, 23–6 (1967) for a description of *Miranda*'s impact in three cities.

ty's rule was that, given the reduction in confessions it was likely to produce, a substantial number of crimes would go unsolved or unpunished. The New Haven study and other research suggests otherwise. Relying on their own evaluation as well as that of the police officers, the participants in the New Haven study concluded that interrogation was necessary to solve a crime in less than ten percent of the felony cases where arrests were made. And confessions were needed to convict in an even smaller percentage of the cases. These findings have been replicated in other studies.[64] Thus, assuming *Miranda has* reduced the proportion of confessions obtained by 10 to 20%, it is probable that the warnings prevent conviction in far less than 2% of all felony cases.

A related argument made by Justice Harlan in dissent was that *Miranda* would bring more lawyers to the stationhouse and that those lawyers would urge their clients to remain silent. In fact, the New Haven study found that when suspects did ask for a lawyer and a lawyer came, he most often advised the suspect to cooperate with the police.

(3) The conceptual importance of Miranda. While the nature of *Miranda's* impact on the conduct and efficacy of interrogations is still open to some debate,[65] it is clear the decision represented a significant modification of the law of confessions in at least two ways. First, it completed the gradual shift of focus from concern over the reliability of confessions to concern over whether the police practices used to obtain them are coercive. *Miranda* is designed to counteract the "inherently coercive" nature of custodial interrogation; any improvement in the reliability of confessions it might produce was clearly of secondary importance to the majority.

Second, *Miranda* represented a repudiation of the due process case-by-case analysis; as had *Massiah,* it relied on a rule-oriented mode of decisionmaking. Indeed, the decision appeared to have announced the most straightforward rule possible: proper warnings and a valid waiver—meaning an express statement that one wants to talk and does not want an attorney beforehand—are required before any "custodial interrogation," or any statements made are not admissible for any purpose.

However, *Miranda* has not eliminated the need for fact specific analysis. Because much of *Miranda* could be said to be dicta or was ambiguous, it left many questions unanswered. And, as subsequent discussion develops, the post-Warren Court's efforts at

64. Seeburger & Wettick, supra note 63, at 26; Medalie, et al., "Custodial Police Interrogation in Our Nation's Capital: The Attempt to Implement Miranda," 66 Mich.L.Rev. 1347 (1968).

65. See articles collected in Bibliography.

answering these questions have diminished its prophylactic thrust significantly.

(e) Other Approaches. As noted above, *Miranda* stated that its warnings requirement could be replaced by "other fully effective means" of informing "accused persons of their right of silence." Both before and after *Miranda,* several alternative approaches were proposed or implemented, some of which provide less protection than *Miranda* and some of which might provide more.

(1) The congressional voluntariness test. In 1968, the same congressional provision that repealed the *McNabb–Mallory* rule attempted to repeal *Miranda* and *Massiah* as well, at least in the federal courts. In the Crime Control Act of that year, Congress provided that in federal cases a confession "shall be admissible in evidence if it is voluntarily given," [66] thus essentially endorsing the due process voluntariness test. While the giving of warnings, the presence of counsel, and the accused's request for counsel were all to be considered in deciding voluntariness, these factors "need not be conclusive on the issue. . . ." [67]

Because the Act did not provide a "fully effective" mechanism for informing suspects of their right to remain silent, it clearly did not meet *Miranda's* stipulation and thus would seem to be ineffective. But some have argued that *Miranda's* stipulation is itself not of constitutional status, since it describes a requirement that "overprotects" the constitutional right to prevent use of coerced confessions.[68] This notion was perhaps reinforced by the Court's decision in *Michigan v. Tucker,*[69] which stated that *Miranda* "recognized that [its] procedural safeguards were not themselves rights protected by the Constitution but were instead measures to insure that the right against compulsory self-incrimination was protected." [70]

Assuming there is some validity to the notion that rules which the Court applies to the states need not be based on the Constitution,[71] it must be admitted that not every unwarned statement is "coerced" or "compelled" in the sense used by the Court prior to *Miranda.* But *Miranda* can be seen as indulging in the reasonable assumption that the typical person subjected to custodial

66. 18 U.S.C.A. § 3401(a).

67. Id. § 3501(b).

68. Grano, "Miranda's Constitutional Difficulties: A Reply to Professor Schulhofer," 55 U.Chi.L.Rev. 174 (1988).

69. 417 U.S. 433, 94 S.Ct. 2357 (1974).

70. These comments of the Court must be taken with a grain of salt, however, since *Tucker* involved the is-

sue of whether an officer should have foreseen the need to give the full warnings prior to *Miranda;* the quoted statement was designed to support a conclusion that *Miranda* could not have been foreseen.

71. For the argument that the notion is nonsensical, see Strauss, "The Ubiquity of Prophylactic Rules," 55 U.Chi.L.Rev. 190 (1988).

interrogation either is not aware of his right to remain silent, or will be led to believe he does not have one, despite what he "knows." Absent such certainty that he can remain silent, the unwarned individual *thinks* he is faced with the very "trilemma" the Fifth Amendment is meant to prevent: a choice between self-accusation, perjury, or some type of sanction for silence (i.e., a contempt citation or some other extrajudicial punishment).[72] The warnings tell him that this trilemma does not exist. If this analysis is correct, the warnings requirement in *Miranda* should have constitutional stature and statutory attempts to nullify it are themselves a nullity.[73]

(2) The New York approach. In New York, as a matter of state law, police may not question a suspect once a complaint or indictment against the defendant issues, unless there is an affirmative waiver in the presence of counsel.[74] This rule clearly provides more protection than either the Fifth or Sixth Amendment rights, both of which can be waived in the absence of counsel.[75] At the same time, it does nothing more than *Miranda* for suspects questioned prior to formal charging. In this situation, New York courts again have a special rule: uncounseled waiver is invalid if, at the time of the waiver, defense counsel has become involved in the case.[76] This rule provides more protection than *Miranda* for those uncharged suspects who have alert attorneys (like the one in *Escobedo*) or who have been able to contact an attorney, but not for those who do not have and do not ask for one. No other state has adopted this approach.

(3) Judicial questioning. In the early years of the republic, most questioning of suspects was conducted by justices of the peace. But this practice fell into disuse as judicial officers took on other roles and police investigatory powers grew.[77] In 1932, Professor Kauper made a proposal to reinstate the practice with some modifications.[78] As he described it, "[t]he remedy proposed consists of two essentials: (1) That the accused be promptly produced before a magistrate for interrogation; and, (2) That the interroga-

---

72. See Stuntz, "Self–Incrimination and Excuse," 88 Colum.L.Rev. 1227 (1988). The "trilemma," described in *Malloy v. Hogan,* 378 U.S. 1, 84 S.Ct. 1489 (1964), is discussed in the Introduction to Part III.

73. But see, *United States v. Crocker,* 510 F.2d 1129 (10th Cir. 1975).

74. *People v. Samuels,* 49 N.Y.2d 218, 424 N.Y.S.2d 892, 400 N.E.2d 1344 (1980).

75. *Miranda* stated so explicitly with respect to the Fifth Amendment.

With respect to Sixth Amendment waiver, see *Brewer v. Williams,* 430 U.S. 387, 97 S.Ct. 1232 (1977), discussed in § 16.04(c).

76. *People v. Rogers,* 48 N.Y.2d 167, 422 N.Y.S.2d 18, 397 N.E.2d 709 (1979).

77. Pound, Criminal Justice in America 88 (1930).

78. Kauper, "Judicial Examination of the Accused—A Remedy for the Third Degree," 30 Mich.L.Rev. 1224 (1932).

tion be supported by the threat that refusal to answer questions of the magistrate will be used against the accused at trial."

Subsequent developments in Fifth Amendment jurisprudence might invalidate the latter method of compelling answers from suspects.[79] But even without this device, there may still be some validity to Professor Kauper's claim that "inauguration of a scheme of magisterial interrogation will greatly weaken the police motive for private interrogation" and ensure that questioning is carried out by "officers who are better qualified to exercise the power of interrogation fairly and effectively." While the number of confessions produced under such a system, particularly in combination with *Miranda* type warnings, would probably fall, its proximity to the time of arrest would mean that those who do talk would "not have time to work out a coherent fabricated story of defense alibi." Unclear under Kauper's proposal is the admissibility of confessions obtained outside of the judicial setting.

16.03   The Elements of Miranda

Of the many different approaches to the regulation of interrogation, *Miranda's* holding has assumed the most importance. The primary issues raised by that decision are: (1) the definition of custody; (2) the definition of interrogation; (3) the content and necessity of the warnings; and (4) the circumstances under which a waiver of the rights to silence and counsel is valid. These issues are addressed here. It is fair to say that every one of *Miranda's* pronouncements on these issues has been undercut to at least some extent by subsequent decisions.

(a) Custody. The *Miranda* Court limited its holding to situations in which "a person has been taken into custody or otherwise deprived of his freedom of action in any significant way." It further explained that this point in the criminal process is what was meant in *Escobedo* when it spoke of an investigation which has focused on the accused. Subsequent developments have made clear that the definition of custody is narrower than suggested by either statement in *Miranda.* In short, the Court's more recent cases indicate that a person is in custody only if the circumstances would indicate to a reasonable suspect that he was under arrest or its functional equivalent. If such circumstances exist, then any interrogation, even if it is about a different crime than the one which led to the arrest, triggers *Miranda.*[80] On the other hand, interrogation during a detention short of arrest or its equivalent is not enough to require warnings, even when the police have clearly

---

79. See *Griffin v. California,* 380 U.S. 609, 85 S.Ct. 1229 (1965), discussed in § 15.02(c). *Griffin,* however, only prevented comments on silence *at trial,* because of the negative effect on the fairness and accuracy of the trial. See § 28.03(c)(1).

80. *Mathis v. United States,* 391 U.S. 1, 88 S.Ct. 1503 (1968).

"focused" on the person detained. As with analysis of when an arrest has occurred for Fourth Amendment purposes,[81] determination of whether a person is in custody depends in large part on the location of the confrontation, and its duration and purpose.

(1) Field stops. The first decision to put forth explicitly the proposition that arrest and "custody" are congruent was *Berkemer v. McCarty,*[82] in which the Court held that warnings need be given only before interrogation of a person whose freedom of action has been curtailed to a "degree associated with formal arrest." The Court also established that neither the beliefs of the officer or the suspect are pertinent in deciding whether this test is met: "the only relevant inquiry is how a reasonable man in the suspect's position would have understood his situation." In *Berkemer,* an officer stopped the defendant for weaving in and out of a highway lane. When he noticed the defendant was having difficulty standing, he decided the defendant would have to be charged with a traffic offense and that he would not be allowed to leave the scene, but did not so inform the defendant. When the defendant could not perform a field sobriety test without falling, the officer asked him if he had been using intoxicants, to which the defendant replied that he had consumed two beers and had smoked marijuana a short time before. The officer then formally arrested the defendant.

The Court's opinion, written by Justice Marshall, admitted that a traffic stop does curtail the motorist's freedom of action and that the Court had on several occasions labeled such a stop a "seizure" for Fourth Amendment purposes. However, because the detention resulting from such a stop is "presumptively temporary and brief" and because the typical traffic stop is public, the motorist should not feel unduly coerced. Here, only a short period of time elapsed between the stop and the arrest and at no time was the defendant informed his detention would be more than temporary. The officer's unexpressed intention to detain the defendant was irrelevant: "From all that appears in the stipulation of facts, a single police officer asked [the defendant] a modest number of questions and requested him to perform a simple balancing test at a location visible to passing motorists."

On the more general question of whether *Miranda* warnings are required after an investigative stop of the type authorized by *Terry v. Ohio,*[83] *Miranda* itself declared that "[g]eneral on-the-scene questioning as to facts surrounding a crime or other general questioning of citizens in the factfinding process is not affected by our holding." Consistent with this statement, the *Berkemer* Court

---

81. See § 3.02.

82. 468 U.S. 420, 104 S.Ct. 3138 (1984).

83. 392 U.S. 1, 88 S.Ct. 1868 (1968), discussed in § 11.01.

stated that "[t]he comparatively nonthreatening character of [investigative] detentions explains the absence of any suggestion in our opinions that *Terry* stops are subject to the dictates of *Miranda*." However, if the stop becomes prolonged, or in any other way takes on aspects of an arrest (such as handcuffing or persistent questioning in an isolated setting), then a finding of custody is more likely.[84] The same can be said for questioning at the border: routine questions do not implicate *Miranda,* but once a person is taken to a private room, or questioned for a prolonged period, a different result might be required.[85]

(2) Questioning in the home. In *Orozco v. Texas,*[86] the Court found that *Miranda* was implicated when four police officers woke up the accused in his own bedroom at 4 a.m. and began questioning him about a murder. The Court focused on the testimony of one of the officers that the accused was not free to leave, a subjective factor which has since been discounted in *Berkemer*; however, the holding could also be supported by the objectively coercive nature of the confrontation. In contrast, in *Beckwith v. United States,*[87] a daytime interview by a number of IRS agents in a private home was found to be noncustodial. The defendant claimed that the questioning should have been preceded by full *Miranda* warnings (rather than the modified warning he received) because he was the "focus" of a criminal investigation and was placed under "'psychological restraints' which are the functional, and therefore, the legal equivalent of custody." Chief Justice Burger, writing for the majority, dismissed this argument, noting that "Miranda specifically defined 'focus,' for its purposes, as 'questioning initiated by law enforcement officers *after* a person has been taken into custody or otherwise deprived of his freedom of action in any significant way.'" After *Beckwith,* routine investigative questioning in the home is unlikely to implicate *Miranda* unless it becomes prolonged or is particularly intrusive, as in *Orozco.*[88] Of course, if there is a formal arrest in the home, then failure to give the warnings violates *Miranda.*[89]

84. See, e.g., *State v. Myers,* 118 Idaho 608, 798 P.2d 453 (1990) (normal traffic stop turned into custody when four police cars participated in stop and officer asked the defendant if he was carrying any drugs or syringes); *United States v. Beraun–Panez,* 812 F.2d 578 (9th Cir.1987) (custody where stop took place away from public view where no passersby would likely be present and defendant repeatedly accused of lying).

85. *United States v. Salinas,* 439 F.2d 376 (5th Cir.1971).

86. 394 U.S. 324, 89 S.Ct. 1095 (1969).

87. 425 U.S. 341, 96 S.Ct. 1612 (1976).

88. See, e.g., *United States v. Griffin,* 922 F.2d 1343 (8th Cir.1990) (robbery suspect in custody when agents sent family members to another part of the house and followed suspect into another room when he went there to get cigarettes).

89. See also, *Rawlings v. Kentucky,* 448 U.S. 98, 100 S.Ct. 2556 (1980) (three house occupants in custody when police detained them for 45 minutes while warrant sought).

(3) Questioning at the stationhouse or its equivalent. In looking at the custody question in the stationhouse setting, the Court has adhered to the arrest analogy. In *Oregon v. Mathiason*,[90] the police initiated contact with Mathiason, a parolee, when an officer left a note at his apartment saying "I'd like to discuss something with you." When Mathiason called in response to this note and expressed no preference as to a meeting place, the officer chose the state patrol office about two blocks from the defendant's apartment. Ninety minutes later, the two met in the hallway adjacent to the office, where the officer assured the defendant he was not under arrest. Once in the office with the door closed, the officer told the defendant he wanted to talk to him about a burglary and that his truthfulness would possibly be considered by the district attorney or judge. He further advised Mathiason that the police believed he was involved in the burglary and then stated, falsely, that the defendant's fingerprints were found at the scene. A few minutes after these statements, and a total of five minutes after he had come into the room, the defendant admitted to taking the property. He then received *Miranda* warnings, made a full confession, and was allowed to leave.

In overturning the Oregon Supreme Court's finding that Mathiason's incriminating statement was made in a "coercive environment," the Court stated:

> Any interview of one suspected of a crime by a police officer will have coercive aspects to it, simply by virtue of the fact that the police officer is part of a law enforcement system which may ultimately cause the suspect to be charged with a crime. But police officers are not required to administer *Miranda* warnings to everyone whom they question. Nor is the requirement of warnings to be imposed simply because the questioning takes place in the station house, or because the questioned person is one whom the police suspect.

Consistent with its focus on coercion, the Court also held that the officer's false statement about the fingerprints was irrelevant to the custody question under *Miranda*.

In a later case, *California v. Beheler*,[91] the Court stated that *Mathiason* stands for the proposition that *Miranda* is not implicated "if the suspect is not placed under arrest, voluntarily comes to the police station, and is allowed to leave unhindered by the police after a brief interview." In *Beheler* itself, the Court relied on this proposition in finding that warnings were not required where the defendant voluntarily confessed over the phone, confessed again at the stationhouse after agreeing to come there, and then was allowed to leave.

90.　429 U.S. 492, 97 S.Ct. 711 (1977).　　**91.**　463 U.S. 1121, 103 S.Ct. 3517 (1983).

Even when the defendant is under considerable pressure to meet with police, the fact of custody is not necessarily established. In *Minnesota v. Murphy,*[92] a probationer was ordered to meet with his probation officer, as part of the probation supervision process; during their interview he confessed to a rape and a murder. The Court held that *Miranda* did not apply because, as in *Berkemer,* Murphy's "freedom of movement [was] not restricted to the degree associated with formal arrest." While "[c]ustodial arrest is said to convey to the suspect a message that he has no choice but to submit to the officers' will and to confess . . . [i]t is unlikely that a probation interview, arranged by appointment at a mutually convenient time, would give rise to a similar impression." The Court continued:

> Many of the psychological ploys discussed in *Miranda* capital-ize on the suspect's unfamiliarity with the officers and the environment. Murphy's regular meetings with his probation officer should have served to familiarize him with her and her office and to insulate him from psychological intimidation that might overbear his desire to claim the privilege. Finally, the coercion inherent in custodial interrogation derives in large measure from an interrogator's insinuation that the interrogation will continue until a confession is ob-tained. . . . Since Murphy was not physically restrained and could have left the office, any compulsion he might have felt from the possibility that terminating the meeting would have led to revocation of probation was not comparable to the pressure on a suspect who is painfully aware that he literally cannot escape a persistent custodial interrogator.

Although the fact that the suspect was allowed to leave (as in *Mathiason* and *Beheler*), or could have left (as in *Murphy*), has only a tenuous connection to what a reasonable suspect would have felt *during* the interrogation, these cases indicate that Court places great emphasis on it.

On the other hand, when a reasonable suspect clearly would not feel "free to leave," he is in custody. In *Mathis v. United States,*[93] the Court held that an accused interrogated by I.R.S. officers while in jail serving a sentence on a state charge was in custody for *Miranda* purposes. Because the accused was clearly detained against his will, the fact that the questioning concerned a crime different from the one for which he was serving time was irrelevant. Similarly, in *Estelle v. Smith,*[94] the Court held that a post-arrest, court-ordered psychiatric evaluation requested by the state must be preceded by *Miranda* warnings when its results are

92. 465 U.S. 420, 104 S.Ct. 1136 (1984).

93. 391 U.S. 1, 88 S.Ct. 1503 (1968).

94. 451 U.S. 454, 101 S.Ct. 1866 (1981).

used for adjudication of guilt or capital sentencing; otherwise, a psychiatrist who later testifies based on such an examination is "essentially like . . . an agent of the State recounting unwarned statements made in a post-arrest custodial setting." [95]

(4) Minor crimes. Consistent with the arrest analogy, sufficient coercion to trigger the warnings requirement exists *whenever* a person is in custody, regardless of the crime. This was a second aspect of *Berkemer,* which, it will be remembered, involved a traffic stop. Although the Court found that custody did not occur there, it also unanimously rejected a "misdemeanor exception" to *Miranda* for persons who are in custody. To the state's argument that police would have no reason to subject those arrested for a traffic offense to strenuous interrogation, the Court noted that police sometimes have difficulty obtaining evidence relating to certain types of misdemeanors, such as driving under the influence of narcotic drugs, and that "[u]nder such circumstances, the incentive for police to try to induce the defendant to incriminate himself may well be substantial."

In addition to deciding that there was no necessary distinction between serious and minor crimes in terms of the coercive impact of custody, the *Berkemer* Court pointed to several practical reasons for its conclusion. There are many situations, noted Justice Marshall for the Court, in which an officer taking a driver into custody for causing a collision would be unable to tell whether the driver will eventually be charged with a felony or a misdemeanor. Moreover, the nature of the offense may depend upon circumstances unknowable to the police, such as whether the suspect has previously committed a similar offense or has a criminal record, or whether the victim will die. Finally, because officers are accustomed to giving *Miranda* warnings to persons in custody, an across-the-board rule would work no undue hardship, while it would maintain the prophylactic advantage of *Miranda.*

(5) Questioning by non-police. When the interrogator is a government official who is not a police officer, the custody issue can sometimes become murky. Public "civilian" investigators, such as health inspectors and school officials, may not be as intimidating as the police. Moreover, given the nature of their jobs, the questions they ask may not be aimed at obtaining "incriminating" answers.[96] But if a government action amounts to the equivalent of an arrest for a criminal offense, then *Miranda*

---

95. See § 15.03(a) for further discussion of *Smith.* The Court also seems to have accepted the idea that a police confrontation with a hospitalized person, at least one who is non-ambulatory and in some pain, is in custody for purposes of *Miranda. Mincey v. Arizona,* 437 U.S. 385, 98 S.Ct. 2408 (1978).

96. Note that, even when a person is in custody, if his answers will not be used in a "criminal proceeding," either because they are not relevant to any criminal offense, or because immunity has been granted, then *Miranda* does not apply; in such cases, there is no right to remain silent. See § 15.03.

should apply. At least three Supreme Court decisions support this conclusion. In *Mathis,* the Court found that *Miranda* was implicated, even though the questioning was conducted by I.R.S. agents. Similarly, in *Smith,* the Court stated: "That respondent was questioned by a psychiatrist designated by the trial court to conduct a neutral competency examination, rather than by a police officer, government informant, or prosecuting attorney is immaterial." And the Court strongly implied that, had the probationer in *Murphy* been in custody, the warnings should have been given by the probation officer who conducted the questioning in that case.

As with other criminal process rights, *Miranda* requires "state action." Thus, as a general rule, questioning by a private individual (e.g., an employer or a journalist) does not trigger *Miranda*.[97] When a private individual conducts a "custodial interrogation" as an agent of the police, however, the Fifth Amendment is clearly implicated.[98] Even when the interrogator is not a direct agent of the police, a good case for applying *Miranda* exists if he is acting with the primary purpose of enforcing the law and significantly restrains a person's liberty. That is, consistent with the above discussion, it would seem that if the private action amounts to an "arrest" for a crime, then *Miranda* should apply. But most courts, defining state action narrowly, have held that questioning by security guards and the like does not implicate *Miranda,* regardless of its custodial aspects.[99]

(b) Interrogation. The mere fact of custody does not trigger the warnings requirement. The person must be subjected to "interrogation" as well. *Miranda* defined interrogation as "questioning initiated by law enforcement officers." But *Miranda* was also concerned with "techniques of persuasion" that would produce a "compulsion to speak." The Court apparently wanted to regulate any police action which might suggest a response was called for. While later decisions have paid lipservice to this view, they have tended to undermine it in practice.

(1) The Innis formulation. Rhode Island v. Innis,[1] was the Court's first attempt to flesh out the definition of interrogation under *Miranda.* The Court began by stating that interrogation "must reflect a measure of compulsion above and beyond that inherent in custody itself." It then went on to define interrogation to mean not only "express questioning" but also its "functional equivalent," including "any words or actions on the part of the police (other than those normally attendant to arrest and custody)

97. George, supra note 7, at 437–38.

98. See *Wilson v. O'Leary,* 895 F.2d 378 (7th Cir.1990).

99. *City of Grand Rapids v. Impens,* 414 Mich. 667, 327 N.W.2d 278 (1982); George, supra note 7, at 438.

1. 446 U.S. 291, 100 S.Ct. 1682 (1980).

that the police should know are reasonably likely to elicit an incriminating response from the suspect." Using examples from *Miranda,* the Court listed as "functional equivalents" of interrogation situations where the police coach witnesses to identify the defendant in a line-up, suggest to the suspect that he was guilty, or minimize the seriousness of the offense or the perpetrator's role in it.

The apparent breadth of the Court's definition of interrogation was called into question, however, by its application in *Innis.* In that case, police officers, while driving Innis to the police station after arresting him for armed robbery, engaged in a conversation about the danger the missing robbery weapon would present to handicapped children; apparently in response to this conversation, Innis directed them to the hiding place of a shotgun later used as evidence to convict him. The Court's opinion, written by Justice Stewart (a *Miranda* dissenter), found that this exchange did not constitute interrogation. The Court characterized it as "nothing more than a dialogue between the two officers to which no response from the respondent was invited."

In dissent, Justice Stevens argued that evidence in the record suggested the officers' actions were not entirely "innocent." He pointed out that the officer whose statement triggered Innis' response was not regularly assigned to the transport vehicle, that he may have been—the record was unclear—sitting in the back seat next to Innis, and that the triggering statement was particularly emotionally charged ("God forbid" that a "little girl" might find the weapon). He also disputed the majority's implicit assumption that a criminal suspect will not respond to "indirect appeals to his humanitarian impulses." He pointed out that such an assumption "is directly contrary to the teachings of police interrogation manuals, which recommend appealing to a suspect's sense of morality as a standard and often successful interrogation technique."

The Court has continued to define interrogation narrowly. In *Arizona v. Mauro,*[2] after Mauro indicated his desire to remain silent, the police allowed his wife, upon her request, to talk to him. An officer was present during the conversation, and tape-recorded it. The conversation was later used to rebut Mauro's insanity defense. The Supreme Court, in a 5–4 opinion authored by Justice Powell, held that no interrogation had taken place on these facts, because Mauro "was not subjected to compelling influences, psychological ploys, or direct questioning." The Arizona Supreme Court had unanimously concluded that interrogation *did* occur, largely on the ground that the detectives had admitted that they

2. 481 U.S. 520, 107 S.Ct. 1931 (1987).

knew incriminating statements were likely to be made if the conversation took place.[3] But Powell concluded that police "do not interrogate a suspect simply by hoping that he will incriminate himself."

The dissent, again authored by Justice Stevens, admitted that there had been no explicit police subterfuge in the case. But because the police "exploited the custodial situation and the understandable desire of Mrs. Mauro to speak with [her husband]" by arranging for and listening to their conversation, he concluded that "interrogation" had taken place.

The definition of interrogation in *Innis* clearly focused on what the *officers* knew or should have known. This approach might be justified on the ground that police should not be penalized through exclusion of statements which they could not have known would be coerced by their actions. At the same time, however, if the issue is the degree of coercion on the suspect, then coercion must ultimately be measured from the suspect's perspective. Indeed, that is the perspective adopted by the Court in defining "custody," appropriately narrowed by a "reasonableness" requirement.[4] On this view, interrogation would be defined as whether a reasonable suspect would have felt that the officers' actions called for an incriminating response. *Mauro* may have moved toward such a definition with its refusal to consider what the officers' "hoped for." But both *Innis* and *Mauro* are less than sensitive to the fact that a reasonable suspect, who otherwise would remain silent, can be induced to talk through police action short of questioning.

(2) When custodial questioning is not interrogation. According to *Innis,* interrogation must add to the compulsion inherent in custody. Thus, when a person in custody does not know his questioner is a government agent, no interrogation takes place. In *Illinois v. Perkins,*[5] the police placed an undercover agent in the cell of the defendant, who was in custody on a charge of aggravated battery. In response to questions by the agent, the defendant made incriminating statements about a murder unrelated to the battery charge. The Court held, 8–1, that admission of these statements did not violate *Miranda* because they were not made in the type of "police-dominated atmosphere" that concerned the *Miranda* majority.[6]

---

3. State v. Mauro, 149 Ariz. 24, 716 P.2d 393 (1986).

4. See *Berkemer v. McCarty,* 468 U.S. 420, 104 S.Ct. 3138 (1984), discussed in § 16.03(a).

5. 496 U.S. 292, 110 S.Ct. 2394 (1990).

6. Nor was the Sixth Amendment violated, since the defendant had not yet been charged with the murder. See § 16.04(a). However, in a concurring opinion in *Perkins,* Justice Brennan argued that police deception of this sort might violate the Due Process Clause.

The Court has also held that, even when the suspect is subjected to custodial questioning by someone he knows to be an agent, "interrogation" has not occurred if the questions asked are part of a legitimate police procedure, such as booking or field tests, that is "not intended to elicit information for investigatory purposes." In *Pennsylvania v. Muniz,*[7] the defendant, arrested for drunk driving and taken to the stationhouse, was asked seven questions regarding his name, address, height, weight, eye color, date of birth and current age. In addition, he was given instructions as to how to perform various sobriety tests and a breathalyzer test, and then asked whether he understood these instructions. A plurality of four members of the Court joined Justice Brennan's opinion holding that the seven identifying questions came within a "routine booking question" exception to *Miranda,* thus permitting, despite the absence of warnings, use of the defendant's responses (some of which indicated he was confused and incoherent).[8] Eight members of the Court also agreed that statements made by the defendant during the sobriety and breathalyzer tests were not prompted by "interrogation;" the police statements prior to and during these tests either were "not likely to be perceived as calling for any verbal responses" or were "focused inquiries . . . necessarily 'attendant to' the [legitimate] police procedure. . . ."

In dissent, Justice Marshall argued that, without warnings, both the booking questions and the test communications violated *Innis;* given their belief that the defendant was intoxicated, the police should have known that incriminating responses were likely to be elicited. Although technically correct, Marshall's interpretation of *Innis* neglects the spirit of that case, which attempted to define when interrogation adds to the coercion already present in any custodial situation.

When a person *voluntarily* walks into a stationhouse and confesses, he is not only not subjected to interrogation but is not in custody.[9] However, if, after this "spontaneous" confession, he is asked questions that go beyond seeking repetition of his original statements, it would seem he is being subjected to custodial interrogation, since he is not likely to feel free to leave at that point (reasonably so, in light of the probable police reaction to his incriminating declarations). However, some courts have held that further questioning under these circumstances does not comprise

---

7. 496 U.S. 582, 110 S.Ct. 2638 (1990).

8. Four other members of the Court contended that the defendant's answers to the questions were not testimonial in any event, see § 15.04, thus giving clear support to the rule that warnings do not have to precede routine booking questions.

9. Cf. *California v. Beheler,* 463 U.S. 1121, 103 S.Ct. 3517 (1983), discussed in § 16.03(a)(3).

interrogation, on the ground that the police are merely seeking clarification of a volunteered statement.[10]

(c) The Warnings. When the accused is in custody and the police wish to "interrogate" him, *Miranda* requires that the warnings be given. The thrust of the opinion is that the warnings should *always* be given, regardless of context. Thus, *Miranda* specifically held that *all* suspects are to be informed of their rights, with no presumption of any prior awareness of those rights. And, in a footnote, the Court recognized that while the warning concerning the right to appointed counsel is technically unnecessary when the person is known to have an attorney or ample funds to retain one, "giving a warning is too simple and the rights involved too important to engage in *ex post facto* inquiries into financial ability when there is any doubt at all on that score." In short, the Court in *Miranda* seemed determined to fashion an easily applied rule that would cover all custodial interrogation situations.

However, there are at least two caveats to this general rule that the full warnings must be given to every suspect in custody. First, as *Miranda* itself recognized, Fifth Amendment protection during interrogation can be implemented either by the warnings *or* "their fully effective equivalent." Thus, for instance, in the Tenth Circuit, the test is whether the words used by police give a clear understandable warning of all the rights, taking into account the characteristics of the person to whom they are given.[11] Second, there may be some emergency situations where exigency permits abandoning the warnings requirement. The post-*Miranda* Court has addressed both of these issues, in the process significantly detracting from the rule-oriented thrust of the original *Miranda* doctrine.

(1) De minimis variations. In *California v. Prysock,*[12] the Supreme Court emphasized that "Miranda itself indicates that no talismanic incantation was required to satisfy its strictures." In *Prysock*, this notion was interpreted to mean that failure to inform an indigent defendant that he has a right to an appointed lawyer prior to, as well as during, interrogation is not violative of *Miranda*. In *Prysock*, the defendant, a juvenile, was told the following: "You have the right to talk to a lawyer before you are questioned, have him present with you while you are being questioned, and all during the questioning." Shortly thereafter, the defendant was also told he had the right to a *court-appointed* lawyer if he could not afford one, but was not told when such an attorney could be

10. *Bailey v. State,* 153 Ga.App. 178, 264 S.E.2d 710 (1980).

11. See *Coyote v. United States,* 380 F.2d 305 (10th Cir.1967), cert. denied 389 U.S. 992, 88 S.Ct. 489 (1967).

12. 453 U.S. 355, 101 S.Ct. 2806 (1981).

appointed. As Justice Stevens noted in his dissent, the California Court of Appeals found that this warning was constitutionally inadequate because "the minor was not given the crucial information that the services of the free attorney were available *prior* to the impending questioning." The Supreme Court's per curiam decision concluded, however, that the warnings given in *Prysock* were a "fully effective equivalent" to the *Miranda* litany. It intimated that had police improperly associated the right to an appointed attorney solely with some future time in court, the result would have been different.

However, in *Duckworth v. Eagan*,[13] where it was confronted with such a case, it found that this variation in the warnings was also de minimis. In *Eagan*, the following warnings were given to defendant shortly after his arrest:

> Before we ask you any questions, you must understand your rights. You have the right to remain silent. Anything you say can be used against you in court. You have a right to talk to a lawyer for advice before we ask you any questions, and to have him with you during questioning. You have this right to the advice and presence of a lawyer even if you cannot afford to hire one. We have no way of giving you a lawyer, but one will be appointed for you, if you wish, if and when you go to court. If you wish to answer questions now without a lawyer present, you have the right to stop answering questions at any time. You also have the right to stop answering at any time until you've talked to a lawyer.

Although this language suggests that a person who cannot afford an attorney is entitled to one only "if and when [the person] goes to court," the Court held, 5–4, that it "touched all the bases required by *Miranda*." Chief Justice Rehnquist, writing for the Court, noted that, under Indiana procedure, a person who asserts his right to an attorney cannot be questioned until one is appointed for him at the initial appearance in front of a judicial officer. Thus, the "if and when" language was accurate and the warnings, "in their totality", satisfied *Miranda*.

In dissent, Justice Marshall faulted the majority for its assumption that "frightened suspects unlettered in the law" will understand the warnings given in *Eagan* to mean that if they cannot afford an attorney they may ask for one and avoid questioning until one is appointed at the initial appearance. Moreover, as Marshall pointed out, even if a defendant does correctly understand the warnings, he is not told when the court appearance will take place. "The threat of an indefinite deferral of interrogation, in a system like Indiana's, thus constitutes an

---

13. 492 U.S. 195, 109 S.Ct. 2875 (1989).

effective means by which the police can pressure a suspect to speak without the presence of counsel." Finally, Marshall emphasized that the confusion produced by the warnings could easily be eradicated merely by eliminating the sentence with the "if and when" language in it.

This latter point is perhaps the strongest. Any possibly misleading statement ought to be excised from the warnings, because it is so easy to do so. Thus, for instance, lower court holdings permitting the second warning to read that anything said might be used "for or against you" reach the wrong result.[14] This statement's distorting implication that the police want to help the suspect, combined with the ease with which the implication can be removed, should lead to the opposite finding.

(2) Collateral information. A second issue associated with the warnings requirement is whether any information other than that contained in the original *Miranda* litany must be communicated to the defendant in order to ensure a valid waiver. For instance, it has been argued that defendants should be told that their silence cannot be used against them at trial; otherwise, they are less likely to see any benefit to remaining silent.[15] Similarly, defendants have contended that they are entitled to be told the crime which has triggered the investigation.[16]

In *Colorado v. Spring,*[17] however, the Supreme Court seemed to adopt the position that the Fifth Amendment does not require that any collateral information be communicated to the defendant. In *Spring,* the defendant was arrested and questioned on charges of transporting stolen firearms, and then was questioned about a homicide as well. Although admitting that he had been given and understood the *Miranda* warnings, he argued that statements made in response to the homicide-related questions were inadmissible because he was not informed he would be interrogated about the murder. Justice Marshall's dissent in *Spring* supported this stance, contending that "[a]dditional questioning about entirely separate and more serious suspicions of criminal activity can take unfair advantage of the suspect's psychological state, as the unexpected questions cause the compulsive pressures [that the warnings are supposed to dissipate] suddenly to reappear"; moreover, had Spring known the homicide was to be the subject of the interrogation, he might have insisted on consulting with an attorney at the outset.

14. *State v. Melvin,* 65 N.J. 1, 319 A.2d 450 (1974).

15. Elsen & Rossett, "Protections for the Suspect Under Miranda v. Arizona," 67 Col.L.Rev. 645, 654 (1967).

16. See, e.g., *People v. Prude,* 66 Ill. 2d 470, 6 Ill.Dec. 689, 363 N.E.2d 371 (1977), cert. denied 434 U.S. 930, 98 S.Ct. 418 (1977).

17. 479 U.S. 564, 107 S.Ct. 851 (1987).

But the majority found that "a suspect's awareness of all the possible subjects of questioning in advance of interrogation is not relevant to determining whether the suspect voluntarily, knowingly, and intelligently waived his Fifth Amendment privilege." So long as the defendant understands "the basic privilege guaranteed by the Fifth Amendment" and "the consequences of speaking freely to law enforcement officials", as was true in this case, *Miranda* is not violated. While the Court did not explicitly state that the *Miranda* rights are the *only* subjects about which a defendant must be informed prior to interrogation, this language indicates it will be hostile to suggestions that other types of collateral information be included in the pre-interrogation litany.

(3) The "public safety" exception. By far the most significant exception to the general rule that *Miranda* warnings must precede custodial interrogations was created by the Court's decision in *New York v. Quarles.*[18] There the Court held that the warnings need not be given at all if the prosecution can show that warning a suspect could have endangered the public. The "public safety exception" to *Miranda* not only substantially erodes the prophylactic nature of the *Miranda* doctrine but for the first time authorizes the use of clearly coerced statements in the prosecution's case-in-chief.

Quarles aptly illustrates both points. Based on information that a man with a gun had just entered a supermarket, Officer Kraft, assisted by three other officers, entered the store, spotted the defendant, and with gun drawn ordered him to stop and put his hands over his head. After frisking the defendant, and discovering an empty shoulder holster, Kraft handcuffed the defendant and asked him where the gun was. The defendant responded "the gun is over there" while nodding in the direction of some empty cartons, from which Kraft retrieved a loaded revolver. At that point, Kraft formally placed the defendant under arrest and read him his *Miranda* rights. In response to further questioning, the defendant admitted to owning the gun. The trial court and the lower appellate courts excluded the gun on the ground it was obtained in violation of *Miranda* and excluded all of the defendant's statements about the gun on the ground that they were "fruit" of the illegal interrogation.

Justice Rehnquist, in an opinion joined by four other Justices, admitted that the defendant had been in custody at the time Officer Kraft asked him about the location of the gun. But he held that the fear of coerced admissions which led to *Miranda* no longer justified reliance on a rigid rule; rather this concern must be balanced against the needs of the public. He then concluded:

18. 467 U.S. 649, 104 S.Ct. 2626 (1984).

[T]he need for answers to questions in a situation posing a threat to the public safety outweighs the need for the prophylactic rule protecting the Fifth Amendment's privilege against self-incrimination. We decline to place officers such as Officer Kraft in the untenable position of having to consider, often in a matter of seconds, whether it best serves society for them to ask the necessary questions without the Miranda warnings and render whatever probative evidence they uncover inadmissible, or for them to give the warnings in order to preserve the admissibility of evidence they might uncover but possibly damage or destroy their ability to obtain that evidence and neutralize the volatile situation confronting them.

Justice Rehnquist also made it clear that the public safety exception is a purely objective standard. Given the "kaleidoscopic situation" confronting officers when public safety is threatened, "where spontaneity rather than adherence to a police manual is necessarily the order of the day, the application of the [public safety] exception . . . should not be made to depend on *post hoc* findings at a suppression hearing concerning the subjective motivation of the arresting officer." To the majority, the events in the supermarket clearly presented such an objectively threatening situation. So long as the whereabouts of the gun remained unknown, "it obviously posed more than one danger to the public safety: an accomplice might make use of it, a customer or employee might later come upon it." The existence of these dangers outweighed, in the majority's eyes, the fact that the defendant had been handcuffed and confronted by four officers with guns drawn when he was asked, without being told he could remain silent, about the gun.

Quarles is a questionable decision at best, both as to the rule it announced and as to the manner in which it applied the rule. With respect to the latter issue, Justice Marshall pointed out, in dissent, that since the defendant's apprehension took place after the store was closed and there was no known accomplice, the threat to the public in *Quarles* was miniscule. In fact, the New York Court of Appeals had specifically found "no evidence in the record before us that there were exigent circumstances posing a risk to public safety . . . ." Thus, even assuming the validity of a public safety exception to *Miranda, Quarles* seems an inappropriate case in which to apply it.

The divergence between the New York court's conclusion concerning the facts and the majority's characterization of them also illustrates the danger of departing from the prophylactic rule in the first place. Police and courts will no longer have the relative clarity offered by *Miranda* but will disagree, as they did in *Quarles,* over when the public is threatened. The majority recognized this possibility but argued that, at least with respect to police, the public safety exception "will not be difficult . . . to apply" because "officers can and will distinguish almost instinctively between questions to secure their own safety or the safety of the public and questions designed solely to elicit testimonial evidence from a suspect." Justice O'Connor, who agreed with the result reached by the Court [19] but dissented with respect to the adoption of the public safety exception, seemed more realistic about the consequences of *Quarles:* "The end result will be a finespun new doctrine on public safety exigencies incident to custodial interrogation, complete with the hair-splitting distinctions that currently plague our Fourth Amendment jurisprudence." [20] As an illustration of Justice O'Connor's point, imagine that the police in *Innis* had *directly* interrogated the accused about the location of the robbery weapon. Presumably, prior to *Quarles,* the evidence thus obtained would have been excluded because no warning preceded the questioning. But now courts must decide: given the apparent danger the gun represented to neighborhood children, does the public safety exception to the warnings requirement apply? [21]

More importantly, as this example illustrates, *Quarles* totally disregards the underlying premise of *Miranda.* Justice O'Connor once again put the matter succinctly when she stated:

> *Miranda* has never been read to prohibit the police from asking questions to secure the public safety. Rather, the critical question *Miranda* addresses is who shall bear the cost of securing the public safety when such questions are asked and answered: the defendant or the State. *Miranda,* for better or worse, found the resolution of that question implicit in the prohibition against compulsory self-incrimination and placed the burden on the State.

Quarles, on the other hand, ignores the issue of coercion in favor of ensuring that evidence obtained under exigent circumstances is not excluded but rather used to convict the guilty.

(d) Waiver: Generally. *Miranda* stated that if a person talks after the warnings, "a heavy burden rests on the government to demonstrate that the defendant knowingly and intelligently waived his privilege against self-incrimination and his right to

19. O'Connor felt that the gun should have been admitted because it was "nontestimonial" in nature and thus, under *Schmerber v. California,* 384 U.S. 757, 86 S.Ct. 1826 (1966), discussed in § 15.04, not covered by the Fifth Amendment.

20. See generally, Note, "The Public Safety Exception to *Miranda*: Careen-

ing Through the Lower Courts," 40 Fla. L.Rev. 989 (1988).

21. The Court did indicate that its decision in *Orozco v. Texas,* 394 U.S. 324, 89 S.Ct. 1095 (1969), involving questioning at home about a gun used in a murder several hours earlier, was not affected by its holding.

retained or appointed counsel." Moreover, "a valid waiver will not be presumed simply from the silence of the accused after warnings are given or simply from the fact that a confession was in fact eventually obtained:"

> Whatever the testimony of the authorities as to waiver of rights by an accused, the fact of lengthy interrogation or incommunicado incarceration before a statement is made is strong evidence that the accused did not validly waive his rights. In these circumstances the fact that the individual eventually made a statement is consistent with the conclusion that the compelling influence of the interrogation finally forced him to do so. It is inconsistent with any notion of a voluntary relinquishment of the privilege. Moreover, any evidence that the accused was threatened, tricked, or cajoled into a waiver will, of course, show that the defendant did not voluntarily waive his privilege.

Since *Miranda,* this language has been interpreted narrowly. Although the Court has been careful to insist that the government bears the burden on the waiver issue,[22] it has also held, in *Colorado v. Connelly,*[23] that the government need only prove the validity of a waiver by a "preponderance of the evidence." [24] This is obviously not a particularly "heavy" burden. Further, the Court's cases suggest that, ultimately, waiver analysis after the warnings have been given will be very similar to the voluntariness analysis found in the Court's due process cases.[25] Indeed, in *Fare v. Michael C.,*[26] the Court explicitly held that the "totality of the circumstances approach is adequate to determine whether there has been a waiver" under *Miranda.* This development has resulted in substantial modification of *Miranda's* wide-ranging dictum.

(1) Express v. implied waiver. Most significant in this regard is the post-*Miranda* Court's rejection of a requirement that the government prove that the defendant expressly waived his rights; rather, circumstantial proof of waiver is sufficient. *Miranda's* statement that "a valid waiver will not be presumed" from the fact that a confession was eventually obtained, together with the holding in *Westover v. United States* (one of the cases joined in *Miranda*) that an "articulated waiver" is required before a confession will be considered admissible, suggested that the *Miranda* majority strongly favored an express written or oral waiver. But in *North Carolina v. Butler,*[27] the Court held otherwise. Justice

---

22. *Tague v. Louisiana,* 444 U.S. 469, 100 S.Ct. 652 (1980) (overturning state court decision placing burden on defendant to show lack of capacity).

23. 479 U.S. 157, 107 S.Ct. 515 (1986).

24. See § 16.06(b).

25. See generally, § 16.02(a).

26. 442 U.S. 707, 99 S.Ct. 2560 (1979).

27. 441 U.S. 369, 99 S.Ct. 1755 (1979).

Stewart, a dissenter in *Miranda,* reasoned for the Court that "[t]he question is not one of form, but rather whether the defendant in fact knowingly and voluntarily waived his rights delineated in the *Miranda* case." A "course of conduct *indicating* waiver" (emphasis added) is sufficient grounds for such a finding. As the three dissenters noted, this decision undermines the prophylactic effect of *Miranda* and runs counter to its premise that, in the "inherently coercive" atmosphere of custodial interrogation, ambiguity should be resolved in favor of the defendant.

The *Butler* majority did not resolve whether the waiver in that case was valid, but merely overruled the state court's decision that an express waiver was required. Butler had been read his rights and also read an "Advice of Rights" form, which he said he understood. However, he also refused to sign the form and made no statement about whether he wanted to waive the right to remain silent or the right to counsel. He then indicated he was willing to talk. The difficulty of determining, after the event, whether this conduct "indicates" a voluntary and intelligent waiver, or instead a misunderstanding on the part of the defendant as to the importance of his signature, illustrates the usefulness of an express waiver requirement. Under it, the burden would be on the government to ascertain what the defendant's ambiguous actions meant and provide proof of a clear decision from Butler with respect to his rights. Under the Court's test, on the other hand, the government's burden is to prove the more amorphous proposition that there was a voluntary waiver in light of "the particular facts and circumstances surrounding [the] case, including the background, experience, and conduct of the accused."

(2) The knowing and intelligent requirement. While *Miranda* insisted that all waivers be "knowing and intelligent," the Court has since indicated that full understanding of the warnings is not necessary for a waiver to be valid. In *Connecticut v. Barrett,*[28] the defendant explicitly refused to give police any written statements before he talked to counsel but just as unequivocally stated that he had "no problem" *talking* with them. The most reasonable interpretation of Barrett's post-warning behavior was that he erroneously believed that only written statements could be used against him.[29] The Court itself admitted Barrett's actions might have been "illogical." But, emphasizing that Barrett had said he understood the warnings, it held that his oral statements were admissible. The result in *Barrett* suggests that, had it reached the

28. 479 U.S. 523, 107 S.Ct. 828 (1987).

29. According to one study, 45 percent of defendants given the warnings mistakenly believed that oral statements could not be used against them. Leiken, "Police Interrogation in Colorado: The Implementation of Miranda," 47 Denver L.J. 1, 15–16, 33 (1970).

issue, the Court would have found in the government's favor in *Butler* (where the defendant also said he understood the warnings), despite the apparent confusion of the defendant in that case.[30]

Sometimes the defendant alleges confusion about the duration of a waiver. In *Wyrick v. Fields,*[31] the defendant, who had retained counsel, agreed in his counsel's absence to take a polygraph examination. Before doing so, he signed a consent form, including a waiver of his right to counsel, and was read a statement informing him of his right to refuse to answer questions at any time. After taking the examination, the defendant answered questions from the examiner about his reactions toward the examination, which eventually led to damaging disclosures. To Fields' contention that neither he nor his attorney believed the procedure would involve post-test questioning, the Court responded, "it would have been unreasonable for Fields and his attorney to assume that Fields would not be informed of the polygraph readings and asked to explain any unfavorable result." The Court also concluded that "the questions put to Fields after the examination would not have caused him to forget the rights of which he had been advised and which he had understood moments before." Thus, despite the absence of proof of actual awareness that the waiver applied to post-test questioning, the Court found the waiver valid.

The related issue of whether, under *Miranda,* the police may use "trickery" to procure a statement has also arisen. In *Colorado v. Spring,*[32] the Court declined to apply this term to a police failure to inform the defendant that he would be questioned about a crime other than the one for which he was arrested. It further suggested that trickery does not occur unless police engage in "affirmative representation," and even as to this situation it was coy about how the matter should be decided.[33] This position is reminiscent of that taken in the due process cases, where trickery, by itself, does not lead to a finding that a confession was involuntary.[34] It is in marked contrast to the language in *Miranda* quoted above, in which the Court stated that "any evidence that the accused was . . . tricked . . . into a waiver will, of course, show that the defendant did not voluntarily waive his privilege."

30. Compare *McDonald v. Lucas,* 677 F.2d 518 (5th Cir.1982) (merely talking to police after refusing to sign a waiver is not, by itself, evidence of a course of conduct implying waiver).

31. 459 U.S. 42, 103 S.Ct. 394 (1982).

32. 479 U.S. 564, 107 S.Ct. 851 (1987).

33. The Court stated that it need "not reach the question whether a waiver of *Miranda* rights would be valid in such a circumstance."

34. See *Frazier v. Cupp,* 394 U.S. 731, 89 S.Ct. 1420 (1969), discussed in § 16.02(a)(1).

"Trickery" was also at issue in *Moran v. Burbine,*[35] where the police assured the defendant's attorney that the defendant would not be questioned until the next day, but then proceeded to question the defendant about a murder, without telling him the attorney had called. The Court held, 6–3, that, so long as he was given the warnings, the fact that the police kept the defendant ignorant of his attorney's effort to reach him was irrelevant to whether the confessions were coerced. As Justice O'Connor pointed out for the Court, "the same defendant, armed with the same information and confronted with precisely the same police conduct, would have knowingly waived his *Miranda* rights had a lawyer not telephoned the police station to inquire about his status."[36] The purpose of *Miranda,* O'Connor emphasized, was to dissipate compulsion directed toward the defendant, not monitor how police treat the defendant's attorney.[37] The same term as *Burbine,* the Court vacated the judgments of two state courts excluding confessions made after counsel present at the stationhouse had been refused permission to see their clients.[38]

To help in understanding, if not justifying, the Court's decisions in this area, it may be useful to make a distinction between trickery as to the contents of the warnings and trickery as to other aspects of the case. If the police lead the defendant to believe he has no right to remain silent or right to counsel, despite the warnings, then he is faced with the "trilemma" against which the Fifth Amendment is meant to protect; as far as he is aware, he must either confess, commit perjury, or face some penalty for remaining silent. On the other hand, if instead of leading the defendant to believe there is no point in remaining silent, the police fail to correct a misimpression about how to assert the right (as in *Butler* or *Barrett*), do not make clear how they plan to proceed (as in *Fields* or *Spring*), or fail to inform him of all possible facts relevant to his decision (as in *Burbine*), the trilemma is not resurrected. Any confession which may occur in the latter situations could be said to be "voluntary," even if not completely "knowing."[39]

35. 475 U.S. 412, 106 S.Ct. 1135 (1986).

36. The Court also found no violation of the Sixth Amendment right to counsel, since the interrogation took place before arraignment. See § 16.04(a).

37. As to a possible due process claim against the police action, the Court held this too would fail, because the conduct of the police did not "shock the conscience."

38. *Maryland v. Lodowski,* 475 U.S. 1078, 106 S.Ct. 1452 (1986); *Florida v. Haliburton,* 475 U.S. 1078, 106 S.Ct. 1452 (1986). Although these cases are similar in some respects to *Escobedo v. Illinois,* 378 U.S. 478, 84 S.Ct. 1758 (1964), discussed in § 16.02(c), Escobedo knew his attorney was trying to reach him and asked to see his attorney.

39. Stuntz, "Self–Incrimination and Excuse," 88 Colum.L.Rev. 1227 (1988).

(3) The voluntariness requirement. As the above discussion makes clear, separating the voluntariness component of waiver analysis from the knowing and intelligent component is somewhat artificial. The only point to be made here is that, just as physical force, threats, promises and prolonged, incommunicado questioning are prohibited under due process analysis, they are impermissible under *Miranda* after the warnings are given.[40] By the same token, as with due process analysis, if the police do not "cause" the confession through some sort of conduct, proof that it was not the product of "free and deliberate choice" because of the defendant's mental condition will not suffice to show an "involuntary" waiver.[41]

An example of the Court's post-*Miranda* treatment of the voluntariness idea is found in *Fare v. Michael C.*,[42] where the Court held, 5–4, that a post-warning confession by a 16½ year-old was not involuntary. Justice Powell, in dissent, emphasized the Court's long tradition of solicitude toward juveniles,[43] and noted that the juvenile here "was immature, emotional, and uneducated, and therefore was likely to be vulnerable to the skillful, two-on-one, repetitive style of interrogation to which he was subjected." The record also showed that the defendant had cried during the interrogation and had indicated on several occasions that he could not or would not answer the police's questions. But the majority concluded that the defendant understood his rights, especially in light of his extensive previous involvement with the criminal justice system, and that the officers did not prolong the questioning nor "intimidate or threaten respondent in any way."

(e) Waiver: After Assertion of Rights. When the defendant's reaction to the warnings is not an express or implied waiver of his rights, but rather an assertion of them, the Supreme Court has developed special waiver rules, albeit different from those apparently intended by the *Miranda* Court. According to *Miranda:*

> If the individual indicates in any manner, at any time prior to or during questioning, that he wishes to remain silent, the interrogation must cease. . . . Without the right to cut off questioning, the setting of in-custody interrogation operates on the individual to overcome free choice in producing a statement after the privilege has been once invoked. If the individual states that he wants an attorney, the interrogation must cease until an attorney is present. . . . If the individual cannot obtain an attorney and he indicates that he wants

40. See, Note, 10 Rutgers Camden L.J. 109 (1978).

41. *Colorado v. Connelly,* 479 U.S. 157, 107 S.Ct. 515 (1986), discussed in § 16.02(a)(2).

42. 442 U.S. 707, 99 S.Ct. 2560 (1979).

43. See *Haley v. Ohio,* 332 U.S. 596, 68 S.Ct. 302 (1948), discussed in 16.02(a) (2).

one before speaking to police, they must respect his decision to remain silent. . . . If authorities conclude that they will not provide counsel during a reasonable period of time in which investigation in the field is carried out, they may refrain from doing so without violating the person's Fifth Amendment privilege so long as they do not question him during that time.

This passage strongly suggests that if a suspect states either that he wishes to remain silent or that he wants an attorney, questioning must cease and may not resume. While the post-*Miranda* Court has been unwilling to give this language its fullest reach, it has indicated that, as discussed further below, a suspect who invokes his right to counsel is entitled to special solicitude. When the suspect merely states he wishes to remain silent, the appropriate waiver analysis is not as clear, but is also likely to make police efforts to resume questioning more difficult.

The leading case on the latter issue is *Michigan v. Mosley*,[44] in which the Court permitted questioning after an assertion of the right to remain silent, but only under special circumstances. There, two hours after the defendant stated he did not want to talk, a different officer confronted him in a different room about another crime and gave him a second set of warnings, after which he gave incriminating statements. The Court held, 7–2, that, on these facts, the "right to cut off questioning" referred to in the above passage from *Miranda* had been "scrupulously honored." The majority was impressed with the facts that "the police here immediately ceased the interrogation, resumed questioning only after the passage of a significant period of time and the provision of a fresh set of warnings, and restricted the second interrogation to a crime that had not been a subject of the earlier interrogation."

The key issue after *Mosley* was whether later questioning on the *same* crime is permissible after an assertion of the right to remain silent. Justice White, concurring in the decision, felt that, at the least, new information further implicating the defendant for that crime could be communicated to him. But this type of recurring confrontation might tend to "wear down" the defendant in the manner feared by the *Miranda* majority, which expressly noted that references to the strength of the evidence against the defendant should be seen as "interrogation."[45] At a minimum, the police should refrain from such confrontation unless the defendant initiates the contact with the police.

This, at least, was the compromise the Court adopted in *Edwards v. Arizona*,[46] which dealt with the allowable limits of

44. 423 U.S. 96, 96 S.Ct. 321 (1975).
45. See § 16.03(b)(1).
46. 451 U.S. 477, 101 S.Ct. 1880 (1981).

interrogation after an assertion of the right to *counsel*. In *Edwards*, the Court held that an accused, "having expressed his desire to deal with the police only through counsel, is not subject to further interrogation by the authorities until counsel has been made available to him, unless the accused himself initiates further communication, exchanges or conversation with the police." The defendant in *Edwards* told the officer who initially interrogated him that he wanted to see an attorney "before making a deal." The next day, two detectives arrived at Edwards' cell to question him further. When the detention officer told Edwards about the detectives, he refused to talk to them. The officer told Edwards he "had" to talk to them, and took him to meet the detectives. After receiving *Miranda* warnings from the detectives, Edwards implicated himself on robbery and murder charges. The Court held that, on these facts, Edwards had not validly waived his Fifth Amendment right to counsel; the police interrogation had not taken place "at his suggestion or request."

Edwards raises three issues: (1) when has the defendant asserted his right to counsel, thus triggering *Edwards?;* (2) what protection does *Edwards* afford after such an assertion and prior to any initiation of contact by the defendant?; and (3) what is initiation and how does it affect subsequent waiver analysis? Although not yet clear, it may be that, in most respects, the Court's treatment of these issues will be replicated in situations where the suspect merely asserts his right to remain silent.

(1) Asserting the right. The Court has established that *Edwards* is not triggered unless: (a) the *suspect;* (b) requests *counsel;* (c) during *interrogation.* Relevant to the first point is *Moran v. Burbine.*[47] There, the police assured the suspect's attorney they would not question her client until the next morning. They then proceeded to question the suspect without telling him about his attorney's call. The Court held that *Edwards* was not implicated because the suspect had been given the warnings and voluntarily signed a form indicating he did not want to talk to an attorney. *Burbine* indicates that a third party cannot invoke the right to counsel.

Relevant to the issue of who must be requested to trigger *Edwards* is *Fare v. Michael C.*[48] There, the suspect, a juvenile, did ask for assistance after receiving the warnings, but from his probation officer. The Court found, 5–4, that this request was not an invocation of the right to counsel. The majority stated that *Miranda's* right to counsel is "based on the unique role the lawyer plays in the adversary system of criminal justice in this country." A probation officer is not legally trained nor trained in advocacy,

---

47. 475 U.S. 412, 106 S.Ct. 1135 (1986).   **48.** 442 U.S. 707, 99 S.Ct. 2560 (1979).

nor is he obligated to keep confidences as is an attorney; moreover, he is an employee of the state who, at the least, would be subject to conflicting pressure at a police-conducted interrogation. The majority rejected the dissenters' contention that a request for a probation officer "constitutes both an attempt to obtain advice and a general invocation of the right to silence." Although *Fare* preceeded *Edwards,* it is obviously relevant to the application of that case. Whether the Court would reach the same result when a parent or minister is requested remains open.

In *McNeil v. Wisconsin,*[49] the Court further constricted the *Edwards* rule by holding that it is not triggered unless the defendant requests an attorney during *interrogation.* In *McNeil,* the defendant appeared with an attorney at a bail hearing on robbery charges. Later the police approached him regarding a murder. After receiving *Miranda* warnings, the defendant agreed to talk about the murder and made statements linking him to it. He subsequently sought to exclude these statements on the ground that his request for an attorney at the hearing triggered the *Edwards* rule, thus barring the police's unsolicited interrogation about the murder. But the Supreme Court held, 6–3, that *Edwards* "requires, at a minimum, some statement that can reasonably be construed to be expression of a desire for the assistance of an attorney *in dealing with custodial interrogation by the police* (emphasis in original)," and that requesting the assistance of an attorney at a bail hearing did not constitute such an expression.[50] According to the Court, *Edwards* was designed to prevent badgering of defendants who have expressed an unwillingness to talk to police in the absence of counsel, a situation not present on the facts of *McNeil.*

A final issue with respect to invoking the right to counsel is how clear the invocation must be. In *Smith v. Illinois,*[51] the Court divided 6–3 over whether *Edwards* had been invoked. After the defendant in *Smith* was given the first two *Miranda* warnings and had indicated that he understood them, the following colloquy took place:

Q. You have a right to consult with a lawyer and to have a lawyer present with you when you're being questioned. Do you understand that?

A. Uh, yeah. I'd like to do that.

49. 501 U.S. ——, 111 S.Ct. 2204 (1991).

50. Requesting a hearing attorney does trigger the *Sixth Amendment* right to counsel during subsequent confrontations with the police, but only with respect to those crimes for which the defendant has been formally charged. See *Michigan v. Jackson* and *Moran v. Burbine,* discussed in § 16.04(a).

51. 469 U.S. 91, 105 S.Ct. 490 (1984).

Q. Okay. . . . If you want a lawyer and you're unable to pay for one a lawyer will be appointed to represent you free of cost, do you understand that?

A. Okay.

Q. Do you wish to talk to me at this time without a lawyer being present?

A. Yeah and no, uh, I don't know what's what, really.

Q. Well. You either have to talk to me this time without a lawyer being present and if you do agree to talk with me without a lawyer being present you can stop at any time you want to.

A. All right. I'll talk to you.

The defendant subsequently made incriminating statements which were used to convict him.

The Illinois Supreme Court held that Smith's statements after his statement, "I'd like to do that" were ambiguous with respect to his desire for an attorney and that therefore *Edwards* was not invoked and the defendant's confession could be admitted. The United States Supreme Court reversed, finding that "post-request responses to further interrogation may not be used to cast retrospective doubt on the clarity of the initial request itself."

This conclusion makes sense in the abstract; it merely repeats *Edwards'* holding that once there is an actual request for counsel, the police may not question the defendant unless he has initiated contact. But using it to find that there was a request for counsel on the facts of *Smith* is more problematic. As Justice Rehnquist pointed out in dissent, "[c]ommon sense suggests that the police should both complete reading [a suspect] his rights and then ask him to state clearly what he elects to do, even if he indicated a tentative desire while he was being informed of his rights." Completing the warnings in this way is not "interrogation" as defined by *Miranda* or later decisions, but merely ascertaining what the suspect wishes to do. Of course, the government should bear a "heavy" burden of showing any waiver at the end of the warnings was knowing and voluntary.

(2) Protection afforded by assertion of rights. If the suspect does request an attorney during interrogation, *Edwards* directs the police to refrain from questioning the suspect until an attorney arrives or the defendant initiates contact. Contrary to the rule when the right to remain silent is asserted, this prohibition applies even if the questioning concerns a different offense than the one for which the defendant is originally detained. In *Arizona v. Roberson*,[52] the defendant was arrested for burglary and given the warnings, at which point he stated that he wanted a lawyer

---

52. 486 U.S. 675, 108 S.Ct. 2093 (1988).

"before answering any questions." Three days later, while still in custody and as yet without counsel, he was questioned by another officer about another burglary. Although he was given warnings before this second interrogation, the Court held that *Edwards* barred admission of the inculpatory statements he made at this point.

The state argued that *Roberson*'s request for counsel had been limited to provision of an attorney for the first burglary. To this the Court responded by noting that Roberson had refused to answer "any" questions; more generally, it held that "the presumption raised by a suspect's request for counsel—that he considers himself unable to deal with the pressures of custodial interrogation without legal assistance—does not disappear simply because the police have approached the suspect, still in custody, still without counsel, about a separate investigation." Thus, this case was different from *Mosley,* where the Court found that the defendant's assertion of the right to remain silent did not prohibit police from a second interrogation on a separate crime, because there the defendant had asserted *only* his right to remain silent, not signalled an inability to proceed without a lawyer's advice. The state also argued that when the police are pursuing truly independent investigations, the chance that the defendant will feel coerced by the second interrogation is more remote than on the *Edwards* facts. But the Court did not agree, "especially in a case such as this, in which a period of three days elapsed between the unsatisfied request for counsel and the interrogation about a second offense."

The Court has also made clear that, once an attorney is requested (and assuming no reinitiation of contact by the defendant), mere consultation with the attorney prior to questioning is insufficient under *Edwards;* according to *Minnick v. Mississippi,*[53] the attorney must be present during the questioning. In *Minnick,* the defendant, after answering some questions during interrogation, stopped the interview by stating, "Come back Monday when I have a lawyer." Counsel was then appointed and consulted with the defendant on three separate occasions. On Monday, the police returned and, without the attorney, the defendant made statements later used at trial. The Supreme Court, in an opinion by Justice Kennedy, held that the statements should have been excluded because interrogation took place in the absence of counsel. According to the Court, "[a] single consultation with an attorney does not remove the suspect from persistent attempts by officials to persuade him to waive his rights, or from the coercive pressures that accompany custody and that may increase as custo-

53. 498 U.S. ——, 111 S.Ct. 486 (1990).

410

dy is prolonged." The Court was unwilling to endorse a rule which would make the protection afforded by *Edwards* dependent upon the defendant resignalling his desire for an attorney after every consultation with one, especially since defining "consultation" might prove difficult.

(3) Initiation and waiver. Roberson and *Minnick* combined indicate that once an attorney's presence at interrogation is requested, *no* unsolicited questioning may take place in the absence of counsel, even about separate offenses and even if a new set of warnings are given. However, as described above, *Edwards* permits questioning to resume if the defendant initiates contact with the police after his request for an attorney. A plurality of the Court has indicated that it takes very little to "initiate" contact for purposes of *Edwards*. In *Oregon v. Bradshaw*,[54] the defendant was given the *Miranda* warnings while being questioned in a homicide case and again after being arrested on a related charge. After denying guilt on both charges, he asked for his attorney. While being transferred to jail, and in the absence of his attorney, he asked an officer, "[w]ell, what is going to happen to me now?" The officer advised him that they did not have to talk; the defendant said he understood. The officer then described the charge against the defendant. He also suggested that the defendant take a polygraph test, which he did, after again being given his *Miranda* rights. When the polygraph examiner told the defendant he did not believe the defendant's story, the defendant admitted his guilt. Justice Rehnquist, writing for the plurality of four justices, admitted the ambiguity of the defendant's initial question, but concluded that it "evinced a willingness and a desire for a generalized discussion about the investigation; it was not merely a necessary inquiry arising out of the incidents of the custodial relationship." He gave as examples of the latter type of communication requests for water or access to a telephone. Here, on the other hand, the question "could reasonably have been interpreted by the officer as relating generally to the investigation." The four dissenters seem much closer to the mark with their conclusion "that respondent's only 'desire' was to find out where the police were going to take him."

Both the plurality and the dissent in *Bradshaw* agreed that a finding that initiation has occurred does not end the analysis under *Edwards*.[55] It must still be decided whether, in the totality of the circumstances, including the fact of initiation, the suspect voluntarily and intelligently waived his rights. This question feeds back into the general waiver analysis discussed earlier. On

---

54. 462 U.S. 1039, 103 S.Ct. 2830 (1983).

55. Justice Powell, in concurrence, felt that separating the initiation and waiver issues would confuse the lower courts; as noted below, he voted with the plurality on the ground that a valid waiver occurred.

this issue, the plurality and the four dissenters once again disagreed. But Justice Powell joined the plurality in holding that Bradshaw's post-initiation actions constituted a valid waiver.

16.04 The Resurgence of the Sixth Amendment Approach

The holding in *Massiah v. United States* [56]—that police may not deliberately elicit information from an indicted defendant in the absence of counsel—lay dormant for over a decade. In analyzing the admissibility of confessions, the Supreme Court and the lower courts virtually ignored the Sixth Amendment perspective endorsed in that case, focusing instead on the application of *Miranda.* But then, in *Brewer v. Williams* [57] and subsequent cases, the Supreme Court reaffirmed the continuing significance of *Massiah,* and even seemed to expand its scope.

In *Williams,* the defendant was suspected of killing a 10 year old girl. Before the defendant was to be taken by police officers to another city, the defendant's lawyers advised him not to make any statements during the trip and extracted a promise from the police that they would not question the defendant during the journey. Nonetheless, during the trip, a detective who knew that Williams was a former mental patient and deeply religious suggested that the girl deserved a "Christian burial." Addressing the defendant as "Reverend," the detective mentioned the possibility that an upcoming snow storm would make it difficult to locate the girl's body unless the defendant assisted police in finding it soon. He then said: "I do not want you to answer me. I don't want to discuss it further. Just think about it as we're riding down the road." Some hours later the defendant made incriminating statements and directed police to the body.

The Court, in a 5–4 decision by Justice Stewart, reversed the defendant's subsequent conviction. The detective had "deliberately and designedly set out to elicit information from Williams just as surely as—and perhaps more effectively than—if he had formally interrogated him," yet had not told Williams of his right to have counsel present and "made no effort at all to ascertain whether Williams wished to relinquish that right." Thus, Williams had been denied his right to counsel and the state had failed to sustain its burden of showing that he had waived his constitutional protection.

In dissent, Justice White, joined by Justices Blackmun and Rehnquist, argued that Williams' revelations had been spontaneous and that, even if they had not been, there was no evidence of coercion by the police. The "Christian burial speech" had been "accompanied by a request that respondent not respond to it; and

56. 377 U.S. 201, 84 S.Ct. 1199 (1964), discussed in § 16.02(c).   **57.** 430 U.S. 387, 97 S.Ct. 1232 (1977).

it was delivered hours before respondent decided to make any statement. Respondent's waiver was thus knowing and intentional."

The most important aspect of *Williams* is the analytical basis of the decision. Although the same result could have been reached under *Miranda*, neither the majority or the dissent discussed the applicability of that case. Instead, the focus in *Williams* was entirely on the Sixth Amendment. While there were obvious differences among members of the Court as to whether "deliberate elicitation" had taken place and a valid waiver had occurred, only Chief Justice Burger, who wrote a separate dissenting opinion, appeared to question the necessity of the original *Massiah* ruling. And three years later, in *United States v. Henry,*[58] even he evidenced a willingness to apply *Massiah* to at least some situations. (In *Henry*, as discussed below, Burger wrote the majority opinion finding inadmissible under *Massiah* an indicted person's incriminating statements, made while in jail, that were encouraged by a cellmate in the government's employ.)

Several issues have arisen under the rejuvenated *Massiah* doctrine: (1) at what point in the criminal process is the Sixth Amendment right to counsel triggered?; (2) when has the government engaged in "deliberate elicitation;"? and (3) when is such elicitation permissible because the defendant has waived his Sixth Amendment right?

(a) The Initiation of Criminal Prosecution. *Massiah* is based on the Sixth Amendment's guarantee of counsel in "all criminal prosecutions." Because the case involved an indicted defendant, lower court decisions interpreting *Massiah* initially defined prosecution as beginning with an indictment.[59] However, eight years after *Massiah,* in *Kirby v. Illinois,*[60] the Supreme Court established that the Sixth Amendment is implicated whenever the "adverse positions of the government and defendant have solidified" so that "a defendant finds himself faced with the prosecutorial forces of organized society, and immersed in the intricacies of substantive and procedural criminal law." Quoting from *Kirby*, the Court in *Williams* held that the *Massiah* right is triggered by any event which indicates that the government has committed itself to prosecute, "whether by way of formal charge, preliminary hearing, indictment, information, or arraignment." In *Williams* itself, no indictment had been issued, but the defendant had been arraigned on an arrest warrant.

58. 447 U.S. 264, 100 S.Ct. 2183 (1980).

59. See *United States ex rel. Forella v. Follette,* 405 F.2d 680 (2d Cir.1969).

60. 406 U.S. 682, 92 S.Ct. 1877 (1972).

Before such time, however, *Massiah* is not applicable. Thus, the mere fact that the defendant has an attorney is not dispositive. In *Moran v. Burbine,*[61] the Court discounted "the fortuity of whether the suspect or his family happens to have retained counsel." Rather, the important question is whether "the government's role [has] shift[ed] from investigation to accusation." In *Burbine,* police interference with the attorney's attempts to see her client did not violate the Sixth Amendment because no charges had yet been brought. A similar result was reached in *Maine v. Moulton,*[62] where a surreptitious investigation of the defendant (obviously undertaken in the absence of counsel), revealed evidence of two crimes, only one of which had been formally charged at the time. The Court excluded evidence pertaining to the crime for which the defendant had been indicted, but admitted evidence concerning the crime for which no formal proceedings had begun. According to the majority, "to exclude evidence pertaining to charges as to which the Sixth Amendment right to counsel had not attached at the time the evidence was obtained, simply because other charges were pending at that time, would unnecessarily frustrate the public's interest in the investigation of criminal activities."[63]

It may seem somewhat artificial to use formal charging as the demarcation for the Sixth Amendment right. But that stage in the process may serve as the best proxy for determining when a suspect needs an attorney's "assistance" in a "criminal prosecution." Before that point, an attorney is useful primarily to combat police compulsion, a need that *Miranda* is designed to meet. It is after that point that the special qualifications of counsel are most likely to be called upon in confrontations with the government.

(b) Deliberate Elicitation. The phrase "deliberate elicitation," found in both *Massiah* and *Williams,* suggests that the Sixth Amendment is implicated by any government attempt, after formal charging, to get information from the defendant in the absence of counsel. In *Henry,* the Court reinforced this notion by referring to whether officers "intentionally create[d] a situation likely to induce Henry to make incriminating statements without the assistance of counsel." There, the incriminating evidence was obtained by one Nichols, an inmate at the jail in which Henry was confined. Government agents working on a robbery case had approached Nichols shortly after Henry was incarcerated, and told him to be alert to any statements Henry might make about the

61. 475 U.S. 412, 106 S.Ct. 1135 (1986).

62. 474 U.S. 159, 106 S.Ct. 477 (1985).

63. See also, *Hoffa v. United States,* 385 U.S. 293, 87 S.Ct. 408 (1966) (Sixth Amendment not violated where undercover work concerned charges unrelated to those on which defendant was tried); *McNeil v. Wisconsin,* 501 U.S. —, 111 S.Ct. 2204 (1991), discussed in § 16.03(e)(1).

robbery. However, they also cautioned Nichols not to initiate any conversation with Henry regarding the crime. Despite this last caveat, the Court found that the officers had "created a situation likely to induce" incriminating statements. It noted that Nichols had been a paid government informant for over a year, that the government agent who contacted Nichols had known he would be able to engage Henry in conversation, and that Nichols had incentive to encourage conversation because he knew he would be paid only if he produced useful information.

However, when the government merely "plants" an informant in the same cell as the defendant, deliberate elicitation does not occur, the Court concluded in *Kuhlmann v. Wilson.*[64] Whereas in *Henry* the informant had "stimulated" conversations with the defendant, in *Kuhlmann* the informant asked no questions concerning the pending charges and, in the words of the state court, "only listened" to the defendant's "spontaneous" and "unsolicited" statements, which had been triggered by a meeting with his brother. The dissent argued that "elicitation" had occurred, as the informant had tried to develop a relationship with the defendant, responded to his initial denial of guilt by saying his story "didn't sound too good," and, as in *Henry,* was paid for his efforts. In any event, *Kuhlmann* explicitly allows "passive" means of obtaining information from uncounseled defendants. After that decision, electronic bugs positioned in a jail cell clearly would not violate the Sixth Amendment.

The "deliberate elicitation" concept introduced in *Massiah,* as refined in later cases, appears to differ in two ways from the "custodial interrogation" which triggers Fifth Amendment analysis. First, as *Henry* and *Kuhlmann* indicate, it does not require custody; questioning by undercover agents who exert no "compulsion," as that term is used in Fifth Amendment cases, may still implicate the Sixth Amendment. Second, even when a person is in custody, police conduct that would not be interrogation may nonetheless constitute deliberate elicitation. A comparison of the facts and results of *Williams* and *Rhode Island v. Innis,*[65] makes the point: the "Christian burial speech" in the former case was enough to implicate the Sixth Amendment, but *Innis* refused to find that the police comments made there—about the danger posed by a hidden weapon, in the presence of a similarly suggestible defendant—amounted to interrogation.

These differences are explicable if one considers the differing purposes of the Fifth and Sixth Amendments. The privilege against self-incrimination is meant to protect against state compulsion, while the Sixth Amendment, *inter alia,* is meant to

64. 477 U.S. 436, 106 S.Ct. 2616 (1986).

65. 446 U.S. 291, 100 S.Ct. 1682 (1980), discussed in § 16.03(b).

prevent state interference with the attorney-client relationship.[66] Thus, at the least, government attempts to induce statements after the right to counsel attaches should implicate the latter Amendment, even if the "inherent coercion" of custodial interrogation is not present. Indeed, an argument can be made that *any* "elicitation" requirement unduly narrows Sixth Amendment protection because, as *Kuhlmann* illustrates, police attempts to avoid having to deal with a counseled defendant can involve "passive" as well as "active" techniques.

(c) **Waiver.** *Williams* recognized that the Sixth Amendment right to counsel may be waived in the absence of counsel, but, as in *Miranda,* required that the waiver be knowing, intelligent and voluntary. Of course, in "undercover cases" like *Henry* and *Kuhlmann,* a "knowing" waiver is impossible; the focus in these cases is entirely on whether there has been deliberate elicitation. But in cases like *Williams,* where the suspect is aware he is dealing with the police, a knowing waiver might occur. Some language in *Williams* suggested that waiver would be harder to show in this setting than under *Miranda.* In particular, the *Williams* Court at one point stated that the "strict standard" associated with waiver of trial counsel should also apply to a waiver during questioning that takes place after the Sixth Amendment attaches.[67] But a complete differentiation between the Fifth and Sixth Amendment rights to counsel has not come to pass.

The first intimation that this would be the case came in *Michigan v. Jackson,*[68] which held that, under the Sixth Amendment, a request for counsel at arraignment does not prevent subsequent questioning by the police if the defendant initiates the contact. Thus, instead of preventing all questioning of a counselless defendant whose Sixth Amendment right has attached, the Court announced a rule virtually identical to the rule of *Edwards v. Arizona,*[69] followed when the Fifth Amendment right to counsel is invoked. Two years later, in *Patterson v. Illinois,*[70] the Court explicitly held that, when a suspect does not yet have counsel, the analysis for determining whether a Sixth Amendment waiver has occurred mimics Fifth Amendment analysis. According to *Patterson,* the stringent waiver of counsel standard adopted at trial is

---

66. See § 32.04(a)(3).

67. For a discussion of the waiver of trial counsel standard, see § 31.04(a).

68. 475 U.S. 625, 106 S.Ct. 1404 (1986).

69. 451 U.S. 477, 101 S.Ct. 1880 (1981), discussed in § 16.03(e). There may be some differences between *Edwards* and *Jackson.* To the state's argument that *Jackson* would penalize police who may not know of the request

for counsel at arraignment, the Court responded: "Sixth Amendment principles require that we impute the State's knowledge from one state actor to another." Such imputation may not be required under the Fifth Amendment. See *Michigan v. Mosley,* 423 U.S. 96, 96 S.Ct. 321 (1975), discussed in § 16.03(e).

70. 487 U.S. 285, 108 S.Ct. 2389 (1988).

not apposite during pretrial questioning by the police "because the full 'dangers and disadvantages of self-representation' during questioning are less substantial and more obvious to an accused than they are at trial." Further, "[b]ecause the role of counsel at questioning is relatively simple and limited, we see no problem in having a waiver procedure at that stage which is likewise simple and limited." Thus, when the defendant does not yet have an attorney, administration of the *Miranda* warnings and a waiver satisfactory for purposes of *Miranda* are also sufficient for Sixth Amendment purposes.

However, *Patterson* also stated that "once an accused has a lawyer, a distinct set of constitutional safeguards aimed at preserving the sanctity of the attorney-client relationship take effect." Most concretely, the Court noted that, whereas police efforts to prevent attorney access to a client do not violate the Fifth Amendment,[71] they would violate the Sixth Amendment once it has attached. *Patterson* may also mean that, in contrast to waiver of the Fifth Amendment right to counsel, waiver of Sixth Amendment counsel, once he has been appointed, must be explicit.[72]

Arguably, *Patterson* did not go far enough. As suggested above, the further a case moves in the criminal process, the more complicated it becomes. Immediately after arrest, the police are usually interested only in getting information about the alleged crime. After arraignment the government is more likely to want to engage in quasi-plea bargaining and other legally technical matters. Under such circumstances, it is more difficult for the defendant to understand what he is giving up by talking. A rule which prohibited waiver after the defendant is formally charged, whether or not he has counsel, would make some sense from this perspective.[73] It would also avoid the inequality created by *Patterson* of affording greater Sixth Amendment protection to those who already have an attorney or are fortunate to have one appointed at the time of formal charging.

16.05 Confessions and the Exclusionary Rule

As in the Fourth Amendment context, the fact that police conduct was unconstitutional under *Miranda, Massiah* or due process analysis does not automatically lead to exclusion of evidence obtained by that conduct.[74] The three most significant

---

71. See *Moran v. Burbine*, 475 U.S. 412, 106 S.Ct. 1135 (1986), discussed in § 16.03(d)(2).

72. *People v. Kidd*, 129 Ill.2d 432, 136 Ill.Dec. 18, 544 N.E.2d 704 (1989). Compare to cases discussed in § 16.03(d)(1).

73. See discussion of New York's approach in § 16.02(d)(2).

74. This is true even though the Fifth Amendment, by prohibiting compulsion of testimony, arguably contains its own exclusionary rule, whereas the Fourth Amendment and Due Process

issues relating to the exclusionary rule as applied to confessions are the scope of the standing requirement, use of illegally obtained evidence for impeachment purposes, and the scope of the derivative evidence, or fruit of the poisonous tree, rule.

(a) Standing. As a general proposition, a person may not exclude evidence obtained in violation of another person's rights.[75] Moreover, the Supreme Court has specifically held that the Fifth Amendment privilege against self-incrimination, upon which *Miranda* is based, is a personal right.[76] Thus, one person cannot bring a Fifth Amendment challenge against the confession of another, or evidence derived from it, even if that confession was obtained in flagrant violation of *Miranda.*[77] There is no reason to think the same analysis would not hold true if a confession were obtained in violation of the Sixth Amendment or the due process clause; when a third party's rights are at issue, the defendant has no standing to claim they were violated.

Two very narrow constitutional limitations on the use of such third party evidence may remain. First, the Confrontation Clause prohibits use of a person's statements against a defendant who does not have the opportunity to cross-examine the declarant before or during trial (a scenario which most commonly occurs when the declarant is a co-defendant who has "taken the Fifth" at trial).[78] Thus, a third party's confession may occasionally be inadmissible against the defendant on Sixth Amendment grounds. Second, a confession which is the product of coercion so intense that it is likely to be "untrustworthy" may be inadmissible.[79] But this rule only bars use of the confession itself; fruit of the confession is likely to have independent indicia of reliability.

(b) The Impeachment Exception. *Miranda's* only reference to use of statements on cross-examination occurred in its discussion of "exculpatory statements." The Court noted that because such statements are often used to "impeach" trial testimony, they "may not be used without the full warnings and effective waiver required for any other statement." *Miranda* thus appeared to hold that a confession obtained in violation of its rules should be rendered inadmissible for any purpose. But in subsequent decisions, the Court has rejected this interpretation in favor

Clause do not. See generally, Loewy, "Police Obtained Evidence and the Constitution: Distinguishing Unconstitutionally Obtained Evidence from Unconstitutionally Used Evidence," 87 Mich.L.Rev. 907 (1989).

75. *Tileston v. Ullman,* 318 U.S. 44, 63 S.Ct. 493 (1943).

76. *Couch v. United States,* 409 U.S. 322, 93 S.Ct. 611 (1973), discussed in § 15.05.

77. *People v. Varnum,* 66 Cal.2d 808, 59 Cal.Rptr. 108, 427 P.2d 772 (1967), appeal dism'd 390 U.S. 529, 88 S.Ct. 1208 (1968).

78. See *Bruton v. United States,* 391 U.S. 123, 88 S.Ct. 1620 (1968), discussed in § 28.04(d).

79. Cf. *Harris v. New York,* 401 U.S. 222, 91 S.Ct. 643 (1971), discussed in § 16.05(b)(1).

of one which permits use of confessions which are "voluntary," in the due process sense, to challenge statements made by the defendant at trial, even if obtained in contravention of *Miranda.*

(1) Use of statements. *Harris v. New York* [80] was the first case to carve an exception out of *Miranda's* total exclusion policy. In *Harris,* the defendant denied in court that he had made a sale of heroin to an undercover agent. On cross examination he was asked if he had made certain statements following his arrest that were inconsistent with this testimony. Although the prosecution conceded that the statements were obtained in violation of *Miranda,* the trial judge instructed the jury that they could be considered in passing on the defendant's credibility. The Supreme Court agreed that confessions obtained in violation of *Miranda's* warnings requirements, but otherwise voluntary, may be used to impeach the testimony of a defendant who takes the stand. It rejected as dicta any language in *Miranda* suggesting otherwise. The primary rationale for the decision was the belief that the privilege against self-incrimination should not "be construed to include the right to commit perjury." Further, the Court noted that the police were unlikely to violate *Miranda* in reliance on its decision: "sufficient deterrence flows when the evidence in question is made unavailable to the prosecution in its case in chief."

The same could not be said in support of the Court's decision in *Oregon v. Hass,*[81] in which the police violated *Miranda* by continuing to question the defendant after he had requested his attorney. As the dissent pointed out, unless statements made in response to such questioning were excluded for any purpose, the police would have very little to lose by always continuing to question a person who has asked for counsel (since otherwise they are unlikely to get *any* information) [82] and everything to gain (i.e., statements that could be used to impeach). However, the Court, by a 7–2 margin, permitted their use for impeachment purposes. As in *Harris,* the Court feared that barring this evidence for all purposes would pervert the shield provided by *Miranda* "to a license to testify inconsistently, or even perjuriously, free from the risk of confrontation with prior inconsistent utterances." The Court stressed the importance of "the search for truth in a criminal case," and found that since there was no evidence of coercion in this case, the statements should be admitted to further the truth-finding function of criminal adjudication.

80. 401 U.S. 222, 91 S.Ct. 643 (1971).

81. 420 U.S. 714, 95 S.Ct. 1215 (1975).

82. The dissent's criticism is diminished only minimally by the fact that, after *Hass*, the Court decided *Edwards* *v. Arizona,* 451 U.S. 477, 101 S.Ct. 1880 (1981), discussed in § 16.03(e), which held that police may resume questioning of a defendant who invokes the right to counsel *if* he initiates contact.

Harris and *Hass* adopt a different definition of "voluntariness" than that fashioned by the majority in *Miranda.* The latter decision assumed that unwarned statements and statements obtained after a request for an attorney were coerced, if not directly, than by the subtle pressures of the custodial setting. *Harris* and *Hass,* on the other hand, revert to the old totality of the circumstances analysis to determine whether a confession is voluntary for purposes of use on cross-examination. However, it is also important to emphasize that the decisions allowing confessions to be used for impeachment purposes apply only when the confession *is* voluntary under the totality of the circumstances. The state may not use a confession which is "involuntary" in the due process sense for any purpose, even if it may be reliable and expose perjury.

The Supreme Court has made this clear on at least two occasions. In *New Jersey v. Portash,*[83] the state argued that *Harris* permits the use of immunized testimony to impeach a witness. The Court disagreed, noting that statements given in response to a grant of legislative immunity are "the essence of coerced testimony." The witness is told simply to testify or face a conviction for contempt. Since this situation invokes "the constitutional privilege against compulsory self-incrimination in its most pristine form," any balancing of the need to deter unsavory police practice and the need to prevent perjury is "impermissible." The Court came to a similar conclusion in *Mincey v. Arizona.*[84] In *Mincey,* the defendant was hospitalized and barely able to speak when the police questioned him, on several different occasions and despite his requests for an attorney. The state's use of inculpatory statements he made during this questioning were found inadmissible for any purpose, despite his receipt of *Miranda* warnings.

When the statements sought to be used for impeachment were obtained in violation of the Sixth Amendment, a slightly different analysis may apply. In *Michigan v. Harvey,*[85] the police procured statements in violation of *Michigan v. Jackson,*[86] which prohibits questioning after a request for counsel at arraignment unless the defendant initiates contact with the police. The Court held, 5–4, that the statements could be used for impeachment purposes, but only because there had otherwise been a knowing and voluntary waiver of the right to counsel. The Court left open the possibility that, had there been no such waiver, a statement might be inadmissible for impeachment purposes even if it is not coerced in

---

83. 440 U.S. 450, 99 S.Ct. 1292 (1979).

84. 437 U.S. 385, 98 S.Ct. 2408 (1978), discussed in § 16.02(a)(2).

85. 494 U.S. 344, 110 S.Ct. 1176 (1990).

86. 475 U.S. 625, 106 S.Ct. 1404 (1986), discussed in § 16.04(c).

the due process sense.[87]   At the same time, the Court clearly rejected Justice Stevens' argument in dissent that because it is designed to ensure a fair trial, the Sixth Amendment, unlike the Fifth Amendment, is violated at the time uncounseled statements are introduced at trial (whether in the prosecution's case-in-chief or in rebuttal), not at the time of their elicitation.   Instead, as it has with the *Miranda* rules, the Court in *Harvey* characterized *Jackson* as a prophylactic rule that should not "be perverted into a license to use perjury by way of a defense. . . ."

   (2) Use of silence.   A different line of cases concerns use of the defendant's *silence* for impeachment purposes.   In *Doyle v. Ohio*,[88] the defendants, who were given *Miranda* warnings after their arrest, took the stand and told an exculpatory story that they had not previously told the police or the prosecutor.   Over their counsel's objection, they were asked on cross-examination why they had not given the arresting officer their explanations.   The defendant's post-arrest "silence" on this issue would seem to be "voluntary," and therefore admissible for impeachment purposes under *Harris* and *Hass*.   But, relying on a due process fairness notion rather then the Fifth Amendment, the Court held that a suspect's post-arrest silence is "insolubly ambiguous" once he has been assured by the *Miranda* warnings that silence will carry no penalty, and thus it is not admissible for the purpose of impugning the suspect's credibility.   Similarly, in *Wainwright v. Greenfield*,[89] the Court found unconstitutional a prosecutor's closing argument that the defendant's repeated post-warning refusals to answer questions without first consulting an attorney demonstrated a degree of comprehension inconsistent with the defendant's insanity plea at trial.   Efforts to prove the defendant's mental state at the time of arrest must be made without reference to the invocation of rights he has been expressly told he has.[90]

   On the other hand, if the defendant did talk after the warnings, the prosecutor may ask the defendant why he didn't tell his current, trial story to the police instead of the one he did tell them after his arrest.   According to the Court in *Anderson v. Charles*,[91] "[s]uch questioning makes no unfair use of silence because a defendant who voluntarily speaks after receiving *Miranda* warnings has not been induced to remain silent."   Further, if the suspect is silent *before* receiving his *Miranda* warnings, that

---

87. For discussion of possible differences between an waiver analysis under the Sixth Amendment and under the due process clause or *Miranda*, see § 16.04(c).

88. 426 U.S. 610, 96 S.Ct. 2240 (1976).

89. 474 U.S. 284, 106 S.Ct. 634 (1986).

90. However, if a prosecutor's question about post-warning silence is followed by a sustained objection and an instruction to disregard the question, no *Doyle* violation occurs.   *Greer v. Miller*, 483 U.S. 756, 107 S.Ct. 3102 (1987).

91. 447 U.S. 404, 100 S.Ct. 2180 (1980).

silence may be used against him. In *Jenkins v. Anderson*,[92] the Court so held, on the ground that such a defendant has not yet been told that he has a right to remain silent and thus his silence is less ambiguous than after such a warning has been given. Whether such silence is sufficiently probative on the issue of the defendant's credibility during his trial testimony is solely a matter of state law. In *Jenkins*, for instance, the Court held that the fact that the defendant waited two weeks to report his commission of a homicide could be used to impeach his self-defense testimony if, under state evidentiary law, such pre-arrest "silence" is considered relevant. It stressed that, since Jenkins had not been in contact with police prior to the time he confessed, his silence was not in response to any warning received from the police.[93]

Doyle was also at issue in *South Dakota v. Neville*,[94] where the defendant was stopped for drunk driving. He was told that he could refuse a blood alcohol test but that, if he did so, he would lose his license. The Court first held that the defendant had no right to refuse to take the test under the Fourth or Fifth Amendments because it was "safe, painless and commonplace," and did not compel testimonial evidence.[95] It then rejected his next argument: that the Due Process Clause, as construed in *Doyle*, prevented use of his refusal to take the test at trial because he had, in effect, been told it would not be used (by virtue of the fact that the police had only mentioned loss of license as an adverse consequence). The Court found it "unrealistic" that the defendant believed his refusal was otherwise harmless: "[i]mportantly, the warning that he could lose his driver's license made it clear that refusing the test was not a 'safe harbor,' free of adverse consequences."

(c) Derivative Evidence. The admissibility of evidence obtained as a result of an arrest made in violation of the Fourth Amendment is judged under so-called "fruit of the poisonous tree" analysis.[96] But when the illegality is an improperly obtained confession, the Supreme Court has been reluctant to apply its "fruits" doctrine. Instead, similar to its treatment of the impeachment issue, it has held that a violation of *Miranda*, not rising to a due process-type violation, will generally not lead to exclusion of subsequently obtained evidence, even if that evidence was clearly derived from the violation. Only evidence which results from "coercion" will be excluded under the Fifth Amendment. Wheth-

92. 447 U.S. 231, 100 S.Ct. 2124 (1980).

93. See also, *Fletcher v. Weir*, 455 U.S. 603, 102 S.Ct. 1309 (1982).

94. 459 U.S. 553, 103 S.Ct. 916 (1983).

95. See § 15.04 for further discussion of the testimonial evidence requirement.

96. See § 2.04 for a discussion of the doctrine in the Fourth Amendment setting.

er the same restrictive rule will apply to violations of the Sixth Amendment remains unclear.

The Court's first clear indication that it would treat "poisonous" confessions differently from "poisonous" searches came in 1947, in *United States v. Bayer.*[97] There the Court stated that its Fourth Amendment fruit of the poisonous tree cases "did not control" the admissibility of evidence derived from an illegally obtained confession because they dealt with a "quite different category" of evidence. In *Michigan v. Tucker,*[98] the Court intimated that its intervening decision in *Miranda* had not changed this position. *Miranda* had stated that "no evidence obtained as a result of interrogation [conducted in violation of *Miranda*] can be used against him." But *Tucker* treated this language as dictum. In *Tucker,* a suspect was arrested for rape and questioned without being told of his right to counsel. During the interrogation he stated that he had been with a friend during the time of the crime. The police later obtained incriminating information from the friend. Although this information was clearly derived from the illegally conducted interrogation, the Court stated that "[t]he police conduct at issue here did not abridge respondent's constitutional privilege against compulsory self-incrimination, but departed only from the prophylactic standards later laid down by this Court in *Miranda* to safeguard this privilege." The Court thus saw no reason to exclude the friend's statement.

Tucker was of limited force, however, because the interrogation in that case took place before *Miranda* was decided; accordingly, the decision could be seen as an effort to avoid penalizing good faith actions by the police who were following practice considered acceptable at that time. But in *Oregon v. Elstad,*[99] the Court made clear that it would continue to treat *Miranda* as a "prophylactic rule," at least for most types of derivative evidence. According to *Elstad, Miranda* created a "presumption of compulsion" which is irrebuttable when the state seeks to introduce unwarned statements in its case-in-chief, but which may be rebutted when the state's objective is to introduce evidence derived from the statements.[1] Such a rebuttal is accomplished if the prosecution can show that the police conduct leading to discovery of the evidence was not "coercive," which the majority defined as action constituting "physical violence or other deliberate means calculated to break the suspect's will."

---

97. 331 U.S. 532, 67 S.Ct. 1394 (1947). A still earlier decision, *Lyons v. Oklahoma,* 322 U.S. 596, 64 S.Ct. 1208 (1944), presaged *Bayer* in holding that the admissibility of a subsequent confession depended on whether it was "voluntary." Fruits doctrine was not mentioned.

98. 417 U.S. 433, 94 S.Ct. 2357 (1974).

99. 470 U.S. 298, 105 S.Ct. 1285 (1985).

1. The Court noted that the same analysis also explained its impeachment decisions, discussed in § 16.05(b).

Whether evidence derived from a Sixth Amendment violation would be admissible under the *Elstad* reasoning is debatable. Although the *Massiah* rule can be termed "prophylactic," the Court appears to believe that it is more closely tied to the assistance of counsel provision in the Sixth Amendment than is *Miranda* to the privilege against self-incrimination.[2] Thus, the typical fruit of the poisonous tree analysis may apply in such situations. The Court may have intimated as much in *Nix v. Williams*,[3] in which it held that the admissibility of evidence derived from a Sixth Amendment violation can depend upon whether its discovery was in any event "inevitable," a concept which has been applied in Fourth Amendment cases. With this in mind, the discussion below focuses on the admissibility of different types of evidence derived from a *Miranda* or due process violation.

(1) Other confessions. In *Elstad,* the police interrogated the defendant and obtained an incriminating statement from him after they had arrested him in his home. The defendant received no warnings, however, until he arrived at the stationhouse. After he was warned, he signed a written confession. The Oregon Court of Appeals concluded that because of the brief period separating the defendant's initial, unwarned statement and his subsequent confession, the "cat was sufficiently out of the bag to exert a coercive impact" on the defendant and render his second confession inadmissible. In other words, the court felt that the defendant's second confession may well have resulted from his inaccurate conclusion that his first confession could be used against him and that thus no further harm could come from making further incriminating statements. In a 6–3 decision written by Justice O'Connor, the Court reversed the Oregon court, finding it "an unwarranted extension of *Miranda* to hold that a simple failure to administer the warnings, unaccompanied by any actual coercion or other circumstances calculated to undermine the suspect's ability to exercise his free will so taints the investigatory process that a subsequent voluntary and informed waiver is ineffective for some indeterminate period." Here, the psychological pressure exerted by the previous confession on the decision to make the second confession was "speculative and attenuated at best."

As Justice Brennan pointed out in dissent, there is little to distinguish what occurred in *Elstad* from the typical Fourth Amendment "fruit" case in which only a short period of time and *Miranda* warnings separate an illegal *arrest* and a signed confession.[4] If anything, an arrest would seem to exert less of an impact on subsequent behavior by the defendant than would a confession.

---

2. See, e.g., discussion of *Patterson v. Illinois,* 487 U.S. 285, 108 S.Ct. 2389 (1988), in § 16.04(c).

3. 467 U.S. 431, 104 S.Ct. 2501 (1984), discussed in § 2.04(d).

4. See § 2.04(b)(1).

Yet, he noted, the Court has refused to presume that a post-warning confession obtained after arrest is "sufficiently an act of free will to purge the primary taint of the unlawful invasion." [5] Brennan argued that derivative evidence analysis in Fifth Amendment cases should be governed by considerations similar to those applied in the Fourth Amendment area. In successive confession cases such as *Elstad,* the relevant criteria should be the second confession's proximity in time and place to the first confession, intervening factors such as consultation with friends or a lawyer, and the purpose and flagrancy of the police misconduct resulting in the first confession.

Another factor Brennan thought should be considered in deciding whether a subsequent confession should be admissible is whether the suspect was told his earlier statements might not be admissible. The majority had held that it would be too burden-some to require such a warning, given the "murky and difficult" state of Fifth Amendment jurisprudence. But Brennan disagreed, because "the vast majority of confrontations implicating this question involve obvious *Miranda* violations." To Justice Brennan's point can be added the observation that *Miranda* warnings must be given at some point if *any* statements are to be admissible; surely it is not that difficult to tell the suspect, after these warnings are read to him, that if similar warnings were not given him prior to his last statements, those statements will not be admissible. If police are not required to do so, there is little to inhibit them from pursuing improper questioning prior to every "formal" interrogation in an effort to create "momentum" toward a usable confession.

After *Elstad,* however, the admissibility of statements by the defendant after an improper interrogation has taken place now depends solely upon whether they are considered "voluntary" in light of "the surrounding circumstances and the entire course of police conduct with respect to the suspect." "Highly probative" to this analysis is whether such statements were preceded by warnings. Given the Court's pronouncement that the "cat's out of the bag" rationale is "speculative and attenuated," the police can thus insulate most confessions from the poison of previous *Miranda* violations simply by giving the *Miranda* warnings. The *Elstad* majority did make favorable reference to *Westover v. United States,* [6] one of the cases decided with *Miranda. Westover* had held inadmissible a confession made after warnings were given because prior to the warnings the accused had been subjected to intermit-tent interrogations over a fourteen hour period, none of which was preceded by warnings. But the more typical case today will

5. *Wong Sun v. United States,* 371 U.S. 471, 83 S.Ct. 407 (1963).

6. For the lower court opinion, see 342 F.2d 684 (9th Cir.1965).

involve a much shorter pre-warning interrogation period which is unlikely to render "coerced" in the due process sense any statements made after the warnings.

(2) Witnesses. In speaking of *Tucker, Elstad* stressed the conclusion in that decision that the officer's conduct—which led to discovery of a witness against the defendant—involved no "actual compulsion." Thus, this type of derivative evidence will usually be admissible as well, so long as the interrogation which results in the discovery of a witness is not designed to "break the suspect's will." Even in the latter situation, exclusion may not be mandated, if Fourth Amendment cases are any guide. When the witness' identity is discovered through an illegal search, the Court has been reluctant to hold that witnesses are "tainted" by police conduct, given the fact that witnesses, unlike tangible evidence, can make themselves known to police, thus making it more likely they would have been discovered in any event.[7]

When the testimony "discovered" is from the defendant himself, an earlier case may have created a limited exception to the *Tucker–Elstad* rule. In *Harrison v. United States,*[8] the government introduced three confessions, improperly obtained under the now defunct *McNabb–Mallory* rule,[9] at the defendant's first trial. The defendant then took the stand and made an admission of guilt. After reversal of the conviction based on the unlawfulness of the admitted confessions, a new trial took place at which the prosecutor read into evidence the admission made during the first trial. The Supreme Court noted that, had the three confessions not been admitted, the defendant might not have testified at all at the first trial, and in any event probably would not have admitted guilt. Thus, stated the Court, the admission was "fruit of the poisonous tree."

Despite this language, *Harrison* may not diverge from *Elstad's* reasoning. Although confessions obtained in violation of the *McNabb–Mallory* rule are not necessarily the result of efforts to break the suspect's will, the *Harrison* Court emphasized that the "fruit" of those confessions—the defendant's testimony—was itself "impelled" by the tactical situation in which the defendant found himself. Thus, consistent with *Elstad, Harrison* could be read to hold that a defendant's testimony is not inadmissible "fruit" of an improperly obtained confession unless its use somehow "coerces" him to testify.

(3) Searches. When the "fruit" of an illegally obtained confession is the probable cause necessary to support a search, the

7. *United States v. Ceccolini,* 435 U.S. 268, 98 S.Ct. 1054 (1978), discussed in § 2.04(b)(2).

8. 392 U.S. 219, 88 S.Ct. 2008 (1968).

9. See § 16.02(b) for a discussion of this rule.

implications of *Elstad* are not quite as clear. But it appears that, as with other confessions and witnesses, tangible evidence which is the fruit of an illegally obtained confession will usually be admissible.

This conclusion stems from the rationale of *Elstad*. There, the majority refused to analogize *Miranda* to Fourth Amendment jurisprudence for derivative evidence purposes because of its conclusion, noted above, that violation of the former rule merely creates a "presumption" that Fifth Amendment interests have been infringed. Those interests, as Justice O'Connor defined them for the Court, are the avoidance of unreliable statements and the prevention of coercion. And, she continued, where derivative, as opposed to primary, evidence is concerned, admissibility rules need only be governed by these interests. Thus, for example, in justifying *Elstad's* holding with respect to successive confessions, she contended that it would neither allow untrustworthy evidence at trial nor encourage "coercive" police conduct prior to trial.

Although it ignores entirely *Miranda's* view of the Fifth Amendment, the same justification even more readily permits a rule allowing introduction of any derivative tangible evidence that is not the product of interrogation calculated to break the suspect's will, since such evidence is never "untrustworthy."[10] The only counter to this interpretation of *Elstad* is Justice Brennan's observation, made in his dissent in that case, that despite the majority's distinction between Fourth and Fifth Amendment jurisprudence, it still felt the need to analyze whether there was a sufficient "gap" between the first and second confessions, suggesting that a fruits analysis might be applied where tangible evidence is involved.

16.06 Assessing the Admissibility and Credibility of a Confession

From the foregoing, it should be obvious that despite the *Miranda* Court's efforts to construct an easily applied rule that does not require case-by-case analysis, judging the admissibility of a confession will often be a difficult endeavor. This section discusses the procedures for determining the admissibility issue. It also addresses the evidentiary rules governing assessment of a confession's credibility once it has been found admissible.

(a) The Decisionmaker. Before *Miranda*, when the validity of confessions was analyzed under the Due Process Clause, at least three different procedures were devised for determining whether a

---

10. One could also make the argument that such evidence is "nontestimonial" and therefore admissible in any event. See Justice O'Connor's concurring opinion in *New York v. Quarles*, 467 U.S. 649, 104 S.Ct. 2626 (1984), summarized in note 19 supra.

confession was voluntarily made. Two of these procedures are still in use today. In states following the so-called orthodox rule, the trial judge alone determines the issue of voluntariness. Under the Massachusetts rule, the trial judge makes an independent judgment regarding voluntariness, but if he concludes that the confession was voluntary, the jury may reconsider the issue and conclude otherwise. Before 1964, many states, including New York, followed a third procedure under which the question of voluntariness of the confession was put to the jury unless the trial judge in a preliminary determination found that under no circumstances could the confession be deemed voluntary.

In *Jackson v. Denno* [11], decided in that year, the Supreme Court found this latter procedure unconstitutional. The trial court in *Jackson* had submitted the issue of voluntariness to the jury in accordance with state practice. The jury members were instructed to disregard the confession if they found it was involuntary, but if they found it voluntary they were to determine its truth or reliability and weigh it accordingly. In rejecting this procedure, the Supreme Court held that the admissibility of a confession must be decided prior to its submission to the jury. Under the New York procedure, the Court observed, prejudice could result in two ways. First, the jury could impermissibly base its decision regarding the voluntariness of the confession on its assessment of its truthfulness. Second, even if the jury found the confession involuntary, it would be unable to disregard it in determining guilt.

In a footnote, the Court indicated that the trial judge, another judge, or another jury may make the voluntariness decision; only the jury that decides guilt or innocence may not do so. Although not required in most states, the Court's reasoning in *Jackson* suggests that the same practice should govern admissibility determinations in bench trials. At least when he finds a confession involuntary, a judge should refrain from trying the case; knowing the defendant has confessed is likely to affect his deliberations no matter how involuntary the confession.

The orthodox rule and the Massachusetts rule obviously survived the Court's holding in *Jackson*. However, now that *Miranda* and *Massiah* have for the most part replaced the totality of the circumstances test with technical legal rules, a good argument can be made that the Massachusetts approach, which allows the legally unsophisticated jury to make the "admissibility" decision a second time after the judge's determination, is not appropriate. Given the complexity of modern confessions law, the best proce-

11. 378 U.S. 368, 84 S.Ct. 1774 (1964).

dure is the judge-based orthodox rule, which is followed in the federal courts.[12]

Even under the orthodox rule, the jury is prohibited only from *making* the ultimate admissibility decision, not from *hearing* the evidence which is relevant to that decision. In *Pinto v. Pierce,*[13] for instance, the trial judge permitted the jury to be present during a voluntariness hearing and then ruled the confession admissible. The Supreme Court held that because the defendant didn't object to this procedure and because the confession was ruled admissible in any event, the jury's verdict should stand. So limited, *Pinto* may be unobjectionable. But had the confession been ruled inadmissible, the same type of prejudice concerns which led to the Court's holding in *Jackson* should have required reversal. In many jurisdictions, juries are forbidden to hear evidence presented in a voluntariness hearing for this reason.[14]

(b) Burden and Standard of Proof. It seems clear that, whether a claim about a confession is based on the Due Process Clause, *Miranda* or the Sixth Amendment, the burden is on the government to show that no violation occurred. In *Miranda,* for instance, the Court spoke of the "heavy burden" on the prosecution of demonstrating the validity of any waiver of *Miranda* rights. If the burden is on the state in these cases, then it is presumably on the government when the defendant makes a due process or Sixth Amendment claim—claims the current Court takes even more seriously.

The more controversial issue has been the standard of proof imposed on the government. *Miranda's* statement that the burden is a "heavy" one suggested that the government should have to show a confession was invalid beyond a reasonable doubt. But in *Lego v. Twomey,*[15] the Court held that the prosecution need only prove voluntariness under the Due Process Clause by a preponderance of the evidence. And in *Colorado v. Connelly,*[16] the Court found that the same standard applies to *Miranda* claims as well, on the ground that if "the voluntariness of a confession need be established only by a preponderance of the evidence, than a waiver of the auxiliary protections established in *Miranda* should require no higher burden of proof."

Lego in particular is questionable, since an involuntary confession may also be unreliable, yet, if given to the jury, still prove highly persuasive. In response to this argument, the *Lego* Court simply stated that, while the reasonable doubt standard "is necessary . . . to ensure against unjust convictions by giving substance to the presumption of innocence[, a] guilty verdict is not

12.　18 U.S.C.A. § 3501(a).

13.　389 U.S. 31, 88 S.Ct. 192 (1967).

14.　See, e.g., Fed.R.Evid. 104(c).

15.　404 U.S. 477, 92 S.Ct. 619 (1972).

16.　479 U.S. 157, 107 S.Ct. 515 (1986).

rendered any less reliable . . . simply because the admissibility of a confession is determined by a less stringent standard." Given this reasoning, it is probable that the government's burden in the face of a Sixth Amendment claim can be met by a preponderance of the evidence showing as well.

Relevant to the government's burden with respect to proving the admissibility of confessions is the common law rule that an uncorroborated confession, even if voluntary, is not sufficient to support a conviction. In most jurisdictions, unless the government produces independent proof of the *corpus delicti* (i.e., proof that the criminal act occurred), the confession is not admissible.[17] As *Miranda* noted, the court must be careful not to let this independent evidence influence the ultimate determination of the confession's admissibility.

(c) **Challenging the Confession at Trial.** Assuming a confession is found to be admissible, the defendant may still attack its *reliability* at trial. In both *Jackson* and *Lego* the Court made clear that its decision in *Jackson* was not meant to undercut the defendant's prerogative to challenge the confession's credibility once found admissible. In *Crane v. Kentucky,*[18] the Court conferred constitutional status on the rule that testimony calling into question a confession's reliability is not limited to the initial voluntariness determination but may also be presented at trial if the confession is found voluntary. Left unresolved by *Crane,* however, is what type of testimony is permitted. Some jurisdictions will allow the defendant to attack a confession's reliability by presenting to the trial jury all of the evidence adduced at the voluntariness hearing, so that the jury can make an independent judgment of the weight to be accorded to the confession;[19] other jurisdictions only permit the jury to hear "controverted testimony" (that is, evidence that was challenged by the prosecution during the hearing).[20]

Of course, the defendant can also decide to take the stand and try to convince the jury that his confession was involuntary. Doing so might entail the risk of questioning about other issues. But most jurisdictions, in an effort to prevent undue inhibition of defendants seeking to impeach their confession, either directly forbid prosecution questions on matters collateral to the voluntari-

17. Imwinkelreid, et al. Criminal Evidence 320 (1979).

18. 476 U.S. 683, 106 S.Ct. 2142 (1986).

19. See, e.g., *People v. Carroll,* 4 Cal. App.3d 52, 84 Cal.Rptr. 60 (Ct.App. 1970); *Karl v. Commonwealth,* 288 S.W.2d 628 (Ky.1956). Note that this procedure does not permit the jury to address the admissibility question, as does the Massachusetts rule, see § 16.06(a), but only the reliability issue.

20. See, e.g., *Malone v. State,* 452 So. 2d 1386 (Ala.Crim.App.1984); *Taylor v. State,* 337 So.2d 1368 (Ala.App.1976).

ness issue,[21] or enforce the so-called "American" (or federal) rule pertaining to the scope of cross-examination, which generally restricts cross-examination to subjects covered on direct examination and to matters affecting credibility.[22]　Thus, if the defendant's testimony on direct addresses only the circumstances surrounding his confession, the prosecution may not question him about the alleged offense itself.

16.07　Conclusion

The original *Miranda* doctrine has been substantially eroded by decisions limiting the situations to which it applies and the extent to which it need be enforced by an exclusionary policy. But despite these inroads, or perhaps because of them, the prophylactic core of *Miranda* seems firmly ensconced.　While more recent Court decisions have harkened back to the case-by-case approach associated with the Due Process Clause, a full retreat to the law of voluntariness is unlikely.

As the jurisprudence of confessions stands today:

(1) Disclosures made to the police before an individual is in "custody" or which are not the product of "interrogation" are admissible for any purpose, at least under the Fifth Amendment. Custody occurs when an individual is placed under arrest or in any similar way is significantly restrained by law enforcement officials.　Interrogation includes not only express questioning but also any words or actions on the part of the police other than those normally attendant to arrest and custody that the police should know are reasonably likely to elicit an incriminating response from the suspect.　Under this definition, interrogation has not occurred if the questions asked are part of a legitimate police procedure, such as booking or a field test, that is not intended to elicit information for investigatory purposes.　Moreover, interrogation must involve coercion beyond that inherent in custody itself.　Thus, questioning by an undercover agent is not interrogation.

(2) Disclosures made in response to custodial interrogation are not admissible in the prosecution's case-in-chief for any criminal offense unless (a) they are preceded by warnings, or the fully effective equivalent of warnings, telling the suspect he has the right to remain silent, that anything he says may be used against him, that he has the right to an attorney before and during police

21.　*Calloway v. Wainwright,* 409 F.2d 59 (5th Cir.1968) (applying Florida law), cert. denied 395 U.S. 909, 89 S.Ct. 1752 (1969); *State v. Lovett,* 345 So.2d 1139 (La.1977); *Washington v. Commonwealth,* 214 Va. 737, 204 S.E.2d 266 (1974).

22.　Fed.R.Evid. 611(b); cf. *Tucker v. United States,* 5 F.2d 818 (8th Cir.1925) (breach of American rule held to violate privilege against self-incrimination). See generally McCormick's Handbook of the Law of Evidence § 21 (2d ed. 1972).

questioning, and that an attorney will be appointed for him if he cannot afford one; or unless (b) they result from questioning triggered by exigent circumstances suggesting an objective threat to police or public safety. Warnings about the subject matter of the interrogation need not be given.

(3) Disclosures made after receipt of the warnings described above are admissible in the prosecution's case-in-chief if they are the product of a valid waiver of the right to remain silent and the right to have an attorney present during questioning. Any statement or course of conduct indicating a willingness to talk to police will suffice as a valid waiver if it is voluntary and intelligent given the totality of the circumstances surrounding the interrogation. Relevant circumstances are the conduct of the police, including their use of physical or psychological pressure, and the age, education and intelligence of the suspect. Disclosures procured through use of physical violence and other deliberate means calculated to break the suspect's will are not the product of a valid waiver. On the other hand, statements which are not "caused" by the police are admissible, even if "compelled" by the defendant's mental condition.

(4) Custodial interrogation may not begin or, if begun, must end if the suspect in any way asserts his right to remain silent or requests an attorney during interrogation. However, a person can waive his right to remain silent after asserting it so long as police scrupulously honor his decision to stop the questioning, which at the least requires waiting a significant period of time before attempting any new interrogation and rewarning the person before this interrogation. Similarly, a person can waive his right to an attorney after asserting it if he initiates further communication with the police by evincing a willingness and desire for a discussion about the investigation. In either case, the waiver must of course be voluntary and intelligent as assessed in the totality of the circumstances.

(5) Although not admissible in the prosecution's case-in-chief, disclosures made prior to the receipt of warnings, or disclosures made after a request for an attorney and before the suspect's initiation of any further communication with the police, are admissible for impeachment purposes if they were voluntarily made in the totality of the circumstances. The suspect's "silence" may be used for impeachment purposes only when it is clearly not the result of being informed he has the right to remain silent and it is relevant under local evidentiary rules.

(6) Disclosures by the defendant, and evidence provided by witnesses, derived from earlier disclosures of the defendant are admissible in the prosecution's case-in-chief if the original disclosures were not obtained through physical violence or other deliber-

ate means calculated to break the suspect's will, and if the derivative evidence is otherwise admissible. Tangible evidence discovered as a result of illegally obtained disclosures is probably admissible under the same circumstances.

(7) In a jury trial, the admissibility of a confession must be determined by someone other than the jury itself. The government bears the burden of proving a confession is admissible by a preponderance of the evidence. The defendant has a due process right to challenge at trial the credibility of a confession found to be admissible.

(8) Disclosures which are admissible under the above rules may nonetheless be inadmissible under the Sixth Amendment, if: (a) they occur in the absence of counsel; (b) after the initiation of adversary proceedings (e.g., arraignment, indictment or preliminary hearing); (c) which concerned the charge which is the subject of the disclosure; and (d) are deliberately elicited by police either directly or by intentionally creating a situation likely to induce incriminating statements; and (e) are not the product of a valid waiver. Waiver rules under the Sixth Amendment are identical to those described in (3) and (4), except that a "knowing" waiver cannot be made if police do not tell a suspect of his attorney's attempts to contact him. The Sixth Amendment may also require a more express waiver than the Fifth Amendment.

BIBLIOGRAPHY

Benner, Laurence. Requiem for Miranda: The Rehnquist Court's Voluntariness Doctrine in Historical Perspective. 67 Wash. U.L.Q. 59 (1989).

Berger, Mark. Compromise and Continuity: Miranda Waivers, Confession Admissibility, and the Retention of Interrogation Protections. 49 U.Pitt.L.Rev. 1007 (1988).

Caplan, Gerald. Questioning Miranda. 38 Vand.L.Rev. 1417 (1985).

Dershowitz, Alan and John H. Ely. Harris v. New York: Some Anxious Observations on the Candor and Logic of the Emerging Nixon Majority. 80 Yale L.J. 1198 (1971).

Driver, Edwin D. Confessions and the Social Psychology of Coercion. 82 Harv.L.Rev. 42 (1968).

Edwards, George B., Jr., B.J. George, Jr., A. Kenneth Pye, Thomas C. Lynch, Richard H. Kuh, Michael W. Hogan, Osmond K. Fraenkel, and Evelle J. Younger. Interrogation of Criminal Defendants—Some Views on Miranda v. Arizona. 35 Fordham L.Rev., 169, 181, 193, 199, 221, 233, 243, 249, 255 (1966).

Gardner, Martin R. The Emerging Good Faith Exception to the Miranda Rule—A Critique. 35 Hastings L.J. 429 (1984).

Grano, Joseph. Selling the Idea to Tell the Truth: The Professional Interrogator and Modern Confessions Law. 84 Mich.L. Rev. 662 (1986).

——. Voluntariness, Free Will and the Law of Confessions. 65 Va.L.Rev. 859 (1979).

——. Rhode Island v. Innis: A Need to Reconsider the Constitutional Premises Underlying the Law of Confessions. 17 Am. Crim.L.Rev. 1 (1979).

Hogan, James, and Snee, Joseph. The McNabb-Mallory Rule: Its Rise, Rationale, and Rescue. 47 Geo.L.J. 1 (1958).

Inbau, Fred E. Overreaction—The Mischief of Miranda v. Arizona. 73 J.Crim.L. & Criminol. 797 (1982).

Interrogations in New Haven: The Impact of *Miranda*. 76 Yale L.J. 1521 (1967).

Kamisar, Yale. A Dissent from the *Miranda* Dissents: Some Comments on the "New" Fifth Amendment and the Old "Voluntariness" Test. 65 Mich.L.Rev. 59 (1966).

——. Equal Justice in the Gatehouses and Mansions of American Criminal Procedure. In: Criminal Justice in our Time, ed. by A.E. Howard. Charlottesville: University of Virginia Press, 1965.

——. Brewer v. Williams, Massiah and Miranda: What Is "Interrogation?" When Does It Matter? 67 Georgetown L.J. 1 (1978).

Robinson, Cyril D. Police and Prosecutor Practices and Attitudes Relating to Interrogation as Revealed by Pre- and Post-Miranda Questionnaires: A Construct of Policy Capacity to Comply. 1968 Duke L.J. 425 (1968).

Rosenberg, Irene and Yale Rosenberg. A Modest Proposal for the Abolition of Custodial Interrogation. 68 N.Car.L.Rev. 69 (1989).

Saltzburg, Stephen. Miranda v. Arizona Revisited: Constitutional Law or Judicial Fiat. 26 Washburn L.J. 1 (1986).

Schulhofer, Stephen. Reconsidering Miranda. 54 U.Chi.L.Rev. 435 (1987).

Stone, Geoffrey. The Miranda Doctrine in the Burger Court. 1977 Sup.Ct.Rev. 99.

Tomkovicz, James. An Adversary System Defense of the Right to Counsel Against Informants: Truth, Fair Play, and the *Massiah* Doctrine. 22 U.C.Davis L.Rev. 1 (1988).

Uviller, H. Richard. Evidence from the Mind of the Criminal Suspect. 87 Colum.L.Rev. 1137 (1987).

White, Welsh S. Police Trickery in Inducing Confessions. 127 U.Pa.L.Rev. 581 (1979).

____. Defending Miranda: A Reply to Professer Caplan. 39 Vand.L.Rev. 1 (1986).

Part C

IDENTIFICATION PROCEDURES

Procedures for identifying the perpertator of a crime can take many forms: lineups, photo arrays, one-on-one confrontations, fingerprinting, blood tests, voice exemplars, and handwriting exemplars are among the most common. The primary focus in this Part will be on the first three procedures, which make use of eyewitness identifications. An eyewitness identification is a particularly powerful piece of evidence in a criminal prosecution. Few scenarios in a criminal trial are more convincing than that in which a witness points to the defendant and says "He's the one." Yet, for reasons described below, such identifications can easily be wrong, whether they are made soon after the crime or in court. The potentially devastating impact of such identifications, combined with their suspect reliability, has made them a special concern of the courts.

Chapter 17 provides an overview of the constitutional constraints on the admissibility of both pretrial and in-court identifications. Chapter 18 then examines in detail the proper methods for conducting pretrial identification procedures.

Chapter Seventeen

GENERAL RESTRICTIONS ON IDENTIFICATION PROCEDURES

17.01 Introduction

Judges and jurors naturally assume that an eyewitness to a crime can accurately discern and remember the physical characteristics of the person who committed the crime.[1] Yet extensive research indicates that both our ability to observe what someone looks like under the type of circumstances likely to be present during a crime and our capacity to recall what we observe is surprisingly deficient.[2] Many factors can cause faulty perception.[3] Aside from the obvious ones of lighting conditions and distance, for instance, there are proven problems with cross-racial identifications, which are notoriously inaccurate, and identifications in crimes involving weapons, which often draw the witness' attention away from the assailant. Even assuming optimum observation conditions, our inability to process more than a few stimuli at any given moment, *especially* when under stress, leads to difficulty in observing multiple details. Recall of an event is also often faulty.[4] Memory of what we perceive decays very rapidly—beginning within minutes of the event.

If people readily recognized and admitted to these failures of perception and memory, then reliance on eyewitness evidence might not be problematic: not only would there be less of it, but any eyewitness testimony that is presented would be discounted appropriately. Unfortunately, eyewitnesses are often not aware of how inaccurate their perceptions and memory are. Worse, they often unknowingly "fill in" their perceptual and recall gaps with possibly unreliable information obtained from other sources (e.g., preconceptions about criminals, newspaper accounts, what other

1. See P. Wall, Eyewitness Identification in Criminal Cases 19–13 (1965) (detailing numerous cases in which jurors disregarded convincing alibi evidence in convicting defendant on the basis of less impressive eyewitness identification testimony).

2. One of the best known examples of inaccurate identification is the "New York City television" study conducted by Dr. Robert Buckhout. In this study, viewers of the nightly news on a New York City TV station were shown a videotape of a mugging incident, and then a lineup of six men. They were then asked to phone in their opinion as to who committed the mugging. Less than 15% of the more than 2,000 respondents, or a percentage equal to random selection, correctly identified the culprit. Buckhout, "Nearly 2,000 Witnesses Can Be Wrong," Soc.Act. & L. at 7 (May, 1975).

3. A summary of the studies on perception is found in Note, "Did Your Eyes Deceive You? Expert Psychological Testimony on the Unreliability of Eyewitness Identification," 29 Stanford L.Rev. 969, 969–79 (1977).

4. Studies are summarized in Note, supra note 3, at 969–89.

witnesses say, or leading questions by the police). The ironic result, according to research, is that sincere confidence in one's identification, especially if it grows over time, may be negatively correlated with accuracy.[5]

These and other problems with eyewitness identification cannot be fully rectified by the legal system. In particular, the law cannot have much of an effect on witness' perceptual and recall capabilities. But it can try to control any conscious or unconscious attempt by the police or the prosecution to supply what perception and memory cannot. The Supreme Court has indicated that both the Sixth Amendment right to counsel and the Due Process Clause place some constraints on the use of such techniques.[6] This chapter discusses these constraints, as well as the applicability of the Fourth Amendment and the privilege against self-incrimination to identification procedures. It also examines how the courts have analyzed the admissibility of identifications which are the "fruit" of a constitutional violation and the procedures for determining the admissibility of identification evidence.

17.02 The Right to Counsel

In *United States v. Wade,*[7] the defendant participated in a lineup conducted without notice to and in the absence of his counsel after he had been indicted. The Supreme Court held that the Sixth Amendment invalidated his subsequent conviction because the post-indictment lineup was a "critical stage",[8] at which "the presence of counsel is necessary to preserve the defendant's basic right to a fair trial." The Court pointed to two factors which made the lineup in *Wade* deserving of Sixth Amendment protection. First, "substantial prejudice to defendant's rights" could result from the confrontation because "the trial which might determine the accused's fate may well be not that in the courtroom but at the pretrial confrontation." Second, counsel could help avoid that prejudice by observing the lineup and using what he observed at trial to contest its results. The Court was not comfortable forcing the attorney to rely on other sources of information about the lineup. In particular, it noted that the defendant is unlikely to know what to look for even if he is calm enough to do so, and will in any event often be an unwilling or relatively unconvincing witness at trial (at least compared to the police). The eyewitness too will probably be impervious to subtle sugges-

---

5. Id. at 985.

6. Other techniques for combatting the vagaries of eyewitness testimony, not derived from the constitution, include cautionary instructions to the jury, see *United States v. Telfaire,* 469 F.2d 552 (D.C.Cir.1972), and expert psychological testimony pointing out the various problems with eyewitness evidence. See, e.g., *State v. Chapple,* 135 Ariz. 281, 660 P.2d 1208 (1983).

7. 388 U.S. 218, 87 S.Ct. 1926 (1967).

8. See § 31.03(a)(1) for a detailed discussion of critical stage analysis.

tions, and thus also an inadequate source of information. To the Court's observations can be added the likely fact that neither the eyewitness or the police who conduct the lineup will be highly motivated to cooperate with the defense.

The Court's apparent concern that counsel have sufficient information to mount an effective subsequent challenge of a lineup procedure suggested that *Wade* was based as much on the Sixth Amendment right to effective cross-examination and confrontation of one's accusers [9] as it was on a Sixth Amendment right to assistance of counsel at the identification. So construed, *Wade* would stand in contrast to cases like *Miranda v. Arizona* [10] and *Massiah v. United States,* [11] which required counsel during police questioning primarily to assist the defendant in dealing with police conduct at the time it occurs, rather than in exposing its impropriety in future proceedings. But *Wade* also talks about counsel's ability to "avert prejudice" at the lineup. As subsequent discussion develops, the scope of the right to counsel could differ significantly, depending upon which conceptual basis for *Wade* is chosen. In any event, both *Wade* and subsequent cases have indicated that its holding is a narrow one, heavily dependent upon the type of procedure at issue and the stage of the criminal process at which it takes place.

(a) Type of Procedure. Certain types of identification procedures do not, by their nature, trigger the Sixth Amendment right to counsel. *Wade* itself distinguished the lineup from "various other preparatory steps, such as systematized or scientific analyzing of the accused's fingerprints, blood sample, clothing, hair and the like." In such cases, counsel is not required because

> [k]nowledge of the techniques of science and technology is sufficiently available, and the variables in techniques few enough, that the accused has the opportunity for a meaningful confrontation of the Government's case at trial through the ordinary processes of cross-examination of the Government's expert witnesses and the presentation of the evidence of his own experts.

Thus, in *Gilbert v. California,* [12] a companion case to *Wade,* the Court held that the taking of handwriting exemplars is not a "critical stage" of the criminal proceeding requiring counsel because such exemplars can easily be duplicated and analyzed at trial. As the Court's reasoning suggests, *Gilbert* and the other cases of "systematized" identification procedures mentioned in *Wade* are more easily explained on right to effective cross-exami-

---

9. See § 28.05(b) for a discussion of the right to cross-examine witnesses.

10. 384 U.S. 436, 86 S.Ct. 1602 (1966), discussed in § 16.02(d).

11. 377 U.S. 201, 84 S.Ct. 1199 (1964), discussed in § 16.02(c).

12. 388 U.S. 263, 87 S.Ct. 1951 (1967).

nation grounds than assistance-of-counsel grounds: while one might require counsel if the objective were to ensure that no police misconduct occurs during the taking of the sample or its analysis, the opposite result is supportable because the accuracy of the procedure can be adequately tested even if counsel does not observe it while it occurs.

Because photo identification is not a "systematized" procedure, the effective cross-examination interpretation of *Wade* and *Gilbert* would suggest that counsel be afforded at such sessions. But in *United States v. Ash,*[13] the Court held there is no such right, relying in part on the dubious assertion that the ability to preserve the photo array makes such a procedure easier to reconstruct than a lineup. As *Wade* indicated, counsel is required at a lineup not just to observe its composition (which, it should be noted, can just as easily be "preserved" by a photograph) but to witness police and eyewitness conduct during the procedure. With a photo array, an attorney is arguably even more necessary, since, in contrast to a lineup, the defendant is not present and cannot provide any information about what happened.

Perhaps realizing this, the *Ash* majority relied more heavily on another justification: the conclusion that, because photo arrays do not involve situations in which the defendant must deal with the "intricacies of the law and the advocacy of the public prosecutor," they do not call for counsel's presence. This so-called "trial-like confrontation" analysis marked a significant departure from previous right to counsel jurisprudence, which had recognized that counsel can provide the defendant non-technical as well as legal aid.[14] More importantly for present purposes, it failed to distinguish the result in *Ash* from the Court's other identification decisions. *Wade* required counsel at lineups, yet a defendant's participation in a lineup does not involve an "adversarial" confrontation with the prosecutor, nor require an understanding of the legal process. While the defendant in a lineup has an interest in ensuring that the procedure is properly conducted, an interest which counsel can help protect, this is also true of a photo procedure, and is not related to the defendant's presence. Thus, *Ash* and *Wade* can be reconciled only if one accepts the notion that the defendant's presence alone decides the Sixth Amendment issue. But, if that is the case, then one would also have to conclude that counsel is required when police seek a handwriting exemplar from the defendant, in contrast to the outcome in *Gilbert.*[15]

13. 413 U.S. 300, 93 S.Ct. 2568 (1973).

14. See, e.g., *Miranda v. Arizona,* 384 U.S. 436, 86 S.Ct. 1602 (1966), discussed in § 16.02(d).

15. Perhaps the best explanation for *Ash* is found in the Court's insinuation that, had it found otherwise, it would have also been required to find a right to counsel during routine government

Ash left unresolved whether the right to counsel applied to the third type of eyewitness identification procedure, the one-on-one confrontation or showup. Not surprisingly, given the fact that such an event is both difficult to reconstruct and requires the defendant's presence, the Court later held, in *Moore v. Illinois,*[16] that a defendant is entitled to an attorney in such situations. Under current law, then, lineups and showups are the only identification procedures which implicate the right to counsel.

(b) Timing of the Procedure. Not every lineup or showup implicates the right to counsel. Consistent with the Court's movement away from an effective cross-examination analysis and toward its "trial-like confrontation" assistance-of-counsel approach, the Court in *Kirby v. Illinois*[17] held that a defendant has no right to an attorney during identification procedures that take place before "prosecution has commenced." This holding derived both from the language of the Sixth Amendment, which speaks of the assistance of counsel in all "criminal prosecutions," and the perception, later echoed in *Ash,* that only after the initiation of "adversary judicial criminal proceedings" is a defendant "faced with the prosecutorial forces of organized society, and immersed in the intricacies of substantive and procedural criminal law." Thus, until such proceedings are initiated, "by way of formal charge, preliminary hearing, indictment, information, or arraignment," a person is not entitled to counsel at lineups or showups. In *Moore,* the Court reaffirmed *Kirby,* making clear, however, that the right to counsel can be triggered *during* arraignment on the warrant, as well as after.

Kirby can be subjected to the same type of criticism as *Ash:* a post-charge identification is no more (or less) likely than a pre-charge identification to involve the defendant in the "intricacies of substantive or procedural law;" at the same time, the substantial degree of prejudice which can result from a pretrial identification procedure exists *whenever* it takes place. The *Kirby* Court may have had in mind the practical reality that obtaining counsel for persons subjected to identifications at an early stage of the criminal process might be very difficult. Police often use showups, and to a lesser extent lineups, to eliminate, as well as identify, suspects soon after a crime is committed; appointing counsel for every person so displayed would be impractical. If this was the Court's concern, however, a better rule might have been to create an

interviews with witnesses, despite the defendant's absence and despite the concomitant interference with the prosecution's development of its case. For discussion of this point, in the context of the Court's other cases dealing with the right to counsel, see § 31.03(a)(2).

16. 434 U.S. 220, 98 S.Ct. 458 (1977).

17. 406 U.S. 682, 92 S.Ct. 1877 (1972).

"exigency" exception for emergency identifications,[18] rather than artificially limiting counsel to identifications conducted at or after arraignment proceedings.

Along these lines, *Wade* indicated that, even after formal charging, "substitute counsel" might be sufficient "where notification and presence of the suspect's own counsel would result in prejudicial delay." While the majority in *Wade* apparently had in mind a "human" substitute, in some cases, particularly lineups or showups conducted at the stationhouse, a videotape of the identification might prove adequate in emergency circumstances. Indeed, as suggested in the next chapter,[19] videotaping the identification might meet Sixth Amendment requirements even when there is no emergency.

(c) Waiver and Alternatives to Counsel. A confrontation theory of the right to counsel would suggest that the right can never be waived. Because the defendant's direct involvement in the procedure makes him less observant and because he may not witness all phases of the identification process, it could be argued that counsel, or some "substitute" for counsel, must be present to ensure an opportunity for adequate reconstruction at trial. But, under the ascendant "assistance" approach, waiver would seem permissible, since a defendant might reasonably feel that he can confront the "intricacies" of the adversary system on his own. *Wade* itself, perhaps somewhat contradictorily given its primary emphasis on the right to effective cross-examination, indicated that a defendant subjected to a lineup could waive counsel, if the waiver is "intelligent." Presumably, this language requires, at the least, that a person be told he has a right to counsel, and that an explicit waiver be obtained.[20]

Wade also stated that "legislation or other regulations, such as those of local police departments, which eliminate the risks of abuse and unintentional suggestion at lineup proceedings and the impediments to meaningful confrontation at trial may . . . remove the basis for regarding the stage as 'critical.'" Here, the Court seemed to be saying that the right to counsel would be eliminated if standardized procedures: (1) minimize the suggestiveness of the procedure; and (2) make adequate reconstruction of the identification possible without the attorney being present. The methods of accomplishing these goals derive in large part from due process analysis, to which we now turn.

---

18. See § 18.03(b) for examples of emergencies where counsel might not be required.

19. See § 18.02(e).

20. *People v. Coleman,* 43 N.Y.2d 222, 401 N.Y.S.2d 57, 371 N.E.2d 819

(1977); cf. *Patterson v. Illinois,* 487 U.S. 285, 108 S.Ct. 2389 (1988) (discussing waiver of Sixth Amendment right to counsel during questioning), discussed in § 16.04(c).

17.03 Due Process

In *Stovall v. Denno,*[21] a companion case of *Wade* and *Gilbert*, the Supreme Court made clear that, in addition to the safeguards provided by the Sixth Amendment, the accused is entitled to protection under the Fifth Amendment against an identification procedure "so unnecessarily suggestive and conducive to irreparable mistaken identification" as to amount to denial of due process of law. Unlike the Sixth Amendment right to counsel, this due process standard applies to identification procedures without regard to whether adversary judicial criminal proceedings have begun.[22]

Stovall established that the totality of circumstances must be examined to determine whether the accused was deprived of the due process of law. In *Stovall*, for instance, the Court held that the identification challenged (a one-on-one emergency confrontation between the accused and an injured witness in a hospital room) did not violate the Fifth Amendment because it was not *unnecessarily* suggestive, and there was not a substantial likelihood of misidentification. To elucidate the *Stovall* rule, the three elements of suggestiveness, necessity and likelihood of misidentification must be examined.

(a) Suggestiveness. An identification procedure is suggestive if it, in effect, dictates to the witness, "this is the man." For example, a lineup is suggestive if the accused is the only one who faintly resembles the person who committed the offense or if the police point out the accused to the suspect. A one-on-one confrontation in which the police present a suspect to a witness is, of course, highly suggestive.[23] The use of suggestive identification procedures is disapproved because it is feared that the suggestion, and not the remembrance, will trigger an identification.

Illustrative is *Moore v. Illinois,*[24] where the Court relied not only on the Sixth Amendment right to counsel, but also seemed to base its reversal on due process grounds. The majority opinion's description of the facts suggests the dual basis for holding Moore's identification unconstitutional:

> It is difficult to imagine a more suggestive manner in which to present a suspect to a witness for their critical first confrontation than was employed in this case. The victim, who had seen her assailant for only 10 to 15 seconds, was asked to make her identification after she was told that she was going

---

21. 388 U.S. 293, 87 S.Ct. 1967 (1967).

22. *Kirby v. Illinois*, 406 U.S. 682, 92 S.Ct. 1877 (1972).

23. See *United States v. Wade*, 388 U.S. 218, 87 S.Ct. 1926 (1967) (delineat-ing other types of suggestive lineups). See also, *United States ex rel Kirby v. Sturges*, 510 F.2d 397 (7th Cir.1975), cert. denied 421 U.S. 1016, 95 S.Ct. 2424 (1975).

24. 434 U.S. 220, 98 S.Ct. 458 (1977).

to view a suspect, after she was told his name and heard it called as he was led before the bench, and after she heard the prosecutor recite the evidence believed to implicate petitioner. Had petitioner been represented by counsel, some or all of this suggestiveness could have been avoided.

Suggestiveness alone will not automatically render a particular identification procedure unconstitutional, however. The Court has indicated that if a suggestive procedure was "necessary" and did not create a substantial likelihood of misidentification, it will withstand a due process challenge. More recently, it has indicated that even an unnecessarily suggestive procedure is permissible if the resulting identification has indicia of reliability.

(b) Necessity. The Supreme Court has on several occasions sanctioned the use of a suggestive procedure on the grounds of exigent circumstances. As noted earlier, *Stovall* found a one-man confrontation at a hospital constitutionally permissible because the witness was in danger of dying. In *Simmons v. United States*,[25] a bank robbery had been committed and the felons were still at large. The police showed six snapshots to witnesses of the robbery, from which the defendants were identified. Although the Supreme Court found that the photo display of the snapshots fell "short of the ideal," "[i]t was essential for the FBI agents swiftly to determine whether they were on the right track, so that they could properly deploy their forces in Chicago and, if necessary, alert officials in other cities." This justification, and the Court's finding that there had been little danger of misidentification, led to a conclusion that the procedure did not deny the accused due process of law. Thus, the Warren Court indicated that a suggestive procedure may be upheld if its use was unavoidable, especially if there is no indication that the resulting identification was unreliable.

(c) Reliability. More recent cases indicate that the most critical factor in the totality of the circumstances is the reliability of the identification. *Stovall* had seemed to suggest that the results of an unnecessarily suggestive procedure should be inadmissible, regardless of its reliability. But in *Neil v. Biggers*,[26] decided five years later, the Court intimated that reliability and not suggestiveness should govern admissibility analysis. In *Biggers*, the accused was identified at a station-house showup conducted seven months after the crime. Although the Court conceded that the procedure had been unnecessarily suggestive, it held that the accused had not been denied due process of law. It is "the likelihood of misidentification which violates a defendant's right to due process." The Court offered a list of factors to be considered in evaluating the likelihood of misidentification, including:

25. 390 U.S. 377, 88 S.Ct. 967 (1968).   **26.** 409 U.S. 188, 93 S.Ct. 375 (1972).

The opportunity of the witness to view the criminal at the time of the crime, the witness' degree of attention, the accuracy of the witness' prior description of the criminal, the level of certainty demonstrated by the witness at the confrontation, and the length of time between the crime and the confrontation.

The Supreme Court reaffirmed the precept that reliability is the "linchpin" in the analysis of pretrial identification procedures in *Manson v. Brathwaite.*[27] In *Manson,* an undercover police officer purchased heroin from a seller while standing near him in a well-lit hallway for two to three minutes. A few minutes after the sale was consummated, the officer described the seller to another officer, who suspected the respondent and gave the undercover officer a picture of him. Two days after receiving the picture, the undercover officer identified it as a picture of the person from whom he had bought heroin. The Supreme Court, in an opinion by Justice Blackmun, held that the single-photograph display did not create a substantial likelihood of irreparable misidentification in the "totality of the circumstances". The witness was a trained police officer, had a sufficient opportunity to view the suspect, accurately described him, positively identified his photograph, and made the photographic identification only two days after the crime. These factors counterbalanced the suggestiveness of the identification procedure used and the fact that less suggestive alternatives were readily available.

If the reliability of identifications could be adequately gauged there would be little problem with the *Biggers-Manson* rule that unnecessarily suggestive identification procedures are permissible. But as the discussion in the introduction to this chapter suggests, difficult-to-discern perceptual and memory deficiencies often affect the accuracy of identifications. And even if such deficiencies are "recognized," their magnitude may not be apparent to courts assessing the admissibility of identification evidence. Thus, when a suggestive procedure is *unnecessary,* it should not be premitted.[28]

17.04 Other Constitutional Considerations

Identification procedures could arguably implicate both the Fourth Amendment and the privilege against self-incrimination, as well as the Sixth Amendment and the Due Process Clause. Taking a handwriting sample, for instance, could be viewed as both a "seizure" and as coercing the production of incriminating information. But the Supreme Court has indicated challenges on Fourth or Fifth Amendment grounds will rarely succeed.

27. 432 U.S. 98, 97 S.Ct. 2243 (1977).

28. The necessity principle is discussed further in §§ 18.02(e) and 18.03(a).

(a) Fourth Amendment. With respect to the Fourth Amendment, the Court has held that one has no "reasonable expectation of privacy" in characteristics that are exposed to the public such as one's visage, one's handwriting and the sound of one's voice.[29] Thus, only the seizure of the person necessary to obtain such identifying information need meet the reasonableness requirement of that Amendment; subsequently viewing a face or taking a handwriting sample is not a "seizure" and need not be justified by probable cause or even reasonable suspicion that it will produce evidence.

Fourth Amendment restrictions on the seizure of the person necessary to obtain identifying information depend upon the entity doing the seizing. When the grand jury is the investigating body, the Supreme Court has held that, so long as the requirements for a subpoena are met, a person can be required to appear for purposes of providing voice and handwriting exemplars.[30] Presumably, the same rule would apply to grand jury efforts to obtain other types of identifying information. As discussed elsewhere in this book,[31] generally a subpoena cannot be quashed unless it requests information clearly irrelevant to the investigation or is overbroad.

When the *police* want to seize a person for the purpose of obtaining identifying information, the Fourth Amendment imposes more onerous requirements, although probably not at the level required for seizures motivated by other objectives. Typically, probable cause is required for an arrest or any other prolonged detention.[32] But in *Hayes v. Florida,*[33] the Court stated in dictum: "There is . . . support in our cases for the view that the Fourth Amendment would permit seizures for the purpose of fingerprinting, if there is reasonable suspicion that the suspect has committed a criminal act, if there is a reasonable basis for believing that fingerprinting will establish or negate the suspect's connection with that crime, and if the procedure is carried out with dispatch."[34] The majority also stated that, while such a seizure would require judicial authorization if it involved entry into the home or removal to the police station, the police could act on their own for an "identification-only" seizure on the street. The appar-

29. See, e.g., *United States v. Dionisio,* 410 U.S. 1, 93 S.Ct. 764 (1973), discussed in § 4.03(b). Note that when the identifying "information" is not exposed to the public, as is true with blood, then a seizure requires probable cause. *Schmerber v. California,* 384 U.S. 757, 86 S.Ct. 1826 (1966), discussed in § 9.02.

30. *United States v. Dionisio,* 410 U.S. 1, 93 S.Ct. 764 (1973); *United States v. Mara,* 410 U.S. 19, 93 S.Ct. 774 (1973).

31. See § 23.05(a)(1).

32. See § 3.02 for a discussion of the types of detentions which require probable cause.

33. 470 U.S. 811, 105 S.Ct. 1643 (1985).

34. See also, *Davis v. Mississippi,* 394 U.S. 721, 89 S.Ct. 1394 (1969).

ent rationale for both these conclusions was the temporary, relatively unintrusive nature of the fingerprinting process. In his concurring opinion in *Hayes*, Justice Brennan argued in favor of the traditional probable cause standard. With respect to on-site fingerprinting in particular, Brennan noted that it might take place "in full view of any passerby" and thus "would involve a singular intrusion on the suspect's privacy, an intrusion that would not be justifiable . . . as necessary for the officer's protection."

The reasoning of the dictum in Hayes would also justify seizures from the home for the purpose of a line-up or showup, based solely on a judicial finding of reasonable suspicion. Further, again assuming reasonable suspicion, Hayes would allow police to act on their own in arranging on-the-scene lineups or showups. On the other hand, suspicionless or random seizures of a person for such identification procedures would be impermissible.

(b) Fifth Amendment. In *Wade*, the Court made clear that the privilege against self-incrimination does not limit the use of identification procedures. Although incriminating evidence can result from these procedures, such evidence is "real" or "physical," not "testimonial"; therefore it is not protected by the Fifth Amendment.[35] Thus, *Wade* found no violation of the privilege when the state requires the accused to exhibit himself for observation in a lineup. Nor, according to *Wade*, is there a Fifth Amendment violation when a lineup participant is required to utter words purportedly uttered by the perpetrator of the crime, because "his voice [is used] as an identifying physical characteristic, not to speak his guilt." On the same rationale, *Gilbert* held that the taking of handwriting exemplars does not violate the privilege. Compelled fingerprinting and other identification procedures could be justified similarly.

17.05 Identifications as Fruit

(a) Of Previous Illegal Identifications. A trial identification is made under extremely suggestive circumstances. Not only is it a one-on-one confrontation, but the eyewitness knows that the prosecution has identified the defendant as the suspect. Nonetheless, most courts routinely permit such identifications,[36] perhaps in part to avoid hearsay concerns,[37] but primarily because there has

35. See § 15.04 on the "testimonial evidence" requirement.

36. See *State v. White*, 160 Ariz. 24, 770 P.2d 328 (1989); *State v. Hannah*, 312 N.C. 286, 322 S.E.2d 148 (1984).

37. Traditionally, evidence of pretrial identification was viewed as inadmissible hearsay. However, most courts today allow such evidence to corroborate an in-court identification or under a hearsay exception. See Mauet, "Prior Identifications in Criminal Cases: Hearsay and Confrontation Issues," 24 Ariz.L.Rev. 29 (1982).

almost always been a previous, properly conducted identification of the defendant.[38] If this previous identification is invalid on Sixth Amendment, due process, or Fourth Amendment grounds, how is the in-court identification affected? The answer to this question depends upon whether the latter identification is "tainted" by the previous illegality. In such cases, analogous to analysis under the Fourth Amendment, one must decide whether the in-court identification is "fruit of the poisonous tree." [39]

In *Wade*, the Supreme Court explicitly recognized the analogy to its Fourth Amendment cases, and held that an illegally conducted lineup does not invalidate subsequent identifications if the subsequent identification derives from an "independent source." The majority mentioned several factors, many of them picked up later in *Biggers'* reliability test, which a court should consider in determining whether an in-court identification derives from an independent source. These include:

> the prior opportunity to observe the alleged criminal act, the existence of any discrepancy between any pre-lineup description and the defendant's actual description, any identification prior to lineup of another person, the identification by picture of the defendant prior to the lineup, failure to identify the defendant on a prior occasion, and the lapse of time between the alleged act and the lineup identification.

Courts have also considered other factors in making the independent source determination. For example, the fact that a witness did not experience extreme anxiety or extraordinary pressure during the event he allegedly witnessed has been found to create a lesser likelihood of distorted observation and to increase the probability that an in-court identification was based on the original observation and not a tainted pretrial identification.[40]

While conceptually the independent source test may make sense, in practice it seems impossible to implement. As pointed out in the introduction to this chapter, a person's "memory" of an event is composed not just of perceptions registered at the time the event occurs but also of subsequent "data" which helps fill in gaps as the recall of the event inevitably decays. Asking a judge to discern the extent to which a new identification is the product of the original perceptions instead of the new "filler" data is a futile task, especially since the witness is likely to be unaware of this substitution process himself.

38. If the in-court identification is the first identification, it is more likely to be found invalid. See § 18.03(a)(6).

39. See § 2.04.

40. *United States v. Johnson*, 412 F.2d 753 (1st Cir.1969), cert. denied 397 U.S. 944, 90 S.Ct. 959 (1970).

Nonetheless, the lower courts have had little trouble applying the independent source doctrine to validate subsequent identifications, often reciting nothing more than a conclusion that the witness had a "good" opportunity to view the incident in question.[41] The better rule might well be to bar from evidence all identifications made subsequent to an identification which is found to be unreliable. An alternative to such a rule is the practice, discussed below,[42] of permitting the reliability of an identification to be challenged in front of the jury even after it is found admissible on independent source grounds. As matters stand now, violation of the right to counsel and due process guarantees during the pretrial process seldom prejudice the prosecution, since an in-court identification is usually found "independent" of the previous identification.

(b) Of Other Illegalities. Suppose that the defendant is illegally arrested and then placed in a lineup. Or suppose that he is subjected to an unconstitutionally coercive interrogation during which he names a person who later identifies him as the perpetrator. If the identification procedure in these cases is conducted properly—that is, if the defendant is provided with counsel and unnecessary suggestivity is avoided—then the identification will very likely be reliable. Should such an identification nonetheless be excluded from evidence, on the ground that it is fruit of the poisonous arrest or confession, actions which should be deterred through application of the exclusionary rule?

In *United States v. Crews,*[43] the Court addressed, but did not definitively resolve, this issue. In *Crews,* the police originally detained the defendant based on the general descriptions of three separate robbery victims, and a tentative face-to-face identification by a fourth person who had seen the defendant on the day of the first robbery "hanging around" the area in which all three crimes were committed. While at police headquarters, Crews was briefly questioned, photographed, and then released. On the following day, the police showed the victim of the first robbery an array of eight photographs, including one of the defendant. Although she had previously viewed over one hundred pictures without identifying the assailant, she immediately selected Crews' photograph on this occasion. Three days later, one of the other victims made a similar identification. Crews was again taken into custody and positively identified by the two women who had made the photographic identifications.

41. See Note, 55 Minn.L.Rev. 779 (1971) (courts have "easily found an 'independent source' for an in-court identification"). See also, *United States v. Dring,* 930 F.2d 687 (9th Cir.1991); *United States v. Lewin,* 900 F.2d 145 (8th Cir.1990); *United States ex rel.*

Kosik v. Napoli, 814 F.2d 1151 (7th Cir. 1987).

42. See § 17.06.

43. 445 U.S. 463, 100 S.Ct. 1244 (1980).

The trial judge found that Crews' initial detention had been an arrest without probable cause and that the products of that arrest—the photographic and lineup identifications—could not be introduced at trial. But he also concluded that the victims would still be able to identify the defendant in court based upon recollection untainted by these identifications. At trial, all three victims identified Crews as their assailant. Crews was convicted of the first armed robbery, but found not guilty of the other two robberies. The lower federal courts reversed the conviction, finding that, under the "fruit of the poisonous tree" doctrine, the in-court identification which led to the conviction was at least indirectly the product of official misconduct (the illegal arrest).

The Supreme Court, while agreeing the arrest was illegal, unanimously upheld the conviction, although the reasons for doing so varied. Justice Brennan, writing for three members of the Court, noted that "[i]n the typical fruit of the poisonous tree case . . . the challenged evidence was acquired by the police *after* some initial Fourth Amendment violation." Here no new evidence was acquired through the illegal arrest; the "fruit" had already been obtained by the time the illegal detention took place. Brennan reached this conclusion by dividing a victim's in-court identification into three components: (1) the victim's presence in the courtroom; (2) the victim's ability to give an accurate identification based on observations made at the time of the crime; and (3) the physical presence of the defendant in the courtroom. He concluded that, in *Crews,* none of these elements " 'ha[d] been come at by exploitation' of the violation of the defendant's Fourth Amendment rights." The victim's identity had been known to the police before the defendant's illegal arrest. The trial court "expressly found that the witness's courtroom identification rested on an independent recollection of her initial encounter with the assailant." Finally, given the fact that the police had already known Crews' identity and had some basis for suspecting his involvement before the illegal arrest, Brennan argued that the Court did not need to decide whether the defendant's visage was "fruit" of the police misconduct.

Five members of the Court, in two separate opinions, diverged from the last part of this analysis, relying on *Frisbie v. Collins,*[44] which held that an illegal arrest does not alone bar prosecution or conviction. As one of the two opinions put it, this ruling "forecloses the claim that [a defendant's] face can be suppressible as a fruit of the unlawful arrest." In practice, this holding means that a properly obtained courtroom identification by an eyewitness is virtually never suppressible as fruit of an illegal arrest (or an

44. 342 U.S. 519, 72 S.Ct. 509 (1952), discussed in § 3.01.

illegal interrogation), even if the defendant's "visage" is in court solely because of the illegal action.[45]

This reading of *Crews* must be considered in conjunction with the holding in *Davis v. Mississippi,*[46] which suppressed the fingerprints of a person who had been illegally detained as part of a dragnet roundup of scores of individuals during a rape investigation. Fingerprints are even more trustworthy than a properly obtained eyewitness identification. The only significant difference between *Davis* and *Crews,* therefore, is the nature of the Fourth Amendment violation. The Court may generally abide by the non-exclusionary approach taken by the five justices in *Crews,* but require exclusion when the illegality underlying the identification is egregious, as it was in *Davis.*

17.06   Procedure for Determining Admissibility

Wade and *Stovall* make clear that evidence of an identification found to violate the defendant's rights to counsel or due process, and any subsequent "tainted" identification, must be suppressed. Generally, the state bears the burden of establishing the presence of counsel or an intelligent waiver by the accused,[47] while the defendant must prove a violation of due process.[48] In some jurisdictions, if the defendant can show that an identification procedure was suggestive, the burden shifts to the state to show the justification of exigent circumstance.[49] The prosecution bears the burden of showing in-court identification testimony derives from an origin independent of tainted pretrial identification.[50]

Normally the suppression hearing is held prior to trial or, if during trial, in the absence of the jury. However, in *Watkins v. Sowders,*[51] the Supreme Court held that these procedures are not constitutionally mandated. The Court recognized that hearings to determine the admissibility of *confessions* should generally be held with the jury excused, given the effect a confession found to be inadmissible can have on the jury's deliberations even when they

---

45. The one caveat to this conclusion might be if the illegal arrest (or interrogation) of the defendant also produced the name of the eyewitness who eventually identified him (Brennan's first component of an identification). But see, *United States v. Ceccolini,* 435 U.S. 268, 98 S.Ct. 1054 (1978), discussed in § 2.04(b)(2), which suggests that when the fruit of an illegality is a witness, exclusion will usually not occur.

46. 394 U.S. 721, 89 S.Ct. 1394 (1969).

47. *United States v. Garner,* 439 F.2d 525 (D.C.Cir.1970). See also, Sobel, Eyewitness Identification § 85 (New York 1972).

48. *Stovall v. Denno,* 388 U.S. 293, 87 S.Ct. 1967 (1967); *Allen v. Rhay,* 431 F.2d 1160 (9th Cir.1970), cert. denied 404 U.S. 834, 92 S.Ct. 116 (1971).

49. See *Sanchell v. Parratt,* 530 F.2d 286 (8th Cir.1976); Sobel, supra note 47, § 85. See generally, *Clemons v. United States,* 408 F.2d 1230 (D.C.Cir.1968), cert. denied 394 U.S. 964, 89 S.Ct. 1318 (1969) (discussion of *Wade-Stovall* hearing).

50. *United States v. Wade,* 388 U.S. 218, 87 S.Ct. 1926 (1967).

51. 449 U.S. 341, 101 S.Ct. 654 (1981).

are instructed to disregard it.[52]   But Justice Stewart, writing for the Court, argued that even if this procedure were constitutionally required when confessions are involved, identification hearings are distinguishable.   He pointed out that the admissibility of a confession depends upon more than its reliability;   the police conduct involved may require its exclusion regardless of how accurate it is. Where identifications are concerned, on the other hand, reliability is the principal determinant of admissibility.   Thus, judging the admissibility of an identification involves "the very task our system must assume juries can perform," and need not require the jury's dismissal.   This reasoning ignores the fact that an identification is as powerful as a confession in its effect on jurors;   as with a confession, once an identification is found inadmissible, every effort should be made to keep them from knowing about it.   Since the identifications in *Watkins* were admissible, the Court did not have to confront this problem in that case.   But it conceded that a judicial determination with the jury excused "may often be advisable," [53] and acknowledged that "[i]n some circumstances such a determination may be constitutionally necessary."

As *Watkins* recognized, if identification evidence is found admissible, then its credibility is for the jury to decide.   A determination by the judge that an identification is reliable does not foreclose the issue.   Thus, for instance, even though a suggestive procedure may have been justified by exigent circumstances, its unreliability may be argued to the jury.   It should also be noted that equivocation or indefiniteness on the part of the identifying party affects the weight of the evidence and not its admissibility.[54]   For example, in *United States v. Hines*,[55] a witness inspecting a police book of photographs stated that one of the pictures looked like, but was not, the assailant.   The court held that evidence of the "looks like" description was relevant to the issue of identification.   The probative value of the evidence was a matter for the jury.

17.07 Conclusion

The vagaries of eyewitness identifications have led the courts to place several restrictions on the means used to obtain them. These restrictions are summarized at the conclusion of the next chapter, after a closer look at the various identification techniques.   The bibliography also appears at the end of the next chapter.

52. See § 16.06(a).

53. The Court suggested that if the defendant could show specific instances when the presence of the jury inhibited his attorney's cross-examination, a due process claim might lie.

54. See, e.g. *United States v. Peterson*, 435 F.2d 192 (7th Cir.1970), cert. denied 403 U.S. 907, 91 S.Ct. 2212 (1971); *Russell v. United States*, 408 F.2d 1280 (D.C.Cir.1969), cert. denied 395 U.S. 928, 89 S.Ct. 1786 (1969).

55. 460 F.2d 949 (D.C.Cir.1972).

Chapter Eighteen

EYEWITNESS IDENTIFICATION TECHNIQUES

18.01 Introduction

The discussion in the previous chapter treated the various pretrial identification techniques together in an effort to provide an overview of the Supreme Court's approach to identification issues. This chapter will examine separately those identification techniques which rely on eyewitnesses—specifically, lineups, show-ups and confrontations, and photographic identifications—so as to better focus on the special problems associated with each. To some extent, this will necessitate repeating the holdings discussed in the last chapter.

18.02 Lineups

Of the three identification techniques discussed in this chapter, properly conducted lineups are the least likely to result in misidentification. As such, they can help police apprehend suspects, relieve the innocent and provide valuable trial evidence. But they can also be unnecessarily suggestive and produce unreliable results. The rules governing the conduct of lineups that are described below are aimed at preventing misidentifications while at the same time permitting full prosecutorial exploitation of lineups.

(a) **Compelling Participation.** In *United States v. Wade,*[1] the Supreme Court held that the privilege against self-incrimination is not violated by forcing a person to participate in a lineup, because the procedure requires only the exhibition of physical characteristics and thus is not testimonial in nature. For the same reason, a person in a lineup can be "required to use his voice as an identifying characteristic." Because the privilege is not implicated, a refusal to participate in a court ordered lineup can subject a person to contempt sanctions.[2] Further, a defendant who refuses to participate may be asked about his refusal or, if he does not take the stand, subject to prosecutorial comment about his failure to participate.[3]

1. 388 U.S. 218, 87 S.Ct. 1926 (1967), this aspect of which is discussed in § 17.04(b).

2. *Doss v. United States,* 431 F.2d 601 (9th Cir.1970).

3. *United States v. Parhms,* 424 F.2d 152 (9th Cir.1970), cert. denied 400 U.S. 846, 91 S.Ct. 92 (1970); *United States v. Franks,* 511 F.2d 25 (6th Cir.1975), cert. denied 422 U.S. 1042, 95 S.Ct. 2656 (1975) (refusal to comply with court order to give voice exemplar admissible to show guilt).

The Fourth Amendment may prohibit indiscriminate use of a person as a lineup subject in some cases. When the person is not already in custody, the Supreme Court has suggested that, unless there is a reasonable suspicion that the person has committed the crime being investigated, "seizing" that person for the purpose of placing him in a lineup is unconstitutional.[4] On the other hand, several lower courts have held that, if a person is already in custody, he may be made to stand in a lineup for any crime as "filler material," without judicial authorization or any showing of suspicion.[5]

(b) Defense Request for a Lineup. The defendant may ask for a lineup prior to trial in an attempt to counteract the results of a previous, more suggestively conducted identification procedure, or merely to prove that the eyewitness cannot identify him. At least one lower court has held that due process requires granting a defense motion for a lineup where "eyewitness identification is shown to be a material issue and there exists a reasonable likelihood of a mistaken identification which a lineup would tend to resolve."[6] Most lower courts have held, however, that the matter is solely within the discretion of the trial court. In *United States v. Ravich*,[7] for instance, the court rejected the defendant's contention that he was constitutionally entitled to a lineup when the prosecution had chosen not to conduct one. Rather, it directed the trial court to consider carefully the defense request, taking into account a number of factors, including:

> the length of time between the crime or arrest and the request, the possibility that the defendant may have altered his appearance . . ., the extent of inconvenience to prosecution witnesses, the possibility that revealing the identity of the prosecution witnesses will subject them to intimidation, the propriety of other identification procedures used by the prosecution, and the degree of doubt concerning the identification.

The court found that the trial court had not abused its discretion in denying the defendant's request, in particular because prior photo identifications of the defendant had been conducted properly.

---

4. *Hayes v. Florida*, 470 U.S. 811, 105 S.Ct. 1643 (1985), discussed in § 17.04(a). See also, *United States v. Allen*, 408 F.2d 1287 (D.C.Cir.1969) (forced participation in lineup for crime other than that for which defendant arrested permissible given that the similarity in modus operandi created a reasonable suspicion that he was responsible).

5. *United States v. Anderson*, 490 F.2d 785 (D.C.Cir.1974).

6. *Evans v. Superior Court*, 11 Cal.3d 617, 114 Cal.Rptr. 121, 522 P.2d 681 (1974).

7. 421 F.2d 1196 (2d Cir.1970), cert. denied 400 U.S. 834, 91 S.Ct. 69 (1970).

A defense request for a lineup *at* trial is arguably on stronger ground. An in-court identification is often inherently suggestive, mainly because the defendant is seated conspicuously at the defense table. Indeed, in *Moore v. Illinois*,[8] the Supreme Court suggested that, at least when the in-court identification is the first confrontation between the witness and the defendant, counsel could postpone the proceeding until a lineup is arranged. But, again, many lower courts have left a ruling on such a request up to the trial court.[9] Thus, wide variation in practice exists. In *United States v. Moss*,[10] the court granted a continuance so that the defense attorney could bring in other members of the defendant's race to sit with him. But in *Dent v. State*,[11] the appellate court found that an in-court identification was not improper simply because the defendant was the only member of his race in the courtroom.

A slightly different argument was raised, and rejected, in *United States v. Hamilton.*[12] There, the defendant contended that the admissibility of an in-court identification derived from an initial photo identification should be conditioned upon an additional confirmatory procedure, such as a lineup. Although emphasizing the greater relative reliability of lineups and acknowledging the merit of the defendant's proposal, the court concluded that "confirmation of a photographic identification is not an imperative of due process." The court also declined to exercise its supervisory process to require such a confirmation. *Hamilton* would seem to follow from the Supreme Court's reliance on reliability as the "linchpin" of due process analysis, without regard to the suggestiveness or necessity of the identification procedure used.

(c) The Role of Counsel. The holding in *United States v. Wade* with respect to the right to counsel was based on the premise that "the presence of . . . counsel [at a post-indictment lineup] is necessary to preserve the defendant's basic right to a fair trial as affected by his right meaningfully to cross-examine the witnesses against him and to have effective assistance of counsel at the trial itself." This language suggests that counsel for the defendant should serve primarily as an observer of the identification procedure. As such, he will be able to reconstruct the circumstances of the pretrial lineup or confrontation at a suppression hearing or at trial. At the suppression hearing, the attorney may argue that the procedure violated the defendant's right to due process of law. At trial, counsel may, by cross-

---

8. 434 U.S. 220, 98 S.Ct. 458 (1977).

9. *Commonwealth v. Small,* 10 Mass. App.Ct. 606, 411 N.E.2d 179 (1980); *United States v. Williams,* 436 F.2d 1166 (9th Cir.1970), cert. denied 402 U.S. 912, 91 S.Ct. 1392 (1971).

10. 410 F.2d 386 (3d Cir.1969), cert. denied 396 U.S. 993, 90 S.Ct. 488 (1969).

11. 423 So.2d 327 (Ala.Cr.App.1982).

12. 420 F.2d 1292 (D.C.Cir.1969).

examination of witnesses or by argument, cast doubt on the credibility of the pretrial identification or an in-court identification.[13]

Other language in *Wade,* however, suggests a more active role. For instance, the opinion speaks of counsel's ability to "avert prejudice" and assist the police "by preventing the infiltration of taint in the prosecution's identification evidence." This conflicting language raises the issue, discussed in the previous chapter,[14] of whether the right to counsel should be based on a cross-examination/confrontation theory, or an assistance of counsel theory. Under the latter theory, counsel would not only observe, but might also be under an obligation to object to improper police procedures. The lower courts appear to take a middle tack. They have permitted counsel to make suggestions about the composition of the lineup, but do not require the police to follow them.[15] This stance has the practical advantage of minimizing attorney interference with police work, at the same time avoiding a subsequent claim by the prosecution that the defense attorney waived any due process claim by not raising it at the time of the lineup. Ideally, of course, the very presence of counsel will "avert prejudice" without the need for strenuous objections.

The assistance of counsel theory also apparently limits counsel to situations in which the defendant is present.[16] Because the actual identification at a lineup (as opposed to the process of viewing it) can take place in the absence of the defendant, it may not be unconstitutional to bar counsel at this point. Under a right to confrontation interpretation of *Wade,* on the other hand, just the opposite result would be required, since government manipulation, conscious or not, may have its most significant impact at the time the witness communicates a decision. Again, the lower courts have taken a middle ground, allowing counsel to be present during the viewing and the actual identification,[17] but not during questioning of the identifying witnesses after the identification.[18]

(d) Substitute Counsel. *Wade* held that use of substitute counsel is permissible, if waiting for the suspect's counsel would result in "prejudicial delay." Given the time it takes to construct

---

13. The attorney might also testify as to what he saw, but this action raises difficult ethical issues. See ABA Code of Professional Responsibility, DR 5–102 (lawyer who is to testify in client's case should withdraw, unless doing so "would work a substantial hardship," given possible conflicts of interest).

14. See § 17.02.

15. *People v. Borrego,* 668 P.2d 21 (Colo.App.1983); *United States v. Eley,* 286 A.2d 239 (D.C.App.1972); *United*

States v. Allen, 408 F.2d 1287 (D.C.Cir. 1969).

16. See discussion of *United States v. Ash,* 413 U.S. 300, 93 S.Ct. 2568 (1973), in § 17.02(a).

17. *People v. Williams,* 3 Cal.3d 853, 92 Cal.Rptr. 6, 478 P.2d 942 (1971).

18. Id.; see also, *United States v. Cunningham,* 423 F.2d 1269 (4th Cir. 1970).

a good lineup, there will usually be enough time to contact the client's counsel, if he is available. If substitute counsel is used, however, then appointed or retained counsel is under a duty to discover what he observed.[19] One court has suggested that the burden is on the government to provide trial counsel with a report of the substitute counsel's observations, and that failure to meet that burden should result in suppression of the identification.[20]

(e) Unnecessary Suggestiveness and Lineups. The "totality of circumstances" due process analysis discussed in the preceding chapter provides the touchstone for the determination of whether a lineup is unnecessarily suggestive.[21] The Court in *Wade* noted that lineup procedures have been suggestive when, for example,

> all in the lineup but the suspect were known to the identifying witness, . . . the other participants in a lineup were grossly dissimilar in appearance to the suspect, . . . only the suspect was required to wear distinctive clothing which the culprit allegedly wore, . . . the suspect is pointed out before or during a lineup, and . . . the participants in the lineup are asked to try on an article of clothing which fits only the suspect.

Another example of a suggestive lineup procedure is provided by *Foster v. California*.[22] There, the manager of a robbed Western Union office viewed a three-person lineup in which the defendant was the only one wearing a leather jacket similar to that worn by the robber and was a half-foot taller than the other two persons. Even so, the manager's identification was only tentative. The police then arranged a one-on-one confrontation with the defendant; again the identification was tentative. Finally, ten days later, the police arranged a second lineup in which the defendant was the only person who appeared in the first lineup. At this point, the manager became "convinced" that the defendant was the perpetrator. The Supreme Court reversed the conviction, noting that "[i]n effect, the police repeatedly said to the witness, '*This* is the man.'"

To minimize the risk of suggestiveness, the Model Rules for Law Enforcement[23] propose the following procedures:

    a.   All lineups should consist of at least 4 persons in addition to the suspect.

19. *United States v. Estes*, 485 F.2d 1078 (D.C.Cir.1973), cert. denied 415 U.S. 923, 94 S.Ct. 1426 (1974).

20. *Marshall v. United States*, 436 F.2d 155 (D.C.Cir.1970).

21. See § 17.03.

22. 394 U.S. 440, 89 S.Ct. 1127 (1969).

23. Arizona State University and Police Foundation, Model Rules for Law Enforcement, Eyewitness Identification 52 (1974) [hereinafter cited as Model Rules].

b. Persons in the lineup should have approximately similar physical characteristics.

c. The suspect should be permitted to select his own place in the line.

d. All persons should be required to take whatever special action is required such as making gestures, speaking, showing profile or donning distinctive clothing.

e. Persons present at the lineup should be warned to conduct themselves so as not to single out the suspect.

f. Each lineup should be photographed or videotaped.[24]

Additionally, multiple witnesses should not be present at the same time, and the police should of course refrain from indicating who the suspect is.

The utilization of such procedures might, as a practical matter, eliminate a due process challenge. Additionally, *Wade* suggested that this type of procedural standardization would obviate the Sixth Amendment right to counsel at the lineup. In particular, the videotaping provision of the Model Rules could ensure that counsel is provided with a representation of how the procedure was conducted. However, the actual identification, as well as the lineup session, should be videotaped if the tape is to provide a substitute for counsel.

18.03 Showups

On-the-scene "showups" and other types of witness-suspect "confrontations" differ from lineups in that the victim or witness is exposed to only one person for identification. The constitutional requirements relating to due process and the right to counsel should apply with even more force to these more suggestive types of pretrial identification.

(a) **When Permissible.** As a general rule, police should use lineups when feasible because confrontations are inherently suggestive.[25] However, the "totality of circumstances" still determines whether due process is violated in any individual case, and the courts have made it clear that there are several circumstances in which one-on-one encounters are not only permissible but to be encouraged.

(1) Immobility or loss of witness. In *Stovall v. Denno,*[26] the Supreme Court approved a showup at the hospital where the victim of an assault was being treated for serious wounds. "Faced with the responsibility for identifying the attacker, with the need

---

24. See, also *United States v. Smallwood,* 473 F.2d 98 (D.C.Cir.1972).

25. *Foster v. California,* 394 U.S. 440, 89 S.Ct. 1127 (1969).

26. 388 U.S. 293, 87 S.Ct. 1967 (1967).

for immediate action and with the knowledge that [the victim] could not visit the jail, the police followed the only feasible procedure and took [the accused] to the hospital room." When the victim is on the verge of dying or in some other way will soon be unable to identify the perpetrator, a showup is clearly permissible. When there is no danger of losing the witness, but he is confined to the hospital, a showup may also be permissible.[27] But if a lineup or photo array can be arranged in the hospital, a showup may not be necessary; if so, it should be avoided, given its suggestive nature.

(2) Inaccessibility of suspect. The *suspect* may also be hospitalized, in which case a lineup is usually impossible.[28] A harder question arises when the police do not have the reasonable suspicion necessary to seize a person for an appearance in a lineup.[29] In such cases, it might be argued that the police are justified in taking the witness to the person's place of work,[30] or to any other place the suspect can be found. While this practice is suggestive, it does not involve a seizure and may be the only way in which the police can obtain a positive or negative identification. The possibility of a photo array should be considered, however.

(3) On-the-scene identifications. Courts have also been reluctant to overturn convictions based upon "on the scene" showups, despite their inherent suggestivity, for two reasons. Prompt identification is generally viewed as reasonable police procedure aimed at the quick solution of crime. In addition, the short lapse of time between the crime and the showup supports the reliability of the identification. Thus, the D.C. Circuit Court of Appeals, in *United States v. Perry,*[31] commented that a police regulation restricting on-the-scene confrontations to those instances where the suspect is arrested near the scene and within sixty minutes of the alleged offense represented a commendable effort "to balance the freshness of such a confrontation against its inherent suggestiveness, and to balance both factors against the need to pick up the trail while fresh if the suspect is not the offender." Another proposal would allow the suspect to be shown to the witness at any appropriate place if the apprehension occurs within two hours of the crime.[32]

27. *People v. Taylor,* 52 Ill.2d 293, 287 N.E.2d 673 (1972).

28. *Jackson v. United States,* 412 F.2d 149 (D.C.Cir.1969).

29. See § 17.04(a) for a discussion of the reasonable suspicion requirement.

30. Cf. *People v. Bradley,* 12 Ill.App. 3d 783, 299 N.E.2d 99 (1973).

31. 449 F.2d 1026 (D.C.Cir.1971).

32. *Model Rules,* supra note 23, Rule 202. See also, *Johnson v. Dugger,* 817 F.2d 726 (11th Cir.1987) ("immediate confrontations allow identification before the suspect has altered his appearance and while the witness' memory is fresh, and permit the quick release of innocent persons.")

It is debatable whether a short lapse of time between the crime and the identification automatically justifies a one-on-one confrontation. The suggestion that "this is the perpetrator" may well inaccurately fill in the perceptual and memory gaps which can plague any observer. But, properly conducted, a show-up within a short period after the offense may be permissible. For instance, in *United States v. McCoy*,[33] suspects were taken to the scene of a robbery within forty-eight minutes of its commission. A witness identification made at the on-the-scene showup was held admissible because a number of factors supported the reliability of the identification: the witness had had a good opportunity to observe the robber; the time lapse was short; the police refused to reply to inquiries by the witness as to whether the suspects were the robbers and whether the stolen property had been recovered; the witness identification was firmly positive; and the witness had previously refused to identify another man as the robber. In *United States v. Hines*,[34] the court held that an on-the-scene showup of a suspect in handcuffs did not automatically violate due process when four of five witnesses simultaneously identified him only ten minutes after the crime.

(4) Non-emergency showups. Even when no emergency exists, and there is no possibility of a prompt on-the-scene showup, a one-on-one encounter may be permissible if the identification it produces is considered reliable in the totality of the circumstances. In *Neil v. Biggers*,[35] the Supreme Court sanctioned an arranged stationhouse encounter which was not necessitated by exigency; the victim was not in *extremis* and the encounter took place seven months after the crime had occurred. Although the justification for the confrontation was somewhat weak—police claimed to be unable to find other individuals with the defendant's "unique" characteristics and thus did not hold a lineup—the Court found the identification reliable. The victim had viewed her assailant for almost one-half hour, under adequate lighting conditions. She had also given police, prior to the showup, a description of her assailant that loosely fit the defendant. Furthermore, she had "no doubt" the defendant was the person who had attacked her. Finally, the victim had made no previous identifications of any person, despite repeated opportunities to do so. Under these circumstances, the Court could find "no substantial likelihood of misidentification."

(5) Accidental confrontations. When a confrontation occurs accidentally, the possibility of improper police action is removed, and courts are understandably even more reluctant to find a

---

33. 475 F.2d 344 (D.C.Cir.1973).

34. 455 F.2d 1317 (D.C.Cir.1971), cert. denied 406 U.S. 975, 92 S.Ct. 2427 (1972).

35. 409 U.S. 188, 93 S.Ct. 375 (1972).

violation of due process in an ensuing identification. In *United States v. Pollack*,[36] the witness had been unable to identify the defendant in photographs but unexpectedly encountered and recognized the defendant in a courthouse corridor. A subsequent in-court identification was held admissible. In *United States v. Evans*,[37] a chance street encounter between the witness and the defendant led to the identification of the defendant. A police officer assisted the witness in re-identifying the defendant a few minutes after the initial confrontation. The court, finding the police conduct to be reasonable and in good faith, approved the identification.[38]

(6) In-court identifications. Probably the most suggestive type of showup is the in-court identification. The defendant is clearly labelled as such, and the witness is under considerable public pressure not to contradict the state's decision to prosecute. Where there has been a previous, properly conducted identification of the same person, this course of action might be justifiable.[39] However, when the in-court identification is the first identification, courts should be more cautious.[40] As the Supreme Court recognized in *Moore v. Illinois*,[41] a case involving a first-time identification at a preliminary hearing, it "is difficult to imagine a more suggestive manner in which to present a suspect to a witness for their critical first confrontation." *Moore* suggested that, in this situation, the court should consider a lineup or seating the defendant in the courtroom with the audience. Yet one court has indicated that, at trial at least, a first-time in-court identification need not be avoided, since the "defendant's protection against the obvious suggestiveness in any courtroom identification confrontation is his right to cross-examine." [42]

(b) The Right to Counsel. After *Kirby v. Illinois*,[43] it was clear that a showup which occurs once prosecution has commenced, "by way of formal charge, preliminary hearing, indictment, information, or arraignment," requires counsel. Most showups, however, usually occur prior to this point in the process. For those that don't, the same exigencies that justify a showup, described above, may justify foregoing notification of counsel.[44] If

---

36. 427 F.2d 1168 (5th Cir.1970), cert. denied 400 U.S. 831, 91 S.Ct. 63 (1970).

37. 438 F.2d 162 (D.C.Cir.1971), cert. denied 402 U.S. 1010, 91 S.Ct. 2196 (1971).

38. Note that an identification resulting from an accidental confrontation may still be excluded as unreliable.

39. As to the proper result when the previous identification was not properly conducted, see § 17.05(a).

40. Cf. *United States ex rel. Haywood v. O'Leary,* 827 F.2d 52 (7th Cir. 1987).

41. 434 U.S. 220, 98 S.Ct. 458 (1977).

42. *State v. Smith,* 200 Conn. 465, 512 A.2d 189 (1986).

43. 406 U.S. 682, 92 S.Ct. 1877 (1972)

44. Cf. the lower court decision in *United States ex rel. Stovall v. Denno,* 355 F.2d 731 (2d Cir.1966).

there is no time to arrange a lineup, then there may be no time to contact counsel, if the suspect has one, or to appoint counsel, if the suspect does not. On the other hand, when the showup is due solely to the immobility of the witness or the suspect, counsel or a substitute should be present. And, of course, when the showup occurs in-court during or after charging, *Moore* requires counsel.

The role of counsel at such showups is presumably similar to his role at lineups. The conduct of the police and the witness should be observed with an eye to challenging the credibility of the identification at a later stage. Counsel might also be able to persuade the police to conduct a less suggestive identification procedure. When the showup occurs in court, *Moore* suggests that counsel may be even more active and argue for alternative procedures, including a lineup.

18.04 Photograph Identification

Law enforcement officers often use photographic displays to identify suspects prior to arrest. Usually, analogous to a lineup, the police use a photo array, in which pictures of several individuals are displayed. Occasionally, however, the photo version of a showup—a showing of one photograph—is relied upon. The Supreme Court has approved both techniques, despite the likelihood that they are less reliable than their in-person counterparts.[45] In *Simmons v. United States,*[46] the Court noted that identification by photographs "has been used widely and effectively in criminal law" and approved use of an array in that case. In *Manson v. Brathwaite,*[47] it refused to find invalid an in-court identification based on an earlier identification from a single photograph, since the totality of the circumstances indicated the earlier determination was reliable. Further, the Court has held, in contrast to lineups and showups, that there is no right to counsel at a photo identification procedure.[48]

(a) **When Permissible.** Given its lesser reliability, a photo array should not be used when a lineup is possible. For instance, the Model Rules for Law Enforcement suggest that photo displays only be relied upon when the suspect has not been apprehended, the suspect threatens to be disruptive, or there is a lack of suitable persons for a lineup.[49] The Supreme Court lent some credence to this view in *Simmons,* when it emphasized that a swift identification was necessary to apprehend the suspect, who was still at large. However, most courts do not make the admissibility of a photo identification dependent upon whether a lineup was feasi-

---

45. P. Wall, Eyewitness Identification in Criminal Cases 83 (1965).

46. 390 U.S. 377, 88 S.Ct. 967 (1968).

47. 432 U.S. 98, 97 S.Ct. 2243 (1977).

48. *United States v. Ash,* 413 U.S. 300, 93 S.Ct. 2568 (1973), discussed in § 17.02(a).

49. Model Rules, supra note 23, Rule 305.

ble; instead, they focus on the danger of mistaken identification in light of the way in which the photo identification was conducted.[50]

(b) Due Process Requirements. As a general rule, suggestiveness varies inversely with the number of pictures displayed. Most obviously, if the police show the witness a single picture of the suspect, the potential for suggestiveness is quite high. The Model Rules for Law Enforcement recommend that photographs of at least seven individuals of substantially similar appearance be displayed to avoid suggestiveness.[51]

As *Manson* demonstrates, however, the display of a single photograph has been permitted in particular circumstances. In *Chaney v. State,*[52] a rapist had mentioned to his victims that he had previously been jailed on a rape charge. Thus, the police were justified in showing the victim a single photograph of a suspect in another rape case. In *United States v. Cox,*[53] the flight of the criminal presented urgent circumstances dictating that no time be spent on arranging a display. In both *Chaney* and *Cox,* the witnesses' good opportunity to view the individual was also important in negating the defendant's due process claims. But this factor alone should not be dispositive. Thus, the decision in *Virgin Islands v. Petersen*[54] is highly questionable. There a photo identification was held admissible even though it consisted of only two photographs, both of defendant, because the witness had stood within a few feet of the defendant for ½ hour during which time her attention was drawn to him.

Assuming a full display is used, it should not be arranged so that a particular individual's picture is in some way emphasized. In *People v. Citrino,*[55] the court disapproved a photo array, shown to a witness shortly before trial, in which the defendant was pictured three times in a five-picture display. In another case, an alteration of only the suspect's photograph to show a "fu manchu" was disapproved.[56] The danger of the misidentification may be exacerbated by other factors as well. Multiple witnesses should be separated during the viewing of a display. The police should not indicate to the witness that a particular individual pictured in a display has been implicated in the crime by other evidence.[57] Showing a number of photograph arrays in which the suspect is

50. *State v. Emerson,* 149 Vt. 171, 541 A.2d 466 (1987).

51. *Model Rules,* supra note 23, Rule 306.

52. 267 So.2d 65 (Fla.1972).

53. 428 F.2d 683 (7th Cir.1970), cert. denied 400 U.S. 881, 91 S.Ct. 127 (1970).

54. 553 F.2d 324 (3d Cir.1977).

55. 90 Cal.Rptr. 80, 11 Cal.App.3d 778 (1970).

56. *State v. Alexander,* 108 Ariz. 556, 503 P.2d 777 (1972). Compare *Rudd v. State,* 477 F.2d 805 (5th Cir. 1973) (each photo was altered).

57. See *People v. Brown,* 52 Ill.2d 94, 285 N.E.2d 1 (1972), for an arguably appropriate method of proceeding in such situations.

the only repeater may also single out the suspect to the witness.[58] As with the single photo display cases, however, the courts generally indicate that none of these practices automatically invalidate an identification; instead, the "linchpin" of the analysis is whether the identification is reliable.[59]

18.05 Conclusion

The rules governing the conduct of identification procedures and use of their results that have been discussed in this and the preceding chapter can be summarized as follows:

(1) The accused has a right to his own counsel at any pretrial lineup or showup which occurs at or after the initial appearance before a judicial officer, unless waiting for counsel would cause "prejudicial delay." Under the latter circumstance, substitute counsel is permitted. There is no right to counsel at accidental or spontaneous confrontations, photographic displays, or "scientific" identification procedures which do not rely on eyewitnesses, such as fingerprinting or the taking of handwriting exemplars. Further, regulations governing the conduct of identification procedures along the lines provided in (3) below could eliminate the need for, and thus the right to, counsel in those situations where it attaches.

(2) In addition to meeting any Sixth Amendment requirement, an identification procedure must meet the demands of due process. Reliability is the linchpin of due process analysis. Thus, a lineup, showup, or photo display which suggests a particular result, even if unnecessarily so, is not unconstitutional if the identification it produces is considered reliable after evaluating the totality of the circumstances. Factors to be considered in evaluating reliability include (a) the opportunity of the witness to view the criminal at the time of the crime; (b) the witness' degree of attention; (c) the accuracy of the witness' prior description of the criminal; (d) the level of certainty demonstrated by the witness at the confrontation; (e) the length of time between the crime and the confrontation; and (f) any discrepancies in identifications, if there is more than one.

(3) Although suggestivity is not dispositive of the due process issue, every effort should be made to avoid suggestive procedures. Lineups and photo displays should include a number of alternatives to the suspect, of approximately similar physical characteristics, and should avoid singling out the suspect in any way. Show-

---

58. See *King v. State*, 18 Md.App. 266, 306 A.2d 258 (1973).

59. See, e.g., *Nicholson v. State*, 523 So.2d 68 (Miss.1988) (fact that defendant was the only person in display to have tattoo was suggestive in light of earlier description, but no risk of misidentification); *State v. Pigott*, 320 N.C. 96, 357 S.E.2d 631 (1987) (only one of 9 other pictures similar to defendant's, but no risk of misidentification).

ups and one-photo displays should be avoided unless emergency circumstances dictate their use. There is no right to demand the least suggestive procedure available, however.

(4) If evidence of an identification is found inadmissible under the above rules, then not only this identification but also any later identification by the same person must be excluded, unless the prosecution can show that evidence of the subsequent identification is derived from a source independent of the tainted identification. Factors to be considered in gauging the degree of taint in a subsequent identification are virtually identical to those considered in evaluating reliability, including: (a) the witness' prior opportunity to observe the alleged criminal act; (b) any discrepancy between the witness' pre-identification descriptions and the defendant's actual description; (c) any pre-identification naming of another person by the witness; (d) any failure to identify the defendant on a prior occasion, and (e) the lapse of time between the alleged act and the identification alleged to be tainted.

(5) The admissibility of a pretrial or incourt identification is determined by the judge, although the jury may be present during the hearing, at least when its presence does not significantly inhibit the defendant's cross-examination and when the identification is ultimately found admissible.

BIBLIOGRAPHY

Decker, John F., Richard Moriarty, and Edward Albert. The Demise of Procedural Protections in Laywitness Identifications: Who is the Culprit? 9 Loy.U.L.Rev. 335 (1978).

Did Your Eyes Deceive You? Expert Psychological Testimony on the Reliability of Eyewitness Identification. [note] 29 Stan.L. Rev. 969 (1977).

Grano, Joseph. Kirby, Biggers, and Ash: Do Any Constitutional Safeguards Remain Against the Danger of Convicting the Innocent? 72 Mich.L.Rev. 717 (1974).

Gross, Samuel. Loss of Innocence: Eyewitness Identification and Proof of Guilt. 16 J.Leg.Studies 395 (1987).

Grossman, Steven P. Suggestive Identifications: The Supreme Court's Due Process Test Fails to Meet Its Own Criteria. 11 U.Balt.L.Rev. 53 (1981).

Jonakait, Randolph. Reliable Identification: Could the Supreme Court Tell in Manson v. Braithwaite? 52 U.Colo.L.Rev. 511 (1981).

Levine, Felice J. and June L. Tapp. The Psychology of Criminal Identification: The Gap from Wade to Kirby. 121 U.Pa.L. Rev. 1079 (1973).

Project on Law Enforcement Policy and Rulemaking. Eyewitness Identification. Tempe, Arizona: 1974 (Model Rules for Law Enforcement Series).

Read, Frank T. Lawyers at Lineups: Constitutional Necessity or Avoidable Extravagance? 17 UC.L.A.L.Rev. 339 (1969) [appendices reprinting police regulations for various jurisdictions].

Rosenberg, Benjamin. Rethinking the Right to Due Process in Connection With Pretrial Identification Procedures: An Analysis and a Proposal. 79 Ken.L.J. 259 (1990/91).

Sobel, Nathan R. Eyewitness Identification: Legal and Practical Problems. New York: Clark Boardman Co., Ltd., 1972; Supplement, 1984.

Uviller, Richard H. The Role of the Defense Lawyer at a Lineup in Light of the Wade, Gilbert and Stovall Decisions. 4 Crim.L. Bull. 273 (1968).

Wall, Patrick M. Eyewitness Identification in Criminal Cases. Springfield, Illinois: Charles C. Thomas, 1971.

Part D

ENTRAPMENT

The defense of entrapment arises when a defendant, who has admittedly committed a crime, can prove that the actions of law enforcement authorities caused him to it. As presently interpreted by the Supreme Court, the defense is "substantive" rather than procedural in nature, in the sense that it focuses on the defendant's mental state at the time of the offense rather than on the nature of the police conduct prior to and during commission of the crime. It is included in this book because the minority view of the defense holds that it should be construed as a constraint on police practices. As such, the entrapment defense operates like the exclusionary rule to deter police engaging in particularly egregious behavior.

Chapter Nineteen

THE ENTRAPMENT DEFENSE

19.01 Introduction

The defense of entrapment is grounded in the belief that the government should not be able to convict a person of a crime which the government itself instigated. But this simple idea can be framed in many different ways. In deciding whether the government has been an "instigator," some courts consider only whether the defendant was predisposed to commit the crime at the time of the instigation (the "predisposition" or "subjective" test). If he was, then regardless of how coercive or egregious the government conduct, he is not entitled to a defense.[1] Other courts have considered the predisposition of the defendant relatively insignificant, and focused instead on the conduct of the government (the "conduct of the authorities" or "objective" test).[2] As described in the American Law Institute's Model Penal Code, if the government "employ[ed] methods of persuasion or inducement which create a substantial risk that such an offense will be committed by persons other than those who are ready to commit it," then a defense will lie regardless of the particular defendant's willingness to commit the offense.[3] This test has also been called the "hypothetical person" test, because it looks at whether the reasonable innocent person would give in to the government's blandishments. Still other courts combine the two approaches, looking first at whether the conduct of the authorities was improper and, if not, then looking at whether the defendant was predisposed to commit the crime (the "hybrid" test).[4]

Finally, several courts have held that, regardless of the test used in the typical case, if the government conduct is so "outrageous" as to shock the conscience, then acquittal should result as a matter of constitutional due process (the due process test).[5] Although this last test is similar to the conduct of authorities standard, it is both broader and narrower. It is broader because it covers any government conduct which is outrageous, whether or not it might encourage crime; it is narrower because, to the extent

1. *Hampton v. United States,* 425 U.S. 484, 96 S.Ct. 1646 (1976) (plurality opinion); *United States v. Rey,* 811 F.2d 1453 (11th Cir.1987) (defendant who was predisposed to commit crime cannot be entrapped, regardless of how outrageous or overreaching government's conduct may be).

2. *People v. Barraza,* 23 Cal.3d 675, 153 Cal.Rptr. 459, 591 P.2d 947 (1979).

3. ALI Model Penal Code § 2.13 (1962).

4. *Moore v. State,* 534 So.2d 557 (Miss.1988).

5. *United States v. Twigg,* 588 F.2d 373 (3d Cir.1978), discussed in § 19.03(a).

it does cover government instigation, it applies only to the most egregious official conduct. Under this test and the conduct of authorities test, the burden of proof is usually on the defendant, whereas the government must prove predisposition beyond a reasonable doubt.[6]

As the first section of this chapter indicates, the Supreme Court has consistently applied the predisposition test, although some members of the Court have argued strongly for the conduct of authorities approach, and a few have contended that a very limited due process defense should also be recognized. As the second section demonstrates, because the Supreme Court has refused to constitutionalize the defense, the lower courts have been much more diverse in their approach.

19.02 Supreme Court Cases

(a) **The Statutory Basis of the Defense.** A consistent majority of the Court has held that the availability of the entrapment defense is purely a matter of statutory interpretation, and does not derive from the Constitution. The Court's first explicit entrapment decision, the 1932 decision of *Sorrells v. United States*,[7] laid down what remains today the Court's approach to entrapment. Chief Justice Hughes stated: "We are unable to conclude that it was the intention of Congress in enacting [the National Prohibition Act] that its processes of detection or enforcement should be abused by the instigation by government officials of an act on the part of persons otherwise innocent in order to lure them to its commission and punish them." The idea that the defense is derived purely from legislative intent was repeated over twenty-five years later by Chief Justice Warren in *Sherman v. United States*,[8] and was restated by Justice Rehnquist in *United States v. Russell*,[9] where he noted that the defense is rooted "in the notion that Congress could not have intended criminal punishment for a defendant who has committed all the elements of a proscribed offense, but was induced to commit them by the Government."

In *Sorrells*, Chief Justice Hughes noted that one consequence of this interpretation of the defense was that certain defendants may not be able to claim it. In particular, he cautioned that a defendant who has committed "heinous" or "revolting" crimes may not assert the defense. Apparently, this limitation is based on the idea that, whatever legislative intent is with respect to other offenses, the legislature would not permit acquittal of some-

---

6. *Jacobson v. United States*, ___ U.S. ___, 112 S.Ct. 1535 (1992). Note also that, in federal court, a defendant may plead both guilty and "guilty but entrapped." *Mathews v. United States*, 485 U.S. 58, 108 S.Ct. 883 (1988).

7. 287 U.S. 435, 53 S.Ct. 210 (1932).
8. 356 U.S. 369, 78 S.Ct. 819 (1958).
9. 411 U.S. 423, 93 S.Ct. 1637 (1973).

one who could be persuaded to commit a violent crime, regardless of the strength of the persuasion or the original innocence of the perpetrator. Furthermore, as the language in both *Sorrells* and *Russell* indicates, the entrapment defense has been limited to situations in which the instigator was a government official or agent. Although an "innocent" person could just as easily be induced to commit crime by a private individual (indeed, as far as the offender is concerned, there is no difference between a private and governmental instigator), the Court has again justified this limitation as a matter of legislative intent.

Justice Frankfurter, in his concurring opinion in *Sherman*, argued that the legislative intent rationale for the entrapment defense is "sheer fiction." In his opinion, "the Courts refuse to convict an entrapped defendant, not because his conduct falls outside the proscription of the statute, but because, even if his guilt be admitted, the methods employed on behalf of the Government to bring about conviction cannot be countenanced." But Frankfurter too avoided a constitutional view of entrapment. Rather, he felt that the defense derived from the federal courts' "supervisory jurisdiction over the administration of criminal justice." This latter position has been the usual stance of those members of the Court who prefer the conduct of the authorities test. No member of the Court has viewed the entrapment defense as constitutionally based, although some have recognized the narrow due process defense, which they view as separate and apart from the entrapment test.[10]

(b) Predisposition v. Conduct of Authorities. The Court's few decisions on entrapment demonstrate a deep split among its members. In each case, the majority focused primarily, if not entirely, on the predisposition of the defendant to commit the act alleged, while the minority view opted for the conduct of the authorities approach.

In *Sorrells*, the defendant was charged with selling whiskey to a prohibition agent in violation of the National Prohibition Act. The agent was introduced to the defendant at the latter's house. After two unsuccessful attempts, the agent finally convinced the defendant to sell him whiskey by "taking advantage of the sentiment aroused by reminiscences of their experiences as companions in arms in the World War." The lower courts ruled as a matter of law that there was no entrapment.

Chief Justice Hughes concluded in the majority opinion that the issue of entrapment should have been submitted to the jury. He described the case as one in which "the criminal design originates with the officials of the Government and they implant in the mind of an innocent person the disposition to commit the

10. See § 19.02(d).

alleged offense and induce its commission in order that they may prosecute." But, in discussing the conduct of the prohibition agent, he was careful to point out that in several cases decided by the Court "artifice and stratagem" were found to be permissible methods of catching those engaged in criminal enterprise. Most importantly, he noted that, in addition to evidence tending to show reprehensible conduct by the authorities, testimony relevant to the defendant's inclination to commit the alleged act is admissible in such cases: "[I]f the defendant seeks acquittal by reason of entrapment, he cannot complain of an appropriate and searching inquiry into his own conduct and predisposition as bearing upon that issue."

In a concurring opinion, Justice Roberts, joined by Justice Brandeis and Justice Stone, clearly set out for the first time the "conduct of authorities" test.[11] The basis for this view of entrapment is "the public policy which protects the purity of government and its processes." The government should not use its machinery to consummate a wrong. Neither should it be allowed to introduce evidence showing "that the defendant had a bad reputation or had previously transgressed. . . ." Allowing the authorities' conduct to be "rendered innocuous" by such evidence "in effect, pivots convictions in such cases, not on the commission of the crime charged, but on the prior reputation or some former act or acts of the defendant not mentioned in the indictment." Thus, according to the minority view, where entrapment is raised, only the conduct of the authorities should be examined. Furthermore, Roberts concluded, it is the province of the court, not the jury, to determine whether there was entrapment. This role falls to the court because it is a necessary step in the "preservation of the purity" of the judicial process, a duty obviously belonging to the court. The court may seek the jury's help in resolving the facts, but must make the ultimate determination.

The Supreme Court next addressed the entrapment defense in *Sherman*, where a government informant met the defendant at a doctor's office where both were being treated to cure narcotics addiction. Thereafter, the two met accidentally several times at the office or at a pharmacy. After progressing in conversation from mere greetings to discussions of mutual experiences and problems, the informant first asked the defendant if he knew a supplier of drugs and then whether the defendant himself could supply the narcotics. The defendant attempted to avoid the issue,

---

11. The Roberts opinion restated and refined a dissent by Justice Brandeis in *Casey v. United States*, 276 U.S. 413, 48 S.Ct. 373 (1928), which stated in part: "This prosecution should be stopped, not because some right of [the defendant's] has been denied, but in order to protect the Government. To protect it from illegal conduct of its officers. To preserve the purity of its courts."

but after repeated requests, apparently predicated on the informant's suffering and his failure to respond to institutionalized
treatment, the defendant agreed. Thereafter, the defendant procured drugs and shared them with the informant several times, at
a cost approximately equal to the defendant's expenses incurred
when obtaining the drug. The defendant was arrested after
government agents observed several of these transactions. The
defendant was convicted by a jury over his claim of entrapment
and the circuit court of appeals affirmed.

The Supreme Court reversed, finding entrapment was "patently clear" as a matter of law. But Chief Justice Warren's
majority opinion adhered to the predisposition test. According to
Warren, in determining whether entrapment has occurred, "a line
must be drawn between the trap for the unwary innocent and the
trap for the unwary criminal." As for the propriety of adopting
Justice Roberts' conduct of the authorities standard, he noted that
the issue had not been argued. But he ventured that such a test
was too broad; if the government could not reply to a claim of
improper inducement with a showing that the conduct was due to
the defendant's "own readiness," the prosecution would suffer a
"handicap [that] is obvious." He then quoted Judge Learned
Hand from the court below, to the effect that, under the official
conduct test, "it would be impossible ever to secure convictions of
any offences which consist of transactions that are carried on in
secret." Although this point is certainly exaggerated, it is true
that judging the conduct of undercover agents can be difficult
without knowing how predisposed the defendant was. Conduct
that may seem impermissible with respect to an "unwary innocent" might be justifiable in connection with a "wary criminal,"
who is familiar with sting operations and the like. The Court also
refused to address Roberts' contention that entrapment issues
should be decided by the court, but noted that all of the circuit
courts of appeals had held otherwise.

Undaunted, Justice Frankfurter, in a concurring opinion, argued that the official conduct test would best serve the "tran-
scending value at stake," which he defined as "public confidence
in the fair and honorable administration of justice, upon which
ultimately depends the rule of law." He noted that if the predisposition test were the correct standard, then encouragement by
private individuals, as well as entrapment by government officials,
should also be a defense for the "unwary innocent." The inquiry
should instead be "whether the police conduct revealed in the
particular case falls below standards, to which common feelings
respond, for the proper use of governmental power." Echoing
Roberts, he contended that this test would avoid the "grave
prejudice that a defendant suffers if hearsay and other reputation

evidence is admitted to show predisposition." [12] Further, he stated that the subjective test would produce inconsistent results: "surely if two suspects have been solicited at the same time in the same manner, one should not go to jail simply because he has been convicted before and is said to have a criminal disposition." He also expressed concern that the predisposition test might encourage police abuse of those defendants who are predisposed; he noted "the possibility that no matter what his past crimes and general disposition the defendant might not have committed the particular crime unless confronted with inordinate inducements."

But the minority view was definitively discarded by the Court in its next entrapment case, *Russell*. There, a government narcotics agent posed as a narcotics manufacturer and distributor who was interested in controlling the manufacture and distribution of methamphetamine. He offered to supply the defendants with one of the difficult-to-obtain ingredients for manufacture of the drug in return for half of the drug produced. This offer was accepted. There was also testimony that the defendants had obtained from another source the scarce ingredient both before and after they obtained it from the narcotics agent. The court of appeals overturned the conviction, saying that there had been "an intolerable degree of governmental participation in the criminal enterprise," on either of two alternative theories: (1) that there is entrapment as a matter of law whenever the government supplies contraband to defendants,[13] or (2) that there is entrapment whenever the government is so enmeshed in the criminal activity that the prosecution was held to be repugnant to the American criminal justice system.[14]

Justice Rehnquist's majority opinion dismissed both theories, finding that there was sufficient predisposition on the part of the defendants to invalidate an entrapment defense. Though acknowledging that "we may some day be presented with a situation in which the conduct of law enforcement agents is so outrageous that due process principles would absolutely bar the government from invoking judicial processes to obtain a conviction," he concluded that the present case was "distinctly not of that breed" because the government had merely supplied a legal and harmless substance to a person who had previously been "an active participant in an illegal drug manufacturing enterprise." Two dissents, by Justices Stewart and Douglas, argued that the majority applied the wrong standard. Stewart contended that the courts *must* look

---

12. Note that reputation evidence need not be admissible in entrapment cases. Rather, the government could be forced to rely on the defendant's behavior between the time of government contact and the commission of the offense. Park, "The Entrapment Controversy," 60 Minn.L.Rev. 163, 272 (1976). But see § 19.02(c).

13. Citing *United States v. Bueno*, 447 F.2d 903 (5th Cir.1971).

14. Citing *Greene v. United States*, 454 F.2d 783 (9th Cir.1971).

at official conduct in order to ensure that the conduct does not drop to a level "not to be tolerated by an advanced society." At the least, he suggested, the predisposition test should not be applicable when the substance provided the defendants is "wholly unobtainable from . . . sources" other than the government.

In a fourth Supreme Court entrapment case, *Hampton v. United States*,[15] the defendant was convicted of distributing heroin supplied to the defendant by a government informant, and sold by the defendant to two government agents. Justice Rehnquist's plurality opinion again reaffirmed the *Sorrells-Sherman* predisposition approach and rejected the governmental conduct approach. In its strongest statment to date against the latter test, the Court averred that its previous decisions had ruled out the "possibility that the defense of entrapment could ever be based upon governmental misconduct . . . where the predisposition of the defendant to commit the crime was established." In response to petitioner's argument that the government's provision of contraband should be ruled a *per se* denial of due process, Rehnquist admitted that "[t]he Government obviously played a more significant role in enabling petitioner to sell contraband in this case than it did in *Russell*." But "[i]f the police engage in illegal activity in concert with a defendant beyond the scope of their duties the remedy lies, not in freeing the equally culpable defendant, but in prosecuting the police under the applicable provisions of state or federal law."

The dissent, authored this time by Justice Brennan and joined by two others, expressed the by now firmly entrenched minority approach and called for reversal of the conviction because "[t]he Government is doing nothing less than buying contraband from itself through an intermediary and jailing the intermediary." The dissent felt that this type of governmental activity could not be tolerated and that, at a minimum, the Court should adopt the principle that there is entrapment "as a matter of law where the subject of the criminal charge is the sale of contraband provided to the defendant by a government agent."

(c) **The Definition of Predisposition.** By the time of the *Hampton* decision, the Court had clearly settled on the subjective, predisposition test for entrapment. But it had yet to offer guidance on the contours of this test. In the three cases in which it came to a definite decision on the entrapment issue—*Sherman, Russell,* and *Hampton*—the existence of predisposition, or the absence thereof, was obvious. In *Sherman,* where the Court found entrapment as a matter of law, the defendant had apparently never engaged in selling drugs prior to his contact with the government agent, only reluctantly became involved after repeat-

---

15.   425 U.S. 484, 96 S.Ct. 1646 (1976).

ed government inducements, and even then did so only as a favor and not in an effort to gain money. In the latter two cases, on the other hand, the defendants were known to have previously been involved in illegal drug activity.

In *Jacobson v. United States*,[16] the Court was more explicit about its views on the predisposition issue, in the process apparently adopting an expansive view of the entrapment doctrine. First, it held that predisposition to commit the crime must pre-exist the government's initial contact with the defendant. Second, it suggested that proof of predisposition requires more than showing a mere "inclination" to engage in the illegal activity.

In *Jacobson*, the defendant was convicted of knowingly receiving child pornography through the mails. Over a two and one-half year period prior to his arrest, the government had sent him various mailings, from five fictitious organizations, asking about his sexual attitudes toward boys, extolling the value of free sexual expression, and suggesting that government laws banning pornography were unconstitutional. The defendant responded to many of these mailings, disclosing an interest in seeing pictures of pre-teen sex and in supporting a (fictitious) group lobbying to change pornography laws. However, on only two occasions, at the end of the two and one-half year period, did he order child pornography materials; the first order was never filled, the second resulted in his arrest. Furthermore, there was no evidence that the defendant ordered any similar material from any other organization during this time. Prior to this period, on the other hand, he had ordered two child pornography magazines from a private organization (apparently thinking they would only contain pictures of boys 18 and older), at a time when possession of child pornography was not a crime under either federal or state law.

A five-member majority held that the defendant was entrapped as a matter of law. Justice White, who wrote the majority opinion, stated that "although [the defendant] had become predisposed to break the law [by the time of the arrest], it is our view that the Government did not prove that this predisposition was independent and not the product of the attention that the Government had directed at petitioner [over the two and-one-half years preceding the arrest]." Rejecting the argument that the defendant's pre-contact purchase of magazines met the government's burden, he stated that "[e]vidence of predisposition to do what once was lawful is not, by itself, sufficient to show predisposition to do what is now illegal, for there is a common understanding that most people obey the law even when they disapprove of it." Quoting from *Sorrells*, he concluded that "[l]aw enforcement

16. __ U.S. __, 112 S.Ct. 1535 (1992).

officials go too far when they 'implant in the mind of an innocent person the *disposition* to commit the alleged offense and induce its commission in order that they may prosecute.'"

Justice O'Connor, in dissent, argued that the majority's definition of predisposition might lead lower courts to require the government to show that it had a "reasonable suspicion of criminal activity before it begins an investigation," which would run counter to the Court's cases holding that the Fourth Amendment does not apply to undercover activity.[17] While the majority explicitly denied it was imposing such a requirement, O'Connor is right that showing the existence of predisposition prior to the initial contact will be difficult in connection with some types of government sting operations, such as advertising campaigns aimed at culling from the general population those who are interested in pornography and similar types of illegal activity. Yet such random inducement operations probably *should* be inhibited, if only because they are likely to cause crime that otherwise would never have occurred.[18] The FBI itself provides that inducement to commit a crime should not be offered unless "(a) there is a reasonable indication, based on information developed through informants or other means, that the subject is engaging, has engaged, or is likely to engage in illegal activity of a similar type; or (b) the opportunity for illegal activity has been structured so that there is reason for believing that persons drawn to the opportunity, or brought to it, are predisposed to engage in the contemplated illegal activity."[19]

A second aspect of *Jacobson* may ultimately have greater impact on entrapment law. To bolster the conclusion that the defendant lacked predisposition independent of the government's blandishments, White not only discounted his original magazine purchases but also refused to characterize the defendant's conduct during the two and one-half year inducement period as evidence of a desire to commit crime; as he put it, "[p]etitioner's responses to the many communications prior to the ultimate criminal act were at most indicative of certain personal inclinations, including a predisposition to view photographs of preteen sex and a willingness to promote a given agenda by supporting lobbying organizations." Justice O'Connor did not see any difference between an

17. See § 4.02(a).

18. Cf. *United States v. Valdovinois–Valdovinois*, 588 F.Supp. 551 (N.D.Cal. 1984), rev'd 743 F.2d 1436 (9th Cir.1984) (finding a due process violation where the INS set up an undercover telephone, disseminated the number in Mexico, and advised Mexican nationals to violate U.S. law.).

19. Attorney General's Guidelines on FBI Undercover Operations (Dec. 31, 1908), reprinted in S.Rep. No. 97–682, p. 551 (1982). To date, however, no federal court has adopted a reasonable suspicion requirement. In *United States v. Luttrell*, 889 F.2d 806 (9th Cir.1989), a panel of the Ninth Circuit adopted such a requirement, but the full court later rejected it. 923 F.2d 764 (1991).

"inclination to view photographs of preteen sex" and a predisposition to commit the crime of possessing child pornography. In fact, there is a difference: for instance, a desire to use illegal drugs is not the same as a desire to commit the crime of buying illegal drugs. Yet in many cases the difference between an "inclination" to do something that is criminal and a "predisposition" to commit the crime will undoubtedly be subtle.

Jacobson may make the government's burden more difficult in entrapment cases. At the same time, given the relatively harmless nature of the offense involved in that case,[20] and the prolonged, intense nature of the government's inducement, it may be readily distinguished from more typical entrapment cases.

(d) A Due Process Test? Although the minority view of entrapment is clearly disfavored, it is important to note that a majority of the Court has not accepted Justice Rehnquist's position that the government's conduct is irrelevant if the government can prove predisposition on the part of the defendant. In his concurring opinion in *Hampton,* Justice Powell, joined by Justice Blackmun, argued that under *Rochin v. California,*[21] a case in which police used brutal physical means to obtain evidence, behavior which shocks the conscience should permit a finding for the defendant on due process grounds, regardless of predisposition. In a footnote, Powell quoted Judge Friendly in *United States v. Archer:* [22]

> [T]here is certainly a [constitutional] limit to allowing governmental involvement in crime. It would be unthinkable, for example, to permit government agents to instigate robberies and beatings merely to gather evidence to convict other members of a gang of hoodlums. Governmental 'investigation' involving participation in activities that result in injury to the rights of its citizens is a course that courts should be extremely reluctant to sanction.

Powell also noted that the Court's earlier cases had not required the Court "to consider whether overinvolvement of Government agents in contraband offenses could ever reach such proportions as to bar conviction of a predisposed defendant as a matter of due process."

Presumably, the three dissenters in *Hampton* would agree with these views. However, Justice Powell emphasized that

---

20. Cf. *United States v. Bogart,* 783 F.2d 1428 (9th Cir.1986) ("where the police control and manufacture a victimless crime, it is difficult to see how anyone is actually harmed, and thus punishment ceases to be a response, but becomes an end in itself—to secure the conviction of a private criminal. . . . [U]nder such circumstances, the criminal justice system infringes upon personal liberty and violates due process.").

21. 342 U.S. 165, 72 S.Ct. 205 (1952), discussed in § 9.02.

22. 486 F.2d 670 (2d Cir.1973).

"[p]olice overinvolvement in crime would have to reach a demonstrable level of outrageousness before it could bar conviction." He also preferred treating due process "outrageousness" claims separately from "entrapment" cases, reserving the latter term for those situations where a non-predisposed defendant was lured into committing crime. This distinction might explain, although it does not necessarily justify, the apparent contradiction between Powell's willingness, under the Due Process Clause, to consider the defense when the government instigates violence, and *Sorrell's* admonition that the entrapment defense should not be available for "heinous" crimes. It also makes clear that, in the federal courts, the conduct of the authorities is relevant only to the extent it coincides with due process concerns. To this limited extent, then, the minority view of an "encouragement" defense may remain viable at the Supreme Court level.

19.03   Entrapment in the Lower Courts

(a) **The Conduct of Authorities and Due Process Tests.** As noted above, the official conduct and due process standards both focus on the government's actions. Although the latter test, as characterized by Justice Powell in *Hampton,* is harder to meet, they raise sufficiently similar issues that they will be treated together here. A growing number of state courts, persuaded by Justice Frankfurter's arguments in *Sherman,* have adopted the official conduct, or "objective" test.[23] And many federal courts, although apparently prohibited from adopting that test by *Hampton,* have nonetheless recognized a due process defense.[24] But very few courts, regardless of the test used, have found the defense to exist in a particular case.

United States v. Twigg[25] is one of the few federal court decisions that has found entrapment as a matter of law on governmental misconduct/due process grounds. There, the entrapment process began when Drug Enforcement Administration agents sought out a convicted felon, Kubica, and offered to reduce the severity of his sentence if he agreed to cooperate with them. At the request of DEA officials, Kubica contacted an acquaintance, Neville, and suggested setting up a laboratory to manufacture speed. Neville expressed an interest and later introduced Kubica to Twigg, who became involved in the operation to repay a debt to Neville. The government supplied Kubica with glassware and a difficult to find ingredient indispensable to the manufacture of speed. The DEA also made arrangements with chemical supply houses to facilitate the purchase of the rest of the necessary

---

23. See cases listed in *State v. Wilkins,* 144 Vt. 22, 473 A.2d 295 (1983).

24. See, e.g., *United States v. Bogart,* 783 F.2d 1428 (9th Cir.1986); *United States v. Twigg,* 588 F.2d 373 (3d Cir. 1978); United States v. Pardue, 765 F.Supp. 513 (W.D.Ark.1991).

25. 588 F.2d 373 (3d Cir.1978).

materials. In addition, the government provided an isolated farm-house in which to set up the laboratory. During the production process, Kubica was completely in charge and furnished all the technical laboratory expertise.

The court found that the only evidence that Neville was predisposed to commit the crime was his receptivity to Kubica's proposal and Kubica's testimony that he had worked with Neville in a similar laboratory several years earlier. The court also considered the fact that the plan did not originate with the defendants. When Kubica, at the insistence of the DEA, had first reestablished contact with Neville, the latter was not engaged in any illegal activity. In fact, found the court, Kubica had im-planted the criminal plan in Neville's mind. In addition, the court found that neither of the defendants had the technical expertise as chemists to have accomplished the criminal enterprise without Kubica.

While the court thus suggested a lack of predisposition on the defendants' part, it did not explicitly reject the jury's finding that there had been predisposition. Instead, its principal focus was the conduct of the authorities. It concluded that the government's involvement in the crime reached a "demonstrable level of outra-geousness," substantial enough to bar prosecution of the defen-dants as a matter of due process. The court thus seemed not only to reject Justice Rehnquist's approach and endorse Justice Pow-ell's, but to broaden Powell's exception to the majority doctrine beyond its original scope. Powell's concurrence in *Hampton* had specifically noted that the level of outrageousness he had in mind "would be especially difficult to show with respect to contraband offenses, which are so difficult to detect in the absence of under-cover Government involvement."

Yet the facts in *Twigg* do suggest egregious conduct by the police. Both *Russell* and *Hampton* are distinguishable. The labo-ratory in *Russell* was already in existence at the time the govern-ment approached the defendants, whereas the government was totally responsible for the establishment of the drug facility in *Twigg.* And although the government instigated the crime in *Hampton,* its involvement was not nearly as pervasive in that case as it was in *Twigg;* the crime in the latter case would have been inconceivable without the substantial government participation that occurred. If due process ever provides an entrapment de-fense in narcotics cases, *Twigg* is a good case for its application.

Only a few other decisions have held government conduct has, as a matter of law, exceeded reasonable bounds. Some courts, for instance, have held that acquittal should result when a person is induced to commit crime by an informant who is offered a contingent fee to implicate him.[26] But this holding is generally limited to situations in which payment is made upon a *conviction,* an arrangement which can encourage perjury by the informant. If the contingency agreement, like other deals with an informant, merely encourages action designed to lead to arrest, the matter is said to be one for the jury.[27] Another police practice found objectionable was a decoy operation in a high-crime area using an officer posing as a "drunk" with money sticking out of his pocket. According to *Cruz v. State,*[28] this conduct "carries with it the 'substantial risk that . . . an offense will be committed by persons other than those who are ready to commit it." Finally, a few courts have considered adopting, as a matter of due process, a reasonable suspicion requirement like the dissent accused the majority of adopting in *Jacobson.*[29]

(b) The Predisposition Test. A few lower courts have found entrapment as a matter of law under the predisposition test. In *United States v. Lard,*[30] two undercover agents and one government informant told defendant Rigsby that they needed guns and asked him if he knew anyone who would sell them guns. Rigsby subsequently took the undercover agents to defendant Lard's home. Once inside, the agents asked Lard if his shotgun was for sale; Lard answered no. An agent then asked Lard if he had any other firearms for sale and Lard replied that he only had a small detonator. The agent, however, implored Lard that to accomplish his purpose he needed a pipe bomb. Lard persisted in trying to sell merely the detonator and some shotgun shells. The agent argued these items were not worth the price. Lard then said he could make a pipe bomb and that it would be ready in three hours. The agents later returned and completed the sale.

The Eighth Circuit found that no reasonable juror could have found beyond a reasonable doubt that Lard was predisposed to commit the crime and that the agents simply gave him the opportunity to do so. The court considered the fact that Lard had no prior criminal record and no record of making or dealing in firearms. It also noted that Lard's possession of and attempt to sell the detonator and shotgun shells were not unlawful acts. The pipe bomb idea was raised only after the agent repeatedly insisted

---

26. *United States v. Yater,* 756 F.2d 1058 (5th Cir.1985), cert. denied 474 U.S. 901, 106 S.Ct. 225 (1985). See also, *People v. Isaacson,* 44 N.Y.2d 511, 406 N.Y.S.2d 714, 378 N.E.2d 78 (1978) (informant tricked into believing he would receive a stiff prison sentence entrapped defendant with no prior criminal record).

27. *United States v. Valona,* 834 F.2d 1334 (7th Cir.1987); *United States v. Gentry,* 839 F.2d 1065 (5th Cir.1988).

28. 465 So.2d 516 (Fla.1985).

29. See supra note 19. Arguably, *Twigg* adopted such a requirement as well, given its emphasis on the fact that, in that case, the defendant was "lawfully and peacefully minding his own affairs" when the government made contact.

30. 734 F.2d 1290 (8th Cir.1984).

he needed something more powerful than these items. The court concluded: "Law enforcement officials may not arbitrarily select an otherwise law abiding person, gain his confidence, and then lure him into committing a crime."

In one of the few other lower court cases in which an entrapment claim was viewed favorably, *United States v. Borum*,[31] the Circuit Court of Appeals for the District of Columbia held that the defendant was entitled to an instruction on entrapment given the evidence of government inducement and lack of predisposition. The case arose out of an undercover fencing operation in which policemen bought stolen goods and contraband from individuals and recorded the transactions on video tape. The primary aim of the fencing operation was to get unregistered and stolen guns off the street. Borum visited the fencing operation twenty-seven times; on twenty of those occasions the agents asked him for guns. Borum repeatedly told them he refused to handle guns, because, given a previous felony conviction, he faced a stiff penalty if caught with firearms. Even after explaining why he was unwilling to deal in guns, the police rejected his offers of other contraband, insisting on firearms. Borum, in need of money to support his drug habit, then brought the fence operators a stolen pistol.

The court of appeals concluded that there was sufficient evidence for a jury to find inducement by government agents and lack of predisposition on Borum's part. While recognizing that entrapment is not a defense when the defendant merely shows that an agent made an offer and the defendant acquiesced, here the government initiated and repeated solicitations for guns, and the evidence suggested both Borum's unwillingness to deal in guns and his avoidance of firearms in the past.

In contrast to *Twigg, Lard* and *Borum,* most lower court decisions have rejected entrapment claims, taking their cue from the Supreme Court. Probably the best known such cases are the series of holdings which arose from the "ABSCAM sting."[32] ABSCAM was an extensive undercover operation aimed at exposing political corruption. FBI agents posed as representatives of wealthy Arab sheiks who wanted to emigrate to the United States and invest in American real estate and businesses. Their aim was to attract public officials into accepting generous bribes in exchange for furthering the "sheiks'" objectives. Through Melvin Weinberg, a reputed "con" man who received probation and a salary for his cooperation with the government, word of "big money" was spread in various circles, including the United States

31. 584 F.2d 424 (D.C.Cir.1978).

32. For an extensive factual description of ABSCAM (Short for (ABdul SCAM), see *United States v. Myers,* 527 F.Supp. 1206 (E.D.N.Y.1981).

Congress. The FBI planned to take appropriate action if any criminal proposals resulted from this "offer."

When the FBI finally terminated the operation, one U.S. Senator, at least seven U.S. representatives, and several lesser officials had been indicted. Although the facts in each indictment varied, each defendant was recorded and filmed accepting money in return for some political favor concerning investments, immigration matters, or both.

While many of the public officials readily accepted payments, FBI agents had more difficulty with Senator Williams of New Jersey and Congressman Kelly of Florida. Over a period of one year, the "sheiks" met with Senator Williams seven times.[33] Williams initially repeatedly refused to exploit his position as a public official. He also rejected plans to conceal profits from the Internal Revenue Service. At a final meeting, however, he consented to a deal and accepted a bribe. Although Williams raised an entrapment defense at trial, the court refused to find entrapment as a matter of law and the jury convicted him of bribery. His conviction was confirmed at the appellate level.[34]

Congressman Kelly also, at first, rejected the idea of payments.[35] At the initial meeting, he expressed interest only in the legitimate aspects of the Arab ventures. He rejected the bribes a second and third time as well, insisting he was only interested in legitimate projects that would benefit his district. But the agents persisted; more pressure and the display of $25,000 spread on a table in stacks of one hundred dollar bills finally persuaded Kelly to take the bribe.

Although Kelly was also convicted by the jury, the trial judge overturned the jury's verdict. He stated that the government may not tempt an individual beyond that which he "is likely to encounter in the ordinary course." The agents should have stopped when Kelly rejected the first bribe since it was unrealistic for a Congressman to receive further bribe offers once the first one had been refused. The D.C. Circuit Court of Appeals reversed and remanded, however, with instructions to reinstate the jury verdict.[36] Considering the genuine need to detect corrupt public officials and the difficulties inherent in doing so, the court concluded that the government's conduct did not reach an intolerable degree of outrageousness nor did Kelly show a suitable lack of predisposition. Interestingly, this was the same court that decided *Borum.*

33. *United States v. Williams,* 529 F.Supp. 1085 (E.D.N.Y.1981) describes the facts of the case.

34. 705 F.2d 603 (2d Cir.1983), cert. denied 464 U.S. 1007, 104 S.Ct. 524 (1983).

35. *United States v. Kelly,* 539 F.Supp. 363 (D.D.C.1982).

36. 707 F.2d 1460 (D.C.Cir.1983), cert. denied 464 U.S. 908, 104 S.Ct. 264 (1983), appeal after remand 748 F.2d 691 (D.C.Cir.1984).

These cases show that, inevitably, the courts consider both government conduct and defendant predisposition in assessing entrapment claims. Unless the government conduct is clearly outrageous, however, any predisposition on the part of the defendant will usually mean entrapment will not be found as a matter of law.

19.04 Conclusion

The law of entrapment can be summarized as follows:

(1) The two major competing interpretations of the entrapment defense are the predisposition, or subjective, test and the conduct of the authorities, or objective, test. Under the former, entrapment exists only if the defendant was not predisposed to commit the crime. Under the latter, entrapment exists only if the government conduct was such that a reasonable person would have been induced to commit the crime.

(2) The Supreme Court and the federal courts have adopted the predisposition test. Under the Court's interpretation of this test, the prosecution must show beyond a reasonable doubt that the defendant was predisposed to commit the offense prior to its initial contract with him. The conduct of the government is irrelevant. Furthermore, the defense may not exist for "heinous" or violent crimes.

(3) Some federal courts, and perhaps a majority of the Supreme Court as well, also recognize a due process defense, which leads to acquittal if the government conduct was outrageous. Although rare, some situations which might give rise to such a due process defense are: (a) when police use physical violence to create and gather evidence of criminal activity; (b) when the government supplies contraband wholly unobtainable from other sources; or (c) when, in a "criminal enterprise" situation, the government initiates, finances and exercises control over the operations of the enterprise.

It should also be remembered that even if undercover work does not give rise to an entrapment claim it may implicate the right to counsel [37] and, rarely, the Fourth Amendment's protection against unreasonable searches and seizures.[38]

BIBLIOGRAPHY

Carlson, Jonathan. The Act Requirement and the Foundations of the Entrapment Defense. 73 Va.L.Rev. 1011 (1987).

Daniels, Richard. "Outrageousness!" What Does It Really Mean—An Examination of the Outrageous Conduct Defense. 18 Southwestern U.L.Rev. 105 (1988).

37. See § 16.04(b).   **38.** See § 4.02(a).

Dix, George E.   Undercover Investigations and Police Rulemaking. 53 Tex.L.Rev. 203 (1975).

Dunham, Daniel.   Hampton v. United States: Last Rites for the "Objective" Theory of Entrapment?   9 Colum.Hum.Rts.L.Rev. 223 (1977).

Gershman, Bennett L.   Abscam, the Judiciary, and the Ethics of Entrapment, 91 Yale L.J. 1565 (1982).

———.   Entrapment, Shocked Consciences, and the Staged Arrest. 66 Minn.L.Rev. 567 (1982).

Marcus, Paul.   The Development of Entrapment Law.   33 Wayne L.Rev. 5 (1986).

Murchison, Kenneth M.   The Entrapment Defense in Federal Courts: Emergence of a Legal Doctrine.   47 Miss.L.J. 211 (1976).

Park, Roger.   The Entrapment Controversy.   60 Minn.L.Rev. 163 (1976).

Rossum, Ralph A.   The Entrapment Defense and the Teaching of Political Responsibility: The Supreme Court as Republican Schoolmaster.   6 Am.J.Crim.L. 287 (1978).

Seidman, L.M.   The Supreme Court, Entrapment, and Our Criminal Justice Dilemma.   1981 Sup.Ct.Rev. 111.

Whelan, Maura F.J.   Lead Us Not Into (Unwarranted) Temptation: A Proposal to Replace the Entrapment Defense with a Reasonable Suspicion Requirement.   133 U.Pa.L.Rev. 1193 (1985).

Part E

THE PRETRIAL PROCESS

Up to this point, the primary focus of this book has been on the types of constraints the Constitution places on the conduct of law enforcement authorities as they pursue their investigatory duties. This portion of the book examines the formal process by which the criminally accused is moved from arrest to adjudication of the charges against him. Each state has erected a multi-stage procedure designed to afford the accused some type of hearing regarding issues such as the legality of his arrest, the advisability of bail, and whether there is probable cause to prosecute. The following chapters examine these various stages, as well as other aspects of the pretrial process, with particular emphasis on how the constitutional mandates of the Fourth, Fifth and Sixth Amendments apply at each stage.

It would be impossible to describe accurately the "typical" pretrial process, since the states vary so widely in their practices and because certain types of cases are handled differently from others.[1] For example, although the Federal Rules of Criminal Procedure provide for a "preliminary examination" to investigate whether there is probable cause to prosecute the accused,[2] several states do not provide for such a proceeding. As a second example, some cases, such as those involving governmental corruption, are usually pursued initially through grand jury indictment, while in the typical criminal case, where apprehension occurs soon after commission of the crime, indictment *follows* arrest, if it occurs at all. Indeed, most states do not normally proceed by indictment in the typical case, but rather make use of the prosecutor's "information," a document subscribed by the prosecutor that recites the charge. These and other differences are discussed here, but no attempt has been made to describe all existing variations.

The following chapters are arranged to reflect the most likely chronological order in the usual pretrial process. Chapter Twenty discusses the initial custodial decisions—most prominently the so-called "bail" determination—which are made immediately following the arrest of a suspect. Chapter Twenty-One addresses the rules governing the prosecutor's charging decision, including joinder rules; while some sort of charge must of course be brought to initiate the criminal process, the types of decisions discussed in this chapter are normally not formalized until the evidence can be

---

1. For a brief description of the "Ordinary Model" of the criminal process, see § 1.03.

2. Fed.R.Crim.P. 5.

sifted, which usually occurs after the bail determination. The preliminary hearing—the procedure many jurisdictions have established to check this formal charging decision—is the subject of Chapter Twenty-Two. There follows, in Chapter Twenty-Three, an examination of the grand jury, which as noted above, performs not only a prearrest investigative function but also, in many jurisdictions, a post-arrest function similar to the preliminary hearing in that it formalizes the charges against the accused. Chapter Twenty-Four discusses the discovery process, which usually begins, at least informally, soon after arrest and continues through to adjudication of the charges. Finally, placing a time limit on these proceedings is the right to speedy trial, discussed in Chapter Twenty-Five. Other pretrial issues are examined elsewhere in this book, including suppression hearings for the purpose of assessing the admissibility of evidence gathered by the police [3] and hearings to evaluate competency to stand trial.[4]

3. See, e.g., §§ 4.05(e), 16.07, 17.04.   4. See § 28.02(b).

Chapter Twenty

INITIAL CUSTODIAL DECISIONS: PRETRIAL DETENTION AND RELEASE

20.01 Introduction

In most jurisdictions, once an individual is arrested, he is taken before a judicial officer for his "initial appearance" or "first appearance" in court. In misdemeanor cases, trial of the accused may occur at this point.[1] In serious cases, the judicial officer, who is usually either a magistrate or a lower court judge without jurisdiction to hear felony crimes, will merely tell the accused his charges, warn him of his right to refrain from self-incrimination, and appoint counsel. The official may also set preliminary bail, although normally a separate hearing is reserved for the formal determination of this issue.

At the bail hearing, for those crimes which are "bailable," the judicial officer decides what conditions to impose on the accused to assure his appearance at trial and at any preliminary proceedings. These conditions may range from merely extracting a promise to reappear to a hefty cash deposit with the court. In some cases, the defendant is unable to meet the imposed conditions, with the result that he is detained pending adjudication of his charges. And in some jurisdictions, if the prosecution can prove the accused is unlikely to remain in the community or is likely to commit a crime if released, the accused may be explicitly subject to "preventive detention."

Logically precedent to both the initial appearance and the pretrial release decision, of course, is a determination that the state has the right to detain the accused in the first place. In cases where arrest was authorized by a warrant or grand jury indictment, an official determination of probable cause has already been made, and these preliminary proceedings may take place without further findings. But when, as is common, an arrest is made "in the street," the only pre-arrest determination of probable cause is the police officer's. As described below, the Supreme Court has held that a judicial check of the officer's decision is required in this situation. In cases where it is necessary, many states combine this probable cause assessment with the initial appearance described above.

The first section of this chapter discusses further the rationale for and nature of the probable cause to detain determination. The

1. Usually, a "complaint" filed by the prosecutor is sufficient basis for such a proceeding. Only felony prosecutions normally require an information or an indictment.

487

second section examines the bail system. The third section deals with preventive detention. Finally, the chapter discusses the legal privileges of those who are detained pending trial.

20.02   The Probable Cause Hearing

(a) **When a Hearing Is Required.** *Gerstein v. Pugh* [2] involved a challenge of the preliminary hearing system used in Florida at the time. Under that system, prosecutors could charge all crimes, other than capital offenses, by information, without a prior preliminary examination and without obtaining leave of court. Only through a special statute allowing a preliminary hearing after 30 days, or during arraignment, which often took place a month or more after arrest, could a suspect obtain a judicial determination of probable cause.

The Supreme Court held this scheme unconstitutional, concluding that the Fourth Amendment requires as a condition for any significant pretrial restraint on liberty a judicial determination of probable cause made either before or promptly after arrest. While the Court recognized the practical necessity of allowing warrantless arrests so long as they are supported by probable cause, it pointed out that exigent circumstances no longer exist once a suspect is taken into custody. At that time, a suspect's rights to be free from unlawful detention becomes paramount:

> [W]hile the State's reasons for taking summary action subside, the suspect's need for a neutral determination of probable cause increases significantly. The consequences of prolonged detention may be more serious than the interference occasioned by arrest. Pretrial confinement may imperil the suspect's job, interrupt his source of income, and impair his family's relationship. . . . Even pretrial release may be accompanied by burdensome conditions that effect a significant restraint of liberty. . . . When the stakes are this high, the detached judgment of a neutral magistrate is essential if the Fourth Amendment is to furnish meaningful protection from unfounded interference with liberty.

Gerstein rejected the contention that the prosecutor's decision to file an information is itself a sufficient determination of probable cause to detain a defendant pending trial. But it also made clear that a probable cause hearing is not required after every arrest. The return of a grand jury indictment satisfies the probable cause determination required to detain a suspect pending trial. Likewise, a person arrested under a warrant has received an adequate prior judicial determination of probable cause. Under these circumstances, therefore, a preliminary hearing is not constitutionally required. *Gerstein* stands only for the proposition

---

2. 420 U.S. 103, 95 S.Ct. 854 (1975).

that before a suspect may be detained some official entity other than a law enforcement officer must make a determination of probable cause.

Moreover, this probable cause determination is required only when a "significant pretrial restraint on liberty" is to be imposed by the state. *Gerstein* explained that the restraint must be something other than the mere condition that the suspect appear for trial, but offered nothing else by way of defining when a restraint might be "significant." It would seem that any imposition of bail would constitute enough restraint to justify a *Gerstein* hearing; even release on personal recognizance can result in a significant infringement on liberty if any conditions are attached to release. Given these facts, the simpler approach would be to hold a *Gerstein* hearing in the absence of a warrant or indictment.

A final limitation on *Gerstein,* noted in the decision, is that, like other constitutional rights, the right to a *Gerstein* hearing may be waived by the accused.

(b) Procedural Protections. The lower courts in *Gerstein* held that the determination of probable cause must be accompanied by the full scheme of adversary safeguards—counsel, confrontation, cross-examination, and compulsory process for witnesses. The Supreme Court reversed the lower courts on this issue, finding that the probable cause determination was not a "critical stage" that would require appointed counsel, because the consequences of the proceeding—although possibly a significant restraint on liberty—do not approximate the possible consequences of trial, sentencing and other stages of the criminal process where counsel has been found necessary.[3] The Court conceded that confrontation and cross-examination might enhance the reliability of probable cause determinations in some cases. But it concluded that the value of such actions would be too slight to justify a constitutional mandate that these formalities be employed in making the Fourth Amendment determination of probable cause; this determination, it pointed out, is always made without benefit of counsel on those occasions when the police approach a magistrate for an arrest warrant *prior* to arrest.

For the same reasons, the Court also approved informal modes of proof at the hearing, including hearsay and written testimony. The standard of proof is simply whether there is probable cause to believe the suspect has committed a crime. As such, there need be only a reasonable belief in guilt, not proof beyond a reasonable doubt or by a preponderance of the evidence. The lesser standard of proof does not call for the "fine resolution of conflicting evidence" that an adversary proceeding seeks to provide.

3. See § 31.03(a) for a discussion of critical stage analysis.

The Court had administrative concerns in mind as well. A footnote explained:

> Criminal justice is already overburdened by the volume of cases and the complexities of our system. The processing of misdemeanors, in particular, and the early stages of prosecution generally are marked by delays that can seriously affect the quality of justice. A constitutional doctrine requiring adversary hearings for all persons detained pending trial could exacerbate the problem of pretrial delay.

Given the Court's eschewal of the full panoply of procedural protections during a *Gerstein* hearing, such a hearing may and often does consist merely of a brief appearance in front of a magistrate after arrest. The proceeding will often be *ex parte* and, in effect, rarely be a "hearing" in anything but name. Since it serves the same purpose as a hearing to secure an arrest warrant, the *Gerstein* hearing will resemble such proceedings.

(c) Timing of the Hearing. *Gerstein* required that the hearing it mandated take place "promptly after arrest." But *Gerstein* did not attempt to define this phrase further. In *Riverside County v. McLaughlin*,[4] the Supreme Court held, 5–4, that a hearing which takes place within 48 hours of arrest will be presumptively reasonable. Although such a hearing might still violate *Gerstein* if it is delayed "unreasonably," [5] "unavoidable delays in transporting arrested persons from one facility to another, handling late-night bookings where no magistrate is readily available, obtaining the presence of an arresting officer who may be busy processing other suspects or securing the premises of an arrest, and other practical realities" are valid excuses for postponement within the two-day period. Moreover, Justice O'Connor, who wrote the Court's opinion, indicated that administrative efficiency is another legitimate reason for delay; relying on *Gerstein's* statement that flexibility during the pretrial stages of the criminal process is important as a means of promoting state experimentation, she referred favorably to a scheme which routinely defers the *Gerstein* hearing for up to 48 hours in order to combine it with other types of proceedings, such as bail determinations.

Justice Scalia in dissent argued that *Gerstein's* language about experimentation focused on the *procedures* for conducting the hearing, not its timing, and that the need to avoid incarceration of an innocent individual far outweighs the state's interest in efficient processing. He also contended that the majority's approach violated the common law notion that judicial review of an arrest

4. 500 U.S. —, 111 S.Ct. 1661 (1991).

5. E.g., "delays for the purpose of gathering additional evidence to justify the arrest, a delay motivated by ill will against the arrested individual, or delay for delay's sake."

must take place as soon after arrest as possible.[6] He concluded that, at most, the Fourth Amendment allows a 24–hour delay between arrest and the *Gerstein* hearing. Justice Marshall, joined by Justices Blackmun and Stevens, wrote a separate dissent which did not mention Scalia's 24–hour rule, but agreed that "a probable cause hearing is sufficiently 'prompt' under *Gerstein* only when provided immediately upon completion of the 'administrative steps incident to arrest.' "

20.03   Bail and Other Pretrial Release Conditions

(a) The History of Pretrial Release. Once a person has been arrested pursuant to a warrant or indictment, or has been found detainable at a *Gerstein* hearing, the question becomes whether he should be released pending the next judicial proceeding. Pretrial release, traditionally known as release on "bail," facilitates preparation of a defense and prevents incarceration of a possibly innocent person. At the same time, it may allow the defendant to flee the jurisdiction, tamper with evidence, or harm others. As the history of pretrial release shows, several different approaches to pretrial release have been devised.

(1) English antecedents. In England, the practice of bail developed as an alternative to holding accused persons for prolonged periods of time in diseased-ridden jails. Bail literally meant the bailment or delivery of an accused from the jail to third parties of his own choosing. If the third party could not produce the accused for trial, he had to surrender himself to custody, or in later times, surrender property or money. Given the size of the community, the releasing sheriff or justice of the peace knew most bailed offenders, as well as their sureties.[7]

(2) The money bail and bondsman system. The practice of pretrial release was carried over to the United States. In 1789, the federal government provided, by statute, that "upon all arrests in criminal cases, bail shall be admitted, except where the punishment may be death."[8] Most states followed suit in their own constitutions or statutes.[9] For instance, California's constitution, in language which is widely copied, provides that "all persons shall be bailable by sufficient sureties, unless for capital offenses when the proof is evident or the presumption great."[10]

As the United States grew, its system for ensuring appearance of a person diverged significantly from English practice, which

---

6. See, e.g., Wright v. Court, 107 Eng.Rep. 1181 (K.B.1825) ("[I]t is the duty of a person arresting any one on suspicion of felony to take him before a justice as soon as he reasonably can.")

7. P. Freed & P. Wald, Bail in the United States 1–3 (1964).

8. 18 U.S.C.A. § 3142 (originally in Judiciary Act of 1789).

9. Freed & Wald, supra note 7, at 2. See, e.g., N.J. Const.Art. I, par. 11.

10. Cal. Const.Art. I, § 6.

functioned in a much smaller community. First, the principal hold on the accused came to be a money deposit, as opposed to the surety himself or his property. Second, as a "supplement" to the private surety known to the sheriff or judge, a professional "bondsman" took on the job of surety.[11] The premise of this money bail system was and continues to be that risk of a sufficiently high financial loss will provide a deterrent to flight and assure the accused's presence at trial.

There are several practical difficulties connected with the money bail system. The first of these weaknesses results from the method by which magistrate sets the amount of bail. Instead of being an informed, individualized decision based on a calculation of the proper financial deterrent, the process is often mechanical— the amount of bail is set according to the offense charged.[12] Because this process makes no allowance for the accused's ability to pay, the great majority of indigent defendants must submit to detention.[13]

Another problem with the money bail system is the role of the bondsman. In most jurisdictions, the bondsman puts up the financial security required by the magistrate for a percentage fee paid by the accused. If the accused fails to appear at trial, the bondsman's security is forfeited, providing incentive for the bondsman to locate the defendant. But if the defendant appears for trial, no portion of the fee paid to the bondsman is refunded to the defendant (otherwise, the bond profession would be singularly unremunerative). This widespread practice removes any deterrent effect from money bail. Whether he appears at trial or not, the defendant loses the same amount of money, i.e., the fee he paid to the bondsman. Thus, the premise on which the system is grounded is seriously undermined. More importantly, this system places the bondsman, rather than the judge, in the position of jailkeeper. Those able to meet the bondsman's fee buy their freedom while those who cannot, or those whom he deems "bad risks" (for he is ostensibly risking forfeiture), remain in jail. The courts are relegated to the rather ministerial role of fixing the amount of bail and holding such deposits as are made.[14]

A final practical problem with the money bail system is the fact that so many people are detained under it. Not only does this overload the jails; it also causes significant hardship for many people. Families are left without financial support and jobs are lost. Moreover, for a number of reasons, including their inability

11. Freed & Wald, supra note 7, at 4.

12. Paulsen, "Pre-Trial Release in the United States," 66 Col.L.Rev. 109, 113 (1966); Ares, Rankin & Sturz, The Manhattan Bail Project: An Interim Report on the Use of Pre-Trial Parole, 38 N.Y.U.L.Rev. 67, 71 (1963).

13. Ares, Rankin & Sturz, supra note 12, at 71.

14. *Pannell v. United States*, 320 F.2d 698 (D.C.Cir.1963).

to contact witnesses, make amends with victims, and continue their connections in the community, pretrial detainees are more likely than others to be convicted and to receive a severe sentence upon conviction.[15]

(3) The first reform movement: personal recognizance. Dissatisfaction with the money bail system led to nationwide recognition of the need for reform in bail procedures. The primary aim of the reform movement was to abolish the money bail system and to seek alternative approaches through which detention could be minimized and release on recognizance maximized.

The pilot bail reform project was conducted by the Vera Institute in New York City. The Manhattan Bail Project, as it was called, focused on indigent defendants who, according to a carefully selected and weighted set of criteria, presented a low risk of flight if release were granted. Among the factors considered important in determining whether an accused would be recommended for release on recognizance were previous convictions, roots in the community, employment history, and the gravity of the charge. The Project achieved a high degree of success. Over the first three years of its operation, from 1961–1964, only 1.6 percent of those defendants recommended for release willfully failed to appear at trial. During the same period, three percent of those released under the traditional system of bail failed to appear, nearly twice as many as had been released without bail.[16]

These results spurred the reform effort in other cities.[17] But the culmination of the reform movement came in 1966. In that year, Congress passed the Federal Bail Reform Act,[18] which furnished a model for several state statutes.[19] The Act provided that any person charged with a non-capital offense "be ordered released pending trial on his personal recognizance or upon the execution of an unsecured appearance bond in an amount specified by the judicial officer, unless the officer determines . . . that such a release will not reasonably assure the appearance of the person as required." If the latter determination was made, the officer could impose, in addition to the above conditions, any other conditions which would assure the appearance of the accused, including placing the person in another's custody, restrictions on travel or association, the execution of a secured appearance bond with a percentage deposited with the court, or other condition the officer might consider necessary.[20] Note that under this statute

15. Rankin, "The Effect of Pretrial Detention," 39 N.Y.U.L.Rev. 641 91964).

16. Vera Institute of Justice, Programs in Criminal Justice Reform, Ten Year Report, 1961–1971, 35 (1972).

17. Over 100 Vera-type projects exist nationwide. C. Thomas, Pretrial Release Programs (1977).

18. 18 U.S.C.A. §§ 3146–3152.

19. See, e.g. Mass.Gen.Laws Annot., 276, §§ 58, 82A (1970).

20. 18 U.S.C.A. § 3146(a).

and its state counterparts money bail is only one of the conditions to be considered; further, when money *is* used as assurance, it is deposited directly with the court, not through a bondsman.

More importantly, in deciding which conditions to impose, the Act provided that "the judge shall . . . take into account the available information concerning: the nature and the circumstances of the offense charged, the weight of evidence against the accused, the accused's family ties, employment, financial resources, character and mental condition, the length of his residence in the community, his record of convictions, and his record of appearances at court proceedings or of flight to avoid prosecution or failure to appear at court proceedings." [21] This list of considerations requires much greater individualization than the mechanical reference to schedules under the money bail system, which sets the amount of bail according to the offense charged.

The Act had a significant impact on the release rate of federal defendants, which increased by as much as 40%.[22] State jurisdictions which reduced their reliance on financial incentives also reduced substantially the number of state defendants detained from arrest to disposition.[23] At the same time, the nonappearance rate in jurisdictions with these new laws was low, and may often have been related more to the time between arrest and disposition than to the seriousness of the penalty involved.[24]

(4) The second reform movement: preventive detention. Under the 1966 Act, the pretrial release decision focused solely on whether the defendant would return for trial. But public concern over crimes committed by defendants on pretrial release eventually led to modification of the original reforms.[25] In 1970, the District of Columbia passed the first explicit "preventive detention" statute, authorizing denial of bail to "dangerous" persons charged with certain offenses for a period of up to 60 days.[26] The Act was infrequently used,[27] and no state followed the District's lead for some time. But fourteen years later, the U.S. Congress passed the

---

21. Id. § 3146(b).

22. See W. Thomas, Bail Reform in America 27 (1976).

23. Id. at 37–39 (over a 10-year period, the percentage of felony defendants detained from arrest to disposition dropped from 52% to 33%, the percentage of misdemeanants detained from 40% to 28%).

24. Id. at 103 (percentage of defendants who failed to appear was roughly five percent across all offenses).

25. Estimates of crimes committed by arrestees on release vary from 10 to 15% of all crimes, Moore, et al. Danger-

ous Offenders: The Elusive Target of Justice 126 (1984), to a finding that only 5% of all those released were rearrested within 60 days. Note, "Preventive Detention: An Empirical Analysis," 6 Harv.Civ.Rts–Civ.Lib.L.Rev. 291 (1971).

26. D.C.Code 1970, § 23–1322.

27. Out of the first 600 felony defendants to enter the criminal justice system in the year following the Act's passage, only ten persons were preventively detained, five of whom had their detention orders reversed. Wice, P., Freedom for Sale: A National Study of Pre–Trial Release 1–3, 164 (1974).

Federal Bail Reform Act of 1984.[28] This Act continued to express a preference for individualized pretrial release and specifically stated that the "judicial officer may not impose a financial condition that results in pretrial detention of the person." [29] But it also authorized preventive detention of dangerous individuals, and amended the 1966 Act in several other ways as well.

First, the 1984 Act permits the judge making the pretrial release decision to impose conditions on the accused which are only tangentially related to assuring reappearance and are obviously designed to inhibit the commission of crime. Under the new Act, for instance, release may be revoked (if the judge so indicates when permitting pretrial release) for possession of a firearm or other destructive device; failure to maintain or commence employment, an educational program, or a treatment program; failure to report to a local agency; failure to comply with a specified curfew; and failure to return to custody for employment, schooling or other limited purposes.[30] Second, the Act permits detention for not more than ten days of any person: (1) who is, and was at the time the alleged offense was committed, on release pending trial for a felony, pending sentencing or appeal, or pursuant to a grant of probation or parole; or (2) who "may flee or pose a danger to any other person or the community." [31] The latter is to be presumed if the accused is charged with certain drug offenses.[32]

Third, and most controversially, the Act permits continued detention after the ten-day period if, after a hearing, it appears that no condition "will reasonably assure the appearance of the person as required and the safety of any other person and the community." [33] This hearing must be held upon motion of the government in any case involving a crime of violence, an offense punishable by life imprisonment or death, a drug-related offense for which the penalty is greater than ten years, or a felony committed by a person who has already been convicted of two of the above-described offenses. A hearing is also to be held if, on motion of the government or the judge's own motion, the case "involves a serious risk that the person will flee; [or] a serious risk that the person will obstruct or attempt to obstruct justice, or threaten, injure, or intimidate, or attempt to threaten, injure, or intimidate, a prospective witness or jury." [34] If the judge finds, apparently by a preponderance of the evidence, that "no condition or combination of conditions will reasonably assure the appearance of the person," or by clear and convincing evidence that "no condition or combination of conditions will reasonably assure the

28. 18 U.S.C.A. § 3141–3150 (1984).

29. Id. § 3142(c).

30. Id. at § 3142(c)(2).

31. Id. at § 3142(d).

32. Id. Of course, the presumption is rebuttable.

33. Id. at § 3142(e).

34. Id. at 3142(f).

safety of any other person and the community," detention until trial is appropriate. The accused is entitled to counsel during the hearing, but "[t]he rules concerning admissibility of evidence in criminal trials do not apply to the presentation and consideration of information at the hearing."[35] Several states have enacted similar statutes.[36]

The Act increased the number of federal prisoners by 32 percent in 1985.[37] The provision allowing preventive detention of "dangerous" offenders was successfully invoked over 1600 times per month over a one year period.[38] Thus, the Act has clearly put a strain on correctional and judicial resources. There is no evidence to date concerning its effect on the crime rate.

(b) The "Right" to Pretrial Release. The Eighth Amendment states that "[e]xcessive bail shall not be required." One might argue that a denial of pretrial freedom subjects an accused to "excessive" constraints in violation of the Eighth Amendment because it entails incarceration without conviction and hampers preparation of his defense. But this argument has never succeeded; as noted above, for instance, from the beginning bail has always been denied in capital cases when the "proof is evident or the presumption great." As the Supreme Court stated in *Carlson v. Landon:* [39]

> [i]n England, [the Bail] clause has never been thought to accord a right to bail in all cases, but merely to provide that bail shall not be excessive in those cases where it is proper to grant bail. When this clause was carried over into our Bill of Rights, nothing was said that indicated any different concept.

Another, similar argument for an absolute right to pretrial release could derive from the presumption of innocence. As argued by Professor Tribe, one could contend that a denial of pretrial release infringes the presumption because it takes away the freedom to which an innocent person is entitled.[40] But in *Bell v. Wolfish,*[41] the Court held that the presumption of innocence is merely "a doctrine that allocates the burden of proof in criminal trials," telling the factfinder to judge the defendant on the evidence rather than on the fact that he has been charged; thus, according to the Court, it has no effect outside of the trial context.

(c) Constitutional Criteria for Pretrial Release. Since there is no constitutional right to bail, the question becomes:

---

35. Id.

36. See, e.g., West's Fla.Stat.Ann. § 907.041 (1984).

37. Kurtz, Detention Law, Further Crowds Prisons, The Washington Post, January 9, 1986, at A4. As of early 1986, the federal prison system was 42% over capacity. Id.

38. Id.

39. 342 U.S. 524, 72 S.Ct. 525 (1952).

40. Tribe, "An Ounce of Prevention: Preventive Justice in the World of John Mitchell," 56 Va.L.Rev. 371, 404 (1970).

41. 441 U.S. 520, 99 S.Ct. 1861 (1979).

under what circumstances may bail be denied? As the historical discussion illustrates, statutory pretrial release criteria are wide-ranging. Addressed here are the three most prominent reasons for denying release: likelihood of flight, dangerousness to others, and lack of financial resources. The Supreme Court's early cases indicated that assuring appearance for trial was the only constitutionally acceptable criterion for evaluating pretrial release. However, the Court has more recently held that other "regulatory" goals are permissible as well, including prevention of harm to the public. In analyzing the constitutionality of the various criteria, the courts have looked not only at the Eighth Amendment's language but also considered the implications of substantive due process and the Equal Protection Clause.

(1) Likelihood of flight. In *Stack v. Boyle*,[42] the Supreme Court stressed that the purpose of bail is to permit pretrial release of an accused with the assurance that he will return for trial:

> Like the ancient practice of securing the oaths of responsible persons to stand as sureties for the accused, the modern practice of requiring a bail bond or the deposit of a sum of money subject to forfeiture serves as additional assurance of the presence of an accused. . . . Since the function of bail is limited, the fixing of bail for any individual defendant must be based upon standards relevant to the purpose of assuring the presence of that defendant.

Not surprisingly, given this language, lower courts concluded that, in setting bail or other pretrial release conditions, the sole consideration was preventing flight from the jurisdiction.[43] Clearly, the Bail Reform Act of 1966 reflected this view.

Further, *Stack* indicated that the language of the Eighth Amendment meant that bail should rarely be set so high as to prevent release under this criterion:

> Admission to bail always involves a risk that the accused will take flight. That is a calculated risk which the law takes as the price of our system of justice. . . . In allowance of bail, the duty of the judge is to reduce the risk by fixing an amount reasonably calculated to hold the accused available for trial and its consequence. But the judge is not free to make the sky the limit, because the Eighth Amendment to the Constitution says: "Excessive bail shall not be required."

In *Stack,* the Court held that a uniform bond of $50,000 for each of several unregistered Communist Party members needed to be reconsidered by the trial court. On remand, each defendant's bail was to be set in light of "the nature and circumstances of the

---

42. 342 U.S. 1, 72 S.Ct. 1 (1951). **43.** See P. Freed & P. Wald, supra note 7, at 6–7.

offense charged, the weight of the evidence against him, the financial ability of the defendant to give bail and the character of the defendant." This language presaged the federal Act of 1966 and parallel state legislation which put emphasis on an individualized assessment of the accused's likelihood of returning for trial.

(2) Dangerousness. Although, for at least three decades after *Stack,* prevention of flight was the only avowed aim of the bail system, several commentators have pointed out that the money bail system was often used, *sub rosa,* to detain "dangerous" individuals.[44] And, of course, once preventive detention statutes like the 1984 Bail Reform Act were passed, courts could openly consider such factors as danger to the community or witnesses. Both of these practices appeared to be in violation of *Stack.* But in *United States v. Salerno,*[45] the Supreme Court rejected a facial challenge of the Bail Reform Act of 1984, finding that *Stack* provided "far too slender a reed on which to rest" the argument that detention for the purpose of preventing crime by arrestees was unconstitutional:

> Nothing in the text of the Bail Clause limits permissible government considerations solely to questions of flight. The only arguable substantive limitation of the Bail Clause is that the Government's proposed conditions of release or detention not be 'excessive' in light of the perceived evil. . . . [W]hen the government has admitted that its only interest is in preventing flight, bail must be set by a court at a sum designed to ensure that goal, and no more. . . . We believe that when Congress has mandated detention on the basis of a compelling interest other than prevention of flight, as it has here, the Eighth Amendment does not require release on bail.

The defendants in *Salerno* also challenged the preventive detention portion of the statute on substantive due process grounds, claiming that such detention amounted to punishment without trial. A similar argument had been made and rejected in the earlier case of *Schall v. Martin,*[46] where the Court upheld a state statute authorizing detention of juveniles who were charged with a delinquent act and posed a "serious risk" of committing a crime before their adjudicatory hearing. The Court in *Schall* had reasoned that whether a government action is "punishment" depends upon whether the government's intent is to punish or, if it is not, whether the action "appears excessive in relation to [a legitimate] alternative purpose."[47] Using these criteria, the Court

44. See, e.g., Mitchell, "Bail Reform and the Constitutionality of Preventive Detention," 55 Val.L.Rev. 1223, 1235 (1969).

45. 481 U.S. 739, 107 S.Ct. 2095 (1987).

46. 467 U.S. 253, 104 S.Ct. 2403 (1984).

47. Relying on *Bell v. Wolfish,* 441 U.S. 520, 99 S.Ct. 1861 (1979), discussed in § 20.04.

found that children confined under the statute were not punished: the duration of detention could be no longer than 17 days and even those children kept in "secure detention" wore street clothes, participated in education and recreational programs, and were disciplined for misbehavior solely by confinement in their rooms. This type of confinement did not indicate an intent to punish and was not excessive in relation to the important government interest of protecting the public from such juveniles.

Similarly, in *Salerno,* the Court found the government's interests to be "regulatory" rather than punishment oriented.[48] Confinement under the Act is not meant to be punishment, because it is limited by the Speedy Trial Act,[49] and must occur in a facility separate, "to the extent practicable," from those who have been convicted. As to the justification for this regulatory confinement, the Court pointed to the strong government interest in preventing crime by arrestees. It also noted that the Act focuses on those charged with serious offenses, and requires clear and convincing proof "that no conditions of release can reasonably assure the safety of the community or any person." By implication, a preventive detention statute which does not impose these two limitations may not pass constitutional muster.

Perhaps the weakest aspect of the Court's due process analysis in *Schall* and *Salerno* is its assumption that the government's interests can be reasonably implemented. In both opinions it stated that, "from a legal point of view[,] there is nothing inherently unattainable about a prediction of future criminal conduct," given the traditional reliance on such predictions in many other context, such as sentencing, parole and probation. But research indicates that a prediction that someone will recidiviate is likely to be wrong more often that it is right.[50] If this is so, preventive detention will not effectuate the government's purpose of detaining those most likely to commit crime.[51] At the same time, it is likely to detain a large number of people who are not dangerous. Further, it provides the government with a means of manipulating defendants. As Justice Marshall pointed out in his *Salerno* dis-

---

48. The Court noted several other instances where pretrial detention was permitted for "regulatory" purposes, among them *Jackson v. Indiana,* 406 U.S. 715, 92 S.Ct. 1845 (1972) (pretrial detention of incompetent defendants), discussed in § 28.03(b)(4); *Gerstein v. Pugh,* 420 U.S. 103, 95 S.Ct. 854 (1975) (temporary detention pending probable cause hearing), discussed in § 20.02(a).

49. The Act usually limits the time between arrest and trial to 100 days, but there are several exceptions. See § 25.05(c) and (d). The Court did indi-

cate that if confinement became prolonged, it might be deemed "punitive." See *United States v. Hare,* 873 F.2d 796 (5th Cir.1989).

50. Monahan, J., The Clinical Prediction of Violent Behavior 54 (1971).

51. The prevention of flight criterion also calls for a speculative prediction. But as noted in § 20.03(a)(3), these predictions tend to be wrong in only a very small percentage of the cases (under 5%).

sent, one of the defendants in that case who had been preventively detained because he was "dangerous" was released when he agreed to be a covert government agent, suggesting that the Act might be used for purposes other than protecting the community. Aware of these difficulties, many lower courts have required fairly stringent proof of dangerousness.[52]

(3) *Lack of financial resources.* As noted in the historical account,[53] pretrial release was, and still is in some states, often denied simply because a person is poor and cannot produce any money (or enough money to meet the bondsman's requirements). The lower courts have, on the whole, found nothing wrong with this result. As one court put it, bail "is not excessive merely because the defendant is unable to pay it." [54] This position makes sense only in those situations where one can predict that no amount of money will assure the defendant's presence (a scenario which may often be true with drug kingpins, for instance),[55] or that the defendant is dangerous. When such predictions cannot be made, even a modest bail may be "excessive" for many indigent defendants, in the sense that a smaller, affordable amount, as low as it might be, will still assure appearance for trial. The federal Reform Act of 1984 seems to recognize this fact by prohibiting imposition of "a financial condition that results in pretrial detention of the person."

The few courts that have found unconstitutional a failure to take into account financial circumstances when setting bail have generally done so on equal protection rather than Eighth Amendment grounds. For instance, in *Ackies v. Purdy,*[56] the court held that setting bail solely according to the nature of the offense would lead to an irrational distinction between the rich and the poor, as "a poor man with strong ties in the community may be more likely to appear than a man with some cash and no community involvement." With the advent of alternatives to money bail, a different type of equal protection might also be made. The federal court in *Pugh v. Rainwater,*[57] upheld a challenge to the Florida bail system, concluding that equal protection standards require that nonfinancial means of assuring appearance should be considered before money bail. As the court put it, "[r]equiring a presumption in favor of non-money bail accommodates the State's

52. See, e.g., *United States v. Townsend,* 897 F.2d 989 (9th Cir.1990) (doubts regarding propriety of release to be resolved in favor of defendant); *United States v. Jackson,* 845 F.2d 1262 (5th Cir.1988) (mere fact that defendant in a drug ring was member of a notorious motorcycle gang not enough); *United States v. Ploof,* 851 F.2d 7 (1st Cir.1988) (generalized danger to the community insufficient).

53. See § 20.03(a)(2) & (3).

54. *Hodgdon v. United States,* 365 F.2d 679 (8th Cir.1966).

55. See *United States v. Jessup,* 757 F.2d 378 (1st Cir.1985).

56. 322 F.Supp. 38 (S.D.Fla.1970).

57. 557 F.2d 1189 (5th Cir.1977).

interest in assuring the defendant's appearance at trial as well as the defendant's right to be free pending trial, regardless of his financial status."

But the Supreme Court has not viewed the equal protection argument favorably in another context. In *Schilb v. Kuebel*,[58] it upheld a state statute which provided that a defendant who was not released on his own recognizance could be required either to deposit cash equal to 10% of the bond set by the court, 10% of which would be forfeited as "bail bond costs" even if the defendant reappeared, or to deposit the full amount of bail, all of which would be refunded if the defendant returned. The defendant argued, in effect, that this statute unfairly taxed the indigent accused, who was forced to pick the first alternative and thus lose money. But the Court found the statute did not necessarily discriminate against the poor, since "[i]t should be obvious that the poor man's real hope and avenue for relief is the personal recognizance provision" and since, given "these days of high interest rates," "it is by no means clear that [the second route] is more attractive to the affluent defendant." Neither of these conclusions addressed the defendant's claim; the dissent argued that, at the least, the state should have to impose a similar retention fee on those who paid the full deposit.

(d) The Pretrial Release Hearing. *Stack* indicated that the Eighth Amendment would be violated if a court set bail according to some predetermined schedule, without considering "the nature and circumstances of the offense charged, the weight of the evidence against [the defendant], the financial ability of the defendant to give bail and the character of the defendant." In upholding preventive detention, *Schall* and *Salerno* also seemed to find important that the statutes in question provided for "case-by-case" determinations of dangerousness at a pretrial hearing presided over by a judge. These cases suggest that each defendant should be afforded, as a matter of procedural due process, some sort of hearing before the longterm pretrial release decision, at which an individualized assessment is made. Thus, they also suggest that the bail schedules frequently used under the money bail system are unconstitutional.[59]

These conclusions are bolstered by the type of reasoning found in *Hunt v. Roth*,[60] where the Eighth Circuit struck down a Nebraska constitutional amendment which denied bail in cases of "sexual offenses involving penetration by force or against the will of the

---

58. 404 U.S. 357, 92 S.Ct. 479 (1971).

59. Preliminary bail, applicable only for a few days, can probably be set according to a schedule, however. *Ackies v. Purdy,* 322 F.Supp. 38 (S.D.Fla. 1970).

60. 648 F.2d 1148 (8th Cir.1981), vac'd for mootness 455 U.S. 478, 102 S.Ct. 1181 (1982).

victim . . . where the proof is evident or the presumption great."
The court concluded:

> The fatal flaw in the . . . amendment is that the state has
> created an irrebuttable presumption that every individual
> charged with this particular offense is incapable of assuring
> his appearance by conditioning it upon reasonable bail or is
> too dangerous to be granted release. . . . The state may be
> free to consider the nature of the charge and the degree of
> proof in granting or denying bail but it cannot give these
> factors conclusive force.

Note that *Hunt's* reasoning applies with equal force to the most
time-honored exception to bail practices, capital cases "where the
proof is evident or the presumption great." [61]   While, on the
whole, a person charged with a capital offense may be more likely
to flee the jurisdiction than other defendants, the state should not
be able to assume that is the case.

If a hearing is held, it should be far more formal than the
nonadversarial probable cause hearing approved in *Gerstein v.
Pugh*,[62] despite the fact that it may take place at approximately
the same point in the criminal process.   Research indicates that
counsel can have a significant effect on whether release occurs
and on what terms.[63]   Further, the Supreme Court's cases require
counsel at any stage after "prosecution commences" and the
defendant is "immersed in the intricacies of substantive and
procedural criminal law." [64]   A post-arrest bail hearing appears to
meet both of these requirements.   Additionally, because the information relevant to this proceeding can come from many sources,
the defendant should have the right to present evidence and cross-
examine the government's witnesses.

However, it should be pointed out that, in *Salerno,* the Supreme Court found the federal preventive detention statute's provision for counsel, evidence presentation, and cross-examination
rights acceptable because it "far exceed[ed] what we found necessary" in *Gerstein*.   It is not clear that this language *requires* that
these various rights be accorded a defendant subject to preventive
detention.   Also noteworthy in this regard is a later holding of the
Court that, despite the federal statute's "prompt hearing" provision, a delayed hearing is harmless error where the person is

---

61. In those states which had their
capital punishment statutes by constitutional developments, some eliminated
this exception, see e.g., *Martinez v.
State,* 26 Ariz.App. 386, 548 P.2d 1198
(1976), while others continue to apply it
those offenses which once were designated capital. *Jones v. Sheriff, Washoe
County,* 89 Nev. 175, 509 P.2d 824
(1973).

62. 420 U.S. 103, 95 S.Ct. 854 (1975),
discussed in § 20.02(b).

63. P. Wice, Freedom for Sale 49
(1974).

64. *Kirby v. Illinois,* 406 U.S. 682, 92
S.Ct. 1877 (1972), discussed in
§ 31.03(a)(3).

subsequently found eligible for detention.[65] Finally, it remains uncertain, despite the emphasis the Court placed on it in *Salerno,* whether the statute's requirement that proof of dangerousness be by "clear and convincing evidence" is constitutionally mandated.[66]

(e) Trial and Post–Conviction Bail. The focus to this point has been on the scope of pretrial release. Similar release questions can arise during trial or after conviction pending appeal. In *Bitter v. United States,*[67] the Supreme Court held that, if granted prior to trial, bail may be revoked during trial "only when and to the extent justified by danger which the defendant's conduct presents or by danger of significant interference with the progress or order of the trial." Bail revocation at trial may not be based, as was the case in *Bitter,* on "a single, brief incident of tardiness." Thus, pretrial release establishes a strong preference for continued release during trial.

With respect to bail after conviction and pending appeal, many states merely leave the issue to the discretion of the trial judge. But the federal Bail Reform Act of 1966, which at the pretrial stage focused purely on assuring appearance for trial, at the post-conviction stage also allowed detention if the person would pose a danger to the community.[68] Under the Bail Reform Act of 1984, post-conviction release is even harder to obtain, as the judge must find by clear and convincing evidence that the offender will *not* pose a danger or flee.[69]

(f) Appealing the Pretrial Release Decision. Most jurisdictions have statutes authorizing an interlocutory appeal from a decision denying pretrial release.[70] If there is no such statute, habeas corpus is considered the proper remedy for review.[71] Furthermore, a state defendant who is unable to make bail before trial may seek habeas review in federal court when the state appellate court docket is so backlogged that effective relief would otherwise be denied.[72] However, it is unlikely that any appellate court, federal or state, will overrule a lower court pretrial release decision, unless a gross abuse of discretion can be proved. Moreover, the Supreme Court has held that, unless the defendant brings a class action in favor of all pretrial detainees similarly situated, an appeal of a pretrial bail decision is moot once the defendant is convicted.[73]

---

65. *United States v. Montalvo–Murillo,* 495 U.S. 711, 110 S.Ct. 2072 (1990).

66. See *United States v. Salerno,* 829 F.2d 345 (2d Cir.1987).

67. 389 U.S. 15, 88 S.Ct. 6 (1967).

68. 18 U.S.C.A. § 3148.

69. 18 U.S.C.A. § 3143(b).

70. See § 29.03(a) for a discussion of interlocutory appeals generally.

71. *Ex parte Brumback,* 46 Cal.2d 810, 299 P.2d 217 (1956).

72. *Boyer v. City of Orlando,* 402 F.2d 966 (5th Cir.1968); see 28 U.S.C.A. § 2254(b).

73. *Murphy v. Hunt,* 455 U.S. 478, 102 S.Ct. 1181 (1982).

20.04 Disposition of Pretrial Detainees

Relevant to the debate over the scope of pretrial detention are the conditions in which the detention occurs. The Supreme Court has been confronted with several cases claiming that particular government practices at detention facilities are unconstitutional. To date, it has rejected all of these claims.

The leading case is *Bell v. Wolfish*,[74] where the Court analyzed a number of rules promulgated by New York City's Metropolitan Correctional Center (MCC), a federally-operated short-term facility used primarily to house pretrial detainees. The majority opinion, by Justice Rehnquist, decided that the issue was whether these rules constituted "punishment" of unconvicted individuals, in which case due process was violated, or were instead "reasonably related to [another] legitimate governmental objective." Using this expansive test, the Court sanctioned: a "publisher-only" rule prohibiting detainees from receiving books or magazines from anyone other than the publisher, book clubs, or bookstores;[75] a prohibition against packages from outside (except a package of food at Christmas); unannounced searches of living areas at irregular intervals; and visual body cavity searches after contact visits. All of these practices were viewed as legitimate means of ensuring the security of the prison and preventing smuggling of weapons and contraband. In *Block v. Rutherford*,[76] the Court relied on the same reasoning in upholding a pretrial detention center's blanket prohibition of contact visits.

Although arising out of the post-conviction prison setting, the Court's decision in *Hudson v. Palmer*[77] is also of relevance here. In that case, Palmer sought damages under § 1983 for an arbitrary "shakedown" of his cell by a prison guard who intentionally destroyed some of his property, including legal materials and letters. Accepting these factual allegations as true, the majority found that the guard's actions violated neither the Due Process Clause or the Fourth Amendment. The Due Process Clause was not implicated because intentional misconduct of this sort could not be prevented by the state and the state provided adequate postconduct remedies.[78] The Fourth Amendment's prohibition of unreasonable searches and seizures was not implicated because prisoners have no reasonable expectation of privacy in their cells. Balancing society's interest in prison security against the prisoner's interest in privacy, Chief Justice Burger concluded for the

---

74. 441 U.S. 520, 99 S.Ct. 1861 (1979).

75. The Court also found that this rule did not violate the First Amendment, especially since it was usually limited to a maximum sixty day detention period.

76. 468 U.S. 576, 104 S.Ct. 3227 (1984).

77. 468 U.S. 517, 104 S.Ct. 3194 (1984).

78. See *Parratt v. Taylor*, 451 U.S. 527, 101 S.Ct. 1908 (1981), discussed in § 2.05(a)(3).

majority that "society would insist that the prisoner's expectation of privacy always yield to what must be considered the paramount interest in institutional security." Therefore, "unfettered access" to prison cells is permissible and prison officials may seize "any articles which, in their view, disserve legitimate institutional interests," including, apparently, Palmer's letters and legal materials. To Palmer's argument that without the reasonableness guarantee incorporated in the Fourth Amendment prisoners would be subject to harassment by prison officials, Chief Justice Burger pointed out that the Eighth Amendment protected against cruel and unusual punishments and that state tort and common-law remedies were available.

Justice Stevens, joined by Justices Brennan, Marshall and Blackmun, agreed that random searches of a prisoner's cell are reasonable in order to ensure that it contains no contraband or dangerous weapons. But the dissenters saw "no need for seizure and destruction of noncontraband items found during such searches." As the dissent pointed out, *Palmer* reinforces the impression that the Court has adopted a "hands-off" attitude toward prison administration.

20.05 Conclusion

The initial custodial decisions made after arrest are relatively unregulated by the Constitution. Set out below are the few Supreme Court pronouncements and some of the more common statutory rules which govern these decisions.

(1) If arrest is not authorized by either an arrest warrant or a grand jury indictment, the Fourth Amendment requires a prompt post-arrest judicial assessment of whether probable cause to detain exists. The assessment may be *ex parte,* in the absence of counsel, and informal in nature—in short, similar to the pre-arrest determination of probable cause when a warrant is sought. If such a hearing takes place within 48 hours of arrest, it is presumptively reasonable.

(2) After arrest, the typical procedure is to determine whether the individual is eligible for bail or other type of pretrial release. While the money bail system is still in force in many states, the trend is to require an individualized assessment of the likelihood an accused will appear for trial and to encourage release of defendants on their own recognizance or on other non-financial conditions. However, a countertrend is developing which permits the state to detain "preventively" suspects who are likely to commit crimes while on pretrial release.

(3) Neither the Eighth Amendment's prohibition of excessive bail nor the Due Process Clause prohibits a denial of pretrial release, so long as the denial is related to a legitimate government

objective, is not disproportionate to the perceived danger, and is not intended as punishment. Thus, the federal Bail Reform Act of 1984, which permits pretrial detention when no reasonable pretrial release condition can assure reappearance at trial, prevent harm to witnesses, or prevent the commission of a crime, is constitutional. However, the Equal Protection Clause may prohibit denial of pretrial release solely on the grounds of indigency, even if the Eighth Amendment or the Due Process Clause do not.

(4) Procedural due process probably requires a judicial hearing, with counsel and the right to call and cross-examine witnesses, prior to a pretrial release determination which can have long-term consequences.

(5) The government has wide-ranging authority to administer pretrial detention facilities, so long as its practices are related to legitimate security rationale.

BIBLIOGRAPHY

Berg, Kenneth. The Bail Reform Act of 1984. 34 Emory L.J. 685 (1985).

Carbone, June. Seeing Through the Emperor's New Clothes: Rediscovery of Basic Principles in the Administration of Bail. 34 Syracuse L.Rev. 517 (1983).

Clarke, Stevens H., Jean L. Freeman, Gary G. Koch. Bail Risk: A Multivariate Analysis. 5 J. of Legal Stud. 340 (1976).

Cohen, Richard A. Wealth, Bail and Equal Protection of the Laws. 23 Vill.L.Rev. 977 (1978).

Dill, Forest. Discretion, Exchange and Social Control: Bail Bondsmen in Criminal Courts. 9 L. & Soc'y Rev. 639 (1975).

Foote, Caleb. The Coming Constitutional Crisis in Bail: I and II. 113 U.Pa.L.Rev. 959, 1125 (1965).

———, ed. Studies on Bail. Philadelphia: University of Pennsylvania Law School, 1966.

Goldkamp, John S. Questioning the Practice of Pretrial Detention: Some Empirical Evidence from Philadelphia. 74 J. of Crim.L. and Crimin. 1556 (1983).

———. Danger and Detention: A Second Generation of Bail Reform. 76 J.Crim.L. & C. 1 (1985).

Landes, William M. The Bail System: An Economic Approach. 2 J. of Legal Stud. 79 (1973).

Miller, Marc & Martin Guggenheim. Pretrial Detention and Punishment. 75 Minn.L.Rev. 335 (1990).

National Center for State Courts. An Evaluation of Policy Related Research on the Effectiveness of Pretrial Release Programs. Denver: National Center for State Courts, 1975.

_____. Policymakers' Views Regarding Issues in the Operation and Evaluation of Pretrial Release and Diversion Programs: Findings from a Questionnaire Survey. Denver: The Center, 1975.

Thomas, W. Bail Reform in America. University of California Press, 1976.

Tribe, Laurence H. An Ounce of Detention: Preventive Justice in the World of John Mitchell. 56 Va.L.Rev. 371 (1970).

Uviller, Richard H., James D. Hopkins, Peter D. Andreoli, Irving Land, and Harold J. Rothwax. Bail, Preventive Detention and Speedy Trials. 8 Colum.J. of L. & Soc.Probs. 1 (1971).

Wice, P. Freedom for Sale: A National Survey of Pretrial Release. U.S. Govt. Printing Office (1974).

Chapter Twenty-One

CONSTRAINTS ON PROSECUTORIAL DISCRETION: CHARGING AND JOINDER RULES

21.01 Introduction

Article II, Section 3 of the United States Constitution provides that the executive branch of the federal government "shall take Care that the Laws be faithfully executed." Similar provisions are found in most state constitutions. Where the criminal law is concerned, the obligation to "execute the law," on both the federal and state levels, falls primarily on the prosecutor.[1] Its principal manifestation is the charging decision, the determination whether a particular individual should formally be accused of crime and, if so, on precisely what charge or charges.

Traditionally, the prosecutor has been vested with wide-ranging authority in making this decision. As the Supreme Court stated in *Bordenkircher v. Hayes*,[2] "so long as the prosecutor has probable cause to believe that the accused committed an offense defined by statute, the decision whether or not to prosecute, and what charge to file or bring before a grand jury, generally rests entirely in his discretion."

Prosecutorial discretion in this area is not unfettered, however. Some constraints derive from the Constitution, some come from statutory regulation, and many are self-imposed by the executive branch itself. The first two sections of this chapter examine the constitutional limitations, as well as some exemplary legislative and administrative restrictions, on the prosecutor's authority to decide who to prosecute and on what charges. The third section discusses the rules regulating joinder of charges and joinder of parties; these rules also tend to restrict the prosecutor's control over the charging process. The intent of this chapter is to give an overview of the complex nature of the charging decision and the law's attempts to regulate it.

The procedural devices which review the validity of a charge once it has been chosen by the prosecutor—the preliminary hearing and the grand jury review process—are discussed in the following chapters.

1. Of course, the police exercise considerable discretion in the field when making the initial arrest decision. See generally, K. Davis, Police Discretion (1975).

2. 434 U.S. 357, 98 S.Ct. 663 (1978).

21.02   The Decision to Forego Prosecution

The prosecutor has the authority to dismiss charges even over the complainant-victim's objection. Additionally, through the plea bargaining process,[3] she has the ability to accept a guilty plea on a lesser charge than that originally brought. Both of these privileges are exercised frequently. In the federal courts, approximately seventy-five percent of all criminal cases brought to the attention of the prosecutor result in dismissal;[4] the proportion of nonprosecutions in state jurisdictions is probably closer to fifty percent,[5] but is obviously still sizeable. Of those cases which are prosecuted, perhaps 90% in both federal and state jurisdictions result in a conviction by guilty plea, often on a charge lower than that originally brought.[6]

(a) **Reasons for Non-Prosecution.** The most obvious, and most justifiable, reason for not prosecuting an individual on a particular charge is insufficient evidence. A dismissal on lack of evidence grounds could involve an assessment that the individual is in fact innocent of the charge, or it could mean that, while the prosecutor believes the defendant is guilty, she also believes certain crucial evidence is inadmissible because of police misconduct or evidentiary rules. Another evidentiary reason for not proceeding is an inability to secure the cooperation of a key witness, who might not want to undergo the inconvenience or possible harassment associated with testimony in court.

Even when the prosecutor has access to sufficient admissible evidence to convict, however, she may decide to forego prosecution or to agree to a plea bargain on a lesser charge than the evidence would support. The reasons for such a decision are legion;[7] only a few will be mentioned here.

The prosecutor may reach the conclusion that, despite the ability to make out a prima facie case, she will have a particularly difficult time obtaining a conviction, given the strength of the defense's evidence or the likely reaction of a jury to the defendant's plight, and thus that her time is better spent focusing on other cases. She may feel that particular charges, although legitimate under prevailing law, are not appropriately brought

3. The procedures normally followed during plea bargaining, and the constitutional restrictions placed on the prosecutor once a bargain has been reached, are discussed in Chapter Twenty-Six. Here plea bargaining will be discussed only from the standpoint of the prosecutor's authority to reduce charges.

4. Frase, "The Decision to File Federal Criminal Charges: A Quantitative Study of Prosecutorial Discretion," 47 U.Chi.L.Rev. 246 (1980).

5. P. Greenwood, et. al., Prosecution of Adult Felony Defendants in Los Angeles County: A Policy Perspective (prosecution rate varies from 46% to 55%).

6. See § 26.01.

7. See LaFave, "The Prosecutor's Discretion in the United States," 18 Am. J.Comp.L. 532, 533–35 (1970) for a detailed discussion of the reasons a prosecutor might decide not to prosecute.

because of the minor nature of the crime, alternative methods of redressing the harm (e.g. restitution), or societal condonation of the behavior involved (as in adultery cases).[8] Or she may believe that application of the law at issue would impose a draconian penalty under the circumstances (e.g., a statute allowing imposition of a mandatory life sentence on a person with three felonies regardless of degree). The characteristics of the potential defendant—that is, her age, prior record, or family situation—may also influence the prosecutor to treat her leniently,[9] either through outright dismissal, charge reduction, or referral to a so-called "pretrial diversion program" designed to help the defendant deal with the problems that allegedly precipitated the criminal activity.[10]

More practical concerns may dictate prosecutorial decisions as well. Charge reduction or dismissal may meet a perceived need to develop informants or to reward the defendant for helping to apprehend others. If prosecution requires a complicated extradition process, it may be dropped. Federal prosecutors may dismiss charges which can also be tried in state court, on the ground that the federal interest in prosecuting the case is minimal.[11]

An underlying consideration in all of these instances is economic. While the conscientious prosecutor may want to convict every individual who has committed crime on the charge which best describes the illegal conduct, lack of attorney time and investigative and other resources may force her to consider lenient treatment of defendants. In particular, the institution of plea bargaining has received powerful impetus because of the belief that, if not offered concessions, defendants will seldom choose a guilty plea over trial, thus severely overburdening the criminal justice system.

Although there is a sense in which all of the reasons for nonprosecution and charge reduction given above are "legitimate," one can argue that, to the extent prosecutors are dismissing or downgrading charges for reasons unrelated to the

8. In the Frase study, supra note 4, federal attorneys cited the minor nature of the crime as the principal reason for declining prosecution in 44% of the cases, while insufficiency of the evidence was responsible for nonprosecution in only 22% of the cases.

9. See Kuh, "Plea Bargaining: Guidelines for the Manhattan District Attorney's Office," 11 Crim.L.Bull 48 (1975) (listing as "mitigating factors" to be taken into account when charging: the defendant's prior criminal record, age, military and work record and the "genuineness of the defendant's contri-

tion"). In the Frase study, supra note 4, federal attorneys cited characteristics of the defendant as the principal reason for declining prosecution in 21% of the cases.

10. For a useful description of pretrial diversion programs, see Zimring, "Measuring the Impact of Pretrial Diversion from the Criminal Justice System," 41 U.Chi.L.Rev. 224 (1974).

11. In the Frase study, supra note 4, the availability of state prosecution was cited as a reason for declining federal prosecution in 26% of the cases.

available evidence, they are failing to "execute" the laws of the state. At the least, it must be admitted that the decision to dismiss or reduce charges for other than evidentiary reasons will often be a complex one. As a result, prosecutorial leniency may frustrate legislative and public will and is susceptible of abuse.

(b) Limitations on Non–Prosecution. Judicial and legislative response to the possible abuses of non-prosecution has not been energetic. A failure to pursue charges may occasionally be overridden by a court on a writ of mandamus [12] or by the prosecutor's superior,[13] and in extremely rare instances, a private party may be able to bring prosecution [14] or the prosecutor may be removed.[15] But none of these devices provides an institutional approach to the everyday problem of arbitrary nonprosecution.

In some jurisdictions, more comprehensive schemes for avoiding arbitrary exercise of discretion to dismiss or reduce charges have been developed. Many prosecutorial offices have taken it upon themselves to develop guidelines for prosecutors to follow. One district attorney's office, for example, has established criteria which tell prosecutors when to seek the lesser of two possible sentences authorized by the legislature.[16] Unlike prosecutorial rules dictating when charges should be dismissed outright (e.g., "cases involving less than a gram of cocaine will not be prosecuted," "defendants with no prior record and a job shall normally have misdemeanor charges dismissed"), such criteria do not ignore legislative intent, since the applicable statute explicitly authorizes the lesser sentence. There remains a question as to the impact these and other types of guidelines have on actual practice; unless they are made known to the public, they may be inconsistently applied by the prosecutor. On the other hand, their publication would tend to lessen the deterrent effect of the law and encourage time-consuming litigation over whether they are rational and equitably applied.

Another approach to the practice of charge dismissal or reduction when sufficient evidence to convict exists is to forbid it. In West Germany, for instance, if a file is closed it must include a written statement of reasons for the dismissal which, in important

12. See *NAACP v. Levi,* 418 F.Supp. 1109 (D.C.D.C.1976), dismissed as moot, *NAACP v. Bell,* 76 F.R.D. 134 (D.D.C.1977). But see, *Inmates of Attica Correctional Facility v. Rockefeller,* 477 F.2d 375 (2d Cir.1973).

13. "Many states by statute confer upon the attorney general the power to initiate prosecution in cases where the local prosecutor has failed to act. In practice, however, attorneys general have seldom exercised much control over local prosecuting attorneys."

Kamisar, LaFave, Israel, Modern Criminal Procedure 931 (5th ed. 1981).

14. Annot., 66 A.L.R.3d 732 (1975). But see *Tonkin v. Michael,* 349 F.Supp. 78 (D.V.I.1972) (holding that notwithstanding a court rule permitting private prosecution, it should not be allowed over the prosecutor's objection).

15. *Kamisar,* et al., supra note 13, at 906.

16. *Greenwood,* et al., supra note 5, at 60.

cases, must be approved by the prosecutor's superior.[17]   Apparently, only reasons having to do with evidentiary insufficiency are acceptable in most instances.   It has been suggested that West German prosecutors may dismiss cases for the same reasons American prosecutors do, but conceal this fact with claims of incomplete evidence.[18]   Even if this is true, the written justification requirement presumably facilitates review of the prosecutor's decision and discourages dismissals based on improper considerations.

A similar approach has been adopted, at least technically, by those American jurisdictions which provide for judicial approval of a *nolle prosequi,* the formal prosecutorial declaration that no prosecution will be sought on a particular charge.[19]   In order to protect against excessive use of this device, these jurisdictions require the prosecutor to explain to the court in writing her reasons for failing to prosecute when the failure occurs after an indictment has been issued or an information filed.   If routinely and conscientiously applied, such a requirement would act as a significant check on prosecutorial charging and plea bargaining decisions.

The requirement does not seem to be routinely applied, however.[20]   Indeed, the "principal object" of this judicial review is not to protect the public's interest but "is apparently to protect a defendant against prosecutorial harassment, e.g., charging, dismissing and recharging, when the Government moves to dismiss an indictment over the defendant's objection." [21]   Moreover, the Supreme Court itself has expressed misgivings about judicial supervision of the charging process.   In *Wayte v. United States* [22] it gave two reasons for avoiding such supervision.   First, "[s]uch factors as the strength of the case, the prosecution's general deterrence value, the Government's enforcement priorities, and the case's relationship to the Government's overall enforcement plan are not readily susceptible to the kind of analysis the courts are competent to make."   Second, law enforcement might be "chilled" if the prosecutor's motives and actions are subjected to outside scrutiny and the government's enforcement policies revealed publicly.

17. See K. Davis, Discretionary Justice: A Preliminary Inquiry 188–196 (1969).

18. Goldstein & Marcus, "The Myth of Judicial Supervision in Three 'Inquisitorial' Systems: France, Italy, and Germany," 87 Yale L.J. 240, 275–6 (1977).

19. See Note, 103 U.Pa.L.Rev. 1057, 1064–67 (1955).

20. Note, 65 Yale L.J. 209, 214 (1955).

21. *Rinaldi v. United States,* 434 U.S. 22, 98 S.Ct. 81 (1977).

22. 470 U.S. 598, 105 S.Ct. 1524 (1985).

Despite these concerns, the benefits of judicial monitoring of the charging process may well outweigh the costs, especially if the court's evaluation is not a rigid one. The focus should be on whether there is sufficient evidence to bring charges and if so, whether the government's failure to bring them is due to factors which are part of a rational law enforcement policy.[23] The prosecution is already subject to some judicial oversight when disposition is by guilty plea;[24] theoretically, even under the present system it should be ready to justify any reduction in charge resulting from the plea bargaining process. When the prosecutorial action being evaluated is dismissal rather than charge reduction, the judicial assessment need not be public, which should reduce the state's reluctance to reveal its policies to the court.

(c) Agreements Not to Prosecute. On occasion, a prosecutor will agree to dismiss criminal charges if the defendant waives any civil claims that might arise from the arrest or prosecution. In *Town of Newton v. Rumery*,[25] the Supreme Court sanctioned such an agreement, so long as the defendant is not coerced into it. Here, the defendant's agreement to forego a civil suit in exchange for dismissal of witness tampering charges against him was found to be voluntary, because he had been released from custody and consulted his attorney beforehand. The Court pointed out that the agreement not only protected the state against suit, but also saved the witness who had allegedly been intimidated from having to testify in criminal and civil court, something she had indicated she did not want to do. The four dissenters argued that such agreements should usually be declared invalid, even if voluntary, because they placed the prosecutor in a conflict of interest between his public duty to prosecute criminal offenses and his desire to protect the police and municipality from civil suit.

21.03 Constraints on Bringing Charges

If the prosecutor does decide to prosecute an individual for a particular act, she possesses wideranging authority with respect to the precise charge or charges to be brought. For instance, if the evidence indicates that X, intending to kill Y, fires at Y and hits her in the leg, in many jurisdictions X could be charged with attempted murder, malicious wounding, or unlawful wounding, or equivalent crimes, each carrying a significantly different penalty. In addition to being able to choose the severity of the charge, the

23. The National Advisory Commission on Criminal Justice Standards, in its 1973 Report on Courts, recommended that a decision not to prosecute (as opposed to a decision to prosecute) be subject to review at the instance of the police or the complainant, under a standard for review which contemplates whether the decision "was so unreasonable as to constitute an abuse of discretion."

24. See § 26.04(c).

25. 480 U.S. 386, 107 S.Ct. 1187 (1987).

prosecutor is often able to charge a number of crimes based on the same incident if the appropriate statutory authority exists. For instance, a robbery of six men at a poker game can result in six separate robbery charges.[26] Theft from a house can result in a burglary charge (for breaking in with intent to steal) and a theft charge.

Generally, the choice the prosecutor makes with respect to these options is unchallengeable. In rare cases, as discussed above, an especially lenient charge might be called into question by the courts, government entities or the public. Equally rarely, the *defendant* may be able to challenge a prosecution, even though based on a valid statute and even though the defendant appears to come within its terms. There are essentially three grounds for a challenge by the defendant: selective prosecution, vindictive prosecution, or a prosecution in apparent disregard of legislative will. This section discusses the legal restrictions that have developed in response to these three possibilities.

(a) Discriminatory Prosecution. The Supreme Court has recognized that, in limited circumstances, a prosecutor's decision to prosecute can violate the Equal Protection Clause. As early as 1886, in *Yick Wo v. Hopkins,*[27] the Court stated:

> Though the law itself be fair on its face and impartial in appearance, yet, if it is applied and administered by public authority with an evil eye and an unequal hand, so as practically to make unjust and illegal discriminations between persons in similar circumstances, material to their rights, the denial of equal justice is still within the prohibition of the Constitution.

Yick Wo was convicted under a city ordinance making it unlawful for any person to maintain a laundry in the city of San Francisco without first obtaining the permission of the board of supervisors, unless the laundry was located in a building constructed of brick or stone. The Court admitted that the statute was, on its face, a reasonable exercise of the police power. But the evidence indicated that those refused permission to continue using wooden facilities were principally Chinese. On this evidence, the Court held that criminal enforcement of the law was illegal. Since *Yick Wo,* the courts have refined the equal protection analysis considerably.

(1) The three-prong test. In *Oyler v. Boles,*[28] the Supreme Court emphasized that selective prosecution has to be both intentional and the result of an arbitrary classification before an equal protection claim will succeed. In *Oyler,* the defendant presented statistics showing that, of the six men sentenced in the Taylor

---

26. See *Ashe v. Swenson,* 397 U.S. 436, 90 S.Ct. 1189 (1970), discussed in § 30.04(a)(1).

27. 118 U.S. 356, 6 S.Ct. 1064 (1886).

28. 368 U.S. 448, 82 S.Ct. 501 (1962).

County Circuit Court who should have been sentenced to life imprisonment under West Virginia's habitual offender statute, only he was so sentenced. The Court rejected his equal protection claim, finding that these statistics did not show whether the failure to sentence the other five individuals as habitual offenders was due to ignorance concerning their prior offenses or "the result of a deliberate policy of proceeding only in a certain class of cases or against specific persons." Only in the latter instance would there be proof of an equal protection violation. "Moreover," the Court stated:

> the conscious exercise of some selectivity in enforcement is not in itself a federal constitutional violation. Even though the statistics in this case might imply a policy of selective enforcement, it was not stated that the selection was deliberately based upon an unjustifiable standard such as race, religion, or other arbitrary classification.

Courts since *Oyler* have devised a three-prong test for determining whether a given prosecution has been discriminatory. The defendant must show: (1) a failure to prosecute those who are similarly situated (2) that is intentionally based on (3) an arbitrary rather than a rational classification.[29] As *Oyler* indicates, a showing that no one else in the defendant's position has been prosecuted under the same statute is not enough. The defendant must also show that this state of affairs is by design, not due to ignorance or inadvertence. And even if the discrimination is intentional, it is not a violation of equal protection unless the reason for the discrimination is race, religion or some other impermissible or irrational classification. Even so limited, the discriminatory prosecution claim can arise in many different contexts. This section will look at a few of the recurring issues.

(2) Prosecution of conspicuous lawbreakers. Several courts have held that "[s]elective enforcement may . . . be justified when a striking example or a few examples are sought in order to deter other violators." [30] Since such prosecutions intentionally select from among many who are similarly situated, the justification for this type of decision is that the classification is not arbitrary; the courts find the deterrence rationale a rational basis for selective prosecution. Even when the "example" is selected because she publicizes her violation as a protest of the law, thus

---

29. See, e.g., *Commonwealth v. Franklin,* 376 Mass. 885, 385 N.E.2d 227 (1978). See also, Reiss, "Prosecutorial Intent in Constitutional Criminal Procedure," 135 U.Pa.L.Rev. 1365 (1987).

30. *People v. Utica Daw's Drug Co.,* 16 A.D.2d 12, 225 N.Y.S.2d 128 (1962).

See also, *Falls v. Town of Dyer, Indiana,* 875 F.2d 146 (7th Cir.1989) ("A government legitimately could enforce its law against a few persons (even just one) to establish a precedent, ultimately leading to widespread compliance.").

implicating the First Amendment, courts generally find no constitutional problem. For instance, in *United States v. Catlett*,[31] a prosecution under an IRS policy targeting cases "involving . . . individuals who have achieved notoriety as tax protesters" was upheld.

Catlett and similar protester-prosecution cases can be justified on the ground that the mere fact of protest should not immunize lawbreakers from prosecution and that, so long as other people who break the same law are prosecuted, no invidious discrimination has occurred.[32] The Supreme Court appeared to adopt this type of reasoning in *Wayte v. United States*.[33] The defendant there was one of 674,000 men who refused to register for the draft: some had actively protested against the Selective Service laws; some, like the defendant, had submitted letters to the government declaring their refusal to register and giving reasons; some indicated their refusal in less dramatic ways; some had been reported by others; some had neither reported themselves nor been reported by anyone else. The defendant was among a handful of these individuals prosecuted under a "passive" enforcement policy which targeted the nonregistrants who were easiest to identify—those who somehow publicly disclosed their unwillingness to register. In rejecting the defendant's equal protection claim, the Court, in an opinion by Justice Powell, concluded that the defendant had "not shown that the enforcement policy selected nonregistrants for prosecution on the basis of their speech." He noted that the government did not prosecute those protesters who eventually registered; at the same time, Powell asserted, of those who never registered, the government prosecuted not only "vocal" nonregistrants, such as the defendant, but also "people who reported themselves or were reported by others but who did not publicly protest." [34]

The Court went on to say that even if vocal nonregistrants were discriminated against, there was no evidence of discriminatory purpose. Quoting from equal protection cases in other contexts,[35] it defined such purpose as "more than . . . awareness of consequences." Intentional discrimination "implies that the decisionmaker . . . selected or reaffirmed a particular course of

---

31. 584 F.2d 864 (8th Cir.1978).

32. See also, *United States v. Bassford*, 812 F.2d 16 (1st Cir.1987) (prosecution for violating marijuana laws not impermissibly selective even though defendant may have been chosen for prosecution in part because he was vocally against drug laws).

33. 470 U.S. 598, 105 S.Ct. 1524 (1985).

34. Contrary to the Court's assertion, the district court appeared to have found that all of those being prosecuted were "vocal" nonregistrants (meaning those who declared their intent not to register via letter or public pronouncement). *United States v. Wayte*, 549 F.Supp. 1376 (D.C.Cal.1982).

35. See *Personnel Administrator of Massachusetts v. Feeney*, 442 U.S. 256, 99 S.Ct. 2282 (1979).

action at least in part 'because of,' not merely 'in spite of,' its adverse effects upon an identifiable group." Here there was no showing that the government prosecuted Wayte *"because"* of his protest activities; rather he was prosecuted because his speech made him more easily identifiable.

The Court also concluded that the defendant's prosecution did not violate the First Amendment, because the "speech" affected (i.e., protesting the draft) was combined with "nonspeech" (i.e., the failure to register) in the same course of conduct, and the government interest in regulating the latter was sufficiently important to justify incidental infringement of the former. Applying the test of *United States v. O'Brien,*[36] Powell concluded that prosecuting nonregistrants was a strong governmental interest in light of its constitutional duty to secure the nation's defense, and that the government's "passive" enforcement policy was a cost effective way of implementing this interest, given the difficulty of identifying all draft evaders and the danger that "failing to proceed against publicly known offenders would encourage others to violate the law." Further the policy was merely an "interim enforcement system," pending development of a method of identifying all nonregistrants.

When it can be shown, contrary to the Court's finding in *Wayte,* that the defendant was selected solely "on the basis of speech," a different result may be called for. In *Federov v. United States,*[37] the defendants, demonstrators being prosecuted for unlawful entry, offered to prove that all other first time offenders charged with unlawful entry had been found eligible for pretrial diversion rather than prosecuted. The trial court ruled that this proffer was insufficient to warrant discovery and an evidentiary hearing on the selective prosecution claim, because the correct comparative group was not all others charged with trespass but other *demonstrators* charged with trespass; the court noted, for instance, that demonstrators might be more disruptive than other trespassers and thus merit greater sanction.

But the appellate court reversed this ruling, noting that *Wayte* had "treated all those who refused to register [i.e. vocal and nonvocal nonregistrants] as members of a single class and considered whether those selected from the class for prosecution were selected on an impermissible basis." Thus, in this case, the defendants' focus on the larger group of all first-time trespassers

---

36. 391 U.S. 367, 88 S.Ct. 1673 (1968). *O'Brien* permits government regulation of speech "if it is within the constitutional power of the Government; if it furthers an important or substantial governmental interest; if the government interest is unrelated to the suppression of free expression; and if the incidental restriction of alleged First Amendment freedoms is no greater than is essential to the furtherance of that interest."

37. 580 A.2d 600 (D.C.App.1990), aff'd 600 A.2d 370 (D.C.App.1991).

was appropriate. Since, based on the record, it appeared that the only difference between this group and the defendants' was that the former's "alleged conduct was not associated with the expression of views protected by the First Amendment," a colorable claim of selective prosecution was made out. "To conclude otherwise is to maintain that persons whose trespass had First Amendment ramifications have, as a result of that fact alone, committed a crime of greater 'magnitude' than persons whose trespass was not politically motivated." *Federov* illustrates how the result in a selective prosecution case can be determined by the choice of the group to which the defendant must be similarly situated.

(3) Prosecution of "significant" offenders. To be distinguished from "conspicuous lawbreaker" prosecution just discussed is a governmental policy which results in prosecution of one offender but not her colleague in crime, on the ground that the former poses the more significant threat to the community. For example, one court has upheld a policy which enforces gambling laws against bookmakers but not against those placing bets with them.[38] A variant of this policy is one which focuses on the most egregious offenders. Thus, a policy of enforcing a law prohibiting sale of securities without a license only against those who sell more than ten securities was upheld.[39] Although these policies all intentionally select certain offenders from among a pool of "similarly situated" offenders, they can be said to do so on a rational rather than arbitrary ground, and thus do not violate the Equal Protection Clause. As one court put it, "the prosecutor may conserve resources for more important cases."[40]

However, as with the conspicuous offender cases, when a suspect classification is connected with a "significant offender" enforcement policy, courts are less reluctant to recognize a selective prosecution claim, even when the government can proffer "rational" reasons for the policy. For instance, in *State v. McCollum*,[41] the court dismissed prostitution charges against female nude dancers who, during a private party at a club, received money for sexual conduct with male patrons, pointing out that the males involved were not also arrested despite Wisconsin's law that criminalized behavior of both the payor and payee in a prostitution arrangement. The court rejected the government's arguments that it was harder to develop evidence against the males and that prosecution of the females would result in "maximum deterrence."[42]

38. *People v. Garner,* 72 Cal.App.3d 214, 139 Cal.Rptr. 838 (1977).

39. *State v. Steurer,* 37 Ohio App.2d 51, 66 O.O.2d 89, 306 N.E.2d 425 (1973), cert. denied 416 U.S. 940, 94 S.Ct. 1943 (1974).

40. *Falls v. Town of Dyer, Indiana,* 875 F.2d 146 (7th Cir.1989).

41. 159 Wis.2d 184, 464 N.W.2d 44 (App.1990).

42. See also, *Commonwealth v. King,* 374 Mass. 5, 372 N.E.2d 196 (1977).

Even when no suspect classification is involved, if there is *no* rational basis for selective prosecution, the courts will dismiss the prosecution. Thus, in *United States v. Robinson,*[43] the court refused to uphold a policy of prosecuting only private detectives, and not government officials, for illegal wiretapping. The court noted that the degree of intrusion occasioned by a wiretap and the divulgence of what is discovered does not depend on who conducts it. In effect, the court concluded that the significance of the crime was the same in both instances and thus differentiation based on the type of perpetrator was unconstitutional.

(4) Pretextual prosecution. Occasionally, a defendant will contend that prosecution for one crime occurred solely because the prosecutor has been unable to obtain sufficient evidence on another, more serious offense. For instance, in *United States v. Sacco,*[44] the court assumed that the government targeted the defendant for investigation under the alien registration laws "based on his suspected role in organized crime." Nonetheless, the court went on to conclude that "[i]t cannot be said that [such a] standard for selection is not rationally related to the purposes of the various criminal laws [under which the defendant] was being investigated, including the alien registration laws." However, in *United States v. Cammisano,*[45] a case involving prosecution under the Federal Meat Inspection Act of a person allegedly associated with "organized crime," the district court stated that "not all classifications used by the government may be found rationally related to the purpose of the particular criminal law being invoked," and held that a colorable claim of selective prosecution had been made out sufficient to grant discovery against the prosecution.

Perhaps the difference between these two cases is that in *Sacco* there was strong evidence of organised crime activity by the defendant, whereas in *Cammisano* there was a suggestion that the defendant was selected purely because of his Italian ancestry, which "would obviously be an impermissible and arbitrary classification." Some have argued that a pretextual prosecution might be impermissible even when there is some evidence of involvement in other criminal activity on the part of the defendant. Professor Freedman, for instance, notes that "few of us . . . have led such unblemished lives as to prevent a determined prosecutor from finding some basis for an indictment or an information." From this, he argues that "to say that the prosecutor's motive is immaterial, is to justify making virtually every citizen the potential victim of arbitrary discretion."[46]

43. 311 F.Supp. 1063 (W.D.Mo.1969).

44. 428 F.2d 264 (9th Cir.1970).

45. 413 F.Supp. 886 (W.D.Mo.1976), mod'd 546 F.2d 238 (8th Cir.1976).

46. Freedman, "The Professional Responsibility of the Prosecuting Attorney," 55 Geo.L.J. 1030, 1034 (1967). But see, Braun, "Ethics in Criminal

(5) Discovery. As the discussion above illustrates, a number of the reported cases focus not on the ultimate issue of whether selective prosecution has occurred, but rather on whether the defendant has made out a good enough case to merit discovery and an evidentiary hearing on the claim. In *Wayte,* the two dissenters took the majority to task for proceeding directly to the merits without considering whether the trial court's discovery order should have been upheld. As the dissenters pointed out, a selective prosecution claim is difficult to make out without such discovery, since "most of the relevant proof in [such] cases will normally be in the Government's hands."

The crucial question is when such discovery should be granted. The *Wayte* dissent argued for the standard adopted by most Courts of Appeal, which grants discovery when the defendant can show her selective prosecution claim has a "colorable basis" which takes "the question past the frivolous state." [47] According to the dissent, "[t]his standard . . . is consistent with our exhortation that '[t]he need to develop all relevant facts in the adversary system is both fundamental and comprehensive . . . [a]t the same time [it] protects the Government from attempts by the defense to seek discovery as a means of harassment or of delay."

State v. Kennedy [48] presents an interesting example of how this standard might be applied. There the public defenders' office produced a survey which disclosed that, over a three-year period, it had represented 43 persons for traffic violations on the road on which the defendants, both non-caucasians, were stopped for speeding. Of these individuals, 70% were African–Americans, 7% were Hispanics and 23% were Caucasians. In contrast, the office's caseload for all crimes committed in the county comprised 76% Caucasians and 17% African–Americans. The court recognized that this study was deficient because it did not provide information as to the racial composition of all those who travelled this particular road, and did not state the race of those who were arrested, as opposed to formally charged, with crimes. But, stressing that only a "colorable basis," not a prima facie showing, was necessary, it held the survey "raises disturbing questions concerning whether . . . members of minority groups are being targeted or singled out for prosecution of traffic infractions," sufficient to warrant discovery of State Police logs, reports, training materials, and names of instructors. It ordered that these materials be submitted to the court for in camera inspection to determine "their relevance and the State's need for confidentiali-

Cases: A Response," 44 Geo.L.J. 1048 (1967).

47. See, e.g., *United States v. Hazel,* 696 F.2d 473 (6th Cir.1983); *United*

States v. Murdock, 548 F.2d 599 (5th Cir.1977).

48. 247 N.J.Super. 21, 588 A.2d 834 (A.D.1991).

ty," and noted that the state could apply for a protective order as it deemed necessary.

(b) Vindictive Prosecution. The Due Process Clause imposes a limited prohibition on prosecutorial use of the charging prerogative to the extent that prerogative is used to penalize the exercise of legal rights. This principle was first announced in *Blackledge v. Perry.*[49] There the defendant was convicted in misdemeanor court on the misdemeanor charge of assault with a deadly weapon, and sentenced to six months. After the defendant filed notice of appeal to a county superior court for a trial *de novo,* which under North Carolina law annuls the previous conviction and requires a new trial, the prosecutor obtained an indictment covering the same conduct at issue in the misdemeanor trial but charging Perry with the *felony* of assault with intent to kill. Perry pleaded guilty in the superior court and was sentenced to a term of five to seven years.

In overturning the new sentence, the Supreme Court relied on *North Carolina v. Pearce,*[50] which held that "vindictiveness against a defendant for having successfully attacked his first conviction must play no part in the sentence he receives after a new trial." Although *Pearce* had involved judicial imposition of a harsher sentence after a successful appeal, the Court found the rationale of that decision relevant to prosecutorial charging decisions after the defendant indicates a desire to appeal a conviction. It emphasized the prosecution's possible motivation to "up the ante" in such situations and the consequent chilling effect on the right to pursue the statutory appellate remedy. Given the "realistic likelihood of vindictiveness" when a felony charge is brought against a convicted misdemeanant who is appealing the conviction, the Court held that any new punishment must be overturned unless, analogous to what it had held in *Pearce,* the prosecutor can identify specific reasons explaining the increased charge. In other words, it established a "presumption of vindictiveness" in such situations.[51]

The types of reasons that can overcome this presumption are not clear. In *Blackledge,* the Court noted that one such reason would be where "it was impossible to proceed on the more serious charge at the outset," because, for instance, the victim of an assault did not die until after charges were filed. Those courts

49. 417 U.S. 21, 94 S.Ct. 2098 (1974).

50. 395 U.S. 711, 89 S.Ct. 2072 (1969) discussed in § 29.02(d).

51. *Thigpen v. Roberts,* 468 U.S. 27, 104 S.Ct. 2916 (1984) involved substantially the same factual situation as *Blackledge* except that the prosecuting agent responsible for the stiffer charge at the defendant's *de novo* trial was not involved in the initial prosecution. In vacating the defendant's sentence, the Court noted that a district attorney faced with the retrial of an already-convicted defendant might be vindictive even if he did not bring the initial prosecution.

which allow other types of reasons are split on whether proffer of any non-vindictive explanation will suffice or whether, instead, new conduct by the defendant justifying the new charge is required.[52] To be of practical use to a defendant, the presumption should be hard to overcome, given the difficulty of evaluating the validity of any proffered prosecutorial reason.

The situations in which the *Blackledge* presumption arises are very limited. First, it applies only when the change in charge occurs after exercise of a legal right, such as the right to appeal, which would otherwise be "chilled." Second, it does not apply if the prosecutor "ups the ante" during the pretrial process. This is because, as explained by the Supreme Court in *United States v. Goodwin,*[53] during this process, "the prosecutor's assessment of the proper extent of prosecution may not have crystallized." New evidence, or a different interpretation of already existing evidence, might lead to an honest reappraisal of the original charge. Thus, in *Goodwin,* a pretrial adjustment of the defendant's charge from a misdemeanor to a felony after the defendant chose to be tried by a jury rather than a judge did not implicate the *Blackledge* presumption.

The *Goodwin* Court noted that, while the *presumption* would not apply in the pretrial setting, there was still "the possibility that a defendant in an appropriate case might prove objectively that the prosecutor's [pretrial] charging decision was motivated by a desire to punish him for doing something that the law plainly allowed him to do." But it found no such proof there, where the defendant's decision to seek a jury trial meant the case was transferred from the magistrate to a district court and the prosecutor who charged the felony was different from the one who charged the misdemeanor.[54] Moreover, it approved the state's observation that, while the "defendant is free to tender evidence to the court to support a claim that enhanced charges are a direct and unjustifiable penalty for the exercise of a procedural right . . . only in a rare case [will] a defendant be able to overcome the presumptive validity of the prosecutor's actions through such a demonstration." In short, when the change in charge takes place prior to trial, the presumption shifts from vindictiveness to non-vindictiveness.

Furthermore, when the change in charge is part of the plea negotiation process, the defendant will apparently never be able to

52. *United States v. Andrews,* 633 F.2d 449 (6th Cir.1980), cert. denied 450 U.S. 927, 101 S.Ct. 1382 (1981). In the sentencing context, the Supreme Court has held that *any* "new information," not just new conduct by the defendant, overcomes the presumption. *Texas v. McCullough,* 475 U.S. 134, 106 S.Ct. 976 (1986), discussed in § 29.02(d)(2).

53. 457 U.S. 368, 102 S.Ct. 2485 (1982).

54. Compare to *Thigpen,* supra note 51.

make out a vindictiveness claim. In *Bordenkircher v. Hayes*,[55] the prosecutor offered Hayes a five-year term on a forged check charge; he also made clear that if Hayes (who had two prior forgery convictions) did not accept the offer, he would be prosecuted as an habitual offender, a charge which carried a mandatory life sentence. Although the Court suggested that there are some limits on the prosecutor's broad discretion to plea bargain, it held that due process is not violated when, as here, the "conduct engaged in by the prosecutor . . . no more than openly presented the defendant with the unpleasant alternatives of foregoing trial or facing charges on which he was plainly subject to prosecution."

Prohibiting a due process claim in such cases seems extreme. As Justice Blackmun, with two others, stated in dissent, "[p]rosecutorial vindictiveness in any context is still prosecutorial vindictiveness." Justice Powell, in a separate dissent, focused on a slightly different proposition:

> Only in the most exceptional case should a court conclude that the scales of the bargaining are so unevenly balanced as to arouse suspicion. In this case, the prosecutor's actions denied respondent due process because their admitted purpose was to discourage and then to penalize with unique severity his exercise of constitutional rights. Implementation of a strategy calculated solely to deter the exercise of constitutional rights is not a constitutionally permissible exercise of discretion.

A different situation arises when the prosecutor dismisses a charge (perhaps because of defects in the investigatory process), and then recharges the defendant after the defendant has complained about or sued concerning the investigation or original charge. Here, the *Blackledge* presumption should be available, since the new charge is very likely vindictive and a reaction to exercise of a legal right.[56] On the other hand, it may not be applicable when the defendant is charged *for the first time* after exercising a right (say, complaining about the prosecutor's office), because the prosecutor's action would not be an attempt to reinstate a successfully challenged decision affecting that person. At least this is the type of analysis employed by the Court in supporting its holding in *Goodwin:*

> A prosecutor has no "personal stake" in a bench trial and thus no reason to engage in "self-vindication" upon a defendant's request for a jury trial. Perhaps most importantly, the institutional bias against the retrial of a decided question that supported the decisions in *Pearce* and *Blackledge* simply has no counterpart in this case.

55. 434 U.S. 357, 98 S.Ct. 663 (1978).   **56.** Cf. *Dixon v. District of Columbia*, 394 F.2d 966 (D.C.Cir.1968).

In such cases, either actual vindictiveness or what may amount to the same thing—an equal protection violation [57]—will have to be shown.[58]

(c) Duplicative Statutes. The legislature will occasionally provide two different maximum sentences, under two different statutes, for the same conduct.[59] Whether this duplication is intended or due to carelessness is not always clear. Whatever the reason for the duplication, it appears that the federal constitution does not dictate under which statute the prosecutor may proceed.

In *United States v. Batchelder,*[60] the defendant received a sentence of five years under a statute which prohibited various persons, including those previously convicted of a crime "punishable by imprisonment for a term exceeding one year," from receiving firearms that have travelled in interstate commerce. In reversing his conviction, the court of appeals pointed out that another federal statute imposed a maximum of two years on those who have been convicted of a "felony" who receive, possess or transport any firearm in interstate commerce. It concluded that Congressional intent had been to limit the punishment for the defendant's conduct to the latter term.

The Supreme Court could find no evidence of such intent. Nor did it think that duplicative statutes gave the prosecutor "unfettered discretion." It could find "no appreciable difference between the discretion a prosecutor exercises when deciding whether to charge under one of two statutes with different elements and the discretion he exercises when choosing one of two statutes with identical elements." Although in the latter situation the prosecutor may be influenced by the penalties available, the defendant has neither a due process nor equal protection right to choose the penalty scheme under which she will be sentenced. Finally, the Court did not agree with the court of appeals' suggestion that duplicative statutes might impermissibly delegate to the executive branch the legislative function, since the statutes plainly demarcated the range of penalties available.

After *Batchelder,* a federal constitutional challenge of a prosecutor's charging decision when duplicative statutes are involved is

57. See § 21.03(a)(2).

58. Related to the *Blackledge* line of cases are those cases where the prosecutor has promised not to prosecute on a particular charge, but then proceeds to prosecute. These decisions have more to do with fair play than with "vindictiveness," and are discussed in this book's treatment of plea bargaining. See § 26.03(b).

59. This situation is thus distinguishable from that involved in *Hayes,* which involved a prosecutorial choice between a forgery statute and an habitual offender statute providing enhanced penalties for various crimes, including forgery, *if* the offender had two other convictions.

60. 442 U.S. 114, 99 S.Ct. 2198 (1979).

unlikely to be successful. But a state court could still find a violation of equal protection as a matter of state constitutional law. In *People v. Marcy,*[61] the Colorado Supreme Court concluded that

> equal protection of the laws requires that statutory classification of crimes be based on differences that are real in fact and reasonably related to the general purposes of criminal legislation. [Such protection is lacking] if different statutes proscribe the same criminal conduct with disparate criminal sanctions.

The implication of this reasoning for prosecutors confronted with two statutes covering precisely the same conduct may be that, barring a clear showing of contrary legislative intent, they should only prosecute under the most recent statute.

21.04   Joinder

Every jurisdiction has rules which dictate when a defendant may be tried on more than one charge at the same trial, and when more than one defendant may be tried at the same trial. These rules are discussed here because they may affect the types of charges the prosecutor brings against a particular defendant or defendants.

(a) Joinder Analysis. Joinder analysis under the typical statute proceeds in two stages. The first stage asks whether joinder—of charges or of defendants—is permissible. If so, the second stage asks whether the joinder would nonetheless prejudice one or both of the parties, in which case severance is granted. It appears that the party seeking joinder, usually the prosecution, bears the burden of showing joinder is proper, while the party seeking severance, usually the defendant, bears the burden of showing prejudice.[62]

This simple framework is complicated by the fact that a misjoinder finding often comes after trial. When this occurs, some courts have held that new, separate trials must be held automatically; to require a showing of prejudice at this point, they reason, would mean the trial court would have little incentive to consider carefully the first stage of the analysis, because whether or not joinder rules were followed, the ultimate question on appeal would be whether the parties were prejudiced.[63] Most courts, however, hold that misjoinder is subject to harmless error analysis. In *United States v. Lane,*[64] for instance, the Supreme Court held that, on appeal in federal court, the question is whether the

---

61. 628 P.2d 69 (Colo.1981).

62. *Johnson v. United States,* 356 F.2d 680 (8th Cir.1966).

63. *United States v. Graci,* 504 F.2d 411 (3d Cir.1974).

64. 474 U.S. 438, 106 S.Ct. 725 (1986).

misjoinder "had a substantial and injurious effect or influence in determining the jury's verdict," language taken from its cases discussing harmless error analysis.[65]

It is probable that this post-trial, harmless error test is equivalent to the prejudice test applied prior to trial. In any event, the discussion below on joinder of charges and joinder of defendants does not distinguish between the two tests.

(b) Joinder of Charges. Under the federal rules, charges against the same defendant may be joined as separate counts in the same indictment or information under a number of circumstances: (1) when the charges arise out of the same transaction (e.g., burglary of a house, theft in the same house, and assault while escaping); (2) when they arise out of two different transactions that are "connected together" or part of a "common scheme or plan" (e.g., burglarizing a gun store to obtain a gun later used in a bank robbery); and (3) when they arise out of two or more different acts that are "the same or similar in character" (e.g., two robberies committed in a similar way).[66] Virtually all states have rules akin to the first two, and about a third of the states have rules similar to the last rule.

The primary justification for these rules is efficiency. Joinder clearly avoids duplication of effort on the part of the prosecution and the witnesses. The defendant too may want a joint trial, to "eliminate the harassment, trauma, expense, and prolonged publicity of multiple trials . . . increase the possibility of concurrent sentences in the event of conviction, and . . . prevent the application of enhanced sentencing statutes."[67] At the same time, as noted above, every jurisdiction also permits severance of properly joined charges if prejudice would otherwise result. For example, under the federal rules, "[i]f it appears that a defendant or the government is prejudiced by a joinder of offenses . . . the court may order an election or separate trials of counts . . . or provide whatever other relief justice requires."[68]

Most severance motions are by the defendant, who usually claims that joinder will cause one of three types of prejudice: (1) the factfinder will simply infer criminal disposition from the number and types of crimes charged, rather than consider the specific evidence against the accused; (2) the factfinder will "cumulate" the evidence, rather than compartmentalize it according to each charge; or (3) the defendant will be inhibited in

65. See *Kotteakos v. United States,* 328 U.S. 750, 66 S.Ct. 1239 (1946), discussed in § 29.05(b).

66. Fed.R.Crim.P. 8(a).

67. 2 ABA Standards for Criminal Justice § 13–2.1, Commentary (2d ed. 1980).

68. Fed.R.Crim.P. 14.

presenting separate defenses.[69] These various objections are considered below.

(1) Inferring criminal disposition. This potential source of prejudice arises most often with the third type of joinder: joinder of similar offenses. The fear is that the factfinder will decide the defendant is guilty of one crime and then, because the crimes are similar, blithely decide she is also guilty of the others without considering specific evidence. A worse scenario is that the factfinder decides that a person charged with so many offenses must be guilty of something and convict accordingly.

Drew v. United States[70] provides a good illustration of how a court might resolve this dilemma. There, the defendant was tried jointly for a robbery and an attempted robbery. The evidence underlying the first charge indicated that a black male wearing sun glasses had announced to a lone sales clerk in a neighborhood convenience store that he was robbing the store. When the clerk hesitated, the man pulled a gun from his pocket. She gave him money and he left. In a lineup seventeen days later, she identified Drew as the offender. Prior to the identification of Drew, another store in the same convenience chain was unsuccessfully robbed. The sales clerk testified that a black man wearing sun glasses asked to buy some peanuts, then demanded the store's money. The sales clerk refused the demand and the robber left. The police apprehended Drew in the store's vicinity shortly thereafter and returned him to the store, where the clerk identified him as the person who attempted to rob her.

The court agreed with Drew that the trial judge had erred in not granting Drew's motion for severance of these two charges. As a guideline for determining when two similar crimes can be joined, the court found applicable the rules governing the admissibility of *evidence* about other crimes. Such evidence is generally admissible when relevant to motive, intent, absence of mistake, the existence of a common plan, a particular *modus operandi*, or the identification of the accused. Yet even if relevant, such evidence may not be admitted if its probative value is substantially outweighed by the risk that its admission will result in unfair prejudice to the defendant.[71] In *Drew,* the evidence concerning the attempted robbery was at most only barely suggestive of a *modus operandi* similar to that involved in the robbery, yet could easily have prejudiced the defendant by suggesting criminal disposition and inhibiting individualized consideration of the charges. Indeed, the record showed repeated confusion as to which of the two crimes involved was being referred to during trial. Thus, the

69. *Drew v. United States,* 331 F.2d 85 (D.C.Cir.1964).

70. 331 F.2d 85 (D.C.Cir.1964).

71. See Wright & Graham, Federal Practice and Procedure, § 5235 (1978).

court held, the probative value of the additional crime was outweighed by the possibility that it prejudiced the defendant and joinder was inapposite.

This kind of analysis suggests that same or similar crimes should rarely be joined. It is reinforced by clear research evidence that, even when limiting instructions are given, conviction rates are higher when a jury has knowledge of multiple offenses, especially when they are the same or similar in nature.[72] In contrast to the federal rules, many states prohibit joinder of such offenses, allowing simultaneous trial only when the crimes arise from the same episode or transaction or series of transactions.[73] The American Bar Association's Criminal Justice Standards accomplish essentially the same result by providing for unlimited joinder, but permitting severance as of right for either party as to those offenses which are not "based upon the same conduct, upon a single episode, or upon a common plan."[74] If joinder of same or similar crimes is allowed, as suggested in *Drew*, prejudice should be minimized by joining only those crimes that meet an exception to the general rule barring evidence of other crimes (e.g., similarity in *modus operandi*).

(2) Cumulation of evidence. The prejudice associated with cumulation of evidence—that is, the danger that the jury will decide that sufficient evidence on one charge means there is probably sufficient evidence on another joined charge—is closely related to the type of prejudice just discussed. But it usually arises when the joined charges reflect crimes stemming from the *same* episode or transaction; in this situation, the jury might see evidence of one crime as dispositive of liability on the other.

Courts rarely consider the possibility of cumulation ground for reversal however. In *United States v. Adams,*[75] the defendant allegedly bought heroin and sold it to an undercover policeman. Nine months later, when he was arrested for the sale, he was found in possession of heroin. The defendant was tried and convicted of selling heroin and of possession of heroin. On appeal, the defendant argued that joinder was inappropriate under Rule 8(a) and that, even if it were proper, the jury's deliberations on the first charge could easily have been unduly influenced by the fact of possession. The Second Circuit disagreed on both points. Despite the fact that the sale and the possession were separated by nine months, the court approved the trial judge's recognition "as matter of common knowledge that the pattern here was typical of

---

72. See Wisler & Saks, "On the Inefficacy of Limiting Instructions: When Jurors Use Prior Conviction Evidence to Decide on Guilt," 9 Law & Human Behavior 37 (1985).

73. See e.g., Fla.R.Crim.Pro. 3.150(a) (1984).

74. See 2 ABA Standards for Criminal Justice §§ 13–2.1, 13–3.1, 13–1.2.

75. 434 F.2d 756 (2d Cir.1970).

conduct in the narcotics traffic," and thus could be joined as parts of "a common scheme or plan." It then went on to hold that the defendant was not prejudiced by the joinder. The court emphasized that the trial judge had instructed the jury to delineate carefully the factors essential to each charge and to find the defendant guilty only if the specific charge had been proven. The court also noted that the evidence supporting each charge was substantial and "simple."

The Second Circuit's conclusion that joinder of the two counts was permissible is questionable, but not unusual.[76] The court's prejudice analysis is more difficult to assess. The deficiencies of instructions in correcting for jury confusion has been noted. It may be, however, that joinder situations involving offenses arising out of the same episode or transaction are not as inherently prejudicial as those involving same or similar offenses. The research on the effect of limiting instructions is most critical of multiple crime evidence when the crimes are similar in nature; in "same transaction" joinder, on the other hand, the crimes involved are often quite different (e.g., possession as contrasted with sale). Jurors may be more likely to assume a criminal disposition toward robbery when confronted with evidence of several robberies than they are likely to assume guilt for a greater crime (i.e., drug sale) from a finding of guilt on a lesser crime (i.e., mere possession).

(3) Inhibition of defenses. The situation most likely to give rise to this problem is when the defendant wishes to testify concerning one charge but not another. In *Cross v. United States*,[77] for instance, the defendant was charged with robbery of a church rectory in one count and robbery of a tourist home in a second count. He obtained an acquittal on the second robbery charge as a result of his alibi testimony, but "to avoid the damaging implication of testifying on only one of the two joined counts," he offered "dubious testimony" about the first robbery, which included admissions about prior convictions and other "unsavory activities." He was ultimately convicted on that charge. The court held that joinder had "embarassed and confounded Cross in making his defense," and thus was prejudicial under Rule 14.[78]

If, in an attempt to avoid the type of "dubious testimony" given in *Cross,* the defendant decides not to testify about one of the counts, may the prosecutor comment on his silence? Generally, adverse reference to a defendant's failure to take the stand is a

76. *Kindred v. State,* 524 N.E.2d 279 (Ind.1988) (perjury properly joined with forgery a month later because necessary to obtain false identification used in forgery).

77. 335 F.2d 987 (D.C.Cir.1964).

78. As an aside, it is not clear that the two charges should have been joined in the first place, given the interpretation of the "similar act" joinder provision by *Drew,* decided the same term by the same court.

violation of the Fifth Amendment, since a defendant's knowledge that such a reference will occur might "compel" self-incriminating testimony.[79] But some courts have held that the government may force a defendant to "elect to testify as to both charges or to none at all." [80] A more discriminating approach was taken in *People v. Perez*,[81] where the California Supreme Court permitted prosecutorial comment about the defendant's failure to testify about two of the four counts joined against him because the crimes charged in those counts exhibited similar *modus operandi* to the first two charges; under California's rules of evidence, these charges could have been referred to during cross-examination even had they not been joined. Had the crimes not carried a similar "signature," on the other hand, the prosecutorial comment may have violated the Fifth Amendment. Thus, as with prejudice that might result from inferring criminal disposition, this type of prejudice might be defined by the rules of evidence.

(4) Double jeopardy concerns. The Double Jeopardy Clause, found in the Fifth Amendment, protects a person from being "twice put in jeopardy" for the "same offense." As developed in detail elsewhere in this book,[82] despite its apparent meaning, the term "same offense" may include more than one crime on a given set of facts. When two or more crimes are the "same offense" for double jeopardy purposes, the prosecutor must join them, or forfeit the ability to try whichever charges are not joined. Any attempt to try these charges separately would mean the defendant would be "twice put in jeopardy." However, an exception to this rule occurs when the second trial on the same offense results from a severance motion by the defendant.[83] As common sense would seem to dictate, if the defendant successfully argues that severance is necessary because prejudice would result from the simultaneous trial of two charges, the Double Jeopardy Clause does not prevent the government from prosecuting on the second charge.

(c) Joinder of Defendants. Generally, a prosecutor may join two or more defendants in the same indictment or information, and thus try them jointly, if they are alleged to have participated in an offense or offenses arising out of the same course of conduct. Federal Rule of Criminal Procedure 8(b) is illustrative:

> Two or more defendants may be charged in the same indictment or information if they are alleged to have participated in

79. *Griffin v. California,* 380 U.S. 609, 85 S.Ct. 1229 (1965), discussed in § 15.02(c).

80. *Holmes v. Gray,* 526 F.2d 622 (7th Cir.1975), cert. denied 434 U.S. 907, 98 S.Ct. 308 (1977).

81. 65 Cal.2d 615, 55 Cal.Rptr. 909, 422 P.2d 597 (1967), cert. granted 390 U.S. 942, 88 S.Ct. 1055 (1968).

82. See § 30.04.

83. See *Jeffers v. United States,* 432 U.S. 137, 97 S.Ct. 2207 (1977), discussed in § 30.04(b)(2).

the same act or transaction or in the same series of acts or transactions constituting an offense or offenses.

Joinder of defendants is most likely to occur with alleged co-conspirators or co-defendants.

The principal reason for allowing such joinder is prosecutorial efficiency.[84] Unlike joinder of charges, joinder of defendants seldom provides any benefit to the defendant.[85] Furthermore, such joinder can often be extremely prejudicial, in a number of ways. For example: (1) a co-defendant's confession which implicates the defendant as well as the co-defendant might be introduced despite the defendant's inability to challenge it effectively, because the co-defendant refuses to take the stand under the Fifth Amendment; [86] (2) also for Fifth Amendment reasons, a co-defendant's testimony tending to *exculpate* the defendant may *not* be introduced; [87] (3) the factfinder may convict merely out of the confusion or disgust created by conflicting defense strategies (e.g., the defendants accuse one another of the crime); [88] or (4) the factfinder may convict merely because the defendant is associated with other clearly guilty defendants.[89]

As discussed elsewhere in this book, the first situation may run afoul of the Sixth Amendment's Confrontation Clause and often results in severance.[90] When confronted by the other three situations, the courts sometimes grant severance motions. But they are usually reluctant to do so.[91] In part, this may be due to a valid concern that severance will allow defendants to prevent accurate factfinding. For instance, granting severance in an attempt to avoid the second type of prejudice (exclusion of exculpatory information) might occasionally present an opportunity for defendants to "swap alibis" (e.g., X falsely exculpating Y at Y's trial, and then Y—now acquitted and protected against retrial by the Double Jeopardy Clause—returning the favor at X's trial). Similarly, severance to avoid the third type of prejudice (contradictory defenses) runs counter to the notion that differing stories are

84. Even this assumption can be questioned, since evidence suggests that, if the defendants are tried separately, the second defendant will plead guilty after conviction of the first. Langrock, "Joint Trials: A Short Lesson From Little Vermont," 9 Crim.L.Bull. 612 (1973).

85. See Dawson, "Joint Trials of Defendants in Criminal Cases: An Analysis of Efficiencies and Prejudices," 77 Mich.L.Rev. 1379, 1381–97 (1979).

86. See *Bruton v. United States*, 391 U.S. 123, 88 S.Ct. 1620 (1968).

87. *United States v. Ford*, 870 F.2d 729 (D.C.Cir.1989).

88. *People v. Boyde*, 46 Cal.3d 212, 250 Cal.Rptr. 83, 758 P.2d 25 (1988).

89. *Krulewitch v. United States*, 336 U.S. 440, 69 S.Ct. 716 (1949) ("It is difficult for the individual to make his own case stand on its own merits in the minds of jurors who are ready to believe that birds of a feather are flocked together.")

90. See § 28.04(d).

91. See generally, Dawson, supra note 85, and cases cited supra, notes 83–85.

most effectively tested when all of the players put on their best defense in the same room. As one court put it, "conflicting versions of what took place, or the extent to which [the defendants] participated in it," is "a reason for rather than against a joint trial" because "it is easier for the truth to be determined if all are required to be tried together." [92] These possibilities make evaluation of the prejudicial impact of joinder very difficult.

The Supreme Court's decision in *Schaffer v. United States* [93] provides a typical illustration of how prejudice of the fourth, "guilt-by-association" type is evaluated by the courts. *Schaffer* involved a trial with seven defendants. Four of these defendants, the two Schaffer brothers and Marco and Karp, appealed the joinder of their cases with the case against the other three, the Stracuzzas. The latter three had been the "brains" of a group which had transported stolen clothing across state lines. They and the Schaffers had transported goods to New York. They and Marco had transported goods to Pennsylvania. And they had joined with Karp in transporting goods to Massachusetts.

Justice Clark, writing for the majority, found that even though the conspiracy charge linking these defendants together was dismissed after presentation of the State's case, there was insufficient prejudice to warrant severance. He noted that proof of the common scheme was competent as to all the petitioners and that during trial proof of each shipment was related to a specific petitioner and proven by different witnesses with respect to each shipment. Thus, the evidence against each petitioner "was carefully compartmentalized." Furthermore, the judge's instructions "meticulously set out separately the evidence as to each of the petitioners and admonished the jury that they were 'not to take into consideration any proof against one defendant and apply it by inference or otherwise to any other defendant.'" The Court also refused to fashion a hard and fast rule that when a conspiracy count fails, joinder is error as a matter of law.

In addition to challenging this last holding, the four-member dissent, written by Justice Douglas, questioned the usefulness of instructions as a means of separating the defendants:

> [W]here, as here, there is no nexus between the several crimes, the mounting proof of the guilt of one is likely to affect another. There is no sure way to protect against it except by separate trials, especially where, as here, the several defendants, though unconnected, commit the crimes charged by dealing with one person, one house, one establishment. By a joint trial of such separate offenses, a subtle bond

---

92. *Ware v. Commonwealth,* 537 S.W.2d 174 (Ky.1976).   **93.** 362 U.S. 511, 80 S.Ct. 945 (1960).

is likely to be created between the several defendants though they have never met nor acted in unison[.]

Schaffer illustrates that, in analyzing joinder of defendants, concrete concerns about judicial economy may often override speculative concerns about prejudice.

21.05 Conclusion

The various rules discussed in this chapter which govern the prosecutor's charging decision can be summarized as follows:

(1) A prosecutor's decision not to prosecute on a particular charge is rarely challenged. A few jurisdictions require the prosecutor who dismisses a case to justify her action in writing if the dismissal occurs after the information or indictment has been filed. The only other realistic controls on a prosecutor's decision to dismiss or drop charges are those imposed by the prosecutor's office on itself. This state of affairs conforms with the Supreme Court's expressed preference against judicial review of most prosecutorial decisions.

(2) A prosecutor's decision to prosecute is subject to two types of constitutional constraints, both narrowly construed. Equal protection is violated if a defendant is (a) intentionally selected for prosecution (b) from among similarly situated offenders (c) for an arbitrary reason or based on a suspect classification connected with race, gender, expression or the like. Due process is violated if the prosecutor's charging decision is a vindictive response to exercise of a legal right (such as the right to appeal) which challenges a previous decision by the prosecutor, under the following conditions: (a) there is a "presumption" of vindictiveness if the prosecutor raises the initial charge after the defendant has exercised the right during or after trial; (b) there may be such a presumption if the prosecutor reinstates a *dismissed* charge after the exercise of the right; (c) imposition of a higher, legitimate charge during plea bargaining, in response to the defendant's rejection of the prosecutor's offer, cannot be challenged on vindictiveness grounds; (d) in other situations in which a charging decision appears to have been made in response to exercise of a legal right, there is, in effect, a presumption against vindictiveness.

(3) Joinder of charges and parties is governed by statute or rule. In the federal courts, the prosecutor may join charges (a) of the same or similar character; or those based on (b) the same act or transaction; or on (c) two or more acts or transactions connected together or constituting parts of a common scheme or plan. Many states permit joinder only in the latter two situations. Joinder of defendants is permitted in virtually all jurisdictions if they participated in the same act or transaction or in the same

series of acts or transactions constituting an offense or offenses. Once joinder is found to be proper, the defendant(s) bears the burden of proving that joinder would prejudice her interests by making it difficult for the factfinder to give each charge or defendant individualized consideration. On appeal, misjoinder is usually subject to harmless error analysis, although some jurisdictions may require automatic reversal.

BIBLIOGRAPHY

Abrams, Norman. Internal Policy: Guiding the Exercise of Prosecutorial Discretion. 19 UCLA L.Rev. 1 (1971).

Amsterdam, Anthony. The One-Sided Sword: Selective Prosecution in Federal Courts. 6 Rutgers-Camden L.J. 1 (1974).

Davis, Kenneth C. Discretionary Justice: A Preliminary Inquiry. Baton Rouge: Louisiana State University Press: 1969.

Dawson, Robert O. Joint Trials of Defendants in Criminal Cases: An Analysis of Efficiencies and Prejudices. 77 Mich.L.Rev. 1379 (1979).

Decker, John F. Joinder and Severance in Federal Criminal Cases: An Examination of Judicial Interpretation of the Federal Rules. 53 Notre Dame Lawyer 147 (1977).

Frase, Richard S. The Decision to File Federal Criminal Charges: A Quantitative Study of Prosecutorial Discretion. 47 U.Chi.L. Rev. 246 (1980).

Gifford, Donald. Equal Protection and the Prosecutor's Charging Decision: Enforcing an Ideal. 49 Geo.Wash.L.Rev. 659 (1981).

Givelber, Daniel J. The Application of Equal Protection Principles to Selective Enforcement of the Criminal Law. 1973 U.Ill.L.F. 88.

LaFave, Wayne. The Prosecutor's Discretion in the United States. 18 Am.J.Comp.L. 532 (1970).

Mellon, Leonard R., Jacoby, Joan E., Brewer, Marion A. The Prosecutor Constrained By His Environment: A New Look at Discretionary Justice in the United States. 72 J.Crim. L. & C. 52 (1981).

Miller, Frank W. Prosecution—The Decision to Charge a Suspect with a Crime. Boston: Little Brown, 1969. (American Bar Foundation, Administration of Criminal Justice Series). See pp. 64–149.

Rethinking Selective Enforcement in the First Amendment Context [note]. 84 Colum.L.Rev. 144 (1984).

Rosett, Arthur. Discretion, Severity and Legality in Criminal Justice. 46 S.Cal.L.Rev. 12 (1972).

Schwartz, Barbara A. The Limits of Prosecutorial Vindictiveness. 69 Iowa L.Rev. 127 (1983).

Trowbridge, James A. Restraining the Prosecutor: Restrictions on Threatening Prosecution for Civil Ends. 37 Maine L.Rev. 41 (1985).

Uviller, H. Richard. The Virtuous Prosecutor in Quest of an Ethical Standard: Guidance from the A.B.A. 71 Mich.L.Rev. 1145 (1973).

Viera, Norman. Registration, Protest, and the Rationale of Wayte v. United States. 40 Ark.L.Rev. 841 (1987).

Vorenberg, James. Decent Restraint of Prosecutorial Power. 94 Harv.L.Rev. 1521 (1981).

Chapter Twenty-Two

THE PRELIMINARY HEARING

22.01 Introduction

The preliminary hearing or examination is to be distinguished from the initial appearance,[1] the *Gerstein* determination,[2] and the bail hearing.[3] The preliminary hearing normally takes place after all of these proceedings, is adversary in nature, and is designed primarily to assess the propriety of the prosecutor's charging decision. In particular, it is meant to prevent "hasty, malicious, improvident, and oppressive prosecutions" and to assure "there are substantial grounds upon which a prosecution may be based."[4] The hearing may also provide an opportunity for discovery, obtaining statements for impeachment purposes, perpetuating testimony and facilitating pretrial release.[5]

This chapter addresses three issues concerning the preliminary hearing: (1) when it is required; (2) the appropriate standard for determining whether the prosecution has a case; and (3) the procedural rights accorded at the hearing, including the extent to which the hearing should be used for discovery purposes.

22.02 When Required

(a) **Under the Federal Constitution.** Despite the important functions associated with the preliminary hearing, the Supreme Court, in *Lem Woon v. Oregon,*[6] has held that the Constitution does not entitle the defendant to a preliminary hearing of this sort. In *Lem Woon*, the Court noted that it had already refused to apply to the states the Fifth Amendment's requirement that serious crimes be tried only on grand jury indictment,[7] and found no relevant distinction between the functions served by the preliminary hearing and the grand jury indictment process. *Lem Woon* was reaffirmed in *Gerstein v. Pugh,*[8] which required a nonadversarial hearing to determine probable cause to detain when no warrant or indictment has authorized arrest. The Court in *Gerstein* specifically recognized that this prompt post-arrest determination is required by the Fourth Amendment and is thus distinguishable

1. See § 20.01.

2. See § 20.02.

3. See § 20.03.

4. *Thies v. State*, 178 Wis. 98, 189 N.W. 539 (1922).

5. See *Coleman v. Alabama*, 399 U.S. 1, 90 S.Ct. 1999 (1970).

6. 229 U.S. 586, 33 S.Ct. 783 (1913).

7. *Hurtado v. California*, 110 U.S. 516, 4 S.Ct. 111 (1884), discussed in § 23.01.

8. 420 U.S. 103, 95 S.Ct. 854 (1975), discussed in § 20.02.

from judicial oversight of the decision to prosecute, which is not constitutionally mandated.

(b) Under Federal and State Statutes. Although the preliminary hearing is not constitutionally required, most jurisdictions make some provision for it by statute or court rule. Assuming the hearing is not waived,[9] the availability of the preliminary hearing in these jurisdictions is contingent upon the prosecutor's ability and desire to proceed by grand jury indictment. In "indictment jurisdictions"—jurisdictions which *require* prosecution by indictment (including the federal courts, which must abide by the Fifth Amendment)—the defendant is entitled to a preliminary hearing to determine whether to bind his case over to the grand jury, *unless* the prosecutor first secures, normally within a certain time period, an indictment. For example under the federal rules,[10] the "preliminary examination" must be held not later than 10 days after the initial appearance if the defendant is in custody and no later than 20 days if he is not in custody, unless the defendant is indicted before that time. In those jurisdictions which allow prosecution by either information or indictment ("information jurisdictions"), if the prosecutor proceeds by information the defendant is usually entitled to a preliminary hearing before the information is filed. As in indictment jurisdictions, however, in most of these information jurisdictions the prosecutor may proceed by indictment, in which case no hearing is necessary.

This ability to "moot" the hearing by obtaining an indictment has meant that, in some jurisdictions, a preliminary examination is a rare event. In response, some courts have specifically disapproved the practice of granting a prosecutor's request to postpone the preliminary hearing so that he can obtain an indictment.[11] One California court has even found the "mooting" practice illegal under the state constitution's equal protection clause, on the ground that the disparity between the rights accorded a defendant during a grand jury proceeding and a preliminary hearing is "considerable." [12] (As developed below and in the next chapter,[13] the defendant has a right to counsel and an opportunity to challenge the prosecution's case at the preliminary hearing, but does not even have a right to be present during a grand jury proceeding).

---

9. One study found that waiver can occur in as many as 50% of the cases in some jurisdictions. L. Katz, L. Letwin, & R. Bamberger, Justice is the Crime 46–47 (1972).

10. Fed.R.Crim.P. 5(c).

11. See e.g., *United States ex rel. Wheeler v. Flood,* 269 F.Supp. 194 (E.D. N.Y.1967); *United States v. Pollard,* 335 F.Supp. 868 (D.D.C.1971).

12. *Hawkins v. Superior Court,* 22 Cal.3d 584, 150 Cal.Rptr. 435, 586 P.2d 916 (1978). *Hawkins,* however, was overruled by an amendment to article I, section 7 of the California Constitution in 1990.

13. Compare § 22.04 with § 23.04.

If the hearing is supposed to take place, but does not, the defendant is entitled to release from custody.[14] Although the defendant may also be able to have his charges dismissed, the prosecution is not prevented from refiling the charges, assuming the statute of limitations has not expired. Moreover, if the prosecution successfully obtains an indictment in the meantime, neither release nor dismissal is usually required.

22.03 The "Probable Cause" Standard

(a) **Definition.** The prosecution bears the burden of showing that a case should be "bound over" to the grand jury or for trial. The standard of proof required, usually referred to as "probable cause," is not easily defined. Clearly, the prosecution should not have to show guilt beyond a reasonable doubt at this preliminary stage of the proceedings. On the other hand, merely requiring the probable cause determination necessary to issue an arrest warrant, as some courts do,[15] seems to serve no useful purpose, since this determination has presumably already been made at least by the time of the initial appearance in front of a judicial officer. Moreover, as one court put it, "probable cause to arrest does not automatically mean that the Commonwealth has sufficient competent legal evidence to justify the costs both to the defendant and to the Commonwealth of a full trial." [16]

Thus, a growing number of courts require the state to make out a "prima facie" case at the preliminary hearing stage.[17] This standard means the prosecutor must present enough evidence to convince the magistrate that a directed verdict for the defendant would not be necessary after the state rests at trial. But even this standard does not necessarily require the prosecution to present the case it would at trial; for instance, hearsay inadmissible at trial might nonetheless be allowed at the preliminary hearing if there is a showing that the out-of-court declarant will be available for trial.[18]

A question which has troubled the courts is the extent to which the implausibility of the prosecution's witnesses, or the strength of various defenses, such as entrapment or self-defense, should influence the magistrate. If the standard is probable cause to arrest, the magistrate can justifiably disregard such matters completely. Even if the issue is whether the prosecution has a prima facie case, one might conclude that assessment of both credibility and the validity of defenses should be left to the jury.

---

14. See, e.g., 18 U.S.C.A. § 3060(d).

15. *State v. Morrissey,* 295 N.W.2d 307 (N.D.1980).

16. *Myers v. Commonwealth,* 363 Mass. 843, 298 N.E.2d 819 (1973).

17. Id.; *Commonwealth v. Beatty,* 281 Pa.Super. 85, 421 A.2d 1159 (1980); *People v. Veal,* 101 Mich.App. 772, 300 N.W.2d 516 (1980); *State v. Anderson,* 612 P.2d 778 (Utah 1980).

18. See § 22.04(b).

As discussed below,[19] based on this assumption, some courts have limited the defense's ability to cross-examine and present witnesses. However, whether so limited or not, if the defense is able to show that the prosecution's witnesses are entirely implausible, or that a defense would make the state's case completely untenable, many courts seem willing to permit dismissal of the case.[20]

(b) **Consequences of Probable Cause Finding.** If probable cause is not found and the charges are dismissed, the defendant is released. But in many states, dismissal after a preliminary hearing does not prohibit a second information and preliminary hearing on the same charge or different charges.[21] Other states require a showing of new evidence before refiling of an information is permitted.[22] In any event, the prosecutor whose case has been dismissed at the preliminary hearing can usually secure an indictment and proceed against the defendant on that basis.[23] One study found that, in such cases, grand juries virtually always indict, but only 50% of the indicted cases end in conviction.[24]

If probable cause is found, the defendant is bound over to the grand jury in indictment jurisdictions and tried on the information in information jurisdictions. If interlocutory appeal of the decision is permitted, it is rarely successful. Even if it is successful, however, the prosecutor presumably has the same options described above with respect to seeking an indictment or refiling. If the bindover decision is not challenged until *after* trial, a conviction usually moots the issue, although some courts have held that the absence of probable cause means the trial court was without jurisdiction and that a new trial is required.[25]

22.04 Procedural Rights

(a) **Right to Counsel.** In *Coleman v. Alabama,*[26] the Supreme Court held that when the state does provide the defendant with a preliminary hearing, it must also provide him with counsel if he is indigent. The Alabama Court of Appeals had sanctioned the denial of counsel, reasoning that the accused is not foreclosed from advancing defenses at trial which were not raised at the preliminary hearing and that, given the Supreme Court's decision

19. See § 22.04(c).

20. On witness credibility, see decisions discussed in *Hunter v. District Court,* 190 Colo. 48, 543 P.2d 1265 (1975). On defenses, see *Jennings v. Superior Court,* 66 Cal.2d 867, 59 Cal. Rptr. 440, 428 P.2d 304 (1967).

21. See, e.g., *State v. Bloomer,* 197 Kan. 668, 421 P.2d 58 (1966), cert. denied 387 U.S. 911, 87 S.Ct. 1697 (1967); *Commonwealth v. Hetherington,* 460 Pa. 17, 331 A.2d 205 (1975).

22. *Jones v. State,* 481 P.2d 169 (Okl. Crim.1971).

23. *People v. Uhlemann,* 9 Cal.3d 662, 108 Cal.Rptr. 657, 511 P.2d 609 (1973).

24. Gilboy, "Prosecutors' Discretionary Use of the Grand Jury to Initiate or to Reinitiate Prosecution," 1984 Am.B. Found.Res.Journ. 1.

25. *People v. Martinovich,* 18 Mich. App. 253, 170 N.W.2d 899 (1969).

26. 399 U.S. 1, 90 S.Ct. 1999 (1970).

in *Pointer v. Texas*,[27] testimony at the hearing which is not subject to cross-examination could not be used at trial in any event. The Supreme Court nonetheless found the hearing a "critical stage"[28] of the criminal process: "Plainly the guiding hand of counsel at the preliminary hearing is essential to protect the indigent accused against an erroneous or improper prosecution."

The Court's opinion listed four ways in which the presence of counsel at the preliminary hearing may protect the accused. First, a lawyer's skill in examining and cross-examining witnesses may turn up weaknesses in the case that could lead the magistrate to refuse to bind the accused over for trial. Second, even if the case goes to trial, the lawyer may use witnesses' answers to impeach their testimony at trial or to preserve favorable testimony. Third, discovery of the state's case may take place, enabling the lawyer to prepare a more effective defense at trial. Finally, the lawyer might make effective arguments for the accused with respect to fixing bail[29] or determining the necessity for a psychiatric examination.[30]

If the state does not provide counsel at the preliminary hearing, however, reversal of conviction is not automatic. The Court in *Coleman* remanded the case to determine whether the denial of counsel prejudiced preparation of the defendant's defense or instead was harmless error. The usual inquiry in such situations, suggested by Justice White in *Coleman*, is whether "important testimony of witnesses unavailable at the trial could have been preserved had counsel been present to cross-examine opposing witnesses or to examine witnesses for the defense."

(b) Rules of Evidence. The federal rules provide that "[t]he finding of probable cause [at the preliminary examination] may be based upon hearsay evidence in whole or in part."[31] Moreover, although the rules do not explicitly state whether the probable cause determination may be based on illegally obtained evidence, they do state "[o]bjections to evidence on the ground that it was acquired by unlawful means are not properly made at the preliminary examination."[32] At least eleven state jurisdictions bar use of both hearsay and illegally-obtained evidence,[33] presumably on the ground that the preliminary hearing should test the prosecution's case as it will be presented at trial.

27. 380 U.S. 400, 85 S.Ct. 1065 (1965). See § 28.04(a).

28. See § 31.03(a)(1) for a discussion of critical stage analysis.

29. Usually, however, the bail decision takes place at an earlier stage of the proceedings. See § 20.01.

30. See § 28.03(b)(2).

31. Fed.R.Crim.P. 5.1.

32. Id.

33. Peterson, "The Preliminary Hearing: A Time for Modification," Prosecutor's Brief (July-Aug. 1983), at 13, 17, 20. See also, *Myers v. Commonwealth*, 363 Mass. 843, 298 N.E.2d 819 (1973).

As suggested above, even if the prosecution must make out a prima facie case at the preliminary hearing, it does not follow that all of the evidence he presents there must be admissible at trial, so long as that evidence convinces the magistrate there will be sufficient admissible evidence to make out such a case when trial occurs. Thus, admitting the out-of-court declarations of a witness who will be available at trial is not necessarily inconsistent with the prima facie standard. Two other reasons can be advanced in favor of the use of hearsay at such proceedings. First, as recognized by a 1990 California constitutional amendment which specifically provides that hearsay is admissible at preliminary hearings,[34] such a rule might help "protect victims and witnesses in criminal cases" because they will not be required to appear. Second, it is firmly established that the grand jury may consider hearsay.[35] Thus, given the prosecutor's ability to obtain an indictment regardless of the outcome of the preliminary hearing, it may make little sense to bar use of hearsay. Some courts adopt an intermediate position, holding that the probable cause determination is much more suspect if founded *solely* on hearsay testimony.[36]

Basing a bindover decision in whole or in large part on illegally obtained evidence excludable at trial is supported on somewhat different grounds. As with hearsay, such evidence may be considered by the grand jury.[37] More importantly, by the time of the hearing the suppression decision may have yet to be made, and the magistrate may not want to delay the hearing to make such a determination. As noted above, the federal rule specifically provides that the magistrate need not consider a suppression motion at this stage.

(c) Right to Cross–Examine and Subpoena Witnesses. Under the Sixth Amendment, the defendant subject to a trial has the right to confront and cross-examine material prosecution witnesses who are available, and to use compulsory process to subpoena his own witnesses.[38] The usual rule at the preliminary hearing is not as broad. While every jurisdiction allows, by rule or statute, some cross-examination of the witnesses the prosecution proffers, the Supreme Court has held there is no federal constitutional right to cross-examination at the preliminary hearing.[39] Thus, cross-examination may be limited by the magistrate if it goes beyond challenging the prima facie case. For example,

34. Cal. Const. Art. I., § 30(b).

35. See § 23.06(a)(1).

36. See, e.g., *Commonwealth ex rel. Buchanan v. Verbonitz,* 525 Pa. 413, 581 A.2d 172 (1990), cert. denied 500 U.S. ___, 111 S.Ct. 1108 (1991) (commonwealth failed to make prima facie showing where only evidence presented was hearsay testimony of investigating police officer).

37. See § 23.06(a)(2).

38. See §§ 28.05; 28.06.

39. *Goldsby v. United States,* 160 U.S. 70, 16 S.Ct. 216 (1895).

questioning designed to prove affirmative defenses may be prohibited.[40] For the same reason, the defense's ability to call its own witnesses and question them may be limited.[41] Furthermore, the defense may be prohibited from calling *prosecution* witnesses that the prosecution did not call.[42] Of course, the magistrate has discretion to relax these rules; they are most strictly enforced when defense tactics will be time-consuming.[43]

Occasionally, a court has suggested that the defense is entitled to greater latitude at the preliminary hearing. One such decision is *Myers v. Commonwealth.*[44] There, the court relied heavily on *Coleman,* which had indicated that counsel's role at the hearing was not only to expose weaknesses in the prosecution's case, but also to preserve testimony for use as an impeachment device and to discover other elements of the prosecution's case. According to *Myers,* while preliminary hearing cross-examination should be limited, as at trial, to relevant issues in dispute, the defendant should have "reasonable latitude" in questioning prosecution witnesses "in order to effectuate the ancillary discovery and impeachment functions of the hearing noted in *Coleman.*" Further, the magistrate should not be able to decide when to limit defendants' ability to "present testimony in their own behalf," not only because *Coleman* suggested that presentation of evidence was a right, but also because allowing such an exercise of discretion "would create a situation where some defendants would be afforded a full adversary hearing upon demand while others received summary hearings," in possible violation of equal protection principles. The court went on to admonish the hearing judge for preventing defense counsel's attempts to ask the sole prosecution witness in a rape case about her beliefs in witchcraft and to present the results of a psychiatric evaluation showing the witness had a hysterical neurosis which might lead her to make up stories about people. The appellate court held that both cross-examination and the introduction of the additional evidence should have been allowed because "the examining magistrate could not have possibly made an informed judgment on the question of whether there was sufficient credible evidence of the defendant's guilt to support a bind-over until he had considered all of this evidence."

Weighed against the valid reasons for permitting trial-like confrontation and compulsory process at the preliminary hearing

---

40. *State v. Altman,* 107 Ariz. 93, 482 P.2d 460 (1971).

41. Id.

42. See *Schiermeister v. Riskedahl,* 449 N.W.2d 566 (N.D.1989) (accused not entitled to cross-examine complaining witness at preliminary hearing where complaining witness did not testify).

43. Graham & Letwin, "The Preliminary Hearing in Los Angeles: Some Field Findings and Legal–Policy Observations," 28 U.C.L.A.L.Rev. 916, 922 (1971).

44. 363 Mass. 843, 298 N.E.2d 819 (1973).

are two concerns. First, as the prosecution argued in *Myers,* permitting these rights at the preliminary hearing might transform the hearing "into a full-blown trial." To this argument the *Myers* court responded: "past experience indicates that trial strategy usually prevents such a result as both the prosecution and the defense wish to withhold as much of their case as possible." Defense attorneys prefer to save attacks on credibility for trial, "rather than tip their hand at this early stage." Further, "defense tactics usually mitigate against putting the defendant on the stand or presenting exculpatory testimony at the preliminary hearing unless defense counsel believes this evidence is compelling enough to overcome the prosecution's case."

The second concern with a more open approach to the preliminary hearing is the fear that the defense attorney will use confrontation and compulsory process mechanisms to convert the hearing into a discovery device. Several courts have forcefully stated that the sole purpose of the preliminary hearing is making the screening determination.[45] As one court put it, "the accused may lay claim to the benefit of only so much discovery as may become incidental to a properly conducted inquiry into probable cause." [46] This attitude seems sensible to the extent formal discovery devices provide the defense with a good picture of the prosecution's case.[47] But in those jurisdictions where discovery procedures are lacking, as Judge Weinsten observed in *United States ex rel. Wheeler v. Flood,*[48] the preliminary hearing "may provide the defendant with the most valuable discovery technique available to him."

California's approach, adopted in 1990, tries to address the tension between the defendant's right to a meaningful screening and the state's desire to conserve resources. The state's statutes provide that the defendant may call any witness, including the declarant of a hearsay statement offered by the prosecutor, provided that, if the prosecutor so requests, the defendant makes an offer of proof to the satisfaction of the magistrate "that the testimony of that witness, if believed, would be reasonably likely to establish an affirmative defense, negate an element of a crime charged, or impeach the testimony of a prosecution witness or the statement of a declarant testified to by a prosecution witness." [49] This approach prevents the defense from engaging in a fishing expedi-

---

45. See, e.g., *United States ex rel. Haywood v. O'Leary,* 827 F.2d 52 (7th Cir.1987); *Hennigan v. State,* 746 P.2d 360 (Wyo.1987). But see, *Avery v. State,* 555 So.2d 1039 (Miss.1990) (The purposes of a preliminary hearing under Mississippi's criminal rules include discovery and the confrontation of witnesses, as well as determining probable cause and setting bond.).

46. *Coleman v. Burnett,* 477 F.2d 1187 (D.C.Cir.1973).

47. See § 24.03(b).

48. 269 F.Supp. 194 (E.D.N.Y.1967).

49. West's Ann.Cal.Evid.Code § 1203.1; West's Ann.Cal.Penal Code § 872.

tion, at the same time it appears to give counsel in cases like *Myers* the power to force the prosecution to prove it has a solid case.

22.05 Conclusion

The preliminary hearing is designed to act as a check on the prosecutor's charging decision. Its essential elements can be summarized as follows:

(1) Although not constitutionally required, the preliminary hearing is available by statute or court rule in almost every state, unless waived by the defendant or unless the prosecutor procures an indictment within the statutory time limit.

(2) To obtain a bindover decision in some jurisdictions, the prosecutor need merely show probable cause sufficient to arrest and his evidence need not be admissible at trial. In a growing number of states, however, the prosecutor must make out a prima facie case.

(3) The defendant has a right to counsel at the hearing under the Sixth Amendment. But the extent to which the defendant may prevent use of hearsay and illegally obtained evidence, cross-examine prosecution witnesses, and subpoena witnesses at the preliminary hearing depends upon the jurisdiction's standard of proof, and its attitude toward use of the preliminary hearing as a discovery device. On the latter score, the usual position appears to be that discovery incidental to challenging the prosecution's case is permissible, but that otherwise discovery should be conducted through other means.

BIBLIOGRAPHY

Amsterdam, Anthony G. Trial Manual for the Defense of Criminal Cases (3d. ed.). Philadelphia: American Law Institute (1974). Chapter IX (The Preliminary Hearing).

Anderson, Gary L. The Preliminary Hearing—Better Alternatives or More of the Same? 35 Mo.L.Rev. 281 (1971).

Arenella, Peter. Reforming the Federal Grand Jury and the State Preliminary Hearing to Prevent Conviction Without Adjudication. 78 Mich.L.Rev. 463 (1980).

Cantrell, Charles L. An Overview of the Preliminary Hearing in Oklahoma. 39 Okla.L.Rev. 457 (1986).

Graham, Kenneth and Leon Letwin. The Preliminary Hearing in Los Angeles: Some Field Findings and Legal-Policy Observations. 18 U.C.L.A. L.Rev. 635 and 916 (1971).

Hammer, William J. Preliminary Hearings in Virginia. 20 Wm. & Mary L.Rev. 625 (1979).

McIntyre, Donald M.   A Study of Judicial Dominance of the Charging Process.   59 J.Crim.L.C. & P.S. 463 (1968).

Miller, Frank W. and Robert O. Dawson.   Non-Use of the Preliminary Examination: A Study of Current Practices.   1964 Wisc. L.Rev. 252 (1964).

Rosenthal, Kenneth S.   Connecticut's New Preliminary Hearing: Perspectives on Pretrial Proceedings in Criminal Law.   5 U.Bridge L.Rev. 1 (1983).

Theis, William H.   Preliminary Hearings in Homicide Cases: A Hearing Delayed is a Hearing Denied.   62 J.Crim.L.C. & P.S. 17 (1971).

Weinberg, Patricia W. and Robert L. Weinberg.   The Congressional Invitation to Avoid the Preliminary Hearing: An Analysis of Section 303 of the Federal Magistrate's Act of 1968.   67 Mich.L.Rev. 1361 (1969).

Chapter Twenty-Three

THE GRAND JURY

23.01 Introduction

The Fifth Amendment states in part: "No person shall be held to answer for a capital, or otherwise infamous crime, unless on a presentment or indictment of a grand jury." The eighteenth century English grand jury, usually consisting of 23 persons and acting in secret, was able to charge both on its own (an accusation called a "presentment") and based on a prosecutor's recommendation (an accusation called an "indictment").[1] The framers of the American Constitution included the grand jury provision in the Bill of Rights because the grand jury was perceived to be a "bulwark against oppression," in terms both of its ability to investigate the government and its authority to deny the government an indictment. For example, during the Revolution the grand jury often charged British soldiers and other royal officers with crimes against the citizenry; at the same time it refused to indict colonists for perceived "political" crimes and frequently issued reports critical of England's colonial policies.[2]

Today, the grand jury is much more dependent upon the prosecutor than it was two centuries ago. But it still performs both an investigative and a screening function. As an investigating body, it has wide-ranging powers—including subpoena, immunity and contempt authority—that can be used not only to develop evidence against individual offenders but also to conduct broad-based examinations of organized crime, or "watchdog" inquiries into government operations. As a screening body, it has the authority, although seldom exercised,[3] to refuse to return an indictment (or to find "no bill"). Because it has so much power, and at the same time, is often perceived as merely a tool of the prosecutor, it has become the focus of considerable controversy.[4]

Perhaps wisely, then, the Supreme Court, in the 1884 decision of *Hurtado v. California*,[5] held that indictment by grand jury is not guaranteed by the Fourteenth Amendment, making the Indictment Clause one of the few Bill of Rights' provisions that is not applicable to the states. After emphasizing the need to encourage

1. Great Britain has since abolished the grand jury.

2. See generally, R. Younger, The People's Panel (1963).

3. In 1976, .1% of indictments sought from federal grand juries were refused, while approximately 10% of indictments sought from New York grand juries were refused. Hearings before the Subcommittee on Immigration, Citizenship, and International Law of the House Committee on Judiciary in H.R. 94, 95th Cong., 1st Sess (1977), at 738, 525.

4. See in particular, § 23.07.

5. 110 U.S. 516, 4 S.Ct. 111 (1884).

experimentation among the states and noting that historically the preliminary hearing had often served as a check on the charging decision, the Court stated "we are unable to say that the substitution for a presentment or indictment by a grand jury of [a] proceeding by information after examination and commitment by a magistrate, certifying to the probable guilt of the defendant, with the right on his part to the aid of counsel, and to the cross-examination of the witnesses produced for the prosecution, is not due process of law." Thus, at least in those states which have the type of preliminary hearing described in the previous chapter, the Constitution does not require a grand jury indictment to prosecute.

However, several state constitutions provide that, with certain limited exceptions, felonies are to be prosecuted solely by indictment.[6] Many other states follow the same practice pursuant to statute.[7] The rest, perhaps thirty in all, allow prosecution either by indictment or information.[8] In these latter states, the prosecutor usually performs his own investigation (aided by the police) and proceeds by information, the validity of which is tested at a preliminary hearing presided over by a judicial officer.[9] Apparently, prosecutors view the grand jury process to be cumbersome and time-consuming. However, occasionally indictments from a grand jury are sought in these "information" jurisdictions as well.[10] Most commonly, an indictment is sought when: (1) the case is of great public interest and the prosecutor, for political reasons, wants to share the charging responsibility with a group of citizens; (2) the investigative powers of the grand jury are useful, as in antitrust, fraud, organized crime and political corruption cases; (3) the grand jury process would be speedier than a preliminary hearing, as in cases involving multiple defendants; (4) a scared or reluctant witness can be coaxed to testify because of the secrecy shrouding grand jury proceedings or, more coercively, because of the immunity-granting and contempt powers the grand jury possesses.[11]

6. The states are Alaska, Delaware, Hawaii, Illinois, Kentucky, Maine, Mississippi, New Jersey, New York, North Carolina, Ohio, Oregon, Pennsylvania, South Carolina, Tennessee, and Texas. The Connecticut, Florida, and Louisiana constitutions require indictment for capital offenses.

7. See, e.g., Va.Code § 19.2–217 (1983 Repl.Vol); W.Va.Code, 62–2–1 (1977 Repl.Vol.); Mass.Gen.Laws Ann. 263, § 4 (1985).

8. Some states allow use of the judicial-inquest or "one-man grand jury." See, e.g., Kan.Stat.Ann. 22–3101 (1974). Florida requires neither a grand jury

nor a preliminary hearing in noncapital cases, so long as an information is filed within 21 days of arrest. West's Fla. S.A.R.Crim.Proc. 3.133(b).

9. See Chapter Twenty-Two.

10. In California, for instance, indictments are obtained in roughly 5% of the cases. Bureau of Criminal Statistics, Crime and Delinquency in California 90 (1968) (indictment procedure employed in 4.3% of the cases in 1968).

11. Comment, "The California Grand Jury—Two Current Problems," 52 Calif.L.Rev. 116 (1964).

This chapter addresses the following issues: (1) the structure and selection of the grand jury; (2) the extent to which grand jury deliberations should be kept secret; (3) the rights of a grand jury witness; (4) the grand jury's investigative powers; (5) the grand jury's screening power, including the common grounds for challenging an indictment; and (6) the value of the grand jury as presently utilized.

23.02 Structure and Composition

(a) Creation and Duration. In most states, the court is the entity charged with deciding whether a grand jury is necessary for investigative or screening purposes and with summoning the grand jury. However, the court is usually prodded in this regard by the prosecutor and, in an increasing number of jurisdictions, the prosecutor may directly impanel a grand jury.[12] Some states also allow a specified number of the electorate to force its creation for particular types of investigations.[13] In large jurisdictions, several grand juries may be impanelled, with some designated as "regular" grand juries which handle everyday investigation and screening, while others are designated "special" grand juries, whose job is to focus on particular cases.[14]

Once summoned, a grand jury sits for a specified term, although this term may be cut short if the court believes further deliberation is unnecessary. A term can last from a month to as long as three years for special grand juries.[15] Under the federal rules, a "regular" grand jury may serve no longer than 18 months, unless the court extends the service of the grand jury for a period of six months "upon a determination that such extension is in the public interest."[16] During its term, the grand jury usually meets several days each month.

(b) Size and Voting Requirements. The large size of the English grand jury (24 or 23) allowed a majority vote larger than the unanimous verdict by twelve individuals that was required of the petit jury at trial. Most American jurisdictions have reduced the size and changed the voting requirement for the grand jury. At the federal level, a grand jury is composed of from sixteen to twenty-three jurors (a range which allows up to seven jurors to be excused during the long grand jury term), with twelve votes necessary for an indictment.[17] One state (Tennessee) has a thirteen-member grand jury, twelve of whom must concur for an indictment,[18] while another (Virginia) sits grand juries of from five

---

12. See, e.g., West's Ann.Cal.Penal Code § 913.

13. See, e.g., Neb.Rev.Stat. § 29–1401.

14. Cf. 18 U.S.C.A. § 3332.

15. See 18 U.S.C.A. § 3334.

16. Fed.R.Crim.P. 6(g).

17. Fed.R.Crim.P. 6.

18. Tenn.Code.Ann. § 40–13–105.

to seven members, with four votes needed for a true bill.[19] There are many other variations.[20]

As with petit juries, each grand jury has a foreman, whose duties vary. Under federal practice, the court appoints both a foreman (as well as a "deputy" foreman), who is to administer oaths and sign all indictments, as well as keep a record of all votes by the grand jury.[21]

(c) Selection. Parallel to the selection process for petit juries,[22] the selection of a grand jury proceeds in two stages. The first involves choosing the jury pool or venire, the second selecting a grand jury from that pool. Various constitutional and statutory rules govern both stages of the process. Under most circumstances, an indictment issued by an unconstitutionally selected grand jury may be quashed, and a conviction based on it overturned.[23]

(1) The venire. Prospective grand jurors are normally selected from the same pool as petit jurors. Most jurisdictions draw this pool randomly from voting lists, tax returns or telephone directories, although a few still use the "key-man" system, which relies on designated individuals to nominate prospective jurors. Either of these selection methods, but in particular the latter, is subject to two different types of constitutional challenges.

The first is grounded on the Equal Protection Clause and requires a showing that the defendant's racial group was purposefully excluded from the grand jury venire. In *Castaneda v. Partida*,[24] the Supreme Court held that, to make out such a claim, actual discriminatory intent need not be proven, but rather may be presumed if there is a significant disparity between the group's representation in the community and its representation in the grand jury pool, particularly when the selection procedure used provides an opportunity for abuse. In *Castaneda*, the Court found that a 40% disparity between the proportion of Mexican–Americans in the community and the proportion summoned for grand jury service, combined with an easily abused "key-man" procedure, established a prima facie case of discrimination. The Court also held that the presumption of discrimination, once established, may be overcome by evidence showing the selection procedure was not abused. In *Castaneda*, however, no rebuttal evidence was offered.

The second constitutional basis for challenging the grand jury selection process derives by analogy from the "fair cross-section"

19. Va.Code §§ 19.2–194; 19.2–202.

20. See Van Dyke, "The Grand Jury: Representative or Elite?" 28 Hastings L.J. 37 (1976).

21. Fed.R.Crim.P. 6(c).

22. See § 27.03.

23. See § 23.06(c).

24. 430 U.S. 482, 97 S.Ct. 1272 (1977), discussed in detail in § 27.03(b).

requirement for petit juries announced in *Taylor v. Louisiana.*[25] In that case, the Court held that "systematic exclusion" of a "large, distinct group" from the pool or venire from which the petit jury is chosen violates the Sixth Amendment, because it infringes upon the defendant's right to have a representative jury and the community's interest in participating in the criminal justice system. This fair cross-section claim has several advantages over an equal protection claim. Most significantly, it does not require a showing of purposeful exclusion but only that it be "systematic" (e.g., via statute), and can be based on exclusion of groups defined by other than racial characteristics (e.g., women).

Three members of the Court, in a dissenting opinion in *Castaneda,* indicated that they would find *Taylor's* cross-section requirement inapplicable to grand jury venires because the Sixth Amendment speaks only of petit juries and the Fifth Amendment's grand jury clause does not apply to the states. But in *Hobby v. United States*[26] it appeared that a majority of the Court was willing to apply the cross-section requirement to the grand jury as a matter of due process, as several lower courts had done.[27] Although *Hobby* focused on the constitutionality of a judge's selection of the grand jury foreman, the Court's opinion also stated that the selection of the grand jury panel must meet the requirement that "no 'large and identifiable segment of the community [be] excluded from jury service.'"

(2) The jury. Once a jury pool is selected, the grand jury is selected through a process of exclusion. Those who do not meet residency, citizenship, or other statutory requirements are excused. Further, a large number of people are excluded on hardship grounds, given the long duration of the grand jury term.[28] If a person who was not legally qualified to be on the grand jury somehow slips through, any subsequent indictment still stands if there were a sufficient number of legally qualified grand jurors voting for the indictment.[29]

Under the Court's petit jury jurisprudence, a defendant can challenge the makeup of the jury that sits on his case on equal protection grounds, or on the ground that the jury was not impartial.[30] Both of these claims can also be raised in the grand jury setting.[31] In *Rose v. Mitchell,*[32] the Court held that a defendant has "a right to equal protection of the laws [which is] denied

25. 419 U.S. 522, 95 S.Ct. 692 (1975), discussed in § 27.03(c).

26. 468 U.S. 339, 104 S.Ct. 3093 (1984).

27. See, e.g., *State v. Jenison,* 122 R.I. 142, 405 A.2d 3 (1979). But see, *Commonwealth v. Bastarache,* 382 Mass. 86, 414 N.E.2d 984 (1980).

28. Van Dyke, supra note 20, at 58–62.

29. See, e.g., Fed.R.Crim.P. 6(b)(2).

30. See § 27.04.

31. A lack of representativeness claim might also be possible, although

32. See note 32 on page 551.

when he is indicted by a grand jury from which members of a racial group purposefully have been excluded." The majority in *Rose* also "assume[d], without deciding" that the selection of the grand jury foreperson could raise an equal protection claim, if a pattern of racial exclusion from that position could be shown.[33]

The ability to challenge a grand jury on lack of impartiality grounds is not as firmly grounded. In *Beck v. Washington,*[34] the Court stated that "[i]t may be that the Due Process Clause of the Fourteenth Amendment requires the State, having once resorted to a grand jury procedure, to furnish an unbiased grand jury." The Court went on to hold that, if so, the trial judge in *Beck* had discharged his obligations under the Clause when he asked prospective jurors if they were conscious of any prejudice due to pretrial publicity and excused three jurors on the ground of possible bias. The problem here is that, in contrast to the petit jury selection process, no state allows the defense to conduct a pre-indictment voir dire of the grand jury. At most, as in *Beck,* the defendant may request that the judge question grand jurors and remind them of their oath not to base their decisions merely on antipathy toward the defendant. Further, a post-indictment voir dire is unlikely to be granted, especially since such an inquiry might reveal the grand juror's vote, supposedly cast in secrecy. Finally, most courts hold that, without proof of actual bias on the part of one or more grand jurors whose vote was necessary for the indictment, a conviction by an impartial petit jury moots the grand jury impartiality issue.[35]

23.03 Secrecy

(a) **Rationale.** Although the original reason for maintaining the secrecy of grand jury proceedings is in some dispute,[36] the modern justifications for confidentiality are fairly widely agreed

the Supreme Court has yet to settle whether this type of claim may be raised even against a petit jury (as opposed to the jury pool), when the jury is otherwise impartial. See *Lockhart v. McCree,* 476 U.S. 162, 106 S.Ct. 1758 (1986), discussed in § 27.04(c).

32. 443 U.S. 545, 99 S.Ct. 2993 (1979).

33. On the other hand, the Due Process Clause is not implicated by the selection of a foreperson, at least where, as is true at the federal level and most states, he is picked from a duly constituted grand jury panel and has mostly clerical duties, rather than added to the panel by judicial appointment and giv-

en power to issue subpoenas. Compare *Rose,* where the latter was the case, to *Hobby v. United States,* 468 U.S. 339, 104 S.Ct. 3093 (1984).

34. 369 U.S. 541, 82 S.Ct. 955 (1962).

35. *United States v. Brien,* 617 F.2d 299 (1st Cir.1980), cert. denied 446 U.S. 919, 100 S.Ct. 1854 (1980). See also, *United States v. Mechanik,* 475 U.S. 66, 106 S.Ct. 938 (1986), discussed in § 23.06(b) & (c).

36. Compare G. Edwards, The Grand Jury 21 (1906) with Calkins, "Grand Jury Secrecy," 63 Mich.L.Rev. 455, 458 (1965).

upon. These were spelled out by the Supreme Court in *Pittsburgh Plate Glass Co. v. United States*: [37]

> (1) to prevent the escape of those whose indictment may be contemplated; (2) to insure the utmost freedom to the grand jury in its deliberations, and to prevent persons subject to indictment or their friends from importuning the grand jurors; (3) to prevent subornation of perjury or tampering with the witnesses who may testify before the grand jury and later appear at the trial of those indicted by it; (4) to encourage free and untrammeled disclosures by persons who have information with respect to the commission of crimes; (5) to protect the innocent accused who is exonerated from disclosure of the fact that he has been under investigation, and from the expense of standing trial where there was no probability of guilt.

An additional, practical reason for secrecy, at least until recently, was that most grand jury proceedings were not transcribed.

Prior to the 1960's, reasons like these were invoked to deny the defendant and third parties access to evidence produced for the grand jury. Since that time, however, most jurisdictions have provided for recording grand jury testimony and have developed some exceptions to the general rule that this record may not be divulged outside the grand jury room.

(b) Disclosure By Witnesses. Probably the most widely adopted exception to grand jury secrecy is that witnesses at the proceeding may disclose their own testimony.[38] By making such a public disclosure, the witness could bring about all the dangers which secrecy is designed to avert, including alerting the suspect to the fact that he is being investigated, wrongfully stigmatizing that person, endangering other witnesses mentioned in the testimony, or creating a situation which might lead to intimidation of the grand jury. But most jurisdictions apparently believe that preventing witnesses from talking is too difficult, and might also prevent monitoring how the grand jury is treating its witnesses.[39]

In *Butterworth v. Smith*,[40] the Supreme Court indicated that the First Amendment may provide another reason for this exception to the secrecy requirement. *Smith* held that a Florida statute which barred a grand jury witness from recounting his own testimony, or its "content, gist, or import," violated freedom of speech to the extent it operated after the grand jury's term has

37. 360 U.S. 395, 79 S.Ct. 1237 (1959).

38. See, e.g., Fed.R.Crim.P. 6(e)(2) (prohibiting disclosure only by grand jurors, prosecutors, and those who record the proceedings).

39. Soroky, "Grand Jury Secrecy: Should Witnesses Have Access to Their Grand Jury Testimony as a Matter of Right?," 20 U.C.L.A.L.Rev. 804, 819 (1973).

40. 494 U.S. 624, 110 S.Ct. 1376 (1990).

ended. Chief Justice Rehqnuist, writing for a unanimous Court, pointed out that by the end of the grand jury term the target of the investigation will usually either have been arrested or exonerated; thus, secrecy is not needed to prevent the target from fleeing or to avoid manipulation of grand jury deliberations. And while removing a secrecy requirement might allow a defendant to learn a witness' identity, modern discovery rules often permit this in any event. Finally, while such a requirement might help avoid unfair stigmatization of an exonerated defendant, "reputational interests alone cannot justify the proscription of truthful speech." Balanced against these interests, Rehnquist pointed out, was the fact that the statute's broad proscription against revealing the content, gist or import of the testimony could keep vital information from the public forever, especially if there is no trial. In *Smith,* it had the effect of enjoining a newspaper reporter from writing about discoveries made while investigating alleged misconduct of government officials.

Smith does not prevent muzzling a witness while the grand jury is still in session. Nor, as Justice Scalia pointed out in a concurring opinion, does it prevent a state from prohibiting a witness from disclosing the testimony of other witnesses at the grand jury session. Finally, Scalia asserted, a state might still be able to prevent a witness from revealing what he *said* at the grand jury proceeding, as opposed to what he *knows* about the events in question.

(c) **Disclosure to the Defendant.** Most jurisdictions permit disclosure of grand jury proceedings to the defendant when, to use the words of the federal rule, the defendant makes "a showing that grounds may exist for a motion to dismiss the indictment because of matters occurring before the grand jury." [41] Having mostly to do with prosecutorial misconduct, these grounds are very limited, as discussed further later in this chapter.[42] Thus disclosure for this purpose rarely occurs.

Much more frequent is disclosure to the defendant for discovery purposes, although the extent and timing of the disclosure varies considerably. With the exception of the defendant's own testimony,[43] in many states and the federal courts only testimony by witnesses who will testify at trial is provided the defendant.[44] Moreover, apparently out of fear that witnesses might otherwise be intimidated, this testimony is usually not disclosed until after the witness testifies at trial.[45] Other states are even more restric-

41. See, e.g., Fed.R.Crim.P. 6(e)(3)(C)(ii).

42. See § 23.06(b).

43. See, e.g., Fed.R.Crim.P. 16(a)(3) (defendant to be provided with transcript of his own testimony).

44. See 18 U.S.C.A. § 3500(e); *State v. CPS Chemical Co., Inc.,* 198 N.J. Super. 236, 486 A.2d 944 (1985).

45. 18 U.S.C.A. § 3500(e). The federal provision has been strictly construed to authorize pretrial disclosure

tive, requiring a special showing of need before any grand jury testimony is divulged.[46] Only about ten states automatically give the defendant the entire transcript.[47] If one agrees with *Smith* that, after indictment, many of the dangers associated with disclosure are mitigated, then the more restrictive approaches seem inappropriate. As the Supreme Court stated in *Dennis v. United States,*[48] in the course of reversing a decision denying a request at trial for the grand jury testimony of four key prosecution witnesses, "[i]n our adversary system for determining guilt or innocence, it is rarely justifiable for the prosecution to have exclusive access to a storehouse of relevant fact. Exceptions to this are justifiable only by the clearest and most compelling considerations."

(d) Disclosure to Third Parties. Any number of parties other than the prosecutor and the defendant in a given case might seek access to parts or all of the grand jury proceeding. The general rule as to disclosure in this situation, at least at the federal level, comes from *Douglas Oil Co. of California v. Petrol Stops Northwest.*[49] There, the Supreme Court stated that the parties requesting disclosure "must show that the material they seek is needed to avoid a possible injustice to another judicial proceeding, that the need for disclosure is greater than the need for continued secrecy, and that their request is structured to cover only material so needed." *Douglas Oil* also noted, presaging *Smith,* that a factor militating in favor of disclosure is that the grand jury has finished its deliberations, although it cautioned that courts must still be careful to consider the impact of disclosure on the behavior of witnesses at *future* grand jury proceedings.

A much earlier case, *United States v. Procter & Gamble Co.,*[50] demonstrates how the *Douglas Oil* calculus might be applied. There, the defendants in an antitrust suit sought disclosure of transcripts from grand jury proceedings of which they had been the target (but which had not resulted in an indictment). The Supreme Court upheld the district court's denial of the request, finding that there had been no showing of "particularized need." The Court noted that the request was not specifically aimed at information designed "to impeach a witness, to refresh his recollection, to test his credibility and the like," and thus impermissibly asked for "*wholesale* discovery." Further, some of the witnesses at the grand jury proceedings were employees and customers of

only at the option of the prosecutor. See § 24.03(b). See, e.g., *United States v. Algie,* 667 F.2d 569 (6th Cir.1982).

46. *Valles v. State,* 90 N.M. 347, 563 P.2d 610 (1977); *Silbert v. State,* 12 Md. App. 516, 280 A.2d 55 (1971).

47. See, e.g., West's Ann.Cal.Penal Code § 938.1; Nev.Rev.Stat. § 172.225.

48. 384 U.S. 855, 86 S.Ct. 1840 (1966).

49. 441 U.S. 211, 99 S.Ct. 1667 (1979).

50. 356 U.S. 677, 78 S.Ct. 983 (1958).

the defendant companies, who might face some sort of retaliation if their identities became known (an event which would certainly intimidate witnesses in future cases). The Court also noted that alternatives to discovery were available and that the savings in time and expense that would come from disclosure of grand jury transcripts did not by itself establish the requisite need.

When the party requesting the information is the government, the Supreme Court has taken a more generous stance toward disclosure. First, it seems clear that the prosecutor should be able to disclose information to those who are assisting him in the prosecution of the case being considered by the grand jury. Indeed, the federal rules require no showing of "particularized need" in such cases.[51] When disclosure is sought by government attorneys who are not assisting in "prosecutorial duties" connected with the federal criminal law, the Supreme Court has held, in *United States v. Sells Engineering, Inc.,*[52] that a showing of need does have to be made, despite language in the federal rules suggesting otherwise.[53] But *Sells* also characterized as having "some validity" the statement that "disclosure of grand jury materials to government attorneys typically implicates few, if any, of the concerns that underlie the policy of grand jury secrecy." More specifically, *Sells* stated that such disclosure might pose "less risk of further leakage or improper use than would disclosure to private parties or the general public."

Also supporting a less stringent approach to disclosure when the supplicant is the government is the Court's decision in *United States v. John Doe, Inc. I.*[54] In interesting contrast to its reasoning in *Proctor & Gamble* (which had counted as one consideration in "particularized need" analysis the availability of other sources of information when private litigants make a request), the Court there pointed out that disclosure to government officials (here lawyers in the Justice Department's antitrust division) could "sav[e] the Government, the potential defendants, and witnesses, the pains of costly and time consuming depositions and interrogatories which might later have turned out to be wasted if the Government decided not to file a civil action after all." The Court

---

51. Fed.R.Crim.P. 6(e)(3)(A)(B) (automatic disclosure to "government personnel (including personnel of a state or subdivision of a state) as are deemed necessary by an attorney for the government to assist . . . in the performance of such attorney's duty to enforce federal criminal law.").

52. 463 U.S. 418, 103 S.Ct. 3133 (1983).

53. The same day that *Sells* was decided, the Court decided that need must

also be shown by state attorneys seeking federal grand jury transcripts. *Illinois v. Abbott & Associates, Inc.,* 460 U.S. 557, 103 S.Ct. 1356 (1983). *Abbott* triggered a congressional amendment to Rule 6(e), which now allows disclosure to state attorneys if a federal attorney shows that "such matters may disclose a violation of state criminal law." Fed. R.Crim.P. 6(e)(3)(C)(iv).

54. 481 U.S. 102, 107 S.Ct. 1656 (1987).

also noted that such disclosure might prevent the government from abusing other investigative techniques. On the other hand, it indicated some concern over whether, when their civil counterparts are making the request, federal grand jury lawyers might be tempted to "manipulate the grand jury's powerful investigative tools to root out additional evidence useful in the civil suit." Of importance to the Court's holding in *Doe*—granting the antitrust division's request for a portion of a grand jury transcript from a case brought by the Justice Department's criminal division—was the fact that the grand jury attorneys had submitted an affidavit attesting to their good faith in conducting the investigation (despite the fact that it had ended without an indictment).[55]

23.04 Rights of Grand Jury Witnesses

Whether conducting its own investigation or screening the prosecutor's decision to prosecute, the grand jury relies heavily on witnesses. The scope of the constitutional rights accorded a grand jury witness differs significantly from those granted a trial witness, a defendant at a preliminary hearing, or a suspect during custodial interrogation.

(a) **Right to Testify.** At trial, the defendant has a constitutional right to testify.[56] The same is probably true of the defendant at a preliminary hearing.[57] But few states grant the target of a grand jury investigation the right to appear before the grand jury.[58] Apparently, this practice is justified on two grounds: (1) the need for secrecy during such an investigation; and (2) the fact that the target may not become known until the conclusion of the proceeding.[59] Of course, in those jurisdictions where a preliminary proceeding precedes the grand jury, neither of these reasons make sense. Where the grand jury is the sole charging mechanism, a failure to inform the target may, in some cases, be justified to prevent his escape. But, at least where a person who is clearly

---

55. A final limitation under the federal rules is that the requested information be relevant to pending *judicial proceedings.* Fed.R.Crim.P. 6(e)(3)(C)(i). This provision has been strictly construed by the Supreme Court. *United States v. Baggot,* 463 U.S. 476, 103 S.Ct. 3164 (1983) (IRS not entitled to disclosure for purpose of assessing tax liability when no litigation pending).

56. *Rock v. Arkansas,* 479 U.S. 1079, 107 S.Ct. 1276 (1987) (basing the right on the Due Process Clause, the Sixth Amendment right to call witnesses in the defendant's favor, and the Fifth Amendment's protection of silence unless the defendant "chooses to speak."), discussed in § 28.06(a).

57. See § 22.04(c).

58. Most jurisdictions allow the grand jury to grant or deny a request at its discretion. A few require that a *requesting* accused be heard, Okla.Stat. Ann. tit. 22, § 335, and others require that certain individuals be informed of an impending indictment and given the opportunity to appear. Ga.Code Ann. §§ 45-15-11, 44-11-4 (public officials accused of misconduct).

59. See, e.g., *State v. Salazar,* 81 N.M. 512, 469 P.2d 157 (1970) (also giving a third reason: that the right to appear under New Mexico constitution only attaches during "criminal prosecution," which has not yet commenced).

a target of the investigation requests an appearance, a strong argument can be made that he should be given the same right that he would have during a preliminary hearing.[60]

(b) Warnings. When a person does appear in front of the grand jury (either voluntarily or under subpoena), he has a right to refuse to answer any question put to him by the grand jury if the answer would be self-incriminating. A frequently litigated question is whether the grand jury witness must be told he may remain silent (and that anything he says may be used against him), by analogy to the Court's decision in *Miranda v. Arizona* [61] requiring that such warnings be given to persons subjected to custodial interrogation. Analysis of this issue boils down to whether questioning by the grand jury is more like interrogation by the police or cross-examination at trial. At trial and the preliminary hearing, a witness who decides to testify is not warned that he has the right to remain silent, on the sensible ground that, because he has counsel, he already knows about and can effectively assert the right; further, such a witness is undoubtedly aware the prosecution is after incriminating information.[62] In contrast, as discussed below,[63] a grand jury witness may not have counsel in the grand jury room with him, if he has one at all, and is less likely to know when he is the target of an investigation. Moreover, the secrecy of the grand jury process makes it more akin to a stationhouse interrogation than a publicly conducted trial or preliminary hearing.

Perhaps for these reasons, many states have mandated warnings by statute, either just for targets,[64] or for all witnesses.[65] But, as a matter of constitutional law, most courts have held that prosecutorial questioning of a grand jury witness does not implicate *Miranda* because the grand jury atmosphere is not as "inherently coercive" as custodial interrogation.[66] A few have adopted the position that once the grand jury's investigation focuses on a witness, the Fifth Amendment requires that he be told of his right to remain silent.[67] The Supreme Court has yet to rule on the issue, although it has indicated its reluctance to require such a warning as a constitutional matter.[68]

---

60. But see, *People v. Newton*, 8 Cal. App.3d 359, 87 Cal.Rptr. 394 (1970) (rejecting an equal protection claim on this ground).

61. 384 U.S. 436, 86 S.Ct. 1602 (1966), discussed in § 16.02(d).

62. See generally § 15.02(a).

63. See § 23.04(c).

64. See, e.g., New Mex.Stat.Ann., § 31–6–12.

65. Idaho Code § 19–1121.

66. See, e.g., *Gollaher v. United States*, 419 F.2d 520 (9th Cir.1969), cert. denied 396 U.S. 960, 90 S.Ct. 434 (1969); *United States v. Corallo*, 413 F.2d 1306 (2d Cir.1969), cert. denied 396 U.S. 958, 90 S.Ct. 431 (1969).

67. *United States v. Reed*, 631 F.2d 87 (6th Cir.1980); *State v. Falcone*, 292 Minn. 365, 195 N.W.2d 572 (1972).

68. See § 15.02(a)(3). See also, *United States v. Mandujano*, 425 U.S. 564, 96 S.Ct. 1768 (1976) (distinguishing the grand jury setting from the "inherently

The Supreme Court *has* clearly held that a putative defendant need not be told that he is being investigated by the grand jury. In *United States v. Washington,*[69] the defendant was informed of his right to remain silent and that anything he said could be used against him. But he was not told that his testimony could lead to his indictment by the grand jury. The Supreme Court held that the defendant's status as a target did not affect his constitutional protections. Because he "knew better than anyone else" whether his answers would be incriminating, and was not compelled to answer, the Fifth Amendment was not violated, despite the absence of a "target warning."

(c) Right to Counsel. Whatever the necessity of informing a grand jury witness of his right to remain silent, it seems clear that the second half of the *Miranda* warnings concerning the right to counsel need not be given, for the simple reason that there is no such right, at least at the typical grand jury proceeding. In *In re Groban's Petition,*[70] the Supreme Court stated, in dictum, that a grand jury "witness cannot insist, as a matter of constitutional right, on being represented by counsel." This dictum was repeated in the Court's opinion in *United States v. Mandujano,*[71] where four members of the Court concluded that a grand jury proceeding takes place before the initiation of adversary criminal proceedings, and thus is not part of the "criminal prosecution" which the Sixth Amendment indicates is the threshold for application of the right to counsel. On the reasoning of the plurality in *Mandujano,* a person who has already been formally charged (through a warrant or an information) might have a right to counsel in the grand jury room,[72] but such persons are usually not the targets of grand jury investigations.

Although the Sixth Amendment probably does not require counsel in the grand jury room, one could still argue, as Justice Brennan did in his dissent in *Mandujano,* that the *Fifth* Amendment mandates that result. Analogous to the reasoning in *Miranda* concluding that counsel must be provided the person subjected to custodial interrogation, Brennan contended that the counselless grand jury witness cannot effectively exercise the right to remain silent. A number of courts have, in effect, accepted this analysis, but concluded, contrary to Brennan, that it merely entitles a grand jury witness to consult with counsel *outside* the grand jury room.[73]

coercive" atmosphere of custodial interrogation).

69. 431 U.S. 181, 97 S.Ct. 1814 (1977).

70. 352 U.S. 330, 77 S.Ct. 510 (1957).

71. 425 U.S. 564, 96 S.Ct. 1768 (1976).

72. See *Kirby v. Illinois,* 406 U.S. 682, 92 S.Ct. 1877 (1972), which held that the Sixth Amendment attaches "by way of formal charge, preliminary hearing, indictment, information, or arraignment." See § 31.03(a).

73. See, e.g., *United States v. Corallo,* 413 F.2d 1306 (2d Cir.1969), cert.

The rationale for limiting the right to counsel to periodic consultation in the grand jury anteroom are several. If counsel is present during the actual questioning, he might: (1) obstruct the investigation by consulting with the witness after each question and, in effect, putting words in the witness' mouth (something even trial counsel cannot do once his client is on the stand); (2) disrupt the proceeding through objections or arguments; and (3) breach grand jury secrecy. On the other hand, when counsel is relegated to the anteroom, a witness may feel reluctant to leave the room more than occasionally, and thus make unwise decisions concerning assertion of the right to remain silent or other privileges or rights.[74] And even if consultation occurs, the witness may not be able to report accurately to the lawyer what has transpired in the grand jury room. Some legislatures have allowed counsel to accompany target witnesses into the grand jury room, but limit them to giving advice; no questions or objections may be raised.[75]

23.05　Investigative Powers

As the Supreme Court stated in *Branzburg v. Hayes*,[76] the grand jury has "a right to every man's evidence," meaning it may compel testimony and documents subject only to "constitutional, common law or statutory privilege." This "right" exists, the Court later explained in *United States v. Dionisio*,[77] because the "obligation of every person to appear and give testimony [to the grand jury is] indispensible to the administration of justice." In the absence of such an obligation, the grand jury process would become a series of "mini-trials," replete with constitutional and evidentiary objections that would impede the investigative process. Thus, as the Court stated in *United States v. Calandra*,[78] a grand jury "may compel the production of evidence or the testimony of witnesses as it considers appropriate, and its operation generally is unrestrained by the technical procedural and evidentiary rules governing the conduct of criminal trials."

In concrete terms, the courts' insistence on the grand jury's right to "every man's evidence" has provided it with three related investigative tools: (1) the power to subpoena testimony and tangible evidence deemed useful to its investigation; (2) the power to grant immunity from prosecution; and (3) the power to hold in contempt a person who refuses to comply with a subpoena or to testify after being immunized. In modern times the utilization of

denied 396 U.S. 958, 90 S.Ct. 431 (1969); *People v. Ianniello,* 21 N.Y.2d 418, 288 N.Y.S.2d 462, 235 N.E.2d 439 (1968), cert. denied 393 U.S. 827, 89 S.Ct. 90 (1968).

74. Steele, "Right to Counsel at the Grand Jury Stage of Criminal Proceedings," 36 Mo.L.Rev. 193, 203 (1971).

75. See, e.g., Mich.Comp.Laws.Ann. § 767.3; *Commonwealth v. Griffin,* 404 Mass. 372, 535 N.E.2d 594 (1989).

76. 408 U.S. 665, 92 S.Ct. 2646 (1972).

77. 410 U.S. 1, 93 S.Ct. 764 (1973).

78. 414 U.S. 338, 94 S.Ct. 613 (1974).

these powers is largely controlled by the prosecutor and, to a much smaller extent, the court. This section describes the grand jury's investigative authority, and the roles of the prosecutor and the court in implementing it.

(a) The Subpoena Power. There are two types of subpoenas available to the grand jury—the subpoena *ad testificandum,* which compels witness attendance, and the subpoena *duces tecum,* which compels production of tangible evidence. There are very few limitations, constitutional or otherwise, on the use of either of these devices.

(1) Fourth Amendment limitations. In the companion cases of *United States v. Dionisio* and *United States v. Mara,*[79] the Court held that a summons to appear before a grand jury and provide evidence was not a "seizure" under the Fourth Amendment because it did not involve the degree of compulsion, stigma, or abruptness of an arrest or an investigative stop. The Court admitted that such an appearance might be "inconvenient" or "burdensome," but this was incidental to the "historically grounded obligation of every person to appear and give his evidence before the grand jury." Further, the imposition of Fourth Amendment strictures on the grand jury "would assuredly impede its investigation and frustrate the public's interest in the fair and expeditious administration of the laws." Thus, the grand jury "could exercise its 'broad investigative powers' on the basis of 'tips, rumors, evidence offered by the prosecutor, or [the jurors'] own personal knowledge' " without making any preliminary showing.

Although *Dionisio* and *Mara* settled that a subpoena *ad testificandum* is not a Fourth Amendment seizure, and need not be based on any showing of suspicion,[80] they did not specifically address the Fourth Amendment's application to subpoenas *duces tecum* for documents or other tangible evidence found in the home or office. In its 1886 decision of *Boyd v. United States,*[81] the Court appeared to hold that the government could not use such a subpoena to seize "mere evidence," as opposed to contraband or instrumentalities or fruits of crime. This conclusion, based in part on privacy concerns underlying the Fourth Amendment, and in part on Fifth Amendment concerns about the compulsion of testimony, would have placed a significant limitation on the subpoena *duces tecum.* Largely for this reason, the Supreme Court

79. 410 U.S. 1, 93 S.Ct. 764 (1973) (*Dionisio*); 410 U.S. 19, 93 S.Ct. 774 (1973) (*Mara*).

80. *Dionisio* did caution that subpoenas may not be "too sweeping." But it went on to find that the subpoena of approximately 20 persons for voice exemplars, which the lower court had characterized as a "dragnet procedure," did not violate this prohibition.

81. 116 U.S. 616, 6 S.Ct. 524 (1886).

soon retreated from this position. In *Hale v. Henkel,*[82] the Court held that the Fourth Amendment's requirement that a search and seizure be reasonable did not bar subpoenas of documents, at least those possessed by corporations.

However, *Hale* also held that these subpoenas may not be "too sweeping." Like a search warrant, a subpoena must state with "particularity" the items to be produced. The Court found that this requirement was not met in *Hale,* where the subpoena required production of numerous different records, delivery of which might have prevented the defendant corporation from carrying on its business (there being no capacity for photocopying).

Despite their general antipathy toward Fourth Amendment limitations on subpoenas, *Dionisio* and *Mara* too could be read as suggesting that subpoenas *duces tecum* should be treated differently than subpoenas *ad testificandum.* The witnesses summoned in *Dionisio* were required to provide voice exemplars and the witness summoned in *Mara* was directed to provide a handwriting exemplar. The Court found that these identification procedures were not "seizures," because they merely obtained physical characteristics "constantly exposed to the public," and thus invaded no privacy interest.[83] The Court also indicated, however, that a different result might be called for if the grand jury sought a blood sample, given its greater intrusiveness. Although a subpoena *duces tecum* is not as intrusive or as "abrupt" as a search conducted by police, it does require the production of documents or other items which are not "exposed to the public" and may be very private. Thus, such a subpoena could be characterized as a "search," albeit a minimal one, for Fourth Amendment purposes.

In short, while probable cause or reasonable suspicion may not be necessary to support a subpoena *duces tecum,* some showing of need might be constitutionally required for this type of subpoena. Many lower courts follow the rule announced in *United States v. Gurule,*[84] which identifies three components of "reasonableness" that must be met by such a subpoena:

(1) the subpoena may command only the production of things relevant to the investigation being pursued;

(2) specification of things to be produced must be made with reasonable particularity; and

(3) production of records covering only a reasonable period of time may be required.

Some courts read into the second component a requirement that the subpoena not result in the party being "harassed or oppressed

---

82. 201 U.S. 43, 26 S.Ct. 370 (1906).   **84.** 437 F.2d 239 (10th Cir.1970).

83. See § 4.03(b) for further discussion of this point.

to the point that he experiences an unreasonable business detriment," [85] which would seem to follow from the Court's holding in *Hale*.[86]

Although it did not address the constitutional issue, the Supreme Court's decision in *United States v. R. Enterprises, Inc.,*[87] is consonant with this approach. There, the Court construed Rule 17(c) of the Federal Rules of Criminal Procedure, which permits quashing of a subpoena on motion "if compliance would be unreasonable or oppressive." Emphasizing the special investigative role of the grand jury, the Court rejected the Court of Appeals' holding that a subpoena would be "unreasonable" under this provision unless it could be shown the evidence it requested was "relevant" to its investigation in the sense required at trial.[88] Rather, it concluded that, to quash a subpoena under Rule 17(c), the subpoenaed party must show "that there is no reasonable possibility that the category of materials the Government seeks will produce information relevant to the general subject of the grand jury's investigation." While this standard sets an extremely low threshold, it does recognize that there must be some connection between the evidence sought and the subject of the grand jury investigation.[89] Further, the Court suggested that there might be a duty on the part of the government to apprise the court, *in camera,* of the subject of the investigation, "so that the court may determine whether the motion to quash has a reasonable prospect for success before it discloses the subject matter to the challenging party." *R. Enterprises* also acknowledged, as does the *Gurule* formulation, that a subpoena can be challenged on two other grounds as well: that it is "too indefinite" or that it would be "overly burdensome."

(2) Fifth Amendment limitations. Clearly, both types of subpoenas compel the subpoenaed party to produce evidence. Occasionally, that evidence may be self-incriminating. Nonetheless, a Fifth Amendment claim will rarely lead to the quashing of a subpoena.

As discussed previously, a grand jury witness, like a trial witness, may refuse to answer questions on Fifth Amendment

---

85. *In re Grand Jury Subpoena Duces Tecum (Corrado Brothers),* 367 F.Supp. 1126 (D.Del.1973).

86. See also *Donovan v. Lone Star, Inc.,* 464 U.S. 408, 104 S.Ct. 769 (1984) (stating that the Fourth Amendment protects against "an unreasonably burdensome . . . subpoena requiring the production of documents).

87. 500 U.S. ___, 111 S.Ct. 722 (1991).

88. The relevant case on trial subpoenas is *United States v. Nixon,* 418

U.S. 683, 94 S.Ct. 3090 (1974), which the Court in *R. Enterprises* held was inapplicable to grand jury subpoenas.

89. The Court refused to express a view on the respondents' further contention that the records sought related to First Amendment activities and thus could be subpoenaed only if the government demonstrated that they were "particularly relevant to its investigation."

grounds.[90] But most courts agree that, unlike a defendant at trial (who can avoid the prejudicial effect of continually claiming the privilege by avoiding taking the stand), a person subpoenaed by a grand jury may not refuse to appear as a witness, even if it is clear he is the object of the grand jury inquiry and will claim the privilege in its presence.[91] This conclusion follows from the premise that the grand jury must be given broad scope in its efforts to ferret out crime. To fulfill this obligation, the grand jury needs a crack at "every man" who might have evidence, including a target who, even if he refuses to provide *self-incriminating* information, may provide exculpatory information or information inculpating others. Further, prospective witnesses cannot know precisely what questions the grand jury will ask and thus cannot make an intelligent assertion of the right before they've made an appearance.[92]

A subpoena *duces tecum* is more likely to implicate the Fifth Amendment, but only in very narrow circumstances. As discussed in detail in this book's treatment of the Fifth Amendment,[93] the Supreme Court has held, in *Fisher v. United States*,[94] that the contents of documents are not protected by the privilege against self-incrimination, because they are voluntarily created. A subpoena compels only the act of producing the documents, which is usually not incriminating. Even if the fact of production does somehow incriminate the custodian of the records (because, for instance, it proves the source of those records, which is an element of the prosecution's case), *Fisher* held that, if the prosecution grants immunity with respect to use of this fact, the records may be compelled via subpoena.

(3) Miscellaneous limitations. Although seldom successful, a number of other grounds for resisting a subpoena have been recognized. For instance, some courts have indicated that if a party can show that the grand jury is investigating matters entirely unrelated to criminal activity, an objection may be sus-

---

90. See § 23.04(a). Note, however, that some types of self-incriminating evidence can be compelled from a grand jury witness because it is considered "non-testimonial." Thus, in *Dionisio* and *Mara* the Court found the Fifth Amendment was not implicated by compelled disclosure of voice and handwriting because this was "noncommunicative" evidence. See § 15.04.

91. See *United States v. Friedman*, 445 F.2d 1076 (9th Cir.1971), cert. denied 404 U.S. 958, 92 S.Ct. 326 (1971); *United States v. Capaldo*, 402 F.2d 821 (2d Cir.1968), cert. denied 394 U.S. 989, 89 S.Ct. 1476 (1969).

92. Nonetheless, the American Bar Association has recommended that the court should prohibit the prosecution from compelling a target to take the stand if he states he intends to assert the privilege in response to its questions, on the ground that otherwise he will be "prejudice[d] . . . in the eyes of the grand jury." ABA Standards Relating to the Prosecution Function 90 (1971).

93. See § 15.06(c).

94. 425 U.S. 391, 96 S.Ct. 1569 (1976).

tained.[95] But these challenges are usually denied on the authority of the Supreme Court's decision in *Blair v. United States,*[96] which concluded that, given the broad investigative powers of the grand jury, a witness should not be allowed "to set limits to the investigation that the grand jury may conduct." Another sometimes successful challenge to a subpoena is to show that the grand jury is being manipulated by the prosecutor. For instance, if the subpoena power is being used for the purpose of obtaining discovery for civil litigation,[97] in order to obtain evidence of crime that should normally be obtained in other ways,[98] or, most commonly, for the purpose of getting more information on an already-indicted defendant,[99] a subpoena may be quashed. Finally, courts recognize that subpoenas used purely for harassment purposes must be quashed.[1]

(b) The Immunity Power. As noted above, a grand jury witness who validly exercises his right to remain silent cannot be sanctioned. But the grand jury is not necessarily stymied in this situation. It retains the power to grant immunity to any person asserting the privilege, in an effort to force him to testify. Immunity is of two types. The broadest form, "transactional" immunity, bars the witness' future prosecution as to any transaction to which he has testified. "Use and derivate use" immunity bars the use, or derivative use, of his own testimony in a prosecution against him. Thus, under the latter type of immunity, later prosecution is possible if independent evidence of the witness' crime is found. In *Kastigar v. United States,*[2] the Supreme Court upheld the constitutionality of use immunity, despite its lesser protection.

However, *Kastigar* also held that, in a subsequent prosecution of a witness granted use immunity, the burden of proof would be on the government to show that the evidence had been derived from "a legitimate source wholly independent of the compelled testimony." Generally, therefore, in those states that provide for use immunity (i.e., a substantial majority of the states), those who are immunized are either "minor players" who are given immunity in exchange for information about other suspects, or individuals concerning whom the prosecution has already developed consider-

95. See, e.g., *Franzi v. Superior Court,* 139 Ariz. 556, 679 P.2d 1043 (1984).

96. 250 U.S. 273, 39 S.Ct. 468 (1919).

97. *United States v. Procter & Gamble Co.,* 356 U.S. 677, 78 S.Ct. 983 (1958) (use for civil discovery would be "flouting the policy of the law.").

98. *In re Grand Jury Subpoena (Kiefaber),* 774 F.2d 969 (9th Cir.1985) (subpoenas quashed because prosecutor used them to obtain evidence for police, in circumvention of Rule 6(e)), vac'd 823 F.2d 383 (1987).

99. *United States v. Star,* 470 F.2d 1214 (9th Cir.1972); *United States v. Dardi,* 330 F.2d 316 (2d Cir.1964), cert. denied 379 U.S. 845, 85 S.Ct. 50 (1964).

1. *Branzburg v. Hayes,* 408 U.S. 665, 92 S.Ct. 2646 (1972).

2. 406 U.S. 441, 92 S.Ct. 1653 (1972).

able evidence, which can be sealed and delivered to the court as proof of its "independence" from any admissions made during immunized testimony.[3]

(c) **The Contempt Power.** The grand jury's ability to issue subpoenas and grant immunity is backed up by the authority to impose civil and criminal contempt citations for those who refuse to respond. If held in civil contempt, which is the usual sanction, the individual may be fined or jailed until he "purges" himself of contempt by producing the evidence or testifying.[4] He is released at the end of the grand jury's term if he has not purged himself by then, although a subsequent grand jury may once again subpoena or immunize him.[5] If civil contempt fails, the grand jury may resort to criminal contempt, which results in a fixed sentence or fine.

The contempt device is not unlimited. In *Wood v. Georgia,*[6] the Supreme Court held unconstitutional, under the First Amendment, a contempt order against a sheriff who had publicly criticized as racist a recently initiated grand jury investigation of bloc voting by blacks; according to the Court, the sheriff's statements had not presented a "clear and present danger" to the grand jury's deliberations. Although the contempt order in *Wood* was not initiated by the grand jury itself, but by the judges who convened it, presumably a contempt order requested by the grand jury attempting to suppress criticism of its actions would be analyzed similarly.

(d) **The Role of the Prosecutor and the Court.** In medieval England, the grand jury initiated investigations either on its own or, most commonly, at the behest of the local justice of the peace. A refusal to indict, at least in the latter instance, had to be explained to the court. Later, in both England and colonial America, the grand jury was occasionally able to distance itself further from both the government and the court.[7] But, in the United States today, the grand jury's independence, especially vis-a-vis the prosecutor, is minimal.

Almost every state makes the prosecutor the primary "legal adviser" of the grand jury, and requires or allows him to be present during all grand jury sessions.[8] Theoretically, the grand

---

3. For further discussion of immunity grants, see § 15.03(c).

4. *Shillitani v. United States,* 384 U.S. 364, 86 S.Ct. 1531 (1966).

5. The Ninth Circuit has rejected claims that successive jailings for civil contempt constitute double jeopardy, a denial of due process, or cruel and unusual punishment. *United States v. Duncan,* 456 F.2d 1401 (9th Cir.1972),

vac'd on other grounds 409 U.S. 814, 93 S.Ct. 161 (1972).

6. 370 U.S. 375, 82 S.Ct. 1364 (1962).

7. R. Younger, The People's Panel 84 (1963).

8. See, e.g., West's Fla.Stat.Ann. § 905.19. But see North Carolina Gen. Stat. § 15A–62.

jury can choose who or what it wants to investigate, issue its own subpoenas, and decide who to immunize. But, in most cases, these decisions are actually made by the prosecutor, who in any event is usually granted independent authority to exercise these functions to assist the grand jury in its deliberations.[9] Even the grand jurors' right to ask questions of witnesses, recognized in every jurisdiction, is diminished by the prosecutor's role of primary inquisitor.

As the prosecutor's dominance over the grand jury has increased, the court's has diminished. Although the grand jury has traditionally been seen as an arm of the court, it is usually impanelled either directly or at the request of the prosecutor. After impanelment, the judge's role is primarily ministerial. He "charges" the grand jury, usually speaking of the nature and tradition of grand jury investigation, and the grand jury's independence from the prosecutor. He may also provide legal advice. Most importantly, he enforces the grand jury's subpoena, immunity, and contempt powers. But because he is not present during the grand jury's deliberations,[10] the judge exerts very little practical control over them. Even when possible abuses are brought to his attention, a judge usually does not intercede. Many courts endorse the view that "there should be no curtailment of the inquisitorial power of the grand jury except in the clearest case of abuse, and mere inconvenience not amounting to harassment does not justify judicial interference with the functions of the grand jury." [11]

23.06 Grand Jury Screening: Challenges to the Indictment

The second major function of the grand jury is to decide, based on the evidence before it, whether an indictment should be issued, or whether instead it should find "no bill." As discussed in the introduction, in the federal system and a little over a third of the states, an indictment by grand jury is required, whereas in the remainder of the states the prosecutor has the option of proceeding via information and the preliminary hearing. Below are discussed the major grounds upon which an indictment may be quashed: (1) evidentiary insufficiency; (2) prosecutorial misconduct; (3) discriminatory practices in the selection of the grand jury; and (4) variance from the indictment. With the exception of the third claim, these claims seldom result in an overturned indictment. Indeed, decisions by the Supreme Court narrowing

9. See, e.g., Fed.R.Crim.P. 17(c).

10. See Fed.R.Crim.P. 6(d), Va.Code § 19.2–199.

11. *United States v. Johns–Manville Corp.*, 213 F.Supp. 65 (E.D.Pa.1962). See also, *United States v. Williams,* ___

U.S. ___, 112 S.Ct. 1735 (1992) (court has no authority to sanction prosecutorial conduct not expressly prohibited by Constitution, statute, or rule), discussed in § 23.06(b).

the grounds upon which an indictment may be challenged seem to emasculate many of the rules governing the grand jury process, at least at the federal level.

(a) Sufficiency and Admissibility of Evidence. As with the preliminary hearing,[12] jurisdictions diverge on the proper standard for indictment. In some states, the statutory test is whether there is "probable cause" to believe the accused committed a crime.[13] Others use a prima facie standard.[14] This latter standard is phrased in various ways. For instance, in Arkansas, the grand jury is to return an indictment "when all the evidence before [it], taken together, would in [its] judgement, if unexplained, warrant a conviction by the trial jury."[15] In Utah, "[a]n indictment may not be found unless the grand jurors who vote in favor of the indictment find there is clear and convincing evidence to believe the crime to be charged was committed and the person to be charged committed it."[16]

Ultimately, the standard applied matters very little as far as indictment challenges are concerned. In *Costello v. United States*,[17] the Supreme Court inveighed against evidentiary challenges of grand jury indictments, primarily on efficiency grounds. According to the majority, "[i]f indictments were to be held open to challenge on the ground that there was inadequate or incompetent evidence before the grand jury, the resulting delay would be great indeed." Although an indictment might be challengeable when it is based on "no substantial or rationally persuasive evidence,"[18] the lower courts generally follow *Costello's* lead on this issue.

(1) Application of evidentiary rule. Closely related to the standard of proof question is whether an indictment may be quashed if it is based on evidence that would be inadmissible at trial. In distinct contrast to the typical preliminary hearing,[19] grand juries in most states usually ignore the rules of evidence, whether based on common law, statute, or the Constitution. Again, *Costello* is the leading case upholding this practice. The Court's explicit ruling in *Costello* was that admitting hearsay evidence at grand jury proceedings does not violate the Fifth Amendment's Indictment Clause. But the Court used broad language suggesting that other types of evidence inadmissible at trial could be considered by the grand jury as well, at one point stating,

12. See § 22.03(a).

13. Wash.Code Ann. § 10.27.150.

14. See, e.g., West's Ann.Cal.Penal Code § 939.8.

15. Ark.Stat. § 16–85–513.

16. Utah Code Ann. § 77–10a–14.

17. 350 U.S. 359, 76 S.Ct. 406 (1956).

18. See *Costello* (Burton, J., concurring). Even this basis for challenge is unlikely to succeed in the federal courts, given the Court's decision in *United States v. Mechanik*, 475 U.S. 66, 106 S.Ct. 938 (1986), discussed in § 23.06(b).

19. See § 22.04(b).

"an indictment returned by a legally constituted and unbiased grand jury, . . . if valid on its face, is enough to call for a trial of the charge on the merits."

The Court reached this conclusion based on several factors: (1) inadmissible evidence does not necessarily lack probative value; (2) many of the rules of evidence, such as the hearsay rule, are rooted in and dependent upon an adversary proceeding and cross-examination, which is antithetical to the grand jury process; (3) any infringement of the accused's right may be remedied by operation of the evidentiary rules at trial; and (4) a contrary result would require grand jurors to apply the evidentiary rules and subject their judgment to the court's review, thereby delaying the grand jury proceeding and sacrificing their independence to the court. Some state legislatures apparently disagree with this reasoning, requiring the grand jury to consider only admissible evidence under the rules of evidence,[20] while at least one federal court has held that hearsay evidence may not serve as a basis for an indictment when better evidence is readily available.[21]

(2) Application of exclusionary rules. The Supreme Court has also held that evidence which is inadmissible for constitutional reasons may be considered by the grand jury. In *Lawn v. United States,*[22] the Court, repeating *Costello's* statement that an indictment valid on its face is a sufficient basis for trial, held that the grand jury could consider statements obtained in violation of the privilege against self-incrimination.[23] And in *United States v. Calandra,*[24] again relying heavily on *Costello,* the Court concluded that an indictment cannot be quashed simply because it is based on illegally seized evidence. To the argument that this situation differed from *Costello* because the Fourth Amendment exclusionary rule was designed to punish and deter unconstitutional conduct, the Court responded that application of the rule at trial would sufficiently advance its deterrent purpose.

Calandra also held that the Fourth Amendment does not provide protection against questions based on illegally seized evidence; thus, answers to such questions may form the basis for an indictment. A narrow exception to this rule was announced in *Gelbard v. United States,*[25] which held that, under Title III, the federal wiretapping statute, a grand jury witness is a "party aggrieved" and thus may refuse to answer questions based on conversations obtained through an illegal wiretap, even if immu-

---

20. N.M.Stat.Ann. § 31–6–11; Nev. Rev.Stat. § 172.135; N.Y.—McKinney's Crim.Pro.Law § 190.30.

21. *United States v. Arcuri,* 282 F.Supp. 347 (E.D.N.Y.1968), aff'd 405 F.2d 691 (1968), cert. denied 395 U.S. 913, 89 S.Ct. 1760 (1969).

22. 355 U.S. 339, 78 S.Ct. 311 (1958).

23. See also, *United States v. Blue,* 384 U.S. 251, 86 S.Ct. 1416 (1966).

24. 414 U.S. 338, 94 S.Ct. 613 (1974), also discussed in § 2.03(a).

25. 408 U.S. 41, 92 S.Ct. 2357 (1972).

nized. *Calandra* made clear that *Gelbard* was not the product of constitutional doctrine but rather stemmed from an interpretation of Title III, which explicitly bars the use of evidence obtained or derived from an illegal wiretap at trial *or* at a grand jury proceeding.[26]

(b) Prosecutorial Misconduct. Many courts have recognized that egregious prosecutorial conduct—such as, for instance, knowing use of perjured testimony,[27] or failure to provide the grand jury with clearly exculpatory evidence[28]—can lead to a successful challenge of the resulting indictment. These rulings can be squared with *Costello*, despite its presumption in favor of facially valid indictments, if one construes the premise of that decision to be an "unbiased" grand jury; prosecutorial malfeasance can create a "biased" indictment that must be quashed despite its facial validity.

However, in *United States v. Williams*,[29] the Supreme Court held that, in federal jurisdictions at least, a court cannot dismiss an indictment for prosecutorial misconduct unless the misconduct violates a pre-existing constitutional, legislative, or procedural rule. In *Williams*, the prosecutor withheld from the grand jury exculpatory information that might have led to a "no bill" finding. While the prosecutor clearly has an obligation, grounded in the Due Process Clause, to provide exculpatory information to the defendant prior to trial,[30] there is no constitutional obligation to give the grand jury such information; as the *Williams* majority stated, "requiring the prosecutor to present exculpatory as well as inculpatory evidence would alter the grand jury's historical role, transforming it from an accusatory to an adjudicatory body." Nor does federal legislation or the Federal Rules of Criminal Procedure require such disclosure. Thus, according to Justice Scalia, who wrote the opinion for a five-member majority, a trial court has no authority to sanction this type of misconduct. "Because the grand jury is an institution separate from the courts, over whose functioning the courts do not preside, we think it clear that, as a general matter at least, no such 'supervisory' judicial authority exists."

Even when the prosecutorial misconduct violates a clearly established rule, indictment challenges will rarely succeed, especially if made after conviction. In *United States v. Mechanik*,[31] the Supreme Court appeared to hold that virtually all such post-

26. 18 U.S.C.A. § 2515. For further discussion of this point, see § 14.03(g).

27. *United States v. Basurto*, 497 F.2d 781 (9th Cir.1974).

28. *Johnson v. Superior Court*, 15 Cal.3d 248, 124 Cal.Rptr. 32, 539 P.2d 792 (1975).

29. ___ U.S. ___, 112 S.Ct. 1735 (1992).

30. See § 24.04.

31. 475 U.S. 66, 106 S.Ct. 938 (1986).

conviction challenges will be denied on harmless error grounds. Although *Mechanik* involved only a violation of federal rule 6(d), which limits the types of individuals who may attend a grand jury hearing, the Court's rationale for holding that violation harmless was broadly applicable:

> Both [of the lower courts] observed that Rule 6(d) was designed, in part, "to ensure that grand jurors, sitting without the direct supervision of a judge, are not subject to undue influence that may come with the presence of an unauthorized person." The Rule protects against the danger that a defendant will be required to defend against a charge for which there is no probable cause to believe him guilty. . . . But the petit jury's subsequent guilty verdict not only means that there was probable cause to believe that the defendants were guilty as charged, but that they are in fact guilty as charged beyond a reasonable doubt. Measured by the petit jury's verdict, then, any error in the grand jury proceeding connected with the charging decision was harmless beyond a reasonable doubt. . . .
>
> [Further], there is no simple way after the verdict to restore the defendant to the position in which he would have been had the indictment been dismissed before trial. He will already have suffered whatever inconvenience, expense, and opprobrium that a proper indictment may have spared him.

Most courts have followed this reasoning in rejecting indictment challenges based on other types of prosecutorial misconduct.[32]

Because *Mechanik's* harmless error analysis depends upon the "mooting" effect of a conviction, a challenge to the indictment brought *before* trial occurs is somewhat more likely to prevail, so long as, per *Williams*, it is based on violation of an established rule. Here, too, however, the Supreme Court has required the defendant to meet a heavy burden in federal court. In *Bank of Nova Scotia v. United States*,[33] the Court held that dismissal of the indictment in this situation "is appropriate only 'if it is established that the violation substantially influenced the grand jury's decision to indict,' or if there is 'grave doubt' that the decision to indict was free from the substantial influence of such violations." Applying this standard in *Bank of Nova Scotia*, the Court found that the following illegal actions by the prosecutor were not grounds for quashing the indictment, since they did not prejudice the grand jury's decision: (1) use of the grand jury to gather evidence for use in civil matters; (2) public identification of the

32. See, e.g., *United States v. Fountain*, 840 F.2d 509 (7th Cir.1988). But see, *United States v. Taylor*, 798 F.2d 1337 (10th Cir.1986).

33. 487 U.S. 250, 108 S.Ct. 2369 (1988).

targets; (3) imposition of secrecy oaths on witnesses; and (4) failure to prevent two witnesses from appearing in front of the grand jury simultaneously.

Mechanik and *Bank of Nova Scotia* send prosecutors the message that most of the rules governing the conduct of grand jury proceedings are precatory only. The latter decision is particularly questionable, since a contrary result would not have required a new trial, but merely resubmission of the case to another grand jury. The opinion in *Bank of Nova Scotia* did indicate that if the prosecutorial misconduct "overreached or deceived in some significant way" or spanned several cases and was "so systematic and pervasive as to raise a substantial question about the fundamental fairness of the process which resulted in the indictment," then prejudice might be found. For what it is worth, it should also be noted that the Court borrowed its prejudice standard in *Bank of Nova Scotia* from *Kotteakos v. United States*,[34] a petit jury harmless error case, which eschewed looking at whether there was sufficient evidence to convict after deleting the error, but rather focused on whether the error influenced the jury's decision.

(c) Discrimination in the Selection Process. As discussed earlier in this chapter,[35] both the Equal Protection Clause and the Due Process Clause may provide a basis for challenging the grand jury's indictment. In contrast to cases involving evidentiary insufficiency and prosecutorial misconduct, the Supreme Court has indicated that these types of claims, if proven, will lead to quashing of the indictment whether raised before or after conviction. Because it "strikes at the fundamental values of our judicial system and our society as a whole," the Court has held, in two different decisions,[36] that discrimination in the selection of a grand jury can never be harmless, even when the person has been convicted by a fairly selected and impartial petit jury.[37]

This notion was reiterated in *Mechanik*, which distinguished these cases on the ground that "racial discrimination in the selection of grand jurors is so pernicious and other remedies so impractical, that the remedy of automatic reversal was necessary as a prophylactic means of deterring grand jury discrimination in the future." Similarly, with respect to a pre-trial challenge on due process representativeness grounds, *Bank of Nova Scotia* explained that a proven violation should result in automatic

34. 328 U.S. 750, 66 S.Ct. 1239 (1946), discussed in § 29.05(b).

35. See § 23.02(c).

36. *Rose v. Mitchell*, 443 U.S. 545, 99 S.Ct. 2993 (1979); *Vasquez v. Hillery*, 474 U.S. 254, 106 S.Ct. 617 (1986).

37. As a result, a resulting conviction must apparently be reversed and a new trial held, although another alternative would be to reinstate the conviction if a duly constituted grand jury reindicts the defendant. See Stacy and Dayton, "Rethinking Harmless Constitutional Error," 88 Colum.L.Rev. 79 (1988).

reversal because the "nature of the violation allow[s] a presumption that the defendant was prejudiced, and any inquiry into harmless error would . . . require[ ] ungrounded speculation."

(d) Variance. Fairly frequently, the proof offered by the prosecution at trial will be at "variance" with the allegations in the grand jury's indictment. If the variance between the indictment and the proof at trial is minimal, modern courts typically take no notice of the fact. However, as the Supreme Court noted in *Russell v. United States*,[38] if a defendant is "convicted on the basis of facts not found by, and perhaps not even presented to, the grand jury which indicted him," he is deprived "of a basic protection which the guaranty of the intervention of the grand jury was designed to secure." Thus, a substantial variance can result in the quashing of an indictment and the reversal of a conviction based on it, on the ground that it violates the Indictment Clause of the Fifth Amendment.

As an extension of this reasoning, federal courts sometimes overturned convictions based on some but not all of the material allegations in the indictment, concluding that if the grand jury had heard only the evidence related to the proven allegations, it might have failed to indict. In *United States v. Miller*,[39] however, the Supreme Court held that when the indictment facts which the prosecution fails to prove are "in no way essential to the offense on which the jury convicted," they can be regarded as "surplusage."[40] This was the case in *Miller*, where the indictment had specified that the defendant had fraudulently used the mails to obtain insurance proceeds by (1) consenting to a "burglary" which resulted in the "loss" of his property and (2) misrepresenting the value of the loss to his insurance company. The government was unable to have the first allegation stricken from the indictment and was unable to prove it at trial. But the second allegation was a sufficient basis for, and led to, a conviction. Thus, concluded the Court, the indictment should be upheld.

Two other traditional rules regarding variance between the proof at trial and the indictment were reaffirmed by *Miller:* new allegations cannot be added to an indictment except by the grand jury and a defendant cannot be convicted on the basis of evidence proving matters not alleged in the indictment. Presumably, if either of these two rules are violated, any resulting conviction must be overturned in violation of the Indictment Clause.

38. 369 U.S. 749, 82 S.Ct. 1038 (1962). See also, *Stirone v. United States,* 361 U.S. 212, 80 S.Ct. 270 (1960).

39. 471 U.S. 130, 105 S.Ct. 1811 (1985).

40. See Fed.R.Crim.P. 7(d) (surplusage in the indictment or information may be stricken).

23.07 An Assessment of the Grand Jury

Should the grand jury continue as an investigative and screening body? Looking first at the grand jury as an investigative device, it is important to note that the power now vested there does not have to be. In Florida, for instance, in all noncapital cases the prosecutor may seek subpoenas, grants of immunity, and contempt citations on his own.[41] He does not need to impanel a grand jury to avail himself of these tools. Thus, a better way to focus on the usefulness of the grand jury as an investigative body is to ask whether its retention, at least as an option, offers any advantages over a system which depends entirely on prosecutor- and police-conducted investigations, assuming each system has the same investigative powers.

At least three possible advantages for an optional system can be advanced. First, the fact that the grand jury is composed of laypeople may have some benefits. As is said about the petit jury,[42] the institution of the grand jury may promote a sense of citizen participation in the criminal process that improves the reputation and credibility of the system as a whole. And the lay nature of the grand jury may make it willing to pursue certain types of investigations—e.g., of political corruption—that the prosecutor would be reluctant to initiate, either because he himself may be involved somehow, or because the targets of the investigation control his future. Most importantly, reliance on a panel of citizens, rather than the prosecutor's office, could be fairer and less partisan, in fact as well as symbolically; the grand jury's mere existence may serve to hold the prosecutor in check from vindictive or ill-advised investigations.

Second, both because of its lay make-up and its history, the investigative scope of the grand jury is likely to be more wide-ranging than the prosecutor's. The prosecutor, for legal or ethical reasons, may feel constrained about using the subpoena process to investigate people who have not yet been formally charged, or who have not at least been targeted by a complaint from a citizen or the police. The grand jury, on the other hand, may engage in virtual fishing expeditions. The most potent evidence of this difference is the fact that, in many states, the grand jury may issue reports on various matters—ranging from conditions in local jails [43] to recommendations on matters of criminal justice policy [44]—without rendering any criminal charges. In support of these reports, it is said the grand jury's investigative authority extends to "all that is comprehended in the police power of the

---

41. F.S. 914.04. In many states, the prosecutor has subpoena power, but only in connection with a pending proceeding, such as a grand jury inquest, a preliminary hearing, or trial.

42. See § 27.01.

43. Ohio Rev.Code § 2939.21.

44. Ga.Code Ann. §§ 15–12–79, 15–12–76.

state." [45] The modern trend is to limit the use of these reports in a number of ways, most notably by requiring that they not be issued unless the individuals implicated are allowed to testify before the grand jury and append a response to the report.[46] Courts may also order such reports expunged if they draw conclusions beyond the bounds of a legitimate investigation.[47] But, even so limited, they represent a power unlikely to be given to the prosecutor's office, which traditionally has focused on enforcing the criminal law.

A third reason the grand jury might be usefully retained as an investigative option is that a witness may be more likely to talk in front of a grand jury than at the stationhouse or the prosecutor's office, for a number of reasons. Because, in contrast to the person subjected to custodial interrogation, a grand jury witness is not entitled to counsel and may not be entitled to reminders about the right to remain silent,[48] he may feel more compelled to talk. Additionally, the grand jury may provide more secrecy than a prosecutorial investigation, which can encourage disclosures. Finally, if the witness does talk, he is more likely to do so truthfully, since, unlike a stationhouse encounter, he is under oath and can be tried for perjury if he lies.

It can be questioned whether these differences justify maintaining the grand jury as an investigative body. The fact that an unwarned, uncounselled person is less likely to remain silent is not necessarily a reason for favoring grand juries. And it is questionable whether a grand jury proceeding is more likely than an interview with the prosecutor to remain confidential,[49] or disclose truthful information.[50] Most importantly, the potential benefits of the grand jury's lay nature and its ability to engage in wide-ranging investigations are undercut significantly by the previously discussed realities that the prosecutor dominates the grand jury and the court seldom steps in. Indeed, these facets of the grand jury mean it can easily serve as a shield for prosecutors who would be unwilling to pursue certain illegitimate or questionable investigations on their own.[51] Only if the grand jury is granted

45. *In re Report of Grand Jury,* 152 Fla. 154, 11 So.2d 316 (1943).

46. N.Y.—McKinney's Crim.P.Law §§ 190.85–90.

47. In *Hammond v. Brown,* 323 F.Supp. 326 (N.D.Ohio 1971), aff'd 450 F.2d 480 (6th Cir.1971), the court expunged a grand jury report finding "beyond doubt" that twenty-five persons it had indicted for the events at Kent State University in May, 1970 had committed the charged offenses.

48. See § 23.04.

49. See § 23.03 for a discussion of the many exceptions to the secrecy prohibition.

50. In the federal courts, for instance, a witness can be punished for intentionally making false statements to a police officer. 18 U.S.C.A. § 1001.

51. See Fine, "Federal Grand Jury Investigations of Political Dissidents," 7 Harv.Civ.Rts.—Civ.Lib.L.Rev. 432 (1972).

more of its traditional independence (through the mechanism of allowing it to hire its own attorney, for instance),[52] and is more closely monitored by the court, is it likely to provide any positive advantages over the prosecutor and the police as an investigative device.

Similar comments can be made about the grand jury's efficacy as a screening mechanism. Here, the alternative is a preliminary hearing, presided over by a judge. As a theoretical matter, it may be useful to have citizens involved in deciding who should be charged with crime or criticized for wrongdoing. But if, in practice, the prosecutor largely controls the evidence which informs these decisions, it is not clear that the grand jury is preferable (especially where, as is true in federal jurisdictions, prosecutorial misconduct is often immune from challenge, in the rare instances when grand jury secrecy allows it to be discovered).[53] In contrast to the grand jury, the preliminary hearing is conducted in open court, with the defendant and counsel present, and allows consideration of evidence for the defendant, as well as against him.[54] While several jurisdictions require both a preliminary hearing and a grand jury proceeding, the prosecutor has the authority, as discussed in the previous chapter,[55] to avoid the preliminary hearing by first obtaining an indictment. Perhaps the opposite rule would make the most sense: the preliminary hearing should be mandatory, with the grand jury used solely as an investigative body *prior* to the hearing, if it is used at all.[56]

23.08   Conclusion

The grand jury indictment may be issued as an authorization to arrest, or serve as a formalization of the prosecutor's decision to arrest. In either case, the following comments about the grand jury process are applicable.

(1) The federal system and slightly over one-third of the states require that prosecution in felony cases proceed by indictment. In most of the remaining states, prosecution may proceed by either indictment or information; in the latter case, a preliminary hearing usually serves the charging function.

(2) The size of the grand jury and the number of votes necessary for an indictment vary considerably among the states. In federal jurisdictions, the grand jury is composed of from 16 to 23 people, with twelve votes needed for an indictment. Neither

---

52. See, e.g., Hawaii Const. art. 1, § 11.

53. See § 23.06(b).

54. See generally, Chapter Twenty-Two.

55. See § 22.02(b).

56. This was the practice in California, under *Hawkins v. Superior Court,* 22 Cal.3d 584, 150 Cal.Rptr. 435, 586 P.2d 916 (1978), until 1990, when a statewide proposition eliminated the right to a preliminary hearing. West's Ann.Cal. Const. Art. I, § 14.1.

the pool from which the grand jury is chosen or the grand jury itself may result from a procedure which purposefully discriminates against the defendant's racial group. Further, the grand jury pool may not result from a procedure which systematically excludes a significant, identifiable segment of society. Finally, the grand jury must be impartial, although ensuring impartiality is difficult, since the defendant is entitled neither to pre- or post-indictment voir dire.

(3) In order to encourage witnesses to come forward, prevent disclosure of derogatory information, avoid premature disclosure of the investigation to a potential defendant, and protect grand jurors from intimidation or reprisal by the government or targets, neither evidence heard by the grand jury nor the grand jury's deliberations are a matter of public record. However, disclosure of this information may be made under the following circumstances: (a) in most jurisdictions, a witness may disclose his own testimony; after the grand jury's term has ended, he *must* be allowed to do so under the First Amendment; (b) in most jurisdictions, the defendant is entitled to the grand jury testimony of witnesses who testify at trial; (c) the validity of other disclosures requires balancing the need for secrecy (including the impact that disclosure may have on future grand juries) against the specificity and strength of the third party's request, with government agencies more likely to obtain grand jury transcripts than private third parties.

(4) Under the federal Constitution, a putative defendant or target apparently has no right (a) to appear in front of the grand jury; (b) to counsel, either in the grand jury room or outside for consultation; (c) to be told he is a target, or (d) to a reminder that he has the right to remain silent. However, most jurisdictions, statutorily or by judicial decision, provide all of these rights in one form or another.

(5) The grand jury has wide-ranging investigative powers, in order to implement its "right to every-man's evidence." Use of subpoenas *ad testificandum* appears to be unrestricted, at least constitutionally. A subpoena *duces tecum* must be reasonable, meaning that: (a) it must state with some particularity what is requested; (b) it must avoid being overly burdensome; and (c) the items it requests must be at least minimally related to the investigation. The latter type of subpoena can also be quashed in the rare event that the act of production it compels is self-incriminating and cannot be immunized. The grand jury's authority to grant immunity allows it to force a witness to testify upon a promise that no future prosecution will be based on that testimony, or on any evidence derived from it. Both the subpoena and immunity powers are enforced by civil and criminal contempt,

imposed by the court. In practice, the prosecutor often suggests to the grand jury who to subpoena and immunize, and when the contempt penalty is appropriate.

(6) In the federal courts, a grand jury indictment probably cannot be quashed for insufficient evidence, or on the ground that the evidence considered by the grand jury would be inadmissible at trial. Egregious prosecutorial conduct during the grand jury investigation will only furnish grounds for quashing an indictment if it violates an established rule, and even then a motion for dismissal will usually succeed only if it is made prior to trial and the defendant establishes that the violation substantially influenced the grand jury's decision to indict. An indictment from a grand jury that was selected unconstitutionally will normally be quashed. Further, a defendant's conviction will be overturned if it is based on facts not found by the grand jury which indicted him.

BIBLIOGRAPHY

American Bar Association. Section of Criminal Justice. Policy on the Grand Jury. Washington, D.C.: American Bar Association, Section of Criminal Justice, 1977.

Arenella, Peter. Reforming the Federal Grand Jury and the State Preliminary Hearing to Prevent Conviction Without Adjudication. 7 Natl.J.Crim.Def. 299 (1981).

Berman, Douglas. Coercive Contempt and the Federal Grand Jury. 79 Colum.L.Rev. 735 (1979).

Boudin, Leonard B. The Federal Grand Jury. 61 Geo.L.J. 1 (1972).

Braun, Richard L. The Grand Jury—Spirit of the Community. 15 Ariz.L.Rev. 893 (1973).

Brown, Robert. The Witness and Grand Jury Secrecy. 11 Am.J.Crim.L. 169 (1983).

Calkins, Richard M. Grand Jury Secrecy. 63 Mich.L.Rev. 455 (1965).

Clark, Leroy D. The Grand Jury: The Use and Abuse of Political Power. New York: Quadrangle, 1975.

Frankel, Marvin E. The Grand Jury: An Institution on Trial. New York: Hill and Wang, 1977.

Hixson, Mary Emma. Bringing Down the Curtain on the Absurd Drama of Entrances and Exits—Witness Representation in the Grand Jury Room. 15 Am.Crim.L.Rev. 307 (1978).

Holderman, James F. Pre-Indictment Prosecutorial Conduct in the Federal System. 71 J.Crim.L. & Criminol. 1 (1980).

Keeney, John C. and Paul R. Walsh. The American Bar Association's Grand Jury Principles: A Critique from a Federal Criminal Justice Perspective. 14 Idaho L.Rev. 545 (1978).

Knudsen, William J., Jr. Pretrial Disclosure of Federal Grand Jury Testimony. 60 Federal Rules Decisions 237 (1974).

National Lawyers Guild. Representation of Witnesses before Federal Grand Juries. New York: Clark Boardman Co., 1976, v. 1 [Looseleaf].

Rief, James. The Grand Jury Witness and Compulsory Testimony Legislation. 10 Am.Crim.L.Rev. 829 (1972).

Schwartz, Helene. Demythologizing the Historic Role of the Grand Jury. Am.Crim.L.Rev. 701 (1972).

Silbert, Earl J. Defense Counsel in the Grand Jury—The Answer to the White Collar Criminal's Prayers. 15 Am.Crim.L.Rev. 293 (1978).

Sullivan, Thomas and Nachman, Robert. If It Ain't Broke, Don't Fix It: Why the Grand Jury's Accusatory Function Should Not Be Changed. 75 J.Crim.L. & Criminol. 1047 (1984).

Van Dyke, John. The Grand Jury: Representative or Elite? 28 Hastings L.J. 37 (1976).

Younger, Richard. The People's Panel. Brown University Press (1963).

Zwerling, Matthew. Federal Grand Juries v. Attorney Independence and the Attorney Client Privilege. 27 Hastings L.J. 1263 (1976).

Chapter Twenty-Four

DISCOVERY

24.01 Introduction

As in the civil system, broad discovery in criminal cases might accomplish several goals: (1) more rational decisionmaking during pretrial negotiations; (2) better prepared adversaries at trial; (3) conservation of attorney resources that will otherwise be diverted to discovering information; and (4) avoidance of surprise, and the trial disruption and continuances that surprise causes. Until the middle of this century, however, there were few formal provisions permitting discovery in criminal cases. In most jurisdictions, both the defendant and the prosecutor had to rely on the information they could glean from pretrial proceedings.

Beginning with the adoption, in 1946, of Rule 16 in the Federal Rules of Criminal Procedure, and the proliferation of similar rules at the state level, the scope of discovery has expanded considerably however. Rule 16 permits the defendant, upon request, to discover from the prosecution: (1) any written statements or transcriptions of oral statements made by the defendant that are in the prosecution's possession; (2) the defendant's prior criminal record; and (3) documents, photographs, tangible objects, results of physical and mental examinations, and test reports in the prosecution's possession that the prosecution intends to use as evidence or that is deemed "material" to the defense's trial preparation.[1] If the defendant requests any of the items in the latter two categories, the prosecutor is granted "reciprocal discovery;" he may request inspection of documents, objects, and test results which the defense intends to introduce at trial.[2] The "work product" of both sides is protected, however.[3]

Some state rules are even broader in scope. For example, over half the states not only provide for discovery of the items covered in Rule 16, but also require the prosecution to provide names and addresses of all persons known to have information relevant to the offense charged, as well as any statements about the offense these persons have made.[4] In several of these states, the defense must reciprocate, either by providing a list of all persons whom the defense expects to call as witnesses and any recorded statements they have made,[5] or by simply providing a list

---

1. Fed.R.Crim.P. 16(a)(1).

2. Id. 16(b)(1).

3. Id. 16(a)(2) and 16(b)(2).

4. Moore's Federal Practice 216 (1982).

5. See, e.g., West's Fla.S.A.R.Crim. Pro. 3.220(b)(3).

of witnesses.[6] In many states, the defense must provide this information even if it has *not* requested information from the prosecution.[7]

The typical statute also provides for protective orders, and for sanctions if the rules are not followed. For instance, under the federal rules the court has discretion, after making an *in camera* inspection of a requested item, to deny, restrict or defer its disclosure.[8] Upon finding that a party has failed to comply with a discovery rule, a protective order, or other court order regarding discovery, the court may either grant a continuance until compliance occurs, "prohibit the party from introducing evidence not disclosed," or "enter such other order as it deems just under the circumstances." [9] One type of "order" sometimes relied upon is a charge to the jury telling it that the party has not produced a requested piece of evidence, and that it may draw whatever conclusion it wishes from that fact.

As this brief description indicates, modern discovery rules enable the defense to obtain a substantial amount of information from the prosecution that may otherwise have been difficult to procure prior to trial. At the same time, it should be apparent that discovery under federal and state rules is not a one-way street: the defendant is *required*, under certain circumstances, to disclose information to the prosecution. This chapter will first discuss issues associated with prosecution discovery of the defense's case. It will then address the prosecution's obligations under today's discovery legislation. Finally, it will examine the prosecutor's duty, under the *Constitution*, to disclose exculpatory information and to preserve evidence.

24.02 Discovery by the Prosecution

When disclosure is sought from the defense, there are three possible limitations on discovery: the Fifth Amendment's privilege against self-incrimination, the Sixth Amendment's right to counsel (and the associated work product doctrine), and, in some states, the requirement that the defense ask for information from the prosecution first. These limitations are discussed here, as well as limitations on sanctions that may be imposed on the defense for violating discovery rules.

(a) **Fifth Amendment Limitations.** As a general proposition, the prosecution cannot compel the defendant to provide inculpatory statements from his own mouth. But the defendant can waive the Fifth Amendment privilege. He can also be granted immunity and forced to talk. Finally, the Fifth Amendment

---

6. See, e.g., Hawaii R.Crim.Pro. 16(c)(2)(i).

7. See infra note 30.

8. Fed.R.Crim.P. 16(d)(1).

9. Fed.R.Crim.P. 16(d)(2).

only prohibits compelled *self*-incrimination.[10] These principles have varying application to discovery rules, depending upon the type of discovery at issue.

(1) Notice of alibi and other defenses. In *Williams v. Florida*,[11] the Court was faced with a "notice-of-alibi" statute. Such statutes, which exist in every jurisdiction (usually independent of the discovery provisions described earlier), require the defendant to give pretrial notice of an alibi defense and a list of witnesses who will support it.[12] The majority in *Williams* found that this type of statute does not violate the Fifth Amendment, because it exerts no more compulsion to produce alibi evidence than does the need to avoid conviction at trial itself, and the latter type of pressure has never been found to implicate the Fifth Amendment. The one difference between the command of a notice-of-alibi statute and the "command" that one produce evidence in one's defense at trial is that the former compels the defendant to accelerate the disclosure. In response to this observation, the Court responded: "Nothing in the Fifth Amendment privilege entitles a defendant as a matter of constitutional right to await the end of the State's case before announcing the nature of his defense, any more than it entitles him to await the jury's verdict on the State's case-in-chief before deciding whether or not to take the stand himself." This reasoning would also seem to support statutes which require notification of other defenses, such as insanity or self-defense.[13]

In dissent, Justice Black pointed out that identification of hitherto unknown defense witnesses prior to trial could provide incriminating information or investigative leads. For instance, such a witness could help the prosecution establish that the defendant was in the vicinity of the crime at the time it happened (even though the witness may insist the defendant was not at the precise spot the crime occurred). Or the witness might provide the government with information about other potential witnesses or crimes committed by the defendant. Finally, as occurred in *Williams* itself, pretrial notice might also help the prosecution gather evidence that can be used to impeach the alibi witness.

The problem with Black's objection is that the state will eventually find out about the alibi witness at trial, at which time it can ask for a continuance which will give it the same investigative advantages. Unless continuances are barred (which would be unfair to the prosecution), notice-of-alibi statutes (and other no-

---

10. For a discussion of the scope of the Fifth Amendment, see Chapter Fifteen.

11. 399 U.S. 78, 90 S.Ct. 1893 (1970).

12. See, e.g., Fed.R.Crim.P. 12.1.

13. See Fed.R.Crim.P. 12.2(b). However, as discussed in § 24.03(a), a notice-of-defense statute which does not also require the prosecution to provide equivalent information about its rebuttal evidence is unconstitutional.

tice-of-defense statutes) are likely to result in no more infringement of the defendant's interests than would occur without one, at
least if the defendant is first given adequate discovery of the
prosecution's case, so that he can make an intelligent decision
about possible defenses. At the same time notice-of-defense statutes are clearly more likely to result in efficient use of judicial
resources (a point the *Williams* majority emphasized).

In favor of Black's position, however, is the possibility that the
defendant may decide to forego the defense after notice is given.
In such cases, the court could impose a ban on prosecutorial use of
evidence derived from the reneged-upon notice, but determining
when such use has occurred can be very difficult. More is said on
the "change-of-defense" problem below.

(2) Witness lists and statements. As noted in the introduction, many states require the defendant to provide the prosecution
with lists of all witnesses (rather than just witnesses who will
support a specific affirmative defense), as well as statements from
those witnesses. A few jurisdictions even require the defendant to
create such statements if they do not exist.[14] Clearly, any of this
information might prove incriminating or provide investigative
leads (for instance, a witness list might lead the prosecution to the
sole eyewitness to a crime). But, after *Williams,* these provisions
are probably justifiable on the ground that the prosecution will
obtain this information at trial in any event. Perhaps the best
compromise is to allow the defendant to seek a protective order
when he can show that disclosure of certain information will be
harmful to him and is not likely to be useful at trial.[15] Thus, the
court might decide to protect the identity of a witness who has
evidence about other crimes committed by the defendant.

The one piece of information regarding witnesses which the
defendant may be able to withhold is whether he himself will
testify. In *Brooks v. Tennessee,*[16] the Supreme Court held invalid a
state statute requiring that, if the defendant chose to testify, he
must do so at the beginning of his case, just after the state has
rested. The Court found that the statute violated both the privilege against self-incrimination and the due process right to "the
guiding hand of counsel," because it forced the defendant to assess
the extent to which his own testimony would be useful or necessary to his defense at the end of the state's case, rather than after
he'd had the opportunity to evaluate the impact of his own

14. See, e.g., R.I. Super.Ct.R.Crim.
Pro. 413(d)(i) (if no statement for witness available, defense shall provide "a
summary of the testimony such person
is expected to give at trial.").

15. Cf. *Prudhomme v. Superior
Court,* 2 Cal.3d 320, 85 Cal.Rptr. 129,

466 P.2d 673 (1970) (disclosure may be
barred depending upon the "incriminating effect" of the item).

16. 406 U.S. 605, 92 S.Ct. 1891
(1972).

evidence. Arguably, if a defendant cannot be forced to make a choice about his own testimony after he's seen the state's case, he should not be required to make the choice prior to trial.

However, *Brooks* is not easily reconciled with *Williams,* which upheld a rule forcing the defendant to make an important choice prior to viewing the *state's* evidence at trial. Perhaps the Court considers the right to testify (or remain silent) to be more fundamental than the opportunity to raise an alibi defense or other defenses.[17] Or perhaps the Court is less worried about the element of "surprise" to the prosecution in the *Brooks* context, since the general outline of what a defendant will say at his own trial can usually be anticipated. A final explanation is that *Brooks* merely recognizes the defendant's right to control the presentation of his case, and has no implications for discovery rules. If so, the state *could* force the defendant to reveal prior to trial whether he plans to testify.

The *Williams* "accelerated disclosure" rationale would not seem to justify forcing the defendant to reveal statements which he does *not* intend to use at trial. Yet, under limited circumstances, the defendant may also be compelled to provide such statements. In *United States v. Nobles,*[18] the defendant attempted to call as a witness a private investigator retained by the defense; his testimony would have cast doubt on two eyewitnesses for the prosecution. The trial judge ruled that the investigator could not testify until the prosecution received the portion of his investigative report that contained alleged statements from these two witnesses (as determined by the judge *in camera*). Defense counsel refused to submit the report and the investigator was not allowed to testify. On appeal, the defendant argued that the trial court's attempt to compel the disclosure of the investigator's report violated his privilege against self-incrimination.

The Supreme Court did not agree. Emphasizing that the Fifth Amendment is a "personal right,"[19] a unanimous Supreme Court found that it was not implicated here because "[t]he court's order was limited to statements allegedly made by third parties who were available as witnesses to both the prosecution and the defense." Thus, had the court order been implemented, the prosecution would not have received any "personal communications" from the defendant, or any statements from witnesses unknown to the prosecution.

---

17. See Mosteller, "Discovery Against the Defense: Tilting the Adversarial Balance," 74 Calif.L.Rev. 1567, 1626 (1986).

18. 422 U.S. 225, 95 S.Ct. 2160 (1975).

19. See *Couch v. United States,* 409 U.S. 322, 93 S.Ct. 611 (1973), discussed in § 15.05.

Nobles establishes that the privilege is not violated when the defendant is compelled to provide, at trial, prior recorded statements from witnesses the prosecution knows about and which will further adversarial testing of those witnesses. *Nobles* does not make clear whether the defendant can be forced to do so prior to trial. However, in light of *Williams'* finding that accelerated disclosure of items that can be "compelled" at trial is not violative of the Fifth Amendment, there does not appear to be any barrier to such a practice. Thus, a rule allowing prosecution discovery of statements the defendant takes from prospective government witnesses, adopted in several jurisdictions,[20] does not appear to violate the Fifth Amendment. Recordings of unfavorable statements from the defense's own witnesses can presumably be obtained as well, at least if the prosecution knows of their existence.

(3) Identities of non-witnesses. Whether the Fifth Amendment prohibits forced disclosure of the identity of a person whom the defense will not call as a witness depends upon the source of the information. In *Fisher v. United States,*[21] the Court held that the Fifth Amendment prohibits the state from compelling the defendant to disclose the existence of evidence against him, and that the attorney-client privilege prohibits compelling the defendant's attorney from surrendering such information (the Fifth Amendment would not prevent the latter disclosure, because, as *Nobles* affirmed, it is concerned only with defendant-directed compulsion). Thus, the state cannot force the defendant or his attorney to disclose the identity of a non-witness (such as a co-perpetrator) whose existence is known because of the *defendant.* On the other hand, if the defense's knowledge about the existence of incriminating information does not come from the defendant, it is not protected by either the Fifth Amendment or the attorney-client privilege. Thus, if awareness of a non-witness is the result of the *attorney's* efforts (as is the case with most experts, for instance), his identity might be discoverable, at least as far as the Fifth Amendment is concerned.[22]

(4) Tangible and documentary evidence. After *Williams* and *Nobles,* the Fifth Amendment is unlikely to be infringed by the typical rule allowing the prosecution access to any documents, photographs, and other tangible objects, as well as any results of physical examinations, psychological evaluations, and scientific tests, that the defendant plans to use at trial. As with other types of information, the more difficult issue is whether the state may

---

20. See, e.g., Minn.R.Crim.P. 9.02–1(3)(b); Wis.R.Crim.P. 971.24.

21. 425 U.S. 391, 96 S.Ct. 1569 (1976), discussed in § 15.05.

22. However, as discussed below, see § 24.03(b), there may be Sixth Amend-

ment or work product limitations on the disclosure of such information. See also, *People ex rel. Bowman v. Woodward,* 63 Ill.2d 382, 349 N.E.2d 57 (1976).

discover evidence of this type which the defendant will *not* use at trial (e.g., a murder weapon, or business records).

Fisher settled that the prosecution cannot force the defendant to admit to the existence of those items that are in the defendant's possession (or are given to his attorney). But *Fisher* also indicated that if the prosecution already knows of their existence, then the Fifth Amendment is not violated by a demand for them, so long as the prosecution is barred from revealing their source. This conclusion derives from the following reasoning: a subpoena for documents or other tangible evidence only compels the act of producing the evidence, not its creation, and this act is incriminating only when the source of the subpoenaed item is a crucial element of the prosecution's case. By barring the prosecution from revealing the source (in effect, "immunizing" the defendant with respect to the fact of production), even this potential for self-incrimination is removed.[23]

Accepting this argument does not mean that all subpoenas for tangible or documentary evidence must be honored by the defense, however. First, as *Fisher* noted, the subpoena cannot, in effect, demand if a document or object exists; rather, it can only compel production of items known to exist. This limitation is bolstered by the Fourth Amendment, which prohibits overbroad or indefinite subpoenas *duces tecum*.[24] Second, even with "immunity" as to the source of the item, subpoenas for certain types of objects, such as contraband or stolen goods, would be invalid, because the factfinder will assume that the source was the defendant regardless of what it is told.[25] Third, some subpoenas may be barred for non-constitutional reasons. Several jurisdictions prohibit use of grand jury subpoenas after an indictment has been returned,[26] apparently on the ground that otherwise they will be abused by evidence-greedy prosecutors.

(b) Sixth Amendment Limitations. In addition to his Fifth Amendment argument, the defendant in *Nobles* argued that the court's order deprived him of his right to compulsory process (i.e., the right to call the investigator) and his right to effective confrontation of the prosecution's witnesses. This contention too the Court rejected: "The Sixth Amendment does not confer the right to present testimony free from the legitimate demands of the adversarial system; one cannot invoke the Sixth Amendment as a justification for presenting what might have been a half-truth."

23. See § 15.06 for further discussion of this point. Note also that barring information about the source also protects against violation of the attorney-client privilege in those cases where the defense attorney turns over evidence given to him by the defendant in the course of their relationship. See *State ex rel. Sowers v. Olwell,* 64 Wash. 2d 828, 394 P.2d 681 (1964).

24. See § 23.05(a)(1).

25. Tomlinson, "Constitutional Limitations on Prosecutorial Discovery," 23 San Diego L.Rev. 923 (1986).

26. See Fed.R.Crim.P. 17(c).

In effect, the Court held that once the defense indicated an intent to call the investigator to the stand and ask questions about statements that were contained in his report, it "waived" protection of those portions of the report.

The Court even more explicitly applied waiver analysis to the defendant's claim that the trial court's action denied him effective assistance of counsel and violated the work product doctrine by compromising his ability to investigate and prepare his defense. As to the Sixth Amendment claim that the disclosure contemplated by the trial court would "inhibit other members of the 'defense team' from gathering information essential to the effective preparation of the case," the Court stated: "The short answer is that the disclosure order resulted form respondent's voluntary election to make testimonial use of his investigator's report." Similarly, while the Court stated that the role of the work-product privilege is "even more vital" in the criminal justice system than it is in the civil system, and must "protect material prepared by agents for the attorney as well as those prepared by the attorney himself," it concluded that the respondent, "by electing to present the investigator as a witness, waived the privilege with respect to matters covered in his testimony."

The Court's emphasis on waiver *at trial* suggests that the Sixth Amendment and the work product doctrine might protect against pretrial discovery of certain types of information, in particular those normally subsumed under the work product doctrine. In fact, most jurisdictions extend protection to "internal memoranda" prepared by either side.[27] But statements *within* those documents may still be discoverable prior to trial under the rules discussed above. And there appears to be no recognition of the argument, based on the Sixth Amendment, that extensive pretrial disclosure of witnesses the defendant plans to use might deter defense attorneys from thoroughly investigating a case, or at least deter them from recording that investigation.

Some lower courts have held that discovery rules which require disclosure of persons or statements the defense does *not* intend to use at trial violate the defendant's right to effective assistance of counsel or the work product doctrine.[28] However, the reasoning of these decisions would prevent disclosure only of information the defense developed in preparation for trial; it would not apply to documents or other tangible objects possessed by the defendant prior to being charged. Thus, the Sixth Amend-

27. See, e.g., Fed.R.Crim.P. 16(b)(2).

28. *State v. Williams,* 80 N.J. 472, 404 A.2d 34 (1979) (no discovery of statements not used); *United States v.* *Alvarez,* 519 F.2d 1036 (3d Cir.1975) (expert psychiatrists); *State v. Mingo,* 77 N.J. 576, 392 A.2d 590 (1978) (expert reports).

ment would not prohibit otherwise valid subpoenas for the latter items.[29]

(c) **Reciprocity Limitations.** At one time, virtually every jurisdiction had adopted the rule that the prosecution could not obtain discovery from the defense unless the defense first requested disclosure from the prosecution. But the clear trend today is to grant the prosecution independent discovery, unconditioned on any requests by the defense (although typically limited to the kinds of information the defense would be authorized to receive had it made a request).[30] The question thus arises whether reciprocity is constitutionally required or whether, instead, it is permissible for the prosecution to obtain information from the defense even when the defense refrains from requesting discovery.

The reciprocity idea apparently is based on a waiver notion; that is, the defense should be able to control its information until it waives that control by requesting information from the prosecution. But if the rationale for discovery is the avoidance of surprise and the thorough preparation of adversaries, then the prosecution should not be barred from obtaining information simply because the defense decides it does not need anything from the prosecution. Or, if the concern is that the defense will otherwise be unable to protect unfavorable information, protective orders are available. In short, independent discovery, as a general matter, would not seem violative of any constitutional provision, provided that, as applied, it does not infringe upon the defendant's Fifth or Sixth Amendment rights.

(d) **Sanctions on Defense.** The particular sanction to be imposed for violation of a discovery rule is usually left to the trial court's discretion and will not implicate constitutional issues. In *Taylor v. Illinois*,[31] however, the Supreme Court was confronted with the argument that the ultimate sanction of excluding evidence, when imposed on the defense, violates the defendant's right to present evidence on his behalf (under the Compulsory Process Clause of the Sixth Amendment). The trial court in *Taylor* had excluded the testimony of a defense witness who had not been listed prior to trial as required by the rules of discovery, despite counsel's awareness of his existence at least a week prior to trial. The Court found both that exclusion of evidence does not, per se,

---

29. For a discussion of Fifth Amendment restrictions on such subpoenas, see § 24.02(a)(4).

30. As of 1986, fourteen states require the defense to disclose names and addresses of all defense witnesses, twelve states give the prosecution an independent right to obtain the statements of all defense witnesses, sixteen states make documents and tangible objects independently available, and twenty-two states similarly allow discovery of expert reports. Mosteller, supra note 17, at 1580–82.

31. 484 U.S. 400, 108 S.Ct. 646 (1988).

violate the Compulsory Process Clause, and then found the sanction in this case was appropriate.

The Court first noted that the right to present evidence is not absolute, pointing to its decision in *Nobles,* where exclusion was permitted because of the attorney's failure to cooperate at trial. The defendant in *Taylor* argued that this type of case was different, because the court had available to it a less drastic sanction—such as a continuance or disciplinary action against the attorney—that would still preserve the adversarial process emphasized in *Nobles.* But the Supreme Court noted that less drastic sanctions might also be less effective. Because a primary purpose of the discovery rules is to "minimize the risk that fabricated testimony will be believed," and because it is "reasonable to assume that there is something suspect about a defense witness who is not identified until after the eleventh hour has passed," exclusion might be appropriate, particularly where, as here, the failure to list the witness was found to be "willful and blatant" by the trial judge.

The Court did not consider important the fact that allowing the unlisted witness to testify probably would not have prejudiced the prosecution in this case (because the trial judge, prior to ordering exclusion, had conducted a voir dire of the witness in the presence of the prosecutor). According to the Court, "[m]ore is at stake than possible prejudice to the prosecution;" also important is "the impact of this conduct on the integrity of the judicial process itself." Nor did the Court accept the argument of the three dissenters that the sins of the lawyer should not be visited on the client, since "it would be highly impracticable to require an investigation into the . . . relative responsibility [of the attorney and the client] before applying the sanction of preclusion."

24.03 Discovery by the Defense

In the typical case, the defense is more in need of discovery than the prosecution. The government is usually the first on the crime scene, has quality investigative expertise, and possesses formidable financial resources. Operating on its own, the defense team, often court appointed, will normally not have the same access to evidence or the same ability to interpret it as the government. Because it helps equalize the contest between the state and the defendant, extensive discovery by the defense is seen by some as a particularly important aspect of the criminal justice system,[32] and could be said to be required by either the Due

---

32. Goldstein, "The State and the Accused: Balance of Advantage in   Criminal Procedure," 69 Yale L.J. 1149 (1960).

Process Clause, the Compulsory Process Clause, or the right to effective assistance of counsel.[33]

Yet a constitutional basis for extensive defense discovery has not developed. Illustrative is the Supreme Court's decision in *Cicenia v. La Gay*,[34] which held that, while it may be "better practice" to give the defense a record of the defendant's confession prior to trial, failing to do so does not violate due process. As discussed in the next section, the courts have recognized a constitutional right to exculpatory information. And, as discussed below, the prosecution is also required by the Due Process Clause to make reciprocal disclosure under some circumstances. But many jurisdictions remain cautious about permitting defense discovery of evidence beyond these minima. This is unfortunate, not only because it impairs defense preparation for plea negotiation and trial, but also because, to the extent the reciprocity doctrine operates, it limits prosecutorial discovery as well.

(a) Mandatory Reciprocal Disclosure by the Prosecution. In *Wardius v. Oregon*,[35] the Supreme Court struck down a notice-of-alibi statute which did not require, in return, that the prosecution notify the defense of any witnesses it intended to offer in rebuttal to the alibi:

> [I]n the absence of a strong showing of state interests to the contrary, discovery must be a two-way street. The State may not insist that trial be run as a "search for truth" so far as defense witnesses are concerned, while maintaining "poker game" secrecy for its own witnesses. It is fundamentally unfair to require a defendant to divulge the details of his own case while at the same time subjecting him to the hazard of surprise concerning refutation of the very pieces of evidence which he disclosed to the State.

This language would seem to extend beyond notice-of-alibi statutes to require prosecutorial disclosure of rebuttal witnesses whenever the state requires the defense to divulge its witnesses supporting a particular defense.

(b) Limitations on Defense Discovery. *Wardius* could perhaps be stretched to stand for the proposition that the scope of discovery by the defense should be, at a minimum, as extensive as prosecution discovery, at least unless the state makes "a strong showing of state interests to the contrary." But even assuming the defense is generally entitled to discovery equivalent to that provided the prosecution, broad discovery is not guaranteed. The

33. See, e.g., Westen, "The Compulsory Process Clause," 73 Mich.L.Rev. 71, 121–32 (1974).

34. 357 U.S. 504, 78 S.Ct. 1297 (1958).

35. 412 U.S. 470, 93 S.Ct. 2208 (1973).

scope of defense discovery can still be kept narrow, either by limiting prosecution discovery or by readily finding a "strong state interest" in non-disclosure.

The state interests ranged against granting the defense substantial access to the prosecution's files were summarized by the court in *State v. Eads:* [36]

> (1) It would afford the defendant increased opportunity to produce perjured testimony and to fabricate evidence to meet the State's case; (2) witnesses would be subject to bribe, threat and intimidation; (3) since the State cannot compel the defendant to disclose . . . evidence [protected by the Fifth Amendment], disclosure by the State would afford the defendant an unreasonable advantage at trial; and (4) disclosure is unnecessary in any event because of the other sources of information which defendant has under existing law.

These types of concerns have led some jurisdictions to curtail defense discovery in various ways. For instance, the reciprocity doctrine can be seen as a means of inhibiting scattershot discovery requests by the defense. Additionally, to prevent perjury and witness intimidation, many jurisdictions do not permit witness depositions for discovery purposes, but only to preserve testimony.[37] For the same reasons, the federal courts, pursuant to the so-called Jencks Act, prohibit disclosure of witness identities and statements until the witness has testified at trial,[38] a rule followed by many states.[39]

The limitation on witness-related information is particularly damaging to the defense. It ensures that this information will be unavailable during plea negotiations. It hampers preparation for trial. And it disrupts the trial process, since the defense may need a continuance to analyze the pretrial statements obtained for the first time at trial. As noted in the introduction to this chapter, many states now have provisions calling for disclosure of such information prior to trial. And some courts have softened the impact of the Jencks Act and similar provisions by permitting pretrial disclosure when the defendant can show hardship would otherwise result.[40]

36. 166 N.W.2d 766 (Iowa 1969).

37. See, e.g., Fed.R.Crim.P. 15(a); Wyo.R.Crim.P. 17. But see, West's Fla. S.A.R.Crim.P. 3.220(d).

38. 18 U.S.C.A. § 3500. See also, Fed.R.Crim.P. 16(a)(2) and 26.2. The type of "statement" to which the defense is entitled includes only those which are "signed or otherwise adopted or approved" by the witness. *Goldberg v. United States,* 425 U.S. 94, 96 S.Ct. 1338 (1976).

39. See, e.g., N.Y.—McKinney's Crim.P.Law § 240.45. Many of these states also bar *all* prosecution access to statements of defense witnesses, apparently due to the reciprocity notion, but this merely compounds the misery. See § 24.02(c).

40. For an example of such a decision, and a good description of the injustice and inefficiency caused by the Jencks Act, see *United States v. Algie,* 503 F.Supp. 783 (E.D.Ky.1980). The

These efforts at broadening defense discovery are warranted, since the points made in *Eads* do not withstand close analysis. The danger that pretrial discovery will increase perjury is exaggerated: even with no pretrial discovery, the dishonest defendant will be able to change his story to fit the prosecution's facts, because he hears the prosecution's case before he puts on his own evidence. In any event, rather than shackling defense discovery in all cases, the best way to deal with the possibility of perjury is on a case-by-case basis through protective orders and the threat of perjury prosecution. Similarly, intimidation or bribery of witnesses not already known to the defendant is a rare event which can be inhibited through protective orders, letting the defense know the prosecution already has signed statements by the witness, and the threat of criminal and disciplinary action. The defendant's right to remain silent is a fundamental tenet of the accusatorial system which should not work to deny the defendant access to information; moreover, as the preceding section made clear,[41] the Fifth Amendment only prevents prosecution access to *self*-incriminating material possessed by the defense, and does not preclude discovery of most material the defense plans to use at trial. And finally, other sources of "discovery," such as the preliminary hearing, the suppression hearing, or the bill of particulars, are neither dependable nor routine and, in any event, should not be manipulated when fairer, more straightforward discovery devices can be devised.[42]

Some have even argued that the defense's need for information is so great and the prosecution's so minimal that unconditional discovery by the defense is warranted. As explained by the American Bar Association's advisory committee on discovery:

> If disclosure to the accused promotes finality, orderliness, and efficiency in prosecution generally, these gains should not depend upon the possible capricious willingness of the accused to make reciprocal discovery. . . . Certainly, the usual reasons for denying disclosure to the accused—dangers of "perjury of intimidation of witness"—are not alleviated by forcing the defendant to make discovery, nor are they heightened by his failure to disclose.[43]

Given the fear that the prosecution would be unfairly disadvantaged if reciprocal disclosure were denied, the courts and legislatures have not supported the ABA's idea.

Sixth Circuit, construing the Jencks Act strictly, reluctantly reversed the district court. 667 F.2d 569 (6th Cir.1982).

41. See § 24.02(a).

42. Note that many courts specifically reject use of the preliminary hearing as a discovery device, citing the existence of more formal discovery mechanisms. See § 22.04(c).

43. ABA Standards Relating to Discovery and Procedure Before Trial, Commentary to § 1.2, at 45 (Approved Draft 1970).

24.04 The Constitutional Duty to Disclose Exculpatory Information

The discovery rules discussed previously are concerned primarily with ensuring that each party knows what the other side will present at trial. With a few exceptions, they do not require revelation of material unfavorable to the disclosing side. This pattern follows the paradigm of discovery in civil cases. But, in a departure from that paradigm, the Supreme Court has held that the Constitution requires the prosecution to reveal exculpatory information, a duty which goes far beyond any constitutional or statutory obligation on the part of the defense to provide incriminating items.[44] This section discusses the scope of this prosecutorial duty to disclose.

(a) The Duty to Reveal False Testimony. The broad duty to disclose exculpatory information was presaged by a series of decisions requiring the prosecutor to reveal perjured testimony by a prosecution witness. In *Mooney v. Holohan*,[45] the prosecutor allegedly procured perjured testimony to convict the defendant. The Court had no trouble finding that due process was violated when the government "has contrived a conviction through the pretense of a trial which in truth is but used as a means of depriving a defendant of liberty through a deliberate deception of court and jury by the presentation of testimony known to be perjured." In its next case, *Alcorta v. Texas*,[46] the Court made clear that solicitation of perjured testimony was not necessary in order to find a due process violation; even perjury that is purely the witness' must be corrected if discovered by the prosecutor.

In *Napue v. Illinois*,[47] the Court held that due process is violated not only by perjury concerning the facts of the case (as in *Mooney* and *Alcorta*), but also by fabrication relating to the credibility of the witness. In *Napue*, a witness falsely stated that the prosecutor had not promised him lenient treatment for his testimony. The Court concluded that the prosecutor's failure to correct this statement required reversal of the conviction, since "[t]he jury's estimate of the truthfulness and reliability of a given witness may well be determinative of guilt or innocence, and it is upon such subtle factors as the possible interest of the witness in testifying falsely that a defendant's life or liberty may depend." The facts in *Giglio v. United States*[48] were similar to *Napue* except

44. Note that ethical guidelines may impose further obligations on the defense attorney. Compare, e.g., the cases described in § 24.04(a) with ABA Model Rules of Professional Conduct § 3.3(a)(4) (prohibiting lawyer from offering evidence he knows to be false and requiring correction of evidence he later finds to have been false).

45. 294 U.S. 103, 55 S.Ct. 340 (1935).

46. 355 U.S. 28, 78 S.Ct. 103 (1957).

47. 360 U.S. 264, 79 S.Ct. 1173 (1959).

48. 405 U.S. 150, 92 S.Ct. 763 (1972).

that the promise of leniency came from another prosecutor, unbeknownst to the examining attorney. Even here, the Court required reversal, since "a promise made by one attorney must be attributed, for these purposes, to the Government." These cases expressed strong support for the notion that any use of false testimony requires reversal, at least when the testimony is important to the case.[49]

(b) The Brady–Agurs–Bagley Materiality Test. In *Brady v. Maryland*,[50] the Court announced a rule that, in effect, subsumed the false testimony cases, by making unconstitutional the failure to provide any "exculpatory" information to the defendant. As Justice Douglas stated for the Court: "Society wins not only when the guilty are convicted but when criminal trials are fair; our system of the administration of justice suffers when any accused is treated unfairly." Thus, "the suppression by the prosecution of evidence favorable to an accused upon request violates due process where the evidence is material either to guilt or to punishment, irrespective of the good faith or bad faith of the prosecution."

In *Brady*, this test was applied to require reversal of the defendant's death sentence for murder. Prior to trial, Brady's attorney had requested that the prosecution provide the pretrial statements of Brady's co-defendant. While the prosecution did hand over most of the statements, for some reason it did not provide the portion in which the co-defendant had asserted that he committed the murder. This statement would have made no difference at trial, since co-defendants in a murder case were equally guilty under state law, regardless of who pulled the trigger. But, finding that this information could easily have affected the sentencing body, the Supreme Court required a new sentencing proceeding.

Several questions were left unanswered by *Brady*, including how "material" information must be before due process requires its disclosure, and whether the defense has to make a request for the information in order to trigger the prosecution's duty to disclose. In *United States v. Agurs*,[51] the Court clarified both of these points to some extent. In *Agurs*, the defendant had stabbed and killed a male companion with the latter's knife during a brief interlude at a motel. She pleaded self-defense, but was convicted of second degree murder. In arguing for reversal, the defense noted that the prosecutor had failed to disclose that the victim had a prior criminal record (including guilty pleas to charges of assault and carrying a deadly weapon).

49. See also, *Giles v. Maryland*, 386 U.S. 66, 87 S.Ct. 793 (1967).

50. 373 U.S. 83, 83 S.Ct. 1194 (1963).

51. 427 U.S. 97, 96 S.Ct. 2392 (1976).

The Supreme Court found that this information did not have to be disclosed under *Brady* because it was not "material" enough, which in turn depended in part on the fact that the defense made no request for it. Justice Stevens, who wrote the Court's opinion, divided the due process duty to disclose into three types. The first was represented by the *Mooney* line of cases. When the prosecutor relies on perjured testimony, he must disclose it if "there is any reasonable likelihood that the false testimony could have affected the judgment of the jury," i.e., most of the time. The second type of duty was represented by *Brady,* where the defense made a specific request for the allegedly exculpatory information. Here again disclosure should be the normal response, because a specific request puts the prosecution on notice that the evidence may be exculpatory. When there is a request, "it is reasonable to require the prosecutor to respond either by furnishing the information or by submitting the problem to the trial judge," and "the failure to make any response is seldom, if ever, excusable." Although Stevens did not explicitly say so, the materiality standard for these first two situations appeared similar to the standard the Court had earlier adopted for determining whether constitutional error is harmless in *Chapman v. California.*[52]

The third situation occurs when the defense makes either no request (as in *Agurs*) or a general request for "all *Brady* material" or "anything exculpatory," requests which Stevens equated with no request. Here, Stevens stated, a conviction will be overturned for failure to provide information only if it creates a reasonable doubt in the mind of the trial judge as to the defendant's guilt. This standard apparently gives more leeway to the prosecutor than the *Chapman* standard, since it depends upon what the judge thinks about the defendant's guilt, not on how the jury would have voted had it had the evidence in front of it. Stevens seemed to believe this difference was justified because, in a no request situation, the prosecutor will have more difficulty deciding what evidence may be exculpatory.

Assuming there is a realistic difference between the two materiality tests developed in *Agurs,* that decision's emphasis on the existence of a specific request can be questioned, given the fact that the defense often has no idea what kind of information the prosecutor may possess. In the Court's next major decision interpreting *Brady, United States v. Bagley,*[53] this distinction was apparently eliminated. At the same time, however, the Court seemed to reject the *Chapman*/harmless error as the test of "materiality," and instead adopted a narrower definition of that

---

52. 386 U.S. 18, 87 S.Ct. 824 (1967), discussed in § 29.05(c).

53. 473 U.S. 667, 105 S.Ct. 3375 (1985).

central aspect of *Brady,* regardless of the type of information involved or the existence of a request.

In *Bagley,* there was a specific request for information about "any deals, promises or inducements made to [government] witnesses in exchange for their testimony." Yet the prosecution not only failed to inform the defense that such financial inducements had been made to two witnesses, it also forwarded affidavits from those witnesses that concluded with the statement that they were made without any threats or rewards or promises of reward. Nonetheless, five members of the Court found no violation of *Brady,* applying a standard of whether "there is a reasonable probability that, had the evidence been disclosed to the defense, the result of the proceeding would be different." [54] Justice Blackmun, in an opinion joined by Justice O'Connor, explicitly equated this standard with that developed in *Agurs* for no request and general request situations. Three other members of the Court appeared to agree with this equation, and stated further that this standard "is sufficiently flexible to cover all instances of prosecutorial failure to disclose evidence favorable to the accused," including, apparently, the use of perjured testimony. Thus, after *Bagley,* the prosecutor is governed by the "reasonable probability" test in all situations; the "any reasonable likelihood" or harmless error test used in *Agurs* for false testimony and specific requests has been abandoned.

In dissent, Justice Marshall argued that the majority's test created an incentive for prosecutors "to gamble, to play the odds, and to take a chance that evidence will later turn out not to have been potentially dispositive." As Marshall noted, the government's legitimate interest in nondisclosure prior to trial is "minimal;" after trial, its interest in avoiding a retrial because of nondisclosure is greater, but should not be given so much weight that it encourages failure to disclose prior to trial.[55] The proper test, at least when the prosecutor has a sufficient idea of what the defense is seeking, should be the *Chapman*/harmless error standard, because it is more likely to encourage disclosure of information when there is any doubt as to its exculpatory nature and to ensure that the subsequent adjudication will be truly "fair."

---

54. In developing this standard, Blackmun relied on the rule for determining when government deportation of witnesses constitutes a denial of the right to present evidence, *United States v. Valenzuela–Bernal,* 458 U.S. 858, 102 S.Ct. 3440 (1982), discussed in § 28.06(b), and the rule for determining when effective assistance of counsel has been denied. *Strickland v. Washington,* 466 U.S. 668, 104 S.Ct. 2052 (1984), discussed in § 32.03(b).

55. Cf. *United States v. Oxman,* 740 F.2d 1298 (3d Cir.1984), judgment vac'd 473 U.S. 922, 105 S.Ct. 3550 (1985) (discussing "disturbing" prosecutorial tendency to withhold information because of later opportunity to argue, with the benefit of hindsight, that information was not "material.").

The facts of *Bagley* illustrate the point. As the Court noted in *Napue*, "such subtle factors as the possible interest of the witness in testifying falsely" can affect the jury's determination. Thus, the prosecution should not only be required, as in *Napue*, to correct false testimony denying incentives to testify were offered, but also to provide information about such incentives. This is especially so when the defense has made a specific request, both because such a request indicates a belief that the information may be important and because a failure to respond will mislead the defense into believing that investigation (and cross-examination) is unnecessary on this point.[56] Although Blackmun's opinion recognized this latter problem, it contended that the "reasonable probability" test is flexible enough to take such possibilities into account. The fact that Blackmun concluded due process was not violated in *Bagley* suggests otherwise.[57]

The Court has also made clear that, just as good faith on the part of the prosecutor normally does not affect materiality analysis (per its decision in *Giglio*),[58] neither does bad faith conduct. *Brady* itself stated that the rule it announced was aimed at assuring a fair trial, not at correcting prosecutorial misconduct. This point was reemphasized in *Smith v. Phillips*,[59] in which the Court refused to reverse a conviction by a jury which had included a juror who had actively pursued a job with the prosecutor's office throughout the trial. Noting that the trial judge had found no evidence of actual bias on the part of the juror, the Court stated that while it could not condone the failure of the prosecutor to discover and report the juror's activities in a timely fashion, "the touchstone of due process analysis [in *Brady*] cases is the fairness of the trial, not the culpability of the prosecutor."

(c) **The Decisionmaker.** Three different decisionmakers could make the materiality determination: defense counsel, the trial judge, or the prosecutor. Clearly, the defense attorney is the person best equipped to make the decision as to what is "material" to his case. But such an approach would subvert an important

---

56. Cf. *People v. Vilardi*, 76 N.Y.2d 67, 556 N.Y.S. 518, 555 N.E.2d 915 (1990) (rejecting *Bagley's* reasonable probability standard and adopting, as a matter of state law, a "reasonable possibility" definition of materiality when there is a specific request).

57. Automatic disclosure of some types of impeachment evidence might deter witnesses from being completely forthcoming with the prosecutor. But even assuming this is a concern that should trump the defendant's (and the state's) interest in a fair trial, it does not apply in *Bagley*, where the impeach-

ment evidence was a prosecutorial promise, not compromising statements by the witness.

58. See § 24.04(a). The courts have not yet resolved the extent to which the prosecutor is responsible for divulging information known by another law enforcement entity. See, e.g., *Johnson v. Bennett*, 386 F.2d 677 (8th Cir.1967), vac'd 393 U.S. 253, 89 S.Ct. 436 (1968); *Grant v. Alldredge*, 498 F.2d 376 (2d Cir.1974).

59. 455 U.S. 209, 102 S.Ct. 940 (1982).

premise of *Brady:* that the prosecution need not turn over its entire file to the defense. The Supreme Court has reiterated this premise in *Pennsylvania v. Ritchie.*[60] There, the Pennsylvania Supreme Court had ordered the state child welfare agency to provide defense counsel with files concerning the defendant's daughter, who was allegedly raped by the defendant; under the order, counsel would then make arguments in favor of disclosure at trial. The Supreme Court reversed, holding that the "defendant's right to discover exculpatory evidence does not include the unsupervised authority to search through the Commonwealth's files." As the Court pointed out, "[s]ettled practice is to the contrary," particularly where, as here, confidentiality concerns are significant.

The Court did order that the case be remanded, with the suggestion that the trial judge review the files *in camera* and decide what information, if any, was material to the defendant's case. Apparently the Court felt this suggestion appropriate because the file did contain statements by the victim, as well as other possibly highly significant information. However, *Ritchie* did not hold, and most courts are reluctant to hold, that such *in camera* review *must* take place upon defense request. The typical holding is that the *Brady* rule "does not make it incumbent upon the trial judge to rummage through the file on behalf of the defendant."[61] In *Ritchie* itself, the Court stated in a footnote that the defendant "may not require the trial court to search through the . . . file without first establishing a basis for his claim that it contains material evidence."

As this language suggests, however, if the defendant is able to make a particularized showing that the prosecution may have exculpatory information, a hearing may be required. In *DeMarco v. United States,*[62] the Supreme Court directed that an evidentiary hearing be held on the defendant's claim that the prosecutor had made an undisclosed promise of leniency to a witness prior to his testimony, based on proof of certain remarks the prosecutor made during the sentencing proceeding. Upon being presented with this type of information, the Court concluded, the trial court should investigate the issue. Presumably, had the same remarks been made prior to trial, the defense could have obtained court intervention as well, if the prosecutor had not cooperated.

When the defense is unable to make such a showing that exculpatory information may exist, the prosecutor generally makes the decision on the materiality issue. This arrangement

---

60. 480 U.S. 39, 107 S.Ct. 989 (1987).

61. *United States v. Frazier,* 394 F.2d 258 (4th Cir.1968), cert. denied 393 U.S. 984, 89 S.Ct. 457 (1968). See also, *United States v. Gonzalez,* 466 F.2d 1286 (5th Cir.1972).

62. 415 U.S. 449, 94 S.Ct. 1185 (1974).

might not be troubling if, as recommended by the dissent in *Bagley*, the prosecutor resolves doubtful questions in favor of disclosure. But, for reasons discussed above, the majority opinion in *Bagley* is likely to encourage stinginess on the part of the prosecution.

(d) Timing of the Disclosure. As noted in the introduction to this chapter, many jurisdictions are moving toward pretrial disclosure of routine discovery items. But most courts hold that a *Brady* disclosure need not be made prior to trial. To some extent, this is based on the familiar fear that extensive pretrial disclosure might damage the adversary nature of the system.[63] Further, at least one court has contended that the materiality standard "can only be sensibly applied to the suppression of evidence throughout the trial." [64]

Ultimately, however, courts which have limited *Brady* to disclosure at trial do so not on conceptual grounds but in the belief that, on the facts of the case before them, the defense still had an opportunity to make use of any information revealed. In *United States v. Baxter,*[65] for example, the government's failure to supply the defense with certain evidence prior to trial did not constitute a denial of due process, because the defendants had at least two weeks prior to the conclusion of the trial to examine, evaluate, and introduce any evidence which had come to their attention. Similarly, in *United States v. Harris,*[66] the Third Circuit held that the disclosure of the prosecution's agreement to help one of its witnesses was made in "timely fashion" so long as such disclosure occurred before the conclusion of the witness' trial testimony.

The Supreme Court itself has held that, in at least one type of situation, the prosecution has no duty to reveal favorable information until the day of trial. In *Weatherford v. Bursey,*[67] a federal undercover agent had been arrested with the respondent for vandalism and later met with the respondent and his counsel at strategy sessions. On the day of trial, the prosecutor called the agent to testify as to the events surrounding the vandalism. The defendant contended that the concealment of the agent's identity until the day of trial violated *Brady*. But the Court upheld the prosecutor's conduct on the ground that nothing in the language or analysis of *Brady* requires the prosecutor to disclose before trial the names of all witnesses who will testify unfavorably to the accused.

63. See, e.g., *United States v. Evans,* 454 F.2d 813 (8th Cir.1972).

64. *United States v. McPartlin,* 595 F.2d 1321 (7th Cir.1979).

65. 492 F.2d 150 (9th Cir.1973), cert. denied 416 U.S. 940, 94 S.Ct. 1945 (1974).

66. 498 F.2d 1164 (3d Cir.1974), cert. denied 419 U.S. 1069, 95 S.Ct. 655 (1974).

67. 429 U.S. 545, 97 S.Ct. 837 (1977).

Most of the courts that have not limited *Brady* to disclosure at trial focus on the importance of possibly exculpatory information to defense trial preparation. Illustrative is *Grant v. Alldredge.*[68] There, the government did not disclose until trial that an eyewitness had identified a photograph of someone other than the defendant as the perpetrator of the crime. After speculating that, armed with this information, the defense could have learned more about the identified person, the Second Circuit ordered a new trial, concluding that skilled counsel may have been able to induce a reasonable doubt in the minds of the jurors had it come by the information earlier in the proceedings.[69]

Unless there is fear of witness intimidation, information which is clearly "material" to the defendant's case under *Agurs* and *Bagley* should be disclosed early enough to allow the defense adequate preparation time to make use of it. Disclosure at trial will rarely meet this test. The courts' fear that pretrial disclosure will somehow disadvantage the prosecutor is exaggerated and contrary to the spirit of *Brady.*

24.05 The Constitutional Duty to Preserve Evidence

Obviously related to the prosecutorial duty to disclose exculpatory evidence is the duty to preserve such evidence for possible use by the defendant. However, as Justice Marshall pointed out for the Court in *California v. Trombetta,*[70] when evidence has been destroyed, not only is its exculpatory value more difficult to evaluate, but a decision in favor of the defendant will bar further prosecution rather than, as in the typical *Brady* situation, merely call for a new trial with the suppressed evidence. Thus, when the defendant makes the claim that exculpatory evidence was destroyed, he has a heavier burden then in the typical *Brady* case. He must not only show that the evidence might have been "expected to play a significant role in the suspect's defense," and that it was of "such a nature that the defendant would be unable to obtain comparable evidence by other reasonably available means," but he must also show that the failure to preserve the evidence resulted from "official animus toward [the defendant] or . . . a conscious effort to suppress exculpatory evidence." This latter requirement obviously departs from the *Brady* standard, which considered prosecutorial intent irrelevant.

In *Trombetta* the state failed to preserve a breath sample taken by police from a suspected drunk driver and tested by them on an instrument that analyzes breath-alcohol levels. The California Court of Appeal ruled that due process required police officers

68. 498 F.2d 376 (2d Cir.1974).

69. See also *United States v. Donatelli,* 484 F.2d 505 (1st Cir.1973).

70. 467 U.S. 479, 104 S.Ct. 2528 (1984).

to "establish and follow rigorous and systematic procedures to preserve the captured evidence or its equivalent for the use of the defendant." But a unanimous Supreme Court rejected this rule and found that the defendant here was able to demonstrate neither exculpatory value or official animus. According to the Court, tests of the breath samples by the defendant would normally merely confirm the results obtained by the state; if inaccuracies in the state's results did occur, they could be shown by other means, such as proof that the machine malfunctioned or that the officer who administered the test erred in operating the machine. Nor was there evidence the police acted in bad faith when they destroyed the breath samples; rather they did so according to routine practice.

While the *Trombetta* Court considered the absence of bad faith relevant, it appeared to put the most stress on the failure of the defendant to prove the evidence destroyed had a unique exculpatory value. In *Arizona v. Youngblood,*[71] however, the Court held that "unless a criminal defendant can show bad faith on the part of the police, failure to preserve potentially useful evidence does not constitute due process of law." Chief Justice Rehnquist, writing for the Court, justified this ruling on two grounds. First, he noted, as had the *Trombetta* Court, "the treacherous task of divining the import of materials whose contents are unknown and, very often, disputed." Second, he expressed an "unwillingness to read the 'fundamental fairness' requirement of the Due Process Clause . . . as imposing on the police an undifferentiated and absolute duty to retain and to preserve all material that might be of conceivable evidentiary significance in a particular prosecution." Thus, the behavior of the police now appears to be the key issue in preservation of evidence cases, at least when there is doubt as to the exculpatory significance of the lost or destroyed evidence.

In *Youngblood,* the defendant was convicted of sexual assault of a ten-year old boy. On appeal the defendant argued that the state's failure to perform tests of semen samples taken from the victim shortly after they were obtained, and to refrigerate the boy's clothing (in order to preserve the semen on it), violated due process. Experts at trial had testified that prompt tests might have exonerated the defendant had they been performed. But the Supreme Court found that at most the failure to preserve and test the semen samples was "negligent." In a concurring opinion, Justice Stevens emphasized the latter point, asserting that the interest of the police and the prosecution in preserving the evidence during the investigation phase of a case is "at least as great" as the accused's. He also noted that the defense attorney

71. 488 U.S. 51, 109 S.Ct. 333 (1988).

had emphasized the state's failure to preserve the evidence at trial, and that the court had told the jury that if it found the state "had allowed [the evidence] to be lost or destroyed," it could infer the evidence was exculpatory.

In dissent, Justice Blackmun rejected the Court's focus on police behavior. He asserted that "it makes no sense to ignore the fact that a defendant has been denied a fair trial because the State allowed evidence that was material to the defense to deteriorate beyond the point of usefulness, simply because police were inept rather than malicious." He also questioned the ability of the courts to determine when police have in fact acted in bad faith, as opposed to recklessly or negligently. Instead he proposed the following test: "where no comparable evidence is likely to be available to the defendant, police must preserve physical evidence of a type that they reasonably should know has the potential, if tested, to reveal immutable characteristics of the criminal, and hence to exculpate a defendant charged with crime." On the facts of *Youngblood,* Blackmun argued that this test was met; he also noted that the only evidence implicating the defendant was the testimony of the ten-year old victim.

24.06 Conclusion

Pretrial disclosure of information can facilitate preparation for trial, avoid surprise, and promote efficiency. It may also serve to equalize an investigative process normally weighted in favor of the state. The following observations can be made about statutory and constitutional pretrial disclosure rules.

(1) The typical jurisdiction at a minimum permits defense discovery of the defendant's statements in the prosecutor's possession, as well as documents, tangible objects and test results in the prosecution's possession which are material to the defendant's case, on condition that the defense reciprocate with like items (other than the defendant's statements) which it intends to introduce at trial. The defense is also typically entitled to any pretrial statements of government witnesses either at the time they testify or at some earlier point.

(2) Although the Fifth Amendment generally protects against compelled disclosure of incriminating information from the defendant, the defendant may be compelled to give notice of witnesses he intends to call in support of an alibi defense, so long as the prosecution is also required to disclose rebuttal witnesses. This accelerated disclosure rationale probably also permits requiring the defendant to reveal most other evidence he plans to use at trial. Moreover, neither the Fifth nor Sixth Amendment permits the defendant to withhold statements, other than his own, the existence of which the prosecution is aware and which might

assist in challenging the defendant's evidence at trial. However, the Sixth Amendment may prevent pretrial disclosure of the identity of, or statements from, persons the defendant does not plan to use at trial.

(3) In addition to the state's statutory obligations outlined in (1), the Due Process Clause imposes a limited duty upon the state to provide the defense with any other information "material" to its case. Specifically, a new trial is required if: (a) the prosecutor fails to disclose that a prosecution witness perjured himself, and there is a reasonable probability the perjured testimony would have affected the factfinder's verdict; (b) the prosecutor fails to disclose other information, whether specifically requested by the defense or not, and there is a reasonable probability that, had the information been disclosed to the defense, the result of the proceeding would have been different; or (c) the state intentionally and in bad faith destroys evidence possessing an exculpatory value apparent before the evidence was destroyed and of such a nature that the defendant would be unable to obtain comparable evidence by other reasonably available means.

(4) It is normally up to the prosecutor to decide whether particular information should be disclosed under the above standards, although a colorable claim that he possesses exculpatory information should require an *in camera* perusal of the prosecutor's files by the trial court. If it is decided information should be disclosed, the best practice will normally be to do so prior to trial in order to permit the defense adequate time to prepare its case, although many courts have sanctioned disclosure at trial so long as the defendant has some time to evaluate the evidence.

BIBLIOGRAPHY

Blumenson, Eric. Constitutional Limitations on Prosecutorial Discovery. 18 Harv.Civ.R.-Civ.L. 122 (1983).

Brennan, William. The Criminal Prosecution: Sporting Event or Quest for Truth? 1963 Wash.U.L.Q. 279.

Burkland, Mark E. Federal Rule of Criminal Procedure 26.2: The Impact on Unsettled Jencks Act Issues. 1981 U.Ill.L.F. 897 (1981).

Capra, Daniel J. Access to Exculpatory Evidence: Avoiding the *Agurs* Problems of Prosecutorial Discretion and Retrospective Review. 53 Ford.L.Rev. 391 (1984).

Feldman, Steven W. The Work Product Rule in Criminal Practice and Procedure. 50 U.Cin.L.Rev. 495 (1981).

Fleming, Susan. Defendant Access to Prosecution Witness Statements in Federal and State Criminal Cases. 61 Wash.U.L.Q. 471 (1983).

Imwinkelreid, Edward J. The Applicability of the Attorney-Client Privilege to Non-Testifying Experts. 68 Wash.U.L.Q. 19 (1990).

Lawry, Robert P. Lying, Confidentiality, and the Adversary System of Justice. 1977 Utah L.Rev. 653 (1977).

Mosteller, Robert P. Discovery Against the Defense: Tilting the Adversarial Balance. 74 Cal.L.Rev. 1567 (1986).

Nakell, Barry. Criminal Discovery for the Defense and the Prosecution—The Developing Constitutional Considerations. 50 N.C.L.Rev. 437 (1972).

Nimmer, Raymond T. Prosecutor Disclosure and Judicial Reform: The Omnibus Hearing in Two Courts. Chicago: American Bar Foundation, 1975.

Tomlinson, Edward A. Constitutional Limitations on Prosecutorial Discovery. 23 San Diego L.Rev. 923 (1986).

Traynor, Robert. Ground Lost and Found in Criminal Discovery. 39 N.Y.U.L.Rev. 228 (1964).

Van Kessel, Gordon. Prosecutorial Discovery and the Privilege Against Self-Incrimination: Accommodation or Capitulation? 4 Hast.Const.L.Q. 855 (1977).

Weninger, Robert A. Criminal Discovery and Omnibus Procedure in a Federal Court: A Defense View. 49 S.Cal.L.Rev. 514 (1976).

Wyrsch, James and Susan Hunt. Specific Requests for Exculpatory Evidence After United States v. Bagley. 55 U.M.K.C.L. Rev. 50 (1986).

Chapter Twenty-Five

THE RIGHT TO SPEEDY TRIAL

25.01 Introduction

The right to speedy trial is explicitly guaranteed by the Sixth Amendment [1] and is applicable to the states through the Fourteenth Amendment.[2] In most jurisdictions, it is also given fairly detailed statutory implementation.[3]

The defendant's interest in securing a speedy trial was first articulated by the Supreme Court in *United States v. Ewell.*[4] There the Court noted that a prompt trial promotes three interests: it (1) prevents undue incarceration; (2) minimizes the anxiety accompanying public accusation; and (3) prevents impairment of the defendant's case due to delay. In *Barker v. Wingo,*[5] the Court elaborated on these points. It noted that if the defendant is detained, the time spent in jail disrupts family life and employment, and hinders the defendant's ability to gather evidence, contact witnesses, and otherwise prepare his case. For defendants on pretrial release, the denial of a speedy trial is less oppressive, but, given the possibility of conditional restraints on liberty, can also result in loss of employment or difficulty in finding work. In either case, noted *Barker*, delay in resolving criminal charges increases the drain on resources, the constraints on associating with others, and the exposure to public obloquy. Most importantly, whether the defendant is in or out of jail, delay may lead to loss of exculpatory evidence: witnesses may die or their memories fade, and tangible evidence may disappear.

Society too has an interest in prompt adjudication, an interest which occasionally may run counter to the defendant's. In *Barker* the Court articulated a number of reasons why society may desire speedy disposition of criminal cases, only one of which is directly associated with concern over the defendant's welfare. First, the Court noted, ensuring speedy trials reduces the likelihood of crimes being committed by those who are free on pretrial release programs. A second concern is the potential damage to the criminal justice system when delay weakens the prosecution's case and a plea bargain or dismissal results. Thirdly, to the extent that rehabilitative measures are put off by lengthy pretrial delays, the chances for success are diminished. Finally, there is substan-

---

1. The Sixth Amendment to the United States Constitution reads in relevant part: "In all criminal prosecutions, the accused shall enjoy the right to a speedy and public trial . . .."

2. *Klopfer v. North Carolina,* 386 U.S. 213, 87 S.Ct. 988 (1967).

3. See § 25.05.

4. 383 U.S. 116, 86 S.Ct. 773 (1966).

5. 407 U.S. 514, 92 S.Ct. 2182 (1972).

tial financial cost and administrative burden associated with lengthy pretrial detention. Indeed, it is probable that the impetus behind speedy trial legislation comes as much from fiscal concerns as it does from a desire to protect the defendant's interests.

Whether the state may *force* a speedy trial on a defendant, as is possible with other Sixth Amendment rights such as the right to jury trial,[6] is not clear. But it should not be overlooked that the accused may suffer from a trial that takes place too quickly. The defendant must be given sufficient time to prepare his case. That this need is sometimes ignored is borne out by the history of the "mass-production" misdemeanor courts.[7] As the Supreme Court put it in *Ewell*: "The essential ingredient is orderly expedition and not mere speed."

The next three sections of this chapter discuss three aspects of the constitutional right to speedy trial: (1) when it attaches; (2) the appropriate remedy for its violation; and (3) the criteria to be considered in deciding whether the right has been violated. The final section examines statutory attempts to implement the speedy trial ideal, focusing in particular on the Federal Speedy Trial Act.

25.02 When the Right Is Implicated

(a) The Post–Accusation Rule. In *United States v. Marion*,[8] the defendants moved to dismiss the indictment against them on speedy trial grounds, claiming that the government had known of their identities for three years prior to the indictment. The Supreme Court rejected their claim, holding that the constitutional guarantee of a speedy trial is applicable only after a person has been "accused" of a crime. According to the Court, an accusation for this purpose does not have to be by way of indictment, information or formal charge, but must at least involve "the actual restraints imposed by arrest and holding to answer on a criminal charge." This result followed from the Sixth Amendment's wording (guaranteeing a right to speedy trial in all "criminal *prosecutions*") as well as the fact that the detention, anxiety, and public obloquy which the right is designed to avoid generally do not occur until this point. The Court also noted that, traditionally, statutes of limitations are designed to prevent the prejudice that might flow from pre-accusation delay.

Even after arrest, the defendant must *remain* charged for the right to speedy trial to be implicated. This was established in *United States v. MacDonald*,[9] where almost four years of delay occurred between the dismissal of the first charges against the

---

6. See § 27.02(g)(2).

7. See Whitebread, C., Mass Production Justice and the Constitutional Ideal (1969).

8. 404 U.S. 307, 92 S.Ct. 455 (1971).

9. 456 U.S. 1, 102 S.Ct. 1497 (1982).

defendant and reindictment on the same charges. Analogizing to the facts of *Marion,* the Court held, 5–4, that "[f]ollowing dismissal of charges, any restraint on liberty, disruption of employment, strain on financial resources, and exposure to public obloquy, stress and anxiety is not greater than it is upon anyone openly subject to a criminal investigation." During the hiatus between the charges, MacDonald had been "free to go about his affairs, to practice his profession, and to continue his life," and thus could not claim Sixth Amendment protection for that period.

In *United States v. Loud Hawk,*[10] the Court held, in another 5–4 decision, that the time period between dismissal of an indictment and its reinstatement should not be considered even if, during that time, the government is pursuing an appeal of the dismissal. Again, because the defendants had been unconditionally released during this period, the Court held that a 46–month period between dismissal and the retrial which followed an appellate court decision in the prosecution's favor was irrelevant to speedy trial analysis. The mere fact that the government's desire to prosecute was a matter of public record did not constitute actual restraint under *Marion.* In dissent, Justice Marshall pointed out that here, unlike in *Marion* and *MacDonald,* the defendants did not have the protection against prolonged pre-accusation delay that is provided by the statute of limitations, since the statute was tolled by the appeal. In further contrast to those cases, the trial court here had the authority, at any time during the appeal, to impose conditions on the defendants' release.

The majority's result is also contrary to the Court's pre-*Marion* decision of *Klopfer v. North Carolina,*[11] in which the Court held that a prosecutorial *nolle prosequi* does not terminate the period of time to be considered for speedy trial purposes. The *nolle prosequi* device is not a dismissal, in that the defendant remains formally accused and can be brought to trial at the whim of the prosecution throughout the time it is in effect. But, functionally, such a defendant is in the same position as the defendants in *Loud Hawk:* he is not under any "actual restraint" and is subject to no more anxiety than the latter defendants suffered awaiting the outcome of the prosecution's appeal. At the same time, in both cases, the defendants were the focus not merely of an investigation but of a formal prosecution, a fact which should implicate the Sixth Amendment.

While the Court has been unwilling to apply the Speedy Trial Clause when no charges are pending, it has also held that, when charges are pending, the Clause is triggered even if the defendant does not know about them and is thus not restrained in any way.

---

10. 474 U.S. 302, 106 S.Ct. 648 (1986).   **11.** 386 U.S. 213, 87 S.Ct. 988 (1967).

This was the unusual situation in *Doggett v. United States,*[12] in which the Court upheld, 5–4, the defendant's speedy trial claim. Doggett had left the country just prior to government attempts to arrest him. Apparently unaware that an indictment on drug dealing charges had been issued against him, he returned to the country two and one-half years later, found a job, and was carrying on a law-abiding life when the government discovered his location through a routine computer check and arrested him 8 and one-half years after the indictment.

In holding that this entire period counted for purposes of speedy trial analysis despite the absence of restraint on the defendant, the majority, in an opinion by Justice Souter, distinguished *Marion, MacDonald,* and *Loudhawk* on the ground that those cases "support nothing beyond the principle . . . that the Sixth Amendment right of the accused to a speedy trial has no application beyond the confines of a formal criminal prosecution." This construction of the caselaw clearly undermines the "actual restraint" rule the Court had been developing as the test for when the Speedy Trial Clause applies. But, in defense of its divergent approach, the majority noted that the Clause is meant to protect against not only pretrial detention and the anxiety associated with criminal charges (effects the defendant in *Doggett* obviously could not claim), but also impairment of the defendant's case. This latter form of prejudice, the majority concluded, must be measured from the time the "criminal prosecution" to which the Sixth Amendment refers begins.

Although, after *Doggett,* arrest or accusation alone triggers the Speedy Trial Clause, it is unlikely this rule will affect the outcome of many cases beyond those which would also implicate the Clause under an actual restraint rule. Defendants are rarely unaware they've been indicted for any length of time, and in those situations where they do know of the charges but evade restraint by avoiding arrest, the resulting delay will be their fault and thus unlikely to help a speedy trial claim.[13] *Doggett* is likely to have an independent impact only in those rare cases where, like *Doggett* itself, the defendant does not know about the charges for a prolonged period, or in cases where the defendant is aware of the indictment and takes no evasive action, but the government inexplicably makes no effort to effectuate arrest.

(b) Pre–Accusation Delay. As *Marion* noted, statutes of limitations may require the state to bring charges within a certain time after an offense occurs. The statute on misdemeanors can range from one to five years, while the limit for felonies may vary from three to ten years. Usually, very serious crimes, such as

12. 505 U.S. ___, 112 S.Ct. 2686 (1992).   **13.** See § 25.04(b).

murder, have no applicable limitation period.[14] Like the speedy trial right, these statutes are designed to ensure that prosecutions are based on reasonably "fresh" evidence.

Marion also recognized, however, that these statutes might not provide sufficient protection against prejudicial pre-accusation delay, in which case due process might be implicated. In the later decision of *United States v. Lovasco,*[15] the Court affirmed that, even if the relevant limitations period has not expired, the Due Process Clause is violated if the delay transgresses "the community's sense of fair play and decency." At the same time, the Court's application of this due process right to the facts of *Lovasco* indicated that it will rarely lead to dismissal of a charge.

In *Lovasco,* two material witnesses died during an eighteen-month delay between the time the government developed sufficient evidence to indict the defendants and the actual indictment. The apparent reason for the delay was a desire to obtain more evidence, even though little new evidence was in fact obtained. The Court held that because thorough investigation can assure against unwarranted prosecutions and relieves the courts of trying insubstantial claims, the government is not obligated to file formal charges as soon as it has probable cause, or even when it has "evidence sufficient to establish guilt." Rather, investigative delay will be unconstitutional only if it is intended "to gain tactical advantage over the accused," or is carried out "in reckless disregard of circumstances . . . suggesting that there existed an appreciable risk that delay would impair the ability to mount an effective defense."

Lovasco's due process test—requiring both prejudice to the defendant's case and prosecutorial bad faith—is not only unduly stringent but incomplete. An important aspect of pre-accusation delay is the extent to which it subjects the individual to the "public obloquy" to which *Barker* refers. A person under public investigation can suffer as much damage to reputation and financial and occupational interests as an arrested person. It would be preferable to allow the individual under investigation (including persons in MacDonald's position, where charges have been dismissed) to force the prosecution either to arrest or to announce it is foregoing prosecution within a reasonable period of time after an investigation becomes public knowledge.

25.03 The Dismissal Remedy

The sole remedy recognized for violation of the constitutional right to speedy trial is dismissal, a fact which has important consequences for the scope of the right. In *Strunk v. United*

14. See West's Fla.S.A.Stat. § 775.15 for an example of typical limitations.

15. 431 U.S. 783, 97 S.Ct. 2044 (1977).

States,[16] the defendant was found guilty of interstate transportation of a stolen vehicle after a ten-month delay between indictment and arraignment. On appeal, the Seventh Circuit Court of Appeals held that the defendant had been denied a speedy trial, but went on to hold that the extreme remedy of dismissal was not warranted, since no loss of evidence had been alleged by the defendant. The case was remanded to the district court for reduction of the defendant's sentence by 259 days to compensate for the unnecessary delay between indictment and arraignment. The United States Supreme Court reversed, holding that when a defendant has been denied a speedy trial, dismissal must remain the *only* possible remedy. The Court based its decision on the rationale that failure to afford a defendant a speedy trial, unlike other guarantees of the Sixth Amendment such as public trial, an impartial jury or compulsory service, cannot be cured by granting a new trial. In particular, the Court noted, the prolonged "emotional stress" suffered while awaiting trial and the possible adverse effect on rehabilitation cannot be rectified through a new proceeding.

As the next section makes clear, the severity of the dismissal remedy, and the concern that it will allow dangerous criminals freedom on a technicality, has made courts loathe to find a deprivation of the speedy trial right in all but the most extreme circumstances. One commentator has contended that the dismissal remedy has converted the speedy trial right from the right of any criminal defendant to have a speedy trial into the right of a few defendants—those most egregiously denied a speedy trial—to have the criminal charges against them dismissed.[17] A more flexible approach would make the remedy depend on which of the three interests protected by the speedy trial right is violated: release if prolonged detention is the concern, dismissal without prejudice if the public obloquy associated with formal charges is at issue, and outright dismissal only if prejudice has occurred.

25.04 The Constitutional Criteria

The Supreme Court's most comprehensive treatment of the Sixth Amendment's speedy trial guarantee came in *Barker v. Wingo*.[18] In that case, the defendant did not explicitly raise his speedy trial right until the prosecution had asked for the last of sixteen continuances, which had stretched over five and one-half years from July, 1958 to October, 1963. The delay, all of which was countable under *Marion*, had resulted from the prosecution's

16. 412 U.S. 434, 93 S.Ct. 2260 (1973).

17. Amsterdam, "Speedy Criminal Trial: Rights and Remedies." 27 Stanford L.Rev. 525 (1975).

18. 407 U.S. 514, 92 S.Ct. 2182 (1972).

repeated attempts to convict Barker's co-defendant (who would otherwise have been able to claim the privilege against self-incrimination when asked to testify against Barker) and, following that conviction in February, 1963, the illness of the chief investigating officer (a key witness). In finding that the defendant's right to speedy trial had not been violated despite the extremely long delay, the Supreme Court articulated a four-factor balancing test to be used in determining whether the right to a speedy trial has been denied a defendant:

> (1) the length of the delay; (2) the reason for the delay (e.g. whether the defense or prosecution caused the delay and, if the latter, the degree of good faith effort expended in bringing the case to trial as soon as possible); (3) whether and when the defendant asserted his right; and (4) whether any actual prejudice to the defendant resulted from the delay due to destruction or staleness of evidence, oppressive pretrial incarceration or the creation of excessive anxiety.

None of these factors are to be considered determinative; they are to be balanced against one another in deciding whether the delay is unconstitutional.[19]

(a) Length of Delay. In *Doggett v. United States*,[20] the Supreme Court suggested that a delay of one year might be "presumptively prejudicial" and trigger judicial review. Nonetheless, as *Barker* indicates, the length of the delay can be quite long without violating the Constitution. In *United States v. Loud Hawk*,[21] the delay was two years longer than that in *Barker*—seven and one-half years [22]—and yet the Court still found no violation of the speedy trial right. In *United States v. Eight Thousand Eight Hundred & Fifty Dollars*,[23] a delay of eighteen months prior to a forfeiture proceeding was deemed "quite significant" but again was constitutionally insufficient. In all of these cases, other factors, such as the reason for delay, or the degree of prejudice, counteracted the length of the delay. At most, it appears that the longer the delay, the greater showing the government must make with respect to these other factors.

---

19. The elements set forth in *Barker* are usually applied to each case after trial has been completed, since the fourth element of the *Barker* test—the degree to which the defendant has been prejudiced by the delay—cannot accurately be determined unless there is a trial record available for review. *United States v. MacDonald*, 435 U.S. 850, 98 S.Ct. 1547 (1978), discussed in § 29.03(a).

20. 505 U.S. ___, 112 S.Ct. 2686 (1992).

21. 474 U.S. 302, 106 S.Ct. 648 (1986).

22. At least, this was the Court's computation, although in fact, 46 months of this period did not involve "actual restraint" and should not have been counted. See discussion of *Loud Hawk* in § 25.02(a).

23. 461 U.S. 555, 103 S.Ct. 2005 (1983).

(b) Reasons for Delay. *Barker* described three different types of reasons for a delay:

> A deliberate attempt to delay the trial in order to hamper the defense should be weighted heavily against the government. A more neutral reason such as negligence or overcrowded courts should be weighted less heavily but nevertheless should be considered since the ultimate responsibility for such circumstances must rest with government rather than the defendant. [Finally,] a valid reason, such as a missing witness . . . should serve to justify appropriate delay.

This language indicates that, analogous to due process analysis of pre-accusation delay, even delay designed to hamper the defense is not an automatic Sixth Amendment violation; at the least some prejudice to the defendant must be shown. At the same time, given the multi-factor nature of the *Barker* test, a so-called "valid reason" for delay does not mean that the delay is constitutionally justifiable; if prejudice is shown, for instance, the speedy trial right may still be infringed. In *Barker,* the Court was confronted with both the first and third type of reason for delay. The Court indicated that the delay caused by the illness of a witness was for a "valid reason," and that some delay in order to convict Barker's co-defendant was also permissible, but that the four years it took to achieve the latter purpose was not justifiable and should count against the government.

In *Loud Hawk,* the Court focused primarily on the second type of reason for delay, since much of the period under consideration resulted from government appeal of decisions by the trial court. In assessing the reasonableness of such appeals, the Court stated that the courts should consider "the strength of the Government's position on the appealed issue, the importance of the issue in the posture of the case, and—in some cases—the seriousness of the crime." [24] Applying these factors in *Loud Hawk,* the Court found no bad faith on the government's part, noting that the strength of the government's positions on appeal had been borne out by the court of appeals' reversals of the trial court. The dissenters, quoting the above language from *Barker,* argued that when delay is due to the courts, whether or not it is deliberate, the government, not the defendant, should pay the cost. Here the court of appeals had taken over five years to hear two appeals, which the dissent viewed as "patently unreasonable."

When the delay is the direct result of prosecutorial negligence, on the other hand, a speedy trial claim is more likely to be successful. In *Doggett,* a six year hiatus between the defendant's

---

24. With respect to this latter criterion, the Court stated: "[T]he charged offense usually must be sufficiently serious to justify restraints that may be imposed on the defendant pending the outcome of the appeal."

return to the country and his arrest was due to the government's failure to continue tracking the defendant after it lost him in Panama. These facts alone (there being no proof of particularized prejudice) led five members of the Court to find a violation of the Sixth Amendment. According to the Court:

> Although negligence is obviously to be weighed more lightly than a deliberate intent to harm the accused's defense, it still falls on the wrong side of the divide between acceptable and unacceptable reasons for delaying a criminal prosecution once it has begun. And such is the nature of the prejudice presumed that the weight we assign to official negligence compounds over time as the presumption of evidentiary prejudice grows. Thus, our toleration of such negligence varies inversely with its protractedness, and its consequent threat to the fairness of the accused's trial. Condoning prolonged and unjustifiable delays in prosecution would both penalize many defendants for the state's fault and simply encourage the government to gamble with the interests of criminal suspects assigned a low prosecutorial priority.

Occasionally, the delay will be due to the defendant rather than the government, in which case the persuasiveness of a speedy trial claim will presumably be undermined. One obvious example of such "culpable" delay is when the defendant escapes from custody.[25] At other times, defense-produced prolongation of the pretrial period will be less deliberate. Some of the delay in *Loud Hawk*, for instance, resulted from defense appeals. The majority concluded that this type of delay usually should not count against the government. According to the Court, where the defendant's claim on appeal is frivolous, as was the case here, he cannot complain about appellate delay; further, even when a claim is "meritorious," he "normally should not be able upon return to the district court to reap the reward of dismissal for failure to receive a speedy trial." The dissent once again disagreed, stating that when the appellate delay is "patently unreasonable" it should not matter that the appeal was initiated by the defense rather than the prosecution.

(c) Assertion of the Right. While *Barker* held that failure to assert the right to speedy trial does not constitute a waiver, it emphasized that the "frequency and force of the objections" to delay should be taken into account. The Court noted that "delay is not an uncommon defense tactic," and thus a failure to object could normally be construed as a determination by the defendant that it was not harmful.[26] Indeed, in contrast to its treatment of

---

25. See, e.g., *United States v. Taylor*, 487 U.S. 326, 108 S.Ct. 2413 (1988), discussed in § 25.05(e)(1).

26. However, the Court was careful to distinguish between a situation in which the defendant knowingly failed to assert the right and "a situation in

most other criminal procedure rights, which must be affirmatively waived, the Court stated that "failure to assert the [speedy trial] right will make it difficult for a defendant to prove that he was denied a speedy trial." Accordingly, in *Barker,* the defendant's failure to demand a trial for a substantial period of time (which the Court viewed as a tactical maneuver based on the hope that his co-defendant would be acquitted), weighed heavily against him. Similarly, in *Eight Thousand Eight Hundred & Fifty Dollars,* the defendant's failure to demand an early forfeiture proceeding counted against her.

In *Loud Hawk,* in contrast, the defendants repeatedly moved for dismissal on speedy trial grounds. Nonetheless, concluded the majority, "that finding alone does not establish that [they] had appropriately asserted their rights." The defendants' numerous other repetitive and often frivolous motions at the trial level suggested to the Court that the defendants' speedy trial motions were dilatory rather than motivated by sincere concern over pretrial delay. It appears, then, that to have a chance at successfully claiming a speedy trial violation, the defendant must not only assert the right but must do so in a "sincere" fashion.

(d) Prejudice. As discussed in the introduction, the right to speedy trial exists to prevent oppressive pretrial incarceration, the anxiety and concern accompanying public accusation, and impairment of the defendant's ability to defend himself as evidence disappears or grows stale. If any of these detriments occur due to unnecessary delay, then the right could be said to be violated. But, as with the other factors, the defendant's burden of showing prejudice is, in practice, quite heavy.

In one pre-*Barker* case, *Dickey v. Florida,*[27] the Court found that a seven-year delay, during which two defense witnesses died and a third one became unavailable, merited dismissal. And in *Doggett,* as noted above, the Court was willing to assume prejudice after an eight and one-half year delay, six years of which was attributable to government negligence. But *Doggett* involved a relatively minor crime and a sympathetic defendant (who had lived a law-abiding life during the six years). Other Court decisions have been much stricter in evaluating claims of prejudice. For instance, in *Barker,* while admitting that loss of memory is extremely hard to prove, the Court found no significant prejudice resulted from the 66–month delay; nor was a ten-month period of incarceration considered unconstitutionally oppressive. And in *Loud Hawk,* the Court found that the "possibility" that witnesses had disappeared or suffered memory loss during the seven-and-a-

which his attorney acquiesces in long delay without adequately informing his client," or "a situation in which no counsel is appointed."

27. 398 U.S. 30, 90 S.Ct. 1564 (1970).

half year hiatus was "not sufficient" to sustain the speedy trial claim. Additionally, the Court stressed that the *government's* case might also be impaired by the passage of time, a curious, if not illogical, attempt at minimizing the possible harm the delay might cause to the defendant's case.

Because prejudice, especially that associated with memory loss, is often difficult to prove, the Court's apparent requirement that substantial, concrete detriment be shown is unrealistic and, together with its prosecution-oriented treatment of the other factors in *Barker's* test, emasculates the right to speedy trial. The better approach would be to presume prejudice if, after a prolonged delay (of over twelve months or so), the defendant asks for a trial, at which point the government must provide a substantial justification for the delay; when there is no assertion of the right, on the other hand, the defendant should prevail only if he can show the delay prejudiced his case.

25.05 Legislation: The Federal Speedy Trial Act

Barker made no effort to establish explicit time requirements defining the speedy trial right. That task it held constitutionally reserved for the legislatures. The legislatures lost little time in responding to the challenge. Within ten years of *Barker,* over two-thirds of the states had enacted provisions setting time limits on the adjudication process.[28] The model for many of these provisions was the Federal Speedy Trial Act of 1974,[29] which was enacted two years after *Barker.* The rest of this chapter will focus on the Act as the best illustration of attempts to implement legislatively the speedy trial right.

(a) **An Overview.** The Act requires each federal district court to establish a plan for trying criminal cases within 100 days of arrest or receipt of summons. Failure to abide by the plan can result in dismissal of the indictment; additionally, deliberate dilatory tactics may be sanctioned by fines (in the case of prosecutors), forfeiture of a percentage of compensation (in the case of defense attorneys), suspension (of either attorney, for up to 90 days), or the filing of a report to the appropriate disciplinary body.[30]

Despite these provisions, speedy adjudication is far from assured. The latter sanctions are likely to be infrequently imposed

---

28. See generally, Misner, Speedy Trial: Federal and State Practice 330–735 (1983). From Misner's research, it appears that only Alabama, Connecticut, Kentucky, Maine, Michigan, Montana, New Hampshire, New Jersey, North Dakota, Oklahoma, South Dakota, Tennessee, Vermont and Wyoming do not have time limits, although they all have constitutional and/or statutory provisions forbidding unnecessary delay.

29. 18 U.S.C.A. § 3161 et. seq.

30. 18 U.S.C.A. § 3162.

since they require proof of intentional delay, and in any event "are totally ineffective against general institutional delay." [31] Even the dismissal remedy is not a strong incentive against delay, since dismissal may be "without prejudice" (meaning the defendant may be reindicted on the same charge).[32] Moreover, the Act permits several types of delay to be excluded from the time computation and allows both sides to seek continuances under certain circumstances. Thus, while the Act is probably more effective than the Sixth Amendment at pressuring the courts and lawyers to resolve criminal cases promptly,[33] it is no guarantee against prolonged adjudication.

(b) Specific Time Limits. The Act specifies three separate time periods:

(1) Any information or indictment must be filed within thirty days from the date of arrest or service of summons. If no grand jury is in session within that thirty days, an extension of thirty days will be granted for felony cases.[34] In contrast to the constitutional analysis,[35] several courts have determined that if a person is arrested, but no formal charges are filed, the speedy trial time limits are not activated at the time of arrest.[36] Moreover, the arrest must be by *federal* officers, not officers of another sovereign, in order to trigger the Act's provisions.[37]

(2) Trial must take place within seventy days from the filing date of the indictment or information, or from the date the defendant first appears before a judicial officer, whichever is later.[38] Trial is deemed to begin when voir dire commences.[39]

(3) Trial cannot take place less than thirty days from the date on which the defendant first appears through counsel or expressly waives counsel and elects to proceed *pro se,* unless the defendant consents to earlier trial in writing.[40]

31. Misner, supra note 28, at 303.

32. See § 25.05(e).

33. But see Bridges, "The Speedy Trial Act of 1974: Effect on Delays in Federal Criminal Litigation," 73 J.Crim.L. & Criminol. 50, 53 (1982) (finding insignificant increase in speed since Act).

34. 18 U.S.C.A. § 3161(b).

35. See § 25.02(a).

36. See, e.g., *United States v. Sanchez,* 722 F.2d 1501 (11th Cir.1984), cert. denied 467 U.S. 1208, 104 S.Ct. 2396 (1984); *United States v. Boles,* 684 F.2d 534 (8th Cir.1982). A particularly bothersome decision is *United States v. Reme,* 738 F.2d 1156 (11th Cir.1984), which held that, even if the offense for which the defendant is indicted is only slightly different from that for which he was arrested, time spent in custody between arrest and indictment is excludable.

37. *United States v. Manuel,* 706 F.2d 908 (9th Cir.1983) (initial arrest by tribal authorities did not trigger Act); *United States v. Iaquinta,* 674 F.2d 260 (4th Cir.1982) (initial arrest by state authorities did not trigger Act even though state officers were assisted by federal officers).

38. 18 U.S.C.A. § 3161(c)(1).

39. *United States v. Richmond,* 735 F.2d 208 (6th Cir.1984); *United States v. Manfredi,* 722 F.2d 519 (9th Cir.1983).

40. 18 U.S.C.A. § 3161(c)(2).

(c) Exemptions. Certain periods of delay are excluded from the computation of time limitations.[41] These include:

(1) Delays caused by proceedings relating to the defendant, such as hearings on competency to stand trial, hearings on pretrial motions, trials on other charges and interlocutory appeals. The most controversial issue involving this provision is whether the entire postponement resulting from a pretrial motion is always excludable or whether some outer limit must be observed. Until *Henderson v. United States*,[42] several courts had permitted exclusion only of that time found to be "reasonably necessary" to effectuate the purpose of the motion.[43] In *Henderson*, however, the Supreme Court held that neither the statutory language nor the legislative history of the Act called for such a rule. Thus, both the five month delay between the filing of the suppression motion and the hearing on the motion, and the ten month delay between the hearing and the court's final decision (resulting largely from prosecution delay in submitting posthearing material requested by the court) was excludable.

(2) Delays caused by deferred prosecution upon agreement of defense counsel, prosecutor, and the court.

(3) Delays caused by the absence or unavailability of the defendant or an essential witness.

(4) Delays resulting from the defendant's mental incompetence or physical unfitness to stand trial.

(5) Delays resulting from treatment of the defendant pursuant to the Narcotics Addict Rehabilitation Act.

(6) Analogous to the holding in *United States v. MacDonald*,[44] delays between the dropping of a charge and filing of a new charge for the same or related offense.

(7) Reasonable periods of delay when the defendant is joined for trial with a co-defendant.

(8) Any delay resulting from a continuance granted by the court to serve the ends of justice.

(d) Continuances. As the final exemption provision above makes clear, periods of delay resulting from a continuance are exempted from computation of the time limits if the continuance serves the ends of justice. The reasons for any continuance must be set forth in the record or the continuance will not be so exempted. In considering whether to grant a continuance, the

---

41. 18 U.S.C.A. § 3161(h)(1)–(9).

42. 476 U.S. 321, 106 S.Ct. 1871 (1986).

43. See, e.g., *United States v. Novak*, 715 F.2d 810 (3d Cir.1983); *United States v. Cobb*, 697 F.2d 38 (2d Cir.1982).

44. 456 U.S. 1, 102 S.Ct. 1497 (1982), discussed in § 25.02(a).

statute states that the following factors are to be taken into account: [45]

(1) Whether failure to grant a continuance would be likely to make a continuation of the proceedings impossible or result in a miscarriage of justice. Thus, in *United States v. Martin* [46] the Ninth Circuit permitted a continuance when the validity of a defense raised by the defendant was soon to be considered by the United States Supreme Court, and the Court's decision could conceivably have overruled two Ninth Circuit cases finding contrary to the defendant's position.

(2) Whether the case is so "unusual or complex" that it is unreasonable to expect adequate preparation within the time limits. *United States v. Perez-Reveles* [47] held that a mere conclusory finding by the trial judge that a case is "complex," when the trial took only two days to complete, involved a single defendant and raised no unusual issues will not constitute an excludable continuance.

(3) Whether, in a case where arrest precedes indictment, delay in the filing of the indictment occurs because the arrest occurred at a time which made convening a grand jury and obtaining an indictment within the period specified difficult or because the facts upon which the grand jury had to base its determination are unusual or complex.

(4) Whether the failure to grant a continuance would deny the defendant reasonable time to obtain counsel, would unreasonably deny the defendant or the government continuity of counsel, or would deny counsel for either party reasonable time for effective preparation. For example, the court in *United States v. Nance* [48] exempted three successive continuances totalling three months because they were granted, respectively, when (a) the defendant's lawyer was unavailable due to a death in the family and continuity of representation was considered important; (b) a co-defendant's counsel was unavailable because of his involvement in another trial; and (c) an unrelated trial scheduled by the judge to fill the docket slot left open by the defendant's continued trial took a few days longer than expected. The last continuance was considered justified because it was aimed at taking full advantage of judicial resources and the delay was unforeseeable.

(5) Whether the continuance was granted for an "inappropriate" reason, such as general congestion of the court's calendar, or lack of diligent preparation or failure to obtain witnesses on the

45. 18 U.S.C.A. § 3161(h)(8)(B)(i–iv).

46. 742 F.2d 512 (9th Cir.1984).

47. 715 F.2d 1348 (9th Cir.1983).

48. 666 F.2d 353 (9th Cir.1982), cert. denied 456 U.S. 918, 102 S.Ct. 1776 (1982).

part of the government's attorney. No continuance granted on such grounds will qualify as excludable.

(e) Dismissal/Reprosecution. Failure to comply with the time limit requirements, after subtracting the allowable exclusions and continuances, results in dismissal of the prosecution. However, discretion is vested in the trial judge to dismiss with or without prejudice. In doing so, the judge is to consider three factors: (1) the seriousness of the offense; (2) the circumstances leading to dismissal (e.g., who is responsible for the delay); and (3) the effect of reprosecution on the administration of the Act and the administration of justice.[49]

(1) The courts' approach. The one Supreme Court decision reaching this issue suggests that the Court believes the harsher dismissal remedy should be used sparingly. In *United States v. Taylor,*[50] the government was prepared to try the defendant one day before expiration of the 70–day deadline established by the statute, but was unable to do so because the defendant had escaped from custody. However, after the defendant was apprehended in another jurisdiction, the government delayed trial for well over a month (at least 15 days of which were nonexcludable), in large part because it was inconvenient for the United States Marshal Service to transfer the defendant to the appropriate jurisdiction at an earlier time. The trial court, applying the three statutory factors noted above, dismissed the charges against the defendant with prejudice. It found that the charges (federal narcotics felonies) were serious. But, with respect to the "circumstances leading to the dismissal" factor, it found that the government's attitude toward reinitiating prosecution had been "lackadaisical." And it concluded that the administration of the Act would be "seriously impaired if the court were not to respond sternly to the instant violation." The Ninth Circuit affirmed.

The Supreme Court held that the dismissal should have been without prejudice. Justice Blackmun, writing for a six-member majority, began by stressing that while the type of dismissal ordered in a particular case is in the discretion of the trial judge, appellate courts should make sure the judge has devoted adequate attention to the three factors set out in the Act, as well as the degree of prejudice to the defendant occasioned by the nonexcludable delay. He included the last consideration based on a reading of the Act's legislative history, which he asserted indicated Congress' desire to have courts consider prejudice in determining a remedy even though it was not specifically included in the statute.

Blackmun then concluded that the trial judge in *Taylor* had failed to explain adequately how she had evaluated these four

---

49. 18 U.S.C.A. § 3162.   **50.** 487 U.S. 326, 108 S.Ct. 2413 (1988).

variables. In particular, the trial court had not sufficiently explained its conclusion, relevant to the second and third statutory factors, that the government was so "lackadaisical" as to deserve the dismissal with prejudice sanction. Blackmun found no evidence in the trial court's opinion that the government had acted in "bad faith", or exhibited "a pattern of neglect" or "antipathy toward a recaptured fugitive." He found the court's determination that there was "no excuse" for the government's conduct insufficient. Additionally, while admitting that the defendant's escape did not restart the clock for purposes of the Act, Blackmun felt the trial court had overlooked the relevance of the escape as a causative factor in the failure of the government to meet the deadline.

Finally, Blackmun stated that the trial court had given insufficient weight to the prejudice issue. He noted that neither the district court nor the circuit court had found that the defendant had been prejudiced by the delay, but that this fact had not seemed to influence either court. Concluded the Supreme Court: "At bottom, the District Court appears to have decided to dismiss with prejudice in this case in order to send a strong message to the Government that unexcused delays will not be tolerated. That factor alone, by definition implicated in almost every Speedy Trial Act case, does not suffice to justify barring reprosecution in light of all the other circumstances present."

The speedy trial claim in *Taylor* was not a particularly strong one. The delay was not very long, and apparently did not prejudice the defendant; moreover, the government probably did not act in "bad faith" and the defendant hardly had "clean hands." However, the Court's willingness to overturn the lower court's decision rather than remand it for further consideration, along with its clearly demonstrated unwillingness to countenance as the sole ground for prohibiting reprosecution a nonchalant attitude on the part of the government, suggests a desire to deter use of the dismissal with prejudice sanction. Additionally, the Court took pains to emphasize that dismissal without prejudice "is not a toothless sanction;" it forces the government to seek a new indictment which, given the time lapse, will be harder to obtain and may be dismissed on statute of limitations grounds.

One can at least conclude that *Taylor* will do nothing to diminish the tendency of most lower courts to rely on the dismissal without prejudice sanction. Although a few courts have held that there is a presumption in favor of dismissal with prejudice,[51] most have decided otherwise.[52] Most have also been willing to

51. See, e.g., *United States v. Angelini,* 553 F.Supp. 367 (D.Mass.1982), aff'd on other grounds 678 F.2d 380 (1st Cir. 1982).

52. See, e.g., *United States v. Russo,* 741 F.2d 1264 (11th Cir.1984).

interpret the three statutory factors in the prosecution's favor. For instance, many courts are apparently willing to dismiss without prejudice for any type of felony.[53] Similarly, even when it is clear that the delay is the fault of the prosecution, the courts often grant dismissal without prejudice if the violation was not in bad faith,[54] or was justified by a need for further investigation.[55] Even a failure to provide a reason does not necessarily hurt the prosecution.[56] As with the Court's holding in *Taylor,* many of these holdings rely heavily on the finding that the defendant did not appear to be prejudiced by the delay.

(2) An alternative approach. The ability to dismiss without prejudice substantially detracts from the original purpose of the Act, which was to adopt relatively finite rules governing the duration of adjudication. As one judge stated: "If dismissal without prejudice is permitted, then the defendant has achieved nothing but the privilege of being tried a second time."[57] Indeed, given the authority to dismiss without prejudice, a violation of the statute may result in *longer* delay than would have occurred had the statute never been passed, since the defendant must be reindicted before retrial can take place and the statutory period begins anew.[58]

The preferable approach would be to dismiss with prejudice all cases involving statutory violations which are not clearly the product of defense-caused delay. When non-excludable delay is due to the government or some other entity over which the defense has no control, the government should bear the cost. Given the large number of exemptions to which the prosecution can resort, this approach would not unfairly burden the government; rather, it would encourage the diligence and efficiency necessary to ensure defendants are not detained or made to wait in the community for prolonged periods of time prior to having their case resolved. When, on the other hand, delay is the result of defense tactics or lack of diligence, a dismissal without prejudice might be proper, at least when serious crimes are involved. While the defendant should not be penalized for an attorney's incompetence or miscalculations, neither should the government be forced to dismiss a case which it has attempted to adjudicate promptly.

53. See, e.g., *United States v. Kiszewski,* 877 F.2d 210 (2d Cir.1989) (perjury to grand jury); *United States v. Bittle,* 699 F.2d 1201 (D.C.Cir.1983) (possession of stolen mail); *United States v. Hawthorne,* 705 F.2d 258 (7th Cir.1983) (possession of government checks).

54. *United States v. Kiszewski,* 877 F.2d 210 (2d Cir.1989).

55. *United States v. Godoy,* 821 F.2d 1498 (11th Cir.1987).

56. *United States v. May,* 819 F.2d 531 (5th Cir.1987).

57. *United States v. Mehrmanesh,* 652 F.2d 766 (9th Cir.1980) (Fletcher, J. dissenting).

58. Further, the Act permits the trial judge to extend the period before retrial to 180 days. 18 U.S.C.A. § 3161(d)(2).

Only if delay caused by the defense attorney results in actual prejudice to the defendant's case should dismissal with prejudice be considered.

(f) Burden of Proof. The burden of proving the time limits in the Act have been exceeded is on the defendant, although when the exemption at issue is that having to do with the absence or unavailability of the defendant or an essential witness, the government bears the burden of coming forward with sufficient evidence to raise the question. Significantly, failure of the defendant to move for dismissal prior to trial or the entry of a plea of guilty or nolo contendere is a waiver of the statutory right.[59]

(g) Sixth Amendment Rights. The Speedy Trial Act does not displace the constitutional right of speedy trial. Section 3173 provides: "No provision of this chapter shall be interpreted as a bar to any claim of denial of speedy trial as required by Amendment VI of the Constitution." If a defendant for some reason cannot make out a violation of his statutory right to speedy trial, he may still argue his constitutional claim, although he is unlikely to be successful.[60]

25.06   Conclusion

The right to speedy disposition of one's charges is embodied both in the Sixth Amendment and legislation in every jurisdiction. The nature of the right varies depending upon its source.

(1) Under the Sixth Amendment, the right does not attach until arrest or indictment (whichever comes first), although the Due Process Clause provides limited protection against excessive and prejudicial pre-accusation delay which is intended to hamper the defense or recklessly causes that result. If the charge or indictment is dismissed and reinstated, the period of dismissal is not relevant to Sixth Amendment analysis unless, during that period, the defendant is subject to restriction on his liberty greater than the *possibility* of pretrial detention or bond.

(2) In deciding whether post-accusation delay as defined in (1) violates the Sixth Amendment, four factors should be considered: (a) the length of the delay; (b) the reason for the delay (e.g. whether the defense or prosecution caused the delay and, if the latter, the degree of good faith effort expended in bringing the case to trial as soon as possible); (c) whether and when the defendant asserted his right; and (d) whether any actual prejudice to the defendant resulted from the delay due to destruction or staleness of evidence, oppressive pretrial incarceration or the creation of excessive anxiety. Even when delay is extraordinary,

---

59. 18 U.S.C.A. § 3162(a)(2).

60. Cf. *Misner*, supra note 28, at 325. ("A violation of the Act itself generally will not offend the Sixth Amendment.")

the Supreme Court requires strong proof concerning the other factors before it will find a violation of the Sixth Amendment.

(3) Statutory implementation of the speedy trial concept tends to place more concrete time limits on the period between arrest and adjudication. The federal act, for instance, presumes that if this period exceeds 100 days, the statutory right is violated. However, several types of delays, including time spent dealing with defense motions, delays resulting from the defendant's incompetence to stand trial, and delays resulting from continuances granted to serve the ends of justice do not count toward the 100-day limit. The number of exceptions to the time limit requirements of the Act illustrates the difficulty of achieving speedy disposition of cases given the realities of the criminal justice system.

(4) The remedy for violation of the constitutional right is dismissal with prejudice (i.e., prohibition of reprosecution). A violation of the federal act can result in dismissal with or without prejudice, depending upon: (a) the seriousness of the offense; (b) the circumstances leading to dismissal; and (c) the effect of reprosecution on the administration of the Act and the administration of justice.

BIBLIOGRAPHY

Amsterdam, A.G. Speedy Criminal Trials: Rights and Remedies. 27 Stan.L.Rev. 525 (1975).

Bridges, George. The Speedy Trial Act of 1974: Effects on Delays in Federal Criminal Litigation, 73 J.Crim.L. & Criminol. 50 (1982).

Frase, R.S. The Speedy Trial Act of 1974. 43 U.Chi.L.Rev. 667 (1976).

Godbold, J.C. Speedy Trial—Major Surgery for a National Ill. 24 Ala.L.Rev. 265 (1972).

Hansen, Vagn, and William Reed. The Speedy Trial Act of 1974 in Constitutional Perspective. 47 Miss.L.J. 365 (1976).

Joseph, Gregory. Speedy Trial Rights in Application. 48 Fordham L.Rev. 611 (1980).

Katz, Lewis. Justice is the Crime: Pretrial Delay in Felony Cases. Cleveland: Case Western Reserve University, 1972.

Misner, R.L. District Court Compliance with the Speedy Trial Act of 1974. 1977 Ariz.St.L.J. 1 (1977).

——. Speedy Trial: Federal and State Practice. Charlottesville, Va.: Michie Co., 1983.

Poulos, J.W. Speedy Trial, Slow Implementation: The ABA Standards in Search of a Statehouse. 28 Hastings L.J. 357 (1976).

Rudstein, David S. Barker v. Wingo in the Lower Courts. 1975 U.Ill.L.F. 11.

Uviller, H. Richard. Barker v. Wingo: Speedy Trial Gets a Fast Shuffle. 72 Colum.L.Rev. 1376 (1972).

Part F

ADJUDICATION OF GUILT

Police investigation, the subject of Parts A through D, and the pretrial process, examined in Part E, share a common goal: they both are aimed at identifying those cases which have a good chance of ending in conviction. As a result, most defendants who enter the adjudication phase of the criminal process have committed some crime. But a number of complex mechanisms have been developed in an effort to assure that *only* those defendants who are culpable "beyond a reasonable doubt"[1] are convicted. This Part describes this adjudication process.

Chapter Twenty-Six describes the rules associated with guilty pleas and plea bargaining, phenomena little known to the public but responsible for most criminal convictions. If the defendant pleads not guilty, he has the right to be tried by a jury, the subject of Chapter Twenty-Seven. Chapter Twenty-Eight discusses a number of matters connected with the conduct of trial itself, all stemming from the defendant's constitutionally-based prerogative to confront his accusers. If trial results in conviction, every jurisdiction gives the defendant a statutory right to appeal, the various aspects of which are covered in Chapter Twenty-Nine. If, on the other hand, the defendant is acquitted, at either the trial or the appellate stage, he is protected from retrial on the same offense by the Double Jeopardy Clause, discussed in Chapter Thirty. The right to counsel at the guilty plea, trial and appellate stages is discussed in Part G (in Chapter Thirty-One), which deals with the right to counsel generally.

1. Beyond a reasonable doubt is typically defined as "a belief to a moral certainty which does not exclude all possible or imaginary doubt, but which is of such convincing character that a reasonable person would not hesitate to rely and act upon it in the most important of his own affairs." See Smith & Blackmore, Federal Jury Practice and Instructions, § 11.14.

Chapter Twenty-Six

GUILTY PLEAS AND PLEA BARGAINING

26.01 Introduction

For many years, most convictions in the United States have been the result of a guilty plea rather than a bench or jury trial. Some estimates indicate that as many as ninety-five percent of all criminal cases are disposed of through guilty pleas.[1] Most of these pleas are the result of "plea bargaining" between the prosecution and the defense, in which the former makes charge or sentencing concessions in exchange for a plea of guilty.

The response to the guilty plea process has been mixed. Most commentators and courts have assumed that as judicial resources become increasingly burdened, guilty pleas and plea bargaining are essential to the efficient administration of criminal justice. As one Manhattan prosecutor stated: "Our office keeps eight courtrooms extremely busy trying 5% of the cases. If even 10% of the cases ended in a trial, the system would break down."[2] As a result, most criticisms of guilty pleas and plea bargains do not call for their elimination, but rather focus on the manner by which they are obtained and the lack of openness surrounding the process.[3]

But some have argued that the outcome of criminal cases should not be affected by lack of resources and that the degree of discretion plea bargaining gives the prosecution produces inappropriate results.[4] It is well known that, of two defendants with identical charges, the one who pleads guilty is likely to receive a less severe sentence than the one who goes to trial.[5] Further, the plea bargaining process encourages the prosecutor to overcharge as a negotiating ploy, and may lead to less individualized dispositions, especially in busy urban areas, where bargaining often appears to proceed according to a pre-set "schedule." The end

---

1. Newman, "Reshape the Deal," 9 Trial 11 (March/April (1973) (90% of convictions for serious crimes are the result of guilty pleas; 98% of all convictions result from pleas if misdemeanors are included); ABA Project on Standards for Criminal Justice, Pleas of Guilty, at 1–2 (1968) [hereafter cited as ABA Standards].

2. Quoted in Alschuler, "The Prosecutor's Role in Plea Bargaining," 36 Chi.L.Rev. 50, 54 (1968).

3. See, e.g., ABA Standards, supra note 1, at 305–07, 309–12 (1974); Kuh,

Plea Bargaining: Guidelines for the Manhattan District Attorney's Office, 11 Crim.L.Bull. 48–65 (1975).

4. See, e.g., National Advisory Commission on Criminal Justice Standards and Goals, *Courts* Standard 3.1 (1973); Kipnis, "Criminal Justice and the Negotiated Plea," 86 Ethics 93 (1976).

5. Zeisel, The Anatomy of Law Enforcement, ch. 12 (average increase of sentence between plea and trial stages was 136%); *Frank v. Blackburn*, 646 F.2d 873 (5th Cir.1980), mod'd 646 F.2d 902 (5th Cir.1981).

result, it is contended, is inaccuracy.[6] Even the administrative need for plea bargaining has been challenged. The bargaining process, it is asserted, actually contributes to inefficiency, for "defense attorneys commonly devise strategies whose only utility lies in the threat they pose to the court's and prosecutor's time."[7] A few jurisdictions have forbidden plea bargaining except in unusual circumstances. One study conducted in Alaska after plea bargaining was severely curtailed in that state concluded that "the efficient operation of Alaska's criminal justice system did not depend upon plea bargaining."[8]

There are several points to be made in favor of guilty pleas reached through plea bargaining, however. On the disparity issue, it has been argued that a person who pleads guilty is often deserving of leniency, since the plea may indicate repentance, a potential for rehabilitation, cooperation with the authorities in bringing to justice other offenders, or a willingness to help the state avoid the delay associated with trial. Indeed, the ABA encourages such leniency in its recommendations concerning plea bargaining.[9] With respect to the potential for "inaccurate" dispositions, it is noted that, given the myriad shades of personal culpability, plea bargaining can, at least theoretically, result in more "just" solutions than a trial, which must proceed based on specified charges connected with specific penalties.[10] Finally, the empirical studies indicating that abolition of plea bargaining can "work" also usually show that the discretion once permitted by that practice has merely been shifted to other points in the process, such as charging or sentencing, with not necessarily more just results.[11]

In any event, the courts have come to accept guilty pleas and plea bargaining as a necessary and established part of the criminal justice system. In *Brady v. United States*,[12] the Supreme Court expressed caution about, but still recognized the validity of, the plea bargain system:

6. Gifford, "Meaningful Reform of Plea Bargaining: The Control of Prosecutorial Discretion," 1983 U.Ill.L.Rev. 37.

7. Alschuler, supra note 2, at 56.

8. Rubinstein & Clark, Conclusions, in The Effect of the Official Prohibition of Plea Bargaining on the Disposition of Felony Cases in Alaska Criminal Courts 219 (Alaska Judicial Council, 1978). See also, Parnas & Atkins, "Abolishing Plea Bargaining: A Proposal," 14 Crim. L.Bull. 101, 110–114 (1978).

9. ABA Standards, supra note 1, § 1.8(a).

10. Church, "In Defense of Bargain Justice," 13 Law & Soc.Rev. 509, 511 (1979).

11. Feeley, "Perspectives on Plea Bargaining," 13 Law & Soc.Rev. 199, 204 (1979). See also, Weninger, "The Abolition of Plea Bargaining: A Case Study of El Paso County, Texas," 35 U.C.L.A.L.Rev. 265 (1987); Callan, "An Experiment in Justice Without Plea Negotiation," 13 Law & Soc.Rev. 327 (1979).

12. 397 U.S. 742, 90 S.Ct. 1463 (1970).

Of course, that the prevalence of guilty pleas is explainable does not necessarily validate those pleas or the system which produces them. But we cannot hold that it is unconstitutional for the State to extend a benefit to a defendant who in turn extends a substantial benefit to the State. . . .

One year later in *Santobello v. New York,* [13] the Court was even more affirmative:

The disposition of criminal charges by agreement between the prosecutor and the accused, sometimes loosely called "plea bargaining," is an essential component of the administration of justice. Properly administered, it is to be encouraged.

This chapter examines: (1) the plea bargaining process; (2) the effect of a bargain once it is made; (3) the rules regarding the "arraignment," or proceeding at which the plea is taken; and (4) the circumstances under which a plea may be challenged.

26.02   The Plea Bargaining Process

(a) **Types of Bargains and Pleas.** With the few exceptions noted above, every jurisdiction has explicitly provided that the prosecution and the defense may engage in discussions with a view toward reaching a plea agreement.[14] Typically, the prosecution offers one or more of the following concessions: (1) a reduction in charge; (2) dismissal of other pending charges; (3) a promise to recommend or not contest a particular sentence or range of sentences; or (4) a stipulation that a particular sentence is the appropriate disposition. The prosecution may also agree to other conditions, such as maintaining confidentiality about the dismissed charges.

The defendant in return agrees to plead guilty to the proferred charge or charges. In many states, as well as federal court,[15] there are actually two different types of guilty pleas: a straight guilty plea and a plea of nolo contendere.[16] The nolo plea (or plea non vult) means literally: "I do not contest this." In effect, it is identical to the guilty plea, except that it cannot be used against a defendant as an admission of guilt in a subsequent civil case. Thus, it is particularly popular among defendants charged with criminal antitrust violations and the like, since civil litigation often follows the criminal adjudication.[17] In addition to agreeing to plead guilty in one of these ways, the defendant may agree to

13. 404 U.S. 257, 92 S.Ct. 495 (1971).

14. See, e.g., Fed.R.Crim.P. 11(e)(1).

15. See *Hudson v. United States,* 272 U.S. 451, 47 S.Ct. 127 (1926).

16. In most states, the defendant can also plead not guilty by reason of insanity, which is also a form of guilty plea, in that the defendant admits he committed the crime, but claims that he should not be held responsible for it.

17. See Wright, Federal Practice and Procedure § 177.

testify against a co-defendant, forego asserting certain rights, or provide other benefits to the prosecution.

(b) Rights During Bargaining. Plea bargaining is, in effect, the adjudicatory process for defendants who eventually plead guilty. But the rights accorded a defendant during the bargaining process are not as extensive as those enjoyed by the defendant at trial.

(1) The right to effective counsel. The Supreme Court has held that the Sixth Amendment right to counsel attaches whenever, after the initiation of criminal proceedings, "a defendant finds himself faced with the prosecutorial forces of organized society, and immersed in the intricacies of substantive and procedural criminal law." [18] Accordingly, it seems clear that the defendant is entitled to counsel during the bargaining process, as well as during arraignment. The prosecutor should not bargain directly with the defendant, unless there has been a waiver of counsel.[19]

If counsel does perform the bargaining, the Sixth Amendment also requires that he do so effectively. Counsel should carry out sufficient investigation of the case to permit him to advise his client as to various charging and sentencing options. He should also ensure that his client understands the options available. The Supreme Court has held, however, that failing to fulfill these tasks is not necessarily ineffective assistance of counsel under the Sixth Amendment. In *Hill v. Lockhart,*[20] it concluded that such a claim will not lie unless the defendant can show "a reasonable probability that, but for counsel's errors, he would not have pleaded guilty and would have insisted on going to trial." In *Hill,* the defendant, who pleaded guilty pursuant to a bargain, claimed that his attorney should have told him that, due to a previous felony conviction, he would not be eligible for parole until he had served one-half of his sentence, rather than one-third of his sentence, as was true of first-time offenders. The Court concluded that the defendant failed to allege "any special circumstances that might support the conclusion that he placed particular emphasis on his parole eligibility in deciding whether or not to plead guilty."

(2) The right to exculpatory evidence. By analogy to the trial process,[21] defense counsel should also receive any "exculpatory" information in the prosecution's possession before a final bargain is struck. But, as with ineffective assistance of counsel claims, it is likely that information will be considered exculpatory only if there is a reasonable probability it would have changed the

---

18. *Kirby v. Illinois,* 406 U.S. 682, 92 S.Ct. 1877 (1972).

19. Ethical rules also prohibit such contact. See, e.g., ABA Code of Professional Responsibility, DR 7–104.

20. 474 U.S. 52, 106 S.Ct. 366 (1985).

21. See § 24.04.

defendant's plea.[22]   Further, some courts have distinguished between specific exculpatory evidence, which must be disclosed, and weaknesses in the prosecution's case that would come out at trial (such as a missing witness), which need not be.[23]

(3) The right to be present.   Although the defendant has the right to be present at his trial and other "critical" proceedings,[24] no court has been willing to grant defendants this right during the bargaining process.   From a doctrinal perspective, this conclusion can be supported on the ground that bargaining does not involve confrontation of prosecution witnesses, and thus does not implicate the Sixth Amendment right from which the right to be present derives.   It could also be based on the practical difficulty of conducting negotiations when the defendant is in jail.   On the other hand, the present approach leans heavily on counsel's ability to recall and report accurately all discussions with the prosecution.   Some commentators have suggested that the accused be present during negotiations to improve his understanding of the stakes involved, as well as the attorneys' performance.[25]

(c) Permissible Inducements and Concessions.   *Brady v. United States* [26] is important not only because it was the first Supreme Court opinion which explicitly condoned plea bargaining, but also because it provided the theoretical basis for analyzing the validity of various types of bargains.   While indicating that a guilty plea that is "compelled" by the government is invalid under the Fifth Amendment because a defendant is thereby forced to "testify" against himself, it was careful to distinguish between a compelled plea, on the one hand, and a plea which is merely "caused" by a legitimately posed offer.   This approach has meant that the Constitution places very few limitations on the types of inducements the state may use to encourage guilty pleas.

(1) Causation v. compulsion.   The defendant in *Brady* was charged with kidnapping under a statute which permitted imposition of the death penalty if a jury so recommended, but provided for a maximum of life at a bench trial.   Brady first pleaded not guilty and opted for a jury trial, "apparently because the trial judge was unwilling to try the case without a jury."   However, Brady subsequently changed his plea to guilty and was sentenced

---

22.   See *United States v. Bagley,* 473 U.S. 667, 105 S.Ct. 3375 (1985), discussed in § 24.04(b).

23.   See, e.g., *People v. Jones,* 44 N.Y.2d 76, 404 N.Y.S.2d 85, 375 N.E.2d 41 (1978), cert. denied 439 U.S. 846, 99 S.Ct. 145 (1978).   On the other hand, at least one court has held that if counsel is denied full discovery and as a result is unable to evaluate its wisdom, the plea is not valid. *Stano v. Dugger,* 889 F.2d 962 (11th Cir.1989), rehr'g decided on other grounds 901 F.2d 898 (1990).

24.   See § 28.03(a).

25.   See, e.g., Morris, N., The Future of Imprisonment 54 (1974) (proposing a pretrial conference at which the attorneys, the judge, the accused and the victim are present).

26.   397 U.S. 742, 90 S.Ct. 1463 (1970).

to 50 years (later reduced to 30 years). Although the trial judge twice questioned him as to the voluntariness of his plea, Brady later argued that it was coerced by the kidnapping statute and, more particularly, by fear of the death penalty.

The Supreme Court, in an opinion by Justice White, rejected this claim. While recognizing that Brady may have been affected by the possibility of a heavier sentence had he gone to trial, White pointed out that this fact would merely prove the statute "caused" the plea, not that it "coerced" the plea. Actual or threatened "physical harm" or "mental coercion overbearing the will of the defendant" would result in a violation of the Fifth Amendment, as would proof that "Brady was so gripped by fear of the death penalty or hope of leniency that he did not or could not, with the help of counsel, rationally weigh the advantages of going to trial against the advantages of pleading guilty." But here White found that at most the spectre of capital punishment influenced Brady's decision. He also pointed out that prior to changing his plea from not guilty to guilty, Brady had discovered that his codefendant had agreed to testify against him at trial, suggesting that factors other than the potential death sentence had played a more significant role in encouraging the changed plea.

White concluded by quoting a Fifth Circuit opinion which he suggested stated the voluntariness standard in the guilty plea context.

> [A] plea of guilty entered by one fully aware of the direct consequences, including the actual value of any commitments made to him by the court, prosecutor, or his own counsel, must stand unless induced by threats (or promises to discontinue improper harassment), misrepresentation (including unfulfilled or unfulfillable promises), or perhaps by promises that are by their nature improper as having no proper relationship to the prosecutor's business (e.g. bribes).[27]

Two other decisions handed down the same day as *Brady*, *McMann v. Richardson*[28] and *Parker v. North Carolina*[29] similarly emphasized the difference between "causation" and "coercion." In each case, the defendant urged that he had been coerced into giving a confession to the police and that his guilty plea was the result of the confession. Justice White, writing for the Court in *McMann*, conceded that if the coercion leading to a confession also tainted the plea, a valid Fifth Amendment claim would exist. But here the defendants were merely alleging a "but for" relationship

---

27. *Shelton v. United States,* 246 F.2d 571 (5th Cir.1957) (en banc), reversed on other grounds 356 U.S. 26, 78 S.Ct. 563 (1958).

28. 397 U.S. 759, 90 S.Ct. 1441 (1970).

29. 397 U.S. 790, 90 S.Ct. 1458 (1970).

between the confession and the guilty plea which did not make out a valid involuntariness claim.

(2) Prosecutorial inducements. While *Brady* made clear that a plea is not compelled merely because it results from a difficult choice, it did not address the constitutionality of inducements consciously offered by the state to obtain a plea. In *Bordenkircher v. Hayes,*[30] the Court applied the reasoning of the "*Brady* trilogy" to sanction direct prosecutorial pressure on the defendant during the plea bargaining process, so long as the choices offered by the prosecutor are authorized by law. *Bordenkircher* involved a defendant indicted by a state grand jury for forging a check for $88.30, punishable by 2 to 10 years in prison. The prosecutor offered to recommend a maximum of five years if the petitioner agreed to plead guilty, but also threatened to seek an indictment under the Kentucky Habitual Criminal Act if the petitioner (who had two prior felony convictions) refused to accept his offer. Notwithstanding the mandatory life sentence which would result from a conviction under the recidivist statute, Hayes rejected the offer. He was subsequently indicted and convicted as a habitual criminal. On federal habeas, petitioner did not contest his culpability under the recidivist statute; rather, he argued that his reindictment and conviction for the greater offense was an unconstitutional punishment, under *North Carolina v. Pearce,*[31] for the exercise of his right to plead not guilty and move to trial.

In a 5–4 decision, the Supreme Court reasserted that an action taken by a defendant in plea negotiations passes constitutional muster if it represents a choice among known alternatives. While reiterating *Pearce's* holding that punishing a defendant "because he has done what the law plainly allows him to do is a due process violation of the most basic sort," the majority, in an opinion by Justice Stewart, concluded that in the " 'give-and-take' of plea bargaining, there is no such element of punishment or retaliation so long as the accused is free to accept or reject the prosecution's offer." The Court emphasized that, while a defendant in petitioner's situation may be discouraged from exercising his right to plead not guilty, "the imposition of these difficult choices [is] an inevitable '—and permissible—' attribute of any legitimate system which tolerates and encourages the negotiation of pleas." By implication, had Hayes pleaded guilty as a result of the prosecutor's threat (rather than proceeded to trial despite the threat), his plea would have been voluntary.

One dissent, written by Justice Blackmun and joined by Justices Brennan and Marshall, alleged the prosecutor had been vindictive in seeking the habitual offender indictment and

30. 434 U.S. 357, 98 S.Ct. 663 (1978).   **31.** 395 U.S. 711, 89 S.Ct. 2072 (1969), discussed in § 29.02(d).

found his actions unconstitutional under *Pearce*. Blackmun argued that, in the plea bargaining context, the prosecutor should be required to adhere to the charge in his original offer rather than allowed to "up the ante" whenever a defendant refused his offer. Justice Powell, who wrote a second dissent, opted for a voluntariness inquiry. Although prosecutorial discretion should be overridden only in the "most exceptional case," he found that this exception applied here, because the prosecutor "penalize[d] with unique severity [the defendant's] exercise of constitutional rights."

After *Bordenkircher*, it appears that virtually all prosecutorial attempts to "persuade" a defendant to plead guilty through the spectre of higher charges are permissible, so long as: (1) the higher charges are legitimate and (2) they are "openly presented" to the defendant (to use the majority's phrase) so that he knows precisely his choices. Short of abolishing plea bargaining, this may be the only reasonable approach to such threats. As Blackmun recognized, his requirement that prosecutors stick to their original charge might encourage them to choose the higher charge initially, in detriment to defendants seeking pleas. Powell's approach avoids this problem, but requires the courts to engage in proportionality analysis (i.e., was the threat "uniquely severe"?), a very difficult task.[32]

Prosecutors occasionally resort to other types of inducements, some of which may not be permissible. For instance, the majority in *Bordenkircher* cautioned that the case did not "involve the constitutional implications of a prosecutor's offer during plea bargaining of adverse or lenient treatment for some person *other* than the accused, which might pose a greater danger of inducing a false guilty plea by skewing the assessment of the risks a defendant must consider." The Supreme Court has also indicated that use of deception to obtain a guilty plea is unconstitutional,[33] as are threats to manufacture evidence or rumors against the defendant if he does not plead guilty.[34] And, of course, as the Court stated in *Brady*, "the State may not produce a plea by actual or threatened physical harm or by mental coercion overbearing the will of the defendant." On the other hand, offering a charge or sentencing concession in return for agreeing not to pursue an appeal or claim some other constitutional right has been found not to violate due process or the Fifth Amendment, on the ground that such waiver

---

32. Some have suggested, nonetheless, that Powell's approach is not very different from the "unconscionability analysis" used by civil courts in contracts cases. See F. Zimring & R. Frase, The Criminal Justice System 587 (1980).

33. *Walker v. Johnston*, 312 U.S. 275, 61 S.Ct. 574 (1941).

34. *Waley v. Johnston*, 316 U.S. 101, 62 S.Ct. 964 (1942).

is no different than the waiver of the right to jury trial and other rights which occurs with a guilty plea.[35]

(3) Statutory inducements. At times, the threat of a greater sentence if no plea is forthcoming comes not from the prosecutor but via statute. In *Corbitt v. New Jersey*,[36] the defendant was tried and convicted of first degree murder and sentenced to life imprisonment, as required by a state statute. Had he pleaded guilty, the same statute permitted the judge to sentence him to either life imprisonment or 30 years (the term for second degree murder). The Supreme Court upheld this scheme against a due process claim, concluding that it could not permit bargaining by a prosecutor, as it had in *Bordenkircher*, "and yet hold that the legislature may not openly provide for the possibility of leniency in return for a plea."

Corbitt does not necessarily approve all "legislative bargaining." As the dissent pointed out, this type of bargaining should be distinguished from prosecutorial bargaining, since the former is not based on individualized factors. Justice Stewart, the author of *Bordenkircher*, argued further in a separate opinion that encouraging plea bargaining is not a legislative, but an executive function. Thus, a legislative provision which automatically gives significant benefits to a person who pleads guilty rather than goes to trial should be "clearly unconstitutional." For example, the legislature should not be able to provide "that the penalty for every criminal offense to which a defendant pleads guilty is to be one-half the penalty to be imposed upon a defendant convicted of the same offense after a not guilty plea." The majority in *Corbitt* seemed to agree with this latter conclusion when it reaffirmed the pre-*Bordenkircher* decision of *United States v. Jackson*,[37] which found unconstitutional, on the ground that it "needlessly encourage[d]" guilty pleas, a statute permitting imposition of the death penalty for a particular offense only after a jury trial. Thus, if a statute does not permit the greater punishment at the guilty plea as well as trial stage, it may violate due process.

(4) Judicial inducements. Traditionally, judges have been barred from involvement in the bargaining process, on the grounds that they might be unduly intimidating to the defendant and could have difficulty remaining neutral if they ended up trying him.[38] But in some jurisdictions this practice has gradually given way to limited judicial participation in plea bargaining, as a means of monitoring the process and providing the parties with

---

35. *People v. Seaberg*, 74 N.Y.2d 1, 543 N.Y.S.2d 968, 541 N.E.2d 1022 (1989); see also, § 26.05(e)(1).

36. 439 U.S. 212, 99 S.Ct. 492 (1978).

37. 390 U.S. 570, 88 S.Ct. 1209 (1968).

38. See, e.g., ABA, Advisory Committee on the Criminal Trial, Standards Relating to Pleas of Guilty 71–74 (1968); Fed.R.Crim.P. 11(e)(1).

more information as to potential sentences. Illustrative are the American Bar Association standards, which allow judicial participation at the request of the parties, provided the judge indicates only what charge or sentence concessions would be acceptable, and "never through word or demeanor, either directly or indirectly, communicate[s] to the defendant or defense counsel that a plea agreement should be accepted or that a guilty plea should be entered." [39] Some commentators have gone further, arguing that bargaining should not take place *except* in front of a judge, who, at a transcribed pretrial conference, would hear evidence from both sides, as well as consider a pre-sentence report, and indicate the sentence he would impose if the defendant pleads guilty.[40]

If the judge makes clear at a pretrial conference that a greater sentence will be imposed if the defendant does not plead, is a subsequent plea coerced? Some courts have answered this question affirmatively, on the ground that "[t]he unequal positions of the judge and the accused, one with the power to commit to prison and the other deeply concerned to avoid prison, at once raise a question of fundamental fairness." [41] But, in light of *Bordenkircher* and *Corbitt,* the Supreme Court would presumably answer this question in the negative.[42] Indeed, because defendants know that courts often accept the prosecutor's sentencing recommendations in any event, there is little functional difference, in "inequality" terms, between judicial and prosecutorial threats of this type.[43]

If judicial involvement is permissible, then, as *Bordenkircher* required of prosecutors, the judge should be required to state with some precision the sentence which will be imposed if a plea of not guilty is entered and conviction follows at trial. Otherwise, there is a grave danger that a judge whose offer is refused will react vindictively and, unconstrained by specific promises, impose a greater sentence than he would have had he not been involved in the negotiations. Alternatively, trial of the defendant who refuses to plead should be assigned to another judge.[44]

(d) Admission of Statements Made In Connection With Bargaining. Under the federal rules, and in most states, "any statement made in the course of plea discussions with an attorney

39. ABA Criminal Justice Standard 14–3.3 (amending the ABA standard cited supra note 38).

40. See Alschuler, "The Trial Judge's Role in Plea Bargaining, Part I," 76 Colum.L.Rev. 1059 (1976).

41. *United States ex rel. Elksnis v. Gilligan,* 256 F.Supp. 244 (S.D.N.Y. 1966).

42. Note also that, in *Brady,* judicial "unwillingness" to hear Brady's capital charge without a jury was not viewed as unconstitutionally coercive, despite the fact that it meant the defendant could only avoid the possibility of a death sentence if he pleaded guilty.

43. See, e.g., *Frank v. Blackburn,* 646 F.2d 873 (5th Cir.1980) (upholding judicial bargaining).

44. This is the suggestion of Alschuler, supra note 40.

for the government which do not result in a plea of guilty or which result in a plea of guilty later withdrawn" are inadmissible in subsequent proceedings.[45] This rule is obviously designed to encourage bargaining. Note, however, that it is does not cover statements made to the police or other individuals who are not attorneys for the government. The admissibility of these admissions is governed by the law of confessions, even when made under the impression that the non-attorney had bargaining authority.[46] Note further that statements made *after* "plea discussions" and the taking of the plea may be admissible in subsequent proceedings if the plea is later withdrawn.[47]

26.03 The Legal Effect of a Bargain

(a) **On the Court.** As a general rule, the court is not bound by a plea bargain reached by the parties.[48] The one obvious exception is when the court participated in the bargaining process and promised the bargain would be fulfilled.[49] Additionally, when the bargain is a "charge bargain" rather than a "sentence bargain," some courts have held, on the theory that charging is a prosecutorial prerogative, that the judge has no authority to reject it unless the dismissal of charges thereby contemplated is "an abuse of prosecutorial discretion."[50] This distinction between the two types of bargains is somewhat problematic, since most charge reductions are sought precisely because of their effect on sentencing. In any event, when the bargain explicitly seeks a particular sentencing disposition, then the court clearly has authority to reject it.[51]

(b) **On the Prosecution.** Once the court accepts a bargain, the prosecutor must fulfill any remaining obligations under it (although occasionally disputes arise over what those obligations are and the remedy for breach). Before the court accepts the bargain, on the other hand, the bargain rarely has binding power on the prosecution.

(1) Post-arraignment. In *Santobello v. New York*,[52] the defendant was indicted on two felony counts. He first entered a plea of not guilty to both counts. After negotiations the prosecutor agreed to allow the defendant to plead guilty to a lesser-included

---

45. Fed.R.Crim.P. 11(e)(6).

46. See § 16.03(d)(2) for a discussion of trickery and confessions cases.

47. *Hutto v. Ross*, 429 U.S. 28, 97 S.Ct. 202 (1976).

48. See, e.g., Fed.R.Crim.P. 11(e)(4). In the federal courts, the nolo plea is accepted "only after due consideration of the views of the parties *and* the interest of the public in the effective ad-

ministration of justice." Fed.R.Crim.P. 11(b) (emphasis added).

49. See § 26.02(c)(4).

50. *United States v. Ammidown*, 497 F.2d 615 (D.C.Cir.1973).

51. As to the consequences for the defendant of such a rejection, see § 26.05(b).

52. 404 U.S. 257, 92 S.Ct. 495 (1971).

offense, conviction of which would carry a maximum sentence of one year, and to make no recommendation as to sentence. Accordingly, the defendant withdrew his plea of not guilty and agreed to plead guilty to the lesser charge. The court accepted the plea. At sentencing, a new prosecutor, unaware of the plea negotiations, requested the maximum one-year sentence. The defense counsel objected on the ground that the first prosecutor had promised to make no recommendation as to sentence. The judge, who stated that he was uninfluenced by the recommendation, imposed the maximum sentence.

The Supreme Court held that the plea should be voided as a matter of due process. The Court noted the many benefits associated with disposing of charges after plea discussions, but added that the utilization of this process presupposes fairness in securing agreement between an accused and a prosecutor. The Court concluded that "when a plea rests in any significant degree on a promise or agreement of the prosecutor, so that it can be said to be part of the inducement or consideration, such promise must be fulfilled." Significantly, it was immaterial to the Court that the prosecution claimed its breach of the agreement had been inadvertent.

In deciding whether a due process violation has occurred under *Santobello,* the precise terms of the agreement must be considered. In *United States v. Benchimol,*[53] the plea agreement included a promise by the government that it would recommend probation with restitution. Instead of making this recommendation, the government's presentence report was silent as to recommendation. When defense counsel pointed out this error, the government's attorney agreed that the promise had been made. The court, however, sentenced the defendant to a term of six years under the Youth Corrections Act. After serving some time, the defendant, arguing that the government had not kept its bargain, moved to have his sentence vacated and be resentenced to time served or to be allowed to withdraw his guilty plea. The court of appeals granted relief, finding that the U.S. Attorney should have stated his grounds for making the lenient recommendation and that, by failing to do so, he "left an impression of less-than-enthusiastic support for leniency." The Supreme Court, in a per curiam opinion, reversed, holding that unless the government agrees to support a particular recommendation "enthusiastically," or to give its reasons for a lenient recommendation, it need not do so.

(2) Pre-arraignment. The prosecutor is given considerably more leeway with respect to adhering to a bargain *before* the

53. 471 U.S. 453, 105 S.Ct. 2103 (1985).

defendant pleads to the court. In *Mabry v. Johnson,*[54] when the defendant's attorney called to accept a dispositional arrangement suggested by the deputy prosecutor, the prosecutor told him that a mistake had been made and withdrew the offer. The prosecutor then proposed a significantly harsher arrangement to which the defendant eventually agreed and which the trial judge accepted at arraignment. The Supreme Court unanimously rejected the court of appeals' reasoning that "fairness" precluded the prosecution's withdrawal of the original plea proposal once it was accepted by the defendant. It pointed out that while the defendant in *Santobello* had pleaded guilty on the false assurance by the state that he had bargained for a specific prosecutorial stance toward sentencing, the defendant's ultimate plea in this case was made with full awareness of the consequences and "was thus in no sense the product of governmental deception; it rested on no 'unfulfilled promise' and fully satisfied the test for voluntariness and intelligence." The Court thus declared irrelevant whether the prosecution was negligent in first making and then withdrawing the original offer.

Mabry did not deal with a pre-arraignment defendant who did *not* accept a second offer after the first, accepted offer is withdrawn. But, in a footnote, the Court suggested that this type of defendant would not be entitled to specific performance either, an issue discussed further below, in connection with remedies. Most lower courts have held that the prosecutor should be allowed to withdraw an accepted offer up to the time a plea is entered unless the defendant has "detrimentally relied" on the agreement before it is withdrawn (by, for instance, testifying against a co-defendant pursuant to the agreement).[55] While this rule runs counter to traditional contract doctrine, so does the well-accepted principle that the defendant may refuse to plead guilty at the time of arraignment despite any previous bargains.[56] Thus, the rule has a reciprocal fairness to it.

(3) Remedy for breach. Of the seven justices who deliberated in *Santobello,* four appeared to agree that if the prosecution fails to abide by an agreement accepted by the court, the defendant is entitled either to specific performance of the agreement (which, in *Santobello,* would have required the prosecutor to make the agreed-upon recommendation to a different judge), or to withdraw the plea. The other three justices appeared to leave the choice of remedy up to the trial court, although they also stated that one or the other remedy might be "required" under some, unspecified circumstances.

54. 467 U.S. 504, 104 S.Ct. 2543 (1984).

55. See *People v. Heiler,* 79 Mich. App. 714, 262 N.W.2d 890 (1977). But

see, *Cooper v. United States,* 594 F.2d 12 (4th Cir.1979).

56. See, e.g., Fed.R.Crim.P. 11(c)(3).

If the choice of remedy is the defendant's, it will usually be in favor of specific performance, since a plea withdrawal requires the parties to begin the bargaining process over again, with unclear results. However, in *Mabry,* the Court intimated that the choice may not be the defendant's. In a footnote, the Court stated that "*Santobello* expressly declined to hold that the Constitution compels specific performance of a broken prosecutorial promise . . .; the Court made it clear that permitting Santobello to replead was within the range of constitutionally appropriate remedies." This somewhat cryptically phrased passage suggests that the defendant can be forced, either pre- *or* post-arraignment, to replead or go to trial rather than be allowed to demand specific performance of an agreed-upon bargain that has been broken.

While, as discussed above, this approach is usually justifiable for pre-arraignment breaches, it is inappropriate after a plea has been entered, for two reasons. First, after a plea is entered, the defendant is usually not permitted to withdraw it unless the agreement is not fulfilled or an error of constitutional or near constitutional magnitude has occurred.[57] Thus, the "reciprocal fairness" argument in favor of allowing pre-arraignment breaches does not apply here. Second, although in many cases there may be no more "concrete" detrimental reliance on a post-plea bargain than on a pre-plea bargain, allowing the prosecution to breach with impunity an agreement that has been endorsed by the court damages the integrity of the system, not only in the eyes of the defendant but of the public at large as well. Nonetheless most courts hold that the defendant is not entitled to specific performance for post-arraignment breaches.[58]

(c) On the Defendant. As already noted, up until the time of arraignment, the defendant may plead not guilty despite a previous agreement to plead guilty. But if he wants the benefits of the bargain, he may have certain obligations beyond merely pleading guilty at the arraignment. Some courts have reasonably held, for instance, that the prosecution need not abide by an agreement based on inaccurate information provided by the defendant.[59] The agreement itself may also impose obligations on the defendant beyond simply pleading guilty. For instance, one common type of bargain already mentioned is a reduction in charges in exchange for testimony against a codefendant. If the defendant refuses to provide the testimony, the plea might be vacated.

57. See § 26.05(b).

58. See, e.g., *United States v. Moscahlaidis,* 868 F.2d 1357 (3d Cir.1989). Occasionally, of course, specific performance is not possible, as when the prosecutor has promised to recommend a sentence which is not legally authorized.

59. Hamlin v. Barrett, 335 So.2d 898 (Miss.1976).

The Supreme Court had occasion to address the latter situation in *Ricketts v. Adamson*.[60] There, the defendant did testify against his two codefendants and helped secure their convictions, in exchange for a reduction in charge from first to second degree murder. However, after he had been sentenced on the latter charge, the codefendants' convictions were overturned on appeal. When the prosecution sought the defendant's testimony at the retrial, the defendant told the prosecution that he believed his obligation to testify had terminated when he had been sentenced and that he would testify again only if the state would release him from custody following the retrial. The prosecution informed the defendant that he was in breach of the agreement and eventually filed an information recharging him with first degree murder. The defendant challenged the validity of the information in state court, arguing it violated the Double Jeopardy Clause. The Arizona Supreme Court found that the defendant had breached the agreement and ordered that he be tried on the original first degree murder charge. Despite his indication that he was now willing to testify against the codefendants, the defendant was tried on the charge and sentenced to death.

The Court, in a 5–4 decision authored by Justice White, held that double jeopardy did not bar the first degree murder prosecution because the plea agreement specifically stated that in the event the defendant refused to testify "this entire agreement is null and void and the original charge will be automatically reinstated." The dissent, authored by Justice Brennan, did not contest the notion that the double jeopardy right could be waived through a plea agreement. However, Brennan argued that under the terms of the agreement at issue in *Adamson* the defendant could reasonably have believed he was required to testify only prior to his sentencing (indeed, the express wording of the agreement spoke of the defendant being sentenced "at the conclusion of his testimony");[61] thus, his communication to the state of the terms under which he would testify after sentencing was not *necessarily* a breach of the agreement. The proper procedure, Brennan contended, would have been to submit the disagreement about the interpretation of the plea to the court which accepted the plea; the state should be able to try the defendant on the greater charge only if the court decided the defendant's interpretation was in error and the defendant continued to refuse to testify.

Adamson, like *Mabry*, indicates that the defendant cannot demand specific performance of a broken bargain. Defendants

60. 483 U.S. 1, 107 S.Ct. 2680 (1987).

61. Contrast the Court's unwillingness to countenance the defendant's literal reading of the plea agreement here with its willingness to allow such a reading when it favors the state. *United States v. Benchimol*, 471 U.S. 453, 105 S.Ct. 2103 (1985), discussed in § 26.03(b)(1).

who disagree with the state's interpretation of a plea agreement now do so at the risk of having the entire plea vacated if the prosecution can convince a court its interpretation is correct, regardless of the defendant's subsequent willingness to abide by the agreement as construed by the court.

26.04 Taking the Plea

If a defendant decides to plead guilty, whether pursuant to a plea bargain or not, the arraignment judge must ensure that the plea meets constitutional and statutory standards. According to the Supreme Court's decision in *Boykin v. Alabama*,[62] it is constitutional error "for the trial judge to accept [a] guilty plea without an affirmative showing that it is intelligent and voluntary." Additionally, local rules often require the judge to inquire into various matters, including, most importantly, the nature of any bargains reached.

Very often this procedure will be pro forma, since the parties, through the plea bargaining process, have usually already agreed to and understand the charges involved, the penalties that they would like imposed, and any other relevant quid pro quo. Nonetheless, the Supreme Court has indicated that a direct interview of the defendant by the arraignment judge is important, if not constitutionally required. In *McCarthy v. United States*,[63] it stated:

> By personally interrogating the defendant, not only will the judge be better able to ascertain the plea's voluntariness, but he also will develop a more complete record to support his determination in a subsequent post-conviction attack. . . .
> Both of these goals are undermined in proportion to the degree the district court judge resorts to "assumptions" not based upon recorded responses to his inquiries.

Summarizing these various requirements, the arraignment judge should address the defendant to ensure: (1) that the plea is "intelligent," i.e., that the defendant understands the elements of the plea and any associated bargain; and (2) that the plea is "voluntary," i.e., that the defendant was not coerced into the plea. Additionally, to ensure that the plea is "accurate," the judge should make some affort to ascertain (3) that there is some sort of factual basis for the plea. These aspects of the arraignment are discussed here.

(a) The Intelligent Plea Requirement. Federal Rule 11(c), which has served as a model for many states, provides that the court may not accept a guilty plea until it has determined that the defendant understands: (1) the nature of the charge or charges to

---

62. 395 U.S. 238, 89 S.Ct. 1709 (1969).

63. 394 U.S. 459, 89 S.Ct. 1166 (1969).

which a plea is offered; (2) the possible sentence for each offense to which a plea is offered; and (3) the rights he will be waiving if he pleads guilty, i.e. the rights to: be tried by a jury, the assistance of counsel at trial, confront and cross-examine witnesses against him, and avoid compelled self-incrimination. Rule 11(e) imposes further requirements with respect to ensuring the defendant understands the nature of any plea bargain he has entered into. The discussion here focuses on which, if any, of these requirements are constitutionally necessary, and whether they recognize all the crucial aspects of the case which the defendant must understand in order to ensure a constitutionally adequate plea.

(1) Understanding the charge. In *Henderson v. Morgan,*[64] the defendant was indicted for first-degree murder, but pleaded guilty to second-degree murder on the advice of counsel and with the agreement of the prosecutor. Five years later he attempted to vacate the conviction on the ground that at the time of his plea he had not known that intent to cause death was an element of second-degree murder. The Supreme Court held that "since respondent did not receive adequate notice of the offense to which he pleaded guilty, his plea was involuntary and the judgment of conviction was entered without due process of law." Because the intent element of a murder charge is a "critical" element of the charge, the fact that neither the judge nor the defense attorney explained this element to the defendant invalidated the plea.

Two things remain unclear after *Henderson.* First is the definition of "critical." In a footnote, the Court stated:

> There is no need in this case to decide whether notice of the true nature, or substance, of a charge always requires a description of the offense; we assume it does not. Nevertheless, intent is such a critical element of the offense of second-degree murder that notice of that element is required.

It would seem that any element knowledge of which might have the effect of changing the plea of the defendant should be described. Thus, for instance, the defendant should have notice of every element which has the effect of differentiating the charged offense from a lesser included offense. On the other hand, most courts have held that inquiry into "defenses" would require too much guesswork, especially if dependent upon individualized factors, and are more appropriately the province of the attorney.[65]

---

64. 426 U.S. 637, 96 S.Ct. 2253 (1976).

65. *United States v. Lumpkins,* 845 F.2d 1444 (7th Cir.1988) (statute of limitations); *Dismuke v. United States,* 864 F.2d 106 (11th Cir.1989) (good faith); *United States ex rel. Salisbury v. Blackburn,* 792 F.2d 498 (5th Cir.1986) (insanity).

The second issue left unclear after *Henderson* is the precise obligation of the judge with respect to notice of those elements which are "critical." Arguably, to ensure an intelligent plea, the judge should inquire into the defendant's understanding of these elements. Yet *Henderson* suggests that even if the judge makes no such inquiry, "a representation [on the record] by defense counsel that the nature of the offense has been explained to the accused" will suffice. Indeed, "it may be appropriate to presume that in most cases defense counsel routinely explain the nature of the offense in sufficient detail to give the accused notice of what he is being asked to admit." Thus, the Constitution may only require the judge to ask defense counsel if the defendant understands the charge against him.

Henderson also suggests that, even if such a certification by counsel is not made, a plea is valid if the defendant provides a "factual statement or admission necessarily implying that he [met all critical elements]." In such a situation, the judge is again apparently absolved for failing to inquire into the defendant's understanding of the charges. The problem here is that an admission of guilt does not necessarily mean the defendant has thought through whether the prosecution would be able to prove the relevant elements at trial; without information as to the nature of these elements, either from the attorney or the judge, an intelligent decision about whether to plead cannot be made. Nonetheless, lower courts tend to follow this aspect of *Henderson*.[66]

(2) Understanding of consequences. Prior to 1975, Rule 11(c)(1) of the federal rules required the court to inform the defendant of the "consequences of the plea." In that year, the Rule was amended to require disclosure concerning the minimum and maximum sentences that might be received, as well as the effect of any special parole term (which can result in confinement beyond the maximum term otherwise provided). In 1989, the Rule was further amended to ensure the defendant is informed of any applicable sentencing guidelines (which replaced the previous system of flexible sentences and "ordinary" parole[67]), as well as any possibility that the court may order the defendant to make restitution to a victim of the offense.

Despite the breadth of the federal rule, other dispositional information might also be considered important. For instance, the ABA Standards[68] require the judge to inform the defendant of any different or additional punishment that might be authorized

---

66. See, e.g., *Commonwealth v. Colantoni*, 396 Mass. 672, 488 N.E.2d 394 (1986).

67. See 28 U.S.C.A. § 994(a) (establishing guidelines); 18 U.S.C.A. § 3624(a)(b) (abolishing parole).

68. See ABA, supra note 1, Standard 14-1.4(a)(iii).

by reason of the defendant's previous conviction of an offense. In addition, they require that a defendant be informed of special circumstances relating to release or probation. On the other hand, there is agreement among the lower courts that "collateral" consequences of a plea, such as loss of the right to vote, need not be described.[69] And the Supreme Court has indicated it would not require the pleading defendant to be told of his parole eligibility under ordinary parole provisions. In *Hill v. Lockhart,*[70] the Court stated: "We have never held that the United States Constitution requires the State to furnish a defendant with information about parole eligibility in order for the defendant's plea of guilty to be voluntary." Although this holding is irrelevant in federal court now that federal parole has been abolished, it obviously is still pertinent in states which have parole provisions.

Indeed, for *constitutional* purposes, it may not be necessary to show the judge informed the defendant about any of the consequences of his plea. As with the necessity of informing the defendant about the nature of the charge against him, it may be sufficient to show on the record that defense counsel has apprised the defendant of the plea's consequences.[71] However, given the ease with which minimum and maximum penalties can be described, and *Boykin's* requirement that there be "an affirmative showing" that the plea was intelligently and understandingly made, an explicit discourse by the judge on the significant consequences flowing from a plea should be mandatory.

(3) Understanding rights waived by a plea. Prior to 1975, Rule 11 did not require the judge to inform the defendant of the rights waived by a plea, apparently on the highly dubious assumption that simply telling the defendant a guilty plea waives his right to trial is sufficient notice of the other rights he is waiving. The Court's decision in *Boykin* suggests that the new rule's explicit notice of the rights waived is constitutionally required. There, the accused, represented by appointed counsel, pleaded guilty to five indictments for common law robbery. So far as the record showed, the judge asked no questions of the accused concerning his plea, and the accused did not address the court. The Supreme Court overturned his convictions because the record did not disclose that the defendant had voluntarily and intelligently entered pleas of guilty. The Court stressed that a guilty plea waives the privilege against self-incrimination, the right to trial by jury and

69. See, e.g., *People v. Thomas,* 41 Ill.2d 122, 242 N.E.2d 177 (1968) (loss of right to vote); *Moore v. Hinton,* 513 F.2d 781 (5th Cir.1975) (loss of driver's license); *Steinsvik v. Vinzant,* 640 F.2d 949 (9th Cir.1981) (deportation).

70. 474 U.S. 52, 106 S.Ct. 366 (1985).

71. Some courts appear to take this tack with respect to determining understanding of sentencing guidelines, despite the Rule's requirement in this regard. See, e.g., *United States v. Alvarez-Quiroga,* 901 F.2d 1433 (7th Cir. 1990).

the right to confront one's accusers. It concluded: "We cannot presume a waiver of these three important federal rights from a silent record." This language strongly supports the notion that the judge must determine whether these specific rights are understood, which can usually best be effectuated simply by describing them to the defendant as required by Rule 11.[72]

(4) Understanding the bargain. Before *Brady,* the fact that the parties had bargained was seldom admitted to in open court, given its uncertain legal status. Now that plea bargaining is accepted, most jurisdictions require that the agreement be clearly revealed on the record at the time the guilty plea is taken. The federal rules, for instance, stipulate that the agreement must be disclosed at the time the plea is offered in court (though, on a showing of good cause, the disclosure may be made *in camera*).[73] This type of rule helps ensure that all the parties to the bargain are aware of its terms and agree upon them, and also facilitates later review of the bargain.

The facts of *Blackledge v. Allison,*[74] which involved a plea accepted before *Brady* was decided, are illustrative. There, the only record of the plea was an executed "plea form" from which the judge had read a number of questions, including whether anyone had "made any promises or threats" that influenced the defendant. The defendant later claimed on habeas that his attorney had told him to give a negative answer to this question, but that in fact he had been promised a lesser sentence than he received; in support of this claim, he provided precise information as to the nature of the promise and when it was made. The Supreme Court, taking note of the defendant's proof, and speculating that defense counsel may have advised the defendant to lie at the arraignment given "the ambiguous status of the process of plea bargaining at the time the guilty plea was made," found that the defendant was entitled to a hearing on his claim.

More importantly, the Court went on to note that North Carolina, the state in which the plea took place, had recently reformed its plea practices to require the judge, on the record, to make "specific inquiry" of both the defendant and the attorneys about whether a plea bargain had been struck and, if so, the nature of the bargain. "Had these commendable procedures been followed in the present case," continued the Court, "Allison's petition would have been cast in a very different light." *Allison* does not constitutionalize disclosure requirements, but provides a strong rationale for them. If procedures like these are followed, it

---

72. However, the Court later upheld a guilty plea from a defendant who had not been advised of these rights, with no discussion of the point. *Brady v.* *United States,* 397 U.S. 742, 90 S.Ct. 1463 (1970).

73. Fed.R.Crim.P. 11(e)(2).

74. 431 U.S. 63, 97 S.Ct. 1621 (1977).

will be difficult for the defendant to later claim that either the prosecutor or his own counsel misled him as to elements of the bargain.

A second requirement relating to the defendant's understanding of the plea bargain has to do with alerting him to the court's possible reaction to the bargain. As discussed later in this chapter,[75] although judicial rejection of agreed-upon terms usually allows the defendant to withdraw his plea, in some jurisdictions a plea of guilty at arraignment may not be withdrawn if the court merely fails to follow, at a subsequent sentencing proceeding, a sentencing recommendation or request made as part of the agreement between the parties. Because this rule is founded on the assumption that the defendant knows the court may arrive at a stiffer sentence, the federal rules require the arraignment judge to inform the defendant who has entered into such a bargain that he may not back out of the plea if, after consideration of the presentence report and other matters, the court decides not to endorse the recommendation or request.[76]

(5) Competence. Occasionally, a person's mental status will be so suspect that he is incapable of understanding the various aspects of a guilty plea and any associated bargain. Typically, such an individual will be found incompetent prior to arraignment and treated to restore his competency. If his competency is restored, he will be given the option, as with any other defendant, of going to trial or pleading guilty. If not restorable, he will normally be hospitalized or released.[77]

Although a competency hearing thus need not be a routine part of the arraignment, a plea can be invalidated if the judge fails to inquire into the effects of obvious mental disability or other disabilities.[78] In most states, no distinction is made between the standard for determining incompetence to plead guilty and the test for determining incompetence to stand trial. Some have argued that this equation is inappropriate. A plea of guilty not only requires an understanding of the legal situation and an ability to communicate with the attorney (which is all that is required before a finding of competence to stand trial),[79] but, as noted above, also requires an understanding of the rights being waived by not going to trial. Additionally, it is argued, a guilty plea requires more "competence" because the defendant, not a jury, is making the dispositive decision.[80]

75. See § 26.05(b).

76. Fed.R.Crim.P. 11(e)(2).

77. This is the procedure applied to those found incompetent to stand trial, described in § 28.03(b).

78. *Fontaine v. United States*, 411 U.S. 213, 93 S.Ct. 1461 (1973).

79. See § 28.03(b)(1).

80. See *Sieling v. Eyman*, 478 F.2d 211 (9th Cir.1973).

In response, it has been noted that a higher competency standard for guilty pleas might "create a class of semi-competent defendants who are not protected from prosecution because they have been found competent to stand trial, but who are denied the leniency of the plea bargaining process because they are not competent to plead guilty." [81] Further, it can be assumed that a guilty plea is usually in the best interests of the defendant who has adequate counsel. Thus, it has been argued, the counselled defendant who is "barely" competent to stand trial (and thus perhaps not, technically speaking, competent to plead guilty), should nonetheless be allowed to plead guilty if he wants to.[82]

(b) The Voluntariness Requirement. *Boykin* emphasized that a plea may be rendered constitutionally invalid not only by "ignorance" or "incomprehension," but also by "coercion, terror, inducements, [and] subtle or blatant threats." Rule 11(d), similar to most state rules, attempts to protect against the danger of such coercion by requiring the judge to address the defendant personally in court and determine that any offered plea is "voluntary and not the result of force or threats or of promises apart from a plea agreement." As discussed in detail earlier,[83] threats or promises within the context of the bargaining process are unlikely to be deemed coercive.

(c) The Factual Basis Requirement. Rule 11 not only requires the court to ensure that a plea is intelligently and voluntarily given, but also that it make "such inquiry as shall satisfy it that there is a factual basis for the plea." [84] The Advisory Committee notes on this rule state that the factual basis should be developed on the record, "for example, by having the accused describe the conduct that gave rise to the charge." [85] As the Supreme Court stated in *McCarthy v. United States*,[86] "[r]equiring this examination of the relation between the law and the acts the defendant admits having committed is designed to 'protect a defendant who is in the position of pleading voluntarily with an understanding of the nature of the charge but without realizing that his conduct does not actually fall within the charge.'"

McCarthy merely construed Rule 11; it did not explicitly hold that the factual basis inquiry was constitutionally required. However, in *North Carolina v. Alford* [87] the Court appeared to give the

81. Note, "Competence to Plead Guilty: A New Standard 1974 Duke L.J. 149, 170.

82. Winick, "Incompetency to Stand Trial: An Assessment of Costs and Benefits, and a Proposal for Reform," 39 Rutgers L.Rev. 243 (1987).

83. See § 26.02(c).

84. Fed.R.Crim.P. 11(f).

85. Quoting *Santobello v. New York,* 404 U.S. 257, 92 S.Ct. 495 (1971).

86. 394 U.S. 459, 89 S.Ct. 1166 (1969).

87. 400 U.S. 25, 91 S.Ct. 160 (1970).

McCarthy holding constitutional status under at least one specific circumstance: when the defendant refuses to admit his guilt. The defendant in *Alford* pleaded guilty to a 30–year term, but insisted on his innocence. The Court first held that "an express admission of guilt . . . is not a constitutional requisite to the imposition of criminal penalty. An individual accused of crime may voluntarily, knowingly, and understandingly consent to the imposition of a prison sentence even if he is unwilling or unable to admit his participation in the acts constituting the crime." The Court then upheld the plea, "[i]n view of the strong factual basis for the plea demonstrated by the State and Alford's clearly expressed desire to enter it despite his professed belief in his innocence." In a footnote, the Court continued:

> Because of the importance of protecting the innocent and of insuring that guilty pleas are a product of free and intelligent choice, various state and federal court decisions properly caution that pleas coupled with claims of innocence should not be accepted unless there is a factual basis for the plea . . . and until the judge taking the plea has inquired into and sought to resolve the conflict between the waiver of trial and the claim of innocence.

Conversely, if such a factual basis is established, a court should not be prevented from accepting an otherwise intelligent and voluntary guilty plea from an individual merely because he refuses to admit his guilt.

26.05   Challenging a Guilty Plea

(a) Substantive and Procedural Options. Although the types of claims that can be raised in an effort to nullify or overturn a guilty plea are numerous, they can be divided into three categories: (1) allegations that the plea is invalid because it was not voluntary or intelligent ("direct" challenges of the plea);[88] (2) allegations that the plea should be nullified because the bargain upon which it was based was breached by the prosecution or was not fully carried out by the court ("breach-of-bargain" challenges);[89] and (3) allegations that the conviction represented by the plea should be overturned because of other defects in the pretrial process, such as an illegal search and seizure or an indictment by an illegally constituted grand jury ("independent" challenges).

The likely success of each type of claim depends in part upon the procedure used to assert them. There are several ways of attacking a guilty plea. The first involves making a "motion to withdraw" a plea. The second is through filing a direct appeal

---

88. See § 26.02(c) and § 26.04.   **89.** See § 26.03(a) & (b).

challenging the plea. The third is via a writ of habeas corpus or other collateral relief.

(b) Withdrawal of the Plea. After a plea is entered, it may be withdrawn under various circumstances, depending upon the jurisdiction. Under the federal rules, withdrawal is permitted only prior to the formal imposition of sentence; after the sentencing proceeding the plea may be challenged solely on direct appeal or habeas.[90] The federal standard governing withdrawal asks whether the defendant can show "any fair and just reason" for overturning the plea, which also approximates the test used in most state jurisdictions that limit withdrawals to pre-sentence motions. Under this standard, the defendant must make a plausible showing that one of the three grounds described above are satisfied, i.e. (1) that the plea was coerced, "unintelligent," or in some other way deficient; (2) that the bargain upon which the plea was based has been breached by the prosecution or not endorsed by the court; or, (3) that, for "good reason," [91] a defense was overlooked prior to the plea that the defendant now seeks to raise.

One further word is necessary regarding pre-sentence withdrawals based on the second-type of claim, the "breach-of-bargain" claim. Out of a concern for fairness to defendants, the general rule is that the defendant may withdraw a plea if the court fails to endorse a bargained-for charge or sentence; every jurisdiction probably follows the federal practice of permitting withdrawal when the judge rejects a sentence (or a charge) that the parties have agreed is the "appropriate disposition." [92] But, under the federal rules and the rules of several states,[93] a withdrawal motion need not be granted if the court rejects a sentence that the government merely agreed to "recommend or not oppose," provided the government carried out its obligation and the judge indicated at arraignment that this action would not be binding on him. This stance is justified on the assumption that the defendant "knew the nonbinding character of the recommendation or request." [94] Other courts reject this position, on the ground that the defendant, in effect, has been falsely induced to plead when the sentence does not coincide with that bargained for.[95]

In some state jurisdictions, a plea may also be withdrawn after the sentencing hearing. Here, however, the prosecution is

90. Fed.R.Crim.P. 32(d).

91. *United States v. Barker,* 514 F.2d 208 (D.C.Cir.1975), cert. denied 421 U.S. 1013, 95 S.Ct. 2420 (1975).

92. See Fed.R.Crim.P. 11(e)(1), (2) & (4).

93. Fed.R.Crim.P. 11(e)(2). See, *United States v. Henderson,* 565 F.2d 1119 (9th Cir.1977); *People v. Lambrechts,* 69 Ill.2d 544, 14 Ill.Dec. 445, 372 N.E.2d 641 (1977).

94. Advisory Committee Note to Rule 11(e)(2), as amended in 1979.

95. See, e.g., *King v. State,* 553 P.2d 529 (Okl.Crim.1976).

more likely to be prejudiced by withdrawal and a motion is more likely to reflect second thoughts about a validly entered plea rather than a legitimate challenge. Thus, the defendant is usually required to meet the more stringent "manifest injustice" standard, a term borrowed from the ABA Criminal Justice Standards.[96] For instance, with respect to "independent" challenges to the plea, a "good reason" for not discovering a defense by the time of the plea may be insufficient; rather, the defendant may have to demonstrate that defense counsel error of constitutional magnitude was the cause of the oversight.[97]

(c) **Appeal.** The defendant may always appeal denial of a withdrawal motion. But once the time for withdrawal has passed (which, as noted above, in many jurisdictions occurs once sentence has been imposed), only "direct" appeal of the plea is possible. Unlike either a withdrawal motion made at the trial level or a habeas petition, an appeal may only raise issues that can be addressed from the trial court transcript (which in the case of a direct appeal of a plea usually consists solely of the arraignment proceedings). Thus, claims which require proof of events beyond the arraignment (e.g., virtually all independent claims and any bargain challenges that require proof of a dispute over the nature of plea discussions) are generally not justiciable on direct appeal.

A few states and the federal government have created a "conditional plea" mechanism, which allows an appeal on specified pretrial motions involving independent challenges (e.g., Fourth Amendment claims).[98] Under these statutes, a defendant is permitted to plead guilty but preserve for appeal (usually on a stipulated factual record) the independent claim; if the appeal prevails, the defendant is allowed to withdraw his plea. The conditional plea procedure is meant to encourage guilty pleas by "factually guilty" defendants who otherwise would go to trial (in the process costing the state time and money) merely to sustain a claim that they are not "legally guilty."

Appeals under such statutes aside, the guilty plea challenge most likely to be heard on appeal is of the "direct" variety, since it can often be based on the arraignment transcript. The typical question on these appeals is whether arraignment procedures were followed and, if not, what the remedy should be. In *McCarthy v. United States,*[99] the Supreme Court held that, in the federal system, failure to comply *strictly* with Rule 11's arraignment procedures required reversal on appeal. The Court gave two

---

96. ABA Criminal Justice Standard 14–2.1(a).

97. Cf. § 26.05(d) (discussing independent claims on habeas).

98. See, e.g., Fed.R.Crim.P. 11(a)(2); *Lefkowitz v. Newsome,* 420 U.S. 283, 95 S.Ct. 886 (1975) (discussing such statutes).

99. 394 U.S. 459, 89 S.Ct. 1166 (1969).

reasons for this holding: (1) the procedure "is designed to assist the district judge in making the constitutionally required determination that a defendant's guilty plea is truly voluntary;" and (2) "the more meticulously the Rule is adhered to, the more it tends to discourage, or at least to enable more expeditious disposition of, the numerous and often frivolous post-conviction attacks on the constitutional validity of guilty pleas." In *McCarthy,* the arraignment judge's failure to inform the defendant that the crime to which he pleaded guilty required proof of specific intent invalidated the plea, despite the absence of clear proof that the defendant misunderstood this point.

McCarthy's "strict adherence" approach may no longer be good law, however. Rule 11 has since been amended to provide that "[a]ny variance from the procedures required by this rule which does not affect substantial rights shall be disregarded." [1] This amendment was adopted because of the current complexity of the rule, and the difficulty of perfect compliance.[2] It is probable that most state appellate courts adopt this "harmless error" approach to such claims as well, especially since the Court has indicated that, under the *Constitution,* failure to follow even the most important aspects of arraignment procedure does not render a plea invalid if there was other evidence the defendant understood the consequences of the plea.[3]

(d) Federal Habeas: Direct and Bargain Challenges. While a guilty plea by a state defendant can be challenged collaterally at the state level, this discussion will focus solely on federal habeas review, as representative of the usual approach. To best understand this approach, a distinction should be made between direct and bargain challenges, on the one hand, and independent challenges on the other.

Most relevant to the first two types of challenges is the requirement that a federal defendant's claim on habeas involve "a complete miscarriage of justice" or "an omission inconsistent with the rudimentary demands of fair procedure." [4] Thus, when making a direct or bargain challenge, such a defendant must show significantly more prejudice than he would have to on appeal (or on a pre-sentence withdrawal motion). For example, in *United States v. Timmreck,*[5] the Supreme Court noted that the arraignment judge's failure to inform the defendant of a special parole provision (which ended up adding 5 years to his sentence) would probably have required reversal on appeal under *McCarthy.* But

1. Fed.R.Crim.P. 11(h).

2. Advisory Committee Note, Rule 11(h).

3. *Henderson v. Morgan,* 426 U.S. 637, 96 S.Ct. 2253 (1976), discussed in § 26.04(a)(1).

4. *Hill v. United States,* 368 U.S. 424, 82 S.Ct. 468 (1962).

5. 441 U.S. 780, 99 S.Ct. 2085 (1979).

it concluded that, absent a showing that the defendant would have acted differently had he been so informed, relief should not be granted now that the case was in a post-appeal posture. The extent to which a state defendant can challenge a plea in federal habeas court is even more limited, since his claim must generally be based on federal constitutional grounds.[6]

(e) Federal Habeas: Independent Challenges. Many independent challenges of guilty pleas cannot be raised on habeas at all. According to the Supreme Court, "a guilty plea represents a break in the chain of events which has preceded it in the criminal process."[7] Thus, while the voluntariness of the plea or its adherence to a previous bargain is subject to attack on habeas, a plea that is valid in these two senses precludes most other claims.

(1) The general rule. The Supreme Court first addressed the preclusive effect of guilty pleas in a trilogy of cases decided in 1970. In *McMann v. Richardson,*[8] the defendants asserted that their guilty pleas many years earlier had been motivated by coerced confessions. The Court of Appeals held that this type of claim could be heard on habeas, at least when, as was true at the time of the defendants' pleas, state law provided that the voluntariness of a confession was to be decided by the jury, not the judge; it reasoned that the defendants may have been deterred from going to trial by this practice, which had subsequently been found unconstitutional in *Jackson v. Denno,*[9] and applied retroactively to defendants who had gone to trial. The Supreme Court reversed, holding that a defendant who pleads guilty "is in a different posture" than one who goes to trial. Had the defendants gone to trial and their confessions erroneously been admitted against them, the Court explained, the basis for conviction might well have been their confessions, and it is this "conviction and the confession on which it rests that the defendant later attacks in collateral proceedings." In contrast, the sole basis for a defendant's guilty plea is a "counseled admission in open court that he committed the crime charged against him." The confession "is not the basis for the judgment, has never been offered in evidence at a trial, and may never be offered in evidence."[10]

The Court conceded that, had the defendants had the benefit of *Jackson,* their confessions might have been found coerced and kept from the jury (thus obviating the need to plead guilty). But it characterized this possibility as "a highly speculative matter in

---

6. See generally, § 33.02.

7. *Tollett v. Henderson,* 411 U.S. 258, 93 S.Ct. 1602 (1973).

8. 397 U.S. 759, 90 S.Ct. 1441 (1970).

9. 378 U.S. 368, 84 S.Ct. 1774 (1964), discussed in § 16.05(c).

10. Note, however, that the distinction between guilty pleas and trial verdicts is no longer as broad as the Court suggests; even defendants who go to trial cannot use habeas to vindicate claims not raised at the time of trial. See § 33.03(c).

any particular case and not an issue promising a meaningful and productive evidentiary hearing long after entry of the guilty plea." Further, noted the Court, finding for the defendant would invalidate all pleas motivated by confessions prior to *Jackson*. This "would be an improvident invasion of the State's interest in maintaining the finality of guilty plea convictions which were valid under constitutional standards applicable at the time." The Court might have added, as one commentator has noted, that "the entry of the plea itself may . . . impair[ ] the state's ability thereafter to prove the defendant guilty at trial." [11]

Similarly, in *Brady v. United States*,[12] a companion case to *McMann*, the Court refused to overturn a guilty plea of a defendant charged under a statute which the Court later found unconstitutional because it "needlessly encouraged guilty pleas." [13] To the defendant's argument that his plea was not "intelligent" given this subsequent decision,[14] the Court stated "[t]he rule that a plea must be intelligently made to be valid does not require that a plea be vulnerable to later attack if the defendant did not correctly assess every relevant factor entering into his decision." In the third case of the trilogy, *Parker v. North Carolina*,[15] the Court likewise held that the defendant's coerced confession claim was barred by his guilty plea.

In a later case, *Tollett v. Henderson*,[16] the Court stated its position even more forcefully: "When a criminal defendant has solemnly admitted in open court that he is in fact guilty of the offense with which he is charged, he may not thereafter raise independent claims relating to the deprivation of constitutional rights that occurred prior to the entry of the guilty plea." The Court then held that a defendant who had pleaded guilty could not subsequently challenge on habeas the racial composition of the grand jury which indicted him, a claim which has received very generous treatment from the Court in other contexts.[17] *Tollett* and the cases leading up to it suggested that any claim which does not directly attack the voluntariness or accuracy of the plea would be barred on habeas.

(2) Ineffective assistance. There are three narrow caveats to *Tollett's* preclusion rule, however. The first was expressed in

11. Westen, "Away From Waiver: A Rationale for the Forfeiture of Constitutional Rights in Criminal Procedure," 75 Mich.L.Rev. 1214, 1236 (1977).

12. 397 U.S. 742, 90 S.Ct. 1463 (1970).

13. *United States v. Jackson*, 390 U.S. 570, 88 S.Ct. 1209 (1968), discussed in § 26.02(c)(3).

14. As to the defendant's argument that his plea was not "voluntary," see § 26.02(c)(1).

15. 397 U.S. 790, 90 S.Ct. 1458 (1970).

16. 411 U.S. 258, 93 S.Ct. 1602 (1973).

17. See § 23.06(c) (discussing challenges of grand jury indictments); § 29.05(c)(2) (discussing harmless error analysis).

McMann: if the defendant can show that the reason he did not raise the "independent claim" at the time of the plea was that he had received advice from counsel outside "the range of competence demanded of attorneys in criminal cases," then it could be heard on habeas. The Court made clear in *McMann* that mere failure to raise a claim that might have been successful did not mean incompetence under this standard. For instance, it stated, "[t]hat this Court might hold a defendant's confession inadmissible in evidence, possibly by a divided vote, hardly justifies a conclusion that the defendant's attorney was incompetent or ineffective when he thought the admissibility of the confession sufficiently probable to advise a plea of guilty."

The facts of *Parker* concretely illustrate this point. There the defendant, a 15 year-old Afro–American, was questioned for one to two hours late at night, and then questioned again the next morning after receiving a drink of water. Soon thereafter, he confessed to a burglary and rape. Although there was some evidence that the defendant was not given food, was promised "help" if he confessed, and was denied access to an attorney, counsel decided not to challenge the admissibility of the confession after the defendant denied being frightened or receiving any threats or promises. The Court stated that "even if Parker's counsel was wrong in his assessment of Parker's confession, it does not follow his error was sufficient to render the plea unintelligent and entitle Parker to disavow his admission in open court that he committed the offense with which he was charged."

The Court's subsequent decision in *Hill v. Lockhart*[18] has further narrowed this aspect of *McMann* and *Parker* to require that the defendant show not just that counsel's performance was "seriously" deficient, but also that there is "a reasonable probability that, but for counsel's errors, [the defendant] would not have pleaded guilty and would have insisted on going to trial." For instance, the Court stated in *Hill,* if the claim is that counsel failed to advise the defendant of an affirmative defense, the defendant must also show that "the affirmative defense would likely have succeeded at trial."

This stringent test for ineffective assistance does not foreclose an independent claim against a guilty plea. An extremely persuasive claim, for instance, would both suggest that counsel was derelict for not raising it at a trial and indicate that the verdict at trial might have been acquittal had it been asserted. But most claims will not qualify for the ineffective assistance exception to the general rule that a guilty plea forecloses independent challenges of guilty pleas.[19]

18. 474 U.S. 52, 106 S.Ct. 366 (1985).

19. For further discussion of ineffective assistance of counsel claims, see § 32.04(c).

(3) "Incurable" defects. The second caveat to the *McMann–Tollett* rule was recognized in two subsequent cases. *Blackledge v. Perry*,[20] involved a habeas claim that the prosecutor had acted vindictively in violation of due process, by changing the defendant's charge from a misdemeanor to a felony after he had asserted his right to a trial de novo upon conviction of the misdemeanor. The Court was willing to consider (and ultimately upheld) this claim, despite the fact that the defendant had pleaded guilty to the felony charge. Unlike the claims involved in *Tollett* and previous cases, the Court explained, this claim "went to the very power of the State to bring the defendant into court to answer the charge brought against him." Similarly, in *Menna v. New York*,[21] the Court held that a double jeopardy claim against the prosecution leading to a guilty plea could be heard because this type of claim, if sustained, precludes the state "from hailing a defendant into court on a charge." [22]

Contrary to the Court's assertion, the claim in *Tollett*, concerning the legitimacy of the indicting grand jury, also went to the "power of the state to bring the defendant into court." Thus, it has been argued,[23] the better way of explaining *Blackledge* and *Menna* is that they involved "incurable" constitutional claims which, if sustained, would prevent the state from *ever* trying a defendant on the charge to which he pleaded guilty.[24] On the other hand, a finding for the defendant on the grand jury claim in *Tollett* (and on the assertions in the *McMann–Brady–Parker* trilogy) would not prevent the state from subsequently trying the defendant on the charge (although in *Tollett* the state would have to convene a new grand jury to proceed against the defendant).

(4) Conditional pleas. The third caveat to *Tollett* was recognized in *Lefkowitz v. Newsome*,[25] where the Supreme Court held that even "curable" claims can be heard on habeas if they are raised pursuant to a conditional plea statute of the type described earlier.[26] In *Lefkowitz*, the defendant pleaded guilty in state court but preserved a search and seizure claim for appeal under New York's conditional plea statute. The claim was rejected on direct appeal, and the federal habeas court, on authority of *McMann* and *Brady*, refused to hear it. The Supreme Court directed the lower federal court to hold a hearing on the claim, concluding that it should be heard so as not to frustrate New York's policy of

20. 417 U.S. 21, 94 S.Ct. 2098 (1974), discussed in § 21.03(b).

21. 423 U.S. 61, 96 S.Ct. 241 (1975).

22. In *United States v. Broce,* 488 U.S. 563, 109 S.Ct. 757 (1989), the Court limited *Menna* to those cases where the double jeopardy claim can be based on the existing record and does not require an evidentiary hearing.

23. Westen, supra note 11, at 1220–21.

24. Another claim that fits this category is a claim that the right to speedy trial has been violated. Id. at 1255.

25. 420 U.S. 283, 95 S.Ct. 886 (1975).

26. See § 26.05(c).

providing post-guilty plea review of pretrial motions.[27] It should be noted, however, that where conditional plea statutes do not exist, the logic of *Tollett* would preclude independent challenges of guilty pleas on appeal as well as on habeas review.

(f) The Effect of an Overturned Plea. If the defendant successfully challenges a guilty plea, his remedy depends upon the type of claim asserted. As discussed earlier,[28] if he wins a "bargain challenge" alleging breach by the prosecution, he should normally obtain specific performance of the bargain (although he may only be entitled to replead). In all other situations, if the prosecution persists in prosecuting, the defendant may either go to trial or plead again. The primary issue that arises in this situation is whether the prosecutor and judge are bound by the charge and sentence in the original plea bargain or whether, instead, a higher charge or sentence may be imposed.

After a *trial* conviction and a successful appeal, retrial on a higher charge is barred by the Double Jeopardy Clause, on the ground that the trial verdict represents an "implied acquittal" of the greater charge.[29] In the analogous situation in the guilty plea context, however, there has been no such "implied acquittal," but merely a determination by the prosecutor, endorsed by the judge, that an offer on the lesser charge or sentence is more likely to get the defendant to plead guilty. Thus, the Double Jeopardy Clause probably does not bar reprosecution on a greater charge or imposition of a greater sentence than that associated with the challenged guilty plea.[30]

Only slightly more likely to be successful is the claim that, under *Blackledge v. Perry*[31] and *North Carolina v. Pearce*,[32] the higher charge or sentence is a vindictive reaction against the defendant for asserting his right to withdraw or otherwise challenge the plea. In order to avoid chilling the right to appeal after a *trial*, these cases established a "presumption of vindictiveness" when the prosecutor raises the charge or the judge imposes a higher sentence after an appeal is taken. But, in *Alabama v. Smith*,[33] the Court held that, because "the relevant sentencing information available to the judge after the plea will usually be considerably less than that available after trial," and because "the

27. Note that, one year after *Lefkowitz, Stone v. Powell,* 428 U.S. 465, 96 S.Ct. 3037 (1976), held that *no* Fourth Amendment claim (the type of claim at issue in *Lefkowitz*) is reviewable on federal habeas if it received a full and fair hearing in state court. See § 33.02(b).

28. See § 26.03(b)(3).

29. *Green v. United States*, 355 U.S. 184, 78 S.Ct. 221 (1957), discussed in § 30.03(a).

30. For further discussion of this point, see § 30.03(a)(1).

31. 417 U.S. 21, 94 S.Ct. 2098 (1974).

32. 395 U.S. 711, 89 S.Ct. 2072 (1969), discussed in § 29.02(d).

33. 490 U.S. 794, 109 S.Ct. 2201 (1989).

factors that may have indicated leniency as consideration for the guilty plea are no longer present," the presumption does not apply when the first charge and sentence occur in the guilty plea context, the defendant successfully appeals the plea, and then decides to go to trial. The prosecutor may charge the original pre-plea bargain offense and the sentencing judge may impose a higher sentence than originally bargained for.

Smith does not foreclose a finding of vindictiveness in this situation; it merely refuses to apply the *Pearce–Blackledge* presumption. In favor of this rule, it has been argued that if the defendant can always be assured of obtaining the same bargain after seeking to overturn a plea, he will often have nothing to lose and much to gain (including a possible dismissal because of passage of time) by challenging it, at considerable cost to the efficiency of the system.[34] Moreover, a higher post-appeal sentence can be justified on the ground that courts often impose more lenient sentences on those who plead guilty than on those who go to trial. On the other hand, if, after a successful challenge, the prosecutor is typically allowed to bring a higher charge or the judge able to impose a higher sentence than was contemplated in the original bargain, the defendant's right to challenge the plea may be chilled, and prosecutors (if not judges) may be encouraged "to coerce a plea in the knowledge that the defendant may be reluctant to risk a successful appeal." [35] At the least, by analogy to the holding in *Blackledge,* unless some "identifiable conduct" other than the successful plea challenge and the decision to go to trial would justify different treatment, the original bargain should form the basis for further prosecution.

26.06　Conclusion

In terms of case dispositions, guilty pleas—and the plea bargaining process that leads to them—are far more important than trials. Yet, relative to its caselaw on trial adjudication, the Supreme Court has devoted little attention to these topics. As a result, the constitutional limitations on the guilty plea process are still somewhat vague, as the following summary illustrates.

(1) Today virtually every jurisdiction permits the defendant and the prosecution to plea bargain, a process which usually involves an agreement by the defendant to plead guilty in exchange for charge concessions or recommendations regarding sentence by the prosecution. The prosecutor may use the threat of significantly higher charges or sentencing recommendations to

---

34. *United States ex rel. Williams v. McMann,* 436 F.2d 103 (2d Cir.1970).

35. Borman, "The Chilled Right to Appeal From a Plea Bargain Convic-tion: A Due Process Cure," 69 Nw.U.L. Rev. 663, 713 (1974).

induce the defendant to plead guilty, so long as the options presented are legitimate and are openly described to the defendant. The legitimacy of judicial involvement in plea bargaining is not clear, although it is probably constitutional and, properly conducted, perhaps even a preferred method of ensuring the process is monitored and the defendant is given accurate information as to the effect of a plea.

(2) The court need not accept a plea bargain, unless it has previously agreed to its provisions. After a plea is accepted by the court, a breach of the agreement by either the prosecution or the defendant should generally lead to specific performance whenever possible, although it is apparently constitutional, after either type of breach, to force the defendant to replead to a different offer or to go to trial. Either party may withdraw from the bargain prior to the arraignment.

(3) To be valid under the Due Process Clause, a guilty plea must be intelligently and voluntarily made, as affirmatively shown on a record developed by the judge who takes the plea. Ideally, this would require the arraignment judge to develop on the record: (a) that the defendant understands the critical elements of the charges against him, including any elements that differentiate the charges to which he is pleading from lesser included offenses; (b) that he understands the penalties and any other non-"collateral" consequences associated with the charges; (c) that he understands that by pleading guilty he is waiving his rights to jury trial, confrontation, and trial counsel and his privilege against self-incrimination; (d) that his plea is not the product of coercion other than that associated with having to choose between known alternatives legitimately offered by the prosecutor or by the relevant law; and (e) that there is a factual basis for his plea. All of these requirements are fully incorporated in Rule 11 of the Federal Rules of Criminal Procedure, with the possible exception of (c). The Constitution appears to require that the judge personally determine (d) and (e), and that he at least obtain general representations of counsel as to (a), (b) and (c). An express admission of guilt is not a constitutional requisite to the acceptance of a guilty plea and imposition of a criminal penalty, although the judge should take particular care to obtain a factual basis for the plea when the defendant maintains his innocence.

(4) In most jurisdictions, prior to formal imposition of sentence, a plea may be withdrawn for any just and fair reason, including proof that the plea was not voluntary or intelligent, that the bargain upon which it was based was breached by the prosecutor or not endorsed by the court, or that a previously overlooked defense is now available to the defendant. After the sentencing proceeding, a plea may be withdrawn only if manifest injustice

would otherwise result, which probably encompasses grounds similar to those recognized on federal habeas, described below. Direct appeal of a guilty plea is generally limited to claims that can be based on the arraignment transcript (such as whether arraignment procedures or the plea bargain was followed), although some jurisdictions allow conditional pleas, under which the defendant can preserve specified pretrial motions for appeal. A federal habeas corpus hearing on the guilty plea is usually granted only in cases which assert (a) that the plea was not voluntary or intelligent; (b) that there was a significant breach of a plea bargain; (c) that counsel was ineffective; (d) that the state lacks power to bring the charge to which the defendant pleaded; or (e) a claim that was preserved via a conditional plea procedure.

BIBLIOGRAPHY

Abrams, Howard E. Systemic Coercion: Unconstitutional Conditions in the Criminal Law. 72 J.Crim.L. & Criminol. 128 (1981).

Adelstein, Richard P. The Negotiated Guilty Plea: A Framework for Analysis. 53 N.Y.U.L.Rev. 783 (1978).

Alschuler, Albert W. The Defense Attorney's Role in Plea Bargaining. 84 Yale L.J. 1179 (1975).

——. Implementing the Criminal Defendant's Right to Trial: Alternatives to the Plea Bargaining System. 50 U.Chi.L.Rev. 931 (1983).

——. The Prosecutor's Role in Plea Bargaining. 36 U.Chi.L.Rev. 50 (1968).

——. The Trial Judge's Role in Plea Bargaining, Part I. 76 Colum.L.Rev. 1059 (1976).

Barkai, John L. Accuracy Inquiries for All Felony and Misdemeanor Pleas: Voluntary Pleas but Innocent Defendants? 126 U.Pa.L.Rev. 88 (1977).

Borman, Paul D. The Chilled Right to Appeal from a Plea Bargain Conviction: A Due Process Cure. 69 Nw.L.Rev. 663 (1974).

Bond, James Edward. Plea Bargaining and Guilty Pleas. New York: Clark Boardman Co., 1982.

Brunk, Conrad. The Problem of Voluntariness and Coercion in the Negotiated Plea. 13 Law & Soc.Rev. 527 (1979).

Finkelstein, Michael O. A Statistical Analysis of Guilty Plea Practices in the Federal Courts. 89 Harv.L.Rev. 293 (1975).

Freedman, Monroe. The Professional Responsibility of the Prosecuting Attorney. 55 Geo.L.J. 1030 (1967).

Gifford, Donald G. Meaningful Reform of Plea Bargaining: The Control of Prosecutorial Discretion. 1983 U.Ill.L.Rev. 37 (1983).

Heumann, Milton. Plea Bargaining. Chicago: University of Chicago Press, 1978.

Jones, J.B. Prosecutors and the Disposition of Criminal Cases: An Analysis of Plea Bargaining Rates. 69 J.Crim.L. and Criminol. 402 (1978).

Lagoy, Stephen P., Joseph J. Senna, and Larry J. Siegel. An Empirical Study on Information Usage for Prosecutorial Decision Making in Plea Negotiations. 13 Am.Crim.L.Rev. 435 (1976).

Langbein, John H. Torture and Plea Bargaining. 46 U.Chi.L. Rev. 3 (1978).

Lefstein, Norman. Plea Bargaining and the Trial Judge, the New ABA Standards, and the Need to Control Judicial Discretion. 59 N.Car.L.Rev. 476 (1981).

Nagel, Stuart S. and Marian Neef. Plea Bargaining, Decision Theory, and Equilibrium Models. 51 Ind.L.J. 987 (1976).

Rosett, Arthur I. and Donald R. Cressey. Justice by Consent: Plea Bargains in the American Courthouse. Philadelphia: J.B. Lippincott, Co., 1976.

Ryan, John P. and James Alfini. Trial Judges' Participation in Plea Bargaining: An Empirical Perspective. 13 Law & Soc. Rev. 479 (1979).

Saltzburg, Stephen A. Pleas of Guilty and the Loss of Constitutional Rights: The Current Price of Pleading Guilty. 76 Mich.L.Rev. 1265 (1978).

Schulhofer, Stephen. Is Plea Bargaining Inevitable? 97 Harv.L. Rev. 1037 (1984).

Scott, Robert E. and William J. Stuntz. Plea Bargaining as Contract. 101 Yale L.J. 1909 (1992).

Uviller, H. Richard. Pleading Guilty: A Critique of Four Models. 41 Law and Contemp. Probs. 102 (1977).

Weninger, Robert A. The Abolition of Plea Bargaining: A Case Study of El Paso County, Texas. 35 U.C.L.A.L.Rev. 265 (1987).

Westen, Peter and David Westin. A Constitutional Law of Remedies for Broken Plea Bargains. 66 Calif.L.Rev. 471 (1978).

Westen, Peter. Away From Waiver: A Rationale for the Forfeiture of Constitutional Rights in Criminal Procedure. 75 Mich.L.Rev. 1214 (1977).

White, Welsh S. A Proposal for Reform of the Plea Bargaining Process. 119 U.Pa.L.Rev. 439 (1971).

Chapter Twenty-Seven

THE RIGHT TO AN IMPARTIAL JURY AND JUDGE

27.01 Introduction

Constitutional doctrine governing the identity and role of the decisionmaker at a criminal proceeding has flowed from two premises. Most important has been the belief that the decisionmaker must be neutral (thus helping to assure, it is assumed, accuracy of judgment). The Sixth Amendment guarantees a trial "by an impartial jury" in all criminal prosecutions, and the Due Process Clause has been found to require an impartial trial judge.[1] Further, to ensure that both the jury and the judge are subject to some outside monitoring, the Sixth Amendment guarantees a "public" trial, and the First Amendment's protection of freedom of press has been applied to most stages of the criminal process.[2]

The second premise concerning the decisionmaker is that the community should be involved in the decisionmaking process, as a matter of participatory democracy and as a protection against government-dominated justice. The right to jury trial is the most direct attempt at realizing this goal. Additionally, the public trial, attended by the media, assures that interested members of the public will be able to evaluate the decisionmaker and the system in which it operates, and provide feedback.

The impartiality and community participation premises can sometimes conflict. A jury composed of laypeople may not be the most impartial decisionmaker, and the most neutral decisionmaker may not represent the community. Press coverage may improperly influence prospective jurors, disrupt the trial process and distort the deliberations of the judge or the jury. This chapter explores these tensions. The first three sections examine the most significant aspects of the right to jury trial: its scope; the selection of the jury venire; and the selection of the petit jury from the venire. The fourth section looks at the selection of the presiding judge. The final section discusses the role of a free press at a jury or bench trial.

27.02 The Scope of the Right to Jury Trial

(a) **History and Rationale of the Right.** The right to a trial by jury has roots deep in the common law. As early as the Magna Carta, the right was recognized as essential, although in somewhat different form than its modern version: to the barons

---

1. See § 27.05.   2. See § 27.06.

who drafted that document, a "jury of peers" was a means of ensuring they would be tried by other members of the aristocracy rather than those in the lower classes.[3] Further, the jury in medieval days functioned more like the grand jury of modern times and could be punished if its verdict was contrary to law. By the end of the seventeenth century, however, it had acquired its three essential elements: (1) a group of twelve lay citizens (2) whose unanimous verdict (3) was given exclusive effect.

During the American Revolution the jury was seen as a bulwark against oppression. Colonists considered the jury trial "a valuable safeguard of liberty" and "the palladium of free government." [4] The jury was idealized as a group of citizens acting as a buffer between the criminal accused and the state. Accordingly, the framers of the Constitution were committed to making the jury an integral part of the criminal justice system. Article II, Section 2 provides that "the trial of all crimes, except in cases of impeachment, shall be by jury." And, as noted above, the Sixth Amendment states: "In all criminal prosecutions, the accused shall enjoy the right to a . . . trial, by an impartial jury . . . .."

While the Sixth Amendment guarantee has always been honored in the federal courts, it was not applied to the states until 1968 in *Duncan v. Louisiana.*[5] The tensions which may have contributed to this delay, and which would later form the basis for diminishing the scope of the jury trial right, are reflected in Justice White's majority opinion in *Duncan* and Justice Harlan's dissent in that case. As it had in earlier cases construing the scope of the right at the federal level,[6] the majority emphasized that the jury not only provides "an inestimable safeguard against the corrupt or overzealous prosecutor and against the compliant, biased, or eccentric judge," but also reflects an "insistence upon community participation in the determination of guilt and innocence." Justice Harlan argued, on the other hand, that the danger of "tyrannous judges" that had so exercised the colonists was largely a relic of the past. And he criticized the lay jury process as cumbersome, costly, and likely to result in defective verdicts, at least in complex legal cases. The majority did not directly respond to Harlan's assertion that the jury is an inefficient decisionmaking institution, but it did state that "we hold no constitutional doubts about the practices, common in both federal and state courts, of accepting waivers of jury trial and prosecuting petty crimes without extending a right to jury trial." As to the

---

3. See F. Pollock and F. Maitland, The History of English Law Before the Time of Edward I, Vol. I, at 173 n. 3 (2d ed. 1899).

4. F. Heller, The Sixth Amendment 21–22, 25–26 (1951).

5. 391 U.S. 145, 88 S.Ct. 1444 (1968).

6. *Patton v. United States,* 281 U.S. 276, 50 S.Ct. 253 (1930); *Thompson v. Utah,* 170 U.S. 343, 18 S.Ct. 620 (1898).

claim of erroneous jury verdicts, White noted the results of a "recent and exhaustive study" [7] which had found that, when juries reach a different decision than the judge in a particular case, "it is usually because they are serving some of the very purposes for which they were created and for which they are now employed."

Although the *Duncan* majority strongly endorsed the concept of the jury trial, it did not explicitly decide whether all of the common law attributes of the jury were required as a matter of due process. In defining the scope of the right in later cases, Harlan's arguments in dissent—particularly those having to do with the jury's cumbersome and costly nature—heavily influenced the Court. Additionally, the optimistic view of lay decisionmaking abilities which supported the holding in *Duncan* would later bolster decisions allowing experimentation with its size and voting requirements.

(b) **The Right in Noncriminal Proceedings.** The Sixth Amendment clearly governs all "criminal prosecutions," and the Seventh Amendment guarantees a right to jury trial in all civil cases in which non-equitable relief is sought.[8] But many types of proceedings do not fit cleanly into either category. In *McKeiver v. Pennsylvania,*[9] the Court held that juveniles charged with delinquent acts do not have a right to trial by jury. Although the Court had been quite willing to import other adult criminal process rights into this quasi-criminal process,[10] it found that granting the right to jury trial to those charged with delinquent acts would introduce the "clamor" of the adversary process and thus undermine the "intimacy" that many states consider important in arriving at an appropriate disposition in cases involving children.

Justice Brennan concurred with this conclusion in one of the two cases joined in *McKeiver,* because the state involved (Pennsylvania) permitted public trials, with press coverage, when requested. In the other case, however, Brennan dissented because the proceedings in that jurisdiction (North Carolina) were routinely closed; thus, without a jury, there was no way the "community conscience" could protect against oppression by the courts. The lower courts have generally disregarded Brennan's distinction, extending the holding in *McKeiver* to civil commitment and similar proceedings which are also often closed at the behest of the state.[11]

---

7. H. Kalven & H. Zeisel, "The American Jury" (1966).

8. See, e.g., *Beacon Theatres, Inc. v. Westover,* 359 U.S. 500, 79 S.Ct. 948 (1959).

9. 403 U.S. 528, 91 S.Ct. 1976 (1971).

10. See *Application of Gault,* 387 U.S. 1, 87 S.Ct. 1428 (1967) (juveniles

have right to adequate notice and counsel, and the privilege against self-incrimination); *Breed v. Jones,* 421 U.S. 519, 95 S.Ct. 1779 (1975) (double jeopardy).

11. See, e.g., *Lynch v. Baxley,* 386 F.Supp. 378 (M.D.Ala.1974).

(c) The Petty Crime Exception. Based on historical precedent, *Duncan* specifically exempted from the jury requirement trials of "petty crimes or offenses." Two years later, in *Baldwin v. New York*,[12] the Court explained that the "disadvantages, onerous though they may be," of punishment for a petty crime are "outweighed by the benefits that result from speedy and inexpensive nonjury adjudication." Several issues arise in connection with the "petty offense" exception.

(1) The six-month imprisonment rule. Duncan did not define "petty" offense, other than to suggest that the primary factor in determining crime seriousness should be the nature of the penalty authorized. *Baldwin* reiterated this criterion and concluded that a crime which can bring imprisonment of more than six months implicates the Sixth Amendment. The six-month dividing line was chosen because only one state at the time absolutely prohibited a jury trial for crimes associated with a longer punishment, and because other alternatives—such as the felony-misdemeanor distinction—did not lend themselves to clear definition.

Note that, in contrast to the right to counsel,[13] the right to jury trial depends upon the punishment that is *possible,* not that which is actually imposed. But when, as in criminal contempt cases, the legislature has not spoken as to the possible punishment, the Court has held that the penalty actually imposed is the correct yardstick.[14] Thus, in *Frank v. United States*,[15] the defendant was not entitled to a jury trial when he received three years probation for contempt, because had he violated the probation terms he would, at most, have been imprisoned for six months.

(2) Relevance of other factors. *Baldwin* left open the possibility that, under some circumstances, a prison term of six months or less, in combination with *other* penalties, might be considered serious for purposes of the right to jury trial. But subsequent decisions have indicated that this possibility is a small one. Most significantly, in *Blanton v. City of North Las Vegas*,[16] the Court held that a defendant is entitled to a jury trial in such a situation "only if he can demonstrate that any additional statutory penalties, viewed in conjunction with the maximum authorized period of incarceration, are so severe that they clearly reflect a legislative determination that the offense in question is a 'serious' one." In *Blanton*, the Court considered a driving while intoxicated statute which authorized a maximum term of six months or, in lieu of a prison sentence, 48 hours of community work while wearing garb identifying the person as a DWI offender. In addition, a person

---

12. 399 U.S. 66, 90 S.Ct. 1886 (1970).

13. See § 31.02(b).

14. See *Bloom v. Illinois*, 391 U.S. 194, 88 S.Ct. 1477 (1968).

15. 395 U.S. 147, 89 S.Ct. 1503 (1969).

16. 489 U.S. 538, 109 S.Ct. 1289 (1989).

given either penalty suffers an automatic 90–day loss of driver's license, and is required to pay a $200 to $1000 fine and to attend an alcohol abuse education course. A unanimous Court held that the penalties under this statute were not "serious" for purposes of the Sixth Amendment. In a footnote, it concluded that even if the sentence and the license suspension were not concurrent—so that the suspension might occur after six months in jail—"we cannot say that a 90–day suspension is that significant as a Sixth Amendment matter, particularly when a restricted license may be obtained after only 45 days."

Blanton is consistent with previous Court decisions. In *Frank,* the contempt case noted above, the Court suggested that a potential penalty of six months plus a fine would not implicate the Sixth Amendment. And in *Muniz v. Hoffman,*[17] also involving a contempt penalty, the Court held that a fine of $10,000 would not trigger the right to jury trial, at least when, as in *Muniz,* the defendant (a labor union) was an organization. Such a large fine levied on an individual might require a different result, however.

Blanton is also important in establishing that, with the exception of contempt cases, where the penalty is judicially defined, only the legislatively imposed penalty is to be considered in determining whether a crime is serious or petty. According to the Court, "[t]he judiciary should not substitute its judgment as to seriousness for that of a legislature, which is 'far better equipped to perform the task, and . . . likewise more responsive to changes in attitude and more amenable to the recognition and correction of . . . misperceptions in this respect.' " This holding rendered irrelevant, for constitutional purposes, several pre-*Duncan* decisions which had looked at such factors as the morally offensive nature of the offense, in addition to its potential penalty, in deciding the reach of the right to jury trial in federal cases.[18]

(3) Aggregation of imprisonment sanctions. In *Codispoti v. Pennsylvania,*[19] the two defendants were tried on several different counts of contempt arising from their criminal trial, in a bench proceeding separate from the trial. Although no single sentence imposed during the contempt proceeding amounted to more than six months, the aggregate sentence received by each was well over six months. In this situation, the Court held that the defendants were entitled to a jury trial, reasoning that, despite the petty nature of each offense, "the salient fact remains that the contempts arose from a single trial, were charged by a single judge and were tried in a single proceeding." Although *Codispoti* dealt

17. 422 U.S. 454, 95 S.Ct. 2178 (1975).

18. See, e.g., *District of Columbia v. Clawans,* 300 U.S. 617, 57 S.Ct. 660 (1937).

19. 418 U.S. 506, 94 S.Ct. 2687 (1974).

with contempt citations, nothing in the decision suggested a distinction should be made for a trial involving more than one *statutory* offense where the aggregate possible penalty is greater than six months.

Ironically, in the typical contempt case, the *Codispoti* rule is unlikely to be applicable. That is because the Court also indicated in that decision (in dictum) that, if the contempt penalties are imposed "summarily"—that is, for in-court contemptuous conduct as it occurs rather than in a separate proceeding as was the case in *Codispoti*—no jury would be required for individual contempt penalties of six months or less, even if, over the course of the trial, the contempt penalties aggregated to more than six months imprisonment. This position was justified by the "need to maintain order" in the courtroom.[20] Additionally, in *Taylor v. Hayes*,[21] decided the same day as *Codispoti*, the Court held that, even when a separate contempt proceeding is held, as in *Codispoti*, if an appellate court later reduces the aggregate sentence to six months or less, the Sixth Amendment is not violated by a bench proceeding.

(d) Jury Size. Traditionally, the jury was twelve strong. In *Williams v. Florida*,[22] the Court held that this number was "a historical accident," and "unnecessary to effect the purposes of the jury system." On the latter point, it declared that reducing the size of the jury would impair neither of the functions of the jury recognized by *Duncan:* such a jury would still interpose "the common-sense judgment of a group of laymen" between the accused and his accuser, and still promote "the community participation and shared responsibility that results from the group's determination of guilt or innocence." To the argument that the smaller group could not as effectively incorporate the community's or the defendant's interests, the Court responded that a six-person jury would provide "a fair possibility for obtaining a representative cross-section of the community," at least "[a]s long as arbitrary exclusions of a particular class from the jury rolls are forbidden." Further, it would not necessarily favor the prosecution, since it reduced the chance of a holdout juror for *both* sides.

Research subsequent to *Williams* has questioned the assumptions underlying each of these points. Progressively smaller groups are less likely to represent the community; less likely to foster deliberation among members of the group; less likely to listen to a minority (since the minority, if any, will be smaller); more likely to harm the defendant, since the number of hung juries (along with the concomitant retrials) would diminish; and

---

20. Thus, for contemptuous conduct that occurs outside the courtroom (e.g., refusal to obey a discovery order), this rule would not apply.

21. 418 U.S. 488, 94 S.Ct. 2697 (1974).

22. 399 U.S. 78, 90 S.Ct. 1893 (1970).

less likely to be reliable.[23] That this research had some persuasive force was borne out by the Court's decision in *Ballew v. Georgia,*[24] which relied heavily on it in concluding that a five-member jury violated the Constitution. Justice Blackmun, who wrote for the Court, found it unlikely that five persons could engage "in meaningful deliberation, . . . remember all the facts and arguments, and truly represent[ ] the common sense of the entire community." He conceded, in light of this conclusion, that the distinction between six and five members was arbitrary. But he also noted that, while the reduction from twelve to six members resulted in substantial savings, the reduction from six to five did not.

(e) Voting Requirements. In two companion cases, *Johnson v. Louisiana,*[25] and *Apodaca v. Oregon,*[26] the Court allowed further experimentation by approving the use of non-unanimous jury verdicts in criminal trials. In *Johnson,* the Court refused to strike down a Louisiana statute which authorized a 9–3 verdict of guilty in cases where the crime is necessarily punishable by hard labor. In *Apodaca,* the Court sustained three convictions, two of which were based on 11–1 verdicts and one which resulted from a 10–2 decision, the minimum requirement for a conviction under Oregon law.

In *Johnson,* the defendant relied on Fourteenth Amendment claims, since *Duncan's* application of the Sixth Amendment to the states occurred after his trial had commenced and was not applied retroactively. His principal argument was that a non-unanimous verdict failed to meet the standard of proving guilt beyond a reasonable doubt and therefore violated due process. Justice White's majority opinion disagreed:

> In our view, disagreement of three jurors does not alone establish reasonable doubt, particularly when such a heavy majority of the jury, after having considered the dissenters' views, remained convinced of guilt . . .. That want of jury unanimity is not to be equated with the existence of reasonable doubt emerges even more clearly from the fact that when a jury in a federal court, which operates under the unanimity rule and is instructed to acquit a defendant if it has a reasonable doubt . . . cannot agree unanimously upon a verdict, the defendant is not acquitted, but is merely given a new trial.

---

23. See M. Saks, Jury Verdicts 207 (1977); Zeisel, "And Then There Were None: The Dimunition of the Federal Jury," 38 U.Chi.L.Rev. 710 (1971).

24. 435 U.S. 223, 98 S.Ct. 1029 (1978).

25. 406 U.S. 356, 92 S.Ct. 1620 (1972).

26. 406 U.S. 404, 92 S.Ct. 1628 (1972).

Of course, this statement overlooks the fact that, under the statutes in question, the result of a hung jury could be conviction, not a new trial.

In *Apodaca* the Court reached the same result even though the defendant's claim was based directly on the Sixth Amendment. Justice White, again speaking for the Court, pointed out that the Sixth Amendment does not speak to the reasonable doubt standard at all. And, with respect to *Duncan's* requirement that the jury interpose the commonsense judgment of a group representative of a cross-section of the community, he put forward the same generous perception of how juries function that was articulated in *Williams* to justify six-person juries:

> We cannot assume that the majority of the jury will refuse to weigh the evidence and reach a decision upon rational grounds, just as it must do now in order to obtain unanimous verdicts, or that a majority will deprive a man of his liberty on the basis of prejudice when a minority is presenting a reasonable argument in favor of acquittal.

Nor would White accept the "assumption" that the minority, believing it will easily be outvoted, would refrain from making its views known at all.

Justice Douglas vigorously attacked this view of how juries operate in his dissent to both *Johnson* and *Apodaca*. He argued that permitting non-unanimous verdicts diminishes jury reliability because jurors will not debate and deliberate as fully. As soon as the requisite majority is obtained, Douglas contended, further consideration will be precluded. "Indeed, if a necessary majority is immediately obtained, then no deliberation at all is required." In contrast, where unanimity is required, Douglas continued, the majority must win the dissenters over to its side. The ultimate result, even if a guilty verdict, may still reflect the reservations of the uncertain jurors who may force compromise verdicts on lesser-included offenses and lesser sentences. As Douglas put it, "even though a minority may not be forceful enough to carry the day, their doubts may nonetheless cause a majority to exercise caution."

In both *Johnson* and *Apodaca*, the justices were split 4–4 between the views of White and Douglas, leaving Justice Powell as the swing vote. Although Powell agreed that the Sixth Amendment mandates unanimity in a federal jury trial, he concluded that unanimity is not a fundamental aspect of the right to jury trial applicable to the states. Thus, unanimity is only required at the federal level.

Burch v. Louisiana,[27] raised the question of how *Williams,* which permitted six person juries, interrelated with *Johnson* and *Apodaca,* which allowed non-unanimous verdicts. There, the Court unanimously found a Louisiana statute which allowed non-unanimous verdicts by six-member juries unconstitutional. It saw little merit to Louisiana's contention that the provision "saved time," especially since only one other state had a similar provision. Thus, *Burch,* like *Ballew,* indicated that the Court was unwilling to carry the administrative convenience rationale to the point where the states are completely free to devise their own jury systems.

Read in conjunction with *Ballew,* the *Burch* decision permits six member juries only if the state additionally requires that decisions by such juries be unanimous. Despite this creation of a "lower limit," the Court's decisions concerning the scope of the jury trial right principally stand for the notion that the unanimous verdict by a twelve-member jury model is an "historical accident" and can be significantly curtailed. Thus, as the law stands today, it is conceivable that a 7–3 verdict by a ten-member jury is permissible.[28]

(f) Trials De Novo. Many states require trial of minor crimes to take place before a judge, but then allow a conviction at this first tier to be "appealed" to a higher trial court, at which a trial *de novo* (i.e., a new proceeding at which evidence from the first trial is inadmissible) takes place in front of a jury. This system allows expedited handling of a large number of less serious offenses. In *Ludwig v. Massachusetts,*[29] the defendant challenged such a system as an impermissible burden on the right to jury trial. The Supreme Court rejected the challenge, emphasizing that a Massachusetts defendant who insists on a jury can proceed "immediately" to the jury trial by "admitting sufficient findings of fact" at the first "trial" (resulting in a conviction which would trigger the *de novo* proceeding). In any event, the Court stated, the defendant had "not presented any evidence to show that there is a greater delay in obtaining a jury in Massachusetts than there would be if the Commonwealth abandoned its two-tier system."

The fact remains that the Massachusetts system requires certain defendants who want a jury trial to jump through hoops not normally required, perhaps leading those with fewer resources or less energy to forego their Sixth Amendment right. Further, as the four-member dissent pointed out, if *de novo* appeal is sought, the first trial, whether abbreviated or not, and despite the "inad-

27. 441 U.S. 130, 99 S.Ct. 1623 (1979).

28. Cf. Justice Stewart's dissent in *Johnson* (contending that an 8–4 verdict

would be constitutional under the majority's reasoning).

29. 427 U.S. 618, 96 S.Ct. 2781 (1976).

missibility" of its outcome in subsequent proceedings, will have an impact on the jury trial, since the judge, as well as any members of the jury familiar with the system, will know a conviction has taken place. The dissenters cogently argued that "[a]ll of the legitimate benefits of the two-tier system could be obtained by giving the defendant the right to waive the first-tier trial completely." [30]

(g) Waiver. A defendant might want to waive the right to jury trial for several reasons. Most obviously, community sentiment against him or the crime he allegedly committed may be so strong that a trial by members of that community could distort the decisionmaking process. Although changes of venue can be sought in such situations, they are rarely granted.[31] Further, some defendants or crimes may be so repulsive that trial by any group of laypeople, no matter where located, poses more of a risk than a proceeding presided over by a less naive judge. Or the case may be a particularly complex one which the defense believes a jury could not easily comprehend.

(1) When waiver may occur. In *Patton v. United States,*[32] the defendants made the relatively novel argument that their waiver of the right to a twelve-member jury at the federal level was invalid because they lacked the power to waive the right. But the Supreme Court held that, as is true with other rights, the right to jury trial may be surrendered. The Court concluded that since defendants routinely waive the right to jury trial when they plead guilty, waiver at trial should be permitted as well. Further, as *Patton* itself illustrated, a defendant can agree to a trial by a jury composed of fewer members that normally required (if, for instance, a juror becomes ill). Although *Patton* was decided before *Duncan* and applied only to federal trials, *Duncan* indicated that *Patton's* holding would apply to the states.

Patton required that the waiver be "express and intelligent." In *United States v. Jackson,*[33] the Court also required that it be voluntary. There the Court found unconstitutional the death penalty provision of the Federal Kidnapping Act, because it permitted imposition of capital punishment only after a jury trial. The Court stated that "the evil in the federal statute is not that it necessarily coerces guilty pleas and jury waivers but simply that it needlessly encourages them." In later cases,[34] however, the Court

30. Justice Powell, following his reasoning in *Apodaca,* found that the Sixth Amendment prohibited a de novo system at the federal level but not at the state level, and thus joined the majority. For the federal rule, see *Callan v. Wilson,* 127 U.S. 540, 8 S.Ct. 1301 (1888).

31. See § 27.06(b)(2).

32. 281 U.S. 276, 50 S.Ct. 253 (1930).

33. 390 U.S. 570, 88 S.Ct. 1209 (1968).

34. See, e.g., *Parker v. North Carolina,* 397 U.S. 790, 90 S.Ct. 1458 (1970); *Brady v. United States,* 397 U.S. 742, 90 S.Ct. 1463 (1970).

limited *Jackson* to its facts. Assuming the potential penalties after a jury and non-jury adjudication are the same, choosing the latter is voluntary if it represents a choice between known alternatives.[35]

(2) "Veto" of waiver. The more controversial issue with respect to waiver of jury trial is whether it may be conditioned on the consent of the court and the prosecution. Most jurisdictions, including the federal courts, allow the judge or the prosecutor to "veto" a defendant's waiver of jury trial.[36] In *Singer v. United States*,[37] the Supreme Court upheld the federal provision, reasoning that "[a] defendant's only constitutional right concerning the method of trial is to an impartial trial by jury." Prosecutorial or judicial refusal to allow waiver simply subjects the defendant to a jury trial, "the very thing that the Constitution guarantees him."

The Court did caution that there might be circumstances, particularly those involving "passion, prejudice [or] public feeling," "where the defendant's reasons for wanting to be tried by a judge alone might be so compelling that the Government's insistence on trial by jury would result in the denial to a defendant of an impartial trial." But it appears that the proof required to meet the Court's "compelling reasons" test is very difficult to produce. One survey of federal cases during an eight-year period after *Singer* found that the prosecutor's decision to block a waiver had never been overruled.[38]

27.03   Selection of Prospective Jurors

(a) The Selection Process and Its Rationale. The selection of the jury is a several stage process. First, a list of names, normally designated the "jury pool", "jury list," or "master jury wheel," is compiled. The pool is usually drawn from voter registration lists (as is the case in the federal courts)[39] or telephone directories.[40] Some states, however, still operate under a jury commissioner, or "key man," system, in which individuals appointed by a judge are responsible for selecting and maintaining jury lists.[41] Generally, these individuals are directed to pick persons of "known integrity" or who have a "reputation for honesty and intelligence." The result can often be a pool that is not as representative as one chosen by purely random methods.

---

35. For further discussion on this point, see § 26.02(c).

36. See, e.g., Fed.R.Crim.P. 23(a).

37. 380 U.S. 24, 85 S.Ct. 783 (1965).

38. Note, "Waiving the Right to Jury Trial in the Federal Courts: The Burden of Prejudice," 7 Suffolk L.Rev. 973 (1973).

39. See, e.g., the federal practice, 28 U.S.C.A. § 1863(b).

40. See generally, J. Van Dyke, Jury Selection Procedures 258–62 (1977) for a description of state procedures.

41. See, e.g. Ala.Code § 12–16–60 (1984); O.Code Ga.Ann. 15–12–40 (1984); Tenn.Code Ann. §§ 22–2–302, 22–2–304 (1984).

From the jury pool of eligible jurors, a much smaller "venire" or "panel" is selected, typically through a random process. Again, however, in jurisdictions with a selection procedure which utilizes commissioners, this stage has often been decidedly non-random in nature. As discussed below, such systems have frequently come under constitutional attack.

Once a venire is selected, those qualified for statutory exemption are excused, usually relying on juror qualification forms they have filled out. Typically exempted are (1) aliens; (2) those unable to speak English; (3) those under 18; (4) persons charged with a felony or serving a felony sentence; (5) and those who are suffering from mental or physical incapacity. Additionally, a prospective juror may normally request exemption from duty if he has previously served as a juror, is engaged in a "critical occupation" (often specified by statute and including military, government and professional jobs), or can show that service on a jury would work undue hardship or inconvenience.[42]

The venirepersons not exempted (a group which is still usually called the venire or panel) are further whittled down to jury size through *voir dire*. This process permits the parties to inform themselves about members of the panel so as to be able to exclude, through "challenges," those they find unsuitable.

In describing the ideal jury selection process, the Supreme Court most often speaks of a procedure which seeks a "fair cross-section" of the community and produces, as required by the language of the Sixth Amendment, an "impartial" jury.[43] It should be apparent that these two goals are not necessarily complementary: merely because a jury represents a number of groups in the community does not mean it is impartial, and fashioning an "impartial" jury may often produce one fairly homogenous in composition. Nor are these objectives equally achievable at each stage of the selection process. While the jury pool, and perhaps the venire, are large enough to include members of most significant groups in the community, a twelve or six-member jury cannot be expected to incorporate such diversity, a fact which the Supreme Court has recognized.[44] Conversely, by its very nature, "impartiality," if obtainable at all, can only be approached after *voir dire* has taken place and individual biases of potential jurors are exposed. Thus, the cross-section goal is most effectively implemented early in the jury selection process while impartiality can only be achieved toward the end of that process.

42. See, e.g., 28 U.S.C.A. §§ 1865(b), 1866(c); ABA Criminal Justice Standard 15–2.1(c).

43. See, e.g., *Strauder v. West Virginia,* 100 U.S. (10 Otto) 303 (1880); *Williams v. Florida,* 399 U.S. 78, 90 S.Ct. 1893 (1970); *Taylor v. Louisiana,* 419 U.S. 522, 95 S.Ct. 692 (1975).

44. *Taylor v. Louisiana,* 419 U.S. 522, 95 S.Ct. 692 (1975); *Fay v. New York,* 332 U.S. 261, 67 S.Ct. 1613 (1947).

Ultimately, these realities serve the jury system well. As will become clear in this section, the ideal of a fair cross-section exists as much for the community's and the government's benefit as the defendant's, indeed perhaps more so. Without the cross-section requirement, the community's sense of participation in the criminal justice system would be minimal; concomitantly, the legitimacy of the government could be diminished. On the other hand, a *particular* jury need not reflect an exact cross-section of the community in order to meet public and governmental needs; so long as the jury *pool* includes a cross-section of the locality, over time the diverse segments of that locality will be represented on actual juries. This eventual representation should satisfy any sense of participation the public at large might seek, and any citizen involvement the government desires to achieve.

For his part, the defendant, like the community at large, is not particularly concerned about whether his particular jury reflects a cross-section of the community. Indeed, although he might wish to have members of certain groups on his jury, he will want to *avoid* a jury composed of people whose differences may make it difficult for them to empathize with his story. His primary concern is not whether the jury is representative of the community but whether the group which considers his case is impartial—if not actively partial—toward him. Closely related, but not identical, to this concern is a desire, shared by the barons who signed the Magna Charta,[45] to seek a jury consisting of individuals similar to him, a jury of his "peers." These objectives, ideally, are achieved through *voir dire.*[46]

The remainder of this section considers those stages of the jury selection process concerned primarily with ensuring various segments of the community have a chance at serving on the jury. The next section discusses those aspects of the selection process more clearly aimed at achieving an impartial jury of the defendant's peers, in particular the *voir dire* procedure.

(b) Equal Protection Challenges. Most litigation about the selection of the venire today focuses on application of the Sixth Amendment's "fair cross-section" requirement, discussed in the next subsection. But, prior to the mid–1970's, the only constitutional means of attacking state venire selection procedure was an argument based on the Equal Protection Clause. The theory behind these cases was that intentional exclusion from the venire of members of a "suspect class"—meaning African–Americans and other racial minorities—violated both the right of class members

---

45. See text at note 3 supra.

46. See generally, Massaro, "Peremptories or Peers? Rethinking Sixth

Amendment Doctrine, Images and Procedures," 64 N.Car.L.Rev. 501 (1986).

who were tried by a jury selected from that venire and the right of the persons excluded to be in the venire.[47]

Today, as a result of a series of decisions beginning with *Holland v. Illinois*,[48] the Court has made clear that the equal protection challenge is based solely on the second ground; that is, as the Court stated in *Holland*, "a juror's right to equal protection is violated when he is excluded because of his race." The defendant is allowed to make an equal protection challenge not to vindicate any personal right but because the juror has "little incentive or resources to set in motion the arduous process needed to vindicate his own rights." The practical consequence of this holding is that, whereas originally an equal protection claim could be raised only by defendants who belonged to the suspect class excluded, now any defendant may raise the claim.

The standing issue aside, the most difficult aspect of an equal protection claim has always been proving an intent to discriminate. The first equal protection attack on selection of the jury, the 1880 decision of *Strauder v. Virginia*,[49] presented no problem in this regard, since it involved a statute which explicitly excluded blacks from jury service. But, after *Strauder*, discrimination took much subtler forms. For the next 85 years, the Court essentially failed to recognize this fact, insisting either on explicit proof of intent to discriminate, or on a showing of "virtual exclusion" of all blacks from the venire, in which case the burden shifted to the state to show that the disparity was not intentional.[50]

The obtuse character of the Court's approach was starkly illustrated in *Swain v. Alabama*,[51] decided by the Warren Court. In *Swain*, the Court had neither evidence of virtual exclusion nor direct confirmation of discriminatory intent. The evidence merely showed that, over a several year period, 26% of eligible jurors in the jurisdiction were black, while jury panels averaged 10–15% black. Furthermore, stressed the Court, the jury commissioners "denied that racial considerations entered into their selections of either their contacts in the community or the names of prospective jurors." Under these circumstances, the Court could find no violation of the Equal Protection Clause.[52] It explained away the disparity shown by petitioner's statistics as the result of "an

47. *Carter v. Jury Commission of Greene County*, 396 U.S. 320, 90 S.Ct. 518 (1970).

48. 493 U.S. 474, 110 S.Ct. 803 (1990); see also, *Powers v. Ohio*, 499 U.S. ___, 111 S.Ct. 1364 (1991); *Georgia v. McCollum*, ___ U.S. ___, 112 S.Ct. 931 (1992), discussed further in § 27.04(d)(2).

49. *Strauder v. West Virginia*, 100 U.S. (10 Otto) 303 (1880).

50. See, e.g., *Cassell v. Texas*, 339 U.S. 282, 70 S.Ct. 629 (1950) (finding proof of actual intent); *Avery v. Georgia*, 345 U.S. 559, 73 S.Ct. 891 (1953) (finding virtual exclusion plus an opportunity to discriminate).

51. 380 U.S. 202, 85 S.Ct. 824 (1965).

52. *Swain* also rejected a challenge to the prosecutor's use of peremptories, discussed in § 27.04(d)(1).

imperfect" but not purposefully discriminatory system which neither excluded nor limited proportionally black representation:

> Neither the jury roll nor the venire need be a perfect mirror of the community or accurately reflect the proportionate strength of every identifiable group. . . . We cannot say that purposeful discrimination based on race alone is satisfactorily proved by showing that an identifiable group in a community is underrepresented by as much as 10%.

The naivete of this language was soon exposed in an article by Professor Finkelstein which showed that the disproportionate and persistent under-representation proven in *Swain* could have resulted by chance only in one out of 100 million trillion venires chosen from the population of Talladega County.[53]

Subsequent decisions showed a Court more sophisticated in its statistical analysis and less willing to give credence to the statements of jury commissioners. Rather than requiring complete or virtual exclusion of African-Americans plus an opportunity to discriminate, the Court was willing to find a prima facie violation of equal protection whenever a "significant" disparity between the proportion of blacks on the jury panels and the proportion in the community existed, and some opportunity to discriminate was shown. For example, in *Whitus v. Georgia*,[54] the Court found a prima facie case of purposeful discrimination when, in a county where 42.6% of males over 21 were black, only 3 of 33 prospective grand jurors were black and only seven of 90 persons selected for the petit jury venire were black, and evidence showed that the jury lists had been made up from an earlier list compiled from tax returns which indicated the taxpayer's race. Testimony by the jury commissioners that race was not a factor in compiling the lists did not overcome this presumption; the Court noted that, while unnecessary to the decision, it was "interesting" that, under Finkelstein's analysis, the probability that the venire would randomly contain the number of blacks it did was .000006. Later decisions reached similar results.[55]

In *Castaneda v. Partida*,[56] the Court for the first time applied the equal protection formula to a group other than blacks and may also have further expanded its scope. The respondent's statistics showed that use of the "key man" system in Texas had produced, over an 11-year period, a 40% disparity (79.1% to 39%) between the proportion of those with Spanish surnames in the community and the proportion summoned for grand jury service.

53. Finkelstein, "The Application of Statistical Decision Theory to the Jury Discrimination Cases," 80 Harv.L.Rev. 338, 356–58 (1966).

54. 385 U.S. 545, 87 S.Ct. 643 (1967).

55. See *Turner v. Fouche*, 396 U.S. 346, 90 S.Ct. 532 (1970); *Alexander v. Louisiana*, 405 U.S. 625, 92 S.Ct. 1221 (1972).

56. 430 U.S. 482, 97 S.Ct. 1272 (1977).

After finding that Mexican-Americans are an identifiable class protected by the Equal Protection Clause, five members of the Court, in an opinion by Justice Blackmun, concluded that these statistics made out a prima facie case of discrimination. "Supporting this conclusion" was the fact that the key man selection procedures, although facially constitutional, were highly subjective and susceptible to abuse against Mexican-Americans, since Spanish surnames are easily identifiable. Because the state "inexplicably" produced no evidence from the grand jury commissioners as to their method of selection, the presumption of discrimination was not rebutted. The Court also rejected the state's contention that since Mexican-Americans were the "governing majority" in the county, it must be presumed that governmental discrimination could not have occurred.

The dissent, not unreasonably, argued that relying on gross population statistics rather than "jury-eligible" population statistics as the baseline for judging the disparity was inappropriate, given the fact that neither "tokenism nor absolute exclusion" was involved. But even had the relevant difference in representation been smaller, the majority seemed to indicate that, "in the absence of evidence to the contrary," a finding of discrimination is proper. Unconstitutional disparity exists when it is "sufficiently large [that] it is unlikely [to be] due solely to chance or accident" (a disparity which the Court defined as "more than two or three standard deviations" from the expected representation of the group in question). The Court also stressed that "a selection procedure that is susceptible of abuse or is not racially neutral supports the presumption of discrimination raised by the statistical showing." *Castaneda* thus suggests that when a procedure susceptible of abuse exists, the disparity necessary to show purposeful discrimination may be smaller than would otherwise be required. It also suggests that when the disparity is large, one may presume discrimination regardless of whether the procedure appears to be racially neutral.

(c) The Fair Cross–Section Requirement. As early as 1942, in *Glasser v. United States*,[57] the Supreme Court interpreted the Sixth Amendment to require a selection process which comports "with the concept of the jury as a cross-section of the community." But that decision applied only to the federal courts. In subsequent years, while relying on the cross-section concept to invalidate federal selection procedures which excluded day laborers[58] and women,[59] the Court refused to consider constitutional

57. 315 U.S. 60, 62 S.Ct. 457 (1942).

58. *Thiel v. Southern Pacific Co.*, 328 U.S. 217, 66 S.Ct. 984 (1946).

59. *Ballard v. United States*, 329 U.S. 187, 67 S.Ct. 261 (1946).

challenges against state selection procedures on any grounds other than equal protection.[60]

When *Duncan* applied the Sixth Amendment to the states, however, the stage was set for a new approach. Seven years later, in *Taylor v. Louisiana*,[61] the Court explicitly stated: "We accept the fair cross-section requirement as fundamental to the jury trial guaranteed by the Sixth Amendment." In providing an alternative to equal protection analysis, *Taylor* facilitated challenge of state petit jury selection procedures in three ways. First, it required only a showing of "systematic exclusion;" according to the Court, proving the existence of discriminatory intent is not necessary to show a violation of the fair cross-section requirement. Second, it signalled that the Constitution banned unjustifiable systematic exclusion of *any* significant, distinct group in the community, not just racial minorities. Third, unlike equal protection analysis at the time, *Taylor* permitted a defendant who is not a member of the excluded group to challenge its exclusion. Although, as noted above, this latter difference has since been eliminated,[62] the first two differences remain. Whether they are significant will be examined further below.

The statute in question in *Taylor* automatically exempted women from jury service unless they filed in advance a written notice of their desire to serve as a juror.[63] As a result, women comprised less than 10% of the persons in the jury wheel, despite comprising 53% of the populace. Relying on its earlier decision in *Peters v. Kiff*,[64] the Court first held that Taylor, a male, had standing to challenge this state of affairs. As Justice Marshall's opinion in *Peters* had stated, "[i]llegal and unconstitutional jury selection procedures cast doubt on the integrity of the whole judicial process," and thus should be challengeable by any defendant. The Court then explained why the fair cross-section requirement it had previously applied only to federal cases now applied, post-*Duncan*, to the state jury selection process as well. According to the majority, the jury cannot fulfill its intended purpose of guarding against the exercise of arbitrary power "if the jury pool is made up of only segments of the populace or if large, distinctive groups are excluded from the pool." The Court also emphasized the public's interest in enforcing a cross-section requirement. "Community participation in the criminal law . . . is not only consistent with our democratic heritage but is also

60. See e.g., *Fay v. New York*, 332 U.S. 261, 67 S.Ct. 1613 (1947).

61. 419 U.S. 522, 95 S.Ct. 692 (1975).

62. See *Holland v. Illinois*, 493 U.S. 474, 110 S.Ct. 803 (1990), discussed in § 27.03(b).

63. Prior to *Duncan*, the Supreme Court had upheld an identical state statute against a cross-section claim in *Hoyt v. Florida*, 368 U.S. 57, 82 S.Ct. 159 (1961).

64. 407 U.S. 493, 92 S.Ct. 2163 (1972).

critical to public confidence in the fairness of the criminal justice system."

Applying this reasoning to the facts, the Court held that women compose the type of large, distinctive group which needs to be included in the jury selection process to guard against arbitrariness and foster a sense of community participation. In addition to their obviously significant numbers, women impart "a flavor, a distinct quality" to a jury. In support of this latter statement, the Court pointed to sociological studies reporting that women brought different perspectives and values to jury service than did men. Thus, any "systematic exclusion" of this group, such as occurred under the Louisiana statute, violated the Sixth Amendment.

The Court also rejected the state's argument that making women as eligible for jury service as men would so interfere with their "distinctive role in society" that the state was justified in excluding them except when they affirmatively requested to serve. The systematic exclusion of all women under a "special hardship or incapacity" category is impermissible since it is "untenable" to suggest that it would be a special hardship for all women to serve. At the same time, the Court sanctioned the granting of individualized exemptions in the cases "of special hardship or incapacity and to those engaged in particular occupations the uninterrupted performance of which is critical to the community's welfare."

Finally, *Taylor* emphasized that while the lists from which jurors are chosen must be representative, the juries chosen from these lists need not mirror the community exactly or reflect every community group. For reasons suggested earlier,[65] this holding is not only practically necessary, but also preferable theoretically. A jury which represents the community may not be impartial. At the same time, the community's interest in participating in and feeling confident about the criminal justice system is adequately taken into account by prohibiting the exclusion of distinctive groups from the panel from which juries are ultimately selected.

The best summary of *Taylor's* holding is found in a later case, *Duren v. Missouri.*[66] There the Court held that a fair cross-section challenge of the jury venire as established in *Taylor* requires the defendant to prove three elements:

> (1) that the group alleged to be excluded is a "distinctive" group in the community; (2) that the representation of this group in venires from which juries are selected is not fair and reasonable in relation to the number of such persons in the community; and (3) that this underrepresentation is due to systematic exclusion of the group in the jury-selection process.

These three elements are discussed in more detail below.

---

65. See § 27.03(a).   **66.** 439 U.S. 357, 99 S.Ct. 664 (1979).

(1) Distinctive group.   There appear to be three requirements a "group" must meet before it comes within the ambit of the Sixth Amendment fair cross-section requirement established in *Taylor* and *Duren.*   First, the group must be "large."   Second, it must be identifiable.   Third, its inclusion in the venire must significantly advance the systemic and community objectives associated with the jury trial right.   As summarized by the Court in *Lockhart v. McCree,*[67] these objectives are "(1) 'guard[ing] against the exercise of arbitrary power' and ensuring that the 'commonsense judgment of the community' will act as a 'hedge against the overzealous or mistaken prosecutor;' (2) preserving 'public confidence in the fairness of the criminal justice system;'   and (3) implementing our belief that 'sharing in the administration of justice is a phase of civic responsibility.' "   If the group, in *Taylor's* words, imparts a "flavor, a distinct quality" to the jury deliberation process, then it presumably meets these latter three objectives.   On the other hand, the group need not "act or tend to act as a class" in the jury room for it to be "distinctive."

The types of exemptions described in the beginning of this section—having to do with aliens, felons, and so on—systematically exclude from jury service identifiable groups which may be large and perhaps even "distinctive" in the sense just described. But, as *Taylor* emphasized, group exemptions based on a valid state justification will continue to be recognized.[68]   Thus, even an exemption which falls predominately on women may not violate the Sixth Amendment if enacted for legitimate reasons.   In *Duren,* for instance, the Court suggested that so long as the state exercised "proper caution" in excusing those members of the family responsible for the care of children, a non-gender-based provision to this effect would not violate the Constitution given the important state interest in assuring proper child care.

Valid exemptions aside, there are many groups other than women potentially eligible under *Taylor's* distinctiveness test.   In *McCree* the Court indicated, not surprisingly, that the Sixth Amendment requires inclusion of racial groups such as African-Americans and Mexican-Americans in the jury pool (thereby specifically incorporating the equal protection cases into fair cross-section jurisprudence).   As Justice Rehnquist wrote for the Court, exclusion of these groups from the venire could produce juries which might be "arbitrarily skewed in such a way as to deny criminal defendants the benefit of the common-sense judgment of the community."   Furthermore, such exclusion creates an appearance of unfairness by basing exclusion not on inability to serve but

67.   476 U.S. 162, 106 S.Ct. 1758 (1986).

68.   See, e.g., *State v. Brewer,* 247 N.W.2d 205 (Iowa 1976) (state's exemp- tion of those over 65 has a rational basis).

on "some immutable characteristic such as race, gender, or ethnic background," and "improperly deprives members of these often historically disadvantaged groups of their right as citizens to serve on juries in criminal cases."

In applying the *Taylor–McCree* test, lower courts have held that other ethnic groups, including Native Americans [69] and Jews,[70] are "distinct" groups for Sixth Amendment purposes. In contrast, non-ethnic groups, such as blue collar workers [71] and young adults,[72] are generally not included in this category. In short, the courts have not strayed very far beyond traditional equal protection doctrine (which has focused on oppressed minorities and gender) in developing this aspect of the fair cross-section doctrine. One of the cases involving young adults, *Barber v. Ponte*,[73] illustrates the difficulties of extending the doctrine beyond racial, ethnic, and gender lines.

The original decision in *Barber* came from two members of a three-judge panel, which found, in contrast to most precedent, that young adults between the ages of 18 and 34 are a cognizable group (and found further that this group had been systematically underrepresented in the jury pool by a factor of between 19 and 22%). In reaching the conclusion that young adults are distinctive for Sixth Amendment purposes, the judges relied heavily on sociological research, as had the Court in *Taylor*. This research indicated that younger adults have differing opinions from older adults on such matters as "the inference of guilt from silence; the presumption of innocence; the predisposition of the young to break the law; and the performance and prerogatives of the police." [74] The judges concluded that "a gross underrepresentation of young people could be expected to affect a large number of cases, particularly those involving young people."

However, on rehearing en banc, the First Circuit reversed, giving two significant reasons. First, it asserted that the Court in *Taylor* and *Duren* had "wanted to give heightened scrutiny to groups needing special protection, not to all groups generally." The court continued: "[I]f age classification is adopted, surely blue-collar workers, yuppies, Rotarians, Eagle Scouts, and an endless variety of other classifications will be entitled to similar

69. *United States v. Herbert*, 698 F.2d 981 (9th Cir.1983); *United States v. Brady*, 579 F.2d 1121 (9th Cir.1978), cert. denied 439 U.S. 1074, 99 S.Ct. 849 (1979).

70. *United States v. Gelb*, 881 F.2d 1155 (2d Cir.1989).

71. *Anaya v. Hansen*, 781 F.2d 1 (1st Cir.1986).

72. *Ford v. Seabold*, 841 F.2d 677 (6th Cir.1988); *Brown v. Harris*, 666

F.2d 782 (2d Cir.1981), cert. denied 456 U.S. 948, 102 S.Ct. 2017 (1982); *United States v. Test*, 550 F.2d 577 (10th Cir. 1976).

73. 772 F.2d 982 (1st Cir.1985), cert. denied 475 U.S. 1050, 106 S.Ct. 1272 (1986).

74. Quoting Zeigler, "Young Adults as a Cognizable Group in Jury Selection," 76 Mich.L.Rev. 1045 (1978).

treatment." Second, the majority concluded that the age group identified by the three-judge panel decision was arbitrary.[75] In terms of "specific common characteristics," the court asserted, there are no "clear lines of demarcation" between the 18–34 group and any other group within or overlapping with that range; further, the diversity within that range might be substantial.

Both rationales can be questioned. The first argument seems heavily tinged with equal protection concerns not necessarily relevant to fair cross-section analysis. The Court's Sixth Amendment cases do not speak of "protecting" groups from discrimination, but of ensuring that groups with a distinctive voice can both contribute to the "common sense" of the jury and experience a sense of participation in the criminal justice process.[76] The majority's concern that this approach will open the door to a wide diversity of claims is understandable. But some of the groups named by the majority may not bring a "distinct flavor" to the jury, and, even assuming they do, they may not be large enough (e.g., Eagle Scouts or Rotarians) or discernible (e.g., "yuppies"), thus failing the other aspects of *Taylor's* distinctive group test.

Lack of discernability is the *Barber* majority's second rationale for its decision. There is certainly some strength to the point that the group of "young adults" is not "identifiable." But as the dissent (written by one member of the original two-judge majority) noted, "amorphousness is not confined to age groups. In what generation does a Mexican–American or Puerto Rican become simply a Texas [sic] or New Yorker and cease to be part of a cognizable group?" Conundrums such as these make the distinctive group aspect of *Taylor* particularly problematic.

(2) Underrepresentation. In *Taylor,* the Court had no difficulty finding the requisite degree of underrepresentation: while women comprised 53% of the persons eligible for jury service in the relevant jurisdictions, no more than 10% of the persons on the jury wheel were women and no women were on the venire from which the petit jury in the defendant's case was drawn. In *Duren,* the defendant presented statistics that only 15% of the persons on venires were women while 54% of the adults in the county were women. Again the Court found the underrepresentation substantial enough to violate the Sixth Amendment.

One might argue that, because *Taylor* was concerned with ensuring a fair cross-section in the jury venire and not with

---

75. *Barber v. Ponte,* 772 F.2d 892 (1st Cir.1985).

76. Indeed, in *Hamling v. United States,* 418 U.S. 87, 94 S.Ct. 2887 (1974), the Supreme Court assumed, without deciding, that the young do constitute a "cognizable group," but went on to hold that, because "[s]ome play in the joints of the jury selection process is necessary," California's scheme of refilling the jury list every four years (and thus failing to include those who reached 18 in the intervening years) did not violate the Constitution.

preventing purposeful discrimination, a very small differential should trigger the Sixth Amendment. But among the lower courts, the disparity between a group's representation in the community and on the venire must usually be over 10% to be sufficient under the Sixth Amendment.[77] Note that this definition of underrepresentation is, at best, no broader than that applied in equal protection cases (indeed, the Court's equal protection decision in *Swain,* which was roundly criticized, involved a 10% disparity, albeit over a several year period).[78] Furthermore, it should be remembered that mere proof of a sufficient disparity does not necessarily conclude the case. If the state can give a legitimate reason for the underrepresentation, then the Sixth Amendment is not violated.

(3) Systematic exclusion. The facts of *Taylor* and *Duren* both illustrate that the Sixth Amendment does not require proof of purposeful exclusion. In *Taylor,* the statute struck down in that case permitted any otherwise qualified woman to serve if she indicated a willingness to do so. No state official prevented women from volunteering for jury service and there was no evidence that the legislature intended to exclude women from such service. In *Duren,* the challenged statutes required women to opt out of service rather than "opt in," arguably a system even less likely to deter female participation in the jury system. Yet the fact that the statutes made opting out especially easy for women (and that local practice was to excuse any woman who failed to appear for jury service), when combined with the statistical showing described above, led the Court to invalidate the Missouri provisions as well.

Despite these decisions, it is misleading to say, as the Court did in *Duren,* that "[i]n contrast [to the equal protection cases], in Sixth Amendment fair-cross-section cases, systematic disproportion itself demonstrates an infringement of the defendant's interest in a jury chosen from a fair cross section." As noted above, both theories require a fairly high degree of unjustified disparity to make out a prima facie case, suggesting that the Sixth Amendment requires something more than systematic exclusion of members of a distinct group.[79] The one difference between the two

77. See, e.g., *United States v. Rodriguez,* 776 F.2d 1509 (11th Cir.1985) ("a prima facie case of underrepresentation has not been made where the absolute disparity . . . does not exceed 10%); *People Porter v. Freeman,* 577 F.2d 329 (5th Cir.1978) (women underrepresented by 20%).

78. Of course, if a group comprises less than 10% of the population, the analysis must be adjusted somewhat, suggesting that the standard deviation

approach of *Castenada* is preferable. See § 27.03(b). Note, however, that a group this small may not be "distinct" under *Taylor.*

79. See Alschuler, "The Supreme Court and the Jury: Voir Dire, Peremptory Challenges and the Review of Jury Verdicts," 56 U.Chi.L.Rev. 153, 184–85 (1989) ("Neither concept appears to encompass 'accidental' exclusion (however frequently it may occur), and random selection appears to satisfy both Sixth

theories may lie in the grounds which will justify a disparity once it is found. For instance, if it is shown that a group is significantly underrepresented in the venire because it is underrepresented on the voter registration lists from which the jury pool is randomly selected (which might be true of Mexican–Americans, for example), an equal protection claim would presumably lose (because the exclusion is accidental, not intentional), while a fair cross-section claim might require that some other means of selecting the pool be found that more accurately represents the excluded group.

(d) **The Right to the Jury List.** In *Test v. United States*,[80] the Supreme Court held that a federal defendant has the right to inspect and copy jury lists in order to prepare challenges to petit and grand jury selection procedures. Relying on the Federal Jury Selection and Service Act, the Court found an unqualified right to inspection in the plain text of the statute and in the statute's overall purpose of assuring that juries are selected at random from a fair cross-section of the community.

Since the decision was based on a federal statute, *Test* has no direct implications for the states. Without an unreasonable extension, however, this right of inspection could be seen as part of the constitutional right to have a jury pool and panel selected from a fair cross-section of the community.

27.04 Voir Dire

(a) **The Basic Structure.** After the jury pool or venire is selected, effort is focused on choosing the members of the jury who will hear the case. At this point, the principal goal is no longer obtaining a cross-section of the community, but rather assuring that the members of the jury are "impartial," as guaranteed by the Sixth Amendment. The principal mechanism for accomplishing this objective is "*voir dire*," literally, "to see what is said."

Depending upon the jurisdiction, *voir dire* questioning—designed to elicit possible biases among the venirepersons—may be conducted by the judge, the attorneys, or by both.[81] When the judge alone conducts the process, the attorneys typically are allowed to suggest questions to the judge. The advantage of judicial questioning is that attorneys will be prevented from using *voir dire* to "indoctrinate" the jury. The disadvantage is that judicial questioning is seldom probing (and may be directed at the entire panel rather than individual jurors). The better practice, probably, is to allow the attorneys to conduct questioning, monitored closely by the judge and other attorney.

and Fourteenth Amendment requirements.")

80. 420 U.S. 28, 95 S.Ct. 749 (1975).

81. The federal rule leaves the matter up to the judge. Fed.R.Civ.P. 24(a).

In addition to questioning at *voir dire,* attorneys may conduct outside research about prospective jurors. This typically consists of culling demographic information from jury lists.[82] But the attorneys may also pursue more detailed investigation of prospective jurors by interviewing their acquaintances and searching records,[83] or even hiring social scientists to anticipate their attitudes on various issues.[84]

Based on the results of the questioning and other information they have acquired, the defense and the prosecution decide which individuals they would like to exclude from the jury. Each side has an unlimited number of for cause challenges, which permit striking from the jury any venireperson who admits or appears to be biased. Each side also has a limited number of peremptories (from 3 to 20 or more, depending upon the jurisdiction, the size of the jury and the type of crime) which it can use to strike any venireperson without explanation.[85]

The following three subsections explore in more depth the questioning process which occurs during *voir dire,* the nature of for cause challenges and the nature of peremptory challenges.

(b) Voir Dire Questioning. Litigation over *voir dire* questioning is most likely to occur when the judge conducts it and refuses to ask questions proffered by the defense. The Supreme Court has held that, under certain circumstances, the judge must ask specific questions about racial prejudice and attitudes toward the death penalty. But otherwise, failure on the part of the judge to ask individualized questions at the defendant's request will not constitute error unless the defendant can show that the failure produced a jury that was prejudiced. This latter burden is very difficult to meet.

(1) Questions about racial prejudice. The Supreme Court has held that specific questions about racial prejudice must be asked if racial issues are "inextricably bound with the conduct of the trial." *Ham v. South Carolina* [86] involved a black tried in South Carolina for the possession of marijuana. The defendant was well known in the locale of his trial as a civil rights activist, and his defense was that law enforcement officials had framed him on the narcotics charge to "get him" for those activities. The Court, in an opinion by Justice Rehnquist, unanimously found that Ham's reputation as an activist and the defense he interposed likely intensified any prejudice that individual members of the jury

---

82. See § 27.03(d).

83. Extrajudicial communication with veniremen prior to trial is considered unethical. ABA Model Code of Professional Responsibility EC 7–29.

84. For a critique of this latter practice, see Saks, "The Limits of Scientific

Jury Selection: Ethical and Empirical," 17 Jurimetrics J. 3 (1976).

85. See e.g., Fed.R.Crim.P. 24(b).

86. 409 U.S. 524, 93 S.Ct. 848 (1973).

might have harbored against blacks and that, in such circumstances, the defendant was entitled to questioning specifically directed to racial prejudice in order to meet the constitutional requirement that an impartial jury be impaneled. The routine questions asked by the trial court (i.e., "Have you formed or expressed any opinion as to the guilt or innocence of the defendant, Gene Ham?; Are you conscious of any bias or prejudice for or against him?; and Can you give the State and the defendant a fair and impartial trial?) were insufficient for this purpose.

But the Court strictly limited *Ham* in *Ristaino v. Ross*,[87] in which a black was convicted in state court of violent crimes against a white security guard. The trial judge denied the defendant's motion that a question specifically directed to racial prejudice be asked during *voir dire*, finding the customary questions directed to general bias and prejudice sufficient. The Court upheld the trial judge's decision, construing *Ham* to mean that it is in the trial judge's discretion to determine whether there is a constitutionally significant likelihood that, absent questioning about racial prejudice, the jurors selected would be less indifferent about the race issue than a jury selected after such questioning. In *Ristaino,* the racial issue was seen as collateral compared to the situation in *Ham;* racial issues did not "permeate" the trial and were not "bound up" with its conduct. Thus questioning about general bias was sufficient.[88]

In the federal courts, the rule concerning questioning about racial prejudice is somewhat more generous toward the defendant. The defendant in *Rosales-Lopez v. United States*[89] was convicted of participating in a plan to bring Mexican aliens across the border from Tijuana to California. Prior to *voir dire*, the defendant's counsel had requested the trial judge to ask potential jury members a list of 26 questions, one of which read: "Would you consider the race or Mexican descent of Humber Rosales-Lopez in your evaluation of this case? How would it affect you?" The Supreme Court found no violation, constitutional or otherwise, in the trial judge's refusal to ask this type of question on *voir dire*, given the failure of the petitioner to show that racial issues were a significant aspect of the trial. However, the plurality opinion went on to create, under its supervisory power over the federal courts, a federal rule calling for such questions when there is "a reasonable possibility that racial or ethnic prejudice might have influenced the jury." The plurality also found, after an analysis of the

87. 424 U.S. 589, 96 S.Ct. 1017 (1976).

88. A narrow exception to the *Ham/Ristaino* rule was announced in *Turner v. Murray,* 476 U.S. 28, 106 S.Ct. 1683 (1986), where the Court held that a *capital sentencing* jury must be asked racial prejudice questions *whenever* the crime involves racial violence.

89. 451 U.S. 182, 101 S.Ct. 1629 (1981).

Court's previous decisions, that such a "reasonable possibility" would exist whenever the defendant is "accused of a violent crime [unlike the instant case] and where the defendant and the victim are members of different racial or ethnic groups." But it cautioned that, in most cases, "whether the total circumstances suggest a reasonable possibility that racial or ethnic prejudice will affect the jury remains primarily with the trial court."

(2) Questions about attitudes toward the death penalty. In order to implement its decisions attempting to maintain jury impartiality in capital sentencing cases, to be discussed below,[90] the Court has required trial judges, at the request of a party, to ask specific questions designed to determine attitudes about the death penalty. The explicit rule announced in *Morgan v. Illinois* [91] was that capital defendants may require potential jurors to disclose whether they would automatically impose the death penalty upon conviction. Six members of the Court, in an opinion by Justice White, concluded that individuals who would do so are unlikely to be discovered by general questions concerning fairness and impartiality, because they might be unwilling to admit a reluctance to abide by the law, or might, "in good conscience, swear to uphold that law and yet be unaware that maintaining such dogmatic beliefs about the death penalty would prevent [them] from doing so." Although not necessary to its holding, the *Morgan* Court also strongly suggested that the *prosecution* can require the judge to ask specific questions as to whether a potential juror would refuse to impose the death penalty under any circumstances. As White stated, "[w]ere *voir dire* not available to lay bare" those who would automatically impose the death penalty, the "right not to be tried by such jurors would be rendered as nugatory and meaningless as the State's right, in the absence of questioning, to strike those who would *never* do so."

(3) Questions about other matters. As to *voir dire* questioning on issues other than racial prejudice or the death penalty, it seems clear that constitutional obligations are minimal. For instance, in rejecting Ham's argument that the trial court should also have examined jurors about possible prejudice engendered by his beard, Rhenquist stated "[g]iven the traditionally broad discretion accorded to the trial judge in conducting *voir dire* . . . and our inability to distinguish possible prejudice against beards from a host of other possible similar prejudices, we do not believe the petitioner's constitutional rights were violated when the trial judge refused to put this question." Much the same thing could be said about *voir dire* questioning directed at most other types of possible prejudices.

90. See § 27.04(c).

91. ___ U.S. ___, 112 S.Ct. 295 (1992).

Post–*Ham* cases do not dispel this notion. In *Hamling v. United States,*[92] the Court held that the trial judge in an obscenity case is not required to inquire into the "whether the jurors' educational, political, and religious beliefs might affect their views on the question of obscenity." And in *Mu'Min v. Virginia,*[93] it concluded that, although there was "a certain common sense appeal" to the argument that the effect of pretrial publicity could not be gauged unless each venireperson was asked specifically what he had heard or read, the judge did not violate the Sixth Amendment by merely asking potential jurors, in groups of four, general questions about whether they had foreknowledge of the case and were able to avoid a fixed opinion about it.

The Court's reasoning in *Mu'Min* suggests that, outside of racial and death penalty issues, the Sixth Amendment imposes few constraints on *voir dire* questioning. Chief Justice Rehnquist characterized as "speculative" the assumption that questioning about the precise content of foreknowledge would cause jurors to consider more carefully whether they were open-minded about the case. He also pointed out that, to prevent other jurors from hearing about the content of the pretrial publicity, the type of *voir dire* proposed by the defendant would necessitate questioning each prospective juror individually, which would be inefficient and might make those questioned feel that they themselves were on trial. Yet Justice Kennedy, one of four dissenters, seemed more realistic when he wrote that, at least when prejudicial pretrial publicity is involved, "findings of impartiality must be based on something more than the mere silence of the individual in response to questions asked *en masse.*"

(c) For Cause Challenges. Typical statutory grounds for challenging jurors include a blood relationship to one of the litigants, a pecuniary interest in the outcome of the case, and previous service on a jury which considered a similar crime or a grand jury which considered the same crime. Additionally, even if not specifically provided for by statute, each party can exclude for cause any juror who has "a state of mind . . . which will prevent him from acting impartially."[94]

Challenges on the latter basis are rarely granted, however. First, as noted in the previous subsection, judges are not normally required to ask *voir dire* questions designed to probe into prejudices involving such matters as race or appearance. Second, judges usually accept at face value a potential juror's statement that he will abide by the oath of impartiality. Prejudice is seldom implied, on the reasonable ground that individuals who say they

---

92. 418 U.S. 87, 94 S.Ct. 2887 (1974).

93. 500 U.S. ___, 111 S.Ct. 1899 (1991).

94. See e.g., ABA Standards for Criminal Justice 15–58 and 15–59 (2d Ed.1980).

can be impartial should be trusted to abide by their oath. The question of when bias *should* be implied, as a matter of constitutional law, is discussed first, followed by a discussion of the special for cause challenge jurisprudence that has developed in death penalty cases.

(1) Implied bias. All of the Supreme Court's decisions dealing with implied juror bias have involved convicted defendants; interlocutory appeal of *voir dire* decisions are rare.[95] This fact may explain why only a few Court decisions have concluded that the trial court erred in not excluding a particular venireperson for cause; such a finding has always required reversal of conviction. If, instead, implying bias merely necessitated obtaining a replacement juror, the Court might be more willing to make such a finding. In any event, except for a few decisions involving the impact of pretrial publicity (which, as discussed later in this chapter,[96] have since been significantly limited in scope), there is only one decision in which the Court held that exclusion for cause should have occurred because of implied bias. In *Leonard v. United States,*[97] the Court held that prospective jurors who had heard the trial court announce the defendant's guilty verdict in his first trial should have been automatically disqualified from sitting at his second trial on similar charges, regardless of whether they vowed impartiality.

In other cases, the Court has been hostile to implied bias claims, requiring instead a showing of "actual bias." In *Dennis v. United States,*[98] the defendant claimed that his conviction on criminal contempt charges for failure to appear before the Committee on UnAmerican Activities was inherently tainted, because his jury had been composed primarily of employees of the federal government who were subject to a regulation providing for their discharge if they were disloyal to the government. The Court dismissed the claim, observing that "[p]reservation of the opportunity to prove actual bias is a guarantee of a defendant's right to an impartial jury," an opportunity which the defendant had failed to exercise. Similarly, in *Remmer v. United States,*[99] while the Court ruled that an attempt to bribe a juror during the trial in an effort to affect the outcome should be deemed "presumptively prejudicial," it remanded the case to determine "the circumstances, the impact thereof upon the jury, and whether or not [they were] prejudicial."

95. Given the "independence" of *voir dire* issues from trial issues, however, such appeal might be allowed on occasion. See § 29.03(a). See also, *Georgia v. McCollum,* ___ U.S. ___, 112 S.Ct. 931 (1992) (considering interlocutory appeal by prosecution of a trial court order permitting use of peremptories to exclude African–Americans from the jury).

96. See § 27.06(b)(1).

97. 378 U.S. 544, 84 S.Ct. 1696 (1964).

98. 339 U.S. 162, 70 S.Ct. 519 (1950).

99. 347 U.S. 227, 74 S.Ct. 450 (1954).

In a more recent case, the Court adhered to the view that actual bias must generally be shown before the Impartiality Clause is violated. In *Smith v. Phillips*,[1] the Court was unwilling to imply bias from the fact that one of the jurors at the defendant's trial was actively seeking employment with the prosecutor's office before and during the trial. Noting that the trial court had concluded, after a post-trial hearing, that the juror had not been biased, the six-member majority considered irrelevant the federal district court's finding on habeas that "the average man in Smith's position would believe that the verdict of the jury would directly affect the evaluation of his job application." Nor was it impressed with the dissent's argument that post-trial hearings to determine bias were ineffective because they relied primarily, if not entirely, on the suspect juror's testimony. Indeed, five members of the majority appeared to believe that bias can *never* be implied from a juror's circumstances. Of the majority, only Justice O'Connor, in a concurring opinion, insisted that prejudice could still be implied in appropriate circumstances, such as those present in *Leonard.*

(2) Death penalty cases. As noted above,[2] in *Morgan v. Illinois* the Court held that the defendant charged with a capital crime is entitled to specific *voir dire* questions designed to determine whether any potential jurors would automatically impose the death penalty were conviction to result. The obvious predicate to this holding was the Court's conclusion that the defendant has the right to remove such people from the capital sentencing jury; because a person who would automatically vote for the death penalty "will fail in good faith to consider the evidence of aggravating and mitigating circumstances as the instructions require him to do," the Court held that the defendant must be able to excuse him for cause. Although this holding resonates with the Impartiality Clause, the majority had to base its decision on the Due Process Clause, because the Sixth Amendment applies only to "criminal prosecutions."

Justice Scalia, joined by Chief Justice Rehnquist and Justice Thomas, argued in dissent that a juror who automatically imposes the death penalty after conviction of a capital crime does not violate the law, at least in Illinois. That state's capital sentencing statute merely provides that a juror *may* reject the death penalty if mitigating circumstances are present, and does not define mitigation. Accordingly, concluded Scalia, a juror who automatically imposes the death penalty "does not 'fail . . . to consider the evidence'; he simply fails to give it the effect the defendant desires."

1. 455 U.S. 209, 102 S.Ct. 940 (1982).   2. See § 27.04(b)(2).

Morgan was decided against the backdrop of several cases which dealt with prosecution use of for cause challenges in the death penalty context. In these cases, the Court was concerned not with whether the failure to excuse for cause results in a biased jury, but rather with whether the *exercise* of such challenges by the prosecution undermined jury impartiality. This issue was first addressed in *Witherspoon v. Illinois,*[3] which involved a statute providing for exclusion, in all capital cases, of any venireperson who "expressed scruples" against the death penalty. The Supreme Court held that a death sentence imposed by a jury so selected could not stand, because the for cause exclusions would result in a tribunal "organized to return a verdict of death," or at least "uncommonly willing to condemn a man to die." The Court also concluded that such a jury could not express the conscience of the community, since those who do not harbor doubts about the wisdom of capital punishment are "a distinct and dwindling minority."

Witherspoon noted that the state may continue to exclude jurors in capital cases who indicate that they would *never* consider returning a verdict of death, regardless of the evidence. Several later decisions refined the scope of the for cause challenge in this context. While a juror cannot be excluded merely because he refuses to take an oath that the mandatory penalty of death or life imprisonment would not "affect his deliberations on any issue of fact,"[4] he can be excluded if the prospect of the death penalty would "interfere" with his judgment of guilt or innocence,[5] or if he indicates that imposing the death penalty is against his "principles."[6] These latter two decisions come close to allowing exclusion based on a finding of "implied bias" against the state, in interesting contrast to *Smith* and like cases prohibiting exclusion by the defendant on such a basis.

Witherspoon invalidated only the defendant's death sentence, not his conviction. Although the defendant had presented what he called "competent scientific evidence" that "death-qualified juries" are partial to the prosecution not only on the sentencing issue but also with respect to guilt, the Court found the data "too tentative and fragmentary" to require reversal of every conviction returned by such juries. In response to this conclusion, several methodologically improved studies were conducted which indicated that even juries which are selected under *Witherspoon's new* standard (excluding only those who would not impose the death penalty) are more conviction-prone than juries which are not so

3. 391 U.S. 510, 88 S.Ct. 1770 (1968).

4. *Adams v. Texas,* 448 U.S. 38, 100 S.Ct. 2521 (1980).

5. *Wainwright v. Witt,* 469 U.S. 412, 105 S.Ct. 844 (1985).

6. *Darden v. Wainwright,* 477 U.S. 168, 106 S.Ct. 2464 (1986).

selected;[7] this research led at least one lower federal court to reverse a conviction by a "death-qualified" jury.[8] However, in *Lockhart v. McCree*,[9] the Supreme Court held that even if research can conclusively prove that death qualified juries are more conviction prone than ordinary juries, no constitutional violation occurs when the prosecution excludes those who cannot impose the death penalty from capital trial juries.

The defendant in *McCree* advanced two separate constitutional grounds for overturning his conviction by a death-qualified jury. The first was that death-qualification results in a jury which violates the Sixth Amendment's fair cross-section requirement because it excludes a "distinctive group," and thus runs afoul of *Taylor v. Louisiana*.[10] In rejecting this argument, Justice Rehnquist's majority opinion first noted that *Taylor* had resisted applying the cross-section requirement to the petit jury, as opposed to the venire. But assuming, without deciding, that *Taylor* covered this situation,[11] the majority concluded that the jurors excluded through the death-qualification process are different from women and the racial groups contemplated by the cross-section requirement, since they are fairly excluded for their inability to be impartial, not because of an "immutable characteristic," and because they can serve in other juries not involving a capital charge, unlike minority groups prevented by exclusion from participating at all in the criminal process.

McCree's second argument was that the death-qualification process made his jury more predisposed to convict than the average jury and thus violated the Impartiality Clause. Rehnquist also rejected this argument. First, he noted that the individual members of McCree's jury were impartial, in the sense they had all promised to abide by their oath. "[E]xactly the same twelve individuals could have ended up on his jury through the 'luck of the draw,' without in any way violating the constitutional guarantee of impartiality." McCree conceded this point, but argued that *Witherspoon* had held that the state may not "slant" a jury by excluding a group of individuals more likely than the population

---

7. See in particular, Cowan, Thompson & Ellsworth, "The Effects of Death Qualification on Jurors' Predisposition to Convict and on the Quality of Deliberation," 8 Law & Hum. Behav. 53 (1984); Winick, "Prosecutorial Preemptory Challenge Practices in Capital Cases: An Empirical Study and a Constitutional Analysis," 81 Mich.L.Rev. 1 (1982); Jurow, "New Data on the Effect of a 'Death Qualified' Jury on the Guilty Determination Process," 84 Harv.L.Rev. 567 (1971).

8. *Grigsby v. Mabry*, 758 F.2d 226 (8th Cir.1985).

9. 476 U.S. 162, 106 S.Ct. 1758 (1986).

10. 419 U.S. 522, 95 S.Ct. 692 (1975), discussed in § 27.03(c).

11. As Justice Marshall pointed out in dissent, if the systematic exclusion of a given group takes place at *voir dire*, then, for practical purposes, the infringement of the Sixth Amendment is the same as if it had occurred during selection of the jury pool.

at large to favor the criminal defendant even if, on an individual-by-individual basis, it is "impartial." But Rehnquist distinguished *Witherspoon* on two grounds. First, whereas there had been no legitimate state interest supporting the prosecution's exclusion of scrupled venirepersons from the jury in *Witherspoon*, here the removal of those who could not impose the death penalty served the "entirely proper interest in obtaining a single jury that could impartially decide all the issues in McCree's case." Because the guilt and penalty issues in a capital case are interwoven, duplication of evidence would be required if separate juries were required. Second, *Witherspoon* dealt with "the special context of capital sentencing, where the range of jury discretion necessarily gave rise to far greater concern over the possible effects of an 'imbalanced' jury."

In dissent, Justice Marshall, joined by Justices Brennan and Stevens, argued that, in light of the research, the Court's decision gives "the prosecution license to empanel a jury especially likely to return [a guilty] verdict." The state's efficiency and financial interests in a unitary jury, Marshall continued, did not overcome the jury's predisposition toward the prosecution. Capital cases resulting in conviction are a very small proportion of all criminal cases, and in those cases where a new jury is required, alternate jurors can replace any "automatic life imprisonment" jurors on the sentencing jury or evidence can be presented in stipulated summaries rather than re-presented wholesale.

The Court reaffirmed and expanded the reach of *McCree* in *Buchanan v. Kentucky*.[12] There, six justices upheld a death-qualified jury for a joint trial of a capital defendant and a *non*capital co-defendant, in light of the state's interest in avoiding duplicate trials and sentencing proceedings. The Court did not pause to consider Marshall's suggestion in dissent that death-qualified alternates sit during the joint trial and replace any "*Witherspoon*-excludables" at the capital defendant's sentencing proceeding if he is convicted.

If *McCree* and *Buchanan* are wrong, it is mostly because they unreasonably inflate the government's needs rather than unfairly characterize the defendant's interests. Rehnquist's assertion in *McCree* that the conviction-proneness of a jury is not determinative of its ability to weigh the evidence fairly is difficult to dispute. Assuming its members have agreed to abide by the law, such a jury may be just as "accurate" as other juries even if it is more "conviction-prone." A stronger argument can be made that a death-qualified jury does not represent "community sentiment." But the Court's decision in *Morgan* now appears to neutralize, at

12. 483 U.S. 402, 107 S.Ct. 2906 (1987).

least to some extent,[13] any prosecution advantage gained by *Mc-Cree* in this regard, by allowing the defendant to exclude from trial (as well as sentencing) the persons who are most likely "conviction-prone." At the same time, building on Marshall's arguments, the burden the state would incur if it were required to seat both types of jurors through trial and replace them at sentencing does not seem particularly significant. Given the *possibility* of bias and lack of community representation that otherwise results, it would seem this burden should be borne.[14]

(d) Peremptory Challenges. In contrast to for cause challenges, peremptory challenges allow removal of a venireperson without explanation; no proof of actual or implied bias is necessary. For example, the defense may use a peremptory challenge to remove a person who glares at the defendant during *voir dire*, while the prosecution may exclude a long-haired college student. Neither of these individuals could typically be excluded from the jury "for cause" (assuming they agree to abide by their oath to consider the evidence impartially) because the reason for exclusion is merely a suspicion based on amorphous assumptions about their attitudes. As the Supreme Court has stated,[15] the peremptory challenge "is often exercised upon the 'sudden impressions and unaccountable prejudices we are apt to conceive upon the bare looks and gestures of another,' upon a juror's 'habits and associations,' or upon the feeling that the 'bare questioning [of a juror's] indifference may sometimes provoke a resentment.' " Peremptory challenges can best be analyzed by looking separately at prosecutorial and defense use.

(1) By the prosecution. The most controversial issue associated with prosecutorial use of peremptories is whether they may be used to exclude potential jurors because of their race. In *Swain v. Alabama,*[16] the defendant argued that the prosecutor's use of peremptory challenges to strike all prospective black jurors violated the Equal Protection Clause. In rejecting this claim, the Court stressed that the function of the peremptory challenge required that its use not be subject to inquiry:

> [The peremptory challenge] is frequently exercised on grounds normally thought irrelevant to legal proceedings or official action, namely, the race, religion, nationality, occupation or affiliations of people summoned for jury duty. For the ques-

---

13. It should be noted, however, that there are many more *Witherspoon*-excludables in the community then there are "automatic death penalty" individuals. See studies cited supra note 7.

14. Of course, even if this approach were adopted, the parties could still use peremptory challenges to remove individuals with the "wrong" attitude about the death penalty. Cf. *Gray v. Mississippi*, 481 U.S. 648, 107 S.Ct. 2045 (1987), where five members of the Court contended the prosecution could do so.

15. *Swain v. Alabama*, 380 U.S. 202, 85 S.Ct. 824 (1965).

16. 380 U.S. 202, 85 S.Ct. 824 (1965).

tion a prosecutor or defense counsel must decide is not whether a juror of a particular race or nationality is in fact partial, but whether one from a different group is less likely to be. . . . Hence veniremen are not always judged solely as individuals for the purpose of exercising peremptory challenges. Rather they are challenged in light of the limited knowledge counsel has of them, which may include their group affiliations, in the context of the case to be tried.

The Court acknowledged, however, that a constitutional violation might be established if it could be shown that the prosecutor systematically used the peremptory challenge to exclude blacks from all juries on the basis of race. On this point the Court found the record deficient, despite uncontradicted evidence that no black within memory of anyone living had ever served in any civil or criminal case tried in Talladega county, Alabama, and verified evidence that no black had served there since 1950.

Twenty-one years later, in *Batson v. Kentucky*,[17] the Court reconsidered the *Swain* ruling and partially overruled it by requiring prosecutors to explain their use of peremptories upon a showing by the defendant that they have been used to exclude members of his race. The primary ground for veering from *Swain's* reluctance to limit use of peremptories was that it had led the *Swain* Court to conclude that only proof of repeated striking of blacks over a number of cases would establish an equal protection violation. Terming this "a crippling burden of proof" which in effect made prosecutors' peremptory challenges of blacks "largely immune from constitutional scrutiny," Justice Powell, joined by six other members of the Court (including Justice White, the author of *Swain*), arrived at a new "evidentiary formulation." Borrowing from the Court's equal protection analysis in cases involving selection of jury pools,[18] he concluded that a defendant could make out a prima facie case that use of peremptory challenges has violated the Constitution if he shows (1) that he is a member of a cognizable racial group, (2) that the prosecutor has exercised peremptories to remove members of the defendant's race, and (3) that "these facts and any other relevant circumstances raise an inference that the prosecutor used [peremptories] to exclude the veniremen from the petit jury on account of their race." "Other relevant circumstances" might include a "pattern" of strikes against blacks, and the prosecutor's questions and statements during *voir dire*. Once a prima facie case is established, the prosecution may rebut it by coming forward "with a neutral explanation for challenging black jurors [which] need not rise to the level justifying exercise of a challenge for cause." However,

17. 476 U.S. 79, 106 S.Ct. 1712   **18.** See § 27.03(b).
(1986).

merely stating blacks were excluded on the assumption or intuitive judgment that they would be partial to the defendant because of shared race is insufficient.

Since the prosecutor in *Batson* had not been given the opportunity to explain his peremptory challenges of blacks, the Court had no occasion to apply these guidelines there. The first Court case to do so suggested that the prosecutor's burden under *Batson* will be minimal. In *Hernandez v. New York*,[19] the prosecutor challenged the only three prospective jurors with Hispanic surnames, as well as an additional Latino. Two of the exclusions were explained on the ground that the individuals had relatives involved in criminal activity; in these cases, the defendant did not press his *Batson* objection. The prosecutor explained the other two exclusions by noting that both of those excluded had looked away from him and been hesitant when stating that they would not consider their own translations of testimony by Spanish-speaking witnesses, but rather follow the court interpreter's version.

Emphasizing the need to prove intentional discrimination, the Court held, 6–3, that the prosecutor's explanation was race neutral. In response to the defendant's argument that there is a high correlation between Spanish-language ability and race in New York, the Court, in an opinion by Justice Kennedy, noted that the prosecutor relied on the jurors' demeanor as well as their language ability. Moreover, Kennedy asserted, even assuming that most Spanish-speaking individuals would act the same way in such a situation, "[n]othing in the prosecutor's explanation shows that he chose to exclude jurors who hesitated in answering questions about following the interpreter *because* he wanted to prevent bilingual Latinos from serving on the jury."

Kennedy did state that, in a different case, prosecutorial exclusions on grounds of language-ability which had a disproportionate impact on Latinos might not survive a *Batson* claim. But here, stated the Court, the trial court legitimately believed the prosecutor's explanation that he was concerned about the jurors' ability to rely on the interpreter's version of testimony, in light of the prosecutor's sincere demeanor, his willingness to explain his exclusions before the defense made out a prima facie case of discrimination, his statement that he did not know the jurors were Latino (as opposed to people who spoke Spanish), and the fact that many of the victims and prosecution witnesses were Latino (thus suggesting, apparently, that the prosecution would have preferred Latinos on the jury, all else being equal). What was not explained is the rationale for excluding jurors who might consider their own

19. 500 U.S. ___, 111 S.Ct. 1859 (1991).

694

interpretation of a Spanish-speaking person's testimony rather than the interpreter's; if it has any effect on the jury verdict, it is most likely to increase its accuracy.

While the Court's treatment of the prosecution's burden in *Hernandez* may signal a desire to limit the impact of *Batson,* its decision in *Powers v. Ohio* [20] increases the number of cases in which that burden must be met. Affirming the view that five justices had expressed in the earlier case of *Holland v. Illinois,* [21] *Powers* held, 7–2, that *any* defendant, not just a member of the excluded group, may bring an equal protection claim under *Batson.* The *Powers* Court first found, as it had already held with respect to selection of the jury pool, [22] that preventing exclusion of racial minorities is necessary to ensure fairness in jury selection, promote public confidence in the jury system, and protect "the right not to be excluded from [the jury] on account of race." According to Justice Kennedy, author of the majority opinion, this latter right exists in order to give excluded jurors the opportunity "to participate in the democratic process," prevent "arbitrary use or abuse" of the judicial system, and develop civic mindedness. The Court then concluded that the criminal defendant has standing to trigger *Batson* regardless of his race. Applying its well-established three-part test for determining when a party has standing to contest a certain issue, [23] Kennedy concluded that: (1) a criminal defendant suffers "injury-in-fact [from discriminatory exclusion] because an improperly composed trier of fact may affect the fairness of his trial;" (2) the defendant "will be a motivated, effective advocate for the excluded venireperson's rights;" and (3) the excluded juror is unlikely to have any other meaningful means of redress.

In dissent, Justice Scalia, joined by Chief Justice Rehnquist, cogently argued that the *Batson* rule could not reasonably be construed as stemming from the rights of excluded jurors rather than the rights of defendants: "Unlike the categorical exclusion of a group from jury service, which implies that all its members are incompetent or untrustworthy, a peremptory strike on the basis of group membership implies nothing more than the undeniable reality (upon which the peremptory strike system is largely based) that all groups tend to have particular sympathies and hostilities—most notably, sympathies towards their own group members." Nor, asserted Scalia, is the excluded juror deprived of a benefit, since he can sit on other juries. And limiting peremptories can have a significant adverse impact "[i]n a criminal-law system in which a single biased juror can prevent a deserved

---

20. 499 U.S. ___, 111 S.Ct. 1364 (1991).

21. 493 U.S. 474, 110 S.Ct. 803 (1990).

22. See § 27.03(b).

23. See *Singleton v. Wulff,* 428 U.S. 106, 96 S.Ct. 2868 (1976).

conviction or a deserved acquittal." With respect to the majority's standing analysis, Scalia focused on the injury-in-fact issue, arguing that while exclusion of blacks might injure a white defendant, the injury was much more speculative than the Court had required in other cases. In particular, he noted that the Court had consistently refused to recognize third party standing in connection with Fourth and Fifth Amendment rights,[24] despite the fact that, in contrast to the situation in *Powers,* denying standing in such cases very often *ensures* a defendant's conviction. One might also note that, with respect to the second prong of the standing analysis, a white defendant's willingness to protect the equal protection interests of black jurors is unlikely to exist in every case in which exclusion results.

Still unresolved by the Court is whether *Batson* applies to exclusion of groups other than racial minorities. Although traditionally only these groups have been protected by the Equal Protection Clause, the majority opinion in *Powers* relied not just on its Fourteenth Amendment cases but also on the community participation rationale in its Sixth Amendment fair cross-section cases,[25] which prohibit exclusion of other groups, such as women (and presumably white males), from the jury pool. Furthermore, decisions of the Court in other contexts have suggested that discrimination against whites may be protected by the Equal Protection Clause.[26]

The ultimate wisdom of *Batson* and its progeny depends upon the goal of *voir dire.* If its primary goal is to create an impartial jury, then *Batson,* with its attendant difficulties, is arguably unnecessary. Exclusion of racial minorities through peremptories does not automatically create a biased jury, even when the defendant is of the same race (especially if *voir dire* questioning about racial prejudice is allowed).[27] But if, as argued earlier,[28] another goal of *voir dire* is to ensure that defendants have a jury of their "peers," then the holding in *Batson* itself is more easily justified. In effect, *Batson* told prosecutors that they may not construct, through use of peremptories, an all-white jury for the trial of a black defendant. Regardless of how impartial the jury actually is, neither the defendant or the public is likely to think such a trial is fair, and the integrity of the system is thereby undermined. Of course, this analysis suggests that *Batson* should be limited, as it originally was, to those cases in which the defendant and the excluded jurors are of the same race. Finally, if the goal is to

---

24. See §§ 4.04; 16.05(a).

25. In particular, it relied on *Peters v. Kiff,* 407 U.S. 493, 92 S.Ct. 2163 (1972), discussed in § 27.03(c).

26. See, e.g., *University of California Regents v. Bakke,* 438 U.S. 265, 98 S.Ct. 2733 (1978) (strict scrutiny standard applies to discrimination against "innocent" whites as well as blacks).

27. See § 27.03(b)(1).

28. See § 27.03(a).

prevent actual and symbolic discrimination against minorities during the *voir dire* process, then *Batson*, as well as *Powers'* expansion of *Batson*, is obviously required. The advisability of this latter goal can be questioned, however, both along the lines suggested by Scalia and because, as discussed below, it leads to a limitation on *defense* use of peremptories as well, a rule which may undermine the protections afforded by the Impartiality Clause.

(2) By the defense. Despite the usefulness of peremptory challenges in terms of ensuring an impartial jury, the Supreme Court has made clear that they are not guaranteed by the Constitution.[29] Thus, so long as the relevant federal or state law is followed, the defendant's use of peremptories can normally be abridged significantly. For instance, the government may require codefendants to be treated as a single defendant so that each has only a small portion of the number of peremptories he would have if tried separately.[30] Or a defendant may be required by statute to exercise his challenges prior to the state, even though this practice means that some may be wasted on jurors whom the state would have challenged.[31] The state may also require the defendant to use a peremptory to excuse a juror who the judge should have excluded for cause.[32] The basis for these decisions appears to be that, so long as the defendant is permitted for cause challenges to remove those obviously biased against him, he will receive the impartial jury to which he is entitled regardless of how his peremptories are restricted.

There is also at least one circumstance where the defendant is prohibited from exercising a peremptory challenge that is *authorized* by law. In *Georgia v. McCollum,*[33] the Court held that the defendant may not use peremptories to exclude potential jurors on the basis of race. The defendants in *McCollum*, who were whites charged with assaulting African–Americans, had indicated an intention to use their peremptories to exclude all the blacks on their panel, and appeared to have sufficient peremptories to do so. In response to a prosecution motion contesting this anticipated action, the trial court entered an order allowing them to use their challenges as they saw fit. On interlocutory appeal, the prosecution argued that this ruling would violate *Powers v. Ohio,* which, as discussed above,[34] held that the Equal Protection Clause prevents prosecution exclusion of racial minorities unless, as established in *Batson v. Kentucky,* a race-neutral explanation is provid-

29. See, e.g., *Gray v. Mississippi,* 481 U.S. 648, 107 S.Ct. 2045 (1987).

30. *Stilson v. United States,* 250 U.S. 583, 40 S.Ct. 28 (1919).

31. *Pointer v. United States,* 151 U.S. 396, 14 S.Ct. 410 (1894).

32. *Ross v. Oklahoma,* 487 U.S. 81, 108 S.Ct. 2273 (1988).

33. ___ U.S. ___, 112 S.Ct. 931 (1992).

34. See § 27.04(d)(1).

ed. The prosecution contended that the same rule should apply to defendants. The defendants, on the other hand, put forward three principal reasons why the interest of the excluded juror and the community in avoiding discriminatory selection processes should not affect defense use of peremptories: (1) defense use of peremptories does not constitute state action in violation of the Fourteenth Amendment; (2) the prosecution lacks standing to assert an equal protection claim; and (3) a defendant's interest in an impartial trial outweighs the interests of the excluded jurors and the community in avoiding exclusion on the basis of race.

The Supreme Court, in an opinion by Justice Blackmun, rejected all three defense arguments. On the first issue, Blackmun concluded that because peremptories are a creation of state law, and because "a criminal defendant is wielding the power to choose a quintessential governmental body," the defendant's exercise of peremptories is state action.[35] With respect to the prosecution's standing, he noted that "[a]s the representative of all its citizens, the State is the logical and proper party to assert the invasion of the constitutional rights of the excluded jurors in a criminal trial." And while not denying the defendant the right to an impartial trial, Blackmun found "a distinction between exercising a peremptory challenge to discriminate invidiously against jurors on account of race and exercising a peremptory challenge to remove an individual juror who harbors racial prejudice." Thus, analogous to *Batson,* if the prosecution makes out a prima facie case of discriminatory use of peremptories, the defendant must provide a race-neutral reason for exclusion.

In dissent, Justice O'Connor was particularly critical of the majority's state action analysis. As she noted, "[t]he government in no way influences the defense's decision to use a peremptory challenge to strike a particular juror." Perhaps more telling was Justice Thomas' concurrence, in which he reluctantly joined the Court because of precedent. Asserting that the original purpose of applying the Equal Protection Clause to jury selection was to prevent racial bias on the jury, he pointed out that the Court's decision "exalt[s] the right of citizens to sit on juries over the rights of the criminal defendant," and predicted that black defendants in particular "will rue the day this court ventured down this road."

McCollum highlights the tension between the Equal Protection and Impartiality Clauses. As Thomas suggests, while the aspiration to have a discrimination-free society is obviously commendable, making an innocent criminal defendant pay for that

---

35. Here Blackmun relied heavily on *Edmonson v. Leesville Concrete Co.,* 500 U.S. ____, 111 S.Ct. 2077 (1991), which the same term as *Powers* had held that *Batson* also applied to private litigants.

aspiration with his liberty or life is not. Admittedly, allowing defendants to use peremptories to remove all African–Americans from the jury may produce a biased decisionmaker, especially in the type of case involved in *McCollum,* where the defendants were white and the victims black. But the opposite may also be true: failing to exclude such persons could lead to a slanted verdict. Furthermore, the defendant is arguably entitled, much more so than the prosecution, to unrestricted peremptories to ensure that he is "comfortable" with the jury that will decide his fate.[36] Finally, *McCollum* will eventually require the Court to decide whether a black defendant can be prevented from excluding whites on the basis of race (for instance, in a case where the victim is white), a case which will raise racial hackles regardless of how it is decided.

Some have argued that abolition of peremptory challenges (for the prosecution as well as the defense) is the only effective way to eliminate their discriminatory abuse against racial and other minorities; at the same time, it would avoid the difficult issues associated with deciding when *Batson* applies.[37] In light of the Court's previous decisions concerning peremptories, this scheme would probably be "constitutional." But it would seriously undermine the defendant's ability to maintain impartiality, given the Court's other *voir dire* cases. Specifically, the Court's reluctance to allow individualized questions during *voir dire,* [38] combined with its unwillingness to imply bias from circumstances,[39] means that in many jurisdictions peremptory challenges may be the only way a defendant can remove from the venire individuals strongly suspected of bias. Unless the grounds for challenges for cause and the means of developing those grounds are relaxed considerably, some entitlement to peremptories is necessary. Again, limiting *Batson's* application to prosecution attempts to remove jurors of the defendant's race may be the best way of reconciling the desire to maintain impartiality with the desire to avoid the appearance of invidious discrimination. An alternative would be to apply *Batson* to both the defense and prosecution, but *only* when racial issues "permeate" the trial.

36. Goldwasser, "Limiting a Criminal Defendant's Use of Peremptory Challenges: On Symmetry and the Jury in a Criminal Trial," 102 Harv.L.Rev. 808, 829–831 (1989). Goldwasser also argues that applying *Batson* to defense peremptories may require revelation of confidential communications between attorney and client. Id. at 831–33. In *McCollum,* Blackmun discounted this problem by noting that *Batson* explanations may be made *in camera.*

37. See, e.g., Justice Marshall's concurrence in *Batson*; Singer, "Peremptory Holds: A Suggestion (Only Half Specious) of a Solution to the Discriminatory Use of Peremptory Challenges," 62 U.Det.L.Rev. 275, 286–87 (1985).

38. See § 27.04(b)(3).

39. See § 27.04(c)(1).

27.05 The Right to an Impartial Judge

(a) The Constitutional Right. Although the Sixth Amendment speaks only of juries, the Supreme Court has held that the Due Process Clause guarantees the defendant an impartial judge as well, whether he sits with or without a jury. The leading case is *Tumey v. Ohio*,[40] where the judge of a municipal court, who was also the mayor, received the fees and costs he levied against violators. The Court had no trouble finding that a defendant is deprived of due process when the judge "has a direct, personal, substantial pecuniary interest in reaching a conclusion against him in his case." *Tumey* was extended in *Ward v. Monroeville*,[41] where the fees collected by the mayor-judge did not go directly to him, but rather provided a substantial portion of the town's funds. Due process was violated here as well because "the mayor's executive responsibilities for village finances may make him partisan to maintain the high level of contribution from the mayor's court." On the other hand, if the mayor who levies the town's fees is one of only several members of a city commission, as was the case in *Dugan v. Ohio*,[42] then the conflict of interest is not direct enough.

The judicial impartiality issue often arises in contempt cases, where the judge is involved in assessing penalties on a defendant who may have directly insulted him. The Supreme Court has held that, while a judge may normally act summarily in the face of vilification by a party,[43] when a separate contempt proceeding is held at the end of trial, due process may require that another judge preside. This was the holding in both *Mayberry v. Pennsylvania*,[44] where the trial judge gave a defendant who had repeatedly insulted him during the trial a contempt sentence of 11–22 years, and *Johnson v. Mississippi*,[45] where the trial judge had lost to the defendant in a related civil rights suit just prior to the contempt proceeding. Similarly, in *Taylor v. Hayes*,[46] a defense attorney was entitled to a new judge at his separate contempt proceeding when the record showed that there had been "marked personal feelings . . . present on both sides." But unless, as *Mayberry* put it, there has been the "sting of slanderous remarks," a new judge is not necessary under the Due Process Clause even when the contempt proceeding is separate. Merely possessing previous knowledge about a case does not disqualify the judge.[47]

---

40. 273 U.S. 510, 47 S.Ct. 437 (1927).

41. 409 U.S. 57, 93 S.Ct. 80 (1972).

42. 277 U.S. 61, 48 S.Ct. 439 (1928).

43. Note that when the judge acts summarily, he may only impose sentences of six months or less. See § 27.02(c)(3).

44. 400 U.S. 455, 91 S.Ct. 499 (1971).

45. 403 U.S. 212, 91 S.Ct. 1778 (1971).

46. 418 U.S. 488, 94 S.Ct. 2697 (1974).

47. *Withrow v. Larkin,* 421 U.S. 35, 95 S.Ct. 1456 (1975).

(b) Mechanisms for Assuring Impartiality. There are three mechanisms for assuring an impartial judge. The first two mimic the *voir dire* process in jury selection. In most jurisdictions, a judge can be excused for cause, if it is shown that he is biased for or against a particular party.[48] Additionally, in some jurisdictions, either party can also peremptorily remove a judge, in which case the trial is automatically transferred to another judge (although this second judge can usually only be removed for cause).[49]

Finally, the judicial code of ethics requires a judge to "recuse" or disqualify himself if: (1) "he has a personal bias or prejudice concerning a party, or personal knowledge of disputed evidentiary facts concerning the proceeding;" (2) he or a former partner served as a lawyer or a material witness in the controversy; (3) he or a close relative has a financial or other "substantial interest" in the outcome of the proceeding; or (4) he is related, directly or by marriage, to one of the parties or lawyers.[50]

27.06 Fair Proceedings and Media Access

(a) The Effects of Publicity. The First Amendment guarantees freedom of speech and of the press. In many cases, these provisions do not conflict with the defendant's right to a fair, impartial trial. Indeed, they often protect that right. Out-of-court statements by trial participants and press accounts of criminal proceedings can energize public opinion against unfair prosecutions. Reports in the media may also lead to the discovery of evidence or witnesses. Additionally, as discussed further in the next chapter,[51] the right to a public trial, guaranteed to the defendant by the Sixth Amendment as well as to the public by the First, protects against "star chamber" proceedings in which the state metes out justice in private.

However, when extensive or dramatic publicity occurs before or during trial, the possibility of a fair proceeding can diminish appreciably. Detailed newspaper accounts of a grisly crime, television depictions of a pretrial confession, or descriptions of the defendant's prior offenses can irredeemably infect the minds of both jurors and judges. Additionally, the mere presence of the media in the courtroom may be disruptive or change the behavior of the parties in ways that could lead to unfairness. As a result, various mechanisms have developed for curtailing the impact of publicity or preventing it altogether.

48. See, e.g., 28 U.S.C.A. § 144.

49. See, e.g., West's Fla.S.A.R.Crim. P. 3.230 (requiring automatic disqualification if motion is accompanied by two affidavits which are judged to state legally sufficient grounds for disqualification, regardless of their credibility).

50. American Bar Association, Code of Judicial Conduct, Canon 3–C.

51. See § 28.02.

(b) Alleviating the Effects of Publicity. There are several ways a court might be able to diminish the impact of inflammatory press coverage. In rare cases where the effects of the publicity are likely to die out quickly, a continuance might be useful. To counteract more extensive or on-going publicity, the courts typically resort to one of three methods: (1) *voir dire* inquiry; (2) changes of venue; and (3) jury sequestration.

(1) Voir dire inquiry. Ideally, the *voir dire* process is the perfect antidote for damaging pretrial publicity. That process could ensure that the jurors who sit on the defendant's case either have not seen or heard the publicity or, if they have, that it has not biased them one way or the other. The Supreme Court, for one, has assumed that this is possible.[52] But empirical research suggests that *voir dire* usually cannot identify all of the potential jurors who have been prejudiced against the defendant by pretrial publicity.[53] Unfortunately, jurors may not recognize their bias or, if they do, may adopt a defensive stance or even lie when the judge or attorneys delve into their attitudes.[54]

Furthermore, whatever chance *voir dire* does have of identifying and excluding prejudiced jurors has been seriously diminished by the Court's own decisions. As discussed earlier in this chapter,[55] the Court has held that the Constitution does not require the trial court to question each juror about the content of publicity he may have heard, even when the publicity has been extensive. Rather, the judge need only ask general questions, to the venire as a whole, inquiring as to whether the venirepersons have a "fixed opinion" about the case. Yet individualized content questioning may be the only way to make a juror realize he is prejudiced. Further, even if, for reasons discussed above, he does not admit to his bias, such questioning can be very useful. The juror's answers about what he has read and heard will allow the defense to exercise more intelligently its for cause and peremptory challenges.

Even in a jurisdiction which allows detailed questioning, however, the usefulness of the information so acquired is significantly limited by other Court decisions addressing the scope of the for cause challenge in high publicity cases. Although Warren Court cases seemed to take the view that extensive publicity allows an

---

52. See, e.g., *Nebraska Press Ass'n v. Stuart,* 427 U.S. 539, 96 S.Ct. 2791 (1976), discussed in § 27.06(c)(1); *Press–Enterprise Co. v. Superior Court,* 478 U.S. 1, 106 S.Ct. 2735 (1986), discussed in § 27.06(c)(3).

53. Kerr, Kramer, Carroll & Alfini, "On the Effectiveness of Voir Dire in Criminal Cases with Prejudicial Pretri-

al Publicity: An Empirical Study," 40 Amer.U.L.Rev. 665 (1991).

54. Minow & Cate, "Who is an Impartial Juror in an Age of Mass Media?," 40 Amer.U.L.Rev. 631, 650–54 (1991).

55. See *Mu'Min v. Virginia,* 500 U.S. ___, 111 S.Ct. 1899 (1991), discussed in § 27.04(b)(2).

assumption of bias on the part of jurors who have been exposed to it (and thus allows excuse for cause), more recent Court opinions have held that, unless an *express* admission of bias is made, a defendant can be forced to use his limited number of peremptory challenges to excuse what may turn out to be a large number of potentially biased jurors.

The Warren Court approach is represented by *Marshall v. United States*[56] and *Irvin v. Dowd.*[57] In *Marshall,* the Court held that "persons who have learned from news sources of a defendant's prior record are presumed to be prejudiced," a holding which would seem to flow from the rules of evidence.[58] And in *Irvin,* the Court held that publicity can be so inflammatory that even statements of impartiality can be discounted. In the county in which the *Irvin* trial took place, newspaper, radio and television media reported, just before trial, his conviction for arson 20 years before, his refusal to take a lie detector test and his offer to plead guilty if he received a 99 year sentence. He was described as a confessed slayer of six, a parole violator and a fraudulent check artist by a newspaper that was delivered to 95% of the homes in the county. During a *voir dire* which lasted four weeks, 268 of 430 people examined were excused because they admitted they had made up their minds about the defendant's guilt. Of the 12 jurors selected, eight stated they thought the defendant was guilty, but all said they could render an impartial verdict. The Court stressed that, given the advent of modern communication systems, "[t]o hold that the mere existence of any preconceived notion as to the guilt or innocence of an accused, without more, is sufficient to rebut the presumption of a prospective juror's impartiality would be to establish an impossible standard." Here, however, the expressions of impartiality could "be given little weight" because the *voir dire* transcript reflected a "pattern of deep and bitter prejudice" in the county.

Later decisions of the Court, however, significantly undercut both *Marshall* and *Irvin.* Like these two cases, *Murphy v. Florida,*[59] involved extensive publicity about the defendant's prior crimes, one a murder. But the Court, in an opinion by Justice Marshall, refused to rely on *Marshall's* holding, pointing out that it did not rest on the Due Process Clause, but on the Court's supervisory power over the federal courts. And it distinguished *Irvin* by noting that, whereas the publicity in that case had immediately preceded the trial and created a "circus atmosphere,"

---

56. 360 U.S. 310, 79 S.Ct. 1171 (1959).

57. 366 U.S. 717, 81 S.Ct. 1639 (1961). See also, *Rideau v. Louisiana,* 373 U.S. 723, 83 S.Ct. 1417 (1963), discussed in § 27.06(b)(2).

58. See Fed.R.Evid. 608 (barring introduction of prior crimes except for impeachment purposes or to rebut character evidence).

59. 421 U.S. 794, 95 S.Ct. 2031 (1975).

almost all the news articles in *Murphy* had appeared seven months before the jury was selected and were "largely factual in nature." Marshall also contrasted the fact that whereas 268 of the 430 venirepersons in *Irvin* had been excused for cause, only 20 of the 78 persons examined in *Murphy* were excluded because they indicated an opinion as to his guilt. According to Rehnquist: "This may indeed be 20 more than would occur in the trial of a totally obscure person, but it by no means suggests a community with sentiment so poisoned against petitioner as to impeach the indifference of jurors who displayed no hostile animus of their own."

In dissent, Justice Brennan disputed Rehnquist's characterization of the jury as non-hostile. He argued that there had been a "daily buildup of prejudice against Murphy" and that several seated jurors had admitted during *voir dire* that they were predisposed against the defendant (one stated that comments about Murphy by other venirepersons had made him "sick to [his] stomach"). In light of these facts, stated Brennan, "[i]t is of no moment that several jurors ultimately testified that they would try to exclude from their deliberations their knowledge of petitioner's past misdeeds and of his community reputation." *Irvin* had settled that "little weight could be attached to such self-serving protestations."

In *Patton v. Yount*,[60] all but 2 of the 162 venirepersons had heard about the case, and 126 of them (a higher percentage than in *Irvin*) were excluded after admitting that they remembered the defendant's first conviction for a gruesome murder and that they "would carry an opinion into the box." Additionally, similar to *Irvin,* of the 14 jurors (including two alternates) who sat on the case, 8 admitted that at some time they had formed an opinion as to the defendant's guilt. One juror and both alternates also stated, in an apparent reluctance to presume innocence, that they would require evidence to overcome their beliefs. The court of appeals held that, even though four years had elapsed between the first conviction (which was reversed on appeal) and the second trial, the passage of time had not served "to erase highly unfavorable publicity from the memory of the community." Additionally, it noted that the publicity just prior to the trial revealed the defendant's prior conviction, his confession and his prior plea of temporary insanity (none of which was admitted at trial).

The Supreme Court reversed by a 6–2 margin (Justice Marshall not participating). The Court held that the fact that the community might remember the first conviction was "essentially irrelevant;" rather, the important question was "whether the

---

60. 467 U.S. 1025, 104 S.Ct. 2885 (1984).

jurors at Yount's trial had such fixed opinions that they could not judge impartially the guilt of the defendant." On this point, it first noted that *voir dire* questioning (which was conducted by the attorneys) had revealed that the four-year lapse in time "had a profound effect on the community and, more important, on the jury, in softening or effacing opinion." It also asserted that more recent publicity had not been inflammatory. It concluded that *voir dire* had "resulted in selecting those who had forgotten [that they thought the defendant was guilty] or would need to be persuaded again."

The Court's cases indicate that bias due to pretrial publicity cannot be a basis for a constitutional challenge unless a juror candidly admits to bias, or unless recent publicity has been extraordinary in its inflammatory nature and pervasiveness. These requirements probably flow from the fact, recognized in *Irvin,* that very few people in the community will not have heard something about highly publicized cases before trial begins. At the same time, when a large proportion of the venire admits to having strong reactions to a case, as in *Irvin* and *Yount,* and the pretrial publicity includes inadmissible, prejudicial information, as in *Murphy* and *Yount,* the impartiality of those who are seated as jurors cannot be assumed merely because they say they can keep an open mind despite what they have heard. An alternative to the Court's approach, suggested by Judge Stern (a concurring judge on the court of appeals in *Yount*), is to excuse any juror who admits an opinion as to guilt and to refuse to empanel a jury where more than 25% of the veniremen state that they hold an opinion concerning the defendant's guilt (in which case, a change of venue may be appropriate).

(2) Change of venue. If *voir dire* exposes overwhelming bias against the defendant, or if the trial court is willing to recognize, even without the assistance of *voir dire* questioning, that publicity has been extensive and probably prejudicial, a change of venue can be granted. Illustrative is *Rideau v. Louisiana,*[61] in which the Supreme Court overturned a death sentence because the trial court refused to grant the defendant's motion for a venue change. Two months before trial, Rideau had confessed to a sheriff on film. Within the next two days, the film was broadcast on local television to audiences of 24,000, 53,000 and 29,000 in a 150,000 person parish. Three members of the jury admitted seeing or hearing the interview, but testified they could return an impartial verdict. Calling the defendant's trial "an empty formality" after the television showings, the Supreme Court stated that regardless of the particular responses of the individual jurors during *voir dire,* "due

61. 373 U.S. 723, 83 S.Ct. 1417 (1963).

process of law in this case required a trial before a jury drawn from a community of people who had not seen and heard Rideau's interview." In other words, according to the Court, bias should have been presumed with respect to all potential jurors, and Rideau's change of venue motion granted.

Whether *Rideau* would have been decided the same way today, in light of *Murphy* and *Yount,* is unclear. Further complicating the matter, of course, is the fact that pretrial publicity does not necessarily end at the jurisdiction's borders. With respect to widely known criminal defendants, a careful *voir dire* may be the only option available. On the other hand, when the "media community" is a small one, a change of venue will usually be the best way to ensure a fair trial in cases of extensive publicity, given the inadequacies of *voir dire.*

(3) Sequestration of the jury. Finding an impartial venue and jury may not be sufficient protection for the defendant, since publicity usually continues, and indeed intensifies, once trial starts. Instructions to members of the jury, warning them that media accounts are not to be taken as evidence, are probably to little avail and may actually stimulate interest in press reports. Thus, the Supreme Court has recognized that sequestration of the jury is a permissible option.[62] If sequestration occurs, however, there is a danger that the jury will resent whichever side it believes is responsible for its confinement (which will usually be the defense). It may be good practice for the judge to tell the jury that its sequestration is by order of the court.

(c) **Preventing Pretrial Publicity.** Given the problems with alleviating the effects of prejudicial publicity, the courts have attempted various means of inhibiting or preventing media reporting and access to the criminal process, including: (1) "gag orders" on the press; (2) "gag orders" on the participants; and (3) closed proceedings. Of course, these mechanisms do not prevent the press from printing facts that are already a matter of public record. More importantly, the First Amendment, as construed by the Supreme Court, severely limits their usefulness.

(1) Gag orders on the media. In *Nebraska Press Ass'n v. Stuart,*[63] the trial judge prohibited media dissemination of certain incriminating information about the defendant (including his confession) that came out in court and from out-of-court statements by the participants. He based the order on a finding that, otherwise, there would be a "clear and present danger that pretrial publicity could impinge on the defendant's right to a fair trial." The Supreme Court firmly repudiated, as an impermissible prior restraint, any bar on media coverage of an open hearing. It further

---

62. *Sheppard v. Maxwell,* 384 U.S. 333, 86 S.Ct. 1507 (1966).

63. 427 U.S. 539, 96 S.Ct. 2791 (1976).

indicated that preventing publication of information from other sources would be permissible only in extreme circumstances, after consideration of: "(a) the nature and extent of pretrial coverage; (b) whether other measures [such as changes of venue, continuances, *voir dire*, and admonitions to the jury] would be likely to mitigate the effects of unrestrained pretrial publicity; and (c) how effectively a restraining order would operate to prevent the threatened danger." Here, the impact of the press coverage was "speculative," the alternatives to the gag order had not been carefully considered, and the order might have merely encouraged rumors that "could well be more damaging than reasonably accurate news accounts." The Court also stressed the difficulty of "managing and enforcing pretrial restraining orders," in particular noting the possibility that such an order will inhibit proper coverage of the proceedings.

Subsequent Court decisions in analogous contexts have energetically followed *Nebraska Press*. For instance, in *Smith v. Daily Mail Publishing Co.*,[64] the Court struck down a state statute which criminally penalized publishing, without written order of the juvenile court, the name of any youth charged as a juvenile offender.[65] On the other hand, the Court's opinion in *Nebraska Press* did not rule out the possibility of a restraining order under appropriate circumstances. Particularly in light of the inadequacy of *voir dire* as a corrective device, a narrowly framed order aimed at preventing a "clear and present danger" of prejudicial publicity might pass constitutional muster.[66]

(2) Gag orders on the participants. Given the difficulty of stopping the press from reporting information it obtains, courts have sometimes resorted to muffling its source. This practice has been approved, at least tangentially, by the Supreme Court. *Sheppard v. Maxwell*[67] involved such extensive and persistent media coverage that the Court characterized the proceedings as a "Roman holiday." Blaming this state of affairs in part on the participants in the trial, the Court suggested that, under appropriate circumstances, the trial judge has an obligation "to control the release of leads, information, and gossip to the press by police officers, witnesses and the counsel for both sides."

This language could be read to mean that a gag order on trial participants is less likely to run afoul of the First Amendment

64. 443 U.S. 97, 99 S.Ct. 2667 (1979).

65. See also, *Landmark Communications, Inc. v. Virginia,* 435 U.S. 829, 98 S.Ct. 1535 (1978).

66. Cf., *Cable News Network, Inc. v. Noriega,* ___ U.S. ___, 111 S.Ct. 451 (1990), where the Court denied certiorari on an Eleventh Circuit opinion upholding a district court restraining order on the media, over a strong dissent by Justices Marshall and O'Connor.

67. 384 U.S. 333, 86 S.Ct. 1507 (1966).

than a restraining order on the press. Alternatively, *Sheppard* could merely represent a situation where comments by the participants in the trial constituted a "clear and present danger" to the fairness and integrity of the trial. In support of this second interpretation, it could be argued that the concerns the Court later expressed in *Nebraska Press*—i.e., that suppressing dissemination of information by the media might inhibit proper press coverage, and may often be based on mere "speculation" that other alternatives cannot alleviate the effect of publicity—are equally applicable when the gag order is imposed on trial participants. Moreover, there is an additional First Amendment concern in the latter situation: such a restraining order not only inhibits press coverage but also prevents the speech of those who are most intimately involved in the trial process and thus most likely to provide useful criticism of it. Many, but not all, lower courts appear to apply some version of the "clear and present danger" test before granting a gag order.[68]

The professional ethical rules, however, appear to restrict speech (at least by attorney) to a much greater extent than these lower court decisions contemplate. For instance, while the ABA Rules of Professional Responsibility prohibit a lawyer from making any "extrajudicial statement" that "will have a substantial likelihood of materially prejudicing an adjudicative proceeding," this provision is broadly interpreted to include statements relating to "the character, credibility, reputation or criminal record of a party, suspect . . . or witness," the identity of a witness, "the expected testimony of a party or witness," the "possibility of a plea of guilty, . . . the performance or results of any examination or test, [and] . . . any opinion as to . . . guilt or innocence."[69] The rules specifically permit an attorney to furnish only a description of the charges and defenses, the schedule of proceedings, and the identity of the defendant and the victim.[70] Whatever the validity of these ethical restrictions on attorneys, they clearly do not apply to witnesses or to the defendant himself.

(3) Closure of the proceedings. A second way of preventing media access to information is to close the relevant proceedings. Here again, however, the First Amendment presents a significant obstacle to the defendant seeking closure in an effort to avoid the effects of negative publicity. The Court's cases indicate that, unless a showing of significant prejudice is made, closure is not appropriate.

---

68. See, e.g., *United States v. Regan,* 878 F.2d 67 (2d Cir.1989); *United States v. Ford,* 830 F.2d 596 (6th Cir.1987).

69. ABA Rule 3.6(a)(b). See also, ABA Code of Professional Responsibility, DR 7–107(D).

70. ABA Rules, Rule 3.6(c).

The Court's first modern decision on this issue, *Gannett Co., Inc. v. DePasquale,*[71] held that the trial judge may, at the request of the defendant, close a pretrial suppression hearing to avoid a "reasonable probability of prejudice" to the defendant's right to a fair trial. But this holding was based solely on an interpretation of the Sixth Amendment's guarantee of a "public" trial which, the Court rightly noted, is a right of the defendant's and thus may be waived by him. One year later, in *Richmond Newspapers, Inc. v. Virginia,*[72] the Court indicated that, when a First Amendment right is asserted by the press or the public, a defendant will seldom be able to close the proceeding, at least when it is a trial.

The defendant in *Richmond Newspapers* sought closure of his trial because he had been through four previous mistrials, one of which occurred after a prospective juror told jurors who sat on the case about press reports concerning the previous trials. Eight members of the Court found closure under these circumstances inappropriate (with Justice Rehnquist dissenting on the ground that closure agreed to by the parties should be constitutional). Although there were several concurring opinions, the essential rationale of the decision was expressed in an opinion by Chief Justice Burger. Noting that criminal trials "had long been presumptively open," he concluded that "the right to attend criminal trials is implicit in the guarantees of the First Amendment; without the freedom to attend such trials, which people have exercised for centuries, important aspects of freedom of speech and of the press could be eviscerated." A later decision by a full majority of the Court elaborated upon this notion, stating that the public access guaranteed by the First Amendment serves "to ensure that the individual citizen can effectively participate in and contribute to our republican system of self-government," and also "fosters an appearance of fairness, thereby heightening public respect for the judicial process."[73]

As suggested by the reference to trial openness as "presumptive," several members of the Court in *Richmond Newspapers* indicated that a trial could be closed at the defendant's request if "overriding" interests could be shown. But the only specific such interest mentioned in any of the opinions was an allusion to "reasonable restrictions" so as to assure "quiet and orderly" trials and prevent overcrowding in the courtroom. As to the need to avoid the tainting impact of publicity about the trial, the Court pointed out that sequestration of the jury was always possible. Thus, it appears that, for this purpose, closure of trial at the defendant's request will seldom be granted.

71. 443 U.S. 368, 99 S.Ct. 2898 (1979).

72. 448 U.S. 555, 100 S.Ct. 2814 (1980).

73. *Globe Newspaper Co. v. Superior Court,* 457 U.S. 596, 102 S.Ct. 2613 (1982).

Because it dealt with a trial, *Richmond Newspapers* did not explicitly resolve whether *Gannett's* holding concerning a pretrial proceeding would withstand a First Amendment challenge. In *Press–Enterprise Co. v. Superior Court II,*[74] the defendant, with the consent of the state, obtained closure of what turned out to be a 41–day preliminary hearing. Upon challenge by the press, the California Supreme Court upheld the closure, finding a "reasonable likelihood" that the defendant, who was charged with murdering 12 nurses with drug overdoses, would have been prejudiced at trial had the hearing been open to the media. The Supreme Court, in a 7–2 opinion written by Chief Justice Burger, rejected the California court's standard, holding that the defendant must show a "substantial probability" of prejudice from the proceeding. Additionally, it required a showing that other "reasonable" alternatives to closure (such as *voir dire*) will not preserve the accused's right to an unbiased jury.

In justifying this decision, the Court relied on several factors. As it had in *Richmond Newspapers,* the Court stressed that, historically, the preliminary hearing had been open to the public. Further, because many cases end in a guilty plea, "the preliminary hearing is often the final and most important step in the criminal proceeding," especially given its adversarial nature. Finally, Burger noted the absence of public representatives at the preliminary hearing (in contrast, for instance, to the grand jury). Given this reasoning, the grand jury process is clearly not covered by *Press–Enterprise II;* unlike the preliminary hearing, it has a tradition of secrecy,[75] and, as Burger pointed out, involves members of the public. Other pretrial hearings (e.g., suppression hearings), vary both in their history and function from the preliminary hearing, but the lower courts tend to allow press access to most such hearings, as well as associated documents, unless the "substantial probability" test is met.[76]

As to the meaning of this test, *Press–Enterprise II* clearly refused to equate it with the California courts "reasonable likelihood" standard, a standard virtually identical to that used by the trial judge (and approved by the Court) in *Gannett.* At the same time, the Court did not adopt a "clear and present danger" rubric. Thus, closure of pretrial proceedings may be permissible in situations where closure of trial and gag orders on the press are not. Differentiating between closure of pretrial proceedings and trial makes some sense, since *voir dire* is not likely to be as successful at alleviating the effects of pretrial prejudicial publicity on potential jurors as sequestration will be at preventing juror access to

74. 478 U.S. 1, 106 S.Ct. 2735 (1986).

75. See § 23.03.

76. See, e.g., *In re Search Warrant for Secretarial Area,* 855 F.2d 569 (8th Cir.1988).

publicity about the trial.[77] Whether differentiating between closure of pretrial proceedings and gag orders on the press makes sense depends upon whether one accepts the assumption, perhaps implicit in *Sheppard,* that preventing the media from broadcasting information already in its possession is more of a "prior restraint" than preventing the source from providing it in the first instance. It should be noted in this regard that if a transcript of the closed proceeding is provided to the press as soon as practicable, a practice approved by the Court in *Gannett,* the infringement of First Amendment interests can be minimized.

(d) The Media in the Courtroom. The mere presence of the public and the media in the courtroom can have an impact on the fairness of a trial, independent of any new reports thereby generated. In *Sheppard,* for instance, the courtroom was packed with members of the public and the media for all nine weeks of the trial, making it "difficult for the witnesses and counsel to be heard," and for Sheppard and his counsel to talk together confidentially. Newsmen also handled and took pictures of exhibits. In reversing Sheppard's conviction on due process grounds, the Court held that this "carnival atmosphere" should have been prevented by limiting the number of reporters in the courtroom and more closely regulating their conduct.

A similar issue arose in *Estes v. Texas,*[78] where pretrial hearings were televised, as well as much of the trial. The Court reversed the defendant's conviction, again on due process grounds, noting that the presence of television cameras could distract the jurors, decrease the quality of testimony, unduly burden the judge and subject him to greater political pressure, and distract the defendant, as well as his attorney. The Court's plurality opinion did not address the First Amendment implications of its decision, although Justice Harlan, who cast the fifth vote, limited his conclusion to the facts of the case and noted that television could be of educational and informational value to the public.

Estes notwithstanding, several states persisted in developing guidelines for permitting television in the courtroom. In *Chandler v. Florida,*[79] the Supreme Court in effect nullified *Estes* and upheld Florida's rule allowing electronic media and still photography coverage of public judicial proceedings, although without specifically addressing First Amendment concerns. The Court instead merely noted that technological advances had diminished many of the distractions originally associated with television coverage (such as bright lighting, numerous technicians and cumber-

77. See discussion of *voir dire,* § 27.06(b)(1).

78. 381 U.S. 532, 85 S.Ct. 1628 (1965).

79. 449 U.S. 560, 101 S.Ct. 802 (1981).

some equipment), that the Florida rule provided significant procedural safeguards for the defendant, and that there was little empirical data showing that the presence of the broadcast media had an adverse effect on the trial process. Under these circumstances, television coverage was permissible, subject only to a showing by the defendant that "the media's coverage of his case—be it printed or broadcast—compromised the ability of the particular jury that heard the case to adjudicate fairly." In the case before it, the Court concluded that the defendants were unable to show that television coverage "impaired the ability of the jurors to decide the case on only the evidence before them or that their trial was affected adversely by the impact on any of the participants of the presence of cameras and the prospect of broadcast."

27.07 Conclusion

The various aspects of the right to trial by an impartial jury and judge can be summarized as follows:

(1) A defendant has the right to a trial by jury whenever the legislated sentence could result in imprisonment of more than six months or, in contempt cases, whenever the actual punishment imposed at one time (whether summarily or at a separate proceeding) is more than six months. The federal model of a twelve-person jury which must vote unanimously for conviction or acquittal is not constitutionally required. Six-person juries which vote unanimously, and twelve-person juries which reach a 9–3 verdict meet constitutional requirements. The right to jury trial may be waived, but can be conditioned on the consent of the prosecution and the court, unless such veto will unduly prejudice the defendant.

(2) Under the Equal Protection Clause, a jury pool and panel may not be the result of purposeful discrimination against members of a suspect class. Purposeful discrimination is presumed if the disparity between the proportion of the group in the community and the proportion of the group in the jury pool or panel is significant (i.e., over two or three standard deviations) and the jury selection procedures used offer an opportunity to discriminate. Under the Sixth Amendment, a defendant is entitled to a jury pool and panel representing a fair cross-section of the community (although the jury itself need not mirror the community). This requirement is violated whenever (1) a large, identifiable, distinctive group is (2) substantially underrepresented in the pool or panel as a result of (3) systematic exclusion. Distinctiveness is defined primarily not in terms of attitudes possessed by a particular group but by more neutral characteristics, such as race and gender. Although the exclusion of group members apparently need not be intentional to be systematic, proof of underrepresenta-

tion similar to that required in equal protection cases will probably be required.

(3) At *voir dire*, the judge is not constitutionally required to ask any particular questions about prospective juror biases beyond general inquiries about prejudice, except when: (a) racial issues are "inextricably bound up" with issues at trial; or (b) the defendant is charged with a capital offense, necessitating questions about attitudes toward the death penalty. Challenges for cause are generally allowed only in circumstances specified by statute or if an identifiable bias becomes apparent during *voir dire*. Thus, bias will not normally be implied due to pretrial publicity about the defendant or a prospective juror's employment with the government. Nor may the prosecution use its challenges to fashion a capital sentencing jury devoid of individuals who have merely expressed scruples against the death penalty, since their bias is not clear and such a jury is organized to return a verdict of death. However, the prosecution may exclude from a capital sentencing jury and trial venirepersons who state that under no circumstances would they impose the death penalty, just as the defense may exclude those who would automatically impose the death penalty at the sentencing stage. Peremptory challenges may be used to exclude venirepersons as the parties see fit, except that neither the prosecution or the defense may use them to exclude blacks or other racial minorities solely on the basis of race. If a prima facie case can be made that peremptories have been used in this way, the party using peremptories must convince the court that it sought exclusion on other, reasonable grounds.

(4) The criminal defendant is entitled, under the Due Process Clause, to an impartial judge, which means the judge may not have a direct, personal, substantial pecuniary interest in reaching a conclusion against him, or in any other way be prejudiced against him.

(5) The prejudicial impact of publicity can be alleviated through (a) continuances; (b) exclusion, at *voir dire*, of jurors with a fixed opinion against the defendant; (c) changes of venue, when publicity has been extraordinarily inflammatory and extensive; and (d) jury sequestration. Media dissemination of prejudicial information can be prevented through gag orders on the press or the trial participants, but probably only when there is a clear and present danger that the trial will otherwise be unfair. Additionally, publicity may be prevented by closing pretrial proceedings, if there is a substantial probability of prejudice from the proceeding and there are no other reasonable alternatives to closure (such as *voir dire*). Closure of *trial* to prevent juror exposure to publicity will rarely, if ever, be permissible, given the availability of sequestration.

BIBLIOGRAPHY

Alschuler, Albert. The Supreme Court and the Jury: Voir Dire, Peremptory Challenges and the Review of Jury Verdicts. 56 U.Chi.L.Rev. 153 (1989).

Ares, Charles E. Chandler v. Florida: Television, Criminal Trials, and Due Process. 1981 Sup.Ct.Rev. 157 (1982).

Babcock, Barbara. Voir Dire: Preserving "Its Wonderful Power." 27 Stan.L.Rev. 545 (1975).

Beale, Sara S. Integrating Statistical Evidence and Legal Theory to Challenge the Selection of Grand and Petit Jurors. 46 Law & Contemp. Probs. 269 (1983).

Brewster, Stanley Farrar. Twelve Men in a Box. Chicago: Callahan and Co., 1934.

Chief Justice Earl Warren Conference on Advocacy in the United States, Cambridge, Massachusetts, 1977. The American Jury System: Final Report. Cambridge, Mass.: The Foundation, 1977.

Crump, Susan W. Lockhart v. McCree: The "Biased But Unbiased Juror," What Are the States' Legitimate Interests? 65 Denver L.Rev. 1 (1988).

Finkelstein, Michael O. The Application of Statistical Decision Theory to the Jury Discrimination Cases. 80 Harv.L.Rev. 338 (1966).

Goldwasser, Katherine. Limiting a Criminal Defendant's Use of Peremptory Challenges: On Symmetry and the Jury in a Criminal Trial. 102 Harv.L.Rev. 808 (1989).

Isaacson, Robert. Fair Trial and Free Press: An Opportunity for Co-Existence. 29 Stan.L.Rev. 561 (1977).

Johnson, Sheri. Black Innocence and the White Jury. 83 Mich.L. Rev. 1611 (1985).

Kalven, Harry and Harry Zeisel. The American Jury. Boston: Little Brown, 1966.

Lermack, Paul, compiler. Materials on Juries and Jury Research; an Annotated Bibliography. Chicago: American Judicature Society, 1977.

Massaro, Toni. Peremptories or Peers? Rethinking Sixth Amendment Doctrine, Images and Procedures. 64 N.Car.L.Rev. 501 (1986).

Minow, Newton and Fred Cate. Who is an Impartial Juror in an Age of Mass Media? 40 Amer.L.Rev. 631 (1991).

Nagel, Stuart S. and Marian Neef. Deductive Modeling to Determine an Optimum Jury Size and Fraction Required to Convict. 1975 Wash.U.L.Q. 933 (1975).

Pizzi, William. Batson v. Kentucky: Curing the Disease But Killing the Patient. 1987 Sup.Ct.Rev. 97.

Sack, Robert D. Principle and Nebraska Press Association v. Stuart. 29 Stan.L.Rev. 411 (1977).

Saks, Michael J. Jury Verdicts: The Role of Group Size and Social Decision Rule. Lexington, Massachusetts: Lexington Books, 1977.

Saltzburg, Stephen A. and Mary Ellen Powers. Peremptory Challenges and the Clash Between Impartiality and Group Representation. 41 Md.L.Rev. 337 (1982).

Simon, Rita J. The Jury System in America: A Critical Overview. Sage: 1975.

Sperlich, Peter W. Trial by Jury: It May Have a Future. 1978 Sup.Ct.Rev. 191 (1978).

Van Dyke, Jon M. Jury Selection Procedures: Our Uncertain Commitment to Representative Jury Panels. Cambridge, Massachusetts: Ballinger Publishing Co., 1977.

Winick, Bruce. Prosecutorial Peremptory Challenge Practices in Capital Cases: An Empirical Study and a Constitutional Analysis. 81 Mich.L.Rev. 1 (1982).

Chapter Twenty-Eight

ADVERSARIAL RIGHTS: OPENNESS, CONFRONTATION, AND COMPULSORY PROCESS

28.01 Introduction

The Sixth Amendment provides in part: "In all criminal prosecutions, the accused shall enjoy the right to . . . public trial[,] to be confronted with the witnesses against him [and] to have compulsory process for obtaining witnesses in his favor." The three rights guaranteed by this language, applied to the states in *In re Oliver*[1] (Public Trial Clause), *Pointer v. Texas*[2] (Confrontation Clause) and *Washington v. Texas*[3] (Compulsory Process Clause), are designed to equalize the contest between the state and the accused and ensure that it is adversarial rather than inquisitional.

The first section of this chapter examines the right to a "public trial," which is meant to promote fair adjudication by bringing the process into the open. The following three sections address the central aspects of an accused's right to confront her accusers: the right to be present, both physically and mentally; the right to force the prosecution to rely on live testimony rather than out-of-court statements; and the right to face and cross-examine those accusers who testify in court. These guarantees help ensure that the defendant is given adequate opportunity to hear and challenge the state's case against her. The final section of the chapter describes the operation of the compulsory process guarantee, which supplements the Confrontation Clause by providing means for the defendant to muster her own evidence against the state's case. Although this chapter focuses primarily on these provisions as they affect the trial process, it also examines their application to other criminal proceedings.

28.02 The Right to Public Adjudication

(a) **Rationale and Scope.** As the Supreme Court recognized in *In re Oliver*,[4] "[t]he knowledge that every criminal trial is subject to contemporaneous review in the forum of public opinion is an effective restraint on possible abuse of power. . . . Without publicity, all other checks are insufficient; in comparison of publicity, all other checks are of small account." The Court explained further that "the presence of interested spectators may

1. 333 U.S. 257, 68 S.Ct. 499 (1948). 3. 388 U.S. 14, 87 S.Ct. 1920 (1967).
2. 380 U.S. 400, 85 S.Ct. 1065 (1965). 4. 333 U.S. 257, 68 S.Ct. 499 (1948).

keep [the accused's] triers keenly alive to a sense of their responsibility and to the importance of their functions."

Although *Oliver* speaks only of trial, its rationale would seem to apply to any formal proceeding where important decisions about the defendant's fate are made. This surmise was affirmed in *Waller v. Georgia*,[5] where the Court held that the right to public trial encompassed the right to an open suppression hearing. The right probably applies to most other pretrial proceedings as well, with the exception of the grand jury, which has traditionally operated in secret.[6]

(b) Closure of Normally Open Proceedings. For the reasons given above, the defendant will usually want an open proceeding. Occasionally, however, she may seek closure, perhaps to mitigate the effects of publicity or to protect privacy interests. Under such circumstances, the Sixth Amendment may be waived.[7] However, the First Amendment's guarantee of a free press permits the public to override this waiver in a number of situations. This issue is discussed elsewhere in this book.[8]

Discussed here are those situations where the defendant (as well as, perhaps, the press) want an open proceeding, but the *state* wishes to close it. In *Waller*, the Court set forth the test for determining when the state may prevail in such circumstances. According to the majority, closure may occur over a Sixth Amendment objection by the defendant only if: (1) the state proves that an overriding interest requires protection (such as the need to protect juror or witness privacy); (2) the closure is no broader than necessary to protect that interest; (3) reasonable alternatives are considered; and (4) findings adequate to support the closure are made.

In *Waller* itself the Court found that this test was not met. There, the state requested that the suppression hearing be closed because it would be playing a tape that referred to persons not yet indicted. Granting the motion, the judge closed all seven days of the hearing, despite the fact that less than 2½ hours of this period were devoted to playing the tape, and few of the conversations mentioned or involved parties not then before the court. The Supreme Court held that, because the state failed to identify specifically "whose privacy interests might be infringed, how they would be infringed, what portions of the tape might infringe them, and what portion of the evidence consisted of the tapes," and because the closure went far beyond that necessary to protect

---

5. *Waller v. Georgia*, 467 U.S. 39, 104 S.Ct. 2210 (1984).

6. See § 23.03.

7. *Gannett Co., Inc. v. DePasquale*, 443 U.S. 368, 99 S.Ct. 2898 (1979) (permitting closure of suppression hearing when there is "reasonable possibility" that pretrial publicity will affect fairness of trial).

8. See § 27.06(c)(3).

against inappropriate disclosure, the Sixth Amendment was violated. Accordingly, the defendants were entitled to a new suppression hearing and, if the results of the hearing were significantly different from the first suppression hearing, a new trial.

Globe Newspaper Co. v. Superior Court,[9] a First Amendment case decided before *Waller,* provides another illustration of the Supreme Court's probable approach in this area. There, the Court found unconstitutional a state-requested closure of trial under a statute which automatically denied access to the public in cases involving sex offenses against minors. The Court did not prohibit closure under all such circumstances, however; rather it held that, upon a motion by the state, the trial court should "determine on a case-by-case basis whether closure is necessary," taking into account "the minor victim's age, psychological maturity and understanding, the nature of the crime, the desires of the victim, and the interests of parents and relatives."[10]

28.03 The Right to be Present

As the Supreme Court stated in *Illinois v. Allen,*[11] "[o]ne of the most basic of the rights guaranteed by the Confrontation Clause is the accused's right to be present in the courtroom at every stage of his trial." The right of confrontation would be meaningless if the defendant were not present to hear and view the state's evidence. It would also be an empty right if the defendant, though present, could not understand and respond to what she observes in the courtroom. Thus the right to be present actually encompasses two different aspects: physical presence and mental competence. The Supreme Court has also indicated that the right to be present may not be burdened unnecessarily, either through prosecutorial comment about the defendant's failure to take the stand or through manipulating the defendant's appearance. These three concepts are discussed here.

(a) Physical Presence. The defendant's right to be physically present during the proceedings against him is limited in several ways. First, it only applies to "critical" proceedings. Second, it can be voluntarily waived, or forfeited (that is, "involuntarily" sacrificed), by the absence of the defendant. Third, it can be forefeited through misconduct of the defendant at the proceeding.

(1) Proceedings at which applicable. Allen speaks of the right to be present "at every stage of [the] trial." In *United States v.*

---

9. 457 U.S. 596, 102 S.Ct. 2613 (1982).

10. See also, *Press–Enterprise Co. v. Superior Court I,* 464 U.S. 501, 104 S.Ct. 819 (1984) (finding unconstitutional, on First Amendment grounds, closure of all but three days of a six-week *voir dire,* without specific findings as to how closure would protect juror privacy).

11. 397 U.S. 337, 90 S.Ct. 1057 (1970).

Gagnon,[12] the Court made clear that, because the right to presence has due process as well as confrontation origins, it is not limited to proceedings at which witnesses appear to offer testimony against the defendant but also to all other proceedings at which the defendant's presence " 'has a relation, reasonably substantial, to the fullness of his opportunity to defend against the charge.' " In *Kentucky v. Stincer,*[13] the Court reiterated this principle, finding a right to presence at any stage of the criminal proceeding which is "critical," in the sense that the accused's presence there "would contribute to the fairness of the prosecution."

However, in both *Gagnon* and *Stincer* the Court held that the proceedings at issue did not implicate the right. In *Gagnon,* the judge met in chambers with a juror who had noticed, and apparently become bothered by, the fact that the defendant was sketching the jury; the judge determined that the sketching did not prejudice the juror against the defendant and allowed the juror to continue sitting. The Court held that the absence of the defendants at this "minor occurrence" did not violate due process, since the defendants "could have done nothing had they been present nor would they have gained anything by attending." In *Stincer,* the proceeding involved a pretrial determination of the testimonial competence of children the prosecution planned to offer as witnesses. Here, the questions asked concerned the witnesses' mental competency, not their account of the offense, thus making it unlikely the defendant could have pointed to any discrepancies in their testimony. Furthermore, the children were subject to cross-examination at trial (at which the defendant was present), and many of the questions asked at the pretrial proceeding were replicated at trial.

Even when the right to be present is violated, it may be such a *de minimis* violation that reversal is not required. For instance, in *Rushen v. Spain,*[14] the trial judge failed to disclose *ex parte* communications between himself and a juror regarding the juror's reaction to impeachment evidence concerning the murder of an acquaintance of hers. The Supreme Court acknowledged that this *in camera* interview was a violation of the right to be present, as well as the right to counsel at critical stages of trial, but ultimately found it harmless in view of the trial judge's post-trial finding of fact that the jury's deliberations were not biased by the *ex parte* communication. A different holding, stated the Court, would "undermine[ ] society's interest in the administration of criminal justice."

12. 470 U.S. 522, 105 S.Ct. 1482 (1985).

13. 479 U.S. 1028, 107 S.Ct. 870 (1987).

14. 464 U.S. 114, 104 S.Ct. 453 (1983).

(2) Waiver/forfeiture through absence. In contrast to *Rushen,* in both *Gagnon* and *Stincer* defense attorneys had been present during the proceeding which the defendant missed. Thus, an additional argument in favor of those decisions might have been that the attorneys waived their clients' right to be present. But this argument is likely to be given short shrift by the Court, since, in *Taylor v. Illinois,*[15] it held that the right cannot be waived by the attorney "without the fully informed and publicly acknowledged consent of the defendant."

On the other hand, the defendant himself can waive the right, or forfeit it through misconduct, in a number of situations. As early as 1912, the Court held that the right to be present may be waived by the defendant. In *Diaz v. United States,*[16] the defendant twice voluntarily absented himself from trial after the trial had begun. The accused also sent a message to the court expressly consenting to the trial continuing in his absence. The Supreme Court held that on these facts waiver of the right to be present was valid. However, it also held that when an accused is charged with a capital offense and is in custody (i.e., has not escaped), the right to be present can never be waived.

The Court has also permitted *implied* waiver of the right to be present. In *Taylor v. United States,*[17] the defendant failed to return to his trial after a noon recess. The jury was admonished that Taylor's absence should not lead to an inference of guilt, but returned a guilty verdict. Taylor was eventually arrested and sentenced, but appealed on the ground that his right to confrontation was violated because he had not "intentionally relinquished a known right." The Court rejected this argument, concluding:

> It is wholly incredible to suggest that [Taylor] . . . entertained any doubts about his right to be present at every stage of the trial. It seems equally incredible to us, as it did to the Court of Appeals, 'that a defendant who flees from a courtroom in the midst of a trial—where judge, jury, witnesses and lawyers are present and ready to continue—would not know that as a consequence the trial could continue in his absence.

Taylor suggests that once trial has already commenced with the defendant present, an uncoerced absence will be construed as a forfeiture of the right to be present regardless of whether the defendant has been informed of the consequences of that absence.[18]

15. 484 U.S. 400, 108 S.Ct. 646 (1988).

16. 223 U.S. 442, 32 S.Ct. 250 (1912).

17. 414 U.S. 17, 94 S.Ct. 194 (1973).

18. The current Fed.R.Crim.Proc. 43 states that a "defendant shall be considered to have waived his right to be present whenever a defendant, initially present . . . voluntarily absents himself after the trial has commenced (whether or not he has been informed by the court of his obligation to remain during the trial).

Finally, the Court has implied that even when the defendant *never* appears for trial, a waiver may be assumed under appropriate circumstances. In *Tacon v. Arizona,*[19] the defendant claimed to be unable to travel from New York to his trial in Arizona because he couldn't afford the trip. The Court granted certiorari to decide whether a state may try a defendant who is *in absentia* for financial reasons. Ultimately, however, it dismissed the writ as improvidently granted, concluding that the only issue raised below was whether the defendant's conduct, which suggested that in fact he could afford the trip, amounted to a "knowing and intelligent" waiver. With this language, the Court strongly indicated that, even in cases not involving escape from custody, one can forfeit one's right to presence without ever appearing at trial.

(3) Forfeiture through conduct. A third exception to the right to be present arises when the defendant makes it impossible to conduct an orderly proceeding. In *Illinois v. Allen,*[20] the defendant did not voluntarily leave the courtroom but rather was removed after repeated warnings from the judge that the defendant's abusive and disruptive behavior would result in his removal. The Supreme Court sanctioned this action, holding that the right to be present may be forfeited if the defendant, after being warned, continues to act "in a manner so disorderly, disruptive, and disrespectful of the court that his trial cannot be carried on with him in the courtroom." The Court also noted, however, that this lost right may be reclaimed when an accused is "willing to conduct himself consistently with the decorum and respect inherent in the concept of courts and judicial proceedings."

The Court recognized alternatives to removal from the courtroom but refused to require their use as a substitute, given the disadvantages associated with them. One alternative—binding and gagging the defendant—would ensure the defendant's presence but might also "have a significant effect on the jury's feelings about the defendant [and act as] something of an affront to the very dignity and decorum of judicial proceedings that the judge is seeking to uphold." Moreover, this approach would severely curtail the defendant's ability to communicate with her attorney, thus denigrating the defendant's right to confront her accusers. The second alternative, a contempt citation, would allow attorney-client communication but would not stop the misconduct of those defendants determined to be disruptive and those charged with serious offenses for whom a contempt sanction might mean little. Thus, held the Court, removal, restraints, and contempt are all permissible solutions to the disruptive defendant, to be used in the judge's discretion.

19. 410 U.S. 351, 93 S.Ct. 998 (1973) (per curiam).　　**20.** 397 U.S. 337, 90 S.Ct. 1057 (1970).

(b) Competency to Proceed. The Supreme Court has held that conviction of an "incompetent" person violates the Constitution.[21] Two very different reasons support this holding. Most clearly, physical presence without some ability to process events in the courtroom and communicate with one's attorney would be a useless prerogative. A second rationale for the competency requirement is the damage to societal integrity that would occur if the state could convict and sentence individuals who are unaware of what is being done to them.[22] Both rationale support the proposition that the defendant's competence should be assured at *any* proceeding, not just at trial. Thus, this discussion speaks of "competency to proceed" rather than competency to stand trial.

(1) The standard. The test for determining a defendant's competency to proceed is often said to have been established in the Supreme Court's per curiam decision in *Dusky v. United States*.[23] There the district court judge found the defendant competent because he was "oriented to time and place and [had] some recollection of events." The Solicitor General found this an insufficient basis for a competency determination and suggested to the Court that the test be whether a defendant "has sufficient present ability to consult with his lawyer with a reasonable degree of rational understanding—and whether he has a rational as well as factual understanding of the proceedings against him." The Court adopted the Solicitor General's suggestion and the *Dusky* test has since been treated as setting forth the appropriate criteria for competency to stand trial in the federal courts; most states have followed suit.[24] The Court has since held that a state may place the burden of proving incompetency on the defendant.[25]

It is important to note the distinction between incompetency to proceed and the insanity defense; the two concepts are often confused. The first concerns the defendant's mental condition at the time of the relevant proceeding, while the second involves the defendant's mental state at the time of the offense. Additionally, the competency test focuses on the defendant's mental capacity with respect to two narrowly defined areas: (1) her ability to understand the proceedings against her and (2) her ability to communicate with her lawyer. The insanity defense contemplates

21. *Pate v. Robinson*, 383 U.S. 375, 86 S.Ct. 836 (1966); *Bishop v. United States*, 350 U.S. 961, 76 S.Ct. 440 (1956). In reaching this holding, the Court has relied on the Due Process Clause, but its reasoning resonates with right to confrontation concerns.

22. See Note, "Incompetency to Stand Trial," 81 Harv.L.Rev. 454, 458 (1967).

23. 362 U.S. 402, 80 S.Ct. 788 (1960).

24. See, e.g., West's Fla.S.A.R.Crim. Pro. 3.211(a)(1).

25. *Medina v. California*, ___ U.S. ___, 112 S.Ct. 2572 (1992).

a broader inquiry designed to determine the extent of *any* cognitive *or* volitional impairment at the time of the offense.[26]

A final point worth making about the competency test is that, at least as applied, it is an extremely low standard. Studies indicate that of those who are referred for a competency evaluation (and who thus presumably evidence some degree of mental deficiency), only between ten and thirty percent are found incompetent by the courts.[27] In contrast, the standards for competency to plead guilty and competency to waive one's attorney, both of which contemplate that the defendant will make a particular *decision*, may be more difficult to meet. Competency to plead guilty contemplates the knowing waiver of a number of rights which are not necessarily relevant to the competency to stand trial assessment.[28] And in *Westbrook v. Arizona*,[29] the Supreme Court suggested that a finding of competency to stand trial is insufficient for the purpose of determining whether a defendant can waive the right to counsel, by holding that, before Westbrook could proceed *pro se,* an inquiry concerning his competency to conduct his own defense might be necessary in addition to the assessment of competency to stand trial which had already taken place.[30]

(2) Raising the competency issue. In *Pate v. Robinson* [31] the Court held that a hearing to determine the defendant's competency to stand trial must be held whenever "a sufficient doubt exists as to his present competence." In *Pate,* the trial judge had not held a hearing on the issue despite Robinson's history of mental illness and his assertion of an insanity defense. The Illinois Supreme Court affirmed this denial in light of the mental alertness and understanding displayed in Robinson's "colloquies" with the trial judge. But the Supreme Court required a hearing, stating:

> [The Illinois courts'] reasoning offers no justification for ignoring the uncontradicted testimony of Robinson's history of pronounced irrational behavior. While Robinson's demeanor at trial might be relevant to the ultimate decision as to his [present] sanity, it cannot be relied upon to dispense with a hearing on that very issue.

26. For a general exposition of these matters, see LaFave & Scott, Criminal Law, §§ 36–39 (1982).

27. Roesch, R. & S. Golding, Competency to Stand Trial 48 (1980). The authors note that variations in the rate exist because "many defendants are inappropriately referred, . . . and confusion exists about the proper criteria necessary for a determination of incompetency." Id. at 51.

28. See § 26.04(a)(5).

29. 384 U.S. 150, 86 S.Ct. 1320 (1966).

30. See § 31.04(a). See also *Massey v. Moore,* 348 U.S. 105, 75 S.Ct. 145 (1954) ("One might not be insane in the sense of being incapable of standing trial and yet lack the capacity to stand trial without benefit of counsel.")

31. 383 U.S. 375, 86 S.Ct. 836 (1966).

As Justice Harlan pointed out in dissent, the pattern of Robinson's illness "may best indicate that Robinson did function adequately during most of his life interrupted by periods of severe derangement that would have been quite apparent had they occurred at trial." Moreover, the trial judge was obviously satisfied as to Robinson's competence and even his attorneys never moved to have his competency examined. Given these facts, the majority decision in *Pate* suggests that a hearing of some sort should be held whenever there is a history of mental aberration, regardless of what other indicia of present mental state may reveal.

This notion is supported by the Court's holding in *Drope v. Missouri*,[32] in which the defendant was charged, along with four others, in the rape and sexual abuse of his wife. During trial, the wife testified that the defendant would sometimes roll down the stairs when he was upset and that the night before trial the defendant had tried to choke her. The second day of trial, the defendant's attorney announced that the defendant had shot himself in the stomach. On these facts, the Court held that the trial judge had an obligation to inquire into the defendant's competency to stand trial despite his apparent lucidity prior to and during the first day of trial.

Pate and *Drope* make clear that the competency issue may be raised at any time prior to or during the proceeding. They further imply, and many states provide, that any party—the defense, the prosecution, or the judge—may raise the issue when a bona fide doubt as to competency exists. If, as suggested above, society too has an interest in trying only competent defendants, this latter rule makes sense. But some commentators believe that only the defense should be able to raise the issue, on the ground that prosecutors and judges may abuse the hospital-based competency evaluation process as an alternative disposition and a means of obtaining discovery.[33]

(3) Self-incrimination and the competency evaluation. As just noted, when the competency issue is raised, most states provide for an evaluation of the defendant's competency by a mental health professional at a state hospital.[34] In *Estelle v. Smith*,[35] the results of such an evaluation were used not only to address the defendant's competency, but also as the basis for testimony at the defendant's sentencing proceeding to the effect that he was dangerous, a finding which permitted the sentencing jury to impose

---

32. 420 U.S. 162, 95 S.Ct. 896 (1975).

33. Eizenstadt, "Mental Competency to Stand Trial," 4 Harv.Civ.Rts.Civ.Lib. L.Rev. 379 (1969).

34. Winick, B., Incompetency to Stand Trial 9–11, in Monahan, J. & H.

Steadman, Mentally Disordered Offenders: Perspectives from Law and Social Science (1983).

35. 451 U.S. 454, 101 S.Ct. 1866 (1981).

the death penalty on the defendant. The Supreme Court held that because the defense did not initiate the evaluation nor introduce psychiatric testimony of its own at the sentencing proceeding, the admission of the dangerousness testimony violated the Fifth Amendment. Comparing the evaluation in *Smith* to the custodial interrogation setting at issue in *Miranda v. Arizona*,[36] the Court concluded that the only way the state could have introduced such testimony under these circumstances was if the psychiatrist performing the evaluation had informed Smith of his right to remain silent and of the possible uses of any disclosures he might make. Here, there had been no such warnings. On the other hand, the Court noted, had Smith been given the warnings and refused to talk, "the validly ordered competency examination nevertheless could have proceeded upon the condition that the results would be applied solely for that purpose." The Court also held that the prosecution's failure to notify the defendant's attorneys about the evaluation violated the Sixth Amendment as construed by *Massiah v. United States*,[37] since the evaluation took place after indictment. But, as with the right to remain silent, the Court concluded that this "right-to-notice" could be waived as well.

After *Estelle*, it appears that if a defendant is told about the right to remain silent and the right to notice of counsel, and then *agrees* to submit to an evaluation on issues other than competency, his disclosures can be used for any purpose designated in the warnings. Given the difficulty of determining when a defendant whose mental capacity is presumably in question has validly waived her Fifth and Sixth Amendment rights, the better approach would be to prohibit use of disclosures made during a court-ordered competency evaluation for any purpose other than the determination of competency itself.[38]

(4) Disposition of the incompetent defendant. In most jurisdictions, if a defendant is found incompetent to proceed, she is usually hospitalized in an effort to restore her to competency. This practice can lead to indeterminate confinement well beyond the sentence associated with the defendant's charge.[39] In *Jackson v. Indiana*,[40] the Supreme Court held that the Constitution places some limitations on the length of hospitalization of individuals found incompetent.

36. 384 U.S. 436, 86 S.Ct. 1602 (1966), discussed in pertinent part in § 16.03(a)(3).

37. 377 U.S. 201, 84 S.Ct. 1199 (1964), discussed in § 16.02(b).

38. Slobogin, *Estelle v. Smith:* "The Constitutional Contours of the Forensic Evaluation Process," 31 Emory L.J. 71, 87–95 (1982).

39. *Winick*, supra note 34, at 19–20.

40. 406 U.S. 715, 92 S.Ct. 1845 (1972).

In *Jackson*, the defendant, a 27 year-old deaf mute with a mental level of a pre-school child, was charged with two robberies, one involving property valued at four dollars and the other involving five dollars in cash. The trial court found Jackson incompetent and committed him to a state hospital until the hospital staff considered him "sane." Since there was very little likelihood the defendant's condition would ever improve, this disposition "amounted to a commitment for life," in the words of Justice Blackmun, who wrote the unanimous Court opinion.

The Court found Indiana's practice unconstitutional on two grounds. First, it violated the equal protection principle. Because Jackson had not been convicted of crime, he should presumptively be able to avoid involuntary hospitalization unless he met the normal criteria for civil commitment of mentally disabled individuals. Yet, under Indiana laws dealing with those found incompetent to stand trial, he was subject to "a more lenient commitment and to a more stringent standard of release" than those subjected to civil commitment. Second, the Due Process Clause "[a]t the least, . . . requires that the nature and duration of commitment bear some reasonable relation to the purpose for which the individual is committed." The duration of the commitment to which Jackson would be subject under Indiana law—a possible lifetime confinement—would not reasonably relate to its purpose.

In effect combining these two lines of reasoning, Blackmun concluded:

> We hold, consequently, that a person charged by a State with a criminal offense who is committed solely on account of his incapacity to proceed to trial cannot be held more than the reasonable period of time necessary to determine whether there is a substantial probability that he will attain that capacity in the foreseeable future. If it is determined that this is not the case, then the State must either institute the customary civil commitment proceeding that would be required to commit indefinitely any other citizen, or release the defendant.

The Court further held that if a defendant is found potentially "restorable" to competency, "his continued commitment must be justified by progress toward that goal."

The Court did not place any outer time limit on the duration of hospitalization authorized by *Jackson*, but did hold that Jackson himself should either be released or civilly committed, given the fact that he had now been confined for three and one-half years "on a record that sufficiently establishes the lack of a substantial probability that he will ever be able to participate fully in a trial." Some jurisdictions have attempted to designate the period after which an unrestorably incompetent defendant must be released or civil committed. For instance, the federal practice is to limit hospitalization on incompetency grounds to 18 months.[41] Michigan limits commitment to 90 days for those charged with misdemeanors and to two-thirds of the maximum sentence for all others.[42]

(c) Prejudicial Aspects of Presence. The defendant's presence in the courtroom could prove prejudicial in two ways. First, if the defendant fails to testify during the proceeding when she is allowed to, the jury may draw adverse conclusions. Second, the defendant's physical appearance may have the same effect. To the extent the state takes advantage of, or manipulates, these aspects of presence, the Fifth Amendment's prohibition of compelled self-incrimination or analogous due process concerns may be implicated.

(1) Refusal to testify. Under the Fifth Amendment, the state may not force the defendant to testify.[43] In *Griffin v. California*,[44] the Supreme Court held further that the prosecution may not call attention to the fact that the defendant exercises the right to remain silent, because such statements would make assertion of the Fifth Amendment "costly" and thus constitute "constitutionally impermissible compulsion." [45] While the majority recognized that the jury might assume the non-testifying defendant is guilty in any event, it distinguished that possibility from prosecutorial comment which "solemnizes the silence of the accused into evidence against him." It also pointed out that there are many reasons an *innocent* defendant might not testify, including fear that she will be impeached with prior crimes, "[e]xcessive timidity [or] nervousness when facing others and attempting to explain transactions of a suspicious character," or confusion and embarrassment "to such a degree as to increase rather than remove prejudices against [her]."

In light of these considerations, the Court's later holding in *Carter v. Kentucky* [46]—that the trial court must, at the defendant's request,[47] instruct the jury to draw no adverse inferences from the defendant's failure to take the stand—was not surprising. Fur-

41. *Drendel v. United States*, 403 F.2d 55 (5th Cir.1968).

42. N.Y.Code Crim.Pro. § 730.50(1), (5).

43. *Malloy v. Hogan*, 378 U.S. 1, 84 S.Ct. 1489 (1964); see also, *Wilson v. United States*, 149 U.S. 60, 13 S.Ct. 765 (1893).

44. 380 U.S. 609, 85 S.Ct. 1229 (1965).

45. For further discussion of *Griffin's* compulsion theory, see § 15.02(c).

46. 450 U.S. 288, 101 S.Ct. 1112 (1981).

47. In *James v. Kentucky*, 466 U.S. 341, 104 S.Ct. 1830 (1984) the Court defined "request" broadly to include a request for an "admonition" as well as a request for an instruction, despite state law distinguishing the two.

ther, in *Lakeside v. Oregon,*[48] it held that the defendant cannot *prevent* such an instruction. Finding speculative the defendant's argument that the instruction might call his refusal to testify to the attention of the jury, the Court stated, "[i]t would be strange indeed to conclude that this cautionary instruction violates the very constitutional provision it is intended to protect."

There is also at least one exception to the holding in *Griffin* forbidding prosecutorial comments about failure to take the stand. Such comments may be made if necessary to counteract defense suggestions that the state is responsible for the failure. In *United States v. Robinson,*[49] defense counsel made numerous charges during closing argument that the government had denied the defendant the opportunity to explain his side of the case. Although, according to the defense, these comments had to do with the government's actions during the investigation stage of the proceedings, they may have left the impression that the government had somehow prevented the defendant from taking the stand. The prosecutor, who was permitted to respond to these comments during his closing statement, noted the several occasions prior to trial at which the defendant could have explained himself and ended by saying "[he] could have taken the stand and explained it to you, anything he wanted to. The United States of America has given him, throughout, the opportunity to explain." The Court felt that, in context, this statement was not a violation of *Griffin* but rather a "fair response" to the defense's assertions.

(2) Prejudicial physical appearance. Related to the *Griffin* line of cases is *Estelle v. Williams,*[50] which held that the state may not compel a defendant to wear jail garb in the courtroom. The fact that the "constant reminder of the accused's condition implicit in such distinctive, identifiable attire may affect a juror's judgment," together with the finding that "compelling an accused to wear jail clothing furthers no essential state policy," led the Court to conclude that such a practice violated the Due Process Clause. However, if, as occurred in *Williams,* the defendant does not object to the clothing, then no constitutional violation occurs, on the assumption that no compulsion has occurred.

28.04 The Right to Live Testimony: When Hearsay Is Permitted

The Confrontation Clause might be read to require the prosecution to produce all of its witnesses in the courtroom, so that the defendant can face and cross-examine them. But, as early as 1895, the Supreme Court concluded, in *Mattox v. United States,*[51]

---

48. 435 U.S. 333, 98 S.Ct. 1091 (1978).

49. 485 U.S. 25, 108 S.Ct. 864 (1988).

50. 425 U.S. 501, 96 S.Ct. 1691 (1976).

51. 156 U.S. 237, 15 S.Ct. 337 (1895).

that the right of confrontation is "subject to exceptions, recognized long before the adoption of the Constitution." There, it upheld the introduction of testimony given at the defendant's first trial by a witness who died before the defendant's second trial. As the majority elaborated, "[t]o say that a criminal, after having once been convicted by the testimony of a certain witness, should go scot free simply because death has closed the mouth of that witness, would be carrying his constitutional protection to an unwarrantable extent."

Since *Mattox,* the Court has recognized a number of situations in which the prosecution may introduce "hearsay"—i.e., testimony about what a "declarant" who is not in court has said—without violating the Confrontation Clause (of course, the hearsay must also be admissible under the relevant evidentiary rules). Although the Court has not done so, its decisions in admitting hearsay can be organized into three categories: (1) when the unavailability of the declarant is required; (2) when the availability of the declarant is irrelevant because the hearsay is admissible under a firmly rooted hearsay exception, or otherwise seems particularly reliable; and (3) when the availability of the declarant is required. Also discussed here is the application of these rules to a special group of cases involving use of extrajudicial statements by one defendant which implicate another defendant.

(a) Declarant Unavailability Required. A declarant might be "unavailable" for courtroom testimony for a number of reasons. As *Mattox* recognized, death of the declarant prior to trial is one such reason. The Court has also held that a declarant becomes unavailable for Confrontation Clause purposes when she permanently transfers to a foreign country,[52] cannot be located after a diligent search by the prosecution,[53] or suffers a loss of memory.[54]

Early Court decisions examining the relationship between the Confrontation Clause and hearsay—virtually all of which involved the admissibility of previous testimony—suggested that the Clause prohibited the introduction of hearsay statements unless the government could show the declarant was "unavailable" in one of these ways. For instance, although the Court in *Mattox* upheld the admissibility of prior trial testimony (and suggested that dying declarations could be admitted as well), it stressed that its holding

---

52. *Mancusi v. Stubbs,* 408 U.S. 204, 92 S.Ct. 2308 (1972).

53. *Ohio v. Roberts,* 448 U.S. 56, 100 S.Ct. 2531 (1980) (prosecution showed that mother's last contact with witness was by phone several months before trial, during which witness said she was "travelling" and did not reveal whereabouts).

54. *California v. Green,* 399 U.S. 149, 90 S.Ct. 1930 (1970). See also, *Idaho v. Wright,* 497 U.S. 805, 110 S.Ct. 3139 (1990) (recognizing that incompetency of witness makes her unavailable).

was based on "the necessities of the case, and to prevent a manifest failure of justice." According to the Court:

> [t]he primary object of the [Confrontation Clause] was to prevent depositions or ex parte affidavits, such as were sometimes admitted in civil cases, being used against the prisoner in lieu of a personal examination and cross-examination of the witness in which the accused has an opportunity, not only of testing the recollection and sifting the conscience of the witness, but of compelling him to stand and face the jury in order that they may look at him, and judge by his demeanor upon the stand and the manner in which he gives his testimony whether he is worthy of belief.

Five years later, in *Motes v. United States*,[55] the Court was even more direct, stating that it was inconsistent with the Confrontation Clause "to permit the deposition or statement of an absent witness (taken at an examining trial) to be read at the final trial when it does not appear that the witness was absent by the suggestion, connivance, or procurement of the accused, but does appear that this absence was due to the negligence of the prosecution."

The necessity threshold for hearsay was reinforced in the much later case of *Barber v. Page*,[56] where a unanimous Court, in an opinion by Justice Marshall, held that introduction of preliminary hearing testimony by a declarant who was not shown to be unavailable violates the Confrontation Clause. The declarant in *Barber* was in federal prison at the time of the trial. While admitting that the federal authorities had discretion to deny his release for a state trial, Marshall noted that the state had not even forwarded a request for his presence. He concluded that "a witness is not 'unavailable' for purposes of the [prior testimony] exception to the confrontation requirement unless the prosecutorial authorities have made a good-faith effort to obtain his presence at trial."

Barber also held that a showing of unavailability was not enough to gain admissibility under the Confrontation Clause. In particular, it noted that, as the earlier case of *Pointer v. Texas*[57] had held, when the prior testimony was not subject to cross-examination because the defendant lacked counsel at the time, it was inadmissible under any circumstances. However, two years later, in *California v. Green*,[58] the Court concluded that preliminary hearing testimony is sufficiently reliable for Confrontation Clause purposes if defense counsel is present and is given an

55. 178 U.S. 458, 20 S.Ct. 993 (1900).

56. 390 U.S. 719, 88 S.Ct. 1318 (1968).

57. 380 U.S. 400, 85 S.Ct. 1065 (1965).

58. 399 U.S. 149, 90 S.Ct. 1930 (1970).

"opportunity to cross-examine" the declarant, over a vigorous dissent by Justice Brennan arguing that, unlike the prior *trial* testimony involved in *Mattox,* the defense might not want or be permitted to cross-examine such testimony aggressively.[59] Since *Green* involved a declarant who was unavailable because of a memory loss at trial, its relaxed standard could have been attributable to the fact that the declarant could be subjected to at least some cross-examination at trial. But, in *Ohio v. Roberts,*[60] the Court held that pretrial testimony may also be used when a witness is physically unavailable, so long as there was an opportunity to cross-examine at the pretrial hearing. In *Roberts,* the Court found this latter requirement met even though the *defense* had called the declarant as a witness at the preliminary hearing, because defense counsel had been allowed to ask several leading questions during the hearing.

While *Roberts* may have broadened the prior testimony exception, its sweeping language continued to give lipservice to the necessity threshold for hearsay. Specifically, it stated that unavailability of the declarant must be demonstrated unless "the utility of confrontation [is] remote."[61] Furthermore, *Roberts* stressed that even if unavailability were shown, the hearsay could not be admitted unless it showed "indicia of reliability." The latter could be "presumed" if a "firmly rooted exception" to the hearsay rule applied, but in all cases reliability, and not the existence of a hearsay exception, was the basic requirement.

(b) Availability Irrelevant. Since *Roberts,* the Court has significantly shifted position, concluding that unavailability need be shown only under narrow circumstances. Further, the Court's most recent decisions indicate that the prosecution may use hearsay whenever a firmly rooted hearsay exception applies, even if its "indicia of reliability" are not evident, and that hearsay that does not fit within an exception is still admissible if "particularized guarantees of trustworthiness" can be shown. In other words, the Confrontation Clause has come to offer little protection against extrajudicial statements outside of that afforded by the traditional hearsay rules.

(1) Firmly rooted exceptions. The first case to attack directly the unavailability requirement was *United States v. Inadi.*[62]

---

59. See § 22.04(c) for a discussion of the scope of cross-examination at the preliminary hearing.

60. 448 U.S. 56, 100 S.Ct. 2531 (1980).

61. Here the Court cited *Dutton v. Evans,* 400 U.S. 74, 91 S.Ct. 210 (1970). *Dutton* was the only Court decision up to that time allowing introduction of hearsay when the declarant was availa-

ble, and its meaning was ambiguous, since at least three members of the five-member majority appeared to prefer considering admission of the hearsay harmless error in light of its "perihpheral" nature.

62. 475 U.S. 387, 106 S.Ct. 1121 (1986). See also, *Bourjaily v. United States,* 479 U.S. 881, 107 S.Ct. 268 (1986).

There, the Court essentially limited *Roberts* to cases involving prior testimony and suggested that the Confrontation Clause would normally be satisfied if the hearsay was admissible under a "firmly rooted" hearsay exception, many of which do not require a showing of unavailability.[63]   According to Justice Powell, who wrote the majority opinion in *Inadi,* the necessity rationale endorsed by *Roberts* and its predecessors could be explained by the fact that prior testimony is not the "best evidence" when the declarant is available for trial.   On the other hand, the type of hearsay involved in *Inadi*—co-conspirator statements made during the course of the conspiracy—"derive much of their value from the fact that they are made in a context very different from trial, and therefore are usually irreplaceable as substantive evidence." Statements admitted under this "firmly rooted" hearsay exception "provide evidence of the conspiracy's context that cannot be replicated, even if the declarant testifies to the same matters in court."

An additional reason given for admitting co-conspirator hearsay without having to produce the declarant was that the declarant "is not likely to produce much testimony that adds anything to the 'truth-determining process' over and above what would be produced without such a rule."   Either the prosecution, or the defendant through use of compulsory process, will usually produce co-conspirators who are material to the case.   Further, an unavailability requirement would make the prosecution locate and keep continuously available each declarant, even when neither party has an interest in calling them.

A unanimous Court relied on similar reasoning in *White v. Illinois,*[64] where it found that the Confrontation Clause was not violated when the out-of-court statements of a four year-old were introduced in an aggravated assault trial in which she did not testify.   The statements there were admitted under the hearsay exceptions for spontaneous declarations and securing medical treatment.   The Court noted that, whereas the factors that make a preliminary hearing statement reliable (such as cross-examination and formal proceedings) can be replicated at trial, thus obviating the need for the pretrial testimony, the "same factors that contribute to the [hearsay] statements' reliability [in *White*] cannot be recaptured . . . by later in-court testimony."

A statement that has been offered in a moment of excitement—without the opportunity to reflect on the consequences of one's exclamation—may justifiably carry more weight with

---

63. See, e.g., the various hearsay exceptions in Fed.R.Evid. 803. It is interesting to note that, at the time the Sixth Amendment was drafted, hearsay evidence was admissible only if the declarant was "unavailable," e.g., dead or mentally disabled. J. Thayer, A Preliminary Treatise on Evidence at the Common Law 501 (1898).

64. ___ U.S. ___, 112 S.Ct. 736 (1992).

a trier of fact than a similar statement offered in the relative calm of the courtroom. Similarly, a statement made in the course of procuring medical services, where the declarant knows that a false statement may cause misdiagnosis or mistreatment, carries special guarantees of credibility that a trier of fact may not think replicated by courtroom testimony.

The Court's assessment in *Inadi* and *White* of the truth-value of co-conspirator statements, spontaneous declarations and statements to secure medical treatment are open to question. For instance, the co-conspirator exception to the hearsay rule, while admittedly "firmly rooted," is based on the legal fiction that the statement of one co-conspirator may be imputed to all co-conspirators, not on an assessment that such statements are reliable. As Justice Marshall pointed out in his dissent in *Inadi,* during the course of a conspiracy, "the conspirator's interest is likely to lie in misleading the listener into believing the conspiracy stronger with more members (and different members) and other aims than it in fact has." Similarly, it is not clear that the four year-old in *White* would respond accurately when "excited" or understand the incentives undergirding the reliability of statements made to secure medical treatment.

But even assuming the Court's conclusions in this regard are accurate, its characterization of the issue is misleading. Requiring the prosecution to produce witnesses who have made hearsay statements does not mean that those statements have to be *replaced* by live testimony. The Confrontation Clause merely speaks of confronting accusers, not of barring all out-of-court statements. The danger in the Court's reasoning is that the defendant might be denied cross-examination of key witnesses against her.

Of course, as *Inadi* indicated, the Compulsory Process Clause permits the defendant to subpoena such witnesses and have them declared "hostile" so that cross-examination may take place.[65] But this solution is not necessarily as fair as it might appear. First, this approach allows the prosecution to put the burden, financial and otherwise, on the defendant to produce the witnesses against her. Second, it puts the defense in the difficult tactical situation of deciding whether it wants to cross-examine the declarant before it has heard her direct testimony. Finally, it allows the prosecution to place the defendant in this tactical quandary any time it is not sure the live testimony will be as favorable to the state as the hearsay testimony. Illustrating the last two points, if a child such as the one in *White* exhibits confusion about the

65. See § 28.06(b) for further discussion of this aspect of the Compulsory Process Clause.

incident subsequent to her hearsay statements, under the Court's approach the prosecution can decide to present only the latter statements, in the hopes that the defense, unaware of the confusion,[66] will refrain from calling a witness who might merely repeat the content of the statements on the stand. The matter is exacerbated if the hearsay is "state-created:" that is, if—as was true of some of the "spontaneous declarations" in *White* —the original hearsay statement is made to a police officer or other government official who has some incentive to manipulate it.[67]

This analysis is not meant to deny the fact that, for many types of hearsay that fit into a traditional exception, the utility of confrontation, to use *Roberts'* language, will be remote. Consider, for instance, hearsay exceptions involving business entries, public records, ancient documents, commercial publications, or learned treatises.[68] As Professor Lilly suggests, requiring a showing of unavailability any time the prosecution seeks to rely on such sources would be unduly burdensome; rather admissibility should depend upon the "particular circumstances" of the case. Thus, "[a] business record containing important test results about blood or narcotics is likely to be treated differently from a business entry showing that an individual had a telephone installed and was assigned a certain number." [69]

(2) Other indicia of reliability. The above cases all involved firmly rooted hearsay exceptions. They did not address the holding in *Roberts* that, even if no firmly rooted hearsay exception is applicable, hearsay is admissible if it evidences other indicia of reliability. In *Idaho v. Wright,*[70] the Court held that, in such circumstances, there is a "presumption" of *in*admissibility which can only be overcome by "particularized guarantees of trustworthiness."

In *Wright,* the Court found inadmissible the out-of-court statements of the 2½ year-old daughter of the two defendants charged with abusing her. The trial court had admitted the statements, made to a pediatrician with considerable experience in abuse cases, on the ground that they appeared to be reliable,[71] and thus

---

66. Only if the confusion rises to a recantation that the prosecutor, in her judgment, considers "exculpatory," need it be revealed to the defense. See § 24.04(b).

67. Two members of the Court in *White*—Thomas and Scalia—tangentially recognized this latter point in a concurring opinion, but only in the course of arguing that application of the Confrontation Clause should be limited *solely* to statements to the government that are "contained in formalized testimonial materials, such as affidavits, deposi-

tions, prior testimony, or confessions." Thomas added the quoted limitation because otherwise the rule would be "difficult to apply."

68. See, e.g., Fed.R.Evid. 803(6)(8) (10)(16) & (18).

69. Lilly, "Notes on the Confrontation Clause and *Ohio v. Roberts,*" 37 U.Fla.L.Rev. 207 (1984).

70. 497 U.S. 805, 110 S.Ct. 3139 (1990).

71. The key statement, made in response to a question asking whether her

were admissible under Idaho's "residual exception" to the hearsay rule.[72] More specifically, the trial court found that (1) the child had no motive to make up a story about her parents; (2) the statements were not of the kind that would have been fabricated by one so young; (3) there was corroborating physical evidence of abuse; (4) the defendants had the opportunity to commit the abuse; and (5) the older daughter also identified the parents as the abusers. The state supreme court, applying *Roberts,* reversed the conviction on the ground that the statements lacked indicia of reliability because the doctor who conducted the interview had failed to videotape it, had asked leading questions, and had a preconceived idea of what the child should be disclosing.

The Supreme Court upheld the state appellate court, 5–4, but on different grounds. Justice O'Connor, writing for the Court, began by assuming that the residual hearsay exception under which the child's hearsay statement was admitted was not, "almost by definition," firmly rooted, given the lack of "longstanding judicial and legislative experience in assessing the trustworthiness" of statements admitted under this exception. O'Connor then concluded that, in light of the Confrontation Clause's purpose of assuring adversarial testing of the state's case, the only factors which should be considered in deciding the reliability question when a firmly rooted hearsay exception is not involved are "those that surround the making of the statement;" extrinsic evidence should not be relevant. She noted, for instance, that firmly rooted hearsay exceptions such as the excited utterance and dying declaration exceptions do not focus on the presence of corroborating evidence but rather on the circumstances attendant to the statement. When these circumstances indicate reliability, then adversarial testing is only of "marginal utility." On the other hand, she implied, when reliability of hearsay depends solely upon the amount of corroborating evidence, the adversary process might still be necessary to expose fabrication or inaccuracy on the part of the declarant, and the hearsay should be excluded.

Applying this analysis to the lower court's approach, O'Connor concluded that the final three factors considered by the trial court were irrelevant to the reliability determination, since they consisted of corroborating items. The presence of this supporting extrinsic evidence, although perhaps relevant to whether the admission of a particular statement was harmless, "would be no substitute for cross-examination of the declarant at trial." By

daddy touched her with his "pee-pee," was that "daddy does do this with me, but he does it a lot more with my sister than with me." According to the pediatrician, the child initially "sort of clammed-up" before responding to the question.

72. The exception, patterned on Federal Rule of Evidence 803(24), permits admission of "a statement not specifically covered by any of the foregoing exceptions but having equivalent circumstantial guarantees of trustworthiness. . . ."

the same token, the appellate court's emphasis on the lack of procedural protections during the doctor's interview was also of only tangential importance. While the way in which out-of-court statements are obtained may be relevant to the reliability assessment, courts should not impose "a preconceived and artificial litmus test for the procedural propriety of professional interviews in which children make hearsay statements against a defendant."

Instead, the primary considerations in this type of case should include the first two identified by the trial court and such factors as the spontaneity and consistency of the statements, the mental state of the declarant, and the type of terminology used. But even some of these factors might be suspect; for instance, O'Connor noted that spontaneity might be an inaccurate indicator of trustworthiness when, as here, there was evidence of prompting by adults. The Court concluded by stating that "given the presumption of inadmissibility accorded accusatory hearsay statements not admitted pursuant to a firmly rooted hearsay exception," the daughter's incriminating statements should have been excluded under the Confrontation Clause.

The dissent, written by Justice Kennedy, and joined by Chief Justice Rehnquist and Justices White and Blackmun, concentrated on the majority's refusal to consider corroborating evidence in assessing reliability. It pointed out that judging a statement in isolation might not only lead to exclusion of a statement which extrinsic evidence strongly suggests is reliable, but also might lead to admission of a statement which other evidence suggests is inaccurate. Moreover, Kennedy questioned whether the Court's analysis could be meaningfully applied *without* considering corroborating evidence. For instance, noting that motive to falsify was one of the majority's factors, he argued that "if the suspect charges that a third person concocted a false case against him and coached the child, surely it is relevant to show that the third person had no contact with the child or no opportunity to suggest false testimony."

(c) Availability of Declarant Required. If the prosecution does present the maker of out-of-court statements in the courtroom, and she is able to remember making the statements, the Confrontation Clause does not bar introduction of the hearsay (although state evidentiary rules might). In such cases, the Court does not require *any* assessment of reliability, given the availability of the declarant for cross-examination.

The first case to contemplate this conclusion was *California v. Green*,[73] which involved not only the admissibility of prior testimony by one of the prosecution's trial witnesses (discussed earlier),

73. 399 U.S. 149, 90 S.Ct. 1930 (1970).

but also the admissibility of prior out-of-court statements made to a police officer by that witness. Although the latter statements were not admissible under the prior testimony rule because they had not been subject to cross-examination, the majority suggested that they might nonetheless be admissible under some circumstances; it noted that neither the lower courts nor the parties had addressed whether the witness' "apparent lapse of memory so affected Green's right to cross-examine as to make a critical difference in the application of the Confrontation Clause." And Justice Harlan, in his concurring opinion, stated outright that, if a witness is subject to cross-examination, her out-of-court statement should not be barred merely because she is unable to "recall either the underlying events that are the subject of an extra-judicial statement or previous testimony or recollect the circumstances under which the statement was given."

In *United States v. Owens,*[74] the issue discussed in *Green* was directly confronted. There the victim of an assault, one Foster, could remember very little about the assault, or the conditions under which he made a pretrial statement about it to an FBI agent, because of head injuries suffered during the incident. In holding that Foster's pretrial statement, which implicated the defendant in the assault, was admissible, the Court followed Justice Harlan's reasoning in *Green.* Justice Scalia, writing for a six-member majority, concluded that the Confrontation Clause guarantees only the "opportunity to cross-examine" witnesses, not the right to an effective cross-examination. Here, that opportunity was afforded. During defense counsel's examination, Scalia noted, Foster had admitted that he could not remember: (1) seeing his assailant; (2) having visitors at the hospital other than the FBI agent (although he had had several other visitors); (3) hearing anyone suggest to him that the defendant was the assailant; or (4) attributing the assault to someone other than the defendant, as one hospital record suggested he had. Justice Brennan in dissent pointed out that none of this allowed the jury to evaluate the trustworthiness or reliability of the pretrial identification of the defendant as the assailant; neither Foster's perception at the time of the offense nor his memory of the offense at the time of his statement to the agent could be explored because he simply could not remember either event. But Scalia rejected the contention that the Confrontation Clause requires hearsay such as this to be examined for "indicia of reliability" or "particularized guarantees of trustworthiness". Echoing the Court's opinion in *Green* with respect to the admissibility of pretrial testimony, Scalia stated: "the traditional protections of the oath, cross-examination, and

74. 484 U.S. 554, 108 S.Ct. 838 (1988).

opportunity for the jury to observe the witness's demeanor satisfy the constitutional requirements."

It should be noted, however, that the declarant in *Owens* was "competent" and able to remember making the hearsay statements (although not able to remember their content). These facts might pose important limitations on the admissibility of hearsay by a declarant who is physically "available" to be cross-examined.

(d) Co–Defendant Confessions. A special type of confrontation case occurs when two or more co-defendants are tried together and the prosecution seeks to convict one of them by introducing her out-of-court stationhouse confession, which also happens to implicate one or more of the co-defendants. If, as is often the case, the maker of the statement refuses to testify (as is her right under the Fifth Amendment),[75] the other defendant or defendants have no "opportunity to cross-examine" her about the confession. Furthermore, although the assertion of the right to remain silent could be said to make the declarant "unavailable," that part of her out-of-court statement implicating another fits no firmly-rooted hearsay exception,[76] and is of questionable reliability, given the possible desire to avoid or reduce liability by placing blame on others.

When first confronted with this prosecutorial practice in the 1957 case of *Delli Paoli v. United States,*[77] the Court found no constitutional infirmity, provided that the jury is given a precautionary instruction directing it to consider the confession as evidence only against the defendant who made it. But eleven years later *Delli Paoli* was overruled in *Bruton v. United States.*[78] There, the Court concluded that the jury could not be expected to follow a precautionary instruction of the type mandated in *Delli Paoli,* and that, in any event, the infringement on the defendant's right of confrontation could not be cured by such an instruction.

The *Bruton* majority apparently contemplated that the prosecutor who wishes to use a confession implicating more than one defendant would have to try the defendants separately. Although Justice White argued in dissent that this solution would place a significant burden on witnesses, prosecutors and courts, it is not clear that this is so: if the confessing defendant is tried first and convicted (and thus no longer able to claim the Fifth Amendment), the second defendant, if really guilty, will often see the advantage of pleading to the charge rather than going to a trial at which the first defendant testifies.

75. See § 28.02(c).

76. That part of the statement which implicates its maker is admissible under the party admission doctrine. See, e.g., Fed.R.Evid. 801(d)(2)(A).

77. 352 U.S. 232, 77 S.Ct. 294 (1957).

78. 391 U.S. 123, 88 S.Ct. 1620 (1968). See also, *Douglas v. Alabama,* 380 U.S. 415, 85 S.Ct. 1074 (1965).

Nonetheless, resistance to the severance option has persisted. Two other solutions to the *"Bruton* problem," of questionable worth,[79] include bifurcated trials, in which the defendants are tried jointly but a verdict is reached with respect to the non-confessing defendant before the confession is introduced, and multiple trials, in which a separate jury is selected for each defendant and the jury for the non-confessing defendant does not hear the confession. Furthermore, since *Bruton,* the Court has indicated that there are several situations in which neither severance nor these other "separating" options are required.

(1) Redaction. In his *Bruton* dissent, Justice White noted that one alternative to severance was to delete (if the confession is in writing) or prohibit testimony about (if the statement is described by a witness) all references to defendants other than the maker. He also pointed out that this option would normally be of limited use, since very often the remaining segments of the confession will either make no sense or strongly suggest the participation of another individual, who the factfinder is likely to suspect is a co-defendant in the courtroom.

Nonetheless, in *Richardson v. Marsh,*[80] the Court sanctioned this practice so long as a proper limiting instruction is given and the confession is redacted to eliminate not only the defendant's name but any reference to her existence.[81] Justice Scalia, writing for the Court, admitted that members of the jury hearing such a confession might have difficulty obeying an instruction to disregard its possible inferences about the defendant, but "there does not exist the overwhelming probability of their inability to do so that is the foundation of *Bruton's* exception to the general rule."

The three dissenters disagreed with this conclusion, supporting their position by pointing to the facts of *Marsh,* which involved a prosecution for assault and murder, committed in the course of a robbery. The redacted confession in *Marsh* described a conversation between Marsh's two co-defendants that took place in a car on the way to the scene of the robbery and murder. During the conversation, one of the co-defendants stated that the victims would have to be killed after the robbery. Although the confession did not mention Marsh, other trial evidence made clear she was in the car with the two co-defendants at the time of this conversation. Thus, the jury was sure to infer that Marsh knew about the plans to commit murder unless she could show she did not hear the conversation. Although she so testified (apparently

79. See Gaynes, "Two Juries/One Trial: Panacea of Judicial Economy or Personification of Murphy's Law?" 5 Am.J.Trial Advoc. 285 (1981).

80. 481 U.S. 200, 107 S.Ct. 1702 (1987).

81. The Court did not express an opinion on the admissibility of a confession in which the defendant's name has been replaced with a symbol or neutral pronoun, so these practices may still violate the Confrontation Clause.

stating that she was in the backseat and that the radio was on), she was prevented from questioning the two co-defendants as to whether they thought she had heard their conversation because they refused to testify.

(2) Testimony by the maker of the confession. Not surprisingly, given the confrontation basis of *Bruton,* the Court has found that *Bruton* is not controlling when the confessing defendant takes the stand and denies the inculpatory admission. The majority in *Nelson v. O'Neil* [82] concluded that the opportunity to cross-examine the declarant at trial, at least when she repudiates the confession, sufficiently protects the non-confessing defendant's right of confrontation. Given the Court's more recent holding in *Owens,* discussed above, it would seem that the crucial issue under current confrontation analysis is whether the declarant is subject to cross-examination; whether she repudiates the out-of-court statements is probably no longer dispositive.

(3) Interlocking confessions. Another situation in which *Bruton* is not violated by a joint trial is when the defendant implicated by another's statement has also confessed, and the confessions are very similar in material detail. In *Parker v. Randolph,* [83] which first announced this rule, a plurality of the Court reasoned that, when "interlocking" confessions are involved, a precautionary instruction like that endorsed in *Delli Paoli* was sufficient to protect the defendant's confrontation right. But in *Cruz v. New York,* [84] five members of the Court, in an opinion by Justice Scalia, found "illogical" the notion that juries are more likely to obey limiting instructions in interlocking confession cases than in other cases. Instead, the Court upheld use of interlocking confessions by borrowing from the *Roberts–Inadi* analysis; Scalia reasoned that the similarity of the confessions is relevant in deciding whether a co-defendant's confession has sufficient "indicia of reliability" to be *directly* admissible against the defendant (in either a joint *or* a severed trial).

While interlocking confessions may thus be admissible despite the absence of confrontation, *Lee v. Illinois,* [85] which was decided between *Parker* and *Cruz* but was affirmed by *Cruz,* suggests that the similarity between the two confessions must be significant for this doctrine to be triggered. *Lee* involved prosecution use of a confession by one Thomas against the petitioner Lee, during a joint trial of Lee and Thomas for a double murder. While many of the facts in Thomas' and Lee's confessions were identical, Justice Brennan's opinion for five members of the Court concluded that

---

82. 402 U.S. 622, 91 S.Ct. 1723 (1971).

83. 442 U.S. 62, 99 S.Ct. 2132 (1979).

84. 481 U.S. 186, 107 S.Ct. 1714 (1987).

85. 476 U.S. 530, 106 S.Ct. 2056 (1986).

they diverged with respect to Lee's participation in the planning of one victim's death, her facilitation of the murder of the other victim, and the factual circumstances relevant to the premeditation exhibited by the two perpetrators. Thus, "[t]he subjects upon which these two confessions do not 'interlock' cannot in any way be characterized as irrelevant or trivial."

As Professor Kirst points out, there are several good reasons for prohibiting introduction of an accomplice's confession against another defendant even when the confessions are entirely identical. First, the hearsay here is "created" by the government, and thus is more subject to manipulation. Relatedly, the mere fact that confessions coincide does not mean they are "reliable." Third, and most importantly in terms of the image associated with "confrontation," *Cruz* comes close to allowing the type of trial by "affidavit" which *Mattox* denigrated. If the police can obtain "identical" confessions from two codefendants, they can both be convicted solely on documentary evidence, a significant part of which was created *ex parte;* unlike other hearsay situations, even compulsory process will not avoid this possibility, given the Fifth Amendment barrier.[86]

(4) Non-hearsay use. A final exception to *Bruton* was formulated in *Tennessee v. Street,*[87] where the defendant claimed that his confession was entitled to no weight because it was a coerced imitation of his accomplice's confession. To rebut this claim, the state called the sheriff to read the accomplice's confession to the jury, which was significantly different than the defendant's. The judge allowed the confession to be read, instructing the jury that it was to be considered only to rebut the defendant's imitation claim, not prove the truth of its contents (which implicated the defendant). A unanimous Court upheld this ruling, pointing out that the accomplice's confession was introduced for the nonhearsay purpose of comparing the confessions and proving the defendant's confession was not coerced; accordingly, unlike the typical *Bruton* situation, cross-examination of the alleged accomplice would serve no purpose.

28.05 Challenging Witnesses in the Courtroom

When a prosecution witness does appear in court, two issues arise: when, if ever, the defendant may be denied a face-to-face encounter with that witness, and the extent to which cross-examination of the witness may be limited.

(a) The Right to a Face-to-Face Encounter. In lay terms, one does not "confront" another unless there is a face-to-face

---

86. Kirst, "The Procedural Dimension of the Confrontation Doctrine," 66 Neb.L.Rev. 485 (1987).

87. 471 U.S. 409, 105 S.Ct. 2078 (1985).

encounter. Nonetheless, under narrow circumstances, the state may prevent the accused from confronting prosecution witnesses who appear in court. In *Coy v. Iowa*,[88] the Court found unconstitutional a state law which permitted a large screen to be placed between the defendant and two 13 year-old girls who testified that he had sexually assaulted him. Justice Scalia, writing for the Court, emphasized that "the Confrontation Clause guarantees the defendant a face-to-face meeting with witnesses appearing before the trier of fact." But two members of the six-member majority appeared to disagree with this latter statement. Justice O'Connor wrote a concurring opinion, joined by Justice White, which noted that the statute in *Coy presumed* that trauma would occur any time a youthful victim testified in such a case. She suggested that had there been an individualized finding that the child witnesses needed special protection, she might support a different result.

In *Maryland v. Craig*,[89] such a finding was made by the trial court pursuant to a Maryland statute which permits a one-way television procedure if the judge determines that face-to-face testimony "will result in the child suffering serious emotional distress such that the child cannot reasonably communicate." Under the statute, once this finding is made, the witness, prosecutor, and defense counsel withdraw to a separate room; the judge, jury, and defendant remain in the courtroom. The defendant can watch direct and cross-examination of the child over the video hookup and remains in electronic communication with his counsel. In a 5–4 decision, the Court upheld this procedure, in an opinion written by O'Connor.

Although recognizing that requiring a face-to-face encounter between defendant and witness forms the "core" of the Confrontation Clause, the majority concluded that the "central concern" of the Clause "is to ensure the reliability of the evidence against a criminal defendant by subjecting it to rigorous testing in the context of an adversary proceeding before the trier of fact." According to O'Connor, this goal can be met even without a face-to-face encounter if other elements of confrontation—physical presence of the accused, oath, cross-examination of the witness, and observation of the witness' demeanor by the trier of fact—are present. Thus actual confrontation, although important, is not an "absolute" requirement.

On the other hand, she cautioned, it may be dispensed with only if "necessary to further an important public policy and only where the reliability of the testimony is otherwise assured." Since the Maryland procedure provided the defendant with all the above-described components of confrontation except the face-to-

88. 487 U.S. 1012, 108 S.Ct. 2798 (1988).

89. 497 U.S. 836, 110 S.Ct. 3157 (1990).

face encounter, and consequently "does not impinge upon the truth-seeking or symbolic purposes of the Confrontation Clause," the "critical inquiry" here was the importance of the state's interest in protecting child witnesses. On this point, the Court relied heavily on the fact that a "significant majority" of the states had enacted statutes similar to Maryland's, reflecting the states' traditional interest in protecting the welfare of children and "a growing body of academic literature documenting the psychological trauma suffered by child abuse victims who must testify in court." Accordingly, so long as the trial court determines on a case-by-case basis that such trauma will result if the child is faced with the defendant, the Confrontation Clause is not violated. The Court further held that this individualized decision need not be based on observation of the child in the presence of the defendant. Nor need the trial court explore less restrictive alternatives than the one-way television procedure permitted under Maryland law.

In dissent, Justice Scalia, joined by Justices Brennan, Marshall and Stevens, quoted from his opinion in *Coy:* "[F]ace-to-face presence may, unfortunately, upset the truthful rape victim or abused child; but by the same token it may confound and undo the false accuser, or reveal the child coached by a malevolent adult." He found the state's interest in protecting children more than offset by the defendant's interest in exposing erroneous testimony by children, who are especially manipulable by other adults or likely to confuse fact with fantasy.

(b) The Right to Cross–Examine. As the Supreme Court stated in *Pointer v. Texas,*[90] the decision which applied the Confrontation Clause to the states, "probably no one, certainly no one with experience in the trial of lawsuits, would deny the value of cross-examination in exposing falsehood and bringing out the truth in the trial of a criminal case." Of course, the Court's cases permitting prosecution use of hearsay have seriously undermined the defendant's ability to cross-examine the witnesses against her.[91] But, when the prosecution does present a witness, significant state or court imposed limitations on cross-examination have consistently been rejected by the Court. At the same time, the Court has carefully distinguished between such limitations and other reasons why cross-examination may not be effective.

(1) State-imposed limitations. A number of cases demonstrate the Court's consistent willingness to safeguard the defendant's right to cross-examine prosecution witnesses against court rulings or state evidentiary rules which inhibit the right. In

90. 380 U.S. 400, 85 S.Ct. 1065 (1965).   **91.** See § 28.04.

Smith v. Illinois,[92] for instance, the Court reversed the conviction of a defendant when a prosecution witness who was also a police informant was allowed to conceal his true identity during cross-examination. Although cross-examination was otherwise permitted, this identifying information was viewed as basic material which "opens countless avenues of in-court examination and out-of-court investigation." Moreover, reasoned the Court, such information and the cross-examination it provokes are necessary for jurors to test properly the weight and credibility of a witness' testimony. These factors outweighed any government interest in avoiding revelation of an informant's identity.

Similarly, a state's interest in protecting the anonymity of juvenile criminal offenders does not outweigh a defendant's right to cross-examine witnesses. In *Davis v. Alaska,*[93] the state's chief witness at the defendant's burglary trial was a juvenile who was himself on probation for two burglaries at the time of the crime and at the time of his identification of the accused. Defense counsel sought to bring out this information for the purpose of showing that the witness may have made a hasty and faulty identification of the defendant in order to shift suspicion away from himself or in order to avoid revocation of probation by police who felt he was being uncooperative. But the trial court prohibited him from doing so under authority of a state rule which bars introduction of any juvenile court adjudication except where the trial judge views its use as appropriate. In the Supreme Court, the state argued that this rule protected against further delinquent acts by juvenile offenders and improved their chances for rehabilitation because it prevented potential employers and associates from discovering their youthful transgressions. But the Court, concluding that "[s]erious damage to the strength of the State's case would have been a real possibility had petitioner been allowed to pursue [his] line of inquiry," held by a 7–2 margin that "the right of confrontation is paramount to the State's policy of protecting a juvenile offender."

While cross-examination was merely inhibited in *Smith* and *Davis, Chambers v. Mississippi,*[94] involved a state rule which operated to deny any cross-examination. There, the defendant sought to cross-examine one MacDonald, who had confessed on three separate occasions to the murder with which the defendant was charged (although he later repudiated the confessions). Because the state did not put MacDonald on the state, the defense had to call him. When the defense sought to treat MacDonald as an adverse witness, the trial court judge prohibited cross-examina-

92. 390 U.S. 129, 88 S.Ct. 748 (1968).

93. 415 U.S. 308, 94 S.Ct. 1105 (1974).

94. 410 U.S. 284, 93 S.Ct. 1038 (1973).

tion, on the authority of the state's "voucher" rule, which assumed that the party calling a witness vouches for her credibility. The Supreme Court unanimously reversed the ensuing conviction, reasoning that because MacDonald's confessions tended to exculpate the defendant, his repudiation tended to inculpate the defendant; thus, the trial court's application of the voucher rule abridged the right to cross-examine a clearly adverse witness. As Justice Powell stated for the Court: "The availability of the right to confront and cross-examine those who give damaging testimony against the accused has never been held to depend on whether the witness was initially put on the stand by the accused or by the State."

(2) Discovery for impeachment purposes. An argument could be made that the government abridges the right to cross-examine its witnesses when it fails to provide impeachment material. In *United States v. Augenblick,*[95] the defendant contended that his right of confrontation (as well as his prerogative under the Jencks Act[96]) was denied when the government failed to produce tapes containing previous statements of a person who had testified at the defendant's trial. The Court found no constitutional or statutory violation occurred because the government had made a diligent effort to find the tapes. But it added that, "in some situations, denial of production of a Jencks Act type of a statement might be a denial of a Sixth Amendment right."

In *United States v. Bagley,*[97] however, the Court held that the Sixth Amendment does not entitle the defendant to any impeachment evidence beyond what the prosecution must already surrender under the Court's Due Process Clause cases, which limit the prosecutorial duty of discovery disclosure to those items which have "exculpatory" significance.[98] As the Court stated in *Bagley,* "failure [of the prosecutor] to assist the defense by disclosing information that might have been helpful in conducting . . . cross-examination . . . amounts to a constitutional violation . . . only if the evidence is material in the sense that its suppression undermines confidence in the outcome of the trial." The Court went on to hold that no constitutional violation occurred when the prosecution intentionally withheld from the defense the fact that two of its witnesses signed an agreement, giving them money in return for their testimony and "the accomplishment of the objective sought to be obtained by use of such information."

Similarly, in *Pennsylvania v. Ritchie,*[99] the Court held that refusal on the part of a state child welfare agency to provide

95. 393 U.S. 348, 89 S.Ct. 528 (1969).

96. 18 U.S.C.A. § 3500 (providing for disclosure to the defense of prior testimony of any government witness testifying at trial). See § 24.01.

97. 473 U.S. 667, 105 S.Ct. 3375 (1985).

98. See § 24.04.

99. 480 U.S. 39, 107 S.Ct. 989 (1987).

defense counsel with copies of a report on the defendant's daughter, who was allegedly molested by the defendant, did not violate the Sixth Amendment. Although the rationale for this refusal was similar to that given by the trial court in *Davis* for limiting defense cross-examination of a juvenile witness, the Court distinguished the cases by noting that here the defense's cross-examination at trial was not restricted in any way.[1] Justice Blackmun argued in dissent that the state should not be able to avoid the Confrontation Clause "simply by deciding to hinder the defendant's right to effective cross-examination . . . at the pretrial, rather than at the trial, stage."

(3) Witness-created limitations. When the inability to cross-examine is due to something other than a court ruling or state rule, the Court has been even more unwilling to find the Confrontation Clause implicated. For instance, in *Delaware v. Fensterer,*[2] the defendant was convicted in part on the testimony of the state's expert witness, who could not remember the scientific test he had used to form his opinion. Because this lack of memory was not the fault of the state or the trial court, the Court found no Sixth Amendment violation, despite the deleterious effect it had on defense counsel's ability to discredit the expert's testimony. Borrowing from its hearsay cases,[3] the Court concluded that the Confrontation Clause guarantees only the "opportunity" to cross-examine, not an effective cross-examination.

Similarly, in *United States v. Owens,*[4] discussed earlier in connection with the admission of hearsay, the Court held irrelevant to confrontation analysis the fact that the prosecution witness, who was the victim of the assault for which the defendant was tried, could not remember the assault or any of the surrounding events. So long as the defendant was not denied the opportunity to cross-examine the witness and was thus able to point out to the jury the fact of the memory loss, no Sixth Amendment violation occurred.

28.06 Compulsory Process and the Right to Present Evidence

In *Washington v. Texas,*[5] the decision which applied the Compulsory Process Clause to the states, the Supreme Court stated that this Sixth Amendment provision implicates "[t]he right to offer the testimony of witnesses, and to compel their attendance

1. However, the majority did remand the case to the trial court for the purpose of determining whether the report contained "material" information that should have been revealed to the defense. For further discussion of this aspect of *Ritchie,* see § 24.04(c).

2. 474 U.S. 15, 106 S.Ct. 292 (1985).

3. See, e.g., *California v. Green,* 399 U.S. 149, 90 S.Ct. 1930 (1970), discussed in § 28.04(c).

4. 484 U.S. 554, 108 S.Ct. 838 (1988).

5. 388 U.S. 14, 87 S.Ct. 1920 (1967).

[and] the right to present the defendant's version of the facts as well as the prosecution's to the jury so that it may decide where the truth lies." In short, the Compulsory Process Clause implements the right of the defendant to present a defense. Echoing *Washington,* subsequent cases have found that the Clause, either by itself or in conjunction with other constitutional provisions, guarantees the defendant the right to testify, the right to subpoena witnesses, and the right to examine those witnesses. These three aspects of the Compulsory Process Clause are discussed here.

(a) **The Defendant's Right to Testify.** Although as recently as the 18th century, English courts refused to allow defendants to testify on the ground that such testimony would be self-serving, this rule fell into disrepute by the next century.[6] On several recent occasions, the Supreme Court appeared to recognize a right to testify in one's own behalf.[7] However, the constitutional status of the right was not explicitly established until 1987, in *Rock v. Arkansas.*[8] In *Rock,* Justice Blackmun, writing for the Court, found that the right derived from three different constitutional provisions: the Due Process Clause's guarantee of fairness, the Compulsory Process Clause's guarantee that the defendant may call witnesses in her favor, and the Fifth Amendment's protection of silence unless the defendant "chooses to speak in the unfettered exercise of his own will." Underlying all of these provisions, Blackmun concluded, is the notion that the right to testify is necessary to facilitate the truth-seeking function of trial.[9]

Blackmun also stressed that the right to testify is not absolute. It may be restricted to accommodate "legitimate interests in the criminal trial process," so long as the restrictions are not "arbitrary or disproportionate to the purposes they are designed to serve." The question before the Court in *Rock* was whether a state rule barring post-hypnosis testimony was a permissible restriction on the right to testify. Conceding that memories induced through hypnosis can be fabricated or distorted, Blackmun found nonetheless that a *per se* rule such as Arkansas' is unconstitutional because it does not take into account the reasons for undergoing hypnosis, the circumstances under which it took place, or any independent verification of the information it produced. Nor does it recognize that cross-examination, expert testimony and cautionary instructions might counteract the inadequacies of post-hypnotic testimony. A case-by-case approach is mandated, held Black-

---

6. See, e.g., *McVeigh v. United States,* 78 U.S. (11 Wall.) 259 (1870).

7. *Faretta v. California,* 422 U.S. 806, 95 S.Ct. 2525 (1975); *Brooks v. Tennessee,* 406 U.S. 605, 92 S.Ct. 1891 (1972); *Harris v. New York,* 401 U.S. 222, 91 S.Ct. 643 (1971).

8. 479 U.S. 1079, 107 S.Ct. 1276 (1987).

9. For similar reasons, once the defendant takes the stand, she may not avoid cross-examination. See § 15.02(a) (4).

mun, unless the state can show "that hypnotically enhanced testimony is always so untrustworthy and so immune to the traditional means of evaluating credibility that it should disable a defendant from presenting her version of the events for which she is on trial." In dissent, Chief Justice Rehnquist, joined by three others, argued that "until there is a much more general consensus on the use of hypnosis than there is now, the Constitution does not warrant this Court's mandating its own view of how to deal with the issue."

(b) The Right to Subpoena Witnesses. The Compulsory Process Clause guarantees the defendant the use of subpoenas to obtain witnesses, documents and objects that are useful to her defense. Each state has statutory rules implementing this right,[10] used primarily to procure evidence the defense will present in its case-in-chief. But subpoenas may also be relied upon to obtain prosecution witnesses whom the prosecution does not have to present in court; indeed, recent Supreme Court cases allowing the prosecution to introduce hearsay have justified their holdings in part on the defendant's ability to subpoena available witnesses that the prosecution has decided not to present.[11] Although, for reasons discussed earlier in this chapter,[12] placing the burden on the defense to produce prosecution witnesses is both conceptually and practically flawed, the Sixth Amendment subpoena power is likely to be used increasingly as a means of ensuring that key components of the prosecution's case are not based on extrajudicial statements. Thus the scope of the subpoena power is more important than ever.

The Supreme Court has adopted a balancing test in deciding whether the right to subpoena has been infringed, weighing the government's interest in avoiding the cost or inconvenience of helping to produce the witness against the defendant's need for the witness in question. In *Roviaro v. United States*,[13] the government refused to disclose to the defendant, who was charged with transportation of narcotics, the true identity of an informer who had not only received from the defendant a package allegedly containing heroin but had been the only witness to the transaction. The Supreme Court took notice of the government's need to withhold the identity of informants in order to maintain the flow of information from undercover sources, but found it outweighed by the defendant's interest in the testimony of this informant, who

---

10. The federal rules, for instance, grant the indigent defendant power to subpoena any witness "necessary to an adequate defense." Fed.R.Crim.P. 17(b).

11. See, e.g., *United States v. Inadi*, 475 U.S. 387, 106 S.Ct. 1121 (1986);

White v. Illinois, 502 U.S. ___, 112 S.Ct. 736 (1992).

12. See § 28.04(b)(1).

13. 353 U.S. 53, 77 S.Ct. 623 (1957).

"might have disclosed an entrapment . . . thrown doubt upon petitioner's identity or on the identity of the package, [or] testified to petitioner's lack of knowledge of the contents of the package that he 'transported.' "

Perhaps undercutting *Roviaro* to some extent is the Court's holding in *United States v. Valenzuela-Bernal*,[14] where the defendant was charged with transporting illegal aliens. Upon the arrest of the defendant and the three individuals in his car, the immigration authorities determined that two of the three passengers were not needed for the prosecution's case and deported them pursuant to immigration bureau policy. The defendant argued that since this deportation made it impossible for him to interview these witnesses prior to trial and to subpoena them for trial he was denied his right to compulsory process.

The Supreme Court, in an opinion authored by Justice Rehnquist, noted that the government had an obligation to deport illegal aliens and that holding cells for illegal aliens were extremely overcrowded. Balanced against these reasons for deporting the individuals seized with the defendant was the defendant's right to witnesses favorable and material to his defense, which Rehnquist found to be weak. Rehnquist rejected the materiality test developed by the court of appeals, which asked whether any "conceivable benefit" might accrue from the deported individuals' presence at trial. Instead, he opted for a standard requiring that defendants provide "some explanation of how [absent witnesses] would have been favorable and material." Here, he found this test not met because the defendant had offered no plausible reason why he would need the two deported individuals in addition to the one who remained. To convict the defendant, the government needed only to show that the defendant knew the third, remaining individual was an alien who had entered the country in the past three years; that individual, Rehnquist pointed out, was fully available for examination. The fact that the other two individuals were eyewitnesses to the incident was not enough.

In dissent, Justice Brennan, joined by Justice Marshall, noted that no inordinate delay in pursuing immigration policies would have been occasioned by postponing the deportation of the first two individuals found in the defendant's car. He also pointed out that in *Roviaro* the Court had not required the defendant to explain how the informant would be useful to him but had merely suggested how he *might* have been helpful. Finally, he noted that the defendant could not be counted upon to give anything more than speculative reasons for requiring the presence of the witnesses when he had not been able to interview them. Indulging in

14. 458 U.S. 858, 102 S.Ct. 3440 (1982).

such speculation, Brennan reasoned, that the deported individuals could have testified as to the defendant's lack of knowledge with respect to their identity and perhaps concerning whether they had helped entrap the defendant.

Valenzuela-Bernal may have heightened the materiality showing required by the Compulsory Process Clause. It would seem that the government interest in protecting informants (at issue in *Roviaro*) is more important than its interest in reducing the number of aliens incarcerated in this country, especially since, as Brennan points out, deportation can take place after trial. Thus, the proof of materiality necessary to outweigh the government's interest in *Valenzuela-Bernal* should have been correspondingly lower than was necessary in *Roviaro*. But the Court's application of its "some explanation" test in that case appeared to require a *greater* showing of materiality than did the *Roviaro* Court. Put another way, *Valenzuela-Bernal* gives more power to the prosecution to decide what is "material" to the defense's case, a tendency also evident in the Court's confrontation cases.[15]

(c) **The Right to Present Evidence.** Literally read, the Compulsory Process Clause guarantees only the power to subpoena witnesses, not the right to have those witnesses testify. But the Supreme Court has rejected that interpretation of the Clause; in *Washington v. Texas,*[16] for instance, the Court stated that "[t]he Framers of the Constitution did not intend to commit the futile act of giving to a defendant the right to secure the attendance of witnesses whose testimony he had no right to use."[17] Instead, analogous to its confrontation cases dealing with cross-examination, the Court has generally disapproved government rules or practices inhibiting or prohibiting direct examination or presentation of other evidence, unless the defense has engaged in misconduct. A separate issue is whether the Clause permits the defendant to immunize witnesses who may have testimony favorable to the defense.

(1) State-imposed limitations; generally. Several cases illustrate the Court's willingness to protect the defendant's opportunity to present evidence on her behalf, regardless of state rules to the contrary. In *Washington,* for instance, the Court struck down a statute which prohibited accomplices from testifying for each

---

15. See, e.g., *United States v. Bagley,* 473 U.S. 667, 105 S.Ct. 3375 (1985), discussed in § 28.05(b)(2). Compare also the minimal showing the government must make to obtain a subpoena, discussed in § 23.05(a)(1).

16. 388 U.S. 14, 87 S.Ct. 1920 (1967).

17. But see, *Taylor v. Illinois,* 484 U.S. 400, 108 S.Ct. 646 (1988) (affirming *Washington,* but finding the argument that the Clause guarantees only subpoena power "supported by the plain language of the Clause, by the historical evidence . . . by some scholarly comment, and by a brief excerpt from the legislative history of the Clause.").

other, a rule apparently based on the theory that accomplices are likely to perjure themselves in an effort to gain acquittal for their colleagues in crime.　Noting that perjury is more likely to be committed by accomplices who testify for the prosecution in an effort to shift blame to others, the Court concluded that the statute was "absurd."　It was also found arbitrary, because it prevented "whole categories of defense witnesses from testifying on the basis of *a priori* categories that presume them worthy of unbelief."　Instead, stated the Court, the state must allow the defendant to present a witness "who was physically and mentally capable of testifying to events that he had personally observed, and whose testimony would have been relevant and material to his defense."

The Court's implicit trust of the jury system's ability to gauge credibility was reaffirmed in *Webb v. Texas,*[18] where it reversed, on due process grounds, the conviction of a defendant whose sole witness refused to testify after the trial judge harshly admonished him not to lie on the stand.　Holding that the judge's lengthy comments "effectively drove the witness off the stand," the Court concluded that, whatever the judge's belief as to the veracity of the witness, the jury should have been allowed to determine "where the truth lies."　For much the same reason, the same term the Court held, in *Cool v. United States,*[19] that a defendant was deprived of his right to compulsory process when the trial court instructed the jury that exculpatory testimony of an accomplice should be disregarded unless the jury decided that such testimony was true beyond a reasonable doubt.　The Court also noted that the instruction reduced the government's burden below the reasonable doubt standard.

Other Court cases have also conflated compulsory process and due process concerns in upholding defense attempts to put on material evidence.　For instance, in *Chambers v. Mississippi,*[20] discussed earlier in connection with the Confrontation Clause, the defendant sought to prove that one MacDonald had actually committed the murder with which the defendant was charged. Part of his proof in this regard was to be the testimony of three individuals to whom MacDonald had confessed that he had committed the murder (although all of these confessions were later repudiated).　The trial court refused to allow this testimony on the ground that it was hearsay and that Mississippi law did not recognize an exception for declarations against penal interest (although it did recognize an exception for declarations against pecuniary interest).　A unanimous Court overturned Chambers' conviction, noting that each of MacDonald's confessions had been

---

18.　409 U.S. 95, 93 S.Ct. 351 (1972).　　**20.**　410 U.S. 284, 93 S.Ct. 1038

19.　409 U.S. 100, 93 S.Ct. 354 (1972).　　(1973).

made spontaneously to a close acquaintance shortly after the murder, that the confessions were corroborated (by, e.g., testimony that MacDonald had been seen with a gun shortly after the shooting), that in this case MacDonald stood to gain little and to lose much by confessing, and that in any event he was in the courtroom and could be cross-examined by the state. Holding that "the hearsay rule may not be applied mechanistically to defeat the ends of justice," the Court concluded that "the exclusion of this critical evidence, coupled with the State's refusal to permit Chambers to cross-examine MacDonald,[21] denied him a trial in accord with traditional and fundamental standards of due process." Although framed in due process terms, the compulsory process overtones are apparent.

Similarly, in *Crane v. Kentucky,*[22] the Court held that the state may not exclude "competent, reliable evidence bearing on the credibility of a confession when such evidence is central to the defendant's claim of innocence," because "[w]hether rooted directly in the Due Process Clause . . . or in the Compulsory Process or Confrontation Clauses . . . the Constitution guarantees criminal defendants a 'meaningful opportunity to present a complete defense.' " In *Crane* the defendant wanted to produce extrinsic evidence suggesting his confession was unreliable because it had been obtained when the defendant, a young, uneducated boy, had allegedly been kept against his will in a small, windowless room for a protracted period of time until he confessed to every unsolved crime in the county, including the one he was tried for. The state courts had rejected this testimony on the ground that it was relevant only to the admissibility of the confession, not its credibility once the confession was found voluntary. Noting that there was no physical evidence connecting the defendant to the crime and that the state offered no rational justification for the exclusion of this body of evidence, the Court unanimously reversed the state courts.

When, in contrast to the type of evidence involved in *Chambers* and *Crane,* the evidence the defense seeks to introduce cannot easily be characterized as "competent" and "reliable," the result may be different. In *United States v. Salerno,*[23] the defendant sought to introduce hearsay statements made at his grand jury proceeding by two individuals who refused to repeat the testimony at trial on Fifth Amendment grounds. The prosecution sought to exclude the hearsay on the authority of Federal Rule of Evidence 804(a)(1), which permits introduction of testimony given at another hearing only when the "party against whom the testimony is

---

21. See discussion of *Chambers* in § 28.05(b)(1).

22. 476 U.S. 683, 106 S.Ct. 2142 (1986).

23. 502 U.S. ___, 112 S.Ct. 2503 (1992).

now offered . . . had an opportunity and similar motive to develop the testimony by direct, cross, or redirect examination." While remanding the case to determine whether the prosecution had had "an opportunity and similar motive" to cross-examine the two individuals during the grand jury hearing,[24] the Court, with only one member dissenting, rejected the defendant's contention that "adversarial fairness" permits the trial court to ignore the similar motive limitation at the defendant's request. The Court based this ruling on its interpretation of the rule rather than on constitutional grounds, but the tone of the opinion suggests that neither the Sixth Amendment nor the Due Process Clause requires admission of hearsay which does not fit within a hearsay exception or at least bears some other indicia of reliability.[25]

(2) Sanctions for defense misconduct. When the state seeks to exclude defense evidence as a sanction, the Court has veered away from the general rule that the defense should be permitted to present relevant and competent information on its behalf. The first case endorsing this view was *Taylor v. Illinois*,[26] where the Court approved the trial court's exclusion of a defense witness in an attempted murder case because he had not been listed on the defense's witness list, in violation of state discovery rules. The Court, in an opinion by Justice Stevens, emphasized that the violation had been "willful and blatant," in that the defense attorney had not mentioned the witness until the second day of trial, even though he had visited the witness a week before and had known his name for much longer. Stevens also asserted that trial courts have a "vital interest in protecting the trial process from the pollution of perjured testimony," and noted the trial judge's statement, after conducting a *voir dire* of the witness, doubting his veracity.[27]

As Justice Brennan, joined by two others, pointed out in dissent, the possibility that a witness might lie had never before been thought to prohibit competent witnesses from testifying for the defense. Rather, cases like *Washington* and *Webb* had left that determination up to the jury. A continuance would have

---

24. Justice Stevens, in dissent, argued that the remand was unnecessary, since the prosecution always has the "opportunity and motive" to cross-examine hostile witnesses at a grand jury proceeding, even if that opportunity is not exercised due to a fear of undermining grand jury secrecy or a decision to undermine the witness in other ways.

25. Compare § 28.04(b)(2).

26. 484 U.S. 400, 108 S.Ct. 646 (1988). Earlier cases had avoided the issue. See, e.g., *Williams v. Florida,*

399 U.S. 78, 90 S.Ct. 1893 (1970); *Wardius v. Oregon,* 412 U.S. 470, 93 S.Ct. 2208 (1973).

27. Apparently, the basis for the judge's doubt about the witness, aside from the "eleventh hour" nature of his appearance, was that he claimed to have warned the defendant just prior to the shooting that the victim had weapons and was out to get him, but also admitted that he had not formally met the defendant until two years after the incident.

been less inimical to the truth-finding process than exclusion, while preventing any prejudice to the prosecution (indeed, in this case even a continuance might not have been necessary, since the prosecution participated in the witness' *voir dire*).[28]   As to the need to sanction discovery violations, Brennan noted that the violation here was by the attorney, not the defendant; direct punishment of the attorney would have been much fairer.   The majority had anticipated this point by concluding that the defendant should be bound by his lawyer's "tactical" decisions.[29]   But here, as Brennan pointed out, the judge was dealing with obvious misconduct, not a tactical error that becomes clearly so only in hindsight and thus can more fairly bind the client.[30]

Despite these arguments, three years later the Court reinforced *Talyor's* message that a defendant can be prevented from presenting material evidence as a sanction for his attorney's misconduct.   In *Michigan v. Lucas,*[31] the trial judge in a rape trial excluded evidence about the victim's past sexual conduct with the defendant because the defendant had failed to give notice within ten days of arraignment that he planned to present the evidence, as required by statute.   Although the Supreme Court remanded the case to determine whether exclusion was appropriate on the facts of *Lucas,* it held that, in principle, such exclusion was permissible.   Citing *Taylor,* it stated that the exclusion sanction, despite its severity, might be imposed if, for instance, the court found the defendant's failure was "willful misconduct" designed to obtain "a tactical advantage."   According to the Court, this rule was justified because the notice requirement at issue in *Lucas,* which is designed to allow the trial court to conduct a hearing considering the admissibility of the evidence, "serves legitimate state interests in protecting against surprise, harassment, and undue delay."[32]

As Justice Blackmun reminded in an opinion concurring with the result, the state also has an interest "in the full and truthful disclosure of critical facts."   He continued: "[I]t may be that, in most cases, preclusion will be 'disproportionate to the purposes

---

28. For further discussion of this point in the context of sanctions for discovery violations, see § 24.02(d).

29. In support of this notion, Stevens also noted the difficulty of determining who is responsible for a violation, since defendants can mislead attorneys about the identity or location of material witnesses.   Whatever the validity of this point generally, it did not apply here, since the defendant had told the attorney about the witness sometime before trial.

30. See § 32.04(c) for further discussion of tactical versus fundamental errors by the attorney.

31. ___ U.S. ___, 111 S.Ct. 1743 (1991).

32. The Court did not assess the constitutionality of the Michigan statute, but noted that "[i]t is not inconceivable" that its 10–day notice rule might be "overly restrictive."   It also reminded, however, that it had upheld other notice statutes.   See, e.g., Williams v. Florida, 399 U.S. 78, 90 S.Ct. 1893 (1970), discussed in § 24.02(a).

[the rule is] designed to serve.'" This would seem so in *Lucas,* where the discovery violation could not be attributed to the defendant, the excluded evidence was clearly relevant, and the prosecution could have been granted a continuance if necessary to counter prejudice to its case.

(3) Immunity for defense witnesses. In *Washington,* the Court cautioned that its decision guaranteeing the defendant the right to present a defense should not be construed "as disapproving testimonial privileges, such as the privilege against self-incrimination." This passage suggests that, in contrast to the power granted the prosecution,[33] the defense cannot seek to immunize witnesses who refuse to provide relevant information on Fifth Amendment grounds. This inequity can be justified on the ground that the prosecution grants immunity to further legitimate societal ends (e.g., as a means of obtaining evidence against more significant offenders), while giving the defense unfettered discretion to grant immunity might have the opposite effect (e.g., immunizing a significant offender to protect a minor offender). On the other hand, when the defendant can show that immunization will likely produce highly relevant information for the defense, and the prosecution cannot show a "strong countervailing interest" in preventing immunization, due process, if not the Compulsory Process Clause, might require that immunity be granted.[34]

28.07   Conclusion

This chapter discussed the various rights, most of them derived from the Sixth Amendment, that are meant to assure that trial and related proceedings arrive at just results. They can be summarized as follows:

(1) Under the Sixth Amendment, the defendant is entitled to insist that her trial, and most pretrial proceedings (other than the grand jury), be conducted in public. However, closure may be allowed (over First Amendment as well as Sixth Amendment objections) if the prosecution can show that: (a) an overriding interest requires protection (such as the need to protect witness privacy); (b) the closure is no broader than necessary to protect that interest; (c) reasonable alternatives are considered; and (d) findings adequate to support the closure are made.

(2) The Confrontation and Due Process Clauses guarantee the defendant the right to be present, while competent, at trial and at all other critical proceedings at which her presence would contribute to the fairness of the prosecution. However, a conviction in absentia is permissible if the defendant intentionally avoids trial

33. See § 15.03(c).

34. See, e.g., *Government of Virgin Islands v. Smith,* 615 F.2d 964 (3d Cir. 1980).

or is disruptive in the courtroom. The prosecution may not comment on the defendant's failure to take the stand (under the Fifth Amendment) or force her to wear jail garb over her objection (under the Due Process Clause).

(3) The right of confrontation does not bar prosecution reliance on hearsay evidence when (a) the hearsay is pretrial testimony by an unavailable declarant who the defendant, through counsel, had the opportunity to subject to cross-examination; (b) the hearsay is admissible under a firmly rooted hearsay exception (e.g., the dying declaration, co-conspirator or spontaneous utterance exceptions), or otherwise seems particularly reliable; or (c) the declarant is subject to cross-examination at trial.

(4) Under the Confrontation Clause, the prosecution must sever the trials of co-defendants when it plans to use a confession from one defendant that implicates both unless: (a) the confessing defendant testifies, repudiates the confession, and is subject to cross-examination; (b) the name and references to the non-confessing defendant are deleted from the confession and the jury is instructed to disregard possible inferences about the defendant; (c) both defendants confess and the confessions are virtually identical (in which case both confessions are admissible in a severed trial as well); or (d) the confession is used solely for a non-hearsay purposes.

(5) The Confrontation Clause guarantees the defendant a face-to-face encounter with accusers whom the prosecution presents unless separation is necessary to further an important public policy, such as protection of child witnesses who have been found in need of protection, and the reliability of the testimony is otherwise assured. The Clause also prevents the state from inhibiting the defendant's opportunity to cross-examine prosecution witnesses. Concealing the identity of a witness, assuring confidentiality of juvenile records and maintaining the viability of a state voucher rule have all been found insufficient reasons for preventing the defendant from developing information through cross-examination. However, the state need not disclose impeachment evidence unless it decides its use would probably affect the outcome of trial.

(6) Under the Compulsory Process Clause, the Due Process Clause and the Fifth Amendment, the defendant has the right to testify in her own behalf, subject to limitations that are not arbitrary or disproportionate to the purposes they are designed to serve. The Compulsory Process Clause also guarantees the defendant the right to subpoena material and relevant witnesses on her behalf, although the burden is on the defendant to offer a plausible explanation of the witness' relevance when the state asserts an countervailing interest (such as protection of witness identity).

756

Finally, the Compulsory Process Clause and the Due Process Clause protect against state restrictions on defense examination of its witnesses, except when those restrictions are imposed as a sanction for willful and blatant misconduct by the defense.

BIBLIOGRAPHY

Ashley, George L. The Uncertain Relationship Between the Hearsay Rule and the Confrontation Clause. 52 Tex.L.Rev. 1167 (1974).

Bradley, Craig. Griffin v. California: Still Viable After All These Years. 79 Mich.L.Rev. 1290 (1981).

Churchwell, Steven G. The Constitutional Right to Present Evidence: Progeny of Chambers v. Mississippi. 19 Crim.L.Bull. 131 (1983).

Cohen, Neil P. Can They Kill Me If I'm Gone: Trial in Absentia in Capital Cases. 36 U.Fla.L.Rev. 273 (1984).

Gobert, J. Competency to Stand Trial: A Pre- and Post-Jackson Analysis. 40 Tenn.L.Rev. 659 (1973).

Graham, Michael H. The Confrontation Clause, the Hearsay Rule, and the Forgetful Witness. 56 Tex.L.Rev. 151 (1978).

Garcia, Alfredo. The Compulsory Process Clause and the "Sporting Theory of Justice:" The Supreme Court Evens the Score. 28 Duq.L.Rev. 619 (1990).

Lilly, G. Notes on the Confrontation Clause and Ohio v. Roberts. 36 U.Fla.L.Rev. 207 (1984).

Luka-Hopson, Diana. The Existing Conflict Between the Defendant's Right of Confrontation and the Witness' Right to Avoid Self-Incrimination. 38 Cath.U.L.Rev. 245 (1989).

Marcus, Paul M. The Confrontation Clause and Co-Defendant Confessions: The Drift from *Bruton* to Parker v. Randolph. 1979 U.Ill.L.Forum 559.

Roesch, R. and S. Golding. Competency to Stand Trial. Univ. of Ill. Press, 1980.

Seidelson, David E. The Confrontation Clause, the Right Against Self-Incrimination and the Supreme Court: A Critique and Some Modest Proposals. 20 Duq.L.Rev. 429 (1982).

Starkey, James G. Trial in Absentia. 53 St. John's L.Rev. 721 (1979).

Westen, Paul. Confrontation and Compulsory Process: A Unified Theory of Evidence for Criminal Cases. 91 Harv.L.Rev. 567 (1978).

____. The Compulsory Process Clause. 73 Mich.L.Rev. 71 (1974).

Chapter Twenty-Nine

APPEALS

29.01 Introduction

An "appeal" usually involves an examination of the trial court record by an appellate court in an effort to ascertain whether the relevant substantive and procedural law was properly applied by the lower court. It might also consist of a trial *de novo*, in which the appellate proceeding is actually a new, independent trial in a Superior Court.[1] In either case, the appeal procedure assures that a convicted offender is "afforded the opportunity to obtain one judicial review of his conviction by a tribunal other than that in which he was tried."

As significant as the opportunity to appeal is, the Supreme Court has never given it constitutional status. In the late 19th century case of *McKane v. Durston*,[2] the Court stated:

> A review by an appellate court of the final judgment in a criminal case, however grave the offense of which the accused is convicted, was not at common law, and is not now, a necessary element of due process of law. It is wholly within the discretion of the state to allow or not to allow such a review.

Although the passage was dictum, it has been continually affirmed by the Court.[3]

The Court's stance on the constitutional status of the right to appeal is unlikely ever to be challenged, because every state, as well as the federal system, provides at least one appeal as of right after conviction, as well as at least one discretionary appeal to a higher level appellate court. In the federal system, for instance, federal convictions may be appealed as of right to the circuit courts of appeal. Further appeal to the Supreme Court is usually dependent upon whether the Court grants a writ of certiorari.[4]

State litigants have somewhat more elaborate appellate opportunities, since they may resort not only to the relevant state courts, but to the United States Supreme Court as well, under certain narrow circumstances. Once the case of a state defendant has been reviewed by the highest available state court, direct appeal to the Supreme Court may be had if the state court ruling invalidated a federal statute or upheld a state statute in the face

---

1. See *Blackledge v. Perry,* 417 U.S. 21, 94 S.Ct. 2098 (1974), described in § 29.02(d)(1).

2. 153 U.S. 684, 14 S.Ct. 913 (1894).

3. See *Abney v. United States,* 431 U.S. 651, 97 S.Ct. 2034 (1977); *Ross v. Moffitt,* 417 U.S. 600, 94 S.Ct. 2437 (1974).

4. See 28 U.S.C.A. § 1254.

of a challenge that it was invalid under the federal Constitution.[5] Further, a writ of certiorari from the Court is available where the decision by the highest available state court "draw[s] into question the validity" of a federal or state statute or "where any title, right, privilege or immunity is specially set up or claimed under the Constitution, treaties or statutes of, or commission held or authority exercised under, the United States." [6]

This chapter discusses some of the legal issues that have arisen as a result of the appeals system. Specifically, it addresses (1) constitutional rights designed to ensure a meaningful appeal; (2) the statutory final judgment requirement; (3) limitations on appeals by the prosecution; (4) the harmless error doctrine; and (5) the retroactivity doctrine.

29.02 Assuring a Meaningful Appeal

A number of Supreme Court decisions stand for the proposition that, while a state need not provide an appeals process, if it does so it may not unfairly inhibit use of that process. This notion has been implemented in a number of ways, discussed below.

(a) **The Right to Trial Transcripts.** The first case to consider constitutional issues in connection with appeals was *Griffin v. Illinois*.[7] There, the Supreme Court held that Illinois appellate procedure violated equal protection because it required defendants to produce transcripts of their trial in order to obtain appellate review, but failed to provide one free of charge to indigent defendants. As the Court put it, the state may not grant the right to appeal "in a way that discriminates against some convicted defendants on account of their poverty."

The Court has vigorously affirmed *Griffin* on several occasions. For example, in *Entsminger v. Iowa*,[8] the Court unanimously held that *Griffin* was violated by a state procedure which provided the indigent defendant with less than a complete record. The procedure in *Entsminger* allowed defense counsel to choose between an appeal based on the full record and an appeal based solely on a "clerk's transcript" that contained grand jury minutes, the trial court's instructions, and various court orders. The defendant's counsel chose the latter procedure, apparently believing the appeal was weak, but the Court held that only the defendant could make such a decision. Absent such a waiver, the defendant "was precluded from obtaining a complete and effective appellate review of his conviction by the operation of the clerk's transcript

5. See 28 U.S.C.A. § 1257(1)(2). While appeal is permitted, the Court may dismiss the claim if no "substantial federal question" is presented. 16 Wright, Miller & Cooper, Jurisdiction: Civil § 4014.

6. 28 U.S.C.A. § 1257(3).

7. 351 U.S. 12, 76 S.Ct. 585 (1956).

8. 386 U.S. 748, 87 S.Ct. 1402 (1967).

procedure." The Court has also held that conditioning production of a transcript on the trial judge's assessment of whether "justice will thereby be promoted" violates equal protection.[9]

(b) The Right to Counsel. The Sixth Amendment guarantee of the right to assistance of counsel applies only to "criminal prosecutions," which does not include the appellate process. Thus, the Court has looked to the Equal Protection and Due Process Clauses in defining the scope of the right to counsel on appeal. The watershed case in this regard was *Douglas v. California*,[10] where the Court relied on *Griffin* and equal protection analysis in concluding that the state must provide the indigent defendant with counsel on appeals as of right to provide "meaningful access" to the appellate courts. According to Justice Douglas' majority opinion, "where the merits of the *one and only* appeal an indigent has as of right are decided without benefit of counsel . . . an unconstitutional line has been drawn between rich and poor."

To reach the result in *Douglas,* the Court in effect had to assume that the state cannot prevent *non*-indigent defendants from having appellate counsel. But it was not until *Evitts v. Lucey*,[11] over twenty years later, that the Court firmly guaranteed a right to counsel on appeal for these defendants as well. Justice Brennan's majority opinion based this conclusion both on the "meaningful access" language underlying *Douglas* and on the notion developed in previous due process and Sixth Amendment cases that lawyers are "necessities, not luxuries."[12]

At the same time, the Court has refused to find that either equal protection or due process guarantees a right to counsel on discretionary appeals. In *Ross v. Moffitt*,[13] the majority held that the Equal Protection Clause does not require precisely equal advantages between rich and poor; further, the counselless discretionary review procedure at issue in *Ross* was sufficiently fair because the indigent defendant was able to present both his trial transcript and the appellate briefs (written by a lawyer) submitted at his appeal as of right. *Ross* notwithstanding, most jurisdictions provide counsel to indigents on all appeals.[14]

9. *Draper v. Washington,* 372 U.S. 487, 83 S.Ct. 774 (1963); see also *Mayer v. Chicago,* 404 U.S. 189, 92 S.Ct. 410 (1971) (transcript must be provided for appeal of crime punishable only by a fine). Both *Draper* and *Mayer* also suggested, however, that "alternative methods of reporting trial proceedings" would be permissible if they were equivalent to a transcript.

10. 372 U.S. 353, 83 S.Ct. 814 (1963).

11. 469 U.S. 387, 105 S.Ct. 830 (1985).

12. Quoting *Gideon v. Wainwright,* 372 U.S. 335, 83 S.Ct. 792 (1963), discussed in § 31.02(b).

13. 417 U.S. 600, 94 S.Ct. 2437 (1974).

14. See commentary to ABA, Criminal Justice Standard 21–1.1.

The underlying right to counsel also determines the extent to which counsel must be "effective" on appeal. In *Evitts,* the Court held that counsel's failure to meet a technical filing deadline for an appeal as of right deprived the defendant of effective assistance, and reinstated the appeal. In contrast, in *Wainwright v. Torna,*[15] counsel's failure to make timely application for discretionary review did not require reinstatement of the appeal, since the lawyer's incompetence did not deprive the defendant of any constitutional right to counsel. These and other cases concerning appellate counsel are discussed further in the context of the Court's effective assistance jurisprudence.[16]

(c) The Right to Pursue "Non–Frivolous" Arguments. Counsel will sometimes perfect an appeal but then decide that there are no substantial appellate claims and withdraw from the case. In *Anders v. California,*[17] the Supreme Court held that withdrawal under these circumstances may take place only after counsel has filed a "brief referring to anything in the record that might arguably support the appeal," the defendant is given a chance to add to this brief, and the appellate court, after reviewing the brief, has determined that the appeal is "wholly frivolous." This procedure was found necessary to assure that appointed counsel thought carefully about deciding to withdraw. Furthermore, violation of this rule can never be harmless error, and cannot be avoided through showing a lack of prejudice, as is the case with most ineffective assistance claims.[18]

However, the Court has also upheld a state rule requiring counsel to submit, in addition to this "*Anders* brief," a statement as to why any issues that might support an appeal lack merit. The defendant in *McCoy v. Wisconsin*[19] argued that this rule forced the appellate attorney to make arguments against her client's case; moreover, unlike the wealthy client, the indigent cannot avoid such damaging submissions by hiring another attorney. But the majority held that, rather than rendering counsel ineffective, the statute furthered the aims underlying *Anders* by encouraging diligent research by counsel and assisting the appellate court in assessing frivolousness. The Court has also held, in *Jones v. Barnes,*[20] that if counsel does decide to argue the case on appeal, she, not the defendant, is the arbiter of what will be

15. 455 U.S. 586, 102 S.Ct. 1300 (1982).

16. For further discussion of the right to counsel on appeal, see § 31.03(c)(1) & (3); for effective assistance issues, see § 32.04(c).

17. 386 U.S. 738, 87 S.Ct. 1396 (1967).

18. *Penson v. Ohio,* 488 U.S. 75, 109 S.Ct. 346 (1988).

19. 486 U.S. 429, 108 S.Ct. 1895 (1988).

20. 463 U.S. 745, 103 S.Ct. 3308 (1983), discussed further in § 32.04(c).

argued, even if some of the arguments she discards are not frivolous.

(d) The Right to Appeal Without Fear of Retaliation. In *North Carolina v. Pearce,*[21] a defendant who had been reconvicted after a successful appeal received a greater punishment than had been imposed after his original conviction. Although the Supreme Court did not explicitly find that the increase in sentence was in retaliation for the appeal, it concluded that, to prevent the right of appeal from being chilled, due process required that a "defendant be freed of apprehension of such a retaliatory motivation on the part of the sentencing judge." Accordingly, when a sentence is increased after a successful appeal, vindictiveness should be assumed unless the trial judge can provide a reasonable explanation for the increase, consisting of "identifiable conduct occurring after the time of the original sentencing proceeding."

(1) When the presumption of vindictiveness applies. In effect, *Pearce* created what has since come to be called a "presumption of vindictiveness"[22] whenever the sentencing judge imposes a heavier sentence after a successful appeal. In *Blackledge v. Perry,*[23] the Court found the presumption also applies to *prosecutorial* decisions that may chill the right to appeal. There the prosecutor raised the charge against the defendant from a misdemeanor to a felony after the defendant had been convicted on the misdemeanor and filed notice of appeal for a trial *de novo* in a higher court. The Supreme Court held that "upping the ante" in this way after a defendant has exercised her right to appeal is presumptively vindictive.

On the other hand, when the sentencing or charging authority lacks the motivation to be vindictive, *Pearce's* presumption of vindictiveness does not apply. For example, in *Colten v. Kentucky,*[24] the Court refused to apply the presumption when the defendant's sentence after a trial *de novo* was higher than the one received at his earlier trial on the same charge. Because *de novo* appeals are fresh determinations of guilt in front of a different judge, the sentencing court is not being asked, as it was in *Pearce,* "to do over what it had thought it had already done correctly," nor even to "overrule" what another court has done. Similarly, the Court found in *Chaffin v. Stynchcombe*[25] that a harsher postappeal sentence imposed by a jury did not violate due process, because the jury lacked knowledge of the first sentence and

21. 395 U.S. 711, 89 S.Ct. 2072 (1969).

22. See, e.g., *United States v. Goodwin,* 457 U.S. 368, 102 S.Ct. 2485 (1982).

23. 417 U.S. 21, 94 S.Ct. 2098 (1974).

24. 407 U.S. 104, 92 S.Ct. 1953 (1972).

25. 412 U.S. 17, 93 S.Ct. 1977 (1973).

because the jury would "have no personal stake in the prior convictions and no motivation to engage in self-vindication."

In *Texas v. McCullough* [26] the second sentencer was the same judge who presided over the first trial. However, the sentence after the first trial was imposed by a jury and the second trial came about because the trial judge herself concluded that certain conduct by the prosecutor required it. Thus, the Court asserted, "unlike the judge who has been reversed, the trial judge here had no motivation to engage in self-vindication." Neither was there "justifiable concern about 'institutional interests that might occasion higher sentences by a judge desirous of discouraging what he regards as meritless appeals.'" The majority rejected as too "speculative" the dissent's argument that the judge may have been vindictive toward the defendant because she was forced to sit through a new trial whose result was a "foregone conclusion."

In possible contrast to these cases is *Thigpen v. Roberts*,[27] where the Court suggested that, in the *Blackledge* context, the presumption of vindictiveness is triggered even when the increase in charge is by a different prosecutor. However, the Court noted that the first prosecutor in this case had assisted the prosecutor at the second adjudication and held that "we need not decide the correct result when independent prosecutors are involved." In light of the Court's subsequent decision in *McCullough,* if the second prosecutor does not know of the first charge, or is from a different office, the Court may find that the institutional pressure to discourage "meritless appeals" does not exist, and thus that the presumption should not apply.

The Court has also held that, even where the charging or sentencing authority is the same before and after the appeal, the presumption of vindictiveness is not triggered where the first charge and sentence occurred in the plea bargaining/guilty plea context and the second charge and sentence occur in connection with trial. The Court reached this conclusion (in *Alabama v. Smith*[28]) because "relevant sentencing information available to the judge after the plea will usually be considerably less than that available at trial," and because "the facts that may have indicated leniency as consideration for the guilty plea [such as the defendant's willingness to forego trial] are no longer present." Thus, a defendant who successfully overturns a guilty plea may be charged with the original, pre-plea bargain charge and, if convicted on it, subjected to a higher sentence than she received after the plea. The presumption of vindictiveness would apply, however, if

26. 475 U.S. 134, 106 S.Ct. 976 (1986).

27. 468 U.S. 27, 104 S.Ct. 2916 (1984).

28. 490 U.S. 794, 109 S.Ct. 2201 (1989).

the new charge was greater than the charge originally brought by the prosecutor.[29]

(2) Overcoming the presumption. If the presumption does apply, *Pearce* held that an increased sentence or charge after the exercise of the right to appeal will stand only if the state provides proof of "identifiable conduct occurring after the time of the original sentencing proceeding." Subsequent cases have made clear that this language is not to be interpreted literally. In *Wasman v. United States,*[30] the judge imposed a higher sentence after a successful appeal because of an intervening conviction on another charge. The charge had been pending at the time of the original sentencing, but the judge had stated that he would consider only prior convictions, not pending charges, in imposing sentence. A unanimous Court upheld the new sentence, concluding that although the conviction did not represent new "conduct" by the defendant since the first sentencing, it was a new "event" which could be considered in showing a nonvindictive motive.

Similarly, in *McCullough,* discussed above, the Court concluded that even if, contrary to its apparent holding, vindictiveness should be presumed, the presumption was overcome in that case. There the judge's sentence after the second trial was thirty years longer than the sentence imposed by the jury after the first trial.[31] The judge justified this differential on the ground that the second trial had presented two new state witnesses who had added to the credibility of the state's case, shed new light on the defendant's personality, and revealed for the first time that he had been released from prison only four months before the murder. She also noted that the defendant had done nothing to rehabilitate himself between trials. According to Chief Justice Burger, this "new objective information . . . amply justified McCullough's increased sentence."

In dissent, Justice Marshall, joined by two others, pointed out that, with the exception of the latter reason, the judge relied on neither "new" conduct or events to justify her decision. As Marshall noted: "If a court on retrial could justify an increased sentence on the ground that it now had additional knowledge concerning the defendant's participation in the offense, then the *Pearce* limitation could be evaded in almost every case." Put another way, if *McCullough* does stand for the proposition that a higher sentence may be imposed anytime the judge can proffer a

29. It would also probably apply when the prosecutor recharges for the originally charged offense, if the reason the guilty plea was overturned was not involuntariness, but because the prosecution breached the plea bargain agreement. For further discussion of the vindictiveness issue in the guilty plea context, see § 26.05(f).

30. 468 U.S. 559, 104 S.Ct. 3217 (1984).

31. The sentence (50 years) equalled the sentence the same judge had given the defendant's two co-defendants.

"new" explanation for the increase, and defendants know this, the right to appeal may be significantly chilled. The likelihood of a higher charge after a successful appeal (or after filing for a trial *de novo,* as in *Blackledge*) is probably lower, but by no means *de minimis,* if prosecutors need merely discover "new information" about the details of the defendant's crime in order to up the ante.

29.03   The Final Judgment Rule

(a) **Defense Appeals.** In addition to appeals after conviction and sentence, interlocutory appeals of decisions reached preliminary to adjudication of guilt may occasionally be attempted by the defendant. The procedural viability of these appeals is governed by the final judgment rule, which is observed in some form or other in virtually every jurisdiction.[32] The rule attempts to discourage piecemeal and time-consuming pretrial litigation by providing, as the relevant federal legislation puts it,[33] that only "final decisions" of the trial court are appealable.

A final judgment is not always required to perfect an appeal, however. In *Cohen v. Beneficial Industrial Loan Corp.,*[34] the Supreme Court articulated an exception to the final judgment rule which permits appeal of "a small class [of pretrial judgments] which finally determine claims of right separable from, and collateral to, rights asserted in the action, too important to be denied review and too independent of the cause itself to require that appellate consideration be deferred until the whole case is adjudicated." *Cohen* identified several factors that must be present before a claim may be appealed as a "collateral order." First, a trial court must have made a final determination on the issue, not leaving it open, unfinished or inconclusive. Second, the issue must involve an important right which would "be lost, probably irreparably," if review had to await final judgment. Third, the appealed right must not be an ingredient of the main cause of action. Relatedly, an appeals court must not be required to consider the main cause of action while reviewing the collateral issue. Although *Cohen* was a civil case, it was based on a construction of 28 U.S.C.A. § 1291, which covers both criminal and civil cases, and its reasoning has been applied in a number of Supreme Court cases involving criminal litigation. Many state courts utilize its test in interpreting their own final judgment rules.[35]

Not surprisingly, given the efficiency concerns underlying the final judgment rule, the Supreme Court has found that only a few

---

32. See 15 Wright, Miller & Cooper, Jurisdiction § 3918.

33. 28 U.S.C.A. § 1291.

34. 337 U.S. 541, 69 S.Ct. 1221 (1949).

35. See e.g., *Commonwealth v. Bolden,* 472 Pa. 602, 373 A.2d 90 (1977).

types of judicial orders in criminal cases fit within the *Cohen* test. In *Stack v. Boyle*,[36] the Court held, in line with the current federal statute,[37] that the defendant may pursue a pretrial appeal of a judicial decision rejecting an argument that bail was excessive under the Eighth Amendment. It found that the judge's bail determination was sufficiently independent of the main cause of action to be considered a final judgment for appeal purposes, that the issue would be moot if raised after conviction, and that failing to preserve the bail right at the pretrial stage would render the presumption of innocence and the right to an unhampered preparation of one's defense meaningless. Similarly, a pretrial order denying a motion to dismiss an indictment on double jeopardy grounds has been found to fit within the *Cohen* class of cases. As the Court noted in *Abney v. United States*,[38] if a criminal defendant is to avoid exposure to jeopardy a second time and thereby enjoy full protection of the right, his double jeopardy challenge must normally be heard before the second adjudication.[39]

On the other hand, the Court has indicated that most claims do not come within the collateral order exception. In *Carroll v. United States*,[40] the Court denied the appealability of orders on post-indictment search and seizure motions because such orders are not "independent" of the ongoing case against the defendant.[41] And in *DiBella v. United States*,[42] the Court held that a ruling on a *pre*-indictment order to suppress evidence under the Fourth Amendment normally does not constitute a final judgment either, even though it is less clear that the order is part of the ongoing litigation. The Court, in an opinion by Justice Frankfurter, saw little practical difference between pre- and post-indictment rulings of this sort. First, unlike a bail determination, in neither case is the Fourth Amendment ruling "fairly severable" from the rest of the litigation, because it may well determine the conduct of the trial. Second, an appeal could "entail serious disruption" of the litigation process, perhaps becoming "an instrument of harassment, jeopardizing by delay the availability of other essential evidence." Third, "appellate intervention makes for truncated presentation of the issue of admissibility, because the legality of

---

36. 342 U.S. 1, 72 S.Ct. 1 (1951).

37. 18 U.S.C.A. § 3147(b).

38. 431 U.S. 651, 97 S.Ct. 2034 (1977).

39. However, in *Illinois v. Vitale,* 447 U.S. 410, 100 S.Ct. 2260 (1980), the Court found that in certain "rare" instances it might be necessary to proceed with the second trial despite the double jeopardy claim in order to determine whether the evidence the prosecution intends to use is sufficiently similar to the evidence it relied upon in the first

trial to justify a finding that the "same offense" is involved. Given recent developments in double jeopardy doctrine, these instances may no longer be rare. See § 30.04(a)(2).

40. 354 U.S. 394, 77 S.Ct. 1332 (1957).

41. The Court found such orders non appealable whether the appeal is brought by the defense *or* the prosecution. But see § 29.04.

42. 369 U.S. 121, 82 S.Ct. 654 (1962).

the search too often cannot truly be determined until the evidence at the trial has brought all circumstances to light."

The Court also acknowledged, however, that forcing a litigant to wait until after trial to seek return of property seized by the government may be an insufficient remedy, in that one's right to one's property prior to the post-trial appeal would be "irreparably lost." Thus, the Court held that suppression orders *are* appealable "if the motion is solely for return of property and is in no way tied to a criminal prosecution *in esse* [in being] against the movant." The federal courts have construed this language to permit appeals of denied motions whose "primary purpose" was to seek the return of seized property, if the order occurs in the early phases of the investigatory process.[43] This latter limitation makes sense, since the closer to trial the appeal occurs the more likely it will disrupt the prosecution, result from insincere motives, and not afford relief substantially different from a post-trial appeal.

Also resolved under the *Cohen* criteria was *United States v. MacDonald,*[44] in which the Court held that a defendant may not bring a pretrial appeal of a court's order denying a motion to dismiss an indictment on speedy trial grounds. The Court stressed that the review of such an order normally requires an appeals court to view not just the circumstances leading up to trial, but the quality and amount of evidence at trial itself.[45] Even more important, vacating the defendant's conviction provides an adequate remedy for violation of her Sixth Amendment right; unlike, for instance, the double jeopardy prohibition, the speedy trial right is not a "right not to be tried" but a right to avoid pretrial delay, which in fact could be harmed by allowing pretrial appeal. Finally, if a right to immediate appeal were recognized, "any defendant" could raise such a claim as a dilatory tactic since "nothing about . . . a speedy trial claim . . . inherently limits [its] availability."

Less persuasively, the Court held, in *United States v. Hollywood Motor Car Co.,*[46] that the pretrial appeal of an order

---

43. The courts are split as to whether a pre-indictment post-arrest suppression order of the type at issue in *DiBella* is part of a prosecution *in esse.* Compare *United States v. One Residence and Attached Garage,* 603 F.2d 1231 (7th Cir.1979) to *Standard Drywall, Inc. v. United States,* 668 F.2d 156 (2d Cir. 1982), cert. denied 456 U.S. 927, 102 S.Ct. 1973 (1982), rehearing denied 457 U.S. 1112, 102 S.Ct. 2917 (1982) (order pending grand jury investigation is nonappealable).

44. 435 U.S. 850, 98 S.Ct. 1547 (1978).

45. See § 25.04. Similarly, in *Flanagan v. United States,* 465 U.S. 259, 104 S.Ct. 1051 (1984), the Court held nonappealable an order disqualifying defendants' attorney because the "effect of the disqualification on the defense, and hence whether the asserted right had been violated, cannot be fairly assessed until the substance of the prosecution's and defendant's case is known."

46. 458 U.S. 263, 102 S.Ct. 3081 (1982).

denying a motion to dismiss an indictment based on prosecutorial vindictiveness was improper. As in *MacDonald,* the Court found there were adequate post-trial means of protecting the *Pearce-Blackledge* right,[47] specifically, reversal of the conviction and a new trial on charges not tainted by prosecutorial vindictiveness. The Court gave short shrift to the petitioner's argument that, like a double jeopardy violation, *Pearce* and *Blackledge* guaranteed the defendant a right not to be tried on particular charges (here the higher charge motivated by vindictiveness). Rather, it asserted that there is a "crucial distinction between a right not to be tried and a right whose remedy requires the dismissal of charges." Pretrial vindication of the latter type of right usually merely *delays* trial (albeit, in this case, on a different charge), and thus need not be allowed.[48]

As Justice Blackmun pointed out in dissent, *Hollywood* is not easily reconciled with the Court's past cases. First, the majority's reasoning notwithstanding, a *Pearce-Blackledge* claim arguably does contemplate a right not to be tried, and thus a post-trial remedy for prosecutorial vindictiveness may be insufficient. The rationale of *Pearce* and *Blackledge* is preservation of the right to appeal by removing inhibitions to its exercise. Allowing the prosecutor to try the defendant on increased charges could create such an inhibition, even if any subsequent conviction could be overturned, since a *third* trial would then be required. Furthermore, unlike determination of a speedy trial claim, whether increased charges are vindictive can be determined from facts already available at the time of the pretrial appeal and collateral to the case against the defendant. Finally, unlike a speedy trial challenge or most other claims, the class of defendants who could plausibly assert a vindictiveness claim is inherently limited and easily ascertained because it is based on an increased charge or sentence; thus, the fear of dilatory tactics raised in *MacDonald* is inapposite here.

A more general consideration is that *Hollywood,* like the Court's decisions in this area generally, may have taken insufficient account of the possibility that immediate correction of an erroneous pretrial ruling, particularly if it disposes of the case, will be more efficient than requiring the case to proceed through adjudication before appeal is possible. In civil litigation, for instance, 28 U.S.C.A. § 1292(b) allows district court judges to certify for appeal pretrial rulings which involve "a controlling

---

47. See § 29.02(d).

48. See also, *Midland Asphalt Corp. v. United States,* 489 U.S. 794, 109 S.Ct. 1494 (1989) (likelihood that violation of rules governing grand jury process will be found harmless on post-conviction appeal, see § 23.06(b), does not mean interlocutory appeal is permissible, because the only remedy granted by such an appeal would be dismissal of charges, which does not foreclose a new indictment).

question of law as to which there is substantial ground for difference of opinion" if immediate appeal would "materially advance the ultimate termination of the litigation."

(b) Prosecution Appeals. The final judgment rule may not apply as forcefully to the prosecution as it does to the defense. For instance, as discussed in the next section, some states provide by statute that certain pretrial rulings that the defendant cannot appeal on an interlocutory basis (e.g., suppression hearing rulings) may be appealable by the prosecution. This stance can be justified on the ground that, analogous to the Court's rationale in *Cohen,* the prosecution might otherwise be "irreparably" barred from any appellate review of the judgment; if, because of the pretrial ruling, charges are dismissed for lack of evidence or the prosecution fails to obtain a conviction, the Double Jeopardy Clause would bar appeal on the pretrial ruling. Not only might this prevent justice in the individual case; it might also lead to the proliferation of "erroneous" rulings at the trial court level. Furthermore, it might be argued, the prosecution is less likely than the defense to use such appeals as a dilatory tactic.

Of course, even if all of these points are true, pretrial appeals by the prosecution can significantly abridge the defendant's right to a speedy resolution of the charges against her. Nonetheless, most speedy trial statutes exclude any pretrial appeal period from speedy trial calculations.[49] Further, the Supreme Court has suggested it would find no constitutional infirmities in this practice, so long as the prosecution's case is not frivolous.[50]

(c) Third Party Appeals. Third parties may seek to appeal a pretrial ruling in a criminal case in two different contexts. First, the third party may allege that she should not have to follow a given court order, such as a subpoena. In this situation, the Supreme Court held in *Cobbledick v. United States,*[51] the order is not appealable unless the third party refuses to comply and has been held in contempt by the court. However, if a contempt citation is issued, then an appeal is appropriate; a contrary holding "would forever preclude review of the witness' claim, for his alternatives are to abandon the claim or languish in jail."

The second way in which a third party might seek to challenge a criminal trial court ruling is when the ruling is not directed at her, but it nonetheless infringes a legal interest of hers. The most obvious example of such a case is when the press protests a closure order or a gag order. In this situation, the third party is usually allowed an interlocutory appeal, on the grounds

---

49. See § 25.05(c) for a description of the federal statute on this point.

50. See *United States v. Loud Hawk,* 474 U.S. 302, 106 S.Ct. 648 (1986), discussed in § 25.04(b).

51. 309 U.S. 323, 60 S.Ct. 540 (1940).

that its claim is "independent" of the criminal action, even though it may work to delay that action.

29.04 Appeals by the Prosecution

Generally, as Chapter Thirty explains,[52] the Double Jeopardy Clause bars government appeal of any acquittal at a jury or bench trial, as well as any other judicial judgment which involves a finding that there is insufficient evidence to convict the defendant. However, other rulings may be appealed by the prosecution, *provided* it has statutory duty to do so. As the Supreme Court stated in *Carroll v. United States:* [53]

> [A]ppeals by the government in criminal cases are something unusual, exceptional, not favored. The history shows resistance of the Court to the opening of an appellate route for the Government until it was plainly provided by the Congress, and after that a close restriction of its uses to those authorized by the statute.

The most common situation covered by such statutes is prosecutorial appeal of a pretrial motion to suppress evidence. For example, on the federal level, 18 U.S.C.A. § 3731 provides for prosecutorial appeal of a district court decision to suppress or exclude evidence having a substantial bearing on the case. As noted in the previous section, such provisions are popular because, if the defendant is acquitted at trial (which could easily occur if the suppressed evidence is crucial to the prosecution's case), the Double Jeopardy Clause will bar the prosecution from appealing the adverse pretrial ruling after trial. A pretrial appeal, on the other hand, occurs before jeopardy has attached and thus is not barred.[54]

The Supreme Court has also held that the prosecution may appeal *post*-jeopardy rulings that do not involve a finding that the evidence was insufficient to convict.[55] While this stance can be questioned in some contexts,[56] it seems appropriate when the appealed order is a post-conviction finding by the trial judge "arresting" or "vacating" the jury's guilty verdict on the ground that it is not supported by the evidence. Statutes permitting such appeals do not violate the double jeopardy prohibition because a successful prosecutorial appeal does not subject the defendant to a new trial and additional jeopardy, but merely reinstates the jury verdict.[57]

---

52. See in particular, § 30.03(a)(2).

53. 354 U.S. 394, 77 S.Ct. 1332 (1957).

54. See § 30.02(b).

55. *United States v. Scott,* 437 U.S. 82, 98 S.Ct. 2187 (1978).

56. See § 30.03(b).

57. Compare *Tibbs v. Florida,* 457 U.S. 31, 102 S.Ct. 2211 (1982), in which the Florida Supreme Court characterized its reversal of the defendant's conviction as a decision that the jury's ver-

Finally, the state of the law with respect to prosecution appeals of sentence will be summarized briefly.[58] Because capital sentencing procedure resembles a trial, the Supreme Court has held that the Double Jeopardy Clause prohibits an appeal arguing that a life sentence imposed by a judge or a jury should be reconsidered at a new sentencing proceeding and converted into a death sentence.[59] On the other hand, because the typical non-capital sentencing proceeding does not resemble a trial either procedurally or in terms of the factors the sentencing tribunal must consider, a prosecution appeal which leads to resentencing in the non-capital context usually does not implicate the Clause, provided, once again, that a statute authorizes the appeal.[60]

29.05 Harmless Error

(a) **Various Approaches.** When an appellate court finds that error has occurred at the trial level, its simplest option would be reversal of the judgment below, regardless of the type of error involved or the overall strength of the case. For some time during the nineteenth century, "automatic reversal" was, in effect, the rule in England. The so-called Exchequer Rule presumed prejudice from any trial defect, and thus virtually always required a new trial when error was found.[61] But, as might be imagined, this system bred numerous retrials and sometimes multiple retrials in the same case, at considerable damage to judicial economy, the witnesses and the litigants.[62] The lesson of the British experience was not lost on American courts. As one American court later put it, treating every error as reversible can be seen as "archaic formalism and . . . watery sentiment that obstructs, delays, and defeats the prosecution of crime." [63]

Accordingly every American jurisdiction has adopted some kind of "harmless error" rule, which allows an appellate court to hold that error is so insignificant that the trial court verdict should stand.[64] While this authority avoids the drawbacks of an

dict was against the weight of the evidence. According to the United States Supreme Court, this finding was not an "acquittal" for double jeopardy purposes. Thus, reprosecution was permitted. See § 30.03(a)(3).

58. A fuller discussion of this issue is found in § 30.05(a).

59. *Bullington v. Missouri,* 451 U.S. 430, 101 S.Ct. 1852 (1981).

60. *United States v. DiFrancesco,* 449 U.S. 117, 101 S.Ct. 426 (1980).

61. See R. Traynor, The Riddle of Harmless Error (1970), at 6–10.

62. See Goldberg, "Harmless Error, Constitutional Sneak Thief," 71 J.Crim. L. & C. 421, 422 (1980).

63. *United States v. Garsson,* 291 Fed. 646 (S.D.N.Y.1923).

64. To be distinguished from the harmless error doctrine is the plain error rule, which determines when an appellate court can hear claims that were not raised at trial. In contrast to harmless error, plain error involves only "defects affecting substantial rights," see, e.g., Fed.R.Crim.P. 52(b), whose recognition is necessary to avoid "a miscarriage of justice." *United States v. Frady,* 456 U.S. 152, 102 S.Ct. 1584 (1982).

automatic reversal rule, it can require very speculative assessments about the impact of error. Further, because harmless error analysis is likely to vary in each case, depending upon the idiosyncracies of the record, it is difficult to describe in a way that is helpful to courts or litigants. But because the number of harmless error findings today is significant,[65] some understanding of its contours is important.

At least four different definitions of harmless error can be discerned from the cases.[66] The broadest is the so-called "correct ruling" test, which finds an error harmless if the appellate court believes, based on an assessment of all the evidence, that the trial court's verdict is correct. This approach has been criticized because it places the appellate court in the position of second-guessing the trial factfinder, which is not its function and may run afoul of the right to jury trial.[67] The remaining three approaches attempt to correct for this problem. The "overwhelming evidence" test requires looking at all of the "left-over" evidence to determine whether it is so overwhelmingly supportive of the verdict, and the relative significance of the error so small, that the factfinder could not have been affected by the error. Next there is the "cumulative evidence" test, which does not consider all of the untainted evidence, but instead permits a finding of harmlessness only if the factfinder was presented with admissible information that proved the same facts the tainted evidence proved; the theory here is that only in this situation is the factfinder not likely to have placed weight on the error in its deliberations.[68] Finally, there is the "effect of the error" test, which pays no attention to the other evidence, focusing entirely on whether the error could have had any effect on the factfinder.

In practice, there may be very little difference between these tests, since each is subject to manipulation by appellate judges, especially in terms of the degree of certainty required (compare, for example, a test which requires the appellate court to find, "beyond a reasonable doubt," that the trial court reached the correct result and a test which requires the appellate court to find that the error "probably" had no effect on the factfinder).[69] Assuming there is a practical difference between the tests, other problems arise. For instance, because they focus on the effect of the error on the factfinder, the last three tests may not be very

65. Allen, "A Serendipitous Trek Through the Advance–Sheet Jungle: Criminal Justice in the Courts of Review," 70 Iowa L.Rev. 311, 329–332 (1985).

66. To a large extent, these approaches are adapted from Traynor, supra note 61.

67. Id. at 13.

68. For the most forceful support of this approach, see Field, "Assessing the Harmlessness of Federal Constitutional Error—A Process in Need of a Rationale," 125 U.Pa.L.Rev. 15 (1976).

69. Saltzburg, "The Harm of Harmless Error," 59 Va.L.Rev. 988, 1014 (1973).

useful when the error is "non-evidentiary," such as is the case with a violation of the right to counsel. The fourth test can also be criticized on the ground that analyzing the impact of the error in the abstract is a meaningless endeavor. And, as already noted, the first test is thought to be deficient because it places the appellate court in the role of the jury or trial judge.

(b) **The Federal Rule for Non–Constitutional Error.** In *Kotteakos v. United States*,[70] the Supreme Court deliberated upon the harmless error standard to be applied in the federal courts to non-constitutional error. It specifically rejected a "correct result" test, reasoning that "it is not the appellate court's function to determine guilt or innocence[, n]or is it to speculate upon probable reconviction and decide according to how the speculation comes out." Instead, the Court held error is harmless only when "the error did not influence the jury, or had but very slight effect." Thus, "if one cannot say, with fair assurance, after pondering all that happened without stripping the erroneous action from the whole, that the judgment was not substantially swayed by the error, it is impossible to conclude that substantial rights were not affected." In short, for the purpose of assessing the harmlessness of non-constitutional error in federal court, the Court appeared to adopt a version of the "overwhelming evidence" test, and require a "fair assurance" that it is met.

(c) **Constitutional Error.** *Kotteakos* specifically declined to apply its test to departures from "a constitutional norm." Thus, the possibility remained that the Court would adopt a more stringent test, or a rule of automatic reversal, when the error was of constitutional magnitude. The first intimation that the latter approach would not be taken came in *Fahy v. Connecticut*,[71] where the error involved was the introduction of evidence illegally seized under the Fourth Amendment. The Court in *Fahy* held that constitutional error could be harmless where there was no "reasonable possibility" that the error "might have contributed to the verdict," although it eventually concluded that the error in this case was not harmless.[72] Justice Harlan disagreed with the majority's result but agreed that the type of constitutional error involved in *Fahy* should not be exempted from harmless error analysis. As he explained, "[s]ince the harmless error rule plainly affords no shield under which prosecutors might use damaging evidence, unconstitutionally obtained, to secure a conviction, there is no danger that application of the rule will undermine the prophylactic function of the rule of admissibility."

---

70. 328 U.S. 750, 66 S.Ct. 1239 (1946).

71. 375 U.S. 85, 84 S.Ct. 229 (1963).

72. For further discussion of *Fahy*, see § 29.05(c)(1) below.

Four years later, in *Chapman v. California*,[73] the Court formally adopted a harmless error test for constitutional error, reframing *Fahy's* language to require the prosecution to prove "beyond a reasonable doubt that the error complained of did not contribute to the verdict obtained." This formulation obviously rejected the "correct result" test, given its emphasis on the effect the error has on the factfinder. Furthermore, it clearly established that the absence of such an effect must be demonstrated by the prosecution, beyond a reasonable doubt, before a harmless error finding will be made, which conforms with the prosecution's burden and standard of proof in criminal cases.[74] But the opinion did not make clear whether the Court meant to adopt an "overwhelming evidence" test, a "cumulative evidence" test, or an "effect of the error" test. Subsequent Court cases seem to have vacillated between the first two standards, and occasionally may even have applied the correct result approach. On the other hand, other Court cases have made clear that *certain* types of constitutional error must result in automatic reversal, regardless of its effect on the factfinder. These two lines of cases are discussed below.

(1) The reasonable doubt test. Many of the Court's cases, especially prior to the 1970's, appeared to subscribe to relatively restrictive definitions of harmless error. For instance, in *Fahy,* the Court found that the trial court's admission of illegally obtained evidence (consisting of paint and brushes that the defendant used to paint a swastika on a synagogue) was not harmless, even though there was substantial independent evidence against the defendant, including several admissions and a confession. The majority stressed that the evidence made the arresting officer's testimony "far more damaging than it would otherwise have been," and was used to "forg[e] another link between the accused and the crime charged."

In *Chapman,* the prosecutor's closing argument repeatedly referred to the defendant's failure to take the stand and the judge instructed the jury that it could draw an adverse inference from this failure, clearly violations of the Fifth Amendment rule announced in *Griffin v. California*.[75] The Court found reversal necessary, stating that "though the case in which this occurred presented a reasonably strong 'circumstantial web of evidence' against petitioners, it was also a case in which, absent the constitutionally forbidden comments, honest fair-minded jurors might very well have brought in not-guilty verdicts." The Court found it

---

73. 386 U.S. 18, 87 S.Ct. 824 (1967).

74. *In re Winship,* 397 U.S. 358, 90 S.Ct. 1068 (1970).

75. 380 U.S. 609, 85 S.Ct. 1229 (1965), discussed in § 28.03(c)(1).

"completely impossible" to say beyond a reasonable doubt that the error did not contribute to the verdict.

The error in *Harrington v. California* [76] was a violation of *Bruton v. United States,* [77] occurring because the trial court had admitted the confessions of two codefendants who did not take the stand and thus were not subject to confrontation by the defendant, who was implicated by both confessions. In finding this error harmless, Justice Douglas stressed that the confessions were merely "cumulative." Although they placed the defendant at the scene of the crime, so did the defendant's own admissions, the statements of several eyewitnesses, and the statements of a third codefendant who did take the stand. Thus, concluded Douglas, it was extremely unlikely the illegally introduced confessions contributed to the verdict. He also remarked that the untainted evidence was "so overwhelming" that to reverse the conviction would amount to making a *Bruton* violation an automatic reversal error.

All of these decisions focused primarily on the nature of the tainted evidence and its possible effect on the jury. Arguably, all of them are also consistent with the relatively restrictive "cumulative evidence" test for harmless error. In contrast, many of the Court's cases subsequent to *Harrington* focused almost entirely on the nature and quality of the *legally* admitted evidence and adopted either an "overwhelming evidence" test or a "correct result" approach.

For instance, the error in *Schneble v. Florida,* [78] a capital murder prosecution, again involved a *Bruton* violation, this time the admission of testimony from an officer recounting statements of a codefendant suggesting that Schneble strangled the victim. Because "the independent evidence of guilt [was] overwhelming"—in particular Schneble's own "minute and grisly" confession and rope burns on his hands—the Court, in a 6–3 decision authored by Justice Rehnquist, held that the admission of the tainted evidence was harmless beyond a reasonable doubt. In dissent, Justice Marshall, joined by Justice Douglas, the author of *Harrington,* and Justice Brennan, pointed out that the petitioner had originally placed the blame for the murder on his codefendant and had confessed only after "a series of bizarre acts by the police designed to frighten him into making incriminating statements." Although the trial judge had made a threshold finding that Schneble's confession was voluntary, he had instructed the jury that if it doubted the voluntariness of the confession it should disregard it.

76. 395 U.S. 250, 89 S.Ct. 1726 (1969).

77. 391 U.S. 123, 88 S.Ct. 1620 (1968), discussed in § 28.04(d).

78. 405 U.S. 427, 92 S.Ct. 1056 (1972).

Marshall argued that there was at least a reasonable possibility that the jury had indeed found Schneble's confession, or at least that part of it stating that he had strangled the victim, involuntary and thus irrelevant, but had convicted him anyway on the strength of the other evidence in the case, including the tainted evidence.

The same term as *Schneble* the Court decided *Milton v. Wainwright,*[79] where the defendant alleged that a confession, obtained by a police officer who posed as a fellow prisoner of the defendant's, should not have been admitted at his trial. Without squarely addressing whether this admission was error, the Court went on to hold that it was harmless in any event, given the fact that three other confessions made by the defendant were *validly* admitted into evidence. Although this result could have been reached under a "cumulative evidence" test, the Court spoke solely of the "overwhelming amount of independent evidence."

Similarly, in *United States v. Hasting,*[80] the Court assumed, without definitively deciding, that the prosecutor had violated *Griffin,*[81] and then declared the error harmless based on an assessment of the remaining evidence, using language which sounded like a correct result test. As Chief Justice Burger stated for the majority, "[t]he question a reviewing court must ask is this: absent the prosecutor's allusion to the failure of the defense to proffer evidence to rebut the testimony of the victims, is it clear beyond a reasonable doubt that the jury would have returned a verdict of guilty?" This formulation subtly rearranges the inquiry from one which focuses on the effect of the error on the jury, as *Chapman* required, to one which looks at whether the remaining evidence supports the jury's guilty verdict.

But the Supreme Court's approach to harmless error is not easily pinned down, perhaps because harmless error analysis is so context-dependent. The same term as *Hasting,* the plurality opinion in *Connecticut v. Johnson*[82] refused to find harmless an erroneous jury instruction, despite overwhelming evidence against the defendant, because of the possible effect of the instruction on the jury. The judge had instructed the jury, in a case where the defendant was charged with a specific intent crime, that every person is "conclusively presumed to intend the natural and necessary consequences of his acts," in clear violation of the Court's

79. 407 U.S. 371, 92 S.Ct. 2174 (1972).

80. 461 U.S. 499, 103 S.Ct. 1974 (1983).

81. As Justice Stevens argued in a concurring opinion, the Court could easily have held no violation occurred, since the prosecutor did not comment on the defendant's failure to take the stand, but only on his failure to present evidence challenging certain aspects of the prosecution's case.

82. 460 U.S. 73, 103 S.Ct. 969 (1983).

ruling in *Sandstrom v. Montana.*[83] The four-member dissent pointed out that the facts of the case definitively established the defendant committed the crime, and argued from this that the jury "could have regarded these facts as dispositive of intent and not relied on the presumption." But the plurality, in an opinion by Justice Blackmun, held that the instruction "permitted the jury to convict respondent without ever examining the evidence concerning an element of the crime charged," and thus could not be considered harmless beyond a reasonable doubt. Justice Stevens joined the result reached by the plurality because he felt the case did not raise a federal question.

It may be that the distinction between *Hasting* and *Johnson* is that the latter involved a jury instruction, the impact of which is difficult to gauge regardless of the evidence against the defendant. This surmise receives some support from *Yates v. Evatt,*[84] where the Court, as it had in *Johnson,* again analyzed the impact of an instruction erroneously telling the jury to presume intent. In a unanimous opinion written by Justice Souter, the Court took to task the South Carolina Supreme Court for finding that the instruction was harmless error, particularly because the test that court applied was whether the other evidence in the case established beyond a reasonable doubt that the jury "would have found it unnecessary to rely" on the unconstitutional presumption. Souter pointed out that this inquiry "will not tell us whether the jury's verdict did rest on that evidence as well as on the presumptions, or whether that evidence was of such compelling force as to show beyond a reasonable doubt that the presumptions must have made no difference in reaching the verdict obtained." It is the latter issue that must be addressed, according to the Court. Although admitting that discerning what the jury actually considered was impossible, the Court emphasized that the reviewing court should conduct harmless error analysis with this ultimate goal in mind.[85] As noted above, this, was not the message sent in cases like *Hasting* and *Schneble,* involving evidentiary errors.

(2) Errors requiring automatic reversal. In *Chapman,* the Court cautioned that certain constitutional errors may involve "rights so basic to a fair trial that their infraction can never be treated as harmless error." It then cited cases involving a coerced

83. 442 U.S. 510, 99 S.Ct. 2450 (1979) (prohibiting presumptive intent instructions because they violate the proof beyond a reasonable doubt requirement).

84. 500 U.S. ___, 111 S.Ct. 1884 (1991).

85. The lower courts also generally find that instructions that misstate the prosecution's burden are not harmless, regardless of the evidence presented. See, e.g., *United States v. Jones,* 909 F.2d 533 (D.C.Cir.1990); *Hall v. Kelso,* 892 F.2d 1541 (11th Cir.1990); *Reid v. Warden,* 708 F.Supp. 730 (W.D.N.C. 1989); *Groesbeck v. Housewright,* 657 F.Supp. 798 (D.Nev.1987).

confession,[86] the right to trial counsel,[87] and the right to an impartial judge.[88]   In other decisions, the Court has suggested that violation of the right to speedy trial,[89] the Double Jeopardy Clause,[90] and the right to a representative jury [91] and grand jury [92] should never be deemed harmless.

The Court's first attempt to explain in general terms why these types of errors require automatic reversal rather than analysis under the reasonable doubt standard came in *Arizona v. Fulminante,*[93] in the course of "reversing" *Payne v. Arkansas,*[94] the case which *Chapman* cited in support of its statement that admission of a coerced confession is never harmless error.   In *Fulminante,* Chief Justice Rehnquist contended for a five-member majority that the "common thread" connecting post-*Chapman* cases permitting a harmless error finding was that they involved "trial error."   This type of error, according to Rehnquist, is "error which occurred during the presentation of the case to the jury, and which may therefore be quantitatively assessed in the context of other evidence presented in order to determine whether its admission was harmless beyond a reasonable doubt."   Calling admission of an involuntary confession a "classic" trial error, Rehnquist distinguished it from the two other examples *Chapman* gave of automatic reversal situations—"total deprivation of the right to counsel at trial" and a trial judge who was not impartial.   These "structural defects" infect the entire trial and thus "defy analysis by 'harmless error' standards."

This conceptualization of harmless error doctrine has some appeal.   As noted earlier, the most commonly advocated harmless error standards all focus on the effect of the error on the factfinder, assessment of which is always difficult, but particularly so when the error is "structural."   Whether the trial-versus-structural error dichotomy explains all of the Court's cases is not

86.   *Payne v. Arkansas,* 356 U.S. 560, 78 S.Ct. 844 (1958) ("where, as here, a coerced confession constitutes a part of the evidence before the jury and a general verdict is returned, no one can say what credit and weight the jury gave to the confession.").

87.   *Gideon v. Wainwright,* 372 U.S. 335, 83 S.Ct. 792 (1963), discussed in § 31.02(b).

88.   *Tumey v. Ohio,* 273 U.S. 510, 47 S.Ct. 437 (1927), discussed in § 27.05(a).

89.   *Strunk v. United States,* 412 U.S. 434, 93 S.Ct. 2260 (1973).

90.   *Price v. Georgia,* 398 U.S. 323, 90 S.Ct. 1757 (1970).

91.   *Taylor v. Louisiana,* 419 U.S. 522, 95 S.Ct. 692 (1975).

92.   *Vasquez v. Hillery,* 474 U.S. 254, 106 S.Ct. 617 (1986).

93.   499 U.S. ___, 111 S.Ct. 1246 (1991).

94.   356 U.S. 560, 78 S.Ct. 844 (1968). The majority in *Fulminante* denied that it was reversing *Payne,* since at the time of the latter decision the harmless error test was whether there was sufficient evidence in the absence of the error to support a conviction. According to the *Fulminante* majority, all *Payne* held was that admission of a coerced confession calls for automatic reversal under this more lenient, pre–*Chapman* test.

clear, however. For instance, while faulty jury instructions have generally been subject to harmless error analysis,[95] in congruence with *Fulminante's* notion that trial errors can be found harmless, the Court has rejected use of that analysis when the judge fails to instruct the jury on the reasonable doubt standard.[96] Further, while *Fulminante* reaffirmed *Chapman's* holding that deprivation of the right to trial counsel should bring automatic reversal, deprivation of that right at pretrial proceedings can be harmless.[97]

Perhaps these decisions can be reconciled with *Fulminante's* categories. As an alternatve to *Fulminante's* framework, or as a supplement to it, one might consider Justice Harlan's argument, in his dissents in *Fahy* and *Chapman,* that automatic reversal should be reserved for those errors which significantly detract from the public's image of fairness. This "public intolerance" rationale might better justify the distinction between the reasonable doubt instruction and other instructions and between deprivations of trial and pretrial counsel. It is also echoed in some of the Court's decisions requiring automatic reversal. For instance, in *Vasquez v. Hillery,*[98] where five members of the Court held that racial discrimination in the selection of the grand jury can never be harmless, the primary justification given was that such discrimination "strikes at the fundamental values of our judicial system and our society as a whole." Harlan's public intolerance rationale might also call into question *Fulminante's* explicit holding, at least to the extent it would allow the introduction of a confession which has been beaten out of a suspect to be labelled harmless error.[99]

Finally, some types of error require automatic reversal because they can only occur if the defendant has been prejudiced. For instance, a denial of ineffective assistance of counsel cannot be found unless the attorney's incompetence is shown to have "deprive[d] the defendant of a fair trial."[1] Similarly, prosecutorial failure to provide material evidence to the defense is not a constitutional violation unless "there is a reasonable probability that, had the evidence been disclosed to the defense, the result of the proceeding would be different."[2] Given the way in which these

95. See, e.g., *Yates v. Evatt,* 500 U.S. ___, 111 S.Ct. 1884 (1991) (presumed intent instruction); *Kentucky v. Whorton,* 441 U.S. 786, 99 S.Ct. 2088 (1979) (presumption of innocence instruction).

96. See *Jackson v. Virginia,* 443 U.S. 307, 99 S.Ct. 2781 (1979). Cf. note 85 supra.

97. See, e.g., *Coleman v. Alabama,* 399 U.S. 1, 90 S.Ct. 1999 (1970) (preliminary hearing counsel); *United States v. Wade,* 388 U.S. 218, 87 S.Ct. 1926 (1967) (counsel at lineups).

98. 474 U.S. 254, 106 S.Ct. 617 (1986).

99. Note that the "coercion" involved in *Fulminante* was not physical, but consisted primarily of veiled threats. See § 16.02(a)(1).

1. *Strickland v. Washington,* 466 U.S. 668, 104 S.Ct. 2052 (1984), discussed in § 32.03(b)(2).

2. *United States v. Bagley,* 473 U.S. 667, 105 S.Ct. 3375 (1985), discussed in § 24.04(b).

rights are defined, if a court finds that they have been violated, it cannot rationally decide that the violation is harmless.

29.06   Retroactivity

Two issues which have given the Supreme Court considerable difficulty are whether a new ruling by an appellate or habeas court should be given retroactive application, and if so, to what extent. Prior to the 1965 decision of *Linkletter v. Walker,*[3] the Court applied *each* of its new constitutional holdings to *all* cases that were on appeal or habeas review at the time of the ruling. The principal practical problem with this approach, as the Court recognized in *Linkletter,* was that a new ruling could impose enormous costs on the criminal justice system. Not only would there need to be numerous retrials, but some cases might even have to be dismissed, given the length of time between many convictions and habeas review. Furthermore, commentators noted,[4] this potential cost might in turn deter the creation of new rules.

Since 1965, the Court has embarked on an attempt to narrow the retroactivity doctrine, with several vacillations and false starts. In *Linkletter* and its progeny, the Court indicated that whether a constitutional ruling should be given retroactive effect depended upon the nature of the rule at issue, and denied retroactive application in a number of cases; at the same time, all rules that were declared retroactive continued to be given "full" effect (i.e. they were applied to all cases on post-conviction review). Then, beginning in 1982 with *United States v. Johnson,*[5] the Court began to collapse the issue of when a rule is retroactive into the issue of how retroactive the rule should be by shifting its analysis from the nature of the rule in question to the stage at which one seeks to have it applied. As a result, today every new rule, regardless of its nature, is available to litigants seeking appellate review at the time it was announced. In contrast, litigants seeking collateral review will seldom benefit from retroactivity. These developments are discussed here, although they are also briefly treated in the context of habeas review.[6]

(a) **The Linkletter-Stovall Rule.** The decision considered in *Linkletter* was *Mapp v. Ohio,*[7] which had ruled that the Fourth Amendment exclusionary rule should apply to the states. The defendant's conviction had occurred one year prior to *Mapp,* and the contested search had obviously occurred even earlier. Yet

3. 381 U.S. 618, 85 S.Ct. 1731 (1965).

4. See Allen, "The Judicial Quest for Penal Justice: The Warren Court and the Criminal Cases," 1975 U.Ill.L.F. 518.

5. 457 U.S. 537, 102 S.Ct. 2579 (1982).

6. See § 33.02(c).

7. 367 U.S. 643, 81 S.Ct. 1684 (1961), discussed in § 2.02.

because the defendant was seeking collateral relief at the time *Mapp* was decided, the pre-*Linkletter* approach to retroactivity would have required reversal of his conviction.

The Supreme Court advanced several reasons for not following the traditional approach. First, the exclusionary rule was a judicially created remedy, rather than a direct outgrowth of the Fourth Amendment, and thus more subject to judicial (i.e., the Court's) manipulation. Second, state officials in the defendant's case had reasonably relied on the Court's decision in *Wolf v. Colorado*,[8] which had explicitly held that although the Fourth Amendment applied to the states, the exclusionary rule did not. Third, and perhaps most importantly, the Court noted that to apply *Mapp* retroactively would flood the courts with retrials and present problems in determining the materiality of lost or deteriorating evidence. Finally, the Court pointed out that, unlike other rights given retroactive application, an illegal search or seizure has no direct bearing on the guilt or innocence of the defendant or on the integrity of the trial.

(1) Retroactive rules: definition. Although *Linkletter* signalled a new approach to retroactivity analysis, it was not until two years later, in *Stovall v. Denno*,[9] that the Court formalized its new approach. There the Court indicated that retroactivity analysis required assessment of "(a) the purpose to be served by the new standards [meaning the effect the standards had on the accuracy of the truth-finding process], (b) the extent of the reliance by law enforcement authorities on the old standards, and (c) the effect on the administration of justice of a retroactive application of the new standards." In *Stovall*, the Court applied these criteria to find non-retroactive the ruling in *United States v. Wade*[10] that the Sixth Amendment requires counsel at pretrial lineups. While it acknowledged that counsel played some role in assuring the reliability of identifications, the Court noted that *Wade* established a prophylactic rule that applied without regard to the fairness of a particular lineup. Moreover, any suggestivity in an identification procedure could always be challenged on due process grounds. Additionally, law enforcement officials had relied in good faith on accepted doctrine that counsel was not required at lineups. Finally, the Court noted that reopening those cases implicated by the *Wade* ruling would saddle the courts with numerous hearings to determine whether the violation was harmless error and, if not, whether a new trial could proceed using evidence that could easily be stale.

8.　338 U.S. 25, 69 S.Ct. 1359 (1949), discussed in § 2.02.

9.　388 U.S. 293, 87 S.Ct. 1967 (1967).

10.　388 U.S. 218, 87 S.Ct. 1926 (1967), discussed in § 17.02(a).

For similar reasons, in *Desist v. United States*,[11] the Court refused to render retroactive the ruling in *Katz v. United States* [12] that non-consensual electronic eavesdropping constitutes a search under the Fourth Amendment; it also held nonretroactive its holdings that jury trials are required for serious contempt charges,[13] that due process prohibits vindictive sentencing after a successful appeal,[14] and that the exclusion of women from jury venires violates the Sixth Amendment.[15] On the other hand, the Court's rulings finding unconstitutional the failure to provide counsel in misdemeanor cases,[16] the use of un-cross-examined preliminary hearing testimony at trial,[17] and non-unanimous six-member juries [18] were given retroactive application, primarily because they were said to affect the truth-finding function. Additionally, in the last two cases, the Court noted that the rulings had been foreshadowed by earlier decisions and thus could have been anticipated by government officials.[19]

This latter type of reasoning dovetailed with the idea, first expressed in *Desist,* that the retroactivity issue is moot if the constitutional ruling is not "new." According to *Desist,* a ruling which "simply applie[s] a well-established constitutional principle to govern a case which is closely analogous to those which have been previously considered in the prior caselaw" should apply to all cases subject to judicial review at the time of the rule.[20] If, on the other hand, the decision overrules a previous Supreme Court precedent (as did the *Katz* decision considered in *Desist*), or rejects a practice which the lower courts had generally followed, then a more careful analysis, along the lines suggested in *Linkletter* and *Stovall,* was warranted.

11. 394 U.S. 244, 89 S.Ct. 1030 (1969).

12. 389 U.S. 347, 88 S.Ct. 507 (1967), discussed in § 4.02.

13. *DeStefano v. Woods,* 392 U.S. 631, 88 S.Ct. 2093 (1968) (finding non-retroactive *Bloom v. Illinois,* discussed in § 27.02(c)(1)).

14. *Michigan v. Payne,* 412 U.S. 47, 93 S.Ct. 1966 (1973) (finding non-retroactive *North Carolina v. Pearce,* discussed in § 29.02(d)).

15. *Daniel v. Louisiana,* 420 U.S. 31, 95 S.Ct. 704 (1975) (finding non-retroactive *Taylor v. Louisiana,* discussed in § 27.03(c)).

16. *Berry v. Cincinnati,* 414 U.S. 29, 94 S.Ct. 193 (1973) (finding retroactive *Argersinger v. Hamlin,* discussed in § 31.02(b)).

17. *Berger v. California,* 393 U.S. 314, 89 S.Ct. 540 (1969) (finding retroactive *Barber v. Page,* discussed in § 28.04(a)).

18. *Brown v. Louisiana,* 447 U.S. 323, 100 S.Ct. 2214 (1980) (finding retroactive *Burch v. Louisiana,* discussed in § 27.02(e)).

19. *Barber,* the confrontation case, had been foreshadowed by *Pointer v. Texas,* discussed in § 28.04(a). *Burch,* the jury voting ruling, had been foreshadowed by *Ballew v. Georgia,* discussed in § 27.02(d).

20. See, e.g., *Lee v. Missouri,* 439 U.S. 461, 99 S.Ct. 710 (1979), holding that *Duren v. Missouri* was merely an "extrapolation" of *Taylor v. Louisiana* (both discussed in § 27.03(c)), and therefore required full retroactive application.

(2) The effect of retroactive rules. While the *Linkletter/ Stovall* approach to retroactivity limited the types of cases given retroactive status, it did not change the *effect* of a ruling on retroactivity. *Stovall* affirmed that when a ruling was found retroactive, it generally applied to all cases subject to judicial review at the time of the ruling, even to those being collaterally attacked. When a ruling was found nonretroactive, then it applied only to those cases where the right in question was violated after the ruling. Thus, in the latter instance, when the right applied to trial proceedings, the Court's ruling only affected trials commenced after the ruling. If it concerned a police practice, the Court's holding only applied to those cases in which the practice (e.g. a search) occurred after the ruling.

The one major exception to the latter rule was *Johnson v. New Jersey*,[21] which decided the retroactivity of *Miranda v. Arizona*.[22] Although the Court acknowledged the minimal relationship between the *Miranda* requirements and the reliability of a confession, as well as the numerous retrials and releases that retroactive application would require, it gave *Miranda* partial retroactivity, limiting its application to all *trials* which commenced after the date of the decision. This meant that confessions obtained in violation of *Miranda* before that decision was handed down could still be challenged, if the trial using those confessions did not take place until after *Miranda*.

(b) Cases on Appeal. Not all members of the Court agreed with the *Linkletter/Stovall* approach during the seventeen years it held sway. For instance, in *Brown v. Louisiana*,[23] the case which held retroactive the Court's ruling in *Burch v. Louisiana*[24] that unanimity is required for six person juries, two members of the Court joined the majority, but refused to endorse the *Stovall* analysis it used. Rather, Justices Powell and Stevens simply noted that the petitioner should prevail because his case at been on "direct review," or appeal, at the time *Burch* was decided. To find otherwise, they argued, would mean that whenever a right was found nonretroactive, one defendant—the one whose case happened to be chosen by the Court—would fortuitously benefit from the rule announced in her case while others, equally situated on the appellate ladder, would be denied relief. Thus, their allegiance with the majority was not based on retroactivity analysis *per se*, but on a fairness rationale approaching an equal protection stance. This position had actually originated with Justice Harlan, in his opinion in *Desist*. Harlan had contended that application of a new rule to cases pending on direct review is

---

21. 384 U.S. 719, 86 S.Ct. 1772 (1966).

22. 384 U.S. 436, 86 S.Ct. 1602 (1966), discussed in § 16.02(d).

23. 447 U.S. 323, 100 S.Ct. 2214 (1980).

24. 441 U.S. 130, 99 S.Ct. 1623 (1979).

always necessary, not only to assure equality of treatment, but also to avoid turning the Court into a "super-legislature" which announced rules of prospective impact only.

In part to resolve this disagreement, the Court, in *United States v. Johnson*,[25] announced that "retroactivity must be rethought." In a 5–4 opinion written by Justice Blackmun, the Court purported to lay down a new framework for examining the question. It began by setting out three "threshold" inquiries designed to determine the applicability of retroactivity analysis. First, as it had in *Desist,* the Court noted that when an opinion "merely has applied settled precedents to new and different factual situations," no retroactivity question arises. Second, departing somewhat from *Desist,* if the new opinion is a "clear break with the past," it should almost always be applied *prospectively* only, because government officials will have reasonably relied upon the earlier rule and because retroactive application will require intolerable disruption of the justice system. Third, however, if the new rule goes to the very authority of the trial court to convict or punish a criminal, then the rule must be applied retroactively even if it is a "clear break". Here the Court was merely affirming the good sense of earlier decisions such as *Robinson v. Neil*,[26] which had applied *Waller v. Florida* [27] retroactively on the ground that after that decision a state court does not have jurisdiction to prosecute a person who had already been prosecuted for the same offense under a municipal ordnance.

The *Johnson* Court focused on distinguishing the second, "clear break" category from the first, "application-of-old-doctrine-to-new-law" category. The clear break cases were seen to fall into three types: (1) those that explicitly overruled a past decision; (2) those that "disapproved a practice this Court arguably has sanctioned in prior cases," and (3) those which overturn[ed] a longstanding and widespread practice to which this Court ha[d] not spoken but which a near-unanimous body of lower court authority ha[d] expressly approved." As noted above, the Court asserted that if a rule met any of these definitions, then it should generally not be applied retroactively. Yet Blackmun also pointed out, in a footnote, that when a rule's "purpose is to overcome an aspect of the criminal trial that substantially impairs its truth-finding function" it had always been given "complete retroactive effect." Thus, he implied that even a clear break rule, if it affects truth-finding, is to be given retroactive effect.

25. 457 U.S. 537, 102 S.Ct. 2579 (1982).

26. 409 U.S. 505, 93 S.Ct. 876 (1973).

27. 397 U.S. 387, 90 S.Ct. 1184 (1970), discussed in § 30.06(c).

The rule before the *Johnson* Court was that announced in *Payton v. New York*,[28] requiring an arrest warrant to effect a non-exigent home arrest. The Court felt that *Payton* neither explicitly overruled a past decision nor disapproved a practice which the Court had sanctioned, and noted that the lower courts had been split on the warrantless house arrest issue. Thus, the rule fit neither the first or second "threshold" categories—it was neither a mere application of past precedent to new facts, nor a clear break with the past. In this situation, the pre-*Johnson* approach would have mandated application of the *Stovall* criteria to ascertain whether retroactive effect should be given; under these criteria and the precedent construing them, such as *Desist*, the rule probably would not have been applied retroactively, since it derived from the Fourth Amendment. But the *Johnson* Court took a different tack. It applied *Payton* to all cases on direct review, agreeing with Harlan that a different holding would increase the risk the Court would "mete out different constitutional protection to defendants simultaneously subjected to identical police conduct."

Thus, *Johnson* suggested that rules that are not clear breaks with the past will always be given retroactive application, at least to cases on appeal. Although *Johnson* was carefully confined to Fourth Amendment cases, nothing in its reasoning logically limited it to those types of claims (which, after all, are the *least* likely to challenge the accuracy of the verdict). Indeed, in *Shea v. Louisiana*,[29] the Court held that *Johnson* applied to Fifth Amendment cases as well. There the Court first held that *Edwards v. Arizona*,[30] which prohibited police from questioning a defendant who has requested counsel, was an "in-between" case like *Payton*—it was neither a straightforward application of *Miranda v. Arizona* nor a clear break from that case.[31] It then concluded that "[t]here is nothing about a Fourth Amendment rule that suggests that in this context it should be given greater retroactive effect than a Fifth Amendment rule." Accordingly, all defendants on direct review at the time *Edwards* was decided should be able to benefit from it.

Johnson and *Shea* left retroactivity analysis in a state of confusion. They appeared to endorse Harlan's approach to cases on direct review, except when the ruling was a "clear break with the past" that did not affect the truth-finding function. Why the latter exception should exist was unclear, if the Court agreed with

28. 445 U.S. 573, 100 S.Ct. 1371 (1980), discussed in § 3.04(b).

29. 470 U.S. 51, 105 S.Ct. 1065 (1985).

30. 451 U.S. 477, 101 S.Ct. 1880 (1981), discussed in § 16.03(e).

31. The Court had actually reached this conclusion earlier, in *Solem v. Stumes*, 465 U.S. 638, 104 S.Ct. 1338 (1984), discussed below.

Harlan's sentiment that all cases on direct review should be treated alike. In *Griffith v. Kentucky*[32] the Court finally explicitly adopted Harlan's approach for such cases. Justice Blackmun, writing for six members of the Court, reiterated Harlan's two reasons for applying *any* new constitutional ruling to all cases on direct appeal. First, to refrain from doing so would put the Court in the position of acting like a legislature rather than a court, because its rule would have the effect only of prospective legislation rather than backward-looking adjudication. Second, failing to apply all new rulings retroactively would unfairly allow the petitioner whose case was selected by the Court to benefit from the rule while others similarly situated might not, simply because their case was not chosen for review by the Court. After *Griffith,* every rule announced on direct review, even one which is a clear break with the past, applies retroactively to all other cases on direct review.

(c) **Cases on Habeas Review.** *Johnson* appeared to hold that habeas litigants should not have the benefit of a "clear break" rule unless it dealt with the truth-finding function, and should have the benefit of an "in-between" rule, such as *Payton's* holding, only if *Stovall's* criteria were met. This approach seemed to be affirmed two years later in *Solem v. Stumes.*[33] There, the Court refused to apply the *Edwards* rule (which would later be applied to cases on direct review in *Shea*) to cases on collateral review, because the *Stovall* criteria were not met. Neither *Shea* nor *Griffith,* both of which were decided after *Solem* but which focused on retroactive application to those on appeal, addressed the validity of this approach. But two years after *Griffith,* in *Teague v. Lane,*[34] the Court completely revamped this aspect of retroactivity analysis as well, again relying on an approach suggested by Justice Harlan.

In *Desist* and *Mackey v. United States,*[35] Harlan had argued that retroactivity analysis for decisions reached on collateral review should depend not on the purpose or content of the rule at issue (as the *Stovall* criteria do), but rather on "the purposes for which the writ of habeas corpus is made available." Emphasizing that the writ is a *collateral* remedy, the scope of which can be narrowed in the interest of promoting finality of judgment, he concluded in *Desist:*

> [T]he threat of habeas serves as a necessary incentive for trial and appellate judges throughout the land to conduct their proceedings in a manner consistent with established constitu-

---

32. 479 U.S. 314, 107 S.Ct. 708 (1987).

33. 465 U.S. 638, 104 S.Ct. 1338 (1984).

34. 489 U.S. 288, 109 S.Ct. 1060 (1989).

35. 401 U.S. 667, 91 S.Ct. 1160 (1971) (separate opinion of Harlan, J.).

tional principles. In order to perform this function, the habeas court need only apply the constitutional standards that prevailed at the time the original proceedings took place.

For these reasons, a new rule should not be applied retroactively to habeas petitioners. However, given the remedial purposes of the writ, Harlan was willing to recognize two exceptions to this approach, both outlined in *Mackey*. A new rule should be applied to habeas petitioners, he concluded, if it places "certain kinds of primary, private individual conduct beyond the power of the criminal law-making authority to proscribe," or if it involves "procedures that . . . are 'implicit in the concept of ordered liberty.'"

In *Teague*, seven members of the Court agreed to adopt the Harlan approach. Implicitly rejecting *Johnson*, which had not distinguished between cases on direct and collateral review, the majority held that only those rules meeting one of Harlan's two exceptions should be applied in habeas cases. Four justices, in an opinion by Justice O'Connor, also voted to circumscribe the ability of federal courts to grant relief even in the case before them when the claim is raised collaterally rather than on direct review. Relying on the type of reasoning used to justify the holding in *Griffith*, O'Connor stated that "the harm caused by the failure to treat similarly situated defendants alike cannot be exaggerated." Thus, she concluded that "habeas corpus cannot be used as a vehicle to create new constitutional rules of criminal procedure unless those rules would be applied retroactively to *all* defendants on collateral review through one of the two exceptions we have articulated."

The final step taken by the plurality was to circumscribe the authority of federal habeas courts even to *consider* the merits of a habeas claim. If the habeas court decides that the proposed rule, if adopted, would not apply retroactively under *Teague*, then, held the plurality, it should refrain from addressing the merits of the proposed rule. According to O'Connor, this approach avoids the danger of advisory opinions, as well as "the inequity" of treating similarly situated defendants differently. This conclusion was the central focus of Justice Brennan's dissent:

> Out of an exaggerated concern for treating similarly situated habeas petitioners the same, the plurality would for the first time preclude the federal courts from considering on collateral review a vast range of important constitutional challenges; where those challenges have merit, it would bar the vindication of personal constitutional rights and deny society a check against further violations until the same claim is presented on direct review.

But the plurality was more impressed with its perception that the previous approach to retroactivity, which Brennan advocated, "*continually* forces the States to marshall resources to keep in prison defendants whose trials and appeals conformed to then-existing constitutional standards."

As Brennan indicated, the plurality's holding in *Teague* (since affirmed by a majority of the Court [36]) will make challenging the constitutionality of state criminal procedures in federal court much more difficult. State criminal defendants' only avenue of federal relief is the writ of habeas corpus or, as indicated in the introduction to this chapter, a direct appeal or writ of certiorari to the United States Supreme Court. If these defendants are not able to meet *Teague's* requirements for gaining access to a federal habeas court, they are limited to Supreme Court review, which is infrequently granted and is based solely on the state court record (unlike a federal habeas case, for which there is often an additional evidentiary hearing).[37]

Thus, understanding *Teague's* scope is important not only for retroactivity purposes but also in order to delineate its impact on the development of federal constitutional law. This objective necessitates looking at two factors: (1) whether the claim at issue merely requires application of clear precedent or instead envisions a "new rule;" and, if the latter, (2) whether it meets one of the two exceptions advanced by Harlan and endorsed in *Teague*.

(1) The definition of "new rule." Consistent with *Desist* and other early retroactivity decisions, nothing in *Teague* prevents a federal habeas court from applying settled law to vindicate a state (or federal) petitioner's claim. But if the claim contemplates what *Teague* calls a "new rule," then relief may not be granted (or even considered) unless one of the two exceptions are met. In defining the "new rule" concept, *Teague* could have adopted *Johnson's* definition of a "clear break" rule; this notion, it will be remembered, was defined as a holding which overruled a past decision, disapproved a practice the Court had arguably sanctioned, or overturned a longstanding practice which a near-unanimous body of lower court authority had approved. But *Johnson* is not mentioned in the plurality opinion. Rather, O'Connor announced another test, seemingly much broader than the clear break standard: "a case announces a new rule if the result was not *dictated* by precedent existing at the time the defendant's conviction became final."

As Justice Brennan argued in dissent, "[f]ew decisions on appeal or collateral review are '*dictated*' by what came before. Most such cases involve a question of law that is at least debata-

---

36. See, e.g., *Penry v. Lynaugh,* 492 U.S. 302, 109 S.Ct. 2934 (1989).

37. See § 33.02(d).

ble, permitting a rational judge to resolve the case in more than one way." This observation was borne out by the Court's post-*Teague* treatment of the rule in *Arizona v. Roberson*,[38] which had held that the holding in *Edwards v. Arizona* (the same ruling at issue in *Shea* and *Stumes*) governed cases where the subsequent police questioning is about a different offense than the one for which the defendant requests counsel. Although the majority in *Roberson* had stated that its rule was within the "logical compass" of and "directly controlled" by *Edwards,* five members of the Court concluded, in *Butler v. McKellar*,[39] that *Roberson's* holding should not be given retroactive effect to habeas litigants. The *McKellar* Court emphasized that since there had been a significant division among lower courts about whether *Edwards* applied to separate offenses, the rule in *Roberson* was "susceptible to debate among reasonable minds," and thus should be seen as "new" for retroactivity purposes. Other Court decisions have continued to define the new rule concept very broadly.[40]

(2) Exceptions to non-retroactivity of new rules. According to *Teague,* a claim which asks a federal habeas court to adopt a new rule may nonetheless be considered, following Justice Harlan's formulation, if it would place "certain kinds of primary, private individual conduct beyond the power of the criminal law-making authority to proscribe," or involves procedures that are "implicit in the concept of ordered liberty." As examples of the first exception, Harlan cited cases involving First and Fifth Amendment claims which, once vindicated, rendered unconstitutional the criminal statute under which the petitioner was prosecuted.[41] In *Penry v. Lynaugh*,[42] the Court also included within this exception claims that place "certain conduct beyond the State's power to punish at all;" it then went on to consider (but ultimately reject) a habeas claim that execution of the mentally retarded is unconstitutional. Other claims which might fit this category are those which would eliminate the state's ability to prosecute certain offenses (such as *Pearce–Blackledge* vindictiveness claims,[43] and double jeopardy claims of the type recognized by *Johnson* in its third "threshold" inquiry).

With respect to the second exception, the four-member plurality in *Teague* concluded that it should be confined to procedures

---

38. 486 U.S. 675, 108 S.Ct. 2093 (1988), discussed in § 16.03(e)(1).

39. 494 U.S. 407, 110 S.Ct. 1212 (1990).

40. See, e.g., *Saffle v. Parks,* 494 U.S. 484, 110 S.Ct. 1257 (1990); *Stringer v. Black,* 503 U.S. __, 112 S.Ct. 1130 (1992) (holding that *Teague* even bars hearing claims dictated by precedent, if relief "would effectively create a new rule by extending the precedent to a novel context").

41. See, e.g., *Stanley v. Georgia,* 394 U.S. 557, 89 S.Ct. 1243 (1969) (invalidating obscenity statute).

42. 492 U.S. 302, 109 S.Ct. 2934 (1989).

43. See § 29.02(d).

"without which the likelihood of an accurate conviction is serious-ly diminished." Harlan had argued in *Mackey* against such a definition, in large part because he found "inherently intractable the purported distinctions between those new rules that are de-signed to improve the factfinding process and those designed principally to further other values." But O'Connor justified the narrower test, subsequently approved by a majority of the Court,[44] by pointing to more recent cases which made factual innocence the touchstone of analysis in deciding the scope of habeas review.[45] Thus, as currently framed, this exception appears to present issues similar to the first of *Stovall's* three criteria.

The petitioner's argument in *Teague* was that *Taylor v. Loui-siana's* [46] requirement that jury venires represent a cross-section of the community should also apply to the jury itself. Since *Taylor* had stated that its cross-section requirement should *not* apply to the petit jury, this claim clearly requested a "new rule," which, under *Teague's* new approach, could only be considered by the Supreme Court on habeas review if it met one of the exceptions. The claim clearly did not fit within the first exception, and the Court found that it did not rest on accuracy concerns either, but rather on a desire to foster community participation in the adjudi-cation process. Since the proposed rule would thus not be applied retroactively, it was not considered on its merits.

29.07 Conclusion

The following summarizes those aspects of the appeals process discussed in this chapter.

(1) The federal Constitution does not guarantee a right to appeal of a criminal conviction. However, if an appeal process is provided, as is the case in every jurisdiction, then: (a) indigent defendants are entitled to complete trial transcripts, free of charge, to perfect the appeal; (b) all defendants are entitled to effective assistance of counsel on appeals as of right (but not on discretionary appeals); (c) counsel may withdraw from representa-tion on an appeal as of right only if she files a brief with the appellate court referring to anything in the record that might arguably support the appeal, the defendant is given a chance to add to the brief, and the appellate court, after reviewing the brief, has determined that the appeal is wholly frivolous; and (d) the state may not retaliate against defendants who successfully ap-peal. With respect to the latter issue, a retaliatory motive is presumed when the post-appeal sentence or charge is higher than

44. See, e.g., *Butler v. McKellar,* 494 U.S. 407, 110 S.Ct. 1212 (1990).

45. See, e.g., *Murray v. Carrier,* 477 U.S. 478, 106 S.Ct. 2639 (1986), dis-cussed in § 33.03(e).

46. 419 U.S. 522, 95 S.Ct. 692 (1975), discussed in § 27.03(c).

the pre-appeal sentence or charge, unless the post-appeal decisionmaker lacks the motivation to be vindictive. This presumption can be overcome by showing that the new sentence or charge is plausibly based on an event subsequent to the previous sentence or charge, or on "new" information.

(2) In order to avoid piecemeal, disruptive litigation, defense appeals of pretrial rulings are permissible only if the ruling: (a) is final from the trial court's point of view; (b) involves an important right which would be lost, probably irreparably, if review were to await conviction; (c) involves an issue which is independent of the main cause of action, so that elements of the latter will not have be considered by the appellate court before they are considered by the trial court; and (d) concerns an issue which is inherently limited, rather than one which could be raised by any defendant as a dilatory tactic. Under this analysis, rulings regarding bail and double jeopardy are usually appealable prior to trial, whereas rulings regarding the Fourth Amendment, speedy trial, vindictive sentencing, and grand jury matters generally are not. The prosecution is not as firmly bound by the final judgment rule, and may appeal many types of pretrial rulings so long as it meets the requirements in (3). Third parties may appeal a pretrial ruling holding them in contempt, or involving a legal right, such as First Amendment access to the court, which is independent of the proceedings.

(3) The Double Jeopardy Clause bars the prosecution from appealing any judgment which determines there is insufficient evidence to convict the defendant. However, given statutory authorization to do so, the prosecution may appeal any other ruling without violating the Clause, including pretrial rulings which may have a significant impact on its case, post-jeopardy rulings, and sentences.

(4) Constitutional error which constitutes a structural defect (e.g., a corrupt judge or violation of the right to trial counsel) requires automatic reversal. Constitutional error which can be labelled trial error—error which occurred during the presentation of the case to the jury and may therefore be quantitatively assessed in the context of other evidence presented (e.g., introduction of illegally seized evidence or a coerced confession)—may be found harmless. To be found harmless, the prosecution must show beyond a reasonable doubt that the error did not contribute to the verdict. Non-constitutional error, in federal court at least, is harmless if it did not influence the jury or only slightly did so.

(5) A new constitutional ruling is applicable to all cases on direct appeal at the time of the ruling. For a habeas claim which asks the court to adopt a "new" rule (i.e., a rule that is not dictated by precedent), retroactivity analysis is governed by

whether the proposed rule (a) places primary, private individual conduct beyond the power of the criminal law-making authority to proscribe or (b) is closely associated with accurate factfinding. If the proposed rule fits one of these latter two criteria, then it should be considered on its merits and, if adopted, should be given retroactive application to all other habeas petitioners. If the proposed rule fits neither criterion, then, because it would not be applicable retroactively to other petitioners, the habeas petitioner is not entitled to relief and her claim should not be ruled upon.

BIBLIOGRAPHY

Bilaisis, Vilija. Harmless Error: Abettor of Courtroom Misconduct. 74 J.Crim.L. & Criminol. 457 (1983).

Carr, John B. Retroactivity: A Study in Supreme Court Doctrine "As Applied." 61 N.C.L.Rev. 745 (1983).

Erlinder, C. Peter and David C. Thomas. Prohibiting Prosecutorial Vindictiveness While Protecting Prosecutorial Discretion. 76 J.Crim.L. & Criminol. 341 (1985).

Fallon, Richard H. and Daniel J. Meltzer. New Law, Non–Retroactivity, and Constitutional Remedies. 104 Harv.L.Rev. 1733 (1991).

Field, Martha A. Assessing the Harmlessness of Federal Constitutional Error—A Process in Need of a Rationale. 125 U.Pa.L. Rev. 15 (1976).

Hermann, Robert. Frivolous Criminal Appeals. 47 N.Y.U.L.Rev. 701 (1972).

Junkin, Frederick J. The Right to Counsel in "Frivolous" Appeals: A Reevaluation of the Guarantees of Anders v. California. 67 Tex.L.Rev. 181 (1988).

Mishkin, Paul J. Foreword: The High Court, The Great Writ, and Due Process of Time and Law. 79 Harv.L.Rev. 56 (1965).

Saltzburg, Stephen. The Harm of Harmless Error. 59 Va.L.Rev. 988 (1973).

Schwartz, Herman. Retroactivity, Reliability, and Due Process: A Reply to Professor Mishkin. 33 U.Chi.L.Rev. 719 (1966).

Stacy, Tom and Kim Dayton. Rethinking Harmless Error. 88 Colum.L.Rev. 79 (1988).

The Sixth Amendment Speedy Trial Guarantee: Delay Resulting from Interlocutory Appeals [note]. 60 B.U.L.Rev. 664 (1980).

Traynor, Roger J. The Riddle of Harmless Error. Ohio State Univ. Press.: 1970.

Chapter Thirty

DOUBLE JEOPARDY

30.01 Introduction

Both the civil and criminal law have developed doctrines which render legal proceedings conclusive and binding. In civil cases, the doctrine of *res judicata* is based upon the maxim that "no man shall be twice vexed for one and the same cause." Its criminal analogue is the prohibition on double jeopardy.

The common law very early developed two pleas which form the basis for the modern theory of double jeopardy. The plea of *autrefois acquit* forbids retrial of a defendant for the same offense after he has been acquitted. Its counterpart, *autrevois convict* disallows retrial after a prior conviction for the same offense. These rules were adopted by the American colonies, many of which, following the lead of Massachusetts, included double jeopardy provisions in their constitutions.[1]

According to the Supreme Court in *Ex parte Lange*,[2] both the *autrefois acquit* and *autrefois convict* notions were meant to be incorporated by that part of the Fifth Amendment which states: "nor shall any person be subject for the same offence to be twice put in jeopardy of life or limb." The Court emphasized that "[t]he 'twice put in jeopardy' language of the Constitution . . . relates to a potential, i.e., the risk that an accused for a second time will be convicted of the 'same offense' for which he was initially tried." Furthermore, stated the Court, the Double Jeopardy Clause not only incorporates the two common law rules but also applies "to all cases where a second punishment is attempted to be inflicted for the same offence by a judicial sentence." Later cases indicated that the Clause also protects the defendant's "valued right to have his trial completed by a particular tribunal," at least to the extent it does not interfere with the "public's interest in fair trials."[3] Thus, the Double Jeopardy Clause, as construed by the Court, is meant to protect against: (1) reprosecution after acquittal; (2) reprosecution after conviction; (3) separate punishments for the same offense; and, in some circumstances, (4) reprosecution after an aborted trial.

In *Palko v. Connecticut*,[4] the Supreme Court refused to hold that the protection from double jeopardy was a fundamental right

1. For more on the history of double jeopardy, see Sigler, Double Jeopardy: The Development of a Legal and Social Policy 13-37 (1969); M. Friedland, Double Jeopardy 3-17 (1969).

2. 85 U.S. (18 Wall.) 163 (1873).

3. *Wade v. Hunter*, 336 U.S. 684, 69 S.Ct. 834 (1949).

4. 302 U.S. 319, 58 S.Ct. 149 (1937).

requiring application to the states. But over thirty years later, in *Benton v. Maryland*,[5] the Court reversed itself, finding the Double Jeopardy Clause applicable to the states through the Fourteenth Amendment. Justice Black, in *Green v. United States*,[6] provided the classic description of why the Clause embodies a fundamental principle of justice:

> The underlying idea, one that is deeply engrained in at least the Anglo-American system of jurisprudence, is that the State with all its resources and power should not be allowed to make repeated attempts to convict an individual for an alleged offense, thereby subjecting him to embarrassment, expense and ordeal and compelling him to live in a continuing state of anxiety and insecurity, as well as enhancing the possibility that even though innocent he may be found guilty.

As this chapter illustrates, this avoidance-of-repeated-prosecutions rationale has receded into the background in more recent Supreme Court interpretations of the Clause; in its place, the Court has focused on whether the criminal defendant asserting a double jeopardy claim has been once subjected to a *determination* as to his guilt. Under the Court's new approach, regardless of the number of jeopardizing events to which the individual is exposed (see § 30.02), he is not entitled to the protection afforded by the Clause until he is either convicted, acquitted, or deprived of a chance for acquittal by prosecutorial action (see § 30.03), and then tried again for the "same offense" (see § 30.04) by the same governmental entity or "sovereign" (see § 30.05).

30.02 When Jeopardy Attaches

(a) **Type of Proceeding.** Although the Fifth Amendment speaks of "jeopardy of life and limb," *Ex parte Lange* established that the Double Jeopardy Clause governs all criminal prosecutions. In support of this holding, the Court noted that when the pleas of *autrefois acquit* and *autrefois convict* were established, they applied to most crimes despite the life or limb limitation, because virtually all were punishable by death or corporeal punishment. Further, common law courts continued to apply these doctrines even when other punishment was involved.

In *Breed v. Jones*,[7] the Court extended the reach of the Clause to juvenile delinquency proceedings, on the ground that "the risk to which the term jeopardy refers is that traditionally associated with 'actions intended to authorize criminal punishment to vindicate public justice.'" Under this reasoning, the fact that a juvenile proceeding might be denominated "civil" was not dispositive. Rather, most important to the Court's conclusion was the fact,

---

5. 395 U.S. 784, 89 S.Ct. 2056 (1969).   **7.** 421 U.S. 519, 95 S.Ct. 1779 (1975).
6. 355 U.S. 184, 78 S.Ct. 221 (1957).

already noted in previous Court decisions,[8] that delinquency proceedings are similar to criminal proceedings in terms of stigma and deprivation of liberty. Thus, the Fifth Amendment prohibits a delinquency proceeding after a criminal prosecution for the same offense, and vice versa.

In contrast, where the intention of the government is not to punish "criminally," but rather to seek rough compensation from the individual, the Clause is usually not implicated. *Helvering v. Mitchell*[9] upheld the constitutionality of a tax proceeding, following an acquittal on criminal fraud charges, which resulted in the government recovering the tax deficiency as well as a 50% additional amount specified by statute on account of the fraud. The Court found that, as a matter of statutory interpretation, the additional 50% penalty was meant to be a "remedial sanction" designed to reimburse the government for investigatory and other costs. Similarly, in *United States ex rel. Marcus v. Hess*,[10] the Court upheld a $2,000 per-count civil penalty plus double damages and costs—imposed on individuals who had already been convicted and fined criminally for the same fraud—amounting to almost $50,000 more than the government's actual damages. The Court reasoned that the fine and double damages "do no more than afford the government complete indemnity for the injuries done it," including the costs of detection and investigation. And in *One Lot Emerald Cut Stones v. United States*,[11] the Court found that a civil forfeiture proceeding seeking return of goods the defendant had allegedly smuggled into the country did not put a defendant in jeopardy.

However, in *United States v. Halper*,[12] the Court stated that "a defendant who already has been punished in a criminal prosecution may not be subjected to an additional civil sanction to the extent that the second sanction may not fairly be characterized as remedial, but only as a deterrent or retribution." In *Halper*, the defendant, who had been convicted of welfare fraud and sentenced to prison, was also assessed $130,000 in civil fines under the provisions of the federal False Claims Act, which is designed to compensate the government for investigating and prosecuting persons convicted of welfare fraud. Noting that this fine amounted to a sum roughly eight times the government's actual costs, a unanimous Court found that the civil penalty constituted "punishment" for purposes of the Double Jeopardy Clause to the extent it bore no "rational relation" to the government's expenses, and

---

8. See, e.g., *Application of Gault,* 387 U.S. 1, 87 S.Ct. 1428 (1967).

9. 303 U.S. 391, 58 S.Ct. 630 (1938).

10. 317 U.S. 537, 63 S.Ct. 379 (1943). See also, *Rex Trailer Co. v. United States,* 350 U.S. 148, 76 S.Ct. 219 (1956).

11. 409 U.S. 232, 93 S.Ct. 489 (1972) (per curiam).

12. 490 U.S. 435, 109 S.Ct. 1892 (1989).

remanded for a determination as to how much the fines should be reduced.

(b) Point in the Proceedings. Assuming a proceeding at which jeopardy can attach, the second issue concerning the threshold of the Double Jeopardy Clause is at what point during that process jeopardy occurs. If the purpose of the Clause is to prevent the embarrassment and harassment from repeated prosecutions, one could argue that jeopardy should attach with the institution of formal charges. If, on the other hand, the primary purpose of the Clause is to prevent the prosecution from honing its case against the defendant, jeopardy might not exist until the prosecution has completed its case against the accused or until the case terminates in a verdict. Under the federal Constitution, the rule falls between these two extremes.

In *Crist v. Bretz*,[13] the Supreme Court held that, under the Fifth Amendment, jeopardy attaches at jury trials when the jury is empaneled and sworn, which had been the federal practice up to that time. To the state's argument that the federal practice was an "arbitrarily chosen rule of convenience" and that, as a constitutional matter, jeopardy should attach when the first witness is sworn, the Court placed emphasis on the defendant's "valued right to have his trial completed before a particular tribunal," and contended that the federal rule has "roots deep in the historic development of trial by jury in the Anglo–American system of criminal justice." According to the Court, "double jeopardy . . . concerns—the finality of judgments, the minimization of harassing exposure to the harrowing experience of a criminal trial, and the valued right to continue with the chosen jury—have combined to produce the federal law that in a jury trial jeopardy attached when the jury is empaneled and sworn." In a concurring opinion, Justice Blackmun added that "the possibility of prosecutorial overreaching in the opening statement" was another reason for rejecting the government's approach.

The latter type of reason has not been persuasive in nonjury cases, however. When trial is in front of a judge alone, jeopardy attaches when the first witness is sworn, despite the fact that opening arguments have been completed at that point.[14] When conviction is by guilty plea, jeopardy attaches when the judge accepts the plea,[15] despite the fact that prior to that event evidence is often presented against the defendant to provide a factual basis for the plea.[16]

If a case is terminated before jeopardy attaches, then reprosecution is possible, even if the termination is on grounds similar to

---

13. 437 U.S. 28, 98 S.Ct. 2156 (1978).
14. Id.

15. See *Ohio v. Johnson,* 467 U.S. 493, 104 S.Ct. 2536 (1984).

16. See § 26.04(c).

an acquittal. As the Court stated in *Serfass v. United States,*[17] a judicial action labelled an "acquittal" still "has no significance in the [double jeopardy] context unless jeopardy has once attached and an accused has been subjected to the risk of conviction." Furthermore, the Double Jeopardy Clause does not prevent prosecution appeals of pre-jeopardy judicial rulings (although other rules might limit prosecution appeals in this context).[18] Finally, even after jeopardy attaches, if the court is not competent to hear the case on jurisdictional grounds, then reprosecution in an appropriate court is permissible.[19]

30.03 Exceptions to the Double Jeopardy Prohibition

A strict interpretation of the Double Jeopardy Clause would contemplate that once jeopardy has attached, the government would be prohibited from subjecting the defendant to jeopardy again for the same offense. Thus, for instance, not only would a judge or jury verdict bar retrial, but so would any decision by the trial judge to abort the trial before it is complete. Out of concern that the government be assured one fair chance to convict the accused, this interpretation of the Clause has never been favored. The Supreme Court has recognized that the general rule barring retrial on the same charge by the same sovereign after jeopardy has attached may be relaxed in three different situations. The first situation occurs when the defendant has successfully appealed his conviction or otherwise managed to have his conviction overturned. The second arises when the trial judge "dismisses" the case against the defendant prior to verdict. The third occurs when the judge declares a mistrial. In each situation, retrial on the same charge is permitted under certain circumstances.

(a) Reprosecution After Reversal of Conviction. A defendant who is convicted and does not appeal that conviction or challenges the conviction and loses cannot be retried on the same charge. But when his appeal of the conviction is successful or the defendant is able to overturn his conviction through some other procedural mechanism, it has long been recognized that the government is generally not barred from reprosecution on the original charge.[20] The Supreme Court explained in *Green v. United States*[21] that this result can be justified either on the ground that the defendant has "waived" his plea of former jeopardy by challenging the conviction or, alternatively, that the original jeopardy is "continued" since the first conviction was not final. A better

---

17. 420 U.S. 377, 95 S.Ct. 1055 (1975). See also, *United States v. Sanford,* 429 U.S. 14, 97 S.Ct. 20 (1976).

18. See § 29.04.

19. *Kepner v. United States,* 195 U.S. 100, 24 S.Ct. 797 (1904).

20. *Ball v. United States,* 163 U.S. 662, 16 S.Ct. 1192 (1896) (reversal on appeal); *United States v. Tateo,* 377 U.S. 463, 84 S.Ct. 1587 (1964) (reversal by trial judge or habeas court).

21. 355 U.S. 184, 78 S.Ct. 221 (1957).

rationale for this rule was provided by Justice Harlan in *United States v. Tateo.*[22] As he noted:

> [I]t would be a high price indeed for society to pay were every accused granted immunity from punishment because of any defect sufficient to constitute reversible error in the proceedings leading to conviction. From the standpoint of a defendant, it is at least doubtful that appellate courts would be as zealous as they now are in protecting against the effects of improprieties at the trial or pretrial stage if they knew that reversal of a conviction would put the accused irrevocably beyond the reach of further prosecution. In reality, therefore, the practice of retrial serves defendants' rights as well as society's interest.

Although reprosecution after a successful appeal is thus generally permissible, there are two limitations on this rule.

(1) The "implied acquittal" doctrine. The first limitation was announced in *Green,* where the defendant was tried for first-degree murder but convicted of second degree murder, a conviction which he successfully appealed. He was then tried on the original first degree murder charge. The Court held that retrial on the greater charge violated the double jeopardy prohibition, because the first jury "was given a full opportunity to return a verdict [on the first degree murder charge] and no extraordinary circumstances appeared which prevented it from doing so." Thus, after the appeal, jeopardy "continued" only for the lesser offense. *Green* stands for the proposition that, when the prosecution presents the factfinder with evidence of a charge and its lesser included offense, conviction on the lesser charge operates as an "implied acquittal" of the greater charge and prosecution on the latter charge is forever barred. The Court has also held that if a prosecution in violation of *Green* takes place, the defendant is entitled to a new trial even if he is convicted only of the lesser offense the second time, since the greater charge against the defendant might have "induced the jury to find him guilty of the less serious offense [rather] than continue to debate his innocence." [23]

When the conviction that is appealed was obtained through a guilty plea, then a different analysis is thought to apply. As one commentator notes:

22. 377 U.S. 463, 84 S.Ct. 1587 (1964).

23. *Price v. Georgia,* 398 U.S. 323, 90 S.Ct. 1757 (1970). But see, *Morris v. Mathews,* 475 U.S. 237, 106 S.Ct. 1032 (1986). Note also that where the appellate court reverses because the defendant was tried under the wrong statute, the defendant may be retried under a different statute because there is no "implied acquittal" for a statutory charge the jury did not consider. *Montana v. Hall,* 481 U.S. 400, 107 S.Ct. 1825 (1987).

Unlike the jury in *Green,* the [judge who] is tendered a plea of guilty to the lesser offense does not have the opportunity to convict on the greater offense. Hence, it does not follow from his acceptance of that plea that he has declined the opportunity to convict on the greater charge thus giving rise to an implication of acquittal.[24]

The defendant's only recourse in such a situation is a due process claim arguing that the new charge is a vindictive response to his appeal.[25]

(2) The evidentiary insufficiency exception: rationale. There is also one situation in which reprosecution after appeal is barred even on the same charge. As established in *Burks v. United States* [26] this occurs when the appellate court finds that the prosecution has failed as a matter of law to meet its burden of persuasion. In *Burks* the federal appellate court found that the prosecution's evidence had been insufficient to rebut the defendant's prima facia defense of insanity. The Supreme Court saw no reason to distinguish between the defendant who is acquitted pursuant to a directed verdict that the prosecution's evidence is insufficient to warrant submitting the case to the jury (which would clearly bar reprosecution), and the defendant whose conviction is reversed by an appellate judge because the evidence is insufficient to support the jury verdict.

Contrary to the Court's assertion, there is a difference between directed verdicts and appellate reversals: the prosecution might be able to present additional evidence after a motion for directed verdict during trial, whereas it cannot on appeal. But, as the Court stated in *Burks,* appellate reversal on evidentiary sufficiency grounds, like a directed verdict, does "constitute a decision to the effect that the government has failed to prove its case." In contrast, appellate reversals based on procedural errors (e.g., incorrect receipt or rejection of evidence, incorrect instructions or prosecutorial misconduct) "impl[y] nothing with respect to the guilt or innocence of the defendant." Thus, the *Burks* exception is unlikely to protect guilty persons or deter proper appellate decisionmaking, the two reasons given by Harlan in *Tateo* for permitting reprosecution after successful appeals.

(3) Defining evidentiary insufficiency. Several subsequent decisions have fleshed out the *Burks* holding. In *Hudson v. Louisiana,* [27] the Court emphasized that *Burks* requires only that the evidence against the defendant be *insufficient* to support the

---

24. Note, "Upping the Ante Against the Defendant Who Successfully Attacks His Guilty Plea: Double Jeopardy and Due Process Implications," 50 Notre Dame Law. 857, 878 (1975).

25. See § 29.02(d).

26. 437 U.S. 1, 98 S.Ct. 2141 (1978). *Burks* was given constitutional status in *Greene v. Massey,* 437 U.S. 19, 98 S.Ct. 2151 (1978).

27. 450 U.S. 40, 101 S.Ct. 970 (1981).

conviction, not that there be *no* evidence to support the verdict. In *Hudson,* the defendant moved for a second trial after his conviction, such motion being the only way he could challenge the sufficiency of the evidence under Louisiana law. The trial judge granted the motion, stating: "I heard the same evidence the jury did[;] I'm convinced that there was no evidence, certainly not evidence beyond a reasonable doubt, to sustain the verdict of the homicide committed by this defendant of this particular victim." Justice Powell, writing for a unanimous Court, emphasized that "nothing in *Burks* suggests, as the Louisiana Supreme Court seemed to believe, that double jeopardy protections are violated only when the prosecution has adduced no evidence at all of the crime or an element thereof." Since the trial judge in *Hudson* had ruled that the state had failed to prove its case as a matter of law in the original trial, there were "no significant facts which distinguish [*Hudson*] from *Burks,* and the Double Jeopardy Clause barred the state from prosecuting petitioner a second time."

On the other hand, the Court has also held, in *Tibbs v. Florida,*[28] that a second trial is not barred by the Double Jeopardy Clause when the reversal of the jury's verdict is based on the *weight* of the evidence rather than its sufficiency. Such a reversal could occur pursuant to a state rule authorizing the trial judge to grant a new trial when he finds the jury verdict against the weight of the evidence[29] or, as was true in *Tibbs* itself, after the defendant convinces an appellate court that the jury verdict was against the weight of the evidence. In either case, the *Tibbs* Court held, the second trial does not violate *Burks*.

Justice O'Connor, who wrote the 5–4 opinion, reasoned that *Burks* was based on two policies: (1) that an acquittal, or any action which has the effect of an acquittal, should bar retrial; and (2) that the Double Jeopardy Clause "forbids a second trial for the purpose of affording the prosecution another opportunity to supply evidence which it failed to muster in the first proceeding." She found that a reversal based on a finding by the trial judge (or, as occurred in *Tibbs* itself, an appellate court) that the jury's verdict was not supported by the weight of the evidence does not implicate either of these policies. First, in such cases the judge is merely sitting as a "thirteenth juror" who disagrees with the jury's resolution of the conflicting testimony; "[t]his difference of opinion no more signifies acquittal than does a disagreement among the jurors themselves." Second, in such cases, the state has presented sufficient evidence to persuade a jury to convict; giving the defendant a second chance to seek acquittal under such circumstances does not create "'an unacceptably high risk that

---

28. 457 U.S. 31, 102 S.Ct. 2211 (1982).

29. See e.g., West's Fla.S.A.R.Crim. Pro. 3.600(a)(2).

the Government, with its superior resources, [will] wear down [the] defendant and obtain conviction' solely through its persistence."

Yet, as the dissent pointed out with respect to *Tibbs* itself, "[w]ere the state to present this same evidence again, we must assume that once again the state courts would reverse any conviction that was based on it." Since the state was not prevented from producing any of its evidence in the first trial, "the only point of any second trial in this case is to allow the state to present additional evidence to bolster its case." If it does not have such evidence, "reprosecution can serve no purpose other than harassment." As the dissent suggests, *Tibbs* holds that some types of *de facto* acquittals will not bar retrial. On the other hand, a contrary ruling might significantly diminish new trial orders, to the detriment of defendants.

An implementation question which arises under *Burks* is whether the Double Jeopardy Clause bars retrial when an appellate court decides that certain evidence should not have been admitted by the trial court, and in addition decides that the remaining evidence is insufficient to support the verdict. *Burks* might be read to prohibit retrial in this situation. But in *Lockhart v. Nelson*,[30] the Supreme Court held that a determination of sufficiency for purposes of *Burks* must be based on a review of *all* the evidence, including that found inadmissible by the appellate court. According to Chief Justice Rehnquist, who wrote the 6–3 opinion for the Court,

> The basis for the *Burks* exception . . . is that a reversal for insufficiency of the evidence should be treated no differently than a trial court's granting judgment of acquittal at the close of all the evidence. A trial court in passing on such a motion considers all the evidence it has admitted, and to make the analogy complete it must be this same quantum of evidence which is considered by the reviewing court.

The majority also pointed out that, had the trial court excluded the inadmissible evidence, the prosecution would have had the opportunity to introduce other evidence on the same point, and thus should be allowed to do so via a retrial when the inadmissibility decision is made for the first time by an appellate court. In *Nelson* itself, the Court permitted the state to resentence the defendant as an habitual offender even though his original habitual offender sentence had been overturned after one of the four felonies upon which the sentence had been based was determined to have been nullified by pardon prior to the original sentencing; had this determination been made at the original proceeding, the Court noted, another felony might have been substituted.

---

30. 488 U.S. 33, 109 S.Ct. 285 (1988).

(4) The termination requirement. Even if the defendant can show that the evidence was insufficient to convict him, the Double Jeopardy Clause affords him no protection against retrial unless the holding favorable to the defendant occurs at the "termination" of the first proceeding against him. In *Justices of Boston Municipal Court v. Lydon,*[31] the defendant chose a bench trial over a jury trial, which under Massachusetts law meant that his first appeal would be a trial *de novo.* After his conviction at the bench trial and pending his trial *de novo,* Lydon motioned for dismissal on the ground that no evidence of criminal intent had been adduced at the bench trial and that retrial was thus barred under *Burks.* Although the state courts denied the motion, he was successful on federal habeas corpus at both the district court and court of appeals levels. The Supreme Court rejected his claim that double jeopardy barred a retrial, however. It pointed out that at the time he raised his double jeopardy claim, Lydon, in contrast to Burks, had not yet been acquitted but was merely asserting he should have been. Thus, his situation was no different from the defendant appealing a conviction through normal appellate channels; in both cases jeopardy had not yet "terminated." In essence, the *Lydon* Court endorsed the "continuing jeopardy" concept described above and applied it to permit the second trial in the Massachusetts system because it resembled an appeal.

(b) Dismissals Which Are Not "Acquittals". *Burks* clearly established that an acquittal by a trial judge or appellate court, even in the face of an adverse jury verdict, bars retrial on the same offense. But what if a judge dismisses the case before the jury returns a verdict? The Court's decisions on this issue at first endorsed, but then rejected the traditional rationale for the Double Jeopardy Clause—i.e. avoidance of the anxiety and harassment associated with a second trial—and adopted in its place an approach analogous to *Burks,* allowing retrial after every dismissal which is not the equivalent of an acquittal.

In *United States v. Jenkins,*[32] a 1975 decision, the Court held that the Double Jeopardy Clause may bar retrial of a case that has been dismissed even when the dismissal is not "on the merits." In *Jenkins,* the trial court dismissed the indictment on draft evasion charges midway through trial, when it became clear that the defendant's application for conscientious objector status had not been considered by the selective service board before the charges were brought. The prosecution appealed the dismissal. The Supreme Court noted that it was unclear whether the trial court had resolved the factual issues in the case before dismissing the indictment, but held that, regardless, the jeopardy bar applied so

31. 466 U.S. 294, 104 S.Ct. 1805   32. 420 U.S. 358, 95 S.Ct. 1006
(1984).   (1975).

long as a successful prosecution appeal would require any further proceedings to resolve the case. In *Jenkins,* the trial court would have had to hear additional evidence, or, at a minimum, make supplemental findings of fact if the government prevailed on appeal, and thus the jeopardy bar prohibited a government appeal of the dismissal.

In a companion case, *United States v. Wilson,*[33] the Court applied the logic behind *Jenkins* in holding that a government appeal was not barred when reversal of the dismissal would *not* necessitate further proceedings. In *Wilson,* the trial court dismissed the indictment after the jury had returned a guilty verdict. Since reversal of the dismissal would result in reinstatement of the jury verdict, rather than retrial, the Double Jeopardy Clause did not apply and prosecution appeal of the dismissal was permissible.

In *Jenkins* and *Wilson,* the Court tried to establish two propositions. First, it differentiated between a mistrial, which it described as a ruling by the trial court that the present trial cannot proceed and that a new one must be held, and a dismissal, which, like an acquittal by verdict, involves a finding favoring the defendant. Second, it refused to distinguish, for purposes of double jeopardy analysis, between dismissals on the merits and those on procedural grounds; according to *Jenkins* and *Wilson,* the Double Jeopardy Clause automatically bars any appeal of a dismissal if its reversal on appeal would require additional proceedings.

Three years later, however, the Court rejected both propositions and overruled *Jenkins. United States v. Scott*[34] held that there is *no* functional distinction between a dismissal which is not on the merits and a mistrial. In *Scott,* the defendant moved successfully for dismissal of two counts of his indictment on the ground of prejudicial pretrial delay. The Supreme Court permitted prosecution appeal of this ruling, over a four-member dissent arguing that if the government fails "for any reason to persuade the court not to enter a final judgment favorable to the accused, the constitutional policies underlying the ban against multiple trials become compelling." Instead, Justice Rehnquist's majority opinion found that the appeal sought by the prosecution was a "far cry" from "an all-powerful state relentlessly pursuing a defendant who had either been found guilty or who had at least insisted on having the issue of guilt submitted to the first trier of fact." Rather, here the defendant chose "to seek termination of the proceedings against him on a basis unrelated to factual guilt or innocence of the offense of which he is accused." The Court also emphasized that its holding was not based on the assumption

33. 420 U.S. 332, 95 S.Ct. 1013 (1975).   **34.** 437 U.S. 82, 98 S.Ct. 2187 (1978).

that the defendant waived his double jeopardy protection when he made the dismissal motion, but rather on the finding that there was no double jeopardy right to waive.

Thus, just as reprosecution is permitted after the defense obtains reversal of a trial ruling not related to guilt, the prosecution is permitted to appeal any judicial ruling that is not an "acquittal" (and, of course, reprosecute if the appeal is successful). As with the exception established in *Burks* (decided the same term as *Scott*), the central question after *Scott* is the definition of "acquittal." In *Scott*, Rehnquist quoted the year-old language in *United States v. Martin Linen Supply Co.*,[35] to the effect that an acquittal occurs "only upon a jury verdict of not guilty [or when] the ruling of the judge, whatever its label, actually represents a resolution [in the defendant's favor], correct or not, of some or all of the factual elements of the offense charged." According to Rehnquist, for example, judicial dismissal predicated on a finding of insanity (which was the case in *Burks*) or entrapment is an acquittal. "By contrast, the dismissal of an indictment for preindictment delay represents a legal judgment that a defendant, although criminally culpable, may not be punished because of a supposed constitutional violation." Thus, the prosecution may not appeal the former but may appeal the latter. The dissent questioned this distinction between "factual" and "legal" innocence, noting that the applicability of the pretrial delay rule depends as much on an evaluation of the trial evidence as does the validity of an insanity or entrapment defense.[36]

Given *Scott's* emphasis on factual matters, it is not clear whether a judicial dismissal based purely on a ruling of law would be appealable. In *Sanabria v. United States*,[37] decided the same term as *Scott*, the Court held that a dismissal based on a finding that the dismissed charge was not in the indictment bars reprosecution. In doing so, it stated that, "when a defendant has been acquitted at trial, he may not be retried on the same offense, even if the legal rulings underlying the acquittal were erroneous." At least one other Court decision supports the idea that acquittals based on interpretations of law, however erroneous, bar reprosecution.[38] But, given the fact that barring retrial in such circumstances might prevent retrial of a person for whom the prosecution has produced sufficient evidence to convict, the Court might ultimately decide otherwise. Alternatively, it might allow prosecution appeals of legal rulings but insulate the particular defendant from an adverse finding, as a way of facilitating review of lower court determinations of law.

---

35. 430 U.S. 564, 97 S.Ct. 1349 (1977).

36. See § 25.02(b) for a discussion of the pretrial delay rule.

37. 437 U.S. 54, 98 S.Ct. 2170 (1978).

38. See *Arizona v. Rumsey*, 467 U.S. 203, 104 S.Ct. 2305 (1984), discussed in § 30.05(a).

In any event, it is clear that a dismissal which *is* based on an assessment of the sufficiency of the prosecution's case against the defendant, whatever its label, is not appealable by the prosecution. In *Smalis v. Pennsylvania*,[39] the Court affirmed that a trial court dismissal on the ground that the prosecution had failed to establish the defendant's guilt beyond a reasonable doubt bars appeal and reprosecution, finding it irrelevant that the state appellate court described the defendant's "demurrer" motion as one which required a legal judgment rather than a factual determination.

As Rehnquist pointed out in *Scott*, one way of avoiding the situation giving rise to both *Scott* and *Jenkins* is to defer the dismissal decision until after the jury has returned a verdict (as in *Wilson*). If the verdict is acquittal, dismissal will of course be unnecessary. If it is a conviction, and the trial judge decides that it cannot stand, the verdict can be reinstated after successful prosecutorial appeal of that decision without violating even *Jenkins'* conception of double jeopardy.

(c) Mistrials. As the Court's discussion in *Jenkins* and *Scott* illustrates, there has been some confusion over the terms "mistrial" and "dismissal." Indeed, in some jurisdictions the terms are nearly interchangeable. But the Court's suggested definition of the two concepts is fairly straightforward. As outlined in *Scott*, the word "dismissal" should be used only to designate judicial decisions which are meant to dispose of the case either legally or factually, whereas a mistrial is abortion of trial for any other reason. The most common cause of a mistrial, as that term is traditionally understood, is the inability of the jury to arrive at a unanimous verdict. A mistrial could also be declared when the judge believes a violation of evidentiary or procedural rules, or some other circumstance, has so influenced the jury that a fair trial, for either the defendant or the government, is impossible.

In *Oregon v. Kennedy*,[40] Justice Stevens helpfully organized the Court's double jeopardy cases involving mistrials into two categories. The first category concerns mistrials declared over the defendant's objection; here retrial is permitted only when the mistrial was a "manifest necessity." The second category includes mistrials to which the defendant consented, or which result from the defendant's own motion; here retrial is permitted unless the mistrial motion was provoked by prosecutorial "overreaching" designed to secure a second trial. The manifest necessity and prosecutorial overreaching notions are discussed below.

---

39. 476 U.S. 140, 106 S.Ct. 1745 (1986).

40. 456 U.S. 667, 102 S.Ct. 2083 (1982) (Stevens, J., concurring).

(1) The manifest necessity doctrine.   At least since 1824, when it decided *United States v. Perez,* [41] the Supreme Court has recognized that retrial after a mistrial is constitutionally permissible if the mistrial is dictated by "manifest necessity, or the ends of public justice would otherwise be defeated."   A more modern formulation of this idea was put forward in *Illinois v. Somerville,* [42] where the Court stated that the double jeopardy ban does not apply when "the defendant's interest in proceeding to verdict is outweighed by the competing and equally legitimate demand for public justice."   Further defining the manifest necessity rule is difficult, given the many different reasons for which a mistrial might be granted.

The classic example of "manifest necessity" occurs when the judge declares a mistrial because the jury is unable to reach a unanimous or otherwise legal verdict.   As *Perez* indicated, other than dismissing the case permanently, the trial court is left with no other option in such circumstances.   Over one and a half centuries later, in *Richardson v. United States,* [43] the Court reaffirmed *Perez* with the following language:

> Without exception, the courts have held that the trial judge may discharge a genuinely deadlocked jury and require the defendant to submit to a second trial.   This rule accords recognition to society's interest in giving the prosecution one complete opportunity to convict those who have violated its laws.

The majority rejected Justice Brennan's argument in dissent that the Court's decision in *Burks* barred retrial if a reviewing court felt the jury was deadlocked because of insufficiency in the prosecution's case.   Rather, it construed *Burks* as prohibiting retrial only if an appellate court found the prosecution's evidence to be insufficient upon review of a *conviction;* when there is no conviction, but only a hung jury, the prosecution may, in the trial judge's discretion, retry the defendant.   Thus, the manifest necessity doctrine sanctions reprosecution following a hung jury even if the majority of the jurors vote to acquit or an appellate court believes the evidence before the jury was insufficient to support conviction.

The Court has also found that manifest necessity justified mistrials declared when the trial judge learned that one of the jurors had served on the indicting grand jury,[44] and when wartime exigencies intervened.[45]   Sometimes manifest necessity is

---

41.   22 U.S. (9 Wheat.) 579 (1824).

42.   410 U.S. 458, 93 S.Ct. 1066 (1973).

43.   468 U.S. 317, 104 S.Ct. 3081 (1984).

44.   *Thompson v. United States,* 155 U.S. 271, 15 S.Ct. 73 (1894).

45.   *Wade v. Hunter,* 336 U.S. 684, 69 S.Ct. 834 (1949).

found in more subtle circumstances. For instance, in *Gori v. United States*,[46] the Court allowed a second trial of the defendant after the judge, apparently prematurely assuming that the prosecutor's questioning of a witness was calculated to inform the jury of the defendant's prior convictions, declared a mistrial without the defendant's consent. In a 5–4 decision, the Court upheld the conviction obtained in a subsequent trial. The Court emphasized that the trial judge declared the mistrial out of "extreme solicitude—an overeager solicitude, it may be—in favor of the accused." The Court may also have been influenced by the fact that the prosecutor probably had not actually committed error at the time the mistrial was declared. It quoted the circuit court opinion in the case to the effect that "the prosecutor did nothing to instigate the declaration of a mistrial and . . . was only performing his assigned duty under trying conditions."

On the other hand, some judicial actions may be so precipitous and so clearly reflect a failure to take into account the alternatives or the defendant's interests that they are not justified under the manifest necessity rule. In *United States v. Jorn*,[47] the trial judge abruptly declared a mistrial after becoming convinced that five government witnesses had not been warned of their constitutional rights, despite the prosecution's assurances that the witnesses had been sufficiently warned. A plurality of the Court held that the trial judge had abused his discretion in not considering the less drastic alternative of a continuance or permitting the defense to object to the mistrial and that, in these circumstances, the Double Jeopardy Clause prohibited reprosecution, the government's claim of undeserved benefit to the defendant notwithstanding.

Several cases concern application of the manifest necessity rule in the more "suspicious" situation created when the mistrial motion originates by the prosecution rather than the court. In *Downum v. United States*,[48] for instance, the prosecution requested that the jury be discharged just after it had been empaneled, because one of the government's key witnesses was not available. The defendant motioned to proceed with trial on the five counts for which the witness was irrelevant, but the court denied the motion and declared a mistrial. Here, unlike in *Gori*, the error leading to abortion of the first trial was at least negligent; apparently understaffing in the prosecutor's office had led to the failure to discover the absence of the witness. Moreover, again in contrast to *Gori*, the first jury was discharged out of concern for the prosecution, not the defense. On these facts, the Court, in a 5–4

---

46. 367 U.S. 364, 81 S.Ct. 1523 (1961).

47. 400 U.S. 470, 91 S.Ct. 547 (1971).

48. 372 U.S. 734, 83 S.Ct. 1033 (1963).

decision, reversed the conviction. However, in *Illinois v. Somerville*,[49] the state was permitted to convict the defendant after a mistrial resulting from a defect in the prosecution's indictment. Here the prosecutor's error was grossly negligent, yet the Supreme Court allowed a second trial under a cured indictment.

One possible explanation for the seeming inconsistency between *Downum* and *Somerville* was that in the first case the state could easily have moved for a continuance and avoided the drastic action of a mistrial, while in the latter case, given Illinois' "archaic mode of reading indictments," a mistrial was the only course.[50] In other words, in *Downum* there was a less drastic means of curing the alleged defect, and thus a mistrial was not a "manifest necessity." [51] Second, it has been argued that the type of error in *Downum* is more subject to prosecutorial manipulation:

> If a witness is willing to testify without a subpoena, an unscrupulous prosecutor might indeed fail to subpoena the witness, knowing that he could exploit the witness's unavailability as grounds for a mistrial if the trial proceeded unfavorably. On the other hand, a prosecutor is unlikely to create uncorrectable error in the indictment to preserve the mistrial option because any conviction is automatically reversible.[52]

Downum and *Somerville* might also be distinguished by looking at the extent to which different results in those cases would allow the *defendant* to manipulate the system. Arguably, the defendant is better able to determine prior to trial when an indictment is defective than when the prosecution is missing a key witness; thus, in the former instance, his objection to a mistrial motion after jeopardy has attached is more likely to be a cynical attempt to take advantage of a "technicality" to avoid conviction, rather than a sincere effort to prevent the prosecution from honing its case.

Relatedly, the Court has suggested that one factor to consider in determining whether "manifest necessity" exists is whether the defense is responsible for the mistrial declaration. In *Arizona v. Washington*, [53] the defendant's first conviction was reversed because the prosecutor had failed to disclose exculpatory information to the defense. In his opening statement at the second trial, the defense counsel referred to this lapse on the part of the prosecu-

---

49. 410 U.S. 458, 93 S.Ct. 1066 (1973).

50. See Katz, "Double Jeopardy," 2 Pub.Def.Rep. 1, 6 (1979).

51. Note that *Crist v. Bretz*, 437 U.S. 28, 98 S.Ct. 2156 (1978), discussed in § 29.02(b), also involved a dismissal due to a defective charging instrument, and that there a continuance was possible.

However, in that case, the parties stipulated that, if jeopardy were found to have attached when the mistrial was declared, retrial would be barred.

52. Thomas, "An Elegant Theory of Double Jeopardy," 1988 U.Ill.L.Rev. 827, 864.

53. 434 U.S. 497, 98 S.Ct. 824 (1978).

tion. The judge declared a mistrial, on the prosecution's motion, on the ground of possible jury bias. The Supreme Court upheld the defendant's conviction at his third trial despite his argument that the judge had made no express finding that the abortion of the second trial was a manifest necessity. In justifying its decision, the Court noted that the judge allowed both sides to offer arguments pertaining to the mistrial motion, and emphasized that the judge's familiarity with the situation "requires that we accord the highest degree of respect to the judge's evaluation." But the most significant reason for the Court's decision may have been the fact that the mistrial was triggered by defense misconduct.[54] Supporting this interpretation is the Court's statement that a mistrial order is not entitled to the same deference when the prosecution is the cause of the order.

(2) Prosecutorial overreaching. When the defense consents to a mistrial order, or makes the motion itself, the Court has usually permitted retrial over a double jeopardy objection. Illustrative is *United States v. Dinitz,* [55] where the Court concluded that so long as "the defendant retains primary control over the course to be followed in the event of . . . error," the Fifth Amendment will rarely be implicated. There, the defendant's first attorney was expelled from the courtroom for repeated misconduct, and co-counsel was unprepared to proceed with the case. From several alternatives offered by the judge (including a continuance), the defendant asked for a mistrial, to permit him to obtain new counsel. Although conceding that the defendant was confronted with a "Hobson's choice" (i.e., continuing with unprepared counsel or undergoing a new trial), the Court rejected the lower appellate court's conclusion that trial should have been precluded:

> The defendant may reasonably conclude that a continuation of the tainted proceeding would result in a conviction followed by a lengthy appeal and, if a reversal is secured, by a second prosecution. In such circumstances, a defendant's mistrial request has objectives not unlike the interest served by the Double Jeopardy Clause—the avoidance of the anxiety, expense, and delay occasioned by multiple prosecutions.

When the event which precipitates a defense motion for mistrial is prosecutorial error, however, a more discerning analysis is necessary. Some hypothetical scenarios suggest why.[56] For instance, a prosecutor might commit repeated prejudicial error merely to subject a defendant he knows he cannot convict to the harassment of multiple trials. Or a prosecutor might try to inject enough unfair prejudice into a trial to ensure a conviction but not

---

54. Katz, supra note 50, at 7.

55. 424 U.S. 600, 96 S.Ct. 1075 (1976).

56. These examples are taken from Justice Stevens concurring opinion in *Oregon v. Kennedy,* 456 U.S. 667, 102 S.Ct. 2083 (1982).

so much as to cause a reversal of that conviction. Under such circumstances, the Court's earlier cases suggested, in dictum, that retrial after a mistrial would be barred, to prevent prosecutorial manipulation of the system.[57]

However, the only Court cases to address directly the prosecutorial overreaching issue suggest that retrial might be permitted even under the circumstances described. In *Lee v. United States*,[58] the defendant, just prior to trial, moved to dismiss the information for theft on the grounds that it did not allege the necessary specific intent. The court tentatively denied the motion and defendant's counsel did not object to going forward with the trial. At the close of the evidence, the trial court decided to grant the defendant's motion to dismiss but observed that his guilt had been proved beyond a reasonable doubt. On the facts in *Lee,* the Court held that a retrial was not barred by former jeopardy. The Court viewed the dismissal as functionally indistinguishable from a mistrial, noting that it was not predicated on any determination that the defendant should be acquitted of the crime with which he was charged. It then found: (1) that there was no prosecutorial bad faith, only negligence; (2) that the proceedings continued at the defendant's request and with his consent; and (3) that the trial court's failure to postpone taking evidence was reasonable in light of the last-minute timing of the motion and defense counsel's failure to request a continuance. *Lee* made clear that whether a trial may take place after a mistrial is declared is not merely dependent upon the culpability of the prosecutor, but on the relative culpability of the prosecution, the defense, and the judge.

In *Oregon v. Kennedy*[59] the Court went a step further by holding that merely negligent prosecutorial action resulting in mistrial will not bar retrial even when the defense does not contribute to the mistrial order. During Kennedy's trial for theft, the state's expert witness, who testified during direct examination concerning the value of the stolen property, admitted on cross-examination that he had once filed a criminal complaint against Kennedy, but that no action had been taken on the complaint. On redirect, the prosecutor tried to rehabilitate her witness by establishing why the witness had filed the complaint, but the defense repeatedly and successfully objected to her questions. Finally, however, having elicited from the witness that he had never done business with the defendant, the prosecutor asked "Is that because he is a crook?" On defendant's motion, the court declared a

---

57. See, e.g., *Arizona v. Washington,* 434 U.S. 497, 98 S.Ct. 824 (1978) (prohibiting "using the superior resources of the State to harass or to achieve a tactical advantage over the accused"); *United States v. Tateo,* 377 U.S. 463, 84 S.Ct. 1587 (1964) (prohibit- ing "prosecutorial . . . impropriety . . . result[ing] from a fear that the jury was likely to acquit the accused").

58. 432 U.S. 23, 97 S.Ct. 2141 (1977).

59. 456 U.S. 667, 102 S.Ct. 2083 (1982).

mistrial and the defendant claimed that his subsequent trial violated the Double Jeopardy Clause.

The Supreme Court rejected the defendant's suggestion that the test for applying the Clause in such situations should be whether the prosecutor "overreached." Rather, after concluding that the dicta in earlier cases offered "no standards for their application," the Court announced that the test should be whether the prosecutor "*intended* to 'goad' the defendant into moving for a mistrial" [emphasis added]. Since the state courts found this intent did not exist in *Kennedy*,[60] the defendant could not invoke the double jeopardy prohibition. Indeed, *Kennedy's* test will seldom ever be met since, as Justice Stevens concurrence pointed out, "[i]t is almost inconceivable that a defendant could prove that the prosecutor's deliberate misconduct was motivated by an intent to provoke a mistrial instead of an intent simply to prejudice the defendant." [61]

30.04 The "Same Offense" Prohibition

If jeopardy has attached on a particular charge and one of the exceptions to the double jeopardy ban described in the previous section does not apply, then reprosecution is generally barred not only on that charge but also on any other charges which are considered the "same offense." Put another way, those offenses which are the "same" for double jeopardy purposes must usually be joined in the same proceeding if the state wishes to prosecute them. This section discusses the definition of "same offense," the exceptions to the same offense prohibition, and the different definition of "same offense" that is applied when the issue is cumulative punishments rather than multiple prosecutions.

(a) **Defining Same Offense.** The Fifth Amendment phrase "same offense" has always been defined more broadly than the precise charge involved at the first proceeding; otherwise, the prosecution could repeatedly try the defendant despite the double jeopardy ban, given the wide array of crimes that any given act might trigger.[62] The courts have devised a number of different standards for determining when related offenses must be joined

---

60. As Justice Stevens noted in his concurring opinion:

> The isolated prosecutorial error occurred early in the trial, too early to determine whether the case was going badly for the prosecution. If anyone was being harassed at that trial, it was the prosecutor, who was frustrated by improper defense objections . . . .

61. For further development of this point, see Reiss, "Prosecutorial Intent

in Constitutional Criminal Procedure," 135 U.Pa.L.Rev. 1365 (1987).

62. For instance, one commentator noted that a single sale of narcotics could, at least in 1958, elicit nine counts under separate federal statutes. Note, "Consecutive Sentences in Single Prosecutions: Judicial Multiplication of Statutory Penalties," 67 Yale L.J. 916, 928 n. 43 (1958).

rather than tried separately. The Supreme Court has vacillated on which standard to use, and has also granted constitutional status to the collateral estoppel principle, which in some instances will bar a second prosecution where the same offense prohibition, at least under some of its guises, would not.

(1) Various approaches. The test which defines "same offense" most narrowly could be called the "identical evidence" test. The basic thrust of this approach is captured by the original American version, formulated in *Morey v. Commonwealth:* [63] "A conviction or acquittal upon one indictment is no bar to a subsequent conviction and sentence upon another, unless the evidence required to support a conviction upon one of them would have been sufficient to warrant a conviction upon the other." In essence, this test places little limitation on reprosecution beyond prohibiting a trial for any lesser included offense of a crime on which the defendant has already been acquitted or convicted. Under a literal application of *Morey's* standard, for instance, if a person is first convicted of the *lesser* offense, he could still be prosecuted for the greater offense, unless the jury in the first trial was presented evidence relating to the greater offense and could be said to have "impliedly acquitted" the defendant by choosing the lesser charge.[64]

A test which appears to be slightly broader than the identical evidence test could be called the "same element" test. As described by the Supreme Court in *Blockburger v. United States,*[65] this test states that "[w]here the same act or transaction constitutes a violation of two distinct statutory provisions, the test to be applied to determine whether there are two offenses or only one, is whether each provision requires proof of an additional fact which the other does not." Under this type of test, second-degree murder and manslaughter are the "same offense," as are larceny and robbery, and an attempt and the completed offense.[66] It bars consecutive prosecution of an offense and its lesser included offenses regardless of the order of prosecution, and without resort to the implied acquittal idea.

On the other hand, under either the same evidence or same element tests, a single criminal act or transaction may result in a number of "offenses" for double jeopardy purposes. For example, a single criminal act involving three victims can be considered three separate offenses.[67] A single act might also be in violation

---

63. 108 Mass. 433 (1871).

64. Cf. § 30.03(a)(1).

65. 284 U.S. 299, 52 S.Ct. 180 (1932).

66. See Annotation, "What Constitutes Lesser Offense 'Necessarily Included' in Offense Charged, under Rule

31(c) of Federal Rules of Criminal Procedure," 11 ALR Fed. 173 (1972).

67. See, e.g. *State v. Hoag,* 21 N.J. 496, 122 A.2d 628 (1956), aff'd 356 U.S. 464, 78 S.Ct. 829 (1958). However, if the defendant is acquitted at a trial relating to the first victim, *collateral*

of overlapping statutes which require different elements, such as burglary and larceny.[68]   Finally, a single transaction may be separable into acts which are chronologically discrete, and thus are separate offenses under the same evidence approach.   For instance, a person who steals a gun, possesses it while breaking and entering a house, and then murders the occupant may, under the same evidence or *Blockburger* approaches, be subjected to three separate trials.[69]   In many instances, dissecting a crime into such components is anathema to the values traditionally associated with the protection against double jeopardy.

For this reason, some jurisdictions have developed other approaches to the same offense issue.   The broadest category of tests in this regard are the so-called "same transaction" tests, which focus not upon the evidence or elements needed to prove each offense but upon the incident which led to apprehension and prosecution; under a same transaction test, multiple prosecutions based on the number of victims involved in a crime or the number of overlapping statutory offenses it implicates would usually be prohibited.   The most vigorous proponent of the transactional approach in the federal constitutional context was Justice Brennan.   In his view, as he explained in *Ashe v. Swenson*,[70] "[t]he Double Jeopardy Clause requires the prosecution, except in most limited circumstances, to join at one trial all the charges against a defendant that grow out of a single criminal act, occurrence, episode, or transaction."   Juridictions which have adopted such an approach [71] have chosen to more actively protect against multiple prosecutions.

However, there are problems with the transaction approach as well.   As one court inquired:

> Assume that one breaks and enters a building to commit larceny of an automobile, does thereafter in fact steal the automobile and drive away, killing the night watchman in the process, and two blocks away runs a red light which brings about his arrest by the municipal police.   Could it be said with any logic that a plea of guilty to breaking and entering would bar a subsequent prosecution for murder?   If so, pre-

estoppel may bar subsequent prosecutions, if the acquittal represents a determination that the defendant was not the perpetrator of the crime.   See § 30.04(a)(3).

68. See Comment, Twice in Jeopardy, 75 Yale L.J. 262, 273 (1965).

69. See *Johnson v. Commonwealth*, 201 Ky. 314, 256 S.W. 388 (1923), where

75 hands of poker were considered to be separate offenses.

70. 397 U.S. 436, 90 S.Ct. 1189 (1970) (Brennan, J., concurring).

71. See, e.g., *Boyette v. State*, 172 Ga. App. 683, 324 S.E.2d 540 (1984); *Cowart v. State*, 461 So.2d 21 (Ala.Crim.App. 1984).

sumably a plea of guilty to the traffic offense would likewise, since all arise out of the "same transaction." [72]

Although the effect of the same transaction test in such a scenario can be circumscribed to some extent,[73] the concerns voiced above have led others to propose a "same conduct" test, which falls somewhere in-between the same element and same transaction approaches.[74] This test looks at the conduct that will be shown to prove each offense to determine whether two offenses are the same. Thus, in the above hypothetical, under a same conduct test the breaking and entering and the theft of the automobile would probably be the same offense, because the prosecution would present testimony about the breaking and entering to prove the theft, but the traffic violation and homicide would not be. Under a same element test, on the other hand, none of the crimes would be the same offense; despite their similarity, the breaking and entering and theft charges each include elements the other does not.

(2) The Supreme Court's approach. The Supreme Court's earliest cases appeared to adopt a same element test. Although the *Blockburger* rule quoted above was developed solely as a guide to when multiple punishments may be imposed (an issue discussed below [75]), in *Brown v. Ohio* [76] the Court relied on the rule in deciding when separate prosecutions for related offenses are permitted. In *Brown*, the defendant had taken another person's car and was apprehended nine days later. He pleaded guilty to "joyriding" and was jailed and fined. Upon his release, he was returned to the county where he first gained possession of the automobile and was indicted for auto theft. Although, as the three-member dissent pointed out, this second prosecution was based on a different part of the nine-day period than the original prosecution, the majority characterized the joyriding charge as a single continuing offense.[77] On this assumption, the majority held that the second prosecution was barred because the joyriding charge (which in essence involves operating a car without the owner's consent) did not require proof of any fact that is not also required to prove auto theft.

72. *State v. Conrad,* 243 So.2d 174 (Fla.App.1971).

73. For instance, as developed in § 30.04(b)(3), if the traffic court lacked jurisdiction to hear the other charges, double jeopardy would not bar a subsequent prosecution on those charges.

74. See Thomas, "Successive Prosecutions for the Same Offense: In Search of a Definition," 71 Iowa L.Rev. 323, 377–88 (1986).

75. See § 30.04(c).

76. 432 U.S. 161, 97 S.Ct. 2221 (1977).

77. However, it noted that had Ohio law provided that joyriding was a separate offense for each day in which a motor vehicle is operated without the owner's consent, a different result would have been required.

Although *Brown* resulted in a finding for the defendant, it clearly adopted the relatively narrow *Blockburger* definition of same offense. The same term as *Brown,* however, the Court created an exception to *Blockburger.* In *Harris v. Oklahoma,* [78] the defendant was convicted of felony-murder for his participation in a robbery during which a grocery store clerk was killed. He was later tried and convicted of robbery with firearms. The *Blockburger* test would have permitted the robbery prosecution, since robbery does not require proof of a killing, and felony murder does not require proof of *robbery,* but only some felony. Despite this, the Court reversed the robbery conviction, holding that where a conviction for a greater crime, in this case felony murder, cannot be had without conviction for a lesser crime, here the underlying felony, the Double Jeopardy Clause bars prosecution for the lesser crime after conviction of the greater.

Three years later the Court decided *Illinois v. Vitale,* [79] which further called into question the continued vitality of the *Blockburger* rule. There the defendant allegedly caused a fatal car accident. He was issued a ticket charging him with failure to reduce speed, and convicted of that offense. The day after his conviction, the state charged him with two counts of involuntary manslaughter based on his reckless driving. The Supreme Court held that, under the *Blockburger* rule, the second prosecution was not barred. But it also stated in dictum that if, to prove the homicide charges, the prosecution *had* to prove a failure to slow or "conduct necessarily involving such failure," then "his claim of double jeopardy would be substantial."

In *Grady v. Corbin,* [80] the Court held, 5–4, that *Vitale's* dictum should become law. The Court reminded that *Blockburger's* rule had originally been devised purely as a method of determining when multiple punishments for similar offenses are permitted. It then concluded that the definition of same offense for determining when multiple trials may take place must be broader, to prevent reprosecutions which give "the State an opportunity to rehearse its presentation of proof, thus increasing the risk of an erroneous conviction for one or more of the offenses charged." Specifically, the Court held, double jeopardy concerns require a "same conduct" definition of "same offense," prohibiting "any . . . prosecution in which the government, to establish an essential element of an offense charged in that prosecution, will prove conduct that constitutes an offense for which the defendant has already been prosecuted."

78. 433 U.S. 682, 97 S.Ct. 2912 (1977).

79. 447 U.S. 410, 100 S.Ct. 2260 (1980).

80. 495 U.S. 508, 110 S.Ct. 2084 (1990).

Although this language is broader than the *Blockburger* rule, it appears to bar reprosecution only when the second offense *requires* proof of conduct for which the defendant has already been prosecuted. The Court's treatment of the facts in *Grady*, which were substantially similar to *Vitale's*, illustrates the point. In *Grady*, the defendant was involved in a car accident which caused a death, as well as a serious injury. Corbin pleaded guilty to tickets charging him with driving while intoxicated and failing to keep to the right of the median.[81] He was later indicted on a number of other charges arising out of the same incident, including homicide and assault. The *Blockburger* rule did not bar the second set of prosecutions because the ticket charges did not require proof of death or injury, and manslaughter and assault do not require proof of driving while intoxicated or failing to keep to the right. However, the Court held that the second prosecution was barred because, according to the prosecution's bill of particulars, the state planned to prove manslaughter and assault by proving the same conduct which had been at issue in the ticket offenses (i.e., operating a vehicle in an intoxicated condition and failing to keep right). At the same time, the Court stated, prosecution on the second set of charges might still be possible, if the bill of particulars were amended so as not to rely on conduct for which Corbin had already been convicted (i.e., "if the State relied solely on Corbin's driving too fast in heavy rain to establish recklessness or negligence").

In dissent, Justice Scalia wondered what would happen under the majority's rule if, during a new trial under the amended bill of particulars, a witness testifies that the defendant had been weaving across the line: would the trial have to be aborted at this point, because the prosecution has now introduced conduct previously used to convict the defendant on another charge? This question has yet to be answered by the Court, and demonstrates the type of confusion application of the same conduct test may generate. It would seem, however, that the trial hypothesized by Scalia could proceed, since the crucial issue under the majority's approach appears to be whether the second prosecution is *based* on conduct that has already led to conviction or acquittal and, under an amended bill of particulars as described by the majority, it is clear that such is not the case.

Scalia also queried whether *Grady* would necessitate, contrary to common practice, joint trial of a substantive offense and conspiracy to commit that offense when, as is usually the case, the

---

81. The judge who accepted the plea had not been informed of the pending homicide investigation against Corbin stemming from the accident. The Court did not address the concern ex- pressed by some judges in the lower courts that the defendant had engaged in a material misrepresentation of fact when pleading guilty to the two ticket offenses.

overt act required to prove the conspiracy is the same conduct that led to the substantive offense. This question was soon answered in the negative, in *United States v. Felix.*[82] There, two years after being convicted of attempting to manufacture methamphetamine in Missouri, the defendant was tried and convicted in Oklahoma on one count of conspiring to manufacture, possess and distribute the same drug, and on five substantive counts relating to manufacture and distribution of the drug. Among the overt acts alleged in furtherance of the conspiracy was the conduct upon which the Missouri conviction was based. Furthermore, evidence of the conduct supporting the five substantive counts (which had taken place prior to the Missouri incident), had been introduced at the Missouri trial to prove criminal intent in that case. Nonetheless, a unanimous Court found that the previous conviction did not bar trial on either the conspiracy or the substantive offenses.

As to the latter counts, the Court stressed that using some of the same evidence in two separate trials did not necessarily violate *Grady;* here, the first trial "did not in any way *prosecute* Felix for the Oklahoma methamphetamine transactions [but] simply introduced those transactions as prior acts evidence." The Court's opinion, written by Chief Justice Rehnquist, characterized this situation as a "mere overlap in proof," rather than two prosecutions which both required proof of the same conduct.[83]

With respect to the contention that *Grady* prohibited trial on the conspiracy charge (which did appear to require proof of the same conduct proven at the Missouri trial), Rehnquist admitted that here "there exists more than a mere overlap in evidence." But he concluded that, in light of *Grady's* failure to question "long established precedent" to the contrary, the Double Jeopardy Clause did not ban prosecution on the conspiracy charge either. In particular, he noted the forty-six year-old decision in *United States v. Bayer,*[84] which had held that a conspiracy and the conspired offense are distinct for double jeopardy purposes because the "essence" of a conspiracy offense "is in the agreement or confederation to commit a crime." Justice Stevens, joined by Justice Blackmun, found this aspect of the Court's opinion overly broad. He concurred in the judgment on the ground that "the overt acts at issue here did not meaningfully 'establish' an essential element of the conspiracy because there is no overt act requirement in the federal drug conspiracy statute and the overt acts did not establish an agreement between Felix and his cocon-

---

82. 503 U.S. ___, 112 S.Ct. 1377 (1992).

83. Here the Court relied heavily on *Dowling v. United States,* 493 U.S. 342, 110 S.Ct. 668 (1990), discussed in § 30.04(a)(3).

84. 331 U.S. 532, 67 S.Ct. 1394 (1947). See also, *Pinkerton v. United States,* 328 U.S. 640, 66 S.Ct. 1180 (1946).

spirators;" thus, he argued, the literal language of *Grady* was not violated.

(3) Collateral estoppel. Closely related to the definition of same offense under the Double Jeopardy Clause is the application of the collateral estoppel principle, which was given constitutional status by the Supreme Court in *Ashe v. Swenson.*[85] Under limited circumstances, this principle can provide as much protection against reprosecution as the same transaction or same conduct tests.

The resolution of *Ashe* illustrates this point. There the state alleged that the defendant had been one of four gunmen to hold up six other men. However, at his trial for robbery of one of the six victims, the defendant was able to cast serious doubt on the reliability of testimony identifying him as a perpetrator and was acquitted. He was then indicted for the robbery of a second member of the group of six victims, and this time he was convicted, the eyewitnesses now being more certain of his identity. This second prosecution would not have been barred under the *Blockburger* rule extant at that time. But the Supreme Court found it unconstitutional on collateral estoppel grounds. After examining the trial record, it concluded that the original acquittal must have turned upon a finding that the defendant had not been a participant in the robbery and that, under the collateral estoppel principle, "when an issue of ultimate fact has once been determined by a valid and final judgment, that issue cannot again be litigated between the same parties in any future lawsuit." That this result was required under the Fifth Amendment as well as customary practice was also clear to the Court, "[f]or whatever else that constitutional guarantee may embrace, ... it surely protects a man who has been acquitted from having to 'run the gauntlet' a second time."

The use of collateral estoppel is quite limited, however. First, there must be, as in *Ashe,* clear evidence that the issue sought to be precluded in the second proceeding was resolved in favor of the defendant in the first proceeding. Because an acquittal can usually rely on a number of different factors, ranging from prosecution failure to prove the various elements of the crime to the defendant's success with one or more defenses, determining whether a particular issue was resolved favorably to the defendant can be very difficult. While use of special verdicts could assuage this problem, they may not always be useful to the defendant. For instance, in *Turner v. Arkansas,*[86] the defendant was charged, along with his brother, of robbing and murdering a fellow poker player, on a felony murder theory. After being acquitted at this

85. 397 U.S. 436, 90 S.Ct. 1189
(1970).

86. 407 U.S. 366, 92 S.Ct. 2096
(1972).

trial, the state courts allowed a second trial of the defendant on the robbery charge, on the assumption that the first jury may have acquitted him of felony murder solely because he did not commit the actual killing. Although this assumption was plausible, the Supreme Court held that the second trial should have been prohibited because the judge at the first trial had instructed the jury to find the defendant guilty of felony murder even if he was only involved in the robbery and not the killing. Had there been a special verdict in this case to determine the rationale for the verdict, it may have revealed that the jury did disregard the instruction, and acquitted the defendant despite his participation in the robbery (thus presumably eliminating the verdict's collateral estoppel value). Worse for the defendant, a special verdict procedure may have deterred the first jury from acquitting him in the first place, knowing that a nullification of the instruction would eventually be discovered.

Even if the finding upon which the jury based its verdict can be determined through a special verdict procedure or otherwise, it must be precisely identical to the issue sought to be precluded in order for the collateral estoppel doctrine to apply. For example, in *United States v. Smith,*[87] the defendant was acquitted on one count of uttering a forged check. A subsequent trial charging him with forgery of that check was permitted by the Fifth Circuit, since the jury in the first trial could have based its acquittal on the identity of the person who uttered the check rather than on the identity of the person who forged it.

Third, a finding in a previous proceeding will not be given preclusive effect unless it involved, in *Ashe's* language, an "ultimate" issue. Thus, while a finding that the defendant was not the perpetrator of a multi-victim crime, such as was involved in *Ashe,* will bar subsequent prosecution for the same transaction, a finding by the jury that the prosecution's key witness was not "credible" would probably not be given preclusive effect.[88] Note, however, that if the issue resolved at the first proceeding is "ultimate," it can have an estoppel effect even if the final verdict was not an acquittal. For instance, one court found that a defendant may not be prosecuted for an assault which occurred during a robbery if he has already been convicted of receiving the property stolen during the robbery.[89]

Finally, collateral estoppel may be used only against a party which lost on the issue sought to be estopped, by at least the standard of proof required in the second proceeding. Given the identity of parties requirement, collateral estoppel cannot be used

---

87. 470 F.2d 1299 (5th Cir.1973).

88. See *Schleiss v. State,* 71 Wis.2d 733, 239 N.W.2d 68 (1976).

89. *Hinton v. State,* 36 Md.App. 52, 373 A.2d 39 (1977).

in a proceeding brought by a different sovereign.[90]   And given the identity of proof requirement, a finding in a criminal trial that there is a reasonable doubt on a particular issue usually cannot be used to estop a civil proceeding where stronger proof is required. For instance, in *United States v. One Assortment of 89 Firearms,*[91] the Supreme Court held that an acquittal on criminal charges did not bar, in a subsequent forfeiture proceeding, a finding by a preponderance of the evidence that the defendant engaged in the same criminal activity.   And in *One Lot Emerald Cut Stones and One Ring v. United States,*[92] the Court disallowed the defendant's use of his acquittal on smuggling charges in a forfeiture proceeding where the government did not have to show criminal intent.[93]

Nor does the collateral estoppel doctrine bar use of conduct for which the defendant was acquitted in a subsequent *criminal* proceeding, so long as the evidence has some credibility and the proceeding is for a different offense (thus avoiding the double jeopardy prohibition).   This was the holding of *Dowling v. United States,*[94] where the state used eyewitness testimony at the defendant's robbery trial which linked the defendant to a separate robbery for which he had been acquitted, in an attempt to show, *inter alia,* that the defendant used the same modus operandi in both.   The Court pointed out that, according to prior caselaw,[95] such prior act evidence is admissible under Federal Rule of Evidence 404(b) (dealing with prior bad acts) if the jury can reasonably conclude that the act occurred and that the defendant was the actor.   Thus, merely because the defendant had managed to raise a reasonable doubt as to whether he was guilty of the first robbery did not bar evidence of that robbery at a trial for another robbery.

The question might arise whether the *state* can estop the defendant from asserting a defense which has proven unsuccessful in a previous trial.   For instance, if the prosecution in *Ashe* had convicted the defendant in the first trial, could it claim that this verdict showed beyond a reasonable doubt that the defendant was also involved in the robbery of the other five victims?   Although the technical requirements of collateral estoppel might be met in this situation, two objections can be raised to its use on these facts. First, it might run afoul of the right to jury trial for each offense.[96]

90. See § 30.06 for further discussion of the different sovereign doctrine.

91. 465 U.S. 354, 104 S.Ct. 1099 (1984).

92. 409 U.S. 232, 93 S.Ct. 489 (1972).

93. Note that if the proceedings are reversed—that is, the civil proceeding precedes the criminal action—collateral estoppel could apply (because a finding by a preponderance of the evidence would certainly suggest a reasonable doubt).   However, application of the estoppel doctrine is not *constitutionally* required in this situation, since jeopardy has not attached at the civil proceeding.   See § 30.02(a).

94. 493 U.S. 342, 110 S.Ct. 668 (1990).

95. *Huddleston v. United States,* 485 U.S. 681, 108 S.Ct. 1496 (1988).

96. See *Simpson v. Florida,* 403 U.S. 384, 91 S.Ct. 1801 (1971).

Second, under current double jeopardy jurisprudence, which defines "same offense" using a "same conduct" standard, the Double Jeopardy Clause might bar the second prosecution altogether.

(b) Exceptions to the Same Offense Prohibition. There are at least four exceptions to the general rule that a prosecution will be barred if the defendant can show that he has already been "acquitted," convicted or provoked into a mistrial motion for a charge constituting the "same offense." They occur when the second prosecution: (1) is based on conduct or events which have occurred after the first prosecution; (2) results from the defendant's own motion; (3) is based on a charge over which the court for the original prosecution did not have jurisdiction; or (4) is based on a charge which was originally filed by the prosecution, but which was dismissed by the arraignment judge over the prosecution's objection in the course of taking a guilty plea.

(1) New conduct or event. The first exception to the same offense prohibition occurs when an essential element of an offense does not develop until after prosecution of a lesser offense. This exception is illustrated by *Diaz v. United States.*[97] The defendant in *Diaz* was convicted of assault and battery, but the victim later died. In rejecting the defendant's attempt to interpose a double jeopardy bar on the subsequent homicide prosecution, the Court stated:

> The death of the injured person was the principal element of the homicide, but was no part of the assault and battery. At the time of the trial for the latter the death had not ensued, and not until it did ensue was the homicide committed. Then, and not before, was it possible to put the accused in jeopardy for the offense.

In *Garrett v. United States,*[98] the Court reaffirmed the *Diaz* rule, at the same time expanding its scope. There, the defendant pleaded guilty to one count of importing marijuana. Two months later, the government indicted the defendant under the "continuing criminal enterprise" (CCE) provision of the Comprehensive Drug Abuse Prevention and Control Act of 1970. The defendant's prior conviction was introduced at his trial on the CCE charge as proof of one of the three predicate offenses which must be proven to authorize the enhanced penalties of the Act. Five members of the Court concluded that the prosecution on the CCE charge was not barred because that charge was based on new conduct after the first prosecution. To the dissent's argument that the government had enough evidence at the time of the first prosecution to bring a CCE charge (albeit one of shorter duration), a plurality of four justices responded that "one who at the time the first indict-

97. 223 U.S. 442, 32 S.Ct. 250 (1912).   **98.** 471 U.S. 773, 105 S.Ct. 2407 (1985).

ment is returned is continuing to engage in other conduct found criminal" cannot object to multiple prosecutions; the fact that a CCE charge could have been brought at the time of the first prosecution was irrelevant to double jeopardy analysis. Justice O'Connor saw "merit" to the dissent's position, but joined the plurality given her belief that the government should be allowed to decide when to prosecute criminal activity that continues after prosecution for a predicate offense, so long as there is no evidence of "governmental oppression of the sort against which the Double Jeopardy Clause was intended to protect."

Diaz permitted a second prosecution for the "same offense" when the offense involved was impossible to charge at the time of the first prosecution. *Garrett* obviously extends the *Diaz* rationale to permit such prosecutions even when the second charge could have been joined at the first trial, so long as the relevant conduct continues after the first indictment. This ruling might have particularly significant consequences in cases involving crimes defined as a continuing course of conduct (such as CCE charges, "racketeering" or "RICO" charges, and conspiracies).[99] But now that *United States v. Felix* [1] has decided that a conspiracy and the associated substantive offense are not the "same" for double jeopardy purposes, *Garrett's* broadening of the *Diaz* exception is likely to add little to the prosecution's arsenal.

(2) Severance by the defendant. In *Jeffers v. United States,*[2] a plurality of the Court announced another exception to the same offense prohibition. In *Jeffers,* a grand jury returned two separate indictments against the defendant, one charging him, along with nine others, of conspiring to distribute narcotics, and the other charging him individually with a CCE violation. Prior to the trial on the conspiracy charge, the government made a motion to join the CCE charge, to which the defendant and his co-conspirators successfully objected. But he and six of the co-conspirators were found guilty of the conspiracy offense, and the defendant was then tried and convicted on the severed CCE charge.

The Court assumed that the conspiracy and the CCE charge were the same offense for double jeopardy purposes. But it went on to uphold the second conviction on grounds analogous to its mistrial jurisprudence.[3] According to the plurality opinion, because the defendant "was solely responsible for the successive prosecutions," he could not prevent the second one. As the dissent pointed out, however, the defendant could not "be held responsible for the fact that two separate indictments were re-

---

99. Thomas, "An Elegant Theory of Double Jeopardy," 1988 U.Ill.L.Rev. 827, 878.

1. 503 U.S. ___, 112 S.Ct. 1377 (1992), discussed in § 30.04(a)(2).

2. 432 U.S. 137, 97 S.Ct. 2207 (1977).

3. See *United States v. Dinitz,* 424 U.S. 600, 96 S.Ct. 1075 (1976), discussed in § 30.03(c)(2).

turned, or for the fact that other defendants were named in the earlier indictment, or for the fact that the Government elected to proceed to trial first on the lesser charge." The plurality's only response to this argument was to suggest that had there been "proof" that joinder would have so severely prejudiced the defendant that his "Sixth Amendment right to a fair trial" would be abridged, a different result might have been necessary. Assuming this degree of prejudice is not shown, when joinder and double jeopardy principles clash, *Jeffers* requires the defendant, not the government, to make the hard choice.

(3) Jurisdictional bar. The third exception to the same offense prohibition occurs when the lesser charge is tried to an inferior court with no jurisdiction over the greater charge. In such a case, jeopardy does not attach for the greater offense. In *Waller v. Florida,*[4] the Supreme Court intimated otherwise when it held that a municipal proceeding upon the lesser offense would bar a state action on the greater. But that decision was premised on a finding that municipalities and the state in which they are located are not separate sovereigns for purposes of the Double Jeopardy Clause. The jurisdictional issue was not explicitly addressed. In *Fugate v. New Mexico,*[5] on the other hand, an evenly divided Court (Justice Powell not participating) let stand a New Mexico Supreme Court decision holding that a defendant's conviction in municipal court on charges of driving while intoxicated and careless driving did not bar his subsequent prosecution, in higher court, for vehicular homicide based on the same incident, because the lower court had no jurisdiction to hear the greater charge. (Note that in *Grady*, involving similar facts, the court in which the first prosecution took place had jurisdiction over both charges).

Assuming the prosecution has, or should have had, possession of all the relevant evidence at the time of the first prosecution (in other words, assuming the *Diaz* exception does not apply), it is not clear why multiple prosecutions should be allowed merely because the prosecution made the mistake of trying the less serious crime first, in a court of limited jurisdiction. Apparently *Fugate* is based on the idea, similar to that voiced in *Garrett, Jeffers* and the Court's mistrial cases, that the prosecution should not be penalized by the same offense prohibition when it has not *intentionally* sought to subject the defendant to multiple trials. Again, the defendant is made to suffer multiple prosecutions due to the prosecution's oversight or inefficiency. If a jurisdictional bar exception is necessary, a more sensible version, suggested by

4. 397 U.S. 387, 90 S.Ct. 1184 (1970).   **5.** 471 U.S. 1112, 105 S.Ct. 2349
See § 30.06(c).   (1985).

Justice Brennan, would permit multiple prosecutions only if no single court had jurisdiction over both offenses.[6]

(4) Guilty pleas over prosecution objection. A final exception to the same offense prohibition occurs in the relatively rare situation represented in *Ohio v. Johnson.*[7] There the defendant, over the prosecution's objection, successfully moved to dismiss murder and aggravated robbery charges after pleading guilty to the lesser included offenses, respectively, of manslaughter and grand theft. The Supreme Court reversed the Ohio Supreme Court's ruling that the Double Jeopardy Clause barred trial on the murder and aggravated robbery charges, pointing out that the defendant "had not been exposed to conviction on the charges to which he pleaded not guilty, nor has the state had the opportunity to marshall its evidence and resources more than once or to hone its presentation of its case through a trial." The situation in *Johnson* "has none of the implications of an 'implied acquittal' which results from a verdict convicting a defendant on lesser included offenses rendered by a jury charged to consider both greater and lesser included offenses." Further, the Court stressed that the defendant "should not be entitled to use the Double Jeopardy Clause as a sword to prevent the State from completing its prosecution on the remaining charges."

This exception too is questionable. It is true, as noted earlier,[8] that when a judge accepts a plea to which the prosecution agrees, the resulting conviction cannot be seen as an "implied acquittal" of any greater charge, because the judge never considered the greater charge. But the judge in *Johnson* clearly did consider, and decided to dismiss, the greater charges. Arguably, the fact that the prosecution disagreed with this dismissal has no more relevance for double jeopardy purposes than its disagreement with a jury verdict; in both cases jeopardy has attached and a final disposition of the "same offense" reached. Only if it can be said that judges do not have "jurisdiction" to dismiss charges over prosecutorial objection might there be support for the *Johnson* holding, for in that case it could be said that jeopardy never attached.[9]

(c) Cumulative Punishments. Whether two offenses constituting the "same offense" are tried successively, as permitted by the above exceptions to the same offense prohibition, or together, as is more normally the case, a central question is whether the punishment for each may be imposed cumulatively or whether the government is limited to seeking the stiffest penalty from among

6. See *Ashe v. Swenson,* 397 U.S. 436, 90 S.Ct. 1189 (1970) (Brennan, J., concurring).

7. 467 U.S. 493, 104 S.Ct. 2536 (1984).

8. See § 30.03(a)(1).

9. Cf. *Kepner v. United States,* 195 U.S. 100, 24 S.Ct. 797 (1904), noted in § 30.02(b).

those available. If the definition of same offense used to determine the validity of multiple prosecutions were also used to determine the validity of multiple punishments, it is clear that the latter approach would be constitutionally required. But the Supreme Court has held that whether cumulative punishment for two offenses is barred by the Double Jeopardy Clause depends in the first instance on what the legislature intended when it enacted the two offenses, not on whether the offenses are the "same offense" as that term is used in determining whether multiple prosecutions are permissible.

The Court alluded to this position in *Albernaz v. United States*,[10] in which it stated that the *Blockburger* rule, although originally developed in the multiple punishments context, merely "serves as a means of discerning congressional purpose [and] should not be controlling where, for example, there is a clear indication of contrary legislative intent." But this language was not necessary to the decision in *Albernaz*. There, the Court held that the two punishments imposed—for conspiracy to import marijuana and conspiracy to distribute marijuana—were not the same offense even under *Blockburger*.

In *Missouri v. Hunter*,[11] the Court specifically held that legislative intent, if clear, determines the scope of "same offense" analysis for purposes of determining when cumulative punishments may be imposed. In *Hunter*, the defendant was convicted at one trial under two separate Missouri statutes, one proscribing robbery in the first degree, the second prohibiting "armed criminal action" (i.e., "use a gun, go to jail"). He received consecutive terms of ten years for the robbery and fifteen years for the armed criminal action even though the former offense is a lesser included offense of the latter. The Court's majority opinion, written by Chief Justice Burger, conceded that the Court was bound by the Missouri Supreme Court's ruling that the two statutes at issue defined the same crime under *Blockburger*. But the Chief Justice went on to conclude that *Blockburger* was irrelevant in this case because the Missouri legislature had made "crystal clear" that it intended the penalty imposed for violation of the armed criminal action statute to be in addition to any other penalty imposed for crimes committed simultaneously with it. In such a situation, "a court's task of statutory construction is at an end and the prosecutor may seek and the trial court or jury may impose cumulative punishment under such statutes in a single trial." As it had suggested in *Albernaz*, the Court held that *Blockburger* merely provided a rule for statutory construction which becomes unnecessary when the legislature's actions are unambiguous.

10. 450 U.S. 333, 101 S.Ct. 1137 (1981).

11. 459 U.S. 359, 103 S.Ct. 673 (1983).

Hunter's holding was limited to multiple punishments imposed at a single trial. It is not implausible to suggest that, on those occasions when two different crimes constituting the same offense are tried separately (as in the four situations discussed above), punishment should have to be imposed concurrently. As the Court has recognized in a different double jeopardy context, "it might be argued that the defendant perceives the length of his sentence as finally determined when he begins to serve it, and that the trial judge should be prohibited from thereafter increasing the sentence." [12] But in *Garrett,* where the defendant received five years and a $15,000 fine after his first trial on the marijuana importation charge, the Court cited *Hunter* in upholding an additional 40 years imprisonment and $100,000 in fines on the CCE charge, based on its assessment of the CCE statute's legislative history.[13] Thus, it appears that the cumulative punishment rule announced in *Hunter* is the same whether charges which constitute the "same offense" are tried together or separately. The sole limitation on legislative discretion with respect to cumulation of sentences is the Eight Amendment's ban on disproportionate, cruel and unusual punishment.[14]

30.05 Resentencing

To be distinguished from cumulation of separate sentences for more than one statutory offense is the practice of increasing a single sentence imposed after conviction on a specific charge. One could argue that the Double Jeopardy Clause prohibits this practice, by analogy to the implied acquittal doctrine, which provides that a conviction on one charge bars subsequent prosecution on a greater charge when the factfinder had the opportunity to consider evidence on the latter charge.[15] But the Supreme Court has indicated that there are a number of situations where a sentence for a particular charge may be increased after it has been imposed. The law of resentencing is best considered by dividing it into the three contexts in which it can occur.

(a) **After Reversal of Conviction.** In *North Carolina v. Pearce,*[16] the defendant successfully appealed his conviction, was retried on the same charge, and received a harsher sentence than

12. *United States v. DiFrancesco,* 449 U.S. 117, 101 S.Ct. 426 (1980) (rejecting this argument, however, when the defendant is on notice that his sentence can be appealed by the prosecution).

13. The *Garrett* Court also characterized as "reasonabl[e]" the conclusion in *Jeffers* that Congress had *not* meant to cumulate the *conspiracy* and CCE penalties involved there, since in contrast to the offenses involved in *Garrett,* "the dangers posed by a conspiracy and a CCE were similar and thus there would be little purpose in cumulating the penalties."

14. And this limitation is virtually non-existent. See *Solem v. Helm,* 463 U.S. 277, 103 S.Ct. 3001 (1983).

15. See § 30.03(a)(1).

16. 395 U.S. 711, 89 S.Ct. 2072 (1969).

the one he received after his first conviction. While the Court held that due process might be implicated if the harsher sentence were vindictively imposed as a penalty for appealing the conviction,[17] it concluded that the Double Jeopardy Clause does not bar the stiffer penalty, so long as it is legally authorized, and so long as the defendant is given credit for time served. The Court reasoned that the original conviction had, "at the defendant's behest, been wholly nullified and the slate wiped clean."

Of course, this latter statement contradicts the sense of the Court's earlier holding in *Green v. United States*,[18] to the effect that a defendant who has successfully appealed cannot be reprosecuted on the original charge if the jury rejected it at the first trial. In a later decision affirming *Pearce*, the Court provided a better (although not necessarily persuasive) reason for rejecting the idea that "the imposition of a particular sentence is an 'implied acquittal' of any greater sentence." In *United States v. DiFrancesco*,[19] discussed further below in connection with prosecution appeals of sentences, the Court pointed out that many of the traditional reasons for barring reprosecution—i.e., saving the defendant the expense and anxiety of another trial, and preventing the prosecution from securing an unwarranted conviction by wearing the defendant down with a well-practiced case—are not implicated by normal resentencing, because no formal proceeding is involved.

However, in *Bullington v. Missouri*,[20] the Court held that when the sentencing process *is* more formalized, the *Pearce–DiFrancesco* reasoning does not apply. In *Bullington*, the defendant, after being convicted of capital murder and sentenced in a separate sentencing proceeding to life imprisonment, moved for a judgment of acquittal or, in the alternative, a new trial. The latter motion was granted because his trial and sentencing jury had been unconstitutionally selected. The prosecution then informed the defendant that, at the second trial, it planned to once again seek the death penalty.

In holding that the prosecution was limited to obtaining life imprisonment, the Court emphasized the similarity between the capital sentencing procedures under Missouri law and a trial on the issue of the defendant's guilt or innocence. Justice Blackmun, writing for a majority of five justices, pointed out that, after *Burks v. United States*,[21] a defendant may not be retried if he obtains a reversal of his conviction on the ground that the prosecution lacked sufficient evidence to prove its case. He then noted that,

17. See § 29.02(d).

18. 355 U.S. 184, 78 S.Ct. 221 (1957).

19. 449 U.S. 117, 101 S.Ct. 426 (1980).

20. 451 U.S. 430, 101 S.Ct. 1852 (1981).

21. 437 U.S. 1, 98 S.Ct. 2141 (1978), discussed in § 30.02(b).

while, in "the usual sentencing proceeding . . . it is impossible to conclude that a sentence less than the statutory maximum 'constitute[s] a decision to the effect that the government has failed to prove its case,' " the procedure established by Missouri's capital sentencing statute "*explicitly requires* the jury to determine whether the prosecution has 'proved its case.' " In particular, Blackmun pointed to the fact that, under Missouri law, the capital "presentence hearing resembled and, indeed, in all relevant respects was like the immediately preceding trial on the issue of guilt or innocence," including the requirement that the prosecution prove its case in support of the death penalty beyond a reasonable doubt.

Bullington was applied in *Arizona v. Rumsey,*[22] which involved a capital sentencing proceeding similar to the Missouri procedure at issue in *Bullington* except that the judge, rather than the jury, had sentencing authority. In *Rumsey,* the judge sentenced the defendant to life imprisonment. The defendant appealed to the Arizona Supreme Court and the prosecution cross-appealed. While it rejected the defendant's claim, the Arizona court agreed with the state that the judge had misconstrued an aggravating circumstance permitting imposition of the death penalty and remanded the case for a new penalty hearing. Upon receiving a death sentence at the new hearing, the defendant again appealed, this time on double jeopardy grounds. The Supreme Court found that the trial judge's first ruling was an implied acquittal of the death penalty even though erroneous. "Reliance on an error of law . . . does not change the double jeopardy effects of a judgment that amounts to an acquittal on the merits."

On the other hand, where the sentencing judge *imposes* the death penalty and a reviewing court finds the sentence erroneous because an aggravating circumstance identified by the judge does not exist, the sentencing court may reimpose capital punishment even if it has previously rejected the remaining aggravating circumstances. In *Poland v. Arizona,*[23] the sentencing judge imposed the death penalty on the ground the defendant's crime had been particularly "heinous" but specifically held that it had not been committed for pecuniary gain, another aggravating circumstance. The Arizona Supreme Court held that the crime had not been heinous but that the sentencing judge had misinterpreted the pecuniary gain provision, and remanded for resentencing. Despite *Poland's* similarity to *Rumsey*, the Court refused to find that the defendant had been "acquitted" by the sentencing judge of the pecuniary gain circumstance, on the ground that *Bullington* prohibits resentencing only when a court has found the death penalty

22. 467 U.S. 203, 104 S.Ct. 2305 (1984).　　**23.** 476 U.S. 147, 106 S.Ct. 1749 (1986).

"inappropriate" and that here no court had done so; since the sentencing court had imposed the death penalty and the reviewing court had indicated it did not consider the matter closed, the state was allowed a "clean slate" hearing on the pecuniary gain circumstance.

It is not clear whether the *Bullington* exception will be applicable to *non*-capital sentencing proceedings which resemble a trial to the same extent Missouri's capital sentencing scheme does.[24] On the one hand, the *Bullington* Court did not specifically limit its holding to capital cases. Moreover, Blackmun cited the Court's decision in *Specht v. Patterson*,[25] which involved noncapital sentencing under a sexual psychopath statute, as an example of a case which, like *Bullington* extended due process protections normally associated with trial to sentencing proceedings. On the other hand, the Court has frequently noted the "unique" nature of the death penalty and imposed procedural protections in such cases that it has not imposed in other situations.[26]

The key variable would seem to be whether the sentencing proceeding is sufficiently structured so that one can point to a specific "case" the prosecution must make out to secure a particular sentence. In such a system, one could justifiably conclude that the sentencing body has "acquitted" the defendant of that sentence if the prosecution fails to obtain it. Note that this same analysis would apply if, as might occur under the sentencing schemes of many states,[27] the defendant appeals the *sentence* he receives (rather than the conviction) and it is overturned on insufficient proof grounds (analogous to *Burks*) rather than on procedural grounds.

(b) After Prosecution Appeal of Sentence. As discussed earlier in this chapter,[28] the prosecution usually may not appeal an acquittal, or a dismissal which is the equivalent of an acquittal. But in those situations just discussed where a particular sentence does not represent an "acquittal" on any greater sentence, the prosecution may appeal a sentence, so long as there is statutory authorization to do so. This was the holding in *United States v. DiFrancesco*,[29] where the Court upheld a federal provision authorizing prosecution appeal of sentences imposed under a "dangerous special offender" statute. In addition to noting that a successful prosecutorial appeal under this provision did not subject the

24. See e.g., Lagoy, Hussey, Kramer, "A Comparative Assessment of Determinative Sentencing in Four Pioneer States," 24 Crime & Delinqu. 387 (1978).

25. 386 U.S. 605, 87 S.Ct. 1209 (1967).

26. See, e.g., *Gardner v. Florida*, 430 U.S. 349, 97 S.Ct. 1197 (1977).

27. See, e.g., West's Fla.S.A.R.Crim. Pro. 3.850.

28. See § 30.03(a) & (b).

29. 449 U.S. 117, 101 S.Ct. 426 (1980).

defendant to the ordeal of a new trial-like proceeding, the Court emphasized that because the defendant was aware that his special offender sentence was subject to appellate review, his legitimate expectations would not be defeated should his sentence be increased. Adhering to the rationale of *Missouri v. Hunter*,[30] the Court also held that an increased sentence as a result of the appeal would not violate the ban on cumulative punishments, because the new sentence would still be within specified legislative limits, of which the defendant was, or should have been, aware.

DiFrancesco's emphasis on the fact that the defendant was on notice that his sentence could be changed suggests that a defendant's expectations with respect to his sentence may be important for double jeopardy purposes. The same theme was sounded in *Pennsylvania v. Goldhammer*,[31] where the defendant appealed a multicount conviction. The state appellate court, after reversing the one count against the defendant which carried a term of imprisonment and affirming the other counts (which carried a suspended sentence), refused on double jeopardy grounds to remand for resentencing on the affirmed counts. Disagreeing with the state court's reasoning, the Supreme Court remanded the case for reconsideration in light of *DiFrancesco,* and directed the state court to consider "whether the Pennsylvania laws in effect at the time allowed the State to obtain review of the sentences on the counts for which the sentence had been suspended." The implication was that, if there were no such review procedure, the defendant's expectation of finality in his sentence could not be upset by reimposing part or all of the suspended sentence.

(c) After Discovery of a Defect in the Sentence. A final resentencing situation involves neither resentencing after a reversal of a conviction or a prosecutorial attempt to increase the sentence. Rather, it occurs when the sentencing judge seeks to redress a legal error in the original sentence. For instance, in *Ex parte Lange*,[32] the trial court imposed the maximum one-year term of imprisonment and the maximum $200 fine, under a statute which authorized only imprisonment *or* a fine. After paying the fine, the defendant petitioned for release, but the trial court instead ordered the refund of the defendant's money and reimposed the imprisonment term of one year. The Supreme Court held that this solution violated the Double Jeopardy Clause's ban on multiple punishments, because the $200 was now beyond the reach of the judiciary (since it was in the state treasury), and the new one-year term was added to the five days the defendant had already served. *In re Bradley*,[33] involved a very similar fact

---

30. 459 U.S. 359, 103 S.Ct. 673 (1983), discussed in § 30.04(c).

31. 474 U.S. 28, 106 S.Ct. 353 (1985).

32. 85 U.S. (18 Wall.) 163 (1873).

33. 318 U.S. 50, 63 S.Ct. 470 (1943).

pattern, except the judge, after returning the fine, was careful to avoid imposing more than the maximum prison term. Nonetheless, the Court once again found that the new sentence was barred, because the defendant had fully satisfied one of the two sentencing alternatives.

The Court has not considered the Double Jeopardy Clause a shield against correction of all judicial errors, however. For instance, in *Bozza v. United States*,[34] the Court upheld an increase in sentence designed to meet the mandatory minimum required by statute. The Court noted that the correction was made within hours of announcing the original sentence, and that it merely provided what was required by law, before the defendant had satisfied the sentence. This holding conforms with the usual mandate that the trial judge may correct an illegal sentence at any time before it is satisfied.[35]

A different scenario confronted the Court in *Jones v. Thomas*.[36] There, the defendant was convicted of felony murder and the underlying felony of attempted robbery and sentenced to consecutive terms of life imprisonment and 15 years respectively. Some years later, after the defendant had already served sufficient time to satisfy the latter sentence, a state appellate court held that the felony murder statute did not authorize separate punishments for the murder and the underlying felony. While the defendant argued that, under *Bradley,* he should thus be freed, the Supreme Court upheld the trial court's conclusion that it only needed to credit the time served against his life sentence for felony murder. The Court distinguished *Bradley* on two grounds. First, in *Bradley* the legislature had obviously conceived of the penalties involved as alternative punishments for the crime, whereas the penalty for robbery could not be seen as an alternative for the felony murder sentence, and thus was not a legitimate substitute. Second, while crediting was possible in *Jones,* because both penalties involved imprisonment, it had not been possible to credit the fine against the imprisonment penalty in *Bradley.*

Echoing the expectation theme from *DiFrancesco* and *Goldhammer,* the Court also noted that Jones could not have expected to serve only an attempted robbery sentence, given his original sentence. At the same time, it implied that, under normal circumstances, a defendant has a "legitimate expectation of finality" in the sentence he receives, at least once he has served it, and perhaps even once he has started serving it.[37] Thus, it may

---

34. 330 U.S. 160, 67 S.Ct. 645 (1947).

35. See, e.g., Fed.R.Crim.P. 35(a).

36. 491 U.S. 376, 109 S.Ct. 2522 (1989).

37. The Court noted this was the federal practice, but ventured "no comment on this limitation."

be that, except in those situations described in this section, a sentence cannot be changed once imposed.

30.06 The Dual Sovereignty Doctrine

Even when the defendant is acquitted at trial, or is convicted and does not appeal, there is one situation in which he can be reprosecuted for the identical offense. That is when the entity which brings the second prosecution is a separate sovereign from the first prosecuting entity. The basis for this rule is that separate sovereigns have the right to enforce their own laws, irrespective of the impact that prerogative may have on the individual defendant. While this reasoning has some appeal when dealing with international crime, it makes less sense within the United States, even acknowledging the federal nature of our system.

(a) **Federal-State Prosecutions.** The first exposition of the dual sovereignty doctrine arose in the context of federal and state prosecutions for the same crime.[38] As articulated in *United States v. Lanza*,[39] the doctrine states that "an act denounced as a crime by both national and state sovereignties is an offense against the peace and dignity of both and may be punished by each." This rule was reaffirmed in two 1959 decisions, *Bartkus v. Illinois*[40] and *Abbate v. United States*.[41] In *Bartkus,* the defendant was tried first in federal court for robbery of a federally insured savings and loan bank. After a federal acquittal, he was tried and convicted in state court for the same act. The reverse situation occurred in *Abbate* (i.e., a state trial was followed by federal trial for the same act) but both prosecutions ended in conviction. Both instances of multiple trials were upheld, given the possibility that the defendant's acts "may impinge more seriously on a federal [state] interest than a state [federal] interest." Illustrating this point in *Bartkus*, the Court noted that a contrary ruling could allow a defendant who has been convicted of a federal civil rights offense, carrying no more than a few years sentence, to prevent state prosecution on homicide charges. Similarly, in *Abbate*, the Court pointed out that the defendants were arguing that their state convictions, "resulting in three months' prison sentences[,] should bar this federal prosecution which could result in a sentence of up to five years."

Two decades later, the Court affirmed the reasoning of these cases in *United States v. Wheeler*.[42] There, the defendant asserted that Navaho Tribal court proceedings which resulted in his conviction for contributing to the delinquency of a minor were a bar to

38. See *Moore v. Illinois*, 55 U.S. (14 How.) 13 (1852).

39. 260 U.S. 377, 43 S.Ct. 141 (1922).

40. 359 U.S. 121, 79 S.Ct. 676 (1959).

41. 359 U.S. 187, 79 S.Ct. 666 (1959).

42. 435 U.S. 313, 98 S.Ct. 1079 (1978).

federal prosecution for the same offense. The Court rejected his claim, holding that the Tribe, like a state, constitutes a sovereign independent of the United States because "the ultimate source of the power under which the respective prosecutions were undertaken" is different. The Tribe's authority to prosecute, the Court found, stemmed from its "'primeval sovereignty' rather than a delegation of federal authority."

As several commentators have pointed out, the dual sovereignty notion established in these cases is contrary to the historical development of the Double Jeopardy Clause, the apparent intent of the framers of the Constitution, and the policy, endorsed in virtually all of the Court's other double jeopardy decisions, against subjecting defendants to multiple prosecutions for the same offense.[43] At the least, these factors should not be outweighed by any "interest" a separate sovereign may have in reprosecuting for the same offense unless the interest is extremely significant.[44] The federal government has, in effect, recognized this "independent interest" limitation by barring federal trial "when there has already been a state prosecution for substantially the same act or acts" unless an Assistant Attorney General directs otherwise. The Supreme Court noted this policy in *Petite v. United States*,[45] (with the consequence that it has since come to be called the "*Petite* policy"), and went so far as to hold, in *Rinaldi v. United States*,[46] that a federal district court abused its discretion by refusing to vacate a conviction upon a motion made by the government pursuant to this policy.

(b) **State-State Prosecutions.** Despite the Court's apparent willingness to recognize at least some form of a "separate interests" exception to the dual sovereignty doctrine when one of the sovereigns is willing to endorse it, its most recent decision has flatly refused to adopt the exception as a matter of constitutional law. In *Heath v. Alabama*,[47] the Court upheld the Alabama conviction of the defendant for the hired murder of his wife after he had pleaded guilty to the same crime in Georgia. The Court, in an opinion by Justice O'Connor, first found that:

> The States are no less sovereign with respect to each other than they are with respect to the Federal Government. Their powers to undertake criminal prosecutions derive from separate and independent sources of power and authority original-

43. See Allen, Ferrall, & Ratnaswamy, "The Double Jeopardy Clause, Constitutional Interpretation and the Limits of Formal Logic," 26 Valparaiso U.L.Rev. 281, 300–306 (1991).

44. See, e.g., Fisher, "Double Jeopardy, Two Sovereignties, and the In-

truding Constitution," 28 U.Chi.L.Rev. 591 (1961).

45. 361 U.S. 529, 80 S.Ct. 450 (1960).

46. 434 U.S. 22, 98 S.Ct. 81 (1977).

47. 474 U.S. 82, 106 S.Ct. 433 (1985).

ly belonging to them before admission to the Union and preserved by the Tenth Amendment.

The Court then explicitly rejected the contention that a defendant subject to dual prosecutions should be able to avoid the second unless doing so would frustrate the interests of the second sovereign. Ignoring the rationale underlying *Bartkus* and *Abbate*, it found the states' interest in prosecuting "irrelevant" in assessing whether two states may prosecute the same crime.

In dissent, Justice Marshall, joined by Justice Brennan, argued that allowing two states to prosecute for the same offense differed from federal-state dual prosecution. "[I]n contrast to the federal-state context, barring the second prosecution [in the two state context] would still permit one government to act upon the broad range of sovereign concerns that have been reserved to the States by the Constitution." He also pointed out that in this case Georgia officials, after obtaining a guilty plea from the defendant, had not only cooperated with Alabama officials in securing the defendant's second conviction but played "leading roles as prosecution witnesses in the Alabama trial." He argued that either double jeopardy or due process was violated by this "relentless prosecution."

(c) State–Municipal Prosecutions. In *Waller v. Florida*,[48] the Supreme Court held that contrary to federal, state and tribal governments, municipalities are not sovereign entities, but rather "subordinate governmental instrumentalities created by the State to assist in the carrying out of state governmental functions." Thus, multiple prosecutions for the "same offense" by a city and the state are barred by the Double Jeopardy Clause. However, if the municipal prosecution was not for the same offense,[49] or, as discussed earlier in this chapter,[50] the municipal court lacked jurisdiction over a more serious version of the same offense, then reprosecution in state court is permitted.

30.07 Conclusion

The Double Jeopardy Clause in the Fifth Amendment has spawned a very complex set of rules governing when the government may subject a defendant to separate prosecutions, separate punishments, and increased punishment for the same offense. These rules are summarized below:

(1) Fifth Amendment protection against reprosecution is not triggered unless jeopardy attaches. Jeopardy attaches in all criminal proceedings, and in any other proceeding which results in a

---

48. 397 U.S. 387, 90 S.Ct. 1184 (1970).

49. As the lower court in *Waller* found on remand.

50. See § 30.04(b)(3).

sanction having a retributive or deterrent purpose rather than a remedial one, when the jury is empanelled (in jury trials), when the first witness is sworn (in bench trials), or when a guilty plea is accepted (when conviction is by plea).

(2) Once jeopardy on a particular charge has attached, reprosecution for the same charge is prohibited unless: (a) the defendant is convicted and obtains a reversal on grounds other than evidentiary insufficiency; (b) the charge is dismissed by the judge on grounds not amounting to a factual determination that the defendant is innocent; or (c) a mistrial is declared for reasons of manifest necessity (when declared over the defendant's objection) or on grounds not involving prosecutorial error designed to provoke a mistrial motion from the defendant (when declared on the defendant's motion).

(3) Also barred is prosecution for any offense, not joined in the first prosecution, which requires the state to prove conduct that constitutes the offense involved in the first prosecution, except when: (a) the second prosecution is based in part on new conduct committed or events occurring after the first prosecution; (b) the defendant is responsible for preventing joinder of the second offense with the first offense on grounds that do not amount to unconstitutional prejudice; (c) the court which heard the first prosecution lacked jurisdiction to try the second offense; or (d) the first offense was resolved through a guilty plea which was objected to by the prosecution. The state is barred from cumulating punishments for different offenses unless the relevant statutes or legislative history indicate otherwise or, in the absence of guidance from these sources, each offense requires proof of a fact the other does not.

(4) Increasing a legal sentence for the same charge (as opposed to adding a separate sentence for a different charge) is prohibited when: (a) the sentence was imposed at a proceeding which resembled in all relevant respects a trial on the issue of guilt and innocence; (b) the increase results from an appeal or motion by the prosecution which is not specifically authorized by statute; or (c) the defendant has fully satisfied the sentence, or has begun serving an unappealed sentence, and has a legitimate expectation in its finality.

(5) The foregoing rules barring reprosecution and cumulative sentences are not applicable to prosecutions brought by separate sovereigns. The federal government, each state government, and each Indian tribe is considered a separate sovereign. Municipalities are not sovereign entities for double jeopardy purposes.

BIBLIOGRAPHY

Allen, Ronald and John Ratnaswany. Heath v. Alabama: A Case Study of Doctrine and Rationality in the Supreme Court. 76 J.Crim.L. & Criminol. 801 (1985).

Cantrell, Charles L. Double Jeopardy and Multiple Punishment: An Historical Analysis. 24 S.Tex.L.J. 735 (1983).

Findlater, Janet E. Retrial After a Hung Jury: The Double Jeopardy Problem. 129 U.Pa.L.Rev. 701 (1981).

Fisher, Walter T. Double Jeopardy: Six Common Boners Summarized. 15 UCLA L.Rev. 81 (1967).

———. Double Jeopardy, Two Sovereignties and the Intruding Constitution. 28 U.Chi.L.Rev. 591 (1961).

Holleman, Frank. Mistrials and the Double Jeopardy Clause. 14 Ga.L.Rev. 45 (1980).

McKay, Monroe. Double Jeopardy: Are the Pieces the Puzzle? 23 Washburn L.J. (1983).

Ponsoldt, James F. When Guilt Should Be Irrelevant: Government Overreaching as a Bar to Reprosecution Under the Double Jeopardy Clause After Oregon v. Kennedy. 69 Cornell L.Rev. 76 (1983).

Schulhofer, Stephen J. Jeopardy and Mistrials. 125 U.Pa.L.Rev. 449 (1977).

Thomas, George. An Elegant Theory of Double Jeopardy. 1988 Ill.L.F. 827.

———. Successive Prosecutions for the Same Offense: In Search of a Definition. 71 Iowa L.Rev. 323 (1986).

———. A Unified Theory of Multiple Punishment. 47 U.Pitt.L. Rev. 1 (1985).

Westen, Peter and Richard Drubel. Toward a General Theory of Double Jeopardy. 1978 Sup.Ct.Rev. 81 (1978).

Westen, Peter. The Three Faces of Double Jeopardy: Reflections on Government Appeals of Criminal Sentences. 78 Mich.L. Rev. 1001 (1980).

Part G

THE ROLE OF THE DEFENSE LAWYER

The Sixth Amendment to the United States Constitution provides "in all criminal prosecutions, the accused shall enjoy the right . . . to have the Assistance of Counsel for his defense." This language, applied to the states in *Gideon v. Wainwright*,[1] has raised two central questions. First, what aspects of the criminal process comprise the "criminal prosecution"—that is, when is a criminal defendant entitled to have counsel present, at state expense if necessary? Second, what is "assistance"—that is, what, beyond mere physical presence, does the Constitution require of the attorney representing a criminal defendant?

Chapter Thirty-One discusses the first issue, which has been an important aspect of the Supreme Court's concern over the fairness of the criminal process since the 1930's. It examines not only the Court's treatment of the Sixth Amendment, but also its use of the Fifth and Fourteenth Amendments in determining when the right to counsel attaches.

The second question—which raises what has come to be called the effective assistance of counsel issue—is addressed in Chapter Thirty-Two. The chapter examines the various factors that the courts have looked at in determining whether the acts or omissions of a lawyer rise to the level of a constitutional violation.

1. 372 U.S. 335, 83 S.Ct. 792 (1963).

Chapter Thirty-One

THE RIGHT TO COUNSEL

31.01 Introduction

As fundamental as the right to counsel may seem today, it developed much later than many of the other rights discussed in this book. In England, for instance, while the right to jury trial was mentioned in the thirteenth century Magna Charta, and the antecedents to the double jeopardy prohibition developed at about the same time, a right to counsel was not recognized until the late seventeenth century. Even then, in the Treason Act of 1695, criminal defendants were allowed counsel only if they could afford one, and only when charged with misdemeanors or treason.[1] Accordingly, self-representation was the norm under English common law.[2] In part the resistance to counsel was due to the Crown's fear that presence of an attorney would unduly strengthen the cause of its political enemies in courts of law.[3] But in part it may also have been due to a distaste for lawyers. The West New Jersey Charter of 1676 explicitly guaranteed criminal defendants the right to *avoid* hiring lawyers.[4]

These attitudes changed in this country as counsel came to be seen as an important bulwark against tyranny; a contributory development was the rise of the public prosecutor, who confronted the defendant with a powerful, well-informed adversary familiar with court procedures and personnel.[5] Thus, the Declaration of Independence specifically complained of the denial of counsel, twelve of the original thirteen states guaranteed a right to counsel for felony cases in their constitutions and, of course, the right was included in the Sixth Amendment.[6]

Even with these developments, the right to counsel existed only for those who could afford one. It was not until 1932 that the Supreme Court recognized an entitlement to defense counsel, and even then the entitlement existed only on a case-by-case basis.[7] It took another three decades for the Court to hold, in *Gideon*, that *every* criminal defendant is guaranteed counsel at trial. The first section of this chapter examines the development of the right to

1. F. Heller, The Sixth Amendment to the Constitution of the United States 10 (1951).

2. *Faretta v. California*, 422 U.S. 806, 95 S.Ct. 2525 (1975) (citing 1 F. Pollock & F. Maitland, The History of the English Law 211 (2d ed. 1909)).

3. Heller, supra note 1, at 10 (citing 5 W. Woldsworth, A History of English Law 196 (1927)).

4. Id. at 17.

5. Id. at 21.

6. See *Powell v. Alabama*, 287 U.S. 45, 53 S.Ct. 55 (1932).

7. See § 31.02(a).

trial counsel, while the second section looks at the right to counsel at other stages of the criminal process. The following sections discuss related matters, specifically: waiver of counsel and the right to self-representation; the right to counsel of one's choice; the right to expert assistance other than counsel; and the state's right to require reimbursement for attorney services rendered to a defendant when he was indigent.

31.02 The Right to Counsel at Trial

The right to counsel at trial developed over four decades. For some time, beginning in 1932, the Court relied on the Due Process Clause and analyzed the right on a case-by-case basis. Even after the Sixth Amendment was applied to the states in 1963, it took several decisions to define precisely the types of cases which trigger the right. Today the Sixth Amendment guarantees counsel at any criminal trial which results in deprivation of liberty. The Due Process Clause remains relevant to analysis of those trials which are not seen to be part of the "criminal prosecution."

(a) Due Process Origins. The constitutional right of an indigent defendant to the assistance of court-appointed counsel was first recognized in *Powell v. Alabama.*[8] In that case nine black defendants were charged with the rapes of two white women. No inquiry was made into whether the defendants had, or were able to employ, counsel. The trial court appointed the entire membership of the local bar to represent the defendants at arraignment and assumed it would continue to help if no one counsel came forward. However, no specific lawyer was designated to represent the defendants until the morning of the trial. Eight of the defendants were subsequently convicted and sentenced to death. The Supreme Court reversed the convictions on two separate grounds: (1) the defendants possessed a right to retain their own counsel, which was violated when the trial court denied them an opportunity to seek legal representation; and (2) the defendants had a right to appointed counsel if they could not retain counsel, which was violated by the trial judge's careless manner of appointing their attorneys.

The Court did not base these holdings on the Sixth Amendment, but relied instead on the Due Process Clause. As to a defendant's right to retained counsel, the Court found that the long history of permitting an accused to rely on his own attorney, dating back to colonial times,[9] made this a fundamental guarantee protected by due process. More significantly, the majority held that, even when counsel cannot be retained, defendants like those in *Powell* were entitled to effective legal representation paid for by the state, not only during trial but "during perhaps the most

---

8. 287 U.S. 45, 53 S.Ct. 55 (1932).   **9.** See § 31.01.

critical period of the proceedings," from arraignment to the beginning of trial. Although there was little historical support for this
second right, the Court found it to be a natural corollary to the
due process right to a fair hearing. In the words of Justice
Sutherland:

> The right to be heard would be, in many cases, of little avail if
> it did not comprehend the right to be heard by counsel. Even
> the intelligent and educated layman has small and sometimes
> no skill in the science of law. If charged with crimes, he is
> incapable, generally, of determining for himself whether the
> indictment is good or bad. He is unfamiliar with the rules of
> evidence. Left without the aid of counsel he may be put on
> trial without a proper charge, and convicted upon incompe-
> tent evidence, or evidence irrelevant to the issue or otherwise
> inadmissible. He lacks both the skill and knowledge ade-
> quately to prepare his defense, even though he have a perfect
> one. He requires the guiding hand of counsel at every step in
> the proceedings against him. Without it, though he be not
> guilty, he faces the danger of conviction because he does not
> know how to establish his innocence. . . .

The right to appointed counsel established in *Powell* was
limited to "capital case[s], where the defendant is unable to
employ counsel, and is incapable adequately of making his own
defense because of ignorance, feeble-mindedness, illiteracy or the
like." But the Court's emphasis on the need for the legal expertise and knowledge of a lawyer argued for a more general rule.
Indeed, six years later, in *Johnson v. Zerbst*,[10] the Court recognized
a Sixth Amendment right to appointed trial counsel in all *federal*
criminal prosecutions which sought to deprive the defendant of
life or liberty. Justice Black, echoing *Powell*, stated that the Sixth
Amendment "embodies a realistic recognition of the obvious truth
that the average defendant does not have the professional legal
skill to protect himself."

However, *Johnson* refused to extend its ruling to the states.
This holding was reaffirmed four years later in *Betts v. Brady*,[11]
which held that "[t]he Due Process Clause of the Fourteenth
Amendment does not incorporate, as such, the specific guarantees
found in the Sixth Amendment." The majority in *Betts* opted for
continuing the due process case-by-case approach in state cases,
requiring examination of whether the particular circumstances
indicated that the absence of counsel would result in a lack of
fundamental fairness. In doing so, the Court seemed particularly
concerned that the *Johnson* rule would impose too heavy a burden

10. 304 U.S. 458, 58 S.Ct. 1019   **11.** 316 U.S. 455, 62 S.Ct. 1252
(1938).   (1942).

on the states and perhaps even open the door to requiring counsel in some types of civil cases.[12]

Betts' due process analysis, to which the Court adhered for the next twenty-one years, rarely resulted in upholding a denial of counsel,[13] whether the denial occurred at trial or at equivalent adjudicatory proceedings, such as guilty plea hearings.[14] Nonetheless, it was criticized from its inception; for instance, Justice Black argued in his *Betts* dissent that the due process approach was both unworkable, given the impossibility of assessing how the trial would have come out had counsel been available, and unrealistic, given its refusal to recognize *Powell's* implicit message that a denial of counsel deprives the defendant of a basic tool to his defense.

(b) The Sixth Amendment Actual Imprisonment Threshold. These concerns finally persuaded a majority of the Court to overrule *Betts* in *Gideon v. Wainwright,*[15] which held that the Sixth Amendment's guarantee of counsel for indigent criminal defendants was fully incorporated by the Fourteenth Amendment. The Court, in an opinion by Justice Black, relied heavily on *Powell* in deciding the right was of a fundamental nature. Black reemphasized the need for legal knowledge and expertise at a criminal trial, concluding that "lawyers in criminal courts are necessities, not luxuries." The strongest indications of this "obvious truth," in his view, were the facts "[t]hat government . . . hires lawyers to prosecute and defendants who have money hire lawyers to defend."

Gideon involved a felony prosecution and later cases referred to that decision as establishing the right to counsel only in felony cases.[16] In *Argersinger v. Hamlin,*[17] however, a unanimous Court held the right to counsel applicable to misdemeanors as well, at least where the defendant receives a jail term. The Court squarely rejected the contention that the right to counsel should, like the right to jury trial,[18] apply only to offenses punishable by imprisonment for six months or more. Unlike the jury right, the right to counsel had historically been accorded those charged with minor crimes. Furthermore:

> The requirement of counsel may well be necessary for a fair trial even in petty-offense prosecution. We are by no means

12. At one point, the Court noted that "as the Fourteenth Amendment extends the protection of due process to property as well as to life and liberty, if we hold with the petitioner, logic would require the furnishing of counsel in civil cases involving property."

13. See Israel, "Gideon v. Wainwright: The 'Art' of Overruling," 1963 Sup.Ct.Rev. 211, 249–251.

14. See, e.g., *Moore v. Michigan,* 355 U.S. 155, 78 S.Ct. 191 (1957).

15. 372 U.S. 335, 83 S.Ct. 792 (1963).

16. See, e.g., *Mempa v. Rhay,* 389 U.S. 128, 88 S.Ct. 254 (1967).

17. 407 U.S. 25, 92 S.Ct. 2006 (1972).

18. See § 27.02(c)(1).

convinced that legal and constitutional questions involved in a case that actually leads to imprisonment even for a brief period are any less complex than when a person can be sent off for six months or more.

Indeed, the opinion noted, the greater likely of mass production justice at the petty-offense level might create a special need for counsel in that context.

Conversely, the Court has refused to find a right to counsel at trial where the loss of liberty is merely a *possibility* and does not, in fact, occur. In *Scott v. Illinois,*[19] a five member majority concluded that "the central premise of *Argersinger*—that actual imprisonment is a penalty different in kind from fines or the mere threat of imprisonment—is eminently sound." A finding otherwise would only "create confusion and impose unpredictable, but necessarily substantial, costs on 50 quite diverse states." Thus, where there is no confinement, the right to counsel does not attach. Presumably, however, if the state does not provide an indigent accused counsel in the belief he would only receive a fine, and the accused is later given a jail sentence, the conviction would have to be overturned.

The efficiency argument which is the principal foundation for *Scott* is open to question. As Justice Brennan pointed out in dissent, the defendant in *Scott*—who was charged with a theft offense that carried a maximum penalty of $500 and a year imprisonment, but received only a $50 fine (and thus was not entitled to counsel under the majority's rule)—would have received counsel in 33 states. Brennan also noted that the majority's actual imprisonment test would mandate time-consuming decisions before trial about the likely disposition of the case, occasionally leading to inaccurate predictions which might require retrials, and could also lead to "unequal treatment" because indigents charged with the same offense would not necessarily always be accorded the same "right" to counsel. Thus he advocated an "authorized imprisonment" threshold for the Sixth Amendment.

Even the dissent's authorized imprisonment test does not recognize the Sixth Amendment's application to "all criminal prosecutions," which would include trials involving charges which could bring only a fine. Nor does it take into account the fact that non-incarcerative penalties can carry consequences as harsh as imprisonment. But it may be advisable given the fact that many states still criminalize very minor offenses, such as traffic violations.

19. 440 U.S. 367, 99 S.Ct. 1158 (1979).

Scott's thrust was undercut somewhat in *Baldasar v. Illinois,*[20] which held that an uncounseled misdemeanor conviction valid under *Scott* may not be used to enhance a later sentence to include a term of imprisonment of six months or more. Baldasar, like Scott, had been unrepresented when he received a fine for conviction of a misdemeanor theft that carried a potential penalty of one year's imprisonment and a fine. Later the same year he was again convicted of misdemeanor theft, this time while represented, but sentenced to a prison term of one to three years under an enhancement statute which permitted a second misdemeanor theft conviction to be treated as a felony. Four members of the Court, in two separate opinions, concluded that the Sixth Amendment was violated because Baldasar, in the words of Justice Stewart, "was sentenced to an increased term of imprisonment *only* because he had been convicted in a previous prosecution in which he had *not* had the assistance of appointed counsel in his defense." A fifth member of the Court, Justice Blackmun, reiterated the view he had expressed in *Scott* that indigent defendants should be represented by appointed counsel not only where imprisonment results but also in any case where a sentence exceeding six months is possible. As Justice Powell pointed out in dissent, in states with similar enhancement statutes, *Baldasar* has made it particularly difficult to predict when counsel should be accorded those accused of petty offenses. Thus, the decision has probably had the effect of mandating counsel in all misdemeanor cases covered by such statutes.

(c) **Non–Criminal Trials.** Because the Sixth Amendment applies only to "criminal prosecutions," the Due Process Clause still retains some vitality in determining whether litigants in other types of proceedings are entitled to counsel. In *In re Gault,*[21] the Supreme Court held that juveniles subjected to delinquency proceedings which "may result in commitment to an institution in which the juvenile's freedom is curtailed," are guaranteed counsel as a matter of due process. It is not clear whether, after *Argersinger,* this due process right has been modified by the "actual imprisonment" threshold applied in Sixth Amendment cases. But, aside from this possible limitation, *Gault* established that the right to counsel in delinquency proceedings is not subject to the case-by-case determination approach endorsed in *Betts.*

On the other hand, in *Vitek v. Jones,*[22] the Court held that prisoners subjected to transfers from prisons to mental health facilities are entitled only to "a qualified and independent advisor . . . who may be . . . a licensed psychiatrist or other mental

---

20. 446 U.S. 222, 100 S.Ct. 1585 (1980).

21. 387 U.S. 1, 87 S.Ct. 1428 (1967).

22. 445 U.S. 480, 100 S.Ct. 1254 (1980).

health professional." And in *Parham v. J.R.*,[23] it concluded that children subjected to commitment by their parents are not entitled to any advocate, although commitment must be based on a decision by a "neutral" decisionmaker. Both decisions stemmed in part from the fear that the presence of counsel would make proceedings designed to determine what is "best" for the individual too adversarial and formalistic.

For different reasons, in *Middendorf v. Henry*,[24] the Court found that due process does not require counsel at military summary courts-martial. The Court first concluded that, even though a loss of liberty can result from such proceedings, they are not criminal prosecutions under the Sixth Amendment because they are inquisitorial rather than adversarial in nature and are meant to enforce disciplinary rules. It then held that counsel was not required under the Due Process Clause because: (1) Congress had determined that counsel should not be provided; (2) the hearings were brief and informal; and (3) the "defendant" had the option of selecting a "special" courts-martial proceeding, where counsel would be provided (but which also usually resulted in more serious penalties).[25]

31.03 Counsel at Other Stages of the Criminal Process

Until *Gideon*, the Court's focus in right to counsel cases was primarily on trial and other adjudicatory proceedings. But after that decision, the Court increasingly turned its attention to the extent to which the state must provide counsel at earlier and later stages of the process. The Sixth Amendment was the principal referent for these cases, but given the Court's definition of when a "criminal prosecution" begins and ends, due process, equal protection, and the privilege against self-incrimination have also played a role in these opinions.

(a) Under the Sixth Amendment. The Court's Sixth Amendment treatment of the right to counsel at stages other than trial can be divided into two distinct periods. During the first period, which lasted only six years, the Court employed what it called "critical stage" analysis. The second period, beginning in 1973, continues to use the critical stage rubric, but actually focuses more closely on whether the stage in question is a "trial-like confrontation." Also during this second period, the Court made clear how it would define "criminal prosecution" for pur-

23. 442 U.S. 584, 99 S.Ct. 2493 (1979).

24. 425 U.S. 25, 96 S.Ct. 1281 (1976).

25. Two members of the five-member majority agreed with this analysis

but emphasized as well that the military is a "specialized society" meriting different treatment.

poses of Sixth Amendment analysis. These three issues are discussed below.

(1) Critical stage analysis. The most articulate exposition of the critical stage framework came in *United States v. Wade,*[26] decided four years after *Gideon.* There the Court established a two part test to determine when counsel is required under the Sixth Amendment: (1) "whether potential substantial prejudice to the defendant's rights inheres in the particular confrontation;" and (2) whether counsel can "help avoid that prejudice." The Court then applied this two step analysis in finding a right to counsel at post-indictment lineup procedures. Justice Brennan's majority opinion first noted that lineups are susceptible to rigging and other "innumerable dangers and variable factors which might seriously, even crucially, derogate from a fair trial." At the same time, Brennan stressed, given the impact of eyewitness testimony, "[t]he trial which might determine the accused's fate may well not be that in the courtroom but that at the pretrial confrontation, with the State aligned against the accused, the witness the sole jury, and the accused unprotected against the overreaching, intentional or unintentional, [of the state]." Unless the state, by statute or regulation, establishes procedures "which eliminate the abuse and unintentional suggestion at lineup proceedings and the impediments to meaningful confrontation at trial," counsel must be provided the indigent accused subjected to a post-indictment lineup, to deter use of suggestive procedures and enable counsel to expose any residual suggestivity at a subsequent suppression hearing or at trial.

The *Wade* Court claimed that the critical stage analysis it described explained all of the Court's earlier due process decisions. It noted, for example, that in *Powell* the Court had characterized the period from arraignment to trial as "perhaps the most critical period of the proceedings." Also said to be consistent with critical stage analysis were the Court's earlier due process decisions finding a right to counsel at a preliminary hearing whenever state law provides that defenses not raised at that point are abandoned,[27] and whenever a plea of guilty made at the hearing, though nonbinding, could be used as evidence at a later proceeding.[28] Finally, the *Wade* Court viewed its holding to be consonant with its two recent decisions involving police questioning, *Massiah v. United States*[29] (requiring counsel during any post-indictment questioning) and *Miranda v. Arizona*[30] (requiring counsel during custodial

---

26. 388 U.S. 218, 87 S.Ct. 1926 (1967).

27. *Hamilton v. Alabama,* 368 U.S. 52, 82 S.Ct. 157 (1961).

28. *White v. Maryland,* 373 U.S. 59, 83 S.Ct. 1050 (1963).

29. 377 U.S. 201, 84 S.Ct. 1199 (1964), discussed in § 16.02(c).

30. 384 U.S. 436, 86 S.Ct. 1602 (1966), discussed in § 16.02(d).

interrogation, regardless of when it takes place). This was so because both cases viewed the presence of counsel as an important means not just of ensuring intelligent decisionmaking, but also of deterring police abuse and exposing improprieties at later proceedings.

However in a companion case to *Wade, Gilbert v. California,*[31] the Court made clear that not every stage of the criminal process is "critical." *Gilbert* involved the taking of handwriting exemplars in the absence of counsel. In finding that the Sixth Amendment is not implicated by this investigative procedure, the Court stressed that once the sample is taken, it can be analyzed at any time, by the defense as well as by the prosecution. Moreover, additional samples can be obtained at any time. Thus, the absence of counsel does not seriously impede efforts at challenging the prosecution's evidence: "Knowledge of the techniques of science and technology is sufficiently available, and the variables in techniques few enough, that the accused has the opportunity for a meaningful confrontation of the Government's case at trial through the ordinary processes of cross-examination of the Government's expert witnesses and the presentation of the evidence of his own experts."[32]

The Court continued to employ critical stage analysis for several years after *Wade.* In *Mempa v. Rhay,*[33] decided the same term as *Wade,* the Court found sentencing proceedings to be a critical stage. And in *Coleman v. Alabama*[34] the Court went beyond its earlier due process decisions in holding that *any* preliminary hearing designed to determine whether the prosecution has a prima facie case implicates *Wade's* test, because at the hearing counsel can expose weaknesses in the state's case and thereby protect the accused against an erroneous or improper prosecution.

(2) Trial-like confrontation analysis. Because it believed that critical stage analysis swept too broadly, the post-Warren Court developed a second mode of analyzing the Sixth Amendment right to counsel, first articulated in *United States v. Ash.*[35] The defendant in that case argued that his Sixth Amendment right was violated when his attorney was barred from observing prosecution witnesses study photo displays for purposes of identification prior to trial. This argument was quite plausible under critical stage theory, given the similarity between the lineup in *Wade* and the photo array at issue in *Ash.* But the Court held otherwise, in the

---

31. 388 U.S. 263, 87 S.Ct. 1951 (1967), also discussed in § 17.02(a).

32. See also, *Schmerber v. California,* 384 U.S. 757, 86 S.Ct. 1826 (1966), in which the Court rejected defendant's claim that, in compelling him to submit to a blood test after he objected to it on advice of counsel, police violated his Sixth Amendment right to counsel.

33. 389 U.S. 128, 88 S.Ct. 254 (1967).

34. 399 U.S. 1, 90 S.Ct. 1999 (1970), discussed in § 22.04(a).

35. 413 U.S. 300, 93 S.Ct. 2568 (1973).

process establishing what could be called the "trial-like confrontation" test for the right to counsel. As Justice Blackmun, the author of the majority opinion, described the new test, the key inquiry in determining when the right to counsel attaches is whether—as at trial—the proceeding at issue confronts the accused with the "intricacies of the law and the advocacy of the public prosecutor."

The Court's principal objection to the critical stage test appeared to be its open-endedness. As Justice Blackmun stated, that test, "if applied outside the [trial-like] confrontation context, [would] result in drastic expansion of the right to counsel," including, for instance, a right to counsel at prosecutorial interviews of the victim and other witnesses. This latter example is worth looking at in more detail, given the Court's reference to it. On the one hand, any improper "suggestions" made during such an interview will be less subtle than those that might occur during a photo array, and thus are more likely to come out later even if counsel is not present; in short, it is not clear that critical stage theory would require counsel at such interviews. But if it does (in which case it might also require counsel at analogous events such as *police* interviews of witnesses), *Wade's* approach is admittedly in tension with the adversarial premise of the criminal justice system, which puts limits on the extent to which the defense may discover the prosecution's case prior to trial.[36] *Ash* attempted to avoid that tension by limiting the pretrial right to counsel to those situations where the defendant is faced by government agents and needs aid in coping with legal problems.

Applying this test to the photo display at issue in *Ash,* Blackmun concluded that the Sixth Amendment was not implicated, since the defendant is usually not present during such displays and confrontation with the prosecution thus does not occur. Theoretically, that should have concluded the Court's reasoning. But the majority, perhaps demonstrating some ambivalence about the new test, went on to address the types of concerns that underlie critical stage analysis as well. Anticipating the dissent's argument that a photo display could easily be rigged in the prosecution's favor and that, as assumed in *Wade,* the presence of the defense attorney would deter such a practice, Blackmun made two points. First, he noted that the defense has equal access to the photos and the identifying witnesses after the identification takes place, as well as the opportunity to cross examine the witnesses at trial. Second, he argued that the prosecution could be depended upon to prevent any residual possibility of abuse. "The primary safeguard against abuses of this kind is the ethical responsibility

---

36. See § 24.03(b) on discovery by the defense.

of the prosecutor, who, as so often has been said, may 'strike hard blows' but not 'foul ones.' " As the dissent pointed out, however, the basis of *Wade* was the need to observe police-witness interaction *during* the identification process, a process in which the prosecutor is seldom involved. Indeed, the reasoning of *Ash* would not support *Wade's* holding, since the prosecutor is often not involved in lineups and defense counsel can gain access to the lineup witnesses.

The "trial-like confrontation" threshold for the right to counsel developed in *Ash* was next applied in *Gerstein v. Pugh.*[37] After holding that a person whose arrest is not authorized by a warrant or indictment is entitled to a post-arrest judicial determination that the arrest is founded on probable cause, the Court addressed whether the hearing it had mandated "must be accompanied by the full panoply of adversarial safeguards—counsel, confrontation, cross-examination and compulsory process for witnesses." In finding that the *Gerstein* hearing is not a "critical stage," Justice Powell compared the preliminary hearing at issue in *Coleman v. Alabama* (noted above) to the *Gerstein* hearing:

> First, under Alabama law the function of the preliminary hearing was to determine whether the evidence justified charging the suspect with an offense. A finding of no probable cause could mean that he would not be tried at all. The Fourth Amendment probable cause determination is addressed only to pretrial custody. To be sure, pretrial custody may affect to some extent the defendant's ability to assist in preparation of his defense, but this does not present the high probability of substantial harm identified as controlling in *Wade* and *Coleman.* Second, Alabama allowed the suspect to confront and cross-examine prosecution witnesses at the preliminary hearing. The Court noted that the suspect's defense on the merits could be compromised if he had no legal assistance for exploring or preserving the witnesses' testimony. This consideration does not apply when the prosecution is not required to produce witnesses for cross-examination.

This language, like the opinion in *Ash,* does not entirely ignore the types of concerns which inspired critical stage analysis. But *Gerstein,* like *Ash,* signals a retreat from the latter approach to the Sixth Amendment. Assuming, as Justice Powell asserted, that lack of counsel at the initial appearance will not seriously detract from a defendant's ability to mount a successful defense at trial,[38] it could still result in "the continuing incarceration of a

---

37. 420 U.S. 103, 95 S.Ct. 854 (1975), discussed in § 20.02.

38. But see, *Hamilton v. Alabama,* 368 U.S. 52, 82 S.Ct. 157 (1961), discussed supra note 24; *Moore v. Illinois,* 434 U.S. 220, 98 S.Ct. 458 (1977) (holding that when a showup is conducted during the initial appearance with the prosecutor present, counsel is required).

presumptively innocent person" (in the words of four concurring justices, who felt that the Court did not need to reach the right to counsel issue in *Gerstein* but suggested they might find contrary to the majority). Indeed, *Gerstein's* reasoning could conceivably support the position that there is no right to counsel at the bail hearing, a proceeding which also affects "only" pretrial custody and does not directly compromise "the suspect's defense on the merits." [39] However, given the fact that the bail hearing involves both the prosecutor and the defendant, as well as cross-examination of prosecution witnesses, it is likely to be considered a "critical stage" even under trial-like confrontation analysis. [40]

One other decision illustrates the Court's continuing adherence to the trial-like confrontation approach. In *Estelle v. Smith*,[41] the Court held that the Sixth Amendment requires notice to the defense attorney of a state-requested psychiatric evaluation, but refused to hold that there is a right to counsel *during* such an evaluation. This result can be justified on trial-like confrontation grounds (since the prosecutor is not present during psychiatric evaluations). But it is difficult to reconcile with traditional critical stage analysis, given the impact of psychiatric testimony in criminal cases and the difficulty of reconstructing its basis merely from the defendant's report.[42]

(3) Defining "criminal prosecution." One year before *Ash*, the Court had significantly limited the scope of *Wade* in another way, by holding, in *Kirby v. Illinois*,[43] that criminal prosecution does not begin until indictment, formal charge or the "initiation of adversary proceedings." This holding conforms with the common-sense meaning of the Sixth Amendment's language. But, as Justice Brennan pointed out in dissent, the issue of when criminal prosecution begins is peripheral to the nature of the inquiry under *Wade's* critical stage analysis—whether the defendant's case at trial has been prejudiced by the absence of counsel.[44] Indirectly, then, *Kirby* helped set the stage for *Ash's* later ruling that only

---

39. Note, however, that *Gerstein* was also based on the finding that since it is "reasonable" under the Fourth Amendment to detain a person based on an arrest warrant, issued *ex parte*, it is also reasonable to deny counsel at the initial appearance, reasoning which would not apply to the bail hearing.

40. See § 20.03(d).

41. 451 U.S. 454, 101 S.Ct. 1866 (1981).

42. Slobogin, "Estelle v. Smith: The Constitutional Contours of the Forensic Evaluation Process," 31 Emory L.J. 71, 114–135 (1982).

43. 406 U.S. 682, 92 S.Ct. 1877 (1972).

44. In *United States v. Gouveia*, 467 U.S. 180, 104 S.Ct. 2292 (1984), the Court did indicate that, if a delay in bringing charges (and the consequent delay in obtaining counsel) was a "deliberate device to gain an advantage over [the defendant] and . . . caused him actual prejudice in presenting his defense," a due process claim would lie. See *United States v. Lovasco*, 431 U.S. 783, 97 S.Ct. 2044 (1977), discussed in § 25.02(b).

confrontation with the prosecutor (which will normally occur only after charges have been brought) implicates the right to counsel.

At the other end of the process, the Court has indicated that the "criminal prosecution" concludes with sentencing (at which, as noted earlier, *Mempa v. Rhay* found a Sixth Amendment right to counsel).   In *Gagnon v. Scarpelli*,[45] for instance, the Court held that a post-sentence probation revocation hearing is not part of the criminal prosecution because the only issue presented is whether to revoke probation, which is a determination based on conduct subsequent to commission of the original offense.   And in *Ross v. Moffitt*,[46] the Court excluded appeals from Sixth Amendment coverage because "it is ordinarily the defendant, rather than the state, who initiates the appellate process, seeking not to fend off the efforts of the State's prosecutor but rather to overturn a finding of guilt."   Thus, the defendant on appeal is using counsel as a "sword" to upset the verdict, not "as a shield" to protect him against a prosecution.

(b) Under the Fifth Amendment.   Although pre-charge confrontations with the state do not implicate the Sixth Amendment, *Miranda v. Arizona*[47] held that the Fifth Amendment's privilege against self-incrimination entitles indigent defendants to counsel during *any* custodial interrogation, pre- or post-charge, to counteract the "inherent coerciveness" of such encounters.   Because the Fifth Amendment bars compelled self-incrimination "in any criminal case," *Miranda* avoids *Kirby's* criminal prosecution threshold. Further discussion on the Fifth Amendment right to counsel is found elsewhere in this book.[48]

(c) Under the Equal Protection and Due Process Clauses. Just as the Fifth Amendment has mitigated to some extent the Sixth Amendment's post-charge threshold, equal protection and due process analysis has, under limited circumstances, provided a basis for a right to counsel at post-sentencing stages where the Sixth Amendment does not apply.   In particular, the Court has looked at the right to counsel at appeals as of right, probation and parole revocation proceedings, discretionary appeals and habeas proceedings.

(1) Appeals as of right.   The first case to rely on the Equal Protection Clause as a basis for the right to counsel was *Douglas v. California*,[49] which held, the same term as *Gideon*, that indigents are entitled to counsel on appeals as of right.   *Douglas* built on

---

45. 411 U.S. 778, 93 S.Ct. 1756 (1973).

46. 417 U.S. 600, 94 S.Ct. 2437 (1974).

47. 384 U.S. 436, 86 S.Ct. 1602 (1966).

48. See, in particular, § 16.03(a) & (e).

49. 372 U.S. 353, 83 S.Ct. 814 (1963).

Griffin v. Illinois,[50] which had concluded that the Equal Protection Clause requires the state to provide indigent appellants with a trial transcript when state law requires submission of such a transcript in order to obtain an appeal; otherwise, held the Court, the state would be granting the right to appeal in a way "that discriminates against some convicted defendants on account of their poverty." Similarly, in *Douglas,* the Court held that "where the merits on the *one and only* appeal an indigent has as of right are decided without benefit of counsel, . . . an unconstitutional line has been drawn between rich and poor." The Court added that without counsel "[t]he indigent, where the record is unclear or the errors are hidden, has only the right to a meaningless ritual, while the rich man has a meaningful appeal."

In dissent, Justice Harlan argued that due process should have been the focus of the Court's analysis. Harlan pointed out that, as a practical matter, the criminal process can never fully equalize justice between the rich and the poor. Further, he argued, the focus of equal protection—the provision of equal treatment—is not necessarily relevant to whether an attorney is needed to assure a fair hearing, and thus diverges from the premise of *Powell.* Even under due process analysis, however, Harlan found no right to counsel on the facts of *Douglas,* given the state appellate court's explicit obligation under the California rules to appoint counsel when it found an attorney would be of value.

When it revisited the right to appellate counsel issue over two decades later, the Court adopted Harlan's conceptual approach, but arrived at a different result. *Douglas* had held that indigents were entitled to appellate counsel whenever non-indigent defendants were, but the decision could not, given its equal protection grounding, prohibit denial of counsel to non-indigent defendants in the first instance. In *Evitts v. Lucey,*[51] the Court held, 7–2, that, as a matter of due process, *all* defendants are entitled to counsel on appeals of right. In arriving at this result, Justice Brennan's opinion relied both on *Douglas*' depiction of a counselless appeal as a "meaningless ritual," and *Gideon's* observation that in an "adversarial system of justice . . . lawyers are 'necessities,' not luxuries."

(2) Probation and parole revocations. The Court conformed even more closely to Harlan's analysis in the earlier case of *Gagnon v. Scarpelli,*[52] which held that, as a matter of due process, indigents subject to probation or parole revocation proceedings are

50. 351 U.S. 12, 76 S.Ct. 585 (1956), discussed in § 29.02(a).

51. 469 U.S. 387, 105 S.Ct. 830 (1985), discussed in more detail in § 32.04(c)(4).

52. 411 U.S. 778, 93 S.Ct. 1756 (1973).

entitled to counsel only on a case-by-case basis, depending upon the complexity of the issues and the indigent's capacities. The majority also left the impression that, under this case-by-case analysis, counsel would usually not be provided in such proceedings; it stressed that revocation decisions are typically based on acts which have already been proven in a separate proceeding or are admitted, and that mitigating circumstances, if advanced, often are "not susceptible of proof or [are] so simple as not to require either investigation or exposition by counsel."

Furthermore, as it had in cases limiting or rejecting the right to counsel in non-criminal cases,[53] the Court asserted that the quasi-judicial role thrust upon it by the presence of lawyers might make the factfinding body in probation or parole cases "less tolerant of marginally deviant behavior and feel more pressure to reincarcerate than to continue non-punitive rehabilitation." Indeed, in light of these considerations, the Court reserved the question of whether the state could prohibit reliance on *retained* counsel in such proceedings.[54]

(3) Discretionary appeals. A year after *Scarpelli*, in *Ross v. Moffitt*,[55] the Court evaluated whether indigents were entitled to counsel during a discretionary appeal (as opposed to the appeal as of right at issue in *Douglas* and *Evitts*). Justice Rehnquist began by noting that since appellate counsel is used as a sword rather than a shield, and since there is no constitutional right to appeal,[56] the state "does not automatically . . . act[ ] unfairly by refusing to provide counsel to indigent defendants at every stage of the [appellate process]." Although this language suggested a due process analysis, Rehnquist proceeded to conclude that the issue of whether the state has in fact acted unfairly toward indigent defendants "is more profitably considered under an equal protection analysis." He noted that, under North Carolina's system, the appellate court deciding whether to review a defendant's case automatically receives the trial transcript, the brief filed in the lower appellate court and, if one is issued, the lower appellate decision. These documents, together with any *pro se* offering the defendant might wish to make, provide the poverty-stricken with access to North Carolina's appellate process not appreciably different from that provided nonindigent defendants.[57]

---

53. See § 31.02(c).

54. Note that in some states, revocation of probation comes before the imposition of sentence, and thus is akin to the situation addressed in *Mempa v. Rhay.* See *Ex parte Shivers,* 501 S.W. 2d 898 (Tex.Crim.App.1973). At the federal level, Congress has provided counsel in parole proceedings. 18 U.S. C.A. §§ 3006A(g), 4214.

55. 417 U.S. 600, 94 S.Ct. 2437 (1974).

56. See § 29.01.

57. The Court did not address the issue of whether counsel would be required if an indigent defendant's petition for appellate review were accepted and the case argued in front of the appellate court. Most states provide counsel at this point.

It is not clear why Rehnquist felt the need to resuscitate equal protection doctrine, which Justice Harlan had so roundly criticized in his *Douglas* dissent. In any event, the central question would seem to be whether the absence of counsel led to an unfair hearing, a due process question. On the fairness issue, Justice Douglas' dissent, joined by Justices Brennan and Marshall, pointed out the technical aspects of certiorari and review proceedings and argued that only a lawyer can make an effective and comprehensive presentation of the defendant's case in such situations. Douglas agreed with Judge Haynsworth (who wrote the opinion for a unanimous Fourth Circuit panel in the case) that there is "no logical basis for differentiation between appeals of right and permissive review procedures in the context of the Constitution and the right to counsel."

(4) Habeas proceedings. In *Pennsylvania v. Finley,*[58] the Court relied on the combined due process/equal protection analysis used in *Ross* in holding that there is no constitutional right to counsel at state postconviction proceedings.[59] Chief Justice Rehnquist, writing for the Court, found that a right to habeas counsel is not required by the Due Process Clause because state "[post]conviction relief is even further removed from the criminal trial than is discretionary direct review" (the procedure at issue in *Ross*) and likewise is not a required avenue of relief. Nor, analogous to the reasoning of *Ross,* does the Equal Protection Clause support such a right, so long as the defendant has access to the trial record and the appellate briefs and opinions. The Court did suggest that the Due Process Clause places some obligation on the state to consider a petitioner's habeas claim; here the habeas court's independent review of the record after counsel's withdrawal notification was sufficient, however.

In *Murray v. Giarratano,*[60] the petitioner, on death row in Virginia, argued that *Finley's* rejection of a right to counsel in state postconviction proceedings should be limited to noncapital cases. Chief Justice Rehnquist, writing for a plurality of four, conceded that, because of the penalty involved, the Court's decisions had provided greater procedural protections in capital cases. But he pointed out that all of these decisions involved *trial* procedures. Because he found these safeguards "sufficient to assure the reliability of the process by which the death penalty is imposed," he concluded that any further distinction between capital and noncapital cases is constitutionally unnecessary, especially in postconviction proceedings, which are "an adjunct to state

58. 481 U.S. 551, 107 S.Ct. 1990 (1987).

59. The precise issue addressed by the Court was whether a habeas litigant is entitled to an *Anders* brief, see § 29.02(c), which the Court held was dependent upon whether such a litigant is entitled to counsel in the first instance.

60. 492 U.S. 1, 109 S.Ct. 2765 (1989).

criminal proceedings and serve a different and more limited purpose than either trial or appeal."

Justice Kennedy, in a concurring opinion joined by Justice O'Connor (also a member of the plurality), seemed less willing to force state habeas petitioners to proceed without counsel. He noted that a substantial proportion of such petitioners succeed in vacating their death sentences; moreover, he pointed out that the complexity of the law in this area "makes it unlikely that capital defendants will be able to file successful petitions for collateral relief without the assistance of persons learned in the law." However, he joined the Court's judgment because he felt that mechanisms other than counsel might provide "meaningful access" to the courts.[61] He concluded by saying:

> While Virginia has not adopted procedures for securing representation that are as far reaching and effective as those available in other States, no prisoner on death row in Virginia has been unable to obtain counsel to represent him in postconviction proceedings, and Virginia's prison system is staffed with institutional lawyers to assist in preparing petitions for postconviction relief. I am not prepared to say that this scheme violates the Constitution.

Given Kennedy's opinion, state habeas petitioners may be entitled to counsel if they can show the state is not providing an adequate substitute.

Although there is no right to counsel at state postconviction proceedings, the Constitution does entitle prisoners to some aid in raising claims through habeas. In *Johnson v. Avery,*[62] the Court ruled that a state may not prohibit inmates from helping each other in preparing habeas corpus petitions unless it provides some reasonable alternative to assist illiterate or poorly educated inmates. And in *Bounds v. Smith,*[63] the Court held that the fundamental constitutional right of access to the courts requires that prison authorities assist inmates in preparation and filing of meaningful legal papers by providing prisoners with adequate law libraries, adequate assistance from persons trained in the law, or other means of assuring adequate access to the courts.

31.04 Waiver of the Right to Counsel

(a) **Defining Waiver.** In *Johnson v. Zerbst,*[64] the Supreme Court held that an individual may waive his right to counsel only so long as his waiver is "competent and intelligent." As a general

61. Here he referred to *Bounds v. Smith,* infra note 63, which held that prisoners are guaranteed such access under the Due Process Clause.

62. 393 U.S. 483, 89 S.Ct. 747 (1969).

63. 430 U.S. 817, 97 S.Ct. 1491 (1977).

64. 304 U.S. 458, 58 S.Ct. 1019 (1938).

rule, *Johnson* held, courts should "indulge every reasonable presumption against waiver." In *Carnley v. Cochran,*[65] the Court added that presuming waiver of counsel from a silent record is impermissible. To sustain a claim that counsel was waived, "the record must show, or there must be an allegation and evidence must show, that an accused was offered counsel but intelligently and understandingly rejected the offer. Anything less is not waiver."

Although the standard is purportedly the same whether the defendant waives counsel at a pretrial stage of the prosecution or at the adjudication stage itself, the Court has suggested that the prosecution's burden in proving a valid waiver is particularly heavy in the latter situation. In *Von Moltke v. Gillies,*[66] a four justice plurality opinion stressed that the judge deciding whether to allow waiver of counsel at trial "must investigate as long and as thoroughly as the circumstances of the case before him demand." Justice Black's opinion continued:

> To be valid such waiver must be made with an apprehension of the nature of the charges, the statutory offenses included within them, the range of allowable punishments thereunder, possible defenses to the charges and circumstances in mitigation thereof, and all other facts essential to a broad understanding of the whole matter. A judge can make certain that an accused's professed waiver of counsel is understandingly and wisely made only from a penetrating and comprehensive examination of all the circumstances.

The lower appellate courts have not always followed *Von Moltke's* formulation precisely, but they have at least considered the critical issue to be "what the defendant understood—not what the [trial] court said." [67]

With respect to waiver at other stages of the criminal process, the Supreme Court has indicated that a less incisive inquiry into the defendant's thought processes is often permissible. For instance, the Court has held that, while the defendant subjected to police questioning must be told about his right to counsel (whether derived from the Fifth or Sixth Amendment),[68] waiver of that right can be found in the absence of an express statement that the right is understood and waived,[69] and under circumstances suggesting that the defendant does not completely understand the consequences of the waiver.[70]

---

65. 369 U.S. 506, 82 S.Ct. 884 (1962).

66. 332 U.S. 708, 68 S.Ct. 316 (1948).

67. *United States v. Harris,* 683 F.2d 322 (9th Cir.1982).

68. *Patterson v. Illinois,* 487 U.S. 285, 108 S.Ct. 2389 (1988).

69. Cf. *North Carolina v. Butler,* 441 U.S. 369, 99 S.Ct. 1755 (1979), discussed in § 16.03(d)(1).

70. See, e.g., *Connecticut v. Barrett,* 479 U.S. 523, 107 S.Ct. 828 (1987) (finding a valid waiver of Fifth Amendment right to counsel, despite defendant's ap-

(b) The Right to Self-Representation. Although a defendant may waive trial counsel, the question of whether he may then proceed without one was not settled until *Faretta v. California*,[71] Faretta was charged with grand theft. At arraignment a public defender was appointed to represent him, but well before trial he requested permission to act as his own lawyer. The trial court at first accepted his waiver of counsel but later revoked it, at least in part because Faretta's answers to questions about the hearsay rule and *voir dire* challenges did not satisfy the judge. Faretta's subsequent request for leave to act as counsel was denied as were his attempted motions on his own behalf. Throughout the subsequent trial, the judge required that Faretta's defense be conducted only through his appointed attorney. At the conclusion of the trial, the jury found the defendant guilty. The California court of appeal affirmed the trial court's ruling that Faretta had no federal or state constitutional right to represent himself.

The United States Supreme Court vacated judgment in a 6–3 opinion authored by Justice Stewart. In establishing the right to self-representation, Stewart found support in English and early American history, and the fact that some state constitutions recognized the right. But he also concluded that the privilege of self-representation could be derived from the Sixth Amendment itself, which guarantees counsel to the "accused:"

> The language and spirit of the Sixth Amendment contemplate that counsel, like the other defense tools guaranteed by the Amendment, shall be an aid to a willing defendant—not an organ of the State interposed between an unwilling defendant and his right to defend himself personally. . . . An unwanted counsel "represents" the defendant only through a tenuous and unacceptable legal fiction. Unless the accused has acquiesced in such representation, the defense presented is not the defense guaranteed him by the Constitution, for in a very real sense, it is not his defense.

The Court acknowledged the validity of the dissent's point that recognizing a right to self-representation "seems to cut against the grain" of the basic premise in *Powell, Gideon,* and *Argersinger* that the lawyer is essential to a fair trial. But the majority asserted that the framers placed the "inestimable worth of free choice" above the right to counsel, and noted that, in some cases, *pro se* representation may be more effective. Moreover, while it:

parent assumption that only a written admission was admissible at trial). Other Court decisions have suggested that analysis of waiver under the Sixth Amendment will not vary significantly from Fifth Amendment cases. See generally, § 16.04(c).

71. 422 U.S. 806, 95 S.Ct. 2525 (1975).

is undeniable that in most criminal prosecutions defendants could better defend with counsel's guidance than by their own unskilled efforts . . . where the defendant will not voluntarily accept representation by counsel, the potential advantage of a lawyer's training and experience can be realized, if at all, only imperfectly. To force a lawyer on a defendant can only lead him to believe that the law contrives against him.

The majority also rejected the dissent's argument that the state's strong societal interest in providing a fair trial permitted it to insist upon representation by counsel: "Although [the defendant] may conduct his own defense ultimately to his own detriment, his choice must be honored out of 'that respect for the individual which is the lifeblood of the law.' "

The Court did stress that the waiver of counsel must be voluntary, knowing and intelligent. In line with *Von Moltke*, the Court noted that the person who proceeds *pro se* must "be made aware of the dangers and disadvantages of self-representation, so that the record will establish that he 'knows what he is doing and his choice is made with eyes open.' " But the majority also indicated that a valid waiver can occur even if the defendant is not well versed in legal technicalities. Although it remanded the case to the lower courts, the Court strongly implied it would find Faretta competent to waive counsel. Stewart noted that Faretta had unequivocally, and in a timely fashion, asked to represent himself, that he appeared to be "literate, competent and understanding," and that he acted freely in making his request. The Court felt that assessing how well Faretta understood the hearsay rule and *voir dire*, as the trial judge had done, was inappropriate, "[f]or his technical legal knowledge, as such, was not relevant to an assessment of his knowing exercise of the right to defend himself."

(c) Standby Counsel. Establishment of a right to self-representation has created a number of issues. Most prominent among these are whether the trial court may force "standby counsel" on a defendant who has been found capable of proceeding *pro se* and, if so, (or assuming the defendant *requests* standby counsel), what the relationship between standby counsel and the defendant should be. Both questions were addressed by the Supreme Court in *McKaskle v. Wiggins*.[72] Although it divided on other matters relating to the role of standby counsel, the Court unanimously agreed with the proposition that, even when it occurs over the *pro se* defendant's objection, a court may appoint standby counsel "to relieve the judge of the need to explain and enforce basic rules of courtroom protocol or to assist the defendant in overcoming rou-

72. 465 U.S. 168, 104 S.Ct. 944 (1984).

tine obstacles that stand in the way of the defendant's achievement of his own clearly indicated goals."

This conclusion helped redress a problem possibly created by *Faretta,* where the Court had stated, in a footnote, that "[t]he right of self representation is not a license . . . not to comply with relevant rules of procedural and substantive law." From this the majority concluded that "whatever else may or may not be open to him on appeal, a defendant who elects to represent himself cannot thereafter complain that the quality of his own defense amounted to a denial of 'effective assistance of counsel.' " The lower courts have adhered to this view.[73] But in his *Faretta* dissent, Chief Justice Burger pointed out that such a position was "totally unrealistic," at least when the defendant had represented himself so poorly that he may have been erroneously convicted. Through recognizing the institution of standby counsel, *Wiggin's* holding helps strike an accommodation between the right to self-representation and the spectre of *pro se* defendants attacking their own conduct as a means of obtaining retrial.

While the entire Court agreed that standby counsel may be appointed to fulfill the minimum role specified above over the defendant's objection, it could not reach a consensus as to the propriety of further actions by standby counsel. Six members of the Court concluded that actions of standby counsel do not violate *Faretta* so long as: (1) the defendant retains actual control over the case presented to the jury; and (2) the jury retains the perception that he represents himself. The three dissenting members, on the other hand, found this test unworkable, as well as violative of *Faretta:* the actual control standard placed "the burden . . . on the *pro se* defendant to comprehend counsel's submissions" and assert they were contrary to his objectives, and the jury perception prong was inconsistent with *Faretta's* emphasis on the "defendant's own perception of the criminal justice system." The dissent preferred the test adopted by the lower court, allowing the trial judge to direct the defendant to consult with counsel on procedural and evidentiary matters, but requiring that standby counsel be "seen and not heard" until the defendant expressly asks for his assistance.

The difference between these tests is illustrated by the way their proponents applied them to the facts in *Wiggins.* The defendant there agreed to the participation of two standby counsel provided by the court, but then frequently changed his mind as to the extent of their participation, sometimes asking the attorneys to make objections directly to the court without consulting him,

---

73. See, e.g., *Green v. State,* 759 P.2d 219 (Okl.Crim.1988); *Commonwealth v. Celijewski,* 324 Pa.Super. 185, 471 A.2d 525 (1984); *State v. Brown,* 33 Wash. App. 843, 658 P.2d 44 (1983).

sometimes conferring with them during his cross-examination of witnesses, and sometimes requesting that they not be present even for consultation. On several occasions, one of the attorneys engaged in "acrimonious" exchanges with the defendant and made objections or motions without consulting the defendant. The majority concluded that "[o]nce a *pro se* defendant invites or agrees to any substantial participation by counsel, subsequent appearances by counsel must be presumed to be with the defendant's acquiescence, at least until the defendant expressly and unambiguously renews his request that standby counsel be silenced." The Court found no such request; applying the two-part test described above, it concluded that since most of the incidents of which the defendant complained occurred when the jury was not in the courtroom, and that since all conflicts between the defendant and counsel which did occur in front of the jury were resolved in the defendant's favor, no violation of *Faretta* occurred. The dissenters, on the other hand concluded that their test would prohibit the actions taken by the standby attorneys in this case, since they had "distracted Wiggins and usurped his prerogatives, altered the tenor of the defense, disrupted the trial, undermined Wiggins perception that he controlled his own fate[,] . . . induced a belief—most assuredly unfounded, but sincerely held nevertheless—that 'the law contrived against him' [citing *Faretta*,] and undoubtedly reduced Wiggins' credibility and prejudiced him in the eyes of the jury."

The majority in *Wiggins* also stated, in dictum, that "*Faretta* does not require a trial judge to permit 'hybrid' representation of the type Wiggins was actually allowed." This language suggests that, once a defendant has decided to proceed *pro se,* he may not depend on standby counsel taking over the role of representing him; that is, while he may ask standby counsel for advice about law and tactics, he is not *entitled* to have the attorney perform other functions. Although this notion may require some fine distinctions between what standby counsel is allowed to do and what he is required to do, several courts have adopted it. For instance, one court upheld a trial court's denial of a *pro se* defendant's request to have standby counsel argue a motion in *limine,* on the ground that such conduct would amount to "hybrid" representation not guaranteed under *Faretta.*[74]

31.05   The Right to Counsel of One's Choice

(a) **The Indigent's Right.** The right to counsel does not guarantee the indigent accused a right to a particular attorney. Ideally, perhaps, the state should provide the indigent with

---

74. *State v. Cooley,* 468 N.W.2d 833 . (Iowa App.1991); see also, *State v.* *Gethers,* 197 Conn. 369, 497 A.2d 408 (1985).

enough money to hire the counsel of his choice. But in *Wheat v. United States,*[75] the Supreme Court stated that "a defendant may not insist on representation by an attorney he cannot afford." Some lower courts have also held, primarily for economic and administrative reasons, that the indigent defendant is not even entitled to his choice from among those on the court appointed list or in the public defender's office.[76]

Once an indigent has appointed counsel, he can obtain a replacement if he shows "good cause, such as a conflict of interest, a complete breakdown of communication, or an irreconcilable conflict" for believing that an "unjust verdict" would otherwise result.[77] As might be imagined, however, such cause is very difficult to show, and may not consist solely of a showing that the defendant does not have a "meaningful relationship" with his attorney.[78]

(b) The Non–Indigent's Right. When the defendant has sufficient financial resources, the government may not, generally speaking, prevent him from retaining the attorney of his choice. One exception to this rule was announced in *Wheat,* where the Court held that a trial court may override the defendant's choice of counsel whenever the court believes that, in light of that attorney's other clients, a serious potential for conflict of interest may develop.[79] Another is where the defendant's attorney is not qualified to practice law.[80] A third exception, one which is likely to have a much more significant impact on defendants' ability to select counsel, occurs when the provisions of a "forfeiture statute" are met, the effect of which is to render the defendant unable to pay for the attorney of his choice because his assets are frozen and made subject to later forfeiture.

In *Caplin & Drysdale v. United States,*[81] the Supreme Court rejected a Sixth Amendment challenge to such a statute. The Comprehensive Forfeiture Act of 1984[82] authorizes the trial court, in cases involving certain federal offenses, to issue a restraining order prohibiting transfer of any of the defendant's assets it believes to be derived from drug-law violations, and further authorizes forfeiture of those assets upon conviction of the defendant. The petitioner in *Caplin and Drysdale* was a law firm representing

---

75. 486 U.S. 153, 108 S.Ct. 1692 (1988).

76. See Tague, "An Indigent's Right to the Attorney of His Choice," 27 Stan. L.Rev. 73, 79 (1974).

77. *McKee v. Harris,* 649 F.2d 927 (2d Cir.1981), cert. denied 456 U.S. 917, 102 S.Ct. 1773 (1982).

78. See *Morris v. Slappy,* 461 U.S. 1, 103 S.Ct. 1610 (1983), discussed in § 32.04(c)(1).

79. This aspect of *Wheat* is discussed in § 32.04(d)(4), which deals with conflicts of interest.

80. Cf. *Leis v. Flynt,* 439 U.S. 438, 99 S.Ct. 698 (1979).

81. 491 U.S. 617, 109 S.Ct. 2646 (1989).

82. 21 U.S.C.A. § 853.

a defendant who had been tried under the federal continuing criminal enterprise (CCE) statute and whose assets had been forfeited under the Forfeiture Act. The firm's primary contention was that the Act impermissibly burdens a criminal defendant's Sixth Amendment right to counsel because it deprives him of funds with which to pay for private legal representation.[83] In a 5–4 opinion, the court rejected this claim. Justice White, who wrote the majority opinion, concluded that "[a] defendant has no Sixth Amendment right to spend another person's money for services rendered by an attorney, even if those funds are the only way that that defendant will be able to retain the attorney of his choice."

The petitioner had argued that his assets were not "another's," in the same way stolen property is and that, in any event, allowing payment of drug-related proceeds to an attorney would not transgress the objective of the Forfeiture Act because the defendant would still be dispossessed of the assets. But White pointed to three reasons why the government has an interest in gaining control over *all* the defendant's assets: (1) the money raised under the Act provides financial support for law enforcement efforts; (2) the Act ensures that property belonging to others will be preserved for later reclamation; and (3) the Act, at least as applied in CCE cases, "lessen[s] the economic power of organized crime and drug enterprises." These interests, concluded the Court, override any Sixth Amendment interest in permitting defendants to use forfeitable assets in their defense.

In dissent, Justice Blackmun characterized as "weak" the government interests identified by the majority, especially since at the time a restraining order is issued the government has only made a probable cause showing that the defendant has violated the law.[84] He also contended that the effect of the Court's decision would be to deny the defendant the right to retain counsel "he has chosen and trusts." Blackmun pointed out that a defendant whose assets are frozen could be forced to accept a public defender or court-appointed attorney who may lack the experience necessary for CCE litigation, which is often lengthy and complex. Even if the defendant is able to retain a private attorney, the quality of his representation may be sullied by concern over finances. The

83. In a case decided the same day as *Caplin & Drysdale,* the Court held that nothing in the language or legislative history of the Act suggested that Congress meant to exempt from its scope sufficient proceeds to pay for legal representation. *United States v. Monsanto,* 491 U.S. 600, 109 S.Ct. 2657 (1989).

84. In *Monsanto,* supra note 83, the majority responded to this point by stat-

ing that if the government may restrain persons prior to trial based on a probable cause showing, as it may do under *United States v. Salerno,* 479 U.S. 1026, 107 S.Ct. 867 (1987) (discussed in § 20.03(c)(2)), then it may restrain the transfer of property on such a showing as well. However, the Court reserved the question as to whether a hearing must be held before a restraining order under the Forfeiture Act may be issued.

attorney may be reticent about investigating the case thoroughly because of the Act's provision that only bona fide purchasers of forfeitable property (i.e., people with no reason to believe that the property is subject to forfeiture) may keep it.   Moreover, the "attorney who fears for his fee will be tempted to make the Government's waiver of fee-forfeiture the *sine qua non* for any plea agreement, a position which conflicts with his client's best interests."

Blackmun also conjectured on the long-term effects of the Court's holding:

> The long-term effects of the fee-forfeiture practice will be to decimate the private criminal-defense bar. As the use of the forfeiture mechanism expands to new categories of federal crimes and spreads to the States, only one class of defendants will be free routinely to retain private counsel: the affluent defendant accused of a crime that generates no economic gain. As the number of private clients diminishes, only the most idealistic and the least skilled of young lawyers will be attracted to the field, while the remainder seek greener pastures elsewhere.

Echoing Blackmun, some commentators have argued that forfeiture statutes such as those involved in *Caplin & Drysdale,* together with other aggressive prosecutorial maneuvers (e.g., law office searches and subpoenas of attorney records) will have a detrimental impact on the quality and morale of the defense bar.[85]

31.06   The Right to Expert Assistance

Many issues which might be raised during a criminal trial—e.g., the interpretation of forensic tests, the defendant's sanity at the time of the offense, proper accounting practices (in fraud and tax cases)— are often beyond the competence of the lawyer as well as the competence of the defendant.   Defense counsel may also find it difficult to track down exculpatory evidence without the aid of a trained investigator.   Most jurisdictions authorize support for the indigent defendant and his counsel in obtaining such expert assistance.[86]   For example, 18 U.S.C.A. § 3007A(e)(1) requires the trial court to provide for "investigative, expert, or other services" upon a showing that the service is "necessary for an adequate defense."

In *Ake v. Oklahoma,*[87] the Supreme Court held that when the service requested is psychiatric assessment of either the defendant's sanity at the time of the offense, or his future dangerousness when that issue is relevant under a state's capital sentencing

---

85. Genego, "The New Adversary," 54 Brooklyn L.Rev. 781 (1988).

86. See N. Lefstein, Criminal Defense Services for the Poor, App. B. (1982).

87. 470 U.S. 68, 105 S.Ct. 1087 (1985).

statute, government support is constitutionally mandated by the Due Process Clause, at least when the defendant can make a preliminary showing that these issues are likely to be a "significant factor" at trial or sentencing. In arriving at these conclusions, Justice Marshall, writing for the Court looked at three factors—the "private interest" in obtaining the safeguard sought, the state interests that will be affected if the safeguard is provided, and the probable value of the safeguard sought. He found the criminal defendant's interest in an accurate resolution of the criminal responsibility and dangerousness issues compelling. Conversely, the only state interest he could identify in the case of psychiatric assistance was financial in nature, and this interest, concluded Marshall, was minimal given the fact that many states, as well as the federal government, provide such assistance. Finally, Marshall noted the "pivotal role" played by psychiatry in criminal proceedings. In insanity cases, the expertise of psychiatrists in identifying the " 'elusive and deceptive' symptoms of insanity," when combined with the complex and foreign nature of the issue, made psychiatrists " 'a virtual necessity if an insanity plea is to have any chance at success.' " Similarly, in capital cases a psychiatrist could be useful at exposing the shortcomings of the dangerousness predictions made by the state's experts.

Ake has potentially far-reaching consequences for the defense of criminal cases. It could be read to hold that if the defendant can show an issue will be a "significant factor" in his case and that expert assistance could play a "pivotal role" in the resolution of this issue, the state will not be able to deny such assistance on the ground of financial burden. Some of Justice Marshall's language is quite sweeping: "We recognized long ago that mere access to the courthouse doors does not by itself assure a proper functioning of the adversary process, and that a criminal trial is fundamentally unfair if the State proceeds against an indigent defendant without making certain that he has access to the raw materials integral to the building of an effective defense."

On the other hand, the Court specifically limited its holding to the provision of *one* psychiatrist for the defendant; it also stated, consistent with its right to counsel holdings, that it did not mean "that the indigent defendant has a constitutional right to choose a psychiatrist of his personal liking or to receive funds to hire his own." Thus, assuming the appropriate showing by the defendant, the state may be able to satisfy *Ake* by providing the defendant with one *state-employed* expert, so long as that expert is not so closely tied to the prosecution that his "neutrality" is questionable.[88] Furthermore, it is unlikely that a defendant will be entitled

---

88. Of course, it could be argued that a state-employed clinician should never been seen as "impartial," given the source of his employment and institutional pressures favoring the prosecu-

to an expert in non-psychiatric fields, state-employed or otherwise, merely upon a showing that the expert's area of competence will be a "significant factor" in his case.[89]   Rather, like the federal statute described above, the courts will probably impose a requirement that the defendant show a "particularized need" for the expertise in question.   For instance, merely because ballistics testimony will be pivotal in a case does not necessarily mean that the defendant is entitled to a ballistics expert.   A court may well find that the state's experts can be trusted to arrive at generally accurate conclusions, and that cross-examination will adequately expose any possible inadequacies in their testimony.[90]

31.07   Reimbursement of Defense Fees

Many states require indigent defendants to reimburse the state for the costs of their legal defense if they become financially able to make such reimbursement.   While the Court has held that such programs may not discriminate arbitrarily against particular defendants or groups of defendants, it has refused to invalidate them altogether.

Rinaldi v. Yeager[91] involved a New Jersey statute that required unsuccessful criminal appellants who were incarcerated to reimburse the state, to the extent possible, for expenses incurred in providing trial transcripts.   The statute was attacked as a violation of *Griffin v. Illinois*,[92] because forcing the indigent to pay for the cost of a transcript chilled his right to appeal while the rich defendant would not be so discouraged.   The Supreme Court struck down the statute, but not on this ground;   rather it held that applying the statute only to incarcerated defendants but not to those on probation or suspended sentence constituted invidious discrimination in violation of equal protection principles.

James v. Strange[93] involved a Kansas statute permitting the state to recover attorney's fees and other legal defense costs expended for the benefit of indigent defendants.   Any debt incurred under the statute became a lien on the real estate of the defendant and could be executed by garnishment or any other statutory method.   The indigent defendant was not, however, accorded the same limitations on wage garnishment and other

tion. See Slobogin, supra note 42, at 132–34.

89. Indeed, a number of courts have held that even obtaining a psychiatrist requires a greater showing, perhaps fearful that experts would contribute to speculative defenses. See, e.g., *Clark v. Dugger*, 834 F.2d 1561 (11th Cir.1987); *Sabiar v. State*, 526 So.2d 661 (Ala. Crim.App.1988).

90. See, e.g., *Moore v. Kemp*, 809 F.2d 702 (11th Cir.1987) (en banc) (defendant not entitled to expert to review tests performed by state crime lab).

91. 384 U.S. 305, 86 S.Ct. 1497 (1966).

92. 351 U.S. 12, 76 S.Ct. 585 (1956), discussed in § 29.02(a).

93. 407 U.S. 128, 92 S.Ct. 2027 (1972).

exemptions afforded other civil judgment debtors. The district court invalidated the statute on the grounds that it "needlessly encourages indigents to do without counsel and consequently infringes on the right to counsel as explicated in *Gideon v. Wainwright.*" The Supreme Court again affirmed on different grounds, holding that, by depriving indigent defendants of the protective exemptions enjoyed by other civil judgment debtors, the state had violated the Equal Protection Clause.

In *Fuller v. Oregon,*[94] the Court finally squarely addressed the constitutionality of a recoupment statute that requires reimbursement of legal expenses by indigent defendants who are found guilty and are later able to repay. In *Fuller,* appointed counsel represented the defendant on his guilty plea and at other court proceedings. The defendant was sentenced to five years probation, conditioned upon compliance with the requirements of a work-release program and upon reimbursement to the county for the fees of the attorney and an investigator. The Court held the Oregon scheme did not violate equal protection principles because the convicted defendant from whom reimbursement was sought was accorded all the exemptions enjoyed by other judgment debtors and because remission was allowed in the case of manifest hardship. The Court refused to invalidate the statute because of its distinction between those defendants ultimately convicted and those acquitted. This distinction, stated the Court, "reflects no more than an effort to achieve elemental fairness and is a far cry from . . . invidious discrimination . . .." The opinion stressed the serious imposition by society upon a defendant who is forced to submit to a prosecution that results in acquittal. The effort to make up for the imposition by releasing acquitted defendants from reimbursement liability met the constitutional standard of objective rationality.

Fuller also rejected the argument that the recoupment scheme infringed on the defendant's right to counsel. As in *Strange,* the appellant had argued that knowledge that he might be required to repay the expenses of his defense might encourage him to decline the services of an appointed attorney and thus chill his exercise of his constitutional right to counsel. In rejecting that contention, the Court reasoned that the Oregon statute was carefully tailored to impose an obligation only upon those who actually become capable of repaying the government without hardship. The Court further observed that a defendant who is just above the indigency line must often make substantial financial sacrifices to retain a lawyer: "We cannot say that the Constitution requires that those only slightly poorer must remain forev-

94. 417 U.S. 40, 94 S.Ct. 2116 (1974).

er immune from any obligation to shoulder the expenses of their legal defense, even when they are able to pay without hardship."

31.08 Conclusion

The several aspects of the right to counsel discussed in this chapter can be summarized as follows:

(1) Under the Sixth Amendment, a criminal defendant has the right to counsel at any criminal trial which actually results in the loss of liberty.

(2) The right to counsel at other stages of the criminal process is governed by several different constitutional provisions. Those stages considered part of the criminal prosecution (i.e., from formal charging to sentencing) are governed by the Sixth Amendment, which today appears to require counsel only at those stages: (a) which involve a trial-like confrontation involving the prosecutor and the intricacies of the law; and (b) which can cause substantial prejudice to defendant's rights which counsel can help avoid. Until 1973 only the latter showing was required. Under the Sixth Amendment, there is a right to counsel at post-charging lineups, preliminary hearings to determine probable cause, guilty plea arraignments, and sentencing, but not at handwriting samplings, photo array identifications, preliminary hearings to determine probable cause to detain, and psychiatric evaluations.

For stages not considered part of the criminal prosecution, the Court has employed either Fifth Amendment, due process, or equal protection analysis. Under the Fifth Amendment, there is a right to counsel at all custodial interrogations. Under the Due Process and Equal Protection Clauses, there is a right to counsel at appeals as of right, and under the Due Process Clause a limited right to counsel (depending upon the complexity of the issues and the defendant's capacities) at parole and probation revocation proceedings. Except perhaps in extraordinary circumstances (such as a capital case), there is no right to counsel at discretionary appeals or petitions for collateral review.

(3) A waiver of the right to counsel is valid only if made voluntarily, knowingly and intelligently. The burden of showing a valid waiver is on the state, and is heavier when the defendant is waiving trial counsel. However, the defendant does have a constitutional right, under the Sixth Amendment, to represent himself at trial, and need not demonstrate technical knowledge of trial rules and procedures in order to exercise this right. At the same time, the trial court may appoint standby counsel to assist the defendant; such counsel may participate in the case, even over the defendant's objection, so long as the defendant retains actual control over the case presented to the jury and the jury retains the perception that he represents himself.

(4) An indigent defendant is not entitled to any particular attorney. A non-indigent defendant's choice of attorney may constitutionally be limited by: (a) conflict of interest considerations; (b) attorney qualification rules; or (c) forfeiture statutes which operate to deprive him of resources to pay for the attorney of his choice.

(5) An indigent defendant has the right, under the Due Process Clause, to psychiatric consultation whenever he can show that his sanity or dangerousness is likely to be a significant factor at trial. However, the defendant is entitled to only one psychiatrist for such evaluations, and he is not necessarily entitled to the psychiatrist of his choice. Whether other types of expert assistance need be provided by the state may depend upon a number of factors, including (a) whether experts normally play a pivotal role in the resolution of the issue on which the defendant seeks expert assistance and (b) whether the alternatives to providing the defendant with expert assistance—e.g., cross-examination of the state's experts—provide adequate expertise to the defendant.

(6) The state may require indigent defendants to reimburse the state for the costs of their legal defense once they become financially able to do so, so long as the reimbursement statute does not discriminate arbitrarily against particular defendants or groups of defendants. Requiring defendants who are convicted to reimburse the state while relieving those who are acquitted from this obligation does not constitute such arbitrary discrimination.

BIBLIOGRAPHY

Berger, Vivian O. The Supreme Court and Defense Counsel: Old Roads, New Paths—A Dead End? 86 Colum.L.Rev. 9 (1986).

Chused, Richard H. *Faretta* and the Personal Defense. The Role of a Represented Defendant in Trial Tactics. 65 Cal.L.Rev. 636 (1977).

Duke, S.B. The Right to Assigned Counsel: Argersinger and Beyond. 12 Am.Crim.L.Rev. 601 (1975).

Enker, A.N. and S.H. Elsen. Counsel for the Suspect: Massiah v. United States and Escobedo v. Illinois. 49 Minn.L.Rev. 47 (1964).

Genego, W. The New Adversary. 54 Brooklyn L.Rev. 781 (1988).

Herman, L. and C.H. Thompson. Scott v. Illinois and the Right to Counsel: A Decision in Search of a Doctrine? 17 Am.Crim.L. Rev. 71 (1979).

Israel, Jerold H. Gideon v. Wainwright: The "Art" of Overruling. 1963 Sup.Ct.Rev. 211 (1963).

Kamisar, Y. Reimbursement of Defense Costs as a Condition of Probation for Indigents. 67 Mich.L.Rev. 1404 (1969).

Rosenberg, D. Self-representation and the Criminally Accused— Its Evolution and Scope. 13 Cal.W.L.Rev. 46 (1976).

Scott, Teresa A. The Role of Standby Counsel: The Road from *Faretta* to *Wiggins.* 27 How.L.J. 1799 (1984).

Tague, P. An Indigent's Right to the Attorney of his Choice. 27 Stan.L.Rev. 73 (1974).

Winick, Bruce. Forfeiture of Attorney's Fees Under RICO and CCE and the Right to Counsel of Choice. 43 U.Miami L.Rev. 763 (1989).

Chapter Thirty-Two

EFFECTIVE ASSISTANCE OF COUNSEL

32.01 Introduction

The right to counsel is empty unless counsel adequately represents his clients. An attorney who does not investigate the factual basis of his client's charges, assert the relevant defenses, or attempt to cross-examine witnesses at trial can hardly be said to provide "counsel" at all. Following this reasoning, courts have interpreted the Sixth Amendment to prohibit "ineffective" counsel, i.e., attorney conduct that fails to provide "assistance" to the accused as required by the Right to Counsel Clause. Ineffective assistance claims are not malpractice actions; they cannot result in money damages payable by the attorney. Rather, the remedy for failing to abide by the demands of the Sixth Amendment is reversal of the conviction resulting from the ineffective assistance.

At least three phenomena have led to a vast increase in ineffective assistance claims since the early 1960's. First, the Supreme Court's announcement in *Gideon v. Wainwright*[1] that the Sixth Amendment right to counsel is applicable to all state felony prosecutions predictably resulted in a proliferation of such claims. Compounding this increase was the simultaneous rise of the public defender movement, which relied primarily upon young and inexperienced practitioners.[2] A final factor that has stimulated ineffective assistance claims has been the Supreme Court's recent efforts to limit habeas corpus actions. As detailed elsewhere in this book, the Court has significantly curbed the ability of federal habeas courts to declare "new rules,"[3] to rule on *any* Fourth Amendment claim,[4] and to grant post-conviction relief on constitutional claims which were not raised at trial.[5] When a habeas petition is denied on any of these grounds, the only alternative remaining to the aggrieved prisoner is to claim that his counsel did not effectively deal with the alleged constitutional violation before or during trial.

Thus, despite recent attempts to narrow its scope, the right to effective assistance of counsel has become an issue of substantial concern and is the most common claim presented in federal habeas corpus petitions. This chapter discusses when the right applies, past and present standards defining the right, and ways of improving representation by defense counsel.

1. 372 U.S. 335, 83 S.Ct. 792 (1963).

2. See generally, Finer "Ineffective Assistance of Counsel," 58 Cornell L.Rev. 1077 (1973).

3. See *Teague v. Lane,* 489 U.S. 288, 109 S.Ct. 1060 (1989), discussed in § 33.03(c).

4. See *Stone v. Powell,* 428 U.S. 465, 96 S.Ct. 3037 (1976), discussed in § 33.02(b)(1).

5. *Wainwright v. Sykes,* 433 U.S. 72, 97 S.Ct. 2497 (1977), discussed in § 33.03(c).

32.02 When the Right Applies

(a) Linkage to Right to Counsel. The right to effective assistance of counsel is linked to the right to counsel. Only when the right to counsel attaches is there a constitutionally-based right to effective assistance. Thus, in *Wainwright v. Torna,*[6] the Supreme Court held that failure to make a timely application for a discretionary appeal could not constitute ineffective assistance of counsel, since there was no right to counsel at discretionary appeals.[7] Similarly, in *Pennsylvania v. Finley,*[8] the Court first concluded that there is no right to counsel at state post-conviction proceedings and then held that, given this finding, no claim of ineffective assistance of counsel can be made in connection with such proceedings.

(b) Retained Counsel. If there is a right to counsel at the proceeding in question, then the right to effective assistance does not vary depending upon whether counsel is retained or appointed. For some time, most courts held otherwise, on one of two theories. According to some courts, if defense counsel was privately retained the defendant was held to be estopped from asserting a claim of ineffective assistance, because he was bound, on an agency rationale, by the conduct of the attorney whom he employed. The theory was explained by the Supreme Court of California in *People v. Stevens.*[9] Rejecting a claim that a mistrial should have been declared because of the alleged gross incompetence of the defendant's retained attorney, the court observed: "If there was any error in this regard, it was merely an error of judgment on the part of the defendant in the selection of counsel to represent him."

The courts also rejected claims of ineffective assistance of retained counsel by saying that there was no "state action" depriving the defendant of life or liberty without due process of law. In the words of the First Circuit in *Farrell v. Lanagan:* [10]

> The petitioner's claim that his counsel was so inadequate as to constitute . . . [a] violation of his constitutional rights is . . . not borne out. Counsel was selected and paid for by the petitioner's family, and accepted by him. [E]ven if incompetency of counsel so selected be assumed, it would not follow from that that the state deprived petitioner of any constitutional right in his trial and conviction.

6. 455 U.S. 586, 102 S.Ct. 1300 (1982).

7. See *Ross v. Moffitt,* 417 U.S. 600, 94 S.Ct. 2437 (1974), discussed in § 31.03(c)(3).

8. 481 U.S. 551, 107 S.Ct. 1990 (1987), discussed in § 31.03(c)(4).

9. 5 Cal.2d 92, 53 P.2d 133 (1935).

10. 166 F.2d 845 (1st Cir.1948). See also *Dusseldorf v. Teets,* 209 F.2d 754 (9th Cir.1954).

In *Cuyler v. Sullivan*,[11] however, the Supreme Court firmly held that the performance of the retained attorney is to be judged by the same standards as the conduct of the appointed attorney. In doing so, it quickly dispensed with the absence of state action argument:

> The vital guarantee of the Sixth Amendment would stand for little if the often uninformed decision to retain a particular lawyer could reduce or forfeit the defendant's entitlement to constitutional protection. Since the State's conduct of a criminal trial itself implicates the State in the defendant's conviction, we see no basis for drawing a distinction between retained and appointed counsel that would deny equal justice to defendants who must choose their own lawyers.

Although *Cuyler* did not directly debunk the agency argument, its holding has led the lower courts to reject that rationale as well and find that, for purposes of ineffective assistance claims, there is no distinction between retained and appointed counsel.[12] The fallacy of the agency analogy is easily exposed. Agency theory presupposes a principal capable of supervising the agent. Yet the assumption underlying the Court's right to counsel decisions is that the person accused of a crime engages counsel to conduct his defense because he is not able to defend himself. Presumably, such a person is *not* in a position to guide and control the conduct of his lawyer. Moreover, agency theory developed primarily as a means of compensating innocent third parties for the actions of a principal's agent. In the counsel context, there is no innocent third party who will benefit from making the defendant liable for his attorney's incompetence.[13]

32.03 The Substantive Standard

(a) **Differing Approaches in the Lower Courts.** Until the 1960s, most courts would reject an ineffective assistance of counsel claim unless counsel's efforts were so incompetent as to render the trial "a farce or mockery of justice." [14] On its face, this standard put an unduly heavy burden on the defendant. Moreover, the "farce and mockery" standard was extremely vague, and seemed unfair in light of the more exacting requirements demanded of other professions.

11. 446 U.S. 335, 100 S.Ct. 1708 (1980).

12. See e.g., *Scott v. Wainwright,* 698 F.2d 427 (11th Cir.1983); *Perez v. Wainwright,* 640 F.2d 596 (5th Cir. 1981).

13. Waltz, "Inadequacy of Trial Defense Representation as a Ground for Post–Conviction Relief in Criminal Cases," 59 Nw.U.L.Rev. 289, 297 (1964).

14. See, e.g., *Edwards v. United States,* 103 U.S.App.D.C. 152, 256 F.2d 707 (1958), cert. denied 358 U.S. 847, 79 S.Ct. 74 (1958).

Beginning in the early 1960's, most courts attempted to articulate a more rigorous standard. For instance, the United States Court of Appeals for the District of Columbia held that the appropriate test for ineffective assistance of counsel is whether gross incompetence "blotted out the essence of a substantial defense." [15] Other courts adopted a malpractice-type standard. The Third Circuit, in *Moore v. United States*,[16] declared: "The standard of the adequacy of legal services as in other professions is the exercise of the customary skill and knowledge which normally prevails at the time and place." Still other courts, finding *Moore's* test too demanding (on the ground that performance which falls below the norm is not necessarily negligent or incompetent), adopted variations on the notion of "reasonable" competence.[17] Under each of these tests, the defendant also had to show that any incompetence was detrimental to his case.

Although these attempts at clarifying the definition of ineffective assistance improved upon the old farce and mockery test, they too were ambiguous and, in the words of one judge, provided the courts with little more than a "semantic merry-go-round." [18] Recognizing this problem, Judge Bazelon, in his opinion for the D.C. Circuit Court of Appeals in *United States v. DeCoster* (*DeCoster I*),[19] borrowed from the American Bar Association's Standards for the Defense Function in an attempt to define more succinctly some of the duties counsel owes his client. Based on the Standards, Bazelon concluded, for instance, that "[c]ounsel should confer with his client without delay and as often as necessary to elicit matters of defense, or to ascertain that potential defenses are unavailable." In addition, "[c]ounsel should promptly advise his client of his rights and take all actions necessary to preserve them." Failure to perform functions such as these did not automatically lead to a finding of ineffective assistance. Rather the defendant first had to show that any violation of these standards was "substantial," which required showing that the violation was egregious or repeated. Secondly, the prosecution was given an opportunity to establish that the defendant was not prejudiced by the violation. But, taken as a whole, the definition of ineffective assistance in *DeCoster I* was not only more refined, but more stringent, than

---

15. *Scott v. United States*, 427 F.2d 609 (D.C.Cir.1970).

16. 432 F.2d 730, 736 (3d Cir.1970).

17. See, e.g., *Cooper v. Fitzharris*, 586 F.2d 1325 (9th Cir.1978) ("reasonably competent attorney acting as a diligent conscientious advocate"); *United States v. Easter*, 539 F.2d 663 (8th Cir. 1976) ("customary skills and diligence that a reasonably competent attorney would perform under similar circumstances"); *Beasley v. United States*, 491 F.2d 687 (6th Cir.1974) ("counsel reasonably likely to render and rendering reasonably effective assistance").

18. *Cooper v. Fitzharris*, 551 F.2d 1162 (9th Cir.1977) (Duniway, J., concurring), vacated 586 F.2d 1325 (9th Cir. 1978) (en banc).

19. 487 F.2d 1197 (D.C.Cir.1973).

earlier definitions. As Judge Bazelon later stated,[20] the approach taken in *DeCoster I* "gave content to what previously had been empty verbal formulations."

Greater clarity for attorneys and judges was not the only purpose behind the *DeCoster I* standard. According to Bazelon's subsequent characterization of it, this standard was meant to focus on the "quality of counsel's performance rather than looking to the effect of counsel's actions on the outcome of the case," a perspective which had two advantages. First, it would go further toward eliminating "second-class justice for the poor," because it would "proscribe second-class performances by counsel, whatever the consequences in a particular case." Second, it would "reduce[ ] the likelihood that any particular defendant will be prejudiced by counsel's shortcomings," and thus reduce the need to engage in "the inherently difficult task of speculating about the precise effect of each error or omission by an attorney." Although the prejudice inquiry would still be made when error was found, it would be "distinct from the determination of whether the defendant has received effective assistance," and "considered only in order to spare defendants, prosecutors and the courts alike a truly futile repetition of the pretrial and trial process."

Ultimately, however, Judge Bazelon's approach did not find favor in the lower courts, or even in his own court. *DeCoster I* was overruled three years after it was decided. In *United States v. DeCoster (DeCoster III)*,[21] the majority intentionally avoided setting forth *any* definitive standards beyond requiring a finding of "serious incompetency," on the ground that it is impossible to define "effectiveness" without reference to the facts of the specific case. As Judge Leventhal wrote:

> [The court] must be wary lest its inquiry and standards undercut the sensitive relationship between attorney and client and tear the fabric of the adversary system. A defense counsel's representation of a client encompasses an almost infinite variety of situations that call for the exercise of professional judgment. . . .

Leventhal offered several reasons in favor of rejecting what he called the "categorical" approach in favor of a flexible "judgmental" approach. The latter approach "preserves the freedom of counsel to make quick judgments," at the same time it deters intentional inadequacy as a means of obtaining reversal in a weak case. The judgmental approach also "avoids the possibility that there will be frequent and wide-ranging inquiries into the information and reasoning that prompted counsel to pursue a given

---

20. *United States v. DeCoster*, 624 F.2d 196 (D.C.Cir.1976) (Bazelon, J., dissenting).

21. 624 F.2d 196 (D.C.Cir.1976).

course." Such inquiries are problematic not only because they might inhibit counsel's behavior, but because they are time-consuming and may require revelation of attorney-client discussions. Furthermore, to avoid the post-trial reviews the categorical approach would require, the court and even the prosecution might begin monitoring counsel's trial behavior. And "[a]n even more difficult problem would be posed by the supervision of defense counsel's development of the case before trial." In short, "[e]fforts to improve the performance of defense counsel should not imperil [the] protection [of the adversary system]." The *DeCoster III* court also required, contrary to *DeCoster I* but in line with the majority stance, that the *defendant* show that any alleged ineffective assistance prejudiced his defense.

(b) The Supreme Court's Approach. Until 1984 the United States Supreme Court provided the lower courts with very little guidance on the ineffective assistance of counsel issue. The one decision in which it made any type of generalized pronouncement prior to that time was in the narrow context of representation during the pleading process. In *McMann v. Richardson,*[22] a 1970 decision, the Court stated that an attorney's performance at the guilty plea stage was effective so long as the advice he rendered was "within the range of competence demanded of attorneys in criminal cases." Arguably, this standard is an exacting one, since the measuring stick it establishes is not attorney performance generally, but the performance of attorneys in *criminal cases.* But for fourteen years the Court did little to elucidate this language,[23] with the result that the lower courts continued to debate the appropriate ineffective assistance standard.

When the Court finally did make its first direct statement on the scope of the ineffective assistance doctrine, it opted for a "judgmental" approach similar to that taken in *DeCoster III*, by a margin of 8–1. At several points in *Strickland v. Washington,*[24] the Court echoed Judge Leventhal's rejection of "mechanical rules" as a means of defining the Sixth Amendment. It also held, as had *DeCoster III*, that, except in a few types of cases where prejudice is presumed, the defendant bears the burden on this issue. Thus, Justice O'Connor, in her majority opinion, set forth a test with two components:

> First, the defendant must show that counsel's performance was deficient. This requires showing that counsel made errors so serious that counsel was not functioning as the "counsel" guaranteed the defendant by the Sixth Amendment.

22. 397 U.S. 759, 90 S.Ct. 1441 (1970).

23. The one significant exception was *Tollett v. Henderson,* 411 U.S. 258,

93 S.Ct. 1602 (1973), discussed in § 32.04(b)(2).

24. 466 U.S. 668, 104 S.Ct. 2052 (1984).

Second, the defendant must show that the deficient performance prejudiced the defense. This requires showing that counsel's errors were so serious as to deprive the defendant of a fair trial, a trial whose result is unreliable.

A year later, in *Hill v. Lockhart,*[25] the Court held that *Strickland's* two-prong test also applied to guilty plea cases, although the prejudice prong was defined somewhat differently to require the defendant to show that "there is a reasonable probability that, but for counsel's errors, he would not have pleaded guilty and would have insisted on going to trial." And one year after *Hill,* it applied *Strickland* to appeals as of right.[26]

(1) The performance prong. In elaborating on the first prong announced in *Strickland,* Justice O'Connor repeated *McMann's* language and stated that "[t]he proper measure of attorney performance remains simply reasonableness under prevailing professional norms." O'Connor posited three such norms: (1) a duty to avoid conflicts of interest; (2) a duty "to advocate the defendant's cause," which includes the duties "to consult with the defendant on important decisions and to keep the defendant informed of important developments"; and (3) a duty "to bring to bear such skill and knowledge as will render the trial a reliable adversarial testing process." Elsewhere in the opinion she stated that "counsel has a duty to make reasonable investigations or to make a reasonable decision that makes particular investigations unnecessary." This was the extent of the Court's effort to develop guidelines. And in analyzing whether an attorney met these standards, Justice O'Connor wrote, "[j]udicial scrutiny of counsel's performance must be highly deferential." Moreover, "counsel is strongly presumed to have rendered adequate assistance and made all significant decisions in the exercise of reasonable professional judgment."

The Court reasons for this relatively undemanding definition of attorney error were similar to those advanced in *Decoster III.* According to the Court, "[i]ntrusive post-trial inquiry into attorney performance or . . . detailed guidelines for its evaluation would encourage the proliferation of ineffectiveness challenges." Further:

> Criminal trials resolved unfavorably to the defendant would increasingly come to be followed by a second trial, this one of counsel's unsuccessful defense. Counsel's performance and even willingness to serve could be adversely affected. Intensive scrutiny of counsel and rigid requirements for acceptable assistance could dampen the ardor and impair the independence of defense counsel, discourage the acceptance of as-

---

25. 474 U.S. 52, 106 S.Ct. 366 (1985).   **26.** *Smith v. Murray,* 477 U.S. 527, 106 S.Ct. 2661 (1986).

signed cases, and undermine the trust between attorney and client.

It is worth noting at this point that, although the Court has refused to develop rigid guidelines for attorneys, it has suggested that conduct which is ethical under the professional codes of responsibility cannot be error for purposes of the Sixth Amendment. In *Nix v. Whiteside,*[27] the five-member majority stated that since the attorney's conduct in that case (i.e., threatening to withdraw if the defendant committed perjury) did not breach "any recognized professional duty, it follows that there can be no deprivation of the right to assistance of counsel under the *Strickland* standard." At the same time, the *Nix* majority was quick to state that it was not adopting a categorical approach; a mere breach of an ethical canon would not mean the performance prong has been violated. According to the Court, "a court must be careful not to narrow the wide range of conduct acceptable under the Sixth Amendment so restrictively as to constitutionalize particular standards of professional conduct and thereby intrude into the State's proper authority to define and apply the standards of professional conduct applicable to those it admits to practice in its courts."[28]

(2) The prejudice prong. With respect to the prejudice prong, the majority in *Strickland* first noted that certain situations are so likely to be prejudicial to the defendant that prejudice is presumed. Here it referred to decisions, discussed in more detail below,[29] which found ineffective assistance in cases involving government rules or rulings which inhibit the functioning of counsel, and conflicts of interest occasioned by dual representation. But in all other situations, the defendant must affirmatively prove that "there is a reasonable probability that, but for counsel's unprofessional errors, the result of the proceeding would have been different." Similar to its generous view of attorney conduct under the performance prong, the Court cautioned that in analyzing the degree of prejudice to the defendant, the court "should presume, absent challenge to the judgment on grounds of evidentiary insufficiency, that the judge or jury acted according to law." In short, the Court's definition of prejudice in those cases where prejudice is not presumed requires the defendant to make a strong showing of "innocence" on either factual or technical "legal" grounds.[30]

---

27. 475 U.S. 157, 106 S.Ct. 988 (1986), discussed in more detail in § 32.03(b)(3).

28. The remaining four members of the Court concurred only in the judgment, criticizing in particular the majority's linkage between the rules of professional conduct and proper conduct under the Sixth Amendment.

29. See § 32.04(a) & (b).

30. Note that in *Kimmelman v. Morrison,* 477 U.S. 365, 106 S.Ct. 2574 (1986), Justice Powell wrote a concurring opinion suggesting that *Strickland's* prejudice prong should be limited solely to cases of factual innocence, an argument which has yet to be squarely addressed by the Court.

In justifying its decision to place the burden on the defendant to prove prejudice rather than on the prosecution to show its absence, the majority reasoned that "[t]he government is not responsible for, and hence not able to prevent, attorney errors that will result in reversal of conviction or sentence." Although this statement is true in the individual case, it is the government which, in the case of indigents, appoints and pays for the attorney; thus, the government's inadequate funding of its legal defense system could be "responsible" for attorney error in an indirect sense. Further, of course, the defendant often has no more control over the attorney than does the government. At the same time, it might be pointed out that the defense is usually in the best position to prove the facts relevant to the prejudice inquiry, and thus should bear the burden on this issue.

With respect to its definition of prejudice, the Court explained that it chose to focus on the error's effect on the outcome of the case because the purpose of the Sixth Amendment's guarantee is "to ensure that a defendant has the assistance necessary to justify reliance on the outcome of the proceeding." Responding to the defendant's proposal to base the prejudice inquiry on whether the error "impaired presentation of the defense," Justice O'Connor stated: "Since any error, if it is indeed an error, 'impairs' the presentation of the defense, the proposed standard is inadequate because it provides no way of deciding what impairments are sufficiently serious to warrant setting aside the outcome of the proceeding." As this latter statement suggests, under the Court's "judgmental" approach the prejudice inquiry may well determine when a particular act or omission fails to meet the performance prong (e.g., failure to raise a certain defense may be "error" when it results in an unjust conviction, but not "error" when the defense was weak.) This is in distinct contrast to the categorical approach, which attempts to pre-define the type of conduct that is deficient and engages in the prejudice inquiry only after error has been found.

32.04 Application of the Standard

As noted above, *Strickland* outlined three general categories of ineffective assistance claims. The first involved state interference with counsel's ability to represent his client, the second concerned conflicts of interest, and the third included most attorney-produced errors. This section adopts *Strickland's* general organization of the cases.

(a) **State Interference Cases.** In *Strickland*, the Court stated that "[a]ctual or constructive denial of the assistance of counsel" and "various kinds of state interference with counsel's assistance" are "legally presumed to result in prejudice." The reason for this presumption in state interference cases, according to the majority, is that "prejudice in these circumstances is so likely that case-by-case inquiry into prejudice is not worth the cost." Furthermore, "such circumstances involve impairments of the Sixth Amendment right that are easy to identify and, for that reason and because the prosecution is directly responsible, easy for the government to prevent." It should also be noted that, in contrast to the "categorical" approach criticized by Judge Leventhal in *DeCoster III*,[31] a rule which treats government interference as presumptively violative of the Sixth Amendment is not likely to inhibit defense tactics, occasion judicial or prosecutorial monitoring of counsel, or "reward" inept conduct designed to ensure a reversal.

The Court's cases involving state interference can be divided into three categories: (1) denial or late appointment of counsel; (2) obstruction of counsel's performance; and (3) intrusion into the attorney-client relationship. Although prejudice is often presumed in these situations, in each the Court has identified some situations where official intermeddling with the right to counsel does not eliminate the need to inquire into its effect on the defendant's case.

(1) Denial or late appointment of counsel. The clearest example of state action which results in ineffective assistance of counsel is when the government fails to provide or denies counsel at a stage of the proceeding at which the right to counsel attaches.[32] Here, as *Strickland* makes clear, prejudice must be presumed.

A related situation—what *Strickland* labelled "constructive denial" of counsel—occurs when an attorney is appointed at such a belated point in the process that the defendant is, in effect, denied counsel. An example is *Avery v. Alabama*,[33] where the court appointed the entire local bar to assist a lone attorney, appearing for the first time on the day of trial, in representing nine defendants. Without bothering to assess counsel's performance at trial, the Court concluded that "such designation of counsel as was attempted was either so indefinite or so close upon the trial as to amount to a denial of effective and substantial aid in that regard."

However, tardy appointment of counsel is not always a violation of the Sixth Amendment. In *Avery v. Alabama*,[34] eight years after *Powell*, the Court upheld a conviction in a capital case when counsel was appointed only three days before trial, on the ground that, despite counsel's statement to the contrary, three days was not unreasonably short under the circumstances. And in *Cham-*

---

31. See § 32.03(a).

32. See §§ 31.02 and 31.03.

33. 287 U.S. 45, 53 S.Ct. 55 (1932), discussed in § 31.02(a).

34. 308 U.S. 444, 60 S.Ct. 321 (1940).

bers v. Maroney,[35] the Court explicitly refused to adopt "a per se rule requiring reversal of every conviction following tardy appointment of counsel," in a case where the late appointment at most prevented counsel from making pretrial suppression motions that would have failed in any event.

Following these decisions, but before *Strickland,* some lower courts had held that a late appointment should establish a presumption of prejudice which the prosecution must overcome.[36] But in *United States v. Cronic,*[37] a companion case to *Strickland,* the Court indicated that the usual late appointment case should be treated no differently than cases in which no state negligence was involved; in other words, the burden of showing prejudice should still be on the defendant. In *Cronic,* the Court refused to find ineffective assistance of counsel when the attorney was allowed only twenty-five days to investigate a case which took the government four-and-one-half years to prepare; the majority concluded that "the period of 25 days . . . is not so short that it even arguably justifies a presumption that no lawyer could provide the respondent with the effective assistance of counsel required by the Constitution." It went on to note that while the government's prolonged investigation was necessary because the check kiting scheme with which the defendant was charged involved banks in several jurisdictions and thousands of documents, the defendant's only defense was the absence of an intent to defraud; viewed in this light, the preparation time allowed did not prejudice the defendant.

A lower court decision which probably summarizes the law on this issue is the pre-*Strickland* case of *Moore v. United States,*[38] where the court stated that "[t]he question necessarily involves a comparison of the time of the appointment with all the attendant circumstances, such as the gravity of the charge, the experience of appointed counsel, the extent of his knowledge and participation in similar cases, his opportunity for preparation and even what he may have been told by the defendant which may reduce the area of necessary preparation." *Moore* specifically disapproved an earlier case suggesting that lateness of appointment creates a burden-shifting presumption of inadequate representation,[39] but it also held that untimely appointment of counsel raises a "strong inference of prejudice."

(2) Obstruction of counsel's performance. Assuming counsel has been retained or appointed with sufficient time to prepare,

35. 399 U.S. 42, 90 S.Ct. 1975 (1970).

36. See, e.g., *Coles v. Peyton,* 389 F.2d 224 (4th Cir.1968).

37. 466 U.S. 648, 104 S.Ct. 2039 (1984).

38. 432 F.2d 730 (3d Cir.1970).

39. See *United States ex rel. Mathis v. Rundle,* 394 F.2d 748 (3d Cir.1968).

there are any number of ways the state can obstruct his effectiveness. The Supreme Court's cases appear to hold that if the obstruction of counsel prevents him from carrying out a well-established prerogative, then prejudice is presumed. On the other hand, other limitations on counsel are subjected to the same analysis as other ineffectiveness claims.

In *Cronic,* the Court listed several decisions which it depicted as cases where prejudice was presumed because of state interference with retained or appointed counsel. *Ferguson v. Georgia,*[40] decided before *Gideon,* held that due process was violated by a state statute barring the defendant from having his testimony elicited by counsel through direct examination. Post–*Gideon* cases cited in *Cronic* were *Brooks v. Tennessee,*[41] which held unconstitutional a statute that restricted counsel's choice of when to put the defendant on the stand; *Herring v. New York,*[42] which struck down a statute giving the judge in a non-jury trial the power to deny defense counsel closing summation; *Davis v. Alaska,*[43] which found the Confrontation Clause violated by a prohibition on defense counsel's attempt to use a juvenile record to impeach a witness; and *Geders v. United States,*[44] which held unconstitutional a judge's order directing a defendant not to consult with his attorney during an overnight recess that fell between direct and cross-examination. In each of these cases, the state action, in *Herring's* words, interfered with "the traditions of the adversary factfinding process," and thus required reversal even when actual prejudice was not shown by the defendant.

Two later cases indicate that the Court is willing to place significant limitations on this analysis, however. In *United States v. Bagley,*[45] the Court refined *Davis* by indicating that where the infringement on counsel's cross-examination results not from a prohibition on using evidence already obtained but from a state refusal to *provide* impeachment evidence, and that refusal is justifiable under the Court's due process analysis in discovery cases,[46] no automatic Sixth Amendment violation occurs. And in *Perry v. Leeke,*[47] which upheld a judge's prohibition on communication between the defendant and his attorney during a 15–minute recess in his testimony, the Court distinguished *Geders* by noting

---

40. 365 U.S. 570, 81 S.Ct. 756 (1961).

41. 406 U.S. 605, 92 S.Ct. 1891 (1972), discussed in § 24.02(a)(2).

42. 422 U.S. 853, 95 S.Ct. 2550 (1975).

43. 415 U.S. 308, 94 S.Ct. 1105 (1974).

44. 425 U.S. 80, 96 S.Ct. 1330 (1976).

45. 473 U.S. 667, 105 S.Ct. 3375 (1985), discussed in § 28.05(b)(1).

46. As *Bagley* also held, the prosecution need disclose only "exculpatory" information, i.e., information that will have a "reasonable probability" of changing the "result of the proceeding." See § 24.04(b).

47. 488 U.S. 272, 109 S.Ct. 594 (1989).

that the overnight gag order there could have prevented discussion of "matters that the defendant [has] a constitutional right to discuss with his lawyer," such as overall strategy. In *Leeke,* on the other hand, there was "a virtual certainty that any conversation between the witness and the lawyer would relate to ongoing testimony;" thus, the order in that case treated the defendant like any other witness (in light of the traditional rule that witnesses are not permitted to talk to others during testimony), and should not lead to a presumption of prejudice.

(3) Intrusion into the attorney-client relationship. Several cases involve government eavesdropping on attorney-client conversations through the use of undercover agents or other devices. It appears to be established, as *Strickland* suggested, that the government may not use information gained in such exchanges against the defendant.[48] But if the government avoids using such information, then the invasion, by itself, probably does not violate the Sixth Amendment unless some other type of prejudice is shown. In effect, barring such prejudice, the state has not actually "interfered" with the defense's case.

In *Weatherford v. Bursey,*[49] an undercover police officer had been arrested with the defendant for vandalizing a selective service office. Trying to maintain his undercover stature, the officer met with the defendant and his attorney at two strategy sessions convened at the defendant's request. He also told the defendant that he would not testify at the defendant's trial, apparently in the honest belief that he would continue to be undercover. At the time of trial, however, his value as an agent had diminished and he was called by the prosecution to testify as to his undercover activities and the events on the day of the vandalizing. Emphasizing that the agent had not testified about the attorney-client conversations and that none of the state's evidence or strategy was based on those conversations, the Court held that no per se violation of the Sixth Amendment right to counsel occurred. The defendant's desire for private conversations with his attorney, by itself, did not outweigh the state's need to protect the identity of its agents.

In *United States v. Morrison,*[50] the Court suggested that it would reach the same result, at least functionally, even when a state intrusion does not result from the need to prevent the "unmasking" of an agent. In *Morrison,* the agent gratuitously met with the defendant and disparaged defense counsel. The Court assumed, without deciding, that this action was a violation

48. See, e.g., *O'Brien v. United States,* 386 U.S. 345, 87 S.Ct. 1158 (1967).

49. 429 U.S. 545, 97 S.Ct. 837 (1977).

50. 449 U.S. 361, 101 S.Ct. 665 (1981).

of the Sixth Amendment. But it went on to hold that the lower court's dismissal of the charge against the defendant, with prejudice, was not warranted, given the absence of any showing that the agent's contact with the defendant prejudiced representation of her case.[51]

(b) Conflict of Interests Cases. The second category of ineffective assistance claims identified in *Strickland* involves conflicts between the attorney's and the client's interests. Such conflicts can stem from an attorney's attempt to represent more than one co-defendant in the same trial, the attorney's prior representation of a prosecution witness in the current trial, the fact that the attorney's fee is coming from a third party, an attorney's contract with a publishing company for the defendant's story, and a host of other situations, most of which are dealt with by the professional codes of conduct.[52]

The Court has held that, as with state interference cases, cases where such conflict is shown often do not require a showing of prejudice in order to implicate the Sixth Amendment. Again, *Strickland* provides the Court's best summary of its reasons for this rule. First, "the duty of loyalty [is] perhaps the most basic of counsel's duties." Second, "it is difficult to measure the precise effect on the defense of representation corrupted by conflicting interests." Third, and perhaps most importantly, the courts have the "ability . . . to make early inquiry in certain situations likely to give rise to conflicts" and thus avoid them.[53] When the court fails to avert obvious conflicts, in a sense the state is once again "interfering" with the defendant's right to counsel.

Even so, as with cases involving direct state interference with counsel, an irrebuttable presumption of prejudice is not ironclad in conflicts cases. For the presumption to operate, it must be shown that the trial court should have been alerted to the potential for conflict prior to trial. If the latter showing is not made, then an ineffective assistance claim will succeed only if there is proof that an "actual" conflict "adversely affected" the lawyer's performance, a standard which appears to come close to requiring a showing of prejudice. Further, the presumption does not oper-

51. The lower courts are divided on the issue, with some still finding a per se violation when the prosecution "improperly" obtains information relating to a confidential defense strategy, see, e.g., *United States v. Costanzo,* 740 F.2d 251 (3d Cir.1984); others requiring the prosecution to show no prejudice, see, e.g., *United States v. Mastroianni,* 749 F.2d 900 (1st Cir.1984); and others requiring the defense to show prejudice, see, e.g., *United States v. Irwin,* 612 F.2d 1182 (9th Cir.1980).

52. See, e.g., American Bar Association, Model Code of Professional Responsibility, Canon 5; ABA Model Rules of Professional Conduct, Rules 1.7–1.9.

53. Here the Court made reference to the federal rule dealing with the court's duty to inquire into possible conflicts in joint representation cases and to apprise defendants of the dangers of joint representation. See Fed.R.Crim.P. 44(c).

ate unless the conflict is between "legitimate" interests. These principles are discussed here. Also examined is the somewhat countervailing notion of whether a defendant can waive his right to conflict-free counsel.

(1) The judicial notice requirement. In *Glasser v. United States*,[54] the trial court had insisted that the same attorney represent co-defendants in a conspiracy prosecution. In evaluating the case, the Court did not require a specific showing of prejudice, but only proof that the accused's defense was rendered less effective by the joint appointment than it would have been had the defendants had separate attorneys. This threshold was met by a showing that arguably inadmissible evidence was admitted without objection against one defendant, and that the attorney failed to cross-examine witnesses who might have helped one defendant but would have hurt the other.

In *Holloway v. Arkansas*,[55] the majority read *Glasser* as holding that requiring joint representation over timely objection demands automatic reversal, unless the court first satisfies itself that no conflict exists. When no such inquiry is made, prejudice is presumed, because a rule requiring proof of prejudice after trial would not be susceptible to "intelligent, even-handed application." *Holloway* also suggested that even an unsupported request for separate counsel should usually be granted since, as Chief Justice Burger pointed out for the majority, "compelled disclosure" of the reasons for such a request might risk revelation of confidential information and "creates significant risks of unfair prejudice, especially when the disclosure is to a judge who may be called upon later to impose sentences on the attorney's clients." Not surprisingly in light of this language, *Holloway* had the effect of imposing a duty on trial courts to appoint separate counsel virtually any time defense counsel makes a conflict of interest claim, at least in multiple representation cases.[56]

More difficult are those cases where a pretrial request for separate counsel is not made. In *Cuyler v. Sullivan*,[57] the Court held that, under such circumstances, the trial court has a duty to inquire into possible conflicts only in the presence of "special circumstances." These circumstances were found not to exist in *Sullivan*: despite the fact that the same attorneys represented three defendants, the conflicts issue was not only not raised prior to trial, but the defendants were tried at separate trials, and counsel for Sullivan presented a defense that was compatible with

54. 315 U.S. 60, 62 S.Ct. 457 (1942).

55. 435 U.S. 475, 98 S.Ct. 1173 (1978).

56. See, e.g., *Smith v. Anderson*, 689 F.2d 59 (6th Cir.1982); *Bishop v. Par-*

ratt, 509 F.Supp. 1140 (D.Neb.1981); *Brooks v. Hooper*, 597 F.2d 57 (5th Cir. 1979).

57. 446 U.S. 335, 100 S.Ct. 1708 (1980).

the view that none of the three defendants were connected with the crime.

As the dissent pointed out, a rule putting the burden on the trial court to inquire into possible conflicts in all joint representation cases would not be unduly burdensome; indeed, the federal rules soon thereafter adopted this practice.[58] But the majority refused to constitutionalize such a rule. However, in *Wood v. Georgia*[59] the Court did emphasize that "*Sullivan* mandated a reversal when the trial court has failed to make an inquiry even though 'it knows or reasonably should know that a particular conflict exists.'" Thus, an inquiry would seem to be required not only when the defense raises the conflict issue prior to trial but also when the record otherwise suggests a "potential" for conflict.

Wood itself involved a different kind of conflict than the multiple representation cases. There, the record disclosed that the defendants, "adult bookstore" employees, were fined substantial sums for selling indecent literature, in the belief that their employer would pay the fines. Their attorney, who was paid by the employer, sought to argue merely that fines in such cases should be limited by the defendant/employee's ability to pay. Although the Court ultimately remanded the case for further proceedings, it suggested that, under *Sullivan,* reversal was appropriate in this case because the trial court should have been on notice of the potential conflict between employer and employee interests, especially in light of the fact that the prosecutor had raised the conflict problem.

(2) The actual conflict requirement. A second holding in *Sullivan* was that in those situations, discussed above, in which the trial court does not have an obligation to inquire into possible conflicts, a postconviction ineffective assistance claim will not be successful based merely on a "potential" conflict, but only when the defendant can show an "actual conflict of interest adversely affected his lawyer's performance." Although the Court did not have occasion to apply this test in *Sullivan* (the case was remanded on the issue), it did interpret the actual conflict standard in *Burger v. Kemp.*[60] There two lawyers from the same firm represented Burger and his co-defendant Stevens, both of whom were charged with capital murder. Assuming, without holding, that two attorneys can be considered as one for purposes of the Sixth Amendment, the Court found no constitutional violation in *Burger.* It was admitted that the two lawyers consulted together frequently on both cases and that Burger's lawyer wrote the appellate brief for Stevens as well. Burger argued that this

---

58. See Fed.R.Crim.P. 44(c).

59. 450 U.S. 261, 101 S.Ct. 1097 (1981).

60. 483 U.S. 776, 107 S.Ct. 3114 (1987).

relationship created an actual conflict of interest, as shown by his attorney's failure to make a "lesser culpability" argument at the plea negotiation and appellate stages, despite Burger's relative youth and evidence from Burger and another witness suggesting that Burger originally resisted Stevens' plan to commit murder. The Court called this evidence weak, especially since it was Burger who eventually committed the murder. It also concluded that even if there had been an actual conflict of interest, the joint representation did not "adversely" affect Burger's case. In particular, leaning heavily on counsel's explanations of his actions, it noted that Burger's counsel attempted to portray Stevens as the principal architect of the crime throughout Burger's trial.

As the dissent reiterated, however, the lesser culpability argument was *not* pressed at plea bargaining or on appeal, despite the relevance of such information under the state's death penalty statute. It was during these two phases of the process that Burger was most likely to be harmed by a fear on the part of his lawyer that the lesser culpability argument would damage Stevens' case, since the plea negotiations for the two defendants went on simultaneously and their appeals were combined, whereas their trials were severed. While the majority's insinuation that the outcome of Burger's case was not affected by any conflict that existed may be correct, that factor is supposedly irrelevant in conflict of interest cases.

Burger illustrates the fine line between *Sullivan's* "actual conflict" test and the prejudice inquiry. Similar in tone to *Burger* are most lower court decisions dealing with post-conviction conflicts claims. For instance, in *Riley v. State*,[61] the court found that joint representation (not objected to prior to trial) had no adverse effect on counsel's performance despite evidence that he failed to develop the defendant's "social history," and instead chose to emphasize the co-defendant's greater culpability.[62] Addressing a different type of conflict, *State v. Stephani*[63] held that prior representation of a victim by a public defender's office will generally not support a post-conviction claim of ineffective assistance.[64]

(3) *The legitimate interest requirement.* There may be circumstances where even an actual conflict of interest does not lead

---

61. 585 A.2d 719 (Del.1990).

62. But see, *Armstrong v. State*, 573 So.2d 1329 (Miss.1990) (lack of mitigating evidence in 14 year-old's sentencing proceeding compared to evidence presented by same attorney for co-defendant demonstrated an actual conflict of interest adversely affecting representation).

63. 369 N.W.2d 540 (Minn.App. 1985). See also, *People v. Wilkins*, 28

N.Y.2d 53, 320 N.Y.S.2d 8, 268 N.E.2d 756 (1971).

64. However, a minority of courts presume prejudice in cases where the defense counsel has represented a victim or complaining witness. See, e.g., *People v. Pinkins*, 222 Cal.App.3d 897, 272 Cal.Rptr. 100 (Cal.App.1990); *People v. Stoval*, 40 Ill.2d 109, 239 N.E.2d 441 (1968).

to a Sixth Amendment violation. In *Nix v. Whiteside,*[65] the defendant, charged with murder, insisted on testifying that he had seen "something metallic" in the victim's hand, although none of the eyewitnesses to the event had seen a gun and no gun was found. Counsel told the defendant that if he testified falsely, counsel would feel obligated to advise the court that he felt the defendant was committing perjury; moreover, counsel would seek to withdraw from representing the defendant and might be allowed to impeach any false testimony given. As a result, the defendant made no mention of a gun in his testimony; he was convicted of second degree murder. He subsequently sought federal habeas relief, alleging denial of effective assistance.

The circuit court of appeals upheld the claim, in part on the ground that *Sullivan* required prejudice be presumed when there is an actual conflict of interest. The Supreme Court unanimously rejected this reasoning. As Chief Justice Burger stated for the Court, "[i]f a 'conflict' between a client's proposal and counsel's ethical obligation gives rise to a presumption that counsel's assistance was prejudicially ineffective, every guilty criminal's conviction would be suspect if the defendant had sought to obtain an acquittal by illegal means." Elsewhere in the opinion, Burger elaborated on the interests involved:

> [The lawyer's] admonitions to his client can in no sense be said to have forced respondent into an *impermissible* choice between his right to counsel and his right to testify as he proposed for there was no *permissible* choice to testify falsely. For a defense counsel to take steps to persuade a criminal defendant to testify truthfully, or to withdraw, deprives the defendant of neither his right to counsel nor the right to testify truthfully. . . . A defendant who informed his counsel that he was arranging to bribe or threaten witnesses or members of the jury would have no "right" to insist on counsel's assistance or silence. Counsel would not be limited to advising against that conduct.

In a similar vein, the four concurring justices noted that whereas the Court's other conflicts cases had involved a conflict between a legitimate interest of the client and other interests, here, on the assumption that the attorney's assessment of the defendant's story was correct, the defendant had no legitimate interest to protect.[66] When such is the case, the presumption of prejudice normally associated with conflicts cases does not apply.

65. 475 U.S. 157, 106 S.Ct. 988 (1986).

66. However, the concurring members were unwilling to join the majority in finding that the Sixth Amendment could never be violated in such circumstances. Rather it merely held that, on the facts of the case, the defendant was not prejudiced by being prevented from testifying falsely.

(4) Waiver. Occasionally, a defendant will be aware of a possible adverse interest on the part of his attorney but nonetheless want to "waive" his right to conflict-free counsel, perhaps because he believes the attorney is his best advocate and that the conflict will not affect that advocacy. In *Wheat v. United States,*[67] the Supreme Court held that such waivers were possible. But it also held that the trial judge may, in his discretion, override the defendant's choice of counsel whenever it finds an "actual" conflict or a "serious potential" for conflict. Perhaps more importantly, the Court held that, in light of the fact that allowing waiver of the right to conflict-free counsel might subject trial courts to assertions of error "no matter which way they rule," the judge's decision as to when a "serious" potential for conflict has developed should be given "substantial latitude" by the appellate courts.

Wheat requested the trial judge to substitute for his counsel an attorney named Iredale, who also represented his two codefendants. Although all three defendants indicated they were willing to waive their right to conflict-free counsel, the trial judge rejected the request. The Supreme Court upheld the judge's decision. The entire Court agreed that the presumption in favor of defendant's counsel of choice could be overcome by either an actual conflict or a serious potential for conflict, because the integrity of the trial process and the "ethical standards of the profession" might otherwise be compromised. However, the Court split 5–4 over whether the trial judge should be allowed "substantial latitude" in deciding whether serious potential conflict existed; it also split by a like margin over whether such potential existed in this particular case.

The facts in *Wheat* illustrate the difficulty of gauging the "potential for conflict." One of Wheat's two codefendants had completed plea negotiations at the time Wheat's request for Iredale occurred, although the court had not yet accepted the plea. The second codefendant was to testify at Wheat's trial. The majority asserted that if the first codefendant's plea had not been accepted and Wheat had testified at his trial, or if the second codefendant had needed to be vigorously cross-examined during Wheat's trial, then Iredale would have been faced with difficult and perhaps impossible-to-reconcile ethical conflicts. Thus the judge's finding that the potential for conflict was serious was proper. The dissent asserted, on the other hand, that at the time of the request for Iredale, it was clear that the first codefendant's plea would be accepted (in fact it was). It was also clear that, while the second codefendant would testify at Wheat's trial, he would not mention Wheat because he had never met him and

67. 486 U.S. 153, 108 S.Ct. 1692 (1988).

could not identify him (which turned out to be the case; indeed, because of the general nature of the testimony there was no cross-examination). Moreover, had cross-examination been necessary, Wheat's initial counsel, who indicated a willingness to stay with Wheat's case, could have conducted it, thereby avoiding the conflict.

It should be emphasized that *Wheat's* willingness to give broad discretion to the trial judge insulates not only decisions to appoint separate counsel, but also decisions to allow waiver. The Court noted that, although it was sustaining the trial court's judgment in the case, another court might have allowed waiver, "with equal justification," and neither would necessarily be right. Any waiver of conflict which is proferred must of course be intelligent and voluntary and requires careful analysis by the court.[68] It also should be noted that *Wheat's* analysis could apply to other types of conflicts claims which the defendant wants to waive (e.g., counsel's prior representation of the victim, counsel's obligation to testify as a witness at trial).

(c) Attorney Errors: Relevant Considerations. When state interference with counsel or conflicts of interests are not involved, *Strickland* required that the defendant making an ineffective assistance claim "affirmatively prove" a reasonable probability that attorney error affected the outcome of the case. The prejudice inquiry is necessary in such cases, the Court explained, because "[a]ttorney errors come in an infinite variety and are as likely to be utterly harmless in a particular case as they are to be prejudicial. They cannot be classified according to likelihood of causing prejudice."

Although the Court is correct that attorney errors are not susceptible to classification, its decisions do reveal some common threads of analysis. The factors that seem to be most important to the Court in determining whether an attorney's conduct constitutes ineffective assistance of counsel are: (1) the specificity of the ineffective assistance claim; (2) whether a "reasonable" explanation for the attorney's conduct exists (which encompasses the performance prong); (3) the extent to which the conduct affected the outcome of the case (which operationalizes the prejudice prong); and (4) the extent to which the defendant should have control of the action taken by the attorney.

(1) Specification of the error. In *United States v. Cronic*,[69] the companion case to *Strickland,* the Court strongly suggested that ineffective assistance claims based on the "overall performance" or character of the defendant will rarely succeed. In *Cronic,* the Tenth Circuit Court of Appeals had overturned a conviction for a

---

68. See, e.g., *United States v. Petz,* 764 F.2d 1390 (11th Cir.1985).

69. 466 U.S. 648, 104 S.Ct. 2039 (1984).

"check" kiting scheme after "inferring" that the defendant's counsel was ineffective. This inference was based on a number of factors, including the youth and inexperience of the attorney (whose expertise was real estate and who had never tried a jury case), and the short period of time (25 days) he had to prepare for what appeared to be a serious, complex charge involving thousands of documents. A unanimous Court reversed the Tenth Circuit's judgment, finding that while these factors "may affect what a reasonably competent attorney could be expected to have done under the circumstances, . . . none identifies circumstances that in themselves make it unlikely that respondent received the effective assistance of counsel." On remand, the Court noted, the defendant would be able to make out a claim of ineffective assistance "only by pointing to specific errors made by trial counsel."

The Court's insistence that ineffectiveness claims not rest on inferences but rather be based on findings of specific attorney error is consistent with most lower court decisions. For instance, well before *Cronic* courts usually concluded that a showing of defense counsel's general inexperience or youth, without more, is not sufficient under the Sixth Amendment.[70] Similarly, lack of experience in the trial of criminal cases has been deemed immaterial without a showing of specific prejudice.[71] A number of older cases take an identical attitude toward claims that defense counsel's effectiveness was impeded by mental illness,[72] advanced age,[73] deafness,[74] or intoxication.[75] And, as already noted, most courts are in line with *Cronic* in being unwilling to assume that late appointment, by itself, leads to a violation of the Sixth Amendment.[76]

A defendant might take a slightly different tack by arguing that he could not work with counsel given personal antagonisms or disagreements (falling short of a potential conflict of interest of the type described earlier).[77] For instance, in *Morris v. Slappy*,[78] the Ninth Circuit Court of Appeals held that the right to effective assistance would "be without substance if it did not include the right to a meaningful attorney-client relationship." But the Supreme Court's reaction to this holding, although only dictum, made clear that it would not constitutionalize such a rule: "No court could possibly guarantee that a defendant will develop the

70. See, e.g., *Spaulding v. United States*, 279 F.2d 65 (9th Cir.1960).

71. *State v. Crowe*, 190 Kan. 658, 378 P.2d 89 (1963).

72. *Hagan v. United States*, 9 F.2d 562 (8th Cir.1925).

73. *United States v. Estep*, 151 F.Supp. 668 (D.C.Tex.1957), aff'd 251 F.2d 579 (5th Cir.1958).

74. *People v. Butterfield*, 37 Cal.App. 2d 140, 99 P.2d 310 (1940).

75. *State v. Keller*, 57 N.D. 645, 223 N.W. 698 (1929).

76. See § 32.04(a)(1).

77. See § 32.04(b).

78. 461 U.S. 1, 103 S.Ct. 1610 (1983).

kind of rapport with his attorney—privately retained or provided by the public—that the Court of Appeals thought part of the Sixth Amendment guarantee to counsel." A poor attorney-client relationship, without proof of specific instances of deficient conduct, is unlikely to lead to reversal.

(2) Existence of a reasonable explanation. Assuming a specific "error" is identified, it will still not violate the performance prong of *Strickland* if there is a "reasonable" explanation for the action. Occasionally, there will be no such explanation. For instance, on remand in *Cronic*, the Tenth Circuit found that the Sixth Amendment was violated because counsel's failure to argue lack of intent, the one obvious defense to the check-kiting charge, could not be explained under any rational strategy.[79] Similarly, in *Kimmelman v. Morrison* [80] the Supreme Court found the incompetence prong of *Strickland* violated by counsel's "total failure" to conduct pretrial discovery. This failure prevented him from finding out about a warrantless search of his client's apartment until trial, at which time it was too late, under New Jersey rules, to make a motion for suppression. Because counsel could offer only "implausible," non-strategic, explanations for the lack of preparation (e.g., counsel said he thought the state was obligated to provide the defense with all inculpatory information), the Court found it "unreasonable."

In the majority of the Court's decisions, however, either a reasonable explanation was offered for the alleged "error" or the Court was able to hypothesize one. In *Strickland,* for instance, the Court came up with its own explanation for why, despite significant evidence of mental dysfunction in the defendant, counsel failed to obtain a psychiatric examination and develop and present character evidence at the defendant's capital sentencing proceeding. The Court speculated that, given the strength of the case against the defendant, trial counsel "could reasonably surmise" that such evidence would have been "of little help." Further, defendant's testimony at the earlier plea colloquy had revealed the substance of what there was to know about his emotional problems; restricting character testimony to this information ensured that contrary psychological evidence, and the defendant's criminal history (which counsel had successfully moved to exclude) would not be introduced by the state. Similarly, in *Burger v. Kemp,*[81] the failure to discover and introduce evidence of the defendant's personality and unhappy childhood at a capital sentencing proceeding was not ineffective assistance

79. *United States v. Cronic*, 839 F.2d 1401 (10th Cir.1988).

80. 477 U.S. 365, 106 S.Ct. 2574 (1986).

81. 483 U.S. 776, 107 S.Ct. 3114 (1987).

when based on a conclusion that such evidence may have harmed the defendant as much as it may have helped him.[82]

A different type of explanation surfaced in *Hill v. Lockhart*,[83] involving counsel's advice to plead guilty. There the majority found that the defendant was not prejudiced by his attorney's failure to discover, prior to the plea, a previous felony conviction, which under state law acted to postpone defendant's parole eligibility. Two members of the Court joined in the decision on the ground that the attorney's failure was not defective performance in any event, since the defendant had signed a "plea statement" indicating he had no prior felonies and the attorney was entitled to rely on this information. This type of reasoning is buttressed by *Strickland*, which stated that counsel need not pursue a particular line of investigation when the "defendant has given counsel reason to believe that [such action] would be fruitless or even harmful."

The reasonableness of the attorney's conduct has also been construed in connection with appellate counsel. In *Smith v. Murray*,[84] the Court found that counsel's failure to advance a particular claim on appeal (later upheld by the Supreme Court) was not ineffective assistance. The fact that an amicus brief submitted at the time of appeal had focused on that claim and that other courts had recognized similar claims was not dispositive. Quoting from *Strickland*, the Court emphasized that "[a] fair assessment of attorney performance requires that every effort be made to eliminate the distorting effects of hindsight, to reconstruct the circumstances of counsel's challenged conduct, and to evaluate the conduct from counsel's perspective at the time." Here counsel had researched a number of issues and decided that the claim in question was not supportable under prevailing law, and had vigorously argued several other issues on the appeal. *Smith* illustrates *Strickland's* conclusion that, when counsel conducts a reasonable investigation and decides to advance only one of several arguments, his choice is "virtually unchallengeable."

Pre-*Strickland* cases, decided under *McMann's* "performance-of-attorneys-in-criminal cases" standard, provide additional examples of how the Court evaluates the performance standard. In *Parker v. North Carolina*,[85] the Court found that a failure to challenge the voluntariness of a confession did not constitute ineffective assistance of counsel. Although there had been con-

---

82. See also, *Darden v. Wainwright,* 477 U.S. 168, 106 S.Ct. 2464 (1986) (reliance solely on a plea of mercy at sentencing explicable by a desire to prevent prosecution use of prior criminal record, an unfavorable psychiatric report, and information about defendant's mistress).

83. 474 U.S. 52, 106 S.Ct. 366 (1985).

84. 477 U.S. 527, 106 S.Ct. 2661 (1986).

85. 397 U.S. 790, 90 S.Ct. 1458 (1970).

flicting evidence as to whether the interrogating officers had given the defendant food, promised "help" if he confessed, and denied him access to a lawyer, the defendant told his lawyer that he had not been threatened or promised help and that he had not been frightened during the interrogation. The Court stated:

> [E]ven, if Parker's counsel was wrong in his assessment of Parker's confession, it does not follow that his error was sufficient to render the plea unintelligent and entitle Parker to disavow his admission in open court that he committed the offense with which he was charged. Based on the facts of record relating to Parker's confession and guilty plea . . ., we think the advice he received was well within the range of competence required of attorneys representing defendants in criminal cases.

A second pre-*Strickland* case, *Tollett v. Henderson*,[86] involved counsel's failure to challenge the racial composition of the grand jury which indicted the defendant, who pleaded guilty on counsel's advice. Although, as the dissent pointed out, there was strong evidence suggesting that counsel was not even aware that such a claim could have been made, the Court found that the attorney's omission may have been dictated by tactical considerations:

> Often the interests of the accused are not advanced by challenges that would only delay the inevitable date of prosecution, or by contesting all guilt. A prospect of plea bargaining, the expectation or hope of a lesser sentence, or the convincing nature of the evidence against the accused are considerations that might well suggest the advisability of a guilty plea without elaborate consideration of whether pleas in abatement, such as unconstitutional grand jury selection procedures, might be factually supported.

This language suggests that the Court is willing to go to some length in providing reasons supporting counsel's allegedly deficient conduct.[87]

Several lower court decisions provide examples of similar analysis, applied to attorney conduct which, on its face, appeared inadequate. In *DeCoster III*,[88] for instance, the court refused to find ineffective assistance when defense counsel, among other things, did not interview the three principal prosecution witnesses prior to trial and waived opening statement. It pointed out that defense counsel had heard one of the three witnesses at the

---

86. 411 U.S. 258, 93 S.Ct. 1602 (1973).

87. The Court may have also been influenced by the rather dubious assumption that some attorneys would be willing to be labelled "ineffective" if failing to raise a grand jury challenge would allow retrial after conviction. See § 33.03(c).

88. 624 F.2d 196 (D.C.Cir.1979), discussed in § 32.03(a).

preliminary hearing describe what he and the other two witnesses saw at the time of the offense, and thus may not have felt it necessary to conduct personal interviews. It also called waiver of opening statement "a tactical decision." In *United States v. Clayborne*,[89] defense counsel did not interview the sole eyewitness to a murder and did not cross-examine her at trial, in part because he believed that further testimony might give a factual basis to support a charge of attempted robbery, needed for a felony murder conviction. The court found no ineffective assistance on these facts, noting that the defendants were convicted of second degree murder rather than felony murder. And in *State v. Ondrak*,[90] counsel's failure at sentencing to ask for probation or make any other recommendation with respect to a burglary defendant's sentence did not constitute inadequate representation, because the defendant had violated probation before and his attorney might have felt that arguing for probation would be futile, as well as "offensive" to the sentencing judge.

In contrast, a number of lower court cases have found defective performance when there is no reasonable explanation for the attorney's conduct. Many of them, like *Kimmelman*, are bottomed on a finding that counsel's ignorance of the law was inexcusable. For instance, attorney error has been found when counsel did not challenge the legality of a search that produced heroin because he was unaware of the rule that allowed him to do so;[91] counsel failed to object to illegally seized evidence because he misread the leading case on the issue;[92] counsel advised a plea of guilty to the charge of forgery, unaware that under the controlling law the defendant could be prosecuted only under a statute proscribing misuse of credit cards, which carried a lighter penalty;[93] and "counsel induced the defendant to plead guilty on the *patently erroneous* advice that if he does not do so he may be subject to a sentence six times more severe than that which the law would really allow."[94]

A number of other cases finding inadequate performance focus on the fact that counsel, although apparently knowledgeable about the law, failed to perform basic investigation or make obvious arguments for no apparent reason. For instance, in *Brooks v. Texas*,[95] the court found attorney error when counsel did not uncover prior commitments of the defendant to three different mental institutions, and consequently failed to raise an insanity

---

89. 509 F.2d 473 (D.C.Cir.1974).

90. 186 Neb. 838, 186 N.W.2d 727 (1971).

91. *People v. Ibarra*, 60 Cal.2d 460, 34 Cal.Rptr. 863, 386 P.2d 487 (1963).

92. *People v. Coffman*, 2 Cal.App.3d 681, 82 Cal.Rptr. 782 (1969).

93. *In re Williams*, 1 Cal.3d 168, 81 Cal.Rptr. 784, 460 P.2d 984 (1969).

94. *Cooks v. United States*, 461 F.2d 530 (5th Cir.1972).

95. 381 F.2d 619 (5th Cir.1967).

defense. And in *Henderson v. Sargent,*[96] the court found that there was "no reasonable professional judgment" that would support trial counsel's failure to interview three individuals who "were among the last to see the victim alive" and who all had possible motivations to commit the murder with which his client was charged.

(3) The prejudice inquiry. Of course, after *Strickland,* even if attorney error is found, there must also be a "reasonable probability" that it affected the outcome of the case. For instance, while finding that there was no excuse for the attorney's ignorance of state discovery rules in *Kimmelman,* the Court remanded the case for an inquiry into whether the unargued Fourth Amendment claim was meritorious and, if so, whether exclusion of the evidence would have affected the outcome of the trial. This resolution of the case makes clear that a lack of prejudice will defeat an ineffective assistance of counsel claim even if there is no reasonable explanation for the attorney's act or omission.

Furthermore, the *Strickland* majority emphasized that a reviewing court need not always determine whether an attorney's performance was defective before evaluating prejudice: "If it is easier to dispose of an ineffectiveness claim on the ground of lack of sufficient prejudice, which we expect will often be so, that course should be followed." In *Hill,* for example, the majority saw no need to address whether the attorney's failure to discover the defendant's prior conviction was error, since it found there was no "reasonable probability" that the defendant's "ignorance" about the conviction and its effect on his parole eligibility would have changed the decision to plead guilty.

Note that, under the Court's cases, the converse of *Strickland's* proposition is not true: a clear showing of prejudice does not eliminate the requirement that it be caused by attorney conduct that is "deficient." This fact is illustrated by *Smith v. Murray,* where, it will be remembered, the attorney failed to raise a claim on appeal that probably would have resulted in reversal. Despite the impact of the attorney's omission on the outcome of the case, the Court found, as noted above, that it did not constitute unreasonable behavior under the performance prong of *Strickland,* and thus did not violate the Sixth Amendment.[97]

(4) The defendant's control over the decision. In *Faretta v. California,*[98] the Supreme Court held that defendants have the right to represent themselves. This holding suggested that, even

96. 926 F.2d 706 (8th Cir.1991).

97. But see, *Bouchillon v. Collins,* 907 F.2d 589 (5th Cir.1990) (counsel's failure to investigate the defendant's incompetency to plead, despite clear evidence that the defendant had a clinically recognized mental disorder, demonstrated prejudice, obviating the need to determine whether error occurred).

98. 422 U.S. 806, 95 S.Ct. 2525 (1975), discussed in § 31.04(b).

when represented, defendants should have some control of their case. Indeed, construed broadly, the *Faretta* principle would mean that an attorney commits "error" anytime he acts against his client's wishes or fails to consult him on a particular decision. But in *Jones v. Barnes*,[99] the Court rejected this interpretation of *Faretta*. At the same time, it indicated that an attorney's failure to follow his client's wishes on certain "fundamental" issues might violate the Sixth Amendment.

The specific holding in *Jones* was that a defendant cannot compel his attorney to argue particular claims on appeal, even claims which are concededly "nonfrivolous," when the attorney has decided, in the exercise of his professional judgment, not to present them to the court. A contrary finding, ruled the majority, would undermine counsel's ability to choose the most effective arguments. Justice Brennan's dissent contended that *Faretta* allowed only those "restrictions on individual autonomy and dignity . . . necessary to vindicate the State's interest in a speedy, effective prosecution;" thus, the appellate attorney's role should be limited to giving advice on appropriate arguments, which the defendant is free to accept or reject. But the majority rejected this conclusion, reasoning that counsel's decision to override the defendant's wishes, "far from being evidence of incompetence, is the hallmark of effective appellate advocacy."

Jones appears to hold that most tactical aspects of the defense are the attorney's domain. In particular, decisions about what claims to investigate and pursue—the focus of virtually all of the "attorney error" cases discussed to this point—are ultimately the attorney's, and thus cannot form the basis for an ineffective assistance claim unless they are unreasonable and affected the outcome of the case. Although he did not go as far as the majority, even Brennan, in his *Jones* dissent, conceded that defense counsel must be given "decisive authority" in making "the hundreds of decisions that must be made quickly in the course of a trial."

However, in a footnote, the majority in *Jones* also quoted approvingly from the ABA Model Rules of Professional Conduct to the effect that the client should hold the ultimate authority to make certain "fundamental" decisions, such as whether to plead guilty, waive the right to jury trial, testify on his own behalf, or forego an appeal.[1] It is not entirely clear why these decisions might be considered "fundamental," and other decisions, such as whether to raise a certain defense, call a particular witness, or request the exclusion of the public from trial, are not. The best explanation may be that the former decisions are thought to go

99. 463 U.S. 745, 103 S.Ct. 3308   **1.** Rule 2.1(a).
(1983).

beyond pure "strategy" and involve issues that are so closely tied to a person's sense of autonomy that the defendant should be allowed to make them regardless of their tactical impact.[2] In any event, *Jones'* dictum may mean that when an attorney fails either to discover or follow a defendant's wishes with respect to such a "fundamental" decision, he automatically commits error.[3]

Subsequent Court decisions, involving attorney incompetence in connection with raising an appeal (one of the four "fundamental" issues noted in *Jones*), indicate that this type of error may also be presumptively prejudicial. In *Evitts v. Lucey,*[4] counsel failed to file a "statement of appeal" along with his motion for an appeal, an omission which resulted in the dismissal of the action and was presumably not in accordance with the defendant's wishes. The Court found, 7–2, that this failure constituted ineffective assistance, without attempting to assess the validity of the foreclosed claims. The majority recognized that its ruling might prevent the state from enforcing a wide range of procedural rules, but stated that "[a] State may not extinguish [the right to appeal] because another right of the appellant—the right to effective assistance of counsel—has been violated."

Although *Evitts* intimated that incompetence of the type involved in that case is presumptively prejudicial, it explicitly avoided so deciding, given the state's concession in that case that the attorney's failure had a "drastic" impact on the defendant. In *Penson v. Ohio,*[5] the Court addressed the prejudice issue more directly. There, the Court considered whether either the harmless error doctrine or the prejudice prong of *Strickland* should apply when the rule announced in *Anders v. California*[6] is breached. *Anders* required that appellate counsel who wish to withdraw from an appeal in the belief it would be frivolous must nonetheless file a brief noting possible arguments. In *Penson,* the Court held, 8–1, that failure to file an "*Anders* brief" requires reversal of the appellate court judgment even when the appellate court scrutinized the record and had the benefit of briefs from co-defendants' counsel. Justice Stevens, writing for the Court, stated: "Because the fundamental importance of the assistance of counsel does not cease as the prosecutorial process moves from the trial to the

2. See, Friedman, "Personal Responsibility in a Professional System," 27 Cath.U.L.Rev. 191 (1978).

3. Note, however, that the defendant's wishes with respect to "fundamental" decisions may be limited in some ways. For instance, in *Nix v. Whiteside,* 475 U.S. 157, 106 S.Ct. 988 (1986), discussed in § 32.04(b)(3), the Court held that, while the defendant

has the right to testify, he does not have the right to testify "falsely" and the attorney may take steps to prevent such testimony.

4. 469 U.S. 387, 105 S.Ct. 830 (1985).

5. 488 U.S. 75, 109 S.Ct. 346 (1988).

6. 386 U.S. 738, 87 S.Ct. 1396 (1967), discussed in § 29.02(c).

appellate stage, the presumption of prejudice must extend as well to the denial of counsel on appeal."

This language may require an ineffective assistance finding any time appeal, and thus representation by an attorney on appeal, is prevented by an attorney's act or omission. If a Sixth Amendment violation occurs when a presumptively "frivolous" appeal is thwarted by counsel's misconduct, then presumably one also occurs when a non-frivolous appeal is prevented through a procedural error by the attorney. Moreover, if prejudice is not presumed in such a situation, the reviewing court (usually a federal habeas court) would be placed in the awkward position of having to determine whether counsel's error affected the "outcome" of the case, by prematurely judging the validity of appellate claims which might well be based on state law.

Of course, even if this reading of *Penson* is correct, the reasoning in that case is tied to the special context of appellate counsel, and does not necessarily imply anything with respect to attorney conduct regarding other "fundamental" decisions, such as whether to plead guilty, waive jury trial or testify. But the very fact that these decisions are considered "fundamental" may require a presumption of prejudice when they are made without the defendant's voluntary and intelligent consent.

32.05 Methods of Improving Representation

In rejecting a "categorical" approach to ineffective assistance claims, the Supreme Court's opinion in *Strickland* emphasized that "the purpose of the effective assistance guarantee is not to improve the quality of legal representation." At the same time, it added that this goal is "of considerable importance to the legal system." Of particular concern is the quality of representation provided the indigent, who are often saddled with court appointed attorneys with little knowledge of the criminal system, or public defenders with little experience of any kind.

To rectify this situation, various proposals have been made. For instance, several commentators have argued that inadequate representation could be greatly reduced by creating a separate criminal bar. One proposal advocates the following measures: (1) a special examination dealing with criminal procedure, evidence, and trial tactics; (2) previous misdemeanor experience as a prerequisite to representing a defendant in a felony case; (3) providing counsel with a checklist of functions that he must perform preparatory to a trial or guilty plea; (4) increased compensation for appointed attorneys; and (5) limitations on the number of cases public defender offices may deal with each year.[7]

7. Finer, "Ineffective Assistance of Counsel," 58 Cornell L.Rev. 1077 (1973).

Several other proposals might supplement, or provide alternatives to, the creation of a separate bar.   For instance, in his dissent in *United States v. DeCoster III*,[8] Judge Bazelon suggested that "[b]efore trial—or before a guilty plea is accepted—defense counsel could submit an investigative checklist certifying that he has conducted a complete investigation and reviewing the steps he has taken in pretrial preparation, including what records were obtained, which witnesses were interviewed, when the defendant was consulted, and what motions were filed."   Bazelon believed that this "worksheet" would "heighten defense counsel's sensitivity to the need for adequate investigation," which, together with judicial oversight of the attorney's conduct at trial, would prevent deprivation of constitutional rights.   To the majority's argument that this intrusive inquiry might "tear the fabric of the adversary system," Bazelon responded "for so very many indigent defendants, the adversary system is already in shreds."   Another proposal is to impose immediate sanctions on attorneys whose assistance has been found ineffective.[9]   Additionally, defendants who are unable to obtain appellate or habeas relief due to a failure to meet the prejudice prong under *Strickland* could be encouraged to sue attorneys under a "malpractice" standard, which does not require a prejudice showing.[10]

Of course, the latter type of suit could not be brought under § 1983, since that avenue of relief is only available for a *constitutional* violation,[11] which would require a showing of prejudice. Even if prejudice could be shown, however, the courts have restricted § 1983 actions against defense attorneys.   The Fourth Circuit has held that court-appointed attorneys, in the performance of their duties, enjoy absolute immunity from such suits.[12] And the Supreme Court has held that public defenders also enjoy absolute immunity from suit under § 1983,[13] except when the attorney has intentionally conspired with state officials to deprive the defendant of federal constitutional rights.[14]

On the other hand, at least one court has recognized the viability of injunctive relief under § 1983 designed to improve representation.   *Luckey v. Harris*[15] involved a suit asking for various changes in Georgia's system for appointing counsel, alleging that "inadequate resources, delays in the appointment of counsel, pressure on attorneys to hurry their clients' case to trial or to enter a guilty plea, and inadequate supervision," denied

---

8.   624 F.2d 196 (D.C.Cir.1976).

9.   Bines, "Remedying Ineffective Representation in Criminal Cases: Departures from Habeas Corpus," 50 Va. L.Rev. 927 (1973).

10.   Id.

11.   See § 2.05(a)(3).

12.   *Minns v. Paul*, 542 F.2d 899 (4th Cir.1976).

13.   *Polk County v. Dodson*, 454 U.S. 312, 102 S.Ct. 445 (1981).

14.   *Tower v. Glover*, 467 U.S. 914, 104 S.Ct. 2820 (1984).

15.   860 F.2d 1012 (11th Cir.1988).

indigent criminal defendants their Sixth Amendment, Eighth Amendment and due process rights. The district court dismissed the suit for failure to state a claim upon which relief could be granted, in part because the plaintiffs did not allege and prove the "future inevitability of ineffective assistance" under the state system. But the Eleventh Circuit reversed and remanded, concluding that even though the alleged deficiencies might not inevitably affect the outcome of the plaintiffs' trials (and therefore would not result in prejudice to them), they might still routinely lead to poor attorney performance and thus cause "ineffectiveness" cognizable under the Sixth Amendment. It further noted that *Strickland's* deferential scrutiny of ineffective assistance claims derived in large part from concerns that a more exacting standard would reduce finality, create post-trial burdens that would discourage counsel from accepting cases, and diminish the independence of counsel, considerations which do not apply when only prospective relief is being sought.

32.06 Conclusion

The Sixth Amendment right to effective assistance of counsel can be summarized as follows:

(1) The right attaches only at proceedings at which the right to counsel attaches. Thus, for instance, there is no right to effective assistance of counsel at discretionary appeals or post-conviction proceedings. At those proceedings at which the right attaches, both retained and appointed counsel must be effective.

(2) To establish an ineffective assistance claim, the defendant must normally show: (a) that counsel's performance was so deficient that he violated his duties to avoid conflicts of interest, consult with the defendant on important decisions, keep the defendant informed of important developments, and bring to bear such skill and knowledge as will render the trial a reliable adversarial testing process; and (b) that there is a reasonable probability that, but for counsel's unprofessional errors, the result of the proceeding would have been different.

(3) Prejudice, as defined in 2(b) above, is presumed when: (a) the government denies or constructively denies counsel to the defendant; (b) the government interferes with counsel's traditionally recognized roles, such as conducting cross-examination, conferring with his client, or making closing arguments; (c) the trial court fails to inquire into a conflict of interest which it knows or should have known existed; (d) the defendant can show the existence of an actual conflict between his legitimate interests and his attorney's interests which adversely affected his attorney's performance; and (e) the attorney overrides the defendant's decision respecting fundamental issues such as whether to plead

guilty, waive the jury, testify, or appeal. In all other cases, the defendant must show prejudice, caused by a specific act or omission on the part of the attorney for which there is no reasonable explanation.

(4) Methods of improving representation beyond that afforded by the Sixth Amendment include creation of a separate criminal defense bar, performance checklists, more vigorous judicial oversight, sanctions and civil suits against attorneys who commit non-prejudicial error, and injunctive actions designed to correct systemic deficiencies.

BIBLIOGRAPHY

American Bar Association. Advisory Committee on the Prosecution and Defense Functions. Standards Relating to the Prosecution Function and the Defense Function. New York: American Bar Association, 1970.

Appel, Brent R. The Limited Impact of Nix v. Whiteside on Attorney-Client Relations. 136 U.Pa.L.Rev. 1413 (1988).

Atkins, Burton M. and Emily W. Boyle. Prisoner Satisfaction with Defense Counsel. 12 Crim.L.Bull. 427 (1976).

Burger, Vivian O. The Supreme Court and Defense Counsel: Old Roads, New Paths—A Dead End? 86 Colum.L.Rev. 9 (1986).

Chused, Richard H. *Faretta* and the Personal Defense: The Role of a Represented Defendant in Trial Tactics. 65 Cal.L.Rev. 636 (1977).

Geer, John S. Conflicts of Interest and the Professional Responsibilities of the Defense Attorney. 62 Minn.L.Rev. 119 (1978).

Genego, William J. The Future of Effective Assistance of Counsel: Performance Standards and Competent Representation. 22 Am.Crim.L.Rev. 181 (1984).

Goodpaster, Gary. The Trial for Life: Effective Assistance of Counsel in Death Penalty Cases. 58 N.Y.U.L.Rev. 299 (1983).

Klein, Richard. The Emperor Gideon Has No Clothes: The Empty Promise of the Constitutional Right to Effective Assistance of Counsel. 13 Hasting Const.L.Q. 625 (1987).

Levine, Barbara R. Preventing Defense Counsel Error—An Analysis of Some Ineffective Assistance of Counsel Claims and Their Implications for Professional Regulation. 15 U.Tol.L. Rev. 1275 (1984).

Lowenthal, Gary T. Joint Representation in Criminal Cases: A Critical Appraisal. 64 Va.L.Rev. 939 (1978).

Rotatori, Arthur J. *Decoster III*: New Issues in Ineffective Assistance of Counsel. 71 J.Crim.L. & Criminol. 275 (1980).

Simon, William H. The Ideology of Advocacy: Procedural Justice and Professional Ethics. 1978 Wis.L.Rev. 30 (1978).

Smithburn, Eric J. and Teresa L. Springman. Effective Assistance of Counsel: In Quest of a Uniform Standard of Review. 17 Wake Forest L.Rev. 497 (1981).

Strazella, James A. Ineffective Assistance of Counsel Claims: New Uses, New Problems. 19 Ariz.L.Rev. 443 (1977).

Tague, Peter W. Multiple Representation and Conflicts of Interest in Criminal Cases. 67 Geo.L.J. 1075 (1979).

Waltz, Jon R. Inadequacy of Trial Defense Representation as a Ground for Post-conviction Relief in Criminal Cases. 59 Nw. U.L.Rev. 289 (1964).

Wanat, Daniel E. Conflicts of Interest in Criminal Cases and the Right of Effective Assistance of Counsel—The Need for Change. 10 Rut.-Cam.L.J. 57 (1978).

Part H

THE RELATIONSHIP BETWEEN THE FEDERAL AND STATE COURTS

As the contents of this book attest, since the 1950s the Supreme Court has increasingly focused its attention on the substantive constitutional rights of the criminally accused. But a substantive right is of no value unless its possessor has a forum in which to vindicate it. As the Warren Court expanded the scope of the Bill of Rights, it became clear that the state courts, which did not always agree with the new federal standards and were often opposed to federal intervention in the area of criminal procedure, could effectively nullify the Court's work by failing to provide a fair assessment of the newly created rights. Thus the ability of the state criminal defendant to obtain review in federal court became a pressing concern. Chapter Thirty-Three is devoted to the issue of when federal relief should be granted to such defendants.

While many state courts in the 1960's were reluctant to enforce the standards announced by the Warren Court, more recently a countertrend has emerged. As the post-Warren Court slowed the extension of federal constitutional rights, some state courts have rejected its pronouncements by interpreting their state constitutions to require more precise procedures than the federally-announced constitutional minimum. Chapter Thirty-Four analyzes this modern state court reaction to the retrenchment of the post-Warren Court.

902

Chapter Thirty-Three

FEDERAL HABEAS CORPUS: THE CLOSING DOOR

33.01 Introduction

Generally, a state criminal defendant can gain access to the federal courts only when an error of federal constitutional dimension is alleged. Such access can be achieved, after appeal through the state system, in either of two ways. Either the defendant can petition the Supreme Court for direct review of the alleged constitutional errors,[1] or he can petition a United States district court to issue a "writ of habeas corpus," a "collateral" remedy challenging the legitimacy of the detention.[2] The tremendous number of criminal cases generated each year prevents direct review by the Supreme Court from being an effective remedy for state prisoners. The Court's entire criminal docket consists of from twenty to forty cases in each term,[3] which is an extremely small percentage of the total number of cases decided by the state supreme courts. Thus, the only realistic access to further federal review of state court decisions is through the vehicle of habeas corpus petitions to the lower federal courts.

The writ of habeas corpus has a long history. It appears to have originated in thirteenth century England as a means of ensuring that a party would appear before the court; literally, "habeas corpus" means "you have the body."[4] During the fifteenth and sixteenth centuries, in the midst of the common law courts' struggle to assert power, it developed into a device for challenging the jurisdiction of another court to detain a person.[5] But it was not until the seventeenth century that the "Great Writ," as Blackstone called it,[6] became a vehicle for challenging arbitrary confinements by the Crown. Under the Habeas Corpus Act of 1679, Parliament attempted to undercut the king's persistent detention of persons in the absence of probable cause by giving the courts statutory authority to recognize the writ. Although the Act specifically dealt only with arrested persons (rath-

1. See § 29.01.

2. As used in this chapter, the "writ of habeas corpus" refers to the writ of habeas corpus *as subjiciendum*, which examines the legality of detentions, and not other habeas corpus writs. See *Fay v. Noia*, 372 U.S. 391, 83 S.Ct. 822 (1963).

3. In the 1976 Term, for example, of the 142 cases disposed of with a full opinion, the Court decided 14 state criminal cases and 9 habeas corpus cases involving state prisoners. "The Supreme Court, 1976 Term," 91 Harv.L. Rev. 70, 299–301.

4. "Developments in the Law—Federal Habeas Corpus," 83 Harvard L.Rev. 1038, 1042 (1970).

5. Id. at 1042–43.

6. 3 Blackstone Commentaries at 129.

er than those who had been convicted), it appears that the courts used the writ to release convicted individuals as well, at least when the detaining court lacked jurisdiction.[7]

In the United States, most colonies recognized the writ, and the United States Constitution specifically provided that the "privilege of the Writ of Habeas Corpus shall not be suspended." [8] However, the Habeas Clause was probably meant to refer only to the suspension of habeas in *state* courts for *federal* prisoners (virtually all of whom, at that time, were kept in state prisons).[9] Thus, the more important early development in American habeas law was the federal Judiciary Act of 1789,[10] which provided that *federal* courts could issue the writ for federal prisoners. Nearly eight decades later, Congress enacted the Habeas Corpus Act of 1867,[11] which authorized federal courts to issue a writ of habeas corpus in "all cases where any person may be restrained of his or her liberty in violation of the constitution, or of any treaty or law of the United States." This language extended the federal writ to state prisoners as well.

The modern successor to the Act of 1867, found in 28 U.S.C.A. §§ 2241–2255, continues to grant the federal writ to "any prisoner," who is "in custody in violation of the Constitution or laws or treaties of the United States." [12] But the congressional enactments are otherwise silent as to the substantive scope of the writ. The statutes' provisions concerning procedures connected with the writ are only slightly more detailed. While federal law prohibits "abuse of the writ," [13] requires exhaustion of state remedies before it may be used,[14] and provides that a state court's findings with respect to findings of fact are "presumed to be correct," [15] the precise reach of these provisions has been left up to the courts.

In construing these provisions, the Supreme Court has fluctuated in its approach. The history of the writ up to the 1970's reflects a constant expansion of its scope, to the point where it became available to virtually any prisoner asserting a constitutional claim that had not been deliberately waived at trial or on direct review. Since that time, however, the Court has significantly reduced the availability of the writ, both substantively and procedurally. In the course of doing so, it has sought to reinvigorate state systems of review as the final arbiter of most federal

---

7. *Bushell's Case,* 124 Eng.Rep. 1006 (C.P.1670).

8. U.S. Const., Art. I, § 9, cl. 2.

9. W. Duker, A Constitutional History of Habeas Corpus 129 (1980).

10. 1 Stat. 81–82 (1789).

11. 14 Stat. 385 (1867).

12. 28 U.S.C.A. § 2241(c)(3).

13. Id. § 2244.

14. Id. § 2254(b)(c).

15. Id. § 2254(d).

constitutional claims, a development which has been dubbed the "New Federalism." [16]

The member of the Court who most vigorously pushed for a broad, easily pursued writ of habeas corpus was Justice Brennan. In *Sanders v. United States,*[17] for instance, he stated:

> Conventional notions of finality of litigation have no place where life or liberty is at stake and infringement of constitutional rights is alleged. If "government [is] always [to] be accountable to the judiciary for a man's imprisonment," access to the courts on habeas must not be thus impeded.

Along the same lines, in *Kaufman v. United States,*[18] he argued that federal habeas review of both federal and state court convictions is necessary to provide "adequate protection of constitutional rights."

When a state (as opposed to a federal) conviction was involved, the Warren Court cited additional reasons for expanding federal review. In *Kaufman,* for instance, the Court stated that "federal courts [should] have the 'last say' with respect to questions of federal law." Further, Brennan later asserted, "[s]tate judges popularly elected may have difficulty resisting popular pressures not experienced by federal judges given lifetime tenure designed to immunize them from such influences." [19] Others have pointed to differences in the means of selection, salary, workload, and attitudes of federal and state judges as reasons for entrusting the ultimate decision about constitutional issues to federal judges.[20] Undoubtedly underlying these arguments was the fear that, without federal review of state decisions, the impact of the "revolution" in criminal procedure that occurred during the 1960's would be blunted in many states.

The post-Warren Court's restriction of access to the federal courts has been fueled by several countering concerns. Perhaps foremost among these is a desire for "finality." As Justice O'Connor stated, convictions that are reversed on habeas can exact significant costs on society, since "[p]assage of time, erosion of memory, and dispersion of witnesses may render retrial difficult, even impossible." [21] Further, according to Justice Powell, open-ended collateral review tends to distract prisoners from seeking rehabilitation, and undermines society's "psychological" desire to

16. See, e.g., Michael, "The 'New Federalism' and the Burger Court's Deference to the States in Federal Habeas Proceedings," 64 Iowa L.Rev. 233 (1979).

17. 373 U.S. 1, 83 S.Ct. 1068 (1963).

18. 394 U.S. 217, 89 S.Ct. 1068 (1969).

19. *Stone v. Powell,* 428 U.S. 465, 96 S.Ct. 3037 (1976) (Brennan, J., dissenting).

20. See, e.g., Neuborne, "The Myth of Parity," 90 Harv.L.Rev. 1105 (1977).

21. *Engle v. Isaac,* 456 U.S. 107, 102 S.Ct. 1558 (1982).

have a final conclusion to criminal matters.[22]   A related limiting rationale cited by the post-Warren Court is efficiency.   Habeas review places a heavy burden on the federal courts; in 1970, for instance, there were over 9,000 federal habeas petitions filed.[23] Consideration of these claims, Justice Powell has noted, detracts from the federal courts' ability to decide other issues, yet rarely results in reversal of an earlier decision.[24]

Focusing on the claim that federal review of state cases is an important means of ensuring quality justice, the post-Warren Court has two responses.   First, it manifests greater faith in the capabilities of state court judges.   As the Court stated in *Stone v. Powell*,[25] "[d]espite differences in institutional environment and the unsympathetic attitude to federal constitutional claims of some state judges in years past, we are unwilling to assume that there now exists a general lack of appropriate sensitivity to constitutional rights in the trial and appellate courts of the several States."   Similarly, Justice O'Connor, a former state appellate judge, has noted (in an article written before she became a justice) that many state judges are not elected, thus reducing their sensitivity to "majoritarian pressures."   She also asserted that many lawyers see "no great difference in the quality of judges or justice between the state and federal courts." [26]   The second response to the argument that federal courts must be the ultimate arbiter of federal rights has been an emphasis on the concept of "comity," or respect for the judgment of state courts.   According to Justice O'Connor, this concern is not just symbolic.   She has argued that federal review (by a single-judge district court) of state appellate decisions undermines "morale" at the state level; this in turn leaves state judges less willing to enforce constitutional rights, to the detriment of the majority of state litigants, who never seek federal habeas review.[27]

22. *Stone v. Powell*, 428 U.S. 465, 96 S.Ct. 3037 (1976).

23. "Federal Habeas Corpus and Its Reform: An Empirical Analysis," 13 Rutgers L.J. 675, 677 n. 2 (1982). Note that, by 1980, after the post-Warren Court had significantly reduced the scope of the writ, the number of petitions was still slightly over 7,000 and much of this reduction could have been due to the increased availability of § 1983 claims. Id.

24. *Schneckloth v. Bustamonte*, 412 U.S. 218, 93 S.Ct. 2041 (1973) (Powell, J., concurring).

25. 428 U.S. 465, 96 S.Ct. 3037 (1976).

26. O'Connor, "Trends in the Relationship Between the Federal and State Courts from the Perspective of a State Court Judge," 22 Wm. & Mary L.Rev. 801 (1981). The latter assertion was based on a study which showed that significantly more lawyers preferred to file their claims in state rather than federal court. However, the survey also showed that although 125 lawyers saw no difference between the quality of state and federal judges, 95 felt that federal judges were more qualified, while only 25 felt the opposite. Id. at 817.

27. Id. at 801.

This chapter discusses how these various perspectives on the writ of habeas corpus have influenced its substantive and procedural scope. Specifically, it will address: (1) the types of claims which may be heard pursuant to the writ; (2) the extent to which claims can be foreclosed pursuant to state rules; (3) the exhaustion requirement; (4) limitations on successive petitions; (5) the custody requirement; and (6) special provisions for indigent habeas petitioners.

33.02 The Substantive Scope of the Writ

(a) From *Watkins* to *Brown:* **Expansion of the Writ.** As noted in the introduction, the common law writ of habeas corpus focused on whether the detaining court had "jurisdiction" over the defendant. This concept was given a narrow definition by Chief Justice Marshall in *Ex parte Watkins,*[28] decided in 1830. Federal habeas review was denied in that case, despite a claim that the indictment failed to state a crime, because the trial court had "general jurisdiction of the subject;" the fact that the state court's decision may have been erroneous was irrelevant.

Gradually, however, the jurisdiction concept expanded to encompass claims that were not purely "jurisdictional." In the 1879 decision of *Ex parte Siebold,*[29] for instance, the Court permitted habeas review of a conviction based on a statute alleged to be unconstitutional, despite the state court's technical jurisdiction over the matter, on the ground that a conviction based on such a law would be "not merely erroneous, but . . . illegal and void." Some 35 years later, in *Frank v. Mangum,*[30] the Court indicated that a conviction rendered by a mob-dominated tribunal was a violation of due process and subject to federal habeas review, unless the state provided an adequate post-conviction "corrective process."[31] And in *Johnson v. Zerbst,*[32] the Court held that a federal trial court's failure to provide counsel in violation of the Sixth Amendment resulted in a loss of "jurisdiction," thus allowing habeas review as a remedial measure.

Finally, in the 1942 decision of *Waley v. Johnston,*[33] the Court explicitly dispensed with jurisdictional analysis, concluding that the writ extended "to those exceptional cases where the conviction has been in disregard of the constitutional rights of the accused." However, like *Frank, Waley* limited use of the writ to those situations where it was "the only effective means of preserving his

---

28. 28 U.S. (3 Pet.) 193 (1830).

29. 100 U.S. (10 Otto) 371 (1880).

30. 237 U.S. 309, 35 S.Ct. 582 (1915).

31. In *Frank,* the Court found that such process was present and denied relief. However, in *Moore v. Dempsey,* 261 U.S. 86, 43 S.Ct. 265 (1923), it grant-ed relief, apparently on the ground that post-conviction state procedure had been inadequate.

32. 304 U.S. 458, 58 S.Ct. 1019 (1938).

33. 316 U.S. 101, 62 S.Ct. 964 (1942).

rights." This formulation appeared to give a federal habeas court discretion to hear any federal constitutional claim, but only if, to use *Frank's* phrase, the "corrective process" provided below was inadequate.

Then, in 1953, the Court decided *Brown v. Allen*,[34] which apparently eliminated the latter half of this formulation. There, the Court held that a federal habeas court could consider a jury discrimination claim and a coerced confession claim even though both had been fully litigated and rejected by the state courts. While stating that the federal court should generally accord conclusive weight to state court findings of fact (unless there was a "vital flaw" in its procedure), the Court stressed that the federal habeas court should reach its own conclusion on the law. For roughly twenty years after it was decided, *Brown* held the federal courtroom door wide open to prisoners, both state and federal,[35] who sought review of constitutional claims that had previously been raised at the trial level.[36]

(b) The Full and Fair Hearing Exception. The first inroad into the broad reach of habeas established in *Brown* came in *Stone v. Powell*.[37] There the Court held that "where the State has provided an opportunity for full and fair litigation of a Fourth Amendment claim," a federal court should not grant review of the claim. According to the Court, affording habeas review of Fourth Amendment claims would provide little benefit, at great cost. Justice Powell, writing for a six-member majority, noted first that the deterrent effect of excluding illegally seized evidence at trial is unlikely to be "enhanced" by permitting exclusion after conviction and appeal, "years after incarceration of the defendant." Nor did the Court believe that habeas review was necessary to keep state courts in line; it rejected "a basic mistrust of state courts as fair and competent forums for adjudication of constitutional rights." At the same time, habeas review undermines the government's interest in conserving judicial resources, and in promoting finality and comity. Furthermore, even a successful Fourth Amendment claim exacts a cost, because it "deflects the truthfinding process and often frees the guilty." *Stone* established, then, that adequate state process could bar certain types of claims from habeas review.

(1) The scope of the exception. *Stone* was not, however, a reversion to the pre-*Brown* rule that provision of adequate "corrective processes" by the state would bar federal habeas review of *any*

34. 344 U.S. 443, 73 S.Ct. 397 (1953).

35. In *Kaufman v. United States*, 394 U.S. 217, 89 S.Ct. 1068 (1969), the Court made clear that *Brown* extended to federal prisoners as well.

36. When the petitioner did not raise the claim at the guilt adjudication stage, a different analysis—based on the scope of procedural default—applied. See § 33.03.

37. 428 U.S. 465, 96 S.Ct. 3037 (1976).

constitutional claim.   In *Stone* itself, the Court made clear that it was only applying the "full and fair hearing" exception to Fourth Amendment petitions.   And, after *Stone,* the Court accepted jurisdiction in a number of habeas cases, involving a variety of claims, without reference to whether *Stone* applied.[38]

Moreover, three years after *Stone,* in *Jackson v. Virginia,*[39] the Court explicitly refused to apply the full and fair hearing exception to a claim alleging that a conviction was not based on proof beyond a reasonable doubt.   The Court concluded that, given its prior holding in *In re Winship*[40] requiring state prosecutions to meet the reasonable doubt burden for each essential element of the offense, a state prisoner is entitled to have a federal court determine not only "whether the jury was properly instructed but [also] whether the record evidence could reasonably support a finding of guilt beyond a reasonable doubt."   Justice Stewart's majority opinion specifically rejected application of *Stone* to this type of claim, asserting that federal courts would not be unduly burdened by such review, and that "[t]he constitutional issue presented in this case is far different from the kind of issue" present in *Stone.*

Jackson, together with *Stone,* suggested that the post-Warren Court would not apply the full and fair hearing requirement across the board, but might eventually limit federal habeas to review of claims related to the guilt of the petitioner.   But the same term as *Jackson,* the Court decided *Rose v. Mitchell,*[41] which refused to apply *Stone* to bar consideration of discrimination in the grand jury selection process, a claim unrelated to guilt.   Justice Blackmun's majority opinion distinguished equal protection petitions from Fourth Amendment claims on several grounds. First, while the latter claim focuses on police behavior, a claim concerning the operation of the grand jury system involves allegations that the *judiciary* has violated the Constitution; in this situation, the Court doubted that state courts would give the claim a full and fair hearing.   As Blackmun put it, "[t]here is a need in such cases to ensure that an independent means of obtaining review by a federal court is available on a broader basis than review only by this Court will permit."   Second, collateral review of equal protection claims is less likely to cause "friction" with state courts because it is of less recent vintage and more firmly grounded in the Constitution than the judicially created exclusion-

38. See, e.g., *Crist v. Bretz,* 437 U.S. 28, 98 S.Ct. 2156 (1978) (double jeopardy claim); *Manson v. Brathwaite,* 432 U.S. 98, 97 S.Ct. 2243 (1977) (due process photo-identification claim).

39. 443 U.S. 307, 99 S.Ct. 2781 (1979).

40. 397 U.S. 358, 90 S.Ct. 1068 (1970).

41. 443 U.S. 545, 99 S.Ct. 2993 (1979).

ary rule. Third, whereas applying the exclusionary rule at the habeas stage is unlikely to have much of a deterrent effect, the "educative" effect of quashing indictments on racial discrimination grounds "is likely to be great," and yet cost society little, because reindictment is usually possible. Finally, the Court noted that a racial discrimination claim seeks to vindicate interests that "are substantially more compelling than those at issue in *Stone.*"

Rose left the Court's approach to the substantive scope of the writ of habeas corpus unclear. Blackmun's first rationale for the holding in that case—that, for institutional reasons, state courts may not fairly adjudicate claims against the grand jury selection process—is probably the strongest. The other three reasons all rest, at bottom, on the somewhat dubious assertion that discrimination claims are inherently more important than the privacy rights protected by the Fourth Amendment. Further, the first reason is consistent with the focus in *Stone* and earlier Court cases on the quality of the state's corrective processes (although, as an empirical matter, it is not clear that state courts lack objectivity in evaluating discrimination claims lodged against the grand jury selection process). A number of other constitutional claims alleging even more direct misconduct by state court judges would presumably be reviewable on habeas under this theory.[42]

The Court's next case dealing with the substantive scope of habeas, *Kimmelman v. Morrison,*[43] did little to clear up confusion as to whether the substantive scope of the writ would focus on the guilt-relatedness of the claim, the adequacy of state corrective processes, or a mixture of the two. There defense counsel failed to seek exclusion of evidence that may have been illegally seized from the defendant's apartment. The claim on habeas was not based directly on the Fourth Amendment,[44] but rather focused on the ineffectiveness of counsel. Justice Brennan's opinion for the Court distinguished this case from *Stone* by stressing that the exclusionary rule is a judicially created right "designed to safeguard Fourth Amendment rights generally," while the Sixth Amendment right to effective assistance is a trial-related, "personal" right. Thus, the latter right is deserving of the added protection of federal review whenever it is raised. Furthermore, Brennan pointed out, prohibiting federal habeas review of such claims would often foreclose their review altogether, because defendants may not discover counsel's incompetence before state review is

---

42. See, e.g., *North Carolina v. Pearce,* 395 U.S. 711, 89 S.Ct. 2072 (1969) (vindictive sentencing by judge), discussed in § 29.02(d); *Chambers v. Mississippi,* 405 U.S. 1205, 92 S.Ct. 754 (1972) (judicial infringement of confrontation and compulsory process rights), discussed in §§ 28.05(b)(1), 28.06(b).

43. 477 U.S. 365, 106 S.Ct. 2574 (1986).

44. Given the Court's procedural default decisions, see § 33.03(c), such a claim probably would have been barred procedurally as well as substantively.

exhausted (although in *Morrison* itself, the petitioner did raise the ineffectiveness claim at both the appeal and habeas stages in state court).

Justice Brennan also rejected the state's argument that the Court's holding would emasculate *Stone* by allowing petitioners to raise Fourth Amendment claims in the guise of Sixth Amendment arguments. Brennan emphasized that the two-prong incompetence and prejudice standard for ineffective assistance, as outlined in *Strickland v. Washington*,[45] was a "rigorous" one, requiring a strong presumption of attorney competence and a strong presumption that, even if counsel's inadequacy is established, the attorney's conduct did not affect the outcome of the proceeding. Thus, for instance, a strategic decision not to assert a Fourth Amendment claim, or a concededly incompetent failure to assert such a claim that does not affect the outcome of the trial, would not amount to ineffective assistance and would not lead to reversal by a federal habeas court. In *Morrison* itself, the Court found that the attorney's failure to make the suppression motion, which apparently resulted from his ignorance of state discovery and motion rules, was incompetent. But it remanded the case for a determination as to whether the Fourth Amendment claim was meritorious and, if so, whether excluding the evidence would have affected the outcome of the trial.

Brennan's disclaimers notwithstanding, the Court's disposition of *Morrison* makes clear that, when framed as part of a Sixth Amendment violation, the validity of a Fourth Amendment claim will now have to be considered by the federal habeas court. Perhaps concerned about this undermining of *Stone,* Justice Powell, the author of that decision, wrote a concurring opinion (joined by Chief Justice Burger and Justice Rehnquist) which argued that failure to raise a Fourth Amendment claim should *never* constitute prejudice under *Strickland.* Powell contended that only if the claim underlying a Sixth Amendment petition relates to the accuracy of the guilt adjudication should a federal habeas court hear the claim.

If Powell's position is adopted, then the post-Warren Court will have made a strong move toward a guilt-related definition of the writ's substantive scope. But since six members of the Court did not join Powell's opinion in *Morrison,* this is not yet the Court's stance. Nor is *Morrison's* holding, at least on the surface, consistent with the inadequate state process approach to the writ, since, as *Morrison* itself demonstrates, full state review of an ineffective assistance claim is often available. However, to the extent Brennan is right that ineffective assistance claims tend to

45. 466 U.S. 668, 104 S.Ct. 2052 (1984), discussed in § 32.03(b).

evade discovery until after much or all of the state process is complete, *Morrison* resonates with the lack of corrective process approach. Furthermore, one might argue that, as the Court subsequently recognized in another context,[46] ineffective assistance is "imputed" to inadequate monitoring by the state courts, and is thus less likely to be fairly considered by them.

The type of claim most likely to be barred from habeas review after *Stone* is a claim arguing that the prophylactic rule established in *Miranda v. Arizona*[47] was violated. In contrast to *Jackson,* such a claim is not related to the guilt of the petitioner and, in contrast to *Rose* and *Morrison,* it does not implicate the state's judiciary. Several justices have indicated they might reach such a conclusion.[48] If so, a *Miranda* claim could be heard by a federal habeas court only as part of an ineffective assistance challenge, as in *Morrison.*

(2) Criteria for a full and fair hearing. Under *Stone,* a Fourth Amendment claim must be accorded federal habeas review only when the state fails to provide a "full and fair opportunity to litigate the claim." Whether this language is meant to be a modern version of *Frank's* relatively narrowly conceived *lack*-of-corrective-process standard is not clear.[49] Most lower courts seem to construe the phrase more broadly than *Frank's* mob-domination fact pattern might suggest. For instance, in *Lee v. Winston,*[50] the Fourth Circuit permitted federal review of a surgical attempt to obtain a bullet because the state court had given defense counsel only three days to prepare for the pre-surgery hearing, and had repeatedly refused to grant counsel's requests for a continuance to obtain expert medical assistance, despite his "obviously diligent effort to obtain" such assistance.[51]

However, assuming adequate process, the mere fact that the state court erroneously applied the Fourth Amendment will generally not suffice to meet the full and fair hearing requirement. Otherwise, *Stone* would be emasculated. In *Stone* itself the Court denied relief even though it noted that, in one of the two cases at

---

46. See *Murray v. Carrier,* 477 U.S. 478, 106 S.Ct. 2639 (1986), discussed in § 33.03(d).

47. 384 U.S. 436, 86 S.Ct. 1602 (1966), discussed in § 16.02(d).

48. See, e.g., *Wainwright v. Sykes,* 433 U.S. 72, 97 S.Ct. 2497 (1977) (Rehnquist, J.); *Brewer v. Williams,* 430 U.S. 387, 97 S.Ct. 1232 (1977) (Burger, C.J., dissenting; Powell, J., concurring).

49. The *Stone* Court made reference to *Townsend v. Sain,* 372 U.S. 293, 83 S.Ct. 745 (1963), which developed the somewhat looser standard determining when federal habeas courts may hold an evidentiary hearing. See § 33.02(d)(1). However, this reference was preceded by a "Cf." signature, which makes *Townsend's* relevance to the issue ambiguous.

50. 717 F.2d 888 (4th Cir.1983).

51. The Supreme Court subsequently accepted the case, noting that the state did not challenge the lack-of-fair-hearing finding. *Winston v. Lee,* 470 U.S. 753, 105 S.Ct. 1611 (1985).

issue there, the state court had incorrectly applied the law.[52] Most lower courts have reached similar conclusions.[53]

(c) The New Rule Exception. As described in more detail elsewhere in this book,[54] independently of its attempts to define the "jurisdiction" of federal habeas courts, the Court has also developed an approach to retroactivity doctrine which, in its most recent guise, effectively bars federal habeas review of most claims seeking a "new" constitutional ruling. This exception to federal habeas jurisdiction has had a significant impact not only on the scope of habeas review, but also on the development of federal constitutional law, since many of the Supreme Court's groundbreaking pronouncements, both for the defense and for the government, have come on habeas review.[55]

For many years, the extent to which a constitutional rule was applied to other pending cases depended upon a complicated analysis examining the extent to which government officials could have anticipated the rule, the purpose of the rule, and the effect its retroactive application would have on the administration of justice.[56] But in two decisions handed down in the late 1980's, the Court held that retroactivity doctrine would no longer depend upon these types of factors, but rather on whether the rule was announced on direct review or on habeas. The first decision was *Griffith v. Kentucky*,[57] which involved the retroactivity of a rule announced on direct review by the Court. There, the Court stressed the frequent inequity caused by the claim-oriented approach to retroactivity, which granted relief to the petitioner whose case happened to be selected by the Court, but often denied it to others similarly situated, simply because their case was not chosen for review. Accordingly, the Court held that any rule it announced on direct review of state or federal cases, regardless of its "purpose" or the affect on the administration of justice, should apply to all other cases pending on direct review.

Two years later, in *Teague v. Lane*,[58] the Court reached quite a different result with respect to habeas review. The Court first asserted that the principal purpose of federal habeas review is to deter state courts from misapplying federal law prevailing at the

---

52. The Nebraska Supreme Court had referred to information not available to the magistrate, a practice which the U.S. Supreme Court noted it had found inappropriate "several times."

53. Halpern, "Federal Habeas Corpus and the Mapp Exclusionary Rule After Stone v. Powell," 82 Colum. L.Rev. 1, 17–18 (1982).

54. See § 29.06(c).

55. See Justice Brennan's dissent in *Teague v. Lane*, 489 U.S. 288, 109 S.Ct.

1060 (1989) (listing cases that would not have been decided had the new rule exception been in effect).

56. See, e.g., *Brown v. Louisiana*, 447 U.S. 323, 100 S.Ct. 2214 (1980), discussed in § 29.06(a)(1).

57. 479 U.S. 314, 107 S.Ct. 708 (1987).

58. 489 U.S. 288, 109 S.Ct. 1060 (1989).

time of trial and appeal. From this, it concluded that there was no purpose in giving retroactive effect to "new" rules announced by a federal habeas court; such an approach would have no deterrent effect on the state courts. Thus, only those rules which are "dictated by precedent" at the time of conviction should affect other cases on collateral review. More importantly for present purposes, the Court then relied on *Griffith's* "equity" idea in deciding that, because the "harm caused by the failure to treat similarly situated defendants alike cannot be exaggerated," the habeas court confronted with a "new" claim should not even consider its merits in the case before it; to permit such consideration would unjustly be favoring the petitioner.

In short, *Teague* held that unless a claim is "dictated by precedent," it cannot be heard by a federal habeas court. *Teague* did announce two exceptions to this rule, however. The first is when the claim goes to the ability of the court to hear the case (e.g., a claim that the statute upon which conviction is based is unconstitutional, or a claim that the prosecution was barred by double jeopardy). This exception is similar to the view of habeas "jurisdiction" recognized by the Court in cases like *Siebold*. The second exception is when the claim implicates procedures "central to an accurate determination of innocence or guilt." This exception resurrects *Stone's* emphasis on the guilt-relatedness of the claim. Given the narrowness of these exceptions, the extent to which *Teague* affects habeas review will depend largely on how the Court determines whether a rule is "dictated by precedent." To date, its interpretation of this phrase has been relatively narrow.[59]

(d) Evidentiary Hearings. In *Brown*, it will be remembered, the Court contemplated that the federal habeas court hearing a state case would arrive at an independent conclusion of law, but would normally rely on the state court's findings of fact unless its proceedings suffered a "vital flaw." As Justice Frankfurter explained in one of the two majority opinions in *Brown*, this distinction between the credence given a state court's findings of fact, as opposed to its findings of law, rested on the premise that the former "may have been made after hearing witnesses no longer available or whose recollection later may have been affected by the passage of time." Yet *Brown* clearly contemplated that the federal habeas court had the authority to convene an evidentiary hearing when there were "unusual circumstances." This "procedural" issue is discussed here because the Supreme Court's treatment of it may work to preclude, on "substantive" grounds, many

---

59. See, e.g., *Butler v. McKellar,* 494 U.S. 407, 110 S.Ct. 1212 (1990), discussed in § 29.06(c)(1).

types of claims, particularly those that are essentially factual in nature.

(1) When held. In *Townsend v. Sain,*[60] the Court undertook to define more carefully the circumstances under which a separate federal hearing should take place, in the process seemingly going well beyond the "vital flaw"/"unusual circumstances" threshold outlined in *Brown.* According to Chief Justice Warren's opinion in *Townsend,* a hearing is required whenever:

> (1) the merits of the factual dispute were not resolved in the state hearing; (2) the state factual determination is not fairly supported by the record as a whole; (3) the fact-finding procedure employed by the state court was not adequate to afford a full and fair hearing; (4) there is a substantial allegation of newly discovered evidence; (5) material facts were not adequately developed at the state court hearing; or (6) for any reason it appears that the state trier of fact did not afford the habeas applicant a full and fair hearing.

As the Supreme Court later stated, *Townsend* "substantially increased the availability of evidentiary hearings in habeas corpus proceedings and made mandatory much of what had previously been within the broad discretion of the District Court." [61]

However, in *Keeney v. Tamayo–Reyes,*[62] the Court significantly reduced the availability of such hearings. *Townsend* had held that the one circumstance in which a defendant who met one of its six criteria would *not* obtain a federal hearing was when he "deliberately bypassed" an opportunity to develop the facts at the state level. The deliberate bypass language was taken from *Fay v. Noia,*[63] a case decided the same term which held that a federal constitutional claim not raised at the state level could still be heard on federal habeas unless the defendant had intentionally bypassed the claim in the state courts. As discussed in detail later in this chapter,[64] the Court subsequently replaced *Fay's* deliberate bypass rule with the "cause and prejudice" rule, which requires a defendant who fails to raise a claim at the state level to show, in effect, that the reason for the failure was either ineffective assistance of counsel or state interference with the defendant's ability to raise the claim ("i.e., cause"), and that the claim would have affected the outcome of the case (i.e., "prejudice"). In *Tamayo–Reyes,* the Court, by a 5–4 margin, applied the cause and prejudice rule to failures to raise factual issues as well. As Justice White stated for the majority, "it is . . . irrational to distinguish

60. 372 U.S. 293, 83 S.Ct. 745 (1963).

61. *Smith v. Yeager,* 393 U.S. 122, 89 S.Ct. 277 (1968).

62. ___ U.S. ___, 112 S.Ct. 1715 (1992).

63. 372 U.S. 391, 83 S.Ct. 822 (1963).

64. See § 33.03.

between failing to properly assert a federal claim in state court and failing in state court to properly develop such a claim, and to apply to the latter a remnant of a decision that is no longer upheld with regard to the former."

The impact of *Tamayo–Reyes* is illustrated by the facts and resolution of that case. The defendant, an immigrant who understood very little English, entered a nolo contendere plea in state court to manslaughter. He later collaterally attacked the plea in state court on the ground that the mens rea element of the crime had not been properly translated for him prior to the plea. His attorney in the state post-conviction proceeding failed to call either the defendant or any other witnesses in an effort to bolster the involuntariness claim. Rejected by the state court, the defendant sought an evidentiary hearing in federal habeas court on the ground that *Townsend's* fifth criterion—inadequate development of the facts—was met. While the Supreme Court remanded the case to determine whether the defendant could satisfy the cause and prejudice standard, the chances of making such a showing are almost eliminated by other Court decisions. As Justice O'Connor pointed out in dissent, proving cause based on "ineffective assistance of counsel" grounds is impossible for someone like Tamayo–Reyes, in light of the Court's previous holding that there is no right to counsel at state post-conviction proceedings, and thus no right to effective counsel at that stage.[65] Thus, unless such a person can show that the state caused the failure to develop the facts (because, for instance, it did not provide a forum), or unless he can make a claim of "actual innocence," an exception to the cause and prejudice standard which the Court has interpreted very narrowly,[66] he cannot present additional evidence in federal court. This inability to have a hearing is especially significant in light of the requirement, discussed below, that the habeas court presume the correctness of all state court factual findings.

(2) The presumption of correctness. Even when a federal court may hold a hearing, its ability to find the facts is circumscribed. In 1966, in the aftermath of *Townsend,* Congress added subsection (d) to § 2254. This section provides that factual findings by a state court "shall be presumed to be correct" by the federal habeas court unless the state proceeding was deficient in one of eight ways. Most of these are identical to the *Townsend* criteria. However, there are a few differences between the two sets of criteria. Because the § 2254 provisions are not meant to determine whether a new hearing should be held, but only whether state court factual findings are presumed correct, they do not include *Townsend's* "new evidence" criterion. At the same time,

---

65. See *Pennsylvania v. Finley,* 481 U.S. 551, 107 S.Ct. 1990 (1987), discussed in § 32.02(a).

66. See § 33.03(3).

the statute defines as "deficient" for purposes of the presumption of correctness some situations which *Townsend* does not specifically mention but which may also be relevant to whether a federal hearing should be held, i.e., when the state court lacked jurisdiction over the subject matter, and when the petitioner was indigent and was denied counsel.

While § 2254(d)'s criteria are not meant to affect when a hearing can be held or the types of legal claims a federal habeas court may address, their interpretation by the Supreme Court has sometimes had that effect. In *LaVallee v. Delle Rose*,[67] for instance, the lower federal courts held that the state court failed "to resolve" a factual dispute over the voluntariness of a confession, because it did not indicate the extent to which it relied on the petitioner's own description of how the confession was obtained; accordingly, the state court's findings with respect to the facts surrounding the confession could not be "presumed correct." The Supreme Court reversed in a 5–4 judgment. Finding that the petitioner's testimony could be reconstructed from the state record, it concluded that the district court should have presumed that the trial judge took into account and legitimately rejected that testimony. Further, given this presumption, the defendant could overturn the state court's finding of involuntariness only by "convincing evidence" independent of the petitioner's account, effectively precluding the confessions claim.

Other Court decisions reached similar results. In *Maggio v. Fulford*,[68] the Court refused to sustain a federal habeas court's overruling of a state court's finding that the petitioner was competent to stand trial, because the federal court, in reaching its conclusion, had relied heavily on trial testimony of a psychiatrist that had been explicitly discounted by the state court. And in *Marshall v. Lonberger*[69] the Court again chastised a federal court's reassessment of witness credibility, this time in refusing to sustain a reversal of a guilty plea conviction that rested on the petitioner's state court testimony that he had not understood the consequences of his plea. The majority reasoned that since the state court was familiar with the circumstances surrounding the defendant's guilty plea, including the fact that he was represented, was intelligent, and had been informed of his charges, his testimony that he had thought he was pleading guilty only to battery, and not to attempted murder as well, must have been rejected by the state court; therefore, it should not have been considered by the federal court. In both of these cases, the Court's application of the

67. 410 U.S. 690, 93 S.Ct. 1203 (1973).

68. 462 U.S. 111, 103 S.Ct. 2261 (1983).

69. 459 U.S. 422, 103 S.Ct. 843 (1983).

presumption of correctness rule had the effect of resolving the case against the petitioner.

Of potentially even more significant impact on the substantive scope of the writ are the Court's decisions defining what is a "fact" and what is a legal conclusion for purposes of the presumption of correctness. In *Fulford,* for instance, the four-member dissent argued that the state court's finding that the defendant was competent to stand trial was a legal determination that should not be accorded a presumption of correctness. The majority, however, characterized the disagreement between the federal and state court as one having to do with the weight of the psychiatric testimony, not the ultimate conclusion as to competency. The same type of reasoning occurred in *Sumner v. Mata,*[70] dealing with the constitutionality of a photo identification by eyewitnesses whose ability to perceive what occurred at the time of the crime was questioned. There, the Court held that "whether the witnesses in this case had an opportunity to observe the crime or were too distracted; whether the witnesses gave a detailed, accurate description; and whether the witnesses were under pressure from prison officials or others are all questions of fact as to which the statutory presumption applies." But as Justice Brennan pointed out in an earlier manifestation of the *Sumner v. Mata* case,[71] characterizing these issues as "factual" is problematic. For instance, important to whether an identification is constitutionally adequate is the *extent* to which the witnesses had an "opportunity to observe the crime" and the *degree* of official "pressure," neither of which would be fully evaluated under the Court's approach to the presumption of correctness provision.[72]

Perhaps backing away from the full implications of *Mata* (as well as *Delle Rose*), the Court subsequently found that the "voluntariness" of a confession is a legal issue that is not subject to the presumption of correctness. The Court's decision in *Miller v. Fenton,*[73] written by Justice O'Connor, appeared to rest on three separate grounds. The first was the long tradition of treating the voluntariness issue as a legal, as opposed to factual, question in appeals and habeas cases. The second was the recognition that voluntariness involves a "hybrid" assessment, but one which is ultimately probably more properly characterized as "legal": it contemplates deciding whether the techniques involved in obtaining a confession (a factual issue) "are compatible with a system that presumes innocence and assures that a conviction will not be secured by inquisitorial means" (a legal issue). Finally, on

---

70. 455 U.S. 591, 102 S.Ct. 1303 (1982).

71. 449 U.S. 539, 101 S.Ct. 764 (1981).

72. See § 18.04(b) for a discussion of the factors relevant to due process analysis in photo identification cases.

73. 474 U.S. 104, 106 S.Ct. 445 (1985).

a more practical level was the question of whether "one judicial actor is better positioned than another to decide the issue." Questions of credibility of witnesses or jurors and evaluations of state of mind are better left to the trial court, while appellate review is appropriate when the trier of fact may have been biased or "the relevant legal principle can be given meaning only through its application to the particular circumstances of a case." In assessing voluntariness, the "subsidiary" findings on things like the length and circumstances of the interrogation, the defendant's prior experience with the legal process and his familiarity with the *Miranda* warnings are entitled to a presumption of correctness on habeas review. But in making the determination of whether, in the totality of the circumstances, the confession was obtained in a constitutional manner, "the state-court judge is not in an appreciably better position than the federal habeas court." Moreover, while credibility assessments are made in open court, confessions are obtained "in a secret and invariably more coercive environment" which, "together with the inevitable and understandable reluctance to exclude an otherwise reliable admission of guilt . . . elevate[s] the risk that erroneous resolution of the voluntariness question might inadvertently frustrate the protection of the federal right."[74]

33.03 The Effect of Default Under State Procedural Rules

Virtually every state prohibits defendants from raising a claim on appeal or other post-conviction proceedings if it was not raised when the error occurred or within a certain time after trial. The subject addressed here is the extent to which such "procedural default" rules act to bar habeas review. The Supreme Court has taken at least four different approaches to the issue. At first, a failure to abide by the state rule was an absolute bar to habeas review unless the state rule was not an "adequate and independent" basis for the dismissal. The Warren Court soon rejected this approach, substituting a much more defendant-oriented "deliberate bypass" rule which focused on whether the defendant's default was an intentional waiver of the claim. The post-Warren Court, finding the deliberate bypass rule too generous to habeas petitioners, largely replaced it with a requirement that the defendant show "cause" as to why he failed to raise the claim, and show further that failure to vindicate the claim would "prejudice" his case. Most recently, the Court has created an "actual innocence" exception to the cause and prejudice requirement which allows review of defaulted claims which are guilt-related.

---

74. In *Wright v. West,* ___ U.S. ___, 112 S.Ct. 2482 (1992), three justices indicated a willingness to overrule *Miller,* or at least undermine it, by applying the presumption of correctness to "mixed" claims as well as factual claims, but the Court as a whole avoided the issue.

(a) **The Adequate and Independent Requirement.** In *Daniels v. Allen*,[75] a companion case to *Brown v. Allen*,[76] the Supreme Court held that when a defendant has defaulted at the state level, federal habeas review is barred as well, so long as the state rule is adequate and independent. The effect of this rule was made apparent in *Daniels*, where the defendant raised the same types of arguments as Brown (i.e., coerced confession and jury selection claims), but was denied federal relief because his attorney failed to perfect his state appeal. As Justice Black stated in dissent, this result, combined with *Brown's* holding that any properly raised constitutional claim could be raised on habeas, meant that the Court would "grant a second review where the state has granted one but . . . deny any review at all where the state has granted none."

The only hope for a defendant under *Daniels* was to show that the state default rule was either "inadequate" or that it was not the basis for the dismissal of his claim, in which case there might not be any "independent" state ground for the dismissal. Neither showing was easily made. The adequacy inquiry appeared to boil down to whether the rule served any legitimate purpose. Only a procedural rule which is an "arid ritual of meaningless form" was likely to be found inadequate.[77] With respect to the second issue, only if the state court ignored the procedural default, and decided the claim despite it, could one argue that the rule was not the basis for the dismissal.[78]

Because the Court's current habeas jurisprudence still views state procedural default rules as a limitation on habeas review, these considerations remain relevant today. On the "adequacy" issue, as recently as 1989 at least four members of the Court seemed willing to hold that a procedural rule which is not "consistently or regularly applied" would not be a legitimate ground for barring habeas review.[79] This position seems defensible, at least when the state uses its rule as means of punishing particular defendants or thwarting federal review by simply refusing to hear a claim.[80] A number of other recent decisions have endorsed the idea that a state court's consideration of a defaulted claim excuses the litigant's failure to abide by the rule. In *Ulster County Court v. Allen*,[81] for instance, the Court stated that if state courts

75. 344 U.S. 443, 73 S.Ct. 397 (1953).

76. 344 U.S. 443, 73 S.Ct. 397 (1953), discussed in § 33.02(a).

77. *Staub v. City of Baxley*, 355 U.S. 313, 78 S.Ct. 277 (1958).

78. See *Irvin v. Dowd*, 359 U.S. 394, 79 S.Ct. 825 (1959).

79. *Dugger v. Adams*, 489 U.S. 401, 109 S.Ct. 1211 (1989) (Blackmun, J., dissenting).

80. Cf. *NAACP v. Alabama ex rel. Flowers*, 377 U.S. 288, 84 S.Ct. 1302 (1964).

81. 442 U.S. 140, 99 S.Ct. 2213 (1979).

themselves bypass a procedural default, a federal court "implies no disrespect" to state interests if it does the same.

Other relatively recent cases deal with the second, "independence" prong, having to do with determining whether the state's default rule was really the basis for the state court decision. After *Harris v. Reed,*[82] it appeared that, as a means of easing the determination of this issue, the state court wanting to avoid federal review would have to make a "plain statement" that its default rule was an independent ground for its ruling, a phrase borrowed from Court's cases describing the circumstances under which the Court can review state court decisions against the prosecution.[83] However, in *Coleman v. Thompson,*[84] the Court held that federal habeas review is presumptively barred simply if it "fairly appears" on the record that the state court's dismissal was based "primarily" on the state procedural rule. The Court rejected a plain statement requirement because such a requirement would evidence a "loss of respect" for state court decisions and "put too great a burden on the state courts." Thus, in *Coleman,* the Court refused to allow federal review of a claim that was dismissed on procedural grounds, even though the state court did so only after deciding its action would not abridge one of the petitioner's federal constitutional rights, and without plainly stating the dismissal was on procedural grounds. In *Ylst v. Nunnemaker,*[85] the Court moved even further from a plain statement rule by holding that when an upper level state court does not indicate the ground for dismissal, federal courts should "presume" that the basis for dismissal is the same ground that lower state courts explicitly relied upon (which may often be procedural default).

(b) The Deliberate Bypass Rule. *Daniels'* holding that federal habeas review was barred by a default under a state rule which is adequate and independent retained vitality until 1963. In that year, the Court decided *Fay v. Noia,*[86] which held that the importance of preventing unconstitutional detentions outweighed the state's interest in an "airtight system" of procedural rules, and that habeas review should therefore usually be available to those state defendants who violate them. Justice Harlan, with two others, wrote in dissent that with this reasoning the Court "turned its back on history and struck a heavy blow at the foundations of our federal system." But the majority opinion, authored by Justice Brennan, contended that sufficient deference to state rules was evidenced by the denial of direct review to the noncomplying

82. 489 U.S. 255, 109 S.Ct. 1038 (1989).

83. See *Michigan v. Long,* 463 U.S. 1032, 103 S.Ct. 3469 (1983), discussed in § 34.04.

84. 501 U.S. ___, 111 S.Ct. 2546 (1991).

85. 501 U.S. 85, 111 S.Ct. 2590 (1991).

86. 372 U.S. 391, 83 S.Ct. 822 (1963).

defendant, who then had the burden of seeking habeas relief. According to Brennan, "the only concrete impact the assumption of federal habeas jurisdiction in the face of a procedural default has on the state interest [in orderly criminal procedure] is that it prevents the State from closing off the convicted defendant's last opportunity to vindicate his constitutional rights, thereby punishing him for his default and deterring others who might commit similar defaults in the future."

The majority did admit, however, that its holding could lead to occasional abuse by state defendants who might withhold claims until habeas as a means of obtaining a retrial after conviction. Thus, it held that "the federal judge may in his discretion deny relief to any applicant who has deliberately bypassed the orderly procedure of the state courts and in so doing has forfeited his state court remedies." At the same time, the majority made clear that it expected this discretion to be rarely exercised. In defining the deliberate bypass concept, it placed emphasis on *Johnson v. Zerbst*,[87] which had described waiver as "an intentional relinquishment or abandonment of a known right or privilege." Furthermore, the Court held that the relinquishment of state remedies must be "the considered choice of the petitioner;" thus, "a choice made by counsel not participated in by the petitioner does not automatically bar relief." Finally, its disposition of the case before it indicated that even some intentional defaults by the petitioner would not constitute a "deliberate bypass;" the Court granted review of Noia's coerced confession claim even though he had affirmatively decided not to appeal, because his decision was based on financial considerations and fear that he might receive the death penalty on a retrial.

The Court later modified somewhat its stance that the defendant be personally involved in every waiver: in *Henry v. Mississippi*,[88] it held that, for certain types of constitutional claims involving tactical decisions, intentional bypass by counsel alone would be sufficient.[89] Moreover, a few lower courts were quite willing to presume waiver from a silent record, or give great weight to an attorney's explanations as to why he did not pursue a particular claim.[90] Nonetheless, *Fay* was a major step, at least as significant as *Brown*, toward creating federal oversight of the state court system. It provided ready access to the federal courts for state prisoners whose counsel was unaware of, or insensitive to, constitutional issues.

---

87. 304 U.S. 458, 58 S.Ct. 1019 (1938).

88. 379 U.S. 443, 85 S.Ct. 564 (1965).

89. See also, *Murch v. Mottram*, 409 U.S. 41, 93 S.Ct. 71 (1972).

90. See Note, "Federal Habeas Corpus and the Doctrine of Waiver Through the Deliberate Bypass of State Procedures," 31 La.L.Rev. 601, 606–08 (1971).

(c) Development of the Cause and Prejudice Standard.
Ten years after *Fay,* the Court began the process of dismantling
the deliberate bypass rule and replacing it with the so-called
"cause and prejudice" standard. Today, unless a claim goes to the
"actual innocence" of the petitioner,[91] the latter analysis determines whether a defaulted claim will be heard on habeas review.

The first case to endorse the cause and prejudice standard was
Davis v. United States,[92] which involved an allegation by a federal
prisoner that the grand jury which indicted him had been selected
in a racially discriminatory manner. Although the claim had not
been raised either prior to trial or on appeal, the petitioner argued
that it should be heard on habeas because there had been no
deliberate bypass. The Court held, in essence, that even if the
latter assertion were true, relief should not be granted. While the
Court conceded that *Fay* had been applied to federal prisoners,[93] it
ignored that decision and chose to decide whether § 2255, the
federal prisoner analogue to § 2254, allowed collateral review in
the circumstances presented in *Davis.*

The majority first noted that, had Davis brought his claim on
direct review, it would have been barred by Federal Rule 12(b)(2),
which provides that an appeal does not lie for a federal defendant
unless he can show "cause" why an objection was not made prior
to trial. The Court then concluded that it was "inconceivable that
Congress, having in the criminal proceeding foreclosed the raising
of a claim such as this after the commencement of trial in the
absence of a showing of 'cause' for relief from waiver, nonetheless
intended to perversely negate the Rule's purpose by permitting an
entirely different but much more liberal requirement of waiver in
federal habeas proceedings." Thus, as a matter of statutory
interpretation, the Rule 12(b) standard should apply under § 2255
as well. Furthermore, the Court held, in addition to showing
cause, the defendant must show "actual prejudice" to his case
should the court fail to grant relief, a stipulation which went
beyond the terms of Rule 12(b) but which had been developed in
earlier cases construing the rule.[94] Since Davis had neither explained his failure to make a pretrial motion nor shown any
"actual" prejudice to his case resulting from the improper selection process,[95] he was denied relief. This disposition of the case
strongly suggested that mere proof that there had been no "deliberate bypass" would seldom satisfy the "cause" prong.

---

91. See § 33.03(e).

92. 411 U.S. 233, 93 S.Ct. 1577
(1973).

93. *Kaufman v. United States,* 394
U.S. 217, 89 S.Ct. 1068 (1969).

94. See, e.g., *Shotwell Mfg. Co. v.
United States,* 371 U.S. 341, 83 S.Ct. 448
(1963).

95. The Court noted that, while
prejudice is presumed when racial discrimination of the grand jury is shown
upon timely objection, it must be prov-
en when such objection is not made.

Three years later, without mentioning the deliberate bypass standard, the Court applied the cause and prejudice rule to a habeas petition by a *state* prisoner. In *Francis v. Henderson,*[96] the petitioner alleged the same type of claim—racial discrimination in the selection of his grand jury—at issue in *Davis.* Citing "considerations of comity and concern for the orderly administration of criminal justice," the Court held that the rule developed in *Davis* should apply here as well, and denied relief.

Although *Davis* and *Francis* established the cause and prejudice standard as an alternative to the deliberate bypass rule, their impact could have been quite limited, given the fact that both involved claims against the indictment process. As Justice Stewart wrote for the Court in *Francis,* applying the state's procedural default rule to such claims would be useful because "[i]f its time limits are followed, inquiry into an alleged defect may be concluded and, if necessary, cured before the court, the witnesses and the parties have gone to the burden and expense of a trial." On the other hand, if the rule is denigrated by allowing habeas review even when it is violated, "there would be little incentive to comply with its terms when a successful attack might simply result in a new indictment prior to trial." These points do not apply to defaults at trial or on appeal, nor do they apply to pretrial defaults involving claims that might prevent trial altogether.

However, in *Wainwright v. Sykes,*[97] the Court indicated that the cause and prejudice standard would govern analysis of virtually all defaulted claims. There, the Court held that habeas review was barred because the defense had failed to make a "contemporaneous objection" during trial to the admission of a confession allegedly obtained in violation of *Miranda.* In denying habeas review of this claim, the Court made clear that, while it was not overturning *Fay's* result on the facts of that case, in the more typical case a failure to raise a claim within the period allowed by state law would foreclose habeas review unless the cause and prejudice standard was met.

Justice Rehnquist's opinion for the Court justified this rejuvenation of the procedural default principle on several grounds. First, he emphasized the valid state interests protected by default rules, including the desire to develop the factual record when recollections "are freshest," and the goal of encouraging finality by forcing the parties to put their best case forward at the time the motion should be made. Second, he asserted that the cause and prejudice standard would make less likely the "sandbagging" alluded to in *Francis,* whereby lawyers intentionally defer raising

96. 425 U.S. 536, 96 S.Ct. 1708 (1976).   **97.** 433 U.S. 72, 97 S.Ct. 2497 (1977).

a constitutional claim at the state level in the hope that a federal court will later decide the question favorably and require a retrial. Relatedly, the cause and prejudice standard better served the adversarial process, because the narrowly-defined deliberate bypass standard had the tendency, Rehnquist asserted, of making federal habeas the "determinative" proceeding, thus minimizing the importance of trial as a "decisive and portentous event."

The rationale underlying *Sykes* are open to serious question, even accepting the Court's objectives of promoting comity, efficiency and finality. Because the deliberate bypass standard presumably deters any intentional failure to raise a claim at the state level, the only additional purpose served by the cause and prejudice standard is to penalize inadvertent attorney error. Accordingly, *Sykes* does not increase the chance an objection will be made at or prior to trial, and makes "the choice between *Fay* and *Sykes* . . . neutral with respect to the goals of promoting determinations based on fresh evidence and deciding all issues in one proceeding." [98] As Justice Brennan put it in his dissent, the assertion that a "meaningful number of lawyers" would risk the sandbagging feared by the majority "offends common sense," and in any event is deterred by the deliberate bypass standard as well. Perhaps more importantly, as subsequent discussion makes clear, the refusal to recognize attorney error as automatic "cause" has not stymied habeas petitioners, as the *Sykes* majority apparently hoped, but merely transformed the procedural default issue into an ineffective assistance of counsel issue, which continues to require federal habeas review and second-guessing of state court determinations.

Nonetheless, the Court has maintained its adherence to the cause and prejudice standard, and extended its scope to apply to all defaults at the state level. In *Murray v. Carrier,* [99] the petitioner argued that habeas review of a claim presented at trial and not defaulted until appeal should not be governed by the *Sykes* rule— or at least should be subject to a "lesser" cause requirement— because its effect on the state's interests is relatively minimal. Unlike habeas review of a claim defaulted prior to or during trial, he argued, review of a defaulted appellate claim does not detract from the significance of trial, nor does it deter development of a full trial record or affect the trial court's ability to correct the error during trial. Moreover, while the fast pace of trial may make it necessary to bind a defendant to his counsel's acts or omissions, the more reflective process on appeal does not require such a rule.

---

98. The Supreme Court, 1976 Term, 91 Har.L.Rev. 70, 214–221 (1977).

99. 477 U.S. 478, 106 S.Ct. 2639 (1986).

But the Court, in an opinion by Justice O'Connor, found that appellate default rules still promoted significant state objectives, including "the opportunity to resolve the issue shortly after trial, while evidence is still available both to assess the defendant's claim and to retry the defendant effectively if he prevails in his appeal." Perhaps revealing the real rationale behind the *Sykes* rule, she also stated that the difference between a failure to detect a colorable claim and a deliberate decision not to raise it "is much too tenuous a distinction to justify a regime of evidentiary hearings into counsel's state of mind in failing to raise a claim on appeal." For much the same reasons, the Court has also held that the cause and prejudice standard governs defaults on appeal of state post-conviction determinations.[1]

The one type of default left untouched by *Carrier* and previous decisions was that involved in *Fay*: a failure to bring any appeal at all. In *Sykes*, the majority opinion had been careful to state that it was only "the sweeping language of *Fay*, going far beyond the facts of the case eliciting it, which we today reject." As Chief Justice Burger's concurring opinion explained, *Fay* "applied the 'deliberate bypass' standard to a case where the critical procedural decision—whether to take a criminal appeal—was entrusted to a convicted defendant." The case for holding that only the deliberate bypass standard need be met in this situation was strengthened by the Court's recognition, in another context,[2] that the decision to forego an appeal (along with the decisions to plead guilty, waive jury trial, and testify) is a "fundamental" one that belongs to the defendant. One could thus argue that when this decision is made by counsel alone, or over the objection of the defendant, and claims are thereby defaulted, habeas review of those claims should automatically be allowed.

But in *Coleman v. Thompson*[3] the Court held that "there is no reason that the [cause and prejudice] standard should not apply to a failure to appeal at all." According to the Court, "[a]ll of the State's interests—in channeling the resolution of claims to the most appropriate forum, in finality, and in having an opportunity to correct is own errors—are implicated whether a prisoner defaults one claim or all of them." Justice O'Connor, who wrote the majority opinion, also noted that by applying the cause and prejudice standard to all default situations, "we . . . eliminate inconsistency between the respect federal courts show for state procedural rules and the respect they show for their own." Thus, *Fay's* deliberate bypass rule has apparently been eliminated alto-

1. *Coleman v. Thompson*, 501 U.S. ___, 111 S.Ct. 2546 (1991).

2. See *Jones v. Barnes*, 463 U.S. 745, 103 S.Ct. 3308 (1983), discussed in § 32.04(c)(4).

3. 501 U.S. ___, 111 S.Ct. 2546 (1991).

gether as a means of evaluating the impact of default on habeas review.[4]

(d) Defining Cause and Prejudice. The adoption of the cause and prejudice standard in *Sykes* and later cases has occasioned considerable litigation as to the definition of cause. In *Carrier,* the Court summarized a number of decisions on this issue by stating that "cause for procedural default must ordinarily turn on whether the prisoner can show that some objective factor external to the defense impeded counsel's efforts to comply with the State's procedural rule." It then gave three illustrations of such "external impediments:" (1) when the factual or legal basis of the claim was not reasonably available at the time the claim should have been made; (2) when state officials interfere with counsel's ability to avoid default; and (3) when default is the result of attorney error rising to the level of ineffective assistance of counsel. (The Court was able to characterize the latter type of cause as an "external impediment" by "imputing" to the state the responsibility for a trial conducted without adequate defense counsel.) These three types of cause, as well as the possible definitions of prejudice in this context, are discussed below.

(1) Cause: novel claims. Cause deriving from the novel legal basis of the claim is illustrated by two pre-*Carrier* decisions. In *Engle v. Isaac,*[5] the defendants were tried and convicted of homicide under an Ohio instruction placing the burden of proving self-defense on the defense. On habeas, the defendants challenged this instruction for the first time, claiming that there was "cause" for not objecting earlier because at the time of their trial both Ohio law and the federal law in their circuit clearly placed the burden of proving self-defense on the defense. But the Court, in an opinion by Justice O'Connor, rejected this argument by concluding that "the futilty of presenting an objection to the state courts cannot alone constitute cause for a failure to object at trial. . . . Even a state court that has previously rejected a constitutional argument may decide, upon reflection, that the contention is valid." The Court also pointed out that, well before the defendant's trial, the Court's decision in *In re Winship*[6] had required the prosecution to prove beyond a reasonable doubt every

---

4. The one possible exception to this statement may involve "jurisdictional" claims. In the guilty plea context, for instance, the Court has indicated that such claims (e.g., double jeopardy claims, or claims of vindictive prosecution) may be raised on habeas even after a voluntary and intelligent plea by a competently represented defendant, because they go to the "very power of the State to bring the defendant into court to answer the charge brought against him." *Blackledge v. Perry,* 417 U.S. 21, 94 S.Ct. 2098 (1974), discussed in § 26.05(e)(3). Note also that attorney failure to raise an appeal may constitute ineffective assistance, thus meeting the cause and prejudice test. See § 33.03(d)(3).

5. 456 U.S. 107, 102 S.Ct. 1558 (1982).

6. 397 U.S. 358, 90 S.Ct. 1068 (1970).

essential element of the crime charged, and dozens of courts outside the defendants' circuit had found *Winship* required the prosecution to bear the burden on affirmative defenses. The Court concluded that "[w]here the basis of a constitutional claim is available, and other defense counsel have perceived and litigated that claim, the demands of comity and finality counsel against labelling alleged unawareness of the objection" sufficient cause for purposes of earning federal review.

In contrast, in *Reed v. Ross,*[7] which involved the same type of instruction at issue in *Engle* but concerned a trial that took place *before Winship,* the Court found cause present. Justice Brennan's majority opinion concluded that the Court's own previous sanction of the prevailing practice,[8] the pervasive support for the instruction in most jurisdictions, and the minimal number of lower court cases supporting its unconstitutionality (a total of two), justified this result. The four dissenters, in an opinion by Justice Rehnquist, disagreed, finding that "it has long been assumed that proof of a criminal charge beyond a reasonable doubt is constitutionally required."

Even if a claim is shown to be "novel," this aspect of cause is likely to be of minimal use to habeas petitioners, given the Court's more recent decision in *Teague v. Lane.*[9] As discussed earlier in this chapter,[10] *Teague* held that a federal habeas court may not consider a "new" rule unless it involves the trial court's jurisdiction to hear the claim or an allegation relating to factual innocence. Thus, a petitioner who meets the cause prong by showing his claim is "novel" will automatically be barred from habeas review under *Teague,* unless he meets one of that case's two exceptions (i.e., a claim that goes to the state court's jurisdiction or a claim that suggests factual innocence). Most claims will not meet either exception; indeed, although the question of what the prosecution must show to prove guilt, at issue in *Engle* and *Reed,* would seem to come under *Teague's* second exception, language in *Engle* suggests it would not reach that conclusion.[11]

To be distinguished from novel legal claims are claims based on newly discovered facts. *Teague* would not affect such claims, because it is based on the retroactive effect of new legal rules. However, to meet this aspect of cause, the Court will probably require strong proof that the fact could not have been discovered prior to trial, thus merging this type of cause with either the state interference aspect of cause (when the information was withheld

---

7. 468 U.S. 1, 104 S.Ct. 2901 (1984).

8. In *Leland v. Oregon,* 343 U.S. 790, 72 S.Ct. 1002 (1952), the Court upheld a statute requiring the defendant to bear the burden of proving insanity.

9. 489 U.S. 288, 109 S.Ct. 1060 (1989).

10. See § 33.02(c).

11. See § 33.03(e).

by the state) or the ineffective assistance aspect of cause (when the information could have been discovered by the defense).

(2) Cause: state interference. The second type of cause identified in *Carrier* requires proof that the state has somehow caused the default. This could occur in at least three different ways. First, state officials might inhibit or actually prevent filing of the objection. In *Carrier,* the Court illustrated this scenario by reference to a case in which a prison official had suppressed the petitioner's appeal papers.[12] Second, state officials might make early objection impossible because they prevent discovery of crucial information. In *Amadeo v. Zant,*[13] for instance, the Court found cause for not raising a jury selection claim, after it was shown that the district attorney's office concealed a memorandum which seemed to encourage underrepresentation of blacks and women on the master list from which all grand and petit juries were drawn.

A third way in which the state action could result in "cause" is when the state's judiciary applies its default rules so inconsistently that the default is more a matter of state arbitrariness than defense inadvertence. This type of state interference involves the same types of actions that are relevant in determining whether a state procedural rule provides an "adequate" basis for dismissal of the claim.[14] Numerous other examples of all three types of state interference can be culled from the cases.[15]

(3) Cause: ineffective assistance. Unless a claim is so novel that even competent attorneys would not be aware of it, or unless the state interferes with a competent attorney's ability to develop or raise a claim, *Carrier* suggests that cause will exist only upon a showing of ineffective assistance of counsel. According to that decision, except where counsel is ineffective as defined in *Strickland v. Washington* [16] (the Court's leading case on the issue), "the question of cause for a procedural default does not turn on whether counsel erred or on the kind of error counsel may have made."

Strickland's two-prong "deficient performance-and-prejudice" standard for determining when counsel has been ineffective is discussed in detail elsewhere in this book,[17] and will not be elaborated upon here. However, three points are worth emphasizing in this context. First, given the narrow definition of "deficient performance" found in *Strickland* and its progeny, only egregious

12. *Dowd v. United States ex rel. Cook,* 340 U.S. 206, 71 S.Ct. 262 (1951).

13. 486 U.S. 214, 108 S.Ct. 1771 (1988).

14. See § 33.03(a).

15. See Amsterdam, "Search, Seizure, and Section 2255: A Com-

ment," 112 U.Pa.L.Rev. 378, at 385 n. 34 (1964).

16. 466 U.S. 668, 104 S.Ct. 2052 (1984).

17. See § 32.03(b).

error for which there is no reasonable explanation will constitute cause. For example, in *Smith v. Murray*,[18] the Court found that counsel's failure to raise a particular Fifth Amendment claim on appeal did not constitute cause even though the claim was argued in an amicus brief and later sustained by the Court in a subsequent case. The Court concluded that the attorney was "reasonable" in his assessment that the claim was weak, given the law at that time, and in his desire to focus on other appellate claims. *Carrier* provides another illustration of the Court's approach. There, counsel in a rape and abduction trial failed to argue on appeal the trial court's rejection of two pretrial discovery motions requesting the victim's statements. According to the Court, while this failure "is more easily described as an oversight" rather than a "misjudgment," it did not justify delving into counsel's state of mind and did not establish cause.

The second point with respect to the ineffective assistance aspect of cause follows from the first. Consistent with *Sykes'* rejection of the deliberate bypass rule, even if counsel's error is not attributable to the defendant in any way, it does not establish cause unless it constitutes ineffective assistance. As the Court stated in *Carrier*, "[s]o long as the defendant is represented by counsel whose performance is not constitutionally ineffective, we discern no inequity in requiring him to bear the risk of attorney error that results in a procedural default." The one exception to this rule may occur when counsel decides not to take a direct appeal. Although *Coleman* made clear that the cause and prejudice standard applies in this situation, an attorney's failure to consult with his client on the "fundamental" decision to forego an appeal may automatically constitute ineffective assistance of counsel,[19] and therefore also constitute cause.

Finally, the Court has held that attorney error at proceedings at which the right to counsel does not attach can never amount to cause, because the right to effective assistance is not implicated. This was another conclusion reached in *Coleman*, where the petitioner argued that his attorney incompetently defaulted a claim on an appeal of a state habeas decision. The Court first noted that, while there is a right to counsel on direct appeal of a conviction,[20] it had also held that there is no constitutional right to an attorney in state postconviction proceedings.[21] From this, it concluded that the right to counsel could not attach at *appeal* of such proceedings either. Accordingly, the error claimed by the petitioner "cannot be constitutionally ineffective." As the Court

---

18. 477 U.S. 527, 106 S.Ct. 2661 (1986).

19. See § 32.04(c)(4).

20. See *Evitts v. Lucey*, 469 U.S. 387, 105 S.Ct. 830 (1985).

21. See, e.g., *Pennsylvania v. Finley*, 481 U.S. 551, 107 S.Ct. 1990 (1987), discussed in § 33.05.

put it, for purposes of establishing cause, "it is not the gravity of the attorney's error that matters, but that it constitutes a violation of petitioner's right to counsel, so that the error must be seen as an external factor, i.e. 'imputed to the State.'" When such is not the case, the Court reiterated its stand in *Carrier* that "the petitioner bears the risk in federal habeas for all attorney errors made in the course of the representation."

(4) Prejudice. Until *United States v. Frady*,[22] a companion case to *Engle*, none of the Court's cases had directly addressed the "prejudice" prong of the cause and prejudice standard. *Frady* did not produce a clear definition of the term either, but it did reject at least one possible interpretation of it. The petitioner's contention in *Frady* was that prejudice should be equated with the "plain error" rule applicable in cases on direct appeal, which under the federal rules allows the appellate court to decide a claim "affecting substantial rights" even when it has not been brought to the attention of the court.[23] But the Court, in another opinion by Justice O'Connor, held that a habeas petitioner must clear a "significantly higher hurdle" than the litigant on direct review in order to obtain relief.

The Court was ambiguous as to what that hurdle might be. But it did find that the error raised by Frady—an erroneous instruction on "malice" at his homicide trial—would not be heard on habeas review because it did not inflict "actual and substantial disadvantage, infecting his entire trial with error of constitutional dimension," and thus was not prejudicial under the cause and prejudice standard. In reaching this conclusion, the Court stressed that the trial judge and nine appellate judges, over the course of several different proceedings, had found that the evidence of intent in Frady's case clearly supported his conviction. This treatment suggested that the Court might conduct the prejudice inquiry in line with an "overwhelming evidence" version of the harmless error test;[24] under this approach, the prejudice prong would not be met if the untainted evidence against the defendant clearly proved his guilt.

However, it is more likely that the eventual definition of prejudice in default cases will mimic the slightly narrower (i.e., more prosecution-oriented) formulation of the prejudice inquiry found in ineffective assistance and discovery cases.[25] That test looks at whether there is a "reasonable probability" that the error affected the "outcome of the proceeding." Besides having the advantage of consistency, this standard would facilitate analysis

---

22. 456 U.S. 152, 102 S.Ct. 1584 (1982).

23. Fed.R.Crim.P. 52(b).

24. See § 29.05(a).

25. See, e.g., *Strickland v. Washington*, 466 U.S. 668, 104 S.Ct. 2052 (1984), discussed in § 32.03(b)(2); *United States v. Bagley*, 473 U.S. 667, 105 S.Ct. 3375 (1985), discussed in § 24.04(b).

under the cause and prejudice standard whenever (as will usually be the case) the asserted cause is ineffective assistance: if both the deficient performance and prejudice prongs of the ineffective assistance standard are shown, cause and prejudice for purposes of habeas review would then be automatically established; if proof of one or the other prong is absent, then the *Sykes* test will not be met.

(e) The Actual Innocence Exception. In *Engle,* the Court stated that "[w]hile the nature of a constitutional claim may affect the calculation of cause and actual prejudice, it does not alter the need to make that threshold showing." Nonetheless, perhaps spurred by the dissent's argument that requiring proof of cause in every case would result in "miscarriages of justice," the *Engle* Court also stated that "[i]n appropriate cases," the principles of comity and finality that underlie the cause and prejudice standard "must yield to the imperative of correcting a fundamentally unjust incarceration." In *Carrier,* the Court made this point more explicit, by admitting that there might be "extraordinary" cases where a fundamental miscarriage of justice would result if the cause prong had to be met before habeas review were granted. It went on to hold that "where a constitutional violation has probably resulted in the conviction of one who is actually innocent," the level of "prejudice" is sufficient by itself to entitle the petitioner to federal review. In the companion case of *Kuhlmann v. Wilson,*[26] the Court elaborated on the actual innocence standard as follows: "the prisoner must show a fair probability that, in light of all the evidence, including that alleged to have been illegally admitted (but with due regard to any unreliability of it) and evidence tenably claimed to have been wrongly excluded or to have become available only after the trial, the trier of the facts would have entertained a reasonable doubt of his guilt." [27]

The scope of this exception appears to be very narrow. First, the language in *Kuhlmann* suggests that it focuses entirely on claims that adduce facts proving innocence; unlike a harmless error test,[28] for instance, the impact of instructions on the accuracy of a verdict may well be irrelevant.[29] Second, the factual claims must go to essential elements of the prosecution's cases. In *Carrier,* for example, the Court indicated that the failure to turn over victim statements would result in relief only if the statements included exculpatory information "*establish[ing]* actual in-

---

26. 477 U.S. 436, 106 S.Ct. 2616 (1986).

27. Quoting Friendly, "Is Innocence Irrelevant? Collateral Attack on Criminal Judgments," 38 U.Chi.L.Rev. 142, 160 (1970).

28. See § 29.05(c)(1).

29. Although both pre-*Carrier* cases, it is noteworthy that relief was denied in both *Engle,* involving an erroneous burden of proof instruction, and *Frady,* involving an erroneous malice instruction. See also, *Dugger v. Adams,* discussed below.

nocence." Further suggesting the narrow scope of the exception is the Court's statement in *Sawyer v. Whitley* [30] that a "prototypical" example of actual innocence is "where the State has convicted the wrong person of the crime."

Sawyer also set forth the Court's definition of "actual innocence" where the defendant claims that his death sentence was unwarranted. The majority opinion, written by Chief Justice Rehnquist, rejected the state's contention that a capital defendant is only "innocent" of a death penalty if he should not have been convicted for intentional murder. At the same time, it found overbroad petitioner's contention that review should always be granted if the claimed constitutional error caused "a fair probability that the admission of false evidence, or the preclusion of true mitigating evidence . . . resulted in a sentence of death." Although this standard is analogous to *Kuhlmann's* definition of actual innocence in the trial context, the Court noted that, given the breadth of mitigating factors that are relevant at capital sentencing proceedings, this test would have a damaging effect on "finality" in capital cases. Instead, the Court held that "[s]ensible meaning is given to the the term 'innocent of the death penalty' by allowing a showing in addition to innocence of the capital crime itself a showing that there was no aggravating circumstance or that some other condition of eligibility had not been met." Thus, the petitioner must "show by clear and convincing evidence that . . . no reasonable juror would have found [him] eligible for the death penalty."

The Court made clear that, under this standard, merely showing that mitigating evidence was not presented due to ineffective assistance of counsel or some other reason would be insufficient, because mitigating evidence, no matter how powerful, does not focus on the petitioner's "eligibility" for the death sentence. Furthermore, it strongly suggested that unless the petitioner's claims undermine *all* of the aggravating circumstances found by the sentencing jury, the actual innocence exception is not met. In *Sawyer* itself, the petitioner had been convicted and sentenced to death for torturing a woman and then setting her on fire, in concert with one Charles Lane. The petitioner claimed that the prosecution withheld evidence that would have impeached its principal witness (Sawyer's girlfriend), as well as a hearsay statement by the girlfriend's four year-old son that suggested Sawyer had "tried to help the lady" at the time the fire was lit but was pushed backed in a chair by Lane. The Court found that, in light of other facts adduced at trial, as well as the relevant state law, this evidence, even if credited, did not show Sawyer was "inno-

30. __ U.S. __, 112 S.Ct. 2514 (1992).

cent" of the jury's findings in aggravation that the crime was heinous and committed during an aggravated arson; undisputed evidence showed that Sawyer had helped his co-defendant beat and kick the victim, submerge her in a bathtub and pour scalding water on her prior to the burning, and Louisiana law held liable principals who "aid and abet in [the crime's] commission, or directly or indirectly counsel or procure another to commit the crime." [31]

Earlier Court cases dealing with capital sentencing claims are consonant with *Sawyer.* In *Smith v. Murray,*[32] for instance, the claim involved the admissibility of psychiatric testimony to the effect that the defendant was "dangerous." Although the Court conceded that this testimony was obtained in violation of the Fifth Amendment,[33] it found that, because the testimony had not been false or misleading, and because the evaluation on which it was based "neither precluded the development of true facts nor result-ed in the admission of false ones," admission of the testimony did not lead to the imposition of capital punishment on one who was actually "nondangerous." Similarly, in *Dugger v. Adams,*[34] the Court held that an erroneous instruction to the jury that the judge had the ultimate "responsibility" for imposing the death penalty was not reviewable under the actual innocence exception, given the fact that the trial judge found an equal number of aggravating and mitigating circumstances in affirming the jury's death sen-tence. According to the Court, "[d]emonstrating that an error is by its nature the kind of error that might have affected the accuracy of a death sentence is far from demonstrating that an individual defendant probably is 'actually innocent' of the sen-tence he or she received."

33.04   Other Procedural Hurdles

(a) **The Exhaustion Requirement.** Generally, state prison-ers must seek vindication of their federal constitutional rights in state court before proceeding to federal court. According to the Supreme Court, this "exhaustion" requirement is based on the comity principle. It "serves to minimize friction between our federal and state systems of justice" by preventing disruption of state proceedings and giving state courts an opportunity to correct federal violations before a federal court does.[35] Justice O'Connor

31. The three dissenters agreed with this result, but argued that the Court should define actual innocence in the capital sentencing context to require the defendant to show that "the alleged error more likely than not created a manifest miscarriage of justice."

32. 477 U.S. 527, 106 S.Ct. 2661 (1986).

33. See *Estelle v. Smith,* 451 U.S. 454, 101 S.Ct. 1866 (1981), discussed in § 28.03(b)(3).

34. 489 U.S. 401, 109 S.Ct. 1211 (1989).

35. *Duckworth v. Serrano,* 454 U.S. 1, 102 S.Ct. 18 (1981).

has further asserted that ensuring state court review of habeas claims will improve competence among state courts since they will "become increasingly familiar with and hospitable toward federal constitutional issues." [36]

Some commentators, however, believe the exhaustion requirement "is at best a nuisance and a wasted effort, and at worst offends comity interests rather than advancing them." [37] By the time most non-exhausted claims are presented in federal court, they are defaulted in any event; returning the claim to a state court to have it confirm that fact is inefficient. In the few cases where the state court does reach the merits of a non-exhausted claim, the federal court will still often reconsider the case from scratch, resulting in further inefficiency; furthermore, as Justice Blackmun has pointed out, "[r]emitting a habeas petitioner to state court to exhaust a patently frivolous claim . . . hardly demonstrates respect for state courts." [38] As to Justice O'Connor's hope that the requirement increases state court competence, one commentator has argued that "state courts have been addressing federal constitutional issues for a long time, . . . and it is condescending at best to suggest that with more practice they might improve their ability to recognize and respect federal rights." [39]

For some time, the Supreme Court seemed willing merely to express a preference against habeas review when review by state courts remained available,[40] but by 1944 the Court considered it well settled that "ordinarily an application for habeas corpus by one detained under a state court judgment of conviction will be entertained . . . only after all state remedies available, including all appellate remedies in the state courts and in this Court by appeal or writ of certiorari have been exhausted." [41] The current federal habeas statute, § 2254(b), summarizes current law with respect to exhaustion. It states that the writ is not available to the applicant "unless it appears that the applicant has exhausted the remedies available in the courts of the State, or that there is either an absence of available State corrective process or the existence of circumstances rendering such process ineffective to protect the rights of the prisoner." The Supreme Court has adhered to this formulation in virtually all cases, although it

36. *Rose v. Lundy*, 455 U.S. 509, 102 S.Ct. 1198 (1982).

37. Friedman, "A Tale of Two Habeas," 73 Minn.L.Rev. 247, 310 (1988). See also, Bator, "Finality in Criminal Law and Federal Habeas Corpus for State Prisoners," 76 Harv.L. Rev. 441, 483 (1963).

38. *Rose v. Lundy*, 455 U.S. 509, 102 S.Ct. 1198 (1982) (Blackmun, J., concurring).

39. Friedman, supra note 37, at 312–13.

40. See e.g., *Ex parte Royall*, 117 U.S. 241, 6 S.Ct. 734 (1886).

41. *Ex parte Hawk*, 321 U.S. 114, 64 S.Ct. 448 (1944).

continues to affirm the idea that the exhaustion requirement is not "jurisdictional" and thus can occasionally be waived by a federal court when "the interest of comity and federalism will be better served by addressing the merits forthwith." [42]

Discussed here are four issues which arise with some frequency in connection with the exhaustion requirement: (1) the meaning of § 2254's phrase "remedies available in the courts of the state;" (2) the meaning of that section's "ineffective" state "corrective process;" (3) the extent to which the precise claim raised on federal habeas must have been presented in state court; and (4) the correct procedure when a habeas petition contains both exhausted and non-exhausted claims.

(1) Available state remedies. In *Brown v. Allen* [43] the Court held that a state prisoner who has fully pursued direct review at the state and Supreme Court level need not seek state collateral remedies in order to meet the exhaustion requirement. And in *Fay v. Noia,*[44] the Court eliminated the need to pursue a direct appeal to the Supreme Court before exhaustion occurs. Thus only state appellate remedies need be sought to meet the exhaustion requirement. However, review must normally be sought up through the highest court level, which usually means the state supreme court.

Fay also stressed that only *available* state remedies need be pursued to satisfy the exhaustion requirement. In *Fay,* the state used Noia's confession, over his objection that it was coerced, to convict him of felony murder. After the statutory period for appeal had run, Noia learned that the similarly produced confessions of his co-defendants were found to have been coerced and sought federal habeas review. The district court dismissed his claim, for failing to exhaust the state remedy. But the Supreme Court was unanimous in holding that the exhaustion requirement in § 2254 "is limited in its application to failure to exhaust state remedies still open to the habeas applicant at the time he files his application in the federal courts." It added: "conventional notions of finality in criminal litigation cannot be permitted to defeat the manifest federal policy that federal constitutional rights of personal liberty shall not be denied without the fullest opportunity for plenary federal judicial review." *Fay's* holding with respect to the exhaustion requirement, unlike its deliberate bypass rule, is still good law.

(2) Ineffective corrective processes. The last clause of § 2254(b) makes clear that even exhaustion of available remedies is not required when circumstances render the state process "inef-

42. *Granberry v. Greer*, 481 U.S. 129, 107 S.Ct. 1671 (1987).

43. 344 U.S. 443, 73 S.Ct. 397 (1953).

44. 372 U.S. 391, 83 S.Ct. 822 (1963).

fective to protect the rights of the prisoner." In *Duckworth v. Serrano*,[45] the Court construed this language to mean that an exception to the exhaustion requirement exists only if there is no opportunity to obtain redress in state court or if the corrective process is so clearly deficient as to render futile any effort to obtain relief." Under this definition of ineffective process, few situations will merit suspension of the exhaustion requirement. Inadequate process may be found, however, when there has been an inordinate delay at the state level,[46] or where "procedural snarls or obstacles preclude an effective state remedy." [47]

(3) The fair presentation requirement. If adequate process was available in the state appellate courts, the habeas petitioner must not only have presented his case to them but also have given them a "fair opportunity" to consider the same issues presented in the habeas petition. Otherwise considerations of comity require dismissal of the petition.[48] The post-Warren Court has strictly construed this requirement.

For example, in *Anderson v. Harless* [49] the petitioner was convicted of murder by a jury which may have been improperly instructed about the burden of proof as required by the Court's decision in *Sandstrom v. Montana*.[50] In his state appeals, the petitioner argued simply that the instruction was erroneous, citing to a state case but not *Sandstrom*. The Supreme Court, in a 6–3 opinion, held that the petition could not be heard on habeas because the *Sandstrom* claim had not been presented in state court. According to the Court:

> [I]t is not enough that all the facts necessary to support the federal claim were before the state courts . . . or that a somewhat similar state-law claim was made. . . . [T]he habeas petitioner must have 'fairly presented' to the state courts the 'substance' of his federal habeas corpus claim.

Where the petitioner merely supplements the *evidence*, rather than adding a new claim, however, the fair presentation requirement is not necessarily violated. In *Vasquez v. Hillery*,[51] the petitioner, at the federal district court's request, presented statistical evidence showing discrimination in the selection of his grand jury that had not been available in state court. Although the state argued that introduction of this evidence rendered the petitioner's claim a "wholly different animal," the Supreme Court

45. 454 U.S. 1, 102 S.Ct. 18 (1981).

46. See e.g., *Lowe v. Duckworth*, 663 F.2d 42 (7th Cir.1981).

47. *Bartone v. United States*, 375 U.S. 52, 84 S.Ct. 21 (1963).

48. *Picard v. Connor*, 404 U.S. 270, 92 S.Ct. 509 (1971).

49. 459 U.S. 4, 103 S.Ct. 276 (1982).

50. 442 U.S. 510, 99 S.Ct. 2450 (1979).

51. 474 U.S. 254, 106 S.Ct. 617 (1986).

pointed out that the new information did not change the nature of the discrimination claim but merely provided more sophisticated data which improved the reliability of the district court's decision. Whether the same holding would be required in a case in which the federal court did not make a request for the supplemental evidence is not clear. As the Court stated, "the circumstances present no occasion for the Court to consider a case in which the prisoner has attempted to expedite federal review by deliberately withholding essential facts from the state courts."

In addition to considering whether the precise claims raised on federal habeas were presented fairly at the state level, one must consider the *type* of state proceeding at which the claims were presented. In *Pitchess v. Davis,*[52] for instance, the Supreme Court found that motions to the California Court of Appeal and the California Supreme Court for a pretrial writ of prohibition were not sufficient, by themselves, to exhaust state remedies, because such writs are granted only when "extraordinary relief" is required, and thus did accurately represent the typical state review process. Similarly, in *Castille v. Peoples,*[53] a unanimous Court found that the fair presentation requirement was not met when the only state court consideration of the claims in the petitioner's federal habeas petition was on a petition for "allocatur review," which under Pennsylvania law is not a matter of right but is granted "only when there are special and important reasons therefor."

(4) Mixed petitions. Frequently, a habeas petition will include both exhausted and non-exhausted claims, the latter involving issues not litigated at the state level because the state court focused on other claims or because the defendant later appended them to the petition as it worked its way up the appellate ladder. Until the Court's decision in *Rose v. Lundy,*[54] the majority of circuits had held that a federal district court confronted with a "mixed" petition must pass upon the fully exhausted claims immediately (if they can be separated from the non-exhausted claims), on the ground that the federal interest in safeguarding the rights of prisoners and swiftly adjudicating disputes outweighed any federal-state comity concerns that might force delayed consideration of a properly presented issue.[55] In *Lundy,* however, the Supreme Court decided that district courts must *dismiss* habeas petitions containing both unexhausted and exhausted claims, in order to "encourage state prisoners to seek full relief first from the

52. 421 U.S. 482, 95 S.Ct. 1748 (1975) (per curiam).

53. 489 U.S. 346, 109 S.Ct. 1056 (1989).

54. 455 U.S. 509, 102 S.Ct. 1198 (1982).

55. See, e.g., *Miller v. Hall,* 536 F.2d 967 (1st Cir.1976); *Tyler v. Swenson,* 483 F.2d 611 (8th Cir.1973); *Hewett v. State of North Carolina,* 415 F.2d 1316 (4th Cir.1969).

state courts, thus giving those courts the first opportunity to review all claims of constitutional error." This holding applies even when the exhausted claims are based on allegations or facts entirely separate from those forming the basis for the non-exhausted claims. A majority of the Court also held, however, that the defendant who has mixed claims can amend his petition to delete the non-exhausted claims and proceed with federal review of his exhausted claims.[56]

(b) **Successive Petitions.** Prisoners will often file more than one habeas petition in the course of their imprisonment. These successive petitions raise two different issues: (1) what is the preclusive effect of having raised the same claim in a previous petition?; and (2) what is the preclusive effect of not having raised a claim in a previous petition?[57]

(1) Raising the same claim. The common law position with respect to successive petitions was that res judicata does not apply to habeas petitions; thus, the petitioner who failed on one habeas petition could go to another habeas court. In the 1924 decision of *Salinger v. Loisel,*[58] the Supreme Court suggested that this rule rested on the fact that appeal of a decision by a habeas court had not been available at common law. Now that such appeal was available, the Court concluded, the previous presentation of a habeas claim should be "considered, and even given controlling weight." However, the Court continued to adhere to the rule that a previous petition on the same claim should not automatically preclude renewed consideration.

In *Sanders v. United States,*[59] the Warren Court reaffirmed *Salinger,* but stressed the part of that decision which refused to apply res judicata principles to habeas. Echoing its other habeas decisions, it held that "[t]he inapplicability of res judicata to habeas . . . is inherent in the very role and function of the writ," because "[c]onventional notions of finality have no place where life or liberty is at stake and infringement of constitutional rights is alleged." Thus, only if "the ends of justice would not be served by reaching the merits of the subsequent application" should a successive petition be denied. Although the petitioner bore the burden of proving that "justice" required review of his second petition, this burden could be met by showing, for example, that the earlier hearing was not "full or fair," or that there had been

56. The drawback to this approach, discussed in § 33.04(b)(2), is that the Court might consider a subsequent petition raising the deleted (and now exhausted) claims an "abuse of the writ" and deny relief.

57. Note that the preclusive effect of *Teague v. Lane,* discussed in § 33.02(c),

has narrowed the cases in which these issues are relevant to those involving claims dictated by precedent at the time of conviction or those meeting one of *Teague's* two exceptions.

58. 265 U.S. 224, 44 S.Ct. 519 (1924).

59. 373 U.S. 1, 83 S.Ct. 1068 (1963).

"an intervening change in law or some other justification for having failed to raise a crucial point or argument in the prior application."

The "ends of justice" language in *Sanders* came from the provision on successive petitions in the 1948 version of § 2244. In 1966, three years after *Sanders,* Congress deleted reference to the "ends of justice" in § 2244, and added subsection (b), which provided that a successive application "need not be entertained [unless it contains a] factual or other ground not adjudicated in the hearing on the earlier application." In *Kuhlmann v. Wilson,*[60] the Court held that this amendment did not eliminate *Sander's* "ends of justice" rule. But, a plurality of the Court went on to reconstrue the meaning of that rule. The plurality emphasized that, at the time of the 1966 amendment, Congress had been concerned with the "heavy burden" created by successive petitions, and had wanted to introduce "a greater degree of finality of judgments in habeas corpus proceedings." To "accommodate Congress' intent . . . with the historic function of habeas corpus to provide relief from unjust incarceration," the plurality held that the "ends of justice" test is met only when the petitioner "supplements his constitutional claim with a colorable showing of factual innocence."

Although only four justices supported this holding, only three dissented from it. The other two justices, White and Blackmun, found it unnecessary to address the successive petition issue, since they felt the petitioner's claim was unmeritorious in any event. It is likely that when the Court is given the opportunity, a majority will support the factual innocence standard endorsed by the plurality in *Kuhlmann,* since it is consistent with the Court's other recent decisions interpreting the scope of the writ.[61] Subsequent decisions have characterized *Kuhlmann* as requiring, at the least, a showing of cause and prejudice akin to what is required in procedural default cases.[62]

(2) Raising a different claim. Sanders also addressed the converse of the issue just discussed: the appropriate disposition of a petition that includes a claim *not* raised in a previous petition. *Sanders* held that the proper response in such a situation depends upon whether there has been "abuse of the writ." Purporting to summarize a number of cases on the issue, it concluded that such abuse normally occurs only when the government can show that there has been a deliberate decision to avoid asserting the claim in the previous petition or hearing.[63] Obviously borrowing from its

60. 477 U.S. 436, 106 S.Ct. 2616 (1986).

61. See, e.g., *Murray v. Carrier,* 477 U.S. 478, 106 S.Ct. 2639 (1986), discussed in § 33.03(e).

62. See *Sawyer v. Whitley,* __ U.S. __, 112 S.Ct. 2514 (1992).

63. Here the Court referred to *Wong Doo v. United States,* 265 U.S. 239, 44 S.Ct. 524 (1924), where the Court up-

reasoning in *Fay v. Noia*,[64] the Court reasoned that any other standard would be "unfair," particularly since such writs are often brought by a petitioner "typically unlearned in the law and unable to procure legal assistance in drafting his application."

Not surprisingly, given the repudiation of *Fay* in its later procedural default cases,[65] the Court subsequently rejected this approach. In *McCleskey v. Zant*,[66] the Court broadened the definition of writ abuse to include any situation where the petitioner making a new claim in a successive petition is unable to meet the narrowly defined cause and prejudice standard developed in those cases. In other words, even inadvertent failure to raise the claim in the first petition will usually prevent it being considered in a subsequent petition. And even if the petitioner can overcome this hurdle, unless he can also show that the claimed error affected the outcome of his trial (i.e. "prejudice"), the claim will usually not be heard.[67] Justice Kennedy, who wrote the majority opinion, first found that the federal habeas statute, which provides that a new ground in a successive petition shall be dismissed if "the applicant has . . . on the earlier application deliberately withheld the newly asserted ground *or* otherwise abused the writ," [68] was ambiguous as to the rule to be followed. He then rejected the deliberate bypass rule in favor of the cause and prejudice standard, given the need to promote finality and efficiency in the collateral review process.

Zant's analogy between successive petition and procedural default cases seems inapt. As Justice Marshall argued in dissent, one of the major reasons earlier decisions had adoped the narrow cause and prejudice standard was to protect against federal encroachment of *state* procedural rules, a concern that is not implicated when the relevant previous petition was in federal court. Furthermore, as *Sanders* noted, usually the habeas petitioner is unassisted by counsel, unlike the litigants in the Court's procedural default cases, who all had counsel, albeit possibly incompetent ones, at the stage they defaulted.[69] Justice Marshall also contended that the Court's new rule will decrease efficiency, because petitioners will now assert all conceivable claims in their first petition, however weak, rather than hold back an as-yet unrecog-

held dismissal of a due process claim that was raised in a previous petition, but not argued at the hearing on the petition.

64. 372 U.S. 391, 83 S.Ct. 822 (1963), discussed in § 33.03(b).

65. See, e.g., *Wainwright v. Sykes*, 433 U.S. 72, 97 S.Ct. 2497 (1977), discussed in § 33.03(c).

66. 499 U.S. —, 111 S.Ct. 1454 (1991).

67. However, consistent with its other habeas cases, see e.g., § 33.03(e), the Court held that the petitioner can always obtain review if he can make a plausible case that the error he is claiming permitted the conviction of an innocent person.

68. 28 U.S.C.A. § 2254(b).

69. See § 33.05.

nized claim in the hopes that future caselaw will give it more credibility. Finally, the majority's apparent assumption that the deliberate bypass standard does not provide an effective barrier to abuses of the writ seems unfounded.[70]

Zant also has implications for the petitioner who brings a petition with both exhausted and non-exhausted claims. In *Rose v. Lundy*,[71] it will be remembered, the Court held that such a petition should be dismissed, and that the petitioner then had the option of returning to state court to obtain review of the non-exhausted claims or deleting those claims from the petition and proceeding with the exhausted claims. A plurality in *Lundy,* in an opinion by Justice O'Connor, went on to suggest that a petitioner who chose the second route might be barred, on abuse of writ grounds, from raising the deleted claims (now presumably exhausted) in a subsequent petition. *Zant's* application of the cause and prejudice standard to successive petitions makes it probable that the plurality view in *Lundy* is now the law.

(c) The Custody Requirement. Historically, the writ of habeas corpus directed the prisoner's jailer to "bring forth the body" of the prisoner to the court. Accordingly, the federal habeas statutes have all provided that the writ extends only to those "in custody." But the legislation has never defined this phrase. While "custody" clearly encompasses those petitioners who are actually imprisoned on criminal charges, it has been defined more broadly by the Supreme Court in decisions construing the habeas statutes.

Jones v. Cunningham,[72] a Warren Court decision, marked the first major decision expanding the custody concept. Noting that the writ had been made available to aliens seeking entry into the United States despite their ability to go anywhere else in the world, Justice Black's majority opinion stated:

> Of course, [the] writ always could and still can reach behind prison walls and iron bars. But it can do more. It is not now and never has been a static, narrow, formalistic remedy; its scope has grown to achieve its grand purpose—the protection of individuals against erosion of their rights to be free from wrongful restraints upon their liberty.[73]

---

70. See, e.g., *Woodard v. Hutchins,* 464 U.S. 377, 104 S.Ct. 752 (1984) (applying deliberate bypass rule in refusing to hear new claims raised immediately after Supreme Court denied writ of certiorari on old claims); *Antone v. Dugger,* 465 U.S. 200, 104 S.Ct. 962 (1984) (applying bypass rule in refusing to hear new claims previously raised in state courts).

71. 455 U.S. 509, 102 S.Ct. 1198 (1982), discussed in § 33.04(b)(4).

72. 371 U.S. 236, 83 S.Ct. 373 (1963).

73. Black also noted that the lower courts had permitted habeas relief in cases involving induction into the military and child custody disputes.

This language suggested that many types of non-prison restrictions other than parole could satisfy the custody requirement. Indeed, in *Hensley v. Municipal Court*,[74] the Court appeared to do away with the custody requirement almost entirely by hearing collaterally the claim of a petitioner who was released on his own recognizance pending execution of his sentence for a misdemeanor conviction. As one justification for this action, the Court pointed out, quoting *Jones*, that the petitioner was subject to "restraints not shared by the public generally." However, the Court also noted that here petitioner's imprisonment was not remote but certain and immediate if habeas relief were denied; due to a number of stays, he had been able to complete the appeals process at the state level. Thus, ultimately *Hensley* may stand only for the proposition that when a petitioner who has been released on his own recognizance has exhausted his state remedies, and imprisonment is accordingly impending, he is entitled to habeas relief.

The Court affirmed this interpretation of *Hensley* in *Justices of Boston Municipal Court v. Lydon*.[75] In *Lydon*, the petitioner was convicted of a misdemeanor and released on his own recognizance pending a trial de novo which, under Massachusetts law, functions as an appeal of misdemeanor cases. He then sought dismissal of the second prosecution, on the ground that the evidence at his first trial had been insufficient and that double jeopardy therefore barred the second trial. Upon rejection of this argument by the de novo court, he was permitted interlocutory appeal of his double jeopardy claim through the state appellate system and was denied relief. The Supreme Court permitted his subsequent habeas petition because he had exhausted his state remedies, although on an interlocutory basis rather than, as in *Hensley*, after final judgment on direct appeal. The Court made clear that the rationale for finding Lydon was in custody was not his release terms alone but the fact that "there are no more state procedures of which Lydon may avail himself to avoid an allegedly unconstitutional second trial."

As a general rule, of course, once a person completes a particular sentence, he is no longer in "custody." In *Maleng v. Cook*,[76] however, a petitioner who had finished his sentence argued that he should still be able to challenge the underlying conviction because it was being used to enhance a sentence he had yet to serve. The majority rejected the broad proposition that a petitioner who has served his sentence remains in custody any time there is the "possibility" that the underlying conviction will be used to

---

74. 411 U.S. 345, 93 S.Ct. 1571 (1973).

75. 466 U.S. 294, 104 S.Ct. 1805 (1984).

76. 490 U.S. 488, 109 S.Ct. 1923 (1989).

enhance a subsequent sentence; under the Court's prior decisions, such a case was "moot." [77] But it granted relief in *Maleng* because the petitioner was already subject to a state detainer, designed to ensure that he would be available to serve an enhanced sentence which was based in part on the conviction underlying his expired prison term.[78]

33.05   The Right to Assistance on Collateral Review

Because the Supreme Court has concluded that criminal prosecution ends at sentencing,[79] the Sixth Amendment's guarantee of the "assistance of counsel in all criminal prosecutions" does not apply to habeas proceedings. Nor does due process or equal protection analysis support a right to counsel on habeas. In *Evitts v. Lucey*,[80] the Court held that due process guarantees assistance of counsel for the indigent accused on direct appeal. But in *Ross v. Moffitt*,[81] it concluded that there is no entitlement to counsel on subsequent discretionary appeals because the petitioner has access to the briefs and other documents from the direct appeal. In *Pennsylvania v. Finley*,[82] the Court applied the same reasoning in denying a right to counsel at state post-conviction proceedings, and in *Murray v. Giarratano* [83] it refused to make an exception to *Finley* for capital cases.[84]

Because *Ross* and *Finley* are based on the assumption that the petitioner has had at least one counseled post-conviction review, one might argue that, with respect to claims that were not or could not have been brought on direct appeal, a right to counsel should exist at collateral proceedings. For instance, in *Coleman v. Thompson*,[85] state law did not allow the petitioner to bring his claims of ineffective trial, sentencing and appellate counsel until state habeas review. Under these circumstances, the majority recognized that there might "be an exception to the rule of *Finley* and *Girratano* in those cases where state collateral review is the first place a prisoner can present a challenge to his conviction." But the Court was able to avoid a final determination on this

77. See *Carafas v. LaVallee,* 391 U.S. 234, 88 S.Ct. 1556 (1968).

78. See *Braden v. 30th Judicial Circuit Court,* 410 U.S. 484, 93 S.Ct. 1123 (1973).

79. See § 31.03(a)(3).

80. 469 U.S. 387, 105 S.Ct. 830 (1985).

81. 417 U.S. 600, 94 S.Ct. 2437 (1974).

82. 481 U.S. 551, 107 S.Ct. 1990 (1987).

83. 492 U.S. 1, 109 S.Ct. 2765 (1989). However, six justices indicated that habeas counsel might be required in capital cases where there was no adequate substitute. See § 31.03(c)(4).

84. The right to counsel at federal post-conviction proceedings has not been addressed, perhaps because federal regulations provide that counsel is automatically provided when an evidentiary hearing is to be held or counsel's participation is deemed "necessary" for utilization of various procedures. See § 2254 Rule 6(a), 8(c).

85. 501 U.S. ___, 111 S.Ct. 2546 (1991).

issue, because the petitioner was asserting he had a right to counsel at the *appeal* of the state habeas proceeding, and he had had counsel at the latter proceeding. As the Court pointed out, the petitioner has thus had "his 'one and only appeal,' if that is what a state collateral proceeding may be considered."

Counterbalancing its refusal to recognize a right to habeas counsel, the Court has held, in *Bounds v. Smith*,[86] that state and federal prisoners have a "constitutional right of access to the courts." Justice Marshall's majority opinion concluded that this right requires prison authorities to assist inmates in the preparation and filing of meaningful legal papers by providing them with adequate law libraries, adequate assistance from persons trained in the law, or some other equivalent. The majority rejected the state's claim that provision of libraries would be useless because prisoners are not competent to make use of such resources. In an earlier case, *Johnson v. Avery*,[87] the Court also ruled that a state may not prohibit inmates from assisting each other in preparing habeas corpus petitions, at least without providing some reasonable alternative to assist illiterate or poorly educated individuals. Finally, building on its holding in *Griffin v. Illinois*,[88] the Court has held that the indigent habeas petitioner is entitled, under the Equal Protection Clause, to a free transcript of his trial proceeding, at least when a lower court certifies that his claim is not "wholly frivolous."[89]

33.06　Conclusion

The current availability of the writ of habeas corpus as a device for seeking federal court post-conviction review of constitutional claims can be summarized as follows:

(1) The following claims are not cognizable on habeas: (a) Fourth Amendment claims for which there has been a full and fair hearing in state court; (b) claims which advance a rule that is not dictated by precedent and do not go to the jurisdiction of the trial court or the innocence of the petitioner; (c) claims that are strictly factual in nature, when the facts have been fully and fairly litigated at the state level. A petitioner's entitlement to a federal evidentiary hearing on a cognizable claim depends upon whether the state provided an adequate opportunity to develop the facts, which in turn depends on whether the petitioner can meet the cause and prejudice standard in (2) below when explaining why the facts were not developed at the state level.

---

86. 430 U.S. 817, 97 S.Ct. 1491 (1977).

87. 393 U.S. 483, 89 S.Ct. 747 (1969).

88. 351 U.S. 12, 76 S.Ct. 585 (1956), discussed in § 29.02(a).

89. *United States v. MacCollom*, 426 U.S. 317, 96 S.Ct. 2086 (1976); see also, *Smith v. Bennett*, 365 U.S. 708, 81 S.Ct. 895 (1961).

(2) In most cases, a claim, even though cognizable, will not be heard on federal habeas if a state procedural default rule barred it from being heard at the trial, appeal, or post-conviction level, and the petitioner is unable to show cause as to why the claim was not raised, as well as prejudice to his case if the claim is not vindicated. Cause exists only if: (a) the legal or factual basis of the claim was novel at the time of the default; (b) the state interfered with counsel's ability to raise the claim; or (c) the default resulted from ineffective assistance of counsel under the Sixth Amendment. Prejudice probably will exist only if there is a reasonable probability that vindicating the claim would affect the outcome of the state proceeding. The cause and prejudice standard does not apply, however, when: (a) the state default rule is inconsistently applied; (b) the state rule is not the true basis for the dismissal at the state level; or (c) the claim alleges a violation which has probably resulted in the conviction of one who is actually innocent or in the imposition of a death sentence for which there is no aggravating circumstance or other condition of eligibility.

(3) A non-defaulted cognizable claim may still not be heard if: (a) the petitioner has not fairly presented the claim to all available state appellate courts; (b) the claim was included in a previous habeas petition and is not related to factual innocence; (c) the claim was not included in a previous habeas petition and cause and prejudice, as defined in (2), cannot be shown; or (d) the petitioner is not in custody, with custody meaning that there is some restraint on his freedom, either presently or impending, beyond a release on his own recognizance.

(4) There is no right to counsel at habeas proceedings, although state and federal prisons are under an obligation to provide legal assistance to prisoners to ensure adequate access to habeas review, and the courts must provide free transcripts to indigent petitioners, at least for non-frivolous petitions.

BIBLIOGRAPHY

Bator, Paul M. Finality in Criminal Law and Federal Habeas Corpus for State Prisoners. 76 Harv.L.Rev. 441 (1963).

Chemerinsky, Erwin. Thinking About Habeas Corpus. 37 Case West.Res.L.Rev. 748 (1987).

Cover, Robert M. and T.A. Aleinikoff. Dialectical Federalism: Habeas Corpus and the Court. 86 Yale L.J. 1035 (1977).

Friedman, Barry. A Tale of Two Habeas. 73 Minn.L.Rev. 247 (1988).

Friendly, Henry. Is Innocence Irrelevant? Collateral Attack on Criminal Judgments. 38 U.Chi.L.Rev. 142 (1970).

Goldstein, Steven M. Application of Res Judicata Principles to Successive Federal Habeas Corpus Petitions in Capital Cases: The Search for an Equitable Approach. 21 U.C.Davis L.Rev. 45 (1987).

Halpern, Philip. Federal Habeas Corpus and the Mapp Exclusionary Rule After Stone v. Powell. 82 Colum.L.Rev. (1982).

Hill, Alfred. The Inadequate State Ground. 65 Colum.L.Rev. 943 (1965).

Hoffman, Joseph L. Retroactivity and the Great Writ How Congress Should Respond to Teague v. Lane. 1990 B.Y.U.L.Rev. 183.

Hughes, Graham. Sandbagging, Constitutional Rights, Federal Habeas Corpus and the Procedural Default Principle. 16 N.Y.U. Rev.Law & Social Change 321 (1988).

Jeffries, John and William Stuntz. Ineffective Assistance and Procedural Default in Federal Habeas Corpus. 57 U.Chi.L. Rev. 681 (1990).

Michael, Richard A. The "New Federalism" and the Burger Court's Deference to the States in Federal Habeas Proceedings. 64 Iowa L.Rev. 233 (1979).

Patchel, Kathleen. The New Habeas. 42 Hastings L.J. 939 (1991).

Rosenberg, Yale L. Jettisoning Fay v. Noia: Procedural Defaults by Reasonably Incompetent Counsel. 62 Minn.L.Rev. 341 (1978).

Solimine, Michael E. and James L. Walker. Constitutional Litigation In Federal and State Courts: An Empirical Analysis of Judicial Parity. 10 Hast.L.J. 213 (1984).

Tague, Peter W. Federal Habeas Corpus and Ineffective Representation of Counsel: The Supreme Court Has Work to Do. 31 Stan. Law Review 2 (1979).

Yackle, L. Post-Conviction Remedies. Lawyers Cooperative Pub. Co. 1981 (1991 Supp.).

____. Explaining Habeas Corpus. 60 N.Y.U.L.Rev. 991 (1985).

Chapter Thirty-Four

STATE CONSTITUTIONS AS AN INDEPENDENT SOURCE OF RIGHTS

34.01 Introduction

This book has concentrated on developments in federal constitutional law, primarily at the Supreme Court level, and on federal and state statutes that regulate criminal procedure. Until now, little attention has been given to state court efforts to put their own stamp on the criminal process. As the preceding chapters amply demonstrate, since the early 1970's the Supreme Court has narrowed the thrust of Bill of Rights protections established by the Warren Court. Some state courts have accepted this retrenchment with little or no visible reaction, adhering to the Supreme Court's rulings. But many state courts have rejected post-Warren Court holdings, relying on state constitutions as an independent source of rights. These latter decisions represent a new field of criminal procedure deserving of examination here.

The rationale for these state-law decisions is inherent in the language of the Tenth Amendment, which states that "[t]he powers not delegated to the United States by the Constitution, nor prohibited by it to the States, are reserved to the States respectively, or to the people." Although not relying on this provision, the Supreme Court itself has, on several occasions, explicitly endorsed the idea that state law restrictions on state action may exceed those under federal law. For instance, in *Cooper v. California*,[1] the Court reminded: "Our holding, of course, does not affect the State's power to impose higher standards on searches and seizures than required by the Federal Constitution if it chooses to do so.[2]

The first section of this chapter examines state constitutional lawmaking from an historical perspective. The second section then analyzes the various approaches depicted in the historical account, and advocates that state courts assert a cautious independence from federal doctrine.[3] The third section describes the Supreme Court's reaction to state court rejection of its holdings.

---

1. 386 U.S. 58, 87 S.Ct. 788 (1967). See also, *City of Mesquite v. Aladdin's Castle, Inc.*, 455 U.S. 283, 102 S.Ct. 1070 (1982).

2. By the same token, state courts can develop rules based on state law that are not as protective as federal law, although these rules will not go into effect unless the federal courts modify their interpretation of the relevant constitutional provision so as to allow the state rule.

3. This thesis is taken from Slobogin, "State Adoption of Federal Law: Exploring the Limits of Florida's 'Forced Linkage' Amendment," 39 Fla. L.Rev. 653 (1987).

34.02   The Four Phases of State–Federal Judicial Interplay

State court views on the relative importance of state and federal law can be divided into four historical phases, the last three of which overlap considerably.[4] The first phase, from the founding of the republic until approximately the middle of this century, has been called the "dual federalism" period, since the Bill of Rights had no binding effect on state courts. The second phase, which peaked during the early 1970s, might be called the "co-option" period, because the advent of the incorporation doctrine, combined with the activism of the United States Supreme Court, created the impression that federal law stated the exclusive standard on constitutional issues. The third phase, from the early 1970s to the present, has been called the "New Federalism" period because, as noted in the introduction, state courts have been much more willing to diverge from the federal standard. The final phase, still nascent, could be called the "forced-linkage" era. This term is meant to describe the impact of electoral decisions requiring state courts to equate state constitutional law with federal constitutional law.

(a) **Dual Federalism.** During the first 150 years under the federal Constitution, the criminal process guarantees found in the Fourth, Fifth, Sixth, and Eighth amendments applied only to federal cases. Since its ratification in 1868, the Fourteenth Amendment has provided a vehicle for guaranteeing these rights to state criminal defendants through the "incorporation" principle. But as described elsewhere in this book, it was not until well into the twentieth century that the Supreme Court indicated any willingness to find the various criminal process rights so fundamental that the states could not abridge them.[5] Only after the Warren Court invigorated the incorporation idea, beginning with *Mapp v. Ohio*,[6] in 1961, could the state criminal defendant depend upon Fourth Amendment protections, the privilege against self-incrimination, the Double Jeopardy Clause, Sixth Amendment trial rights, and protection against cruel and unusual punishment.

Before the 1960s, then, state courts were almost entirely free to develop their own rules of criminal procedure, despite the fact that state constitutional provisions were usually similar or identical to the analogous federal provisions. State courts interpreted their provisions in one of three ways. They either explicitly

---

4. The first three phases described below duplicate phases described by Collins, "Reliance on State Constitutions: Some Random Thoughs," 54 Miss.L.J. 371, 378–79 (1984).

5. See § 1.01. The first Supreme Court case that relied on the federal Constitution to overturn a state criminal conviction was *Powell v. Alabama*, 287 U.S. 45, 53 S.Ct. 55 (1932), discussed in § 31.02(a).

6. 367 U.S. 643, 81 S.Ct. 1684 (1961).

followed federal court interpretations of federal provisions;[7] viewed federal case law as a helpful guidepost, but not dispositive;[8] or ignored it altogether.[9] Often, the latter two approaches resulted in state standards that were more prosecution-oriented than those applied at the federal level. For example, numerous state courts refused to follow *Weeks v. United States,*[10] which required that illegally seized evidence be excluded from federal prosecutions.[11] But occasionally state courts were more energetic than the federal courts in protecting the rights of criminal defendants. For instance, at least one state court found a right to counsel at criminal trials well before *Johnson v. Zerbst*[12] guaranteed that right at the federal level.[13] In any event, during this phase, the independence of state and federal law was an accepted fact.

(b) Co–Option. In the 1960s, the Supreme Court's activism significantly altered the pattern of state constitutional interpretation. The Warren Court not only applied most federal criminal rights guarantees to the states, but also interpreted those guarantees so as to radically restructure the criminal process. Within a decade of its decision in *Mapp* requiring the states to exclude evidence obtained in violation of the Fourth Amendment, the Court had expanded tremendously the types of searches requiring exclusion.[14] Within seven years of its finding in *Gideon v. Wainwright*[15] that the Sixth Amendment's counsel guarantee applied to the states, the Court extended the right beyond trial proceedings to police questioning, lineups, preliminary hearings, and sentencing.[16] And two years after the Court found the privilege against self-incrimination to be a fundamental right,[17] it decided *Miranda v. Arizona,*[18] causing an upheaval in the law of confessions.

This revolution in criminal procedure made state constitutional interpretation seem irrelevant. State litigants and courts were inclined to view the federal standards as the sole source of crimi-

---

7. See, e.g., *Griggs v. Hanson,* 86 Kan. 632, 121 P. 1094 (1912).

8. See, e.g., *State v. Miles,* 29 Wash.2d 921, 190 P.2d 740 (1948) (relying in part on *United States v. Di Re,* 332 U.S. 581, 68 S.Ct. 222 (1948)); *People v. Exum,* 382 Ill. 204, 47 N.E.2d 56, 59 (1943) (relying in part on *Haywood v. United States,* 268 Fed. 795 (7th Cir.1920)).

9. See Abrahamson, "Criminal Law and State Constitutions: The Emergence of State Constitutional Law," 63 Tex.L.Rev. 1141, 1144–46 (1985).

10. 232 U.S. 383, 34 S.Ct. 341 (1914).

11. See, e.g., *Elkins v. United States,* 364 U.S. 206, 80 S.Ct. 1437 (1960) (ap-

pendix listing state decisions following and rejecting *Weeks*).

12. 304 U.S. 458, 58 S.Ct. 1019 (1938).

13. See *Carpenter v. County of Dane,* 9 Wis. 274 (1859).

14. See, e.g., §§ 6.04(a); 14.02(d).

15. 372 U.S. 335, 83 S.Ct. 792 (1963).

16. See § 31.03(a)(1).

17. *Malloy v. Hogan,* 378 U.S. 1, 84 S.Ct. 1489 (1964).

18. 384 U.S. 436, 86 S.Ct. 1602 (1966).

nal procedure law.[19] State courts either interpreted similar federal and state standards similarly, or more commonly, simply neglected to consider the independent significance of state constitutional law. For instance, in Florida between 1961 and 1983, over two-thirds of the state courts' search and seizure decisions made no mention of the state constitutional provision,[20] even though during the last fifteen years of this period an amendment to this provision made it different in significant respects from the Fourth Amendment.[21] On those rare occasions when Florida courts did refer to the state provision, they almost always interpreted it to coincide with federal standards. Indeed, in 1980, the Florida Supreme Court adopted as its own a lower court opinion concluding that "the search and seizure provision of the Florida Constitution imposes no higher standard than that of the Fourth Amendment to the United States Constitution." [22]

(c) **New Federalism.** Developments at the Supreme Court level also prompted the third phase in state constitutional interpretation. The post-Warren Court's retrenchment on the Warren Court's groundbreaking decisions has made clear that federal standards do not necessarily represent the most "progressive" approach to criminal procedure. As the Court has constricted the scope of the Bill of Rights, state courts have disinterred state law and increasingly adopted standards more rigorous than those announced by the Supreme Court. For instance, between 1970 and 1986 over 300 state decisions went beyond Supreme Court pronouncements, and more than half of those decisions involved criminal procedure.[23]

State court reaction against the Supreme Court has been particularly energetic with respect to search and seizure, perhaps because the post–1970 Supreme Court has been especially antagonistic to the Fourth Amendment. Indeed, the first Supreme Court criminal procedure decision to encounter significant state court resistance involved a search and seizure issue. In *United States v. Robinson*,[24] the Supreme Court held that a full search is permissible after a lawful custodial arrest, regardless of the crime giving rise to the arrest. Within four years of *Robinson*, four different state courts had held, based on state constitutional language, that the nature of the offense is relevant to whether a full search is

19. See Howard, "State Courts and Constitutional Rights in the Day of the Burger Court," 62 Va.L.Rev. 873–86 (1976).

20. See Slobogin, supra note 3, at 668.

21. The 1968 version of Florida's search and seizure provision specifically protected "communications" as well as persons, papers, houses and effects, and explicitly stated that illegally seized evidence should be excluded.

22. *State v. Hetland,* 366 So.2d 831 (Fla.App.1979), aff'd 387 So.2d 963 (Fla. 1980).

23. Collins & Galie, The Methodology, Nat'l L.J., Sept. 29, 1986, at S–8 (collecting over 300 such cases decided since 1970).

24. 414 U.S. 218, 94 S.Ct. 467 (1973).

justified.[25]   Similarly, the courts of four states have refused to follow *United States v. White*[26] on state law grounds, finding untenable the Court's opinion that monitoring a private conversation with a body bug is not a search.[27]   At least three states' courts,[28] again relying on their constitutions, have declined to adopt the Supreme Court's totality of the circumstances approach to the probable cause inquiry established in *Illinois v. Gates.*[29] Other Supreme Court Fourth Amendment decisions that at least one state court has found unpersuasive include *New York v. Belton,*[30] allowing searches of cars and containers in them when the occupant has been lawfully arrested;[31] *Smith v. Maryland,*[32] holding that a person does not have a reasonable expectation of privacy in the identity of phone numbers called;[33] and *United States v. Leon,*[34] establishing that a search pursuant to an invalid warrant is lawful if the searching officer believed in objective good faith that the warrant was valid.[35]   These examples far from exhaust the list of issues on which state courts have come to independent conclusions on search and seizure issues.[36]

Nor is the New Federalism limited to rejecting the Supreme Court's Fourth Amendment decisions. For instance, several state courts have rejected the Court's decision in *Harris v. New York*[37] permitting use of statements obtained in violation of *Miranda* for impeachment purposes.[38]   Decisions holding inapplicable other Supreme Court rulings concerning the interrogation process are

---

25. See *Zehrung v. State,* 569 P.2d 189 (Alaska 1977); *People v. Brisendine,* 13 Cal.3d 528, 119 Cal.Rptr. 315, 531 P.2d 1099 (1975); *People v. Clyne,* 189 Colo. 412, 541 P.2d 71 (1975); *State v. Kaluna,* 55 Hawaii 361, 520 P.2d 51 (1974).   The Oregon Supreme Court joined this group in 1982. *State v. Caraher,* 293 Or. 741, 653 P.2d 942 (1982).

26. 401 U.S. 745, 91 S.Ct. 1122 (1971).

27. *State v. Glass,* 583 P.2d 872 (Alaska 1978); *State v. Sarmiento,* 397 So.2d 643 (Fla.1981); *People v. Beavers,* 393 Mich. 554, 227 N.W.2d 511 (1975); *State v. Brackman,* 178 Mont. 105, 582 P.2d 1216 (1978).

28. *State v. Kimbro,* 197 Conn. 219, 496 A.2d 498 (1985); *Commonwealth v. Upton II,* 394 Mass. 363, 476 N.E.2d 548 (1985); *People v. Johnson,* 66 N.Y.2d 398, 497 N.Y.S.2d 618, 488 N.E.2d 439 (1985).

29. 462 U.S. 213, 103 S.Ct. 2317 (1983).

30. 453 U.S. 454, 101 S.Ct. 2860 (1981).

31. *State v. Hernandez,* 410 So.2d 1381 (La.1982).

32. 442 U.S. 735, 99 S.Ct. 2577 (1979).

33. See *People v. Blair,* 25 Cal.3d 640, 159 Cal.Rptr. 818, 602 P.2d 738 (1979); *People v. Sporleder,* 666 P.2d 135 (Colo.1983); *State v. Hunt,* 91 N.J. 338, 450 A.2d 952 (1982).

34. 468 U.S. 897, 104 S.Ct. 3405 (1984).

35. *State v. Novembrino,* 105 N.J. 95, 519 A.2d 820 (1987); *People v. Bigelow,* 66 N.Y.2d 417, 497 N.Y.S.2d 630, 488 N.E.2d 451 (1985).

36. See list of cases in Collins & Galie, *supra* note 23, at S–9, S–12.

37. 401 U.S. 222, 91 S.Ct. 643 (1971).

38. *People v. Disbrow,* 16 Cal.3d 101, 127 Cal.Rptr. 360, 545 P.2d 272 (1976); *Commonwealth v. Triplett,* 462 Pa. 244, 341 A.2d 62 (1975); *State v. Santiago,* 53 Hawaii 254, 492 P.2d 657 (1971).

numerous.[39] Court holdings on issues as disparate as double jeopardy [40] and the right to jury trial [41] have also been repudiated. Measuring the extent of the New Federalism with a different gauge, at least thirty-five courts have flexed state constitutional muscle on at least one issue of criminal procedure.[42]

The New Federalism phase is neither insignificant nor isolated, and is likely to continue in the criminal procedure area. Factors that will fuel further state constitutional developments include the Supreme Court's likely persistence in its prosecution-oriented tendencies and state courts' unwillingness to relinquish the power they have discovered and come to enjoy since the 1970's. A factor that could severely curtail the New Federalism, however, is the hostile reaction of state citizens to their courts' activism. Chief Justice Burger, for one, sought to encourage this reaction while he was on the Court. In a concurring opinion to a dismissal of a writ of certiorari, he stated that "when state courts interpret state law to require more than the Federal Constitution requires, the citizens of the state must be aware that they have the power to amend state law to ensure rational law enforcement." [43] As discussed below, in at least two states, the electorate has exercised this power.

(d) Forced Linkage. Linkage of federal and state standards can occur in two ways. Linkage most frequently occurs when state courts interpret their constitutional provisions to conform with the federal courts' interpretation of similar federal provisions.[44] This approach does not force linkage on the courts, because state judges control conformity with federal interpretation

39. See, e.g., *People v. Harris,* 77 N.Y.2d 434, 568 N.Y.S.2d 702, 570 N.E.2d 1051 (1991) (rejecting *New York v. Harris,* discussed in § 2.03(d)); *People v. Houston,* 42 Cal.3d 595, 230 Cal.Rptr. 141, 724 P.2d 1166 (1986) (rejecting *Moran v. Burbine,* discussed in § 16.04(a)); *People v. Pettingill,* 21 Cal.3d 231, 145 Cal.Rptr. 861, 578 P.2d 108 (1978) (rejecting *Michigan v. Mosley,* discussed in § 16.03(e)).

40. See, e.g., *State v. Kennedy,* 295 Or. 260, 666 P.2d 1316 (1983) (rejecting *Oregon v. Kennedy,* discussed in § 30.03(c)(2); *People v. Paulsen,* 198 Colo. 458, 601 P.2d 634 (1979) (rejecting *United States v. Scott,* discussed in § 30.03(b)).

41. See, e.g., *Baker v. City of Fairbanks,* 471 P.2d 386 (Alaska 1970) (rejecting *Baldwin v. New York,* discussed in § 27.02(c); *State v. Becker,* 130 Vt. 153, 287 A.2d 580 (1972) (same); *Holland v. State,* 91 Wis.2d 134, 280

N.W.2d 288 (1979) (rejecting *Apodaca v. Oregon,* discussed in § 27.02(e); *Gilbreath v. Wallace,* 292 Ala. 267, 292 So. 2d 651 (1974) (rejecting *Williams v. Florida,* discussed in § 27.02(d)).

42. See Collins & Galie, supra note 23, at S–9, S–12. The supreme courts of Washington, Alaska, California and New Jersey have been particularly active. Some state legislatures have also repudiated Supreme Court holdings. See Arons and Katsh, "Reclaiming the Fourth Amendment in Massachusetts," 2 Civ.Liberties Rev. 82 (Winter 1975) (legislation overturning *Robinson*).

43. *Florida v. Casal,* 462 U.S. 637, 103 S.Ct. 3100 (1983) (Burger, C.J., concurring).

44. See, e.g., *State v. Jackson,* 206 Mont. 338, 672 P.2d 255 (1983); *Brown v. State,* 657 S.W.2d 797 (Tex.Crim.App. 1983) (en banc).

and can selectively apply it as they see fit. This form of linkage is merely a judicially adopted aid to judicial decisionmaking.

The second type of linkage is that which the electorate imposes on the courts.[45] Many state constitutions provide for amendment through initiative or referendum.[46] The citizens of two states, California and Florida, have used the amendment process to require their courts to follow certain aspects of federal law. The California provision accomplishes this objective indirectly by stating that all "relevant evidence" is admissible in criminal proceedings.[47] Under this provision, California courts remain free to develop the substantive law as they see fit, but the exclusionary remedy is available only in those situations dictated by federal law.[48] The Florida provision differs in two ways. First, it focuses solely on search and seizure law, rather than impinging on every substantive area where exclusion may be the sought-after remedy. Second, it provides that the state search and seizure provision "shall be construed in conformity with the 4th Amendment to the United States Constitution as interpreted by the United States Supreme Court."[49] Thus, in contrast to the California provision, the Florida amendment eliminates the power of the Florida courts to develop their own substantive law in the search and seizure area.

The impetus for these two provisions was the same. In California, law enforcement groups were primarily responsible for the drafting of a number of constitutional measures, ultimately proposed in 1982, which came to be called the Victims' Bill of Rights.[50] The pre-vote literature devoted considerable attention to the exclusionary rule provision, describing it as a means of counteracting the California courts' tendency to be "too concerned with rights of defendants."[51] Thus, approval of the provision was probably in large part a reaction to perceived state court activism in search and seizure law.

---

45. The discussion here focuses on direct action by the electorate. The legislature may also impose linkage on the courts. See, e.g., Fla.Stat. § 933.19(1) (1985) (providing that the opinion in *Carroll v. United States,* 267 U.S. 132, 45 S.Ct. 280 (1925), is "adopted as the statute law of the state applicable to searches and seizures under § 12, Art. 1 of the State Constitution").

46. See, e.g., Alaska Const. art. XIII, § 1; Fla. Const. art. XI, §§ 1, 3, 5; N.Y. Const. art. XIX, § 1. "Initiative" refers to a proposal initiated by the populace. "Referendum" refers to a proposal initiated by the legislature and submitted to the electorate.

47. Cal. Const. art. I, § 28(d).

48. In *California v. Greenwood,* 486 U.S. 35, 108 S.Ct. 1625 (1988), the Supreme Court rejected the argument that this provision violated the Due Process Clause because it permits introduction of evidence seized in violation of state law.

49. Fla. Const., art. I, § 12.

50. Wilkes, "First Things Last: Amendomania and State Bills of Rights," 54 Miss.L.J. 223, 253–54 (1984).

51. Id. at 254, n. 168.

Law enforcement groups also initiated Florida's amendment, which was even more clearly the result of dissatisfaction with a specific state court ruling. Although, as noted earlier,[52] Florida courts had tended to mimic federal law, the one significant decision which did not track Supreme Court precedent (*State v. Sarmiento,*[53] rejecting the Supreme Court's ruling that use of a bugged undercover agent was not a search) immediately led law enforcement groups to propose the amendment. Within two years, after receiving vigorous backing from the Governor, it was passed.[54]

34.03 An Assessment of the Different Approaches to State Constitutional Interpretation

Of the various approaches that state courts could take to federal constitutional law, a cautious version of the New Federalism probably best balances the tradition of federalism with principles of judicial decisionmaking. Co-option is clearly an inappropriate response to the need for a policy governing state court consideration of federal law. Linkage, while attractive in some respects, is ultimately repugnant to our notion of parallel systems of government. Forced linkage of the type California and Florida have adopted is especially so. On the other hand, wide-open state activism runs counter to judicial decisionmaking goals of clarity, efficiency, and principled reasoning. In short, under a balanced approach to judicial regulation of criminal procedure, state courts would have the authority to develop standards more protective than those the federal courts have produced, but they would be circumspect in doing so.

(a) **Differences in Local Law.** The justification for state court independence is most clear when the organic state law is different from federal law. Most commentators and jurists agree that interpretive variance is permissible when based on something uniquely local.[55] Thus, a significant difference in the state constitutional provision's language or its legislative history may be a proper justification for departure from the federal interpretation of the analogous federal provision. For instance, New York's constitution speaks of a right to counsel "in any trial in any court whatever,"[56] language which on its face appears to be broader than the Supreme Court's holding that the Sixth Amendment guarantees counsel only at proceedings which result in imprison-

52. See § 34.02(b).

53. 397 So.2d 643 (Fla.1981).

54. Slobogin, supra note 3, at 671–73.

55. See, e.g., Shapiro, "State Constitutional Doctrine and the Criminal Pro-

cess," 16 Seton Hall L.Rev. 630, 650–54 (1986); Developments in the Law, "The Interpretation of State Constitutional Rights," 95 Harv.L.Rev. 1324, 1361 (1982).

56. N.Y. Const. art. I, § 6.

ment.[57] Similarly, judicial history indicating state court adoption of a standard more expansive than a subsequently established federal standard is clearly a proper basis for ignoring the federal standard.[58]

Finally, a distinct "local morality" is generally a valid reason for diverging from federal standards. A good example of this latter idea is *Ravin v. State,*[59] in which the Alaska Supreme Court established a state constitutional right to private, in-home possession and use of marijuana by adults. The court relied in part on the observation that Alaska "has traditionally been the home of people who prize their individuality and who have chosen to settle or to continue living here in order to achieve a measure of control over their own life style which is now unattainable in many of our sister states."

(b) When Local Factors Are Absent: The Cases For and Against Linkage. Beyond these relatively rare "local factor" situations, the value of the New Federalism is much in dispute. Three arguments have been advanced to support the proposition that, despite their technical independence from federal law, state constitutional provisions should not be interpreted any differently from analogous federal provisions when local textual, historical or cultural differences are absent. First is a desire to avoid the uncertainty and confusion among state officials that might result from having two interpretations of the same text. Second is the notion that having two sets of courts address the same issue is unnecessary unless the state courts offer unique insight on the issue based on local factors. Third is the complaint that state activism that is not based on local factors is a result-oriented reaction to federal precedent and therefore unprincipled. The following discussion suggests that, while these arguments carry some weight, at most they support a "presumptive linkage" between federal and state constitutional interpretations, not "forced linkage."

(1) Uncertainty. Jurists frequently make the uncertainty argument. For instance, Chief Justice Erickson of the Colorado Supreme Court has contended that police should be able to rely on United States Supreme Court decisions as the final word.[60] In the Fourth Amendment context, the Arizona Supreme Court has expressed a similar sentiment, stating "one of the few things worse

---

57. *Argersinger v. Hamlin,* 407 U.S. 25, 92 S.Ct. 2006 (1972), discussed in § 31.02(b).

58. See, e.g., *People v. Paulsen,* 198 Colo. 458, 601 P.2d 634 (1979) (rejecting *United States v. Scott,* 437 U.S. 82, 98 S.Ct. 2187 (1978), on the basis of state precedent).

59. 537 P.2d 494 (Alaska 1975).

60. *People v. Sporleder,* 666 P.2d 135 (Colo.1983) (Erickson, C.J., dissenting).

than a single exclusionary rule is two different exclusionary rules." [61]

The uncertainty argument may be a reason for leaning toward linkage. But it does not persuasively support the conclusion that linkage should be required, as is the case in Florida and California. Uncertainty is a fact of constitutional adjudication, particularly in the criminal procedure area. Even if state courts were bound to the federal standard, disputes would arise over the meaning of most decisions. State officers would still be confronted with a complex array of rules in these cases. Further, even when clear standards are attainable, the claim that uncertainty results when two different court systems address the same issue is easily exaggerated. Unless a state court announces a more protective standard, the federal minimum applies. In those rare instances when the state court arrives at a different standard, that standard will control. In short, only one standard will apply to state officials at any given time.

(2) Duplication of review. The second argument against state court activism, that the dual review contemplated under the New Federalism unnecessarily shackles state legislatures and officials, is most forcefully presented by Professor Maltz.[62] The dual layer of review is unnecessary, he argues, because state courts are no better situated than federal courts to interpret constitutional language, except when textual differences, legislative history, or local morality create special considerations under state law. In all other circumstances, contends Maltz, neither the competence nor the institutional traits of the state courts distinguish them from the federal courts enough to merit allowing them independent review of constitutional issues and burdening state legislation with another judicial hurdle.

Like the uncertainty argument, the "duplication-of-review" argument might predispose one toward linkage, but it is not a persuasive reason for requiring it. As Maltz concedes, the duplication argument loses its force when the text of the state constitution is significantly different from the federal text, when state legislative history differs from the intent behind the federal provision, or when local morality diverges from national morality. More importantly, forced linkage is inappropriate even when differences between federal and state language or between federal and state history are minimal. Admittedly, in this situation state courts may be no better equipped to exercise judicial review than federal courts, and should therefore be inclined to accept federal interpretation. But there are three related reasons for permit-

61. *State v. Bolt,* 142 Ariz. 260, 689 P.2d 519 (1984).

62. Maltz, "The Dark Side of State Court Activism," 63 Tex.L.Rev. 995, 1005–06 (1985).

ting, if not encouraging, state courts to diverge from federal precedent even when the reason for doing so is not among those Maltz identifies.

First, federal courts, and especially the Supreme Court, may be constrained in interpreting particular constitutional language because their rulings govern more than one state. For example, the Supreme Court might construe the Fourth Amendment quite differently if freed from the spectre of requiring exclusion in all fifty states every time it announces a new search and seizure principle. Professor Sager has persuasively argued that the underenforcement that may result from this type of institutional pressure on the Supreme Court justifies more expansive state court interpretations.[63] Non-judicial considerations that are irrelevant to the state should not drive state constitutional law.

Second, linkage denies federal and state courts the benefit of the state court's reasoning on the proper interpretation of particular language. Such reasoning has played a valuable role in the past. At times, state court reasoning has proven influential even at the United State Supreme Court level.[64]

Finally, linkage prevents the experimentation of which Justice Brandeis spoke so fondly in *New State Ice Co. v. Liebmann.*[65] According to Brandeis:

> Denial of the right to experiment may be fraught with serious consequences to the Nation. It is one of the happy incidents of the federal system that a single courageous State may, if its citizens choose, serve as a laboratory; and try novel social and economic experiments without risk to the rest of the country.

This refrain, which has appeared in many Supreme Court opinions,[66] is particularly germane when speaking of the rights of the criminally accused. As Judge Abrahamson of the Wisconsin Supreme Court has pointed out, state constitutional provisions concerning criminal procedure are "less encrusted with layers of court decisions" than their federal counterparts and thus allow state courts "to rethink the fundamental issues." [67]

(3) Result-oriented decisionmaking. For these reasons, duplicative review can fulfill an important role, even when local interpretation factors are absent. But it still might be viewed as

---

63. See Sager, "Fair Measure: The Legal Status of Underenforced Constitutional Norms," 91 Harv.L.Rev. 1212, 1242–63 (1978).

64. See Utter, "Swimming in the Jaws of the Crocodile: State Court Comment on Federal Constitutional Issues When Disposing of Cases on State Constitutional Grounds," 63 Tex.L.Rev. 1025, 1040 (1985).

65. 285 U.S. 262, 52 S.Ct. 371 (1932).

66. See, e.g., *Chandler v. Florida,* 449 U.S. 560, 101 S.Ct. 802 (1981); *Reeves, Inc. v. Stake,* 447 U.S. 429, 100 S.Ct. 2271 (1980).

67. Abrahamson, supra note 9, at 1181.

improper because it encourages unprincipled decisionmaking. The third argument against state court activism, that it is often result-oriented, is the most prevalent. Many commentators view the current renaissance in state constitutional litigation as an ideological reaction to the retrenchment of the United States Supreme Court, rather than as an objective effort to develop state constitutional doctrine.[68]

The claim that state court activism is result-oriented overlooks the possibility that a judicial decision can be principled simply because it is analytically persuasive. A state court decision need not rely on state constitutional language, history, or precedent to meet this requirement. Admittedly, a state court that strikes out on its own path without giving due deliberation to relevant federal precedent is also likely to be forsaking judicial neutrality. This type of decisionmaking is much more likely to create uncertainty and suggest the type of institutional deficiency that prompts criticism of duplicative review.[69] But if the state court deals with federal precedent and persuasively demonstrates that federal court reasoning is unacceptable, its result can no more be called unprincipled than can the original federal holding. In short, while linkage with federal law should probably be "presumed," that presumption should be one that can be overcome if the state court gives careful attention to federal doctrine before rejecting it.

(c) A Case Study. The Mississippi Supreme Court's original opinion in *Stringer v. State (Stringer I)*[70] illustrates the type of reasoning that can legitimize state repudiation of a federal standard. The opinion, written by Justice Robertson, declined as a matter of state law to adopt the United States Supreme Court's holding in *United States v. Leon,*[71] which interpreted the Fourth Amendment to allow the introduction of evidence seized pursuant to an invalid warrant if, at the time of its seizure, the seizing officer believed in good faith that the warrant was valid. Justice Robertson's opinion offered at least three different bases for rejecting *Leon's* holding.

---

68. See, e.g., Deukmejian & Thompson, "All Sail and No Anchor–Judicial Review Under the California Constitution," 6 Hastings Const. L.Q. 975 (1979); Martineau, "Review Essay, The Status of State Government Law in Legal Education," 53 U.Cin.L.Rev. 511, 516 (1984).

69. For a somewhat contrary position, arguing for a "self-reliant" approach to state constitutional interpretation, see Collins, "Reliance on State Constitutions—Away From a Reactionary Approach," 9 Hastings Const. L.Q. 1 (1981).

70. No. 54,805 (Miss.1985) (LEXIS, States library, Miss. file). On petition for rehearing, the Mississippi Supreme Court withdrew its original opinion in *Stringer* and substituted a second opinion upholding the result, but on a different ground. 491 So.2d 837 (Miss. 1986). The original opinion, written by Justice Robertson, became the concurring opinion in the second Stringer decision.

71. 468 U.S. 897, 104 S.Ct. 3405 (1984), discussed in § 2.03(c)(2).

The first ground advanced in *Stringer I* for repudiating *Leon* focused on explicit differences between federal and state law. Justice Robertson noted that the exclusionary rule has been a recognized facet of Mississippi law since 1922,[72] and that state cases since then had continuously affirmed, even after *Mapp*, the availability of the exclusionary sanction under state law. These facts alone justified a decision to reject *Leon's* good faith exception to the exclusionary rule. Mississippi's pre-*Mapp* judicial history established the state's independent interest in excluding illegally seized evidence, regardless of how federal courts chose to sanction illegal searches.

The *Stringer I* court also based its position on a perception that local systemic tendencies differed from those influencing the United States Supreme Court. Justice Robertson found that the good faith exception in *Leon* "more reflects a shift in judicial/ political ideology than a judicial response to demonstrable and felt societal needs." In Mississippi, at least, no such societal needs were demonstrable. Justice Robertson noted that only once in thirteen years had the Mississippi Supreme Court used the exclusionary rule to keep out evidence police had seized under a groundless warrant. He also pointed out that the effect of *Leon* could be particularly insidious in Mississippi "where most judges issuing warrants have had no formal legal training."

Finally, *Stringer I* attacked *Leon's* logic. The majority in *Leon* justified its holding with a cost-benefit analysis. On the one hand, it reasoned, the loss of convictions due to a blanket exclusionary rule is significant. On the other hand, exclusion would not deter officers acting in good faith reliance on a warrant, and would be unnecessary to deter the magistrate issuing the warrant, assuming the necessary detachment from the law enforcement process. This analysis did not persuade Justice Robertson. He pointed to the Supreme Court's own statistics for the proposition that exclusion of evidence actually aborts few prosecutions.[73] He also noted that the benefit of exclusion is substantial because it motivates the magistrate to be careful in calculating probable cause. Conversely, if the good faith rule of *Leon* were adopted, the magistrate would have little incentive to act properly. A warrant is obtained in an *ex parte* proceeding from which there is no appeal. Moreover, because of judicial immunity, the magistrate does not experience even the slim deterrent effect that fear of civil liability produces.

72. *Tucker v. State,* 128 Miss. 211, 90 So. 845 (1922).

73. The Leon Court had noted that the exclusionary rule "results in the nonprosecution of between 0.6% and 2.35% of individuals arrested for felonies."

Ultimately, however, the *Stringer I* court grounded its decision not on cost-benefit concerns but on what it considered the "fundamental logic of the exclusionary rule." Justice Robertson asserted that the exclusionary rule is meant to leave the state no better or worse off than if the illegal search and seizure had not occurred, citing *Nix v. Williams*,[74] a recent United States Supreme Court decision that had relied on this proposition in addressing the scope of the exclusionary rule in the derivative evidence context. He then reasoned that because the good faith exception violates this precept by allowing the state to benefit from an illegal search, it cannot be countenanced. The *Stringer I* court also restated its adherence to the rationale for the exclusionary rule advanced in *Weeks v. United States*,[75] and endorsed by the Mississippi Supreme Court when it established the state exclusionary rule in 1922: admitting illegally obtained evidence "would be to affirm by judicial decision a manifest neglect if not an open defiance of the prohibitions of the Constitution."

Stringer I exemplifies a state court's use of state precedent, local morality, and logical refutation to justify a position different from the United States Supreme Court's. The logical component of its attack on *Leon* is of particular interest. Justice Robertson's opinion evaluated the good faith exception in terms already recognized by the federal courts. He engaged in cost-benefit analysis, as had *Leon*, and relied on the reasoning not only of *Weeks*, but of the Court's recent decision in *Nix v. Williams*. The opinion thus reaches its contrary decision within the parameters previous federal law had sketched out. Although concern about creating uncertainty and engaging in unnecessary duplication of review might make a state court cautious about rejecting federal precedent, it should not prevent principled state court analysis of the type *Stringer I* illustrates.

34.04 The Supreme Court's Reaction to the New Federalism

Because the Supreme Court will not review a decision resting on adequate state grounds,[76] a state court which bases its ruling on the state constitution effectively precludes Supreme Court oversight, so long as the ruling meets the minimum federal constitutional standard. This policy insulates those state court decisions which construe the state bill of rights to provide greater protection than the federal Bill of Rights. The result is that law enforcement officials who feel burdened by the broader state constitutional requirements are unable to seek remedies in a federal forum.

---

74. 467 U.S. 431, 104 S.Ct. 2501 (1984), discussed in § 2.04(d).

75. 232 U.S. 383, 34 S.Ct. 341 (1914).

76. *Herb v. Pitcairn*, 324 U.S. 117, 65 S.Ct. 459 (1945). See generally, Wright, Federal Courts, § 39 (1983).

Apparently frustrated by this fact, the Burger Court indicated that the state ruling must *clearly* rest on a state constitutional ground before that ground will be considered adequate and independent. In *Michigan v. Long*,[77] for instance, despite the fact that the Michigan Supreme Court held a vehicle search invalid because it was "proscribed by the Fourth Amendment to the United States Constitution *and* art. 1, § 11 of the Michigan Constitution," the Court remained "unconvinced that the lower court's decision rests upon an independent state ground." Justice O'Connor, writing for the majority, noted that although the Michigan Constitution had been cited twice by the Michigan Supreme Court, the lower court had relied exclusively on federal cases. Justice Stevens, in a vigorous dissent to this part of the opinion, argued that historically the presumption has always been against asserting jurisdiction over cases where there may be an independent state ground. He cautioned against the issuance of advisory opinions: "We do not sit to expound our understanding of the Constitution to interested listeners in the legal community; we sit to resolve disputes. If it is not apparent that our views would affect the outcome of a particular case, we cannot presume to interfere."

But the Court appears to have put the burden on the state court to show its decision rests on independent grounds. As Justice O'Connor wrote for the majority, "[i]f a state court chooses merely to rely on federal precedents as it would on the precedents of all other jurisdictions, then it need only make clear by a plain statement in its judgment or opinion that the federal cases are being used only for the purpose of guidance, and do not themselves compel the result that the court has reached." If the state court fails to make such a "plain statement," the Supreme Court is not precluded from reviewing the decision.

34.05 Conclusion

State court reliance on state constitutions as an independent source of rights is widespread. This chapter's assessment of this development can be summarized as follows:

(1) State courts have always had the authority to interpret state law differently from federal precedent. With the advent of incorporation, many states simply followed federal law. But, as the U.S. Supreme Court has retrenched on Warren Court precedent, many state courts have repudiated federal law in favor of more protective rules based on state constitutions. In response to this development, the electorates in a few states have adopted constitutional amendments requiring linkage between state consti-

---

77. 463 U.S. 1032, 103 S.Ct. 3469 (1983). See also *Montana v. Jackson*, 460 U.S. 1030, 103 S.Ct. 1418 (1983) (per curiam).

tutional law and Supreme Court precedent in certain areas of criminal procedure.

(2) Forced linkage between analogous federal and state constitutional provisions is bad policy because it undercuts state court analytical independence, thus compromising the ability of state courts to reflect local legal and moral preferences, fully enforce constitutional guarantees, stimulate thought among other courts, and experiment with important concepts. Unlimited state activism is also bad policy because it promotes uncertainty, questionable duplication of review, and result-oriented jurisprudence. Presumptive linkage is the preferable approach to state court treatment of federal law. State courts should not lightly repudiate a federal ruling, but they should be free to do so when state precedent, local morality, or careful analysis suggests that the federal standard should not be adopted as the state standard.

(3) State court decisions which do not include a plain statement that federal cases in the opinion are being used only for the purpose of guidance and do not themselves compel the result that the court has reached are not based on an adequate and independent state ground and may be reviewed and overturned by the federal courts.

BIBLIOGRAPHY

Abrahamson, Shirley S. Criminal Law and State Constitutions: The Emergence of State Constitutional Law. 63 Tex.L.Rev. 1141 (1985).

Brennan, W. State Constitutions and the Protection of Individual Rights. 90 Harv.L.Rev. 489 (1977).

Collins, Ronald & Peter J. Galie. Models of Post-Incorporation Judicial Review: 1985 Survey of State Constitutional Individual Rights Decisions. 55 U.Cin.L.Rev. 317 (1986).

Developments in State Constitutional Law. 21 Rutgers L.Rev. 90 (1990) (Survey of Cases).

Gruhl, John. State Supreme Courts and the U.S. Supreme Court's Post-Miranda Rulings. 72 J.Crim.L. & Criminol. 886 (1981).

Howard, A.E. State Courts and Constitutional Rights in the Day of the Burger Court. 62 Va.L.Rev. 873 (1976).

———. The Supreme Court of California, 1974–75. 64 Calif.L.Rev. 286 (1976).

Maltz, Earl M. The Dark Side of State Court Activism. 63 Tex.L. Rev. 995 (1985).

Robinson At Large in the Fifty States: A Continuation of the State Bills of Rights Debate in the Search and Seizure Context [note]. 5 Gold.Gate L.Rev. 5 (1974).

Slobogin, Christopher. State Adoption of Federal Law: Exploring the Limits of Florida's "Forced Linkage" Amendment. 39 U.Fla.L.Rev. 653 (1987).

Welsh, Robert C. Whose Federalism? The Burger Court's Treatment of State Civil Liberties Judgments. 10 Hast.L.Q. 819 (1983).

Wilkes, D.E. First Things Last: Amendomania and State Bills of Rights. 54 Miss.L.J. 223 (1984).

——. The New Federalism in Criminal Procedure: State Court Evasion of the Burger Court. 62 Ky.L.J. 421 (1974).

TABLE OF CASES

References are to Pages.

TABLE OF CASES
References are to Pages

967

TABLE OF CASES
References are to Pages

972

TABLE OF CASES
References are to Pages

974

975

TABLE OF CASES
References are to Pages

*

INDEX

References are to Pages

†

						8A (18)
	3	4	−3	−2	−1	
	3A (13)	4A (14)	5A (15)	6A (16)	7A (17)	Helium 2 **He** 4.0026
	Boron 5 **B** 10.811	Carbon 6 **C** 12.011	Nitrogen 7 **N** 14.0067	Oxygen 8 **O** 15.9994	Fluorine 9 **F** 18.9984	Neon 10 **Ne** 20.1797
2B (12)	Aluminum 13 **Al** 26.9815	Silicon 14 **Si** 28.0855	Phosphorus 15 **P** 30.9738	Sulfur 16 **S** 32.066	Chlorine 17 **Cl** 35.4527	Argon 18 **Ar** 39.948
Zinc 30 **Zn** 65.38	Gallium 31 **Ga** 69.723	Germanium 32 **Ge** 72.61	Arsenic 33 **As** 74.9216	Selenium 34 **Se** 78.96	Bromine 35 **Br** 79.904	Krypton 36 **Kr** 83.80
Cadmium 48 **Cd** 112.411	Indium 49 **In** 114.818	Tin 50 **Sn** 118.710	Antimony 51 **Sb** 121.760	Tellurium 52 **Te** 127.60	Iodine 53 **I** 126.9045	Xenon 54 **Xe** 131.29
Mercury 80 **Hg** 200.59	Thallium 81 **Tl** 204.3833	Lead 82 **Pb** 207.2	Bismuth 83 **Bi** 208.9804	Polonium 84 **Po** (208.98)	Astatine 85 **At** (209.99)	Radon 86 **Rn** (222.02)
— 112 — Discovered 1996	— 113 — Discovered 2004	— 114 — Discovered 1999	— 115 — Discovered 2004	— 116 — Discovered 1999		— 118 — Discovered 2002

Terbium 65 **Tb** 158.9254	Dysprosium 66 **Dy** 162.50	Holmium 67 **Ho** 164.9303	Erbium 68 **Er** 167.26	Thulium 69 **Tm** 168.9342	Ytterbium 70 **Yb** 173.054	Lutetium 71 **Lu** 174.9668
Berkelium 97 **Bk** (247.07)	Californium 98 **Cf** (251.08)	Einsteinium 99 **Es** (252.08)	Fermium 100 **Fm** (257.10)	Mendelevium 101 **Md** (258.10)	Nobelium 102 **No** (259.10)	Lawrencium 103 **Lr** (262.11)

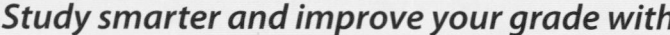
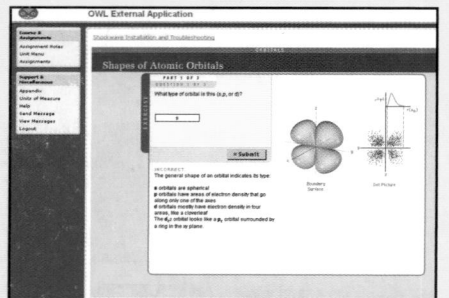
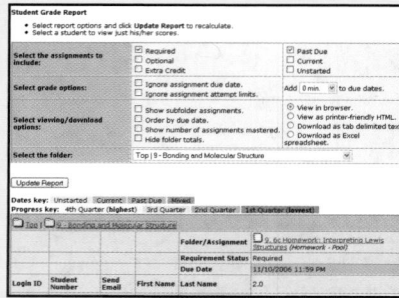
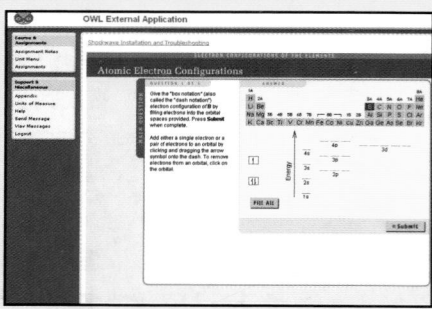

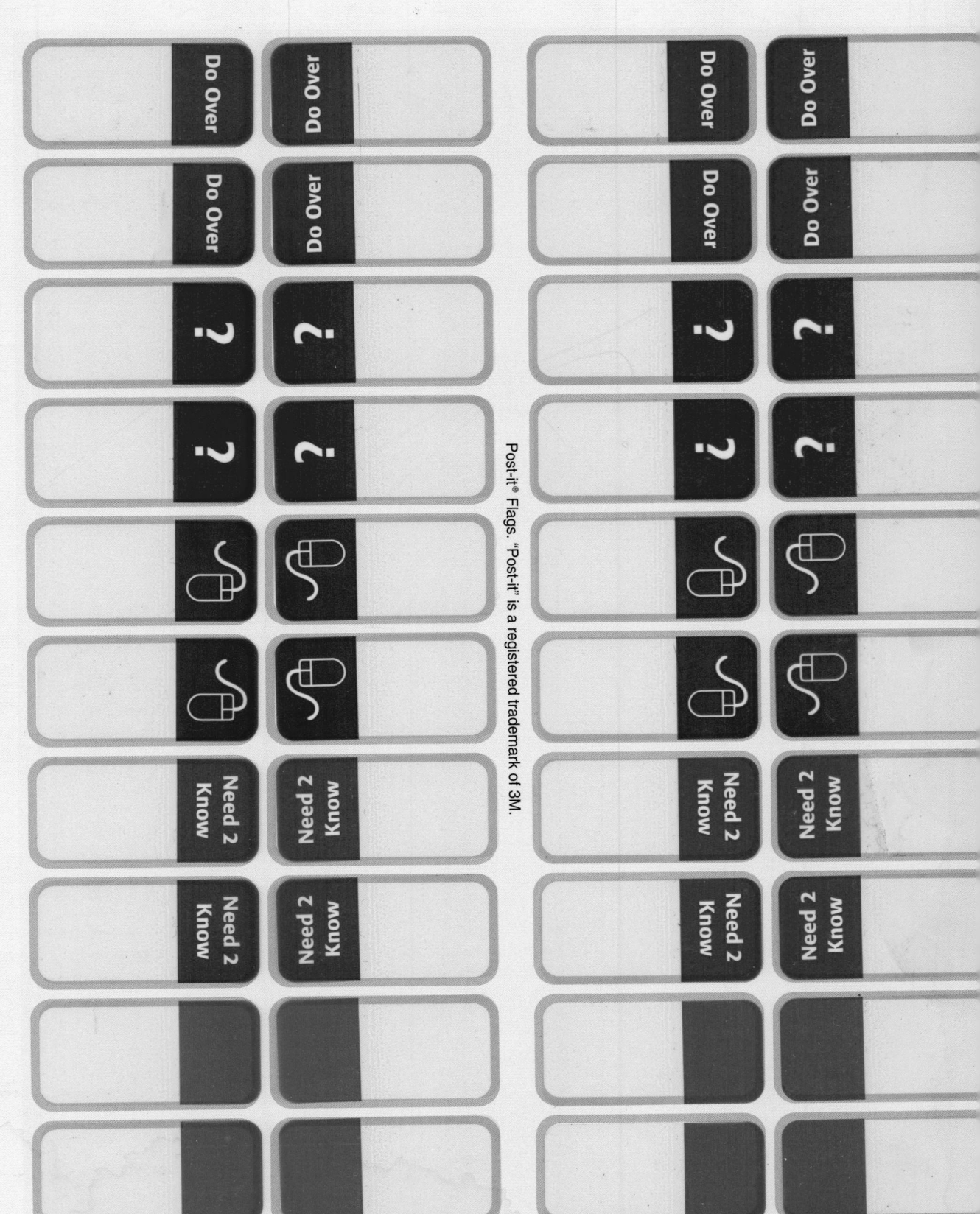

Post-it® Flags. "Post-it" is a registered trademark of 3M.

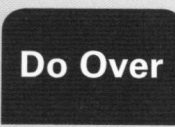

Do Over

Do you need to review something? Try again? Work it out on your own after class? Tab it.

?

Got a question for office hours? Do you need to review an example on your own to get a full understanding? Do you need to look something up before moving on? Tab it.

Check out an online source? Complete your online homework? Tab it.

Need 2 Know

Is this going to be on the test? Need to mark a key formula? Do you need to memorize these steps? Tab it.

Do you have your own study system? Do you need to make a note? Do you want to express yourself? Tab it.

Tab it. Do it. Ace it.

SBN 13: 978-0-495-56095-1

SEVENTH EDITION

CHEMISTRY

& Chemical Reactivity

Enhanced Edition

John C. Kotz

SUNY Distinguished Teaching Professor
State University of New York
College of Oneonta

Paul M. Treichel

Professor of Chemistry
University of Wisconsin–Madison

John R. Townsend

Professor of Chemistry
West Chester University of Pennsylvania

BROOKS/COLE
CENGAGE Learning

Australia • Brazil • Japan • Korea • Mexico • Singapore • Spain • United Kingdom • United States

BROOKS/COLE
CENGAGE Learning™

Chemistry & Chemical Reactivity, Enhanced Edition
John C. Kotz, Paul M. Treichel, and John R. Townsend

Publisher: Mary Finch

Senior Acquisitions Editor: Lisa Lockwood

Senior Development Editor: Peter McGahey

Assistant Editor: Ashley Summers

Editorial Assistant: Liz Woods

Technology Project Manager: Lisa Weber

Marketing Manager: Amee Mosley

Marketing Assistant: Elizabeth Wong

Marketing Communications Manager: Talia Wise

Project Manager, Editorial Production: Teresa L. Trego

Creative Director: Rob Hugel

Art Director: John Walker

Print Buyer: Rebecca Cross

Permissions Editor: Mari Masalin-Cooper

Production Service: Graphic World Inc.

Text Designer: Brian Salisbury

Photo Researcher: Marcy Lunetta

Copy Editor: Graphic World Inc.

Illustrators: Patrick A. Harman and Graphic World Inc.

OWL Producers: Stephen Battisti, Cindy Stein, David Hart (Center for Educational Software Development, University of Massachusetts, Amherst)

Cover Designer: John Walker

Cover Image: Felice Frankel, Harvard University

Compositor: Graphic World Inc.

For product information and technology assistance, contact us at
Cengage Learning Customer & Sales Support, 1-800-354-9706.
For permission to use material from this text or product, submit all requests online at **www.cengage.com/permissions.**
Further permissions questions can be e-mailed to **permissionrequest@cengage.com.**

Library of Congress Control Number: 2007940546

ISBN-13: 978-0-495-38703-9
ISBN-10: 0-495-38703-7

Paper Edition:
ISBN-13: 978-0-495-39029-9
ISBN-10: 0-495-39029-1

Brooks/Cole
10 Davis Drive
Belmont, CA 94002-3098
USA

Cengage Learning is a leading provider of customized learning solutions with office locations around the globe, including Singapore, the United Kingdom, Australia, Mexico, Brazil, and Japan. Locate your local office at: **www.cengage.com/international.**

Cengage Learning products are represented in Canada by Nelson Education, Ltd.

To learn more about Brooks/Cole, visit **www.cengage.com/brookscole**

Purchase any of our products at your local college store or at our preferred online store **www.ichapters.com.**

CREDITS

This page constitutes an extension of the copyright page. We have made every effort to trace the ownership of all copyrighted material and to secure permission from copyright holders. In the event of any question arising as to the use of any material, we will be pleased to make the necessary corrections in future printings. Thanks are due to the following authors, publishers, and agents for permission to use the material indicated.

264: Based on L. Schlarbach and A. Zuttle: Nature, Vol. 414, pp. 353-358, 2001;

667: Reprinted with permission of Dr. Klaus Hermann of the Fritz Haber Institution;

961: From www.acs.org. Copyright © American Chemical Society. Reprinted with permission from the American Chemical Society.

Printed in Canada
1 2 3 4 5 6 7 13 12 11 10 09

Brief Contents

Contents

The interchapters found in the standard edition are available on this book's companion website at www.cengage.com/chemistry/kotz

This text is available in these student versions:
- Complete text ISBN 978-0-495-38703-9 • Volume 1 (Chapters 1–11) ISBN 978-0-495-38711-4
- Volume 2 (Chapters 11–23) ISBN 978-0-495-38712-1 • Complete Enhanced Edition ISBN 978-0-495-39029-9

Go Chemistry Modules

The new Go Chemistry modules are mini video lectures included in ChemistryNow that are designed for portable use on video iPods, iPhones, MP3 players, and iTunes. Modules are referenced in the text and may include animations, problems, or e-Flashcards for quick review of key concepts. Modules may also be purchased at **www.ichapters.com**.

Chapter 1	Basic Concepts of Chemistry	Module 1	Exploring the Periodic Table
Chapter 2	Atoms, Molecules, and Ions	Module 2	Ion Charges
		Module 3	Naming: Names to Formulas of Ionic Compounds
		Module 4	The Mole
Chapter 3	Chemical Reactions	Module 5	Solubility of Ionic Compounds
		Module 6	Net Ionic Equations
Chapter 4	Stoichiometry: Quantitative Information About Chemical Reactions	Module 7	Simple Stoichiometry
		Module 8a	Limiting Reactants – part 1
		Module 8b	Limiting Reactants – part 2
		Module 9a	pH – part 1
		Module 9b	pH – part 2
Chapter 5	Principles of Chemical Reactivity: Energy and Chemical Reactions	Module 10	Using Hess's Law
Chapter 7	The Structure of Atoms and Periodic Trends	Module 11	Periodic Trends
Chapter 8	Bonding and Molecular Structure	Module 12	Lewis Electron Dot Structures
		Module 13	Molecular Polarity
Chapter 9	Bonding and Molecular Structure: Orbital Hybridization and Molecular Orbitals	Module 14	Hybrid Orbitals
Chapter 10	Carbon: More Than Just Another Element	Module 15	Naming Organic Compounds
Chapter 11	Gases and Their Properties	Module 16	The Gas Laws and Kinetic Molecular Theory
Chapter 12	Intermolecular Forces and Liquids	Module 17	Identifying Intermolecular Forces
Chapter 13	The Chemistry of Solids	Module 18	Unit Cells and Compound Formulas
Chapter 14	Solutions and Their Behavior	Module 19	Colligative Properties
Chapter 15	Chemical Kinetics: The Rates of Chemical Reactions	Module 20	Half-Life and the Integrated First Order Equation
Chapter 16	Principles of Reactivity: Chemical Equilibria	Module 21	Solving an Equilibrium Problem
Chapter 17	The Chemistry of Acids and Bases	Module 22	Equilibrium – pH of a Weak Acid
Chapter 18	Principles of Reactivity: Other Aspects of Aqueous Equilibria	Module 23	Understanding Buffers
Chapter 19	Principles of Reactivity: Entropy and Free Energy	Module 24	Free Energy and Equilibrium
Chapter 20	Principles of Reactivity: Electron Transfer Reactions	Module 25	Balancing Redox Equations

Preface

The authors of this book have more than 100 years of experience teaching general chemistry and other areas of chemistry at the college level. Although we have been at different institutions during our careers, we share several goals in common. One is to provide a broad overview of the principles of chemistry, the reactivity of the chemical elements and their compounds, and the applications of chemistry. To reach that goal with our students, we have tried to show the close relation between the observations chemists make of chemical and physical changes in the laboratory and in nature and the way these changes are viewed at the atomic and molecular level.

Another of our goals has been to convey a sense of chemistry as a field that not only has a lively history but also one that is currently dynamic, with important new developments occurring every year. Furthermore, we want to provide some insight into the chemical aspects of the world around us. Indeed, a major objective of this book is to provide the tools needed for you to function as a chemically literate citizen. Learning something of the chemical world is just as important as understanding some basic mathematics and biology and as important as having an appreciation for history, music, and literature. For example, you should know what materials are important to our economy, some of the reactions in plants and animals and in our environment, and the role that chemists play in protecting the environment.

These goals and our approach have been translated into *Chemistry & Chemical Reactivity*, a book that has been used by more than 1 million students in its first six editions. We are clearly gratified by this success. But, at the same time, we know that the details of our presentation and organization can always be improved. In addition, there are significant advances in the technology of communicating information, and we want to take advantage of those new approaches. These have been the impetus behind the preparation of this new edition, which incorporates a new organization of material, new ways to describe contemporary uses of chemistry, new technologies, and improved integration with existing technologies.

Enhanced Edition

Why an Enhanced Review Edition?

As authors and publishers we are in constant conversation with instructors and students about their textbooks and courses. To accommodate requests for less costly alternatives to the standard book, we sought a manner in which we could reduce manufacturing costs and pass the savings on to students. Similarly, many users have mentioned a desire for exam preparation materials and study tools in the test itself that better integrate with the book and media. The Enhanced Edition is an attempt to satisfy these requests.

What Is an Enhanced Edition?

The Enhanced Edition of *Chemistry & Chemical Reactivity*, Seventh Edition, is an alternative version that can be used in place of the standard seventh edition. Students and instructors can choose either the standard seventh edition or the Enhanced Edition without loss of continuity between versions. Although we believe the changes for the Enhanced Edition will provide a better learning tool for those who choose it, the new book's alterations are not substantial enough to warrant it being called a new edition because the core chapters and appendices remain unchanged. The standard hardbound seventh edition remains available for purchase and classroom use.

Four new *Let's Review* sections have been added. These cumulative review sections in four of the book parts offer students review aids and questions that bring together material from the several chapters and are similar to those they may see on an exam. The review questions are keyed to text and media material to assist students in preparing for an exam. In order to include these sections, the four supplemental interchapters in the standard seventh edition are available on the book's companion website (**www.cengage.com/chemistry/kotz**) where they are accessible to users of the Enhanced Edition.

What's New in This Edition

1. *New chapter introductions* on topics such as altitude sickness (page 514) and the contribution of ethanol to environmental goals (page 860). Each of these chapter-opening topics has a question or two that is answered in Appendix Q.

2. One or more **Case Studies** are presented in each chapter. These cover practical chemistry and pose questions that can be answered using the concepts of that chapter. Case Studies cover such topics as silver in washing machines (page 148), using isotopes to catch cheaters (page 58), aquarium chemistry (page 992), why garlic stinks (page 541), what is in those French fries (page 96), why Beethoven died at an early age (page 989), and many others.

3. New and completely revised *Interchapters*. John Emsley, a noted science writer, revised the interchapter on the environment (page 949) and wrote a new interchapter on the history of chemistry (page 338).

4. *Reorganization/addition of material:*
   - The first four chapters in particular have been revised and condensed.
   - The "moles of reaction" concept is used in thermodynamics.
   - The material on intermolecular forces (Chapter 12) has been separated from solids (Chapter 13).
   - The chapter on entropy and free energy (Chapter 19) has been thoroughly revised.

- A brief discussion of modern organometallic chemistry has been added to Chapter 22.
- Additional challenging questions have been added to each chapter.
- Additional *Chemical Perspectives* and *Case Studies* boxes have been authored by Jeffrey Kaeffaber (University of Florida) and Eric Scerri (UCLA).

5. **OWL** The *OWL* (Online Web-based Learning) system has been used by over 100,000 students. The contents of OWL are the contents and organization of *Chemistry & Chemical Reactivity*. For the sixth edition, about 20 end-of-chapter questions were assignable in OWL. That number has been approximately doubled for the seventh edition. In addition, the assets of ChemistryNow—Exercises, Tutorials, and Simulations that allow students to practice chemistry—are now fully incorporated in OWL.

6. The new *e-Book in OWL* is a complete electronic version of the text, fully assignable and linked to OWL homework. The e-book can be purchased with the printed book or as an independent text replacement.

7. *Go Chemistry* modules. There are 27 mini-lectures that can be played on an iPod or other personal video player or on a computer. The modules feature narrated examples of the most important material from each chapter and focus on areas in which we know from experience that students may need extra help.

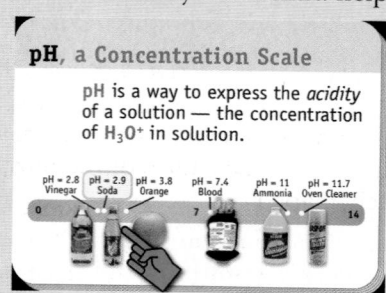

pH, a Concentration Scale

pH is a way to express the *acidity* of a solution — the concentration of H_3O^+ in solution.

| pH = 2.8 Vinegar | pH = 2.9 Soda | pH = 3.8 Orange | pH = 7.4 Blood | pH = 11 Ammonia | pH = 11.7 Oven Cleaner |

9. *How Do I Solve It?* modules in OWL help students learn how to approach the types of questions asked in each chapter.

8. *In the Laboratory* end-of-chapter Study Questions. These questions pertain directly to situations that the student may confront in a typical laboratory experiment.

The Enhanced Edition is offered with a soft paper binding. The subsequent reduction in manufacturing costs allows us to offer this version at a reduced price compared to the standard edition.

Emerging Developments in Content Usage and Delivery: OWL, the e-Book, and Go Chemistry™

The use of media, presentation tools, and homework management tools has expanded significantly in the last 3 years. More than 10 years ago we incorporated electronic media into this text with the first edition of our interactive CD-ROM, a learning tool used by thousands of students worldwide.

Multimedia technology has evolved over the past 10 years, and so have our students. Our challenge as authors and educators is to use our students' focus on assessment as a way to help them reach a higher level of conceptual understanding. In light of this we have made major changes in our integrated media program. We have redesigned the media so that students now have the opportunity to interact with media based on clearly stated chapter goals that are correlated to end-of-chapter questions. This has been achieved through **OWL (Online Web-based Learning)**, a system developed at the University of Massachusetts and in use by general chemistry students for more than 10 years. In the past few years the system has been used successfully by over 100,000 students.

In addition, as outlined in *What's New in this Edition*, the *electronic book (e-book)* has been enhanced for this edition, and we have developed new *Go Chemistry* modules that consist of mini-lectures of the most important aspect in each chapter.

Audience for *Chemistry & Chemical Reactivity* and OWL

The textbook and OWL are designed for introductory courses in chemistry for students interested in further study in science, whether that science is chemistry, biology, engineering, geology, physics, or related subjects. Our assumption is that students beginning this course have had some preparation in algebra and in general science. Although undeniably helpful, a previous exposure to chemistry is neither assumed nor required.

Philosophy and Approach of the Chemistry & Chemical Reactivity Program

We have had several major, but not independent, objectives since the first edition of the book. The first was to write a book that students would enjoy reading and that would offer, at a reasonable level of rigor, chemistry and chemical principles in a format and organization typical of college and university courses today. Second, we wanted to convey the utility and importance of chemistry by introducing the properties of the elements, their compounds, and their reactions as early as possible and by focusing the discussion as much as possible on these subjects. Finally, with the new *Go Chemistry* modules and even more complete integration of *OWL*, we wanted to give students new and proven tools to bring them to a higher level of conceptual understanding.

The American Chemical Society has been urging educators to put "chemistry" back into introductory chemistry courses. We agree wholeheartedly. Therefore, we have tried to describe the elements, their compounds, and their reactions as early and as often as possible by:

- Using numerous **color photographs** of reactions occurring, of the elements and common compounds, and of common laboratory operations and industrial processes.
- Bringing **material on the properties of elements and compounds** as early as possible into the Exercises and Study Questions and to introduce new principles using realistic chemical situations.
- Introducing each chapter with a **problem in practical chemistry**—a short discussion of the color of an aurora borealis or ethanol in gasoline—that is relevant to the chapter.
- Introducing *Case Studies* on practical chemistry.

General Organization of the Book and Its Features

Chemistry & Chemical Reactivity has two overarching themes: *Chemical Reactivity* and *Bonding and Molecular Structure*. The chapters on *Principles of Reactivity* introduce the factors that lead chemical reactions to be successful in converting reactants to products. Thus, under this topic there is a discussion of common types of reactions, the energy involved in reactions, and the factors that affect the speed of a reaction. One reason for the enormous advances in chemistry and molecular biology in the last several decades has been an understanding of molecular structure. Therefore, sections of the book on *Principles of Bonding and Molecular Structure* lay the groundwork for understanding these developments. Particular attention is paid to an understanding of the structural aspects of such biologically important molecules as DNA.

Flexibility of Chapter Organization

A glance at the introductory chemistry texts currently available shows that there is a generally common order of topics used by educators. With a few minor variations, we have followed that order as well. That is not to say that the chapters in our book cannot be used in some other order. We have written it to be as flexible as possible. The most important example is the chapter on the behavior of gases (Chapter 11), which is placed with chapters on liquids, solids, and solutions (Chapters 12–14) because it logically fits with these topics. It can easily be read and understood, however, after covering only the first four or five chapters of the book.

Similarly, chapters on atomic and molecular structure (Chapters 6–9) could be used before the chapters on stoichiometry and common reactions (Chapters 3 and 4). Also, the chapters on chemical equilibria (Chapters 16–18) can be covered before those on solutions and kinetics (Chapters 14 and 15).

Organic chemistry (Chapter 10) is often left to one of the final chapters in chemistry textbooks. However, we believe the importance of organic compounds in biochemistry and in consumer products means we should present that material earlier in the sequence of chapters. Therefore, it follows the chapters on structure and bonding because organic chemistry nicely illustrates the application of models of chemical bonding and molecular structure. However, one can use the remainder of the book without including this chapter.

The order of topics in the text was also devised to introduce as early as possible the background required for the laboratory experiments usually performed in introductory chemistry courses. For this reason, chapters on chemical and physical properties, common reaction types, and stoichiometry begin the book. In addition, because an understanding of energy is so important

in the study of chemistry, thermochemistry is introduced in Chapter 5.

Interchapters

In addition to the regular chapters, uses and applications of chemistry are described in more detail in supplemental chapters on *The Chemistry of Fuels and Energy Sources; Milestones in the Development of Chemistry and the Modern View of Atoms and Molecules; The Chemistry of Life: Biochemistry; The Chemistry of Modern Materials;* and *The Chemistry of the Environment.*

(The interchapters found in the standard edition are available on this book's companion website accessible from **www.cengage.com/chemistry/kotz.**)

Other Book Sections

As in the sixth edition, we continue with boxed sections titled *Chemical Perspectives, Historical Perspectives, A Closer Look* (for a more in-depth look at relevant material), and *Problem Solving Tips.* As described in "What's New . . ." we have now introduced one or more *Case Studies* in each chapter.

Organization and Purposes of the Sections of the Book

Part 1: The Basic Tools of Chemistry

There are basic ideas and methods that are the basis of all chemistry, and these are introduced in Part 1. Chapter 1 defines important terms, and the accompanying *Let's Review* section reviews units and mathematical methods. Chapter 2 introduces basic ideas of atoms, molecules, and ions, and the most important organizational device in chemistry, the periodic table. In Chapters 3 and 4 we begin to discuss the principles of chemical reactivity and to introduce the numerical methods used by chemists to extract quantitative information from chemical reactions. Chapter 5 is an introduction to the energy involved in chemical processes. The supplemental chapter *The Chemistry of Fuels and Energy Sources,* available on the book's website, uses many of the concepts developed in the preceding chapters.

Part 2: The Structure of Atoms and Molecules

The goal of this section is to outline the current theories of the arrangement of electrons in atoms (Chapters 6 and 7). This discussion is tied closely to the arrangement of elements in the periodic table so that these properties can be recalled and predictions made. In Chapter 8 we discuss for the first time how the electrons of atoms in a molecule lead to chemical bonding and the properties of these bonds. In addition, we show how to derive the three-dimensional structure of simple molecules. Finally, Chapter 9 considers the major theories of chemical bonding in more detail.

This part of the book is completed with a discussion of organic chemistry (Chapter 10), primarily from a structural point of view.

This section includes the interchapter on *Milestones in the Development ...*, and *The Chemistry of Life: Biochemistry* available on the book's website provides an overview of some of the most important aspects of biochemistry.

Part 3: States of Matter

The behavior of the three states of matter—gases, liquids, and solids—is described in that order in Chapters 11–14. The discussion of liquids and solids is tied to gases through the description of intermolecular forces in Chapter 12, with particular attention given to liquid and solid water. In Chapter 14 we describe the properties of solutions, intimate mixtures of gases, liquids, and solids.

The supplemental chapter on *The Chemistry of Modern Materials* is available on the book's website. Designing and making new materials with useful properties is one of the most exciting areas of modern chemistry.

Part 4: The Control of Chemical Reactions

This section is wholly concerned with the *Principles of Reactivity*. Chapter 15 examines the important question of the rates of chemical processes and the factors controlling these rates. With this in mind, we move to Chapters 16-18, chapters that describe chemical reactions at equilibrium. After an introduction to equilibrium in Chapter 16, we highlight the reactions involving acids and bases in water (Chapters 17 and 18) and reactions leading to slightly soluble salts (Chapter 18). To tie together the discussion of chemical equilibria, we again explore thermodynamics in Chapter 19. As a final topic in this section we describe in Chapter 20 a major class of chemical reactions, those involving the transfer of electrons, and the use of these reactions in electrochemical cells.

The Chemistry of the Environment supplemental chapter is available on the book's website. This chapter uses ideas from kinetics and chemical equilibria, in particular, as well as principles described in earlier chapters in the book.

Part 5: The Chemistry of the Elements and Their Compounds

Although the chemistry of the various elements has been described throughout the book to this point, Part 5 considers this topic in a more systematic way. Chapter 21 is devoted to the chemistry of the representative elements, whereas Chapter 22—which has been expanded to include an introduction to organometallic chemistry—is a discussion of the transition elements and their compounds. Finally, Chapter 23 is a brief discussion of nuclear chemistry.

Supporting Materials for the Instructor

Supporting instructor materials are available to qualified adopters. Please consult your local Cengage Learning, Brooks/Cole representative for details. Visit **www.cengage.com/chemistry/kotz** to:

- See samples of materials
- Request a desk copy
- Locate your local representative
- Download electronic files of the *Instructor's Manual*, the *Test Bank*, and other helpful materials for instructors and students

Instructor's Resource Manual
by Susan Young, Hartwick College
ISBN-10: 0-495-38705-3; ISBN-13: 978-0-495-38705-3

Contains worked-out solutions to *all* end-of-chapter Study Questions and features ideas for instructors on how to fully utilize resources and technology in their courses. The *Manual* provides questions for electronic response systems, suggests classroom demonstrations, and emphasizes good and innovative teaching practices. Electronic files of the *Instructor's Resource Manual* are available for download on the PowerLecture DVD-ROM and on the instructor's companion site at **www.cengage .com/chemistry/kotz**.

OWL: Online Web-based Learning
by Roberta Day and Beatrice Botch of the University of Massachusetts, Amherst, and William Vining of the State University of New York at Oneonta

OWL Instant Access (2 Semesters) ISBN-10: 0-495-05099-7; ISBN-13: 978-0-495-05099-5

e-Book in OWL Instant Access (2 Semesters) ISBN-10: 0-495-55499-5; ISBN-13: 978-0-495-55499-8

Used by more than 300 institutions and proven reliable for tens of thousands of students, OWL offers an online homework and quizzing system with unsurpassed ease of use, reliability, and dedicated training and service. OWL makes homework management a breeze and helps students improve their problem-solving skills and visualize concepts, providing instant analysis and feedback on a variety of homework problems, including tutors, simulations, and chemically and/or numerically parameterized short-answer questions. OWL is the only system specifically designed to support mastery learning, where students work as long as they need to master each chemical concept and skill. To view an OWL demo and for more information, visit **www.cengage.com/owl** or contact your Brooks/Cole representative.

New to OWL!

For the seventh edition, approximately 20 new end-of-chapter questions (marked in the text with ■) can be assigned in OWL for a total of approximately 40 end-of-chapter Study Questions for each chapter available in OWL.

The **e-Book in OWL** is a complete electronic version of the text, fully assignable and linked to OWL homework. This exclusive option is available to students with instructor permission. Instructors can consult their Brooks/Cole representative for details and to determine the best option: access to the e-book can be bundled with the text and/or ordered as a text replacement.

Learning Resources allow students to quickly access valuable help to master each homework question with integrated e-book readings, tutors, simulations, and exercises that accompany each question. Learning Resources are configurable by instructors.

More new OWL features:

- New student Learning Resources and Toolbars
- New Answer Input tool for easy subscript and superscript formatting
- Enhanced reports that give instant snapshots of your class progress
- Easier grading access for quick report downloads
- New Survey and Authoring features for creating your own content
- Enhanced security to help you comply with FERPA regulations

A fee-based access code is required for OWL.

Instructor's PowerLecture DVD-ROM with Exam-View® and JoinIn™ for *Chemistry & Chemical Reactivity*

ISBN-10: 0-495-38706-1; ISBN-13: 978-0-495-38706-0

PowerLecture is a dual platform, one-stop digital library and presentation tool that includes:

- Prepared Microsoft® PowerPoint® Lecture Slides covering all key points from the text in a convenient format that you can enhance with your own materials or with additional interactive video and animations on the DVD-ROM for personalized, media-enhanced lectures.
- Image Libraries in PowerPoint and in JPEG format that contain electronic files for all text art, most photographs, and all numbered tables in the text. These files can be used to print transparencies or to create your own PowerPoint lectures.
- Electronic files for the complete *Instructor's Resource Manual* and *Test Bank*.
- Sample chapters from the *Student Solutions Manual* and *Study Guide*.
- ExamView testing software, with all the test items from the printed *Test Bank* in electronic format, enables you to create customized tests of up to 250 items in print or online.
- JoinIn "clicker" questions written specifically for the use of *Chemistry & Chemical Reactivity* with the classroom response system of your choice that allows you to seamlessly display student answers.

Test Bank

by David Treichel, Nebraska Wesleyan University
ISBN-10: 0-495-38709-6; ISBN-13: 978-0-495-38709-1

A printed test bank of more than 1250 questions in a range of difficulty and variety are correlated directly to the chapter sections found in the main text. Numerical, open-ended, or conceptual problems are written in multiple choice, fill-in-the-blank, or short-answer formats. Both single- and multiple-step problems are presented for each chapter. Electronic files of the *Test Bank* are included on the PowerLecture DVD-ROM. WebCT and Blackboard versions of the test bank are available on the instructor's companion site at **www.cengage .com/chemistry/kotz**.

Transparencies

ISBN-10: 0-495-38714-2; ISBN-13: 978-0-495-38714-5

A collection of 150 full-color transparencies of key images selected from the text by the authors. The Power Lecture DVD-ROM includes all text art and many photos to aid in preparing transparencies for material not present in this set.

Supporting Materials for the Student

Visit the student companion website at **www.cengage .com/chemistry/kotz** to see samples of selected student supplements. Students can purchase any Brooks/ Cole products at your local college store or at our preferred online store **www.ichapters.com**.

Student Solutions Manual

by Alton J. Banks, North Carolina State University
ISBN-10: 0-495-38707-X; ISBN-13: 978-0-495-38707-7

This manual contains detailed solutions to the text's blue-numbered end-of-chapter Study Questions that match the problem-solving strategies from the text. Sample chapters are available for review on the PowerLecture CD and on the student companion website at **www .cengage.com/chemistry/kotz.**

Study Guide

by John R. Townsend and Michael J. Moran, West Chester University of Pennsylvania
ISBN-10: 0-495-38708-8; ISBN-13: 978-0-495-38708-4

This study guide contains chapter overviews, key terms with definitions, and sample tests explicitly linked to the goals introduced in each chapter. Emphasis is placed on the text's chapter goals by means of further commentary, study tips, worked examples, and direct references back to the text. Sample chapters are available for review on the student companion website at **www.cengage .com/chemistry/kotz.**

ChemistryNow   Chemistry.Now™

ChemistryNow's online self-assessment tools give you the choices and resources you need to study smarter. You can explore a variety of tutorials, exercises, and simulations (cross-referenced throughout the text by margin annotations), view Active Figure interactive versions of key pieces of art from the text, or take chapter-specific Pre-Tests and get a Personalized Study Plan that directs you to specific interactive materials that can help you master the areas in which you need additional work. Includes access to one-on-one tutoring and Go Chemistry mini video lectures. Access to ChemistryNow for two semesters may be included with each new textbook or can be purchased at **www.ichapters.com** using ISBN 0-495-39431-9.

Go Chemistry for General Chemistry

27-Module Set ISBN-10: 0-495-38228-0; ISBN-13: 978-0-495-38228-7

These new mini video lectures, playable on video iPods, iPhones, and personal video players as well as on iTunes, include animations and problems for a quick summary of key concepts. In selected Go Chemistry modules, e-Flashcards briefly introduce a key concept and then test student understanding of the basics with a series of questions. Modules are also available separately. Go Chemistry is included in ChemistryNow and in OWL. To purchase, enter ISBN 0-495-38228-0 at **www.ichapters.com.**

OWL for General Chemistry   ᴓWL

See the above description in the instructor support materials section.

Essential Math for Chemistry Students, Second Edition by David W. Ball, Cleveland State University
ISBN-10: 0-495-01327-7; ISBN-13: 978-0-495-01327-3

This short book is intended for students who lack confidence and/or competency in the essential mathematical skills necessary to survive in general chemistry. Each chapter focuses on a specific type of skill and has worked-out examples to show how these skills translate to chemical problem solving.

Survival Guide for General Chemistry with Math Review, Second Edition by Charles H. Atwood, University of Georgia
ISBN-10: 0-495-38751-7; ISBN-13: 978-0-495-38751-0

Intended to help you practice for exams, this "survival guide" shows you how to solve difficult problems by dissecting them into manageable chunks. The guide includes three levels of proficiency questions—A, B, and minimal—to quickly build confidence as you master the knowledge you need to succeed in your course.

For the Laboratory

Brooks/Cole Lab Manuals

Brooks/Cole offers a variety of printed manuals to meet all general chemistry laboratory needs. Visit the chemistry site at **www.cengage.com/chemistry** for a full listing and description of these laboratory manuals and laboratory notebooks. All Brooks/Cole lab manuals can be customized for your specific needs.

Signature Labs . . . for the customized laboratory

Signature Labs (**www.signaturelabs.com**) combines the resources of Brooks/Cole, CER, and OuterNet Publishing to provide you unparalleled service in creating your ideal customized lab program. Select the experiments and artwork you need from our collection of content and imagery to find the perfect labs to match your course. Visit **www.signaturelabs.com** or contact your Brooks/Cole representative for more information.

Acknowledgments

Because significant changes have been made from the sixth edition, preparing this new edition of *Chemistry & Chemical Reactivity* took almost 3 years of continuous effort. However, as in our work on the first six editions, we have had the support and encouragement of our families and of some wonderful friends, colleagues, and students.

CENGAGE LEARNING Brooks/Cole

The sixth edition of this book was published by Thomson Brooks/Cole. As often happens in the modern publishing industry, that company was recently acquired by another group and the new name is Cengage Learning Brooks/Cole. In spite of these changes in ownership, we continue with the same excellent team we have had in place for the previous several years.

The sixth edition of the book was very successful, in large part owing to the work of David Harris, our publisher. David again saw us through much of the development of this new edition, but Lisa Lockwood recently assumed his duties as our acquisitions editor; she has considerable experience in textbook publishing and was also responsible for the success of the sixth edition. We will miss David but are looking forward to a close association with Lisa.

Peter McGahey has been our the Development Editor for the fifth and sixth editions and again for this edition. Peter is blessed with energy, creativity, enthusiasm, intelligence, and good humor. He is a trusted friend and confidant and cheerfully answers our many questions during almost-daily phone calls.

No book can be successful without proper marketing. Amee Mosley was a great help in marketing the sixth edition and she is back in that role for this edition. She is knowledgeable about the market and has worked tirelessly to bring the book to everyone's attention.

Our team at Brooks/Cole is completed with Teresa Trego, Production Manager, and Lisa Weber, Technology Project Manager. Schedules are very demanding in textbook publishing, and Teresa has helped to keep us on schedule. We certainly appreciate her organizational skills. Lisa Weber directed the development of the Instructor's PowerLecture DVD-ROM, the *Go Chemistry* modules, and our expanded use of OWL.

People outside of publishing often do not realize the number of people involved in producing a textbook.

Anne Williams of Graphic World Inc. guided the book through its almost year-long production. Marcy Lunetta was the photo researcher for the book and was successful in filling our sometimes offbeat requests for a particular photo.

Photography, Art, and Design

Most of the color photographs for this edition were again beautifully created by Charles D. Winters. He produced several dozen new images for this book, always with a creative eye. Charlie's work gets better and better with each edition. We have worked with Charlie for more than 20 years and have become close friends. We listen to his jokes, both new and old—and always forget them. When we finish the book, we look forward to a kayaking trip.

When the fifth edition was being planned, we brought in Patrick Harman as a member of the team. Pat designed the first edition of the *General ChemistryNow* CD-ROM, and we believe its success is in no small way connected to his design skill. For the fifth edition of the book, Pat went over almost every figure, and almost every word, to bring a fresh perspective to ways to communicate chemistry and he did the same for the sixth edition. Once again he has worked on designing and producing new illustrations for the seventh edition, and his creativity is obvious in their clarity and beauty. Finally, Pat also designed and produced the Go Chemistry modules. As we have worked together so closely for so many years, Pat has become a good friend, as well, and we share interests not only in beautiful books but in interesting music.

Other Collaborators

We have been fortunate to have a number of other colleagues who have played valuable roles in this project.

- Bill Vining (State University of New York, Oneonta), was the lead author of the *General ChemistryNow* CD-ROM and of the media assets in OWL. He has been a friend for many years and recently took the place of one of the authors at SUNY-Oneonta. Bill has again applied his considerable energy and creativity in preparing many more OWL questions with tutorials.
- Susan Young (Hartwick College) has been a good friend and collaborator through five editions and has again prepared the *Instructor's Resource Manual*. She has always been helpful in proofreading, in answering questions on content, and in giving us good advice.
- Alton Banks (North Carolina State University) has also been involved for a number of editions preparing the *Student Solutions Manual*. Both Susan

and Alton have been very helpful in ensuring the accuracy of the Study Question answers in the book, as well as in their respective manuals.

- Michael Moran (West Chester University) has updated and revised the *Study Guide* that was written by John Townsend for the sixth edition. This book has had a history of excellent study guides, and this manual follows that tradition.
- We also wish to acknowledge the support of George Purvis and Fujitsu for use of the CAChe Scientific software for molecular modeling. All the molecular models and the electrostatic potential surfaces in the book were prepared using CAChe software.
- Jay Freedman once again did a masterful job compiling the index/glossary for this edition.

A major task is proofreading the book after it has been set in type. The book is read in its entirety by the authors and accuracy reviewers. After making corrections, the book is read a second time. Any errors remaining at this point are certainly the responsibility of the authors, and students and instructors should contact the authors by email to offer their suggestions. If this is done in a timely manner, corrections can be made when the book is reprinted.

We want to thank the following accuracy reviewers for their invaluable assistance. The book is immeasurably improved by their work.

- William Broderick, Montana State University
- Stephen Z. Goldberg, Adelphi University
- Jeffrey Alan Mack, California State University, Sacramento
- Clyde Metz, College of Charleston
- David Shinn, University of Hawaii, Manoa
- Scott R. White, Southern Arkansas University, Magnolia

Reviewers for the Seventh Edition

- Gerald M. Korenowski, Rensselaer Polytechnic Institute
- Robert L. LaDuca, Michigan State University
- Jeffrey Alan Mack, California State University, Sacramento
- Armando M. Rivera-Figueroa, East Los Angeles College
- Daniel J. Williams, Kennesaw State University
- Steven G. Wood, Brigham Young University
- Roger A. Hinrichs, Weill Cornell Medical College in Qatar (reviewed the Energy interchapter)
- Leonard Fine, Columbia University (reviewed the Materials interchapter)

Advisory Board for the Seventh Edition

As the new edition was being planned, this board listened to some of our ideas and made other suggestions. We hope to continue our association with these energetic and creative chemical educators.

- Donnie Byers, Johnson County Community College
- Sharon Fetzer Gislason, University of Illinois, Chicago
- Adrian George, University of Nebraska
- George Grant, Tidewater Community College, Virginia Beach Campus
- Michael Hampton, University of Central Florida
- Milton Johnston, University of South Florida
- Jeffrey Alan Mack, California State University, Sacramento
- William Broderick, Montana State University
- Shane Street, University of Alabama
- Martin Valla, University of Florida

About the Authors

JOHN C. KOTZ, a State University of New York Distinguished Teaching Professor, Emeritus, at the College at Oneonta, was educated at Washington and Lee University and Cornell University. He held National Institutes of Health postdoctoral appointments at the University of Manchester Institute for Science and Technology in England and at Indiana University.

He has coauthored three textbooks in several editions (*Inorganic Chemistry, Chemistry & Chemical Reactivity,* and *The Chemical World*) and the *General ChemistryNow CD-ROM.* His research in inorganic chemistry and electrochemistry also has been published.

He was a Fulbright Lecturer and Research Scholar in Portugal in 1979 and a Visiting Professor there in 1992. He was also a Visiting Professor at the Institute for Chemical Education (University of Wisconsin, 1991-1992), at Auckland University in New Zealand (1999), and at Potchefstroom University in South Africa in

Left to right: Paul Treichel, John Townsend, and John Kotz.

2006. He has been an invited speaker on chemical education at conferences in South Africa, New Zealand, and Brazil. He also served 3 years as a mentor for the U.S. National Chemistry Olympiad Team.

He has received several awards, among them a State University of New York Chancellor's Award (1979), a National Catalyst Award for Excellence in Teaching (1992), the Estee Lecturership at the University of South Dakota (1998), the Visiting Scientist Award from the Western Connecticut Section of the American Chemical Society (1999), the Distinguished Education Award from the Binghamton (NY) Section of the American Chemical Society (2001), the SUNY Award for Research and Scholarship (2005), and the Squibb Lectureship in Chemistry at the University of North Carolina-Asheville (2007). He may be contacted by email at kotzjc@oneonta.edu.

PAUL M. TREICHEL received his B.S. degree from the University of Wisconsin in 1958 and a Ph.D. from Harvard University in 1962. After a year of postdoctoral study in London, he assumed a faculty position at the University of Wisconsin-Madison. He served as department chair from 1986 through 1995 and was awarded a Helfaer Professorship in 1996. He has held visiting faculty positions in South Africa (1975) and in Japan (1995). Retiring after 44 years as a faculty member in 2007, he is currently Emeritus Professor of Chemistry. During his faculty career he taught courses in general chemistry, inorganic chemistry, organometallic chemistry, and scientific ethics. Professor Treichel's research in organometallic and metal cluster chemistry and in mass spectrometry, aided by 75 graduate and undergraduate students, has led to more than 170 papers in scientific journals. He may be contacted by email at treichel@chem.wisc.edu.

JOHN R. TOWNSEND, Professor of Chemistry at West Chester University of Pennsylvania, completed his B.A. in Chemistry as well as the Approved Program for Teacher Certification in Chemistry at the University of Delaware. After a career teaching high school science and mathematics, he earned his M.S. and Ph.D. in biophysical chemistry at Cornell University. At Cornell he also performed experiments in the origins of life field and received the DuPont Teaching Award. After teaching at Bloomsburg University, Dr. Townsend joined the faculty at West Chester University, where he coordinates the chemistry education program for prospective high school teachers and the general chemistry lecture program for science majors. His research interests are in the fields of chemical education and biochemistry. He may be contacted by email at jtownsend@wcupa.edu.

Contributors

When we designed this edition, we decided to seek chemists outside of our team to author some of the supplemental chapters and other materials.

John Emsley, University of Cambridge
Milestones in the Development of Chemistry and the Modern View of Atoms and Molecules and *The Chemistry of the Environment*

After 22 years as a chemistry lecturer at King's College London, John Emsley became a full-time science writer in 1990. As the Science Writer in Residence at Imperial College London from 1990 to 1997, he wrote the "Molecule of the Month" column for *The Independent* newspaper. Emsley's main activity is writing popular science books that feature chemistry and its role in everyday life. Recent publications include *The Consumer's Good Chemical Guide*, which won the Science Book Prize of 1995; *Molecules at an Exhibition; Was it Something You Ate?; Nature's Building Blocks; The Shocking History of Phosphorus; Vanity, Vitality & Virility;* and *The Elements of Murder.* His most recent book, published in 2007, is *Better Looking, Better Living, Better Loving.*

Jeffrey J. Keaffaber, University of Florida
Case Study: A Healthy Aquarium and the Nitrogen Cycle

Jeffrey J. Keaffaber received his B.S. in biology and chemistry at Manchester College, Indiana, and his Ph.D. in physical organic chemistry at the University of Florida. After finishing his doctoral work, Keaffaber joined the environmental research and development arm of Walt Disney Imagineering. He has worked as a marine environmental consultant and has taught chemistry and oceanography in the California Community College system. His research is in the fields of marine environmental chemistry and engineering, and his contributions have included the design of nitrate reduction and ozone disinfection processes for several large aquarium projects.

Eric Scerri, University of California, Los Angeles
Historical Perspectives: The Story of the Periodic Table

Eric Scerri is a continuing lecturer in the Department of Chemistry and Biochemistry at University of California, Los Angeles. After obtaining an undergraduate degree from the University of London, and a master's degree from the University of Southampton, he obtained his Ph. D. in the history and philosophy of science from King's College, London, focusing on the question of the reduction of chemistry to quantum mechanics. Scerri is the founder and editor of the international journal *Foundations of Chemistry* and recently authored *The Periodic Table: Its Story and Its Significance* (Oxford University Press, 2007), which has been described as the definitive book on the periodic table. He is also the author of more than 100 articles on the history and philosophy of chemistry, as well as chemical education. At UCLA, Scerri regularly teaches general chemistry classes of 350 students and smaller classes in the history and philosophy of science.

Felice Frankel, Harvard University

Cover photograph

As a senior research fellow, Felice Frankel heads the Envisioning Science program at Harvard University's Initiative in Innovative Computing (IIC). Frankel's images have appeared in more than 300 articles and covers in journals and general audience publications. Her awards include the 2007 Lennart Nilsson Award for Scientific Photography, a Guggenheim Fellowship, and grants from the National Science Foundation, the National Endowment for the Arts, the Alfred P. Sloan Foundation, the Graham Foundation for the Advanced Studies in the Fine Arts, and the Camille and Henry Dreyfus Foundation. Frankel's books include *On the Surface of Things, Images of the Extraordinary in Science,* and *Envisioning Science: The Design and Craft of the Science Image,* and she has a regularly appearing column, "Sightings," in *American Scientist* magazine.

About the Cover

© narcisa - floricica buzlea/istockphoto.com

The lotus is the national flower of India and Vietnam. The flowers, seeds, young leaves, and rhizomes of the plant are edible and have been used for centuries in Asia and India. Hindus associate the lotus blossom with the story of creation, and Buddhists believe it represents purity of body, speech, and mind. These ideas have come in part from the fact that the lotus flower grows in a muddy, watery environment, but, when the flower and leaves open, the mud and water are completely shed to leave a clean surface. Chemists recently discovered the underlying reasons for this phenomenon. First, the surface of the leaves is not smooth; it is covered with micro- and nanostructured wax crystals, and these tiny bumps allow only minimal contact between the leaf surface and the water droplet. Thus, only about 2% to 3% of the droplet's surface is actually in contact with the leaf. Second, the surface of the leaf itself is hydrophobic, that is, the forces of attraction between water molecules and the surface of the leaf are relatively weak. Because of strong hydrogen bonding, water molecules within a droplet are strongly attracted to one another instead of the leaf's surface and so form spherical droplets. As these droplets roll off of the surface, any dirt on the surface is swept away. On less hydrophobic surfaces, water molecules interact more strongly with the surface and drops glide off rather than roll off. This self-cleaning property of lotus leaves has been called the "lotus effect," an effect beautifully illustrated by the photograph on the cover of this book. Chemists are now trying to mimic this in new materials that can be incorporated into consumer products such as self-cleaning textiles, paint, and roofing tiles.

1 | Basic Concepts of Chemistry

Charles D. Winters

Sports Drinks

Sports drinks are popular among athletes and nonathletes alike. The original sports drink, Gatorade, contained sucrose, glucose-fructose syrup, citric acid, sodium chloride, sodium citrate, potassium dihydrogen phosphate, and flavoring and coloring agents. This is not unlike the usual soft drink, but the carbohydrates in the sports drink provide only about half of the calories in fruit juice or in an ordinary soda or soft drink. To understand the chemistry behind sports drinks, we have to know the names and composition of the various organic and inorganic compounds in the drink and understand such important areas of chemistry as thermodynamics and colligative properties. As you study chemistry you will learn about these compounds, their structures, and their functions, and you will come to understand more about the ingredients in sports drinks, among other things. For now, think how you would describe a sports drink.

Questions:
1. What are its physical properties? Is it a homogeneous or heterogeneous mixture? Is the density of a sports drink more or less than that of water?
2. What is the volume of a bottle of a typical sports drink in milliliters? In liters? In deciliters?

Answers to these questions are in Appendix Q.

In February 2006 an athlete from the U.S. was sent home from the Winter Olympics Games in Italy because he had used a common treatment for his baldness. The reason was, as the Olympic committee stated, that the remedy can also be used to mask other, illegal drugs. Similarly, athletes were banned from the Summer Olympics Games in Greece in 2004 and the winner of the 2006 Tour de France was stripped of his title for using banned steroids. How can these drugs be detected or identified?

On June 13, 2003, a colorless liquid arrived at the Olympic Analytical Laboratory (OAL) in Los Angeles, California. This laboratory annually tests about 25,000 samples for the presence of illegal drugs. Among its clients are the U.S. Olympic Committee, the National Collegiate Athletic Association, and the National Football League.

About the time of the U.S. Outdoor Track and Field Championships in the summer of 2003, a coach in Colorado tipped off the U.S. Anti-Doping Agency (USADA) that several athletes were using a new steroid. The coach had found a syringe containing an unknown substance and had sent it to the USADA. The USADA chemists dissolved the contents of the syringe in a few milliliters of an alcohol and sent the solution to the OAL. That submission initiated weeks of intense work that led to the identification of a previously unknown steroid that was presumably being used by athletes (Figure 1.1).

Chemistry⚛Now™

Throughout the text this icon introduces an opportunity for self-study or to explore interactive tutorials by signing in at **www.cengage.com/login**.

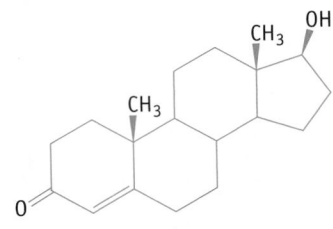

The steroid testosterone. All steroids, including cholesterol, have the same four-ring structure.

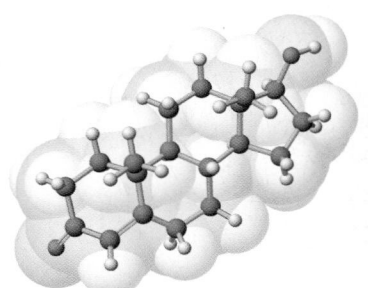

A molecular model of testosterone.

Royalty-free/Photodisc

A photo of crystals of the steroid cholesterol taken with a microscope using polarized light.

FIGURE 1.1 The steroid testosterone. The unknown compound discussed in the text is a steroid closely related to testosterone.

Dr. Donald Catlin, the director of the Olympic Analytical Laboratory in Los Angeles, California.

To identify the unknown substance, chemists at the Olympic Analytical Laboratory used a GC-MS, an instrument widely employed in forensic science work (Figure 1.2). They first passed the sample through a gas chromatograph (GC), an instrument that can separate different chemical compounds in a mixture. A GC has a small-diameter, coiled tube (a typical inside diameter is 0.025 mm) in which the inside surface has been specially treated so that chemicals are attracted to the surface. This tube is placed in an oven and heated to temperatures of 200 °C or higher. The substances in a sample are swept along the tube with a stream of helium gas. Because each component in the sample binds differently to the material on the inside surface of the tube, each component moves through the column at a different rate and exits from the end of the column at a different time. Thus, separation of the components in the mixture is achieved.

After exiting the GC, each compound is routed directly into a mass spectrometer (MS). In a mass spectrometer, the compounds are bombarded with high-energy electrons and each compound is turned into ions, a chemical species with an electric charge. These ions are then passed through a strong magnetic field, causing the ions to be deflected. The path an ion takes in the magnetic field (the extent of deflection) is related to its mass. The masses of the ions are a key piece of information that helps to identify the compound.

Such a straightforward process: separate the compounds in a GC and identify them in an MS. What can go wrong? In fact, many things can go wrong that require ingenuity to overcome. In this case, the unknown steroid did not survive the high temperatures of the GC. It broke apart into pieces, and so it was only possible to study the pieces of the original molecule. However, this gave enough evidence to convince scientists that the compound was indeed a steroid. But what steroid? Dr. Catlin, the director of OAL, said that one hypothesis was that "the new steroid was made by people who knew it was not going to be detectable," that the molecule had been designed in a way that would guarantee that it would not be detected by the standard GC-MS procedure.

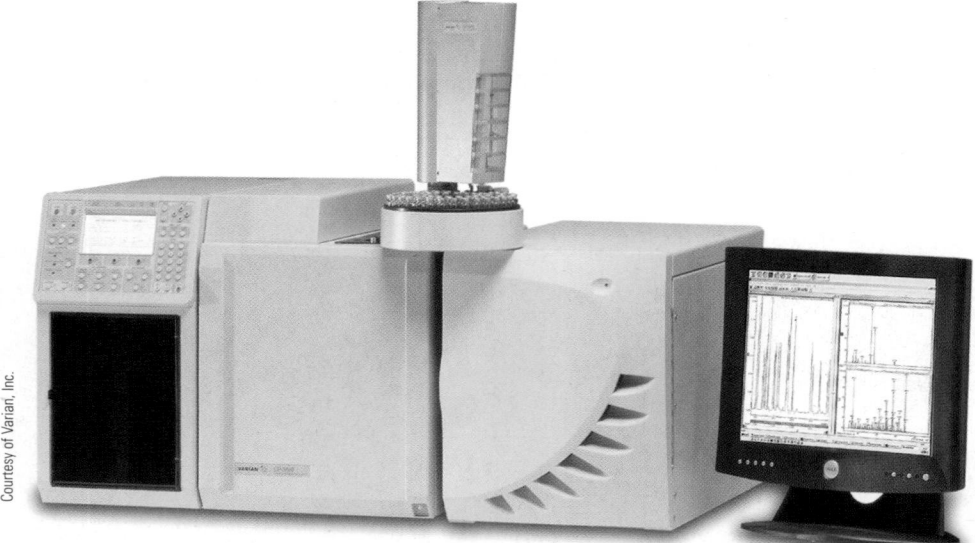

FIGURE 1.2 A GC-MS (gas chromatograph-mass spectrometer). A GC-MS is one of the major tools used in forensic chemistry. The GC portion of the instrument separates the components in a mixture of volatile compounds, and the MS portion then analyzes and identifies them. The GC-MS pictured here has an automated sample changer (carousel, center). An operator will load dozens of samples into the carousel, and the instrument will then process the samples automatically, with the data recorded and stored in a computer.

So, Catlin and his colleagues set out to identify the steroid. The first thing they did was to make the molecule stable during the analysis. This was done by attaching new atoms to the molecule to make what chemists call a *derivative*. A number of approaches to making derivatives were tested, and, within a few weeks, they believed they knew the identity of the unknown steroid.

The final step in solving the mystery was to try to make a sample of the compound in the laboratory and then to use the gas chromatograph and mass spectrometer on this sample. If the material behaved the same way as the unknown sample, then they could be as certain as possible they knew the identify of what they had received from the track coach. These experiments worked, confirming the identity of the compound. It was an entirely new steroid, never seen before in nature or in the laboratory. Its formula is $C_{21}H_{28}O_2$, and its name is tetrahydrogestrinone or THG. It resembled two well-known steroids: gestrinone, used to treat gynecological problems, and trenbolone, a steroid used by ranchers to beef up cattle.

There are two sequels to the story. First, a scientific problem is not solved until it has been verified in another laboratory. Not only was this done, but a test was soon devised to find THG in urine samples. Second, with new analytical procedures, the USADA asked OAL to retest 550 urine samples—and THG was found in several.

Throughout this mystery, chemistry played a critical role, from using the analytical technique of mass spectrometry, to using chemical intuition to determine possible arrangements of the molecular fragments, and finally to synthesizing the derivative and the proposed compound. A knowledge of chemistry is crucial to solving problems not only like this one but many others as well.

■ **Athletes and Steroids** What is the problem with athletes taking steroids? THG is one of a class of steroids called anabolic steroids. They elevate the body's natural testosterone levels and increase body mass, muscle strength, and muscle definition. They can also improve an athlete's capacity to train and compete at the highest levels. Aside from giving steroid users an illegal competitive advantage, the potential side effects of steroids are liver damage, heart disease, anxiety, and rage.

A check of the internet shows that there are hundreds of sources of steroids for athletes. The known performance-enhancing drugs can be detected and their users banned from competitive sports. But what about as-yet unknown steroids? The director of the OAL, Dr. Donald Catlin, believes there are other steroids out in the market, made by secret labs without safety standards, a problem he calls horrifying.

1.1 Chemistry and Its Methods

Chemistry is about change. It was once only about changing one natural substance into another—wood and oil burn; grape juice turns into wine; and cinnabar (Figure 1.3), a red mineral from the earth, changes ultimately into shiny quicksilver (mercury). Chemistry is still about change, but now chemists focus on the change of one pure substance, whether natural or synthetic, into another (Figure 1.4).

(a)

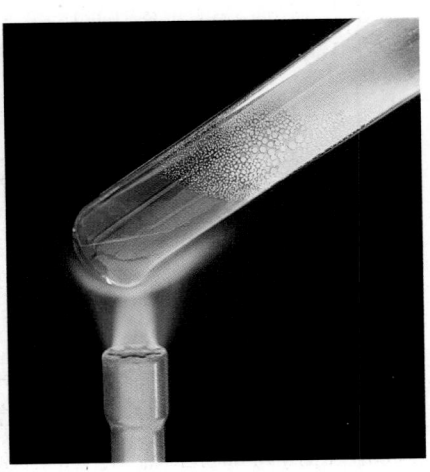
(b)

Charles D. Winters

FIGURE 1.3 Cinnabar and mercury. (a) The red crystals of cinnabar are the chemical compound mercury(II) sulfide. (b) It is heated in air to change it into orange mercury oxide, which, on further heating, is decomposed to the elements oxygen and mercury metal. (The droplets you see on the inside of the test tube wall are mercury.)

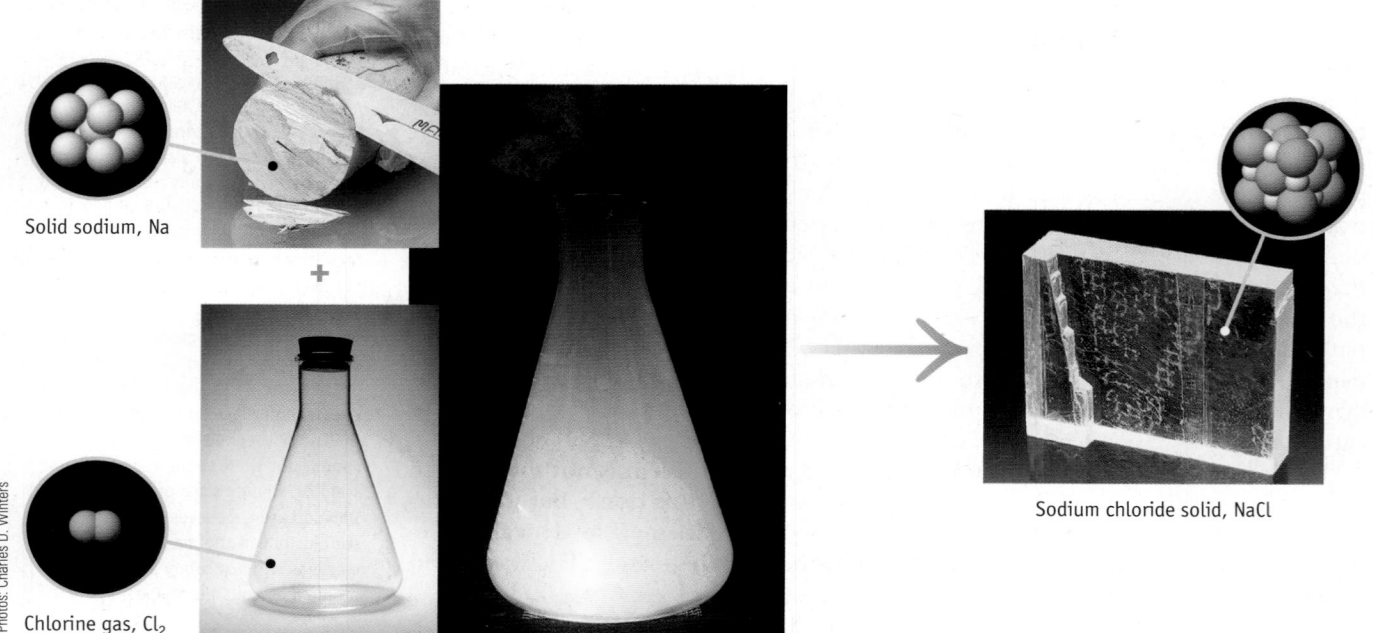

Solid sodium, Na

Chlorine gas, Cl$_2$

Sodium chloride solid, NaCl

FIGURE 1.4 Forming a chemical compound. Sodium chloride, table salt, can be made by combining sodium metal (Na) and yellow chlorine gas (Cl$_2$). The result is a crystalline solid, common salt. (The tiny spheres show how the atoms are arranged in the substances. In the case of the salt crystal, the spheres represent electrically charged sodium and chlorine ions.)

Although chemistry is endlessly fascinating—at least to chemists—why should you study chemistry? Each person probably has a different answer, but many students take a chemistry course because someone else has decided it is an important part of preparing for a particular career. Chemistry is especially useful because it is central to our understanding of disciplines as diverse as biology, geology, materials science, medicine, physics, and many branches of engineering. In addition, chemistry plays a major role in the economy of developed nations, and chemistry and chemicals affect our daily lives in a wide variety of ways. Furthermore, a course in chemistry can help you see how a scientist thinks about the world and how to solve problems. The knowledge and skills developed in such a course will benefit you in many career paths and will help you become a better-informed citizen in a world that is becoming technologically more complex—and more interesting.

Hypotheses, Laws, and Theories

As scientists, we study questions of our own choosing or ones that someone else poses in the hope of finding an answer or of discovering some useful information. In the story of the banned steroid, THG, the chemists at the Olympic Analytical Laboratory were handed a problem to solve, and they followed the usual methods of science to get to the answer. After some preliminary tests they recognized that the mystery substance was probably a steroid. That is, they formed a **hypothesis**, a tentative explanation or prediction based on experimental observations.

After formulating one or more hypotheses, scientists perform experiments designed to give results that confirm or invalidate these hypotheses. In chemistry this usually requires that both quantitative and qualitative information be collected.

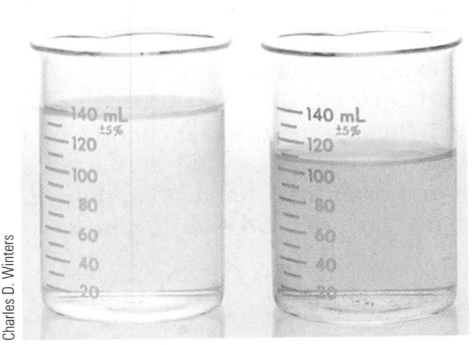 

FIGURE 1.5 Qualitative and quantitative observations. A new substance is formed by mixing two known substances in solution. We can make several observations about the substances involved. *Qualitative* observations: The solutions before mixing are colorless and yellow; a yellow, fluffy solid is formed on mixing. *Quantitative* observations: Mixing measured volumes of the solutions produces a measureable mass of solid.

Quantitative information is numerical data, such as the temperature at which a chemical substance melts or its mass (Figure 1.5). **Qualitative** information, in contrast, consists of nonnumerical observations, such as the color of a substance or its physical appearance.

The chemists at the OAL assembled a great deal of qualitative and quantitative information on various drugs. Based on their experience, and on published reports of experiments done in the past by other chemists who study steroids, they became more certain that they knew the identity of the substance. Their preliminary experiments led them to perform still more experiments, such as looking for a way to stabilize the molecule so it would not decompose, and they looked for a way to make the molecule in the laboratory. Final confirmation came when their work was reproduced by scientists in other laboratories.

After scientists have done a number of experiments and the results have been checked to ensure they are reproducible, a pattern of behavior or results may emerge. At this point it may be possible to summarize the observations in the form of a general rule or conclusion. After making a number of experimental observations, the chemists at OAL could conclude, for example, that the unknown substance was a steroid because it had properties characteristic of many other steroids they had observed.

Finally, after numerous experiments by many scientists over an extended period of time, the original hypothesis may become a **law**—a concise verbal or mathematical statement of a behavior or a relation that is consistently observed in nature without contradiction. An example might be the *law of mass conservation* in chemical reactions.

We base much of what we do in science on laws because they help us predict what may occur under a new set of circumstances. For example, we know from experience that if the chemical element sodium comes in contact with water, a violent reaction occurs and new substances are formed (Figure 1.6), and we know that the mass of the substances produced in the reaction is exactly the same as the mass of sodium and water used in the reaction. That is, *mass is always conserved in chemical reactions.* But the result of an experiment might be different from what is expected based on a general rule. When that happens, chemists get excited because experiments that do not follow our expectations are often the most interesting. We know that understanding the exceptions almost invariably gives new insights.

FIGURE 1.6 The metallic element sodium reacts with water.

Once enough reproducible experiments have been conducted, and experimental results have been generalized as a law or general rule, it may be possible to conceive a theory to explain the observations. A **theory** is a well-tested, unifying principle that explains a body of facts and the laws based on them. It is capable of suggesting new hypotheses that can be tested experimentally.

Sometimes nonscientists use the word "theory" to imply that someone has made a guess and that an idea is not yet substantiated. But, to scientists, a theory is based on carefully determined and reproducible evidence. Theories are the cornerstone of our understanding of the natural world at any given time. Remember, though, that theories are inventions of the human mind. Theories can and do change as new facts are uncovered.

Goals of Science

The sciences, including chemistry, have several goals. Two of these are prediction and control. We do experiments and seek generalities because we want to be able to predict what may occur under a given set of circumstances. We also want to know how we might control the outcome of a chemical reaction or process.

A third goal is explanation and understanding. We know, for example, that certain elements such as sodium will react vigorously with water. But why should this be true? To explain and understand this, we turn to theories such as those developed in Chapters 6 and 7.

Dilemmas and Integrity in Science

You may think research in science is straightforward: Do an experiment; draw a conclusion. But, research is seldom that easy. Frustrations and disappointments are common enough, and results can be inconclusive. Experiments sometimes contain some level of uncertainty, and spurious or contradictory data can be collected. For example, suppose you do an experiment expecting to find a direct relation between two experimental quantities. You collect six data sets. When plotted, four of the sets lie on a straight line, but two others lie far away from the line. Should you ignore the last two points? Or should you do more experiments when you know the time they take will mean someone else could publish their results first and thus get the credit for a new scientific principle? Or should you consider that the two points not on the line might indicate that your original hypothesis is wrong, and that you will have to abandon a favorite idea you have worked on for a year? Scientists have a responsibility to remain objective in these situations, but it is sometimes hard to do.

It is important to remember that scientists are human and therefore subject to the same moral pressures and dilemmas as any other person. To help ensure integrity in science, some simple principles have emerged over time that guide scientific practice:

- Experimental results should be reproducible. Furthermore, these results should be reported in the scientific literature in sufficient detail that they can be used or reproduced by others.
- Conclusions should be reasonable and unbiased.
- Credit should be given where it is due.

■ **The Stem Cell Scandal of 2005** In 2004–2005 researchers at Seoul National University in South Korea published several papers in which they claimed to have cloned DNA from human embryonic stem cells. Because it was such an important discovery, scientists around the world examined the data closely. Within months, however, it was discovered that many of the reported results were based on fabricated data, and the results were retracted. Misrepresentation of information does great harm because it misleads scientists into spending time, energy, and funds in trying to replicate the information and using that information in other experiments. The stem cell scandal illustrates, however, the ways in which the scientific community ensures that scientific research is correct and accurate.

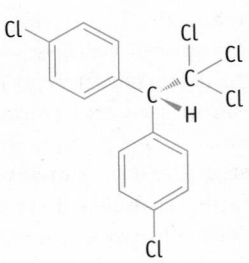
(a) The molecular structure of DDT.

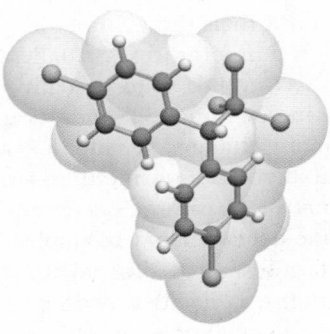
(b) A molecular model of DDT.

(c) DDT can be used to control malaria-carrying insects such as mosquitos.

1.2 Classifying Matter

This chapter begins our discussion of how chemists think about science in general and about matter in particular. After looking at a way to classify matter, we will turn to some basic ideas about elements, atoms, compounds, and molecules and describe how chemists characterize these building blocks of matter.

States of Matter and Kinetic-Molecular Theory

An easily observed property of matter is its **state**—that is, whether a substance is a solid, liquid, or gas (Figure 1.7). You recognize a material as a solid because it has a rigid shape and a fixed volume that changes little as temperature and pressure

Active Figure 1.7 States of matter—solid, liquid, and gas. Elemental bromine exists in all three states near room temperature. The tiny spheres represent bromine (Br) atoms. In elemental bromine, two Br atoms join to form a Br_2 molecule. (See Section 1.3 and Chapter 2.)

Chemistry ⚛ Now™ Sign in at www.cengage.com/login and go to the Chapter Contents menu to explore an interactive version of this figure accompanied by an exercise.

Photos: Charles D. Winters

| Solid | Liquid | Gas |

Bromine solid and liquid   Bromine gas and liquid

■ **Water—Changes in Volume on Freezing** Water is an exception to the general statement that a given mass of a substance has a smaller volume as a solid than as a liquid. Water is almost unique in that, for a given mass, the volume *increases* on changing from a liquid to a solid. (That is, its density decreases. See page 15.)

■ **Gases, Liquids, and Solids** Gases and kinetic-molecular theory are discussed in detail in Chapter 11, liquids in Chapter 12, and solids in Chapter 13.

change. Like solids, liquids have a fixed volume, but a liquid is fluid—it takes on the shape of its container and has no definite shape of its own. Gases are fluid as well, but the volume of a gas is determined by the size of its container. The volume of a gas varies more than the volume of a liquid with temperature and pressure.

At low enough temperatures, virtually all matter is found in the solid state. As the temperature is raised, solids usually melt to form liquids. Eventually, if the temperature is high enough, liquids evaporate to form gases. Volume changes typically accompany changes in state. For a given mass of material, there is usually a small increase in volume on melting—water being a significant exception—and then a large increase in volume occurs upon evaporation.

The **kinetic-molecular theory of matter** helps us interpret the properties of solids, liquids, and gases. According to this theory, all matter consists of extremely tiny particles (atoms, molecules, or ions), which are in constant motion.

- In solids these particles are packed closely together, usually in a regular array. The particles vibrate back and forth about their average positions, but seldom does a particle in a solid squeeze past its immediate neighbors to come into contact with a new set of particles.
- The atoms or molecules of liquids are arranged randomly rather than in the regular patterns found in solids. Liquids and gases are fluid because the particles are not confined to specific locations and can move past one another.
- Under normal conditions, the particles in a gas are far apart. Gas molecules move extremely rapidly because they are not constrained by their neighbors. The molecules of a gas fly about, colliding with one another and with the container walls. This random motion allows gas molecules to fill their container, so the volume of the gas sample is the volume of the container.

An important aspect of the kinetic-molecular theory is that the higher the temperature, the faster the particles move. The energy of motion of the particles (their **kinetic energy**) acts to overcome the forces of attraction between particles. A solid melts to form a liquid when the temperature of the solid is raised to the point at which the particles vibrate fast enough and far enough to push one another out of the way and move out of their regularly spaced positions. As the temperature increases even more, the particles move even faster until finally they can escape the clutches of their comrades and enter the gaseous state. *Increasing temperature* *corresponds to faster and faster motions of atoms and molecules*, a general rule you will find useful in many future discussions.

Matter at the Macroscopic and Particulate Levels

The characteristic properties of gases, liquids, and solids are observed by the unaided human senses. They are determined using samples of matter large enough to be seen, measured, and handled. Using such samples, we can also determine, for example, what the color of a substance is, whether it dissolves in water, or whether it conducts electricity or reacts with oxygen. Observations such as these generally take place in the **macroscopic** world of chemistry (Figure 1.8). This is the world of experiments and observations.

Now let us move to the level of atoms, molecules, and ions—a world of chemistry we cannot see. Take a macroscopic sample of material and divide it, again and again, past the point where the amount of sample can be seen by the naked eye, past the point where it can be seen using an optical microscope. Eventually you reach the level of individual particles that make up all matter, a level that chemists refer to as the **submicroscopic** or **particulate** world of atoms and molecules (Figures 1.7 and 1.8).

Chemists are interested in the structure of matter at the particulate level. Atoms, molecules, and ions cannot be "seen" in the same way that one views the macroscopic world, but they are no less real. Chemists imagine what atoms must look like and how they might fit together to form molecules. They create models to represent atoms and molecules (Figures 1.7 and 1.8)—where tiny spheres are used to represent atoms—and then use these models to think about chemistry and to explain the observations they have made about the macroscopic world.

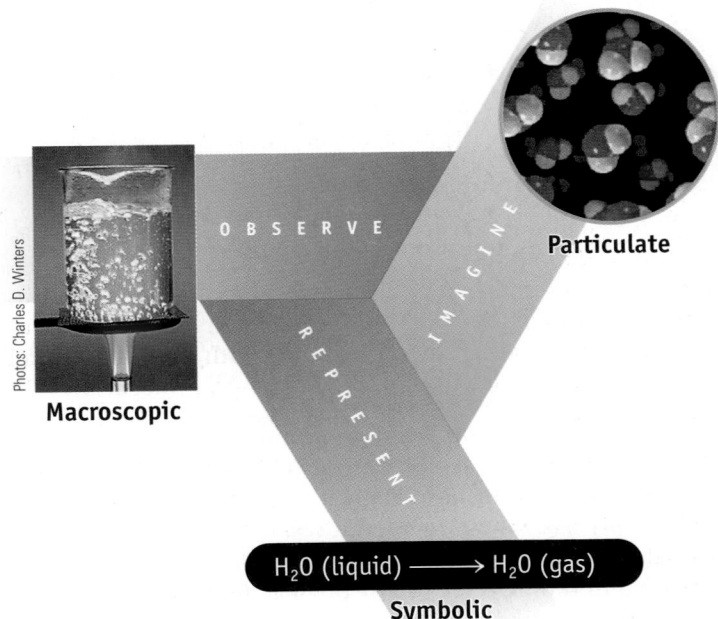

Photos: Charles D. Winters

Macroscopic

OBSERVE

IMAGINE

REPRESENT

Particulate

H₂O (liquid) ⟶ H₂O (gas)

Symbolic

Active Figure 1.8 **Levels of matter.** We observe chemical and physical processes at the macroscopic level. To understand or illustrate these processes, scientists often try to imagine what has occurred at the particulate atomic and molecular levels and write symbols to represent these observations. A beaker of boiling water can be visualized at the particulate level as rapidly moving H_2O molecules. The process is symbolized by the chemical equation $H_2O(liquid) \longrightarrow H_2O(gas)$.

Chemistry.Now™ Sign in at **www.cengage.com/login** and go to the Chapter Contents menu to explore an interactive version of this figure accompanied by an exercise.

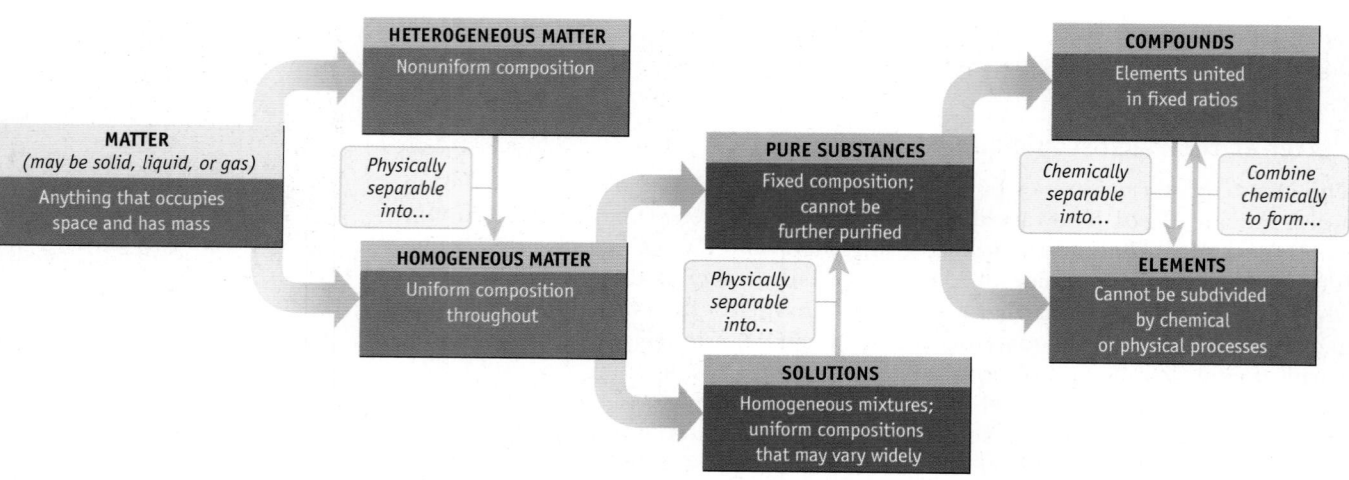

It has been said that chemists carry out experiments at the macroscopic level, but they think about chemistry at the particulate level. They then write down their observations as "symbols," the letters (such as H_2O for water or Br_2 for bromine molecules) and drawings that signify the elements and compounds involved. This is a useful perspective that will help you as you study chemistry. Indeed, one of our goals is to help you make the connections in your own mind among the symbolic, particulate, and macroscopic worlds of chemistry.

Pure Substances

A chemist looks at a glass of drinking water and sees a liquid. This liquid could be the pure chemical compound water. More likely, though, the liquid is a *homogeneous* mixture of water and dissolved substances—that is, a **solution.** It is also possible the water sample is a *heterogeneous* mixture, with solids suspended in the liquid. These descriptions represent some of the ways we can classify matter (Figure 1.9).

Every substance has a set of unique properties by which it can be recognized. Pure water, for example, is colorless and odorless and certainly does not contain suspended solids. If you wanted to identify a substance conclusively as water, you would have to examine its properties carefully and compare them against the known properties of pure water. Melting point and boiling point serve the purpose well here. If you could show that the substance melts at 0 °C and boils at 100 °C at atmospheric pressure, you can be certain it is water. No other known substance melts and boils at precisely these temperatures.

A second feature of a pure substance is that it generally cannot be separated into two or more different species by any physical technique at ordinary temperatures. If it could be separated, our sample would be classified as a mixture.

(a)

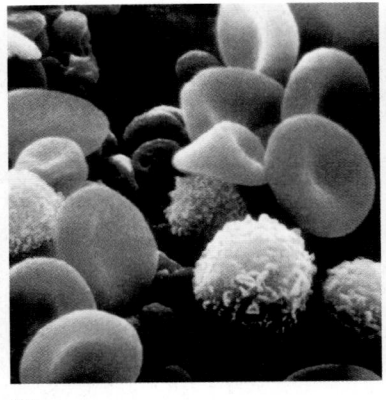
(b)

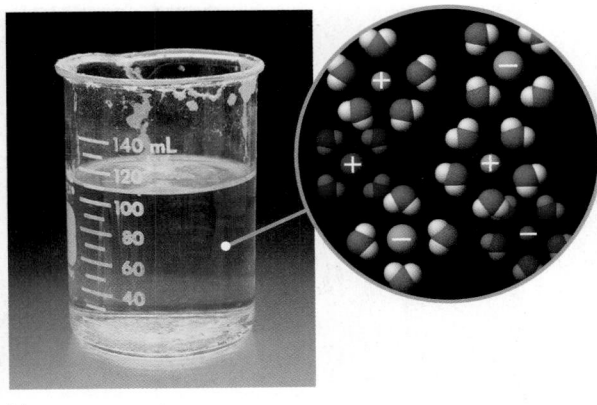
(c)

a and c, Charles D. Winters; b, Kenneth Eward/BioGrafx/Photo Researchers, Inc.

FIGURE 1.10 Mixtures. (a) A cup of noodle soup is a heterogeneous mixture. (b) A sample of blood may look homogeneous, but examination with an optical microscope shows it is, in fact, a heterogeneous mixture of liquids and suspended particles (blood cells). (c) A homogeneous mixture, here consisting of salt in water. The model shows that salt in water consists of separate, electrically charged particles (ions), but the particles cannot be seen with an optical microscope.

Mixtures: Homogeneous and Heterogeneous

A cup of noodle soup is obviously a mixture of solids and liquids (Figure 1.10a). A mixture in which the uneven texture of the material can be detected is called a **heterogeneous** mixture. Heterogeneous mixtures such as blood may appear completely uniform but on closer examination are not (Figure 1.10b). Milk, for example, appears smooth in texture to the unaided eye, but magnification would reveal fat and protein globules within the liquid. In a heterogeneous mixture the properties in one region are different from those in another region.

A **homogeneous** mixture consists of two or more substances in the same phase (Figure 1.10c). No amount of optical magnification will reveal a homogeneous mixture to have different properties in different regions. Homogeneous mixtures are often called **solutions.** Common examples include air (mostly a mixture of nitrogen and oxygen gases), gasoline (a mixture of carbon- and hydrogen-containing compounds called *hydrocarbons*), and an unopened soft drink.

When a mixture is separated into its pure components, the components are said to be **purified.** Efforts at separation are often not complete in a single step, however, and repetition almost always gives an increasingly pure substance. For example, soil particles can be separated from water by filtration (Figure 1.11). When the mixture is passed through a filter, many of the particles are removed. Repeated filtrations will give water a higher and higher state of purity. This purification process uses a property of the mixture, its clarity, to measure the extent of purification. When a perfectly clear sample of water is obtained, all of the soil particles are assumed to have been removed.

Chemistry ⚛ Now™

Sign in at **www.cengage.com/login** and go to Chapter 1 Contents to see:
- Screen 1.5 for an exercise on **identifying pure substances and types of mixtures**
- Screen 1.6 to watch a video on **heterogeneous mixtures**

a, Charles D. Winters; b, Littleton, Massachusetts, Spectacle Pond Iron and Manganese Treatment Facility

(a)

(b)

FIGURE 1.11 Purifying water by filtration. (a) A laboratory setup. A beaker full of muddy water is passed through a paper filter, and the mud and dirt are removed. (b) A water treatment plant uses filtration to remove suspended particles from the water.

Module 1

1.3 Elements and Atoms

Passing an electric current through water can decompose it to gaseous hydrogen and oxygen (Figure 1.12a). Substances like hydrogen and oxygen that are composed of only one type of atom are classified as **elements.** Currently, 117 elements are known. Of these, only about 90—some of which are illustrated in Figure 1.12—are found in nature. The remainder have been created by scientists. The name and symbol for each element are listed in the tables at the front and back of this book. Carbon (C), sulfur (S), iron (Fe), copper (Cu), silver (Ag), tin (Sn), gold (Au), mercury (Hg), and lead (Pb) were known to the early Greeks and Romans and to the alchemists of ancient China, the Arab world, and medieval Europe. However,

Photos: Charles D. Winters

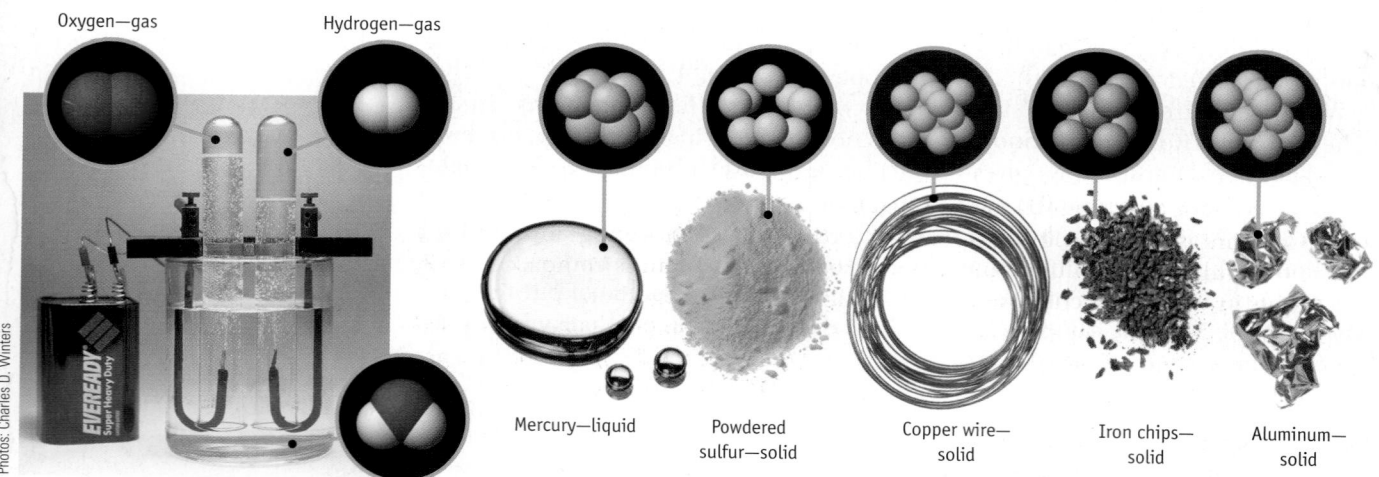

Oxygen—gas   Hydrogen—gas

Water—liquid

Mercury—liquid   Powdered sulfur—solid   Copper wire—solid   Iron chips—solid   Aluminum—solid

(a)

(b)

FIGURE 1.12 Elements. (a) Passing an electric current through water produces the elements hydrogen (test tube on the right) and oxygen (test tube on the left). (b) Chemical elements can often be distinguished by their color and their state at room temperature.

Sign in at **www.cengage.com/login** to download the Go Chemistry module for this section or go to **www.ichapters.com** to purchase modules.

many other elements—such as aluminum (Al), silicon (Si), iodine (I), and helium (He)—were not discovered until the 18th and 19th centuries. Finally, scientists in the 20th and 21st centuries have made elements that do not exist in nature, such as technetium (Tc), plutonium (Pu), and americium (Am).

The table inside the front cover of this book, in which the symbol and other information for the elements are enclosed in a box, is called the **periodic table.** We will describe this important tool of chemistry in more detail beginning in Chapter 2.

An **atom** is the smallest particle of an element that retains the characteristic chemical properties of that element. Modern chemistry is based on an understanding and exploration of nature at the atomic level (▶ Chapters 6 and 7).

Chemistry ⚛ Now™

Sign in at **www.cengage.com/login** and go to Chapter 1 Contents to see Screen 1.7 for a self-study module on **Elements and Atoms,** and the Periodic Table tool on this screen or in the Toolbox.

EXERCISE 1.1 Elements

Using the periodic table inside the front cover of this book:

(a) Find the names of the elements having the symbols Na, Cl, and Cr.

(b) Find the symbols for the elements zinc, nickel, and potassium.

1.4 Compounds and Molecules

A pure substance like sugar, salt, or water, which is composed of two or more different elements held together by **chemical bonds,** is referred to as a **chemical compound.** Even though only 117 elements are known, there appears to be no limit to the number of compounds that can be made from those elements. More than 20 million compounds are now known, with about a half million added to the list each year.

When elements become part of a compound, their original properties, such as their color, hardness, and melting point, are replaced by the characteristic properties of the compound. Consider common table salt (sodium chloride), which is composed of two elements (see Figure 1.4):

- Sodium is a shiny metal that reacts violently with water. Its solid state structure has sodium atoms tightly packed together.
- Chlorine is a light yellow gas that has a distinctive, suffocating odor and is a powerful irritant to lungs and other tissues. The element is composed of Cl_2 units in which two chlorine atoms are tightly bound together.
- Sodium chloride, or common salt, is a colorless, crystalline solid composed of sodium and chloride ions bound tightly together (NaCl). Its properties are completely unlike those of the two elements from which it is made.

It is important to distinguish between a mixture of elements and a chemical compound of two or more elements. Pure metallic iron and yellow, powdered sulfur (Figure 1.13a) can be mixed in varying proportions. In the chemical compound iron pyrite (Figure 1.13b), however, there is no variation in composition. Not only does iron pyrite exhibit properties peculiar to itself and different from those of either iron or sulfur, or a mixture of these two elements, but it also has a definite percentage composition by mass (46.55% Fe and 53.45% S). Thus, two

■ **Writing Element Symbols** Notice that only the first letter of an element's symbol is capitalized. For example, cobalt is Co, not CO. The notation CO represents the chemical compound carbon monoxide. Also note that the element name is not capitalized, except at the beginning of a sentence.

■ **Origin of Element Names and Symbols** Many elements have names and symbols with Latin or Greek origins. Examples include helium (He), from the Greek word *helios* meaning "sun," and lead, whose symbol, Pb, comes from the Latin word for "heavy," *plumbum.* More recently discovered elements have been named for their place of discovery or for a person or place of significance. Examples include americium (Am), californium (Cf), and curium (Cm; for Marie Curie).

■ **Periodic Tables Online** Sign in at **www.cengage.com/login** and go to Chapter 1 Contents to see Screen 1.7 or the Toolbox. See also the extensive information on the periodic table and the elements at the American Chemical Society website:
- acswebcontent.acs.org/games/pt.html

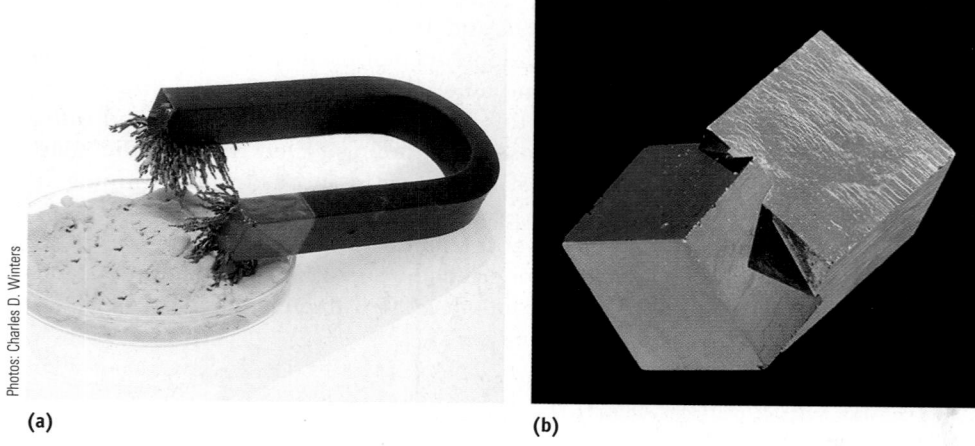

FIGURE 1.13 Mixtures and compounds. (a) The material in the dish is a mixture of iron chips and sulfur. The iron can be removed easily by using a magnet. (b) Iron pyrite is a chemical compound composed of iron and sulfur. It is often found in nature as perfect, golden cubes.

Photos: Charles D. Winters

(a) (b)

major differences exist between mixtures and pure compounds: Compounds have distinctly different characteristics from their parent elements, and they have a definite percentage composition (by mass) of their combining elements.

Some compounds—such as table salt, NaCl—are composed of **ions,** which are electrically charged atoms or groups of atoms [▶ Chapter 2]. Other compounds—such as water and sugar—consist of **molecules,** the smallest discrete units that retain the composition and chemical characteristics of the compound.

The composition of any compound is represented by its **chemical formula.** In the formula for water, H_2O, for example, the symbol for hydrogen, H, is followed by a subscript "2" indicating that two atoms of hydrogen occur in a single water molecule. The symbol for oxygen appears without a subscript, indicating that one oxygen atom occurs in the molecule.

As you shall see throughout this book, molecules can be represented with models that depict their composition and structure. Figure 1.14 illustrates the names, formulas, and models of the structures of a few common molecules.

1.5 Physical Properties

You recognize your friends by their physical appearance: their height and weight and the color of their eyes and hair. The same is true of chemical substances. You can tell the difference between an ice cube and a cube of lead of the same size not only because of their appearance (one is clear and colorless, and the other is a lustrous metal) (Figure 1.15), but also because one is more dense (lead) than the other (ice). Properties such as these, which can be observed and measured without changing the composition of a substance, are called **physical properties.** The chemical elements in Figure 1.12, for example, clearly differ in terms of their color,

FIGURE 1.14 Names, formulas, and models of some common molecules. Models of molecules appear throughout this book. In such models, C atoms are gray, H atoms are white, N atoms are blue, and O atoms are red.

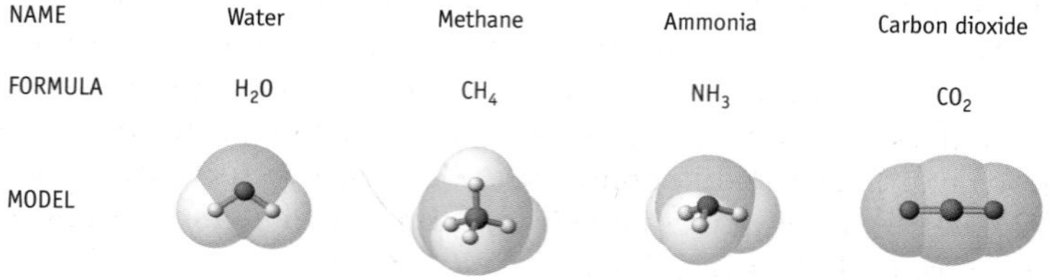

NAME	Water	Methane	Ammonia	Carbon dioxide
FORMULA	H_2O	CH_4	NH_3	CO_2
MODEL				

TABLE 1.1 Some Physical Properties

Property	Using the Property to Distinguish Substances
Color	Is the substance colored or colorless? What is the color, and what is its intensity?
State of matter	Is it a solid, liquid, or gas? If it is a solid, what is the shape of the particles?
Melting point	At what temperature does a solid melt?
Boiling point	At what temperature does a liquid boil?
Density	What is the substance's density (mass per unit volume)?
Solubility	What mass of substance can dissolve in a given volume of water or other solvent?
Electric conductivity	Does the substance conduct electricity?
Malleability	How easily can a solid be deformed?
Ductility	How easily can a solid be drawn into a wire?
Viscosity	How easily will a liquid flow?

FIGURE 1.15 Physical properties. An ice cube and a piece of lead can be differentiated easily by their physical properties (such as density, color, and melting point).

appearance, and state (solid, liquid, or gas). Physical properties allow us to classify and identify substances. Table 1.1 lists a few physical properties of matter that chemists commonly use.

EXERCISE 1.2 Physical Properties

Identify as many physical properties in Table 1.1 as you can for the following common substances: (a) iron, (b) water, (c) table salt (chemical name is sodium chloride), and (d) oxygen.

Density, the ratio of the mass of an object to its volume, is a physical property useful for identifying substances.

$$\text{Density} = \frac{\text{mass}}{\text{volume}} \tag{1.1}$$

For example, you can readily tell the difference between an ice cube and a cube of lead of identical size (Figure 1.15). Lead has a high density, 11.35 g/cm^3 (11.35 grams per cubic centimeter), whereas the density of ice is slightly less than 0.917 g/cm^3. An ice cube with a volume of 16.0 cm^3 has a mass of 14.7 g, whereas a cube of lead with the same volume has a mass of 182 g.

The **temperature** of a sample of matter often affects the numerical values of its properties. Density is a particularly important example. Although the change in water density with temperature seems small (Table 1.2), it affects our environment profoundly. For example, as the water in a lake cools, the density of the water increases, and the denser water sinks (Figure 1.16a). This continues until the water temperature reaches 3.98 °C, the point at which water has its maximum density $(0.999973 \text{ g/cm}^3)$. If the water temperature drops further, the density decreases slightly, and the colder water floats on top of water at 3.98 °C. If water is cooled below about 0 °C, solid ice forms. Water is unique among substances in the universe: Ice is less dense than water, so the solid ice floats on liquid water.

Because the density of liquids changes with temperature, the volume of a given mass of liquid also changes with temperature. This is the reason laboratory glassware used to measure precise volumes of solutions always specifies the temperature at which it was calibrated (Figure 1.16b).

■ **Units of Density** As described on page 25, the SI unit of mass is the kilogram and the SI unit of length is the meter. Therefore, the SI unit of density is kg/m^3. In chemistry, the more commonly used unit is g/cm^3. To convert from kg/m^3 to g/cm^3, divide by 1000.

■ **Calculations Involving Density and Mathematics Review** See *Let's Review* beginning on page 24 for a review of some of the mathematics used in introductory chemistry.

■ **Temperature Scales** Scientists use the Celsius (°C) and Kelvin scales (K) for temperature. See page 26.

TABLE 1.2 Temperature Dependence of Water Density

Temperature (°C)	Density of Water (g/cm³)
0 (ice)	0.917
0 (liq water)	0.99984
2	0.99994
4	0.99997
10	0.99970
25	0.99707
100	0.95836

When you think of chemistry, you probably think of colored liquids bubbling in flasks and maybe a fire or even an explosion. That is not what we usually see in a university laboratory, but pay a visit to Yellowstone National Park in Wyoming (or to areas of the North Island of New Zealand) and you will see just that: bubbling, steaming hot water springs with colorful substances in a natural "laboratory."

Yellowstone Park is unique in having one of the highest concentrations of geysers, hot springs, steam vents, and mudpots on the planet. The reason rests in the geology of the area—the earth's crust is thinner here (about 64 km) compared with the crust covering the rest of the earth (144 km). Hot magma lies not far below Yellowstone's surface (6–16 km), and it heats the rocks above and the reservoirs of water closer to the surface (a physical process). The superheated water dissolves some of the minerals (another physical process), and it is forced upwards through fissures in the rocks and sometimes explodes through the surface as geysers and hot springs.

The hot water shooting to the surface carries with it dissolved minerals such as limestone (calcium carbonate), and they are deposited around the geysers and hot springs as limestone and travertine.

Once the hot water reaches the surface, it can harbor thermophilic or "heat-loving" bacteria. These can grow in enormous colonies

with brilliant colors. Different bacteria grow at different temperatures, usually in the range of 50 °C to 70 °C, and the colors of the pools and streams can change with temperature. In the Grand Prismatic Spring shown in the photo, you can see that bacteria grow in the slightly cooler water around the edge of the spring, but the deep blue, very hot water in

© James Cowlin

A travertine formation in Yellowstone National Park. The formation consists largely of limestone (calcium carbonate) mixed with silica.

the center is devoid of living organisms. The bacteria growing around the hot springs are single-cell organisms ranging in size from 0.2 to 50 μm in diameter. They are often highly colored, owing to pigments such as carotenoids and chlorophylls, and different organisms with different colors grow at different temperatures. Some are anaerobic bacteria and use sulfur instead of oxygen for respiration (a chemical process).

A study of the hot springs of Yellowstone National Park is a good example of the intersection of chemistry, geology, and biology and of all of their subdisciplines (biochemistry, geochemistry, bacteriology, and mineralogy, among others). Our goal in this book is to introduce the chemistry background you will need to study more chemistry or to carve out a career in another field of science.

Stephen Hoerold

Grand Prismatic Spring, Yellowstone National Park.

Extensive and Intensive Properties

Extensive properties depend on the amount of a substance present. The mass and volume of the samples of elements in Figure 1.12, or the amount of heat obtained from burning gasoline, are extensive properties, for example. In contrast, **intensive properties** do *not* depend on the amount of substance. A sample of ice will melt at 0 °C, no matter whether you have an ice cube or an iceberg. Density is also an intensive property. The density of gold, for example, is the same (19.3 g/cm^3 at 20 °C) whether you have a flake of pure gold or a solid gold ring. Intensive properties are often useful in identifying a material. For example, the temperature at which a material melts (its melting point) is often so characteristic that it can be used to identify the solid (Figure 1.17).

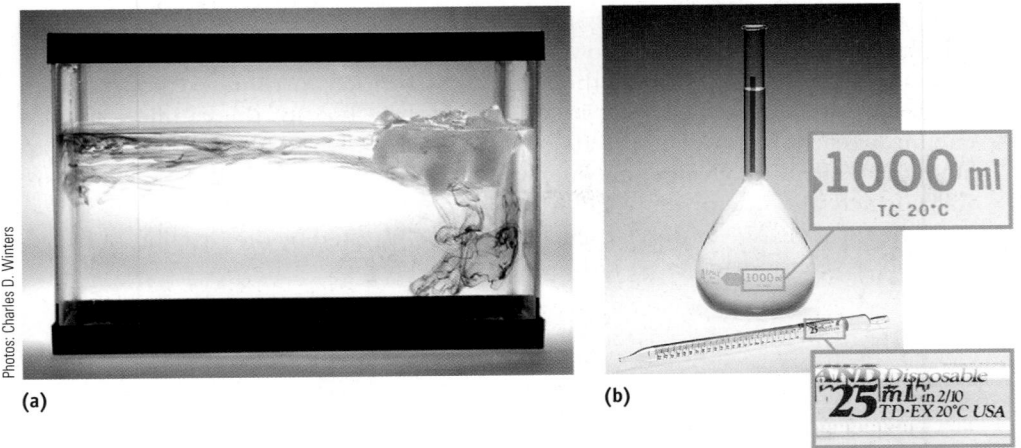

(a) (b)

FIGURE 1.16 Temperature dependence of physical properties. (a) Change in density with temperature. Ice cubes were placed in the right side of the tank and blue dye in the left side. The water beneath the ice is cooler and denser than the surrounding water, so it sinks. The convection current created by this movement of water is traced by the dye movement as the denser, cooler water sinks. (b) Temperature and calibration. Laboratory glassware is calibrated for specific temperatures. The pipet will deliver and the volumetric flask will contain the specified volume at the indicated temperature.

1.6 Physical and Chemical Changes

Changes in physical properties are called **physical changes.** In a physical change, the identity of a substance is preserved even though it may have changed its physical state or the gross size and shape of its pieces. A physical change does not result in a new chemical substance being produced. The substances (atoms, molecules, or ions) present before and after the change are the same. An example of a physical change is the melting of a solid (Figure 1.17). In the case of ice melting, the molecules present both before and after the change are H_2O molecules. Their chemical identity has not changed; they are now simply able to flow past one another in the liquid state instead of being locked in position in the solid.

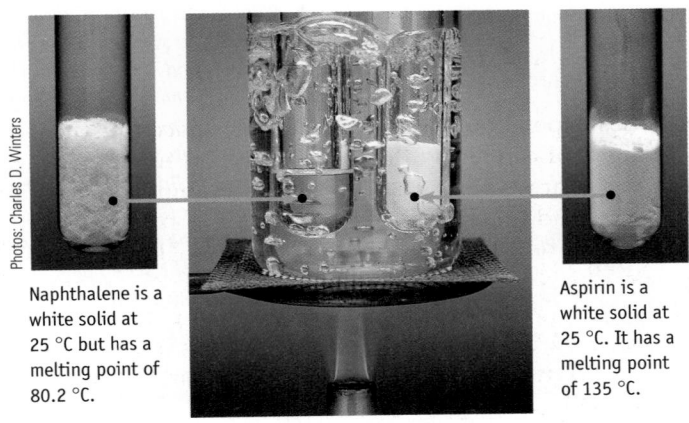

Naphthalene is a white solid at 25 °C but has a melting point of 80.2 °C.

Aspirin is a white solid at 25 °C. It has a melting point of 135 °C.

FIGURE 1.17 A physical property used to distinguish compounds. Aspirin and naphthalene are both white solids at 25 °C. You can tell them apart by, among other things, a difference in physical properties. At the temperature of boiling water, 100 °C, naphthalene is a liquid (left), whereas aspirin is a solid (right).

A physical property of hydrogen gas (H_2) is its low density, so a balloon filled with H_2 floats in air. Suppose, however, that a lighted candle is brought up to the balloon. When the heat causes the skin of the balloon to rupture, the hydrogen combines with the oxygen (O_2) in the air, and the heat of the candle sets off a chemical reaction, producing water, H_2O (Figure 1.18). This reaction is an example of a **chemical change,** in which one or more substances (the **reactants**) are transformed into one or more different substances (the **products**).

A chemical change at the particulate level is illustrated by the reaction of hydrogen and oxygen molecules to form water molecules.

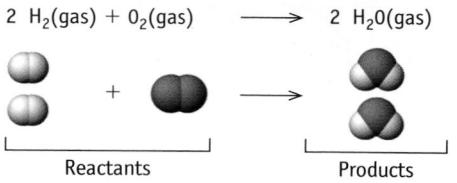

$$2\ H_2(gas) + O_2(gas) \longrightarrow 2\ H_2O(gas)$$

Reactants   Products

Case Study   Ancient and Modern Hair Coloring

Humankind has always been interested in pigments for artistic uses and to decorate their bodies. One of the oldest pigments is galena, PbS (Figure 1), which was first brought from Asia to Egypt thousands of years ago. When powdered, it is black and has been widely used as a cosmetic, particularly for dyeing hair. Some evidence for this is that small piles of galena were found next to the skeleton of a young Egyptian woman whose remains were buried in 3080 BC ± 110 years. Analysis by chemical archeologists found that the galena in this tomb was not from Asia, though. Instead, using modern forensic techniques, they found it came from nearby cities on the Red Sea.

According to recent research, the same effect on hair that galena has could be achieved by applying a mixture of the chemical compounds PbO and $Ca(OH)_2$. This was originally described by Claudius Galen, a Roman physician who lived between about 130 and 200 AD. Similar formulations have been used through the centuries for dyeing wool, and the present-day hair-coloring product Grecian Formula™ still uses this technique.

In recent research, chemists in France found that only a few hours after applying the PbO and $Ca(OH)_2$ mixture to hair (Figure 2a), the hair was blackened (Figure 2b), and that the blackening came from tiny particles of PbS (about 5 nanometers in diameter).

But where did the sulfur in PbS come from? The French research found it came from the amino acids in hair. (The amino acids cysteine and methionine both have sulfur as part of their structure.)

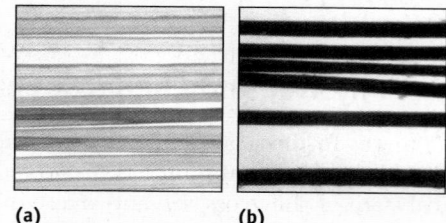

(a)   (b)

FIGURE 2 Photographs of strands of hair before (a) and after (b) treating with a mixture of PbO and $Ca(OH)_2$. From *C & EN,* Vol. 84, No. 37, p. 12, 2006, "Still Dyeing After 2,000 Years," Dr. B. Halford. Copyright © 2006 American Chemical Society. Used with permission.

Questions:

1. *What is the name of the element Pb? Of Ca?*
2. *What is the density of Pb?*
3. *What is the symbol for the element sulfur?*
4. *Can you find (on the World Wide Web, for example) the common name for the compound $Ca(OH)_2$?*
5. *A particulate view of galena is illustrated in Figure 1b. Briefly describe the shape of this tiny piece of PbS.*
6. *Compare the particulate view of galena with that of NaCl on page 4. Are there similarities? Any differences?*

Answers to these questions are in Appendix Q.

Charles D. Winters

— Pb^{2+} ion

— S^{2-} ion

(a)   (b)

FIGURE 1 **Lead sulfide, galena.** (a) Small crystal of the mineral galena, PbS. (b) The particulate view of PbS (where the gray spheres are Pb and the yellow spheres are S).

References: Nano Letters, 2006, p. 2215; J. L. Lambert, *Traces of the Past,* Addison-Wesley, 1997, p. 80.

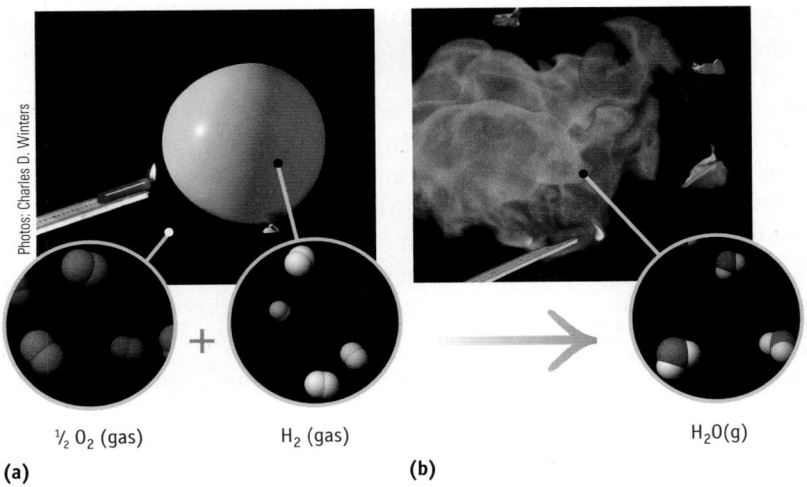

FIGURE 1.18 A chemical change—
the reaction of hydrogen and oxygen.
(a) A balloon filled with molecules of
hydrogen gas and surrounded by molecules of oxygen in the air. (The balloon
floats in air because gaseous hydrogen
is less dense than air.) (b) When ignited
with a burning candle, H_2 and O_2 react to
form water, H_2O.

Chemistry Now™ Sign in at
www.cengage.com/login and go to
Chapter 1 Contents to see Screen 1.11
Chemical Change, for a video of this
reaction.

½ O_2 (gas) H_2 (gas) $H_2O(g)$

(a)   (b)

The representation of the change using chemical formulas is called a **chemical
equation.** It shows that the substances on the left (the reactants) produce the substances on the right (the products). As this equation shows, there are four atoms
of H and two atoms of O before *and* after the reaction, but the molecules before
the reaction are different from those after the reaction.

A **chemical property** indicates whether and sometimes how readily a material
undergoes a chemical change with another material. For example, a chemical
property of hydrogen gas is that it reacts vigorously with oxygen gas.

Chemistry Now™

Sign in at **www.cengage.com/login** and go to Chapter 1 Contents to see:
- Screen 1.12 for an exercise on **identifying physical and chemical changes**
- Screen 1.13 to watch a video and view an animation of the **molecular changes when chlorine gas and
  solid phosphorus react**

EXERCISE 1.3 Chemical Reactions and Physical Changes

When camping in the mountains, you boil a pot of water on a campfire. What physical and chemical
changes take place in this process?

Chemical and physical changes. A pot of
water has been put on a campfire. What
chemical and physical changes are occurring here (Exercise 1.3)?

Chapter Goals Revisited

Now that you have studied this chapter, you should ask whether you have met the chapter goals. In particular, you should be able to:

Understand the nature of hypotheses, laws, and theories
a. Recognize the difference between a hypothesis and a theory and describe how laws are established.

Apply the kinetic-molecular theory to the properties of matter
a. Understand the basic ideas of the kinetic-molecular theory (Section 1.2).

Classify matter
a. Recognize the different states of matter (solids, liquids, and gases) and give their characteristics (Section 1.2).
b. Appreciate the difference between pure substances and mixtures and the difference between homogeneous and heterogeneous mixtures (Section 1.2).
c. Recognize the importance of representing matter at the macroscopic level and at the particulate level (Section 1.2).

Recognize elements, atoms, compounds, and molecules
a. Identify the name or symbol for an element, given its symbol or name (Section 1.3). Study Question(s) assignable in OWL: 2, 4; Go Chemistry Module 1.
b. Use the terms atom, element, molecule, and compound correctly (Sections 1.3 and 1.4).

Identify physical and chemical properties and changes
a. List commonly used physical properties of matter (Section 1.5).
b. Identify several physical and chemical properties of common substances (Sections 1.5 and 1.6). Study Question(s) assignable in OWL: 8, 10, 13, 14, 31, 37.
c. Relate density to the volume and mass of a substance (Section 1.5). Study Question(s) assignable in OWL: 18, 19, 21, 23, 29, 30, 34.
d. Explain the difference between chemical and physical changes (Section 1.6). Study Question(s) assignable in OWL: 8, 13, 33.
e. Understand the difference between extensive and intensive properties and give examples of them (Section 1.5). Study Question(s) assignable in OWL: 11.

KEY EQUATIONS

Equation 1.1 (page 15)   Density. In chemistry the common unit of density is g/cm³, whereas kg/m³ is common in geology and oceanography.

$$\text{Density} = \frac{\text{mass}}{\text{volume}}$$

STUDY QUESTIONS

🦉**WL** Online homework for this chapter may be assigned in OWL.

▲ denotes challenging questions.

■ denotes questions assignable in OWL.

Blue-numbered questions have answers in Appendix O and fully-worked solutions in the *Student Solutions Manual*.

Practicing Skills

Matter: Elements and Atoms, Compounds, and Molecules
(See Exercise 1.1)

1. Give the name of each of the following elements:
   (a) C   (c) Cl   (e) Mg
   (b) K   (d) P   (f) Ni

2. ■ Give the name of each of the following elements:
   (a) Mn   (c) Na   (e) Xe
   (a) Cu   (d) Br   (f) Fe

3. Give the symbol for each of the following elements:
   (a) barium   (c) chromium   (e) arsenic
   (b) titanium   (d) lead   (f) zinc

4. ■ Give the symbol for each of the following elements:
   (a) silver   (c) plutonium   (e) technetium
   (b) aluminum   (d) tin   (f) krypton

5. In each of the following pairs, decide which is an element and which is a compound.
   (a) Na and NaCl
   (b) Sugar and carbon
   (c) Gold and gold chloride

6. ■ In each of the following pairs, decide which is an element and which is a compound.
   (a) $Pt(NH_3)_2Cl_2$ and Pt
   (b) Copper or copper(II) oxide
   (c) Silicon or sand

Physical and Chemical Properties
(See Exercises 1.2 and 1.3)

7. In each case, decide if the underlined property is a physical or chemical property.
   (a) The color of elemental bromine is <u>orange-red</u>.
   (b) Iron <u>turns to rust</u> in the presence of air and water.
   (c) Hydrogen can <u>explode</u> when ignited in air (Figure 1.18).
   (d) The <u>density</u> of titanium metal is 4.5 g/cm^3.
   (e) Tin metal <u>melts</u> at 505 K.
   (f) Chlorophyll, a plant pigment, is <u>green</u>.

8. ■ In each case, decide if the change is a chemical or physical change.
   (a) A cup of household bleach changes the color of your favorite T-shirt from purple to pink.
   (a) Water vapor in your exhaled breath condenses in the air on a cold day.
   (b) Plants use carbon dioxide from the air to make sugar.
   (c) Butter melts when placed in the sun.

9. Which part of the description of a compound or element refers to its physical properties and which to its chemical properties?
   (a) The colorless liquid ethanol burns in air.
   (b) The shiny metal aluminum reacts readily with orange-red bromine.

10. ■ Which part of the description of a compound or element refers to its physical properties and which to its chemical properties?
    (a) Calcium carbonate is a white solid with a density of 2.71 g/cm^3. It reacts readily with an acid to produce gaseous carbon dioxide.
    (b) Gray, powdered zinc metal reacts with purple iodine to give a white compound.

General Questions
These questions are not designated as to type or location in the chapter. They may combine several concepts.

11. ■ A piece of turquoise is a blue-green solid; it has a density of 2.65 g/cm^3 and a mass of 2.5 g.
    (a) Which of these observations are qualitative and which are quantitative?
    (b) Which of the observations are extensive and which are intensive?
    (c) What is the volume of the piece of turquoise?

12. Give a physical property and a chemical property for the elements hydrogen, oxygen, iron, and sodium. (The elements listed are selected from examples given in Chapter 1.)

13. ■ Eight observations are listed below. What observations identify chemical properties?
    (a) Sugar is soluble in water.
    (b) Water boils at 100 °C.
    (c) Ultraviolet light converts O_3 (ozone) to O_2 (oxygen).
    (d) Ice is less dense than water.
    (e) Sodium metal reacts violently with water.
    (f) CO_2 does not support combustion.
    (g) Chlorine is a green gas.
    (i) Heat is required to melt ice.

14. ■ Azurite, a blue, crystalline mineral, is composed of copper, carbon, and oxygen.

Charles D. Winters

Azurite is a deep blue crystalline mineral. It is surrounded by copper pellets and powdered carbon (in the dish).

    (a) What are the symbols of the three elements that combine to make the mineral azurite?
    (b) Based on the photo, describe some of the physical properties of the elements and the mineral. Are any the same? Are any properties different?

15. The mineral fluorite contains the elements calcium and fluorine and has colors that range from blue, to violet, to green and yellow.

Charles D. Winters

The mineral fluorite, calcium fluoride.

    What are the symbols of these elements? How would you describe the shape of the fluorite crystals in the photo? What can this tell us about the arrangement of the particles (ions) inside the crystal?

16. Small chips of iron are mixed with sand (see the following photo). Is this a homogeneous or heterogeneous mixture? Suggest a way to separate the iron from the sand.

Chips of iron mixed with sand.

17. In Figure 1.4 you see a piece of salt and a representation of its internal structure. Which is the macroscopic view and which is the particulate view? How are the macroscopic and particulate views related?

18. ■ The following photo shows copper balls, immersed in water, floating on top of mercury. What are the liquids and solids in this photo? Which substance is most dense? Which is least dense?

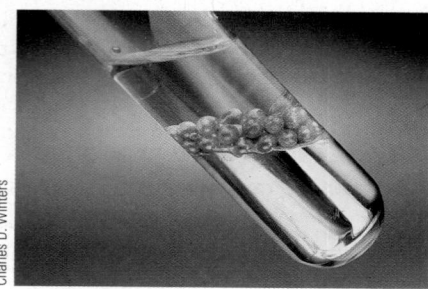

Water, copper, and mercury.

19. ■ Carbon tetrachloride, CCl_4, a common liquid compound, has a density of 1.58 g/cm^3. If you place a piece of a plastic soda bottle ($d = 1.37 \text{ g/cm}^3$) and a piece of aluminum ($d = 2.70 \text{ g/cm}^3$) in liquid CCl_4, will the plastic and aluminum float or sink?

20. ▲ You have a sample of a white crystalline substance from your kitchen. You know that it is either salt or sugar. Although you could decide by taste, suggest another property that you could use to decide. (Hint: You may use the World Wide Web or a handbook of chemistry in the library to find some information.)

21. ■ Hexane (C_6H_{14}, density = 0.766 g/cm^3), perfluorohexane (C_6F_{14}, density = 1.669 g/cm^3), and water are immiscible liquids; that is, they do not dissolve in one another. You place 10 mL of each in a graduated cylinder, along with pieces of high-density polyethylene (HDPE, density 0.97 g/cm^3), polyvinyl chloride (PVC, density = 1.36 g/cm^3), and Teflon (density = 2.3 g/cm^3). None of these common plastics dissolves in these liquids. Describe what you expect to see.

22. Milk in a glass bottle was placed in the freezing compartment of a refrigerator overnight. By morning, a column of frozen milk emerged from the bottle. Explain this observation.

Frozen milk in a glass bottle.

23. ■ You can figure out whether a substance floats or sinks if you know its density and the density of the liquid. In which of the liquids listed below will high-density polyethylene (HDPE) float. (HDPE, a common plastic, has a density of 0.97 g/cm^3. It does not dissolve in any of these liquids.)

Substance	Density (g/cm³)	Properties, Uses
Ethylene glycol	1.1088	Toxic; the major component of automobile antifreeze
Water	0.9997	
Ethanol	0.7893	The alcohol in alcoholic beverages
Methanol	0.7914	Toxic; gasoline additive to prevent gas line freezing
Acetic acid	1.0492	Component of vinegar
Glycerol	1.2613	Solvent used in home care products

24. Describe an experimental method that can be used to determine the density of an irregularly shaped piece of metal.

25. ▲ Make a drawing, based on the kinetic-molecular theory and the ideas about atoms and molecules presented in this chapter, of the arrangement of particles in each of the cases listed here. For each case, draw 10 particles of each substance. It is acceptable for your diagram to be two dimensional. Represent each atom as a circle, and distinguish each different kind of atom by shading.
(a) A sample of solid iron (which consists of iron atoms)
(b) A sample of *liquid* water (which consists of H_2O molecules)
(c) A sample of water *vapor*

▲ more challenging   ■ in OWL   Blue-numbered questions answered in Appendix O

26. ▲ Make a drawing, based on the kinetic-molecular theory and the ideas about atoms and molecules presented in this chapter, of the arrangement of particles in each of the cases listed here. For each case, draw 10 particles of each substance. It is acceptable for your diagram to be two dimensional. Represent each atom as a circle, and distinguish each different kind of atom by shading.
    (a) A homogeneous mixture of water vapor and helium gas (which consists of helium atoms)
    (b) A heterogeneous mixture consisting of liquid water and solid aluminum; show a region of the sample that includes both substances
    (c) A sample of brass (which is a homogeneous solid mixture of copper and zinc)

27. You are given a sample of a silvery metal. What information would you seek to prove that the metal is silver?

28. Suggest a way to determine if the colorless liquid in a beaker is water. If it is water, does it contain dissolved salt? How could you discover if there is salt dissolved in the water?

29. ■ Diabetes can alter the density of urine, and so urine density can be used as a diagnostic tool. Diabetics can excrete too much sugar or excrete too much water. What do you predict will happen to the density of urine under each of these conditions? (*Hint*: Water containing dissolved sugar is more dense than pure water.)

30. ■ Three liquids of different densities are mixed. Because they are not miscible (do not form a homogeneous solution with one another), they form discrete layers, one on top of the other. Sketch the result of mixing carbon tetrachloride (CCl_4, $d = 1.58$ g/cm^3), mercury ($d = 13.546$ g/cm^3), and water ($d = 1.00$ g/cm^3).

31. ■ The following photo shows the element potassium reacting with water to form the element hydrogen, a gas, and a solution of the compound potassium hydroxide.

Charles D. Winters

Potassium reacting with water to produce hydrogen gas and potassium hydroxide.

    (a) What states of matter are involved in the reaction?
    (b) Is the observed change chemical or physical?
    (c) What are the reactants in this reaction, and what are the products?
    (d) What qualitative observations can be made concerning this reaction?

32. A copper-colored metal is found to conduct an electric current. Can you say with certainty that it is copper? Why or why not? Suggest additional information that could provide unequivocal confirmation that the metal is copper.

33. ■ What experiment can you use to:
    (a) Separate salt from water?
    (b) Separate iron filings from small pieces of lead?
    (c) Separate elemental sulfur from sugar?

34. ■ Four balloons are each filled with a different gas of varying density:

    Helium, $d = 0.164$ g/L

    Neon, $d = 0.825$ g/L

    Argon, $d = 1.633$ g/L

    Krypton, $d = 4.425$ g/L

    If the density of dry air is 1.12 g/L, which balloon or balloons float in air?

35. Many foods are fortified with vitamins and minerals. Some breakfast cereals have elemental iron added. Iron chips are used instead of iron compounds because the compounds can be converted by the oxygen in air to a form of iron that is not biochemically useful. Iron chips, on the other hand, are converted to useful iron compounds in the gut, and the iron can then be absorbed. Outline a method by which you could remove the iron (as iron chips) from a box of cereal and determine the mass of iron in a given mass of cereal. (*See ChemistryNow Screens 1.1 and 1.18, Chemical Puzzler*.)

36. Study the animation of the conversion of P_4 and Cl_2 molecules to PCl_3 molecules in *ChemistryNow*, Screen 1.12 (*Chemical Change on the Molecular Scale*).
    (a) What are the reactants in this chemical change? What are the products?
    (b) Describe how the structures of the reactant molecules differ from the structures of the product molecules.

37. ■ The photo below shows elemental iodine dissolving in ethanol to give a solution. Is this a physical or chemical change?

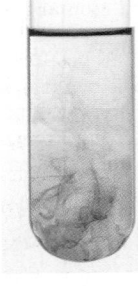

Charles D. Winters

Elemental iodine dissolving in ethanol.

(*See also the ChemistryNow Screen 1.12, Exercise, Physical Properties of Matter*)

Let's Review | The Tools of Quantitative Chemistry

John Katz

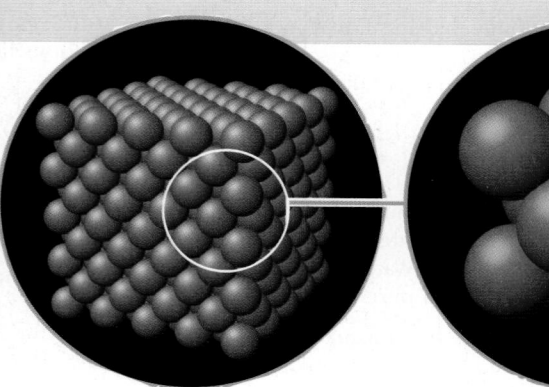

Copper

Copper (Cu) is the 26th element in abundance in the Earth's crust (not too different from its near neighbors nickel and zinc in the periodic table), but it and its minerals are widely distributed, and it is relatively easy to obtain the metal from its ores. As a result, elemental copper is used around the world for many useful items, from cooking pots to electric wires. The photo at the left above shows large copper pots on sale in a market in southwestern China.

Pure copper (often called *native copper*) is found in nature, but more commonly it is found combined with other elements in minerals such as cuprite, azurite, or malachite. Copper metal is relatively soft but, when combined in a ratio of about 2 to 1 with tin, it forms bronze. Bronze was important in early civilizations and gave its name to an epoch of human development, the Bronze Age, which started around 3000 BC and lasted until about 1000 BC. The development of bronze was significant because bronze is stronger than copper and can be shaped into a sharper edge. This improved the cutting edges

of plows and weapons, thus giving cultures that possessed bronze advantages over those that did not.

Copper is now used in wiring because it conducts electricity well, and it is used in cooking pots because it conducts heat well. It is also described as one of the "coinage metals" (along with silver and gold) because it has been used in coins for centuries.

Compounds of copper are common, and copper is one of the eight essential metals in our bodies, where it is needed for some enzymes to use oxygen more effectively. Fortunately, it is found in common foods (in meats such as lamb, duck, pork, and beef, and in almonds and walnuts). The average person has about 72 mg of copper in his or her body.

The figure above also shows what happens as we zoom into copper at the particulate level. We begin to see atoms arranged in a regular array, or *lattice,* as chemists call it. Zooming in even closer, we see the smallest repeating unit of the crystal.

You can learn more about copper and its properties by answering the Study Questions 56 and 57 at the end of this *Let's Review* section.

At its core, chemistry is a quantitative science. Chemists make measurements of, among other things, size, mass, volume, time, and temperature. Scientists then manipulate that information to search for relationships among properties and to provide insight into the molecular basis of matter.

This section reviews the units used in chemistry, briefly describes the proper treatment of numerical data, and reviews some mathematical skills you will need in chemical calculations. After studying this section you should be able to:

- use the common units for measurements in chemistry and make unit conversions (such as liters to milliliters).
- express and use numbers in exponential or scientific notation.
- express quantitative information in an algebraic expression and solve that expression.
- read information from graphs.
- prepare a graph of numerical information. If the graph produces a straight line, find the slope and equation of the line.
- recognize and express uncertainties in measurements.

1 Units of Measurement

Doing chemistry requires observing chemical reactions and physical changes. We make qualitative observations—such as changes in color or the evolution of heat—and quantitative measurements of temperature, time, volume, mass, and length or size. To record and report measurements, the scientific community has chosen a modified version of the **metric system.** This decimal system, used internationally in science, is called the Système International d'Unités (International System of Units), abbreviated **SI.**

All SI units are derived from base units, some of which are listed in Table 1. Larger and smaller quantities are expressed by using appropriate prefixes with the base unit (Table 2). The nanometer (nm), for example, is 1 billionth of a meter. That is, it is equivalent to 1×10^{-9} m (meter). Dimensions on the nanometer scale are common in chemistry and biology because a typical molecule is about 1 nm across and a bacterium is about 1000 nm in length. The prefix *nano-* is also used in the name for a new area of science, *nanotechnology* (▶ *Materials Chemistry,* pages 656–669) which involves the synthesis and study of materials around this tiny size.

TABLE 1 Some SI Base Units

Measured Property	Name of Unit	Abbreviation
Mass	kilogram	kg
Length	meter	m
Time	second	s
Temperature	kelvin	K
Amount of substance	mole	mol
Electric current	ampere	A

■ Common Conversion Factors
1000 g = 1 kg
1×10^9 nm = 1 m
10 mm = 1 cm
100 cm = 10 dm = 1 m
1000 m = 1 km

Conversion factors for SI units are given in Appendix C and inside the back cover of this book.

TABLE 2 Selected Prefixes Used in the Metric System

Prefix	Abbreviation	Meaning	Example
giga-	G	10^9 (billion)	1 gigahertz = 1×10^9 Hz
mega-	M	10^6 (million)	1 megaton = 1×10^6 tons
kilo-	k	10^3 (thousand)	1 kilogram (kg) = 1×10^3 g
deci-	d	10^{-1} (tenth)	1 decimeter (dm) = 1×10^{-1} m
centi-	c	10^{-2} (one hundredth)	1 centimeter (cm) = 1×10^{-2} m
milli-	m	10^{-3} (one thousandth)	1 millimeter (mm) = 1×10^{-3} m
micro-	μ	10^{-6} (one millionth)	1 micrometer (μm) = 1×10^{-6} m
nano-	n	10^{-9} (one billionth)	1 nanometer (nm) = 1×10^{-9} m
pico-	p	10^{-12}	1 picometer (pm) = 1×10^{-12} m
femto-	f	10^{-15}	1 femtometer (fm) = 1×10^{-15} m

Temperature Scales

Two temperature scales are commonly used in scientific work: Celsius and Kelvin (Figure 1). The Celsius scale is generally used worldwide for measurements in the laboratory. When calculations incorporate temperature data, however, the Kelvin scale must be used.

The Celsius Temperature Scale

The size of the Celsius degree is defined by assigning zero as the freezing point of pure water (0 °C) and 100 as its boiling point (100 °C). You may recognize that a comfortable room temperature is around 20 °C and your normal body temperature is 37 °C. And we find that the warmest water we can stand to immerse a finger in is about 60 °C.

Active Figure 1 A comparison of Fahrenheit, Celsius, and Kelvin scales. The reference, or starting point, for the Kelvin scale is absolute zero (0 K = −273.15 °C), which has been shown theoretically and experimentally to be the lowest possible temperature.

Chemistry ⚗ Now™ Sign in at www.cengage.com/login and go to the Chapter Contents menu to explore an interactive version of this figure accompanied by an exercise.

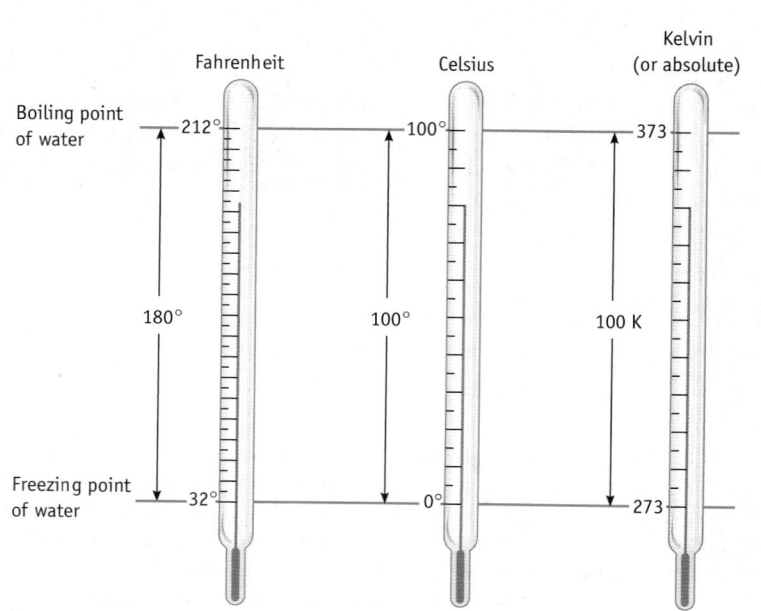

The Kelvin Temperature Scale

William Thomson, known as Lord Kelvin (1824–1907), first suggested the temperature scale that now bears his name. The Kelvin scale uses the same size unit as the Celsius scale, but it assigns zero as the lowest temperature that can be achieved, a point called **absolute zero.** Many experiments have found that this limiting temperature is -273.15 °C (-459.67 °F). *Kelvin units and Celsius degrees are the same size.* Thus, the freezing point of water is reached at 273.15 K; that is, 0 °C = 273.15 K. The boiling point of pure water is 373.15 K. Temperatures in Celsius degrees are readily converted to kelvins, and vice versa, using the relation

$$T \text{ (K)} = \frac{1 \text{ K}}{1 \text{ °C}} (T \text{ °C} + 273.15 \text{ °C}) \tag{1}$$

Thus, a common room temperature of 23.5 °C is

$$T \text{ (K)} = \frac{1 \text{ K}}{1 \text{ °C}} (23.5 \text{ °C} + 273.15 \text{ °C}) = 296.7 \text{ K}$$

Finally, notice that the degree symbol (°) is not used with Kelvin temperatures. The name of the unit on this scale is the *kelvin* (not capitalized), and such temperatures are designated with a capital K.

EXERCISE 1 Temperature Scales

Liquid nitrogen boils at 77 K. What is this temperature in Celsius degrees?

■ **Lord Kelvin** William Thomson (1824–1907), known as Lord Kelvin, was a professor of natural philosophy at the University in Glasgow, Scotland, from 1846 to 1899. He was best known for his work on heat and work, from which came the concept of the absolute temperature scale.

E. F. Smith Collection/Van Pelt Library/University of Pennsylvania

■ **Temperature Conversions** When converting 23.5 °C to kelvins, adding 273.15 gives 296.65. However, the rules of "significant figures" (page 35) tell us that the sum or difference of two numbers can have no more decimal places than the number with the fewest decimal places. Thus, we round the answer to 296.7 K, a number with one decimal place.

Length, Volume, and Mass

The meter is the standard unit of *length*, but objects observed in chemistry are frequently smaller than 1 meter. Measurements are often reported in units of centimeters (cm), millimeters (mm), or micrometers (μm) (Figure 2), and objects on the atomic and molecular scale have dimensions of nanometers (nm; 1 nm = 1×10^{-9} m) or picometers (pm; 1 pm = 1×10^{-12} m) (Figure 3).

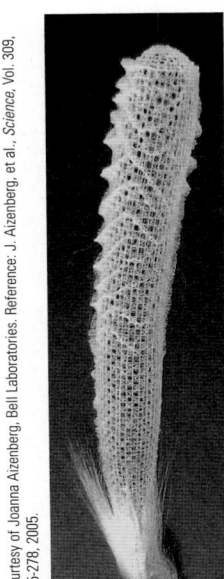

(a)

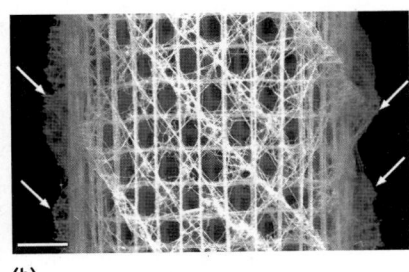

(b)

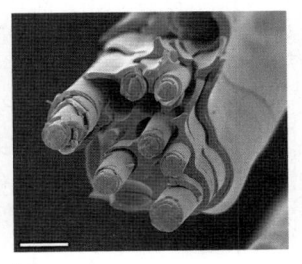

(c)

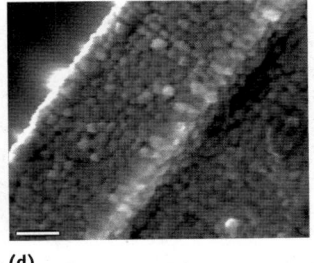

(d)

Photos courtesy of Joanna Aizenberg, Bell Laboratories. Reference: J. Aizenberg, et al., *Science*, Vol. 309, pages 275-278, 2005.

FIGURE 2 Dimensions in chemistry and biology. (a) Photograph of the glassy skeleton of a sea sponge, *Euplectella*. Scale bar = 5 cm. (b) Fragment of the structure showing the square grid of the lattice with diagonal supports. Scale bar = 1 mm. (c) Scanning electron microscope (SEM) image of a single strand showing its ceramic-composite structure. Scale bar = 20 μm. (d) SEM image of the surface of a strand showing that is it composed of nanoscale spheres of hydrated silica. Scale bar = 500 nm.

FIGURE 3 Dimensions in the molecular world. Dimensions on the molecular scale are often given in terms of nanometers (1 nm = 1 × 10⁻⁹ m) or picometers (1 pm = 1 × 10⁻¹² m). Here, the distance between C atoms in diamond is 0.154 nm or 154 pm. An older, but often-used non-SI unit is the Ångstrom unit (Å), where 1 Å = 1.0 × 10⁻¹⁰ m. The C–C distance in diamond would be 1.54 A.

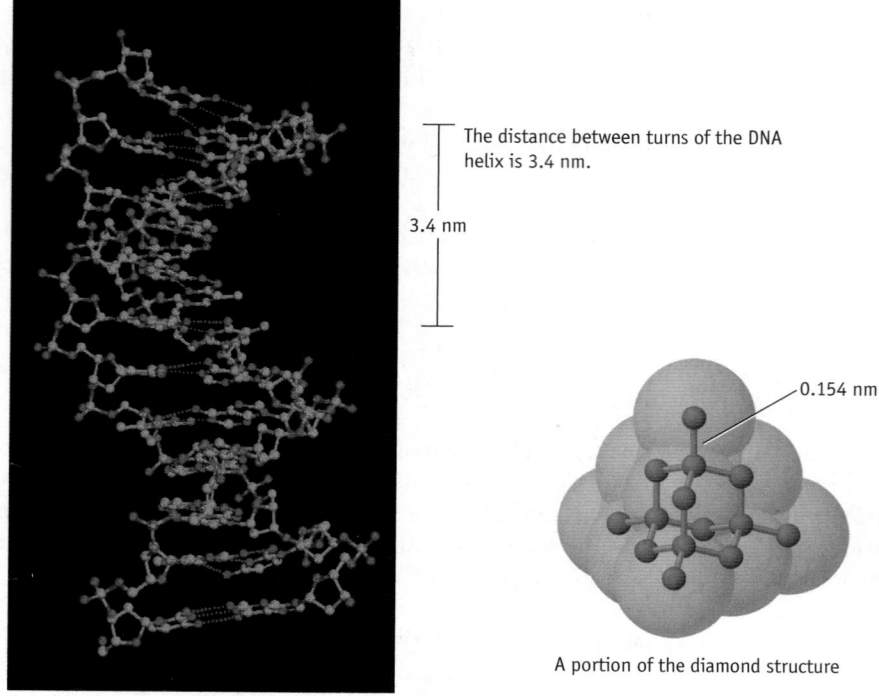

The distance between turns of the DNA helix is 3.4 nm.

3.4 nm

0.154 nm

A portion of the diamond structure

To illustrate the range of dimensions used in science, let us look at a recent study of the glassy skeleton of a sea sponge. The sea sponge in Figure 2a is about 20 cm long and a few centimeters in diameter. A closer look (Figure 2b) shows more detail of the lattice-like structure. Scientists at Bell Laboratories found that each strand of the lattice is a ceramic-fiber composite of silica (SiO₂) and protein less than 100 μm in diameter (Figure 2c). These strands are composed of "spicules," which, at the nanoscale level, consist of silica nanoparticles just a few nanometers in diameter (Figure 2d).

■ **EXAMPLE 1 Distances on the Molecular Scale**

Problem The distance between an O atom and an H atom in a water molecule is 95.8 pm. What is this distance in meters (m)? In nanometers (nm)?

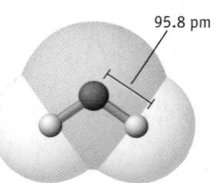

95.8 pm

Strategy You can solve this problem by knowing the relationship or conversion factor between the units in the information you are given (picometers) and the desired units (meters or nanometers). (For more about conversion factors and their use in problem solving, see page 38.) There is no conversion factor given in Table 2 to change nanometers to picometers directly, but relationships are listed between meters and picometers and between meters and nanometers. Therefore, we first convert picometers to meters, and then we convert meters to nanometers.

$$\text{Picometers} \xrightarrow{\text{x } ^{m}/_{pm}} \text{Meters} \xrightarrow{\text{x } ^{nm}/_{m}} \text{Nanometers}$$

Solution Using the appropriate conversion factors (1 pm = 1×10^{-12} m and 1 nm = 1×10^{-9} m), we have

$$95.8 \text{ pm} \times \frac{1 \times 10^{-12} \text{ m}}{1 \text{ pm}} = 9.58 \times 10^{-11} \text{ m}$$

$$9.58 \times 10^{-11} \text{ m} \times \frac{1 \text{ nm}}{1 \times 10^{-9} \text{ m}} = 9.58 \times 10^{-2} \text{ nm} \text{ or } 0.0958 \text{ nm}$$

Comment Notice how the units cancel to leave an answer whose unit is that of the numerator of the conversion factor. The process of using units to guide a calculation is called *dimensional analysis*. It is explored further on pages 38–39.

EXERCISE 2 Using Units of Length

A platinum sheet is 2.50 cm square and has a thickness of 0.25 mm. What is the volume of the platinum sheet (in cm^3)?

Chemists often use glassware such as beakers, flasks, pipets, graduated cylinders, and burets, which are marked in volume units (Figure 4). The SI unit of volume is the cubic meter (m^3), which is too large for everyday laboratory use. Chemists usually use the liter, symbolized by L, for volume measurements. One liter is equivalent to the volume of a cube with sides equal to 10 cm [= $(0.1 \text{ m})^3$ = 0.001 m^3].

$$1 \text{ liter (L)} = 1000 \text{ cm}^3 = 1000 \text{ mL} = 0.001 \text{ m}^3$$

The liter is a convenient unit to use in the laboratory, as is the milliliter (mL). Because there are exactly 1000 mL (= 1000 cm^3) in a liter, this means that

$$1 \text{ mL} = 0.001 \text{ L} = 1 \text{ cm}^3$$

The units *milliliter and cubic centimeter* (or "cc") *are interchangeable*. Therefore, a flask that contains exactly 125 mL has a volume of 125 cm^3.

Although not widely used in the United States, the cubic decimeter (dm^3) is a common unit in the rest of the world. A length of 10 cm is called a decimeter (dm). Because a cube 10 cm on a side defines a volume of 1 liter, *a liter is equivalent to a cubic decimeter*. 1 L = 1 dm^3. Products in Europe, Africa, and other parts of the world are often sold by the cubic decimeter.

The *deciliter, dL,* which is exactly equivalent to 0.100 L or 100 mL, is widely used in medicine. For example, standards for concentrations of environmental contaminants are often set as a certain mass per deciliter. The state of Massachusetts recommends that children with more than 10 micrograms (10×10^{-6} g) of lead per deciliter of blood undergo further testing for lead poisoning.

FIGURE 4 Some common laboratory glassware. Volumes are marked in units of milliliters (mL). Remember that 1 mL is equivalent to 1 cm^3.

EXERCISE 3 Volume

(a) A standard wine bottle has a volume of 750 mL. What volume, in liters, does this represent? How many deciliters?

(b) One U.S. gallon is equivalent to 3.7865 L. What is the volume in liters of a 2.0-quart carton of milk? (There are 4 quarts in a gallon.) How many cubic decimeters?

Finally, when chemists prepare chemicals for reactions, they often take given quantities or masses of materials. The *mass* of a body is the fundamental measure of the quantity of matter, and the SI unit of mass is the kilogram (kg). Smaller masses are expressed in grams (g) or milligrams (mg).

$$1 \text{ kg} = 1000 \text{ g } and \text{ 1 g} = 1000 \text{ mg}$$

2 Making Measurements: Precision, Accuracy, Experimental Error, and Standard Deviation

The **precision** of a measurement indicates how well several determinations of the same quantity agree. This is illustrated by the results of throwing darts at a target. In Figure 5a, the dart thrower was apparently not skillful, and the precision of the dart's placement on the target is low. In Figures 5b and 5c, the darts are clustered together, indicating much better consistency on the part of the thrower—that is, greater precision.

Accuracy is the agreement of a measurement with the accepted value of the quantity. Figure 5c shows that our thrower was accurate as well as precise—the average of all shots is close to the targeted position, the bull's eye.

Figure 5b shows it is possible to be precise without being accurate—the thrower has consistently missed the bull's eye, although all the darts are clustered precisely around one point on the target. This is analogous to an experiment with some flaw (either in design or in a measuring device) that causes all results to differ from the correct value by the same amount.

The accuracy of a result in the laboratory is often expressed in terms of percent error, whereas the precision is expressed as a standard deviation.

■ **Accuracy and NIST** The National Institute for Standards and Technology (NIST) is an important resource for the standards used in science. Comparison with NIST data is a test of the accuracy of the measurement. See www.nist.gov.

Experimental Error

If you measure a quantity in the laboratory, you may be required to report the error in the result, the difference between your result and the accepted value,

$$\text{Error} = \text{experimentally determined value} - \text{accepted value}$$

(a) Poor precision and poor accuracy

(b) Good precision and poor accuracy

(c) Good precision and good accuracy

Charles D. Winters

FIGURE 5 Precision and accuracy.

or the **percent error.**

$$\text{Percent error} = \frac{\text{error in measurement}}{\text{accepted value}} \times 100\%$$

■ **Percent Error** Percent error can be positive or negative, indicating whether the experimental value is too high or too low compared to the accepted value. In Example 2, Student B's error is −0.2%, indicating it is 0.2% lower than the accepted value.

■ **EXAMPLE 2** **Precision, Accuracy, and Error**

Problem A coin has an "accepted" diameter of 28.054 mm. In an experiment, two students measure this diameter. Student A makes four measurements of the diameter of the coin using a precision tool called a micrometer. Student B measures the same coin using a simple plastic ruler. The two students report the following results:

Student A	Student B
28.246 mm	27.9 mm
28.244	28.0
28.246	27.8
28.248	28.1

What is the average diameter and percent error obtained in each case? Which student's data are more accurate?

Strategy For each set of values, we calculate the average of the results and then compare this average with 28.054 mm.

Solution The average for each set of data is obtained by summing the four values and dividing by 4.

Average value for Student A = 28.246 mm
Average value for Student B = 28.0 mm

Although Student A has four results very close to one another (and so of high precision), student A's result is less accurate than that of Student B. The average diameter for Student A differs from the "accepted" value by 0.192 mm and has a percent error of 0.684%:

$$\text{Percent error} = \frac{28.246 \text{ mm} - 28.054 \text{ mm}}{28.054 \text{ mm}} \times 100\% = 0.684\%$$

Student B's measurement has a percent error of only about −0.2%.

Comment We noted that Student A had precise results; the standard deviation calculated as described below is 2×10^{-3}. In contrast, Student B had less precise results (standard deviation = 0.14). Possible reasons for the error in Students A's result are incorrect use of the micrometer or a flaw in the instrument.

Standard Deviation

Laboratory measurements can be in error for two basic reasons. First, there may be "determinate" errors caused by faulty instruments or human errors such as incorrect record keeping. So-called "indeterminate" errors arise from uncertainties in a measurement where the cause is not known and cannot be controlled by the lab worker. One way to judge the indeterminate error in a result is to calculate the standard deviation.

The **standard deviation** of a series of measurements is equal to the square root of the sum of the squares of the deviations for each measurement from the average divided by one less than the number of measurements. It has a precise statistical significance: assuming a large number of measurements is used to calculate the average, 68% of the values collected are expected to be within one standard deviation of the value determined, and 95% are within two standard deviations.

Suppose you carefully measured the mass of water delivered by a 10-mL pipet. (A pipet containing a green solution is shown in Figure 4.) For five attempts at the measurement (shown in column 2 of the table below), the standard deviation is found as follows: First, the average of the measurements is calculated (here, 9.984). Next, the deviation of each individual measurement from this value is determined (column 3). These values are squared, giving the values in column 4, and the sum of these values is determined. The standard deviation is then calculated by dividing this sum by 4 (the number of determinations minus 1) and taking the square root of the result.

Determination	Measured Mass (g)	Difference between Average and Measurement (g)	Square of Difference
1	9.990	−0.006	4×10^{-5}
2	9.993	−0.009	8×10^{-5}
3	9.973	0.011	12×10^{-5}
4	9.980	0.004	2×10^{-5}
5	9.982	0.002	0.4×10^{-5}

Average mass = 9.984 g

Sum of squares of differences = 26×10^{-5}

$$\text{Standard deviation} = \sqrt{\frac{26 \times 10^{-5}}{4}} = \pm 0.008$$

Based on this calculation, it would be appropriate to represent the measured mass as 9.984 ± 0.008 g. This would tell a reader that if this experiment were repeated, a majority of the values would fall in the range of 9.976 g to 9.992 g.

EXERCISE 5 Accuracy, Error, and Standard Deviation

Two students measured the freezing point of an unknown liquid. Student A used an ordinary laboratory thermometer calibrated in 0.1 °C units. Student B used a thermometer certified by NIST (National Institute for Standards and Technology) and calibrated in 0.01 °C units. Their results were as follows:

Student A: −0.3 °C; 0.2 °C; 0.0 °C; and −0.3 °C

Student B: −0.02 °C, +0.02 °C, 0.00 °C, and +0.04 °C

Calculate the average value, and, knowing that the liquid was water, calculate the percent error and standard deviation for each student. Which student has the more precise values? Which has the smaller error?

FIGURE 6 Lake Otsego. This lake, with a surface area of 2.33×10^7 m², is located in northern New York State. Cooperstown is a village at the base of the lake where the Susquehanna River originates. To learn more about the environmental biology and chemistry of the lake, go to **www.oneonta.edu/academics/biofld**

3 Mathematics of Chemistry

Exponential or Scientific Notation

Lake Otsego in northern New York is also called *Glimmerglass*, a name suggested by James Fenimore Cooper (1789–1851), the great American author and an early resident of the village now known as Cooperstown. Extensive environmental studies have been done along this lake (Figure 6), and some quantitative information useful to chemists, biologists, and geologists is given in the following table:

Lake Otsego Characteristics	Quantitative Information
Area	2.33×10^7 m^2
Maximum depth	505 m
Dissolved solids in lake water	2×10^2 mg/L
Average rainfall in the lake basin	1.02×10^2 cm/year
Average snowfall in the lake basin	198 cm/year

FIGURE 7 Exponential numbers in astronomy. The spiral galaxy M-83 is 3.0×10^6 parsecs away from Earth and has a diameter of 9.0×10^3 parsecs. The unit used in astronomy, the parsec (pc), is equivalent to 206265 AU (astronomical units) where 1 AU is 1.496×10^8 km. What is the distance between Earth and M-83 in km?

All of the data collected are in metric units. However, some data are expressed in **fixed notation** (505 m, 198 cm/year), whereas other data are expressed in **exponential,** or **scientific, notation** (2.33×10^7 m^2). Scientific notation is a way of presenting very large or very small numbers in a compact and consistent form that simplifies calculations. Because of its convenience, scientific notation is widely used in sciences such as chemistry, physics, engineering, and astronomy (Figure 7).

In scientific notation a number is expressed as a product of two numbers: $N \times 10^n$. N is the digit term and is a number between 1 and 9.9999. . . . The second number, 10^n, the exponential term, is some integer power of 10. For example, 1234 is written in scientific notation as 1.234×10^3, or 1.234 multiplied by 10 three times:

$$1234 = 1.234 \times 10^1 \times 10^1 \times 10^1 = 1.234 \times 10^3$$

Conversely, a number less than 1, such as 0.01234, is written as 1.234×10^{-2}. This notation tells us that 1.234 should be divided twice by 10 to obtain 0.01234:

$$0.01234 = \frac{1.234}{10^1 \times 10^1} = 1.234 \times 10^{-1} \times 10^{-1} = 1.234 \times 10^{-2}$$

When converting a number to scientific notation, notice that the exponent n is positive if the number is greater than 1 and negative if the number is less than 1. The value of n is the number of places by which the decimal is shifted to obtain the number in scientific notation:

$$1 \ 2 \ 3 \ 4 \ 5. = 1.2345 \times 10^4$$

(a) Decimal shifted four places to the left. Therefore, n is positive and equal to 4.

$$0.0 \ 0 \ 1 \ 2 = 1.2 \times 10^{-3}$$

(b) Decimal shifted three places to the right. Therefore, n is negative and equal to 3.

If you wish to convert a number in scientific notation to one using fixed notation (that is, not using powers of 10), the procedure is reversed:

$$6 \ . \ 2 \ 7 \ 3 \times 10^2 = 627.3$$

(a) Decimal point moved two places to the right because n is positive and equal to 2.

$$0 \ 0 \ 6.273 \times 10^{-3} = 0.006273$$

(b) Decimal point shifted three places to the left because n is negative and equal to 3.

Two final points should be made concerning scientific notation. First, be aware that calculators and computers often express a number such as 1.23×10^3 as 1.23E3

Using Your Calculator

You will be performing a number of calculations in general chemistry, most of them using a calculator. Many different types of calculators are available, but this problem-solving tip describes several of the kinds of operations you will need to perform on a typical calculator. Be sure to consult your calculator manual for specific instructions to enter scientific notation and to find powers and roots of numbers.

1. Scientific Notation

When entering a number such as 1.23×10^{-4} into your calculator, you first enter 1.23 and then press a key marked EE or EXP (or something similar). This enters the "$\times 10$" portion of the notation for you. You then complete the entry by keying in the exponent of the number, -4. (To change the exponent from $+4$ to -4, press the "$+/-$" key.)

A common error made by students is to enter 1.23, press the multiply key ($\times$), and then key in 10 before finishing by pressing EE or EXP followed by -4. This gives you an entry that is 10 times too large.

2. Powers of Numbers

Electronic calculators often offer two methods of raising a number to a power. To square a number, enter the number and then press the x^2 key. To raise a number to any power, use the y^x (or similar key such as ^). For example, to raise 1.42×10^2 to the fourth power:

1. Enter 1.42×10^2.
2. Press y^x.
3. Enter 4 (this should appear on the display).
4. Press $=$, and 4.0659×10^8 appears on the display.

3. Roots of Numbers

A general procedure for finding any root is to use the y^x key. For a square root, x is 0.5 (or 1/2), whereas it is 0.3333 (or 1/3) for a cube root, 0.25 (or 1/4) for a fourth root, and so on. For example, to find the fourth root of 5.6×10^{-10}:

1. Enter the number.
2. Press the y^x key.
3. Enter the desired root. Because we want the fourth root, enter 0.25.
4. Press $=$. The answer here is 4.9×10^{-3}.

To make sure you are using your calculator correctly, try these sample calculations:

1. $(6.02 \times 10^{23})(2.26 \times 10^{-5})/367$
   (Answer $= 3.71 \times 10^{16}$)
2. $(4.32 \times 10^{-3})^3$
   (Answer $= 8.06 \times 10^{-8}$)
3. $(4.32 \times 10^{-3})^{1/3}$
   (Answer $= 0.163$)

---

or 6.45×10^{-5} as 6.45E-5. Second, some electronic calculators can readily convert numbers in fixed notation to scientific notation. If you have such a calculator, you may be able to do this by pressing the EE or EXP key and then the "$=$" key (but check your calculator manual to learn how your device operates).

In chemistry, you will often have to use numbers in exponential notation in mathematical operations. The following five operations are important:

- *Adding and Subtracting Numbers Expressed in Scientific Notation*
  When adding or subtracting two numbers, first convert them to the same powers of 10. The digit terms are then added or subtracted as appropriate:

$$(1.234 \times 10^{-3}) + (5.623 \times 10^{-2}) = (0.1234 \times 10^{-2}) + (5.623 \times 10^{-2})$$
$$= 5.746 \times 10^{-2}$$

- *Multiplication of Numbers Expressed in Scientific Notation*
  The digit terms are multiplied in the usual manner, and the exponents are added algebraically. The result is expressed with a digit term with only one nonzero digit to the left of the decimal:

$$(6.0 \times 10^{23}) \times (2.0 \times 10^{-2}) = (6.0)(2.0 \times 10^{23-2}) = 12 \times 10^{21} = 1.2 \times 10^{22}$$

- *Division of Numbers Expressed in Scientific Notation*
  The digit terms are divided in the usual manner, and the exponents are subtracted algebraically. The quotient is written with one nonzero digit to the left of the decimal in the digit term:

$$\frac{7.60 \times 10^3}{1.23 \times 10^2} = \frac{7.60}{1.23} \times 10^{3-2} = 6.18 \times 10^1$$

■ **Comparing the Earth and a Plant Cell—Powers of Ten**
Earth $= 12,760,000$ meters wide
$\quad = 12.76$ million meters
$\quad = 1.276 \times 10^7$ meters
Plant cell $= 0.00001276$ meter wide
$\quad\quad = 12.76$ millionths of a meter
$\quad\quad = 1.276 \times 10^{-5}$ meters

- *Powers of Numbers Expressed in Scientific Notation*
  When raising a number in exponential notation to a power, treat the digit term in the usual manner. The exponent is then multiplied by the number indicating the power:

$$(5.28 \times 10^3)^2 = (5.28)^2 \times 10^{3 \times 2} = 27.9 \times 10^6 = 2.79 \times 10^7$$

- *Roots of Numbers Expressed in Scientific Notation*
  Unless you use an electronic calculator, the number must first be put into a form in which the exponent is exactly divisible by the root. For example, for a square root, the exponent should be divisible by 2. The root of the digit term is found in the usual way, and the exponent is divided by the desired root:

$$\sqrt{3.6 \times 10^7} = \sqrt{36 \times 10^6} = \sqrt{36} \times \sqrt{10^6} = 6.0 \times 10^3$$

Significant Figures

In most experiments, several kinds of measurements must be made, and some can be made more precisely than others. It is common sense that a result calculated from experimental data can be no more precise than the least precise piece of information that went into the calculation. This is where the rules for significant figures come in. **Significant figures** are the digits in a measured quantity that were observed with the measuring device.

Determining Significant Figures

Suppose we place a U.S. dime on the pan of a standard laboratory balance such as the one pictured in Figure 8 and observe a mass of 2.265 g. This number has four significant figures or digits because all four numbers are observed. However, you will learn from experience that the final digit (5) is somewhat uncertain because you may notice the balance readings can change slightly and give masses of 2.264, 2.265, and 2.266, with the mass of 2.265 observed most of the time. Thus, of the four significant digits (2.265) the last (5) is uncertain. In general, *in a number representing a scientific measurement, the last digit to the right is taken to be inexact.* Unless stated otherwise, it is common practice to assign an uncertainty of ±1 to the last significant digit.

Suppose you want to calculate the density of a piece of metal (Figure 9). The mass and dimensions were determined by standard laboratory techniques. Most of these data have two digits to the right of the decimal, but they have different numbers of significant figures.

Charles D. Winters

FIGURE 8 Standard laboratory balance and significant figures. Such balances can determine the mass of an object to the nearest milligram. Thus, an object may have a mass of 13.456 g (13456 mg, five significant figures), 0.123 g (123 mg, three significant figures), or 0.072 g (72 mg, two significant figures).

Measurement	Data Collected	Significant Figures
Mass of metal	13.56 g	4
Length	6.45 cm	3
Width	2.50 cm	3
Thickness	3.1 mm = 0.31 cm	2

The quantity 0.31 cm has two significant figures. That is, the 3 in 0.31 is exactly known, but the 1 is uncertain. This means the thickness of the metal piece may have been as small as 0.30 cm or as large as 0.32 cm, but it is most likely 0.31 cm.

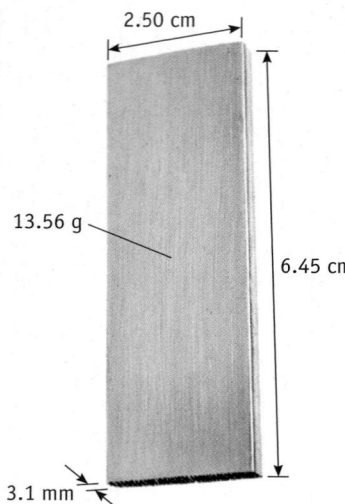

2.50 cm

13.56 g

6.45 cm

3.1 mm

FIGURE 9 Data used to determine the density of a metal.

■ **Zeroes and Common Laboratory Mistakes** We often see students find the mass of a chemical on a balance and fail to write down trailing zeroes. For example, if you find the mass is 2.340 g, the final zero is significant and must be reported as part of the measured value. The number 2.34 g has only three significant figures and implies the 4 is uncertain, when in fact the balance reading indicated the 4 is certain.

In the case of the width of the piece, you found it to be 2.50 cm, where 2.5 is known with certainty, but the final 0 is uncertain. There are three significant figures in 2.50.

When you first read a number in a problem, or collect data in the laboratory, how do you determine how many significant figures it contains?

First, is the number an exact number or a measured quantity? If it is an exact number, you don't have to worry about the number of significant figures. For example, there are exactly 100 cm in 1 m. We could add as many zeros after the decimal place, and the expression would still be true. Using this number in a calculation will not affect how many significant figures you can report in your answer.

If, however, the number is a measured value, you must take into account significant figures. The number of significant figures in our data above is clear, with the possible exception of 0.31 and 2.50. Are the zeroes significant?

1. *Zeroes between two other significant digits are significant.* For example, the zero in 103 is significant.
2. *Zeroes to the right of a nonzero number and also to the right of a decimal place are significant.* For example, in the number 2.50 cm, the zero is significant.
3. *Zeroes that are placeholders are not significant.* There are two types of numbers that fall under this rule.
   a) The first are decimal numbers with zeroes that occur *before* the first nonzero digit. For example, in 0.0013, only the 1 and the 3 are significant; the zeroes are not. This number has two significant figures.
   b) The second are *numbers with trailing zeroes* that must be there to indicate the magnitude of the number. For example, the zeroes in the number 13,000 may or may not be significant; it depends on whether they were measured or not. To avoid confusion with regard to such numbers, we *shall assume in this book that trailing zeroes are significant when there is a decimal point to the right of the last zero.* Thus, we would say that 13,000 has only two significant figures but that 13,000. has five. We suggest that the best way to be unambiguous when writing numbers with trailing zeroes is to use scientific notation. For example 1.300×10^4 clearly indicates four significant figures, whereas 1.3×10^4 indicates two and 1.3000×10^4 indicates five.

Using Significant Figures in Calculations

When doing calculations using measured quantities, we follow some basic rules so that the results reflect the precision of all the measurements that go into the calculations. *The rules used for significant figures in this book are as follows:*

Rule 1. When adding or subtracting numbers, the number of decimal places in the answer is equal to the number of decimal places in the number with the fewest digits after the decimal.

0.12	2 decimal places	2 significant figures
+ 1.9	1 decimal place	2 significant figures
+10.925	3 decimal places	5 significant figures
12.945	3 decimal places	

The sum should be reported as 12.9, a number with one decimal place, because 1.9 has only one decimal place.

Rule 2. In multiplication or division, the number of significant figures in the answer is determined by the quantity with the fewest significant figures.

$$\frac{0.01208}{0.0236} = 0.512, \text{ or in scientific notation, } 5.12 \times 10^{-1}$$

Because 0.0236 has only three significant digits, while 0.01208 has four, the answer should have three significant digits.

Rule 3. When a number is rounded off, the last digit to be retained is increased by one only if the following digit is 5 or greater.

Full Number	Number Rounded to Three Significant Digits
12.696	12.7
16.349	16.3
18.35	18.4
18.351	18.4

Now let us apply these rules to calculate the density of the piece of metal in Figure 9.

$$\text{Length} \times \text{width} \times \text{thickness} = \text{volume}$$

$$6.45 \text{ cm} \times 2.50 \text{ cm} \times 0.31 \text{ cm} = 5.0 \text{ cm}^3$$

$$\text{Density} = \frac{\text{mass (g)}}{\text{volume (cm}^3)} = \frac{13.56 \text{ g}}{5.0 \text{ cm}^3} = 2.7 \text{ g/cm}^3$$

The calculated density has two significant figures because *a calculated result can be no more precise than the least precise data used*, and here the thickness has only two significant figures.

One last word on significant figures and calculations: When working problems, you should do the calculation with all the digits allowed by your calculator and round off only at the end of the calculation. *Rounding off in the middle of a calculation can introduce errors.*

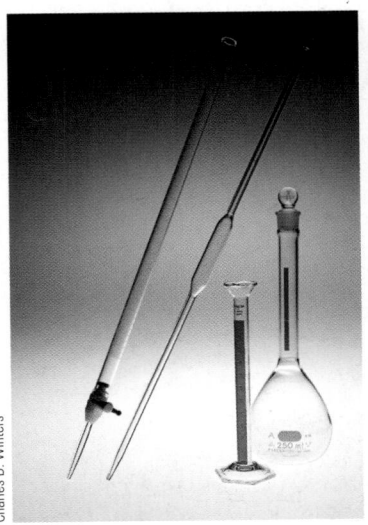

Glassware and significant figures. The 10-mL graduated cylinder is marked in 0.1-mL increments. Graduated cylinders are not considered precision glassware, so, at best, you can expect no more than two significant figures when reading a volume. Conversely, a 50-mL buret is marked in 0.10-mL increments, so it can be read to the nearest 0.01 mL. A volumetric flask is meant to be filled to the mark on the neck. When you have this volume, it is known to the nearest 0.01 mL, so a 250-mL volumetric flask contains 250.00 mL when full to the mark (or five significant figures). Finally, a pipet is like a volumetric flask in that the volume is known to the nearest 0.01 mL.

Charles D. Winters

Chemistry ⚛ Now™

Sign in at **www.cengage.com/login** and go to Screen 1.17 for a self-study module on **using numerical information.**

■ EXAMPLE 3 Using Significant Figures

Problem An example of a calculation you will do later in the book (Chapter 11) is

$$\text{Volume of gas (L)} = \frac{(0.120)(0.08206)(273.15 + 23)}{(230/760.0)}$$

Calculate the final answer to the correct number of significant figures.

Strategy Let us first decide on the number of significant figures represented by each number and then apply Rules 1–3.

■ To Multiply or to Add? Take the number 4.68.
(a) Take the sum of $4.68 + 4.68 + 4.68$. The answer is 14.04, a number with four significant figures.
(b) Multiply 4.68 times 3. The answer can have only three significant figures (14.0). You should recognize that different outcomes are possible, depending on the type of mathematical operation.

Solution

Number	Number of Significant Figures	Comments
0.120	3	The trailing 0 is significant.
0.08206	4	The first 0 to the immediate right of the decimal is not significant.
$273.15 + 23 = 296$	3	23 has no decimal places, so the sum can have none.
$230/760.0 = 0.30$	2	230 has two significant figures because the last zero is not significant. In contrast, there is a decimal point in 760.0, so there are four significant digits. The quotient may have only two significant digits.

Analysis shows that one of the pieces of information is known to only two significant figures. Therefore, the volume of gas is 9.6 L, a number with two significant figures.

EXERCISE 6 Using Significant Figures

(a) How many significant figures are indicated by 2.33×10^7, by 50.5, and by 200?

(b) What are the sum and the product of 10.26 and 0.063?

(c) What is the result of the following calculation?

$$x = \frac{(110.7 - 64)}{(0.056)(0.00216)}$$

Problem Solving by Dimensional Analysis

Figure 9 illustrated the data that were collected to determine the density of a piece of metal. The thickness was measured in millimeters, whereas the length and width were measured in centimeters. To find the volume of the sample in cubic centimeters, we first had to have the length, width, and thickness in the same units and so converted the thickness to centimeters.

$$3.1 \text{ mm} \times \frac{1 \text{ cm}}{10 \text{ mm}} = 0.31 \text{ cm}$$

Here, we multiplied the number we wished to convert (3.1 mm) by a *conversion factor* (1 cm/10 mm) to produce the result in the desired unit (0.31 cm). Notice that units are treated like numbers. Because the unit "mm" was in both the numerator and the denominator, dividing one by the other leaves a quotient of 1. The units are said to "cancel out." Here, this leaves the answer in centimeters, the desired unit.

This approach to problem solving is often called **dimensional analysis** (or sometimes the **factor-label method**). It is a general problem-solving approach that uses the dimensions or units of each value to guide us through calculations. And, it is often the case that conversion factors are used to change measured quantities to chemically useful information.

A **conversion factor** expresses the equivalence of a measurement in two different units (1 cm ≡ 10 mm; 1 g ≡ 1000 mg; 12 eggs ≡ 1 dozen; 12 inches ≡ 1 foot). Because the numerator and the denominator describe the same quantity, the conversion factor is equivalent to the number 1. Therefore, multiplication by this factor does not change the measured quantity, only its units. A conversion factor is always written so that it has the form "new units divided by units of original number."

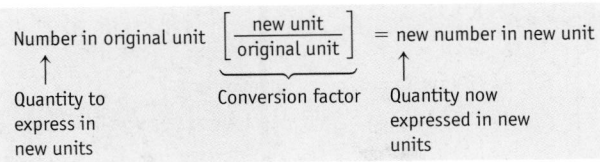

$$\text{Number in original unit} \left[\frac{\text{new unit}}{\text{original unit}}\right] = \text{new number in new unit}$$

Quantity to express in new units

Conversion factor

Quantity now expressed in new units

Chemistry .ȯ. Now™

Sign in at **www.cengage.com/login** and go to Screen 1.17 for a self-study module on **dimensional analysis and using numerical information.**

■ **Using Conversion Factors and Doing Calculations** As you work problems in this book and read Example problems, notice that proceeding from given information to an answer very often involves a series of multiplications. That is, we multiply the given data by a conversion factor, multiply that answer of that step by another factor, and so on to the answer.

■ **EXAMPLE 4 Using Conversion Factors and Dimensional Analysis**

Problem Oceanographers often express the density of sea water in units of kilograms per cubic meter. If the density of sea water is 1.025 g/cm^3 at 15 °C, what is its density in kilograms per cubic meter?

Strategy To simplify this problem, break it into three steps. First, change the mass in grams to kilograms. Next, convert the volume in cubic centimeters to cubic meters. Finally, calculate the density by dividing the mass in kilograms by the volume in cubic meters.

Solution First convert the mass in grams to a mass in kilograms.

$$1.025 \text{ g} \times \frac{1 \text{ kg}}{1000 \text{ g}} = 1.025 \times 10^{-3} \text{ kg}$$

No conversion factor is available in one of our tables to directly change units of cubic centimeters to cubic meters. You can find one, however, by cubing (raising to the third power) the relation between the meter and the centimeter:

$$1 \text{ cm}^3 \times \left(\frac{1 \text{ m}}{100 \text{ cm}}\right)^3 = 1 \text{ cm}^3 \times \left(\frac{1 \text{ m}^3}{1 \times 10^6 \text{ cm}^3}\right) = 1 \times 10^{-6} \text{ m}^3$$

Therefore, the density of sea water is

$$\text{Density} = \frac{1.025 \times 10^{-3} \text{ kg}}{1 \times 10^{-6} \text{ m}^3} = \boxed{1.025 \times 10^3 \text{ kg/m}^3}$$

EXERCISE 7 Using Dimensional Analysis

(a) The annual snowfall at Lake Otsego is 198 cm each year. What is this depth in meters? In feet (where 1 foot = 30.48 cm)?

(b) The area of Lake Otsego is 2.33×10^7 m^2. What is this area in square kilometers?

(c) The density of gold is 19,320 kg/m^3. What is this density in g/cm^3?

(d) See Figure 7. Show that 9.0×10^3 pc is 2.8×10^{17} km.

■ **Who Is Right—You or the Book?**
If your answer to a problem in this book does not quite agree with the answers in Appendix N through Q, the discrepancy may be the result of rounding the answer after each step and then using that rounded answer in the next step. This book follows these conventions:
(a) Final answers to numerical problems in this book result from retaining four or more digits past the decimal place throughout the calculation and rounding only at the end.
(b) In Example problems, the answer to each step is given to the correct number of significant figures for that step, but a number of digits are carried to the next step. The number of significant figures in the final answer is dictated by the number of significant figures in the original data.

Graphing

In a number of instances in this text, graphs are used when analyzing experimental data with a goal of obtaining a mathematical equation that may help us predict new results. The procedure used will often result in a straight line, which has the equation

$$y = mx + b$$

FIGURE 10 Plotting data. Data for the variable x are plotted on the horizontal axis (abscissa), and data for y are plotted on the vertical axis (ordinate). The slope of the line, m in the equation $y = mx + b$, is given by $\Delta y / \Delta x$. The intercept of the line with the y-axis (when $x = 0$) is b in the equation.

Using Microsoft Excel with these data, and doing a linear regression analysis, we find $y = -0.525x + 1.87$.

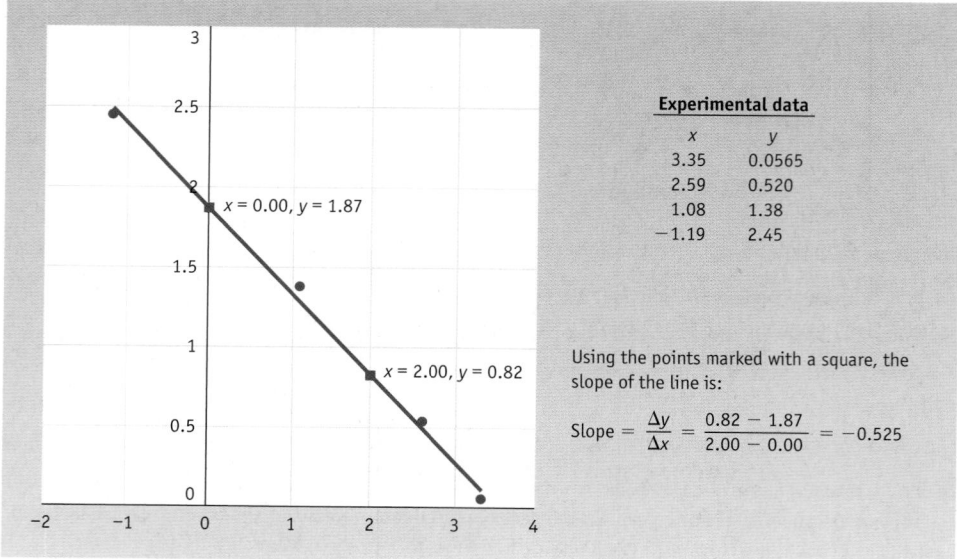

Experimental data

x	y
3.35	0.0565
2.59	0.520
1.08	1.38
−1.19	2.45

Using the points marked with a square, the slope of the line is:

$$\text{Slope} = \frac{\Delta y}{\Delta x} = \frac{0.82 - 1.87}{2.00 - 0.00} = -0.525$$

■ **Determining the Slope with a Computer Program—Least-Squares Analysis** Generally, the easiest method of determining the slope and intercept of a straight line (and thus the line's equation) is to use a program such as Microsoft Excel. These programs perform a "least squares" or "linear regression" analysis and give the best straight line based on the data. (This line is referred to in Excel as a trendline.)

In this equation, y is usually referred to as the dependent variable; its value is determined from (that is, is dependent on) the values of x, m, and b. In this equation, x is called the independent variable, and m is the slope of the line. The parameter b is the y-intercept—that is, the value of y when $x = 0$. Let us use an example to investigate two things: (a) how to construct a graph from a set of data points, and (b) how to derive an equation for the line generated by the data.

A set of data points to be graphed is presented in Figure 10. We first mark off each axis in increments of the values of x and y. Here, our x-data are within the range from −2 to 4, so the x-axis is marked off in increments of 1 unit. The y-data falls within the range from 0 to 2.5, so we mark off the y-axis in increments of 0.5. Each data point is marked as a circle on the graph.

After plotting the points on the graph (round circles), we draw a straight line that comes as close as possible to representing the trend in the data. (Do not connect the dots!) Because there is always some inaccuracy in experimental data, this line will not pass exactly through every point.

To identify the specific equation corresponding to our data, we must determine the y-intercept (b) and slope (m) for the equation $y = mx + b$. The y-intercept is the point at which $x = 0$. (In Figure 10, $y = 1.87$ when $x = 0$). The slope is determined by selecting two points *on the line* (marked with squares in Figure 10) and calculating the difference in values of y ($\Delta y = y_2 - y_1$) and x ($\Delta x = x_2 - x_1$). The slope of the line is then the ratio of these differences, $m = \Delta y / \Delta x$. Here, the slope has the value −0.525. With the slope and intercept now known, we can write the equation for the line

$$y = -0.525x + 1.87$$

and we can use this equation to calculate y-values for points that are not part of our original set of x–y data. For example, when $x = 1.50$, we find $y = 1.08$.

EXERCISE 8 Graphing

To find the mass of 50 jelly beans, we weighed several samples of beans.

Number of Beans	Mass (g)
5	12.82
11	27.14
16	39.30
24	59.04

Plot these data with the number of beans on the horizontal or *x*-axis, and the mass of beans on the vertical or *y*-axis. What is the slope of the line? Use your equation of a straight line to calculate the mass of exactly 50 jelly beans.

Case Study

Out of Gas!

On July 23, 1983, a new Boeing 767 jet aircraft was flying at 26,000 ft from Montreal to Edmonton as Air Canada Flight 143. Warning buzzers sounded in the cockpit. One of the world's largest planes was now a glider—the plane had run out of fuel!

How did this modern airplane, having the latest technology, run out of fuel? A simple mistake had been made in calculating the amount of fuel required for the flight!

Like all Boeing 767s, this plane had a sophisticated fuel gauge, but it was not working properly. The plane was still allowed to fly, however, because there is an alternative method of determining the quantity of fuel in the tanks. Mechanics can use a stick, much like the oil dipstick in an automobile engine, to measure the fuel level in each of the three tanks. The mechanics in Montreal read the dipsticks, which were calibrated in centimeters, and translated those readings to a volume in liters. According to this, the plane had a total of 7682 L of fuel.

Pilots always calculate fuel quantities in units of mass because they need to know the total mass of the plane before take-off. Air Canada pilots had always calculated the quantity of fuel in pounds, but the new 767's fuel consumption was given in kilograms. The pilots knew that 22,300 kg of fuel was required for the trip. If 7682 L of fuel remained in the tanks, how much had to be added? This involved using the fuel's density to convert 7682 L to a mass in kilograms. The mass of fuel to be added could then be calcu-

lated, and that mass converted to a volume of fuel to be added.

The First Officer of the plane asked a mechanic for the conversion factor to do the volume-to-mass conversion, and the mechanic replied "1.77." Using that number, the First Officer and the mechanics calculated that 4917 L of fuel should be added. But later calculations showed that this is only about one fourth of the required amount of fuel! Why? Because no one thought about the units of the number 1.77. They realized later that 1.77 has units of pounds per liter and not kilograms per liter.

Out of fuel, the plane could not make it to Winnipeg, so controllers directed them to the town of Gimli and to a small airport abandoned by the Royal Canadian Air Force. After gliding for almost 30 minutes, the plane approached the

Gimli runway. The runway, however, had been converted to a race course for cars, and a race was underway. Furthermore, a steel barrier had been erected across the runway. Nonetheless, the pilot managed to touch down very near the end of the runway. The plane sped down the concrete strip; the nose wheel collapsed; several tires blew—and the plane skidded safely to a stop just before the barrier. The Gimli glider had made it! And somewhere an aircraft mechanic is paying more attention to units on numbers.

Question:

1. *What is the fuel density in units of kg/L?*
2. *What mass and what volume of fuel should have been loaded? (1 lb = 453.6 g) (See Study Question 58, page 48.)*

Answers to these questions are in Appendix Q.

© Wayne Glowacki/Winnipeg Free Press, July 23, 1987, reproduced with permission.

The Gimli glider. After running out of fuel, Air Canada Flight 143 glided 29 minutes before landing on an abandoned airstrip at Gimli, Manitoba, near Winnipeg.

Problem Solving and Chemical Arithmetic

Problem-Solving Strategy

Some of the calculations in chemistry can be complex. Students frequently find it is helpful to follow a definite plan of attack as illustrated in examples throughout this book.

Step 1: Problem. State the problem. Read it carefully—and then read it again.

Step 2: Strategy. What key principles are involved? What information is known or not known? What information might be there just to place the question in the context of chemistry? Organize the information to see what is required and to discover the relationships among the data given. Try writing the information down in table form. If it is numerical information, be sure to include units.

One of the greatest difficulties for a student in introductory chemistry is picturing what is being asked for. Try sketching a picture of the situation involved. For example, we sketched a picture of the piece of metal whose density we wanted to calculate, and put the dimensions on the drawing (page 36).

Develop a plan. Have you done a problem of this type before? If not, perhaps the problem is really just a combination of several simpler ones you have seen before. Break it down into those simpler components. Try reasoning backward from the units of the answer. What data do you need to find an answer in those units?

Step 3: Solution. Execute the plan. Carefully write down each step of the problem, being sure to keep track of the units on numbers. (Do the units cancel to give you the answer in the desired units?) Don't skip steps. Don't do anything except the simplest steps in your head. Students often say they got a problem wrong because they "made a stupid mistake." Your instructor—and book authors—make them, too, and it is usually because they don't take the time to write down the steps of the problem clearly.

Step 4: Comment and Check Answer. As a final check, ask yourself whether the answer is reasonable.

EXAMPLE 5 Problem Solving

Problem A mineral oil has a density of 0.875 g/cm³. Suppose you spread 0.75 g of this oil over the surface of water in a large dish with an inner diameter of 21.6 cm. How thick is the oil layer? Express the thickness in centimeters.

Strategy It is often useful to begin solving such problems by sketching a picture of the situation.

21.6 cm

This helps recognize that the solution to the problem is to find the volume of the oil on the water. If we know the volume, then we can find the thickness because

Volume of oil layer = (thickness of layer) × (area of oil layer)

So, we need two things: (a) the volume of the oil layer and (b) the area of the layer.

Solution First, calculate the volume of oil. The mass of the oil layer is known, so combining the mass of oil with its density gives the volume of the oil used:

$$0.75 \text{ g} \times \frac{1 \text{ cm}^3}{0.875 \text{ g}} = 0.86 \text{ cm}^3$$

Next, calculate the area of the oil layer. The oil is spread over a circular surface, whose area is given by

$$\text{Area} = \pi \times (\text{radius})^2$$

The radius of the oil layer is half its diameter (= 21.6 cm) or 10.8 cm, so

$$\text{Area of oil layer} = (3.142)(10.8 \text{ cm})^2 = 366 \text{ cm}^2$$

With the volume and the area of the oil layer known, the thickness can be calculated.

$$\text{Thickness} = \frac{\text{Volume}}{\text{Area}} = \frac{0.86 \text{ cm}^3}{366 \text{ cm}^2} = 0.0023 \text{ cm}$$

Comment In the volume calculation, the calculator shows 0.857143. . . . The quotient should have two significant figures because 0.75 has two significant figures, so the result of this step is 0.86 cm³. In the area calculation, the calculator shows 366.435. . . . The answer to this step should have three significant figures because 10.8 has three. When these interim results are combined in calculating thickness, however, the final result can have only two significant figures. Premature rounding can lead to errors.

EXERCISE 9 Problem Solving

A particular paint has a density of 0.914 g/cm³. You need to cover a wall that is 7.6 m long and 2.74 m high with a paint layer 0.13 mm thick. What volume of paint (in liters) is required? What is the mass (in grams) of the paint layer?

STUDY QUESTIONS

⏱WL Online homework for this chapter may be assigned in OWL.

▲ denotes challenging questions.

■ denotes questions assignable in OWL.

Blue-numbered questions have answers in Appendix O and fully-worked solutions in the *Student Solutions Manual*.

Practicing Skills
Temperature Scales
(Exercise 1)

1. Many laboratories use 25 °C as a standard temperature. What is this temperature in kelvins?

2. The temperature on the surface of the sun is 5.5×10^3 °C. What is this temperature in kelvins?

3. ■ Make the following temperature conversions:

	°C	K
(a)	16	____
(b)	____	370
(c)	40	____

4. Make the following temperature conversions:

	°C	K
(a)	____	77
(b)	63	____
(c)	____	1450

Length, Volume, Mass, and Density
(See Example 1 and Exercises 2–4)

5. A marathon distance race covers a distance of 42.195 km. What is this distance in meters? In miles?

6. ■ The average lead pencil, new and unused, is 19 cm long. What is its length in millimeters? In meters?

7. A standard U.S. postage stamp is 2.5 cm long and 2.1 cm wide. What is the area of the stamp in square centimeters? In square meters?

8. ■ A compact disc has a diameter of 11.8 cm. What is the surface area of the disc in square centimeters? In square meters? [Area of a circle = $(\pi)(\text{radius})^2$.]

9. A typical laboratory beaker has a volume of 250. mL. What is its volume in cubic centimeters? In liters? In cubic meters? In cubic decimeters?

10. ■ Some soft drinks are sold in bottles with a volume of 1.5 L. What is this volume in milliliters? In cubic centimeters? In cubic decimeters?

11. A book has a mass of 2.52 kg. What is this mass in grams?

12. A new U.S. dime has a mass of 2.265 g. What is its mass in kilograms? In milligrams?

13. ■ Ethylene glycol, $C_2H_6O_2$, is an ingredient of automobile antifreeze. Its density is 1.11 g/cm^3 at 20 °C. If you need 500. mL of this liquid, what mass of the compound, in grams, is required?

14. ■ A piece of silver metal has a mass of 2.365 g. If the density of silver is 10.5 g/cm^3, what is the volume of the silver?

15. ■ You can identify a metal by carefully determining its density (d). An unknown piece of metal, with a mass of 2.361 g, is 2.35 cm long, 1.34 cm wide, and 1.05 mm thick. Which of the following is the element?
(a) Nickel, $d = 8.91$ g/cm^3
(b) Titanium, $d = 4.50$ g/cm^3
(c) Zinc, $d = 7.14$ g/cm^3
(d) Tin, $d = 7.23$ g/cm^3

16. ■ Which occupies a larger volume, 600 g of water (with a density of 0.995 g/cm^3) or 600 g of lead (with a density of 11.35 g/cm^3)?

Accuracy, Precision, Error, and Standard Deviation
(See Example 2 and Exercise 5)

17. You and your lab partner are asked to determine the density of an aluminum bar. The mass is known accurately (to four significant figures). You use a simple metric ruler to measure its dimensions and find the results in A. Your partner uses a precision micrometer, and obtains the results in B.

Method A (g/cm³)	Method B (g/cm³)
2.2	2.703
2.3	2.701
2.7	2.705
2.4	5.811

The accepted density of aluminum is 2.702 g/cm^3.
(a) Calculate the average density for each method. Should all the experimental results be included in your calculations? If not, justify any omissions.
(b) Calculate the percent error for each method's average value.
(c) Calculate the standard deviation for each set of data.
(d) Which method's average value is more precise? Which method is more accurate?

18. ■ The accepted value of the melting point of pure aspirin is 135 °C. Trying to verify that value, you obtain 134 °C, 136 °C, 133 °C, and 138 °C in four separate trials. Your partner finds 138 °C, 137 °C, 138 °C, and 138 °C.
(a) Calculate the average value and percent error for you and your partner.
(b) Which of you is more precise? More accurate?

Exponential Notation and Significant Figures
(See Example 3)

19. ■ Express the following numbers in exponential or scientific notation, and give the number of significant figures in each.
(a) 0.054 g   (c) 0.000792 g
(b) 5462 g   (d) 1600 mL

20. ■ Express the following numbers in fixed notation (e.g., $1.23 \times 10^2 = 123$), and give the number of significant figures in each.
(a) 1.623×10^3 (c) 6.32×10^{-2}
(b) 2.57×10^{-4} (d) 3.404×10^3

21. ■ Carry out the following operations. Provide the answer with the correct number of significant figures.
(a) $(1.52)(6.21 \times 10^{-3})$
(b) $(6.217 \times 10^3) - (5.23 \times 10^2)$
(c) $(6.217 \times 10^3) \div (5.23 \times 10^2)$
(d) $(0.0546)(16.0000)\left[\dfrac{7.779}{55.85}\right]$

22. Carry out the following operations. Provide the answer with the correct number of significant figures.
(a) $(6.25 \times 10^2)^3$
(b) $\sqrt{2.35 \times 10^{-3}}$
(c) $(2.35 \times 10^{-3})^{1/3}$
(d) $(1.68)\left[\dfrac{23.56 - 2.3}{1.248 \times 10^3}\right]$

Graphing
(See Exercise 8)

23. To determine the average mass of a popcorn kernel, you collect the following data:

Number of kernels	Mass (g)
5	0.836
12	2.162
35	5.801

Plot the data with number of kernels on the *x*-axis and mass on the *y*-axis. Draw the best straight line using the points on the graph (or do a least-squares or linear regression analysis using a computer program), and then write the equation for the resulting straight line. What is the slope of the line? What does the slope of the line signify about the mass of a popcorn kernel? What is the mass of 20 popcorn kernels? How many kernels are there in a handful of popcorn with a mass of 20.88 g?

▲ more challenging   ■ in OWL   Blue-numbered questions answered in Appendix O

24. Using the graph below:
(a) What is the value of x when $y = 4.0$?
(b) What is the value of y when $x = 0.30$?
(c) ■ What are the slope and the y-intercept of the line?
(d) What is the value of y when $x = 1.0$?

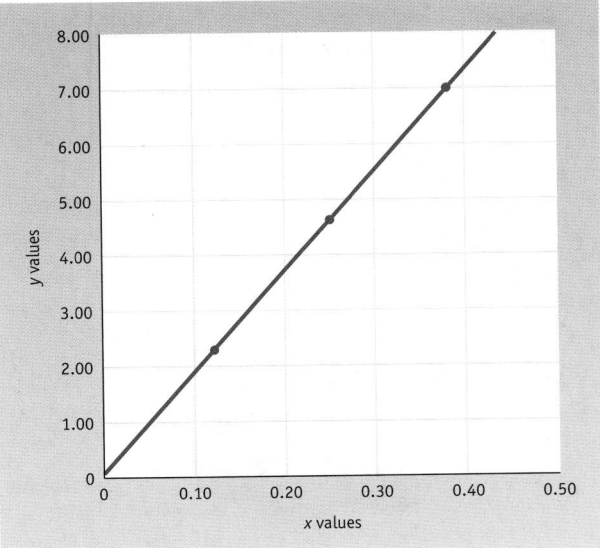

25. ■ Use the graph below to answer the following questions.
(a) Derive the equation for the straight line, $y = mx + b$.
(b) What is the value of y when $x = 6.0$?

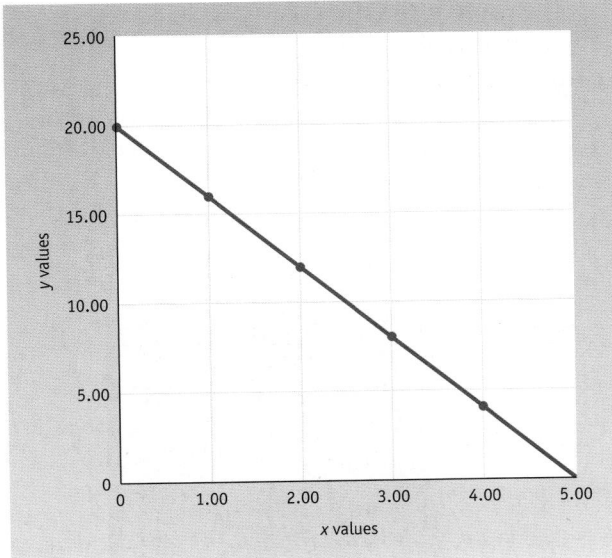

26. The following data were collected in an experiment to determine how an enzyme works in a biochemical reaction.

Amount of H_2O_2	Reaction Speed (amount/second)
1.96	4.75×10^{-5}
1.31	4.03×10^{-5}
0.98	3.51×10^{-5}
0.65	2.52×10^{-5}
0.33	1.44×10^{-5}
0.16	0.585×10^{-5}

(a) Plot these data as 1/amount on the y-axis and 1/speed on the x-axis.
(b) Determine the equation for the data, and give the values of the y-intercept of the slope. (*Note: in biochemistry this is known as a Lineweaver-Burk plot, and the y-intercept is related to the maximum speed of the reaction.*)

Solving Equations

27. Solve the following equation for the unknown value, C.
$$(0.502)(123) = (750.)C$$

28. Solve the following equation for the unknown value, n.
$$(2.34)(15.6) = n(0.0821)(273)$$

29. Solve the following equation for the unknown value, T.
$$(4.184)(244)(T - 292.0) + (0.449)(88.5)(T - 369.0) = 0$$

30. Solve the following equation for the unknown value, n.
$$-246.0 = 1312\left[\frac{1}{2^2} - \frac{1}{n^2}\right]$$

General Questions
These questions are not designated as to type or location in the chapter. They may combine several concepts.

31. Molecular distances are usually given in nanometers (1 nm $= 1 \times 10^{-9}$ m) or in picometers (1 pm $= 1 \times 10^{-12}$ m). However, the angstrom (Å) unit is sometimes used, where 1 Å $= 1 \times 10^{-10}$ m. (The angstrom unit is not an SI unit.) If the distance between the Pt atom and the N atom in the cancer chemotherapy drug cisplatin is 1.97 Å, what is this distance in nanometers? In picometers?

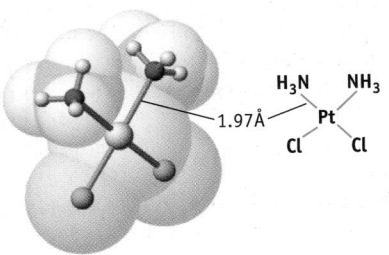

Cisplatin.

32. ■ The separation between carbon atoms in diamond is 0.154 nm. What is their separation in meters? In picometers (pm)? In Angstroms (Å)? (See Study Question 31.)

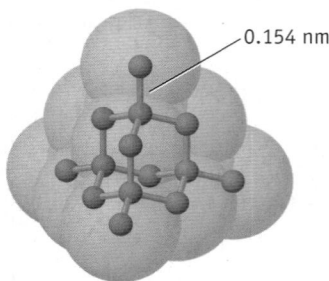

0.154 nm

A portion of the diamond structure.

33. ■ A red blood cell has a diameter of 7.5 μm (micrometers). What is this dimension in (a) meters, (b) nanometers, and (c) picometers?

34. ■ The platinum-containing cancer drug *cisplatin* (Study Question 31) contains 65.0 mass-percent of the metal. If you have 1.53 g of the compound, what mass of platinum (in grams) is contained in this sample?

35. ■ The anesthetic procaine hydrochloride is often used to deaden pain during dental surgery. The compound is packaged as a 10.% solution (by mass; $d = 1.0$ g/mL) in water. If your dentist injects 0.50 mL of the solution, what mass of procaine hydrochloride (in milligrams) is injected?

36. ■ You need a cube of aluminum with a mass of 7.6 g. What must be the length of the cube's edge (in cm)? (The density of aluminum is 2.698 g/cm³.)

37. ■ You have a 250.0-mL graduated cylinder containing some water. You drop 3 marbles with a total mass of 95.2 g into the water. What is the average density of a marble?

(a)   (b)

Determining density. (a) A graduated cylinder with 61 mL of water. (b) Three marbles are added to the cylinder.

38. ■ You have a white crystalline solid, known to be one of the potassium compounds listed below. To determine which, you measure its density. You measure out 18.82 g and transfer it to a graduated cylinder containing kerosene (in which salts will not dissolve). The level of liquid kerosene rises from 8.5 mL to 15.3 mL. Calculate the density of the solid, and identify the compound from the following list.
(a) KF, $d = 2.48$ g/cm³
(b) KCl, $d = 1.98$ g/cm³
(c) KBr, $d = 2.75$ g/cm³
(d) KI, $d = 3.13$ g/cm³

39. ■ ▲ The smallest repeating unit of a crystal of common salt is a cube (called a unit cell) with an edge length of 0.563 nm.

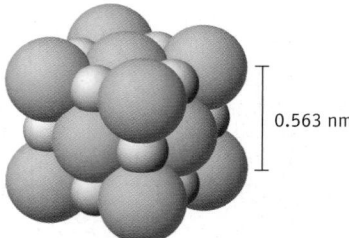

0.563 nm

Sodium chloride, NaCl.

(a) What is the volume of this cube in cubic nanometers? In cubic centimeters?
(b) The density of NaCl is 2.17 g/cm³. What is the mass of this smallest repeating unit ("unit cell")?
(c) Each repeating unit is composed of four NaCl "molecules." What is the mass of one NaCl molecule?

40. ■ Diamond has a density of 3.513 g/cm³. The mass of diamonds is often measured in "carats," where 1 carat equals 0.200 g. What is the volume (in cubic centimeters) of a 1.50-carat diamond?

41. The element gallium has a melting point of 29.8 °C. If you held a sample of gallium in your hand, should it melt? Explain briefly.

Gallium metal.

▲ more challenging   ■ in OWL   Blue-numbered questions answered in Appendix O

42. ■ ▲ The density of pure water is given at various temperatures.

t (°C)	d (g/cm³)
4	0.99997
15	0.99913
25	0.99707
35	0.99406

Suppose your laboratory partner tells you the density of water at 20 °C is 0.99910 g/cm³. Is this a reasonable number? Why or why not?

43. When you heat popcorn, it pops because it loses water explosively. Assume a kernel of corn, with a mass of 0.125 g, has a mass of only 0.106 g after popping.
   (a) What percentage of its mass did the kernel lose on popping?
   (b) ■ Popcorn is sold by the pound in the United States. Using 0.125 g as the average mass of a popcorn kernel, how many kernels are there in a pound of popcorn? (1 lb = 453.6 g)

44. ■ ▲ The aluminum in a package containing 75 ft² of kitchen foil weighs approximately 12 ounces. Aluminum has a density of 2.70 g/cm³. What is the approximate thickness of the aluminum foil in millimeters? (1 oz = 28.4 g)

45. ■ ▲ The fluoridation of city water supplies has been practiced in the United States for several decades. It is done by continuously adding sodium fluoride to water as it comes from a reservoir. Assume you live in a medium-sized city of 150,000 people and that 660 L (170 gal) of water is consumed per person per day. What mass of sodium fluoride (in kilograms) must be added to the water supply each year (365 days) to have the required fluoride concentration of 1 ppm (part per million)—that is, 1 kilogram of fluoride per 1 million kilograms of water? (Sodium fluoride is 45.0% fluoride, and water has a density of 1.00 g/cm³.)

46. ■ ▲ About two centuries ago, Benjamin Franklin showed that 1 teaspoon of oil would cover about 0.5 acre of still water. If you know that 1.0×10^4 m² = 2.47 acres, and that there is approximately 5 cm³ in a teaspoon, what is the thickness of the layer of oil? How might this thickness be related to the sizes of molecules?

47. ■ ▲ Automobile batteries are filled with an aqueous solution of sulfuric acid. What is the mass of the acid (in grams) in 500. mL of the battery acid solution if the density of the solution is 1.285 g/cm³ and if the solution is 38.08% sulfuric acid by mass?

48. ■ A 26-meter-tall statue of Buddha in Tibet is covered with 279 kg of gold. If the gold was applied to a thickness of 0.0015 mm, what surface area is covered (in square meters)? (Gold density = 19.3 g/cm³)

49. At 25 °C, the density of water is 0.997 g/cm³, whereas the density of ice at −10 °C is 0.917 g/cm³.
   (a) If a soft-drink can (volume = 250. mL) is filled completely with pure water at 25 °C and then frozen at −10 °C, what volume does the solid occupy?
   (b) Can the ice be contained within the can?

50. ■ Suppose your bedroom is 18 ft long, 15 ft wide, and the distance from floor to ceiling is 8 ft, 6 in. You need to know the volume of the room in metric units for some scientific calculations.
   (a) What is the room's volume in cubic meters? In liters?
   (b) What is the mass of air in the room in kilograms? In pounds? (Assume the density of air is 1.2 g/L and that the room is empty of furniture.)

51. ■ A spherical steel ball has a mass of 3.475 g and a diameter of 9.40 mm. What is the density of the steel? [The volume of a sphere = $(4/3)\pi r^3$ where r = radius.]

52. ■ ▲ The substances listed below are clear liquids. You are asked to identify an unknown liquid that is known to be one of these liquids. You pipet a 3.50-mL sample into a beaker. The empty beaker had a mass of 12.20 g, and the beaker plus the liquid weighed 16.08 g.

Substance	Density at 25 °C (g/cm³)
Ethylene glycol	1.1088 (the major component of antifreeze)
Water	0.9971
Ethanol	0.7893 (the alcohol in alcoholic beverages)
Acetic acid	1.0492 (the active component of vinegar)
Glycerol	1.2613 (a solvent, used in home care products)

   (a) Calculate the density and identify the unknown.
   (b) If you were able to measure the volume to only two significant figures (that is, 3.5 mL, not 3.50 mL), will the results be sufficiently accurate to identify the unknown? Explain.

53. ■ ▲ You have an irregularly shaped piece of an unknown metal. To identify it, you determine its density and then compare this value with known values that you look up in the chemistry library. The mass of the metal is 74.122 g. Because of the irregular shape, you measure the volume by submerging the metal in water in a graduated cylinder. When you do this, the water level in the cylinder rises from 28.2 mL to 36.7 mL.
   (a) What is the density of the metal? (Use the correct number of significant figures in your answer.)
   (b) The unknown is one of the seven metals listed below. Is it possible to identify the metal based on the density you have calculated? Explain.

Metal	Density (g/cm³)	Metal	Density (g/cm³)
zinc	7.13	nickel	8.90
iron	7.87	copper	8.96
cadmium	8.65	silver	10.50
cobalt	8.90		

54. ■ ▲ There are 5 hydrocarbon compounds (compounds of C and H) that have the formula C_6H_{14}. (These are isomers; they differ in the way that C and H atoms are attached. See Chapters 8 and 10.) All are liquids at room temperature but have slightly different densities.

Hydrocarbon	Density (g/mL)
hexane	0.6600
2,3-dimethylbutane	0.6616
1-methylpentane	0.6532
2,2-dimethylbutane	0.6485
2-methylpentane	0.6645

(a) You have a pure sample of one of these hydrocarbons, and to identify it you decide to measure its density. You determine that a 5.0-mL sample (measured in a graduated cylinder) has a mass of 3.2745 g (measured on an analytical balance.) Assume that the accuracy of the values for mass and volume is expressed by the number of significant figures, that is, plus or minus one (± 1) in the last significant figure. What is the density of the liquid?

(b) Express the estimated uncertainty of your value in two other ways:
  i) The value you have calculated for the density is uncertain to ____ g/mL.
  ii) The value calculated for density is between x g/mL and y g/mL.

(c) Can you identify the unknown hydrocarbon based on your experiment?

(d) Can you eliminate any of the five possibilities based on the data? If so, which one(s)?

(e) You need a more accurate volume measurement to solve this problem, and you redetermine the volume to be 4.93 mL. Based on these new data, what is the unknown compound?

55. ■ ▲ Suppose you have a cylindrical glass tube with a thin capillary opening, and you wish to determine the diameter of the capillary. You can do this experimentally by weighing a piece of the tubing before and after filling a portion of the capillary with mercury. Using the following information, calculate the diameter of the capillary.

Mass of tube before adding mercury = 3.263 g

Mass of tube after adding mercury = 3.416 g

Length of capillary filled with mercury = 16.75 mm

Density of mercury = 13.546 g/cm³

Volume of cylindrical capillary filled with mercury = $(\pi)(\text{radius})^2(\text{length})$

56. ■ **COPPER:** Copper has a density of 8.96 g/cm³. An ingot of copper with a mass of 57 kg (126 lb) is drawn into wire with a diameter of 9.50 mm. What length of wire (in meters) can be produced? [Volume of wire = $(\pi)(\text{radius})^2(\text{length})$]

57. ▲ COPPER: See the illustration of the copper lattice on page 24.

(a) Suppose you have a cube of copper metal that is 0.236 cm on a side with a mass of 0.1206 g. If you know that each copper atom (radius = 128 pm) has a mass of 1.055×10^{-22} g (you will learn in Chapter 2 how to find the mass of one atom), how many atoms are there in this cube? What fraction of the cube is filled with atoms? (Or conversely, how much of the lattice is empty space?) Why is there "empty" space in the lattice?

(b) Now look at the smallest, repeating unit of the crystal lattice of copper. Knowing that an edge of this cube is 361.47 pm and the density of copper is 8.960 g/cm³, estimate the number of copper atoms in this smallest, repeating unit.

58. ■ ▲ CASE STUDY: In July 1983, an Air Canada Boeing 767 ran out of fuel over central Canada on a trip from Montreal to Edmonton. (The plane glided safely to a landing at an abandoned airstrip.) The pilots knew that 22,300 kg of fuel were required for the trip, and they knew that 7682 L of fuel were already in the tank. The ground crew added 4916 L of fuel, which was only about one fifth of what was required. The crew members used a factor of 1.77 for the fuel density—the problem is that 1.77 has units of pounds per liter and not kilograms per liter! What is the fuel density in units of kg/L? What mass and what volume of fuel should have been loaded? (1 lb = 453.6 g)

In the Laboratory

59. ■ A sample of unknown metal is placed in a graduated cylinder containing water. The mass of the sample is 37.5 g, and the water levels before and after adding the sample to the cylinder are as shown in the figure. Which metal in the following list is most likely the sample? (d is the density of the metal.)
(a) Mg, d = 1.74 g/cm³   (d) Al, d = 2.70 g/cm³
(b) Fe, d = 7.87 g/cm³   (e) Cu, d = 8.96 g/cm³
(c) Ag, d = 10.5 g/cm³   (f) Pb, d = 11.3 g/cm³

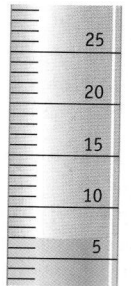 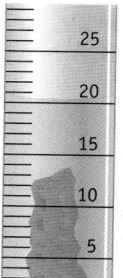

Graduated cylinders with unknown metal (right).

60. ■ Iron pyrite is often called "fool's gold" because it looks like gold (see page 14). Suppose you have a solid that looks like gold, but you believe it to be fool's gold. The sample has a mass of 23.5 g. When the sample is lowered into the water in a graduated cylinder (see Study Question 37), the water level rises from 47.5 mL to 52.2 mL. Is the sample fool's gold ($d = 5.00$ g/cm^3) or "real" gold ($d = 19.3$ g/cm^3)?

61. You can analyze for a copper compound in water using an instrument called a spectrophotometer. In this technique, the light passing through an aqueous solution of a compound can be absorbed, and the amount of light absorbed (at a given wavelength of light) depends directly on the amount of compound per liter of solution. To calibrate the spectrophotometer, you collect the following data:

Absorbance (A)	Concentration of Copper Compound (g/L)
0.000	0.000
0.257	1.029×10^{-3}
0.518	2.058×10^{-3}
0.771	3.087×10^{-3}
1.021	4.116×10^{-3}

Plot the absorbance (A) against the mass of copper compound per liter (g/L), and find the slope (m) and intercept (b) (assuming that A is y and the amount in solution is x in the equation for a straight line, $y = mx + b$). What is the amount of copper compound in the solution in g/L and mg/mL when the absorbance is 0.635?

62. A gas chromatograph (page 2) is calibrated for the analysis of isooctane (a major gasoline component) using the following data:

Percent Isooctane (x-data)	Instrument Response (y-data)
0.352	1.09
0.803	1.78
1.08	2.60
1.38	3.03
1.75	4.01

If the instrument response is 2.75, what percentage of isooctane is present? (Data are taken from *Analytical Chemistry, An Introduction*, by D.A. Skoog, D.M. West, F. J. Holler, and S. R. Crouch, Thomson-Brooks/Cole, Belmont, CA, 7th Edition, 2000.)

2 | Atoms, Molecules, and Ions

The Periodic Table, the Central Icon of Chemistry

Nineteenth-century chemists such as Newlands, Chancourtois, Mayer, and others devised ways to organize the chemistry of the elements with varying degrees of success. However, it was Dmitri Mendeleev in 1870 who first truly recognized the periodicity of the chemistry of the elements, who proposed the first periodic table, and who used this to predict the existence of yet-unknown elements.

Mendeleev placed the elements in a table in order of increasing atomic weight. In doing so Li, Be, B, C, N, O, and F became the first row of the table. The next element then known, sodium (Na), had properties quite similar to those of lithium (Li), so Na began the next row of the table. As additional elements were added in order of increasing atomic weight, elements with similar properties fell in columns or groups.

If you compare the periodic table published by Mendeleev in 1871 (shown here) with the table in the front of this book, you will see that many elements are missing in the 1871 table. Mendeleev's genius was that he recognized there must be yet-undiscovered elements, and so he left a place for them in the table (marking the empty places with a —). For example, Mendeleev concluded that "Gruppe IV" was missing an element between silicon (Si) and tin (Sn) and marked its position as "— = 72." He called the missing element *eka-silicon* and predicted the element would have, for example, an atomic weight of 72 and a density of 5.5 g/cm^3. Based on this and other predictions, chemists knew what to look for in mineral samples, and soon many of the missing elements were discovered.

Charles D. Winters

TABELLE II.

REIHEN	GRUPPE I. — R^2O	GRUPPE II. — RO	GRUPPE III. — R^2O^3	GRUPPE IV. RH^4 RO^2	GRUPPE V. RH^3 R^2O^5	GRUPPE VI. RH^2 RO^3	GRUPPE VII. RH R^2O^7	GRUPPE VIII. — RO^4
1	H = 1							
2	Li = 7	Be = 9,4	B = 11	C = 12	N = 14	O = 16	F = 19	
3	Na = 23	Mg = 24	Al = 27,3	Si = 28	P = 31	S = 32	Cl = 35,5	
4	K = 39	Ca = 40	— = 44	Ti = 48	V = 51	Cr = 52	Mn = 55	Fe = 56, Co = 59, Ni = 59, Cu = 63.
5	(Cu = 63)	Zn = 65	— = 68	— = 72	As = 75	Se = 78	Br = 80	
6	Rb = 85	Sr = 87	?Yt = 88	Zr = 90	Nb = 94	Mo = 96	— = 100	Ru = 104, Rh = 104, Pd = 106, Ag = 108.
7	(Ag = 108)	Cd = 112	In = 113	Sn = 118	Sb = 122	Te = 125	J = 127	
8	Cs = 133	Ba = 137	?Di = 138	?Ce = 140	—	—	—	— — — —
9	(—)							
10	—	—	?Er = 178	?La = 180	Ta = 182	W = 184	—	Os = 195, Ir = 197, Pt = 198, Au = 199.
11	(Au = 199)	Hg = 200	Tl = 204	Pb = 207	Bi = 208			
12	—	—	—	Th = 231	—	U = 240	—	— — — —

Questions:

1. What is eka-silicon, and how close were Mendeleev's predictions to the actual values for this element?
2. How many of the missing elements can you identify?

Answers to these questions are in Appendix Q.

Chapter Goals

See Chapter Goals Revisited (page 72) for Study Questions keyed to these goals and assignable in OWL.

- Describe atomic structure, and define atomic number and mass number.
- Understand the nature of isotopes, and calculate atomic weights from the isotopic masses and abundances.
- Know the terminology of the periodic table.
- Interpret, predict, and write formulas for ionic and molecular compounds.
- Name ionic and molecular compounds.
- Understand some properties of ionic compounds.
- Explain the concept of the mole, and use molar mass in calculations.
- Calculate percent composition for a compound and derive formulas from experimental data.

Chapter Outline

The chemical elements are forged in stars, and from these elements molecules such as water and ammonia are made in outer space. These simple molecules and much more complex ones such as DNA and hemoglobin are found on earth. To comprehend the burgeoning fields of molecular biology, as well as all modern chemistry, we have to understand the nature of the chemical elements and the properties and structures of molecules. This chapter begins our exploration of the chemistry of the elements, the building blocks of chemistry, and of the compounds they form.

Chemistry.Now™

Throughout the text this icon introduces an opportunity for self-study or to explore interactive tutorials by signing in at **www.cengage.com/login**.

2.1 Atomic Structure—Protons, Electrons, and Neutrons

Around 1900, a series of experiments done by scientists such as Sir John Joseph Thomson (1856–1940) and Ernest Rutherford (1871–1937) in England established a model of the atom that is still the basis of modern atomic theory. Three subatomic particles make up all atoms: electrically positive protons, electrically neutral neutrons, and electrically negative electrons. The model places the more massive protons and neutrons in a very small nucleus (Figure 2.1), which contains all the positive charge and almost all the mass of an atom. Electrons, with a much smaller mass than protons or neutrons, surround the nucleus and occupy most of the volume.

The chemical properties of elements and molecules depend largely on the electrons of the atoms involved. We shall look more carefully at their arrangement and how they influence the properties of atoms in Chapters 6 and 7. In this chapter, however, we first want to describe how the composition of the atom relates to its mass and then to the mass of molecules. This is crucial information when we consider the quantitative aspects of chemical reactions in later chapters.

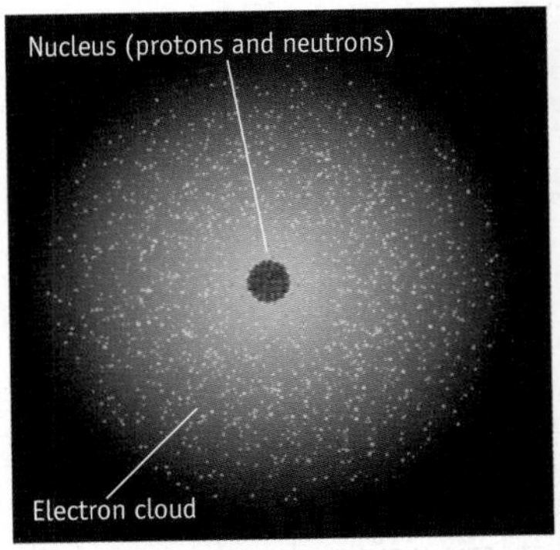

2.2 Atomic Number and Atomic Mass

Atomic Number

All atoms of a given element have the same number of protons in the nucleus. Hydrogen is the simplest element, with one nuclear proton. All helium atoms have two protons, all lithium atoms have three protons, and all beryllium atoms have four protons.

Nucleus (protons and neutrons)

Electron cloud

FIGURE 2.1 The structure of the atom. All atoms contain a nucleus with one or more protons (positive electric charge) and, except for H atoms, neutrons (no charge). Electrons (negative electric charge) are found in space as a "cloud" around the nucleus. In an electrically neutral atom, the number of electrons equals the number of protons. Note that this figure is not drawn to scale. If the nucleus were really the size depicted here, the electron cloud would extend over 200 m. The atom is mostly empty space!

■ **How Small Is an Atom?** The radius of the typical atom is between 30 and 300 pm (3×10^{-11} m to 3×10^{-10} m). To get a feeling for the incredible smallness of an atom, consider that one teaspoon of water (about 1 cm³) contains about three times as many atoms as the Atlantic Ocean contains teaspoons of water.

■ **Periodic Table Entry for Copper**

Copper
29 ------- Atomic number
Cu ---- Symbol

■ **Historical Perspective on the Development of Our Understanding of Atomic Structure** A brief history of important experiments and the scientists involved in developing the modern view of the atom is on pages 338–347. See also ChemistryNow Screens 2.3–2.10.

The number of protons in the nucleus of an element is its **atomic number**, which is generally given the symbol **Z**.

Currently known elements are listed in the periodic table inside the front cover of this book and on the list inside the back cover. The integer number at the top of the box for each element in the periodic table is its atomic number. A sodium atom (Na), for example, has an atomic number of 11, so its nucleus contains 11 protons. A uranium atom (U) has 92 nuclear protons and $Z = 92$.

Atomic Weight and the Atomic Mass Unit

With the quantitative work of the great French chemist Antoine Laurent Lavoisier (1743–1794), chemistry began to change from medieval alchemy to a modern field of study. As 18th- and 19th-century chemists tried to understand how the elements combined, they carried out increasingly quantitative studies aimed at learning, for example, how much of one element would combine with another. Based on this work, they learned that the substances they produced had a constant composition, and so they could define the relative masses of elements that would combine to produce a new substance. At the beginning of the 19th century, John Dalton (1766–1844) suggested that the combinations of elements involve atoms, and so he proposed a relative scale of atom masses. Apparently for simplicity, Dalton chose a mass of 1 for hydrogen on which to base his scale.

The atomic weight scale has changed since 1800, but like the 19th-century chemists, we still use *relative* masses. Our standard today, however, is carbon-12. A carbon atom having six protons and six neutrons in the nucleus is assigned a mass value of exactly 12. From chemical experiments and physical measurements, we know an oxygen atom having eight protons and eight neutrons has 1.3329 times the mass of carbon, so it has a relative mass of 15.9949. Masses of atoms of other elements have been assigned in a similar manner.

Masses of fundamental atomic particles are often expressed in **atomic mass units (u)**. *One atomic mass unit, 1 u, is one twelfth of the mass of an atom of carbon with six protons and six neutrons.* Thus, such a carbon atom has a mass of 12.000 u. The atomic mass unit can be related to other units of mass using the conversion factor $1 \text{ u} = 1.66054 \times 10^{-24}$ g.

Mass Number

Protons and neutrons have masses very close to 1 u (Table 2.1). The mass of an electron, in contrast, is only about 1/2000 of this value. Because proton and neutron masses are so close to 1 u, the approximate mass of an atom can be estimated if the

TABLE 2.1 Properties of Subatomic Particles*

Particle	Mass		Charge	Symbol
	Grams	*Atomic Mass Units*		
Electron	9.109383×10^{-28}	0.0005485799	1−	$_{-1}^{0}e$ or e^-
Proton	1.672622×10^{-24}	1.007276	1+	$_1^1p$ or p^+
Neutron	1.674927×10^{-24}	1.008665	0	$_0^1n$ or n

* These values and others in the book are taken from the National Institute of Standards and Technology website at http://physics.nist.gov/cuu/Constants/index.html

number of neutrons and protons is known. The sum of the number of protons and neutrons for an atom is called its **mass number** and is given the symbol *A*.

$$A = \text{mass number} = \text{number of protons} + \text{number of neutrons}$$

For example, a sodium atom, which has 11 protons and 12 neutrons in its nucleus, has a mass number of $A = 23$. The most common atom of uranium has 92 protons and 146 neutrons, and a mass number of $A = 238$. Using this information, we often symbolize atoms with the notation

$$\text{Mass number} \rightarrow {}^{A}_{Z}X \leftarrow \text{Element symbol}$$
$$\text{Atomic number} \rightarrow$$

The subscript *Z* is optional because the element's symbol tells us what the atomic number must be. For example, the atoms described previously have the symbols ${}^{23}_{11}\text{Na}$ or ${}^{238}_{92}\text{U}$, or just ${}^{23}\text{Na}$ or ${}^{238}\text{U}$. In words, we say "sodium-23" or "uranium-238."

Chemistry⚛Now™

Sign in at **www.cengage.com/login** and go to Chapter 2 Contents to see Screen 2.11 for a tutorial on **the notation for symbolizing atoms.**

■ **EXAMPLE 2.1 Atomic Composition**

Problem What is the composition of an atom of phosphorus with 16 neutrons? What is its mass number? What is the symbol for such an atom? If the atom has an actual mass of 30.9738 u, what is its mass in grams? Finally, what is the mass of this phosphorus atom relative to the mass of a carbon atom with a mass number of 12?

Strategy All P atoms have the same number of protons, 15, which is given by the atomic number. The mass number is the sum of the number of protons and neutrons. The mass of the atom in grams can be obtained from the mass in atomic mass units using the conversion factor 1 u = 1.66054 × 10^{-24} g.

Solution A phosphorus atom has 15 protons and, because it is electrically neutral, also has 15 electrons. A P atom with 16 neutrons has a mass number of 31.

$$\text{Mass number} = \text{number of protons} + \text{number of neutrons} = 15 + 16 = \boxed{31}$$

The atom's complete symbol is ${}^{31}_{15}\text{P}$.

$$\text{Mass of one } {}^{31}\text{P atom} = (30.9738 \text{ u}) \times (1.66054 \times 10^{-24} \text{ g/u}) = \boxed{5.14332 \times 10^{-23} \text{ g}}$$

An atom of ${}^{31}\text{P}$ is 2.58115 times heavier than an atom of ${}^{12}\text{C}$: 30.9738/12.0000 = 2.58115

EXERCISE 2.1 Atomic Composition

(a) What is the mass number of an iron atom with 30 neutrons?

(b) A nickel atom with 32 neutrons has a mass of 59.930788 u. What is its mass in grams?

(c) How many protons, neutrons, and electrons are in a ${}^{64}\text{Zn}$ atom?

(d) What is the mass of ${}^{64}\text{Zn}$ (63.929 u) relative to ${}^{12}\text{C}$?

2.3 Isotopes

In only a few instances (for example, aluminum, fluorine, and phosphorus) do all atoms in a naturally occurring sample of a given element have the same mass. Most elements consist of atoms having several different mass numbers. For example, there are two kinds of boron atoms, one with a mass of about 10 u (${}^{10}\text{B}$) and a second with a mass of about 11 u (${}^{11}\text{B}$). Atoms of tin can have any of 10 different masses. Atoms with the same atomic number but different mass numbers are called **isotopes**.

■ **Atomic Masses of Some Isotopes**

Atom	Relative Mass
${}^{4}\text{He}$	4.0092603
${}^{13}\text{C}$	13.003355
${}^{16}\text{O}$	15.994915
${}^{58}\text{Ni}$	57.935346
${}^{60}\text{Ni}$	59.930788
${}^{79}\text{Br}$	78.918336
${}^{81}\text{Br}$	80.916289
${}^{197}\text{Au}$	196.966543
${}^{238}\text{U}$	238.050784

Solid H₂O
Liquid H₂O
Solid D₂O

Charles D. Winters

FIGURE 2.2 Ice made from "heavy water." Water containing ordinary hydrogen ($^1_1$H, protium) forms a solid that is less dense ($d = 0.917$ g/cm³ at 0 °C) than liquid H_2O ($d = 0.997$ g/cm³ at 25 °C) and so floats in the liquid. (Water is unique in this regard. The solid phase of virtually all other substances sinks in the liquid phase of that substance.) Similarly, "heavy ice" (D_2O, deuterium oxide) floats in "heavy water." D_2O-ice is denser than liquid H_2O, however, so cubes made of D_2O sink in liquid H_2O.

All atoms of an element have the same number of protons—five in the case of boron. To have different masses, isotopes must have different numbers of neutrons. The nucleus of a ^{10}B atom ($Z = 5$) contains five protons and five neutrons, whereas the nucleus of a ^{11}B atom contains five protons and six neutrons.

Scientists often refer to a particular isotope by giving its mass number (for example, uranium-238, ^{238}U), but the isotopes of hydrogen are so important that they have special names and symbols. All hydrogen atoms have one proton. When that is the only nuclear particle, the isotope is called *protium*, or just "hydrogen." The isotope of hydrogen with one neutron, $^2_1$H, is called *deuterium*, or "heavy hydrogen" (symbol = D). The nucleus of radioactive hydrogen-3, $^3_1$H, or *tritium* (symbol = T), contains one proton and two neutrons.

The substitution of one isotope of an element for another isotope of the same element in a compound sometimes can have an interesting effect (Figure 2.2). This is especially true when deuterium is substituted for hydrogen because the mass of deuterium is double that of hydrogen.

Isotope Abundance

A sample of water from a stream or lake will consist almost entirely of H_2O where the H atoms are the ^{1}H isotope. A few molecules, however, will have deuterium (^{2}H) substituted for ^{1}H. We can predict this outcome because we know that 99.985% of all hydrogen atoms on earth are ^{1}H atoms. That is, the **percent abundance** of ^{1}H atoms is 99.985%.

$$\text{Percent abundance} = \frac{\text{number of atoms of a given isotope}}{\text{total number of atoms of all isotopes of that element}} \times 100\% \quad \text{(2.1)}$$

The remainder of naturally occurring hydrogen is deuterium, whose abundance is only 0.015% of the total hydrogen atoms. Tritium, the radioactive ^{3}H isotope, occurs naturally in only trace amounts.

Consider again the two isotopes of boron. The boron-10 isotope has an abundance of 19.91%; the abundance of boron-11 is 80.09%. Thus, if you could count out 10,000 boron atoms from an "average" natural sample, 1991 of them would be boron-10 atoms, and 8009 of them would be boron-11 atoms.

Chemistry Now™

Sign in at **www.cengage.com/login** and go to Chapter 2 Contents to see Screen 2.12, **Isotopes.**

EXERCISE 2.2 Isotopes

Silver has two isotopes, one with 60 neutrons (percent abundance = 51.839%) and the other with 62 neutrons. What is the mass number and symbol of the isotope with 62 neutrons, and what is its percent abundance?

Determining Atomic Mass and Isotope Abundance

The masses of isotopes and their percent abundances are determined experimentally using a mass spectrometer (Figure 2.3). A gaseous sample of an element is introduced into the evacuated chamber of the spectrometer, and the atoms or

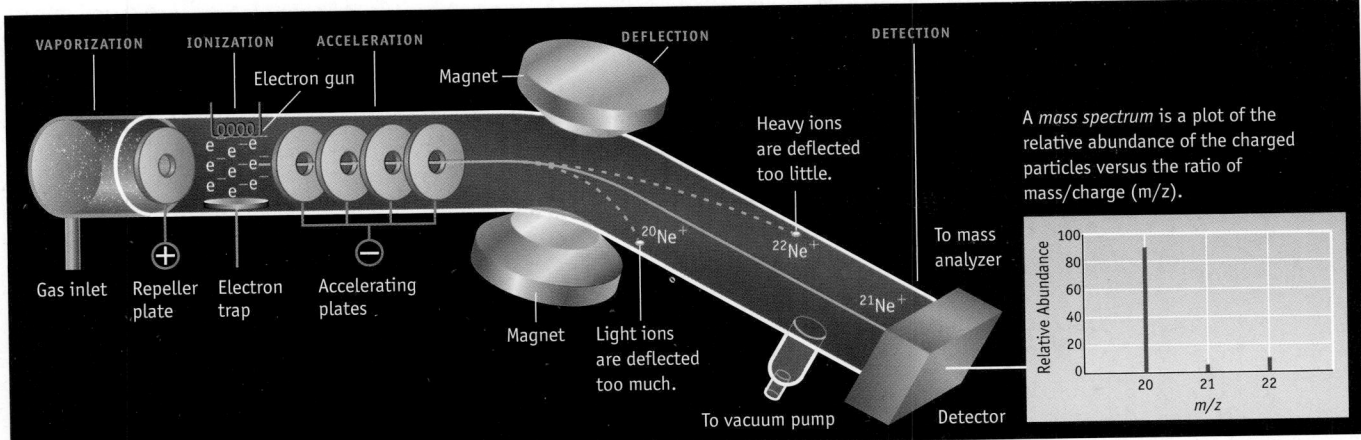

VAPORIZATION **IONIZATION** **ACCELERATION** **DEFLECTION** **DETECTION**

Electron gun   Magnet

Heavy ions
are deflected
too little.

$^{20}Ne^+$ $^{22}Ne^+$

$^{21}Ne^+$

To mass
analyzer

Gas inlet   Repeller   Electron   Accelerating
plate   trap   plates

Magnet   Light ions
          are deflected
          too much.

To vacuum pump   Detector

A *mass spectrum* is a plot of the relative abundance of the charged particles versus the ratio of mass/charge (m/z).

Relative Abundance — 100, 80, 60, 40, 20, 0 vs m/z (20, 21, 22)

1. A sample is introduced as a vapor into the ionization chamber.

There it is bombarded with high-energy electrons that strip electrons from the atoms or molecules of the sample.

2. The resulting positive particles are accelerated by a series of negatively charged accelerator plates into an analyzing chamber.

3. This chamber is in a magnetic field, which is perpendicular to the direction of the beam of charged particles.

The magnetic field causes the beam to curve. The radius of curvature depends on the mass and charge of the particles (as well as the accelerating voltage and strength of the magnetic field).

4. Here, particles of $^{21}Ne^+$ are focused on the detector, whereas beams of ions of $^{20}Ne^+$ and $^{22}Ne^+$ (of lighter or heavier mass) experience greater and lesser curvature, respectively, and so fail to be detected.

By changing the magnetic field, charged particles of different masses can be focused on the detector to generate the observed spectrum.

Active Figure 2.3 **Mass spectrometer.**

Chemistry Now™ Sign in at www.cengage.com/login and go to the Chapter Contents menu to explore an interactive version of this figure accompanied by an exercise.

molecules of the sample are converted to positively charged particles (called *ions*). A beam of these ions is injected into a magnetic field, which causes the paths of the ions to be deflected. The extent of deflection depends on particle mass: The less massive ions are deflected more, and the more massive ions are deflected less. The ions, now separated by mass, are detected at the end of the chamber. Chemists using modern instruments (Figure 1.2) can measure isotopic masses to as many as nine significant figures.

Except for carbon-12, whose mass is defined to be exactly 12 u, isotopic masses do not have integer values. However, the isotopic masses are always very close to the mass numbers for the isotope. For example, the mass of an atom of boron-11 (^{11}B, 5 protons and 6 neutrons) is 11.0093 u, and the mass of an atom of iron-58 (^{58}Fe, 26 protons and 32 neutrons) is 57.9333 u.

■ **Isotopic Masses and the Mass Defect** Actual masses of atoms are always less than the sum of the masses of subatomic particles composing that atom. This is called the *mass defect,* and the reason for it is discussed in Chapter 23.

2.4 Atomic Weight

Because every sample of boron has some atoms with a mass of 10.0129 u and others with a mass of 11.0093 u, the average atomic mass must be somewhere between these values. The **atomic weight** of an element is the average mass of a representa-

TABLE 2.2 Isotope Abundance and Atomic Weight

Element	Symbol	Atomic Weight	Mass Number	Isotopic Mass	Natural Abundance (%)
Hydrogen	H	1.00794	1	1.0078	99.985
	D*		2	2.0141	0.015
	T†		3	3.0161	0
Boron	B	10.811	10	10.0129	19.91
			11	11.0093	80.09
Neon	Ne	20.1797	20	19.9924	90.48
			21	20.9938	0.27
			22	21.9914	9.25
Magnesium	Mg	24.3050	24	23.9850	78.99
			25	24.9858	10.00
			26	25.9826	11.01

*D = deuterium; †T = tritium, radioactive.

■ **Atomic Mass, Relative Atomic Mass, and Atomic Weight** The atomic mass is the mass of an atom at rest. The relative atomic mass, also known as the atomic weight or the average atomic weight, is the average of the atomic masses of all of the element's isotopes. The term "atomic weight" is slowly being phased out in favor of "relative atomic mass."

tive sample of atoms. For boron, for example, the atomic weight is 10.811. If isotope masses and abundances are known, the atomic mass of an element can be calculated using Equation 2.2.

$$\text{Atomic weight} = \left(\frac{\%\ \text{abundance isotope 1}}{100}\right)(\text{mass of isotope 1})$$
$$+ \left(\frac{\%\ \text{abundance isotope 2}}{100}\right)(\text{mass of isotope 2}) + \ldots \tag{2.2}$$

For boron with two isotopes (^{10}B, 19.91% abundant; ^{11}B, 80.09% abundant), we find

$$\text{Atomic weight} = \left(\frac{19.91}{100}\right) \times 10.0129 + \left(\frac{80.09}{100}\right) \times 11.0093 = 10.81$$

Equation 2.2 gives an average mass, weighted in terms of the abundance of each isotope for the element. As illustrated by the data in Table 2.2, *the atomic mass of an element is usually closer to the mass of the most abundant isotope or isotopes.*

The atomic weight of each stable element has been determined experimentally, and these numbers appear in the periodic table inside the front cover of this book. In the periodic table, each element's box contains the atomic number, the element symbol, and the atomic weight. For unstable (radioactive) elements, the atomic weight or mass number of the most stable isotope is given in parentheses.

Chemistry ☊ Now™

Sign in at **www.cengage.com/login** and go to Chapter 2 Contents to see Screen 2.13 for an exercise and a tutorial on **mass spectrometers and on calculating atomic mass.**

EXAMPLE 2.2 Calculating Atomic Weight from Isotope Abundance

Problem Bromine has two naturally occurring isotopes. One has a mass of 78.918338 and an abundance of 50.69%. The other isotope, of mass 80.916291, has an abundance of 49.31%. Calculate the atomic weight of bromine.

Strategy The atomic weight of any element is the weighted average of the masses of the isotopes in a representative sample. To calculate the atomic weight, multiply the mass of each isotope by its percent abundance divided by 100 (Equation 2.2).

Solution

Atomic weight of bromine = (50.69/100)(78.918338) + (49.31/100)(80.916291)
= 79.90

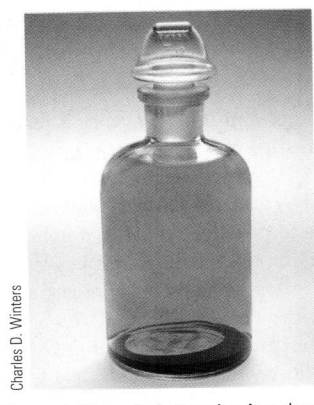

Elemental bromine. Bromine is a deep orange, volatile liquid at room temperature. It consists of Br_2 molecules in which two bromine atoms are chemically bonded together. There are two, stable, naturally-occurring isotopes of bromine atoms: ^{79}Br (50.69% abundant) and ^{81}Br (49.31% abundant).

Charles D. Winters

EXAMPLE 2.3 Calculating Isotopic Abundances

Problem Antimony, Sb, has two stable isotopes: ^{121}Sb, 120.904 u, and ^{123}Sb, 122.904 u. What are the relative abundances of these isotopes?

Strategy The atomic mass of antimony is 121.760 u (see the periodic table). Before we do the calculation we can infer that the lighter isotope (^{121}Sb) must be the more abundant because the atomic weight is closer to 121 than to 123. Next, to calculate the abundances we recognize there are two unknown but related quantities, and we can write the following expression (where the fractional abundance of an isotope is the percent abundance of the isotope divided by 100):

Atomic weight = 121.760

= (fractional abundance of ^{121}Sb)(120.904) + (fractional abundance of ^{123}Sb)(122.904)

or

121.760 = x(120.904) + y(122.904)

where x = fractional abundance of ^{121}Sb and y = fractional abundance of ^{123}Sb. Because we know that the sum of the fractional abundances of the isotopes must equal 1, $x + y = 1$, and we can solve the simultaneous equations for x and y.

Solution

Because y = fractional abundance of ^{123}Sb = $1 - x$, we can make a substitution for y.

121.760 = x(120.904) + (1 − x)(122.904)

Expanding this equation, we have

121.760 = 120.904x + 122.904 − 122.904x

Finally, solving for x, we find

121.760 − 122.904 = (120.904 − 122.904)x

x = 0.5720

The fractional abundance of ^{121}Sb is 0.5720, and its percent abundance is 57.20%. This means that the percent abundance of ^{123}Sb must be 42.80%. The result confirms our initial inference that the lighter isotope is the more abundant of the two.

EXERCISE 2.3 Calculating Atomic Weight

Verify that the atomic weight of chlorine is 35.45, given the following information:

^{35}Cl mass = 34.96885; percent abundance = 75.77%

^{37}Cl mass = 36.96590; percent abundance = 24.23%

Case Study

Catching Cheaters with Isotopes

The U.S. Anti-Doping Agency is responsible for testing for performance-enhancing drugs such as synthetic testosterone that has been used by athletes (page 1). But, if an athlete were to take this synthetic steroid, how can chemists tell the difference between that and the testosterone normally occurring in a male athlete's body?

Testosterone (T) and epitestosterone (E) are closely related steroids, and both are produced naturally. (The latter is an *isomer* of testosterone, a compound with an identical formula to testosterone but with a difference in the way the molecule fills space.) In most adult men the compounds are found in about equal amounts, although the natural T/E ratio can be as high as 4/1. To allow for elevated natural testosterone levels, the Anti-Doping Agency considers that a ratio of 6/1 is an indication an athlete must be using synthetic testosterone. This situation arose when the winner of the 2006 Tour de France bicycle race, Floyd Landis, was found to have a ratio of T/E = 11/1 based on a urine test after one stage of the race.

When the race was over, and the drug-testing results were announced, Landis strongly denied taking testosterone. He

© Robert Houser/Index Stock Imagery

argued that his body may have produced more testosterone than normal because of the rigors of the race. This prompted the doping-control laboratory for the Tour to seek additional evidence. They used a technique developed by the U.S. Anti-Doping Agency called "isotope ratio mass spectrometry," which measures the ratio of carbon isotopes, ^{12}C and ^{13}C, in compounds.

Carbon-13 is a naturally occurring isotope of carbon. When most plants grow using CO_2 from the atmosphere, about 1% of the C atoms incorporated in the plant are ^{13}C. The ^{13}C is ingested either directly by humans when eating plants or indirectly when eating meat

from grazing animals, and it is then incorporated into the carbon-containing molecules, including testosterone, that our bodies build.

Synthetic testosterone is made from wild yams and soy, plants that are so-called warm climate "C3 plants" that take up atmospheric CO_2 differently than temperate-zone "C4 plants." One important result of this difference is that C3 plants have a lower $^{13}C/^{12}C$ ratio than C4 plants. Because diets in most industrialized countries derive from a mixture of C3 and C4 plants, the natural testosterone in male athletes in most countries will have a different $^{13}C/^{12}C$ ratio than synthetic testosterone. A skilled scientist with a mass spectrometer (Figure 2.3), can relatively easily detect the difference. In the Tour de France case, the $^{13}C/^{12}C$ ratio added further evidence to the case that illegal steroid use had occurred.

Questions:

1. *How many neutrons are there in atoms of ^{13}C?*
2. *^{14}C is a radioactive isotope of carbon that occurs in trace amounts in all living materials. How many neutrons are in a ^{14}C atom?*
3. *Use your library or the World Wide Web to find the source of ^{14}C in living materials.*

Answers to these questions are in Appendix Q.

 Module 1

2.5 The Periodic Table

The periodic table of elements is one of the most useful tools in chemistry. Not only does it contain a wealth of information, but it can also be used to organize many of the ideas of chemistry. It is important to become familiar with its main features and terminology.

Developing the Periodic Table

■ **About the Periodic Table**
For more information on the periodic table, we recommend the following:
- The American Chemical Society has a description of every element on its website (http://pubs.acs.org/cen/80th/elements.html).
- J. Emsley: *Nature's Building Blocks—An A–Z Guide to the Elements*, New York, Oxford University Press, 2001.
- O. Sacks: *Uncle Tungsten—Memories of a Chemical Boyhood*, New York, Alfred A. Knopf, 2001.

Although the arrangement of elements in the periodic table is now understood on the basis of atomic structure (▶ Chapters 6 and 7), the table was originally developed from many experimental observations of the chemical and physical properties of elements and is the result of the ideas of a number of chemists in the 18th and 19th centuries.

In 1869, at the University of St. Petersburg in Russia, Dmitri Ivanovitch Mendeleev (1834–1907) was pondering the properties of the elements as he wrote a textbook on chemistry. On studying the chemical and physical properties of the elements, he realized that, if the elements were arranged in order of increasing atomic weight, elements with similar properties appeared in a regular pattern. That is, he saw a **periodicity** or periodic repetition of the properties of elements. Mendeleev organized the known elements into a table by lining them up in a horizontal row in

by Eric R. Scerri, UCLA

Dimitri Mendeleev was probably the greatest scientist produced by Russia. The youngest of 14 children, he was taken by his mother on a long journey, on foot, in order to enroll him into a university. However, several attempts initially proved futile because, as a Siberian, Mendeleev was barred from attending certain institutions. His mother did succeed in enrolling him in a teacher training college, thus giving Mendeleev a lasting interest in science education, which contributed to his eventual discovery of the periodic system that essentially simplified the subject of inorganic chemistry.

After completing a doctorate, Mendeleev headed to Germany for a postdoctoral fellowship and then returned to Russia, where he set about writing a book aimed at summarizing all of inorganic chemistry. It was while writing this book that he identified the organizing principle with which he is now invariably connected—the periodic system of the elements.

More correctly, though, the periodic system was developed by Mendeleev, as well as five other scientists, over a period of about 10 years, after the Italian chemist Cannizzaro had published a consistent set of atomic weights in 1860. It appears that Mendeleev was unaware of the work of several of his co-discoverers, however.

In essence, the periodic table groups together sets of elements with similar properties into vertical columns. The underlying idea is that if the elements are arranged in order of increasing atomic weights, there are approximate repetitions in their chemical properties after certain intervals. As a result of the existence of the periodic table, students and even professors of chemistry were no longer obliged to learn the properties of all the elements in a disorganized fashion. Instead, they could concentrate on the properties of representative members of the eight columns or groups in the early short-form periodic table, from which they could predict properties of other group members.

Mendeleev is justly regarded as the leading discoverer of the periodic table since he continued to champion the finding and drew out its consequences to a far greater extent than any of his contemporaries. First, he accommodated the 65 or so elements that were known at the time into a coherent scheme based on ascending order of atomic weight while also reflecting chemical and physical similarities. Next, he noticed gaps in his system, which he reasoned would eventually be filled by elements that had not yet been discovered. In addition, by judicious interpolation between the properties of known elements, Mendeleev predicted the

John Kotz

Statue of Dmitri Mendeleev and a periodic table mural. This statue and mural are at the Institute for Metrology in St. Petersburg, Russia.

nature of a number of completely new elements. Within a period of about 20 years, three of these elements—subsequently called gallium, scandium, and germanium—were isolated and found to have almost the exact properties that Mendeleev had predicted.

What is not well known is that about half of the elements that Mendeleev predicted were never found. But given the dramatic success of his early predictions, these later lapses have largely been forgotten.

Eric Scerri, The Periodic Table: Its Story and Its Significance, Oxford University Press, New York, 2007.

order of increasing atomic weight (page 50). Every time he came to an element with properties similar to one already in the row, he started a new row. For example, the elements Li, Be, B, C, N, O, and F were in a row. Sodium was the next element then known; because its properties closely resembled those of Li, Mendeleev started a new row. As more and more elements were added to the table, new rows were added, and elements with similar properties (such as Li, Na, and K) were found in the same vertical column.

An important feature of Mendeleev's table—and a mark of his genius—was that he left an empty space in a column when an element was not known but should exist and have properties similar to the element above it in his table. He deduced that these spaces would be filled by undiscovered elements. For example, he left a space between Si (silicon) and Sn (tin) in Group 4A for an element he called *eka-silicon*. Based on the progression of properties in this group, Mendeleev was able to predict the properties of this missing element. With the discovery of germanium (Ge) in 1886, Mendeleev's prediction was confirmed.

■ **Mendeleev and Atomic Numbers**
Mendeleev developed the periodic table based on atomic weights because the concept of atomic numbers was not known until after the development of the structure of the atom in the early 20th century.

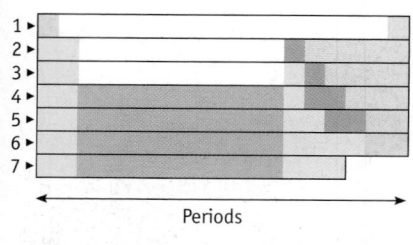

Periods

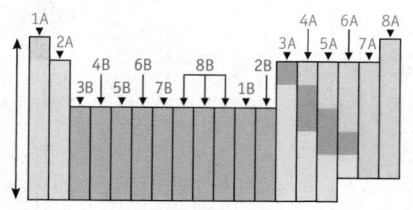

Groups or Families

Periods and groups in the periodic table. One way to designate periodic groups is to number them 1 through 18 from left to right. This method is generally used outside the United States. The system predominant in the United States labels main group elements as Groups 1A–8A and transition elements as Groups 1B–8B. This book uses the A/B system.

In Mendeleev's table, the elements were ordered by increasing mass. A glance at a modern table, however, shows that, if some elements (such as Ni and Co, Ar and K, and Te and I) were ordered by mass and not chemical and physical properties, they would be reversed in their order of appearance. Mendeleev recognized these discrepancies and simply assumed the atomic weights known at that time were inaccurate—not a bad assumption based on the analytical methods then in use. In fact, his order is correct, and what was wrong was his assumption that element properties were a function of their mass.

In 1913, H. G. J. Moseley (1887–1915), a young English scientist working with Ernest Rutherford (1871–1937), corrected Mendeleev's assumption. Moseley was doing experiments in which he bombarded many different metals with electrons in a cathode-ray tube (page 343) and examined the x-rays emitted in the process. In seeking some order in his data, he realized that the wavelength of the x-rays emitted by a given element was related in a precise manner to the atomic number of the element. Indeed, once the concept of an atomic number was recognized early in the 20th century, chemists realized that organizing the elements in a table by increasing atomic number corrected the inconsistencies in the Mendeleev table. The **law of chemical periodicity** is now stated as *the properties of the elements are periodic functions of atomic number.*

Features of the Periodic Table

The main organizational features of the periodic table are the following:

- Elements are arranged so those with similar chemical and physical properties lie in vertical columns called **groups** or **families**. The periodic table commonly used in the United States has groups numbered 1 through 8, with each number followed by a letter: A or B. The A groups are often called the **main group elements,** and the B groups are the **transition elements**.
- The horizontal rows of the table are called **periods**, and they are numbered beginning with 1 for the period containing only H and He. For example, sodium, Na, in Group 1A, is the first element in the third period. Mercury, Hg, in Group 2B, is in the sixth period (or sixth row).

The periodic table can be divided into several regions according to the properties of the elements. On the table inside the front cover of this book, elements that behave as *metals* are indicated in purple, those that are *nonmetals* are indicated in yellow, and elements called *metalloids* appear in green. Elements gradually become less metallic as one moves from left to right across a period, and the metalloids lie along the metal–nonmetal boundary. Some elements are shown in Figure 2.4.

You are probably familiar with many properties of **metals** from everyday experience (Figure 2.5a). Metals are solids (except for mercury), can conduct electricity, are usually ductile (can be drawn into wires) and malleable (can be rolled into sheets), and can form alloys (solutions of one or more metals in another metal). Iron (Fe) and aluminum (Al) are used in automobile parts because of their ductility, malleability, and low cost relative to other metals. Copper (Cu) is used in electric wiring because it conducts electricity better than most other metals.

The **nonmetals** lie to the right of a diagonal line that stretches from B to Te in the periodic table and have a wide variety of properties. Some are solids (carbon, sulfur, phosphorus, and iodine). Five elements are gases at room temperature (hydrogen, oxygen, nitrogen, fluorine, and chlorine). One nonmetal, bromine, is a liquid at room temperature (Figure 2.5b). With the exception of carbon in the form of graphite, nonmetals do not conduct electricity, which is one of the main features that distinguishes them from metals.

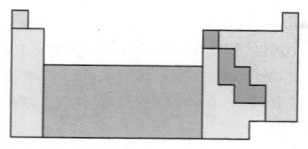

☐ Main Group Metals
■ Transition Metals
■ Metalloids
☐ Nonmetals

Active Figure 2.4 Some of the known 117 elements.

Chemistry ⚛ Now™ Sign in at www.cengage.com/login and go to the Chapter Contents menu to explore an interactive version of this figure accompanied by an exercise.

Group 1A
Lithium—Li (top)
Potassium—K (bottom)

Group 2A
Magnesium—Mg

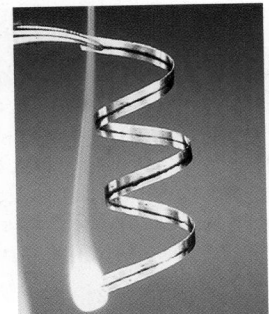

Transition Metals
Titanium—Ti, Vanadium—V, Chromium—Cr, Manganese—Mn, Iron—Fe, Cobalt—Co, Nickel—Ni, Copper—Cu

Group 2B
Zinc—Zn (top)
Mercury—Hg (bottom)

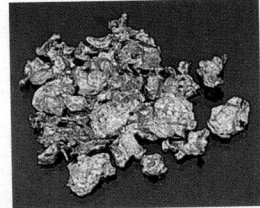

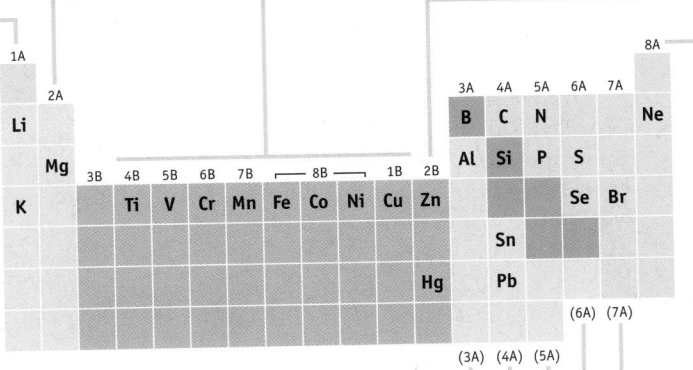

Group 8A, Noble Gases
Neon—Ne

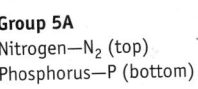

Photos: Charles D. Winters

Group 3A
Boron—B (top)
Aluminum—Al (bottom)

Group 4A
Carbon—C (top)
Lead—Pb (left)
Silicon—Si (right)
Tin—Sn (bottom)

Group 5A
Nitrogen—N_2 (top)
Phosphorus—P (bottom)

Group 6A
Sulfur—S (top)
Selenium—Se (bottom)

Group 7A
Bromine—Br

(a) Metals

Bromine, Br₂ Iodine, I₂

(b) Nonmetals

Forms of silicon

(c) Metalloids

FIGURE 2.5 Metals, nonmetals, and metalloids. (a) Molybdenum (Mo, wire), bismuth (Bi, center object), and copper (Cu) are metals. Metals can generally be drawn into wires, and they conduct electricity. (b) Only 15 or so elements can be classified as nonmetals. Here are orange liquid bromine and purple solid iodine. (c) Only six elements are generally classified as metalloids or semimetals. This photograph shows solid silicon in various forms, including a wafer that holds printed electronic circuits.

The elements next to the diagonal line from boron (B) to tellurium (Te) have properties that make them difficult to classify as metals or nonmetals. Chemists call them **metalloids** or, sometimes, **semimetals** (Figure 2.5c). You should know, however, that chemists often disagree about which elements fit into this category. We will define a metalloid as an element that has some of the physical characteristics of a metal but some of the chemical characteristics of a nonmetal; we include only B, Si, Ge, As, Sb, and Te in this category. This definition reflects the ambiguity in the behavior of these elements. Antimony (Sb), for example, conducts electricity as well as many elements that are true metals. Its chemistry, however, resembles that of the nonmetal phosphorus.

A Brief Overview of the Periodic Table and the Chemical Elements

The metals in the leftmost column, **Group 1A**, are known as the **alkali metals**. All are metals and are solids at room temperature. They are all very reactive. For example, they react with water to produce hydrogen and alkaline solutions (Figure 2.6). Because of their reactivity, these metals are only found in nature combined in compounds (such as NaCl) (Figure 1.4), never as the free element.

The second group in the periodic table, **Group 2A**, is also composed entirely of metals that occur naturally only in compounds. Except for beryllium (Be), these elements react with water to produce alkaline solutions, and most of their oxides (such as lime, CaO) form alkaline solutions; hence, they are known as the **alkaline earth metals**. Magnesium (Mg) and calcium (Ca) are the seventh and fifth most abundant elements in the earth's crust, respectively (Table 2.3). Calcium is one of the important elements in teeth and bones, and it occurs naturally in vast limestone deposits. Calcium carbonate ($CaCO_3$) is the chief constituent of limestone and of corals, sea shells, marble, and chalk. Radium (Ra), the heaviest alkaline earth element, is radioactive and is used to treat some cancers by radiation.

■ **Alkali and Alkaline** The word "alkali" comes from the Arabic language; ancient Arabian chemists discovered that ashes of certain plants, which they called al-qali, gave water solutions that felt slippery and burned the skin. These ashes contain compounds of Group 1A elements that produce alkaline (basic) solutions.

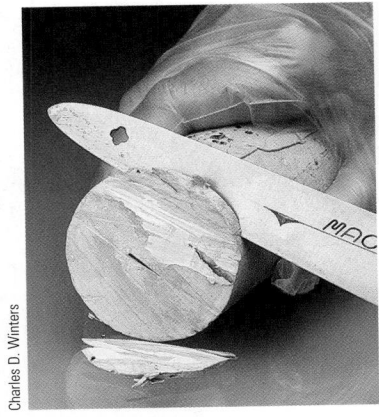

(a) Cutting sodium.

(b) Potassium reacts with water.

FIGURE 2.6 Alkali metals. (a) Cutting a bar of sodium with a knife is about like cutting a stick of cold butter. (b) When an alkali metal such as potassium is treated with water, a vigorous reaction occurs, giving an alkaline solution and hydrogen gas, which burns in air.

Charles D. Winters

TABLE 2.3 The 10 Most Abundant Elements in the Earth's Crust

Rank	Element	Abundance (ppm)*
1	Oxygen	474,000
2	Silicon	277,000
3	Aluminum	82,000
4	Iron	41,000
5	Calcium	41,000
6	Sodium	23,000
7	Magnesium	23,000
8	Potassium	21,000
9	Titanium	5,600
10	Hydrogen	1,520

*ppm = g per 1000 kg.

Group 3A contains one element of great importance, aluminum (see Figure 2.4). This element and three others (gallium, indium, and thallium) are metals, whereas boron (B) is a metalloid. Aluminum (Al) is the most abundant metal in the earth's crust at 8.2% by mass. It is exceeded in abundance only by the nonmetal oxygen and metalloid silicon. These three elements are found combined in clays and other common minerals. Boron occurs in the mineral borax, a compound used as a cleaning agent, antiseptic, and flux for metal work.

As a metalloid, boron has a different chemistry than the other elements of the group, all of which are metals. Nonetheless, all form compounds with analogous formulas such as BCl_3 and $AlCl_3$, and this similarity marks them as members of the same periodic group.

Thus far, all the elements we have described, except boron, have been metals. Beginning with **Group 4A**, however, the groups contain more and more nonmetals. In Group 4A, there are a nonmetal, carbon (C), two metalloids, silicon (Si) and germanium (Ge), and two metals, tin (Sn) and lead (Pb) (Figure 2.4). Because of the change from nonmetallic to metallic character, more variation occurs in the properties of the elements of this group than in most others. Nonetheless, there are similarities. For example, these elements form compounds with analogous formulas such as CO_2, SiO_2, GeO_2, and PbO_2.

Carbon is the basis for the great variety of chemical compounds that make up living things. It is found in Earth's atmosphere as CO_2, on the surface of the earth in carbonates like limestone and coral (calcium carbonate, $CaCO_3$), and in coal, petroleum, and natural gas—the fossil fuels.

One interesting aspect of the chemistry of the nonmetals is that a particular element can often exist in several different and distinct forms, called **allotropes**, each having its own properties. Carbon has a number of allotropes, the best known of which are graphite and diamond. Graphite consists of flat sheets in which each carbon atom is connected to three others (Figure 2.7a). Because the sheets of carbon atoms cling only weakly to one another, one layer can slip easily over another. This explains why graphite is soft, is a good lubricant, and is used in pencil lead. (Pencil "lead" is not the element lead (Pb) but a composite of clay and graphite that leaves a trail of graphite on the page as you write.)

Charles D. Winters

Liquid gallium. Bromine and mercury are the only elements that are liquids under ambient conditions. Gallium (29.8 °C) and cesium (28.4 °C) melt slightly above room temperature. Here gallium melts when held in the hand.

(a) Graphite   **(b)** Diamond   **(c)** Buckyballs

FIGURE 2.7 The allotropes of carbon. (a) Graphite consists of layers of carbon atoms. Each carbon atom is linked to three others to form a sheet of six-member, hexagonal rings. (b) In diamond, the carbon atoms are also arranged in six-member rings, but the rings are not planar because each C atom is connected tetrahedrally by four other C atoms. (c) Buckyballs. A member of the family called buckminsterfullerenes, C_{60} is an allotrope of carbon. Sixty carbon atoms are arranged in a spherical cage that resembles a hollow soccer ball. Notice that each six-member ring shares an edge with three other six-member rings and three five-member rings. Chemists call this molecule a "buckyball." C_{60} is a black powder; it is shown here in the tip of a pointed glass tube.

■ **Special Group Names** Some groups have common and widely used names. (See Figure 2.4)
Group 1A: Alkali metals
Group 2A: Alkaline earth metals
Group 7A: Halogens
Group 8A: Noble gases

In diamond, each carbon atom is connected to four others at the corners of a tetrahedron, and this extends throughout the solid (see Figure 2.7b). This structure causes diamonds to be extremely hard, denser than graphite ($d = 3.51$ g/cm³ for diamond and $d = 2.22$ g/cm³ for graphite), and chemically less reactive. Because diamonds are not only hard but are excellent conductors of heat, they are used on the tips of metal- and rock-cutting tools.

In the late 1980s, another form of carbon was identified as a component of black soot, the stuff that collects when carbon-containing materials are burned in a deficiency of oxygen. This substance is made up of molecules with 60 carbon atoms arranged as a spherical "cage" (Figure 2.7c). You may recognize that the surface is made up of five- and six-member rings and resembles a hollow soccer ball. The shape also reminded its discoverers of an architectural dome conceived several decades ago by the American philosopher and engineer, R. Buckminster Fuller. This led to the official name of the allotrope, buckminsterfullerene, although chemists often simply call these C_{60} molecules "buckyballs."

Oxides of silicon are the basis of many minerals such as clay, quartz, and beautiful gemstones like amethyst (Figure 2.8). Tin and lead have been known for centuries because they are easily obtained from their ores. Tin alloyed with copper makes bronze, which was used in ancient times in utensils and weapons. Lead has been used in water pipes and paint, even though the element is toxic to humans.

Nitrogen in **Group 5A** occurs naturally in the form of the diatomic molecule N_2 (Figure 2.9) and makes up about three fourths of Earth's atmosphere. It is also incorporated in biochemically important substances such as chlorophyll, proteins, and DNA. Therefore, scientists have long sought ways to make compounds from atmospheric nitrogen, a process referred to as "nitrogen fixation." Nature accomplishes this easily in some prokaryotic organisms, but severe conditions (high temperatures, for example) must be used in the laboratory and in industry to cause N_2 to react with other elements (such as H_2 to make ammonia, NH_3, which is widely used as a fertilizer).

FIGURE 2.8 Compounds containing silicon. Ordinary clay, sand, and many gemstones are based on compounds of silicon and oxygen. Here, clear, colorless quartz and dark purple amethyst lie in a bed of sand. All are silicon dioxide, SiO_2. The different colors are due to impurities.

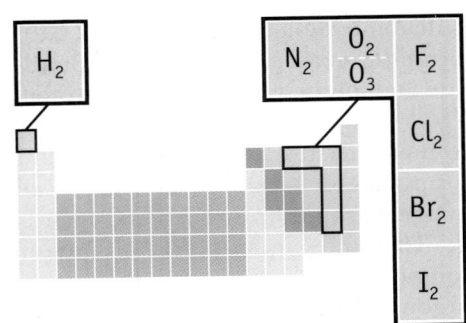

FIGURE 2.9 Elements that exist as diatomic or triatomic molecules. Seven of the elements in the periodic table exist as diatomic, or two-atom, molecules. Oxygen has an additional allotrope, ozone, with three O atoms in each molecule. See also ChemistryNow Screen 2.16, Elements that Exist as Molecules.

■ **Placing H in the Periodic Table** Where to place H? Tables often show it in Group 1A even though it is clearly not an alkali metal. However, in its reactions it forms a 1+ ion just like the alkali metals. For this reason, H is often placed in Group 1A.

Phosphorus is also essential to life. It is an important constituent in bones, teeth, and DNA. The element glows in the dark if it is exposed to air (owing to its reaction with O_2), and its name, based on Greek words meaning "light-bearing," reflects this. This element also has several allotropes, the most important being white (Figure 2.4) and red phosphorus. Both forms of phosphorus are used commercially. White phosphorus ignites spontaneously in air and so is normally stored under water. When it does react with air, it forms P_4O_{10}, which can react with water to form phosphoric acid (H_3PO_4), a compound used in food products such as soft drinks. Red phosphorus is used in the striking strips on match books. When a match is struck, potassium chlorate in the match head mixes with some red phosphorus on the striking strip, and the friction is enough to ignite this mixture.

As with Group 4A, we again see nonmetals (N and P), metalloids (As and Sb), and a metal (Bi, Figure 2.5a) in Group 5A. In spite of these variations, they also form analogous compounds such as the oxides N_2O_5, P_2O_5 and As_2O_5.

Oxygen, which constitutes about 20% of Earth's atmosphere and which combines readily with most other elements, is at the top of **Group 6A**. Most of the energy that powers life on Earth is derived from reactions in which oxygen combines with other substances.

Sulfur has been known in elemental form since ancient times as brimstone or "burning stone" (Figure 2.10). Sulfur, selenium, and tellurium are often referred to collectively as **chalcogens** (from the Greek word, *khalkos*, for copper) because most copper ores contain these elements. Their compounds can be foul smelling and poisonous; nevertheless, sulfur and selenium are essential components of the human diet. By far the most important compound of sulfur is sulfuric acid (H_2SO_4), which is manufactured in larger amounts than any other compound.

As in Group 5A, the second- and third-period elements of Group 6A have different structures. Like nitrogen, oxygen is also a diatomic molecule (see Figure 2.9). Unlike nitrogen, however, oxygen has an allotrope, the triatomic molecule ozone, O_3. Sulfur, which can be found in nature as a yellow solid, has many allotropes. The most common allotrope consists of eight-member, crown-shaped rings of sulfur atoms (see Figure 2.10).

Polonium, a radioactive element in Group 6A, was isolated in 1898 by Marie and Pierre Curie, who separated it from tons of a uranium-containing ore and named it for Madame Curie's native country, Poland.

In Group 6A, we once again observe a variation of properties. Oxygen, sulfur, and selenium are nonmetals; tellurium is a metalloid; and polonium is a metal. Nonetheless, there is a family resemblance in their chemistries. All form oxygen-containing compounds such as SO_2, SeO_2, and TeO_2 and sodium-containing compounds (Na_2O, Na_2S, Na_2Se, and Na_2Te).

At the far right of the periodic table are two groups composed entirely of nonmetals. The **Group 7A** elements—fluorine, chlorine, bromine, iodine, and radioac-

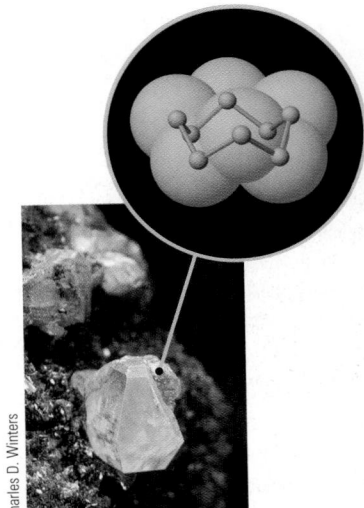

Charles D. Winters

FIGURE 2.10 Sulfur. The most common allotrope of sulfur consists of S atoms arranged in eight-member, crown-shaped rings.

tive astatine—are nonmetals, and all exist as diatomic molecules (see Figure 2.9). At room temperature, fluorine (F_2) and chlorine (Cl_2) are gases. Bromine (Br_2) is a liquid, and iodine (I_2) is a solid, but bromine and iodine vapor are clearly visible over the liquid or solid (see Figure 2.5b).

The Group 7A elements are among the most reactive of all elements, and all combine violently with alkali metals to form salts such as table salt, NaCl (see Figure 1.4). The name for this group, the **halogens**, comes from the Greek words *hals*, meaning "salt," and *genes*, for "forming." The halogens also react with other metals and with most nonmetals to form compounds.

The **Group 8A** elements—helium, neon, argon, krypton, xenon, and radioactive radon—are the least reactive elements (Figure 2.11). All are gases, and none is abundant on Earth or in Earth's atmosphere. Because of this, they were not discovered until the end of the 19th century. Helium, the second most abundant element in the universe after hydrogen, was detected in the sun in 1868 by analysis of the solar spectrum. (The name of the element comes from the Greek word for the sun, *helios*.) It was not found on Earth until 1895, however. Until 1962, when a compound of xenon was first prepared, it was believed that none of these elements would combine chemically with any other element. The name **noble gases** for this group, a term meant to denote their general lack of reactivity, derives from this fact. For the same reason, they are sometimes called the *inert gases* or, because of their low abundance, the *rare gases*.

Stretching between Groups 2A and 3A is a series of elements called the **transition elements.** These fill the B-groups (1B through 8B) in the fourth through the seventh periods in the center of the periodic table. All are metals (see Figure 2.4), and 13 of them are in the top 30 elements in terms of abundance in the earth's crust. Some, like iron (Fe), are abundant in nature (Table 2.3). Most occur naturally in combination with other elements, but a few—copper (Cu), silver (Ag), gold (Au), and platinum (Pt)—are much less reactive and so can be found in nature as pure elements.

Virtually all of the transition elements have commercial uses. They are used as structural materials (iron, titanium, chromium, copper); in paints (titanium, chromium); in the catalytic converters in automobile exhaust systems (platinum and rhodium); in coins (copper, nickel, zinc); and in batteries (manganese, nickel, cadmium, mercury).

A number of the transition elements play important biological roles. For example, iron, a relatively abundant element (see Table 2.3), is the central element in the chemistry of hemoglobin, the oxygen-carrying component of blood.

FIGURE 2.11 The noble gases. This kit is sold for detecting the presence of radioactive radon in the home. Neon gas is used in advertising signs, and xenon-containing headlights are increasingly popular on automobiles.

Charles D. Winters

Two rows at the bottom of the table accommodate the **lanthanides** [the series of elements between the elements lanthanum ($Z = 57$) and hafnium ($Z = 72$)] and the **actinides** [the series of elements between actinium ($Z = 89$) and rutherfordium ($Z = 104$)]. Some lanthanide compounds are used in color television picture tubes; uranium ($Z = 92$) is the fuel for atomic power plants, and americium ($Z = 95$) is used in smoke detectors.

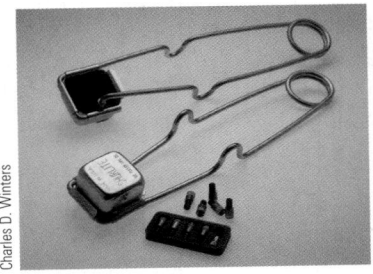

Lanthanides. If you use a Bunsen burner in the lab, you may light it with a "flint" lighter. The flints are composed of iron and "mischmetal," a mixture of lanthanide elements, chiefly Ce, La, Pr, and Nd with traces of other lanthanides. (The word "mischmetal" comes from the German for "mixed metals.") It is produced by the electrolysis of a mixture of lanthanide oxides.

Chemistry ⊙ Now™

Sign in at **www.cengage.com/login** and go to Chapter 2 Contents to see:
- Screen 2.14 for an exercise on **periodic table organization**
- Screen 2.15 for an exercise on **chemical periodicity**

EXERCISE 2.4 The Periodic Table

How many elements are in the third period of the periodic table? Give the name and symbol of each. Tell whether each element in the period is a metal, metalloid, or nonmetal.

2.6 Molecules, Compounds, and Formulas

A molecule is the smallest identifiable unit into which a pure substance like sugar or water can be divided and still retain the composition and chemical properties of the substance. Such substances are composed of identical molecules consisting of atoms of two or more elements bound firmly together. For example, atoms of the element aluminum, Al, combine with molecules of the element bromine, Br_2, to produce the compound aluminum bromide, Al_2Br_6 (Figure 2.12).

$$2\ Al(s) + 3\ Br_2(\ell) \rightarrow Al_2Br_6(s)$$
aluminum + bromine → aluminum bromide

(a)   (b)   (c)

Active Figure 2.12 **Reaction of the elements aluminum and bromine.** (a) Solid aluminum and (in the beaker) liquid bromine. (b) When the aluminum is added to the bromine, a vigorous chemical reaction produces white, solid aluminum bromide, Al_2Br_6 (c).

Chemistry ⊙ Now™ Sign in at **www.cengage.com/login** and go to the Chapter Contents menu to explore an interactive version of this figure accompanied by an exercise.

To describe this chemical change (or chemical reaction) on paper, the composition of each element and compound is represented by a symbol or formula. Here, one molecule of Al_2Br_6 is composed of two Al atoms and six Br atoms.

How do compounds differ from elements? When a compound is produced from its elements, the characteristics of the constituent elements are lost. Solid, metallic aluminum and red-orange liquid bromine, for example, react to form Al_2Br_6, a white solid.

Formulas

For molecules more complicated than water, there is often more than one way to write the formula. For example, the formula of ethanol (also called ethyl alcohol) can be represented as C_2H_6O (Figure 2.13). This **molecular formula** describes the composition of ethanol molecules—two carbon atoms, six hydrogen atoms, and one atom of oxygen occur per molecule—but it gives us no structural information. Structural information—how the atoms are connected and how the molecule fills space—is important, however, because it helps us understand how a molecule can interact with other molecules, which is the essence of chemistry.

To provide some structural information, it is useful to write a **condensed formula**, which indicates how certain atoms are grouped together. For example, the condensed formula of ethanol, CH_3CH_2OH (see Figure 2.13), informs us that the molecule consists of three "groups": a CH_3 group, a CH_2 group, and an OH group. Writing the formula as CH_3CH_2OH also shows that the compound is not dimethyl ether, CH_3OCH_3, a compound with the same molecular formula but with a different structure and distinctly different properties.

That ethanol and dimethyl ether are different molecules is further apparent from their **structural formulas** (Figure 2.13). This type of formula gives us an even higher level of structural detail, showing how all of the atoms are attached within a molecule. The lines between atoms represent the chemical bonds that hold atoms together in this molecule (▶ Chapter 8).

■ **Writing Formulas** When writing molecular formulas of organic compounds (compounds with C, H, and other elements), the convention is to write C first, then H, and finally other elements in alphabetical order. For example, acrylonitrile, a compound used to make consumer plastics, has the condensed formula CH_2CHCN. Its molecular formula is C_3H_3N.

■ **Ethanol and Dimethyl Ether Are Isomers** Compounds having the same molecular formula but different structures are called isomers. (See Chapter 10, and sign in to ChemistryNow and see Screen 2.17, Representing Compounds.)

Chemistry ⚛ Now™

Sign in at **www.cengage.com/login** and go to Chapter 2 Contents to see Screen 2.17 for an exercise and tutorial on **representations of molecules**.

NAME	MOLECULAR FORMULA	CONDENSED FORMULA	STRUCTURAL FORMULA	MOLECULAR MODEL
Ethanol	C_2H_6O	CH_3CH_2OH	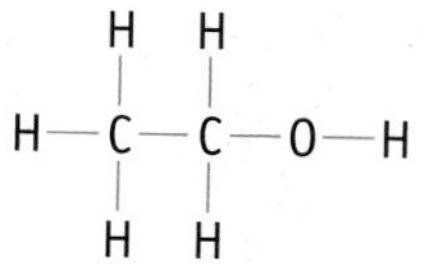	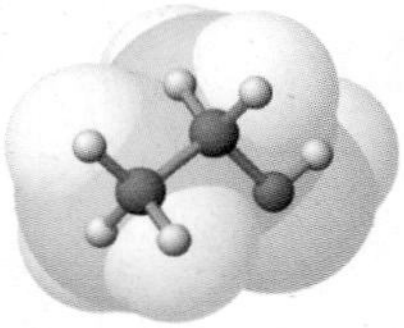
Dimethyl ether	C_2H_6O	CH_3OCH_3	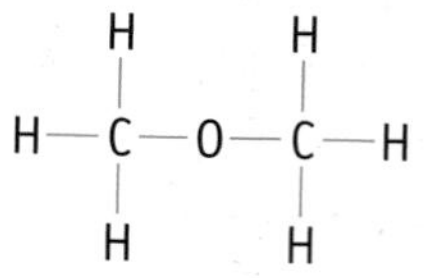	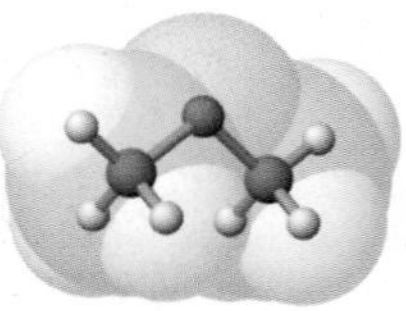

FIGURE 2.13 Four approaches to showing molecular formulas. Here, the two molecules have the same molecular formula. Condensed or structural formulas, and a molecular model, show that these molecules are different.

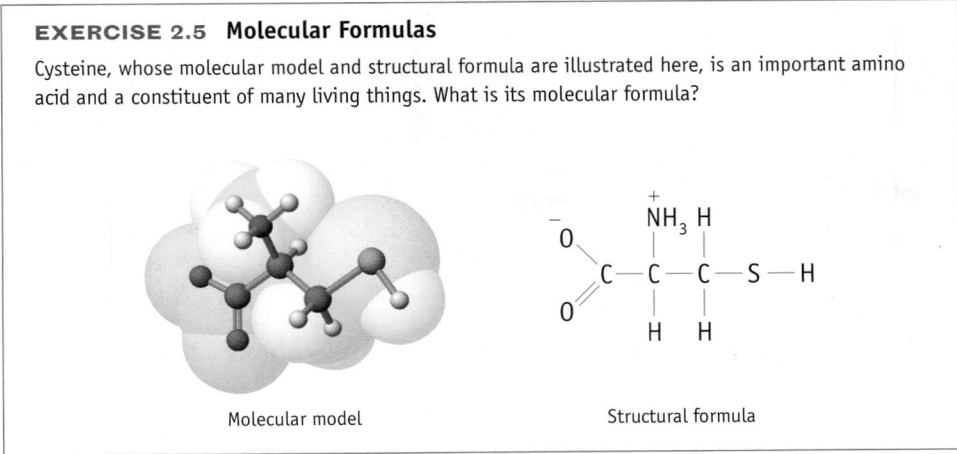
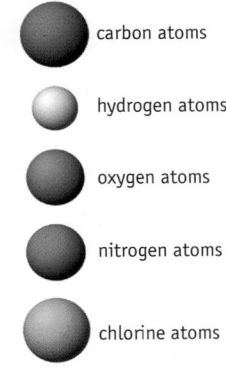

■ **Standard Colors for Atoms in Molecular Models** The colors listed here are used for molecular models in this book and are generally used by chemists. Note that Cl and S atoms have the same color, but it is usually apparent what atom is being designated.

carbon atoms

hydrogen atoms

oxygen atoms

nitrogen atoms

chlorine atoms

Molecular Models

Molecular structures are often beautiful in the same sense that art is beautiful, and there is something intrinsically beautiful about the pattern created by water molecules assembled in ice (Figure 2.14).

More important, however, is the fact that the physical and chemical properties of a molecular compound are often closely related to its structure. For example, two well-known features of ice are related to its structure. The first is the shape of ice crystals: The sixfold symmetry of macroscopic ice crystals also appears at the particulate level in the form of six-sided rings of hydrogen and oxygen atoms. The second is water's unique property of being less dense when solid than it is when liquid. The lower density of ice, which has enormous consequences for Earth's climate, results from the fact that molecules of water are not packed together tightly.

Because molecules are three-dimensional, it is often difficult to represent their shapes on paper. Certain conventions have been developed, however, that help represent three-dimensional structures on two-dimensional surfaces. Simple perspective drawings are often used (Figure 2.15).

FIGURE 2.14 Ice. Snowflakes are six-sided structures, reflecting the underlying structure of ice. Ice consists of six-sided rings formed by water molecules, in which each side of a ring consists of two O atoms and an H atom.

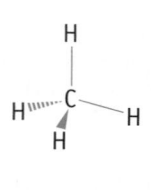
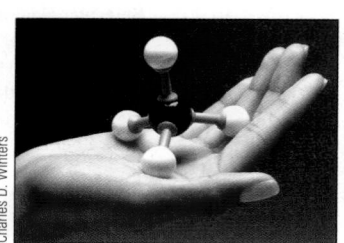
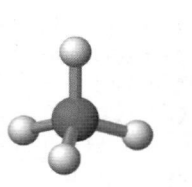
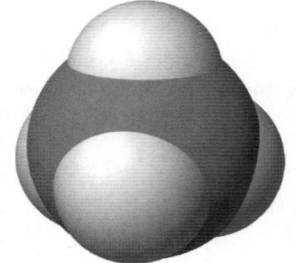
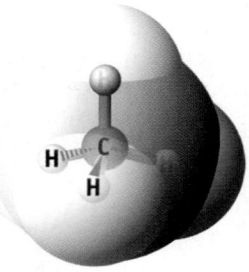

| Simple perspective drawing | Plastic model | Ball-and-stick model | Space-filling model | All visualizing techniques represent the same molecule. |

Active Figure 2.15 Ways of depicting a molecule, here the methane (CH_4) molecule.

Chemistry ☼ Now™ Sign in at www.cengage.com/login and go to the Chapter Contents menu to explore an interactive version of this figure accompanied by an exercise.

Several kinds of molecular models exist. In the **ball-and-stick model**, spheres, usually in different colors, represent the atoms, and sticks represent the bonds holding them together. These models make it easy to see how atoms are attached to one another. Molecules can also be represented using **space-filling models**. These models are more realistic because they offer a better representation of relative sizes of atoms and their proximity to each other when in a molecule. A disadvantage of pictures of space-filling models is that atoms can often be hidden from view.

 **Module 2**
Module 3

2.7 Ionic Compounds: Formulas, Names, and Properties

The compounds you have encountered so far in this chapter are **molecular compounds**—that is, compounds that consist of discrete molecules at the particulate level. **Ionic compounds** constitute another major class of compounds. They consist of **ions**, atoms or groups of atoms that bear a positive or negative electric charge. Many familiar compounds are composed of ions (Figure 2.16). Table salt, or sodium chloride (NaCl), and lime (CaO) are just two. To recognize ionic compounds, and to be able to write formulas for these compounds, it is important to know the formulas and charges of common ions. You also need to know the names of ions and be able to name the compounds they form.

FIGURE 2.16 Some common ionic compounds.

Common Name	Name	Formula	Ions Involved
Calcite	Calcium carbonate	$CaCO_3$	Ca^{2+}, CO_3^{2-}
Fluorite	Calcium fluoride	CaF_2	Ca^{2+}, F^-
Gypsum	Calcium sulfate dihydrate	$CaSO_4 \cdot 2\,H_2O$	Ca^{2+}, SO_4^{2-}
Hematite	Iron(III) oxide	Fe_2O_3	Fe^{3+}, O^{2-}
Orpiment	Arsenic sulfide	As_2S_3	As^{3+}, S^{2-}

Hematite, Fe_2O_3
Calcite, $CaCO_3$
Gypsum, $CaSO_4 \cdot 2\,H_2O$
Fluorite, CaF_2
Orpiment, As_2S_3

Ions

Atoms of many elements can gain or lose electrons in the course of a chemical reaction. To be able to predict the outcome of chemical reactions (▶ Sections 3.1–3.9), you need to know whether an element will likely gain or lose electrons and, if so, how many.

Cations

If an atom loses an electron (which is transferred to an atom of another element in the course of a reaction), the atom now has one fewer negative electrons than it has positive protons in the nucleus. The result is a positively charged ion called a **cation** (Figure 2.17). (The name is pronounced "cat'-ion.") Because it has an excess of one positive charge, we write the cation's symbol as, for example, Li^+:

$$Li \text{ atom} \longrightarrow e + Li^+ \text{ cation}$$

$$\text{(3 protons and 3 electrons)} \qquad \text{(3 protons and 2 electrons)}$$

Anions

Conversely, if an atom gains one or more electrons, there is now a greater number of negatively charged electrons than protons. The result is an **anion** (Figure 2.17). (The name is pronounced "ann'-ion.")

$$O \text{ atom} + 2 e^- \longrightarrow O^{2-} \text{ anion}$$

$$\text{(8 protons and 8 electrons)} \qquad \text{(8 protons and 10 electrons)}$$

Here, the O atom has gained two electrons, so we write the anion's symbol as O^{2-}.

How do you know whether an atom is likely to form a cation or an anion? It depends on whether the element is a metal or a nonmetal.

- Metals generally lose electrons in the course of their reactions to form cations.
- Nonmetals frequently gain one or more electrons to form anions in the course of their reactions.

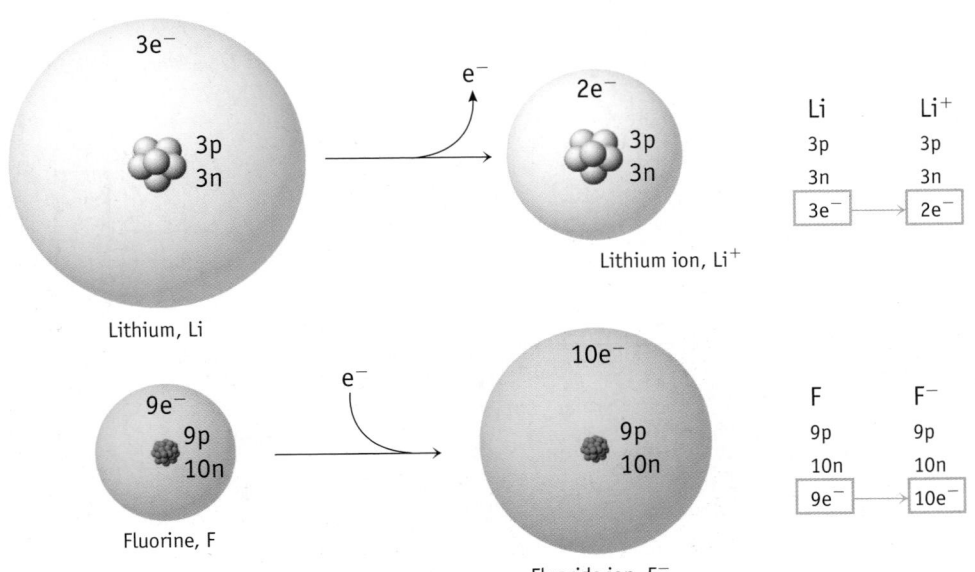

Lithium, Li
Lithium ion, Li^+

Fluorine, F
Fluoride ion, F^-

	Li	Li^+
	3p	3p
	3n	3n
	$3e^-$	$2e^-$

	F	F^-
	9p	9p
	10n	10n
	$9e^-$	$10e^-$

Active Figure 2.17 Ions. A lithium-6 atom is electrically neutral because the number of positive charges (three protons) and negative charges (three electrons) are the same. When it loses one electron, it has one more positive charge than negative charge, so it has a net charge of 1+. We symbolize the resulting lithium cation as Li^+. A fluorine atom is also electrically neutral, having nine protons and nine electrons. A fluorine atom can acquire an electron to produce an F^- anion. This anion has one more electron than it has protons, so it has a net charge of 1−.

Chemistry ⚗ Now™ Sign in at **www.cengage.com/login** and go to the Chapter Contents menu to explore an interactive version of this figure accompanied by an exercise.

Monatomic Ions

Monatomic ions are single atoms that have lost or gained electrons. As indicated in Figure 2.18, metals typically lose electrons to form monatomic cations, and nonmetals typically gain electrons to form monatomic anions.

How can you predict the number of electrons gained or lost? Like lithium in Figure 2.17, *metals of Groups 1A–3A form positive ions having a charge equal to the group number of the metal.*

■ **Writing Ion Formulas** When writing the formula of an ion, the charge on the ion must be included.

Group	Metal Atom	Electron Change		Resulting Metal Cation
1A	Na (11 protons, 11 electrons)	-1	$\rightarrow$	Na^+ (11 protons, 10 electrons)
2A	Ca (20 protons, 20 electrons)	-2	$\rightarrow$	Ca^{2+} (20 protons, 18 electrons)
3A	Al (13 protons, 13 electrons)	-3	$\rightarrow$	Al^{3+} (13 protons, 10 electrons)

Transition metals (B-group elements) also form cations. Unlike the A-group metals, however, no easily predictable pattern of behavior occurs for transition metal cations. In addition, transition metals often form several different ions. An iron-containing compound, for example, may contain either Fe^{2+} or Fe^{3+} ions. Indeed, 2+ and 3+ ions are typical of many transition metals (see Figure 2.18).

Group	Metal Atom	Electron Change		Resulting Metal Cation
7B	Mn (25 protons, 25 electrons)	-2	$\rightarrow$	Mn^{2+} (25 protons, 23 electrons)
8B	Fe (26 protons, 26 electrons)	-2	$\rightarrow$	Fe^{2+} (26 protons, 24 electrons)
8B	Fe (26 protons, 26 electrons)	-3	$\rightarrow$	Fe^{3+} (26 protons, 23 electrons)

Nonmetals often form ions having a negative charge equal to the group number of the element minus 8. For example, nitrogen is in Group 5A, so it forms an ion having a 3− charge because a nitrogen atom can gain three electrons.

Group	Nonmetal Atom	Electron Change		Resulting Nonmetal Anion
5A	N (7 protons, 7 electrons)	$+3$	$\rightarrow$	N^{3-} (7 protons, 10 electrons) Charge = 5 − 8
6A	S (16 protons, 16 electrons)	$+2$	$\rightarrow$	S^{2-} (16 protons, 18 electrons) Charge = 6 − 8
7A	Br (35 protons, 35 electrons)	$+1$	$\rightarrow$	Br^- (35 protons, 36 electrons) Charge = 7 − 8

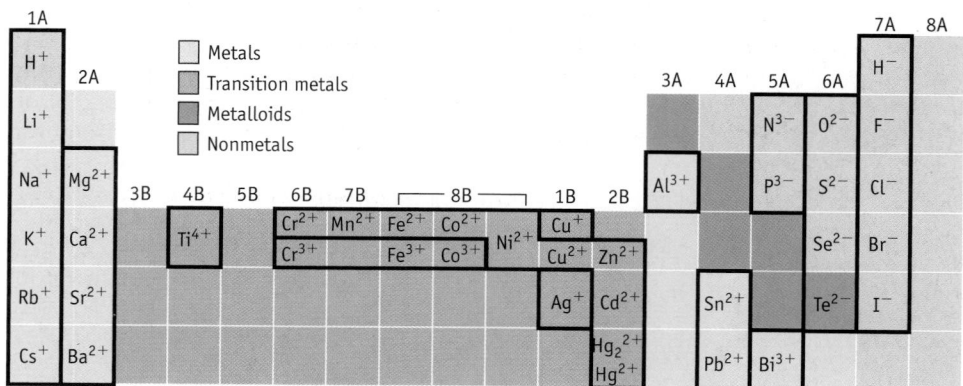

FIGURE 2.18 Charges on some common monatomic cations and anions. Metals usually form cations, and nonmetals usually form anions. (The boxed areas show ions of identical charge.)

Notice that hydrogen appears at two locations in Figure 2.18. The H atom can either lose or gain electrons, depending on the other atoms it encounters.

Electron lost: H (1 proton, 1 electron) $\rightarrow$ H$^+$ (1 proton, 0 electrons) + e$^-$
Electron gained: H (1 proton, 1 electron) + e$^-$ $\rightarrow$ H$^-$ (1 proton, 2 electrons)

Finally, the noble gases *very* rarely form monatomic cations or anions in chemical reactions.

Ion Charges and the Periodic Table

The metals of Groups 1A, 2A, and 3A form ions having 1+, 2+, and 3+ charges (Figure 2.18); that is, their atoms lose one, two, or three electrons, respectively. *For Group 1A and 2A metals and aluminum, the number of electrons remaining on the cation is the same as the number of electrons in an atom of the noble gas that precedes it in the periodic table.* For example, Mg^{2+} has 10 electrons, the same number as in an atom of the noble gas neon (atomic number 10).

An atom of a nonmetal near the right side of the periodic table would have to lose a great many electrons to achieve the same number as a noble gas atom of lower atomic number. (For instance, Cl, whose atomic number is 17, would have to lose seven electrons to have the same number of electrons as Ne.) If a nonmetal atom were to gain just a few electrons, however, it would have the same number as a noble gas atom of higher atomic number. For example, an oxygen atom has eight electrons. By gaining two electrons per atom, it forms O^{2-}, which has ten electrons, the same number as neon. *Anions having the same number of electrons as the noble gas atom succeeding it in the periodic table are commonly observed in chemical compounds.*

Cation charges and the periodic table

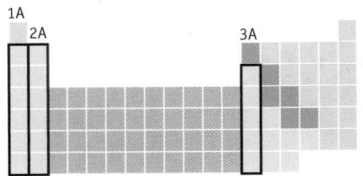

Group 1A, 2A, 3A metals form
M^{n+} cations where n = group number.

Chemistry ⚛ Now™

Sign in at **www.cengage.com/login** and go to Chapter 2 Contents to see Screen 2.18 for an exercise and tutorial on **ion charge.**

EXERCISE 2.6 Predicting Ion Charges

Predict formulas for monatomic ions formed from **(a)** K, **(b)** Se, **(c)** Ba, and **(d)** Cs. In each case, indicate the number of electrons gained or lost by an atom of the element in forming the anion or cation, respectively. For each ion, indicate the noble gas atom having the same total number of electrons.

Polyatomic Ions

Polyatomic ions are made up of two or more atoms, and the collection has an electric charge (Figure 2.19 and Table 2.4). For example, carbonate ion, CO$_3$$^{2-}$, a common polyatomic anion, consists of one C atom and three O atoms. The ion has two units of negative charge because there are two more electrons (a total of 32) in the ion than there are protons (a total of 30) in the nuclei of one C atom and three O atoms.

The ammonium ion, NH$_4$$^+$, is a common polyatomic cation. In this case, four H atoms surround an N atom, and the ion has a 1+ electric charge. This ion has 10 electrons, but there are 11 positively charged protons in the nuclei of the N and H atoms (seven and one each, respectively).

Chemistry ⚛ Now™

Sign in at **www.cengage.com/login** and go to Chapter 2 Contents to see Screen 2.19 for a tutorial on **polyatomic ions.**

CO_3^{2-}

Calcite, $CaCO_3$
Calcium carbonate

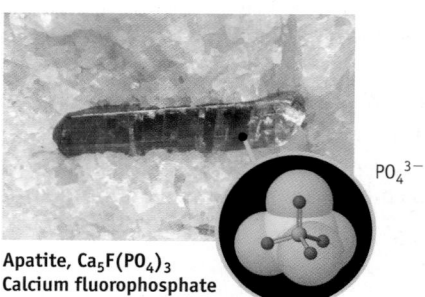

PO_4^{3-}

Apatite, $Ca_5F(PO_4)_3$
Calcium fluorophosphate

SO_4^{2-}

Celestite, $SrSO_4$
Strontium sulfate

Active Figure 2.19 Common ionic compounds based on polyatomic ions.

Chemistry ☉ Now™ Sign in at www.cengage.com/login and go to the Chapter Contents menu to explore an interactive version of this figure accompanied by an exercise.

Formulas of Ionic Compounds

Compounds are electrically neutral; that is, they have no net electric charge. Thus, in an ionic compound, the numbers of positive and negative ions must be such that the positive and negative charges balance. In sodium chloride, the sodium ion has a 1+ charge (Na^+), and the chloride ion has a 1− charge (Cl^-). These ions must be present in a 1 : 1 ratio, and the formula is NaCl.

TABLE 2.4   Formulas and Names of Some Common Polyatomic Ions

Formula	Name	Formula	Name
CATION: Positive Ion			
NH_4^+	ammonium ion		
ANIONS: Negative Ions			
Based on a Group 4A element		**Based on a Group 7A element**	
CN^-	cyanide ion	ClO^-	hypochlorite ion
$CH_3CO_2^-$	acetate ion	ClO_2^-	chlorite ion
CO_3^{2-}	carbonate ion	ClO_3^-	chlorate ion
HCO_3^-	hydrogen carbonate ion (or bicarbonate ion)	ClO_4^-	perchlorate ion
Based on a Group 5A element		**Based on a transition metal**	
NO_2^-	nitrite ion	CrO_4^{2-}	chromate ion
NO_3^-	nitrate ion	$Cr_2O_7^{2-}$	dichromate ion
PO_4^{3-}	phosphate ion	MnO_4^-	permanganate ion
HPO_4^{2-}	hydrogen phosphate ion		
$H_2PO_4^-$	dihydrogen phosphate ion		
Based on a Group 6A element			
OH^-	hydroxide ion		
SO_3^{2-}	sulfite ion		
SO_4^{2-}	sulfate ion		
HSO_4^-	hydrogen sulfate ion (or bisulfate ion)		

The gemstone ruby is largely the compound formed from aluminum ions (Al^{3+}) and oxide ions (O^{2-}) (but the color comes from a trace of Cr^{3+} ions.) Here, the ions have positive and negative charges that are of different absolute value. To have a compound with the same number of positive and negative charges, two Al^{3+} ions [total charge = $2 \times (3+) = 6+$] must combine with three O^{2-} ions [total charge = $3 \times (2-) = 6-$] to give a formula of Al_2O_3.

Calcium is a Group 2A metal, and it forms a cation having a 2+ charge. It can combine with a variety of anions to form ionic compounds such as those in the following table:

Compound	Ion Combination	Overall Charge on Compound
$CaCl_2$	$Ca^{2+} + 2\ Cl^-$	$(2+) + 2 \times (1-) = 0$
$CaCO_3$	$Ca^{2+} + CO_3^{2-}$	$(2+) + (2-) = 0$
$Ca_3(PO_4)_2$	$3\ Ca^{2+} + 2\ PO_4^{3-}$	$3 \times (2+) + 2 \times (3-) = 0$

In writing formulas of ionic compounds, the convention is that *the symbol of the cation is given first, followed by the anion symbol*. Also notice the use of parentheses when more than one of a given polyatomic ion is present.

Chemistry ❂ Now™

Sign in at **www.cengage.com/login** and go to Chapter 2 Contents to see Screen 2.20 for a video of the **sodium and chlorine reaction** and for a simulation on the **relationship between cations and anions in ionic compounds.**

■ EXAMPLE 2.4 Ionic Compound Formulas

Problem For each of the following ionic compounds, write the symbols for the ions present, and give the number of each: (a) Li_2CO_3, and (b) $Fe_2(SO_4)_3$.

Strategy Divide the formula of the compound into the cation and the anion. To accomplish this, you will have to recognize, and remember, the composition and charges of common ions.

Solution

(a) Li_2CO_3 is composed of two lithium ions, Li^+, and one carbonate ion, CO_3^{2-}. Li is a Group 1A element and always has a 1+ charge in its compounds. Because the two 1+ charges balance the negative charge of the carbonate ion, the latter must be 2−.

(b) $Fe_2(SO_4)_3$ contains two iron ions, Fe^{3+}, and three sulfate ions, SO_4^{2-}. The way to recognize this is to recall that sulfate has a 2− charge. Because three sulfate ions are present (with a total charge of 6−), the two iron cations must have a total charge of 6+. This is possible only if each iron cation has a charge of 3+.

Comment Remember that the formula for an ion must include its composition and its charge. Formulas for ionic compounds are always written with the cation first and then the anion, but ion charges are not included.

■ EXAMPLE 2.5 Ionic Compound Formulas

Problem Write formulas for ionic compounds composed of aluminum cations and each of the following anions: (a) fluoride ion, (b) sulfide ion, and (c) nitrate ion.

Strategy First decide on the formula of the Al cation and the formula of each anion. Combine the Al cation with each type of anion to form an electrically neutral compound.

Solution An aluminum cation is predicted to have a charge of 3+ because Al is a metal in Group 3A.

(a) Fluorine is a Group 7A element. The charge of the fluoride ion is predicted to be 1− (from $7 - 8 = -1$). Therefore, we need 3 F^- ions to combine with one Al^{3+}. The formula of the compound is AlF_3.

(b) Sulfur is a nonmetal in Group 6A, so it forms a 2− anion. Thus, we need to combine two Al^{3+} ions [total charge is $6+ = 2 \times (3+)$] with three S^{2-} ions [total charge is $6- = 3 \times (2-)$]. The compound has the formula Al_2S_3.

■ Balancing Ion Charges in Formulas

Aluminum, a metal in Group 3A, loses three electrons to form the Al^{3+} cation. Oxygen, a nonmetal in Group 6A, gains two electrons to form an O^{2-} anion. Notice that in the compound formed from these ions, the charge on the cation is the subscript on the anion, and vice versa.

$$2\ Al^{3+} + 3\ O^{2-} \rightarrow Al_2O_3$$

This often works well, but there are exceptions. For example, the formula of titanium (IV) oxide is TiO_2, the simplest ratio, and not Ti_2O_4.

$$Ti^{4+} + 2\ O^{2-} \rightarrow TiO_2$$

(c) The nitrate ion has the formula NO_3^- (see Table 2.4). The answer here is therefore similar to the AlF_3 case, and the compound has the formula $Al(NO_3)_3$. Here, we place parentheses around NO_3 to show that three polyatomic NO_3^- ions are involved.

Comment The most common error students make is not knowing the correct charge on an ion.

EXERCISE 2.7   Formulas of Ionic Compounds

(a) Give the number and identity of the constituent ions in each of the following ionic compounds: NaF, $Cu(NO_3)_2$, and $NaCH_3CO_2$.

(b) Iron, a transition metal, forms ions having at least two different charges. Write the formulas of the compounds formed between chloride ions and the two different iron cations.

(c) Write the formulas of all neutral ionic compounds that can be formed by combining the cations Na^+ and Ba^{2+} with the anions S^{2-} and PO_4^{3-}.

Names of Ions

Naming Positive Ions (Cations)

With a few exceptions (such as NH_4^+), the positive ions described in this text are metal ions. Positive ions are named by the following rules:

■ **"-ous" and "-ic" Endings** An older naming system for metal ions uses the ending -ous for the ion of lower charge and -ic for the ion of higher charge. For example, there are cobaltous (Co^{2+}) and cobaltic (Co^{3+}) ions, and ferrous (Fe^{2+}) and ferric (Fe^{3+}) ions. We do not use this system in this book, but some chemical manufacturers continue to use it.

1. For a monatomic positive ion (that is, a metal cation) the name is that of the metal plus the word "cation." For example, we have already referred to Al^{3+} as the aluminum cation.
2. Some cases occur, especially in the transition series, in which a metal can form more than one type of positive ion. In these cases, the charge of the ion is indicated by a Roman numeral in parentheses immediately following the ion name. For example, Co^{2+} is the cobalt(II) cation, and Co^{3+} is the cobalt(III) cation.

Finally, you will encounter the ammonium cation, NH_4^+, many times in this book and in the laboratory. Do not confuse the ammonium cation with the ammonia molecule, NH_3, which has no electric charge and one less H atom.

Naming Negative Ions (Anions)

There are two types of negative ions: those having only one atom (*monatomic*) and those having several atoms (*polyatomic*).

1. A monatomic negative ion is named by adding *-ide* to the stem of the name of the nonmetal element from which the ion is derived (Figure 2.20). The anions of the Group 7A elements, the halogens, are known as the fluoride, chloride, bromide, and iodide ions and as a group are called **halide ions**.
2. Polyatomic negative ions are common, especially those containing oxygen (called **oxoanions**). The names of some of the most common oxoanions are given in Table 2.4. Although most of these names must simply be learned, some guidelines can help. For example, consider the following pairs of ions:

NO_3^- is the nitrate ion, whereas NO_2^- is the nitrite ion
SO_4^{2-} is the sulfate ion, whereas SO_3^{2-} is the sulfite ion

The oxoanion having the greater number of oxygen atoms is given the suffix *-ate*, and the oxoanion having the smaller number of oxygen atoms has the suffix *-ite*. For a series of oxoanions having more than two members, the ion with the largest number of oxygen atoms has the prefix *per-* and the suffix *-ate*. The ion

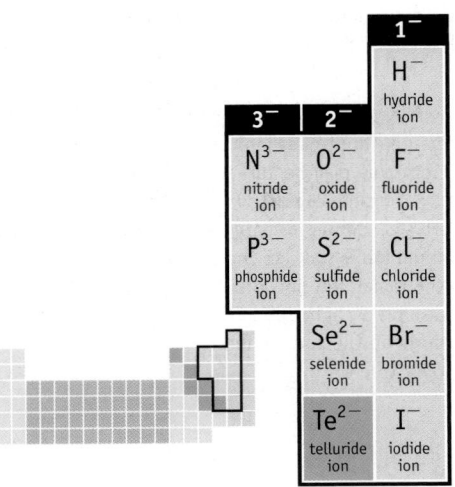

FIGURE 2.20 Names and charges of some common monatomic anions.

having the smallest number of oxygen atoms has the prefix *hypo-* and the suffix *-ite*. The chlorine oxoanions are the most commonly encountered example.

ClO_4^-	*per*chlor*ate* ion
ClO_3^-	chlor*ate* ion
ClO_2^-	chlor*ite* ion
ClO^-	*hypo*chlor*ite* ion

Oxoanions that contain hydrogen are named by adding the word "hydrogen" before the name of the oxoanion. If two hydrogens are in the anion, we say "dihydrogen." Many hydrogen-containing oxoanions have common names that are used as well. For example, the hydrogen carbonate ion, HCO_3^-, is called the bicarbonate ion.

Ion	Systematic Name	Common Name
HPO_4^{2-}	hydrogen phosphate ion	
$H_2PO_4^-$	dihydrogen phosphate ion	
HCO_3^-	hydrogen carbonate ion	bicarbonate ion
HSO_4^-	hydrogen sulfate ion	bisulfate ion
HSO_3^-	hydrogen sulfite ion	bisulfite ion

Names of Ionic Compounds

The name of an ionic compound is built from the names of the positive and negative ions in the compound. The name of the positive cation is given first, followed by the name of the negative anion. Examples of ionic compound names are given below.

Ionic Compound	Ions Involved	Name
$CaBr_2$	Ca^{2+} and 2 Br^-	calcium bromide
$NaHSO_4$	Na^+ and HSO_4^-	sodium hydrogen sulfate
$(NH_4)_2CO_3$	2 NH_4^+ and CO_3^{2-}	ammonium carbonate
$Mg(OH)_2$	Mg^{2+} and 2 OH^-	magnesium hydroxide
$TiCl_2$	Ti^{2+} and 2 Cl^-	titanium(II) chloride
Co_2O_3	2 Co^{3+} and 3 O^{2-}	cobalt(III) oxide

■ **Naming Oxoanions**

increasing oxygen content ↑

per . . . ate

. . . ate

. . . ite

hypo . . . ite

■ **Names of Compounds Containing Transition Metal Cations** Be sure to notice that the charge on a transition metal cation is indicated by a Roman numeral and is included in the name.

Problem Solving Tip 2.1

Formulas for Ions and Ionic Compounds

Writing formulas for ionic compounds takes practice, and it requires that you know the formulas and charges of the most common ions. The charges on monatomic ions are often evident from the position of the element in the periodic table, but you simply have to remember the formula and charges of polyatomic ions—especially the most common ones such as nitrate, sulfate, carbonate, phosphate, and acetate.

If you cannot remember the formula of a polyatomic ion, or if you encounter an ion you have not seen before, you may be able to figure out its formula. For example, suppose you are told that $NaCHO_2$ is sodium formate. You know that the sodium ion is Na^+, so the formate ion must be the remaining portion of the compound; it must have a charge of $1-$ to balance the $1+$ charge on the sodium ion. Thus, the formate ion must be CHO_2^-.

Finally, when writing the formulas of ions, you *must* include the charge on the ion (except in the formula of an ionic compound). Writing Na when you mean sodium ion is incorrect. There is a vast difference in the properties of the element sodium (Na) and those of its ion (Na^+).

Chemistry　Now™

Sign in at **www.cengage.com/login** and go to Chapter 2 Contents to see Screens 2.20 and 2.21 for a tutorial, an exercise, and a simulation on **ionic compounds.**

EXERCISE 2.8 Names of Ionic Compounds

1. Give the formula for each of the following ionic compounds. Use Table 2.4 and Figure 2.20.

(a) ammonium nitrate

(b) cobalt(II) sulfate

(c) nickel(II) cyanide

(d) vanadium(III) oxide

(e) barium acetate

(f) calcium hypochlorite

2. Name the following ionic compounds:

(a) $MgBr_2$

(b) Li_2CO_3

(c) $KHSO_3$

(d) $KMnO_4$

(e) $(NH_4)_2S$

(f) $CuCl$ and $CuCl_2$

Properties of Ionic Compounds

When a substance having a negative electric charge is brought near a substance having a positive electric charge, there is a force of attraction between them (Figure 2.21). In contrast, there is a repulsive force when two substances with the same charge—both positive or both negative—are brought together. These forces are called **electrostatic** forces, and the force of attraction between ions is given by **Coulomb's law** (Equation 2.3)

$$\text{Force of attraction} = k \, \frac{(n^+e)\,(n^-e)}{d^2}$$

(2.3)

charge on $+$ and $-$ ions — charge on electron

proportionality constant — distance between ions

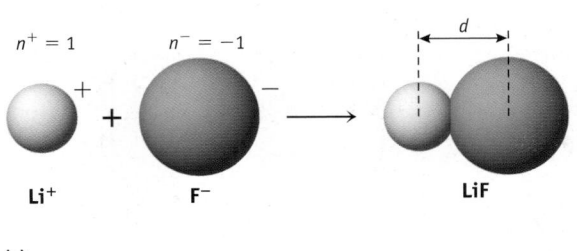

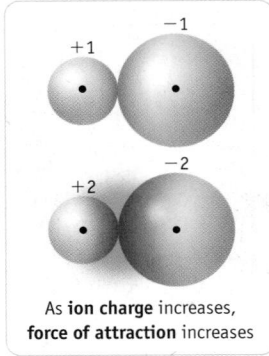

As **ion charge** increases, **force of attraction** increases

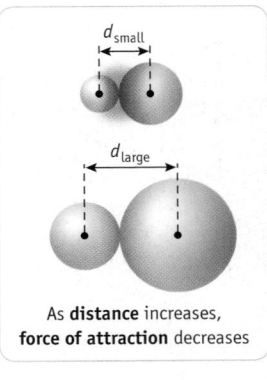

As **distance** increases, **force of attraction** decreases

(a)

(b)

Active Figure 2.21 Coulomb's law and electrostatic forces. (a) Ions such as Li$^+$ and F$^-$ are held together by an electrostatic force. Here, a lithium ion is attracted to a fluoride ion, and the distance between the nuclei of the two ions is d. (b) Forces of attraction between ions of opposite charge increase with increasing ion charge and decrease with increasing distance (d).

Chemistry. Now™ Sign in at www.cengage.com/login and go to the Chapter Contents menu to explore an interactive version of this figure accompanied by an exercise.

where, for example, n^+ is 3 for Al^{3+} and n^- is -2 for O^{2-}. Based on Coulomb's law, the force of attraction between oppositely charged ions increases:

- As the ion charges (n^+ and n^-) increase. Thus, the attraction between ions having charges of 2+ and 2− is greater than that between ions having 1+ and 1− charges (Figure 2.21).
- As the distance between the ions becomes smaller (Figure 2.21).

Ionic compounds do not consist of simple pairs or small groups of positive and negative ions. The simplest ratio of cations to anions in an ionic compound is represented by its formula, but an ionic solid consists of millions upon millions of ions arranged in an extended three-dimensional network called a **crystal lattice.** A portion of the lattice for NaCl, illustrated in Figure 2.22, illustrates a common way of arranging ions for compounds that have a 1:1 ratio of cations to anions.

Ionic compounds have characteristic properties that can be understood in terms of the charges of the ions and their arrangement in the lattice. Because each ion is surrounded by oppositely charged nearest neighbors, it is held tightly in its allotted location. At room temperature, each ion can move just a bit around its average position, but considerable energy must be added before an ion can escape the attraction of its neighboring ions. Only if enough energy is added will the lattice structure collapse and the substance melt. Greater attractive forces mean that ever more energy—higher and higher temperatures—is required to cause melting. Thus, Al$_2$O$_3$, a solid composed of Al^{3+} and O^{2-} ions, melts at a much higher temperature (2072 °C) than NaCl (801 °C), a solid composed of Na$^+$ and Cl$^-$ ions.

Most ionic compounds are "hard" solids. That is, the solids are not pliable or soft. The reason for this characteristic is again related to the lattice of ions. The nearest neighbors of a cation in a lattice are anions, and the force of attraction makes the lattice rigid. However, a blow with a hammer can cause the lattice to break cleanly along a sharp boundary. The hammer blow displaces layers of ions just enough to cause ions of like charge to become nearest neighbors, and the repulsion between these like-charged ions forces the lattice apart (Figure 2.23).

Photo: Charles D. Winters; model, S. M. Young

FIGURE 2.22 Sodium chloride. A crystal of NaCl consists of an extended lattice of sodium ions and chloride ions in a 1 : 1 ratio. (Sign in to ChemistryNow, and see Screen 2.20, Ionic Compounds, to view an animation on the formation of a sodium chloride crystal lattice.)

(a)

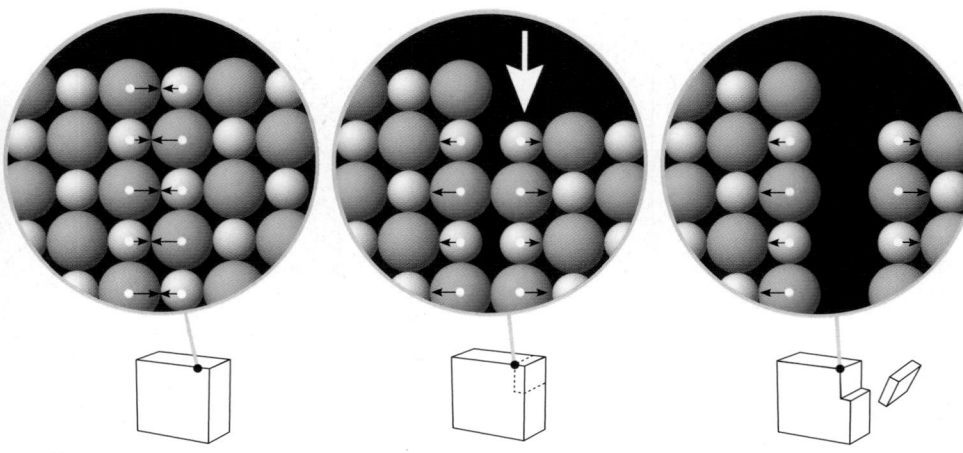

(b)

FIGURE 2.23 Ionic solids. (a) An ionic solid is normally rigid, owing to the forces of attraction between oppositely charged ions. When struck sharply, however, the crystal can cleave cleanly. (b) When a crystal is struck, layers of ions move slightly, and ions of like charge become nearest neighbors. Repulsions between ions of similar charge cause the crystal to cleave. (Sign in to ChemistryNow, and see Screen 2.23, Properties of Ionic Compounds, to watch a video of cleaving a crystal.)

Chemistry₊Ȯ₊Now™

Sign in at **www.cengage.com/login** and go to Chapter 2 Contents to see:
- Screen 2.22 for a simulation on **Coulomb's Law**
- Screen 2.23 for an exercise and a simulation on **properties of ionic compounds**

EXERCISE 2.9 Coulomb's Law

Explain why the melting point of MgO (2830 °C) is much higher than the melting point of NaCl (801 °C).

2.8 Molecular Compounds: Formulas and Names

Many familiar compounds are not ionic; they are molecular: the water you drink, the sugar in your coffee or tea, or the aspirin you take for a headache.

Problem Solving Tip 2.2

Is a Compound Ionic?

Students often ask how to know whether a compound is ionic. Here are some useful guidelines.

1. Most metal-containing compounds are ionic. So, if a metal atom appears in the formula of a compound, a good first guess is that it is ionic. (There are interesting exceptions, but few come up in introductory chemistry.) It is helpful in this regard to recall trends in metallic behavior: All

elements to the left of a diagonal line running from boron to tellurium in the periodic table are metallic.
2. If there is no metal in the formula, it is likely that the compound is not ionic. The exceptions here are compounds composed of polyatomic ions based on nonmetals (e.g., NH_4Cl or NH_4NO_3).
3. Learn to recognize the formulas of polyatomic ions (see Table 2.4). Chemists write

the formula of ammonium nitrate as NH_4NO_3 (not as $N_2H_4O_3$) to alert others to the fact that it is an ionic compound composed of the common polyatomic ions NH_4^+ and NO_3^-.

As an example of these guidelines, you can be sure that $MgBr_2$ (Mg^{2+} with Br^-) and K_2S (K^+ with S^{2-}) are ionic compounds. On the other hand, the compound CCl_4, formed from two nonmetals, C and Cl, is not ionic.

WATER

FIGURE 2.24 Molecular compounds.
Ionic compounds are generally solids at room temperature. In contrast, molecular compounds can be gases, liquids, or solids. The molecular models are of caffeine (in coffee), water, and citric acid (in lemons).

Ionic compounds are generally solids, whereas molecular compounds can range from gases to liquids to solids at ordinary temperatures (see Figure 2.24). As size and molecular complexity increase, compounds generally exist as solids. We will explore some of the underlying causes of these general observations in Chapter 12.

Some molecular compounds have complicated formulas that you cannot, at this stage, predict or even decide if they are correct. However, there are many simple compounds you will encounter often, and you should understand how to name them and, in many cases, know their formulas.

Let us look first at molecules formed from combinations of two nonmetals. These "two-element" compounds of nonmetals, often called **binary compounds**, can be named in a systematic way.

Hydrogen forms binary compounds with all of the nonmetals except the noble gases. For compounds of oxygen, sulfur, and the halogens, the H atom is generally written first in the formula and is named first. The other nonmetal is named as if it were a negative ion.

Compound	Name
HF	hydrogen fluoride
HCl	hydrogen chloride
H_2S	hydrogen sulfide

■ **Formulas of Binary Nonmetal Compounds Containing Hydrogen** Simple hydrocarbons (compounds of C and H) such as methane (CH_4) and ethane (C_2H_6) have formulas written with H following C, and the formulas of ammonia and hydrazine have H following N. Water and the hydrogen halides, however, have the H atom preceding O or the halogen atom. Tradition is the only explanation for such irregularities in writing formulas.

Although there are exceptions, *most binary molecular compounds are a combination of nonmetallic elements from Groups 4A–7A with one another or with hydrogen.* The formula is generally written by putting the elements in order of increasing group number. When naming the compound, the number of atoms of a given type in the compound is designated with a prefix, such as "di-," "tri-," "tetra-," "penta-," and so on.

Compound	Systematic Name
NF_3	nitrogen trifluoride
NO	nitrogen monoxide
NO_2	nitrogen dioxide
N_2O	dinitrogen monoxide
N_2O_4	dinitrogen tetraoxide
PCl_3	phosphorus trichloride
PCl_5	phosphorus pentachloride
SF_6	sulfur hexafluoride
S_2F_{10}	disulfur decafluoride

■ **Hydrocarbons** Compounds such as methane, ethane, propane, and butane belong to a class of hydrocarbons called alkanes. (Sign in to ChemistryNow, and see Screen 2.24, Alkanes.).

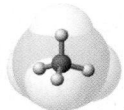

methane, CH_4

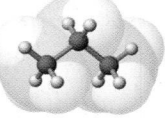

propane, C_3H_8

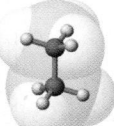

ethane, C_2H_6

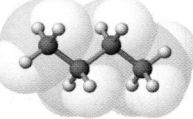

butane, C_4H_{10}

Finally, many of the binary compounds of nonmetals were discovered years ago and have common names.

Compound	Common Name	Compound	Common Name
CH_4	methane	N_2H_4	hydrazine
C_2H_6	ethane	PH_3	phosphine
C_3H_8	propane	NO	nitric oxide
C_4H_{10}	butane	N_2O	nitrous oxide ("laughing gas")
NH_3	ammonia	H_2O	water

Chemistry Now™

Sign in at **www.cengage.com/login** and go to Chapter 2 Contents to see:
• Screen 2.25 for a tutorial on **naming compounds of the nonmetals**
• Screen 2.26 for an exercise on **naming alkanes**

EXERCISE 2.10 Naming Compounds of the Nonmetals

1. Give the formula for each of the following binary, nonmetal compounds:

(a) carbon dioxide   **(d)** boron trifluoride

(b) phosphorus triiodide   **(e)** dioxygen difluoride

(c) sulfur dichloride   **(f)** xenon trioxide

2. Name the following binary, nonmetal compounds:

(a) N_2F_4 **(c)** SF_4 **(e)** P_4O_{10}

(b) HBr   **(d)** BCl_3 **(f)** ClF_3

 Module 4

2.9 Atoms, Molecules, and the Mole

One of the most exciting aspects of chemical research is the discovery of some new substance, and part of this process of discovery involves quantitative experiments. When two chemicals react with each other, we want to know how many atoms or molecules of each are used so that formulas can be established for the reaction products. To do so, we need some method of counting atoms and molecules. That is, we must discover a way of connecting the macroscopic world, the world we can see, with the particulate world of atoms, molecules, and ions. The solution to this problem is to define a unit of matter that contains a known number of particles. That chemical unit is the mole.

The **mole** (abbreviated mol) is the SI base unit for measuring an *amount of a substance* and is defined as follows:

A mole is the amount of a substance that contains as many elementary entities (atoms, molecules, or other particles) as there are atoms in exactly 12 g of the carbon-12 isotope.

The key to understanding the concept of the mole is recognizing that *one mole always contains the same number of particles, no matter what the substance.* One mole of sodium contains the same number of atoms as one mole of iron or as the number of mol-

■ **An Important Difference between the Terms "Amount" and "Quantity"** The terms "amount" and "quantity" are used in a specific sense by chemists. The amount of a substance is the number of moles of that substance. Quantity refers, for example, to the mass or volume of the substance. (See W. G. Davies and J. W. Moore. *Journal of Chemical Education*, Vol. 57, p. 303, 1980.)

Historical Perspectives — Amedeo Avogadro and His Number

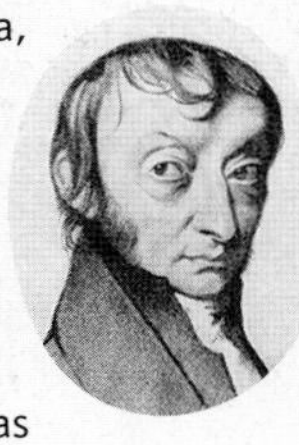

Amedeo Avogadro, conte di Quaregna, (1776–1856) was an Italian nobleman and a lawyer. In about 1800, he turned to science and was the first professor of mathematical physics in Italy.

Avogadro did not himself propose the notion of a fixed number of particles in a chemical unit. Rather, the number was named in his honor because he had performed experiments in the 19th century that laid the groundwork for the concept.

Just how large is Avogadro's number? One mol of unpopped popcorn kernels would cover the continental United States to a depth of about 9 miles. One mole of pennies divided equally among every man, woman, and child in the U.S. would allow each person to pay off the national debt (\$9.1 trillion or 9.1×10^{12} dollars), and still have trillions of dollars left over!

Is the number a unique value like π? No. It is fixed by the definition of the mole as exactly 12 g of carbon-12. If one mole of carbon were defined to have some other mass, then Avogadro's number would have a different value.

Photo: E. F. Smith Collection/Van Pelt/Library/University of Pennsylvania

---

ecules in one mole of water. How many particles? Many, many experiments over the years have established that number as

$$\textbf{1 mole} = \textbf{6.0221415} \times \textbf{10}^{23} \textbf{ particles}$$

This value is known as **Avogadro's number** in honor of Amedeo Avogadro, an Italian lawyer and physicist (1776–1856) who conceived the basic idea (but never determined the number).

■ **The "Mole"** The term "mole" was introduced about 1895 by Wilhelm Ostwald (1853–1932), who derived the term from the Latin word *moles*, meaning a "heap" or a "pile."

Atoms and Molar Mass

The mass in grams of one mole of any element (6.0221415×10^{23} atoms of that element) is the **molar mass** of that element. Molar mass is conventionally abbreviated with a capital italicized *M*, and it has units of grams per mole (g/mol). *An element's molar mass is the quantity in grams numerically equal to its atomic weight.* Using sodium and lead as examples,

Molar mass of sodium (Na) = mass of 1.000 mol of Na atoms
= 22.99 g/mol
= mass of 6.022×10^{23} Na atoms

Molar mass of lead (Pb) = mass of 1.000 mol of Pb atoms
= 207.2 g/mol
= mass of 6.022×10^{23} Pb atoms

Figure 2.25 shows the relative sizes of a mole of some common elements. Although each of these "piles of atoms" has a different volume and different mass, each contains 6.022×10^{23} atoms.

The mole concept is the cornerstone of quantitative chemistry. It is essential to be able to convert from moles to mass and from mass to moles. Dimensional analysis, which is described in *Let's Review*, page 38, shows that this can be done in the following way:

MASS ⟷ MOLES CONVERSION

Moles to Mass

$$\text{Moles} \times \frac{\text{grams}}{1\text{ mol}} = \text{grams}$$

↑ molar mass

Mass to Moles

$$\text{Grams} \times \frac{1\text{ mol}}{\text{grams}} = \text{moles}$$

↑ 1/molar mass

Charles D. Winters

Copper
63.546 g

Sulfur
32.066 g

Magnesium
24.305 g

Tin
118.71 g

Silicon
28.086 g

For example, what mass, in grams, is represented by 0.35 mol of aluminum? Using the molar mass of aluminum (27.0 g/mol), you can determine that 0.35 mol of Al has a mass of 9.5 g.

$$0.35 \text{ mol Al} \times \frac{27.0 \text{ g Al}}{1 \text{ mol Al}} = 9.5 \text{ g Al}$$

Molar masses are generally known to at least four significant figures. The convention followed in calculations in this book is to use a value of the molar mass with one more significant figure than in any other number in the problem. For example, if you weigh out 16.5 g of carbon, you use 12.01 g/mol for the molar mass of C to find the amount of carbon present.

$$16.5 \text{ g C} \times \frac{1 \text{ mol C}}{12.01 \text{ g C}} = 1.37 \text{ mol C}$$

↑
Note that four significant figures are used in the molar mass, but there are three in the sample mass.

Using one more significant figure for the molar mass means the precision of this value will not affect the precision of the result.

Chemistry ⚛ Now™

Sign in at **www.cengage.com/login** and go to Chapter 2 Contents to see:
• Screen 2.25 for a tutorial on **moles and atoms conversion**
• Screen 2.26 for two tutorials on **molar mass conversion**

Problem Consider two elements in the same vertical column of the periodic table, lead and tin.

(a) What mass of lead, in grams, is equivalent to 2.50 mol of lead (Pb, atomic number = 82)?

(b) What amount of tin, in moles, is represented by 36.6 g of tin (Sn, atomic number = 50)? How many atoms of tin are in the sample?

Strategy The molar masses of lead (207.2 g/mol) and tin (118.7 g/mol) are required and can be found in the periodic table inside the front cover of this book. Avogadro's number is needed to convert the amount of each element to number of atoms.

Solution

(a) Convert the amount of lead in moles to mass in grams.

$$2.50 \text{ mol Pb} \times \frac{207.2 \text{ g}}{1 \text{ mol Pb}} = \boxed{518 \text{ g Pb}}$$

(b) First convert the mass of tin to the amount in moles.

$$36.6 \text{ g Sn} \times \frac{1 \text{ mol Sn}}{118.7 \text{ g Sn}} = \boxed{0.308 \text{ mol Sn}}$$

Finally, use Avogadro's number to find the number of atoms in the sample.

$$0.308 \text{ mol Sn} \times \frac{6.022 \times 10^{23} \text{ atoms Sn}}{1 \text{ mol Sn}} = \boxed{1.85 \times 10^{23} \text{ atoms Sn}}$$

Lead. A 150-mL beaker containing 2.50 mol or 518 g of lead.

Tin. A sample of tin having a mass of 36.6 g (or 1.85×10^{23} atoms).

EXERCISE 2.11 Mass/Mole Conversions

(a) What is the mass, in grams, of 1.5 mol of silicon?

(b) What amount (moles) of sulfur is represented by 454 g? How many atoms?

EXERCISE 2.12 Atoms

The density of gold, Au, is 19.32 g/cm³. What is the volume (in cubic centimeters) of a piece of gold that contains 2.6×10^{24} atoms? If the piece of metal is a square with a thickness of 0.10 cm, what is the length (in centimeters) of one side of the piece?

Molecules, Compounds, and Molar Mass

The formula of a compound tells you the type of atoms or ions in the compound and the relative number of each. For example, one molecule of methane, CH_4, is made up of one atom of C and four atoms of H. But suppose you have Avogadro's number of C atoms (6.022×10^{23}) combined with the proper number of H atoms. The compound's formula tells us that four times as many H atoms are required ($4 \times 6.022 \times 10^{23}$ H atoms). What masses of atoms are combined, and what is the mass of this many CH_4 molecules?

C	+	4 H	→	CH_4
6.022×10^{23} C atoms		$4 \times 6.022 \times 10^{23}$ H atoms		6.022×10^{23} CH_4 molecules
= 1.000 mol of C		= 4.000 mol of H atoms		= 1.000 mol of CH_4 molecules
= 12.01 g of C atoms		= 4.032 g of H atoms		= 16.04 g of CH_4 molecules

■ **Molar Mass or Molecular Weight**
Although chemists often use the term "molecular weight," the more correct term is molar mass. The SI unit of molar mass is kg/mol, but chemists worldwide usually express it in units of g/mol. See "NIST Guide to SI Units" at www.NIST.gov

Because we know the number of moles of C and H atoms, we know the masses of carbon and hydrogen that combine to form CH_4. It follows that the mass of CH_4 is the sum of these masses. That is, 1 mol of CH_4 has a mass equivalent to the mass of 1 mol of C atoms (12.01 g) plus 4 mol of H atoms (4.032 g). Thus, the *molar mass*, M, of CH_4 is 16.04 g/mol. The molar masses of some substances are:

Molar and Molecular Masses

Element or Compound	Molar Mass, M (g/mol)	Average Mass of One Molecule (g/molecule)
O_2	32.00	5.314×10^{-23}
NH_3	17.03	2.828×10^{-23}
H_2O	18.02	2.992×10^{-23}
$NH_2CH_2CO_2H$ (glycine)	75.07	1.247×10^{-22}

Ionic compounds such as NaCl do not exist as individual molecules. Thus, we write the simplest formula that shows the relative number of each kind of atom in a "formula unit" of the compound, and the molar mass is calculated from this formula (M for NaCl = 58.44 g/mol). To differentiate substances like NaCl that do not contain molecules, chemists sometimes refer to their *formula weight* instead of their molecular weight.

Figure 2.26 illustrates 1-mole quantities of several common compounds. To find the molar mass of any compound, you need only to add up the atomic masses for each element in one formula unit. As an example, let us find the molar mass of aspirin, $C_9H_8O_4$. In 1 mole of aspirin, there are 9 mol of carbon atoms, 8 mol of

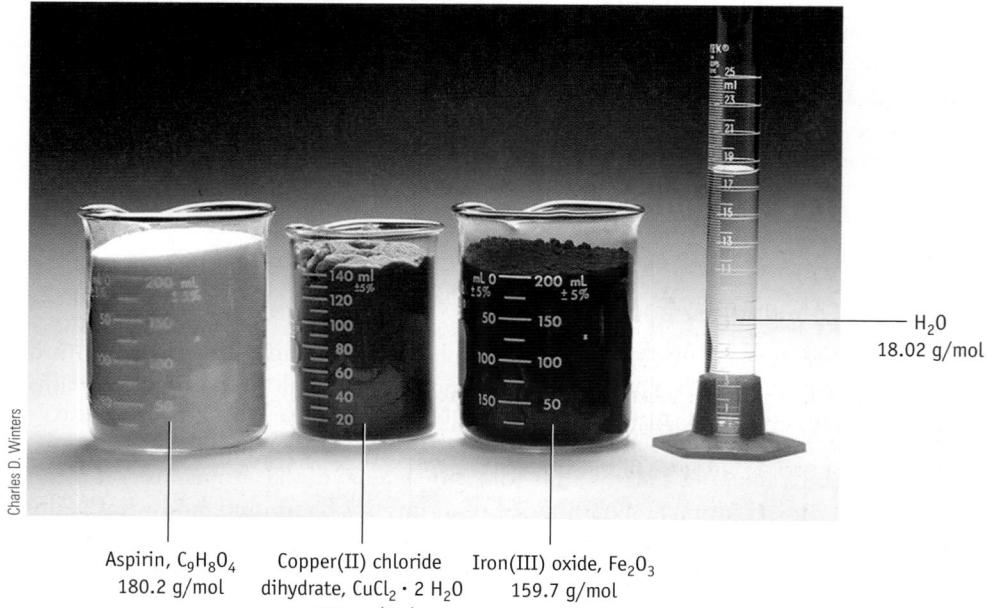

Charles D. Winters

H_2O
18.02 g/mol

Aspirin, $C_9H_8O_4$
180.2 g/mol

Copper(II) chloride dihydrate, $CuCl_2 \cdot 2 H_2O$
170.5 g/mol

Iron(III) oxide, Fe_2O_3
159.7 g/mol

FIGURE 2.26 One-mole quantities of some compounds. Notice the molar mass for $CuCl_2 \cdot 2H_2O$. This is called a *hydrated compound* because water is associated with the $CuCl_2$ (see page 96). Thus, one "formula unit" consists of one Cu^{2+} ion, two Cl^- ions, and two water molecules. The molar masses are the sum of the mass of 1 mol of Cu, 2 mol of Cl, and 2 mol of H_2O.

hydrogen atoms, and 4 mol of oxygen atoms, which add up to 180.2 g/mol of aspirin:

$$\text{Mass of C in 1 mol } C_9H_8O_4 = 9 \text{ mol C} \times \frac{12.01 \text{ g C}}{1 \text{ mol C}} = 108.1 \text{ g C}$$

$$\text{Mass of H in 1 mol } C_9H_8O_4 = 8 \text{ mol H} \times \frac{1.008 \text{ g H}}{1 \text{ mol H}} = 8.064 \text{ g H}$$

$$\text{Mass of O in 1 mol } C_9H_8O_4 = 4 \text{ mol O} \times \frac{16.00 \text{ g O}}{1 \text{ mol O}} = 64.00 \text{ g O}$$

$$\text{Total mass of 1 mol of } C_9H_8O_4 = \text{molar mass of } C_9H_8O_4 = 180.2 \text{ g}$$

As was the case with elements, it is important to be able to convert between amounts (moles) and mass (grams). For example, if you take 325 mg (0.325 g) of aspirin in one tablet, what amount of the compound have you ingested? Based on a molar mass of 180.2 g/mol, there are 0.00180 mol of aspirin per tablet.

$$0.325 \text{ g aspirin} \times \frac{1 \text{ mol aspirin}}{180.2 \text{ g aspirin}} = 0.00180 \text{ mol aspirin}$$

Using the molar mass of a compound, it is possible to determine the number of molecules in any sample from the sample mass and to determine the mass of one molecule. For example, the number of aspirin molecules in one tablet is

$$0.00180 \text{ mol aspirin} \times \frac{6.022 \times 10^{23} \text{ molecules}}{1 \text{ mol aspirin}} = 1.08 \times 10^{21} \text{ molecules}$$

and the mass of one molecule is

$$\frac{180.2 \text{ g aspirin}}{1 \text{ mol aspirin}} \times \frac{1 \text{ mol aspirin}}{6.022 \times 10^{23} \text{ molecules}} = 2.99 \times 10^{-22} \text{ g/molecule}$$

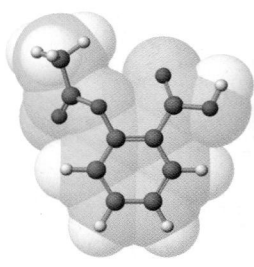

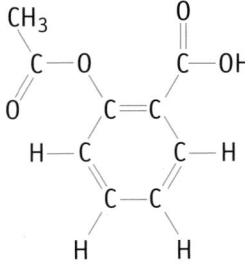

Aspirin formula. Aspirin has the molecular formula $C_9H_8O_4$ and a molar mass of 180.2 g/mol. Aspirin is the common name of the compound acetylsalicylic acid.

Chemistry ⚛ Now™

Sign in at **www.cengage.com/login** and go to Chapter 2 Contents to see:
• Screen 2.27 for a simulation on **compounds and moles** and a tutorial on **determining molar mass**
• Screen 2.28 for tutorials on **using molar mass**

■ EXAMPLE 2.7 Molar Mass and Moles

Problem You have 16.5 g of oxalic acid, $H_2C_2O_4$.

(a) What amount (moles) is represented by 16.5 g of oxalic acid?

(b) How many molecules of oxalic acid are in 16.5 g?

(c) How many atoms of carbon are in 16.5 g of oxalic acid?

(d) What is the mass of one molecule of oxalic acid?

Strategy The first step in any problem involving the conversion of mass and moles is to find the molar mass of the compound in question. Then you can perform the other calculations as outlined by the scheme shown here to find the number of molecules from the amount of substance and the number of atoms of a particular kind:

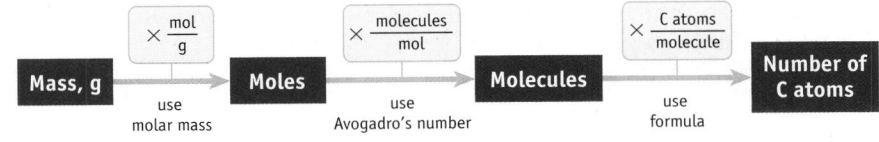

What amount of water is in a snow-flake? According to K. G. Libbrecht, there are about a billion billion water molecules in a snowflake. Given that this is 1×10^{18} molecules, how many moles of water are in a snowflake and what mass of water? Libbrecht also calculates that "each of us on Earth has contributed by exhalation and evaporation about 1,000 of the molecules in each snowflake." (D. Overbye, *New York Times*, December 23, 2003, page F3. See also K. G. Libbrecht, *American Scientist*, Vol. 95, pages 52–59, January-February 2007.)

Solution

(a) *Moles represented by 16.5 g*

Let us first calculate the molar mass of oxalic acid:

$$2 \text{ mol C per mol } H_2C_2O_4 \times \frac{12.01 \text{ g C}}{1 \text{ mol C}} = 24.02 \text{ g C per mol } H_2C_2O_4$$

$$2 \text{ mol H per mol } H_2C_2O_4 \times \frac{1.008 \text{ g H}}{1 \text{ mol H}} = 2.016 \text{ g H per mol } H_2C_2O_4$$

$$4 \text{ mol O per mol } H_2C_2O_4 \times \frac{16.00 \text{ g O}}{1 \text{ mol O}} = 64.00 \text{ g O per mol } H_2C_2O_4$$

Molar mass of $H_2C_2O_4$ = 90.04 g per mol $H_2C_2O_4$

Now calculate the amount in moles. The molar mass (expressed in units of 1 mol/90.04 g) is the conversion factor in all mass-to-mole conversions.

$$16.5 \text{ g } H_2C_2O_4 \times \frac{1 \text{ mol}}{90.04 \text{ g } H_2C_2O_4} = 0.183 \text{ mol } H_2C_2O_4$$

(b) *Number of molecules*

Use Avogadro's number to find the number of oxalic acid molecules in 0.183 mol of $H_2C_2O_4$.

$$0.183 \text{ mol} \times \frac{6.022 \times 10^{23} \text{ molecules}}{1 \text{ mol}} = 1.10 \times 10^{23} \text{ molecules}$$

(c) *Number of C atoms*

Because each molecule contains two carbon atoms, the number of carbon atoms in 16.5 g of the acid is

$$1.10 \times 10^{23} \text{ molecules} \times \frac{2 \text{ C atoms}}{1 \text{ molecule}} = 2.20 \times 10^{23} \text{ C atoms}$$

(d) *Mass of one molecule*

Use the molar mass and Avogadro's number to carry out this calculation.

$$\frac{90.04 \text{ g}}{1 \text{ mol}} \times \frac{1 \text{ mol}}{6.0221 \times 10^{23} \text{ molecules}} = 1.495 \times 10^{-22} \text{ g/molecule}$$

EXERCISE 2.13 Molar Mass and Moles-to-Mass Conversions

(a) Calculate the molar masses of citric acid ($H_3C_6H_5O_7$) and $MgCO_3$.

(b) If you have 454 g of citric acid, what amount (moles) does this represent?

(c) To have 0.125 mol of $MgCO_3$, what mass (g) must you have?

2.10 Describing Compound Formulas

Given a sample of an unknown compound, how can its formula be determined? The answer lies in *chemical analysis*, a major branch of chemistry that deals with the determination of formulas and structures.

Percent Composition

Any sample of a pure compound always consists of the same elements combined in the same proportion by mass. This means molecular composition can be expressed in at least three ways:

- In terms of the number of atoms of each type per molecule or per formula unit—that is, by giving the formula of the compound

88 **Chapter 2** | Atoms, Molecules, and Ions

- In terms of the mass of each element per mole of compound
- In terms of the mass of each element in the compound relative to the total mass of the compound—that is, as a mass percent

Suppose you have 1.0000 mol of NH_3 or 17.031 g. This mass of NH_3 is composed of 14.007 g of N (1.0000 mol) and 3.0237 g of H (3.0000 mol). If you compare the mass of N to the total mass of compound, 82.244% of the total mass is N (and 17.755% is H).

$$\text{Mass of N per mole of } NH_3 = \frac{1 \text{ mol N}}{1 \text{ mol } NH_3} \times \frac{14.007 \text{ g N}}{1 \text{ mol N}} = 14.007 \text{ g N}/1 \text{ mol } NH_3$$

$$\text{Mass percent N in } NH_3 = \frac{\text{mass of N in 1 mol } NH_3}{\text{mass of 1 mol } NH_3}$$

$$= \frac{14.007 \text{ g N}}{17.031 \text{ g } NH_3} \times 100\%$$

$$= 82.244\% \text{ (or 82.244 g N in 100.000 g } NH_3)$$

$$\text{Mass of H per mole of } NH_3 = \frac{3 \text{ mol H}}{1 \text{ mol } NH_3} \times \frac{1.0079 \text{ g H}}{1 \text{ mol H}}$$

$$= 3.0237 \text{ g H}/1 \text{ mol } NH_3$$

$$\text{Mass percent H in } NH_3 = \frac{\text{mass of H in 1 mol } NH_3}{\text{mass of 1 mol } NH_3} \times 100\%$$

$$= \frac{3.0237 \text{ g H}}{17.031 \text{ g } NH_3} \times 100\%$$

$$= 17.755\% \text{ (or 17.755 g H in 100.000 g } NH_3)$$

These values represent the mass percent of each element, or percent composition by mass. They tell you that in a 100.000-g sample there are 82.244 g of N and 17.755 g of H.

Chemistry ☼ Now™

Sign in at **www.cengage.com/login** and go to Chapter 2 Contents to see Screen 2.29 for a tutorial on **using percent composition.**

■ EXAMPLE 2.8 Using Percent Composition

Problem What is the mass percent of each element in propane, C_3H_8? What mass of carbon is contained in 454 g of propane?

Strategy First, find the molar mass of C_3H_8, and then calculate the mass percent of C and H per mole of C_3H_8. Using the mass percent of C, calculate the mass of carbon in 454 g of C_3H_8.

Solution

(a) The molar mass of C_3H_8 is 44.097 g/mol (= 3 mol C + 8 mol H = 36.03 g + 8.064 g).

(b) Mass percent of C and H in C_3H_8:

$$\frac{3 \text{ mol C}}{1 \text{ mol } C_3H_8} \times \frac{12.01 \text{ g C}}{1 \text{ mol C}} = 36.03 \text{ g C}/1 \text{ mol } C_3H_8$$

$$\text{Mass percent of C in } C_3H_8 = \frac{36.03 \text{ g C}}{44.097 \text{ g } C_3H_8} \times 100\% = \boxed{81.71\% \text{ C}}$$

$$\frac{8 \text{ mol H}}{1 \text{ mol } C_3H_8} \times \frac{1.008 \text{ g H}}{1 \text{ mol H}} = 8.064 \text{ g H}/1 \text{ mol } C_3H_8$$

$$\text{Mass percent of H in } C_3H_8 = \frac{8.064 \text{ g H}}{44.097 \text{ g } C_3H_8} \times 100\% = \boxed{18.29\% \text{ H}}$$

■ **Molecular Composition** Molecular composition can be expressed as a percent (mass of an element in a 100-g sample). For example, NH_3 is 82.244% N. Therefore, it has 82.244 g of N in 100.000 g of compound.

82.244% of NH_3 mass is **nitrogen**.

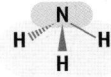

17.755% of NH_3 mass is **hydrogen**.

2.10 | Describing Compound Formulas **89**

(c) Mass of C in 454 g of C_3H_8:

$$454 \text{ g } C_3H_8 \times \frac{81.71 \text{ g C}}{100.0 \text{ g } C_3H_8} = \boxed{371 \text{ g C}}$$

EXERCISE 2.14 Percent Composition

(a) Express the composition of ammonium carbonate, $(NH_4)_2CO_3$, in terms of the mass of each element in 1.00 mol of compound and the mass percent of each element.

(b) What is the mass of carbon in 454 g of octane, C_8H_{18}?

Empirical and Molecular Formulas from Percent Composition

Now let us consider the reverse of the procedure just described: using relative mass or percent composition data to find a molecular formula. Suppose you know the identity of the elements in a sample and have determined the mass of each element in a given mass of compound by chemical analysis (▶ Section 4.4). You can then calculate the relative amount (moles) of each element and from this the relative number of atoms of each element in the compound. For example, for a compound composed of atoms of A and B, the steps from percent composition to a formula are

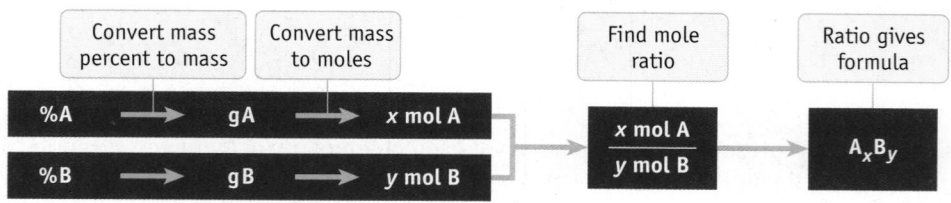

■ **Deriving a Formula** Percent composition gives the mass of an element in 100 g of sample. However, in deriving a formula, any amount of sample is appropriate if you know the mass of each element in that sample mass.

Let us derive the formula for hydrazine, a compound used to remove oxygen from water in heating and cooling systems. It is composed of 87.42% N and 12.58% H and is a close relative of ammonia.

Step 1: *Convert mass percent to mass.* The mass percentages of N and H in hydrazine tell us there are 87.42 g of N and 12.58 g of H in a 100.00 g sample.

Step 2: *Convert the mass of each element to moles.* The amount of each element in the 100.00-g sample is

$$87.42 \text{ g N} \times \frac{1 \text{ mol N}}{14.007 \text{ g N}} = 6.241 \text{ mol N}$$

$$12.58 \text{ g H} \times \frac{1 \text{ mol H}}{1.0079 \text{ g H}} = 12.48 \text{ mol H}$$

■ **Deriving a Formula—Mole Ratios** When finding the ratio of moles of one element relative to another, *always* divide the larger number by the smaller one.

Step 3: *Find the mole ratio of elements.* Use the amount (moles) of each element in the 100.00 g of sample to find the amount of one element relative to the other. For hydrazine, this ratio is 2 mol of H to 1 mol of N,

$$\frac{12.48 \text{ mol H}}{6.241 \text{ mol N}} = \frac{2.00 \text{ mol H}}{1.00 \text{ mol N}} \longrightarrow NH_2$$

showing that there are 2 mol of H atoms for every 1 mol of N atoms in hydrazine. Thus, in one molecule, two atoms of H occur for every atom of N; that is, the formula is NH_2. This simplest, whole-number ratio of atoms in a formula is called the **empirical formula**.

Percent composition data allow us to calculate the atom ratios in a compound. A *molecular formula*, however, must convey two pieces of information: (1) the relative numbers of atoms of each element in a molecule (the atom ratios) and (2) the total number of atoms in the molecule. For hydrazine, there are twice as many H atoms as N atoms, so the molecular formula could be NH_2. Recognize, however, that percent composition data give only the simplest possible ratio of atoms in a molecule. The empirical formula of hydrazine is NH_2, but the true molecular formula could be NH_2, N_2H_4, N_3H_6, N_4H_8, or any other formula having a 1:2 ratio of N to H.

To determine the molecular formula from the empirical formula, the molar mass must be obtained from experiment. For example, experiments show that the molar mass of hydrazine is 32.0 g/mol, twice the formula mass of NH_2, which is 16.0 g/mol. Thus, the molecular formula of hydrazine is two times the empirical formula of NH_2, that is, N_2H_4.

Chemistry ⚛ Now™

Sign in at **www.cengage.com/login** and go to Chapter 2 Contents to see:
- Screen 2.30 for a tutorial on **determining empirical formulas**
- Screen 2.31 for a tutorial on **determining molecular formulas**

■ EXAMPLE 2.9 Calculating a Formula from Percent Composition

Problem Eugenol is the major component in oil of cloves. It has a molar mass of 164.2 g/mol and is 73.14% C and 7.37% H; the remainder is oxygen. What are the empirical and molecular formulas of eugenol?

Strategy To derive a formula, we need to know the mass percent of each element. Because the mass percents of all elements must add up to 100.0%, we find the mass percent of O from the difference between 100.0% and the mass percents of C and H. Next, we assume that the mass percent of each element is equivalent to its mass in grams, and convert each mass to moles. Finally, the ratio of moles gives the empirical formula. The mass of a mole of compound having the calculated empirical formula is compared with the actual, experimental molar mass to find the true molecular formula.

Problem Solving Tip 2.3   Finding Empirical and Molecular Formulas

- The experimental data available to find a formula may be in the form of percent composition or the masses of elements combined in some mass of compound. No matter what the starting point, the first step is always to convert masses of elements to moles.
- Be sure to use *at least* three significant figures when calculating empirical formulas. Using fewer significant figures can give a misleading result.
- When finding mole ratios, always divide the larger number of moles by the smaller one.
- Empirical and molecular formulas can differ for molecular compounds. In contrast, the formula of an ionic compound is generally the same as its empirical formula.
- Determining the molecular formula of a compound after calculating the empirical formula requires knowing the molar mass.
- When *both* the percent composition and the molar mass are known for a compound, the alternative method mentioned in the comment to Example 2.9 could be used.

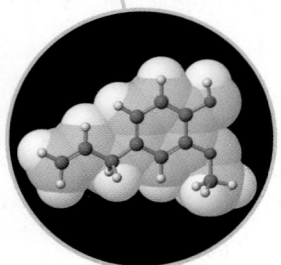

Eugenol, $C_{10}H_{12}O_2$, is an important component in oil of cloves.

Solution The mass of oxygen in a 100.00 g sample of eugenol is

$$100.00 \text{ g} = 73.14 \text{ g C} + 7.37 \text{ g H} + \text{mass of O}$$
$$\text{Mass of O} = 19.49 \text{ g}$$

The amount of each element is

$$73.14 \text{ g C} \times \frac{1 \text{ mol C}}{12.011 \text{ g C}} = 6.089 \text{ mol C}$$

$$7.37 \text{ g H} \times \frac{1 \text{ mol H}}{1.008 \text{ g H}} = 7.31 \text{ mol H}$$

$$19.49 \text{ g O} \times \frac{1 \text{ mol O}}{15.999 \text{ g O}} = 1.218 \text{ mol O}$$

To find the mole ratio, the best approach is to base the ratios on the smallest number of moles present—in this case, oxygen.

$$\frac{\text{mol C}}{\text{mol O}} = \frac{6.089 \text{ mol C}}{1.218 \text{ mol O}} = \frac{4.999 \text{ mol C}}{1.000 \text{ mol O}} = \frac{5 \text{ mol C}}{1 \text{ mol O}}$$

$$\frac{\text{mol H}}{\text{mol O}} = \frac{7.31 \text{ mol H}}{1.218 \text{ mol O}} = \frac{6.00 \text{ mol H}}{1.000 \text{ mol O}} = \frac{6 \text{ mol H}}{1 \text{ mol O}}$$

Now we know there are 5 mol of C and 6 mol of H per 1 mol of O. Thus, the empirical formula is C_5H_6O.

The experimentally determined molar mass of eugenol is 164.2 g/mol. This is twice the molar mass of C_5H_6O (82.1 g/mol).

$$\frac{164.2 \text{ g/mol of eugenol}}{82.10 \text{ g/mol of } C_5H_6O} = 2.000 \text{ mol } C_5H_6O \text{ per mol of eugenol}$$

The molecular formula is $C_{10}H_{12}O_2$.

Comment There is another approach to finding the molecular formula here. Knowing the percent composition of eugenol and its molar mass, we could calculate that in 164.2 g of eugenol there are 120.1 g of C (10 mol of C), 12.1 g of H (12 mol of H), and 32.00 g of O (2 mol of O). This gives us a molecular formula of $C_{10}H_{12}O_2$. However, you must recognize that *this approach can only be used when you know both the percent composition and the molar mass.*

EXERCISE 2.15 Empirical and Molecular Formulas

(a) What is the empirical formula of naphthalene, $C_{10}H_8$?

(b) The empirical formula of acetic acid is CH_2O. If its molar mass is 60.05 g/mol, what is the molecular formula of acetic acid?

EXERCISE 2.16 Calculating a Formula from Percent Composition

Isoprene is a liquid compound that can be polymerized to form synthetic rubber. It is composed of 88.17% carbon and 11.83% hydrogen. Its molar mass is 68.11 g/mol. What are its empirical and molecular formulas?

EXERCISE 2.17 Calculating a Formula from Percent Composition

Camphor is found in "camphor wood," much prized for its wonderful odor. It is composed of 78.90% carbon and 10.59% hydrogen. The remainder is oxygen. What is its empirical formula?

Determining a Formula from Mass Data

The composition of a compound in terms of mass percent gives us the mass of each element in a 100.0-g sample. In the laboratory, we often collect information on the composition of compounds slightly differently. We can:

1. Combine known masses of elements to give a sample of the compound of known mass. Element masses can be converted to moles, and the ratio of moles gives the combining ratio of atoms—that is, the empirical formula. This approach is described in Example 2.10.
2. Decompose a known mass of an unknown compound into "pieces" of known composition. If the masses of the "pieces" can be determined, the ratio of moles of the "pieces" gives the formula. An example is a decomposition such as

$$Ni(CO)_4(\ell) \rightarrow Ni(s) + 4\ CO(g)$$

The masses of Ni and CO can be converted to moles, whose 1 : 4 ratio would reveal the formula of the compound. We will describe this approach in Chapter 4 (▶ Section 4.4).

EXAMPLE 2.10 Formula of a Compound from Combining Masses

Problem Gallium oxide, Ga_xO_y, forms when gallium is combined with oxygen. Suppose you allow 1.25 g of gallium (Ga) to react with oxygen and obtain 1.68 g of Ga_xO_y. What is the formula of the product?

Strategy Calculate the mass of oxygen in 1.68 g of product (which you already know contains 1.25 g of Ga). Next, calculate the amounts of Ga and O (in moles), and find their ratio.

Solution The masses of Ga and O combined in 1.68 g of product are

$$1.68\ g\ product\ -\ 1.25\ g\ Ga = 0.43\ g\ O$$

Next, calculate the amount of each reactant:

$$1.25\ g\ Ga \times \frac{1\ mol\ Ga}{69.72\ g\ Ga} = 0.0179\ mol\ Ga$$

$$0.43\ g\ O \times \frac{1\ mol\ O}{16.0\ g\ O} = 0.027\ mol\ O$$

Find the ratio of moles of O to moles of Ga:

$$Mole\ ratio = \frac{0.027\ mol\ O}{0.0179\ mol\ Ga} = \frac{1.5\ mol\ O}{1.0\ mol\ Ga}$$

It is 1.5 mol O/1.0 mol Ga, or 3 mol O to 2 mol Ga. Thus, the product is gallium oxide, Ga_2O_3.

EXAMPLE 2.11 Determining a Formula from Mass Data

Problem Tin metal (Sn) and purple iodine (I_2) combine to form orange, solid tin iodide with an unknown formula.

$$Sn\ metal\ +\ solid\ I_2 \rightarrow solid\ Sn_xI_y$$

Weighed quantities of Sn and I_2 are combined, where the quantity of Sn is more than is needed to react with all of the iodine. After Sn_xI_y has been formed, it is isolated by filtration. The mass of excess tin is also determined. The following data were collected:

Mass of tin (Sn) in the original mixture	1.056 g
Mass of iodine (I_2) in the original mixture	1.947 g
Mass of tin (Sn) recovered after reaction	0.601 g

Strategy The first step is to find the masses of Sn and I that are combined in Sn_xI_y. The masses are then converted to moles, and the ratio of moles reveals the compound's empirical formula.

(a) Weighed samples of tin (left) and iodine (right).

(b) The tin and iodine are heated in a solvent.

(c) The hot reaction mixture is filtered to recover unreacted tin.

(d) When the solvent cools, solid, orange tin oxide forms and is isolated.

Charles D. Winters

The formula of a compound of tin and iodine can be found by determining the mass of iodine that combines with a given mass of tin.

Solution First, let us find the mass of tin that combined with iodine

Mass of Sn in original mixture	1.056 g
Mass of Sn recovered	− 0.601 g
Mass of Sn combined with 1.947 g I_2	0.455 g

Now convert the mass of tin to the amount of tin.

$$0.455 \text{ g Sn} \times \frac{1 \text{ mol Sn}}{118.7 \text{ g Sn}} = 0.00383 \text{ mol Sn}$$

No I_2 was recovered; it all reacted with Sn. Therefore, 0.00383 mol of Sn combined with 1.947 g of I_2. Because we want to know the amount of I that combined with 0.00383 mol of Sn, we calculate the amount of I from the mass of I_2.

$$1.947 \text{ g } I_2 \times \frac{1 \text{ mol } I_2}{253.81 \text{ g } I_2} \times \frac{2 \text{ mol I}}{1 \text{ mol } I_2} = 0.01534 \text{ mol I}$$

Finally, we find the ratio of moles.

$$\frac{\text{mol I}}{\text{mol Sn}} = \frac{0.01534 \text{ mol I}}{0.00383 \text{ mol Sn}} = \frac{4.01 \text{ mol I}}{1.00 \text{ mol Sn}} = \frac{4 \text{ mol I}}{1 \text{ mol Sn}}$$

There are four times as many moles of I as moles of Sn in the sample. Therefore, there are four times as many atoms of I as atoms of Sn per formula unit. The empirical formula is SnI_4.

EXERCISE 2.18 Determining a Formula from Combining Masses

Analysis shows that 0.586 g of potassium metal combines with 0.480 g of O_2 gas to give a white solid having a formula of K_xO_y. What is the empirical formula of the compound?

Determining a Formula by Mass Spectrometry

We have described chemical methods of determining a molecular formula, but there are many instrumental methods as well. One of them is *mass spectrometry* (Figure 2.27). We introduced this technique where it was used to describe the existence of isotopes and to measure their relative abundance (Figure 2.3). If a compound can be turned into a vapor, the vapor can be passed through an electron beam in a mass spectrometer where high energy electrons collide with the gas phase molecules. These high energy collisions cause the molecule to lose electrons and turn the molecules into positive ions. These ions usually break apart or fragment into smaller pieces. As illustrated in Figure 2.27, the cation created from

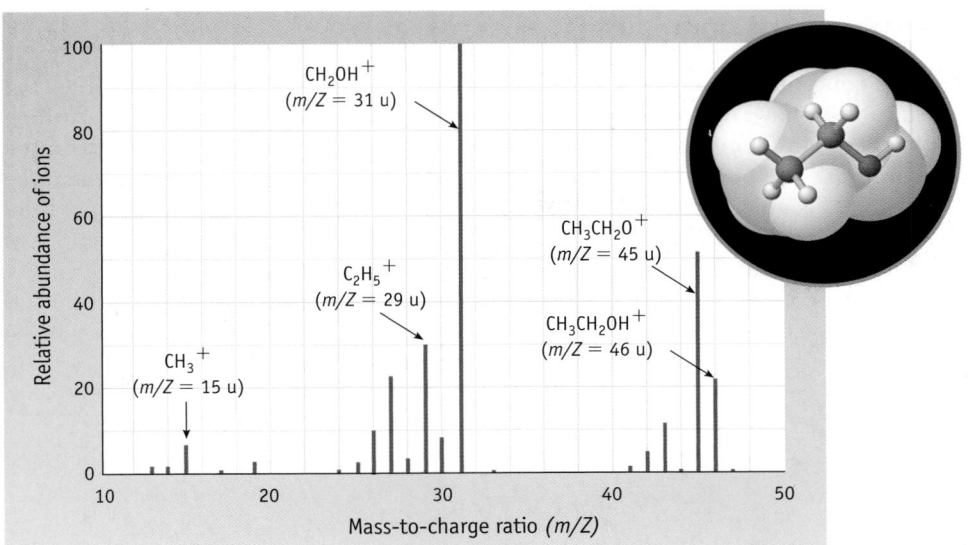

FIGURE 2.27 Mass spectrum of ethanol, CH₃CH₂OH. A prominent peak or line in the spectrum is the "parent" ion ($CH_3CH_2OH^+$) at mass 46. (The "parent" ion is the heaviest ion observed.) The mass designated by the peak for the "parent" ion confirms the formula of the molecule. Other peaks are for "fragment" ions. This pattern of lines can provide further, unambiguous evidence of the formula of the compound. (The horizontal axis is the mass-to-charge ratio of a given ion. Because almost all observed ions have a charge of $Z = +1$, the value observed is the mass of the ion.) (See *A Closer Look: Mass Spectrometry, Molar Mass, and Isotopes.*)

ethanol ($CH_3CH_2OH^+$) fragments (losing an H atom) to give another cation ($CH_3CH_2O^+$), which further fragments. A mass spectrometer detects and records the masses of the different particles. Analysis of the spectrum can help identify a compound and can give an accurate molar mass.

A Closer Look

Mass Spectrometry, Molar Mass, and Isotopes

Bromobenzene, C_6H_5Br, has a molar mass of 157.010 g/mol. Why, then, are there two prominent lines at a mass-to-charge ratio (*m/Z*) 156 and 158 in the mass spectrum of the compound (when $Z = 1$)? The answer shows us the influence of isotopes on molar mass.

Bromine has two naturally occurring isotopes, ^{79}Br and ^{81}Br. They are 50.7% and 49.3% abundant, respectively. What is the mass of C_6H_5Br based on each isotope? If we use the most abundant isotopes of C and H (^{12}C and ^1H), the mass of the molecule having only the ^{79}Br isotope, $C_6H_5{}^{79}Br$, is 156. The mass of the molecule containing only the ^{81}Br isotope, $C_6H_5{}^{81}Br$, is 158.

The calculated molar mass of bromobenzene is 157.010, a value derived from the atomic masses of the elements. Atomic masses reflect the abundances of all of the isotopes. In contrast, the mass spectrum has a line for each possible combination of isotopes. This explains why there are small lines at the mass-to-charge ratios of 157 and 159. They arise from various combinations of ^1H, ^{12}C, ^{13}C, ^{79}Br, and ^{81}Br atoms. In fact, careful analysis of such patterns can identify a molecule unambiguously.

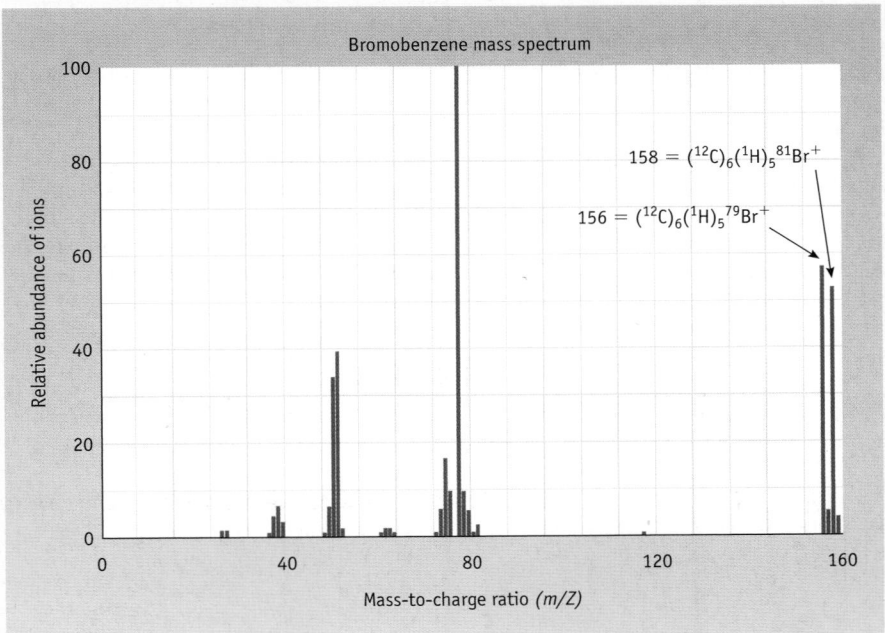

Bromobenzene mass spectrum

$$158 = (^{12}C)_6(^1H)_5{}^{81}Br^+$$
$$156 = (^{12}C)_6(^1H)_5{}^{79}Br^+$$

2.11 Hydrated Compounds

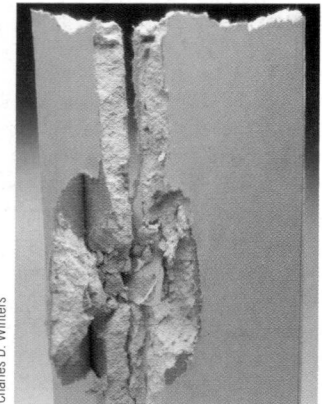

FIGURE 2.28 Gypsum wallboard. Gypsum is hydrated calcium sulfate, $CaSO_4 \cdot 2H_2O$.

If ionic compounds are prepared in water solution and then isolated as solids, the crystals often have molecules of water trapped in the lattice. Compounds in which molecules of water are associated with the ions of the compound are called **hydrated compounds.** The beautiful blue copper(II) compound in Figure 2.26, for example, has a formula that is conventionally written as $CuCl_2 \cdot 2 H_2O$. The dot between $CuCl_2$ and $2 H_2O$ indicates that 2 mol of water are associated with every mole of $CuCl_2$; it is equivalent to writing the formula as $CuCl_2(H_2O)_2$. The name of the compound, copper(II) chloride dihydrate, reflects the presence of 2 mol of water per mole of $CuCl_2$. The molar mass of $CuCl_2 \cdot 2 H_2O$ is 134.5 g/mol (for $CuCl_2$) plus 36.0 g/mol (for $2 H_2O$) for a total mass of 170.5 g/mol.

Hydrated compounds are common. The walls of your home may be covered with wallboard, or "plaster board" (Figure 2.28) These sheets contain hydrated calcium sulfate, or gypsum ($CaSO_4 \cdot 2 H_2O$), as well as unhydrated $CaSO_4$, sandwiched between

Case Study

What's in Those French Fries?

The U.S. Environmental Protection Agency (EPA) maintains a database of toxicities of chemicals. One compound on that list is acrylamide, $CH_2{=}CHCONH_2$, which is listed as a possible human carcinogen (cancer-causing substance). Although not confirmed by human data, carcinogenicity has been observed in rats. Based on the animal studies, the EPA suggests that the "Reference Dose" (RfD) of acrylamide should be 0.0002 mg per kilogram of body weight per day. (The RfD is a numerical estimate of a daily oral exposure to the human population, including sensitive subgroups such as children, that is not likely to cause harmful effects during a lifetime.)

In 2002, Swedish chemists announced that they had found previously undetected acrylamide in foods that many find appealing: french fries and potato chips (or chips and crisps as they are called in other countries).

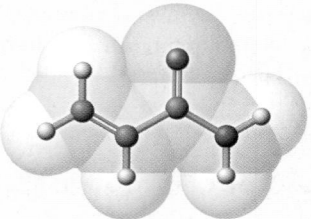

Acrylamide

Not only was acrylamide present, but it was in concentrations hundreds of times higher than what the EPA and the World Health Organization (WHO) consider safe. And soon thereafter it was also found in coffee, pastries, cookies, cereals, rolls, and toasted bread.

Where does the acrylamide come from, and can the amount be reduced? Chemists soon understood that the likely source was an interaction between the naturally occurring amino acid asparagine and a simple sugar such as fructose or glucose when the food was cooked. However, the level of acrylamide in food can vary widely with cooking time and temperature.

Can acrylamide levels be reduced in foods? Recent work in England indicates that if 0.39% by weight each of glycine (an amino acid) and citric acid are added before cooking, acrylamide levels can be reduced by 40%.

Should we give up french fries? Before acting precipitously, a closer look is called for. Even the report from the Swedish government's National Food Administration counseled that "...there is not sufficient data to

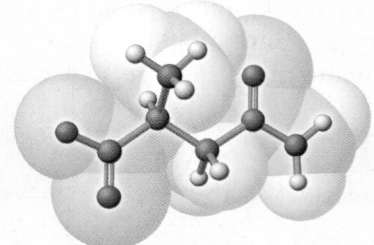

Asparagine, an amino acid

warrant changing the current dietary recommendation." Other scientists who study carcinogenic compounds point out that acrylamide is not a proven human carcinogen and that the dose of acrylamide from fried foods is 700 times less that the dose that causes cancer in rodents. Furthermore, many common foods that we eat regularly—among them cantaloupe, carrots, cauliflower, cherries, chocolate, and coffee—have substances that have been proven to cause cancer in rodents.

Nonetheless, the warning is there. Clearly, more information is needed, and chemists are the ones with the background to do such studies.

Questions:

1. *Which has the higher mass percent of nitrogen, acrylamide or asparagine?*
2. *If you weigh 150 pounds (1 pound = 453.6 g), how many molecules of acrylamide are you consuming per day if you consume 0.0002 mg per kilogram?*

Answers to these questions are in Appendix Q.

Charles D. Winters

Active Figure 2.29

Dehydrating hydrated cobalt(II) chloride, CoCl₂ · 6 H₂O. *(left)* Cobalt (II) chloride hexahydrate [CoCl₂ · 6 H₂O] is a deep red compound. *(left and center)* When it is heated, the compound loses the water of hydration and forms the deep blue compound CoCl₂.

Chemistry ⚛ Now™ Sign in at **www.cengage.com/login** and go to the Chapter Contents menu to explore an interactive version of this figure accompanied by an exercise.

paper. Gypsum is a mineral that can be mined. Now, however, it is usually obtained as a byproduct in the manufacture of hydrofluoric acid and phosphoric acid.

If gypsum is heated between 120 and 180 °C, the water is partly driven off to give $CaSO_4 \cdot \frac{1}{2} H_2O$, a compound commonly called "plaster of Paris." If you have ever broken an arm or leg and had to have a cast, the cast may have been made of this compound. It is an effective casting material because, when added to water, it forms a thick slurry that can be poured into a mold or spread out over a part of the body. As it takes on more water, the material increases in volume and forms a hard, inflexible solid. These properties also make plaster of Paris a useful material for artists, because the expanding compound fills a mold completely and makes a high-quality reproduction.

Hydrated cobalt(II) chloride is the red solid in Figure 2.29. When heated, it turns purple and then deep blue as it loses water to form anhydrous $CoCl_2$; "anhydrous" means a substance without water. On exposure to moist air, anhydrous $CoCl_2$ takes up water and is converted back into the red hydrated compound. It is this property that allows crystals of the blue compound to be used as a humidity indicator. You may have seen them in a small bag packed with a piece of electronic equipment.

There is no simple way to predict how much water will be present in a hydrated compound, so it must be determined experimentally. Such an experiment may involve heating the hydrated material so that all the water is released from the solid and evaporated. Only the anhydrous compound is left. The formula of hydrated copper(II) sulfate, commonly known as "blue vitriol," is determined in this manner in Example 2.12.

■ **Invisible Ink** CoCl₂ · 6 H₂O also makes a good "invisible ink." A solution of cobalt(II) chloride in water is red, but if you write on paper with the solution, it cannot be seen. When the paper is warmed, however, the cobalt compound dehydrates to give the deep blue anhydrous compound, and the writing becomes visible.

White CuSO₄

Blue CuSO₄ · 5 H₂O

Charles D. Winters

Heating a hydrated compound. The formula of a hydrated compound can be determined by heating a weighed sample enough to cause the compound to release its water of hydration. Knowing the mass of the hydrated compound before heating and the mass of the anhydrous compound after heating, we can determine the mass of water in the original sample.

■ **EXAMPLE 2.12** **Determining the Formula of a Hydrated Compound**

Problem You want to know the value of *x* in blue, hydrated copper(II) sulfate, $CuSO_4 \cdot x\ H_2O$; that is, the number of water molecules for each unit of $CuSO_4$. In the laboratory, you weigh out 1.023 g of the solid. After heating the solid thoroughly in a porcelain crucible (see Figure), 0.654 g of nearly white, anhydrous copper(II) sulfate, $CuSO_4$, remains.

$$1.023\ g\ CuSO_4 \cdot x\ H_2O + heat \rightarrow 0.654\ g\ CuSO_4 + ?\ g\ H_2O$$

Strategy To find *x*, we need to know the amount of H_2O per mole $CuSO_4$. Therefore, first find the mass of water lost by the sample from the difference between the mass of hydrated compound and the anhydrous form. Finally, find the ratio of the amount of water lost (moles) to the amount of anhydrous $CuSO_4$.

Solution Find the mass of water.

Mass of hydrated compound	1.023 g
— Mass of anhydrous compound, $CuSO_4$	−0.654
Mass of water	0.369 g

Next, convert the masses of $CuSO_4$ and H_2O to moles.

$$0.369 \text{ g } H_2O \times \frac{1 \text{ mol } H_2O}{18.02 \text{ g } H_2O} = 0.0205 \text{ mol } H_2O$$

$$0.654 \text{ g } CuSO_4 \times \frac{1 \text{ mol } CuSO_4}{159.6 \text{ g } CuSO_4} = 0.00410 \text{ mol } CuSO_4$$

The value of x is determined from the mole ratio.

$$\frac{0.0205 \text{ mol } H_2O}{0.00410 \text{ mol } CuSO_4} = \frac{5.00 \text{ mol } H_2O}{1.00 \text{ mol } CuSO_4}$$

The water-to-$CuSO_4$ ratio is 5-to-1, so the formula of the hydrated compound is $CuSO_4 \cdot 5\,H_2O$. Its name is copper(II) sulfate pentahydrate.

EXERCISE 2.19 Determining the Formula of a Hydrated Compound

Hydrated nickel(II) chloride is a beautiful, green, crystalline compound. When heated strongly, the compound is dehydrated. If 0.235 g of $NiCl_2 \cdot x\,H_2O$ gives 0.128 g of $NiCl_2$ on heating, what is the value of x?

Chapter Goals Revisited

Now that you have studied this chapter, you should ask whether you have met the chapter goals. In particular, you should be able to:

Describe atomic structure, and define atomic number and mass number

a. Describe electrons, protons, and neutrons, and the general structure of the atom (Section 2.1). Study Question(s) assignable in OWL: 2.

b. Understand the relative atomic weight scale and the atomic mass unit (Section 2.2).

Understand the nature of isotopes, and calculate atomic weight from isotopic abundances and isotopic masses

a. Define isotope and give the mass number and number of neutrons for a specific isotope (Sections 2.2 and 2.3). Study Question(s) assignable in OWL: 4, 5, 8.

b. Do calculations that relate the atomic weight of an element and isotopic abundances and masses (Section 2.4). Study Question(s) assignable in OWL: 10, 12, 15, 86, 88.

Know the terminology of the periodic table

a. Identify the periodic table locations of groups, periods, metals, metalloids, nonmetals, alkali metals, alkaline earth metals, halogens, noble gases, and the transition elements (Section 2.5). Study Question(s) assignable in OWL: 20, 21, 23, 92; Go Chemistry Module 1.

b. Recognize similarities and differences in properties of some of the common elements of a group.

Interpret, predict, and write formulas for ionic and molecular compounds

a. Recognize and interpret molecular formulas, condensed formulas, and structural formulas (Section 2.6).

b. Recognize that metal atoms commonly lose one or more electrons to form positive ions, called cations, and nonmetal atoms often gain electrons to form negative ions, called anions (see Figure 2.7).

c. Recognize that the charge on a metal cation in Groups 1A, 2A, and 3A is equal to the group number in which the element is found in the periodic table (M^{n+}, n = Group number) (Section 2.7). Charges on transition metal cations are often 2+ or 3+, but other charges are observed. Study Question(s) assignable in OWL: 29, 33, 35; Go Chemistry Module 2.

d. Recognize that the negative charge on a single-atom or monatomic anion, X^{n-}, is given by n = Group number − 8 (Section 2.7).

e. Write formulas for ionic compounds by combining ions in the proper ratio to give no overall charge (Section 2.7).

Name ionic and molecular compounds

a. Give the names or formulas of polyatomic ions, knowing their formulas or names, respectively (Table 2.4 and Section 2.7).

b. Name ionic compounds and simple binary compounds of the nonmetals (Sections 2.7 and 2.8). Study Question(s) assignable in OWL: 41, 43, 49, 51; Go Chemistry Module 3.

Understand some properties of ionic compounds

a. Understand the importance of Coulomb's law (Equation 2.3), which describes the electrostatic forces of attraction and repulsion of ions. Coulomb's law states that the force of attraction between oppositely charged species increases with electric charge and with decreasing distance between the species (Section 2.7). Study Question(s) assignable in OWL: 48.

Explain the concept of the mole, and use molar mass in calculations

a. Understand that the molar mass of an element is the mass in grams of Avogadro's number of atoms of that element (Section 2.9). Study Question(s) assignable in OWL: 53, 55, 57, 89, 93, 96.

b. Know how to use the molar mass of an element and Avogadro's number in calculations (Section 2.9). Study Question(s) assignable in OWL: 55, 57, 93, 98.

c. Understand that the molar mass of a compound (often called the molecular weight) is the mass in grams of Avogadro's number of molecules (or formula units) of a compound (Section 2.9). For ionic compounds, which do not consist of individual molecules, the sum of atomic masses is often called the formula mass (or formula weight).

d. Calculate the molar mass of a compound from its formula and a table of atomic masses (Section 2.9). Study Question(s) assignable in OWL: 59, 61, 105.

e. Calculate the number of moles of a compound that is represented by a given mass, and vice versa (Section 2.9). Study Question(s) assignable in OWL: 63; Go Chemistry Module 4.

Derive compound formulas from experimental data

a. Express the composition of a compound in terms of percent composition (Section 2.10). Study Question(s) assignable in OWL: 67, 69.

b. Use percent composition or other experimental data to determine the empirical formula of a compound (Section 2.10). Study Question(s) assignable in OWL: 71, 76, 77, 79, 81, 120.

c. Understand how mass spectrometry can be used to find a molar mass (Section 2.10).

d. Use experimental data to find the number of water molecules in a hydrated compound (Section 2.11) Study Question(s) assignable in OWL: 141.

KEY EQUATIONS

Equation 2.1 (page 54)   Percent abundance of an isotope

$$\text{Percent abundance} = \frac{\text{number of atoms of a given isotope}}{\text{total number of atoms of all isotopes of that element}} \times 100\%$$

Equation 2.2 (page 56)   Calculate the average atomic mass (atomic weight) from isotope abundances and the exact atomic mass of each isotope of an element.

$$\text{Atomic weight} = \left(\frac{\%\ \text{abundance isotope 1}}{100}\right)(\text{mass of isotope 1})$$
$$+ \left(\frac{\%\ \text{abundance isotope 2}}{100}\right)(\text{mass of isotope 2}) + \ ...$$

Equation 2.3 (page 78)   **Coulomb's Law,** the force of attraction between oppositely charged ions.

$$\text{Force of attraction} = k\ \frac{(n^+ e)\,(n^- e)}{d^2}$$

charge on + and − ions / charge on electron

proportionality constant   distance between ions

STUDY QUESTIONS

OWL Online homework for this chapter may be assigned in OWL.

▲ denotes challenging questions.

■ denotes questions assignable in OWL.

Blue-numbered questions have answers in Appendix O and fully-worked solutions in the *Student Solutions Manual*.

Practicing Skills

Atoms: Their Composition and Structure
(See ChemistryNow Screen 2.11.)

1. What are the three fundamental particles from which atoms are built? What are their electric charges? Which of these particles constitute the nucleus of an atom? Which is the least massive particle of the three?

2. ■ If a gold atom has a radius of 145 pm and you could string gold atoms like beads on a thread, how many atoms would you need to have a necklace 36 cm long?

3. Give the complete symbol ($_Z^A X$), including atomic number and mass number, for each of the following atoms: (a) magnesium with 15 neutrons, (b) titanium with 26 neutrons, and (c) zinc with 32 neutrons.

4. ■ Give the complete symbol ($_Z^A X$), including atomic number and mass number, of (a) a nickel atom with 31 neutrons, (b) a plutonium atom with 150 neutrons, and (c) a tungsten atom with 110 neutrons.

5. ■ How many electrons, protons, and neutrons are there in each of the following atoms?
(a) magnesium-24, ^{24}Mg (d) carbon-13, ^{13}C;
(b) tin-119, ^{119}Sn (e) copper-63, ^{63}Cu
(c) thorium-232, ^{232}Th (f) bismuth-205, ^{205}Bi

6. Atomic Structure
(a) The synthetic radioactive element technetium is used in many medical studies. Give the number of electrons, protons, and neutrons in an atom of technetium-99.
(b) Radioactive americium-241 is used in household smoke detectors and in bone mineral analysis. Give the number of electrons, protons, and neutrons in an atom of americium-241.

Isotopes
(See ChemistryNow Screen 2.12.)

7. Cobalt has three radioactive isotopes used in medical studies. Atoms of these isotopes have 30, 31, and 33 neutrons, respectively. Give the symbol for each of these isotopes.

8. ■ Which of the following are isotopes of element X, the atomic number for which is 9: $^{19}_9X$, $^{20}_9X$, $^9_{18}X$ and $^{21}_9X$?

Isotope Abundance and Atomic Weight
(See Examples 2.2 and 2.3, Exercises 2.2 and 2.3, and ChemistryNow Screens 2.12 and 2.13.)

9. Thallium has two stable isotopes, ^{203}Tl and ^{205}Tl. Knowing that the atomic weight of thallium is 204.4, which isotope is the more abundant of the two?

10. ■ Strontium has four stable isotopes. Strontium-84 has a very low natural abundance, but ^{86}Sr, ^{87}Sr, and ^{88}Sr are all reasonably abundant. Knowing that the atomic weight of strontium is 87.62, which of the more abundant isotopes predominates?

11. Verify that the atomic weight of lithium is 6.94, given the following information:
^6Li, mass = 6.015121 u; percent abundance = 7.50%
^7Li, mass = 7.016003 u; percent abundance = 92.50%

12. ■ Verify that the atomic weight of magnesium is 24.31, given the following information:
^{24}Mg, mass = 23.985042 u; percent abundance = 78.99%
^{25}Mg, mass = 24.985837 u; percent abundance = 10.00%
^{26}Mg, mass = 25.982593 u; percent abundance = 11.01%

13. Silver (Ag) has two stable isotopes, ^{107}Ag and ^{109}Ag. The isotopic weight of ^{107}Ag is 106.9051, and the isotopic mass of ^{109}Ag is 108.9047. The atomic weight of Ag, from the periodic table, is 107.868. Estimate the percent of ^{107}Ag in a sample of the element.
(a) 0%   (b) 25%   (c) 50%   (d) 75%

14. Copper exists as two isotopes: ^{63}Cu (62.9298 u) and ^{65}Cu (64.9278 u). What is the approximate percent of ^{63}Cu in samples of this element?
(a) 10%   (c) 50%   (e) 90%
(b) 30%   (d) 70%

15. ■ Gallium has two naturally occurring isotopes, ^{69}Ga and ^{71}Ga, with masses of 68.9257 u and 70.9249 u, respectively. Calculate the percent abundances of these isotopes of gallium.

16. Europium has two stable isotopes, ^{151}Eu and ^{153}Eu, with masses of 150.9197 u and 152.9212 u, respectively. Calculate the percent abundances of these isotopes of europium.

The Periodic Table
(See Section 2.5 and Exercise 2.4. See also the Periodic Table Tool on the ChemistryNow website.)

17. Titanium and thallium have symbols that are easily confused with each other. Give the symbol, atomic number, atomic weight, and group and period number of each element. Are they metals, metalloids, or nonmetals?

18. In Groups 4A–6A, there are several elements whose symbols begin with S. Name these elements, and for each one give its symbol, atomic number, Group number, and period. Describe each as a metal, metalloid, or nonmetal.

19. How many periods of the periodic table have 8 elements; how many have 18 elements, and how many have 32 elements?

20. ■ How many elements occur in the seventh period? What is the name given to the majority of these elements, and what well-known property characterizes them?

21. ■ Select answers to the questions listed below from the following list of elements whose symbols start with the letter C: C, Ca, Cr, Co, Cd, Cl, Cs, Ce, Cm, Cu, and Cf. (You should expect to use some symbols more than once.)
(a) Which are nonmetals?
(b) Which are main group elements?
(c) Which are lanthanides?
(d) Which are transition elements?
(e) Which are actinides?
(f) Which are gases?

22. Give the name and chemical symbol for the following.
(a) a nonmetal in the second period
(b) an alkali metal in the fifth period
(c) the third-period halogen
(d) an element that is a gas at 20°C and 1 atmosphere pressure

23. ■ Classify the following elements as metals, metalloids, or nonmetals: N, Na, Ni, Ne, and Np.

24. Here are symbols for five of the seven elements whose names begin with the letter B: B, Ba, Bk, Bi, and Br. Match each symbol with one of the descriptions below.
(a) a radioactive element
(b) a liquid at room temperature
(c) a metalloid
(d) an alkaline earth element
(e) a Group 5A element

Molecular Formulas and Models
(See Exercise 2.5.)

25. A model of sulfuric acid is illustrated here. Write the molecular formula for sulfuric acid, and draw the structural formula. Describe the structure of the molecule. Is it flat? That is, are all the atoms in the plane of the paper? (Color code: sulfur atoms are yellow; oxygen atoms are red; and hydrogen atoms are white.)

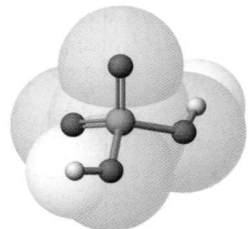

26. A model of the platinum-based chemotherapy agent cisplatin is given here. Write the molecular formula for the compound, and draw its structural formula.

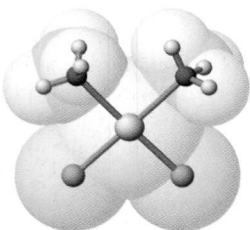

Ions and Ion Charges
(See Exercise 2.6, Figure 2.18, Table 2.4, and ChemistryNow Screens 2.18 and 2.19.)

27. What charges are most commonly observed for monatomic ions of the following elements?
    (a) magnesium   (c) nickel
    (b) zinc   (d) gallium

28. What charges are most commonly observed for monatomic ions of the following elements?
    (a) selenium   (c) iron
    (b) fluorine   (d) nitrogen

29. ■ Give the symbol, including the correct charge, for each of the following ions:
    (a) barium ion   (e) sulfide ion
    (b) titanium(IV) ion   (f) perchlorate ion
    (c) phosphate ion   (g) cobalt(II) ion
    (d) hydrogen carbonate ion (h) sulfate ion

30. Give the symbol, including the correct charge, for each of the following ions:
    (a) permanganate ion   (d) ammonium ion
    (b) nitrite ion   (e) phosphate ion
    (c) dihydrogen phosphate ion   (f) sulfite ion

31. When a potassium atom becomes a monatomic ion, how many electrons does it lose or gain? What noble gas atom has the same number of electrons as a potassium ion?

32. When oxygen and sulfur atoms become monatomic ions, how many electrons does each lose or gain? Which noble gas atom has the same number of electrons as an oxide ion? Which noble gas atom has the same number of electrons as a sulfide ion?

Ionic Compounds
(See Examples 2.4 and 2.5 and ChemistryNow Screen 2.20.)

33. ■ Predict the charges of the ions in an ionic compound containing the elements barium and bromine. Write the formula for the compound.

34. What are the charges of the ions in an ionic compound containing cobalt(III) and fluoride ions? Write the formula for the compound.

35. ■ For each of the following compounds, give the formula, charge, and the number of each ion that makes up the compound:
    (a) K_2S (d) $(NH_4)_3PO_4$
    (b) $CoSO_4$ (e) $Ca(ClO)_2$
    (c) $KMnO_4$ (f) $NaCH_3CO_2$

36. For each of the following compounds, give the formula, charge, and the number of each ion that makes up the compound:
    (a) $Mg(CH_3CO_2)_2$ (d) $Ti(SO_4)_2$
    (b) $Al(OH)_3$ (e) KH_2PO_4
    (c) $CuCO_3$ (f) $CaHPO_4$

37. Cobalt forms Co^{2+} and Co^{3+} ions. Write the formulas for the two cobalt oxides formed by these transition metal ions.

38. Platinum is a transition element and forms Pt^{2+} and Pt^{4+} ions. Write the formulas for the compounds of each of these ions with (a) chloride ions and (b) sulfide ions.

39. Which of the following are correct formulas for ionic compounds? For those that are not, give the correct formula.
    (a) $AlCl_2$ (c) Ga_2O_3
    (b) KF_2 (d) MgS

40. Which of the following are correct formulas for ionic compounds? For those that are not, give the correct formula.
    (a) Ca_2O (c) Fe_2O_5
    (b) $SrBr_2$ (d) Li_2O

Naming Ionic Compounds
(See Exercise 2.8 and ChemistryNow Screen 2.21.)

41. ■ Name each of the following ionic compounds:
    (a) K_2S
    (b) $CoSO_4$
    (c) $(NH_4)_3PO_4$
    (d) $Ca(ClO)_2$

42. Name each of the following ionic compounds:
    (a) $Ca(CH_3CO_2)_2$
    (b) $Ni_3(PO_4)_2$
    (c) $Al(OH)_3$
    (d) KH_2PO_4

43. ■ Give the formula for each of the following ionic compounds:
    (a) ammonium carbonate
    (b) calcium iodide
    (c) copper(II) bromide
    (d) aluminum phosphate
    (e) silver(I) acetate

44. Give the formula for each of the following ionic compounds:
    (a) calcium hydrogen carbonate
    (b) potassium permanganate
    (c) magnesium perchlorate
    (d) potassium hydrogen phosphate
    (e) sodium sulfite

45. Write the formulas for the four ionic compounds that can be made by combining each of the cations Na^+ and Ba^{2+} with the anions CO_3^{2-} and I^-. Name each of the compounds.

46. Write the formulas for the four ionic compounds that can be made by combining the cations Mg^{2+} and Fe^{3+} with the anions PO_4^{3-} and NO_3^-. Name each compound formed.

Coulomb's Law
(See Equation 2.3, Figure 2.21, and ChemistryNow Screen 2.22.)

47. Sodium ions, Na^+, form ionic compounds with fluoride ions, F^-, and iodide ions, I^-. The radii of these ions are as follows: $Na^+ = 116$ pm; $F^- = 119$ pm; and $I^- = 206$ pm. In which ionic compound, NaF or NaI, are the forces of attraction between cation and anion stronger? Explain your answer.

48. ■ Consider the two ionic compounds NaCl and CaO. In which compound are the cation–anion attractive forces stronger? Explain your answer.

Naming Binary, Nonmetal Compounds
(See Exercise 2.10 and ChemistryNow Screens 2.24 and 2.25.)

49. ■ Name each of the following binary, nonionic compounds:
    (a) NF_3
    (b) HI
    (c) BI_3
    (d) PF_5

50. Name each of the following binary, nonionic compounds:
    (a) N_2O_5
    (b) P_4S_3
    (c) OF_2
    (d) XeF_4

51. ■ Give the formula for each of the following compounds:
    (a) sulfur dichloride
    (b) dinitrogen pentaoxide
    (c) silicon tetrachloride
    (d) diboron trioxide (commonly called boric oxide)

52. Give the formula for each of the following compounds:
    (a) bromine trifluoride
    (b) xenon difluoride
    (c) hydrazine
    (d) diphosphorus tetrafluoride
    (e) butane

Atoms and the Mole
(See Example 2.6, Exercises 2.11 and 2.12, and ChemistryNow Screens 2.25 and 2.26.)

53. ■ Calculate the mass, in grams, of each the following:
    (a) 2.5 mol of aluminum
    (b) 1.25×10^{-3} mol of iron
    (c) 0.015 mol of calcium
    (d) 653 mol of neon

54. Calculate the mass, in grams, of each the following:
    (a) 4.24 mol of gold
    (b) 15.6 mol of He
    (c) 0.063 mol of platinum
    (d) 3.63×10^{-4} mol of Pu

55. ■ Calculate the amount (moles) represented by each of the following:
    (a) 127.08 g of Cu
    (b) 0.012 g of lithium
    (c) 5.0 mg of americium
    (d) 6.75 g of Al

56. Calculate the amount (moles) represented by each of the following:
    (a) 16.0 g of Na
    (b) 0.876 g of tin
    (c) 0.0034 g of platinum
    (d) 0.983 g of Xe

57. ■ You are given 1.0 g samples of He, Fe, Li, Si, and C. Which sample contains the largest number of atoms? Which contains the smallest?

58. A semiconducting material is composed of 52 g of Ga, 9.5 g of Al, and 112 g of As. Which element has the largest number of atoms in the final mixture?

Molecules, Compounds, and the Mole
(See Example 2.7 and ChemistryNow Screens 2.27 and 2.28.)

59. ■ Calculate the molar mass of each of the following compounds:
    (a) Fe_2O_3, iron(III) oxide
    (b) BCl_3, boron trichloride
    (c) $C_6H_8O_6$, ascorbic acid (vitamin C)

60. Calculate the molar mass of each of the following compounds:
    (a) $Fe(C_6H_{11}O_7)_2$, iron(II) gluconate, a dietary supplement
    (b) $CH_3CH_2CH_2CH_2SH$, butanethiol, has a skunk-like odor
    (c) $C_{20}H_{24}N_2O_2$, quinine, used as an antimalarial drug

61. ■ Calculate the molar mass of each hydrated compound. Note that the water of hydration is included in the molar mass. (See Section 2.11.)
(a) $Ni(NO_3)_2 \cdot 6\ H_2O$
(b) $CuSO_4 \cdot 5\ H_2O$

62. Calculate the molar mass of each hydrated compound. Note that the water of hydration is included in the molar mass. (See Section 2.11.)
(a) $H_2C_2O_4 \cdot 2\ H_2O$
(b) $MgSO_4 \cdot 7\ H_2O$, Epsom salts

63. ■ What mass is represented by 0.0255 mol of each of the following compounds?
(a) C_3H_7OH, propanol, rubbing alcohol
(b) $C_{11}H_{16}O_2$, an antioxidant in foods, also known as BHA (butylated hydroxyanisole)
(c) $C_9H_8O_4$, aspirin
(d) $(CH_3)_2CO$, acetone, an important industrial solvent

64. Assume you have 0.123 mol of each of the following compounds. What mass of each is present?
(a) $C_{14}H_{10}O_4$, benzoyl peroxide, used in acne medications
(b) Dimethylglyoxime, used in the laboratory to test for nickel(II) ions

$$
\begin{array}{c}
CH_3 \\
| \\
C{=}N{-}OH \\
| \\
C{=}N{-}OH \\
| \\
CH_3
\end{array}
$$

(c) The compound below is responsible for the "skunky" taste in poorly made beer.

$$
\begin{array}{c}
CH_3\ H\ \ H \\
|\ \ |\ \ | \\
C{=}C{-}C{-}S{-}H \\
|\ \ \ \ | \\
CH_3\ \ \ H
\end{array}
$$

(d) DEET, a mosquito repellent

65. Sulfur trioxide, SO_3, is made industrially in enormous quantities by combining oxygen and sulfur dioxide, SO_2. What amount (moles) of SO_3 is represented by 1.00 kg of sulfur trioxide? How many molecules? How many sulfur atoms? How many oxygen atoms?

66. An Alka-Seltzer tablet contains 324 mg of aspirin ($C_9H_8O_4$), 1904 mg of $NaHCO_3$, and 1000. mg of citric acid ($H_3C_6H_5O_7$). (The last two compounds react with each other to provide the "fizz," bubbles of CO_2, when the tablet is put into water.)
(a) Calculate the amount (moles) of each substance in the tablet.
(b) If you take one tablet, how many molecules of aspirin are you consuming?

Percent Composition
(See Example 2.8 and ChemistryNow Screen 2.29.)

67. ■ Calculate the mass percent of each element in the following compounds:
(a) PbS, lead(II) sulfide, galena
(b) C_3H_8, propane
(c) $C_{10}H_{14}O$, carvone, found in caraway seed oil

68. Calculate the mass percent of each element in the following compounds:
(a) $C_8H_{10}N_2O_2$, caffeine
(b) $C_{10}H_{20}O$, menthol
(c) $CoCl_2 \cdot 6\ H_2O$

69. ■ Calculate the mass percent of copper in CuS, copper(II) sulfide. If you wish to obtain 10.0 g of copper metal from copper(II) sulfide, what mass of CuS (in grams) must you use?

70. Calculate the mass percent of titanium in the mineral ilmenite, $FeTiO_3$. What mass of ilmenite (in grams) is required if you wish to obtain 750 g of titanium?

Empirical and Molecular Formulas
(See Example 2.9 and ChemistryNow Screens 2.31 and 2.32.)

71. ■ Succinic acid occurs in fungi and lichens. Its empirical formula is $C_2H_3O_2$, and its molar mass is 118.1 g/mol. What is its molecular formula?

72. An organic compound has the empirical formula C_2H_4NO. If its molar mass is 116.1 g/mol, what is the molecular formula of the compound?

73. Complete the following table:

	Empirical Formula	Molar Mass (g/mol)	Molecular Formula
(a)	CH	26.0	_____
(b)	CHO	116.1	_____
(c)	_____	_____	C_8H_{16}

74. Complete the following table:

	Empirical Formula	Molar Mass (g/mol)	Molecular Formula
(a)	$C_2H_3O_3$	150.0	_____
(b)	C_3H_8	44.1	_____
(c)	_____	_____	B_4H_{10}

▲ more challenging ■ in OWL Blue-numbered questions answered in Appendix O

75. Acetylene is a colorless gas used as a fuel in welding torches, among other things. It is 92.26% C and 7.74% H. Its molar mass is 26.02 g/mol. What are the empirical and molecular formulas of acetylene?

76. ■ A large family of boron-hydrogen compounds has the general formula B_xH_y. One member of this family contains 88.5% B; the remainder is hydrogen. What is its empirical formula?

77. ■ Cumene is a hydrocarbon, a compound composed only of C and H. It is 89.94% carbon, and its molar mass is 120.2 g/mol. What are the empirical and molecular formulas of cumene?

78. In 2006, a Russian team discovered an interesting molecule they called "sulflower" because of its shape and because it was based on sulfur. It is composed of 57.17% S and 42.83% C and has a molar mass of 448.70 g/mol. Determine the empirical and molecular formulas of "sulflower."

79. ■ Mandelic acid is an organic acid composed of carbon (63.15%), hydrogen (5.30%), and oxygen (31.55%). Its molar mass is 152.14 g/mol. Determine the empirical and molecular formulas of the acid.

80. Nicotine, a poisonous compound found in tobacco leaves, is 74.0% C, 8.65% H, and 17.35% N. Its molar mass is 162 g/mol. What are the empirical and molecular formulas of nicotine?

Determining Formulas from Mass Data
(See Examples 2.10 and 2.11 and ChemistryNow Screens 2.30 and 2.31.)

81. ■ A new compound containing xenon and fluorine was isolated by shining sunlight on a mixture of Xe (0.526 g) and excess F_2 gas. If you isolate 0.678 g of the new compound, what is its empirical formula?

82. Elemental sulfur (1.256 g) is combined with fluorine, F_2, to give a compound with the formula SF_x, a very stable, colorless gas. If you have isolated 5.722 g of SF_x, what is the value of x?

83. Zinc metal (2.50 g) combines with 9.70 g of iodine to produce zinc iodide, Zn_xI_y. What is the formula of this ionic compound?

84. You combine 1.25 g of germanium, Ge, with excess chlorine, Cl_2. The mass of product, Ge_xCl_y, is 3.69 g. What is the formula of the product, Ge_xCl_y?

General Questions
These questions are not designed as to type or location in the chapter. They may combine several concepts.

85. Fill in the blanks in the table (one column per element).

Symbol	^{58}Ni	^{33}S	___	___
Number of protons	___	___	10	___
Number of neutrons	___	___	10	30
Number of electrons in the neutral atom	___	___	___	25
Name of element	___	___	___	___

86. ■ Potassium has three naturally occurring isotopes (^{39}K, ^{40}K, and ^{41}K), but ^{40}K has a very low natural abundance. Which of the other two isotopes is the more abundant? Briefly explain your answer.

87. Crossword Puzzle: In the 2 × 2 box shown here, each answer must be correct four ways: horizontally, vertically, diagonally, and by itself. Instead of words, use symbols of elements. When the puzzle is complete, the four spaces will contain the overlapping symbols of 10 elements. There is only one correct solution.

1	2
3	4

Horizontal
1–2: Two-letter symbol for a metal used in ancient times
3–4: Two-letter symbol for a metal that burns in air and is found in Group 5A

Vertical
1–3: Two-letter symbol for a metalloid
2–4: Two-letter symbol for a metal used in U.S. coins

Single squares: All one-letter symbols
1: A colorful nonmetal
2: Colorless, gaseous nonmetal
3: An element that makes fireworks green
4: An element that has medicinal uses

Diagonal
1–4: Two-letter symbol for an element used in electronics
2–3: Two-letter symbol for a metal used with Zr to make wires for superconducting magnets

This puzzle first appeared in *Chemical & Engineering News*, p. 86, December 14, 1987 (submitted by S. J. Cyvin) and in *Chem Matters*, October 1988.

88. ■ *The abundance of the elements in the solar system from H to Zn.* The chart shows a general decline in abundance with increasing mass among the first 30 elements. The decline continues beyond zinc. (Notice that the scale on the vertical axis is logarithmic, that is, it progresses in powers of 10. The abundance of nitrogen, for example, is 1/10,000 (1/10^4) of the abundance of hydrogen. All abundances are plotted as the number of atoms per 10^{12} atoms of H. (The fact that the abundances of Li, Be, and B, as well as those of the elements near Fe, do not follow the general decline is a consequence of the way that elements are synthesized in stars.)

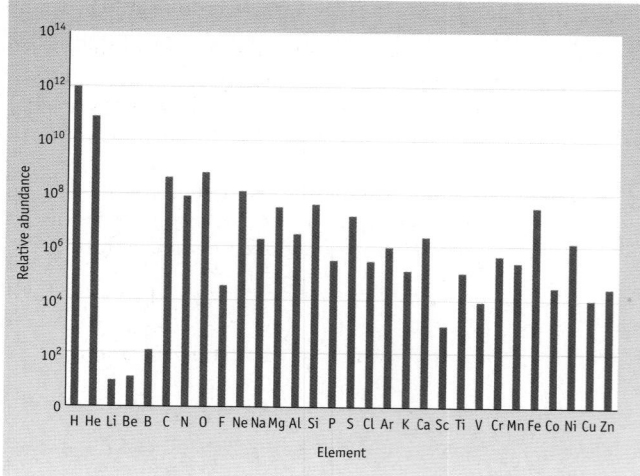

(a) What is the most abundant main group metal?
(b) What is the most abundant nonmetal?
(c) What is the most abundant metalloid?
(d) Which of the transition elements is most abundant?
(e) Which halogens are included on this plot, and which is the most abundant?

89. Copper atoms
(a) ■ What is the average mass of one copper atom?
(b) Students in a college computer science class once sued the college because they were asked to calculate the cost of one atom and could not do it. But you are in a chemistry course, and you can do this. (See E. Felsenthal, *Wall Street Journal*, May 9, 1995.) If the cost of 2.0 mm diameter copper wire (99.999% pure) is currently $41.70 for 7.0 g, what is the cost of one copper atom?

90. Which of the following is impossible?
(a) silver foil that is 1.2×10^{-4} m thick
(b) a sample of potassium that contains 1.784×10^{24} atoms
(c) a gold coin of mass 1.23×10^{-3} kg
(d) 3.43×10^{-27} mol of S_8 molecules

91. Reviewing the periodic table.
(a) Name the element in Group 2A and the fifth period.
(b) Name the element in the fifth period and Group 4B.
(c) Which element is in the second period in Group 4A?
(d) Which element is in the fourth period in Group 5A?
(e) Which halogen is in the fifth period?
(f) Which alkaline earth element is in the third period?
(g) Which noble gas element is in the fourth period?
(h) Name the nonmetal in Group 6A and the third period.
(i) Name a metalloid in the fourth period.

92. ■ Give two examples of nonmetallic elements that have allotropes. Name those elements, and describe the allotropes of each.

93. ■ In each case, decide which represents more mass:
(a) 0.5 mol of Na, 0.5 mol of Si, or 0.25 mol of U
(b) 9.0 g of Na, 0.50 mol of Na, or 1.2×10^{22} atoms of Na
(c) 10 atoms of Fe or 10 atoms of K

94. The recommended daily allowance (RDA) of iron in your diet is 15 mg. How many moles is this? How many atoms?

95. Put the following elements in order from smallest to largest mass:
(a) 3.79×10^{24} atoms Fe   (e) 9.221 mol Na
(b) 19.921 mol H_2 (f) 4.07×10^{24} atoms Al
(c) 8.576 mol C   (g) 9.2 mol Cl_2
(d) 7.4 mol Si

96. ■ ▲ When a sample of phosphorus burns in air, the compound P_4O_{10} forms. One experiment showed that 0.744 g of phosphorus formed 1.704 g of P_4O_{10}. Use this information to determine the ratio of the atomic weights of phosphorus and oxygen (mass P/mass O). If the atomic weight of oxygen is assumed to be 16.000 u, calculate the atomic weight of phosphorus.

97. ▲ Although carbon-12 is now used as the standard for atomic weights, this has not always been the case. Early attempts at classification used hydrogen as the standard, with the weight of hydrogen being set equal to 1.0000 u. Later attempts defined atomic weights using oxygen (with a weight of 16.0000). In each instance, the atomic weights of the other elements were defined relative to these masses. (To answer this question, you need more precise data on current atomic weights: H, 1.00794 u; O, 15.9994 u.)
(a) If H = 1.0000 u was used as a standard for atomic weights, what would the atomic weight of oxygen be? What would be the value of Avogadro's number under these circumstances?
(b) Assuming the standard is O = 16.0000, determine the value for the atomic weight of hydrogen and the value of Avogadro's number.

▲ more challenging ■ in OWL Blue-numbered questions answered in Appendix O

98. ■ A reagent occasionally used in chemical synthesis is sodium–potassium alloy. (Alloys are mixtures of metals, and Na-K has the interesting property that it is a liquid.) One formulation of the alloy (the one that melts at the lowest temperature) contains 68 atom percent K; that is, out of every 100 atoms, 68 are K and 32 are Na. What is the mass percent of potassium in sodium–potassium alloy?

99. Write formulas for all of the compounds that can be made by combining the cations NH_4^+ and Ni^{2+} with the anions CO_3^{2-} and SO_4^{2-}.

100. How many electrons are in a strontium atom (Sr)? Does an atom of Sr gain or lose electrons when forming an ion? How many electrons are gained or lost by the atom? When Sr forms an ion, the ion has the same number of electrons as which one of the noble gases?

101. Which of the following compounds has the highest mass percent of chlorine?
    (a) BCl_3 (d) $AlCl_3$
    (b) $AsCl_3$ (e) PCl_3
    (c) $GaCl_3$

102. Which of the following samples has the largest number of ions?
    (a) 1.0 g of $BeCl_2$ (d) 1.0 g of $SrCO_3$
    (b) 1.0 g of $MgCl_2$ (e) 1.0 g of $BaSO_4$
    (c) 1.0 g of CaS

103. The structure of one of the bases in DNA, adenine, is shown here. Which represents the greater mass: 40.0 g of adenine or 3.0×10^{23} molecules of the compound?

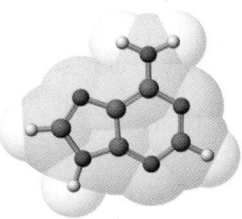

104. Ionic and molecular compounds of the halogens.
    (a) What are the names of BaF_2, $SiCl_4$, and $NiBr_2$?
    (b) Which of the compounds in part (a) are ionic, and which are molecular?
    (c) Which has the larger mass, 0.50 mol of BaF_2, 0.50 mol of $SiCl_4$, or 1.0 mol of $NiBr_2$?

105. ■ A drop of water has a volume of about 0.050 mL. How many molecules of water are in a drop of water? (Assume water has a density of 1.00 g/cm³.)

106. Capsaicin, the compound that gives the hot taste to chili peppers, has the formula $C_{18}H_{27}NO_3$.
    (a) Calculate its molar mass.
    (b) If you eat 55 mg of capsaicin, what amount (moles) have you consumed?
    (c) Calculate the mass percent of each element in the compound.
    (d) What mass of carbon (in milligrams) is there in 55 mg of capsaicin?

107. Calculate the molar mass and the mass percent of each element in the blue solid compound $Cu(NH_3)_4SO_4 \cdot H_2O$. What is the mass of copper and the mass of water in 10.5 g of the compound?

108. Write the molecular formula, and calculate the molar mass for each of the molecules shown here. Which has the larger percentage of carbon? Of oxygen?
    (a) Ethylene glycol (used in antifreeze)

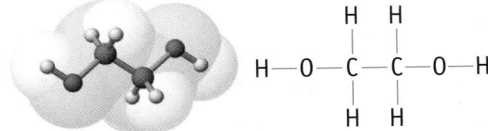

    (b) Dihydroxyacetone (used in artificial tanning lotions)

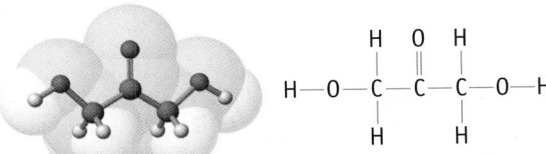

    (c) Ascorbic acid, commonly known as vitamin C

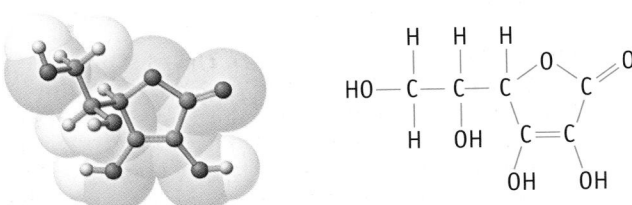

109. Malic acid, an organic acid found in apples, contains C, H, and O in the following ratios: $C_1H_{1.50}O_{1.25}$. What is the empirical formula of malic acid?

110. Your doctor has diagnosed you as being anemic—that is, as having too little iron in your blood. At the drugstore, you find two iron-containing dietary supplements: one with iron(II) sulfate, $FeSO_4$, and the other with iron(II) gluconate, $Fe(C_6H_{11}O_7)_2$. If you take 100. mg of each compound, which will deliver more atoms of iron?

111. A compound composed of iron and carbon monoxide, $Fe_x(CO)_y$, is 30.70% iron. What is the empirical formula for the compound?

112. Ma huang, an extract from the ephedra species of plants, contains ephedrine. The Chinese have used this herb for more than 5000 years to treat asthma. More recently, the substance has been used in diet pills that can be purchased over the counter in herbal medicine shops. However, very serious concerns have been raised regarding these pills following reports that their use led to serious heart problems.
  (a) Write the molecular formula for ephedrine, and calculate its molar mass.
  (b) What is the weight percent of carbon in ephedrine?
  (c) Calculate the amount (moles) of ephedrine in a 0.125 g sample.
  (d) How many molecules of ephedrine are there in 0.125 g? How many C atoms?

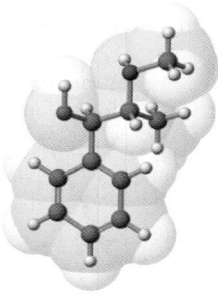

113. Saccharin is more than 300 times sweeter than sugar. It was first made in 1897, a time when it was common practice for chemists to record the taste of any new substances they synthesized.
  (a) Write the molecular formula for the compound, and draw its structural formula. (S atoms are yellow.)
  (b) If you ingest 125 mg of saccharin, what amount (moles) of saccharin have you ingested?
  (c) What mass of sulfur is contained in 125 mg of saccharin?

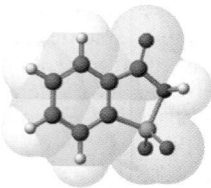

114. Name each of the following compounds, and tell which ones are best described as ionic:
  (a) ClF_3
  (b) NCl_3
  (c) $SrSO_4$
  (d) $Ca(NO_3)_2$
  (e) XeF_4
  (f) OF_2
  (g) KI
  (h) Al_2S_3
  (i) PCl_3
  (j) K_3PO_4

115. Write the formula for each of the following compounds, and tell which ones are best described as ionic:
  (a) sodium hypochlorite
  (b) boron triiodide
  (c) aluminum perchlorate
  (d) calcium acetate
  (e) potassium permanganate
  (f) ammonium sulfite
  (g) potassium dihydrogen phosphate
  (h) disulfur dichloride
  (i) chlorine trifluoride
  (j) phosphorus trifluoride

116. Complete the table by placing symbols, formulas, and names in the blanks.

Cation	Anion	Name	Formula
_____	_____	ammonium bromide	_____
Ba^{2+}	_____	_____	BaS
_____	Cl^-	iron(II) chloride	_____
_____	F^-	_____	PbF_2
Al^{3+}	$CO_3{}^{2-}$	_____	_____
_____	_____	iron(III) oxide	_____

117. Empirical and molecular formulas.
  (a) Fluorocarbonyl hypofluorite is composed of 14.6% C, 39.0% O, and 46.3% F. If the molar mass of the compound is 82 g/mol, determine the empirical and molecular formulas of the compound.
  (b) Azulene, a beautiful blue hydrocarbon, is 93.71% C and has a molar mass of 128.16 g/mol. What are the empirical and molecular formulas of azulene?

118. Cacodyl, a compound containing arsenic, was reported in 1842 by the German chemist Robert Wilhelm Bunsen. It has an almost intolerable garlic-like odor. Its molar mass is 210 g/mol, and it is 22.88% C, 5.76% H, and 71.36% As. Determine its empirical and molecular formulas.

119. The action of bacteria on meat and fish produces a compound called cadaverine. As its name and origin imply, it stinks! (It is also present in bad breath and adds to the odor of urine.) It is 58.77% C, 13.81% H, and 27.40% N. Its molar mass is 102.2 g/mol. Determine the molecular formula of cadaverine.

120. ■ ▲ Transition metals can combine with carbon monoxide (CO) to form compounds such as $Fe_x(CO)_y$ (Study Question 2.111). Assume that you combine 0.125 g of nickel with CO and isolate 0.364 g of $Ni(CO)_x$. What is the value of x?

121. ▲ A major oil company has used a gasoline additive called MMT to boost the octane rating of its gasoline. What is the empirical formula of MMT if it is 49.5% C, 3.2% H, 22.0% O, and 25.2% Mn?

122. ▲ Elemental phosphorus is made by heating calcium phosphate with carbon and sand in an electric furnace. What is the mass percent of phosphorus in calcium phosphate? Use this value to calculate the mass of calcium phosphate (in kilograms) that must be used to produce 15.0 kg of phosphorus.

123. ▲ Chromium is obtained by heating chromium(III) oxide with carbon. Calculate the mass percent of chromium in the oxide, and then use this value to calculate the quantity of Cr_2O_3 required to produce 850 kg of chromium metal.

124. ▲ Stibnite, Sb_2S_3, is a dark gray mineral from which antimony metal is obtained. What is the mass percent of antimony in the sulfide? If you have 1.00 kg of an ore that contains 10.6% antimony, what mass of Sb_2S_3 (in grams) is in the ore?

125. ▲ Direct reaction of iodine (I_2) and chlorine (Cl_2) produces an iodine chloride, I_xCl_y, a bright yellow solid. If you completely consume 0.678 g of I_2 (when reacted with excess Cl_2) and produce 1.246 g of I_xCl_y, what is the empirical formula of the compound? A later experiment showed that the molar mass of I_xCl_y was 467 g/mol. What is the molecular formula of the compound?

126. ▲ In a reaction, 2.04 g of vanadium combined with 1.93 g of sulfur to give a pure compound. What is the empirical formula of the product?

127. ▲ Iron pyrite, often called "fool's gold," has the formula FeS_2. If you could convert 15.8 kg of iron pyrite to iron metal, what mass of the metal would you obtain?

128. Which of the following statements about 57.1 g of octane, C_8H_{18}, is (are) *not* true?
(a) 57.1 g is 0.500 mol of octane.
(b) The compound is 84.1% C by weight.
(c) The empirical formula of the compound is C_4H_9.
(d) 57.1 g of octane contains 28.0 g of hydrogen atoms.

129. The formula of barium molybdate is $BaMoO_4$. Which of the following is the formula of sodium molybdate?
(a) Na_4MoO (c) Na_2MoO_3 (e) Na_4MoO_4
(b) $NaMoO$ (d) Na_2MoO_4

130. ▲ A metal M forms a compound with the formula MCl_4. If the compound is 74.75% chlorine, what is the identity of M?

131. Pepto-Bismol, which helps provide soothing relief for an upset stomach, contains 300. mg of bismuth subsalicylate, $C_{21}H_{15}Bi_3O_{12}$, per tablet. If you take two tablets for your stomach distress, what amount (in moles) of the "active ingredient" are you taking? What mass of Bi are you consuming in two tablets?

132. ▲ The weight percent of oxygen in an oxide that has the formula MO_2 is 15.2%. What is the molar mass of this compound? What element or elements are possible for M?

133. The mass of 2.50 mol of a compound with the formula ECl_4, in which E is a nonmetallic element, is 385 g. What is the molar mass of ECl_4? What is the identity of E?

134. ▲ The elements A and Z combine to produce two different compounds: A_2Z_3 and AZ_2. If 0.15 mol of A_2Z_3 has a mass of 15.9 g and 0.15 mol of AZ_2 has a mass of 9.3 g, what are the atomic masses of A and Z?

135. ▲ Polystyrene can be prepared by heating styrene with tribromobenzoyl peroxide in the absence of air. A sample prepared by this method has the empirical formula $Br_3C_6H_3(C_8H_8)_n$, where the value of n can vary from sample to sample. If one sample has 10.46% Br, what is the value of n?

136. A sample of hemoglobin is found to be 0.335% iron. If hemoglobin contains one iron atom per molecule, what is the molar mass of hemoglobin? What is the molar mass if there are four iron atoms per molecule?

137. ▲ Consider an atom of ^{64}Zn.
(a) Calculate the density of the nucleus in grams per cubic centimeter, knowing that the nuclear radius is 4.8×10^{-6} nm and the mass of the ^{64}Zn atom is 1.06×10^{-22} g. (Recall that the volume of a sphere is $[4/3]\pi r^3$.)
(b) Calculate the density of the space occupied by the electrons in the zinc atom, given that the atomic radius is 0.125 nm and the electron mass is 9.11×10^{-28} g.
(c) Having calculated these densities, what statement can you make about the relative densities of the parts of the atom?

138. ▲ Estimating the radius of a lead atom.
(a) You are given a cube of lead that is 1.000 cm on each side. The density of lead is 11.35 g/cm³. How many atoms of lead are in the sample?
(b) Atoms are spherical; therefore, the lead atoms in this sample cannot fill all the available space. As an approximation, assume that 60% of the space of the cube is filled with spherical lead atoms. Calculate the volume of one lead atom from this information. From the calculated volume (V) and the formula $(4/3)\pi r^3$ for the volume of a sphere, estimate the radius (r) of a lead atom.

139. A piece of nickel foil, 0.550 mm thick and 1.25 cm square, is allowed to react with fluorine, F_2, to give a nickel fluoride.
(a) How many moles of nickel foil were used? (The density of nickel is 8.902 g/cm³.)
(b) If you isolate 1.261 g of the nickel fluoride, what is its formula?
(c) What is its complete name?

140. ▲ Uranium is used as a fuel, primarily in the form of uranium(IV) oxide, in nuclear power plants. This question considers some uranium chemistry.

(a) A small sample of uranium metal (0.169 g) is heated to between 800 and 900°C in air to give 0.199 g of a dark green oxide, U_xO_y. How many moles of uranium metal were used? What is the empirical formula of the oxide, U_xO_y? What is the name of the oxide? How many moles of U_xO_y must have been obtained?

(b) The naturally occurring isotopes of uranium are ^{234}U, ^{235}U, and ^{238}U. Knowing that uranium's atomic weight is 238.02 g/mol, which isotope must be the most abundant?

(c) If the hydrated compound $UO_2(NO_3)_2 \cdot z\ H_2O$ is heated gently, the water of hydration is lost. If you have 0.865 g of the hydrated compound and obtain 0.679 g of $UO_2(NO_3)_2$ on heating, how many waters of hydration are in each formula unit of the original compound? (The oxide U_xO_y is obtained if the hydrate is heated to temperatures over 800°C in the air.)

In the Laboratory

141. ■ If Epsom salt, $MgSO_4 \cdot x\ H_2O$, is heated to 250°C, all the water of hydration is lost. On heating a 1.687-g sample of the hydrate, 0.824 g of $MgSO_4$ remains. How many molecules of water occur per formula unit of $MgSO_4$?

142. The "alum" used in cooking is potassium aluminum sulfate hydrate, $KAl(SO_4)_2 \cdot x\ H_2O$. To find the value of x, you can heat a sample of the compound to drive off all of the water and leave only $KAl(SO_4)_2$. Assume you heat 4.74 g of the hydrated compound and that the sample loses 2.16 g of water. What is the value of x?

143. ■ In an experiment, you need 0.125 mol of sodium metal. Sodium can be cut easily with a knife (Figure 2.6), so if you cut out a block of sodium, what should the volume of the block be in cubic centimeters? If you cut a perfect cube, what is the length of the edge of the cube? (The density of sodium is 0.97 g/cm³.)

144. Mass spectrometric analysis showed that there are four isotopes of an unknown element having the following masses and abundances:

Isotope	Mass Number	Isotope Mass	Abundance (%)
1	136	135.9090	0.193
2	138	137.9057	0.250
3	140	139.9053	88.48
4	142	141.9090	11.07

Three elements in the periodic table that have atomic weights near these values are lanthanum (La), atomic number 57, atomic weight 139.9055; cerium (Ce), atomic number 58, atomic weight 140.115; and praeseodymium (Pr), atomic number 59, atomic weight 140.9076. Using the data above, calculate the atomic weight, and identify the element if possible.

145. ▲ Most standard analytical balances can measure accurately to the nearest 0.0001 g. Assume you have weighed out a 2.0000-g sample of carbon. How many atoms are in this sample? Assuming the indicated accuracy of the measurement, what is the largest number of atoms that can be present in the sample?

146. ▲ When analyzed, an unknown compound gave these experimental results: C, 54.0%; H, 6.00%; and O, 40.0%. Four different students used these values to calculate the empirical formulas shown here. Which answer is correct? Why did some students not get the correct answer?

(a) $C_4H_5O_2$ (c) $C_7H_{10}O_4$
(b) $C_5H_7O_3$ (d) $C_9H_{12}O_5$

147. ▲ Two general chemistry students working together in the lab weigh out 0.832 g of $CaCl_2 \cdot 2\ H_2O$ into a crucible. After heating the sample for a short time and allowing the crucible to cool, the students determine that the sample has a mass of 0.739 g. They then do a quick calculation. On the basis of this calculation, what should they do next?

(a) Congratulate themselves on a job well done.
(b) Assume the bottle of $CaCl_2 \cdot 2\ H_2O$ was mislabeled; it actually contained something different.
(c) Heat the crucible again, and then reweigh it.

148. The mass spectrum of CH_3Cl is illustrated here. You know that carbon has two stable isotopes, ^{12}C and ^{13}C with relative abundances of 98.9% and 1.1%, respectively, and chlorine has two isotopes, ^{35}Cl and ^{37}Cl with abundances of 75.77% and 24.23%, respectively.

(a) What molecular species gives rise to the lines at m/Z of 50 and 52? Why is the line at 52 about 1/3 the height of the line at 50?
(b) What species might be responsible for the line at $m/Z = 51$?

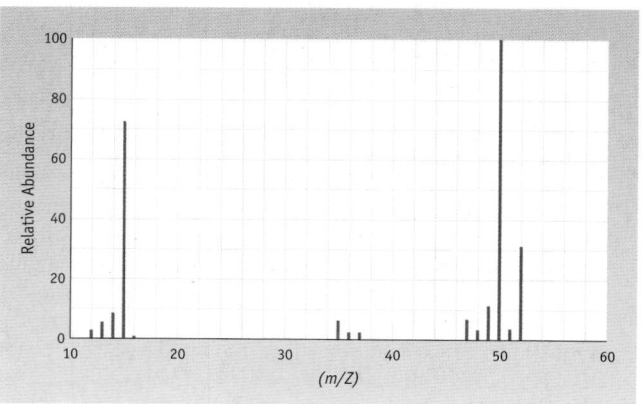

▲ more challenging   ■ in OWL   Blue-numbered questions answered in Appendix O

Summary and Conceptual Questions

The following questions may use concepts from this and the previous chapter.

149. ▲ Identify, from the list below, the information needed to calculate the number of atoms in 1.00 cm³ of iron. Outline the procedure used in this calculation.
    (a) the structure of solid iron
    (b) the molar mass of iron
    (c) Avogadro's number
    (d) the density of iron
    (e) the temperature
    (f) iron's atomic number
    (g) the number of iron isotopes

150. Consider the plot of relative element abundances on page 106. Is there a relationship between abundance and atomic number? Is there any difference between the relative abundance of an element of even atomic number and the relative abundance of an element of odd atomic number?

151. The photo here depicts what happens when a coil of magnesium ribbon and a few calcium chips are placed in water.
    (a) Based on their relative reactivities, what might you expect to see when barium, another Group 2A element, is placed in water?
    (b) Give the period in which each element (Mg, Ca, and Ba) is found; what correlation do you think you might find between the reactivity of these elements and their positions in the periodic table?

Magnesium *(left)* and calcium *(right)* in water.

152. A jar contains some number of jelly beans. To find out precisely how many are in the jar, you could dump them out and count them. How could you estimate their number without counting each one? (Chemists need to do just this kind of "bean counting" when they work with atoms and molecules. They are too small to count one by one, so they have worked out other methods to "count atoms.")

How many jelly beans are in the jar?

153. Cobalt(II) chloride hexahydrate, dissolves readily in water to give a red solution. If we use this solution as an "ink," we can write secret messages on paper. The writing is not visible when the water evaporates from the paper. When the paper is heated, however, the message can be read. Explain the chemistry behind this observation.

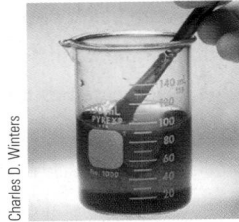

A solution of CoCl₂ · 6 H₂O.

Using the secret ink to write on paper.

Heating the paper reveals the writing.

3 | Chemical Reactions

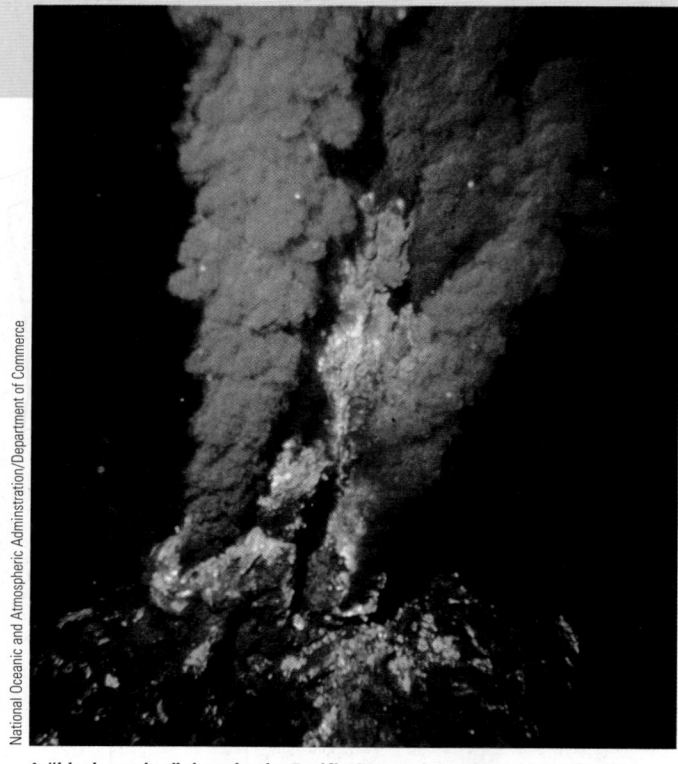

A "black smoker" deep in the Pacific Ocean along the East Pacific Rise.

National Oceanic and Atmospheric Administration/Department of Commerce

Black Smokers

In 1977, scientists were exploring the junction of two of the tectonic plates that form the floor of the Pacific Ocean. There they found thermal springs gushing a hot, black soup of minerals. Seawater seeps into cracks in the ocean floor, and, as it sinks deeper into the earth's crust, the water is superheated to between 300 and 400 °C by the magma of the earth's core. This superhot water dissolves minerals in the crust and is pushed back to the surface. When this hot water, now laden with dissolved metal cations and rich in anions such as sulfide and sulfate, gushes through the surface, it cools, and metal sulfates, such as calcium sulfate, and sulfides—such as those of copper, manganese, iron, zinc, and nickel—precipitate. Many metal sulfides are black, and the plume of material coming from the sea bottom looks like black "smoke"; thus, the vents have been called "black smokers." The solid sulfides and other minerals settle around the edges of the vent on the sea floor and eventually form a "chimney" of precipitated minerals.

Question:
1. Write balanced, net ionic equations for the reactions of Fe^{2+} and Bi^{3+} with H_2S and for Ca^{2+} with sulfate ions.

Answer to this question is in Appendix Q.

Chapter Goals

 *See Chapter Goals Revisited (page 151) for Study Questions keyed to these goals and assignable in OWL.*

- Balance equations for simple chemical reactions.
- Understand the nature and characteristics of chemical equilibria.
- Understand the nature of ionic substances dissolved in water.
- Recognize common acids and bases, and understand their behavior in aqueous solution.
- Recognize the common types of reactions in aqueous solution.
- Write chemical equations for the common types of reactions in aqueous solution.
- Recognize common oxidizing and reducing agents, and identify oxidation-reduction reactions.

Chapter Outline

Chemical reactions are the heart of chemistry. We begin a chemical reaction with one set of materials and end up with different materials. Just reading this sentence involves an untold number of chemical reactions in your body. Indeed, every activity of living things depends on carefully regulated chemical reactions. Our objective in this chapter is to introduce you to the symbolism used to represent chemical reactions and to describe various types of common chemical reactions.

Chemistry.⚛.Now™

Throughout the text this icon introduces an opportunity for self-study or to explore interactive tutorials by signing in at **www.cengage.com/login**.

3.1 Introduction to Chemical Equations

When a stream of chlorine gas, Cl_2, is directed onto solid phosphorus, P_4, the mixture bursts into flame, and a chemical reaction produces liquid phosphorus trichloride, PCl_3 (Figure 3.1). We can depict this reaction using a **balanced chemical equation**.

$$P_4(s) + 6\ Cl_2(g) \longrightarrow 4\ PCl_3(\ell)$$

Reactants   Product

$$P_4(s) + 6\ Cl_2(g) \longrightarrow 4\ PCl_3(\ell)$$

REACTANTS   PRODUCT

Charles D. Winters

FIGURE 3.1 Reaction of solid white phosphorus with chlorine gas. The product is liquid phosphorus trichloride.

On Monday, August 7, 1774, the Englishman Joseph Priestley (1733–1804) isolated oxygen. (The Swedish chemist Carl Scheele [1742–1786] also discovered the element, perhaps in 1773 or earlier.) Priestley heated solid mercury(II) oxide, HgO, causing the oxide to decompose to mercury and oxygen.

$$2\ HgO(s) \longrightarrow 2\ Hg(\ell) + O_2(g)$$

He did not immediately understand the significance of the discovery, but he mentioned it to the French chemist Antoine Lavoisier in October, 1774. One of Lavoisier's contributions to science was his recognition of the importance of exact scientific measure-

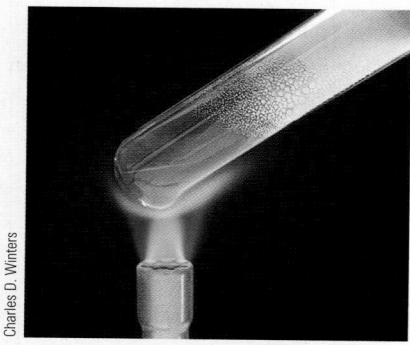

The decomposition of red mercury(II) oxide. The decomposition reaction gives mercury metal and oxygen gas. The mercury is seen as a film on the surface of the test tube.

ments and of carefully planned experiments, and he applied these methods to the study of oxygen. From this work, Lavoisier proposed that oxygen was an element, that it was one of the constituents of the compound water, and that burning involved a reaction with oxygen. He also mistakenly came to believe Priestley's gas was present in all acids, and so he named it "oxygen," from the Greek words meaning "to form an acid."

In other experiments, Lavoisier observed that the heat produced by a guinea pig when exhaling a given amount of carbon dioxide is similar to the quantity of heat produced by burning carbon to give the same amount of carbon dioxide. From these and other experiments he concluded that, "Respiration is a combustion, slow it is true, but otherwise perfectly similar to that of charcoal." Although he did not understand the details of the process, this was an important step in the development of biochemistry.

Lavoisier was a prodigious scientist, and the principles of naming chemical substances that he introduced are still in use today. Further, he wrote a textbook in which he applied the principles of the conservation of matter to chemistry, and he used the idea to write early versions of chemical equations.

Because Lavoisier was an aristocrat, he came under suspicion during the Reign of Terror of the French Revolution. He was an investor in the Ferme Générale, the infamous

tax-collecting organization in 18th-century France. Tobacco was a monopoly product of the Ferme Générale, and it was common to cheat the purchaser by adding water to the tobacco, a practice that Lavoisier opposed. Nonetheless, because of his involvement with the Ferme, his career was cut short by the guillotine on May 8, 1794, on the charge of "adding water to the people's tobacco."

Lavoisier and his wife, as painted in 1788 by Jacques-Louis David. Lavoisier was then 45, and his wife, Marie Anne Pierrette Paulze, was 30. (The Metropolitan Museum of Art, Purchase, Mr. and Mrs. Charles Wrightsman gift, in honor of Everett Fahy, 1997. Photograph © 1989 The Metropolitan Museum of Art.)

■ **Information from Chemical Equations**
The same number of atoms must exist after a reaction as before it takes place. However, these atoms are arranged differently. In the phosphorus/chlorine reaction, for example, the P atoms were in the form of P_4 molecules before reaction but appear in the PCl_3 molecules after reaction.

In a chemical equation, the formulas for the **reactants** (the substances combined in the reaction) are written to the left of the arrow, and the formulas of the **products** (the substances produced) are written to the right of the arrow. The physical states of reactants and products can also be indicated. The symbol (s) indicates a solid, (g) a gas, and (ℓ) a liquid. A substance dissolved in water, that is, an *aqueous* solution of a substance, is indicated by (aq).

In the 18th century, the French scientist Antoine Lavoisier (1743–1794) introduced the **law of conservation of matter**, which states that *matter can neither be created nor destroyed*. This means that if the total mass of reactants is 10 g, and if the reaction completely converts reactants to products, you must end up with 10 g of products. This also means that if 1000 atoms of a particular element are contained in the reactants, then those 1000 atoms must appear in the products in some fashion.

When applied to the reaction of phosphorus and chlorine, the law of conservation of matter tells us that 1 molecule of phosphorus, P_4 (with 4 phosphorus atoms) and 6 diatomic molecules of Cl_2 (with 12 atoms of Cl) are required to produce

$$2\ Fe(s)\ +\ 3\ Cl_2(g)\ \longrightarrow\ 2\ FeCl_3(s)$$

REACTANTS   PRODUCT

FIGURE 3.2 The reaction of iron and chlorine. Here, hot iron gauze is inserted into a flask containing chlorine gas. The heat from the reaction causes the iron gauze to glow, and brown iron(III) chloride forms.

four molecules of PCl_3. Because each PCl_3 molecule contains 1 P atom and 3 Cl atoms, the four PCl_3 molecules are needed to account for 4 P atoms and 12 Cl atoms in the product.

$$
\begin{array}{ccc}
6 \times 2 = & & 4 \times 3 = \\
12\ \text{Cl atoms} & & 12\ \text{Cl atoms}
\end{array}
$$

$$P_4(s)\ +\ 6\ Cl_2(g)\ \longrightarrow\ 4\ PCl_3(\ell)$$

4 P atoms   4 P atoms

Next, consider the balanced equation for the reaction of iron and and chlorine (Figure 3.2). In this case, there are two iron atoms and six chlorine atoms on both sides of the equation.

$$2\ Fe(s)\ +\ 3\ Cl_2(g)\ \longrightarrow\ 2\ FeCl_3(s)$$

stoichiometric coefficients

The numbers in front of formulas in balanced chemical equations are required by the law of conservation of matter. They can be read as a number of atoms (2 atoms of Fe), molecules (3 molecules of Cl_2), or formula units (2 formula units of the ionic compound $FeCl_3$). They can refer equally well to amounts of reactants and products: 2 moles of solid iron combine with 3 moles of chlorine gas to produce 2 moles of solid $FeCl_3$. The relationship between the quantities of chemical reactants and products is called **stoichiometry** (pronounced "stoy-key-AHM-uh-tree") (▶ Chapter 4), and the coefficients in a balanced equation are the **stoichiometric coefficients**.

Chemistry.Now™

Sign in at **www.cengage.com/login** and go to Chapter 3 Contents to see Screens 3.2 and 3.3 for exercises on **the conservation of mass in reactions.**

EXERCISE 3.1 Chemical Reactions

The reaction of aluminum with bromine is shown on page 67. The equation for the reaction is

$$2\ Al(s) + 3\ Br_2(\ell) \rightarrow Al_2Br_6(s)$$

(a) What are the stoichiometric coefficients in this equation?

(b) If you were to use 8000 atoms of Al, how many molecules of Br_2 are required to consume the Al completely?

3.2 Balancing Chemical Equations

Balancing a chemical equation ensures that the same number of atoms of each element appears on both sides of the equation. Many chemical equations can be balanced by trial and error, although some will involve more trial than others.

One general class of chemical reactions is the reaction of metals or nonmetals with oxygen to give oxides of the general formula M_xO_y. For example, iron reacts with oxygen to give iron(III) oxide (Figure 3.3a).

$$4\ Fe(s) + 3\ O_2(g) \rightarrow 2\ Fe_2O_3(s)$$

The nonmetals sulfur and oxygen react to form sulfur dioxide (Figure 3.3b),

$$S(s) + O_2(g) \rightarrow SO_2(g)$$

and phosphorus, P_4, reacts vigorously with oxygen to give tetraphosphorus decaoxide, P_4O_{10} (Figure 3.3c).

$$P_4(s) + 5\ O_2(g) \rightarrow P_4O_{10}(s)$$

The equations written above are balanced. The same number of iron, sulfur, or phosphorus atoms and oxygen atoms occurs on each side of these equations.

The **combustion**, or burning, of a fuel in oxygen is accompanied by the evolution of energy. You are familiar with combustion reactions such as the burning of octane, C_8H_{18}, a component of gasoline, in an automobile engine:

$$2\ C_8H_{18}(\ell) + 25\ O_2(g) \rightarrow 16\ CO_2(g) + 18\ H_2O(g)$$

FIGURE 3.3 Reactions of a metal and two nonmetals with oxygen. (See ChemistryNow, Screen 3.4, Balancing Chemical Equations, for a video of the phosphorus and oxygen reaction.)

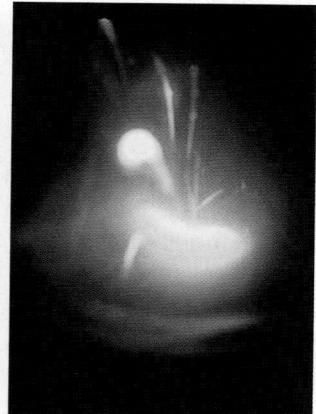

(a) Reaction of iron and oxygen to give iron(III) oxide, Fe_2O_3.

(b) Reaction of sulfur (in the spoon) with oxygen.

(c) Reaction of phosphorus and oxygen to give tetraphosphorus decaoxide, P_4O_{10}.

In all combustion reactions, some or all the elements in the reactants end up as oxides, compounds containing oxygen. When the reactant is a hydrocarbon (a compound such as gasoline, natural gas, or propane that contains only C and H), the products of complete combustion are always just carbon dioxide and water.

When balancing chemical equations, there are two important things to remember.

- Formulas for reactants and products must be correct, or the equation is meaningless.
- Subscripts in the formulas of reactants and products cannot be changed to balance equations. Changing the subscripts changes the identity of the substance. For example, you cannot change CO_2 to CO to balance an equation; carbon monoxide, CO, and carbon dioxide, CO_2, are different compounds.

As an example of equation balancing, let us write the balanced equation for the complete combustion of propane, C_3H_8.

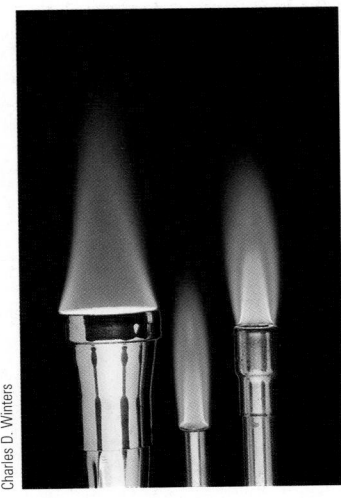

A combustion reaction. Here, propane, C_3H_8, burns to give CO_2 and H_2O. These simple oxides are always the products of the complete combustion of a hydrocarbon.

Step 1. *Write correct formulas for the reactants and products.*

$$C_3H_8(g) + O_2(g) \xrightarrow{\text{unbalanced equation}} CO_2(g) + H_2O(\ell)$$

Here, propane and oxygen are the reactants, and carbon dioxide and water are the products.

Step 2. *Balance the C atoms.* In combustion reactions such as this, it is usually best to balance the carbon atoms first and leave the oxygen atoms until the end (because the oxygen atoms are often found in more than one product). In this case, three carbon atoms are in the reactants, so three must occur in the products. Three CO_2 molecules are therefore required on the right side:

$$C_3H_8(g) + O_2(g) \xrightarrow{\text{unbalanced equation}} 3\ CO_2(g) + H_2O(\ell)$$

Step 3. *Balance the H atoms.* Propane, the reactant, contains 8 H atoms. Each molecule of water has two hydrogen atoms, so four molecules of water account for the required eight hydrogen atoms on the right side:

$$C_3H_8(g) + O_2(g) \xrightarrow{\text{unbalanced equation}} 3\ CO_2(g) + 4\ H_2O(\ell)$$

Step 4. *Balance the O atoms.* Ten oxygen atoms are on the right side ($3 \times 2 = 6$ in CO_2 plus $4 \times 1 = 4$ in H_2O). Therefore, five O_2 molecules are needed to supply the required 10 oxygen atoms:

$$C_3H_8(g) + 5\ O_2(g) \rightarrow 3\ CO_2(g) + 4\ H_2O(\ell)$$

Step 5. *Verify that the number of atoms of each element is balanced.* The equation shows three carbon atoms, eight hydrogen atoms, and ten oxygen atoms on each side.

Chemistry.Now™

Sign in at **www.cengage.com/login** and go to Chapter 3 Contents to see Screen 3.4 for an exercise and a tutorial on **balancing the chemical equations for a series of combustion reactions.**

EXAMPLE 3.1 Balancing an Equation for a Combustion Reaction

Problem Write the balanced equation for the combustion of ammonia ($NH_3 + O_2$) to give NO and H_2O.

Strategy First, write the unbalanced equation. Next, balance the N atoms, then the H atoms, and finally, balance the O atoms.

Solution

Step 1. Write correct formulas for the reactants and products. The unbalanced equation for the combustion is

$$NH_3(g) + O_2(g) \xrightarrow{\text{unbalanced equation}} NO(g) + H_2O(\ell)$$

Step 2. *Balance the N atoms.* There is one N atom on each side of the equation. The N atoms are in balance, at least for the moment.

$$NH_3(g) + O_2(g) \xrightarrow{\text{unbalanced equation}} NO(g) + H_2O(\ell)$$

Step 3. *Balance the H atoms.* There are three H atoms on the left and two on the right. To have the same number on each side, let us use two molecules of NH_3 on the left and three molecules of H_2O on the right (which gives us six H atoms on each side).

$$2\ NH_3(g) + O_2(g) \xrightarrow{\text{unbalanced equation}} NO(g) + 3\ H_2O(\ell)$$

Notice that when we balance the H atoms, the N atoms are no longer balanced. To bring them into balance, let us use 2 NO molecules on the right.

$$2\ NH_3(g) + O_2(g) \xrightarrow{\text{unbalanced equation}} 2\ NO(g) + 3\ H_2O(\ell)$$

Step 4. *Balance the O atoms.* After Step 3, there are two O atoms on the left side and five on the right. That is, there are an even number of O atoms on the left and an odd number on the right. Because there cannot be an odd number of O atoms on the left (O atoms are paired in O_2 molecules), multiply each coefficient on both sides of the equation by 2 so that an even number of oxygen atoms (10) can now occur on the right side:

$$4\ NH_3(g) + O_2(g) \xrightarrow{\text{unbalanced equation}} 4\ NO(g) + 6\ H_2O(\ell)$$

Now the oxygen atoms can be balanced by having five O_2 molecules on the left side of the equation:

$$4\ NH_3(g) + 5\ O_2(g) \xrightarrow{\text{balanced equation}} 4\ NO(g) + 6\ H_2O(\ell)$$

Step 5. *Verify the result.* Four N atoms, 12 H atoms, and 10 O atoms occur on each side of the equation.

Comment An alternative way to write this equation is

$$2\ NH_3(g) + {}^5\!/_2\ O_2(g) \rightarrow 2\ NO(g) + 3\ H_2O(\ell)$$

where a fractional coefficient has been used. This equation is correctly balanced and will be useful under some circumstances. In general, however, we balance equations with whole-number coefficients.

EXERCISE 3.2 Balancing the Equation for a Combustion Reaction

(a) Butane gas, C_4H_{10}, can burn completely in air [use $O_2(g)$ as the other reactant] to give carbon dioxide gas and water vapor. Write a balanced equation for this combustion reaction.

(b) Write a balanced chemical equation for the complete combustion of liquid tetraethyllead, $Pb(C_2H_5)_4$ (which was used until the 1970s as a gasoline additive). The products of combustion are $PbO(s)$, $H_2O(\ell)$, and $CO_2(g)$.

3.3 Introduction to Chemical Equilibrium

To this point, we have treated chemical reactions as proceeding in one direction only, with reactants being converted completely to products. Nature, however, is more complex than this. Chemical reactions are reversible, and many reactions lead to incomplete conversion of reactants to products.

A good example of a reversible reaction that does not proceed completely to products is the reaction of nitrogen with hydrogen to form ammonia gas, a

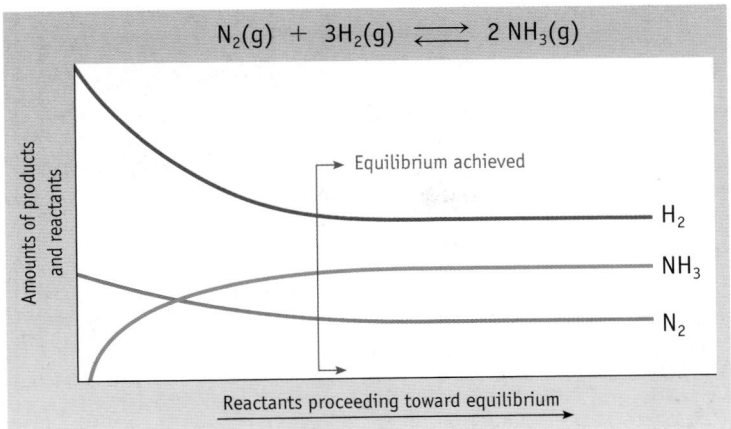

$$N_2(g) + 3H_2(g) \rightleftharpoons 2\,NH_3(g)$$

Equilibrium achieved

H₂
NH₃
N₂

Amounts of products and reactants

Reactants proceeding toward equilibrium

FIGURE 3.4 The reaction of N_2 and H_2 to produce NH_3. N_2 and H_2 in a 1:3 mixture react to produce some NH_3. As the reaction proceeds, the rate or speed of NH_3 production slows, as does the rate of consumption of N_2 and H_2. Eventually, the amounts of N_2 and H_2, and NH_3 no longer change. At this point, the reaction has reached equilibrium. Nonetheless, the forward reaction to produce NH_3 continues, as does the reverse reaction (the decomposition of NH_3).

compound used extensively both as a fertilizer and in the production of other fertilizers.

$$N_2(g) + 3\,H_2(g) \rightarrow 2\,NH_3(g)$$

Nitrogen and hydrogen react to form ammonia, but, under the conditions of the reaction, the product ammonia also breaks down into nitrogen and hydrogen in the reverse reaction.

$$2\,NH_3(g) \rightarrow N_2(g) + 3\,H_2(g)$$

Let us consider what would happen if we mixed nitrogen and hydrogen in a closed container under the proper conditions for the reaction to occur. At first, N_2 and H_2 react to produce some ammonia. As the ammonia is produced, however, some NH_3 molecules decompose to re-form nitrogen and hydrogen in the reverse reaction. At the beginning of the process, the forward reaction to give NH_3 predominates, but, as the reactants are consumed, the rate of the forward reaction is progressively slower. At the same time, the reverse reaction speeds up as the amount of ammonia increases. Eventually, the rate or speed of the forward reaction will equal the rate of the reverse reaction. Once this occurs, no further *macroscopic* change is observed; the amounts of nitrogen, hydrogen, and ammonia in the container stop changing (Figure 3.4). We say the system has reached **chemical equilibrium**. The reaction vessel will contain all three substances: nitrogen, hydrogen, and ammonia. Because both the forward and reverse processes are still occurring (but at equal rates), we refer to this state as a **dynamic equilibrium**. We represent a system at dynamic equilibrium by writing a double arrow symbol ($\rightleftharpoons$) connecting the reactants and products.

$$N_2(g) + 3\,H_2(g) \rightleftharpoons 2\,NH_3(g)$$

The formation of stalactites and stalagmites in a limestone cave is another example of a system that depends on the reversibility of a chemical reaction (Figure 3.5). Stalactites and stalagmites are made chiefly of calcium carbonate, a mineral found in underground deposits in the form of limestone, a leftover from ancient oceans. If water seeping through the limestone contains dissolved CO_2, a reaction occurs in which the mineral dissolves, giving an aqueous solution of $Ca(HCO_3)_2$.

$$CaCO_3(s) + CO_2(aq) + H_2O(\ell) \rightarrow Ca(HCO_3)_2(aq)$$

■ **Progression Toward Equilibrium**
Reactions always proceed spontaneously toward equilibrium. A reaction will never proceed on its own in a direction that takes a system further from equilibrium.

Dr. Arthur N. Palmer

FIGURE 3.5 Cave chemistry. Calcium carbonate stalactites cling to the roof of a cave, and stalagmites grow up from the cave floor. The chemistry producing these formations is a good example of the reversibility of chemical reactions.

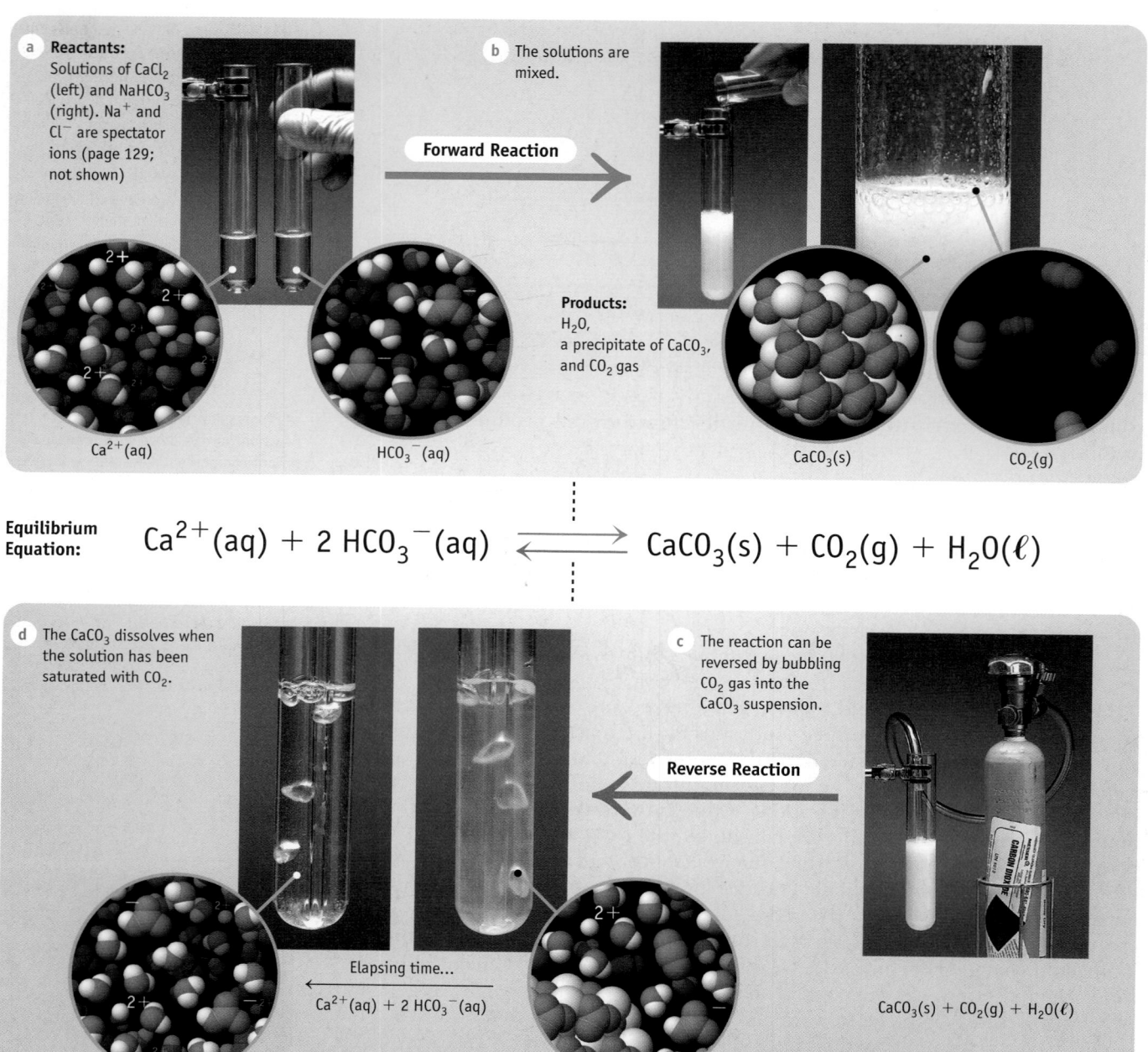

a **Reactants:**
Solutions of $CaCl_2$ (left) and $NaHCO_3$ (right). Na^+ and Cl^- are spectator ions (page 129; not shown)

b The solutions are mixed.

Forward Reaction

Products:
H_2O, a precipitate of $CaCO_3$, and CO_2 gas

Ca^{2+}(aq)

HCO_3^-(aq)

$CaCO_3$(s)

CO_2(g)

Equilibrium Equation:

$$Ca^{2+}(aq) + 2\ HCO_3^-(aq) \rightleftharpoons CaCO_3(s) + CO_2(g) + H_2O(\ell)$$

d The $CaCO_3$ dissolves when the solution has been saturated with CO_2.

c The reaction can be reversed by bubbling CO_2 gas into the $CaCO_3$ suspension.

Reverse Reaction

Elapsing time...
$Ca^{2+}(aq) + 2\ HCO_3^-(aq)$

$CaCO_3(s) + CO_2(g) + H_2O(\ell)$

FIGURE 3.6 The nature of chemical equilibrium. The experiments here demonstrate the reversibility of chemical reactions. (*top*) Solutions of $CaCl_2$ (a source of Ca^{2+} ions) and $NaHCO_3$ (a source of HCO_3^- ions) are mixed (a) and produce a precipitate of $CaCO_3$ and CO_2 gas (b). (*bottom*) If CO_2 gas is bubbled into a suspension of $CaCO_3$ (c), the reverse of the reaction displayed in the top panel occurs. That is, solid $CaCO_3$ and gaseous CO_2 produce Ca^{2+} and HCO_3^- ions (d).

Photos: Charles D. Winters

When the mineral-laden water reaches a cave, the reverse reaction occurs, with CO_2 being evolved into the cave and solid $CaCO_3$ being deposited as stalagmites and stalactites.

$$Ca(HCO_3)_2(aq) \longrightarrow CaCO_3(s) + CO_2(g) + H_2O(\ell)$$

Cave chemistry can be done in a laboratory (Figure 3.6) using reactions that further demonstrate the reversiblity of the reactions involved.

A key question that arises is, "When a reaction reaches equilibrium, will the reactants be converted largely to products, or will most of the reactants still be present?" The answer will depend on the nature of the compounds involved, the temperature, and other factors, and that is the subject of later chapters (▶ Chapters 16–18). For the present, though, it is useful to define **product-favored reactions** as *reactions in which reactants are completely or largely converted to products at equilibrium.* The combustion reactions we have been studying are examples of reactions that are product-favored at equilibrium, in contrast to the N_2/H_2 reaction in Figure 3.4. In fact, most of the reactions that we shall study in the rest of this chapter are product-favored reactions at equilibrium. We usually write the equations for reactions that are very product-favored using only the single arrows we have been using up to this point.

The opposite of a product-favored reaction is one that is **reactant-favored** at equilibrium. Such reactions lead to the conversion of only a small amount of the reactants to products. An example of such a reaction is the ionization of acetic acid in water, in which only a tiny fraction of the acid reacts to produce ions.

$$CH_3CO_2H(aq) + H_2O(\ell) \rightleftharpoons H_3O^+(aq) + CH_3CO_2^-(aq)$$

■ **Quantitative Description of Chemical Equilibrium** As you shall see in Chapters 16–18, the extent to which a reaction is product-favored can be described by a simple mathematical expression, called the equilibrium constant expression. Each chemical reaction has a numerical value for the equilibrium constant, symbolized by K. Product-favored reactions have large values of K; small K values indicate reactant-favored reactions. For the ionization of acetic acid in water, $K = 1.8 \times 10^{-5}$.

■ **Acetic Acid, a Weak Acid** Acetic acid is an example of a large number of acids called "weak acids" because only a few percent of the molecules ionize to form ionic products.

3.4 Chemical Reactions in Aqueous Solution

Many of the reactions you will study in your chemistry course and the reactions that occur in living systems are carried out in aqueous solution. Because reactions in aqueous solution are so important, the remainder of this chapter is an introduction to the behavior of compounds in solution and to some of the types of reactions you will observe.

A **solution** is a homogeneous mixture of two or more substances. One substance is generally considered the **solvent**, the medium in which another substance—the **solute**—is dissolved. In the human body, the solvent for chemical reactions is usually water. Water assists in transporting nutrients and waste products in and out of cells and is necessary for digestive, absorption, circulatory, and excretory functions. In fact, the human body is two-thirds water. Water is an excellent solvent to use for biochemical reactions and also for many other chemical reactions. For the next several sections of this chapter, we shall study chemical reactions that occur in **aqueous solutions** where water is the solvent.

So that you are familiar with types of reactions as you work through the book, we also want to introduce you to four major categories of reactions in aqueous solution: precipitation, acid-base, gas-forming, and oxidation-reduction reactions. As you learn about these reactions, it will be useful to look for patterns that allow you to predict the reaction products. You will notice that many of the reactions are **exchange reactions** in which *the ions of the reactants change partners.*

$$A^+B^- \ + \ C^+D^- \longrightarrow A^+D^- \ + \ C^+B^-$$

FIGURE 3.7 **Precipitation of silver chloride.** (a) Mixing aqueous solutions of silver nitrate and potassium chloride produces white, insoluble silver chloride, AgCl. In (b) through (d), you see a model of the process at the molecular and ionic level.

Photo, a, Charles D. Winters; b–d, model from an animation by Roy Tasker, University of Western Sydney, Australia

(a)

(b) Initially, the Ag$^+$ ions (silver color) and Cl$^-$ ions (green) are widely separated.

(c) Ag$^+$ and Cl$^-$ ions approach and form ion pairs.

(d) As more and more Ag$^+$ and Cl$^-$ ions come together, a precipitate of solid AgCl forms.

For example, aqueous solutions of silver nitrate and potassium chloride react to produce solid silver chloride and aqueous potassium nitrate. (Figure 3.7a)

$$AgNO_3(aq) + KCl(aq) \rightarrow AgCl(s) + KNO_3(aq)$$

Recognizing that cations exchange anions in many chemical reactions gives us a good way to predict the products of precipitation, acid-base, and many gas-forming reactions.

Module 5

3.5 Ions and Molecules in Aqueous Solution

To understand reactions occurring in aqueous solution, it is important first to understand something about the behavior of compounds in water. The water you drink every day, the oceans, and the aqueous solutions in your body contain many ions, most of which result from dissolving solid materials present in the environment (Table 3.1).

TABLE 3.1   Concentrations of Some Cations and Anions in the Environment and in Living Cells

Element	Dissolved Species	Sea Water	*Valonia*†	Red Blood Cells	Blood Plasma
Chlorine	Cl$^-$	550	50	50	100
Sodium	Na$^+$	460	80	11	160
Magnesium	Mg^{2+}	52	50	2.5	2
Calcium	Ca^{2+}	10	1.5	10^{-4}	2
Potassium	K$^+$	10	400	92	10
Carbon	HCO$_3^-$, CO$_3^{2-}$	30	<10	<10	30
Phosphorus	H$_2$PO$_4^-$, HPO$_4^{2-}$	<1	5	3	<3

*Data are taken from J. J. R. Fraústo da Silva and R. J. P. Williams: *The Biological Chemistry of the Elements*, Oxford, England, Clarendon Press, 1991. Concentrations are given in millimoles per liter. (A millimole is 1/1000 of a mole.)
†*Valonia* are single-celled algae that live in sea water.

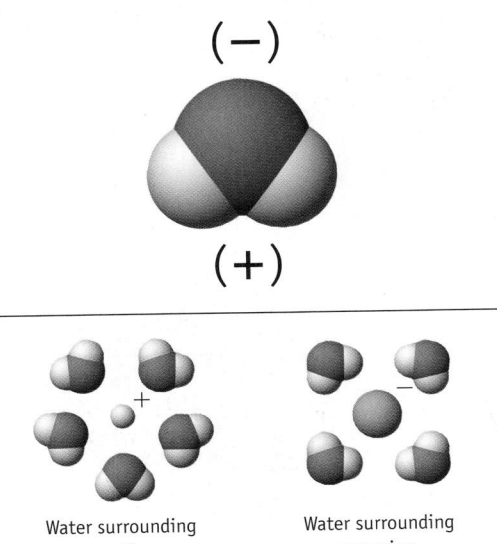

A water molecule is electrically positive on one side (the H atoms) and electrically negative on the other (the O atom). These charges enable water to interact with negative and positive ions in aqueous solution.

(−)

(+)

Water surrounding a cation

Water surrounding an anion

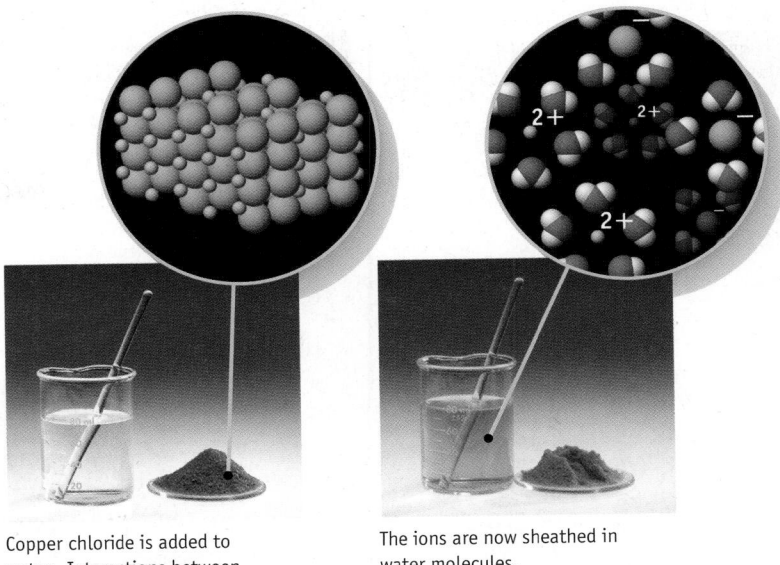

Photos: Charles D. Winters

Copper chloride is added to water. Interactions between water and the Cu^{2+} and Cl^- ions allow the solid to dissolve.

The ions are now sheathed in water molecules.

FIGURE 3.8 Water as a solvent for ionic substances. (a) Water molecules are attracted to both positive cations and negative anions in aqueous solution. (b) When an ionic substance dissolves in water, each ion is surrounded by water molecules. (The number of water molecules around an ion is often 6.)

Dissolving an ionic solid requires separating each ion from the oppositely charged ions that surround it in the solid state. Water is especially good at dissolving ionic compounds because each water molecule has a positively charged end and a negatively charged end (Figure 3.8). When an ionic compound dissolves in water, each negative ion becomes surrounded by water molecules with the positive end of water molecules pointing toward it, and each positive ion becomes surrounded by the negative ends of several water molecules.

The water-encased ions produced by dissolving an ionic compound are free to move about in solution. Under normal conditions, the movement of ions is random, and the cations and anions from a dissolved ionic compound are dispersed uniformly throughout the solution. However, if two **electrodes** (conductors of electricity such as copper wire) are placed in the solution and connected to a battery, ion movement is no longer random. Positive cations move through the solution to the negative electrode, and negative anions move to the positive electrode (Figure 3.9). If a light bulb is inserted into the circuit, the bulb lights, showing that ions are available to conduct charge in the solution just as electrons conduct charge in the wire part of the circuit. Compounds whose aqueous solutions conduct electricity are called **electrolytes.** *All ionic compounds that are soluble in water are electrolytes.*

For every mole of NaCl that dissolves, 1 mol of Na^+ and 1 mol of Cl^- ions enter the solution.

$$NaCl(s) \rightarrow Na^+(aq) + Cl^-(aq)$$

100% Dissociation ≡ strong electrolyte

Because the solute has dissociated (broken apart) completely into ions, the solution will be a good conductor of electricity. Substances whose solutions are good

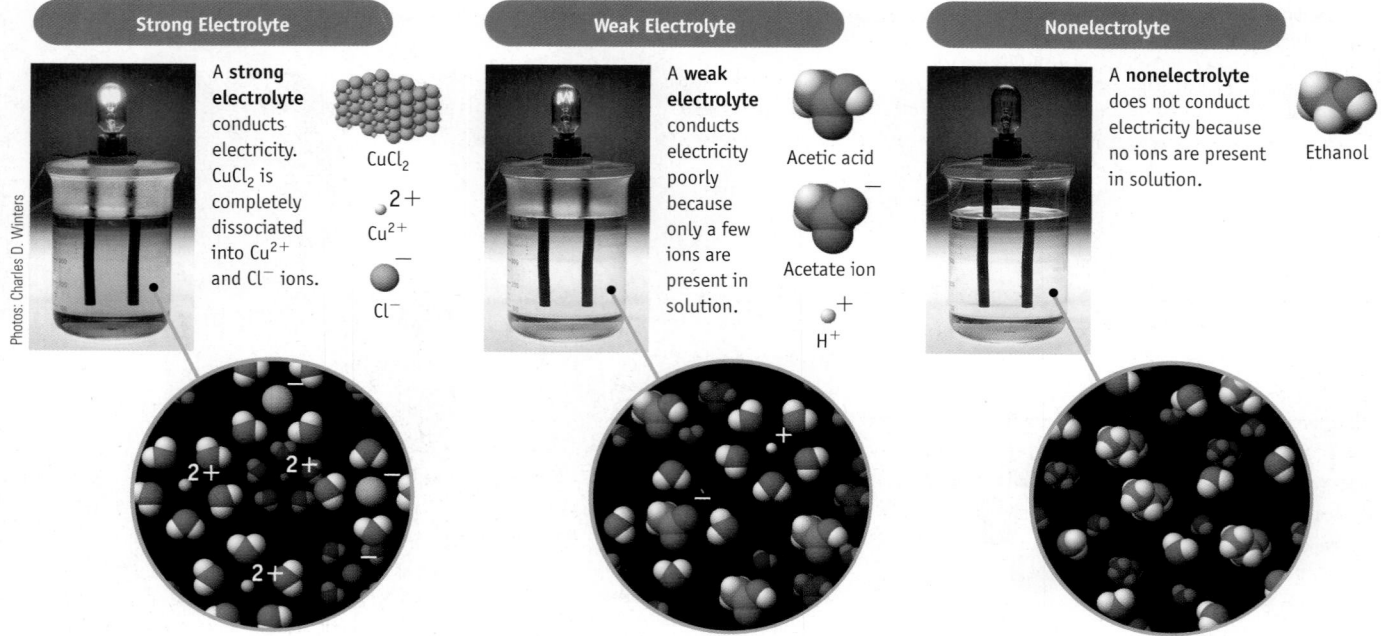

Strong Electrolyte	Weak Electrolyte	Nonelectrolyte

A **strong electrolyte** conducts electricity. $CuCl_2$ is completely dissociated into Cu^{2+} and Cl^- ions.

$CuCl_2$

Cu^{2+} 2+

Cl^- −

A **weak electrolyte** conducts electricity poorly because only a few ions are present in solution.

Acetic acid

Acetate ion −

H^+ +

A **nonelectrolyte** does not conduct electricity because no ions are present in solution.

Ethanol

Photos: Charles D. Winters

Active Figure 3.9 Classifying solutions by their ability to conduct electricity.

Chemistry Now™ Sign in at www.cengage.com/login and go to the Chapter Contents menu to explore an interactive version of this figure accompanied by an exercise.

electrical conductors owing to the presence of ions are **strong electrolytes** (see Figure 3.9). The ions into which an ionic compound will dissociate are given by the compound's name, and the relative amounts of these ions are given by its formula. For example, as we have seen, sodium chloride yields sodium ions (Na^+) and chloride ions (Cl^-) in solution in a 1:1 ratio. The ionic compound barium chloride, $BaCl_2$, is also a strong electrolyte. In this case, there are two chloride ions for each barium ion in solution.

$$BaCl_2(s) \rightarrow Ba^{2+}(aq) + 2\ Cl^-(aq)$$

■ **Dissolving Halides** When an ionic compound with halide ions dissolves in water, the halide ions are released into aqueous solution. Thus, $BaCl_2$ produces two Cl^- ions for each Ba^{2+} ion (and not Cl_2 or Cl_2^{2-} ions).

Notice also that the chloride ions do not stay together as one unit but separate from each other into two separate chloride ions. In yet another example, the ionic compound barium nitrate yields barium ions and nitrate ions in solution. For each Ba^{2+} ion in solution, there are two NO_3^- ions.

$$Ba(NO_3)_2(s) \rightarrow Ba^{2+}(aq) + 2\ NO_3^-(aq)$$

Notice that the polyatomic ion stays together as one unit, NO_3^-, and that the two nitrate ions separate from each other.

Compounds whose aqueous solutions do not conduct electricity are called **nonelectrolytes**. The solute particles present in these aqueous solutions are molecules, not ions. *Most molecular compounds that dissolve in water are nonelectrolytes.* For example, when the molecular compound ethanol (C_2H_5OH) dissolves in water, each molecule of ethanol stays together as a single unit. We do not get ions in the solution.

$$C_2H_5OH(\ell) \rightarrow C_2H_5OH(aq)$$

Other examples of nonelectrolytes are sucrose ($C_{12}H_{22}O_{11}$) and antifreeze (ethylene glycol, $HOCH_2CH_2OH$).

Some molecular compounds (strong acids, weak acids, and weak bases) (▶ Section 3.7), however, react with water to form ions and are thus electrolytes. Hydrogen chloride is a molecular compound, but it reacts with water to form ions, and the solution is referred to as *hydrochloric acid*.

$$HCl(g) + H_2O(\ell) \rightarrow H_3O^+(aq) + Cl^-(aq)$$

This reaction is very product-favored. Each molecule of HCl produces ions in solution so hydrochloric acid is a strong electrolyte.

A **weak electrolyte** is a molecular substance in whose aqueous solutions some of the molecules react with water to form ions but where some of the molecules (usually most) remain as molecules. Their aqueous solutions are poor conductors of electricity (see Figure 3.9). As described on page 135, the interaction of acetic acid with water is very reactant-favored. In vinegar, an aqueous solution of acetic acid, fewer than 100 molecules in every 10,000 molecules of acetic acid are ionized to form acetate and hydronium ions. Thus, aqueous acetic acid is a weak electrolyte.

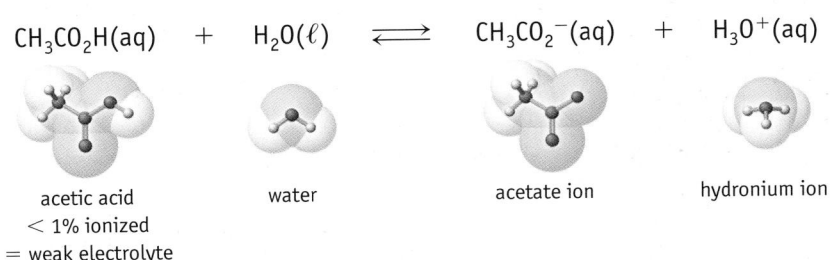

$$CH_3CO_2H(aq) \quad + \quad H_2O(\ell) \quad \rightleftharpoons \quad CH_3CO_2^-(aq) \quad + \quad H_3O^+(aq)$$

acetic acid
< 1% ionized
= weak electrolyte

water

acetate ion

hydronium ion

■ **H⁺ Ions in Water** As illustrated for acetic acid in Figure 3.9, the H^+ ions from the acid are surrounded by water molecules. When writing an equation for acid ionization, we symbolize this with the H_3O^+ or hydronium ion. For more on this, see page 134.

Chemistry.⚛.Now™

Sign in at **www.cengage.com/login** and go to Chapter 3 Contents to see:
• Screen 3.5 for exercises on **the dissolving of an ionic compound**
• Screen 3.6 for information on **the types of electrolytes**

EXERCISE 3.3 Electrolytes

Epsom salt, $MgSO_4 \cdot 7\ H_2O$, is sold in drugstores and, as a solution in water, is used for various medical purposes. Methanol, CH_3OH, is dissolved in gasoline in the winter in colder climates to prevent the formation of ice in automobile fuel lines. Which of these compounds is an electrolyte, and which is a nonelectrolyte?

Solubility of Ionic Compounds in Water

Many ionic compounds dissolve completely in water, but some dissolve only to a small extent, and still others are essentially insoluble. Fortunately, we can make some general statements about which ionic compounds are water soluble. In this chapter, we consider solubility as an "either–or" question, referring to those materials that are soluble beyond a certain extent as "soluble" and to those that do not dissolve to that extent as "insoluble." To get a better idea of the amounts that will actually dissolve in a given quantity of water, we could do an experiment or perform a calculation that uses the concept of equilibrium (▶ Chapter 18).

■ **Solubility Guidelines** Observations such as those shown in Figure 3.10 were used to create the solubility guidelines. Note, however, that these are general guidelines and not rules followed under all circumstances. There are exceptions, but the guidelines are a good place to begin. See B. Blake, *Journal of Chemical Education*, Vol. 80, pp. 1348–1350, 2003.

Figure 3.10 lists broad guidelines that help predict whether a particular ionic compound is soluble in water. For example, sodium nitrate, $NaNO_3$, contains both an alkali metal cation, Na^+, and the nitrate anion, NO_3^-. The presence of either of these ions ensures that the compound is soluble in water. By contrast, calcium hydroxide is poorly soluble in water. If a spoonful of solid $Ca(OH)_2$ is added to 100 mL of water, only 0.17 g, or 0.0023 mol, will dissolve at 10 °C. Nearly all of the $Ca(OH)_2$ remains as a solid (Figure 3.10c).

Chemistry ⚛ Now™

Sign in at **www.cengage.com/login** and go to Chapter 3 Contents to see Screen 3.7 for a tutorial and simulation on **the solubility of ionic compounds in water.**

SILVER COMPOUNDS

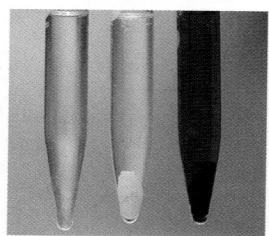

AgNO₃   AgCl   AgOH

(a) Nitrates are generally soluble, as are chlorides (except AgCl). Hydroxides are generally not soluble.

SULFIDES

(NH₄)₂S   CdS   Sb₂S₃   PbS

(b) Sulfides are generally not soluble (exceptions include salts with NH_4^+ and Na^+).

HYDROXIDES

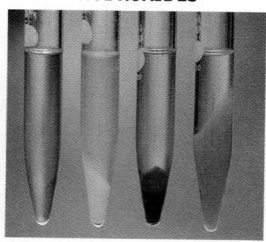

Photos: Charles D. Winters

NaOH   Ca(OH)₂   Fe(OH)₃   Ni(OH)₂

(c) Hydroxides are generally not soluble, except when the cation is a Group 1A metal.

SOLUBLE COMPOUNDS	EXCEPTIONS
Almost all salts of Na^+, K^+, NH_4^+	
Salts of nitrate, NO_3^- chlorate, ClO_3^- perchlorate, ClO_4^- acetate, $CH_3CO_2^-$	
Almost all salts of Cl^-, Br^-, I^-	Halides of Ag^+, Hg_2^{2+}, Pb^{2+}
Salts containing F^-	Fluorides of Mg^{2+}, Ca^{2+}, Sr^{2+}, Ba^{2+}, Pb^{2+}
Salts of sulfate, SO_4^{2-}	Sulfates of Ca^{2+}, Sr^{2+}, Ba^{2+}, Pb^{2+}

INSOLUBLE COMPOUNDS	EXCEPTIONS
Most salts of carbonate, CO_3^{2-} phosphate, PO_4^{3-} oxalate, $C_2O_4^{2-}$ chromate, CrO_4^{2-} sulfide, S^{2-}	Salts of NH_4^+ and the alkali metal cations
Most metal hydroxides and oxides	Alkali metal hydroxides and $Ba(OH)_2$

Active Figure 3.10 Guidelines to predict the solubility of ionic compounds. If a compound contains one of the ions in the column on the left in the top chart, it is predicted to be at least moderately soluble in water. There are exceptions, which are noted at the right. Most ionic compounds formed by the anions listed at the bottom of the chart are poorly soluble (with the exception on compounds with NH_4^+ and the alkali metal cations).

Chemistry ⚛ Now™ Sign in at www.cengage.com/login and go to the Chapter Contents menu to explore an interactive version of this figure accompanied by an exercise.

Problem Predict whether the following ionic compounds are likely to be water-soluble. List the ions present in solution for soluble compounds.

(a) KCl

(b) MgCO$_3$

(c) Fe$_2$O$_3$

(d) Cu(NO$_3$)$_2$

Strategy You must first recognize the cation and anion involved and then decide the probable water solubility based on the guidelines outlined in Figure 3.10.

Solution

(a) KCl is composed of K$^+$ and Cl$^-$ ions. The presence of *either* of these ions means that the compound is likely to be soluble in water. The solution contains K$^+$ and Cl$^-$ ions dissolved in water.

$$KCl(s) \rightarrow K^+(aq) + Cl^-(aq)$$

(The solubility of KCl is about 35 g in 100 mL of water at 20 °C.)

(b) Magnesium carbonate is composed of Mg^{2+} and CO$_3^{2-}$ ions. Salts containing the carbonate ion are usually insoluble, unless combined with an ion like Na$^+$ or NH$_4^+$. Therefore, MgCO$_3$ is predicted to be insoluble in water. (The solubility of MgCO$_3$ is less than 0.2 g/100 mL of water.)

(c) Iron(III) oxide is composed of Fe^{3+} and O^{2-} ions. Oxides are soluble only when O^{2-} is combined with an alkali metal ion; Fe^{3+} is a transition metal ion, so Fe$_2$O$_3$ is insoluble.

(d) Copper(II) nitrate is composed of Cu^{2+}(aq) and NO$_3^-$(aq) ions. Nitrate salts are soluble, so this compound dissolves in water, giving ions in solution as shown in the equation below

$$Cu(NO_3)_2(s) \rightarrow Cu^{2+}(aq) + 2 NO_3^-(aq)$$

EXERCISE 3.4 Solubility of Ionic Compounds

Predict whether each of the following ionic compounds is likely to be soluble in water. If it is soluble, write the formulas of the ions present in aqueous solution.

(a) LiNO$_3$

(b) CaCl$_2$

(c) CuO

(d) NaCH$_3$CO$_2$

3.6 **Precipitation Reactions**

 **Module 6**

A **precipitation reaction** produces a water-insoluble solid product, known as a **precipitate**. The reactants in such reactions are generally water-soluble ionic compounds. When these substances dissolve in water, they dissociate to give the appropriate cations and anions. If the cation from one compound can form an insoluble compound with the anion from the other compound in the solution, precipitation occurs. As described earlier, both silver nitrate and potassium chloride are water-soluble ionic compounds. When combined in water, they undergo an *exchange reaction* to produce insoluble silver chloride and soluble potassium nitrate (Figure 3.7).

$$AgNO_3(aq) + KCl(aq) \rightarrow AgCl(s) + KNO_3(aq)$$

Reactants	Products
Ag$^+$(aq) + NO$_3^-$(aq)	Insoluble AgCl(s)
K$^+$(aq) + Cl$^-$(aq)	K$^+$(aq) + NO$_3^-$(aq)

Predicting the Outcome of a Precipitation Reaction

Many combinations of positive and negative ions give insoluble substances (see Figure 3.10). For example, the solubility guidelines indicate that most compounds containing the chromate ion are not soluble (alkali metal chromates and ammonium chromate are exceptions). Thus, we can predict that yellow, solid lead(II)

Charles D. Winters

FIGURE 3.11 Precipitation reactions. Many ionic compounds are insoluble in water. Guidelines for predicting the solubilities of ionic compounds are given in Figure 3.10.

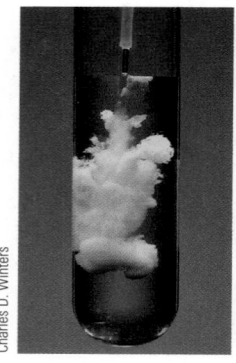

(a) $Pb(NO_3)_2$ and K_2CrO_4 produce yellow, insoluble $PbCrO_4$ and soluble KNO_3.

(b) $Pb(NO_3)_2$ and $(NH_4)_2S$ produce black, insoluble PbS and soluble NH_4NO_3.

(c) $FeCl_3$ and NaOH produce red, insoluble $Fe(OH)_3$ and soluble NaCl.

(d) $AgNO_3$ and K_2CrO_4 produce red, insoluble Ag_2CrO_4 and soluble KNO_3. See Example 3.3.

chromate will precipitate when a water-soluble lead(II) compound is combined with a water-soluble chromate compound (Figure 3.11a).

$$Pb(NO_3)_2(aq) + K_2CrO_4(aq) \rightarrow PbCrO_4(s) + 2\ KNO_3(aq)$$

Reactants	Products
$Pb^{2+}(aq) + 2\ NO_3^-(aq)$	Insoluble $PbCrO_4(s)$
$2\ K^+(aq) + CrO_4^{2-}(aq)$	$2\ K^+(aq) + 2\ NO_3^-(aq)$

Similarly, we know from the solubility guidelines that almost all metal sulfides are insoluble in water (Figure 3.11b). If a solution of a soluble metal compound comes in contact with a source of sulfide ions, the metal sulfide precipitates.

$$Pb(NO_3)_2(aq) + (NH_4)_2S(aq) \rightarrow PbS(s) + 2\ NH_4NO_3(aq)$$

Reactants	Products
$Pb^{2+}(aq) + 2\ NO_3^-(aq)$	Insoluble PbS(s)
$2\ NH_4^+(aq) + S^{2-}(aq)$	$2\ NH_4^+(aq) + 2\ NO_3^-(aq)$

In still another example, the solubility guidelines indicate that with the exception of the alkali metal cations (and Ba^{2+}), all metal cations form insoluble hydroxides. Thus, water-soluble iron(III) chloride and sodium hydroxide react to give insoluble iron(III) hydroxide (Figures 3.10c and 3.11c).

$$FeCl_3(aq) + 3\ NaOH(aq) \rightarrow Fe(OH)_3(s) + 3\ NaCl(aq)$$

Reactants	Products
$Fe^{3+}(aq) + 3\ Cl^-(aq)$	Insoluble $Fe(OH)_3(s)$
$3\ Na^+(aq) + 3\ OH^-(aq)$	$3\ Na^+(aq) + 3\ Cl^-(aq)$

Charles D. Winters

Black tongue. Pepto-Bismol™ has anti-diarrheal, antibacterial, and antacid effects in the digestive tract, and has been used for over 100 years as an effective remedy. However, some people find their tongues blackened after taking this over-the-counter medicine. The active ingredient in Pepto-Bismol is bismuth subsalicylate. (It also contains pepsin, zinc salts, oil of wintergreen, and salol, a compound related to aspirin.) The tongue blackening comes from the reaction of bismuth ions with traces of sulfide ions found in saliva to form black Bi_2S_3. The discoloration is harmless and lasts only a few days.

Chemistry⚛Now™

Sign in at **www.cengage.com/login** and go to Chapter 3 Contents to see:
- Screen 3.8 for a self-study module on **types of reactions in aqueous solutions**
- Screen 3.9 for a tutorial and simulation on **precipitation reactions**

■ **EXAMPLE 3.3** **Writing the Equation for a Precipitation Reaction**

Problem Is an insoluble product formed when aqueous solutions of potassium chromate and silver nitrate are mixed? If so, write the balanced equation.

Strategy First, decide what ions are formed in solution when the reactants dissolve. Then use information in Figure 3.10 to determine whether a cation from one reactant will combine with an anion from the other reactant to form an insoluble compound.

Solution Both reactants—$AgNO_3$ and K_2CrO_4—are water-soluble. The ions Ag^+, NO_3^-, K^+, and CrO_4^{2-} are released into solution when the compounds are dissolved.

$$AgNO_3(s) \rightarrow Ag^+(aq) + NO_3^-(aq)$$
$$K_2CrO_4(s) \rightarrow 2\ K^+(aq) + CrO_4^{2-}(aq)$$

Here, Ag^+ could combine with CrO_4^{2-}, and K^+ could combine with NO_3^-. Based on the solubility guidelines, we know that the former combination, Ag_2CrO_4, is an insoluble compound, whereas KNO_3 is soluble in water. Thus, the balanced equation for the reaction of silver nitrate and potassium chromate is

$$2\ AgNO_3(aq) + K_2CrO_4(aq) \rightarrow Ag_2CrO_4(s) + 2\ KNO_3(aq)$$

Comment This reaction is illustrated in Figure 3.11d.

EXERCISE 3.5 **Precipitation Reactions**

In each of the following cases, does a precipitation reaction occur when solutions of the two water-soluble reactants are mixed? Give the formula of any precipitate that forms, and write a balanced chemical equation for the precipitation reactions that occur.

(a) Sodium carbonate and copper(II) chloride

(b) Potassium carbonate and sodium nitrate

(c) Nickel(II) chloride and potassium hydroxide

Net Ionic Equations

We have seen that when aqueous solutions of silver nitrate and potassium chloride are mixed, insoluble silver chloride forms, leaving potassium nitrate in solution (see Figure 3.7). The balanced chemical equation for this process is

$$AgNO_3(aq) + KCl(aq) \rightarrow AgCl(s) + KNO_3(aq)$$

We can represent this reaction in another way by writing an equation in which we show that the soluble ionic compounds are present in solution as dissociated ions. An aqueous solution of silver nitrate contains Ag^+ and NO_3^- ions, and an aqueous solution of potassium chloride contains K^+ and Cl^- ions. In the products, the potassium nitrate is present in solution as K^+ and NO_3^- ions. The silver chloride, however, is insoluble and thus is not present in the solution as dissociated ions. It is shown in the equation by its entire formula, AgCl.

$$\underbrace{Ag^+(aq) + NO_3^-(aq) + K^+(aq) + Cl^-(aq)}_{\text{before reaction}} \rightarrow \underbrace{AgCl(s) + K^+(aq) + NO_3^-(aq)}_{\text{after reaction}}$$

This type of equation is called a **complete ionic equation**.

The K^+ and NO_3^- ions are present in solution before and after reaction and so appear on both the reactant and product sides of the complete ionic equation. Such ions are often called **spectator ions** because they do not participate in the net reaction; they only "look on" from the sidelines. Little chemical information is lost if the equation is written without them, and so we can simplify the equation to

$$Ag^+(aq) + Cl^-(aq) \rightarrow AgCl(s)$$

Writing Net Ionic Equations

Net ionic equations are commonly written for chemical reactions in aqueous solution because they describe the actual chemical species involved in a reaction. To write net ionic equations, we must know which compounds exist as ions in solution.

1. Strong acids, strong bases, and soluble salts exist as ions in solution. Examples include the acids HCl and HNO_3, a base such as NaOH, and salts such as NaCl and $CuCl_2$.
2. All other species should be represented by their complete formulas. Weak acids such as acetic acid (CH_3CO_2H) exist in solutions primarily as molecules. (See Section 3.7.) Insoluble salts such as $CaCO_3(s)$ or insoluble bases such as $Mg(OH)_2(s)$ should not be written in ionic form, even though they are ionic compounds.

The best way to approach writing net ionic equations is to follow precisely a set of steps:

1. Write a complete, balanced equation. Indicate the state of each substance (aq, s, ℓ, g).
2. Next, rewrite the whole equation, writing all strong acids, strong bases, and soluble salts as ions. (Consider only species labeled with an "(aq)" suffix in this step.)
3. Some ions may remain unchanged in the reaction (the ions that appear in the equation both as reactants or products). These "spectator ions" are not part of the chemistry that is going on. You can cancel them from each side of the equation.
4. Like molecular equations, net ionic equations must be balanced. The same number of atoms must appear on each side of the arrow, and the sum of the ion charges on the two sides must also be equal.

■ **Net Ionic Equations** All chemical equations, including net ionic equations, must be balanced. The same number of atoms of each kind must appear on both the product and reactant sides. In addition, the sum of positive and negative charges must be the same on both sides of the equation.

The balanced equation that results from leaving out the spectator ions is the **net ionic equation** for the reaction. *Only the aqueous ions, insoluble compounds, and weak- or nonelectrolytes* (which can be soluble molecular compounds such as sugar, weak acids, weak bases, or gases) *that participate in a chemical reaction are included in the net ionic equation.*

Leaving out the spectator ions does not imply that K^+ and NO_3^- ions are unimportant in the $AgNO_3 + KCl$ reaction. Indeed, Ag^+ ions cannot exist alone in solution; a negative ion, in this case NO_3^-, must be present to balance the positive charge of Ag^+. Any anion will do, however, as long as it forms a water-soluble compound with Ag^+. Thus, we could have used $AgClO_4$ instead of $AgNO_3$. Similarly, there must be a positive ion present to balance the negative charge of Cl^-. In this case, the positive ion present is K^+ in KCl, but we could have used NaCl instead of KCl. The net ionic equation would have been the same.

Finally, notice that there must always be a *charge balance* as well as a mass balance in a balanced chemical equation. Thus, in the $Ag^+ + Cl^-$ net ionic equation, the cation and anion charges on the left add together to give a net charge of zero, the same as the zero charge on AgCl(s) on the right.

Sign in at **www.cengage.com/login** and go to Chapter 3 Contents to see Screen 3.10 for a tutorial on **writing net ionic equations.**

Precipitation reaction. The reaction of barium chloride and sodium sulfate produces insoluble barium sulfate and water-soluble sodium chloride.

Charles D. Winters

■ **EXAMPLE 3.4 Writing and Balancing Net Ionic Equations**

Problem Write a balanced, net ionic equation for the reaction of aqueous solutions of $BaCl_2$ and Na_2SO_4.

Strategy Follow the strategy outlined in Problem Solving Tip 3.1.

Solution

Step 1. First, notice that this is an *exchange reaction*. That is, the Ba^{2+} and Na^+ cations exchange anions (Cl^- and SO_4^{2-}) to give $BaSO_4$ and NaCl. Now that the reactants and products are known, we can write an equation for the reaction. To balance the equation, we place a 2 in front of the NaCl.

$$BaCl_2 + Na_2SO_4 \rightarrow BaSO_4 + 2\ NaCl$$

Step 2. Decide on the solubility of each compound (Figure 3.10). Compounds containing sodium ions are always water-soluble, and those containing chloride ions are almost always soluble. Sulfate salts are also usually soluble, one important exception being $BaSO_4$. We can therefore write

$$BaCl_2(aq) + Na_2SO_4(aq) \rightarrow BaSO_4(s) + 2\ NaCl(aq)$$

Step 3. Identify the ions in solution. All soluble ionic compounds dissociate to form ions in aqueous solution.

$$BaCl_2(s) \rightarrow Ba^{2+}(aq) + 2\ Cl^-(aq)$$

$$Na_2SO_4(s) \rightarrow 2\ Na^+(aq) + SO_4^{2-}(aq)$$

$$NaCl(s) \rightarrow Na^+(aq) + Cl^-(aq)$$

This results in the following complete ionic equation:

$$Ba^{2+}(aq) + 2\ Cl^-(aq) + 2\ Na^+(aq) + SO_4^{2-}(aq) \rightarrow BaSO_4(s) + 2\ Na^+(aq) + 2\ Cl^-(aq)$$

Step 4. Identify and eliminate the spectator ions (Na^+ and Cl^-) to give the net ionic equation.

$$Ba^{2+}(aq) + SO_4^{2-}(aq) \rightarrow BaSO_4(s)$$

Comment Notice that the sum of ion charges is the same on both sides of the equation. On the left, 2+ and 2− give zero; on the right, the charge on $BaSO_4$ is also zero.

EXERCISE 3.6 Net Ionic Equations

Write a balanced net ionic equation for each of the following reactions:

(a) $AlCl_3 + Na_3PO_4 \rightarrow AlPO_4 + NaCl$ (not balanced)

(b) Solutions of iron(III) chloride and potassium hydroxide give iron(III) hydroxide and potassium chloride when combined. See Figure 3.10c.

(c) Solutions of lead(II) nitrate and potassium chloride give lead(II) chloride and potassium nitrate when combined.

3.7 Acids and Bases

Acids and bases are two important classes of compounds. You may already be familiar with some common properties of acids. They produce bubbles of CO_2 gas when added to a metal carbonate such as $CaCO_3$ (Figure 3.12a), and they react with many metals to produce hydrogen gas (H_2) (Figure 3.12b). Although tasting substances is *never* done in a chemistry laboratory, you have probably experienced the sour taste of acids such as acetic acid in vinegar and citric acid (commonly found in fruits and added to candies and soft drinks). Acids and bases have some related properties. Solutions of acids or bases, for example, can change the colors of vegetable pigments (Figure 3.12c). You may have seen acids change the color of litmus, a dye derived from certain lichens, from blue to red. If an acid has made blue litmus paper turn red, adding a base reverses the effect, making the litmus blue again. Thus, acids and bases seem to be opposites. A base can neutralize the effect of an acid, and an acid can neutralize the effect of a base. See Table 3.2 for a list of common acids and bases.

Over the years, chemists have examined the properties, chemical structures, and reactions of acids and bases and have proposed different definitions of the terms "acid" and "base." In this section, we shall examine the two most commonly used definitions, one proposed by Svante Arrhenius (1859–1927) and another proposed by Johannes N. Brønsted (1879–1947) and Thomas M. Lowry (1874–1936).

(a) A piece of coral (mostly CaCO₃) dissolves in acid to give CO₂ gas.

(b) Zinc reacts with hydrochloric acid to produce zinc chloride and hydrogen gas.

(c) The juice of a red cabbage is normally blue-purple. On adding acid, the juice becomes more red. Adding base produces a yellow color.

FIGURE 3.12 Some properties of acids and bases. (a) Acids react readily with coral ($CaCO_3$) and other metal carbonates to produce gaseous CO_2 (and a salt). (b) Acids react with many metals to produce hydrogen gas (and a metal salt). (c) The colors of natural dyes, such as the juice from a red cabbage, are affected by acids and bases.

Acids and Bases: The Arrhenius Definition

The Swedish chemist Svante Arrhenius made a number of important contributions to chemistry, but he is perhaps best known for his studies of the properties of solutions of salts, acids, and bases. In the late 1800s, Arrhenius proposed that these compounds dissolve in water and ultimately form ions. This theory of electrolytes

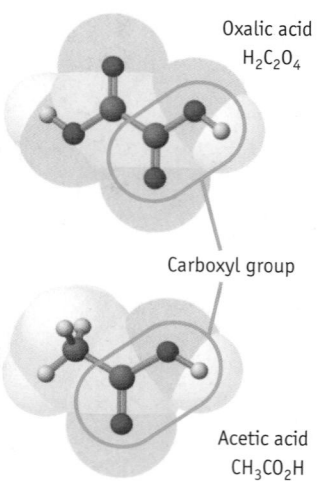

Oxalic acid
$H_2C_2O_4$

Carboxyl group

Acetic acid
CH_3CO_2H

■ **Weak Acids** Common acids and bases are listed in Table 3.2. There are numerous other weak acids and bases, and many of these are natural substances. Oxalic and acetic acid are among them. Many of these natural acids contain CO_2H groups. (The H of this group is lost as H^+.)

TABLE 3.2   Common Acids and Bases in Aqueous Solution

Strong Acids (Strong Electrolytes)		Soluble Strong Bases	
HCl (aq)	Hydrochloric acid	LiOH	Lithium hydroxide
HBr (aq)	Hydrobromic acid	NaOH	Sodium hydroxide
HI (aq)	Hydroiodic acid	KOH	Potassium hydroxide
HNO_3	Nitric acid	$Ba(OH)_2$	Barium hydroxide
$HClO_4$	Perchloric acid		
H_2SO_4	Sulfuric acid		
Weak Acids (Weak Electrolytes) *		**Weak Base (Weak Electrolyte)**	
H_3PO_4	Phosphoric acid	NH_3	Ammonia
H_2CO_3	Carbonic acid		
CH_3CO_2H	Acetic acid		
$H_2C_2O_4$	Oxalic acid		
$H_2C_4H_4O_6$	Tartaric acid		
$H_3C_6H_5O_7$	Citric acid		
$HC_9H_7O_4$	Aspirin		

* These are representative of hundreds of weak acids.

predated any knowledge of the composition and structure of atoms and was not well accepted initially. With a knowledge of atomic structure, however, we now take it for granted.

The Arrhenius definitions for acids and bases derives from his theory of electrolytes and focuses on formation of H^+ and OH^- ions in aqueous solutions.

- An acid is a substance that, when dissolved in water, increases the concentration of hydrogen ions, H^+ in solution.

$$HCl(g) \rightarrow H^+(aq) + Cl^-(aq)$$

- A base is a substance that, when dissolved in water, increases the concentration of hydroxide ions, OH^-, in the solution.

$$NaOH(s) \rightarrow Na^+(aq) + OH^-(aq)$$

- The reaction of an acid and a base produces a salt and water. Because the characteristic properties of an acid are lost when a base is added, and vice versa, acid–base reactions were logically described as resulting from the combination of H^+ and OH^- to form water.

$$HCl(aq) + NaOH(aq) \rightarrow NaCl(aq) + H_2O(\ell)$$

Arrhenius further proposed that acid strength was related to the extent to which the acid ionized. Some acids such as hydrochloric acid (HCl) and nitric acid (HNO_3) ionize completely in water; they are strong electrolytes, and we now call them **strong acids**. Other acids such as acetic acid and hydrofluoric acid are incompletely ionized; they are weak electrolytes and are **weak acids**. Weak acids exist in solution primarily as acid molecules, and only a fraction of these molecules ionize to produce $H^+(aq)$ ions along with the appropriate anion in solution.

Water-soluble compounds that contain hydroxide ions, such as sodium hydroxide (NaOH) or potassium hydroxide (KOH), are strong electrolytes and strong bases.

Aqueous ammonia, $NH_3(aq)$, is a weak electrolyte. Even though it does not have an OH^- ion as part of its formula, it does produce ammonium ions and hydroxide ions from its reaction with water and so is a base (Figure 3.13). The fact that this is a weak electrolyte indicates that only a fraction of ammonia molecules react with water to form ions; most of the base remains in solution in molecular form.

Although the Arrhenius theory is still used to some extent and is interesting in an historical context, modern concepts of acid–base chemistry such as the Brønsted–Lowry theory have gained preference among chemists.

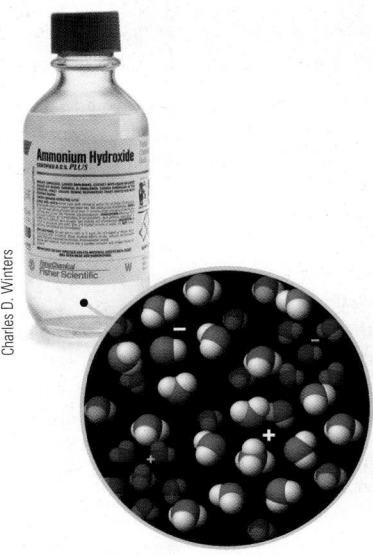

Charles D. Winters

FIGURE 3.13 Ammonia, a weak electrolyte. Ammonia, NH_3, interacts with water to produce a very small number of NH_4^+ and OH^- ions per mole of ammonia molecules. (The name on the bottle, ammonium hydroxide, is misleading. The solution consists almost entirely of NH_3 molecules dissolved in water. It is better referred to as "aqueous ammonia.")

EXERCISE 3.7 Acids and Bases

(a) What ions are produced when nitric acid dissolves in water?

(b) Barium hydroxide is moderately soluble in water. What ions are produced when it dissolves in water?

Acids and Bases: The Brønsted-Lowry Definition

In 1923, Brønsted in Copenhagen (Denmark) and Lowry in Cambridge (England) independently suggested a new concept of acid and base behavior. They viewed acids and bases in terms of the transfer of a proton (H^+) from one species to an-

The Hydronium Ion—The H⁺ Ion in Water

The H^+ ion is a hydrogen atom that has lost its electron. Only the nucleus, a proton, remains. Because a proton is only about 1/100,000 as large as the average atom or ion, water molecules can approach closely, and the proton and water molecules are strongly attracted. In fact, the H^+ ion in water is better represented as H_3O^+, called the **hydronium ion.** This ion is formed by combining H^+ and H_2O. Experiments also show that other forms of the ion exist in water, one example being $[H_3O(H_2O)_3]^+$.

There will be instances when, for simplicity, we will use $H^+(aq)$. However, we will usually use the H_3O^+ symbol to represent the hydrogen ion in water in this book. Thus, hydrochloric acid is better represented as a solution of H_3O^+ and Cl^-.

hydronium ion
$H_3O^+(aq)$

chloride ion
$Cl^-(aq)$

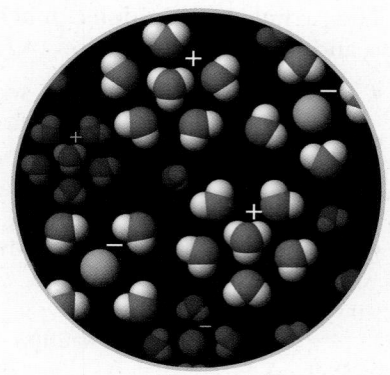

When HCl ionizes in aqueous solution, it produces the hydronium ion, H_3O^+, and the chloride ion, Cl^-.

other, and they described all acid–base reactions in terms of equilibria. The Brønsted–Lowry theory expanded the scope of the definition of acids and bases and helped chemists make predictions of product or reactant favorability based on acid and base strength. We will describe this theory here qualitatively; a more complete discussion will be given in Chapter 17.

The main concepts of the Brønsted-Lowry theory are the following:

- *An acid is a proton donor.* This is similar to the Arrhenius definition.
- *A base is a proton acceptor.* This definition includes the OH^- ion, but it also broadens the number and type of bases.
- *An acid–base reaction involves the transfer of a proton from an acid to a base to form a new acid and a new base. The reaction is written as an equilibrium reaction, and the equilibrium favors the weaker acid and base.* This allows the prediction of product- or reactant-favored reactions based on acid and base strength.

From the point of view of the Brønsted–Lowry theory, the behavior of acids such as HCl or CH_3CO_2H in water is seen to involve an acid–base reaction. Both species (both Brønsted acids) donate a proton to water (a Brønsted base), forming $H_3O^+(aq)$. Hydrochloric acid, HCl(aq), is a strong electrolyte because it ionizes completely in aqueous solution; it is thus classified as a strong acid.

Hydrogen chloride, a strong acid. 100% ionized. Equilibrium strongly favors products.

$$HCl(aq) \quad + \quad H_2O(\ell) \quad \rightleftharpoons \quad H_3O^+(aq) \quad + \quad Cl^-(aq)$$

hydrochloric acid
strong electrolyte
= 100% ionized

water

hydronium ion

chloride ion

For many years, sulfuric acid has been the chemical produced in the largest quantity in the United States (and in many other industrialized countries). About 40–50 billion kilograms (40–50 million metric tons) are made annually in the United States. The acid is so important to the economy of industrialized nations that some economists have said sulfuric acid production is a measure of a nation's industrial strength.

Sulfuric acid is a colorless, syrupy liquid with a density of 1.84 g/mL and a boiling point of 337 °C. It has several desirable properties that have led to its widespread use: it is generally less expensive to produce than other acids, is a strong acid, can be handled in steel containers, reacts readily with many organic compounds to produce useful prod-

Sulfur. Much of the sulfur used in the U.S. is produced by the Frasch process. This works by injecting superheated water into pockets of the element deep in the earth. The sulfur is forced to the surface in the molten state by compressed air.

ucts, and reacts readily with lime (CaO), the least expensive and most readily available base, to give calcium sulfate, a compound used to make wall board for the construction industry.

The first step in the industrial preparation of sulfuric acid is combustion of sulfur in air to give sulfur dioxide.

$$S(s) + O_2(g) \rightarrow SO_2(g)$$

This gas is then combined with more oxygen, in the presence of a catalyst (a substance that speeds up a reaction), to give sulfur trioxide,

$$2\ SO_2(g) + O_2(g) \rightarrow 2\ SO_3(g)$$

which can give sulfuric acid when absorbed in water.

$$SO_3(g) + H_2O(\ell) \rightarrow H_2SO_4(aq)$$

Currently, over two thirds of the production is used in the fertilizer industry. The remainder is used to make pigments, explosives, alcohol, pulp and paper, and detergents, and is employed as a component in storage batteries.

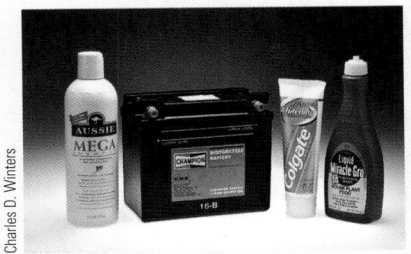

Some products that require sulfuric acid for their manufacture or use.

A sulfuric acid plant.

In contrast, CH_3CO_2H is a weak electrolyte, evidence that it is ionized to a small extent in water and therefore is a weak acid.

Acetic acid, a weak acid, << 100% ionized. Equilibrium favors reactants.

$$CH_3CO_2H(aq) + H_2O(\ell) \rightleftharpoons H_3O^+(aq) + CH_3CO_2^-(aq)$$
Weak Brønsted acid   Brønsted base

The different extent of ionization for these two acids relates to their acid strengths. Hydrochloric acid is a strong acid, and the equilibrium strongly favors the products. In contrast, acetic acid is a weak acid, and equilibrium for its reaction with water is reactant-favored.

Sulfuric acid, a *diprotic acid* (an acid capable of transferring two H$^+$ ions), reacts with water in two steps. The first step strongly favors products, whereas the second step is reactant-favored.

Strong Acid: $H_2SO_4(aq) + H_2O(\ell) \rightleftharpoons H_3O^+(aq) + HSO_4^-(aq)$
                     sulfuric acid   hydronium ion   hydrogen
                     100% ionized   sulfate ion

Weak Acid: $HSO_4^-(aq) + H_2O(\ell) \rightleftharpoons H_3O^+(aq) + SO_4^{2-}(aq)$
                     hydrogen sulfate ion   hydronium ion   sulfate ion
                     <100% ionized

■ **Acetic Acid** Acetic acid, CH_3CO_2H, is the substance that gives the taste and odor to vinegar. Fermentation of carbohydrates such as sugar produces ethanol (CH_3CH_2OH), and the action of bacteria on the alcohol results in acetic acid. Even a trace of acetic acid will ruin the taste of wine. This is the source of the name vinegar, which comes from the French *vin egar* meaning "sour wine." In addition to its use in food products such as salad dressings, mayonnaise, and pickles, acetic acid is used in hair-coloring products and in the manufacture of cellulose acetate, a commonly used synthetic fiber.

Ammonia, a weak base, reacts with water to produce OH^-(aq) ions. The reaction is reactant-favored at equilibrium.

Ammonia, a weak base, < 100% ionized. Equilibrium favors reactants.

$$NH_3(aq) + H_2O(\ell) \rightleftarrows NH_4^+(aq) + OH^-(aq)$$

| ammonia, base weak electrolyte < 100% ionized | water | ammonium ion | hydroxide ion |

Some species are described as **amphiprotic**, that is, they can function either as acids or as bases depending on the reaction. In the examples above, water functions as a base in reactions with acids (it accepts a proton) and as an acid in its reaction with ammonia (where it donates a proton to ammonia forming the ammonium ion.)

Chemistry⚛Now™

Sign in at **www.cengage.com/login** and go to Chapter 3 Contents to see:
• Screen 3.11 for a simulation on **acid ionization**
• Screen 3.12 for a self-study module on **weak and strong bases**

EXERCISE 3.8 Brønsted Acids and Bases

(a) Write a balanced equation for the reaction that occurs when H_3PO_4, phosphoric acid, donates a proton to water to form the dihydrogen phosphate ion.

(b) Write a net ionic equation showing the dihydrogen phosphate ion acting as a Brønsted acid in a reaction with water. Write another net ionic equation showing the dihydrogen phosphate ion acting as a Brønsted base in a reaction with water. What term is used to describe a species such as dihydrogen phosphate that can act either as an acid or as a base?

(c) Write a balanced net ionic equation for the reaction that occurs when the cyanide ion, CN^-, accepts a proton from water to form HCN. Is CN^- a Brønsted acid or base?

Reactions of Acids and Bases

Acids and bases in aqueous solution react to produce a salt and water. For example (Figure 3.14),

$$\underset{\text{hydrochloric acid}}{HCl(aq)} + \underset{\text{sodium hydroxide}}{NaOH(aq)} \longrightarrow \underset{\text{water}}{H_2O(\ell)} + \underset{\text{sodium chloride}}{NaCl(aq)}$$

The word "salt" has come into the language of chemistry to describe any ionic compound whose cation comes from a base (here Na^+ from NaOH) and whose anion comes from an acid (here Cl^- from HCl). The reaction of any of the acids listed in Table 3.2 with any of the hydroxide-containing bases listed there produces a salt and water.

Hydrochloric acid and sodium hydroxide are strong electrolytes in water (see Figure 3.14 and Table 3.2), so the complete ionic equation for the reaction of HCl(aq) and NaOH(aq) should be written as

$$\underbrace{H_3O^+(aq) + Cl^-(aq)}_{\text{from HCl(aq)}} + \underbrace{Na^+(aq) + OH^-(aq)}_{\text{from NaOH(aq)}} \longrightarrow \underset{\text{water}}{2\,H_2O(\ell)} + \underbrace{Na^+(aq) + Cl^-(aq)}_{\text{from salt}}$$

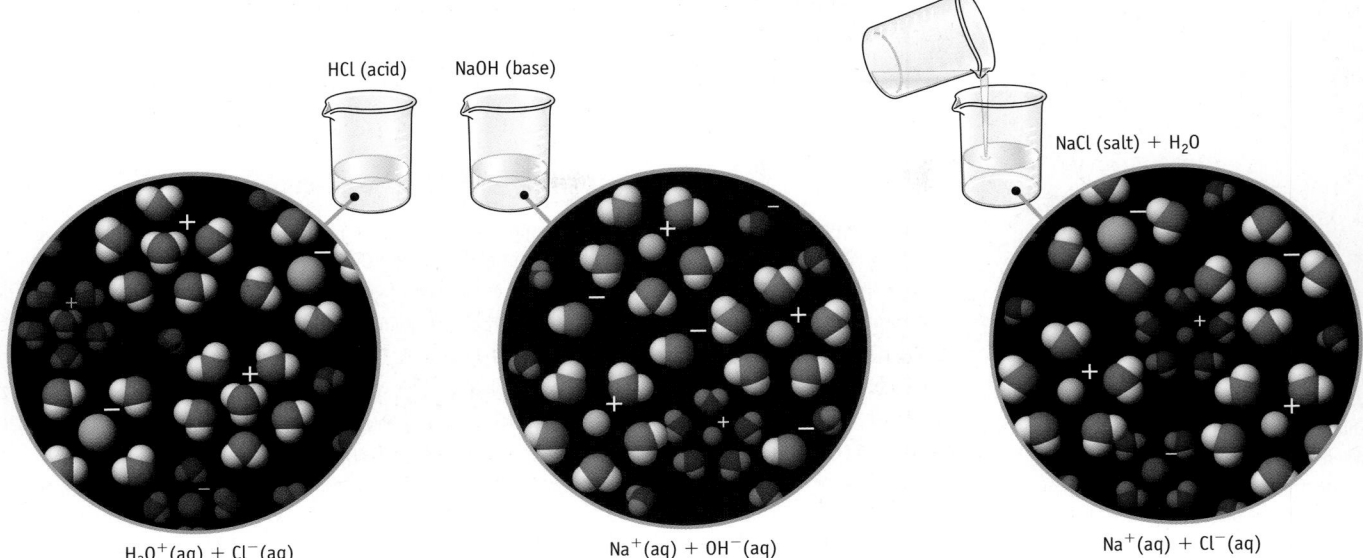

HCl (acid)   NaOH (base)   NaCl (salt) + H₂O

$H_3O^+(aq) + Cl^-(aq)$ $Na^+(aq) + OH^-(aq)$ $Na^+(aq) + Cl^-(aq)$

Active Figure 3.14 **An acid–base reaction, HCl and NaOH.** On mixing, the H_3O^+ and OH^- ions combine to produce H_2O, whereas the ions Na^+ and Cl^- remain in solution.

Chemistry Now™ Sign in at www.cengage.com/login and go to the Chapter Contents menu to explore an interactive version of this figure accompanied by an exercise.

Because Na^+ and Cl^- ions appear on both sides of the equation, the *net ionic equation* is just the combination of the ions H_3O^+ and OH^- to give water.

$$H_3O^+(aq) + OH^-(aq) \rightarrow 2\,H_2O(\ell)$$

This is always the net ionic equation when a strong acid reacts with a strong base.

Reactions between *strong acids* and *strong bases* are called **neutralization reactions** because, on completion of the reaction, the solution is neutral if exactly the same amounts (number of moles) of the acid and base are mixed; that is, it is neither acidic nor basic. The other ions (the cation of the base and the anion of the acid) remain unchanged. If the water is evaporated, however, the cation and anion form a solid salt. In the example above, NaCl can be obtained. If nitric acid, HNO_3, and NaOH were allowed to react, the salt sodium nitrate, $NaNO_3$ (and water) would be obtained.

$$HNO_3(aq) + NaOH(aq) \rightarrow H_2O(\ell) + NaNO_3(aq)$$

If acetic acid and sodium hydroxide are mixed, the following reaction will take place.

$$CH_3CO_2H(aq) + NaOH(aq) \rightarrow H_2O(\ell) + NaCH_3CO_2(aq)$$

Because acetic acid is a weak acid and ionizes to such a small extent (Figure 3.9), the molecular species is the predominant form in aqueous solutions. In ionic equations, therefore, acetic acid is shown as molecular $CH_3CO_2H(aq)$. The *complete ionic equation* for this reaction is

$$CH_3CO_2H(aq) + Na^+(aq) + OH^-(aq) \rightarrow H_2O(\ell) + Na^+(aq) + CH_3CO_2^-(aq)$$

The only spectator ions in this equation are the sodium ions, so the *net ionic equation* is

$$CH_3CO_2H(aq) + OH^-(aq) \rightarrow H_2O(\ell) + CH_3CO_2^-(aq)$$

Charles D. Winters

Reaction of gaseous HCl and NH₃. Open dishes of aqueous ammonia and hydrochloric acid were placed side by side. When gas molecules of NH_3 and HCl escape from solution to the atmosphere and encounter one another, we observe a cloud of solid ammonium chloride, NH_4Cl.

Chemistry⚛Now™

Sign in at **www.cengage.com/login** and go to Chapter 3 Contents to see Screen 3.13 for an exercise on **acid–base reactions**.

■ **EXAMPLE 3.5 Net Ionic Equation for an Acid–Base Reaction**

Problem Ammonia, NH_3, is one of the most important chemicals in industrial economies. Not only is it used directly as a fertilizer but it is the raw material for the manufacture of nitric acid. As a base, it reacts with acids such as hydrochloric acid. Write a balanced, net ionic equation for this reaction.

Strategy Follow the general strategy outlined in Problem Solving Tip 3.1.

Solution The complete balanced equation is

$$NH_3(aq) + HCl(aq) \rightarrow NH_4Cl(aq)$$
ammonia   hydrochloric acid   ammonium chloride

Notice that the reaction produces a salt, NH_4Cl, but not water. An H^+ ion from the acid transfers to ammonia, a weak Brønsted base, to give the ammonium ion. To write the net ionic equation, start with the fact that hydrochloric acid is a strong acid and produces H_3O^+ and Cl^- ions and that NH_4Cl is a soluble, ionic compound. On the other hand, ammonia is a weak base and so is predominantly present in the solution as the molecular species, NH_3.

$$NH_3(aq) + H_3O^+(aq) + Cl^-(aq) \rightarrow NH_4^+(aq) + Cl^-(aq) + H_2O(\ell)$$

Eliminating the spectator ion, Cl^-, we have

$$NH_3(aq) + H_3O^+(aq) \rightarrow NH_4^+(aq) + H_2O(\ell)$$

Comment The net ionic equation shows that the important aspect of the reaction between the weak base ammonia and the strong acid HCl is the transfer of an H^+ ion from the acid to the NH_3. Any strong acid could be used here (HBr, HNO_3, $HClO_4$, H_2SO_4) and the net ionic equation would be the same.

EXERCISE 3.9 Acid–Base Reactions

Write the balanced, overall equation and the net ionic equation for the reaction of magnesium hydroxide with hydrochloric acid. *(Hint: Think about the solubility guidelines.)*

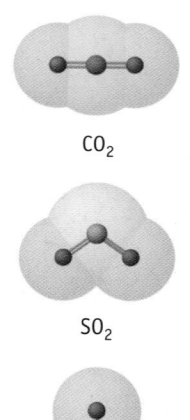

CO_2

SO_2

SO_3

NO_2

Some common nonmetal oxides that form acids in water.

Oxides of Nonmetals and Metals

Each acid shown in Table 3.2 has one or more H atoms in the molecular formula that dissociate in water to form H_3O^+ ions. There are, however, less obvious compounds that form acidic solutions. Oxides of nonmetals, such as carbon dioxide and sulfur trioxide, have no H atoms but react with water to produce H_3O^+ ions. Carbon dioxide, for example, dissolves in water to a small extent, and some of the dissolved molecules react with water to form the weak acid, carbonic acid. This acid then ionizes to a small extent to form the hydronium ion, H_3O^+, and the hydrogen carbonate (bicarbonate) ion, HCO_3^-.

$$CO_2(g) + H_2O(\ell) \rightleftharpoons H_2CO_3(aq)$$

$$H_2CO_3(aq) + H_2O(\ell) \rightleftharpoons HCO_3^-(aq) + H_3O^+(aq)$$

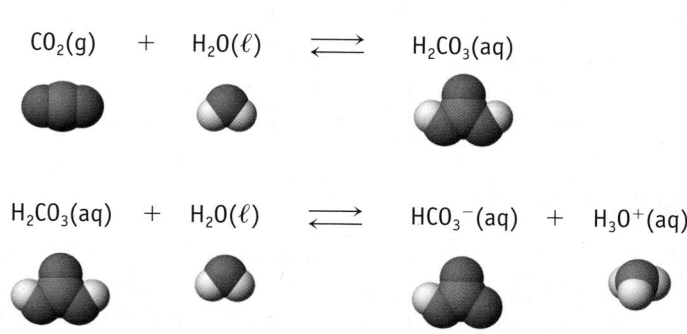

The HCO_3^- ion can also function as an acid, ionizing to produce H_3O^+ and the carbonate ion, CO_3^{2-}.

$$HCO_3^-(aq) + H_2O(\ell) \rightleftharpoons CO_3^{2-}(aq) + H_3O^+(aq)$$

■ **Acid Rain** Oxides of sulfur and nitrogen are the major source of the acid in what is called *acid rain*. These acidic oxides arise from the burning of fossil fuels such as coal and gasoline. The gaseous oxides mix with water and other chemicals in the troposphere, and the rain that falls is more acidic than if it contained only dissolved CO_2. When the rain falls on areas that cannot easily tolerate this greater-than-normal acidity, serious environmental problems can occur.

These reactions are important in our environment and in the human body. Carbon dioxide is normally found in small amounts in the atmosphere, so rainwater is always slightly acidic. In the human body, carbon dioxide is dissolved in body fluids, where the HCO_3^- and CO_3^{2-} ions perform an important "buffering" action (▶ Chapter 18).

Oxides like CO_2 that can react with water to produce H_3O^+ ions are known as **acidic oxides.** Other acidic oxides include those of sulfur and nitrogen. For example, sulfur dioxide, SO_2, from human and natural sources, can react with oxygen to give sulfur trioxide, SO_3, which then reacts with water to form sulfuric acid.

$$2\ SO_2(g) + O_2(g) \rightarrow 2\ SO_3(g)$$

$$SO_3(g) + H_2O(\ell) \rightarrow H_2SO_4(aq)$$

Nitrogen dioxide, NO_2, reacts with water to give nitric and nitrous acids.

$$2\ NO_2(g) + H_2O(\ell) \rightarrow HNO_3(aq) + HNO_2(aq)$$
$$\text{nitric acid}\quad\text{nitrous acid}$$

Oxides of metals are called **basic oxides** because they give basic solutions if they dissolve appreciably in water. Perhaps the best example is calcium oxide, CaO, often called *lime*, or *quicklime*. Almost 20 billion kg of lime is produced annually in the United States for use in the metals and construction industries, in sewage and pollution control, in water treatment, and in agriculture. This metal oxide reacts with water to give calcium hydroxide, commonly called *slaked lime*. Although only slightly soluble in water (about 0.2 g/100 g H_2O at 10 °C), $Ca(OH)_2$ is widely used in industry as a base because it is inexpensive.

$$CaO(s) + H_2O(\ell) \rightarrow Ca(OH)_2(s)$$
$$\text{lime}\text{slaked lime}$$

EXERCISE 3.10 Acidic and Basic Oxides

For each of the following, indicate whether you expect an acidic or basic solution when the compound dissolves in water. Remember that compounds based on elements in the same group usually behave similarly.

(a) SeO_2 **(b)** BaO **(c)** P_4O_{10}

3.8 Gas-Forming Reactions

Several different chemical reactions lead to gas formation (Table 3.3), but the most common are those leading to CO_2 formation. All metal carbonates (and bicarbonates) react with acids to produce carbonic acid, H_2CO_3, which in turn decomposes

FIGURE 3.15 Dissolving limestone (calcium carbonate, CaCO₃) in vinegar. Notice the bubbles of CO₂ rising from the surface of the limestone. This reaction shows why vinegar can be used as a household cleaning agent. It can be used, for example, to clean the calcium carbonate deposited from hard water.

TABLE 3.3   Gas-Forming Reactions

Metal carbonate or bicarbonate + acid → metal salt + $CO_2(g)$ + $H_2O(\ell)$
$Na_2CO_3(aq) + 2\ HCl(aq) \rightarrow 2\ NaCl(aq) + CO_2(g) + H_2O(\ell)$
$NaHCO_3(aq) + HCl(aq) \rightarrow NaCl(aq) + CO_2(g) + H_2O(\ell)$
Metal sulfide + acid → metal salt + $H_2S(g)$
$Na_2S(aq) + 2\ HCl(aq) \rightarrow 2\ NaCl(aq) + H_2S(g)$
Metal sulfite + acid → metal salt + $SO_2(g)$ + $H_2O(\ell)$
$Na_2SO_3(aq) + 2\ HCl(aq) \rightarrow 2\ NaCl(aq) + SO_2(g) + H_2O(\ell)$
Ammonium salt + strong base → metal salt + $NH_3(g)$ + $H_2O(\ell)$
$NH_4Cl(aq) + NaOH(aq) \rightarrow NaCl(aq) + NH_3(g) + H_2O(\ell)$

rapidly to carbon dioxide and water. For example, the reaction of calcium carbonate and hydrochloric acid is:

$$CaCO_3(s) + 2\ HCl(aq) \rightarrow CaCl_2(aq) + H_2CO_3(aq)$$

$$H_2CO_3(aq) \rightarrow H_2O(\ell) + CO_2(g)$$

Overall reaction: $CaCO_3(s) + 2\ HCl(aq) \rightarrow CaCl_2(aq) + H_2O(\ell) + CO_2(g)$

If the reaction is done in an open beaker, most of the CO₂ gas bubbles out of the solution.

Calcium carbonate is a common residue from hard water in home heating systems and cooking utensils. Washing with vinegar is a good way to clean the system or utensils because the insoluble calcium carbonate is turned into water-soluble calcium acetate in the following gas-forming reaction (Figure 3.15).

$$2\ CH_3CO_2H(aq) + CaCO_3(s) \rightarrow Ca(CH_3CO_2)_2(aq) + H_2O(\ell) + CO_2(g)$$

What is the net ionic equation for this reaction? Acetic acid is a weak acid. Calcium carbonate is insoluble in water. Therefore, the reactants are simply $CH_3CO_2H(aq)$ and $CaCO_3(s)$. On the products side, calcium acetate is water-soluble and forms aqueous calcium and acetate ions. Water and carbon dioxide are molecular compounds, so the net ionic equation is

$$2\ CH_3CO_2H(aq) + CaCO_3(s) \rightarrow Ca^{2+}(aq) + 2\ CH_3CO_2^-(aq) + H_2O(\ell) + CO_2(g)$$

There are no spectator ions in this reaction.

Have you ever made biscuits or muffins? As you bake the dough, it rises in the oven (Figure 3.16). But what makes it rise? A gas-forming reaction occurs between an acid and baking soda, sodium hydrogen carbonate (bicarbonate of soda, $NaHCO_3$). One acid used for this purpose is tartaric acid, a weak acid found in many foods. The net ionic equation for a typical reaction would be

FIGURE 3.16 Muffins rise because of a gas-forming reaction. The acid and sodium bicarbonate in baking powder produce carbon dioxide gas. The acid used in many baking powders is $Ca(H_2PO_4)_2$, but tartaric acid and $NaAl(SO_4)_2$ are also common. (Aqueous solutions containing the aluminum ion are acidic.)

$$\underset{\text{tartaric acid}}{H_2C_4H_4O_6(aq)} + \underset{\text{hydrogen carbonate ion}}{HCO_3^-(aq)} \rightarrow \underset{\substack{\text{hydrogen} \\ \text{tartrate ion}}}{HC_4H_4O_6^-(aq)} + H_2O(\ell) + CO_2(g)$$

In dry baking powder, the acid and $NaHCO_3$ are kept apart by using starch as a filler. When mixed into the moist batter, however, the acid and sodium hydrogen carbonate dissolve and come into contact. Now they can react to produce CO_2, causing the dough to rise.

Chemistry.Now™

Sign in at **www.cengage.com/login** and go to Chapter 3 Contents to see Screen 3.14 for a tutorial identifying **the type of reaction that will result from the mixing of solutions** and to watch videos about **four of the most important gases produced in reactions.**

■ **EXAMPLE 3.6 Gas-Forming Reactions**

Problem Write a balanced equation for the reaction that occurs when nickel(II) carbonate is treated with sulfuric acid.

Strategy First, identify the reactants and write their formulas (here $NiCO_3$ and H_2SO_4). Next, recognize this as a typical gas-forming reaction (Table 3.3) between a metal carbonate and an acid. The products are water, CO_2, and a salt. The anion of the salt is the anion from the acid (SO_4^{2-}), and the cation is from the metal carbonate (Ni^{2+}).

Solution The complete, balanced equation is

$$NiCO_3(s) + H_2SO_4(aq) \longrightarrow NiSO_4(aq) + H_2O(\ell) + CO_2(g)$$

EXERCISE 3.11 Gas-Forming Reactions

(a) Barium carbonate, $BaCO_3$, is used in the brick, ceramic, glass, and chemical manufacturing industries. Write a balanced equation that shows what happens when barium carbonate is treated with nitric acid. Give the name of each of the reaction products.

(b) Write a balanced equation for the reaction of ammonium sulfate with sodium hydroxide.

3.9 Oxidation-Reduction Reactions

The terms "oxidation" and "reduction" come from reactions that have been known for centuries. Ancient civilizations learned how to change metal oxides and sulfides into the metal, that is, how to "reduce" ore to the metal. A modern example is the reduction of iron(III) oxide with carbon monoxide to give iron metal (Figure 3.17a).

Fe_2O_3 loses oxygen and is reduced.

$$Fe_2O_3(s) + 3\ CO(g) \longrightarrow 2\ Fe(s) + 3\ CO_2(g)$$

CO is the reducing agent. It gains oxygen and is oxidized.

In this reaction, carbon monoxide is the agent that brings about the reduction of iron ore to iron metal, so carbon monoxide is called the **reducing agent.**

When Fe_2O_3 is reduced by carbon monoxide, oxygen is removed from the iron ore and added to the carbon monoxide. The carbon monoxide, therefore, is "oxidized" by the addition of oxygen to give carbon dioxide. *Any process in which oxygen is added to another substance is an oxidation.* In the reaction of oxygen with magnesium,

FIGURE 3.17 Oxidation-reduction.
(a) Iron ore, which is largely Fe_2O_3, is reduced to metallic iron with carbon or carbon monoxide in a blast furnace, a process done on a massive scale.
(b) Burning magnesium metal in air produces magnesium oxide.

a, Jan Halaska/Photo Researchers, Inc.; b, Charles D. Winters

(a)   (b)

for example (see Figure 3.17b), oxygen is the **oxidizing agent** because it is the agent responsible for the oxidation of magnesium.

Mg combines with
oxygen and is oxidized.

$$2\ Mg(s) + O_2(g) \longrightarrow 2\ MgO(s)$$

O_2 is the oxidizing agent

Oxidation-Reduction Reactions and Electron Transfer

Not all redox reactions involve oxygen, but *all oxidation and reduction reactions can be accounted for by considering them to occur by means of a transfer of electrons between substances.* When a substance accepts electrons, it is said to be **reduced** because there is a reduction in the numerical value of the charge on an atom of the substance. In the net ionic equation for the reaction of a silver salt with copper metal, positively charged Ag^+ ions accept electrons from copper metal and are reduced to uncharged silver atoms (Figure 3.18).

Ag^+ ions accept electrons from Cu and are
reduced to Ag. Ag^+ is the oxidizing agent.
$Ag^+(aq) + e^- \rightarrow Ag(s)$

$$2\ Ag^+(aq) + Cu(s) \longrightarrow 2\ Ag(s) + Cu^{2+}(aq)$$

Cu donates electrons to Ag^+ and is oxidized to Cu^{2+}.
Cu is the reducing agent.
$Cu(s) \rightarrow Cu^{2+}(aq) + 2\ e^-$

Because copper metal supplies the electrons and causes Ag^+ ions to be reduced, Cu is the reducing agent.

When a substance *loses electrons*, the numerical value of the charge on an atom of the substance increases. The substance is said to have been **oxidized**. In our example, copper metal releases electrons on going to Cu^{2+}, so the metal is oxidized. For this to happen, something must be available to accept the electrons from cop-

Pure copper
wire

Copper wire in dilute AgNO₃
solution; after several hours

Blue color due to
Cu²⁺ ions formed
in redox reaction

Silver crystals
formed after
several weeks

FIGURE 3.18 The oxidation of copper metal by silver ions. A clean piece of copper wire is placed in a solution of silver nitrate, $AgNO_3$. Over time, the copper reduces Ag^+ ions, forming silver crystals, and the copper metal is oxidized to copper ions, Cu^{2+}. The blue color of the solution is due to the presence of aqueous copper(II) ions. (Sign in to ChemistryNow and Screen 3.15, Redox Reactions and Electron Transfer, to watch a video of the reaction.)

per. In this case, Ag^+ is the electron acceptor, and its charge is reduced to zero in silver metal. Therefore, Ag^+ is the "agent" that causes Cu metal to be oxidized; that is, Ag^+ is the *oxidizing agent*.

In every oxidation-reduction reaction, one reactant is reduced (and is therefore the oxidizing agent) and one reactant is oxidized (and is therefore the reducing agent). We can show this by dividing the general redox reaction $X + Y \rightarrow X^{n+} + Y^{n-}$ into two parts or *half-reactions*:

Half Reaction	Electron Transfer	Result
$X \rightarrow X^{n+} + n\,e^-$	X transfers electrons to Y	X is oxidized to X^{n+}. X is the reducing agent
$Y + n\,e^- \rightarrow Y^{n-}$	Y accepts electron from X	Y is reduced to Y^{n-}. Y is the oxidizing agent

In the reaction of magnesium and oxygen, O_2 is reduced because it gains electrons (four electrons per molecule) on going to two oxide ions. Thus, O_2 is the oxidizing agent.

Mg releases 2 e⁻ per atom. Mg is oxidized to Mg^{2+}
and is the reducing agent.

$$2\ Mg(s) + O_2(g) \longrightarrow 2\ MgO(s)$$

O_2 gains 4 e⁻ per molecule to form 2 O^{2-}. O_2 is
reduced and is the oxidizing agent.

In the same reaction, magnesium is the reducing agent because it releases two electrons per atom on being oxidized to the Mg^{2+} ion (and so two Mg atoms are required to supply the four electrons required by one O_2 molecule). All redox reactions can be analyzed in a similar manner.

■ **Balancing Equations for Redox Reactions** The notion that a redox reaction can be divided into an oxidizing portion and a reducing portion will lead us to a method of balancing more complex equations for redox reactions described in Chapter 20.

■ **Chemical Safety and Redox Reactions** A strong oxidizing agent and a strong reducing agent may react violently. For this reason, it would not be a good idea to store a strong oxidizing agent next to a strong reducing agent. Certain chemicals are often stored separately from the bulk of the other chemicals. Examples of chemicals that might be stored in their own separate areas are strong oxidizing agents, acids, water-reactive chemicals, and highly flammable materials.

Charles D. Winters

The observations outlined so far lead to several important conclusions:

- If one substance is oxidized, another substance in the same reaction must be reduced. For this reason, such reactions are called oxidation-reduction reactions, or **redox reactions** for short.
- The reducing agent is itself oxidized, and the oxidizing agent is reduced.
- Oxidation is the opposite of reduction. For example, the removal of oxygen is reduction, and the addition of oxygen is oxidation. The gain of electrons is reduction, and the loss of electrons is oxidation.

Oxidation Numbers

How can you tell an oxidation-reduction reaction when you see one? How can you tell which substance has gained or lost electrons and so decide which substance is the oxidizing (or reducing) agent? Sometimes it is obvious. For example, if an uncombined element becomes part of a compound (Mg becomes part of MgO, for example), the reaction is definitely a redox process. If it's not obvious, then the answer is to *look for a change in the oxidation number of an element in the course of the reaction.* The **oxidation number** of an atom in a molecule or ion is defined as the charge an atom has, *or appears to have*, as determined by the following guidelines for assigning oxidation numbers.

1. **Each atom in a pure element has an oxidation number of zero.** The oxidation number of Cu in metallic copper is 0, and it is 0 for each atom in I_2 and S_8.
2. **For monatomic ions, the oxidation number is equal to the charge on the ion.** You know that magnesium forms ions with a 2+ charge (Mg^{2+}); the oxidation number of magnesium in this ion is therefore +2.
3. **When combined with another element, fluorine always has an oxidation number of −1.**
4. **The oxidation number of O is −2 in most compounds.** The exceptions to this rule occur
   a) when oxygen is combined with fluorine (where oxygen takes on a positive oxidation number)
   b) in compounds called peroxides (such as Na_2O_2) and superoxides (such as KO_2) in which oxygen has an oxidation number of −1 and −1/2, respectively
5. **Cl, Br, and I have oxidation numbers of −1 in compounds, except when combined with oxygen and fluorine.** This means that Cl has an oxidation

■ **Writing Charges on Ions** Conventionally, charges on ions are written as (number, sign), whereas oxidation numbers are written as (sign, number). For example, the oxidation number of the Cu^{2+} ion is +2 and its charge is 2+.

■ **Peroxides** In peroxides, the oxidation number of oxygen is −1. For example, in hydrogen peroxide (H_2O_2), each hydrogen atom has an oxidation number of +1. To balance this, each oxygen must have an oxidation number of −1. A 3% aqueous solution of H_2O_2 is sometimes used as an antiseptic.

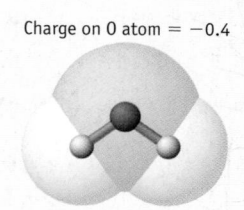

number of -1 in NaCl (in which Na is $+1$, as predicted by the fact that it is an element of Group 1A). In the ion ClO^-, however, the Cl atom has an oxidation number of $+1$ (and O has an oxidation number of -2; see guideline 4).

6. **The oxidation number of H is $+1$ in most compounds.** The key exception to this guideline occurs when H forms a binary compound with a metal. In such cases, the metal forms a positive ion, and H becomes a hydride ion, H^-. Thus, in CaH_2 the oxidation number of Ca is $+2$ (equal to the group number), and that of H is -1.

7. **The algebraic sum of the oxidation numbers for the atoms in a neutral compound must be zero; in a polyatomic ion, the sum must be equal to the ion charge.** For example, in $HClO_4$ the H atom is assigned $+1$, and each O atom is assigned -2. This means the Cl atom must be $+7$.

■ **Why Use Oxidation Numbers?** The reason for learning about oxidation numbers at this point is to be able to identify which reactions are oxidation-reduction processes and to identify the oxidizing agent and the reducing agent in a reaction. We return to a more detailed discussion of redox reactions in Chapter 20.

Chemistry.⬡.Now™

Sign in at **www.cengage.com/login** and go to Chapter 3 Contents to see Screen 3.16 for exercises and a tutorial on **oxidation numbers**.

■ **EXAMPLE 3.7 Determining Oxidation Numbers**

Problem Determine the oxidation number of the indicated element in each of the following compounds or ions:

(a) aluminum in aluminum oxide, Al_2O_3

(b) phosphorus in phosphoric acid, H_3PO_4

(c) sulfur in the sulfate ion, SO_4^{2-}

(d) each Cr atom in the dichromate ion, $Cr_2O_7^{2-}$

Strategy Follow the guidelines in the text, paying particular attention to guidelines 4, 6, and 7.

Solution

(a) Al_2O_3 is a neutral compound. Assuming that O has its usual oxidation number of -2, we can solve the following algebraic equation for the oxidation number of aluminum.

Net charge on $Al_2O_3 =$ sum of oxidation numbers for two Al atoms + three O atoms

$0 = 2(x) + 3(-2)$

$0 = 2x + (-6)$

$+6 = 2x$

$x = +3$

The oxidation number of Al must be $+3$, in agreement with its position in the periodic table.

(b) H_3PO_4 has an overall charge of 0. If each of the oxygen atoms has an oxidation number of -2 and each of the H atoms is $+1$, then we can determine the oxidation number of phosphorus as follows:

Net charge on $H_3PO_4 =$ sum of oxidation numbers for three H atoms + one P atom + four O atoms

$0 = 3(+1) + (x) + 4(-2)$

$x = +5$

The oxidation number of phosphorus in this compound is therefore $+5$.

(c) The sulfate ion, SO_4^{2-}, has an overall charge of $2-$. Oxygen is assigned its usual oxidation number of -2.

Net charge on $SO_4^{2-} =$ sum of oxidation numbers of one S atom + 4 O atoms

$2- = (x) + 4(-2)$

$x = +6$

The sulfur in this ion has an oxidation number of $+6$.

(d) The net charge on the $Cr_2O_7^{2-}$ ion is 2-. Oxygen is assigned its usual oxidation number of -2.

Net charge on $Cr_2O_7^{2-}$ = sum of oxidation numbers for two Cr atoms + seven O atoms

$2- = 2(x) + 7(-2)$

$2- = 2x + (-14)$

$12 = 2x$

$x = +6$

The oxidation number of each chromium in this polyatomic ion is $+6$.

EXERCISE 3.12 Determining Oxidation Numbers

Assign an oxidation number to the underlined atom in each ion or molecule.

(a) $\underline{Fe}_2O_3$ **(b)** $H_2\underline{S}O_4$ **(c)** $\underline{C}O_3^{2-}$ **(d)** $\underline{N}O_2^+$

Recognizing Oxidation-Reduction Reactions

You can always tell if a reaction involves oxidation and reduction by assessing the oxidation number of each element and noting whether any of these numbers change in the course of the reaction. In many cases, however, this will not be necessary. For example, it will be obvious that a redox reaction has occurred if an uncombined element is converted to a compound or if a well-known oxidizing or reducing agent is involved (Table 3.4).

Like oxygen (O_2), the halogens (F_2, Cl_2, Br_2, and I_2) are oxidizing agents in their reactions with metals and nonmetals. An example is the reaction of chlorine with sodium metal (see Figure 1.4).

Na releases 1 e^- per atom.
Oxidation number increases.
Na is oxidized to Na^+ and is the reducing agent.

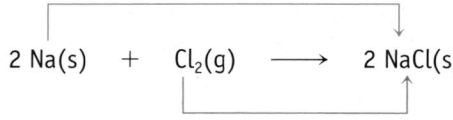

$$2\ Na(s) \quad + \quad Cl_2(g) \quad \longrightarrow \quad 2\ NaCl(s)$$

Cl_2 gains 2 e^- per molecule.
Oxidation number decreases by 1 per Cl.
Cl_2 is reduced to Cl^- and is the oxidizing agent.

NO₂ gas

Copper metal oxidized to green $Cu(NO_3)_2$

Active Figure 3.19 The reaction of copper with nitric acid. Copper (a reducing agent) reacts vigorously with concentrated nitric acid (an oxidizing agent) to give the brown gas NO_2 and a deep green solution of copper(II) nitrate.

Chemistry ⚛ Now™ Sign in at www.cengage.com/login and go to the Chapter Contents menu to explore an interactive version of this figure accompanied by an exercise.

TABLE 3.4 Common Oxidizing and Reducing Agents

Oxidizing Agent	Reaction Product	Reducing Agent	Reaction Product
O_2, oxygen	O^{2-}, oxide ion or O combined in H_2O	H_2, hydrogen	$H^+(aq)$, hydrogen ion or H combined in H_2O or other molecule
Halogen, F_2, Cl_2, Br_2, or I_2	Halide ion, F^-, Cl^-, Br^-, or I^-	M, metals such as Na, K, Fe, and Al	M^{n+}, metal ions such as Na^+, K^+, Fe^{2+} or Fe^{3+}, and Al^{3+}
HNO_3, nitric acid	Nitrogen oxides* such as NO and NO_2	C, carbon (used to reduce metal oxides)	CO and CO_2
$Cr_2O_7^{2-}$, dichromate ion	Cr^{3+}, chromium(III) ion (in acid solution)		
MnO_4^-, permanganate ion	Mn^{2+}, manganese(II) ion (in acid solution)		

* NO is produced with dilute HNO_3, whereas NO_2 is a product of concentrated acid.

A chlorine molecule ends up as two Cl⁻ ions, having acquired two electrons (from two Na atoms). Thus, the oxidation number of each Cl atom has decreased from 0 to −1. This means Cl_2 has been reduced, and therefore it is the oxidizing agent.

Figure 3.19 illustrates the chemistry of another excellent oxidizing agent, nitric acid, HNO_3. Here, copper metal is oxidized to give copper(II) nitrate, and the nitrate ion is reduced to the brown gas NO_2. The net ionic equation for the reaction is

Oxidation number of Cu changes from 0 to +2. Cu
is oxidized to Cu^{2+} and is the reducing agent.

$$Cu(s) + 2\ NO_3^-(aq) + 4\ H_3O^+(aq) \longrightarrow Cu^{2+}(aq) + 2\ NO_2(g) + 6\ H_2O(\ell)$$

N in NO_3^- changes from +5 to +4 in NO_2. NO_3^-
is reduced to NO_2 and is the oxidizing agent.

Nitrogen has been reduced from +5 (in the NO_3^- ion) to +4 (in NO_2); therefore, the nitrate ion in acid solution is the oxidizing agent. Copper metal is the reducing agent; each metal atom has given up two electrons to produce the Cu^{2+} ion.

In the reactions of sodium with chlorine and copper with nitric acid, the metals are oxidized. This is typical of metals. In yet another example of this, aluminum metal, a good reducing agent, is capable of reducing iron(III) oxide to iron metal in a reaction called the *thermite reaction* (Figure 3.20).

$$\underset{\substack{\text{oxidizing} \\ \text{agent}}}{Fe_2O_3(s)} + \underset{\substack{\text{reducing} \\ \text{agent}}}{2\ Al(s)} \rightarrow 2\ Fe(\ell) + Al_2O_3(s)$$

Such a large quantity of energy is evolved as heat in the reaction that the iron is produced in the molten state.

Tables 3.4 and 3.5 may help you organize your thinking as you look for oxidation-reduction reactions and use their terminology.

Chemistry ⚗ Now™

Sign in at **www.cengage.com/login** and go to Chapter 3 Contents to see Screen 3.17 for an exercise on **redox reaction**.

■ EXAMPLE 3.8 Oxidation-Reduction Reaction

Problem For the reaction of iron(II) ion with permanganate ion in aqueous acid,

$$5\ Fe^{2+}(aq) + MnO_4^-(aq) + 8\ H_3O^+(aq) \rightarrow 5\ Fe^{3+}(aq) + Mn^{2+}(aq) + 12\ H_2O(\ell)$$

decide which atoms are undergoing a change in oxidation number, and identify the oxidizing and reducing agents.

TABLE 3.5 Recognizing Oxidation-Reduction Reactions

	Oxidation	Reduction
In terms of oxidation number	Increase in oxidation number of an atom	Decrease in oxidation number of an atom
In terms of electrons	Loss of electrons by an atom	Gain of electrons by an atom
In terms of oxygen	Gain of one or more O atoms	Loss of one or more O atoms

FIGURE 3.20 Thermite reaction.
Here, Fe_2O_3 is reduced by aluminum metal to produce iron metal and aluminum oxide.

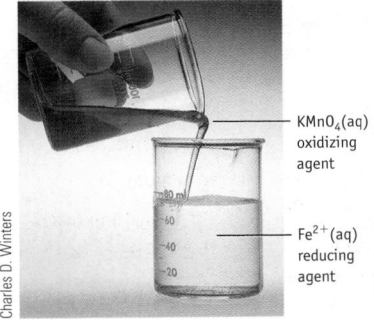

KMnO₄(aq) oxidizing agent

Fe²⁺(aq) reducing agent

The reaction of iron(II) ion and permanganate ion. The reaction of purple permanganate ion (MnO_4^-, the oxidizing agent) with the iron(II) ion (Fe^{2+}, the reducing agent) in acidified aqueous solution gives the nearly colorless manganese(II) ion (Mn^{2+}) and the iron(III) ion (Fe^{3+}).

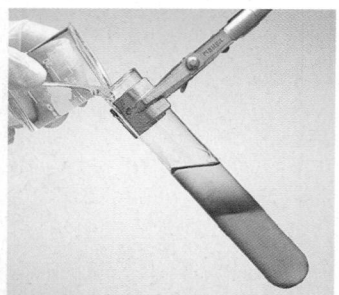

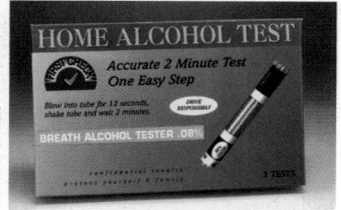

Charles D. Winters

FIGURE 3.21 The redox reaction of ethanol and dichromate ion is the basis of the test used in a Breathalyzer. When ethanol, an alcohol, is poured into a solution of orange-red dichromate ion, it reduces the dichromate ion to green chromium(III) ion. The bottom photo is a breath tester that can be purchased in grocery or drug stores. See Exercise 3.13.

Strategy Determine the oxidation numbers of the atoms in each ion or molecule involved in the reaction. Decide which atoms have increased in oxidation number (oxidation) and which have decreased in oxidation number (reduction).

Solution The Mn oxidation number in MnO_4^- is +7, and it decreases to +2 in the product, the Mn^{2+} ion. Thus, the MnO_4^- ion has been reduced and is the oxidizing agent (see Table 3.4).

$$5\ Fe^{2+}(aq) + MnO_4^-(aq) + 8\ H_3O^+(aq) \rightarrow 5\ Fe^{3+}(aq) + Mn^{2+}(aq) + 12\ H_2O(\ell)$$

| +2 | +7, −2 | +1, −2 | +3 | +2 | +1, −2 |

The oxidation number of iron has increased from +2 to +3, so each Fe^{2+} ion has lost one electron upon being oxidized to Fe^{3+} (see Table 3.5). This means the Fe^{2+} ion is the reducing agent.

Comment If one of the reactants in a redox reaction is a simple substance (here Fe^{2+}), it is usually obvious whether its oxidation number has increased or decreased. Once a species has been established as having been reduced (or oxidized), you know another species has been oxidized (or reduced). It is also helpful to recognize common oxidizing and reducing agents (Table 3.4).

EXERCISE 3.13 Oxidation-Reduction Reactions

The following reaction occurs in a device for testing the breath for the presence of ethanol. Identify the oxidizing and reducing agents, the substance oxidized, and the substance reduced (Figure 3.21).

$$3\ CH_3CH_2OH(aq) + 2\ Cr_2O_7^{2-}(aq) + 16\ H_3O^+(aq) \longrightarrow$$

ethanol   dichromate ion; orange-red

$$3\ CH_3CO_2H(aq) + 4\ Cr^{3+}(aq) + 27\ H_2O(\ell)$$

acetic acid   chromium(III) ion; green

Case Study   Killing Bacteria with Silver

We recently read about a new washing machine that injects silver ions into the wash water, the purpose being to kill bacteria in the wash water. The advertisement told us that 100 quadrillion silver ions are injected. How does this machine work? Is 100 quadrillion silver ions a lot? Does the silver kill bacteria?

The washing machine works by using electrical energy to oxidize silver metal to give silver ions.

$$Ag(s) \rightarrow Ag^+(aq) + e^-$$

This is a simple electrolysis procedure. (More about that in Chapter 20.) And 100 quadrillion silver ions? This is 100×10^{15} ions.

Do silver ions act as a bacteriocide? There is plenty of medical evidence for this property. In fact, when you were born, the physician or nurse may have put drops of a very dilute silver nitrate solution in your eyes to treat neonatal conjunctivitis. And severely burned patients are treated with silver sulfadiazine ($C_{10}H_9AgN_4O_2S$) to prevent bacterial or fungal infections.

Charles D. Winters

Silver ions as a bacteriocide in dental floss.

The use of silver to prevent infections has a long history. Phoenicians kept wine, water, and vinegar in silver vessels. Early settlers in America put silver coins into water barrels. And you might have been born with a "silver spoon in your mouth." Babies in wealthier

homes, who were fed from silver spoons and used a silver pacifier, were found to be healthier.

The historical uses of silver carry over to modern society. One can buy many different kinds of silver-containing water purifiers for the home, and dental floss coated with silver nitrate is available.

Although silver does have health benefits, beware of fraudulent claims. For example, consuming large amounts of "colloidal silver" (nanosized particles of silver suspended in water) is claimed to have health-giving properties. One person who tried this, Stan Jones, ran for the U.S. Congress in 2002 and 2006. From consuming silver, he acquired argyria, a medically irreversible condition in which the skin turns a gray-blue color.

Questions:

1. *How many moles of silver are used in a wash cycle?*
2. *What mass of silver is used?*

Answers to these questions are in Appendix Q.

3.10 Classifying Reactions in Aqueous Solution

One goal of this chapter has been to explore the most common types of reactions that can occur in aqueous solution. This helps you decide, for example, that a gas-forming reaction occurs when an Alka-Seltzer tablet (containing citric acid and $NaHCO_3$) is dropped into water (Figure 3.22).

$$H_3C_6H_5O_7(aq) \quad + \quad HCO_3^-(aq) \quad \longrightarrow$$
citric acid   hydrogen carbonate ion

$$H_2C_6H_5O_7^-(aq) \quad + \quad H_2O(\ell) \quad + \quad CO_2(g)$$
dihydrogen citrate ion

FIGURE 3.22 A gas-forming reaction. An Alka-Seltzer tablet contains an acid (citric acid) and sodium hydrogen carbonate ($NaHCO_3$), the reactants in a gas-forming reaction.

We have examined four types of reactions in aqueous solution: precipitation reactions, acid-base reactions, gas-forming reactions, and oxidation-reduction reactions. Three of these four (precipitation, acid-base, and gas-forming) fall into the category of exchange reactions.

Precipitation Reactions (see Figure 3.11): Ions combine in solution to form an insoluble reaction product.
Overall Equation

$$Pb(NO_3)_2(aq) + 2\ KI(aq) \longrightarrow PbI_2(s) + 2\ KNO_3(aq)$$

Net Ionic Equation

$$Pb^{2+}(aq) + 2\ I^-(aq) \longrightarrow PbI_2(s)$$

Acid–Base Reactions (see Figures 3.12 and 3.14): Water is a product of many acid–base reactions, and the cation of the base and the anion of the acid form a salt.
Overall Equation for the Reaction of a Strong Acid and a Strong Base

$$HNO_3(aq) + KOH(aq) \longrightarrow HOH(\ell) + KNO_3(aq)$$

Net Ionic Equation for the Reaction of a Strong Acid and a Strong Base

$$H_3O^+(aq) + OH^-(aq) \rightarrow 2\ H_2O(\ell)$$

Overall Equation for the Reaction of a Weak Acid and a Strong Base

$$CH_3CO_2H(aq) + NaOH(aq) \rightarrow NaCH_3CO_2(aq) + HOH(\ell)$$

Net Ionic Equation for the Reaction of a Weak Acid and a Strong Base

$$CH_3CO_2H(aq) + OH^-(aq) \rightarrow CH_3CO_2^-(aq) + H_2O(\ell)$$

Gas-Forming Reactions (see Figures 3.15 and 3.22): The most common examples involve metal carbonates and acids, but others exist (see Table 3.3). One product with a metal carbonate is always carbonic acid, H_2CO_3, most of which decomposes to H_2O and CO_2. Carbon dioxide is the gas in the bubbles you see during these reactions.

Overall Equation:

$$CuCO_3(s) + 2\ HNO_3(aq) \rightarrow Cu(NO_3)_2(aq) + CO_2(g) + H_2O(\ell)$$

Net Ionic Equation

$$CuCO_3(s) + 2\ H_3O^+(aq) \rightarrow Cu^{2+}(aq) + CO_2(g) + 3\ H_2O(\ell)$$

Oxidation-Reduction Reactions (see Figure 3.18): These reactions are *not* ion exchange reactions. Rather, electrons are transferred from one material to another.

Overall Equation

$$Cu(s) + 2\ AgNO_3(aq) \rightarrow Cu(NO_3)_2(aq) + 2\ Ag(s)$$

Net Ionic Equation

$$Cu(s) + 2\ Ag^+(aq) \rightarrow Cu^{2+}(aq) + 2\ Ag(s)$$

These four types of reactions are usually easy to recognize, but keep in mind that a reaction may fall into more than one category. For example, barium hydroxide reacts readily with sulfuric acid to give barium sulfate and water, a reaction that is both a precipitation and an acid–base reaction.

$$Ba(OH)_2(aq) + H_2SO_4(aq) \rightarrow BaSO_4(s) + 2\ H_2O(\ell)$$

Chemistry ⚛ Now™

Sign in at **www.cengage.com/login** and go to Chapter 3 Contents to see Screen 3.8 for a self-study module on the **four reaction types.**

EXAMPLE 3.9 **Types of Reactions**

Problem Classify each of the following reactions as precipitation, acid–base, gas-forming, or oxidation-reduction.

(a) $2\ HNO_3(aq) + Ca(OH)_2(s) \rightarrow Ca(NO_3)_2(aq) + 2\ H_2O(\ell)$

(b) $2\ MnO_4^-(aq) + 5\ HSO_3^-(aq) + H_3O^+(aq) \rightarrow 2\ Mn^{2+}(aq) + 5\ SO_4^{2-}(aq) + 4\ H_2O(\ell)$

Strategy An acid–base reaction is usually easy to identify. Next, check the oxidation numbers of each element. If they change, then it is a redox reaction. If there is no change, then check to see if it is a simple precipitation or gas-forming process.

Solution Reaction (a) involves a common acid (nitric acid, HNO_3) and a common base [calcium hydroxide, $Ca(OH)_2$]; it produces a salt, calcium nitrate, and water. It is an acid–base reaction. Reaction (b) is a redox reaction because the oxidation numbers of S and Mn change.

$$2\ MnO_4^-(aq) + 5\ HSO_3^-(aq) + H_3O^+(aq) \rightarrow 2\ Mn^{2+}(aq) + 5\ SO_4^{2-}(aq) + 4\ H_2O(\ell)$$

$$+7, -2 \qquad +1, +4, -2 \qquad +1, -2 \qquad +2 \qquad\quad +6, -2 \qquad\quad +1, -2$$

The oxidation number of S changes from $+4$ to $+6$, and that of Mn changes from $+7$ to $+2$. Therefore, permanganate ion, MnO_4^-, has been reduced (and is the oxidizing agent), and HSO_3^- has been oxidized (and is the reducing agent).

Comment Note that no changes occur in the oxidation numbers of the elements in reaction (a).

$$HNO_3(aq) \quad + \quad Ca(OH)_2(s) \quad \rightarrow \quad Ca(NO_3)_2(aq) \quad + \quad 2\ H_2O(\ell)$$
$$+1, +5, -2 \qquad +2, -2, +1 \qquad\quad +2, +5, -2 \qquad\qquad +1, -2$$

EXERCISE 3.15 Classifying and Predicting Reactions

Classify each of the following reactions as a precipitation, acid–base, gas-forming reaction, or oxidation-reduction reaction. Predict the products of the reaction, and then balance the completed equation. Write the net ionic equation for each.

(a) $CuCO_3(s) + H_2SO_4(aq) \rightarrow$

(b) $Ga(s) + O_2(g) \rightarrow$

(c) $Ba(OH)_2(s) + HNO_3(aq) \rightarrow$

(d) $CuCl_2(aq) + (NH_4)_2S(aq) \rightarrow$

Chapter Goals Revisited

Now that you have studied this chapter, you should ask if you have met the chapter goals. In particular, you should be able to:

Balance equations for simple chemical reactions.
a. Understand the information conveyed by a balanced chemical equation (Section 3.1).
b. Balance simple chemical equations (Section 3.2). Study Question(s) assignable in OWL: 2, 4, 47, 54.

Understand the nature and characteristics of chemical equilibria.
a. Recognize that chemical reactions are reversible (Section 3.3).
b. Describe what is meant by the term dynamic equilibrium.
c. Recognize the difference between reactant-favored and product-favored reactions.

Understand the nature of ionic substances dissolved in water.
a. Explain the difference between electrolytes and nonelectrolytes, and recognize examples of each (Section 3.5 and Figure 3.9).
b. Predict the solubility of ionic compounds in water (Section 3.5 and Figure 3.10). Study Question(s) assignable in OWL: 9, 11, 13, 15, 55, 57, 60, 65, 67; Go Chemistry Module 5.
c. Recognize what ions are formed when an ionic compound or acid or base dissolves in water (Sections 3.5–3.7). Study Question(s) assignable in OWL: 13, 15, 60.

Recognize common acids and bases, and understand their behavior in aqueous solution.
a. Know the names and formulas of common acids and bases (Section 3.7 and Table 3.2). Study Question(s) assignable in OWL: 21, 26, 27.
b. Categorize acids and bases as strong or weak.
c. Define and use the Arrhenius concept of acids and bases.
d. Define and use the Brønsted–Lowry concept of acids and bases.
e. Appreciate when a substance can be amphiprotic.
f. Recognize the Brønsted acid and base in a reaction. Study Question(s) assignable in OWL: 21, 27, 28.

Chemistry ⚛ Now™ Sign in at **www.cengage.com/login** to:
- Assess your understanding with Study Questions in OWL keyed to each goal in the Goals and Homework menu for this chapter
- For quick review, download Go Chemistry mini-lecture flashcard modules (or purchase them at **www.ichapters.com**)
- Check your readiness for an exam by taking the Pre-Test and exploring the modules recommended in your Personalized Study plan.

❓ Access **How Do I Solve It?** tutorials on how to approach problem solving using concepts in this chapter.

For additional preparation for an examination on this chapter see the *Let's Review* section on pages 254–267.

Recognize the common types of reactions in aqueous solution.

a. Recognize the key characteristics of four types of reactions in aqueous solution.

Reaction Type	Key Characteristic
Precipitation	Formation of an insoluble compound
Acid–strong base	Formation of a salt and water; H^+ ion transfer
Gas-forming	Evolution of a water-insoluble gas such as CO_2
Oxidation-reduction	Transfer of electrons (with changes in oxidation numbers)

Study Question(s) assignable in OWL: 47, 48, 51, 52, 70, 76–78.

b. Predict the products of precipitation reactions (Section 3.6), acid–base reactions (Section 3.7), and gas-forming reactions (Section 3.8). These are all examples of exchange reactions, which involve the exchange of anions between the cations involved in the reaction. Study Question(s) assignable in OWL: 17, 19, 21, 27, 37–39, 71.

Write chemical equations for the common types of reactions in aqueous solution.

a. Write overall balanced equations for precipitation, acid–base, and gas-forming reactions.

b. Write net ionic equations (Sections 3.6–3.8). Study Question(s) assignable in OWL: 17, 19, 33, 63, 67, 68; Go Chemistry Module 6.

c. Understand that the net ionic equation for the reaction of a strong acid with a strong base is $H_3O^+(aq) + OH^-(aq) \rightarrow 2\,H_2O(\ell)$ (Section 3.7).

Recognize common oxidizing and reducing agents, and identify oxidation-reduction reactions.

a. Determine oxidation numbers of elements in a compound and understand that these numbers represent the charge an atom has, or appears to have, when the electrons of the compound are counted according to a set of guidelines (Section 3.9). Study Question(s) assignable in OWL: 41, 42, 69.

b. Identify oxidation-reduction reactions (often called redox reactions), and identify the oxidizing and reducing agents and substances oxidized and reduced in the reaction (Section 3.9 and Tables 3.4 and 3.5). Study Question(s) assignable in OWL: 44–46, 61, 73.

STUDY QUESTIONS

OWL Online homework for this chapter may be assigned in OWL.

▲ denotes challenging questions.

■ denotes questions assignable in OWL.

Blue-numbered questions have answers in Appendix O and fully-worked solutions in the *Student Solutions Manual*.

Practicing Skills

Balancing Equations

(See Example 3.1 and ChemistryNow Screen 3.4.)

1. Write a balanced chemical equation for the combustion of liquid pentane, C_5H_{12}.

2. ■ Write balanced chemical equations for the following reactions:
   (a) production of ammonia, $NH_3(g)$, by combining $N_2(g)$ and $H_2(g)$
   (b) production of methanol, $CH_3OH(\ell)$ by combining $H_2(g)$ and $CO(g)$
   (c) production of sulfuric acid by combining sulfur, oxygen, and water

3. Balance the following equations:
   (a) $Cr(s) + O_2(g) \rightarrow Cr_2O_3(s)$
   (b) $Cu_2S(s) + O_2(g) \rightarrow Cu(s) + SO_2(g)$
   (c) $C_6H_5CH_3(\ell) + O_2(g) \rightarrow H_2O(\ell) + CO_2(g)$

4. ■ Balance the following equations:
   (a) $Cr(s) + Cl_2(g) \rightarrow CrCl_3(s)$
   (b) $SiO_2(s) + C(s) \rightarrow Si(s) + CO(g)$
   (c) $Fe(s) + H_2O(g) \rightarrow Fe_3O_4(s) + H_2(g)$

5. Balance the following equations, and name each reactant and product:
(a) $Fe_2O_3(s) + Mg(s) \rightarrow MgO(s) + Fe(s)$
(b) $AlCl_3(s) + NaOH(aq) \rightarrow Al(OH)_3(s) + NaCl(aq)$
(c) $NaNO_3(s) + H_2SO_4(\ell) \rightarrow Na_2SO_4(s) + HNO_3(\ell)$
(d) $NiCO_3(s) + HNO_3(aq) \rightarrow$
$$Ni(NO_3)_2(aq) + CO_2(g) + H_2O(\ell)$$

6. Balance the following equations, and name each reactant and product:
(a) $SF_4(g) + H_2O(\ell) \rightarrow SO_2(g) + HF(\ell)$
(b) $NH_3(aq) + O_2(aq) \rightarrow NO(g) + H_2O(\ell)$
(c) $BF_3(g) + H_2O(\ell) \rightarrow HF(aq) + H_3BO_3(aq)$

Chemical Equilibrium
(See Sections 3.3 and 3.5.)

7. Equal amounts of two acids—HCl and HCO_2H (formic acid)—are placed in solution. When equilibrium has been achieved, the HCl solution has a much greater electrical conductivity than the HCO_2H solution. Which reaction is more product favored at equilibrium?

$$HCl(aq) + H_2O(\ell) \rightleftharpoons H_3O^+(aq) + Cl^-(aq)$$

$$HCO_2H(aq) + H_2O(\ell) \rightleftharpoons H_3O^+(aq) + HCO_2^-(aq)$$

8. Equal amounts of two compounds, AgBr and H_3PO_4, are placed in solution. When equilibrium has been achieved, the H_3PO_4 solution has a greater electrical conductivity than the AgBr solution (which is almost a nonelectrolyte). Which reaction is more product favored at equilibrium?

$$AgBr(s) \rightleftharpoons Ag^+(aq) + Br^-(aq)$$

$$H_3PO_4(aq) + H_2O(\ell) \rightleftharpoons H_3O^+(aq) + H_2PO_4^-(aq)$$

Ions and Molecules in Aqueous Solution
(See Exercise 3.3, Example 3.2, and ChemistryNow Screens 3.5–3.7.)

9. ■ What is an electrolyte? How can you differentiate experimentally between a weak electrolyte and a strong electrolyte? Give an example of each.

10. Name two acids that are strong electrolytes and one acid that is a weak electrolyte. Name two bases that are strong electrolytes and one base that is a weak electrolyte.

11. ■ Which compound or compounds in each of the following groups is (are) expected to be soluble in water?
(a) CuO, $CuCl_2$, $FeCO_3$
(b) AgI, Ag_3PO_4, $AgNO_3$
(c) K_2CO_3, KI, $KMnO_4$

12. Which compound or compounds in each of the following groups is (are) expected to be soluble in water?
(a) $BaSO_4$, $Ba(NO_3)_2$, $BaCO_3$
(b) Na_2SO_4, $NaClO_4$, $NaCH_3CO_2$
(c) $AgBr$, KBr, Al_2Br_6

13. ■ The following compounds are water-soluble. What ions are produced by each compound in aqueous solution?
(a) KOH
(b) K_2SO_4
(c) $LiNO_3$
(d) $(NH_4)_2SO_4$

14. The following compounds are water-soluble. What ions are produced by each compound in aqueous solution?
(a) KI
(b) $Mg(CH_3CO_2)_2$
(c) K_2HPO_4
(d) $NaCN$

15. ■ Decide whether each of the following is water-soluble. If soluble, tell what ions are produced.
(a) Na_2CO_3
(b) $CuSO_4$
(c) NiS
(d) $BaBr_2$

16. Decide whether each of the following is water-soluble. If soluble, tell what ions are produced.
(a) $NiCl_2$
(b) $Cr(NO_3)_3$
(c) $Pb(NO_3)_2$
(d) $BaSO_4$

Precipitation Reactions and Net Ionic Equations
(See Examples 3.3 and 3.4 and ChemistryNow Screens 3.9 and 3.10.)

17. ■ Balance the equation for the following precipitation reaction, and then write the net ionic equation. Indicate the state of each species (s, ℓ, aq, or g).

$$CdCl_2 + NaOH \rightarrow Cd(OH)_2 + NaCl$$

18. Balance the equation for the following precipitation reaction, and then write the net ionic equation. Indicate the state of each species (s, ℓ, aq, or g).

$$Ni(NO_3)_2 + Na_2CO_3 \rightarrow NiCO_3 + NaNO_3$$

19. ■ Predict the products of each precipitation reaction. Balance the completed equation, and then write the net ionic equation.
(a) $NiCl_2(aq) + (NH_4)_2S(aq) \rightarrow ?$
(b) $Mn(NO_3)_2(aq) + Na_3PO_4(aq) \rightarrow ?$

20. Predict the products of each precipitation reaction. Balance the completed equation, and then write the net ionic equation.
(a) $Pb(NO_3)_2(aq) + KBr(aq) \rightarrow ?$
(b) $Ca(NO_3)_2(aq) + KF(aq) \rightarrow ?$
(c) $Ca(NO_3)_2(aq) + Na_2C_2O_4(aq) \rightarrow ?$

Acids and Bases and Their Reactions
(See Exercise 3.8, Example 3.5, Exercise 3.10, and ChemistryNow Screens 3.11–3.13.)

21. ■ Write a balanced equation for the ionization of nitric acid in water.

22. Write a balanced equation for the ionization of perchloric acid in water.

23. Oxalic acid, $H_2C_2O_4$, which is found in certain plants, can provide two hydronium ions in water. Write balanced equations (like those for sulfuric acid on page 135) to show how oxalic acid can supply one and then a second H_3O^+ ion.

24. Phosphoric acid can supply one, two, or three H_3O^+ ions in aqueous solution. Write balanced equations (like those for sulfuric acid on page 135) to show this successive loss of hydrogen ions.

25. Write a balanced equation for reaction of the basic oxide, magnesium oxide, with water.

26. ■ Write a balanced equation for the reaction of sulfur trioxide with water.

27. ■ Complete and balance the following acid–base equations. Name the reactants and products. Decide which is the Brønsted acid and which is the Brønsted base.
(a) $CH_3CO_2H(aq) + Mg(OH)_2(s) \rightarrow$
(b) $HClO_4(aq) + NH_3(aq) \rightarrow$

28. ■ Complete and balance the following acid–base equations. Name the reactants and products. Decide which is the Brønsted acid and which is the Brønsted base.
(a) $H_3PO_4(aq) + KOH(aq) \rightarrow$
(b) $H_2C_2O_4(aq) + Ca(OH)_2(s) \rightarrow$
($H_2C_2O_4$ is oxalic acid, an acid capable of donating two H^+ ions.)

29. Write a balanced equation for the reaction of barium hydroxide with nitric acid.

30. Write a balanced equation for the reaction of aluminum hydroxide with sulfuric acid.

31. Name two strong Brønsted acids and one strong Brønsted base.

32. Name three weak Brønsted acids and one weak Brønsted base.

Writing Net Ionic Equations
(See Examples 3.4 and 3.5 and ChemistryNow Screen 3.10.)

33. ■ Balance the following equations, and then write the net ionic equation.
(a) $(NH_4)_2CO_3(aq) + Cu(NO_3)_2(aq) \rightarrow$
$CuCO_3(s) + NH_4NO_3(aq)$
(b) $Pb(OH)_2(s) + HCl(aq) \rightarrow PbCl_2(s) + H_2O(\ell)$
(c) $BaCO_3(s) + HCl(aq) \rightarrow$
$BaCl_2(aq) + H_2O(\ell) + CO_2(g)$
(d) $CH_3CO_2H(aq) + Ni(OH)_2(s) \rightarrow$
$Ni(CH_3CO_2)_2(aq) + H_2O(\ell)$

34. ■ Balance the following equations, and then write the net ionic equation:
(a) $Zn(s) + HCl(aq) \rightarrow H_2(g) + ZnCl_2(aq)$
(b) $Mg(OH)_2(s) + HCl(aq) \rightarrow MgCl_2(aq) + H_2O(\ell)$
(c) $HNO_3(aq) + CaCO_3(s) \rightarrow$
$Ca(NO_3)_2(aq) + H_2O(\ell) + CO_2(g)$
(d) $(NH_4)_2S(aq) + FeCl_3(aq) \rightarrow NH_4Cl(aq) + Fe_2S_3(s)$

35. Balance the following equations, and then write the net ionic equation. Show states for all reactants and products (s, ℓ, g, aq).
(a) the reaction of silver nitrate and potassium iodide to give silver iodide and potassium nitrate
(b) the reaction of barium hydroxide and nitric acid to give barium nitrate and water
(c) the reaction of sodium phosphate and nickel(II) nitrate to give nickel(II) phosphate and sodium nitrate

36. Balance each of the following equations, and then write the net ionic equation. Show states for all reactants and products (s, ℓ, g, aq).
(a) the reaction of sodium hydroxide and iron(II) chloride to give iron(II) hydroxide and sodium chloride
(b) the reaction of barium chloride with sodium carbonate to give barium carbonate and sodium chloride
(c) the reaction of ammonia with phosphoric acid

Gas-Forming Reactions
(See Example 3.6 and ChemistryNow Screen 3.14.)

37. ■ Siderite is a mineral consisting largely of iron(II) carbonate. Write an overall, balanced equation for its reaction with nitric acid, and name the products.

38. ■ The beautiful red mineral rhodochrosite is manganese(II) carbonate. Write an overall, balanced equation for the reaction of the mineral with hydrochloric acid, and name the products.

Charles D. Winters

Rhodochrosite, a mineral consisting largely of MnCO₃.

39. ■ Write an overall, balanced equation for the reaction of $(NH_4)_2S$ with HBr, and name the reactants and products.

40. Write an overall, balanced equation for the reaction of Na_2SO_3 with CH_3CO_2H, and name the reactants and products.

Oxidation Numbers
(See Example 3.7 and ChemistryNow Screens 3.15 and 3.16.)

41. ■ Determine the oxidation number of each element in the following ions or compounds.
(a) BrO_3^- (d) CaH_2
(b) $C_2O_4^{2-}$ (e) H_4SiO_4
(c) F^- (f) HSO_4^-

42. ■ Determine the oxidation number of each element in the following ions or compounds.
(a) PF_6^- (d) N_2O_5
(b) $H_2AsO_4^-$ (e) $POCl_3$
(c) UO^{2+} (f) XeO_4^{2-}

Oxidation–Reduction Reactions
(See Example 3.8 and ChemistryNow Screen 3.17.)

43. Which two of the following reactions are oxidation–reduction reactions? Explain your answer in each case. Classify the remaining reaction.
(a) $Zn(s) + 2 NO_3^-(aq) + 4 H_3O^+(aq) \rightarrow$
$Zn^{2+}(aq) + 2 NO_2(g) + 6 H_2O(\ell)$
(b) $Zn(OH)_2(s) + H_2SO_4(aq) \rightarrow$
$ZnSO_4(aq) + 2 H_2O(\ell)$
(c) $Ca(s) + 2 H_2O(\ell) \rightarrow Ca(OH)_2(s) + H_2(g)$

44. ■ Which two of the following reactions are oxidation–reduction reactions? Explain your answer briefly. Classify the remaining reaction.
(a) $CdCl_2(aq) + Na_2S(aq) \rightarrow CdS(s) + 2 NaCl(aq)$
(b) $2 Ca(s) + O_2(g) \rightarrow 2 CaO(s)$
(c) $4 Fe(OH)_2(s) + 2 H_2O(\ell) + O_2(g) \rightarrow$
$4 Fe(OH)_3(aq)$

45. ■ In the following reactions, decide which reactant is oxidized and which is reduced. Designate the oxidizing agent and the reducing agent.
(a) $C_2H_4(g) + 3 O_2(g) \rightarrow 2 CO_2(g) + 2 H_2O(\ell)$
(b) $Si(s) + 2 Cl_2(g) \rightarrow SiCl_4(\ell)$

46. ■ In the following reactions, decide which reactant is oxidized and which is reduced. Designate the oxidizing agent and the reducing agent.

(a) $Cr_2O_7^{2-}(aq) + 3\ Sn^{2+}(aq) + 14\ H_3O^+(aq) \rightarrow$
$\qquad\qquad 2\ Cr^{3+}(aq) + 3\ Sn^{4+}(aq) + 21\ H_2O(\ell)$

(b) $FeS(s) + 3\ NO_3^-(aq) + 4\ H_3O^+(aq) \rightarrow$
$\qquad\qquad 3\ NO(g) + SO_4^{2-}(aq) + Fe^{3+}(aq) + 6\ H_2O(\ell)$

Types of Reactions in Aqueous Solution

(See Example 3.9 and ChemistryNow Screen 3.8.)

47. ■ Balance the following equations, and then classify each as a precipitation, an acid–base, or a gas-forming reaction.

(a) $Ba(OH)_2(aq) + HCl(aq) \rightarrow BaCl_2(aq) + H_2O(\ell)$

(b) $HNO_3(aq) + CoCO_3(s) \rightarrow$
$\qquad\qquad Co(NO_3)_2(aq) + H_2O(\ell) + CO_2(g)$

(c) $Na_3PO_4(aq) + Cu(NO_3)_2(aq) \rightarrow$
$\qquad\qquad Cu_3(PO_4)_2(s) + NaNO_3(aq)$

48. ■ Balance the following equations, and then classify each as a precipitation, an acid–base, or a gas-forming reaction.

(a) $K_2CO_3(aq) + Cu(NO_3)_2(aq) \rightarrow$
$\qquad\qquad CuCO_3(s) + KNO_3(aq)$

(b) $Pb(NO_3)_2(aq) + HCl(aq) \rightarrow$
$\qquad\qquad PbCl_2(s) + HNO_3(aq)$

(c) $MgCO_3(s) + HCl(aq) \rightarrow$
$\qquad\qquad MgCl_2(aq) + H_2O(\ell) + CO_2(g)$

49. Balance the following equations, and then classify each as a precipitation, an acid–base, or a gas-forming reaction. Show states for the products (s, ℓ, g, aq), and then balance the completed equation. Write the net ionic equation.

(a) $MnCl_2(aq) + Na_2S(aq) \rightarrow MnS + NaCl$

(b) $K_2CO_3(aq) + ZnCl_2(aq) \rightarrow ZnCO_3 + KCl$

50. Balance the following equations, and then classify each as a precipitation, an acid–base, or a gas-forming reaction. Write the net ionic equation.

(a) $Fe(OH)_3(s) + HNO_3(aq) \rightarrow Fe(NO_3)_3 + H_2O$

(b) $FeCO_3(s) + HNO_3(aq) \rightarrow Fe(NO_3)_2 + CO_2 + H_2O$

51. ■ Balance each of the following equations, and classify them as precipitation, acid–base, gas-forming, or oxidation-reduction reactions.

(a) $CuCl_2 + H_2S \rightarrow CuS + HCl$

(b) $H_3PO_4 + KOH \rightarrow H_2O + K_3PO_4$

(c) $Ca + HBr \rightarrow H_2 + CaBr_2$

(d) $MgCl_2 + H_2O \rightarrow Mg(OH)_2 + HCl$

52. ■ ▲ Complete and balance the equations below, and classify them as precipitation, acid–base, gas-forming, or oxidation-reduction reactions.

(a) $NiCO_3 + H_2SO_4 \rightarrow$?

(b) $Co(OH)_2 + HBr \rightarrow$?

(c) $AgCH_3CO_2 + NaCl \rightarrow$?

(d) $NiO + CO \rightarrow$?

General Questions

These questions are not designated as to type or location in the chapter. They may combine concepts from several chapters.

53. Balance the following equations:

(a) the synthesis of urea, a common fertilizer

$$CO_2(g) + NH_3(g) \rightarrow NH_2CONH_2(s) + H_2O(\ell)$$

(b) reactions used to make uranium(VI) fluoride for the enrichment of natural uranium

$UO_2(s) + HF(aq) \rightarrow UF_4(s) + H_2O(\ell)$
$UF_4(s) + F_2(g) \rightarrow UF_6(s)$

(c) the reaction to make titanium(IV) chloride, which is then converted to titanium metal

$TiO_2(s) + Cl_2(g) + C(s) \rightarrow TiCl_4(\ell) + CO(g)$
$TiCl_4(\ell) + Mg(s) \rightarrow Ti(s) + MgCl_2(s)$

54. ■ Balance the following equations:

(a) reaction to produce "superphosphate" fertilizer

$$Ca_3(PO_4)_2(s) + H_2SO_4(aq) \rightarrow$$
$$Ca(H_2PO_4)_2(aq) + CaSO_4(s)$$

(b) reaction to produce diborane, B_2H_6

$$NaBH_4(s) + H_2SO_4(aq) \rightarrow$$
$$B_2H_6(g) + H_2(g) + Na_2SO_4(aq)$$

(c) reaction to produce tungsten metal from tungsten(VI) oxide

$$WO_3(s) + H_2(g) \rightarrow W(s) + H_2O(\ell)$$

(d) decomposition of ammonium dichromate

$$(NH_4)_2Cr_2O_7(s) \rightarrow N_2(g) + H_2O(\ell) + Cr_2O_3(s)$$

55. ■ Give a formula for each of the following:
(a) a soluble compound containing the bromide ion
(b) an insoluble hydroxide
(c) an insoluble carbonate
(d) a soluble nitrate-containing compound
(e) a weak Brønsted acid

56. Give the formula for the following compounds:
(a) a soluble compound containing the acetate ion
(b) an insoluble sulfide
(c) a soluble hydroxide
(d) an insoluble chloride
(e) a strong Brønsted base

57. ■ Which of the following copper(II) salts are soluble in water and which are insoluble: $Cu(NO_3)_2$, $CuCO_3$, $Cu_3(PO_4)_2$, $CuCl_2$?

58. Name two anions that combine with Al^{3+} ion to produce water-soluble compounds.

59. Identify the spectator ion or ions in the reaction of nitric acid and magnesium hydroxide, and write the net ionic equation. What type of reaction is this?

$$2\ H_3O^+(aq) + 2\ NO_3^-(aq) + Mg(OH)_2(s) \rightarrow$$
$$4\ H_2O(\ell) + Mg^{2+}(aq) + 2\ NO_3^-(aq)$$

60. ■ Identify and name the water-insoluble product in each reaction and write the net ionic equation:
(a) $CuCl_2(aq) + H_2S(aq) \rightarrow CuS + 2\ HCl$
(b) $CaCl_2(aq) + K_2CO_3(aq) \rightarrow 2\ KCl + CaCO_3$
(c) $AgNO_3(aq) + NaI(aq) \rightarrow AgI + NaNO_3$

61. ■ Bromine is obtained from sea water by the following reaction:

$$Cl_2(g) + 2\ NaBr(aq) \rightarrow 2\ NaCl(aq) + Br_2(\ell)$$

(a) What has been oxidized? What has been reduced?
(b) Identify the oxidizing and reducing agents.

62. Identify each of the following substances as a likely oxidizing or reducing agent: HNO_3, Na, Cl_2, O_2, $KMnO_4$.

63. ■ The mineral dolomite contains magnesium carbonate. This reacts with hydrochloric acid.

$$MgCO_3(s) + 2\ HCl(aq) \rightarrow$$
$$CO_2(g) + MgCl_2(aq) + H_2O(\ell)$$

(a) Write the net ionic equation for the reaction of magnesium carbonate and hydrochloric acid, and name the spectator ions.
(b) What type of reaction is this?

64. Ammonium sulfide, $(NH_4)_2S$, reacts with $Hg(NO_3)_2$ to produce HgS and NH_4NO_3.
(a) Write the overall balanced equation for the reaction. Indicate the state (s, aq) for each compound.
(b) Name each compound.
(c) What type of reaction is this?

65. ■ What species (atoms, molecules, or ions) are present in an aqueous solution of each of the following compounds? Decide which are Brønsted acids or bases and whether they are strong or weak.
(a) NH_3 (b) CH_3CO_2H (c) NaOH (d) HBr

66. (a) Name two water-soluble compounds containing the Cu^{2+} ion. Name two water-insoluble compounds based on the Cu^{2+} ion.
(b) Name two water-soluble compounds containing the Ba^{2+} ion. Name two water-insoluble compounds based on the Ba^{2+} ion.

67. ■ Balance equations for these reactions that occur in aqueous solution, and then classify each one as a precipitation, acid–base, or gas-forming reaction. Show states for the products (s, ℓ, g, aq), give their names, and write the net ionic equation.
(a) $K_2CO_3 + HClO_4 \rightarrow KClO_4 + CO_2 + H_2O$
(b) $FeCl_2 + (NH_4)_2S \rightarrow FeS + NH_4Cl$
(c) $Fe(NO_3)_2 + Na_2CO_3(aq) \rightarrow FeCO_3 + NaNO_3$
(d) $NaOH + FeCl_3 \rightarrow NaCl + Fe(OH)_3$

68. ■ For each reaction, write an overall, balanced equation and the net ionic equation.
(a) the reaction of aqueous lead(II) nitrate and aqueous potassium hydroxide
(b) the reaction of aqueous copper(II) nitrate and aqueous sodium carbonate

In the Laboratory

69. ■ The following reaction can be used to prepare iodine in the laboratory.

$$2\ NaI(s) + 2\ H_2SO_4(aq) + MnO_2(s) \rightarrow$$
$$Na_2SO_4(aq) + MnSO_4(aq) + I_2(g) + 2\ H_2O(\ell)$$

(a) Determine the oxidation number of each atom in the equation.
(b) What is the oxidizing agent, and what has been oxidized? What is the reducing agent, and what has been reduced?

(c) Is the reaction observed product-favored or reactant-favored?
(d) Name the reactants and products.

Preparation of iodine. A mixture of NaI and MnO_2 was placed in a flask in a hood *(left)*. On adding concentrated H_2SO_4 *(right)*, brown gaseous I_2 was evolved.

70. ■ ▲ If you have "silverware" in your home, you know it tarnishes easily. Tarnish is from the oxidation of silver in the presence of sulfur-containing compounds (in the atmosphere or in your food) to give black Ag_2S. To remove the tarnish, you can warm the tarnished object with some aluminum foil (in water with a small amount of baking soda). The silver sulfide reacts with aluminum to produce silver as well as aluminum oxide and hydrogen sulfide.

$$3\ Ag_2S(s) + 2\ Al(s) + 3\ H_2O(\ell) \rightarrow$$
$$6\ Ag(s) + Al_2O_3(s) + 3\ H_2S(aq)$$

Hydrogen sulfide is foul smelling, but it is removed by reaction with the baking soda.

$$NaHCO_3(aq) + H_2S(aq) \rightarrow$$
$$NaHS(aq) + H_2O(\ell) + CO_2(g)$$

Classify the two reactions, and identify any acids, bases, oxidizing agents, or reducing agents.

(a) (b)

Removing silver tarnish. A badly tarnished piece of silver (a) is placed in a dish with aluminum foil and aqueous sodium hydrogen carbonate. The portion of the silver in contact with the solution is now free of tarnish (b).

▲ more challenging ■ in OWL Blue-numbered questions answered in Appendix O

71. ■ ▲ Suppose you wish to prepare a sample of magnesium chloride. One way to do this is to use an acid–base reaction, the reaction of magnesium hydroxide with hydrochloric acid.

$$Mg(OH)_2(s) + 2 HCl(aq) \rightarrow MgCl_2(aq) + 2 H_2O(\ell)$$

When the reaction is complete, evaporating the water will give solid magnesium chloride. Can you suggest at least one other way to prepare $MgCl_2$?

72. ▲ Suggest a laboratory method for preparing barium phosphate. (See Question 71 for a way to approach this question.)

73. ■ One way to test for the presence of sugars (say in a urine sample) is to treat the sample with silver ions in aqueous ammonia. (This is called the Tollen's test.) Using glucose, $C_6H_{12}O_6$ to illustrate this test, the oxidation-reduction reaction occurring is

$$C_6H_{12}O_6 \ (aq) + 2 Ag^+(aq) + 2 OH^-(aq) \rightarrow$$
$$C_6H_{12}O_7(aq) + 2 Ag(s) + H_2O(\ell)$$

What has been oxidized, and what has been reduced? What is the oxidizing agent, and what is the reducing agent?

(a)   (b)

Tollen's test. The reaction of silver ions with a sugar such as glucose produces metallic silver. (a) The set up for the reaction. (b) The silvered testtube

Summary and Conceptual Questions

The following questions may use concepts from this and previous chapters.

74. There are many ionic compounds that dissolve in water to a very small extent. One example is lead(II) chloride. Suppose you stir some solid $PbCl_2$ into water. Explain how you would prove that the compound dissolves but to a small extent? Is the dissolving process product-favored or reactant-favored?

$$PbCl_2(s) \rightleftharpoons Pb^{2+}(aq) + 2 Cl^-(aq)$$

75. ▲ Most naturally occurring acids are weak acids. Lactic acid is one example.

$$CH_3CH(OH)CO_2H(s) + H_2O(\ell) \rightleftharpoons$$
$$H_3O^+(aq) + CH_3CH(OH)CO_2^-(aq)$$

If you place some lactic acid in water, it will ionize to a small extent, and an equilibrium will be established eventually. Suggest some experiments to prove that this is a weak acid and that the establishment of equilibrium is a reversible process.

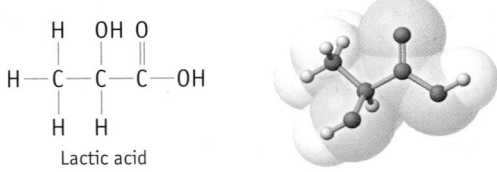

Lactic acid

76. ■ ▲ You want to prepare barium chloride, $BaCl_2$, using an exchange reaction of some type. To do so, you have the following reagents from which to select the reactants: $BaSO_4$, $BaBr_2$, $BaCO_3$, $Ba(OH)_2$, HCl, $HgSO_4$, $AgNO_3$, and HNO_3. Write a complete, balanced equation for the reaction chosen. (*Note: There are several possibilities.*)

77. ■ Describe how to prepare $BaSO_4$, barium sulfate, by (a) a precipitation reaction and (b) a gas-forming reaction. To do so, you have the following reagents from which to select the reactants: $BaCl_2$, $BaCO_3$, $Ba(OH)_2$, H_2SO_4, and Na_2SO_4. Write complete, balanced equations for the reactions chosen. (See page 130 for an illustration of the preparation of a compound.)

78. ■ Describe how to prepare zinc chloride by (a) an acid–base reaction, (b) a gas-forming reaction, and (c) an oxidation-reduction reaction. The available starting materials are $ZnCO_3$, HCl, Cl_2, HNO_3, $Zn(OH)_2$, $NaCl$, $Zn(NO_3)_2$, and Zn. Write complete, balanced equations for the reactions chosen.

4 | Stoichiometry: Quantitative Information About Chemical Reactions

Charles D. Winters

The Chemistry of a Sparkler

This "sparkler," like many forms of fireworks, depends on some very straightforward chemistry. It consists of a mixture of finely powdered metals, such as Al and Fe, other substances such as $KClO_3$, KNO_3, and a binder that holds the mixture onto a wire handle. When ignited, the powdered metal reacts with oxygen in the air (or extracted from $KClO_3$), and the sparks fly!

Questions:
1. What kind of chemical reaction is occurring here?
2. What are the likely products from the reaction of aluminum metal or iron with oxygen in the air or with $KClO_3$?
3. If the sparkler contains 1.0 g of Al, what is the mass of the product of the reaction of aluminum with oxygen?

Answers to these questions are in Appendix Q.

Chapter Goals

OWL *See Chapter Goals Revisited (page 194) for Study Questions keyed to these goals and assignable in OWL.*

- Perform stoichiometry calculations using balanced chemical equations.
- Understand the meaning of a limiting reactant in a chemical reaction.
- Calculate the theoretical and percent yields of a chemical reaction.
- Use stoichiometry to analyze a mixture of compounds or to determine the formula of a compound.
- Define and use concentration in solution stoichiometry.

Chapter Outline

The objective of this chapter is to introduce the quantitative study of chemical reactions. Quantitative studies are needed to determine, for example, how much oxygen is required for the complete combustion of a given quantity of gasoline and what masses of carbon dioxide and water can be obtained. This part of chemistry is fundamental to much of what chemists, chemical engineers, biochemists, molecular biologists, geochemists, and many others do.

Chemistry.Now™

Throughout the text this icon introduces an opportunity for self-study or to explore interactive tutorials by signing in at **www.cengage.com/login**.

4.1 Mass Relationships in Chemical Reactions: Stoichiometry

Module 7

A balanced chemical equation shows the quantitative relationship between reactants and products in a chemical reaction. Let us apply this concept to the reaction of phosphorus and chlorine (◄ Figure 3.1).

$$P_4(s) + 6\ Cl_2(g) \longrightarrow 4\ PCl_3(\ell)$$

Suppose you use 1.00 mol of phosphorus (P_4, 124 g/mol) in this reaction. The balanced equation shows that 6.00 mol (= 425 g) of Cl_2 must be used for complete reaction with 1.00 mol of P_4 and that 4.00 mol (= 549 g) of PCl_3 can be produced. The mole and mass relationships of reactants and products in a reaction can be summarized in an *amounts table.* You will find such tables helpful in identifying the amounts of reactants and products and the changes that occur upon reaction.

Equation	**$P_4(s)$**	+	**$6\ Cl_2(g)$**	→	**$4\ PCl_3(\ell)$**
Initial amount (mol)	1.00 mol (124 g)		6.00 mol (425 g)		0 mol (0 g)
Change in amount upon reaction (mol)	−1.00 mol		−6.00 mol		+4.00 mol
Amount after complete reaction (mol)	0 mol (0 g)		0 mol (0 g)		4.00 mol [549 g = 124 g + 425 g]

The balanced equation for a reaction tells us the correct *mole ratios* of reactants and products. Here, 6 mol of Cl_2 should be used per mole of P_4. Now, what if only 0.0100 mol of P_4 (1.24 g) is available? Six times as many moles of Cl_2 are still required (0.0600 mol of Cl_2; 4.25 g), and 0.0400 mol of PCl_3 (5.49 g) will be formed. The only requirement is that there should be a ratio of 6 to 1 for the amount of Cl_2 relative to the amount of P_4.

■ **Amounts Tables** Amounts tables are useful not only here but will also be used extensively when you study chemical equilibria more thoroughly in Chapters 16–18.

Following this line of reasoning, let us determine (a) what mass of Cl_2 is required to react completely with 1.45 g of phosphorus and (b) what mass of PCl_3 can be produced.

Part (a): Mass of Cl_2 Required

Step 1. *Write the balanced equation* (using correct formulas for reactants and products). This is always the first step when dealing with chemical reactions.

$$P_4(s) + 6\ Cl_2(g) \longrightarrow 4\ PCl_3(\ell)$$

Step 2. *Calculate amount (moles) from mass (grams).* From the mass of P_4, calculate the amount of P_4 available.

$$1.45\ g\ P_4 \times \frac{1\ mol\ P_4}{123.9\ g\ P_4} = 0.0117\ mol\ P_4$$

$$\uparrow$$

$$1/\text{molar mass of } P_4$$

Step 3. *Use a stoichiometric factor.* The amount of Cl_2 required is related by the balanced equation to the amount of the other reactant (P_4) available.

$$0.0117\ mol\ P_4 \times \frac{6\ mol\ Cl_2\ required}{1\ mol\ P_4\ required} = 0.0702\ mol\ Cl_2\ required$$

$$\uparrow$$

stoichiometric factor from balanced equation

To perform this calculation the amount of phosphorus available has been multiplied by a **stoichiometric factor**, a mole ratio based on the coefficients for the two chemicals in the balanced equation. Here, the balanced equation specifies that 6 mol of Cl_2 is required for each mole of P_4, so the stoichiometric factor is (6 mol Cl_2/1 mol P_4). Calculation shows that 0.0702 mol of Cl_2 is required to react with all the available phosphorus (1.45 g, 0.0117 mol).

Problem Solving Tip 4.1   Stoichiometry Calculations

You are asked to determine what mass of product can be formed from a given mass of reactant. It is not possible to calculate the mass of product in a single step. Instead, you must follow a route such as that illustrated here for the reaction of a reactant A to give the product B according to an equation such as x A ⟶ y B.

- The mass (g) of reactant A is converted to the amount (moles) of A.
- Next, using the stoichiometric factor, find the amount (moles) of B.
- Finally, the mass (g) of B is obtained by multiplying amount of B by its molar mass.

When solving a stoichiometry problem, remember that you will always use a stoichiometric factor at some point.

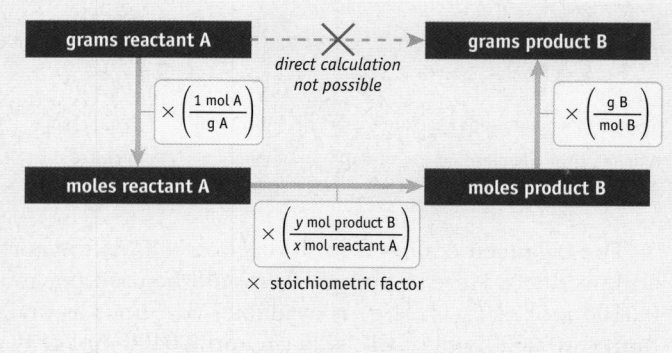

Step 4. *Calculate mass from amount.* Convert the amount (moles) of Cl_2 calculated in Step 3 to mass (in grams) of Cl_2 required.

$$0.0702 \text{ mol } Cl_2 \times \frac{70.91 \text{ g } Cl_2}{1 \text{ mol } Cl_2} = 4.98 \text{ g } Cl_2$$

Part (b) Mass of PCl_3 Produced from P_4 and Cl_2

What mass of PCl_3 can be produced from the reaction of 1.45 g of phosphorus with 4.98 g of Cl_2? From part (a), we know that these masses are the correct quantities needed for complete reaction. Because matter is conserved, the answer can be obtained by adding the masses of P_4 and Cl_2 used (giving 1.45 g + 4.98 g = 6.43 g of PCl_3 produced). Alternatively, Steps 3 and 4 can be repeated, but with the appropriate stoichiometric factor and molar mass.

Step 3b. *Use a stoichiometric factor.* Convert the amount of available P_4 to the amount of PCl_3 produced. Here, the balanced equation specifies that 4 mol PCl_3 is produced for each mole of P_4 used, so the stoichiometric factor is (4 mol PCl_3/1 mol P_4)

$$0.0117 \text{ mol } P_4 \times \frac{4 \text{ mol } PCl_3 \text{ produced}}{1 \text{ mol } P_4 \text{ available}} = 0.0468 \text{ mol } PCl_3 \text{ produced}$$

↑
stoichiometric factor from balanced equation

Step 4b. *Calculate the mass of product from its amount.* Convert the amount of PCl_3 produced to a mass in grams.

$$0.0468 \text{ mol } PCl_3 \times \frac{137.3 \text{ g } PCl_3}{1 \text{ mol } PCl_3} = 6.43 \text{ g } PCl_3$$

Chemistry ⚛ Now™

Sign in at **www.cengage.com/login** and go to Chapter 4 Contents to see:
- Screen 4.2 for (a) a video and animation of **the phosphorus and chlorine reaction discussed in this section,** and (b) an exercise that examines **the reaction between chlorine and elemental phosphorus**
- Screen 4.3 for a tutorial on **yield**

■ **EXAMPLE 4.1 Mass Relations in Chemical Reactions**

Problem Glucose, $C_6H_{12}O_6$, reacts with oxygen to give CO_2 and H_2O. What mass of oxygen (in grams) is required for complete reaction of 25.0 g of glucose? What masses of carbon dioxide and water (in grams) are formed?

Strategy After writing a balanced equation, you can perform the stoichiometric calculations using the scheme in Problem Solving Tip 4.1.

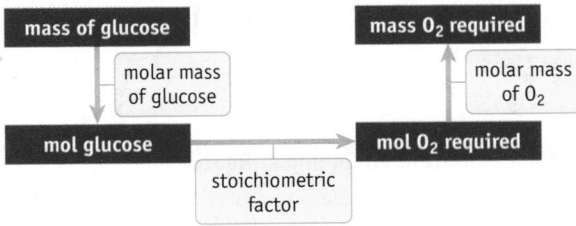

First, find the amount of glucose available; then relate it to the amount of O_2 required using the stoichiometric factor based on the coefficients in the balanced equation. Finally, find the mass of O_2 required from the amount of O_2. Follow the same procedure to calculate the masses of carbon dioxide and water.

■ **Mass Balance and Moles of Reactants and Products** Mass is always conserved in chemical reactions. The total mass of the reactants is always the same as the products. This does not mean, however, that the total amount (moles) of reactants is the same as that of the products. Atoms are rearranged into different "units" (molecules) in the course of a reaction. In the P_4 + Cl_2 reaction, 7 mol of reactants gives 4 mol of product.

Solution

Step 1. Write a balanced equation.

$$C_6H_{12}O_6(s) + 6\ O_2(g) \longrightarrow 6\ CO_2(g) + 6\ H_2O(\ell)$$

Step 2. Convert the mass of glucose to amount.

$$25.0\text{ g glucose} \times \frac{1\text{ mol}}{180.2\text{ g}} = 0.139\text{ mol glucose}$$

Step 3. Use the stoichiometric factor. Here we calculate the amount of O_2 required.

$$0.139\text{ mol glucose} \times \frac{6\text{ mol }O_2}{1\text{ mol glucose}} = 0.832\text{ mol }O_2$$

Step 4. Calculate mass from amount. Convert the required amount of O_2 to a mass in grams.

$$0.832\text{ mol }O_2 \times \frac{32.00\text{ g}}{1\text{ mol }O_2} = 26.6\text{ g }O_2$$

Repeat Steps 3 and 4 to find the mass of CO_2 produced in the combustion. First, relate the amount (moles) of glucose available to the amount of CO_2 produced using a stoichiometric factor. Then convert the amount of CO_2 to its mass in grams.

$$0.139\text{ mol glucose} \times \frac{6\text{ mol }CO_2}{1\text{ mol glucose}} \times \frac{44.01\text{ g }CO_2}{1\text{ mol }CO_2} = \boxed{36.6\text{ g }CO_2}$$

Now, how can you find the mass of H_2O produced? You could go through Steps 3 and 4 again. However, recognize that the total mass of reactants

$$25.0\text{ g }C_6H_{12}O_6 + 26.6\text{ g }O_2 = 51.6\text{ g reactants}$$

must be the same as the total mass of products. The mass of water that can be produced is therefore

$$\text{Total mass of products} = 51.6\text{ g} = 36.6\text{ g }CO_2\text{ produced} + ?\text{ g }H_2O$$

$$\text{Mass of }H_2O\text{ produced} = \boxed{15.0\text{ g}}$$

The results of this calculation can be summarized in an amounts table.

Equation	$C_6H_{12}O_6(s)$	+ 6 $O_2(g)$	$\longrightarrow$ 6 $CO_2(g)$	+ 6 $H_2O(\ell)$
Initial amount (mol)	0.139 mol	6(0.139 mol) = 0.832 mol	0	0
Change (mol)	−0.139 mol	−0.832 mol	+0.832 mol	+0.832 mol
Amount after reaction (mol)	0	0	0.832 mol	0.832 mol

Comment When you know the mass of all but one of the chemicals in a reaction, you can find the unknown mass using the principle of mass conservation (the total mass of reactants must equal the total mass of products; page 114).

EXERCISE 4.1 Mass Relations in Chemical Reactions

What mass of oxygen, O_2, is required to completely combust 454 g of propane, C_3H_8? What masses of CO_2 and H_2O are produced?

4.2 Reactions in Which One Reactant Is Present in Limited Supply

Reactions are often carried out with an excess of one reactant over that required by stoichiometry. This is usually done to ensure that one of the reactants in the reaction is consumed completely, even though some of another reactant remains unused.

Suppose you burn a toy "sparkler," a wire coated with a mixture of aluminum or iron powder and potassium nitrate or chlorate (Figure 4.1 and page 158). The aluminum or iron burns, consuming oxygen from the air or from the potassium salt and producing a metal oxide.

$$4 \, Al(s) + 3 \, O_2(g) \longrightarrow 2 \, Al_2O_3(s)$$

The sparkler burns until the metal powder is consumed completely. What about the oxygen? Four moles of aluminum require three moles of oxygen, but there is much, much more O_2 available in the air than is needed to consume the metal in a sparkler. How much metal oxide is produced? That depends on the quantity of metal powder in the sparkler, not on the quantity of O_2 in the atmosphere. The metal powder in this example is called the **limiting reactant** because its amount determines, or limits, the amount of product formed.

Let us look at an example of a limiting reactant situation using the reaction of oxygen and carbon monoxide to give carbon dioxide. The balanced equation for the reaction is

$$2 \, CO(g) + O_2(g) \longrightarrow 2 \, CO_2(g)$$

Suppose you have a mixture of four CO molecules and three O_2 molecules. The four CO molecules require only two O_2 molecules (and produce four CO_2 molecules). This means that one O_2 molecule remains after reaction is complete.

FIGURE 4.1 Burning aluminum and iron powder. A toy sparkler contains a metal powder such as Al or Fe and other chemicals such as KNO_3 or $KClO_3$. When ignited, the metal burns with a brilliant white light.

Charles D. Winters

Reactants: 4 **CO** and 3 **O₂**   ⟶   Products: 4 **CO₂** and 1 **O₂**

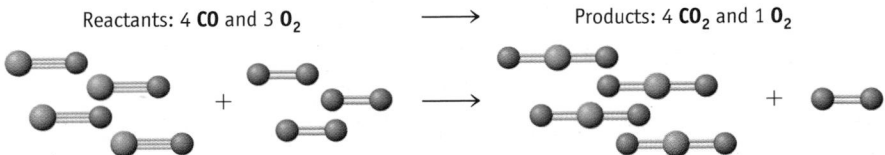

Because more O_2 molecules are available than are required, the number of CO_2 molecules produced is determined by the number of CO molecules available. Carbon monoxide, CO, is therefore the limiting reactant in this case.

A Stoichiometry Calculation with a Limiting Reactant

The first step in the manufacture of nitric acid is the oxidation of ammonia to NO over a platinum-wire gauze (Figure 4.2).

$$4 \, NH_3(g) + 5 \, O_2(g) \longrightarrow 4 \, NO(g) + 6 \, H_2O(\ell)$$

Suppose that equal masses of NH_3 and O_2 are mixed (750. g of each). Are these reactants mixed in the correct stoichiometric ratio, or is one of them in short supply? That is, will one of them limit the quantity of NO that can be produced? How much NO can be formed if the reaction using this reactant mixture goes to completion? And how much of the excess reactant is left over when the maximum amount of NO has been formed?

■ **Comparing Reactant Ratios** For the CO/O_2 reaction, the stoichiometric ratio of reactants should be (2 mol CO/1 mol O_2). However, the ratio of amounts of reactants available in the text example is (4 mol CO/3 mol O_2) or (1.33 mol CO/1 mol O_2). The fact that the CO/O_2 ratio is not large enough tells us that there is not enough CO to react with all of the available O_2. Carbon monoxide is the limiting reactant, and some O_2 will be left over when all of the CO is consumed.

(a)

(b)

Active Figure 4.2 **Oxidation of ammonia.** (a) Burning ammonia on the surface of a platinum wire produces so much heat that the wire glows bright red. (b) Billions of kilograms of HNO_3 are made annually starting with the oxidation of ammonia over a wire gauze containing platinum.

Chemistry.·۞·.Now™ Sign in at www.cengage.com/login and go to the Chapter Contents menu to explore an interactive version of this figure accompanied by an exercise.

Step 1. Find the amount of each reactant.

$$750. \text{ g NH}_3 \times \frac{1 \text{ mol NH}_3}{17.03 \text{ g NH}_3} = 44.0 \text{ mol NH}_3 \text{ available}$$

$$750. \text{ g O}_2 \times \frac{1 \text{ mol O}_2}{32.00 \text{ g O}_2} = 23.4 \text{ mol O}_2 \text{ available}$$

Step 2. What is the limiting reactant? Examine the ratio of amounts of reactants. Are the reactants present in the correct stoichiometric ratio as given by the balanced equation?

$$\text{Stoichiometric ratio of reactants required by balanced equation} = \frac{5 \text{ mol O}_2}{4 \text{ mol NH}_3} = \frac{1.25 \text{ mol O}_2}{1 \text{ mol NH}_3}$$

$$\text{Ratio of reactants } actually \text{ } available = \frac{23.4 \text{ mol O}_2}{44.0 \text{ mol NH}_3} = \frac{0.532 \text{ mol O}_2}{1 \text{ mol NH}_3}$$

Dividing moles of O_2 available by moles of NH_3 available shows that the ratio of available reactants is much smaller than the 5 mol O_2/4 mol NH_3 ratio required by the balanced equation. Thus, there is not sufficient O_2 available to react with all of the NH_3. In this case, oxygen, O_2, is the limiting reactant. That is, 1 mol of NH_3 requires 1.25 mol of O_2, but we have only 0.532 mol of O_2 available.

Step 3. Calculate the mass of product. We can now calculate the expected mass of product, NO, based on the amount of the limiting reactant, O_2.

$$23.4 \text{ mol O}_2 \times \frac{4 \text{ mol NO}}{5 \text{ mol O}_2} \times \frac{30.01 \text{ g NO}}{1 \text{ mol NO}} = 562 \text{ g NO}$$

Step 4. Calculate the mass of excess reactant. Ammonia is the "excess reactant" in this NH_3/O_2 reaction because more than enough NH_3 is available to react with 23.4 mol of O_2. Let us calculate the quantity of NH_3 remaining after all the O_2 has been used. To do so, we first need to know the amount of NH_3 required to consume all the limiting reactant, O_2.

$$23.4 \text{ mol } O_2 \text{ available} \times \frac{4 \text{ mol } NH_3 \text{ required}}{5 \text{ mol } O_2} = 18.8 \text{ mol } NH_3 \text{ required}$$

Because 44.0 mol of NH_3 is available, the amount of excess NH_3 can be calculated,

$$\text{Excess } NH_3 = 44.0 \text{ mol } NH_3 \text{ available} - 18.8 \text{ mol } NH_3 \text{ required}$$
$$= 25.2 \text{ mol } NH_3 \text{ remaining}$$

and then converted to a mass.

$$25.2 \text{ mol } NH_3 \times \frac{17.03 \text{ g } NH_3}{1 \text{ mol } NH_3} = 429 \text{ g } NH_3 \text{ in excess of that required}$$

Finally, because 429 g of NH_3 is left over, this means that 321 g of NH_3 has been consumed (= 750. g − 429 g).

In limiting reactant problems, it is helpful to summarize your results in an amounts table.

Equation	4 NH₃(g)	+	5 O₂(g)	→	4 NO(g)	+	6 H₂O(ℓ)
Initial amount (mol)	44.0		23.4		0		0
Change in amount (mol)	−(4/5)(23.4) = −18.8		−23.4		+(4/5)(23.4) = +18.8		+(6/5)(23.4) = +28.1
After complete reaction (mol)	25.2		0		18.8		28.1

All of the limiting reactant, O_2, is consumed. Of the original 44.0 mol of NH_3, 18.8 mol is consumed and 25.2 mol remains. The balanced equation indicates that the amount of NO produced is equal to the amount of NH_3 consumed, so 18.8 mol of NO is produced from 18.8 mol of NH_3. In addition, 28.1 mol of H_2O is produced.

■ **Conservation of Mass** Mass is conserved in the $NH_3 + O_2$ reaction. The total mass present before reaction (1500. g) is the same as the total mass produced in the reaction plus the mass of NH_3 remaining. That is, 562 g of NO (18.8 mol) and 506 g of H_2O (28.1 mol) are produced. Because 429 g of NH_3 (25.2 mol) remains, the total mass after reaction (562 g + 506 g + 429 g) is the same as the total mass before reaction.

Chemistry ⚛ Now™

Sign in at **www.cengage.com/login** and go to Chapter 4 Contents menu to see:
• Screen 4.4 for a video and animation of **the limiting reactant in the methanol and oxygen reaction**
• Screen 4.5 for (a) an exercise on **zinc and hydrochloric acid in aqueous solution** and (b) a simulation **using limiting reactants**

■ **EXAMPLE 4.2 A Reaction with a Limiting Reactant**

Problem Methanol, CH_3OH, which is used as a fuel, can be made by the reaction of carbon monoxide and hydrogen.

$$CO(g) + 2 H_2(g) \longrightarrow CH_3OH(\ell)$$
$$\text{methanol}$$

Suppose 356 g of CO and 65.0 g of H_2 are mixed and allowed to react.

(a) Which is the limiting reactant?

(b) What mass of methanol can be produced?

(c) What mass of the excess reactant remains after the limiting reactant has been consumed?

A car that uses methanol as a fuel. In this car, methanol is converted to hydrogen, which is then combined with oxygen in a fuel cell. The fuel cell generates electric energy to run the car (see Chapter 20). See Example 4.2.

Strategy There are usually two steps to a limiting reactant problem:

(a) After calculating the amount of each reactant, compare the ratio of reactant amounts to the required stoichiometric ratio, here 2 mol H_2/1 mol CO.

- If [mol H_2 available/mol CO available] > 2/1, then CO is the limiting reactant.
- If [mol H_2 available/mol CO available] < 2/1, then H_2 is the limiting reactant.

(b) Use the amount of limiting reactant to find the masses of product and excess reactant.

Solution

(a) *What is the limiting reactant?* The amount of each reactant is

$$\text{Amount of CO} = 356 \text{ g CO} \times \frac{1 \text{ mol CO}}{28.01 \text{ g CO}} = 12.7 \text{ mol CO}$$

$$\text{Amount of } H_2 = 65.0 \text{ g } H_2 \times \frac{1 \text{ mol } H_2}{2.016 \text{ g } H_2} = 32.2 \text{ mol } H_2$$

Are these reactants present in a perfect stoichiometric ratio?

$$\frac{\text{Mol } H_2 \text{ available}}{\text{Mol CO available}} = \frac{32.2 \text{ mol } H_2}{12.7 \text{ mol CO}} = \frac{2.54 \text{ mol } H_2}{1.00 \text{ mol CO}}$$

The required mole ratio is 2 mol of H_2 to 1 mol of CO. Here, we see that more hydrogen is available than is required to consume all the CO. It follows that not enough CO is present to use up all of the hydrogen. CO is the limiting reactant.

(b) *What is the maximum mass of CH_3OH that can be formed?* This calculation must be based on the amount of limiting reactant.

$$12.7 \text{ mol CO} \times \frac{1 \text{ mol } CH_3OH \text{ formed}}{1 \text{ mol CO available}} \times \frac{32.04 \text{ g } CH_3OH}{1 \text{ mol } CH_3OH} = \boxed{407 \text{ g } CH_3OH}$$

(c) *What mass of H_2 remains when all the CO has been converted to product?* First, we must find the amount of H_2 required to react with all the CO, then calculate the mass from the amount.

$$12.7 \text{ mol CO} \times \frac{2 \text{ mol } H_2}{1 \text{ mol CO}} = 25.4 \text{ mol } H_2 \text{ required}$$

Because 32.2 mol of H_2 is available, but only 25.4 mol is required by the limiting reactant, 32.2 mol − 25.4 mol = 6.8 mol of H_2 is in excess. This is equivalent to 14 g of H_2.

Comment The amounts table for this reaction is

Equation	CO(g)	+	2 H_2(g)	→	$CH_3OH(\ell)$
Initial amount (mol)	12.7		32.2		0
Change (mol)	−12.7		−2(12.7)		+12.7
After complete reaction (mol)	0		6.8		12.7

The mass of product formed plus the mass of H_2 remaining after reaction (407 g CH_3OH produced + 14 g H_2 remaining = 421 g) is equal to the mass of reactants present before reaction (356 g CO + 65.0 g H_2 = 421 g).

Thermite reaction. Iron(III) oxide reacts with aluminum metal to produce aluminum oxide and iron metal. The reaction produces so much heat that the iron melts and spews out of the reaction vessel. See Exercise 4.2.

EXERCISE 4.2 A Reaction with a Limiting Reactant

The thermite reaction produces iron metal and aluminum oxide from a mixture of powdered aluminum metal and iron(III) oxide.

$$Fe_2O_3(s) + 2 Al(s) \longrightarrow 2 Fe(\ell) + Al_2O_3(s)$$

A mixture of 50.0 g each of Fe_2O_3 and Al is used.

(a) Which is the limiting reactant?

(b) What mass of iron metal can be produced?

Moles of Reaction and Limiting Reactants

There is another method of solving stoichiometry problems that applies especially well to limiting reactant problems. This involves the useful concept of "moles of reaction."

One "mole of reaction" is said to have occurred when the reaction has taken place according to the number of moles given by the coefficients in the equation. For example, for the reaction of CO and O_2,

$$2\ CO(g) + O_2(g) \longrightarrow 2\ CO_2(g)$$

one mol of reaction occurs when 2 mol of CO and 1 mol of O_2 produce 2 mol of CO_2. If the reaction mixture consists of only 1 mol of CO and 0.5 mol of O_2, then only 1 mol of CO_2 is produced, and 0.5 mol of reaction has occurred according to this balanced equation.

To pursue this example further, suppose 9.5 g of CO and excess O_2 are combined. What amount of CO_2 (moles) can be produced?

$$9.5\ g\ CO \times \frac{1\ mol\ CO}{28.0\ g\ CO} \times \frac{1\ mol\text{-rxn}}{2\ mol\ CO}$$
$$= 0.34\ mol\text{-rxn}$$

$$0.34\ mol\text{-rxn} \times \frac{2\ mol\ CO_2}{1\ mol\text{-rxn}} = 0.68\ mol\ CO_2$$

You can see in this example that the number of moles of reaction that occurred is calculated by multiplying the amount (moles) of the reactant CO by the factor, 1 mol-rxn/2 mol CO (which amounts to dividing the amount of CO by its stoichiometric coefficient).

All reactants and products involved in a chemical reaction undergo the same number of moles of reaction because the reaction can only occur a certain number of times before the reactants are consumed and the reaction reaches completion.

If one of the reactants is in short supply, the actual number of times a reaction can be carried out—the number of "moles of reaction"—will be determined by the limiting reactant. To use this approach, we first calculate the amount of each reactant initially present and then calculate the **moles of reaction** that could occur with each amount of reactant. (This is equivalent to dividing amount [moles] of each reactant by its stoichiometric coefficient.) The reactant producing the smallest number of moles of reaction is the limiting reactant. Once the limiting reactant is known, we proceed as before.

Consider again the NH_3/O_2 reaction on page 163:

1. *Calculate the moles of reaction predicted for each reactant, and decide on the limiting reactant.*

In the case of the NH_3/O_2 reaction,

$$4\ NH_3(g) + 5\ O_2(g) \longrightarrow 4\ NO(g) + 6\ H_2O(\ell)$$

1 "mole of reaction" uses 4 mol of NH_3 and 5 mol of O_2 and produces 4 mol of NO and 6 mol of H_2O. In the example on page 163, we started with 44.0 mol of NH_3, so 11.0 mol of reaction can result.

$$44.0\ mol\ NH_3 \times \frac{1\ mol\text{-rxn}}{4\ mol\ NH_3} = 11.0\ mol\text{-rxn}$$

Based on the amount of O_2 available, 4.68 mol of reaction can occur.

$$23.4\ mol\ O_2 \times \frac{1\ mol\text{-rxn}}{5\ mol\ O_2} = 4.68\ mol\text{-rxn}$$

Fewer moles of reaction can occur with the amount of O_2 available, so O_2 is the limiting reactant.

2. *Calculate the change in amount and the amount upon completion of the reaction, for each reactant and product.* The number of moles of reaction predicted by the limiting reactant corresponds to the number of moles of reaction that can *actually* occur. Each reactant and product will undergo this number of moles of reaction, 4.68 mol-rxn in this case. To calculate the *change* in amount for a given reactant or product, multiply this number of moles of reaction by the stoichiometric coefficient of the reactant or product. To illustrate this step, for NH_3 this corresponds to the following calculation:

$$4.68\ mol\text{-rxn} \times \left(\frac{4\ mole\ NH_3}{1\ mol\text{-rxn}} \right) =$$
$$18.8\ mol\ NH_3.$$

The amount of each reactant and product after reaction is calculated as usual.

Equation	$4\ NH_3(g)$	$+\ 5\ O_2(g)$	$\longrightarrow 4\ NO(g)$	$+\ 6\ H_2O(g)$
Initial amount (mol)	44.0	23.4	0	0
Moles of reaction based on limiting reactant (mol)	4.68	4.68	4.68	4.68
Change in amount (mol)	−4.68(4)	−4.68(5)	+4.68(4)	+4.68(6)
	= −18.8	= −23.4	= +18.8	= +28.1
Amount remaining after complete reaction (mol)	25.2	0	18.8	28.1

Finally, from the amounts present after completion, we can calculate the masses of the products and of any reactant remaining.

You may find this approach easier to use particularly when there are more than two reactants, each present initially in some designated quantity.

A final note: the concept of "moles of reaction" will be applied in this text in the discussion of thermochemistry in Chapters 5 and 19.

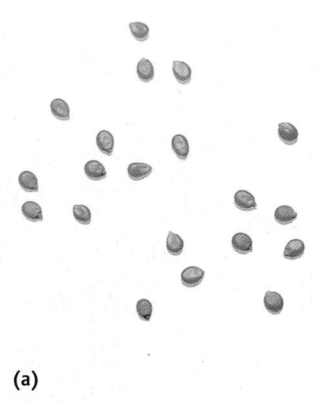

(a)

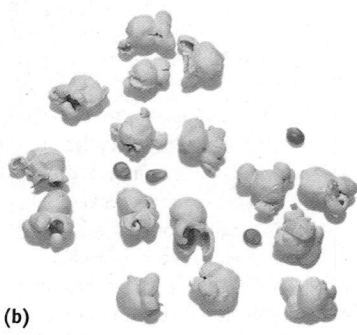

(b)

FIGURE 4.3 Percent yield. Although not a chemical reaction, popping corn is a good analogy to the difference between a theoretical yield and an actual yield. Here, we began with 20 popcorn kernels and found that only 16 of them popped. The percent yield from our "reaction" was (16/20) x 100%, or 80%.

4.3 Percent Yield

The maximum mass of product that can be obtained from a chemical reaction is the **theoretical yield**. Frequently, however, the **actual yield** of the product—the mass of material that is actually obtained in the laboratory or a chemical plant—is less than the theoretical yield. Loss of product often occurs during the isolation and purification steps. In addition, some reactions do not go completely to products, and reactions are sometimes complicated by giving more than one set of products. For all these reasons, the actual yield is almost always less than the theoretical yield (Figure 4.3).

To provide information to other chemists who might want to carry out a reaction, it is customary to report a percent yield. **Percent yield**, which specifies how much of the theoretical yield was obtained, is defined as

$$\text{Percent yield} = \frac{\text{actual yield}}{\text{theoretical yield}} \times 100\% \tag{4.1}$$

Suppose you made aspirin in the laboratory by the following reaction:

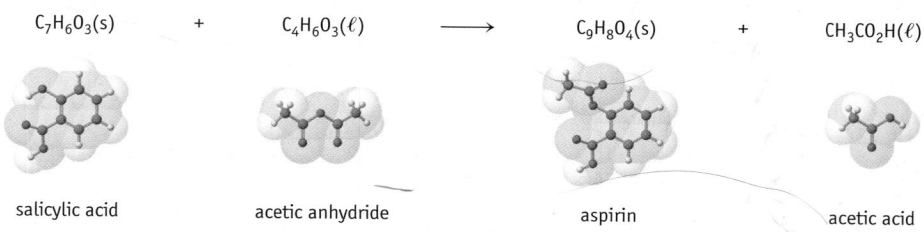

$$C_7H_6O_3(s) \quad + \quad C_4H_6O_3(\ell) \quad \longrightarrow \quad C_9H_8O_4(s) \quad + \quad CH_3CO_2H(\ell)$$

salicylic acid   acetic anhydride   aspirin   acetic acid

and that you began with 14.4 g of salicylic acid and an excess of acetic anhydride. That is, salicylic acid is the limiting reactant. If you obtain 6.26 g of aspirin, what is the percent yield of this product? The first step is to find the amount of the limiting reactant, salicylic acid ($C_6H_4(OH)CO_2H$).

$$14.4 \text{ g } C_6H_4(OH)CO_2H \times \frac{1 \text{ mol } C_6H_4(OH)CO_2H}{138.1 \text{ g } C_6H_4(OH)CO_2H} = 0.104 \text{ mol } C_6H_4(OH)CO_2H$$

Next, use the stoichiometric factor from the balanced equation to find the amount of aspirin expected based on the limiting reactant, $C_6H_4(OH)CO_2H$.

$$0.104 \text{ mol } C_6H_4(OH)CO_2H \times \frac{1 \text{ mol aspirin}}{1 \text{ mol } C_6H_4(OH)CO_2H} = 0.104 \text{ mol aspirin}$$

The maximum amount of aspirin that can be produced—the theoretical yield—is 0.104 mol. Because the quantity you measure in the laboratory is the mass of the product, it is customary to express the theoretical yield as a mass in grams.

$$0.104 \text{ mol aspirin} \times \frac{180.2 \text{ g aspirin}}{1 \text{ mol aspirin}} = 18.7 \text{ g aspirin}$$

Finally, with the actual yield known to be only 6.26 g, the percent yield of aspirin can be calculated.

$$\text{Percent yield} = \frac{6.26 \text{ g aspirin obtained (actual yield)}}{18.7 \text{ g aspirin expected (theoretical yield)}} \times 100\% = 33.5\% \text{ yield}$$

Chemistry Now™

Sign in at **www.cengage.com/login** and go to Chapter 4 Contents to see Screen 4.6 for tutorials on (a) determining the theoretical yield of a reaction and on (b) **determining the percent yield of a reaction.**

FIGURE 4.4 A modern analytical instrument. This nuclear magnetic resonance (NMR) spectrometer is closely related to a magnetic resonance imaging (MRI) instrument found in a hospital. NMR is used to analyze compounds and to decipher their structure. (The instrument is controlled by a computer and console not seen in this photo.)

EXERCISE 4.3 Percent Yield

Aluminum carbide, Al_4C_3, reacts with water to produce methane.

$$Al_4C_3(s) + 12 H_2O(\ell) \longrightarrow 4 Al(OH)_3(s) + 3 CH_4(g)$$

If 125 g of aluminum carbide is decomposed, what is the theoretical yield of methane? If only 13.6 g of methane is obtained, what is the percent yield of this gas?

4.4 Chemical Equations and Chemical Analysis

Analytical chemists use a variety of approaches to identify substances as well as to measure the quantities of components of mixtures. Analytical chemistry is often done now using instrumental methods (Figure 4.4), but classical chemical reactions and stoichiometry still play a central role.

Quantitative Analysis of a Mixture

Quantitative chemical analysis generally depends on one of the following basic ideas:

- A substance, present in unknown amount, can be allowed to react with a known quantity of another substance. If the stoichiometric ratio for their reaction is known, the unknown amount can be determined.
- A material of unknown composition can be converted to one or more substances of known composition. Those substances can be identified, their amounts determined, and these amounts related to the amount of the original, unknown substance.

An example of the first type of analysis is the analysis of a sample of vinegar containing an unknown amount of acetic acid, the ingredient that makes vinegar acidic. The acid reacts readily and completely with sodium hydroxide.

$$CH_3CO_2H(aq) + NaOH(aq) \longrightarrow CH_3CO_2Na(aq) + H_2O(\ell)$$
acetic acid

If the exact amount of sodium hydroxide used in the reaction can be measured, the amount of acetic acid present can be calculated. This type of analysis is the subject of a later section in this chapter (▶ Section 4.7).

The second type of analysis is exemplified by the analysis of a sample of a mineral, thenardite, which is largely sodium sulfate, Na_2SO_4 (Figure 4.5). Sodium sulfate is soluble in water. Therefore, to find the quantity of Na_2SO_4 in an impure mineral sample, we would crush the rock and then wash the powdered sample thoroughly with water to dissolve the sodium sulfate. Next, we would treat this solution of sodium sulfate with barium chloride to precipitate the water-insoluble compound barium sulfate. The barium sulfate is collected on a filter and weighed (Figure 4.6).

$$Na_2SO_4(aq) + BaCl_2(aq) \longrightarrow BaSO_4(s) + 2 NaCl(aq)$$

FIGURE 4.5 Thenardite. The mineral thenardite is sodium sulfate, Na_2SO_4. It is named after the French chemist Louis Thenard (1777–1857), a co-discoverer (with J. L. Gay-Lussac and Humphry Davy) of boron. Sodium sulfate is used in making detergents, glass, and paper.

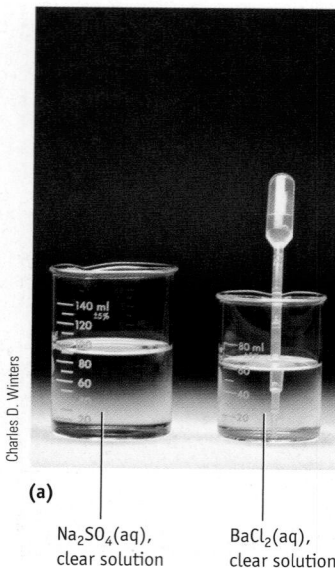

(a)

Na₂SO₄(aq),
clear solution

BaCl₂(aq),
clear solution

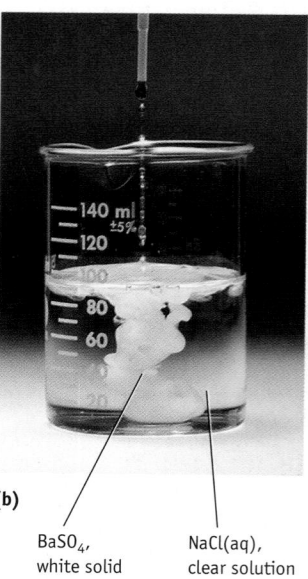

(b)

BaSO₄,
white solid

NaCl(aq),
clear solution

(c)

NaCl(aq),
clear solution

BaSO₄,
white solid
caught in filter

(d)

Mass of dry BaSO₄ determined

Charles D. Winters

Active Figure 4.6 **Analysis for the sulfate content of a sample.** The sulfate ions in a solution of Na_2SO_4 react with barium ions (Ba^{2+}) to form $BaSO_4$. The white, solid precipitate, barium sulfate ($BaSO_4$), is collected on a filter and weighed. The amount of $BaSO_4$ obtained can be related to the amount of Na_2SO_4 in the sample.

Chemistry ⚛ Now™ Sign in at www.cengage.com/login and go to the Chapter Contents menu to explore an interactive version of this figure accompanied by an exercise.

■ **Analysis and 100% Yield** Quantitative analysis requires reactions in which the yield is 100%.

We can then find the amount of sodium sulfate in the mineral sample because it is directly related to the amount of $BaSO_4$.

$$1 \text{ mol } Na_2SO_4(aq) \rightarrow 1 \text{ mol } BaSO_4(s)$$

Example 4.3 illustrates another instance of the analysis of a mineral in this way.

Chemistry ⚛ Now™

Sign in at **www.cengage.com/login** and go to Chapter 4 Contents to see Screen 4.7 for a tutorial on **chemical analysis.**

Photo: Charles D. Winters

A precipitate of nickel with dimethyl-glyoxime. Red, insoluble $Ni(C_4H_7N_2O_2)_2$ precipitates when dimethylglyoxime ($C_4H_8N_2O_2$) is added to an aqueous solution of nickel(II) ions. (See Example 4.3.)

EXAMPLE 4.3 Mineral Analysis

Problem Nickel(II) sulfide, NiS, occurs naturally as the relatively rare mineral millerite. One of its occurrences is in meteorites. To analyze a mineral sample for the quantity of NiS, the sample is dissolved in nitric acid to form a solution of $Ni(NO_3)_2$.

$$NiS(s) + 4 \text{ } HNO_3(aq) \rightarrow Ni(NO_3)_2(aq) + S(s) + 2 \text{ } NO_2(g) + 2 \text{ } H_2O(\ell)$$

The aqueous solution of $Ni(NO_3)_2$ is then treated with the organic compound dimethylglyoxime ($C_4H_8N_2O_2$, DMG) to give the red solid $Ni(C_4H_7N_2O_2)_2$.

$$Ni(NO_3)_2(aq) + 2 \text{ } C_4H_8N_2O_2(aq) \rightarrow Ni(C_4H_7N_2O_2)_2(s) + 2 \text{ } HNO_3(aq)$$

Suppose a 0.468-g sample containing millerite produces 0.206 g of red, solid $Ni(C_4H_7N_2O_2)_2$. What is the mass percent of NiS in the sample?

Strategy The balanced equations for the reactions show the following "road map":

$$1 \text{ mol NiS} \rightarrow 1 \text{ mol } Ni(NO_3)_2 \rightarrow 1 \text{ mol } Ni(C_4H_7N_2O_2)_2$$

If we know the mass of $Ni(C_4H_7N_2O_2)_2$, we can calculate its amount and thus the amount of NiS. The amount of NiS allows us to calculate the mass and mass percent of NiS in the sample.

Solution The molar mass of $Ni(C_4H_7N_2O_2)_2$ is 288.9 g/mol. The amount of this red solid is

$$0.206 \text{ g } Ni(C_4H_7N_2O_2)_2 \times \frac{1 \text{ mol } Ni(C_4H_7N_2O_2)_2}{288.9 \text{ g } Ni(C_4H_7N_2O_2)_2} = 7.13 \times 10^{-4} \text{ mol } Ni(C_4H_7N_2O_2)_2$$

Because 1 mol of $Ni(C_4H_7N_2O_2)_2$ is ultimately produced from 1 mol of NiS, the amount of NiS in the sample must have been 7.13×10^{-4} mol.

With the amount of NiS known, we calculate the mass of NiS.

$$7.13 \times 10^{-4} \text{ mol NiS} \times \frac{90.76 \text{ g NiS}}{1 \text{ mol NiS}} = 0.0647 \text{ g NiS}$$

Finally, the mass percent of NiS in the 0.468-g sample is

$$\text{Mass percent NiS} = \frac{0.0647 \text{ g NiS}}{0.468 \text{ g sample}} \times 100\% = \boxed{13.8\% \text{ NiS}}$$

EXERCISE 4.4 Analysis of a Mixture

One method for determining the purity of a sample of titanium(IV) oxide, TiO_2, an important industrial chemical, is to react the sample with bromine trifluoride.

$$3 \text{ } TiO_2(s) + 4 \text{ } BrF_3(\ell) \longrightarrow 3 \text{ } TiF_4(s) + 2 \text{ } Br_2(\ell) + 3 \text{ } O_2(g)$$

This reaction is known to occur completely and quantitatively. That is, all of the oxygen in TiO_2 is evolved as O_2. Suppose 2.367 g of a TiO_2-containing sample evolves 0.143 g of O_2. What is the mass percent of TiO_2 in the sample?

Determining the Formula of a Compound by Combustion

The empirical formula of a compound can be determined if the percent composition of the compound is known (◀ Section 2.10). But where do the percent composition data come from? One chemical method that works well for compounds that burn in oxygen is analysis by combustion. In this technique, each element in the compound combines with oxygen to produce the appropriate oxide.

Consider an analysis of the hydrocarbon methane, CH_4. A balanced equation for the combustion of methane shows that every atom of C in the original compound appears as CO_2 and every atom of H appears in the form of water. In other words, for every mole of CO_2 observed, there must have been one mole of carbon in the unknown compound. Similarly, for every mole of H_2O observed from combustion, there must have been two moles of H atoms in the unknown carbon-hydrogen compound.

$$CH_4(g) + 2 \text{ } O_2(g) \longrightarrow CO_2(g) + 2 \text{ } H_2O(\ell)$$

In the combustion experiment, gaseous carbon dioxide and water are separated (as illustrated in Figure 4.7) and their masses determined. From these masses, it is possible to calculate the amounts of C and H in CO_2 and H_2O, respectively, and

■ **Finding an Empirical Formula by Chemical Analysis** Finding the empirical formula of a compound by chemical analysis always uses the following procedure:
1. The unknown but pure compound is converted in a chemical reaction into known products.
2. The reaction products are isolated, and the amount of each is determined.
3. The amount of each product is related to the amount of each element in the original compound.
4. The empirical formula is determined from the relative amounts of elements in the original compound.

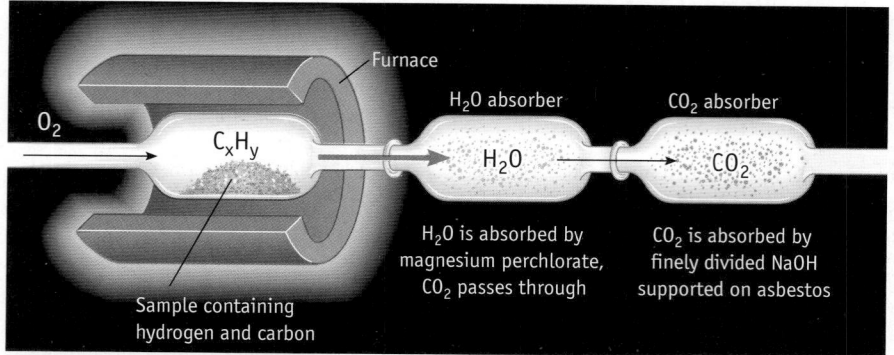

Furnace

O_2

C_xH_y

H₂O absorber

H_2O

CO₂ absorber

CO_2

Sample containing
hydrogen and carbon

H_2O is absorbed by
magnesium perchlorate,
CO_2 passes through

CO_2 is absorbed by
finely divided NaOH
supported on asbestos

Active Figure 4.7   **Combustion analysis of a hydrocarbon.** If a compound containing C and
H is burned in oxygen, CO_2 and H_2O are formed, and the mass of each can be determined. The H_2O is absorbed by
magnesium perchlorate, and the CO_2 is absorbed by finely divided NaOH supported on asbestos. The mass of each
absorbent before and after combustion gives the masses of CO_2 and H_2O. Only a few milligrams of a combustible
compound are needed for analysis.

Chemistry Now™ Sign in at www.cengage.com/login and go to the Chapter Contents menu to explore
an interactive version of this figure accompanied by an exercise.

the ratio of amounts of C and H in a sample of the original compound can then
be found. This ratio gives the empirical formula.

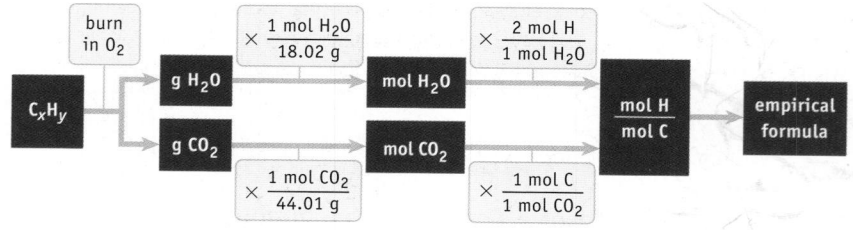

EXAMPLE 4.4 Using Combustion Analysis to Determine the Formula of a Hydrocarbon

Problem When 1.125 g of a liquid hydrocarbon, C_xH_y, was burned in an apparatus like that shown in
Figure 4.7, 3.447 g of CO_2 and 1.647 g of H_2O were produced. The molar mass of the compound was
found to be 86.2 g/mol in a separate experiment. Determine the empirical and molecular formulas for
the unknown hydrocarbon, C_xH_y.

Strategy As outlined in the preceding diagram, we first calculate the amounts of CO_2 and H_2O. These are
then converted to amounts of C and H. The ratio (mol H/mol C) is used to determine the empirical formula of the compound. The molar mass of the compound and the molar mass of the empirical formula are
then used to determine the molecular formula.

Solution The amounts of CO_2 and H_2O isolated from the combustion are

$$3.447 \text{ g } CO_2 \times \frac{1 \text{ mol } CO_2}{44.010 \text{ g } CO_2} = 0.07832 \text{ mol } CO_2$$

$$1.647 \text{ g } H_2O \times \frac{1 \text{ mol } H_2O}{18.015 \text{ g } H_2O} = 0.09142 \text{ mol } H_2O$$

For every mole of CO_2 isolated, 1 mol of C must have been present in the unknown compound.

$$0.07832 \text{ mol } CO_2 \times \frac{1 \text{ mol C in unknown}}{1 \text{ mol } CO_2} = 0.07832 \text{ mol C}$$

For every mole of H_2O isolated, 2 mol of H must have been present in the unknown.

$$0.09142 \text{ mol } H_2O \times \frac{2 \text{ mol H in unknown}}{1 \text{ mol } H_2O} = 0.1828 \text{ mol H}$$

The original 1.125 g sample of compound therefore contained 0.07832 mol of C and 0.1828 mol of H. To determine the empirical formula of the unknown, we find the ratio of moles of H to moles of C (◀ Section 2.10).

$$\frac{0.1828 \text{ mol H}}{0.07832 \text{ mol C}} = \frac{2.335 \text{ mol H}}{1.000 \text{ mol C}}$$

Atoms combine to form molecules in whole-number ratios. The translation of this ratio (2.335/1) to a whole-number ratio can usually be done quickly by trial and error. Multiplying the numerator and denominator by 3 gives 7/3. So, we know the ratio is 7 mol H to 3 mol C, which means the empirical formula of the hydrocarbon is C_3H_7.

Comparing the experimental molar mass with the molar mass calculated for the empirical formula,

$$\frac{\text{Experimental molar mass}}{\text{Molar mass of } C_3H_7} = \frac{86.2 \text{ g/mol}}{43.1 \text{ g/mol}} = \frac{2}{1}$$

we find that the molecular formula is twice the empirical formula. That is, the molecular formula is $(C_3H_7)_2$, or C_6H_{14}.

Comment As noted in Problem Solving Tip 2.3 (page 91), for problems of this type be sure to use data with enough significant figures to give accurate atom ratios. Finally, note that the determination of the molecular formula does not end the problem for a chemist. In this case, the formula C_6H_{14} is appropriate for several distinctly different compounds. Two of the five compounds having this formula are shown here:

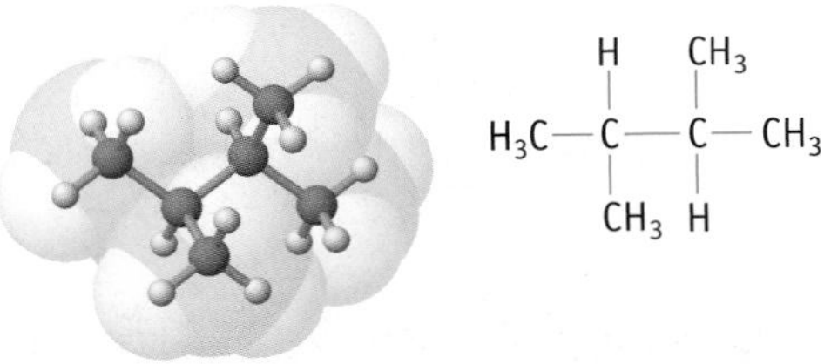

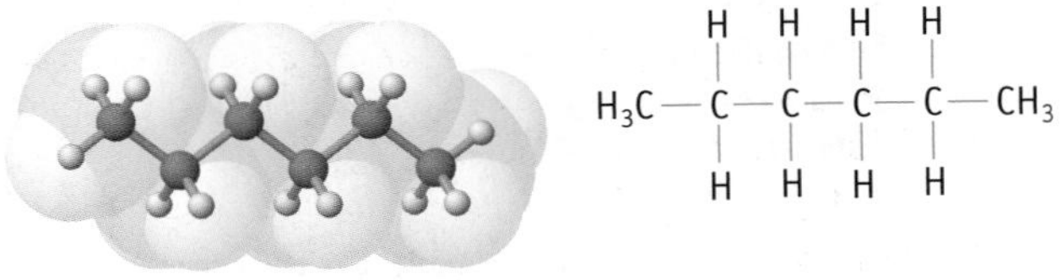

To determine the identity of the unknown compound, more laboratory experiments have to be done. One option is to use an NMR spectrometer such as is pictured in Figure 4.4 or to compare the properties of the unknown with values listed in the chemical literature.

EXERCISE 4.5 Determining the Empirical and Molecular Formulas for a Hydrocarbon

A 0.523-g sample of the unknown compound C_xH_y was burned in air to give 1.612 g of CO_2 and 0.7425 g of H_2O. A separate experiment gave a molar mass for C_xH_y of 114 g/mol. Determine the empirical and molecular formulas for the hydrocarbon.

4.5 Measuring Concentrations of Compounds in Solution

Most chemical studies require quantitative measurements, including experiments involving aqueous solutions. When doing such experiments, we continue to use balanced equations and moles, but we measure volumes of solution rather than masses of solids, liquids, or gases. Solution concentration expressed as molarity relates the volume of solution in liters to the amount of substance in moles.

Solution Concentration: Molarity

The concept of concentration is useful in many contexts. For example, about 5,500,000 people live in Wisconsin, and the state has a land area of roughly 56,000 square miles; therefore, the average concentration of people is about (5.5×10^6 people/5.6×10^4 square miles) or 98 people per square mile. In chemistry, the amount of solute dissolved in a given volume of solution, the concentration of the

■ **Molar and Molarity** Chemists use "molar" as an adjective to describe a solution. We use "molarity" as a noun. For example, we refer to a 0.1 molar solution or say the solution has a molarity of 0.1 mole per liter.

FIGURE 4.8 Volume of solution versus volume of solvent. To make a 0.100 M solution of $CuSO_4$, 25.0 g or 0.100 mol of $CuSO_4 \cdot 5 H_2O$ (the blue crystalline solid) was placed in a 1.00-L volumetric flask.

For this photo, we measured out exactly 1.00 L of water, which was slowly added to the volumetric flask containing $CuSO_4 \cdot 5 H_2O$. When enough water had been added so that the solution volume was exactly 1.00 L, approximately 8 mL (the quantity in the small graduated cylinder) was left over from the original 1.00 L of water. This emphasizes that molar concentrations are defined as moles of solute per liter of solution and not per liter of water or other solvent.

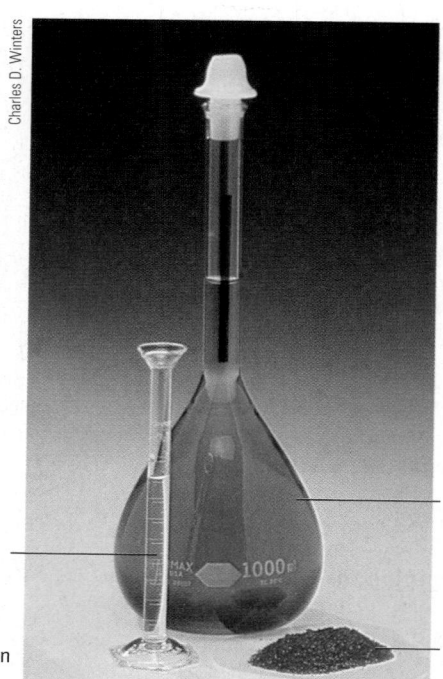

Charles D. Winters

Volume of water remaining when 1.00 L of water was used to make 1.00 L of a solution

1.00 L of 0.100 M $CuSO_4$

25.0 g or 0.100 mol of $CuSO_4 \cdot 5 H_2O$

solution, can be found in the same way. A useful unit of solute concentration, c, is **molarity**, which is defined as amount of solute per liter of solution.

$$\text{Molarity of } x \ (c_x) = \frac{\text{amount of solute } x \text{ (mol)}}{\text{volume of solution (L)}} \qquad (4.2)$$

For example, if 58.4 g (1.00 mol) of NaCl is dissolved in enough water to give a total solution volume of 1.00 L, the concentration, c, is 1.00 mol/L. This is often abbreviated as 1.00 M, where the capital "M" stands for "moles per liter." Another common notation is to place the formula of the compound in square brackets (for example, [NaCl]); this implies that the concentration of the solute in moles of compound per liter of solution is being specified.

$$c_{NaCl} = [NaCl] = 1.00 \ \text{mol/L} = 1.00 \ \text{M}$$

It is important to notice that molarity refers to the amount of solute per liter of solution and not per liter of solvent. If one liter of water is added to one mole of a solid compound, the final volume will not be exactly one liter, and the final concentration will not be exactly one mol/L (Figure 4.8). When making solutions of a given molarity, it is always the case that we dissolve the solute in a volume of solvent smaller than the desired volume of solution, then add solvent until the final solution volume is reached.

Potassium permanganate, $KMnO_4$, which was used at one time as a germicide in the treatment of burns, is a shiny, purple-black solid that dissolves readily in water to give a deep purple solution. Suppose 0.435 g of $KMnO_4$ has been dissolved in enough water to give 250. mL of solution (Figure 4.9). What is the concentration

■ **Volumetric Flask** A volumetric flask is a special flask with a line marked on its neck (see Figures 4.8 and 4.9). If the flask is filled with a solution to this line (at a given temperature), it contains precisely the volume of solution specified.

■ **NIST and Solution Concentration** The guidelines from NIST specify that the term "molarity" with its symbol M are obsolete and should no longer be used. Instead, the preferred name is "amount of substance concentration of X" or "amount concentration of X." The numerical value should be followed by the units mol/L. Thus, a solution of salt would be described as having a concentration of $c_{NaCl} = 1.00 \ \text{mol/L}$. Nonetheless, the use of the symbol M, of square brackets, and of the term molarity is so widespread that we shall continue to use them in this edition of the text. See http://physics.nist.gov/Pubs/SP811/sec08.html

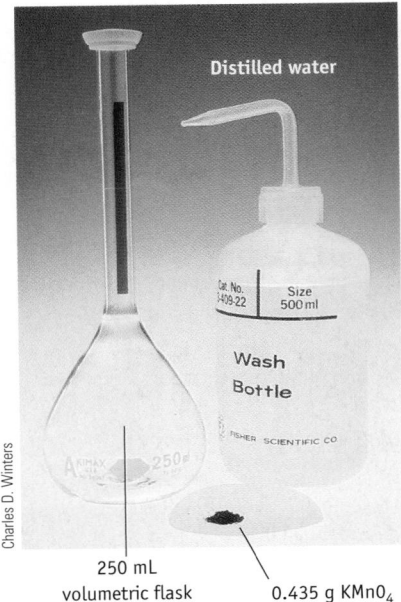

250 mL
volumetric flask   0.435 g $KMnO_4$

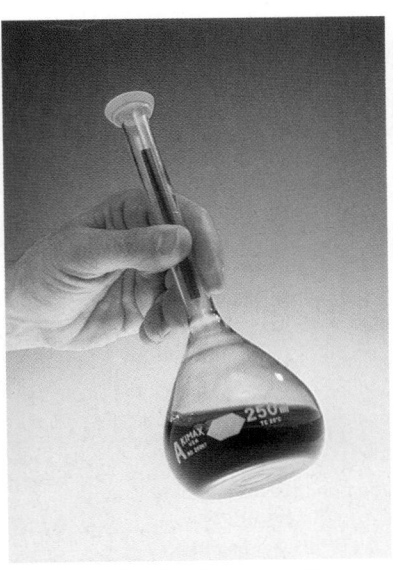

The $KMnO_4$ is first dissolved in a small amount of water.

Distilled water is added to fill the flask with solution just to the mark on the flask.

A mark on the neck of a volumetric flask indicates a volume of exactly 250. mL at 25 °C.

Charles D. Winters

Active Figure 4.9 **Making a solution.** A 0.0110 M solution of $KMnO_4$ is made by adding enough water to 0.435 g of $KMnO_4$ to make 0.250 L of solution.

Chemistry..Now™ **Sign in at www.cengage.com/login and go to the Chapter Contents menu to explore an interactive version of this figure accompanied by an exercise.**

Ion concentrations for a soluble ionic compound. Here, 1 mol of $CuCl_2$ dissociates to 1 mol of Cu^{2+} ions and 2 mol of Cl^- ions. Therefore, the Cl^- concentration is twice the concentration calculated for $CuCl_2$.

of $KMnO_4$? The first step is to convert the mass of $KMnO_4$ to an amount (moles) of solute.

$$0.435 \text{ g KMnO}_4 \times \frac{1 \text{ mol KMnO}_4}{158.0 \text{ g KMnO}_4} = 0.00275 \text{ mol KMnO}_4$$

Now that the amount of $KMnO_4$ is known, this information can be combined with the volume of solution—which must be in liters—to give the concentration. Because 250. mL is equivalent to 0.250 L,

$$\text{Concentration of KMnO}_4 = c_{KMnO_4} = [KMnO_4] = \frac{0.00275 \text{ mol KMnO}_4}{0.250 \text{ L}} = 0.0110 \text{ M}$$

The $KMnO_4$ concentration is 0.0110 mol/L, or 0.0110 M. This is useful information, but it is often equally useful to know the concentration of each type of ion in a solution. Like all soluble ionic compounds, $KMnO_4$ dissociates completely into its ions, K^+ and MnO_4^-, when dissolved in water.

$$KMnO_4(aq) \longrightarrow K^+(aq) + MnO_4^-(aq)$$
100% dissociation

One mole of $KMnO_4$ provides 1 mol of K^+ ions and 1 mol of MnO_4^- ions. Accordingly, 0.0110 M $KMnO_4$ gives a concentration of K^+ in the solution of 0.0110 M; similarly, the concentration of MnO_4^- is also 0.0110 M.

Another example of ion concentrations is provided by the dissociation of $CuCl_2$.

$$CuCl_2(aq) \longrightarrow Cu^{2+}(aq) + 2 Cl^-(aq)$$
100% dissociation

If 0.10 mol of $CuCl_2$ is dissolved in enough water to make 1.0 L of solution, the concentration of the copper(II) ion is $[Cu^{2+}] = 0.10$ M. However, the concentration of chloride ions, $[Cl^-]$, is 0.20 M because the compound dissociates in water to provide 2 mol of Cl^- ions for each mole of $CuCl_2$.

Chemistry Now™

Sign in at **www.cengage.com/login** and go to Chapter 4 Contents to see Screen 4.9 for a tutorial on determining **solution concentration** and for a tutorial on **determining ion concentration.**

EXAMPLE 4.5 Concentration

Problem If 25.3 g of sodium carbonate, Na_2CO_3, is dissolved in enough water to make 250. mL of solution, what is the concentration of Na_2CO_3? What are the concentrations of the Na^+ and CO_3^{2-} ions?

Strategy The concentration of Na_2CO_3 is defined as the amount of Na_2CO_3 per liter of solution. We know the volume of solution (0.250 L). We need the amount of Na_2CO_3. To find the concentrations of the individual ions, recognize that the dissolved salt dissociates completely.

$$Na_2CO_3(s) \rightarrow 2 Na^+(aq) + CO_3^{2-}(aq)$$

Solution Let us first find the amount of Na_2CO_3.

$$25.3 \text{ g Na}_2CO_3 \times \frac{1 \text{ mol Na}_2CO_3}{106.0 \text{ g Na}_2CO_3} = 0.239 \text{ mol Na}_2CO_3$$

and then the concentration of Na_2CO_3,

$$\text{Concentration of Na}_2CO_3 = \frac{0.239 \text{ mol Na}_2CO_3}{0.250 \text{ L}} = \boxed{0.955 \text{ mol/L}}$$

The ion concentrations follow from the concentration of Na_2CO_3 and the knowledge that each mole of Na_2CO_3 produces 2 mol of Na^+ ions and 1 mol of CO_3^{2-} ions.

$$0.955 \text{ M } Na_2CO_3(aq) \equiv 2 \times 0.955 \text{ M } Na^+(aq) + 0.955 \text{ M } CO_3^{2-}(aq)$$

That is, $[Na^+] = 1.91$ M and $[CO_3^{2-}] = 0.955$ M.

EXERCISE 4.7 Concentration

Sodium bicarbonate, $NaHCO_3$, is used in baking powder formulations and in the manufacture of plastics and ceramics, among other things. If 26.3 g of the compound is dissolved in enough water to make 200. mL of solution, what is the concentration of $NaHCO_3$? What are the concentrations of the ions in solution?

Preparing Solutions of Known Concentration

Chemists often have to prepare a given volume of solution of known concentration. There are two common ways to do this.

Combining a Weighed Solute with the Solvent

Suppose you wish to prepare 2.00 L of a 1.50 M solution of Na_2CO_3. You have some solid Na_2CO_3 and distilled water. You also have a 2.00-L volumetric flask (see Figures 4.8 and 4.9). To make the solution, you must weigh the necessary quantity of Na_2CO_3 as accurately as possible, carefully place all the solid in the volumetric flask, and then add some water to dissolve the solid. After the solid has dissolved completely, more water is added to bring the solution volume to 2.00 L. The solution then has the desired concentration and the volume specified.

But what mass of Na_2CO_3 is required to make 2.00 L of 1.50 M Na_2CO_3? First, calculate the amount of Na_2CO_3 required,

$$2.00 \text{ L} \times \frac{1.50 \text{ mol } Na_2CO_3}{1.00 \text{ L solution}} = 3.00 \text{ mol } Na_2CO_3 \text{ required}$$

and then the mass in grams.

$$3.00 \text{ mol } Na_2CO_3 \times \frac{106.0 \text{ g } Na_2CO_3}{1 \text{ mol } Na_2CO_3} = 318 \text{ g } Na_2CO_3$$

Thus, to prepare the desired solution, you should dissolve 318 g of Na_2CO_3 in enough water to make 2.00 L of solution.

EXERCISE 4.8 Preparing Solutions of Known Concentration

An experiment in your laboratory requires 250. mL of a 0.0200 M solution of $AgNO_3$. You are given solid $AgNO_3$, distilled water, and a 250.-mL volumetric flask. Describe how to make up the required solution.

Diluting a More Concentrated Solution

Another method of making a solution of a given concentration is to begin with a concentrated solution and add water until the desired, lower concentration is reached (Figure 4.10). Many of the solutions prepared for your laboratory course are probably made by this dilution method. It is more efficient to store a small volume of a concentrated solution and then, when needed, add water to make a much larger volume of a dilute solution.

Suppose you need 500. mL of 0.0010 M potassium dichromate, $K_2Cr_2O_7$, for use in chemical analysis. You have some 0.100 M $K_2Cr_2O_7$ solution available. To make

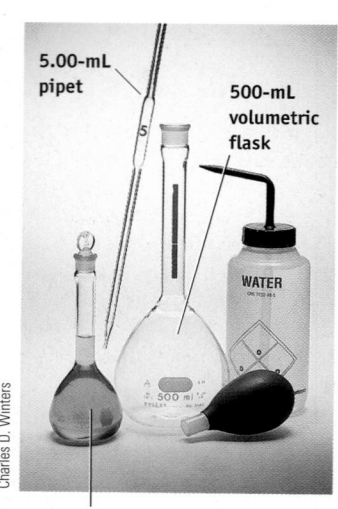

5.00-mL pipet

500-mL volumetric flask

WATER

0.100 M K₂Cr₂O₇

Charles D. Winters

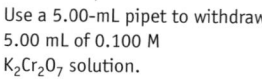

Use a 5.00-mL pipet to withdraw 5.00 mL of 0.100 M K₂Cr₂O₇ solution.

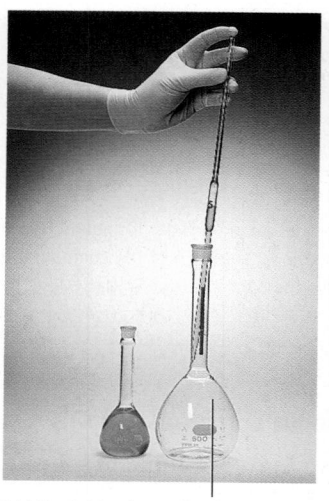

Add the 5.00-mL sample of 0.100 M K₂Cr₂O₇ solution to a 500-mL volumetric flask.

Fill the flask to the mark with distilled water to give 0.00100 M K₂Cr₂O₇ solution.

FIGURE 4.10 Making a solution by dilution. Here, 5.00 mL of a K₂Cr₂O₇ solution is diluted to 500. mL. This means the solution is diluted by a factor of 100, from 0.100 M to 0.00100 M.

■ **Diluting Concentrated Sulfuric Acid** The instruction that one prepares a solution by adding water to a more concentrated solution is correct, except for sulfuric acid solutions. When mixing water and sulfuric acid, the resulting solution becomes quite warm. If water is added to concentrated sulfuric acid, so much heat is evolved that the solution may boil over or splash and burn someone nearby. To avoid this problem, chemists always add concentrated sulfuric acid to water to make a dilute solution.

the required 0.0010 M solution, place a measured volume of the more concentrated K₂Cr₂O₇ solution in a flask, and then add water until the K₂Cr₂O₇ is contained in the appropriate larger volume of water (Figure 4.10).

What volume of a 0.100 M K₂Cr₂O₇ solution must be diluted to make the 0.0010 M solution? If the volume and concentration of a solution are known, the amount of solute is also known. Therefore, the amount of K₂Cr₂O₇ that must be in the final dilute solution is

$$\text{Amount of } K_2Cr_2O_7 \text{ in dilute solution} = c_{K_2Cr_2O_7} \times V_{K_2Cr_2O_7} = \left(\frac{0.0010 \text{ mol}}{L}\right) \times (0.500 \text{ L})$$
$$= 0.00050 \text{ mol } K_2Cr_2O_7$$

A more concentrated solution containing this amount of K₂Cr₂O₇ must be placed in a 500.-mL flask and then be diluted to the final volume. The volume of 0.100 M K₂Cr₂O₇ that must be transferred and diluted is 5.0 mL.

$$0.00050 \text{ mol } K_2Cr_2O_7 \times \frac{1.00 \text{ L}}{0.100 \text{ mol } K_2Cr_2O_7} = 0.0050 \text{ L or } 5.0 \text{ mL}$$

Thus, to prepare 500. mL of 0.0010 M K₂Cr₂O₇, place 5.0 mL of 0.100 M K₂Cr₂O₇ in a 500.-mL flask and add water until a volume of 500. mL is reached (see Figure 4.10).

Chemistry.◯.Now™

Sign in at **www.cengage.com/login** and go to Chapter 4 Contents to see Screen 4.11 for an exercise and a tutorial on **the direct addition method of preparing a solution** and for an exercise and tutorial on **the dilution method of preparing a solution.**

■ EXAMPLE 4.6 Preparing a Solution by Dilution

Problem What is the concentration of iron(III) ion in a solution prepared by diluting 1.00 mL of a 0.236 M solution of iron(III) nitrate to a volume of 100.0 mL?

Strategy First, calculate the amount of iron(III) ion in the 1.00-mL sample. The concentration of the ion in the final, dilute solution is equal to this amount of iron(III) divided by the new volume.

Solution The amount of iron(III) ion in the 1.00 mL sample is

$$\text{Amount of Fe}^{3+} = c_{Fe^{3+}} V_{Fe^{3+}} = \frac{0.236 \text{ mol Fe}^{3+}}{\text{L}} \times 1.00 \times 10^{-3} \text{ L} = 2.36 \times 10^{-4} \text{ mol Fe}^{3+}$$

This amount of iron(III) ion is distributed in the new volume of 100.0 mL, so the final concentration of the diluted solution is

$$c_{Fe^{3+}} = [Fe^{3+}] = \frac{2.36 \times 10^{-4} \text{ mol Fe}^{3+}}{0.100 \text{ L}} = 2.36 \times 10^{-3} \text{ M}$$

EXERCISE 4.9 Preparing a Solution by Dilution

An experiment calls for you to use 250. mL of 1.00 M NaOH, but you are given a large bottle of 2.00 M NaOH. Describe how to make desired volume of 1.00 M NaOH.

4.6 pH, a Concentration Scale for Acids and Bases

 Module 9

Vinegar, which contains the weak acid, acetic acid, has a hydronium ion concentration of only 1.2×10^{-3} M, and "pure" rainwater has $[H_3O^+] = 2.5 \times 10^{-6}$ M. These small values can be expressed using scientific notation, but a more convenient way to express such numbers is the logarithmic pH scale.

The pH of a solution is the negative of the base-10 logarithm of the hydronium ion concentration.

$$pH = -\log[H_3O^+] \qquad (4.3)$$

Taking vinegar, pure water, blood, and ammonia as examples,

pH of vinegar	$= -\log(1.2 \times 10^{-3} \text{ M}) = -(-2.92) = 2.92$
pH of pure water (at 25 °C)	$= -\log(1.0 \times 10^{-7} \text{ M}) = -(-7.00) = 7.00$
pH of blood	$= -\log(4.0 \times 10^{-8} \text{ M}) = -(-7.40) = 7.40$
pH of household ammonia	$= -\log(4.3 \times 10^{-12} \text{ M}) = -(-11.37) = 11.37$

you see that something you recognize as acidic has a relatively low pH, whereas ammonia, a common base, has a very low hydronium ion concentration and a high

■ **pH of Pure Water** Highly purified water, which is said to be "neutral," has a pH of exactly 7 at 25 °C. This is the "dividing line" between acidic substances (pH < 7) and basic substances (pH > 7) at 25 °C.

We often find in the laboratory that a solution is too concentrated for the analytical technique we want to use. You might want to analyze a seawater sample for its chloride ion content, for instance. To obtain a solution with a chloride concentration of the proper magnitude for analysis by the Mohr method (Case Study, page 186), for example, you might want to dilute the sample, not once but several times.

Suppose you have 100.0 mL of a seawater sample that has a NaCl concentration of 0.550 mol/L. You transfer 10.0 mL of that sample to a 100.0-mL volumetric flask and fill to the mark with distilled water. You then transfer 5.00 mL of that diluted sample to another 100.0 mL flask and fill to the mark with distilled water. What is the NaCl concentration in the final 100.0-mL sample?

The original solution contains 0.550 mol/L of NaCl. If you remove 10.00 mL, you have removed

$$0.01000 \text{ L} \times 0.550 \text{ mol/L}$$
$$= 5.50 \times 10^{-3} \text{ mol NaCl}$$

and the concentration in 100.0 mL of the diluted solution is

$$c_{NaCl} = 5.50 \times 10^{-3} \text{ mol/0.100 L}$$
$$= 5.50 \times 10^{-2} \text{ M}$$

or 1/10 of the concentration of the original solution (because we diluted the sample by a factor of 10).

Now we take 5.0 mL of the diluted solution and dilute that once again to 100.0 mL. The final concentration is

$$0.00500 \text{ L} \times 5.50 \times 10^{-2} \text{ mol/L}$$
$$= 2.75 \times 10^{-4} \text{ mol NaCl}$$

$$c_{NaCl} = 2.75 \times 10^{-4} \text{ mol/0.1000 L}$$
$$= 2.75 \times 10^{-3} \text{ M}$$

This is 1/200 of the concentration of the original solution.

A fair question at this point is why we did not just take 1 mL of the original solution and dilute to 200 mL. The answer is that there is less error in using larger pipets such as 5.00- or 10.00-mL pipets rather than a 1.00-mL pipet. And then there is a limitation in available glassware. A 200.00-mL volumetric flask is not often available.

Question: *You have a 100.0-mL sample of a blue dye having a concentration of 0.36 M. You dilute a 10.0-mL sample of this to 100.0 mL and then a 2.00-mL sample of that solution to 100.0 mL. What is the final dye concentration? (Answer: 7.2 × 10⁻⁴ M)*

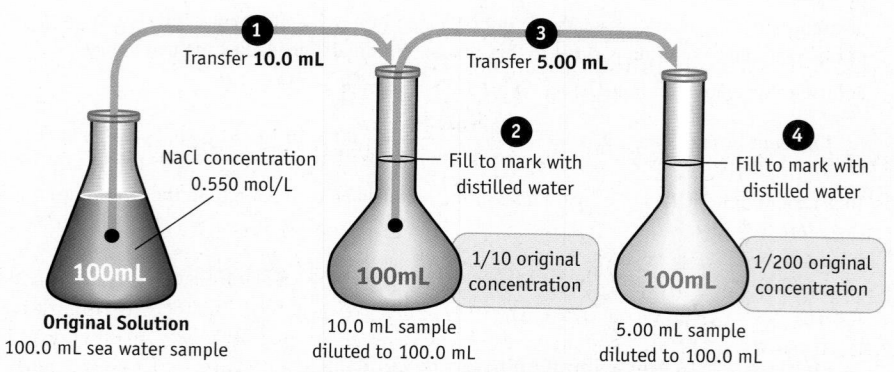

Transfer **10.0 mL**   Transfer **5.00 mL**

①   ③

② Fill to mark with distilled water

④ Fill to mark with distilled water

NaCl concentration 0.550 mol/L

100mL — **Original Solution** 100.0 mL sea water sample

100mL — 1/10 original concentration — 10.0 mL sample diluted to 100.0 mL

100mL — 1/200 original concentration — 5.00 mL sample diluted to 100.0 mL

pH. Blood, which your common sense tells you is likely to be neither acidic nor basic, has a pH near 7. Indeed, for aqueous solutions at 25 °C, we can say that acids will have pH values less than 7, bases will have values greater than 7, and a pH of 7 represents a neutral solution (Figure 4.11).

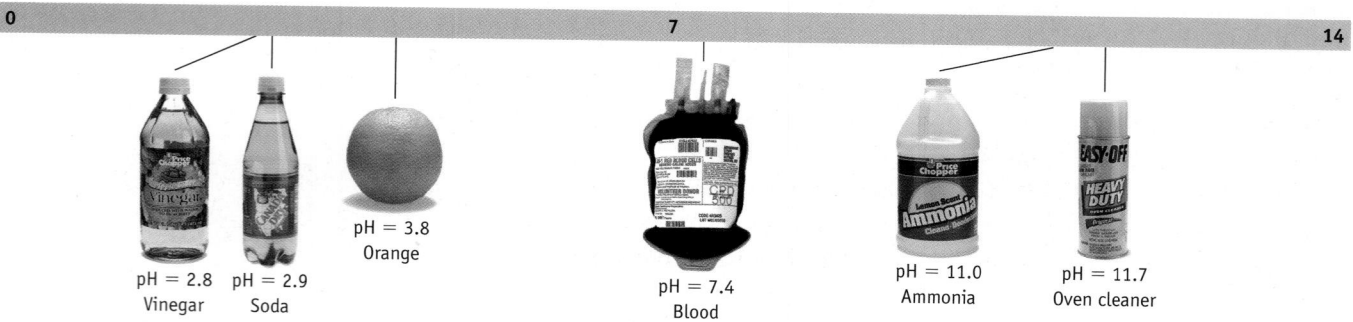

0   7   14

pH = 2.8 Vinegar   pH = 2.9 Soda   pH = 3.8 Orange   pH = 7.4 Blood   pH = 11.0 Ammonia   pH = 11.7 Oven cleaner

Active Figure 4.11 pH values of some common substances. Here, the "bar" is colored red at one end and blue at the other. These are the colors of litmus paper, commonly used in the laboratory to decide whether a solution is acidic (litmus is red) or basic (litmus is blue).

Chemistry Now™ Sign in at www.cengage.com/login and go to the Chapter Contents menu to explore an interactive version of this figure accompanied by an exercise.

(a)

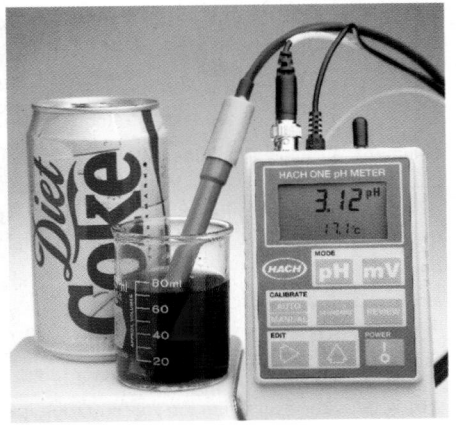
(b)

FIGURE 4.12 Determining pH.
(a) Some household products. Each solution contains a few drops of a universal indicator, a mixture of several acid–base indicators. A color of yellow or red indicates a pH less than 7. A green to purple color indicates a pH greater than 7. (b) The pH of a soda is measured with a modern pH meter. Soft drinks are often quite acidic, owing to the dissolved CO_2 and other ingredients.

Suppose you know the pH of a solution. To find the hydronium ion concentration, you take the antilog of the pH. That is,

$$[H_3O^+] = 10^{-pH} \qquad (4.4)$$

For example, the pH of a diet soda is 3.12, and the hydronium ion concentration of the solution is

$$[H_3O^+] = 10^{-3.12} = 7.6 \times 10^{-4} \text{ M}$$

The approximate pH of a solution may be determined using any of a variety of dyes. Litmus paper contains a dye extracted from a type of lichen, but many other dyes are also available (Figure 4.12a). A more accurate measurement of pH is done with a pH meter such as that shown in Figure 4.12b. Here, a pH electrode is immersed in the solution to be tested, and the pH is read from the instrument.

Chemistry.ᴼ.Now™

Sign in at **www.cengage.com/login** and go to Chapter 4 Contents to see Screen 4.11 for a tutorial on **determining the pH of a solution.**

■ **Logarithms** Numbers less than 1 have negative logs. Defining pH as $-\log[H^+]$ produces a positive number. See Appendix A for a discussion of logs.

■ **Logs and Your Calculator** All scientific calculators have a key marked "log." To find an antilog, use the key marked "10^x" or the inverse log. In determining $[H_3O^+]$ from a pH, when you enter the value of x for 10^x, make sure it has a negative sign.

■ **pH-Indicating Dyes** Many natural substances change color in solution as pH changes. See the extract of red cabbage in Figure 3.12. Tea changes color when acidic lemon juice is added.

■ **EXAMPLE 4.7 pH of Solutions**

Problem

(a) Lemon juice has $[H_3O^+] = 0.0032$ M. What is its pH?

(b) Sea water has a pH of 8.30. What is the hydronium ion concentration of this solution?

(c) A solution of nitric acid has a concentration of 0.0056 mol/L. What is the pH of this solution?

Strategy Use Equation 4.3 to calculate pH from the H_3O^+ concentration. Use Equation 4.4 to find $[H_3O^+]$ from the pH.

Solution

(a) Lemon juice: Because the hydronium ion concentration is known, the pH is found using Equation 4.3.

$$pH = -\log[H_3O^+] = -\log(3.2 \times 10^{-3}) = -(-2.49) = \boxed{2.49}$$

(b) Sea water: Here, pH = 8.30. Therefore,

$$[H_3O^+] = 10^{-pH} = 10^{-8.30} = \boxed{5.0 \times 10^{-9} \text{ M}}$$

(c) Nitric acid: Nitric acid, a strong acid (Table 3.2, page 132), is completely ionized in aqueous solution. Because the concentration of HNO_3 is 0.0056 mol/L, the ion concentrations are

$$[H_3O^+] = [NO_3^-] = 0.0056 \text{ M}$$
$$pH = -\log[H_3O^+] = -\log(0.0056 \text{ M}) = \boxed{2.25}$$

Comment A comment on logarithms and significant figures (Appendix A) is useful. The number to the left of the decimal point in a logarithm is called the *characteristic*, and the number to the right is the *mantissa*. The mantissa has as many significant figures as the number whose log was found. For example, the logarithm of 3.2×10^{-3} (two significant figures) is 2.49 (two numbers to the right of the decimal point).

EXERCISE 4.10 pH of Solutions

(a) What is the pH of a solution of HCl in which $[HCl] = 2.6 \times 10^{-2}$ M?

(b) What is the hydronium ion concentration in orange juice with a pH of 3.80?

4.7 Stoichiometry of Reactions in Aqueous Solution

Solution Stoichiometry

Suppose we want to know what mass of $CaCO_3$ is required to react completely with 25 mL of 0.750 M HCl. The first step in finding the answer is to write a balanced equation. In this case, we have a gas-forming exchange reaction involving a metal carbonate and an aqueous acid (Figure 4.13).

$$CaCO_3(s) + 2\ HCl(aq) \longrightarrow CaCl_2(aq) + H_2O(\ell) + CO_2(g)$$
$$\text{metal carbonate} + \quad \text{acid} \quad \longrightarrow \quad \text{salt} \quad + \text{ water } + \text{ carbon dioxide}$$

This problem can be solved in the same way as all the stoichiometry problems you have seen so far, except that the quantity of one reactant is given as a volume of a solution of known concentration instead of as a mass in grams. The first step is to find the amount of HCl.

$$\text{Amount of HCl} = c_{HCl}V_{HCl} = \frac{0.750 \text{ mol HCl}}{1 \text{ L HCl}} \times 0.025 \text{ L HCl} = 0.019 \text{ mol HCl}$$

This is then related to the amount of $CaCO_3$ required.

$$0.019 \text{ mol HCl} \times \frac{1 \text{ mol CaCO}_3}{2 \text{ mol HCl}} = 0.0094 \text{ mol CaCO}_3$$

Finally, the amount of $CaCO_3$ is converted to a mass in grams.

$$0.0094 \text{ mol CaCO}_3 \times \frac{100. \text{ g CaCO}_3}{1 \text{ mol CaCO}_3} = 0.94 \text{ g CaCO}_3$$

Chemists are likely to do such calculations many times in the course of their work. If you follow the general scheme outlined in Problem Solving Tip 4.4 and pay attention to the units on the numbers, you can successfully carry out any kind of stoichiometry calculations involving concentrations.

Chemistry ∴ Now™

Sign in at **www.cengage.com/login** and go to Chapter 4 Contents to see Screen 4.12 for an exercise on **solution stoichiometry**, for a tutorial on **determining the mass of a product**, and for a tutorial on **determining the volume of a reactant.**

FIGURE 4.13 A commercial remedy for excess stomach acid. The tablet contains calcium carbonate, which reacts with hydrochloric acid, the acid present in the digestive system. The most obvious product is CO_2 gas.

Charles D. Winters

Stoichiometry Calculations Involving Solutions

In Problem Solving Tip 4.1, you learned about a general approach to stoichiometry problems. We can now modify that scheme for a reaction involving solutions such as x A(aq) + y B(aq) ⟶ products.

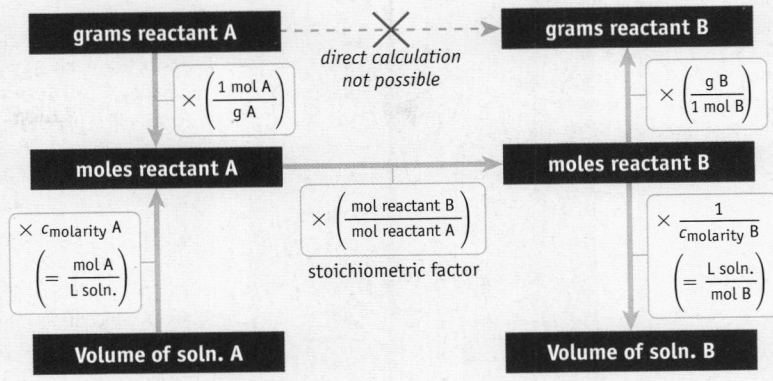

■ **EXAMPLE 4.8 Stoichiometry of a Reaction in Solution**

Problem Metallic zinc reacts with aqueous HCl.

$$Zn(s) + 2\ HCl(aq) \longrightarrow ZnCl_2(aq) + H_2(g)$$

What volume of 2.50 M HCl, in milliliters, is required to convert 11.8 g of Zn completely to products?

Strategy Here, the mass of zinc is known, so you first calculate the amount of zinc. Next, use a stoichiometric factor (= 2 mol HCl/1 mol Zn) to relate amount of HCl required to amount of Zn available. Finally, calculate the volume of HCl from the amount of HCl and its concentration.

Solution Begin by calculating the amount of Zn.

$$11.8\ \text{g Zn} \times \frac{1\ \text{mol Zn}}{65.39\ \text{g Zn}} = 0.180\ \text{mol Zn}$$

Use the stoichiometric factor to calculate the amount of HCl required.

$$0.180\ \text{mol Zn} \times \frac{2\ \text{mol HCl}}{1\ \text{mol Zn}} = 0.360\ \text{mol HCl}$$

Use the amount of HCl and the solution concentration to calculate the volume.

$$0.360\ \text{mol HCl} \times \frac{1.00\ \text{L solution}}{2.50\ \text{mol HCl}} = \boxed{0.144\ \text{L HCl}}$$

The answer is requested in units of milliliters, so we convert the volume to milliliters and find that 144 mL of 2.50 M HCl is required to convert 11.8 g of Zn completely to products.

EXERCISE 4.11 Solution Stoichiometry

If you combine 75.0 mL of 0.350 M HCl and an excess of Na_2CO_3, what mass of CO_2, in grams, is produced?

$$Na_2CO_3(s) + 2\ HCl(aq) \longrightarrow 2\ NaCl(aq) + H_2O(\ell) + CO_2(g)$$

Titration: A Method of Chemical Analysis

Oxalic acid, $H_2C_2O_4$, is a naturally occurring acid. Suppose you are asked to determine the mass of this acid in an impure sample. Because the compound is an acid, it reacts with a base such as sodium hydroxide.

$$H_2C_2O_4(aq) + 2\ NaOH(aq) \longrightarrow Na_2C_2O_4(aq) + 2\ H_2O(\ell)$$

■ **Titrations** Acid–base titrations are discussed in more detail in Chapter 18.

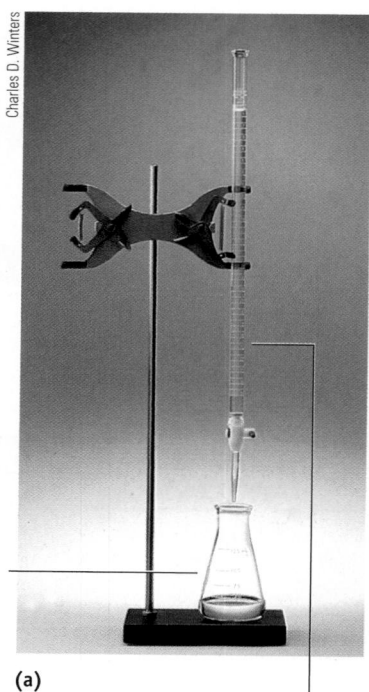

Charles D. Winters

Flask containing aqueous solution of sample being analyzed

(a)
Buret containing aqueous NaOH of accurately known concentration.

(b)
A solution of NaOH is added slowly to the sample being analyzed.

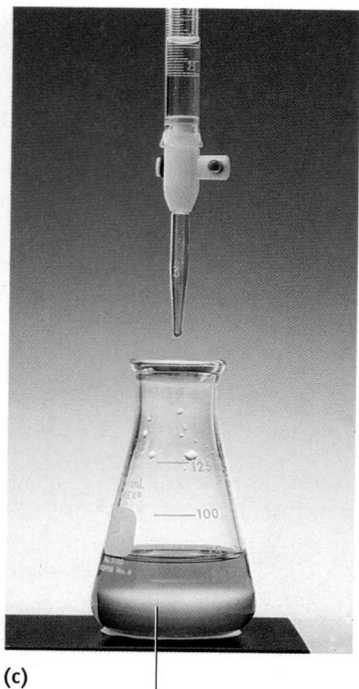

(c)
When the amount of NaOH added from the buret equals the amount of H_3O^+ supplied by the acid being analyzed, the dye (indicator) changes color.

Active Figure 4.14 **Titration of an acid in aqueous solution with a base.** (a) A buret, a volumetric measuring device calibrated in divisions of 0.1 mL, is filled with an aqueous solution of a base of known concentration. (b) Base is added slowly from the buret to the solution containing the acid being analyzed and an indicator. (c) A change in the color of the indicator signals the equivalence point. (The indicator used here is phenolphthalein.)

Chemistry ⚛ Now™ **Sign in at www.cengage.com/login and go to the Chapter Contents menu to explore an interactive version of this figure accompanied by an exercise.**

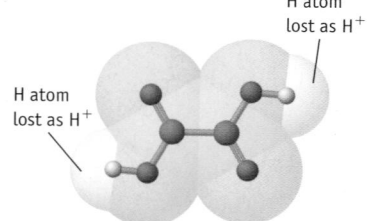

H atom lost as H^+

H atom lost as H^+

Oxalic acid $H_2C_2O_4$

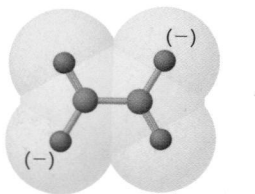

(−)

(−)

Oxalate anion $C_2O_4{}^{2-}$

Oxalic acid. Oxalic acid has two groups that can supply an H^+ ion to solution. Hence, 1 mol of the acid requires 2 mol of NaOH for complete reaction.

You can use this reaction to determine the quantity of oxalic acid present in a given mass of sample if the following conditions are met:

- You can determine when the amount of sodium hydroxide added is just enough to react with all the oxalic acid present in solution.
- You know the concentration of the sodium hydroxide solution and the volume that has been added at the point of complete reaction.

These conditions are fulfilled in a titration, a procedure illustrated in Figure 4.14. The solution containing oxalic acid is placed in a flask along with an acid–base indicator, a dye that changes color when the pH of the reaction solution reaches a certain value. Aqueous sodium hydroxide of accurately known concentration is placed in a buret. The sodium hydroxide in the buret is added slowly to the acid solution in the flask. As long as some acid is present in solution, all the base supplied from the buret is consumed, the solution remains acidic, and the indicator color is unchanged. At some point, however, the amount of OH^- added exactly equals the amount of H_3O^+

that can be supplied by the acid. This is called the **equivalence point**. As soon as the slightest excess of base has been added beyond the equivalence point, the solution becomes basic, and the indicator changes color (see Figure 4.14). The example that follows shows how to use the equivalence point and the other information to determine the percentage of oxalic acid in a mixture.

Chemistry⚛Now™

Sign in at **www.cengage.com/login** and go to Chapter 4 Contents to see Screen 4.13 for a tutorial on the **volume of titrant used,** for a tutorial on **determining the concentration of acid solution,** and for a tutorial on **determining the concentration of an unknown acid.**

EXAMPLE 4.9 **Acid–Base Titration**

Problem A 1.034-g sample of impure oxalic acid is dissolved in water and an acid–base indicator added. The sample requires 34.47 mL of 0.485 M NaOH to reach the equivalence point. What is the mass of oxalic acid, and what is its mass percent in the sample?

Strategy The balanced equation for the reaction of NaOH and $H_2C_2O_4$ is

$$H_2C_2O_4(aq) + 2\ NaOH(aq) \longrightarrow Na_2C_2O_4(aq) + 2\ H_2O(\ell)$$

The concentration and volume of NaOH delivered in the titration are used to determine the amount of NaOH. A stoichiometric factor is used to relate the amount of NaOH to the amount of $H_2C_2O_4$, and the amount of $H_2C_2O_4$ is converted to a mass. The mass percent of acid in the sample is then calculated. See Problem Solving Tip 4.4.

Solution The amount of NaOH is given by

$$\text{Amount of NaOH} = c_{NaOH} \times V_{NaOH} = \frac{0.485\ \text{mol NaOH}}{\text{L}} \times 0.03447\ \text{L} = 0.0167\ \text{mol NaOH}$$

The balanced equation for the reaction shows that 1 mol of oxalic acid requires 2 mol of sodium hydroxide. This is the required stoichiometric factor to obtain the amount of oxalic acid present.

$$0.0167\ \text{mol NaOH} \times \frac{1\ \text{mol } H_2C_2O_4}{2\ \text{mol NaOH}} = 0.00836\ \text{mol } H_2C_2O_4$$

The mass of oxalic acid is found from the amount of the acid.

$$0.00836\ \text{mol } H_2C_2O_4 \times \frac{90.04\ \text{g } H_2C_2O_4}{1\ \text{mol } H_2C_2O_4} = 0.753\ \text{g } H_2C_2O_4$$

This mass of oxalic acid represents 72.8% of the total sample mass.

$$\frac{0.753\ \text{g } H_2C_2O_4}{1.034\ \text{g sample}} \times 100\% = 72.8\%\ H_2C_2O_4$$

EXERCISE 4.12 **Acid–Base Titration**

A 25.0-mL sample of vinegar (which contains the weak acid, acetic acid, CH_3CO_2H) requires 28.33 mL of a 0.953 M solution of NaOH for titration to the equivalence point. What mass of acetic acid, in grams, is in the vinegar sample, and what is the concentration of acetic acid in the vinegar?

$$CH_3CO_2H(aq) + NaOH(aq) \longrightarrow NaCH_3CO_2(aq) + H_2O(\ell)$$

How Much Salt Is There in Seawater?

There is a French legend about a princess who told her father, the king, that she loved him as much as she loved salt. Thinking that this was not a great measure of love, he banished her from the kingdom. Only later did he realize how much he needed, and valued, salt.

Salt has played a key role in history. The earliest written record of salt production dates from around 800 BC, but the sea has always been a source of salt, and there is evidence of the Chinese harvesting salt from seawater by 6000 BC.

The average human body contains about 50 g of salt. Because we continually lose salt in urine, sweat, and other excretions, salt must be a part of our diet. Early humans recognized that salt deficiency causes headaches, cramps, loss of appetite, and, in extreme cases, death. Consuming meat provides salt, but consuming vegetables does not. This is the reason herbivorous animals seek out salt.

Saltiness is one of the basic taste sensations, and a taste of seawater quickly reveals it is salty. How did the oceans become salty? And why is chloride ion the most abundant ion?

A result of the interaction of atmospheric CO_2 and water is hydronium ions and bicarbonate ions.

$$CO_2(g) + H_2O(\ell) \longrightarrow H_2CO_3(aq)$$

$$H_2CO_3(aq) + H_2O(\ell) \rightleftharpoons H_3O^+(aq) + HCO_3^-(aq)$$

Indeed, this is the reason rain is normally acidic, and this slightly acidic rainwater can then cause substances such as limestone or corals to dissolve, producing calcium ions and more bicarbonate ions.

$$CaCO_3(s) + CO_2(g) + H_2O(\ell) \longrightarrow$$
$$Ca^{2+}(aq) + 2\ HCO_3^-(aq)$$

Seawater contains many dissolved salts. Among the ions in seawater are halide anions, alkali metal cations, and anions such as carbonate and hydrogen phosphate. See Table 3.1, page 122.

Sodium ions arrive in the oceans by a similar reaction with sodium-bearing minerals such as albite, $NaAlSi_3O_6$. Acidic rain falling on the land extracts sodium ions that are then carried by rivers to the ocean.

The average chloride content of rocks in the earth's crust is only 0.01%, so only a minute proportion of the chloride ion in the oceans can come from the weathering of rocks and minerals. What then is the origin of the chloride ions in seawater? The answer is volcanoes. Hydrogen chloride gas, HCl, is a constituent of volcanic gases. Early in Earth's history, the planet was much hotter, and volcanoes were much more widespread. The HCl gas emitted from these volcanoes is very soluble in water and is quickly dissolved to give a dilute solution of hydrochloric acid. The chloride ions from dissolved HCl gas and sodium ions from weathered rocks are the source of the salt in the sea.

Suppose you are an oceanographer, and you want to determine the concentration of chloride ions in a sample of seawater. How can you do this? And what results might you find?

There are several ways to analyze a solution for its chloride ion content, among them the classic "Mohr method." Here, a solution containing chloride ions is titrated with standardized silver nitrate. You know that the following reaction should occur,

$$Ag^+(aq) + Cl^-(aq) \longrightarrow AgCl(s)$$

and will continue until the chloride ions have been precipitated completely. To detect the equivalence point of the titration of Cl^- with Ag^+, the Mohr method specifies the addition of a few drops of a solution of potassium chromate. This "indicator" works because silver chromate is slightly more soluble than AgCl, so the red Ag_2CrO_4 precipitates only after all of the AgCl is precipitated.

$$2\ Ag^+(aq) + CrO_4^{2-}(aq) \longrightarrow Ag_2CrO_4(s)$$

The appearance of the red color of Ag_2CrO_4 (see Figure 3.11d) signals the equivalence point.

Question:

1. *Using the following information, calculate the chloride ion concentration in a sample of seawater.*
   a. *Volume of original seawater sample = 100.0 mL.*
   b. *A 10.00 mL sample of the seawater was diluted to 100.0 mL with distilled water.*
   c. *10.00 mL of the diluted sample was again diluted to 100.0 mL.*
   d. *A Mohr titration was done on 50.00 mL of the diluted sample (from step 3) and required 26.25 mL of 0.100 M $AgNO_3$. What was the chloride ion concentration in the original seawater sample?*

Answer to this question is in Appendix Q.

Standardizing an Acid or Base

In Example 4.9, the concentration of the base used in the titration was given. In actual practice, this usually has to be found by a prior measurement. The procedure by which the concentration of an analytical reagent is determined accurately is called **standardization**, and there are two general approaches.

One approach is to weigh accurately a sample of a pure, solid acid or base (known as a *primary standard*) and then titrate this sample with a solution of the base or acid to be standardized (Example 4.10). An alternative approach to standardizing a solution is to titrate it with another solution that is already standardized (Exercise 4.13). This is often done using standard solutions purchased from chemical supply companies.

EXAMPLE 4.10 Standardizing an Acid by Titration

Problem Sodium carbonate, Na_2CO_3, is a base, and an accurately weighed sample can be used to standardize an acid. A sample of sodium carbonate (0.263 g) requires 28.35 mL of aqueous HCl for titration to the equivalence point. What is the concentration of the HCl?

Strategy The balanced equation for the reaction is written first.

$$Na_2CO_3(aq) + 2\ HCl(aq) \longrightarrow 2\ NaCl(aq) + H_2O(\ell) + CO_2(g)$$

The amount of Na_2CO_3 can be calculated from its mass, and then, using the stoichiometric factor, the amount of HCl in 28.35 mL can be calculated. The amount of HCl divided by the volume of solution (in liters) gives its concentration (mol/L).

Solution Convert the mass of Na_2CO_3 used as the standard to amount.

$$0.263\ g\ Na_2CO_3 \times \frac{1\ mol\ Na_2CO_3}{106.0\ g\ Na_2CO_3} = 0.00248\ mol\ Na_2CO_3$$

Use the stoichiometric factor to calculate the amount of HCl in 28.35 mL.

$$0.00248\ mol\ Na_2CO_3 \times \frac{2\ mol\ HCl\ required}{1\ mol\ Na_2CO_3\ available} = 0.00496\ mol\ HCl$$

The 28.35-mL (0.02835-L) sample of aqueous HCl contains 0.00496 mol of HCl, so the concentration of the HCl solution is 0.175 M.

$$[HCl] = \frac{0.00496\ mol\ HCl}{0.02835\ L} = \boxed{0.175\ M}$$

Comment In this example, Na_2CO_3 is a primary standard. Sodium carbonate can be obtained in pure form, can be weighed accurately, and reacts completely with a strong acid.

EXERCISE 4.13 Standardization of a Base

Hydrochloric acid, HCl, can be purchased from chemical supply houses with a concentration of 0.100 M, and this solution can be used to standardize the solution of a base. If titrating 25.00 mL of a sodium hydroxide solution to the equivalence point requires 29.67 mL of 0.100 M HCl, what is the concentration of the base?

Determining Molar Mass by Titration

In Chapter 2 and this chapter, we used analytical data to determine the empirical formula of a compound. The molecular formula could then be derived if the molar mass were known. If the unknown substance is an acid or a base, it is possible to determine the molar mass by titration.

EXAMPLE 4.11 Determining the Molar Mass of an Acid by Titration

Problem To determine the molar mass of an organic acid, HA, we titrate 1.056 g of HA with standardized NaOH. Calculate the molar mass of HA assuming the acid reacts with 33.78 mL of 0.256 M NaOH according to the equation

$$HA(aq) + OH^-(aq) \longrightarrow A^-(aq) + H_2O(\ell)$$

Strategy The key to this problem is to recognize that the molar mass of a substance is the ratio of the mass of a sample (g) to the amount of substance (mol) in the sample. Here, molar mass of HA = 1.056 g HA/x mol HA. Because 1 mol of HA reacts with 1 mol of NaOH in this case, the amount of acid (x mol) is equal to the amount of NaOH used in the titration, which is determined by its concentration and volume.

Solution Let us first calculate the amount of NaOH used in the titration.

$$\text{Amount of NaOH} = c_{NaOH}V_{NaOH} = \frac{0.256\ mol}{L} \times 0.03378\ L = 8.65 \times 10^{-3}\ mol\ NaOH$$

Next, recognize that the amount of NaOH used in the titration is the same as the amount of acid titrated. That is,

$$8.65 \times 10^{-3} \text{ mol NaOH} \times \frac{1 \text{ mol HA}}{1 \text{ mol NaOH}} = 8.65 \times 10^{-3} \text{ mol HA}$$

Finally, calculate the molar mass of HA.

$$\text{Molar mass of acid} = \frac{1.056 \text{ g HA}}{8.65 \times 10^{-3} \text{ mol HA}} = \boxed{122 \text{ g/mol}}$$

EXERCISE 4.14 Determining the Molar Mass of an Acid by Titration

An acid reacts with NaOH according to the net ionic equation

$$HA(aq) + OH^-(aq) \longrightarrow A^-(aq) + H_2O(\ell)$$

Calculate the molar mass of HA if 0.856 g of the acid requires 30.08 mL of 0.323 M NaOH.

Titrations Using Oxidation-Reduction Reactions

Analysis by titration is not limited to acid–base chemistry. Many oxidation-reduction reactions go rapidly to completion in aqueous solution, and methods exist to determine their equivalence point.

■ EXAMPLE 4.12 Using an Oxidation-Reduction Reaction in a Titration

Problem The iron in a sample of an iron ore can be converted quantitatively to the iron(II) ion, Fe^{2+}, in aqueous solution, and this solution can then be titrated with aqueous potassium permanganate, $KMnO_4$. The balanced, net ionic equation for the reaction occurring in the course of this titration is

$$MnO_4^-(aq) + 5 Fe^{2+}(aq) + 8 H_3O^+(aq) \longrightarrow Mn^{2+}(aq) + 5 Fe^{3+}(aq) + 12 H_2O(\ell)$$

purple   colorless   colorless   pale yellow

Case Study

Forensic Chemistry: Titrations and Food Tampering

The U.S. Food and Drug Administration (FDA) has recently discovered cases of product tampering involving the addition of bleach to products such as soup, infant formula, and soft drinks. Household bleach is a dilute solution of sodium hypochlorite (NaClO), a compound that is an oxidizing agent and is dangerous if swallowed.

One method of detecting bleach uses starch-iodide paper. The bleach oxidizes the iodide ion to iodine in an acid solution,

$$2 I^-(aq) + HClO(aq) + H_3O^+(aq) \longrightarrow$$
$$I_2(aq) + 2 H_2O(\ell) + Cl^-(aq)$$

and the I_2 is then detected by a deep blue color in the presence of starch.

This reaction is also used in the quantitative analysis of solutions containing bleach. Excess iodide ion (in the form of KI) is added to the sample. The bleach in the sample (which forms HClO in acid solution) oxidizes

I^- in a ratio of 1 mol HClO to 2 mol I^-. The iodine formed in the reaction is then titrated with sodium thiosulfate, $Na_2S_2O_3$ in another oxidation-reduction reaction (as in Exercise 4.15).

$$I_2(aq) + 2 S_2O_3^{2-}(aq) \longrightarrow$$
$$2 I^-(aq) + S_4O_6^{2-}(aq)$$

The amount of $Na_2S_2O_3$ used in the titration can then be used to determine the amount of NaClO in the sample.

Question:
Excess KI is added to a 100.0 mL sample of a soft drink that had been contaminated with bleach, NaClO. The iodine (I_2) generated in the solution was then titrated with 0.0425 M $Na_2S_2O_3$ and required 25.3 mL to reach the equivalence point. What mass of NaClO was contained in the 100.0-mL sample of adulterated soft drink?

Answer to this question is in Appendix Q.

A distinctive blue color is generated when iodine reacts with water-soluble starch.

Charles D. Winters

A 1.026-g sample of iron-containing ore requires 24.35 mL of 0.0195 M $KMnO_4$ to reach the equivalence point. What is the mass percent of iron in the ore?

Strategy Because the volume and concentration of the $KMnO_4$ solution are known, the amount of $KMnO_4$ used in the titration can be calculated. Using the stoichiometric factor, the amount of $KMnO_4$ is related to the amount of iron(II) ion. The amount of iron(II) is converted to its mass, and the mass percent of iron in the sample is determined.

Solution First, calculate the amount of $KMnO_4$.

$$\text{Amount of } KMnO_4 = c_{KMnO_4} \times V_{KMnO_4} = \frac{0.0195 \text{ mol } KMnO_4}{L} \times 0.02435 \text{ } L = 0.000475 \text{ mol}$$

Use the stoichiometric factor to calculate the amount of iron(II) ion.

$$0.000475 \text{ mol } KMnO_4^- \times \frac{5 \text{ mol } Fe^{2+}}{1 \text{ mol } KMnO_4} = 0.00237 \text{ mol } Fe^{2+}$$

The mass of iron can now be calculated,

$$0.00237 \text{ mol } Fe^{2+} \times \frac{55.85 \text{ g } Fe^{2+}}{1 \text{ mol } Fe^{2+}} = 0.133 \text{ g } Fe^{2+}$$

Finally, the mass percent can be determined.

$$\frac{0.133 \text{ g } Fe^{2+}}{1.026 \text{ g sample}} \times 100\% = \boxed{12.9\% \text{ iron}}$$

Comment This is a useful analytical reaction because it is easy to detect when all the iron(II) ion has reacted. The MnO_4^- ion is a deep purple color, but when it reacts with Fe^{2+}, the color disappears because the reaction product, Mn^{2+}, is colorless. Therefore, $KMnO_4$ solution is added from a buret until the initially colorless, Fe^{2+}-containing solution just turns a faint purple color (due to unreacted $KMnO_4$), the signal that the equivalence point has been reached.

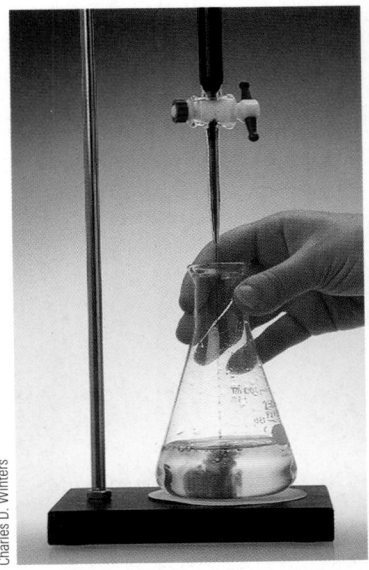

Using an oxidation-reduction reaction for analysis by titration. Purple, aqueous $KMnO_4$ is added to a solution containing Fe^{2+}. As $KMnO_4$ drops into the solution, colorless Mn^{2+} and pale yellow Fe^{3+} form. Here, an area of the solution containing unreacted $KMnO_4$ is seen. As the solution is mixed, this disappears until the equivalence point is reached.

Charles D. Winters

EXERCISE 4.15 Using an Oxidation-Reduction Reaction in a Titration

Vitamin C, ascorbic acid ($C_6H_8O_6$), is a reducing agent. One way to determine the ascorbic acid content of a sample is to mix the acid with an excess of iodine,

$$C_6H_8O_6(aq) + I_2(aq) + 2 H_2O(\ell) \longrightarrow C_6H_6O_6(aq) + 2 H_3O^+(aq) + 2 I^-(aq)$$

and then titrate the iodine that did not react with the ascorbic acid with sodium thiosulfate. The balanced, net ionic equation for the reaction occurring in this titration is

$$I_2(aq) + 2 S_2O_3{}^{2-}(aq) \longrightarrow 2 I^-(aq) + S_4O_6{}^{2-}(aq)$$

Suppose 50.00 mL of 0.0520 M I_2 was added to the sample containing ascorbic acid. After the ascorbic acid/I_2 reaction was complete, the I_2 not used in this reaction required 20.30 mL of 0.196 M $Na_2S_2O_3$ for titration to the equivalence point. Calculate the mass of ascorbic acid in the unknown sample.

4.8 Spectrophotometry, Another Method of Analysis

Solutions of many compounds are colored, a consequence of the absorption of light (Figure 4.15). It is possible to measure, quantitatively, the extent of light absorption and to relate this to the concentration of the dissolved solute. This kind of experiment, called **spectrophotometry**, is an important analytical method.

Every substance absorbs or transmits certain wavelengths of radiant energy but not others (Figures 4.15 and 4.16). For example, nickel(II) ions (and chlorophyll) absorb red and blue/violet light, while transmitting or reflecting green light. Your eyes "see" the transmitted or reflected wavelengths, those not absorbed, as the color

FIGURE 4.15 Light absorption and color. A beam of white light shines on a solution of nickel(II) ions in water, and the light that emerges is green. The color of a solution is due to the color of the light *not* absorbed by the solution. Here, red and blue/violet light was absorbed, and green light is transmitted.

Charles D. Winters

FIGURE 4.16 An absorption spectrophotometer. A beam of white light passes through a prism or diffraction grating, which splits the light into its component wavelengths. After passing through the sample, the light reaches a detector. The spectrophotometer "scans" all wavelengths of light and determines the amount of light absorbed at each wavelength. The output is a *spectrum*, a plot of the amount of light absorbed as a function of the wavelength or frequency of the incoming or incident light. Here, the sample absorbs light in the green-blue part of the spectrum and transmits light in the remaining wavelengths. The sample would appear red to orange to your eye.

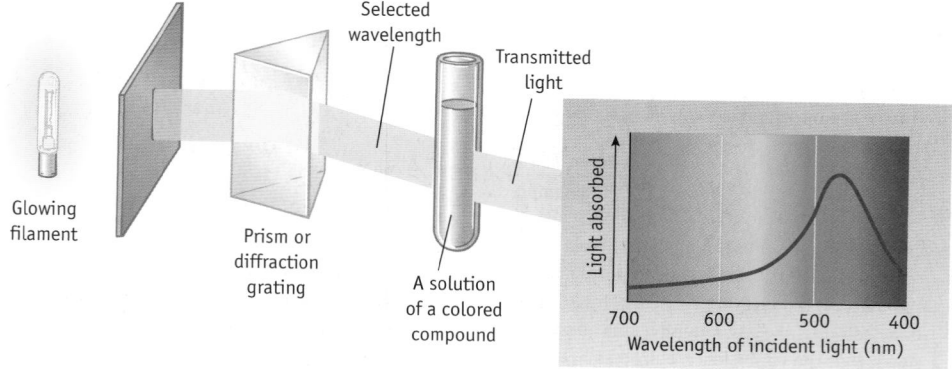

green. Furthermore, the specific wavelengths absorbed and transmitted are characteristic for a substance, and so a spectrum serves as a "fingerprint" of the substance that can help identify an unknown.

Now suppose you look at two solutions of the same substance, one a deeper color than the other. Your common sense tells you that the intensely colored one is the more concentrated (Figure 4.17a). This is true, and the intensity of the color is a measure of the concentration of the material in the solution.

In recent years, spectrophotometry has become one of the most frequently used methods of quantitative analysis. It is applicable to many industrial and clinical problems involving the quantitative determination of compounds that are colored or that react to form a colored product.

Transmittance, Absorbance, and the Beer–Lambert Law

To understand the exact relationship of light absorption and solution concentration, we need to define several terms. **Transmittance** (T) is the ratio of the amount of light transmitted by or passing through the sample relative to the amount of light that initially fell on the sample (the incident light).

$$\text{Transmittance } (T) = \frac{P}{P_0} = \frac{\text{intensity of transmitted light}}{\text{intensity of incident light}}$$

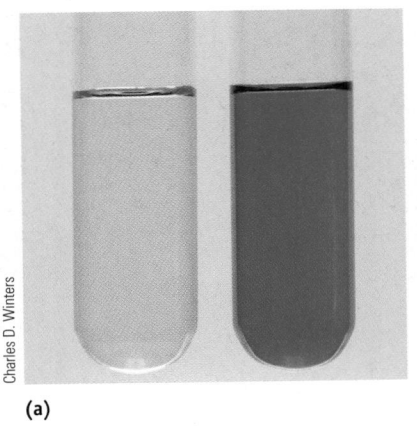

(a)

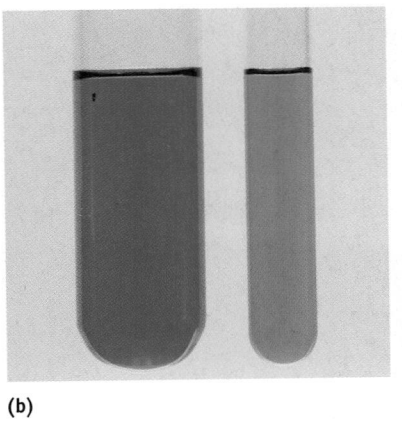

(b)

FIGURE 4.17 Light absorption, concentration, and path length.
(a) The test tube on the left has a solution of copper(II) sulfate with a concentration of 0.05 M. On the right, the concentration is 1.0 M in copper(II) sulfate. More light is absorbed by the more concentrated sample, and it appears more blue.
(b) The amount of light absorbed by a solution depends on the path length. Here, both solutions have the same concentration, but the distance the light travels is longer in one than the other.

Absorbance is defined as the negative logarithm of the transmittance, and you will note that absorbance and transmittance bear an inverse relationship. That is, as the absorbance of a solution increases, the transmittance decreases

$$\text{Absorbance} = -\log T = -\log P/P_0$$

Going back to our example of an aqueous solution of copper(II) ions in Figure 4.17, if you have two colored solutions, you may deduce that the bluer solution appears more blue because it absorbs more of the light falling on it. That is, the *absorbance, A, of a sample increases as the concentration increases.*

Next, suppose that there are two test tubes, both containing the same solution at the same concentration. The only difference is that one of the test tubes has a smaller diameter than the other (Figure 4.17b). We shine light of the same intensity (P_0) on both test tubes. In the first case, the light has to travel only a short distance through the sample, whereas in the second case it has to pass through more of the sample. In the second case more of the light will be absorbed because the path length is longer. In other words, *absorbance increases as path length increases.*

The two observations described above constitute the **Beer–Lambert law**.

$$\text{Absorbance } (A) \propto \text{ path length } (\ell) \times \text{ concentration } (c)$$
$$A = \varepsilon \times \ell \times c \tag{4.5}$$

■ **Beer–Lambert Law** The Beer–Lambert law applies strictly to relatively dilute solutions. At higher solute concentrations, the dependence of absorbance on concentration may not be linear.

where

- A, the absorbance of the sample, is a dimensionless number.
- ε, proportionality constant, is called the *molar absorptivity*. It is a constant for a given substance, provided the temperature and wavelength are constant. It has units of L/mol·cm.
- ℓ and c have the units of length (cm) and concentration (mol/L), respectively.

The Beer–Lambert law shows that *there is a linear relationship between a sample's absorbance and its concentration for a given path length.*

FIGURE 4.18 Spectrophotometers.
The instruments illustrated here are often found in introductory chemistry laboratories. *(left)* Spectronic 20 from Spectronic Instruments. *(right)* Ocean Optics spectrometer (where the digital data are collected by a computer).

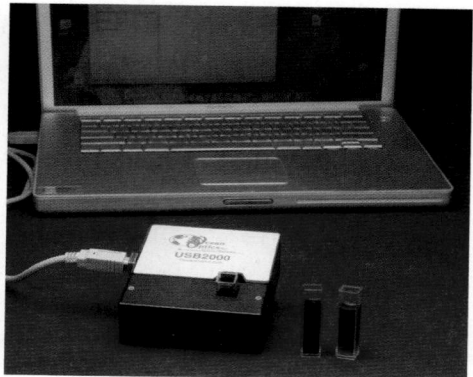

Charles D. Winters

Spectrophotometric Analysis

There are usually four steps in carrying out a spectrophotometric analysis.

- **Record the absorption spectrum of the substance to be analyzed.** In introductory chemistry laboratories, this is often done using an instrument such as the ones shown in Figure 4.18. The result is a spectrum such as that for aqueous permanganate ions (MnO_4^-) in Figure 4.19. The spectrum is a plot of the absorbance of the sample versus the wavelength of incident light. Here, the maximum in absorbance is at about 525 nm.

- **Choose the wavelength for the measurement.** According to the Beer–Lambert Law, the absorbance at each wavelength is proportional to concentration. Therefore, in theory we could choose any wavelength for quantitative estimations of concentration. However, the magnitude of the absorbance is important, especially when you are trying to detect very small amounts of material. In the spectra of permanganate ions in Figure 4.19, note that the difference in absorbance between curves 1 and 2 is at a maximum at about 525 nm, and at this wavelength the change in absorbance is greatest for a given change in concentration. That is, the measurement of concentration as a function of concentration is most sensitive at this wavelength. For this reason, *we generally select the wavelength of maximum absorbance for our measurements.*

- **Prepare a calibration plot.** Once we have chosen the wavelength, the next step is to construct a **calibration curve** or **calibration plot.** This consists of a plot of absorbance versus concentration for a series of standard solutions whose concentrations are accurately known. Because of the linear relation between concentration and absorbance (at a given wavelength and pathlength), this plot is a straight line with a positive slope. Once the plot has been made, and the equation for the line is known, you can find the concentration of an unknown sample from its absorbance.

Example 4.13 illustrates the preparation of a calibration curve and its use in determining the concentration of a species in solution.

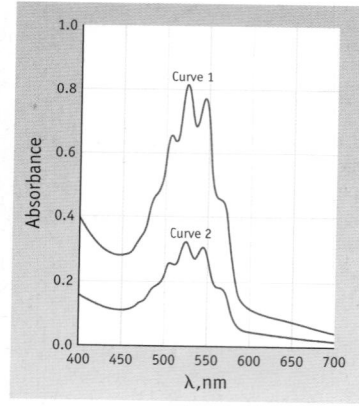

FIGURE 4.19 The absorption spectrum of solutions of potassium permanganate (KMnO₄) at different concentrations. The solution for curve 1 has a higher concentration than that for curve 2.

EXAMPLE 4.13 Using Spectrophotometry in Chemical Analysis

Problem A solution of $KMnO_4$ has an absorbance of 0.539 when measured at 540 nm in a 1.0-cm cell. What is the concentration of the $KMnO_4$?

Prior to determining the absorbance for the unknown solution, the following calibration data were collected for the spectrophotometer.

Concentration of $KMnO_4$ (M)	Absorbance
0.0300	0.162
0.0600	0.330
0.0900	0.499
0.120	0.670
0.150	0.840

Strategy The first step is to prepare a calibration plot from the data above. You can then use the plot to estimate the unknown concentration from the measured absorbance or, better, find the equation for the straight line in the calibration plot (see pages 39 and 40) and calculate the unknown concentration. We shall do the latter.

Solution Using Excel or a calculator, prepare a calibration plot from the experimental data. The equation for the straight line (as determined using Excel) is

$$y = 5.633x - 0.009$$

$$\text{Absorbance} = 5.633 \,(\text{Conc}) - 0.009$$

If we put in the absorbance for the unknown solution,

$$0.539 = 5.633 \,(\text{Conc}) - 0.009$$

$$\text{Unknown concentration} = 0.0973$$

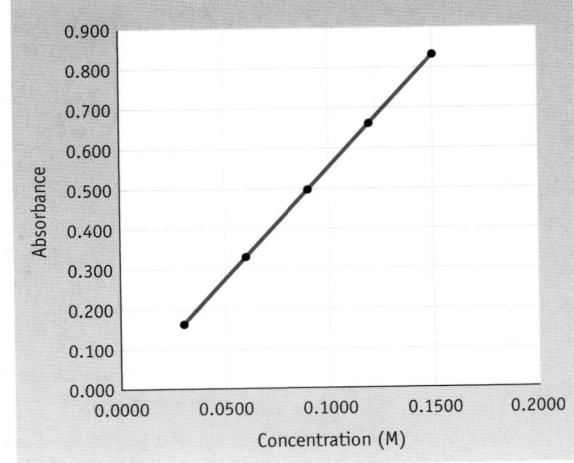

EXERCISE 4.16 Analysis Using Spectrophotometry

Using the following data, calculate the concentration of copper(II) ions in the unknown solution. (The cell pathlength is 1.00 cm in all cases, and the wavelength used in the determination was 645 nm.)

Calibration data

Concentration of Cu^{2+} (M)	Absorbance
0.0562	0.720
0.0337	0.434
0.0281	0.332
0.0169	0.219

Absorbance of unknown solution containing Cu^{2+} ions = 0.418

Chapter Goals Revisited

Chemistry Now™ Sign in at www.cengage.com/login to:

- Assess your understanding with Study Questions in OWL keyed to each goal in the Goals and Homework menu for this chapter
- For quick review, download Go Chemistry mini-lecture flashcard modules (or purchase them at www.ichapters.com)
- Check your readiness for an exam by taking the Pre-Test and exploring the modules recommended in your Personalized Study plan.

❓ Access How Do I Solve It? tutorials on how to approach problem solving using concepts in this chapter.

For additional preparation for an examination on this chapter see the *Let's Review* section on pages 254–267.

Now that you have studied this chapter, you should ask whether you have met the chapter goals. In particular, you should be able to:

Perform stoichiometry calculations using balanced chemical equations

a. Understand the principle of the conservation of matter, which forms the basis of chemical stoichiometry.

b. Calculate the mass of one reactant or product from the mass of another reactant or product by using the balanced chemical equation (Section 4.1). Study Question(s) assignable in OWL: 2, 5, 8, 77, 81, 93, 95, 97, 99, 100; Go Chemistry Module 7.

c. Use amounts tables to organize stoichiometric information. Study Question(s) assignable in OWL: 8.

Understand the meaning of a limiting reactant in a chemical reaction

a. Determine which of two reactants is the limiting reactant (Section 4.2). Study Question(s) assignable in OWL: 12, 14, 96, 132; Go Chemistry Module 8.

b. Determine the yield of a product based on the limiting reactant. Study Question(s) assignable in OWL: 12, 14, 16, 18.

Calculate the theoretical and percent yields of a chemical reaction

Explain the differences among actual yield, theoretical yield, and percent yield, and calculate percent yield (Section 4.3). Study Question(s) assignable in OWL: 19.

Use stoichiometry to analyze a mixture of compounds or to determine the formula of a compound

a. Use stoichiometry principles to analyze a mixture (Section 4.4). Study Question(s) assignable in OWL: 23, 123, 125, 127.

b. Find the empirical formula of an unknown compound using chemical stoichiometry (Section 4.4). Study Question(s) assignable in OWL: 29, 34.

Define and use concentrations in solution stoichiometry

a. Calculate the concentration of a solute in a solution in units of moles per liter (molarity), and use concentrations in calculations (Section 4.5). Study Question(s) assignable in OWL: 37, 39, 41.

b. Describe how to prepare a solution of a given concentration from the solute and a solvent or by dilution from a more concentrated solution (Section 4.5). Study Question(s) assignable in OWL: 46, 47, 51.

c. Calculate the pH of a solution from the concentration of hydronium ion in the solution. Calculate the hydronium ion concentration of a solution from the pH (Section 4.6). Study Question(s) assignable in OWL: 54, 55; Go Chemistry Module 9.

d. Solve stoichiometry problems using solution concentrations (Section 4.7). Study Question(s) assignable in OWL: 59, 62, 106, 107.

e. Explain how a titration is carried out, explain the procedure of standardization, and calculate concentrations or amounts of reactants from titration data (Section 4.7). Study Question(s) assignable in OWL: 67, 71.

f. Understand and use the principles of spectrophotometry to determine the concentration of a species in solution. (Secton 4.8). Study Question(s) assignable in OWL: 75.

KEY EQUATIONS

Equation 4.1 (page 168)   Percent yield

$$\text{Percent yield} = \frac{\text{actual yield}}{\text{theoretical yield}} \times 100\%$$

Equation 4.2 (page 175)   Definition of molarity, a measure of the concentration of a solute in a solution.

$$\text{Molarity of } x \ (c_x) = \frac{\text{amount of solute} \times (\text{mol})}{\text{volume of solution (L)}}$$

A useful form of this equation is

$$\text{Amount of solute } x \ (\text{mol}) = c_x \ (\text{mol/L}) \times \text{volume of solution (L)}$$

Dilution Equation (page 179)   This is a shortcut to find, for example, the concentration of a solution (c_d) after diluting some volume (V_c) of a more concentrated solution (c_c) to a new volume (V_d).

$$c_c \times V_c = c_d \times V_d$$

Equation 4.3 (page 179)   pH. The pH of a solution is the negative logarithm of the hydronium ion concentration.

$$pH = -\log[H_3O^+]$$

Equation 4.4 (page 181)   Calculating $[H_3O^+]$ from pH. The equation for calculating the hydronium ion concentration of a solution from the pH of the solution.

$$[H_3O^+] = 10^{-pH}$$

Equation 4.5 (page 192)   Beer–Lambert Law. The absorbance of light (A) by a substance in solution is equal to the molar absorptivity of the substance (ε), the pathlength of the cell (ℓ), and the concentration of the solute (c).

$$\text{Absorbance } (A) \propto \text{path length } (\ell) \times \text{concentration } (c)$$
$$A = \varepsilon \times \ell \times c$$

STUDY QUESTIONS

OWL Online homework for this chapter may be assigned in OWL.

▲ denotes challenging questions.

■ denotes questions assignable in OWL.

Blue-numbered questions have answers in Appendix O and fully-worked solutions in the *Student Solutions Manual*.

Practicing Skills

Mass Relationships in Chemical Reactions: Basic Stoichiometry
(See Example 4.1 and ChemistryNow Screens 4.2 and 4.3.)

1. Aluminum reacts with oxygen to give aluminum oxide.

$$4 \text{ Al(s)} + 3 \text{ O}_2(g) \rightarrow 2 \text{ Al}_2\text{O}_3(s)$$

What amount of O_2, in moles, is needed for complete reaction with 6.0 mol of Al? What mass of Al_2O_3, in grams, can be produced?

2. ■ What mass of HCl, in grams, is required to react with 0.750 g of $Al(OH)_3$? What mass of water, in grams, is produced?

$$\text{Al(OH)}_3(s) + 3 \text{ HCl(aq)} \rightarrow \text{AlCl}_3(aq) + 3 \text{ H}_2\text{O}(\ell)$$

3. Like many metals, aluminum reacts with a halogen to give a metal halide (see Figure 2.12).

$$2 \text{ Al(s)} + 3 \text{ Br}_2(\ell) \rightarrow \text{Al}_2\text{Br}_6(s)$$

What mass of Br_2, in grams, is required for complete reaction with 2.56 g of Al? What mass of white, solid Al_2Br_6 is expected?

4. The balanced equation for a reaction in the process of the reduction of iron ore to the metal is

$$\text{Fe}_2\text{O}_3(s) + 3 \text{ CO(g)} \rightarrow 2 \text{ Fe(s)} + 3 \text{ CO}_2(g)$$

(a) What is the maximum mass of iron, in grams, that can be obtained from 454 g (1.00 lb) of iron(III) oxide?

(b) What mass of CO is required to react with 454 g of Fe_2O_3?

5. ■ Methane, CH_4, burns in oxygen.
(a) What are the products of the reaction?
(b) Write the balanced equation for the reaction.
(c) What mass of O_2, in grams, is required for complete combustion of 25.5 g of methane?
(d) What is the total mass of products expected from the combustion of 25.5 g of methane?

6. The formation of water-insoluble silver chloride is useful in the analysis of chloride-containing substances. Consider the following *unbalanced* equation:

$$\text{BaCl}_2(aq) + \text{AgNO}_3(aq) \rightarrow \text{AgCl}(s) + \text{Ba(NO}_3)_2(aq)$$

(a) Write the balanced equation.
(b) What mass of $AgNO_3$, in grams, is required for complete reaction with 0.156 g of $BaCl_2$? What mass of AgCl is produced?

Amounts Tables and Chemical Stoichiometry

For each question below, set up an amounts table that lists the initial amount or amounts of reactants, the changes in amounts of reactants and products, and the amounts of reactants and products after reaction. See page 159 and Example 4.1.

7. A major source of air pollution years ago was the metals industry. One common process involved "roasting" metal sulfides in the air:

$$2 \text{ PbS(s)} + 3 \text{ O}_2(g) \rightarrow 2 \text{ PbO(s)} + 2 \text{ SO}_2(g)$$

If you heat 2.50 mol of PbS in the air, what amount of O_2 is required for complete reaction? What amounts of PbO and SO_2 are expected?

8. ■ Iron ore is converted to iron metal in a reaction with carbon.

$$2 \text{ Fe}_2\text{O}_3(s) + 3 \text{ C(s)} \rightarrow 4 \text{ Fe(s)} + 3 \text{ CO}_2(g)$$

If 6.2 mol of Fe_2O_3(s) is used, what amount of C(s) is needed, and what amounts of Fe and CO_2 are produced?

9. Chromium metal reacts with oxygen to give chromium(III) oxide, Cr_2O_3.
(a) Write a balanced equation for the reaction.
(b) If a piece of chromium has a mass of 0.175 g, what mass (in grams) of Cr_2O_3 is produced if the metal is converted completely to the oxide?
(c) What mass of O_2 (in grams) is required for the reaction?

10. Ethane, C_2H_6, burns in oxygen.
(a) What are the products of the reaction?
(b) Write the balanced equation for the reaction.
(c) What mass of O_2, in grams, is required for complete combustion of 13.6 of ethane?
(d) What is the total mass of products expected from the combustion of 13.6 g of ethane?

Limiting Reactants
(See Example 4.2 and Exercise 4.2. See also ChemistryNow Screens 4.4 and 4.5.)

11. Sodium sulfide, Na_2S, is used in the leather industry to remove hair from hides. The Na_2S is made by the reaction

$$\text{Na}_2\text{SO}_4(s) + 4 \text{ C(s)} \rightarrow \text{Na}_2\text{S(s)} + 4 \text{ CO(g)}$$

Suppose you mix 15 g of Na_2SO_4 and 7.5 g of C. Which is the limiting reactant? What mass of Na_2S is produced?

12. ■ Ammonia gas can be prepared by the reaction of a metal oxide such as calcium oxide with ammonium chloride.

$$\text{CaO(s)} + 2 \text{ NH}_4\text{Cl(s)} \rightarrow$$
$$2 \text{ NH}_3(g) + \text{H}_2\text{O}(g) + \text{CaCl}_2(s)$$

If 112 g of CaO and 224 g of NH_4Cl are mixed, what is the limiting reactant, and what mass of NH_3 can be produced?

13. The compound SF_6 is made by burning sulfur in an atmosphere of fluorine. The balanced equation is

$$\text{S}_8(s) + 24 \text{ F}_2(g) \rightarrow 8 \text{ SF}_6(g)$$

If you begin with 1.6 mol of sulfur, S_8, and 35 mol of F_2, which is the limiting reagent?

14. ■ Disulfur dichloride, S_2Cl_2, is used to vulcanize rubber. It can be made by treating molten sulfur with gaseous chlorine:

$$\text{S}_8(\ell) + 4 \text{ Cl}_2(g) \rightarrow 4 \text{ S}_2\text{Cl}_2(\ell)$$

Starting with a mixture of 32.0 g of sulfur and 71.0 g of Cl_2,
(a) Which is the limiting reactant?
(b) What is the theoretical yield of S_2Cl_2?
(c) What mass of the excess reactant remains when the reaction is completed?

▲ more challenging ■ in OWL Blue-numbered questions answered in Appendix O

15. The reaction of methane and water is one way to prepare hydrogen for use as a fuel:

$$CH_4(g) + H_2O(g) \rightarrow CO(g) + 3 H_2(g)$$

If you begin with 995 g of CH_4 and 2510 g of water,
(a) Which reactant is the limiting reactant?
(b) What is the maximum mass of H_2 that can be prepared?
(c) What mass of the excess reactant remains when the reaction is completed?

16. ■ Aluminum chloride, $AlCl_3$, is made by treating scrap aluminum with chlorine.

$$2 Al(s) + 3 Cl_2(g) \rightarrow 2 AlCl_3(s)$$

If you begin with 2.70 g of Al and 4.05 g of Cl_2,
(a) Which reactant is limiting?
(b) What mass of $AlCl_3$ can be produced?
(c) What mass of the excess reactant remains when the reaction is completed?
(d) Set up an amounts table for this problem.

17. Hexane (C_6H_{14}) burns in air (O_2) to give CO_2 and H_2O.
(a) Write a balanced equation for the reaction.
(b) If 215 g of C_6H_{14} is mixed with 215 g of O_2, what masses of CO_2 and H_2O are produced in the reaction?
(c) What mass of the excess reactant remains after the hexane has been burned?
(d) Set up an amounts table for this problem.

18. ■ Aspirin, $C_6H_4(OCOCH_3)CO_2H$, is produced by the reaction of salicylic acid, $C_6H_4(OH)CO_2H$, and acetic anhydride, $(CH_3CO)_2O$ (page 168).

$$C_6H_4(OH)CO_2H(s) + (CH_3CO)_2O(\ell) \rightarrow$$
$$C_6H_4(OCOCH_3)CO_2H(s) + CH_3CO_2H(\ell)$$

If you mix 100. g of each of the reactants, what is the maximum mass of aspirin that can be obtained?

Percent Yield
(See Exercise 4.3 and ChemistryNow Screen 4.3.)

19. ■ In Example 4.2, you found that a particular mixture of CO and H_2 could produce 407 g CH_3OH.

$$CO(g) + 2 H_2(g) \rightarrow CH_3OH(\ell)$$

If only 332 g of CH_3OH is actually produced, what is the percent yield of the compound?

20. Ammonia gas can be prepared by the following reaction:

$$CaO(s) + 2 NH_4Cl(s) \rightarrow$$
$$2 NH_3(g) + H_2O(g) + CaCl_2(s)$$

If 112 g of CaO and 224 g of NH_4Cl are mixed, the theoretical yield of NH_3 is 68.0 g (Study Question 12). If only 16.3 g of NH_3 is actually obtained, what is its percent yield?

21. The deep blue compound $Cu(NH_3)_4SO_4$ is made by the reaction of copper(II) sulfate and ammonia.

$$CuSO_4(aq) + 4 NH_3(aq) \rightarrow Cu(NH_3)_4SO_4(aq)$$

(a) If you use 10.0 g of $CuSO_4$ and excess NH_3, what is the theoretical yield of $Cu(NH_3)_4SO_4$?
(b) If you isolate 12.6 g of $Cu(NH_3)_4SO_4$, what is the percent yield of $Cu(NH_3)_4SO_4$?

22. Black smokers are found in the depths of the oceans (page 112). Thinking that the conditions in these smokers might be conducive to the formation of organic compounds, two chemists in Germany found the following reaction could occur in similar conditions.

$$2 CH_3SH + CO \rightarrow CH_3COSCH_3 + H_2S$$

If you begin with 10.0 g of CH_3SH and excess CO,
(a) What is the theoretical yield of CH_3COSCH_3?
(b) If 8.65 g of CH_3COSCH_3 is isolated, what is its percent yield?

Analysis of Mixtures
(See Example 4.3 and ChemistryNow Screen 4.7.)

23. ■ A mixture of $CuSO_4$ and $CuSO_4 \cdot 5 H_2O$ has a mass of 1.245 g. After heating to drive off all the water, the mass is only 0.832 g. What is the mass percent of $CuSO_4 \cdot 5 H_2O$ in the mixture? (See page 97.)

24. A 2.634-g sample containing impure $CuCl_2 \cdot 2H_2O$ was heated. The sample mass after heating to drive off the water was 2.125 g. What was the mass percent of $CuCl_2 \cdot 2 H_2O$ in the original sample?

25. A sample of limestone and other soil materials was heated, and the limestone decomposed to give calcium oxide and carbon dioxide.

$$CaCO_3(s) \rightarrow CaO(s) + CO_2(g)$$

A 1.506-g sample of limestone-containing material gave 0.558 g of CO_2, in addition to CaO, after being heated at a high temperature. What is the mass percent of $CaCO_3$ in the original sample?

26. At higher temperatures, $NaHCO_3$ is converted quantitatively to Na_2CO_3.

$$2 NaHCO_3(s) \rightarrow Na_2CO_3(s) + CO_2(g) + H_2O(g)$$

Heating a 1.7184-g sample of impure $NaHCO_3$ gives 0.196 g of CO_2. What was the mass percent of $NaHCO_3$ in the original 1.7184-g sample?

27. A pesticide contains thallium(I) sulfate, Tl_2SO_4. Dissolving a 10.20-g sample of impure pesticide in water and adding sodium iodide precipitates 0.1964 g of thallium(I) iodide, TlI.

$$Tl_2SO_4(aq) + 2 NaI(aq) \rightarrow 2 TlI(s) + Na_2SO_4(aq)$$

What is the mass percent of Tl_2SO_4 in the original 10.20-g sample?

28. ▲ The aluminum in a 0.764-g sample of an unknown material was precipitated as aluminum hydroxide, $Al(OH)_3$, which was then converted to Al_2O_3 by heating strongly. If 0.127 g of Al_2O_3 is obtained from the 0.764-g sample, what is the mass percent of aluminum in the sample?

Using Stoichiometry to Determine Empirical and Molecular Formulas
(See Example 4.4, Exercise 4.6, and ChemistryNow Screen 4.8.)

29. ■ Styrene, the building block of polystyrene, consists of only C and H. If 0.438 g of styrene is burned in oxygen and produces 1.481 g of CO_2 and 0.303 g of H_2O, what is the empirical formula of styrene?

30. Mesitylene is a liquid hydrocarbon. Burning 0.115 g of the compound in oxygen gives 0.379 g of CO_2 and 0.1035 g of H_2O. What is the empirical formula of mesitylene?

31. Cyclopentane is a simple hydrocarbon. If 0.0956 g of the compound is burned in oxygen, 0.300 g of CO_2 and 0.123 g of H_2O are isolated.
    (a) What is the empirical formula of cyclopentane?
    (b) If a separate experiment gave 70.1 g/mol as the molar mass of the compound, what is its molecular formula?

32. Azulene is a beautiful blue hydrocarbon. If 0.106 g of the compound is burned in oxygen, 0.364 g of CO_2 and 0.0596 g of H_2O are isolated.
    (a) What is the empirical formula of azulene?
    (b) If a separate experiment gave 128.2 g/mol as the molar mass of the compound, what is its molecular formula?

33. An unknown compound has the formula $C_xH_yO_z$. You burn 0.0956 g of the compound and isolate 0.1356 g of CO_2 and 0.0833 g of H_2O. What is the empirical formula of the compound? If the molar mass is 62.1 g/mol, what is the molecular formula? (See Exercise 4.6.)

34. ■ An unknown compound has the formula $C_xH_yO_z$. You burn 0.1523 g of the compound and isolate 0.3718 g of CO_2 and 0.1522 g of H_2O. What is the empirical formula of the compound? If the molar mass is 72.1 g/mol, what is the molecular formula? (See Exercise 4.6.)

35. Nickel forms a compound with carbon monoxide, $Ni_x(CO)_y$. To determine its formula, you carefully heat a 0.0973-g sample in air to convert the nickel to 0.0426 g of NiO and the CO to 0.100 g of CO_2. What is the empirical formula of $Ni_x(CO)_y$?

36. To find the formula of a compound composed of iron and carbon monoxide, $Fe_x(CO)_y$, the compound is burned in pure oxygen to give Fe_2O_3 and CO_2. If you burn 1.959 g of $Fe_x(CO)_y$ and obtain 0.799 g of Fe_2O_3 and 2.200 g of CO_2, what is the empirical formula of $Fe_x(CO)_y$?

Solution Concentration
(See Example 4.5 and ChemistryNow Screen 4.9.)

37. ■ If 6.73 g of Na_2CO_3 is dissolved in enough water to make 250. mL of solution, what is the molar concentration of the sodium carbonate? What are the molar concentrations of the Na^+ and CO_3^{2-} ions?

38. Some potassium dichromate ($K_2Cr_2O_7$), 2.335 g, is dissolved in enough water to make exactly 500. mL of solution. What is the molar concentration of the potassium dichromate? What are the molar concentrations of the K^+ and $Cr_2O_7^{2-}$ ions?

39. ■ What is the mass of solute, in grams, in 250. mL of a 0.0125 M solution of $KMnO_4$?

40. What is the mass of solute, in grams, in 125 mL of a 1.023×10^{-3} M solution of Na_3PO_4? What is the molar concentration of the Na^+ and PO_4^{3-} ion?

41. ■ What volume of 0.123 M NaOH, in milliliters, contains 25.0 g of NaOH?

42. What volume of 2.06 M $KMnO_4$, in liters, contains 322 g of solute?

43. For each solution, identify the ions that exist in aqueous solution, and specify the concentration of each ion.
    (a) 0.25 M $(NH_4)_2SO_4$
    (b) 0.123 M Na_2CO_3
    (c) 0.056 M HNO_3

44. For each solution, identify the ions that exist in aqueous solution, and specify the concentration of each ion.
    (a) 0.12 M $BaCl_2$
    (b) 0.0125 M $CuSO_4$
    (c) 0.500 M $K_2Cr_2O_7$

Preparing Solutions
(See Exercises 4.7–4.9, Example 4.6, and ChemistryNow Screen 4.10.)

45. An experiment in your laboratory requires 500. mL of a 0.0200 M solution of Na_2CO_3. You are given solid Na_2CO_3, distilled water, and a 500.-mL volumetric flask. Describe how to prepare the required solution.

46. ■ What mass of oxalic acid, $H_2C_2O_4$, is required to prepare 250. mL of a solution that has a concentration of 0.15 M $H_2C_2O_4$?

47. ■ If you dilute 25.0 mL of 1.50 M hydrochloric acid to 500. mL, what is the molar concentration of the dilute acid?

48. If 4.00 mL of 0.0250 M $CuSO_4$ is diluted to 10.0 mL with pure water, what is the molar concentration of copper(II) sulfate in the diluted solution?

49. Which of the following methods would you use to prepare 1.00 L of 0.125 M H_2SO_4?
    (a) Dilute 20.8 mL of 6.00 M H_2SO_4 to a volume of 1.00 L.
    (b) Add 950. mL of water to 50.0 mL of 3.00 M H_2SO_4.

▲ more challenging   ■ in OWL   Blue-numbered questions answered in Appendix O

50. Which of the following methods would you use to prepare 300. mL of 0.500 M $K_2Cr_2O_7$?
(a) Add 30.0 mL of 1.50 M $K_2Cr_2O_7$ to 270. mL of water.
(b) Dilute 250. mL of 0.600 M $K_2Cr_2O_7$ to a volume of 300. mL.

Serial Dilutions
(See A Closer Look: Serial Dilutions, page 180.)

51. ■ You have 250. mL of 0.136 M HCl. Using a volumetric pipet, you take 25.00 mL of that solution and dilute it to 100.00 mL in a volumetric flask. Now you take 10.00 mL of that solution, using a volumetric pipet, and dilute it to 100.00 mL in a volumetric flask. What is the concentration of hydrochloric acid in the final solution?

52. ▲ Suppose you have 100.00 mL a solution of a dye and transfer 2.00 mL of the solution to a 100.00-mL volumetric flask. After adding water to the 100.00 mL mark, you take 5.00 mL of that solution and again dilute to 100.00 mL. If you find the dye concentration in the final diluted sample is 0.000158 M, what was the dye concentration in the original solution?

Calculating and Using pH
(See Example 4.7 and ChemistryNow Screen 4.11.)

53. A table wine has a pH of 3.40. What is the hydronium ion concentration of the wine? Is it acidic or basic?

54. ■ A saturated solution of milk of magnesia, $Mg(OH)_2$, has a pH of 10.5. What is the hydronium ion concentration of the solution? Is the solution acidic or basic?

55. ■ What is the hydronium ion concentration of a 0.0013 M solution of HNO_3? What is its pH?

56. What is the hydronium ion concentration of a 1.2×10^{-4} M solution of $HClO_4$? What is its pH?

57. Make the following conversions. In each case, tell whether the solution is acidic or basic.

pH	$[H_3O^+]$
(a) 1.00	_____
(b) 10.50	_____
(c) _____	1.3×10^{-5} M
(d) _____	2.3×10^{-8} M

58. Make the following conversions. In each case, tell whether the solution is acidic or basic.

pH	$[H_3O^+]$
(a) _____	6.7×10^{-10} M
(b) _____	2.2×10^{-6} M
(c) 5.25	_____
(d) _____	2.5×10^{-2} M

Stoichiometry of Reactions in Solution
(See Example 4.8 and ChemistryNow Screen 4.12.)

59. ■ What volume of 0.109 M HNO_3, in milliliters, is required to react completely with 2.50 g of $Ba(OH)_2$?

$$2\ HNO_3(aq) + Ba(OH)_2(s) \rightarrow 2\ H_2O(\ell) + Ba(NO_3)_2(aq)$$

60. What mass of Na_2CO_3, in grams, is required for complete reaction with 50.0 mL of 0.125 M HNO_3?

$$Na_2CO_3(aq) + 2\ HNO_3(aq) \rightarrow 2\ NaNO_3(aq) + CO_2(g) + H_2O(\ell)$$

61. When an electric current is passed through an aqueous solution of NaCl, the valuable industrial chemicals $H_2(g)$, $Cl_2(g)$, and NaOH are produced.

$$2\ NaCl(aq) + 2\ H_2O(\ell) \rightarrow H_2(g) + Cl_2(g) + 2\ NaOH(aq)$$

What mass of NaOH can be formed from 15.0 L of 0.35 M NaCl? What mass of chlorine is obtained?

62. ■ Hydrazine, N_2H_4, a base-like ammonia, can react with sulfuric acid.

$$2\ N_2H_4(aq) + H_2SO_4(aq) \rightarrow 2\ N_2H_5^+(aq) + SO_4^{2-}(aq)$$

What mass of hydrazine reacts with 250. mL of 0.146 M H_2SO_4?

63. In the photographic developing process, silver bromide is dissolved by adding sodium thiosulfate.

$$AgBr(s) + 2\ Na_2S_2O_3(aq) \rightarrow Na_3Ag(S_2O_3)_2(aq) + NaBr(aq)$$

If you want to dissolve 0.225 g of AgBr, what volume of 0.0138 M $Na_2S_2O_3$, in milliliters, should be used?

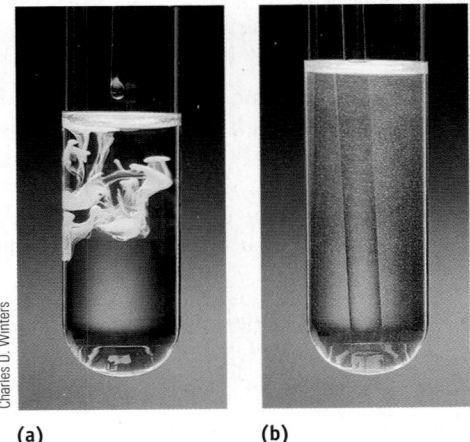

(a)　　　　**(b)**

Silver chemistry. (a) A precipitate of AgBr formed by adding $AgNO_3(aq)$ to KBr(aq). (b) On adding $Na_2S_2O_3(aq)$, sodium thiosulfate, the solid AgBr dissolves.

Charles D. Winters

64. You can dissolve an aluminum soft-drink can in an aqueous base such as potassium hydroxide.

$$2\ Al(s) + 2\ KOH(aq) + 6\ H_2O(\ell) \rightarrow$$
$$2\ KAl(OH)_4(aq) + 3\ H_2(g)$$

If you place 2.05 g of aluminum in a beaker with 185 mL of 1.35 M KOH, will any aluminum remain? What mass of $KAl(OH)_4$ is produced?

65. What volume of 0.750 M $Pb(NO_3)_2$, in milliliters, is required to react completely with 1.00 L of 2.25 M NaCl solution? The balanced equation is

$$Pb(NO_3)_2(aq) + 2\ NaCl(aq) \rightarrow$$
$$PbCl_2(s) + 2\ NaNO_3(aq)$$

66. What volume of 0.125 M oxalic acid, $H_2C_2O_4$ is required to react with 35.2 mL of 0.546 M NaOH?

$$H_2C_2O_4(aq) + 2\ NaOH(aq) \rightarrow$$
$$Na_2C_2O_4(aq) + 2\ H_2O(\ell)$$

Titrations

(See Examples 4.9–4.12 and ChemistryNow Screen 4.13.)

67. ■ What volume of 0.812 M HCl, in milliliters, is required to titrate 1.45 g of NaOH to the equivalence point?

$$NaOH(aq) + HCl(aq) \rightarrow H_2O(\ell) + NaCl(aq)$$

68. What volume of 0.955 M HCl, in milliliters, is required to titrate 2.152 g of Na_2CO_3 to the equivalence point?

$$Na_2CO_3(aq) + 2\ HCl(aq) \rightarrow$$
$$H_2O(\ell) + CO_2(g) + 2\ NaCl(aq)$$

69. If 38.55 mL of HCl is required to titrate 2.150 g of Na_2CO_3 according to the following equation, what is the concentration (mol/L) of the HCl solution?

$$Na_2CO_3(aq) + 2\ HCl(aq) \rightarrow$$
$$2\ NaCl(aq) + CO_2(g) + H_2O(\ell)$$

70. Potassium hydrogen phthalate, $KHC_8H_4O_4$, is used to standardize solutions of bases. The acidic anion reacts with strong bases according to the following net ionic equation:

$$HC_8H_4O_4^-(aq) + OH^-(aq) \rightarrow$$
$$C_8H_4O_4^{2-}(aq) + H_2O(\ell)$$

If a 0.902-g sample of potassium hydrogen phthalate is dissolved in water and titrated to the equivalence point with 26.45 mL of NaOH, what is the molar concentration of the NaOH?

71. ■ You have 0.954 g of an unknown acid, H_2A, which reacts with NaOH according to the balanced equation

$$H_2A(aq) + 2\ NaOH(aq) \rightarrow Na_2A(aq) + 2\ H_2O(\ell)$$

If 36.04 mL of 0.509 M NaOH is required to titrate the acid to the second equivalence point, what is the molar mass of the acid?

72. An unknown solid acid is either citric acid or tartaric acid. To determine which acid you have, you titrate a sample of the solid with aqueous NaOH and from this determine the molar mass of the unknown acid. The appropriate equations are as follows:

Citric acid:

$$H_3C_6H_5O_7(aq) + 3\ NaOH(aq) \rightarrow$$
$$3\ H_2O(\ell) + Na_3C_6H_5O_7(aq)$$

Tartaric acid:

$$H_2C_4H_4O_6(aq) + 2\ NaOH(aq) \rightarrow$$
$$2\ H_2O(\ell) + Na_2C_4H_4O_6(aq)$$

A 0.956-g sample requires 29.1 mL of 0.513 M NaOH to consume the acid completely. What is the unknown acid?

73. To analyze an iron-containing compound, you convert all the iron to Fe^{2+} in aqueous solution and then titrate the solution with standardized $KMnO_4$. The balanced, net ionic equation is

$$MnO_4^-(aq) + 5\ Fe^{2+}(aq) + 8\ H_3O^+(aq) \rightarrow$$
$$Mn^{2+}(aq) + 5\ Fe^{3+}(aq) + 12\ H_2O(\ell)$$

A 0.598-g sample of the iron-containing compound requires 22.25 mL of 0.0123 M $KMnO_4$ for titration to the equivalence point. What is the mass percent of iron in the sample?

74. Vitamin C has the formula $C_6H_8O_6$. Besides being an acid, it is a reducing agent. One method for determining the amount of vitamin C in a sample is therefore to titrate it with a solution of bromine, Br_2, an oxidizing agent.

$$C_6H_8O_6(aq) + Br_2(aq) \rightarrow 2\ HBr(aq) + C_6H_6O_6(aq)$$

A 1.00-g "chewable" vitamin C tablet requires 27.85 mL of 0.102 M Br_2 for titration to the equivalence point. What is the mass of vitamin C in the tablet?

Spectrophotometry
(See Section 4.8. The problems below are adapted from Fundamentals of Analytical Chemistry, 8th ed., by D. A. Skoog, D. M. West, F. J. Holler, and S. R. Crouch, Thomson/Brooks-Cole, Belmont, CA 2004.)

75. ■ A solution of a dye was analyzed by spectrophotometry, and the following calibration data were collected.

Dye Concentration	Absorbance at 475 nm
0.50×10^{-6} M	0.24
1.5×10^{-6} M	0.36
2.5×10^{-6} M	0.44
3.5×10^{-6} M	0.59
4.5×10^{-6} M	0.70

(a) Construct a calibration plot, and determine the slope and intercept.
(b) What is the dye concentration in a solution with $A = 0.52$?

▲ more challenging ■ in OWL Blue-numbered questions answered in Appendix O

76. The nitrite ion is involved in the biochemical nitrogen cycle. You can analyze for the nitrite ion content of a sample using spectrophotometry by first using several organic compounds to create a colored compound from the ion. The following data were collected.

NO_2^- Ion Concentration	Absorbance at 550 nm of Nitrite-Ion Containing Solution
2.00×10^{-6} M	0.065
6.00×10^{-6} M	0.205
10.00×10^{-6} M	0.338
14.00×10^{-6} M	0.474
18.00×10^{-6} M	0.598
Unknown solution	0.402

(a) Construct a calibration plot, and determine the slope and intercept.
(b) What is the nitrite ion concentration in the unknown solution?

General Questions on Stoichiometry

These questions are not designated as to type or location in the chapter. They may combine several concepts from the chapter.

77. ■ Suppose 16.04 g of benzene, C_6H_6, is burned in oxygen.
(a) What are the products of the reaction?
(b) What is the balanced equation for the reaction?
(c) What mass of O_2, in grams, is required for complete combustion of benzene?
(d) What is the total mass of products expected from 16.04 g of benzene?

78. The metabolic disorder diabetes causes a buildup of acetone, CH_3COCH_3, in the blood. Acetone, a volatile compound, is exhaled, giving the breath of untreated diabetics a distinctive odor. The acetone is produced by a breakdown of fats in a series of reactions. The equation for the last step, the breakdown of acetoacetic acid to give acetone and CO_2, is

$$CH_3COCH_2CO_2H \rightarrow CH_3COCH_3 + CO_2$$

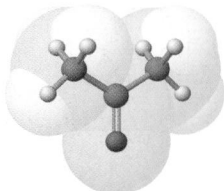

acetone, CH_3COCH_3

What mass of acetone can be produced from 125 mg of acetoacetic acid?

79. Your body deals with excess nitrogen by excreting it in the form of urea, NH_2CONH_2. The reaction producing it is the combination of arginine ($C_6H_{14}N_4O_2$) with water to give urea and ornithine ($C_5H_{12}N_2O_2$).

$$C_6H_{14}N_4O_2 + H_2O \rightarrow NH_2CONH_2 + C_5H_{12}N_2O_2$$
$$\text{Arginine} \qquad\qquad \text{Urea} \qquad \text{Ornithine}$$

If you excrete 95 mg of urea, what mass of arginine must have been used? What mass of ornithine must have been produced?

80. The reaction of iron metal and chlorine gas to give iron(III) chloride is illustrated in Figure 3.2.
(a) Write the balanced chemical equation for the reaction.
(b) Beginning with 10.0 g of iron, what mass of Cl_2, in grams, is required for complete reaction? What mass of $FeCl_3$ can be produced?
(c) If only 18.5 g of $FeCl_3$ is obtained from 10.0 g of iron and excess Cl_2, what is the percent yield?
(d) If 10.0 g each of iron and chlorine are combined, what is the theoretical yield of iron(III) chloride?

81. ■ Some metal halides react with water to produce the metal oxide and the appropriate hydrogen halide (see photo). For example,

$$TiCl_4(\ell) + 2\,H_2O(\ell) \rightarrow TiO_2(s) + 4\,HCl(g)$$

The reaction of TiCl₄ with the water in moist air.

(a) Name the four compounds involved in this reaction.
(b) If you begin with 14.0 mL of $TiCl_4$ ($d = 1.73$ g/mL), what mass of water, in grams, is required for complete reaction?
(c) What mass of each product is expected?

82. The reaction of 750. g each of NH_3 and O_2 was found to produce 562 g of NO (see pages 163–165).

$$4\,NH_3(g) + 5\,O_2(g) \rightarrow 4\,NO(g) + 6\,H_2O(\ell)$$

(a) What mass of water is produced by this reaction?
(b) What mass of O_2 is required to consume 750. g of NH_3?

83. Sodium azide, the explosive chemical used in automobile airbags, is made by the following reaction:

$$NaNO_3 + 3\ NaNH_2 \rightarrow NaN_3 + 3\ NaOH + NH_3$$

If you combine 15.0 g of $NaNO_3$ (85.0 g/mol) with 15.0 g of $NaNH_2$, what mass of NaN_3 is produced?

84. Iodine is made by the following reaction

$$2\ NaIO_3(aq) + 5\ NaHSO_3(aq) \rightarrow$$
$$3\ NaHSO_4(aq) + 2\ Na_2SO_4(aq) + H_2O(\ell) + I_2(aq)$$

(a) Name the two reactants.
(b) If you wish to prepare 1.00 kg of I_2, what mass of $NaIO_3$ is required? What mass of $NaHSO_3$?
(c) What is the theoretical yield of I_2 if you mixed 15.0 g of $NaIO_3$ with 125 mL of 0.853 M $NaHSO_3$?

85. Saccharin, an artificial sweetener, has the formula $C_7H_5NO_3S$. Suppose you have a sample of a saccharin-containing sweetener with a mass of 0.2140 g. After decomposition to free the sulfur and convert it to the SO_4^{2-} ion, the sulfate ion is trapped as water-insoluble $BaSO_4$ (see Figure 4.6). The quantity of $BaSO_4$ obtained is 0.2070 g. What is the mass percent of saccharin in the sample of sweetener?

86. ■▲ Boron forms an extensive series of compounds with hydrogen, all with the general formula B_xH_y.

$$B_xH_y(s) + \text{excess } O_2(g) \rightarrow \frac{x}{2} B_2O_3(s) + \frac{y}{2} H_2O(g)$$

If 0.148 g of B_xH_y gives 0.422 g of B_2O_3 when burned in excess O_2, what is the empirical formula of B_xH_y?

87. ▲ Silicon and hydrogen form a series of compounds with the general formula Si_xH_y. To find the formula of one of them, a 6.22-g sample of the compound is burned in oxygen. All of the Si is converted to 11.64 g of SiO_2, and all of the H is converted to 6.980 g of H_2O. What is the empirical formula of the silicon compound?

88. ▲ Menthol, from oil of mint, has a characteristic odor. The compound contains only C, H, and O. If 95.6 mg of menthol burns completely in O_2, and gives 269 mg of CO_2 and 110 mg of H_2O, what is the empirical formula of menthol?

89. ▲ Quinone, a chemical used in the dye industry and in photography, is an organic compound containing only C, H, and O. What is the empirical formula of the compound if 0.105 g of the compound gives 0.257 g of CO_2 and 0.0350 g of H_2O when burned completely in oxygen?

90. ▲ Iron(II) chloride and sodium sulfide react to form iron(II) sulfide and sodium chloride (ChemistryNow Screen 4.8.)
(a) Write the balanced equation for the reaction.
(b) If you combine 40 g each of Na_2S and $FeCl_2$, what is the limiting reactant?
(c) What mass of FeS is produced?
(d) What mass of Na_2S or $FeCl_2$ remains after the reaction?
(e) What mass of $FeCl_2$ is required to react completely with 40 g of Na_2S?

91. Sulfuric acid can be prepared starting with the sulfide ore, cuprite (Cu_2S). If each S atom in Cu_2S leads to one molecule of H_2SO_4, what is the theoretical yield of H_2SO_4 from 3.00 kg of Cu_2S?

92. ▲ In an experiment, 1.056 g of a metal carbonate, containing an unknown metal M, is heated to give the metal oxide and 0.376 g CO_2.

$$MCO_3(s) + \text{heat} \rightarrow MO(s) + CO_2(g)$$

What is the identity of the metal M?
(a) M = Ni   (c) M = Zn
(b) M = Cu   (d) M = Ba

93. ■▲ An unknown metal reacts with oxygen to give the metal oxide, MO_2. Identify the metal based on the following information:

Mass of metal = 0.356 g

Mass of sample after converting metal completely to oxide = 0.452 g

94. ▲ Titanium(IV) oxide, TiO_2, is heated in hydrogen gas to give water and a new titanium oxide, Ti_xO_y. If 1.598 g of TiO_2 produces 1.438 g of Ti_xO_y, what is the empirical formula of the new oxide?

95. ■▲ Potassium perchlorate is prepared by the following sequence of reactions:

$$Cl_2(g) + 2\ KOH(aq) \rightarrow KCl(aq) + KClO(aq) + H_2O(\ell)$$
$$3\ KClO(aq) \rightarrow 2\ KCl(aq) + KClO_3(aq)$$
$$4\ KClO_3(aq) \rightarrow 3\ KClO_4(aq) + KCl(aq)$$

What mass of $Cl_2(g)$ is required to produce 234 kg of $KClO_4$?

96. ■▲ Commercial sodium "hydrosulfite" is 90.1% $Na_2S_2O_4$. The sequence of reactions used to prepare the compound is

$$Zn(s) + 2\ SO_2(g) \rightarrow ZnS_2O_4(s)$$
$$ZnS_2O_4(s) + Na_2CO_3(aq) \rightarrow ZnCO_3(s) + Na_2S_2O_4(aq)$$

(a) What mass of pure $Na_2S_2O_4$ can be prepared from 125 kg of Zn, 500 g of SO_2, and an excess of Na_2CO_3?
(b) What mass of the commercial product would contain the $Na_2S_2O_4$ produced using the amounts of reactants in part (a)?

97. ■ What mass of lime, CaO, can be obtained by heating 125 kg of limestone that is 95.0% by mass $CaCO_3$?

$$CaCO_3(s) \rightarrow CaO(s) + CO_2(g)$$

98. ▲ The elements silver, molybdenum, and sulfur combine to form Ag_2MoS_4. What is the maximum mass of Ag_2MoS_4 that can be obtained if 8.63 g of silver, 3.36 g of molybdenum, and 4.81 g of sulfur are combined?

▲ more challenging   ■ in OWL   Blue-numbered questions answered in Appendix O

99. ■▲ A mixture of butene, C_4H_8, and butane, C_4H_{10}, is burned in air to give CO_2 and water. Suppose you burn 2.86 g of the mixture and obtain 8.80 g of CO_2 and 4.14 g of H_2O. What are the mass percentages of butene and butane in the mixture?

100. ■▲ Cloth can be waterproofed by coating it with a silicone layer. This is done by exposing the cloth to $(CH_3)_2SiCl_2$ vapor. The silicon compound reacts with OH groups on the cloth to form a waterproofing film (density = 1.0 g/cm³) of $[(CH_3)_2SiO]_n$, where n is a large integer number.

$$n\,(CH_3)_2SiCl_2 + 2n\,OH^- \rightarrow 2n\,Cl^- + n\,H_2O + [(CH_3)_2SiO]_n$$

The coating is added layer by layer, each layer of $[(CH_3)_2SiO]_n$ being 0.60 nm thick. Suppose you want to waterproof a piece of cloth that is 3.00 m square, and you want 250 layers of waterproofing compound on the cloth. What mass of $(CH_3)_2SiCl_2$ do you need?

101. ■▲ Copper metal can be prepared by roasting copper ore, which can contain cuprite (Cu_2S) and copper(II) sulfide.

$$Cu_2S(s) + O_2(g) \rightarrow 2\,Cu(s) + SO_2(g)$$
$$CuS(s) + O_2(g) \rightarrow Cu(s) + SO_2(g)$$

Suppose an ore sample contains 11.0% impurity in addition to a mixture of CuS and Cu_2S. Heating 100.0 g of the mixture produces 75.4 g of copper metal with a purity of 89.5%. What is the weight percent of CuS in the ore? The weight percent of Cu_2S?

102. Which has the larger concentration of hydronium ions, 0.015 M HCl or aqueous HCl with a pH of 1.2?

103. The mineral dolomite contains magnesium carbonate.

$$MgCO_3(s) + 2\,HCl(aq) \rightarrow CO_2(g) + MgCl_2(aq) + H_2O(\ell)$$

(a) Write the net ionic equation for the reaction of $MgCO_3$ and HCl(aq).
(b) What type of reaction is this?
(c) What mass of $MgCO_3$ will react with 125 mL of HCl(aq) with a pH of 1.56?

104. An Alka-Seltzer tablet contains exactly 100. mg of citric acid, $H_3C_6H_5O_7$, plus some sodium bicarbonate. If the following reaction occurs, what mass of sodium bicarbonate must the tablet also contain if citric acid is completely consumed by the following reaction?

$$H_3C_6H_5O_7(aq) + 3\,NaHCO_3(aq) \rightarrow 3\,H_2O(\ell) + 3\,CO_2(g) + Na_3C_6H_5O_7(aq)$$

105. ▲ Sodium bicarbonate and acetic acid react according to the equation

$$NaHCO_3(aq) + CH_3CO_2H(aq) \rightarrow NaCH_3CO_2(aq) + CO_2(g) + H_2O(\ell)$$

What mass of sodium acetate can be obtained from mixing 15.0 g of $NaHCO_3$ with 125 mL of 0.15 M acetic acid?

106. ■ A noncarbonated soft drink contains an unknown amount of citric acid, $H_3C_6H_5O_7$. If 100. mL of the soft drink requires 33.51 mL of 0.0102 M NaOH to neutralize the citric acid completely, what mass of citric acid does the soft drink contain per 100. mL? The reaction of citric acid and NaOH is

$$H_3C_6H_5O_7(aq) + 3\,NaOH(aq) \rightarrow Na_3C_6H_5O_7(aq) + 3\,H_2O(\ell)$$

107. Sodium thiosulfate, $Na_2S_2O_3$, is used as a "fixer" in black-and-white photography. Suppose you have a bottle of sodium thiosulfate and want to determine its purity. The thiosulfate ion can be oxidized with I_2 according to the balanced, net ionic equation

$$I_2(aq) + 2\,S_2O_3^{2-}(aq) \rightarrow 2\,I^-(aq) + S_4O_6^{2-}(aq)$$

If you use 40.21 mL of 0.246 M I_2 in a titration, what is the weight percent of $Na_2S_2O_3$ in a 3.232-g sample of impure material?

108. You have a mixture of oxalic acid, $H_2C_2O_4$, and another solid that does not react with sodium hydroxide. If 29.58 mL of 0.550 M NaOH is required to titrate the oxalic acid in the 4.554-g sample to the second equivalence point, what is the mass percent of oxalic acid in the mixture? Oxalic acid and NaOH react according to the equation

$$H_2C_2O_4(aq) + 2\,NaOH(aq) \rightarrow Na_2C_2O_4(aq) + 2\,H_2O(\ell)$$

109. (a) What is the pH of a 0.105 M HCl solution?
(b) What is the hydronium ion concentration in a solution with a pH of 2.56? Is the solution acidic or basic?
(c) A solution has a pH of 9.67. What is the hydronium ion concentration in the solution? Is the solution acidic or basic?
(d) A 10.0-mL sample of 2.56 M HCl is diluted with water to 250. mL. What is the pH of the dilute solution?

110. A solution of hydrochloric acid has a volume of 125 mL and a pH of 2.56. What mass of $NaHCO_3$ must be added to completely consume the HCl?

111. ▲ One half liter (500. mL) of 2.50 M HCl is mixed with 250. mL of 3.75 M HCl. Assuming the total solution volume after mixing is 750. mL, what is the concentration of hydrochloric acid in the resulting solution? What is its pH?

112. A solution of hydrochloric acid has a volume of 250. mL and a pH of 1.92. Exactly 250. mL of 0.0105 M NaOH is added. What is the pH of the resulting solution?

113. ▲ You place 2.56 g of $CaCO_3$ in a beaker containing 250. mL of 0.125 M HCl. When the reaction has ceased, does any calcium carbonate remain? What mass of $CaCl_2$ can be produced?

$$CaCO_3(s) + 2\,HCl(aq) \rightarrow CaCl_2(aq) + CO_2(g) + H_2O(\ell)$$

▲ more challenging ■ in OWL   Blue-numbered questions answered in Appendix O | **203**

114. The cancer chemotherapy drug cisplatin, $Pt(NH_3)_2Cl_2$, can be made by reacting $(NH_4)_2PtCl_4$ with ammonia in aqueous solution. Besides cisplatin, the other product is NH_4Cl.
(a) Write a balanced equation for this reaction.
(b) To obtain 12.50 g of cisplatin, what mass of $(NH_4)_2PtCl_4$ is required? What volume of 0.125 M NH_3 is required?
(c) ▲ Cisplatin can react with the organic compound pyridine, C_5H_5N, to form a new compound.

$$Pt(NH_3)_2Cl_2(aq) + x\, C_5H_5N(aq) \rightarrow$$
$$Pt(NH_3)_2Cl_2(C_5H_5N)_x(s)$$

Suppose you treat 0.150 g of cisplatin with what you believe is an excess of liquid pyridine (1.50 mL; $d = 0.979$ g/mL). When the reaction is complete, you can find out how much pyridine was not used by titrating the solution with standardized HCl. If 37.0 mL of 0.475 M HCl is required to titrate the excess pyridine,

$$C_5H_5N(aq) + HCl(aq) \rightarrow C_5H_5NH^+(aq) + Cl^-(aq)$$

what is the formula of the unknown compound $Pt(NH_3)_2Cl_2(C_5H_5N)_x$?

115. ▲ You need to know the volume of water in a small swimming pool, but, owing to the pool's irregular shape, it is not a simple matter to determine its dimensions and calculate the volume. To solve the problem, you stir in a solution of a dye (1.0 g of methylene blue, $C_{16}H_{18}ClN_3S$, in 50.0 mL of water). After the dye has mixed with the water in the pool, you take a sample of the water. Using a spectrophotometer, you determine that the concentration of the dye in the pool is 4.1×10^{-8} M. What is the volume of water in the pool?

116. ▲ Calcium and magnesium carbonates occur together in the mineral dolomite. Suppose you heat a sample of the mineral to obtain the oxides, CaO and MgO, and then treat the oxide sample with hydrochloric acid. If 7.695 g of the oxide sample requires 125 mL of 2.55 M HCl,

$$CaO(s) + 2\, HCl(aq) \rightarrow CaCl_2(aq) + H_2O(\ell)$$

$$MgO(s) + 2\, HCl(aq) \rightarrow MgCl_2(aq) + H_2O(\ell)$$

What is the weight percent of each oxide (CaO and MgO) in the sample?

117. ■ Gold can be dissolved from gold-bearing rock by treating the rock with sodium cyanide in the presence of oxygen.

$$4\, Au(s) + 8\, NaCN(aq) + O_2(g) + 2\, H_2O(\ell) \rightarrow$$
$$4\, NaAu(CN)_2(aq) + 4\, NaOH(aq)$$

(a) Name the oxidizing and reducing agents in this reaction. What has been oxidized, and what has been reduced?
(b) If you have exactly one metric ton (1 metric ton = 1000 kg) of gold-bearing rock, what volume of 0.075 M NaCN, in liters, do you need to extract the gold if the rock is 0.019% gold?

118. ▲ You mix 25.0 mL of 0.234 M $FeCl_3$ with 42.5 mL of 0.453 M NaOH.
(a) What mass of $Fe(OH)_3$ (in grams) will precipitate from this reaction mixture?
(b) One of the reactants ($FeCl_3$ or NaOH) is present in a stoichiometric excess. What is the molar concentration of the excess reactant remaining in solution after $Fe(OH)_3$ has been precipitated?

In the Laboratory

119. ■ Suppose you dilute 25.0 mL of a 0.110 M solution of Na_2CO_3 to exactly 100.0 mL. You then take exactly 10.0 mL of this diluted solution and add it to a 250-mL volumetric flask. After filling the volumetric flask to the mark with distilled water (indicating the volume of the new solution is 250. mL), what is the concentration of the diluted Na_2CO_3 solution?

120. ▲ In some laboratory analyses, the preferred technique is to dissolve a sample in an excess of acid or base and then "back-titrate" the excess with a standard base or acid. This technique is used to assess the purity of a sample of $(NH_4)_2SO_4$. Suppose you dissolve a 0.475-g sample of impure $(NH_4)_2SO_4$ in aqueous KOH.

$$(NH_4)_2SO_4(aq) + 2\, KOH(aq) \rightarrow$$
$$2\, NH_3(aq) + 2\, K_2SO_4(aq) + 2\, H_2O(\ell)$$

The NH_3 liberated in the reaction is distilled from the solution into a flask containing 50.0 mL of 0.100 M HCl. The ammonia reacts with the acid to produce NH_4Cl, but not all of the HCl is used in this reaction. The amount of excess acid is determined by titrating the solution with standardized NaOH. This titration consumes 11.1 mL of 0.121 M NaOH. What is the weight percent of $(NH_4)_2SO_4$ in the 0.475-g sample?

121. You wish to determine the weight percent of copper in a copper-containing alloy. After dissolving a 0.251-g sample of the alloy in acid, an excess of KI is added, and the Cu^{2+} and I^- ions undergo the reaction

$$2\, Cu^{2+}(aq) + 5\, I^-(aq) \rightarrow 2\, CuI(s) + I_3^-(aq)$$

The liberated I_3^- is titrated with sodium thiosulfate according to the equation

$$I_3^-(aq) + 2\, S_2O_3^{2-}(aq) \rightarrow S_4O_6^{2-}(aq) + 3\, I^-(aq)$$

(a) Designate the oxidizing and reducing agents in the two reactions above.
(b) If 26.32 mL of 0.101 M $Na_2S_2O_3$ is required for titration to the equivalence point, what is the weight percent of Cu in the alloy?

122. ▲ A compound has been isolated that can have either of two possible formulas: (a) $K[Fe(C_2O_4)_2(H_2O)_2]$ or (b) $K_3[Fe(C_2O_4)_3]$. To find which is correct, you dissolve a weighed sample of the compound in acid and then titrate the oxalate ion ($C_2O_4^{2-}$, which in acid becomes $H_2C_2O_4$) with potassium permanganate, $KMnO_4$ (the source of the MnO_4^- ion). The balanced, net ionic equation for the titration is

$$5\,H_2C_2O_4(aq) + 2\,MnO_4^-(aq) + 6\,H_3O^+(aq) \rightarrow$$
$$2\,Mn^{2+}(aq) + 10\,CO_2(g) + 14\,H_2O(\ell)$$

Titration of 1.356 g of the compound requires 34.50 mL of 0.108 M $KMnO_4$. Which is the correct formula of the iron-containing compound: (a) or (b)?

123. ▲ Chromium(III) ion forms many compounds with ammonia. To find the formula of one of these compounds, you titrate the NH_3 in the compound with standardized acid.

$$Cr(NH_3)_xCl_3(aq) + x\,HCl(aq) \rightarrow$$
$$x\,NH_4^+(aq) + Cr^{3+}(aq) + (x + 3)\,Cl^-(aq)$$

Assume that 24.26 mL of 1.500 M HCl is used to titrate 1.580 g of $Cr(NH_3)_xCl_3$. What is the value of x?

124. ▲ Thioridazine, $C_{21}H_{26}N_2S_2$, is a pharmaceutical agent used to regulate dopamine. (Dopamine, a neurotransmitter, affects brain processes that control movement, emotional response, and ability to experience pleasure and pain.) A chemist can analyze a sample of the pharmaceutical for the thioridazine content by decomposing it to convert the sulfur in the compound to sulfate ion. This is then "trapped" as water-insoluble barium sulfate (see Figure 4.6).

$$SO_4^{2-}(aq,\ from\ thioridazine) + BaCl_2(aq) \rightarrow$$
$$BaSO_4(s) + 2\,Cl^-(aq)$$

Suppose a 12-tablet sample of the drug yielded 0.301 g of $BaSO_4$. What is the thioridazine content, in milligrams, of each tablet?

125. ■▲ A herbicide contains 2,4-D (2,4-dichlorophenoxyacetic acid), $C_8H_6Cl_2O_3$. A 1.236-g sample of the herbicide was decomposed to liberate the chlorine as Cl^- ion. This was precipitated as AgCl, with a mass of 0.1840 g. What is the mass percent of 2,4-D in the sample?

126. ▲ Sulfuric acid is listed in a catalog with a concentration of 95–98%. A bottle of the acid in the stockroom states that 1.00 L has a mass of 1.84 kg. To determine the concentration of sulfuric acid in the stockroom bottle, a student dilutes 5.00 mL to 500. mL. She then takes four 10.00-mL samples and titrates each with standardized sodium hydroxide ($c = 0.1760$ mol/L).

Sample	1	2	3	4
Volume NaOH (mL)	20.15	21.30	20.40	20.35

(a) What is the average concentration of the diluted sulfuric acid sample?
(b) What is the mass percent of H_2SO_4 in the original bottle of the acid?

127. ▲ Anhydrous calcium chloride is a good drying agent as it will rapidly pick up water. Suppose you have stored some carefully dried $CaCl_2$ in a dessicator. Unfortunately, someone did not close the top of the dessicator tightly, and the $CaCl_2$ became partially hydrated. A 150-g sample of this partially hydrated material was dissolved in 80 g of hot water. When the solution was cooled to 20 °C, 74.9 g of $CaCl_2 \cdot 6\,H_2O$ precipitated. Knowing the solubility of calcium chloride in water at 20 °C is 74.5 g $CaCl_2$/100 g water, determine the water content of the 150-g sample of partially hydrated calcium chloride (in moles of water per mole of $CaCl_2$).

128. ▲ A sample consisting of a mixture of iron and iron(III) oxide was dissolved completely in acid (which converted the iron to iron(III) ions.) After adding a reducing agent to ensure that all of the iron was in the form of iron(II) ions, the solution was titrated with the standardized $KMnO_4$ (0.04240 M); 37.50 mL of the $KMnO_4$ solution was required. Calculate the mass percent of Fe and Fe_2O_3 in the 0.5510-g sample. (See Example 4.12 for the reaction of iron(II) and $KMnO_4$.)

129. ▲ Phosphate in urine can be determined by spectrophotometry. After removing protein from the sample, it is treated with a molybdenum compound to give, ultimately, a deep blue polymolybdate. The absorbance of the blue polymolybdate can be measured at 650 nm and is directly related to the urine phosphate concentration. A 24-hour urine sample was collected from a patient; the volume of urine was 1122 mL. The phosphate in a 1.00 mL portion of the urine sample was converted to the blue polymolybdate (P) and diluted to 50.00 mL. A calibration curve was prepared using phosphate-containing solutions.

Solution (mass P/L)	Absorbance at 650 nm in a 1.0 cm cell
1.00×10^{-6} g	0.230
2.00×10^{-6} g	0.436
3.00×10^{-6} g	0.638
4.00×10^{-6} g	0.848
Urine sample	0.518

(a) What are the slope and intercept of the calibration curve?
(b) What is the mass of phosphorus per liter of urine?
(c) What mass of phosphate did the patient excrete per day?

130. ▲ A 4.000-g sample containing KCl and KClO$_4$ was dissolved in sufficient water to give 250.00 mL of solution. A 50.00-mL portion of the solution required 41.00 mL of 0.0750 M AgNO$_3$ in a Mohr titration (page 186). Next, a 25.00-mL portion of the original solution was treated with V$_2$(SO$_4$)$_3$ to reduce the perchlorate ion to chloride,

$$8\ V^{3+}(aq) + ClO_4^-(aq) + 12\ H_2O(\ell) \longrightarrow$$
$$Cl^-(aq) + 8\ VO^{2+}(aq) + 8\ H_3O^+(aq)$$

and the resulting solution was titrated with AgNO$_3$. This titration required 38.12 mL of 0.0750 M AgNO$_3$. What is the mass percent of KCl and KClO$_4$ in the mixture?

Summary and Conceptual Questions

The following questions may use concepts from this and preceding chapters.

131. Two beakers sit on a balance; the total mass is 167.170 g. One beaker contains a solution of KI; the other contains a solution of Pb(NO$_3$)$_2$. When the solution in one beaker is poured completely into the other, the following reaction occurs:

$$2\ KI(aq) + Pb(NO_3)_2(aq) \longrightarrow 2\ KNO_3(aq) + PbI_2(s)$$

Solutions of KI and Pb(NO$_3$)$_2$ before reaction.　Solutions after reaction.

What is the total mass of the beakers and solutions after reaction? Explain completely.

132. ▲ A weighed sample of iron (Fe) is added to liquid bromine (Br$_2$) and allowed to react completely. The reaction produces a single product, which can be isolated and weighed. The experiment was repeated a number of times with different masses of iron but with the same mass of bromine. (See the graph below.)

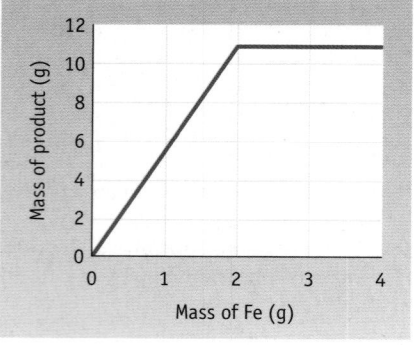

(a) What mass of Br$_2$ is used when the reaction consumes 2.0 g of Fe?
(b) What is the mole ratio of Br$_2$ to Fe in the reaction?
(c) What is the empirical formula of the product?
(d) Write the balanced chemical equation for the reaction of iron and bromine.
(e) What is the name of the reaction product?
(f) Which statement or statements best describe the experiments summarized by the graph?
   (i) When 1.00 g of Fe is added to the Br$_2$, Fe is the limiting reagent.
   (ii) When 3.50 g of Fe is added to the Br$_2$, there is an excess of Br$_2$.
   (iii) When 2.50 g of Fe is added to the Br$_2$, both reactants are used up completely.
   (iv) When 2.00 g of Fe is added to the Br$_2$, 10.0 g of product is formed. The percent yield must therefore be 20.0%.

133. Let us explore a reaction with a limiting reactant. (See ChemistryNow Screens 4.4 and 4.5.) Here, zinc metal is added to a flask containing aqueous HCl, and H$_2$ gas is a product.

$$Zn(s) + 2\ HCl(aq) \longrightarrow ZnCl_2(aq) + H_2(g)$$

The three flasks each contain 0.100 mol of HCl. Zinc is added to each flask in the following quantities.

Flask 1: 7.00 g Zn
Flask 2: 3.27 g Zn
Flask 3: 1.31 g Zn

When the reactants are combined, the H$_2$ inflates the balloon attached to the flask. The results are as follows:

Flask 1: Balloon inflates completely, but some Zn remains when inflation ceases.
Flask 2: Balloon inflates completely. No Zn remains.
Flask 3: Balloon does not inflate completely. No Zn remains.

Explain these results. Perform calculations that support your explanation.

▲ more challenging　■ in OWL　Blue-numbered questions answered in Appendix O

134. The reaction of aluminum and bromine is pictured in Figure 2.12 and below. The white solid on the lip of the beaker at the end of the reaction is Al_2Br_6. In the reaction pictured below, which was the limiting reactant, Al or Br_2? (See ChemistryNow Screen 4.2.)

Before reaction.

After reaction.

135. ▲ Two students titrate different samples of the same solution of HCl using 0.100 M NaOH solution and phenolphthalein indicator (see Figure 4.14). The first student pipets 20.0 mL of the HCl solution into a flask, adds 20 mL of distilled water and a few drops of phenolphthalein solution, and titrates until a lasting pink color appears. The second student pipets 20.0 mL of the HCl solution into a flask, adds 60 mL of distilled water and a few drops of phenolphthalein solution, and titrates to the first lasting pink color. Each student correctly calculates the molarity of an HCl solution. What will the second student's result be?
(a) four times less than the first student's result
(b) four times greater than the first student's result
(c) two times less than the first student's result
(d) two times greater than the first student's result
(e) the same as the first student's result

136. A video on Screen 4.12 of ChemistryNow shows the reaction of Fe^{2+} with MnO_4^- in aqueous solution.
(a) What is the balanced equation for the reaction that occurred?
(b) What is the oxidizing agent, and what is the reducing agent?
(c) Equal volumes of Fe^{2+}-containing solution and MnO_4^--containing solution were mixed. The amount of Fe^{2+} was just sufficient to consume all of the MnO_4^-. Which ion (Fe^{2+} or MnO_4^-) was initially present in larger concentration?

137. In some states, a person will receive a "driving while intoxicated" (DWI) ticket if the blood alcohol level (BAL) is 100 mg per deciliter (dL) of blood or higher. Suppose a person is found to have a BAL of 0.033 mol of ethanol (C_2H_5OH) per liter of blood. Will the person receive a DWI ticket?

5 | Principles of Chemical Reactivity: Energy and Chemical Reactions

©Nicolas Raymond

A Hot Air Balloon

These colorful balloons usually consist of a gas bag or envelope of nylon with a basket suspended below for passengers. A propane burner sits on top of the basket and below the gas envelope. When the air inside the envelope is heated by burning propane, the balloon can ascend (because the density of heated air in the bag is less than that of the cooler surrounding air). Under normal conditions, about 3 m³ of envelope volume is required to lift 1 kg of mass. Thus, to carry one person and the needed equipment, most balloons have a volume of about 1000 m³.

Question:

You have a balloon with a volume of 1100 m³ and want to heat the air inside of the envelope from 22 °C to 110 °C. What mass of propane must you burn to accomplish this? (The specific heat capacity of air is 1.01 J/g · K, and the density of dry air [at sea level] is about 1.2 kg/m³. Other information you need is in this chapter or Appendix L.)

Answer to this question is in Appendix Q.

Chapter Goals

OWL *See Chapter Goals Revisited (page 241) for Study Questions keyed to these goals and assignable in OWL.*

- Assess the transfer of energy as heat associated with changes in temperature and changes of state.
- Understand and apply the first law of thermodynamics.
- Define and understand state functions (enthalpy, internal energy).
- Learn how energy changes are measured.
- Calculate the energy evolved or required for physical changes and chemical reactions using tables of thermodynamic data.

The importance of energy is evident in our daily lives—in heating and cooling our homes, in powering our appliances, and in propelling our vehicles, among other things. Most of the energy we use for these purposes is obtained by carrying out chemical reactions, mostly by burning fossil fuels. We use natural gas for heating, coal and natural gas to generate most of our electric power, and fuels derived from petroleum for automobiles and for heat. In addition, energy is required for all life processes. Chemical reactions in our bodies provide the energy for all body functions, for movement, and to maintain body temperature. It is not surprising that the topic of energy is a prominent part of our discussion of chemistry.

To scientists, however, energy has significance that goes well beyond these many practical uses. In this chapter, we will begin the discussion of **thermodynamics**, the science of heat and work. This subject will provide important insights on the following questions:

- How do we measure and calculate the energy changes that are associated with physical changes and chemical reactions?
- What is the relationship between energy changes, heat, and work?
- How can we determine whether a chemical reaction is product-favored or reactant-favored at equilibrium?
- How can we determine whether a chemical reaction or physical process will occur spontaneously, that is, without outside intervention?

We will concentrate attention on the first two questions in this chapter and address the last two questions in Chapter 19.

5.1 Energy: Some Basic Principles

Energy is defined as the capacity to do work. You do work against the force of gravity when carrying yourself and hiking equipment up a mountain. The energy to do this is provided by the food you have eaten. Food is a source of chemical energy—energy stored in chemical compounds and released when the compounds undergo the chemical reactions of metabolism in your body.

Chemistry.Now™

Throughout the text this icon introduces an opportunity for self-study or to explore interactive tutorials by signing in at **www.cengage.com/login**.

■ **World Energy Consumption** Burning fossil fuels provides about 85% of the total energy used by people on our planet. Nuclear and hydroelectric power each contribute about 6%. The remaining 3% is provided from biomass, solar, wind, and geothermal sources.

James Cowlin

Royalty-Free/Corbis

William James Warren/Corbis

(a) Gravitational energy   (b) Chemical potential energy   (c) Electrostatic energy

Active Figure 5.1 | **Energy and its conversion.** (a) Water at the top of a waterfall represents stored, or potential, energy. As water falls, its potential energy is converted to mechanical energy. (b) Chemical potential energy of the fuel and oxygen is converted to thermal and mechanical energy. (c) Lightning converts electrostatic energy into radiant and thermal energy.

Chemistry ⚛ Now™ Sign in at www.cengage.com/login and go to the Chapter Contents menu to explore an interactive version of this figure accompanied by an exercise.

Energy can be classified as kinetic or potential. **Kinetic energy** is energy associated with motion, such as:

- The motion of atoms, molecules, or ions at the submicroscopic (particulate) level (*thermal energy*). All matter has thermal energy.
- The motion of macroscopic objects like a moving tennis ball or automobile (*mechanical energy*).
- The movement of electrons through a conductor (*electrical energy*).
- The compression and expansion of the spaces between molecules in the transmission of sound (*acoustic energy*).

Potential energy results from an object's position and includes:

- Energy possessed by a ball held above the floor and by water at the top of a waterfall (*gravitational energy*) (Figure 5.1a).
- Energy stored in fuels (*chemical energy*) (Figure 5.1b). All chemical reactions involve a change in chemical energy.
- The energy associated with the separation of two electrical charges (*electrostatic energy*) (Figure 5.1c).

Potential energy and kinetic energy can be interconverted. For example, as water falls over a waterfall, its potential energy is converted into kinetic energy. Similarly, kinetic energy can be converted into potential energy: The kinetic energy of falling water can turn a turbine to produce electricity, which can then be used to convert water into H_2 and O_2 by electrolysis. Hydrogen gas contains stored chemical potential energy because it can be burned to produce heat and light or electricity.

Sign in at **www.cengage.com/login** and go to Chapter 5 Contents to see Screen 5.3 for an exercise that examines examples of **energy transfer.**

Conservation of Energy

Standing on a diving board, you have considerable potential energy because of your position above the water. Once you jump off the board, some of that potential energy is converted into kinetic energy (Figure 5.2). During the dive, the force of gravity accelerates your body so that it moves faster and faster. Your kinetic energy increases, and your potential energy decreases. At the moment you hit the water, your velocity is abruptly reduced, and much of your kinetic energy is transferred to the water as your body moves it aside. Eventually, you float to the surface, and the water becomes still again. If you could see them, however, you would find that the water molecules are moving a little faster in the vicinity of your entry into the water; that is, the kinetic energy of the water molecules is slightly higher.

This series of energy conversions illustrates the **law of conservation of energy**, which states that *energy can neither be created nor destroyed.* Or, to state this law differently, *the total energy of the universe is constant.* The law of conservation of energy summarizes the results of a great many experiments in which the amounts of energy transferred have been measured and in which the total energy content has been found to be the same before and after an event.

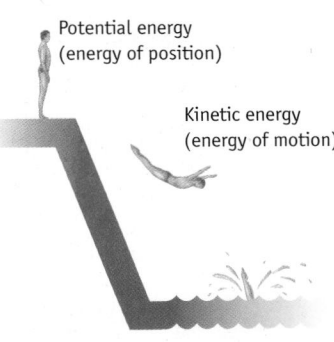

FIGURE 5.2 The law of energy conservation. The diver's potential energy is converted to kinetic energy, and this is then transferred to the water, illustrating the law of conservation of energy. See ChemistryNow Screen 5.2 Energy, to view an animation of this figure.

Temperature and Heat

The temperature of an object is a measure of its ability to transfer energy as heat. When two objects at different temperatures are brought into contact, energy will be transferred as heat from the one at the higher temperature to the one at the lower temperature. One way to measure temperature is with a thermometer containing mercury or some other liquid (Figure 5.3). When the thermometer is placed

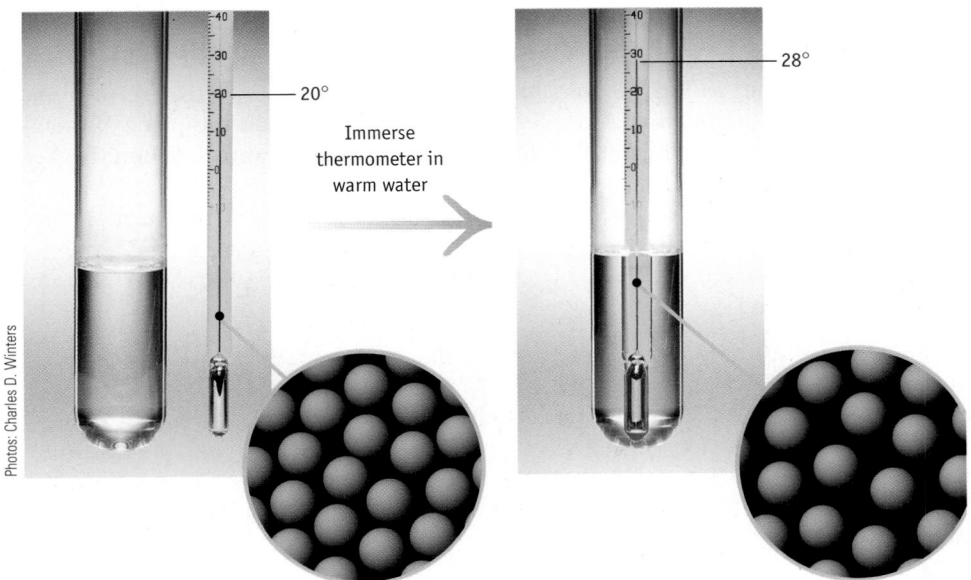

Photos: Charles D. Winters

FIGURE 5.3 Measuring temperature. The volume of liquid mercury in a thermometer increases slightly when immersed in warm water. The volume increase causes the mercury to rise in the thermometer, which is calibrated to give the temperature.

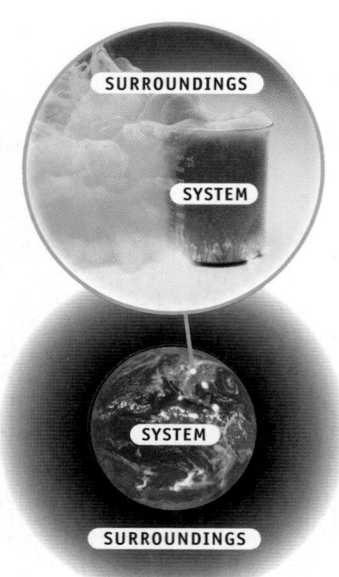

FIGURE 5.4 Systems and their surroundings. Earth can be considered a thermodynamic system, with the rest of the universe as its surroundings. A chemical reaction occurring in a laboratory is also a system, with the laboratory its surroundings.

Photos: (Top) Charles D. Winters; (Bottom) NASA

in hot water, thermal energy is transferred from the water to the thermometer (heating the thermometer and cooling the water). This causes the atoms of liquid mercury to move more rapidly (increasing their kinetic energy) and the space between them to increase slightly. The resulting increase in volume causes the column of liquid to rise higher in the thermometer tube.

Several important aspects of thermal energy and temperature should be recognized:

- Temperature determines the direction of thermal energy transfer.
- The higher the temperature of a given object, the greater the thermal energy (energy associated with molecular motion) of its atoms, ions, or molecules.
- Heating and cooling are processes by which energy is transferred as heat from an object at a higher temperature to one at a lower temperature. Heat is not a substance. (See *A Closer Look: What Is Heat?*)

Systems and Surroundings

In thermodynamics, the terms "system" and "surroundings" have precise and important scientific meanings. A **system** is defined as an object, or collection of objects, being studied (Figure 5.4). The **surroundings** include everything outside the system that can exchange energy and/or matter with the system. In the discussion that follows, we will need to define systems precisely. If we are studying the energy evolved in a chemical reaction carried out in solution, for example, the system might be defined as the reactants, products, and solvent. The surroundings would be the reaction vessel and the air in the room and anything else in contact with the vessel that might exchange energy or matter. At the atomic level, the system could be a single atom or molecule, and the surroundings would be the atoms or molecules in its vicinity. How we choose to define the system and its surroundings for each situation depends on the information we are trying to obtain or convey.

This concept of a system and its surroundings applies to nonchemical situations as well. If we want to study the energy balance on this planet, we might choose to define Earth as the system and outer space as the surroundings. On a cosmic level, the solar system might be defined as the system being studied, and the rest of the galaxy would be the surroundings.

Directionality and Extent of Transfer of Heat: Thermal Equilibrium

Energy is transferred as heat if two objects at different temperatures are brought into contact. In Figure 5.5, for example, the beaker of water and the piece of metal being heated in a Bunsen burner flame have different temperatures. When the hot

FIGURE 5.5 Energy transfer. Energy transfer as heat occurs from the hotter metal bar to the cooler water. Eventually, the water and metal reach the same temperature and are said to be in thermal equilibrium.

See ChemistryNow Screen 5.4, Energy Transfer Between Substances, for a simulation and tutorial.

Charles D. Winters

What Is Heat?

Two hundred years ago, scientists characterized heat as a real substance called a caloric fluid. The caloric hypothesis supposed that when a fuel burned and a pot of water was heated, for example, caloric fluid was transferred from the fuel to the water. Burning the fuel released caloric fluid, and the temperature of the water increased as the caloric fluid was absorbed.

Over the next 50 years, however, the caloric hypothesis lost favor, and we now know it is incorrect. Experiments by James Joule (1818–1889) and Benjamin Thompson (1753–1814) that showed the interrelationship between heat and other forms of energy such as mechanical energy provided the key to dispelling this idea. Even so, some of our everyday language retains the influence of this early theory. For example, we often speak of heat flowing as if it were a fluid.

From our discussion so far, we know one thing that "heat" is not—but what is it? Heat is said to be a "process quantity" as opposed to a "state quantity." That is, heating is a *process* that changes the internal energy of a system. It is the process by which energy is transferred across the boundary of a system owing to a difference in temperature between the two sides of the boundary. In this process, the energy of one object increases, and the energy of another object decreases.

Heating is not the only way to transfer energy. Work is another process by which energy can be transferred between objects.

The idea of energy transfer by the processes of heat and work is embodied in the definition of thermodynamics: the science of heat and work.

Richard Howard

Work and heat. A classic experiment that showed the relationship between work and heat was performed by Benjamin Thompson (also known as Count Rumford) (1753–1814) using an apparatus similar to that shown here. Thompson measured the rise in temperature of water (in the vessel mostly hidden at the back of the apparatus) that resulted from the energy expended to turn the crank.

---

metal is plunged into the cold water, energy is transferred as heat from the metal to the water. The thermal energy (molecular motion) of the water molecules increases; the thermal energy of the metal atoms decreases. Eventually, the two objects reach the same temperature. At that point, the system has reached **thermal equilibrium**. The distinguishing feature of thermal equilibrium is that, on the macroscopic scale, no further temperature change occurs; both the metal and water are at the same temperature.

Putting a hot metal bar into a beaker of water and following the temperature change may seem like a rather simple experiment with an obvious outcome. Illustrated in the experiment, however, are three principles that are important in our further discussion:

- Energy transfer as heat will occur spontaneously from an object at a higher temperature to an object at a lower temperature.
- Transfer of energy as heat continues until both objects are at the same temperature and thermal equilibrium is achieved.
- After thermal equilibrium is attained, the object whose temperature increased has gained thermal energy, and the object whose temperature decreased has lost thermal energy.

For the specific case where energy is transferred as heat within an isolated system (that is, a system that cannot transfer either energy or matter with its surroundings), we can also say that the quantity of thermal energy lost by a hotter object and the quantity of thermal energy gained by a cooler object are numerically equal. (This is required by the law of conservation of energy.) When energy is transferred as

■ **Thermal Equilibrium** Although no change is evident at the macroscopic level when thermal equilibrium is reached, on the molecular level transfer of energy between individual molecules will continue to occur. A general feature of systems at equilibrium is that there is no change on a macroscopic level but that processes still occur at the particulate level. (See Section 3.3, page 118.)

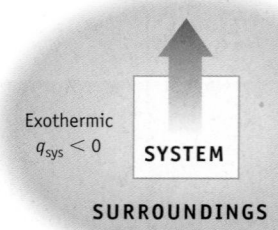
Exothermic
$q_{sys} < 0$ **SYSTEM**

SURROUNDINGS

Exothermic: energy transferred
from system to surroundings

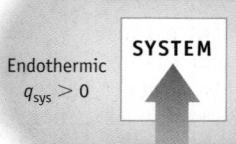
SYSTEM
Endothermic
$q_{sys} > 0$

SURROUNDINGS

Endothermic: energy transferred
from surroundings to system

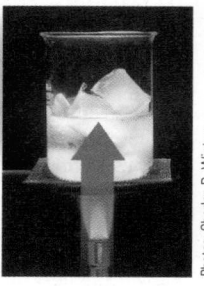

Photos: Charles D. Winters

Active Figure 5.6 **Exothermic and endothermic processes.** The symbol q represents the energy transferred as heat, and the subscript sys refers to the system.

Chemistry Now™ Sign in at www.cengage.com/login and go to the Chapter Contents menu to explore an interactive version of this figure accompanied by an exercise.

■ **Exothermic and Endothermic** The terms "endothermic" and "exothermic" apply specifically to energy transfer as heat. The more general terms "endoergic" and "exoergic" are sometimes used, encompassing any type of energy transfer between system and surroundings.

heat between a system and its surroundings, we describe the directionality of this transfer as exothermic or endothermic (Figure 5.6).

- In an **exothermic process**, energy is transferred as heat from a system to its surroundings. The energy of the system decreases, and the energy of the surroundings increases.
- An **endothermic process** is the opposite of an exothermic process. Energy is transferred as heat from the surroundings to the system, increasing the energy of the system, decreasing the energy of the surroundings.

Energy Units

■ **James Joule** The joule is named for James P. Joule (1818–1889), the son of a wealthy brewer in Manchester, England. The family wealth and a workshop in the brewery gave Joule the opportunity to pursue scientific studies. Among the topics that Joule studied was the issue of whether heat was a massless fluid. Scientists at that time referred to this idea as the caloric hypothesis. Joule's careful experiments showed that heat and mechanical work are related, providing evidence that heat is not a fluid. (See *A Closer Look: What Is Heat?*)

Oesper Collection in the History of Chemistry/University of Cincinnati

When expressing energy quantities, most chemists (and much of the world outside the United States) use the **joule** (J), the SI unit. The joule is related directly to the units used for mechanical energy: 1 J equals 1 kg · m²/s². Because the joule is inconveniently small for most uses in chemistry, the kilojoule (kJ), equivalent to 1000 joules, is often the unit of choice.

To give you some feeling for joules, suppose you drop a six-pack of soft-drink cans, each full of liquid, on your foot. Although you probably will not take time to calculate the kinetic energy at the moment of impact, it is between 4 J and 10 J.

The calorie (cal) is an older energy unit. It is defined as the energy transferred as heat that is required to raise the temperature of 1.00 g of pure liquid water from 14.5 °C to 15.5 °C. A kilocalorie (kcal) is equivalent to 1000 calories. The conversion factor relating joules and calories is

1 calorie (cal) = 4.184 joules (J)

The dietary Calorie (with a capital C) is often used in the United States to represent the energy content of foods. The dietary Calorie (Cal) is equivalent to the kilocalorie or 1000 calories. Thus, a breakfast cereal that gives you 100.0 Calories of nutritional energy per serving provides 100.0 kcal or 418.4 kJ.

Chemistry Now™

Sign in at **www.cengage.com/login** and go to Chapter 5 Contents to see Screen 5.4 to view an animation on **endothermic and exothermic systems** and Screen 5.5 for a tutorial on **converting between different energy units.**

Chemical Perspectives Food and Calories

The U.S. Food and Drug Administration (FDA) mandates that nutritional data, including energy content, be included on almost all packaged food. The Nutrition Labeling and Education Act of 1990 requires that the total energy from protein, carbohydrates, fat, and alcohol be specified. How is this determined? Initially, the method used was calorimetry. In this method, which is described in Section 5.6, a food product is burned, and the energy transferred as heat in the combustion is measured. Now, however, energy contents are estimated using the Atwater system. This specifies the following average values for energy sources in foods:

1 g protein = 4 kcal (17 kJ)
1 g carbohydrate = 4 kcal (17 kJ)
1 g fat = 9 kcal (38 kJ)
1 g alcohol = 7 kcal (29 kJ)

Because carbohydrates may contain some indigestible fiber, the mass of fiber is subtracted from the mass of carbohydrate when calculating the energy from carbohydrates.

As an example, one serving of cashew nuts (about 28 g) has

14 g fat = 126 kcal
6 g protein = 24 kcal
7 g carbohydrates − 1 g fiber = 24 kcal
Total = 174 kcal (728 kJ)

A value of 170 kcal is reported on the package.

You can find data on more than 6000 foods at the Nutrient Data Laboratory website (www.ars.usda.gov/ba/bhnrc/ndl).

Nutrition Facts
Serving Size 1 cup (30g)
Children Under 4 - ¾ cup (20g)
Servings Per Container About 19
Children Under 4 - About 28
Amount Per Serving
Cheerios
with ½ cup skim milk
Cereal for Children Under 4
Calories 110 150 70
Calories from Fat 15 20 10
% Daily Value**
Total Fat 2g* 3% 3% 1g
Saturated Fat 0g 0% 3% 0g
Polyunsaturated Fat 0.5g 0g
Monounsaturated Fat 0.5g 0g
Cholesterol 0mg 0% 1% 0mg
Sodium 210mg 9% 12% 140mg
Potassium 200mg 6% 12% 130mg

Charles D. Winters

Energy and food labels. All packaged foods must have labels specifying nutritional values, with energy given in Calories (where 1 Cal = 1 kilocalorie).

> **EXERCISE 5.1 Energy Units**
>
> **(a)** In an old textbook, you read that the burning 1.00 g of hydrogen to form liquid water produces 3800 calories. What is this energy in units of joules?
>
> **(b)** The label on a cereal box indicates that one serving (with skim milk) provides 250 Cal. What is this energy in kilojoules (kJ)?

■ **Kinetic Energy** Kinetic energy is calculated by the equation KE = $1/2\ mv^2$. One joule is the kinetic energy of a 2.0 kg mass (m) moving at 1.0 m/s (v).
KE = $(1/2)(2.0\ \text{kg})(1.0\ \text{m/s})^2$
= $1.0\ \text{kg} \cdot \text{m}^2/\text{s}^2 = 1.0\ \text{J}$

5.2 Specific Heat Capacity: Heating and Cooling

When an object is heated or cooled, the quantity of energy transferred depends on three things:

- The quantity of material
- The magnitude of the temperature change
- The identity of the material gaining or losing energy

Specific heat capacity (*C*) is defined as *the energy transferred as heat that is required to raise the temperature of 1 gram of a substance by one kelvin.* It has units of joules per gram per kelvin (J/g · K). A few specific heat capacities are listed in Figure 5.7, and a longer list of specific heat capacities is given in Appendix D (Table 11).

The energy gained or lost as heat when a given mass of a substance is warmed or cooled can be calculated using Equation 5.1.

$$q = C \times m \times \Delta T \quad (5.1)$$

Here, q is the energy gained or lost as heat by a given mass of substance (m); C is the specific heat capacity, and ΔT is the change in temperature. The change in temperature, ΔT, is calculated as the final temperature minus the initial temperature.

$$\Delta T = T_{\text{final}} - T_{\text{initial}} \quad (5.2)$$

■ **Change in Temperature, ΔT**

Sign of ΔT	Meaning
Positive	$T_{\text{final}} > T_{\text{initial}}$, so T has increased, and q will be positive. Energy has been transferred to the object under study.
Negative	$T_{\text{initial}} > T_{\text{final}}$, so T has decreased, and q will be negative. Energy has been transferred out of the object under study.

Specific Heat Capacities of Some Elements, Compounds, and Substances

Substances	Specific Heat Capacity (J/g · K)	Molar Heat Capacity (J/mol · K)
Al, aluminum	0.897	24.2
Fe, iron	0.449	25.1
Cu, copper	0.385	24.5
Water (liquid)	4.184	75.4
Water (ice)	2.06	37.1
$HOCH_2CH_2OH(\ell)$, ethylene glycol (antifreeze)	2.39	14.8
Wood	1.8	—
Glass	0.8	—

FIGURE 5.7 Specific heat capacity. Metals have different values of specific heat capacity on a per-gram basis. However, their molar heat capacities are all in the range of 25 J/mol · K. Among common substances, liquid water has the highest specific heat capacity on a per-gram or per-mole basis (except for liquid ammonia), a fact that plays a significant role in Earth's weather and climate.

■ **Molar Heat Capacity** Heat capacities can be expressed on a per-mole basis. The amount of energy that is transferred as heat in raising the temperature of one mole of a substance by one Kelvin is the molar heat capacity. For water, the molar heat capacity is 75.4 J/mol · K. The molar heat capacity of metals at room temperature is always near 25 kJ/mol · K.

Calculating a change in temperature using Equation 5.2 will give a result with an algebraic sign that indicates the direction of energy transfer. For example, we can use the specific heat capacity of copper, 0.385 J/g · K, to calculate the energy that must be transferred as heat to a 10.0-g sample of copper if its temperature is raised from 298 K (25 °C) to 598 K (325 °C).

$$q = \left(0.385 \ \frac{J}{g \cdot K}\right)(10.0 \ g)(598 \ K - 298 \ K) = +1160 \ J$$

T_{final} — Final temp. $T_{initial}$ — Initial temp.

Notice that the answer has a positive sign. This indicates that the thermal energy of the sample of copper has increased by 1160 J, which is in accord with energy being transferred as heat to the copper from the water.

The relationship between energy, mass, and specific heat capacity has numerous implications. The high specific heat capacity of liquid water, 4.184 J/g · K, is a major reason why large bodies of water have a profound influence on weather. In spring, lakes warm up more slowly than the air. In autumn, the energy given off by a large lake as it cools moderates the drop in air temperature. The relevance of specific heat capacity is also illustrated when bread is wrapped in aluminum foil (specific heat capacity 0.897 J/g · K) and heated in an oven. You can remove the foil with your fingers after taking the bread from the oven. The bread and the aluminum foil are very hot, but the small mass of aluminum foil used and its low specific heat capacity result in only a small quantity of energy being transferred to your fingers (which have a larger mass and a higher specific heat capacity) when you touch the hot foil. This is also the reason why a chain of fast-food restaurants warns you that the filling of an apple pie can be much warmer than the paper wrapper or the pie crust. Although the wrapper, pie crust, and filling are at the same temperature, the quantity of energy transferred to your fingers (or your mouth!) from the filling is greater than that transferred from the wrapper and crust.

A practical example of specific heat capacity. The filling of the apple pie has a higher specific heat (and higher mass) than the pie crust and wrapper. Notice the warning on the wrapper.

Chemistry. ○. Now™

Sign in at **www.cengage.com/login** and go to Chapter 5 Contents to see Screen 5.7 for a simulation and exercise on **energy transfer as heat.**

EXAMPLE 5.1 Specific Heat Capacity

Problem How much energy must be transferred to raise the temperature of a cup of coffee (250 mL) from 20.5 °C (293.7 K) to 95.6 °C (368.8 K)? Assume that water and coffee have the same density (1.00 g/mL), and specific heat capacity (4.184 J/g · K).

Strategy Use Equation 5.1. For the calculation, you will need the specific heat capacity for H_2O, the mass of the coffee (calculated from its density and volume), and the change in temperature ($T_{final} - T_{initial}$).

Solution

$$\text{Mass of coffee} = (250 \text{ mL})(1.00 \text{ g/mL}) = 250 \text{ g}$$

$$\Delta T = T_{final} - T_{initial} = 368.8 \text{ K} - 293.7 \text{ K} = 75.1 \text{ K}$$

$$q = C \times m \times \Delta T$$

$$q = (4.184 \text{ J/g} \cdot \text{K})(250 \text{ g})(75.1 \text{ K})$$

$$q = 79,000 \text{ J (or 79 kJ)}$$

Comment The positive sign in the answer indicates that thermal energy has been transferred to the coffee as heat. The thermal energy of the coffee is now higher.

EXERCISE 5.2 Specific Heat Capacity

In an experiment, it was determined that 59.8 J was required to raise the temperature of 25.0 g of ethylene glycol (a compound used as antifreeze in automobile engines) by 1.00 K. Calculate the specific heat capacity of ethylene glycol from these data.

Quantitative Aspects of Energy Transferred as Heat

Like melting point, boiling point, and density, specific heat capacity is a characteristic intensive property of a pure substance. The specific heat capacity of a substance can be determined experimentally by accurately measuring temperature changes that occur when energy is transferred as heat from the substance to a known quantity of water (whose specific heat capacity is known).

Suppose a 55.0-g piece of metal is heated in boiling water to 99.8 °C and then dropped into cool water in an insulated beaker (Figure 5.8). Assume the beaker contains 225 g of water and its initial temperature (before the metal was dropped in) was 21.0 °C. The final temperature of the metal and water is 23.1 °C. What is the specific heat capacity of the metal? Here are the important aspects of this experiment.

- Let us define the metal and the water as the system and the beaker and environment as the surroundings. We will assume that energy is transferred only within the system and not between the system and the surroundings. (This assumption is good, but not perfect; for a more accurate result, we would also want to account for any energy transfer to the surroundings.)
- The water and the metal bar end up at the same temperature. (T_{final} is the same for both.)
- We will also assume energy is transferred *only as heat* within the system.
- The energy transferred as heat from the metal to the water, q_{metal}, has a negative value because the temperature of the metal drops. Conversely, q_{water} has a positive value because its temperature increases.
- The values of q_{water} and q_{metal} are numerically equal but of opposite sign.

Because of the law of conservation of energy, *in an isolated system the sum of the energy changes within the system must be zero.* If energy is transferred only as heat, then

$$q_1 + q_2 + q_3 + \ldots = 0 \qquad (5.3)$$

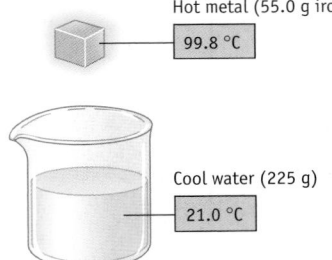

Hot metal (55.0 g iron)

99.8 °C

Cool water (225 g)

21.0 °C

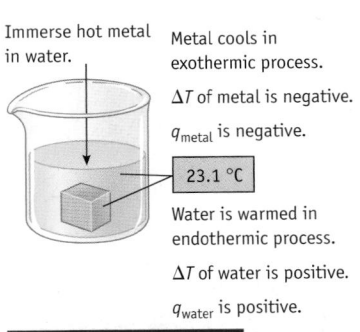

Immerse hot metal in water.

Metal cools in exothermic process.

ΔT of metal is negative.

q_{metal} is negative.

23.1 °C

Water is warmed in endothermic process.

ΔT of water is positive.

q_{water} is positive.

Active Figure 5.8 **Transfer of energy as heat.** When energy is transferred as heat from a hot metal to cool water, the thermal energy of the metal decreases, and that of the water increases. The value of q_{metal} is thus negative, and that of q_{water} is positive.

Chemistry ⚗ Now™ Sign in at **www.cengage.com/login** and go to the Chapter Contents menu to explore an interactive version of this figure accompanied by an exercise.

Calculating ΔT

Specific heat capacity values are given in units of joules per gram per kelvin (J/g · K). Virtually all calculations that involve temperature in chemistry are expressed in kelvins. In calculating ΔT, however, we can use Celsius temperatures because a kelvin and a Celsius degree are the same size. That is, the difference between two temperatures is the same on both scales. For example, the difference between the boiling and freezing points of water is

$$\Delta T, \text{Celsius} = 100\ ^{\circ}C - 0\ ^{\circ}C = 100\ ^{\circ}C$$

$$\Delta T, \text{kelvin} = 373\ K - 273\ K = 100\ K$$

where the quantities q_1, q_2, and so on represent the energies transferred as heat for the individual parts of the system. For this specific problem, there are thermal energy changes associated with water and metal, q_{water} and q_{metal}, the two components of the system; thus

$$q_{\text{water}} + q_{\text{metal}} = 0$$

Each of these quantities is related individually to specific heat capacities, mass, and change of temperature, as defined by Equation 5.1. Thus

$$[C_{\text{water}} \times m_{\text{water}} \times (T_{\text{final}} - T_{\text{initial, water}})] + [C_{\text{metal}} \times m_{\text{metal}} \times (T_{\text{final}} - T_{\text{initial, metal}})] = 0$$

The specific heat capacity of the metal, C_{metal}, is the unknown in this problem. Using the specific heat capacity of water (4.184 J/g · K) and converting Celsius to kelvin temperature gives

$$[(4.184\ \text{J/g} \cdot K)(225\ g)(296.3\ K - 294.2\ K)] + [(C_{\text{metal}})(55.0\ g)(296.3\ K - 373.0\ K)] = 0$$
$$C_{\text{metal}} = 0.469\ \text{J/g} \cdot K$$

Chemistry ⚛ Now™

Sign in at **www.cengage.com/login** and go to Chapter 5 Contents to see Screens 5.8 and 5.10 for exercises, tutorials, and simulations on **energy transfers as heat between substances** and **calculating energy transfer.**

■ **EXAMPLE 5.2** **Using Specific Heat Capacity**

Problem An 88.5-g piece of iron whose temperature is 78.8 °C (352.0 K) is placed in a beaker containing 244 g of water at 18.8 °C (292.0 K). When thermal equilibrium is reached, what is the final temperature? (Assume no energy is lost to warm the beaker and its surroundings.)

Strategy First, define the system as consisting of the iron and water. Within the system, energy is transferred as heat from the metal to the water; the metal thus loses thermal energy, and the water gains thermal energy. The sum of these energy changes must equal zero. Each of these energy changes is related to the specific heat capacity, mass, and temperature change of the substance (Equation 5.1). The specific heat capacities of iron and water are given in Appendix D, and the final temperature is unknown. The change in temperature, ΔT, may be in °C or K (see Problem Solving Tip 5.1).

Solution

$$q_{\text{metal}} + q_{\text{water}} = 0$$
$$[C_{\text{water}} \times m_{\text{water}} \times (T_{\text{final}} - T_{\text{initial, water}})] + [C_{Fe} \times m_{Fe} \times (T_{\text{final}} - T_{\text{initial, }Fe})] = 0$$
$$[(4.184\ \text{J/g} \cdot K)(244\ g)(T_{\text{final}} - 292.0\ K)] + [(0.449\ \text{J/g} \cdot K)(88.5\ g)(T_{\text{final}} - 352.0\ K)] = 0$$
$$T_{\text{final}} = 295\ K\ (22\ ^{\circ}C)$$

Comment Be sure to notice that T_{initial} for the metal and T_{initial} for the water in this problem have different values. Also, the low specific heat capacity and smaller quantity of iron result in the temperature of iron being reduced by about 60 degrees; in contrast, the temperature of the water has been raised by only a few degrees.

> **EXERCISE 5.3 Using Specific Heat Capacity**
>
> A 15.5-g piece of chromium, heated to 100.0 °C, is dropped into 55.5 g of water at 16.5 °C. The final temperature of the metal and the water is 18.9 °C. What is the specific heat capacity of chromium? (Assume no energy as heat is lost to the container or to the surrounding air.)

5.3 Energy and Changes of State

A *change of state* is a change, for example, between solid and liquid or between liquid and gas. When a solid melts, its atoms, molecules, or ions move about vigorously enough to break free of the attractive forces holding them in rigid positions in the solid lattice. When a liquid boils, particles move much farther apart from one another, to distances at which attractive forces are minimal. In both cases, energy must be furnished to overcome attractive forces among the particles.

The energy transferred as heat that is required to convert a substance from a solid at its melting point to a liquid is called the **heat of fusion.** The energy transferred as heat to convert a liquid at its boiling point to a vapor is called the **heat of vaporization.** Heats of fusion and vaporization for many substances are provided along with other physical properties in reference books. Values for a few common substances are given in Appendix D (Table 12).

It is important to recognize that *temperature is constant throughout a change of state* (Figure 5.9). During a change of state, the added energy is used to overcome the forces holding one molecule to another, not to increase the temperature (Figures 5.9 and 5.10).

For water, the heat of fusion at 0 °C is 333 J/g, and the heat of vaporization at 100 °C is 2256 J/g. These values are used to calculate the heat required for a given mass of water to melt or boil, respectively. For example, the energy required to convert 500. g of water from the liquid to gaseous state at 100 °C is

$$(2256 \text{ J/g})(500. \text{ g}) = 1.13 \times 10^6 \text{ J} (= 1130 \text{ kJ})$$

In contrast, to melt the same mass of ice to form liquid water at 0 °C requires only 167 kJ.

$$(333 \text{ J/g})(500. \text{ g}) = 1.67 \times 10^5 \text{ J} (= 167 \text{ kJ})$$

■ **Heats of Fusion and Vaporization for H_2O at the Normal Melting and Boiling Points**
Heat of fusion = 333 J/g
　　　　　　 = 6.00 kJ/mol
Heat of vaporization = 2256 J/g
　　　　　　 = 40.65 kJ/mol

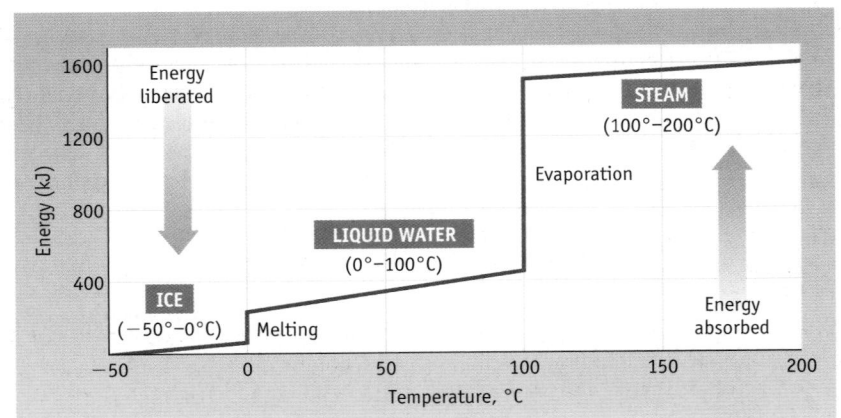

FIGURE 5.9 Energy transfer as heat and the temperature change for water. This graph shows the energy transferred as heat to 500. g of water and the consequent temperature change as the water warms from − 50 °C to 200 °C (at 1 atm).

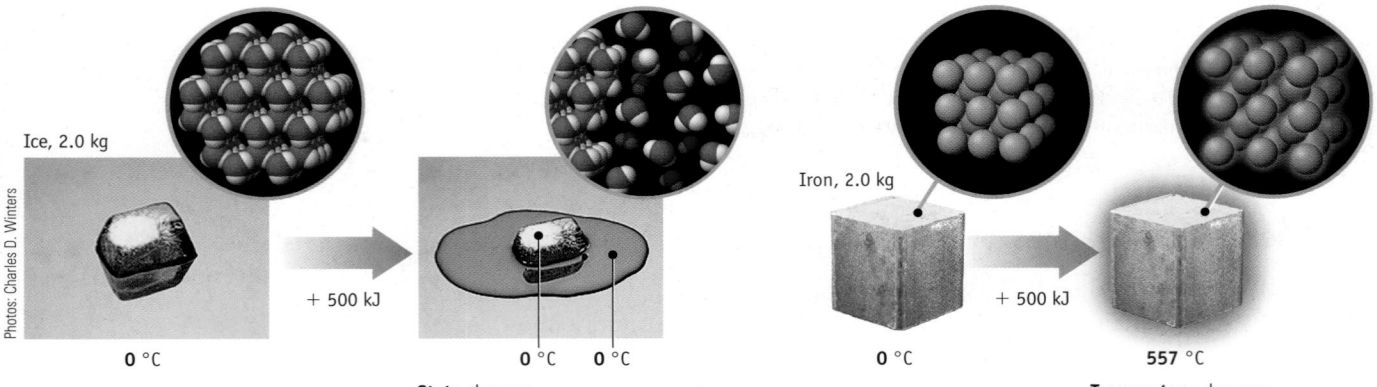

Ice, 2.0 kg

0 °C   + 500 kJ   0 °C   0 °C

State changes.
Temperature does **NOT** change.

Iron, 2.0 kg

0 °C   + 500 kJ   557 °C

Temperature changes.
State does **NOT** change.

Active Figure 5.10 **Changes of state.** (*left*) Transferring 500 kJ of energy as heat to 2.0 kg of ice at 0 °C will cause 1.5 kg of ice to melt to water at 0 °C (and 0.5 kg of ice will remain). No temperature change occurs. (*right*) In contrast, transferring 500 kJ of energy as heat to 2.0 kg of iron at 0 °C will cause the temperature to increase to 557 °C (and the metal to expand slightly).

Chemistry ⚛ Now™ Sign in at www.cengage.com/login and go to the Chapter Contents menu to explore an interactive version of this figure accompanied by an exercise.

Figure 5.9 gives a profile of a process in which 500. g of ice at − 50 °C is converted to water vapor at 200 °C . This process involves a series of steps: (1) warming ice to 0 °C, (2) conversion to liquid water at 0 °C, (3) warming liquid water to 100 °C, (4) evaporation at 100 °C, and (5) warming the water vapor to 200 °C. Each step requires the input of additional energy. The energy transferred as heat to raise the temperature of solid, liquid, and vapor can be calculated with Equation 5.1, using the specific heat capacities of ice, liquid water, and water vapor (which are different), and the energies transferred as heat for the changes of state can be calculated using heats of fusion and vaporization. These calculations are carried out in Example 5.3.

■ **EXAMPLE 5.3 Energy and Changes of State**

Problem Calculate the energy that is transferred as heat to convert 500. g of ice at −50.0 °C to steam at 200.0 °C. (The temperature change occurring in each step is illustrated in Figure 5.9.) The heat of fusion of water is 333 J/g, and the heat of vaporization is 2256 J/g. The specific heat capacities of ice, liquid water, and water vapor are given in Appendix D.

Strategy The problem is broken down into a series of steps as noted above: (1) warm the ice from −50 °C to 0 °C; (2) melt the ice at 0 °C; (3) raise the temperature of the liquid water from 0 °C to 100 °C; (4) boil the water at 100 °C; (5) raise the temperature of the steam from 100 °C to 200 °C. Use Equation 5.1 and the specific heat capacities of solid, liquid, and gaseous water to calculate the energy transferred as heat associated with the temperature changes. Use the heat of fusion and the heat of vaporization to calculate the energy transferred as heat associated with changes of state. The total energy transferred as heat is the sum of the energies of the individual steps.

Solution

Step 1. (to warm ice from −50.0 °C to 0.0 °C)

$$q_1 = (2.06 \text{ J/g} \cdot \text{K})(500. \text{ g})(273.2 \text{ K} − 223.2 \text{ K}) = 5.15 \times 10^4 \text{ J}$$

Step 2. (to melt ice at 0.0 °C)

$$q_2 = (500. \text{ g})(333 \text{ J/g}) = 1.67 \times 10^5 \text{ J}$$

Step 3. (to raise temperature of liquid water from 0.0 °C to 100.0 °C)

$$q_3 = (4.184 \text{ J/g} \cdot \text{K})(500. \text{ g})(373.2 \text{ K} - 273.2 \text{ K}) = 2.09 \times 10^5 \text{ J}$$

Step 4. (to evaporate water at 100.0 °C)

$$q_4 = (2256 \text{ J/g})(500. \text{ g}) = 1.13 \times 10^6 \text{ J}$$

Step 5. (to raise temperature of water vapor from 100.0 °C to 200.0 °C)

$$q_5 = (1.86 \text{ J/g} \cdot \text{K})(500. \text{ g}) (473.2 \text{ K} - 373.2 \text{ K}) = 9.30 \times 10^4 \text{ J}$$

The total energy transferred as heat is the sum of the energies of the individual steps.

$$q_{total} = q_1 + q_2 + q_3 + q_4 + q_5$$

$$q_{total} = 1.65 \times 10^6 \text{ J (or 1650 kJ)}$$

Comment The conversion of liquid water to steam is the largest increment of energy added by a considerable margin. (You may have noticed that it does not take much time to heat water to boiling on a stove, but to boil off the water takes a much greater time.)

■ **EXAMPLE 5.4 Change of State**

Problem What is the minimum amount of ice at 0 °C that must be added to the contents of a can of diet cola (340. mL) to cool the cola from 20.5 °C to 0.0 °C? Assume that the specific heat capacity and density of diet cola are the same as for water.

Strategy It is easiest to define the system as the ice and cola; the calculation will then involve energy transfers between the two components in the system. We need to assume that, within the system, energy transfers only as heat and that there is no transfer of energy between the surroundings and the system. The law of conservation of energy then dictates that $q_{ice} + q_{cola} = 0$. The value of q_{cola} can be calculated using the specific heat capacity of the cola and Equation 5.1, and the energy transferred as heat required to melt ice can be calculated using the heat of fusion for water.

Solution The mass of cola is 340. g [(340. mL)(1.00 g/mL) = 340. g], and its temperature changes from 293.7 K to 273.2 K. The heat of fusion of water is 333 J/g, and the mass of ice is the unknown.

$$q_{cola} + q_{ice} = 0$$

$$C_{cola} \times m \times (T_{final} - T_{initial}) + q_{ice} = 0$$

$$[(4.184 \text{ J/g} \cdot \text{K})(340. \text{ g})(273.2 \text{ K} - 293.7 \text{ K})] + [(333 \text{ J/g}) (m_{ice})] = 0$$

$$m_{ice} = 87.6 \text{ g}$$

Comment This quantity of ice is just sufficient to cool the cola to 0 °C. If more than 87.6 g of ice is added, then the final temperature will still be 0 °C when thermal equilibrium is reached, and some ice will remain (see Exercise 5.4). If less than 87.6 g of ice is added, the final temperature will be greater than 0 °C. In this case, all the ice will melt, and the liquid water formed by melting the ice will absorb additional energy to warm up to the final temperature (an example is given in Study Question 71, page 248).

EXERCISE 5.4 Changes of State

To make a glass of iced tea, you pour 250 mL of tea, whose temperature is 18.2 °C, into a glass containing five ice cubes. Each cube has a mass of 15 g. What quantity of ice will melt, and how much ice will remain to float at the surface in this beverage? Assume that iced tea has a density of 1.0 g/mL and a specific heat capacity of 4.2 J/g · K, that energy is transferred only as heat within the system, that ice is at 0.0 °C, and that no energy is transferred between system and surroundings.

If you put a pot of water on a kitchen stove or a campfire, or if you put the pot in the sun, the water will evaporate. You must supply energy in some form because evaporation requires the input of energy. This well-known principle was applied in a novel way by a young African teacher, Mohammed Bah Abba in Nigeria, to improve the life of his people.

Life is hard in northern Nigerian communities. In this rural semi-desert area, most people eke out a living by subsistence farming. Without modern refrigeration, food spoilage is a major problem. Using a simple thermodynamic principle, Abba developed a refrigerator that cost about 30 cents to make and does not use electricity.

Abba's refrigerator is made of two earthen pots, one inside the other, separated by a layer of sand. The pots are covered with damp cloth and placed in a well-ventilated area. Water seeps through the pot's outer wall and rapidly evaporates in the dry desert air. The water remaining in

Mohammed Bah Abba. Abba earned a college degree in business, and while still in his 20s, became an instructor in a college of business in Jigwa, Nigeria, and a consultant to the United Nations Development Program. That brought him into close contact with rural communities in Northern Nigeria and made him aware of the hardships of the families there.

the pot and its contents drop in temperature, so much so that food in the inner pot can stay cool for days and not spoil.

In the 1990s, at his own expense, Abba made and distributed almost 10,000 pots in the villages of northern Nigeria. He estimates that about 75% of the families in this area are now using his refrigerator. The impact of this simple device has implications not only for the health of his people but also for their economy and their social structure. Prior to the development of the pot-in-pot device for food storage, it was necessary to sell produce immediately upon harvesting. The young girls in the family who sold food on the street daily could now be released from this chore to attend school and improve their lives.

Every two years, the Rolex Company, the Swiss maker of timepieces, gives a series of awards for enterprise. For his pot-in-pot refrigerator, Abba was one of the five recipients of a Rolex Award in 2000.

Questions:

1. *What quantity of energy must be transferred as heat to evaporate 95 g of water at 25°C? (The heat of vaporization at 25 °C is 44.0 kJ/mol.)*
2. *If this quantity of energy is transferred as heat out of 750 g of water, what is the temperature change of the water?*

Answers to these questions are in Appendix Q.

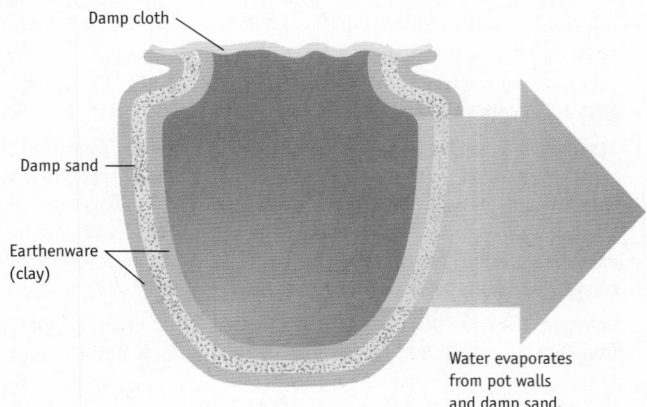

Damp cloth

Damp sand

Earthenware (clay)

Water evaporates from pot walls and damp sand.

The pot-in-pot refrigerator. Water seeps through the outer pot from the damp sand layer separating the pots, or from food stored in the inner pot. As the water evaporates from the surface of the outer pot, the food inside the pot is cooled.

The Rolex Awards for Enterprise/Tomas Bertelsen/Scientific American, Nov. 2000, p. 26

5.4 The First Law of Thermodynamics

To this point, we have only considered energy transfers as heat. Now we need to broaden the discussion. Recall the definition of thermodynamics as *the science of heat and work*. Work is done whenever a mass is moved against an opposing force; some form of energy is required for work to be done.

As described earlier, energy transferred as heat between a system and its surroundings changes the energy of the system. Work done by a system or on a system will also affect the energy in the system. If a system does work on its surroundings, energy must be expended by the system, and the system's energy will decrease. Conversely, if work is done by the surroundings on a system, the energy of the system increases.

A system doing work on its surroundings is illustrated in Figure 5.11. A small quantity of dry ice, solid CO_2, is sealed inside a plastic bag, and a weight (a book) is placed on top of the bag. When energy is transferred as heat from the surround-

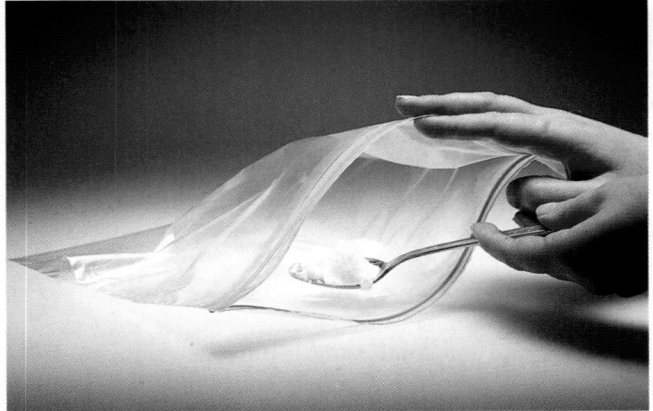

(a) Pieces of dry ice [$CO_2(s)$, $-78\ °C$] are placed in a plastic bag. The dry ice will sublime (change directly from a solid to a gas) upon the input of energy.

(b) Energy is absorbed by $CO_2(s)$ when it sublimes, and the system (the contents of the bag) does work on its surroundings by lifting the book against the force of gravity.

Charles D. Winters

Active Figure 5.11 Energy changes in a physical process.

Chemistry ⚛ Now™ Sign in at www.cengage.com/login and go to the Chapter Contents menu to explore an interactive version of this figure accompanied by an exercise.

ings to the dry ice, the dry ice changes directly from solid to gas at $-78\ °C$, in a process called **sublimation:**

$$CO_2(s,\ -78\ °C) \longrightarrow CO_2(g,\ -78\ °C)$$

As sublimation proceeds, gaseous CO_2 expands within the plastic bag, lifting the book against the force of gravity. The system (the CO_2 inside the bag) is expending energy to do this work.

Even if the book had not been on top of the plastic bag, work would have been done by the expanding gas because the gas must push back the atmosphere when it expands. Instead of raising a book, the expanding gas moves a part of the atmosphere.

Now let us restate this example in terms of thermodynamics. First, we must identify the system and the surroundings. The system is the CO_2, initially a solid and later a gas. The surroundings consist of the objects that exchange energy with the system. This includes the plastic bag, the book, the table-top, and the surrounding air. Thermodynamics focuses on energy transfer. Sublimation of CO_2 requires energy, which is transferred as heat to the system (the CO_2) from the surroundings. At the same time, the system does work on the surroundings by lifting the book. An energy balance for the system will include both quantities, heat and work.

This example can be generalized. For any system, we can identify energy transfers both as heat and as work between system and surroundings. We can express the change of energy in a system explicitly as an equation:

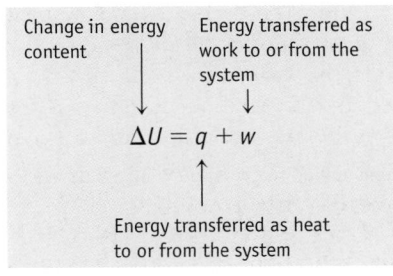

Change in energy content

Energy transferred as work to or from the system

$$\Delta U = q + w$$

Energy transferred as heat to or from the system

(5.4)

Equation 5.4 is a mathematical statement of the **first law of thermodynamics:** The energy change for a system (ΔU) is the sum of the energy transferred as heat between the system and its surroundings (q) and the energy transferred as work between the system and its surroundings (w).

The equation defining the first law of thermodynamics can be thought of as a version of the general principle of conservation of energy. Because energy is conserved, we must be able to account for any change in the energy of the system. All energy transfers between a system and the surroundings occur by the processes of heat and work. Equation 5.4 thus states that the change in the energy of the system is exactly equal to the sum of all of the energy transfers (heat or work) between the system and its surroundings.

The quantity U in Equation 5.4 has a formal name—**internal energy**—and a precise meaning in thermodynamics. The internal energy in a chemical system is the sum of the potential and kinetic energies of the atoms, molecules, or ions in the system. The potential energy here is the energy associated with the attractive and repulsive forces between all the nuclei and electrons in the system. It includes the energy associated with bonds in molecules, forces between ions, and forces between molecules. The kinetic energy is the energy of motion of the atoms, ions, and molecules in the system. Actual values of internal energy are rarely determined or needed. In most instances, we are interested in the *change* in internal energy, and this is a measurable quantity. In fact, Equation 5.4 tells us how to determine ΔU: *Measure the energy transferred as heat and work to or from the system.*

The sign conventions for Equation 5.4 are important. The following table summarizes how the internal energy of a system is affected by energy transferred as heat and work.

Sign Conventions for *q* and *w* of the System

Change	Sign Convention	Effect on U_{system}
Energy transferred as heat to the system (endothermic)	$q > 0 \, (+)$	U increases
Energy transferred as heat from the system (exothermic)	$q < 0 \, (-)$	U decreases
Energy transferred as work done on system	$w > 0 \, (+)$	U increases
Energy transferred as work done by system	$w < 0 \, (-)$	U decreases

The work in the example involving the sublimation of CO_2 (Figure 5.11) is of a specific type, called *P–V* (pressure–volume) work. It is the work (w) associated with a change in volume (ΔV) that occurs against a resisting external pressure (P). For a system in which the external pressure is constant, the value of *P–V* work can be calculated using Equation 5.5:

Work (at constant pressure)   Change in volume

$$w = -P \times \Delta V \tag{5.5}$$

Pressure

Chemistry ⚛ Now™

Sign in at **www.cengage.com/login** and go to Chapter 5 Contents to see Screen 5.11 for a self-study module on **energy changes in a physical process.**

Enthalpy

Most experiments in a chemical laboratory are carried out in beakers or flasks open to the atmosphere, where the external pressure is constant. Similarly, chemical processes that occur in living systems are open to the atmosphere. Because many processes in chemistry and biology are carried out under conditions of constant pressure, it is useful to have a specific measure of the energy transferred as heat under these conditions.

Let us first examine ΔU under conditions of constant pressure:

$$\Delta U = q_p + w_p$$

where the subscript p indicates conditions of constant pressure. If the only type of work that occurs is $P\text{–}V$ work, then

$$\Delta U = q_p - P\Delta V$$

Rearranging this gives

$$q_p = \Delta U + P\Delta V$$

We now introduce a new thermodynamic function called the **enthalpy, H**, which is defined as

$$H = U + PV$$

■ **Energy Transfer Under Conditions of Constant Volume** Under conditions of constant volume, $\Delta V = 0$. If energy is transferred as heat under these conditions and if the only type of work possible is $P\text{–}V$ work, the equation for the first law of thermodynamics simplifies to $\Delta U = q_v$. The subscript v indicates conditions of constant volume. In this case, the energy transferred as heat is equal to ΔU.

A Closer Look

P–V Work

Work is done when an object of some mass is moved against an external resisting force. We know this from common experience, such as when we use a pump to blow up a bicycle tire.

To evaluate the work done when a gas is compressed, we can use, for example, a cylinder with a movable piston, as would occur in a bicycle pump (see figure). The drawing on the left shows the initial position of the piston, and the one on the right shows its final position. To depress the piston, we would have to expend some energy (the energy of this process comes from the energy obtained by food metabolism in our body). The work required to depress the piston is calculated from a law of physics, $w = F \times d$, or work equals the magnitude of the force (F) applied times the distance (d) over which the force is applied.

Pressure is defined as a force divided by the area over which the force is applied: $P = F/A$. In this example, the force is being applied to a piston with an area A. Substituting $P \times A$ for F in the equation gives $w = (P \times A) \times d$. The product of $A \times d$ is equivalent to the change in the volume of the gas in the pump, and, because $\Delta V = V_{final} - V_{initial}$, this change in volume is negative. Finally, because work done on a system is defined as positive, this means that $w = -P\Delta V$.

Pushing down on the piston means we have done work on the system, the gas contained within the cylinder. The gas is now compressed to a smaller volume and has attained a higher energy as a consequence. The additional energy is equal to $-P\Delta V$.

Notice how energy has been converted from one form to another—from chemical energy in food to mechanical energy used to depress the piston, to potential energy stored in a system of a gas at a higher pressure. In each step, energy was conserved, and the total energy of the universe remained constant.

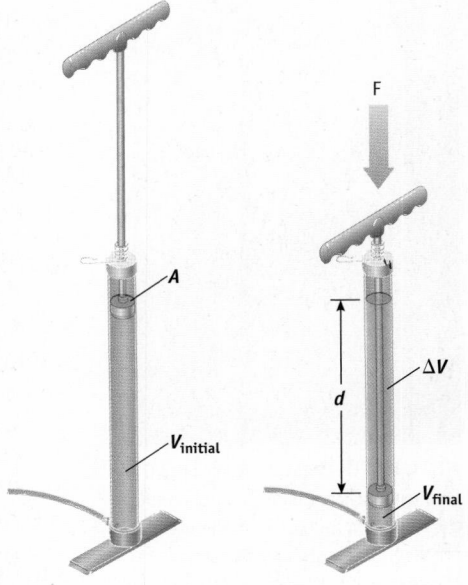

■ Enthalpy and Internal Energy

Differences The difference between ΔH and ΔU will be quite small unless a large volume change occurs. For water at 1 atm pressure and 273 K, for example, the difference between ΔH and ΔU (= $P\Delta V$) is 0.142 J/mol for the conversion of ice to liquid water at 273 K, whereas it is 3, 100 J/mol for the conversion of liquid water to water vapor at 373 K.

Changes in enthalpy for a system at constant pressure would be calculated from the following equation:

$$\Delta H = \Delta U + P\Delta V$$

Thus,

$$\Delta H = q_p$$

Now we see that, for a system where the only type of work possible is $P–V$ work, the change in enthalpy, ΔH, is equal to the energy transferred as heat at constant pressure, often symbolized by q_p.

Under conditions of constant pressure and where the only type of work possible is $P–V$ work, ΔU (= $q_p - P\Delta V$) and ΔH (= q_p) differ by $P\Delta V$ (the energy transferred to or from the system as work). We observe that in many processes—such as the melting of ice—the volume change, ΔV, is small, and hence the amount of work is small. Under these circumstances, ΔU and ΔH have almost the same value. The amount of work will be significant, however, in processes in which the volume change is large. This usually occurs when gases are formed or consumed. In the evaporation or condensation of water, the sublimation of CO_2, and chemical reactions in which the number of moles of gas changes, ΔU and ΔH have significantly different values.

Similar sign and symbol conventions apply to both ΔU and ΔH.

- Negative values of ΔH specify that energy is transferred as heat from the system to the surroundings.
- Positive values of ΔH specify that energy is transferred as heat from the surroundings to the system.

State Functions

Internal energy and enthalpy share a significant characteristic—namely, changes in these quantities that accompany chemical or physical processes depend only on the initial and final states. They do not depend on the path taken to go from the initial state to the final state. No matter how you go from reactants to products in a reaction, for example, the value of ΔH and ΔU for the reaction is always the same. A quantity that has this property is called a **state function**.

Many commonly measured quantities, such as the pressure of a gas, the volume of a gas or liquid, the temperature of a substance, and the size of your bank account, are state functions. You could have arrived at a current bank balance of $25 by having deposited $25 or you could have deposited $100 and then withdrawn $75. You can blow up a balloon to a large volume and then let some air out to arrive at the desired volume. Alternatively, you can blow up the balloon in stages, adding tiny amounts of air at each stage. The change in your bank balance or change in volume of the balloon does not depend on how you got there.

Not all quantities are state functions. For instance, distance traveled is not a state function (Figure 5.12). The travel distance from New York City to Denver depends on the route taken. Nor is the elapsed time of travel between these two locations a state function. In contrast, the altitude above sea level is a state function; in going from New York City (at sea level) to Denver (1600 m above sea level), there is an altitude change of 1600 m, regardless of the route followed.

Significantly, neither the energy transferred as heat nor the energy transferred as work individually is a state function but their sum, the change in internal energy,

FIGURE 5.12 State functions. There are many ways to climb a mountain, but the change in altitude from the base of the mountain to its summit is the same. The change in altitude is a state function. The distance traveled to reach the summit is not.

ΔU, is. The value of ΔU is fixed by $U_{initial}$ and U_{final}. A transition between the initial and final states can be accomplished by different routes having different values of q and w, but the sum of q and w for each path must always give the same ΔU.

Enthalpy is also a state function. The enthalpy change occurring when 1.0 g of water is heated from 20 °C to 50 °C is independent of how the process is carried out.

5.5 Enthalpy Changes for Chemical Reactions

Enthalpy changes accompany chemical reactions. In this book, we shall follow the conventions used by physical chemists and report the **standard reaction enthalpy, $\Delta_r H°$** for reactions. For example, for the decomposition of water vapor to hydrogen and oxygen, with the reactant and products all in their standard states at 25 °C, the standard reaction enthalpy is +241.8 kJ/mol-rxn.

$$H_2O(g) \rightarrow H_2(g) + \tfrac{1}{2} O_2(g) \qquad \Delta_r H° = +241.8 \text{ kJ/mol-rxn}$$

The positive sign of $\Delta_r H°$ in this case indicates that the decomposition is an endothermic process.

There are several important things to know about $\Delta_r H°$.

- The designation of $\Delta_r H°$ as a "standard enthalpy change" means that the pure, unmixed reactants in their standard states have formed pure, unmixed products in their standard states (where the superscript ° indicates standard conditions). The **standard state** of an element or a compound is defined as the most stable form of the substance in the physical state that exists at a pressure of 1 bar and at a specified temperature. [Most sources report standard reaction enthalpies at 25 °C (298 K).]
- The "per mol-rxn" designation in the units for $\Delta_r H°$ means this is the enthalpy change for a "mole of reaction" (where *rxn* is an abbreviation for reaction). For example, for the reaction $H_2O(g) \rightarrow H_2(g) + 1/2\ O_2(g)$, a mole of reaction has occurred when 1 mol of water vapor has been converted completely to 1 mol of H_2 and $1/2$ mol of O_2.

Now consider the opposite reaction, the combination of hydrogen and oxygen to form 1 mol of water. The magnitude of the enthalpy change for this reaction is the same as that for the decomposition reaction, but the sign of $\Delta_r H°$ is reversed. The exothermic formation of 1 mol of water vapor from 1 mol of H_2 and $1/2$ mol of O_2 transfers 241.8 kJ to the surroundings (Figure 5.13).

$$H_2(g) + \tfrac{1}{2} O_2(g) \rightarrow H_2O(g) \qquad \Delta_r H° = -241.8 \text{ kJ/mol-rxn}$$

The value of $\Delta_r H°$ depends on the chemical equation used. For example, $\Delta_r H°$ for 1 mole of the reaction

$$2 H_2(g) + O_2(g) \rightarrow 2 H_2O(g) \qquad \Delta_r H° = -483.6 \text{ kJ/mol-rxn}$$

will be twice that of $\Delta_r H°$ for the reaction

$$H_2(g) + \tfrac{1}{2} O_2(g) \rightarrow H_2O(g) \qquad \Delta_r H° = -241.8 \text{ kJ/mol-rxn}$$

This happens because 1 mole of reaction for the first equation uses twice the amount of reactants and produces twice the amount of product as the second equation.

■ **Notation for Thermodynamic Parameters** NIST and IUPAC (International Union of Pure and Applied Chemistry) specify that parameters such as ΔH should have a subscript, between Δ and the thermodynamic parameter, that specifies the type of process. Among the subscripts you will see are: a lower case r for "reaction," f for "formation," c for "combustion," fus for "fusion," and vap for "vaporization."

■ **Moles of Reaction, Mol-rxn** One "mole of reaction" is said to have occurred when the reaction has occurred according to the number of moles given by the coefficients in the balanced equation. (This concept was described as a way to solve limiting reactant problems on page 167.)

■ **Fractional Stoichiometric Coefficients** When writing balanced equations to define thermodynamic quantities, chemists often use fractional stoichiometric coefficients. For example, to define $\Delta_r H$ for the decomposition or formation of 1 mol of H_2O, the coefficient for O_2 must be 1/2.

(a) A lighted candle is brought up to a balloon filled with hydrogen gas.

(b) When the balloon breaks, the candle flame ignites the hydrogen.

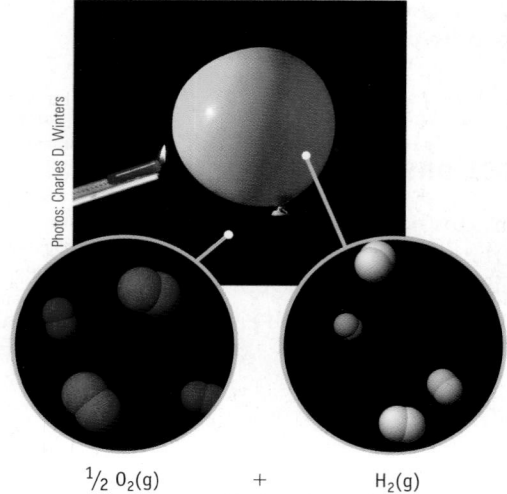
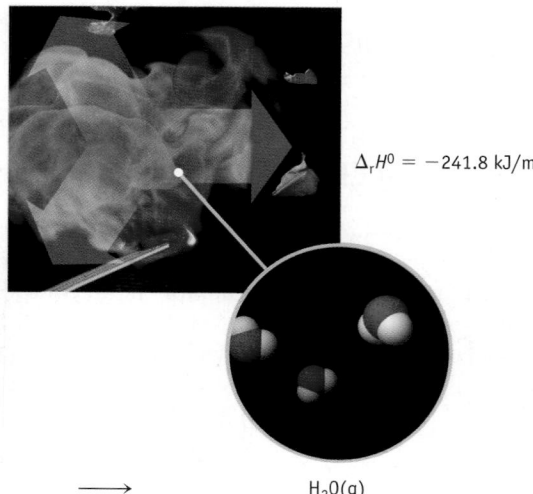

$\Delta_r H^0 = -241.8$ kJ/mol-rxn

$$\tfrac{1}{2}\ O_2(g) \quad + \quad H_2(g) \quad \longrightarrow \quad H_2O(g)$$

Active Figure 5.13 **The exothermic combustion of hydrogen in air.** The reaction transfers energy to the surroundings in the form of heat, work, and light.

Chemistry ⊙ Now™ Sign in at **www.cengage.com/login** and go to the Chapter Contents menu to explore an interactive version of this figure accompanied by an exercise.

■ **Standard Conditions** The superscript ° indicates standard conditions. It is applied to any type of thermodynamic data, such as enthalpy of fusion and vaporization ($\Delta_{fus}H°$ and $\Delta_{vap}H°$) and enthalpy of a reaction ($\Delta_r H°$). Standard conditions refers to reactants and products in their standard states at a pressure of 1 bar. One bar is approximately one atmosphere (1 atm = 1.013 bar; see Appendix B).

It is important to identify the states of reactants and products in a reaction because the magnitude of $\Delta_r H°$ depends on whether they are solids, liquids, or gases. For the formation of 1 mol of *liquid water* from the elements, the enthalpy change is −285.8 kJ.

$$H_2(g) + \tfrac{1}{2}\ O_2(g) \longrightarrow H_2O(\ell) \qquad \Delta_r H° = -285.8 \text{ kJ/mol–rxn}$$

Notice that this value is not the same as $\Delta_r H°$ for the formation of *water vapor* from hydrogen and oxygen. The difference between the two values is equal to the enthalpy change for the condensation of 1 mol of water vapor to 1 mol of liquid water.

These examples illustrate several general features of the enthalpy changes for chemical reactions.

- Enthalpy changes are specific to the reaction being carried out. The identities of reactants and products and their states (s, ℓ, g) are important, as are the amounts of reactants and products.
- The enthalpy change depends on the number of moles of reaction; that is, the number of times the reaction *as written* is carried out.
- $\Delta_r H°$ has a negative value for an exothermic reaction. It has a positive value for an endothermic reaction.
- Values of $\Delta_r H°$ are numerically the same, but opposite in sign, for chemical reactions that are the reverse of each other.

■ **Enthalpy of Fusion and Enthalpy of Vaporization** Previously, we called $\Delta_{fus}H°$ and $\Delta_{vap}H°$ the heat of fusion and heat of vaporization, respectively. You can see now that, based on the way that the process is carried out (at constant pressure) and by the use of H in their symbols, these are more properly referred to as the enthalpy of fusion and the enthalpy of vaporization. From this point on, we will refer to them by these designations.

Standard reaction enthalpies can be used to calculate the quantity of energy transferred as heat under conditions of constant pressure by any given mass of a reactant or product. Suppose you want to know the energy transferred to the surroundings as heat if 454 g of propane, C_3H_8, is burned (at constant pressure), given the equation for the exothermic combustion and the enthalpy change for the reaction.

$$C_3H_8(g) + 5\ O_2(g) \longrightarrow 3\ CO_2(g) + 4\ H_2O(\ell) \qquad \Delta_r H° = -2220 \text{ kJ/mol-rxn}$$

Two steps are needed. First, find the amount of propane present in the sample:

$$454 \text{ g } C_3H_8 \left(\frac{1 \text{ mol } C_3H_8}{44.10 \text{ g } C_3H_8} \right) = 10.3 \text{ mol } C_3H_8$$

Second, multiply $\Delta_r H°$ by the amount of propane:

$$\Delta_r H° = 10.3 \text{ mol } C_3H_8 \left(\frac{1 \text{ mol-rxn}}{1 \text{ mol } C_3H_8} \right) \left(\frac{-2220 \text{ kJ}}{1 \text{ mol-rxn}} \right) = -22,900 \text{ kJ}$$

Chemistry ⚛ Now™

Sign in at **www.cengage.com/login** and go to Chapter 5 Contents to see Screens 5.12 and 5.13 for self-study modules and a tutorial on **enthalpy changes.**

■ **EXAMPLE 5.5 Calculating the Enthalpy Change for a Reaction**

Problem Sucrose (sugar, $C_{12}H_{22}O_{11}$) can be oxidized to CO_2 and H_2O and the enthalpy change for the reaction can be measured (under conditions of constant pressure).

$$C_{12}H_{22}O_{11}(s) + 12 \text{ } O_2(g) \rightarrow 12 \text{ } CO_2(g) + 11 \text{ } H_2O(\ell) \qquad \Delta_r H° = -5645 \text{ kJ/mol-rxn}$$

What is the energy transferred as heat by burning 5.00 g of sugar?

Strategy We will first determine the amount (mol) of sucrose in 5.00 g, then use this with the value given for the enthalpy change for the oxidation of 1 mol of sucrose.

Solution

$$5.00 \text{ g sucrose} \times \frac{1 \text{ mol sucrose}}{342.3 \text{ g sucrose}} = 1.46 \times 10^{-2} \text{ mol sucrose}$$

$$\Delta_r H° = 1.46 \times 10^{-2} \text{ mol sucrose} \left(\frac{1 \text{ mol-rxn}}{1 \text{ mol sucrose}} \right) \left(\frac{-5645 \text{ kJ}}{1 \text{ mol-rxn}} \right)$$

$$\Delta_r H° = -82.5 \text{ kJ}$$

Comment A person on a diet might note that a (level) teaspoonful of sugar (about 3.5 g) supplies about 15 Calories (dietary Calories; the conversion is 4.184 kJ = 1 Cal). As diets go, a single spoonful of sugar doesn't have a large caloric content. But will you use just one level teaspoonful?

■ **Chemical Potential Energy**
Gummi Bears are mostly sugar. See Example 5.5 for a calculation of the energy in a spoonful of sugar, and see ChemistryNow Screen 5.2 for a video of a Gummi bear consumed by an oxidizing agent.

Charles D. Winters

EXERCISE 5.5 Enthalpy Calculation

The combustion of ethane, C_2H_6, has an enthalpy change of -2857.3 kJ for the reaction as written below. Calculate the value of energy transferred as heat when 15.0 g of C_2H_6 is burned.

$$2 \text{ } C_2H_6(g) + 7 \text{ } O_2(g) \rightarrow 4 \text{ } CO_2(g) + 6 \text{ } H_2O(g) \qquad \Delta_r H° = -2857.3 \text{ kJ/mol-rxn}$$

5.6 Calorimetry

The energy evolved or required as heat in a chemical or physical process can be measured by **calorimetry**. The apparatus used in this kind of experiment is a *calorimeter.*

Constant Pressure Calorimetry, Measuring ΔH

A constant pressure calorimeter can be used to measure the energy change for a chemical reaction as energy is transferred as heat under constant pressure conditions, that is, it measures the enthalpy change.

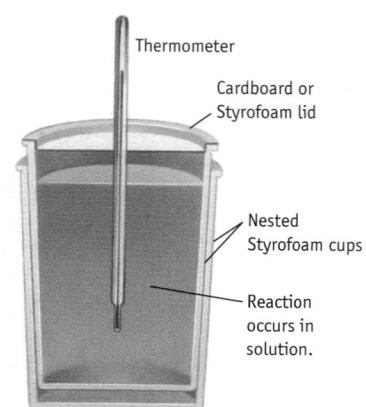

FIGURE 5.14 A coffee-cup calorimeter. A chemical reaction produces a change in temperature of the solution in the calorimeter. The Styrofoam container is fairly effective in preventing the transfer of energy as heat between the solution and its surroundings. Because the cup is open to the atmosphere, this is a constant pressure measurement.

In general chemistry laboratories, a "coffee-cup calorimeter" is often used to estimate enthalpy changes for chemical reactions. This inexpensive device consists of two nested Styrofoam coffee cups with a loose-fitting lid and a temperature-measuring device such as a thermometer (Figure 5.14) or thermocouple. Styrofoam, a fairly good insulator, minimizes energy transfer as heat between the system and the surroundings. The reaction is carried out in solution in the cup. If the reaction is exothermic, it releases energy as heat to the solution, and the temperature of the solution rises. If the reaction is endothermic, energy is absorbed as heat from the solution, and a decrease in the temperature of the solution will be seen. The change in temperature of the solution is measured. Knowing the mass and specific heat capacity of the solution and the temperature change, the enthalpy change for the reaction can be calculated.

In this calorimetry experiment, it will be convenient to define the chemicals and the solution as the system. The surroundings are the cup and everything beyond the cup. As noted above, we assume that there is no energy transfer to the cup or beyond and that energy is transferred only as heat within the system. Two energy changes occur within the system. One is the change that takes place as the chemical reaction occurs, either releasing the potential energy stored in the reactants or absorbing energy and converting it to potential energy stored in the products. We label this energy as q_r. The other energy change is the energy gained or lost as heat by the solution ($q_{solution}$). Based on the law of conservation of energy,

$$q_r + q_{solution} = 0$$

The value of $q_{solution}$ can be calculated from the specific heat capacity, mass, and change in temperature of the solution. The quantity of energy evolved or absorbed as heat for the reaction (q_r) is the unknown in the equation.

The accuracy of a calorimetry experiment depends on the accuracy of the measured quantities (temperature, mass, specific heat capacity). In addition, it depends on how closely the assumption is followed that there is no energy transfer beyond the solution. A coffee-cup calorimeter is an unsophisticated apparatus, and the results obtained with it are not highly accurate, largely because this assumption is poorly met. In research laboratories, calorimeters are used that more effectively limit the energy transfer between system and surroundings. In addition, it is also possible to estimate and correct for the minimal energy transfer that occurs between the system and the surroundings.

■ **EXAMPLE 5.6 Using a Coffee-Cup Calorimeter**

Problem Suppose you place 0.0500 g of magnesium chips in a coffee-cup calorimeter and then add 100.0 mL of 1.00 M HCl. The reaction that occurs is

$$Mg(s) + 2\ HCl(aq) \longrightarrow H_2(g) + MgCl_2(aq)$$

The temperature of the solution increases from 22.21 °C (295.36 K) to 24.46 °C (297.61 K). What is the enthalpy change for the reaction per mole of Mg? Assume that the specific heat capacity of the solution is 4.20 J/g · K and the density of the HCl solution is 1.00 g/mL.

Strategy The energy evolved in the reaction is absorbed by the solution. Solving the problem has three steps. First, calculate $q_{solution}$ from the values of the mass, specific heat capacity, and ΔT using Equation 5.1. Second, calculate q_r, assuming no energy transfer as heat occurs beyond the solution, that is, $q_r + q_{solution} = 0$. Third, use the value of q_r and the amount of Mg to calculate the enthalpy change per mole of Mg.

Solution

Step 1. Calculate $q_{solution}$. The mass of the solution is the mass of the 100.0 mL of HCl plus the mass of magnesium.

$$q_{solution} = (100.0 \text{ g HCl solution} + 0.0500 \text{ g Mg})(4.20 \text{ J/g K})(297.61 \text{ K} - 295.36 \text{ K})$$
$$= 9.45 \times 10^2 \text{ J}$$

Step 2. Calculate q_r.

$$q_r + q_{solution} = 0$$
$$q_r + 9.45 \times 10^2 \text{ J} = 0$$
$$q_r = -9.45 \times 10^2 \text{ J}$$

Step 3. Calculate the value of ΔH per mole of Mg. Note that q_r found in Step 2 resulted from the reaction of 0.0500 g of Mg. The enthalpy change per mole of Mg is therefore

$$\Delta_r H = (-9.45 \times 10^2 \text{ J/0.0500 g Mg})(24.31 \text{ g Mg/1 mol Mg})$$
$$= -4.60 \times 10^5 \text{ J/mol Mg} (= -460. \text{ kJ/mol-rxn Mg})$$

Comment The calculation gives the correct sign of q_r and $\Delta_r H$. The negative sign indicates that this is an exothermic reaction.

EXERCISE 5.6 Using a Coffee-Cup Calorimeter

Assume 200. mL of 0.400 M HCl are mixed with 200. mL of 0.400 M NaOH in a coffee-cup calorimeter. The temperature of the solutions before mixing was 25.10 °C; after mixing and allowing the reaction to occur, the temperature is 27.78 °C. What is the enthalpy change when one mole of acid is neutralized? (Assume that the densities of all solutions are 1.00 g/mL and their specific heat capacities are 4.20 J/g · K.)

Constant Volume Calorimetry: Measuring ΔU

Constant volume calorimetry is often used to evaluate heats of combustion of fuels and the caloric value of foods. A weighed sample of a combustible solid or liquid is placed inside a "bomb," often a cylinder about the size of a large fruit juice can with thick steel walls and ends (Figure 5.15). The bomb is placed in a water-filled container with well-insulated walls. After filling the bomb with pure oxygen, the sample is ignited, usually by an electric spark. The heat generated by the combustion reaction warms the bomb and the water around it. The bomb, its contents, and the water are defined as the system. Assessment of energy transfers as heat within the system shows that

$$q_r + q_{bomb} + q_{water} = 0$$

where q_r is the energy produced by the reaction, q_{bomb} is the energy involved in heating the calorimeter bomb, and q_{water} is the energy involved in heating the water in the calorimeter. Because the volume does not change in a constant volume calorimeter, energy transfer as work cannot occur. Therefore, the energy transferred as heat at constant volume (q_v) is the change in internal energy, ΔU.

■ **Calorimetry, ΔU, and ΔH** The two types of calorimetry (constant volume and constant pressure) highlight the differences between enthalpy and internal energy. The energy transferred as heat at constant pressure, q_p, is, by definition, ΔH, whereas the energy transferred as heat at constant volume, q_v, is ΔU.

Chemistry ⚛ Now™

Sign in at **www.cengage.com/login** and go to Chapter 5 Contents to see Screen 5.14 for a simulation and exercise exploring **reactions in a constant volume calorimeter** and for a tutorial on **calculating the enthalpy change for a reaction from a calorimetry experiment.**

Active Figure 5.15 **Constant volume calorimeter.** A combustible sample is burned in pure oxygen in a sealed metal container or "bomb." Energy released as heat warms the bomb and the water surrounding it. By measuring the increase in temperature, the energy evolved as heat in the reaction can be determined.

Chemistry ̣○̣Now™ Sign in at www. cengage.com/login and go to the Chapter Contents menu to explore an interactive version of this figure accompanied by an exercise.

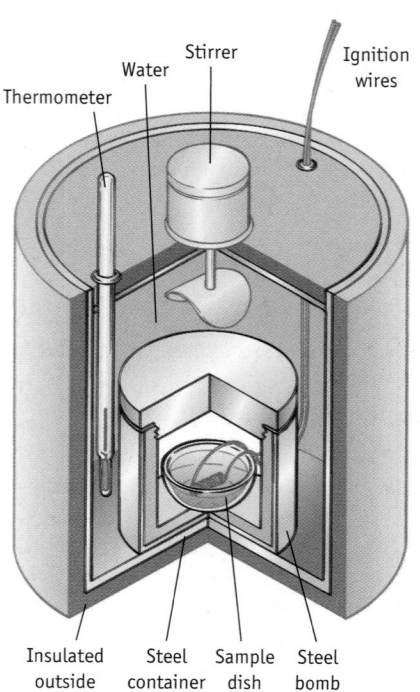

Thermometer   Water   Stirrer   Ignition wires

Insulated outside container   Steel container   Sample dish   Steel bomb

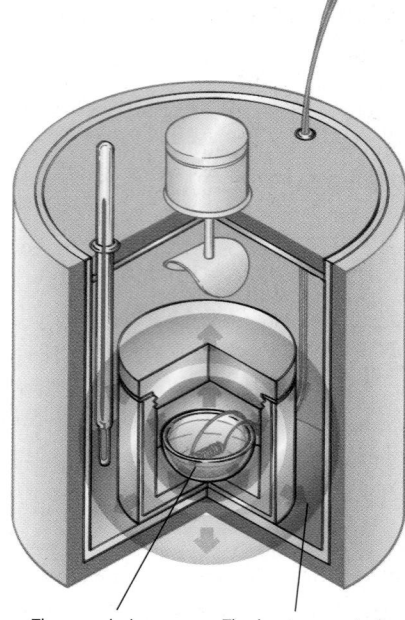

The sample burns in pure oxygen, warming the bomb.   The heat generated warms the water, and ΔT is measured by the thermometer.

■ EXAMPLE 5.7 Constant Volume Calorimetry

Problem Octane, C_8H_{18}, a primary constituent of gasoline, burns in air:

$$C_8H_{18}(\ell) + 25/2\ O_2(g) \longrightarrow 8\ CO_2(g) + 9\ H_2O(\ell)$$

A 1.00-g sample of octane is burned in a constant volume calorimeter similar to that shown in Figure 5.15. The calorimeter is in an insulated container with 1.20 kg of water. The temperature of the water and the bomb rises from 25.00 °C (298.15 K) to 33.20 °C (306.35 K). The heat capacity of the bomb, C_{bomb}, is 837 J/K. (a) What is the heat of combustion per gram of octane? (b) What is the heat of combustion per mole of octane?

Strategy (a) The sum of all the energies transferred as heat in the system will be zero; that is, $q_r + q_{bomb} + q_{water} = 0$. The first term, q_r, is the unknown. The second and third terms in the equation can be calculated from the data given: q_{bomb} is calculated from the bomb's heat capacity and ΔT, and q_{water} is determined from the specific heat capacity, mass, and ΔT for water. (b) The value of q_r calculated in part (a) is the energy evolved in the combustion of 1.00 g of octane. Use this and the molar mass of octane (114.2 g/mol) to calculate the energy evolved as heat per mole of octane.

Solution

(a)
$$q_{water} = C_{water} \times m_{water} \times \Delta T$$
$$= (4.184\ J/g \cdot K)(1.20 \times 10^3\ g)(306.35\ K - 298.15\ K) = +41.2 \times 10^3\ J$$
$$q_{bomb} = (C_{bomb})(\Delta T) = (837\ J/K)(306.35\ K - 298.15\ K) = 6.86 \times 10^3\ J$$
$$q_r + q_{water} + q_{bomb} = 0$$
$$q_r + 41.2 \times 10^3\ J + 6.86 \times 10^3\ J = 0$$
$$q_r = -48.1 \times 10^3\ J\ (or\ -48.1\ kJ)$$

Heat of combustion per gram = −48.1 kJ

(b) Heat of combustion per mol of octane = (-48.1 kJ/g)(114.2 g/mol) = −5.49 × 10³ kJ/mol

Comment Because the volume does not change, no energy transfer in the form of work occurs. The change of internal energy, ΔU, for the combustion of $C_8H_{18}(\ell)$ is −5.49 × 10³ kJ/mol. Also note that C_{bomb} has no mass units. It is the heat required to warm the whole object by 1 kelvin.

5.7 Enthalpy Calculations

Enthalpy changes for an enormous number of chemical and physical processes are available on the World Wide Web and in reference books. These data have been collected by scientists over a number of years from many experiments and are used to calculate enthalpy changes for chemical processes. Now we want to discuss how to use such data.

Hess's Law

The enthalpy change can be measured by calorimetry for many, but not all, chemical processes. Consider, for example, the oxidation of carbon to form carbon monoxide.

$$C(graphite) + \tfrac{1}{2}\, O_2(g) \longrightarrow CO(g)$$

Even if a deficiency of oxygen is used, the primary product of the reaction of carbon and oxygen is CO_2. As soon as CO is formed, it reacts with O_2 to form CO_2. Because the reaction cannot be carried out in a way that allows CO to be the sole product, it is not possible to measure the change in enthalpy for this reaction by calorimetry.

The enthalpy change for the reaction forming CO(g) from C(s) and O_2(g) can be determined indirectly, however, from enthalpy changes for other reactions that can be measured. The calculation is based on **Hess's law**, which states that if a reaction is the sum of two or more other reactions, $\Delta_r H°$ for the overall process is the sum of the $\Delta_r H°$ values of those reactions.

The oxidation of C(s) to CO_2(g) can be viewed as occurring in two steps: first the oxidation of C(s) to CO(g) (Equation 1), and then the oxidation of CO(g) to CO_2(g) (Equation 2). Adding these two equations gives the equation for the oxidation of C(s) to CO_2(g) (Equation 3).

Equation 1:	$C(graphite) + \tfrac{1}{2}\, O_2(g) \longrightarrow CO(g)$	$\Delta_r H_1° = ?$
Equation 2:	$CO(g) + \tfrac{1}{2}\, O_2(g) \longrightarrow CO_2(g)$	$\Delta_r H_2° = -283.0$ kJ/mol-rxn
Equation 3:	$C(graphite) + O_2(g) \longrightarrow CO_2(g)$	$\Delta_r H_3° = -393.5$ kJ/mol-rxn

Hess's law tells us that the enthalpy change for the overall reaction $(\Delta_r H_3°)$ will equal the sum of the enthalpy changes for reactions 1 and 2 $(\Delta_r H_1° + \Delta_r H_2°)$. Both $\Delta_r H_2°$ and $\Delta_r H_3°$ can be measured, and these values are then used to calculate the enthalpy change for reaction 1.

$$\Delta_r H_3° = \Delta_r H_1° + \Delta_r H_2°$$
$$-393.5 \text{ kJ/mol-rxn} = \Delta_r H_1° + (-283.0 \text{ kJ/mol-rxn})$$
$$\Delta_r H_1° = -110.5 \text{ kJ/mol-rxn}$$

Hess's law also applies to physical processes. The enthalpy change for the reaction of H_2(g) and O_2(g) to form 1 mol of H_2O vapor is different from the enthalpy change to form 1 mol of liquid H_2O. The difference is the negative of the *enthalpy of vaporization* of water, $\Delta_r H°_2 \ (= -\Delta_{vap}H°)$ as shown in the following analysis

Equation 1:	$H_2(g) + \frac{1}{2} O_2(g) \rightarrow H_2O(g)$	$\Delta_r H°_1 = -241.8$ kJ/mol-rxn
Equation 2:	$H_2O(g) \rightarrow H_2O(\ell)$	$\Delta_r H°_2 = -44.0$ kJ/mol-rxn
Equation 3:	$H_2(g) + \frac{1}{2} O_2(g) \rightarrow H_2O(\ell)$	$\Delta_r H°_3 = -285.8$ kJ/mol-rxn

Energy Level Diagrams

When using Hess's law, it is often helpful to represent enthalpy data schematically in an energy level diagram. In such drawings, the various substances being studied—the reactants and products in a chemical reaction, for example—are placed on an arbitrary energy scale. The relative enthalpy of each substance is given by its position on the vertical axis, and numerical differences in enthalpy between them are shown by the vertical arrows. Such diagrams provide a visual perspective on the magnitude and direction of enthalpy changes and show how enthalpy changes of the substances are related.

Energy level diagrams that summarize the two examples of Hess's law discussed earlier are shown in Figure 5.16. In Figure 5.16a, the elements, C(s) and $O_2(g)$ are at the highest enthalpy. The reaction of carbon and oxygen to form $CO_2(g)$ lowers the enthalpy by 393.5 kJ. This can occur either in a single step, shown on the left in Figure 5.16a, or in two steps via initial formation of CO(g), as shown on the right. Similarly, in Figure 5.16b, the mixture of $H_2(g)$ and $O_2(g)$ is at the highest enthalpy. Both liquid and gaseous water have lower enthalpies, with the difference between the two being the enthalpy of vaporization.

Chemistry Now™

Sign in at **www.cengage.com/login** and go to Chapter 5 Contents to see Screen 5.15 for a simulation and exercise on **Hess's law.**

Active Figure 5.16 **Energy level diagrams.** (a) Relating enthalpy changes in the formation of $CO_2(g)$. (b) Relating enthalpy changes in the formation of $H_2O(\ell)$. Enthalpy changes associated with changes between energy levels are given alongside the vertical arrows.

Chemistry Now™ Sign in at www.cengage.com/login and go to the Chapter Contents menu to explore an interactive version of this figure accompanied by an exercise.

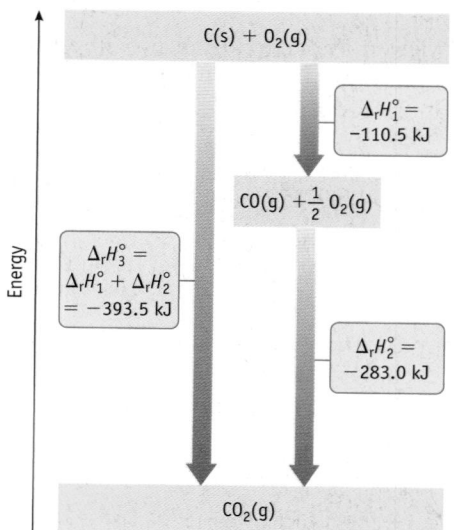

(a) The formation of CO_2 can occur in a single step or in a succession of steps. $\Delta_r H°$ for the overall process is −393.5 kJ, no matter which path is followed.

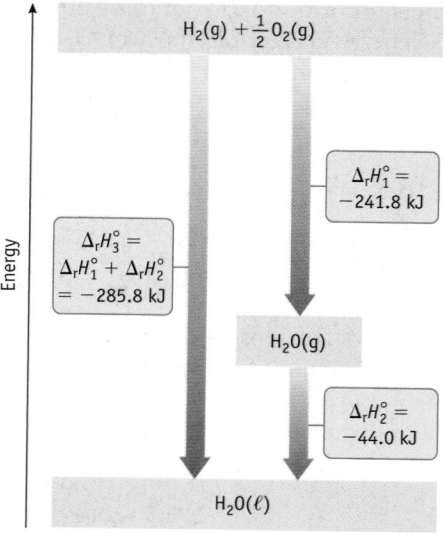

(b) The formation of $H_2O(\ell)$ can occur in a single step or in a succession of steps. $\Delta_r H°$ for the overall process is −285.8 kJ, no matter which path is followed.

Problem Suppose you want to know the enthalpy change for the formation of methane, CH_4, from solid carbon (as graphite) and hydrogen gas:

$$C(s) + 2 H_2(g) \longrightarrow CH_4(g) \qquad \Delta_r H^\circ = ?$$

The enthalpy change for this reaction cannot be measured in the laboratory because the reaction is very slow. We can, however, measure enthalpy changes for the combustion of carbon, hydrogen, and methane.

Equation 1:	$C(s) + O_2(g) \longrightarrow CO_2(g)$	$\Delta_r H^\circ_1 = -393.5$ kJ/mol-rxn
Equation 2:	$H_2(g) + \frac{1}{2} O_2(g) \longrightarrow H_2O(\ell)$	$\Delta_r H^\circ_2 = -285.8$ kJ/mol-rxn
Equation 3:	$CH_4(g) + 2 O_2(g) \longrightarrow CO_2(g) + 2 H_2O(\ell)$	$\Delta_r H^\circ_3 = -890.3$ kJ/mol-rxn

Use this information to calculate $\Delta_r H^\circ$ for the formation of methane from its elements.

Strategy The three reactions (1, 2, and 3), as they are written, cannot be added together to obtain the equation for the formation of CH_4 from its elements. Methane, CH_4, is a product in the reaction for which we wish to calculate $\Delta_r H^\circ$, but it is a reactant in Equation 3. Water appears in two of these equations although it is not a component of the reaction forming CH_4 from carbon and hydrogen. To use Hess's law to solve this problem, we will first have to manipulate the equations and adjust the $\Delta_r H^\circ$ values accordingly before adding equations together. Recall, from Section 5.5, that writing an equation in the reverse direction changes the sign of $\Delta_r H^\circ$ and that doubling the amount of reactants and products doubles the value of $\Delta_r H^\circ$. Adjustments to Equations 2 and 3 will produce new equations that, along with Equation 1, can be combined to give the desired net reaction.

Solution To have CH_4 appear as a product in the overall reaction, we reverse Equation 3, which changes the sign of $\Delta_r H^\circ$.

Equation 3′: $\quad CO_2(g) + 2 H_2O(\ell) \longrightarrow CH_4(g) + 2 O_2(g)$

$\Delta_r H^{\circ\prime}_3 = -\Delta_r H^\circ_3 = +890.3$ kJ/mol-rxn

Next, we see that 2 mol of $H_2(g)$ is on the reactant side in our desired equation. Equation 2 is written for only 1 mol of $H_2(g)$ as a reactant. Therefore we multiply the stoichiometric coefficients in Equation 2 by 2 and multiply the value of $\Delta_r H^\circ$ by 2.

Equation 2′: $\quad 2 H_2(g) + O_2(g) \longrightarrow 2 H_2O(\ell)$

$\Delta_r H^{\circ\prime}_2 = 2 \Delta_r H^\circ_2 = 2 (-285.8$ kJ/mol-rxn$) = -571.6$ kJ/mol-rxn

We now have three equations that, when added together, will give the targeted equation for the formation of methane from carbon and hydrogen. In this summation process, $O_2(g)$, $H_2O(\ell)$, and $CO_2(g)$ all cancel.

Equation 1:	$C(s) + O_2(g) \longrightarrow CO_2(g)$	$\Delta_r H^\circ_1 = -393.5$ kJ/mol-rxn
Equation 2′:	$2 H_2(g) + O_2(g) \longrightarrow 2 H_2O(\ell)$	$\Delta_r H^{\circ\prime}_2 = 2 \Delta_r H^\circ_2 = -571.6$ kJ/mol-rxn
Equation 3′:	$CO_2(g) + 2 H_2O(\ell) \longrightarrow CH_4(g) + 2 O_2(g)$	$\Delta_r H^{\circ\prime}_3 = -\Delta_r H^\circ_3 = +890.3$ kJ/mol-rxn

Net Equation: $\quad C(s) + 2 H_2(g) \longrightarrow CH_4(g) \qquad \Delta_r H^\circ_{net} = \Delta_r H^\circ_1 + 2 \Delta_r H^\circ_2 + (-\Delta_r H^\circ_3)$

$\Delta_r H^\circ_{net} = (-393.5$ kJ/mol-rxn$) + (-571.6$ kJ/mol-rxn$) + (+890.3$ kJ/mol-rxn$)$

$= -74.8$ kJ/mol-rxn

Thus, for the formation of 1 mol of $CH_4(g)$ from the elements, we find $\Delta_r H^\circ = -74.8$ kJ/mol-rxn.

EXERCISE 5.8 **Using Hess's Law**

Use Hess's law to calculate the enthalpy change for the formation of $CS_2(\ell)$ from C(s) and S(s) [$C(s) + 2 S(s) \longrightarrow CS_2(\ell)$] from the following enthalpy values.

$C(s) + O_2(g) \longrightarrow CO_2(g)$	$\Delta_r H^\circ = -393.5$ kJ/mol-rxn
$S(s) + O_2(g) \longrightarrow SO_2(g)$	$\Delta_r H^\circ = -295.8$ kJ/mol-rxn
$CS_2(\ell) + 3 O_2(g) \longrightarrow CO_2(g) + 2 SO_2(g)$	$\Delta_r H^\circ = -1103.9$ kJ/mol-rxn

How did we know how the three equations should be adjusted in Example 5.8? Here is a general strategy for solving this type of problem.

Step 1. Inspect the equation whose $\Delta_r H°$ you wish to calculate, identifying the reactants and products, and locate those substances in the equations available to be added. In Example 5.8, the reactants, C(s) and $H_2(g)$,

are reactants in Equations 1 and 2, and the product, $CH_4(g)$, is a reactant in Equation 3. Equation 3 was reversed to get CH_4 on the product side.

Step 2. Get the correct amount of the substances on each side. In Example 5.8, only one adjustment was needed. There was 1 mol of H_2 on the left (reactant side) in Equation 2. We needed 2 mol of H_2 in the overall equa-

tion; this required doubling the quantities in Equation 2.

Step 3. Make sure other substances in the equations cancel when the equations are added. In Example 5.8, equal amounts of O_2 and H_2O appeared on the left and right sides in the three equations, and so they canceled when the equations were added together.

Standard Enthalpies of Formation

- $\Delta_f H°$ **Values** Consult the National Institute for Standards and Technology website (webbook.nist.gov/chemistry) for an extensive compilation of enthalpies of formation.

Calorimetry and the application of Hess's law have made available a great many $\Delta_r H°$ values for chemical reactions. Often, these values are assembled into tables. The table in Appendix L, for example, lists **standard molar enthalpies of formation, $\Delta_f H°$**. *The standard molar enthalpy of formation is the enthalpy change for the formation of 1 mol of a compound directly from its component elements in their standard states.*

Several examples of standard molar enthalpies of formation will be helpful to illustrate this definition.

$\Delta_f H°$ **for NaCl(s):** At 25 °C and a pressure of 1 bar, Na is a solid, and Cl_2 is a gas. The standard enthalpy of formation of NaCl(s) is defined as the enthalpy change that occurs when 1 mol of NaCl(s) is formed from 1 mol of Na(s) and $\frac{1}{2}$ mol of $Cl_2(g)$.

$$Na(s) + \tfrac{1}{2}\, Cl_2(g) \longrightarrow NaCl(s) \qquad \Delta_f H° = -411.12 \text{ kJ/mol}$$

$\Delta_f H°$ **for NaCl(aq):** The enthalpy of formation for an aqueous solution of a compound refers to the enthalpy change for the formation of a 1 mol/L solution of the compound starting with the elements making up the compound. It is thus the enthalpy of formation of the compound plus the enthalpy change that occurs when the substance dissolves in water.

$$Na(s) + \tfrac{1}{2}\, Cl_2(g) \longrightarrow NaCl(aq) \qquad \Delta_f H° = -407.27 \text{ kJ/mol}$$

- **Units for Enthalpy of Formation** The units for values of $\Delta_f H°$ are usually given simply as kJ/mol where the denominator is really mol-rxn. However, because an enthalpy of formation is defined as the change in enthalpy for the formation of 1 mol of compound, it is understood that "per mol" means "per mol of compound," which, in this case, is the same thing as "per mol-rxn."

$\Delta_f H°$ **for $C_2H_5OH(\ell)$:** At 25 °C and 1 bar, the standard states of the elements are C(s, graphite), $H_2(g)$, and $O_2(g)$. The standard enthalpy of formation of $C_2H_5OH(\ell)$ is defined as the enthalpy change that occurs when 1 mol of $C_2H_5OH(\ell)$ is formed from 2 mol of C(s), 3 mol of $H_2(g)$, and 1/2 mol of $O_2(g)$.

$$2\, C(s) + 3\, H_2(g) + \tfrac{1}{2}\, O_2(g) \longrightarrow C_2H_5OH(\ell) \qquad \Delta_f H° = -277.0 \text{ kJ/mol}$$

Notice that the reaction defining the enthalpy of formation for liquid ethanol is not a reaction that a chemist can carry out in the laboratory. This illustrates an important point: *the enthalpy of formation of a compound does not necessarily correspond to a reaction that can be carried out.*

Appendix L lists values of $\Delta_f H°$ for some common substances, and a review of these values leads to some important observations.

- *The standard enthalpy of formation for an element in its standard state is zero.*
- Most $\Delta_f H°$ values are negative, indicating that formation of most compounds from the elements is exothermic. A very few values are positive, and these

represent compounds that are unstable with respect to decomposition to the elements. (One example is NO(g) with $\Delta_f H^\circ = +90.29$ kJ/mol.)

- Values of $\Delta_f H^\circ$ can often be used to compare the stabilities of related compounds. Consider the values of $\Delta_f H^\circ$ for the hydrogen halides. Hydrogen fluoride is the most stable of these compounds with respect to decomposition to the elements, whereas HI is the least stable (as indicated by $\Delta_f H^\circ$ of HF being the most negative value and that of HI being the most positive).

■ **$\Delta_f H^\circ$ Values of Hydrogen Halides**

Compound	$\Delta_f H^\circ$ (kJ/mol)
HF(g)	−273.3
HCl(g)	−92.31
HBr(g)	−35.29
HI(g)	+25.36

EXERCISE 5.9 Standard Enthalpies of Formation

Write equations for the reactions that define the standard enthalpy of formation of $FeCl_3(s)$ and of solid sucrose (sugar, $C_{12}H_{22}O_{11}$).

Enthalpy Change for a Reaction

Using standard molar enthalpies of formation and Equation 5.6, it is possible to calculate the enthalpy change for a reaction under standard conditions.

$$\Delta_r H^\circ = \Sigma \Delta_f H^\circ \text{(products)} - \Sigma \Delta_f H^\circ \text{(reactants)} \qquad (5.6)$$

■ **Δ = Final − Initial** Equation 5.6 is another example of the convention that a change (Δ) is always calculated by subtracting the value for the initial state (the reactants) from the value for the final state (the products).

In this equation, the symbol Σ (the Greek capital letter sigma) means "take the sum." To find $\Delta_r H^\circ$, add up the molar enthalpies of formation of the products, each multiplied by its stoichiometric coefficient, and subtract from this the sum of the molar enthalpies of formation of the reactants, each multiplied by its stoichiometric coefficient. This equation is a logical consequence of the definition of $\Delta_f H^\circ$ and Hess's law (see *A Closer Look: Hess's Law and Equation 5.6*).

Suppose you want to know how much heat is required to decompose 1 mol of calcium carbonate (limestone) to calcium oxide (lime) and carbon dioxide under standard conditions:

$$CaCO_3(s) \longrightarrow CaO(s) + CO_2(g) \qquad \Delta_r H^\circ = ?$$

You would use the following enthalpies of formation (from Appendix L):

Compound	$\Delta_f H^\circ$ (kJ/mol)
$CaCO_3$(s)	−1207.6
CaO(s)	−635.1
CO_2(g)	−393.5

and then use Equation 5.6 to find the standard enthalpy change for the reaction, $\Delta_r H^\circ$.

$$\Delta_r H^\circ = \left[\left(\frac{1 \text{ mol CaO}}{1 \text{ mol-rxn}}\right)\left(\frac{-635.1 \text{ kJ}}{\text{mol CaO}}\right) + \left(\frac{1 \text{ mol CO}_2}{1 \text{ mol-rxn}}\right)\left(\frac{-393.5 \text{ kJ}}{1 \text{ mol CO}_2}\right)\right]$$
$$- \left[\left(\frac{1 \text{ mol CaCO}_3}{1 \text{ mol-rxn}}\right)\left(\frac{-1207.6 \text{ kJ}}{1 \text{ mol CaCO}_3}\right)\right]$$
$$= +179.0 \text{ kJ/mol-rxn}$$

The decomposition of limestone to lime and CO_2 is endothermic. That is, energy (179.0 kJ) must be supplied to decompose 1 mol of $CaCO_3(s)$ to CaO(s) and $CO_2(g)$.

Chemistry ☼ Now™

Sign in at **www.cengage.com/login** and go to Chapter 5 Contents to see Screen 5.16 for a tutorial on calculating the standard enthalpy change for a reaction.

Equation 5.6 is an application of Hess's law. To illustrate this, let us look further at the decomposition of calcium carbonate.

$$CaCO_3(s) \longrightarrow CaO(s) + CO_2(g) \qquad \Delta_r H^\circ = \; ?$$

Because enthalpy is a state function, the change in enthalpy for this reaction is independent of the route from reactants to products. We can imagine an alternate route from reactant to products that involves first converting the reactant to elements in their standard states, then recombining these elements to give the reaction products. Notice that the enthalpy changes for these processes are the enthalpies of formation of the reactants and products in the equation above:

$CaCO_3(s) \longrightarrow Ca(s) + C(s) + 3/2 \, O_2(g)$ $-\Delta_f H^\circ[CaCO_3(s)] = \Delta_r H_1^\circ$

$C(s) + O_2(g) \longrightarrow CO_2(g)$ $\Delta_f H^\circ[CO_2(g)] = \Delta_r H_2^\circ$

$Ca(s) + \frac{1}{2} O_2(g) \longrightarrow CaO(s)$ $\Delta_f H^\circ[CaO(s)] = \Delta_r H_3^\circ$

$CaCO_3(s) \longrightarrow CaO(s) + CO_2(g)$ $\Delta_r H_{net}^\circ$

$\Delta_r H_{net}^\circ = \Delta_r H_1^\circ + \Delta_r H_2^\circ + \Delta_r H_3^\circ$

$\Delta_r H^\circ = \Delta_f H^\circ[CaO(s)] + \Delta_f H^\circ[CO_2(g)] - \Delta_f H^\circ[CaCO_3(s)]$

That is, the change in enthalpy for the reaction is equal to the enthalpies of formation of products (CO_2 and CaO) minus the enthalpy of formation of the reactant ($CaCO_3$), which is, of course, what one does when using Equation 5.6 for this calculation. The relationship among these enthalpy quantities is illustrated in the energy-level diagram.

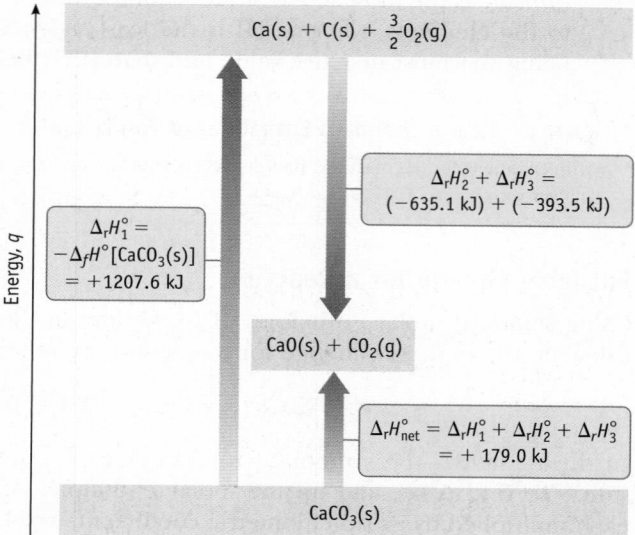

Energy level diagram for the decomposition of $CaCO_3(s)$

$Ca(s) + C(s) + \frac{3}{2}O_2(g)$

$\Delta_r H_1^\circ = -\Delta_f H^\circ[CaCO_3(s)] = +1207.6$ kJ

$\Delta_r H_2^\circ + \Delta_r H_3^\circ = (-635.1 \text{ kJ}) + (-393.5 \text{ kJ})$

$CaO(s) + CO_2(g)$

$\Delta_r H_{net}^\circ = \Delta_r H_1^\circ + \Delta_r H_2^\circ + \Delta_r H_3^\circ = +179.0$ kJ

$CaCO_3(s)$

Energy, q

EXAMPLE 5.9   Using Enthalpies of Formation

Problem Nitroglycerin is a powerful explosive that forms four different gases when detonated:

$$2 \, C_3H_5(NO_3)_3(\ell) \longrightarrow 3 \, N_2(g) + \frac{1}{2} \, O_2(g) + 6 \, CO_2(g) + 5 \, H_2O(g)$$

Calculate the enthalpy change that occurs when 10.0 g of nitroglycerin is detonated. The standard enthalpy of formation of nitroglycerin, $\Delta_f H^\circ$, is −364 kJ/mol. Use Appendix L to find other $\Delta_f H^\circ$ values that are needed.

Strategy Use values of $\Delta_f H^\circ$ for the reactants and products in Equation 5.6 to calculate the enthalpy change produced by one mole of reaction ($\Delta_r H^\circ$). From Appendix L, $\Delta_f H^\circ[CO_2(g)] = -393.5$ kJ/mol, $\Delta_f H^\circ[H_2O(g)] = -241.8$ kJ/mol, and $\Delta_f H^\circ = 0$ for $N_2(g)$ and $O_2(g)$. Determine the amount (mol) represented by 10.0 g of nitroglycerin; then use this value with $\Delta_r H^\circ$ and the balanced chemical equation to obtain the answer.

Solution Using Equation 5.6, we find the enthalpy change for the explosion of 2 mol of nitroglycerin is

$$\Delta_r H^\circ = \left(\frac{6 \text{ mol } CO_2}{1 \text{ mol-rxn}} \right) \Delta_f H^\circ[CO_2(g)] + \left(\frac{5 \text{ mol } H_2O}{1 \text{ mol-rxn}} \right) \Delta_f H^\circ[H_2O(g)]$$

$$- \left(\frac{2 \text{ mol } C_3H_5(NO_3)_3}{1 \text{ mol-rxn}} \right) \Delta_f H^\circ[C_3H_5(NO_3)_3(\ell)]$$

$$\Delta_r H^\circ = \left(\frac{6 \text{ mol } CO_2}{1 \text{ mol-rxn}} \right) \left(\frac{-393.5 \text{ kJ}}{1 \text{ mol } CO_2} \right) + \left(\frac{5 \text{ mol } H_2O}{1 \text{ mol-rxn}} \right) \left(\frac{-241.8 \text{ kJ}}{1 \text{ mol } H_2O} \right)$$

$$- \left(\frac{2 \text{ mol } C_3H_5(NO_3)_3}{1 \text{ mol-rxn}} \right) \left(\frac{-364 \text{ kJ}}{1 \text{ mol } C_3H_5(NO_3)_3} \right) = -2842 \text{ kJ/mol-rxn}$$

The problem asks for the enthalpy change using 10.0 g of nitroglycerin. We next need to determine the amount of nitroglycerin in 10.0 g.

$$10.0 \text{ g nitroglycerin} \left(\frac{1 \text{ mol nitroglycerin}}{227.1 \text{ g nitroglycerin}} \right) = 0.0440 \text{ mol nitroglycerin}$$

The enthalpy change for the detonation of 0.0440 mol of nitroglycerin is

$$\Delta H° = 0.0440 \text{ mol nitroglycerin} \left(\frac{1 \text{ mol-rxn}}{2 \text{ mol nitroglycerin}} \right) \left(\frac{-2842 \text{ kJ}}{1 \text{ mol-rxn}} \right)$$

$$= -62.6 \text{ kJ}$$

Comment The large value of $\Delta H°$ is in accord with the fact that this reaction is highly energetic.

EXERCISE 5.10 Using Enthalpies of Formation

Calculate the standard enthalpy of combustion for benzene, C_6H_6.

$$C_6H_6(\ell) + 15/2 \ O_2(g) \longrightarrow 6 \ CO_2(g) + 3 \ H_2O(\ell) \qquad \Delta_r H° = ?$$

$$\Delta_f H°[C_6H_6(\ell)] = +49.0 \text{ kJ/mol}.$$

Other values needed can be found in Appendix L.

5.8 Product- or Reactant-Favored Reactions and Thermodynamics

At the beginning of this chapter, we noted that thermodynamics would provide answers to four questions. How much energy is evolved or required in physical changes and in chemical reactions, and the relationship of heat and work have been the primary topics of this chapter. The first two questions were addressed in this chapter, but there are two other important questions: How can we determine whether a reaction is product-favored or reactant-favored at equilibrium? And what determines whether a chemical reaction will occur spontaneously; that is, without outside intervention?

In Chapter 3, we learned that chemical reactions proceed toward equilibrium, and spontaneous changes occur in a way that allows a system to approach equilibrium. Reactions in which reactants are largely converted to products when equilibrium is reached are said to be *product-favored*. Reactions in which only a small amount of products are present at equilibrium are called *reactant-favored* (◄ page 121).

Let us look back at the many chemical reactions that we have seen. For example, all combustion reactions are exothermic, and the oxidation of iron (Figure 5.17) is clearly exothermic.

$$4 \ Fe(s) + 3 \ O_2(g) \longrightarrow 2 \ Fe_2O_3(s)$$

$$\Delta_r H° = 2 \ \Delta_f H°[Fe_2O_3(s)] = \left(\frac{2 \text{ mol Fe}_2O_3}{1 \text{ mol-rxn}} \right) \left(\frac{-825.5 \text{ kJ}}{1 \text{ mol Fe}_2O_3} \right) = -1651.0 \text{ kJ/mol-rxn}$$

The reaction has a negative value for $\Delta_r H°$, and it is also spontaneous and product-favored.

Conversely, the decomposition of calcium carbonate is endothermic.

$$CaCO_3(s) \longrightarrow CaO(s) + CO_2(g) \qquad \Delta_r H° = +179.0 \text{ kJ/mol-rxn}$$

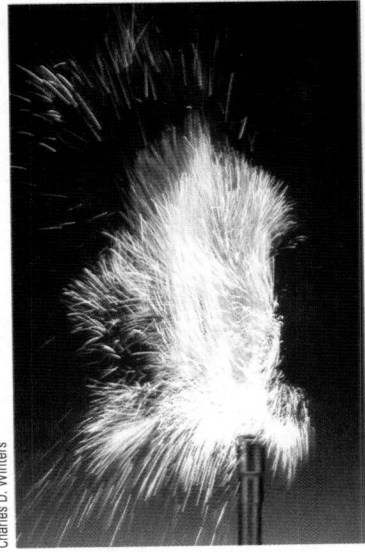

Charles D. Winters

FIGURE 5.17 The product-favored oxidation of iron. Iron powder, sprayed into a bunsen burner flame, is rapidly oxidized. The reaction is exothermic and is product-favored.

It is clear that supplies of fossil fuels are declining, and their price is increasing, just as the nations of the earth have ever greater energy needs. We will have more to say about this in the Interchapter (Energy) that follows. Here, however, let's analyze the debate about replacing gasoline with ethanol (C_2H_5OH).

As Matthew Wald says in the article "Is Ethanol in for the Long Haul?" (*Scientific American*, January 2007), "The U.S. has gone on an ethanol binge." In 2005, the U.S. Congress passed an energy bill stating that ethanol production should be 7.5 billion gallons a year by 2012, up from about 5 billion gallons a year presently. The goal is to at least partially replace gasoline with ethanol.

Is the goal of replacing gasoline with ethanol reasonable? This is a lofty goal, given that present gasoline consumption in the U.S. is about 140 billion gallons annually. Again, according to Matthew Wald, "Even if 100 percent of the U.S. corn supply was distilled into ethanol, it would supply only a small fraction of the fuel consumed by the nation's vehicles." Wald's thesis in his article, which is supported by numerous scientific studies, is that if ethanol is to be pursued as an alternative to gasoline, more emphasis should be placed on deriving ethanol from sources other than corn, such as cellulose from cornstalks and various grasses.

© Stephen Lunetta Photography, 2007

Ethanol available at a service station. E85 fuel is a blend of 85% ethanol and 15% gasoline. Be aware that you can only use E85 in vehicles designed for the fuel. In an ordinary vehicle, the ethanol leads to deterioration of seals in the engine and fuel system.

Beyond this, there are other problems associated with ethanol. One is that it cannot be distributed through a pipeline system as gasoline can. Any water in the pipeline is miscible with ethanol, which causes the fuel value to decline. Instead, ethanol must be trucked to service stations.

Finally, E85 fuel—a blend of 85% ethanol and 15% gasoline—cannot be used in most current vehicles because relatively few vehicles as yet have engines designed for fuels with a high ethanol content (so-called "flexible fuel" engines). The number of these vehicles would need to be increased in order for E85 to have a significant effect on our gasoline usage.

For more information, see the references in Wald's *Scientific American* article.

Questions:

For the purposes of this analysis, let us use octane (C_8H_{18}) as a substitute for the complex mixture of hydrocarbons in gasoline. Data you will need for this question (in addition to Appendix L) are:

$$\Delta_f H° \ [C_8H_{18}(\ell)] = -250.1 \text{ kJ/mol}$$
Density of ethanol = 0.785 g/mL
Density of octane = 0.699 g/mL

1. Calculate $\Delta_r H°$ for the combustion of ethanol and octane, and compare the values per mol and per gram. Which provides more energy per gram?

2. Compare the energy produced per liter of the two fuels. Which produces more energy for a given volume (something useful to know when filling your gas tank)?

3. What mass of CO_2, a greenhouse gas, is produced per liter of fuel (assuming complete combustion)?

4. Now compare the fuels on an energy-equivalent basis. What volume of ethanol would have to be burned to get the same energy as 1.00 L of octane? When you burn enough ethanol to have the same energy as a liter of octane, which fuel produces more CO_2?

5. On the basis of this analysis and assuming the same price per liter, which fuel will propel your car further? Which will produce less greenhouse gas?

Answers to these questions are in Appendix Q.

■ **Reactant-Favored or Product-Favored?** In most—but not all—cases exothermic reactions are product-favored at equilibrium and endothermic reactions are reactant-favored at equilibrium.

The decomposition of $CaCO_3$ proceeds spontaneously to an equilibrium that favors the reactants; that is, it is reactant-favored.

Are all exothermic reactions product-favored and all endothermic reactions reactant-favored? From these examples, we might formulate that idea as a hypothesis that can be tested by experiment and by examination of other examples. We would find that *in most cases, product-favored reactions have negative values of $\Delta_r H°$, and reactant-favored reactions have positive values of $\Delta_r H°$.* But this is not *always* true; there are exceptions.

Clearly, a further discussion of thermodynamics must be tied to the concept of equilibrium. This relationship, and the complete discussion of the third and fourth questions, will be presented in Chapter 19.

Chemistry⚛Now™

Sign in at **www.cengage.com/login** and go to Chapter 5 Contents to see Screen 5.17 Product-Favored Systems, for an exercise on **the reaction when a Gummi Bear is placed in molten potassium chlorate.**

Chapter Goals Revisited

Now that you have studied this chapter, you should ask whether you have met the chapter goals. In particular, you should be able to:

Assess the transfer of energy as heat associated with changes in temperature and changes of state

a. Describe various forms of energy and the nature of energy transfers as heat (Section 5.1).

b. Use the most common energy unit, the joule, and convert between other energy units and joules (Section 5.1). Study Question(s) assignable in OWL: 5.

c. Recognize and use the language of thermodynamics: the system and its surroundings; exothermic and endothermic reactions (Section 5.1). Study Question(s) assignable in OWL: 61, 92.

d. Use specific heat capacity in calculations of energy transfer as heat and of temperature changes (Section 5.2). Study Question(s) assignable in OWL: 8, 10, 12, 13, 16, 18, 83.

e. Understand the sign conventions in thermodynamics.

f. Use enthalpy (heat) of fusion and enthalpy (heat) of vaporization to find the quantity of energy transferred as heat that is involved in changes of state (Section 5.3). Study Question(s) assignable in OWL: 20, 22, 23, 24, 28, 68, 70, 71, 88, 93, 97.

Understand and apply the first law of thermodynamics

a. Understand the basis of the first law of thermodynamics (Section 5.4).

b. Recognize how energy transferred as heat and work done on or by a system contribute to changes in the internal energy of a system (Section 5.4).

Define and understand state functions (enthalpy, internal energy)

a. Recognize state functions whose values are determined only by the state of the system and not by the pathway by which that state was achieved (Section 5.4).

Learn how energy changes are measured

a. Recognize that when a process is carried out under constant pressure conditions, the energy transferred as heat is the enthalpy change, ΔH (Section 5.5). Study Question(s) assignable in OWL: 28, 29, 30, 52, 54.

b. Describe how to measure the quantity of energy transferred as heat in a reaction by calorimetry (Section 5.6). Study Question(s) assignable in OWL: 32, 33, 34, 36, 38, 40, 42.

Calculate the energy evolved or required for physical changes and chemical reactions using tables of thermodynamic data.

a. Apply Hess's law to find the enthalpy change for a reaction (Section 5.7). Study Question(s) assignable in OWL: 44, 73, 74, 79; Go Chemistry Module 10.

b. Know how to draw and interpret energy level diagrams (Section 5.7).

c. Use standard molar enthalpies of formation, $\Delta_f H°$, to calculate the enthalpy change for a reaction $\Delta_r H°$ (Section 5.7). Study Question(s) assignable in OWL: 49, 53, 58.

Chemistry ⚛ Now™ Sign in at **www.cengage.com/login** to:

• Assess your understanding with Study Questions in OWL keyed to each goal in the Goals and Homework menu for this chapter

• For quick review, download Go Chemistry mini-lecture flashcard modules (or purchase them at **www.ichapters.com**)

• Check your readiness for an exam by taking the Pre-Test and exploring the modules recommended in your Personalized Study plan.

❓ Access **How Do I Solve It?** tutorials on how to approach problem solving using concepts in this chapter.

For additional preparation for an examination on this chapter see the *Let's Review* section on pages 254–267.

KEY EQUATIONS

Equation 5.1 (page 215) The energy transferred as heat when the temperature of a substance changes. Calculated from the specific heat capacity (C), mass (m), and change in temperature (ΔT).

$$q(\text{J}) = C(\text{J/g} \cdot \text{K}) \times m(\text{g}) \times \Delta T(\text{K})$$

Equation 5.2 (page 215) Temperature changes are always calculated as final temperature minus initial temperature.

$$\Delta T = T_{final} - T_{initial}$$

Equation 5.3 (page 217) If no energy is transferred between a system and its surroundings and if energy is transferred within the system only as heat, the sum of the thermal energy changes within the system equals zero.

$$q_1 + q_2 + q_3 + \ldots = 0$$

Equation 5.4 (page 223) The first law of thermodynamics: The change in internal energy (ΔU) in a system is the sum of the energy transferred as heat (q) and the energy transferred as work (w).

$$\Delta U = q + w$$

Equation 5.5 (page 224) Work (w) at constant pressure is the product of pressure (P) and change in volume (ΔV)

$$w = -P(\Delta V)$$

Equation 5.6 (page 237) This equation is used to calculate the standard enthalpy change of a reaction ($\Delta_r H°$) when the enthalpies of formation ($\Delta_f H°$) of all of the reactants and products are known.

$$\Delta_r H° = \Sigma \Delta_f H°(\text{products}) - \Sigma \Delta_f H°(\text{reactants})$$

STUDY QUESTIONS

OWL Online homework for this chapter may be assigned in OWL.

▲ denotes challenging questions.

■ denotes questions assignable in OWL.

Blue-numbered questions have answers in Appendix O and fully-worked solutions in the *Student Solutions Manual*.

Practicing Skills

Energy
(See Section 5.1 and ChemistryNow Screen 5.2.)

1. The flashlight in the photo does not use batteries. Instead, you move a lever, which turns a geared mechanism and results finally in light from the bulb. What type of energy is used to move the lever? What type or types of energy are produced?

A hand-operated flashlight.

2. A solar panel is pictured in the photo. When light shines on the panel, it generates an electric current that is used by a small electric motor to propel the car. What types of energy are involved in this setup?

A solar panel operates a toy car.

Energy Units
(See Exercise 5.1 and ChemistryNow Screen 5.5.)

3. You are on a diet that calls for eating no more than 1200 Cal/day. What is this energy in joules?

4. A 2-in. piece of chocolate cake with frosting provides 1670 kJ of energy. What is this in dietary Calories (Cal)?

5. ■ One food product has an energy content of 170 kcal per serving, and another has 280 kJ per serving. Which food provides the greater energy per serving?

6. Which provides the greater energy per serving, a raw apple or a raw apricot? Go to the USDA Nutrient Database on the World Wide Web for the information: http://www.ars.usda.gov/main/site_main.htm?modecode=12354500. Report the energy content of the fruit in kcal and kJ.

Specific Heat Capacity
(See Examples 5.1 and 5.2 and ChemistryNow Screens 5.6–5.10.)

7. The molar heat capacity of mercury is 28.1 J/mol · K. What is the specific heat capacity of this metal in J/g · K?

8. ■ The specific heat capacity of benzene (C_6H_6) is 1.74 J/g · K. What is its molar heat capacity (in J/mol · K)?

9. The specific heat capacity of copper is 0.385 J/g · K. How much energy is required to heat 168 g of copper from -12.2 °C to $+25.6$ °C?

10. ■ How much energy is required to raise the temperature of 50.00 mL of water from 25.52 °C to 28.75 °C? (The density of water at this temperature is 0.997 g/mL.)

11. The initial temperature of a 344-g sample of iron is 18.2 °C. If the sample absorbs 2.25 kJ of energy as heat, what is its final temperature?

12. ■ After absorbing 1.850 kJ of energy as heat, the temperature of a 0.500-kg block of copper is 37 °C. What was its initial temperature?

13. ■ A 45.5-g sample of copper at 99.8 °C is dropped into a beaker containing 152 g of water at 18.5 °C. What is the final temperature when thermal equilibrium is reached?

14. A 182-g sample of gold at some temperature is added to 22.1 g of water. The initial water temperature is 25.0 °C, and the final temperature is 27.5 °C. If the specific heat capacity of gold is 0.128 J/g · K, what was the initial temperature of the gold?

15. One beaker contains 156 g of water at 22 °C, and a second beaker contains 85.2 g of water at 95 °C. The water in the two beakers is mixed. What is the final water temperature?

16. ■ When 108 g of water at a temperature of 22.5 °C is mixed with 65.1 g of water at an unknown temperature, the final temperature of the resulting mixture is 47.9 °C. What was the initial temperature of the second sample of water?

17. A 13.8-g piece of zinc was heated to 98.8 °C in boiling water and then dropped into a beaker containing 45.0 g of water at 25.0 °C. When the water and metal come to thermal equilibrium, the temperature is 27.1 °C. What is the specific heat capacity of zinc?

18. ■ A 237-g piece of molybdenum, initially at 100.0 °C, is dropped into 244 g of water at 10.0 °C. When the system comes to thermal equilibrium, the temperature is 15.3 °C. What is the specific heat capacity of molybdenum?

Changes of State
(See Examples 5.3 and 5.4 and ChemistryNow Screen 5.8.)

19. How much energy is evolved when 1.0 L of water at 0 °C solidifies to ice? (The heat of fusion of water is 333 J/g.)

20. ■ The energy required to melt 1.00 g of ice at 0 °C is 333 J. If one ice cube has a mass of 62.0 g and a tray contains 16 ice cubes, what quantity of energy is required to melt a tray of ice cubes to form liquid water at 0 °C?

21. ■ How much energy is required to vaporize 125 g of benzene, C_6H_6, at its boiling point, 80.1 °C? (The heat of vaporization of benzene is 30.8 kJ/mol.)

22. ■ Chloromethane, CH_3Cl, arises from microbial fermentation and is found throughout the environment. It is also produced industrially and is used in the manufacture of various chemicals and has been used as a topical anesthetic. How much energy is required to convert 92.5 g of liquid to a vapor at its boiling point, -24.09 °C? (The heat of vaporization of CH_3Cl is 21.40 kJ/mol.)

23. The freezing point of mercury is -38.8 °C. What quantity of energy, in joules, is released to the surroundings if 1.00 mL of mercury is cooled from 23.0 °C to -38.8 °C and then frozen to a solid? (The density of liquid mercury is 13.6 g/cm³. Its specific heat capacity is 0.140 J/g · K and its heat of fusion is 11.4 J/g.)

24. ■ What quantity of energy, in joules, is required to raise the temperature of 454 g of tin from room temperature, 25.0 °C, to its melting point, 231.9 °C, and then melt the tin at that temperature? (The specific heat capacity of tin is 0.227 J/g · K, and the heat of fusion of this metal is 59.2 J/g.)

25. Ethanol, C_2H_5OH, boils at 78.29 °C. How much energy, in joules, is required to raise the temperature of 1.00 kg of ethanol from 20.0 °C to the boiling point and then to change the liquid to vapor at that temperature? (The specific heat capacity of liquid ethanol is 2.44 J/g · K, and its enthalpy of vaporization is 855 J/g.)

26. ■ A 25.0-mL sample of benzene at 19.9 °C was cooled to its melting point, 5.5 °C, and then frozen. How much energy as heat was given off in this process? (The density of benzene is 0.80 g/mL; its specific heat capacity is 1.74 J/g · K, and its heat of fusion is 127 J/g.)

Enthalpy Changes
(See Example 5.5 and ChemistryNow Screens 5.12 and 5.13.)

27. Nitrogen monoxide, a gas recently found to be involved in a wide range of biological processes, reacts with oxygen to give brown NO_2 gas.

$$2 NO(g) + O_2(g) \rightarrow 2 NO_2(g)$$
$$\Delta_r H° = -114.1 \text{ kJ/mol-rxn}$$

Is this reaction endothermic or exothermic? What is the enthalpy change if 1.25 g of NO is converted completely to NO_2?

28. ■ Calcium carbide, CaC_2, is manufactured by the reaction of CaO with carbon at a high temperature. (Calcium carbide is then used to make acetylene.)

$$CaO(s) + 3 C(s) \rightarrow CaC_2(s) + CO(g)$$
$$\Delta_r H° = +464.8 \text{ kJ/mol-rxn}$$

Is this reaction endothermic or exothermic? What is the enthalpy change if 10.0 g of CaO is allowed to react with an excess of carbon?

29. ■ Isooctane (2,2,4-trimethylpentane), one of the many hydrocarbons that make up gasoline, burns in air to give water and carbon dioxide.

$$2 C_8H_{18}(\ell) + 25 O_2(g) \rightarrow 16 CO_2(g) + 18 H_2O(\ell)$$
$$\Delta_r H° = -10,922 \text{ kJ/mol-rxn}$$

What is the enthalpy change if you burn 1.00 L of isooctane (density = 0.69 g/mL)?

30. ■ Acetic acid, CH_3CO_2H, is made industrially by the reaction of methanol and carbon monoxide.

$$CH_3OH(\ell) + CO(g) \rightarrow CH_3CO_2H(\ell)$$
$$\Delta_r H° = -355.9 \text{ kJ/mol-rxn}$$

If you produce 1.00 L of acetic acid ($d = 1.044$ g/mL) by this reaction, how much energy as heat is evolved?

Calorimetry
(See Examples 5.6 and 5.7 and ChemistryNow Screens 5.8, 5.9, and 5.14.)

31. Assume you mix 100.0 mL of 0.200 M CsOH with 50.0 mL of 0.400 M HCl in a coffee-cup calorimeter. The following reaction occurs:

$$CsOH(aq) + HCl(aq) \rightarrow CsCl(aq) + H_2O(\ell)$$

The temperature of both solutions before mixing was 22.50 °C, and it rises to 24.28 °C after the acid–base reaction. What is the enthalpy change for the reaction per mole of CsOH? Assume the densities of the solutions are all 1.00 g/mL and the specific heat capacities of the solutions are 4.2 J/g · K.

32. ■ You mix 125 mL of 0.250 M CsOH with 50.0 mL of 0.625 M HF in a coffee-cup calorimeter, and the temperature of both solutions rises from 21.50 °C before mixing to 24.40 °C after the reaction.

$$CsOH(aq) + HF(aq) \rightarrow CsF(aq) + H_2O(\ell)$$

What is the enthalpy of reaction per mole of CsOH? Assume the densities of the solutions are all 1.00 g/mL and the specific heats of the solutions are 4.2 J/g · K.

33. ■ A piece of titanium metal with a mass of 20.8 g is heated in boiling water to 99.5 °C and then dropped into a coffee-cup calorimeter containing 75.0 g of water at 21.7 °C. When thermal equilibrium is reached, the final temperature is 24.3 °C. Calculate the specific heat capacity of titanium.

34. ■ A piece of chromium metal with a mass of 24.26 g is heated in boiling water to 98.3 °C and then dropped into a coffee-cup calorimeter containing 82.3 g of water at 23.3 °C. When thermal equilibrium is reached, the final temperature is 25.6 °C. Calculate the specific heat capacity of chromium.

35. Adding 5.44 g of $NH_4NO_3(s)$ to 150.0 g of water in a coffee-cup calorimeter (with stirring to dissolve the salt) resulted in a decrease in temperature from 18.6 °C to 16.2 °C. Calculate the enthalpy change for dissolving $NH_4NO_3(s)$ in water, in kJ/mol. Assume that the solution (whose mass is 155.4 g) has a specific heat capacity of 4.2 J/g · K. (Cold packs take advantage of the fact that dissolving ammonium nitrate in water is an endothermic process.)

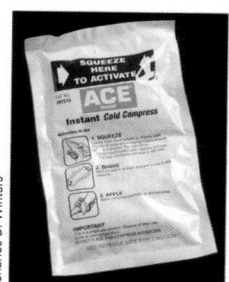

A cold pack uses the endothermic enthalpy of solution of ammonium nitrate.

36. ■ You should use care when dissolving H_2SO_4 in water because the process is highly exothermic. To measure the enthalpy change, 5.2 g $H_2SO_4(\ell)$ was added (with stirring) to 135 g of water in a coffee-cup calorimeter. This resulted in an increase in temperature from 20.2 °C to 28.8 °C. Calculate the enthalpy change for the process $H_2SO_4(\ell) \rightarrow H_2SO_4(aq)$, in kJ/mol.

▲ more challenging ■ in OWL Blue-numbered questions answered in Appendix O

37. Sulfur (2.56 g) is burned in a constant volume calorimeter with excess $O_2(g)$. The temperature increases from 21.25 °C to 26.72 °C. The bomb has a heat capacity of 923 J/K, and the calorimeter contains 815 g of water. Calculate ΔU per mole of SO_2 formed, for the reaction

$$S_8(s) + 8\ O_2(g) \rightarrow 8\ SO_2(g)$$

Sulfur burns in oxygen with a bright blue flame to give $SO_2(g)$.

38. ■ Suppose you burn 0.300 g of C(graphite) in an excess of $O_2(g)$ in a constant volume calorimeter to give $CO_2(g)$.

$$C(graphite) + O_2(g) \rightarrow CO_2(g)$$

The temperature of the calorimeter, which contains 775 g of water, increases from 25.00 °C to 27.38 °C. The heat capacity of the bomb is 893 J/K. Calculate ΔU per mole of carbon.

39. Suppose you burn 1.500 g of benzoic acid, $C_6H_5CO_2H$, in a constant volume calorimeter and find that the temperature increases from 22.50 °C to 31.69 °C. The calorimeter contains 775 g of water, and the bomb has a heat capacity of 893 J/K. Calculate ΔU per mole of benzoic acid.

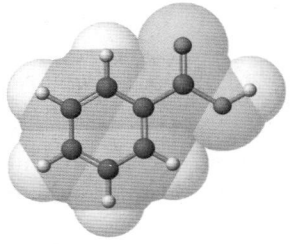

Benzoic acid, $C_6H_5CO_2H$, occurs naturally in many berries. Its heat of combustion is well known, so it is used as a standard to calibrate calorimeters.

40. ■ A 0.692-g sample of glucose, $C_6H_{12}O_6$, is burned in a constant volume calorimeter. The temperature rises from 21.70 °C to 25.22 °C. The calorimeter contains 575 g of water, and the bomb has a heat capacity of 650 J/K. What is ΔU per mole of glucose?

41. An "ice calorimeter" can be used to determine the specific heat capacity of a metal. A piece of hot metal is dropped onto a weighed quantity of ice. The energy transferred from the metal to the ice can be determined from the amount of ice melted. Suppose you heat a 50.0-g piece of silver to 99.8 °C and then drop it onto ice. When the metal's temperature has dropped to 0.0 °C, it is found that 3.54 g of ice has melted. What is the specific heat capacity of silver?

42. ■ A 9.36-g piece of platinum is heated to 98.6 °C in a boiling water bath and then dropped onto ice. (See Study Question 41.) When the metal's temperature has dropped to 0.0 °C, it is found that 0.37 g of ice has melted. What is the specific heat capacity of platinum?

Hess's Law
(See Example 5.8 and ChemistryNow Screen 5.15.)

43. The enthalpy changes for the following reactions can be measured:

$$CH_4(g) + 2\ O_2(g) \rightarrow CO_2(g) + 2\ H_2O(g)$$
$$\Delta_r H° = -802.4\ \text{kJ/mol-rxn}$$

$$CH_3OH(g) + \tfrac{3}{2}\ O_2(g) \rightarrow CO_2(g) + 2\ H_2O(g)$$
$$\Delta_r H° = -676\ \text{kJ/mol-rxn}$$

(a) Use these values and Hess's law to determine the enthalpy change for the reaction

$$CH_4(g) + \tfrac{1}{2}\ O_2(g) \rightarrow CH_3OH(g)$$

(b) Draw an energy-level diagram that shows the relationship between the energy quantities involved in this problem.

44. ■ The enthalpy changes of the following reactions can be measured:

$$C_2H_4(g) + 3\ O_2(g) \rightarrow 2\ CO_2(g) + 2\ H_2O(\ell)$$
$$\Delta_r H° = -1411.1\ \text{kJ/mol-rxn}$$

$$C_2H_5OH(\ell) + 3\ O_2(g) \rightarrow 2\ CO_2(g) + 3\ H_2O(\ell)$$
$$\Delta_r H° = -1367.5\ \text{kJ/mol-rxn}$$

(a) ■ Use these values and Hess's law to determine the enthalpy change for the reaction

$$C_2H_4(g) + H_2O(\ell) \rightarrow C_2H_5OH(\ell)$$

(b) Draw an energy-level diagram that shows the relationship between the energy quantities involved in this problem.

45. Enthalpy changes for the following reactions can be determined experimentally:

$$N_2(g) + 3 H_2(g) \rightarrow 2 NH_3(g)$$
$$\Delta_r H° = -91.8 \text{ kJ/mol-rxn}$$

$$4 NH_3(g) + 5 O_2(g) \rightarrow 4 NO(g) + 6 H_2O(g)$$
$$\Delta_r H° = -906.2 \text{ kJ/mol-rxn}$$

$$H_2(g) + \tfrac{1}{2} O_2(g) \rightarrow H_2O(g)$$
$$\Delta_r H° = -241.8 \text{ kJ/mol-rxn}$$

Use these values to determine the enthalpy change for the formation of NO(g) from the elements (an enthalpy change that cannot be measured directly because the reaction is reactant-favored).

$$\tfrac{1}{2} N_2(g) + \tfrac{1}{2} O_2(g) \rightarrow NO(g) \qquad \Delta_r H° = ?$$

46. You wish to know the enthalpy change for the formation of liquid PCl₃ from the elements.

$$P_4(s) + 6 Cl_2(g) \rightarrow 4 PCl_3(\ell) \qquad \Delta_r H° = ?$$

The enthalpy change for the formation of PCl₅ from the elements can be determined experimentally, as can the enthalpy change for the reaction of PCl₃(ℓ) with more chlorine to give PCl₅(s):

$$P_4(s) + 10 Cl_2(g) \rightarrow 4 PCl_5(s)$$
$$\Delta_r H° = -1774.0 \text{ kJ/mol-rxn}$$

$$PCl_3(\ell) + Cl_2(g) \rightarrow PCl_5(s)$$
$$\Delta_r H° = -123.8 \text{ kJ/mol-rxn}$$

Use these data to calculate the enthalpy change for the formation of 1.00 mol of PCl₃(ℓ) from phosphorus and chlorine.

Standard Enthalpies of Formation
(See Example 5.9 and ChemistryNow Screen 5.16.)

47. Write a balanced chemical equation for the formation of CH₃OH(ℓ) from the elements in their standard states. Find the value for $\Delta_f H°$ for CH₃OH(ℓ) in Appendix L.

48. Write a balanced chemical equation for the formation of CaCO₃(s) from the elements in their standard states. Find the value for $\Delta_f H°$ for CaCO₃(s) in Appendix L.

49. (a) Write a balanced chemical equation for the formation of 1 mol of Cr₂O₃(s) from Cr and O₂ in their standard states. Find the value for $\Delta_f H°$ for Cr₂O₃(s) in Appendix L.
(b) ■ What is the standard enthalpy change if 2.4 g of chromium is oxidized to Cr₂O₃(s)?

50. (a) Write a balanced chemical equation for the formation of 1 mol of MgO(s) from the elements in their standard states. Find the value for $\Delta_f H°$ for MgO(s) in Appendix L.
(b) What is the standard enthalpy change for the reaction of 2.5 mol of Mg with oxygen?

51. Use standard enthalpies of formation in Appendix L to calculate enthalpy changes for the following:
(a) 1.0 g of white phosphorus burns, forming P₄O₁₀(s)
(b) 0.20 mol of NO(g) decomposes to N₂(g) and O₂(g)
(c) 2.40 g of NaCl(s) is formed from Na(s) and excess Cl₂(g)
(d) 250 g of iron is oxidized with oxygen to Fe₂O₃(s)

52. ■ Use standard enthalpies of formation in Appendix L to calculate enthalpy changes for the following:
(a) 0.054 g of sulfur burns, forming SO₂(g)
(b) 0.20 mol of HgO(s) decomposes to Hg(ℓ) and O₂(g)
(c) 2.40 g of NH₃(g) is formed from N₂(g) and excess H₂(g)
(d) 1.05 × 10⁻² mol of carbon is oxidized to CO₂(g)

53. The first step in the production of nitric acid from ammonia involves the oxidation of NH₃.

$$4 NH_3(g) + 5 O_2(g) \rightarrow 4 NO(g) + 6 H_2O(g)$$

(a) Use standard enthalpies of formation to calculate the standard enthalpy change for this reaction.
(b) ■ How much energy as heat is evolved or absorbed in the oxidation of 10.0 g of NH₃?

54. ■ The Romans used calcium oxide, CaO, to produce a strong mortar to build stone structures. The CaO was mixed with water to give Ca(OH)₂, which reacted slowly with CO₂ in the air to give CaCO₃.

$$Ca(OH)_2(s) + CO_2(g) \rightarrow CaCO_3(s) + H_2O(g)$$

(a) Calculate the standard enthalpy change for this reaction.
(b) How much energy as heat is evolved or absorbed if 1.00 kg of Ca(OH)₂ reacts with a stoichiometric amount of CO₂?

55. The standard enthalpy of formation of solid barium oxide, BaO, is −553.5 kJ/mol, and the standard enthalpy of formation of barium peroxide, BaO₂, is −634.3 kJ/mol.
(a) Calculate the standard enthalpy change for the following reaction. Is the reaction exothermic or endothermic?

$$2 BaO_2(s) \rightarrow 2 BaO(s) + O_2(g)$$

(b) Draw an energy-level diagram that shows the relationship between the enthalpy change of the decomposition of BaO₂ to BaO and O₂ and the enthalpies of formation of BaO(s) and BaO₂(s).

56. An important step in the production of sulfuric acid is the oxidation of SO_2 to SO_3.

$$SO_2(g) + \tfrac{1}{2} O_2(g) \rightarrow SO_3(g)$$

Formation of SO_3 from the air pollutant SO_2 is also a key step in the formation of acid rain.

(a) Use standard enthalpies of formation to calculate the enthalpy change for the reaction. Is the reaction exothermic or endothermic?

(b) Draw an energy-level diagram that shows the relationship between the enthalpy change for the oxidation of SO_2 to SO_3 and the enthalpies of formation of $SO_2(g)$ and $SO_3(g)$.

57. The enthalpy change for the oxidation of naphthalene, $C_{10}H_8$, is measured by calorimetry.

$$C_{10}H_8(s) + 12 O_2(g) \rightarrow 10 CO_2(g) + 4 H_2O(\ell)$$
$$\Delta_r H° = -5156.1 \text{ kJ/mol-rxn}$$

Use this value, along with the standard enthalpies of formation of $CO_2(g)$ and $H_2O(\ell)$, to calculate the enthalpy of formation of naphthalene, in kJ/mol.

58. ■ The enthalpy change for the oxidation of styrene, C_8H_8, is measured by calorimetry.

$$C_8H_8(\ell) + 10 O_2(g) \rightarrow 8 CO_2(g) + 4 H_2O(\ell)$$
$$\Delta_r H° = -4395.0 \text{ kJ/mol-rxn}$$

Use this value, along with the standard enthalpies of formation of $CO_2(g)$ and $H_2O(\ell)$, to calculate the enthalpy of formation of styrene, in kJ/mol.

General Questions on Thermochemistry

These questions are not designated as to type or location in the chapter. They may combine several concepts.

59. The following terms are used extensively in thermodynamics. Define each and give an example.
(a) exothermic and endothermic
(b) system and surroundings
(c) specific heat capacity
(d) state function
(e) standard state
(f) enthalpy change, ΔH
(g) standard enthalpy of formation

60. For each of the following, tell whether the process is exothermic or endothermic. (No calculations are required.)
(a) $H_2O(\ell) \rightarrow H_2O(s)$
(b) $2 H_2(g) + O_2(g) \rightarrow 2 H_2O(g)$
(c) $H_2O(\ell, 25 °C) \rightarrow H_2O(\ell, 15 °C)$
(d) $H_2O(\ell) \rightarrow H_2O(g)$

61. ■ For each of the following, define a system and its surroundings, and give the direction of energy transfer between system and surroundings.
(a) Methane is burning in a gas furnace in your home.
(b) Water drops, sitting on your skin after a dip in a swimming pool, evaporate.
(c) Water, at 25 °C, is placed in the freezing compartment of a refrigerator, where it cools and eventually solidifies.
(d) Aluminum and $Fe_2O_3(s)$ are mixed in a flask sitting on a laboratory bench. A reaction occurs, and a large quantity of energy is evolved as heat.

62. What does the term "standard state" mean? What are the standard states of the following substances at 298 K: H_2O, NaCl, Hg, CH_4?

63. Use Appendix L to find the standard enthalpies of formation of oxygen atoms, oxygen molecules (O_2), and ozone (O_3). What is the standard state of oxygen? Is the formation of oxygen atoms from O_2 exothermic? What is the enthalpy change for the formation of 1 mol of O_3 from O_2?

64. See the ChemistryNow website, Screen 5.9, Heat Transfer Between Substances. Use the Simulation section of this screen to do the following experiment: Add 10.0 g of Al at 80 °C to 10.0 g of water at 20 °C. What is the final temperature when equilibrium is achieved? Use this value to estimate the specific heat capacity of aluminum.

65. See the ChemistryNow website, Screen 5.15, Hess's Law. Use the Simulation section of this screen to find the value of $\Delta_r H°$ for

$$SnBr_2(s) + TiCl_4(\ell) \rightarrow SnCl_4(\ell) + TiBr_2(s)$$

66. Which gives up more energy on cooling from 50 °C to 10 °C, 50.0 g of water or 100. g of ethanol (specific heat capacity of ethanol = 2.46 J/g · K)?

67. You determine that 187 J of heat is required to raise the temperature of 93.45 g of silver from 18.5 °C to 27.0 °C. What is the specific heat capacity of silver?

68. ■ Calculate the quantity of energy required to convert 60.1 g of $H_2O(s)$ at 0.0 °C to $H_2O(g)$ at 100.0 °C. The heat of fusion of ice at 0 °C is 333 J/g; the heat of vaporization of liquid water at 100 °C is 2260 J/g.

69. ■ You add 100.0 g of water at 60.0 °C to 100.0 g of ice at 0.00 °C. Some of the ice melts and cools the water to 0.00 °C. When the ice and water mixture has come to a uniform temperature of 0 °C, how much ice has melted?

70. ▲ ■ Three 45-g ice cubes at 0 °C are dropped into 5.00×10^2 mL of tea to make iced tea. The tea was initially at 20.0 °C; when thermal equilibrium was reached, the final temperature was 0 °C. How much of the ice melted, and how much remained floating in the beverage? Assume the specific heat capacity of tea is the same as that of pure water.

71. ▲ ■ Suppose that only two 45-g ice cubes had been added to your glass containing 5.00×10^2 mL of tea (see Study Question 70). When thermal equilibrium is reached, all of the ice will have melted, and the temperature of the mixture will be somewhere between 20.0 °C and 0 °C. Calculate the final temperature of the beverage. (Note: The 90 g of water formed when the ice melts must be warmed from 0 °C to the final temperature.)

72. You take a diet cola from the refrigerator and pour 240 mL of it into a glass. The temperature of the beverage is 10.5 °C. You then add one ice cube (45 g). Which of the following describes the system when thermal equilibrium is reached?
   (a) The temperature is 0 °C, and some ice remains.
   (b) The temperature is 0 °C, and no ice remains.
   (c) The temperature is higher than 0 °C, and no ice remains.

   Determine the final temperature and the amount of ice remaining, if any.

73. ▲ ■ The standard molar enthalpy of formation of diborane, $B_2H_6(g)$, cannot be determined directly because the compound cannot be prepared by the reaction of boron and hydrogen. It can be calculated from other enthalpy changes, however. The following enthalpy changes can be measured.

$$4\ B(s) + 3\ O_2(g) \rightarrow 2\ B_2O_3(s)$$
$$\Delta_r H^\circ = -2543.8 \text{ kJ/mol-rxn}$$

$$H_2(g) + \tfrac{1}{2}\ O_2(g) \rightarrow H_2O(g)\ \ \Delta_r H^\circ = -241.8 \text{ kJ/mol-rxn}$$

$$B_2H_6(g) + 3\ O_2(g) \rightarrow B_2O_3(s) + 3\ H_2O(g)$$
$$\Delta_r H^\circ = -2032.9 \text{ kJ/mol-rxn}$$

   (a) Show how these equations can be added together to give the equation for the formation of $B_2H_6(g)$ from $B(s)$ and $H_2(g)$ in their standard states. Assign enthalpy changes to each reaction.
   (b) Calculate $\Delta_f H^\circ$ for $B_2H_6(g)$.
   (c) Draw an energy-level diagram that shows how the various enthalpies in this problem are related.
   (d) Is the formation of $B_2H_6(g)$ from its elements product-favored or reactant-favored?

74. Chloromethane, CH_3Cl, a compound found ubiquitously in the environment, is formed in the reaction of chlorine atoms with methane.

$$CH_4(g) + 2\ Cl(g) \rightarrow CH_3Cl(g) + HCl(g)$$

   (a) ■ Calculate the enthalpy change for the reaction of $CH_4(g)$ and Cl atoms to give $CH_3Cl(g)$ and $HCl(g)$. Is the reaction product-favored or reactant-favored?
   (b) Draw an energy-level diagram that shows how the various enthalpies in this problem are related.

75. When heated to a high temperature, coke (mainly carbon, obtained by heating coal in the absence of air) and steam produce a mixture called water gas, which can be used as a fuel or as a chemical feedstock for other reactions. The equation for the production of water gas is

$$C(s) + H_2O(g) \rightarrow CO(g) + H_2(g)$$

   (a) Use standard enthalpies of formation to determine the enthalpy change for this reaction.
   (b) Is the reaction product-favored or reactant-favored?
   (c) What is the enthalpy change if 1.0 metric ton (1000.0 kg) of carbon is converted to water gas?

76. Camping stoves are fueled by propane (C_3H_8), butane [$C_4H_{10}(g)$, $\Delta_f H^\circ = -127.1$ kJ/mol], gasoline, or ethanol (C_2H_5OH). Calculate the enthalpy of combustion per gram of each of these fuels. [Assume that gasoline is represented by isooctane, $C_8H_{18}(\ell)$, with $\Delta_f H^\circ = -259.2$ kJ/mol.] Do you notice any great differences among these fuels? Are these differences related to their composition?

A camping stove that uses butane as a fuel.

77. Methanol, CH_3OH, a compound that can be made relatively inexpensively from coal, is a promising substitute for gasoline. The alcohol has a smaller energy content than gasoline, but, with its higher octane rating, it burns more efficiently than gasoline in combustion engines. (It has the added advantage of contributing to a lesser degree to some air pollutants.) Compare the enthalpy of combustion per gram of CH_3OH and C_8H_{18} (isooctane), the latter being representative of the compounds in gasoline. ($\Delta_f H^\circ = -259.2$ kJ/mol for isooctane.)

78. Hydrazine and 1,1-dimethylhydrazine both react spontaneously with O_2 and can be used as rocket fuels.

$$N_2H_4(\ell) + O_2(g) \rightarrow N_2(g) + 2\,H_2O(g)$$
hydrazine

$$N_2H_2(CH_3)_2(\ell) + 4\,O_2(g) \rightarrow$$
1,1-dimethylhydrazine $\qquad 2\,CO_2(g) + 4\,H_2O(g) + N_2(g)$

The molar enthalpy of formation of $N_2H_4(\ell)$ is $+50.6$ kJ/mol, and that of $N_2H_2(CH_3)_2(\ell)$ is $+48.9$ kJ/mol. Use these values, with other $\Delta_f H°$ values, to decide whether the reaction of hydrazine or 1,1-dimethylhydrazine with oxygen provides more energy per gram.

NASA

A control rocket in the Space Shuttle uses hydrazine as the fuel.

79. ■ (a) Calculate the enthalpy change, $\Delta_r H°$, for the formation of 1.00 mol of strontium carbonate (the material that gives the red color in fireworks) from its elements.

$$Sr(s) + C(graphite) + \tfrac{3}{2}\,O_2(g) \rightarrow SrCO_3(s)$$

The experimental information available is

$Sr(s) + \tfrac{1}{2}\,O_2(g) \rightarrow SrO(s) \qquad \Delta_f H° = -592$ kJ/mol-rxn

$SrO(s) + CO_2(g) \rightarrow SrCO_3(s) \quad \Delta_r H° = -234$ kJ/mol-rxn

$C(graphite) + O_2(g) \rightarrow CO_2(g) \quad \Delta_f H° = -394$ kJ/mol-rxn

(b) Draw an energy-level diagram relating the energy quantities in this problem.

80. You drink 350 mL of diet soda that is at a temperature of 5 °C.
(a) How much energy will your body expend to raise the temperature of this liquid to body temperature (37 °C)? Assume that the density and specific heat capacity of diet soda are the same as for water.
(b) Compare the value in part (a) with the caloric content of the beverage. (The label says that it has a caloric content of 1 Calorie.) What is the net energy change in your body resulting from drinking this beverage?

(c) Carry out a comparison similar to that in part (b) for a nondiet beverage whose label indicates a caloric content of 240 Calories.

81. ▲ Chloroform, $CHCl_3$, is formed from methane and chlorine in the following reaction.

$$CH_4(g) + 3\,Cl_2(g) \rightarrow 3\,HCl(g) + CHCl_3(g)$$

Calculate $\Delta_r H°$, the enthalpy change for this reaction, using the enthalpies of formation of $CO_2(g)$, $H_2O(\ell)$, and $CHCl_3(g)$ ($\Delta_f H° = -103.1$ kJ/mol), and the enthalpy changes for the following reactions:

$CH_4(g) + 2\,O_2(g) \rightarrow 2\,H_2O(\ell) + CO_2(g)$
$\qquad\qquad\qquad \Delta_r H° = -890.4$ kJ/mol-rxn

$2\,HCl(g) \rightarrow H_2(g) + Cl_2(g)$
$\qquad\qquad\qquad \Delta_r H° = +184.6$ kJ/mol-rxn

82. Water gas, a mixture of carbon monoxide and hydrogen, is produced by treating carbon (in the form of coke or coal) with steam at high temperatures. (See Question 75.)

$$C(s) + H_2O(g) \rightarrow CO(g) + H_2(g)$$

Not all of the carbon available is converted to water gas since some is burned to provide the heat for the endothermic reaction of carbon and water. What mass of carbon must be burned (to CO_2 gas) to provide the energy to convert 1.00 kg of carbon to water gas?

In the Laboratory

83. ■ A piece of lead with a mass of 27.3 g was heated to 98.90 °C and then dropped into 15.0 g of water at 22.50 °C. The final temperature was 26.32 °C. Calculate the specific heat capacity of lead from these data.

84. A 192-g piece of copper is heated to 100.0 °C in a boiling water bath and then dropped into a beaker containing 751 g of water (density = 1.00 g/cm³) at 4.0 °C. What is the final temperature of the copper and water after thermal equilibrium is reached? (The specific heat capacity of copper is 0.385 J/g · K.)

85. Insoluble $AgCl(s)$ precipitates when solutions of $AgNO_3(aq)$ and $NaCl(aq)$ are mixed.

$$AgNO_3(aq) + NaCl(aq) \rightarrow AgCl(s) + NaNO_3(aq)$$
$$\Delta_r H° = ?$$

To measure the energy evolved in this reaction, 250. mL of 0.16 M $AgNO_3(aq)$ and 125 mL of 0.32 M $NaCl(aq)$ are mixed in a coffee-cup calorimeter. The temperature of the mixture rises from 21.15 °C to 22.90 °C. Calculate the enthalpy change for the precipitation of $AgCl(s)$, in kJ/mol. (Assume the density of the solution is 1.0 g/mL and its specific heat capacity is 4.2 J/g · K.)

86. Insoluble $PbBr_2(s)$ precipitates when solutions of $Pb(NO_3)_2(aq)$ and $NaBr(aq)$ are mixed.

$$Pb(NO_3)_2(aq) + 2\ NaBr(aq) \rightarrow PbBr_2(s) + 2\ NaNO_3(aq)$$
$$\Delta_r H° = ?$$

To measure the enthalpy change, 200. mL of 0.75 M $Pb(NO_3)_2(aq)$ and 200. mL of 1.5 M $NaBr(aq)$ are mixed in a coffee-cup calorimeter. The temperature of the mixture rises by 2.44 °C. Calculate the enthalpy change for the precipitation of $PbBr_2(s)$, in kJ/mol. (Assume the density of the solution is 1.0 g/mL and its specific heat capacity is 4.2 J/g · K.)

87. The value of ΔU in the decomposition of 7.647 g of ammonium nitrate can be measured in a bomb calorimeter. The reaction that occurs is

$$NH_4NO_3(s) \rightarrow N_2O(g) + 2\ H_2O(g)$$

The temperature of the calorimeter, which contains 415 g of water, increases from 18.90 °C to 20.72 °C. The heat capacity of the bomb is 155 J/K. What is the value of ΔU for this reaction, in kJ/mol?

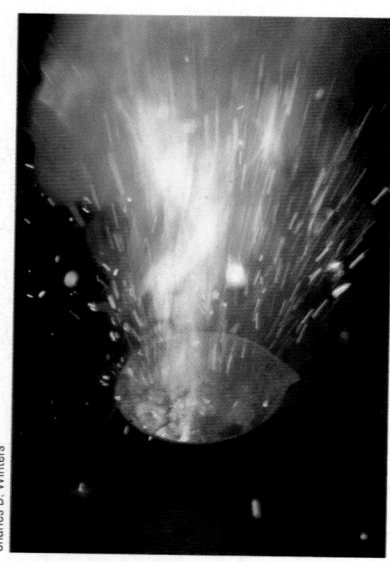

The decomposition of ammonium nitrate is clearly exothermic.

88. ■ A bomb calorimetric experiment was run to determine the heat of combustion of ethanol (a common fuel additive). The reaction is

$$C_2H_5OH(\ell) + 3\ O_2(g) \rightarrow 2\ CO_2(g) + 3\ H_2O(\ell)$$

The bomb had a heat capacity of 550 J/K, and the calorimeter contained 650 g of water. Burning 4.20 g of ethanol, $C_2H_5OH(\ell)$ resulted in a rise in temperature from 18.5 °C to 22.3 °C. Calculate the enthalpy of combustion of ethanol, in kJ/mol.

89. The meals-ready-to-eat (MREs) in the military can be heated on a flameless heater. You can purchase a similar product called "Heater Meals." Just pour water into the heater unit, wait a few minutes, and you have a hot meal. The source of energy in the heater is

$$Mg(s) + 2\ H_2O(\ell) \rightarrow Mg(OH)_2(s) + H_2(g)$$

The "heater meal" uses the reaction of magnesium with water as a source of energy as heat.

Calculate the enthalpy change under standard conditions, in joules, for this reaction. What quantity of magnesium is needed to supply the energy required to warm 25 mL of water ($d = 1.00$ g/mL) from 25 °C to 85 °C? (See W. Jensen: *Journal of Chemical Education,* Vol. 77, pp. 713–717, 2000.)

90. On a cold day, you can warm your hands with a "heat pad," a device that uses the oxidation of iron to produce energy as heat.

$$4\ Fe(s) + 3\ O_2(g) \rightarrow 2\ Fe_2O_3(s)$$

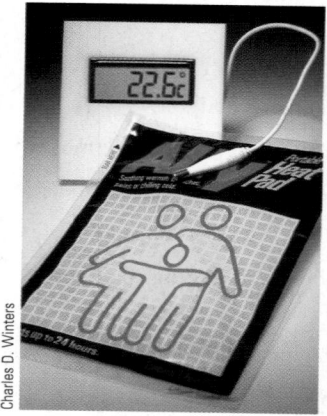 

A hand warmer uses the oxidation of iron as a source of thermal energy.

What mass of iron is needed to supply the energy required to warm 15 mL of water ($d = 1.00$ g/mL) from 23 °C to 37 °C?

▲ more challenging   ■ in OWL   Blue-numbered questions answered in Appendix O

Summary and Conceptual Questions

The following questions may use concepts from this and previous chapters.

91. Without doing calculations, decide whether each of the following is product-favored or reactant-favored.
    (a) the combustion of natural gas
    (b) the decomposition of glucose, $C_6H_{12}O_6$, to carbon and water

92. ■ Which of the following are state functions?
    (a) the volume of a balloon
    (b) the time it takes to drive from your home to your college or university
    (c) the temperature of the water in a coffee cup
    (d) the potential energy of a ball held in your hand

93. ▲ ■ You want to determine the value for the enthalpy of formation of $CaSO_4(s)$.

    $$Ca(s) + S(s) + 2\ O_2(g) \rightarrow CaSO_4(s)$$

    This reaction cannot be done directly. You know, however, that both calcium and sulfur react with oxygen to produce oxides in reactions that can be studied calorimetrically. You also know that the basic oxide CaO reacts with the acidic oxide $SO_3(g)$ to produce $CaSO_4(s)$ with $\Delta_rH° = -402.7$ kJ. Outline a method for determining $\Delta_fH°$ for $CaSO_4(s)$, and identify the information that must be collected by experiment. Using information in Appendix L, confirm that $\Delta_fH°$ for $CaSO_4(s) = -1433.5$ kJ/mol.

94. Prepare a graph of specific heat capacities for metals versus their atomic weights. Combine the data in Figure 5.7 and the values in the following table. What is the relationship between specific heat capacity and atomic weight? Use this relationship to predict the specific heat capacity of platinum. The specific heat capacity for platinum is given in the literature as 0.133 J/g · K. How good is the agreement between the predicted and actual values?

Metal	Specific Heat Capacity (J/g · K)
Chromium	0.450
Lead	0.127
Silver	0.236
Tin	0.227
Titanium	0.522

95. Observe the molar heat capacity values for the metals in Figure 5.7. What observation can you make about these values—specifically, are they widely different or very similar? Using this information, estimate the specific heat capacity for silver. Compare this estimate with the correct value for silver, 0.236 J/g · K.

96. ▲ Suppose you are attending summer school and are living in a very old dormitory. The day is oppressively hot. There is no air-conditioner, and you can't open the windows of your room because they are stuck shut from layers of paint. There is a refrigerator in the room, however. In a stroke of genius, you open the door of the refrigerator, and cool air cascades out. The relief does not last long, though. Soon the refrigerator motor and condenser begin to run, and not long thereafter the room is hotter than it was before. Why did the room warm up?

97. ■ You want to heat the air in your house with natural gas (CH_4). Assume your house has 275 m² (about 2800 ft²) of floor area and that the ceilings are 2.50 m from the floors. The air in the house has a molar heat capacity of 29.1 J/mol · K. (The number of moles of air in the house can be found by assuming that the average molar mass of air is 28.9 g/mol and that the density of air at these temperatures is 1.22 g/L.) What mass of methane do you have to burn to heat the air from 15.0 °C to 22.0 °C?

98. Water can be decomposed to its elements, H_2 and O_2, using electrical energy or in a series of chemical reactions. The following sequence of reactions is one possibility:

    $$CaBr_2(s) + H_2O(g) \rightarrow CaO(s) + 2\ HBr(g)$$
    $$Hg(\ell) + 2\ HBr(g) \rightarrow HgBr_2(s) + H_2(g)$$
    $$HgBr_2(s) + CaO(s) \rightarrow HgO(s) + CaBr_2(s)$$
    $$HgO(s) \rightarrow Hg(\ell) + \tfrac{1}{2}\ O_2(g)$$

    (a) Show that the net result of this series of reactions is the decomposition of water to its elements.
    (b) If you use 1000. kg of water, what mass of H_2 can be produced?
    (c) Calculate the value of $\Delta_rH°$ for each step in the series. Are the reactions predicted to be product-favored or reactant-favored?

    $$\Delta_fH°\ [CaBr_2(s)] = -683.2 \text{ kJ/mol}$$
    $$\Delta_fH°\ [HgBr_2(s)] = -169.5 \text{ kJ/mol}$$

    (e) Comment on the commercial feasibility of using this series of reactions to produce $H_2(g)$ from water.

99. Suppose that an inch of rain falls over a square mile of ground. (Density of water is 1.0 g/cm³.) The enthalpy of vaporization of water at 25 °C is 44.0 kJ/mol. How much energy as heat is transferred to the surroundings from the condensation of water vapor in forming this quantity of liquid water? (The huge number tells you how much energy is "stored" in water vapor and why we think of storms as such great forces of energy in nature. It is interesting to compare this result with the energy given off, 4.2×10^6 kJ, when a ton of dynamite explodes.)

100. ▲ Peanuts and peanut oil are organic materials and burn in air. How many burning peanuts does it take to provide the energy to boil a cup of water (250 mL of water)? To solve this problem, we assume each peanut, with an average mass of 0.73 g, is 49% peanut oil and 21% starch; the remainder is non-combustible. We further assume peanut oil is palmitic acid, $C_{16}H_{32}O_2$, with an enthalpy of formation of -848.4 kJ/mol. Starch is a long chain of $C_6H_{10}O_5$ units, each unit having an enthalpy of formation of -960 kJ. (*See ChemistryNow Screens 5.1 and 5.19: Chemical Puzzler.*)

How many burning peanuts are required to provide the energy to boil 250 mL of water?

101. ▲ Isomers are molecules with the same elemental composition but a different atomic arrangement. Three isomers with the formula C_4H_8 are shown in the models below. The enthalpy of combustion ($\Delta_c H°$) of each isomer, determined using a calorimeter, is:

Compound	$\Delta_{com}H°$ (kJ/mol-rxn)
cis-2 butene	-2687.5
trans-2-butene	-2684.2
1-butene	-2696.7

(a) Draw an energy level diagram relating the energy content of the three isomers to the energy content of the combustion products, $CO_2(g)$ and $H_2O(g)$.

(b) Use the $\Delta_c H°$ data in part (a), along with the enthalpies of formation of $CO_2(g)$ and $H_2O(g)$ from Appendix L, to calculate the enthalpy of formation for each of the isomers.

(c) Draw an energy level diagram that relates the enthalpies of formation of the three isomers to the energy of the elements in their standard states.

(d) What is the enthalpy change for the conversion of *cis*-2-butene to *trans*-2-butene?

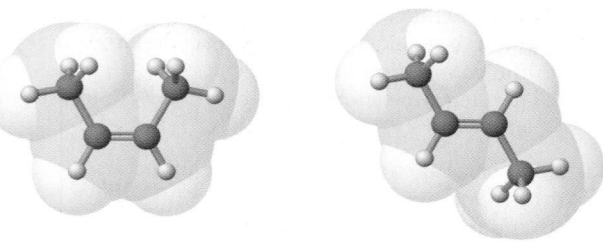

cis-2-butene   *trans*-2-butene

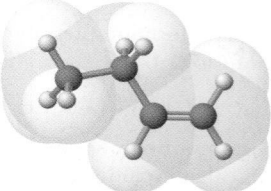

1-butene

102. Several standard enthalpies of formation (from Appendix L) are given below. Use these data to calculate:

(a) The standard enthalpy of vaporization of bromine.

(b) The energy required for the reaction $Br_2(g) \rightarrow 2\ Br(g)$. (This is the Br—Br bond energy.)

Species	$\Delta_f H°$ (kJ/mol)
Br(g)	111.9
$Br_2(\ell)$	0
$Br_2(g)$	30.9

103. When 0.850 g of Mg is burned in oxygen in a constant volume calorimeter, 25.4 kJ of energy as heat is evolved. The calorimeter is in an insulated container with 750. g of water at an initial temperature of 18.6 °C. The heat capacity of the calorimeter is 820. J/K.

(a) Calculate ΔU for the oxidation of Mg (in kJ/mol Mg).

(b) What will be the final temperature of the water and the bomb calorimeter in this experiment?

104. A piece of gold (10.0 g, $C = 0.129$ J/g · K) is heated to 100.0 °C. A piece of copper (also 10.0 g, $C = 0.385$ J/g · K) is chilled in an ice bath to 0 °C. Both pieces of metal are placed in a beaker containing 150. g H_2O at 20 °C. Will the temperature of the water be greater than or less than 20 °C when thermal equilibrium is reached? Calculate the final temperature.

▲ more challenging   ■ in OWL   Blue-numbered questions **answered in Appendix O**

105. Methane, CH_4, can be converted to methanol which, like ethanol, can be used as a fuel. The energy level diagram shown here presents relationships between energies of the fuels and their oxidation products. Use the information in the diagram to answer the following questions. (The energy terms are per mol-rxn.)

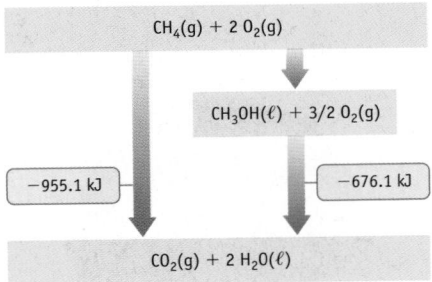

(a) Which fuel, methanol or methane, yields the most energy per mole when burned?
(b) Which fuel yields the most energy per gram when burned?
(c) What is the enthalpy change for the conversion of methane to methanol?
(d) Each arrow on the diagram represents a chemical reaction. Write the equation for the reaction that converts methane to methanol.

106. Calculate $\Delta_r H°$ for the reaction

$2 C(s) + 3 H_2(g) + ½ O_2(g) \rightarrow C_2H_5OH(\ell)$
given the information below.

$C(s) + O_2(g) \rightarrow CO_2(g) \quad \Delta_r H° = -393.5$ kJ/mol-rxn

$2 H_2(g) + O_2(g) \rightarrow 2 H_2O(\ell)$
$\Delta_r H° = -571.6$ kJ/mol-rxn

$C_2H_5OH(\ell) + 3 O_2(g) \rightarrow 2 CO_2(g) + 3 H_2O(\ell)$
$\Delta_r H° = -1367.5$ kJ/mol-rxn

107. You have the six pieces of metal listed below, plus a beaker of water containing 3.00×10^2 g of water. The water temperature is 21.00 °C.

Metals	Specific Heat (J/g K)	Mass (g)
1. Al	0.9002	100.0
2. Al	0.9002	50.0
3. Au	0.1289	100.0
4. Au	0.1289	50.0
5. Zn	0.3860	100.0
6. Zn	0.3860	50.0

(a) In your first experiment you select one piece of metal and heat it to 100 °C, and then select a second piece of metal and cool it to −10 °C. Both pieces of metal are then placed in the beaker of water and the temperatures equilibrated. You want to select two pieces of metal to use, such that the final temperature of the water is as high as possible. What piece of metal will you heat? What piece of metal will you cool? What is the final temperature of the water?
(b) The second experiment is done in the same way as the first. However, your goal now is to cause the temperature to change the least, that is, the final temperature should be be as near to 21.00 °C as possible. What piece of metal will you heat? What piece of metal will you cool? What is the final temperature of the water?

108. In lab, you plan to carry out a calorimetry experiment to determine the $\Delta_r H$ for the exothermic reaction of $Ca(OH)_2(s)$ and $HCl(aq)$. Predict how each of the following will affect the calculated value of $\Delta_r H$. (The value calculated for $\Delta_r H$ for this reaction is a negative value so choose your answer from the following: $\Delta_r H$ will be too low [that is, a larger negative value], $\Delta_r H$ will be unaffected, $\Delta_r H$ will be too high [that is, a smaller negative value.])
(a) You spill a little bit of the $Ca(OH)_2$ on the benchtop before adding it to the calorimeter.
(b) Because of a miscalculation, you add an excess of HCl to the measured amount of $Ca(OH)_2$ in the calorimeter.
(b) $Ca(OH)_2$ readily absorbs water from the air. The $Ca(OH)_2$ sample you weighed had been exposed to the air prior to weighing and had absorbed some water.
(c) After weighing out $Ca(OH)_2$, the sample sat in an open beaker and absorbed water.
(d) You delay too long in recording the final temperature.
(e) The insulation in your coffee cup calorimeter was poor and so some energy as heat was lost to the surroundings during the experiment.
(e) You have ignored the fact that energy as heat also raised the temperature of the stirrer and the thermometer in your system.

Let's Review | Chapters 1–5

Photo source: Charles D. Winters

When solid NH_4Cl is heated it is converted to gaseous NH_3 and HCl. The white "smoke" you see consists of tiny particles of solid NH_4Cl formed by the recombination of gaseous NH_3 and HCl. At this point in your study of chemistry you should be able to:

a) write a balanced chemical equation for the decomposition of NH_4Cl,

b) name each of the compounds involved,

c) calculate the enthalpy change to decompose the NH_4Cl,

d) and determine the mass of product expected if you know the masses of the reactants.

This section, called *Let's Review*, will explore questions about this and other reactions.

THE PURPOSE OF *LET'S REVIEW*

- *Let's Review* provides additional questions for Chapters 1 through 5. Routine questions covering the concepts in a chapter are in the Study Questions at the end of that chapter and are usually identified by topic. In contrast, *Let's Review* questions combine several concepts from one or more chapters. Many come from the examinations given by the authors and others are based on actual experiments or processes in chemical research or in the chemical industries.

- *Let's Review* provides guidance for Chapters 1 through 5 as you prepare for an exam on these chapters. Although this is designated for Chapters 1 through 5, you may choose only material appropriate to the exam in your course.

- To direct your review, **Comprehensive Questions** are correlated with relevant chapter sections and with the OWL online homework system to which you may have purchased access. Some questions may include a screen shot from one of these tools so you see what resources are available to help you review.

PREPARING FOR AN EXAMINATION ON CHAPTERS 1–5

1. Review **Go Chemistry** modules for these chapters. Go Chemistry modules are available at **www.cengage.com/chemistry/kotz** or **www.ichapters.com**.

2. Take the ChemistryNow **Pre-Test** and work through your **Personalized Learning Plan.** Work through ChemistryNow **Exercises, Guided Simulations,** and **Intelligent Tutors.**

3. **OWL** If you subscribe to OWL, use the **Tutorials** in that system.

4. Work on the questions below that are relevant to a particular chapter or chapters. See the solutions to those questions at the end of this section.

5. For background and help answering a question, use the Go Chemistry and OWL questions correlated with it.

KEY POINTS TO KNOW FOR CHAPTERS 1–5

Here are some of the key points you must know to be successful in Chapters 1–5.

- Identify chemical and physical properties.
- Use temperature in kelvins and other units of measurement in chemistry.
- Give the names and symbols of the chemical elements, and understand basic atomic structure and the arrangement of the periodic table.
- Carry out mass to amount (moles) and amount (moles) to mass conversions.
- Calculate the molar mass of a chemical compound.
- Gives names and formulas of chemical compounds.
- Identify empirical and molecular formulas.
- Balance chemical equations.
- Understand and use chemical stoichiometry.
- Know the names and formulas of common cations and anions and of acids and bases.
- Write chemical equations for precipitation, acid-base, and gas-forming reactions.
- Calculate and use solution concentrations.
- Know the terminology of thermochemistry.
- Relate heat, mass, temperature, and specific heat capacity.
- Calculate the enthalpy change for a chemical reaction ($\Delta_r H°$).

EXAMINATION PREPARATION QUESTIONS

▲ denotes more challenging questions.

Important information about the questions that follow:

- See the Study Questions in each chapter for questions on basic concepts.
- Some of these questions arise from recent research in chemistry and the other sciences. They often involve concepts from more than one chapter and may be more challenging than those in earlier chapters. Not all chapter goals or concepts are necessarily addressed in these questions.
- **Assessing Key Points** are short-answer questions covering the Key Points to Know on this page.

- **Comprehensive Questions** bring together concepts from multiple chapters and are correlated with text sections covering that topic, with Go Chemistry modules, and with questions in OWL that may provide additional background.
- The screen shots are largely taken from Go Chemistry modules available at **www.cengage.com/chemistry/kotz** or **www.ichapters.com.**

Assessing Key Points

1. Sulfur is a *(metal)(nonmetal)(metalloid)* _____ and its symbol is _____. The element has _____ protons in the nucleus. Sulfur-32 and sulfur-34 account for 99.2% of all S atoms; _____ is the more abundant of the two. In the sulfur-34 isotope there are _____ neutrons in the nucleus. Sulfur forms a common monatomic ion whose symbol is _____.

2. A flask having 0.0123 g of Ar contains _____ mol and _____ atoms.

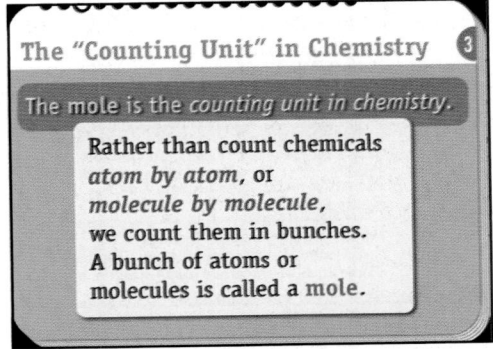

Screen from Go Chemistry module 4 on moles.

3. Fill in the table with the correct formula or name.

Cation	Anion	Name	Formula
NH_4^+		ammonium bromide	
		iron(II) sulfate	
			$Mg(CH_3CO_2)_2$
Al^{3+}	NO_3^-		

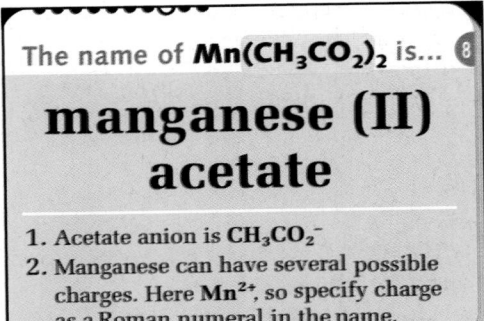

Screen from Go Chemistry module 3 on naming ionic compounds.

4. Which has the greater mass, 0.50 mol of silicon dioxide or 0.50 mol of iron?

5. What is the molar mass of Epsom salt, $MgSO_4 \cdot 7H_2O$?

6. Which formula below is NOT correct?
   (a) $Ba(NO_3)_2$ (d) $Al_2(SO_4)_3$
   (b) $KClO_4$ (e) Ca_2HPO_4
   (c) Na_3N

7. Sodium oxalate has the formula $Na_2C_2O_4$. Based on this information, the formula for iron(III) oxalate is
   (a) FeC_2O_4 (d) $Fe_2(C_2O_4)_3$
   (b) $Fe(C_2O_4)_2$ (e) $Fe_3(C_2O_4)_2$
   (c) $Fe(C_2O_4)_3$

8. Which of the following series contains only *known non-metal anions*?
   (a) S^{2-}, Br^-, Al^{3+} (d) Cl^-, Fe^{3+}, S^{2-}
   (b) N^{2-}, I^-, O^{2-} (e) In^+, Br^{2-}, Te^{2-}
   (c) P^{3-}, F^-, Se^{2-}

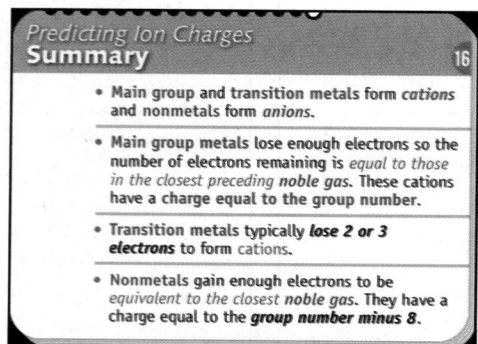

Screen from Go Chemistry module 2 on ion charges.

9. Balance the following chemical equations.
   (a) $Fe_2O_3(s) + Mg(s) \rightarrow MgO(s) + Fe(s)$
   (b) $C_6H_5CH_3(\ell) + O_2(g) \rightarrow H_2O(\ell) + CO_2(g)$

10. The reaction of iron with oxygen produces iron(III) oxide.

$$4\,Fe(s) + 3\,O_2(g) \rightarrow 2\,Fe_2O_3(s)$$

If you have 1.6 mol of Fe, what amount of O_2 is needed for complete reaction and what amount of Fe_2O_3 is produced? What are the masses of the reactants and products involved?

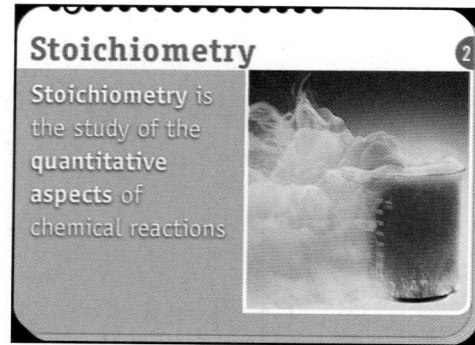

Screen from Go Chemistry module 7 on stoichiometry.

11. Give the oxidation number of each underlined atom:
    (a) $\underline{Br}O_3^-$ (b) $H_2\underline{C}_2O_4$ (c) $\underline{S}O_4^{2-}$

12. Zinc reacts readily with nitric acid to give the metal ion and other products such as NO_2.

$$Zn(s) + 2\,NO_3^-(aq) + 4\,H_3O^+(aq) \rightarrow Zn^{2+}(aq) + 2\,NO_2(g) + 6\,H_2O(\ell)$$

The oxidation number of N in NO_3^- is _____. The substance oxidized is _____ and the oxidizing agent is _____.

13. What mass of Na_2CO_3 (molar mass = 106 g/mol) must be used to make 250. mL of a 0.100 M solution of sodium carbonate? What is the concentration of Na^+ ions in this solution?

14. In the laboratory you added water to 125 mL of 0.160 M H_2SO_4. If the final volume of the diluted solution is 1.00 L, what is the concentration of the acid in the diluted solution?

15. Which of the following ionic compounds are water-soluble?

$BaSO_4$	$Ba(NO_3)_2$	$BaCO_3$	Na_2SO_4
$AgBr$	KCl	$Mg(CH_3CO_2)_2$	

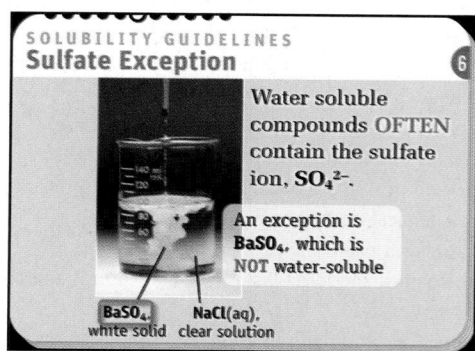

Screen from Go Chemistry module 5 on solubility guidelines.

16. Complete and balance the equation for the following reaction. Describe the reaction as an acid-base, precipitation, gas-forming, or redox reaction:

$$Na_2CO_3(aq) + HNO_3(aq) \rightarrow$$

17. Vinegar has a pH of 4.52. What is the hydronium ion concentration in the vinegar?

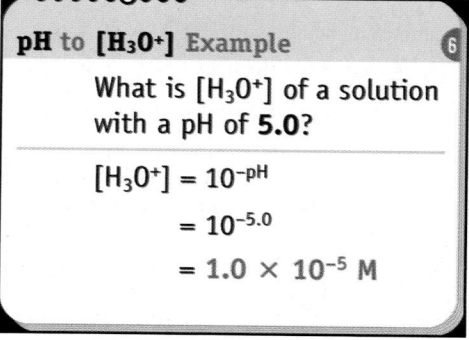

Screen from Go Chemistry module 9b on pH.

18. A sample of Na_2CO_3 (0.412 g) is titrated to the equivalence point with 35.63 mL of HNO_3. What is the concentration of the HNO_3 solution?

19. Write the net ionic equation for the reaction of aqueous solutions of sodium hydroxide and iron(II) chloride.

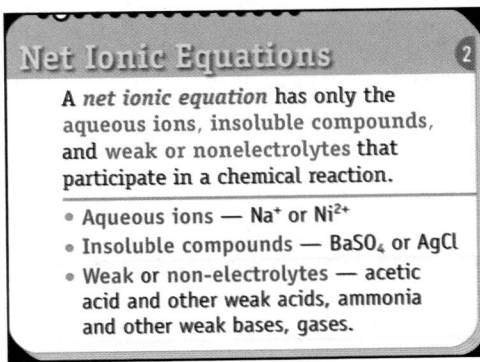

Net Ionic Equations ②

A *net ionic equation* has only the aqueous ions, insoluble compounds, and weak or nonelectrolytes that participate in a chemical reaction.

- Aqueous ions — Na^+ or Ni^{2+}
- Insoluble compounds — $BaSO_4$ or $AgCl$
- Weak or non-electrolytes — acetic acid and other weak acids, ammonia and other weak bases, gases.

Screen from Go Chemistry module 6 on writing net ionic equations.

20. What quantity of energy as heat must be transferred to warm 225 g of water from room temperature (25 °C) to 93 °C?

21. What is the enthalpy change for the combustion of exactly one mole of gaseous propane at 25 °C? Is the reaction exo- or endothermic?

$$C_3H_8(g) + 5\ O_2(g) \rightarrow 3\ CO_2(g) + 4\ H_2O(g)$$

Comprehensive Questions

22. (Chapters 1 and 2) Nanotechnology is a rapidly growing field of chemistry, and much research is being done to discover ways of making particles that have dimensions of only a few nanometers.
   (a) Gold has only one naturally occurring isotope. How many neutrons are there in an atom of gold?
   (b) Gold's density is 19.3 g/cm^3. If you have 0.0125 mol of gold, what is the volume of the piece? How many atoms are contained in the piece?
   (c) ▲ A spherical gold nanoparticle has a diameter of 3.00 nm. If the radius of a gold atom is 0.144 nm, estimate the number of gold atoms in the nanoparticle. [Assume the gold atoms are tiny spheres and that they occupy 74.0% of the available space in the spherical nanoparticle. Volume of a sphere = $(4/3)\pi r^3$]
   Text Sections: Tools of Quantiative Chemistry, 2.1 and 2.3
   OWL Questions: 1.5c, 2.2c

23. (Chapters 1 and 2) Copper is commonly used, in spite of the fact that its abundance on Earth is only 50 parts per million.
   (a) Copper has two isotopes: ^{63}Cu (62.930 u) and ^{65}Cu (64.928 u). Which is more abundant?
   (b) ▲ What are the relative abundances of the two isotopes?

   (c) Two copper-containing compounds are $CuCO_3$ and Cu_2S. Name each compound and give the charge on the copper ion in each.
   (d) What amount of copper (mol) is in a piece of copper wire with a diameter of 2.50 mm and 16.0 cm long? How many copper atoms are contained in the wire? (The density of copper metal is 8.96 g/cm^3.) [Volume of a cylinder = πr^2(length)]
   Text Sections: 2.3, 2.4, and 2.9
   OWL Questions: 1,5c, 2.3a, 2.4b, 2.9b, 2.9g, 2.9h

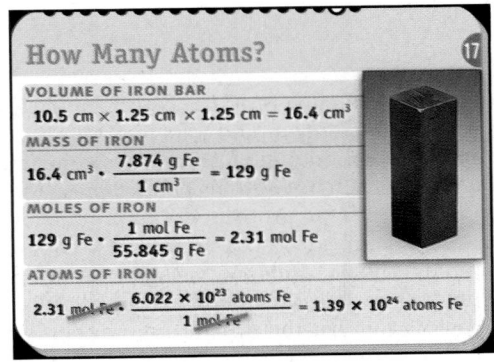

How Many Atoms? ⑰

VOLUME OF IRON BAR
10.5 cm × 1.25 cm × 1.25 cm = 16.4 cm^3

MASS OF IRON
16.4 cm^3 · $\dfrac{7.874\ g\ Fe}{1\ cm^3}$ = 129 g Fe

MOLES OF IRON
129 g Fe · $\dfrac{1\ mol\ Fe}{55.845\ g\ Fe}$ = 2.31 mol Fe

ATOMS OF IRON
2.31 mol Fe · $\dfrac{6.022 \times 10^{23}\ atoms\ Fe}{1\ mol\ Fe}$ = 1.39 × 10^{24} atoms Fe

Screen from Go Chemistry module 4 on moles.

24. (Chapter 2) Nuclear power plants are relatively common in much of the world and most use uranium.
   (a) Natural uranium exists mostly as the ^{238}U isotope, but fissionable uranium is the ^{235}U isotope. Give the number of protons and neutrons in each of these isotopes.
   (b) Several common uranium-containing compounds are (i) UO_2, (ii) $U(SO_4)_2$, and (iii) UF_6. Name each compound, calculate its molar mass, and give the oxydation number of uranium in each.
   Text Sections 2.3, 2.7, 2.9, and 3.9
   OWL Questions: 2.2c, 2.7k, 2.9d

25. (Chapter 2) Silver, a Group 1B element, has two stable isotopes. If one of the silver isotopes has a mass of 106.905 u and an abundance of 51.839%, what is the mass of the other silver isotope? What is its mass number?
   Text Section 2.4
   OWL Questions: 2.4b

26. (Chapters 2–4) The common mineral fluorite has the formula CaF_2.

Violet crystals of the mineral fluorite, CaF_2.

(a) What is the proper chemical name of the mineral?

(b) How many electrons do the ions Ca^{2+} and F^- have? Do these have the same number of electrons as a noble gas? Which of the gases?

(c) Fluorite is the commercial source of hydrogen fluoride. Balance the equation for the reaction of sulfuric acid, H_2SO_4, with CaF_2 to give calcium sulfate and hydrogen fluoride.

(d) If you combine 1.0 kg of CaF_2 with excess sulfuric acid, what mass of hydrogen fluoride can be produced?

Text Sections 2.7, 3.2, and 4.1
OWL Questions: 2.7d, 2.7k, 3.2d, 4.1c

27. (Chapter 2) "Green chemistry" is a movement within the chemistry community to find ways to produce chemicals in a way that does not lead to environmental problems. Caprolactam, used to make nylon, is made in large quantities. One problem is that production of each kilogram of caprolactam results in 4 kilograms of ammonium sulfate. Ammonium sulfate has few commercial uses, so it is often deposited in landfills.

(a) Caprolactam has the structure shown here (where C atoms are gray, H atoms are white, N atoms are blue, and O atoms are red). What is the formula of caprolactam?

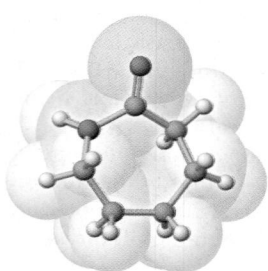

Structure of a molecule of caprolactam

(b) What is the molar mass of caprolactam?

(c) What is the weight percent of each element in caprolactam?

(d) What volume of landfill (in m^3) is required for the ammonium sulfate that is the by-product of the production of 1.00 metric ton (1.00×10^3 kg) of caprolactam? (Density of ammonium sulfate is 1.77 g/cm^3.)

Text Sections 2.9 and 2.10
OWL: 1.5c, 2.6, 2.9d, 2.10b

28. (Chapters 2 and 3) An article by C. M. Johnson and B. L. Beard (*Science*, Vol. 309, page 1025, 2005) described the biogeochemical cycling of iron isotopes. The authors stated that "In terms of isotopic studies of the transition elements, iron has received the most attention because of its high abundance on Earth and its prominent role in biogeochemical processes."

(a) Give the number of electrons and protons in an atom of Fe and in ions Fe^{2+} and Fe^{3+}. Which is the most oxidized form?

(b) Name the following iron compounds: $Fe(CH_3CO_2)_2$, $FePO_4$, $Fe(ClO_4)_3$.

Text Sections 2.7 and 3.9
OWL: 2.2c, 2.7d, 2.7k, 3.9b

29. (Chapter 2) Inorganic nanotubes have been prepared based on tungsten and sulfur. The tungsten content of one such nanotube is 74.14%. What is the empirical formula of these nanotubes?

Text Section 2.10
OWL: 2.10f

30. (Chapter 2) Nepetalactone is the chemical name for catnip. It is one of a family of compounds that sets many cats into a frenzy. It is 72.26% carbon, 8.49% hydrogen, and the remainder is oxygen. It has a molar mass of 166.21 g/mol. What are the empirical and molecular formulas of catnip?

Text Section 2.10
OWL: 2.10f

31. (Chapter 4) There is great interest in finding inexpensive ways to produce hydrogen gas, which can be used as a fuel in homes and cars and trucks. A recently discovered method uses a catalyst to promote the reaction of ethanol, water, and oxygen.

$$2\ C_2H_5OH(g)\ +\ 4\ H_2O(g)\ +\ O_2(g)$$
$$\rightarrow 4\ CO_2(g)\ +\ 10\ H_2(g)$$

(a) What mass of H_2 can be produced from 1.00 kg of ethanol and unlimited amounts of water and oxygen?

(b) What masses of H_2O and O_2 are required to react with 1.00 kg of ethanol?

Text Section 4.1
OWL: 4.1c

32. (Chapters 4 and 5) Methane, CH_4, can be converted to gaseous CH_3OH under special circumstances.

(a) Write a balanced equation for the conversion of O_2 and CH_4 to gaseous CH_3OH.

(b) If you combine 125 g of CH_4 with 145 g of O_2 what mass of CH_3OH would be obtained in theory?

(c) Is the conversion of CH_4 to CH_3OH with O_2 exothermic or endothermic? What is the enthalpy change for the conversion of 1.00 kg of CH_4 to $CH_3OH(g)$?

Text Sections 3.2, 4.1, 4.2, 5.1, and 5.7
OWL: 3.2d, 4.2d, 4.2f, 5.5c, 5.7d

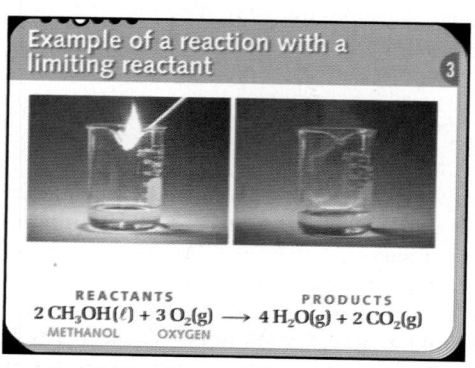

Example of a reaction with a limiting reactant

REACTANTS   PRODUCTS
$2\ CH_3OH(\ell) + 3\ O_2(g) \longrightarrow 4\ H_2O(g) + 2\ CO_2(g)$
METHANOL   OXYGEN

Screen from Go Chemistry module 8a on limiting reactants.

33. (Chapters 2–4) Gold is an important commodity in our economy. Gold (in rocks) dissolves in the presence of CN^- ion (from KCN) and oxygen to form the stable anion $[Au(CN)_2]^-$.

$$4 \, Au(s) + 8 \, CN^-(aq) + O_2(g) + 2 \, H_2O(\ell)$$
$$\rightarrow 4 \, [Au(CN)_2]^-(aq) + 4 \, OH^-(aq)$$

(a) What is the name of the CN^- ion and of KCN?

(b) This is an oxidation-reduction reaction. Describe how you would reach that conclusion and then identify the substance oxidized, the substance reduced, and the oxidizing and reducing agents.

(c) What mass of KCN would be needed to dissolve 1.00 kg of gold?

(d) If the KCN is used as a 0.15 M solution, what volume of solution is required to dissolve 1.00 kg of gold?

Text Sections 2.7, 3.9, 4.1, and 4.5

OWL: 2.7f, 2.7k, 3.9b, 4.1c, 4.5e

34. (Chapters 2 and 4) Linoleic acid is an essential fatty acid and a component of many vegetable oils such as peanut, corn, safflower, and soybean oils.

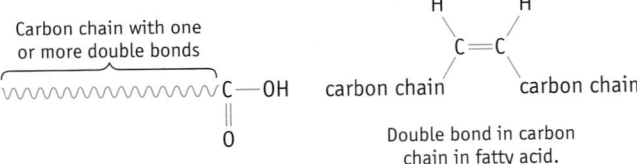

Carbon chain with one or more double bonds

C—OH   carbon chain   carbon chain

O

Double bond in carbon chain in fatty acid.

All fatty acids have a long hydrocarbon chain with an acid group ($-CO_2H$) at one end. The chain consists of carbon atoms bonded mostly by single C—C bonds, but there can be one or more C=C double bonds.

(a) Analysis of linoleic acid indicates it is 77.09% carbon and 11.50% H; the remainder is oxygen. What is the empirical formula of linoleic acid?

(b) A 1.234-g sample is titrated with 0.113 M NaOH. The volume of base required is 38.94 mL. What is the molar mass of the acid? What is its molecular formula?

(c) One can determine the number of double bonds in a fatty acid by reacting it with iodine, I_2. Each double bond reacts with one I_2 molecule. If 0.351 g of linoleic acid requires 0.636 g of I_2, how many double bonds does the fatty acid contain?

Text Sections 2.10, 4.1, 4.5, and 4.7

OWL: 2.10f, 4.7g, 4.7h

35. (Chapter 3 and 4) Oyster beds in the oceans require chloride ions for growth. The minimum concentration is 8 mg/L (8 parts per million). To analyze for the amount of chloride ion in a 50.0-mL sample of water, you add a few drops of aqueous potassium chromate and then titrate the sample with 25.60 mL of 0.001036 M silver nitrate. The silver nitrate reacts with chloride ion and, when the chloride ion is completely removed, the silver nitrate reacts with potassium chromate to give a red precipitate.

(a) Write a balanced net ionic equation for the reaction of silver nitrate with chloride ions.

(b) Write a complete balanced equation and a net ionic equation for the reaction of silver nitrate with potassium chromate, indicating whether each compound is water-soluble or not.

(c) What is the concentration of chloride ions in the sample? Is it sufficient to promote oyster growth?

Text Sections 3.5, 3.6, 4.4, 4.5, and 4.7

OWL: 3.5f, 3.6b, 3.6g, 4.7g, 4.7h

36. ▲ (Chapters 2 and 4) A 0.463-g sample of a compound composed of Ti, Cl, C, and H was burned in air to produce 0.818 g of CO_2 and 0.168 g of H_2O. Aqueous silver nitrate was added to the residue from the combustion and produced 0.533 g of AgCl. What is the empirical formula of the compound?

Text Sections 2.10 and 4.7

OWL: 4.4c

37. (Chapter 3) You have a bottle of solid barium hydroxide and some dilute sulfuric acid. You then dissolve some of the barium hydroxide in water and slowly add sulfuric acid to the mixture. While adding the sulfuric acid, you measure the electrical conductivity of the mixture (as in Active Figure 3.9, page 124).

(a) Write the complete, balanced equation for the reaction occurring when barium hydroxide and sulfuric acid are mixed.

(b) Write the net ionic equation for the barium hydroxide and sulfuric acid reaction.

(c) Which diagram below represents the change in conductivity as the acid is added to the aqueous barium hydroxide? Explain briefly.

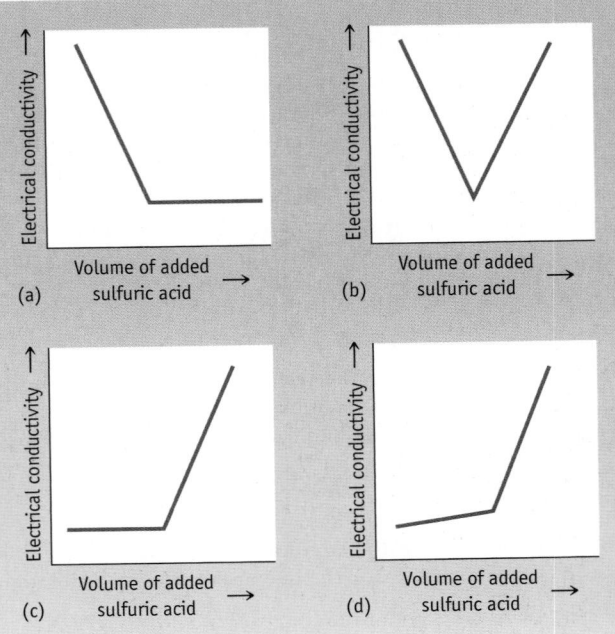

Text Sections 3.2, 3.5, 3.6, and 3.7

OWL: 3.5c, 3.7e

38. (Chapter 5) A 9.40-g sample of KBr was dissolved in 105 g of water at 23.6 °C in a coffee cup calorimeter. After mixing, the temperature of the solution was 20.3 °C. Assume no energy as heat is transferred to the cup or the surroundings. Find the enthalpy of solution, $\Delta_{soln}H$, of KBr. (The specific heat capacity of the solution is assumed to be 4.184 J/g·K.)

Text Section 5.6
OWL: 5.6b

39. (Chapter 5) The enthalpy of combustion of isooctane (C_8H_{18}) is 5.45×10^3 kJ/mol. Calculate the energy transferred as heat per gram of isooctane and per liter of isooctane ($d = 0.688$ g/mL). (Isooctane is one of many hydrocarbons in gasoline, and its enthalpy of combustion will approximate the energy obtained when gasoline burns.)

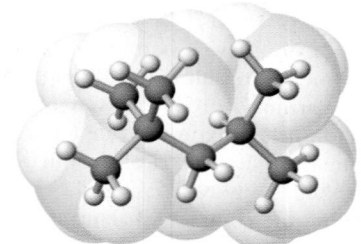

Isooctane
C_8H_{18}

Text Section 5.5
OWL: 1.5c, 2.9g, 2.9h, 3.2d

40. (Chapters 4 and 5) Hydrogen can be produced (along with CO) using the reaction of steam (H_2O) with carbon (as coal), methane, and other hydrocarbons. For example,

$$C(s) + H_2O(g) \rightarrow H_2(g) + CO(g)$$

(a) Compare the mass of H_2 expected from the reaction of steam with 100. g each of methane, petroleum, and coal. (Assume complete reaction in each case. Use CH_2 and C as representative formulas for petroleum and coal, respectively.)
(b) Compare the values of $\Delta_rH°$ for the reactions of 1.00 mol of carbon and 1.00 mol of methane with steam. Which involves more energy?

Text Sections 4.1 and 5.7
OWL: 4.1c, 5.7d

41. (All chapters) On page 254 you see the decomposition of solid NH_4Cl to form gaseous NH_3 and HCl.
(a) Write a balanced chemical equation for the decomposition of NH_4Cl.
(b) When NH_3 and HCl recombine to form NH_4Cl, is this an oxidation-reduction reaction?
(c) Name each of the compounds involved.
(d) Calculate $\Delta_rH°$ for the decomposition of 1.00 mol of NH_4Cl.
(e) Determine the mass of NH_3 expected if you decompose 1.00 g of NH_4Cl.

(f) If the HCl from the decomposition (part e) is absorbed by 126 mL of water, what is the pH of the solution?

Text Sections 3.2, 3.7, 3.9, 4.1, and 5.7
OWL: 2.7k, 3.2d, 3.7a, 3.7e, 3.9b, 4.1c, 4.7g, 4.7h, and 5.7d

42. (Chapter 2) Prussian blue was first made by a German artist in 1704, but the nature of the compound was not understood until well into the 20th century. The formula for Prussian blue is $Fe_4[Fe(CN)_6]_3$.

Preparing Prussian blue from aqueous $FeCl_3$ and $K_4[Fe(CN)_6]$.

(a) ▲ Knowing that the CN group is the cyanide ion, CN^-, what are the charges on the two types of iron ions present in Prussian blue?
(b) What is the weight percent of iron in Prussian blue?

Text Sections 2.7 and 2.10
OWL: 2.7d, 2.10b

43. (Chapter 2) The structures of alanine and phenylalanine are illustrated here.

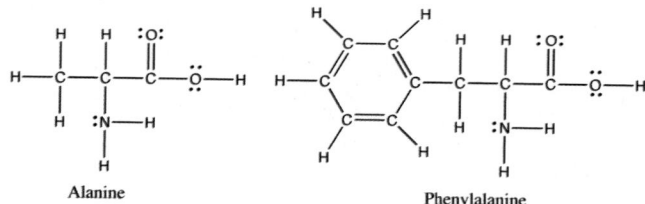

Alanine   Phenylalanine

(a) What is the molecular formula and molar mass of each of these amino acids?
(b) What structural elements do these molecules have in common?
(c) Which molecule has the greater mass percent of N?
(d) If you have 5.12 g of each, which sample has more molecules?

Text Sections 2.6, 2.9, and 2.10
OWL: 2.6, 2.9b, 2.9d, 2.10b

44. (Chapters 3–5) Titanium compounds, especially TiO_2 and $TiCl_4$, are important in industry. The chloride, $TiCl_4$, can be prepared by the reaction of white, solid TiO_2 with chlorine gas and carbon to give liquid $TiCl_4$ and carbon dioxide gas.

(a) Write a balanced chemical equation for this reaction.

(b) Name the compounds TiO_2 and $TiCl_4$.

(c) Calculate the enthalpy change for the reaction. Is the reaction exo- or endothermic?

(d) If 1.000 kg of TiO_2 is treated with 1.000 kg of chlorine gas, what mass of $TiCl_4$ can be produced? If 893 g of $TiCl_4$ are produced, what is the percent yield?

Text Sections 2.7, 3.2, 4.1, 4.2, and 5.7
OWL: 3.2d, 3.9b, 4.2f, 5.7d

45. (Chapter 5) ▲ Calculate the enthalpy change for the reaction

$$CaC_2(s) + 2 H_2O(\ell) \rightarrow Ca(OH)_2(s) + C_2H_2(g)$$

based on the enthalpy changes for the following reactions:

$$H_2(g) + 1/2 O_2(g) \rightarrow H_2O(\ell)$$
$$\Delta_r H° = -285.83 \text{ kJ/mol-rxn}$$

$$C(s) + 1/2 O_2(g) \rightarrow CO(g)$$
$$\Delta_r H° = -110.525 \text{ kJ/mol-rxn}$$

$$2 C(s) + H_2(g) \rightarrow C_2H_2(g) \quad \Delta_r H° = 226.73 \text{ kJ/mol-rxn}$$

$$CaO(s) + H_2O(\ell) \rightarrow Ca(OH)_2(s)$$
$$\Delta_r H° = -65.17 \text{ kJ/mol-rxn}$$

$$CaO(s) + 3 C(s) \rightarrow CaC_2(s) + CO(g)$$
$$\Delta_r H° = 464.77 \text{ kJ/mol-rxn}$$

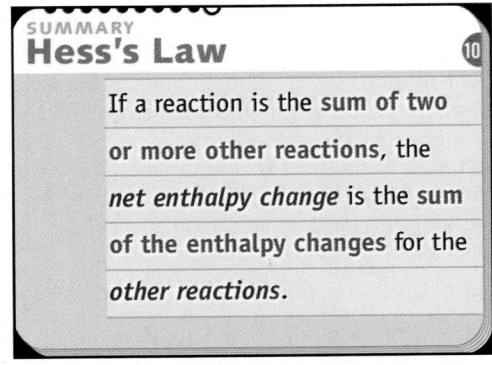

SUMMARY
Hess's Law 10

If a reaction is the sum of two or more other reactions, the net enthalpy change is the sum of the enthalpy changes for the other reactions.

Screen from Go Chemistry module 10 on Hess's law.

Text Section 5.7
OWL: 5.7b

Answers to Assessing Key Points Questions

1. The nonmetal, sulfur (S), has 16 protons. The ^{32}S isotope, with 16 neutrons, is more abundant because the atomic weight is very close to 32. ^{34}S has 18 neutrons. A common ion is S^{2-}.

2. 3.08×10^{-4} mol Ar and 1.85×10^{20} atoms

3. NH_4^+, Br^-, ammonium bromide, NH_4Br

Fe^{2+}, SO_4^{2-}, iron(II) sulfate, $FeSO_4$

Mg^{2+}, $CH_3CO_2^-$, magnesium acetate, $Mg(CH_3CO_2)_2$

Al^{3+}, NO_3^-, aluminum nitrate, $Al(NO_3)_3$

4. 0.50 mol of SiO_2 (with a molar mass of 60.1 g/mol) has more mass (30. g) than 0.50 mol of Fe (55.85 g/mol) (28 g).

5. 246.5 g/mol. **Comment:** Make sure to add in 7 mol of H_2O.

6. (e) The calcium ion is always Ca^{2+}, and the hydrogen phosphate ion is HPO_4^{2-}. The correct formula is $CaHPO_4$.

7. Based on the formula of $Na_2C_2O_4$ you know the oxalate ion has a 2- charge, $C_2O_4^{2-}$. Thus, the correct formula is (d).

8. (c) Answers (a) and (d) also have correct ions, but two of the ions (Al^{3+} and Fe^{3+}) are based on metals.

9. (a) $Fe_2O_3(s) + 3 Mg(s) \rightarrow 3 MgO(s) + 2 Fe(s)$
(b) $C_6H_5CH_3(\ell) + 9 O_2(g) \rightarrow 4 H_2O(\ell) + 7 CO_2(g)$

10. Stoichiometry

$$1.6 \text{ mol Fe} \left(\frac{3 \text{ mol } O_2}{4 \text{ mol Fe}} \right) = 1.2 \text{ mol } O_2 \text{ required}$$

$$1.6 \text{ mol Fe} \left(\frac{2 \text{ mol } Fe_2O_3}{4 \text{ mol Fe}} \right) = 0.80 \text{ mol } Fe_2O_3 \text{ produced}$$

$$1.6 \text{ mol Fe} \left(\frac{55.85 \text{ g Fe}}{\text{mol Fe}} \right) = 89 \text{ g Fe}$$

$$1.2 \text{ mol } O_2 \left(\frac{32.0 \text{ g } O_2}{\text{mol } O_2} \right) = 38 \text{ g } O_2$$

$$0.80 \text{ mol } Fe_2O_3 \left(\frac{159.7 \text{ g } Fe_2O_3}{\text{mol } Fe_2O_3} \right) = 130 \text{ g } Fe_2O_3$$

11. Br = +5; C = +3; S = +6

12. N in NO_3^- is +5. Zn is oxidized (oxidation number goes from 0 to +2) and the oxidizing agent is NO_3^-. (Note that the oxidation number of N goes from +5 to +4.)

13.
$$0.250 \text{ L} \left(\frac{0.100 \text{ mol}}{\text{L}} \right)\left(\frac{106.0 \text{ g } Na_2CO_3}{1 \text{ mol } Na_2CO_3} \right) = 2.65 \text{ g } Na_2CO_3$$

The Na^+ concentration is 2×0.100 M = 0.200 M

14. Here we can use the shortcut equation $c_c \cdot V_c = c_d \cdot V_d$. See Problem-Solving Tip 4.3, page 179.

$$\left(\frac{0.160 \text{ mol } H_2SO_4}{\text{L}} \right)(0.125 \text{ L}) = (c_{dilute})(1.00 \text{ L})$$

$$c_{dilute} = \frac{0.0200 \text{ mol } H_2SO_4}{\text{L}} = 0.0200 \text{ M}$$

15. $Ba(NO_3)_2$, Na_2SO_4, KCl, $Mg(CH_3CO_2)_2$. Nitrates, sodium salts, potassium salts, and acetates are almost always soluble in water.

16. $Na_2CO_3(aq) + 2\ HNO_3(aq)$
$$\rightarrow 2\ NaNO_3(aq) + CO_2(g) + H_2O(\ell)$$

This is a gas-forming reaction.

17. $pH = -\log[H_3O^+]$ or $[H_3O^+] = 10^{-pH}$. See page 179, Equation 4.3 and page 181, Equation 4.4.

$$[H_3O^+] = 1 \times 10^{-4.52} = 3.0 \times 10^{-5}\ M$$

Comment: Don't forget that the power of 10 is a negative number when using the equation $[H_3O^+] = 10^{-pH}$.

18. The first step is to write a balanced equation for the reaction. See the answer to 16 above.

$$0.412\ g\ Na_2CO_3 \left(\frac{1\ mol\ Na_2CO_3}{106.0\ g\ Na_2CO_3}\right)$$
$$= 3.89 \times 10^{-3}\ mol\ Na_2CO_3$$

$$3.89 \times 10^{-3}\ mol\ Na_2CO_3 \left(\frac{2\ mol\ HNO_3}{1\ mol\ Na_2CO_3}\right)$$
$$= 7.77 \times 10^{-3}\ mol\ HNO_3$$

$$\frac{7.77 \times 10^{-3}\ mol\ HNO_3}{0.03563\ L} = 0.218\ M\ HNO_3$$

19. Complete balanced equation:

$$2\ NaOH(aq) + FeCl_2(aq) \rightarrow 2\ NaCl(aq) + Fe(OH)_2(s)$$

Net ionic equation:

$$2\ OH^-(aq) + Fe^{2+}(aq) \rightarrow Fe(OH)_2(s)$$

20. Use Equation 5.1 on page 215.

$q = (225\ g)(4.184\ J/g\cdot K)(366\ K - 298\ K) = 6.40 \times 10^4\ J$

21. Use Equation 5.6 on page 237.

$$\Delta_r H° = 3\ \Delta_f H°[CO_2(g)] + 4\ \Delta_f H°[H_2O(g)]$$
$$- \{\Delta_f H°[C_3H_8(g)] + 5\ \Delta_f H°[O_2(g)]\}$$
$$= (3\ mol\ CO_2/1\ mol\text{-}rxn)(-393.5\ kJ/mol\ CO_2)$$
$$+ (4\ mol\ H_2O/1\ mol\text{-}rxn)(-241.8\ kJ/mol\ H_2O)$$
$$- [(1\ mol\ C_3H_8/1\ mol\text{-}rxn)(-104.7\ kJ/mol\ C_3H_8)$$
$$+ (5\ mol\ O_2/1\ mol\text{-}rxn)(0\ kJ/mol\ O_2)]$$
$$= -2043.0\ kJ/mol\text{-}rxn$$

Reaction is exothermic. The energy transferred as heat per mole of C_3H_8 is 2043.0 kJ.

Solutions to Comprehensive Questions

22. (a) The atomic weight of gold is 196.967, so the mass number of the single gold isotope is 197 ($^{197}_{79}Au$).

Mass number = 197 = No. of protons + no. of neutrons

No. of neutrons = 118

(b) Calculate the volume of the piece of gold. Let us first convert amount of gold (mol) to mass (g) using the atomic weight and then convert the mass to a volume using the density.

$$0.0125\ mol \left(\frac{196.967\ g}{1\ mol}\right) = 2.46\ g$$

$$2.46\ g \left(\frac{1\ cm^3}{19.3\ g}\right) = 0.128\ cm^3$$

Calculate the number of atoms of gold from the amount of gold using Avogadro's number.

$$0.0125\ mol\ Au \left(\frac{6.022 \times 10^{23}\ atoms\ Au}{1\ mol\ Au}\right)$$
$$= 7.53 \times 10^{21}\ atoms\ Au$$

(c) The strategy here is first to calculate the volume of the nanoparticle. Next, we find the volume occupied by gold atoms. The third step is to calculate the volume of one gold atom. Finally, we divide the volume occupied by gold atoms by the volume of one gold atom.

$$\text{Volume of gold nanoparticle} = \frac{4}{3}\pi r^3$$
$$= \frac{4}{3}\pi(1.50\ nm)^3 = 14.1\ nm^3$$

Volume of particle occupied by gold atoms
$$= 14.1\ nm^3\ (0.740) = 10.5\ nm^3$$

$$\text{Volume of one gold atom} = \frac{4}{3}\pi r^3$$
$$= \frac{4}{3}\pi(0.144\ nm)^3 = 0.0125\ nm^3\ per\ atom$$

Number of atoms in the nanoparticle
$$= 10.5\ nm^3 \left(\frac{1\ atom\ Au}{0.0125\ nm^3}\right) = 836\ Au\ atoms$$

23. (a) The atomic weight of an element is the weighted average of the isotopic weights and their abundances. The atomic weight of copper is closer to 63 than to 65 so ^{63}Cu is more abundant than ^{65}Cu.

(b) To calculate the isotopes abundances begin by assuming the percent abundance of ^{63}Cu is X and that of ^{65}Cu is Y. Therefore,

$$63.546\ u = (X/100)(62.930\ u) + (Y/100)(64.928\ u)$$

Because X + Y must equal 100, this means that Y = 100 − X, and so

$$63.546\ u = (X/100)(62.930\ u) + [(100 - X)/100](64.928\ u)$$

Solving for X, we find a percent abundance of 69.17%. This means Y is 30.83%.

(c) $CuCO_3$, copper(II) carbonate, Cu^{2+}
Cu_2S, copper(I) sulfide, Cu^+

(d) The strategy here is to find the volume of the wire (cm^3), convert that volume to a mass (g) using the density, and then find the amount of copper using the molar mass.

$$\text{Volume of wire} = \pi r^2(\text{length})$$
$$= \pi(0.125\ cm)^2(16.0\ cm)$$
$$= 0.785\ cm^3$$

$$\text{Mass of copper} = 0.785 \text{ cm}^3 \left(\frac{8.96 \text{ g Cu}}{1 \text{ cm}^3} \right)$$
$$= 7.04 \text{ g Cu}$$
$$\text{Amount of copper} = 7.04 \text{ g Cu} \left(\frac{1 \text{ mol Cu}}{63.55 \text{ g Cu}} \right)$$
$$= 0.111 \text{ mol Cu}$$

The number of atoms can be found from the amount and Avogadro's number.

Number of atoms in the wire
$$= 0.111 \text{ mol Cu} \left(\frac{6.022 \times 10^{23} \text{ atoms Cu}}{1 \text{ mol Cu}} \right)$$
$$= 6.67 \times 10^{22} \text{ atoms Cu}$$

24. (a) ^{238}U has 92 proton and 146 neutrons. ^{235}U has 92 protons and 143 neutrons.
    (b) Formulas

Formula	Name	Molar Mass (g/mol)	Charge on U
UO_2	uranium(IV) oxide	270.0	+4
$U(SO_4)_2$	uranium(IV) sulfate	430.2	+4
UF_6	uranium(VI) fluoride	352.0	+6

25. This question is similar to question 23b above. Here we want to find the mass of one isotope knowing the mass of the other isotope and the percent abundance of each.

    Atomic mass of silver = 107.868 u
    = (51.839/100)(106.905 u) + [(100 − 51.839)/100] X

    where X = mass of other silver isotope = 108.905 u. The mass number of the isotope is 109 (^{109}Ag).

26. (a) The name of the mineral is calcium fluoride
    (b) Ca^{2+} ions have 18 electrons, the same as the number of electrons in argon, Ar. F^- ions have 10 electrons, the same as the number of electrons in Ne.
    (c) $CaF_2 + H_2SO_4 \rightarrow CaSO_4 + 2 \text{ HF}$
    (d) See Problem-Solving Tip 4.1 on page 160. First convert the mass of CaF_2 to amount (mol). Next, use the stoichiometric factor to calculate the amount of HF expected (the theoretical yield). Finally, convert this amount to mass.

$$1.0 \times 10^3 \text{ g CaF}_2 \left(\frac{1 \text{ mol}}{78.07 \text{ g CaF}_2} \right) = 13 \text{ mol CaF}_2$$
$$13 \text{ ml CaF}_2 \left(\frac{2 \text{ mol HF}}{1 \text{ mol CaF}_2} \right) = 26 \text{ mol HF}$$
$$26 \text{ mol HF} \left(\frac{20.0 \text{ g}}{1 \text{ mol HF}} \right) = 5.1 \times 10^2 \text{ g HF}$$

27. (a) Molecular formula: $C_6H_{11}NO$
       Comment: Note that it is usual to write formulas of compounds having C and H with those elements first. Any other elements follow in alphabetical order.
    (b) Molar mass: 113.2 g/mol
    (c) The mass percent is calculated as on page 89.

       Mass percent of carbon
       $$= \frac{6 \text{ mol C } (12.011 \text{ g/mol C})}{113.2 \text{ g/mol caprolactam}} \times 100\% = 63.66\%$$

       In the same manner, we find 9.80% for H, 12.38% for N, and 14.14% for O.
    (d) The first step is to convert the mass of ammonium sulfate to grams and then use the density to calculate the volume in cubic centimeters. This is used to calculate the volume in units of cubic meters.

       Volume occupied by $(NH_4)_2SO_4$
       $$= 4.00 \times 10^3 \text{ kg} \left(\frac{1 \times 10^3 \text{ g}}{\text{kg}} \right) \left(\frac{1 \text{ cm}^3}{1.77 \text{ g}} \right)$$
       $$= 2.26 \times 10^6 \text{ cm}^3$$
       Volume in cubic meters
       $$= 2.26 \times 10^6 \text{ cm}^3 \left(\frac{1 \text{ m}}{100 \text{ cm}} \right)^3 = 2.26 \text{ m}^3$$

28. (a)

Atom/Ion	Protons	Electrons
Fe	26	26
Fe^{2+}	26	24
Fe^{3+}	26	23

    The most oxidized form is Fe^{3+}.
    Comment: Students occasionally and incorrectly add electrons to make a positive ion and subtract them to make a negative, the opposite of the correct procedure. Remember that the plus or minus sign on the ion indicates its electric charge. Positive ions occur when there are fewer electrons than protons, and negative ions result when there are more electrons than protons.

    (b)

Formula	Name
$Fe(CH_3CO_2)_2$	Iron(II) acetate
$FePO_4$	Iron(III) phosphate
$Fe(ClO_4)_3$	Iron(III) perchlorate

29. We assume that the weight percent of an element is the mass of the element in a 100-g sample. To find the empirical formula, you first find the amount (mol) of each element in the 100-g sample, then compare the amounts of all elements in the 100-g sample. These amounts are in the same ratio as the number of atoms in one molecule or formula unit.

$$74.14 \text{ g W} \left(\frac{1 \text{ mol W}}{183.84 \text{ g}} \right) = 0.4033 \text{ mol W}$$

$$25.86 \text{ g S} \left(\frac{1 \text{ mol S}}{32.066 \text{ g}} \right) = 0.8065 \text{ mol S}$$

$$\frac{0.8065 \text{ mol S}}{0.4033 \text{ mol W}} = \frac{2 \text{ mol S}}{1 \text{ mol W}}$$

The formula of the compound is WS_2.
Comment: When finding a formula from weight percent data, always use as many significant figures as possible (usually at least 3). See Problem-Solving Tip 2.3 on page 91.

30. This follows the same procedure as in question 29.

$$72.26 \text{ g C} \left(\frac{1 \text{ mol C}}{12.011 \text{ g}} \right) = 6.016 \text{ mol C}$$

$$8.49 \text{ g H} \left(\frac{1 \text{ mol H}}{1.008 \text{ g}} \right) = 8.423 \text{ mol H}$$

$$19.25 \text{ g O} \left(\frac{1 \text{ mol O}}{15.999 \text{ g}} \right) = 1.203 \text{ mol O}$$

With the amount of each element in a 100-g sample known, we divide each amount by the amount of the element present in the smallest amount (here oxygen).

$$\frac{6.016 \text{ mol C}}{1.203 \text{ mol O}} = 5 \text{ C to 1 O} \qquad \frac{8.423 \text{ mol H}}{1.203 \text{ mol O}} = 7 \text{ H to 1 O}$$

This leads to an empirical formula of C_5H_7O. Because the experimental molar mass (166.21 g/mol) is twice the empirical formula mass, the molecular formula is $C_{10}H_{14}O_2$. The structure of the active ingredient in catnip is illustrated here.

Nepetalactone, catnip

31. (a) After calculating the amount of C_2H_5OH, we use a stoichiometric factor to relate the amount of H_2 produced to the amount of C_2H_5OH available.

$$1.00 \times 10^3 \text{ g C}_2\text{H}_5\text{OH} \left(\frac{1 \text{ mol C}_2\text{H}_5\text{OH}}{46.07 \text{ g}} \right)$$
$$= 21.7 \text{ mol C}_2\text{H}_5\text{OH}$$

$$21.7 \text{ mol C}_2\text{H}_5\text{OH} \left(\frac{10 \text{ mol H}_2}{2 \text{ mol C}_2\text{H}_5\text{OH}} \right) = 109 \text{ mol H}_2$$

$$109 \text{ mol H}_2 \left(\frac{2.016 \text{ g}}{1 \text{ mol H}_2} \right) = 219 \text{ g H}_2$$

(b) The amount of C_2H_5OH is known from part (a), and this can be related to the amount and mass of H_2O and O_2 required, again using the appropriate stoichiometric factors.

$$21.7 \text{ mol C}_2\text{H}_5\text{OH} \left(\frac{1 \text{ mol O}_2 \text{ required}}{2 \text{ mol C}_2\text{H}_5\text{OH available}} \right)$$
$$= 10.9 \text{ mol O}_2 \text{ required}$$

$$10.9 \text{ mol O}_2 \left(\frac{32.0 \text{ g O}_2}{1 \text{ mol O}_2} \right) = 347 \text{ g O}_2 \text{ required}$$

$$21.7 \text{ mol C}_2\text{H}_5\text{OH} \left(\frac{4 \text{ mol H}_2\text{O required}}{2 \text{ mol C}_2\text{H}_5\text{OH available}} \right)$$
$$= 43.4 \text{ mol H}_2\text{O required}$$

$$43.4 \text{ mol H}_2\text{O} \left(\frac{18.02 \text{ g H}_2\text{O}}{1 \text{ mol H}_2\text{O}} \right) = 782 \text{ g H}_2\text{O required}$$

32. Stoichiometry and thermochemistry of methanol production
(a) $2 \text{ CH}_4(g) + \text{O}_2(g) \rightarrow 2 \text{ CH}_3\text{OH}(g)$
(b) This is a limiting reactant problem, so we first calculate the amounts of each reactant and then determine if they are in the correct stoichiometric ratio or if one is in limited supply.

$$125 \text{ g CH}_4 \left(\frac{1 \text{ mol CH}_4}{16.04 \text{ g CH}_4} \right) = 7.79 \text{ mol CH}_4$$

$$145 \text{ g O}_2 \left(\frac{1 \text{ mol O}_2}{31.999 \text{ g O}_2} \right) = 4.53 \text{ mol O}_2$$

$$\text{Ratio of amounts} = \frac{7.79 \text{ mol CH}_4}{4.53 \text{ mol O}_2} = \frac{1.72 \text{ mol CH}_4}{1.00 \text{ mol O}_2}$$

The balanced equation specifies there should be twice as much CH_4 as O_2. The ratio of amounts available (1.72 mol CH_4 to 1.00 mol O_2) is less than the required 2 to 1, so CH_4 is the limiting reactant and is used in the stoichiometric calculation.

$$7.79 \text{ mol CH}_4 \left(\frac{2 \text{ mol CH}_3\text{OH}}{2 \text{ mol CH}_4} \right) = 7.79 \text{ mol CH}_3\text{OH}$$

$$7.79 \text{ mol CH}_3\text{OH} \left(\frac{32.04 \text{ g CH}_3\text{OH}}{1 \text{ mol CH}_3\text{OH}} \right)$$
$$= 250. \text{ g CH}_3\text{OH}$$

(c) See Equation 5.6 on page 237 for the way to calculate the enthalpy change for a reaction from enthalpies of formation.

$$\Delta_r H^\circ = 2 \Delta_f H^\circ [\text{CH}_3\text{OH}(g)]$$
$$- \{2 \Delta_f H^\circ [\text{CH}_4(g)] + \Delta_f H^\circ [\text{O}_2(g)]\}$$
$$\Delta_r H^\circ = (2 \text{ mol CH}_3\text{OH}/1 \text{ mol-rxn})(-201.0 \text{ kJ/mol CH}_3\text{OH})$$
$$- (2 \text{ mol CH}_4/1 \text{ mol-rxn})(-74.87 \text{ kJ/mol CH}_4)$$
$$\Delta_r H^\circ = -252.3 \text{ kJ/mol-rxn}$$

The reaction is exothermic.

$$1.00 \times 10^3 \text{ g CH}_4 \left(\frac{1 \text{ mol CH}_4}{16.04 \text{ g CH}_4} \right) = 62.3 \text{ mol CH}_4$$

$$62.3 \text{ mol CH}_4 \left(\frac{1 \text{ mol-rxn}}{2 \text{ mol CH}_4} \right) \left(\frac{-252.3 \text{ kJ}}{1 \text{ mol-rxn}} \right)$$
$$= -7860 \text{ kJ for } 1.00 \text{ kg of CH}_4$$

33. (a) CN^- is the cyanide ion and KCN is potassium cyanide.

(b) Oxygen begins with an oxidation number of 0 in O_2 and appears as an O atom with an oxidation number of -2 in H_2O. Thus, the oxygen is reduced and is the oxidizing agent. Gold begins as gold(0), whereas it is the Au^+ ion in the anion $[Au(CN)_2]^-$. This means the gold has been oxidized and is the reducing agent.

(c) Mass of KCN required by 1.00 kg of gold

$$1.00 \times 10^3 \text{ g Au} \left(\frac{1 \text{ mol Au}}{196.97 \text{ g Au}} \right) = 5.08 \text{ mol Au}$$

$$5.08 \text{ mol Au} \left(\frac{8 \text{ mol KCN required}}{4 \text{ mol Au available}} \right)$$
$$= 10.2 \text{ mol KCN required}$$

$$10.2 \text{ mol KCN} \left(\frac{65.12 \text{ g KCN}}{1 \text{ mol KCN}} \right) = 661 \text{ g KCN}$$

(d) Volume of 0.15 M KCN solution required by 1.00 kg of gold

$$10.2 \text{ mol KCN} \left(\frac{1 \text{ L}}{0.15 \text{ mol KCN}} \right) = 68 \text{ L KCN solution}$$

34. (a) Use the percent composition to determine the empirical formula.

$$77.09 \text{ g C} \left(\frac{1 \text{ mol C}}{12.011 \text{ g C}} \right) = 6.418 \text{ mol C}$$

$$11.50 \text{ g H} \left(\frac{1 \text{ mol H}}{1.008 \text{ g H}} \right) = 11.41 \text{ mol H}$$

$$11.41 \text{ g O} \left(\frac{1 \text{ mol O}}{15.999 \text{ g O}} \right) = 0.7132 \text{ mol O}$$

To find the empirical formula, find the ratio of amounts of the elements.

$$\frac{6.418 \text{ mol C}}{0.7132 \text{ mol O}} = \frac{9 \text{ mol C}}{1 \text{ mol O}} \qquad \frac{11.41 \text{ mol H}}{0.7132 \text{ mol O}} = \frac{16 \text{ mol H}}{1 \text{ mol O}}$$

The empirical formula is $C_9H_{16}O$.

(b) Use titration data to determine the molar mass and thus the molecular formula.

$$0.03894 \text{ L NaOH soln} \left(\frac{0.113 \text{ mol NaOH}}{1 \text{ L NaOH}} \right)$$
$$= 4.40 \times 10^{-3} \text{ mol NaOH}$$

Because each molecule of fatty acid has only one acid group to react with a base, the amount of acid in the sample is 4.40×10^{-3} mol. The molar mass is

$$\text{Molar mass} = \frac{\text{sample mass}}{\text{amount of acid in sample}}$$
$$= \frac{1.234 \text{ g}}{4.40 \times 10^{-3} \text{ mol}} = 2.80 \times 10^2 \text{ g/mol}$$

This is twice the molar mass of the empirical formula, so the molecular formula is therefore $C_{18}H_{32}O_2$.

(c) Number of double bonds in the carbon chain.

$$0.636 \text{ g I}_2 \left(\frac{1 \text{ mol I}_2}{253.8 \text{ g I}_2} \right)$$
$$= 2.51 \times 10^{-3} \text{ mol I}_2 \text{ and mol of}$$
$$\text{double bonds in carbon chain}$$

$$0.351 \text{ g fatty acid} \left(\frac{1 \text{ mol fatty acid}}{280.4 \text{ g fatty acid}} \right)$$
$$= 1.25 \times 10^{-3} \text{ mol fatty acid}$$

$$\frac{2.51 \times 10^{-3} \text{ mol double bonds}}{1.25 \times 10^{-3} \text{ mol fatty acid}}$$
$$= 2 \text{ mol double bonds per mol of fatty acid}$$

35. (a) $Ag^+(aq) + Cl^-(aq) \rightarrow AgCl(s)$

(b) Complete equation:

$$2 \text{ AgNO}_3(aq) + K_2CrO_4(aq)$$
$$\rightarrow Ag_2CrO_4(s) + 2 \text{ KNO}_3(aq)$$

Net ionic equation:

$$2 \text{ Ag}^+(aq) + CrO_4^{2-}(aq) \rightarrow Ag_2CrO_4(s)$$

(c) Concentration of chloride ions: From the volume and concentration of silver ions used in the titration, we know the amount of silver used.

$$0.02560 \text{ L AgNO}_3 \left(\frac{1.036 \times 10^{-3} \text{ mol Ag}^+}{1 \text{ L AgNO}_3} \right)$$
$$= 2.652 \times 10^{-5} \text{ mol Ag}^+$$

Because each silver ion reacts with one Cl^- ion, the 50.0-mL sample contained 2.652×10^{-5} mol Cl^-.

$$2.652 \times 10^{-5} \text{ mol Cl}^- \left(\frac{35.453 \text{ g Cl}^-}{1 \text{ mol Cl}} \right) \left(\frac{1000 \text{ mg}}{1 \text{ g}} \right)$$
$$= 0.9403 \text{ mg Cl}^-$$

$$Cl^- \text{ concentration in the water} = \frac{\text{mass of Cl}^-}{\text{sample volume}}$$
$$= \left(\frac{0.9403 \text{ mg Cl}^-}{50.0 \text{ mL}} \right) \left(\frac{1000 \text{ mL}}{\text{L}} \right) = 18.8 \text{ mg/L}$$

The Cl^- concentration is sufficient.

36. From the combustion of the compound we can find the amount and mass of C and H in the 0.463-g sample.

$$0.818 \text{ g CO}_2 \left(\frac{1 \text{ mol CO}_2}{44.01 \text{ g CO}_2} \right)\left(\frac{1 \text{ mol C}}{1 \text{ mol CO}_2} \right)$$
$$= 0.0186 \text{ mol C}$$

$$0.0186 \text{ mol C} \left(\frac{12.011 \text{ g C}}{1 \text{ mol C}} \right) = 0.223 \text{ g C}$$

$$0.168 \text{ g H}_2\text{O} \left(\frac{1 \text{ mol H}_2\text{O}}{18.02 \text{ g H}_2\text{O}} \right)\left(\frac{2 \text{ mol H}}{1 \text{ mol H}_2\text{O}} \right)$$
$$= 0.0186 \text{ mol H}$$

$$0.0186 \text{ mol H} \left(\frac{1.008 \text{ g H}}{1 \text{ mol H}} \right) = 0.0188 \text{ g H}$$

By precipitating the Cl as AgCl, we find the amount and mass of Cl in the sample.

$$0.533 \text{ g AgCl} \left(\frac{1 \text{ mol AgCl}}{143.3 \text{ g AgCl}} \right)\left(\frac{1 \text{ mol Cl}}{1 \text{ mol AgCl}} \right)$$
$$= 0.00372 \text{ mol Cl}$$

$$0.00372 \text{ mol Cl} \left(\frac{35.45 \text{ g Cl}}{1 \text{ mol Cl}} \right) = 0.132 \text{ g Cl}$$

The total mass of C, H, and Cl in the 0.463-g sample is 0.374 g. Thus, the mass of Ti is 0.089 g or 1.9×10^{-3} mol.

$$0.089 \text{ g Ti} \left(\frac{1 \text{ mol Ti}}{47.9 \text{ g Ti}} \right) = 0.0019 \text{ mol Ti}$$

Ratio of amounts:

$$\frac{0.0186 \text{ mol C}}{0.0019 \text{ mol Ti}} = 10 \text{ C to 1 Ti}$$

$$\frac{0.0186 \text{ mol H}}{0.0019 \text{ mol Ti}} = 10 \text{ H to 1 Ti}$$

$$\frac{0.00372 \text{ mol Cl}}{0.0019 \text{ mol Ti}} = 2 \text{ Cl to 1 Ti}$$

The empirical formula of the compound is $C_{10}H_{10}TiCl_2$.

37. (a) $Ba(OH)_2(aq) + H_2SO_4(aq) \rightarrow BaSO_4(s) + 2 H_2O(\ell)$
(b) $Ba^{2+}(aq) + 2 OH^-(aq) + 2 H_3O^+(aq) + SO_4^{2-}(aq)$
$\rightarrow BaSO_4(s) + 4 H_2O(\ell)$
(c) Plot (b). As H_2SO_4 is added to the $Ba(OH)_2$ solution, both are consumed, and the reaction products are both nonconducting. The number of ions in solution declines and so does the conductivity. At some point both of the reactants are completely consumed, so the conductivity drops to a minimum. If addition of H_2SO_4 continues, the conductivity increases due to excess H_2SO_4.

38. Calculate the energy as heat involved in the solution process.

$q_{solution} = (105 \text{ g water} + 9.40 \text{ g KBr})(4.184 \text{ J/g·K})(-3.3 \text{ K})$
$= -1600 \text{ J}$

The sign of the energy transferred as heat in the solution process is negative, indicating that the water has given energy as heat to the KBr.

Now we recognize that

$$q_{solution} + q_{KBr} = 0 \text{ and so } q_{KBr} = +1600 \text{ J}$$

Calculate the amount of KBr.

$$9.40 \text{ g KBr} \left(\frac{1 \text{ mol KBr}}{119.0 \text{ g KBr}} \right) = 0.0790 \text{ mol KBr}$$

Calculate the energy involved per mole.

$$\text{Enthalpy of solution per mol} = \frac{+1600 \text{ J}}{0.0790 \text{ mol KBr}}$$
$$= 2.0 \times 10^4 \text{ J/mol or 20. kJ/mol}$$

Comment: The solution process is endothermic, so the temperature drops when KBr dissolves, and q for the solution ($q_{solution}$) is a negative quantity. This means the heat of solution of KBr is a positive quantity. This can be verified using the enthalpies of formation.

$\Delta_{soln}H° = \Delta_fH°[KBr(aq)] - \Delta_fH°[KBr(s)]$
$= (1 \text{ mol KBr(aq)}/1 \text{ mol-rxn})[-373.9 \text{ kJ/mol KBr(aq)}]$
$\quad - (1 \text{ mol KBr(s)}/1 \text{ mol-rxn})[-393.8 \text{ kJ/mol KBr(s)}]$
$= +19.9 \text{ kJ/mol-rxn}$

39. Burning isooctane.

$$\left(\frac{5.45 \times 10^3 \text{ kJ}}{1 \text{ mol isooctane}} \right)\left(\frac{1 \text{ mol isooctane}}{114.2 \text{ g}} \right) = 47.7 \text{ kJ/g}$$

$$\left(\frac{47.7 \text{ kJ}}{1 \text{ g isooctane}} \right)\left(\frac{0.688 \text{ g isooctane}}{\text{mL}} \right)\left(\frac{1000 \text{ mL}}{\text{L}} \right)$$
$$= 3.28 \times 10^4 \text{ kJ/L}$$

40. (a) Compare the mass of hydrogen obtained from methane, petroleum, and coal.

Methane: $CH_4(g) + H_2O(g) \rightarrow 3 H_2(g) + CO(g)$

$$100. \text{ g} \left(\frac{1 \text{ mol CH}_4}{16.04 \text{ g}} \right)\left(\frac{3 \text{ mol H}_2}{1 \text{ mol CH}_4} \right)\left(\frac{2.016 \text{ g H}_2}{1 \text{ mol H}_2} \right) = 37.7 \text{ g H}_2$$

Petroleum: $CH_2(g) + H_2O(g) \rightarrow 2 H_2(g) + CO(g)$

$$100. \text{ g} \left(\frac{1 \text{ mol CH}_2}{14.03 \text{ g}} \right)\left(\frac{2 \text{ mol H}_2}{1 \text{ mol CH}_2} \right)\left(\frac{2.016 \text{ g H}_2}{1 \text{ mol H}_2} \right) = 28.7 \text{ g H}_2$$

Coal: $C(s) + H_2O(g) \rightarrow H_2(g) + CO(g)$

$$100. \text{ g} \left(\frac{1 \text{ mol C}}{12.01 \text{ g}} \right)\left(\frac{1 \text{ mol H}_2}{1 \text{ mol C}} \right)\left(\frac{2.016 \text{ g H}_2}{1 \text{ mol H}_2} \right) = 16.8 \text{ g H}_2$$

(b) Enthapy changes for the reaction of steam with methane and coal.

Methane:

$\Delta_rH° = \Delta_fH°[CO(g)] + 3 \Delta_fH°[H_2(g)]$
$\quad - \{\Delta_fH°[CH_4(g)] + \Delta_fH°[H_2O(g)]\}$
$= (1 \text{ mol CO}_2/1 \text{ mol-rxn}) (-110.525 \text{ kJ/mol CO}_2)$
$\quad + (3 \text{ mol H}_2/1 \text{ mol-rxn}) (0 \text{ kJ/mol H}_2)$
$\quad - [(1 \text{ mol CH}_4/1 \text{ mol-rxn}) (-74.87 \text{ kJ/mol CH}_4)$
$\quad - (1 \text{ mol H}_2\text{O}/1 \text{ mol-rxn}) (-241.83 \text{ kJ/mol H}_2\text{O})]$
$= +206.18 \text{ kJ/mol-rxn}$

Coal:

$\Delta_r H^\circ = \Delta_f H^\circ \text{ [CO(g)]} + \Delta_f H^\circ \text{ [H}_2\text{(g)]}$
$\qquad - \{\Delta_f H^\circ \text{ [C(s)]} + \Delta_f H^\circ \text{ [H}_2\text{O(g)]}\}$
$\qquad = (1 \text{ mol CO}_2/1 \text{ mol-rxn})(-110.525 \text{ kJ/mol})$
$\qquad\qquad + (1 \text{ mol H}_2/1 \text{ mol-rxn})(0 \text{ kJ/mol})$
$\qquad - \left[\begin{array}{l} (1 \text{ mol C}/1 \text{ mol-rxn})(0 \text{ kJ/mol}) \\ + (1 \text{ mol H}_2\text{O}/1 \text{ mol-rxn})(-241.83 \text{ kJ/mol}) \end{array} \right]$

$\qquad = +131.31 \text{ kJ/mol-rxn}$

Methane requires more energy than coal per mol.

41. (a) $NH_4Cl(s) \rightarrow NH_3(g) + HCl(g)$

(b) The combination of NH_3 and HCl is an acid-base reaction.

(c) Ammonium chloride, ammonia, and hydrogen chloride

(d) $\Delta_r H^\circ = \Delta_f H^\circ [NH_3(g)] + \Delta_f H^\circ \text{ [HCl(g)]}$
$\qquad - \Delta_f H^\circ \text{ [NH}_4\text{Cl(s)]}$
$\qquad = (1 \text{ mol NH}_3/1 \text{ mol-rxn})(-45.90 \text{ kJ/mol})$
$\qquad\quad + (1 \text{ mol HCl}/1 \text{ mol-rxn})(-92.31 \text{ kJ/mol HCl})$
$\qquad\quad - (1 \text{ mol NH}_4\text{Cl}/1 \text{ mol-rxn})$
$\qquad\qquad\qquad\qquad (-314.55 \text{ kJ/mol NH}_4\text{Cl})$

$\qquad = +176.34 \text{ kJ/mol-rxn}$

(e) Mass of ammonia expected from 1.0 g NH_4Cl

$1.00 \text{ g NH}_4\text{Cl} \left(\dfrac{1 \text{ mol NH}_4\text{Cl}}{53.49 \text{ g}} \right) \left(\dfrac{1 \text{ mol NH}_3}{1 \text{ mol NH}_4\text{Cl}} \right) \left(\dfrac{17.03 \text{ g NH}_3}{1 \text{ mol NH}_3} \right)$
$\qquad = 0.318 \text{ g NH}_3$

(f) pH of solution

$1.00 \text{ g NH}_4\text{Cl} \left(\dfrac{1 \text{ mol NH}_4\text{Cl}}{53.49 \text{ g}} \right) \left(\dfrac{1 \text{ mol HCl}}{1 \text{ mol NH}_4\text{Cl}} \right)$
$\qquad = 0.0187 \text{ mol HCl}$

$\text{Concentration of HCl solution} = \dfrac{0.0187 \text{ mol HCl}}{0.126 \text{ L}}$
$\qquad = 0.148 \text{ M}$

Hydrochloric acid is a strong acid, so the concentration of H_3O^+ ion in solution is also 0.148 M. This gives a pH of 0.830.

$\text{pH} = -\log [H_3O^+] = -\log (0.148) = -(-0.830) = 0.830$

42. (a) $Fe_4[Fe(CN)_6]_3$ is composed of four Fe^{3+} ions and, attached to the CN^- ions, a total of three Fe^{2+} ions. (There is one Fe^{2+} ion for each 6 CN^- ions.) That is, the ions are $(Fe^{3+})_4[Fe^{2+}(CN)_6]_3$.

(b) Weight percent iron
$\qquad = \dfrac{7 \text{ mol Fe } (55.845 \text{ g/mol Fe})}{859.2 \text{ g of Prussian blue}} \times 100\% = 45.50\% \text{ Fe}$

43. (a) Alanine, $C_3H_7NO_2$, 89.09 g/mol; phenylalanine, $C_9H_{11}NO_2$, 165.19 g/mol.

(b) Both molecules have the structural element $H_2N-CH-CO_2H$. This is common to all of the α-amino acids that are found in proteins.

(c) Both have 1 N atom per molecule. Because alanine has a lower molar mass, it has a greater weight percent of N (15.72%) than phenylalanine (8.48%).

(d) Because alanine has a lower molar mass than phenylalanine, there are more molecules in a given mass of alanine (5.12 g or 0.0575 mol) than in the same mass of phenylalanine (0.0310 mol).

44. (a) $TiO_2(s) + 2 Cl_2(g) + C(s) \rightarrow TiCl_4(\ell) + CO_2(g)$

(b) $TiO_2 = \text{titanium(IV) oxide}$; $TiCl_4 = \text{titanium(IV) chloride}$

(c) $\Delta_r H^\circ = \Delta_f H^\circ [TiCl_4(\ell)] + \Delta_f H^\circ [CO_2(g)]$
$\qquad - \{\Delta_f H^\circ [TiO_2(s)] + 2 \Delta_f H^\circ [Cl_2(g)] + \Delta_f H^\circ (C)\}$

(c) $\Delta_r H^\circ = (1 \text{ mol TiCl}_4(\ell)/1 \text{ mol-rxn})$
$\qquad\qquad\qquad\qquad (-804.2 \text{ kJ/mol-rxn})$
$\qquad\quad + (1 \text{ mol CO}_2(g)/1 \text{ mol-rxn})$
$\qquad\qquad\qquad\qquad (-393.5 \text{ kJ/mol-rxn})$
$\qquad\quad - (1 \text{ mol TiO}_2(s)/1 \text{ mol-rxn})$
$\qquad\qquad\qquad\qquad (-939.7 \text{ kJ/mol-rxn})$

$\qquad = -258.0 \text{ kJ/mol-rxn}$
The reaction is exothermic.

(d) First, decide on the limiting reactant

$1.000 \times 10^3 \text{ g TiO}_2 = 12.52 \text{ mol}$
$1.000 \times 10^3 \text{ g Cl}_2 = 14.10 \text{ mol}$

Now compare the amounts available:

$\dfrac{\text{mol Cl}_2}{\text{mol TiO}_2} = \dfrac{14.10 \text{ mol Cl}_2}{12.52 \text{ mol TiO}_2} = \dfrac{1.126 \text{ mol Cl}_2}{1 \text{ mol TiO}_2}$

This is less than the 2 to 1 ratio defined by the balanced equation, so Cl_2 is the limiting reactant. Now calculate the theoretical yield of $TiCl_4$.

$(14.10 \text{ mol Cl}_2) \left(\dfrac{1 \text{ mol TiCl}_4}{2 \text{ mol Cl}_2} \right) \left(\dfrac{189.68 \text{ g}}{1 \text{ mol TiCl}_4} \right)$
$\qquad = 1337 \text{ g TiCl}_4$

$\text{Percent yield TiCl}_4 = \left(\dfrac{893 \text{ g}}{1337 \text{ g}} \right) 100\% = 66.8\%$

45. $H_2O(\ell) \rightarrow H_2(g) + 1/2 \ O_2(g)$
$\qquad\qquad\qquad\qquad \Delta_r H^\circ = +285.83 \text{ kJ/mol-rxn}$

$C(s) + 1/2 \ O_2(g) \rightarrow CO(g)$
$\qquad\qquad\qquad\qquad \Delta_r H^\circ = -110.525 \text{ kJ/mol-rxn}$

$2 C(s) + H_2(g) \rightarrow C_2H_2(g) \qquad \Delta_r H^\circ = 226.73 \text{ kJ/mol-rxn}$

$CaC_2(s) + CO(g) \rightarrow CaO(s) + 3 C(s)$
$\qquad\qquad\qquad\qquad \Delta_r H^\circ = -464.77 \text{ kJ/mol-rxn}$

$CaO(s) + H_2O(\ell) \rightarrow Ca(OH)_2(s)$
$\qquad\qquad\qquad\qquad \Delta_r H^\circ = -65.17 \text{ kJ/mol-rxn}$

$CaC_2(s) + 2 H_2O(\ell) \rightarrow Ca(OH)_2(s) + C_2H_2(g)$
$\qquad\qquad\qquad\qquad \Delta_r H^\circ = -127.91 \text{ kJ/mol-rxn}$

6 | The Structure of Atoms

©Arctic-Images/Corbis

Aurora Borealis

The beautiful display of "northern lights" can light up the night sky in the Northern Hemisphere. Colors can range from white to red, green, orange, and others. The display comes from the collision of electrons in the solar wind with atoms and molecules in the upper atmosphere near Earth's poles. This excites the atoms or molecules energetically, and they emit light.

Questions:

This photo shows an aurora with green light.

1. Which has the longer wavelength, red light or green light?
2. Which has the greater energy?
3. How do the colors of light emitted by excited atoms contribute to our understanding of electronic structure?

Answer to these questions are in Appendix Q.

Chapter Goals

- Describe the properties of electromagnetic radiation.
- Understand the origin of light emitted by excited atoms and its relationship to atomic structure.
- Describe the experimental evidence for particle–wave duality.
- Describe the basic ideas of quantum mechanics.
- Define the four quantum numbers (n, ℓ, m_ℓ, and m_s) and recognize their relationship to electronic structure.

Chapter Outline

The work of the Curies, Rutherford, and other scientists early in the 20th century (Chapter 2 and pages 338–347) led to a model for an atom with a small nucleus of neutrons and protons containing most of the mass and with electrons surrounding the nucleus and filling most of the volume. This is still the basic model of the atom. But, at the beginning of the 21st century, is there a more useful model? Will a more complete model help us understand why atoms of different elements have different properties and help us predict properties of an element? To answer these and other questions, we want to probe more deeply into atomic structure in this and the next chapter.

Much of our understanding of atomic structure comes from a knowledge of how atoms interact with light and how excited atoms emit light. The first three sections of this chapter, therefore, describe radiation and its relation to our modern view of the atom.

Chemistry.⊙.Now™

Throughout the text this icon introduces an opportunity for self-study or to explore interactive tutorials by signing in at **www.cengage.com/login**.

6.1 Electromagnetic Radiation

In 1864, James Clerk Maxwell (1831–1879) developed a mathematical theory to describe all forms of radiation in terms of oscillating, or wave-like, electric and magnetic fields (Figure 6.1). Thus, light, microwaves, television and radio signals, x-rays, and other forms of radiation are now called **electromagnetic radiation**.

Electromagnetic radiation is characterized by its wavelength and frequency.

- **Wavelength**, symbolized by the Greek letter *lambda* (λ), is defined as the distance between successive crests or high points of a wave (or between successive troughs or low points). This distance can be given in meters, nanometers, or whatever unit of length is convenient.

- **Frequency**, symbolized by the Greek letter *nu* (ν), refers to the number of waves that pass a given point in some unit of time, usually per second. The unit for frequency, written either as s^{-1} or $1/s$ and standing for 1 per second, is now called a **hertz**.

Wavelength and frequency are related to the speed (c) at which a wave is propagated (Equation 6.1).

$$c \text{ (m/s)} = \lambda \text{ (m)} \times \nu \text{ (1/s)} \qquad (6.1)$$

■ **Heinrich Hertz** Heinrich Hertz (1857–1894) was the first person to send and receive radio waves. He showed that they could be reflected and refracted the same as light, confirming that different forms of radiation such as radio and light waves are related. Scientists now use "hertz" as the unit of frequency.

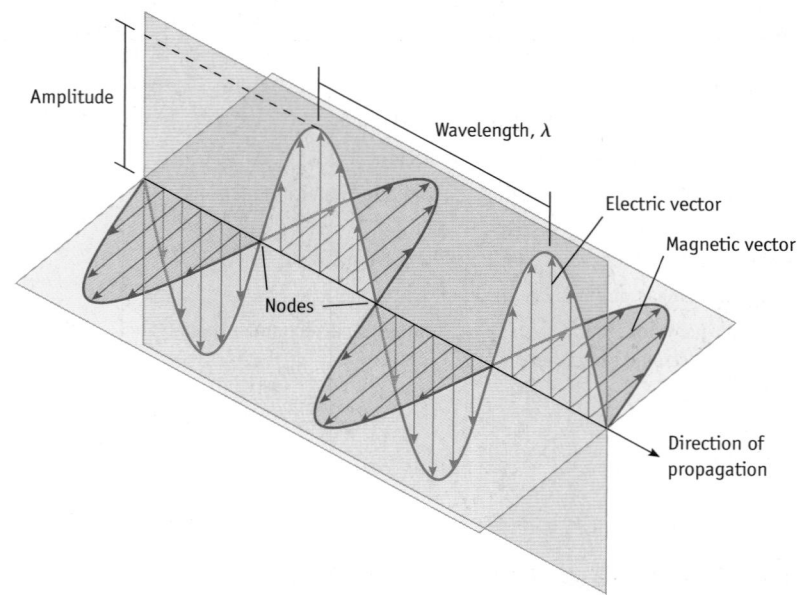

■ **Speed of Light** The speed of light passing through a substance (air, glass, water, for example) depends on the chemical constitution of the substance. It is also dependent on the wavelength of the light. This is the basis for using a glass prism to disperse light and is the explanation for rainbows.

The speed of visible light and all other forms of electromagnetic radiation in a vacuum is a constant, c ($= 2.99792458 \times 10^8$ m/s; approximately 186,000 miles/s or 1.079×10^9 km/h). For calculations, we will generally use the value of c with four or fewer significant figures.

Different types of electromagnetic radiation are related, as shown in Figure 6.2. Notice that visible light is only a very small portion of the total spectrum of electromagnetic radiation. Ultraviolet (UV) radiation, the radiation that can lead to sunburn, has wavelengths shorter than those of visible light. X-rays and γ-rays, the latter emitted in the process of radioactive disintegration of some atoms, have even shorter wavelengths. At wavelengths longer than those of visible light, we first encounter infrared radiation (IR). At even longer wavelengths is the radiation used in microwave ovens and in television and radio transmissions.

Chemistry Now™

■ **EXAMPLE 6.1** **Wavelength–Frequency Conversions**

Problem The frequency of the radiation used in microwave ovens sold in the United States is 2.45 GHz. (GHz stands for "gigahertz"; 1 GHz = 10^9 1/s.) What is the wavelength of this radiation in meters?

Strategy Rearrange Equation 6.1 to solve for λ, and then substitute the appropriate values into this equation.

Solution

$$\lambda = \frac{c}{\nu} = \frac{2.998 \times 10^8 \text{ m/s}}{2.45 \times 10^9 \text{ 1/s}} = 0.122 \text{ m}$$

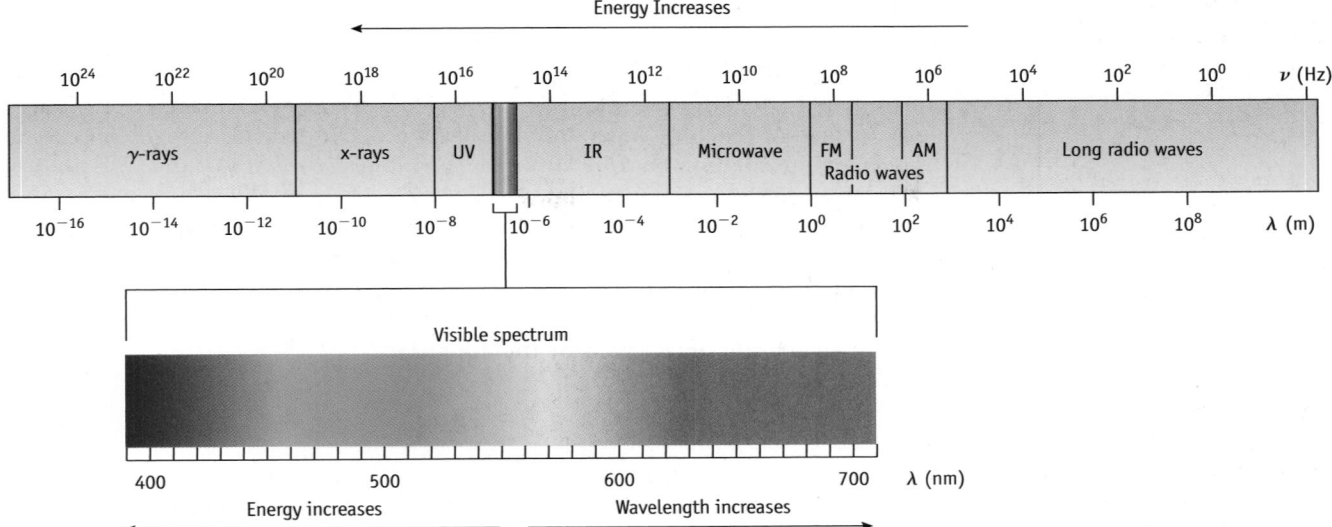

Active Figure 6.2 **The electromagnetic spectrum.** Visible light (enlarged portion) is a very small part of the entire spectrum. The radiation's energy increases from the radio-wave end of the spectrum (low frequency, ν, and long wavelength, λ) to the γ-ray end (high frequency and short wavelength).

Chemistry ⚛ Now™ Sign in at www.cengage.com/login and go to the Chapter Contents menu to explore an interactive version of this figure accompanied by an exercise.

EXERCISE 6.1 Radiation, Wavelength, and Frequency

(a) Which color in the visible spectrum has the highest frequency? Which has the lowest frequency?

(b) Is the frequency of the radiation used in a microwave oven higher or lower than that from your favorite FM radio station (for example, 91.7 MHz), where 1 MHz (megahertz) = 10^6 1/s?

(c) Is the wavelength of x-rays longer or shorter than that of ultraviolet light?

6.2 Quantization: Planck, Einstein, Energy, and Photons

Planck's Equation

If you heat a piece of metal to a high temperature, electromagnetic radiation is emitted with wavelengths that depend on temperature. At lower temperatures, the color is a dull red (Figure 6.3a). As the temperature increases, the red color brightens, and at even higher temperatures a brilliant white light is emitted.

Your eyes detect the radiation that occurs in the visible region of the electromagnetic spectrum. However, radiation with wavelengths both shorter (in the ultraviolet region) and longer (in the infrared region) than those of visible light is also given off by the hot metal (Figure 6.3b). In addition, it is observed that the wavelength of the most intense radiation is related to temperature: as the temperature of the metal is raised, the maximum intensity shifts toward shorter wavelengths (Figure 6.3b). This corresponds to the change in color observed as the temperature is raised.

At the end of the 19th century, scientists were not able to explain the relationship between the intensity and the wavelength for radiation given off by a heated object (often called *blackbody radiation,* Figure 6.3c). Theories available at the time predicted that the intensity should increase continuously with decreasing wavelength, instead of reaching a maximum and then declining as is actually observed. This perplexing situation became known as the *ultraviolet catastrophe* because predictions failed in the ultraviolet region.

In 1900, a German physicist, Max Planck (1858–1947), offered an explanation. Planck assumed that the electromagnetic radiation emitted was caused by vibrating atoms (called *oscillators*) in the heated object. He proposed that each oscillator had a fundamental frequency (ν) of oscillation and that the emitted radiation could have only certain energies, given by the equation

$$E = nh\nu$$

where n is a positive integer. That is, Planck proposed that the energy is *quantized.* **Quantization** means that only certain energies are allowed. The proportionality constant h in the equation is now called **Planck's constant** and its experimental

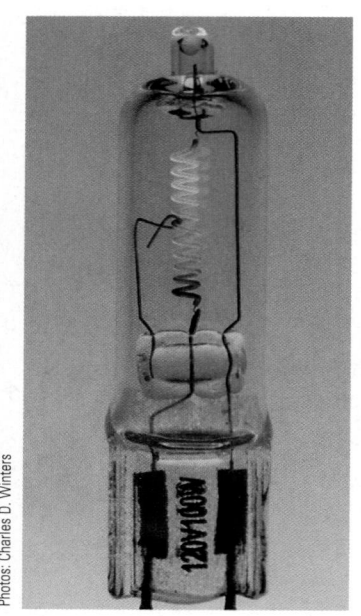

(a) Light emitted by a heated metal.

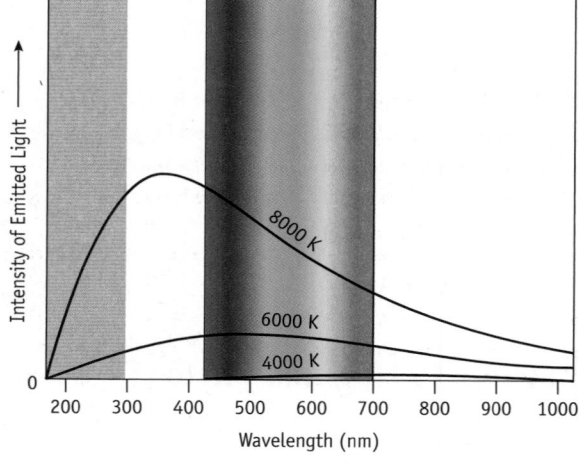

(b) The spectrum of light emitted by a heated metal at different temperatures.

(c) Blackbody radiation from burning charcoal.

FIGURE 6.3 The radiation given off by a heated body. (a) The heated filament of an incandescent bulb emits radiation at the long wavelength or red end of the visible spectrum. (b) When an object is heated, it emits radiation covering a spectrum of wavelengths. For a given temperature, some of the radiation is emitted at long wavelengths and some at short wavelengths. Most, however, is emitted at some intermediate wavelength, the maximum in the curve. As the temperature of the object increases, the maximum moves from the red end of the spectrum to the violet end. At still higher temperatures, intense light is emitted at all wavelengths in the visible region, and the maximum in the curve is in the ultraviolet region. The object is described as "white hot." (Stars are often referred to as "red giants" or "white dwarfs," a reference to their temperatures and relative sizes.) (c) In physics a blackbody is a theoretical concept in which a body absorbs all radiation that falls on it. However, it will emit energy with a temperature-dependent wavelength. The light emanating from the spaces between the burning charcoal briquets in this photo is a close approximation to blackbody radiation. The color of the light depends on the temperature of the briquets.

value is $6.6260693 \times 10^{-34}$ J · s. The unit of frequency is 1/s, so the energy calculated using this equation is in joules (J). If an oscillator changes from a higher energy to a lower one, energy is emitted as electromagnetic radiation, where the difference in energy between the higher and lower energy states is

$$\Delta E = E_{\text{higher } n} - E_{\text{lower } n} = \Delta nh\nu$$

If the value of Δn is 1, which corresponds to changing from one energy level to the next lower one for that oscillator, then the energy change for the oscillator and the electromagnetic radiation emitted would have an energy equal to

$$E = h\nu \qquad\qquad (6.2)$$

This equation is called **Planck's equation.**

Now, assume as Planck did that there must be a *distribution* of vibrations of atoms in an object—some atoms are vibrating at a high frequency; some are vibrating at a low frequency, but most have some intermediate frequency. The few atoms with high-frequency vibrations are responsible for some of the light, as are those few with low-frequency vibrations. However, most of the light must come from the majority of the atoms that have intermediate vibrational frequencies. That is, a spectrum of light is emitted with a maximum intensity at some intermediate wavelength, in accord with experiment. The intensity should not become greater and greater on approaching the ultraviolet region. With this realization, the ultraviolet catastrophe was solved.

Einstein and the Photoelectric Effect

As often happens, the explanation of one fundamental phenomenon leads to other important discoveries. A few years after Planck's work, Albert Einstein (1879–1955) incorporated Planck's ideas into an explanation of the photoelectric effect and in doing so changed the model that described electromagnetic radiation.

In the photoelectric effect, electrons are ejected when light strikes the surface of a metal (Figure 6.4), but only if the frequency of the light is high enough. If light with a lower frequency is used, no electrons are ejected, regardless of the light's intensity (its brightness). If the frequency is at or above a minimum, critical frequency, increasing the light intensity causes more electrons to be ejected.

Einstein decided the experimental observations could be explained by combining Planck's equation ($E = h\nu$) with a new idea, that light has particle-like properties. Einstein characterized these massless particles, now called **photons,** as packets of energy, and stated that the energy of each photon is proportional to the frequency of the radiation as defined by Planck's equation. In the photoelectric effect, photons striking atoms on a metal surface will cause electrons to be ejected only if the photons have high enough energy. The greater the number of photons that strike the surface at or above the threshold energy, the greater the number of electrons dislodged. The metal atoms will not lose electrons, however, if no individual photon has enough energy to dislodge an electron from an atom.

■ **The Photoelectric Effect** The photoelectric effect is put to use in photoelectric cells, light-operated switches that are commonly used in automatic door openers in stores and elevators.

Energy and Chemistry: Using Planck's Equation

Compact disc players use lasers that emit red light with a wavelength of 685 nm. What is the energy of one photon of this light? What is the energy of 1 mole of photons of red light? To answer these questions, first convert the wavelength to the frequency of the radiation, and then use the frequency to calculate the energy per

■ **The Relationship of Energy, Wavelength, and Frequency**

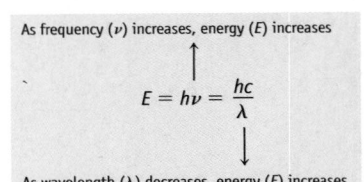

As frequency (ν) increases, energy (E) increases

$$E = h\nu = \frac{hc}{\lambda}$$

As wavelength (λ) decreases, energy (E) increases

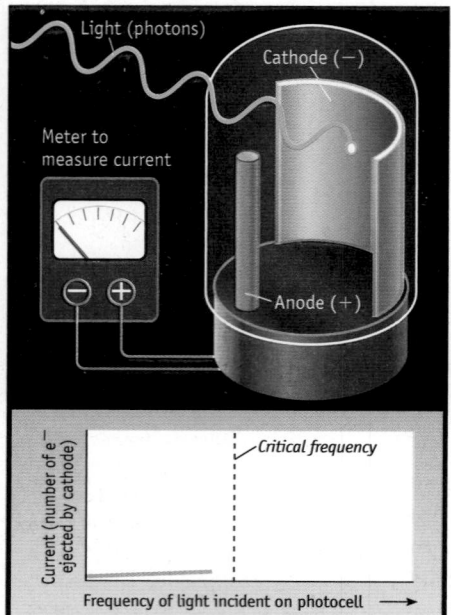

(a) A photocell operates by the photoelectric effect. The main part of the cell is a light-sensitive cathode. This is a material, usually a metal, that ejects electrons if struck by photons of light of sufficient energy. No current is observed until the critical frequency is reached.

FIGURE 6.4 A photoelectric cell.

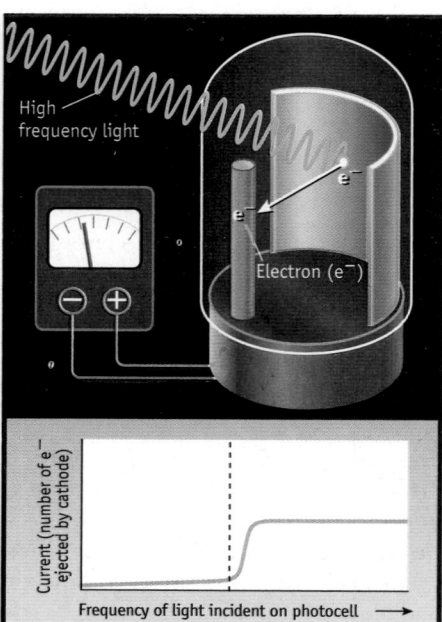

(b) When light of higher frequency than the minimum is used, the excess energy of the photon allows the electron to escape the atom with greater velocity. The ejected electrons move to the anode, and a current flows in the cell. Such a device can be used as a switch in electric circuits.

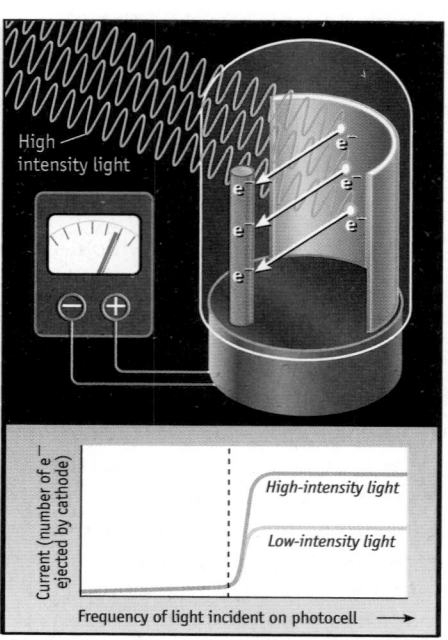

(c) If higher intensity light is used, the only effect is to cause more electrons to be released from the surface. The onset of current is observed at the same frequency as with lower intensity light, but more current flows.

photon. Finally, calculate the energy of a mole of photons by multiplying the energy per photon by Avogadro's number:

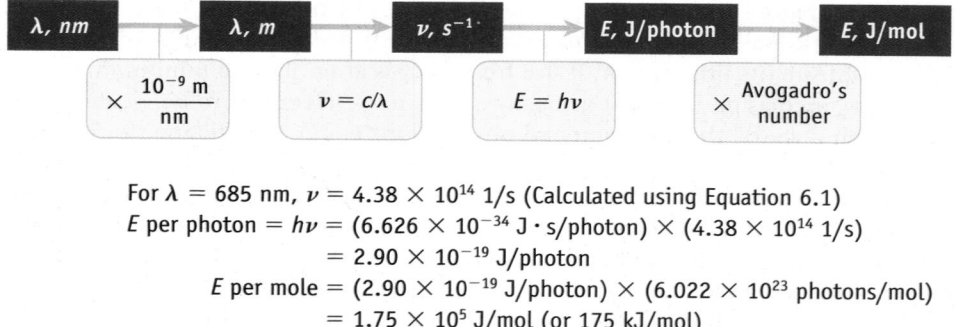

For $\lambda = 685$ nm, $\nu = 4.38 \times 10^{14}$ 1/s (Calculated using Equation 6.1)
E per photon $= h\nu = (6.626 \times 10^{-34}$ J·s/photon$) \times (4.38 \times 10^{14}$ 1/s$)$
$= 2.90 \times 10^{-19}$ J/photon
E per mole $= (2.90 \times 10^{-19}$ J/photon$) \times (6.022 \times 10^{23}$ photons/mol$)$
$= 1.75 \times 10^{5}$ J/mol (or 175 kJ/mol)

The energy of red light photons with a wavelength of 685 nm is 175 kJ/mol, whereas the energy of blue light photons ($\lambda = 400$ nm) is about 300 kJ/mol. The energy of the blue light photons, and of ultraviolet light photons in particular, is in the range of the energies necessary to break the chemical bonds in proteins. This is what happens if you spend too much time unprotected in the sun (Figure 6.5). In contrast, the energy of light at the red end of the spectrum and infrared radiation has a lower energy and, although it is generally not energetic enough to break chemical bonds, it can affect the vibrations of molecules. We sense infrared radiation as heat, such as the heat given off by a glowing burner on an electric stove.

Chemistry ⚛ Now™

Sign in at **www.cengage.com/login** and go to Chapter 6 Contents to see Screen 6.5 for a simulation exploring **the relationship between wavelength, frequency, and photon energy,** and for an exercise on **using Planck's equation to calculate wavelength.**

FIGURE 6.5 Damage from radiation. Various manufacturers have developed mixtures of compounds that protect skin from UVA and UVB radiation. These sunscreens are given "sun protection factor" (SPF) labels that indicate how long the user can stay in the sun without burning. Sunscreens produced by Coppertone, for example, contain the organic compounds 2-ethylhexyl-p-methoxycinnamate and oxybenzene. These molecules absorb UV radiation, preventing it from reaching your skin.

EXERCISE 6.2 Photon Energies

Compare the energy of a mole of photons of orange light (625 nm) with the energy of a mole of photons of microwave radiation having a frequency of 2.45 GHz (1 GHz = 10^9 s^{-1}). Which has the greater energy?

6.3 Atomic Line Spectra and Niels Bohr

If a high voltage is applied to atoms of an element in the gas phase at low pressure, the atoms absorb energy and are said to be "excited." The excited atoms can then emit light, and a familiar example is the colored light from neon advertising signs.

The light falling on Earth from the Sun, or the light emitted by a very hot object, consists of a continuous spectrum of wavelengths (Figures 6.2 and 6.3b). In contrast, the light from excited atoms consists of only a few different wavelengths of light (Figure 6.6). We can demonstrate this by passing a beam of light from excited neon or hydrogen through a prism; only a few colored lines are seen. The spectrum obtained in this manner, such as that for excited H atoms (Figure 6.6), is called a **line emission spectrum.**

The line emission spectra of hydrogen, mercury, and neon are shown in Figure 6.7, and you can see that every element has a unique spectrum. Indeed, the characteristic lines in the emission spectrum of an element can be used in chemical analysis, both to identify the element and to determine how much of it is present.

Neon sign. If a high voltage is applied to a tube containing a gas like neon, light is emitted. Different colors result if different gases are used.

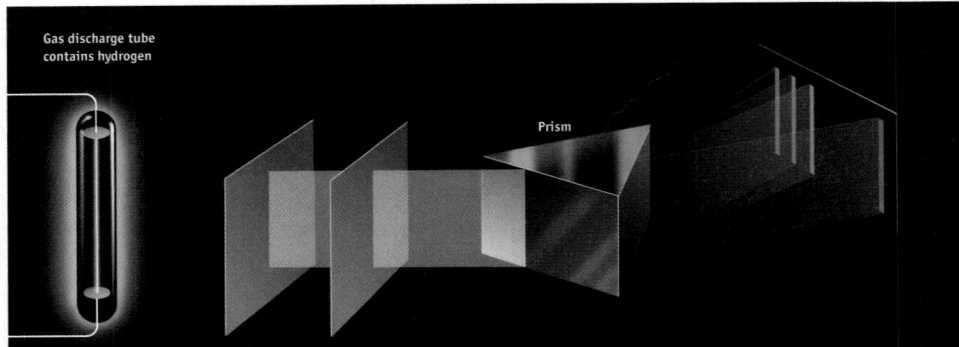

Active Figure 6.6 **The line emission spectrum of hydrogen.** The emitted light is passed through a series of slits to create a narrow beam of light, which is then separated into its component wavelengths by a prism. A photographic plate or photocell can be used to detect the separate wavelengths as individual lines. Hence, the name "line spectrum" for the light emitted by a glowing gas.

Chemistry ⚛ Now™ Sign in at www.cengage.com/login and go to the Chapter Contents menu to explore an interactive version of this figure accompanied by an exercise.

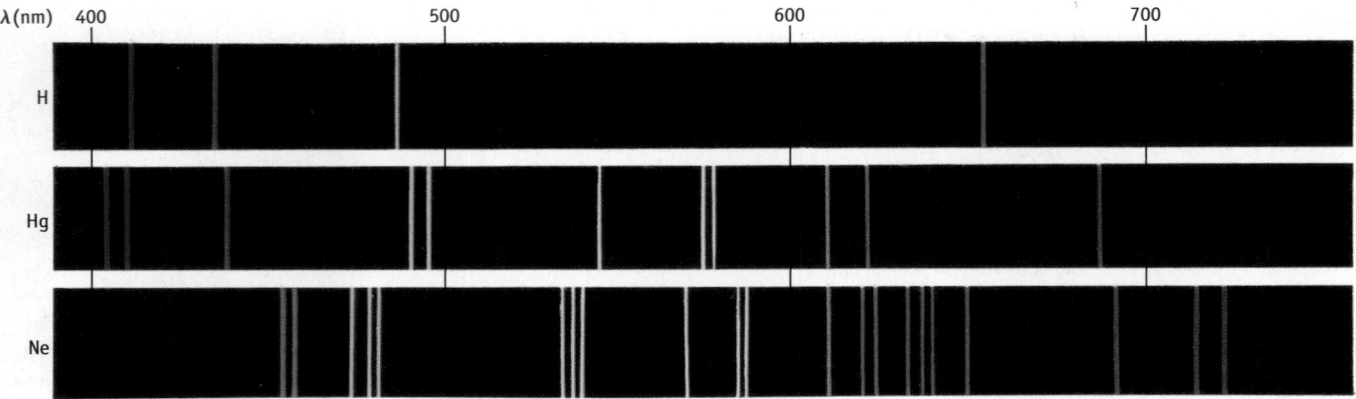

H

Hg

Ne

FIGURE 6.7 Line emission spectra of hydrogen, mercury, and neon. Excited gaseous elements produce characteristic spectra that can be used to identify the elements as well as to determine how much of each element is present in a sample.

A goal of scientists in the late 19th century was to explain why excited gaseous atoms emitted light of only certain frequencies. One approach was to look for a mathematical relationship among the observed frequencies because a regular pattern of information implies a logical explanation. The first steps in this direction were taken by Johann Balmer (1825–1898) and later by Johannes Rydberg (1854–1919). From these studies, an equation—now called the **Balmer equation** (Equation 6.3)— was found that could be used to calculate the wavelength of the red, green, and blue lines in the visible emission spectrum of hydrogen (Figure 6.7).

$$\frac{1}{\lambda} = R\left(\frac{1}{2^2} - \frac{1}{n^2}\right) \qquad \text{when } n > 2 \tag{6.3}$$

In this equation n is an integer, and R, now called the **Rydberg constant,** has the value 1.0974×10^7 m^{-1}. If $n = 3$, the wavelength of the red line in the hydrogen spectrum is obtained (6.563×10^{-7} m, or 656.3 nm). If $n = 4$, the wavelength for the green line is calculated. Using $n = 5$ and $n = 6$ in the equation gives the wavelengths of the blue lines. The four visible lines in the spectrum of hydrogen atoms are now known as the **Balmer series**.

The Bohr Model of the Hydrogen Atom

Early in the 20th century, the Danish physicist Niels Bohr (1885–1962) proposed a model for the electronic structure of atoms and with it an explanation for the emission spectra of excited atoms. Bohr proposed a planetary structure for the hydrogen atom in which the electron moved in a circular orbit around the nucleus, similar to a planet revolving about the sun. In proposing this model, however, he had to contradict the laws of classical physics. According to classical theories, a charged electron moving in the positive electric field of the nucleus should lose energy, and, eventually, the electron should crash into the nucleus. This is clearly not the case; if it were so, matter would eventually self-destruct. To solve this contradiction, Bohr postulated that there are certain orbits corresponding to particular energy levels where this would not occur. As long as an electron is in one of these energy levels, the system is stable. That is, Bohr introduced *quantization* into the description of electronic structure. By combining this quantization postulate with the laws of motion from classical physics, Bohr derived an equation for the energy possessed by the single electron in the *n*th orbit (energy level) of the H atom.

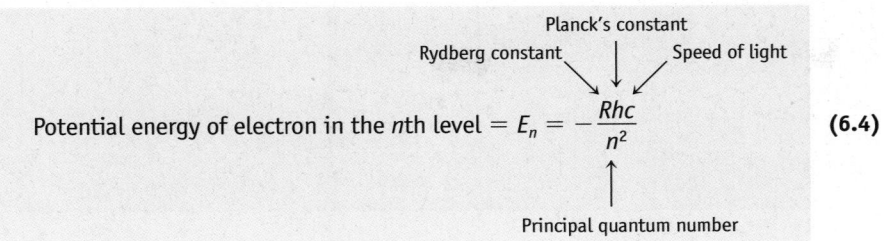

Potential energy of electron in the *n*th level $= E_n = -\dfrac{Rhc}{n^2}$ **(6.4)**

(labels: Planck's constant, Rydberg constant, Speed of light, Principal quantum number)

Here, E_n is the energy of the electron (in J/atom); and R, h, and c are constants (the Rydberg constant, Planck's constant, and the speed of light, respectively). The symbol *n* is a positive, unitless integer called the **principal quantum number**. It can have integral values of 1, 2, 3, and so on.

Equation 6.4 has several important features (which are illustrated in Figure 6.8).

- The quantum number *n* defines the energies of the allowed orbits in the H atom.
- The energy of an electron in an orbit has a negative value. (Because the negative electron is attracted to the positive nucleus, the energy of attraction is a negative value).
- An atom with its electrons in the lowest possible energy levels is said to be in its **ground state**; for the hydrogen atom, this is the level defined by the quantum number $n = 1$. States for the H atom with higher energies (and $n > 1$) are called **excited states**, and, as the value of *n* increases, states have less negative energy values.

Bohr also showed that, as the value of *n* increases, the distance of the electron from the nucleus increases. An electron in the $n = 1$ orbit is closest to the nucleus and has the lowest (most negative) energy. For higher integer values of *n*, the electron is further from the nucleus and has a higher (less negative) energy.

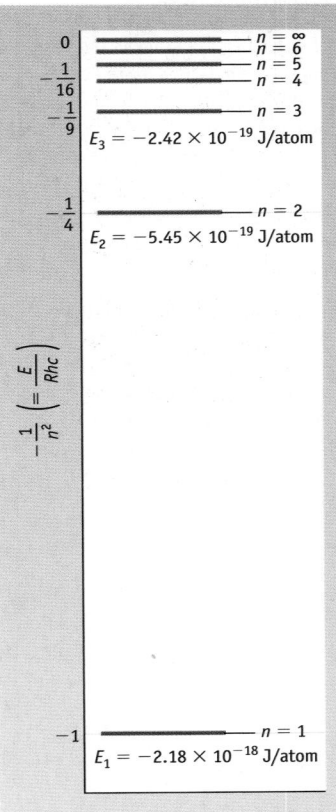

Active Figure 6.8 Energy levels for the H atom in the Bohr model. The energies of the electron in the hydrogen atom depend on the value of the principal quantum number *n* ($E_n = -Rhc/n^2$). The larger the value of *n*, the larger the Bohr radius and the less negative the value of the energy. Energies are given in joules per atom (J/atom). Notice that the difference between successive energy levels becomes smaller as *n* becomes larger.

Chemistry ⬡ Now™ Sign in at www.cengage.com/login and go to the Chapter Contents menu to explore an interactive version of this figure accompanied by an exercise.

EXAMPLE 6.2 Energies of the Ground and Excited States of the H Atom

Problem Calculate the energies of the $n = 1$ and $n = 2$ states of the hydrogen atom in joules per atom and in kilojoules per mole. What is the difference in energy of these two states in kJ/mol?

Strategy Use Equation 6.4 with the following constants: $R = 1.097 \times 10^7$ m^{-1}, $h = 6.626 \times 10^{-34}$ J · s, and $c = 2.998 \times 10^8$ m/s.

Solution When $n = 1$, the energy of an electron in a single H atom is

$E_1 = -Rhc$
$E_1 = -(1.097 \times 10^7 \text{ m}^{-1})(6.626 \times 10^{-34} \text{ J · s})(2.998 \times 10^8 \text{ m/s})$
$\quad = -2.179 \times 10^{-18}$ J/atom

In units of kJ/mol,

$E_1 = \dfrac{-2.179 \times 10^{-18} \text{ J}}{\text{atom}} \times \dfrac{6.022 \times 10^{23} \text{ atoms}}{\text{mol}} \times \dfrac{1 \text{ kJ}}{1000 \text{ J}}$
$\quad = -1312$ kJ/mol

When $n = 2$, the energy is

$E_2 = -\dfrac{Rhc}{2^2} = -\dfrac{E_1}{4} = -\dfrac{2.179 \times 10^{-18} \text{ J/atom}}{4}$
$\quad = -5.448 \times 10^{-19}$ J/atom

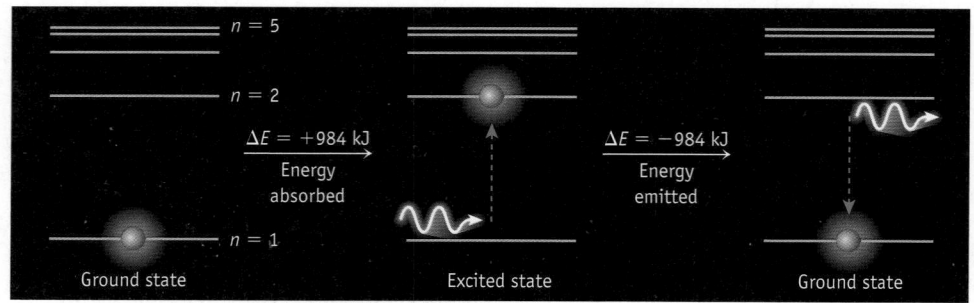

In units of kJ/mol,

$$E_1 = \frac{-5.448 \times 10^{-19} \text{ J}}{\text{atom}} \times \frac{6.022 \times 10^{23} \text{ atoms}}{\text{mol}} \times \frac{1 \text{ kJ}}{1000 \text{ J}}$$

$$= -328.1 \text{ kJ/mol}$$

The difference in energy, ΔE, between the first two energy states of the H atom is

$$\Delta E = E_2 - E_1 = (-328.1 \text{ kJ/mol}) - (-1312 \text{ kJ/mol}) = \boxed{984 \text{ kJ/mol}}$$

Comment The calculated energies are negative, with E_1 more negative than E_2. The $n = 2$ state is higher in energy than the $n = 1$ state by 984 kJ/mol. Also, be sure to notice that 1312 kJ/mol is the value of Rhc multiplied by Avogadro's number N_A (i.e., $N_A Rhc$). This will be useful in future calculations.

EXERCISE 6.3 Electron Energies

Calculate the energy of the $n = 3$ state of the H atom in **(a)** joules per atom and **(b)** kilojoules per mole.

The Bohr Theory and the Spectra of Excited Atoms

Bohr's theory describes electrons as having only specific orbits and energies. If an electron moves from one energy level to another, then energy must be absorbed or evolved. This idea allowed Bohr to relate energies of electrons and the emission spectra of hydrogen atoms.

To move an electron from the $n = 1$ state to an excited state, such as the $n = 2$ state, the atom must absorb energy. When E_{final} has $n = 2$ and E_{initial} has $n = 1$, then 984 kJ of energy must be absorbed (Figure 6.9). This is the difference in energy between final and initial states:

$$\Delta E = E_{\text{final state}} - E_{\text{initial state}} = (-N_A Rhc/2^2) - (-N_A Rhc/1^2) = (0.75)N_A Rhc = 984 \text{ kJ/mol}$$

(where $N_A Rhc/1^2$ is the energy in kJ/mol calculated in Example 6.2 for an electron in the $n = 1$ energy level in the H atom). Moving an electron from the first to the second energy state requires input of 984 kJ/mol of atoms—no more and no less. If $0.7 N_A Rhc$ or $0.8 N_A Rhc$ is provided, a transition between states is not possible. Requiring a specific and precise amount of energy is a consequence of quantization.

Moving an electron from a state of low n to one of higher n requires that energy be absorbed. The opposite process, in which an electron "falls" from a level of higher n to one of lower n, leads to emission of energy (Figure 6.9). For example, for a transition from the $n = 2$ level to $n = 1$ level,

$$\Delta E = E_{\text{final state}} - E_{\text{initial state}} = -984 \text{ kJ/mol}$$

The negative sign indicates energy is evolved; 984 kJ must be *emitted* per mole of H atoms.

We can now visualize the mechanism by which the characteristic line emission spectrum of hydrogen originates according to the Bohr model. Energy is provided to the atoms from an electric discharge or by heating. Depending on how much energy is added, some atoms have their electrons excited from the $n = 1$ state to the $n = 2, 3$, or even higher states. After absorbing energy, these electrons can return to any lower level (either directly or in a series of steps), releasing energy. We observe this released energy as photons of electromagnetic radiation, and, because only certain energy levels are possible, only photons with particular energies and wavelengths are observed. A line spectrum is thus predicted for the emission spectrum of H atoms, which is exactly what is observed.

The energy of any emission line (in kJ/mol) for excited hydrogen atoms can be calculated using Equation 6.5.

$$\Delta E = E_{\text{final}} - E_{\text{initial}} = -N_A Rhc \left(\frac{1}{n_{\text{final}}^2} - \frac{1}{n_{\text{initial}}^2} \right) \qquad \textbf{(6.5)}$$

For hydrogen, a series of emission lines having energies in the ultraviolet region (called the **Lyman series**; Figure 6.10) arises from electrons moving from states with $n > 1$ to the $n = 1$ state. The series of lines that have energies in the visible region—the **Balmer series**—arises from electrons moving from states with $n > 2$ to the $n = 2$ state. There are also series of lines in the infrared spectral region, arising from transitions from higher levels to the $n = 3, 4$ or 5 levels.

Bohr's model, introducing quantization into a description of the atom, tied the unseen (the structure of the atom) to the seen (the observable lines in the hydrogen spectrum). Agreement between theory and experiment is taken as evidence

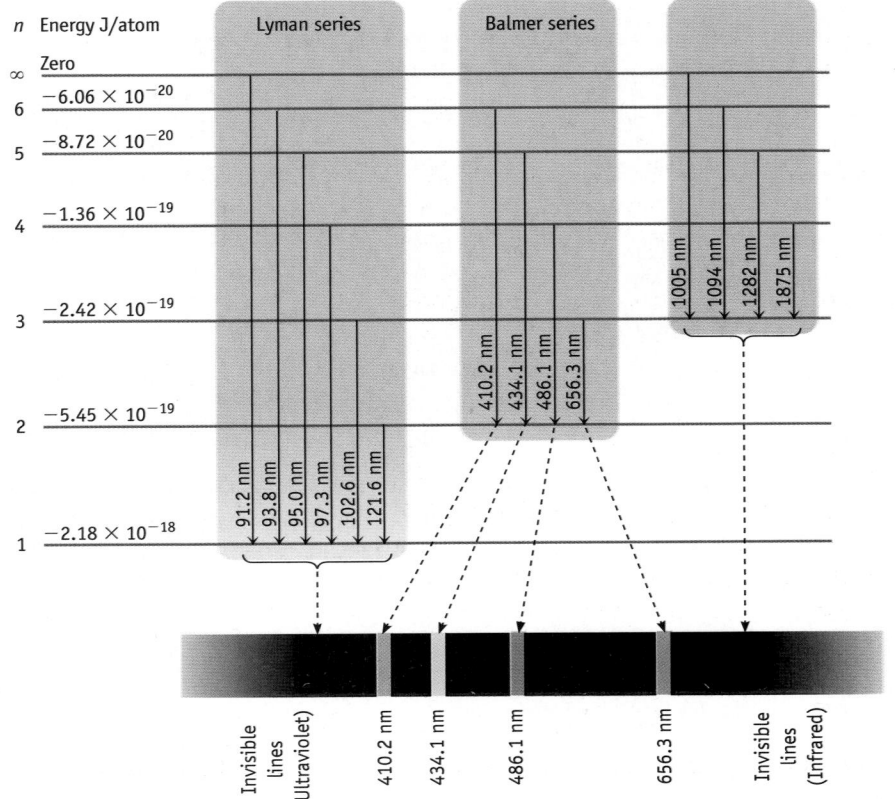

Active Figure 6.10 Some of the electronic transitions that can occur in an excited H atom. The Lyman series of lines in the ultraviolet region results from transitions to the $n = 1$ level. Transitions from levels with values of n greater than 2 to $n = 2$ occur in the visible region (Balmer series; see Figures 6.6 and 6.7). Lines in the infrared region result from transitions from levels with n greater than 3 or 4 to the $n = 3$ or 4 levels. (Only the series ending at $n = 3$ is illustrated.)

Chemistry ⚛ Now™ Sign in at **www.cengage.com/login** and go to the Chapter Contents menu to explore an interactive version of this figure accompanied by an exercise.

that the theoretical model is valid. It was apparent, however, that Bohr's theory was inadequate. This model of the atom explained only the spectrum of hydrogen atoms and of other systems having one electron (such as He⁺), but failed for all other systems. A better model of electronic structure was needed.

Chemistry ⊹ Now™

Sign in at **www.cengage.com/login** and go to Chapter 6 Contents to see Screen 6.6 for a simulation and exercise exploring **the radiation emitted when electrons of excited hydrogen atoms return to the ground state,** and for a tutorial on **calculating the wavelength of radiation emitted when electrons change energy levels.**

■ EXAMPLE 6.3 Energies of Emission Lines for Excited Atoms

Problem Calculate the wavelength of the green line in the visible spectrum of excited H atoms.

Strategy First, locate the green line in Figure 6.10 and determine $n_{initial}$ and n_{final}. Then use Equation 6.5 to calculate the difference in energy, ΔE, between these states. Finally, calculate the wavelength from the value of ΔE.

Solution The green line arises from electrons moving from $n = 4$ to $n = 2$. Using Equation 6.5 where $n_{final} = 2$ and $n_{initial} = 4$, and the value of $N_A Rhc$ (1312 kJ/mol), we have

$$\Delta E = E_{final} - E_{initial} = \left(-\frac{N_A Rhc}{2^2}\right) - \left(-\frac{N_A Rhc}{4^2}\right)$$

$$\Delta E = -N_A Rhc \left(\frac{1}{4} - \frac{1}{16}\right) = -N_A Rhc(0.1875)$$

$$\Delta E = -(1312 \text{ kJ/mol})(0.1875) = -246.0 \text{ kJ/mol}$$

The wavelength can now be calculated. First, the photon energy, E_{photon}, is expressed as J/photon.

$$E_{photon} = \left(246.0 \frac{\text{kJ}}{\text{mol}}\right)\left(1 \times 10^3 \frac{\text{J}}{\text{kJ}}\right)\left(\frac{1 \text{ mol}}{6.022 \times 10^{23} \text{ photons}}\right) = 4.085 \times 10^{-19} \frac{\text{J}}{\text{photon}}$$

Now apply Planck's equation where $E_{photon} = h\nu = hc/\lambda$, and so $\lambda = hc/E_{photon}$.

$$\lambda = \frac{hc}{E_{photon}} = \frac{\left(6.626 \times 10^{-34} \frac{\text{J} \cdot \text{s}}{\text{photon}}\right)\left(2.998 \times 10^8 \text{ m} \cdot \text{s}^{-1}\right)}{4.085 \times 10^{-19} \text{ J/photon}}$$

$$= 4.863 \times 10^{-7} \text{ m}$$

$$= (4.863 \times 10^{-7} \text{ m})(1 \times 10^9 \text{ nm/m})$$

$$= \boxed{486.3 \text{ nm}}$$

Comment The experimental value of 486.1 nm is in excellent agreement with this.

EXERCISE 6.4 Energy of an Atomic Spectral Line

The Lyman series of spectral lines for the H atom, in the ultraviolet region, arises from transitions from higher levels to $n = 1$. Calculate the frequency and wavelength of the least energetic line in this series.

EXERCISE 6.5 Ionization of Hydrogen

Calculate the energy per mole for the process in which hydrogen is ionized [H(g) → H⁺(g) + e⁻(g)]; that is, the energy for the transition from $n = 1$ to $n = \infty$.

The colors of the beautiful fireworks displays you see on holidays such as July 4 in the U.S. are just the emission spectra of excited atoms. But what is their chemistry? What elements are involved?

Typical fireworks have several important chemical components. For example, there must be an oxidizer. Today, this is usually potassium perchlorate ($KClO_4$), potassium chlorate ($KClO_3$), or potassium nitrate (KNO_3). Potassium salts are used instead of sodium salts because the latter have two important drawbacks. They are hygroscopic—they absorb water from the air—and so do not remain dry on storage. Also, when heated, sodium salts give off an intense, yellow light that is so bright it can mask other colors.

The parts of any fireworks display we remember best are the vivid colors and brilliant flashes. White light can be produced by oxidizing magnesium or aluminum metal at high temperatures. The flashes you see at rock concerts or similar events, for example, are typically $Mg/KClO_4$ mixtures.

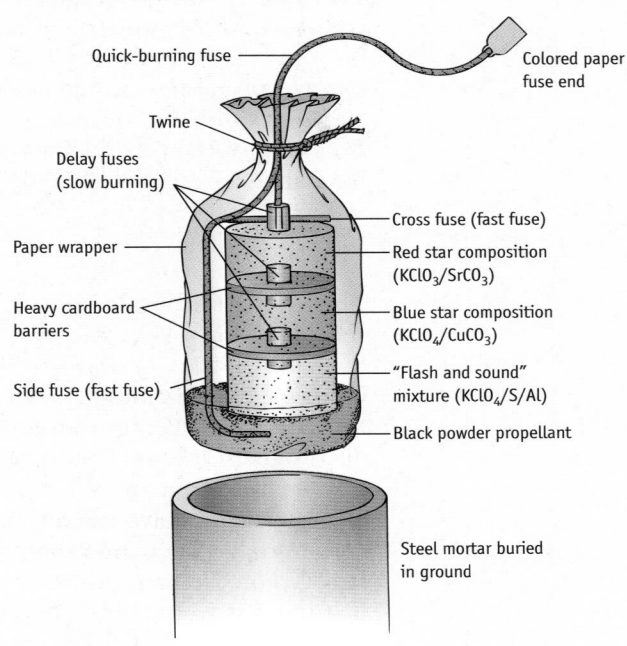

Quick-burning fuse

Colored paper fuse end

Twine

Delay fuses (slow burning)

Paper wrapper

Heavy cardboard barriers

Side fuse (fast fuse)

Cross fuse (fast fuse)

Red star composition ($KClO_3/SrCO_3$)

Blue star composition ($KClO_4/CuCO_3$)

"Flash and sound" mixture ($KClO_4/S/Al$)

Black powder propellant

Steel mortar buried in ground

The design of an aerial rocket for a fireworks display. When the fuse is ignited, it burns quickly to the delay fuses at the top of the red star mixture as well as to the black powder propellant at the bottom. The propellant ignites, sending the shell into the air. Meanwhile, the delay fuses burn. If the timing is correct, the shell bursts high in the sky into a red star. This is followed by a blue burst and then a flash and sound.

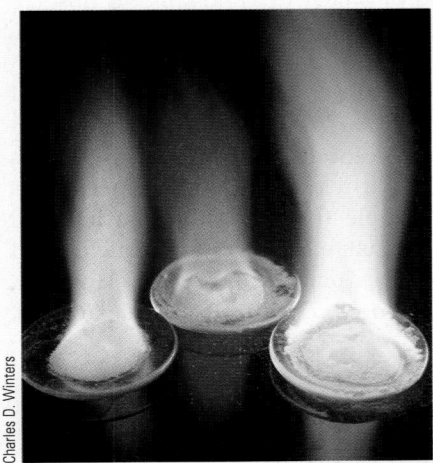

Charles D. Winters

Emission of light by excited atoms. Flame tests are often used to identify elements in a chemical sample. Shown here are the colors produced in a flame (burning methanol) by NaCl (yellow), $SrCl_2$ (red), and boric acid (green).
(See ChemistryNow Screen 6.1, Chemical Puzzler, for a description of colors in fireworks.)

Yellow light is easiest to produce because sodium salts give an intense light with a wavelength of 589 nm. Fireworks mixtures usually contain sodium in the form of non-hygroscopic compounds such as cryolite, Na_3AlF_6. Strontium salts are most often used to produce a red light, and green is produced by barium salts such as $Ba(NO_3)_2$.

The next time you see a fireworks display, watch for the ones that are blue. Blue has always been the most difficult color to produce. Recently, however, fireworks designers have learned that the best way to get a really good "blue" is to decompose copper(I) chloride at low temperatures. To achieve this effect, CuCl is mixed with $KClO_4$, copper powder, and the organic chlorine-containing compound hexachloroethane, C_2Cl_6.

Questions:

1. The main lines in the emission spectrum of sodium are at wavelengths (nm) of 313.5, 589, 590, 818, and 819. Which one or ones are most responsible for the characteristic yellow color of excited sodium atoms?
2. Does the main emission line for $SrCl_2$ (in the photo) have a higher or lower wavelength than that of the yellow line from NaCl?
3. Mg is oxidized by $KClO_4$ to make white flashes. One product of the reaction is KCl. Write a balanced equation for the reaction.

Answers to these questions are in Appendix Q.

6.4 Particle–Wave Duality: Prelude to Quantum Mechanics

The photoelectric effect demonstrated that light, usually considered to be a wave, can also have the properties of particles, albeit without mass. This fact was pondered by Louis Victor de Broglie (1892–1987), who asked if light can have both wave and particle properties, would matter behave similarly? Could an object such as an electron, normally considered a particle, also exhibit wave properties? In 1925, de Broglie proposed that a free electron of mass m moving with a velocity v should have an associated wavelength λ, calculated by the equation

$$\lambda = \frac{h}{mv} \tag{6.6}$$

This revolutionary idea linked the particle properties of the electron (mass and velocity) with a wave property (wavelength). Experimental proof was soon produced. In 1927, C. J. Davisson (1881–1958) and L. H. Germer (1896–1971), working at the Bell Telephone Laboratories in New Jersey, found that a beam of electrons was diffracted like light waves by the atoms of a thin sheet of metal foil and that de Broglie's relation was followed quantitatively. Because diffraction is best explained based on the wave properties of radiation (Figure 6.11), it follows that electrons can be described as having wave properties in certain situations.

De Broglie's equation suggests that any moving particle has an associated wavelength. For λ to be measurable, however, the product of m and v must be very small because h is so small. A 114-g baseball, traveling at 110 mph, for example, has a large mv product (5.6 kg · m/s) and therefore an incredibly small wavelength, 1.2×10^{-34} m! Such a small value cannot be measured with any instrument now available, nor is such a value meaningful. As a consequence, wave properties are never assigned to a baseball or any other massive object. It is possible to observe wave-like properties only for particles of extremely small mass, such as protons, electrons, and neutrons.

Cathode ray tubes, such as were found in television sets before the advent of LCD and plasma TVs, generate a beam of electrons. When the electrons impact the screen, the beam gives rise to tiny flashes of colored light. In contrast to this effect, best explained by assuming electrons are particles, diffraction experiments suggest that electrons are waves. But, how can an electron be both a particle and a wave? In part, we are facing limitations in language; the words "particle" and "wave" accurately describe things encountered on a macroscopic scale. However, they apply less well on the submicroscopic scale associated with subatomic particles.

■ **Cathode Rays** Experiments with cathode rays led to the discovery and understanding of electrons. See the interchapter on *Milestones in the Development of the Modern View of Atoms and Molecules*.

FIGURE 6.11 Diffraction. (a) When two water waves come together, constructive and destructive interference occurs. Similar interference patterns are observed when electrons, which have wave properties, encounter atoms in the gas or solid phase. (b) The pattern observed when a thin film of magnesium oxide diffracts a beam of electrons.

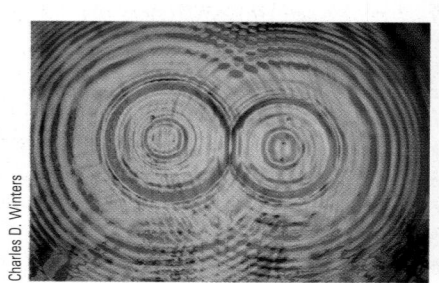

(a) Constructive/destructive interference in water waves.

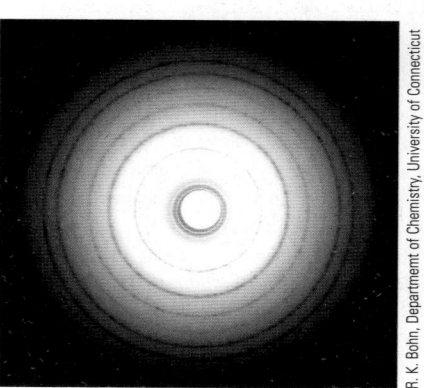

(b) Diffraction of an electron beam by a thin film of magnesium oxide.

In some experiments, electrons behave like particles. In other experiments, we find that they behave like waves. No single experiment can be done to show the electron behaving *simultaneously* as a wave and a particle. Scientists now accept this **wave–particle duality**—that is, the idea that the electron has the properties of both a wave and a particle. Which is observed depends on the experiment.

Chemistry ⚛ Now™

Sign in at **www.cengage.com/login** and go to Chapter 6 Contents to see Screen 6.8 for a tutorial on **calculating the wavelength of a moving electron.**

■ **EXAMPLE 6.4 Using de Broglie's Equation**

Problem Calculate the wavelength associated with an electron of mass $m = 9.109 \times 10^{-28}$ g that travels at 40.0% of the speed of light.

Strategy First, consider the units involved. Wavelength is calculated from h/mv, where h is Planck's constant expressed in units of joule seconds (J · s). As discussed in Chapter 5 (page 214), $1\ J = 1\ kg \cdot m^2/s^2$. Therefore, the mass must be in kilograms and speed in meters per second.

Solution

Electron mass $= 9.109 \times 10^{-31}$ kg

Electron speed (40.0% of light speed) $= (0.400)(2.998 \times 10^8\ m \cdot s^{-1}) = 1.20 \times 10^8\ m \cdot s^{-1}$

Substituting these values into de Broglie's equation, we have

$$\lambda = \frac{h}{mv} = \frac{6.626 \times 10^{-34}\ (kg \cdot m^2/s^2)(s)}{(9.109 \times 10^{-31}\ kg)(1.20 \times 10^8\ m/s)} = 6.07 \times 10^{-12}\ m$$

In nanometers, the wavelength is

$$\lambda = (6.07 \times 10^{-12}\ m)(1.00 \times 10^9\ nm/m) = 6.07 \times 10^{-3}\ nm$$

Comment The calculated wavelength is about 1/12 of the diameter of the H atom.

EXERCISE 6.6 De Broglie's Equation

Calculate the wavelength associated with a neutron having a mass of 1.675×10^{-24} g and a kinetic energy of 6.21×10^{-21} J. (Recall that the kinetic energy of a moving particle is $E = \frac{1}{2}mv^2$.)

6.5 The Modern View of Electronic Structure: Wave or Quantum Mechanics

How does wave–particle duality affect our model of the arrangement of electrons in atoms? Following World War I, German scientists Erwin Schrödinger (1887–1961), Werner Heisenberg (1901–1976), and Max Born (1882–1970) provided the answer.

In Bohr's model of the atom, both the energy and location (the orbit) for the electron in the hydrogen atom can be described accurately. However, Heisenberg determined that, for a tiny object such as an electron in an atom, it is impossible to determine accurately *both* its position and its energy. That is, any attempt to determine accurately either the location or the energy will leave the other uncertain. This is now known as Heisenberg's **uncertainty principle**.

Born proposed the following application of Heisenberg's idea to understand the arrangement of electrons in atoms: *If we choose to know the energy of an electron in an atom with only a small uncertainty, then we must accept a correspondingly large uncertainty*

■ **History of the Modern View of Structure** For the historical background to efforts to understand atomic structure see the interchapter *Milestones in the Development of the Modern View of Atoms and Molecules* (pages 338–347).

in its position. The importance of this idea is that we can assess only the likelihood, or *probability*, of finding an electron with a given energy within a given region of space. Because electron energy is the key to understanding the chemistry of an atom, chemists accept the notion of knowing only the approximate location of the electron.

Erwin Schrödinger (1887–1961) worked on a comprehensive theory of the behavior of electrons in atoms. Starting with de Broglie's hypothesis that an electron could be described as a wave, Schrödinger developed a model for electrons in atoms that has come to be called **quantum mechanics** or **wave mechanics.** This model used the mathematical equations of wave motion to generate a series of equations called wave equations or **wave functions,** which are designated by the Greek letter ψ (psi).

Unlike Bohr's model, Schrödinger's model can be difficult to visualize, and the mathematical approach is complex. Nonetheless, the consequences of the model are important, and understanding its implications is essential to understanding the modern view of the atom. The following points summarize the important issues concerning wave mechanics:

1. An electron in the atom is described as a **standing wave.** If you tie down a string at both ends, as you would the string of a guitar, and then pluck it, the string vibrates as a standing wave (Figure 6.12). A two-dimensional standing wave such as a vibrating string must have two or more points of zero amplitude (called **nodes**), and only certain vibrations are possible. These allowed vibrations have wavelengths of $n(\lambda/2)$, where n is an integer ($n = 1$, 2, 3, ...). In the first vibration illustrated in Figure 6.12, the distance between the ends of the string is half a wavelength, or $\lambda/2$. In the second, the string's length equals one complete wavelength, or $2(\lambda/2)$. In the third vibration, the string's length is $3(\lambda/2)$. That is, for standing waves, vibrations are quantized, and the integer n is a **quantum number.**

2. By defining the electron as a standing wave, quantization is introduced into the description of electronic structure. The mathematics describing a one-dimensional vibrating string requires one "quantum number" (n). Schrödinger's equations for an electron in three-dimensional space requires three quantum numbers: n, ℓ, and m_ℓ, all integers. Only certain combinations of their values are possible as outlined below.

■ **Wave Functions and Energy** In Bohr's theory, the electron energy for the H atom is given by $E_n = -Rhc/n^2$. Schrödinger's electron wave model gives the same result.

FIGURE 6.12 Standing waves. In the first wave, the end-to-end distance is $(1/2)\lambda$; in the second wave, it is λ, and in the third wave, it is $(3/2) \lambda$. (In addition to the nodes marked, there are nodes at the ends of the string.)

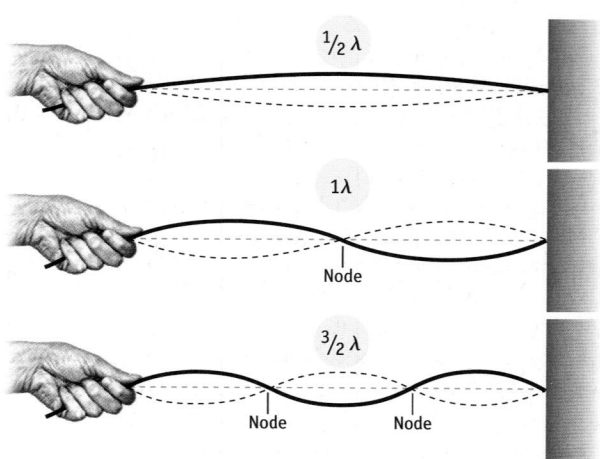

3. Each wave function is associated with an allowed energy value. That is, the energy is quantized because only certain values of energy are possible for the electron.

4. The value of the wave function ψ at a given point in space is the amplitude (height) of the wave. This value has both a magnitude and a sign that can be either positive or negative. (Visualize a vibrating string in a guitar or piano, for example. Points of positive amplitude are above the axis of propagation, and points of negative amplitude are below it.)

5. At any point in space, the square of the value of the wave function (ψ^2) defines the *probability* of finding the electron. Scientists refer to this probability as the **electron density.**

6. Schrödinger's theory defines the energy of the electron precisely. The uncertainty principle, however, tells us there must be uncertainty in the electron's position. Thus, we describe the **probability** of the electron being within a certain region in space when in a given energy state. **Orbitals** define the region of space within which an electron of a given energy is most likely to be located.

Quantum Numbers and Orbitals

Quantum numbers are used to identify the energy states and orbitals available to electrons. We will first describe the quantum numbers and the information they provide and then turn to the connection between quantum numbers and the energies and shapes of atomic orbitals.

n, the Principal Quantum Number (*n* = 1, 2, 3, . . .)

The principal quantum number n can have any integer value from 1 to infinity. The value of n is the primary factor in determining the *energy* of an orbital. It also defines the *size* of an orbital: for a given atom, the greater the value of n, the greater the size of the orbital.

In atoms having more than one electron, two or more electrons may have the same n value. These electrons are then said to be in the same **electron shell.**

■ **Electron Energy and Quantum Numbers** The electron energy in the H atom depends only on the value of n. In atoms with more electrons, the energy depends on both n and ℓ.

ℓ, the Azimuthal Quantum Number (ℓ = 0, 1, 2, 3, . . . , *n* − 1)

Orbitals of a given shell can be grouped into **subshells**, where each subshell is characterized by a different value of the quantum number ℓ. The quantum number ℓ can have any integer value from 0 to a maximum of $n - 1$. This quantum number defines the *characteristic shape of an orbital*; different ℓ values correspond to different orbital shapes.

Because ℓ can be no larger than $n - 1$, the value of n limits the number of subshells possible for each shell. For the shell with $n = 1$, ℓ must equal 0; thus, only one subshell is possible. When $n = 2$, ℓ can be either 0 or 1. Because two values of ℓ are now possible, there are two subshells in the $n = 2$ electron shell.

Subshells are usually identified by letters. For example, an $\ell = 1$ subshell is called a "p subshell," and an orbital in that subshell is called a "p orbital."

■ **Orbital Symbols** Early studies of the emission spectra of elements classified lines into four groups on the basis of their appearance. These groups were labeled sharp, principal, diffuse, and fundamental. From these names came the labels we now apply to orbitals: *s, p, d,* and *f*.

Subshell labels	
Value of ℓ	Subshell Label
0	*s*
1	*p*
2	*d*
3	*f*

■ Subshells and Orbitals

Subshell	Number of Orbitals in Subshell (= 2ℓ + 1)
s	1
p	3
d	5
f	7

m_ℓ, the Magnetic Quantum Number ($m_\ell = 0, \pm 1, \pm 2, \pm 3, \ldots, \pm \ell$)

The magnetic quantum number, m_ℓ, is related to the *orientation in space of the orbitals within a subshell*. Orbitals in a given subshell differ in their orientation in space, not in their energy.

The value of m_ℓ can range from $+\ell$ to $-\ell$, with 0 included. For example, when $\ell = 2$, m_ℓ can have five values: $+2, +1, 0, -1$, and -2. The number of values of m_ℓ for a given subshell ($= 2\ell + 1$) specifies the number of orbitals in the subshell.

Shells and Subshells

Allowed values of the three quantum numbers are summarized in Table 6.1. By analyzing the sets of quantum numbers in this table, you will discover the following:

- n = the number of subshells in a shell.
- $2\ell + 1$ = the number of orbitals in a subshell = the number of values of m_ℓ
- n^2 = the number of orbitals in a shell.

The First Electron Shell, $n = 1$

When $n = 1$, the value of ℓ can only be 0, and so m_ℓ must also have a value of 0. This means that, in the shell closest to the nucleus, only one subshell exists, and that subshell consists of only a single orbital, the 1s orbital.

The Second Electron Shell, $n = 2$

When $n = 2$, ℓ can have two values (0 and 1), so there are two subshells in the second shell. One of these is the 2s subshell ($n = 2$ and $\ell = 0$), and the other is the 2p subshell ($n = 2$ and $\ell = 1$). Because the values of m_ℓ can be -1, 0, and $+1$ when $\ell = 1$, three 2p orbitals exist. All three orbitals have the same shape. However, because each has a different m_ℓ value, the three orbitals differ in their orientation in space.

TABLE 6.1 Summary of the Quantum Numbers, Their Interrelationships, and the Orbital Information Conveyed

Principal Quantum Number	Azimuthal Quantum Number	Magnetic Quantum Number	Number and Type of Orbitals in the Subshell
Symbol = n Values = 1, 2, 3, . . . n = number of subshells	Symbol = ℓ Values = 0 . . . $n - 1$	Symbol = m_ℓ Values = $+\ell$ . . . 0 . . . $-\ell$	Number of orbitals in shell = n^2 and number of orbitals in subshell = $2\ell + 1$
1	0	0	one 1s orbital (one orbital of one type in the $n = 1$ shell)
2	0 1	0 +1, 0, −1	one 2s orbital three 2p orbitals (four orbitals of two types in the $n = 2$ shell)
3	0 1 2	0 +1, 0, −1 +2, +1, 0, −1, −2	one 3s orbital three 3p orbitals five 3d orbitals (nine orbitals of three types in the $n = 3$ shell)
4	0 1 2 3	0 +1, 0, −1 +2, +1, 0, −1, −2 +3, +2, +1, 0, −1, −2, −3	one 4s orbital three 4p orbitals five 4d orbitals seven 4f orbitals (16 orbitals of four types in the $n = 4$ shell)

The Third Electron Shell, $n = 3$

When $n = 3$, three subshells are possible for an electron because ℓ has the values 0, 1, and 2. The first two subshells within the $n = 3$ shell are the $3s$ ($\ell = 0$, one orbital) and $3p$ ($\ell = 1$, three orbitals) subshells. The third subshell is labeled $3d$ ($n = 3$, $\ell = 2$). Because m_ℓ can have five values (-2, -1, 0, $+1$, and $+2$) for $\ell = 2$, there are five d orbitals in this d subshell.

The Fourth Electron Shell, $n = 4$, and Beyond

There are four subshells in the $n = 4$ shell. In addition to $4s$, $4p$, and $4d$ subshells, there is the $4f$ subshell for which $\ell = 3$. Seven such orbitals exist because there are seven values of m_ℓ when $\ell = 3$ (-3, -2, -1, 0, $+1$, $+2$, and $+3$).

Chemistry ⚛ Now™

Sign in at **www.cengage.com/login** and go to Chapter 6 Contents to see:
- Screen 6.9 to view an animation on **the quantum mechanical view of the atom**
- Screen 6.12 for a tutorial on **determining values for the quantum numbers for an orbital**

EXERCISE 6.7 Using Quantum Numbers

Complete the following statements:

(a) When $n = 2$, the values of ℓ can be _____ and _____.

(b) When $\ell = 1$, the values of m_ℓ can be _____ , _____ , and _____ , and the subshell has the letter label _____.

(c) The subshell with $\ell = 2$ is called a _____ subshell.

(d) When a subshell is labeled s, the value of ℓ is _____, and m_ℓ has the value _____.

(e) There are _____ orbitals in the p subshell.

(f) When a subshell is labeled f, there are _____ values of m_ℓ, corresponding to _____ orbitals.

■ **Shells, Subshells, and Orbitals—A Summary** Electrons in atoms are arranged in shells. Within each shell, there can be one or more electron subshells, each comprised of one or more orbitals.

Electron Location	Quantum Number
Shell	n
Subshell	ℓ
Orbital	m_ℓ

6.6 The Shapes of Atomic Orbitals

We often say the electron is assigned to, or "occupies," an orbital. But what does this mean? What is an orbital? What does it look like? To answer these questions, we must examine the wave functions for the orbitals.

s Orbitals

A $1s$ orbital is associated with the quantum numbers $n = 1$ and $\ell = 0$. If we could photograph a $1s$ electron at one-second intervals for a few thousand seconds, the composite picture would look like the drawing in Figure 6.13a. This resembles a cloud of dots, and chemists often refer to such representations of electron orbitals as *electron cloud pictures*. In Figure 6.13a, the density of dots is greater close to the nucleus, that is, the electron cloud is denser close to the nucleus. This indicates that the $1s$ electron is most likely to be found near the nucleus. However, the density of dots declines on moving away from the nucleus and so, therefore, does the probability of finding the electron.

The thinning of the electron cloud at increasing distance is illustrated in a different way in Figure 6.13b. Here we have plotted the square of the wave function for the electron in a $1s$ orbital (ψ^2), times 4π and the distance squared ($4\pi r^2$), as a function of the distance of the electron from the nucleus. This plot represents

■ **Atomic Orbitals for the H Atom** Orbitals and their shapes discussed here are for the H atom, that is, for a one-electron atom. Orbitals for multielectron atoms are approximated by assuming they are hydrogen-like. For most purposes this is a reasonable assumption.

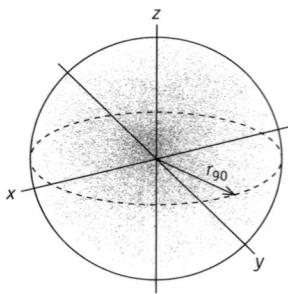

(a) Dot picture of an electron in a 1s orbital. Each dot represents the position of the electron at a different instant in time. Note that the dots cluster closest to the nucleus. r_{90} is the radius of a sphere within which the electron is found 90% of the time.

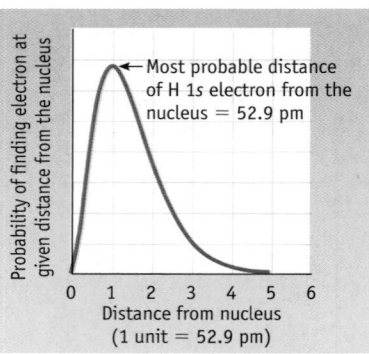

Most probable distance of H 1s electron from the nucleus = 52.9 pm

Probability of finding electron at given distance from the nucleus

0 1 2 3 4 5 6
Distance from nucleus
(1 unit = 52.9 pm)

(b) A plot of the surface density $(4\pi r^2\psi^2)$ as a function of distance for a hydrogen atom 1s orbital. This gives the probability of finding the electron at a given distance from the nucleus.

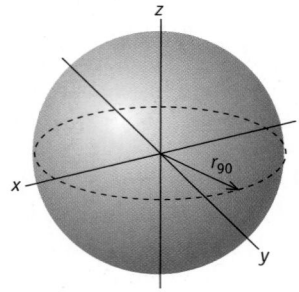

(c) The surface of the sphere within which the electron is found 90% of the time for a 1s orbital. This surface is often called a "boundary surface." (A 90% surface was chosen arbitrarily. If the choice was the surface within which the electron is found 50% of the time, the sphere would be considerably smaller.)

Active Figure 6.13 Different views of a 1s ($n = 1$, $\ell = 0$) orbital.

Chemistry ⊙ Now™ Sign in at www.cengage.com/login and go to the Chapter Contents menu to explore an interactive version of this figure accompanied by an exercise.

■ **Surface Density Plot for 1s** The maximum value of the radial distribution plot for a 1s electron in a hydrogen atom occurs at 52.9 pm. It is interesting to note that this maximum is at exactly the same distance from the nucleus that Niels Bohr calculated for the radius of the orbit occupied by the $n = 1$ electron.

the probability of finding the electron in a thin spherical shell at a distance r from the nucleus. For this reason, the plot of $4\pi r^2\psi^2$ vs. r is sometimes called a **surface density plot** or a **radial distribution plot.** For the 1s orbital, $4\pi r^2\psi^2$ is zero at the nucleus—there is no probability the electron will be exactly at the nucleus—but the probability rises rapidly on moving away from the nucleus, reaches a maximum a short distance from the nucleus (at 52.9 pm), and then decreases rapidly as the distance from the nucleus increases. Notice that the probability of finding the electron approaches but never quite reaches zero, even at very large distances.

Figure 6.13a shows that, for the 1s orbital, the probability of finding an electron is the same at a given distance from the nucleus, no matter in which direction you proceed from the nucleus. Consequently, the *1s orbital is spherical in shape.*

Because the probability of finding the electron approaches but never quite reaches zero, there is no sharp boundary beyond which the electron is never found (although the probability can be incalculably small). Nonetheless, the s orbital (and other types of orbitals as well) is often depicted as having a **boundary surface** (Figure 6.13c), largely because it is easier to draw such pictures. To create Figure 6.13c, we drew a sphere about the nucleus in such a way that the probability of finding the electron somewhere inside the sphere is 90%. The choice of 90% is arbitrary—we could have chosen a different value—and if we do, the shape would be the same, but the size of the sphere would be different.

There are misconceptions about pictures of orbitals. First, there is not an impenetrable surface within which the electron is "contained." Second, the probability of finding the electron is not the same throughout the volume enclosed by the surface. (An electron in the 1s orbital of a H atom has a greater probability of being 52.9 pm from the nucleus than of being closer or farther away.) Third, the terms "electron cloud" and "electron distribution" imply that the electron is a particle, but the basic premise in quantum mechanics is that the electron is treated as a wave, not a particle.

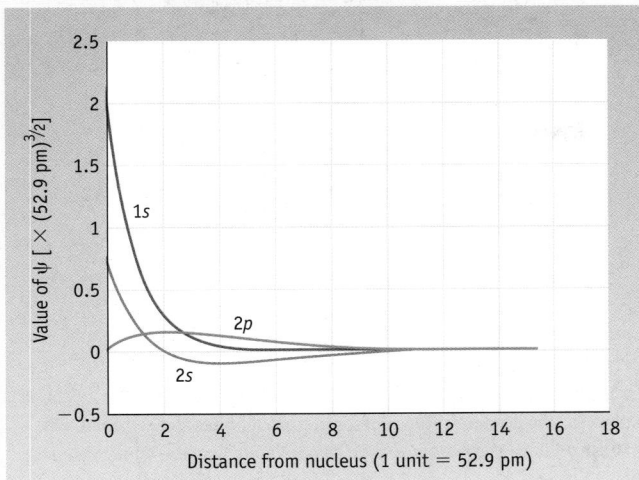

FIGURE A Plot of the wave functions for 1s, 2s, and 2p orbitals versus distance from the nucleus.

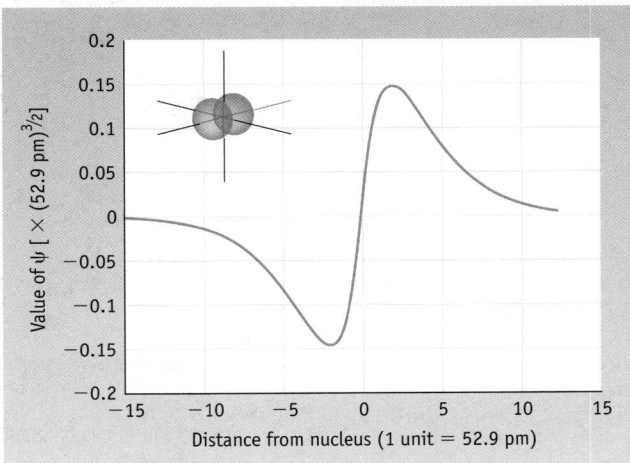

FIGURE B Wave functions for a 2p orbital. The sign of ψ for a 2p orbital is positive on one side of the nucleus and negative on the other (but it has a 0 value at the nucleus). A nodal plane separates the two lobes of this "dumbbell-shaped" orbital. (The vertical axis is the value of ψ, and the horizontal axis is the distance from the nucleus, where 1 unit = 52.9 pm.)

Waves have crests, troughs, and nodes, and these terms can be applied to the description of an electron as a wave. For a 1s orbital of the H atom, the wave function ψ approaches a maximum at the nucleus, but the wave's amplitude declines rapidly at points farther removed from the nucleus (Figure A). The sign of ψ is positive at all points in space.

For a 2s orbital, there is a different profile; the sign of ψ is positive near the nucleus, drops to zero (there is a node at 2 × 52.9 pm), and then becomes negative before approaching zero at greater distances.

For the 2p orbital, the value of ψ is zero at the nucleus because there is a nodal surface passing through the nucleus. Moving away from the nucleus in one direction, say along the x-axis, we see the value of ψ rises to a maximum around 106 pm before falling off at greater distances. Moving away along

the $-x$ direction, the value of ψ is the same but opposite in sign (Figure B). The 2p electron is a wave with a node at the nucleus. (In drawing orbitals, we indicate this with + or − signs or with two different colors as in Figure 6.14 or Figure B.)

For the 2s orbital, there is a node at 105.8 pm when plotting the wave function. However, because ψ has the same value in all directions, this means there is a *spherical nodal surface* surrounding the nucleus as illustrated in Figure C.

As noted on page 290, the number of nodal surfaces passing through the nucleus for any orbital is equal to ℓ. The number of spherical nodes is $n - \ell - 1$. Thus, for a 2s orbital, $2 - 0 - 1 = 1$ spherical nodes, as we have seen. In general, the consequence of this is that electron density in all s orbitals (except 1s) occurs as a series of nested shells.

A possible analogy to this picture is that an s orbital resembles an onion with layers of electron density, the number of layers increasing with n.

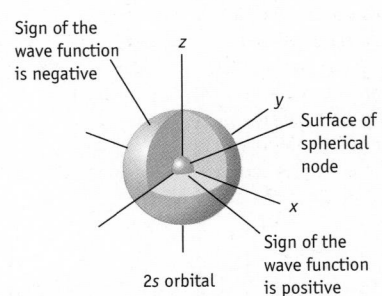

FIGURE C Wave functions for a 2s orbital. A 2s orbital for the H atom showing the spherical node (at 105.8 pm) around the nucleus.

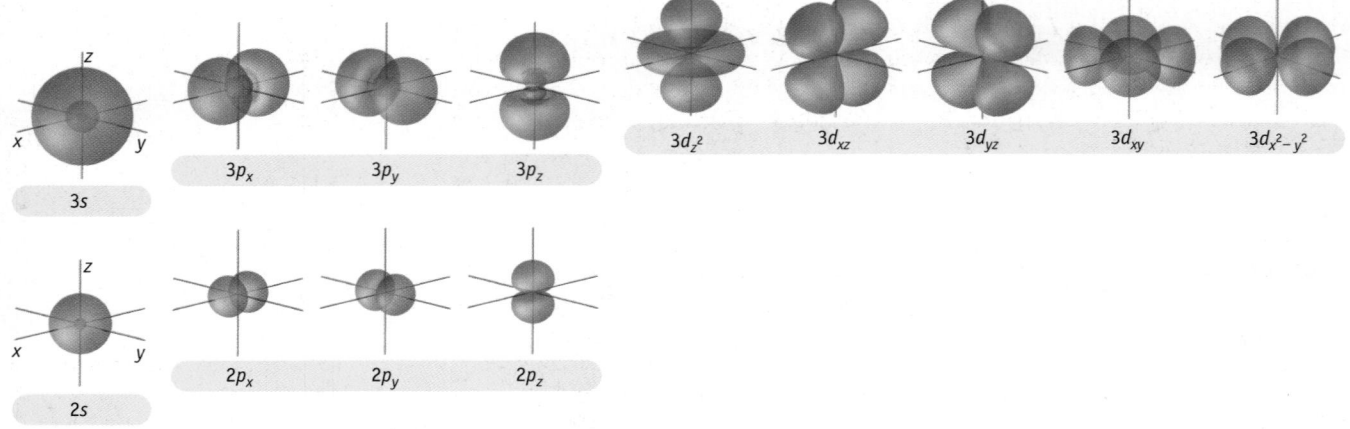

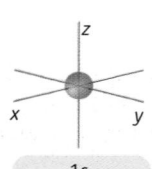

Active Figure 6.14 **Atomic orbitals.** Boundary surface diagrams for electron densities of 1*s*, 2*s*, 2*p*, 3*s*, 3*p*, and 3*d* orbitals for the hydrogen atom. For the *p* orbitals, the subscript letter indicates the cartesian axis along which the orbital lies. For more about orbitals, see *A Closer Look: H Atom Orbital Shapes—Wave Functions and Nodes.*

Chemistry ⊙ Now™ Sign in at www.cengage.com/login and go to the Chapter Contents menu to explore an interactive version of this figure accompanied by an exercise.

All *s* orbitals (1*s*, 2*s*, 3*s* ...) are spherical in shape. However, for any atom, the size of *s* orbitals increases as *n* increases (Figure 6.14). For a given atom, the 1*s* orbital is more compact than the 2*s* orbital, which is in turn more compact than the 3*s* orbital.

p Orbitals

All atomic orbitals for which $\ell = 1$ (*p* orbitals) have the same basic shape. If you enclose 90% of the electron density in a *p* orbital within a surface, the electron cloud has a shape that resembles a weight lifter's "dumbbell," and chemists describe *p* orbitals as having dumbbell shapes (Figures 6.14 and 6.15) because there is a **nodal surface**—a surface on which the electron has no probability—that passes through the nucleus. (The nodal surface is a consequence of the wave function for *p* orbitals,

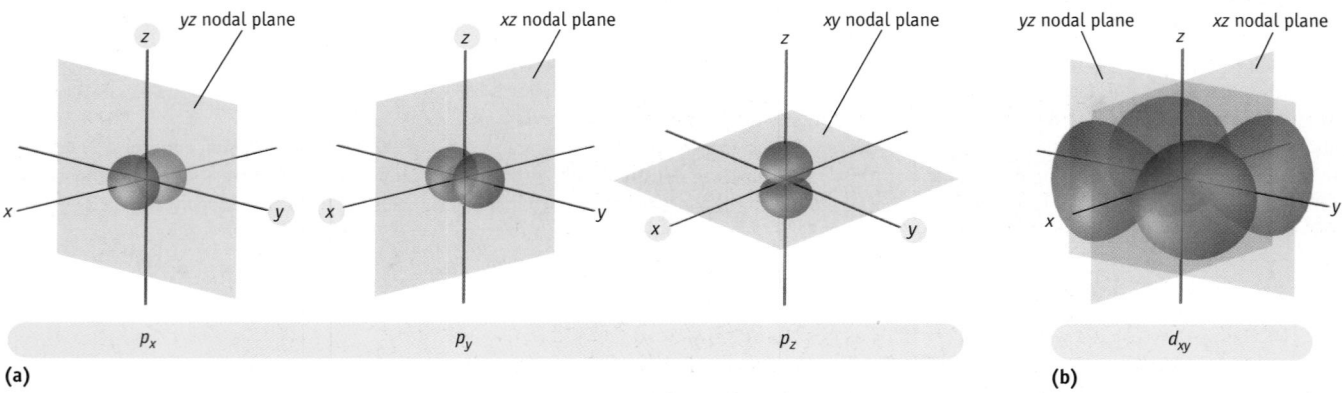

FIGURE 6.15 Nodal surfaces of *p* and *d* orbitals. A plane passing through the nucleus (perpendicular to the axis) is called a nodal surface. (a) The three *p* orbitals each have one nodal surface ($\ell = 1$). (b) The d_{xy} orbital. All five *d* orbitals have two nodal surfaces ($\ell = 2$) through the nucleus. Here, the nodal surfaces are the *xz*- and *yz*-planes, so the regions of electron density lie in the *xy*-plane and between the *x*- and *y*-axes.

which has no value at the nucleus but which rises rapidly in value on moving way from the nucleus. See *A Closer Look: H Atom Orbital Shapes—Wave Functions and Nodes.*)

There are three *p* orbitals in a subshell, and all have the same basic shape with one planar node through the nucleus. Usually, *p* orbitals are drawn along the *x*-, *y*-, and *z*-axes and labeled according to the axis along which they lie (p_x, p_y, or p_z).

d Orbitals

Orbitals with $\ell = 0$, *s* orbitals, have no nodal surfaces through the nucleus, and *p* orbitals, for which $\ell = 1$, have one nodal surface through the nucleus. *The value of ℓ is equal to the number of nodal surfaces slicing through the nucleus.* It follows that the five *d* orbitals, for which $\ell = 2$, have two nodal surfaces through the nucleus, resulting in four regions of electron density. The d_{xy} orbital, for example, lies in the *xy*-plane, and the two nodal surfaces are the *xz*- and *yz*-planes (Figure 6.15). Two other orbitals, d_{xz} and d_{yz}, lie in planes defined by the *xz*- and *yz*-axes, respectively; they also have two, mutually perpendicular nodal surfaces (Figure 6.14).

Of the two remaining *d* orbitals, the $d_{x^2-y^2}$ orbital is easier to visualize. In the $d_{x^2-y^2}$ orbital, the nodal planes bisect the *x*- and *y*-axes, so the regions of electron density lie along the *x*- and *y*-axes. The d_{z^2} orbital has two main regions of electron density along the *z*-axis, and a "doughnut" of electron density also occurs in the *xy*-plane. This orbital has two cone-shaped nodal surfaces.

f Orbitals

Seven *f* orbitals arise with $\ell = 3$. Three nodal surfaces through the nucleus cause the electron density to lie in eight regions of space. One of the *f* orbitals is illustrated in Figure 6.16.

Chemistry ☌ Now™

Sign in at **www.cengage.com/login** and go to Chapter 6 Contents to see Screen 6.13 for exercises on **orbital shapes, quantum numbers, and nodes.**

EXERCISE 6.8 Orbital Shapes

(a) What are the *n* and ℓ values for each of the following orbitals: *6s*, *4p*, *5d*, and *4f*?

(b) How many nodal planes exist for a *4p* orbital? For a *6d* orbital?

FIGURE 6.16 One of the seven possible *f* orbitals. Notice the presence of three nodal planes as required by an orbital with $\ell = 3$.

■ **Nodal Surfaces** Nodal surfaces through the nucleus occur for all *p*, *d*, and *f* orbitals. These surfaces are usually flat, so they are referred to as nodal planes. In some cases (for example, d_{z^2}), however, the "plane" is not flat and so is better referred to as a "surface."

■ **ℓ and Nodal Surfaces** The number of nodal surfaces passing through the nucleus for an orbital = ℓ.

Orbital	ℓ	Number of Nodal Surfaces through the Nucleus
s	0	0
p	1	1
d	2	2
f	3	3

6.7 One More Electron Property: Electron Spin

There is one more property of the electron that plays an important role in the arrangement of electrons in atoms and gives rise to properties of elements you observe every day: electron spin.

The Electron Spin Quantum Number, m_s

In 1921 Otto Stern and Walther Gerlach performed an experiment that probed the magnetic behavior of atoms by passing a beam of silver atoms in the gas phase through a magnetic field. Although the results were complex, they were best interpreted by imagining the electron has a spin and behaves as a tiny magnet that can be attracted or repelled by another magnet (Figure 6.17). If atoms with a single unpaired electron are placed in a magnetic field, the Stern-Gerlach ex-

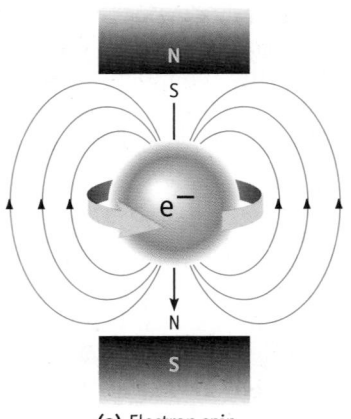

(a) Electron spin

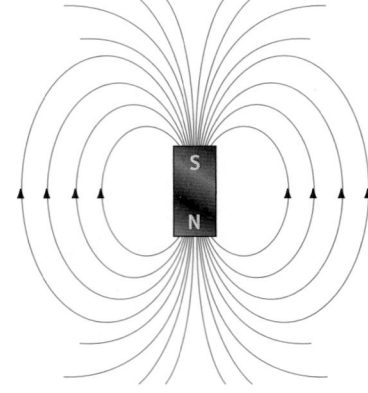

(b) A bar magnet

FIGURE 6.17 Magnetic fields—a bar magnet and an electron. The electron, with its spin and negative electric charge, can be thought of as a small bar magnet. Relative to a magnetic field, only two spin directions are possible for the electron, clockwise or counterclockwise. The north pole of the spinning electron can therefore be either aligned with an external magnetic field or opposed to that field.

A Closer Look

Paramagnetism and Ferromagnetism

Magnetic materials are relatively common, and many are important in our economy. For example, a large magnet is at the heart of the magnetic resonance imaging (MRI) used in medicine, and tiny magnets are found in stereo speakers and in telephone handsets. Magnetic oxides are used in recording tapes and computer disks.

The magnetic materials we use are **ferromagnetic**. The magnetic effect of ferromagnetic materials is much larger than that of paramagnetic ones. Ferromagnetism occurs when the spins of unpaired electrons in a

cluster of atoms (called a *domain*) in the solid align themselves in the same direction. Only the metals of the iron, cobalt, and nickel subgroups, as well as a few other metals such as neodymium, exhibit this property. They are also unique in that, once the domains are aligned in a magnetic field, the metal is permanently magnetized.

Many alloys exhibit greater ferromagnetism than do the pure metals themselves. One example of such a material is Alnico, which is composed of aluminum, nickel, and cobalt as well as copper and iron.

Audio and video tapes are plastics coated with crystals of ferromagnetic oxides such as Fe_2O_3 or CrO_2. The recording head uses an electromagnetic field to create a varying magnetic field based on signals from a microphone. This magnetizes the tape as it passes through the head, with the strength and direction of magnetization varying with the frequency of the sound to be recorded. When the tape is played back, the magnetic field of the moving tape induces a current, which is amplified and sent to the speakers.

Magnets. Many common consumer products such as loud speakers contain permanent magnets.

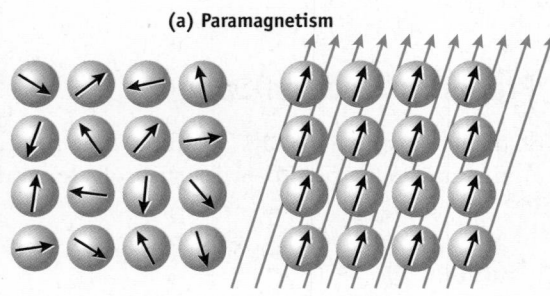

(a) Paramagnetism

No Magnetic Field   External Magnetic Field

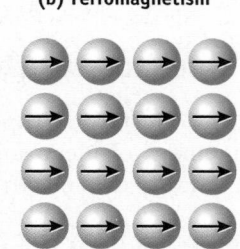

(b) Ferromagnetism

The spins of unpaired electrons align themselves in the same direction

Magnetism. (a) Paramagnetism: In the absence of an external magnetic field, the unpaired electrons in the atoms or ions of the substance are randomly oriented. If a magnetic field is imposed, however, these spins will tend to become aligned with the field. (b) Ferromagnetism: The spins of the unpaired electrons in a cluster of atoms or ions align themselves in the same direction in the absence of a magnetic field.

periment showed there are two orientations for the atoms: with the electron spin aligned with the field or opposed to the field. That is, *the electron spin is quantized,* which introduces another quantum number, the **electron spin quantum number,** m_s. One orientation is associated with a value of m_s of $+\frac{1}{2}$ and the other with m_s of $-\frac{1}{2}$.

When it was recognized that electron spin is quantized, scientists realized that a complete description of an electron in any atom requires four quantum numbers, n, ℓ, m_ℓ, and m_s. The important consequences of this fact are explored in Chapter 7.

Diamagnetism and Paramagnetism

A hydrogen atom has a single electron. If a hydrogen atom is placed in a magnetic field, the magnetic field of the single electron will tend to align with the external field like the needle of a compass. There is an attractive force. Helium atoms, each with two electrons, are not attracted to a magnet, however. In fact, they are slightly repelled by the magnet. To account for this observation, we assume the two electrons of helium have opposite spin orientations. We say their spins are *paired*, and the result is that the magnetic field of one electron can be canceled out by the magnetic field of the second electron with opposite spin. To account for this, the two electrons are assigned different values of m_s.

It is important to understand the relationship between electron spin and magnetism. *Elements and compounds that have unpaired electrons are attracted to a magnet.* These species are referred to as **paramagnetic.** The effect can be quite weak, but, by placing a sample of an element or compound in a magnetic field, it can be observed (Figure 6.18). For example, the oxygen you breathe, is paramagnetic. You can observe this experimentally because liquid oxygen sticks to a magnet of the kind you may have in the speakers of a music player (Figure 6.18b).

Substances in which all electrons are paired (with the two electrons of each pair having opposite spins) experience a slight repulsion when subjected to a magnetic

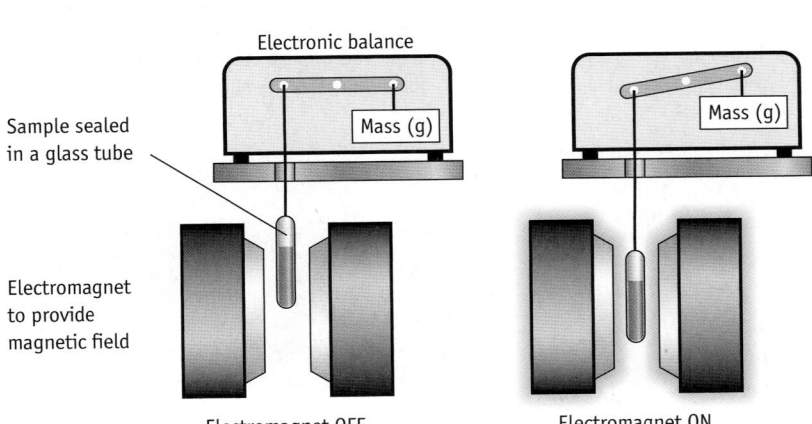

Electronic balance

Sample sealed in a glass tube

Mass (g)

Mass (g)

Electromagnet to provide magnetic field

Electromagnet OFF

Electromagnet ON

(a) Electromagnetic balance

Charles D. Winters

(b) Liquid oxygen clings to a magnet.

Active Figure 6.18 **Observing and measuring paramagnetism.** (a) A magnetic balance is used to measure the magnetism of a sample. The sample is first weighed with the electromagnet turned off. The magnet is then turned on and the sample reweighed. If the substance is paramagnetic, the sample is drawn into the magnetic field, and the apparent weight increases. (b) Liquid oxygen (boiling point 90.2 K) clings to a strong magnet. Elemental oxygen is paramagnetic because it has unpaired electrons. (See Chapter 9.)

Chemistry‿Now™ Sign in at www.cengage.com/login and go to the Chapter Contents menu to explore an interactive version of this figure accompanied by an exercise.

Just as electrons have a spin, so do atomic nuclei. In the hydrogen atom, the single proton of the nucleus spins on its axis. For most heavier atoms, the atomic nucleus includes both protons and neutrons, and the entire entity has a spin. This property is important, because nuclear spin allows scientists to detect these atoms in molecules and to learn something about their chemical environments.

The technique used to detect the spins of atomic nuclei is *nuclear magnetic resonance* (NMR). It is one of the most powerful methods currently available to determine molecular structures. About 20 years ago, it was adapted as a diagnostic technique in medicine, where it is known as *magnetic resonance imaging* (MRI).

Just as electron spin is quantized, so too is nuclear spin. The H atom nucleus can spin in either of two directions. If the H atom is placed in a strong, external magnetic field, however, the spinning nuclear magnet can align itself with or against the external field. If a sample of ethanol (CH_3CH_2OH), for example, is placed in a strong magnetic field, a slight excess of the H atom nuclei (and ^{13}C atom nuclei) is aligned with the lines of force of the field.

The nuclei aligned with the field have a slightly lower energy than when aligned against the field. The NMR and MRI technologies depend on the fact that energy in the radio-frequency region can be absorbed by the sample and can cause the nuclear spins switch alignments—that is, to move to a

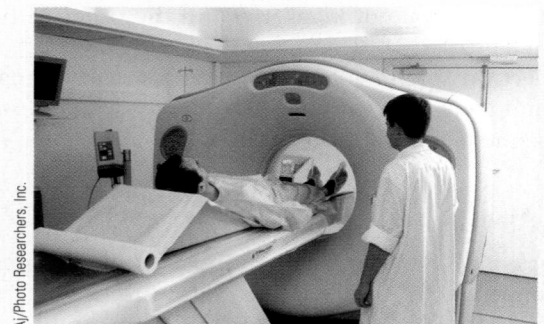
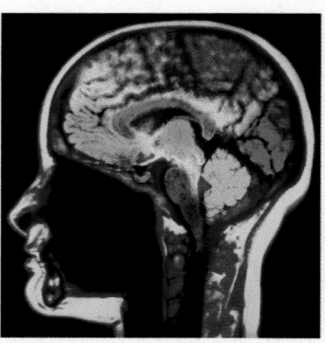

(a)   **(b)**

Magnetic resonance imaging. (a) MRI instrument. The patient is placed inside a large magnet, and the tissues to be examined are irradiated with radio-frequency radiation. (b) An MRI image of the human brain.

higher energy state. This absorption of energy is detected by the instrument.

The most important aspect of the magnetic resonance technique is that the difference in energy between two different spin states depends on the electronic environment of atoms in the molecule. In the case of ethanol, the three CH_3 protons are different from the two CH_2 protons, and both sets are different from the OH proton. These three different sets of H atoms absorb radiation of slightly different energies. The instrument measures the frequencies absorbed, and a scientist familiar with the technique can quickly distinguish the three different environments in the molecule.

The MRI technique closely resembles the NMR method. Hydrogen is abundant in the human body as water and in numerous

organic molecules. In the MRI device, the patient is placed in a strong magnetic field, and the tissues being examined are irradiated with pulses of radio-frequency radiation.

The MRI image is produced by detecting how fast the excited nuclei "relax"; that is, how fast they return to the lower energy state from the higher energy state. The "relaxation time" depends on the type of tissue. When the tissue is scanned, the H atoms in different regions of the body show different relaxation times, and an accurate "image" is built up.

MRI gives information on soft tissue—muscle, cartilage, and internal organs—which is unavailable from x-ray scans. This technology is also noninvasive, and the magnetic fields and radio-frequency radiation used are not harmful to the body.

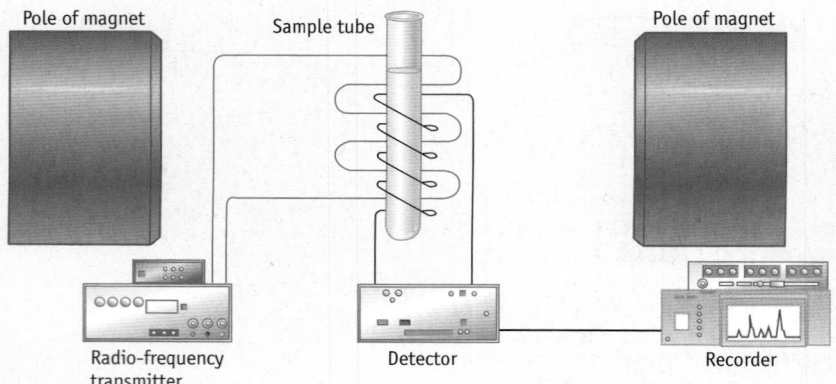

(a) An nmr spectrometer (see Figure 4.4, page 169.)

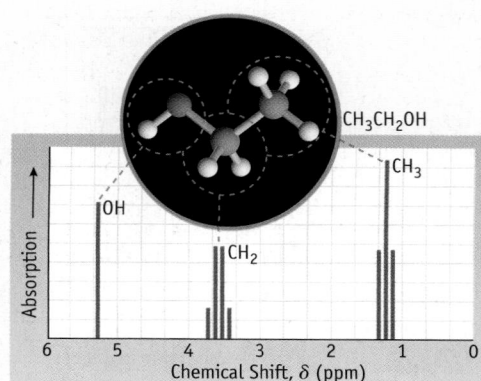

(b) The nmr spectrum of ethanol

Nuclear magnetic resonance. (a) A schematic diagram of an NMR spectrometer. (b) The NMR spectrum of ethanol, showing that the three different types of protons appear in distinctly different regions of the spectrum. The pattern observed for the CH_2 and CH_3 protons is characteristic of these groups of atoms and signals the chemist that they are present in the molecule.

field; they are called **diamagnetic**. Therefore, by determining the magnetic behavior of a substance (see Figure 16.8) we can gain information on the electronic structure.

In summary, *paramagnetism is the attraction to a magnetic field of substances in which the constituent ions or atoms contain unpaired electrons.* Substances in which all electrons are paired with partners of opposite spin are diamagnetic. This explanation opens the way to understanding the arrangement of electrons in atoms with more than one electron.

Chemistry ⚛ Now™

Sign in at **www.cengage.com/login** and go to Chapter 6 Contents to see:
- Screen 6.15 for a self-study module on **electron spin**
- Screen 6.16 for an exercise on **spinning electrons and magnetism**

Chapter Goals Revisited

Now that you have studied this chapter, you should ask whether you have met the chapter goals. In particular, you should be able to:

Describe the properties of electromagnetic radiation

a. Use the terms wavelength, frequency, amplitude, and node (Section 6.1). Study Question(s) assignable in OWL: 3.

b. Use Equation 6.1 ($c = \lambda \nu$), relating wavelength (λ) and frequency (ν) of electromagnetic radiation and the speed of light (c).

c. Recognize the relative wavelength (or frequency) of the various types of electromagnetic radiation (Figure 6.2). Study Question(s) assignable in OWL: 1.

d. Understand that the energy of a photon, a massless particle of radiation, is proportional to its frequency (Planck's equation, Equation 6.2) (Section 6.2). Study Question(s) assignable in OWL: 5, 8, 9, 12, 14, 56, 57, 58, 63, 64, 66, 72, 73, 78, 83.

Understand the origin of light from excited atoms and its relationship to atomic structure

a. Describe the Bohr model of the atom, its ability to account for the emission line spectra of excited hydrogen atoms, and the limitations of the model (Section 6.3).

b. Understand that, in the Bohr model of the H atom, the electron can occupy only certain energy states, each with an energy proportional to $1/n^2$ ($E_n = -Rhc/n^2$), where n is the principal quantum number (Equation 6.4, Section 6.3). If an electron moves from one energy state to another, the amount of energy absorbed or emitted in the process is equal to the difference in energy between the two states (Equation 6.5, Section 6.3). Study Question(s) assignable in OWL: 16, 18, 22, 60.

Describe the experimental evidence for particle-wave duality

a. Understand that in the modern view of the atom, electrons can be described either as particles or as waves (Section 6.4). The wavelength of an electron or any subatomic particle is given by de Broglie's equation (Equation 6.6). Study Question(s) assignable in OWL: 24, 26, 47.

Chemistry ⚛ Now™ Sign in at **www.cengage.com/login** to:
- Assess your understanding with Study Questions in OWL keyed to each goal in the Goals and Homework menu for this chapter
- For quick review, download Go Chemistry mini-lecture flashcard modules (or purchase them at **www.ichapters.com**)
- Check your readiness for an exam by taking the Pre-Test and exploring the modules recommended in your Personalized Study plan.

❓ Access **How Do I Solve It?** tutorials on how to approach problem solving using concepts in this chapter.

For additional preparation for an examination on this chapter see the *Let's Review* section on pages 496–513.

Describe the basic ideas of quantum mechanics

a. Recognize the significance of quantum mechanics in describing atomic structure (Section 6.5).

b. Understand that an orbital for an electron in an atom corresponds to the allowed energy of that electron.

c. Understand that the position of the electron is not known with certainty; only the probability of the electron being at a given point of space can be calculated. This is a consequence of the Heisenberg uncertainty principle.

Define the four quantum numbers (n, ℓ, m_ℓ, and m_s), and recognize their relationship to electronic structure

a. Describe the allowed energy states of the orbitals in an atom using three quantum numbers n, ℓ, and m_ℓ (Section 6.5). Study Question(s) assignable in OWL: 28, 30, 32, 34, 36, 37, 38, 40, 43, 44, 80, 83.

b. Describe the shapes of the orbitals (Section 6.6). Study Question(s) assignable in OWL: 46, 51, 53, 67f.

c. Recognize the spin quantum number, m_s, which has values of $\pm\frac{1}{2}$. Classify substances as paramagnetic (attracted to a magnetic field; characterized by unpaired electron spins) or diamagnetic (repelled by a magnetic field, all electrons paired) (Section 6.7).

KEY EQUATIONS

Equation 6.1 (page 269)   The product of the wavelength (λ) and frequency (ν) of electromagnetic radiation is equal to the speed of light (c).

$$c = \lambda \times \nu$$

Equation 6.2 (page 273)   Planck's equation: the energy of a photon, a massless particle of radiation, is proportional to its frequency (ν). The proportionality constant, h, is called Planck's constant (6.626×10^{-34} J · s).

$$E = h\nu$$

Equation 6.4 (page 277)   In Bohr's theory, the potential energy of the electron, E_n, in the nth quantum level of the H atom is proportional to $1/n^2$, where n is a positive integer (the principal quantum number and $Rhc = 2.179 \times 10^{-18}$ J/atom or $N_A Rhc = 1312$ kJ/mol).

$$E_n = -\frac{Rhc}{n^2}$$

Equation 6.5 (page 279)   The energy change for an electron moving between two quantum levels (n_{final} and $n_{initial}$) in the H atom.

$$\Delta E = E_{final} - E_{initial} = -Rhc \left(\frac{1}{n_{final}^2} - \frac{1}{n_{initial}^2} \right)$$

Equation 6.6 (page 282)   De Broglie's equation: the wavelength of a particle (λ) is related to its mass (m) and speed (v) and to Planck's constant (h).

$$\lambda = \frac{h}{mv}$$

STUDY QUESTIONS

OWL Online homework for this chapter may be assigned in OWL.

▲ denotes challenging questions.

■ denotes questions assignable in OWL.

Blue-numbered questions have answers in Appendix O and fully-worked solutions in the *Student Solutions Manual*.

Practicing Skills

Electromagnetic Radiation

(See Example 6.1, Exercise 6.1, Figure 6.2, and ChemistryNow Screen 6.3.)

1. ■ Answer the following questions based on Figure 6.2:
   (a) Which type of radiation involves less energy, x-rays or microwaves?
   (b) Which radiation has the higher frequency, radar or red light?
   (c) Which radiation has the longer wavelength, ultraviolet or infrared light?

2. Consider the colors of the visible spectrum.
   (a) Which colors of light involve less energy than green light?
   (b) Which color of light has photons of greater energy, yellow or blue?
   (c) Which color of light has the greater frequency, blue or green?

3. ■ Traffic signals are often now made of LEDs (light-emitting diodes). Amber and green ones are pictured here.
   (a) The light from an amber signal has a wavelength of 595 nm, and that from a green signal has wavelength of 500 nm. Which has the higher frequency?
   (b) Calculate the frequency of amber light.

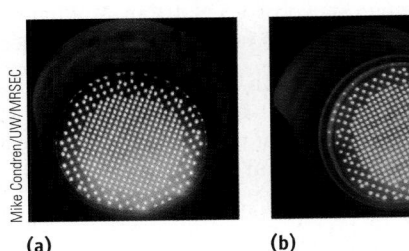

(a)   (b)

4. Suppose you are standing 225 m from a radio transmitter. What is your distance from the transmitter in terms of the number of wavelengths if:
   (a) the station is broadcasting at 1150 kHz (on the AM radio band)? (1 kHz = 1 × 10³ Hz.)
   (b) the station is broadcasting at 98.1 MHz (on the FM radio band)? (1 MHz = 10⁶ Hz.)

Electromagnetic Radiation and Planck's Equation

(See page 274, Exercise 6.2, and ChemistryNow Screens 6.4 and 6.5.)

5. ■ Green light has a wavelength of 5.0×10^2 nm. What is the energy, in joules, of one photon of green light? What is the energy, in joules, of 1.0 mol of photons of green light?

6. Violet light has a wavelength of about 410 nm. What is its frequency? Calculate the energy of one photon of violet light. What is the energy of 1.0 mol of violet photons? Compare the energy of photons of violet light with those of red light. Which is more energetic?

7. The most prominent line in the spectrum of aluminum is at 396.15 nm. What is the frequency of this line? What is the energy of one photon with this wavelength? Of 1.00 mol of these photons?

8. ■ The most prominent line in the spectrum of magnesium is 285.2 nm. Other lines are found at 383.8 and 518.4 nm. In what region of the electromagnetic spectrum are these lines found? Which is the most energetic line? What is the energy of 1.00 mol of photons with the wavelength of the most energetic line?

9. ■ Place the following types of radiation in order of increasing energy per photon:
   (a) yellow light from a sodium lamp
   (b) x-rays from an instrument in a dentist's office
   (c) microwaves in a microwave oven
   (d) your favorite FM music station at 91.7 MHz

10. Place the following types of radiation in order of increasing energy per photon:
    (a) radiation within a microwave oven
    (b) your favorite radio station
    (c) gamma rays from a nuclear reaction
    (d) red light from a neon sign
    (e) ultraviolet radiation from a sun lamp

Photoelectric Effect

(See page 274 and Figure 6.4.)

11. An energy of 2.0×10^2 kJ/mol is required to cause a cesium atom on a metal surface to lose an electron. Calculate the longest possible wavelength of light that can ionize a cesium atom. In what region of the electromagnetic spectrum is this radiation found?

12. ■ You are an engineer designing a switch that works by the photoelectric effect. The metal you wish to use in your device requires 6.7×10^{-19} J/atom to remove an electron. Will the switch work if the light falling on the metal has a wavelength of 540 nm or greater? Why or why not?

Atomic Spectra and the Bohr Atom
(See Examples 6.2 and 6.3, Figures 6.6–6.10, and ChemistryNow Screens 6.6 and 6.7.)

13. The most prominent line in the spectrum of mercury is at 253.652 nm. Other lines are located at 365.015 nm, 404.656 nm, 435.833 nm, and 1013.975 nm.
    (a) Which of these lines represents the most energetic light?
    (b) What is the frequency of the most prominent line? What is the energy of one photon with this wavelength?
    (c) Are any of these lines found in the spectrum of mercury shown in Figure 6.7? What color or colors are these lines?

14. ■ The most prominent line in the spectrum of neon is found at 865.438 nm. Other lines are located at 837.761 nm, 878.062 nm, 878.375 nm, and 1885.387 nm.
    (a) In what region of the electromagnetic spectrum are these lines found?
    (b) Are any of these lines found in the spectrum of neon shown in Figure 6.7?
    (c) Which of these lines represents the most energetic radiation?
    (d) What is the frequency of the most prominent line? What is the energy of one photon with this wavelength?

15. A line in the Balmer series of emission lines of excited H atoms has a wavelength of 410.2 nm (Figure 6.10). What color is the light emitted in this transition? What quantum levels are involved in this emission line? That is, what are the values of $n_{initial}$ and n_{final}?

16. ■ What are the wavelength and frequency of the radiation involved in the least energetic emission line in the Lyman series? What are the values of $n_{initial}$ and n_{final}?

17. Consider only transitions involving the $n = 1$ through $n = 5$ energy levels for the H atom (See Figures 6.8 and 6.10).
    (a) How many emission lines are possible, considering only the five quantum levels?
    (b) Photons of the highest frequency are emitted in a transition from the level with $n = $ ____ to a level with $n = $ ____.
    (c) The emission line having the longest wavelength corresponds to a transition from the level with $n = $ ____ to the level with $n = $ ____.

18. ■ Consider only transitions involving the $n = 1$ through $n = 4$ energy levels for the hydrogen atom (See Figures 6.8 and 6.10).
    (a) How many emission lines are possible, considering only the four quantum levels?
    (b) Photons of the lowest energy are emitted in a transition from the level with $n = $ ____ to a level with $n = $ ____.

    (c) The emission line having the shortest wavelength corresponds to a transition from the level with $n = $ ____ to the level with $n = $ ____.

19. The energy emitted when an electron moves from a higher energy state to a lower energy state in any atom can be observed as electromagnetic radiation.
    (a) Which involves the emission of less energy in the H atom, an electron moving from $n = 4$ to $n = 2$ or an electron moving from $n = 3$ to $n = 2$?
    (b) Which involves the emission of more energy in the H atom, an electron moving from $n = 4$ to $n = 1$ or an electron moving from $n = 5$ to $n = 2$? Explain fully.

20. If energy is absorbed by a hydrogen atom in its ground state, the atom is excited to a higher energy state. For example, the excitation of an electron from the level with $n = 1$ to the level with $n = 3$ requires radiation with a wavelength of 102.6 nm. Which of the following transitions would require radiation of *longer wavelength* than this?
    (a) $n = 2$ to $n = 4$ (c) $n = 1$ to $n = 5$
    (b) $n = 1$ to $n = 4$ (d) $n = 3$ to $n = 5$

21. Calculate the wavelength and frequency of light emitted when an electron changes from $n = 3$ to $n = 1$ in the H atom. In what region of the spectrum is this radiation found?

22. ■ Calculate the wavelength and frequency of light emitted when an electron changes from $n = 4$ to $n = 3$ in the H atom. In what region of the spectrum is this radiation found?

DeBroglie and Matter Waves
(See Example 6.4 and ChemistryNow Screen 6.8.)

23. An electron moves with a velocity of 2.5×10^8 cm/s. What is its wavelength?

24. ■ A beam of electrons ($m = 9.11 \times 10^{-31}$ kg/electron) has an average speed of 1.3×10^8 m/s. What is the wavelength of electrons having this average speed?

25. Calculate the wavelength, in nanometers, associated with a 1.0×10^2-g golf ball moving at 30. m/s (about 67 mph). How fast must the ball travel to have a wavelength of 5.6×10^{-3} nm?

26. ■ A rifle bullet (mass = 1.50 g) has a velocity of 7.00×10^2 mph (miles per hour). What is the wavelength associated with this bullet?

Quantum Mechanics
(See Sections 6.5–6.7 and ChemistryNow Screens 6.9–6.14.)

27. (a) When $n = 4$, what are the possible values of ℓ?
    (b) When ℓ is 2, what are the possible values of m_ℓ?
    (c) For a 4s orbital, what are the possible values of n, ℓ, and m_ℓ?
    (d) For a 4f orbital, what are the possible values of n, ℓ, and m_ℓ?

▲ more challenging   ■ in OWL   Blue-numbered questions answered in Appendix O

28. ■ (a) When $n = 4$, $\ell = 2$, and $m_\ell = -1$, to what orbital type does this refer? (Give the orbital label, such as $1s$.)

(b) How many orbitals occur in the $n = 5$ electron shell? How many subshells? What are the letter labels of the subshells?

(c) If a subshell is labeled f, how many orbitals occur in the subshell? What are the values of m_ℓ?

29. A possible excited state of the H atom has the electron in a $4p$ orbital. List all possible sets of quantum numbers n, ℓ, and m_ℓ for this electron.

30. ■ A possible excited state for the H atom has an electron in a $5d$ orbital. List all possible sets of quantum numbers n, ℓ, and m_ℓ for this electron.

31. How many subshells occur in the electron shell with the principal quantum number $n = 4$?

32. ■ How many subshells occur in the electron shell with the principal quantum number $n = 5$?

33. Explain briefly why each of the following is not a possible set of quantum numbers for an electron in an atom.

(a) $n = 2$, $\ell = 2$, $m_\ell = 0$
(b) $n = 3$, $\ell = 0$, $m_\ell = -2$
(c) $n = 6$, $\ell = 0$, $m_\ell = 1$

34. ■ Which of the following represent valid sets of quantum numbers? For a set that is invalid, explain briefly why it is not correct.

(a) $n = 3$, $\ell = 3$, $m_\ell = 0$ (c) $n = 6$, $\ell = 5$, $m_\ell = -1$
(b) $n = 2$, $\ell = 1$, $m_\ell = 0$ (d) $n = 4$, $\ell = 3$, $m_\ell = -4$

35. ■ What is the maximum number of orbitals that can be identified by each of the following sets of quantum numbers? When "none" is the correct answer, explain your reasoning.

(a) $n = 3$, $\ell = 0$, $m_\ell = +1$ (c) $n = 7$, $\ell = 5$
(b) $n = 5$, $\ell = 1$ (d) $n = 4$, $\ell = 2$, $m_\ell = -2$

36. ■ What is the maximum number of orbitals that can be identified by each of the following sets of quantum numbers? When "none" is the correct answer, explain your reasoning.

(a) $n = 4$, $\ell = 3$ (c) $n = 2$, $\ell = 2$
(b) $n = 5$ (d) $n = 3$, $\ell = 1$, $m_\ell = -1$

37. ■ Explain briefly why each of the following is not a possible set of quantum numbers for an electron in an atom. In each case, change the incorrect value (or values) to make the set valid.

(a) $n = 4$, $\ell = 2$, $m_\ell = 0$, $m_s = 0$

(b) $n = 3$, $\ell = 1$, $m_\ell = -3$, $m_s = -\frac{1}{2}$

(c) $n = 3$, $\ell = 3$, $m_\ell = -1$, $m_s = +\frac{1}{2}$

38. Explain briefly why each of the following is not a possible set of quantum numbers for an electron in an atom. In each case, change the incorrect value (or values) to make the set valid.

(a) $n = 2$, $\ell = 2$, $m_\ell = 0$, $m_s = +\frac{1}{2}$

(b) $n = 2$, $\ell = 1$, $m_\ell = -1$, $m_s = 0$

(c) $n = 3$, $\ell = 1$, $m_\ell = +2$, $m_s = +\frac{1}{2}$

39. State which of the following orbitals cannot exist according to the quantum theory: $2s$, $2d$, $3p$, $3f$, $4f$, and $5s$. Briefly explain your answers.

40. ■ State which of the following are incorrect designations for orbitals according to the quantum theory: $3p$, $4s$, $2f$, and $1p$. Briefly explain your answers.

41. Write a complete set of quantum numbers (n, ℓ, and m_ℓ) that quantum theory allows for each of the following orbitals: (a) $2p$, (b) $3d$, and (c) $4f$.

42. ■ Write a complete set of quantum numbers (n, ℓ, and m_ℓ) for each of the following orbitals: (a) $5f$, (b) $4d$, and (c) $2s$.

43. ■ A particular orbital has $n = 4$ and $\ell = 2$. What must this orbital be: (a) $3p$, (b) $4p$, (c) $5d$, or (d) $4d$?

44. ■ A given orbital has a magnetic quantum number of $m_\ell = -1$. This could *not* be a (an)

(a) f orbital   (c) p orbital
(b) d orbital   (d) s orbital

45. How many planar nodes are associated with each of the following orbitals?

(a) $2s$ (b) $5d$ (c) $5f$

46. ■ How many planar nodes are associated with each of the following atomic orbitals?

(a) $4f$ (b) $2p$ (c) $6s$

General Questions on Atomic Structure

These questions are not designated as to type or location in the chapter. They may combine several concepts.

47. ■ Which of the following are applicable when explaining the photoelectric effect? Correct any statements that are wrong.

(a) Light is electromagnetic radiation.
(b) The intensity of a light beam is related to its frequency.
(c) Light can be thought of as consisting of massless particles whose energy is given by Planck's equation, $E = h\nu$

48. In what region of the electromagnetic spectrum for hydrogen is the Lyman series of lines found? The Balmer series?

49. Give the number of nodal surfaces through the nucleus (planar nodes) for each orbital type: s, p, d, and f.

50. What is the maximum number of s orbitals found in a given electron shell? The maximum number of p orbitals? Of d orbitals? Of f orbitals?

51. ■ Match the values of ℓ shown in the table with orbital type (s, p, d, or f).

ℓ Value	Orbital Type
3	_____
0	_____
1	_____
2	_____

52. Sketch a picture of the 90% boundary surface of an s orbital and the p_x orbital. Be sure the latter drawing shows why the p orbital is labeled p_x and not p_y, for example.

53. ■ Complete the following table.

Orbital Type	Number of Orbitals in a Given Subshell	Number of Nodal Surfaces through the Nucleus
s	_____	_____
p	_____	_____
d	_____	_____
f	_____	_____

54. Excited H atoms have many emission lines. One series of lines, called the Pfund series, occurs in the infrared region. It results when an electron changes from higher energy levels to a level with $n = 5$. Calculate the wavelength and frequency of the lowest energy line of this series.

55. An advertising sign gives off red light and green light.
(a) Which light has the higher-energy photons?
(b) One of the colors has a wavelength of 680 nm, and the other has a wavelength of 500 nm. Which color has which wavelength?
(c) Which light has the higher frequency?

56. ■ Radiation in the ultraviolet region of the electromagnetic spectrum is quite energetic. It is this radiation that causes dyes to fade and your skin to develop a sunburn. If you are bombarded with 1.00 mol of photons with a wavelength of 375 nm, what amount of energy, in kilojoules per mole of photons, are you being subjected to?

57. ■ A cell phone sends signals at about 850 MHz (1 MHz = 1×10^6 Hz or cycles per second).
(a) What is the wavelength of this radiation?
(b) What is the energy of 1.0 mol of photons with a frequency of 850 MHz?
(c) Compare the energy in part (b) with the energy of a mole of photons of blue light (420 nm).
(d) Comment on the difference in energy between 850 MHz radiation and blue light.

58. ■ Assume your eyes receive a signal consisting of blue light, $\lambda = 470$ nm. The energy of the signal is 2.50×10^{-14} J. How many photons reach your eyes?

59. If sufficient energy is absorbed by an atom, an electron can be lost by the atom and a positive ion formed. The amount of energy required is called the ionization energy. In the H atom, the ionization energy is that required to change the electron from $n = 1$ to $n = $ infinity. (See Exercise 6.5, page 280.) Calculate the ionization energy for the He$^+$ ion. Is the ionization energy of the He$^+$ more or less than that of H? (Bohr's theory applies to He$^+$ because it, like the H atom, has a single electron. The electron energy, however, is now given by $E = -Z^2 Rhc/n^2$, where Z is the atomic number of helium.)

60. ■ Suppose hydrogen atoms absorb energy so that electrons are excited to the $n = 7$ energy level. Electrons then undergo these transitions, among others: (a) $n = 7 \rightarrow n = 1$; (b) $n = 7 \rightarrow n = 6$; and (c) $n = 2 \rightarrow n = 1$. Which transition produces a photon with (i) the smallest energy, (ii) the highest frequency, and (iii) the shortest wavelength?

61. Rank the following orbitals in the H atom in order of increasing energy: $3s$, $2s$, $2p$, $4s$, $3p$, $1s$, and $3d$.

62. ■ How many orbitals correspond to each of the following designations?
(a) $3p$ (d) $6d$ (g) $n = 5$
(b) $4p$ (e) $5d$ (h) $7s$
(c) $4p_x$ (f) $5f$

63. ■ Cobalt-60 is a radioactive isotope used in medicine for the treatment of certain cancers. It produces β particles and γ rays, the latter having energies of 1.173 and 1.332 MeV. (1 MeV = 10^6 electron-volts and 1 eV = 9.6485×10^4 J/mol.) What are the wavelength and frequency of a γ-ray photon with an energy of 1.173 MeV?

64. ▲ ■ Exposure to high doses of microwaves can cause tissue damage. Estimate how many photons, with $\lambda = 12$ cm, must be absorbed to raise the temperature of your eye by 3.0 °C. Assume the mass of an eye is 11 g and its specific heat capacity is 4.0 J/g · K.

65. When the Sojourner spacecraft landed on Mars in 1997, the planet was approximately 7.8×10^7 km from Earth. How long did it take for the television picture signal to reach Earth from Mars?

66. ■ The most prominent line in the emission spectrum of chromium is found at 425.4 nm. Other lines in the chromium spectrum are found at 357.9 nm, 359.3 nm, 360.5 nm, 427.5 nm, 429.0 nm, and 520.8 nm.
(a) Which of these lines represents the most energetic light?
(b) What color is light of wavelength 425.4 nm?

67. Answer the following questions as a summary quiz on the chapter.
    (a) The quantum number n describes the _____ of an atomic orbital.
    (b) The shape of an atomic orbital is given by the quantum number _____.
    (c) A photon of green light has _____ (less or more) energy than a photon of orange light.
    (d) The maximum number of orbitals that may be associated with the set of quantum numbers $n = 4$ and $\ell = 3$ is _____.
    (e) The maximum number of orbitals that may be associated with the quantum number set $n = 3$, $\ell = 2$, and $m_\ell = -2$ is _____.
    (f) ■ Label each of the following orbital pictures with the appropriate letter:

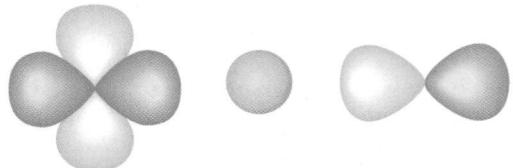

    (g) When $n = 5$, the possible values of ℓ are _____.
    (h) The number of orbitals in the $n = 4$ shell is _____.
    (i) A Co^{2+} ion has three unpaired electrons. A sample of $CoCl_2$ is (paramagnetic)(diamagnetic).

68. Answer the following questions as a summary quiz on this chapter.
    (a) The quantum number n describes the _____ of an atomic orbital, and the quantum number ℓ describes its _____.
    (b) When $n = 3$, the possible values of ℓ are _____.
    (c) What type of orbital corresponds to $\ell = 3$? _____
    (d) For a $4d$ orbital, the value of n is _____, the value of ℓ is _____, and a possible value of m_ℓ is _____.
    (e) Each of the following drawings represents a type of atomic orbital. Give the letter designation for the orbital; give its value of ℓ, and specify the number of nodal surfaces.

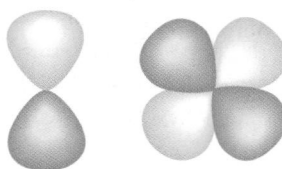

    Letter =   _____   _____
    ℓ value =   _____   _____
    Planar nodes =   _____   _____
    (f) An atomic orbital with three nodal surfaces through the nucleus is _____.
    (g) Which of the following orbitals cannot exist according to modern quantum theory: $2s$, $3p$, $2d$, $3f$, $5p$, $6p$?

(h) Which of the following is not a valid set of quantum numbers?

n	ℓ	m_ℓ	m_s
3	2	1	$-\frac{1}{2}$
2	1	2	$+\frac{1}{2}$
4	3	0	0

(i) What is the maximum number of orbitals that can be associated with each of the following sets of quantum numbers? (One possible answer is "none.")
    (i) $n = 2$ and $\ell = 1$
    (ii) $n = 3$
    (iii) $n = 3$ and $\ell = 3$
    (iv) $n = 2$, $\ell = 1$, and $m_\ell = 0$
(j) A Cu^{2+} ion has one unpaired electron. Is a sample of $CuBr_2$ paramagnetic or diamagnetic?

69. The diagrams below represent a small section of a solid. Each circle represents an atom, and an arrow represents an electron.

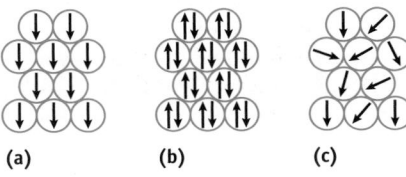

(a) Which represents a diamagnetic solid, which a paramagnetic solid, and which a ferromagnetic solid?
(b) Which is most strongly attracted to a magnetic field? Which is least strongly attracted?

In the Laboratory

70. A solution of $KMnO_4$ absorbs light at 540 nm (page 192). What is the frequency of the light absorbed? What is the energy of one mole of photons with $\lambda = 540$ nm?

71. A large pickle is attached to two electrodes, which are then attached to a 110-V power supply (see the problem on Screen 6.7 of ChemistryNow). As the voltage is increased across the pickle, it begins to glow with a yellow color. Knowing that pickles are made by soaking the vegetable in a concentrated salt solution, describe why the pickle might emit light when electrical energy is added.

Charles D. Winters

The "electric pickle."

72. ■ The spectrum shown here is for aspirin. The vertical axis is the amount of light absorbed, and the horizontal axis is the wavelength of incident light (in nm).

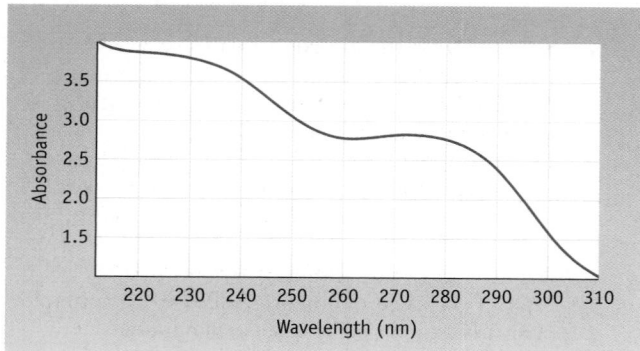

What is the frequency of light with a wavelength of 278 nm? What is the energy of one mole of photons with $\lambda = 278$ nm? What region of the electromagnetic spectrum is covered by the spectrum above? Knowing that aspirin only absorbs light in the region depicted by this spectrum, what is the color of aspirin?

73. ■ The infrared spectrum for methanol, CH_3OH, is illustrated below. It shows the amount of light in the infrared region that methanol transmits as a function of wavelength. The vertical axis is the amount of light transmitted. At points near the top of the graph, most of the incident light is being transmitted by the sample (or, conversely, little light is absorbed.) Therefore, the "peaks" or "bands" that descend from the top indicate light absorbed; the longer the band, the more light is being absorbed (or, conversely, the less is being transmitted). The horizontal scale is in units of "wavenumbers," abbreviated cm^{-1}. The energy of light is given by Planck's law as $E = hc/\lambda$; that is, E is proportional to $1/\lambda$. Therefore, the horizontal scale is in units of $1/\lambda$ and reflects the energy of the light incident on the sample.

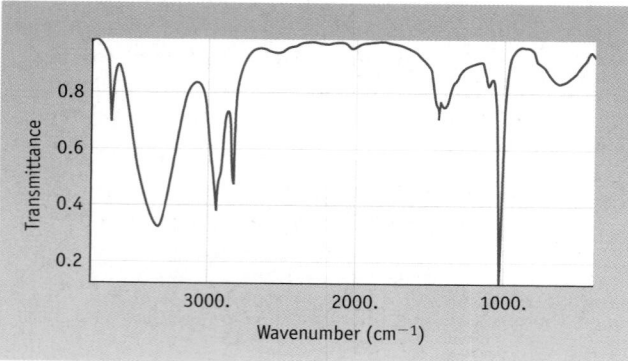

(a) One point on the horizontal axis is marked as 2000 cm^{-1}. What is the wavelength of light at this point?
(b) Which is the low energy end of this spectrum (left or right), and which is the high energy end?
(c) The broad absorption at about 3300–3400 cm^{-1} indicates that infrared radiation is interacting with the OH group of the methanol molecule. The narrower absorptions around 2800–3000 cm^{-1} are for interactions with C—H bonds. Which interaction requires more energy, with O—H or with C—H?

Summary and Conceptual Questions

The following questions use concepts from this and previous chapters.

74. Bohr pictured the electrons of the atom as being located in definite orbits about the nucleus, just as the planets orbit the sun. Criticize this model.

75. Light is given off by a sodium- or mercury-containing streetlight when the atoms are excited. The light you see arises for which of the following reasons?
(a) Electrons are moving from a given energy level to one of higher energy.
(b) Electrons are being removed from the atom, thereby creating a metal cation.
(c) Electrons are moving from a given energy level to one of lower energy.

76. How do we interpret the physical meaning of the square of the wave function? What are the units of $4\pi r^2\psi^2$?

77. What does "wave–particle duality" mean? What are its implications in our modern view of atomic structure?

78. ■ Which of these are observable?
(a) position of an electron in an H atom
(b) frequency of radiation emitted by H atoms
(c) path of an electron in an H atom
(d) wave motion of electrons
(e) diffraction patterns produced by electrons
(f) diffraction patterns produced by light
(g) energy required to remove electrons from H atoms
(h) an atom
(i) a molecule
(j) a water wave

79. In principle, which of the following can be determined?
(a) the energy of an electron in the H atom with high precision and accuracy
(b) the position of a high-speed electron with high precision and accuracy
(c) at the same time, both the position and the energy of a high-speed electron with high precision and accuracy

▲ more challenging   ■ in OWL   Blue-numbered questions answered in Appendix O

80. ▲ ■ Suppose you live in a different universe where a different set of quantum numbers is required to describe the atoms of that universe. These quantum numbers have the following rules:

N, principal	1, 2, 3, . . . , ∞
L, orbital	$= N$
M, magnetic	$-1, 0, +1$

How many orbitals are there altogether in the first three electron shells?

81. A photon with a wavelength of 93.8 nm strikes a hydrogen atom, and light is emitted by the atom. How many emission lines would be observed? At what wavelengths? Explain briefly (see Figure 6.10).

82. Explain why you could or could not measure the wavelength of a golf ball in flight.

83. ■ The radioactive element technetium is not found naturally on earth; it must be synthesized in the laboratory. It is a valuable element, however, because it has medical uses. For example, the element in the form of sodium pertechnetate ($NaTcO_4$) is used in imaging studies of the brain, thyroid, and salivary glands and in renal blood flow studies, among other things.
    (a) In what group and period of the periodic table is the element found?
    (b) The valence electrons of technetium are found in the $5s$ and $4d$ subshells. What is a set of quantum numbers (n, ℓ, and m_ℓ) for one of the electrons of the $5s$ subshell?
    (c) ■ Technetium emits a γ-ray with an energy of 0.141 MeV. (1 MeV = 10^6 electron-volts, where 1 eV = 9.6485×10^4 J/mol.) What are the wavelength and frequency of a γ-ray photon with an energy of 0.141 MeV?
    (d) To make $NaTcO_4$, the metal is dissolved in nitric acid.

    $$7\ HNO_3(aq)\ +\ Tc(s) \rightarrow$$
    $$HTcO_4(aq)\ +\ 7\ NO_2(g)\ +\ 3\ H_2O(\ell)$$

    and the product, $HTcO_4$, is treated with NaOH to make $NaTcO_4$.
    (i) Write a balanced equation for the reaction of $HTcO_4$ with NaOH.
    (ii) If you begin with 4.5 mg of Tc metal, how much $NaTcO_4$ can be made? What mass of NaOH, in grams, is required to convert all of the $HTcO_4$ into $NaTcO_4$?
    (e) If you synthesize 1.5 micromoles of $NaTcO_4$, what mass of compound do you have? If the compound is dissolved in 10.0 mL of solution, what is the concentration?

84. See ChemistryNow Screen 6.1, Chemical Puzzler. This screen shows that light of different colors can come from a "neon" sign or from certain salts when they are placed in a burning organic liquid. ("Neon" signs are glass tubes filled with neon, argon, and other gases, and the gases are excited by an electric current.) What do these two sources of light have in common? How is the light generated in each case?

85. See ChemistryNow Screen 6.7, Bohr's Model of the Hydrogen Atom, Simulation. A photon with a wavelength of 97.3 nm is fired at a hydrogen atom and leads to the emission of light. How many emission lines are emitted? Explain why more than one line is emitted.

7 | The Structure of Atoms and Periodic Trends

Charles D. Winters

The Chromium-Bearing Mineral Crocoite, $PbCrO_4$

Minerals containing the chromate ion are extremely rare. The best example is crocoite, lead(II) chromate, which is found almost exclusively in Tasmania. Although it is nearly insoluble in water, traces will nonetheless dissolve and contaminate groundwater with Pb^{2+} and CrO_4^{2-} ions.

Chromium compounds in groundwater can be a problem. In the United States, 56% of the population relies on groundwater for drinking water, and the shallow aquifers from which the water is often obtained are susceptible to contamination. One such contaminant is chromium in its various ionic forms (Cr^{3+}, CrO_4^{2-}, and $Cr_2O_7^{2-}$). The source of such ions can be mineral deposits, but more significant sources are industries involved in leather tanning [which uses $Cr(OH)SO_4$] or electroplating of chromium for corrosion protection. In a case depicted in the movie *Erin Brockovich*, a gas and electric utility was found to have contaminated groundwater in southern California with chromates that had been used in water-cooling towers to prevent rust.

Chromium compounds can also be biochemically active, although they are not implicated in as many important processes as another element in Group 6B, molybdenum. There is some evidence that chromium is one of the essential elements, and it is implicated in insulin regulation. In fact, the recommended daily dose of chromium is 5–200 μg. A compound called chromium(III) picolinate is marketed as a "nutritional" supplement and is widely used as a weight-loss aid. The majority of research has found, however, that it is neither helpful nor beneficial in weight-loss programs.

Questions:

1. What is the electron configuration for the Cr atom, for the Cr^{3+} ion, and for the chromium in the CrO_4^{2-} ion?
2. Is chromium in any of the ionic forms paramagnetic?
3. What is the electron configuration for the lead ions in $PbCrO_4$?

Answers to these questions are in Appendix Q.

The wave mechanical model of the atom has spinning electrons assigned to orbitals that are best described as matter waves. The orbitals are arranged in subshells that are in turn part of electron shells. One objective of this chapter is to apply this model to the electronic structure of all of the elements.

A second objective is to explore some of the physical properties of elements, among them the ease with which atoms lose or gain electrons to form ions and the sizes of atoms and ions. These properties are directly related to the arrangement of electrons in atoms and thus to the chemistry of the elements and their compounds.

Chemistry.Now™

Throughout the text this icon introduces an opportunity for self-study or to explore interactive tutorials by signing in at **www.cengage.com/login**.

7.1 The Pauli Exclusion Principle

To make the quantum theory consistent with experiment, the Austrian physicist Wolfgang Pauli (1900–1958) stated in 1925 his **exclusion principle:** no two electrons in an atom can have the same set of four quantum numbers (n, ℓ, m_ℓ, and m_s). The consequence of this is that *no atomic orbital can be assigned more than two electrons,* and the two electrons assigned to an orbital must have different values of m_s.

An electron assigned to the $1s$ orbital of the H atom may have the set of quantum numbers $n = 1$, $\ell = 0$, and $m_\ell = 0$, and $m_s = +\frac{1}{2}$. Let us represent an orbital by a box and the electron spin by an arrow ($\uparrow$ or $\downarrow$). A representation of the hydrogen atom is then:

■ **Orbitals Are Not Boxes** Orbitals are not boxes in which electrons are placed. Thus, it is not conceptually correct to talk about electrons being in orbitals or occupying orbitals, although this is commonly done for the sake of simplicity.

Electrons in 1s orbital: $\boxed{\uparrow}$ Quantum number set

$1s$ $n = 1$, $\ell = 0$, $m_\ell = 0$, $m_s = +\frac{1}{2}$

The choice of m_s (either $+\frac{1}{2}$ or $-\frac{1}{2}$) and the direction of the electron spin arrow are arbitrary; that is, we could choose either value, and the arrow may point in either direction. Diagrams such as these are called **orbital box diagrams.**

A *helium* atom has two electrons, both assigned to the $1s$ orbital. The Pauli exclusion principle requires that each electron must have a different set of quantum numbers, so the orbital box diagram now is:

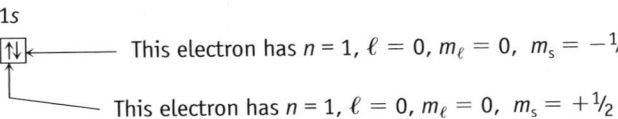

Two electrons in 1s orbital: $1s$ $\boxed{\uparrow\downarrow}$ — This electron has $n = 1$, $\ell = 0$, $m_\ell = 0$, $m_s = -\frac{1}{2}$

— This electron has $n = 1$, $\ell = 0$, $m_\ell = 0$, $m_s = +\frac{1}{2}$

By having opposite spins, the two electrons in the $1s$ orbital of an He atom have different sets of the four quantum numbers.

TABLE 7.1   Number of Electrons Accommodated in Electron Shells and Subshells with $n = 1$ to 6

Electron Shell (n)	Subshells Available	Orbitals Available ($2\ell + 1$)	Number of Electrons Possible in Subshell $[2(2\ell + 1)]$	Maximum Electrons Possible for nth Shell ($2n^2$)
1	s	1	2	2
2	s	1	2	8
	p	3	6	
3	s	1	2	18
	p	3	6	
	d	5	10	
4	s	1	2	32
	p	3	6	
	d	5	10	
	f	7	14	
5	s	1	2	50
	p	3	6	
	d	5	10	
	f	7	14	
	g*	9	18	
6	s	1	2	72
	p	3	6	
	d	5	10	
	f*	7	14	
	g*	9	18	
	h*	11	22	

*These orbitals are not occupied in the ground state of any known element.

■ **Spin Quantum Number and Arrows**
In this book, we arbitrarily use an arrow pointing up (↑) to represent $m_s = +\frac{1}{2}$ and an arrow pointing down (↓) to represent $m_s = -\frac{1}{2}$. We will usually designate the first electron assigned to an orbital as having $m_s = +\frac{1}{2}$ though it could just as readily have $m_s = -\frac{1}{2}$.

Our understanding of orbitals and the knowledge that an orbital can accommodate no more than two electrons tell us the maximum number of electrons that can occupy each electron shell or subshell. For example, because each of the three orbitals in a p subshell can hold two electrons, p subshells can hold a maximum of six electrons. By the same reasoning, the five orbitals of a d subshell can accommodate a total of 10 electrons, and the seven f orbitals can accommodate 14 electrons. Recall that there are n subshells in the nth shell, and that there are n^2 orbitals in that shell (◀ Table 6.1, page 286). Thus, *the maximum number of electrons in any shell is $2n^2$*. The relationship among the quantum numbers and the numbers of electrons is shown in Table 7.1.

7.2 Atomic Subshell Energies and Electron Assignments

Our goal in this section is to understand and predict the orbital distribution of electrons in atoms with many electrons. The procedure by which electrons are assigned to orbitals is known as the *aufbau* principle (aufbau means "building up").

Electrons in an atom are assigned to shells (defined by the quantum number n) and subshells (defined by the quantum number ℓ) in order of increasingly higher energy. In this way, the total energy of the atom is as low as possible.

Order of Subshell Energies and Assignments

Quantum theory and the Bohr model state that the energy of the H atom, with a single electron, depends only on the value of n ($E_n = -Rhc/n^2$). For atoms with more than one electron, however, the situation is more complex. The order of subshell energies for $n = 1$, 2, and 3 in Figure 7.1 shows that subshell energies in multielectron atoms depend on *both n and ℓ*.

Based on theoretical and experimental studies of orbital electron distributions in atoms, chemists have found that there are two general rules that help predict these arrangements:

- Electrons are assigned to subshells in order of increasing "$n + \ell$" value.
- For two subshells with the same value of "$n + \ell$," electrons are assigned first to the subshell of lower n.

The following are examples of these rules:

- Electrons are assigned to the $2s$ subshell ($n + \ell = 2 + 0 = 2$) before the $2p$ subshell ($n + \ell = 2 + 1 = 3$).
- Electrons are assigned to $2p$ orbitals ($n + \ell = 2 + 1 = 3$) before the $3s$ subshell ($n + \ell = 3 + 0 = 3$) because n for the $2p$ electrons is less than for the $3s$ electrons.
- Electrons are assigned to $4s$ orbitals ($n + \ell = 4 + 0 = 4$) before the $3d$ subshell ($n + \ell = 3 + 2 = 5$) because $n + \ell$ is less for $4s$ than for $3d$.

Figure 7.2 summarizes the assignment of electrons according to increasing $n + \ell$ values, and the discussion that follows explores the underlying causes and their consequences and connects atomic electron configurations to the periodic table.

		n	ℓ	$n + \ell$
$3d$ — — — — —		3	2	5
$3p$ — — —		3	1	4
$3s$ — Same $n + \ell$, different n		3	0	3
$2p$ — — —		2	1	3
Same n, different ℓ				
$2s$ —		2	0	2
$1s$ —		1	0	1

Active Figure 7.1 **Order of subshell energies.** Energies of electron shells increase with increasing n, and, within a shell, subshell energies increase with increasing ℓ. (The energy axis is not to scale.) The energy gaps between subshells of a given shell become smaller as n increases.

Chemistry Now™ Sign in at www.cengage.com/login and go to the Chapter Contents menu to explore an interactive version of this figure accompanied by an exercise.

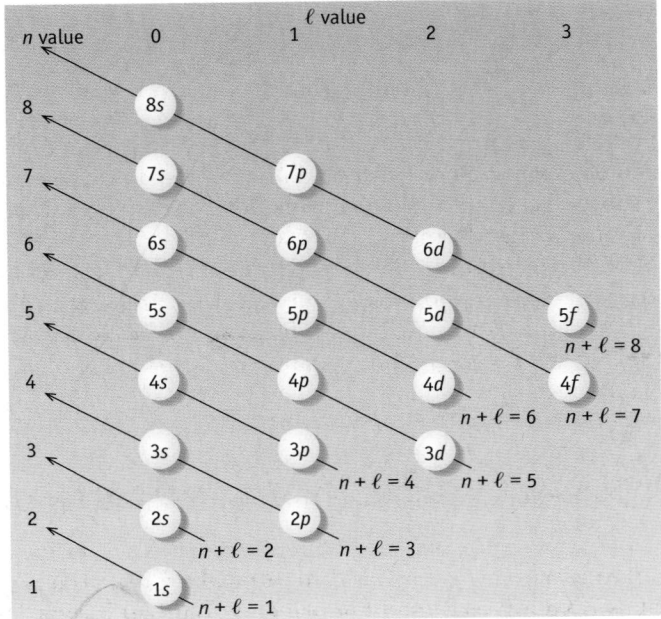

FIGURE 7.2 Subshell filling order. Subshells in atoms are filled in order of increasing $n + \ell$. When two subshells have the same $n + \ell$ value, the subshell of lower n is filled first. To use the diagram, begin at $1s$ and follow the arrows of increasing $n + \ell$. (Thus, the order of filling is $1s \Rightarrow 2s \Rightarrow 2p \Rightarrow 3s \Rightarrow 3p \Rightarrow 4s \Rightarrow 3d$ and so on.)

Effective Nuclear Charge, Z*

■ **More About Z*** For a more complete discussion of effective nuclear charge, see D. M. P. Mingos: *Essential Trends in Inorganic Chemistry*, New York, Oxford University Press, 1998.

The order in which electrons are assigned to subshells in an atom, and many atomic properties, can be rationalized by introducing the concept of **effective nuclear charge** **(Z*)**. This is the net charge experienced by a particular electron in a multielectron atom resulting from the nucleus and the other electrons. Knowing Z^* provides a convenient way to assess the attractive and repulsive forces on that electron by the nucleus and the other electrons and to assess the energy of that electron.

The surface density plot $(4\pi r^2\psi^2)$ for a 2s electron for lithium in plotted in Figure 7.3. (Lithium has three protons in the nucleus, two 1s electrons in the first shell, and a 2s electron in the second shell.) The probability of finding the 2s electron (recorded on the vertical axis) changes as one moves away from the nucleus (horizontal axis). Lightly shaded on this figure is the region in which the two 1s electrons have their highest probability. Observe that the 2s electron wave occurs partly within the region of space occupied by 1s electrons. Chemists say that the 2s orbital *penetrates* the region defining the 1s orbital.

At a large distance from the nucleus, the lithium 2s electron will experience a +1 charge, the net effect of the two 1s electrons (total charge = −2) and the nucleus (+3 charge.) The 1s electrons are said to *screen* the 2s electron from experiencing the full nuclear charge. However, this screening of the nuclear charge varies with the distance of the 2s electron from the nucleus. As the 2s electron wave penetrates the 1s electron region, it experiences an increasingly higher net positive charge. Very near the nucleus, the 1s electrons do not effectively screen the electron from the nucleus, and the 2s electron experiences a charge close to +3. Figure 7.3 shows that a 2s electron has some probability of being both inside and outside the

FIGURE 7.3 **Effective nuclear charge, Z*.** The two 1s electrons of lithium have their highest probability in the shaded region, but this region is penetrated by the 2s electron (whose approximate surface density plot is shown here). As the 2s electron penetrates the 1s region, however, the 2s electron experiences a larger and larger positive charge, to a maximum of +3. On average, the 2s electron experiences a charge, called the effective nuclear charge *(Z*)* that is smaller than +3 but greater than +1.

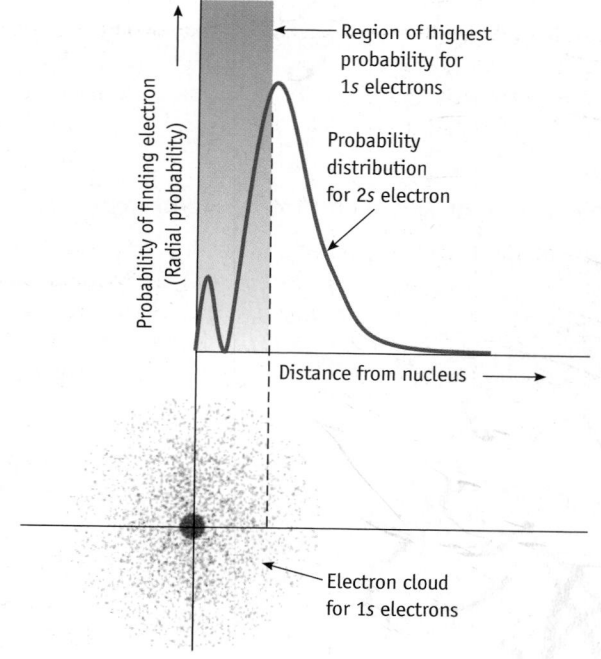

Region of highest probability for 1s electrons

Probability distribution for 2s electron

Probability of finding electron (Radial probability)

Distance from nucleus

Electron cloud for 1s electrons

region occupied by the $1s$ electrons. Thus, on average, a $2s$ electron experiences a positive charge greater than $+1$ but much smaller than $+3$. The *average* charge experienced by the electron is called the *effective nuclear charge* (Z^*).

In the hydrogen atom, with only one electron, the $2s$ and $2p$ subshells have the same energy. However, in atoms with two or more electrons, the energies of the $2s$ and $2p$ subshells are different. Why should this be true? It is observed that the relative extent to which an outer electron penetrates inner orbitals occurs in the order $s > p > d > f$. Thus, the effective nuclear charge experienced by electrons in a multielectron atom is in the order $ns > np > nd > nf$. The values of Z^* for s and p electrons for the second-period elements (Table 7.2) illustrate this. In each case, Z^* is greater for s electrons than for p electrons. In a given shell, s electrons always have a lower energy than p electrons; p electrons have a lower energy than d electrons, and d electrons have a lower energy than f electrons. A consequence of this is that subshells within an electron shell are filled in the order ns before np before nd before nf.

Table 7.2 also shows that for the second-period elements the value of Z^* for the higher energy electrons increases across the period. As you will see in Section 7.5, this effect is important in understanding trends in properties of elements across a period.

What emerges from this analysis is the order of shell and subshell energies for any given atom and the filling order in Figure 7.2. With this as background, we turn to the periodic table and use it as a guide to electron arrangements in atoms.

Chemistry ☐ Now™

Sign in at **www.cengage.com/login** and go to Chapter 7 Contents to see Screen 7.2 and Screen 7.3, as well as Screen 7.4, which has a simulation and exercise exploring **effective nuclear charge and shielding value.**

7.3 Electron Configurations of Atoms

Arrangements of electrons in the elements up to 109—their **electron configurations**—are given in Table 7.3. Specifically, these are the ground state electron configurations, where electrons are found in the shells, subshells, and orbitals that result in the lowest energy for the atom. In general, electrons are assigned to orbitals in order of increasing $n + \ell$. The emphasis here, however, will be to connect the configurations of the elements with their positions in the periodic table (Figure 7.4).

Electron Configurations of the Main Group Elements

Hydrogen, the first element in the periodic table, has one electron in a $1s$ orbital. One way to depict its electron configuration is with the orbital box diagram used earlier, but an alternative and more frequently used method is the *spdf* notation. Using this method, the electron configuration of H is $1s^1$, read "one s one." This indicates that there is one electron (indicated by the superscript) in the $1s$ orbital.

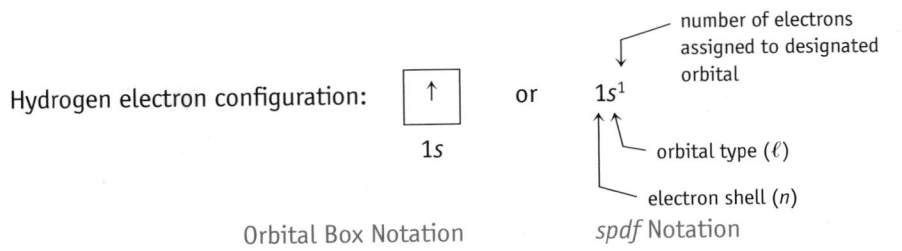

Hydrogen electron configuration:

Orbital Box Notation — *spdf* Notation

■ **Z^* for s and p Subshells** Z^* is greater for s electrons than for p electrons in the same shell. This difference becomes larger as n becomes larger. For example, compare the Group 4A elements.

Atom	$Z^*(ns)$	$Z^*(np)$	Value of n
C	3.22	3.14	2
Si	4.90	4.29	3
Ge	8.04	6.78	4

TABLE 7.2 Effective Nuclear Charges, Z^*, for $n = 2$ Elements

Atom	$Z^*(2s)$	$Z^*(2p)$
Li	1.28	
B	2.58	2.42
C	3.22	3.14
N	3.85	3.83
O	4.49	4.45
F	5.13	5.10

TABLE 7.3 Ground State Electron Configurations

Z	Element	Configuration	Z	Element	Configuration	Z	Element	Configuration
1	H	$1s^1$	37	Rb	$[Kr]5s^1$	74	W	$[Xe]4f^{14}5d^46s^2$
2	He	$1s^2$	38	Sr	$[Kr]5s^2$	75	Re	$[Xe]4f^{14}5d^56s^2$
3	Li	$[He]2s^1$	39	Y	$[Kr]4d^15s^2$	76	Os	$[Xe]4f^{14}5d^66s^2$
4	Be	$[He]2s^2$	40	Zr	$[Kr]4d^25s^2$	77	Ir	$[Xe]4f^{14}5d^76s^2$
5	B	$[He]2s^22p^1$	41	Nb	$[Kr]4d^45s^1$	78	Pt	$[Xe]4f^{14}5d^96s^1$
6	C	$[He]2s^22p^2$	42	Mo	$[Kr]4d^55s^1$	79	Au	$[Xe]4f^{14}5d^{10}6s^1$
7	N	$[He]2s^22p^3$	43	Tc	$[Kr]4d^55s^2$	80	Hg	$[Xe]4f^{14}5d^{10}6s^2$
8	O	$[He]2s^22p^4$	44	Ru	$[Kr]4d^75s^1$	81	Tl	$[Xe]4f^{14}5d^{10}6s^26p^1$
9	F	$[He]2s^22p^5$	45	Rh	$[Kr]4d^85s^1$	82	Pb	$[Xe]4f^{14}5d^{10}6s^26p^2$
10	Ne	$[He]2s^22p^6$	46	Pd	$[Kr]4d^{10}$	83	Bi	$[Xe]4f^{14}5d^{10}6s^26p^3$
11	Na	$[Ne]3s^1$	47	Ag	$[Kr]4d^{10}5s^1$	84	Po	$[Xe]4f^{14}5d^{10}6s^26p^4$
12	Mg	$[Ne]3s^2$	48	Cd	$[Kr]4d^{10}5s^2$	85	At	$[Xe]4f^{14}5d^{10}6s^26p^5$
13	Al	$[Ne]3s^23p^1$	49	In	$[Kr]4d^{10}5s^25p^1$	86	Rn	$[Xe]4f^{14}5d^{10}6s^26p^6$
14	Si	$[Ne]3s^23p^2$	50	Sn	$[Kr]4d^{10}5s^25p^2$	87	Fr	$[Rn]7s^1$
15	P	$[Ne]3s^23p^3$	51	Sb	$[Kr]4d^{10}5s^25p^3$	88	Ra	$[Rn]7s^2$
16	S	$[Ne]3s^23p^4$	52	Te	$[Kr]4d^{10}5s^25p^4$	89	Ac	$[Rn]6d^17s^2$
17	Cl	$[Ne]3s^23p^5$	53	I	$[Kr]4d^{10}5s^25p^5$	90	Th	$[Rn]6d^27s^2$
18	Ar	$[Ne]3s^23p^6$	54	Xe	$[Kr]4d^{10}5s^25p^6$	91	Pa	$[Rn]5f^26d^17s^2$
19	K	$[Ar]4s^1$	55	Cs	$[Xe]6s^1$	92	U	$[Rn]5f^36d^17s^2$
20	Ca	$[Ar]4s^2$	56	Ba	$[Xe]6s^2$	93	Np	$[Rn]5f^46d^17s^2$
21	Sc	$[Ar]3d^14s^2$	57	La	$[Xe]5d^16s^2$	94	Pu	$[Rn]5f^67s^2$
22	Ti	$[Ar]3d^24s^2$	58	Ce	$[Xe]4f^15d^16s^2$	95	Am	$[Rn]5f^77s^2$
23	V	$[Ar]3d^34s^2$	59	Pr	$[Xe]4f^36s^2$	96	Cm	$[Rn]5f^76d^17s^2$
24	Cr	$[Ar]3d^54s^1$	60	Nd	$[Xe]4f^46s^2$	97	Bk	$[Rn]5f^97s^2$
25	Mn	$[Ar]3d^54s^2$	61	Pm	$[Xe]4f^56s^2$	98	Cf	$[Rn]5f^{10}7s^2$
26	Fe	$[Ar]3d^64s^2$	62	Sm	$[Xe]4f^66s^2$	99	Es	$[Rn]5f^{11}7s^2$
27	Co	$[Ar]3d^74s^2$	63	Eu	$[Xe]4f^76s^2$	100	Fm	$[Rn]5f^{12}7s^2$
28	Ni	$[Ar]3d^84s^2$	64	Gd	$[Xe]4f^75d^16s^2$	101	Md	$[Rn]5f^{13}7s^2$
29	Cu	$[Ar]3d^{10}4s^1$	65	Tb	$[Xe]4f^96s^2$	102	No	$[Rn]5f^{14}7s^2$
30	Zn	$[Ar]3d^{10}4s^2$	66	Dy	$[Xe]4f^{10}6s^2$	103	Lr	$[Rn]5f^{14}6d^17s^2$
31	Ga	$[Ar]3d^{10}4s^24p^1$	67	Ho	$[Xe]4f^{11}6s^2$	104	Rf	$[Rn]5f^{14}6d^27s^2$
32	Ge	$[Ar]3d^{10}4s^24p^2$	68	Er	$[Xe]4f^{12}6s^2$	105	Db	$[Rn]5f^{14}6d^37s^2$
33	As	$[Ar]3d^{10}4s^24p^3$	69	Tm	$[Xe]4f^{13}6s^2$	106	Sg	$[Rn]5f^{14}6d^47s^2$
34	Se	$[Ar]3d^{10}4s^24p^4$	70	Yb	$[Xe]4f^{14}6s^2$	107	Bh	$[Rn]5f^{14}6d^57s^2$
35	Br	$[Ar]3d^{10}4s^24p^5$	71	Lu	$[Xe]4f^{14}5d^16s^2$	108	Hs	$[Rn]5f^{14}6d^67s^2$
36	Kr	$[Ar]3d^{10}4s^24p^6$	72	Hf	$[Xe]4f^{14}5d^26s^2$	109	Mt	$[Rn]5f^{14}6d^77s^2$
			73	Ta	$[Xe]4f^{14}5d^36s^2$			

*This table follows the general convention of writing the orbitals in order of increasing n when writing electron configurations. For a given n, the subshells are listed in order of increasing ℓ.

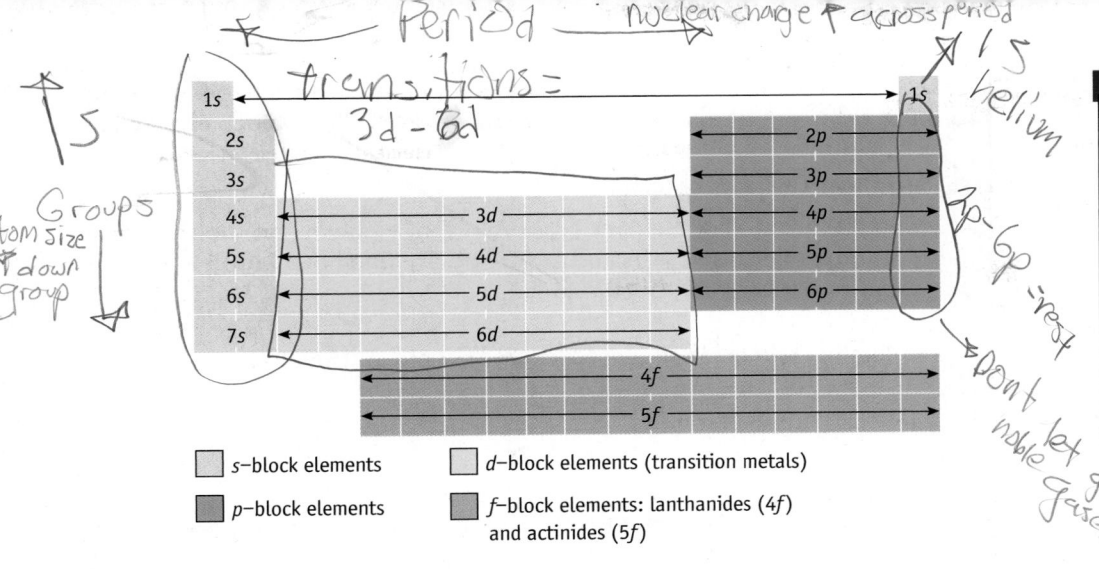

Handwritten annotations around figure:

period — nuclear charge ↑ across period

transitions = 3d - 6d

↑ S · helium

↑ S

Groups
↑Atom Size ↓down group

2p, 6p - rest

→Don't let go of e⁻ noble gases for notation

Active Figure 7.4 Electron configurations and the periodic table. The periodic table can serve as a guide in determining the order of filling of atomic orbitals. As one moves from left to right in a period, electrons are assigned to the indicated orbitals. See Table 7.3.

Chemistry·ᄋ·Now™ Sign in at www.thomsonedu.com/login and go to the Chapter Contents menu to explore an interactive version of this figure accompanied by an exercise.

- □ s–block elements
- □ p–block elements
- □ d–block elements (transition metals)
- □ f–block elements: lanthanides (4f) and actinides (5f)

Lithium (Li) and Other Elements of Group 1A

Lithium, with three electrons, is the first element in the second period of the periodic table. The first two electrons are in the $1s$ subshell, and the third electron must be in the $2s$ subshell of the $n = 2$ shell. The *spdf* notation, $1s^2 2s^1$, is read "one s two, two s one."

Lithium: *spdf* notation $1s^2 2s^1$

Box notation   [↑↓] [↑] [ ][ ][ ]
                $1s$ $2s$ $2p$

Electron configurations are often written in abbreviated form by writing in brackets the symbol for the noble gas preceding the element (called the **noble gas notation**) and then indicating any electrons beyond those in the noble gas by using *spdf* or orbital box notation. In lithium, the arrangement preceding the $2s$ electron is the electron configuration of the noble gas helium, so, instead of writing out $1s^2 2s^1$, using this shorthand lithium's configuration would be written as $[He]2s^1$.

The electrons included in the noble gas notation are often referred to as the **core electrons** of the atom. The core electrons can generally be ignored when considering the chemistry of an element. The electrons beyond the core electrons—the $2s^1$ electron in the case of lithium—are called **valence electrons**; these are the electrons that determine the chemical properties of an element.

All the elements of Group 1A have one electron assigned to an s orbital of the nth shell, for which n is the number of the period in which the element is found (Figure 7.4). For example, potassium is the first element in the $n = 4$ row (the fourth period), so potassium has the electron configuration of the element preceding it in the table (Ar) plus a final electron assigned to the $4s$ orbital: $[Ar]4s^1$.

Beryllium (Be) and Other Elements of Group 2A

All elements of Group 2A have electron configurations of [electrons of preceding noble gas] ns^2, where n is the period in which the element is found in the periodic table. Beryllium, for example, has two electrons in the $1s$ orbital plus two additional electrons.

Beryllium: *spdf* notation $1s^2 2s^2$ or $[He]2s^2$

Box notation   [↑↓] [↑↓] [ ][ ][ ]
                $1s$ $2s$ $2p$

Because all the elements of Group 1A have the valence electron configuration ns^1, and those in Group 2A have ns^2, these elements are called **s-block elements**.

Boron (B) and Other Elements of Group 3A

Boron (Group 3A) is the first element in the block of elements on the right side of the periodic table. Because the $1s$ and $2s$ orbitals are filled in a boron atom, the fifth electron must be assigned to a $2p$ orbital.

Boron: *spdf* notation $1s^22s^22p^1$ or $[He]2s^22p^1$

Box notation

1s   2s   2p

Elements from Group 3A through Group 8A are often called the **p-block elements**. All have the outer shell configuration ns^2np^x, where x varies from 1 to 6. The elements in Group 3A, for example, have two s electrons and one p electron (ns^2np^1) in their outer shells.

Carbon (C) and Other Elements of Group 4A

Carbon (Group 4A) is the second element in the *p*-block, with two electrons assigned to the $2p$ orbitals. You can write the electron configuration of carbon by referring to the periodic table: Starting at H and moving from left to right across the successive periods, you write $1s^2$ to reach the end of period 1 and then $2s^2$ and finally $2p^2$ to bring the electron count to six. For carbon to be in its lowest energy (ground) state, these electrons must be assigned to different p orbitals, and both will have the same spin direction.

Carbon: *spdf* notation $1s^22s^22p^2$ or $[He]2s^22p^2$

Box notation

1s   2s   2p

When assigning electrons to p, d, or f orbitals, each successive electron is assigned to a different orbital of the subshell, and each electron has the same spin as the previous one, until the subshell is half full. Additional electrons must then be assigned to half-filled orbitals. This procedure follows **Hund's rule,** which states that *the most stable arrangement of electrons is that with the maximum number of unpaired electrons, all with the same spin direction.*

All elements in Group 4A have similar outer shell configurations, ns^2np^2, where n is the period in which the element is located in the periodic table.

Nitrogen (N) and Oxygen (O) and Elements of Groups 5A and 6A

Nitrogen (Group 5A) has five valence electrons. Besides the two $2s$ electrons, it has three electrons, all with the same spin, in three different $2p$ orbitals.

Nitrogen: *spdf* notation $1s^22s^22p^3$ or $[He]2s^22p^3$

Box notation

1s   2s   2p

Oxygen (Group 6A) has six valence electrons. Two of these six electrons are assigned to the $2s$ orbital, and the other four electrons are assigned to $2p$ orbitals.

Oxygen: *spdf* notation $1s^2 2s^2 2p^4$ or $[\text{He}]2s^2 2p^4$

Box notation

↑↓		↑↓		↑↓	↑	↑
1s		2s		2p		

The fourth $2p$ electron must pair up with one already present. It makes no difference to which orbital this electron is assigned (the $2p$ orbitals all have the same energy), but it must have a spin opposite to the other electron already assigned to that orbital so that each electron has a different set of quantum numbers.

All elements in Group 5A have an outer shell configuration of $ns^2 np^3$, and all elements in Group 6A have an outer shell configuration of $ns^2 np^4$, where n is the period in which the element is located in the periodic table.

Fluorine (F) and Neon (Ne) and Elements of Groups 7A and 8A

Fluorine (Group 7A) has seven electrons in the $n = 2$ shell. Two of these electrons occupy the $2s$ subshell, and the remaining five electrons occupy the $2p$ subshell.

Fluorine: *spdf* notation $1s^2 2s^2 2p^5$ or $[\text{He}]2s^2 2p^5$

Box notation

↑↓		↑↓		↑↓	↑↓	↑
1s		2s		2p		

All halogen atoms have similar outer shell configurations, $ns^2 np^5$, where n is the period in which the element is located.

Like all the elements in Group 8A, neon is a noble gas. The Group 8A elements (except helium) have eight electrons in the shell of highest n value, so all have the outer shell configuration $ns^2 np^6$, where n is the period in which the element is found. That is, all the noble gases have filled ns and np subshells. The nearly complete chemical inertness of the noble gases is associated with this electron configuration.

Neon: *spdf* notation $1s^2 2s^2 2p^6$ or $[\text{He}]2s^2 2p^6$

Box notation

↑↓		↑↓		↑↓	↑↓	↑↓
1s		2s		2p		

Elements of Period 3

The elements of the third period have valence electron configurations similar to those of the second period, except that the preceding noble gas is neon and the valence shell is the third energy level. For example, silicon has four electrons and a neon core. Because it is the second element in the p block, it has two electrons in $3p$ orbitals. Thus, its electron configuration is

Silicon: *spdf* notation $1s^2 2s^2 2p^6 3s^2 3p^2$ or $[\text{Ne}]3s^2 3p^2$

Box notation

↑↓		↑↓	↑↓	↑↓	↑↓		↑↓		↑	↑	
1s		2s		2p			3s		3p		

Chemistry Now™

Sign in at **www.cengage.com/login** and go to Chapter 7 Contents to see Screen 7.5 for a simulation exploring **the relationship between an element's electron configuration and its position in the periodic table** and for tutorials on **determining an element's box and spdf notations.**

■ EXAMPLE 7.1 Electron Configurations

Problem Give the electron configuration of sulfur, using the *spdf*, noble gas, and orbital box notations.

Strategy Sulfur, atomic number 16, is the sixth element in the third period ($n = 3$) and is in the *p*-block. The last six electrons assigned to the atom, therefore, have the configuration $3s^2 3p^4$. These are preceded by the completed shells $n = 1$ and $n = 2$, the electron arrangement for Ne.

Solution The electron configuration of sulfur is

Complete *spdf* notation: $1s^2 2s^2 2p^6 3s^2 3p^4$

spdf with noble gas notation: $[Ne]3s^2 3p^4$

Orbital box notation: [Ne] ⇅   ⇅ ↑ ↑
                              3s   3p

■ EXAMPLE 7.2 Electron Configurations and Quantum Numbers

Problem Write the electron configuration for Al using the noble gas notation, and give a set of quantum numbers for each of the electrons with $n = 3$ (the valence electrons).

Strategy Aluminum is the third element in the third period. It therefore has three electrons with $n = 3$. Because Al is in the *p*-block of elements, two of the electrons are assigned to 3*s*, and the remaining electron is assigned to 3*p*.

Solution The element is preceded by the noble gas neon, so the electron configuration is $[Ne]3s^2 3p^1$. Using box notation, the configuration is

Aluminum configuration: [Ne] ⇅   ↑ □ □
                                3s   3p

The possible sets of quantum numbers for the two 3*s* electrons are

	n	ℓ	m_ℓ	m_s
For ↑	3	0	0	$+\frac{1}{2}$
For ↓	3	0	0	$-\frac{1}{2}$

For the single 3*p* electron, one of six possible sets is $n = 3$, $\ell = 1$, $m_\ell = 11$, and $m_s = 1\frac{1}{2}$.

EXERCISE 7.2 *spdf* Notation, Orbital Box Diagrams, and Quantum Numbers

(a) Which element has the configuration $1s^2 2s^2 2p^6 3s^2 3p^5$?

(b) Using *spdf* notation and a box diagram, show the electron configuration of phosphorus.

(c) Write one possible set of quantum numbers for the valence electrons of calcium.

Electron Configurations of the Transition Elements

The elements of the fourth through the seventh periods use d and f subshells, in addition to s and p subshells, to accommodate electrons (see Figure 7.4 and Tables 7.3 and 7.4). Elements whose atoms are filling d subshells are called **transition elements.** Those elements for which atoms are filling f subshells are sometimes called the **inner transition elements** or, more usually, the **lanthanides** (filling $4f$ orbitals) and **actinides** (filling $5f$ orbitals).

In a given period in the periodic table, the transition elements are always preceded by two s-block elements. After filling the ns orbital in the period, we begin filling the $(n-1)d$ orbitals. Scandium, the first transition element, has the configuration $[Ar]3d^14s^2$, and titanium follows with $[Ar]3d^24s^2$ (Table 7.4).

The general procedure for assigning electrons would suggest that the configuration of a chromium atom is $[Ar]3d^44s^2$. The actual configuration, however, has one electron assigned to each of the six available $3d$ and $4s$ orbitals: $[Ar]3d^54s^1$. This apparently anomalous configuration is explained by assuming that the $4s$ and $3d$ orbitals have approximately the same energy in Cr, and each of the six valence electrons of chromium is assigned to one of these orbitals.

Following chromium, atoms of manganese, iron, and nickel have the configurations that would be expected from the order of orbital filling in Figure 7.2. Copper ($[Ar]3d^{10}4s^1$) is the second exception in this series; it has a single electron in the $4s$ orbital, and the remaining 10 electrons beyond the argon core are assigned to the $3d$ orbitals. Zinc, with the configuration $[Ar]3d^{10}4s^2$, ends the first transition series.

The fifth period transition elements follow the pattern of the fourth period with minor variations.

■ **Writing Configurations for Transition Metals** We follow the convention of writing configurations with shells listed in order of increasing n and, within a given shell, writing subshells in order of increasing ℓ. Many educators write them as, for example, $[Ar]4s^23d^2$ to reflect the order of orbital filling. In fact, either notation is correct.

TABLE 7.4   Orbital Box Diagrams for the Elements Ca Through Zn

		3d	4s
Ca	$[Ar]4s^2$	☐ ☐ ☐ ☐ ☐	↑↓
Sc	$[Ar]3d^14s^2$	↑ ☐ ☐ ☐ ☐	↑↓
Ti	$[Ar]3d^24s^2$	↑ ↑ ☐ ☐ ☐	↑↓
V	$[Ar]3d^34s^2$	↑ ↑ ↑ ☐ ☐	↑↓
Cr*	$[Ar]3d^54s^1$	↑ ↑ ↑ ↑ ↑	↑
Mn	$[Ar]3d^54s^2$	↑ ↑ ↑ ↑ ↑	↑↓
Fe	$[Ar]3d^64s^2$	↑↓ ↑ ↑ ↑ ↑	↑↓
Co	$[Ar]3d^74s^2$	↑↓ ↑↓ ↑ ↑ ↑	↑↓
Ni	$[Ar]3d^84s^2$	↑↓ ↑↓ ↑↓ ↑ ↑	↑↓
Cu*	$[Ar]3d^{10}4s^1$	↑↓ ↑↓ ↑↓ ↑↓ ↑↓	↑
Zn	$[Ar]3d^{10}4s^2$	↑↓ ↑↓ ↑↓ ↑↓ ↑↓	↑↓

*These configurations do not follow the "$n + \ell$" rule.

Lanthanides and Actinides

The sixth period includes the lanthanide series beginning with lanthanum, La. As the first element in the *d*-block, lanthanum has the configuration $[Xe]5d^16s^2$. The next element, cerium (Ce), is set out in a separate row at the bottom of the periodic table, and it is with the elements in this row (Ce through Lu) that electrons are first assigned to *f* orbitals. Thus, the configuration of cerium is $[Xe]4f^15d^16s^2$. Moving across the lanthanide series, the pattern continues (although with occasional variations in occupancy of the 5*d* and 4*f* orbitals). The lanthanide series ends with 14 electrons being assigned to the seven 4*f* orbitals in the last element, lutetium (Lu, $[Xe]4f^{14}5d^16s^2$) (see Table 7.3).

The seventh period also includes an extended series of elements utilizing *f* orbitals, the actinides, which begin with actinium (Ac, $[Rn]6d^17s^2$). The next element is thorium (Th), which is followed by protactinium (Pa) and uranium (U). The electron configuration of uranium is $[Rn]5f^36d^17s^2$.

EXAMPLE 7.3 Electron Configurations of the Transition Elements

Problem Using the *spdf* and noble gas notations, give electron configurations for (a) technetium, Tc, and (b) osmium, Os.

Strategy Base your answer on the positions of the elements in the periodic table. That is, for each element, find the preceding noble gas, and then note the number of *s*, *p*, *d*, and *f* electrons that lead from the noble gas to the element.

Solution

(a) Technetium, Tc: The noble gas that precedes Tc is krypton, Kr, at the end of the *n* = 4 row. After the 36 electrons of Kr are assigned to the Kr core as [Kr], seven electrons remain. Two of these electrons are in the 5*s* orbital, and the remaining five are in 4*d* orbitals. Therefore, the technetium configuration is $[Kr]4d^55s^2$.

(b) Osmium, Os: Osmium is a sixth-period element and the twenty-second element following the noble gas xenon. Of the 22 electrons to be added after the Xe core, two are assigned to the 6*s* orbital and 14 to 4*f* orbitals. The remaining six are assigned to 5*d* orbitals. Thus, the osmium configuration is $[Xe]4f^{14}5d^66s^2$.

EXERCISE 7.3 Electron Configurations

Using the periodic table and without looking at Table 7.3, write electron configurations for the following elements:

(a) P   (c) Zr   (e) Pb

(b) Zn   (d) In   (f) U

Use the *spdf* and noble gas notations. When you have finished, check your answers with Table 7.4.

7.4 Electron Configurations of Ions

We can also determine electron configurations for ions. To form a cation from a neutral atom, one or more of the valence electrons is removed. Electrons are always removed from the electron shell of highest *n*. If several subshells are present within the *n*th shell, the electron or electrons of maximum ℓ are removed. Thus, a sodium ion is formed by removing the $3s^1$ electron from the Na atom,

$$\text{Na: } [1s^22s^22p^63s^1] \longrightarrow \text{Na}^+ : [1s^22s^22p^6] + e^-$$

A Closer Look

Questions About Transition Element Electron Configurations

Why don't all of the $n = 3$ subshells fill before beginning to fill the $n = 4$ subshells? Why is scandium's configuration [Ar]$3d^14s^2$ and not [Ar]$3d^3$?

Theoretical chemists have calculated that for the atoms from scandium to zinc the energies of the $3d$ orbitals are always lower than the energy of the $4s$ orbital, so for scandium the configuration [Ar]$3d^3$ would seem to be preferred. One way to understand why it is not is to consider the effect of electron–electron repulsion in $3d$ and $4s$ orbitals. The ground state configuration will be the one that most effectively minimizes electron–electron repulsions and that leads to the lowest total energy.

If we prepare plots for $3d$ and $4s$ orbitals such as that in Figure 7.3, we find that the most probable distance of a $3d$ electron from the nucleus is less than that for a $4s$ electron. Being closer to the nucleus, the $3d$ orbitals are more compact than the $4s$ orbital. This means the $3d$ electrons are closer together, and so two $3d$ electrons would repel each other more strongly than two $4s$ electrons, for example. A consequence is that placing electrons in the slightly higher energy $4s$ orbital lessens the effect of electron–electron repulsions and lowers the overall energy of the atom.

For more on this question, and for insight into an interesting scientific debate, see a series of papers in the *Journal of Chemical Education,* and *The Periodic Table* by E. Scerri, Oxford, 2007. For example,

a) F. L. Pilar, "4s is Always Above 3d," *Journal of Chemical Education*, Vol. 55, pages 1–6, 1978.
b) E. R. Scerri, "Transition Metal Configurations and Limitations of the Orbital Approximation," *Journal of Chemical Education*, Vol. 66, pages 481–483, 1989.
c) L. G. Vanquickenborne, K. Pierloot, and D. Devoghel, "Transition Metals and the Aufbau Principle," *Journal of Chemical Education*, Vol. 71, pages 469–471, 1994.
d) M. P. Melrose and E. R. Scerri, "Why the $4s$ Orbital is Occupied before the $3d$," *Journal of Chemical Education*, Vol. 73, pages 498–503, 1996.

and Ge^{2+} is formed by removing two $4p$ electrons from a germanium atom,

$$\text{Ge: [Ar]}3d^{10}4s^24p^2 \longrightarrow \text{Ge}^{2+}\text{: [Ar]}3d^{10}4s^2 + 2\,e^-$$

The same general rule applies to transition metal atoms. This means, for example, that the titanium(II) cation has the configuration [Ar]$3d^2$

$$\text{Ti: [Ar]}3d^24s^2 \longrightarrow \text{Ti}^{2+}\text{: [Ar]}3d^2 + 2\,e^-$$

Iron(II) and iron(III) cations have the configurations [Ar]$3d^6$ and [Ar]$3d^5$, respectively:

$$\text{Fe: [Ar]}3d^64s^2 \longrightarrow \text{Fe}^{2+}\text{: [Ar]}3d^6 + 2\,e^-$$

$$\text{Fe}^{2+}\text{: [Ar]}3d^6 \longrightarrow \text{Fe}^{3+}\text{: [Ar]}3d^5 + e^-$$

Note that in the ionization of transition metals the ns electrons are lost before $(n - 1)d$ electrons. All the common transition metals lose their ns electrons first, and the cations formed have electron configurations of the general type [noble gas core]$(n - 1)d^x$. This point is important to remember because the magnetic properties of transition metal cations are determined by the number of unpaired electrons in d orbitals. For example, the Fe^{3+} ion is paramagnetic to the extent of five unpaired electrons (Figures 6.18, 7.5, and 7.6 and *A Closer Look: Paramagnetism,* page 292). If three $3d$ electrons had been removed instead of two s electrons and one d electron, the Fe^{3+} ion would still be paramagnetic but only to the extent of three unpaired electrons.

Chemistry .ᦺ. Now™

Sign in at **www.cengage.com/login** and go to Chapter 7 Contents to see Screen 7.6 for a simulation of the **changes to an element's electron configuration when it ionizes,** a tutorial on **determining an ion's box notation,** and a tutorial on **determining whether an element is diamagnetic or paramagnetic.**

FIGURE 7.5 Formation of iron(III) chloride. Iron reacts with chlorine (Cl$_2$) to produce FeCl$_3$. The paramagnetic Fe^{3+} ion has the configuration [Ar]$3d^5$.

FIGURE 7.6 Paramagnetism of Transition Metals and Their Compounds. (a) A sample of iron(III) oxide is packed into a plastic tube and suspended from a thin nylon filament. (b) When a powerful magnet is brought near, the paramagnetic iron(III) ions in Fe_2O_3 cause the sample to be attracted to the magnet. (The magnet is made of neodymium, iron, and boron [$Nd_2Fe_{14}B$]. These powerful magnets are used in acoustic speakers.)

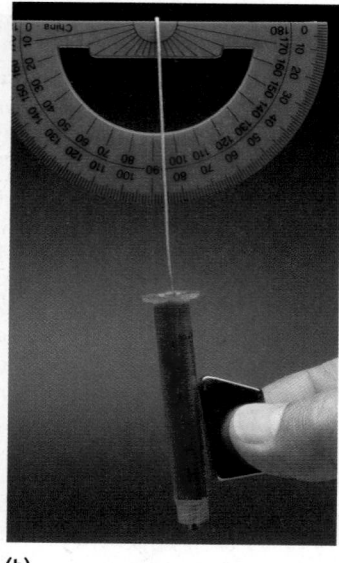

Charles D. Winters

(a)   (b)

■ **EXAMPLE 7.4 Configurations of Transition Metal Ions**

Problem Give the electron configurations for Cu, Cu^+ and Cu^{2+}. Are either of the ions paramagnetic? How many unpaired electrons does each have?

Strategy Observe the configuration of copper in Table 7.4. Recall that s and then d electrons are removed to form a transition metal ion.

Solution Copper has only one electron in the $4s$ orbital and ten electrons in $3d$ orbitals:

Cu: $[Ar]3d^{10}4s^1$ ↑↓ ↑↓ ↑↓ ↑↓ ↑↓   ↑
                              3d   4s

When copper is oxidized to Cu^+, the $4s$ electron is lost.

Cu^+: $[Ar]3d^{10}$ ↑↓ ↑↓ ↑↓ ↑↓ ↑↓   ☐
                              3d   4s

The copper(II) ion is formed from copper(I) by removal of one of the $3d$ electrons.

Cu^{2+}: $[Ar]3d^9$ ↑↓ ↑↓ ↑↓ ↑↓ ↑   ☐
                              3d   4s

A copper(II) ion (Cu^{2+}) has one unpaired electron, so it is paramagnetic. In contrast, Cu^+ is diamagnetic.

EXERCISE 7.4 Metal Ion Configurations

Depict the electron configurations for V^{2+}, V^{3+}, and Co^{3+}. Use orbital box diagrams and the noble gas notation. Are any of the ions paramagnetic? If so, give the number of unpaired electrons.

7.5 Atomic Properties and Periodic Trends

Once electron configurations were understood, chemists realized that *similarities in properties of the elements are the result of similar valence shell electron configurations.* An objective of this section is to describe how atomic electron configurations are related to some of the physical and chemical properties of the elements and why those properties change in a reasonably predictable manner when moving down groups and across periods. This background should make the periodic table an even more useful tool in your study of chemistry. With an understanding of electron configurations and their relation to properties, you should be able to organize and predict many chemical and physical properties of the elements and their compounds.

Atomic Size

An orbital has no sharp boundary (◄ Figure 6.13a), so how can we define the size of an atom? There are actually several ways, and they can give slightly different results.

One of the simplest and most useful ways to define atomic size is to relate it to the distance between atoms in a sample of the element. Let us consider a diatomic molecule such as Cl_2 (Figure 7.7a). The radius of a Cl atom is assumed to be half the experimentally determined distance between the centers of the two atoms (198 pm), so the radius of one Cl atom is 99 pm. Similarly, the C—C distance in diamond is 154 pm, so a radius of 77 pm can be assigned to carbon. To test these estimates, we can add them together to estimate the C—Cl distance in CCl_4. The predicted distance of 176 pm agrees with the experimentally measured C—Cl distance of 176 pm. (Radii determined this way are often called "covalent radii.")

This approach to determining atomic radii applies only if molecular compounds of the element exist (and so it is limited to nonmetals and metalloids). For metals, atomic radii are sometimes estimated from measurements of the atom-to-atom distance in a crystal of the element (Figure 7.7b).

Some interesting periodic trends are seen immediately on looking at a table of radii (Figure 7.8). *For the main group elements, atomic radii generally increase going down*

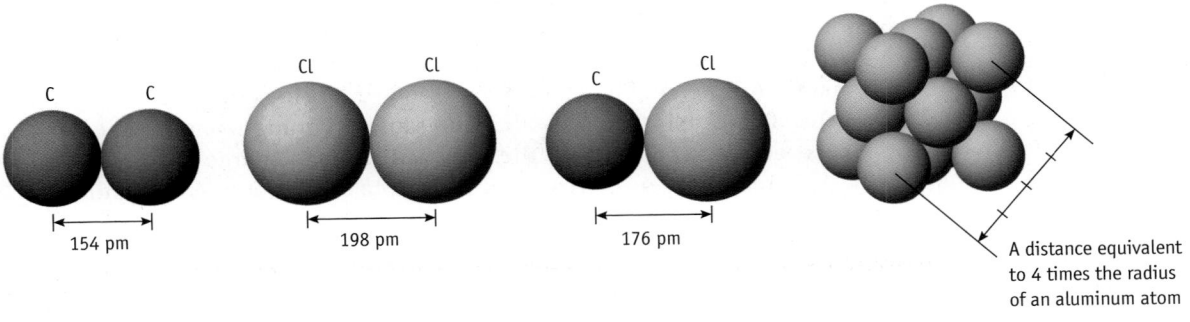

(a)
(b)

FIGURE 7.7 Determining atomic radii. (a) The sum of the atomic radii of C and Cl provides a good estimate of the C–Cl distance in a molecule having such a bond. (b) Pictured here is a tiny piece of an aluminum crystal. Each sphere represents an aluminum atom. Measuring the distance shown allows a scientist to estimate the radius of an aluminum atom.

Sign in at **www.cengage.com/login** to download the Go Chemistry module for this section or go to **www.ichapters.com** to purchase modules.

319

Active Figure 7.8 Atomic radii in picometers for main group elements. 1 pm = 1×10^{-12} m = 1×10^{-3} nm. *(Data taken from J. Emsley: The Elements, Clarendon Press, Oxford, 1998, 3rd ed.)*

Chemistry.⚛.Now™ Sign in at www. cengage.com/login and go to the Chapter Contents menu to explore an interactive version of this figure accompanied by an exercise.

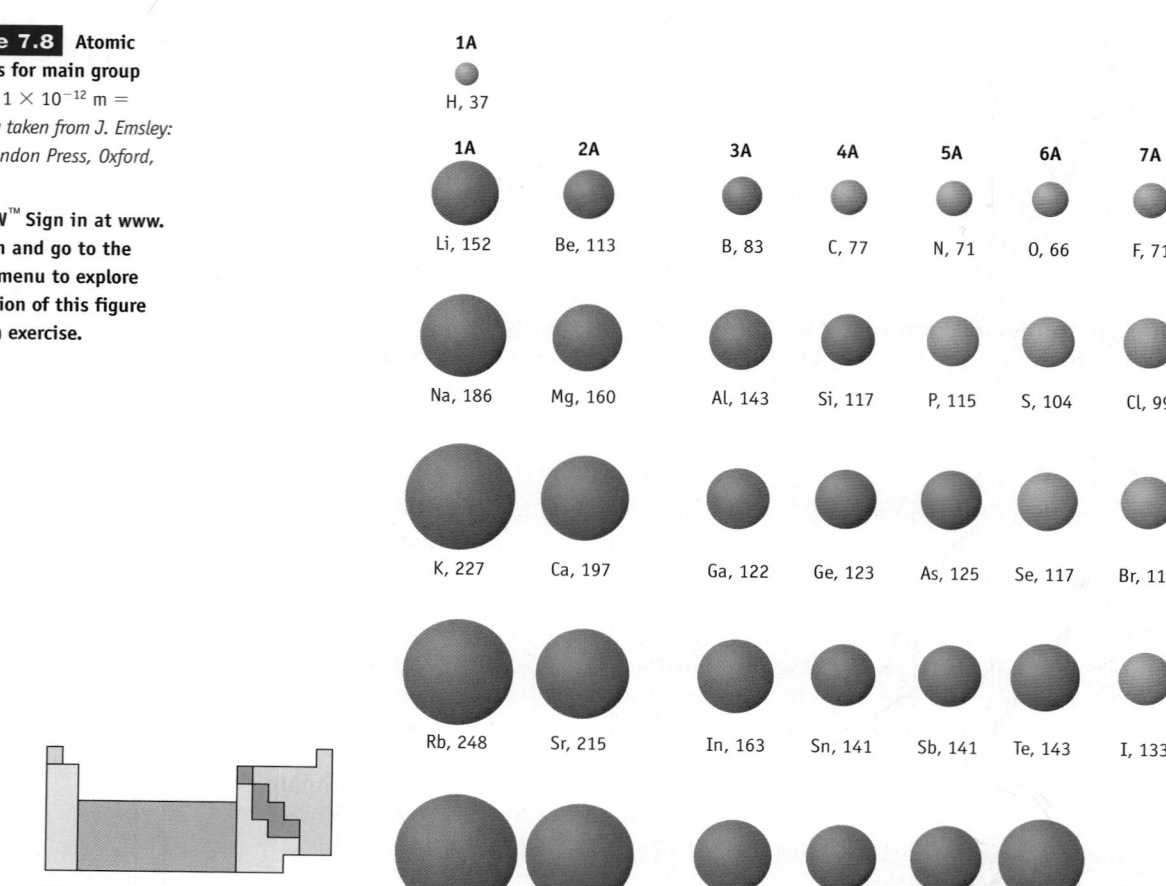

MAIN GROUP METALS   METALLOIDS
TRANSITION METALS   NONMETALS

a group in the periodic table and decrease going across a period. These trends reflect two important effects:

- The size of an atom is determined by the outermost electrons. In going from the top to the bottom of a group in the periodic table, the outermost electrons are assigned to orbitals with increasingly higher values of the principal quantum number, n. Because the underlying electrons require some space, these higher energy electrons are, on average, further from the nucleus.
- For main group elements of a given period, the principal quantum number, n, of the valence electron orbitals is the same. In going from one element to the next across a period, Z^*, the effective nuclear charge increases (Table 7.2). This results in an increased attraction between the nucleus and the valence electrons, and the atomic radius decreases.

The periodic trend in the atomic radii of transition metal atoms (Figure 7.9) across a period is somewhat different from that for main group elements. Going from left to right in a given period, the radii initially decrease. However, the sizes of the elements in the middle of a transition series change very little, and a small increase in size occurs at the end of the series. The size of transition metal atoms is determined largely by electrons in the outermost shell—that is, by the electrons of the ns subshell—but electrons are being added to the $(n - 1)d$ orbitals across the series. The increased nuclear charge on the atoms as one moves from left to

■ **Atomic Radii—Caution** Numerous tabulations of atomic and covalent radii exist, and the values quoted in them often differ somewhat. The variation comes about because several methods are used to determine the radii of atoms.

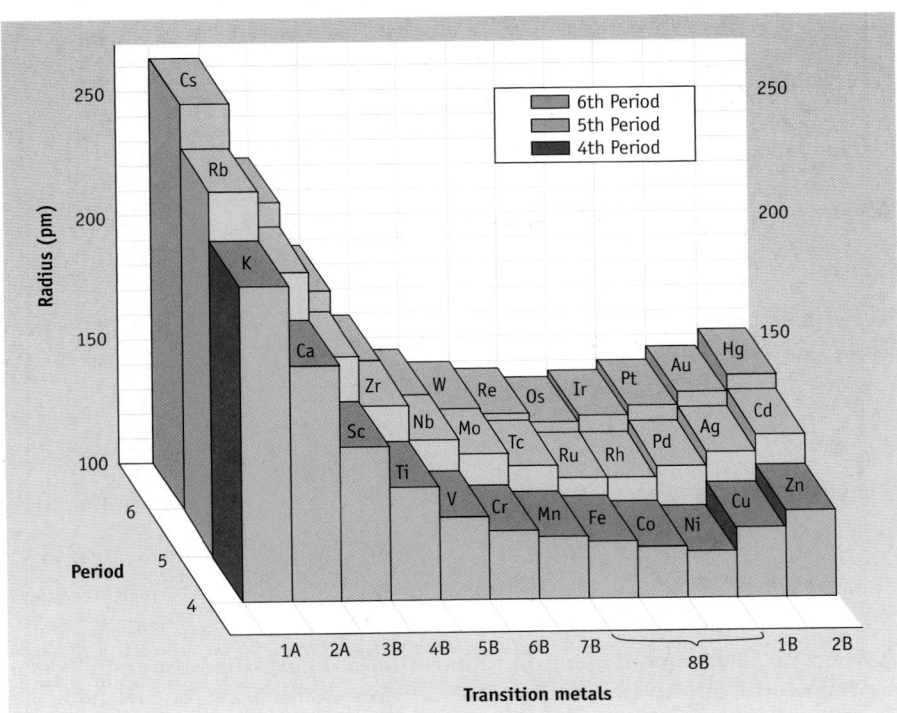

FIGURE 7.9 Trends in atomic radii for the transition elements. Atomic radii of the Group 1A and 2A metals and the transition metals of the fourth, fifth, and sixth periods.

right should cause the radius to decrease. This effect, however, is mostly canceled out by increased electron–electron repulsion. On reaching the Group 1B and 2B elements at the end of the series, the size increases slightly because the *d* subshell is filled and electron–electron repulsions dominate.

Chemistry ⚛ Now™

Sign in at **www.cengage.com/login** and go to Chapter 7 Contents to see:
- Screen 7.8 for a simulation exploring **the trends in atomic size moving across and down the periodic table**
- Screen 7.9 for a simulation exploring **energy levels of orbitals and the ability to retain electrons**

EXERCISE 7.5 Periodic Trends in Atomic Radii

Place the three elements Al, C, and Si in order of increasing atomic radius.

Ionization Energy

Ionization energy *(IE)* is the energy required to remove an electron from an atom in the gas phase.

$$\text{Atom in ground state(g)} \longrightarrow \text{Atom}^+(g) + e^-$$

$$\Delta U \equiv \text{ionization energy, } IE$$

To separate an electron from an atom, energy must be supplied to overcome the attraction of the nuclear charge. Because energy must be supplied, ionization energies always have positive values.

■ **Trends in Atomic Radii** General trends in atomic radii of *s*- and *p*-block elements with position in the periodic table.

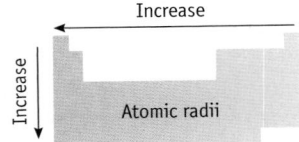

Atoms other than hydrogen have a series of ionization energies as electrons are removed sequentially. For example, the first three ionization energies of magnesium are

■ **Valence and Core Electrons** Removal of core electrons requires much more energy than removal of a valence electron. Core electrons are not lost in chemical reactions.

■ **Measuring Ionization Energy** Ionization energy values can be measured accurately as compared with the estimations that must be made when measuring atomic radii.

First ionization energy, $IE_1 = 738$ kJ/mol

$$\begin{array}{ccc} Mg(g) & \longrightarrow & Mg^+(g) + e^- \\ 1s^22s^22p^63s^2 & & 1s^22s^22p^63s^1 \end{array}$$

Second ionization energy, $IE_2 = 1451$ kJ/mol

$$\begin{array}{ccc} Mg^+(g) & \longrightarrow & Mg^{2+}(g) + e^- \\ 1s^22s^22p^63s^1 & & 1s^22s^22p^6 \end{array}$$

Third ionization energy, $IE_3 = 7732$ kJ/mol

$$\begin{array}{ccc} Mg^{2+}(g) & \longrightarrow & Mg^{3+}(g) + e^- \\ 1s^22s^22p^6 & & 1s^22s^22p^5 \end{array}$$

Removing each subsequent electron requires more energy because the electron is being removed from an increasingly positive ion (Table 7.5), but there is a particularly large increase in ionization energy for removing the third electron to give Mg^{3+}. The first two ionization steps are for the removal of electrons from the outermost or valence shell of electrons. The third electron, however, must come from the $2p$ subshell, which has a much lower energy than the $3s$ subshell. *This large increase is experimental evidence for the electron shell structure of atoms.*

For main group (s- and p-block) elements, *first ionization energies generally increase across a period and decrease down a group* (Figure 7.10, Table 7.5, and Appendix F). The trend across a period corresponds to the increase in effective nuclear charge, Z^*, with increasing atomic number. As Z^* increases, the energy required to remove an electron increases. The general decrease in ionization energy down a group

TABLE 7.5 First, Second, and Third Ionization Energies for the Main Group Elements in Periods 2–4 (kJ/mol)

2nd Period	**Li**	**Be**	**B**	**C**	**N**	**O**	**F**	**Ne**
1st	513	899	801	1086	1402	1314	1681	2080
2nd	7298	1757	2427	2352	2856	3388	3374	3952
3rd	11815	14848	3660	4620	4578	5300	6050	6122
3rd Period	**Na**	**Mg**	**Al**	**Si**	**P**	**S**	**Cl**	**Ar**
1st	496	738	577	787	1012	1000	1251	1520
2nd	4562	1451	1817	1577	1903	2251	2297	2665
3rd	6912	7732	2745	3231	2912	3361	3826	3928
4th Period	**K**	**Ca**	**Ga**	**Ge**	**As**	**Se**	**Br**	**Kr**
1st	419	590	579	762	947	941	1140	1351
2nd	3051	1145	1979	1537	1798	2044	2104	2350
3rd	4411	4910	2963	3302	2735	2974	3500	3565

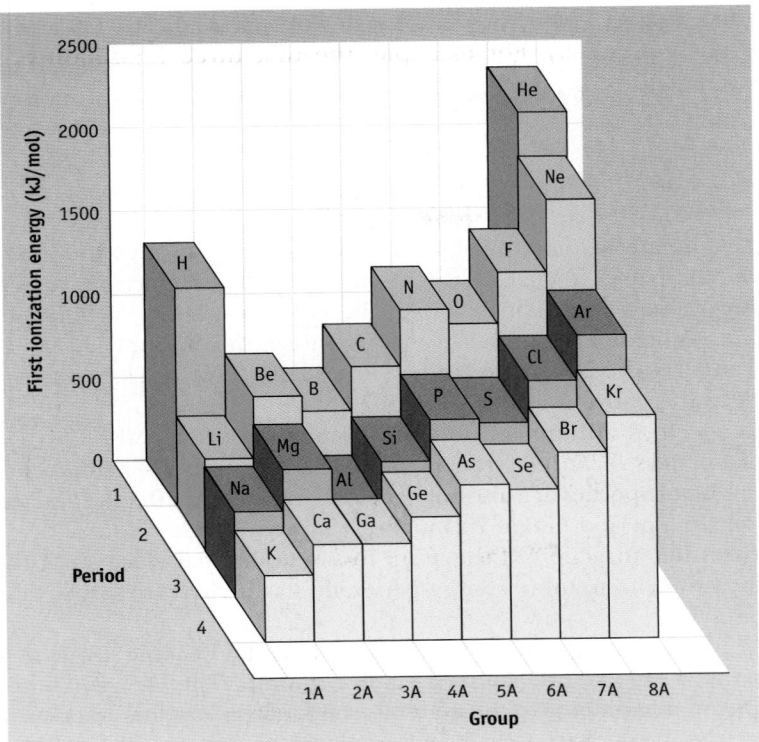

Active Figure 7.10 First
ionization energies of the main group
elements these first four periods. (For
data on these elements see Table 7.5
and Appendix F.)

Chemistry.⚬.Now™ Sign in at www.
cengage.com/login and go to the
Chapter Contents menu to explore
an interactive version of this figure
accompanied by an exercise.

occurs because the electron removed is increasingly farther from the nucleus and thus held less strongly.

Notice that atomic radius and ionization energy are both linked to Z^*. They are inversely related: *as the atomic radius decreases, the ionization energy increases.*

A closer look at ionization energies reveals that there are exceptions to the general trend in a period. One exception occurs on going from s-block to p-block elements—from beryllium to boron, for example. The $2p$ electrons are slightly higher in energy than the $2s$ electrons so the ionization energy for boron is slightly less than that for beryllium. Another dip to lower ionization energy occurs on going from nitrogen to oxygen. No change occurs in either n or ℓ, but electron–electron repulsions increase for the following reason. In Groups 3A–5A, electrons are assigned to separate p orbitals (p_x, p_y, and p_z). Beginning in Group 6A, however, two electrons are assigned to the same p orbital. The fourth p electron shares an orbital with another electron and thus experiences greater repulsion than it would if it had been assigned to an orbital of its own.

■ **Trends in Ionization Energy** General trends in first ionization energies of s- and p-block elements with position in the periodic table.

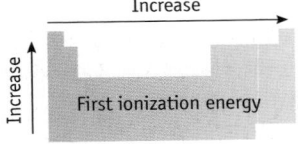

$$\text{O (oxygen atom)} \xrightarrow{\text{+1314 kJ/mol}} \text{O}^+ \text{ (oxygen cation)} + e^-$$

[Ne]⟨↑↓⟩ ⟨↑↓ ↑ ↑⟩   [Ne]⟨↑↓⟩ ⟨↑ ↑ ↑⟩
   $2s$ $2p$ $2s$ $2p$

The greater repulsion experienced by the fourth $2p$ electron makes it easier to remove. The usual trend resumes on going from oxygen to fluorine to neon, however, reflecting the increase in Z^*.

Electron Affinity

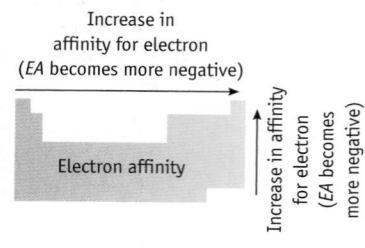

Increase in affinity for electron (*EA* becomes more negative)

Electron affinity

Increase in affinity for electron (*EA* becomes more negative)

The electron affinity, *EA*, of an atom is defined as the energy change for a process in which an electron is acquired by the atom in the gas phase (Figure 7.11 and Appendix F).

$$A(g) + e^-(g) \rightarrow A^-(g) \qquad \Delta U \equiv \text{electron affinity, } EA$$

The greater the affinity an atom has for an electron, the lower the energy of the ion will be compared to that of the atom and the free electron, and the more negative the value of *EA*. For example, the electron affinity of fluorine is −328 kJ/mol, indicating an exothermic reaction to form the anion, F^-, from a fluorine atom and an electron. Boron has a much lower affinity for an electron, as indicated by a much less negative *EA* value of −26.7 kJ/mol.

Because electron affinity and ionization energy represent the energy involved in the gain or loss of an electron by an atom, it is not surprising that periodic trends in these properties are also related. The increase in effective nuclear charge of atoms across a period (Table 7.2) makes it more difficult to ionize the atom and also increases the attraction of the atom for an additional electron. Thus, an element with a high ionization energy generally has a more negative value for its electron affinity.

As seen in Figure 7.11, the values of *EA* generally become more negative on moving across a period, but the trend is not smooth. The elements in Group 2A and 5A appear as variations to the general trend, corresponding to cases where the added electron would start a *p* subshell or would be paired with another electron in the *p* subshell, respectively.

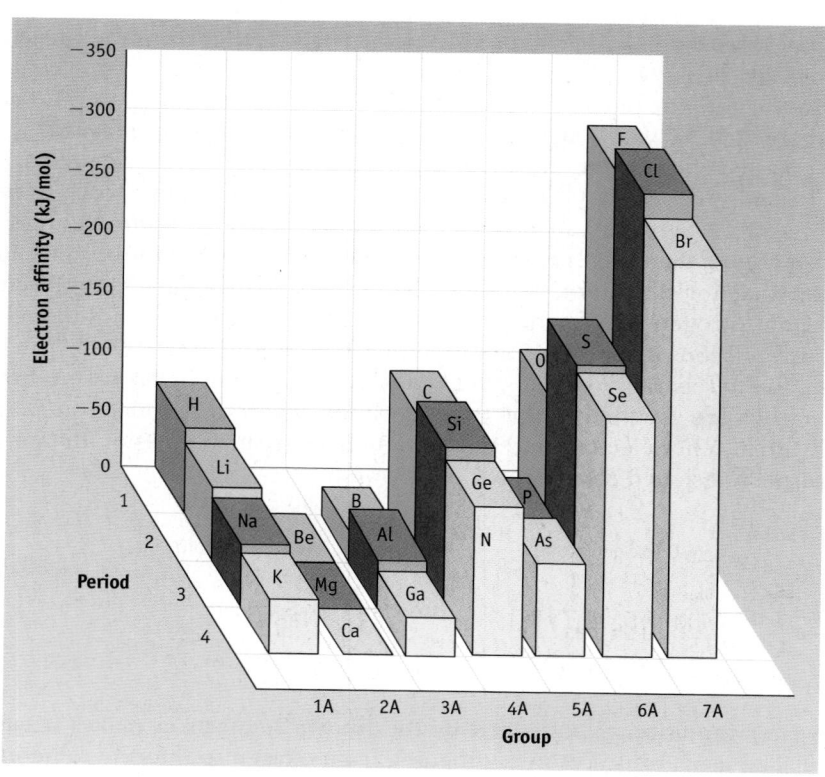

The value of electron affinity usually becomes less negative on descending a group of the periodic table. Electrons are added increasingly farther from the nucleus, so the attractive force between the nucleus and electrons decreases. This general trend does not apply to second period elements, however. For example, the value of the electron affinity of fluorine is higher (less negative) than the *EA* value for chlorine. The same phenomenon is observed in Groups 3A through 6A. One explanation is that significant electron–electron repulsions occur in small anions such as F⁻. That is, adding an electron to the seven electrons already present in the $n = 2$ shell of the small F atom leads to considerable repulsion between electrons. Chlorine has a larger atomic volume than fluorine, so adding an electron does not result in such significant electron–electron repulsions.

A few elements, such as nitrogen and the Group 2A elements, have no affinity for electrons and are listed as having an *EA* value of zero. The noble gases are generally not listed in electron affinity tables. They have no affinity for electrons, because any additional electron must be added to the next higher electron shell.

No atom has a negative electron affinity for a second electron. So what accounts for the existence of ions such as O^{2-} that occur in many compounds? The answer is that doubly charged anions can be stabilized in crystalline environments by electrostatic attraction to neighboring positive ions (see Chapters 8 and 13).

■ **Electron Affinity and Sign Conventions** Changes in sign conventions for electron affinities over the years have caused confusion. For a useful discussion of electron affinity, see J. C. Wheeler: "Electron affinities of the alkaline earth metals and the sign convention for electron affinity," *Journal of Chemical Education*, Vol. 74, pp. 123–127, 1997.

Chemistry ☉ Now™

Sign in at **www.cengage.com/login** and go to Chapter 7 Contents to see Screens 7.8–7.10 for simulations exploring the **periodic trends in these properties.**

EXAMPLE 7.5 Periodic Trends

Problem Compare the three elements C, O, and Si.

(a) Place them in order of increasing atomic radius.

(b) Which has the largest ionization energy?

(c) Which has the more negative electron affinity, O or C?

Strategy Review the trends in atomic properties in Figures 7.8–7.11, Table 7.5, and Appendix F.

Solution

(a) Atomic size: Atomic radius declines on moving across a period, so oxygen must have a smaller radius than carbon. However, the radius increases on moving down a periodic group. Because C and Si are in the same group (Group 4A), Si must be larger than C. The trend is O < C < Si.

(b) Ionization energy: Ionization energies generally increase across a period and decrease down a group. Thus, the trend in ionization energies is Si (787 kJ/mol) < C (1086 kJ/mol) < O (1314 kJ/mol).

(c) Electron affinity: Electron affinity values generally become less negative down a group (except for the second period elements) and more negative across a period. Therefore, the *EA* for O (= −141.0 kJ/mol) has a more negative *EA* than C (= −121.9 kJ/mol).

EXERCISE 7.6 Periodic Trends

Compare the three elements B, Al, and C.

(a) Place the three elements in order of increasing atomic radius.

(b) Rank the elements in order of increasing ionization energy. (Try to do this without looking at Table 7.5; then compare your prediction with the table.)

(c) Which element, B or C, is expected to have the more negative electron affinity value?

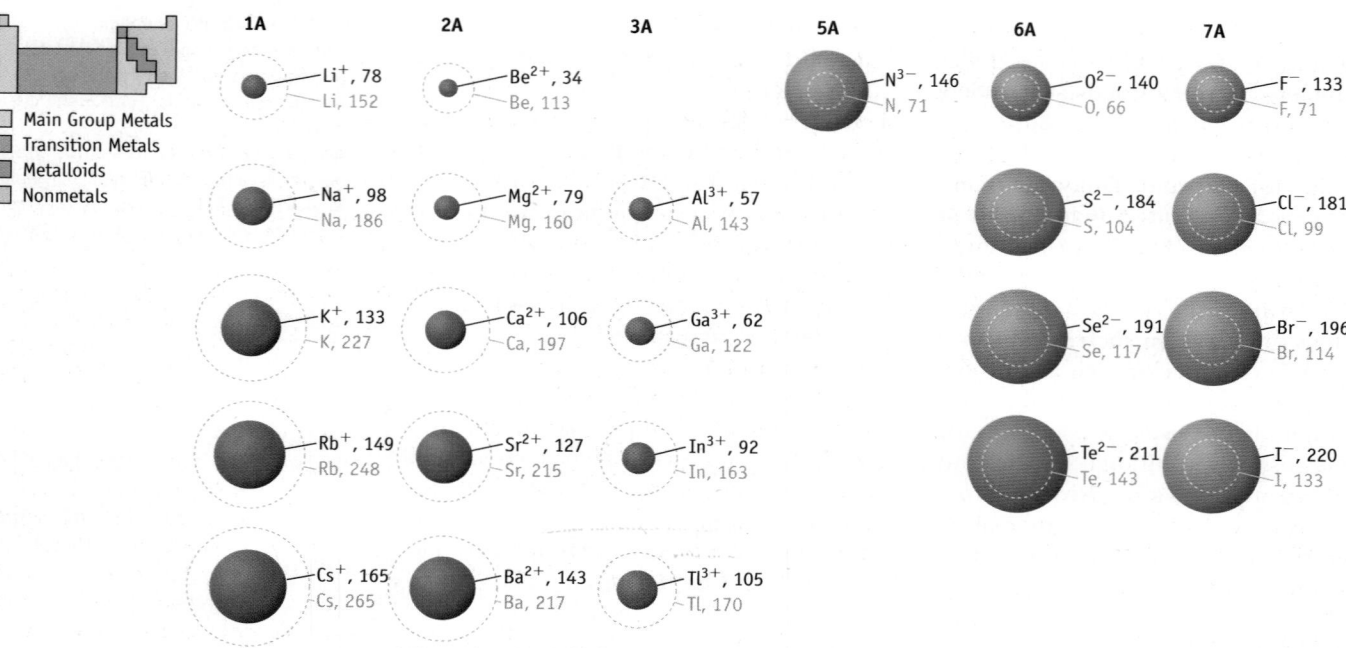

1A	2A	3A	5A	6A	7A
Li⁺, 78 / Li, 152	Be²⁺, 34 / Be, 113		N³⁻, 146 / N, 71	O²⁻, 140 / O, 66	F⁻, 133 / F, 71
Na⁺, 98 / Na, 186	Mg²⁺, 79 / Mg, 160	Al³⁺, 57 / Al, 143		S²⁻, 184 / S, 104	Cl⁻, 181 / Cl, 99
K⁺, 133 / K, 227	Ca²⁺, 106 / Ca, 197	Ga³⁺, 62 / Ga, 122		Se²⁻, 191 / Se, 117	Br⁻, 196 / Br, 114
Rb⁺, 149 / Rb, 248	Sr²⁺, 127 / Sr, 215	In³⁺, 92 / In, 163		Te²⁻, 211 / Te, 143	I⁻, 220 / I, 133
Cs⁺, 165 / Cs, 265	Ba²⁺, 143 / Ba, 217	Tl³⁺, 105 / Tl, 170			

☐ Main Group Metals
☐ Transition Metals
☐ Metalloids
☐ Nonmetals

Active Figure 7.12 **Relative sizes of some common ions.** Radii are given in picometers (1 pm = 1 × 10⁻¹² m). (Data taken from J. Emsley, *The Elements*, Clarendon Press, Oxford, 1998, 3rd edition.)

Chemistry 🔴 Now™ Sign in at **www.cengage.com/login** and go to the Chapter Contents menu to explore an interactive version of this figure accompanied by an exercise.

Trends in Ion Sizes

The trend in the sizes of ions down a periodic group are the same as those for neutral atoms: Positive and negative ions increase in size when descending the group (Figure 7.12). Pause for a moment, however, and compare the ionic radii with the atomic radii, as illustrated in Figure 7.12. When an electron is removed from an atom to form a cation, the size shrinks considerably. The radius of a cation is always smaller than that of the atom from which it is derived. For example, the radius of Li is 152 pm, whereas the radius of Li⁺ is only 78 pm. When an electron is removed from an Li atom, the attractive force of three protons is now exerted on only two electrons, so the remaining electrons are drawn closer to the nucleus. The decrease in ion size is especially great when the last electron of a particular shell is removed, as is the case for Li. The loss of the 2s electron from Li leaves Li⁺ with no electrons in the $n = 2$ shell.

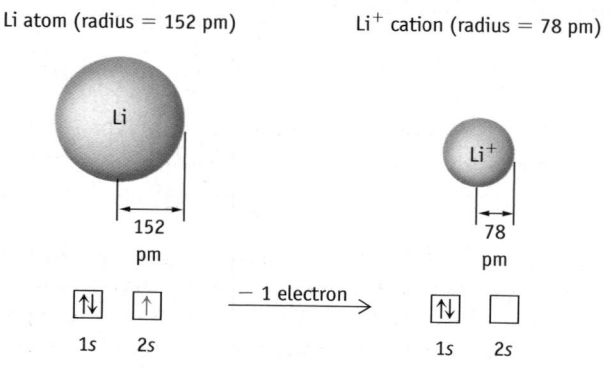

Li atom (radius = 152 pm)   Li⁺ cation (radius = 78 pm)

152 pm   — 1 electron →   78 pm

1s   2s   1s   2s

Metals in Biochemistry and Medicine

Many main group and transition metals play an important role in biochemistry and in medicine. Your body has low levels of the following metals in the form of various compounds: Ca, 1.5%; Na, 0.1%; Mg, 0.05%, and the metals iron, cobalt zinc, and copper, all less than about 0.05%. (Levels are percentages by mass.)

Much of the 3–4 g of iron in your body is found in hemoglobin, the substance responsible for carrying oxygen to cells. Iron deficiency is marked by fatigue, infections, and mouth inflammations.

Iron in your diet can come from eggs, and brewer's yeast has a very high iron content. In addition, foods such as many breakfast cereals are "fortified" with metallic iron [made by the decomposition of $Fe(CO)_5$]. (In an interesting experiment you can do at home, you can remove the iron by stirring the cereal with a strong magnet.) Vitamin pills often contain iron(II) compounds with anions such as sulfate and succinate ($C_4H_4O_4^{2-}$).

The average person has about 75 mg of copper, about one third of which is found in the muscles. Copper is involved in many biological functions, and a deficiency shows up in many ways: anemia, degeneration of the nervous system, and impaired immunity. Wilson's disease, a genetic disorder, leads to the overaccumulation of copper in the body and results in hepatic and neurological damage.

Like silver ions (page 148), copper ions can also act as a bacteriocide. Scientists

Filling a brass water jug for drinking water in India. Copper ions released in tiny amounts from the brass kill bacteria in contaminated water.

from Britain and India recently investigated a long-held belief among people in India that storing water in brass pitchers can ward off illness. (Brass is an alloy of copper and zinc.) They filled brass pitchers with sterile water inoculated with *E. coli* bacteria and filled other brass pitchers with contaminated river water from India. In both cases, they found that fecal bacteria counts dropped from as high as 1,000,000 bacteria per milliliter to zero in two days. In contrast, bacteria levels stayed high in plastic or earthenware pots. Apparently, just enough copper ions are released by the brass to kill the bacteria but not enough to affect humans.

Questions:

1. Give the electron configurations for iron and the iron(II) and iron(III) ions.
2. In hemoglobin, iron can be in the iron(II) or iron(III) state. Are either of these iron ions paramagnetic?
3. Give the electron configurations for copper and the copper(I) and copper(II) ions. Is copper in any of these forms paramagnetic?
4. Why are copper atoms (radius = 128 pm) slightly larger than iron atoms (radius = 124 pm)?
5. In hemoglobin, the iron is enclosed by the porphyrin group, a flat grouping of carbon, hydrogen, and nitrogen atoms. (This is in turn encased in a protein.) When iron is in the form of the Fe^{3+} ion, it just fits into the space within the four N atoms, and the arrangement is flat. Speculate on what occurs to the structure when iron is reduced to the Fe^{2+} ion.

Answers to these questions are in Appendix Q.

A large decrease in size is also expected if two or more electrons are removed. For example, an aluminum ion, Al^{3+}, has a radius of 57 pm; in contrast, the atomic radius of an aluminum atom is 143 pm.

Al atom (radius = 143 pm) Al^{3+} cation (radius = 57 pm)

$[Ne]$ ↑↓ ↑ □ □ —3 electrons→ $[Ne]$ □ □ □ □
      3s   3p   3s   3p

You can also see by comparing Figures 7.8 and 7.12 that anions are always larger than the atoms from which they are derived. Here, the argument is the opposite of that used to explain positive ion radii. The F atom, for example, has nine protons and nine electrons. On forming the anion, the nuclear charge is still +9, but the anion has ten electrons. The F⁻ ion is larger than the F atom because of increased electron–electron repulsions.

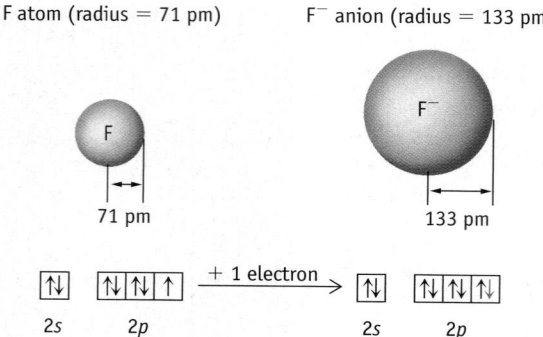

F atom (radius = 71 pm)   F⁻ anion (radius = 133 pm)

71 pm   133 pm

$$2s \quad 2p \quad \xrightarrow{\text{+ 1 electron}} \quad 2s \quad 2p$$

Finally, it is useful to compare the sizes of isoelectronic ions across the periodic table. **Isoelectronic** ions have the same number of electrons (but a different number of protons). One such series of ions is N^{3-}, O^{2-}, F^-, Na^+, and Mg^{2+}:

Ion	N^{3-}	O^{2-}	F^-	Na^+	Mg^{2+}
Number of electrons	10	10	10	10	10
Number of nuclear protons	7	8	9	11	12
Ionic radius (pm)	146	140	133	98	79

All these ions have 10 electrons but they differ in the number of protons. As the number of protons increases in a series of isoelectronic ions, the balance between electron–proton attraction and electron–electron repulsion shifts in favor of attraction, and the radius decreases.

Chemistry⚛Now™

Sign in at **www.cengage.com/login** and go to Chapter 7 Contents to see Screen 7.12 for simulations on **the relationship between ion formation and orbital energies in main group elements** and on the **relationship between orbital energies and electron configurations on the size of the main group element ions.**

EXERCISE 7.7 Ion Sizes

What is the trend in sizes of the ions K^+, S^{2-}, and Cl^-? Briefly explain why this trend exists.

7.6 Periodic Trends and Chemical Properties

Atomic and ionic radii, ionization energies, and electron affinities are properties associated with atoms and their ions. It is reasonable to expect that knowledge of these properties will be useful as we explore the chemistry involving formation of ionic compounds.

The periodic table was created by grouping together elements having similar chemical properties (Figure 7.13). Alkali metals, for example, characteristically form compounds containing a 1+ ion, such as Li^+, Na^+, or K^+. Thus, the reaction

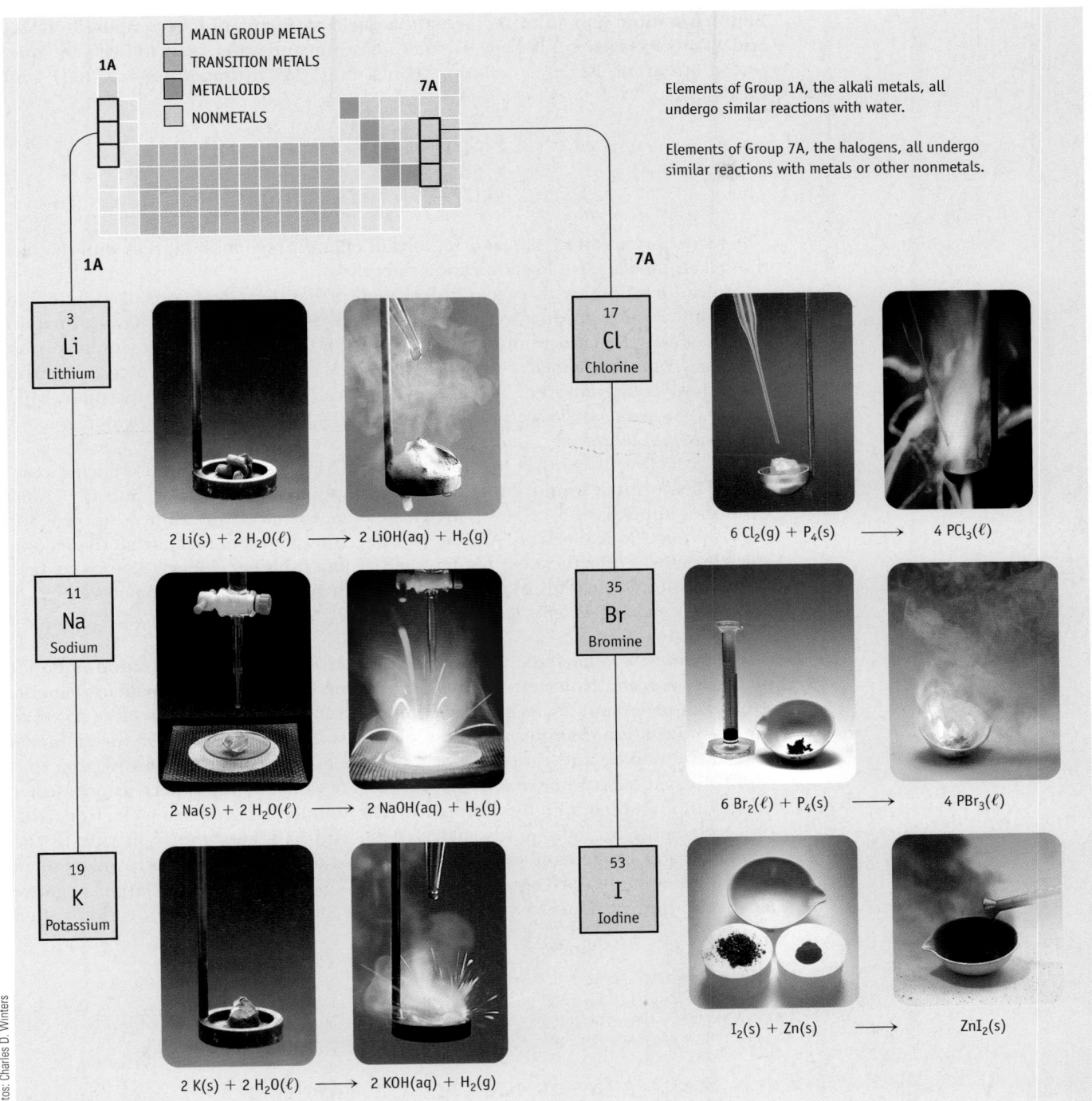

MAIN GROUP METALS
TRANSITION METALS
METALLOIDS
NONMETALS

1A

7A

Elements of Group 1A, the alkali metals, all undergo similar reactions with water.

Elements of Group 7A, the halogens, all undergo similar reactions with metals or other nonmetals.

1A

7A

3
Li
Lithium

$2 Li(s) + 2 H_2O(\ell) \longrightarrow 2 LiOH(aq) + H_2(g)$

11
Na
Sodium

$2 Na(s) + 2 H_2O(\ell) \longrightarrow 2 NaOH(aq) + H_2(g)$

19
K
Potassium

$2 K(s) + 2 H_2O(\ell) \longrightarrow 2 KOH(aq) + H_2(g)$

17
Cl
Chlorine

$6 Cl_2(g) + P_4(s) \longrightarrow 4 PCl_3(\ell)$

35
Br
Bromine

$6 Br_2(\ell) + P_4(s) \longrightarrow 4 PBr_3(\ell)$

53
I
Iodine

$I_2(s) + Zn(s) \longrightarrow ZnI_2(s)$

Photos: Charles D. Winters

Active Figure 7.13 **Examples of the periodicity of Group 1A and Group 7A elements.** Dimitri Mendeleev developed the first periodic table by listing elements in order of increasing atomic weight. Every so often, an element had properties similar to those of a lighter element, and these were placed in vertical columns or groups. We now recognize that the elements should be listed in order of increasing atomic number and that the periodic occurrence of similar properties is related to the electron configurations of the elements.

Chemistry ⚛ Now™ Sign in at www.cengage.com/login and go to the Chapter Contents menu to explore an interactive version of this figure accompanied by an exercise.

between sodium and chlorine gives the ionic compound, NaCl (composed of Na$^+$ and Cl$^-$ ions) [Figure 1.4, page 4], and potassium and water react to form an aqueous solution of KOH, a solution containing the hydrated ions K$^+$(aq) and OH$^-$(aq).

$$2 \text{ Na(s)} + \text{Cl}_2\text{(g)} \rightarrow 2 \text{ NaCl(s)}$$

$$2 \text{ K(s)} + 2 \text{ H}_2\text{O}(\ell) \rightarrow 2 \text{ K}^+\text{(aq)} + 2 \text{ OH}^-\text{(aq)} + \text{H}_2\text{(g)}$$

The facile formation of Na$^+$ and K$^+$ ions in chemical reactions agrees with the fact that alkali metals have low ionization energies.

Ionization energies also account for the fact that these reactions of sodium and potassium do not produce compounds such as NaCl$_2$ or K(OH)$_2$. The formation of an Na^{2+} or K^{2+} ion would be a very unfavorable process. Removing a second electron from these metals requires a great deal of energy because a core electron would have to be removed. The energetic barrier to this process is the underlying reason that *main group metals generally form cations with an electron configuration equivalent to that of the preceding noble gas*.

Why isn't Na$_2$Cl another possible product from the sodium and chlorine reaction? This formula would imply that the compound contains Na$^+$ and Cl^{2-} ions. Chlorine atoms have a relatively negative value for electron affinity, but only for the addition of one electron. Adding two electrons per atom means that the second electron must enter the next higher shell at much higher energy. Anions such as Cl^{2-} are not known. This example leads us to a general statement: *nonmetals generally acquire enough electrons to form an anion with the electron configuration of the next noble gas*.

We can use similar logic to rationalize other observations. Ionization energies increase on going from left to right across a period. We have seen that elements from Groups 1A and 2A form ionic compounds, an observation directly related to the low ionization energies for these elements. Ionization energies for elements toward the middle and right side of a period, however, are sufficiently large that cation formation is unfavorable. Thus, we generally do not expect to encounter ionic compounds containing carbon; instead, we find carbon sharing electrons with other elements in compounds such as CO$_2$ and CCl$_4$. On the right side of the second period, oxygen and fluorine much prefer taking on electrons to giving them up; these elements have high ionization energies and relatively large, negative electron affinities. Thus, oxygen and fluorine form anions and not cations when they react.

Chemistry ⚛ Now™

Sign in at **www.cengage.com/login** and go to Chapter 7 Contents to see Screen 7.13 to watch videos on **the relationship of atomic electron configurations and orbital energies on periodic trends.**

EXERCISE 7.8 Energies and Compound Formation

Give a plausible explanation for the observation that magnesium and chlorine react to form MgCl$_2$ and not MgCl$_3$.

Now that you have studied this chapter, you should ask whether you have met the chapter goals. In particular, you should be able to:

Recognize the relationship of the four quantum numbers (n, ℓ, m_ℓ, and m_s) to atomic structure

a. Recognize that each electron in an atom has a different set of the four quantum numbers, n, ℓ, m_ℓ, and m_s (Sections 6.5–6.7, 7.1, and 7.3). Study Questions assignable in OWL: 11, 13, 35, 37, 52.

b. Understand that the Pauli exclusion principle leads to the conclusion that no atomic orbital can be assigned more than two electrons and that the two electrons in an orbital must have opposite spins (different values of m_s) (Section 7.1).

Write the electron configuration for atoms and monatomic ions

a. Recognize that electrons are assigned to the subshells of an atom in order of increasing subshell energy (Aufbau principle, Section 7.2). In the H atom, the subshell energies increase with increasing n, but, in a many-electron atom, the energies depend on both n and ℓ (see Figure 7.2).

b. Understand effective nuclear charge, Z^*, and its ability to explain why different subshells in the same shell of multielectron atoms have different energies. Also, understand the role of Z^* in determining the properties of atoms (Section 7.2).

c. Using the periodic table as a guide, depict electron configurations of neutral atoms (Section 7.3) and monatomic ions (Section 7.4) using the orbital box or *spdf* notation. In both cases, configurations can be abbreviated with the noble gas notation. Study Question(s) assignable in OWL: 2, 3, 6, 10, 13, 15, 18, 20, 21, 33, 34, 35, 36, 39, 44, 52, 59, 71.

d. When assigning electrons to atomic orbitals, apply the Pauli exclusion principle and Hund's rule (Sections 7.3 and 7.4).

e. Understand the role magnetism plays in revealing atomic structure (Section 7.4). Study Question(s) assignable in OWL: 20, 21, 33, 34, 39, 52.

Rationalize trends in atom and ion sizes, ionization energy, and electron affinity

a. Predict how properties of atoms—size, ionization energy *(IE)*, and electron affinity *(EA)*—change on moving down a group or across a period of the periodic table (Section 7.5). The general periodic trends for these properties are as follows: Study Question(s) assignable in OWL: 24, 26, 28, 30, 32, 40–43, 45–50, 52, 56–58, 64.

(i) Atomic size decreases across a period and increases down a group.

(ii) *IE* increases across a period and decreases down a group.

(iii) The value of *EA* becomes more negative across a period and becomes less negative down a group.

b. Recognize the role that ionization energy and electron affinity play in forming ionic compounds (Section 7.6). Study Question(s) assignable in OWL: 72.

STUDY QUESTIONS

OWL Online homework for this chapter may be assigned in OWL.

▲ denotes challenging questions.

■ denotes questions assignable in OWL.

Blue-numbered questions have answers in Appendix O and fully-worked solutions in the *Student Solutions Manual.*

Practicing Skills

Writing Electron Configurations of Atoms
(See Examples 7.1–7.3; Tables 7.1, 7.3, and 7.4; and Screen 7.5 and the Toolbox in ChemistryNow.)

1. Write the electron configurations for P and Cl using both *spdf* notation and orbital box diagrams. Describe the relationship between each atom's electron configuration and its position in the periodic table.

2. ■ Write the electron configurations for Mg and Ar using both *spdf* notation and orbital box diagrams. Describe the relationship of the atom's electron configuration to its position in the periodic table.

3. ■ Using *spdf* notation, write the electron configurations for atoms of chromium and iron, two of the major components of stainless steel.

4. Using *spdf* notation, give the electron configuration of vanadium, V, an element found in some brown and red algae and some toadstools.

5. Depict the electron configuration for each of the following atoms using *spdf* and noble gas notations.
   (a) Arsenic, As. A deficiency of As can impair growth in animals even though larger amounts are poisonous.
   (b) Krypton, Kr. It ranks seventh in abundance of the gases in Earth's atmosphere.

6. ■ Using *spdf* and noble gas notations, write electron configurations for atoms of the following elements, and then check your answers with Table 7.3.
   (a) Strontium, Sr. This element is named for a town in Scotland.
   (b) Zirconium, Zr. The metal is exceptionally resistant to corrosion and so has important industrial applications. Moon rocks show a surprisingly high zirconium content compared with rocks on Earth.
   (c) Rhodium, Rh. This metal is used in jewelry and in catalysts in industry.
   (d) Tin, Sn. The metal was used in the ancient world. Alloys of tin (solder, bronze, and pewter) are important.

7. Use noble gas and *spdf* notations to depict electron configurations for the following metals of the third transition series.
   (a) Tantalum, Ta. The metal and its alloys resist corrosion and are often used in surgical and dental tools.
   (b) Platinum, Pt. This metal was used by pre-Columbian Indians in jewelry. It is used now in jewelry and for anticancer drugs and catalysts (such as those in automobile exhaust systems).

8. The lanthanides, once called the rare earth elements, are really only "medium rare." Using noble gas and *spdf* notations, depict reasonable electron configurations for the following elements.
   (a) Samarium, Sm. This lanthanide is used in magnetic materials.
   (b) Ytterbium, Yb. This element was named for the village of Ytterby in Sweden, where a mineral source of the element was found.

9. The actinide americium, Am, is a radioactive element that has found use in home smoke detectors. Depict its electron configuration using noble gas and *spdf* notations.

10. ■ Predict reasonable electron configurations for the following elements of the actinide series of elements. Use noble gas and *spdf* notations.
    (a) Plutonium, Pu. The element is best known as a by-product of nuclear power plant operations.
    (b) Curium, Cm. This actinide was named for Marie Curie (page 342).

Quantum Numbers and Electron Configurations
(See Example 7.2 and ChemistryNow Screens 6.12 and 7.2–7.5.)

11. ■ What is the maximum number of electrons that can be identified with each of the following sets of quantum numbers? In one case, the answer is "none." Explain why this is true.
    (a) $n = 4$, $\ell = 3$, $m_\ell = 1$
    (b) $n = 6$, $\ell = 1$, $m_\ell = -1$, $m_s = -\frac{1}{2}$
    (c) $n = 3$, $\ell = 3$, $m_\ell = -3$

12. What is the maximum number of electrons that can be identified with each of the following sets of quantum numbers? In some cases, the answer may be "none." In such cases, explain why "none" is the correct answer.
    (a) $n = 3$
    (b) $n = 3$ and $\ell = 2$
    (c) $n = 4$, $\ell = 1$, $m_\ell = -1$, and $m_s = +\frac{1}{2}$
    (d) $n = 5$, $\ell = 0$, $m_\ell = -1$, $m_s = +\frac{1}{2}$

13. ■ Depict the electron configuration for magnesium using an orbital box diagram and noble gas notation. Give a complete set of four quantum numbers for each of the electrons beyond those of the preceding noble gas.

14. Depict the electron configuration for phosphorus using an orbital box diagram and noble gas notation. Give one possible set of four quantum numbers for each of the electrons beyond those of the preceding noble gas.

15. ■ Using an orbital box diagram and noble gas notation, show the electron configuration of gallium, Ga. Give a set of quantum numbers for the highest-energy electron.

16. Using an orbital box diagram and noble gas notation, show the electron configuration of titanium. Give one possible set of four quantum numbers for each of the electrons beyond those of the preceding noble gas.

**Electron Configurations of Atoms and Ions
and Magnetic Behavior**
*(See Example 7.4, Section 6.7, and ChemistryNow Screens 6.16,
7.5, and 7.6.)*

17. Using orbital box diagrams, depict an electron configuration for each of the following ions: (a) Mg^{2+},
(b) K^+, (c) Cl^-, and (d) O^{2-}.

18. ■ Using orbital box diagrams, depict an electron
configuration for each of the following ions: (a) Na^+,
(b) Al^{3+}, (c) Ge^{2+}, and (d) F^-.

19. Using orbital box diagrams and noble gas notation, depict the electron configurations of (a) V, (b) V^{2+}, and
(c) V^{5+}. Are any of the ions paramagnetic?

20. ■ Using orbital box diagrams and noble gas notation,
depict the electron configurations of (a) Ti, (b) Ti^{2+},
and (c) Ti^{4+}. Are any of the ions paramagnetic?

21. ■ Manganese is found as MnO_2 in deep ocean
deposits.
(a) Depict the electron configuration of this element
using the noble gas notation and an orbital box
diagram.
(b) Using an orbital box diagram, show the electrons
beyond those of the preceding noble gas for the
4+ ion.
(c) Is the 4+ ion paramagnetic?
(d) How many unpaired electrons does the Mn^{4+} ion
have?

22. One compound found in alkaline batteries is NiOOH,
a compound containing Ni^{3+} ions. When the battery is
discharged, the Ni^{3+} is reduced to Ni^{2+} ions [as in
$Ni(OH)_2$]. Using orbital box diagrams and the noble
gas notation, show electron configurations of these
ions. Are either of these ions paramagnetic?

Periodic Properties
*(See Section 7.5, Example 7.5, and ChemistryNow
Screens 7.7–7.13.)*

23. Arrange the following elements in order of increasing
size: Al, B, C, K, and Na. (Try doing it without looking
at Figure 7.8, and then check yourself by looking up
the necessary atomic radii.)

24. ■ Arrange the following elements in order of increasing size: Ca, Rb, P, Ge, and Sr. (Try doing it without
looking at Figure 7.8; then check yourself by looking
up the necessary atomic radii.)

25. Select the atom or ion in each pair that has the larger
radius.
(a) Cl or Cl^- (b) Al or O   (c) In or I

26. ■ Select the atom or ion in each pair that has the
larger radius.
(a) Cs or Rb   (b) O^{2-} or O   (c) Br or As

27. Which of the following groups of elements is arranged
correctly in order of increasing ionization energy?
(a) C < Si < Li < Ne   (c) Li < Si < C < Ne
(b) Ne < Si < C < Li   (d) Ne < C < Si < Li

28. ■ Arrange the following atoms in order of increasing
ionization energy: Li, K, C, and N.

29. Compare the elements Na, Mg, O, and P.
(a) Which has the largest atomic radius?
(b) Which has the most negative electron affinity?
(c) Place the elements in order of increasing ionization
energy.

30. ■ Compare the elements B, Al, C, and Si.
(a) Which has the most metallic character?
(b) Which has the largest atomic radius?
(c) Which has the most negative electron affinity?
(d) Place the three elements B, Al, and C in order of
increasing first ionization energy.

31. Explain each answer briefly.
(a) Place the following elements in order of increasing
ionization energy: F, O, and S.
(b) Which has the largest ionization energy: O, S, or Se?
(c) Which has the most negative electron affinity:
Se, Cl, or Br?
(d) Which has the largest radius: O^{2-}, F^-, or F?

32. ■ Explain each answer briefly.
(a) Rank the following in order of increasing atomic
radius: O, S, and F.
(b) Which has the largest ionization energy: P, Si, S,
or Se?
(c) Place the following in order of increasing radius:
O^{2-}, N^{3-}, and F^-.
(d) Place the following in order of increasing ionization energy: Cs, Sr, and Ba.

General Questions
*These questions are not designated as to type or location in the
chapter. They may combine several concepts.*

33. ■ Using an orbital box diagram and noble gas notation,
show the electron configurations of uranium and of the
uranium(IV) ion. Is either of these paramagnetic?

34. ■ The rare earth elements, or lanthanides, commonly
exist as 3+ ions. Using an orbital box diagram and noble gas notation, show the electron configurations of
the following elements and ions.
(a) Ce and Ce^{3+} (cerium)
(b) Ho and Ho^{3+} (holmium)

35. ■ A neutral atom has two electrons with $n = 1$, eight
electrons with $n = 2$, eight electrons with $n = 3$, and
two electrons with $n = 4$. Assuming this element is in
its ground state, supply the following information:
(a) atomic number
(b) total number of s electrons
(c) total number of p electrons
(d) total number of d electrons
(e) Is the element a metal, metalloid, or nonmetal?

36. ■ Element 109, now named meitnerium (in honor of the Austrian–Swedish physicist, Lise Meitner [1878–1968]), was produced in August 1982 by a team at Germany's Institute for Heavy Ion Research. Depict its electron configuration using *spdf* and noble gas notations. Name another element found in the same group as meitnerium.

Lise Meitner (1878–1968) and Otto Hahn (1879–1968). Element 109 (Mt) was named after Meitner. She earned her Ph.D. in physics under Ludwig Boltzmann at the University of Vienna, the first woman to do so at that university.

37. Which of the following is *not* an allowable set of quantum numbers? Explain your answer briefly. For those sets that are valid, identify an element in which an outermost valence electron could have that set of quantum numbers.

	n	ℓ	m_ℓ	m_s
(a)	2	0	0	$-\frac{1}{2}$
(b)	1	1	0	$+\frac{1}{2}$
(c)	2	1	-1	$-\frac{1}{2}$
(d)	4	2	$+2$	$-\frac{1}{2}$

38. A possible excited state for the H atom has an electron in a $4p$ orbital. List all possible sets of quantum numbers (n, ℓ, m_ℓ, m_s) for this electron.

39. ■ The magnet in the photo is made from neodymium, iron, and boron.

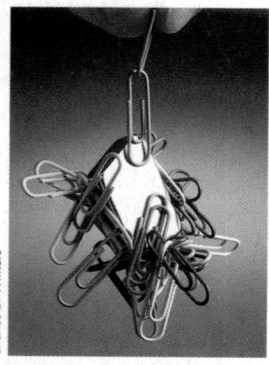

A magnet made of an alloy containing the elements Nd, Fe, and B.

(a) Write the electron configuration of each of these elements using an orbital box diagram and noble gas notation.
(b) Are these elements paramagnetic or diamagnetic?
(c) Write the electron configurations of Nd^{3+} and Fe^{3+} using orbital box diagrams and noble gas notation. Are these ions paramagnetic or diamagnetic?

40. ■ Name the element corresponding to each characteristic below.
(a) the element with the electron configuration $1s^22s^22p^63s^23p^3$
(b) the alkaline earth element with the smallest atomic radius
(c) the element with the largest ionization energy in Group 5A
(d) the element whose 2+ ion has the configuration $[Kr]4d^5$
(e) the element with the most negative electron affinity in Group 7A
(f) the element whose electron configuration is $[Ar]3d^{10}4s^2$

41. ■ Arrange the following atoms in the order of increasing ionization energy: Si, K, P, and Ca.

42. ■ Rank the following in order of increasing ionization energy: Cl, Ca^{2+}, and Cl^-. Briefly explain your answer.

43. ■ Answer the questions below about the elements A and B, which have the electron configurations shown.

$$A = [Kr]5s^1 \quad B = [Ar]3d^{10}4s^24p^4$$

(a) Is element A a metal, nonmetal, or metalloid?
(b) Which element has the greater ionization energy?
(c) Which element has the less negative electron affinity?
(d) Which element has the larger atomic radius?
(e) What is the formula for a compound formed between A and B?

44. ■ Answer the following questions about the elements with the electron configurations shown here:

$$A = [Ar]4s^2 \quad B = [Ar]3d^{10}4s^24p^5$$

(a) Is element A a metal, metalloid, or nonmetal?
(b) Is element B a metal, metalloid, or nonmetal?
(c) Which element is expected to have the larger ionization energy?
(d) Which element has the smaller atomic radius?

45. ■ Which of the following ions are unlikely to be found in a chemical compound: Cs^+, In^{4+}, Fe^{6+}, Te^{2-}, Sn^{5+}, and I^-? Explain briefly.

46. ■ Place the following ions in order of decreasing size: K^+, Cl^-, S^{2-}, and Ca^{2+}.

47. ■ Answer each of the following questions:
(a) Of the elements S, Se, and Cl, which has the largest atomic radius?
(b) Which has the larger radius, Br or Br^-?
(c) Which should have the largest difference between the first and second ionization energy: Si, Na, P, or Mg?
(d) Which has the largest ionization energy: N, P, or As?
(e) Which of the following has the largest radius: O^{2-}, N^{3-}, or F^-?

48. ■ The following are isoelectronic species: Cl^-, K^+, and Ca^{2+}. Rank them in order of increasing (a) size, (b) ionization energy, and (c) electron affinity.

49. ■ Compare the elements Na, B, Al, and C with regard to the following properties:
(a) Which has the largest atomic radius?
(b) Which has the most negative electron affinity?
(c) Place the elements in order of increasing ionization energy.

50. ■ ▲ Two elements in the second transition series (Y through Cd) have four unpaired electrons in their 3+ ions. What elements fit this description?

51. The configuration for an element is given here.

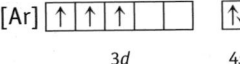

3d   4s

(a) What is the identity of the element with this configuration?
(b) Is a sample of the element paramagnetic or diamagnetic?
(c) How many unpaired electrons does a 3+ ion of this element have?

52. ■ The configuration of an element is given here.

[Ar] ↑ ↑ ↑ | | ↑↓

3d   4s

(a) What is the identity of the element?
(b) In what group and period is the element found?
(c) Is the element a nonmetal, a main group element, a transition metal, a lanthanide, or an actinide?
(d) Is the element diamagnetic or paramagnetic? If paramagnetic, how many unpaired electrons are there?
(e) Write a complete set of quantum numbers (n, ℓ, m_ℓ, m_s) for each of the valence electrons.
(f) What is the configuration of the 2+ ion formed from this element? Is the ion diamagnetic or paramagnetic?

In the Laboratory

53. Nickel(II) formate [$Ni(HCO_2)_2$] is widely used as catalyst precursor and to make metallic nickel. It can be prepared in the general chemistry laboratory by treating readily available nickel(II) acetate with formic acid (HCO_2H).

$$Ni(CH_3CO_2)_2(aq) + 2\ HCO_2H(aq) \rightarrow$$
$$Ni(HCO_2)_2(aq) + 2\ CH_3CO_2H(aq)$$

Green crystalline $Ni(HCO_2)_2$ is precipitated after adding ethanol to the solution.
(a) What is the theoretical yield of nickel(II) formate from 0.500 g of nickel(II) acetate and excess formic acid?
(b) Is nickel(II) formate paramagnetic or diamagnetic? If it is paramagnetic, how many unpaired electrons would you expect?
(c) If nickel(II) formate is heated to 300 °C in the absence of air for 30 minutes, the salt decomposes to form pure nickel powder. What mass of nickel powder should be produced by heating 253 mg of nickel(II) formate? Are nickel atoms paramagnetic?

54. ▲ Spinels are solids with the general formula $M^{2+}(M'^{3+})_2O_4$ (where M^{2+} and M'^{3+} are metal cations of the same or different metals). The best-known example is common magnetite, Fe_3O_4 [which you can formulate as $(Fe^{2+})(Fe^{3+})_2O_4$].

Charles D. Winters

A crystal of a spinel.

(a) Given its name, it is evident that magnetite is ferromagnetic. How many unpaired electrons are there in iron(II) and in iron(III) ions?
(b) Two other spinels are $CoAl_2O_4$ and $SnCo_2O_4$. What metal ions are involved in each? What are their electron configurations? Are the metal ions also paramagnetic, and if so how many unpaired electrons are involved?

Summary and Conceptual Questions
The following questions use concepts from this and previous chapters.

55. Why is the radius of Li^+ so much smaller than the radius of Li? Why is the radius of F^- so much larger than the radius of F?

56. ■ Which ions in the following list are not likely to be found in chemical compounds: K^{2+}, Cs^+, Al^{4+}, F^{2-}, and Se^{2-}? Explain briefly.

57. ■ ▲ Two elements have the following first through fourth ionization energies. Deduce the group in the periodic table to which they probably belong. Explain briefly.

Ionization Energy (kJ/mol)	Element 1	Element 2
1st IE	1086.2	577.4
2nd IE	2352	1816.6
3rd IE	4620	2744.6
4th IE	6222	11575

58. ■ ▲ The ionization of the hydrogen atom can be calculated from Bohr's equation for the electron energy.

$$E = -(N_A Rhc)(Z^2/n^2)$$

where $N_A Rhc$ = 1312 kJ/mol and Z is the atomic number. Let us use this approach to calculate a possible ionization energy for helium. First, assume the electrons of the He experience the full 2+ nuclear charge. This gives us the upper limit for the ionization energy. Next, assume one electron of He completely screens the nuclear charge from the other electrons, so $Z = 1$. This gives us a lower limit to the ionization energy. Compare these calculated values for the upper and lower limits to the experimental value of 2372.3 kJ/mol. What does this tell us about the ability of one electron to screen the nuclear charge?

59. ■ Compare the configurations below with two electrons located in *p* orbitals. Which would be the most stable (have the lowest energy)? Which would be the least stable? Explain your answers.

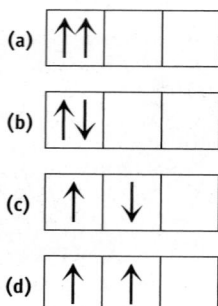

(a)

(b)

(c)

(d)

60. The bond lengths in Cl_2, Br_2, and I_2 are 200, 228, and 266 pm, respectively. Knowing that the tin radius is 141 pm, estimate the bond distances in Sn—Cl, Sn—Br, and Sn—I. Compare the estimated values with the experimental values of 233, 250, and 270 pm, respectively.

61. Write electron configurations to show the first two ionization processes for potassium. Explain why the second ionization energy is much greater than the first.

62. Explain how the ionization energy of atoms changes and why the change occurs when proceeding down a group of the periodic table.

63. (a) Explain why the sizes of atoms change when proceeding across a period of the periodic table.
(b) Explain why the sizes of transition metal atoms change very little across a period.

64. ■ Which of the following elements has the greatest difference between its first and second ionization energies: C, Li, N, Be? Explain your answer.

65. ▲ What arguments would you use to convince another student in general chemistry that MgO consists of the ions Mg^{2+} and O^{2-} and not the ions Mg^+ and O^-? What experiments could be done to provide some evidence that the correct formulation of magnesium oxide is $Mg^{2+}O^{2-}$?

66. Explain why the first ionization energy of Ca is greater than that of K, whereas the second ionization energy of Ca is lower than the second ionization energy of K.

67. The energies of the orbitals in many elements have been determined. For the first two periods they have the following values:

Element	1s (kJ/mol)	2s (kJ/mol)	2p (kJ/mol)
H	−1313		
He	−2373		
Li		−520.0	
Be		−899.3	
B		−1356	−800.8
C		−1875	−1029
N		−2466	−1272
O		−3124	−1526
F		−3876	−1799
Ne		−4677	−2083

(a) ▲ Why do the orbital energies generally become more negative on proceeding across the second period?
(b) How are these values related to the ionization energy and electron affinity of the elements?
(c) Use these energy values to explain the observation that the ionization energies of the first four second-period elements are in the order Li < Be > B < C.

Note that these energy values are the basis for the discussion in the Simulation on ChemistryNow Screen 7.8. (Data from J. B. Mann, T. L. Meek, and L. C. Allen: *Journal of the American Chemical Society*, Vol. 122, p. 2780, 2000.)

68. ▲ The ionization energies for the removal of the first electron in Si, P, S, and Cl are as listed in the table below. Briefly rationalize this trend.

Element	First Ionization Energy (kJ/mol)
Si	780
P	1060
S	1005
Cl	1255

69. Using your knowledge of the trends in element sizes on going across the periodic table, explain briefly why the density of the elements increases from K through V.

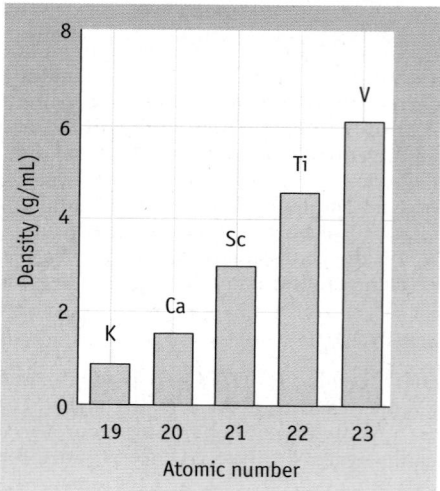

70. The densities (in g/cm³) of elements in Groups 6B, 8B, and 1B are given in the table below.

Period 4	Cr, 7.19	Co, 8.90	Cu, 8.96
Period 5	Mo, 10.22	Rh, 12.41	Ag, 10.50
Period 6	W, 19.30	Ir, 22.56	Au, 19.32

Transition metals in the sixth period all have much greater densities than the elements in the same groups in the fourth and fifth periods. Refer to Figure 7.9, and explain this observation.

▲ more challenging   ■ in OWL   Blue-numbered questions answered in Appendix O

71. ■ The discovery of two new elements (atomic numbers 113 and 115) was announced in February 2004.

Courtesy of Lawrence Livermore National Laboratory

Some members of the team that discovered elements 113 and 115 at the Lawrence Livermore National Laboratory (left to right): Jerry Landrum, Dawn Shaughnessy, Joshua Patin, Philip Wilk, and Kenton Moody.

(a) Use *spdf* and noble gas notations to give the electron configurations of these two elements.

(b) Name an element in the same periodic group as the two elements.

(c) Element 113 was made by firing a light atom at a heavy americium atom. The two combine to give a nucleus with 113 protons. What light atom was used as a projectile?

72. ■ Explain why the reaction of calcium and fluorine does not form CaF_3.

73. ▲ Thionyl chloride, $SOCl_2$, is an important chlorinating and oxidizing agent in organic chemistry. It is prepared industrially by oxygen atom transfer from SO_3 to SCl_2.

$$SO_3(g) + SCl_2(g) \rightarrow SO_2(g) + SOCl_2(g)$$

(a) Give the electron configuration for an atom of sulfur using an orbital box diagram. Do not use the noble gas notation.

(b) Using the configuration given in part (a), write a set of quantum numbers for the highest-energy electron in a sulfur atom.

(c) What element involved in this reaction (O, S, Cl) should have the smallest ionization energy? The smallest radius?

(d) Which should be smaller: the sulfide ion, S^{2-}, or a sulfur atom, S?

(e) If you want to make 675 g of $SOCl_2$, what mass of SCl_2 is required?

(f) If you use 10.0 g of SO_3 and 10.0 g of SCl_2, what is the theoretical yield of $SOCl_2$?

(g) $\Delta_r H°$ for the reaction of SO_3 and SCl_2 is -96.0 kJ/mol $SOCl_2$ produced. Using data in Appendix L, calculate the standard molar enthalpy of formation of SCl_2.

74. Sodium metal reacts readily with chlorine gas to give sodium chloride. *(See ChemistryNow Screen 7.17 Chemical Puzzler.)*

$$Na(s) + \tfrac{1}{2}\,Cl_2(g) \rightarrow NaCl(s)$$

(a) What is the reducing agent in this reaction? What property of the element contributes to its ability to act as a reducing agent?

(b) What is the oxidizing agent in this reaction? What property of the element contributes to its ability to act as an oxidizing agent?

(c) Why does the reaction produce NaCl and not a compound such as Na_2Cl or $NaCl_2$?

75. ▲ Slater's rules are a simple way to estimate the effective nuclear charge experienced by an electron. In this approach, the "shielding constant," σ, is calculated. The effective nuclear charge is then the difference between σ and the atomic number, Z. (Note that the results in Table 7.2 were calculated in a slightly different way.)

$$Z^* = Z - \sigma$$

The shielding constant, σ, is calculated using the following rules:

1. The electrons of an atom are grouped as follows: $(1s)$ $(2s, 2p)$ $(3s, 3p)$ $(3d)$ $(4s, 4p)$ $(4d)$, and so on.

2. Electrons in higher groups (to the right) do not shield those in the lower groups.

3. For ns and np valence electrons
   a) Electrons in the same ns, np group contribute 0.35 (for $1s$ 0.30 works better).
   b) Electrons in the $n - 1$ group contribute 0.85.
   c) Electrons in the $n - 2$ group (and lower) contribute 1.00.

4. For nd and nf electrons, electrons in the same nd or nf group contribute 0.35, and those in groups to the left contribute 1.00.

As an example, let us calculate Z^* for the outermost electron of oxygen:

$$\sigma = (2 \times 0.85) + (5 \times 0.35) = 3.45$$
$$Z^* = 8 - 3.45 = 4.55$$

(a) Calculate Z^* for F and Ne. Relate the Z^* values for O, F, and Ne to their relative atomic radii and ionization energies.

(b) Calculate Z^* for one of the $3d$ electrons of Mn, and compare this with Z^* for one of the $4s$ electrons of the element. Do the Z^* values give us some insight into the ionization of Mn to give the cation?

Milestones in the Development of Chemistry and the Modern View of Atoms and Molecules

John Emsley
University of Cambridge

The journey to our understanding of atoms and molecules began 2500 years ago in ancient Greece and continues today with developments in our understanding of chemical bonding and molecular structure. The journey may have started long ago, but it was only when chemistry developed in the 1700s that real progress was made. Today, we have instruments like the scanning tunneling microscope to help us visualize these tiny objects.

But let us start at the beginning and pay a short visit to the Greeks of 450 BC. Their civilization valued learning, and this led to various schools of philosophy. Their teachers did not engage in scientific research as we know it, so their theories were never more than thought experiments. Nevertheless, they correctly deduced that the world was made up of a few basic elements and that these existed as atoms, but they had no way of knowing which elements existed, or how small atoms were. Today, we know of 117 elements—at the last count—and that atoms are so tiny that the dot at the end of this sentence contains billions of them.

Greek Philosophers and Medieval Alchemists

The early Greek philosophers thought that there would be just one element and debated what it might be. Some favored air, some fire, some water, and some said earth. Eventually, Empedocles (who lived from around 490 to 430 BC) argued that all four were elements. This theory was believed for 2000 years—and yet it was wrong.

What form did these elements take? The first person to give an answer was Leucippus, around 450 BC, who said they must exist as atoms. This idea was developed by his pupil Democritus (460–370 BC), who was the first to use the word "atom," which means un-cut-able or indivisible. Epicurus (341–270 BC) said atoms were spherical, varied in size, and were constantly in motion. This theory remained also unchanged for 2000 years—but it was right.

Alchemy can trace its roots to ancient Egypt. The most famous Egyptian alchemist was Zosimos, who lived around 300 AD. He described such chemical processes as distillation and sublimation, crediting a woman alchemist, Maria the Jewess, with their invention. She lived about 100 AD and experimented with mercury and sulfur, but her best-known invention was the bain-Marie, which is still used in cooking.

Early Muslim rulers encouraged learning, and alchemy flourished. The best-known Arab alchemists were Geber (Jabir ibn Hayyan, 721–815 AD) and Rhazes (Abu Bakr Mohammad ibn Zakariyya al-Razi, 865–925 AD). Geber knew that when mercury and sulfur were combined, the product was a red compound, which we know as mercury (II) sulfide, but he believed that if the recipe were exactly right, then gold would be formed. Rhazes thought that all metals were made from mercury and sulfur, and his influential book, *Secret of Secrets*, contained a long list of chemicals, minerals, and apparatus that a modern chemist would recognize.

In the early Middle Ages, alchemists were at work in Europe, but only a little progress was made. A Spaniard, who also called himself Geber, discovered how to make nitric acid and knew that a mixture of nitric and hydrochloric acids (*aqua regia*) would dissolve gold. The European center for alchemy was Prague, where many alchemists practiced their art while some of their number merely

• **The Alchymist in Search of the Philosophere's Stone, Discovers Phosphorus.** Painted by J. Wright of Derby (1734–1797).

practiced deception, often convincing onlookers that they could turn base metals into gold.

The 1600s saw the gradual emergence of chemistry from alchemy, and in this period we find several men who are now recognized as true scientists but who were also secret alchemists, such as Robert Boyle (1626–1691) and even the great Isaac Newton (1642–1727). Today, Boyle is considered one of the founding fathers of chemistry. His book, *The Sceptical Chymist*, is regarded as the seminal work that broke the link between chemistry and alchemy.

The Philosopher's Stone, a legendary substance that can supposedly turn ordinary substances into gold, was the ultimate prize sought by alchemists. So, when the alchemist Hennig Brandt of Hamburg discovered phosphorus in 1669, he believed it would lead him to the Philosopher's Stone because of the almost miraculous ability of phosphorus to shine in the dark and burst into flames. Some of this new wonder material was shown to Boyle, who eventually was able to make it himself. (It was formed by heating evaporated urine residues to red heat.) What Boyle did next distinguished him as a true chemist: he researched the properties of phosphorus and its reactions with other materials and published his findings, not in the secret language of the alchemists but in plain English, and in a manner that would allow even a modern chemist to repeat what he had done. Phosphorus was a new element although it was not recognized as such for another century.

Boyle too thought about the nature of matter, and he came up with a definition of an element. He wrote:

"I mean by Elements, as those Chymists that speak plainest do by the Principles, certain Primitive and Simple, or perfectly unmingled bodies; which not being made of any other bodies, or of one another, are the ingredients of which all those call'd perfectly mixt Bodies are immediately compounded, and into which they are ultimately resolved."

We can see that Boyle was struggling with the idea of elements and how these can be compounded together.

Chemists of the 18th–19th Centuries

The theory of four elements was dealt its first body blow by a shy but extremely wealthy Englishman, Henry Cavendish (1731–1810), who had his own laboratory near London. There, he investigated gases. In 1784, he discovered hydrogen and observed that when it burned, water was formed. The French chemist Antoine Lavoisier (1743–1794) (◄ page 114) also studied gases, but he went one step further and noted that when a *mixture* of hydrogen

Henry Cavendish (1731–1810, left) and John Dalton (1766–1844, right).

and another newly discovered gas, oxygen, was sparked, it formed only water. Obviously, water was not an element, but hydrogen and oxygen were.

In 1789, Lavoisier wrote his influential book *Elements of Chemistry*, in which he defined a chemical element as something that could not be further broken down, and he listed 33 of them. Most of these are still considered elements today, but some—such as light, heat, and the earths (later shown to be oxides)—are not. His list is given in Table 1. Lavoisier was the founder of modern chemistry, but, as described on page 114, he fell out of favor with the leaders of the French Revolution and was guillotined.

The next major advance in chemical understanding came from a modest school teacher, John Dalton (1766–1844), who lived in Manchester, England. He knew of the *Law of Fixed Proportions*, which said elements combined in definite ratios by weight, and said it could only be so if they were composed of atoms. The idea of atoms had been revived by scientists like Newton in the 1600s, who said elements would cluster together, but nothing had come of such speculations because chemistry was still little more than mystical alchemy.

In 1803, Dalton gave a talk to the Manchester (England) Literary and Philosophical Society on the way gases dis-

TABLE 1 The Elements According to Lavoisier (1789)

Gases	Nonmetals	Metals		Earths
Light	Sulfur	Antimony	Mercury	Lime
Heat	Phosphorus	Arsenic	Molybdenum	Magnesia
Oxygen	Carbon	Bismuth	Nickel	Barytes
Nitrogen	Chloride	Cobalt	Platinum	Alumina
Hydrogen	Fluoride	Copper	Silver	Silica
	Borate	Gold	Tin	
		Iron	Tungsten	
		Lead	Zinc	
		Manganese		

solved in water, and when his talk was published in the Society's Proceedings he included a table of relative atomic weights, which were based on hydrogen having a value of 1. He listed 20 elements with their weights and said they combined to form "compound atoms," his name for what we now call molecules. At a stroke, Dalton not only revived the idea of atoms, but gave them weight. In his book of 1808, *New System of Chemical Philosophy*, he went further, and he said an atom was a "solid, massy, hard, impenetrable, moveable particle." This description was eventually proved wrong on many counts, but he was right that they existed.

Chemists in the early 1800s were puzzled by the fact that most of the new atomic weights were whole numbers. An explanation was suggested in 1815 by William Prout (1785–1850), who went further than Dalton and reasoned that atoms were not indivisible but were composed of hydrogen. If the atomic weight of hydrogen was taken as 1, then it explained why all the other elements had weights that were whole numbers, or nearly so. In fact, most elements have atomic weights that fall within the limits of $\pm$ 0.1 of a whole number, with very few having fractional numbers. Nevertheless, it was the few exceptions that seemed to disprove Prout's theory, which could not explain the atomic weight of chlorine, which was 35.5, or copper, which was 63.5. (The explanation, of course, lies with their isotopic composition, a concept that lay 100 years in the future.)

Prout was almost right. Hydrogen, or at least 99.99% of it, consists of a single proton surrounded by a single electron. The proton is the nucleus, and that accounts for virtually all of the mass. We now classify elements based on how many protons their nuclei contain, with each element on the periodic table differing from the one immediately preceding it by one proton. In some ways, then, they differ according to the nucleus of hydrogen. When the proton was finally identified in 1919, and its importance realized, it took its name from the Greek word *protos* meaning first, although Ernest Rutherford, who made the discovery, also said the name was chosen partly in honor of Prout.

Back in the early 1800s, chemists preferred atomic weights that were calculated relative to that of oxygen because oxygen forms compounds with almost all other elements. (Today, atomic weights are based on the carbon isotope carbon-12, which is taken as exactly 12.) Like Dalton, they believed water consisted of one oxygen and one hydrogen atom, so naturally their scale of atomic weights was of little use.

Inaccurate atomic weights, however, did not hinder the discovery of more and more elements. The 1860s were a particularly fruitful decade with the introduction of the atomic spectroscope, which revealed that each element had a characteristic "fingerprint" pattern of lines in its visible spectrum. As a result, the discoveries of rubidium, cesium, thallium, and indium were announced in the years 1860–1863. The total of known elements was now 65, and chemists were beginning to ask whether there was a limit to their number.

Meanwhile, the Italian chemist Stanislao Cannizzaro (1826–1910) had published a correct list of atomic weights, which he circulated at the First International Chemical Congress, held in Karlsruhe, Germany, in 1860. Dimitri Mendeleev attended the conference and took a copy of Cannizzaro's atomic weights back to St. Petersburg in Russia. What he did with it was to revolutionize chemistry, a story that is told in Chapter 2.

Dalton had suggested ways in which atoms might combine to form larger units. It was clear that the world was composed primarily not of single atoms but of molecules, and chemistry was the science of studying them. The word *molecule* was first given a chemical meaning in 1811; before then, it had simply been a French word for something extremely small. In 1873, its chemical meaning was spelled out by James Clerk Maxwell, who wrote a milestone paper in the journal *Nature* in which he defined a molecule as "the smallest possible portion of a particular substance" beyond which it would no longer have the properties associated with that substance. This is the meaning it still has.

In the 1800s, chemical analysis became quite sophisticated, and the elements in a chemical compound could be identified and expressed as numbers. For example, alcohol was C_2H_6O, but what was it really? And why did dimethyl ether, which was a different substance, have exactly the same formula? The concept of valency could explain how elements combined. Hydrogen had a valency of 1, oxygen of 2 as in H_2O, nitrogen of 3 as in NH_3, and carbon of 4 as in CH_4, but this in itself was not enough to explain what molecules really were. Turning valences into actual molecular arrangements was the next step, and two people were instrumental in doing this: 29-year-old August Kekulé (1829–1896) in 1858, and 22-year-old Jacobus van't Hoff (1852–1911) in 1878.

Kekulé was one of the great chemists of the second half of the 1800s. He is best known for his theory of molecule structures based on valence and especially of organic molecules in which carbon is four-valent and bonds in various ways to other atoms including car-

August Kekulé (1829–1896).

bon atoms. He published his paper only weeks before one by Archibald Scott Couper (1831–1892), a young Scottish chemist, who was studying in Paris. In fact, Couper had written his paper before Kekulé, but his supervisor took rather a long time to read it, so he lost out. In some ways, Scott Couper's paper was even more advanced than Kekulé's because he drew lines between atoms to indicate actual chemical bonds. (Scott Couper's sad life was to end in an insane asylum.)

Kekulé also claimed some undeserved fame for having deduced that benzene, a molecule whose formula, C_6H_6, seemed to violate the laws of valency, consisted of a ring of six carbon atoms each with hydrogen attached. Late in life, he said it had come to him in a dream while he was working in London in the mid-1850s and fell asleep on the bus taking him home one evening. What he had conveniently forgotten was that Johann Loschmidt (1821–1895), a modest high school teacher from Vienna, had deduced the structure as many as 4 years earlier and published it in an essay that Kekulé had read.

Van't Hoff focused on the problem of how two compounds with exactly the same formula and physical properties could differ in two respects: their crystal shapes could vary but were mirror images of each other and the way they rotated a beam of polarized light, one clockwise, the other counterclockwise. He put forward his theory, in 1874, that this could be explained if carbon formed four bonds arranged tetrahedrally. The idea was ridiculed by older chemists as "fantastic foolishness" and the "shallow speculations" of a youth, yet it could not be ignored because it explained why molecules could be left and right handed (▶ page 446). In any event, he had the laugh on them because he was awarded the first ever Nobel Prize in Chemistry in 1901.

Atomic Structure—Remarkable Discoveries—1890s and Beyond

Like the 1860s, the 1890s was another decade of remarkable chemical discovery, the most surprising being that atoms could spontaneously disintegrate. It began in 1896 when Henri Becquerel (1852–1908) started to investigate the mineral potassium uranyl sulfate [$K_2SO_4 \cdot UO_2(SO_4)_2 \cdot 2 H_2O$]. He found by chance that it was emitting invisible rays that caused a photographic plate to produce an image. Other uranium compounds also gave off these rays. What was equally intriguing was the observation that the common uranium ore pitchblende contained something that gave off more of this invisible radiation than could be explained by the uranium it contained. The husband and wife team of Pierre Curie (1859–1906) and Marie Curie (1867–1934) worked for weeks in an old shed in Paris to separate this impurity. Eventually, they succeeded, and in 1898 they an-

Marie Curie (1867–1934) and Pierre Curie (1859–1906). Marie Curie is one of very few people and the only woman to have ever received two Nobel Prizes. She was born in Poland but studied and carried out her research in Paris. In 1903, she shared the Nobel Prize in physics with H. Becquerel and her husband Pierre for their discovery of radioactivity. She received a second Nobel Prize in 1911 for chemistry, for the discovery of two new chemical elements, radium and polonium (the latter named from her homeland, Poland). A unit of radioactivity (curie, Ci) and an element (curium, Cm) are named in her honor. Pierre, who died in an accident in 1906, was also well known for his research on magnetism. One of their daughters, Irène, married Frédéric Joliot, and they shared in the 1935 Nobel Prize in chemistry for their discovery of artificial radioactivity.

Emilio Segre Visual Archives

nounced the discovery of two new, intensely radioactive elements: polonium and radium. Radioactivity was the word they invented to describe the new phenomenon of invisible rays (Figure 1), and they called one of the new elements radium because of its intense rays, and the other polonium after Marie's native country Poland.

In 1897, J. J. Thomson (1856–1940) reported his studies of another type of ray, cathode rays. Cathode ray tubes were glass vacuum tubes containing two metal electrodes. When a high voltage is applied to the electrodes, electricity flows from the negative electrode (cathode) to the positive electrode (anode) even though there is nothing there to conduct it. Thomson showed that there was, in fact, a stream of charged particles moving from the cathode to the anode and that these could be deflected by electric and magnetic fields, which showed they were negatively charged (Figure 2). He deduced they were two thousand times lighter than even the lightest element, hydrogen. They became known as *electrons*, a term already invented to describe the smallest particle of electricity.

Sir Joseph John Thomson (1856–1940). Cavendish Professor of Experimental Physics at Cambridge University in England. In 1896, he gave a series of lectures at Princeton University in the U.S. on the discharge of electricity in gases. It was this work on cathode rays that led to his discovery of the electron, which he announced at a lecture on the evening of Friday, April 30, 1897. He later published a number of books on the electron and was awarded the Nobel Prize in physics in 1906.

Oesper Collection in the History of Chemistry/University of Cincinnati

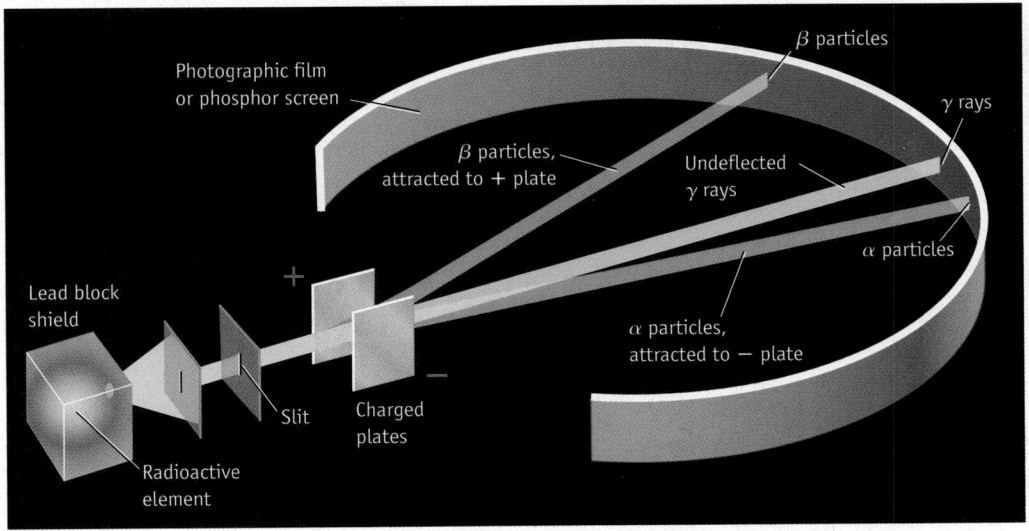

Figure 1 Radioactivity. Alpha (α), beta (β), and gamma (γ) rays from a radioactive element are separated by passing them between electrically charged plates. Positively charged α particles are attracted to the negative plate, and negatively charged β particles are attracted to the positive plate. (Note that the heavier α particles are deflected less than the lighter β particles.) Gamma rays have no electric charge and pass undeflected between the charged plates.

(See ChemistryNow Screen 2.5 for an interactive version of this figure.)

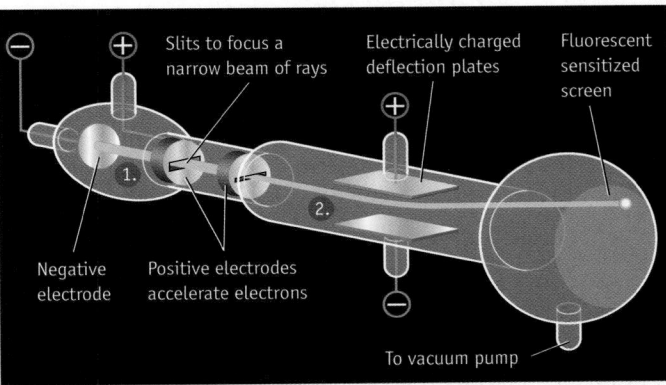

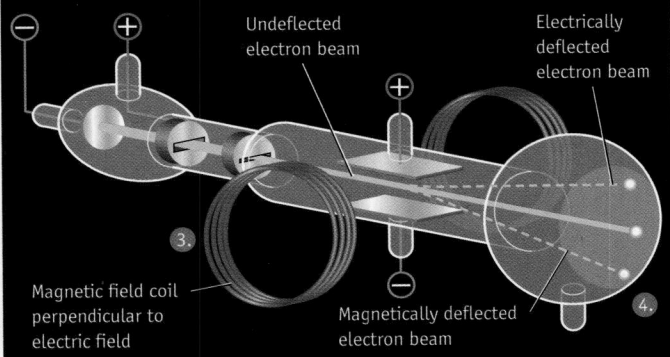

1. A beam of electrons (cathode rays) is accelerated through two focusing slits.

2. When passing through an electric field, the beam of electrons is deflected.

3. The experiment is arranged so that the electric field causes the beam of electrons to be deflected in one direction. The magnetic field deflects the beam in the opposite direction.

4. By balancing the effects of the electrical and magnetic fields, the charge-to-mass ratio of the electron can be determined.

Figure 2 Thomson's experiment to measure the electron's charge-to-mass ratio. This experiment was done by J. J. Thomson in 1896–1897. (See ChemistryNow Screen 2.6 for an interactive version of this figure.)

Thomson reasoned that electrons must originate from the atoms of the cathode, and he suggested that an atom was a uniform sphere of positively charged matter in which negative electrons were embedded. That view of an atom was not to persist for long.

In 1886, a few years before Thomson's report, Eugene Goldstein (1850–1930) had also explored cathode rays and had noticed something rather unexpected. Although negatively charged particles were streaming from the cathode to the anode, there were also positively charged particles moving in the opposite direction, and these could be observed if tiny holes were drilled into the cathode plate. These rays, which he called *Kanalstrahlen* from the German word meaning channel rays, became known as canal rays or anode rays (Figure 3). Goldstein thought he had discovered a basic type of atomic particle, the opposite of the

electron, but his positive particles were just traces of residual gas ions in the cathode-ray tube.

The man most associated with discovering the true nature of the atom was Ernest Rutherford (1871–1937), better known as Lord Rutherford. He contributed to the story of atoms in three important ways: he identified the rays that radioactive atoms emitted; he proved that an atom has a tiny nucleus of positively charged protons; and he split the atom; in other words, he converted one element into another. Rutherford, who was born near Nelson on the South Island of New Zealand, went to Cambridge University in England, where he studied under Thomson. He concerned himself with radioactive phenomena and in the years 1898–1900 he identified the various types of radiation: alpha (α), beta (β), and gamma (γ) rays. Alpha and beta rays were particles, the former with an electric charge (+2) twice as

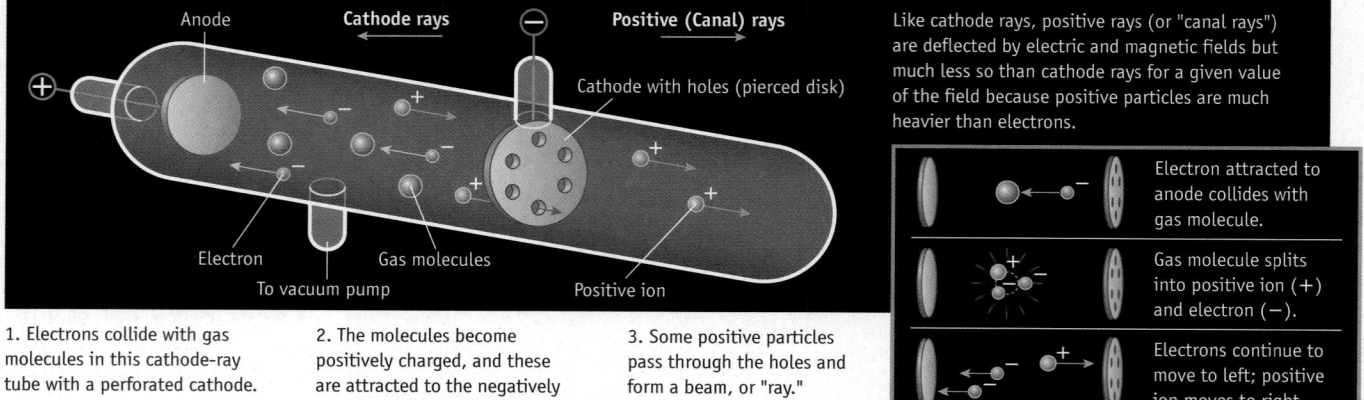

Like cathode rays, positive rays (or "canal rays") are deflected by electric and magnetic fields but much less so than cathode rays for a given value of the field because positive particles are much heavier than electrons.

Electron attracted to anode collides with gas molecule.

Gas molecule splits into positive ion (+) and electron (−).

Electrons continue to move to left; positive ion moves to right.

1. Electrons collide with gas molecules in this cathode-ray tube with a perforated cathode.

2. The molecules become positively charged, and these are attracted to the negatively charged, perforated cathode.

3. Some positive particles pass through the holes and form a beam, or "ray."

Figure 3 Canal rays. In 1886, Eugene Goldstein detected a stream of particles traveling in the direction opposite to that of the negatively charged cathode rays. We now know that these particles are positively charged ions formed by collisions of electrons with gaseous molecules in the cathode-ray tube. (See ChemistryNow Screen 2.8 for an animation of this experiment.)

large as that of the latter, which was negatively charged (−1). We now know that α particles are helium nuclei and that β particles are electrons. Gamma rays are like light rays but with much shorter wavelengths.

Rutherford moved to McGill University in Montreal, Canada, where he collaborated with Frederick Soddy (1877–1956), and together they were able to show that another element, thorium, was radioactive and that it decayed via a series of elements, finally ending up as stable lead. Together, they published their theory of radioactivity in 1908. That same year, Rutherford returned to England to become Professor of Physics at Manchester, where his research was to reveal even more spectacular discoveries about atoms.

Soddy had already returned to England in 1903 and was now working in University College London, where he was able to prove that as radium decayed it formed helium gas. He then moved to Glasgow, Scotland, and there his research showed that atoms of the same element could have more than one atomic mass, and the idea of isotopes was born. These made it possible to explain why an element could have an atomic weight which was not a whole num-

ber. For example, chlorine's was 35.5 because it consisted of 76% the isotope chlorine-35 plus 24% of chlorine-37.

Meanwhile at Manchester, two of Rutherford's students—Hans Geiger (1882–1945) and Ernest Marsden (1889–1970)—bombarded thin gold foil with α particles to test whether Thomson's model of a solid atom with embedded electrons was correct (Figure 4). Almost all the particles passed straight through the gold foil as if there was nothing there. However, they were surprised to find that a few were deflected sideways; some even bounced right back. This experiment proved that an atom of gold is mostly empty space with a tiny nucleus at its center. It was the electrons that accounted for most of its volume. Rutherford calculated that the central nucleus of an atom occupied only 1/10,000th of its volume. He also calculated that a gold nucleus had a positive charge of around 100 units and a radius of about 10^{-12} cm. (The currently accepted values are +79 for atomic charge and 10^{-13} cm for the radius.) Just as Dalton had done more than a century before, Rutherford announced his findings at a meeting of the Manchester Literary and Philosophical Society. The date was March 7, 1911.

In 1908, the American physicist Robert Millikan (1868–1953), based at the California Institute of Technology (Caltech), measured the charge on the electron as 1.592×10^{-19} coulombs, not far from today's accepted value of 1.602×10^{-19} C (Figure 5). Millikan rightly assumed this was the fundamental unit of charge. Knowing this, and the charge-to-mass ratio determined by Thomson, enabled the mass of an electron to be calculated as 9.109×10^{-28} g.

In 1913, Henry G. J. Moseley (1887–1915) realized it was not its atomic weight that defined an element but its atomic number, which he deduced from a study of the wavelengths of lines in x-ray spectra. Moseley was then able to put the periodic table of elements on a more secure footing. (Sadly, his life came to an end when a bullet from a sniper killed him in World War I.) Mendeleev had been

Ernest Rutherford (1871–1937). Rutherford was born in New Zealand in 1871 but went to Cambridge University in England to pursue his Ph.D. in physics in 1895. There, he worked with J. J. Thomson, and it was at Cambridge that he discovered α and β radiation. At McGill University in Canada in 1899, Rutherford did further experiments to prove that α radiation is composed of helium nuclei and that β radiation consists of electrons. He received the Nobel Prize in chemistry for his work in 1908. His research on the structure of the atom was done after he moved to Manchester University in England. In 1919, he returned to Cambridge University, where he took up the position formerly held by Thomson. In his career, Rutherford guided the work of 10 future recipients of the Nobel Prize. Element 104 has been named rutherfordium in his honor.

Oesper Collection in the History of Chemistry/University of Cincinnati

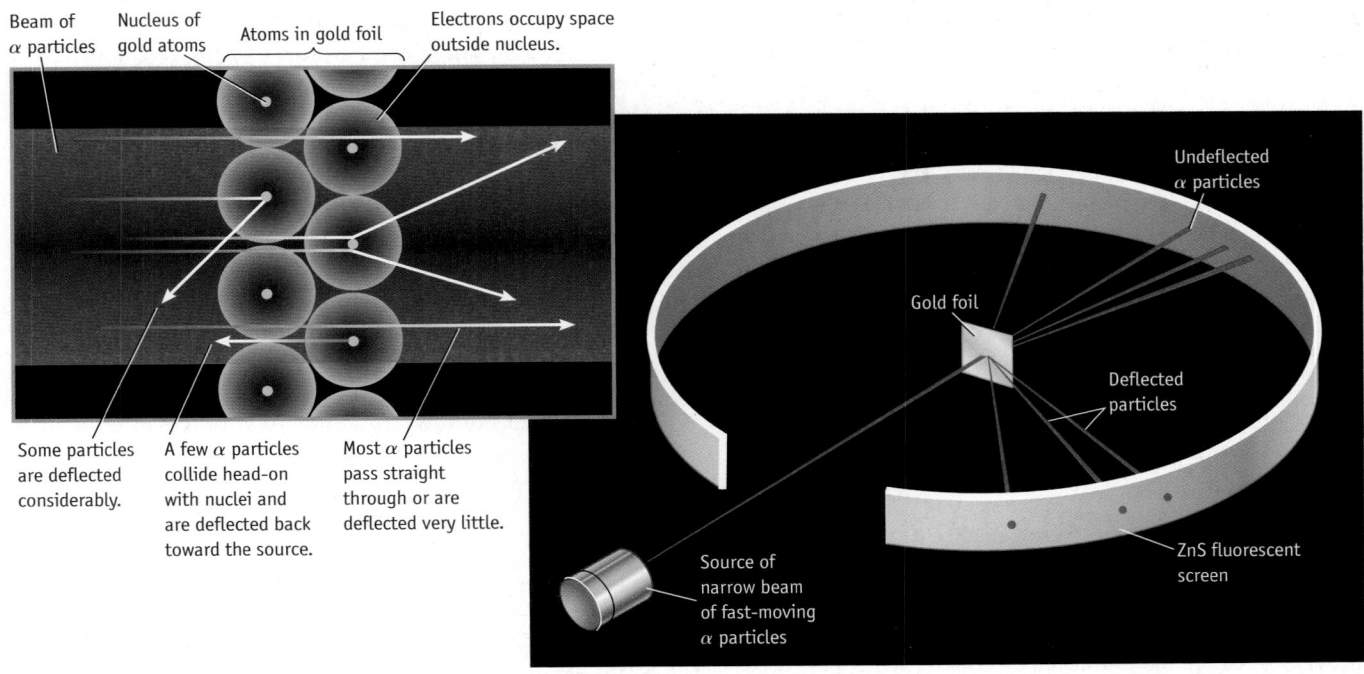

Beam of α particles
Nucleus of gold atoms
Atoms in gold foil
Electrons occupy space outside nucleus.

Some particles are deflected considerably.

A few α particles collide head-on with nuclei and are deflected back toward the source.

Most α particles pass straight through or are deflected very little.

Undeflected α particles

Gold foil

Deflected particles

ZnS fluorescent screen

Source of narrow beam of fast-moving α particles

Figure 4 Rutherford's experiment to determine the structure of the atom. A beam of positively charged α particles was directed at a thin gold foil. A fluorescent screen coated with zinc sulfide (ZnS) was used to detect particles passing through or deflected by the foil. (A flash of light is seen when a particle strikes the screen.) Most of the particles passed through the foil, but some were deflected from their path. A few were even deflected backward. (See ChemistryNow Screen 2.10 to explore an interactive version of this figure accompanied by an exercise.)

perplexed by some elements when he arranged them in order of increasing atomic weight. For example, tellurium has an atomic weight of 127.6, and iodine has an atomic weight of 126.9. The problem was that their properties indicated that tellurium should be placed before iodine in the periodic table. Arranging the elements in order of increasing atomic number, however, removed this problem. Tellurium has an atomic number of 52, and iodine has an atomic number of 53, thus justifying placing tellurium before iodine in the table.

Although he was not to know it, Moseley's atomic number corresponded to the number of protons in the nucleus. In 1919, Rutherford proved there were such things as protons, and these were the positive charges located at the center of an atom. Atoms were at last correctly seen as consisting of positive protons balanced by the same number of negative electrons.

In 1919, Rutherford "split the atom" according to the newspapers of the day. What he had performed was the first-ever successful experiment deliberately designed to

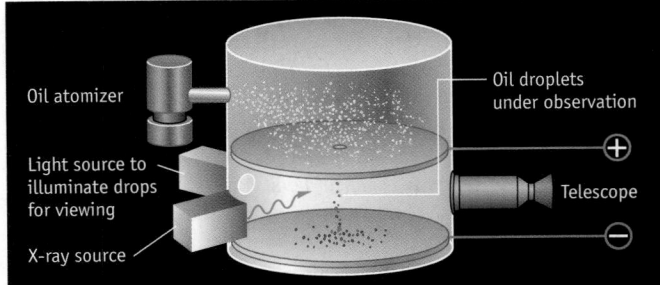

Oil atomizer

Oil droplets under observation

Light source to illuminate drops for viewing

Telescope

X-ray source

1. A fine mist of oil drops is introduced into one chamber.

2. The droplets fall one by one into the lower chamber under the force of gravity.

3. Gas molecules in the bottom chamber are ionized (split into electrons and a positive fragment) by a beam of x-rays. The electrons adhere to the oil drops, some droplets having one electron, some two, and so on.

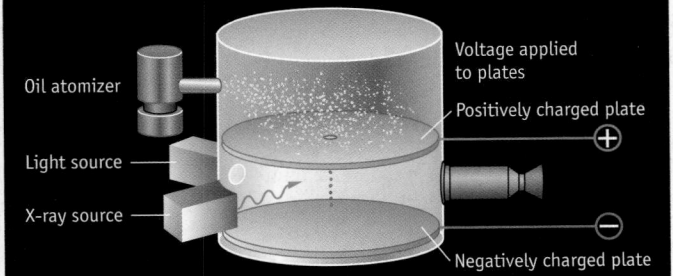

Oil atomizer

Voltage applied to plates

Positively charged plate

Light source

X-ray source

Negatively charged plate

These negatively charged droplets continue to fall due to gravity.

4. By carefully adjusting the voltage on the plates, the force of gravity on the droplet is exactly counterbalanced

by the attraction of the negative droplet to the upper, positively charged plate.

Analysis of these forces led to a value for the charge on the electron.

Figure 5 Millikan's experiment to determine the electron charge. The experiment was done by R. A. Millikan in 1909. (See ChemistryNow Screen 2.7 for an interactive exercise on this experiment.)

convert one element into another. He bombarded nitrogen gas with α particles, and this led to its conversion to oxygen and hydrogen. We can express this as an equation:

$$^{14}N \text{ (7 protons)} + \alpha \text{ particle } (^4He, \text{ 2 protons}) \rightarrow$$
$$^{17}O \text{ (8 protons)} + {}^1H \text{ (1 proton)}$$

By about 1920, the image of an atom was that it consisted of a tight nucleus, where all the protons were located, surrounded by a fuzzy cloud of negatively charged electrons, and that these were circling the nucleus rather like planets orbiting the sun. And just as the planets don't move in a random way, so electrons were confined to particular orbits, some nearer the nucleus, some farther away.

The physical nature of atoms was known, but how could the arrangement of electrons be explained? Niels Bohr (1885–1962) was the scientist who helped solve that puzzle.

He lived in Copenhagen, Denmark, and had trained under J. J. Thomson and Ernest Rutherford in England. It was while studying atomic spectra in England that he began to develop his theory of electrons circulating in orbits around the nucleus and with specific quantized energies (◀ page 276). Bohr postulated that the electrons were confined to specific energy levels called orbits. He could then understand the atomic emission spectrum of hydrogen by postulating that the lines it displayed corresponded to discrete quantities of energy (quanta) that an electron emitted as it jumped from one orbit to another.

Bohr's idea of specific energy levels is still retained, but his idea of orbits at specific distances has been revised to be the orbitals of modern atomic theory (Chapter 6). Also involved in applying quantum theory to electron energies were Erwin Schrödinger (1887–1961), who devised a math-

Historical Perspectives   20th-Century Giants of Science

Many of the advances in science occurred during the early part of the 20th century, as the result of theoretical studies by some of the greatest minds in the history of science.

Max Karl Ernst Ludwig Planck (1858–1947) was raised in Germany, where his father was a professor at a university. While still in his teens, Planck decided to become a physicist, against the advice of the head of the physics department at

Max Planck

Munich, who told him, "The important discoveries [in physics] have been made. It is hardly worth entering physics anymore." Fortunately, Planck did not take this advice and went on to study thermodynamics. This interest led him eventually to consider the ultraviolet catastrophe in explanations of blackbody radiation and to develop his revolutionary hypothesis of quantized energy, which was announced 2 weeks before Christmas in 1900. He was awarded the Nobel Prize in physics in 1918 for this work. Einstein later said it was a longing to find harmony and order in nature, a "hunger in his soul," that spurred Planck on.

Erwin Schrödinger (1887–1961) was born in Vienna, Austria. Following his service as an artillery officer in World War I, he became a professor of physics. In 1928, he succeeded Planck as professor of physics at the University of Berlin. He shared the Nobel Prize in physics in 1933.

Erwin Schrödinger

Niels Bohr (1885–1962) was born in Copenhagen, Denmark. He earned a Ph.D. in physics in Copenhagen in 1911 and then went to work first with J. J. Thomson and later with Ernest Rutherford in England. It was there that he began to develop his theory of atomic structure and his explanation of atomic spectra. (He received the Nobel Prize in physics in 1922 for this work.) Bohr returned to Copenhagen, where he eventually became director of the Institute for Theoretical Physics. Many young physicists worked with him at the Institute, seven of whom eventually received Nobel Prizes in chemistry and physics. Among these scientists were Werner Heisenberg, Wolfgang Pauli, and Linus Pauling. Element 107 was recently named bohrium in Bohr's honor.

Niels Bohr

Werner Heisenberg (1901–1976) studied with Max Born and later with Bohr. He received the Nobel Prize in physics in 1932. The recent play *Copenhagen*, which has been staged in London and New York, centers on the relationship between Bohr and Heisenberg and their involvement in the development of atomic weapons in World War II.

Gilbert Newton Lewis (1875–1946) introduced the theory of the shared electron-pair chemical bond in a paper published in the *Journal of the American Chemical Society* in

Werner Heisenberg

1916. Lewis also made major contributions in acid–base chemistry, thermodynamics, and on the interaction of light with substances.

Lewis was born in Massachusetts but raised in Nebraska. After earning his B. A. and Ph.D. at Harvard, he began his career in 1912 at the University of California at Berkeley. He was not only a productive researcher, but was also an influential teacher. Among his ideas was the use of problem sets in teaching, an idea still in use today.

Gilbert Newton Lewis

Linus Pauling (1901–1994) was born in Portland, Oregon, earned a B.Sc. degree in chemical engineering from Oregon State College in 1922, and completed his Ph.D. in chemistry at the California Institute of Technology in 1925. In chemistry, he is best known for his book *The Nature of the Chemical Bond*. He also studied protein structure, and, in the words of Francis Crick, was "one of the founders of molecular biology." It was this work and his study of chemical bonding that were cited in the award of the Nobel Prize in chemistry in 1954. Although chemistry was the focus of his life, at the urging of his wife, Ava Helen, he was also involved in nuclear disarmament issues, and he received the Nobel Peace Prize in 1962 for the role he played in advocating for the nuclear test ban treaty.

Linus Pauling

ematical equation that described orbitals, and Werner Heisenberg (1901–1976), whose *Uncertainty Principle* said that we cannot ever know exactly both the position and the energy of an electron.

The nucleus of an atom still presented a problem in 1930. How could a large number of positively charged protons co-exist in a nucleus without their repelling one another so much so that the atom falls apart? Lead, for example, had 82 protons. There had to be something else in the nucleus, and it had to be a heavy particle to account for the atomic weight of an element, which was more than double its atomic number and in the case of lead was 207. In 1932, the British physicist James Chadwick (1891–1974) found the missing particles. He directed the very powerful α rays that were released from radioactive polonium towards a beryllium target. The secondary emanations emitted by the latter metal were strange in that they carried no charge but were massive enough to knock protons out of the nuclei of other atoms. These new particles, now known as *neutrons*, had no electric charge and a mass of 1.674927×10^{-24} g, slightly greater than the mass of a proton. (At the same time, Hans Falkenhagen in Germany discovered neutrons also, but he did not publish his results.) Chadwick had found the missing particle. It completed the chemists' picture of an atom. It also made it possible to produce elements heavier than uranium—as well as to create atomic bombs.

The Nature of the Chemical Bond

Molecules presented a more complex problem: how did atoms join together to form them? The first person to provide an answer based on the new view of the atom was the American chemist Gilbert Newton Lewis (1875–1946). In his chemistry lectures at the University of California–Berkeley in the early 1900s, he used dots to symbolize electrons, and he developed this idea so that it became more than just a teaching aid. Lewis said in 1916 that a single chemical bond was the sharing of a pair of electrons between two atoms; a double bond was the sharing of two pairs; and a triple bond the sharing of three pairs. This simple concept explained valency and structure and had enormous influence because it made so much of the chemistry of atoms and molecules understandable.

More sophisticated concepts of bonding were developed based on Max Planck's (1858–1947) theory that energy was quantized. Neils Bohr (1885–1962) and Robert Mulliken (1896–1986) saw that this implied there were only certain energy levels within an atom that its electrons could inhabit. Mulliken proposed a theory of chemical bonding based on combining atomic orbitals into molecular orbitals and showed how the energies of these related to the way the atomic orbitals overlapped. He also developed the theory of electronegativity, which is based on the relative abilities of atoms in molecules to attract electrons, again a concept useful in explaining chemical behavior.

For chemists, the man whose name is most famously linked to bonding was Linus Pauling (1901–1994). He wrote his first paper on the subject when he was only 27 years old, in 1928, and followed it with several more. He brought all his thoughts together in his seminal work *The Nature of the Chemical Bond* in 1939.

Of course, there are still many things to be discovered about atoms and molecules, but as far as chemistry was concerned, the age-old questions of what elements, atoms, and molecules really were had been answered by the mid-twentieth century. The world of the nucleus and of subatomic particles could be left to the physicists to investigate.

SUGGESTED READINGS

1. Eric Scerri, *The Periodic Table: Its Story and Its Significance*, Oxford University Press, New York, 2007.
2. John Emsley, *The 13th Element: The Sordid Tale of Murder, Fire, and Phosphorus*, John Wiley and Sons, New York, 2000.
3. John Emsley, *Nature's Building Blocks*, Oxford University Press, 2002.
4. Arthur Greenberg, *A Chemical History Tour: Picturing Chemistry from Alchemy to Modern Molecular Science*, Wiley-Interscience, New York, 2000.
5. Aaron Ihde, *The Development of Modern Chemistry*, Dover Publications, New York, 1984.
6. L. K. James, ed., *Nobel Laureates in Chemistry, 1901–1992*, American Chemical Society and Chemical Heritage Foundation, 1993.

STUDY QUESTIONS

Blue-numbered questions have answers in Appendix P and fully-worked solutions in the *Student Solutions Manual*.

1. Dalton proposed that an atom was a "solid, massy, hard, impenetrable, moveable particle." Critique this description. How does this description misrepresent atomic structure.

2. Dalton's hypotheses on the structure of atoms was based in part on the observation of a "Law of definite proportions," which said that atoms combined in a definite ratio by weight. Using the formula for water and atomic weights from the current atomic mass scale, calculate the ratio of the mass of hydrogen to the mass of oxygen in water.

3. From cathode ray experiments, J. J. Thomson estimated that the mass of an electron was "about a thousandth" of the mass of a proton. How accurate is that estimate? Calculate the ratio of the mass of an electron to the mass of a hydrogen atom.

4. Goldstein observed positively charged particles moving in the opposite direction to electrons in a cathode ray tube. From their mass, he concluded that these particles were formed from residual gas in the tube. For example, if the cathode ray tube contained helium, the cathode rays consisted of He^+ ions. Describe the process that forms these ions.

8 | Bonding and Molecular Structure

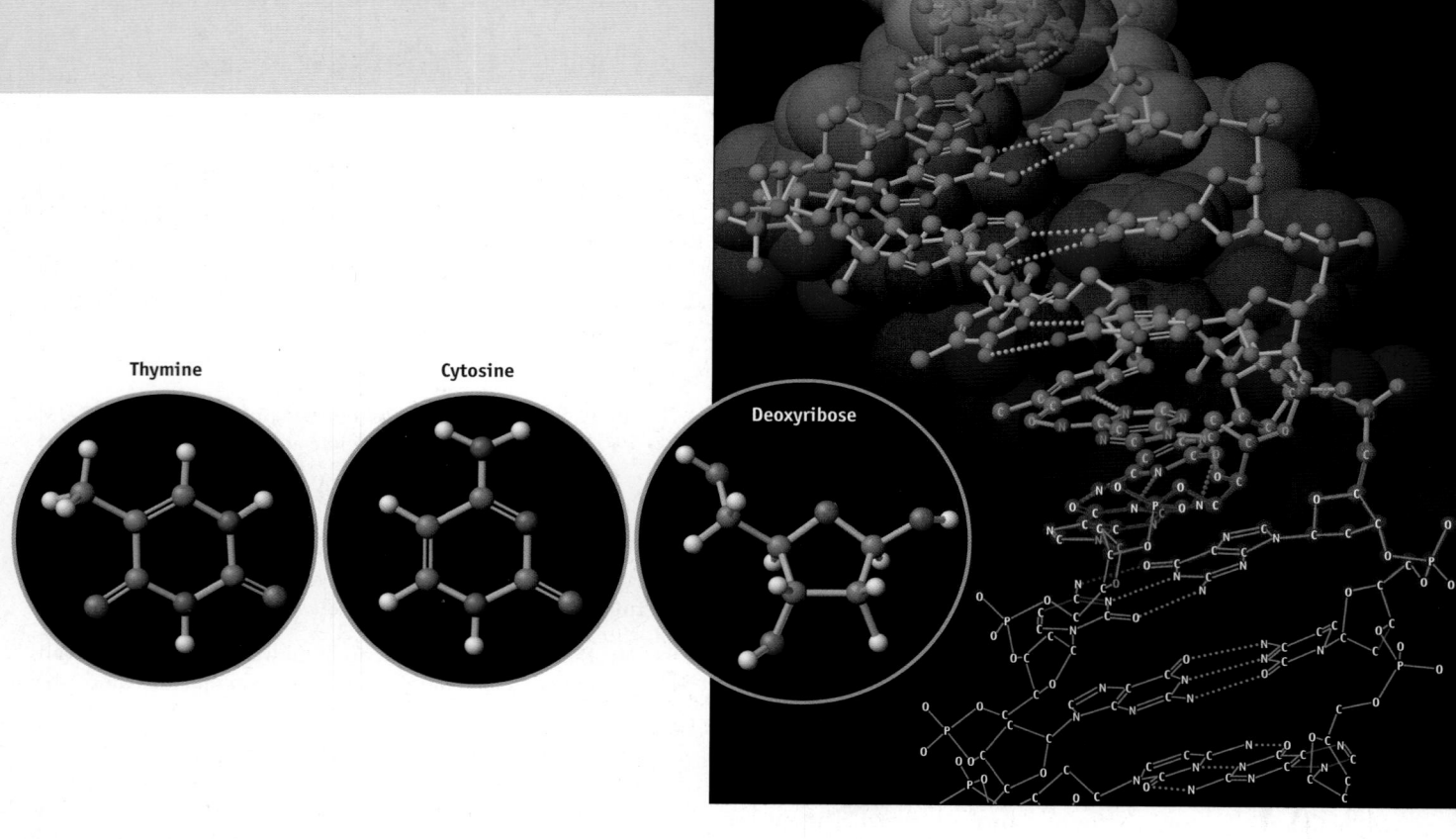

Thymine

Cytosine

Deoxyribose

Chemical Bonding in DNA

The theme of this chapter and the next is molecular bonding and structure, and the subject is well-illustrated by the structure of DNA. This molecule is a helical coil of two chains of tetrahedral phosphate groups and deoxyribose groups. Organic bases (such as thymine and cytosine) on one chain interact with complementary bases on the other chain.

Questions:

Among the many questions you can answer from studying this chapter are the following:

1. Why are there four bonds to carbon and phosphorus?
2. Why are the C atoms and P atoms in the backbone, and the C atoms in deoxyribose, surrounded by other atoms at an angle of 109°?
3. What are the angles in the six-member rings of the bases thymine and cytosine? Why are the six-member rings flat?
4. Are thymine and cytosine polar molecules?

Answers to these questions are in Appendix Q.

Scientists have long known that the key to interpreting the properties of a chemical substance is first to recognize and understand its structure and bonding. **Structure** refers to the way atoms are arranged in space, and **bonding** describes the forces that hold adjacent atoms together.

Our discussion of structure and bonding begins with small molecules and then progresses to larger molecules. From compound to compound, atoms of the same element participate in bonding and structure in a predictable way. This consistency allows us to develop a group of principles that apply to many different chemical compounds, including such complex molecules as DNA.

Chemistry ⚛ Now™

Throughout the text this icon introduces an opportunity for self-study or to explore interactive tutorials by signing in at **www.cengage.com/login**.

8.1 Chemical Bond Formation

When a chemical reaction occurs between two atoms, their valence electrons are reorganized so that a net attractive force—a **chemical bond**—occurs between atoms. There are two general types of bonds, ionic and covalent, and their formation can be depicted using Lewis symbols.

An **ionic bond** forms when *one or more valence electrons is transferred from one atom to another*, creating positive and negative ions. When sodium and chlorine react (Figure 8.1a), an electron is transferred from a sodium atom to a chlorine atom to form Na^+ and Cl^-.

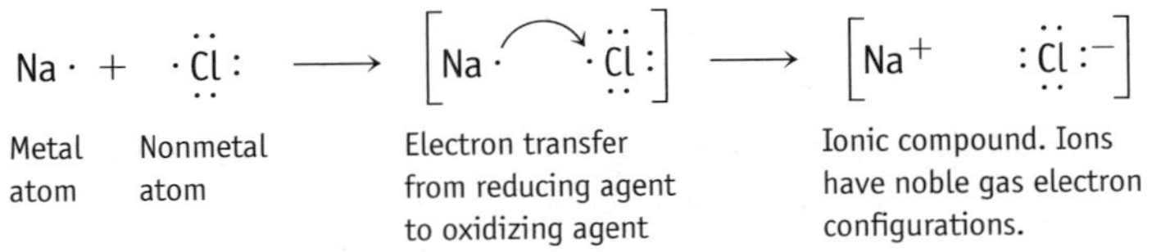

Na· + ·C̤l̤: ⟶ [Na ⤳ ·C̤l̤:] ⟶ [Na$^+$:C̤l̤:$^-$]

| Metal atom | Nonmetal atom | Electron transfer from reducing agent to oxidizing agent | Ionic compound. Ions have noble gas electron configurations. |

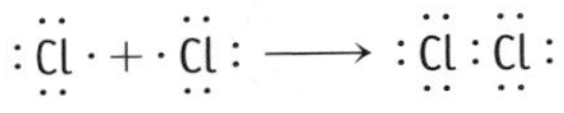

■ **Valence Electron Configurations and Ionic Compound Formation** For the formation of NaCl:

Na changes from $1s^22s^22p^63s^1$ to Na^+ with $1s^22s^22p^6$, equivalent to the Ne configuration.

Cl changes from $[Ne]3s^23p^5$ to Cl^- with $[Ne]3s^23p^6$, equivalent to the Ar configuration.

The "bond" is the attractive force between the positive and negative ions.

Covalent bonding, in contrast, *involves sharing of valence electrons between atoms.* Two chlorine atoms, for example, share a pair of electrons, one electron from each atom, to form a covalent bond.

:C̤l̤· + ·C̤l̤: ⟶ :C̤l̤:C̤l̤:

FIGURE 8.1 Formation of ionic compounds. Both reactions shown here are quite exothermic, as reflected by the very negative molar enthalpies of formation for the reaction products. (See ChemistryNow Screen 8.3 for a video of the formation of sodium chloride from the elements.)

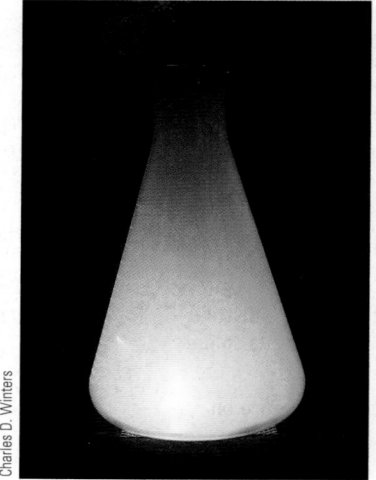

(a) The reaction of elemental sodium and chlorine to give sodium chloride.
$\Delta_f H°$ [NaCl(s)] = −411.12 kJ/mol

(b) The reaction of elemental calcium and oxygen to give calcium oxide.
$\Delta_f H°$ [CaO(s)] = −635.09 kJ/mol

As bonding is described in greater detail, you will discover that the two types of bonding—complete electron transfer and the equal sharing of electrons—are extreme cases. In most chemical compounds, electrons are shared unequally, with the extent of sharing varying widely from very little sharing (largely ionic) to considerable sharing (largely covalent).

Ionic bonding will be described in more detail in Chapter 13, while the present chapter focuses on bonding in covalent compounds.

Module 12

8.2 Covalent Bonding and Lewis Structures

There are many examples of compounds having covalent bonds, including the gases in our atmosphere (O_2, N_2, H_2O, and CO_2), common fuels (CH_4), and most of the compounds in your body. Covalent bonding is also responsible for the atom-to-atom connections in common ions such as CO_3^{2-}, CN^-, NH_4^+, NO_3^-, and PO_4^{3-}. We will develop the basic principles of structure and bonding using these and other small molecules and ions, but the same principles apply to larger molecules from aspirin to proteins and DNA with thousands of atoms.

The molecules and ions just mentioned are composed entirely of *nonmetal* atoms. A point that needs special emphasis is that, in molecules or ions made up *only* of nonmetal atoms, the atoms are attached by covalent bonds. Conversely, the presence of a metal in a formula is often a signal that the compound is likely to be ionic.

Valence Electrons and Lewis Symbols for Atoms

The electrons in an atom are of two types: **valence electrons** and **core electrons.** Chemical reactions result in the loss, gain, or rearrangement of valence electrons. The core electrons are not involved in bonding or in chemical reactions.

For main group elements (elements of the A groups in the periodic table), the valence electrons are the *s* and *p* electrons in the outermost shell (Table 8.1). All electrons in inner shells are core electrons. A useful guideline for *main group elements* is that *the number of valence electrons is equal to the group number.* The fact that all elements in a periodic group have the same number of valence electrons accounts for the similarity of chemical properties among members of the group.

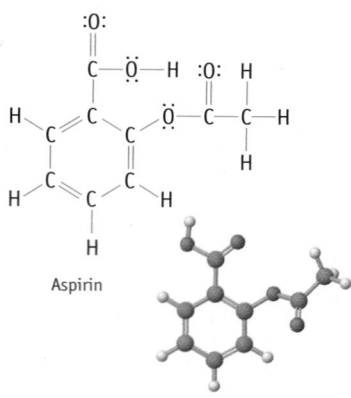

Aspirin

One goal of this chapter is to understand why a molecule such as aspirin has the shape that it exhibits.

TABLE 8.1 Core and Valence Electrons for Several Common Elements

Element	Periodic Group	Core Electrons	Valence Electrons	Total Configuration
Main Group Elements				
Na	1A	$1s^2 2s^2 2p^6 = [\text{Ne}]$	$3s^1$	$[\text{Ne}]3s^1$
Si	4A	$1s^2 2s^2 2p^6 = [\text{Ne}]$	$3s^2 3p^2$	$[\text{Ne}]3s^2 3p^2$
As	5A	$1s^2 2s^2 2p^6 3s^2 3p^6 3d^{10} = [\text{Ar}]3d^{10}$	$4s^2 4p^3$	$[\text{Ar}]3d^{10}4s^2 4p^3$
Transition Elements				
Ti	4B	$1s^2 2s^2 2p^6 3s^2 3p^6 = [\text{Ar}]$	$3d^2 4s^2$	$[\text{Ar}]3d^2 4s^2$
Co	8B	$[\text{Ar}]$	$3d^7 4s^2$	$[\text{Ar}]3d^7 4s^2$
Mo	6B	$[\text{Kr}]$	$4d^5 5s^1$	$[\text{Kr}]4d^5 5s^1$

Valence electrons for transition elements include the electrons in the ns and $(n-1)d$ orbitals (see Table 8.1). The remaining electrons are core electrons. As with main group elements, the valence electrons for transition metals determine the chemical properties of these elements.

The American chemist Gilbert Newton Lewis (1875–1946) introduced a useful way to represent electrons in the valence shell of an atom. The element's symbol represents the atomic nucleus together with the core electrons. Up to four valence electrons, represented by dots, are placed one at a time around the symbol; then, if any valence electrons remain, they are paired with ones already there. Chemists now refer to these pictures as **Lewis electron dot symbols.** Lewis dot symbols for main group elements of the second and third periods are shown in Table 8.2.

Arranging the valence electrons of a main group element around an atom in four groups suggests that the valence shell can accommodate four pairs of electrons. Because this represents eight electrons in all, this is referred to as an **octet** of electrons. An octet of electrons surrounding an atom is regarded as a stable configuration. The noble gases, with the exception of helium, have eight valence electrons and demonstrate a notable lack of reactivity. (Helium, neon, and argon do not undergo any chemical reactions, and the other noble gases have very limited chemical reactivity.) Because chemical reactions involve changes in the valence electron shell, the limited reactivity of the noble gases is taken as evidence of the stability of their noble gas ($ns^2 np^6$) electron configuration. Hydrogen, which in its compounds has two electrons in its valence shell, obeys the spirit of this rule by matching the electron configuration of He.

Chemistry ⚛ Now™

Sign in at **www.cengage.com/login** and go to Chapter 8 Contents to see Screen 8.2 for more on **the correlation of the periodic table and valence electrons.**

TABLE 8.2 Lewis Dot Symbols for Main Group Atoms

1A ns^1	2A ns^2	3A $ns^2 np^1$	4A $ns^2 np^2$	5A $ns^2 np^3$	6A $ns^2 np^4$	7A $ns^2 np^5$	8A $ns^2 np^6$
Li·	·Be·	·B·	·C·	·N·	:O·	:F·	:Ne:
Na·	·Mg·	·Al·	·Si·	·P·	:S·	:Cl·	:Ar:

Lewis Electron Dot Structures and the Octet Rule

In a simple description of covalent bonding, a bond results when one or more
electron pairs are shared between two atoms. The electron pair bond between the
two atoms of an H_2 molecule is represented by a pair of dots or, alternatively, a
line.

Electron pair bond

H:H   H—H

The representation of a molecule in this fashion is called a **Lewis electron dot
structure** or just a **Lewis structure** in honor of G. N. Lewis.

Simple Lewis structures, such as that for F_2, can be drawn starting with Lewis
dot symbols for atoms and arranging the valence electrons to form bonds. Fluorine,
an element in Group 7A, has seven valence electrons. The Lewis symbol shows that
an F atom has a single unpaired electron along with three electron pairs. In F_2,
the single electrons, one on each F atom, pair up in the covalent bond.

Lone pair of
electrons

:F· + ·F: ⟶ :F:F: or   :F—F:

Shared or bonding
electron pair

In the Lewis structure for F_2 the pair of electrons in the F—F bond is the bonding
pair, or **bond pair.** The other six pairs reside on single atoms and are called **lone
pairs.** Because they are not involved in bonding, they are also called **nonbonding
electrons.**

Carbon dioxide, CO_2, and dinitrogen, N_2, are examples of molecules in which
two atoms are multiply bonded; that is, they share more than one electron pair.

■ **H Atoms and Electron Octets**
Hydrogen atoms cannot be surrounded by
an octet of electrons. An atom of H,
which has only a 1s valence electron orbital, can accommodate only a pair of
electrons.

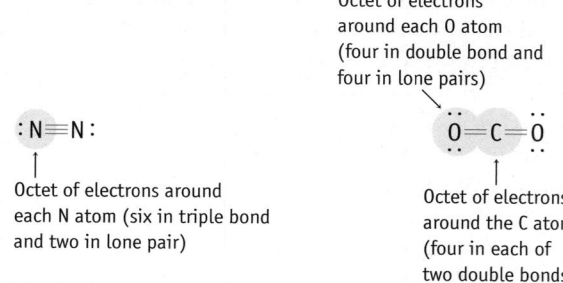

Octet of electrons
around each O atom
(four in double bond and
four in lone pairs)

:N≡N:

Octet of electrons around
each N atom (six in triple bond
and two in lone pair)

O=C=O

Octet of electrons
around the C atom
(four in each of
two double bonds)

■ **Importance of Lone Pairs** Lone pairs
can be important in a structure. Since
they are in the same valence electron shell
as the bonding electrons, they can influence molecular shape. See Section 8.6.

In carbon dioxide, the carbon atom shares two pairs of electrons with each oxygen
and so is linked to each O atom by a double bond. The valence shell of each oxygen atom in CO_2 has two bonding pairs and two lone pairs. In dinitrogen, the two
nitrogen atoms share three pairs of electrons, so they are linked by a triple bond.
In addition, each N atom has a single lone pair.

An important observation can be made about the molecules you have seen so
far: each atom (except H) has a share in four pairs of electrons, so each has achieved
a *noble gas configuration. Each atom is surrounded by an octet of eight electrons.* (Hydrogen
typically forms a bond to only one other atom, resulting in two electrons in its
valence shell.) *The tendency of molecules and polyatomic ions to have structures in which
eight electrons surround each atom* is known as the **octet rule.** As an example, a triple

bond is necessary in dinitrogen in order to have an octet around each nitrogen atom. The carbon atom and both oxygen atoms in CO_2 achieve the octet configuration by forming double bonds.

The octet rule is extremely useful, but keep in mind that it is more a *guideline* than a rule. Particularly for the second period elements C, N, O, and F, a Lewis structure in which each atom achieves an octet is likely to be correct. Although there are a few exceptions, if an atom such as C, N, O, or F in a Lewis structure does not follow the octet rule, you should question the structure's validity. If a structure obeying the octet rule cannot be written, then it is possible an incorrect formula has been assigned to the compound or the atoms have been assembled in an incorrect way.

■ **Exceptions to the Octet Rule** Although the octet rule is widely applicable, there are exceptions. Fortunately, many will be obvious, such as when there are more than four bonds to an element or when an odd number of electrons occur. See Section 8.5.

Drawing Lewis Electron Dot Structures

There is a systematic approach to constructing Lewis structures of molecules and ions. Let us take formaldehyde, CH_2O, as an example.

1. *Determine the arrangement of atoms within a molecule.* The central atom is *usually* the one with the lowest electron affinity. In CH_2O, the central atom is C. You will come to recognize that certain elements often appear as the central atom, among them C, N, P, and S. Halogens are often terminal atoms forming a single bond to one other atom, but they can be the central atom when combined with O in oxoacids (such as $HClO_4$). Oxygen is the central atom in water, but in conjunction with nitrogen, phosphorus, and the halogens it is usually a terminal atom. Hydrogen is a terminal atom because it typically bonds to only one other atom.

2. *Determine the total number of valence electrons in the molecule or ion.* In a neutral molecule, this number will be the sum of the valence electrons for each atom. For an *anion,* add the number of electrons equal to the negative charge; for a *cation,* subtract the number of electrons equal to the positive charge. The number of valence electron pairs will be half the total number of valence electrons. For CH_2O,

■ **Choosing the Central Atom**
1. The electronegativities of atoms can also be used to choose the central atom. Electronegativity is discussed in Section 8.7.
2. For simple compounds, the first atom in a formula is often the central atom (e.g., SO_2, NH_4^+, NO_3^-). This is not always a reliable predictor, however. Notable exceptions include water (H_2O) and most common acids (HNO_3, H_2SO_4), in which the acidic hydrogen is usually written first but where another atom (such as N or S) is the central atom.

$$\text{Valence electrons} = 12 \text{ electrons (or 6 electron pairs)}$$
$$= 4 \text{ for C} + (2 \times 1 \text{ for two H atoms}) + 6 \text{ for O}$$

3. *Place one pair of electrons between each pair of bonded atoms to form a single bond.*

Here, three electron pairs are used to make three single bonds (which are represented by single lines). Three pairs of electrons remain to be used.

4. *Use any remaining pairs as lone pairs around each terminal atom (except H) so that each terminal atom is surrounded by eight electrons.* If, after this is done, there are electrons left over, assign them to the central atom. (If the central atom is an element in the third or higher period, it can have more than eight electrons. See page 364.)

Here, all six pairs have been assigned, but notice that the C atom has a share in only three pairs.

5. *If the central atom has fewer than eight electrons at this point, change one or more of the lone pairs on the terminal atoms into a bonding pair between the central and terminal atom to form a multiple bond.*

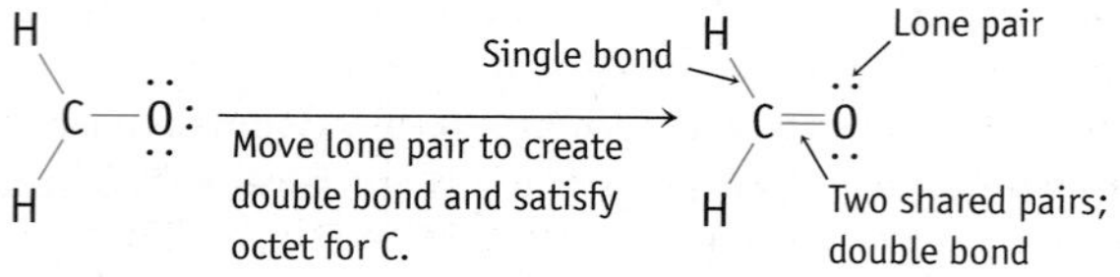

As a general rule, double or triple bonds are most often encountered when *both* atoms are from the following list: C, N, or O. That is, bonds such as C=C, C=N, and C=O will be encountered frequently.

O as a Terminal Atom Oxygen atoms are usually terminal atoms when combined with many other atoms such as B, C, Si, S, N, P, and the halogens.

Chemistry ₒ Now™

Sign in at **www.cengage.com/login** and go to Chapter 8 Contents to see:
• Screen 8.4 for an animation of the **factors influencing bond formation**
• Screen 8.5 for a tutorial on **Lewis structures**
• Screen 8.6 for a tutorial and an exercise on **drawing Lewis structures**

EXAMPLE 8.1 Drawing Lewis Structures

Problem Draw Lewis structures for the chlorate ion (ClO_3^-) and the nitronium ion (NO_2^+).

Strategy Follow the five steps outlined for CH_2O in the preceding text.

Solution for chlorate ion

1. Cl is the central atom, and the O atoms are terminal atoms.
2. Valence electrons = 26 (13 pairs)
   = 7 (for Cl) + 18 (six for each O) + 1 (for the negative charge)
3. Three electron pairs form single bonds from Cl to the O terminal atoms.

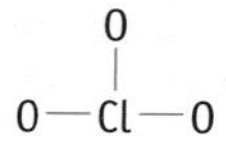

4. Distribute three lone pairs on each of the terminal O atoms to complete the octet of electrons around each of these atoms.

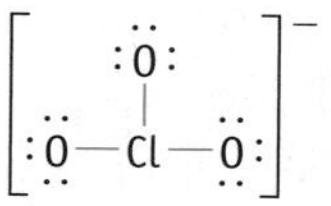

5. One pair of electrons remains, and it is placed on the central Cl atom to complete its octet.

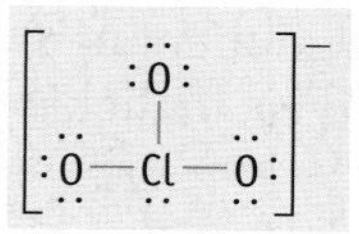

Each atom now has a share in four pairs of electrons, and the Lewis structure is complete.

Solution for nitronium ion

1. Nitrogen is the central atom, because its electron affinity is lower than that of oxygen.

354 Chapter 8 | Bonding and Molecular Structure

2. Valence electrons = 16 (8 valence pairs)

= 5 (for N) + 12 (six for each O) − 1 (for the positive charge)

3. Two electron pairs form single bonds from the nitrogen to each oxygen:

$$O-N-O$$

4. Distribute the remaining six pairs of electrons on the terminal O atoms:

$$\left[:\ddot{O}-N-\ddot{O}: \right]^+$$

5. The central nitrogen atom is two electron pairs short of an octet. Thus, a lone pair of electrons on each oxygen atom is converted to a bonding electron pair to give two N=O double bonds. Each atom in the ion now has four electron pairs. Nitrogen has four bonding pairs, and each oxygen atom has two lone pairs and shares two bond pairs.

$$\left[:\ddot{O}-N-\ddot{O}: \right]^+ \xrightarrow{\text{Move lone pairs to create double bonds and satisfy the octet for N.}} \left[\ddot{O}=N=\ddot{O} \right]^+$$

Comment Why don't we take two lone pairs from one side and none from the other? We shall discuss that after describing charge distribution in molecules and ions (page 377).

EXERCISE 8.1 Drawing Lewis Structures

Draw Lewis structures for NH_4^+, CO, NO^+, and SO_4^{2-}.

Predicting Lewis Structures

Lewis structures are useful in gaining a perspective on the structure and chemistry of a molecule or ion. The guidelines for drawing Lewis structures are helpful, but chemists also rely on patterns of bonding in related molecules.

Hydrogen Compounds

Some common compounds and ions formed from second-period nonmetal elements and hydrogen are shown in Table 8.3. Their Lewis structures illustrate the fact that the Lewis symbol for an element is a useful guide in determining the number of bonds formed by the element. For example, if there is no charge, nitrogen has five valence electrons. Two electrons occur as a lone pair; the other three occur as unpaired electrons. To reach an octet, it is necessary to pair each of the unpaired electrons with an electron from another atom. Thus, N is predicted

---

Problem Solving Tip 8.1

Useful Ideas to Consider When Drawing Lewis Electron Dot Structures

- The octet rule is a useful guideline when drawing Lewis structures.
- Carbon forms four bonds (four single bonds; two single bonds and one double bond; two double bonds; or one single bond and one triple bond). In uncharged species, nitrogen forms three bonds and oxygen forms two bonds. Hydrogen typically forms only one bond to another atom.

- When multiple bonds are formed, both of the atoms involved are usually one of the following: C, N, and O. Oxygen has the ability to form multiple bonds with a variety of elements. Carbon forms many compounds having multiple bonds to another carbon or to N or O.
- Nonmetals may form single, double, and triple bonds but never quadruple bonds.

- Always account for single bonds and lone pairs before determining whether multiple bonds are present.
- Be alert for the possibility the molecule or ion you are working on is isoelectronic (page 358) with a species you have seen before.

TABLE 8.3 Lewis Structures of Common Hydrogen-Containing Molecules and Ions of Second-Period Elements

Group 4A	Group 5A	Group 6A	Group 7A
CH_4 methane	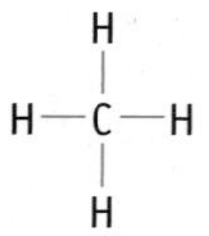 NH_3 ammonia	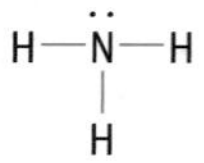 H_2O water	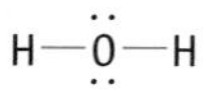 HF hydrogen fluoride 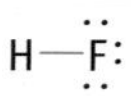
C_2H_6 ethane	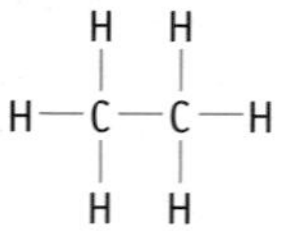 N_2H_4 hydrazine	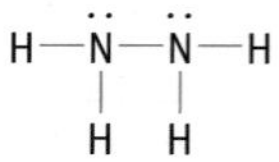 H_2O_2 hydrogen peroxide	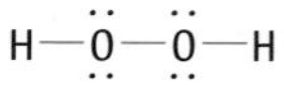
C_2H_4 ethylene	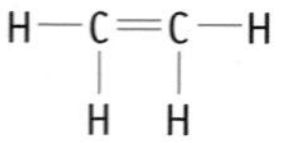 NH_4^+ ammonium ion	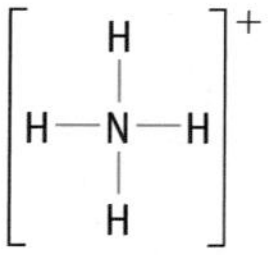 H_3O^+ hydronium ion	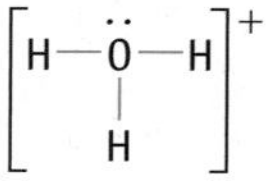
C_2H_2 acetylene	 NH_2^- amide ion	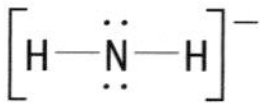 OH^- hydroxide ion	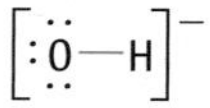

to form three bonds in uncharged molecules, and this is indeed the case. Similarly, carbon is expected to form four bonds, oxygen two, and fluorine one.

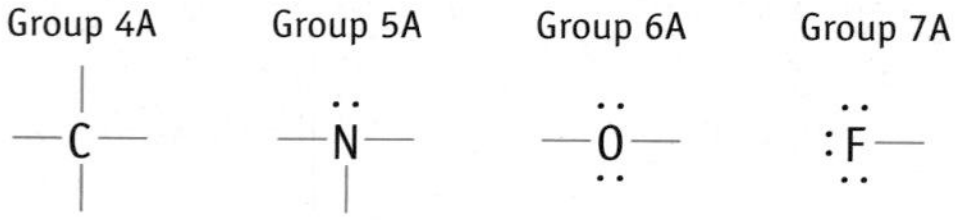

Group 4A	Group 5A	Group 6A	Group 7A
—C—	—N—	—O—	:F—

■ **EXAMPLE 8.2 Predicting Lewis Structures**

Problem Draw Lewis electron dot structures for CCl_4 and NF_3.

Strategy One way to answer this is to recognize that CCl_4 and NF_3 are similar to CH_4 and NH_3 (in Table 8.3), respectively, except that H atoms have been replaced by halogen atoms.

Solution Recall that carbon is expected to form four bonds and nitrogen three bonds to give an octet of electrons. In addition, halogen atoms have seven valence electrons, so both Cl and F can attain an octet by forming one covalent bond, just as hydrogen does.

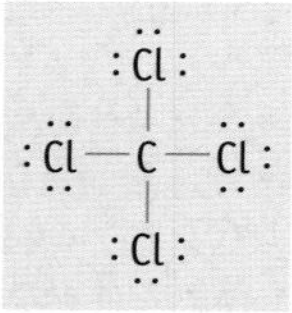

carbon tetrachloride 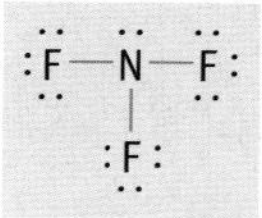   nitrogen trifluoride

As a check, count the number of valence electrons for each molecule, and verify that all are present.

CCl_4: Valence electrons = 4 for C + 4 × 7 (for Cl) = 32 electrons (16 pairs)

The structure shows eight electrons in single bonds and 24 electrons as lone pair electrons, for a total of 32 electrons. The structure is correct.

NF_3: Valence electrons = 5 for N + 3 × 7 (for F) = 26 electrons (13 pairs)

The structure shows six electrons in single bonds and 20 electrons as lone pair electrons, for a total of 26 electrons. The structure is correct.

■ **Lewis Structures for Anions of Oxoacids** Stuctures for oxoanions such as PO_4^{3-}, SO_4^{2-}, and ClO_4^- are sometimes drawn with multiple bonds between the central atom and oxygen. Theory suggests that this does not accurately represent the bonding in these species, and that structures obeying the octet rule are more appropriate. See L. Suidan, J. K. Badenhoop, E. D. Glendening, and F. Weinhold, *Journal of Chemical Education*, Vol. 72, pages 583–585, 1995.

EXERCISE 8.2 Predicting Lewis Structures

Predict Lewis structures for methanol, H_3COH, and hydroxylamine, H_2NOH. (Hint: The formulas of these compounds are written to guide you in choosing the correct arrangement of atoms.)

Oxoacids and Their Anions

Lewis structures of common acids and their anions are illustrated in Table 8.4. In the absence of water, these acids are covalently bonded molecular compounds, a conclusion that we should draw because all elements in the formula are nonmetals. (Nitric acid, for example, has properties that we associate with a covalent compound: it is a colorless liquid with a boiling point of 83 °C.) In aqueous solution, however, HNO_3, H_2SO_4, and $HClO_4$ are ionized to give a hydronium ion and the appropriate anion. A Lewis structure for the nitrate ion, for example, can be created using the guidelines on page 353, and the result is a structure with two N—O single bonds and one N=O double bond. To form nitric acid from the nitrate ion, a hydrogen ion is attached to one of the O atoms that has a single bond to the central N.

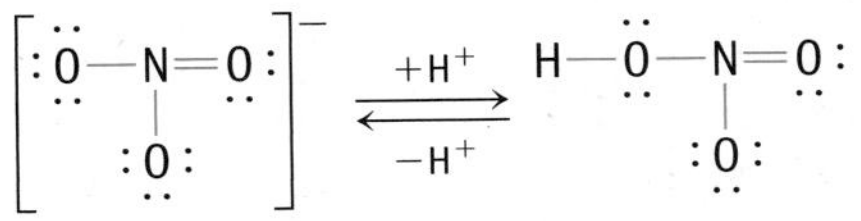

nitrate ion   nitric acid

A characteristic property of acids in aqueous solution is their ability to donate a hydrogen ion (H^+, which combines with water to give the hydronium ion). The NO_3^- anion is formed when the acid, HNO_3, loses a hydrogen ion. The H^+ ion

---

TABLE 8.4 Lewis Structures of Common Oxoacids and Their Anions

HNO_3
nitric acid

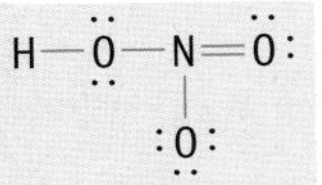

NO_3^-
nitrate ion

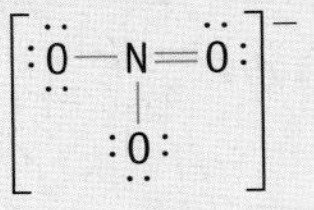

$HClO_4$
perchloric acid

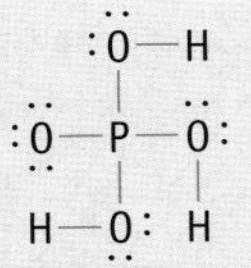

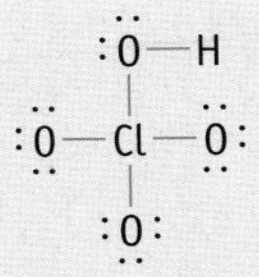

ClO_4^-
perchlorate ion

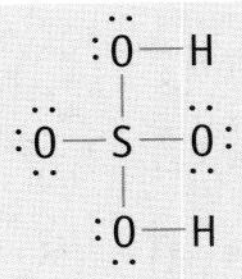

H_3PO_4
phosphoric acid

PO_4^{3-}
phosphate ion

$HOCl$
hypochlorous acid

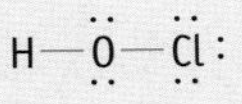

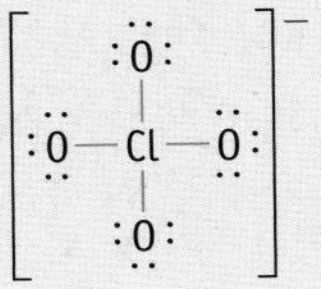

OCl^-
hypochlorite ion

H_2SO_4
sulfuric acid

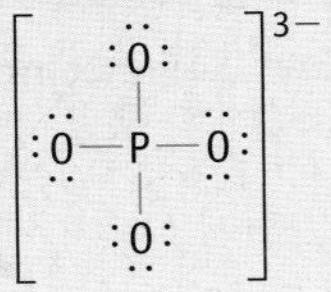

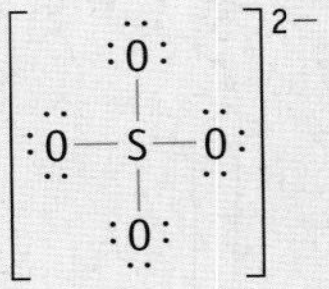

HSO_4^-
hydrogen sulfate ion

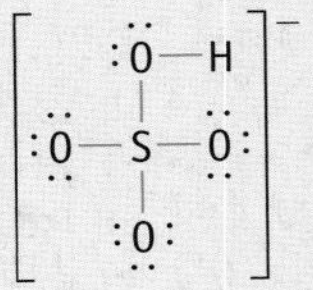

SO_4^{2-}
sulfate ion

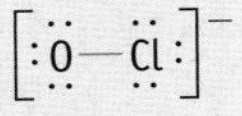

separates from the acid by breaking the H—O bond, the electrons of the bond staying with the O atom. As a result, HNO_3 and NO_3^- have the same number of electrons, 24, and their structures are closely related.

EXERCISE 8.3 Lewis Structures of Acids and Their Anions

Draw a Lewis structure for the anion $H_2PO_4^-$, derived from phosphoric acid.

Isoelectronic Species

■ **Isoelectronic and Isostructural** The term **isostructural** is often used in conjunction with isoelectronic species. Species that are isostructural have the same structure. For example, the PO_4^{3-}, SO_4^{2-}, and ClO_4^- ions in Table 8.5 all have four oxygens bonded to the central atom. In addition, they are isoelectronic in that all have 32 valence electrons.

The species NO^+, N_2, CO, and CN^- are similar in that they each have two atoms and the same total number of valence electrons, 10, which leads to the same Lewis structure for each molecule or ion. The two atoms in each are linked with a triple bond. With three bonding pairs and one lone pair, each atom thus has an octet of electrons.

$$[:N\equiv O:]^+ \qquad :N\equiv N: \qquad :C\equiv O: \qquad [:C\equiv N:]^-$$

Molecules and ions having the *same number of valence electrons and the same Lewis structures* are said to be **isoelectronic** (Table 8.5). You will find it helpful to recognize isoelectronic molecules and ions because this is another way to see relationships in bonding among common chemical substances.

There are similarities and important differences in chemical properties of isoelectronic species. For example, both carbon monoxide, CO, and cyanide ion, CN^-, are very toxic, which results from the fact that they can bind to the iron of hemoglobin in blood and block the uptake of oxygen. They are different, though, in their acid–base chemistry. In aqueous solution, cyanide ion readily adds H^+ to form hydrogen cyanide, whereas CO does not protonate in water.

EXERCISE 8.4 Identifying Isoelectronic Species

(a) Is the acetylide ion, C_2^{2-}, isoelectronic with N_2?

(b) Identify a common molecular (uncharged) species that is isoelectronic with nitrite ion, NO_2^-. Identify a common ion that is isoelectronic with HF.

TABLE 8.5 Some Common Isoelectronic Molecules and Ions

Formulas	Representative Lewis Structure	Formulas	Representative Lewis Structure
BH_4^-, CH_4, NH_4^+	[H—N—H with H above and H below]$^+$	CO_3^{2-}, NO_3^-	[:O—N=O: with :O: below]$^-$
NH_3, H_3O^+	H—N—H with H below (lone pair on N)	PO_4^{3-}, SO_4^{2-}, ClO_4^-	[:O: above, :O—P—O:, :O: below]$^{3-}$
CO_2, OCN^-, SCN^-, N_2O NO_2^+, OCS, CS_2	O=C=O		

8.3 Atom Formal Charges in Covalent Molecules and Ions

You have seen that Lewis structures show how electron pairs are placed in a covalently bonded species, whether it is a neutral molecule or a polyatomic ion. Now we turn to one of the consequences of the placement of electron pairs in this way: individual atoms can be negatively or positively charged or have no electric charge. The location of a positive or negative charge in a molecule or ion will influence, among other things, the atom at which a reaction occurs. For example, does a positive H^+ ion attach itself to the Cl or the O of ClO^-? Is the product HClO or HOCl? It is reasonable to expect H^+ to attach to the more negatively charged atom. We can predict this by evaluating atom formal charges in molecules and ions.

The **formal charge** is the charge on an atom in a molecule or polyatomic ion, and the sum of the formal charges for the atoms in a species equals the overall charge on the ion or is zero (for an uncharged molecule). The formal charge for an atom in a molecule or ion is calculated based on the Lewis structure of the molecule or ion, using Equation 8.1.

$$\text{Formal charge of an atom in a molecule or ion} = \text{group number of the atom} - [\text{LPE} + \tfrac{1}{2}(\text{BE})] \tag{8.1}$$

In this equation:

- The group number gives the number of valence electrons brought by a particular atom to the molecule or ion.
- LPE = number of lone pair electrons on an atom.
- BE = number of bonding electrons around an atom.

The term in square brackets is the number of electrons assigned by the Lewis structure to an atom in a molecule or ion. The difference between this term and the group number is the formal charge. An atom in a molecule or ion will be positive if it "contributes" more electrons to bonding than it "gets back." The atom's formal charge will be negative if the reverse is true.

There are two important assumptions in Equation 8.1. First, lone pairs are assumed to belong to the atom on which they reside in the Lewis structure. Second, bond pairs are assumed to be divided equally between the bonded atoms. (The factor of $\frac{1}{2}$ divides the bonding electrons equally between the atoms linked by the bond.)

The sum of the formal charges on the atoms in a molecule or ion always equals the net charge on the molecule or ion. Consider the hypochlorite ion. Oxygen is in Group 6A and so has six valence electrons. However, oxygen can lay claim to seven electrons (six lone pair electrons and one bonding electron), and so the atom has a formal charge of -1. The O atom has "formally" gained an electron as part of the ion.

Formal charge $= -1 = 6 - [6 + \frac{1}{2}(2)]$

$$\left[:\overset{\cdot\cdot}{\underset{\cdot\cdot}{Cl}} - \overset{\cdot\cdot}{\underset{\cdot\cdot}{O}}: \right]^-$$

Assume a covalent bond, so bonding electrons are divided equally between Cl and O.

Formal charge $= 0 = 7 - [6 + \frac{1}{2}(2)]$

Sum of formal charges $= -1$

The formal charge on the Cl atom in ClO^- is zero. So we have -1 for oxygen and 0 for chlorine, and the sum of these equals the net charge of -1 for the ion. An important conclusion we can draw from the formal charges in ClO^- is that, if an

H⁺ ion approaches the ion, it should attach itself to the negatively charged O atom to give hypochlorous acid, HOCl.

Chemistry ⊙ Now™

Sign in at **www.cengage.com/login** and go to Chapter 8 Contents to see Screen 8.11 for practice **determining formal charge.**

■ **HClO$_x$ Acids and Formal Charge** Both ClO⁻ and ClO$_3$⁻ ions attract a proton to give the corresponding acid, HClO and HClO$_3$. In all of the HClO$_x$ acids, the H⁺ ion is attached to an O atom, owing to the negative formal charge on that atom. See Table 8.4.

■ **EXAMPLE 8.3 Calculating Formal Charges**

Problem Calculate formal charges for the atoms of the ClO$_3$⁻ ion.

Strategy The first step is always to write the Lewis structure for the molecule or ion. (The Lewis structure for the ClO$_3$⁻ ion is in Example 8.1.) Then Equation 8.1 can be used to calculate the formal charges.

Solution

$$\text{Formal charge} = -1 = 6 - [6 + \tfrac{1}{2}(2)]$$

$$\left[\begin{array}{c} \ddot{\underset{\cdots}{O}} \\ | \\ \ddot{\underset{\cdots}{O}} - Cl - \ddot{\underset{\cdots}{O}} \\ | \end{array} \right]^{-}$$

$$\text{Formal charge} = +2 = 7 - [2 + \tfrac{1}{2}(6)]$$

The formal charge on each O atom is −1, whereas for the Cl atom it is +2. The sum of the atom's formal charges is the charge on the ion, which is −1 for ClO$_3$⁻.

EXERCISE 8.5 Calculating Formal Charges

Calculate formal charges on each atom in **(a)** CN⁻ and **(b)** SO$_3$²⁻.

A Closer Look

Comparing Formal Charge and Oxidation Number

In Chapter 3, you learned to calculate the oxidation number of an atom as a way to tell if a reaction involves oxidation and reduction. Are an atom's oxidation number and its formal charge related? To answer this question, let us look at the hydroxide ion. The formal charges are −1 on the O atom and 0 on the H atom. Recall that these formal charges are calculated assuming the O—H bond electrons are shared equally in an O—H covalent bond.

$$\text{Formal charge} = -1 = 6 - [6 + \tfrac{1}{2}(2)]$$

$$\left[\ddot{\underset{\cdots}{O}} - H \right]^{-} \quad \textit{Sum of formal charges} = -1$$

$$\text{Formal charge} = 0 = 1 - [0 + \tfrac{1}{2}(2)]$$

In contrast, in Chapter 3 (page 144), you learned that O has an oxidation number of −2 and H has a number of +1. Oxidation numbers are determined by assuming that the bond between a pair of atoms is ionic, not covalent. For OH⁻ this means the pair of electrons between O and H is located fully on O. Thus, the O atom now has eight valence electrons instead of six and a charge of −2. The H atom now has no valence electrons and a charge of +1.

$$\text{Oxidation number} = -2$$

$$\left[\ddot{\underset{\cdots}{\ddot{O}}} , H \right]^{-} \quad \begin{array}{l} \textit{Sum of oxidation} \\ \textit{numbers} = -1 \end{array}$$

Assume an   Oxidation number = +1
ionic bond

Formal charges and oxidation numbers are calculated using different assumptions. Both are useful, but for different purposes. Oxidation numbers allow us to follow changes in redox reactions. Formal charges provide insight into atom charges in molecules and polyatomic ions.

8.4 Resonance

Ozone, O_3, an unstable, blue, diamagnetic gas with a characteristic pungent odor, protects the earth and its inhabitants from intense ultraviolet radiation from the sun. An important feature of its structure is that the two oxygen–oxygen bonds are the same length, which suggests that the two bonds are equivalent. That is, equal O—O bond lengths imply an equal number of bond pairs in each O—O bond. Using the guidelines for drawing Lewis structures, however, you might come to a different conclusion. There are two possible ways of writing the Lewis structure for the molecule:

Alternative Ways of Drawing the Ozone Structure

Double bond on the left: Ö═Ö—Ö:

Double bond on the right: :Ö—Ö═Ö

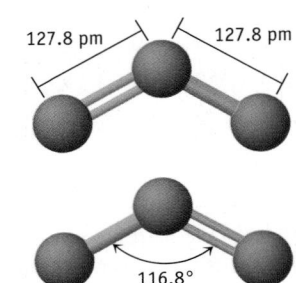

Ozone, O_3, is a bent molecule with oxygen–oxygen bonds of the same length.

These structures are equivalent in that each has a double bond on one side of the central oxygen atom and a single bond on the other side. If either were the actual structure of ozone, one bond (O═O) should be shorter than the other (O—O). The actual structure of ozone shows this is not the case. The inescapable conclusion is that these Lewis structures do not correctly represent the bonding in ozone.

Linus Pauling (1901–1994) proposed the theory of **resonance** to solve the problem. *Resonance structures are used to represent bonding in a molecule or ion when a single Lewis structure fails to describe accurately the actual electronic structure.* The alternative structures shown for ozone are called **resonance structures.** They have identical patterns of bonding and equal energy. The actual structure of this molecule is a *composite,* or **resonance hybrid,** of the equivalent resonance structures. In this hybrid, the bonds between the oxygens are between a single bond and a double bond in length, in this case corresponding to one and a half bonds. This is a reasonable conclusion because we see that the O—O bonds both have a length of 127.8 pm, intermediate between the average length of an O═O double bond (121 pm) and an O—O single bond (132 pm). Because we cannot accurately draw fractions of a bond, chemists draw the resonance structures and connect them with double-headed arrows (⟷) to indicate that the true structure is somewhere in between these extremes.

Lone pair becomes a bond pair.   Bond pair becomes a lone pair.

:Ö—Ö═Ö: ⟷   :Ö═Ö—Ö:

Benzene is the classic example of the use of resonance to represent a structure. The benzene molecule is a six-member ring of carbon atoms with six equivalent carbon–carbon bonds (and a hydrogen atom attached to each carbon atom). The carbon–carbon bonds are 139 pm long, intermediate between the average length of a C═C double bond (134 pm) and a C—C single bond (154 pm).

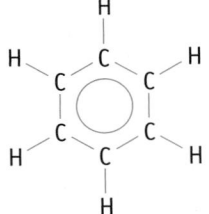

Resonance structures of benzene, C_6H_6

Abbreviated representation of resonance structures

- Resonance is a means of representing the bonding when a single Lewis structure fails to give an accurate picture.
- The atoms must have the same arrangement in each resonance structure. Attaching the atoms in a different fashion creates a different compound.

- Resonance structures differ only in the assignment of electron-pair positions, never atom positions.
- Resonance structures differ in the number of bond pairs between a given pair of atoms.
- Even though the formal process of converting one resonance structure to another seems to move electrons

about, resonance is not meant to indicate the motion of electrons.
- The actual structure of a molecule is a composite or hybrid of the resonance structures.
- There will always be at least one multiple bond (double or triple) in each resonance structure.

Two resonance structures that differ only in double bond placement can be written for the molecule. A hybrid of these two structures, however, will lead to a molecule with six equivalent carbon–carbon bonds.

Let us apply the concepts of resonance to describe bonding in the carbonate ion, CO_3^{2-}, an anion with 24 valence electrons (12 pairs).

Three equivalent structures can be drawn for this ion, differing only in the location of the C=O double bond. This fits the classical situation for resonance, so it is appropriate to conclude that no single structure correctly describes this ion. Instead, the actual structure is the composite of the three structures, in good agreement with experimental results. In the CO_3^{2-} ion, all three carbon–oxygen bond distances are 129 pm, intermediate between C—O single bond (143 pm) and C=O double bond (122 pm) distances.

Formal charges can be calculated for each atom in the resonance structure for a molecule or ion. For example, using one of the resonance structures for the nitrate ion, we find that the central N atom has a formal charge of +1, and the singly bonded O atoms are both −1. The doubly bonded O atom has no charge. The net charge for the ion is thus −1.

Is this a reasonable charge distribution for the nitrate ion? The answer is no. The actual structure of the nitrate ion is a resonance hybrid of three equivalent resonance structures. Because the three oxygen atoms in NO_3^- are equivalent, the charge on one oxygen atom should not be different from the other two. This can be resolved, however, if the formal charges are averaged to give a formal charge of $-\frac{2}{3}$ on the oxygen atoms. Summing the charges on the three oxygen atoms and the +1 charge on the nitrogen atom then gives −1, the charge on the ion.

In the resonance structures for O_3, CO_3^{2-}, and NO_3^-, for example, all the possible resonance structures are equally likely; they are "equivalent" structures. The molecule or ion therefore has a symmetrical distribution of electrons over all the atoms involved—that is, its electronic structure consists of an equal "mixture," or "hybrid," of the resonance structures.

Chemistry.●.Now™

Sign in at **www.cengage.com/login** and go to Chapter 8 Contents to see Screen 8.7 for a tutorial on **drawing resonance structures.**

■ EXAMPLE 8.4 Drawing Resonance Structures

Problem Draw resonance structures for the nitrite ion, NO_2^-. Are the N—O bonds single, double, or intermediate in value? What are the formal charges on the N and O atoms?

Strategy Draw the Lewis structure in the usual manner. If multiple bonds are required, resonance structures may exist. This will be the case if the octet of an atom can be completed by using an electron pair from more than one terminal atom to form a multiple bond. Bonds to the central atom cannot then be "pure" single or double bonds but rather are somewhere between the two.

Solution Nitrogen is the central atom in the nitrite ion, which has a total of 18 valence electrons (nine pairs).

Valence electrons = 5 (for the N atom) + 12 (6 for each O atom) + 1 (for negative charge)

After forming N—O single bonds, and distributing lone pairs on the terminal O atoms, a pair remains, which is placed on the central N atom.

$$\left[:\!\ddot{O}\!-\!\ddot{N}\!-\!\ddot{O}\!: \right]^-$$

To complete the octet of electrons about the N atom, form an N=O double bond.

$$\left[:\!O\!\!=\!\!\ddot{N}\!-\!\ddot{O}\!: \right]^- \longleftrightarrow \left[:\!\ddot{O}\!-\!\ddot{N}\!\!=\!\!O\!: \right]^-$$

Because there are two ways to do this, two equivalent structures can be drawn, and the actual structure must be a resonance hybrid of these two structures. The nitrogen–oxygen bonds are neither single nor double bonds but have an intermediate value.

Taking one of the resonance structures, we find the formal charge for the N atom is 0. The charge on one O atom is 0 and −1 for the other O atom. Because the two resonance structures are of equal importance, however, the net formal charge on each O atom is $-\frac{1}{2}$.

Formal charge =   Formal charge =
$0 = 6 - [4 + \frac{1}{2}(4)]$ $-1 = 6 - [6 + \frac{1}{2}(2)]$

$$\left[\ddot{O}\!\!=\!\!N\!-\!\ddot{O}\!: \right]^-$$

Formal charge $= 0 = 5 - [2 + \frac{1}{2}(6)]$

■ EXERCISE 8.6 Drawing Resonance Structures

Draw resonance structures for the bicarbonate ion, HCO_3^-.

(a) Does HCO_3^- have the same number of resonance structures as the CO_3^{2-} ion?

(b) What are the formal charges on the O and C atoms in HCO_3^-? What is the average formal charge on the O atoms? Compare this with the O atoms in CO_3^{2-}.

(c) What do formal charges predict about the point of attachment of the H atom in HCO_3^-?

8.5 Exceptions to the Octet Rule

Although the vast majority of molecular compounds and ions obey the octet rule, there are exceptions. These include molecules and ions that have fewer than four pairs of electrons on a central atom, those that have more than four pairs, and those that have an odd number of electrons.

Compounds in Which an Atom Has Fewer Than Eight Valence Electrons

Boron, a metalloid in Group 3A, has three valence electrons and so is expected to form three covalent bonds with other nonmetallic elements. This results in a valence shell for boron in its compounds with only six electrons, two short of an octet. Many boron compounds of this type are known, including such common compounds as boric acid $(B(OH)_3)$, borax $(Na_2B_4O_5(OH)_4 \cdot 8\ H_2O)$ (Figure 8.2), and the boron trihalides $(BF_3, BCl_3, BBr_3, \text{ and } BI_3)$.

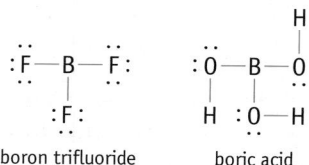

boron trifluoride   boric acid

Boron compounds such as BF_3 that are two electrons short of an octet are quite reactive. The boron atom can accommodate a fourth electron pair when that pair is provided by another atom, and molecules or ions with lone pairs can fulfill this role. Ammonia, for example, reacts with BF_3 to form $H_3N{\rightarrow}BF_3$.

coordinate covalent bond

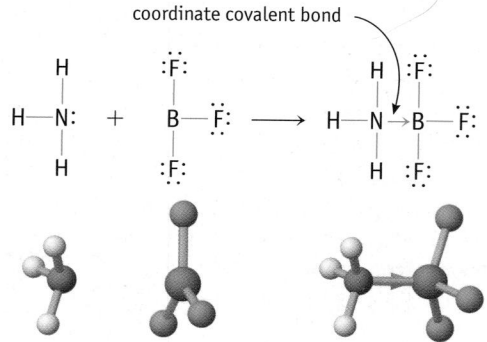

If a bonding pair of electrons originates on one of the bonded atoms, the bond is called a **coordinate covalent bond.** In Lewis structures, a coordinate covalent bond is often designated by an arrow that points away from the atom donating the electron pair.

Compounds in Which an Atom Has More Than Eight Valence Electrons

Elements in the third or higher periods often form compounds and ions in which the central element is surrounded by more than four valence electron pairs (Table 8.6). With most compounds and ions in this category, the central atom is bonded to fluorine, chlorine, or oxygen.

It is often obvious from the formula of a compound that an octet around an atom has been exceeded. As an example, consider sulfur hexafluoride, SF_6, a gas

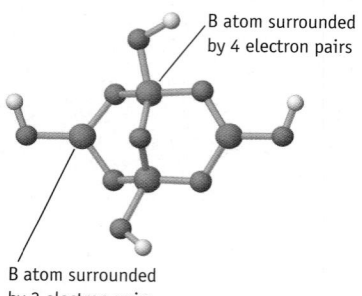

B atom surrounded by 4 electron pairs

B atom surrounded by 3 electron pairs

FIGURE 8.2 The anion in Borax. Borax is a common mineral, which is used in soaps and contains an interesting anion, $B_4O_5(OH)_4^{2-}$. The anion has two B atoms surrounded by four electron pairs, and two B atoms surrounded by only three pairs.

TABLE 8.6 Lewis Structures in Which the Central Atom Exceeds an Octet

Group 4A	Group 5A	Group 6A	Group 7A	Group 8
SiF_5^-	PF_5	SF_4	ClF_3	XeF_2
SiF_6^{2-}	PF_6^-	SF_6	BrF_5	XeF_4

formed by the reaction of sulfur and excess fluorine. Sulfur is the central atom in this compound, and fluorine typically bonds to only one other atom with a single electron pair bond (as in HF and CF_4). Six S—F bonds are required in SF_6, meaning there will be six electron pairs in the valence shell of the sulfur atom.

If there are more than four groups bonded to a central atom, this is a reliable signal that there are more than eight electrons around a central atom. But be careful—the central atom octet can also be exceeded with four or fewer atoms bonded to the central atom. Consider three examples from Table 8.6: the central atom in SF_4, ClF_3, and XeF_2 has five electron pairs in its valence shell.

A useful observation is that *only elements of the third and higher periods in the periodic table may form compounds and ions in which an octet is exceeded.* Second-period elements (B, C, N, O, F) are restricted to a maximum of eight electrons in their compounds. For example, nitrogen forms compounds and ions such as NH_3, NH_4^+, and NF_3, but NF_5 is unknown. Phosphorus, the third-period element just below nitrogen in the periodic table, forms many compounds similar to nitrogen (PH_3, PH_4^+, PF_3), but it also readily accommodates five or six valence electron pairs in compounds such as PF_5 or in ions such as PF_6^-. Arsenic, antimony, and bismuth, the elements below phosphorus in Group 5A, resemble phosphorus in their behavior.

The usual explanation for the contrasting behavior of second- and third-period elements centers on the number of orbitals in the valence shell of an atom. Second-period elements have four valence orbitals (one 2s and three 2p orbitals). Two electrons per orbital result in a total of eight electrons being accommodated around an atom. For elements in the third and higher periods, the d orbitals in the outer shell are traditionally included among valence orbitals for the elements. Thus, for phosphorus, the 3d orbitals are included with the 3s and 3p orbitals as valence orbitals. The extra orbitals provide the element with an opportunity to accommodate up to 12 electrons.

Chemistry Now™

Sign in at **www.cengage.com/login** and go to Chapter 8 Contents to see Screen 8.8 for a tutorial on **identifying electron-deficient compounds.**

■ **Xenon Compounds** Compounds of xenon are among the more interesting entries in Table 8.6 because noble gas compounds were not discovered until the early 1960s. One of the more intriguing compounds is XeF_2, in part because of the simplicity of its synthesis. Xenon difluoride can be made by placing a flask containing xenon gas and fluorine gas in the sunlight. After several weeks, crystals of colorless XeF_2 are found in the flask (see page 404).

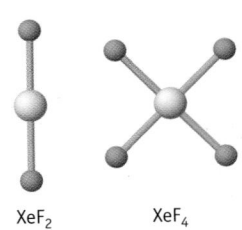

XeF₂   XeF₄

Problem Sketch the Lewis structure of the $[ClF_4]^-$ ion.

Strategy Use the guidelines on page 353.

Solution

1. The Cl atom is the central atom.

2. This ion has 36 valence electrons [= 7 (for Cl) + 4 × 7 (for F) + 1 (for ion charge)] or 18 pairs.

3. Draw the ion with four single covalent Cl—F bonds.

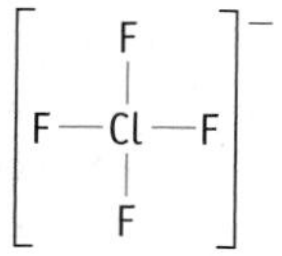

$$\left[\begin{array}{c} F \\ | \\ F - Cl - F \\ | \\ F \end{array} \right]^-$$

4. Place lone pairs on the terminal atoms. Because two electron pairs remain after placing lone pairs on the four F atoms, and because we know that Cl can accommodate more than four pairs, these two pairs are placed on the central Cl atom.

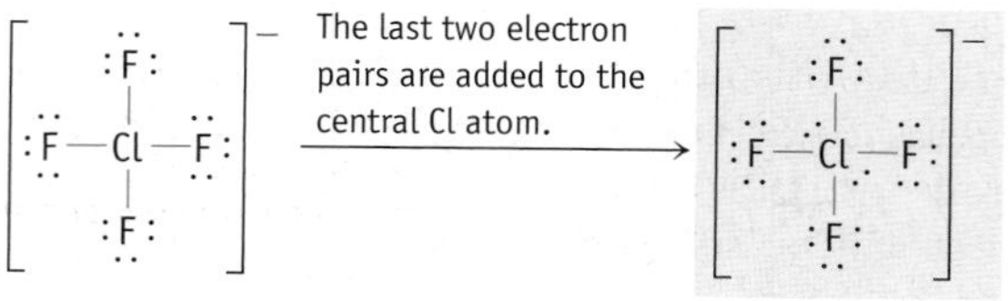

The last two electron pairs are added to the central Cl atom.

EXERCISE 8.7 **Lewis Structures in Which the Central Atom Has More Than Eight Electrons**

Sketch the Lewis structures for $[ClF_2]^+$ and $[ClF_2]^-$. How many lone pairs and bond pairs surround the Cl atom in each ion?

Molecules with an Odd Number of Electrons

Two nitrogen oxides—NO, with 11 valence electrons, and NO_2, with 17 valence electrons—are among a very small group of stable molecules with an odd number of electrons. Because they have an odd number of electrons, it is impossible to draw a structure obeying the octet rule; at least one electron must be unpaired.

Even though NO_2 does not obey the octet rule, an electron dot structure can be written that approximates the bonding in the molecule. This Lewis structure places the unpaired electron on nitrogen. Two resonance structures show that the nitrogen–oxygen bonds are expected to be equivalent.

Experimental evidence for NO indicates that the bonding between N and O is intermediate between a double and a triple bond. It is not possible to write a Lewis structure for NO that is in accord with the properties of this substance, so a different theory is needed to understand bonding in this molecule. We shall return to compounds of this type when molecular orbital theory is introduced in Section 9.3.

The two nitrogen oxides, NO and NO_2, are members of a class of chemical substances called free radicals. **Free radicals** are chemical species—both atomic and molecular—with an unpaired electron. Free radicals are generally quite reac-

Small molecules such as H_2, O_2, H_2O, CO, and CO_2 are among the most important molecules commercially, environmentally, and biologically. Imagine the surprise of chemists and biologists when it was discovered a few years ago that nitrogen monoxide (nitric oxide, NO), which was widely considered toxic, also has an important biological role.

Nitric oxide is a colorless, paramagnetic gas that is moderately soluble in water. In the laboratory, it can be synthesized by the reduction of nitrite ion with iodide ion:

$$KNO_2(aq) + KI(aq) + H_2SO_4(aq) \rightarrow$$
$$NO(g) + K_2SO_4(aq) + H_2O(\ell) + \tfrac{1}{2} I_2(aq)$$

The formation of NO from the elements is an unfavorable, energetically uphill reaction ($\Delta_f H° = 90.2$ kJ/mol). Nevertheless, small quantities of this compound form from nitrogen and oxygen at high temperatures. For example, conditions in an internal combustion engine are favorable for this to happen.

Nitric oxide reacts rapidly with O_2 to form the reddish-brown gas NO_2.

$$2\ NO(\text{colorless, g}) + O_2(g) \rightarrow$$
$$2\ NO_2(\text{brown, g})$$

The result is that compounds such as NO_2 and HNO_3 arising from reactions of NO with O_2 and H_2O are among the air pollutants produced by automobiles.

A few years ago, chemists learned that NO is synthesized in a biological process by animals as diverse as barnacles, fruit flies, horseshoe crabs, chickens, trout, and humans. Even more recently, chemists have found that NO is important in an astonishing range of physiological processes in humans and other animals. These include a role in neurotransmission, blood clotting, and blood pressure control as well as in the immune system's ability to kill tumor cells and intracellular parasites.

Questions: *Oxygen is needed by many living organisms, but some reactions with oxygen can lead to oxidative damage. One species that can produce damage in an organism is the superoxide ion, O_2^-. Fortunately, this ion is removed extremely rapidly by reaction with NO to produce the peroxynitrite ion, $ONOO^-$.*
1. Draw the Lewis structure for the ion.

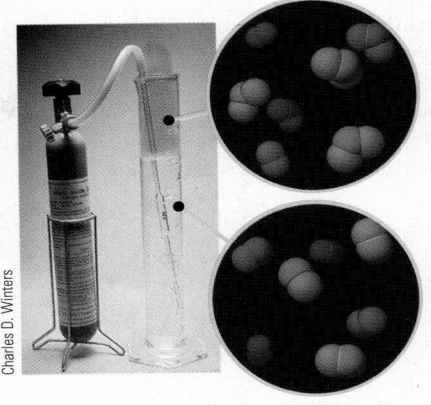

Charles D. Winters

The colorless gas NO is bubbled into water from a high-pressure tank. When the gas emerges into the air, the NO reacts rapidly with O_2 to give brown NO_2 gas.

2. Are there any multiple bonds in the ion?
3. Are there any resonance structures needed?

Answers to these questions are in Appendix Q.

---

tive. Free atoms such as H and Cl, for example, are free radicals and readily combine with each other to give molecules such as H_2, Cl_2, and HCl.

Free radicals are involved in many reactions in the environment. For example, small amounts of NO are released from vehicle exhausts. The NO rapidly forms NO_2, which is even more harmful to human health and to plants. Exposure to NO_2 at concentrations of 50–100 parts per million can lead to significant inflammation of lung tissue. Nitrogen dioxide is also generated by natural processes. For example, when hay, which has a high level of nitrates, is stored in silos on farms, NO_2 can be generated as the hay ferments, and there have been reports of farm workers dying from exposure to this gas in the silo.

The two nitrogen oxides, NO and NO_2, are unique in that they can be isolated and neither has the extreme reactivity of most free radicals. When cooled, however, two NO_2 molecules join or "dimerize" to form colorless N_2O_4; the unpaired electrons combine to form an N—N bond in N_2O_4 (Figure 8.3).

8.6 Molecular Shapes

One reason for drawing Lewis electron dot structures is to be able to predict the three-dimensional geometry of molecules and ions. Because the physical and chemical properties of compounds are tied to their structures, the importance of this subject cannot be overstated.

FIGURE 8.3 Free radical chemistry.
When cooled, the brown gas NO_2, a free radical, forms colorless N_2O_4, a molecule with an N—N single bond. The coupling of two free radicals is a common type of chemical reaction. Because identical free radicals come together, the product is called a dimer, and the process is called a dimerization. (Sign in to ChemistryNow, Screen 8.9, to see a video of this reaction.)

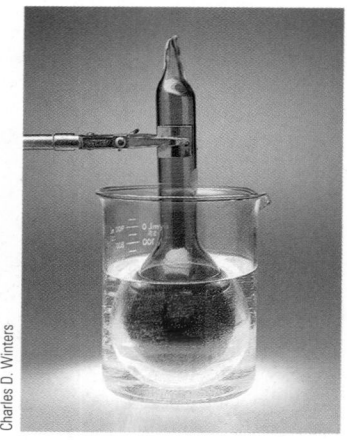

When cooled, NO_2 free radicals couple to form N_2O_4 molecules.

→

N_2O_4 gas is colorless.

A flask of brown NO_2 gas in warm water

A flask of NO_2 gas in ice water

■ **VSEPR Theory** The VSEPR theory was devised by Ronald J. Gillespie (1924–) and Ronald S. Nyholm (1917–1971).

The **valence shell electron-pair repulsion (VSEPR)** model is a reliable method for predicting the shapes of covalent molecules and polyatomic ions. This model is based on the idea that *bond and lone electron pairs in the valence shell of an element repel each other and seek to be as far apart as possible.* The positions assumed by the valence electrons of an atom thus define the angles between bonds to surrounding atoms. VSEPR is remarkably successful in predicting structures of molecules and ions of main group elements. However, it is less effective (and seldom used) to predict structures of compounds containing transition metals.

To have a sense of how valence shell electron pairs repel and determine structure, blow up several balloons to a similar size. Imagine that each balloon represents an electron cloud. When two, three, four, five, or six balloons are tied together at a central point (representing the nucleus and core electrons of a central atom), the balloons naturally form the shapes shown in Figure 8.4. These geometric arrangements minimize interactions between the balloons.

Central Atoms Surrounded Only by Single-Bond Pairs

The simplest application of VSEPR theory is to molecules and ions in which all the electron pairs around the central atom are involved in single covalent bonds. Figure 8.5 illustrates the geometries predicted for molecules or ions with the general formulas AX_n, where A is the central atom and n is the number of X groups bonded to it.

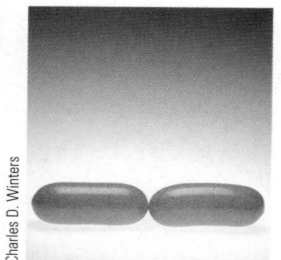

Linear

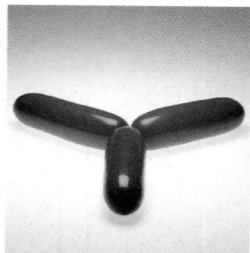

Trigonal planar

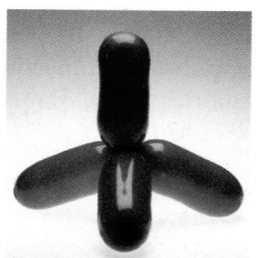

Tetrahedral

Trigonal bipyramidal

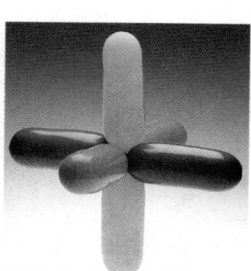

Octahedral

FIGURE 8.4 Balloon models of electron-pair geometries for two to six electron pairs. If two to six balloons of similar size and shape are tied together, they will naturally assume the arrangements shown. These pictures illustrate the predictions of VSEPR.

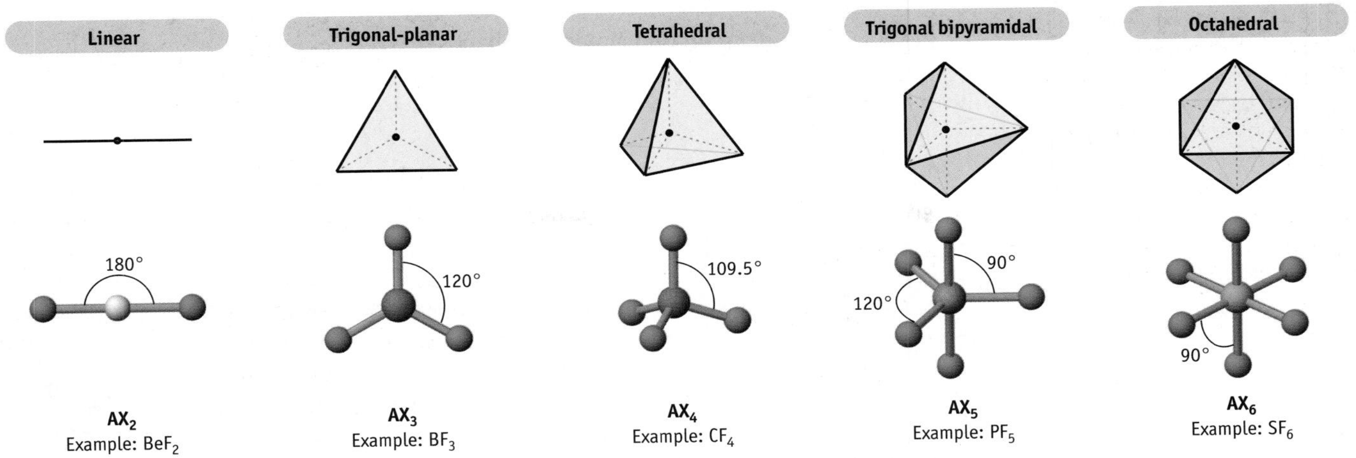

Linear
Trigonal-planar
Tetrahedral
Trigonal bipyramidal
Octahedral
180°
120°
109.5°
90°
120°
90°
AX2
Example: BeF2
AX3
Example: BF3
AX4
Example: CF4
AX5
Example: PF5
AX6
Example: SF6

Active Figure 8.5 Various geometries predicted by VSEPR. Geometries predicted by VSEPR for molecules that contain only single covalent bonds around the central atom.

Chemistry Now™ Sign in at www.cengage.com/login and go to the Chapter Contents menu to explore an interactive version of this figure accompanied by an exercise.

The linear geometry for two bond pairs and the trigonal-planar geometry for three bond pairs involve a central atom that does not have an octet of electrons (see Section 8.5). The central atom in a tetrahedral molecule obeys the octet rule with four bond pairs. The central atoms in trigonal-bipyramidal and octahedral molecules have five and six bonding pairs, respectively, and are expected only when the central atom is an element in Period 3 or higher of the periodic table (▶ page 372).

Chemistry Now™

Sign in at **www.cengage.com/login** and go to Chapter 8 Contents to see:
- Screen 8.13 for an animation of **the electron-pair geometries** and on **identifying geometries**
- Screen 8.14 for practice **predicting molecular geometry**

EXAMPLE 8.6 Predicting Molecular Shapes

Problem Predict the shape of silicon tetrachloride, $SiCl_4$.

Strategy The first step is to draw the Lewis structure. The Lewis structure does not need to be drawn in any particular way because its purpose is only to describe the number of bonds around an atom and to determine if there are any lone pairs. The number of bond and lone pairs of electrons around the central atom determines the molecular shape (Figure 8.5).

Solution The Lewis structure of $SiCl_4$ has four electron pairs, all of them bond pairs, around the central Si atom. Therefore, a tetrahedral structure is predicted for the $SiCl_4$ molecule, with Cl—Si—Cl bond angles of 109.5°. This agrees with the actual structure for $SiCl_4$.

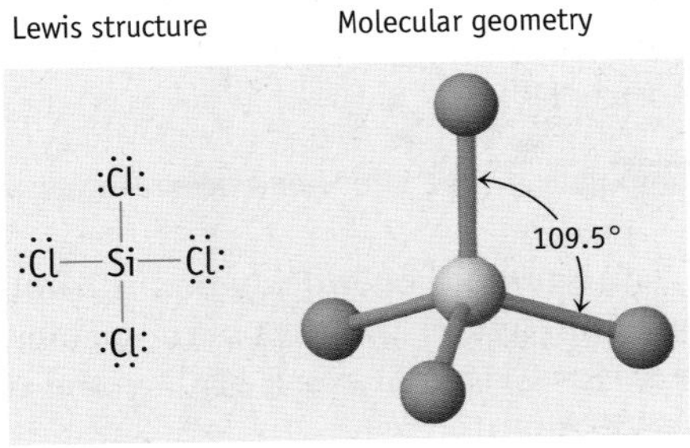

Lewis structure
Molecular geometry
109.5°

■ **Lewis Structures and Molecular Shapes** Drawing the Lewis structure is the first step in determining the shape of a molecule or ion.

Central Atoms with Single-Bond Pairs and Lone Pairs

To see how lone pairs affect the geometry of the molecule or polyatomic ion, return to the balloon models in Figure 8.4. Recall that the balloons represented *all* the electron pairs in the valence shell. The balloon model therefore predicts the "electron-pair geometry" rather than the "molecular geometry." The **electron-pair geometry** is the geometry taken up by *all* the valence electron pairs around a central atom, whereas the **molecular geometry** describes the arrangement in space of the central atom and the atoms directly attached to it. It is important to recognize that *lone pairs of electrons on the central atom occupy spatial positions, even though their location is not included in the verbal description of the shape of the molecule or ion.*

Let us use the VSEPR model to predict the molecular geometry and bond angles in the NH_3 molecule. On drawing the Lewis structure, we see there are four pairs of electrons in the nitrogen valence shell, three bond pairs, and one lone pair. Thus, the predicted *electron-pair geometry* is tetrahedral. The *molecular geometry*, however, is said to be *trigonal pyramidal* because that describes the location of the atoms. The nitrogen atom is at the apex of the pyramid, and the three hydrogen atoms form the trigonal base.

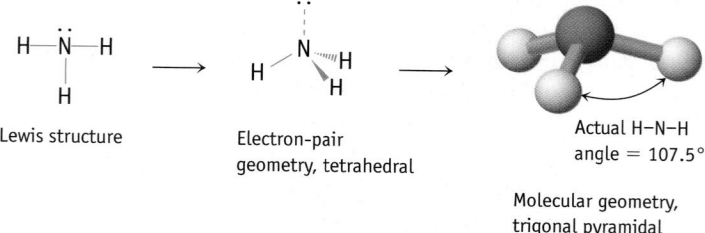

Lewis structure

Electron-pair
geometry, tetrahedral

Actual H–N–H
angle = 107.5°

Molecular geometry,
trigonal pyramidal

Effect of Lone Pairs on Bond Angles

Because the electron-pair geometry in NH_3 is tetrahedral, we would expect the H—N—H bond angle to be 109.5°. However, the experimentally determined bond angles in NH_3 are 107.5°, and the H—O—H angle in water is smaller still (104.5°) (Figure 8.6). These angles are close to the tetrahedral angle but not exactly that value. This highlights the fact that VSEPR is not an accurate model; it can only predict the approximate geometry. Small variations in geometry (e.g., bond angles a few degrees different from predicted) are quite common and often arise because there is a difference between the spatial requirements of lone pairs and bond pairs. Lone pairs of electrons seem to occupy a larger volume than bonding pairs, and the increased volume of lone pairs causes bond pairs to squeeze closer together. In general, the relative strengths of repulsions are in the order

Lone pair–lone pair > lone pair–bond pair > bond pair–bond pair

The different spatial requirements of lone pairs and bond pairs can be used to predict variations in the bond angles in series of molecules. For example, the bond angles decrease in the series CH_4, NH_3, and H_2O as the number of lone pairs on the central atom increases (Figure 8.6).

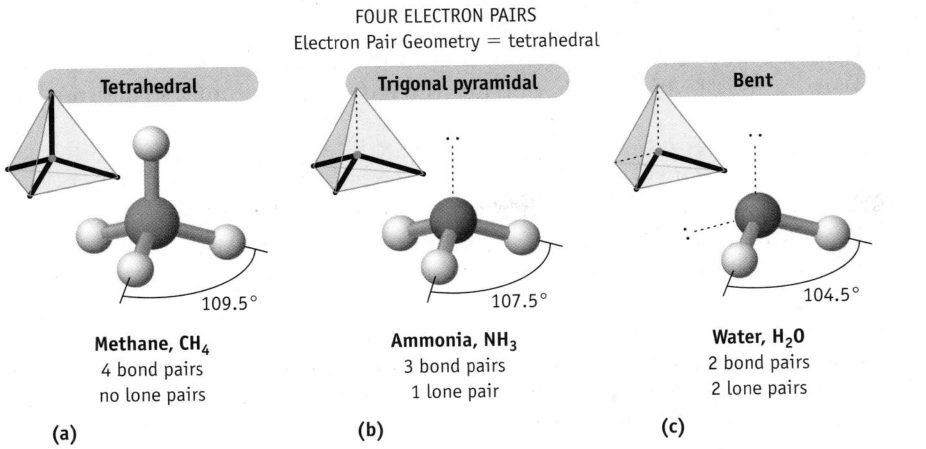

FOUR ELECTRON PAIRS
Electron Pair Geometry = tetrahedral

Tetrahedral   **Trigonal pyramidal**   **Bent**

109.5°   107.5°   104.5°

Methane, CH_4
4 bond pairs
no lone pairs

Ammonia, NH_3
3 bond pairs
1 lone pair

Water, H_2O
2 bond pairs
2 lone pairs

(a)   (b)   (c)

FIGURE 8.6 The molecular geometries of methane, ammonia, and water. All have four electron pairs around the central atom, so all have a tetrahedral electron-pair geometry. (a) Methane has four bond pairs and so has a tetrahedral molecular shape. (b) Ammonia has three bond pairs and one lone pair, so it has a trigonal-pyramidal molecular shape. (c) Water has two bond pairs and two lone pairs, so it has a bent, or angular, molecular shape. The decrease in bond angles in the series can be explained by the fact that the lone pairs have a larger spatial requirement than the bond pairs.

EXAMPLE 8.7 Finding the Shapes of Molecules

Problem What are the shapes of the ions H_3O^+ and ClF_2^+?

Strategy Draw the Lewis structures for each ion. Count the number of lone and bond pairs around the central atom. Use Figure 8.5 to decide on the electron-pair geometry. Finally, the location of the atoms in the ion—which is determined by the bond and lone pairs—gives the geometry of the ion.

Solution

(a) The Lewis structure of the hydronium ion, H_3O^+, shows that the oxygen atom is surrounded by four electron pairs, so the electron-pair geometry is tetrahedral.

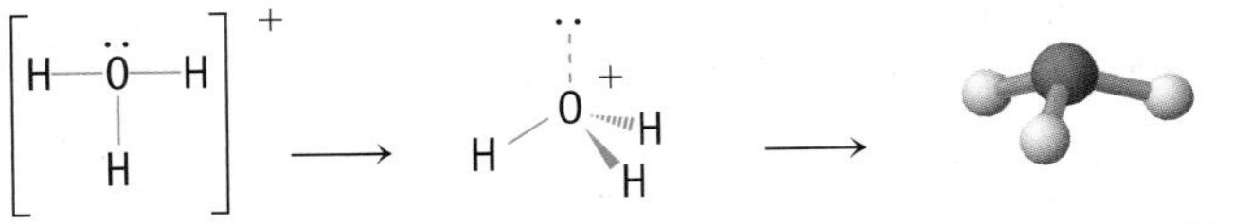

Lewis structure   Electron-pair geometry, tetrahedral   Molecular geometry, trigonal pyramidal

Because three of the four pairs are used to bond terminal atoms, the central O atom and the three H atoms form a trigonal-pyramidal molecular shape like that of NH_3.

(b) Chlorine is the central atom in ClF_2^+. It is surrounded by four electron pairs, so the electron-pair geometry around chlorine is tetrahedral. Because only two of the four pairs are bonding pairs, the ion has a bent geometry.

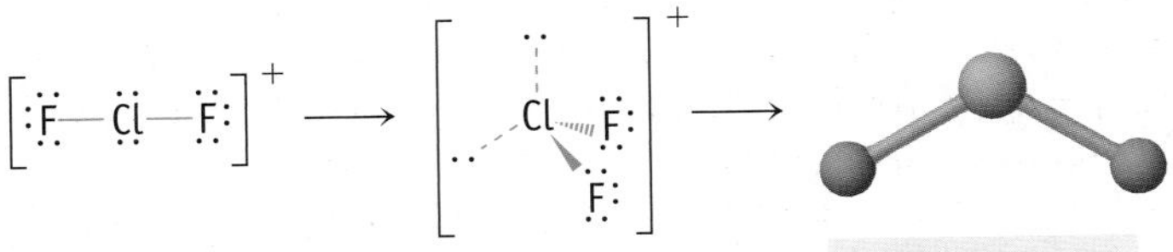

Lewis structure   Electron-pair geometry, tetrahedral   Molecular geometry, bent or angular

---

EXERCISE 8.9 VSEPR and Molecular Shape

Give the electron-pair geometry and molecular shape for BF_3 and BF_4^-. What is the effect on the molecular geometry of adding an F^- ion to BF_3 to give BF_4^-?

■ **"Energized Water" with a Bond Angle of 114°!** There are many dubious products sold over the internet, and one of them claims that water is "energized" by increasing its bond angle. One advertisement said that in the past water had a bond angle of a healthy 110°, but now it is "wimpy" and unhealthy with an angle of only 104°. Further, it is claimed that distilled water only has a bond angle of 101° and is biologically dead. To cure this problem, you can buy a costly machine that "energizes" water and causes a bond angle increase to as much as 114°. Now, it is also claimed, this water has enough energy to destroy pathogens. The old circus master, P. T. Barnum, once said there is a sucker born every minute.

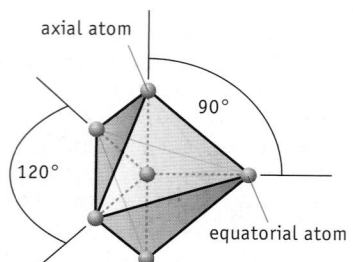

Central Atoms with More Than Four Valence Electron Pairs

The situation becomes more complicated if the central atom has five or six electron pairs, some of which are lone pairs. A trigonal-bipyramidal structure (Figures 8.5 and 8.7) has two sets of positions that are not equivalent. The positions in the trigonal plane lie in the equator of an imaginary sphere around the central atom and are called the *equatorial* positions. The north and south poles in this representation are called the *axial* positions. Each equatorial atom has two neighboring groups (the axial atoms) at 90°, and each axial atom has three groups (the equatorial atoms) at 90°. The result is that the lone pairs, which require more space than bonding pairs, prefer to occupy equatorial positions rather than axial positions.

The entries in the top line of Figure 8.8 show species having a total of five valence electron pairs, with zero, one, two, and three lone pairs. In SF_4, with one lone pair, the molecule assumes a "seesaw" shape with the lone pair in one of the equatorial positions. The ClF_3 molecule has three bond pairs and two lone pairs. The two lone pairs in ClF_3 are in equatorial positions; two bond pairs are axial, and the third is in the equatorial plane, so the molecular geometry is T-shaped. The third molecule shown is XeF_2. Here, all three equatorial positions are occupied by lone pairs so the molecular geometry is linear.

The geometry assumed by six electron pairs is octahedral (see Figure 8.8), and all the angles at adjacent positions are 90°. Unlike the trigonal bipyramid, the octahedron has no distinct axial and equatorial positions; all positions are the same. Therefore, if the molecule has one lone pair, as in BrF_5, it makes no difference which position it occupies. The lone pair is often drawn in the top or bottom posi-

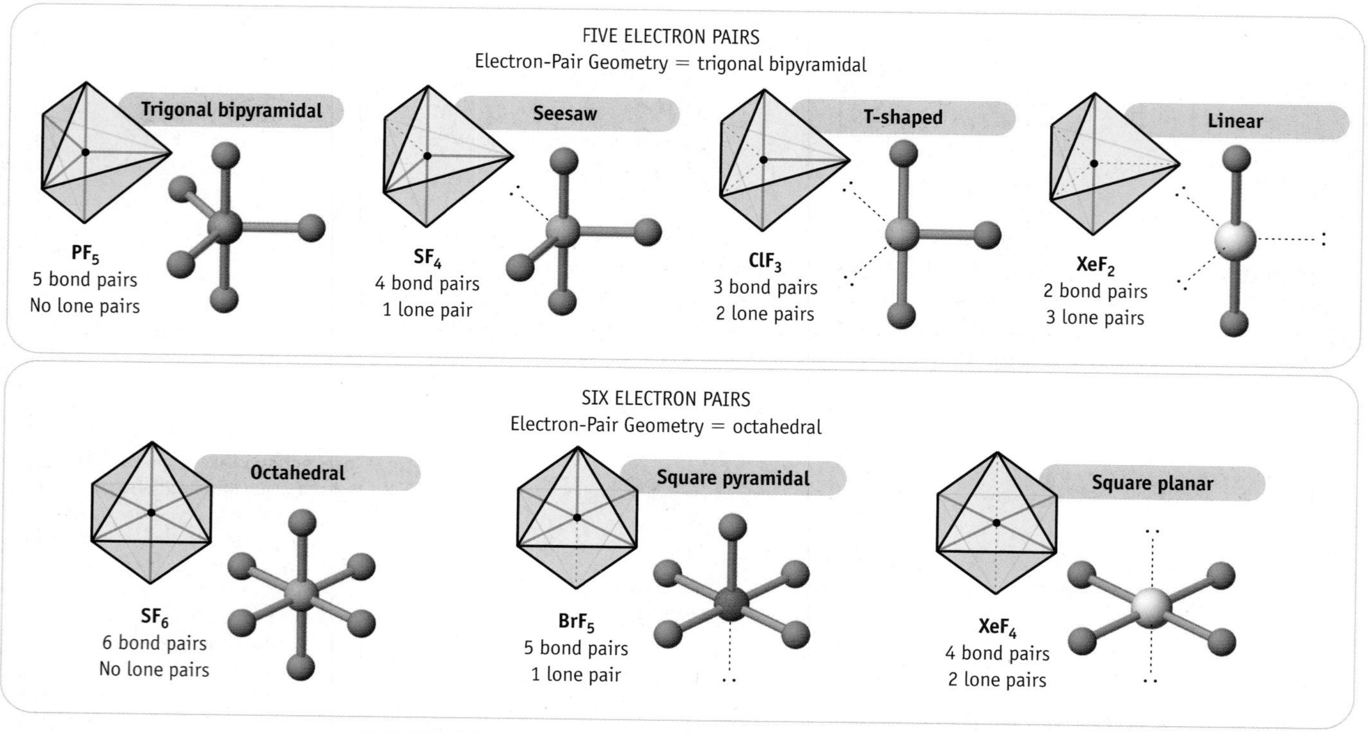

FIVE ELECTRON PAIRS
Electron-Pair Geometry = trigonal bipyramidal

Trigonal bipyramidal

PF_5
5 bond pairs
No lone pairs

Seesaw

SF_4
4 bond pairs
1 lone pair

T-shaped

ClF_3
3 bond pairs
2 lone pairs

Linear

XeF_2
2 bond pairs
3 lone pairs

SIX ELECTRON PAIRS
Electron-Pair Geometry = octahedral

Octahedral

SF_6
6 bond pairs
No lone pairs

Square pyramidal

BrF_5
5 bond pairs
1 lone pair

Square planar

XeF_4
4 bond pairs
2 lone pairs

FIGURE 8.8 Electron-pair geometries and molecular shapes for molecules and ions with five or six electron pairs around the central atom.

tion to make it easier to visualize the molecular geometry, which in this case is square-pyramidal. If two pairs of electrons in an octahedral arrangement are lone pairs, they seek to be as far apart as possible. The result is a square-planar molecule, as illustrated by XeF_4.

■ **EXAMPLE 8.8 Predicting Molecular Shape**

Problem What is the shape of the ICl_4^- ion?

Strategy Draw the Lewis structure, and then decide on the electron-pair geometry. The position of the atoms gives the molecular geometry of the ion. (See Example 8.7 and Figure 8.8.)

Solution A Lewis structure for the ICl_4^- ion shows that the central iodine atom has six electron pairs in its valence shell. Two of these are lone pairs. Placing the lone pairs on opposite sides leaves the four chlorine atoms in a square-planar geometry.

Electron-pair geometry, octahedral

90°

Molecular geometry, square planar

EXERCISE 8.10 Predicting Molecular Shape

Draw the Lewis structure for ICl_2^-, and then decide on the geometry of the ion.

Multiple Bonds and Molecular Geometry

Double and triple bonds involve more electron pairs than single bonds, but this has little effect on the overall molecular shape. All of the electron pairs in a multiple bond are shared between the same two nuclei and therefore occupy the same region of space. Because they must remain in that region, two electron pairs in a double bond (or three pairs in a triple bond) have the same effect on the structure as one electron pair in a single bond. That is, all electron pairs in a multiple bond count as one bond and contribute to molecular geometry the same as a single bond does. For example, the carbon atom in CO_2 has no lone pairs and participates in two double bonds. Each double bond counts as one for the purpose of predicting geometry, so the structure of CO_2 is linear.

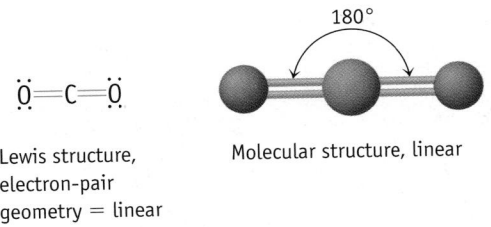

$\ddot{O}{=}C{=}\ddot{O}$

Lewis structure, electron-pair geometry = linear

180°

Molecular structure, linear

When resonance structures are possible, the geometry can be predicted from any of the Lewis resonance structures or from the resonance hybrid structure. For example, the geometry of the CO_3^{2-} ion is predicted to be trigonal planar because the carbon atom has three sets of bonds and no lone pairs.

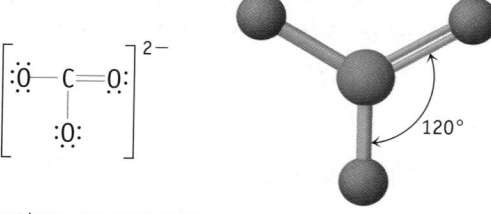

Lewis structure, one resonance
structure, electron-pair
geometry = trigonal planar

Molecular structure,
trigonal planar

The NO_2^- ion also has a trigonal-planar electron-pair geometry. Because there is a lone pair on the central nitrogen atom, and bonds in the other two positions, the geometry of the ion is angular or bent.

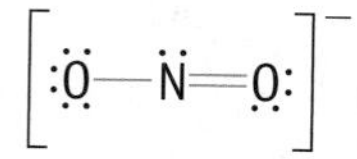

Lewis structure, one
resonance structure,
electron-pair geometry
= trigonal planar

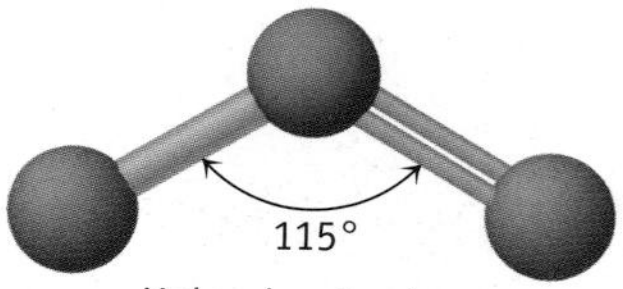

Molecular structure,
angular or bent

The techniques just outlined can be used to find the geometries around the atoms in more complicated molecules. Consider, for example, cysteine, one of the natural amino acids.

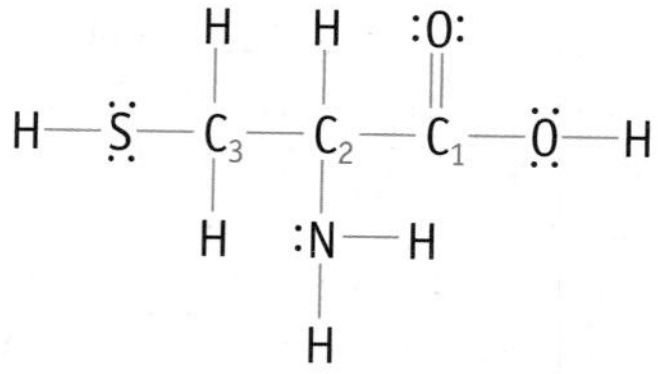

Cysteine, $HSCH_2CH(NH_2)CO_2H$

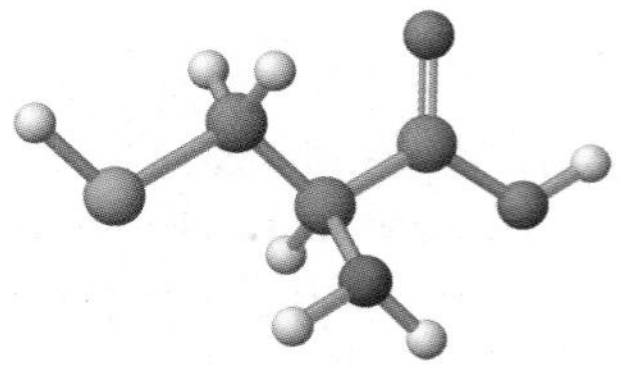

Four pairs of electrons occur around the S, N, C_2, and C_3 atoms, so the electron-pair geometry around each is tetrahedral. Thus, the S—C—H and H—N—H angles are predicted to be approximately 109°. The O atom in the grouping C—O—H and the S atom in the grouping H—S—C are also surrounded by four pairs, and so these angles are likewise approximately 109°. Finally, the angle made by O—C_1—O is 120° because the electron-pair geometry around C_1 is trigonal planar.

EXAMPLE 8.9 Finding the Shapes of Molecules and Ions

Problem What are the shapes of the nitrate ion, NO_3^-, and $XeOF_4$?

Strategy Draw the Lewis structure, and then decide on the electron pair geometry. The position of the atoms gives the molecular geometry of the ion. Follow the procedure used in Examples 8.6–8.8.

Solution

(a) The NO_3^- and CO_3^{2-} ions are isoelectronic. Thus, like the carbonate ion described in the text above, the electron-pair geometry and molecular shape of NO_3^- are trigonal planar.

(b) The $XeOF_4$ molecule has a Lewis structure with a total of six electron pairs about the central Xe atom, one of which is a lone pair. It has a square-pyramidal molecular structure. Two structures are possible, based on the position occupied by the oxygen, but there is no way to predict which is correct. The actual structure is the one shown, with the oxygen in the apex of the square pyramid.

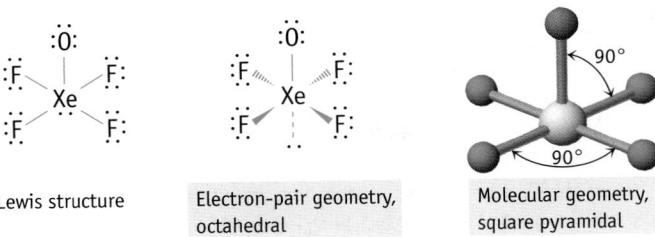

| Lewis structure | Electron-pair geometry, octahedral | Molecular geometry, square pyramidal |

EXERCISE 8.11 Determining Molecular Shapes

Use Lewis structures and the VSEPR model to determine the electron-pair and molecular geometries for **(a)** the phosphate ion, PO_4^{3-}; **(b)** the sulfite ion, SO_3^{2-}; and **(c)** IF_5.

8.7 | Bond Polarity and Electronegativity

The models used to represent covalent and ionic bonding are the extreme situations in bonding. Pure covalent bonding, in which atoms share an electron pair equally, occurs *only* when two identical atoms are bonded. When two dissimilar atoms form a covalent bond, the electron pair will be unequally shared. The result is a **polar covalent bond,** a bond in which the two atoms have residual or partial charges (Figure 8.9).

Bonds are polar because not all atoms hold onto their valence electrons with the same force, nor do atoms take on additional electrons with equal ease. Recall from the discussion of atom properties that different elements have different values of ionization energy and electron affinity (Section 7.5). These differences in behavior for free atoms carry over to atoms in molecules.

If a bond pair is not equally shared between atoms, the bonding electrons are on average nearer to one of the atoms. The atom toward which the pair is displaced has a larger share of the electron pair and thus acquires a partial negative charge. At the same time, the atom at the other end of the bond is depleted in electrons and acquires a partial positive charge. The bond between the two atoms has a positive end and a negative end; that is, it has negative and positive poles. The bond is called a **polar bond.**

In ionic compounds, displacement of the bonding pair to one of the two atoms is essentially complete, and + and − symbols are written alongside the atom symbols in the Lewis drawings. For a polar covalent bond, the polarity is indicated by writing the symbols $\delta+$ and $\delta-$ alongside the atom symbols, where δ (the Greek letter "delta") stands for a *partial* charge. Hydrogen fluoride, water, and ammonia are three simple molecules having polar, covalent bonds.

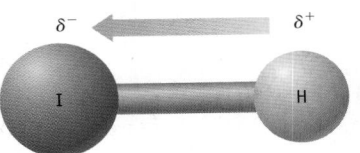

FIGURE 8.9 A polar covalent bond. Iodine has a larger share of the bonding electrons, and hydrogen has a smaller share. The result is that I has a partial negative charge ($\delta-$), and H has a partial positive charge ($\delta+$).

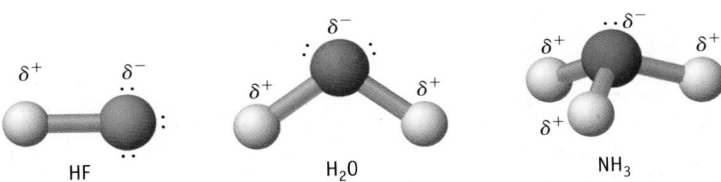

Three simple molecules with polar covalent bonds. In each case, F, O, and N are more electronegative than H.

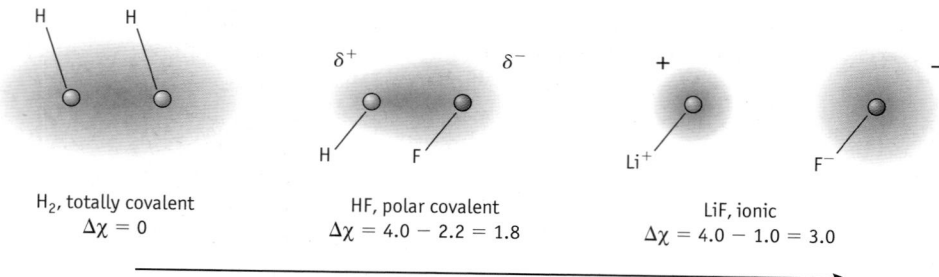

H₂, totally covalent
$\Delta\chi = 0$

HF, polar covalent
$\Delta\chi = 4.0 - 2.2 = 1.8$

LiF, ionic
$\Delta\chi = 4.0 - 1.0 = 3.0$

Increasing ionic character

FIGURE 8.10 Covalent to ionic bonding. As the electronegativity difference increases between the atoms of a bond, the bond becomes increasingly ionic.

With so many atoms to use in covalent bond formation, it is not surprising that bonds between atoms can fall anywhere in a continuum from pure covalent to pure ionic (Figure 8.10). There is no sharp dividing line between an ionic bond and a covalent bond.

In the 1930s, Linus Pauling proposed a parameter called atom electronegativity that allows us to decide if a bond is polar, which atom of the bond is negative and which is positive, and if one bond is more polar than another. The **electronegativity, χ,** of an atom is defined as a measure of *the ability of an atom in a molecule to attract electrons to itself.*

Values of electronegativity are given in Figure 8.11. Several features and periodic trends are apparent. The element with the largest electronegativity is fluorine; it is assigned a value of $\chi = 4.0$. The element with the smallest value is the alkali metal cesium. Electronegativities generally increase from left to right across a period and decrease down a group. This is the opposite of the trend observed for metallic character. Metals typically have low values of electronegativity, ranging from slightly less than 1 to about 2. Electronegativity values for the metalloids are around 2, whereas nonmetals have values greater than 2.

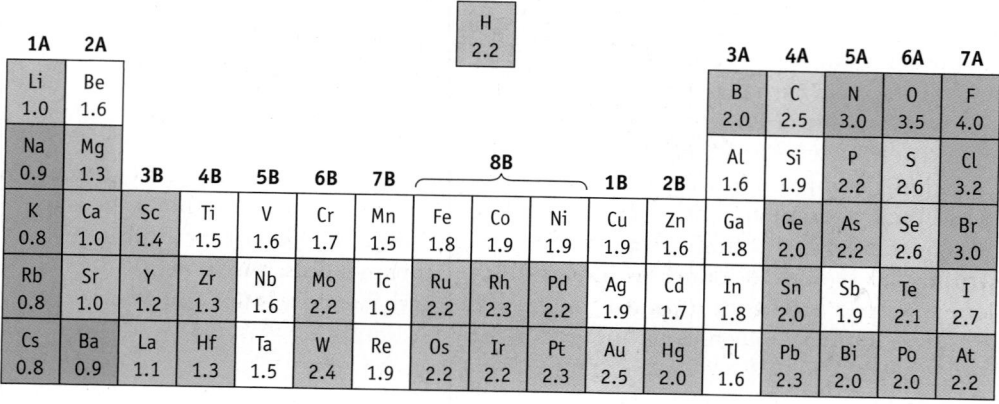

FIGURE 8.11 Electronegativity values for the elements according to Pauling. Trends for electronegativities are the opposite of the trends defining metallic character. Nonmetals have high values of electronegativity; the metalloids have intermediate values, and the metals have low values. Values for these elements as well as for the noble gases and for the lanthanides and actinides are available in the following handbook: Emsley, J., *The Elements,* 3rd edition, Clarendon Press, Oxford, 1998.

There is a large *difference* in electronegativity for atoms from the left- and right-hand sides of the periodic table. For cesium fluoride, for example, the difference in electronegativity values, $\Delta\chi$, is 3.2 [= 4.0 (for F) − 0.8 (for Cs)]. The bond is decidedly ionic in CsF, therefore, with Cs the cation (Cs^+) and F the anion (F^-). In contrast, the electronegativity difference between H and F in HF is only 1.8 [= 4.0 (for F) − 2.2 (for H)]. We conclude that bonding in HF must be more covalent, as expected for a compound formed from two nonmetals. The H—F bond is polar, however, with hydrogen being the positive end of the molecule and fluorine the negative end ($H^{\delta+}$—$F^{\delta-}$).

Chemistry Now™

Sign in at **www.cengage.com/login** and go to Chapter 8 Contents to see Screen 8.15 for **relative electronegativity values.**

Linus Pauling (1901–1994). Linus Pauling was born in Portland, Oregon, earned a B.Sc. degree in chemical engineering from Oregon State College in 1922, and completed his Ph.D. in chemistry at the California Institute of Technology in 1925. In chemistry, he is well known for his book *The Nature of the Chemical Bond.* He also studied protein structure and, in the words of Francis Crick, was "one of the founders of molecular biology." It was this work and his study of chemical bonding that were cited in the award of the Nobel Prize in chemistry in 1954. Although chemistry was the focus of his life, at the urging of his wife, Ava Helen, he was also involved in nuclear disarmament issues, and he received the Nobel Peace Prize in 1962 for the role he played in advocating for the nuclear test ban treaty.

©Ted Streshinsky/Corbis

■ **EXAMPLE 8.10 Estimating Bond Polarities**

Problem For each of the following bond pairs, decide which is the more polar and indicate the negative and positive poles.

(a) B—F and B—Cl

(b) Si—O and P—P

Strategy Locate the elements in the periodic table. Recall that electronegativity generally increases across a period and up a group.

Solution

(a) B and F lie relatively far apart in the periodic table. B is a metalloid, and F is a nonmetal. Here, χ for B = 2.0, and χ for F = 4.0. Similarly, B and Cl are relatively far apart in the periodic table, but Cl is below F in the periodic table (χ for Cl = 3.2) and is therefore less electronegative than F. The difference in electronegativity for B—F is 2.0, and for B—Cl it is 1.2. Both bonds are expected to be polar, with B positive and the halide atom negative, but a B—F bond is more polar than a B—Cl bond.

(b) Because the bond is between two atoms of the same kind, the P—P bond is nonpolar. Silicon is in Group 4A and the third period, whereas O is in Group 6A and the second period. Consequently, O has a greater electronegativity (3.5) than Si (1.9), so the bond is highly polar ($\Delta\chi = 1.6$), with O the more negative atom.

EXERCISE 8.12 Bond Polarity

For each of the following pairs of bonds, decide which is the more polar. For each polar bond, indicate the positive and negative poles. First, make your prediction from the relative atom positions in the periodic table; then check your prediction by calculating $\Delta\chi$.

(a) H—F and H—I   **(b)** B—C and B—F   **(c)** C—Si and C—S

Charge Distribution: Combining Formal Charge and Electronegativity

The way electrons are distributed in a molecule or ion is called its **charge distribution.** The charge distribution can profoundly affect the properties of a molecule. Examples include its physical properties, such as its melting and boiling points, and its chemical properties, such as its susceptibility to attack by an anion or cation or whether it is an acid or a base.

We saw earlier (◄ page 359) that formal charge calculations can locate the site of a charge in a molecule or an ion. However, this can sometimes lead to results that are incorrect because formal charge calculations assume that there is equal sharing of electrons in all bonds. The ion BF_4^- illustrates this point. Boron has a formal charge of −1 in this ion, whereas the formal charge calculated for the fluorine atoms is 0. This is not logical: fluorine is the more electronegative atom so the negative charge should reside on F and not on B.

Electronegativity is a useful, if somewhat vague, concept. It is, however, related to the ionic character of bonds. Chemists have found, as illustrated in the figure, that a correlation exists between the difference in electronegativity of bonded atoms and the degree of ionicity expressed as "% ionic character."

As the difference in electronegativity increases, ionic character increases. Does this trend allow us to say that one compound is ionic and another is covalent? No, we can say only that one bond is more ionic or more covalent than another.

Electron affinity was introduced in Section 7.5. At first glance, it may appear that electronegativity and electron affinity measure the same property, but they do not. Electronegativity is a parameter that applies only to atoms in molecules, whereas electron affinity is a measurable energy quantity for atoms in the gas phase.

Although electron affinity was introduced earlier as a criterion with which to predict the central atom in a molecule, experience indicates that electronegativity is a better choice. That is, *the central atom is generally the atom of lowest electronegativity.*

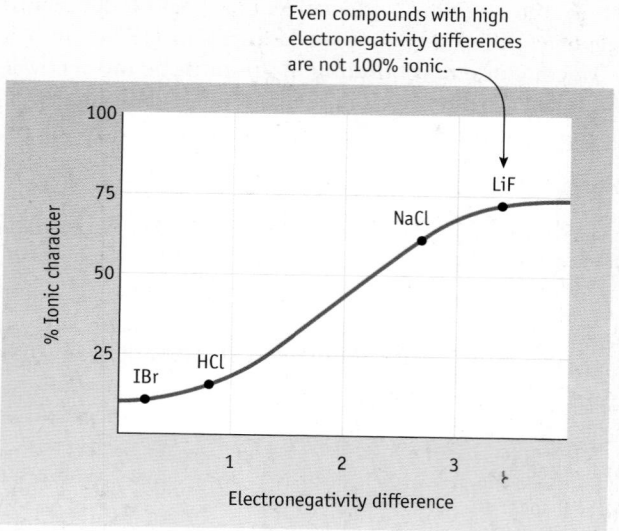

Even compounds with high electronegativity differences are not 100% ionic.

The way to resolve this dilemma is to consider electronegativity in conjunction with formal charge. Based on the electronegativity difference between fluorine and boron ($\Delta\chi = 2.0$), the B—F bonds are expected to be polar, with fluorine being the negative end of the bond, $B^{\delta+}$—$F^{\delta-}$. So, in this instance, predictions based on electronegativity and formal charge work in opposite directions. The formal charge calculation places the negative charge on boron, but the electronegativity difference leads us to say the negative charge on boron is distributed onto the fluorine atoms, effectively spreading it out over the molecule.

Linus Pauling pointed out two basic guidelines to use when describing charge distributions in molecules and ions. The first is the **electroneutrality principle.** This declares that electrons will be distributed in such a way that the charges on all atoms are as close to zero as possible. Second, he noted that if a negative charge is present, it should reside on the most electronegative atoms. Similarly, positive charges are expected on the least electronegative atoms. The effect of these principles is clearly seen in the case of BF_4^-, where the negative charge is distributed over the four fluorine atoms rather than residing on boron.

Considering the concepts of electronegativity and formal charge together can help to decide which of several resonance structures is the more important. For example, Lewis structure A for CO_2 is the logical one to draw. But what is wrong with B, in which each atom also has an octet of electrons?

Formal charge =
$$0 = 7 - [6 + \tfrac{1}{2}(2)]$$

Formal charge =
$$-1 = 3 - [0 + \tfrac{1}{2}(8)]$$

Formal charges for the B and F atoms of the BF$_4^-$ anion.

Formal charges	0 0 0	+1 0 −1
Resonance structures	O=C=O	:O≡C—O:
	A	B

For structure A, each atom has a formal charge of 0, a favorable situation. In B, however, one oxygen atom has a formal charge of +1, and the other has −1. This is contrary to the principle of electroneutrality. In addition, B places a positive charge on the more electronegative O atom. Thus, we can conclude that structure B is a much less satisfactory structure than A.

Now use the logic applied to CO_2 to decide which of the three possible resonance structures for the OCN^- ion is the most reasonable. Formal charges for each atom are given above the element's symbol.

Formal charges

Resonance structures

$$\begin{bmatrix} \overset{-1}{:\ddot{O}} - \overset{0}{C} \equiv \overset{0}{N}: \end{bmatrix}^- \longleftrightarrow \begin{bmatrix} \overset{0}{:\ddot{O}} = \overset{0}{C} = \overset{-1}{\ddot{N}}: \end{bmatrix}^- \longleftrightarrow \begin{bmatrix} \overset{+1}{:O} \equiv \overset{0}{C} - \overset{-2}{\ddot{N}}: \end{bmatrix}^-$$

A   B   C

Structure C will not contribute significantly to the overall electronic structure of the ion. It has a -2 formal charge on the N atom and a $+1$ formal charge on the O atom. Not only is the charge on the N atom high, but O is more electronegative than N and would be expected to take on a negative charge. Structure A is more significant than structure B because the negative charge in A is placed on the most electronegative atom (O). We predict, therefore, that structure A is the best representation for this ion and that the carbon–nitrogen bond will resemble a triple bond. The result for OCN^- also allows us to predict that protonation of the ion will lead to HOCN and not HNCO. That is, an H^+ ion will add to the more negative oxygen atom.

■ **EXAMPLE 8.11 Calculating Formal Charges**

Problem Boron-containing compounds often have a boron atom with only three bonds (and no lone pairs). Why not form a double bond with a terminal atom to complete the boron octet? To answer this, consider possible resonance structures of BF_3, and calculate the atoms' formal charges. Are the bonds polar in BF_3? If so, which is the more negative atom?

Strategy Calculate the formal charges on each atom in the resonance structures. The preferred structure will have atoms with low formal charges. Negative formal charges should be on the most electronegative atoms.

Solution The two possible structures for BF_3 are illustrated here with the calculated formal charges on the B and F atoms.

Formal charge = 0
$= 7 - [6 + \frac{1}{2}(2)]$

Formal charge = +1
$= 7 - [4 + \frac{1}{2}(4)]$

$:\ddot{F}:$

$:\ddot{F} - B - \ddot{F}:$

Formal charge = 0
$= 3 - [0 + \frac{1}{2}(6)]$

$:\ddot{F}:$

$:\ddot{F} - B - \ddot{F}:$

Formal charge = -1
$= 3 - [0 + \frac{1}{2}(8)]$

The structure on the left is strongly preferred because all atoms have a zero formal charge and the very electronegative F atom does not have a charge of $+1$.

F ($\chi = 4.0$) is more electronegative than B ($\chi = 2.0$), so the B—F bond is highly polar, the F atom being partially negative and the B atom partially positive.

EXERCISE 8.13 Formal Charge, Bond Polarity, and Electronegativity

Consider all possible resonance structures for SO_2. What are the formal charges on each atom in each resonance structure? What are the bond polarities? Do they agree with the formal charges?

8.8 Bond and Molecular Polarity

The term "polar" was used in Section 8.7 to describe a bond in which one atom has a partial positive charge and the other a partial negative charge. Because most molecules have polar bonds, molecules as a whole can also be polar. In a polar molecule, electron density accumulates toward one side of the molecule, giving that side a partial negative charge, $\delta-$, and leaving the other side with a partial positive charge of equal value, $\delta+$ (Figure 8.12a).

Before describing the factors that determine whether a molecule is polar, let us look at the experimental measurement of the polarity of a molecule. When placed in an electric field, polar molecules experience a force that tends to align them with the field (Figure 8.12). When the electric field is created by a pair of oppositely charged plates, the positive end of each molecule is attracted to the negative plate, and the negative end is attracted to the positive plate (Figure 8.12b). The extent to which the molecules line up with the field depends on their **dipole moment, μ,** which is defined as the product of the magnitude of the partial charges ($\delta+$ and $\delta-$) on the molecule and the distance by which they are separated. The SI unit of the dipole moment is the coulomb-meter, but dipole moments have traditionally been given using a derived unit called the *debye* (D; $1\text{ D} = 3.34 \times 10^{-30}\text{ C} \cdot \text{m}$). Experimental values of some dipole moments are listed in Table 8.7.

To predict if a molecule is polar, we need to consider if the molecule has polar bonds and how these bonds are positioned relative to one another. Diatomic molecules composed of two atoms with different electronegativities are always polar (see Table 8.7); there is one bond, and the molecule has a positive and a negative end. But what happens with a molecule with three or more atoms, in which there are two or more polar bonds?

Consider first a linear triatomic molecule such as carbon dioxide, CO_2 (Figure 8.13). Here, each C=O bond is polar, with the oxygen atom the negative end of the bond dipole. The terminal atoms are at the same distance from the C atom; they both have the same $\delta-$ charge, and they are symmetrically arranged around the central C atom. Therefore, CO_2 has no molecular dipole, even though each

■ Dipole–Dipole Forces The force of attraction between the negative end of one polar molecule and the positive end of another (called a dipole–dipole force and discussed in Section 12.2) affects the properties of polar compounds. Intermolecular forces (forces between molecules) influence the temperature at which a liquid freezes or boils, for example.

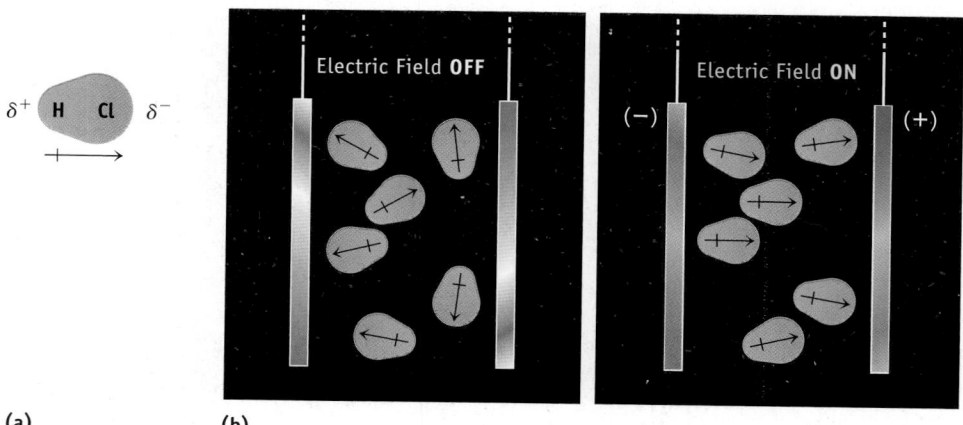

(a) **(b)**

FIGURE 8.12 Polar molecules in an electric field. (a) A representation of a polar molecule. To indicate the direction of molecular polarity, an arrow is drawn with the head pointing to the negative side and a plus sign placed at the positive end. (b) When placed in an electric field (between charged plates), polar molecules experience a force that tends to align them with the field. The negative end of the molecules is drawn to the positive plate, and vice versa. The orientation of the polar molecule affects the electrical capacitance of the plates (their ability to hold a charge), and this provides a way to measure experimentally the magnitude of the dipole moment.

TABLE 8.7 Dipole Moments of Selected Molecules

Molecule (AX)	Moment (μ, D)	Geometry	Molecule (AX$_2$)	Moment (μ, D)	Geometry
HF	1.78	linear	H_2O	1.85	bent
HCl	1.07	linear	H_2S	0.95	bent
HBr	0.79	linear	SO_2	1.62	bent
HI	0.38	linear	CO_2	0	linear
H_2	0	linear			

Molecule (AX$_3$)	Moment (μ, D)	Geometry	Molecule (AX$_4$)	Moment (μ, D)	Geometry
NH_3	1.47	trigonal pyramidal	CH_4	0	tetrahedral
NF_3	0.23	trigonal pyramidal	CH_3Cl	1.92	tetrahedral
BF_3	0	trigonal planar	CH_2Cl_2	1.60	tetrahedral
			$CHCl_3$	1.04	tetrahedral
			CCl_4	0	tetrahedral

bond is polar. This is analogous to a tug-of-war in which the people at opposite ends of the rope are pulling with equal force.

In contrast, water is a bent triatomic molecule. Because O has a larger electronegativity ($\chi = 3.5$) than H ($\chi = 2.2$), each of the O—H bonds is polar, with the H atoms having the same $\delta+$ charge and oxygen having a negative charge ($\delta-$) (Figure 8.13). Electron density accumulates on the O side of the molecule, making the molecule electrically "lopsided" and therefore polar ($\mu = 1.85$ D).

In trigonal-planar BF_3, the B—F bonds are highly polar because F is much more electronegative than B (χ of B = 2.0 and χ of F = 4.0) (Figure 8.14). The molecule is nonpolar, however, because the three terminal F atoms have the same $\delta-$ charge, are the same distance from the boron atom, and are arranged symmetrically and in the same plane as the central boron atom. In contrast, the trigonal-planar molecule phosgene is polar (Cl_2CO, $\mu = 1.17$ D) (Figure 8.14). Here, the angles are all about 120°, so the O and Cl atoms are symmetrically arranged around the C atom. The

■ **Peter Debye and Dipoles** The commonly used unit of dipole moments is named in honor of Peter Debye (1884–1966). He was born in The Netherlands, but attended university in Germany and later studied for his Ph.D. in physics in Munich. He developed a theory on the diffraction of x-rays by solids, a new concept for magnetic cooling, and (with E. Hückel) a model for interionic attractions in aqueous solution. As his interests turned more to chemistry, he worked on methods of determining the shapes of polar molecules. Debye received the Nobel Prize in chemistry in 1936.

Rare Book & Manuscript Collections/Carl A. Knoch Library/Cornell University

Peter Debye (1884–1966)

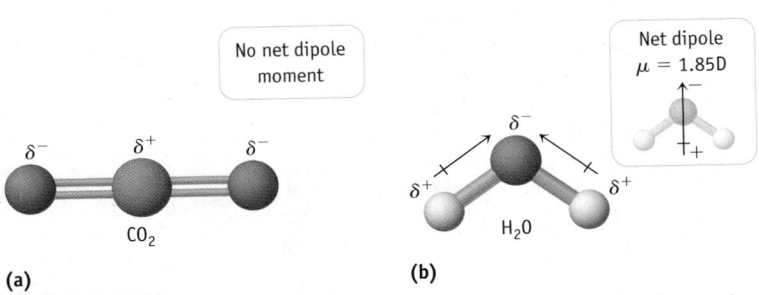

No net dipole moment

CO_2

(a)

Net dipole $\mu = 1.85$D

H_2O

(b)

Active Figure 8.13 Polarity of triatomic molecules, AX$_2$. For CO_2, the CO bonds are polar, but the electron density is distributed evenly over the molecule, and the charges of $\delta-$ lie 180° apart. (Charges calculated using advanced molecular modeling software: C = +0.42 and O = −0.21.) The molecule has no net dipole. In the water molecule, the O atom is negative, and the H atoms are positive. (Calculated charges: H = +0.19 and O = −0.38.) However, the positively charged H atoms lie on one side of the molecule, and the negatively charged O atom is on the other side. The molecule is polar. (The calculated dipole of 1.86 D is in good agreement with experiment.)

Chemistry ⊙Now™ Sign in at www.cengage.com/login and go to the Chapter Contents menu to explore an interactive version of this figure accompanied by an exercise.

Visualizing Charge Distributions and Molecular Polarity— Electrostatic Potential Surfaces and Partial Charge

In Chapter 6, you saw atomic orbitals, regions of space within which an electron is most probably found. The boundary surface of these orbitals was created in such a way that the electron wave amplitude at all points of the surface was the same value (◄ page 288). Using advanced molecular modeling software, we can generate the same type of pictures for molecules, and in Figure A you see a surface defining the electron density in the HF molecule. The electron density surface, calculated using software from CAChe, is made up of all of the points in space around the HF molecule where the electron density is at least 0.002 $e^-/Å^3$ (where 1 Å = 0.1 nm). You can see that the surface bulges toward the F end of the molecule, an indication of the larger size of the F atom. The larger size of the F atom here is mainly related to the fact that it has more valence electrons than H, and to a lesser extent to the fact that H—F bond is polar and electron density in that bond is shifted toward the F atom.

We can add another layer of information. The electron density surface can be colored according to the *electrostatic potential*. (Hence, this figure is called an *electrostatic potential surface*.) The computer program calculates the electrostatic potential that would be observed by a proton (H^+) on the surface. This is the sum of the attractive and repulsive forces on that proton due to the nuclei and the electrons in the molecule. Regions of the molecule in which there is an attractive potential are colored red. That is, this is a region of negative charge on the molecule. Repulsive potentials occur in regions where the molecule is positively charged; these regions are colored blue. As might be expected, the net electrostatic potential will change continuously as one moves from a negative portion of a molecule to a positive portion, and this is indicated by a progression of colors from blue to red (from positive to negative).

The electrostatic potential surface for HF shows the H atom is positive (the H atom end of the molecule is blue), and the F atom is

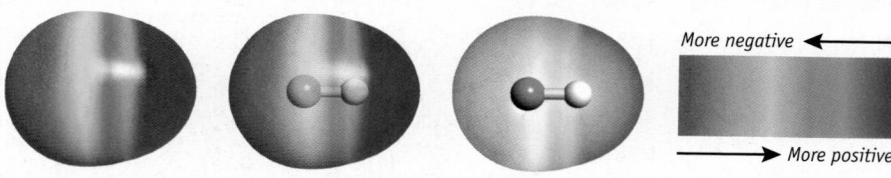

FIGURE A Three views of the electrostatic potential surface for HF.

(*left*) The electron density surface around HF. The F atom is at the left. The surface is made up of all of the points in space around the HF molecule where the electron density is 0.002 $e^-/Å^3$ (where 1 Å = 0.1 nm).

(*middle*) The surface is made more transparent, so you can see the HF atom nuclei inside the surface.

(*right*) The front of the electron density surface has been "peeled away" for a view of the HF molecule inside.

Color scheme: The colors on the electron density surface reflect the charge in the different regions of the molecule   384. Colors to the blue end of the spectrum indicate a positive charge, whereas colors to the red end of the spectrum indicate a negative charge.

negative (the F atom end is red). This is, of course, what we would predict based on electronegativity.

Our program also calculated that the F atom has a charge of −0.29 and H has a charge of +0.29. Finally, the calculated dipole moment for the molecule is 1.74 D, in good agreement with the experimental value in Table 8.7.

Other examples of electrostatic potential surfaces illustrate the polarity of water and methylamine, CH_3NH_2.

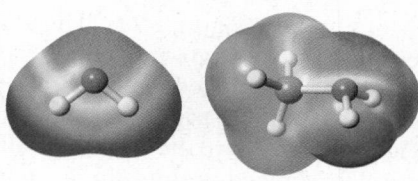

Water   Methylamine

The surface shows the O atom of the water molecule bears a partial negative charge and the H atoms are positive. The surface for the amine clearly shows the molecule is polar and that the region around the N atom is also negative. Indeed, we know from experiment that an H^+ ion will attack the N atom to give the cation $CH_3NH_3^+$.

Electrostatic potential surfaces are becoming more widely used, particularly in organic chemistry and biochemistry, to probe the reactive sites of more and more complex molecules. One example is the dipeptide glycylglycine.

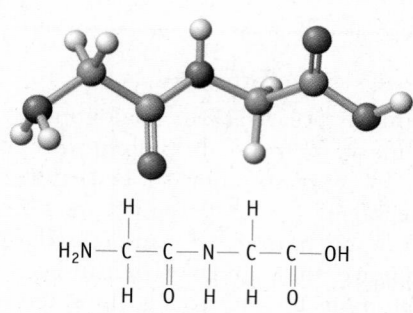

$$H_2N—\overset{\overset{\displaystyle H}{|}}{C}—\overset{\overset{\displaystyle \|}{O}}{C}—\overset{\overset{\displaystyle H}{|}}{N}—\overset{\overset{\displaystyle H}{|}}{C}—\overset{\overset{\displaystyle \|}{O}}{C}—OH$$

The electrostatic surface for the molecule shows that the O atoms of the C=O groups have a partial negative charge as does the N of the NH_2 group. Positive regions of the molecule include the H atom of the C(O)—NH grouping (the amide grouping) and the H atom of the OH group. Such pictures can help you see quickly the regions of a molecule that may be a proton donor (an acid) or a proton acceptor (a base).

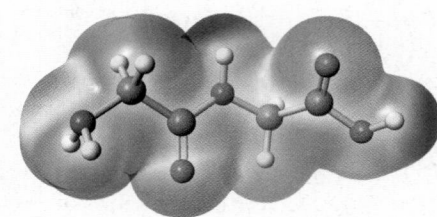

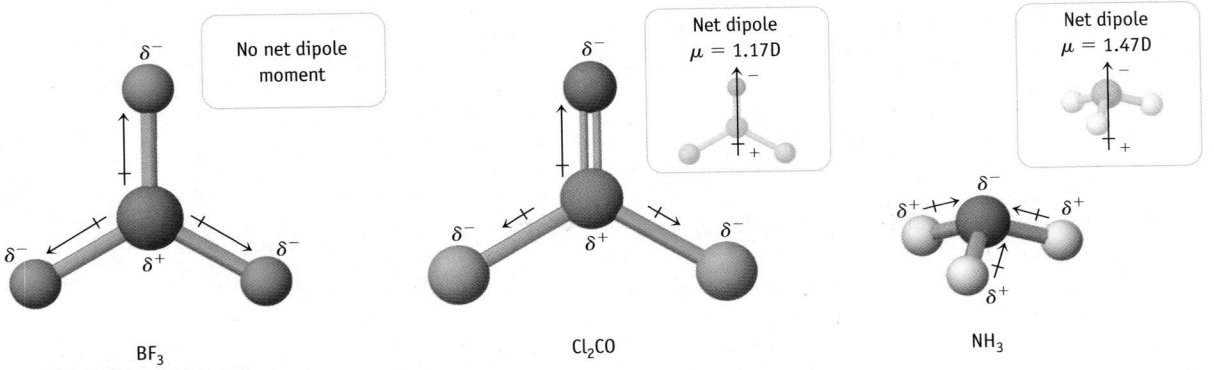

BF₃

Cl₂CO

NH₃

No net dipole moment

Net dipole
$\mu = 1.17D$

Net dipole
$\mu = 1.47D$

Active Figure 8.14 **Polar and nonpolar molecules of the type AX₃.** In BF_3, the negative charge on the F atoms is distributed symmetrically, so the molecular dipole is zero. In contrast, in Cl_2CO and NH_3, the negative charge in the molecules is shifted to one side and the positive charge to the other side.

Molecule	Calculated Partial Charges	Calculated dipole
BF_3	B = 0.44, F = −0.15	0
Cl_2CO	O = −0.21, C = 0.23, Cl = −0.01	1.25
NH_3	N = −0.40, H = 0.13	1.58

The calculated dipoles are in reasonable agreement with experimentally measured dipoles. (Calculations were done with molecular modeling software from CACHe.)

Chemistry ☼ Now™ Sign in at www.cengage.com/login and go to the Chapter Contents menu to explore an interactive version of this figure accompanied by an exercise.

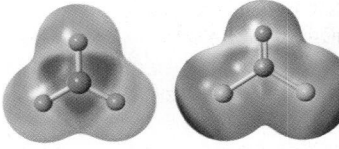

■ **Electrostatic Potential Surfaces for BF₃ and Cl₂CO** Notice that the charge distribution for BF_3 (left) is symmetrical whereas that for Cl_2CO (right) has a partial negative charge on the O atom and much less negative charges on the Cl atoms.

electronegativities of the three atoms in the molecule differ, however: $\chi(O) > \chi(Cl) > \chi(C)$. There is therefore a net displacement of electron density away from the center of the molecule, more toward the O atom than the Cl atoms.

Ammonia, like BF_3, has AX₃ stoichiometry and polar bonds. In contrast to BF_3, however, NH_3 is a trigonal-pyramidal molecule. The positive H atoms are located in the base of the pyramid, and the negative N atom is on the apex of the pyramid. As a consequence, NH_3 is polar (Figure 8.14). Indeed, trigonal-pyramidal molecules are generally polar.

Molecules like carbon tetrachloride, CCl_4, and methane, CH_4, are nonpolar, owing to their symmetrical, tetrahedral structures. The four atoms bonded to C have the same partial charge and are the same distance from the C atom. Tetrahedral molecules with both Cl and H atoms ($CHCl_3$, CH_2Cl_2, and CH_3Cl) are polar, however (Figure 8.15). The electronegativity for H atoms (2.2) is less than that of Cl atoms (3.2), and the carbon–hydrogen distance is different from the carbon–chlorine distances. Because Cl is more electronegative than H, the Cl atoms are on the more negative side of the molecule. This means the positive end of the molecular dipole is toward the H atom.

To summarize this discussion of molecular polarity, look again at Figure 8.5 (page 369). These are sketches of molecules of the type AX_n where A is the central atom and X is a terminal atom. You can predict that a molecule AX_n will *not* be polar, regardless of whether the A—X bonds are polar, if

- All the terminal atoms (or groups), X, are identical, and
- All the X atoms (or groups) are arranged symmetrically around the central atom, A.

On the other hand, if one of the X atoms (or groups) is different in the structures in Figure 8.5 (as in Figures 8.14 and 8.15), or if one of the X positions is occupied by a lone pair, the molecule will be polar.

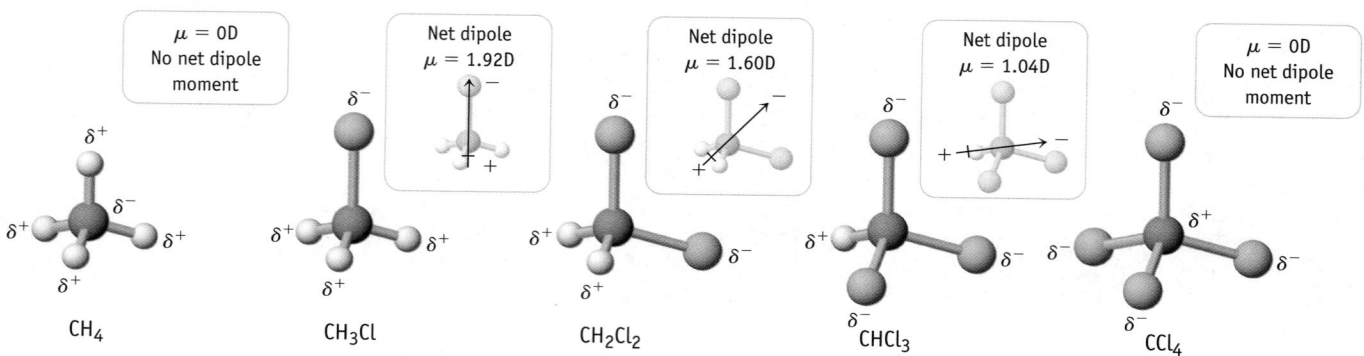

CH$_4$ $\mu = 0D$ No net dipole moment

CH$_3$Cl   Net dipole $\mu = 1.92D$

CH$_2$Cl$_2$ Net dipole $\mu = 1.60D$

CHCl$_3$ Net dipole $\mu = 1.04D$

CCl$_4$ $\mu = 0D$ No net dipole moment

FIGURE 8.15 Polarity of tetrahedral molecules. The electronegativities of the atoms involved are in the order Cl (3.2) > C(2.5) > H (2.2). This means the C—H and C—Cl bonds are polar with a net displacement of electron density away from the H atoms and toward the Cl atoms [H $^{\delta+}$—C $^{\delta-}$ and C $^{\delta+}$—Cl $^{\delta-}$]. Although the electron-pair geometry around the C atom in each molecule is tetrahedral, only in CH$_4$ and CCl$_4$ are the polar bonds totally symmetrical in their arrangement. Therefore, CH$_3$Cl, CH$_2$Cl$_2$, and CHCl$_3$ are polar molecules, with the negative end toward the Cl atoms and the positive end toward the H atoms.

Chemistry.̤Now™

Sign in at **www.cengage.com/login** and go to Chapter 8 Contents to see Screen 8.16 for practice **determining polarity.**

■ **EXAMPLE 8.12 Molecular Polarity**

Problem Are nitrogen trifluoride (NF$_3$) and sulfur tetrafluoride (SF$_4$) polar or nonpolar? If polar, indicate the negative and positive sides of the molecule.

Strategy You cannot decide if a molecule is polar without determining its structure. Therefore, start with the Lewis structure, decide on the electron-pair geometry, and then decide on the molecular geometry. If the molecular geometry is one of the highly symmetrical geometries in Figure 8.5, the molecule is not polar. If it does not fit one of these categories, it will be polar.

Solution

(a) NF$_3$ has the same trigonal-pyramidal structure as NH$_3$. Because F is more electronegative than N, each bond is polar, the more negative end being the F atom. Because this molecule contains polar bonds and because the geometry is not symmetrical but has instead three positions of the tetrahedron occupied by bonding groups and one by a lone pair, the NF$_3$ molecule as a whole is expected to be polar.

    You will notice, however, that the dipole moment for NF$_3$ is quite small (0.23 D in Table 8.7), much smaller than that of NH$_3$. This illustrates that *lone pairs have an effect on polarity*. For NH$_3$, the N-atom lone pair adds to the overall polarity of the molecule. (The lone electron pair extends into space beyond the N atom and increases the charge separation in NH$_3$; this enhances the dipole.) For NF$_3$, however, the effect of the lone pair on the nitrogen atom of the molecule is counterbalanced by the highly polar N—F bonds on the other side and the magnitude of the dipole pointing toward the side with the F atoms is reduced.

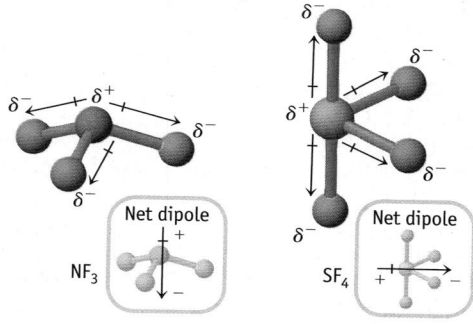

NF$_3$ Net dipole

SF$_4$ Net dipole

(b) The S—F bonds in sulfur tetrafluoride, SF_4, are highly polar, the bond dipole having F as the negative end (χ for S is 2.6 and χ for F is 4.0). The molecule has an electron-pair geometry of a trigonal bipyramid (see Figure 8.8). Because the lone pair occupies one of the positions, the S—F bonds are not arranged symmetrically. The axial S—F bond dipoles cancel each other because they point in opposite directions. The equatorial S—F bonds, however, both point to one side of the molecule.

Comment In general, we do not consider lone pair effects on molecular dipoles. Nonetheless, they do have an effect, as seen when comparing the dipole moment for NF_3 (0.23 D) with that for NH_3 (1.47 D).

This is a case in which electrostatic potential surfaces and calculated atom charges are useful in showing the difference between these molecules. The N atom in NH_3 is decidedly negative (-0.40), and the H atoms are positive ($+0.13$). In contrast, in NF_3 the N atom is positively charged, and the F atoms are negatively charged (N $= +0.3$ and F $= -0.1$). The difference in charge between N and F is not as great as between N and H in NH_3.

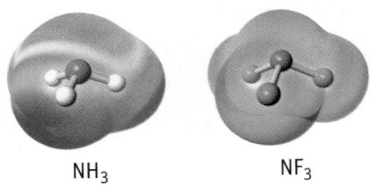

NH$_3$ NF$_3$

Electrostatic potential maps.

■ **EXAMPLE 8.13 Molecular Polarity**

Problem 1,2-Dichloroethylene can exist in two forms. Is either of these planar molecules polar?

$$
\begin{array}{ccc}
\text{H} & & \text{H} \\
 & \text{C}=\text{C} & \\
\text{Cl} & & \text{Cl} \\
 & \text{A} &
\end{array}
\qquad
\begin{array}{ccc}
\text{Cl} & & \text{H} \\
 & \text{C}=\text{C} & \\
\text{H} & & \text{Cl} \\
 & \text{B} &
\end{array}
$$

Strategy To decide if a molecule is polar, we first sketch the structure and then, using electronegativity values, decide on the bond polarity. Finally, we decide if the electron density in the bonds is distributed symmetrically or if it is shifted to one side of the molecule.

Solution Here, the H and Cl atoms are arranged around the C=C double bonds with all bond angles 120° (and all the atoms lie in one plane). The electronegativities of the atoms involved are in the order Cl(3.2) $>$ C(2.5) $>$ H (2.2). This means the C—H and C—Cl bonds are polar with a net displacement of electron density away from the H atoms and toward the Cl atoms [$H^{\delta+}$—$C^{\delta-}$ and $C^{\delta+}$—$Cl^{\delta-}$]. In structure A, the Cl atoms are located on one side of the molecule, so electrons in the H—C and C—Cl bonds are displaced toward the side of the molecule with Cl atoms and away from the side with the H atoms. Molecule A is polar. In molecule B, the displacement of electron density toward the Cl atom on one end of the molecule is counterbalanced by an opposing displacement on the other end. Molecule B is not polar.

Overall displacement of bonding electrons

$$
\begin{array}{ccc}
H^{\delta+} & & H^{\delta+} \\
 & C=C & \\
Cl^{\delta-} & & Cl^{\delta-}
\end{array}
$$

A, polar, diplacement of bonding electrons to one side of the molecule

Displacement of bonding electrons

$$
\begin{array}{ccc}
Cl^{\delta-} & & H^{\delta+} \\
 & C=C & \\
H^{\delta+} & & Cl^{\delta-}
\end{array}
$$

(Displacement of bonding electrons

B, not polar, no net displacement of bonding electrons to one side of the molecule

Comment The electrostatic potential surfaces reflect the fact that molecule A is polar because the electron density is shifted to one side of the molecule. Molecule B is not polar because the electron density is distributed symmetrically.

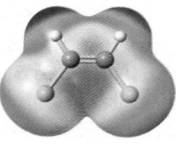

Molecule A

Molecule B

EXERCISE 8.14 Molecular Polarity

For each of the following molecules, decide whether the molecule is polar and which side is positive and which negative: $BFCl_2$, NH_2Cl, and SCl_2.

EXERCISE 8.15 Molecular Polarity

The electrostatic potential surface for $OSCl_2$ is pictured here.

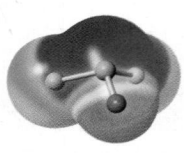

(a) Draw a Lewis electron dot picture for the molecule, and give the formal charge of each atom.

(b) What is the molecular geometry of $OSCl_2$?

(c) Is the molecule polar? If so, locate the positive and negative charges and the direction of the dipole.

8.9 Bond Properties: Order, Length, Energy

Bond Order

The **order of a bond** is the number of bonding electron pairs shared by two atoms in a molecule (Figure 8.16). You will encounter bond orders of 1, 2, and 3, as well as fractional bond orders.

When the bond order is 1, there is only a single covalent bond between a pair of atoms. Examples are the bonds in molecules such as H_2, NH_3, and CH_4. The bond order is 2 when two electron pairs are shared between atoms, such as the C=O bonds in CO_2 and the C=C bond in ethylene, H_2C=CH_2. The bond order is 3 when two atoms are connected by three bonds. Examples include the carbon–oxygen bond in carbon monoxide, CO and the nitrogen–nitrogen bond in N_2.

Fractional bond orders occur in molecules and ions having resonance structures. For example, what is the bond order for each oxygen–oxygen bond in O_3? Each resonance structure of O_3 has one O—O single bond and one O=O double bond, for a total of three shared bonding pairs accounting for two oxygen–oxygen links.

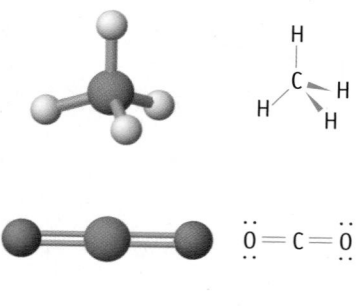

FIGURE 8.16 Bond order. The four C—H bonds in methane each have a bond order of 1. The two C=O bonds of CO_2 each have a bond order of two, whereas the nitrogen–nitrogen bond in N_2 has an order of 3.

Bond order = 1

Bond order = 2

Bond order for each oxygen–oxygen bond = $\frac{3}{2}$, or 1.5

One resonance structure

We can define the bond order between any bonded pair of atoms X and Y as

$$\text{Bond order} = \frac{\text{number of shared pairs in all X—Y bonds}}{\text{number of X—Y links in the molecule or ion}} \qquad (8.2)$$

For ozone, there are three bond pairs involved in two oxygen-oxygen links, so the bond order for each oxygen–oxygen bond is ³⁄₂, or 1.5.

Chemistry Now™

Sign in at **www.cengage.com/login** and go to Chapter 8 Contents to see Screen 8.17 to see **how bond order, bond length, and bond energy are related.**

Bond Length

Bond length is the distance between the nuclei of two bonded atoms. Bond lengths are therefore related to the sizes of the atoms (Section 7.5), but, for a given pair of atoms, the order of the bond also plays a role.

Table 8.8 lists average bond lengths for a number of common chemical bonds. It is important to recognize that these are *average* values. Neighboring parts of a molecule can affect the length of a particular bond. For example, Table 8.8 specifies that the average C—H bond has a length of 110 pm. In methane, CH_4, the measured bond length is 109.4 pm, whereas the C—H bond is only 105.9 pm long in acetylene, H—C≡C—H. Variations as great as 10% from the average values listed in Table 8.8 are possible.

TABLE 8.8 Some Average Single- and Multiple-Bond Lengths in Picometers (pm)*

Single Bond Lengths

	1A	4A	5A	6A	7A	4A	5A	6A	7A	7A	7A
	H	C	N	O	F	Si	P	S	Cl	Br	I
H	74	110	98	94	92	145	138	132	127	142	161
C		154	147	143	141	194	187	181	176	191	210
N			140	136	134	187	180	174	169	184	203
O				132	130	183	176	170	165	180	199
F					128	181	174	168	163	178	197
Si						234	227	221	216	231	250
P							220	214	209	224	243
S								208	203	218	237
Cl									200	213	232
Br										228	247
I											266

Multiple Bond Lengths

C=C	134	C≡C	121
C=N	127	C≡N	115
C=O	122	C≡O	113
N=O	115	N≡O	108

*1 pm = 10^{-12} m.

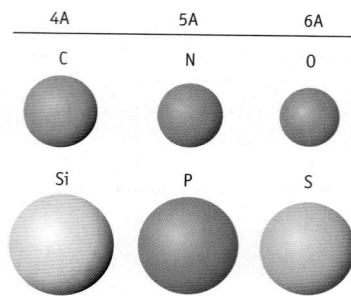

	4A	5A	6A
	C	N	O
	Si	P	S

Relative sizes of some atoms of Groups 4A, 5A, and 6A.

Bond lengths are related to atom sizes.

C—H	N—H	O—H
110	98	94 pm
Si—H	**P—H**	**S—H**
145	138	132 pm

Because atom sizes vary in a regular fashion with the position of the element in the periodic table (Figure 7.8), predictions of trends in bond length can be made quickly. For example, the H—X distance in the hydrogen halides increases in the order predicted by the relative sizes of the halogens: H—F < H—Cl < H—Br < H—I. Likewise, bonds between carbon and another element in a given period decrease going from left to right, in a predictable fashion; for example, C—C > C—N > C—O > C—F. Trends for multiple bonds are similar. A C=O bond is shorter than a C=S bond, and a C=N bond is shorter than a C=C bond.

The effect of bond order is evident when bonds between the same two atoms are compared. For example, the bonds become shorter as the bond order increases in the series C—O, C=O, and C≡O:

Bond	C—O	C=O	C≡O
Bond Order	1	2	3
Bond Length (pm)	143	122	113

Double bonds are shorter than single bonds between the same set of atoms, and triple bonds between those same atoms are shorter still.

The carbonate ion, CO_3^{2-}, has three equivalent resonance structures. Each CO bond has a bond order of 1.33 (or 4/3) because four electron pairs are used to form three carbon–oxygen links. The CO bond distance (129 pm) is intermediate between a C—O single bond (143 pm) and a C=O double bond (122 pm).

$$\begin{bmatrix} :\!O\!: \\ \| \\ C \\ :\!O \quad O\!: \end{bmatrix}^{2-}$$

Bond order = 2
Bond order = 1
Bond order = 1

Average bond order = 4/3, or 1.33
Bond length = 129 pm

EXERCISE 8.16 Bond Order and Bond Length

(a) Give the bond order of each of the following bonds, and arrange them in order of decreasing bond distance: C=N, C≡N, and C—N.

(b) Draw resonance structures for NO_2^-. What is the NO bond order in this ion? Consult Table 8.8 for N—O and N=O bond lengths. Compare these with the NO bond length in NO_2^- (124 pm). Account for any differences you observe.

Bond Dissociation Enthalpy

The **bond dissociation enthalpy** is the enthalpy change for breaking a bond in a molecule with the reactants and products in the gas phase.

$$\text{Molecule (g)} \underset{\text{Energy released} = \Delta H < 0}{\overset{\text{Energy supplied} = \Delta H > 0}{\rightleftharpoons}} \text{Molecular fragments (g)}$$

Suppose you wish to break the carbon–carbon bonds in ethane (H_3C—CH_3), ethylene (H_2C=CH_2), and acetylene (HC≡CH). The carbon–carbon bond orders in these molecules are 1, 2, and 3, respectively, and these bond orders are reflected in the bond dissociation enthalpies. Carbon–carbon bond breaking in ethane requires the least energy in this group, and acetylene requires the most energy.

$$H_3C-CH_3(g) \rightarrow H_3C(g) + CH_3(g) \qquad \Delta_r H = +368 \text{ kJ/mol-rxn}$$

$$H_2C=CH_2(g) \rightarrow H_2C(g) + CH_2(g) \qquad \Delta_r H = +682 \text{ kJ/mol-rxn}$$

$$HC\equiv CH(g) \rightarrow HC(g) + CH(g) \qquad \Delta_r H = +962 \text{ kJ/mol-rxn}$$

Because ΔH represents the energy transferred to the molecule from its surroundings, ΔH has a positive value; that is, *the process of breaking bonds in a molecule is always endothermic.*

The energy supplied to break carbon–carbon bonds must be the same as the energy released when the same bonds form. *The formation of bonds from atoms or radicals in the gas phase is always exothermic.* This means, for example, that $\Delta_r H$ for the formation of H_3C-CH_3 from two $CH_3(g)$ radicals is -368 kJ/mol-rxn.

$$H_3C \cdot (g) + \cdot CH_3(g) \rightarrow H_3C-CH_3(g) \qquad \Delta_r H = -368 \text{ kJ/mol-rxn}$$

Generally, the bond energy for a given type of bond (a C—C bond, for example) varies somewhat, depending on the compound, just as bond lengths vary from one molecule to another. They are sufficiently similar, however, so it is possible to create a table of *average bond dissociation enthalpies* (Table 8.9). The values in such tables may be used to *estimate* the enthalpy change for a reaction, as described below.

■ **Variability in Bond Dissociation Enthalpies** The values of $\Delta_r H$ for ethane, ethylene, and acetylene in the text are for those molecules in particular. The bond dissociation enthalpies in Table 8.9 are average values for a range of molecules containing the indicated bond.

TABLE 8.9 Some Average Bond Dissociation Enthalpies (kJ/mol)*

Single Bonds

	H	C	N	O	F	Si	P	S	Cl	Br	I
H	436	413	391	463	565	328	322	347	432	366	299
C		346	305	358	485	—	—	272	339	285	213
N			163	201	283	—	—	—	192	—	—
O				146	—	452	335	—	218	201	201
F					155	565	490	284	253	249	278
Si						222	—	293	381	310	234
P							201	—	326	—	184
S								226	255	—	—
Cl									242	216	208
Br										193	175
I											151

Multiple Bonds

N=N	418	C=C	610
N≡N	945	C≡C	835
C=N	615	C=O	745
C≡N	887	C≡O	1046
O=O (in O_2)	498		

*Sources of dissociation enthalpies: I. Klotz and R. M. Rosenberg: *Chemical Thermodynamics*, 4th Ed., p. 55, New York, John Wiley, 1994; and J. E. Huheey, E. A. Keiter, and R. L. Keiter: *Inorganic Chemistry* 4th Ed., Table E. 1, New York, Harper-Collins, 1993. See also Lange's *Handbook of Chemistry*, J. A. Dean (ed.), McGraw-Hill Inc., New York.

■ **Bond Energy and Electronegativity**
Linus Pauling derived electronegativity values from a consideration of bond energies. He recognized that the energy required to break a bond between two different atoms is often greater than expected, based on an assumption that bond electrons are shared equally. He postulated that the "extra energy" arises from the fact that the atoms do not share electrons equally. One atom is slightly positive and the other slightly negative. This means there is a small coulombic force of attraction involving oppositely charged ions in addition to the force of attraction arising from the sharing of electrons. This coulombic force enhances the overall force of attraction.

In reactions between molecules, bonds in reactants are broken; new bonds are formed as products form. If the total energy released when new bonds form exceeds the energy required to break the original bonds, the overall reaction is exothermic. If the opposite is true, then the overall reaction is endothermic. Let us see how this works in practice.

Let us use bond dissociation enthalpies to estimate the enthalpy change for the hydrogenation of propene to propane:

propene   propane

The first step is to examine the reactants and product to see what bonds are broken and what bonds are formed. In this case, the C=C bond in propene and the H—H bond in hydrogen are broken. A C—C bond and two C—H bonds are formed.

Bonds broken: 1 mol of C=C bonds and 1 mol of H—H bonds

Energy required = 610 kJ for C=C bonds + 436 kJ for H—H bonds = 1046 kJ/mol-rxn

Bonds formed: 1 mol of C—C bonds and 2 mol of C—H bonds

Energy evolved = 346 kJ for C—C bonds + 2 mol × 413 kJ/mol for C—H bonds = 1172 kJ/mol-rxn

By combining the energy required to break bonds and the energy evolved in making bonds, we can estimate $\Delta_r H$ for the hydrogenation of propene and see that the reaction is exothermic.

$$\Delta_r H = 1046 \text{ kJ/mol-rxn} - 1172 \text{ kJ/mol-rxn} = -126 \text{ kJ/mol-rxn}$$

The example of the propene–hydrogen reaction illustrates the fact that the enthalpy change for any reaction can be estimated using the equation

■ **Hydrogenation Reactions** Adding hydrogen to a double (or triple) bond is called a hydrogenation reaction. It is commonly done to convert vegetable oils, whose molecules contain C=C double bonds, to solid fats.

■ **$\Delta_r H$ from Enthalpies of Formation** Using $\Delta_f H°$ values for propane and propene, we calculate $\Delta_r H$ for the reaction of −125.1 kJ/mol-rxn. The bond dissociation enthalpy calculation is in excellent agreement with that from enthalpies of formation.

$$\Delta_r H = \Sigma \Delta H(\text{bonds broken}) - \Sigma \Delta H(\text{bonds formed}) \qquad \textbf{(8.3)}$$

To use this equation, first identify all the bonds in the reactants that are broken, and add up their bond dissociation enthalpies. Then, identify all the new bonds formed in the products, and add up their bond dissociation enthalpies. The difference between the energy required to break bonds [= $\Sigma \Delta H(\text{bonds broken})$] and the energy evolved when bonds are made $[= \Sigma \Delta H(\text{bonds formed})]$ gives the estimated enthalpy change for the reaction. Such calculations can give acceptable results in many cases.

Chemistry ⚛ Now™

Sign in at **www.cengage.com/login** and go to Chapter 8 Contents to see Screen 8.18 to explore **how reactant and product bond energies influence the energy of reaction.**

■ **EXAMPLE 8.14 Using Bond Dissociation Enthalpies**

Problem Acetone, a common industrial solvent, can be converted to isopropanol, rubbing alcohol, by hydrogenation. Calculate the enthalpy change for this reaction using bond energies.

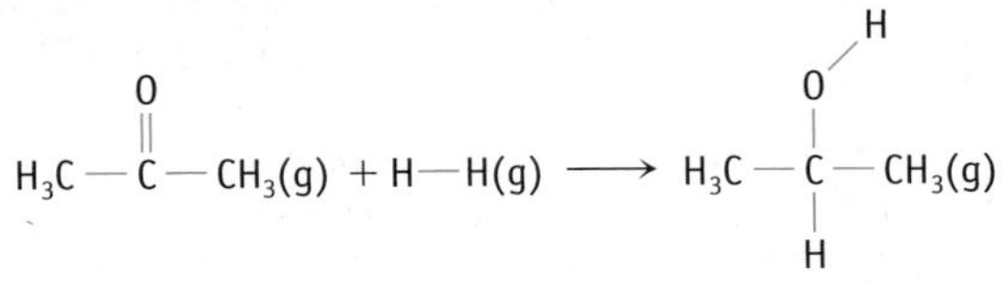

acetone   isopropanol

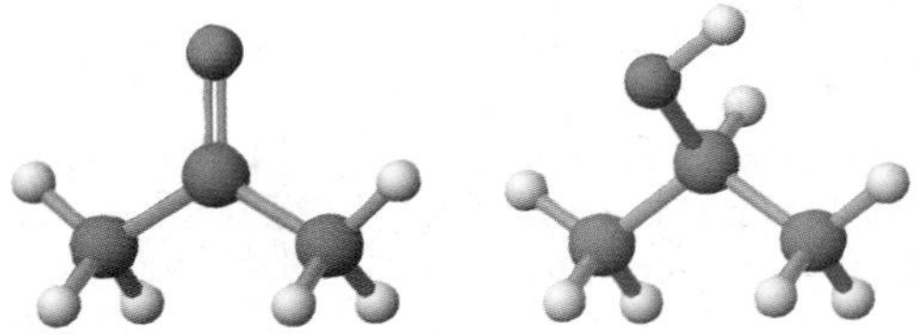

Strategy Examine the reactants and products to determine which bonds are broken and which are formed. Add up the energies required to break bonds in the reactants and the energy evolved to form bonds in the product. The difference in the sums of bond dissociation enthalpies is an estimate of the enthalpy change of the reaction (Equation 8.3).

Solution

Bonds broken: 1 mol of C=O bonds and 1 mol of H—H bonds

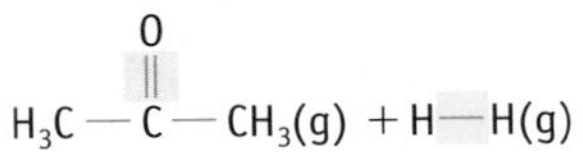

$\Sigma \Delta H(\text{bonds broken})$ = 745 kJ for C=O bonds + 436 kJ for H—H bonds = 1181 kJ/mol-rxn

Bonds formed: 1 mol of C—H bonds, 1 mol of C—O bonds, and 1 mol of O—H bonds

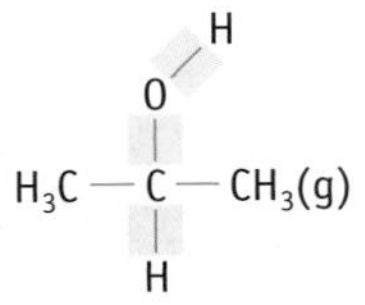

$\Sigma \Delta H(\text{bonds formed})$ = 413 kJ for C—H + 358 kJ for C—O + 463 kJ for O—H = 1234 kJ/mol-rxn

$\Delta_r H = \Sigma \Delta H(\text{bonds broken}) - \Sigma \Delta H(\text{bonds formed})$

$\Delta_r H$ = 1181 kJ − 1234 kJ = −53 kJ/mol-rxn

Comment The overall reaction is predicted to be exothermic by 53 kJ per mol of product formed. This is in good agreement with the value calculated from $\Delta_f H°$ values (= −55.8 kJ/mol-rxn).

EXERCISE 8.17 Using Bond Dissociation Enthalpies

Using the bond dissociation enthalpies in Table 8.9, estimate the enthalpy of combustion of gaseous methane, CH_4. That is, estimate $\Delta_r H$ for the reaction of methane with O_2 to give water vapor and carbon dioxide gas.

DNA is the substance in every plant and animal that carries the exact blueprint of that plant or animal. The structure of this molecule, the cornerstone of life, was uncovered in 1953, and James D. Watson, Francis Crick, and Maurice Wilkins shared the 1962 Nobel Prize in medicine and physiology for the work. It was one of the most important scientific discoveries of the 20th century, and the story

James D. Watson and Francis Crick. In a photo taken in 1953, Watson (left) and Crick (right) stand by their model of the DNA double helix. Together with Maurice Wilkins, Watson and Crick received the Nobel Prize in medicine and physiology in 1962. (A Barrington Brown/Science/Photo Researchers, Inc.)

has been told by Watson in his book *The Double Helix*.

When Watson was a graduate student at Indiana University, he had an interest in the gene and said he hoped that its biological role might be solved "without my learning any chemistry." Later, however, he and Crick found out just how useful chemistry can be when they began to unravel the structure of DNA.

Solving important problems requires teamwork among scientists of many kinds, so Watson went to Cambridge University in England in 1951. There he met Crick, who, Watson said, talked louder and faster than anyone else. Crick shared Watson's belief in the fundamental importance of DNA, and the pair soon learned that Maurice Wilkins and Rosalind Franklin at King's College in London were using a technique called x-ray crystallography to learn more about DNA's structure. Watson and Crick believed that understanding this structure was crucial to understanding genetics. To solve the structural problem, however, they needed experimental data of the type that could come from the experiments at King's College.

The King's College group was initially reluctant to share their data; and, what is more, they did not seem to share Watson and Crick's sense of urgency. There was also an ethical dilemma: Could Watson and Crick work on a problem that others had claimed as

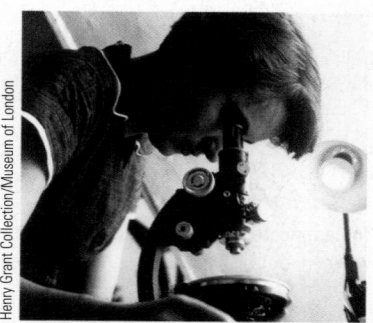

Rosalind Franklin of King's College, London. She died in 1958 at the age of 37. Because Nobel Prizes are never awarded posthumously, she did not share in this honor with Watson, Crick, and Wilkins. For more on Rosalind Franklin, read *Rosalind Franklin: The Dark Lady of DNA* by Brenda Maddox.

theirs? "The English sense of fair play would not allow Francis to move in on Maurice's problem," said Watson.

Watson and Crick approached the problem through a technique chemists now use frequently—model building. They built models of the pieces of the DNA chain, and they tried various chemically reasonable ways of fitting them together. Finally, they discovered that one arrangement was "too pretty not to be true." Ultimately, the experimental evidence of Wilkins and Franklin confirmed the "pretty structure" to be the real DNA structure.

8.10 DNA, Revisited

This chapter opened with some questions about the structure of DNA, one of the key molecules in all biological systems. The tools are now in place to say more about the structure of this important molecule and why it looks the way it does.

As shown in Figure 8.17, each strand of the double-stranded DNA molecule consists of three units: a phosphate, a deoxyribose molecule (a sugar molecule with a five-member ring), and a nitrogen-containing base. (The bases in DNA can be one of four molecules: adenine, guanine, cytosine, and thymine; in Figure 8.17, the base is adenine.) Two units of the backbone (without the adenine on the deoxyribose ring) are also illustrated in Figure 8.17.

The important point here is that the repeating unit in the backbone of DNA consists of the atoms O—P—O—C—C—C. Each atom has a tetrahedral electron-pair geometry. Therefore, the chain cannot be linear. In fact, the chain twists as one moves along the backbone. This twisting gives DNA its helical shape.

Why are there two strands in DNA with the O—P—O—C—C—C backbone on the outside and the nitrogen-containing bases on the inside? This structure arises from the polarity of the bonds in the base molecules attached to the backbone.

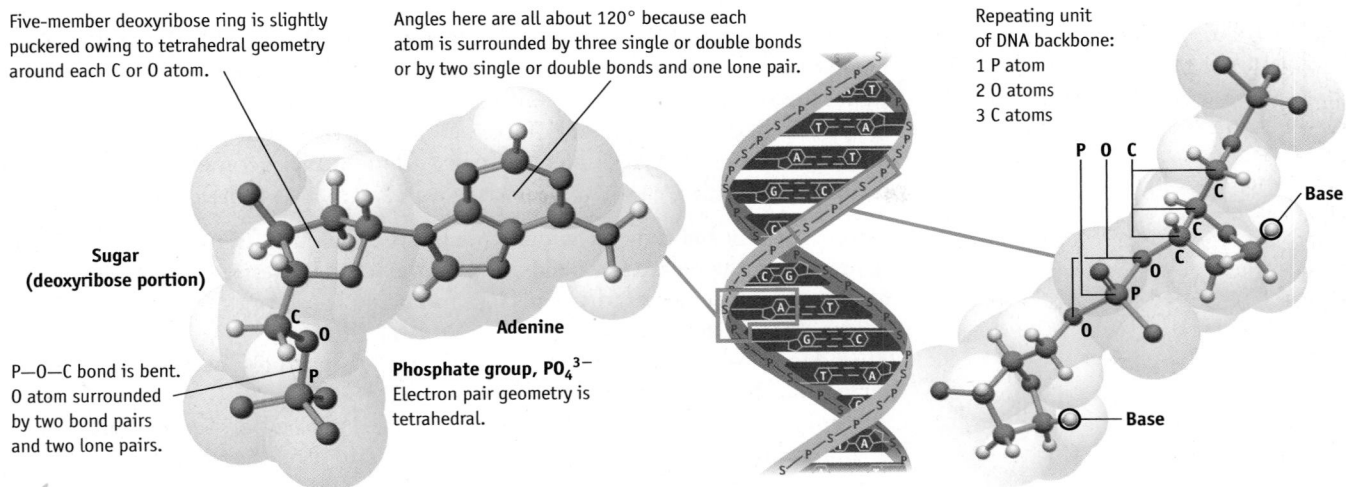

Five-member deoxyribose ring is slightly puckered owing to tetrahedral geometry around each C or O atom.

Angles here are all about 120° because each atom is surrounded by three single or double bonds or by two single or double bonds and one lone pair.

Repeating unit of DNA backbone:
1 P atom
2 O atoms
3 C atoms

P O C

Base

Sugar (deoxyribose portion)

Adenine

Base

P—O—C bond is bent. O atom surrounded by two bond pairs and two lone pairs.

Phosphate group, PO_4^{3-}
Electron pair geometry is tetrahedral.

FIGURE 8.17 A portion of the DNA molecule. A repeating unit consists of a phosphate portion, a deoxyribose portion (a sugar molecule with a five-member ring), and a nitrogen-containing base (here adenine) attached to the deoxyribose ring.

For example, the N-H bonds in the adenine molecule are very polar, which leads to a special form of intermolecular forces—hydrogen bonding—to the base molecule in the neighboring chain. More about this in Chapter 12 when we explore intermolecular forces and again in *The Chemistry of Life: Biochemistry* (pages 496–512).

Chapter Goals Revisited

Now that you have studied this chapter, you should ask whether you have met the chapter goals. In particular, you should be able to:

Understand the difference between ionic and covalent bonds

a. Describe the basic forms of chemical bonding—ionic and covalent—and the differences between them, and predict from the formula whether a compound has ionic or covalent bonding, based on whether a metal is part of the formula (Section 8.1).

b. Write Lewis symbols for atoms (Section 8.2).

Draw Lewis electron dot structures for small molecules and ions

a. Draw Lewis structures for molecular compounds and ions (Section 8.2). Study Question(s) assignable in OWL: 6, 8, 10.

b. Understand and apply the octet rule; recognize exceptions to the octet rule (Sections 8.2–8.5). Study Question(s) assignable in OWL: 6, 8, 10, 12, 56.

c. Write resonance structures, understand what resonance means, and how and when to use this means of representing bonding (Section 8.4). Study Question(s) assignable in OWL: 10.

Chemistry.⚛.Now™ Sign in at **www.cengage.com/login** to:

- Assess your understanding with Study Questions in OWL keyed to each goal in the Goals and Homework menu for this chapter
- For quick review, download Go Chemistry mini-lecture flashcard modules (or purchase them at **www.ichapters.com**)
- Check your readiness for an exam by taking the Pre-Test and exploring the modules recommended in your Personalized Study plan.

❓Access **How Do I Solve It?** tutorials on how to approach problem solving using concepts in this chapter.

For additional preparation for an examination on this chapter see the *Let's Review* section on pages 496–513.

Use the valence shell electron-pair repulsion theory (VSEPR) to predict the shapes of simple molecules and ions and to understand the structures of more complex molecules.

a. Predict the shape or geometry of molecules and ions of main group elements using VSEPR theory (Section 8.6). Table 8.10 shows a summary of the relation between valence electron pairs, electron-pair and molecular geometry, and molecular polarity. Study Question(s) assignable in OWL: 18, 20, 22, 24, 86, 88; Go Chemistry Module 12.

Use electronegativity and formal charge to predict the charge distribution in molecules and ions, to define the polarity of bonds, and to predict the polarity of molecules.

a. Calculate formal charges for atoms in a molecule based on the Lewis structure (Section 8.3). Study Question(s) assignable in OWL: 14, 16, 36.
b. Define electronegativity and understand how it is used to describe the unequal sharing of electrons between atoms in a bond (Section 8.7).
c. Combine formal charge and electronegativity to gain a perspective on the charge distribution in covalent molecules and ions (Section 8.7). Study Question(s) assignable in OWL: 28, 29, 31, 32, 34, 71.
d. Understand why some molecules are polar whereas others are nonpolar (Section 8.8). See Table 8.7. Study Question(s) assignable in OWL: 38.
e. Predict the polarity of a molecule (Section 8.8). Study Question(s) assignable in OWL: 38, 40, 78, 79, 81, 86; Go Chemistry Module 13.

Understand the properties of covalent bonds and their influence on molecular structure

a. Define and predict trends in bond order, bond length, and bond dissociation energy (Section 8.9). Study Question(s) assignable in OWL: 27, 42, 44, 45, 48, 58, 81.
b. Use bond dissociation enthalpies in calculations (Section 8.9 and Example 8.14). Study Question(s) and assignable in OWL: 50, 51, 52, 69.

TABLE 8.10   Summary of Molecular Shapes and Molecular Polarity

Valence Electron Pairs	Electron-Pair Geometry	Number of Bond Pairs	Number of Lone Pairs	Molecular Geometry	Molecular Dipole?*	Examples
2	linear	2	0	linear	no	$BeCl_2$
3	trigonal planar	3	0	trigonal planar	no	BF_3, BCl_3
		2	1	bent	yes	$SnCl_2(g)$
4	tetrahedral	4	0	tetrahedral	no	CH_4, BF_4^-
		3	1	trigonal pyramidal	yes	NH_3, PF_3
		2	2	bent	yes	H_2O, SCl_2
5	trigonal bipyramidal	5	0	trigonal bipyramidal	no	PF_5
		4	1	seesaw	yes	SF_4
		3	2	T-shaped	yes	ClF_3
		2	3	linear	no	XeF_2, I_3^-
6	octahedral	6	0	octahedral	no	SF_6, PF_6^-
		5	1	square pyramidal	yes	ClF_5
		4	2	square planar	no	XeF_4

*For molecules of the AX_n, where the X atoms are identical.

KEY EQUATIONS

Equation 8.1 (page 359) Calculating the formal charge on an atom in a molecule

Formal charge of an atom in a molecule or ion = Group Number − [LPE + ½(BE)]

Equation 8.2 (page 387) Calculating bond order

$$\text{Bond order} = \frac{\text{number of shared pairs in all X—Y bonds}}{\text{number of X—Y links in the molecule or ion}}$$

Equation 8.3 (page 390) Estimating the enthalpy change for a reaction using bond dissociation enthalpies

$$\Delta_r H = \Sigma \Delta H(\text{bonds broken}) - \Sigma \Delta H(\text{bonds formed})$$

STUDY QUESTIONS

OWL Online homework for this chapter may be assigned in OWL.

▲ denotes challenging questions.

■ denotes questions assignable in OWL.

Blue-numbered questions have answers in Appendix O and fully-worked solutions in the *Student Solutions Manual*.

Practicing Skills

Valence Electrons and the Octet Rule
(See Section 8.1 and ChemistryNow Screen 8.2.)

1. Give the periodic group number and number of valence electrons for each of the following atoms.
   (a) O   (d) Mg
   (b) B   (e) F
   (c) Na   (f) S

2. Give the periodic group number and number of valence electrons for each of the following atoms.
   (a) C   (d) Si
   (b) Cl   (e) Se
   (c) Ne   (f) Al

3. For elements in Groups 4A–7A of the periodic table, give the number of bonds an element is expected to form if it obeys the octet rule.

4. Which of the following elements are capable of forming compounds in which the indicated atom has more than four valence electron pairs?
   (a) C   (d) F   (g) Se
   (b) P   (e) Cl   (h) Sn
   (c) O   (f) B

Lewis Electron Dot Structures
(See Examples 8.1, 8.2, 8.4, and 8.5, and ChemistryNow Screens 8.5–8.11.)

5. Draw a Lewis structure for each of the following molecules or ions.
   (a) NF_3 (c) HOBr
   (b) ClO_3^- (d) SO_3^{2-}

6. ■ Draw a Lewis structure for each of the following molecules or ions:
   (a) CS_2
   (b) BF_4^-
   (c) HNO_2 (where the bonding is in the order HONO)
   (d) $OSCl_2$ (where S is the central atom)

7. Draw a Lewis structure for each of the following molecules:
   (a) Chlorodifluoromethane, $CHClF_2$ (C is the central atom)
   (b) Acetic acid, CH_3CO_2H. Its basic structure is pictured.

   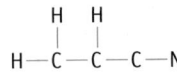

   (c) Acetonitrile, CH_3CN (the framework is H_3C—C—N)
   (d) Allene, H_2CCCH_2

8. ■ Draw a Lewis structure for each of the following molecules:
   (a) Methanol, CH_3OH
   (b) Vinyl chloride, H_2C=CHCl, the molecule from which PVC plastics are made.
   (c) Acrylonitrile, H_2C=CHCN, the molecule from which materials such as Orlon are made

9. Show all possible resonance structures for each of the following molecules or ions:
(a) SO_2
(b) HNO_2
(c) SCN^-

10. ■ Show all possible resonance structures for each of the following molecules or ions:
(a) Nitrate ion, NO_3^-
(b) Nitric acid, HNO_3
(c) Nitrous oxide (laughing gas), N_2O (where the bonding is in the order N-N-O)

11. Draw a Lewis structure for each of the following molecules or ions:
(a) BrF_3
(b) I_3^-
(c) XeO_2F_2
(d) XeF_3^+

12. ■ Draw a Lewis structure for each of the following molecules or ions:
(a) BrF_5
(b) IF_3
(c) IBr_2^-
(d) BrF_2^+

Formal Charge
(See Example 8.3 and ChemistryNow Screen 8.11.)

13. Determine the formal charge on each atom in the following molecules or ions:
(a) N_2H_4
(b) PO_4^{3-}
(c) BH_4^-
(d) NH_2OH

14. ■ Determine the formal charge on each atom in the following molecules or ions:
(a) SCO
(b) HCO_2^- (formate ion)
(c) CO_3^{2-}
(d) HCO_2H (formic acid)

15. Determine the formal charge on each atom in the following molecules and ions:
(a) NO_2^+
(b) NO_2^-
(c) NF_3
(d) HNO_3

16. ■ Determine the formal charge on each atom in the following molecules and ions:
(a) SO_2
(b) $OSCl_2$
(c) O_2SCl_2
(d) FSO_3^-

Molecular Geometry
(See Examples 8.6 and ChemistryNow Screens 8.12–8.14. Note that many of these molecular structures are available in ChemistryNow.)

17. Draw a Lewis structure for each of the following molecules or ions. Describe the electron-pair geometry and the molecular geometry around the central atom.
(a) NH_2Cl
(b) Cl_2O (O is the central atom)
(c) SCN^-
(d) HOF

18. ■ Draw a Lewis structure for each of the following molecules or ions. Describe the electron-pair geometry and the molecular geometry around the central atom.
(a) ClF_2^+
(b) $SnCl_3^-$
(c) PO_4^{3-}
(d) CS_2

19. The following molecules or ions all have two oxygen atoms attached to a central atom. Draw a Lewis structure for each one, and then describe the electron-pair geometry and the molecular geometry around the central atom. Comment on similarities and differences in the series.
(a) CO_2
(b) NO_2^-
(c) O_3
(d) ClO_2^-

20. ■ The following molecules or ions all have three oxygen atoms attached to a central atom. Draw a Lewis structure for each one, and then describe the electron-pair geometry and the molecular geometry around the central atom. Comment on similarities and differences in the series.
(a) CO_3^{2-}
(b) NO_3^-
(c) SO_3^{2-}
(d) ClO_3^-

21. Draw a Lewis structure for each of the following molecules or ions. Describe the electron-pair geometry and the molecular geometry around the central atom.
(a) ClF_2^-
(b) ClF_3
(c) ClF_4^-
(d) ClF_5

22. ■ Draw a Lewis structure of each of the following molecules or ions. Describe the electron-pair geometry and the molecular geometry around the central atom.
(a) SiF_6^{2-}
(b) PF_5
(c) SF_4
(d) XeF_4

23. Give approximate values for the indicated bond angles.
(a) O—S—O in SO_2
(b) F—B—F angle in BF_3
(c) Cl—C—Cl angle in Cl_2CO
(d) H—C—H (angle 1) and C—C≡N (angle 2) in acetonitrile

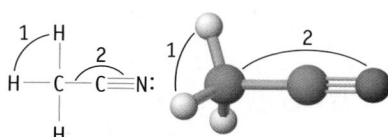

24. ■ Give approximate values for the indicated bond angles.
(a) Cl—S—Cl in SCl_2
(b) N—N—O in N_2O
(c) Bond angles 1, 2, and 3 in vinyl alcohol (a component of polymers and a molecule found in outer space).

396

25. Phenylalanine is one of the natural amino acids and is a "breakdown" product of aspartame. Estimate the values of the indicated angles in the amino acid. Explain why the —CH_2—$CH(NH_2)$—CO_2H chain is not linear.

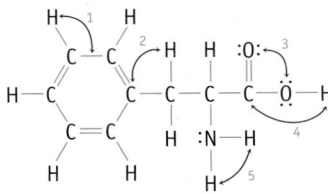

26. ■ Acetylacetone has the structure shown here. Estimate the values of the indicated angles.

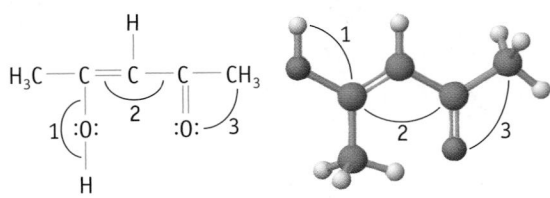

Bond Polarity, Electronegativity, and Formal Charge
(See Examples 8.10 and 8.11 and ChemistryNow Screens 8.11 and 8.15.)

27. ■ For each pair of bonds, indicate the more polar bond, and use an arrow to show the direction of polarity in each bond.
   (a) C—O and C—N
   (b) P—Br and P—Cl
   (c) B—O and B—S
   (d) B—F and B—I

28. ■ For each of the bonds listed below, tell which atom is the more negatively charged.
   (a) C—N
   (b) C—H
   (c) C—Br
   (d) S—O

29. ■ Acrolein, C_3H_4O, is the starting material for certain plastics.

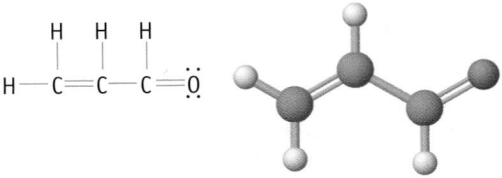

   (a) Which bonds in the molecule are polar, and which are nonpolar?
   (b) Which is the most polar bond in the molecule? Which is the more negative atom of this bond?

30. Urea, $(NH_2)_2CO$, is used in plastics and fertilizers. It is also the primary nitrogen-containing substance excreted by humans.
   (a) Which bonds in the molecule are polar, and which are nonpolar?

   (b) Which is the most polar bond in the molecule? Which atom is the negative end of the bond dipole?

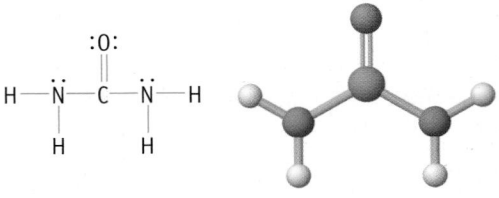

31. ■ Considering both formal charges and bond polarities, predict on which atom or atoms the negative charge resides in the following anions:
   (a) OH^-
   (b) BH_4^-
   (c) $CH_3CO_2^-$

32. ■ Considering both formal charge and bond polarities, predict on which atom or atoms the positive charge resides in the following cations.
   (a) H_3O^+
   (b) NH_4^+
   (c) NO_2^+
   (d) NF_4^+

33. Three resonance structures are possible for dinitrogen monoxide, N_2O.
   (a) Draw the three resonance structures.
   (b) Calculate the formal charge on each atom in each resonance structure.
   (c) Based on formal charges and electronegativity, predict which resonance structure is the most reasonable.

34. ■ Compare the electron dot structures of the carbonate (CO_3^{2-}) and borate (BO_3^{3-}) ions.
   (a) Are these ions isoelectronic?
   (b) How many resonance structures does each ion have?
   (c) What are the formal charges of each atom in these ions?
   (d) If an H^+ ion attaches to CO_3^{2-} to form the bicarbonate ion, HCO_3^-, does it attach to an O atom or to the C atom?

35. The chemistry of the nitrite ion and HNO_2:
   (a) Two resonance structures are possible for NO_2^-. Draw these structures, and then find the formal charge on each atom in each resonance structure.
   (b) If an H^+ ion is attached to NO_2^- (to form the acid HNO_2), it attaches to the O atom and not the N atom. Explain why you would predict this structure.
   (c) Two resonance structures are possible for HNO_2. Draw these structures, and then find the formal charge on each atom in each resonance structure. Is either of these structures strongly preferred over the other?

36. ■ Draw the resonance structures for the formate ion, HCO_2^-, and find the formal charge on each atom. If an H^+ ion is attached to HCO_2^- (to form formic acid), does it attach to C or O?

Molecular Polarity
(*See Examples 8.12 and 8.13 and ChemistryNow Screen 8.16.*)

37. Consider the following molecules:
   (a) H_2O (c) CO_2 (e) CCl_4
   (b) NH_3 (d) ClF
   (i) In which compound are the bonds most polar?
   (ii) Which compounds in the list are *not* polar?
   (iii) Which atom in ClF is more negatively charged?

38. ■ Consider the following molecules:
   (a) CH_4 (c) BF_3
   (b) NH_2Cl (d) CS_2
   (i) Which compound has the most polar bonds?
   (ii) Which compounds in the list are *not* polar?

39. Which of the following molecules is (are) polar? For each polar molecule, indicate the direction of polarity— that is, which is the negative end, and which is the positive end of the molecule.
   (a) $BeCl_2$ (c) CH_3Cl
   (b) HBF_2 (d) SO_3

40. ■ Which of the following molecules is (are) not polar? Which molecule has bonds with the largest polarity?
   (a) CO (d) PCl_3
   (b) BCl_3 (e) GeH_4
   (c) CF_4

Bond Order and Bond Length
(*See Exercise 8.16 and ChemistryNow Screen 8.17.*)

41. Give the bond order for each bond in the following molecules or ions:
   (a) CH_2O (c) NO_2^+
   (b) SO_3^{2-} (d) NOCl

42. ■ Give the bond order for each bond in the following molecules or ions:
   (a) CN^- (c) SO_3
   (b) CH_3CN (d) $CH_3CH{=}CH_2$

43. In each pair of bonds, predict which is shorter.
   (a) B—Cl or Ga—Cl (c) P—S or P—O
   (b) Sn—O or C—O (d) C=O or C≡N

44. ■ In each pair of bonds, predict which is shorter.
   (a) Si—N or Si—O
   (b) Si—O or C—O
   (c) C—F or C—Br
   (d) The C—N bond or the C≡N bond in $H_2NCH_2C{≡}N$

45. ■ Consider the nitrogen–oxygen bond lengths in NO_2^+, NO_2^-, and NO_3^-. In which ion is the bond predicted to be longest? In which is it predicted to be shortest? Explain briefly.

46. Compare the carbon–oxygen bond lengths in the formate ion (HCO_2^-), in methanol (CH_3OH), and in the carbonate ion (CO_3^{2-}). In which species is the carbon–oxygen bond predicted to be longest? In which is it predicted to be shortest? Explain briefly.

Bond Strength and Bond Dissociation Enthalpy
(*See Table 8.9, Example 8.14, and ChemistryNow Screen 8.18.*)

47. ■ Consider the carbon–oxygen bond in formaldehyde (CH_2O) and carbon monoxide (CO). In which molecule is the CO bond shorter? In which molecule is the CO bond stronger?

48. ■ Compare the nitrogen–nitrogen bond in hydrazine, H_2NNH_2, with that in "laughing gas," N_2O. In which molecule is the nitrogen–nitrogen bond shorter? In which is the bond stronger?

49. Hydrogenation reactions, which involve the addition of H_2 to a molecule, are widely used in industry to transform one compound into another. For example, 1-butene (C_4H_8) is converted to butane (C_4H_{10}) by addition of H_2.

Use the bond dissociation enthalpies in Table 8.9 to estimate the enthalpy change for this hydrogenation reaction.

50. ■ Phosgene, Cl_2CO, is a highly toxic gas that was used as a weapon in World War I. Using the bond dissociation enthalpies in Table 8.9, estimate the enthalpy change for the reaction of carbon monoxide and chlorine to produce phosgene. (*Hint:* First draw the electron dot structures of the reactants and products so you know the types of bonds involved.)

$$CO(g) + Cl_2(g) \rightarrow Cl_2CO(g)$$

51. ■ The compound oxygen difluoride is quite reactive, giving oxygen and HF when treated with water:

$$OF_2(g) + H_2O(g) \rightarrow O_2(g) + 2\,HF(g)$$
$$\Delta_rH° = -318\ kJ/mol\text{-rxn}$$

Using bond dissociation enthalpies, calculate the bond dissociation energy of the O—F bond in OF_2.

52. ■ Oxygen atoms can combine with ozone to form oxygen:

$$O_3(g) + O(g) \rightarrow 2\,O_2(g)$$
$$\Delta_rH° = -394\ kJ/mol\text{-rxn}$$

Using $\Delta_rH°$ and the bond dissociation enthalpy data in Table 8.9, estimate the bond dissociation enthalpy for the oxygen–oxygen bond in ozone, O_3. How does your estimate compare with the energies of an O—O single bond and an O=O double bond? Does the oxygen–oxygen bond dissociation enthalpy in ozone correlate with its bond order?

▲ more challenging ■ in OWL Blue-numbered questions answered in Appendix O

General Questions on Bonding and Molecular Structure

These questions are not designated as to type or location in the chapter. They may combine several concepts.

53. ■ Specify the number of valence electrons for Li, Ti, Zn, Si, and Cl.

54. In boron compounds, the B atom often is not surrounded by four valence electron pairs. Illustrate this with BCl_3. Show how the molecule can achieve an octet configuration by forming a coordinate covalent bond with ammonia (NH_3).

55. Which of the following compounds or ions do not have an octet of electrons surrounding the central atom: BF_4^-, SiF_4, SeF_4, BrF_4^-, XeF_4?

56. ■ In which of the following does the central atom obey the octet rule: NO_2, SF_4, NH_3, SO_3, ClO_2, and ClO_2^-? Are any of these species odd-electron molecules or ions?

57. Draw resonance structures for the formate ion, HCO_2^- and then determine the C—O bond order in the ion.

58. ■ Consider a series of molecules in which carbon is bonded by single bonds to atoms of second-period elements: C—O, C—F, C—N, C—C, and C—B. Place these bonds in order of increasing bond length.

59. To estimate the enthalpy change for the reaction

$$O_2(g) + 2\,H_2(g) \rightarrow 2\,H_2O(g)$$

what bond dissociation enthalpies do you need? Outline the calculation, being careful to show correct algebraic signs.

60. What is the principle of electroneutrality? Use this rule to exclude a possible resonance structure of CO_2.

61. Draw Lewis structures (and resonance structures where appropriate) for the following molecules and ions. What similarities and differences are there in this series?
    (a) CO_2 (b) N_3^- (c) OCN^-

62. Draw resonance structures for the SO_2 molecule, and indicate the partial charges on the S and O atoms. Are the S—O bonds polar, and is the molecule as a whole polar? If so, what is the direction of the net dipole in SO_2? Is your prediction confirmed by the electrostatic potential surface? Explain briefly.

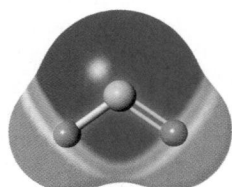

Electrostatic potential surface for sulfur dioxide.

63. What are the orders of the N—O bonds in NO_2^- and NO_2^+? The nitrogen–oxygen bond length in one of these ions is 110 pm and 124 pm in the other. Which bond length corresponds to which ion? Explain briefly.

64. Which has the greater O—N—O bond angle, NO_2^- or NO_2^+? Explain briefly.

65. Compare the F—Cl—F angles in ClF_2^+ and ClF_2^-. Using Lewis structures, determine the approximate bond angle in each ion. Decide which ion has the greater bond angle, and explain your reasoning.

66. Draw an electron dot structure for the cyanide ion, CN^-. In aqueous solution, this ion interacts with H^+ to form the acid. Should the acid formula be written as HCN or CNH?

67. Draw the electron dot structure for the sulfite ion, SO_3^{2-}. In aqueous solution, the ion interacts with H^+. Predict whether a H^+ ion will attach to the S atom or the O atom of SO_3^{2-}.

68. Dinitrogen monoxide, N_2O, can decompose to nitrogen and oxygen gas:

$$2\,N_2O(g) \rightarrow 2\,N_2(g) + O_2(g)$$

Use bond dissociation enthalpies to estimate the enthalpy change for this reaction.

69. ▲ ■ The equation for the combustion of gaseous methanol is

$$2\,CH_3OH(g) + 3\,O_2(g) \rightarrow 2\,CO_2(g) + 4\,H_2O(g)$$

(a) Using the bond dissociation enthalpies in Table 8.9, estimate the enthalpy change for this reaction. What is the enthalpy of combustion of one mole of gaseous methanol?

(b) Compare your answer in part (a) with a calculation of $\Delta_rH°$ using thermochemical data and the methods of Chapter 5 (see Equation 5.6).

70. ▲ Acrylonitrile, C_3H_3N, is the building block of the synthetic fiber Orlon.

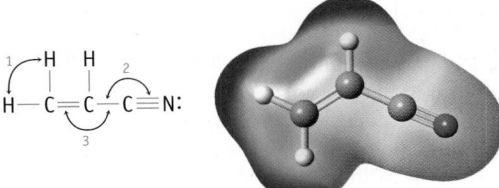

Electrostatic potential surface for acrylonitrile.

(a) Give the approximate values of angles 1, 2, and 3.
(b) Which is the shorter carbon–carbon bond?
(c) Which is the stronger carbon–carbon bond?
(d) Based on the electrostatic potential surface, where are the positive and negative charges located in the molecule?
(e) Which is the most polar bond?
(f) Is the molecule polar?

71. ▲ ■ The cyanate ion, NCO⁻, has the least electronegative atom, C, in the center. The very unstable fulminate ion, CNO⁻, has the same formula, but the N atom is in the center.
  (a) Draw the three possible resonance structures of CNO⁻.
  (b) On the basis of formal charges, decide on the resonance structure with the most reasonable distribution of charge.
  (c) Mercury fulminate is so unstable it is used in blasting caps. Can you offer an explanation for this instability? (*Hint:* Are the formal charges in any resonance structure reasonable in view of the relative electronegativities of the atoms?)

72. Vanillin is the flavoring agent in vanilla extract and in vanilla ice cream. Its structure is shown here:

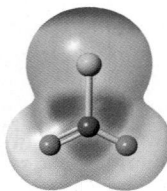

  (a) Give values for the three bond angles indicated.
  (b) Indicate the shortest carbon–oxygen bond in the molecule.
  (c) Indicate the most polar bond in the molecule.

73. ▲ Given that the spatial requirement of a lone pair is greater than that of a bond pair, explain why
  (a) XeF₂ has a linear molecular structure and not a bent one.
  (b) ClF₃ has a T-shaped structure and not a trigonal-planar one.

74. The formula for nitryl chloride is ClNO₂.
  (a) Draw the Lewis structure for the molecule, including all resonance structures.
  (b) What is the N—O bond order?
  (c) Describe the electron-pair and molecular geometries, and give values for all bond angles.
  (d) What is the most polar bond in the molecule? Is the molecule polar?
  (e) ▲ The computer program used to calculate electrostatic potential surfaces gave the following charges on atoms in the molecule: A = −0.03, B = −0.26, and C = +0.56. Identify the atoms A, B, and C. Are these calculated charges in accord with your predictions?

Electrostatic potential surface for ClNO₂.

75. Hydroxyproline is a less-common amino acid.

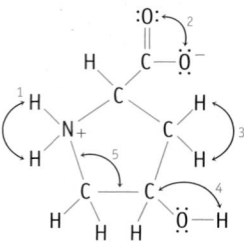

  (a) ■ Give approximate values for the indicated bond angles.
  (b) Which are the most polar bonds in the molecule?

76. Amides are an important class of organic molecules. They are usually drawn as sketched here, but another resonance structure is possible.

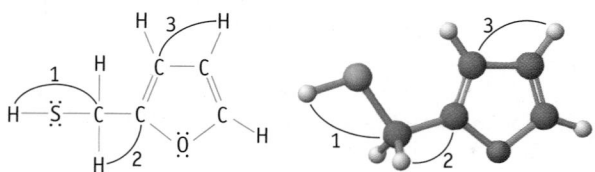

  (a) Draw that structure, and then suggest why it is usually not pictured.
  (b) Suggest a reason for the fact that the H—N—H angle is close to 120°.

77. Use the bond dissociation enthalpies in Table 8.9 to calculate the enthalpy change for the decomposition of urea (Study Question 30) to hydrazine, H₂N—NH₂, and carbon monoxide. (Assume all compounds are in the gas phase.)

78. The molecule shown here, 2-furylmethanethiol, is responsible for the aroma of coffee:

  (a) What are the formal charges on the S and O atoms?
  (b) ■ Give approximate values of angles 1, 2, and 3.
  (c) Which are the shorter carbon–carbon bonds in the molecule?
  (d) Which bond in this molecule is the most polar?
  (e) Is the molecule as a whole polar or nonpolar?
  (f) The molecular model makes it clear that the four C atoms of the ring are all in a plane. Is the O atom in that same plane (making the five-member ring planar), or is the O atom bent above or below the plane?

79. ▲ ■ Dihydroxyacetone is a component of quick-tanning lotions. (It reacts with the amino acids in the upper layer of skin and colors them brown in a reaction similar to that occurring when food is browned as it cooks.)
    (a) Supposing you can make this compound by treating acetone with oxygen, use bond dissociation enthalpies to estimate the enthalpy change for the following reaction (which is assumed to occur in the gas phase). Is the reaction exothermic or endothermic?

$$H-\overset{\overset{H}{|}}{\underset{\underset{H}{|}}{C}}-\overset{:O:}{\overset{||}{C}}-\overset{\overset{H}{|}}{\underset{\underset{H}{|}}{C}}-H + O_2 \longrightarrow H-\ddot{O}-\overset{\overset{H}{|}}{\underset{\underset{H}{|}}{C}}-\overset{:O:}{\overset{||}{C}}-\overset{\overset{H}{|}}{\underset{\underset{H}{|}}{C}}-\ddot{O}-H$$

        acetone   dihydroxyacetone

    (b) Is acetone polar?
    (c) Positive H atoms can sometimes be removed (as H⁺) from molecules with strong bases (which is in part what happens in the tanning reaction). Which H atoms are the most positive in dihydroxyacetone?

80. Nitric acid, HNO_3, has three resonance structures. One of them, however, contributes much less to the resonance hybrid than the other two. Sketch the three resonance structures, and assign a formal charge to each atom. Which one of your structures is the least important?

81. ▲ ■ Acrolein is used to make plastics. Suppose this compound can be prepared by inserting a carbon monoxide molecule into the C—H bond of ethylene.

$$\overset{\overset{H}{|}\quad\overset{H}{|}}{\underset{\underset{H}{|}\ \underset{H}{|}}{C=C}} + :C\equiv O: \longrightarrow \overset{\overset{H}{|}\ \ \overset{C=\ddot{O}}{}}{\underset{\underset{H}{|}\ \underset{H}{|}}{C=C}}$$

        ethylene   acrolein

    (a) Which is the stronger carbon–carbon bond in acrolein?
    (b) Which is the longer carbon–carbon bond in acrolein?
    (c) Is ethylene or acrolein polar?
    (d) Is the reaction of CO with C_2H_4 to give acrolein endothermic or exothermic?

82. Molecules in space:
    (a) In addition to molecules such as CO, HCl, H_2O, and NH_3, glycolaldehyde has been detected in outer space. Is the molecule polar?

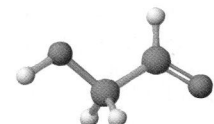

HOCH₂CHO, glycolaldehyde.

    (b) Where do the positive and negative charges lie in the molecule?
    (c) One molecule found in the 1995 Hale-Bopp comet is HC_3N. Suggest a structure for this molecule.

83. 1,2-Dichloroethylene can be synthesized by adding Cl_2 to the carbon–carbon triple bond of acetylene.

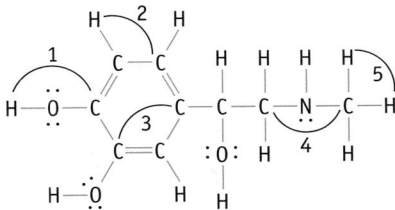

    Using bond dissociation enthalpies, estimate the enthalpy change for this reaction in the gas phase.

84. The molecule pictured below is epinephrine, a compound used as a bronchodilator and antiglaucoma agent.

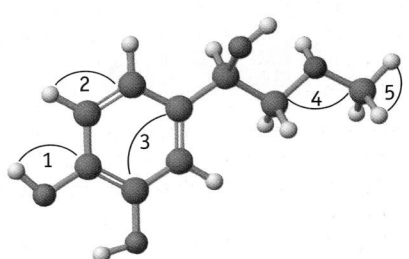

    (a) ■ Give a value for each of the indicated bond angles.
    (b) What are the most polar bonds in the molecule?

In the Laboratory

85. You are doing an experiment in the laboratory and want to prepare a solution in a polar solvent. Which solvent would you choose, methanol (CH_3OH) or toluene ($C_6H_5CH_3$)? Explain your choice.

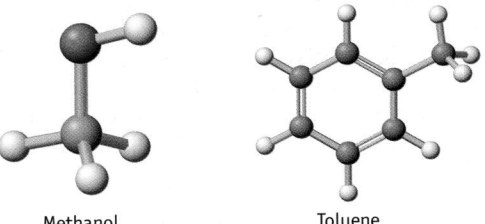

    Methanol   Toluene
    Methanol (left) and toluene (right).

86. ■ Methylacetamide, $CH_3CONHCH_3$, is a small molecule with an amide link (CO—NH), the group that binds one amino acid to another in proteins.
    (a) Is this molecule polar?
    (b) Where do you expect the positive and negative charges to lie in this molecule? Does the electrostatic potential surface confirm your predictions?. (Compare this with the dipeptide model in the *A Closer Look* box on page 382.)

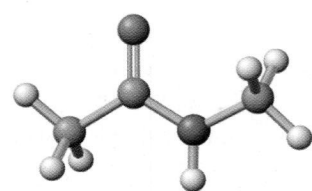

Methylacetamide
Ball-and-stick model.

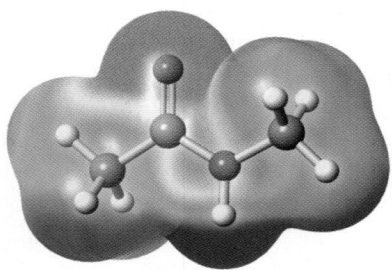

Electrostatic potential surface.

87. ▲ A paper published in the research journal *Science* in 2007 (S. Vallina and R. Simo, *Science*, Vol. 315, page 506, January 26, 2007) reported studies of dimethylsulfide (DMS), an important greenhouse gas that is released by marine phytoplankton. This gas "represents the largest natural source of atmospheric sulfur and a major precursor of hygroscopic (i.e., cloud-forming) particles in clean air over the remote oceans, thereby acting to reduce the amount of solar radiation that crosses the atmosphere and is absorbed by the ocean."
    (a) Sketch the Lewis structure of dimethylsulfide, CH_3SCH_3, and give the unique bond angles in the molecule.
    (b) Use electronegativities to decide where the positive and negative charges lie in the molecule. Is the molecule polar?
    (c) The mean seawater concentration of DMS in the ocean in the region between 15° north latitude and 15° south latitude is 2.7 nM (nanomolar). How many molecules of DMS are present in 1.0 m³ of seawater?

88. ■ Uracil is one of the bases in DNA.

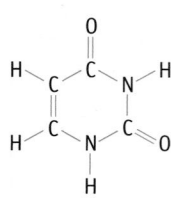

Uracil, $C_4H_4N_2O_2$.

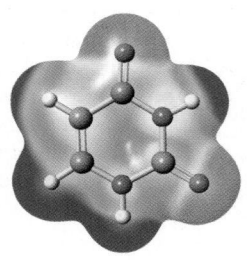

Electrostatic potential surface for uracil.

    (a) What are the values of the O—C—N and C—N—H angles?
    (b) There are two carbon–carbon bonds in the molecule. Which is predicted to be shorter?
    (c) If a proton attacks the molecule, decide on the basis of the electrostatic potential surface to which atom or atoms it could be attached.

Summary and Conceptual Questions

The following questions may use concepts from this and previous chapters.

89. Bromine-containing species play a role in environmental chemistry. For example, they are evolved in volcanic eruptions.
    (a) The following molecules are important in bromine environmental chemistry: HBr, BrO, and HOBr. Which are odd-electron molecules?
    (b) Use bond dissociation enthalpies to estimate $\Delta_r H$ for three reactions of bromine:

$$Br_2(g) \rightarrow 2\ Br(g)$$

$$2\ Br(g) + O_2(g) \rightarrow 2\ BrO(g)$$

$$BrO(g) + H_2O(g) \rightarrow HOBr(g) + OH(g)$$

    (c) Using bond dissociation enthalpies, estimate the standard enthalpy of formation of HOBr(g) from $H_2(g)$, $O_2(g)$, and $Br_2(g)$.
    (d) Are the reactions in parts (b) and (c) exothermic or endothermic?

90. Acrylamide, $H_2C=CHC(=O)NH_2$, is a known neurotoxin and possible carcinogen. It was a shock to all consumers of potato chips and french fries a few years ago when it was found to occur in those products (page 90).
    (a) Sketch the molecular structure of acrylamide, showing all unique bond angles.
    (b) Indicate which carbon–carbon bond is the stronger of the two.
    (c) Is the molecule polar or nonpolar?
    (d) The amount of acrylamide found in potato chips is 1.7 mg/kg. If a serving of potato chips is 28 g, how many moles of acrylamide are you consuming?

91. See ChemistryNow Screen 8.16, Molecular Polarity. Use the Molecular Polarity tool on this screen to explore the polarity of molecules.
    (a) Is BF_3 a polar molecule? Does the molecular polarity change as the F atoms of BF_3 are replaced by H atoms?
    (b) Is $BeCl_2$ a polar molecule? Does the polarity change when Cl is replaced by Br?

92. Locate the molecules in the table shown here in the Molecular Models available in ChemistryNow. Measure the carbon–carbon bond length in each, and complete the table. (Note that the bond lengths are given in angstrom units, where 1 Å = 0.1 nm.)

Formula	Measured Bond Distance (Å)	Bond Order
ethane, C_2H_6	_____	_____
butane, C_4H_{10}	_____	_____
ethylene, C_2H_4	_____	_____
acetylene, C_2H_2	_____	_____
benzene, C_6H_6	_____	_____

What relationship between bond order and carbon–carbon bond length do you observe?

9 | Bonding and Molecular Structure: Orbital Hybridization and Molecular Orbitals

The Chemistry of the Noble Gases

It was a shock when, in 1962, we learned that the noble gases were not chemically inert as our chemistry professors had taught us. Xenon at the very least was found to form compounds! The first was an ionic compound, now known to be $XeF^+Pt_2F_{11}^-$. However, this was followed shortly thereafter with the discovery of a large number of covalently bonded compounds, including XeF_4, XeF_6, $XeOF_4$, and XeO_3.

Since 1962, the field of noble gas chemistry has expanded with the discovery of such interesting molecules as FXeOXeF and, at low temperatures, species such as HArF, HXeH, HXeCl, and even HKrF.

Initially, xenon compounds were thought to form only under the most severe conditions. Therefore, it was again a surprise when it was learned that irradiating a mixture of xenon and fluorine gases at room temperature gave crystals of XeF_2 (as seen in the photo).

©Gary J. Schrobilgen

White crystals of xenon difluoride, XeF_2, form when a mixture of Xe and F_2 gases is irradiated with UV light.

Questions:

1. What is the most reasonable structure of XeF_2? Does knowing that the molecule has no dipole moment confirm your structural choice? Why or why not?
2. Describe the bonding in XeF_2 using valence bond theory.
3. Predict a structure for FXeOXeF.

Answers to these questions are in Appendix Q.

Chapter Goals

OWL *See Chapter Goals Revisited (page 433) for Study Questions keyed to these goals and assignable in OWL.*

- Understand the differences between valence bond theory and molecular orbital theory.
- Identify the hybridization of an atom in a molecule or ion.
- Understand the differences between bonding and antibonding molecular orbitals and be able to write the molecular orbital configurations for simple diatomic molecules.

Just how are molecules held together? How can two molecules with distinctly different properties have the same formula? Why is oxygen paramagnetic, and how is this property connected with bonding in the molecule? These are just a few of the fundamental and interesting questions that are raised in this chapter and that require us to take a more advanced look at bonding.

Chemistry⚛Now™

Throughout the text this icon introduces an opportunity for self-study or to explore interactive tutorials by signing in at **www.cengage.com/login**.

9.1 Orbitals and Theories of Chemical Bonding

From Chapter 6, you know that the location of the valence electrons in atoms is described by an orbital model. It seems reasonable that an orbital model could also be used to describe electrons in molecules.

Two common approaches to rationalizing chemical bonding based on orbitals are **valence bond (VB) theory** and **molecular orbital (MO) theory.** The former was developed largely by Linus Pauling (page 377) and the latter by another American scientist, Robert S. Mulliken (1896–1986). The valence bond approach is closely tied to Lewis's idea of bonding electron pairs between atoms and lone pairs of electrons localized on a particular atom. In contrast, Mulliken's approach was to derive molecular orbitals that are "spread out," or *delocalized*, over the molecule. One way to do this is to combine atomic orbitals to form a set of orbitals that are the property of the molecule, and then distribute the electrons of the molecule within these orbitals.

Why are two theories used? Is one more correct than the other? Actually, both give good descriptions of the bonding in molecules and polyatomic ions, but they are used for different purposes. Valence bond theory is generally the method of choice to provide a qualitative, visual picture of molecular structure and bonding. This theory is particularly useful for molecules made up of many atoms. In contrast, molecular orbital theory is used when a more quantitative picture of bonding is needed. Furthermore, valence bond theory provides a good description of bonding for molecules in their ground, or lowest, energy state. On the other hand, MO theory is essential if we want to describe molecules in higher energy, excited states. Among other things, this is important in explaining the colors of compounds. Finally, for a few molecules such as NO and O_2, MO theory is the only theory that can describe their bonding accurately.

■ **Bonds Are a "Figment of Our Own Imagination"** C. A. Coulson, a prominent theoretical chemist at the University of Oxford, England, has said that "Sometimes it seems to me that a bond between atoms has become so real, so tangible, so friendly, that I can almost see it. Then I awake with a little shock, for a chemical bond is not a real thing. It does not exist. No one has ever seen one. No one ever can. It is a figment of our own imagination" (*Chemical and Engineering News,* January 29, 2007, page 37). Nonetheless, bonds are a useful figment, and this chapter will present some of these useful ideas.

9.2 Valence Bond Theory

The Orbital Overlap Model of Bonding

What happens if two atoms at an infinite distance apart are brought together to form a bond? This process is often illustrated with H_2 because, with two electrons and two nuclei, this is the simplest molecular compound known (Figure 9.1). Initially, when two hydrogen atoms are widely separated, they do not interact. If the atoms move closer together, however, the electron on one atom begins to experience an attraction to the positive charge of the nucleus of the other atom. Because of the attractive forces, the electron clouds on the atoms distort as the electron of one atom is drawn toward the nucleus of the second atom, and the potential energy of the system is lowered. Calculations show that when the distance between the H atoms is 74 pm, the potential energy reaches a minimum and the H_2 molecule is most stable. Significantly, 74 pm corresponds to the experimentally measured bond distance in the H_2 molecule.

Individual hydrogen atoms each have a single electron. In H_2 the two electrons pair up to form the bond. There is a net stabilization, representing the extent to which the energies of the two electrons are lowered from their value in the free atoms. The net stabilization (the extent to which the potential energy is lowered) can be calculated, and the calculated value approximates the experimentally determined bond energy. Agreement between theory and experiment on both bond distance and energy is evidence that this theoretical approach has merit.

Bond formation is depicted in Figures 9.1 and 9.2 as occurring when the electron clouds on the two atoms interpenetrate or overlap. This **orbital overlap** increases the probability of finding the bonding electrons in the region of space between the two nuclei. *The idea that bonds are formed by overlap of atomic orbitals is the basis for valence bond theory.*

■ **Bonds in Valence Bond Theory** In the language of valence bond theory, a pair of electrons of opposite spin located between a pair of atoms constitutes a bond.

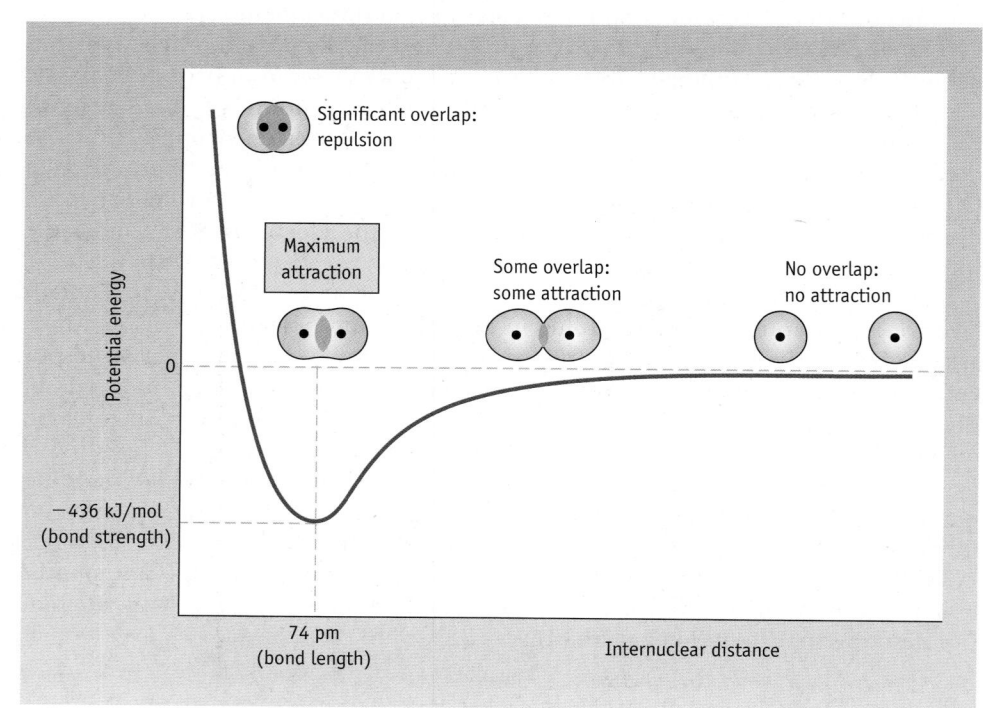

Active Figure 9.1 Potential energy change during H—H bond formation from isolated hydrogen atoms. The lowest energy is reached at an H—H separation of 74 pm, where there is overlap of 1s orbitals. At greater distances, the overlap is less, and the bond is weaker. At H—H distances less than 74 pm, repulsions between the nuclei and between the electrons of the two atoms increase rapidly, and the potential energy curve rises steeply.

Chemistry .Now™ Sign in at www. cengage.com/login and go to the Chapter Contents menu to explore an interactive version of this figure accompanied by an exercise.

When the single covalent bond is formed in H_2, the $1s$ electron cloud of each atom is distorted in a way that gives the electrons a higher probability of being in the region between the two hydrogen atoms (Figure 9.2a). This makes sense because this distortion results in the electrons being situated so they can be attracted equally to the two positively charged nuclei. Placing the electrons between the nuclei also matches the Lewis electron dot model.

The covalent bond that arises from the overlap of two s orbitals, one from each of two atoms as in H_2, is called a **sigma (σ) bond.** *The electron density of a sigma bond is greatest along the axis of the bond.*

In summary, the main points of the valence bond approach to bonding are:

- Orbitals overlap to form a bond between two atoms.
- Two electrons, *of opposite spin*, can be accommodated in the overlapping orbitals. Usually, one electron is supplied by each of the two bonded atoms.
- Because of orbital overlap, the bonding electrons have a higher probability of being found within a region of space influenced by both nuclei. Both electrons are simultaneously attracted to both nuclei.

What happens for elements beyond hydrogen? In the Lewis structure of HF, for example, a bonding electron pair is placed between H and F, and three lone pairs of electrons are depicted as localized on the F atom (Figure 9.2b). To use an orbital approach, look at the valence shell electrons and orbitals for each atom that can overlap. The hydrogen atom will use its $1s$ orbital in bond formation. The electron configuration of fluorine is $1s^2 2s^2 2p^5$, and the unpaired electron for this atom is assigned to one of the $2p$ orbitals. A sigma bond results from overlap of the hydrogen $1s$ and the fluorine $2p$ orbital.

Formation of the H—F bond is similar to formation of an H—H bond. A hydrogen atom approaches a fluorine atom along the axis containing the $2p$ orbital with

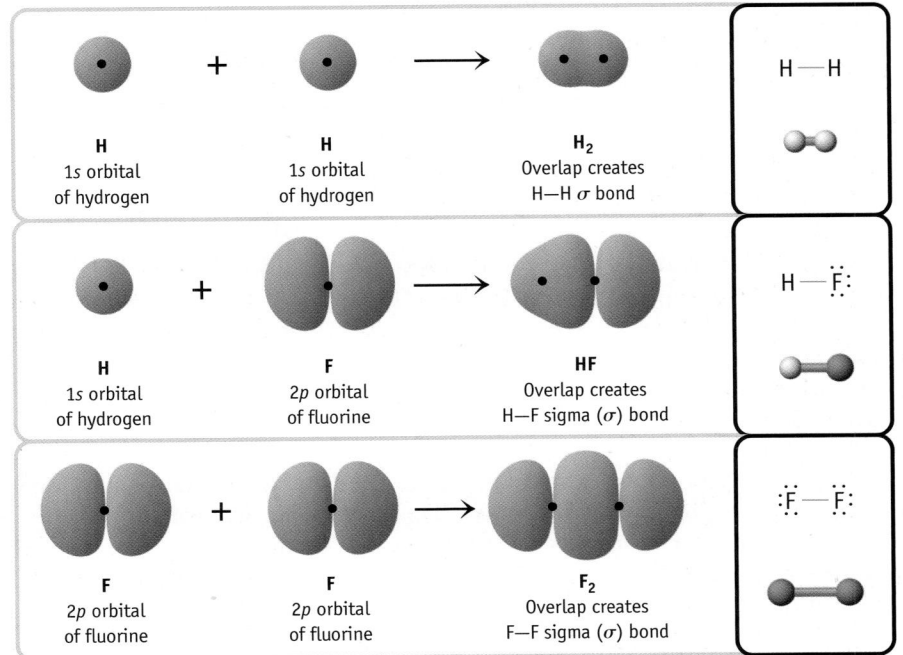

FIGURE 9.2 Covalent bond formation in H_2, HF, and F_2.

(a) Overlap of hydrogen $1s$ orbitals to form the H—H sigma (σ) bond.

(b) Overlap of hydrogen $1s$ and fluorine $2p$ orbitals to form the sigma (σ) bond in HF.

(c) Overlap of $2p$ orbitals on two fluorine atoms forming the sigma (σ) bond in F_2.

a single electron. The orbitals (1s on H and 2p on F) distort as each atomic nucleus influences the electron and orbital of the other atom. Still closer together, the 1s and 2p orbitals overlap, and the two electrons, with opposite spins, pair up to give a σ bond (Figure 9.2b). There is an optimum distance (92 pm) at which the energy is lowest, and this corresponds to the bond distance in HF. The net stabilization achieved in this process is the energy for the H—F bond.

The remaining electrons on the fluorine atom (a pair of electrons in the 2s orbital and two pairs of electrons in the other two 2p orbitals) are not involved in bonding. They are nonbonding electrons, the lone pairs associated with this element in the Lewis structure.

Extension of this model gives a description of bonding in F_2. The 2p orbitals on the two atoms overlap, and the single electron from each atom is paired in the resulting σ bond (Figure 9.2c). The 2s and the 2p electrons not involved in the bond are the lone pairs on each atom.

Chemistry‧Now™

Sign in at **www.cengage.com/login** and go to Chapter 9 Contents to see Screen 9.3 for an exercise on **bond formation**.

Hybridization of Atomic Orbitals

The simple picture using orbital overlap to describe bonding in H_2, HF, and F_2 works well, but we run into difficulty when molecules with more atoms are considered. For example, a Lewis dot structure of methane, CH_4, shows four C—H covalent bonds. VSEPR theory predicts, and experiments confirm, that the electron-pair geometry of the C atom in CH_4 is tetrahedral, with an angle of 109.5° between the bond pairs. The hydrogens are identical in this structure. This means that four equivalent bonding electron pairs occur around the C atom. An orbital picture of the bonds should convey both the geometry and the fact that all C—H bonds are the same.

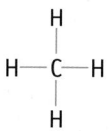
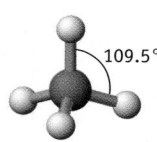
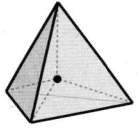

Lewis structure   Molecular model   Electron-pair geometry

If we apply the orbital overlap model used for H_2 and F_2 without modification to describe the bonding in CH_4, a problem arises. The three orbitals for the 2p valence electrons of carbon are at right angles, 90° (Figure 9.3), and do not match the tetrahedral angle of 109.5°. The spherical 2s orbital could bond in any direction. Furthermore, a carbon atom in its ground state ($1s^2 2s^2 2p^2$) has only two unpaired electrons (in the 2p orbitals), not the four that are needed to allow formation of four bonds.

To describe the bonding in methane and other molecules, Linus Pauling proposed the theory of **orbital hybridization** (Figure 9.4). He suggested that a new set of orbitals, called **hybrid orbitals,** could be created by mixing the s, p, and (when required) d atomic orbitals on an atom. There are three important principles that govern the outcome.

- The number of hybrid orbitals is always equal to the number of atomic orbitals that are mixed to create the hybrid orbital set.

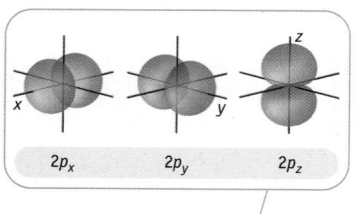

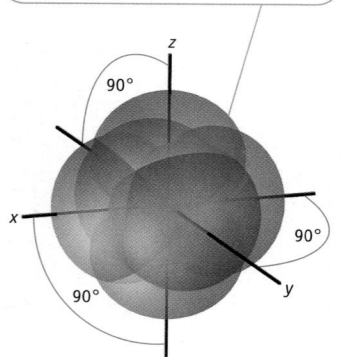

FIGURE 9.3 The 2p orbitals of an atom. The $2p_x$, $2p_y$, and $2p_z$ orbitals lie along the x-, y-, and z-axes, 90° to each other.

Charles D. Winters

FIGURE 9.4 Hybridization: an analogy. Atomic orbitals can mix, or hybridize, to form hybrid orbitals. When two atomic orbitals on an atom combine, two new orbitals are produced on that atom. The new orbitals have a different direction in space than the original orbitals. An analogy is mixing two different colors (left) to produce a third color, which is a "hybrid" of the original colors (center). After mixing, there are still two beakers (right), each containing the same volume of solution as before, but the color is a "hybrid" color.

- Hybrid orbital sets are always built by combining an s orbital with as many p orbitals (and d orbitals if necessary) to have enough hybrid orbitals to accommodate the bond and lone pairs on the central atom.
- The hybrid orbitals are directed toward the terminal atoms, leading to better orbital overlap and a stronger bond between the central and terminal atoms.

Chemistry Now™

Sign in at **www.cengage.com/login** and go to Chapter 9 Contents to see:
- Screen 9.4 for exercises on **hybrid orbitals**
- Screen 9.6 for a tutorial on **determining hybrid orbitals**

The sets of hybrid orbitals that arise from mixing s, p, and d atomic orbitals are illustrated in Figure 9.5. *The hybrid orbitals required by an atom in a molecule or ion are chosen to match the electron pair geometry of the atom* because a hybrid orbital is required for each sigma bond electron pair and each lone pair. The following types of hybridization are important:

- **sp**: If the valence shell s orbital on the central atom in a molecule or ion is mixed with a valence shell p orbital on that same atom, two sp hybrid orbitals are created. They are separated by 180°.
- **sp^2**: If an s orbital is combined with two p orbitals, all in the same valence shell, three sp^2 hybrid orbitals are created. They are in the same plane and are separated by 120°.
- **sp^3**: When the s orbital in a valence shell is combined with three p orbitals, the result is four hybrid orbitals, each labeled sp^3. The hybrid orbitals are separated by 109.5°, the tetrahedral angle.
- **sp^3d and sp^3d^2**: If one or two d orbitals are combined with s and p orbitals in the same valence shell, two other hybrid orbital sets are created. These are utilized by the central atom of a molecule or ion with a trigonal-bipyramidal or octahedral electron-pair geometry, respectively.

Valence Bond Theory for Methane, CH₄

In methane, four orbitals directed to the corners of a tetrahedron are needed to match the electron-pair geometry on the central carbon atom. By mixing the four valence shell orbitals, the $2s$ and all three of the $2p$ orbitals on carbon, a new set of

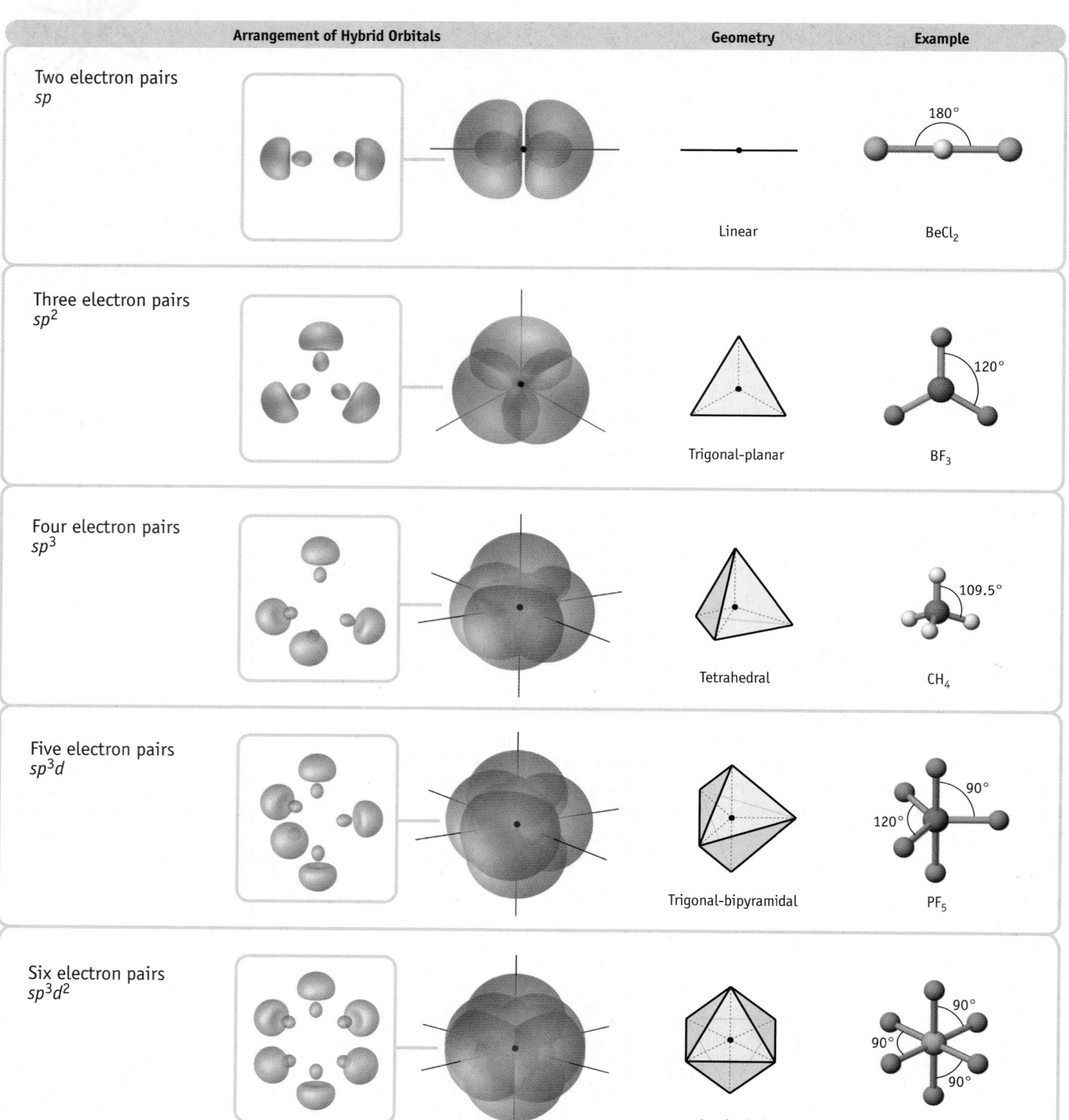

Arrangement of Hybrid Orbitals	Geometry	Example

Two electron pairs
sp

Linear

$BeCl_2$

180°

Three electron pairs
sp^2

Trigonal-planar

BF_3

120°

Four electron pairs
sp^3

Tetrahedral

CH_4

109.5°

Five electron pairs
sp^3d

Trigonal-bipyramidal

PF_5

90°
120°

Six electron pairs
sp^3d^2

Octahedral

SF_6

90°
90°
90°

Active Figure 9.5 **Hybrid orbitals for two to six electron pairs.** The geometry of the hybrid orbital sets for two to six valence shell electron pairs is given in the right column. In forming a hybrid orbital set, the s orbital is always used, plus as many p orbitals (and d orbitals) as are required to give the necessary number of σ-bonding and lone-pair orbitals.

Chemistry Now™ Sign in at www.cengage.com/login and go to the Chapter Contents menu to explore an interactive version of this figure accompanied by an exercise.

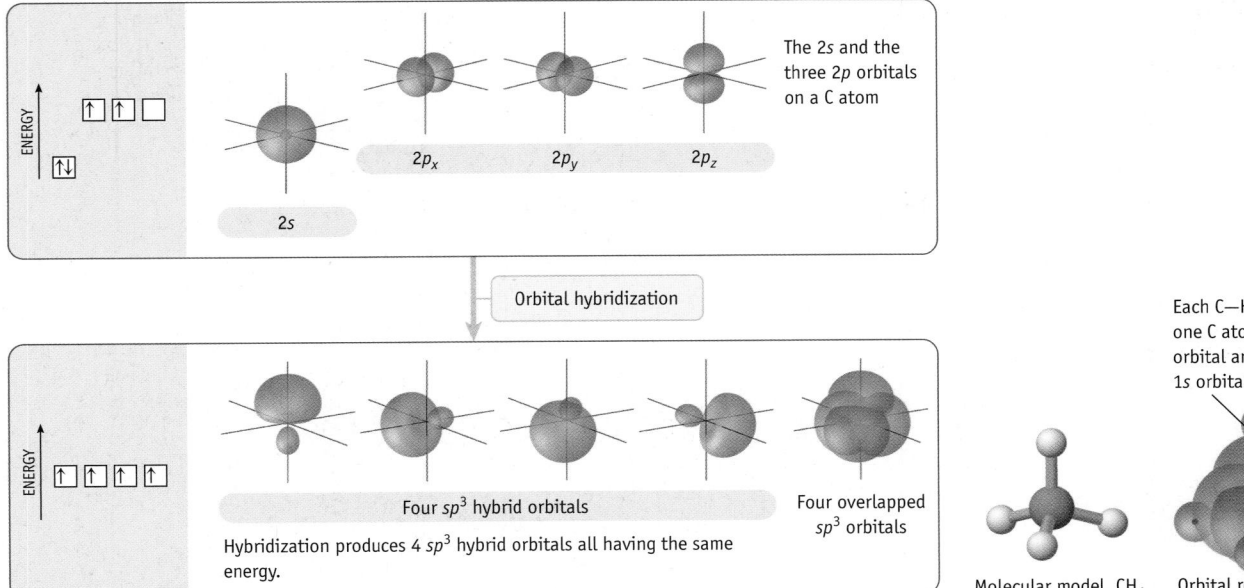

The 2s and the three 2p orbitals on a C atom

Orbital hybridization

Four sp³ hybrid orbitals

Hybridization produces 4 sp³ hybrid orbitals all having the same energy.

Four overlapped sp³ orbitals

Each C—H bond uses one C atom sp³ hybrid orbital and a H atom 1s orbital

Molecular model, CH₄   Orbital representation

Active Figure 9.6 Bonding in the methane (CH₄) molecule.

Chemistry⚛Now™ Sign in at www.cengage.com/login and go to the Chapter Contents menu to explore an interactive version of this figure accompanied by an exercise.

four hybrid orbitals is created that has tetrahedral geometry (Figures 9.5 and 9.6). Each of the four hybrid orbitals is labeled sp^3 to indicate the atomic orbital combination (an s orbital and three p orbitals) from which they are derived. All four sp^3 orbitals have an identical shape, and the angle between them is 109.5°, the tetrahedral angle. Because the orbitals have the same energy, one electron can be assigned to each according to Hund's rule (see Section 7.3 [page 312]). Then, each C—H bond is formed by overlap of one of the carbon sp^3 hybrid orbitals with the 1s orbital from a hydrogen atom; one electron from the C atom is paired with an electron from an H atom.

■ **Hybrid and Atomic Orbitals** Be sure to notice that *four* atomic orbitals produce *four* hybrid orbitals. The number of hybrid orbitals produced is always the same as the number of atomic orbitals used.

Valence Bond Theory for Ammonia, NH₃

The Lewis structure for ammonia shows there are four electron pairs in the valence shell of nitrogen: three bond pairs and a lone pair (Figure 9.7). VSEPR theory predicts a tetrahedral electron-pair geometry and a trigonal-pyramidal molecular geometry. The actual structure is a close match to the predicted structure; the H—N—H bond angles are 107.5° in this molecule.

Based on the electron-pair geometry of NH₃, we predict sp^3 hybridization to accommodate the four electron pairs on the N atom. The lone pair is assigned to one of the hybrid orbitals, and each of the other three hybrid orbitals is occupied by a single electron. Overlap of each of the singly occupied, sp^3 hybrid orbitals with a 1s orbital from a hydrogen atom, and pairing of the electrons in these orbitals, create the N—H bonds.

Valence Bond Theory for Water, H₂O

The oxygen atom of water has two bonding pairs and two lone pairs in its valence shell, and the H—O—H angle is 104.5° (Figure 9.7). Four sp^3 hybrid orbitals are created from the 2s and 2p atomic orbitals of oxygen. Two of these sp^3 orbitals are

FIGURE 9.7 Bonding in ammonia, NH₃, and water, H₂O.

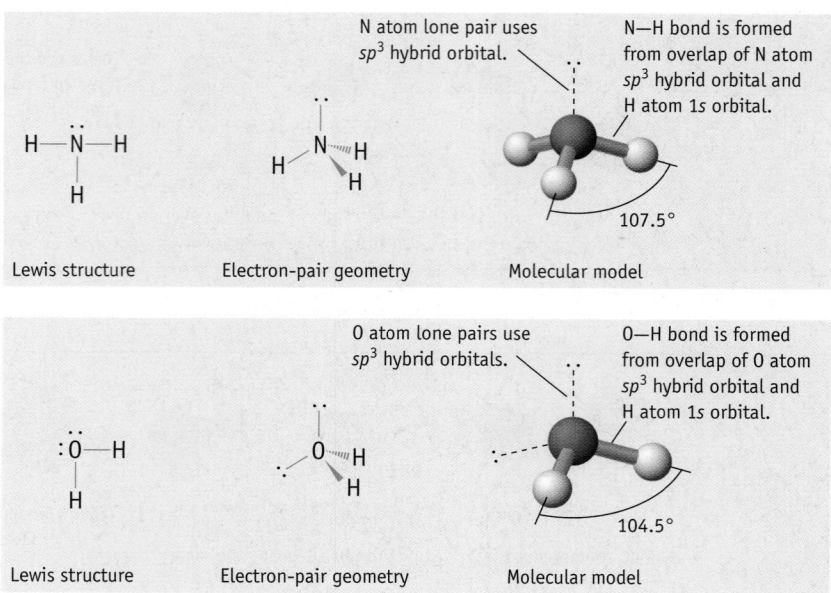

N atom lone pair uses *sp³* hybrid orbital.

N—H bond is formed from overlap of N atom *sp³* hybrid orbital and H atom 1*s* orbital.

Lewis structure   Electron-pair geometry   Molecular model

107.5°

O atom lone pairs use *sp³* hybrid orbitals.

O—H bond is formed from overlap of O atom *sp³* hybrid orbital and H atom 1*s* orbital.

Lewis structure   Electron-pair geometry   Molecular model

104.5°

occupied by unpaired electrons and are used to form O—H bonds. Lone pairs occupy the other two hybrid orbitals.

Chemistry Now™

Sign in at **www.cengage.com/login** and go to Chapter 9 Contents to see:
- Screen 9.4 for exercises on **hybrid orbitals**
- Screen 9.5 for a tutorial on **sigma bonding**
- Screen 9.6 for a tutorial on **determining hybrid orbitals**

■ **Hybridization and Geometry**
Hybridization reconciles the electron-pair geometry with the orbital overlap criterion of bonding. A statement such as "the atom is tetrahedral because it is *sp³* hybridized" is backward. That the electron-pair geometry around the atom is tetrahedral is a fact. Hybridization is one way to rationalize that fact.

■ **EXAMPLE 9.1 Valence Bond Description of Bonding in Ethane**

Problem Describe the bonding in ethane, C₂H₆, using valence bond theory.

Strategy First, draw the Lewis structure, and predict the electron-pair geometry at both carbon atoms. Next, assign a hybridization to these atoms. Finally, describe covalent bonds that arise based on orbital overlap, and place electron pairs in their proper locations.

Solution Each carbon atom has an octet configuration, sharing electron pairs with three hydrogen atoms and with the other carbon atom. The electron pairs around carbon have tetrahedral geometry, so carbon is assigned *sp³* hybridization. The C—C bond is formed by overlap of *sp³* orbitals on each C atom, and each of the C—H bonds is formed by overlap of an *sp³* orbital on carbon with a hydrogen 1*s* orbital.

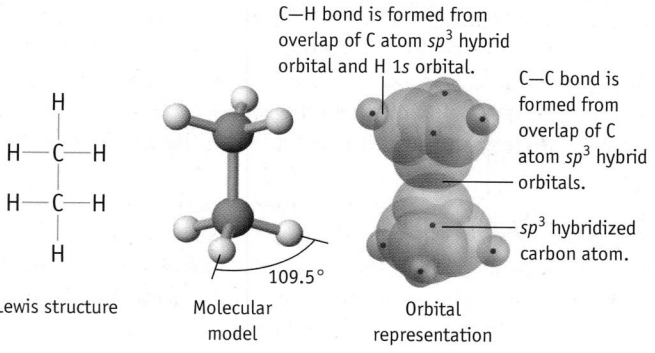

C—H bond is formed from overlap of C atom *sp³* hybrid orbital and H 1*s* orbital.

C—C bond is formed from overlap of C atom *sp³* hybrid orbitals.

sp³ hybridized carbon atom.

Lewis structure   Molecular model   Orbital representation

109.5°

EXAMPLE 9.2 Valence Bond Description of Bonding in Methanol

Problem Describe the bonding in the methanol molecule, CH_3OH, using valence bond theory.

Strategy First, construct the Lewis structure for the molecule. The electron pair geometry around each atom determines the hybrid orbital set used by that atom.

Solution The electron-pair geometry around both the C and O atoms in CH_3OH is tetrahedral. Thus, we may assign sp^3 hybridization to each atom, and the C—O bond is formed by overlap of sp^3 orbitals on these atoms. Each C—H bond is formed by overlap of a carbon sp^3 orbital with a hydrogen 1s orbital, and the O—H bond is formed by overlap of an oxygen sp^3 orbital with the hydrogen 1s orbital. Two lone pairs on oxygen occupy the remaining sp^3 orbitals on the atom.

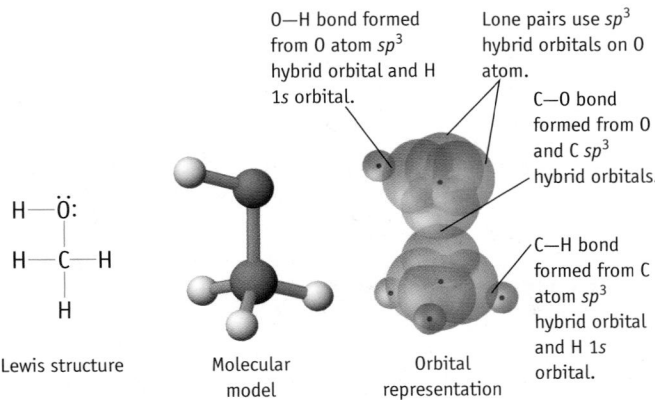

O—H bond formed from O atom sp^3 hybrid orbital and H 1s orbital.

Lone pairs use sp^3 hybrid orbitals on O atom.

C—O bond formed from O and C sp^3 hybrid orbitals.

C—H bond formed from C atom sp^3 hybrid orbital and H 1s orbital.

Lewis structure   Molecular model   Orbital representation

Comment Notice that one end of the CH_3OH molecule (the CH_3 or methyl group) is just like the CH_3 group in the methane molecule, and the OH group resembles the OH group in water. It is helpful to recognize pieces of molecules and their bonding descriptions.

This example also shows how to predict the structure and bonding in a complicated molecule by looking at each atom separately. This is an important principle that is essential when dealing with molecules made up of many atoms.

EXERCISE 9.1 Valence Bond Description of Bonding

Use valence bond theory to describe the bonding in the hydronium ion, H_3O^+, and methylamine, CH_3NH_2.

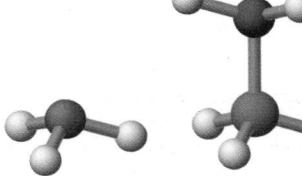

Hydronium ion, H_3O^+ Methylamine, CH_3NH_2

Hybrid Orbitals for Molecules and Ions with Trigonal-Planar Electron Pair Geometries

The central atoms in species such as BF_3, O_3, NO_3^-, and CO_3^{2-} all have a trigonal-planar electron-pair geometry, which requires a central atom with three hybrid orbitals in a plane, 120° apart. Three hybrid orbitals mean three atomic orbitals must be combined, and the combination of an s orbital with two p orbitals is appropriate (Figure 9.8). If p_x and p_y orbitals are used in hybrid orbital formation, the three hybrid sp^2 orbitals will lie in the xy-plane. The p_z orbital not used to form these hybrid orbitals is perpendicular to the plane containing the three sp^2 orbitals (Figure 9.8).

Boron trifluoride has a trigonal-planar electron-pair and molecular geometry. Each boron–fluorine bond in this compound results from overlap of an sp^2 orbital on boron with a p orbital on fluorine. Notice that the p_z orbital on boron, which is not used to form the sp^2 hybrid orbitals, is not occupied by electrons.

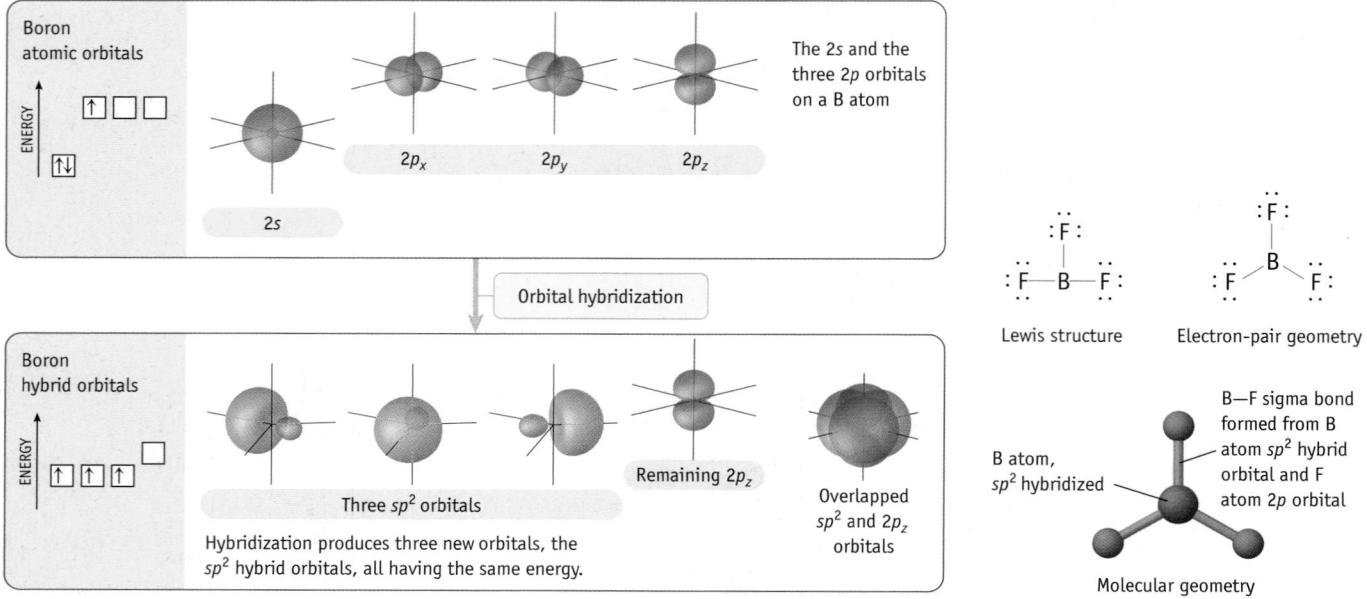

FIGURE 9.8 **Bonding in a trigonal-planar molecule.**

Hybrid Orbitals for Molecules and Ions with Linear Electron-Pair Geometries

For molecules in which the central atom has a linear electron-pair geometry, two hybrid orbitals, 180° apart, are required. One s and one p orbital can be hybridized to form two sp hybrid orbitals (Figure 9.9). If the p_z orbital is used, then the sp orbitals are oriented along the z-axis. The p_x and p_y orbitals are perpendicular to this axis.

Beryllium dichloride, $BeCl_2$, is a solid under ordinary conditions. When it is heated to over 520 °C, however, it vaporizes to give $BeCl_2$ vapor. In the gas phase, $BeCl_2$ is a linear molecule, so sp hybridization is appropriate for the beryllium atom in this species. Combining beryllium's $2s$ and $2p_z$ orbitals gives the two sp hybrid orbitals that lie along the z-axis. Each Be—Cl bond arises by overlap of an sp hybrid orbital on beryllium with a $3p$ orbital on chlorine. In this molecule, there are only two electron pairs around the beryllium atom, so the p_x and p_y orbitals are not occupied (Figure 9.9).

Hybrid Orbitals for Molecules and Ions with Trigonal-Bipyramidal or Octahedral Electron-Pair Geometries

Bonding in compounds having five or six electron pairs on a central atom (such as PF_5 or SF_6) requires the atom to have five or six hybrid orbitals, which must be created from five or six atomic orbitals. This is possible if additional atomic orbitals from the d subshell are used in hybrid orbital formation. The d orbitals are considered to be valence shell orbitals for main group elements of the third and higher periods.

To accommodate six electron pairs in the valence shell of an element, six sp^3d^2 hybrid orbitals can be created from one s, three p, and two d orbitals. The six sp^3d^2 hybrid orbitals are directed to the corners of an octahedron (Figure 9.5). Thus, they are oriented to accommodate the valence electron pairs for a compound that has an octahedral electron-pair geometry. Five coordination and trigonal-bipyramidal electron-pair geometry are matched to sp^3d hybridization. One s, three p, and one d orbital combine to produce five sp^3d hybrid orbitals.

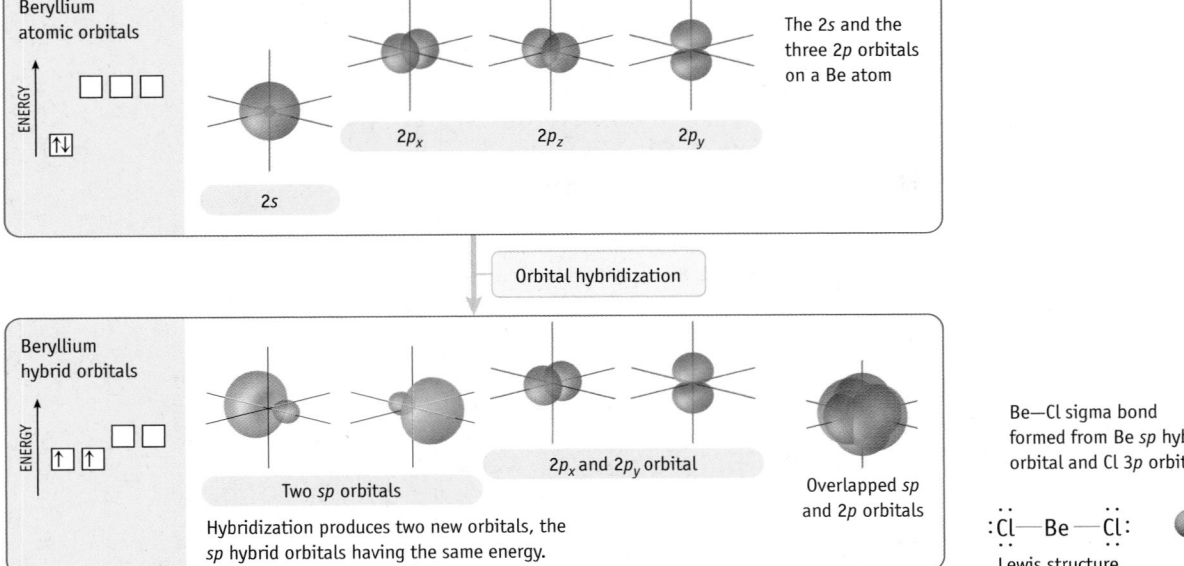

FIGURE 9.9 Bonding in a linear molecule. Because only one *p* orbital is incorporated in the hybrid orbital, two *p* orbitals remain unhybridized. These orbitals are perpendicular to each other and to the axis along which the two *sp* hybrid orbital lies.

EXAMPLE 9.3 Hybridization Involving *d* Orbitals

Problem Describe the bonding in PF_5 using valence bond theory.

Strategy The first step is to establish the electron-pair and molecular geometry of PF_5. The electron-pair geometry around the P atom gives the number of hybrid orbitals required. If five hybrid orbitals are required, the combination of atomic orbitals is sp^3d.

Solution Here, the P atom is surrounded by five electron pairs, so PF_5 has a trigonal-bipyramidal electron-pair and molecular geometry. The hybridization scheme is therefore sp^3d.

■ **Do $(n − 1)d$ orbitals participate in bonding?** Because the $(n − 1)d$ orbitals are at a relatively high energy their involvement in bonding is believed to be minimal. Using molecular orbital theory, it is possible to describe the bonding in compounds with expanded octets without using *d* orbitals to form hybrid orbital sets.

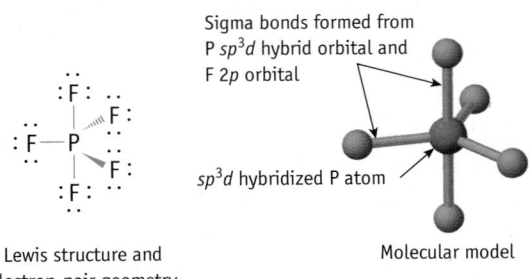

Sigma bonds formed from
P sp^3d hybrid orbital and
F 2*p* orbital

sp^3d hybridized P atom

Lewis structure and
electron-pair geometry

Molecular model

EXAMPLE 9.4 Recognizing Hybridization

Problem Identify the hybridization of the central atom in the following compounds and ions:

(a) SF_3^+ **(c)** SF_4 **(b)** SO_4^{2-} **(d)** I_3^-

Strategy The hybrid orbitals used by a central atom are determined by the electron-pair geometry (see Figure 9.5). Thus, to answer this question first write the Lewis structure, and then predict the electron-pair geometry.

Solution The Lewis structures for SF_3^+, and SO_4^{2-} are written as follows:

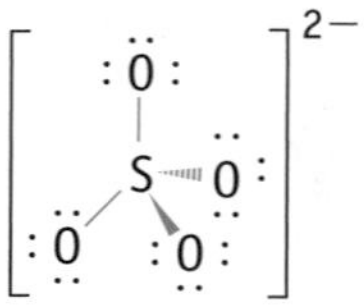

Four electron pairs surround the central atom in each of these ions, and the electron-pair geometry for these atoms is tetrahedral. Thus, *sp³ hybridization* for the central atom is used to describe the bonding. For SF_4 and I_3^-, five pairs of electrons are in the valence shell of the central atom. For these, *sp³d hybridization* is appropriate for the central S or I atom.

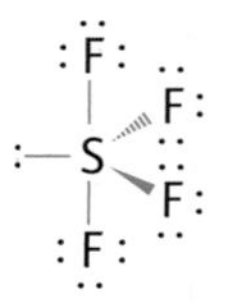

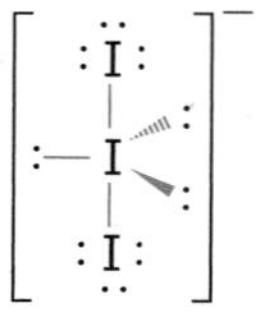

EXERCISE 9.2 Recognizing Hybridization

Identify the hybridization of the underlined central atom in the following compounds and ions:

(a) $\underline{B}H_4^-$ (d) $\underline{Cl}F_3$

(b) $\underline{S}F_5^-$ (e) $\underline{B}Cl_3$

(c) $OS\underline{F}_4$ (f) $\underline{Xe}O_6^{4-}$

Multiple Bonds

■ **Multiple Bonds**

C=C

Double bond requires two sets of overlapping orbitals and two pairs of electrons.

C≡C

Triple bond requires three sets of overlapping orbitals and three pairs of electrons.

According to valence bond theory, bond formation requires that two orbitals on adjacent atoms overlap. Many molecules have two or three bonds between pairs of atoms. Therefore, according to valence bond theory, a double bond requires *two* sets of overlapping orbitals and *two* electron pairs. For a triple bond, *three* sets of atomic orbitals are required, each set accommodating a pair of electrons.

Double Bonds

Consider ethylene, $H_2C=CH_2$, a common molecule with a double bond. The molecular structure of ethylene places all six atoms in a plane, with H—C—H and H—C—C angles of approximately 120°. Each carbon atom has trigonal-planar geometry, so *sp²* hybridization is assumed for these atoms. Thus, a description of bonding in ethylene starts with each carbon atom having three *sp²* hybrid orbitals in the molecular plane and an unhybridized *p* orbital perpendicular to that plane. Because each carbon atom is involved in four bonds, a single unpaired electron is placed in each of these orbitals.

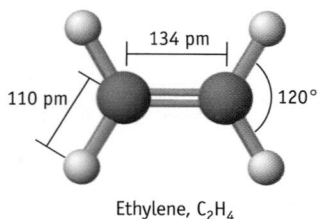

110 pm   134 pm   120°

Ethylene, C_2H_4

 Unhybridized *p* orbital. Used for π bonding in C_2H_4.

 Three *sp²* hybrid orbitals. Used for C—H and C—C σ bonding in C_2H_4.

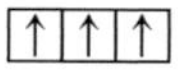

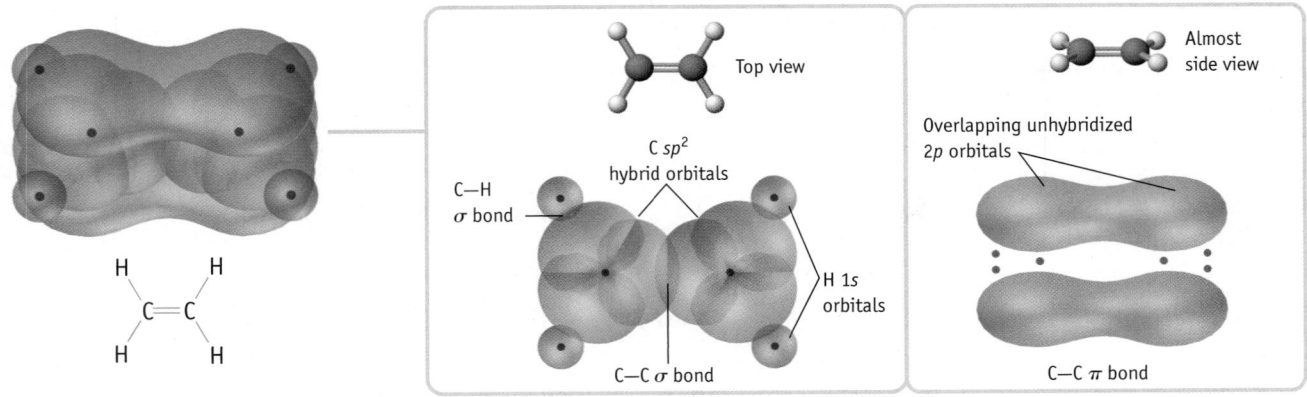

(a) Lewis structure and bonding of ethylene, C_2H_4.

(b) The C—H σ bonds are formed by overlap of C atom sp^2 hybrid orbitals with H atom $1s$ orbitals. The σ bond between C atoms arises from overlap of sp^2 orbitals.

(c) The carbon–carbon π bond is formed by overlap of an unhybridized $2p$ orbital on each atom. Note the lack of electron density along the C—C bond axis from this bond.

Active Figure 9.10 The valence bond model of bonding in ethylene, C_2H_4. Each C atom is assumed to be sp^2 hybridized.

Chemistry Now™ Sign in at www.cengage.com/login and go to the Chapter Contents menu to explore an interactive version of this figure accompanied by an exercise.

Now we can visualize the C—H bonds, which arise from overlap of sp^2 orbitals on carbon with hydrogen $1s$ orbitals. After accounting for the C—H bonds, one sp^2 orbital on each carbon atom remains. These orbitals point toward each other and overlap to form one of the bonds linking the carbon atoms (Figure 9.10). This leaves only one other orbital unaccounted for on each carbon, an unhybridized p orbital, and it is these orbitals that can be used to create the second bond between carbon atoms in C_2H_4. If they are aligned correctly, the unhybridized p orbitals on the two carbons can overlap, allowing the electrons in these orbitals to be paired. The overlap does not occur directly along the C—C axis, however. Instead, the arrangement compels these orbitals to overlap sideways, and the electron pair occupies an orbital with electron density above and below the plane containing the six atoms.

This description results in two types of bonds in C_2H_4. One type is the C—H and C—C bonds that arise from the overlap of atomic orbitals so that the bonding electrons that lie along the bond axes form sigma (σ) bonds. The other is the bond formed by sideways overlap of p atomic orbitals, called a **pi (π) bond.** In a π bond, the overlap region is above and below the internuclear axis, and the electron density of the π bond is above and below the bond axis.

Be sure to notice that a π bond can form *only* if (a) there are unhybridized p orbitals on adjacent atoms and (b) the p orbitals are perpendicular to the plane of the molecule and parallel to one another. This happens only if the sp^2 orbitals of both carbon atoms are in the same plane. A consequence of this is that both atoms involved in the π bond have trigonal-planar geometry, and the six atoms in and around the π bond (the two atoms involved in the π bond and the four atoms attached to the π-bonded atoms) lie in one plane.

Double bonds between carbon and oxygen, sulfur, or nitrogen are quite common. Consider formaldehyde, CH_2O, in which a carbon–oxygen π bond occurs

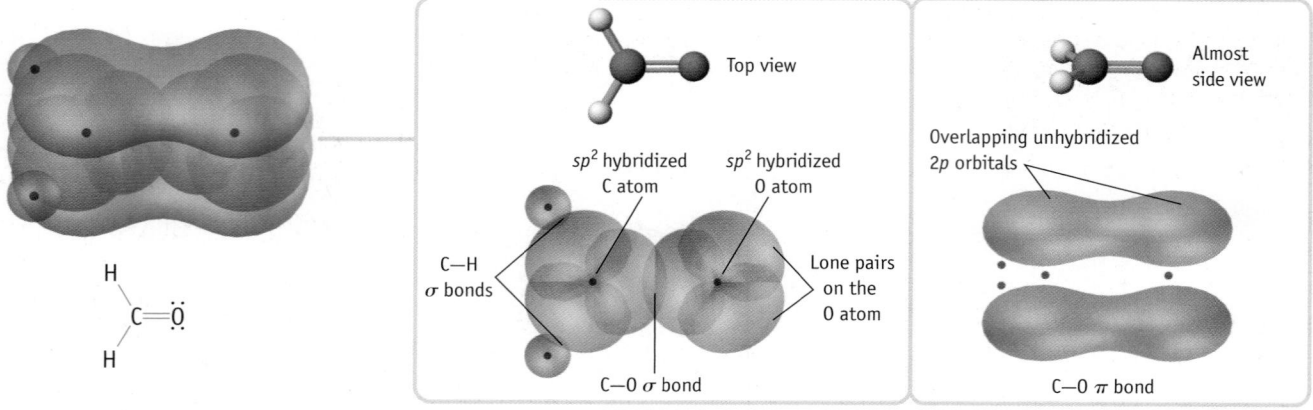

(a) Lewis structure and bonding of formaldehyde, CH_2O.

(b) The C—H σ bonds are formed by overlap of C atom sp^2 hybrid orbitals with H atom $1s$ orbitals. The σ bond between C and O atoms arises from overlap of sp^2 orbitals.

(c) The C—O π bond comes from the side-by-side overlap of p orbitals on the two atoms.

FIGURE 9.11 Valence bond description of bonding in formaldehyde, CH_2O.

■ **Alternative View of the C—O π Bond in CH₂O** An alternative but still satisfactory explanation of the C—O π bond is to assume the O atom is unhybridized and that the π bond is constructed from an unhybridized $2p$ oxygen orbital overlapping with a p orbital on the carbon atom.

(Figure 9.11). A trigonal-planar electron-pair geometry indicates sp^2 hybridization for the C atom. The σ bonds from carbon to the O atom and the two H atoms form by overlap of sp^2 hybrid orbitals with half-filled orbitals from the oxygen and two hydrogen atoms. An unhybridized p orbital on carbon is oriented perpendicular to the molecular plane (just as for the carbon atoms of C_2H_4). This p orbital is available for π bonding, this time with an oxygen orbital.

What orbitals on oxygen are used in this model? The approach in Figure 9.11 assumes sp^2 hybridization for oxygen. This uses one O atom sp^2 orbital in σ bond formation, leaving two sp^2 orbitals to accommodate lone pairs. The remaining p orbital on the O atom participates in the π bond.

Chemistry ⚛ Now™

Sign in at **www.cengage.com/login** and go to Chapter 9 Contents menu to see Screen 9.7 for exercises and a tutorial on **hybrid orbitals and σ and π bonding**.

■ **EXAMPLE 9.5 Bonding in Acetic Acid**

Problem Using valence bond theory, describe the bonding in acetic acid, CH_3CO_2H, the important ingredient in vinegar.

Strategy Write a Lewis electron dot structure, and determine the geometry around each atom using VSEPR theory. Use this geometry to decide on the hybrid orbitals used in σ bonding. If unhybridized p orbitals are available on adjacent C and O atoms, then C—O π bonding can occur.

Solution The carbon atom of the CH_3 group has tetrahedral electron-pair geometry, which means it is sp^3 hybridized. Three sp^3 orbitals are used to form the C—H bonds. The fourth sp^3 orbital is used to bond to the adjacent carbon atom. This carbon atom has a trigonal-planar electron-pair geometry; it must be sp^2 hybridized. The C—C bond is formed using one of these hybrid orbitals, and the other two sp^2 orbitals are used to form the σ bonds to the two oxygens. The oxygen of the O—H group has four electron pairs; it must be tetrahedral and sp^3 hybridized. Thus, this O atom uses two sp^3 orbitals to bond to the adjacent carbon and the hydrogen, and two sp^3 orbitals accommodate the two lone pairs.

Finally, the carbon–oxygen double bond can be described by assuming the C and O atoms are both sp^2 hybridized (like the C—O π bond in formaldehyde, Figure 9.11). The unhybridized p orbital remaining on each atom is used to form the carbon–oxygen π bond, and the lone pairs on the O atom are accommodated in sp^2 hybrid orbitals.

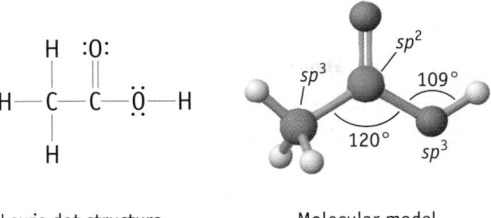

Lewis dot structure   Molecular model

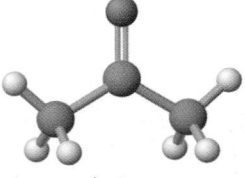

Acetone

EXERCISE 9.3 Bonding in Acetone

Use valence bond theory to describe the bonding in acetone, CH_3COCH_3.

Triple Bonds

Acetylene, H—C≡C—H, is an example of a molecule with a triple bond. VSEPR theory predicts that the four atoms lie in a straight line with H—C—C angles of 180°. This implies that the carbon atom is sp hybridized (Figure 9.12). For each carbon atom, there are two sp orbitals, one directed toward hydrogen and used to create the C—H σ bond, and the second directed toward the other carbon and used to create a σ bond between the two carbon atoms. Two unhybridized p orbitals remain on each carbon, and they are oriented so that it is possible to form *two* π bonds in HC≡CH.

⟦↑|↑⟧ Two unhybridized p orbitals. Used for π bonding in C_2H_2.

⟦↑|↑⟧ Two sp hybrid orbitals. Used for C—H and C—C σ bonding in C_2H_2.

These π bonds are perpendicular to the molecular axis and perpendicular to each other. Three electrons on each carbon atom are paired to form the triple bond consisting of a σ bond and two π bonds (Figure 9.12).

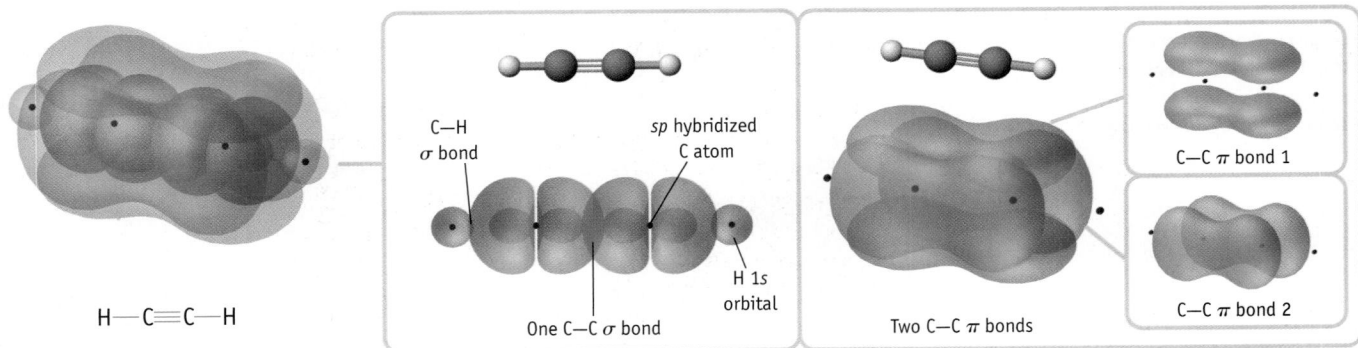

H—C≡C—H

FIGURE 9.12 Bonding in acetylene.

Now that we have examined two cases of multiple bonds, let us summarize several important points:

- In valence bond theory a double bond always consists of a σ bond and a π bond. Similarly, a triple bond always consists of a σ bond and *two* π bonds.
- A π bond may form only if unhybridized p orbitals remain on the bonded atoms.
- If a Lewis structure shows multiple bonds, the atoms involved must therefore be either sp^2 or sp hybridized. Only in this manner will unhybridized p orbitals be available to form a π bond.

EXERCISE 9.4 Triple Bonds Between Atoms

Describe the bonding in a nitrogen molecule, N_2.

EXERCISE 9.5 Bonding and Hybridization

Estimate values for the H—C—H, H—C—C, and C—C—N angles in acetonitrile, $CH_3C\equiv N$. Indicate the hybridization of both carbon atoms and the nitrogen atom, and analyze the bonding using valence bond theory.

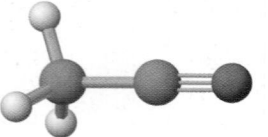

Acetonitrile, CH_3CN

Cis-Trans Isomerism: A Consequence of π Bonding

Ethylene, C_2H_4, is a planar molecule, a geometry that allows the unhybridized p orbitals on the two carbon atoms to line up and form a π bond (see Figure 9.13b). Let us speculate on what would happen if one end of the ethylene molecule were twisted relative to the other end. This action would distort the molecule away from planarity, and the p orbitals would rotate out of alignment. Rotation would diminish the extent of overlap of these orbitals, and, if a twist of 90° were achieved, the two p orbitals would no longer overlap at all; the π bond would be broken. However, so much energy is required to break this bond (about 260 kJ/mol) that rotation around a C=C bond is not expected to occur at room temperature.

Active Figure 9.13 Rotation around bonds.

Chemistry.Now™ Sign in at www.cengage.com/login and go to the Chapter Contents menu to explore an interactive version of this figure accompanied by an exercise.

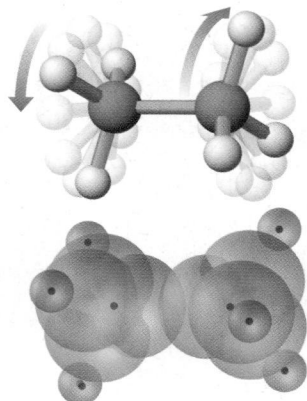

(a) In ethane nearly free rotation can occur around the axis of a single (σ) bond.

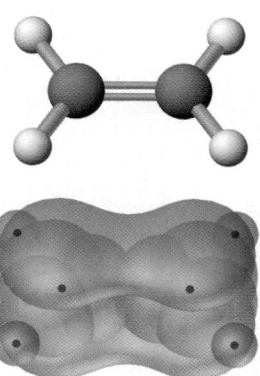

(b) Ethylene rotation is severely restricted around double bonds because doing so would break the π bond, a process generally requiring a great deal of energy.

A consequence of restricted rotation is that isomers occur for many compounds containing a C=C bond. **Isomers** are compounds that have the same formula but different structures. In this case, the two isomeric compounds differ with respect to the orientation of the groups attached to the carbons of the double bond. Two isomers of $C_2H_2Cl_2$ are *cis*- and *trans*-1,2-dichloroethylene. Their structures resemble ethylene, except that two hydrogen atoms have been replaced by chlorine atoms. Because a large amount of energy is required to break the π bond, the *cis* compound cannot rearrange to the *trans* compound under ordinary conditions. Each compound can be obtained separately, and each has its own identity. *Cis*-1,2-dichloroethylene boils at 60.3 °C, whereas *trans*-1,2-dichloroethylene boils at 47.5 °C.

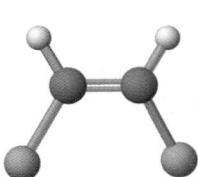

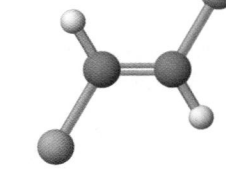

cis-1,2-dichloroethylene   trans-1,2-dichloroethylene

■ *Cis* and *Trans* Isomers Compounds having the same formula, but different structures, are isomers. *Trans* isomers have distinguishing groups on opposite sides of a double bond. *Cis* isomers have these groups on the same side of the double bond.

Although *cis* and *trans* isomers do not interconvert at ordinary temperatures, they will do so at higher temperatures. If the temperature is sufficiently high, the molecular motions can become sufficiently energetic that rotation around the C=C bond can occur. This may also occur under other special conditions, such as when the molecule absorbs light energy.

Chemistry Now™

Sign in at **www.cengage.com/login** and go to Chapter 9 Contents to see Screen 9.8 for an exercise on **isomers and multiple bonds**.

Benzene: A Special Case of π Bonding

Benzene, C_6H_6, is the simplest member of a large group of substances known as *aromatic* compounds, a historical reference to their odor. It occupies a pivotal place in the history and practice of chemistry.

To 19th-century chemists, benzene was a perplexing substance with an unknown structure. Based on its chemical reactions, however, August Kekulé (1829–1896) suggested that the molecule has a planar, symmetrical ring structure. We know now he was correct. The ring is flat, and all the carbon–carbon bonds are the same length, 139 pm, a distance intermediate between the average single bond (154 pm) and double bond (134 pm) lengths. Assuming the molecule has two resonance structures with alternating double bonds, the observed structure is rationalized. The C—C bond order in C_6H_6(1.5) is the average of a single and a double bond.

resonance structures   resonance hybrid

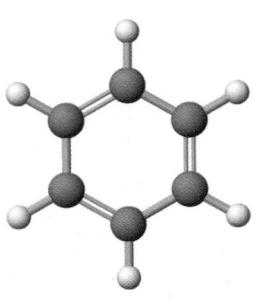

Benzene, C_6H_6

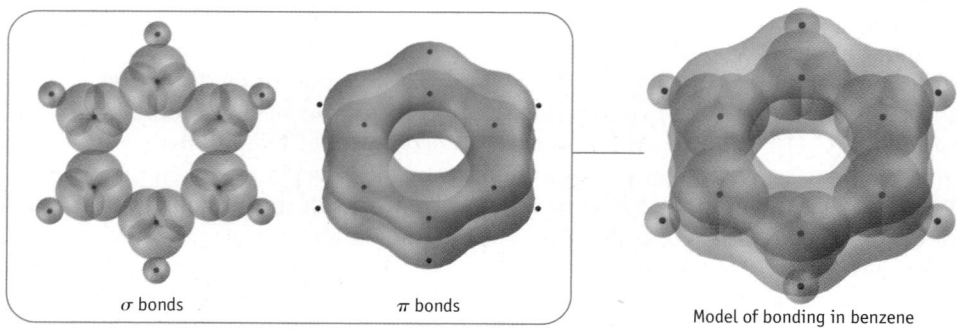

FIGURE 9.14 Bonding in benzene, C_6H_6. (left) The C atoms of the ring are bonded to each other through σ bonds using C atom sp^2 hybrid orbitals. The C—H bonds also use C atom sp^2 hybrid orbitals. The π framework of the molecule arises from overlap of C atom p orbitals not used in hybrid orbital formation. Because these orbitals are perpendicular to the ring, π electron density is above and below the plane of the ring. (right) A composite of σ and π bonding in benzene.

σ bonds π bonds

σ and π bonding in benzene

Model of bonding in benzene

Understanding the bonding in benzene (Figure 9.14) is important because the benzene ring structure occurs in an enormous number of chemical compounds. We assume that the trigonal-planar carbon atoms have sp^2 hybridization. Each C—H bond is formed by overlap of an sp^2 orbital of a carbon atom with a $1s$ orbital of hydrogen, and the C—C σ bonds arise by overlap of sp^2 orbitals on adjacent carbon atoms. After accounting for the σ bonding, an unhybridized p orbital remains on each C atom, and each is occupied by a single electron. These six orbitals and six electrons form π bonds. Because all carbon–carbon bond lengths are the same, each p orbital overlaps equally well with the p orbitals of both adjacent carbons, and the π interaction is unbroken around the six-member ring.

9.3 Molecular Orbital Theory

Molecular orbital (MO) theory is an alternative way to view orbitals in molecules. In contrast to the localized bond and lone pair electrons of valence bond theory, MO theory assumes that pure s and p atomic orbitals of the atoms in the molecule combine to produce orbitals that are spread out, or delocalized, over several atoms or even over an entire molecule. These orbitals are called **molecular orbitals.**

One reason for learning about the MO concept is that it correctly predicts the electronic structures of molecules such as O_2 that do not follow the electron-pairing assumptions of the Lewis approach. The rules of Section 8.2 would guide you to draw the electron dot structure of O_2 with all the electrons paired, which fails to explain its paramagnetism (Figure 9.15). The molecular orbital approach can account for this property, but valence bond theory cannot. To see how MO theory can be used to describe the bonding in O_2 and other diatomic molecules, we shall first describe four principles used to develop the theory.

Principles of Molecular Orbital Theory

In MO theory, we begin with a given arrangement of atoms in the molecule at the known bond distances. We then determine the *sets* of molecular orbitals. One way to do this is to combine available valence orbitals on all the constituent atoms. These molecular orbitals more or less encompass all the atoms of the molecule, and the valence electrons for all the atoms in the molecule are assigned to the molecular orbitals. Just as with orbitals in atoms, electrons are assigned in order of increasing orbital energy and according to the Pauli principle and Hund's rule (see Sections 7.1 and 7.3).

The **first principle of molecular orbital theory** is that *the total number of molecular orbitals is always equal to the total number of atomic orbitals contributed by the atoms that*

(a) Making liquid O_2

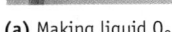

(c) Paramagnetic liquid O_2 clings to a magnet.

(b) Liquid O_2 is a light blue color.

(d) Diamagnetic liquid N_2 is not attracted to a magnet.

FIGURE 9.15 The paramagnetism of liquid oxygen. Oxygen gas condenses (a) to a pale blue liquid at $-183\ °C$ (b). Because O_2 molecules have two unpaired electrons, oxygen in the liquid state is paramagnetic and clings a relatively strong neodymium magnet (c). In contrast, liquid N_2 is diamagnetic and does not stick to the magnet (d). It just splashes on the surface when poured onto the magnet.

have combined. To illustrate this orbital conservation principle, let us consider the H_2 molecule.

Molecular Orbitals for H_2

Molecular orbital theory specifies that when the $1s$ orbitals of two hydrogen atoms overlap, *two* molecular orbitals result. One molecular orbital results from *addition* of the $1s$ atomic orbital wave functions, leading to an increased probability that electrons will reside in the bond region between the two nuclei (Figure 9.16). This is called a **bonding molecular orbital.** It is also a σ orbital because the region of electron probability lies directly along the bond axis. This molecular orbital is labeled σ_{1s}, the subscript $1s$ indicating that $1s$ atomic orbitals were used to create the molecular orbital.

The other molecular orbital is constructed by *subtracting* one atomic orbital wave function from the other (see Figure 9.16). When this happens, the probability of finding an electron between the nuclei in the molecular orbital is reduced, and the probability of finding the electron in other regions is higher. Without significant electron density between them, the nuclei repel one another. This type of orbital is called an **antibonding molecular orbital.** Because it is also a σ orbital, it is labeled σ^*_{1s}. The asterisk signifies that it is antibonding. *Antibonding orbitals have no counterpart in valence bond theory.*

A **second principle of molecular orbital theory** is that *the bonding molecular orbital is lower in energy than the parent orbitals, and the antibonding orbital is higher in energy* (Figure 9.16). This means that the energy of a group of atoms is lower than the energy of the separated atoms when electrons are assigned to bonding molecular orbitals. Chemists say the system is "stabilized" by chemical bond formation.

■ **Orbitals and Electron Waves** Orbitals are characterized as electron waves; therefore, a way to view molecular orbital formation is to assume that two electron waves, one from each atom, interfere with each other. The interference can be constructive, giving a bonding MO, or destructive, giving an antibonding MO.

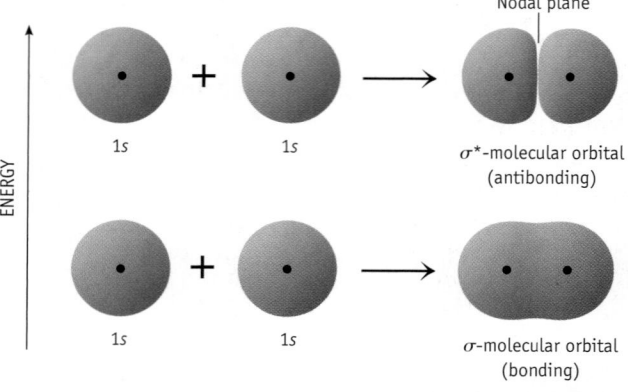

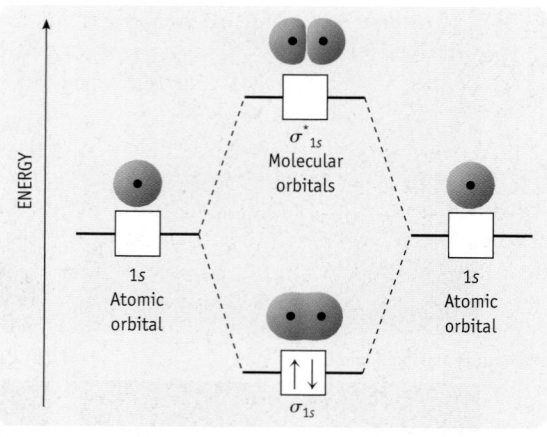

Nodal plane

1s $\quad + \quad$ 1s $\quad \longrightarrow \quad$ σ^*-molecular orbital (antibonding)

1s $\quad + \quad$ 1s $\quad \longrightarrow \quad$ σ-molecular orbital (bonding)

ENERGY

(a)

σ^*_{1s}
Molecular orbitals

1s
Atomic orbital

1s
Atomic orbital

σ_{1s}

ENERGY

(b)

FIGURE 9.16 Molecular orbitals. (a) Bonding and antibonding σ molecular orbitals are formed from two 1s atomic orbitals on adjacent atoms. Notice the presence of a node in the antibonding orbital. (The node is a plane on which there is zero probability of finding an electron.) (b) A molecular orbital diagram for H_2. The two electrons are placed in the σ_{1s} orbital, the molecular orbital lower in energy.

Sign in at **www.cengage.com/login** and go to Chapter 9 Contents to see Screen 9.11 for an animated version of this figure.

Conversely, the system is "destabilized" when electrons are assigned to antibonding orbitals because the energy of the system is higher than that of the atoms themselves.

A **third principle of molecular orbital theory** is that the *electrons of the molecule are assigned to orbitals of successively higher energy* according to the Pauli exclusion principle and Hund's rule. This is analogous to the procedure for building up electronic structures of atoms. Thus, electrons occupy the lowest energy orbitals available, and when two electrons are assigned to an orbital, their spins must be paired. Because the energy of the electrons in the bonding orbital of H_2 is lower than that of either parent 1s electron (see Figure 9.16b), the H_2 molecule is more stable than two separate H atoms. We write the electron configuration of H_2 as $(\sigma_{1s})^2$.

What would happen if we tried to combine two helium atoms to form dihelium, He_2? Both He atoms have a 1s valence orbital that can produce the same kind of molecular orbitals as in H_2. Unlike H_2, however, four electrons need to be assigned to these orbitals (Figure 9.17). The pair of electrons in the σ_{1s} orbital stabilizes He_2. The two electrons in σ^*_{1s}, however, destabilize the He_2 molecule. The energy decrease from the electrons in the σ_{1s}-bonding molecular orbital is offset by the energy increase due to the electrons in the σ^*_{1s}-antibonding molecular orbital. Thus, molecular orbital theory predicts that He_2 has no net stability; two He atoms have no tendency to combine. This confirms what we already know, that elemental helium exists in the form of single atoms and not as a diatomic molecule.

Bond Order

Bond order was defined in Section 8.9 as the net number of bonding electron pairs linking a pair of atoms. This same concept can be applied directly to molecular orbital theory, but now bond order is defined as

Bond order = 1/2 (number of electrons in bonding MOs − number of electrons in antibonding MOs) $\quad$ (9.1)

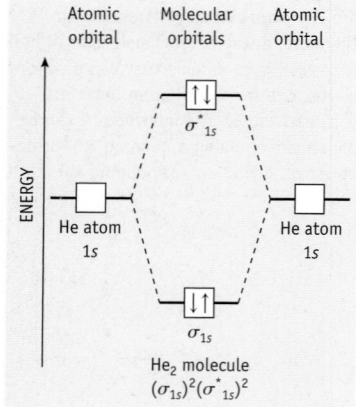

Atomic orbital $\quad$ Molecular orbitals $\quad$ Atomic orbital

σ^*_{1s}

He atom 1s $\qquad$ He atom 1s

σ_{1s}

He_2 molecule $(\sigma_{1s})^2(\sigma^*_{1s})^2$

ENERGY

FIGURE 9.17 A molecular orbital energy level diagram for the dihelium molecule, He_2. This diagram provides a rationalization for the nonexistence of the molecule. In He_2, both the bonding (σ_{1s}) and antibonding orbitals (σ^*_{1s}) would be fully occupied.

In the H_2 molecule, there are two electrons in a bonding orbital and none in an antibonding orbital, so H_2 has a bond order of 1. In contrast, in He_2 the stabilizing effect of the σ_{1s} pair is canceled by the destabilizing effect of the σ^*_{1s} pair, and so the bond order is 0.

Fractional bond orders are possible. Consider the ion He_2^+. Its molecular orbital electron configuration is $(\sigma_{1s})^2(\sigma^*_{1s})^1$. In this ion, there are two electrons in a bonding molecular orbital, but only one in an antibonding orbital. MO theory predicts that He_2^+ should have a bond order of 0.5; that is, a weak bond should exist between helium atoms in such a species. Interestingly, this ion has been identified in the gas phase using special experimental techniques.

Chemistry • Now™

Sign in at **www.cengage.com/login** and go to Chapter 9 Contents to see:
- Screen 9.9 for exercises on **molecular orbital theory**
- Screen 9.10 for a description of **molecular electron configurations**

■ EXAMPLE 9.6 Molecular Orbitals and Bond Order

Problem Write the electron configuration of the H_2^- ion in molecular orbital terms. What is the bond order of the ion?

Strategy Count the number of valence electrons in the ion, and then place those electrons in the MO diagram for the H_2 molecule. Find the bond order from Equation 9.1.

Solution This ion has three electrons (one each from the H atoms plus one for the negative charge). Therefore, its electronic configuration is $(\sigma_{1s})^2(\sigma^*_{1s})^1$, identical with the configuration for He_2^+. This means H_2^- also has a net bond order of 0.5. The H_2^- ion is thus predicted to exist under special circumstances.

EXERCISE 9.6 Molecular Orbitals and Bond Order

What is the electron configuration of the H_2^+ ion? Compare the bond order of this ion with He_2^+ and H_2^-. Do you expect H_2^+ to exist?

Molecular Orbitals of Li₂ and Be₂

A **fourth principle of molecular orbital theory** is that *atomic orbitals combine to form molecular orbitals most effectively when the atomic orbitals are of similar energy.* This principle becomes important when we move past He_2 to Li_2, dilithium, and heavier molecules such as O_2 and N_2.

A lithium atom has electrons in two orbitals of the s type ($1s$ and $2s$), so a $1s \pm 2s$ combination is theoretically possible. Because the $1s$ and $2s$ orbitals are quite different in energy, however, this interaction can be disregarded. Thus, the molecular orbitals come only from $1s \pm 1s$ and $2s \pm 2s$ combinations (Figure 9.18). This means the molecular orbital electron configuration of dilithium, Li_2, is

$$\text{Li}_2 \text{ MO Configuration:} \qquad (\sigma_{1s})^2(\sigma^*_{1s})^2(\sigma_{2s})^2$$

The bonding effect of the σ_{1s} electrons is canceled by the antibonding effect of the σ^*_{1s} electrons, so these pairs make no net contribution to bonding in Li_2. Bonding in Li_2 is due to the electron pair assigned to the σ_{2s} orbital, and the bond order is 1.

The fact that the σ_{1s} and σ^*_{1s} electron pairs of Li_2 make no net contribution to bonding is exactly what you observed in drawing electron dot structures in

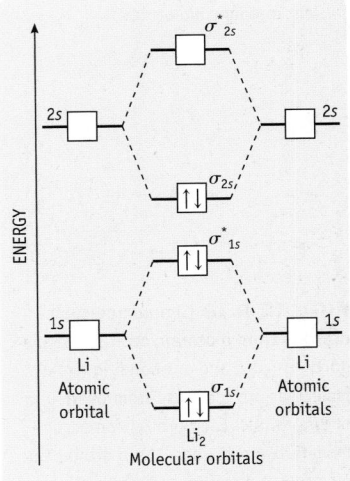

FIGURE 9.18 Energy level diagram for the combination of two Li atoms with 1s and 2s atomic orbitals. Notice that the molecular orbitals are created by combining orbitals of similar energies. The electron configuration is shown for Li₂.

Section 8.2: *core electrons are ignored*. In molecular orbital terms, core electrons are assigned to bonding and antibonding molecular orbitals that offset one another.

A diberyllium molecule, Be$_2$, is not expected to exist. Its electron configuration is

$$\text{Be}_2 \text{ MO Configuration:} \qquad \text{[core electrons]}(\sigma_{2s})^2(\sigma^*_{2s})^2$$

The effects of σ_{2s} and σ^*_{2s} electrons cancel, and there is no net bonding. The bond order is 0, so the molecule does not exist.

EXAMPLE 9.7 Molecular Orbitals in Diatomic Molecules

Problem Be$_2$ does not exist. But what about the Be$_2^+$ ion? Describe its electron configuration in molecular orbital terms, and give the net bond order. Do you expect the ion to exist?

Strategy Count the number of electrons in the ion, and place them in the MO diagram in Figure 9.18. Write the electron configuration, and calculate the bond order from Equation 9.1.

Solution The Be$_2^+$ ion has only seven electrons (in contrast to eight for Be$_2$), of which four are core electrons. (The core electrons are assigned to σ_{1s} and σ^*_{1s} molecular orbitals.) The remaining three electrons are assigned to the σ_{2s} and σ^*_{2s} molecular orbitals, so the MO electron configuration is [core electrons]$(\sigma_{2s})^2(\sigma^*_{2s})^1$. This means the net bond order is 0.5, and so Be$_2^+$ is predicted to exist under special circumstances.

EXERCISE 9.7 Molecular Orbitals in Diatomic Molecules

Could the anion Li$_2^-$ exist? What is the ion's bond order?

Molecular Orbitals from Atomic *p* Orbitals

■ **Diatomic Molecules** Molecules such as H$_2$, Li$_2$, and N$_2$, in which two identical atoms are bonded, are examples of *homonuclear* diatomic molecules.

With the principles of molecular orbital theory in place, we are ready to account for bonding in such important homonuclear diatomic molecules as N$_2$, O$_2$, and F$_2$. To describe the bonding in these molecules, we will have to use both *s* and *p* valence orbitals in forming molecular orbitals.

For *p*-block elements, sigma-bonding and antibonding molecular orbitals are formed by their *s* orbitals interacting as in Figure 9.16. Similarly, it is possible for a *p* orbital on one atom to interact with a *p* orbital on the other atom to produce a pair of σ-bonding and σ^*-antibonding molecular orbitals (Figure 9.19).

In addition, each *p*-block atom has *two p* orbitals in planes perpendicular to the σ bond connecting the two atoms. These *p* orbitals can interact sideways to give π-bonding and π-antibonding molecular orbitals (Figure 9.20). Combining these

FIGURE 9.19 Sigma molecular orbitals from *p* atomic orbitals. Sigma-bonding (σ_{2p}) and antibonding (σ^*_{2p}) molecular orbitals arise from overlap of 2*p* orbitals. Each orbital can accommodate two electrons. The *p* orbitals in electron shells of higher *n* give molecular orbitals of the same basic shape.

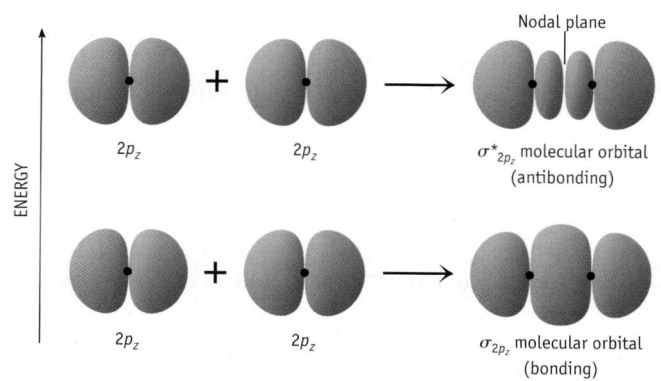

ENERGY

$2p_z$ + $2p_z$ → $\sigma^*_{2p_z}$ molecular orbital (antibonding)

Nodal plane

$2p_z$ + $2p_z$ → σ_{2p_z} molecular orbital (bonding)

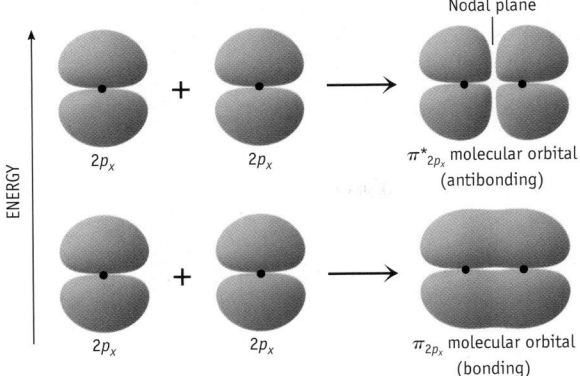

FIGURE 9.20 Formation of π molecular orbitals. Sideways overlap of atomic $2p$ orbitals that lie in the same direction in space gives rise to pi-bonding (π_{2p}) and pi-antibonding (π^*_{2p}) molecular orbitals. The p orbitals in shells of higher n give molecular orbitals of the same basic shape.

two p orbitals on each atom produces *two* π-bonding molecular orbitals (π_p) and *two* π-antibonding molecular orbitals (π^*_p).

Electron Configurations for Homonuclear Molecules for Boron Through Fluorine

Orbital interactions in a second-period, homonuclear, diatomic molecule lead to the energy level diagram in Figure 9.21. Electron assignments can be made using this diagram, and the results for the diatomic molecules B_2 through F_2 are assembled in Table 9.1, which has two noteworthy features.

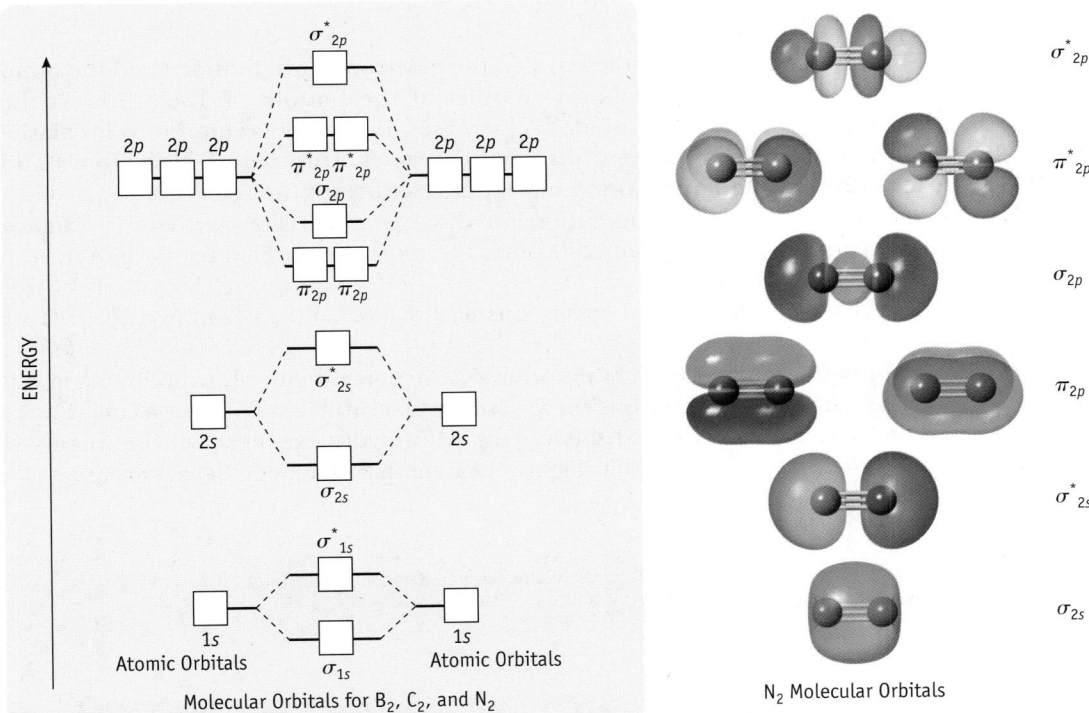

FIGURE 9.21 Molecular orbitals for homonuclear diatomic molecules of second period elements. (left) Energy level diagram. Although the diagram leads to the correct conclusions regarding bond order and magnetic behavior for O_2 and F_2, the energy ordering of the MOs in this figure is correct only for B_2, C_2, and N_2. For O_2 and F_2, the σ_{2p} MO is lower in energy than the π_{2p} MOs. See *A Closer Look*, page 429. (right) Calculated molecular orbitals for N_2. (Color scheme: occupied MOs are blue/green. Unoccupied MOs are red/yellow. The different colors reflect the different phases [positive or negative signs] of the wave functions.)

TABLE 9.1 Molecular Orbital Occupations and Physical Data for Homonuclear Diatomic Molecules of Second-Period Elements

	B_2	C_2	N_2		O_2	F_2
σ^*_{2p}	☐	☐	☐	σ^*_{2p}	☐	☐
π^*_{2p}	☐☐	☐☐	☐☐	π^*_{2p}	↑ ↑	↑↓ ↑↓
σ_{2p}	☐	☐	↑↓	π_{2p}	↑↓ ↑↓	↑↓ ↑↓
π_{2p}	↑ ↑	↑↓ ↑↓	↑↓ ↑↓	σ_{2p}	↑↓	↑↓
σ^*_{2s}	↑↓	↑↓	↑↓	σ^*_{2s}	↑↓	↑↓
σ_{2s}	↑↓	↑↓	↑↓	σ_{2s}	↑↓	↑↓
Bond order	One	Two	Three		Two	One
Bond-dissociation energy (kJ/mol)	290	620	945		498	155
Bond distance (pm)	159	131	110		121	143
Observed magnetic behavior (paramagnetic or diamagnetic)	Para	Dia	Dia		Para	Dia

■ **Highest Occupied Molecular Orbital (HOMO)** Chemists often refer to the highest energy MO that contains electrons as the HOMO. For O_2, this is the π^*_{2p} orbital. Chemists also use the term LUMO for the lowest unoccupied molecular orbital. For O_2, this would be σ^*_{2p}.

First, notice the correlation between the electron configurations and the bond orders, bond lengths, and bond energies at the bottom of Table 9.1. As the bond order between a pair of atoms increases, the energy required to break the bond increases, and the bond distance decreases. Dinitrogen, N_2, with a bond order of 3, has the largest bond energy and shortest bond distance.

Second, notice the configuration for dioxygen, O_2. Dioxygen has 12 valence electrons (six from each atom), so it has the molecular orbital configuration

$$O_2 \text{ MO Configuration:} \quad [\text{core electrons}](\sigma_{2s})^2(\sigma^*_{2s})^2(\sigma_{2p})^2(\pi_{2p})^4(\pi^*_{2p})^2$$

This configuration leads to a bond order of 2 in agreement with experiment, and it specifies two unpaired electrons (in π^*_{2p} molecular orbitals). Thus, molecular theory succeeds where valence bond theory fails. MO theory explains both the observed bond order and as illustrated in Figure 9.15, the paramagnetic behavior of O_2.

Chemistry Now™

Sign in at **www.cengage.com/login** and go to Chapter 9 Contents to see Screen 9.11 for an exercise on **molecular orbital configurations**.

■ **Phases of Atomic Orbitals and Molecular Orbitals** Recall from page 289 in Chapter 6 that electron orbitals are electron waves and as such have positive and negative phases. For this reason, the atomic orbitals in Figures 9.19–9.21 are drawn with two different colors. Looking at the p orbitals in Figure 9.19, you see that a bonding MO is formed when p orbitals with the same wave function sign overlap (+ with +). An antibonding orbital arises if they overlap out of phase (+ with −).

EXAMPLE 9.8 Electron Configuration for a Homonuclear Diatomic Ion

Problem When potassium reacts with O_2, potassium superoxide, KO_2, is one of the products. This is an ionic compound, and the anion is the superoxide ion, O_2^-. Write the molecular orbital electron configuration for the ion. Predict its bond order and magnetic behavior.

Strategy Use the energy level diagram for O_2 in Table 9.1 to generate the electron configuration of this ion, and use Equation 9.1 to determine the bond order.

A Closer Look

Molecular Orbitals for Compounds Formed from *p*-Block Elements

Several features of the molecular orbital energy level diagram in Figure 9.21 should be described in more detail.

(a) The bonding and antibonding σ orbitals from 2s interactions are lower in energy than the σ and π MOs from 2p interactions. The reason is that 2s orbitals have a lower energy than 2p orbitals in the separated atoms.

(b) The energy separation of the bonding and antibonding orbitals is greater for σ_{2p} than for π_{2p}. This happens because

p orbitals overlap to a greater extent when they are oriented head to head (to give σ_{2p} MOs) than when they are side by side (to give π_{2p} MOs). The greater the orbital overlap, the greater the stabilization of the bonding MO and the greater the destabilization of the antibonding MO.

Figure 9.21 shows an energy ordering of molecular orbitals that you might not have expected, but there are reasons for this. A more sophisticated approach takes into

account the "mixing" of s and p atomic orbitals, which have similar energies. This causes the σ_{2s} and σ^*_{2s} molecular orbitals to be lower in energy than otherwise expected, and the σ_{2p} and σ^*_{2p} orbitals to be higher in energy.

The mixing of s and p orbitals is important for B_2, C_2, and N_2, so Figure 9.21 applies strictly only to these molecules. For O_2 and F_2, σ_{2p} is lower in energy than π_{2p}, and Table 9.1 takes this into account.

Solution The MO electron configuration for O_2^- is

O_2^- MO Configuration: [core electrons]$(\sigma_{2s})^2(\sigma^*_{2s})^2(\sigma_{2p})^2(\pi_{2p})^4(\pi^*_{2p})^3$

The ion is predicted to be paramagnetic to the extent of one unpaired electron, a prediction confirmed by experiment. The bond order is 1.5, because there are eight bonding electrons and five antibonding electrons. The bond order for O_2^- is lower than O_2 so we predict the O—O bond length in O_2^- should be longer than the oxygen–oxygen bond length in O_2. The superoxide ion in fact has an O—O bond length of 134 pm, whereas the bond length in O_2 is 121 pm.

Comment You should quickly spot the fact that the superoxide ion (O_2^-), contains an odd number of electrons. This is another diatomic species (in addition to NO and O_2) for which it is not possible to write a Lewis structure that accurately represents the bonding.

> **EXERCISE 9.8 Molecular Electron Configurations**
>
> The cations O_2^+ and N_2^+ are important components of Earth's upper atmosphere. Write the electron configuration of O_2^+. Predict its bond order and magnetic behavior.

Electron Configurations for Heteronuclear Diatomic Molecules

The compounds NO, CO, and ClF, molecules containing two different elements, are examples of **heteronuclear diatomic molecules.** MO descriptions for heteronuclear diatomic molecules generally resemble those for homonuclear diatomic molecules. As a consequence, an energy level diagram like Figure 9.21 can be used to judge the bond order and magnetic behavior for heteronuclear diatomics.

Let us do this for nitrogen monoxide, NO. Nitrogen monoxide has 11 valence electrons. If these are assigned to the MOs for a homonuclear diatomic molecule, the molecular electron configuration is

NO MO Configuration: [core electrons]$(\sigma_{2s})^2(\sigma^*_{2s})^2(\pi_{2p})^4(\sigma_{2p})^2(\pi^*_{2p})^1$

The net bond order is 2.5, in accord with bond length information. The single, unpaired electron is assigned to the π^*_{2p} molecular orbital, and the molecule is paramagnetic, as predicted for a molecule with an odd number of electrons.

Nature is based on millions of chemical compounds, and chemists have created thousands more in the laboratory. In general, we understand their structures and bonding reasonably well, but from time to time nature gives us wonderful mysteries to solve.

Some of the mysteries are about the simplest molecules. One is B_2H_6, diborane, the simplest member of a large class of compounds. When it was discovered in the 1930s, chemists thought it must look like ethane, $H_3C–CH_3$. However, by the 1940s it was known that its structure had B—H—B bridges.

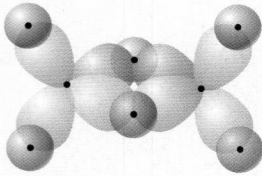

(a)   (b)

There are two mysteries. If each line in the structure represents a two-electron bond, you realize the molecule is "electron-deficient"; two B atoms and six H atoms do not contribute enough electrons for eight two-electron bonds. Also, notice that hydrogen is bonded to two different atoms, something we don't expect to happen because H has only one valence electron. One way to approach this problem is to begin by assuming each B atom is sp^3 hybridized. The four outside or terminal H atoms are then bonded to the B atoms by normal, two-electron bonds using two of the sp^3 hybrid orbitals on each B atom. The remaining two sp^3 hybrid orbitals on each B atom point into the bridging region where H atom $1s$ orbitals overlap with sp^3 orbitals from two different B atoms. Two electrons are assigned to each set of the bridging B—H—B groups, so the bridging bonds are two-electron/three-center bonds.

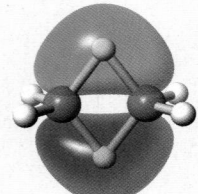

One can also apply molecular orbital theory to the molecule, and the bonding picture that emerges likewise has stable B—H—B bridges. The lowest energy molecular orbital, shown here, shows that electron density is spread over the B_2H_2 portion of the molecule.

The molecular orbital that accounts for B—H—B bridge bonding.

It turns out that hydrogen bridges are also found in many other boron compounds and in other kinds of molecules. William Lipscomb

received the Nobel Prize in Chemistry in 1976 for "his studies of boranes which have illuminated problems with chemical bonding."

Another bonding mystery involves Zeise's salt, a compound first discovered in the 1820s. However, it was not until the 1950s that three chemists (M. Dewar, J. Chatt, and Duncanson) devised a reasonable bonding model. The salt is based on the anion $[(C_2H_4)PtCl_3]^-$. The most interesting aspect of this ion is that the ethylene molecule, C_2H_4, is bonded sideways to the Pt^{2+} ion. How can this occur? As illustrated in the figure below, the π–bonding electrons of ethylene are donated to Pt^{2+} through overlap of the filled π orbital for C_2H_4 with an empty Pt^{2+} orbital. To account for the stability of the ion, however, there is another important aspect: a filled d-orbital on the Pt^{2+} ion donates electron density to the empty π-antibonding LUMO on the ethylene.

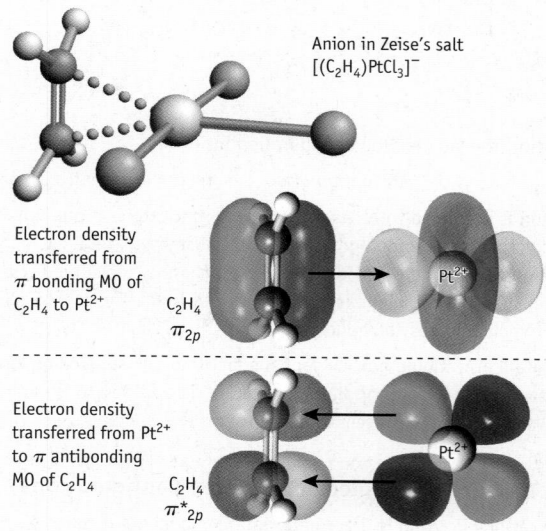

Anion in Zeise's salt $[(C_2H_4)PtCl_3]^-$

Electron density transferred from π bonding MO of C_2H_4 to Pt^{2+} C_2H_4 Pt^{2+}
π_{2p}

Electron density transferred from Pt^{2+} to π antibonding MO of C_2H_4 C_2H_4 Pt^{2+}
π^*_{2p}

An understanding of bonding in Zeise's salt was a seminal event in chemistry because the ion is the model for the binding of other molecules like ethylene to transition metal centers.

Questions:

1. *If you treat each line in the B_2H_6 structure above as a two-electron bond, how many electrons are required for bonding in the molecule? How many electrons are actually available?*

2. *Diborane reacts with molecules such as NH_3 to give, for example, $H_3B–NH_3$. Draw a Lewis structure for this compound, estimate bond angles, and indicate the B and N hybridization. Is the molecule polar? What are the formal charges on the atoms?*

3. *Silver(I) ion is known to bond to ethylene, forming an ion of the formula $[Ag(C_2H_4)_x]^+$. When heated, the reaction $[Ag(C_2H_4)_x]BF_4(s) \rightarrow AgBF_4(s) + x\ C_2H_4(g)$ occurs. If 62.1 mg of the silver(I) complex is heated, 54.3 mg of $AgBF_4$ remains. What is the value of x?*

Answers to these questions are in Appendix Q.

Resonance and MO Theory

Ozone, O_3, is a simple triatomic molecule with equal oxygen–oxygen bond lengths. Equal X—O bond lengths are also observed in other molecules and ions, such as SO_2, NO_2^-, and HCO_2^-. Valence bond theory introduced resonance to rationalize the equivalent bonding to the oxygen atoms in these structures, but MO theory provides another view of this problem.

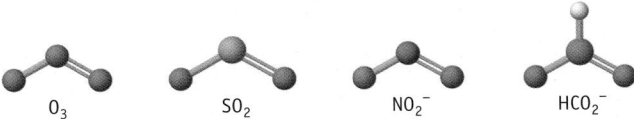

To understand the bonding in ozone, we begin by looking at the valence bond picture. Let us assume that all three O atoms are sp^2 hybridized. The central atom uses its sp^2 hybrid orbitals to form two σ bonds and to accommodate a lone pair. The terminal atoms use their sp^2 hybrid orbitals to form one σ bond and to accommodate two lone pairs. In total, the lone pairs and bonding pairs in the σ framework of O_3 account for seven of the nine valence electron pairs in O_3.

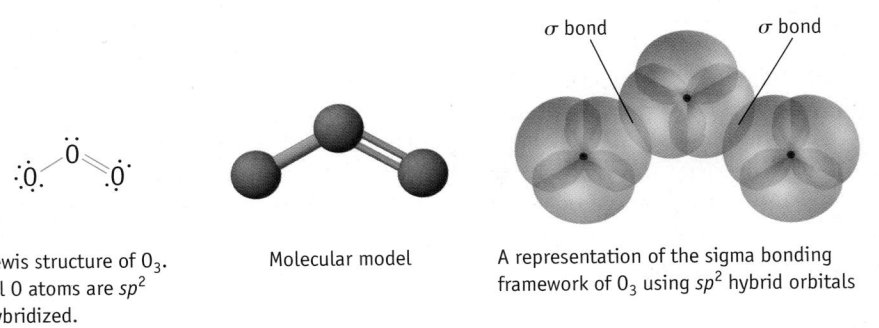

Lewis structure of O_3. All O atoms are sp^2 hybridized.

Molecular model

A representation of the sigma bonding framework of O_3 using sp^2 hybrid orbitals

The π bond in ozone arises from the two remaining pairs (Figure 9.22). Because we have assumed that each oxygen atom in O_3 is sp^2 hybridized, an unhybridized p orbital perpendicular to the O_3 plane remains on each of the three oxygen atoms. The orbitals are in the correct orientation to form π bonds.

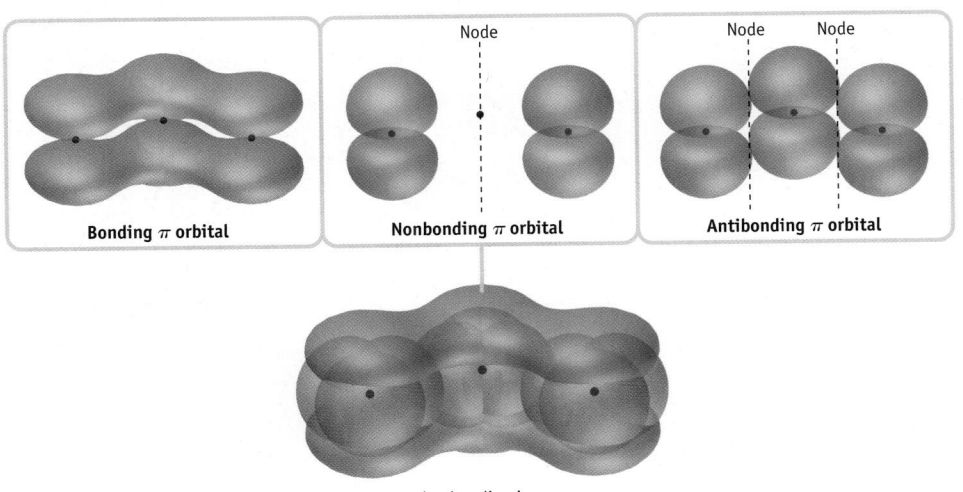

Bonding π orbital

Nonbonding π orbital

Antibonding π orbital

σ and π bonding in ozone

FIGURE 9.22 Pi-bonding in ozone, O_3. Each O atom in O_3 is sp^2 hybridized. The three $2p$ orbitals, one on each atom, are used to create the three π molecular orbitals. Two pairs of electrons are assigned to the orbitals: one pair in the bonding orbital and one pair in the nonbonding orbital. The π bond order is 0.5, as one bonding pair is spread across two bonds.

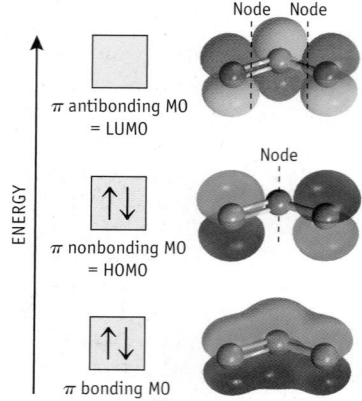

Node Node

π antibonding MO = LUMO

Node

↑↓
π nonbonding MO = HOMO

↑↓
π bonding MO

FIGURE 9.23. The π molecular diagram for ozone. Notice that, as in the other MO diagrams illustrated (especially Figure 9.21), the energy of the molecular orbitals increases as the number of nodes increases.

Now let's apply MO theory to the pi bonds. A principle of MO theory is that the number of molecular orbitals must equal the number of atomic orbitals. Thus, the three $2p$ atomic orbitals must be combined in a way that forms three molecular orbitals.

One π_p MO for ozone is a bonding orbital because the three p orbitals are "in phase" across the molecule. Another π_p MO is an antibonding orbital because the atomic orbital on the central atom that is "out of phase" with the terminal atom p orbitals. The third π_p MO is a nonbonding orbital because the middle p orbital does not participate in the MO. The bonding π_p MO is filled by a pair of electrons that is delocalized, or "spread over," the molecule, just as the resonance hybrid implies. The nonbonding orbital is also occupied, but the electrons in this orbital are concentrated near the two terminal oxygens. As the name implies, electrons in this molecular orbital neither help nor hinder the bonding in the molecule. The π bond order of O_3 is 0.5 (Figure 9.23). Because the σ bond order is 1.0 and the π bond order is 0.5, the net oxygen–oxygen bond order is 1.5—the same value given by valence bond theory.

The observation that two of the π molecular orbitals for ozone extend over three atoms illustrates an important point regarding molecular orbital theory: *Orbitals can extend beyond two atoms.* In valence bond theory, in contrast, all representations for bonding are based on being able to localize pairs of electrons in bonds between two atoms. To further illustrate the MO approach, look again at benzene (Figure 9.24). On page 421, we noted that the π electrons in this molecule were spread out over all six carbon atoms. We can now see how the same case can be made with MO theory. Six p orbitals contribute to the π system. Based on the premise that the number of molecular orbitals must equal the number of atomic orbitals, there must be six π molecular orbitals in benzene. An energy level diagram for benzene shows that the six π electrons reside in the three lowest-energy (bonding) molecular orbitals.

FIGURE 9.24 Molecular orbital energy level diagram for benzene. Because there are six unhybridized p orbitals, six π molecular orbitals can be formed—three bonding and three antibonding. The three bonding molecular orbitals accommodate the six π electrons.

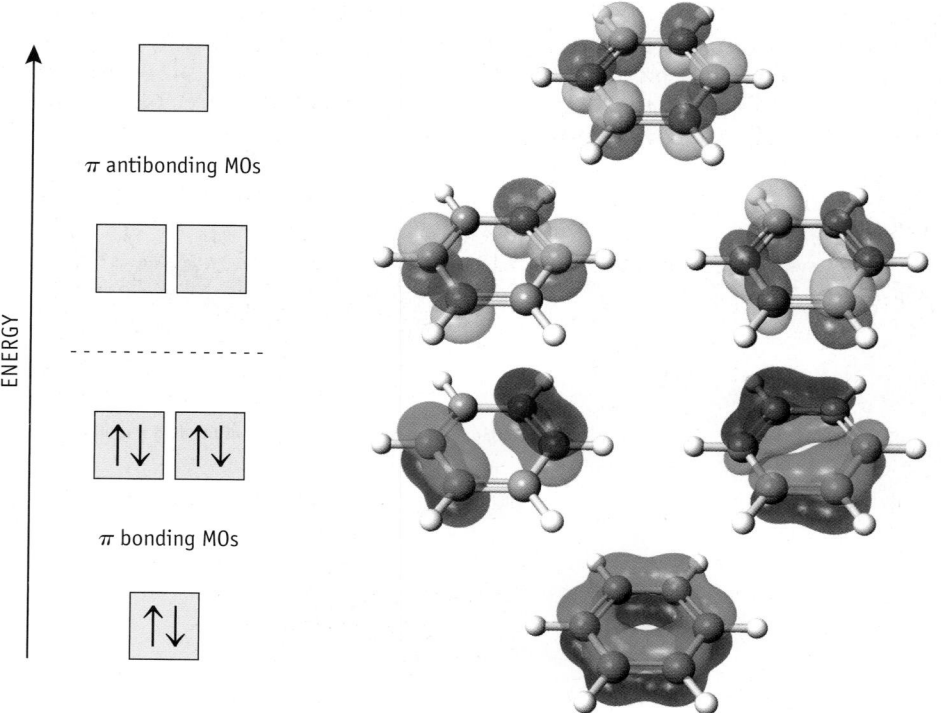

π antibonding MOs

ENERGY

↑↓ ↑↓

π bonding MOs

↑↓

Chapter Goals Revisited

Now that you have studied this chapter, you should ask whether you have met the chapter goals. In particular, you should be able to:

Understand the differences between valence bond theory and molecular orbital theory

a. Describe the main features of valence bond theory and molecular orbital theory, the two commonly used theories for covalent bonding (Section 9.1).

b. Recognize that the premise for valence bond theory is that bonding results from the overlap of atomic orbitals. By virtue of the overlap of orbitals, electrons are concentrated (or localized) between two atoms (Section 9.2).

c. Distinguish how sigma (σ) and pi (π) bonds arise. For σ bonding, orbitals overlap in a head-to-head fashion, concentrating electrons along the bond axis. Sideways overlap of p atomic orbitals results in π bond formation, with electron density above and below the molecular plane (Section 9.2).

d. Understand how molecules having double bonds can have isomeric forms. Study Question(s) assignable in OWL: 14.

Identify the hybridization of an atom in a molecule or ion

a. Use the concept of hybridization to rationalize molecular structure (Section 9.2). Study Question(s) assignable in OWL: 2, 3, 4, 5, 6, 8, 9, 11, 12, 21, 22, 24, 27, 32, 35, 36, 38, 44, 45, 47–50, 51, 52–54; Go Chemistry Module 14.

Hybrid Orbitals	Atomic Orbitals Used	Number of Hybrid Orbitals	Electron-Pair Geometry
sp	$s + p$	2	Linear
sp^2	$s + p + p$	3	Trigonal-planar
sp^3	$s + p + p + p$	4	Tetrahedral
sp^3d	$s + p + p + p + d$	5	Trigonal bipyramidal
sp^3d^2	$s + p + p + p + d + d$	6	Octahedral

Understand the differences between bonding and antibonding molecular orbitals and be able to write the molecular orbital configurations for simple diatomic molecules.

a. Understand molecular orbital theory (Section 9.3), in which atomic orbitals are combined to form bonding orbitals, nonbonding orbitals, or antibonding orbitals that are delocalized over several atoms. In this description, the electrons of the molecule or ion are assigned to the orbitals beginning with the one at lowest energy, according to the Pauli exclusion principle and Hund's rule.

b. Use molecular orbital theory to explain the properties of O_2 and other diatomic molecules. Study Question(s) assignable in OWL: 15–20, 40, 42, 43, 57.

Chemistry⚛Now™ Sign in at **www. cengage.com/login** to:

- Assess your understanding with Study Questions in OWL keyed to each goal in the Goals and Homework menu for this chapter
- For quick review, download Go Chemistry mini-lecture flashcard modules (or purchase them at **www.ichapters.com**)
- Check your readiness for an exam by taking the Pre-Test and exploring the modules recommended in your Personalized Study plan.

Access **How Do I Solve It?** tutorials on how to approach problem solving using concepts in this chapter.

For additional preparation for an examination on this chapter see the *Let's Review* section on pages 496–513.

KEY EQUATIONS

Equation 9.1 (page 424) Calculating the order of a bond from the molecular orbital electron configuration

Bond order = 1/2 (number of electrons in bonding MOs
 — number of electrons in antibonding MOs)

STUDY QUESTIONS

OWL Online homework for this chapter may be assigned in OWL.

▲ denotes challenging questions.

■ denotes questions assignable in OWL.

Blue-numbered questions have answers in Appendix O and fully-worked solutions in the *Student Solutions Manual*.

Practicing Skills

Valence Bond Theory
(See Examples 9.1–9.5 and ChemistryNow Screens 9.2–9.7.)

1. Draw the Lewis structure for chloroform, $CHCl_3$. What are its electron-pair and molecular geometries? What orbitals on C, H, and Cl overlap to form bonds involving these elements?

2. ■ Draw the Lewis structure for NF_3. What are its electron-pair and molecular geometries? What is the hybridization of the nitrogen atom? What orbitals on N and F overlap to form bonds between these elements?

3. ■ Specify the electron-pair and molecular geometry for each underlined atom in the following list. Describe the hybrid orbital set used by this atom in each molecule or ion.
   (a) $\underline{B}Br_3$ (b) $\underline{C}O_2$ (c) $\underline{C}H_2Cl_2$ (d) $\underline{C}O_3^{2-}$

4. ■ Specify the electron-pair and molecular geometry for each underlined atom in the following list. Describe the hybrid orbital set used by this atom in each molecule or ion.
   (a) $\underline{C}Se_2$ (b) $\underline{S}O_2$ (c) $\underline{C}H_2O$ (d) $\underline{N}H_4^+$

5. ■ Describe the hybrid orbital set used by each of the indicated atoms in the molecules below:
   (a) the carbon atoms and the oxygen atom in dimethyl ether, H_3COCH_3
   (b) each carbon atom in propene

$$H_3C-\overset{\overset{\displaystyle H}{|}}{C}=CH_2$$

   (c) the two carbon atoms and the nitrogen atom in the amino acid glycine

$$H-\overset{\overset{\displaystyle H}{|}}{\underset{\underset{\displaystyle H}{|}}{N}}-\overset{\overset{\displaystyle H}{|}}{\underset{\underset{\displaystyle H}{|}}{C}}-\overset{\overset{\displaystyle :O:}{\|}}{C}-\overset{\displaystyle ..}{\underset{\displaystyle ..}{O}}-H$$

6. ■ Give the hybrid orbital set used by each of the underlined atoms in the following molecules.

$$\text{(a) } H-\overset{\overset{\displaystyle H}{|}}{\underset{\underset{\displaystyle ..}{|}}{N}}-\overset{\overset{\displaystyle :O:}{\|}}{\underline{C}}-\overset{\overset{\displaystyle H}{|}}{\underset{\underset{\displaystyle ..}{|}}{N}}-H \qquad \text{(c) } H-\underline{C}=\underline{C}-\underline{C}\equiv N:$$

$$\text{(b) } H_3\underline{C}-\overset{\overset{\displaystyle H}{|}}{\underline{C}}=\overset{\overset{\displaystyle H}{|}}{\underline{C}}-\underline{C}=\overset{\displaystyle ..}{\underset{\displaystyle ..}{O}}$$

7. Draw the Lewis structure, and then specify the electron-pair and molecular geometries for each of the following molecules or ions. Identify the hybridization of the central atom.
   (a) SiF_6^{2-} (b) SeF_4 (c) ICl_2^- (d) XeF_4

8. ■ Draw the Lewis structure, and then specify the electron-pair and molecular geometries for each of the following molecules or ions. Identify the hybridization of the central atom.
   (a) $XeOF_4$ (c) central S in SOF_4
   (b) BrF_5 (d) central Br in Br_3^-

9. ■ Draw the Lewis structures of the acid HPO_2F_2 and its anion $PO_2F_2^-$. What is the molecular geometry and hybridization for the phosphorus atom in each species? (H is bonded to an O atom in the acid.)

10. Draw the Lewis structures of HSO_3F and SO_3F^-. What is the molecular geometry and hybridization for the sulfur atom in each species? (H is bonded to an O atom in the acid.)

11. ■ What is the hybridization of the carbon atom in phosgene, Cl_2CO? Give a complete description of the σ and π bonding in this molecule.

12. ■ What is the hybridization of the sulfur atom in sulfuryl fluoride, SO_2F_2?

13. The arrangement of groups attached to the C atoms involved in a C=C double bond leads to *cis* and *trans* isomers. For each compound below, draw the other isomer.

$$\text{(a)} \quad \underset{H}{\overset{H_3C}{>}}C=C\underset{CH_3}{\overset{H}{<}} \qquad \text{(b)} \quad \underset{H}{\overset{Cl}{>}}C=C\underset{H}{\overset{CH_3}{<}}$$

14. ■ For each compound below, decide whether *cis* and *trans* isomers are possible. If isomerism is possible, draw the other isomer.

$$\text{(a)} \quad \underset{H}{\overset{H_3C}{>}}C=C\underset{CH_2CH_3}{\overset{H}{<}}$$

$$\text{(b)} \quad \underset{H}{\overset{H}{>}}C=C\underset{H}{\overset{CH_3}{<}} \qquad \text{(c)} \quad \underset{H}{\overset{Cl}{>}}C=C\underset{H}{\overset{CH_2OH}{<}}$$

Molecular Orbital Theory
(See Examples 9.6–9.8 and ChemistryNow Screens 9.9–9.12.)

15. ■ The hydrogen molecular ion, H_2^+, can be detected spectroscopically. Write the electron configuration of the ion in molecular orbital terms. What is the bond order of the ion? Is the hydrogen–hydrogen bond stronger or weaker in H_2^+ than in H_2?

16. ■ Give the electron configurations for the ions Li_2^+ and Li_2^- in molecular orbital terms. Compare the Li—Li bond order in these ions with the bond order in Li_2.

17. ■ Calcium carbide, CaC_2, contains the acetylide ion, C_2^{2-}. Sketch the molecular orbital energy level diagram for the ion. How many net σ and π bonds does the ion have? What is the carbon–carbon bond order? How has the bond order changed on adding electrons to C_2 to obtain C_2^{2-}? Is the C_2^{2-} ion paramagnetic?

18. ■ Oxygen, O_2, can acquire one or two electrons to give O_2^- (superoxide ion) or O_2^{2-} (peroxide ion). Write the electron configuration for the ions in molecular orbital terms, and then compare them with the O_2 molecule on the following bases.
(a) magnetic character
(b) net number of σ and π bonds
(c) bond order
(d) oxygen–oxygen bond length

19. ■ Assume the energy level diagram for homonuclear diatomic molecules (Figure 9.21) can be applied to heteronuclear diatomics such as CO.
(a) Write the electron configuration for carbon monoxide, CO.
(b) What is the highest-energy, occupied molecular orbital?
(c) Is the molecule diamagnetic or paramagnetic?
(d) What is the net number of σ and π bonds? What is the CO bond order?

20. ■ The nitrosyl ion, NO^+, has an interesting chemistry.
(a) Is NO^+ diamagnetic or paramagnetic? If paramagnetic, how many unpaired electrons does it have?
(b) Assume the molecular orbital diagram for a homonuclear diatomic molecule (Figure 9.21) applies to NO^+. What is the highest-energy molecular orbital occupied by electrons?
(c) What is the nitrogen–oxygen bond order?
(d) Is the N—O bond in NO^+ stronger or weaker than the bond in NO?

General Questions on Valence Bond and Molecular Orbital Theory

These questions are not designated as to type or location in the chapter. They may combine several concepts from this and other chapters.

21. ■ Draw the Lewis structure for AlF_4^-. What are its electron-pair and molecular geometries? What orbitals on Al and F overlap to form bonds between these elements? What are the formal charges on the atoms? Is this a reasonable charge distribution?

22. ■ Draw the Lewis structure for ClF_3. What are its electron-pair and molecular geometries? What is the hybridization of the chlorine atom? What orbitals on Cl and F overlap to form bonds between these elements?

23. ■ Describe the O—S—O angle and the hybrid orbital set used by sulfur in each of the following molecules or ions:
(a) SO_2 (b) SO_3 (c) SO_3^{2-} (d) SO_4^{2-}

Do all have the same value for the O—S—O angle? Does the S atom in all these species use the same hybrid orbitals?

24. ■ Sketch the Lewis structures of ClF_2^+ and ClF_2^-. What are the electron-pair and molecular geometries of each ion? Do both have the same F—Cl—F angle? What hybrid orbital set is used by Cl in each ion?

25. Sketch the resonance structures for the nitrite ion, NO_2^-. Describe the electron-pair and molecular geometries of the ion. From these geometries, decide on the O—N—O bond angle, the average NO bond order, and the N atom hybridization.

26. Sketch the resonance structures for the nitrate ion, NO_3^-. Is the hybridization of the N atom the same or different in each structure? Describe the orbitals involved in bond formation by the central N atom.

27. ■ Sketch the resonance structures for the N_2O molecule. Is the hybridization of the N atoms the same or different in each structure? Describe the orbitals involved in bond formation by the central N atom.

28. Compare the structure and bonding in CO_2 and CO_3^{2-} with regard to the O—C—O bond angles, the CO bond order, and the C atom hybridization.

29. Numerous molecules are detected in deep space. Three of them are illustrated here.

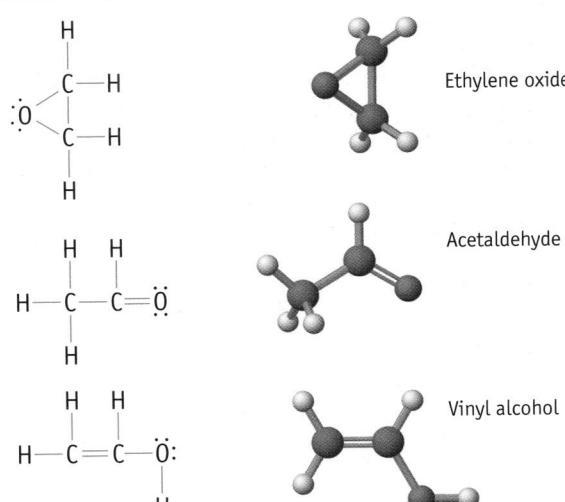

Ethylene oxide

Acetaldehyde

Vinyl alcohol

(a) Comment on the similarities or differences in the formulas of these compounds. Are they isomers?
(b) Indicate the hybridization of each C atom in each molecule.
(c) Indicate the value of the H—C—H angle in each of the three molecules.
(d) Are any of these molecules polar?
(e) Which molecule should have the strongest carbon–carbon bond? The strongest carbon–oxygen bond?

30. Acrolein, a component of photochemical smog, has a pungent odor and irritates eyes and mucous membranes.

$$H-\overset{A}{\underset{1}{C}}=\overset{H}{\underset{2}{C}}-\overset{H}{\underset{B}{C}}\overset{:O:}{\underset{C}{=}}H$$

(a) What are the hybridizations of carbon atoms 1 and 2?
(b) What are the approximate values of angles A, B, and C?
(c) Is *cis-trans* isomerism possible here?

31. The organic compound below is a member of a class known as oximes.

$$H-\overset{H}{\underset{H}{C}}-\overset{:\overset{..}{O}-H}{\underset{H}{C}}=N:$$

(a) What are the hybridizations of the two C atoms and of the N atom?
(b) What is the approximate C—N—O angle?

32. ■ The compound sketched below is acetylsalicylic acid, commonly known as aspirin:

(a) What are the approximate values of the angles marked A, B, C, and D?
(b) What hybrid orbitals are used by carbon atoms 1, 2, and 3?

33. Phosphoserine is a less-common amino acid.

(a) Describe the hybridizations of atoms 1 through 5.
(b) What are the approximate values of the bond angles A, B, C, and D?
(c) What are the most polar bonds in the molecule?

34. ■ Lactic acid is a natural compound found in sour milk.

(a) How many π bonds occur in lactic acid? How many σ bonds?
(b) Describe the hybridization of atoms 1, 2, and 3.
(c) Which CO bond is the shortest in the molecule? Which CO bond is the strongest?
(d) What are the approximate values of the bond angles A, B, and C?

35. ■ Cinnamaldehyde occurs naturally in cinnamon oil.

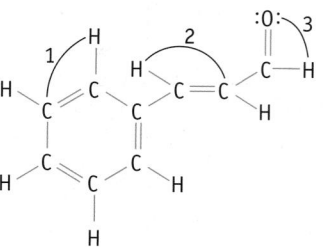

Cinnamaldehyde

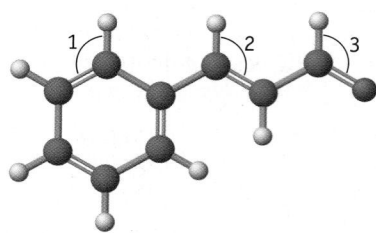

(a) What is the most polar bond in the molecule?
(b) How many sigma (σ) bonds and how many pi (π) bonds are there?
(c) Is *cis-trans* isomerism possible? If so, draw the isomers of the molecule.
(d) Give the hybridization of the C atoms in the molecule.
(e) What are the values of the bond angles 1, 2, and 3?

36. ■ Iodine and oxygen form a complex series of ions, among them IO_4^- and IO_5^{3-}. Draw the Lewis structures for these ions, and specify their electron-pair geometries and the shapes of the ions. What is the hybridization of the I atom in these ions?

37. Antimony pentafluoride reacts with HF according to the equation

$$2\,HF + SbF_5 \rightarrow [H_2F]^+[SbF_6]^-$$

(a) What is the hybridization of the Sb atom in the reactant and product?
(b) Draw a Lewis structure for H_2F^+. What is the geometry of H_2F^+? What is the hybridization of F in H_2F^+?

38. ■ Xenon forms well-characterized compounds (◄ page 404). Two xenon–oxygen compounds are XeO_3 and XeO_4. Draw the Lewis structures of these compounds, and give their electron-pair and molecular geometries. What are the hybrid orbital sets used by xenon in these two oxides?

39. The simple valence bond picture of O_2 does not agree with the molecular orbital view. Compare these two theories with regard to the peroxide ion, O_2^{2-}.
   (a) Draw an electron dot structure for O_2^{2-}. What is the bond order of the ion?
   (b) Write the molecular orbital electron configuration for O_2^{2-}. What is the bond order based on this approach?
   (c) Do the two theories of bonding lead to the same magnetic character and bond order for O_2^{2-}?

40. ■ Nitrogen, N_2, can ionize to form N_2^+ or add an electron to give N_2^-. Using molecular orbital theory, compare these species with regard to (a) their magnetic character, (b) net number of π bonds, (c) bond order, (d) bond length, and (e) bond strength.

41. Which of the homonuclear, diatomic molecules of the second-period elements (from Li_2 to Ne_2) are paramagnetic? Which have a bond order of 1? Which have a bond order of 2? Which diatomic molecule has the highest bond order?

42. ■ Which of the following molecules or molecule ions should be paramagnetic? What is the highest occupied molecular orbital (HOMO) in each one? Assume the molecular orbital diagram in Figure 9.21 applies to all of them.
   (a) NO   (c) O_2^{2-} (e) CN
   (b) OF^- (d) Ne_2^+

43. ■ The CN molecule has been found in interstellar space. Assuming the electronic structure of the molecule can be described using the molecular orbital energy level diagram in Figure 9.21, answer the following questions.
   (a) What is the highest energy occupied molecular orbital (HOMO) to which an electron (or electrons) is (are) assigned?
   (b) What is the bond order of the molecule?
   (c) How many net σ bonds are there? How many net π bonds?
   (d) Is the molecule paramagnetic or diamagnetic?

44. ■ Amphetamine is a stimulant. Replacing one H atom on the NH_2, or amino, group with CH_3 gives methamphetamine, a particularly dangerous drug commonly known as "speed."

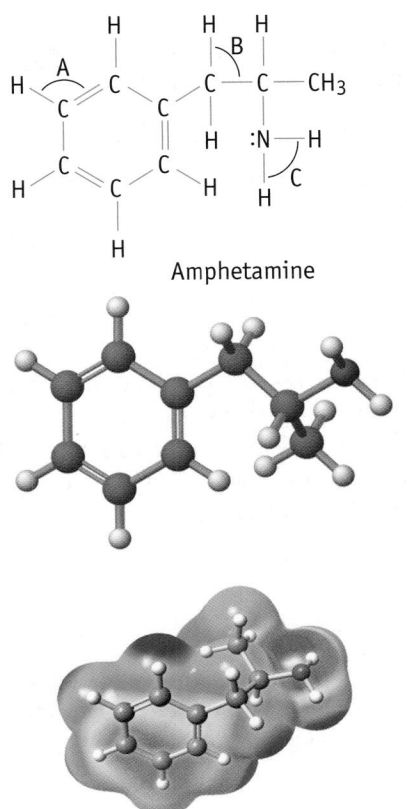

Amphetamine

   (a) What are the hybrid orbitals used by the C atoms of the C_6 ring, by the C atoms of the side chain, and by the N atom?
   (b) Give approximate values for the bond angles *A*, *B*, and *C*.
   (c) How many σ bonds and π bonds are in the molecule?
   (d) Is the molecule polar or nonpolar?
   (e) Amphetamine reacts readily with a proton (H^+) in aqueous solution. Where does this proton attach to the molecule? Does the electrostatic potential map shown above confirm this possibility?

45. ■ Menthol is used in soaps, perfumes, and foods. It is present in the common herb mint, and it can be prepared from turpentine.
   (a) What are the hybridizations used by the C atoms in the molecule?
   (b) What is the approximate C—O—H bond angle?
   (c) Is the molecule polar or nonpolar?
   (d) Is the six-member carbon ring planar or nonplanar? Explain why or why not.

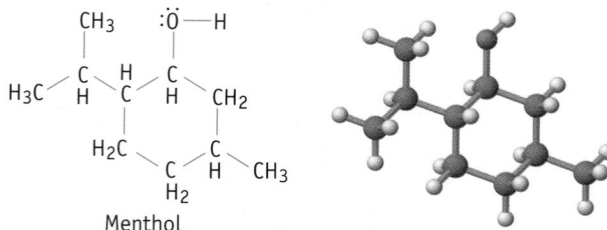

Menthol

46. The elements of the second period from boron to oxygen form compounds of the type X_nE—EX_n, where X can be H or a halogen. Sketch possible molecular structures for B_2F_4, C_2H_4, N_2H_4, and O_2H_2. Give the hybridizations of E in each molecule and specify approximate X—E—E bond angles.

In the Laboratory

47. ■ Suppose you carry out the following reaction of ammonia and boron trifluoride in the laboratory.

$$H-\underset{\underset{H}{|}}{\overset{\overset{H}{|}}{N}}: + \underset{\underset{F}{|}}{\overset{\overset{F}{|}}{B}}-F \longrightarrow H-\underset{\underset{H}{|}}{\overset{\overset{H}{|}}{N}}\rightarrow\underset{\underset{F}{|}}{\overset{\overset{F}{|}}{B}}-F$$

   (a) What is the geometry of the boron atom in BF_3? In $H_3N{\rightarrow}BF_3$?
   (b) What is the hybridization of the boron atom in the two compounds?
   (c) Does the boron atom's hybridization change on formation of the coordinate covalent bond?
   (d) Considering atom electronegativities and the bonding in NH_3 and BF_3, why do you expect the nitrogen on NH_3 to donate an electron pair to the B atom of BF_3?
   (e) BF_3 also reacts readily with water. Based on the ammonia reaction above, speculate on how water can interact with BF_3.

48. ▲ ■ Ethylene oxide is an intermediate in the manufacture of ethylene glycol (antifreeze) and polyester polymers. More than 4 million tons are produced annually

in the U.S. The molecule has a three-member ring of two C atoms and an O atom.

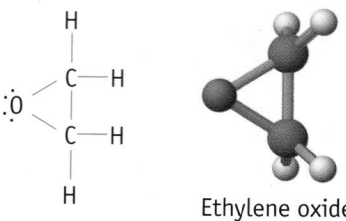

Ethylene oxide

   (a) What are the expected bond angles in the ring?
   (b) What is the hybridization of each atom in the ring?
   (c) Comment on the relation between the bond angles expected based on hybridization and the bond angles expected for a three-member ring.
   (d) Is the molecule polar? Based on the electrostatic potential map shown below, where do the negative and positive charges lie in the molecule?

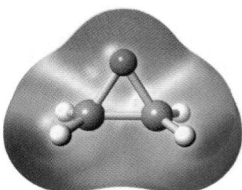

Electrostatic potential map for ethylene oxide.

49. ■ The sulfamate ion, $H_2NSO_3^-$, can be thought of as having been formed from the amide ion, NH_2^-, and sulfur trioxide, SO_3.
   (a) What are the geometries of the amide ion and of SO_3? What are the hybridizations of the N and S atoms, respectively?
   (b) Sketch a structure for the sulfamate ion, and estimate the bond angles.
   (c) What changes in hybridization do you expect for N and S in the course of the reaction

$$NH_2^- + SO_3 \rightarrow H_2N{-}SO_3^-?$$

   (d) Is SO_3 the donor of an electron pair or the acceptor of an electron pair in the reaction with amide ion? Does the electrostatic potential map shown below confirm your prediction?

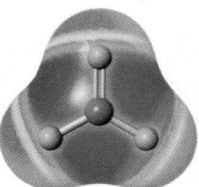

Electrostatic potential map for sulfur trioxide.

▲ more challenging   ■ in OWL   Blue-numbered questions answered in Appendix O

50. ▲ ■ The compound whose structure is shown here is acetylacetone. It exists in two forms: the *enol* form and the *keto* form.

enol form   *keto* form

The molecule reacts with OH^- to form an anion, $[CH_3COCHCOCH_3]^-$ (often abbreviated acac⁻ for acetylacetonate ion). One of the most interesting aspects of this anion is that one or more of them can react with transition metal cations to give stable, highly colored compounds.

(a) Are the *keto* and *enol* forms of acetylacetone resonance forms? Explain your answer.
(b) What is the hybridization of each atom (except H) in the *enol* form? What changes in hybridization occur when it is transformed into the *keto* form?
(c) What are the electron-pair geometry and molecular geometry around each C atom in the *keto* and *enol* forms? What changes in geometry occur when the *keto* form changes to the *enol* form?
(d) Draw three possible resonance structures for the acac⁻ ion.
(e) Is *cis-trans* isomerism possible in either the *enol* or the *keto* form?
(f) Is the enol form of acetylacetone polar? Where do the positive and negative charges lie in the molecule?

Summary and Conceptual Questions
The following questions may use concepts from this and previous chapters.

51. ■ What is the maximum number of hybrid orbitals that a carbon atom may form? What is the minimum number? Explain briefly.

52. ■ Consider the three fluorides BF_4^-, SiF_4, and SF_4.
(a) Identify a molecule that is isoelectronic with BF_4^-.
(b) Are SiF_4 and SF_4 isoelectronic?
(c) What is the hybridization of the central atom in each of these species?

53. ▲ ■ When two amino acids react with each other, they form a linkage called an amide group, or a peptide link. (If more linkages are added, a protein or polypeptide is formed.)
(a) What are the hybridizations of the C and N atoms in the peptide linkage?

(b) Is the structure illustrated the only resonance structure possible for the peptide linkage? If another resonance structure is possible, compare it with the one shown. Decide which is the more important structure.
(c) The computer-generated structure shown here, which contains a peptide linkage, shows that the linkage is flat. This is an important feature of proteins. Speculate on reasons that the CO—NH linkage is planar. What are the sites of positive and negative charge in this dipeptide?

Peptide linkage

54. ■ What is the connection between bond order, bond length, and bond energy? Use ethane (C_2H_6), ethylene (C_2H_4), and acetylene (C_2H_2) as examples.

55. When is it desirable to use MO theory rather than valence bond theory?

56. How do valence bond theory and molecular orbital theory differ in their explanation of the bond order of 1.5 for ozone?

57. ■ Three of the four π molecular orbitals for cyclobutadiene are pictured here. Place them in order of increasing energy. (Remember that orbitals increase in energy in order of an increasing number of nodes. If a pair of orbitals have the same number of nodes, they have the same energy.)

Orbital A

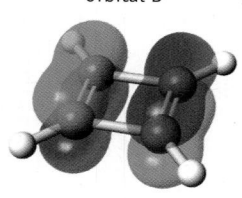

Orbital B

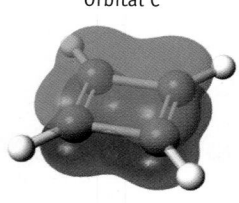

Orbital C

58. Examine the Hybrid Orbitals tool on Screen 9.6 of ChemistryNow. Use this tool to systematically combine atomic orbitals to form hybrid atomic orbitals.

(a) What is the relationship between the number of hybrid orbitals produced and the number of atomic orbitals used to create them?

(b) Do hybrid atomic orbitals form between different p orbitals without involving s orbitals?

(c) What is the relationship between the energy of hybrid atomic orbitals and the atomic orbitals from which they are formed?

(d) Compare the shapes of the hybrid orbitals formed from an s orbital and a p_x orbital with the hybrid atomic orbitals formed from an s orbital and a p_z orbital.

(e) Compare the shape of the hybrid orbitals formed from s, p_x, and p_y orbitals with the hybrid atomic orbitals formed from s, p_x, and p_z orbitals.

59. Screen 9.2 of ChemistryNow shows the change in energy as a function of the H—H distance when H_2 forms from separated H atoms.

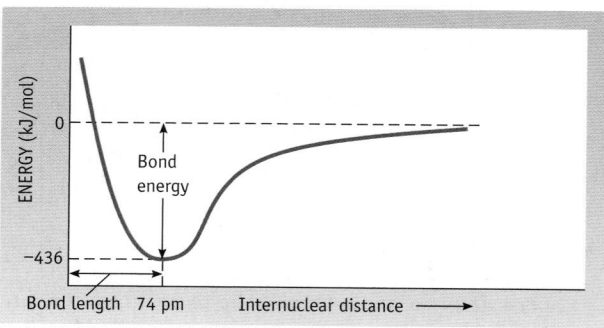

(a) Screen 9.3 describes the attractive and repulsive forces that occur when two atoms approach each other. What must be true about the relative strengths of those attractive and repulsive forces if a covalent bond is to form?

(b) When two atoms are widely separated, the energy of the system is defined as zero. As the atoms approach each other, the energy drops, reaches a minimum, and then increases as they approach still more closely. Explain these observations.

(c) For a bond to form, orbitals on adjacent atoms must overlap, and each pair of overlapping orbitals will contain two electrons. Explain why neon does not form a diatomic molecule, Ne_2, whereas fluorine forms F_2.

60. Examine the bonding in ethylene, C_2H_4, on Screen 9.7 of ChemistryNow and then go to the *A Closer Look* auxiliary screen.

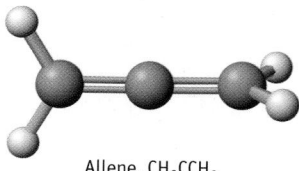

Allene, CH_2CCH_2

(a) Explain why the allene molecule is not flat. That is, explain why the CH_2 groups at opposite ends do not lie in the same plane.

(b) Based on the theory of orbital hybridization, explain why benzene is a planar, symmetrical molecule.

(c) What are the hybrid orbitals used by the three C atoms of allyl alcohol?

$$\underset{3}{C}=\underset{2}{C}-\underset{1}{C}-\overset{..}{\underset{..}{O}}-H$$

with H atoms: H H H on top of C=C-C, and H H on bottom of C=C-C

▲ more challenging   ■ in OWL   Blue-numbered questions answered in Appendix O

61. Screen 9.8 of ChemistryNow describes the motions of molecules.

(a) Observe the animations of the rotations of *trans*-2-butene and butane about their carbon–carbon bonds.

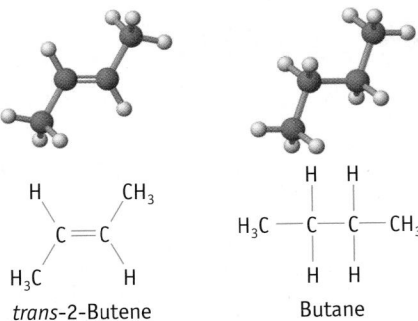

trans-2-Butene   Butane

As one end of *trans*-2-butene rotates relative to the other end, the energy increases about 20-25 kJ/mol and then drops as the rotation produces *cis*-2-butene. In contrast, the rotation of the butane molecule requires much less energy (only 12.5 kJ/mol). When butane has reached the halfway point in its rotation, the energy has reached a maximum. Why does *trans*-2-butene require so much more energy to rotate about the central carbon–carbon bond than does butane?

(b) Can the two CH_2 fragments of allene (see the sidebar of Screen 9.7) rotate with respect to each other? Briefly explain why or why not.

10 | Carbon: More Than Just Another Element

Charles D. Winters

Camphor, an "Aromatic" Molecule

You might know just what this compound smells like! When you were a child and had a cold or cough, your mother might have smeared some Vick's® VapoRub on your chest. This home remedy, now more than 100 years old, contains camphor (5% by weight) as well as eucalyptus oil, turpentine oil, and menthol as active ingredients.

Camphor is said to be the first pure chemical that humans isolated and purified. Beginning in about 3000 BC, it was isolated from the camphor tree (*Cinnamomum camphora*), a native of China, Japan, and Indonesia, by chipping the wood from the tree and then steaming it. Camphor, being quite volatile, readily sublimes, and the solid is collected by cooling the resulting vapor.

An early use for camphor was as a wine additive, but the compound is toxic when taken internally, so this was clearly not a healthy practice. In the Middle Ages, it was said to be an aphrodisiac, but later it was declared an antiaphrodisiac.

Camphor was also used as a treatment during the yellow fever epidemic in 1793 that killed thousands in Philadelphia. Benjamin Rush, a Philadelphia physician, chemist (who published the first American chemistry textbook), and signer of the Declaration of Independence, recommended a mixture of vinegar and camphor to ward off the yellow fever. It did not cure the disease, but it did keep away mosquitoes, the carrier of yellow fever.

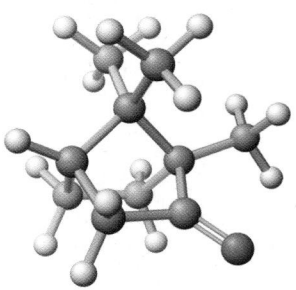

Questions:

1. The structure of camphor is interesting, although it was not known until 1893.
   a) The O atom is attached to a structurally unique C atom. What is the geometry around this atom? What is its hybridization? What are the geometry and hybridization of the other C atoms in the molecule?
   b) The five- and six-carbon rings in the molecule are not flat. Why is this so?
   c) Is there a chiral center in this molecule? (See page 446.)
2. Organic compounds are often classified by their "functional group." To what class does this molecule belong?

Answers to these questions are in Appendix Q.

The vast majority of the millions of chemical compounds currently known are organic; that is, they are compounds built on a carbon framework. Organic compounds vary greatly in size and complexity, from the simplest hydrocarbon, methane, to molecules made up of many thousands of atoms. As you read this chapter, you will see why the range of possible materials is huge.

Chemistry.Now™

Throughout the text this icon introduces an opportunity for self-study or to explore interactive tutorials by signing in at **www.cengage.com/login**.

10.1 Why Carbon?

We begin this discussion of organic chemistry with a question: What features of carbon lead to both the abundance and the complexity of organic compounds? Answers fall into two categories: structural diversity and stability.

Structural Diversity

With four electrons in its outer shell, carbon will form four bonds to reach an octet configuration. In contrast, the elements boron and nitrogen form three bonds in molecular compounds; oxygen forms two bonds; and hydrogen and the halogens form one bond. With a larger number of bonds comes the opportunity to create more complex structures. This will become increasingly evident in this brief tour of organic chemistry.

A carbon atom can reach an octet of electrons in various ways (Figure 10.1):

- *By forming four single bonds.* A carbon atom can bond to four other atoms, which can be either atoms of other elements (often H, N, or O) or other carbon atoms.
- *By forming a double bond and two single bonds.* The carbon atoms in ethylene, $H_2C{=}CH_2$, are linked to other atoms in this way.
- *By forming two double bonds,* as in carbon dioxide $(O{=}C{=}O)$.
- *By forming a triple bond and a single bond,* an arrangement seen in acetylene, $HC{\equiv}CH$.

Recognize, with each of these arrangements, the various possible geometries around carbon: tetrahedral, trigonal planar, and linear. Carbon's tetrahedral

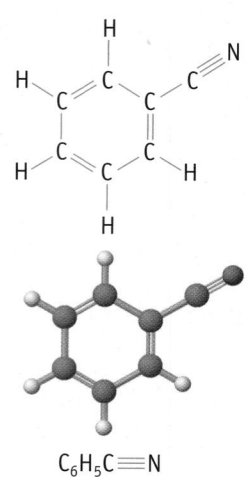

(a) Acetic acid. One carbon atom in this compound is attached to four other atoms by single bonds and has tetrahedral geometry. The second carbon atom, connected by a double bond to one oxygen and by single bonds to the other oxygen and to carbon, has trigonal-planar geometry.

$$CH_3COH$$
(with O double-bonded above C)

(b) Benzonitrile. Six trigonal-planar carbon atoms make up the benzene ring. The seventh C atom, bonded by a single bond to carbon and a triple bond to nitrogen, has a linear geometry.

$$C_6H_5C{\equiv}N$$

(c) Carbon is linked by double bonds to two other carbon atoms in C_3H_4, a linear molecule commonly called allene.

$$CH_2{=}C{=}CH_2$$

FIGURE 10.1 Ways that carbon atoms bond.

geometry is of special significance because it leads to three-dimensional chains and rings of carbon atoms, as in propane and cyclopentane.

propane, C_3H_8 cyclopentane, C_5H_{10}

The ability to form multiple bonds leads to families of compounds with double and triple bonds.

Isomers

A hallmark of carbon chemistry is the remarkable array of isomers that can exist. **Isomers** are compounds that have identical composition but different structures. Two broad categories of isomers exist: structural isomers and stereoisomers.

 Structural isomers are compounds having the same elemental composition, but the atoms are linked together in different ways. Ethanol and dimethyl ether are structural isomers, as are 1-butene and 2-methylpropene.

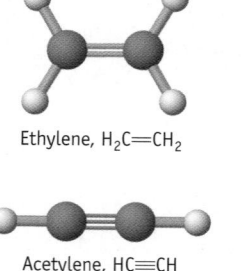

Ethylene, $H_2C{=}CH_2$

Acetylene, $HC{\equiv}CH$

Ethylene and acetylene. These two-carbon hydrocarbons can be the building blocks of more complex molecules. These are their common names, but their systematic names are ethene and ethyne.

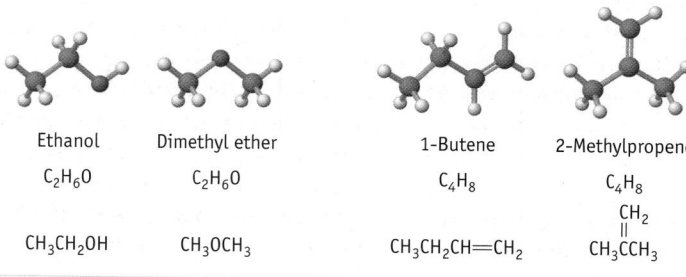

Ethanol

C_2H_6O

CH_3CH_2OH

Dimethyl ether

C_2H_6O

CH_3OCH_3

1-Butene

C_4H_8

$CH_3CH_2CH{=}CH_2$

2-Methylpropene

C_4H_8

CH_3CCH_3 (with CH_2 double-bonded)

In Chapter 2, you learned that there are various ways of presenting structures (page 68). It is appropriate to return to this topic as we look at organic compounds. Consider methane and ethane, for example. We can represent these molecules in several ways:

1. *Molecular formula:* CH_4 or C_2H_6. This type of formula gives information on composition only.
2. *Condensed formula:* For ethane, this would be written CH_3CH_3 (or as H_3CCH_3). This method of writing the formula gives some information on the way atoms are connected.
3. *Structural formula:* You will recognize this formula as the Lewis structure. An elaboration on the condensed formula in (2), this representation defines more clearly how the atoms are connected,

but it fails to describe the shapes of molecules.

Methane, CH_4 Ethane, C_2H_6

4. *Perspective drawings:* These drawings are used to convey the three-dimensional nature of molecules. Bonds extending out of the plane of the paper are drawn with wedges, and bonds behind the plane of the paper are represented as dashed wedges (page 70). Using these guidelines, the structures of methane and ethane could be drawn as follows:

5. *Computer-drawn ball-and-stick and space-filling models.*

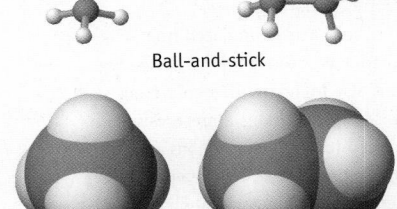

Ball-and-stick

Space-filling

Stereoisomers are compounds with the same formula and in which there is a similar attachment of atoms. However, the atoms have different orientations in space. Two types of stereoisomers exist: geometric isomers and optical isomers.

Cis- and *trans-*2-butene are **geometric isomers.** Geometric isomerism in these compounds occurs as a result of the C=C double bond. Recall that the carbon atom and the attached groups cannot rotate around a double bond (page 420). Thus, the geometry around the C=C double bond is fixed in space. If identical groups occur on the adjacent carbon atoms and on the same side of the double bond, a *cis* isomer is produced. If those groups appear on opposite sides, a *trans* isomer is produced.

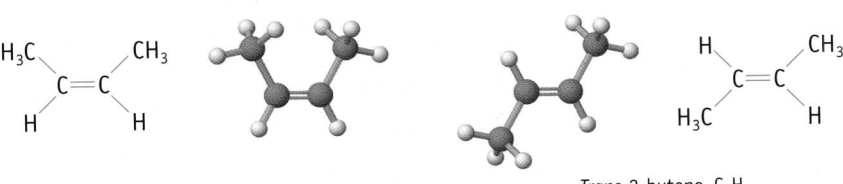

Cis-2-butene, C_4H_8 Trans-2-butene, C_4H_8

Optical isomerism is a second type of stereoisomerism. Optical isomers are molecules that have nonsuperimposable mirror images (Figure 10.2). Molecules (and other objects) that have nonsuperimposable mirror images are termed **chiral.** Pairs of nonsuperimposable molecules are called **enantiomers.**

Pure samples of enantiomers have the same physical properties, such as melting point, boiling point, density, and solubility in common solvents. They differ in one significant way, however: When a beam of plane-polarized light passes through a solution of a pure enantiomer, the plane of polarization rotates. The two enantiomers rotate polarized light to an equal extent, but in opposite directions (Figure 10.3). The term "optical isomerism" is used because this effect involves light.

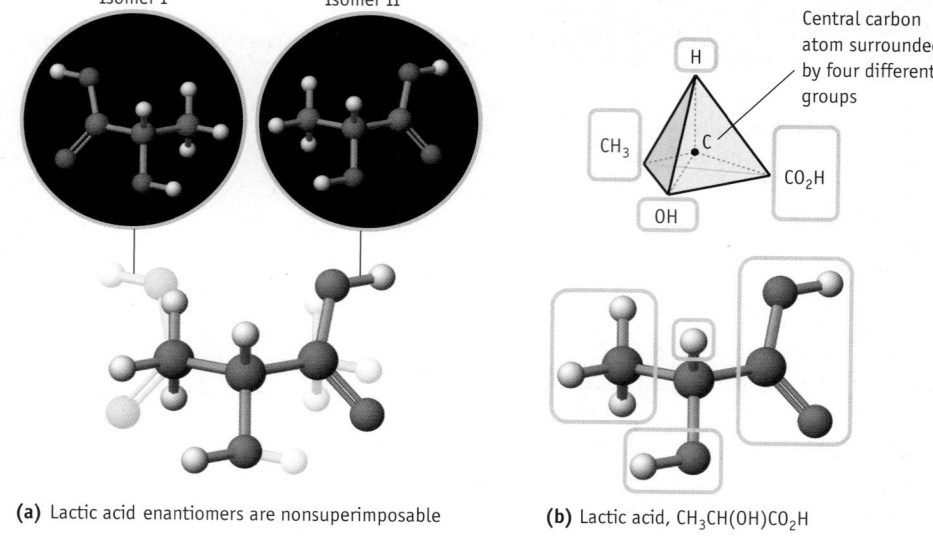

(a) Lactic acid enantiomers are nonsuperimposable

(b) Lactic acid, $CH_3CH(OH)CO_2H$

The most common examples of chiral compounds are those in which four different atoms (or groups of atoms) are attached to a tetrahedral carbon atom. Lactic acid,
found in milk and a product of normal human metabolism, is an example of one
such chiral compound (Figure 10.2). Optical isomerism is particularly important in
the amino acids (▶ *The Chemistry of Life: Biochemistry*) and other biologically important
molecules. Among the many interesting examples is a compound, frontalin, produced
naturally by male elephants (see "Chemical Perspectives: Chirality and Elephants").

Stability of Carbon Compounds

Carbon compounds are notable for their resistance to chemical change. This resistance is a result of two things: strong bonds and slow reactions.

Strong bonds are needed for molecules to survive in their environment.
Molecular collisions in gases, liquids, and solutions often provide enough energy
to break some chemical bonds, and bonds can be broken if the energy associated
with photons of visible and ultraviolet light exceeds the bond energy. Carbon–
carbon bonds are relatively strong, however, as are the bonds between carbon and
most other atoms. The average C—C bond energy is 346 kJ/mol; the C—H bond
energy is 413 kJ/mol; and carbon–carbon double and triple bond energies are even
higher (◀ Section 8.9). Contrast these values with bond energies for the Si—H
bond (328 kJ/mol) and the Si—Si bond (222 kJ/mol). The consequence of high

**FIGURE 10.3 Rotation of plane-
polarized light by an optical isomer.**
Monochromatic light (light of only one
wavelength) is produced by a sodium
lamp. After it passes through a polarizing filter, the light vibrates in only one
direction—it is polarized. A solution of an
optical isomer placed between the first
and second polarizing filters causes rotation of the plane of polarized light. The
angle of rotation can be determined by
rotating the second filter until maximum
light transmission occurs. The magnitude
and direction of rotation are unique
physical properties of the optical isomer
being tested.

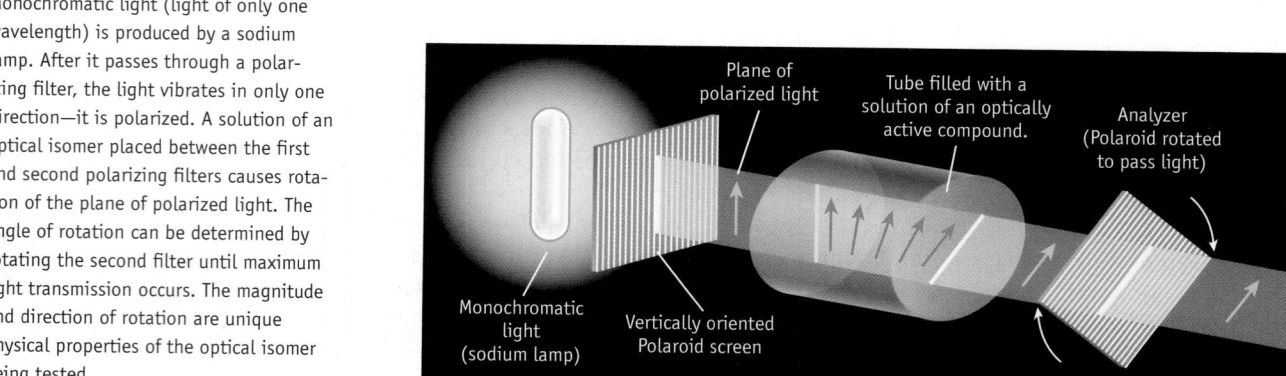

During a period known as musth, male elephants undergo a time of heightened sexual activity. They can become more aggressive and can work themselves into a frenzy. Aside from these physical changes, the males also produce chemical signals. A secretion containing the enantiomers of frontalin ($C_8H_{14}O_2$) is emitted from a gland between the eye and the ear. Young males produce mixtures containing more of one enantiomer than the other, whereas older elephants produce a more balanced and more concentrated mixture. When that occurs in older elephants, other males are repelled, but ovulating female elephants are more highly attracted.

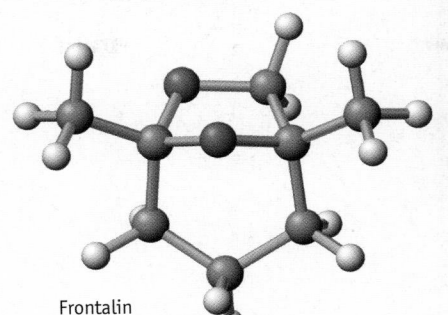

Frontalin

John Katz

An African elephant in musth. Fluid containing the enantiomers of frontalin flows from a gland between the elephant's eye and ear.

bond energies for bonds to carbon is that, for the most part, organic compounds do not degrade under normal conditions.

Oxidation of most organic compounds is strongly product-favored, but most organic compounds survive contact with O_2. The reason is that these reactions occur slowly. Most organic compounds burn only if their combustion is initiated by heat or by a spark. As a consequence, oxidative degradation is not a barrier to the existence of organic compounds.

Module 15

10.2 Hydrocarbons

Hydrocarbons, compounds made of carbon and hydrogen only, are classified into several subgroups: alkanes, cycloalkanes, alkenes, alkynes, and aromatic compounds (Table 10.1). We begin our discussion by considering compounds that have carbon atoms with four single bonds, the alkanes and cycloalkanes.

Chemistry Now™

Sign in at **www.cengage.com/login** and go to Chapter 10 Contents to see Screen 10.3 for a description of the **classes of hydrocarbons.**

TABLE 10.1 Some Types of Hydrocarbons

Type of Hydrocarbon	Characteristic Features	General Formula	Example
alkanes	C—C single bonds and all C atoms have four single bonds	C_nH_{2n+2}	CH_4, methane C_2H_6, ethane
cycloalkanes	C—C single bonds and all C atoms have four single bonds	C_nH_{2n}	C_6H_{12}, cyclohexane
alkenes	C=C double bond	C_nH_{2n}	$H_2C=CH_2$, ethylene
alkynes	C≡C triple bond	C_nH_{2n-2}	HC≡CH, acetylene
aromatics	rings with π bonding extending over several C atoms	—	benzene, C_6H_6

TABLE 10.2 Selected Hydrocarbons of the Alkane Family, C_nH_{2n+2}*

Name	Molecular Formula	State at Room Temperature
methane	CH_4	
ethane	C_2H_6	gas
propane	C_3H_8	
butane	C_4H_{10}	
pentane	C_5H_{12} (pent- = 5)	
hexane	C_6H_{14} (hex- = 6)	
heptane	C_7H_{16} (hept- = 7)	liquid
octane	C_8H_{18} (oct- = 8)	
nonane	C_9H_{20} (non- = 9)	
decane	$C_{10}H_{22}$ (dec- = 10)	
octadecane	$C_{18}H_{38}$ (octadec- = 18)	solid
eicosane	$C_{20}H_{42}$ (eicos- = 20)	

* This table lists only selected alkanes. Liquid compounds with 11 to 16 carbon atoms are also known. Many solid alkanes with more than 20 carbon atoms also exist.

Alkanes

Alkanes have the general formula C_nH_{2n+2}, with n having integer values (Table 10.2). Formulas of specific compounds can be generated from this general formula, the first four of which are CH_4 (methane), C_2H_6 (ethane), C_3H_8 (propane), and C_4H_{10} (butane) (Figure 10.4). Methane has four hydrogen atoms arranged tetrahedrally around a single carbon atom. Replacing a hydrogen atom in methane by a —CH_3 group gives ethane. If an H atom of ethane is replaced by yet another —CH_3 group, propane results. Butane is derived from propane by replacing an H atom of one of the chain-ending carbon atoms with a —CH_3 group. In all of these compounds, each C atom is attached to four other atoms, either C or H, so alkanes are often called **saturated compounds**.

Structural Isomers

Structural isomers are possible for all alkanes larger than propane. For example, there are two structural isomers for C_4H_{10} and three for C_5H_{12}. As the number of carbon atoms in an alkane increases, the number of possible structural isomers

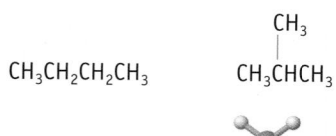

$CH_3CH_2CH_2CH_3$

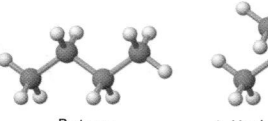

Butane

CH_3CHCH_3 with CH_3 above

2-Methylpropane

Structural isomers of butane, C_4H_{10}.

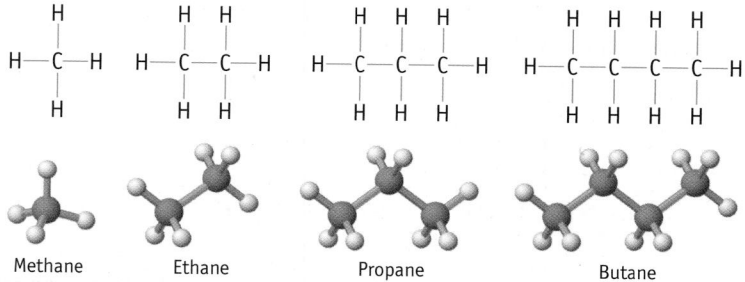

Active Figure 10.4 **Alkanes.** The lowest–molar-mass alkanes, all gases under normal conditions, are methane, ethane, propane, and butane.

Chemistry ⚛ Now™ Sign in at www.cengage.com/login and go to the Chapter Contents menu to explore an interactive version of this figure accompanied by an exercise.

greatly increases; there are five isomers possible for C_6H_{14}, nine isomers for C_7H_{16}, 18 for C_8H_{18}, 75 for $C_{10}H_{22}$, and 366,319 for $C_{20}H_{42}$.

To recognize the isomers corresponding to a given formula, keep in mind the following points:

- Each alkane is built upon a framework of tetrahedral carbon atoms, and each carbon must have four single bonds.
- An effective approach is to create a framework of carbon atoms and then fill the remaining positions around carbon with H atoms so that each C atom has four bonds.
- Nearly free rotation occurs around carbon–carbon single bonds. Therefore, when atoms are assembled to form the skeleton of an alkane, the emphasis is on how carbon atoms are attached to one another and not on how they might lie relative to one another in the plane of the paper.

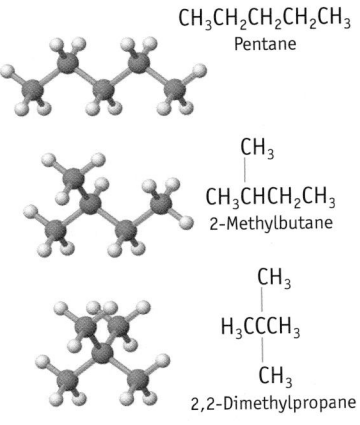

$CH_3CH_2CH_2CH_2CH_3$
Pentane

CH_3
|
$CH_3CHCH_2CH_3$
2-Methylbutane

CH_3
|
H_3CCCH_3
|
CH_3
2,2-Dimethylpropane

Structural isomers of pentane, C_5H_{12}.

■ **EXAMPLE 10.1 Drawing Structural Isomers of Alkanes**

Problem Draw structures of the five isomers of C_6H_{14}. Are any of these isomers chiral?

Strategy Focus first on the different frameworks that can be built from six carbon atoms. Having created a carbon framework, fill hydrogen atoms into the structure so that each carbon has four bonds.

Solution

Step 1. Placing six carbon atoms in a chain gives the framework for the first isomer. Now fill in hydrogen atoms: three on the carbons on the ends of the chain, two on each of the carbons in the middle. You have created the first isomer, hexane.

C — C — C — C — C — C ⟶ H — C — C — C — C — C — C — H

carbon framework of hexane   hexane

Step 2. Draw a chain of five carbon atoms; then add the sixth carbon atom to one of the carbons in the middle of this chain. (Adding it to a carbon at the end of the chain gives a six-carbon chain, the same framework drawn in Step 1.) Two different carbon frameworks can be built from the five-carbon chain, depending on whether the sixth carbon is linked to the 2 or 3 position. For each of these frameworks, fill in the hydrogens.

carbon framework of methylpentane isomers

2-methylpentane

3-methylpentane

■ **Chirality in Alkanes** To be chiral, *a compound must have at least one C atom attached to four different groups.* Thus, the C_7H_{16} isomer here is chiral.

CH_3
|
H — C* — CH_2CH_3
|
$CH_2CH_2CH_3$

We often designate the center of chirality with an asterisk.

Step 3. Draw a chain of four carbon atoms. Add in the two remaining carbons, again being careful not to extend the chain length. Two different structures are possible: one with the remaining carbon atoms in the 2 and 3 positions, and another with both extra carbon atoms attached at the 2 position. Fill in the 14 hydrogens. You have now drawn the fourth and fifth isomers.

carbon atom frameworks for dimethylbutane isomers

2,3-dimethylbutane

2,2-dimethylbutane

None of the isomers of C_6H_{14} is chiral. *To be chiral, a compound must have at least one C atom with four different groups attached.* This condition is not met in any of these isomers.

Comment Should we look for structures in which the longest chain is three carbon atoms? Try it, but you will see that it is not possible to add the three remaining carbons to a three-carbon chain without creating one of the carbon chains already drawn in a previous step. Thus, we have completed the analysis, with five isomers of this compound being identified.

Names have been given to each of these compounds. See the text that follows this Example, and see Appendix E for guidelines on nomenclature.

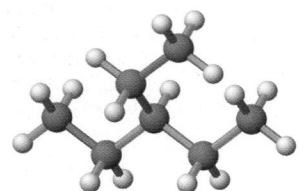

One possible isomer of an alkane with the formula C_7H_{16}.

EXERCISE 10.1 Drawing Structural Isomers of Alkanes

(a) Draw the nine isomers having the formula C_7H_{16}. (Hint: There is one structure with a seven-carbon chain, two structures with six-carbon chains, five structures in which the longest chain has five carbons [one is illustrated in the margin], and one structure with a four-carbon chain.)

(b) Identify the isomers of C_7H_{16} that are chiral.

■ **Naming Guidelines** For more details on naming organic compounds, see Appendix E.

Naming Alkanes

With so many possible isomers for a given alkane, chemists need a systematic way of naming them. The guidelines for naming alkanes and their derivatives follow:

- The names of alkanes end in "-ane."
- The names of alkanes with chains of one to 10 carbon atoms are given in Table 10.2. After the first four compounds, the names are derived from Latin numbers—pentane, hexane, heptane, octane, nonane, decane—and this regular naming continues for higher alkanes.
- When naming a specific alkane, the root of the name corresponds to the longest carbon chain in the compound. One isomer of C_5H_{12} has a three—

An error students sometimes make is to suggest that the three carbon skeletons drawn here are different. They are, in fact, the same. All are five-carbon chains with another C atom in the 2 position.

$$
\begin{array}{ccccc}
& C & & & \\
& | & & & \\
C - & C - & C - & C - & C \\
1 & 2 & 3 & 4 & 5
\end{array}
\qquad
\begin{array}{ccccc}
C & & & & \\
| & & & & \\
C - & C - & C - & C & \\
2 & 3 & 4 & 5 & \\
| & & & & \\
C & & & & \\
1 & & & &
\end{array}
\qquad
\begin{array}{ccccc}
& & C & & \\
& & | & & \\
C - & C - & C - & C - & C \\
5 & 4 & 3 & 2 & 1
\end{array}
$$

Remember that Lewis structures do not indicate the geometry of molecules.

carbon chain with two —CH$_3$ groups on the second C atom of the chain. Thus, its name is based on propane.

$$
\begin{array}{c}
CH_3 \\
| \\
H_3C - C - CH_3 \\
| \\
CH_3
\end{array}
$$

2,2-dimethylpropane

- Substituent groups on a hydrocarbon chain are identified by a name and the position of substitution in the carbon chain; this information precedes the root of the name. The position is indicated by a number that refers to the carbon atom to which the substituent is attached. (Numbering of the carbon atoms in a chain should begin at the end of the carbon chain that allows the substituent groups to have the lowest numbers.) Both —CH$_3$ groups in 2,2-dimethylpropane are located at the 2 position.
- Names of hydrocarbon substituents, called **alkyl groups,** are derived from the name of the hydrocarbon. The group —CH$_3$, derived by taking a hydrogen from methane, is called the methyl group; the C$_2$H$_5$ group is the ethyl group.
- If two or more of the same substituent groups occur, the prefixes di-, tri-, and tetra- are added. When different substituent groups are present, they are generally listed in alphabetical order.

■ **Systematic and Common Names** The IUPAC (International Union of Pure and Applied Chemistry) has formulated rules for systematic names, which are generally used in this book. (See Appendix E.) However, many organic compounds are known by common names. For example, 2,2-dimethylpropane is also called neopentane.

EXAMPLE 10.2 Naming Alkanes

Problem Give the systematic name for

$$
\begin{array}{cc}
CH_3 & C_2H_5 \\
| & | \\
CH_3CHCH_2CH_2CHCH_2CH_3 &
\end{array}
$$

Strategy Identify the longest carbon chain and base the name of the compound on that alkane. Identify the substituent groups on the chain and their locations. When there are two or more substituents (the groups attached to the chain), number the parent chain from the end that gives the lower number to the substituent encountered first. If the substituents are different, list them in alphabetical order. (For more on naming compounds, see Appendix E.)

Solution Here, the longest chain has seven C atoms, so the root of the name is *heptane*. There is a methyl group on C-2 and an ethyl group on C-5. Giving the substituents in alphabetic order and numbering the chain from the end having the methyl group, the systematic name is 5-ethyl-2-methylheptane.

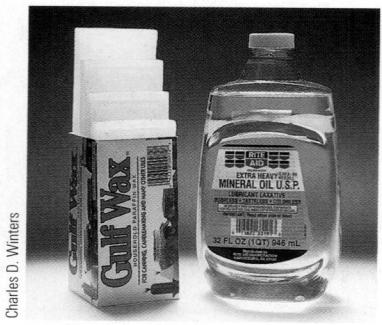

Charles D. Winters

FIGURE 10.5 Paraffin wax and mineral oil. These common consumer products are mixtures of alkanes.

EXERCISE 10.2 Naming Alkanes

Name the nine isomers of C_7H_{16} in Exercise 10.1.

Properties of Alkanes

Methane, ethane, propane, and butane are gases at room temperature and pressure, whereas the higher–molar-mass compounds are liquids or solids (Table 10.2). An increase in melting point and boiling point with molar mass is a general phenomenon that reflects the increased forces of attraction between molecules (▶ Section 12.2).

You already know about alkanes in a nonscientific context because several are common fuels. Natural gas, gasoline, kerosene, fuel oils, and lubricating oils are all mixtures of various alkanes. White mineral oil is also a mixture of alkanes, as is paraffin wax (Figure 10.5).

Pure alkanes are colorless. (The colors seen in gasoline and other petroleum products are due to additives.) The gases and liquids have noticeable but not unpleasant odors. All of these substances are insoluble in water, which is typical of compounds that are nonpolar or nearly so. Low polarity is expected for alkanes because the electronegativities of carbon ($\chi = 2.5$) and hydrogen ($\chi = 2.2$) are not greatly different (◀ Section 8.8).

All alkanes burn readily in air to give CO_2 and H_2O in very exothermic reactions. This is, of course, the reason they are widely used as fuels.

$$CH_4(g) + 2\ O_2(g) \rightarrow CO_2(g) + 2\ H_2O(\ell) \qquad \Delta_r H° = -890.3 \text{ kJ/mol-rxn}$$

Other than in combustion reactions, alkanes exhibit relatively low chemical reactivity. One reaction that does occur, however, is the replacement of the hydrogen atoms of an alkane by chlorine atoms on reaction with Cl_2. It is formally an oxidation because Cl_2, like O_2, is a strong oxidizing agent. These reactions, which can be initiated by ultraviolet radiation, are free radical reactions. Highly reactive Cl atoms are formed from Cl_2 under UV radiation. Reaction of methane with Cl_2 under these conditions proceeds in a series of steps, eventually yielding CCl_4, commonly known as carbon tetrachloride. (HCl is the other product of these reactions.)

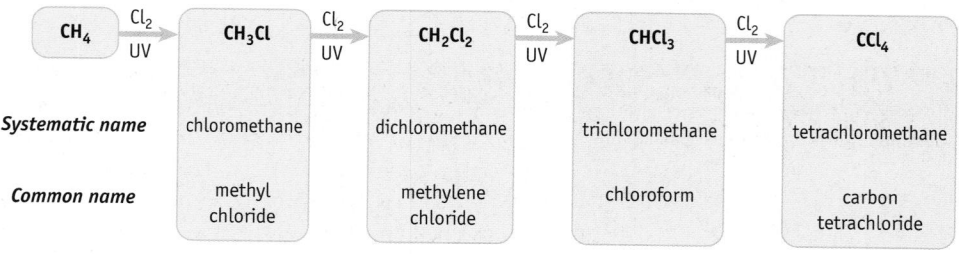

CH₄ →Cl₂/UV→	**CH₃Cl** →Cl₂/UV→	**CH₂Cl₂** →Cl₂/UV→	**CHCl₃** →Cl₂/UV→	**CCl₄**
Systematic name	chloromethane	dichloromethane	trichloromethane	tetrachloromethane
Common name	methyl chloride	methylene chloride	chloroform	carbon tetrachloride

The last three compounds are used as solvents, albeit less frequently today because of their toxicity. Carbon tetrachloride was also once widely used as a dry cleaning fluid and, because it does not burn, in fire extinguishers.

Cycloalkanes, C_nH_{2n}

Cycloalkanes are constructed with tetrahedral carbon atoms joined together to form a ring. For example, cyclopentane, C_5H_{10}, consists of a ring of five carbon atoms. Each carbon atom is bonded to two adjacent carbon atoms and to two hydrogen atoms. Notice that the five carbon atoms fall very nearly in a plane because

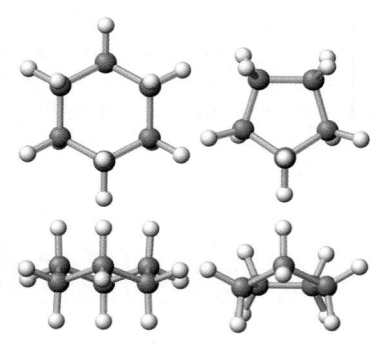

Cyclohexane, top and front views   Cyclopentane, top and front views

The structures of cyclopentane, C_5H_{10}, and cyclohexane, C_6H_{12}. The C_5 ring is nearly planar. In contrast, the tetrahedral geometry around carbon means that the C_6 ring is decidedly puckered.

Flexible Molecules

Most organic molecules are flexible; that is, they can twist and bend in various ways. Few molecules better illustrate this behavior than cyclohexane. Two structures are possible: "chair" and "boat" forms. These forms can interconvert by partial rotation of several bonds.

The more stable structure is the chair form, which allows the hydrogen atoms to remain as far apart as possible. A side view of this form of cyclohexane reveals two sets of hydrogen atoms in this molecule. Six hydrogen atoms, called the equatorial hydrogen atoms,

lie in a plane around the carbon ring. The other six hydrogens are positioned above and below the plane and are called axial hydrogens. Flexing the ring (a rotation around the C—C single bonds) moves the hydrogen atoms between axial and equatorial environments.

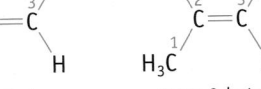

chair form   boat form   chair form

the internal angles of a pentagon, 108°, closely match the tetrahedral angle of 109.5°. The small distortion from planarity allows hydrogen atoms on adjacent carbon atoms to be a little farther apart.

Cyclohexane has a nonplanar ring with six —CH_2 groups. If the carbon atoms were in the form of a regular hexagon with all carbon atoms in one plane, the C—C—C bond angles would be 120°. To have tetrahedral bond angles of 109.5° around each C atom, the ring has to pucker. The C_6 ring is flexible, however, and exists in two interconverting forms (see *A Closer Look: Flexible Molecules*).

Interestingly, cyclobutane and cyclopropane are also known, although the bond angles in these species are much less than 109.5°. These compounds are examples of **strained hydrocarbons,** so named because an unfavorable geometry is imposed around carbon. One of the features of strained hydrocarbons is that the C—C bonds are weaker and the molecules readily undergo ring-opening reactions that relieve the bond angle strain.

Alkenes and Alkynes

The diversity seen for alkanes is repeated with **alkenes,** hydrocarbons with one or more C=C double bonds. The presence of the double bond adds two features missing in alkanes: the possibility of geometric isomerism and increased reactivity.

The general formula for alkenes is C_nH_{2n}. The first two members of the series of alkenes are ethene, C_2H_4 (common name, ethylene), and propene, C_3H_6 (common name, propylene). Only a single structure can be drawn for these compounds. As with alkanes, the occurrence of isomers begins with species containing four carbon atoms. Four alkene isomers have the formula C_4H_8, and each has distinct chemical and physical properties (Table 10.3).

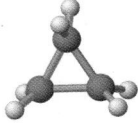

Cyclopropane, C_3H_6 Cyclobutane, C_4H_8

Cyclopropane and cyclobutane. Cyclopropane was at one time used as a general anesthetic in surgery. However, its explosive nature when mixed with oxygen soon eliminated this application. The *Columbia Encyclopedia* states that "cyclopropane allowed the transport of more oxygen to the tissues than did other common anesthetics and also produced greater skeletal muscle relaxation. It is not irritating to the respiratory tract. Because of the low solubility of cyclopropane in the blood, postoperative recovery was usually rapid but nausea and vomiting were common."

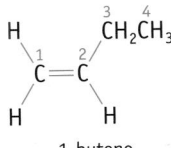

1-butene   2-methylpropene   *cis*-2-butene   *trans*-2-butene

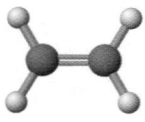

C_2H_4
Systematic name:
Ethene
Common name:
Ethylene

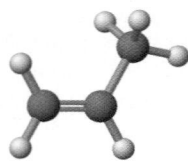

C_3H_6
Systematic name:
Propene
Common name:
Propylene

TABLE 10.3 Properties of Butene Isomers

Name	Boiling Point	Melting Point	Dipole Moment (D)	$\Delta_f H°$ (gas) (kJ/mol)
1-butene	−6.26 °C	−185.4 °C	—	−20.5
2-methylpropene	−6.95 °C	−140.4 °C	0.503	−37.5
cis-2-butene	3.71 °C	−138.9 °C	0.253	−29.7
trans-2-butene	0.88 °C	−105.5 °C	0	−33.0

Alkene names end in "-ene." As with alkanes, the root name for alkenes is that of the longest carbon chain that contains the double bond. The position of the double bond is indicated with a number, and, when appropriate, the prefix *cis* or *trans* is added. Three of the C_4H_8 isomers have four-carbon chains and so are butenes. One has a three-carbon chain and is a propene. Notice that the carbon chain is numbered from the end that gives the double bond the lowest number. In the first isomer at the left, the double bond is between C atoms 1 and 2, so the name is 1-butene and not 3-butene.

■ EXAMPLE 10.3 Determining Isomers of Alkenes from a Formula

Problem Draw structures for the six possible alkene isomers with the formula C_5H_{10}. Give the systematic name of each.

Strategy A procedure that involved drawing the carbon skeleton and then adding hydrogen atoms served well when drawing structures of alkanes (Example 10.1), and a similar approach can be used here. It will be necessary to put one double bond into the framework and to be alert for *cis–trans* isomerism.

Solution

1. A five-carbon chain with one double bond can be constructed in two ways. *Cis–trans* isomers are possible for 2-pentene.

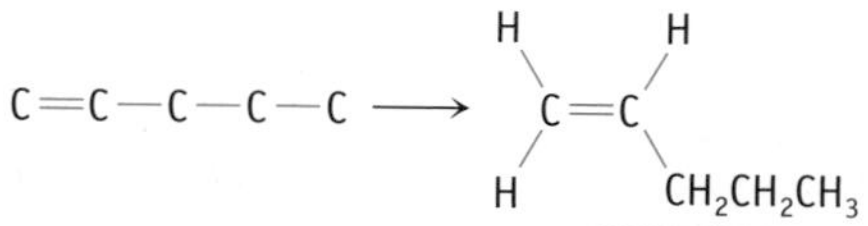

$$C=C-C-C-C \longrightarrow$$

1-pentene

$$C-C=C-C-C$$

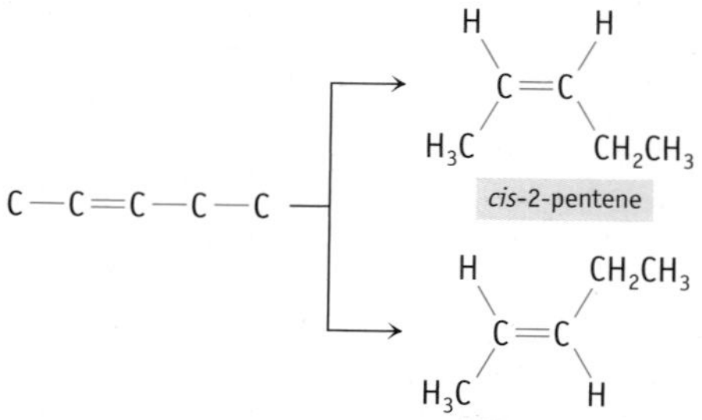

cis-2-pentene

trans-2-pentene

2. Draw the possible four-carbon chains containing a double bond. Add the fifth carbon atom to either the 2 or 3 position. When all three possible combinations are found, fill in the hydrogen atoms. This results in three more structures:

$$\underset{1}{C}=\underset{2}{\overset{\overset{\displaystyle C}{|}}{C}}-\underset{3}{C}-\underset{4}{C} \longrightarrow$$

H   CH₃
  \\   /
   C=C
  /   \\
 H   CH₂CH₃

2-methyl-1-butene

$$\underset{1}{C}=\underset{2}{C}-\underset{3}{\overset{\overset{\displaystyle C}{|}}{C}}-\underset{4}{C} \longrightarrow$$

H   H
  \\   /
   C=C
  /   \\
 H   CHCH₃
              |
             CH₃

3-methyl-1-butene

$$\underset{4}{C}-\underset{3}{C}=\underset{2}{\overset{\overset{\displaystyle C}{|}}{C}}-\underset{1}{C} \longrightarrow$$

H   CH₃
  \\   /
   C=C
  /   \\
 H₃C   CH₃

2-methyl-2-butene

EXERCISE 10.3 Determining Structural Isomers of Alkenes from a Formula

There are 17 possible alkene isomers with the formula C_6H_{12}. Draw structures of the five isomers in which the longest chain has six carbon atoms, and give the name of each. Which of these isomers is chiral? (There are also eight isomers in which the longest chain has five carbon atoms, and four isomers in which the longest chain has four carbon atoms. How many can you find?)

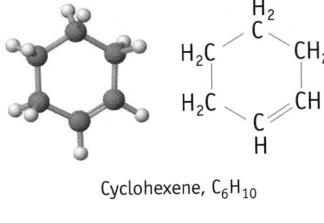

Cyclohexene, C_6H_{10}

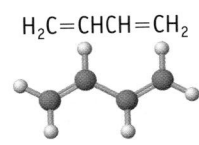

$H_2C=CHCH=CH_2$

1,3-Butadiene, C_4H_6

Cycloalkenes and dienes. Cyclohexene, C_6H_{10} (*top*), and 1,3-butadiene (C_4H_6) (*bottom*).

More than one double bond can be present in a hydrocarbon. Butadiene, for example, has two double bonds and is known as a *diene*. Many natural products have numerous double bonds (Figure 10.6). There are also cyclic hydrocarbons, such as cyclohexene, with double bonds.

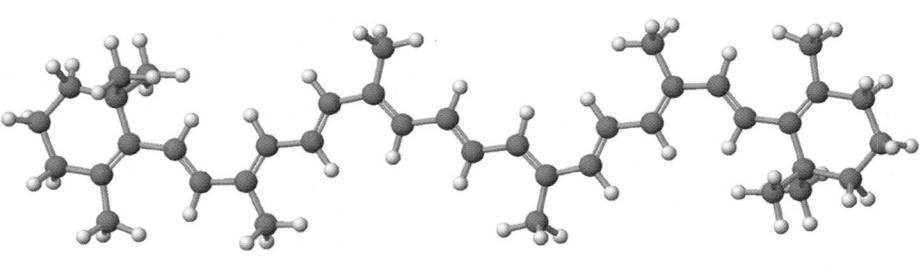

FIGURE 10.6 Carotene, a naturally occurring compound with 11 C=C bonds. The π electrons can be excited by visible light in the blue-violet region of the spectrum. As a result, carotene appears orange-yellow to the observer. Carotene or carotene-like molecules are partnered with chlorophyll in nature in the role of assisting in the harvesting of sunlight. Green leaves have a high concentration of carotene. In autumn, green chlorophyll molecules are destroyed, and the yellows and reds of carotene and related molecules are seen. The red color of tomatoes, for example, comes from a molecule very closely related to carotene. As a tomato ripens, its chlorophyll disintegrates, and the green color is replaced by the red of the carotene-like molecule.

An oxy-acetylene torch. The reaction of ethyne (acetylene) with oxygen produces a very high temperature. Oxy-acetylene torches, used in welding, take advantage of this fact.

TABLE 10.4   Some Simple Alkynes C_nH_{2n-2}

Structure	Systematic Name	Common Name	BP (°C)
$HC\equiv CH$	ethyne	acetylene	−85
$CH_3C\equiv CH$	propyne	methylacetylene	−23
$CH_3CH_2C\equiv CH$	1-butyne	ethylacetylene	9
$CH_3C\equiv CCH_3$	2-butyne	dimethylacetylene	27

Alkynes, compounds with a carbon–carbon triple bond, have the general formula (C_nH_{2n-2}). Table 10.4 lists alkynes that have four or fewer carbon atoms. The first member of this family is ethyne (common name, acetylene), a gas used as a fuel in metal cutting torches.

Properties of Alkenes and Alkynes

Like alkanes, alkenes and alkynes are colorless. Low–molar-mass compounds are gases, whereas compounds with higher molecular weights are liquids or solids. Alkanes, alkenes, and alkynes are also oxidized by O_2 to give CO_2 and H_2O.

In contrast to alkanes, alkenes and alkynes have an elaborate chemistry. We gain an insight into their chemical behavior by noting that they are called **unsaturated compounds.** Carbon atoms are capable of bonding to a maximum of four other atoms, and they do so in alkanes and cycloalkanes. In alkenes, however, the carbon atoms linked by a double bond are bonded to only three atoms; in alkynes, they bond to two atoms. It is possible to increase the number of groups attached to carbon by **addition reactions,** in which molecules with the general formula X—Y (such as hydrogen, halogens, hydrogen halides, and water) add across the carbon–carbon double bond (Figure 10.7). The result is a compound with four groups bonded to each carbon.

$$\underset{H}{\overset{H}{>}}C=C\underset{H}{\overset{H}{<}} + X-Y \longrightarrow \overset{X \quad Y}{H-C-C-H} \underset{H \quad H}{}$$

$X-Y = H_2, Cl_2, Br_2; H-Cl, H-Br, H-OH, HO-Cl$

The products of addition reactions are often substituted alkanes. For example, the addition of bromine to ethylene forms 1,2-dibromoethane.

$$\underset{H}{\overset{H}{>}}C=C\underset{H}{\overset{H}{<}} + Br_2 \longrightarrow \overset{Br \quad Br}{H-C-C-H} \underset{H \quad H}{}$$

1,2-dibromoethane

The addition of 2 mol of chlorine to acetylene gives 1,1,2,2-tetrachloroethane.

$$HC\equiv CH + 2 Cl_2 \longrightarrow \overset{Cl \quad Cl}{Cl-C-C-Cl} \underset{H \quad H}{}$$

1,1,2,2-tetrachloroethane

During the 1860s, a Russian chemist, Vladimir Markovnikov, examined a large number of alkene addition reactions. In cases in which two isomeric products were

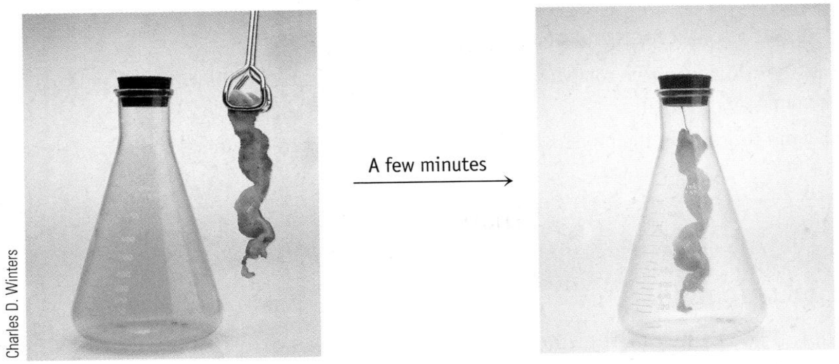
A few minutes
Charles D. Winters

FIGURE 10.7 Bacon fat and addition reactions. The fat in bacon is partially unsaturated. Like other unsaturated compounds, bacon fat reacts with Br_2 in an addition reaction. Here, you see the color of Br_2 vapor fade when a strip of bacon is introduced.

possible, he found that one was more likely to predominate. Based on these results, Markovnikov formulated a rule (now called *Markovnikov's rule*) stating that, when a reagent HX adds to an unsymmetrical alkene, the hydrogen atom in the reagent becomes attached to the carbon that already has the largest number of hydrogens. An example of Markovnikov's rule is the reaction of 2-methylpropene with HCl that results in formation of 2-chloro-2-methylpropane rather than 1-chloro-2-methylpropane.

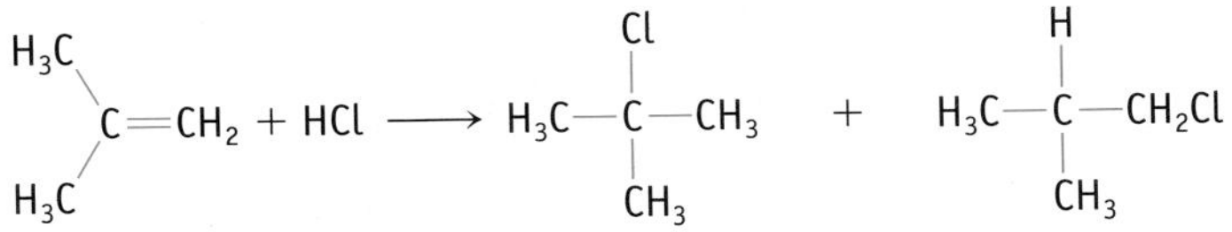
H₃C
C=CH₂ + HCl ⟶ H₃C—C—CH₃ + H₃C—C—CH₂Cl
Cl
H
CH₃

2-methylpropene — 2-chloro-2-methylpropane Sole product — 1-chloro-2-methylpropane NOT formed

■ **Nomenclature of Substituted Alkanes** The substituent groups in substituted alkanes are identified by the name and position of the substituent on the alkane chain.

If the reagent added to a double bond is hydrogen (X—Y = H_2), the reaction is called **hydrogenation.** Hydrogenation is usually a very slow reaction, but it can be speeded up in the presence of a catalyst, often a specially prepared form of a metal, such as platinum, palladium, and rhodium. You may have heard the term hydrogenation because certain foods contain "hydrogenated" or "partially hydrogenated" ingredients. One brand of crackers has a label that says, "Made with 100% pure vegetable shortening . . . (partially hydrogenated soybean oil with hydrogenated cottonseed oil)." One reason for hydrogenating an oil is to make it less susceptible to spoilage; another is to convert it from a liquid to a solid.

■ **Catalysts** A catalyst is a substance that causes a reaction to occur at a faster rate without itself being permanently changed in the reaction. We will describe catalysts in more detail in Chapter 15.

Chemistry Now™

Sign in at **www.cengage.com/login** and go to Chapter 10 Contents to see Screen 10.4 for a simulation and tutorial on **alkene addition reactions.**

EXAMPLE 10.4 Reaction of an Alkene

Problem Draw the structure of the compound obtained from the reaction of Br_2 with propene, and name the compound.

Strategy Bromine adds across the C=C double bond. The name includes the name of the carbon chain and indicates the positions of the Br atoms.

Solution

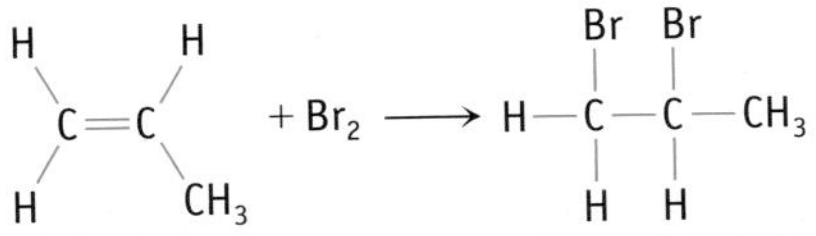
H H
C=C + Br₂ ⟶ H—C—C—CH₃
Br Br
H CH₃
H H

propene — 1,2-dibromopropane

Aromatic Compounds

Benzene, C_6H_6, is a key molecule in chemistry. It is the simplest **aromatic compound**, a class of compounds so named because they have significant, and usually not unpleasant, odors. Other members of this class, which are all based on benzene, include toluene and naphthalene. A source of many aromatic compounds is coal. These compounds, and many other volatile substances, are released when coal is heated to a high temperature in the absence of air (Table 10.5).

benzene   toluene   naphthalene

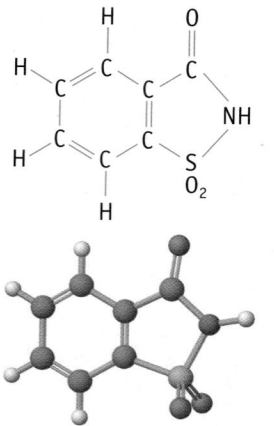

Saccharin ($C_7H_5NO_3S$). This compound, an artificial sweetener, contains an aromatic ring.

Benzene occupies a pivotal place in the history and practice of chemistry. Michael Faraday discovered this compound in 1825 as a by-product of illuminating gas, a fuel produced by heating coal. Today, benzene is an important industrial chemical, usually ranking among the top 25 chemicals in production annually in the United States. It is used as a solvent and is also the starting point for making thousands of different compounds by replacing the H atoms of the ring.

Toluene was originally obtained from tolu balsam, the pleasant-smelling gum of a South American tree, *Toluifera balsamum*. This balsam has been used in cough syrups and perfumes. Naphthalene is an ingredient in "moth balls," although 1,4-dichlorobenzene is now more commonly used. Aspartame and another artificial sweetener, saccharin, are also benzene derivatives.

TABLE 10.5   Some Aromatic Compounds from Coal Tar

Common Name	Formula	Boiling Point (°C)	Melting Point (°C)
benzene	C_6H_6	80	+6
toluene	$C_6H_5CH_3$	111	−95
o-xylene	$1,2\text{-}C_6H_4(CH_3)_2$	144	−25
m-xylene	$1,3\text{-}C_6H_4(CH_3)_2$	139	−48
p-xylene	$1,4\text{-}C_6H_4(CH_3)_2$	138	+13
naphthalene	$C_{10}H_8$	218	+80

The Structure of Benzene

The formula of benzene suggested to 19th-century chemists that this compound should be unsaturated, but, if viewed this way, its chemistry was perplexing. Whereas alkenes readily add Br_2, for example, benzene does not do so under similar conditions. The structural question was finally solved by August Kekulé (1829–1896). We now recognize that benzene's different reactivity relates to its structure and bonding, both of which are quite different from the structure and bonding in alkenes. Benzene has equivalent carbon–carbon bonds, 139 pm in length, intermediate between a C—C single bond (154 pm) and a C=C double bond (134 pm). The π bonds are formed by the continuous overlap of the p orbitals on the six carbon atoms (page 421). Using valence bond terminology, the structure is represented by a hybrid of two resonance structures.

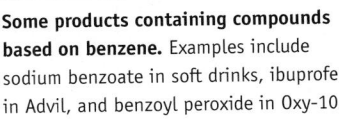

Some products containing compounds based on benzene. Examples include sodium benzoate in soft drinks, ibuprofen in Advil, and benzoyl peroxide in Oxy-10.

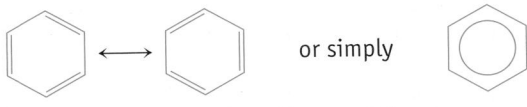

Representations of benzene, C_6H_6

Benzene Derivatives

Toluene, chlorobenzene, benzoic acid, aniline, styrene, and phenol are common examples of benzene derivatives.

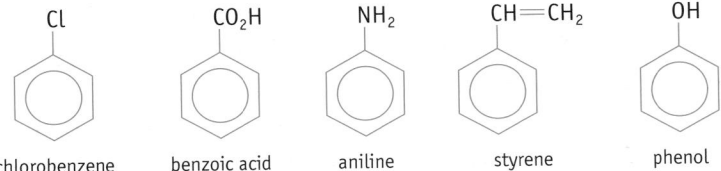

chlorobenzene   benzoic acid   aniline   styrene   phenol

If more than one H atom of benzene is replaced, isomers can arise. Thus, the systematic nomenclature for benzene derivatives involves naming substituent groups and identifying their positions on the ring by numbering the six carbon atoms (▶ Appendix E). Some common names, which are based on an older naming scheme, are also used. This scheme identified isomers of disubstituted benzenes with the prefixes *ortho* (*o*-, substituent groups on adjacent carbons in the benzene ring), *meta* (*m*-, substituents separated by one carbon atom), and *para* (*p*-, substituent groups on carbons on opposite sides of the ring).

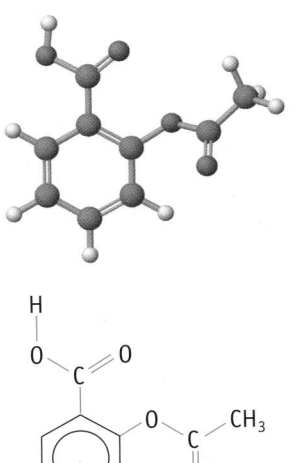

Aspirin, a commonly used analgesic. It is based on benzoic acid with an acetate group, —O_2CCH_3, in the *ortho* position.

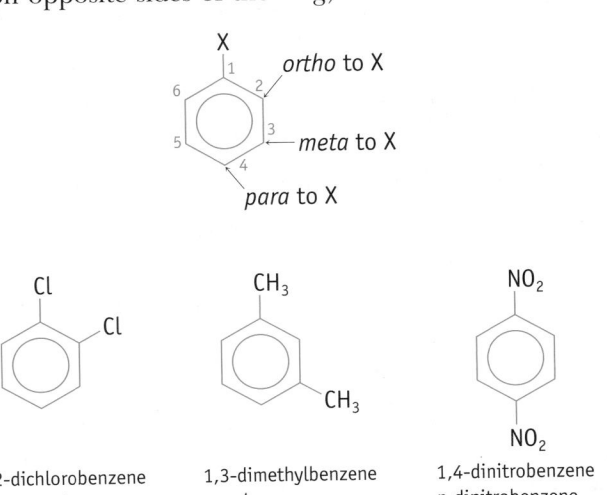

Systematic name:	1,2-dichlorobenzene	1,3-dimethylbenzene	1,4-dinitrobenzene
Common name:	*o*-dichlorobenzene	*m*-xylene	*p*-dinitrobenzene

Problem Draw and name the isomers of $C_6H_3Cl_3$.

Strategy Begin by drawing the structure of C_6H_5Cl. Place a second Cl atom on the ring in the *ortho*, *meta*, and *para* positions. Add the third Cl in one of the remaining positions.

Solution The three isomers of $C_6H_3Cl_3$ are shown here. They are named as derivatives of benzene by specifying the number of substituent groups with the prefix "tri-," the name of the substituent, and the positions of the three groups around the six-member ring.

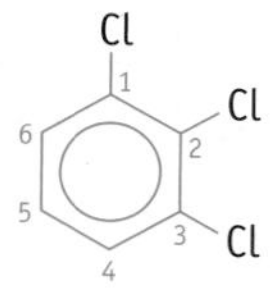

1,2,3-trichlorobenzene

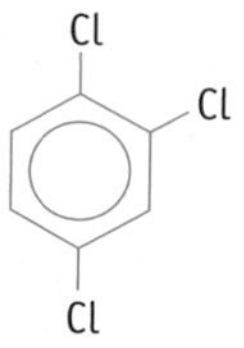

1,2,4-trichlorobenzene

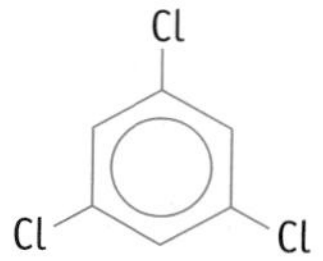

1,3,5-trichlorobenzene

EXERCISE 10.5 Isomers of Substituted Benzenes

Aniline, $C_6H_5NH_2$, is the common name for aminobenzene. Draw a structure for *p*-diaminobenzene, a compound used in dye manufacture. What is the systematic name for *p*-diaminobenzene?

Properties of Aromatic Compounds

Benzene is a colorless liquid, and simple substituted benzenes are liquids or solids under normal conditions. The properties of aromatic hydrocarbons are typical of hydrocarbons in general: They are insoluble in water, soluble in nonpolar solvents, and oxidized by O_2 to form CO_2 and H_2O.

One of the most important properties of benzene and other aromatic compounds is an unusual stability that is associated with the unique π bonding in this molecule. Because the π bonding in benzene is typically described using resonance structures, the extra stability is termed **resonance stabilization.** The extent of resonance stabilization in benzene is evaluated by comparing the energy evolved in the hydrogenation of benzene to form cyclohexane

$$C_6H_6(\ell) + 3\ H_2(g) \xrightarrow{\text{catalyst}} C_6H_{12}(\ell) \qquad \Delta_rH° = -206.7\ \text{kJ/mol-rxn}$$

with the energy evolved in hydrogenation of three isolated double bonds.

$$3\ H_2C{=}CH_2(g) + 3\ H_2(g) \rightarrow 3\ C_2H_6(g) \qquad \Delta_rH° = -410.8\ \text{kJ/mol-rxn}$$

The hydrogenation of benzene is about 200 kJ less exothermic than the hydrogenation of three moles of ethylene. The difference is attributable to the added stability associated with π bonding in benzene.

Much of the world's current technology relies on petroleum. Burning fuels derived from petroleum provides by far the largest amount of energy in the industrial world (see *The Chemistry of Fuels and Energy Sources*, pages 254–267). Petroleum and natural gas are also the chemical raw materials used in the manufacture of plastics, rubber, pharmaceuticals, and a vast array of other compounds.

The petroleum that is pumped out of the ground is a complex mixture whose composition varies greatly, depending on its source. The primary components of petroleum are always alkanes, but, to varying degrees, nitrogen- and sulfur-containing compounds are also present. Aromatic compounds are present as well, but alkenes and alkynes are not.

An early step in the petroleum refining process is distillation, in which the crude mixture is separated into a series of fractions based on boiling point: first a gaseous fraction (mostly alkanes with one to four carbon atoms; this fraction is often burned off), and then gasoline, kerosene, and fuel oils. After distillation, considerable material, in the form of a semi-solid, tar-like residue, remains.

The petrochemical industry seeks to maximize the amounts of the higher-valued fractions of petroleum produced and to make specific compounds for which a particular need exists. This means carrying out chemical reactions involving the raw materials on a huge scale. One process to which petroleum is subjected is known as *cracking*. At very high temperatures, bond breaking or "cracking" can occur, and longer-chain hydrocarbons will fragment into smaller molecular units. These reactions are carried out in the presence of a wide array of catalysts, materials that speed up reactions and direct them toward specific products. Among the important products of cracking are ethylene and other alkenes, which serve as the raw materials for the formation of materials such as polyethylene. Cracking also produces gaseous hydrogen, a widely used raw material in the chemical industry.

Other important reactions involving petroleum are run at elevated temperatures and in the presence of specific catalysts. Such reactions include *isomerization* reactions, in which the carbon skeleton of an alkane rearranges to form a new isomeric species, and *reformation* processes, in which smaller molecules combine to form new molecules. Each process is directed toward achieving a specific goal, such as increasing the proportion of branched-chain hydrocarbons in gasoline to obtain higher octane ratings. A great amount of chemical research has gone into developing and understanding these highly specialized processes.

A modern petrochemical plant.

Thomas Kitchin/Tom Stack & Associates

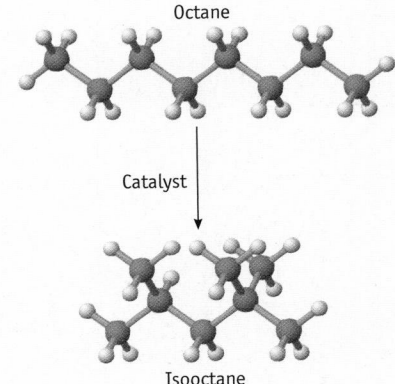

Octane

Catalyst

Isooctane

Producing gasoline. Branched hydrocarbons have a higher octane rating in gasoline. Therefore, an important process in producing gasoline is the isomerization of octane to a branched hydrocarbon such as isooctane, 2,2,4-trimethylpentane.

Although aromatic compounds are unsaturated hydrocarbons, they do not undergo the addition reactions typical of alkenes and alkynes. Instead, *substitution reactions* occur, in which one or more hydrogen atoms are replaced by other groups. Such reactions require a strong Brønsted acid such as H_2SO_4 or a Lewis acid such as $AlCl_3$ or $FeBr_3$.

Nitration: $C_6H_6(\ell) + HNO_3(\ell) \xrightarrow{H_2SO_4} C_6H_5NO_2(\ell) + H_2O(\ell)$

Alkylation: $C_6H_6(\ell) + CH_3Cl(\ell) \xrightarrow{AlCl_3} C_6H_5CH_3(\ell) + HCl(g)$

Halogenation: $C_6H_6(\ell) + Br_2(\ell) \xrightarrow{FeBr_3} C_6H_5Br(\ell) + HBr(g)$

10.3 Alcohols, Ethers, and Amines

Other types of organic compounds arise as elements other than carbon and hydrogen are included in the compound. Two elements in particular, oxygen and nitrogen, add a rich dimension to carbon chemistry.

TABLE 10.6 Common Functional Groups and Derivatives of Alkanes

Functional Group*	General Formula*	Class of Compound	Examples
F, Cl, Br, I	RF, RCl, RBr, RI	haloalkane	CH_3CH_2Cl, chloroethane
OH	ROH	alcohol	CH_3CH_2OH, ethanol
OR′	ROR′	ether	$(CH_3CH_2)_2O$, diethyl ether
NH₂†	RNH₂	(primary) amine	$CH_3CH_2NH_2$, ethylamine
$\overset{\displaystyle O}{\overset{\|}{-CH}}$	RCHO	aldehyde	CH_3CHO, ethanal (acetaldehyde)
$\overset{\displaystyle O}{\overset{\|}{-C-R'}}$	RCOR′	ketone	CH_3COCH_3, propanone (acetone)
$\overset{\displaystyle O}{\overset{\|}{-C-OH}}$	RCO₂H	carboxylic acid	CH_3CO_2H, ethanoic acid (acetic acid)
$\overset{\displaystyle O}{\overset{\|}{-C-OR'}}$	RCO₂R′	ester	$CH_3CO_2CH_3$, methyl acetate
$\overset{\displaystyle O}{\overset{\|}{-C-NH_2}}$	RCONH₂	amide	CH_3CONH_2, acetamide

* R and R′ can be the same or different hydrocarbon groups.
† Secondary amines (R_2NH) and tertiary amines (R_3N) are also possible, see discussion in the text.

Organic chemistry organizes compounds containing elements other than carbon and hydrogen as derivatives of hydrocarbons. Formulas (and structures) are represented by substituting one or more hydrogens in a hydrocarbon molecule by a **functional group.** A functional group is an atom or group of atoms attached to a carbon atom in the hydrocarbon. Formulas of hydrocarbon derivatives are then written as R—X, in which R is a hydrocarbon lacking a hydrogen atom, and X is the functional group that has replaced the hydrogen. The chemical and physical properties of the hydrocarbon derivatives are a blend of the properties associated with hydrocarbons and the group that has been substituted for hydrogen.

Table 10.6 identifies some common functional groups and the families of organic compounds resulting from their attachment to a hydrocarbon.

Chemistry ⚛ Now™

Sign in at **www.cengage.com/login** and go to Chapter 10 Contents to see Screen 10.5 for a description of the **types of organic functional groups** and for tutorials on **their structures, bonding, and chemistry.**

Alcohols and Ethers

If one of the hydrogen atoms of an alkane is replaced by a hydroxyl (—OH) group, the result is an **alcohol,** ROH. Methanol, CH_3OH, and ethanol, CH_3CH_2OH, are the most important alcohols, but others are also commercially important (Table 10.7). Notice that several have more than one OH functional group.

More than 5×10^8 kg of methanol is produced in the United States annually. Most of this production is used to make formaldehyde (CH_2O) and acetic acid

Alcohol racing fuel. Methanol, CH_3OH, is used as the fuel in cars of the type that race in Indianapolis.

David Young/Tom Stack & Associates

TABLE 10.7 Some Important Alcohols

Condensed Formula	BP (°C)	Systematic Name	Common Name	Use
CH_3OH	65.0	methanol	methyl alcohol	fuel, gasoline additive, making formaldehyde
CH_3CH_2OH	78.5	ethanol	ethyl alcohol	beverages, gasoline additive, solvent
$CH_3CH_2CH_2OH$	97.4	1-propanol	propyl alcohol	industrial solvent
$CH_3CH(OH)CH_3$	82.4	2-propanol	isopropyl alcohol	rubbing alcohol
$HOCH_2CH_2OH$	198	1,2-ethanediol	ethylene glycol	antifreeze
$HOCH_2CH(OH)CH_2OH$	290	1,2,3-propanetriol	glycerol (glycerin)	moisturizer in consumer products

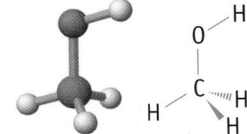

Methanol, CH_3OH, is the simplest alcohol. Methanol is often called "wood alcohol" because it was originally produced by heating wood in the absence of air.

(CH_3CO_2H), both important chemicals in their own right. Methanol is also used as a solvent, as a de-icer in gasoline, and as a fuel in high-powered racing cars. It is found in low concentration in new wine, where it contributes to the odor, or "bouquet." Like ethanol, methanol causes intoxication, but methanol differs in being more poisonous, largely because the human body converts it to formic acid (HCO_2H) and formaldehyde (CH_2O). These compounds attack the cells of the retina in the eye, leading to permanent blindness.

Ethanol is the "alcohol" of alcoholic beverages, in which it is formed by the anaerobic (without air) fermentation of sugar. For many years, industrial alcohol, which is used as a solvent and as a starting material for the synthesis of other compounds, was made by fermentation. In the last several decades, however, it has become cheaper to make ethanol from petroleum by-products—specifically, by the addition of water to ethylene.

■ **Aerobic Fermentation** Aerobic fermentation (in the presence of O_2) of sugar leads to the formation of acetic acid. This is how wine vinegar is made.

$$ \underset{\text{ethylene}}{\text{H}_2\text{C}=\text{CH}_2} \text{ (g) } + \text{ H}_2\text{O(g)} \xrightarrow{\text{catalyst}} \underset{\text{ethanol}}{\text{CH}_3\text{CH}_2\text{OH}(\ell)} $$

Beginning with three-carbon alcohols, structural isomers are possible. For example, 1-propanol and 2-propanol (common name, isopropyl alcohol) are different compounds (Table 10.7).

Ethylene glycol and glycerol are common alcohols having two and three —OH groups, respectively. Ethylene glycol is used as antifreeze in automobiles. Glycerol's most common use is as a softener in soaps and lotions. It is also a raw material for the preparation of nitroglycerin (Figure 10.8).

Systematic name: 1,2-ethanediol   1,2,3-propanetriol
Common name: ethylene glycol   glycerol or glycerin

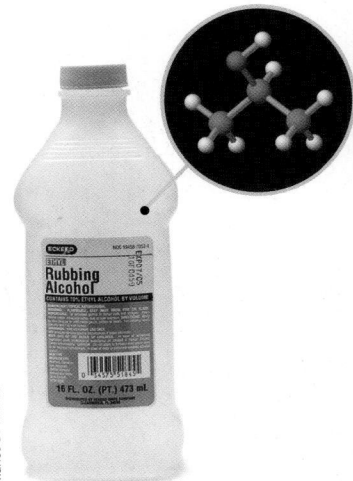

Charles D. Winters

Rubbing alcohol. Common rubbing alcohol is 2-propanol, also called isopropyl alcohol.

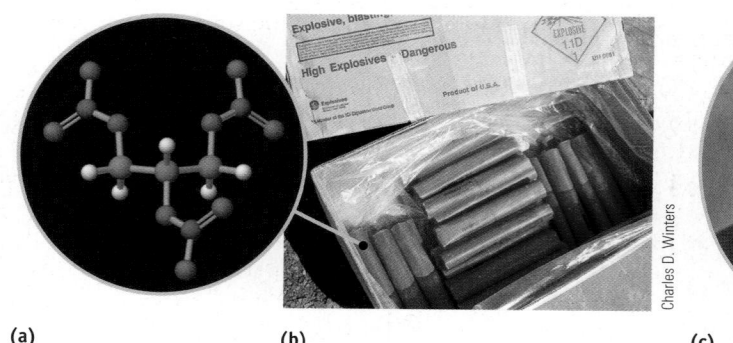

(a)   (b)   (c)

FIGURE 10.8 Nitroglycerin. (a) Concentrated nitric acid and glycerin react to form an oily, highly unstable compound called nitroglycerin, $C_3H_5(ONO_2)_3$. (b) Nitroglycerin is more stable if absorbed onto an inert solid, a combination called dynamite. (c) The fortune of Alfred Nobel (1833–1896), built on the manufacture of dynamite, now funds the Nobel Prizes.

■ **EXAMPLE 10.6 Structural Isomers of Alcohols**

Problem How many different alcohols are derivatives of pentane? Draw structures, and name each alcohol.

Strategy Pentane, C_5H_{12}, has a five-carbon chain. An —OH group can replace a hydrogen atom on one of the carbon atoms. Alcohols are named as derivatives of the alkane (pentane) by replacing the "-e" at the end with "-ol" and indicating the position of the —OH group by a numerical prefix (Appendix E).

Solution Three different alcohols are possible, depending on whether the —OH group is placed on the first, second, or third carbon atom in the chain. (The fourth and fifth positions are identical to the second and first positions in the chain, respectively.)

1-pentanol   2-pentanol

3-pentanol

Comment Additional structural isomers with the formula $C_5H_{11}OH$ are possible in which the longest carbon chain has three C atoms (one isomer) or four C atoms (four isomers).

EXERCISE 10.6 Structures of Alcohols

Draw the structure of 1-butanol and alcohols that are structural isomers of the compound.

Properties of Alcohols and Ethers

Methane, CH_4, is a gas (boiling point, −161 °C) with low solubility in water. Methanol, CH_3OH, by contrast, is a liquid that is *miscible* with water in all proportions. The boiling point of methanol, 65 °C, is 226 °C higher than the boiling point of methane. What a difference the addition of a single atom into the structure can make in the properties of simple molecules!

Alcohols are related to water, with one of the H atoms of H_2O being replaced by an organic group. If a methyl group is substituted for one of the hydrogens of water, methanol results. Ethanol has a —C_2H_5 (ethyl) group, and propanol has a —C_3H_7 (propyl) group in place of one of the hydrogens of water. Viewing alcohols as related to water also helps in understanding the properties of alcohols.

The two parts of methanol, the —CH_3 group and the —OH group, contribute to its properties. For example, methanol will burn, a property associated with hydrocarbons. On the other hand, its boiling point is more like that of water. The temperature at which a substance boils is related to the forces of attraction between molecules, called *intermolecular forces:* The stronger the attractive, intermolecular forces in a sample, the higher the boiling point (▶ Section 12.4). These forces are particularly strong in water, a result of the polarity of the —OH group in this molecule (◀ Section 8.8). Methanol is also a polar molecule, and it is the polar —OH group that leads to a high boiling point. In contrast, methane is nonpolar and its low boiling point is the result of weak intermolecular forces.

It is also possible to explain the differences in the solubility of methane and methanol in water. The solubility of methanol is conferred by the polar —OH portion of the molecule. Methane, which is nonpolar, has low water-solubility.

■ **Hydrogen Bonding** The intermolecular forces of attraction of compounds with hydrogen attached to a highly electronegative atom, like O, N, or F, are so exceptional that they are accorded a special name: hydrogen bonding. We will discuss hydrogen bonding in Section 12.2.

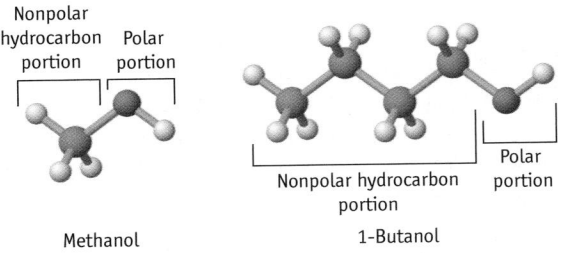

Nonpolar hydrocarbon portion Polar portion

Methanol

Nonpolar hydrocarbon portion   Polar portion

1-Butanol

As the size of the alkyl group in an alcohol increases, the alcohol boiling point rises, a general trend seen in families of similar compounds and related to molar mass (see Table 10.7). The solubility in water in this series decreases. Methanol and ethanol are completely miscible in water, whereas 1-propanol is moderately water-soluble; 1-butanol is less soluble than 1-propanol. With an increase in the size of the hydrocarbon group, the organic group (the nonpolar part of the molecule) has become a larger fraction of the molecule, and properties associated with nonpolarity begin to dominate. Space-filling models show that in methanol, the polar and nonpolar parts of the molecule are approximately similar in size, but in 1-butanol the —OH group is less than 20% of the molecule. The molecule is less like water and more "organic."

Attaching an additional —OH group to a hydrocarbon framework has an effect on water solubility (Figure 10.9). Two —OH groups on a three-carbon framework, as found in propylene glycol, convey complete miscibility with water, in contrast to the limited solubility of 1-propanol and 2-propanol.

Ethers have the general formula ROR′. The best-known ether is diethyl ether, $CH_3CH_2OCH_2CH_3$. Lacking an —OH group, the properties of ethers are in sharp contrast to those of alcohols. Diethyl ether, for example, has a lower boiling point (34.5 °C) than ethanol, CH_3CH_2OH (78.3 °C), and is only slightly soluble in water.

Chemistry ⚛ Now™

Sign in at **www.cengage.com/login** and go to Chapter 10 Contents to see Screen 10.6 for an exercise on **substitution and elimination reactions of alcohols.**

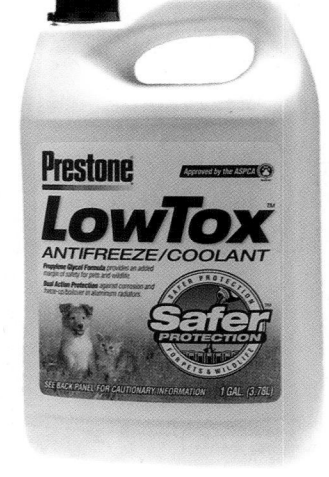

Charles D. Winters

Safe antifreeze—propylene glycol, $CH_3CHOHCH_2OH$. Most antifreeze sold today consists of about 95% ethylene glycol. Cats and dogs are attracted by the smell and taste of the compound, but it is toxic. In fact, only a few milliliters can prove fatal to a small dog or cat. In the first stage of poisoning, an animal may appear drunk, but within 12–36 hours the kidneys stop functioning, and the animal slips into a coma. To avoid accidental poisoning of domestic and wild animals, you can use propylene glycol antifreeze. This compound affords the same antifreeze protection but is much less toxic.

Methanol is often added to automobile gasoline tanks in the winter to prevent fuel lines from freezing. It is soluble in water and lowers the water's freezing point.

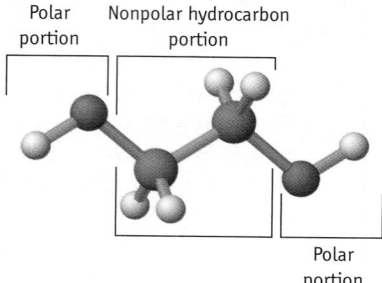

Polar portion — Nonpolar hydrocarbon portion — Polar portion

Ethylene glycol is used in automobile radiators. It is soluble in water, and lowers the freezing point and raises the boiling point of the water in the cooling system. (See Section 14.4.)

Ethylene glycol, a major component of automobile antifreeze, is completely miscible with water.

FIGURE 10.9 Properties and uses of methanol and ethylene glycol.

Amines

It is often convenient to think about water and ammonia as being similar molecules: They are the simplest hydrogen compounds of adjacent second-period elements. Both are polar and exhibit some similar chemistry, such as protonation (to give H_3O^+ and NH_4^+) and deprotonation (to give OH^- and NH_2^-).

This comparison of water and ammonia can be extended to alcohols and amines. Alcohols have formulas related to water in which one hydrogen in H_2O is replaced with an organic group ($R—OH$). In organic **amines,** one or more hydrogen atoms of NH_3 are replaced with an organic group. Amine structures are similar to ammonia's structure; that is, the geometry about the N atom is trigonal pyramidal.

Amines are categorized based on the number of organic substituents as primary (one organic group), secondary (two organic groups), or tertiary (three organic groups). As examples, consider the three amines with methyl groups: CH_3NH_2, $(CH_3)_2NH$, and $(CH_3)_3N$.

CH_3NH_2
Primary amine
Methylamine

$(CH_3)_2NH$
Secondary amine
Dimethylamine

$(CH_3)_3N$
Tertiary amine
Trimethylamine

Properties of Amines

Amines usually have offensive odors. You know what the odor is if you have ever smelled decaying fish. Two appropriately named amines, putrescine and cadaverine, add to the odor of urine, rotten meat, and bad breath.

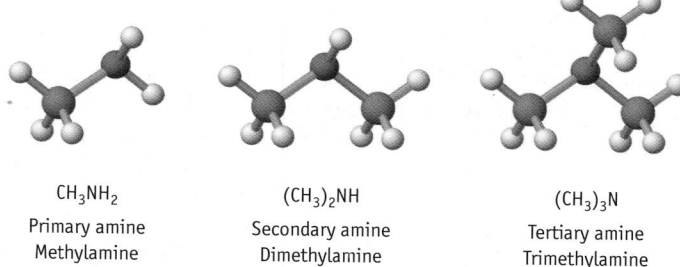

$H_2NCH_2CH_2CH_2CH_2NH_2$
putrescine
1,4-butanediamine

$H_2NCH_2CH_2CH_2CH_2CH_2NH_2$
cadaverine
1,5-pentanediamine

The smallest amines are water-soluble, but most amines are not. All amines are bases, however, and they react with acids to give salts, many of which are water-soluble. As with ammonia, the reactions involve adding H^+ to the lone pair of electrons on the N atom. This is illustrated by the reaction of aniline (aminobenzene) with H_2SO_4 to give anilinium sulfate, a compound of some historical interest (see "Historical Perspectives: Mauvine").

$$C_6H_5NH_2(aq) + H_2SO_4(aq) \longrightarrow C_6H_5NH_3^+(aq) + HSO_4^-(aq)$$

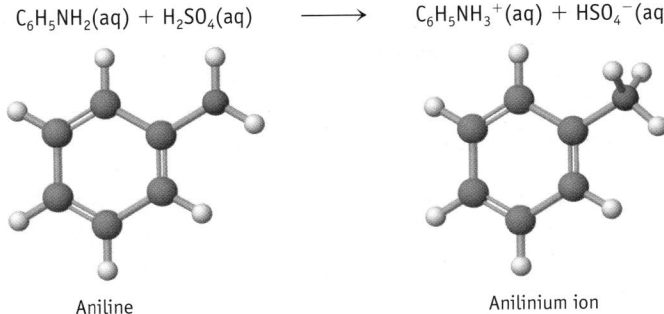

Aniline   Anilinium ion

Historical Perspectives   Mauveine

Among the roots of modern organic chemistry was the synthesis, in 1856, of the compound mauveine (or mauve) by William Henry Perkin (1838–1907). This discovery led to a flourishing dye industry, one of the first chemical industries.

The discovery of mauve is an interesting tale. At the age of 13, Perkin enrolled at the City of London School. His father paid an

Mauveine. The original stoppered bottle of mauveine prepared by Perkin. The structure of the mauveine cation is shown here.

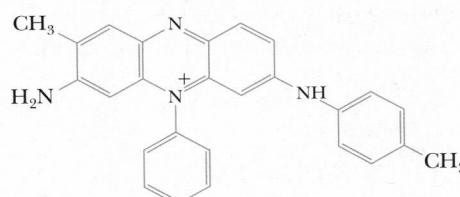

extra fee for him to attend a lunchtime chemistry course and set up a lab at home for him to do experiments. He began attending the public lectures that Michael Faraday gave on Saturdays at the Royal Institution. At 15, Perkin enrolled in the Royal College of Science in London to study chemistry under the school's Director, August Wilhelm von Hofmann. After he completed his studies at age 17, he took a position at the college as Hofmann's assistant, rather a great honor.

Perkin's first project was to synthesize quinine, an antimalarial drug. The route he proposed involved oxidizing anilinium sulfate. From the reaction, he obtained a black solid that dissolved in a water-ethanol mixture to give a purple solution that stained cloth a beautiful purple color. The color didn't wash out, an essential feature for a dye. Later, it was learned that the anilinium sulfate Perkin used had been impure and that the impurity was essential in the synthesis. Had Perkins used a pure sample or his starting reagent, the discovery of mauve would not have happened. A study in 1994 on samples of mauve preserved in museums determined that Perkin's mauve was actually a mixture of two very similar compounds, along with traces of several others.

At the age of 18, Perkin quit his assistantship and, with financial help from his family, set up a dye factory outside of London. By the age of 36, he was a very wealthy man. He

then retired from the dye business and devoted the rest of his life to chemical research on various topics, including the synthesis of fragrances and a study of optical activity. During his lifetime, he received numerous honors for his research, but one honor came many years after his death. In 1972, when The Chemical Society (in England) renamed its journals after famous society members, it chose Perkin's name for the organic chemistry journals. (See *Mauve*, a book on Perkin's life, by S. Garfield, W. W. Norton Publishers, New York.)

A silk dress dyed with Perkin's original sample of mauve in 1862, at the dawning of the synthetic dye industry. From *Mauve*.

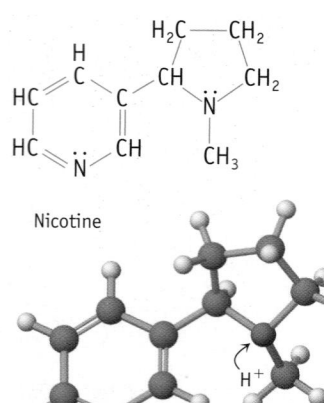

Nicotine

Nicotine. Two nitrogen atoms in the nicotine molecule can be protonated, which is the form in which nicotine is normally found. The protons can be removed, however, by treating it with a base. This "free-base" form is much more poisonous and addictive. See J. F. Pankow: *Environmental Science & Technology,* Vol 31, p. 2428, August 1997.

Primary alcohol: ethanol

Secondary alcohol: 2-propanol

Tertiary alcohol: 2-methyl-2-propanol

The facts that an amine can be protonated and that the proton can be removed again by treating the compound with a base have practical and physiological importance. Nicotine in cigarettes is normally found in the protonated form. (This water-soluble form is often used in insecticides.) Adding a base such as ammonia removes the H^+ ion to leave nicotine in its "free-base" form.

$$NicH_2^{2+}(aq) + 2\ NH_3(aq) \rightarrow Nic(aq) + 2\ NH_4^+(aq)$$

In this form, nicotine is much more readily absorbed by the skin and mucous membranes, so the compound is a much more potent poison.

10.4 Compounds with a Carbonyl Group

Formaldehyde, acetic acid, and acetone are among the organic compounds referred to in previous examples. These compounds have a common structural feature: Each contains a trigonal-planar carbon atom doubly bonded to an oxygen. The C=O group is called the **carbonyl group,** and all of these compounds are members of a large class of compounds called **carbonyl compounds.**

Carbonyl group

Formaldehyde
CH_2O
Aldehyde

Acetic acid
CH_3CO_2H
Carboxylic acid

Acetone
CH_3COCH_3
Ketone

In this section, we will examine five groups of carbonyl compounds (Table 10.6, page 462):

- *Aldehydes* (RCHO) have an organic group (—R) and an H atom attached to a carbonyl group.
- *Ketones* (RCOR′) have two —R groups attached to the carbonyl carbon; they may be the same groups, as in acetone, or different groups.
- *Carboxylic acids* (RCO₂H) have an —R group and an —OH group attached to the carbonyl carbon.
- *Esters* (RCO₂R′) have —R and —OR′ groups attached to the carbonyl carbon.
- *Amides* (RCONR₂′, RCONHR′, and RCONH₂) have an —R group and an amino group (—NH₂, —NHR, —NR₂) bonded to the carbonyl carbon.

Aldehydes, ketones, and carboxylic acids are oxidation products of alcohols and, indeed, are commonly made by this route. The product obtained through oxidation of an alcohol depends on the alcohol's structure, which is classified according to the number of carbon atoms bonded to the C atom bearing the —OH group. *Primary alcohols* have one carbon and two hydrogen atoms attached, whereas *secondary alcohols* have two carbon atoms and one hydrogen atom attached. *Tertiary alcohols* have three carbon atoms attached to the C atom bearing the —OH group.

A *primary alcohol* is oxidized in two steps. It is first oxidized to an aldehyde and then in a second step to a carboxylic acid:

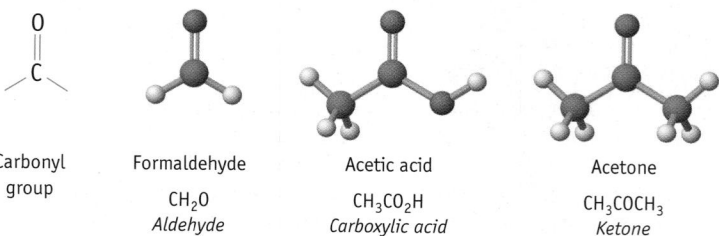

For example, the air oxidation of ethanol in wine produces wine (with excess oxygen) vinegar, the most important ingredient of which is acetic acid.

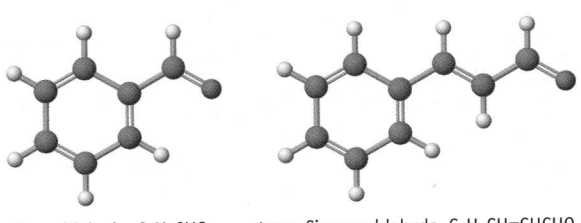

ethanol   acetic acid

FIGURE 10.10 Alcohol tester. This device for testing a person's breath for the presence of ethanol relies on the oxidation of the alcohol. If present, ethanol is oxidized by potassium dichromate, $K_2Cr_2O_7$, to acetaldehyde, and then to acetic acid. The yellow-orange dichromate ion is reduced to green $Cr^{3+}(aq)$, the color change indicating that ethanol was present.

Acids have a sour taste. The word "vinegar" (from the French *vin aigre*) means sour wine. A device to test one's breath for alcohol relies on a similar oxidation of ethanol (Figures 3.21 and 10.10).

In contrast to primary alcohols, oxidation of a *secondary alcohol* produces a ketone:

secondary alcohol   ketone

(—R and —R′ are organic groups. They may be the same or different.)

Common oxidizing agents used for these reactions are reagents such as $KMnO_4$ and $K_2Cr_2O_7$ (Table 3.4).

Finally, tertiary alcohols do *not* react with the usual oxidizing agents.

$$(CH_3)_3COH \xrightarrow{\text{oxidizing agent}} \text{no reaction}$$

Aldehydes and Ketones

Aldehydes and **ketones** have pleasant odors and are often used in fragrances. Benzaldehyde is responsible for the odor of almonds and cherries; cinnamaldehyde is found in the bark of the cinnamon tree; and the ketone 4-(*p*-hydroxyphenyl) 2-butanone is responsible for the odor of ripe raspberries (a favorite of the authors of this book). Table 10.8 lists several simple aldehydes and ketones.

Benzaldehyde, C_6H_5CHO *trans*-Cinnamaldehyde, $C_6H_5CH=CHCHO$

Aldehydes and ketones are the oxidation products of primary and secondary alcohols, respectively. The reverse reactions—reduction of aldehydes to primary alcohols and reduction of ketones to secondary alcohols—are also known.

Charles D. Winters

Aldehydes and odors. The odors of almonds and cinnamon are due to aldehydes, but the odor of fresh raspberries comes from a ketone.

TABLE 10.8 Simple Aldehydes and Ketones

Structure	Common Name	Systematic Name	BP (°C)
$\overset{\displaystyle O}{\overset{\|}{HCH}}$	formaldehyde	methanal	−19
$\overset{\displaystyle O}{\overset{\|}{CH_3CH}}$	acetaldehyde	ethanal	20
$\overset{\displaystyle O}{\overset{\|}{CH_3CCH_3}}$	acetone	propanone	56
$\overset{\displaystyle O}{\overset{\|}{CH_3CCH_2CH_3}}$	methyl ethyl ketone	butanone	80
$\overset{\displaystyle O}{\overset{\|}{CH_3CH_2CCH_2CH_3}}$	diethyl ketone	3-pentanone	102

Commonly used reagents for such reductions are $NaBH_4$ and $LiAlH_4$, although H_2 is used on an industrial scale.

$$R-\overset{\overset{\displaystyle O}{\|}}{C}-H \xrightarrow{\text{NaBH}_4 \text{ or LiAlH}_4} R-\overset{\overset{\displaystyle OH}{|}}{\underset{\underset{\displaystyle H}{|}}{C}}-H$$

aldehyde   primary alcohol

$$R-\overset{\overset{\displaystyle O}{\|}}{C}-R \xrightarrow{\text{NaBH}_4 \text{ or LiAlH}_4} R-\overset{\overset{\displaystyle OH}{|}}{\underset{\underset{\displaystyle H}{|}}{C}}-R$$

ketone   secondary alcohol

EXERCISE 10.7 Aldehydes and Ketones

(a) Draw the structural formula for 2-pentanone. Draw structures for a ketone and two aldehydes that are isomers of 2-pentanone, and name each of these compounds.

(b) What is the product of the reduction of 2-pentanone with $NaBH_4$?

EXERCISE 10.8 Aldehydes and Ketones

Draw the structures, and name the aldehyde or ketone formed upon oxidation of the following alcohols: (a) 1-butanol, (b) 2-butanol, (c) 2-methyl-1-propanol. Are these three alcohols structural isomers? Are the oxidation products structural isomers?

Carboxylic Acids

Acetic acid is the most common and most important **carboxylic acid.** For many years, acetic acid was made by oxidizing ethanol produced by fermentation. Now, however, acetic acid is generally made by combining carbon monoxide and methanol in the presence of a catalyst:

$$CH_3OH(\ell) + CO(g) \xrightarrow{catalyst} CH_3CO_2H(\ell)$$
$$\text{methanol} \qquad\qquad\qquad\quad \text{acetic acid}$$

About 1 billion kilograms of acetic acid are produced annually in the United States for use in plastics, synthetic fibers, and fungicides.

Many organic acids are found naturally (Table 10.9). Acids are recognizable by their sour taste (Figure 10.11) and are found in common foods: Citric acid in fruits, acetic acid in vinegar, and tartaric acid in grapes are just three examples.

Some carboxylic acids have common names derived from the source of the acid (Table 10.9). Because formic acid is found in ants, its name comes from the Latin word for ant (*formica*). Butyric acid gives rancid butter its unpleasant odor, and the name is related to the Latin word for butter (*butyrum*). The systematic names of acids (Table 10.10) are formed by dropping the "-e" on the name of the corresponding alkane and adding "-oic" (and the word "acid").

Because of the substantial electronegativity of oxygen, the two O atoms of the carboxylic acid group are slightly negatively charged, and the H atom of the —OH group is positively charged. This charge distribution has several important implications:

- The polar acetic acid molecule dissolves readily in water, which you already know because vinegar is an aqueous solution of acetic acid. (Acids with larger organic groups are less soluble, however.)

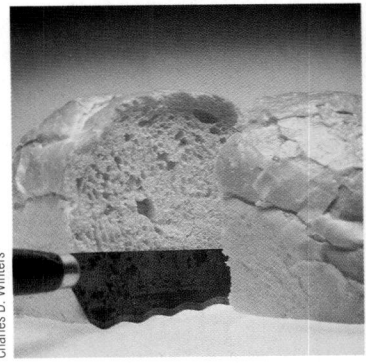

FIGURE 10.11 Acetic acid in bread. Acetic acid is produced in bread when leavened with the yeast *Saccharomyces exigus*. Another group of bacteria, *Lactobacillus sanfrancisco*, contributes to the flavor of sourdough bread. These bacteria metabolize the sugar maltose, excreting acetic acid and lactic acid, $CH_3CH(OH)CO_2H$, thereby giving the bread its unique sour taste.

TABLE 10.9 Some Naturally Occurring Carboxylic Acids

Name	Structure	Natural Source
benzoic acid	⬡—CO₂H	berries
citric acid	HO₂C—CH₂—C(OH)(CO₂H)—CH₂—CO₂H	citrus fruits
lactic acid	H₃C—CH(OH)—CO₂H	sour milk
malic acid	HO₂C—CH₂—CH(OH)—CO₂H	apples
oleic acid	CH₃(CH₂)₇—CH=CH—(CH₂)₇—CO₂H	vegetable oils
oxalic acid	HO₂C—CO₂H	rhubarb, spinach, cabbage, tomatoes
stearic acid	CH₃(CH₂)₁₆—CO₂H	animal fats
tartaric acid	HO₂C—CH(OH)—CH(OH)—CO₂H	grape juice, wine

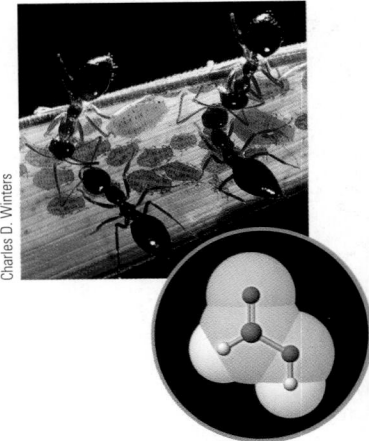

Formic acid, HCO₂H. This acid puts the sting in ant bites.

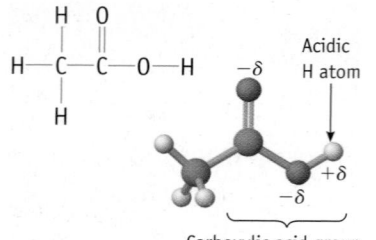

Acetic acid. The H atom of the carboxylic acid group (—CO₂H) is the acidic proton of this and other carboxylic acids.

TABLE 10.10 Some Simple Carboxylic Acids

Structure	Common Name	Systematic Name	BP (°C)
$\overset{\displaystyle O}{\overset{\displaystyle \|}{HCOH}}$	formic acid	methanoic acid	101
$\overset{\displaystyle O}{\overset{\displaystyle \|}{CH_3COH}}$	acetic acid	ethanoic acid	118
$\overset{\displaystyle O}{\overset{\displaystyle \|}{CH_3CH_2COH}}$	propionic acid	propanoic acid	141
$\overset{\displaystyle O}{\overset{\displaystyle \|}{CH_3(CH_2)_2COH}}$	butyric acid	butanoic acid	163
$\overset{\displaystyle O}{\overset{\displaystyle \|}{CH_3(CH_2)_3COH}}$.	valeric acid	pentanoic acid	187

- The hydrogen of the —OH group is the acidic hydrogen. As noted in Chapter 3, acetic acid is a weak acid in water, as are most other organic acids.

Carboxylic acids undergo a number of reactions. Among these is the reduction of the acid (with reagents such as LiAlH₄ or NaBH₄) first to an aldehyde and then to an alcohol. For example, acetic acid is reduced first to acetaldehyde and then to ethanol.

$$CH_3CO_2H \xrightarrow{\text{LiAlH}_4} CH_3CHO \xrightarrow{\text{LiAlH}_4} CH_3CH_2OH$$

acetic acid   acetaldehyde   ethanol

Yet another important aspect of carboxylic acid chemistry is these acids' reaction with bases to give carboxylate anions. For example, acetic acid reacts with sodium hydroxide to give sodium acetate (sodium ethanoate).

$$CH_3CO_2H(aq) + OH^-(aq) \rightarrow CH_3CO_2^-(aq) + H_2O(\ell)$$

Esters

Carboxylic acids (RCO₂H) react with alcohols (R′OH) to form esters (RCO₂R′) in an **esterification** reaction. (These reactions are generally run in the presence of strong acids because acids accelerate the reaction.)

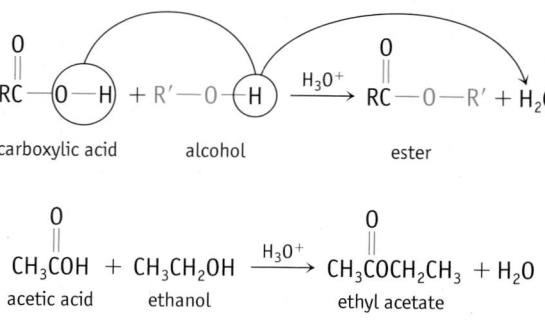

$$\overset{\displaystyle O}{\overset{\displaystyle \|}{RC}}\!-\!\overbrace{O\!-\!H} + R'\!-\!O\!-\!\overbrace{H} \xrightarrow{H_3O^+} \overset{\displaystyle O}{\overset{\displaystyle \|}{RC}}\!-\!O\!-\!R' + H_2O$$

carboxylic acid   alcohol   ester

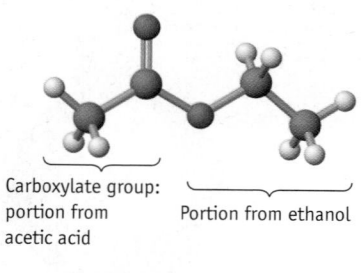

Carboxylate group: portion from acetic acid — Portion from ethanol

Ethyl acetate, an ester
CH₃CO₂CH₂CH₃

$$\overset{\displaystyle O}{\overset{\displaystyle \|}{CH_3COH}} + CH_3CH_2OH \xrightarrow{H_3O^+} \overset{\displaystyle O}{\overset{\displaystyle \|}{CH_3COCH_2CH_3}} + H_2O$$

acetic acid   ethanol   ethyl acetate

Glucose and Sugars

Having described alcohols and carbonyl compounds, we now pause to look at glucose, the most common, naturally occurring carbohydrate.

As their name implies, formulas of carbohydrates can be written as though they are a combination of carbon and water, $C_x(H_2O)_y$. Thus, the formula of glucose, $C_6H_{12}O_6$, is equivalent to $C_6(H_2O)_6$. This compound is a sugar, or, more accurately, a **monosaccharide**.

Carbohydrates are polyhydroxy aldehydes or ketones. Glucose is an interesting molecule that exists in three different isomeric forms. Two of the isomers contain six-member rings; the third isomer features a chain structure. In solution, the three forms rapidly interconvert.

Notice that glucose is a chiral molecule. In the chain structure, four of the carbon atoms are bonded to four different groups.

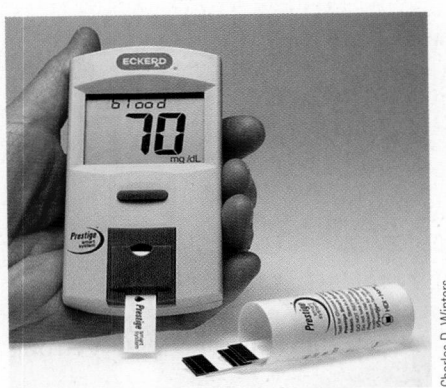

Home test for glucose.

Charles D. Winters

α-D-Glucose   Open-chain form   β-D-Glucose

In nature, glucose occurs in just one of its enantiomeric forms; thus, a solution of glucose rotates polarized light.

Knowing glucose's structure allows one to predict some of its properties. With five polar —OH groups in the molecule, glucose is, not surprisingly, soluble in water.

The aldehyde group is susceptible to chemical oxidation to form a carboxylic acid. Detection of glucose (in urine or blood) takes advantage of this fact; diagnostic tests for glucose involve oxidation with subsequent detection of the products.

Glucose is in a class of sugar molecules called hexoses, molecules having six carbon atoms. 2-Deoxyribose, the sugar in the backbone of the DNA molecule, is a pentose, a molecule with five carbon atoms.

deoxyribose, a pentose,
part of the DNA backbone

Glucose and other monosaccharides serve as the building blocks for larger carbohydrates. Sucrose, a disaccharide, is formed from a molecule of glucose and a molecule of fructose, another monosaccharide. Starch is a polymer composed of many monosaccharide units.

α-D-Glucose

Fructose

The structure of sucrose. Sucrose is formed from α-D-glucose and fructose. An ether linkage is formed by loss of H_2O from two —OH groups.

When a carboxylic acid and an alcohol react to form an ester, the OR group of the alcohol ends up as part of the ester (as shown above). This fact is known because of isotope labeling experiments. If the reaction is run using an alcohol in which the alcohol oxygen is ^{18}O, all of the ^{18}O ends up in the ester molecule.

Table 10.11 lists a few common esters and the acid and alcohol from which they are formed. The two-part name of an ester is given by (1) the name of the hydrocarbon group from the alcohol and (2) the name of the carboxylate group derived from the acid name by replacing "-ic" with "-ate." For example, ethanol (commonly called ethyl alcohol) and acetic acid combine to give the ester ethyl acetate.

An important reaction of esters is their **hydrolysis** (literally, reaction with water), a reaction that is the reverse of the formation of the ester. The reaction, generally

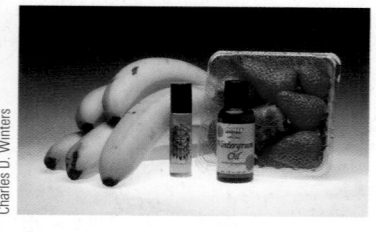

Esters. Many fruits such as bananas and strawberries as well as consumer products (here, perfume and oil of wintergreen) contain esters.

TABLE 10.11 Some Acids, Alcohols, and Their Esters

Acid	Alcohol	Ester	Odor of Ester
CH_3CO_2H acetic acid	$CH_3CHCH_2CH_2OH$ (with CH_3 branch) 3-methyl-1-butanol	$CH_3COCH_2CH_2CHCH_3$ (with C=O and CH_3 branch) 3-methylbutyl acetate	banana
$CH_3CH_2CH_2CO_2H$ butanoic acid	$CH_3CH_2CH_2CH_2OH$ 1-butanol	$CH_3CH_2CH_2COCH_2CH_2CH_2CH_3$ (with C=O) butyl butanoate	pineapple
$CH_3CH_2CH_2CO_2H$ butanoic acid	⬡—CH_2OH benzyl alcohol	$CH_3CH_2CH_2COCH_2$—⬡ (with C=O) benzyl butanoate	rose

■ **Saponification** Fats and oils are esters of glycerol and long-chain acids. When reacted with a strong base (NaOH or KOH), they produce glycerol and a salt of the long-chain acid. Because this product is used as soap, the reaction is called *saponification.* See *A Closer Look: Fats and Oils,* page 476.

done in the presence of a base such as NaOH, produces the alcohol and a sodium salt of the carboxylic acid:

$$\underset{\text{ester}}{RCOR'} + NaOH \xrightarrow[\text{in water}]{\text{heat}} \underset{\text{carboxylate salt}}{RCO^-Na^+} + \underset{\text{alcohol}}{R'OH}$$

$$\underset{\text{ethyl acetate}}{CH_3COCH_2CH_3} + NaOH \xrightarrow[\text{in water}]{\text{heat}} \underset{\text{sodium acetate}}{CH_3CO^-Na^+} + \underset{\text{ethanol}}{CH_3CH_2OH}$$

The carboxylic acid can be recovered if the sodium salt is treated with a strong acid such as HCl:

$$\underset{\text{sodium acetate}}{CH_3CO^-Na^+(aq)} + HCl(aq) \longrightarrow \underset{\text{acetic acid}}{CH_3COH(aq)} + NaCl(aq)$$

Unlike the acids from which they are derived, esters often have pleasant odors (see Table 10.11). Typical examples are methyl salicylate, or "oil of wintergreen," and benzyl acetate. Methyl salicylate is derived from salicylic acid, the parent compound of aspirin.

$$\underset{\substack{\text{salicylic acid}}}{\overset{}{\text{⬡}}-COH} + \underset{\text{methanol}}{CH_3OH} \longrightarrow \underset{\substack{\text{methyl salicylate,}\\\text{oil of wintergreen}}}{\overset{}{\text{⬡}}-COCH_3} + H_2O$$

(salicylic acid has OH substituent; methyl salicylate product has OH substituent)

Benzyl acetate, the active component of "oil of jasmine," is formed from benzyl alcohol ($C_6H_5CH_2OH$) and acetic acid. The chemicals are inexpensive, so synthetic jasmine is a common fragrance in less-expensive perfumes and toiletries.

$$CH_3\overset{\overset{\displaystyle O}{\|}}{C}OH + \langle \text{benzene ring} \rangle - CH_2OH \longrightarrow CH_3\overset{\overset{\displaystyle O}{\|}}{C}OCH_2 - \langle \text{benzene ring} \rangle + H_2O$$

acetic acid   benzyl alcohol   benzyl acetate
oil of jasmine

EXERCISE 10.9 Esters

Draw the structure, and name the ester formed from each of the following reactions:

(a) propanoic acid and methanol

(b) butanoic acid and 1-butanol

(c) hexanoic acid and ethanol

EXERCISE 10.10 Esters

Draw the structure, and name the acid and alcohol from which the following esters are derived:

(a) propyl acetate

(b) 3-methyl-1-pentyl benzoate

(c) ethyl salicylate

Amides

An acid and an alcohol react by loss of water to form an ester. In a similar manner, another class of organic compounds—amides—form when an acid reacts with an amine, again with loss of water.

$$R-\overset{\overset{\displaystyle O}{\|}}{C}-(OH) + (H)-\overset{\overset{\displaystyle R'}{|}}{N}-R' \longrightarrow R-\overset{\overset{\displaystyle O}{\|}}{C}-\overset{\overset{\displaystyle R'}{|}}{N}-R' + H_2O$$

Carboxylic acid   Amine   Amide

Amides have an organic group and an amino group ($-NH_2$, $-NHR'$, or $-NR'R$) attached to the carbonyl group.

The C atom involved in the amide bond has three bonded groups and no lone pairs around it. We would predict it should be sp^2 hybridized with trigonal-planar geometry and bond angles of approximately 120°—and this is what is found. However, the structure of the amide group offers a surprise. The N atom is also observed to have trigonal-planar geometry with bonds to three attached atoms at 120°. Because the amide nitrogen is surrounded by four pairs of electrons, we would have predicted the N atom would have sp^3 hybridization and bond angles of about 109°.

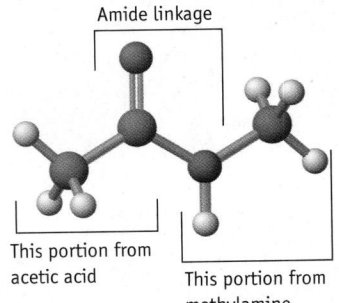

Amide linkage

This portion from acetic acid   This portion from methylamine

An amide, *N*-methylacetamide. The *N*-methyl portion of the name derives from the amine portion of the molecule, where the *N* indicates that the methyl group is attached to the nitrogen atom. The "-acet" portion of the name indicates the acid on which the amide is based.

Fats and Oils

Fats and oils are among the many compounds found in plants and animal tissues. In the body, these substances serve several functions, a primary one being the storage of energy.

Fats (solids) and oils (liquids) are triesters formed from glycerol (1,2,3-propanetriol) and three carboxylic acids that can be the same or different.

$$
\begin{array}{c}
\quad\quad\quad\quad O \\
\quad\quad\quad\quad \| \\
H_2C - O - CR \\
\quad\quad\quad\quad O \\
\quad\quad\quad\quad \| \\
HC - O - CR \\
\quad\quad\quad\quad O \\
\quad\quad\quad\quad \| \\
H_2C - O - CR
\end{array}
$$

The carboxylic acids in fats and oils, known as *fatty acids*, have a lengthy carbon chain, usually containing between 12 and 18 carbon atoms. The hydrocarbon chains can be saturated or may include one or more double bonds. The latter are referred to as monounsaturated or polyunsaturated, depending on the number of double bonds. Saturated compounds are more common in animal products, while unsaturated fats and oils are more common in plants.

About 94% of the fatty acids in olive oil are monounsaturated. The major fatty acid is oleic acid.

Common Fatty Acids

Name	Number of C Atoms	Formula
Saturated Acids		
lauric	C_{12}	$CH_3(CH_2)_{10}CO_2H$
myristic	C_{14}	$CH_3(CH_2)_{12}CO_2H$
palmitic	C_{16}	$CH_3(CH_2)_{14}CO_2H$
stearic	C_{18}	$CH_3(CH_2)_{16}CO_2H$
Unsaturated Acid		
oleic	C_{18}	$CH_3(CH_2)_7CH{=\!=}CH(CH_2)_7CO_2H$

In general, fats containing saturated fatty acids are solids, and those containing unsaturated fatty acids are liquids at room temperature. The difference in melting point relates to the molecular structure. With only single bonds linking carbon atoms in saturated fatty acids, the hydrocarbon group is flexible, allowing the molecules to pack more closely together. The double bonds in unsaturated fats introduce kinks that make the hydrocarbon group less flexible; consequently, the molecules pack less tightly together.

Food companies often hydrogenate vegetable oils to reduce unsaturation. The chemical rationale is that double bonds are reactive and unsaturated compounds are more susceptible to oxidation, which results in unpleasant odors. There are also aesthetic reasons for this practice. Food processors often want solid fats to improve the quality and appearance of the food. If liquid vegetable oil is used in a cake icing, for example, the icing may slide off the cake.

Polar bear fat. Polar bears feed primarily on seal blubber and build up a huge fat reserve during winter. During summer, they maintain normal activity but eat nothing, relying entirely on body fat for sustenance. A polar bear will burn about 1 to 1.5 kg of fat per day.

The conditions under which hydrogenation occurs can also lead to the isomerization of an unsaturated fat to the *trans* configuration. Such "trans-fats" in the diet have been linked to coronary heart disease.

Like other esters, fats and oils can undergo hydrolysis. This process is catalyzed by enzymes in the body. In industry, hydrolysis is carried out using aqueous NaOH or KOH to produce a mixture of glycerol and the sodium salts of the fatty acids. This reaction is called *saponification*, a term meaning "soap making."

$$
\text{Glyceryl stearate, a fat}
$$
$$
R = -(CH_2)_{16}CH_3
$$

$$
\begin{array}{c}
\quad\quad\quad\quad O \\
\quad\quad\quad\quad \| \\
H_2C - O - CR \\
\quad\quad\quad\quad O \\
\quad\quad\quad\quad \| \\
HC - O - CR \;+\; 3\,NaOH \\
\quad\quad\quad\quad O \\
\quad\quad\quad\quad \| \\
H_2C - O - CR
\end{array}
$$

$$
\downarrow
$$

$$
\begin{array}{c}
H_2C - O - H \quad\quad\quad\quad O \\
\quad\quad\quad\quad\quad\quad\quad\quad\quad \| \\
HC - O - H \;+\; 3\,RC - O^- \; Na^+ \\
H_2C - O - H
\end{array}
$$

glycerol   sodium stearate, a soap

Simple soaps are sodium salts of fatty acids. The anion in these compounds has an ionic end (the carboxylate group) and a nonpolar end (the large hydrocarbon tail). The ionic end allows these molecules to interact with water, and the nonpolar end enables them to mix with oily and greasy substances to form an emulsion that can be washed away with water.

Based on the observed geometry of the amide N atom, the atom is assigned sp^2 hybridization. To explain the observed angle and to rationalize sp^2 hybridization, we can introduce a second resonance form of the amide.

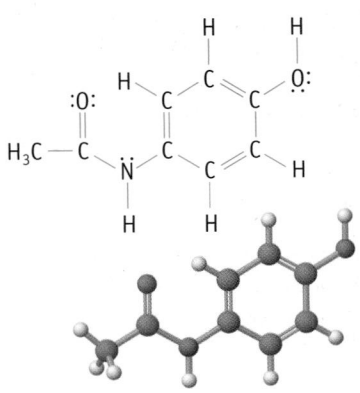

Acetaminophen, N-acetyl-p-aminophenol. This analgesic is an amide. It is used in over-the-counter painkillers such as Tylenol.

Form B contains a C=N double bond, and the O and N atoms have negative and positive charges, respectively. The N atom can be assigned sp^2 hybridization, and the π bond in B arises from overlap of p orbitals on C and N.

The existence of a second resonance structure for an amide link explains why the carbon–nitrogen bond is relatively short, about 132 pm, a value between that of a C—N single bond (149 pm) and a C=N double bond (127 pm). In addition, restricted rotation occurs around the C=N bond, making it possible for isomeric species to exist if the two groups bonded to N are different.

The amide grouping is particularly important in some synthetic polymers (Section 10.5) and in proteins (pages 496–513), where it is referred to as a *peptide link*. The compound N-acetyl-p-aminophenol, an analgesic known by the generic name acetaminophen and sold under the brand names Tylenol, Datril, and Momentum, among others, is another amide. Use of this compound as an analgesic was apparently discovered by accident when a common organic compound called acetanilide (like acetaminophen but without the —OH group) was mistakenly put into a prescription for a patient. Acetanilide acts as an analgesic, but it can be toxic. An —OH group *para* to the amide group makes the compound nontoxic, an interesting example of how a seemingly small structural difference affects chemical function.

■ **Amides, Peptides, and Proteins** When amino acids combine, they form amide or peptide links. Polymers of amino acids are proteins. For more on amino acids and proteins, see *The Chemistry of Life: Biochemistry,* pages 496–513.

Chemistry ⚛ Now™

Sign in at **www.cengage.com/login** and go to Chapter 10 Contents to see Screen 10.5 for a description of the **types of organic functional groups** and for tutorials on **their structures, bonding, and chemistry.**

■ **EXAMPLE 10.7 Functional Group Chemistry**

Problem

(a) Name the product of the reaction between ethylene and HCl.

(b) Draw the structure of the product of the reaction between propanoic acid and 1-propanol. What is the systematic name of the reaction product, and what functional group does it contain?

(c) What is the result of reacting 2-butanol with an oxidizing agent? Give the name, and draw the structure of the reaction product.

Strategy Ethylene is an alkene (page 453); propanoic acid is a carboxylic acid (page 471); and 2-butanol is an alcohol (page 462). Consult the discussion regarding their chemistry.

Solution

(a) HCl will add to the double bond of ethylene to produce chloroethane.

$$H_2C=CH_2 + HCl \longrightarrow H-\overset{\displaystyle H}{\underset{\displaystyle H}{C}}-\overset{\displaystyle H}{\underset{\displaystyle H}{C}}-Cl$$

ethylene   chloroethane

(b) Carboxylic acids such as propanoic acid react with alcohols to give esters.

$$CH_3CH_2\overset{\overset{\displaystyle O}{\|}}{C}OH + CH_3CH_2CH_2OH \longrightarrow CH_3CH_2\overset{\overset{\displaystyle O}{\|}}{C}OCH_2CH_2CH_3 + H_2O$$

propanoic acid   1-propanol   propyl propanoate, an ester

(c) 2-Butanol is a secondary alcohol. Such alcohols are oxidized to ketones.

$$CH_3\overset{\overset{\displaystyle OH}{|}}{C}HCH_2CH_3 \xrightarrow{\text{oxidizing agent}} CH_3\overset{\overset{\displaystyle O}{\|}}{C}CH_2CH_3$$

2-butanol   butanone, a ketone

EXERCISE 10.11 Functional Groups

(a) Name each of the following compounds and its functional group.

1. $CH_3CH_2CH_2OH$ 2. $CH_3\overset{\overset{\displaystyle O}{\|}}{C}OH$ 3. $CH_3CH_2NH_2$

(b) Name the product from the reaction of compounds 1 and 2.

(c) What is the name and structure of the product from the oxidation of 1?

(d) What compound could result from combining compounds 2 and 3?

(e) What is the result of adding an acid (say HCl) to compound 3?

10.5 Polymers

We now turn to the very large molecules known as polymers. These can be either synthetic materials or naturally occurring substances such as proteins or nucleic acids. Although these materials have widely varying compositions, their structures and properties are understandable, based on the principles developed for small molecules.

Classifying Polymers

The word *polymer* means "many parts" (from the Greek, *poly* and *meros*). **Polymers** are giant molecules made by chemically joining many small molecules called **monomers.** Polymer molar masses range from thousands to millions.

Extensive use of synthetic polymers is a fairly recent development. A few synthetic polymers (Bakelite, rayon, and celluloid) were made early in the 20th century, but most of the products with which you are familiar originated in the last 50 years. By 1976, synthetic polymers outstripped steel as the most widely used materials in the United States. The average production of synthetic polymers in the United States is approximately 150 kg per person annually.

The polymer industry classifies polymers in several different ways. One is their response to heating. **Thermoplastics** (such as polyethylene) soften and flow when they are heated and harden when they are cooled. **Thermosetting plastics** (such as Formica) are initially soft but set to a solid when heated and cannot be resoftened. Another classification scheme depends on the end use of the polymer—for example, plastics, fibers, elastomers, coatings, and adhesives.

■ **Biochemical Polymers** Polymer chemistry extends to biochemistry, where chemists study proteins and other large molecules. See *The Chemistry of Life: Biochemistry,* pages 496–513.

Biodiesel, promoted as an alternative to petroleum-based fuels used in diesel engines, is made from plant and animal oils. In the past 7 years, there has been a spectacular increase in its production and use, from under 1 million gallons in 1999 to 75 million gallons in 2005. But what is biodiesel?

Biodiesel, a mixture of long-chain esters of fatty acids.

Chemically, biodiesel is a mixture of esters of long-chain fatty acids. It is prepared from plant and animal fats and oils by *trans-esterification*. This is a reaction between an ester and an alcohol in which the —OR" on the alcohol exchanges with the OR' group of the ester:

$$RCO_2R' + R''OH \rightarrow RCO_2R'' + R'OH$$

Recall that fats and oils are esters (page 476), derivatives of glycerol and high–molar-mass organic acids (fatty acids). Their reaction with methanol (in the presence of a catalyst to speed up the reaction) produces a mixture of the methyl esters of long chain fatty acids and glycerol.

$$
\begin{array}{c}
H_2C-O-\overset{\overset{O}{\|}}{C}-R \\
HC-O-\overset{\overset{O}{\|}}{C}-R' + 3\,CH_3OH \longrightarrow HC-O-H + \\
H_2C-O-\overset{\underset{\|}{}}{C}-R'' \\
O
\end{array}
\quad
\begin{array}{c}
H_2C-O-H \\
HC-O-H \\
H_2C-O-H
\end{array}
\left\{
\begin{array}{c}
H_3C-O-\overset{\overset{O}{\|}}{C}-R \\
H_3C-O-\overset{\overset{O}{\|}}{C}-R' \\
H_3C-O-\overset{\overset{O}{\|}}{C}-R''
\end{array}
\right.
$$

Glycerol, a by-product of the reaction, is a valuable commodity for the health care products industry, so it is separated and sold. The mixture of esters that remains can be used directly as a fuel in existing diesel engines, or it can be blended with petroleum products. In the latter

case, the fuel mixture is identified by a designation such as B20 (B = biodiesel, 20 refers to 20% by volume.) The fuel has the advantage of being clean burning with fewer environmental problems associated with exhaust gases. In particular, there are no SO_2 emissions, one of the common problems associated with petroleum-based diesel fuels.

Proponents of the use of biodiesel note that biodiesel is produced from renewable resources, in contrast to petroleum. Critics point out, however, that growing crops for this purpose brings two problems. The first is that if crops are grown for biodiesel production, this has a negative effect on food supply. The case for biodiesel would be improved significantly, however, if it were possible to convert agricultural waste (corn stalks, for example) into a biofuel. Scientists are now actively trying to do this.

It is also pointed out that it would be impossible to grow enough crops to supply the raw materials to replace all petroleum-based diesel fuel—there isn't enough land available. Economics is also in the picture: Biodiesel is currently more expensive to produce; it is presently competitive only due to government subsidies.

Trans-esterification might seem like another kind of reaction, but it is actually closely related to chemistry we have already seen, the hydrolysis of an ester.

Ester hydrolysis:

$$R-\overset{\overset{O}{\|}}{C}-\boxed{O-R' + H}-O-H \longrightarrow R-\overset{\overset{O}{\|}}{C}-O-H + R'OH$$

Trans-esterification:

$$R-\overset{\overset{O}{\|}}{C}-\boxed{O-R' + H}-O-R'' \longrightarrow R-\overset{\overset{O}{\|}}{C}-O-R'' + R'OH$$

In both reactions, the OR' group on the ester combines with hydrogen of second reagent (water or alcohol) as shown. In drawing this analogy, it is useful to recognize that there are other similarities in the chemistry of alcohols and water. For example, both can be protonated with strong acids (giving H_3O^+ and ROH_2^+) and deprotonated by strong bases (giving OH^- and OR^-).

Questions:
1. *Write a balanced chemical equation for the reaction that occurs when methyl myristate, $C_{13}H_{27}CO_2CH_3(\ell)$, is burned, forming $CO_2(g)$ and $H_2O(g)$.*
2. *Using enthalpy of formation data, calculate the standard enthalpy change per mole in the oxidation of methyl myristate ($\Delta_f H° = -771.0$ kJ/mol).*
3. *Which compound, methyl myristate ($C_{15}H_{30}O_2$) or hexadecane ($C_{16}H_{34}$, one of many hydrocarbons in petroleum based diesel fuel) is predicted to provide the greater energy per mole? Per liter? ($\Delta_f H°$ for $C_{16}H_{34} = -456.1$ kJ/mol) [d(methyl myristate) = 0.86 g/mL, and d($C_{16}H_{34}$) = 0.77 g/mL]*

Answers to these questions are in Appendix Q.

(a)

(b)

(c)

FIGURE 10.12 Common polymer-based consumer products. (a) Packaging materials from high-density polyethylene; (b) from polystyrene; and (c) from polyvinyl chloride. Recycling information is provided on most plastics (often molded into the bottom of bottles). High-density polyethylene is designated with a "2" inside a triangular symbol and the letters "HDPE." PVC is designated with a "3" inside a triangular symbol with the letter "V" below.

A more chemically oriented approach to polymer classification is based on the method of synthesis. **Addition polymers** are made by directly adding monomer units together. **Condensation polymers** are made by combining monomer units and splitting out a small molecule, often water.

Addition Polymers

Polyethylene, polystyrene, and polyvinyl chloride (PVC) are common addition polymers (Figure 10.12). They are built by "adding together" simple alkenes such as ethylene ($CH_2=CH_2$), styrene ($C_6H_5CH=CH_2$), and vinyl chloride ($CH_2=CHCl$). These and other addition polymers (Table 10.12), all derived from alkenes, have widely varying properties and uses.

Chemistry⚛Now™

Sign in at **www.cengage.com/login** and go to Chapter 10 Contents to see Screen 10.9 for an animation of **addition polymerization.**

Polyethylene and Other Polyolefins

Polyethylene is by far the leader in terms of addition polymer production. Ethylene (C_2H_4), the monomer from which polyethylene is made, is a product of petroleum refining and one of the top five chemicals produced in the United States. When ethylene is heated to between 100 and 250 °C at a pressure of 1000 to 3000 atm in the presence of a catalyst, polymers with molar masses up to several million are formed. The reaction can be expressed as a balanced chemical equation:

$$n\ H_2C=CH_2 \longrightarrow \left(\begin{array}{cc} H & H \\ | & | \\ C & C \\ | & | \\ H & H \end{array}\right)_n$$

ethylene   polyethylene

TABLE 10.12 Ethylene Derivatives That Undergo Addition Polymerization

Formula	Monomer Common Name	Polymer Name (Trade Names)	Uses	U.S. Polymer Production (Metric tons/year)*
$H_2C=CH_2$ (H, H / C=C / H, H)	ethylene	polyethylene (polythene)	squeeze bottles, bags, films, toys and molded objects, electric insulation	7 million
(H, H / C=C / H, CH_3)	propylene	polypropylene (Vectra, Herculon)	bottles, films, indoor-outdoor carpets	1.2 million
(H, H / C=C / H, Cl)	vinyl chloride	polyvinyl chloride (PVC)	floor tile, raincoats, pipe	1.6 million
(H, H / C=C / H, CN)	acrylonitrile	polyacrylonitrile (Orlan, Acrilan)	rugs, fabrics	0.5 million
(H, H / C=C / H, benzene ring)	styrene	polystyrene (Styrofoam, Styron)	food and drink coolers, building material insulation	0.9 million
(H, H / C=C / H, O—C—CH_3 with =O)	vinyl acetate	polyvinyl acetate (PVA)	latex paint, adhesives, textile coatings	200,000
(H, CH_3 / C=C / H, C—O—CH_3 with =O)	methyl methacrylate	polymethyl methacrylate (Plexiglass, Lucite)	high-quality transparent objects, latex paints, contact lenses	200,000
(F, F / C=C / F, F)	tetrafluoroethylene	polytetrafluoroethylene (Teflon)	gaskets, insulation, bearings, pan coatings	6,000

* One metric ton = 1000 kg.

The abbreviated formula of the reaction product, $-(CH_2CH_2)_n$, shows that polyethylene is a chain of carbon atoms, each bearing two hydrogens. The chain length for polyethylene can be very long. A polymer with a molar mass of 1 million would contain almost 36,000 ethylene molecules linked together.

Polyethylene formed under various pressures and catalytic conditions has different properties, as a result of different molecular structures. For example, when chromium oxide is used as a catalyst, the product is almost exclusively a linear chain (Figure 10.13a). If ethylene is heated to 230 °C at high pressure, however, irregular branching occurs. Still other conditions lead to cross-linked polyethylene, in which different chains are linked together (Figures 10.13b and c).

The high–molar-mass chains of linear polyethylene pack closely together and result in a material with a density of 0.97 g/cm^3. This material, referred to as

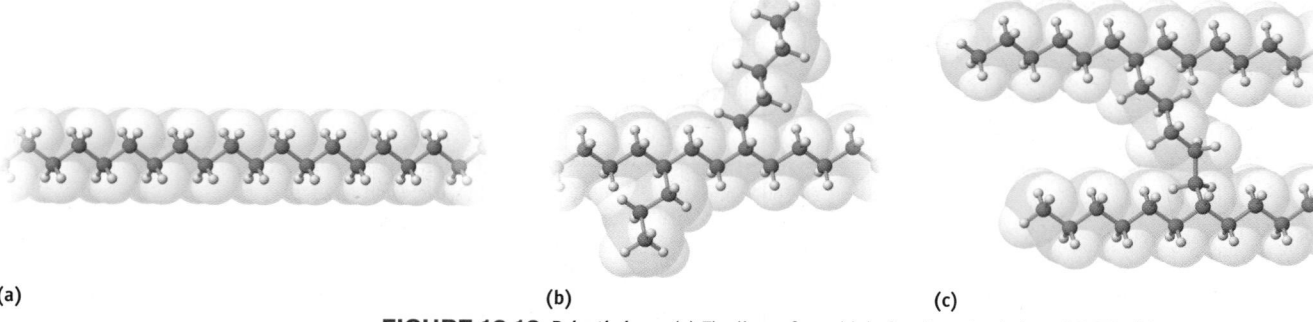

(a)   (b)   (c)

FIGURE 10.13 Polyethylene. (a) The linear form, high-density polyethylene (HDPE). (b) Branched chains occur in low-density polyethylene (LDPE). (c) Cross-linked polyethylene (CLPE).

high-density polyethylene (HDPE), is hard and tough, which makes it suitable for items such as milk bottles. If the polyethylene chain contains branches, however, the chains cannot pack as closely together, and a lower-density material (0.92 g/cm^3) known as low-density polyethylene (LDPE) results. This material is softer and more flexible than HDPE. It is used in plastic wrap and sandwich bags, among other things. Linking up the polymer chains in cross-linked polyethylene (CLPE) causes the material to be even more rigid and inflexible. Plastic bottle caps are often made of CLPE.

Polymers formed from substituted ethylenes (CH$_2$=CHX) have a range of properties and uses (see Table 10.12). Sometimes, the properties are predictable based on the molecule's structure. Polymers without polar substituent groups, such as polystyrene, often dissolve in organic solvents, a property useful for some types of fabrication (Figure 10.14).

Polymers based on substituted ethylenes, H$_2$C=CHX

$$\left(\!-\!CH_2CH\!-\!\right)_n \qquad \left(\!-\!CH_2CH\!-\!\right)_n \qquad \left(\!-\!CH_2CH\!-\!\right)_n$$
OH   OCCH$_3$ ◯
                           ‖
                           O

polyvinyl alcohol   polyvinyl acetate   polystyrene

Polyvinyl alcohol is a polymer with little affinity for nonpolar solvents but an affinity for water, which is not surprising, based on the large number of polar OH groups (Figure 10.15). Vinyl alcohol itself is not a stable compound (it isomerizes to acetaldehyde CH$_3$CHO), so polyvinyl alcohol cannot be made from this compound. Instead, it is made by hydrolyzing the ester groups in polyvinyl acetate.

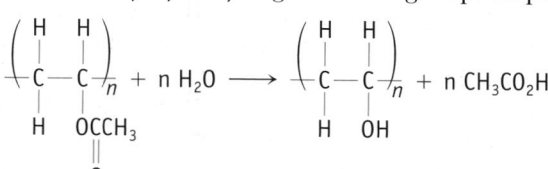

Christopher Springmann/Corbisstockmarket.com

Polyethylene film. The polymer film is produced by extruding the molten plastic through a ring-like gap and inflating the film like a balloon.

Solubility in water or organic solvents can be a liability for polymers. The many uses of polytetrafluoroethylene [Teflon, $\left(\!-\!CF_2CF_2\!-\!\right)_n$] stem from the fact that it does not interact with water or organic solvents.

Polystyrene, with $n = 5700$, is a clear, hard, colorless solid that can be molded easily at 250 °C. You are probably more familiar with the very light, foam-like mate-

482 Chapter 10 | Carbon: More Than Just Another Element

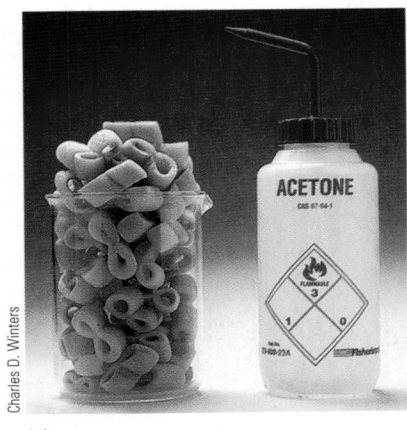

(a) **(b)**

FIGURE 10.14 Polystyrene. (a) The polymer is a clear, hard, colorless solid, but it may be more familiar as a light, foam-like material called Styrofoam. (b) Styrofoam has no polar groups and thus dissolves well in organic solvents such as acetone. See also Figure 10.12b.

rial known as Styrofoam that is used widely for food and beverage containers and for home insulation (Figure 10.14). Styrofoam is produced by a process called "expansion molding." Polystyrene beads containing 4% to 7% of a low-boiling liquid like pentane are placed in a mold and heated with steam or hot air. Heat causes the solvent to vaporize, creating a foam in the molten polymer that expands to fill the shape of the mold.

Natural and Synthetic Rubber

Natural rubber was first introduced in Europe in 1740, but it remained a curiosity until 1823, when Charles Macintosh invented a way of using it to waterproof cotton cloth. The mackintosh, as rain coats are still sometimes called, became popular despite major problems: Natural rubber is notably weak and is soft and tacky when warm but brittle at low temperatures. In 1839, after 5 years of research on natural rubber, the American inventor Charles Goodyear (1800–1860) discovered that heating gum rubber with sulfur produces a material that is elastic, water-repellent, resilient, and no longer sticky.

Rubber is a naturally occurring polymer, the monomers of which are molecules of 2-methyl-1,3-butadiene, commonly called *isoprene*. In natural rubber, isoprene monomers are linked together through carbon atoms 1 and 4—that is, through the end carbon atoms of the C_4 chain (Figure 10.16). This leaves a double bond between carbon atoms 2 and 3. In natural rubber, these double bonds have a *cis* configuration.

In vulcanized rubber, the material that Goodyear discovered, the polymer chains of natural rubber are cross-linked by short chains of sulfur atoms. Cross-linking helps to align the polymer chains, so the material does not undergo a permanent change when stretched and it springs back when the stress is removed. Substances that behave this way are called **elastomers**.

With a knowledge of the composition and structure of natural rubber, chemists began searching for ways to make synthetic rubber. When they first tried to make the polymer by linking isoprene monomers together, however, what they made was sticky and useless. The problem was that synthesis procedures gave a mixture of *cis* and *trans* polyisoprene. In 1955, however, chemists at the Goodyear and Firestone companies discovered special catalysts to prepare the all-*cis* polymer. This synthetic material, which was structurally identical to natural rubber, is now manufactured cheaply. In fact, more than 8.0×10^8 kg of synthetic polyisoprene is produced annually in the United States.

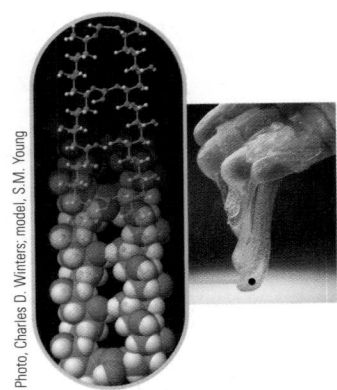

FIGURE 10.15 Slime. When boric acid, $B(OH)_3$, is added to an aqueous suspension of polyvinyl alcohol, $(CH_2CHOH)_n$, the mixture becomes very viscous because boric acid reacts with the —OH groups on the polymer chain, causing cross-linking to occur. (The model shows an idealized structure of a portion of the polymer.)

Isoprene, 2-methyl-1,3-butadiene.

Other kinds of polymers have further expanded the repertoire of elastomeric materials now available. Polybutadiene, for example, is currently used in the production of tires, hoses, and belts. Some elastomers, called **copolymers,** are formed by polymerization of two (or more) different monomers. A copolymer of styrene and butadiene, made with a 1:3 ratio of these raw materials, is the most important synthetic rubber now made; more than about 1 billion kg of styrene-butadiene rubber (SBR) is produced each year in the United States for making tires.

FIGURE 10.16 Natural rubber. The sap that comes from the rubber tree is a natural polymer of isoprene. All the linkages in the carbon chain are *cis*. When natural rubber is heated strongly in the absence of air, it smells of isoprene. This observation provided a clue that rubber is composed of this building block.

$$3n \ \ \underset{\underset{CH_2}{|}}{HC} - \underset{\underset{CH_2}{|}}{CH} \quad + \quad n \ H_2C = \overset{\overset{H}{|}}{C}$$

1,3-butadiene   styrene

styrene-butadiene rubber (SBR)

And a little is left over each year to make bubble gum. The stretchiness of bubble gum once came from natural rubber, but SBR is now used to help you blow bubbles.

Chemistry Now™

Sign in at **www.cengage.com/login** and go to Chapter 10 Contents to see Screen 10.11 for a self-study module on **the polymer used in bubble gum.**

Condensation Polymers

A chemical reaction in which two molecules react by splitting out, or eliminating, a small molecule is called a **condensation reaction.** The reaction of an alcohol with a carboxylic acid to give an ester is an example of a condensation reaction. One way to form a condensation polymer uses *two* different reactant molecules, each containing *two* functional groups. Another route uses a single molecule with two different functional groups. Commercial polyesters are made using both types of reactions.

Chemistry Now™

Sign in at **www.cengage.com/login** and go to Chapter 10 Contents to see Screen 10.10 to view an animation of **condensation polymerization** and to watch a video of **the synthesis of nylon.**

Polyesters

Terephthalic acid contains two carboxylic acid groups, and ethylene glycol contains two alcohol groups. When mixed, the acid and alcohol functional groups at both ends of these molecules can react to form ester linkages, splitting out water. The

Copolymer of styrene and butadiene, SBR rubber. The elasticity of bubble gum comes from SBR rubber.

result is a polymer called polyethylene terephthalate (PET). The multiple ester linkages make this substance a **polyester.**

$$n \; HOC\text{—}\bigcirc\text{—}COH + n \; HOCH_2CH_2OH \longrightarrow \left(\begin{matrix} O \\ \| \\ C \end{matrix}\text{—}\bigcirc\text{—}\begin{matrix} O \\ \| \\ COCH_2CH_2O \end{matrix} \right)_n + 2n \; H_2O$$

terephthalic acid   ethylene glycol   polyethylene terephthalate (PET), a polyester

Polyester textile fibers made from PET are marketed as Dacron and Terylene. The inert, nontoxic, noninflammatory, and non–blood-clotting properties of Dacron polymers make Dacron tubing an excellent substitute for human blood vessels in heart bypass operations, and Dacron sheets are sometimes used as temporary skin for burn victims. A polyester film, Mylar, has unusual strength and can be rolled into sheets one-thirtieth the thickness of a human hair. Magnetically coated Mylar films are used to make audio and video tapes (Figure 10.17).

There is considerable interest in another polyester, polylactic acid (PLA). Lactic acid contains both carboxylic acid and alcohol functional groups, so condensation between molecules of this monomer gives a polymer.

$$n \; HO\text{—}\begin{matrix} H \\ | \\ C \\ | \\ CH_3 \end{matrix}\text{—}\begin{matrix} O \\ \| \\ C \end{matrix}\text{—}OH \longrightarrow \left(O\text{—}\begin{matrix} H \\ | \\ C \\ | \\ CH_3 \end{matrix}\text{—}\begin{matrix} O \\ \| \\ C \end{matrix}\text{—}O \right)_n + n \; H_2O$$

There is interest in polylactic acid for two reasons. First, the monomer used to make this polymer is obtained by biological fermentation of plant materials. (Most of the chemicals used in the manufacture of other types of polymers are derived from petroleum, and there is increased concern about the availability and cost of raw materials in the future.) Second, this polymer, which is currently being used in packaging material, is biodegradable, which has the potential to alleviate land-fill disposal problems.

Polyamides

In 1928, the DuPont Company embarked on a basic research program headed by Wallace Carothers (1896–1937). Carothers was interested in high–molar-mass compounds, such as rubbers, proteins, and resins. In 1935, his research yielded

FIGURE 10.17 Polyesters. Polyethylene terephthalate is used to make clothing and soda bottles. The two students are wearing jackets made from recycled PET soda bottles. Mylar film, another polyester, is used to make recording tape as well as balloons. Because the film has very tiny pores, Mylar can be used for helium-filled balloons; the atoms of gaseous helium move through the pores in the film very slowly.

Active Figure 10.18 Nylon-
6,6. Hexamethylenediamine is dissolved
in water (bottom layer), and adipoyl
chloride (a derivative of adipic acid)
is dissolved in hexane (top layer). The
two compounds react at the interface
between the layers to form nylon, which
is being wound onto a stirring rod.

Chemistry ⚛ Now™ Sign in at www.
cengage.com/login and go to the
Chapter Contents menu to explore
an interactive version of this figure
accompanied by an exercise.

nylon-6,6 (Figure 10.18), a **polyamide** prepared from adipoyl chloride, a derivative of adipic acid, a diacid, and hexamethylenediamine, a diamine:

$$n\ \text{ClC(CH}_2)_4\text{CCl} + 2n\ \text{H}_2\text{N(CH}_2)_6\text{NH}_2 \longrightarrow \left(\!\!\begin{array}{c}\text{C(CH}_2)_4\text{C}-\text{N(CH}_2)_6\text{N}\\ |\quad\quad |\\ \text{H}\quad\quad\text{H}\end{array}\!\!\right)_n + 2n\ \text{HCl}$$

adipoyl chloride   hexamethylenediamine   amide link in nylon-6,6 a polyamide

Nylon can be extruded easily into fibers that are stronger than natural fibers and chemically more inert. The discovery of nylon jolted the American textile industry at a critical time. Natural fibers were not meeting 20th-century needs. Silk was expensive and not durable; wool was scratchy; linen crushed easily; and cotton did not have a high-fashion image. Perhaps the most identifiable use for the new fiber was in nylon stockings. The first public sale of nylon hosiery took place on October 24, 1939, in Wilmington, Delaware (the site of DuPont's main office). This use of nylon in commercial products ended shortly thereafter, however, with the start of World War II. All nylon was diverted to making parachutes and other military gear. It was not until about 1952 that nylon reappeared in the consumer marketplace.

Figure 10.19 illustrates why nylon makes such a good fiber. To have good tensile strength (the ability to resist tearing), the polymer chains should be able to attract one another, albeit not so strongly that the plastic cannot be initially extended to form fibers. Ordinary covalent bonds between the chains (cross-linking) would be too strong. Instead, cross-linking occurs by a somewhat weaker intermolecular force called *hydrogen bonding* (▶ Section 12.2) between the hydrogens of N—H groups on one chain and the carbonyl oxygens on another chain. The polarities of the $\text{N}^{\delta-}\text{—H}^{\delta+}$ group and the $\text{C}^{\delta+}\text{=O}^{\delta-}$ group lead to attractive forces between the polymer chains of the desired magnitude.

■ EXAMPLE 10.8 Condensation Polymers

Problem What is the repeating unit of the condensation polymer obtained by combining $\text{HO}_2\text{CCH}_2\text{CH}_2\text{CO}_2\text{H}$ (succinic acid) and $\text{H}_2\text{NCH}_2\text{CH}_2\text{NH}_2$ (1,2-ethylenediamine)?

Strategy Recognize that the polymer will link the two monomer units through the amide linkage. The smallest repeating unit of the chain will contain two parts, one from the diacid and the other from the diamine.

Solution The repeating unit of this polyamide is

amide linkage

$$\left(\!\!\begin{array}{c}\text{O}\quad\quad\text{O}\\ ||\quad\quad ||\\ \text{CCH}_2\text{CH}_2\text{C}-\text{NCH}_2\text{CH}_2\text{N}\\ |\quad\quad\quad |\\ \text{H}\quad\quad\quad\text{H}\end{array}\!\!\right)_n$$

FIGURE 10.19 Hydrogen bonding
between polyamide chains. Carbonyl
oxygen atoms with a partial negative
charge on one chain interact with an
amine hydrogen with a partial positive
charge on a neighboring chain. (This form
of bonding is described in more detail in
Section 12.3.)

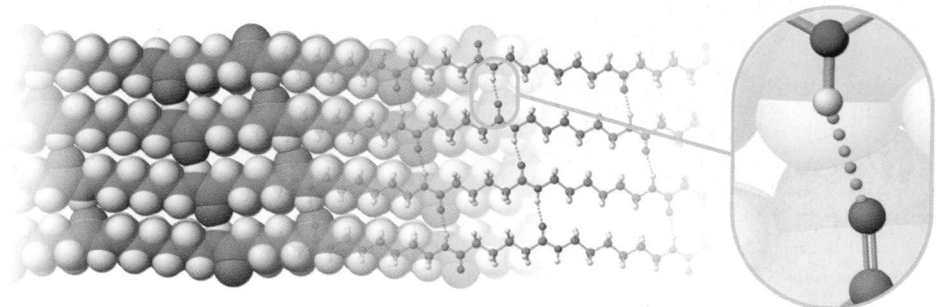

Chemical Perspectives

Super Diapers

Disposable diapers are a miracle of modern chemistry: Most of the materials used are synthetic polymers. The outer layer is mostly microporous polyethylene; it keeps the urine in but remains breathable. The inside layer is polypropylene, a material prized by winter-camping enthusiasts. It stays soft and dry while wicking moisture away from the skin. Sandwiched between these layers is powdered sodium polyacrylate combined with cellulose;

the latter is the only natural part of the materials used. The package is completed with elasticized hydrophobic polypropylene cuffs around the baby's thighs, and Velcro tabs hold the diaper on the baby.

The key ingredient in the diaper is the polyacrylate polymer filling. This substance can absorb up to 800 times its weight in water. When dry, the polymer has a carboxylate group associated with sodium ions. When placed in water, osmotic pressure causes water molecules to enter the polymer (because the ion concentration in the polymer is higher than in water; see Chapter 14). As water enters, the sodium ions dissociate from the polymer, and the polar water molecules are attracted to these positive ions and to the negative carboxylate groups of the polymer. At the same time, the negative carboxylate groups repel one another, forcing them apart and causing the polymer to unwind. Evidence for the unwinding of the polymer is seen as swelling of the diaper. In addition, because it contains so much water, the polymer becomes gel-like.

If the gelled polymer is put into a salt solution, water is attracted to the Na^+ and Cl^- ions and is drawn from the polymer. Thus, the polymer becomes solid once again. The diminished ability of sodium polyacrylate to absorb water in a salt solution is the reason that disposable diapers do not absorb urine as well as pure water.

These kinds of superabsorbent materials—sodium polyacrylate and a related material, polyacrylamide—are useful not only in diapers but also for cleaning up spills in hospitals, for protecting power and optical cables from moisture, for filtering water out of aviation gasoline, and for conditioning garden soil to retain water. You will also find them in the toy store as "gro-creatures."

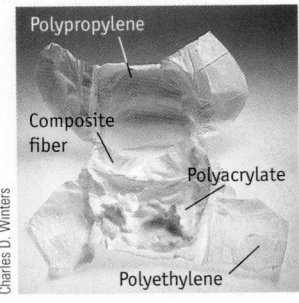

Charles D. Winters

Polypropylene

Composite fiber

Polyacrylate

Polyethylene

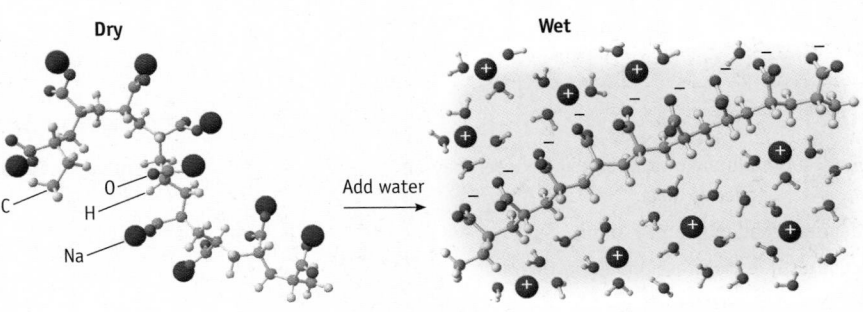

Dry

C   O   H   Na   Add water   Wet

Chapter Goals Revisited

Now that you have studied this chapter, you should ask whether you have met the chapter goals. In particular, you should be able to:

Classify organic compounds based on formula and structure

a. Understand the factors that contribute to the large numbers of organic compounds and the wide array of structures (Section 10.1). Study Question(s) assignable in OWL: 3.

Recognize and draw structures of structural isomers and stereoisomers for carbon compounds

a. Recognize and draw structures of geometric isomers and optical isomers (Section 10.1). Study Question(s) assignable in OWL: 11, 12, 15, 58.

Name and draw structures of common organic compounds

a. Draw structural formulas, and name simple hydrocarbons, including alkanes, alkenes, alkynes, and aromatic compounds (Section 10.2). Study Question(s) assignable in OWL: 1, 5, 7, 28, 67, 69, 70, 96; Go Chemistry Module 15.

b. Identify possible isomers for a given formula (Section 10.2).

c. Name and draw structures of alcohols and amines (Section 10.3). Study Question(s) assignable in OWL: 31, 32, 34.

d. Name and draw structures of carbonyl compounds—aldehydes, ketones, acids, esters, and amides (Section 10.4). Study Question(s) assignable in OWL: 38, 39, 40, 41, 43, 51.

Know the common reactions of organic functional groups

a. This goal applies specifically to the reactions of alkenes, alcohols, amines, aldehydes and ketones, and carboxylic acids. Study Question(s) assignable in OWL: 19, 21, 24, 46, 64, 76, 79, 81, 83–85, 90–92, 97.

Relate properties to molecular structure

a. Describe the physical and chemical properties of the various classes of hydrocarbon compounds (Section 10.2).

b. Recognize the connection between the structures and the properties of alcohols (Section 10.3).

c. Know the structures and properties of several natural products, including carbohydrates (Section 10.4) and fats and oils (Section 10.4). Study Question(s) assignable in OWL: 49, 50.

Identify common polymers

a. Write equations for the formation of addition polymers and condensation polymers, and describe their structures (Section 10.5).

b. Relate properties of polymers to their structures (Section 10.5). Study Question(s) assignable in OWL: 95.

STUDY QUESTIONS

⛭WL Online homework for this chapter may be assigned in OWL.

▲ denotes challenging questions.

■ denotes questions assignable in OWL.

Blue-numbered questions have answers in Appendix O and fully-worked solutions in the *Student Solutions Manual*.

Practicing Skills

Alkanes and Cycloalkanes
(See Examples 10.1 and 10.2 and ChemistryNow Screen 10.3.)

1. ■ What is the name of the straight (unbranched) chain alkane with the formula C_7H_{16}?

2. What is the molecular formula for an alkane with 12 carbon atoms?

3. ■ Which of the following is an alkane? Which could be a cycloalkane?
(a) C_2H_4
(c) $C_{14}H_{30}$
(b) C_5H_{10}
(d) C_7H_8

4. Isooctane, 2,2,4-trimethylpentane, is one of the possible structural isomers with the formula C_8H_{18}. Draw the structure of this isomer, and draw and name structures of two other isomers of C_8H_{18} in which the longest carbon chain is five atoms.

5. ■ Give the systematic name for the following alkane:

$$CH_3$$
$$|$$
$$CH_3CHCHCH_3$$
$$|$$
$$CH_3$$

6. Give the systematic name for the following alkane. Draw a structural isomer of the compound, and give its name.

$$CH_3$$
$$|$$
$$CH_3CHCH_2CH_2CHCH_3$$
$$|$$
$$CH_2CH_3$$

7. ■ Draw the structure of each of the following compounds:
(a) 2,3-dimethylhexane
(b) 2,3-dimethyloctane
(c) 3-ethylheptane
(d) 3-ethyl-2-methylhexane

8. Draw structures for 3-ethylpentane and 2,3-dimethylpentane.

9. Draw Lewis structures, and name all possible compounds that have a seven-carbon chain with one methyl substituent group. Which of these isomers has a chiral carbon center?

10. Draw a structure for cycloheptane. Is the seven-member ring planar? Explain your answer.

11. ■ There are two ethylheptanes (compounds with a seven-carbon chain and one ethyl substituent). Draw the structures, and name these compounds. Is either isomer chiral?

12. ■ Among the 18 structural isomers with the formula C_8H_{18} are two with a five-carbon chain having one ethyl and one methyl substituent group. Draw their structures, and name these two isomers.

13. List several typical physical properties of C_4H_{10}. Predict the following physical properties of dodecane, $C_{12}H_{26}$: color, state (s, ℓ, g), solubility in water, solubility in a nonpolar solvent.

14. Write balanced equations for the following reactions of alkanes.
(a) The reaction of methane with excess chlorine.
(b) Complete combustion of cyclohexane, C_6H_{12}, with excess oxygen.

Alkenes and Alkynes
(See Examples 10.3 and 10.4 and ChemistryNow Screens 10.3 and 10.4.)

15. ■ Draw structures for the *cis* and *trans* isomers of 4-methyl-2-hexene.

16. What structural requirement is necessary for an alkene to have *cis* and *trans* isomers? Can *cis* and *trans* isomers exist for an alkane? For an alkyne?

17. A hydrocarbon with the formula C_5H_{10} can be either an alkene or a cycloalkane.
(a) Draw a structure for each of the isomers possible for C_5H_{10}, assuming it is an alkene. Six isomers are possible. Give the systematic name of each isomer you have drawn.
(b) Draw a structure for a cycloalkane having the formula C_5H_{10}.

18. Five alkenes have the formula C_7H_{14} and a seven-carbon chain. Draw their structures, and name them.

19. ■ Draw the structure, and give the systematic name for the products of the following reactions:
(a) $CH_3CH{=}CH_2 + Br_2 \rightarrow$
(b) $CH_3CH_2CH{=}CHCH_3 + H_2 \rightarrow$

20. Draw the structure, and give the systematic name for the products of the following reactions:

(a)
$$H_3C \qquad\qquad CH_2CH_3$$
$$\diagdown\quad\diagup$$
$$C{=}C \qquad\qquad + H_2 \longrightarrow$$
$$\diagup\quad\diagdown$$
$$H_3C \qquad\qquad H$$

(b) $CH_3C{\equiv}CCH_2CH_3 + 2\,Br_2 \longrightarrow$

21. ■ The compound 2-bromobutane is a product of addition of HBr to an alkene. Identify the alkene and give its name.

22. The compound 2,3-dibromo-2-methylhexane is formed by addition of Br_2 to an alkene. Identify the alkene, and write an equation for this reaction.

23. Draw structures for alkenes that have the formula C_3H_5Cl, and name each compound. (These are derivatives of propene in which a chlorine atom replaces one hydrogen atom.)

24. ■ Elemental analysis of a colorless liquid has given its formula as C_5H_{10}. You recognize that this could be either a cycloalkane or an alkene. A chemical test to determine the class to which this compound belongs involves adding bromine. Explain how this would allow you to distinguish between the two classes.

Aromatic Compounds
(See Example 10.5, Exercise 10.5, and ChemistryNow Screen 10.3.)

25. Draw structural formulas for the following compounds:
(a) 1,3-dichlorobenzene (alternatively called *m*-dichlorobenzene)
(b) 1-bromo-4-methylbenzene (alternatively called *p*-bromotoluene)

26. Give the systematic name for each of the following compounds:

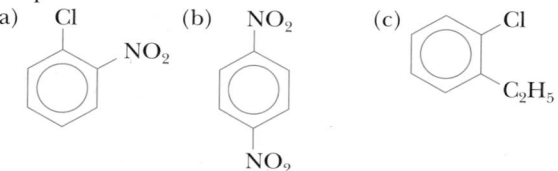

27. Write an equation for the preparation of ethylbenzene from benzene and an appropriate compound containing an ethyl group.

28. ■ Write an equation for the preparation of hexylbenzene from benzene and other appropriate reagents.

29. A single compound is formed by alkylation of 1,4-dimethylbenzene. Write the equation for the reaction of this compound with CH_3Cl and $AlCl_3$. What is the structure and name of the product?

30. Nitration of toluene gives a mixture of two products, one with the nitro group ($-NO_2$) in the *ortho* position and one with the nitro group in the *para* position. Draw structures of the two products.

Alcohols, Ethers, and Amines
(See Example 10.6 and ChemistryNow Screen 10.5.)

31. ■ Give the systematic name for each of the following alcohols, and tell if each is a primary, secondary, or tertiary alcohol:
(a) $CH_3CH_2CH_2OH$
(b) $CH_3CH_2CH_2CH_2OH$

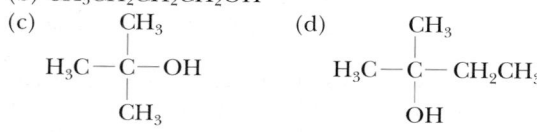

32. ■ Draw structural formulas for the following alcohols, and tell if each is primary, secondary, or tertiary:
(a) 1-butanol
(b) 2-butanol
(c) 3,3-dimethyl-2-butanol
(d) 3,3-dimethyl-1-butanol

33. Write the formula, and draw the structure for each of the following amines:
(a) ethylamine
(b) dipropylamine
(c) butyldimethylamine
(d) triethylamine

34. ■ Name the following amines:
(a) $CH_3CH_2CH_2NH_2$
(b) $(CH_3)_3N$
(c) $(CH_3)(C_2H_5)NH$
(d) $C_6H_{13}NH_2$

35. Draw structural formulas for all the alcohols with the formula $C_4H_{10}O$. Give the systematic name of each.

36. Draw structural formulas for all primary amines with the formula $C_4H_9NH_2$.

37. Complete and balance the following equations:
(a) $C_6H_5NH_2(\ell) + HCl(aq) \rightarrow$
(b) $(CH_3)_3N(aq) + H_2SO_4(aq) \rightarrow$

38. ■ Aldehydes and carboxylic acids are formed by oxidation of primary alcohols, and ketones are formed when secondary alcohols are oxidized. Give the name and formula for the alcohol that, when oxidized, gives the following products:
(a) $CH_3CH_2CH_2CHO$
(b) 2-hexanone

Compounds with a Carbonyl Group
(See Exercises 10.7–10.10 and ChemistryNow Screen 10.5.)

39. ■ Draw structural formulas for (a) 2-pentanone, (b) hexanal, and (c) pentanoic acid.

40. ■ Identify the class of each of the following compounds, and give the systematic name for each:
(a)

$$CH_3\overset{\overset{\displaystyle O}{\|}}{C}CH_3$$

(b)

$$CH_3CH_2CH_2\overset{\overset{\displaystyle O}{\|}}{C}H$$

(c)

$$CH_3\overset{\overset{\displaystyle O}{\|}}{C}CH_2CH_2CH_3$$

41. ■ Identify the class of each of the following compounds, and give the systematic name for each:
(a)

$$CH_3CH_2\overset{\overset{\displaystyle CH_3}{|}}{C}HCH_2CO_2H$$

(b)

$$CH_3CH_2\overset{\overset{\displaystyle O}{\|}}{C}OCH_3$$

(c)

$$CH_3\overset{\overset{\displaystyle O}{\|}}{C}OCH_2CH_2CH_2CH_3$$

(d)

$$Br-\text{⟨benzene ring⟩}-\overset{\overset{\displaystyle O}{\|}}{C}OH$$

42. Draw structural formulas for the following acids and esters:
(a) 2-methylhexanoic acid
(b) pentyl butanoate (which has the odor of apricots)
(c) octyl acetate (which has the odor of oranges)

43. ■ Give the structural formula and systematic name for the product, if any, from each of the following reactions:
   (a) pentanal and $KMnO_4$
   (b) pentanal and $LiAlH_4$
   (c) 2-octanone and $LiAlH_4$
   (d) 2-octanone and $KMnO_4$

44. Describe how to prepare 2-pentanol beginning with the appropriate ketone.

45. Describe how to prepare propyl propanoate beginning with 1-propanol as the only carbon-containing reagent.

46. ■ Give the name and structure of the product of the reaction of benzoic acid and 2-propanol.

47. Draw structural formulas, and give the names for the products of the following reaction:

$$CH_3COCH_2CH_2CH_2CH_3 + NaOH$$

48. Draw structural formulas, and give the names for the products of the following reaction:

   (benzene ring)—C(=O)—O—CH(CH$_3$)—CH$_3$ + NaOH ⟶ ?

49. ■ The Lewis structure of phenylalanine, one of the 20 amino acids that make up proteins, is drawn below (without lone pairs of electrons). The carbon atoms are numbered for the purpose of this question.
   (a) What is the geometry of C_3?
   (b) What is the O—C—O bond angle?
   (c) Is this molecule chiral? If so, which carbon atom is chiral?
   (d) Which hydrogen atom in this compound is acidic?

50. ■ The Lewis structure of vitamin C, whose chemical name is ascorbic acid, is drawn below (without lone pairs of electrons).

   (a) What is the approximate value for the O—C—O bond angle?

(b) There are four OH groups in this structure. Estimate the C—O—H bond angles for these groups. Will they be the same value (more or less), or should there be significant differences in these bond angles?
(c) Is the molecule chiral? How many chiral carbon atoms can be identified in this structure?
(d) Identify the shortest bond in this molecule.
(e) What are the functional groups of the molecule?

Functional Groups
(See Example 10.7 and ChemistryNow Screen 10.5.)

51. ■ Identify the functional groups in the following molecules.
   (a) $CH_3CH_2CH_2OH$
   (b)
   $H_3CCNHCH_3$ (with O double bonded)
   (c)
   CH_3CH_2COH (with O double bonded)
   (d)
   $CH_3CH_2COCH_3$ (with O double bonded)

52. Consider the following molecules:
   1. $CH_3CH_2CCH_3$ (with O double bonded)
   2. CH_3CH_2COH (with O double bonded)
   3. $H_2C=CHCH_2OH$
   4. $CH_3CH_2CHCH_3$ (with OH)

   (a) What is the result of treating compound 1 with $NaBH_4$? What is the functional group in the product? Name the product.
   (b) Draw the structure of the reaction product from compounds 2 and 4. What is the functional group in the product?
   (c) What compound results from adding H_2 to compound 3? Name the reaction product.
   (d) What compound results from adding NaOH to compound 2?

Polymers
(See Example 10.8, Exercise 10.10, and ChemistryNow Screens 10.9 and 10.10.)

53. Polyvinyl acetate is the binder in water-based paints.
   (a) Write an equation for its formation from vinyl acetate.
   (b) Show a portion of this polymer with three monomer units.
   (c) Describe how to make polyvinyl alcohol from polyvinyl acetate.

54. Neoprene (polychloroprene, a kind of rubber) is a polymer formed from the chlorinated butadiene $H_2C=CHCCl=CH_2$.
   (a) Write an equation showing the formation of polychloroprene from the monomer.
   (b) Show a portion of this polymer with three monomer units.

55. Saran is a copolymer of 1,1-dichloroethene and chloroethene (vinyl chloride). Draw a possible structure for this polymer.

56. The structure of methyl methacrylate is given in Table 10.12. Draw the structure of a polymethyl methacrylate (PMMA) polymer that has four monomer units. (PMMA has excellent optical properties and is used to make hard contact lenses.)

General Questions on Organic Chemistry

These questions are not designated as to type or location in the chapter. They may combine several concepts.

57. Three different compounds with the formula $C_2H_2Cl_2$ are known.
   (a) Two of these compounds are geometric isomers. Draw their structures.
   (b) The third compound is a structural isomer of the other two. Draw its structure.

58. ■ Draw the structure of 2-butanol. Identify the chiral carbon atom in this compound. Draw the mirror image of the structure you first drew. Are the two molecules superimposable?

59. Draw Lewis structures, and name three structural isomers with the formula C_6H_{12}. Are any of these isomers chiral?

60. Draw structures, and name the four alkenes that have the formula C_4H_8.

61. Write equations for the reactions of *cis*-2-butene with the following reagents, representing the reactants and products using structural formulas.
   (a) H_2O
   (b) HBr
   (c) Cl_2

62. Draw the structure, and name the product formed if the following alcohols are oxidized. Assume an excess of the oxidizing agent is used. If the alcohol is not expected to react with a chemical oxidizing agent, write NR (no reaction).
   (a) $CH_3CH_2CH_2CH_2OH$
   (b) 2-butanol
   (c) 2-methyl-2-propanol
   (d) 2-methyl-1-propanol

63. Write equations for the following reactions, representing the reactants and products using structural formulas.
   (a) The reaction of acetic acid and sodium hydroxide
   (b) The reaction of methylamine with HCl

64. ■ Write equations for the following reactions, representing the reactants and products using structural formulas.
   (a) The formation of ethyl acetate from acetic acid and ethanol
   (b) The hydrolysis of glyceryl tristearate (the triester of glycerol with stearic acid, a fatty acid)

65. Write an equation for the formation of the following polymers.
   (a) Polystyrene, from styrene ($C_6H_5CH=CH_2$)
   (b) PET (polyethylene terephthalate), from ethylene glycol and terephthalic acid

66. Write equations for the following reactions, representing the reactants and products using structural formulas.
   (a) The hydrolysis of the amide $C_6H_5CONHCH_3$ to form benzoic acid and methylamine
   (b) The hydrolysis $+CO(CH_2)_4CONH(CH_2)_6NH+_n$, (nylon-6, 6, a polyamide) to give a carboxylic acid and an amine

67. ■ Draw the structure of each of the following compounds:
   (a) 2,2-dimethylpentane
   (b) 3,3-diethylpentane
   (c) 3-ethyl-2-methylpentane
   (d) 3-ethylhexane

68. ▲ Structural isomers.
   (a) Draw all of the isomers possible for C_3H_8O. Give the systematic name of each, and tell into which class of compound it fits.
   (b) Draw the structural formulas for an aldehyde and a ketone with the molecular formula C_4H_8O. Give the systematic name of each.

69. ▲ ■ Draw structural formulas for possible isomers of the dichlorinated propane, $C_3H_6Cl_2$. Name each compound.

70. ■ Draw structural formulas for possible isomers with the formula C_3H_6ClBr, and name each isomer.

71. Give structural formulas and systematic names for the three structural isomers of trimethylbenzene, $C_6H_3(CH_3)_3$.

72. Give structural formulas and systematic names for possible isomers of dichlorobenzene, $C_6H_4Cl_2$.

73. Voodoo lilies depend on carrion beetles for pollination. Carrion beetles are attracted to dead animals, and because dead and putrefying animals give off the horrible-smelling amine cadaverine, the lily likewise releases cadaverine (and the closely related compound putrescine) (page 466). A biological catalyst, an enzyme, converts the naturally occurring amino acid lysine to cadaverine.

$$H_2NCH_2CH_2CH_2CH_2 \overset{\overset{\displaystyle H}{|}}{\underset{\underset{\displaystyle O}{\overset{\displaystyle \|}{C-OH}}}{C}} - NH_2$$

lysine

▲ more challenging   ■ in OWL   Blue-numbered questions answered in Appendix O

What group of atoms must be replaced in lysine to make cadaverine? (Lysine is essential to human nutrition but is not synthesized in the human body.)

74. Benzoic acid occurs in many berries. When humans eat berries, benzoic acid is converted to hippuric acid in the body by reaction with the amino acid glycine $H_2NCH_2CO_2H$. Draw the structure of hippuric acid, knowing it is an amide formed by reaction of the carboxylic acid group of benzoic acid and the amino group of glycine. Why is hippuric acid referred to as an acid?

75. ■ Consider the reaction of *cis*-2-butene with H_2 (in the presence of a catalyst).
    (a) Draw the structure, and give the name of the reaction product. Is this reaction product chiral?
    (b) Draw an isomer of the reaction product.

76. ■ Give the name of each compound below, and name the functional group involved.

(a)
$$H_3C-\overset{\overset{\displaystyle OH}{|}}{\underset{\underset{\displaystyle H}{|}}{C}}-CH_2CH_2CH_3$$

(b)
$$H_3C-\overset{\overset{\displaystyle O}{\|}}{C}CH_2CH_2CH_3$$

(c)
$$H_3C-\overset{\overset{\displaystyle H}{|}}{\underset{\underset{\displaystyle CH_3}{|}}{C}}-\overset{\overset{\displaystyle O}{\|}}{C}-H$$

(d)
$$H_3CCH_2CH_2-\overset{\overset{\displaystyle O}{\|}}{C}-OH$$

77. Draw the structure of glyceryl trilaurate. When this triester is saponified, what are the products? (See page 476.)

78. ▲ A well-known company selling outdoor clothing has recently introduced jackets made of recycled polyethylene terephthalate (PET), the principal material in many soft drink bottles. Another company makes PET fibers by treating recycled bottles with methanol to give the diester dimethylterephthalate and ethylene glycol and then repolymerizes these compounds to give new PET. Write a chemical equation to show how the reaction of PET with methanol can give dimethylterephthalate and ethylene glycol.

79. ■ Identify the reaction products, and write an equation for the following reactions of $CH_2=CHCH_2OH$.
    (a) H_2 (hydrogenation, in the presence of a catalyst)
    (b) Oxidation (excess oxidizing agent)
    (c) Addition polymerization
    (d) Ester formation, using acetic acid

80. Write a chemical equation describing the reaction between glycerol and stearic acid to give glyceryl tristearate.

81. ■ The product of an addition reaction of an alkene is often predicted by Markovnikov's rule.
    (a) Draw the structure of the product of adding HBr to propene, and give the name of the product.
    (b) Draw the structure, and give the name of the compound that results from adding H_2O to 2-methyl-1-butene.
    (c) If you add H_2O to 2-methyl-2-butene, is the product the same or different than the product from the reaction in part (b)?

82. An unknown colorless liquid has the formula $C_4H_{10}O$. Draw the structures for the four alcohol compounds that have this formula.

In the Laboratory

83. ■ Which of the following compounds produces acetic acid when treated with an oxidizing agent such as $KMnO_4$?

(a) H_3C-CH_3

(c)
$$H_3C-\overset{\overset{\displaystyle OH}{|}}{\underset{\underset{\displaystyle H}{|}}{C}}-H$$

(b)
$$H_3C-\overset{\overset{\displaystyle O}{\|}}{C}-H$$

(d)
$$H_3C-\overset{\overset{\displaystyle O}{\|}}{C}-CH_3$$

84. ■ Consider the reactions of C_3H_7OH.

$$H_3CCH_2-\overset{\overset{\displaystyle H}{|}}{\underset{\underset{\displaystyle H}{|}}{C}}-O-H \xrightarrow[H_2SO_4]{Rxn\ A} H_3C-\overset{\overset{\displaystyle H}{|}}{C}=\overset{\overset{\displaystyle H}{|}}{\underset{\underset{\displaystyle H}{|}}{C}} + H_2O$$

$$Rxn\ B \downarrow + CH_3CO_2H$$

$$H_3CCH_2-\overset{\overset{\displaystyle H}{|}}{\underset{\underset{\displaystyle H}{|}}{C}}-O-\overset{\overset{\displaystyle O}{\|}}{C}CH_3$$

    (a) Name the reactant C_3H_7OH.
    (b) Draw a structural isomer of the reactant, and give its name.
    (c) Name the product of reaction A.
    (d) Name the product of reaction B.

85. You have a liquid that is either cyclohexene or benzene. When the liquid is exposed to dark-red bromine vapor, the vapor is immediately decolorized. What is the identity of the liquid? Write an equation for the chemical reaction that has occurred.

86. ▲ ■ Hydrolysis of an unknown ester of butanoic acid, $CH_3CH_2CH_2CO_2R$, produces an alcohol A and butanoic acid. Oxidation of this alcohol forms an acid B that is a structural isomer of butanoic acid. Give the names and structures for alcohol A and acid B.

87. ▲ You are asked to identify an unknown colorless, liquid carbonyl compound. Analysis has determined that the formula for this unknown is C_3H_6O. Only two compounds match this formula.
   (a) Draw structures for the two possible compounds.
   (b) To decide which of the two structures is correct, you react the compound with an oxidizing agent and isolate from that reaction a compound that is found to give an acidic solution in water. Use this result to identify the structure of the unknown.
   (c) Name the acid formed by oxidation of the unknown.

88. Describe a simple chemical test to tell the difference between $CH_3CH_2CH_2CH=CH_2$ and its isomer cyclopentane.

89. Describe a simple chemical test to tell the difference between 2-propanol and its isomer methyl ethyl ether.

90. ▲ ■ An unknown ester has the formula $C_4H_8O_2$. Hydrolysis gives methanol as one product. Identify the ester, and write an equation for the hydrolysis reaction.

91. ▲ ■ Addition of water to alkene X gives an alcohol Y. Oxidation of Y produces 3,3-dimethyl-2-pentanone. Identify X and Y, and write equations for the two reactions.

92. ■ 2-Iodobenzoic acid, a tan, crystalline solid, can be prepared from 2-aminobenzoic acid. Other required reagents are $NaNO_2$ and KI (as well as HCl).

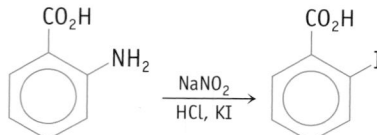

2-aminobenzoic acid   2-iodobenzoic acid

   (a) If you use 4.0 g of 2-aminobenzoic acid, 2.2 g of $NaNO_2$, and 5.3 g of KI, what is the theoretical yield of 2-iodobenzoic acid?
   (b) Are other isomers of 2-iodobenzoic acid possible?
   (c) To verify that you have isolated 2-iodobenzoic acid, you titrate it in water/ethanol. If you use 15.62 mL of 0.101 M NaOH to titrate 0.399 g of the product, what is its molar mass? Is it in reasonable agreement with the theoretical molar mass?

Summary and Conceptual Questions

The following questions may use concepts from this and previous chapters.

93. Carbon atoms appear in organic compounds in several different ways with single, double, and triple bonds combining to give an octet configuration. Describe the various ways that carbon can bond to reach an octet, and give the name, and draw the structure of a compound that illustrates that mode of bonding.

94. There is a high barrier to rotation around a carbon–carbon double bond, whereas the barrier to rotation around a carbon–carbon single bond is considerably smaller. Use the orbital overlap model of bonding (Chapter 9) to explain why there is restricted rotation around a double bond.

95. ■ What important properties do the following characteristics impart on an polymer?
   (a) Cross linking in polyethylene
   (b) The OH groups in polyvinyl alcohol
   (c) Hydrogen bonding in a polyamide like nylon

96. ■ One of the resonance structures for pyridine is illustrated here. Draw another resonance structure for the molecule. Comment on the similarity between this compound and benzene.

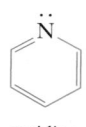

pyridine

97. ■ Write balanced equations for the combustion of ethane gas and liquid ethanol (to give gaseous products).
   (a) Calculate the enthalpy of combustion of each compound. Which has the more negative enthalpy change for combustion per gram?
   (b) If ethanol is assumed to be partially oxidized ethane, what effect does this have on the heat of combustion?

98. Plastics make up about 20% of the volume of landfills. There is, therefore, considerable interest in reusing or recycling these materials. To identify common plastics, a set of universal symbols is now used, five of which are illustrated here. They symbolize low- and high-density polyethylene, polyvinyl chloride, polypropylene, and polyethylene terephthalate.

PETE

HDPE

V

LDPE

PP

▲ more challenging   ■ in OWL   Blue-numbered questions answered in Appendix O

(a) Tell which symbol belongs to which type of plastic.

(b) Find an item in the grocery or drug store made from each of these plastics.

(c) Properties of several plastics are listed in the table. Based on this information, describe how to separate samples of these plastics from one another.

Plastic	Density (g/cm^3)	Melting Point (°C)
Polypropylene	0.92	170
High-density polyethylene	0.97	135
Polyethylene terephthalate	1.34–1.39	245

99. ▲ Maleic acid is prepared by the catalytic oxidation of benzene. It is a dicarboxylic acid; that is, it has two carboxylic acid groups.

(a) Combustion of 0.125 g of the acid gives 0.190 g of CO_2 and 0.0388 g of H_2O. Calculate the empirical formula of the acid.

(b) A 0.261-g sample of the acid requires 34.60 mL of 0.130 M NaOH for complete titration (so that the H ions from both carboxylic acid groups are used). What is the molecular formula of the acid?

(c) Draw a Lewis structure for the acid.

(d) Describe the hybridization used by the C atoms.

(e) What are the bond angles around each C atom?

Chapters 6–10

Everyone enjoys a good fireworks display, and neon signs can be intriguing and even beautiful. Both owe their colorful display to the emission of light by various chemical substances, and these chapters have laid out some of the principles involved in this effect. When you have finished these chapters you will know more about how the colors of a fireworks display and the light emitted by neon signs are produced and what they have in common.

THE PURPOSE OF *LET'S REVIEW*

- *Let's Review* provides additional questions for Chapters 6 through 10. Routine questions covering the concepts in a chapter are in the Study Questions at the end of that chapter and are usually identified by topic. In contrast, *Let's Review* questions combine several concepts from one or more chapters. Many come from the examinations given by the authors and others are based on actual experiments or processes in chemical research or in the chemical industries.

- *Let's Review* provides guidance for Chapters 6 through 10 as you prepare for an exam on these chapters. Although this is designated for Chapters 6 through 10 you may choose only material appropriate to the exam in your course.

- To direct your review, **Comprehensive Questions** are correlated with relevant chapter sections and with the OWL online homework system to which you may have purchased access. Some questions may include a screen shot from one of these tools so you see what resources are available to help you review.

PREPARING FOR AN EXAMINATION ON CHAPTERS 6–10

1. Review **Go Chemistry** modules for these chapters. Go Chemistry modules are available at **www.cengage.com/chemistry/kotz** or **www.ichapters.com**.

Charles D. Winters

Charles D. Winters

2. Take the ChemistryNow **Pre-Test** and work through your **Personalized Learning Plan.** Work through ChemistryNow **Exercises, Guided Simulations,** and **Intelligent Tutors.**

3. **OWL** If you subscribe to OWL, use the **Tutorials** in that system.

4. Work on the questions below that are relevant to a particular chapter or chapters. See the solutions to those questions at the end of this section.

5. For background and help answering a question, use the Go Chemistry and OWL questions correlated with it.

KEY POINTS TO KNOW FOR CHAPTERS 6–10

Here are some of the key points you must know to be successful in Chapters 6–10.

- The properties of electromagnetic radiation.
- The origin of light from excited atoms.
- The quantum numbers and their relation to atomic structure.
- Electron configurations for the elements and common monatomic ions.
- Periodic trends in properties of the elements.
- Concepts of bonding: covalent bonds, octet rule, resonance
- Lewis structures for small molecules and ions.
- VSEPR theory to predict the shapes of simple molecules and ions and to understand the structures of more complex molecules.
- Electronegativity and its relation to bond and molecular polarity.
- Atom hybridization in molecules and ions.
- The principles of molecular orbital theory.
- Classification of organic molecules by functional group.
- Isomerism in organic molecules.
- Structures of common organic compounds
- Reactions of organic functional groups.
- Common polymers.

EXAMINATION PREPARATION QUESTIONS

▲ denotes more challenging questions.

Important information about the questions that follow:

- See the Study Questions in each chapter for questions on basic concepts.
- Some of these questions arise from recent research in chemistry and the other sciences. They often involve concepts from more than one chapter and may be more challenging than those in earlier chapters. Not all chapter goals or concepts are necessarily addressed in these questions.
- **Assessing Key Points** are short-answer questions covering the Key Points to Know on this page.
- **Comprehensive Questions** bring together concepts from multiple chapters and are correlated with text sections covering that topic, with Go Chemistry modules, and with questions in OWL that may provide additional background.
- The screens shots are largely taken from Go Chemistry modules available at **www.cengage.com/chemistry/kotz** or **www.ichapters.com.**

Assessing Key Points

1. Place the following types of radiation in order of increasing energy: (a) x-rays, (b) radio waves, (c) blue light, and (d) light with $\lambda = 520$ nm

2. Radiation called UVB (290–315 nm) is responsible for your sunburn at the beach. Another type of radiation [UVA (315-400 nm)] is also responsible for tissue damage (page 275). Which has the greater energy, UVA or UVB?

3. The quantum number n describes the _____ of an atomic orbital and the quantum number ℓ describes its _____.

4. For a $4d$ orbital, what are the values of n and ℓ? What is one possible value of m_ℓ?

5. What elements have these ground state electron configurations?
   (a) $[Kr]5s^1$ (b) $[Ar]3d^{10}4s^24p^4$

6. Which has the largest first ionization energy: N, P, or As?

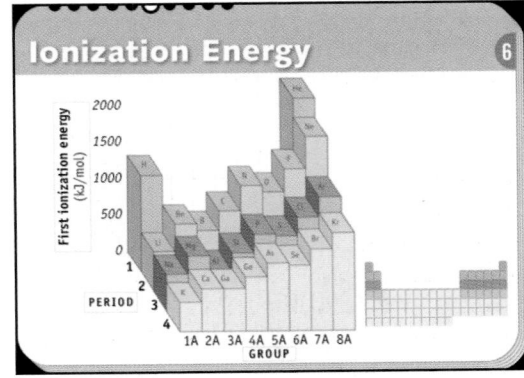

Screen from Go Chemistry module 11 on periodic trends

7. Which of the following is NOT a correct Lewis resonance structure for the N_2O molecule?

   (a) $\ddot{N}=N=\ddot{O}$ (b) $:\ddot{N}-N\equiv O:$

   (c) $:N\equiv N-\ddot{O}:$ (d) $:N\equiv N=\ddot{O}$

8. Consider the N_2O molecule in question 7.
   (a) Is the structure of the molecule bent or linear?
   (b) Is the N—O bond polar? Is the molecule polar?
   (c) What is the hybridization of the central N atom and what is its formal charge?

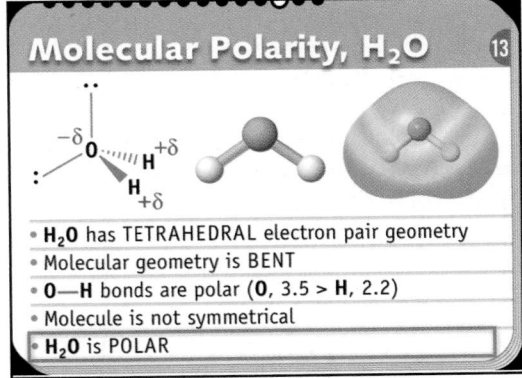

Screen from Go Chemistry module 13 on molecular polarity

9. If, in a molecule, three atomic orbitals combine, how many molecular orbitals will result?

10. To which class of organic molecules does each of these belong?

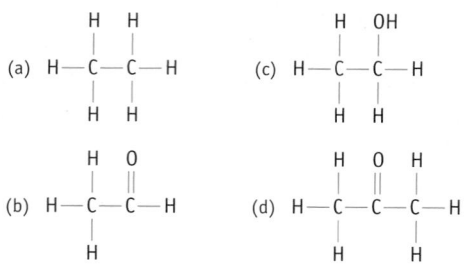

FUNCTIONAL GROUP

A structural fragment found in all members of a class of compounds. Some examples:

- Alcohols
  —OH
- Aldehydes
  —C=O(H)
- Ketones
  —C(=O)—
- Carboxylic Acids
  —C(=O)OH
- Esters
  R—C(=O)—O—(ALCOHOL PORTION)

Screen from Go Chemistry module 15 on organic compounds

11. Name compound (d) in question 10 and draw an isomer of this compound.

12. Name the product of the oxidation with $KMnO_4$ of compound (c) in question 10.

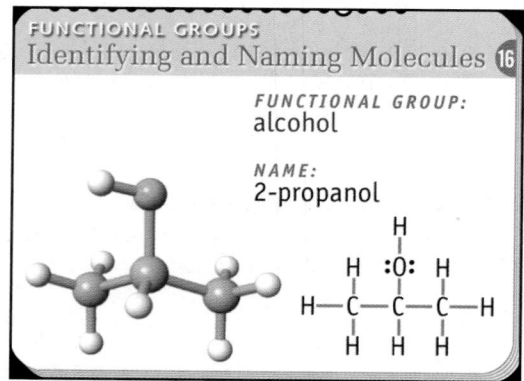

FUNCTIONAL GROUPS
Identifying and Naming Molecules ⑯

FUNCTIONAL GROUP:
alcohol

NAME:
2-propanol

Screen from Go Chemistry module 15 on organic compounds

13. Which compound or compounds could be used to synthesize a polymer?

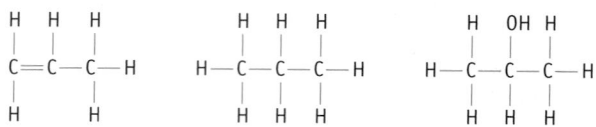

Comprehensive Questions

14. (Chapter 6) Blue light has a wavelength, λ, of 420. nm.
    (a) What is the frequency of the light?
    (b) If the total energy of a signal involving blue light is 2.50×10^{-14} J, how many photons reach your eyes?
    Text Sections: 6.1 and 6.2
    OWL Questions: 6.1e, 6.2d

15. (Chapters 6 and 7) Quantum numbers and electron configurations.
    (a) When $n = 3$, $\ell = 1$, and $m_\ell = -1$, to what orbital does this refer? (Give the orbital label, such as 1s.)
    (b) For the $n = 5$ shell, there are _____ subshells and _____ orbitals. How many electrons can be accommodated in the $n = 5$ shell? _____
    (c) What type of orbital is not possible based on quantum theory: $2p$, $3s$, $5g$, $3f$, $7d$?
    (d) What is the maximum number of orbitals that can be associated with each of the following sets of quantum numbers? (One possible answer is "none.")
      (i) $n = 3$
      (ii) $n = 3$ and $\ell = 3$
      (iii) $n = 2$, $\ell = 1$, and $m_\ell = 0$
    (e) Which ion or ions are unlikely based on your knowledge of electron configurations and ionization energies? Ba^{3+}, Cr^{3+}, Al^{3+}, S^{3-}, Cu^+
    (f) At what element is the $n = 3$ shell just completed?
    Text Sections: 6.5, 6.7, and 7.2–7.4
    OWL Questions: 6.5c, 7.4c

16. (Chapters 5 and 6) To prepare some tea, you want to heat 254 g of water from 12 °C to 90. °C in a microwave oven, which operates at a frequency of 2.45 Gigahertz ($\nu = 2.45 \times 10^9$ sec^{-1}).
    (a) What is the wavelength of microwave radiation?
    (b) Suppose a microwave oven is 48 cm wide. How many wavelengths of the given radiation are equivalent to 48 cm.
    (c) How many moles of these microwave photons must be absorbed to heat your mug of water to 90. °C?
    Text Sections: 5.2, 6.1, and 6.2
    OWL Questions: 5.2e, 6.1e, 6.2d

17. (Chapters 5 and 6) Photosynthesis.
  (a) Calculate the enthalpy change for the production of one mole of glucose by the process of photosynthesis at 25 °C. $\Delta_f H°$ [glucose(s)] = -1273.3 kJ/mol.

  $$6\ CO_2(g) + 6\ H_2O(\ell) \rightarrow C_6H_{12}O_6(s) + 6\ O_2(g)$$

  (b) What is the enthalpy change involved in producing one molecule of glucose by this process?
  (c) Chlorophyll molecules absorb light of various wavelengths. One wavelength absorbed is 650. nm. Calculate the energy of a photon of light having this wavelength.
  (d) How many photons with a wavelength of 650. nm are required to produce one glucose molecule, assuming all of the light energy is converted to chemical energy?
  Text Sections: 5.5, 5.7, 6.1, and 6.2
  OWL Questions: 5.7d, 6.1e, 6.2d

18. (Chapter 6) The energy level diagram in Figure 6.8 (page 277) describes a H atom using the Bohr model.
  (a) What quantum levels are involved in the emission of UV, visible, and infrared light in the hydrogen spectrum?
  (b) What is the energy of the hydrogen atom's electron in its ground state?
  (c) What is the energy of an electron in the $n = 4$ state?
  (d) Calculate the energy of the transition from the $n = 2$ level to the $n = 1$ level.
  (e) Calculate the energy (in kJ/mol) required to ionize 1.0 mole of hydrogen atoms.
  (f) Calculate the wavelength of light required to cause ionization of an H atom. In what region of the electromagnetic spectrum is this radiation found?
  Text Sections: 6.1–6.3
  OWL Questions: 6.1b, 6.1e, 6.2d, 6.3c, 6.3e

19. (Chapter 7) Atom A has the ground state electron configuration [Ne]$3s^2 3p^5$. Atom B has the ground state electron configuration [Ar]$4s^2$. Identify A and B from their electron configurations; then identify the compound formed when these two elements react. Is this compound diamagnetic or paramagnetic? Write an equation for this reaction.
  Text Sections: 6.7, 7.3, and 7.4
  OWL Questions: 7.3g, 7.3h, 7.4c, 7.4e

20. (Chapter 7) Electron configurations and periodic trends.
  (a) What element has the ground state electron configuration [Ar]$3d^6 4s^2$?
  (b) What element has a 2+ ion with the ground state configuration [Ar]$3d^5$? Is the ion paramagnetic or diamagnetic?

  (c) How many unpaired electrons are there in a ground state Ni^{2+} ion?
  (d) The ground state configuration for an element is given here.

  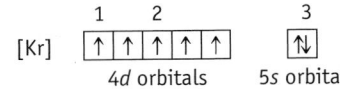

  What is the identity of the element? Is an atom of the element paramagnetic or diamagnetic? How many unpaired electrons does a 3– ion of this element have?
  (e) What element has the following ground state electron configuration?

  [Kr] | ↑ | ↑ | ↑ | ↑ | ↑ | | ↑↓ |
        4d orbitals   5s orbital

  Is the element paramagnetic or diamagnetic? Write a complete set of quantum numbers for electrons labeled 1–3.

Electron	n	ℓ	m_ℓ	m_s
1	____	____	____	____
2	____	____	____	____
3	____	____	____	____

  (f) Answer the questions below about the elements A and B, which have the ground state electron configurations shown.

  $$A = [Kr]5s^2 \qquad B = [Kr]4d^{10}5s^2 5p^5$$

  Is element A a metal, nonmetal, or metalloid?
  Which element has the greater ionization energy?
  Which element has larger atoms?
  Which is more likely to form a cation?
  What is a likely formula for a compound formed between A and B?
  Text Sections: 6.5, 6.7, and 7.3–7.5
  OWL Questions: 6.5c, 7.3g, 7.3h, 7.4c, 7.4e, 7.5b, 7.5e

21. (Chapter 7) Periodic trends.
  Part 1: General Periodic Trends
  (a) Of the elements S, Se, and Cl, which has the largest atomic radius?
  (b) Which has the larger radius, Br or Br^-?
  (c) Which should have the most negative electron affinity: N, O, S, or Cl?
  (d) Which has the largest first ionization energy: B, Al, or C?
  (e) Which of the following has the largest radius: O^{2-}, N^{3-}, or F^-?

Part 2: Consider the elements Al, C, Ca, Mg, K:
Of these elements, _____ has the lowest ionization energy whereas _____ has the most negative electron affinity. The element with the largest radius is _____, and the element with the smallest radius is _____. The element with the largest difference between the first and second ionization energies is _____.

Text Section: 7.5
OWL Questions: 7.5b, 7.5e, 7.5i

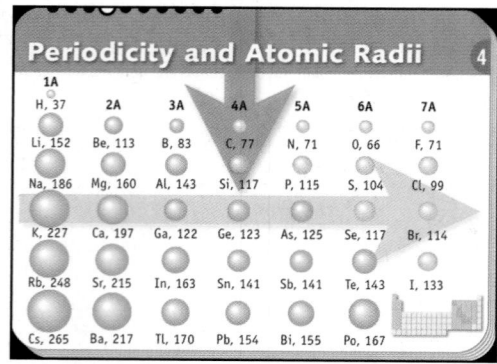

Screen from Go Chemistry module 11 on periodic trends

22. (Chapter 7) Electron configurations.

(a) Using the *spdf* notation [e.g., $1s^2 2s^2$], write ground state electron configurations for each of the following: arsenic, manganese, and plutonium. Use the noble gas notation for all cases.

(b) Using the orbital box notation, write electron configurations for the following atoms or ions: tin(II) ion, cobalt(III) ion, and oxide ion. Use the noble gas notation in all cases.

Text Sections: 7.3 and 7.4
OWL Questions: 7.3g, 7.3h, 7.4c

23. (Chapter 7) Ionization energies.

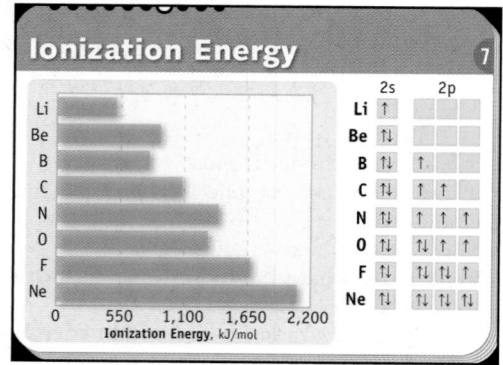

Screen from Go Chemistry module 11 on periodic trends

(a) Generally ionization energies increase on proceeding across a period, but this is not true for magnesium (738 kJ/mol) and aluminum (578 kJ/mol). Explain this observation.

(b) Explain why the ionization energy of phosphorus (1012 kJ/mol) is greater than that of sulfur (1000 kJ/mol) when the general trend in ionization energies in a period would predict the opposite.

Text Section: 7.5
OWL Question: 7.5e

Ionization Energy

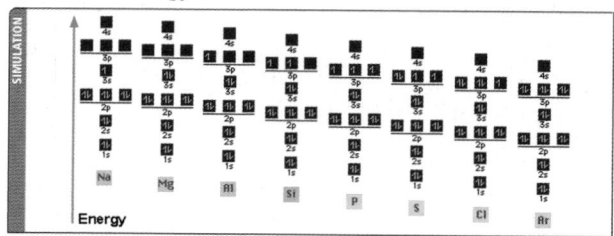

OWL Simulation 7.5d: This simulation illustrates the trend in orbital energies across the third period and allows us to understand trends in ionization energy and electron affinity.

24. (Chapters 8 and 9) Sketch the electron dot structure for each of the following, give the hybridization of the N atom, and arrange them in order of increasing N—O bond length: H_2NOH, NO_3^-, NO_2^-, NO^+.

Text Sections: 8.2, 8.4, 8.9, and 9.2
OWL Questions: 8.4b, 8.5d, 8.9a, 9.2f

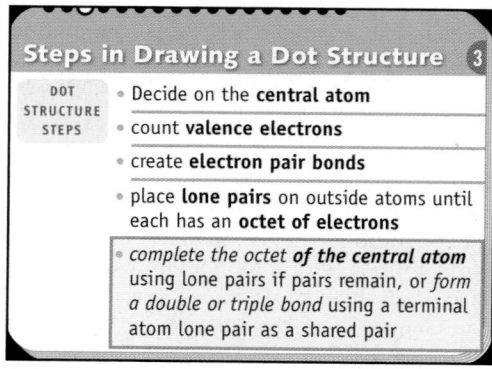

Screen from Go Chemistry module 12 on drawing dot structures

25. (Chapters 5, 8, and 9) Brown NO_2 gas is a product of the reaction of copper with nitric acid. (See Figure 3.19, page 146, and Active Figure 3.19 on ChemistryNow.) Some NO_2 molecules form N_2O_4 where two NO_2 molecules are bonded through an N—N bond.

(a) Draw the Lewis electron dot structure of N_2O_4, specify the formal charges on each atom and the hybridization of the N atoms, indicate the N—O bond order, and give the bond angles.

(b) Is the reaction of NO_2 to form N_2O_4 endothermic or exothermic? (You can answer this by considering bond energies and could confirm it using enthalpies of formation.)

Text Sections: 5.7, 8.2, 8.3, 8.6, 8.9, and 9.2
OWL Questions: 5.7d, 8.3b, 8.5d, 8.6a, 8.6d, 8.6f, 8.9a, 8.9c, 9.2f, 9.2h

26. (Chapters 8 and 9) Sulfur can react with the sulfite ion to give the thiosulfate ion, $S_2O_3^{2-}$.

(a) Draw the Lewis electron dot structure for the sulfite ion, specify the formal charge on each atom and the S atom hybridization, and give the S—O bond order.

(b) Knowing that the thiosulfate ion is analogous with the sulfate ion, where a S atom has replaced an O atom, draw the electron dot structure for thiosulfate ion.

Text Sections: 8.2, 8.3, and 9.2
ChemistryNow Screens: 9.8–9.10, 10.4
OWL Questions: 8.3b, 8.5d, 8.6a, 8.6b, 8.6f, 8.9a, 9.2f, 9.2h

27. (Chapters 8 and 9) Chemistry of chlorine trifluoride.

(a) Sketch the Lewis electron dot structure for ClF_3 and indicate the hybridization of the central Cl atom.

(b) There are several geometries possible for ClF_3. Which is the most reasonable and why?

(c) Liquid ClF_3 is weakly conducting, a behavior attributed to the presence of ClF_2^+ and ClF_4^- ions. Sketch the structures of these two ions and compare their geometries.

Text Sections: 8.2, 8.5, 8.6, and 9.2
OWL Questions: 8.5d, 8.6a, 8.6b, 8.6f, 9.2f, 9.2h

28. (Chapters 8 and 9) Nitrogen chemistry. Draw electron dot structures, and answer the accompanying questions, for nitryl chloride, hydroxylamine, and dinitrogen monoxide.

(a) Nitryl chloride, $ClNO_2$. (N is the central atom.)

(i) What is the electron pair geometry around the central N atom? Describe the molecular geometry of the molecule and specify the O—N—O and Cl—N—O bond angles.

(ii) What is the formal charge and hybridization of the N atom?

(iii) Is the molecule polar?

(b) Hydroxylamine, NH_2OH, is an ammonia derivative. (N is the central atom.)

(i) What is the electron pair geometry around the central N atom? Specify the H—O—N and H—N—H bond angles.

(ii) What is its formal charge and hybridization of the N atom?

(iii) Is the molecule polar?

(c) Dinitrogen monoxide, N_2O, can be obtained from oxidation of ammonia. Draw all the resonance structures for N_2O. Specify the geometry of the molecule, the N—N—O angle, and the formal charge on each atom in each resonance structure.

Text Sections: 8.2–8.8, and 9.2
OWL Questions: 8.3b, 8.4b, 8.6a, 8.6b, 8.6f, 8.8b, 9.2f, 9.2h

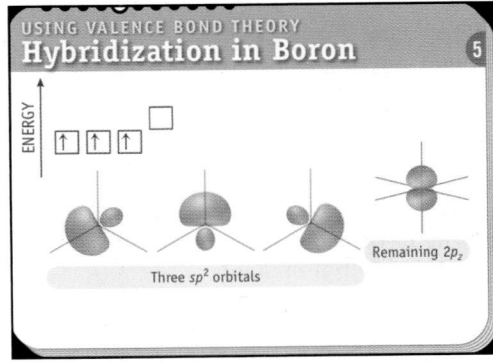

Screen from Go Chemistry module 12 on drawing dot structures

29. (Chapters 8–10) The Lewis structure of asparagine, one of the naturally occurring amino acids, is drawn below. The questions that follow are about this compound. The carbons are labeled with subscripts for the purpose of this question. Questions (a)–(e) refer to the letters accompanying the arrows in the figure.

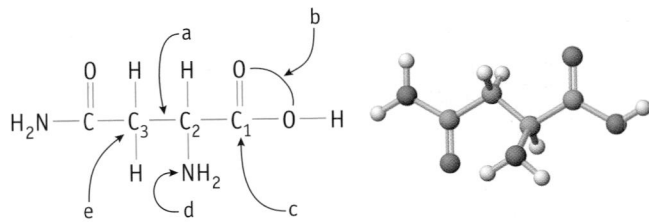

(a) What orbitals overlap to form bond (a)?

(b) What is the O—C—O bond angle labeled (b)?

(c) What hybridization is assigned to C_1?

(d) What is the molecular geometry around this N?

(e) What is this H—C_3—H bond angle?

(f) Identify any chiral carbon atom in this compound.

(g) How many lone pairs are missing in this drawing? Where should they be located?

(h) Name the three functional groups in the molecule.

Text Sections: 8.6, 9.2, 10.3, and 10.4
OWL Questions: 8.5d, 9.2f, 9.2g, 9.2h, 10.1d, 10.4c

30. (Chapters 9 and 10) Organic chemistry and hybridization.
   (a) Naphthalene is an aromatic hydrocarbon. What is the hybridization of the C atoms in naphthalene? How many resonance structures does naphthalene have?

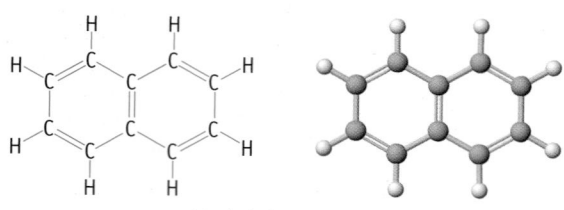

Naphthalene, $C_{10}H_8$

   (b) What is the hybridization of the C atoms in diamond and in graphite? (See Figure 2.7, page 64, for the structures of diamond and graphite.)
   Text Section: 8.4, 9.2, and 10.2
   OWL Questions: 8.4b, 9.2f, 9.2h

31. (Chapter 9) Experimental evidence for the ion Si_2^- was reported in 1996.
   (a) Using molecular orbital theory, predict the electron configuration of the ion.
   (b) What is the predicted bond order?
   (c) Is the ion paramagnetic or diamagnetic?
   (d) What is the highest energy molecular orbital that contains one or more electrons?
   Text Section: 9.3
   OWL Questions: 9.3d, 9.3f

32. (Chapters 8–10) The compound pictured below (anethole) is the substance that gives licorice its odor.

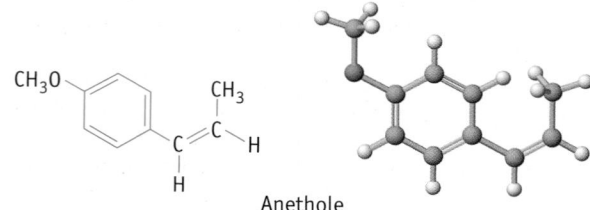

Anethole

   (a) Draw Lewis structures for the following:
      (1) a second resonance structure
      (2) any structural isomer of this compound
      (3) a geometric isomer of this compound
   (b) What orbitals overlap to form a C=C double bond in this compound?
   (c) Describe the π bonding in the C_6H_4 ring using molecular orbital theory.
   Text Sections: 8.2, 8.4, 9.2, and 10.1
   OWL Questions: 8.4b, 8.5d, 9.2o, 10.1c

33. (Chapters 2 and 8) Acetaminophen, which is sold under the tradename Tylenol, among others, has the structure shown here.

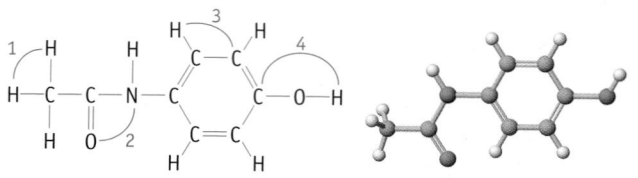

Acetaminophen

   (a) Which is the most polar bond?
   (b) Which is the strongest carbon-oxygen bond?
   (c) Give approximate values for the indicated bond angles in the molecule.
   (d) One Excedrin tablet contains 250 mg of acetaminophen. What amount (moles) of acetaminophen are you consuming in one tablet?
   (e) What is the weight percent of carbon in acetaminophen?
   Text Sections: 2.9, 2.10, 8.7, and 8.9
   OWL Questions: 2.9g, 2.9h, 2.10b, 8.6a, 8.6b, 8.6f, 8.7

34. (Chapters 8 and 9) Hydrazine, N_2H_4, is a useful commercial reducing agent.

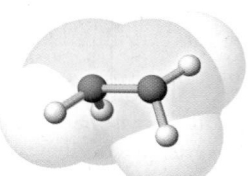

Hydrazine, N_2H_4

   (a) Draw a Lewis electron dot structure for the molecule and specify the bond angles.
   (b) Specify the electron pair geometry around the N atoms and their hybridization.
   (c) Suppose hydrazine, N_2H_4, can be made from ammonia by the reaction

   $$2\ NH_3(g) \rightarrow H_2N{-}NH_2(g) + H_2(g)$$

   Does the geometry around the N atom change in the course of the reaction of ammonia to produce hydrazine?
   (d) Use bond energies to calculate the enthalpy change for this reaction. Is it predicted to be endo- or exothermic?
   Text Sections: 8.2, 8.6, 8.9, and 9.2
   OWL Questions: 8.5d, 8.6a, 8.6b, 8.6f, 8.9c, 9.2f, 9.2h

35. (Chapters 8 and 9) Urea reacts with malonic acid to produce barbituric acid, a member of the class of compounds called phenobarbitals, which are widely prescribed as sedatives.

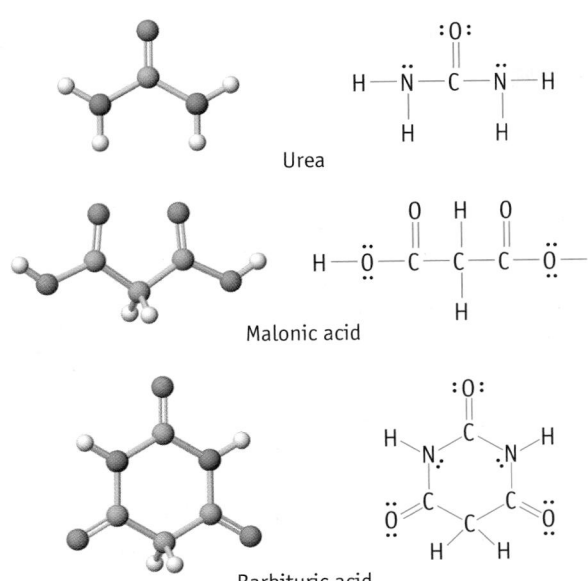

Urea

Malonic acid

Barbituric acid

(a) What bonds are broken and what bonds are made when malonic acid and urea combine to make barbituric acid? Is the reaction predicted to be exo- or endothermic?
(b) Write a balanced equation for the reaction.
(c) Specify the bond angles in malonic acid.
(d) Give the hybridization of the C atoms in barbituric acid.
(e) What is (are) the most polar bond(s) in barbituric acid?
(f) Is barbituric acid polar?

Text Sections: 8.6–8.9 and 9.2
OWL Questions: 8.6a, 8.6b, 8.6f, 8.7, 8.8b, 8.9c, 9.2f, 9.2h

36. (Chapter 10) The alkene *cis*-2-pentene reacts with hydrogen to produce another hydrocarbon.
(a) Draw the structures of the reactants and products.
(b) What type of reaction is illustrated here (addition, elimination, condensation, or esterification)?
(c) Name the product of the reaction.
(d) Sketch a geometric isomer of *cis*-2-pentene.

(e) Draw the structure and give the systematic name of each of the isomers of C_5H_{12}.

Text Section: 10.2
OWL Questions: 10.1c, 10.2a, 10.2c, 10.2e, 10.2g

37. (Chapters 8-10) In order to convert *cis*-2-butene to *trans*-2-butene, it is necessary to heat this compound to around 450 °C. Explain, in a short phrase or sentence, why it is necessary to supply so much energy to cause rotation around a carbon-carbon double bond.

Text Sections: 9.2 and 10.2
OWL Questions: 9.2o, 10.1c

38. (Chapters 8-10) The structure drawn below is for the molecule aspartame, one of several common artificial sweeteners.

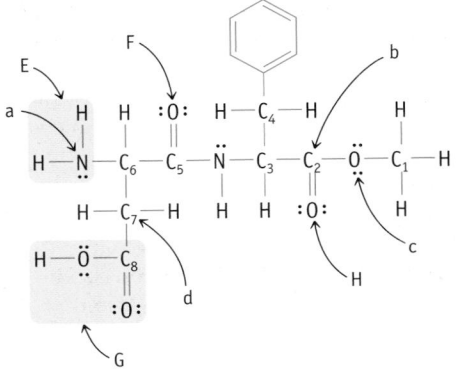

(a) What is the approximate H—N—H bond angle (a)?
(b) What is the geometry of the indicated carbon atom (C_2) (b)?
(c) What is the hybridization of oxygen (c)?
(d) What is the electron pair geometry of carbon (C_7) (d)?
(e) Name the functional group enclosed in box (E).
(f) Name the functional group that contains the carbonyl group (F).
(g) Name the functional group enclosed in box (G).
(h) Name the functional group that contains the carbonyl group (H).
(i) Carbon atoms in this drawing (except those in the C_6H_5— group) are numbered 1–8. Which of these carbons is/are a chiral center?

(j) Hydrolysis of aspartame (reaction with water) will cleave this large molecule into three different compounds. Draw the structures of the products formed by this hydrolysis.
Text Sections: 8.6, 9.2, 10.1, 10.3, and 10.4
OWL Questions: 8.6a, 8.6b, 8.6f, 9.2f, 9.2h, 10.1d, 10.3h, 10.4c

39. (Chapter 10) You have two unlabeled flasks containing colorless liquids. One liquid is *cis*-2-pentene, the other cyclopentane, but you don't know which is which. To determine their identities you add bromine to each flask.
(a) What are the empirical and molecular formulas of *cis*-2-pentene and cyclopentane?
(b) Draw the structure of each compound.
(c) Describe what you observe when you add bromine to these compounds and indicate how the observation will allow you to tell the identity of the liquids in the flasks.
(d) Draw the structure of the product of the reaction with bromine, if any, for the two molecules.
Text Section: 10.2
OWL Questions: 10.2a, 10.2c, 10.2e, 10.2g

40. (Chapter 10) You have two beakers, one containing propanal and the other propanone (acetone). To tell which is which, you add a reagent, aqueous acidic $Na_2Cr_2O_7$.
(a) Draw the structures of propanal and propanone.
(b) Describe what you observe when you treat these compounds with aqueous acidic sodium dichromate and indicate how the observation will allow you to tell the identity of the liquids in the beakers.
(c) Draw the structure of the organic product of each reaction, if any, in each case.
Text Section: 10.4
OWL Questions: 10.4g, 10.4h

41. (Chapter 10) Consider the molecule illustrated below.

```
      H  H  O        CH₃
      |  |  ||        |
  H—C—C—C—O—C—H
      |  |            |
      H  H           CH₃
```

(a) To what class of organic compounds does this belong?
(b) Name the compound.
(c) Draw structures for and name the products that result when the compound reacts with aqueous sodium hydroxide followed by hydrochloric acid.
Text Section: 10.4
OWL Questions: 10.4k, 10.4m

42. (Chapter 10) Organic reactions.

```
      H  H  H
      |  |  |                Reaction B
  H—C—C—C—O—H           +KMnO₄        Compound 3
      |  |  |
      H  H  H
   Compound 1
            ↑ Reaction A
              +H₂O
      H  H  H
      |  |  |                Reaction C
  H—C—C=C                   +HBr         Compound 4
      |     |
      H     H
   Compound 2
```

(a) Name compounds 1 and 2.
(b) Draw structures for the reaction products, compounds 3 and 4, and name each one.
Text Sections: 10.2, 10.3, and 10.4
OWL Questions: 10.2g, 10.3c, 10.4f, 10.4g

43. (Chapter 10) Compound I, aspirin, can be converted to compound III (oil of wintergreen) in two steps. Identify reactants A and B and draw the structure of compound II.

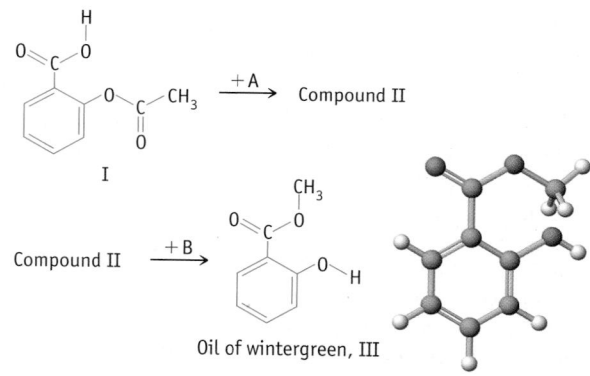

Oil of wintergreen, III

Text Section: 10.4
OWL Question: 10.4k

44. (Chapter 10) Give the structural formula for the product formed by polymerization of $H_2NCH_2CH_2CH_2CH_2CH_2CO_2H$. Is the product an addition polymer or a condensation polymer? Is it a polyester or a polyamide?
Text Section: 10.5
OWL Questions: 10.5c, 10.5d

45. (Chapter 10) The reaction of 1-octene, $C_6H_{13}CH$=CH_2, and water could, potentially, form two different isomeric products.
  (a) Draw their structures and name the two possible isomeric products.
  (b) In fact, only one product is formed in the water reaction. To identify the product, you first add a solution of $Na_2Cr_2O_7$ to this product and observe that a reaction occurs. Next you add aqueous NaOH to the product obtained from the dichromate reaction. There is no evidence of a reaction with NaOH (no heat was evolved and the organic product didn't dissolve in the aqueous solution). Based on these observations, which isomer was formed?
  Text Sections: 10.2 and 10.4
  OWL Questions: 10.3c, 10.4f, 10.4h

46. (Chapter 10) Draw structures and name the following:
  (a) A chiral compound with the formula C_7H_{16}, in which the longest carbon chain contains 5 carbon atoms.
  (b) An ester that is a structural isomer of butanoic acid.
  (c) An aldehyde and a ketone with the formula C_4H_8O.
  (d) An alkene, C_7H_{14}, in which the longest carbon chain is 5 carbons, and there is an ethyl group as a substituent.
  Text Sections: 10.2 and 10.4
  OWL Questions: 10.1d, 10.4c

47. (Chapter 10) In the lab, you have inadvertently spilled some 1.0 M NaOH(aq) on the sleeve of your polyester shirt. About a half an hour later, you notice a hole where the spill was. Explain why the NaOH caused this to happen.
  Text Sections: 10.4 and 10.5
  OWL Questions: 10.4k, 10.5c, 10.5d

48. (Chapter 10) Analysis of an unknown ester has determined that its formula is $C_4H_8O_2$. Hydrolysis of the ester, under acidic conditions, yields methanol. Draw the structure and give the name of the second product of hydrolysis and write a chemical equation for the hydrolysis reaction.
  Text Section: 10.4
  OWL Question: 10.k

49. (Chapter 10) When an acid reacts with an amine, an amide linkage is formed. (See equation on page 475.) Amino acids are characterized by having both a carboxylic acid and an amine functional group, so if an amino acid reacts with another amino acid of the same or different kind, an amide link is formed (and the product is called a peptide). (If many amino acids react, a polymer called a protein is formed.)

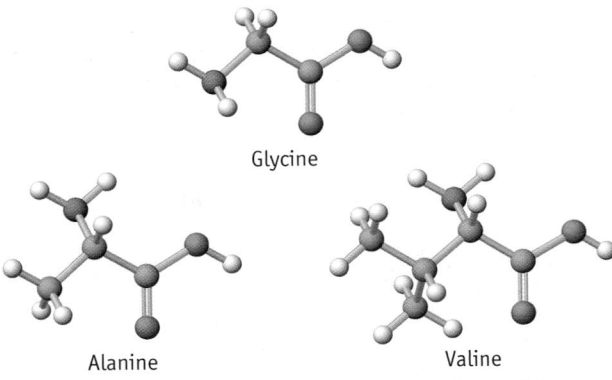

Glycine

Alanine   Valine

  (a) Draw structures for the dipeptides formed by reacting glycine and alanine.
  (b) How many tripeptides are possible when glycine, alanine, and valine react?
  Text Sections: 10.4 and 10.5
  OWL Questions: 10.4n, 10.5c, 10.5d

50. (Chapters 6 and 8) Fireworks and neon signs.
  (a) As described on page 281 fireworks commonly use salts of sodium, strontium, barium, and copper, among other metals. Neon signs are filled with gases such as neon or a mixture of argon with minute particles of mercury. Based on the discussion of atomic spectra in Chapter 6, what do fireworks and neon signs have in common? How do they generate light?
  (b) Chlorate and perchlorate salts are common ingredients in fireworks. After drawing the Lewis structures for these ions, describe their geometry.
  (c) What are the formal charges on the atoms in the perchlorate ion?
  Text Sections: 6.3, 8.2, 8.3, and 8.6
  OWL Questions: 6.3c, 8.3b, 8.5d, 8.6a, 8.6b, 8.6f

51. (Chapters 2, 4, 5, 8, and 9) In 2007 and 2008 there were several international incidents when it was found that food imports from China contained high levels of melamine ($C_3H_6N_6$, 1,3,5-triazine-2,4,6-triamine). It was evidently added to foodstuffs to raise the apparent level of nitrogen, which normally comes from protein.

Melamine

(a) What is the empirical formula of melamine?
(b) What is the mass percent of nitrogen in melamine?
(c) The compound is synthesized starting with urea, which decomposes to cyanic acid and ammonia.

$$(NH_2)_2CO(s) \rightarrow HNCO(g) + NH_3(g)$$

The cyanic acid then forms melamine and carbon dioxide.

$$6\ HNCO(g) \rightarrow C_3H_6N_6 + 3\ CO_2$$

If you begin with 1.000 kg of urea, what is the theoretical yield of melamine?
(d) Is the first step in the synthesis of melamine exo- or endothermic?

Compound	$\Delta_f H°$ (kJ/mol)
$(NH_2)_2CO(s)$	-333.1
$HNCO(g)$	-101.67
$NH_3(g)$	-45.90

(e) Describe the hybridization of the C and N atoms of the melamine ring.
(f) What are the N—C—N and C—N—C bond angles in the melamine ring?
(g) Is melamine a polar molecule?

Text Sections: 2.10, 4.1, 5.7, 8.6, 8.8, 8.9, and 9.2
OWL Questions: 2.10b, 4.1c, 5.7d, 8.8b, 9.2f, 9.2h

Answers to Assessing Key Points Questions

1. See Figure 6.2: radio < 520 nm < blue light < x-rays

2. Energy UVB > energy UVA

3. n describes orbital size and energy and ℓ describes orbital shape. See pages 285–290.

4. For $n = 4$ and $\ell = 2$, m_ℓ could range from -2 to $+2$ including 0.

5. (a) Rb and (b) Se. See Table 7.3, page 310.

6. Nitrogen. See Active Figure 7.10, page 323.

7. (d) Too many electron pairs around the central N atom. The other structures are resonance structures of N_2O.

8. (a) Linear. (b) The N—O bond is polar, and the molecule is polar. (c) The central N atom is sp hybridized and has a +1 formal charge.

9. Three MOs. The number of MOs formed is always equal to the number of combining atomic orbitals. See pages 422–423.

10. (a) alkane (b) aldehyde (c) alcohol (d) ketone

11. (d) is 2-propanone, commonly called acetone. An isomer would be propanal, an aldehyde.

$$\begin{array}{ccccc} & H & H & O & \\ & | & | & || & \\ H- & C- & C- & CH & \\ & | & | & & \\ & H & H & & \end{array}$$

12. Oxidizing (c) (ethanol) first produces (b) in Question 10 (the aldehyde ethanal). Further oxidation gives acetic acid, CH_3CO_2H.

13. Only (a), an alkene, can be used to make a polymer, in this case polypropylene. See Table 10.12, page 481.

Solutions to Comprehensive Questions

14. (a) Convert the wavelength in nm to meters (1 nm = 1×10^{-9} m); then use the relation $\lambda \cdot \nu =$ velocity of light.

$$\text{Frequency} = \frac{\text{Velocity of light}}{\text{Wavelength}} = \frac{2.9979 \times 10^8 \text{ m·s}^{-1}}{4.20 \times 10^{-7} \text{ m}}$$
$$= 7.14 \times 10^{14} \text{ s}^{-1}$$

(b) Use Planck's equation to calculate the energy per photon, then find the number of photons.

E per photon = $h\nu = (6.626 \times 10^{-34} \text{ J·s})(7.14 \times 10^{14} \text{ s}^{-1})$
$E = 4.73 \times 10^{-19}$ J/photon
Number of photons
   $= (2.50 \times 10^{-14} \text{ J})(1 \text{ photon}/4.73 \times 10^{-19} \text{ J})$
   $= 5.29 \times 10^4$ photons

15. (a) One of the $3p$ orbitals
(b) There are 5 subshells and $n^2 = 25$ orbitals (one s, three p, five d, seven f, nine g). Number of electrons = $2 \times 25 = 50$.
(c) $3f$ orbitals are not possible: ℓ would be 3, and n and ℓ cannot be the same.
(d) (i) When $n = 3$ there can be 9 orbitals (one s, three p, five d). (ii) There are no orbitals for $n = 3$ and $\ell = 3$ (as explained in c above). (iii) This refers to one of the $2p$ orbitals.
(e) Barium has the configuration $[Xe]6s^2$, so only two electrons can be removed easily. A 3+ ion is not feasible. The S^{3-} ion is not likely because the S atom would need to acquire three electrons, whereas only two additional electrons can be accommodated in its $3s$ and $3p$ valence orbitals. (S has the ground state configuration $[Ne]3s^23p^4$.)
(f) The $n = 3$ shell is completed with copper.

16. (a) Use the relation $c = \lambda \cdot \nu$ to calculate wavelength from frequency.

$$\lambda = c/\nu = (2.998 \times 10^8 \text{ m·s}^{-1})/(2.45 \times 10^9 \text{ s}^{-1}) = 0.122 \text{ m}$$

(b) Number of wavelengths $= 0.48 \text{ m}/0.122 \text{ m} = 3.9$

(c) We first need to know the energy per mole of photons and the heat needed to warm the water.

E per photon $= h\nu = (6.626 \times 10^{-34} \text{ J·s})(2.45 \times 10^9 \text{ s}^{-1})$
$\qquad = 1.62 \times 10^{-24} \text{ J per photon}$

E per mol of photons $=$
$\qquad = (1.62 \times 10^{-24} \text{ J/photon})(6.022 \times 10^{23} \text{ photons/mol})$
$\qquad = 0.978 \text{ J/mol of photons}$

Energy required $= q = (254 \text{ g})(4.184 \text{ J/g·K})(363 \text{ K} - 285 \text{ K})$
$\qquad = 8.3 \times 10^4 \text{ J}$

Now we can calculate the amount (mol) of photons required.

Amount of photons $= (8.3 \times 10^4 \text{ J})(1 \text{ mol photons}/0.978 \text{ J})$
$\qquad = 8.5 \times 10^4 \text{ mol photons}$

17. (a) Use Hess's law, Equation 5.6 (page 237).

$$\Delta_r H^\circ = \Delta_f H^\circ [\text{glucose}] + 6\, \Delta_f H^\circ [\text{O}_2]$$
$$- \{6\, \Delta_f H^\circ [\text{CO}_2(\text{g})] + 6\, \Delta_f H^\circ [\text{H}_2\text{O}(\ell)]\}$$

Recognizing $\Delta_f H^\circ [\text{O}_2] = 0$,

$\Delta_r H^\circ = (1 \text{ mol glucose}/1 \text{ mol-rxn})(-1273.3 \text{ kJ/mol})$
$\qquad - [(6 \text{ mol CO}_2/1 \text{ mol-rxn})(-393.5 \text{ kJ/mol})$
$\qquad + (6 \text{ mol H}_2\text{O}/1 \text{ mol-rxn})(-285.83 \text{ kJ/mol})]$
$\qquad = +2802.7 \text{ kJ/mol-rxn}$

Thus, $\Delta_r H^\circ = +2802.7$ kJ per mol of glucose because 1 mol of glucose is consumed per mol of reaction.

(b) Energy per molecule $=$
$\qquad = (2802.7 \text{ kJ/mol})(1 \text{ mol}/6.022 \times 10^{23} \text{ molecules})$
$\qquad = 4.654 \times 10^{-21} \text{ kJ/molecule or } 4.654$
$\qquad\qquad\qquad\qquad\qquad\qquad \times 10^{-18} \text{ J/molecule}$

(c) Using the approach in questions 14 and 16, we find light with a wavelength of 650. nm has an energy of 3.06×10^{-19} J/photon.

(d) More than 15 photons with $\lambda = 650.$ nm are required to make one molecule of glucose.

$(4.654 \times 10^{-18} \text{ J/molecule})(1 \text{ photon}/3.06 \times 10^{-19} \text{ J})$
$= 15.2$ photons

18. (a) Emitting light in the UV region would require a transition from a higher level to $n = 1$. Visible light is emitted by transitions to $n = 2$ from higher energy levels. Infrared radiation arises from transitions to $n = 3$ from levels of higher energy. See Figure 6.10.

(b) -2.18×10^{-18} J/atom (Figures 6.8 and 6.10)

(c) E (for $n = 4$) $= -Rhc/n^2$
$\qquad\qquad\qquad = -(2.18 \times 10^{-18} \text{ J/atom})/4^2$
$\qquad E = -1.362 \times 10^{-19}$ J/atom

(d) $\Delta E = E_2 - E_1 = (-5.45 \times 10^{-19} \text{ J})$
$\qquad\qquad\qquad\qquad\qquad - (-2.18 \times 10^{-18} \text{ J})$
$\qquad = -1.64 \times 10^{-18}$ J
or $\Delta E = -(3/4) Rhc$

(e) The energy to ionize the H atom is $+2.18 \times 10^{-18}$ J/atom. Therefore, multiply by Avogadro's number to find the energy per mole ($= 1312$ kJ/mol).

(f) To ionize an H atom requires 2.18×10^{-18} J/atom. Use Planck's equation to calculate the frequency of radiation equivalent to this energy.

$2.18 \times 10^{-18} \text{ J} = (6.626 \times 10^{-34} \text{ J·s})(\nu)$
$\nu = 3.29 \times 10^{15} \text{ s}^{-1}$
$\lambda = c/\nu = (2.998 \times 10^8 \text{ m·s}^{-1})/(3.29 \times 10^{15} \text{ s}^{-1})$
$\qquad = 9.11 \times 10^{-8}$ m (or 91.1 nm)

Radiation of this wavelength is found in the high energy UV region. See Active Figure 6.2.

19. Atom A is Cl and atom B is Ca. The two elements react to give CaCl_2, with Ca^{2+} and Cl^- ions. Neither of these ions has an unpaired electron and so both are diamagnetic.

$$\text{Ca(s)} + \text{Cl}_2(\text{g}) \rightarrow \text{CaCl}_2(\text{s})$$

20. (a) Iron, Fe

(b) Manganese. The Mn^{2+} ion has 5 unpaired electrons and so is paramagnetic.

(c) Ni^{2+} has the electron configuration $[\text{Ar}]3d^8$ and has two unpaired electrons.

(d) The element is arsenic, As. It is paramagnetic but the $3-$ ion has no unpaired electrons $\{[\text{Ar}]3d^{10}4s^24p^6\}$.

(e) Tc, technetium. The element is paramagnetic.

Electron	n	ℓ	m_ℓ	m_s
1	4	2	-2	+1/2
2	4	2	0	+1/2
3	5	0	0	-1/2

Comment: The m_ℓ values for electrons 1 and 2 can have any value from -2 to $+2$ including 0. However, they cannot both have the same value. The m_ℓ value for electron 3, however, is fixed by the fact that $\ell = 0$. Also, m_s can be either $\pm 1/2$ for electrons 1 and 2, but they must have the same value. Finally, whatever the value of m_s for electrons 1 and 2, that for electron 3 must be the opposite because its spin is in the opposite direction.

(f) A is Sr, a metal, and B is I, a nonmetal. Iodine (B) has a higher ionization energy, and its atoms are smaller than those of Sr. (See App. F, page A-21, Table 7.5, and Figure 7.8.) Strontium, Sr, is a metal and so is likely to form cations (here Sr^{2+}). Iodine forms I^- ions, so A and B react to form SrI_2.

21. Part 1
(a) Se (Figure 7.8, page 320)
(b) Anions are always larger than the atoms from which are formed. See Figure 7.12, page 326.
(c) Cl (App. F, page A-21)
(d) C (Figure 7.10, page 323)
(e) These ions are isoelectronic; that is, they have the same number of electrons (here 10 electrons). For such a series, the ion with the largest negative charge and smallest nuclear charge will be the largest ion, here N^{3-}.

Part 2: K has the lowest ionization energy and C the most negative electron affinity. K has the largest radius and C has the smallest radius. K has the largest difference in 1st and 2nd ionization energy (because the 2nd electron comes from an inner shell). See Table 7.5.

22. (a) See Table 7.3 on page 310.

Arsenic: $[Ar]3d^{10}4s^24p^3$
Manganese: $[Ar]3d^54s^2$
Plutonium: $[Rn]4f^67s^2$

(b) Tin(II), Sn^{2+}

[Kr] ⇅ ⇅ ⇅ ⇅ ⇅   ⇅   ☐ ☐ ☐
       4d orbitals   5s orbital 5p orbitals

Cobalt(III), Co^{3+}

[Ar] ⇅ ↑ ↑ ↑ ↑   ☐
       3d orbitals   4s orbital

Oxide ion, O^{2-}. Its ground state electron configuration is isoelectronic with neon.

[He] ⇅   ⇅ ⇅ ⇅
      2s orbital 2p orbitals

23. (a) For Mg one electron is removed from a 3s orbital,

Mg, $1s^22s^22p^63s^2 \rightarrow$ Mg^+, $1s^22s^22p^63s^1$

whereas an Al atom loses an electron from a 3p orbital of slightly *higher* energy.

Al, $1s^22s^22p^63s^23p^1 \rightarrow$ Al^+, $1s^22s^22p^63s^2$

Comment: The orbital energies are graphically illustrated on the OWL Simulation 7.5d. This provides a clear explanation of the effect of orbital energies on ionization energies.

(b) This illustrates the effect on ionization energy of electron-electron repulsion in an electron pair. For S we have

[Ne]   ⇅   ⇅ ↑ ↑
     3s orbital   3p orbitals

The electron lost is one of the pair in the 3p orbitals. Removal of an electron is "assisted" by the loss of electron-electron repulsion when the electron is removed. Such pairing is not present in P.

24. Nitrogen-oxygen bond lengths in increasing order.

Increasing N—O bond length = decreasing bond order

Molecule	N Atom Hybridization
NO^+	sp
NO_2^-	sp^2
NO_3^-	sp^2
H_2NOH	sp^3

25. (a) Dot structure of N_2O_4

formal charge = 0
formal charge = +1
formal charge = −1

The N hybridization is sp^2 and the N—O bond order is 1.5.

(b) $\Delta_r H° = \Delta_f H°[N_2O_4(g)] - 2\,\Delta_f H°[NO_2(g)]$
$= (1\ mol/1\ mol\text{-}rxn)(9.08\ kJ/mol)$
$\qquad - (2\ mol/1\ mol\text{-}rxn)(33.1\ kJ/mol)$
$= -57.1\ kJ/mol$

The reaction involves only the formation of an N—N single bond, and, like the formation of any chemical bond, it is an exothermic process. N—N single bonds are often notably weak, and this is reflected in this value calculated from enthalpies of formation.

26. (a) Sulfite ion, SO_3^{2-}

The formal charge on each O atom is −1, whereas it is +1 on the central S. The SO bond order is 1, and S atom hybridization is sp^3.

(b) Thiosulfate ion, $S_2O_3{}^{2-}$

$$\left[\begin{array}{c} \ddot{\text{:O:}} \\ | \\ \text{:}\ddot{\text{O}}\text{—S—}\ddot{\text{O}}\text{:} \\ | \\ \text{:}\ddot{\text{S}}\text{:} \end{array}\right]^{2-}$$

27. (a) and (b) ClF_3 has trigonal pyramidal electron pair geometry with an sp^3d hybrid Cl atom. The most reasonable structure is T-shaped, adopted to minimize interactions between electron pairs. In the T-shape there are 4 lone pair-atom interactions at 90°. In an alternate structure, trigonal planar, there would be 6 such interactions. See Figure 8.8 and discussion, page 372.

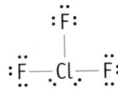   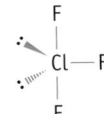

| Dot structure | Most likely structure | Possible alternate structure |

(c) The $ClF_2{}^+$ ion has a tetrahedral electron pair geometry and a bent molecular geometry. The $ClF_4{}^-$ ion has an octahedral electron pair geometry and a square planar molecular geometry.

$$\left[\text{:Cl}\overset{\text{F}}{\underset{\text{F}}{\text{}}}\right]^+ \quad \left[\text{F}\overset{\text{F}}{\underset{\text{F}}{\text{Cl}}}\text{F}\right]^-$$

28. (a) Nitryl chloride has 24 valence electrons.

$$\ddot{\text{O}}\text{=N—}\ddot{\text{Cl}}\text{:}$$
(with $\text{:}\ddot{\text{O}}\text{:}$ above N)

(i) The electron-pair geometry around N is trigonal planar with O—N—O and Cl—N—O bond angles of 120°.
(ii) The sp^2 hybridized N atom has a formal charge of +1. (The single-bonded O atom has a formal charge of −1 and the double bonded O has a formal charge of 0.)
(iii) The molecule is polar.

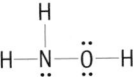

(b) The NH_2OH molecule has 14 valence electrons.

$$\text{H—}\overset{\overset{\text{H}}{|}}{\text{N}}\text{—}\ddot{\text{O}}\text{—H}$$

(i) The electron-pair geometry around the N atom is tetrahedral, and the H—O—N and H—N—H angles are predicted to be about 109°.
(ii) The sp^3 hybridized N atom has a formal charge of 0.
(iii) The molecule is polar.

(c) N_2O has 16 valence electrons.

$$\text{:N}\equiv\text{N—}\ddot{\text{O}}\text{:} \longleftrightarrow \ddot{\text{N}}\text{=N=}\ddot{\text{O}} \longleftrightarrow \text{:}\ddot{\text{N}}\text{—N}\equiv\text{O:}$$
$$\ \ 0\ \ +1\ -1\qquad\quad -1\ +1\ \ 0\qquad\quad -2\ +1\ +1$$

The molecule is linear (N—N—O bond angle 180°) with an sp hybridized N atom. Formal charges suggest that the resonance structure on the left above is predominant.

29. (a) sp^3 orbitals on each C atom overlap to form the C—C bond.
(b) 120°
(c) C_1 carbon is sp^2 hybridized.
(d) Trigonal pyramidal. The N atom is surrounded by two H atoms, a bond to C_2, and a lone pair.
(e) 109°, a tetrahedral angle
(f) C_2 is a chiral carbon. It is surrounded by four *different* groups.
(g) There are 8 lone pairs missing. Each O atom needs two lone pairs and each N atom needs one.
(h) At the left end of the molecule is an amide group (—CONH$_2$), at the right end there is a carboxylic acid group (—CO$_2$H), and the NH$_2$ on C_2 is an amine group.

30. (a) Naphthalene has sp^2 hybridized C atoms and three resonance structures.
(b) The C atoms of graphite are sp^2 hybridized (to account for the trigonal planar C atoms) and the tetrahedral C atoms of diamond are sp^3 hybridized.

31. (a) There are 9 valence electrons (4 for each Si plus 1 for the charge). Assuming that the MOs formed by the valence orbitals (3s and 3p) are identical to those formed by 2s and 2p in Figure 9.21, the configuration would be [core] $(\sigma_{3s})^2(\sigma^*_{3s})^2(\pi_{3p})^4(\sigma_{3p})^1$.

(b) The bond order is 1.5.
(c) Paramagnetic
(d) σ_{3p}

32. (a) Anethole alternate resonance structure and isomers

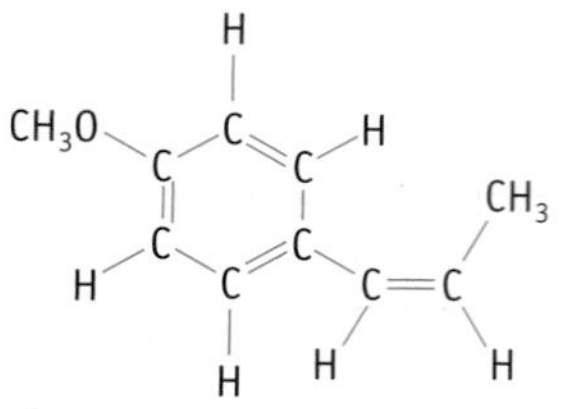

Resonance structure

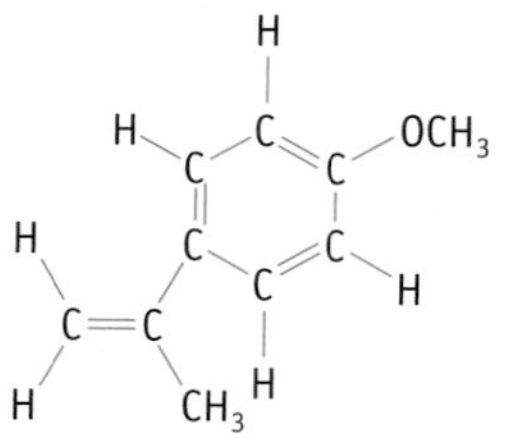

Structural isomer

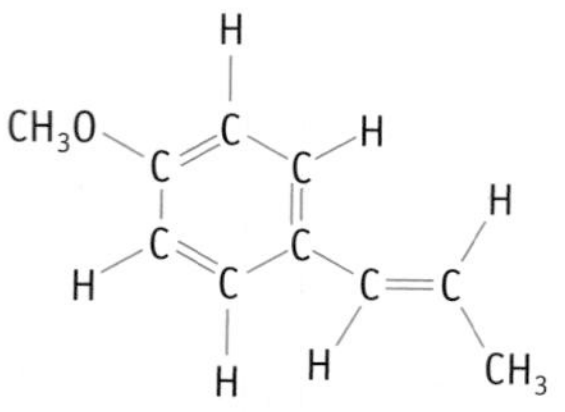

Geometric isomer

(b) See Figure 9.10. C=C bonds consist of one σ bond formed by direct overlap of hybridized sp^2 orbitals and one π bond formed by sideways overlap of un-hybridized p orbitals.

(c) Six p orbitals, one from each of six C atoms, contribute to form 6 molecular orbitals (3 bonding and 3 antibonding). Six electrons, one from each of the C atoms, fill the bonding MOs to give three filled π MOs. See Figure 9.24.

33. (a) Most polar bond, O—H
(b) C=O bond is the strongest bond.
(c) 1 = 109.5°; 2 = 120°; 3 = 120°; 4 = 109.5°
(d) Molar mass of $C_8H_9NO_2$ is 151.165 g/mol. 250 mg is equivalent to 0.0017 mol.
(e) Weight percent C = 63.57%

34. (a) and (b) Electron dot structure of hydrazine

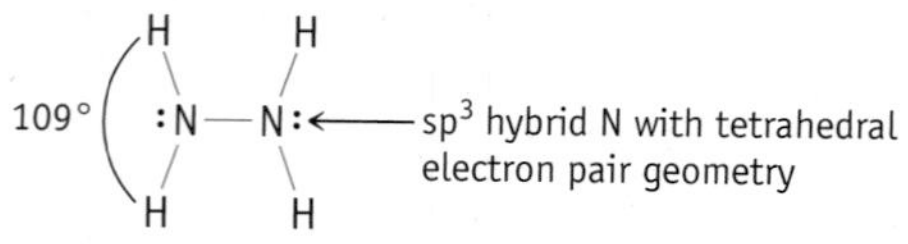

(c) N atom geometry does not change. It has a tetrahedral electron pair geometry (and trigonal pyramidal molecular geometry) in ammonia and hydrazine.

(d) Bonds broken on reaction = 2 NH

ΔH = 2 mol (391 kJ/mol) = 782 kJ
Bonds made = 1 NN + 1 HH
ΔH = 1 mol (163 kJ/mol) + 1 mol (436 kJ/mol)
        = 599 kJ
ΔH = +782 kJ − 599 kJ = +183 kJ

The reaction is endothermic.

35. (a) Two N—H bonds in urea and two C—O bonds and 2 O—H bonds in malonic acid are broken. Two N—C bonds are made in barbituric acid. Two molecules of water form, involving the formation of four O—H bonds.

ΔH for bond breaking
    = 2 NH bonds + 2 CO bonds + 2 OH bonds
    = 2 mol (391 kJ/mol) + 2 mol (358 kJ/mol)
            + 2 mol (463 kJ/mol)
    = 2424 kJ
ΔH for bond making
    = 2 NC bonds + 4 OH bonds
    = 2 mol (305 kJ/mol) + 4 mol (463 kJ/mol)
    = 2462 kJ
ΔH_{net} = +2424 kJ − 2462 kJ = −38 kJ

The reaction is predicted to be exothermic.
(b) $(NH_2)_2CO + CH_2(CO_2H)_2 \rightarrow C_4H_4N_2O_3 + 2\ H_2O$
(c) The H—O—C and H—C—H angles are 109°. The O—C—O and C—C—O angles are 120°.
(d) The CH_2 carbon atom is sp^3 hybridized, and the C atoms bonded to O are sp^2 hybridized.
(e) The CO bonds are the most polar (with a difference in electronegativity of C and O being 1.0).
(f) The molecule is polar.

36. (a) Hydrogenation reaction

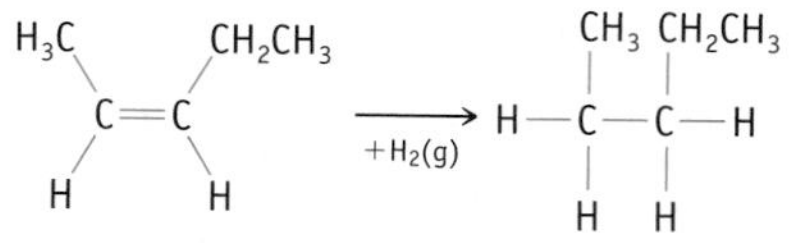

(b) Addition reaction (of H_2)
(c) Pentane
(d) See Example 10.3 on page 454.

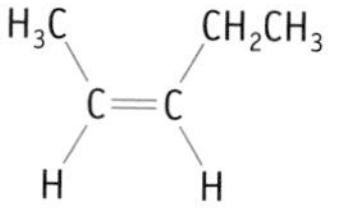

cis-2-pentene 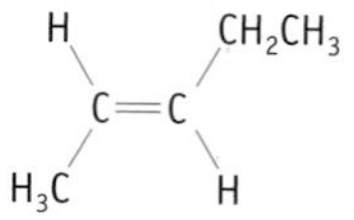   trans-2-pentene

(e) See the pentane isomers in the margin of page 449.

37. Energy must be supplied to break the C=C π bond to allow free rotation of one end of the molecule relative to the other. See page 420.

38. (a) 109°   (f) Amide
(b) Trigonal planar   (g) Carboxylic acid
(c) sp^3 (h) Ester
(d) Tetrahedral   (i) C_3 and C_6 are chiral centers
(e) Amine

(j) Reaction with water breaks the ester and amide links to give three products.

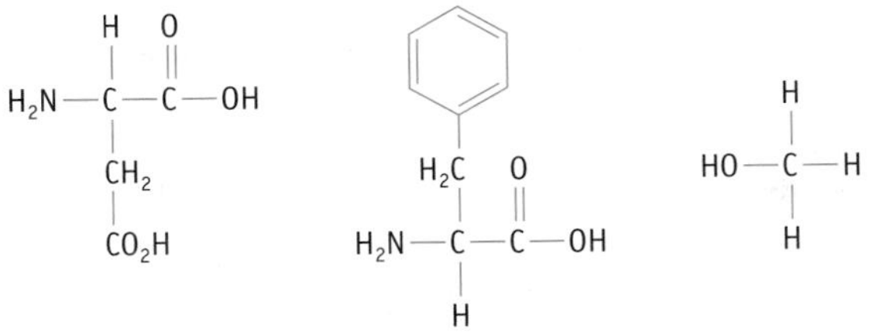

39. (a) Both have the same empirical (CH_2) and molecular formulas (C_5H_{10}).
(b) Structural isomers of C_5H_{10}

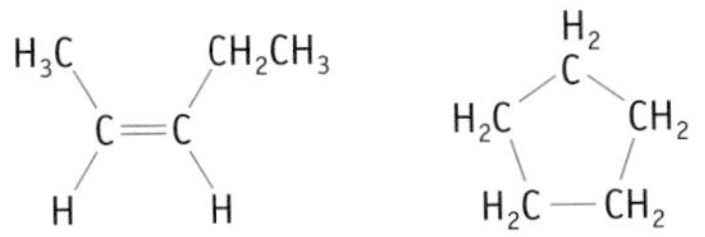

cis-2-pentene   cyclopentane

(c) The alkene, *cis*-2-pentene, will add bromine across the double bond to give 2,3-dibromopentane, and the color of Br_2 will disappear. (See Figure 10.7.) Cyclopentane will not react with bromine. The orange-red color of bromine will therefore remain.
(d) Adding Br_2 to an alkene

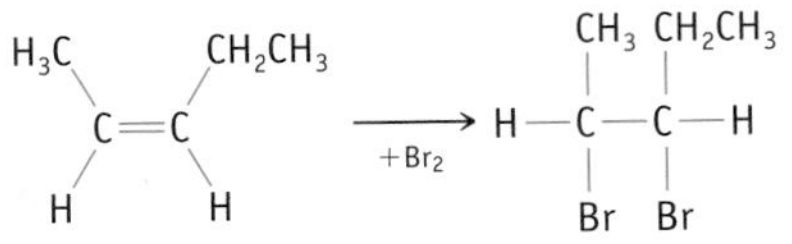

40. (a) and (c) Structures of propanone and propanal and reaction products.

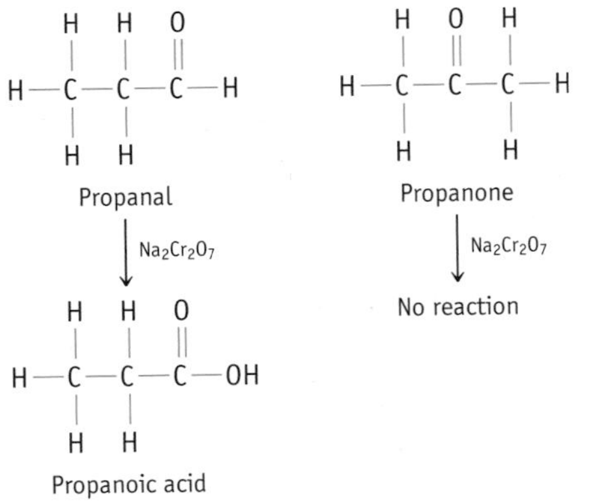

Propanal   Propanone

Propanoic acid

Of the isomers, only propanal reacts with the oxidizing agent in acid. The orange color of $Na_2Cr_2O_7$ fades and is replaced by the green color of Cr^{3+}.

41. (a) Ester
(b) 2-Propyl propanoate
(c) Products of reaction with NaOH followed by HCl.

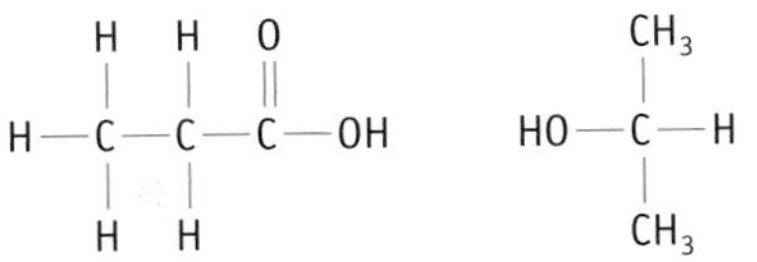

Propanoic acid   2-Propanol

42. (a) 1 is 1-Propanol and 2 is propene
(b) Compounds 3 and 4

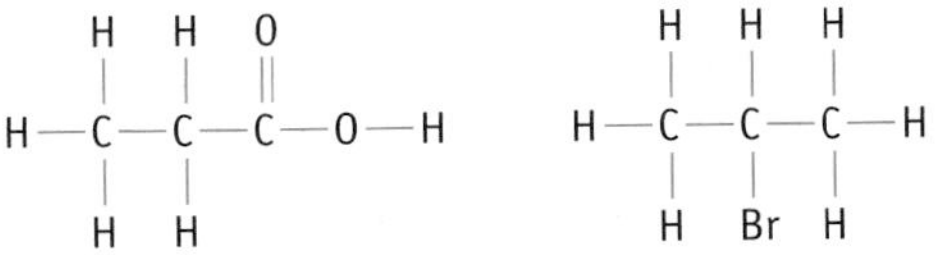

Propanoic acid   2-Bromopropane

Comment: When propene reacts with HBr, the HBr can add in two ways. The H atom could attach to the CH_2 carbon or to the CH carbon. The former is generally observed and is called a Markovnikov addition.

43. The group *ortho* to the carboxylic acid group is an ester. Therefore, first react aspirin with NaOH (followed by acid) to give compound II, 2-hydroxybenzoic acid (but better known as salicylic acid). Second, react II with methanol to give the desired ester (oil of wintergreen).

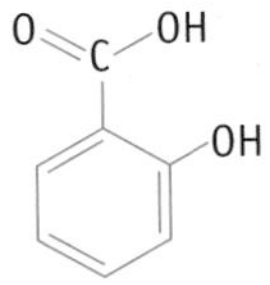

2-hydroxybenzoic acid
or
salicylic acid

44. The compound forms a polyamide, a condensation polymer. See Example 10.8 on page 486.

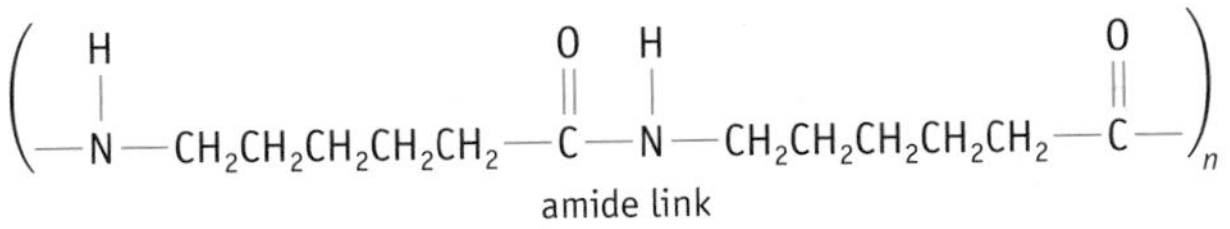

amide link

45. The two possible products from 1-octene with water arise because the OH of water can be found on C(1) or C(2) of the C_8 chain. The product here has OH on C(2). We prove this by oxidizing the resulting alcohol to a ketone, which does not react with NaOH.

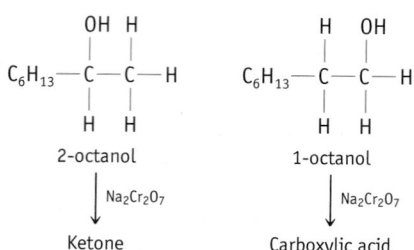

If the OH group was on C(1), the product of oxidation would be a carboxylic acid, which would react with NaOH.

46. (a) Chiral carbon is marked with *.

```
        H   H  CH₃ CH₃ H
        |   |   |   |  |
    H — C — C — C*— C — C — H
        |   |   |   |  |
        H   H   H   H  H
```

(b) Isomer of butanoic acid

```
        H   H   O
        |   |   ||
    H — C — C — C — O — CH₃
        |   |
        H   H
     methyl propanoate
```

(c) Aldehyde and ketone

```
     H   H   H   O              H   O   H   H
     |   |   |   ||             |   ||  |   |
 H — C — C — C — C — H      H — C — C — C — C — H
     |   |   |                  |       |   |
     H   H   H                  H       H   H
       butanal                     butanone
```

(d) One of several isomers of C_7H_{14}

```
     H   H   H       H   H
     |   |   |       |   |
     C = C — C ————— C — C — H
     |       |       |   |
     H      C₂H₅     H   H
          3-ethyl-1-pentene
```

47. An ester can react with NaOH to produce an alcohol and a carboxylic acid, so reaction with NaOH can destroy the polyester in the material. See page 474.

48. Ester hydrolysis. The reaction is, in effect, the addition of water to the reactant, with the ester forming a carboxylic acid and an alcohol.

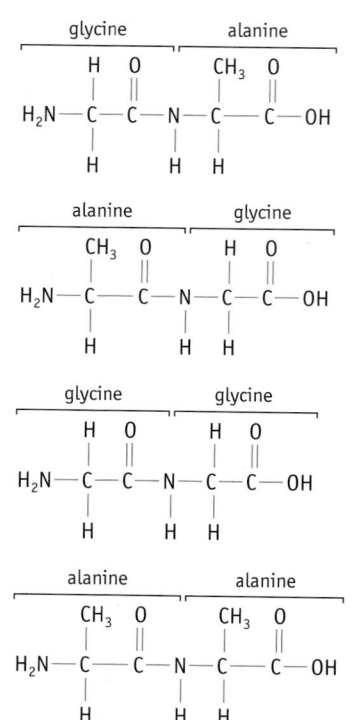

49. (a) Four peptides (2^2) are possible on reacting a mixture of two amino acids.

(b) 3^3 or 27 peptides are possible. One is illustrated here.

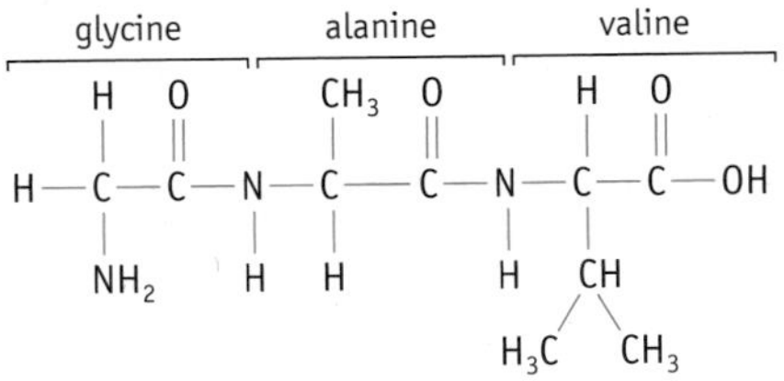

| glycine | alanine | valine |

50. (a) The colors of fireworks and neon signs arise the same way: from excited atoms, whether these are strontium atoms or neon atoms. As the atoms are excited by the input of energy, electrons move to higher quantum levels. Light is emitted as the electrons move back to lower quantum levels.
   (b) Perchlorate and chlorate both have a tetrahedral electron pair geometry. The former has a tetrahedral shape, whereas the latter is trigonal pyramidal.

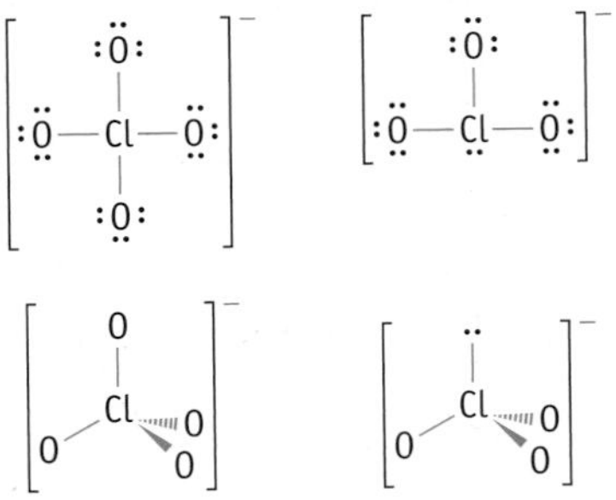

Perchlorate ion   Chlorate ion

(c) The formal charge on each O atom in ClO_4^- is -1, whereas it is $+3$ for Cl.

51. (a) Empirical formula = CH_2N_2
   (b) Mass percent of N = 66.64%

$$\frac{\left[6 \text{ mol N} \left(\frac{14.0067 \text{ g}}{1 \text{ mol N}}\right)\right]}{126.12 \text{ g/mol } C_3H_6N_6} \times 100\% = 66.64\%$$

(c) Theoretical yield of melamine

$$1.000 \times 10^3 \text{ g urea} \left(\frac{1 \text{ mol}}{60.06 \text{ g urea}}\right) = 16.65 \text{ mol urea}$$

$$16.65 \text{ mol urea} \left(\frac{1 \text{ mol HNCO}}{1 \text{ mol urea}}\right)\left(\frac{1 \text{ mol } C_3H_6N_6}{6 \text{ mol HNCO}}\right)$$
$$= 2.775 \text{ mol } C_3H_6N_6$$

$$2.775 \text{ mol } C_3H_6N_6 \left(\frac{126.12 \text{ g}}{1 \text{ mol } C_3H_6N_6}\right) = 345.0 \text{ g } C_3H_6N_6$$

(d) $\Delta_r H° = \Delta_f H°[HCNO(g)] + \Delta_f H°[NH_3(g)]$
$$- \Delta_f H°[(NH_2)_2CO(s)]$$
= (1 mol HNCO(g)/1mol-rxn)(-101.67 kJ/mol)
+ (1 mol NH_3(g)/1 mol-rxn)(-45.90 kJ/mol)
- (1 mol $(NH_2)_2$CO(s)/1 mol-rxn)(-333.1 kJ/mol)
= 185.5 kJ/mol-rxn

The reaction is endothermic.
(e) The C and N atoms in the melamine ring are sp^2 hybridized.
(f) The N—C—N and C—N—C bond angles in the ring are both 120°.
(g) The molecule is not polar.

11 | Gases and Their Properties

The Atmosphere and Altitude Sickness

Some of you may have dreamed of climbing to the summits of the world's tallest mountains, or you may be an avid skier and visit high-mountain ski areas. In either case, "acute mountain sickness" (AMS) is a possibility. AMS is common at higher altitudes and is characterized by a headache, nausea, insomnia, dizziness, lassitude, and fatigue. It can be prevented by a slow ascent, and its symptoms can be relieved by a mild pain reliever.

©Davis Barber/PhotoEdit

AMS and more serious forms of high altitude sickness are generally due to hypoxia or oxygen deprivation. The oxygen concentration in Earth's atmosphere is 21%. As you go higher into the atmosphere, the concentration remains 21%, but the atmospheric pressure drops. When you reach 3000 m (the altitude of some ski resorts), the barometric pressure is about 70% of that at sea level. At 5000 m, barometric pressure is only 50% of sea level, and on the summit of Mt. Everest, it is only 29% of the sea level pressure. At sea level, your blood is nearly saturated with oxygen, but as the partial pressure of oxygen drops, the percent saturation drops as well. At $P(O_2)$ of 50 mm Hg, hemoglobin in the red blood cells is about 80% saturated. Other saturation levels are given in the table (for a pH of 7.4).

$P(O_2)$ (mm Hg)	Approximate Percent Saturation
90	95%
80	92%
70	90%
60	85%
50	80%
40	72%

For more on the atmosphere, see page 534.

Questions:

1. Assume a sea level pressure of 1 atm (760 mm Hg). What are the O_2 partial pressures at a 3000-m ski resort and on Mt. Everest?
2. What are the approximate blood saturation levels under these conditions?

Answers to these questions are in Appendix Q.

Mountain climbers, hot air balloons, SCUBA diving, and automobile air bags (Figure 11.1) depend on the properties of gases. Aside from understanding how these work, there are at least three reasons for studying gases. First, some common elements and compounds (such as oxygen, nitrogen, and methane) exist in the gaseous state under normal conditions of pressure and temperature. Furthermore, many liquids such as water can be vaporized, and the physical properties of these vapors are important. Second, our gaseous atmosphere provides one means of transferring energy and material throughout the globe, and it is the source of life-sustaining chemicals.

The third reason for studying gases is also compelling. Of the three states of matter, gases are reasonably simple when viewed at the molecular level, and, as a result, gas behavior is well understood. It is possible to describe the properties of gases *qualitatively* in terms of the behavior of the molecules that make up the gas. Even more impressive, it is possible to describe the properties of gases *quantitatively* using simple mathematical models. One objective of scientists is to develop precise mathematical and conceptual models of natural phenomena, and a study of gas behavior will introduce you to this approach. To describe gases, chemists have learned that only four quantities are needed: the pressure (P), volume (V), and temperature (T, kelvins) of the gas, and amount (n, mol).

Chemistry Now™

Throughout the text this icon introduces an opportunity for self-study or to explore interactive tutorials by signing in at **www.cengage.com/login**.

FIGURE 11.1. Automobile air bags. Most automobiles are now equipped with airbags to protect the driver and passengers in the event of a head-on or side crash. Such bags are inflated with nitrogen gas, which is generated by the explosive decomposition of sodium azide:

$$2\ NaN_3(s) \longrightarrow 2\ Na(s) + 3\ N_2(g)$$

The airbag is fully inflated in about 0.050 s. This is important because the typical automobile collision lasts about 0.125 s.

See ChemistryNow Screen 11.1 for questions about automobile air bags.

SAAB Car, USA, Inc.

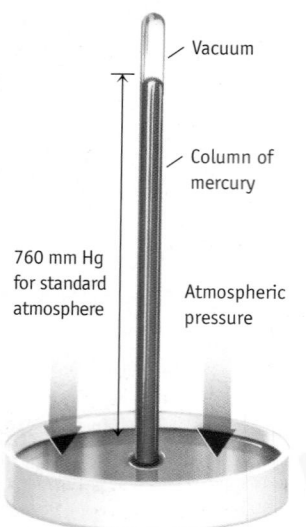

Vacuum

Column of
mercury

760 mm Hg
for standard
atmosphere

Atmospheric
pressure

FIGURE 11.2 A barometer. The pressure of the atmosphere on the surface of the mercury in the dish is balanced by the downward pressure exerted by the column of mercury. The barometer was invented in 1643 by Evangelista Torricelli (1608–1647). A unit of pressure called the torr in his honor is equivalent to 1 mm Hg.

■ **Hectopascals** Meteorologists have long measured atmospheric pressure in millibars. However, after the SI system of units became more widespread, they began to use the unit "hectopascal," which is equivalent to the millibar.
1 hectopascal (hPa) = 100 Pa = 1 mbar
1 kilopascal (kPa) = 1000 Pa = 10 hPa

11.1 Gas Pressure

Pressure is the force exerted on an object divided by the area over which it is exerted, and a barometer depends on this to measure atmospheric pressure. A barometer can be made by filling a tube with a liquid, often mercury, and inverting the tube in a dish containing the same liquid (Figure 11.2). If the air has been removed completely from the vertical tube, the liquid in the tube assumes a level such that the pressure exerted by the mass of the column of liquid in the tube is balanced by the pressure of the atmosphere pressing down on the surface of the liquid in the dish.

Pressure is often reported in units of **millimeters of mercury (mm Hg),** the height (in mm) of the mercury column in a mercury barometer above the surface of the mercury in the dish. At sea level, this height is about 760 mm. Pressures are also reported as **standard atmospheres (atm),** a unit defined as follows:

$$1 \text{ standard atmosphere (1 atm)} = 760 \text{ mm Hg (exactly)}$$

The SI unit of pressure is the **pascal (Pa).**

$$1 \text{ pascal (Pa)} = 1 \text{ newton/meter}^2$$

(The newton is the SI unit of force.) Because the pascal is a very small unit compared with ordinary pressures, the unit kilopascal (kPa) is more often used. Another unit used for gas pressures is the **bar,** where 1 bar = 100,000 Pa. To summarize, the units used in science for pressure are

$$1 \text{ atm} = 760 \text{ mm Hg (exactly)} = 101.325 \text{ kilopascals (kPa)} = 1.01325 \text{ bar}$$

or

$$1 \text{ bar} = 1 \times 10^5 \text{ Pa (exactly)} = 1 \times 10^2 \text{ kPa} = 0.9872 \text{ atm}$$

■ **EXAMPLE 11.1 Pressure Unit Conversions**

Problem Convert a pressure of 635 mm Hg into its corresponding value in units of atmospheres (atm), bars, and kilopascals (kPa).

Strategy Use the relationships between millimeters of Hg, atmospheres, bars, and pascals described earlier in the text.

Solution The relationship between millimeters of mercury and atmospheres is 1 atm = 760 mm Hg.

$$635 \text{ mm Hg} \times \frac{1 \text{ atm}}{760 \text{ mm Hg}} = \boxed{0.836 \text{ atm}}$$

The relationship between atmospheres and bars is 1 atm = 1.013 bar.

$$0.836 \text{ atm} \times \frac{1.013 \text{ bar}}{1 \text{ atm}} = \boxed{0.846 \text{ bar}}$$

The relationship between millimeters of mercury and kilopascals is 101.325 kPa = 760 mm Hg.

$$635 \text{ mm Hg} \times \frac{101.3 \text{ kPa}}{760 \text{ mm Hg}} = \boxed{84.6 \text{ kPa}}$$

A Closer Look

Measuring Gas Pressure

Pressure is the force exerted on an object divided by the area over which the force is exerted:

Pressure = force/area

This book, for example, weighs more than 4 lb and has an area of 82 in², so it exerts a pressure of about 0.05 lb/in² when it lies flat on a surface. (In metric units, the pressure is about 3 g/cm².)

Now consider the pressure that the column of mercury exerts on the mercury in the dish in the barometer shown in Figure 11.2. This pressure exactly balances the pressure of the atmosphere. Thus, the pressure of the atmosphere (or of any other gas) can be measured by relating it to the height of the column of mercury (or any other liquid) the gas can support.

Mercury is the liquid of choice for barometers because of its high density. A barometer filled with water would be over 10 m in height. [The water column is about 13.6 times as high as a column of mercury because mercury's density (13.53 g/cm³) is 13.6 times that of water (density = 0.997 g/cm³, at 25 °C).]

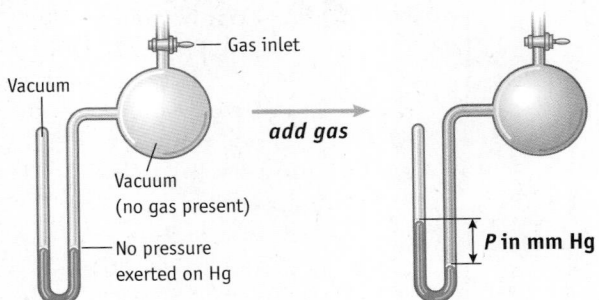

In the laboratory, we often use a U-tube manometer, which is a mercury-filled, U-shaped glass tube. The closed side of the tube has been evacuated so that no gas remains to exert pressure on the mercury on that side. The other side is open to the gas whose pressure we want to measure. When the gas presses on the mercury in the open side, the gas pressure is read directly (in mm Hg) as the difference in mercury levels on the closed and open sides.

You may have used a tire gauge to check the pressure in your car or bike tires. In the U.S., such gauges usually indicate the pressure in pounds per square inch (psi) where 1 atm = 14.7 psi. Some newer gauges give the pressure in kilopascals as well. Be sure to recognize that the reading on the scale refers to the pressure *in excess of atmospheric pressure*. (A flat tire is not a vacuum; it contains air at atmospheric pressure.) For example, if the gauge reads 35 psi (2.4 atm), the pressure in the tire is actually about 50 psi or 3.4 atm.

EXERCISE 11.1 Pressure Unit Conversions

Rank the following pressures in decreasing order of magnitude (from largest to smallest): 75 kPa, 250 mm Hg, 0.83 bar, and 0.63 atm.

11.2 Gas Laws: The Experimental Basis

Boyle's Law: The Compressibility of Gases

When you pump up the tires of your bicycle, the pump squeezes the air into a smaller volume (Figure 11.3). This property of a gas is called its **compressibility**. While studying the compressibility of gases, Robert Boyle (1627–1691) observed that the volume of a fixed amount of gas at a given temperature is inversely proportional to the pressure exerted by the gas. All gases behave in this manner, and we now refer to this relationship as **Boyle's law.**

Boyle's law can be demonstrated in many ways. In Figure 11.4, a hypodermic syringe is filled with air and sealed. When pressure is applied to the movable plunger of the syringe, the air inside is compressed. As the pressure (*P*) increases on the syringe, the gas volume in the syringe (*V*) decreases. When $1/V$ of the gas in the syringe is plotted as a function of *P*, a straight line results. This type of plot demonstrates that the pressure and volume of the gas are inversely proportional; that is, they change in opposite directions.

FIGURE 11.3 A bicycle pump— Boyle's law in action. This works by compressing air into a smaller volume. You experience Boyle's law because you can feel the increasing pressure of the gas as you press down on the plunger.

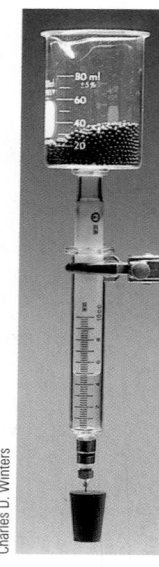
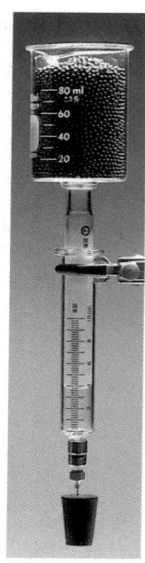
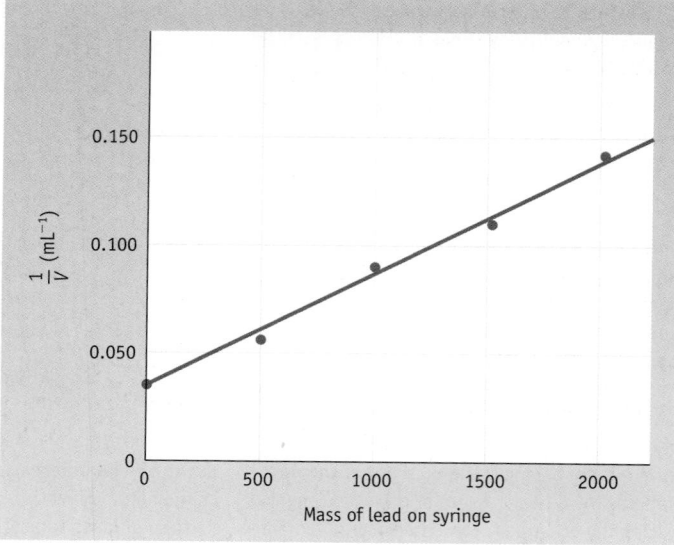

Mass of lead on syringe

$\frac{1}{V}$ (mL^{-1})

0.150

0.100

0.050

0

0   500   1000   1500   2000

Active Figure 11.4 **An experiment to demonstrate Boyle's law.** A syringe filled with air was sealed. Pressure was applied by adding lead shot to the beaker on top of the syringe. As the mass of lead increased, the pressure on the air in the sealed syringe increased, and the gas was compressed. A plot of (1/volume of air in the syringe) versus P (as measured by the mass of lead) is a straight line.

Chemistry..Now™ Sign in at www.cengage.com/login and go to the Chapter Contents menu to explore an interactive version of this figure accompanied by an exercise.

Mathematically, we can write Boyle's law as:

$$P \propto \frac{1}{V} \quad \text{when } n \text{ and } T \text{ are constant}$$

where the symbol $\propto$ means "proportional to."

When two quantities are proportional to each other, they can be equated if a *proportionality constant*, here called C_B, is introduced.

$$P = C_B \times \frac{1}{V} \quad \text{or} \quad PV = C_B \quad \text{when } n \text{ and } T \text{ are constant}$$

This form of Boyle's law expresses the fact that *the product of the pressure and volume of a gas sample is a constant at a given temperature,* where the constant C_B is determined by the amount of gas (in moles) and its temperature (in kelvins). It follows from this that, if the pressure–volume product is known for a gas sample under one set of conditions (P_1 and V_1), then it is known for another set of conditions (P_2 and V_2). Under either set of conditions, the PV product is equal to C_B, so

$$P_1V_1 = P_2V_2 \quad \text{at constant } n \text{ and } T \tag{11.1}$$

This form of Boyle's law is useful when we want to know, for example, what happens to the volume of a given amount of gas when the pressure changes at a constant temperature.

EXAMPLE 11.2 Boyle's Law

Problem A sample of gaseous nitrogen in a 65.0-L automobile air bag has a pressure of 745 mm Hg. If this sample is transferred to a 25.0-L bag at the same temperature, what is the pressure of the gas in the 25.0-L bag?

Strategy Here, we use Boyle's law, Equation 11.1. The original pressure and volume (P_1 and V_1) and the new volume (V_2) are known.

Solution It is often useful to make a table of the information provided.

Initial Conditions	Final Conditions
$P_1 = 745$ mm Hg	$P_2 = ?$
$V_1 = 65.0$ L	$V_2 = 25.0$ L

You know that $P_1V_1 = P_2V_2$. Therefore,

$$P_2 = \frac{P_1V_1}{V_2} = \frac{(745 \text{ mm Hg})(65.0 \text{ L})}{25.0 \text{ L}} = \boxed{1940 \text{ mm Hg}}$$

Comment According to Boyle's law, P and V change in opposite directions. Because the volume has decreased, the new pressure (P_2) must be greater than the original pressure (P_1). A quick way to solve these problems takes advantage of this: if the volume decreases, the pressure must increase, and the original pressure must be multiplied by a volume fraction greater than 1.

$$P_2 = P_1 \left(\frac{65.0 \text{ L}}{25.0 \text{ L}} \right)$$

EXERCISE 11.2 Boyle's Law

A sample of CO_2 with a pressure of 55 mm Hg in a volume of 125 mL is compressed so that the new pressure of the gas is 78 mm Hg. What is the new volume of the gas? (Assume the temperature is constant.)

The Effect of Temperature on Gas Volume: Charles's Law

In 1787, the French scientist Jacques Charles (1746–1823) discovered that the volume of a fixed quantity of gas at constant pressure decreases with decreasing temperature (Figure 11.5).

Figure 11.6 illustrates how the volumes of two different gas samples change with temperature (at a constant pressure). When the plots of volume versus temperature

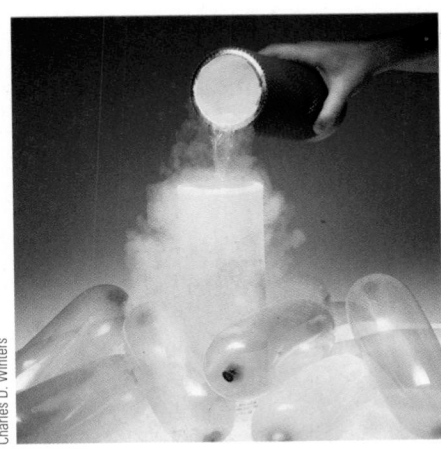
(a)

(b)

(c)

Charles D. Winters

FIGURE 11.5 A dramatic illustration of Charles's law. (a) Air-filled balloons are placed in liquid nitrogen (77 K). The volume of the gas in the balloons is dramatically reduced at this temperature. (b) After all of the balloons have been placed in the liquid nitrogen, (c) they are removed; as they warm to room temperature, they reinflate to their original volume.

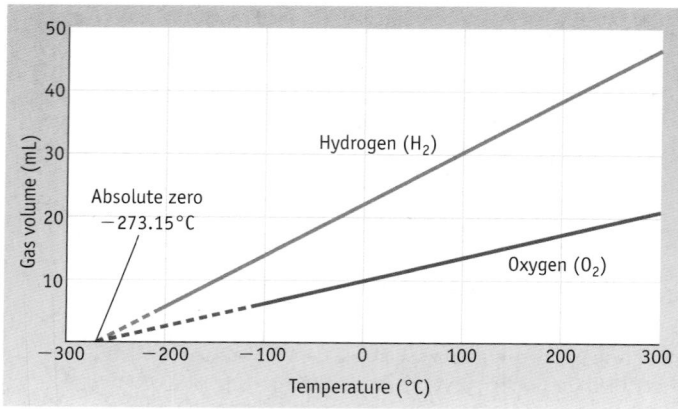

T (°C)	T (K)	Vol. H_2 (mL)	Vol. O_2 (mL)
300	573	47.0	21.1
200	473	38.8	17.5
100	373	30.6	13.8
0	273	22.4	10.1
−100	173	14.2	6.39
−200	73	6.00	—

Active Figure 11.6 **Charles's law.** The solid lines represent the volumes of the samples of hydrogen and oxygen at different temperatures. The volumes decrease as the temperature is lowered (at constant pressure). These lines, if extended, intersect the temperature axis at approximately −273 °C.

Chemistry Now™ Sign in at www.cengage.com/login and go to the Chapter Contents menu to explore an interactive version of this figure accompanied by an exercise.

■ **Boyle's and Charles's Laws** Neither Boyle's law nor Charles's law depends on the identity of the gas being studied. These laws describe the behavior of any gaseous substance, regardless of its identity.

are extended to lower temperatures, they all reach zero volume at the same temperature, −273.15 °C. (Of course, gases will not actually reach zero volume; they liquefy above that temperature.) This temperature is significant, however. William Thomson (1824–1907), also known as Lord Kelvin, proposed a temperature scale—now known as the Kelvin scale—for which the zero point is −273.15 °C (◀ page 27).

When Kelvin temperatures are used with volume measurements, the volume–temperature relationship is

$$V = C_c \times T$$

where C_c is a proportionality constant (which depends on the amount of gas and its pressure). This is **Charles's law,** which states that if a given quantity of gas is held at a constant pressure, its volume is directly proportional to the Kelvin temperature.

Writing Charles's law another way, we have $V/T = C_c$; that is, the volume of a gas divided by the temperature of the gas (in kelvins) is constant for a given sample of gas at a specified pressure. Therefore, if we know the volume and temperature of a given quantity of gas (V_1 and T_1), we can find the volume, V_2, at some other temperature, T_2, using the equation

$$\frac{V_1}{T_1} = \frac{V_2}{T_2} \quad \text{at constant } n \text{ and } P \tag{11.2}$$

Calculations using Charles's law are illustrated by the following example and exercise. Be sure to notice that the temperature T *must always be expressed in kelvins.*

■ **EXAMPLE 11.3 Charles's Law**

Problem A sample of CO_2 in a gas-tight syringe (as in Figure 11.4) has a volume of 25.0 mL at room temperature (20.0 °C). What is the final volume of the gas if you hold the syringe in your hand to raise its temperature to 37 °C?

Strategy Because a given quantity of gas is heated (at a constant pressure), Charles's law applies. Because we know the original V and T, and want to calculate a new volume at a new, but known, temperature, use Equation 11.2.

Solution Organize the information in a table. Remember the temperature must be converted to kelvins.

Initial Conditions

$V_1 = 25.0$ mL

$T_1 = 20.0 + 273.2 = 293.2$ K

Final Conditions

$V_2 = ?$

$T_2 = 37 + 273 = 310.$ K

Substitute the known quantities into Equation 11.2, and solve for V_2:

$$V_2 = T_2\left(\frac{V_1}{T_1}\right) = 310.\ \text{K}\left(\frac{25.0\ \text{mL}}{293.2\ \text{K}}\right) = 26.5\ \text{mL}$$

Comment As expected, the volume of the gas increased with a temperature increase. The new volume (V_2) must equal the original volume (V_1) multiplied by a temperature fraction that is greater than 1 to reflect the effect of the temperature increase. That is,

$$V_2 = V_1\left(\frac{310.\ \text{K}}{293\ \text{K}}\right)$$

EXERCISE 11.3 Charles's Law

A balloon is inflated with helium to a volume of 45 L at room temperature (25 °C). If the balloon is cooled to −10 °C, what is the new volume of the balloon? Assume that the pressure does not change.

Combining Boyle's and Charles's Laws: The General Gas Law

The volume of a given amount of gas is inversely proportional to its pressure at constant temperature (Boyle's law) and directly proportional to the Kelvin temperature at constant pressure (Charles's law). But what if we need to know what happens to the gas when two of the three parameters (P, V, and T) change? For example, what would happen to the pressure of a sample of nitrogen in an automobile air bag if the same amount of gas were placed in a smaller bag and heated to a higher temperature? You can deal with this situation by combining the two equations that express Boyle's and Charles's laws.

$$\frac{P_1 V_1}{T_1} = \frac{P_2 V_2}{T_2} \quad \text{for a given amount of gas, } n \qquad (11.3)$$

This equation is sometimes called the **general gas law** or **combined gas law.** It applies specifically to situations in which the *amount of gas does not change*.

A weather balloon is filled with helium. As it ascends into the troposphere, does the volume increase or decrease?

EXAMPLE 11.4 General Gas Law

Problem Helium-filled balloons are used to carry scientific instruments high into the atmosphere. Suppose a balloon is launched when the temperature is 22.5 °C and the barometric pressure is 754 mm Hg. If the balloon's volume is 4.19×10^3 L (and no helium escapes from the balloon), what will the volume be at a height of 20 miles, where the pressure is 76.0 mm Hg and the temperature is −33.0 °C?

Strategy Here we know the initial volume, temperature, and pressure of the gas. We want to know the volume of the same amount of gas at a new pressure and temperature. It is most convenient to use Equation 11.3, the general gas law.

Solution Begin by setting out the information given in a table.

Initial Conditions

$V_1 = 4.19 \times 10^3$ L

$P_1 = 754$ mm Hg

$T_1 = 22.5$ °C (295.7 K)

Final Conditions

$V_2 = ?$ L

$P_2 = 76.0$ mm Hg

$T_2 = -33.0$ °C (240.2 K)

We can rearrange the general gas law to calculate the new volume V_2:

$$V_2 = \left(\frac{T_2}{P_2}\right) \times \left(\frac{P_1 V_1}{T_1}\right) = V_1 \times \frac{P_1}{P_2} \times \frac{T_2}{T_1}$$

$$= 4.19 \times 10^3 \text{ L} \left(\frac{754 \text{ mm Hg}}{76.0 \text{ mm Hg}}\right)\left(\frac{240.2 \text{ K}}{295.7 \text{ K}}\right)$$

$$= 3.38 \times 10^4 \text{ L}$$

Comment The pressure decreased by almost a factor of 10, which should lead to about a ten-fold volume increase. This increase is partly offset by a drop in temperature that leads to a volume decrease. On balance, the volume increases because the pressure has dropped so substantially.

Notice that the solution was to multiply the original volume (V_1) by a pressure factor larger than 1 (because the volume increases with a lower pressure) and a temperature factor smaller than 1 (because volume decreases with a decrease in temperature).

EXERCISE 11.4 The General Gas Law

You have a 22.-L cylinder of helium at a pressure of 150 atm and at 31 °C. How many balloons can you fill, each with a volume of 5.0 L, on a day when the atmospheric pressure is 755 mm Hg and the temperature is 22 °C?

The general gas law leads to other, useful predictions of gas behavior. For example, if a given amount of gas is held in a closed container, the pressure of the gas will increase with increasing temperature.

$$\frac{P_1}{T_1} = \frac{P_2}{T_2} \text{ when } V_1 = V_2 \text{ and so } P_2 = P_1 \times \frac{T_2}{T_1}$$

■ **Gay-Lussac's Law** Gay-Lussac's law states that, at constant volume, the pressure of a given mass of gas is proportional to the absolute temperature. In 1779 Joseph Lambert proposed a definition of absolute zero of temperature based on this relationship.

That is, when T_2 is greater than T_1, P_2 will be greater than P_1. In fact, this is the reason tire manufacturers recommend checking tire pressures when the tires are cold. After driving for some distance, friction warms a tire and increases the internal pressure. Filling a warm tire to the recommended pressure may lead to an underinflated tire.

Avogadro's Hypothesis

Front and side air bags are now common in automobiles. In the event of an accident, a bag is rapidly inflated with nitrogen gas generated by a chemical reaction. The air bag unit has a sensor that is sensitive to sudden deceleration of the vehicle and will send an electrical signal that will trigger the reaction (Figures 11.1 and 11.7). In many types of air bags, the explosion of sodium azide generates nitrogen gas.

$$2 \text{ NaN}_3(s) \longrightarrow 2 \text{ Na}(s) + 3 \text{ N}_2(g)$$

Driver-side air bags inflate to a volume of about 35–70 L, and passenger air bags inflate to about 60–160 L. The final volume of the bag will depend on the amount of nitrogen gas generated.

The relationship between volume and amount of gas was first noted by Amedeo Avogadro. In 1811, he used work on gases by the chemist (and early experimenter with hot air balloons) Joseph Gay-Lussac (1778–1850) to propose that *equal volumes of gases under the same conditions of temperature and pressure have equal numbers of particles* (either molecules or atoms, depending on the composition of the gas.) This idea came to be known as **Avogadro's hypothesis.** Stated another way, the volume

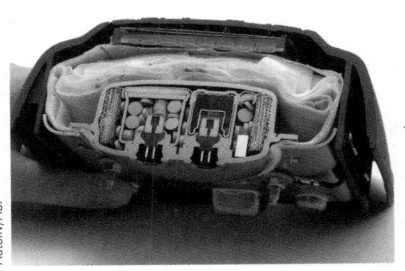

When a car decelerates in a collision, an electrical contact is made in the sensor unit. The propellant (green solid) detonates, releasing nitrogen gas, and the folded nylon bag explodes out of the plastic housing.

Driver-side air bags inflate with 35–70 L of N_2 gas, whereas passenger air bags hold about 60–160 L.

The bag deflates within 0.2 s, the gas escaping through holes in the bottom of the bag.

FIGURE 11.7 Automobile air bags. See ChemistryNow Screen 11.1 for more on air bags.

of a gas at a given temperature and pressure is directly proportional to the amount of gas in moles:

$$V \propto n \text{ at constant } T \text{ and } P$$

Chemistry :Now™

Sign in at **www.cengage.com/login** and go to Chapter 11 Contents to see Screen 11.3 for exercises on **the three gas laws**.

■ **EXAMPLE 11.5 Avogadro's Hypothesis**

Problem Ammonia can be made directly from the elements:

$$N_2(g) + 3 H_2(g) \longrightarrow 2 NH_3(g)$$

If you begin with 15.0 L of $H_2(g)$, what volume of $N_2(g)$ is required for complete reaction (both gases being at the same T and P)? What is the theoretical yield of NH_3, in liters, under the same conditions?

Strategy From Avogadro's law, we know that gas volume is proportional to the amount of gas. Therefore, we can substitute gas volumes for moles in this stoichiometry problem.

Solution Calculate the volumes of N_2 required and NH_3 produced (in liters) by multiplying the volume of H_2 available by a stoichiometric factor (also in units of liters) obtained from the chemical equation:

$$V \text{ (N}_2 \text{ required)} = (15.0 \text{ L } H_2 \text{ available}) \left(\frac{1 \text{ L } N_2 \text{ required}}{3 \text{ L } H_2 \text{ available}} \right) = 5.00 \text{ L } N_2 \text{ required}$$

$$V \text{ (NH}_3 \text{ produced)} = (15.0 \text{ L } H_2 \text{ available}) \left(\frac{2 \text{ L } NH_3 \text{ produced}}{3 \text{ L } H_2 \text{ available}} \right) = 10.0 \text{ L } NH_3 \text{ produced}$$

EXERCISE 11.5 Avogadro's Hypothesis

Methane burns in oxygen to give CO_2 and H_2O, according to the balanced equation

$$CH_4(g) + 2 O_2(g) \longrightarrow CO_2(g) + 2 H_2O(g)$$

If 22.4 L of gaseous CH_4 is burned, what volume of O_2 is required for complete combustion? What volumes of CO_2 and H_2O are produced? Assume all gases have the same temperature and pressure.

11.3 The Ideal Gas Law

Four interrelated quantities can be used to describe a gas: pressure, volume, temperature, and amount (moles). We know from experiments that three gas laws can be used to describe the relationship of these properties (Section 11.2).

Boyle's Law	Charles's Law	Avogadro's Hypothesis
$V \propto (1/P)$	$V \propto T$	$V \propto n$
(constant T, n)	(constant P, n)	(constant T, P)

If all three laws are combined, the result is

$$V \propto \frac{nT}{P}$$

■ **Properties of an Ideal Gas** For ideal gases, it is assumed that there are no forces of attraction between molecules and that the molecules themselves occupy no volume.

This can be made into a mathematical equation by introducing a proportionality constant, now labeled **R.** This constant, called the **gas constant,** is a *universal constant,* a number you can use to interrelate the properties of any gas:

$$V = R\left(\frac{nT}{P}\right)$$

or **(11.4)**

$$PV = nRT$$

The equation $PV = nRT$ is called the **ideal gas law.** It describes the behavior of a so-called ideal gas. As you will learn in Section 11.9, however, there is no such thing as an "ideal" gas. Nonetheless, real gases at pressures around one atmosphere or less and temperatures around room temperature usually behave close enough to the ideal that $PV = nRT$ adequately describes their behavior.

To use the equation $PV = nRT$, we need a value for R. This is readily determined experimentally. By carefully measuring P, V, n, and T for a sample of gas, we can calculate the value of R from these values using the ideal gas law equation. For example, under conditions of **standard temperature and pressure (STP)** (a gas temperature of 0 °C or 273.15 K and a pressure of 1 atm), 1 mol of gas occupies 22.414 L, a quantity called the **standard molar volume.** Substituting these values into the ideal gas law gives a value for R:

■ **STP—What Is It?** A gas is at STP, or standard temperature and pressure, when its temperature is 0 °C or 273.15 K and its pressure is 1 atm. Under these conditions, exactly 1 mol of a gas occupies 22.414 L.

$$R = \frac{PV}{nT} = \frac{(1.0000 \text{ atm})(22.414 \text{ L})}{(1.0000 \text{ mol})(273.15)} = 0.082057 \frac{\text{L} \cdot \text{atm}}{\text{K} \cdot \text{mol}}$$

With a value for R, we can now use the ideal gas law in calculations.

Chemistry ⚛ Now™

Sign in at **www.cengage.com/login** and go to Chapter 11 Contents to see Screen 11.4 for a simulation of the **ideal gas law.**

■ **EXAMPLE 11.6** **Ideal Gas Law**

Problem The nitrogen gas in an automobile air bag, with a volume of 65 L, exerts a pressure of 829 mm Hg at 25 °C. What amount of N_2 gas (in moles) is in the air bag?

Strategy You are given P, V, and T and want to calculate the amount of gas (n). Use the ideal gas law, Equation 11.4.

Solution First, list the information provided.

$P = 829$ mm Hg $V = 65$ L $T = 25$ °C $n = ?$

To use the ideal gas law with R having units of (L·atm/K·mol), the pressure must be expressed in atmospheres and the temperature in kelvins. Therefore,

$$P = 829 \text{ mm Hg} \left(\frac{1 \text{ atm}}{760 \text{ mm Hg}} \right) = 1.09 \text{ atm}$$

$$T = 25 + 273 = 298 \text{ K}$$

Now substitute the values of P, V, T, and R into the ideal gas law, and solve for the amount of gas, n:

$$n = \frac{PV}{RT} = \frac{(1.09 \text{ atm})(65 \text{ L})}{(0.082057 \text{ L} \cdot \text{atm/K} \cdot \text{mol})(298 \text{ K})} = 2.9 \text{ mol}$$

Notice that units of atmospheres, liters, and kelvins cancel to leave the answer in units of moles.

EXERCISE 11.6 Ideal Gas Law

The balloon used by Jacques Charles in his historic balloon flight in 1783 (see page 533) was filled with about 1300 mol of H_2. If the temperature of the gas was 23 °C and its pressure was 750 mm Hg, what was the volume of the balloon?

The Density of Gases

The density of a gas at a given temperature and pressure (Figure 11.8) is a useful quantity. Because the amount (n, mol) of any compound is given by its mass (m) divided by its molar mass (M), we can substitute m/M for n in the ideal gas equation.

$$PV = \left(\frac{m}{M} \right) RT$$

Density (d) is defined as mass divided by volume (m/V). We can rearrange the form of the gas law above to give the following equation, which has the term (m/V) on the left. This is the density of the gas.

$$d = \frac{m}{V} = \frac{PM}{RT} \tag{11.5}$$

FIGURE 11.8 Gas density. (a) The balloons are filled with nearly equal amounts of gas at the same temperature and pressure. One yellow balloon contains helium, a low-density gas ($d = 0.179$ g/L at STP). The other balloons contain air, a higher density gas ($d = 1.2$ g/L at STP). (b) A hot-air balloon rises because the heated air has a lower density than the surrounding air.

(a)   (b)

Charles D. Winters

Greg Gawlowski/Dembinski Associates

FIGURE 11.9 Gas density. Because carbon dioxide from fire extinguishers is denser than air, it settles on top of a fire and smothers it. (When CO_2 gas is released from the tank, it expands and cools significantly. The white cloud is condensed moisture from the air.)

Gas density is directly proportional to the pressure and molar mass and inversely proportional to the temperature. Equation 11.5 is useful because gas density can be calculated from the molar mass, or the molar mass can be found from a measurement of gas density at a given pressure and temperature.

■ **EXAMPLE 11.7 Density and Molar Mass**

Problem Calculate the density of CO_2 at STP. Is CO_2 more or less dense than air?

Strategy Use Equation 11.5, the equation relating gas density and molar mass. Here, we know the molar mass (44.0 g/mol), the pressure ($P = 1.00$ atm), the temperature ($T = 273.15$ K), and the gas constant (R). Only the density (d) is unknown.

Solution The known values are substituted into Equation 11.5, which is then solved for molar mass (M):

$$d = \frac{PM}{RT} = \frac{(1.00 \text{ atm})(44.0 \text{ g/mol})}{(0.082057 \text{ L} \cdot \text{atm/K} \cdot \text{mol})(273 \text{ K})} = \boxed{1.96 \text{ g/L}}$$

The density of CO_2 is considerably greater than that of dry air at STP (1.2 g/L).

EXERCISE 11.7 Gas Density and Molar Mass

The density of an unknown gas is 5.02 g/L at 15.0 °C and 745 mm Hg. Calculate its molar mass.

Gas density has practical implications. From the equation $d = PM/RT$, we recognize that the density of a gas is directly proportional to its molar mass. Dry air, which has an average molar mass of about 29 g/mol, has a density of about 1.2 g/L at 1 atm and 25 °C. Gases or vapors with molar masses greater than 29 g/mol have densities larger than 1.2 g/L under these same conditions (1 atm and 25 °C). Gases such as CO_2, SO_2, and gasoline vapor settle along the ground if released into the atmosphere (Figure 11.9). Conversely, gases such as H_2, He, CO, CH_4 (methane), and NH_3 rise if released into the atmosphere.

The significance of gas density has been revealed in several tragic events. One occurred in the African country of Cameroon in 1984 when Lake Nyos expelled a huge bubble of CO_2 into the atmosphere. Because CO_2 is denser than air, the CO_2 cloud hugged the ground, killing 1700 people nearby (page 630).

Calculating the Molar Mass of a Gas from *P*, *V*, and *T* Data

When a new compound is isolated in the laboratory, one of the first things to be done is to determine its molar mass. If the compound is in the gas phase, a classical method of determining the molar mass is to measure the pressure and volume exerted by a given mass of the gas at a given temperature.

Chemistry.●.Now™

Sign in at **www.cengage.com/login** and go to Chapter 11 Contents to see:
• Screen 11.5 for an exercise on **gas density**
• Screen 11.6 for a tutorial on **using gas laws determining molar mass**

■ **EXAMPLE 11.8 Calculating the Molar Mass of a Gas from *P*, *V*, and *T* Data**

Problem You are trying to determine, by experiment, the formula of a gaseous compound to replace chlorofluorocarbons in air conditioners. You have determined the empirical formula is CHF_2, but now you want to know the molecular formula. To do this, you need the molar mass of the compound. You therefore do another experiment and find that a 0.100-g sample of the compound exerts a pressure of 70.5 mm Hg in a 256-mL container at 22.3 °C. What is the molar mass of the compound? What is its molecular formula?

526 Chapter 11 | Gases and Their Properties

Strategy Here, you know the mass of a gas in a given volume (V), so you can calculate its density, d. Then, knowing the gas pressure and temperature, you can use Equation 11.5 to calculate the molar mass.

Solution Begin by organizing the data:

$$m = \text{mass of gas} = 0.100 \text{ g}$$
$$P = 70.5 \text{ mm Hg, or } 0.0928 \text{ atm}$$
$$V = 256 \text{ mL, or } 0.256 \text{ L}$$
$$T = 22.3 \text{ °C, or } 295.5 \text{ K}$$

The density of the gas is the mass of the gas divided by the volume:

$$d = \frac{0.100 \text{ g}}{0.256 \text{ L}} = 0.391 \text{ g/L}$$

Use this value of density along with the values of pressure and temperature in Equation 11.5 ($d = PM/RT$), and solve for the molar mass (M).

$$M = \frac{dRT}{P} = \frac{(0.391 \text{ g/L})(0.082057 \text{ L} \cdot \text{atm/K} \cdot \text{mol})(295.5 \text{ K})}{0.0928 \text{ atm}} = 102 \text{ g/mol}$$

With this result, you can compare the experimentally determined molar mass with the mass of a mole of gas having the empirical formula CHF_2.

$$\frac{\text{Experimental molar mass}}{\text{Mass of 1 mol } CHF_2} = \frac{102 \text{ g/mol}}{51.0 \text{ g/formula unit}} = 2 \text{ formula units of } CHF_2 \text{ per mol}$$

Therefore, the formula of the compound is $C_2H_2F_4$.

Comment Alternatively, you can use the ideal gas law. Here, you know the P and T of a gas in a given volume (V), so you can calculate the amount of gas (n).

$$n = \frac{PV}{RT} = \frac{(0.0928 \text{ atm})(0.256 \text{ L})}{(0.082057 \text{ L} \cdot \text{atm/K} \cdot \text{mol})(295.5 \text{ K})} = 9.80 \times 10^{-4} \text{ mol}$$

You now know that 0.100 g of gas is equivalent to 9.80×10^{-4} mol. Therefore,

$$\text{Molar mass} = \frac{0.100 \text{ g}}{9.80 \times 10^{-4} \text{ mol}} = 102 \text{ g/mol}$$

EXERCISE 11.8 Molar Mass from *P*, *V*, and *T* Data

A 0.105-g sample of a gaseous compound has a pressure of 561 mm Hg in a volume of 125 mL at 23.0 °C. What is its molar mass?

11.4 Gas Laws and Chemical Reactions

Many industrially important reactions involve gases. Two examples are the combination of nitrogen and hydrogen to produce ammonia,

$$N_2(g) + 3 H_2(g) \longrightarrow 2 NH_3(g)$$

and the electrolysis of aqueous NaCl to produce hydrogen and chlorine,

$$2 NaCl(aq) + 2 H_2O (\ell) \longrightarrow 2 NaOH(aq) + H_2(g) + Cl_2(g)$$

If we want to understand the quantitative aspects of such reactions, we need to carry out stoichiometry calculations. The scheme in Figure 11.10 connects these calculations for gas reactions with the stoichiometry calculations in Chapter 4.

Chemistry⊹Now™

Sign in at **www.cengage.com/login** and go to Chapter 11 Contents to see Screen 11.7 for a tutorial on **gas laws and chemical reactions: stoichiometry.**

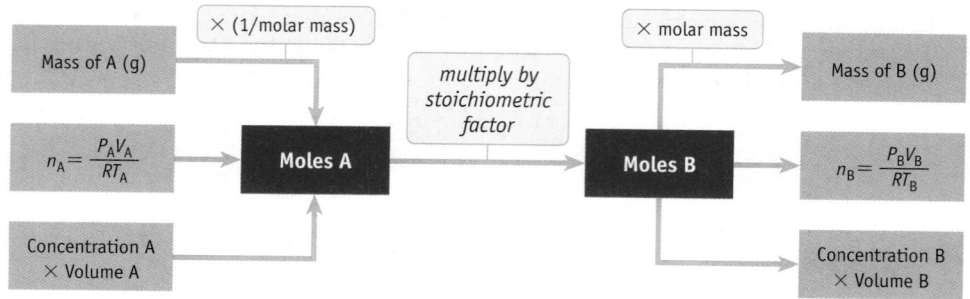

FIGURE 11.10 A scheme for stoichiometry calculations. Here, A and B may be either reactants or products. The amount of A (mol) can be calculated from its mass in grams and its molar mass, from the concentration and volume of a solution, or from P, V, and T data by using the ideal gas law. Once the amount of B is determined, this value can be converted to a mass or solution concentration or volume, or to a volume of gas at a given pressure and temperature.

EXAMPLE 11.9 Gas Laws and Stoichiometry

Problem You are asked to design an air bag for a car. You know that the bag should be filled with gas with a pressure higher than atmospheric pressure, say 829 mm Hg, at a temperature of 22.0 °C. The bag has a volume of 45.5 L. What quantity of sodium azide, NaN_3, should be used to generate the required quantity of gas? The gas-producing reaction is

$$2\ NaN_3(s) \longrightarrow 2\ Na(s) + 3\ N_2(g)$$

Strategy The general logic to be used here follows a pathway in Figure 11.10.

Use $PV = nRT$ with gas data $\longrightarrow$ Amount of N_2 required $\longrightarrow$ Use stoichiometric factor to calculate amount of NaN_3 required $\longrightarrow$ Use molar mass to calculate mass of NaN_3 required

Solution The first step is to find the amount (mol) of gas required so that this can be related to the quantity of sodium azide required:

$$P = 829\ \text{mm Hg (1 atm/760 mm Hg)} = 1.09\ \text{atm}$$

$$V = 45.5\ \text{L}$$

$$T = 22.0\ °\text{C, or } 295.2\ \text{K}$$

$$n = N_2\ \text{required (mol)} = \frac{PV}{RT}$$

$$n = \frac{(1.09\ \text{atm})(45.5\ \text{L})}{(0.082057\ \text{L} \cdot \text{atm/K} \cdot \text{mol})(295.2\ \text{K})} = 2.05\ \text{mol}\ N_2$$

Now that the required amount of nitrogen has been calculated, we can calculate the quantity of sodium azide that will produce 2.05 mol of N_2 gas.

$$\text{Mass of } NaN_3 = 2.05\ \text{mol}\ N_2 \left(\frac{2\ \text{mol}\ NaN_3}{3\ \text{mol}\ N_2}\right)\left(\frac{65.01\ \text{g}}{1\ \text{mol}\ NaN_3}\right) = \boxed{88.8\ \text{g}\ NaN_3}$$

EXAMPLE 11.10 Gas Laws and Stoichiometry

Problem You wish to prepare some deuterium gas, D_2, for use in an experiment. One way to do this is to react heavy water, D_2O, with an active metal such as lithium.

$$2\ Li(s) + 2\ D_2O(\ell) \longrightarrow 2\ LiOD(aq) + D_2(g)$$

What amount of D_2 (in moles) can be prepared from 0.125 g of Li metal in 15.0 mL of D_2O ($d = 1.11$ g/mL). If dry D_2 gas is captured in a 1450-mL flask at 22.0 °C, what is the pressure of the gas in mm Hg? (Deuterium has an atomic weight of 2.0147 g/mol.)

Strategy You are combining two reactants with no guarantee that they are in the correct stoichiometric ratio. This example must therefore be approached as a limiting reactant problem. You have to find the amount of each substance and then see if one of them is present in a limited amount. Once the limiting reactant is known, the amount of D_2 produced and its pressure under the conditions given can be calculated.

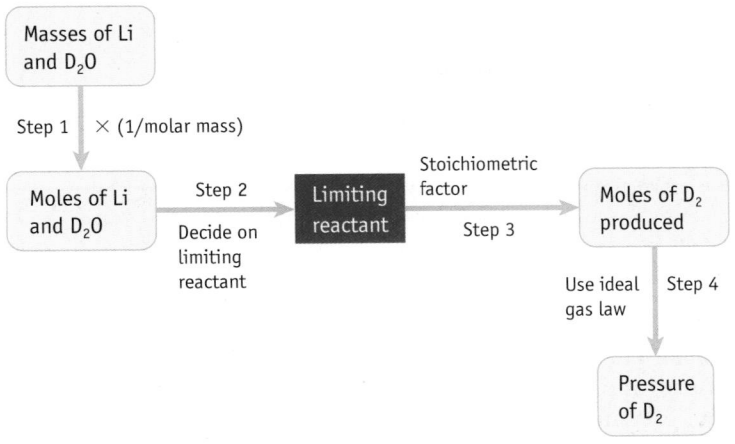

Lithium metal (in the spoon) reacts with drops of water, H_2O, to produce LiOH and hydrogen gas, H_2. If heavy water, D_2O, is used, deuterium gas, D_2, can be produced.

Solution

Step 1. *Calculate the amount (mol) of Li and of D_2O:*

$$0.125 \text{ g Li} \left(\frac{1 \text{ mol Li}}{6.941 \text{ g Li}} \right) = 0.0180 \text{ mol Li}$$

$$15.0 \text{ mL } D_2O \left(\frac{1.11 \text{ g } D_2O}{1 \text{ mL } D_2O} \right) \left(\frac{1 \text{ mol } D_2O}{20.03 \text{ g } D_2O} \right) = 0.831 \text{ mol } D_2O$$

Step 2. *Decide which reactant is the limiting reactant:*

$$\text{Ratio of moles of reactants available} = \frac{0.831 \text{ mol } D_2O}{0.0180 \text{ mol Li}} = \frac{46.2 \text{ mol } D_2O}{1 \text{ mol Li}}$$

The balanced equation shows that the ratio should be 1 mol of D_2O to 1 mol of Li. From the calculated values, we see that D_2O is in large excess, and so Li is the limiting reactant. Therefore, further calculations are based on the amount of Li available.

Step 3. *Use the limiting reactant to calculate the quantity of D_2 produced:*

$$0.0180 \text{ mol Li} \left(\frac{1 \text{ mol } D_2 \text{ produced}}{2 \text{ mol Li}} \right) = 0.00900 \text{ mol } D_2 \text{ produced}$$

Step 4. *Calculate the pressure of D_2:*

$P = ?$ $T = 22.0 \text{ °C, or } 295.2 \text{ K}$

$V = 1450 \text{ mL, or } 1.45 \text{ L}$ $n = 0.00900 \text{ mol } D_2$

$$P = \frac{nRT}{V} = \frac{(0.00900 \text{ mol})(0.082057 \text{ L} \cdot \text{atm/K} \cdot \text{mol})(295.2 \text{ K})}{1.45 \text{ L}} = \boxed{0.150 \text{ atm}}$$

EXERCISE 11.9 Gas Laws and Stoichiometry

Gaseous ammonia is synthesized by the reaction

$$N_2(g) + 3 \text{ } H_2(g) \longrightarrow 2 \text{ } NH_3(g)$$

Assume that 355 L of H_2 gas at 25.0 °C and 542 mm Hg is combined with excess N_2 gas. What amount of NH_3 gas, in moles, can be produced? If this amount of NH_3 gas is stored in a 125-L tank at 25.0 °C, what is the pressure of the gas?

TABLE 11.1 Components of Atmospheric Dry Air

Constituent	Molar Mass*	Mole Percent	Partial Pressure at STP (atm)
N_2	28.01	78.08	0.7808
O_2	32.00	20.95	0.2095
CO_2	44.01	0.0385	0.00033
Ar	39.95	0.934	0.00934

*The average molar mass of dry air = 28.960 g/mol.

11.5 Gas Mixtures and Partial Pressures

The air you breathe is a mixture of nitrogen, oxygen, argon, carbon dioxide, water vapor, and small amounts of other gases (Table 11.1). Each of these gases exerts its own pressure, and atmospheric pressure is the sum of the pressures exerted by each gas. The pressure of each gas in the mixture is called its **partial pressure.**

John Dalton (1766–1844) was the first to observe that the pressure of a mixture of ideal gases is the sum of the partial pressures of the different gases in the mixture. This observation is now known as **Dalton's law of partial pressures** (Figure 11.11). Mathematically, we can write Dalton's law of partial pressures as

$$P_{total} = P_1 + P_2 + P_3 \ldots \tag{11.6}$$

where P_1, P_2, and P_3 are the pressures of the different gases in a mixture, and P_{total} is the total pressure.

In a mixture of gases, each gas behaves independently of all others in the mixture. Therefore, we can consider the behavior of each gas in a mixture separately. As an example, let us take a mixture of three ideal gases, labeled A, B, and C. There are n_A moles of A, n_B moles of B, and n_C moles of C. Assume that the mixture ($n_{total} = n_A + n_B + n_C$) is contained in a given volume (V) at a given temperature (T). We can calculate the pressure exerted by each gas from the ideal gas law equation:

$$P_A V = n_A RT \qquad P_B V = n_B RT \qquad P_C V = n_C RT$$

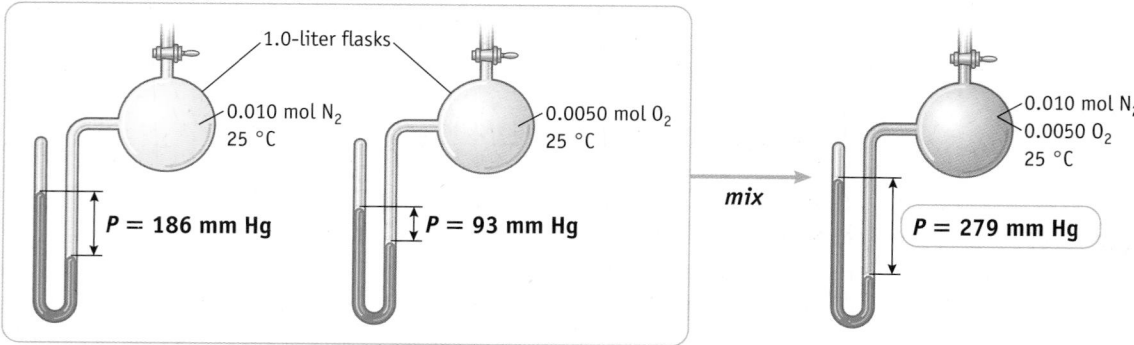

FIGURE 11.11 Dalton's law. In a 1.0-L flask at 25 °C, 0.010 mol of N_2 exerts a pressure of 186 mm Hg, and 0.0050 mol of O_2 in a 1.0-L flask at 25 °C exerts a pressure of 93 mm Hg (left and middle). The N_2 and O_2 samples are mixed in a 1.0-L flask at 25 °C (right). The total pressure, 279 mm Hg, is the sum of the pressures that each gas alone exerts in the flask.

where each gas (A, B, and C) is in the same volume V and is at the same temperature T. According to Dalton's law, the total pressure exerted by the mixture is the sum of the pressures exerted by each component:

$$P_{total} = P_A + P_B + P_C = n_A\left(\frac{RT}{V}\right) + n_B\left(\frac{RT}{V}\right) + n_C\left(\frac{RT}{V}\right)$$

$$P_{total} = (n_A + n_B + n_C)\left(\frac{RT}{V}\right)$$

$$P_{total} = (n_{total})\left(\frac{RT}{V}\right) \tag{11.7}$$

For mixtures of gases, it is convenient to introduce a quantity called the **mole fraction, X**, which is defined as the number of moles of a particular substance in a mixture divided by the total number of moles of all substances present. Mathematically, the mole fraction of a substance A in a mixture with B and C is expressed as

$$X_A = \frac{n_A}{n_A + n_B + n_C} = \frac{n_A}{n_{total}}$$

Now we can combine this equation (written as $n_{total} = n_A/X_A$) with the equations for P_A and P_{total}, and derive the equation

$$P_A = X_A P_{total} \tag{11.8}$$

This equation is useful because it tells us that *the pressure of a gas in a mixture of gases is the product of its mole fraction and the total pressure of the mixture.* For example, the mole fraction of N_2 in air is 0.78, so, at STP, its partial pressure is 0.78 atm or 590 mm Hg.

Chemistry.⚬.Now™

Sign in at **www.cengage.com/login** and go to Chapter 11 Contents to see Screen 11.8 for tutorials on **gas mixtures and partial pressures.**

EXAMPLE 11.11 Partial Pressures of Gases

Problem Halothane, $C_2HBrClF_3$, is a nonflammable, nonexplosive, and nonirritating gas that is commonly used as an inhalation anesthetic.

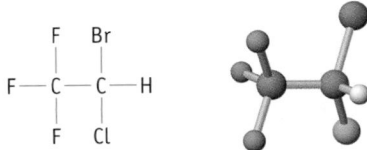

1,1,1-trifluorobromochloroethane, halothane

The total pressure of a mixture of 15.0 g of halothane vapor and 23.5 g of oxygen gas is 855 mm Hg. What is the partial pressure of each gas?

Strategy One way to solve this problem is to recognize that the partial pressure of a gas is given by the total pressure of the mixture multiplied by the mole fraction of the gas.

FIGURE 11.12 A molecular view of gases and liquids. The fact that a large volume of N_2 gas can be condensed to a small volume of liquid indicates that the distance between molecules in the gas phase is very large as compared with the distances between molecules in liquids.

Charles D. Winters

Solution Let us first calculate the mole fractions of halothane and of O_2.

Step 1. *Calculate mole fractions:*

$$\text{Amount of } C_2HBrClF_3 = 15.0 \text{ g}\left(\frac{1 \text{ mol}}{197.4 \text{ g}}\right) = 0.0760 \text{ mol}$$

$$\text{Amount of } O_2 = 23.5 \text{ g}\left(\frac{1 \text{ mol}}{32.00 \text{ g}}\right) = 0.734 \text{ mol}$$

$$\text{Total amount of gas} = 0.0760 \text{ mol } C_2HBrClF_2 + 0.734 \text{ mol } O_2 = 0.810 \text{ mol}$$

$$\text{Mole fraction of } C_2HBrClF_3 = \frac{0.0760 \text{ mol } C_2HBrClF_3}{0.810 \text{ total moles}} = 0.0938$$

Because the sum of the mole fraction of halothane and of O_2 must equal 1.0000, this means that the mole fraction of oxygen is 0.906.

$$X_{\text{halothane}} + X_{\text{oxygen}} = 1.0000$$

$$0.0938 + X_{\text{oxygen}} = 1.0000$$

$$X_{\text{oxygen}} = 0.906$$

Step 2. *Calculate partial pressures:*

$$\text{Partial pressure of halothane} = P_{\text{halothane}} = X_{\text{halothane}} \cdot P_{\text{total}}$$

$$P_{\text{halothane}} = 0.0938 \cdot P_{\text{total}} = 0.0938 \,(855 \text{ mm Hg})$$

$$P_{\text{halothane}} = \boxed{80.2 \text{ mm Hg}}$$

The total pressure of the mixture is the sum of the partial pressures of the gases in the mixture.

$$P_{\text{halothane}} + P_{\text{oxygen}} = 855 \text{ mm Hg}$$

and so

$$P_{\text{oxygen}} = 855 \text{ mm Hg} - P_{\text{halothane}}$$

$$P_{\text{oxygen}} = 855 \text{ mm Hg} - 80.2 \text{ mm Hg} = \boxed{775 \text{ mm Hg}}$$

EXERCISE 11.10 Partial Pressures

The halothane–oxygen mixture described in Example 11.11 is placed in a 5.00-L tank at 25.0 °C. What is the total pressure (in mm Hg) of the gas mixture in the tank? What are the partial pressures (in mm Hg) of the gases?

 Module 16

11.6 The Kinetic-Molecular Theory of Gases

So far, we have discussed the macroscopic properties of gases, properties such as pressure and volume that result from the behavior of a system with a large number of particles. Now we turn to the kinetic-molecular theory (◄ page 7) for a description of the behavior of matter at the molecular or atomic level. Hundreds of experimental observations have led to the following postulates regarding the behavior of gases.

- Gases consist of particles (molecules or atoms) whose separation is much greater than the size of the particles themselves (see Figure 11.12).
- The particles of a gas are in continual, random, and rapid motion. As they move, they collide with one another and with the walls of their container, but they do so without loss of energy.
- The average kinetic energy of gas particles is proportional to the gas temperature. *All gases, regardless of their molecular mass, have the same average kinetic energy at the same temperature.*

Let us discuss the behavior of gases from this point of view.

Robert Boyle (1627–1691) was born in Ireland as the 14th and last child of the first Earl of Cork. In his book *Uncle Tungsten*, Oliver Sacks tells us that "Chemistry as a true science made its first emergence with the work of Robert Boyle in the middle of the seventeenth century. Twenty years [Isaac] Newton's senior, Boyle was born at a time when the practice of alchemy still held sway, and he still maintained a variety of alchemical beliefs and practices, side by side with his scientific ones. He believed gold could be created, and that he had succeeded in creating it (Newton, also an alchemist, advised him to keep silent about this)."

Boyle examined crystals, explored color, devised an acid-base indicator from the syrup of violets, and provided the first modern definition of an element. He was also a physiologist, and was the first to show that the healthy human body has a constant

Robert Boyle (1627–1691).

temperature. Today, Boyle is best known for his studies of gases, which were described in his book *The Sceptical Chymist*, published in 1680.

The French chemist and inventor Jacques Alexandre César Charles began his career as a clerk in the finance ministry, but his real interest was science. He developed several inventions and was best known in

Jacques Alexandre César Charles (1746–1823).

his lifetime for inventing the hydrogen balloon. In August 1783, Charles exploited his recent studies on hydrogen gas by inflating a balloon with this gas. Because hydrogen would escape easily from a paper bag, he made a silk bag coated with rubber. Inflating the bag took several days and required nearly 225 kg of sulfuric acid and 450 kg of iron to produce the H_2 gas. The balloon stayed aloft for almost 45 minutes and traveled about 15 miles. When it landed in a village, however, the people were so terrified they tore it to

Jacques Charles and A. Roberts ascended over Paris on December 1, 1783, in a hydrogen-filled balloon.

shreds. Several months later, Charles and a passenger flew a new hydrogen-filled balloon some distance across the French countryside and ascended to the then-incredible altitude of 2 miles.

Molecular Speed and Kinetic Energy

If your friend walks into your room carrying a pizza, how do you know it? In scientific terms, we know that the odor-causing molecules of food enter the gas phase and drift through space until they reach the cells of your body that react to odors. The same thing happens in the laboratory when bottles of aqueous ammonia (NH_3) and hydrochloric acid (HCl) sit side by side (Figure 11.13). Molecules of the two compounds enter the gas phase and drift along until they encounter one another, at which time they react and form a cloud of tiny particles of solid ammonium chloride (NH_4Cl).

If you change the temperature of the environment of the containers in Figure 11.13 and measure the time needed for the cloud of ammonium chloride to form, you would find the time would be longer at lower temperatures. The reason for this is that the speed at which molecules move depends on the temperature. Let us expand on this idea.

The molecules in a gas sample do not all move at the same speed. Rather, as illustrated in Figure 11.14 for O_2 molecules, there is a distribution of speeds. Figure 11.14 shows the number of particles in a gas sample that are moving at certain speeds at a given temperature, and there are two important observations we can make. First, at a given temperature some molecules have high speeds, and others have low speeds. Most of the molecules, however, have some intermediate speed, and their most probable speed corresponds to the maximum in the curve. For oxygen gas at 25 °C, for example, most molecules have speeds in the range

FIGURE 11.13 The movement of gas molecules. Open dishes of aqueous ammonia and hydrochloric acid are placed side by side. When molecules of NH_3 and HCl escape from solution to the atmosphere and encounter one another, a cloud of solid ammonium chloride, NH_4Cl is observed.

Earth's atmosphere is a fascinating mixture of gases in more or less distinct layers with widely differing temperatures.

Up to the troposphere, there is a gradual decline in temperature (and pressure) with altitude. The temperature climbs again in the stratosphere due to the absorption of energy from the sun by stratospheric ozone, O_3.

Above the stratosphere, the pressure declines because there are fewer molecules present. At still higher altitudes, we observe a dramatic increase in temperature in the thermosphere. This is an illustration of the difference between *temperature* and *thermal energy*. The temperature of a gas reflects the average kinetic energy of the molecules of the gas, whereas the thermal energy present in an object is the *total* kinetic energy of the molecules. In the thermosphere, the few molecules present have a very high temperature, but the thermal energy is exceedingly small because there are so few molecules.

Gases within the troposphere are well mixed by convection. Pollutants that are evolved on Earth's surface can rise into the stratosphere, but it is said that the stratosphere acts as a "thermal lid" on the troposphere and prevents significant mixing of polluting gases into the stratosphere and beyond.

The pressure of the atmosphere declines with altitude, and so the partial pressure of O_2 declines. The figure shows why climbers have a hard time breathing on Mt. Everest, where the altitude is 29,028 ft (8848 m) and the O_2 partial pressure is only 29% of the sea level partial pressure. With proper training, a climber could reach the summit without supplemental oxygen. However, this same feat would not be possible if Everest were farther north. Earth's atmosphere thins toward the poles, and so the O_2 partial pressure would be even less if Everest's summit were in North America, for example.

(See G. N. Eby, *Environmental Geochemistry*, Thomson/Brooks/Cole, 2004.)

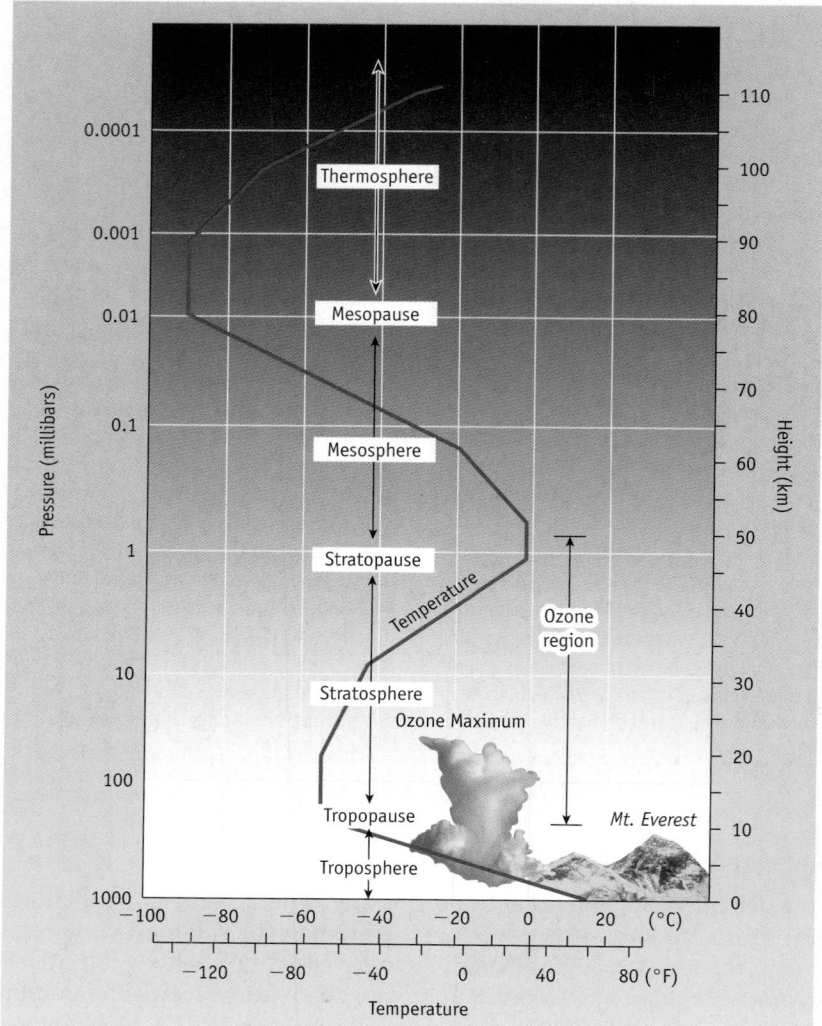

Average Composition of Earth's Atmosphere to a Height of 25 km

Gas	Volume %	Source
N_2	78.08	biologic
O_2	20.95	biologic
Ar	0.93	radioactivity
Ne	0.0018	Earth's interior
He	0.0005	radioactivity
H_2O	0 to 4	evaporation
CO_2	0.0385	biologic, industrial
CH_4	0.00017	biologic
N_2O	0.00003	biologic, industrial
O_3	0.000004	photochemical

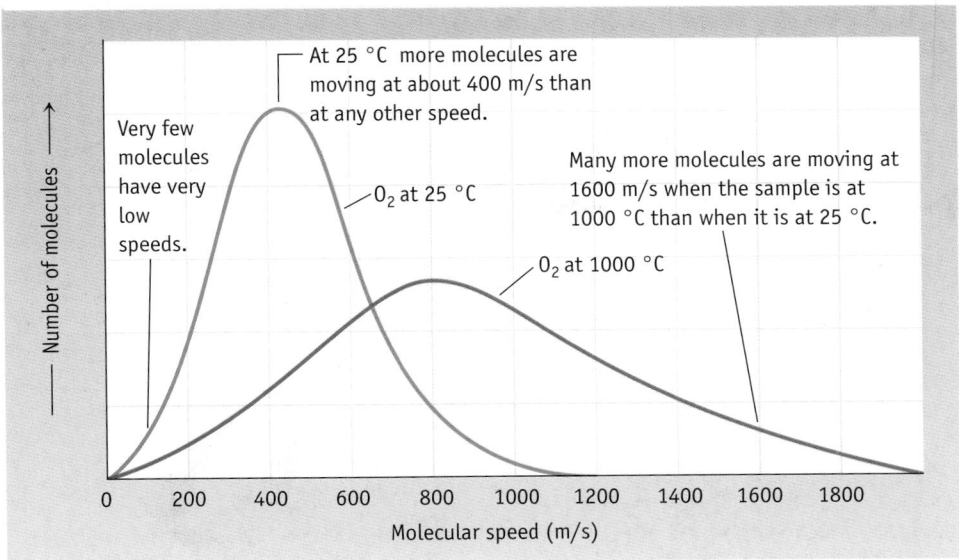

FIGURE 11.14 The distribution of molecular speeds. A graph of the number of molecules with a given speed versus that speed shows the distribution of molecular speeds. The red curve shows the effect of increased temperature. Even though the curve for the higher temperature is "flatter" and broader than the one at a lower temperature, the areas under the curves are the same because the number of molecules in the sample is fixed.

In the figure:
- At 25 °C more molecules are moving at about 400 m/s than at any other speed.
- Very few molecules have very low speeds.
- O_2 at 25 °C
- Many more molecules are moving at 1600 m/s when the sample is at 1000 °C than when it is at 25 °C.
- O_2 at 1000 °C

Axis labels: Number of molecules (vertical); Molecular speed (m/s) (horizontal), with gridlines at 0, 200, 400, 600, 800, 1000, 1200, 1400, 1600, 1800.

from 200 m/s to 700 m/s, and their most probable speed is about 400 m/s. (These are very high speeds, indeed. A speed of 400 m/s corresponds to about 1000 miles per hour!)

A second observation regarding the distribution of speeds is that as the temperature increases the most probable speed increases, and the number of molecules traveling at very high speeds increases greatly.

The kinetic energy of a single molecule of mass m in a gas sample is given by the equation

$$KE = \frac{1}{2}(mass)(speed)^2 = \frac{1}{2}\,mu^2$$

where u is the speed of that molecule. We can calculate the kinetic energy of a single gas molecule from this equation but not of a collection of molecules because not all of the molecules in a gas sample are moving at the same speed. However, we can calculate the average kinetic energy of a collection of molecules by relating it to other averaged quantities of the system. In particular, the average kinetic energy is related to the average speed:

$$\overline{KE} = \frac{1}{2}\,\overline{mu^2}$$

(The horizontal bar over the symbols KE and u indicate an average value.) This equation states that the average kinetic energy of the molecules in a gas sample, $\overline{KE}$, is related to $\overline{u^2}$, the average of the squares of their speeds (called the "mean square speed").

Experiments also show that the average kinetic energy, $\overline{KE}$, of a sample of gas molecules is directly proportional to temperature with a proportionality constant of $\frac{3}{2}R$,

$$\overline{KE} = \frac{3}{2}RT$$

where R is the gas constant expressed in SI units (8.314472 J/K · mol).

Now, because $\overline{KE}$ is proportional to both $\frac{1}{2}\,\overline{mu^2}$ and T, temperature and $\frac{1}{2}\,\overline{mu^2}$ must also be proportional; that is, $\frac{1}{2}\,\overline{mu^2} \propto T$. This relation among

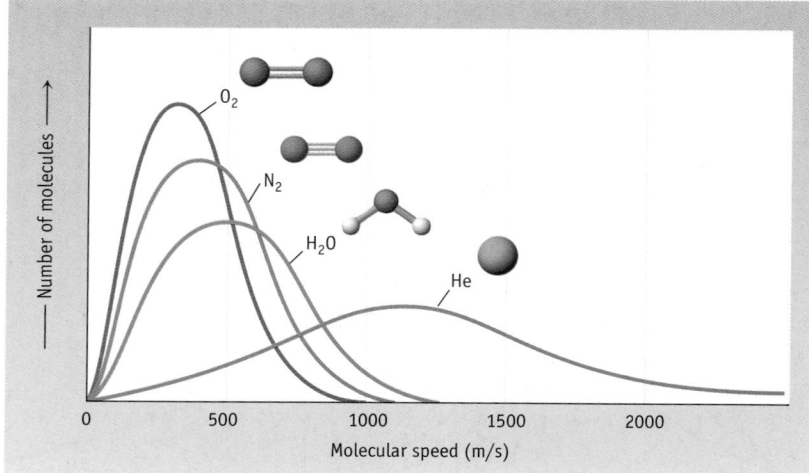

- **Maxwell–Boltzmann Curves** Plots showing the relation between the number of molecules and their speed or energy (Figure 11.14) are often called Maxwell–Boltzmann distribution curves. They are named after James Clerk Maxwell (1831–1879) and Ludwig Boltzmann (1844–1906). The distribution of speeds (or kinetic energies) of molecules (as illustrated by Figures 11.14 and 11.15) is often used when explaining chemical phenomena.

mass, average speed, and temperature is expressed in Equation 11.9. Here, the square root of the mean square speed ($\sqrt{u^2}$, called the **root-mean-square, or rms speed**), the temperature (T, in kelvins), and the molar mass (M) are related.

$$\sqrt{\overline{u^2}} = \sqrt{\frac{3RT}{M}}$$

(11.9)

This equation, sometimes called *Maxwell's equation* after James Clerk Maxwell (Section 6.1), shows that the speeds of gas molecules are indeed related directly to the temperature (Figure 11.14). The rms speed is a useful quantity because of its direct relationship to the average kinetic energy and because it is very close to the true average speed for a sample. (The average speed is 92% of the rms speed.)

All gases have the same average kinetic energy at the same temperature. However, if you compare a sample of one gas with another, say compare O_2 and N_2, this does not mean the molecules have the same average speed (Figure 11.15). Instead, Maxwell's equation shows that the smaller the molar mass of the gas the greater the rms speed.

Chemistry.⚛.Now™

Sign in at **www.cengage.com/login** and go to Chapter 11 Contents to see:
- Screen 11.9 for a self-study module on **gases at different temperatures**
- Screen 11.11 for a tutorial on **Boltzmann distribution and calculation of distribution curves**

■ **EXAMPLE 11.12 Molecular Speed**

Problem Calculate the rms speed of oxygen molecules at 25 °C.

Strategy We must use Equation 11.9 with M in units of kg/mol. The reason for this is that R is in units of J/K · mol, and 1 J = 1 kg · m²/s².

Solution The molar mass of O_2 is 32.0×10^{-3} kg/mol.

$$\sqrt{\overline{u^2}} = \sqrt{\frac{3(8.3145 \text{ J/K} \cdot \text{mol})(298 \text{ K})}{32.0 \times 10^{-3} \text{ kg/mol}}} = \sqrt{2.32 \times 10^5 \text{ J/kg}}$$

To obtain the answer in meters per second, we use the relation $1\ J = 1\ kg \cdot m^2/s^2$. This means we have

$$\sqrt{\overline{u^2}} = \sqrt{2.32 \times 10^5\ kg \cdot m^2/(kg \cdot s^2)} = \sqrt{2.32 \times 10^5\ m^2/s^2} = \boxed{482\ m/s}$$

This speed is equivalent to about 1100 miles per hour!

EXERCISE 11.11 Molecular Speeds

Calculate the rms speeds of helium atoms and N_2 molecules at 25 °C.

Kinetic-Molecular Theory and the Gas Laws

The gas laws, which come from experiment, can be explained by the kinetic-molecular theory. The starting place is to describe how pressure arises from collisions of gas molecules with the walls of the container holding the gas (Figure 11.16). Remember that pressure is related to the force of the collisions (see Section 11.1).

$$\text{Gas pressure} = \frac{\text{force of collisions}}{\text{area}}$$

The force exerted by the collisions depends on the number of collisions and the average force per collision. When the temperature of a gas is increased, we know the average kinetic energy of the molecules increases. This causes the average force of the collisions with the walls to increase as well. (This is much like the difference in the force exerted by a car traveling at high speed versus one moving at only a few kilometers per hour.) Also, because the speed of gas molecules increases with temperature, more collisions occur per second. Thus, the collective force per square centimeter is greater, and the pressure increases. Mathematically, this is related to the direct proportionality between P and T when n and V are fixed, that is, $P = (nR/V)T$.

Increasing the number of molecules of a gas at a fixed temperature and volume does not change the average collision force, but it does increase the number of collisions occurring per second. Thus, the pressure increases, and we can say that P is proportional to n when V and T are constant, that is, $P = n(RT/V)$.

If the pressure is to remain constant when either the number of molecules of gas or the temperature is increased, then the volume of the container (and the area over which the collisions can take place) must increase. This is expressed by stating that V is proportional to nT when P is constant [$V = nT(R/P)$], a statement that is a *combination of Avogadro's hypothesis and Charles's law*.

Finally, if the temperature is constant, the average impact force of molecules of a given mass with the container walls must be constant. If n is kept constant while the volume of the container is made smaller, the number of collisions with the container walls per second must increase. This means the pressure increases, and so P is proportional to $1/V$ when n and T are constant, as stated by *Boyle's law*, that is, $P = (1/V)(nRT)$.

Chemistry ☍ Now™

Sign in at **www.cengage.com/login** and go to Chapter 11 Contents to see Screen 11.10 for simulations of **the gas laws at the molecular level.**

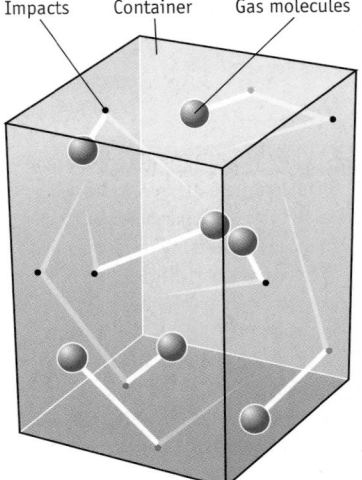

Impacts   Container   Gas molecules

FIGURE 11.16 Gas pressure.
According to the kinetic-molecular theory, gas pressure is caused by gas molecules bombarding the container walls.

Charles D. Winters

(a)   (b)

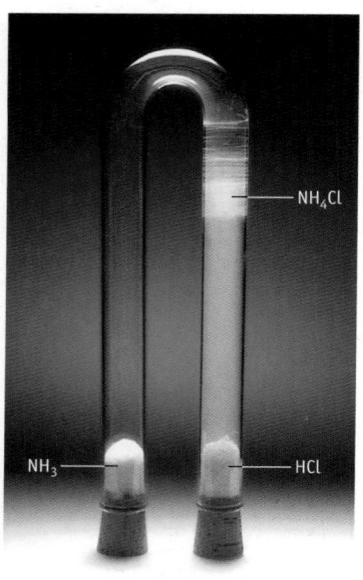

NH₄Cl

NH₃   HCl

Charles D. Winters

Active Figure 11.18 **Gaseous diffusion.** Here, HCl gas (from hydrochloric acid) and ammonia gas (from aqueous ammonia) diffuse from opposite ends of a glass U-tube. When they meet, they produce white, solid NH_4Cl. It is clear that the NH_4Cl is formed closer to the end from which the HCl gas begins because HCl molecules move slower on average than NH_3 molecules. See also Figure 11.13.

Chemistry **Now**™ Sign in at www. cengage.com/login and go to the Chapter Contents menu to explore an interactive version of this figure accompanied by an exercise.

11.7 Diffusion and Effusion

When a pizza is brought into a room, the volatile aroma-causing molecules vaporize into the atmosphere, where they mix with the oxygen, nitrogen, carbon dioxide, water vapor, and other gases present. Even if there were no movement of the air in the room caused by fans or people moving about, the odor would eventually reach everywhere in the room. This mixing of molecules of two or more gases due to their random molecular motions is the result of **diffusion.** Given time, the molecules of one component in a gas mixture will thoroughly and completely mix with all other components of the mixture (Figure 11.17).

Diffusion is also illustrated by the experiment in Figure 11.18. Here, we have placed cotton moistened with hydrochloric acid at one end of a U-tube and cotton moistened with aqueous ammonia at the other end. Molecules of HCl and NH_3 diffuse into the tube, and, when they meet, they produce white, solid NH_4Cl (just as in Figure 11.13).

$$HCl(g) + NH_3(g) \rightarrow NH_4Cl(s)$$

We find that the gases do not meet in the middle. Rather, because the heavier HCl molecules diffuse less rapidly than the lighter NH_3 molecules, the molecules meet closer to the HCl end of the U-tube.

Closely related to diffusion is **effusion**, which is the movement of gas through a tiny opening in a container into another container where the pressure is very low (Figure 11.19). Thomas Graham (1805–1869), a Scottish chemist, studied the effusion of gases and found that the rate of effusion of a gas—the amount of gas moving from one place to another in a given amount of time—is inversely proportional to the square root of its molar mass. Based on these experimental results, the rates of effusion of two gases can be compared:

$$\frac{\text{Rate of effusion of gas 1}}{\text{Rate of effusion of gas 2}} = \sqrt{\frac{\text{molar mass of gas 2}}{\text{molar mass of gas 1}}} \qquad (11.10)$$

The relationship in Equation 11.10—now known as **Graham's law**—is readily derived from Maxwell's equation by recognizing that the rate of effusion depends on

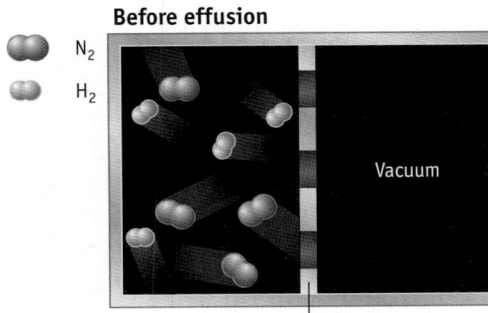

Before effusion

N₂

H₂

Vacuum

Porous barrier

During effusion

FIGURE 11.19 Effusion. H_2 and N_2 gas molecules effuse through the pores of a porous barrier. Lighter molecules (H_2) with higher average speeds strike the barrier more often and pass more often through it than heavier, slower molecules (N_2) at the same temperature. According to Graham's law, H_2 molecules effuse 3.72 times faster than N_2 molecules.

the speed of the molecules. The ratio of the rms speeds is the same as the ratio of the effusion rates:

$$\frac{\text{Rate of effusion of gas 1}}{\text{Rate of effusion of gas 2}} = \frac{\sqrt{u^2 \text{ of gas 1}}}{\sqrt{u^2 \text{ of gas 2}}} = \frac{\sqrt{3RT/(M \text{ of gas 1})}}{\sqrt{3RT/(M \text{ of gas 2})}}$$

Canceling out like terms gives the expression in Equation 11.10.

Chemistry ⬡ Now™

Sign in at **www.cengage.com/login** and go to Chapter 11 Contents to see screen 11.12 for an exercise and tutorial on **diffusion**.

■ **EXAMPLE 11.13 Using Graham's Law of Effusion to Calculate a Molar Mass**

Problem Tetrafluoroethylene, C_2F_4, effuses through a barrier at a rate of 4.6×10^{-6} mol/h. An unknown gas, consisting only of boron and hydrogen, effuses at the rate of 5.8×10^{-6} mol/h under the same conditions. What is the molar mass of the unknown gas?

Strategy From Graham's law, we know that a light molecule will effuse more rapidly than a heavier one. Because the unknown gas effuses more rapidly than C_2F_4 ($M = 100.0$ g/mol), the unknown must have a molar mass less than 100 g/mol. Substitute the experimental data into Graham's law equation (Equation 11.10).

Solution

$$\frac{5.8 \times 10^{-6} \text{ mol/h}}{4.6 \times 10^{-6} \text{ mol/h}} = 1.3 = \sqrt{\frac{100.0 \text{ g/mol}}{M \text{ of unknown}}}$$

To solve for the unknown molar mass, square both sides of the equation and rearrange to find M for the unknown.

$$1.6 = \frac{100.0 \text{ g/mol}}{M \text{ of unknown}}$$

$$M = \boxed{63 \text{ g/mol}}$$

Comment A boron–hydrogen compound corresponding to this molar mass is B_5H_9, called pentaborane.

EXERCISE 11.12 Graham's Law

A sample of pure methane, CH_4, is found to effuse through a porous barrier in 1.50 min. Under the same conditions, an equal number of molecules of an unknown gas effuses through the barrier in 4.73 min. What is the molar mass of the unknown gas?

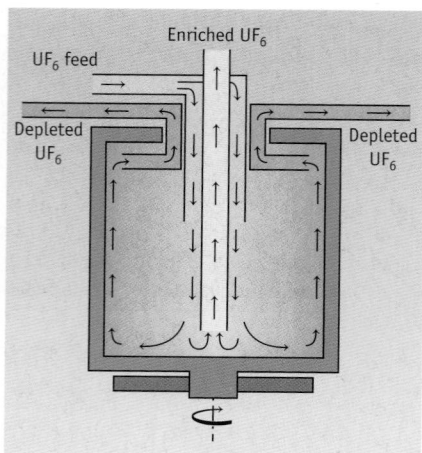

11.8 Some Applications of the Gas Laws and Kinetic-Molecular Theory

Separating Isotopes

The effusion process played a central role in the development of the atomic bomb in World War II and is still in use today to prepare fissionable uranium for nuclear power plants. Naturally occurring uranium exists primarily as two isotopes: ^{235}U (0.720% abundant) and ^{238}U (99.275% abundant). However, because only the lighter isotope, ^{235}U, is suitable as a fuel in reactors, uranium ore must be enriched in this isotope.

Gas effusion is one way to separate the ^{235}U and ^{238}U isotopes. To achieve this, a uranium oxide sample is first converted to uranium hexafluoride, UF_6. This solid fluoride sublimes readily; it has a vapor pressure of 760 mm Hg at 55.6 °C. When UF_6 vapor is placed is a chamber with porous walls, the lighter, more rapidly moving $^{235}UF_6$ molecules effuse through the walls at a greater rate than the heavier $^{238}UF_6$ molecules.

To assess the separation of uranium isotopes, let us compare the rates of effusion of $^{235}UF_6$ and $^{238}UF_6$. Using Graham's law,

$$\frac{\text{Rate of } ^{235}UF_6}{\text{Rate of } ^{238}UF_6} = \sqrt{\frac{238.051 + 6(18.998)}{235.044 + 6(18.998)}} = 1.0043$$

we find that $^{235}UF_6$ will pass through a porous barrier 1.0043 times faster than $^{238}UF_6$. In other words, if we sample the gas that passes through the barrier, the fraction of $^{235}UF_6$ molecules will be larger. If the process is carried out again on the sample now higher in $^{235}UF_6$ concentration, the fraction of $^{235}UF_6$ would again increase in the effused sample, and the separation factor is now 1.0043×1.0043. If the cycle is repeated over and over again, the separation factor is 1.0043^n, where n is the number of enrichment cycles. To achieve a separation of about 99%, hundreds of cycles are required!

Deep Sea Diving

Diving with a self-contained underwater breathing apparatus (SCUBA) is exciting. If you want to dive much beyond about 60 ft (18 m) or so, however, you need to take special precautions.

Do those dirty old sneakers in your closet stink? Did your friends ever tell you you have halitosis, the polite term for bad breath? Did your roommates ever experience flatulence (a malodorous gaseous emission, to say it politely) after eating too many beans? Or have you ever smelled the odor from a paper-making plant or from brackish water? The bad odors in all these cases can come from several gaseous, sulfur-containing compounds. Hydrogen sulfide (H_2S) and dimethylsulfide (CH_3SCH_3) are important contributors, but methyl mercaptan (CH_3SH) is the main culprit.

Methyl mercaptan, also called methane-thiol, heads the list of things that smell bad. Sources say it smells like rotten cabbage, but you already know what it smells like even if you have not smelled rotten cabbage recently. It is a gas at room temperature, but can be condensed to a liquid in an ice bath.

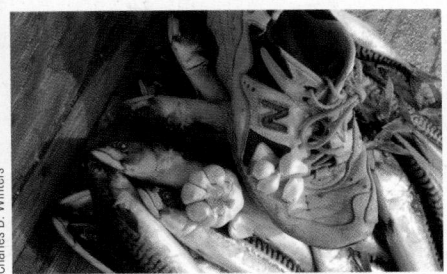

Charles D. Winters

Data for methyl mercaptan

Melting Point	−123 °C
Boiling point	+5.95 °C
Density (gas, 298 K, 1 atm)	1.966 g/L
$\Delta_f H°$	−22.3 kJ/mol

Current OSHA guidelines are that the compound should not exceed concentrations of 10 parts per million (ppm) in air (or about 20 mg/m³). Concentrations over 400 ppm have been known to cause death. However, humans can detect the odor of the compound at levels of a few parts per billion and so would leave the area if possible before concentrations became dangerous.

Bad breath comes from the formation of CH_3SH and similar compounds by the action of enzymes in the mouth on sulfur-containing compounds. Two of these compounds are common amino acids, methionine and cysteine. Methyl mercaptan is also produced when you digest allicin, which is produced when garlic is chopped to put into your pizza or your salad.

How can you get rid of halitosis? One way is to use a mouthwash. This can wash away some sources of sulfur compounds and might mask the odor. A more suitable method, however, is to use a toothpaste that has anti-plaque agents such as zinc and tin salts. It is thought that these interfere with the enzymes that act on something like methionine to produce methyl mercaptan.

Methyl mercaptan is not just a source of bad odors. It is used industrially to make pes-

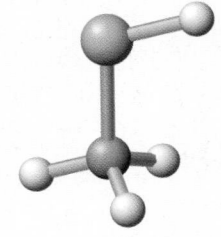

Methyl mercapatan or methanethiol.

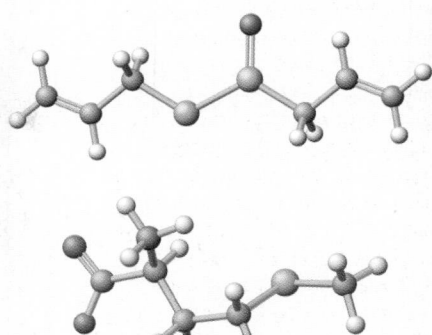

The digestion of allicin (top, from garlic) and methionine (bottom) is a source of CH_3SH in bad breath. Methionine is also made industrially using CH_3SH as one of the starting materials.

ticides, to regenerate catalysts in the petroleum industry, and to make methionine, which is used as a supplement in animal feed. Finally, mercaptans are added to natural gas and tanks of cooking gas. The three hydrocarbons in natural gas and cooking gas are odorless, so if you smell the unmistakable odor of a mercaptan you know there is a gas leak.

Questions:

1. *If an air sample contains CH_3SH with a concentration of 15 mg/m³, what is its partial pressure at 25 °C? How many molecules are there per cubic meter?*
2. *What are the bond angles in CH_3SH?*
3. *Is CH_3SH polar or nonpolar?*
4. *Do you expect CH_3SH gas to behave as an ideal gas? (See Section 11.9.)*
5. *Which gas diffuses most rapidly, CH_3SH, H_2S, or CH_3SCH_3?*

Answers to these questions are in Appendix Q.

When you breathe air from a SCUBA tank (Figure 11.21), the pressure of the gas in your lungs is equal to the pressure exerted on your body. When you are at the surface, atmospheric pressure is about 1 atm, and, because air has an oxygen concentration of 21%, the partial pressure of O_2 is about 0.21 atm. If you are at a depth of about 33 ft, the water pressure is 2 atm. This means the oxygen partial pressure is double the surface partial pressure, or about 0.4 atm. Similarly, the partial pressure of N_2, which is about 0.8 atm at the surface, doubles to about 1.6 atm at a depth of 33 ft. The solubility of gases in water (and in blood) is directly proportional to pressure. Therefore, more oxygen and nitrogen dissolve in blood under these conditions, and this can lead to several problems.

FIGURE 11.21 SCUBA diving.
Ordinary recreational dives can be made with compressed air to depths of about 60 feet or so. With a gas mixture called Nitrox (which has up to 36% O_2), one can stay at such depths for a longer period. To go even deeper, however, divers must breathe special gas mixtures such as Trimix. This is a breathing mixture consisting of oxygen, helium, and nitrogen.

OAR/National Undersea Research Program (NURP)

Nitrogen narcosis, also called "rapture of the deep" or the "martini effect," results from the toxic effect on nerve conduction of N_2 dissolved in blood. Its effect is comparable to drinking a martini on an empty stomach or taking laughing gas (nitrous oxide, N_2O) at the dentist; it makes you slightly giddy. In severe cases, it can impair a diver's judgment and even cause a diver to take the regulator out of his or her mouth and hand it to a fish! Some people can go as deep as 130 ft with no problem, but others experience nitrogen narcosis at 80 ft.

Another problem with breathing air at depths beyond 100 ft or so is oxygen toxicity. Our bodies are regulated for a partial pressure of O_2 of 0.21 atm. At a depth of 130 ft, the partial pressure of O_2 is comparable to breathing 100% oxygen at sea level. These higher partial pressures can harm the lungs and cause central nervous system damage. Oxygen toxicity is the reason deep dives are done not with compressed air but with gas mixtures with a much lower percentage of O_2, say about 10%.

Because of the risk of nitrogen narcosis, divers going beyond about 130 ft, such as those who work for offshore oil drilling companies, use a mixture of oxygen and helium. This solves the nitrogen narcosis problem, but it introduces another. If the diver has a voice link to the surface, the diver's speech sounds like Donald Duck! Speech is altered because the velocity of sound in helium is different from that in air, and the density of gas at several hundred feet is much higher than at the surface.

11.9 Nonideal Behavior: Real Gases

■ **Assumptions of the KMT—Revisited**
The assumptions of the kinetic molecular theory were given on page 532.
1. Gases consist of particles (molecules or atoms) whose separation is much greater than the size of the particles themselves.
2. The particles of a gas are in continual, random, and rapid motion. As they move, they collide with one another and with the walls of their container, but they do so without loss of energy.
3. The average kinetic energy of gas particles is proportional to the gas temperature. All gases, regardless of their molecular mass, have the same average kinetic energy at the same temperature.

If you are working with a gas at approximately room temperature and a pressure of 1 atm or less, the ideal gas law is remarkably successful in relating the amount of gas and its pressure, volume, and temperature. At higher pressures or lower temperatures, however, deviations from the ideal gas law occur. The origin of these deviations is explained by the breakdown of the assumptions used when describing ideal gases, specifically the assumptions that the particles have no size and that there are no forces between them.

At standard temperature and pressure (STP), the volume occupied by a single molecule is *very* small relative to its share of the total gas volume. A helium atom with a radius of 31 pm has relatively about the same space to move about as a pea has inside a basketball. Now suppose the pressure is increased significantly, to 1000 atm. The volume available to each molecule is a sphere with a radius of only about 200 pm, which means the situation is now like that of a pea inside a sphere a bit larger than a Ping-Pong ball.

The kinetic-molecular theory and the ideal gas law are concerned with the volume available to the molecules to move about, not the total volume of the container. The problem is that the volume occupied by gas molecules is not negligible at higher pressures. For example, suppose you have a flask marked with a volume of 500 mL. This does not mean the space available to molecules is 500 mL. Rather, the available volume is less than 500 mL, especially at high gas pressures, because the molecules themselves occupy some of the volume.

Another assumption of the kinetic-molecular theory is that the atoms or molecules of the gas never stick to one another by some type of intermolecular force. This is clearly not true as well. All gases can be liquefied—although some gases require a very low temperature (see Figure 11.12)—and the only way this can happen is if there are forces between the molecules. When a molecule is about to strike the wall of its container, other molecules in its vicinity exert a slight pull on the molecule and pull it away from the wall. The effect of the intermolecular forces is that molecules strike the wall with less force than in the absence of intermolecular attractive forces. Thus, because collisions between molecules in a real gas and the wall are softer, the observed gas pressure is less than that predicted by the ideal gas law. This effect can be particularly pronounced when the temperature is low.

The Dutch physicist Johannes van der Waals (1837–1923) studied the breakdown of the ideal gas law equation and developed an equation to correct for the errors arising from nonideality. This equation is known as the **van der Waals equation:**

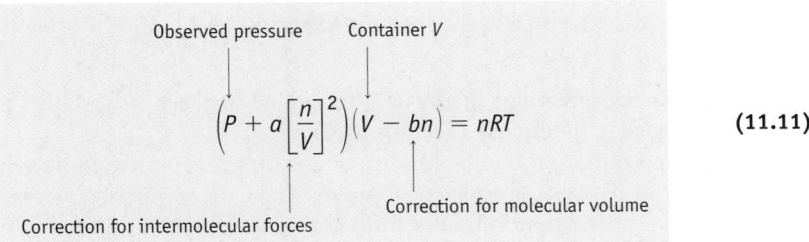

Observed pressure   Container V

$$\left(P + a\left[\frac{n}{V}\right]^2\right)(V - bn) = nRT \qquad (11.11)$$

Correction for intermolecular forces   Correction for molecular volume

where a and b are experimentally determined constants (Table 11.2). Although Equation 11.11 might seem complicated at first glance, the terms in parentheses are those of the ideal gas law, each corrected for the effects discussed previously. The pressure correction term, $a(n/V)^2$, accounts for intermolecular forces. Owing to intermolecular forces, the observed gas pressure is lower than the ideal pressure ($P_{observed} < P_{ideal}$ where P_{ideal} is calculated using the equation $PV = nRT$). Therefore, the term $a(n/V)^2$ is added to the observed pressure. The constant a typically has values in the range 0.01 to 10 atm · L²/mol². The actual volume available to the molecules is smaller than the volume of the container because the molecules themselves take up space. Therefore, an amount is subtracted from the container volume ($= bn$) to take this into account. Here, n is the number of moles of gas, and b is an experimental quantity that corrects for the molecular volume. Typical values of b range from 0.01 to 0.1 L/mol, roughly increasing with increasing molecular size.

As an example of the importance of these corrections, consider a sample of 4.00 mol of chlorine gas, Cl_2, in a 4.00-L tank at 100.0 °C. The ideal gas law would lead you to expect a pressure of 30.6 atm. A better estimate of the pressure, obtained from the van der Waals equation, is 26.0 atm, about 4.6 atm less than the ideal pressure!

TABLE 11.2. van der Waals Constants

Gas	a Values atm · L²/mol²	b Values L/mol
He	0.034	0.0237
Ar	1.34	0.0322
H_2	0.244	0.0266
N_2	1.39	0.0391
O_2	1.36	0.0318
CO_2	3.59	0.0427
Cl_2	6.49	0.0562
H_2O	5.46	0.0305

EXERCISE 11.13 van der Waals's Equation

Using both the ideal gas law and van der Waals's equation, calculate the pressure expected for 10.0 mol of helium gas in a 1.00-L container at 25 °C.

Chapter Goals Revisited

Now that you have studied this chapter, you should ask whether you have met the chapter goals. In particular, you should be able to:

Understand the basis of the gas laws and how to use those laws.

a. Describe how pressure measurements are made and the units of pressure, especially atmospheres (atm) and millimeters of mercury (mm Hg) (Section 11.1). Study Question(s) assignable in OWL: 1.

b. Understand the basis of the gas laws (Boyle's Law, Charles's Law, and Avogadro's Hypothesis) and how to apply them (Section 11.2). Study Question(s) assignable in OWL: 6, 8, 10, 12, 14.

Use the ideal gas law.

a. Understand the origin of the ideal gas law and how to use the equation (Section 11.3). Study Question(s) assignable in OWL: 18, 22, 24, 59, 63, 73, 81, 84, 88, 90, 96.

b. Calculate the molar mass of a compound from a knowledge of the pressure of a known quantity of a gas in a given volume at a known temperature (Section 11.3). Study Question(s) assignable in OWL: 26, 28, 30, 66, 85, 86, 92.

Apply the gas laws to stoichiometric calculations.

a. Apply the gas laws to a study of the stoichiometry of reactions (Section 11.4). Study Question(s) assignable in OWL: 32, 34, 65, 78.

b. Use Dalton's law of partial pressures (Section 11.5). Study Question(s) assignable in OWL: 39, 40, 70, 76, 83.

Understand kinetic molecular theory as it is applied to gases, especially the distribution of molecular speeds (energies) (Section 11.6).

a. Apply the kinetic-molecular theory of gas behavior at the molecular level (Section 11.6). Study Question(s) assignable in OWL: 41, 45, 101; Go Chemistry Module 16.

b. Understand the phenomena of diffusion and effusion and how to use Graham's law (Section 11.7). Study Question(s) assignable in OWL: 47.

Recognize why gases do not behave like ideal gases under some conditions.

a. Appreciate the fact that gases usually do not behave as ideal gases. Deviations from ideal behavior are largest at high pressure and low temperature (Section 11.9). Study Question(s) assignable in OWL: 51, 52.

KEY EQUATIONS

Equation 11.1 (page 518)   Boyle's law (where P is the pressure and V is the volume)

$$P_1V_1 = P_2V_2$$

Equation 11.2 (page 520)   Charles's law (where T is the Kelvin temperature)

$$\frac{V_1}{T_1} = \frac{V_2}{T_2} \quad \text{at constant } n \text{ and } P$$

Equation 11.3 (page 521)   General gas law (combined gas law)

$$\frac{P_1V_1}{T_1} = \frac{P_2V_2}{T_2} \quad \text{for a given amount of gas, } n$$

Equation 11.4 (page 524)   Ideal gas law (where n is the amount of gas (moles) and R is the universal gas constant, $0.082057 \text{ L} \cdot \text{atm/K} \cdot \text{mol}$)

$$PV = nRT$$

Equation 11.5 (page 525)   Density of gases (where d is the gas density in g/L and M is the molar mass of the gas)

$$d = \frac{m}{V} = \frac{PM}{RT}$$

Equation 11.6 (page 530)   Dalton's law of partial pressures. The total pressure of a gas mixture is the sum of the partial pressures of the component gases (P_n).

$$P_{total} = P_1 + P_2 + P_3 + \ldots$$

Equation 11.7 (page 531)   The total pressure of a gas mixture is equal to the total number of moles of gases multiplied by (RT/V).

$$P_{total} = (n_{total})\left(\frac{RT}{V}\right)$$

Equation 11.8 (page 531)   The pressure of a gas (A) in a mixture is the product of its mole fraction (X_A) and the total pressure of the mixture.

$$P_A = X_A P_{total}$$

Equation 11.9 (page 536)   Maxwell's equation relates the rms speed ($\sqrt{\overline{u^2}}$) to the molar mass of a gas (M) and its temperature (T).

$$\sqrt{\overline{u^2}} = \sqrt{\frac{3RT}{M}}$$

Equation 11.10 (page 538)   Graham's law. The rate of effusion of a gas—the amount of material moving from one place to another in a given time—is inversely proportional to the square root of its molar mass.

$$\frac{\text{Rate of effusion of gas 1}}{\text{Rate of effusion of gas 2}} = \sqrt{\frac{\text{molar mass of gas 2}}{\text{molar mass of gas 1}}}$$

Equation 11.11 (page 543)   The van der Waals equation: Relates pressure, volume, temperature, and amount of gas for a nonideal gas.

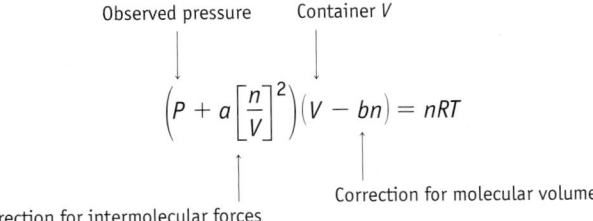

STUDY QUESTIONS

OWL Online homework for this chapter may be assigned in OWL.

▲ denotes challenging questions.

■ denotes questions assignable in OWL.

Blue-numbered questions have answers in Appendix O and fully-worked solutions in the *Student Solutions Manual*.

PRACTICING SKILLS

Pressure
(See Example 11.1 and ChemistryNow Screen 11.2.)

1. ■ The pressure of a gas is 440 mm Hg. Express this pressure in units of (a) atmospheres, (b) bars, and (c) kilopascals.

2. The average barometric pressure at an altitude of 10 km is 210 mm Hg. Express this pressure in atmospheres, bars, and kilopascals.

3. Indicate which represents the higher pressure in each of the following pairs:
   (a) 534 mm Hg or 0.754 bar
   (b) 534 mm Hg or 650 kPa
   (c) 1.34 bar or 934 kPa

4. Put the following in order of increasing pressure: 363 mm Hg, 363 kPa, 0.256 atm, and 0.523 bar.

Boyle's Law and Charles's Law
(See Examples 11.2 and 11.3 and ChemistryNow Screen 11.3.)

5. A sample of nitrogen gas has a pressure of 67.5 mm Hg in a 500.-mL flask. What is the pressure of this gas sample when it is transferred to a 125-mL flask at the same temperature?

6. ■ A sample of CO_2 gas has a pressure of 56.5 mm Hg in a 125-mL flask. The sample is transferred to a new flask, where it has a pressure of 62.3 mm Hg at the same temperature. What is the volume of the new flask?

7. You have 3.5 L of NO at a temperature of 22.0 °C. What volume would the NO occupy at 37 °C? (Assume the pressure is constant.)

8. ■ A 5.0-mL sample of CO_2 gas is enclosed in a gas-tight syringe (see Figure 11.4) at 22 °C. If the syringe is immersed in an ice bath (0 °C), what is the new gas volume, assuming that the pressure is held constant?

The General Gas Law
(See Example 11.4.)

9. You have 3.6 L of H_2 gas at 380 mm Hg and 25 °C. What is the pressure of this gas if it is transferred to a 5.0-L flask at 0.0 °C?

10. ■ You have a sample of CO_2 in a flask A with a volume of 25.0 mL. At 20.5 °C, the pressure of the gas is 436.5 mm Hg. To find the volume of another flask, B, you move the CO_2 to that flask and find that its pressure is now 94.3 mm Hg at 24.5 °C. What is the volume of flask B?

11. You have a sample of gas in a flask with a volume of 250 mL. At 25.5 °C, the pressure of the gas is 360 mm Hg. If you decrease the temperature to −5.0 °C, what is the gas pressure at the lower temperature?

12. ■ A sample of gas occupies 135 mL at 22.5 °C; the pressure is 165 mm Hg. What is the pressure of the gas sample when it is placed in a 252-mL flask at a temperature of 0.0 °C?

13. One of the cylinders of an automobile engine has a volume of 400. cm^3. The engine takes in air at a pressure of 1.00 atm and a temperature of 15 °C and compresses the air to a volume of 50.0 cm^3 at 77 °C. What is the final pressure of the gas in the cylinder? (The ratio of before and after volumes—in this case, 400 : 50 or 8 : 1—is called the compression ratio.)

14. ■ A helium-filled balloon of the type used in long-distance flying contains 420,000 ft^3 (1.2×10^7 L) of helium. Suppose you fill the balloon with helium on the ground, where the pressure is 737 mm Hg and the temperature is 16.0 °C. When the balloon ascends to a height of 2 miles, where the pressure is only 600. mm Hg and the temperature is −33 °C, what volume is occupied by the helium gas? Assume the pressure inside the balloon matches the external pressure. Comment on the result.

Avogadro's Hypothesis
(See Example 11.5 and ChemistryNow Screen 11.3.)

15. Nitrogen monoxide reacts with oxygen to give nitrogen dioxide.

$$2\ NO(g) + O_2(g) \longrightarrow 2\ NO_2(g)$$

   (a) If you mix NO and O_2 in the correct stoichiometric ratio and NO has a volume of 150 mL, what volume of O_2 is required (at the same pressure and temperature)?
   (b) After reaction is complete between 150 mL of NO and the stoichiometric volume of O_2, what is the volume of NO_2 (at the same pressure and temperature)?

16. Ethane, C_2H_6, burns in air according to the equation

$$2\ C_2H_6(g) + 7\ O_2(g) \longrightarrow 4\ CO_2(g) + 6\ H_2O(g)$$

What volume of O_2 (L) is required for complete reaction with 5.2 L of C_2H_6? What volume of H_2O vapor (L) is produced? Assume all gases are measured at the same temperature and pressure.

Ideal Gaw Law
(See Example 11.6 and ChemistryNow Screen 11.4.)

17. A 1.25-g sample of CO_2 is contained in a 750.-mL flask at 22.5 °C. What is the pressure of the gas?

18. ■ A balloon holds 30.0 kg of helium. What is the volume of the balloon if the final pressure is 1.20 atm and the temperature is 22 °C?

19. A flask is first evacuated so that it contains no gas at all. Then, 2.2 g of CO_2 is introduced into the flask. On warming to 22 °C, the gas exerts a pressure of 318 mm Hg. What is the volume of the flask?

20. A steel cylinder holds 1.50 g of ethanol, C_2H_5OH. What is the pressure of the ethanol vapor if the cylinder has a volume of 251 cm^3 and the temperature is 250 °C? (Assume all of the ethanol is in the vapor phase at this temperature.)

21. A balloon for long-distance flying contains 1.2×10^7 L of helium. If the helium pressure is 737 mm Hg at 25 °C, what mass of helium (in grams) does the balloon contain? (See Study Question 14.)

22. ■ What mass of helium, in grams, is required to fill a 5.0-L balloon to a pressure of 1.1 atm at 25 °C?

Gas Density
(See Example 11.8 and ChemistryNow Screen 11.5.)

23. Forty miles above Earth's surface, the temperature is 250 K, and the pressure is only 0.20 mm Hg. What is the density of air (in grams per liter) at this altitude? (Assume the molar mass of air is 28.96 g/mol.)

24. ■ Diethyl ether, $(C_2H_5)_2O$, vaporizes easily at room temperature. If the vapor exerts a pressure of 233 mm Hg in a flask at 25 °C, what is the density of the vapor?

25. A gaseous organofluorine compound has a density of 0.355 g/L at 17 °C and 189 mm Hg. What is the molar mass of the compound?

26. ■ Chloroform is a common liquid used in the laboratory. It vaporizes readily. If the pressure of chloroform vapor in a flask is 195 mm Hg at 25.0 °C and the density of the vapor is 1.25 g/L, what is the molar mass of chloroform?

Ideal Gas Laws and Determining Molar Mass
(See Examples 11.7 and 11.8 and ChemistryNow Screen 11.6.)

27. A 1.007-g sample of an unknown gas exerts a pressure of 715 mm Hg in a 452-mL container at 23 °C. What is the molar mass of the gas?

28. ■ A 0.0125-g sample of a gas with an empirical formula of CHF_2 is placed in a 165-mL flask. It has a pressure of 13.7 mm Hg at 22.5 °C. What is the molecular formula of the compound?

29. A new boron hydride, B_xH_y, has been isolated. To find its molar mass, you measure the pressure of the gas in a known volume at a known temperature. The following experimental data are collected:

Mass of gas = 12.5 mg   Pressure of gas = 24.8 mm Hg

Temperature = 25 °C   Volume of flask = 125 mL

Which formula corresponds to the calculated molar mass?
(a) B_2H_6 (d) B_6H_{10}
(b) B_4H_{10} (e) $B_{10}H_{14}$
(c) B_5H_9

30. ■ Acetaldehyde is a common liquid compound that vaporizes readily. Determine the molar mass of acetaldehyde from the following data:

Sample mass = 0.107 g   Volume of gas = 125 mL

Temperature = 0.0 °C   Pressure = 331 mm Hg

Gas Laws and Stoichiometry
(See Examples 11.9 and 11.10 and ChemistryNow Screen 11.7.)

31. Iron reacts with hydrochloric acid to produce iron(II) chloride and hydrogen gas:

$$Fe(s) + 2\ HCl(aq) \rightarrow FeCl_2(aq) + H_2(g)$$

The H_2 gas from the reaction of 2.2 g of iron with excess acid is collected in a 10.0-L flask at 25 °C. What is the pressure of the H_2 gas in this flask?

32. ■ Silane, SiH_4, reacts with O_2 to give silicon dioxide and water:

$$SiH_4(g) + 2\ O_2(g) \rightarrow SiO_2(s) + 2\ H_2O(\ell)$$

A 5.20-L sample of SiH_4 gas at 356 mm Hg pressure and 25 °C is allowed to react with O_2 gas. What volume of O_2 gas, in liters, is required for complete reaction if the oxygen has a pressure of 425 mm Hg at 25 °C?

33. Sodium azide, the explosive compound in automobile air bags, decomposes according to the following equation:

$$2\ NaN_3(s) \rightarrow 2\ Na(s) + 3\ N_2(g)$$

What mass of sodium azide is required to provide the nitrogen needed to inflate a 75.0-L bag to a pressure of 1.3 atm at 25 °C?

34. ■ The hydrocarbon octane (C_8H_{18}) burns to give CO_2 and water vapor:

$$2\ C_8H_{18}(g) + 25\ O_2(g) \rightarrow 16\ CO_2(g) + 18\ H_2O(g)$$

If a 0.048-g sample of octane burns completely in O_2, what will be the pressure of water vapor in a 4.75-L flask at 30.0 °C? If the O_2 gas needed for complete combustion was contained in a 4.75-L flask at 22 °C, what would its pressure be?

▲ more challenging   ■ in OWL   Blue-numbered questions answered in Appendix O

35. Hydrazine reacts with O_2 according to the following equation:

$$N_2H_4(g) + O_2(g) \rightarrow N_2(g) + 2\ H_2O(\ell)$$

Assume the O_2 needed for the reaction is in a 450-L tank at 23 °C. What must the oxygen pressure be in the tank to have enough oxygen to consume 1.00 kg of hydrazine completely?

36. A self-contained underwater breathing apparatus uses canisters containing potassium superoxide. The superoxide consumes the CO_2 exhaled by a person and replaces it with oxygen.

$$4\ KO_2(s) + 2\ CO_2(g) \rightarrow 2\ K_2CO_3(s) + 3\ O_2(g)$$

What mass of KO_2, in grams, is required to react with 8.90 L of CO_2 at 22.0 °C and 767 mm Hg?

Gas Mixtures and Dalton's Law
(See Example 11.11 and ChemistryNow Screen 11.8.)

37. What is the total pressure in atmospheres of a gas mixture that contains 1.0 g of H_2 and 8.0 g of Ar in a 3.0-L container at 27 °C? What are the partial pressures of the two gases?

38. A cylinder of compressed gas is labeled "Composition (mole %): 4.5% H_2S, 3.0% CO_2, balance N_2." The pressure gauge attached to the cylinder reads 46 atm. Calculate the partial pressure of each gas, in atmospheres, in the cylinder.

39. ■ A halothane–oxygen mixture ($C_2HBrClF_3 + O_2$) can be used as an anesthetic. A tank containing such a mixture has the following partial pressures: P (halothane) = 170 mm Hg and P (O_2) = 570 mm Hg.
(a) What is the ratio of the number of moles of halothane to the number of moles of O_2?
(b) If the tank contains 160 g of O_2, what mass of $C_2HBrClF_3$ is present?

40. ■ A collapsed balloon is filled with He to a volume of 12.5 L at a pressure of 1.00 atm. Oxygen, O_2, is then added so that the final volume of the balloon is 26 L with a total pressure of 1.00 atm. The temperature, which remains constant throughout, is 21.5 °C.
(a) What mass of He does the balloon contain?
(b) What is the final partial pressure of He in the balloon?
(c) What is the partial pressure of O_2 in the balloon?
(d) What is the mole fraction of each gas?

Kinetic-Molecular Theory
(See Section 11.6, Example 11.12, and ChemistryNow Screens 11.9–11.12.)

41. ■ You have two flasks of equal volume. Flask A contains H_2 at 0 °C and 1 atm pressure. Flask B contains CO_2 gas at 25 °C and 2 atm pressure. Compare these two gases with respect to each of the following:
(a) average kinetic energy per molecule
(b) average molecular velocity
(c) number of molecules
(d) mass of gas

42. Equal masses of gaseous N_2 and Ar are placed in separate flasks of equal volume at the same temperature. Tell whether each of the following statements is true or false. Briefly explain your answer in each case.
(a) There are more molecules of N_2 present than atoms of Ar.
(b) The pressure is greater in the Ar flask.
(c) The Ar atoms have a greater average speed than the N_2 molecules.
(d) The N_2 molecules collide more frequently with the walls of the flask than do the Ar atoms.

43. If the speed of an oxygen molecule is 4.28×10^4 cm/s at 25 °C, what is the speed of a CO_2 molecule at the same temperature?

44. Calculate the rms speed for CO molecules at 25 °C. What is the ratio of this speed to that of Ar atoms at the same temperature?

45. ■ Place the following gases in order of increasing average molecular speed at 25 °C: Ar, CH_4, N_2, CH_2F_2.

46. The reaction of SO_2 with Cl_2 gives dichlorine oxide, which is used to bleach wood pulp and to treat wastewater:

$$SO_2(g) + 2\ Cl_2(g) \rightarrow OSCl_2(g) + Cl_2O(g)$$

All of the compounds involved in the reaction are gases. List them in order of increasing average speed.

Diffusion and Effusion
(See Example 11.13 and ChemistryNow Screen 11.12.)

47. ■ In each pair of gases below, tell which will effuse faster:
(a) CO_2 or F_2
(b) O_2 or N_2
(c) C_2H_4 or C_2H_6
(d) two chlorofluorocarbons: $CFCl_3$ or $C_2Cl_2F_4$

48. Argon gas is 10 times denser than helium gas at the same temperature and pressure. Which gas is predicted to effuse faster? How much faster?

49. A gas whose molar mass you wish to know effuses through an opening at a rate one third as fast as that of helium gas. What is the molar mass of the unknown gas?

50. ▲ A sample of uranium fluoride is found to effuse at the rate of 17.7 mg/h. Under comparable conditions, gaseous I_2 effuses at the rate of 15.0 mg/h. What is the molar mass of the uranium fluoride? (*Hint:* Rates must be converted to units of moles per time.)

Nonideal Gases
(See Section 11.9.)

51. ■ In the text, it is stated that the pressure of 4.00 mol of Cl_2 in a 4.00-L tank at 100.0 °C should be 26.0 atm if calculated using the van der Waals equation. Verify this result, and compare it with the pressure predicted by the ideal gas law.

52. ■ You want to store 165 g of CO_2 gas in a 12.5-L tank at room temperature (25 °C). Calculate the pressure the gas would have using (a) the ideal gas law and (b) the van der Waals equation. (For CO_2, $a = 3.59$ atm $\cdot$ L^2/mol^2 and $b = 0.0427$ L/mol.)

General Questions

These questions are not designated as to type or location in the chapter. They may combine several concepts.

53. Complete the following table:

	atm	mm Hg	kPa	bar
Standard atmosphere	____	____	____	____
Partial pressure of N_2 in the atmosphere	____	593	____	____
Tank of compressed H_2	____	____	____	133
Atmospheric pressure at the top of Mount Everest	____	____	33.7	____

54. On combustion, 1.0 L of a gaseous compound of hydrogen, carbon, and nitrogen gives 2.0 L of CO_2, 3.5 L of H_2O vapor, and 0.50 L of N_2 at STP. What is the empirical formula of the compound?

55. ▲ You have a sample of helium gas at −33 °C, and you want to increase the average speed of helium atoms by 10.0%. To what temperature should the gas be heated to accomplish this?

56. If 12.0 g of O_2 is required to inflate a balloon to a certain size at 27 °C, what mass of O_2 is required to inflate it to the same size (and pressure) at 5.0 °C?

57. Butyl mercaptan, C_4H_9SH, has a very bad odor and is among the compounds added to natural gas to help detect a leak of otherwise odorless natural gas. In an experiment, you burn 95.0 mg of C_4H_9SH and collect the product gases (SO_2, CO_2, and H_2O) in a 5.25 L flask at 25 °C. What is the total gas pressure in the flask, and what is the partial pressure of each of the product gases?

58. A bicycle tire has an internal volume of 1.52 L and contains 0.406 mol of air. The tire will burst if its internal pressure reaches 7.25 atm. To what temperature, in degrees Celsius, does the air in the tire need to be heated to cause a blowout?

59. ■ The temperature of the atmosphere on Mars can be as high as 27 °C at the equator at noon, and the atmospheric pressure is about 8 mm Hg. If a spacecraft could collect 10. m^3 of this atmosphere, compress it to a small volume, and send it back to Earth, how many moles would the sample contain?

60. If you place 2.25 g of solid silicon in a 6.56-L flask that contains CH_3Cl with a pressure of 585 mm Hg at 25 °C, what mass of dimethyldichlorosilane, $(CH_3)_2SiCl_2(g)$, can be formed?

$$Si(s) + 2\ CH_3Cl(g) \rightarrow (CH_3)_2SiCl_2(g)$$

What pressure of $(CH_3)_2SiCl_2(g)$ would you expect in this same flask at 95 °C on completion of the reaction? (Dimethyldichlorosilane is one starting material used to make silicones, polymeric substances used as lubricants, antistick agents, and water-proofing caulk.)

61. $Ni(CO)_4$ can be made by reacting finely divided nickel with gaseous CO. If you have CO in a 1.50-L flask at a pressure of 418 mm Hg at 25.0 °C, along with 0.450 g of Ni powder, what is the theoretical yield of $Ni(CO)_4$?

62. The gas B_2H_6 burns in air to give H_2O and B_2O_3.

$$B_2H_6(g) + 3\ O_2(g) \rightarrow B_2O_3(s) + 3\ H_2O(g)$$

(a) Three gases are involved in this reaction. Place them in order of increasing rms speed. (Assume all are at the same temperature.)
(b) A 3.26-L flask contains B_2H_6 at a pressure of 256 mm Hg and a temperature of 25 °C. Suppose O_2 gas is added to the flask until B_2H_6 and O_2 are in the correct stoichiometric ratio for the combustion reaction. At this point, what is the partial pressure of O_2?

63. ■ You have four gas samples:
   1. 1.0 L of H_2 at STP
   2. 1.0 L of Ar at STP
   3. 1.0 L of H_2 at 27 °C and 760 mm Hg
   4. 1.0 L of He at 0 °C and 900 mm Hg
   (a) Which sample has the largest number of gas particles (atoms or molecules)?
   (b) Which sample contains the smallest number of particles?
   (c) Which sample represents the largest mass?

64. Propane reacts with oxygen to give carbon dioxide and water vapor.

$$C_3H_8(g) + 5\ O_2(g) \rightarrow 3\ CO_2(g) + 4\ H_2O(g)$$

If you mix C_3H_8 and O_2 in the correct stoichiometric ratio, and if the total pressure of the mixture is 288 mm Hg, what are the partial pressures of C_3H_8 and O_2? If the temperature and volume do not change, what is the pressure of the water vapor?

65. ■ Iron carbonyl can be made by the direct reaction of iron metal and carbon monoxide.

$$Fe(s) + 5\ CO(g) \rightarrow Fe(CO)_5(\ell)$$

What is the theoretical yield of $Fe(CO)_5$ if 3.52 g of iron is treated with CO gas having a pressure of 732 mm Hg in a 5.50-L flask at 23 °C?

66. ■ Analysis of a gaseous chlorofluorocarbon, CCl_xF_y, shows that it contains 11.79% C and 69.57% Cl. In another experiment, you find that 0.107 g of the compound fills a 458-mL flask at 25 °C with a pressure of 21.3 mm Hg. What is the molecular formula of the compound?

---

67. There are five compounds in the family of sulfur–fluorine compounds with the general formula S_xF_y. One of these compounds is 25.23% S. If you place 0.0955 g of the compound in a 89-mL flask at 45 °C, the pressure of the gas is 83.8 mm Hg. What is the molecular formula of S_xF_y?

68. A miniature volcano can be made in the laboratory with ammonium dichromate. When ignited, it decomposes in a fiery display.

$$(NH_4)_2Cr_2O_7(s) \rightarrow N_2(g) + 4 H_2O(g) + Cr_2O_3(s)$$

If 0.95 g of ammonium dichromate is used and if the gases from this reaction are trapped in a 15.0-L flask at 23 °C, what is the total pressure of the gas in the flask? What are the partial pressures of N_2 and H_2O?

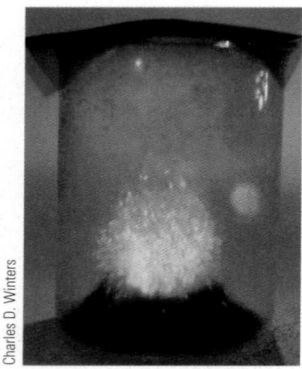

Thermal decomposition of $(NH_4)_2Cr_2O_7$.

69. The density of air 20 km above the earth's surface is 92 g/m³. The pressure of the atmosphere is 42 mm Hg, and the temperature is −63 °C.
    (a) What is the average molar mass of the atmosphere at this altitude?
    (b) If the atmosphere at this altitude consists of only O_2 and N_2, what is the mole fraction of each gas?

70. ■ A 3.0-L bulb containing He at 145 mm Hg is connected by a valve to a 2.0-L bulb containing Ar at 355 mm Hg. (See the accompanying figure.) Calculate the partial pressure of each gas and the total pressure after the valve between the flasks is opened.

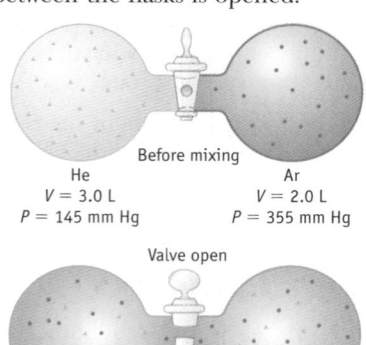

Before mixing

He
V = 3.0 L
P = 145 mm Hg

Ar
V = 2.0 L
P = 355 mm Hg

Valve open

After mixing

He + Ar   He + Ar

71. Chlorine dioxide, ClO_2, reacts with fluorine to give a new gas that contains Cl, O, and F. In an experiment, you find that 0.150 g of this new gas has a pressure of 17.2 mm Hg in a 1850-mL flask at 21 °C. What is the identity of the unknown gas?

72. A xenon fluoride can be prepared by heating a mixture of Xe and F_2 gases to a high temperature in a pressure-proof container. Assume that xenon gas was added to a 0.25-L container until its pressure reached 0.12 atm at 0.0 °C. Fluorine gas was then added until the total pressure reached 0.72 atm at 0.0 °C. After the reaction was complete, the xenon was consumed completely, and the pressure of the F_2 remaining in the container was 0.36 atm at 0.0 °C. What is the empirical formula of the xenon fluoride?

73. ■ A balloon at the circus is filled with helium gas to a gauge pressure of 22 mm Hg at 25 °C. The volume of the gas is 305 mL, and the barometric pressure is 755 mm Hg. What amount of helium is in the balloon? (Remember that gauge pressure = total pressure − barometric pressure. See page 517.)

74. If you have a sample of water in a closed container, some of the water will evaporate until the pressure of the water vapor, at 25 °C, is 23.8 mm Hg. How many molecules of water per cubic centimeter exist in the vapor phase?

75. You are given 1.56 g of a mixture of $KClO_3$ and KCl. When heated, the $KClO_3$ decomposes to KCl and O_2,

$$2 KClO_3(s) \rightarrow 2 KCl(s) + 3 O_2(g)$$

and 327 mL of O_2 with a pressure of 735 mm Hg is collected at 19 °C. What is the weight percentage of $KClO_3$ in the sample?

76. ▲ ■ A study of climbers who reached the summit of Mount Everest without supplemental oxygen showed that the partial pressures of O_2 and CO_2 in their lungs were 35 mm Hg and 7.5 mm Hg, respectively. The barometric pressure at the summit was 253 mm Hg. Assume the lung gases are saturated with moisture at a body temperature of 37 °C [which means the partial pressure of water vapor in the lungs is $P(H_2O) = 47.1$ mm Hg]. If you assume the lung gases consist of only O_2, N_2, CO_2, and H_2O, what is the partial pressure of N_2?

77. Nitrogen monoxide reacts with oxygen to give nitrogen dioxide:

$$2 NO(g) + O_2(g) \rightarrow 2 NO_2(g)$$

    (a) Place the three gases in order of increasing rms speed at 298 K.
    (b) If you mix NO and O_2 in the correct stoichiometric ratio and NO has a partial pressure of 150 mm Hg, what is the partial pressure of O_2?
    (c) After reaction between NO and O_2 is complete, what is the pressure of NO_2 if the NO originally had a pressure of 150 mm Hg and O_2 was added in the correct stoichiometric amount?

▲ more challenging ■ in OWL Blue-numbered questions answered in Appendix O

78. ▲ ■ Ammonia gas is synthesized by combining hydrogen and nitrogen:

$$3 H_2(g) + N_2(g) \rightarrow 2 NH_3(g)$$

(a) If you want to produce 562 g of NH_3, what volume of H_2 gas, at 56 °C and 745 mm Hg, is required?

(b) To produce 562 g of NH_3, what volume of air (the source of N_2) is required if the air is introduced at 29 °C and 745 mm Hg? (Assume the air sample has 78.1 mole % N_2.)

79. Nitrogen trifluoride is prepared by the reaction of ammonia and fluorine.

$$4 NH_3(g) + 3 F_2(g) \rightarrow 3 NH_4F(s) + NF_3(g)$$

If you mix NH_3 with F_2 in the correct stoichiometric ratio, and if the total pressure of the mixture is 120 mm Hg, what are the partial pressures of NH_3 and F_2? When the reactants have been completely consumed, what is the total pressure in the flask? (Assume T is constant.)

80. Chlorine trifluoride, ClF_3, is a valuable reagent because it can be used to convert metal oxides to metal fluorides:

$$6 NiO(s) + 4 ClF_3(g) \rightarrow 6 NiF_2(s) + 2 Cl_2(g) + 3 O_2(g)$$

(a) What mass of NiO will react with ClF_3 gas if the gas has a pressure of 250 mm Hg at 20 °C in a 2.5-L flask?

(b) If the ClF_3 described in part (a) is completely consumed, what are the partial pressures of Cl_2 and of O_2 in the 2.5-L flask at 20 °C (in mm Hg)? What is the total pressure in the flask?

81. ▲ ■ Relative humidity is the ratio of the partial pressure of water in air at a given temperature to the vapor pressure of water at that temperature. Calculate the mass of water per liter of air under the following conditions:
(a) at 20 °C and 45% relative humidity
(b) at 0 °C and 95% relative humidity

Under which circumstances is the mass of H_2O per liter greater? (See Appendix G for the vapor pressure of water.)

82. ■ How much water vapor is present in a dormitory room when the relative humidity is 55% and the temperature is 23 °C? The dimensions of the room are 4.5 m² floor area and 3.5 m ceiling height. (See Study Question 81 for a definition of relative humidity and Appendix G for the vapor pressure of water.)

In the Laboratory

83. ▲ ■ You have a 550.-mL tank of gas with a pressure of 1.56 atm at 24 °C. You thought the gas was pure carbon monoxide gas, CO, but you later found it was contaminated by small quantities of gaseous CO_2 and O_2. Analysis shows that the tank pressure is 1.34 atm (at 24 °C) if the CO_2 is removed. Another experiment shows that 0.0870 g of O_2 can be removed chemically. What are the masses of CO and CO_2 in the tank, and what is the partial pressure of each of the three gases at 25 °C?

84. ▲ ■ Methane is burned in a laboratory Bunsen burner to give CO_2 and water vapor. Methane gas is supplied to the burner at the rate of 5.0 L/min (at a temperature of 28 °C and a pressure of 773 mm Hg). At what rate must oxygen be supplied to the burner (at a pressure of 742 mm Hg and a temperature of 26 °C)?

85. ▲ ■ Iron forms a series of compounds of the type $Fe_x(CO)_y$. In air, they are oxidized to Fe_2O_3 and CO_2 gas. After heating a 0.142-g sample of $Fe_x(CO)_y$ in air, you isolate the CO_2 in a 1.50-L flask at 25 °C. The pressure of the gas is 44.9 mm Hg. What is the empirical formula of $Fe_x(CO)_y$?

86. ▲ ■ Group 2A metal carbonates are decomposed to the metal oxide and CO_2 on heating:

$$MCO_3(s) \rightarrow MO(s) + CO_2(g)$$

You heat 0.158 g of a white, solid carbonate of a Group 2A metal (M) and find that the evolved CO_2 has a pressure of 69.8 mm Hg in a 285-mL flask at 25 °C. Identify M.

87. One way to synthesize diborane, B_2H_6, is the reaction

$$2 NaBH_4(s) + 2 H_3PO_4(aq) \rightarrow$$
$$B_2H_6(g) + 2 NaH_2PO_4(aq) + 2 H_2(g)$$

(a) If you have 0.136 g of $NaBH_4$ and excess H_3PO_4, and you collect the B_2H_6 in a 2.75 L flask at 25 °C, what is the pressure of the B_2H_6 in the flask?

(b) A by-product of the reaction is H_2 gas. If both B_2H_6 and H_2 gas come from this reaction, what is the total pressure in the 2.75-L flask (after reaction of 0.136 g of $NaBH_4$ with excess H_3PO_4) at 25 °C?

88. ■ You are given a solid mixture of $NaNO_2$ and NaCl and are asked to analyze it for the amount of $NaNO_2$ present. To do so, you allow the mixture to react with sulfamic acid, HSO_3NH_2, in water according to the equation

$$NaNO_2(aq) + HSO_3NH_2(aq) \rightarrow$$
$$NaHSO_4(aq) + H_2O(\ell) + N_2(g)$$

What is the weight percentage of $NaNO_2$ in 1.232 g of the solid mixture if reaction with sulfamic acid produces 295 mL of N_2 gas with a pressure of 713 mm Hg at 21.0 °C?

89. ▲ You have 1.249 g of a mixture of $NaHCO_3$ and Na_2CO_3. You find that 12.0 mL of 1.50 M HCl is required to convert the sample completely to NaCl, H_2O, and CO_2.

$$NaHCO_3(aq) + HCl(aq) \rightarrow$$
$$NaCl(aq) + H_2O(\ell) + CO_2(g)$$

$$Na_2CO_3(aq) + 2 HCl(aq) \rightarrow$$
$$2 NaCl(aq) + H_2O(\ell) + CO_2(g)$$

What volume of CO_2 is evolved at 745 mm Hg and 25 °C?

90. ▲ ■ A mixture of $NaHCO_3$ and Na_2CO_3 has a mass of 2.50 g. When treated with HCl(aq), 665 mL of CO_2 gas is liberated with a pressure of 735 mm Hg at 25 °C. What is the weight percent of $NaHCO_3$ and Na_2CO_3 in the mixture? (See Study Question 89 for the reactions that occur.)

91. ▲ Many nitrate salts can be decomposed by heating. For example, blue, anhydrous copper(II) nitrate produces nitrogen dioxide and oxygen when heated. In the laboratory, you find that a sample of this salt produced 0.195 g of mixture of NO_2 and O_2 with a pressure of 725 mm Hg at 35 °C in a 125-mL flask (and black, solid CuO was left as a residue). What is the average molar mass of the gas mixture? What are the mole fractions of NO_2 and O_2? What amount of each gas is in the mixture? Do these amounts reflect the relative amounts of NO_2 and O_2 expected based on the balanced equation? Is it possible that the fact that some NO_2 molecules combine to give N_2O_4 plays a role?

Charles D. Winters

Heating copper(II) nitrate produces nitrogen dioxide and oxygen gas and leaves a residue of copper(II) oxide.

92. ▲ ■ A compound containing C, H, N, and O is burned in excess oxygen. The gases produced by burning 0.1152 g are first treated to convert the nitrogen-containing product gases into N_2, and then the resulting mixture of CO_2, H_2O, N_2, and excess O_2 is passed through a bed of $CaCl_2$ to absorb the water. The $CaCl_2$ increases in mass by 0.09912 g. The remaining gases are bubbled into water to form H_2CO_3, and this solution is titrated with 0.3283 M NaOH; 28.81 mL is required to achieve the second equivalence point. The excess O_2 gas is removed by reaction with copper metal (to give CuO). Finally, the N_2 gas is collected in a 225.0-mL flask, where it has a pressure of 65.12 mm Hg at 25 °C. In a separate experiment, the unknown compound is found to have a molar mass of 150 g/mol. What are the empirical and molecular formulas of the unknown compound?

Summary and Conceptual Questions

The following questions may use concepts from the previous chapters.

93. A 1.0-L flask contains 10.0 g each of O_2 and CO_2 at 25 °C.
   (a) Which gas has the greater partial pressure, O_2 or CO_2, or are they the same?
   (b) Which molecules have the greater average speed, or are they the same?
   (c) Which molecules have the greater average kinetic energy, or are they the same?

94. If equal masses of O_2 and N_2 are placed in separate containers of equal volume at the same temperature, which of the following statements is true? If false, tell why it is false.
   (a) The pressure in the flask containing N_2 is greater than that in the flask containing O_2.
   (b) There are more molecules in the flask containing O_2 than in the flask containing N_2.

95. You have two pressure-proof steel cylinders of equal volume, one containing 1.0 kg of CO and the other containing 1.0 kg of acetylene, C_2H_2.
   (a) In which cylinder is the pressure greater at 25 °C?
   (b) Which cylinder contains the greater number of molecules?

96. ■ Two flasks, each with a volume of 1.00 L, contain O_2 gas with a pressure of 380 mm Hg. Flask A is at 25 °C, and flask B is at 0 °C. Which flask contains the greater number of O_2 molecules?

97. ▲ State whether each of the following samples of matter is a gas. If there is not enough information for you to decide, write "insufficient information."
   (a) A material is in a steel tank at 100 atm pressure. When the tank is opened to the atmosphere, the material suddenly expands, increasing its volume by 10%.
   (b) A 1.0-mL sample of material weighs 8.2 g.
   (c) The material is transparent and pale green in color.
   (d) One cubic meter of material contains as many molecules as 1.0 m³ of air at the same temperature and pressure.

98. Each of the four tires of a car is filled with a different gas. Each tire has the same volume, and each is filled to the same pressure, 3.0 atm, at 25 °C. One tire contains 116 g of air, another tire has 80.7 g of neon, another tire has 16.0 g of helium, and the fourth tire has 160. g of an unknown gas.
   (a) Do all four tires contain the same number of gas molecules? If not, which one has the greatest number of molecules?
   (b) How many times heavier is a molecule of the unknown gas than an atom of helium?
   (c) In which tire do the molecules have the largest kinetic energy? The highest average speed?

▲ more challenging ■ in OWL Blue-numbered questions answered in Appendix 0

99. You have two gas-filled balloons, one containing He and the other containing H_2. The H_2 balloon is twice the size of the He balloon. The pressure of gas in the H_2 balloon is 1 atm, and that in the He balloon is 2 atm. The H_2 balloon is outside in the snow (-5 °C), and the He balloon is inside a warm building (23 °C).
    (a) Which balloon contains the greater number of molecules?
    (b) Which balloon contains the greater mass of gas?

100. The sodium azide required for automobile air bags is made by the reaction of sodium metal with dinitrogen oxide in liquid ammonia:

$$3 N_2O(g) + 4 Na(s) + NH_3(\ell) \rightarrow$$
$$NaN_3(s) + 3 NaOH(s) + 2 N_2(g)$$

    (a) You have 65.0 g of sodium and a 35.0-L flask containing N_2O gas with a pressure of 2.12 atm at 23 °C. What is the theoretical yield (in grams) of NaN_3?
    (b) Draw a Lewis structure for the azide ion. Include all possible resonance structures. Which resonance structure is most likely?
    (c) What is the shape of the azide ion?

101. ■ If the absolute temperature of a gas doubles, by how much does the average speed of the gaseous molecules increase? *(See ChemistryNow Screen 11.9.)*

102. ▲ Chlorine gas (Cl_2) is used as a disinfectant in municipal water supplies, although chlorine dioxide (ClO_2) and ozone are becoming more widely used. ClO_2 is a better choice than Cl_2 in this application because it leads to fewer chlorinated by-products, which are themselves pollutants.
    (a) How many valence electrons are in ClO_2?
    (b) The chlorite ion, ClO_2^-, is obtained by reducing ClO_2. Draw a possible electron dot structure for ClO_2^-. (Cl is the central atom.)
    (c) What is the hybridization of the central Cl atom in ClO_2^-? What is the shape of the ion?
    (d) Which species has the larger bond angle, O_3 or ClO_2^-? Explain briefly.
    (e) Chlorine dioxide, ClO_2, a yellow-green gas, can be made by the reaction of chlorine with sodium chlorite:

$$2 NaClO_2(s) + Cl_2(g) \rightarrow 2 NaCl(s) + 2 ClO_2(g)$$

Assume you react 15.6 g of $NaClO_2$ with chlorine gas, which has a pressure of 1050 mm Hg in a 1.45-L flask at 22 °C. What mass of ClO_2 can be produced?

12 | Intermolecular Forces and Liquids

John Katz

Antarctica Scene—Icebergs, Penguins, Snow, Ice, and Fog

Antarctica is a place of unique wonder and beauty. Aside from the living creatures—many species of penguins, whales, and birds—one mostly thinks of ice and icebergs. Some icebergs are as large as a small state, while others are only the size of a football field. We all know ice floats on water, but what is the reason for this?

Questions:
1. Given the density of seawater ($d = 1.026$ g/mL) and of ice ($d = 0.917$ g/cm³), is most of the volume of an iceberg above or below the waterline?
2. What volume is above or below the waterline?

Answers to these questions are in Appendix Q.

Chemistry ⚬ Now™

Throughout the text this icon introduces an opportunity for self-study or to explore interactive tutorials by signing in at **www.cengage.com/login**.

Hundreds of common compounds can exist in the liquid and vapor states at or near room temperature and under ordinary pressures, and the one that comes to mind immediately is water. Water molecules in the atmosphere can interact at lower temperatures and come together to form clouds or fog, and still larger clusters of molecules eventually can fall as rain drops. At only slightly lower temperatures, the molecules assemble into a crystalline lattice, which you see as snowflakes and ice.

The primary objectives of this chapter are to examine the intermolecular forces that allow molecules to interact and then to look at liquids, a result of such interactions. You will find this a useful chapter because it explains, among other things, why your body is cooled when you sweat and why ice can float on liquid water, a property shared by almost no other substance in its liquid and solid states.

Early morning fog over Lake Champlain in upstate New York.

12.1 States of Matter and Intermolecular Forces

The kinetic-molecular theory of gases (◄ Section 11.6) assumes that gas molecules or atoms are widely separated and that these particles can be considered to be independent of one another. Consequently, we can relate the properties of gases under most conditions by a simple mathematical equation, $PV = nRT$, known as the ideal gas law equation (Equation 11.4). In real gases, however, there are forces between molecules—intermolecular forces—and these require a more complex analysis of gas behavior (◄ page 543). If these intermolecular forces become strong enough, the substance can condense to a liquid and eventually to a solid. For liquids in particular, the existence of intermolecular forces makes the picture more complex, and it is not possible to create a simple "ideal liquid equation."

How different are the states of matter at the particulate level? We can get a sense of this by comparing the volumes occupied by equal numbers of molecules of a material in different states. Figure 12.1a shows a flask containing about 300 mL of liquid nitrogen. If all of the liquid were allowed to evaporate, the gaseous nitrogen, at 1 atm and room temperature, would fill a large balloon (more than 200 L). A great amount of space exists between molecules in a gas, whereas in liquids the molecules are close together.

The increase in volume when converting liquids to gases is strikingly large. In contrast, no dramatic change in volume occurs when a solid is converted to a liquid. Figure 12.1b shows the same amount of liquid and solid benzene, C_6H_6, side by side. As you see, they are not appreciably different in volume. This means that the atoms in the liquid are packed together about as tightly as the atoms in the solid phase.

■ **The Lotus Effect** The photograph on the cover of this book illustrates the importance of intermolecular forces. You can read about the lotus effect on the back of the title page and on the back cover of the book.

FIGURE 12.1 Contrasting gases, liquids, and solids. (a) When a 300-mL sample of liquid nitrogen evaporates, it will produce more than 200 L of gas at 25 °C and 1.0 atm. In the liquid phase, the molecules of N_2 are close together; in the gas phase, they are far apart. (b) The same volume of liquid benzene, C_6H_6, is placed in two test tubes, and one tube (right) is cooled, freezing the liquid. The solid and liquid states have almost the same volume, showing that the molecules are packed together almost as tightly in the liquid state as they are in the solid state.

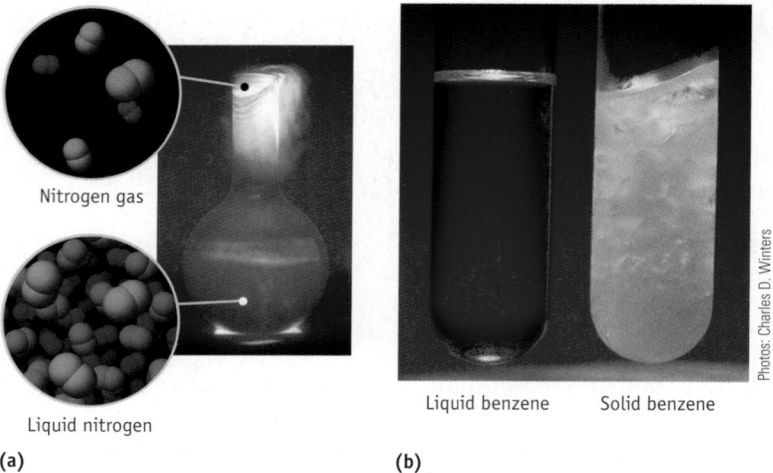

Nitrogen gas

Liquid nitrogen

(a)

Liquid benzene   Solid benzene

(b)

Photos: Charles D. Winters

We know that gases can be compressed easily, a process that involves forcing the gas molecules much closer together. In contrast, the molecules, ions, or atoms in liquid or solid phases strongly resist forces that would push them even closer together. Lack of compressibility is a characteristic property of liquids and solids. For example, the volume of liquid water changes only by 0.005% per atmosphere of pressure applied.

Intermolecular forces influence chemistry in many ways:

- They are directly related to properties such as melting point, boiling point, and the energy needed to convert a solid to a liquid or a liquid to a vapor.
- They are important in determining the solubility of gases, liquids, and solids in various solvents.
- They are crucial in determining the structures of biologically important molecules such as DNA and proteins.

Bonding in ionic compounds depends on the electrostatic forces of attraction between oppositely charged ions. Similarly, the intermolecular forces attracting one molecule to another are electrostatic. By comparison, the attractive forces between the ions in ionic compounds are usually in the range of 700 to 1100 kJ/mol, and most covalent bond energies are in the range of 100 to 400 kJ/mol (Table 8.9). As a rough guideline, intermolecular forces are generally less than about 15% of the values of bond energies. Nonetheless, these interactions can have a profound effect on molecular properties and are the subject of this section.

The sections that follow are organized around the polarity of the molecules involved. We shall first describe forces involving polar molecules and then those involving nonpolar molecules. In Chapter 13, we shall describe ionic and metallic solids and the bonding in those substances.

Chemistry꘎Now™

Sign in at **www.cengage.com/login** and go to Chapter 12 Contents to see:
- Screen 12.2 to view an animation of **gases, liquids, and solids at the molecular level**
- Screen 12.3 for an outline of **the important intermolecular forces**

12.2 Intermolecular Forces Involving Polar Molecules

Interactions Between Ions and Molecules with a Permanent Dipole

The distribution of bonding electrons in a molecule often results in a permanent dipole moment (◄ Section 8.7). Because polar molecules have positive and negative ends, if a polar molecule and an ionic compound are mixed, the negative end of the dipole will be attracted to a positive cation (Figure 12.2). Similarly, the positive end of the dipole will be attracted to a negative anion. Forces of attraction between a positive or negative ion and polar molecules—**ion–dipole forces**—are less than those for ion–ion attractions (which can be on the order of 500 kJ/mol), but they are greater than other types of forces between molecules, whether polar or nonpolar.

Ion–dipole attractions can be evaluated based on Coulomb's law (◄ Equation 2.3), which informs us that the force of attraction between two charged objects depends on the product of their charges divided by the square of the distance between them (◄ Section 2.7). Therefore, when a polar molecule encounters an ion, the attractive forces depend on three factors:

- The distance between the ion and the dipole. The closer the ion and dipole, the stronger the attraction.
- The charge on the ion. The higher the ion charge, the stronger the attraction.
- The magnitude of the dipole. The greater the magnitude of the dipole, the stronger the attraction.

The formation of hydrated ions in aqueous solution is one of the most important examples of the interaction between an ion and a polar molecule (Figure 12.3). The enthalpy change associated with the hydration of ions—which is generally called the **enthalpy of solvation** or, for ions in water, the **enthalpy of hydration**—is substantial. The solvation enthalpy for an individual ion cannot be measured directly, but values can be estimated. For example, the hydration of sodium ions is described by the following reaction:

$$Na^+(g) + x\ H_2O(\ell) \rightarrow [Na(H_2O)_x]^+(aq)\ (x\ probably = 6) \qquad \Delta_r H° = -405\ kJ/mol$$

The enthalpy of hydration depends on $1/d$, where d is the distance between the center of the ion and the oppositely charged "pole" of the dipole.

As the ion radius becomes larger, d increases, and the enthalpy of hydration becomes less exothermic. This trend is illustrated by the enthalpies of hydration of the alkali metal cations (Table 12.1) and by those for Mg^{2+}, Li^+, and K^+ (Figure 12.3). It is interesting to compare these values with the enthalpy of hydration of the

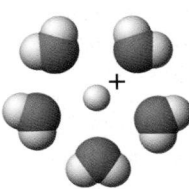

Water surrounding a cation

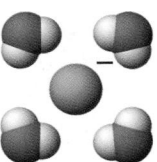

Water surrounding an anion

Active Figure 12.2 **Ion-dipole interactions.** When an ionic compound such as NaCl is placed in water, the polar water molecules surround the cations and anions.

Chemistry ⚛ Now™ Sign in at www.cengage.com/login and go to the Chapter Contents menu to explore an interactive version of this figure accompanied by an exercise.

■ **Coulomb's Law** The **force** of attraction between oppositely charged particles depends directly on the product of their charges and inversely on the square of the distance (d) between the ions ($1/d^2$) (Equation 2.3, page 78). The **energy** of the attraction is also proportional to the charge product, but it is inversely proportional to the distance between them ($1/d$).

FIGURE 12.3 Enthalpy of hydration. The energy evolved when an ion is hydrated depends on the dipole moment of water, the ion charge, and the distance d between centers of the ion and the polar water molecule. The distance d increases as ion size increases.

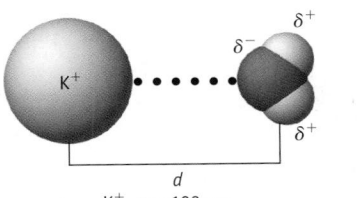

δ^+
δ^-
δ^+
d
$K^+, r = 133\ pm$
$\Delta H = -321\ kJ/mol$

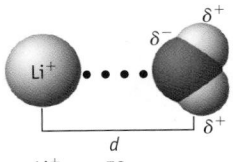

δ^+
δ^-
δ^+
d
$Li^+, r = 78\ pm$
$\Delta H = -515\ kJ/mol$

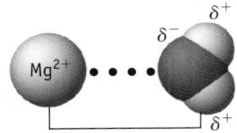

δ^+
δ^-
δ^+
d
$Mg^{2+}, r = 79\ pm$
$\Delta H = -1922\ kJ/mol$

Increasing force of attraction; more exothermic enthalpy of hydration

TABLE 12.1 Radii and Enthalpies of Hydration of Alkali Metal Ions

Cation	Ion Radius (pm)	Enthalpy of Hydration (kJ/mol)
Li^+	78	−515
Na^+	98	−405
K^+	133	−321
Rb^+	149	−296
Cs^+	165	−263

H^+ ion, estimated to be −1090 kJ/mol. This extraordinarily large value is due to the tiny size of the H^+ ion.

Chemistry ⚛ Now™

Sign in at **www.cengage.com/login** and go to Chapter 12 Contents to see Screen 12.4 to view an animation of **ion–dipole forces.**

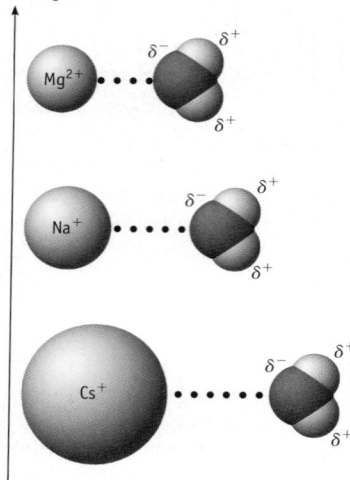

Strong attraction

Weak attraction

■ **EXAMPLE 12.1 Hydration Energy**

Problem Explain why the enthalpy of hydration of Na^+ (−405 kJ/mol) is somewhat more exothermic than that of Cs^+ (−263 kJ/mol), whereas that of Mg^{2+} is much more exothermic (−1922 kJ/mol) than that of either Na^+ or Cs^+.

Strategy The strength of ion–dipole attractions depends directly on the size of the ion charge and the magnitude of the dipole, and inversely on the distance between them. To judge the ion–dipole distance, we need ion sizes from Figure 7.12.

Solution The relevant ion sizes are Na^+ = 98 pm, Cs^+ = 165 pm, and Mg^{2+} = 79 pm. From these values, we can predict that the distances between the center of the positive charge on the metal ion and the negative side of the water dipole will vary in this order: $Mg^{2+} < Na^+ < Cs^+$. The hydration energy varies in the reverse order (with the hydration energy of Mg^{2+} being the most negative value). Notice also that Mg^{2+} has a 2+ charge, whereas the other ions are 1+. The greater charge on Mg^{2+} leads to a greater force of ion–dipole attraction than for the other two ions, which have only a 1+ charge. As a result, the hydration energy for Mg^{2+} is much more negative than for the other two ions.

EXERCISE 12.1 Hydration Energy

Which should have the more negative hydration energy, F^- or Cl^-? Explain briefly.

Interactions Between Molecules with Permanent Dipoles

When a polar molecule encounters another polar molecule, of the same or a different kind, the positive end of one molecule is attracted to the negative end of the other polar molecule.

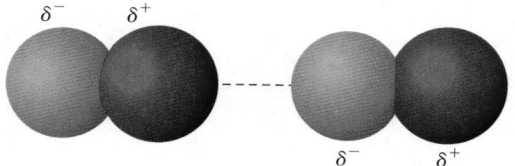

Many molecules have dipoles, and their interactions occur by **dipole–dipole attraction.**

Solid salts with waters of hydration are common. The formulas of these compounds are given by appending a specific number of water molecules to the end of the formula, as in $BaCl_2 \cdot 2\ H_2O$. Sometimes, the water molecules simply fill in empty spaces in a crystalline lattice, but often the cation in these salts is directly associated with water molecules. For example, the compound $CrCl_3 \cdot 6\ H_2O$ is better written as $[Cr(H_2O)_4Cl_2]Cl \cdot 2\ H_2O$. Four of the six water molecules are associated with the Cr^{3+} ion by ion–dipole attractive forces; the remaining two water molecules are in the lattice. Common examples of hydrated salts are listed in the table.

Compound	Common Name	Uses
$Na_2CO_3 \cdot 10\ H_2O$	Washing soda	Water softener
$Na_2S_2O_3 \cdot 5\ H_2O$	Hypo	Photography
$MgSO_4 \cdot 7\ H_2O$	Epsom salt	Cathartic, dyeing and tanning
$CaSO_4 \cdot 2\ H_2O$	Gypsum	Wallboard
$CuSO_4 \cdot 5\ H_2O$	Blue vitriol	Biocide

Photos: Charles D. Winters

Hydrated cobalt(II) chloride, $CoCl_2 \cdot 6\ H_2O$. In the solid state, the compound is best described by the formula $[Co(H_2O)_4Cl_2] \cdot 2\ H_2O$. The cobalt(II) ion is surrounded by four water molecules and two chloride ions in an octahedral arrangement. In water, the ion is completely hydrated, now being surrounded by six water molecules. Cobalt(II) ions and water molecules interact by ion–dipole forces. This is an example of a coordination compound, a class of compounds discussed in detail in Chapter 22.

For polar molecules, dipole–dipole attractions influence, among other things, the evaporation of a liquid and the condensation of a gas (Figure 12.4). An energy change occurs in both processes. Evaporation requires the input of energy, specifically the enthalpy of vaporization ($\Delta_{vap}H°$) [see Section 5.3 and Section 12.4]. The value for the enthalpy of vaporization has a positive sign, indicating that evaporation is an endothermic process. The enthalpy change for the condensation process—the reverse of evaporation—has a negative value.

The greater the forces of attraction between molecules in a liquid, the greater the energy that must be supplied to separate them. Thus, we expect polar compounds to have a higher value for their enthalpy of vaporization than nonpolar compounds with similar molar masses. For example, notice that $\Delta_{vap}H°$ for polar

FIGURE 12.4 Evaporation at the molecular level. Energy must be supplied to separate molecules in the liquid state against intermolecular forces of attraction.

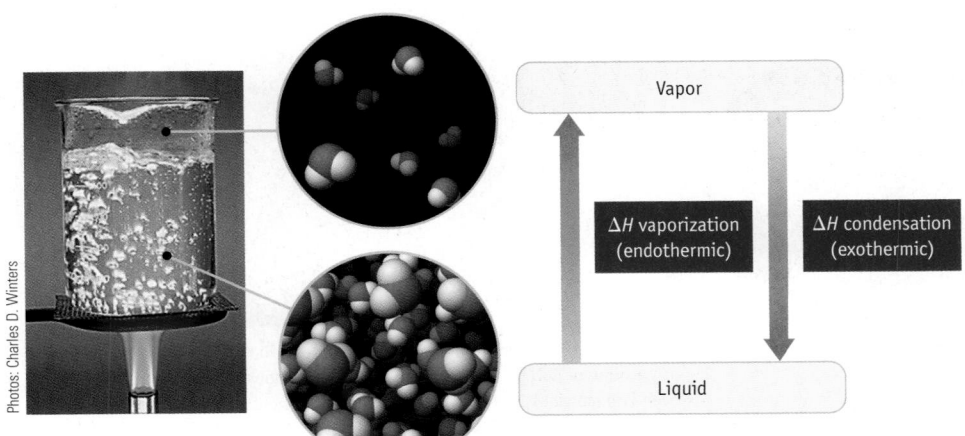

Photos: Charles D. Winters

Vapor

ΔH vaporization (endothermic)

ΔH condensation (exothermic)

Liquid

TABLE 12.2 Molar Masses, Boiling Points, and $\Delta_{vap}H°$ of Nonpolar and Polar Substances

	Nonpolar				Polar		
	M (g/mol)	BP (°C)	$\Delta_{vap}H°$ (kJ/mol)		M (g/mol)	BP (°C)	$\Delta_{vap}H°$ (kJ/mol)
N_2	28	−196	5.57	CO	28	−192	6.04
SiH_4	32	−112	12.10	PH_3	34	−88	14.06
GeH_4	77	−90	14.06	AsH_3	78	−62	16.69
Br_2	160	59	29.96	ICl	162	97	—

molecules is greater than for nonpolar molecules of approximately the same size and mass (Table 12.2).

The boiling point of a liquid also depends on intermolecular forces of attraction. As the temperature of a substance is raised, its molecules gain kinetic energy. Eventually, when the boiling point is reached, the molecules have sufficient kinetic energy to escape the forces of attraction of their neighbors. For molecules of similar molar mass, the greater the polarity, the higher the temperature required for the liquid to boil. In Table 12.2, you see that the boiling point for polar ICl is greater than that for nonpolar Br_2, for example.

Intermolecular forces also influence solubility. A qualitative observation on solubility is that "like dissolves like." In other words, polar molecules are likely to dissolve in a polar solvent, and nonpolar molecules are likely to dissolve in a nonpolar solvent (Figure 12.5) (◄ Chapter 8). The converse is also true; that is, it is unlikely that polar molecules will dissolve in nonpolar solvents or that nonpolar molecules will dissolve in polar solvents.

For example, water and ethanol (C_2H_5OH) can be mixed in any ratio to give a homogeneous mixture. In contrast, water does not dissolve in gasoline to an ap-

Photos: Charles D. Winters

Ethylene glycol

(a) Ethylene glycol ($HOCH_2CH_2OH$), a polar compound used as antifreeze in automobiles, dissolves in water.

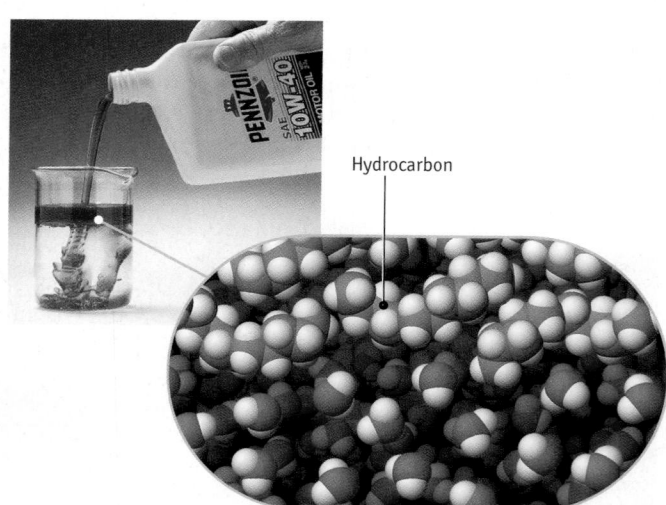

Hydrocarbon

(b) Nonpolar motor oil (a hydrocarbon) dissolves in nonpolar solvents such as gasoline or CCl_4. It will not dissolve in a polar solvent such as water, however. Commercial spot removers use nonpolar solvents to dissolve oil and grease from fabrics.

FIGURE 12.5 "Like dissolves like."

preciable extent. The difference in these two situations is that ethanol and water are polar molecules, whereas the hydrocarbon molecules in gasoline (e.g., octane, C_8H_{18}) are nonpolar. The water–ethanol interactions are strong enough that the energy expended in pushing water molecules apart to make room for ethanol molecules is compensated for by the energy of attraction between the two kinds of polar molecules. In contrast, water–hydrocarbon attractions are weak. The hydrocarbon molecules cannot disrupt the stronger water–water attractions.

Chemistry .ȯ. Now™

Sign in at **www.cengage.com/login** and go to Chapter 12 Contents to see Screen 12.4 to view an animation of **dipole–dipole forces.**

Hydrogen Bonding

Hydrogen fluoride, water, ammonia and many other compounds with O—H and N—H bonds have exceptional properties. Consider, for example, the boiling points for hydrogen compounds of elements in Groups 4A through 7A (Figure 12.6). Generally, the boiling points of related compounds increase with molar mass. This trend is seen in the boiling points of the hydrogen compounds of Group 4A elements, for example ($CH_4 < SiH_4 < GeH_4 < SnH_4$). The same effect is also operating for the heavier molecules of the hydrogen compounds of elements of Groups 5A, 6A, and 7A. The boiling points of NH_3, H_2O, and HF, however, deviate significantly from what might be expected based on molar mass alone. If we extrapolate the curve for the boiling points of H_2Te, H_2Se, and H_2S, the boiling point of water is predicted to be around $-90\ °C$. The boiling point of water is almost 200 °C higher than this value! Similarly, the boiling points of NH_3 and HF are much higher than would be expected based on molar mass. Because the temperature at which a substance boils depends on the attractive forces between molecules, the extraordinarily high boiling points of H_2O, HF, and NH_3 indicate strong intermolecular attractions.

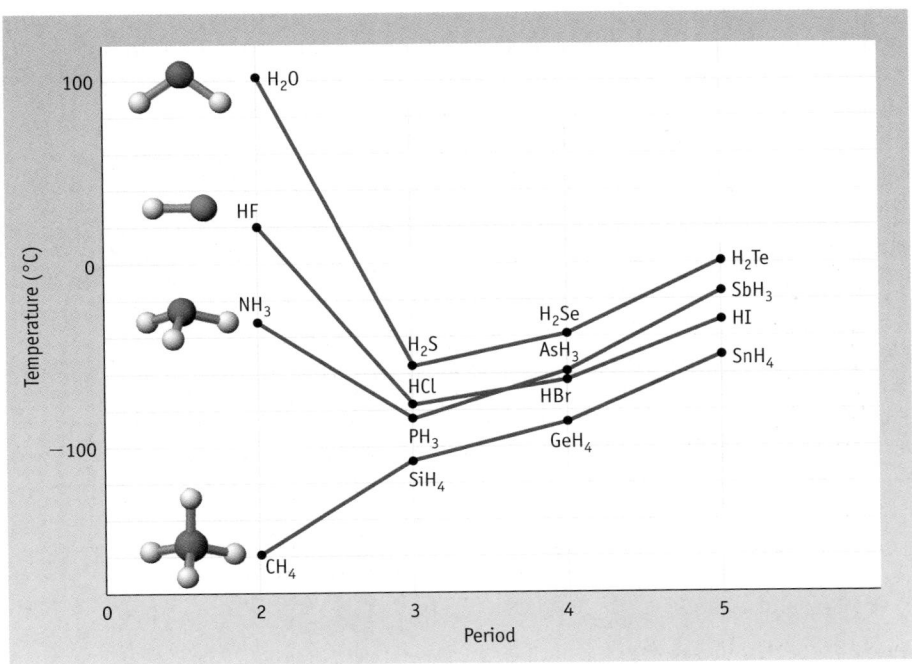

Active Figure 12.6 The boiling points of some simple hydrogen compounds. The effect of hydrogen bonding is apparent in the unusually high boiling points of H_2O, HF, and NH_3. (Also, notice that the boiling point of HCl is somewhat higher than expected based on the data for HBr and HI. It is apparent that some degree of hydrogen bonding also occurs in liquid HCl.)

Chemistry .ȯ. Now™ Sign in at www. cengage.com/login and go to the Chapter Contents menu to explore an interactive version of this figure accompanied by an exercise.

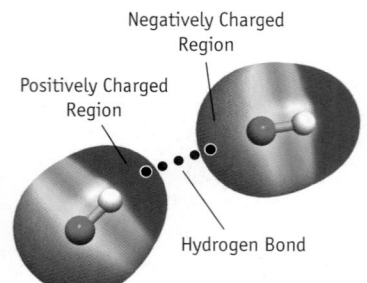

Negatively Charged Region

Positively Charged Region

Hydrogen Bond

Hydrogen bonding between HF molecules. The partially negative F atom of one HF molecule interacts through hydrogen bonding with a neighboring HF molecule. (Red regions of the molecule are negatively charged, whereas blue regions are positively charged. For more on electrostatic potential surfaces, see page 382.)

The electronegativities of N (3.0), O (3.5), and F (4.0) are among the highest of all the elements, whereas the electronegativity of hydrogen is much lower (2.2). This large difference in electronegativity means that N—H, O—H, and F—H bonds are very polar. In bonds between H and N, O, or F, the more electronegative element takes on a significant negative charge (see Figure 8.11), and the hydrogen atom acquires a significant positive charge.

There is an unusually strong attraction between an electronegative atom with a lone pair of electrons (most often, an N, O, or F atom in another molecule or even in the same molecule) and the hydrogen atom of the N—H, O—H, or F—H bond. This type of interaction is known as a **hydrogen bond.** Hydrogen bonds are an extreme form of dipole–dipole interaction where one atom involved is always H and the other atom is highly electronegative, most often O, N, or F. A hydrogen bond can be represented as

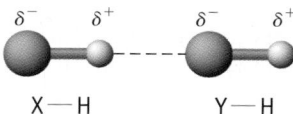

δ^- δ^+ δ^- δ^+

X—H   Y—H

The hydrogen atom becomes a bridge between the two electronegative atoms X and Y, and the dashed line represents the hydrogen bond. The most pronounced effects of hydrogen bonding occur where both X and Y are N, O, or F. Energies associated with most hydrogen bonds involving these elements are in the range of 5 to 30 kJ/mol.

Types of Hydrogen Bonds [X—H - - - :Y]

N—H - - - :N—	O—H - - - :N—	F—H - - - :N—
N—H - - - :O—	O—H - - - :O—	F—H - - - :O—
N—H - - - :F—	O—H - - - :F—	F—H - - - :F—

Hydrogen bonding has important implications for any property of a compound that is influenced by intermolecular forces of attraction. For example, hydrogen bonding affects the structures of molecular solids. In solid acetic acid, CH_3CO_2H, for example, two molecules are joined to one another by hydrogen bonding (Figure 12.7).

Chemistry Now™

Sign in at **www.cengage.com/login** and go to Chapter 12 Contents to see Screen 12.6 for a **description of hydrogen bonding.**

FIGURE 12.7 Hydrogen bonding. Two acetic acid molecules can interact through hydrogen bonds. This photo shows partly solid glacial acetic acid. Notice that the solid is denser than the liquid, a property shared by virtually all substances, the notable exception being water.

Photos: Charles D. Winters

EXAMPLE 12.2 The Effect of Hydrogen Bonding

Problem Ethanol, CH_3CH_2OH, and dimethyl ether, CH_3OCH_3, have the same formula but a different arrangement of atoms. Predict which of these compounds has the higher boiling point.

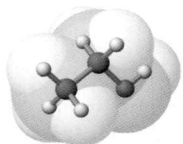

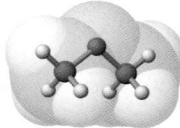

Ethanol, CH_3CH_2OH Dimethyl ether, CH_3OCH_3

Strategy Inspect the structure of each molecule to decide whether each is polar and, if polar, whether hydrogen bonding is possible.

Solution Although these two compounds have identical masses, they have different structures. Ethanol possesses an O—H group, and an electrostatic potential surface in the margin shows it to be polar with a partially negative O atom and a partially negative H atom. The result is that hydrogen bonding between ethanol molecules is possible and makes an important contribution to its intermolecular forces.

$$CH_3CH_2 - \overset{\cdot\cdot}{\underset{|}{O}}\!: \cdots H - \overset{\cdot\cdot}{\underset{|}{O}}\!:$$
$$H CH_2CH_3$$

hydrogen bonding in ethanol, CH_3CH_2OH

In contrast, dimethyl ether, although a polar molecule, presents no opportunity for hydrogen bonding because there is no O—H bond. The H atoms are attached to much less electronegative C atoms. We can predict, therefore, that intermolecular forces will be larger in ethanol than in dimethyl ether and that ethanol will have the higher boiling point. Indeed, ethanol boils at 78.3 °C, whereas dimethyl ether has a boiling point of −24.8 °C, more than 100 °C lower. Under standard conditions, dimethyl ether is a gas, whereas ethanol is a liquid.

EXERCISE 12.2 **Hydrogen Bonding**

Using structural formulas, describe the hydrogen bonding between methanol (CH_3OH) molecules. What physical properties of methanol are likely to be affected by hydrogen bonding?

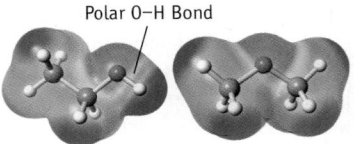

Polar O—H Bond

Electrostatic potential surfaces for ethanol (left) and dimethyl ether (right). The surface for ethanol clearly shows the polar O—H bond. The O atom in dimethyl ether has a partial negative charge, but there is no H atom attached. [Color coding: Red indicates a region of largest negative charge. Colors from yellow to green to turquoise indicate increasing positive charge (or decreasing negative charge). Blue indicates a region of partial positive charge.]

Hydrogen Bonding and the Unusual Properties of Water

One of the most striking differences between our planet and others in our solar system is the presence of large amounts of water on Earth. Three fourths of the planet is covered by oceans; the polar regions are vast ice fields; and even soil and rocks hold large amounts of water. Although we tend to take water for granted, almost no other substance behaves in a similar manner. Water's unique features reflect the ability of H_2O molecules to cling tenaciously to one another by hydrogen bonding.

One reason for ice's unusual structure and water's unusual properties is that each hydrogen atom of a water molecule can form a hydrogen bond to a lone pair of electrons on the oxygen atom of an adjacent water molecule. In addition, because the oxygen atom in water has two lone pairs of electrons, it can form two more hydrogen bonds with hydrogen atoms from adjacent molecules (Figure 12.8a). The result, seen particularly in ice, is a tetrahedral arrangement for the hydrogen atoms around each oxygen, involving two covalently bonded hydrogen atoms and two hydrogen-bonded hydrogen atoms.

As a consequence of the regular arrangement of water molecules linked by hydrogen bonding, ice has an open-cage structure with lots of empty space (Figure 12.8b). The result is that ice has a density about 10% less than that of liquid water, which explains why ice floats. (In contrast, virtually all other solids sink in their liquid phase.) We can also see in this structure that the oxygen atoms are arranged at the corners of puckered, hexagonal rings. Snowflakes are always based on six-sided figures (◄ page 69), a reflection of this internal molecular structure of ice.

When ice melts at 0 °C, the regular structure imposed on the solid state by hydrogen bonding breaks down, and a relatively large increase in density occurs (Figure 12.9). Another surprising thing occurs when the temperature of liquid water is raised from 0 °C to 4 °C: The density of water increases. For almost every other substance known, density decreases as the temperature is raised. Once again, hydrogen bonding is the reason for water's seemingly odd behavior. At a tempera-

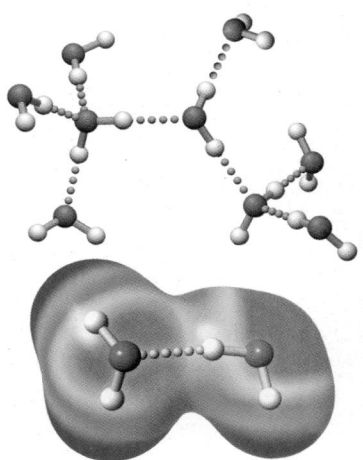

Hydrogen bonding in water. (above) Water readily forms hydrogen bonds. (below) An electrostatic potential surface for two water molecules shows the hydrogen bond involving the negatively charged O atom of one molecule and the positively charged H atom of a neighboring molecule.

FIGURE 12.8 The structure of ice.
(a) The oxygen atom of a water molecule attaches itself to two other water
molecules by hydrogen bonds. Notice
that the four groups that surround an
oxygen atom are arranged as a distorted tetrahedron. Each oxygen atom
is covalently bonded to two hydrogen
atoms and hydrogen bonded to hydrogen atoms from two other molecules.
The hydrogen bonds are longer than
the covalent bonds. (b) In ice, the structural unit shown in part (a) is repeated
in the crystalline lattice. This computer-
generated structure shows a small portion
of the extensive lattice. Notice the six-
member, hexagonal rings. The corners of
each hexagon are O atoms, and each side
is composed of a normal O—H bond and
a slightly longer hydrogen bond.

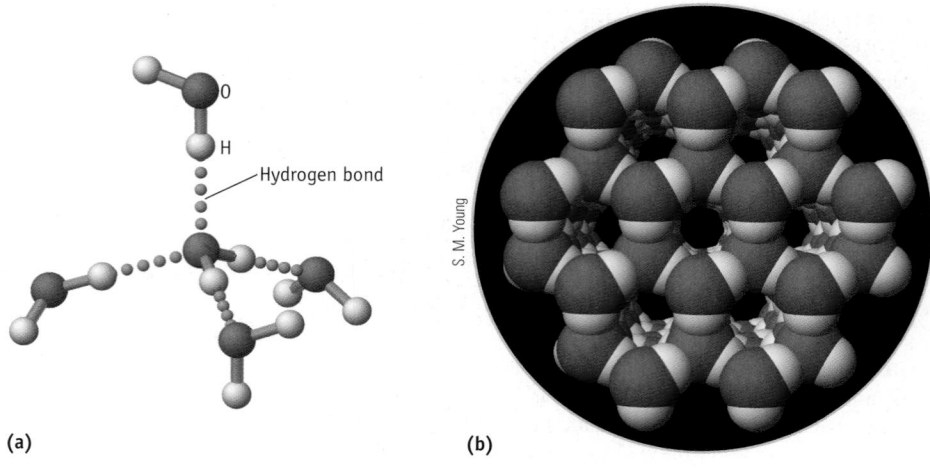

(a)   (b)

ture just above the melting point, some of the water molecules continue to cluster
in ice-like arrangements, which require extra space. As the temperature is raised
from 0 °C to 4 °C, the final vestiges of the ice structure disappear, and the volume
contracts further, giving rise to the increase in density. Water's density reaches a
maximum at about 4 °C. From this point, the density declines with increasing
temperature in the normal fashion.

Because of the way that water's density changes as the temperature approaches
the freezing point, lakes do not freeze solidly from the bottom up in the winter.
When lake water cools with the approach of winter, its density increases, the cooler
water sinks, and the warmer water rises. This "turn over" process continues until
all the water reaches 4 °C, the maximum density. (This is the way oxygen-rich water moves to the lake bottom to restore the oxygen used during the summer and
nutrients are brought to the top layers of the lake.) As the temperature decreases
further, the colder water stays on the top of the lake, because water cooler than
4 °C is less dense than water at 4 °C. With further heat loss, ice can then begin to
form on the surface, floating there and protecting the underlying water and aquatic
life from further heat loss.

Extensive hydrogen bonding is also the origin of the extraordinarily high heat
capacity of water. Although liquid water does not have the regular structure of
ice, hydrogen bonding still occurs. With a rise in temperature, the extent of
hydrogen bonding diminishes. Disrupting hydrogen bonds requires energy. The
high heat capacity of water is, in large part, why oceans and lakes have such an
enormous effect on weather. In autumn, when the temperature of the air is lower
than the temperature of the ocean or lake, the water transfers energy as heat to
the atmosphere, moderating the drop in air temperature. Furthermore, so much
energy is available to be transferred for each degree drop in temperature that
the decline in water temperature is gradual. For this reason, the temperature of
the ocean or of a large lake is generally higher than the average air temperature
until late in the autumn.

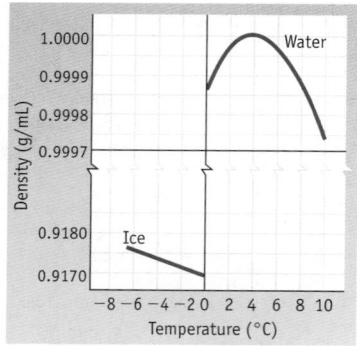

Active Figure 12.9 The temperature dependence of the densities
of ice and water.

Chemistry ⚛ Now™ Sign in at www.
cengage.com/login and go to the
Chapter Contents menu to explore
an interactive version of this figure
accompanied by an exercise.

Chemistry ⚛ Now™

Sign in at **www.cengage.com/login** and go to Chapter 12 Contents to see Screen 12.7 to view an animation
of **the transformation of ice to water** and for a table listing all of the **unusual properties of water.**

It is arguable that our world is what it is because of hydrogen bonding in water and in biochemical systems. Perhaps the most important occurrence is in DNA and RNA where the organic bases adenine, cytosine, guanine, and thymine (in DNA) or uracil (in RNA) are attached to sugar-phosphate chains (**Figure A**). The chains in DNA are joined by the pairing of bases, adenine with thymine and guanine with cytosine.

Figure B illustrates the hydrogen bonding between adenine and thymine. These models show that the molecules naturally fit together to form a six-sided ring, where two of the six sides involve hydrogen bonds. One side consists of a N · · · H—N grouping, and the other side is N—H · · · O. Here, the electrostatic potential surfaces show that the N atoms of adenine and the O atoms of thymine bear partial negative charges, and the H atoms of the N—H groups bear a positive charge. These charges and the geometry of the bases lead to these very specific interactions.

The fact that base pairing through hydrogen bonding leads to the joining of the sugar-phosphate chains of DNA, and to the double helical form of DNA, was first recognized by James Watson and Francis Crick on the basis of experimental work by Rosalind Franklin and Maurice Wilkins in the 1950s. It was this development that was so important in the molecular biology revolution in the last part of the 20th century. See page 392 for more on these scientists.

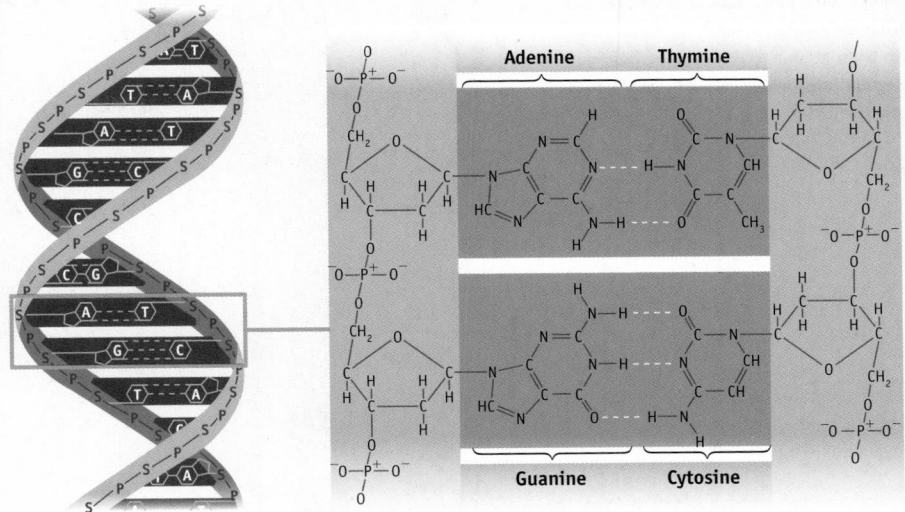

FIGURE A **Hydrogen bonding in DNA.** With the four bases in DNA, the usual pairings are adenine with thymine and guanine with cytosine. This pairing is promoted by hydrogen bonding.

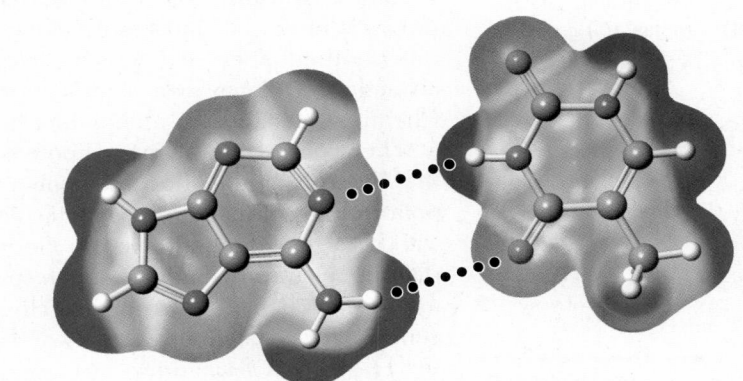

FIGURE B **Hydrogen bonding between adenine and thymine.** Electrostatic potential surfaces show that the polar N—H bond on one molecule can hydrogen bond to an electronegative N atom in a neighboring molecule.

12.3 Intermolecular Forces Involving Nonpolar Molecules

Many important molecules such as O_2, N_2, and the halogens are not polar. Why, then, does O_2 dissolve in polar water? Why can the N_2 of the atmosphere be liquefied (see Figure 12.1)? Some intermolecular forces must be acting between O_2 and water and between N_2 molecules, but what is their nature?

Dipole/Induced Dipole Forces

Polar molecules such as water can induce, or create, a dipole in molecules that do not have a permanent dipole. To see how this situation can occur, picture a polar water molecule approaching a nonpolar molecule such as O_2 (Figure 12.10). The

 Module 17

■ **Van der Waals Forces** The name "van der Waals forces" is a general term applied to attractive intermolecular interactions. (P. W. Atkins: *Quanta: A Handbook of Concepts,* 2nd ed., p. 187, Oxford, Oxford University Press, 2000.)

FIGURE 12.10 Dipole/induced dipole interaction. (a) A polar molecule such as water can induce a dipole in nonpolar O_2 by distorting the molecule's electron cloud. (b) Nonpolar I_2 dissolves in polar ethanol (C_2H_5OH). The intermolecular force involved is a dipole/induced dipole force.

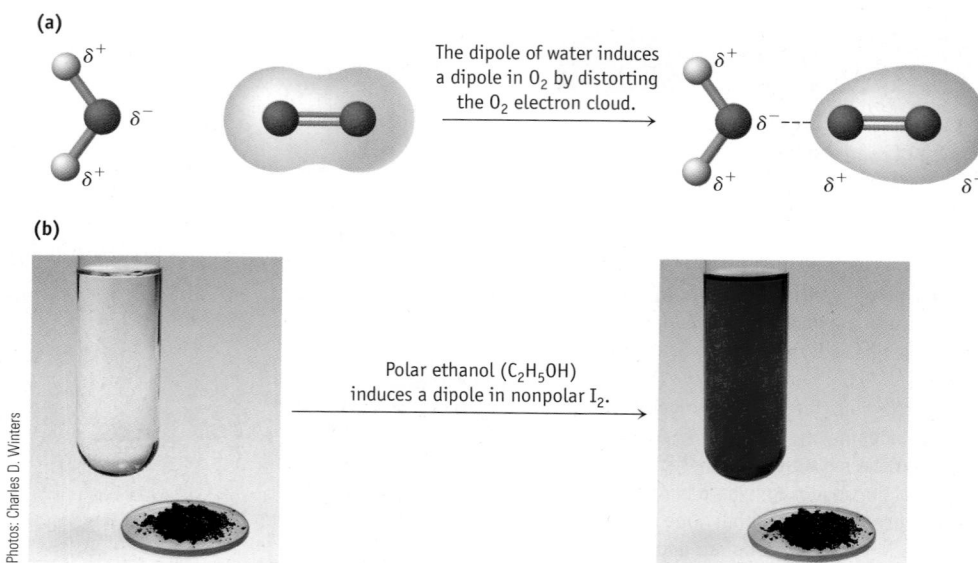

The dipole of water induces a dipole in O_2 by distorting the O_2 electron cloud.

(b)

Photos: Charles D. Winters

Polar ethanol (C_2H_5OH) induces a dipole in nonpolar I_2.

TABLE 12.3 The Solubility of Some Gases in Water*

	Molar Mass (g/mol)	Solubility at 20 °C (g gas/100 g water)†
H_2	2.01	0.000160
N_2	28.0	0.00190
O_2	32.0	0.00434

* Data taken from J. Dean: *Lange's Handbook of Chemistry*. 14th Ed., pp. 5.3–5.8, New York, McGraw-Hill, 1992.
† Measured under conditions where pressure of gas + pressure of water vapor = 760 mm Hg.

TABLE 12.4 Enthalpies of Vaporization and Boiling Points of Some Nonpolar Substances

	$\Delta_{vap}H°$ (kJ/mol)	Element/ Compound BP (°C)
N_2	5.57	−196
O_2	6.82	−183
CH_4 (methane)	8.2	−161.5
Br_2	29.96	+58.8
C_6H_6 (benzene)	30.7	+80.1
I_2	41.95	+185

electron cloud of an isolated (gaseous) O_2 molecule is symmetrically distributed between the two oxygen atoms. As the negative end of the polar H_2O molecule approaches, however, the O_2 electron cloud becomes distorted. In this process, the O_2 molecule itself becomes polar; that is, a dipole is *induced* in the otherwise nonpolar O_2 molecule. The result is that H_2O and O_2 molecules are now attracted to one another, albeit only weakly. Oxygen can dissolve in water because a force of attraction exists between water's permanent dipole and the induced dipole in O_2. Chemists refer to such interactions as **dipole/induced dipole interactions.**

The process of inducing a dipole is called **polarization,** and the degree to which the electron cloud of an atom or a molecule can be distorted depends on the **polarizability** of that atom or molecule. The electron cloud of an atom or molecule with a large, extended electron cloud, such as I_2, can be polarized more readily than the electron cloud in a much smaller atom or molecule, such as He or H_2, in which the valence electrons are close to the nucleus and more tightly held. In general, for an analogous series of substances, say the halogens or alkanes (such as CH_4, C_2H_6, C_3H_8, and so on), *the higher the molar mass, the greater the polarizability of the molecule.*

The solubilities of common gases in water illustrate the effect of interactions between a dipole and an induced dipole. In Table 12.3, you see a trend to higher solubility with increasing mass of the nonpolar gas. As the molar mass of the gas increases, the polarizability of the electron cloud increases and the strength of the dipole/induced dipole interaction increases.

London Dispersion Forces: Induced Dipole/Induced Dipole Forces

Iodine, I_2, is a solid and not a gas around room temperature and pressure, illustrating that nonpolar molecules must also experience intermolecular forces. An estimate of these forces is provided by the enthalpy of vaporization of the substance at its boiling point. The data in Table 12.4 suggest that these forces can range from very weak (N_2, O_2, and CH_4 with low enthalpies of vaporization and very low boiling points) to more substantial (I_2 and benzene).

To understand how two nonpolar molecules can attract each other, recall that the electrons in atoms or molecules are in a state of constant motion. When two

 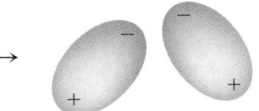 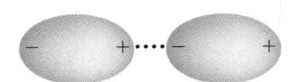

Two nonpolar atoms or molecules (depicted as having an electron cloud that has a time-averaged spherical shape).

Momentary attractions and repulsions between nuclei and electrons in neighboring molecules lead to induced dipoles.

Correlation of the electron motions between the two atoms or molecules (which are now dipolar) leads to a lower energy and stabilizes the system.

FIGURE 12.11 Induced dipole interactions. Momentary attractions and repulsions between nuclei and electrons create induced dipoles and lead to a net stabilization due to attractive forces.

atoms or nonpolar molecules approach each other, attractions or repulsions between their electrons and nuclei can lead to distortions in their electron clouds (Figure 12.11). That is, dipoles can be induced momentarily in neighboring atoms or molecules, and these induced dipoles lead to intermolecular attractions. The intermolecular force of attraction in liquids and solids composed of nonpolar molecules is an **induced dipole/induced dipole force**. Chemists often call them **London dispersion forces**. London dispersion forces actually arise between all molecules, both nonpolar and polar, but *London dispersion forces are the only intermolecular forces that allow nonpolar molecules to interact.*

A Closer Look

Methane Hydrates: An Answer to World Fuel Supplies?

Hydrogen bonds involving water are also responsible for the structure and properties of one of the strangest substances on earth (Figure). When methane (CH_4) is mixed with water at high pressures and low temperatures, solid methane hydrate forms. Although the substance has been known for years, vast deposits of methane hydrate were only recently discovered deep within sediments on the floor of Earth's oceans. How these were formed is a mystery, but what is important is their size. It is estimated that global methane hydrate deposits contain approximately 10^{13} tons of carbon, or about twice the combined amount in all known reserves of coal, oil, and natural gas. Methane hydrate is also an efficient energy storehouse; a liter of methane hydrate releases about 160 liters of methane gas.

But of course there are problems to be solved. One significant problem is how to bring commercially useful quantities to the surface from deep in the ocean. Yet another is the possibility of a large, uncontrolled release of methane. Methane is a very effective greenhouse gas, so the release of a significant quantity into the atmosphere could damage the earth's climate.

Among the many sources of information is: E. Suess, G. Bohrmann, J. Greinert, and E. Lausch, *Scientific American*, November 1999, pp. 76–83.

John Pinkston and Laura Stern/U.S. Geological Survey/*Science News*, 11-9-96

(a) Methane hydrate burns as methane gas escapes from the solid hydrate.

(b) Methane hydrate consists of a lattice of water molecules with methane molecules trapped in the cavity.

Methane hydrate. (a) When a sample is brought to the surface from the depths of the ocean, the methane oozes out of the solid, and the gas readily burns. (b) The structure of the solid methane hydrate consists of methane molecules trapped in a lattice of water molecules. Each point of the lattice shown here is an O atom of an H_2O molecule. The edges are O—H—O hydrogen bonds. Such structures are often called "clathrates." (For more on methane hydrates, see pages 259–260.)

Induced dipole/induced dipole forces.
Br_2 (left) and I_2 (right) both consist of nonpolar molecules. They are a liquid and a solid, respectively, implying that there are forces between the molecules sufficient to cause them to be in a condensed phase. These forces between nonpolar substances are known as London dispersion forces or induced dipole/induced dipole forces.

Geckos use intermolecular forces! A little gecko can climb vertically 1 m up a polished glass surface in 1 s. Geckos have millions of tiny hairs or setae on their feet, and each setae ends in 1000 or more even tinier hairs at the tip. Recent research has found that geckos are unique in that they adhere to a surface through van der Waals forces of attraction between the hairs and the surface. (K. Autumn, "How gecko toes stick." *American Scientist* Vol. 94, pages 124–132, 2006.)

■ **EXAMPLE 12.3 Intermolecular Forces**

Problem Suppose you have a mixture of solid iodine, I_2, and the liquids water and carbon tetrachloride (CCl_4). What intermolecular forces exist between each possible pair of compounds? Describe what you might see when these compounds are mixed.

Strategy First, decide whether each substance is polar or nonpolar. Second, determine the types of intermolecular forces that could exist between the different pairs. Finally, use the "like dissolves like" guideline to decide whether iodine will dissolve in water or CCl_4 and whether CCl_4 will dissolve in water.

Solution Iodine, I_2, is nonpolar. As a molecule composed of large iodine atoms, it has an extensive electron cloud. Thus, the molecule is easily polarized, and iodine could interact with water, a polar molecule, by dipole/induced dipole forces.

Carbon tetrachloride, a tetrahedral molecule, is not polar (see Figure 8.15). As a consequence, it can interact with iodine only by dispersion forces. Water and CCl_4 could interact by dipole/induced dipole forces, but the interaction is expected to be weak.

The photo here shows the result of mixing these three compounds. Iodine does dissolve to a small extent in water to give a brown solution. When this brown solution is added to a test tube containing CCl_4, the liquid layers do not mix. (Polar water does not dissolve in nonpolar CCl_4.) (Notice the more dense CCl_4 layer [$d = 1.58$ g/mL] is underneath the less dense water layer.) When the test tube is shaken, however, nonpolar I_2 dissolves preferentially in nonpolar CCl_4, as evidenced by the disappearance of the color of I_2 in the water layer (top) and the appearance of the purple I_2 color in the CCl_4 layer (bottom).

Nonpolar I_2
Polar H_2O

Nonpolar CCl_4

Shake the test tube

Polar H_2O

Nonpolar CCl_4 and I_2

EXERCISE 12.3 Intermolecular Forces

You mix water, CCl_4, and hexane ($CH_3CH_2CH_2CH_2CH_2CH_3$). What type of intermolecular forces can exist between each pair of these compounds?

Summary of Intermolecular Forces

Intermolecular forces involve molecules that are polar or those in which polarity can be induced (Table 12.5). Furthermore, several types of intermolecular forces can be at work in a single type of molecule (Figure 12.12). Also note in Figure 12.12 that while each individual induced dipole/induced dipole force is usually quite small, the sum of these forces over the entire structure of a molecule can actually be quite great, even in polar molecules.

Chemistry Now™

Sign in at **www.cengage.com/login** and go to Chapter 12 Contents to see Screen 12.5 to view an animation of **induced dipole forces** and for an exercise and tutorial on **intermolecular forces**.

TABLE 12.5 Summary of Intermolecular Forces

Type of Interaction	Factors Responsible for Interaction	Approximate Energy (kJ/mol)	Example
Ion–dipole	Ion change, magnitude of dipole	40–600	$Na^+ \ldots H_2O$
Dipole–dipole	Dipole moment (depends on atom electronegativities and molecular structure)	20–30	$H_2O \ldots CH_3OH$
Hydrogen bonding, X—H . . . :Y	Very polar X—H bond (where X = F, N, O) and atom Y with lone pair of electrons	5–30	$H_2O \ldots H_2O$
Dipole/induced dipole	Dipole moment of polar molecule and polarizability of nonpolar molecule	2–10	$H_2O \ldots I_2$
Induced dipole/induced dipole (London dispersion forces)	Polarizability	0.05–40	$I_2 \ldots I_2$

■ EXAMPLE 12.4 Intermolecular Forces

Problem Decide which are the most important intermolecular forces involved in each of the following, and place them in order of increasing strength of interaction: (a) liquid methane, CH_4; (b) a mixture of water and methanol (CH_3OH); and (c) a solution of bromine in water.

Strategy For each molecule, we consider its structure and decide whether it is polar. If polar, we consider the possibility of hydrogen bonding.

Solution (a) Methane is a covalently bonded molecule. Based on the Lewis structure, we can conclude that it must be a tetrahedral molecule and that it cannot be polar. The only way methane molecules can interact with one another is through induced dipole/induced dipole forces.

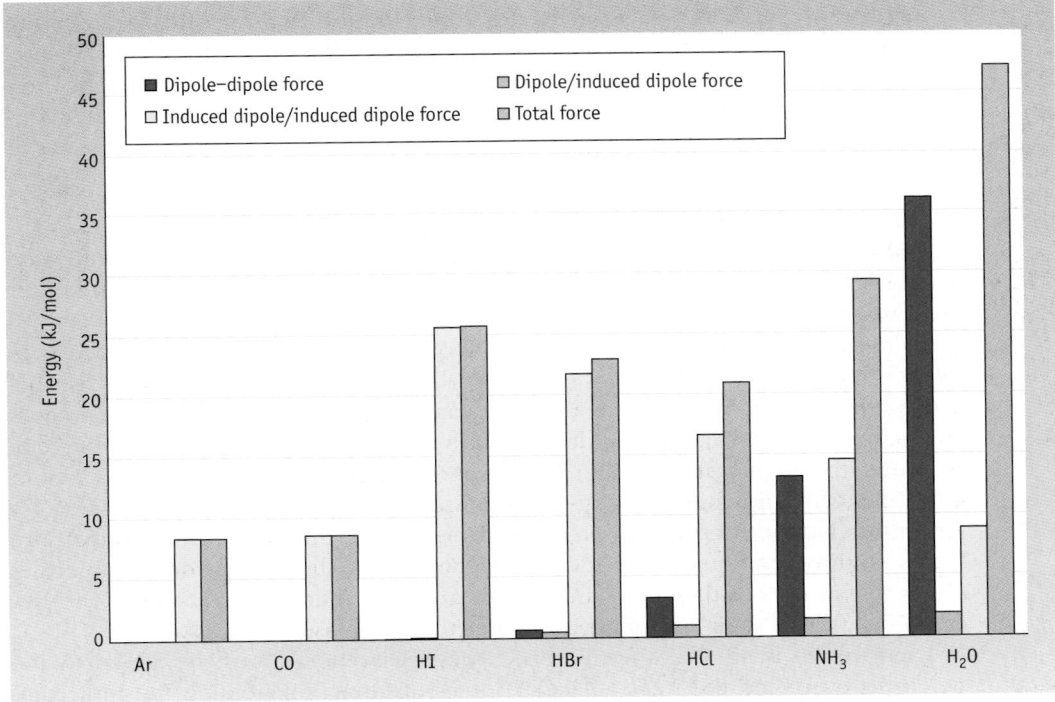

FIGURE 12.12 Energies associated with intermolecular forces.

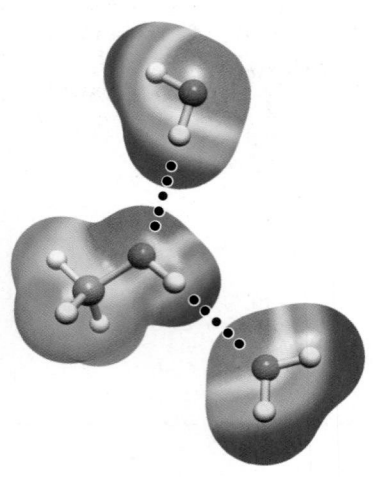

Hydrogen bonding involving methanol (CH₃OH) and water.

(b) Both water and methanol are covalently bonded molecules; both are polar; and both have an O—H bond. They therefore interact through the special dipole–dipole force called hydrogen bonding, as well as by dipole-dipole and London forces.

$$\delta^+ H \diagdown \underset{\delta^+ H}{O} \cdots \overset{\delta^-}{H} — \overset{\delta^+}{O} \underset{CH_3}{} \quad \text{and} \quad \delta^+ H \diagdown \underset{H_3C}{O} \cdots \overset{\delta^-}{H} — \overset{\delta^+}{O} \underset{H^{\delta^+}}{}$$

(c) Nonpolar molecules of bromine, Br₂, interact by induced dipole forces, whereas water is a polar molecule. Therefore, dipole/induced dipole forces (and London forces) are involved when Br₂ molecules interact with water. (This is similar to the I₂–ethanol interaction in Figure 12.10.)

In order of increasing strength, the likely order of interactions is

$$\text{liquid } CH_4 < H_2O \text{ and } Br_2 < H_2O \text{ and } CH_3OH$$

EXERCISE 12.4 Intermolecular Forces

Decide which type of intermolecular force is involved in (a) liquid O_2; (b) liquid CH_3OH; and (c) N_2 dissolved in H_2O. Place the interactions in order of increasing strength.

12.4 Properties of Liquids

Of the three states of matter, liquids are the most difficult to describe precisely. The molecules in a gas under normal conditions are far apart and may be considered more or less independent of one another. The structures of solids can be described readily because the particles that make up solids—atoms, molecules, or ions—are close together and are usually in an orderly arrangement. The particles of a liquid interact with their neighbors, like the particles in a solid, but, unlike in solids, there is little long-range order in their arrangement.

In spite of a lack of precision in describing liquids, we can still consider the behavior of liquids at the molecular level. In the following sections, we will look further at the process of vaporization, at the vapor pressure of liquids, at their boiling points and critical properties, and at the behavior that results in their surface tension, capillary action, and viscosity.

Vaporization and Condensation

Vaporization or evaporation is the process in which a substance in the liquid state becomes a gas. In this process, molecules escape from the liquid surface and enter the gaseous state.

To understand evaporation, we have to look at molecular energies. Molecules in a liquid have a range of energies (Figure 12.13) that closely resembles the distribution of energies for molecules of a gas (see Figure 11.14). As with gases, the average energy for molecules in a liquid depends only on temperature: The higher the temperature, the higher the average energy and the greater the relative number of molecules with high kinetic energy. In a sample of a liquid, at least a few molecules have more kinetic energy than the potential energy of the intermolecular attractive forces holding the liquid molecules to one another. If these high-energy molecules are at the surface of the liquid and if they are moving in the right direction, they can break free of their neighbors and enter the gas phase (Figure 12.14).

Vaporization is an endothermic process because energy must be added to the system to overcome the intermolecular forces of attraction holding the molecules together. The energy required to vaporize a sample is often given as the standard

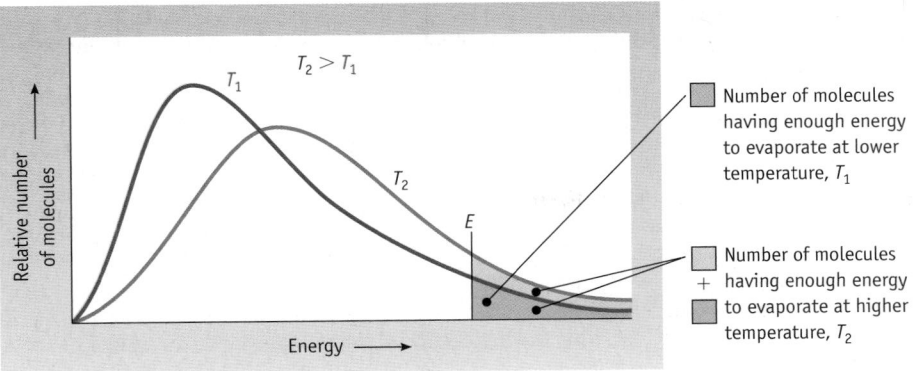

FIGURE 12.13 The distribution of energy among molecules in a liquid sample. T_2 is a higher temperature than T_1, and at the higher temperature, there are more molecules with an energy greater than E.

molar enthalpy of vaporization, $\Delta_{vap}H°$ (in units of kilojoules per mole; see Tables 12.4 and 12.6 and Figure 12.4).

$$\text{Liquid} \xrightarrow[\substack{\text{heat energy absorbed} \\ \text{by liquid}}]{\text{vaporization}} \text{Vapor} \qquad \Delta_{vap}H° = \text{molar heat of vaporization}$$

A molecule in the gas phase can transfer some of its kinetic energy by colliding with slower gaseous molecules and solid objects. If this molecule loses sufficient energy and comes in contact with the surface of the liquid, it can reenter the liquid phase in the process called **condensation**.

$$\text{Vapor} \xrightarrow[\substack{\text{heat energy released} \\ \text{by vapor}}]{\text{condensation}} \text{Liquid}$$

Condensation is the reverse of vaporization. Condensation is exothermic, so energy is transferred to the surroundings. *The enthalpy change for condensation is equal but opposite in sign to the enthalpy of vaporization.* For example, the enthalpy change for the vaporization of 1.00 mol of water at 100 °C is +40.7 kJ. On condensing 1.00 mol of water vapor to liquid water at 100 °C, the enthalpy change is −40.7 kJ.

In the discussion of intermolecular forces, we pointed out the relationship between the $\Delta_{vap}H°$ values for various substances and the temperatures at which they boil (Table 12.6). Both properties reflect the attractive forces between particles in the liquid. The boiling points of nonpolar liquids (e.g., the hydrocarbons, atmospheric gases, and the halogens) increase with increasing atomic or molecular mass,

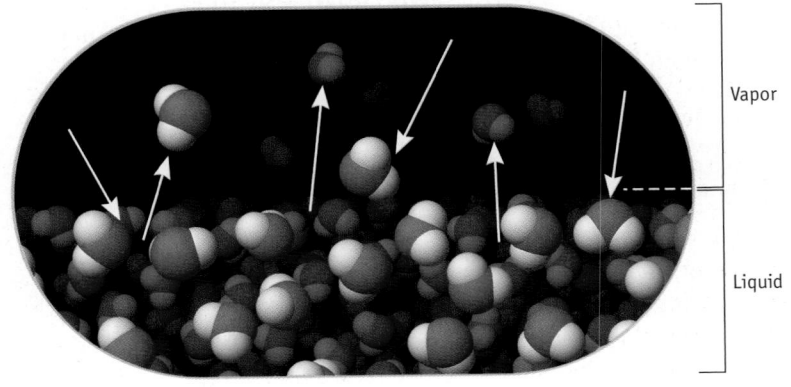

FIGURE 12.14 Evaporation. Some molecules at the surface of a liquid have enough energy to escape the attractions of their neighbors and enter the gaseous state. At the same time, some molecules in the gaseous state can reenter the liquid.

TABLE 12.6   Molar Enthalpies of Vaporization and Boiling Points for Common Substances*

Compound	Molar Mass (g/mol)	$\Delta_{vap}H°$ (kJ/mol)†	Boiling Point (°C) (Vapor pressure = 760 mm Hg)
Polar Compounds			
HF	20.0	25.2	19.7
HCl	36.5	16.2	−84.8
HBr	80.9	19.3	−66.4
HI	127.9	19.8	−35.6
NH_3	17.0	23.3	−33.3
H_2O	18.0	40.7	100.0
SO_2	64.1	24.9	−10.0
Nonpolar Compounds			
CH_4 (methane)	16.0	8.2	−161.5
C_2H_6 (ethane)	30.1	14.7	−88.6
C_3H_8 (propane)	44.1	19.0	−42.1
C_4H_{10} (butane)	58.1	22.4	−0.5
Monatomic Elements			
He	4.0	0.08	−268.9
Ne	20.2	1.7	−246.1
Ar	39.9	6.4	−185.9
Xe	131.3	12.6	−108.0
Diatomic Elements			
H_2	2.0	0.90	−252.9
N_2	28.0	5.6	−195.8
O_2	32.0	6.8	−183.0
F_2	38.0	6.6	−188.1
Cl_2	70.9	20.4	−34.0
Br_2	159.8	30.0	58.8

*Data taken from D. R. Lide: *Basic Laboratory and Industrial Chemicals*, Boca Raton, FL, CRC Press, 1993.
†$\Delta_{vap}H°$ is measured at the normal boiling point of the liquid.

a reflection of increased intermolecular dispersion forces. The alkanes (such as methane) listed in Table 12.6 show this trend clearly. Similarly, the boiling points and enthalpies of vaporization of the heavier hydrogen halides (HX, where X = Cl, Br, and I) increase with increasing molecular mass. For these molecules, hydrogen bonding is not as important as it is in HF, so dispersion forces and ordinary dipole–dipole forces account for their intermolecular attractions (see Figure 12.12). Because dispersion forces become increasingly important with increasing mass, the boiling points are in the order HCl < HBr < HI. Also notice in Table 12.6 the very high enthalpies of vaporization of water and hydrogen fluoride that result from extensive hydrogen bonding.

Chemistry ⊙ Now™

Sign in at **www.cengage.com/login** and go to Chapter 12 Contents to see Screen 12.8 to view an animation of the **vaporization process** and for a table of $\Delta_{vap}H°$ **values.**

◼ **EXAMPLE 12.5   Enthalpy of Vaporization**

Problem You put 925 mL of water (about 4 cupsful) in a pan at 100 °C, and the water slowly evaporates. How much energy must have been transferred as heat to vaporize the water?

Strategy Three pieces of information are needed to solve this problem:

1. $\Delta_{vap}H°$ for water = +40.7 kJ/mol at 100 °C.

2. The density of water at 100 °C = 0.958 g/cm³. (This is needed because $\Delta_{vap}H°$ has units of kilojoules per mole, so you first must find the mass of water and then the amount.)

3. Molar mass of water = 18.02 g/mol.

Solution A volume of 925 mL (or 9.25×10^2 cm³) is equivalent to 886 g, and this mass is in turn equivalent to 49.2 mol of water.

$$925 \text{ mL} \left(\frac{0.958 \text{ g}}{1 \text{ mL}} \right) \left(\frac{1 \text{ mol}}{18.02 \text{ g}} \right) = 49.2 \text{ mol H}_2\text{O}$$

Therefore, the amount of energy required is

$$49.2 \text{ mol H}_2\text{O} \left(\frac{40.7 \text{ kJ}}{\text{mol}} \right) = \mathbf{2.00 \times 10^3 \text{ kJ}}$$

2000 kJ is equivalent to about one quarter of the energy in your daily food intake.

EXERCISE 12.5 Enthalpy of Vaporization

The molar enthalpy of vaporization of methanol, CH_3OH, is 35.2 kJ/mol at 64.6 °C. How much energy is required to evaporate 1.00 kg of this alcohol at 64.6 °C?

Water is exceptional among the liquids listed in Table 12.6 in that an enormous amount of heat is required to convert liquid water to water vapor. This fact is important to your own physical well-being. When you exercise vigorously, your body responds by sweating to rid itself of the excess heat. Energy from your body is transferred to sweat in the process of evaporation, and your body is cooled.

Enthalpies of vaporization and condensation of water also play a role in weather (Figure 12.15). For example, if enough water condenses from the air to fall as an inch of rain on an acre of ground, the heat released exceeds 2.0×10^8 kJ! This is equivalent to about 50 tons of exploded dynamite, the energy released by a small bomb.

Vapor Pressure

If you put some water in an open beaker, it will eventually evaporate completely. Air movement and gas diffusion remove the water vapor from the vicinity of the liquid surface, so many water molecules are not able to return to the liquid.

If you put water in a sealed flask (Figure 12.16), however, the water vapor cannot escape, and some will recondense to form liquid water. Eventually, the masses of liquid and of vapor in the flask remain constant. This is another example of a **dynamic equilibrium** (◀ page 119).

Liquid ⇌ Vapor

Molecules still move continuously from the liquid phase to the vapor phase and from the vapor phase back to the liquid phase. The rate at which molecules move from liquid to vapor is the same as the rate at which they move from vapor to liquid; thus, there is no net change in the masses of the two phases.

When a liquid–vapor equilibrium has been established, the equilibrium vapor pressure (often just called the vapor pressure) can be measured. The **equilibrium vapor pressure** of a substance is the pressure exerted by the vapor in equilibrium with the liquid phase. Conceptually, the vapor pressure of a liquid is a measure of the tendency of its molecules to escape from the liquid phase and enter the vapor

The Image Bank/Getty Images

FIGURE 12.15 Rainstorms release an enormous quantity of energy. When water vapor condenses, energy is evolved to the surroundings. The enthalpy of condensation of water is large, so a large quantity of energy is released in a rainstorm.

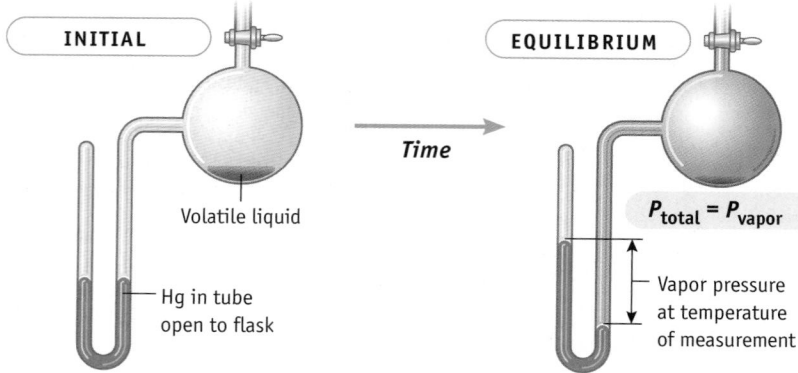

INITIAL

EQUILIBRIUM

Time

Volatile liquid

Hg in tube
open to flask

$P_{total} = P_{vapor}$

Vapor pressure
at temperature
of measurement

phase at a given temperature. This tendency is referred to qualitatively as the
volatility of the compound. The higher the equilibrium vapor pressure at a given
temperature, the more volatile the substance.

As described previously (see Figure 12.13), the distribution of molecular energies
in the liquid phase is a function of temperature. At a higher temperature, more
molecules have sufficient energy to escape the surface of the liquid. The equilibrium vapor pressure must, therefore, increase with temperature.

It is useful to represent vapor pressure as a function of temperature. Figure 12.17
shows the vapor pressure curves for several liquids as a function of temperature.
*All points along the vapor pressure versus temperature curves represent conditions of pressure
and temperature at which liquid and vapor are in equilibrium.* For example, at 60 °C the
vapor pressure of water is 149 mm Hg (Appendix G). If water is placed in an
evacuated flask that is maintained at 60 °C, liquid water will evaporate until the
pressure exerted by the water vapor is 149 mm Hg (assuming enough water is in
the flask so that some liquid remains when equilibrium is reached).

■ **Equilibrium Vapor Pressure** At the
conditions of *T* and *P* given by any point
on a curve in Figure 12.17, the pure liquid
and its vapor are in dynamic equilibrium.
If *T* and *P* define a point not on the curve,
the system is not at equilibrium. See
Appendix G for the equilibrium vapor pressures of water at various temperatures.

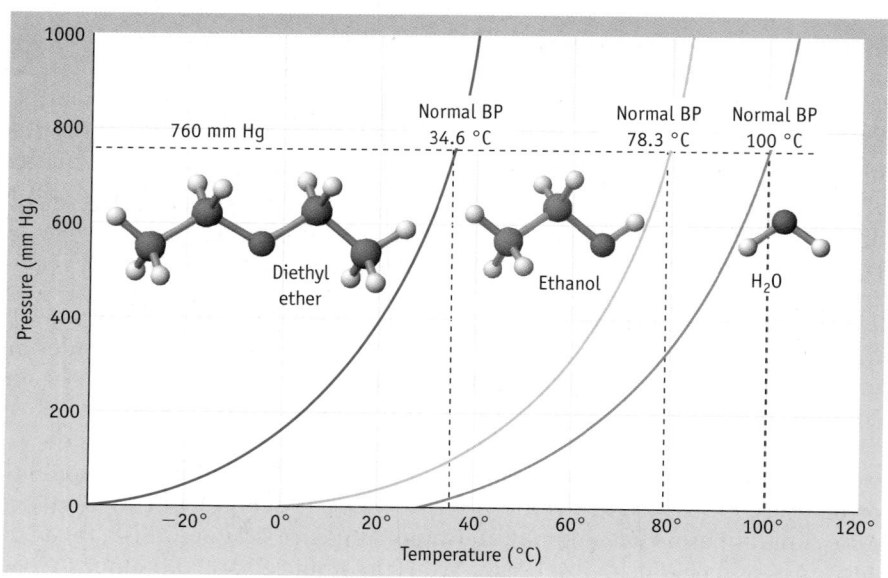

Problem You place 2.00 L of water in an open container in your dormitory room; the room has a volume of 4.25×10^4 L. You seal the room and wait for the water to evaporate. Will all of the water evaporate at 25 °C? (At 25 °C the density of water is 0.997 g/mL, and its vapor pressure is 23.8 mm Hg.)

Strategy One approach to solving this problem is to calculate the quantity of water that must evaporate to exert a pressure of 23.8 mm Hg in a volume of 4.25×10^4 L at 25 °C. We use the ideal gas law for this calculation.

Solution Calculate the amount and then mass and volume of water that fulfills the following conditions: $P = 23.8$ mm Hg, $V = 4.25 \times 10^4$ L, $T = 25$ °C (298 K).

$$P = 23.8 \text{ mm Hg}\left(\frac{1 \text{ atm}}{760 \text{ mm Hg}}\right) = 0.0313 \text{ atm}$$

$$n = \frac{PV}{RT} = \frac{(0.0313 \text{ atm})(4.25 \times 10^4 \text{ L})}{\left(0.082057 \dfrac{\text{L} \cdot \text{atm}}{\text{K} \cdot \text{mol}}\right)(298 \text{ K})} = 54.4 \text{ mol}$$

$$54.4 \text{ mol H}_2\text{O}\left(\frac{18.02 \text{ g}}{1 \text{ mol H}_2\text{O}}\right) = 980. \text{ g H}_2\text{O}$$

$$980. \text{ g H}_2\text{O}\left(\frac{1 \text{ mL}}{0.997 \text{ g H}_2\text{O}}\right) = 983 \text{ mL}$$

Only about half of the available water needs to evaporate to achieve the equilibrium water vapor pressure of 23.8 mm Hg at 25 °C.

EXERCISE 12.6 Vapor Pressure Curves

Examine the vapor pressure curve for ethanol in Figure 12.17.

(a) What is the approximate vapor pressure of ethanol at 40 °C?

(b) Are liquid and vapor in equilibrium when the temperature is 60 °C and the pressure is 600 mm Hg? If not, does liquid evaporate to form more vapor, or does vapor condense to form more liquid?

EXERCISE 12.7 Vapor Pressure

If 0.50 g of pure water is sealed in an evacuated 5.0-L flask and the whole assembly is heated to 60 °C, will the pressure be equal to or less than the equilibrium vapor pressure of water at this temperature? What if you use 2.0 g of water? Under either set of conditions, is any liquid water left in the flask, or does all of the water evaporate?

Vapor Pressure, Enthalpy of Vaporization, and the Clausius–Clapeyron Equation

Plotting the vapor pressure for a liquid at a series of temperatures results in a curved line (Figure 12.17). However, the German physicist R. Clausius (1822–1888) and the Frenchman B. P. E. Clapeyron (1799–1864) showed that, for a pure liquid, a linear relationship exists between the reciprocal of the Kelvin temperature $(1/T)$ and the natural logarithm of vapor pressure $(\ln P)$ (Figure 12.18).

$$\ln P = -(\Delta_{vap}H^{\circ}/RT) + C \tag{12.1}$$

Here, $\Delta_{vap}H^{\circ}$ is the enthalpy of vaporization of the liquid; R is the ideal gas constant ($8.314472 \text{ J/K} \cdot \text{mol}$); and C is a constant characteristic of the liquid in question. This equation, now called the **Clausius-Clapeyron equation,** provides a method of obtaining values for $\Delta_{vap}H^{\circ}$. The equilibrium vapor pressure of a liquid can be measured at several different temperatures, and the logarithm of these pressures

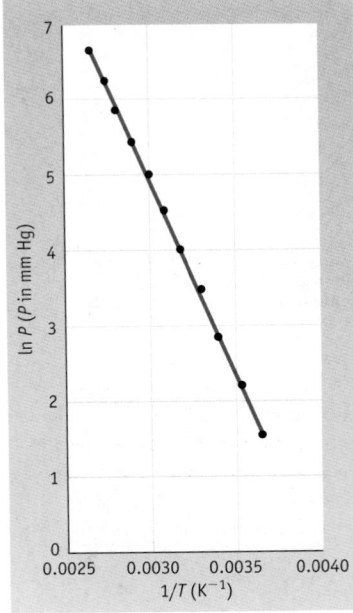

FIGURE 12.18 Clausius–Clapeyron equation. When the natural logarithm of the vapor pressure ($\ln P$) of water at various temperatures (T) is plotted against $1/T$, a straight line is obtained. The slope of the line equals $-\Delta_{vap}H^{\circ}/R$. Values of T and P are from Appendix G.

is plotted versus $1/T$. The result is a straight line with a slope of $-\Delta_{vap}H^\circ/R$. For example, plotting data for water (Figure 12.18), we find the slope of the line is -4.90×10^3, which gives $\Delta_{vap}H^\circ = 40.7$ kJ/mol.

As an alternative to plotting $\ln P$ versus $1/T$, we can write the following equation that allows us to calculate $\Delta_{vap}H^\circ$ knowing the vapor pressure of a liquid at two different temperatures.

$$\ln P_2 - \ln P_1 = \left[\frac{-\Delta_{vap}H^\circ}{RT_2} + C \right] - \left[\frac{-\Delta_{vap}H^\circ}{RT_1} + C \right]$$

This can be simplified to

$$\ln \frac{P_2}{P_1} = -\frac{\Delta_{vap}H^\circ}{R} \left[\frac{1}{T_2} - \frac{1}{T_1} \right]$$

(12.2)

For example, ethylene glycol has a vapor pressure of 14.9 mm Hg (P_1) at 373 K (T_1), and a vapor pressure of 49.1 mm Hg (P_2) at 398 K (T_2).

$$\ln \left(\frac{49.1 \text{ mm Hg}}{14.9 \text{ mm Hg}} \right) = -\frac{\Delta_{vap}H^\circ}{0.0083145 \text{ kJ/K} \cdot \text{mol}} \left[\frac{1}{398 \text{ K}} - \frac{1}{373 \text{ K}} \right]$$

$$1.192 = -\frac{\Delta_{vap}H^\circ}{0.0083145 \text{ kJ/K} \cdot \text{mol}} \left(-\frac{0.000168}{K} \right)$$

$$\Delta_{vap}H^\circ = 59.0 \text{ kJ/mol}$$

Chemistry.⚬.Now™

Sign in at **www.cengage.com/login** and go to Chapter 12 Contents to see Screen 12.9 for three tutorials on using the **Clausius–Clapeyron equation.**

EXERCISE 12.8 Clausius–Clapeyron Equation

Calculate the enthalpy of vaporization of diethyl ether, $(C_2H_5)_2O$ (see Figure 12.17). This compound has vapor pressures of 57.0 mm Hg and 534 mm Hg at -22.8 °C and 25.0 °C, respectively.

Boiling Point

If you have a beaker of water open to the atmosphere, the atmosphere presses down on the surface. If enough energy is added, a temperature is eventually reached at which the vapor pressure of the liquid equals the atmospheric pressure. At this temperature, bubbles of the liquid's vapor will not be crushed by the atmospheric pressure. The bubbles can rise to the surface, and the liquid boils (Figure 12.19).

The boiling point of a liquid is the temperature at which its vapor pressure is equal to the external pressure. If the external pressure is 760 mm Hg, this temperature is called the **normal boiling point.** This point is highlighted on the vapor pressure curves for the substances in Figure 12.17.

The normal boiling point of water is 100 °C, and in a great many places in the United States, water boils at or near this temperature. If you live at higher altitudes, however, such as in Salt Lake City, Utah, where the barometric pressure is about 650 mm Hg, water will boil at a noticeably lower temperature. The curve in Figure 12.19 shows that a pressure of 650 mm Hg corresponds to a boiling temperature of about 95 °C. Food, therefore, has to be cooked a little longer in Salt Lake City to achieve the same result as in New York City at sea level.

FIGURE 12.19 Vapor pressure and boiling. When the vapor pressure of the liquid equals the atmospheric pressure, bubbles of vapor begin to form within the body of liquid, and the liquid boils.

Critical Temperature and Pressure

On first thought, it might seem that vapor pressure–temperature curves (such as shown in Figure 12.17) should continue upward without limit, but this is not so. Instead, when a specific temperature and pressure are reached, the interface between the liquid and the vapor disappears. This point is called the **critical point.** The temperature at which this phenomenon occurs is the **critical temperature, T_c,** and the corresponding pressure is the **critical pressure, P_c** (Figure 12.20). The substance that exists under these conditions is called a **supercritical fluid.** It is like a gas under such a high pressure that its density resembles that of a liquid, while its viscosity (ability to flow) remains close to that of a gas (▶ page 580).

Consider what the substance might look like at the molecular level under these conditions. The molecules have been forced almost as close together as they are in the liquid state, but each molecule has enough kinetic energy to exceed the forces holding molecules together. As a result, the supercritical fluid has a tightly packed molecular arrangement like a liquid, but the intermolecular forces of attraction that characterize the liquid state are less than the kinetic energy of the particles.

For most substances, the critical point is at a very high temperature and pressure (Table 12.7). Water, for instance, has a critical temperature of 374 °C and a critical pressure of 217.7 atm.

Supercritical fluids can have unexpected properties, such as the ability to dissolve normally insoluble materials. Supercritical CO_2 is especially useful. Carbon dioxide is widely available, essentially nontoxic, nonflammable, and inexpensive. It is relatively easy to reach its critical temperature of 30.99 °C and critical pressure of 72.8 atm. One use of supercritical CO_2 is to extract caffeine from coffee. The coffee beans are treated with steam to bring the caffeine to the surface. The beans are then immersed in supercritical CO_2, which selectively dissolves the caffeine but leaves intact the compounds that give flavor to coffee. (Decaffeinated coffee contains less than 3% of the original caffeine.) The solution of caffeine in supercritical CO_2 is poured off, and the CO_2 is evaporated, trapped, and reused.

TABLE 12.7 Critical Temperatures and Pressures for Common Compounds*

Compound	T_c (°C)	P_c (atm)
CH_4 (methane)	−82.6	45.4
C_2H_6 (ethane)	32.3	49.1
C_3H_8 (propane)	96.7	41.9
C_4H_{10} (butane)	152.0	37.3
CCl_2F_2 (CFC-12)	111.8	40.9
NH_3	132.4	112.0
H_2O	374.0	217.7
CO_2	30.99	72.8
SO_2	157.7	77.8

*Data taken from D. R. Lide: *Basic Laboratory and Industrial Chemicals,* Boca Raton, FL, CRC Press, 1993.

■ **Green Chemistry and Supercritical CO_2** It is not surprising that other uses are being sought for supercritical CO_2. One application being investigated is its use as a dry cleaning solvent. More than 10 billion kilograms of organic and halogenated solvents are used worldwide every year in cleaning applications. These cleaning agents can have deleterious effects on the environment, so it is hoped that many can be replaced by supercritical CO_2. (For more about supercritical CO_2 see page 609.)

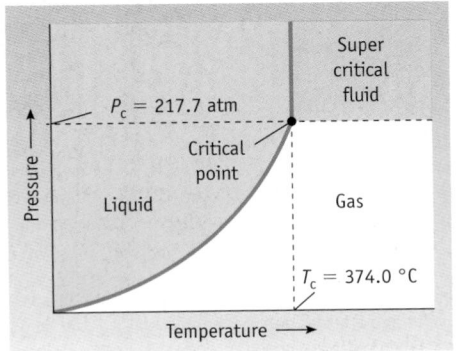

FIGURE 12.20 Critical temperature and pressure for water. The curve representing equilibrium conditions for liquid and gaseous water ends at the critical point; above that temperature and pressure, water becomes a supercritical fluid.

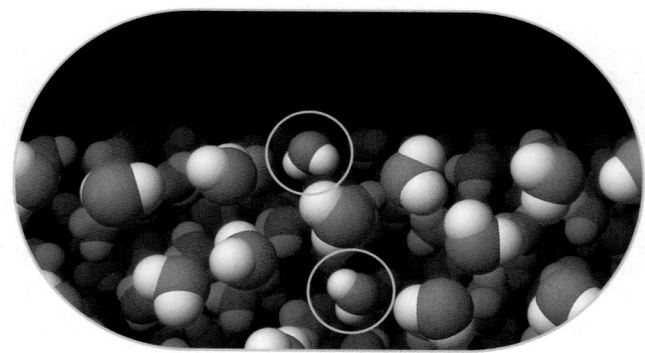

FIGURE 12.21 Intermolecular forces in a liquid. Forces acting on a molecule at the surface of a liquid are different than those acting on a molecule in the interior of a liquid.

Water molecules on the surface are not completely surrounded by other water molecules.

Water molecules under the surface are completely surrounded by other water molecules.

Surface Tension, Capillary Action, and Viscosity

Molecules in the interior of a liquid interact with molecules all around them (Figure 12.21). In contrast, molecules on the surface of a liquid are affected only by those molecules located at or below the surface layer. This leads to a net inward force of attraction on the surface molecules, contracting the surface area and making the liquid behave as though it had a skin. The toughness of this skin is measured by its **surface tension**—the energy required to break through the surface or to disrupt a liquid drop and spread the material out as a film. Surface tension causes water drops to be spheres and not little cubes, for example (Figure 12.22a), because a sphere has a smaller surface area than any other shape of the same volume.

Capillary action is closely related to surface tension. When a small-diameter glass tube is placed in water, the water rises in the tube, just as water rises in a piece of paper in water (Figure 12.22b). Because polar Si—O bonds are present on the

■ **Viscosity** Long chains of atoms, such as those present in oils, are floppy and become entangled with one another in the liquid; the longer the chain, the greater the tangling and the greater the viscosity.

**FIGURE 12.22
Adhesive and cohesive forces.**

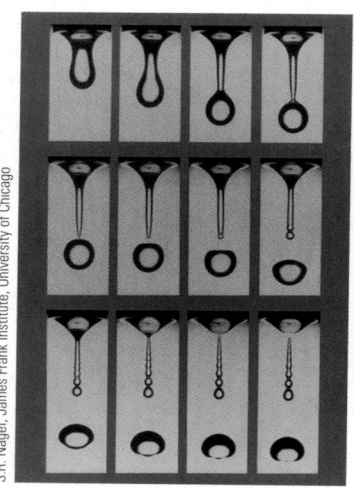

(a) A series of photographs showing the different stages when a water drop falls. The drop was illuminated by a strobe light of 5-ms duration. (The total time for this sequence was 0.05 s.) Water droplets take a spherical shape because of surface tension.

(b) Capillary action. Polar water molecules are attracted to the —OH bonds in paper fibers, and water rises in the paper. If a line of ink is placed in the path of the rising water, the different components of the ink are attracted differently to the water and paper and are separated in a process called chromatography.

(c) Water (top layer) forms a concave meniscus, while mercury (bottom layer) forms a convex meniscus. The different shapes are determined by the adhesive forces of the molecules of the liquid with the walls of the tube and the cohesive forces between molecules of the liquid.

The events of September 11, 2001, are etched in everyone's memory. The possibility of domestic terrorism, however, began almost two years before when a man was apprehended in late December 1999 at the Canadian border with bomb materials and a map of the Los Angeles International Airport. Although he claimed innocence, his fingerprints were on the bomb materials, and he was convicted of an attempt to bomb the airport.

Each of us has a unique fingerprint pattern, as first described by John Purkinji in 1823. Not long after, the English in India began using fingerprints on contracts because they believed it made the contract appear more binding. It was not until late in the 19th century, however, that fingerprinting was used as an identifier. Sir Francis Galton, a British anthropologist and cousin of Charles Darwin, established that a person's fingerprints do not change over the course of a lifetime and that no two prints are exactly the same. Fingerprinting has since become an accepted tool in forensic science.

In 1993 in Knoxville, Tennessee, detective Art Bohanan thought he could use it to solve the case of the kidnapping of a young girl. The girl had been taken from her home and driven away in a green car. The girl soon managed to escape from her attacker and was able to describe the car to the police. After four days, the police found the car and arrested its owner. But had the girl been in that car? Art Bohanan inspected the car for her fingerprints and even used the latest technique, fuming with superglue. No prints were found.

The abductor of the girl was eventually convicted on other evidence, but Bohanan wondered why he had never found her prints in the car. He decided to test the permanence of children's fingerprints compared with adults. To his amazement, he found that chil-

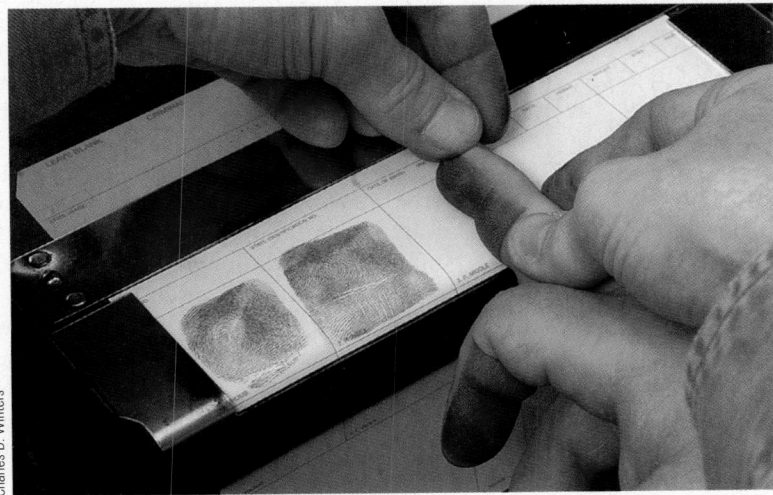

Taking a fingerprint at the local police station.

dren's prints disappear in a few hours, whereas an adult's prints can last for days. Bohanan said, "It sounded like the compounds in children's fingerprints might simply be evaporating faster than adult's."

To answer this, you should know about the nature of fingerprints. The residue deposited by fingerprints is 99% water. The other 1% contains oils, fatty acids, esters, salts, urea $[(NH_2)_2CO]$, and amino acids. An example of a fatty acid is myristic acid: $CH_3(CH_2)_{12}CO_2H$. An ester is the combination of an acid with an alcohol such as ethanol (CH_3CH_2OH), so an ester of myristic acid would be: $CH_3(CH_2)_{12}CO_2CH_2CH_3$

Scientists at Oak Ridge National Laboratory studied the fingerprints of 50 child and adult volunteers, identifying the compounds present by such techniques as mass spectrometry (◄ page 68). What they found clarified the mystery of the disappearing fingerprints.

Children's fingerprints contain more low-molecular-weight fatty acids than adult fingerprints. In contrast, adult fingerprints contain esters of long-chain fatty acids with long-chain alcohols. These are waxes, semi-solid or solid organic compounds with high molecular weights. (Examples of waxes are lanolin, a component of wool, or carnauba wax used in furniture polish.)

Before puberty, children do not produce waxy compounds in their skin. However, sebaceous glands in adult skin produce sebum, a complex mixture of organic compounds (triglycerides, fatty acids, cholesterol, and waxes). There are only a few of these glands on the hands; most are on the mid-back, forehead, and chin. So, when you touch your face, this mixture of compounds is transferred to your fingers, and you can leave a fingerprint that is unique to you.

Question:

Why do children's fingerprints evaporate more readily than adult fingerprints?

Answer to this question is in Appendix Q.

---

surface of glass, polar water molecules are attracted by **adhesive forces** between the two different substances. These forces are strong enough that they can compete with the **cohesive forces** between the water molecules themselves. Thus, some water molecules can adhere to the walls; other water molecules are attracted to them and build a "bridge" back into the liquid. The surface tension of the water (from cohesive forces) is great enough to pull the liquid up the tube, so the water level rises in the tube. The rise will continue until the attractive forces—adhesion between water and glass, cohesion between water molecules—are balanced by the force of gravity pulling down on the water column. These forces lead to the characteristic concave, or downward-curving, meniscus seen with water in a test tube (Figure 12.22c).

In some liquids, cohesive forces (high surface tension) are much greater than adhesive forces with glass. Mercury is one example. Mercury does not climb the walls of a glass capillary. In fact, when it is in a glass tube, mercury will form a convex, or upward-curving, meniscus (Figure 12.22c).

One other important property of liquids in which intermolecular forces play a role is **viscosity,** the resistance of liquids to flow. When you turn over a glassful of water, it empties quickly. In contrast, it takes much more time to empty a glassful of olive oil or honey. Olive oil consists of molecules with long chains of carbon atoms, and it is about 70 times more viscous than ethanol, a small molecule with only two carbons and one oxygen. Longer chains have greater intermolecular forces because there are more atoms to attract one another, with each atom contributing to the total force. Honey (a concentrated aqueous solution of sugar molecules), however, is also a viscous liquid, even though the size of the molecules is fairly small. In this case, the sugar molecules have numerous —OH groups. These lead to greater forces of attraction due to hydrogen bonding.

Chemistry.ⵙ.Now™

Sign in at **www.cengage.com/login** and go to Chapter 12 Contents to see Screen 12.11 to watch videos on **surface tension, capillary action,** and **viscosity.**

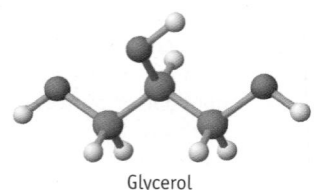

Glycerol

EXERCISE 12.9 Viscosity

Glycerol ($HOCH_2CHOHCH_2OH$) is used in cosmetics. Do you expect its viscosity to be larger or smaller than the viscosity of ethanol, CH_3CH_2OH? Explain briefly.

Chapter Goals Revisited

Chemistry.ⵙ.Now™ Sign in at **www.cengage.com/login** to:
- Assess your understanding with Study Questions in OWL keyed to each goal in the Goals and Homework menu for this chapter
- For quick review, download Go Chemistry mini-lecture flashcard modules (or purchase them at **www.ichapters.com**)
- Check your readiness for an exam by taking the Pre-Test and exploring the modules recommended in your Personalized Study plan.

Access **How Do I Solve It?** tutorials on how to approach problem solving using concepts in this chapter.

Now that you have studied this chapter, you should ask whether you have met the chapter goals. In particular, you should be able to:

Describe intermolecular forces and their effects

a. Describe the various intermolecular forces found in liquids and solids (Sections 12.2 and 12.3). Study Question(s) assignable in OWL: 2, 4, 6, 7, 25–28, 30, 32, 39; Go Chemistry Module 17.

b. Tell when two molecules can interact through a dipole–dipole attraction and when hydrogen bonding may occur. The latter occurs most strongly when H is attached to O, N, or F (Section 12.2). Study Question(s) assignable in OWL: 7–10.

c. Identify instances in which molecules interact by induced dipoles (dispersion forces) (Section 12.3). Study Question(s) assignable in OWL: 7.

Understand the importance of hydrogen bonding

a. Explain how hydrogen bonding affects the properties of water (Section 12.2).

Understand the properties of liquids

a. Explain the processes of evaporation and condensation, and use the enthalpy of vaporization in calculations (Section 12.4). Study Question(s) assignable in OWL: 11, 12, 18, 31, 53.

b. Define the equilibrium vapor pressure of a liquid, and explain the relationship between the vapor pressure and boiling point of a liquid (Section 12.4). Study Question(s) assignable in OWL: 14, 15, 17, 19, 20, 29, 38, 50.

c. Describe the phenomena of the critical temperature, T_c, and critical pressure, P_c, of a substance (Section 12.4). Study Question(s) assignable in OWL: 23.

d. Describe how intermolecular interactions affect the cohesive forces between identical liquid molecules, the energy necessary to break through the surface of a liquid (surface tension), and the resistance to flow, or viscosity, of liquids (Section 12.4). Study Question(s) assignable in OWL: 41.

e. Use the Clausius–Clapeyron equation, which connects temperature, vapor pressure, and enthalpy of vaporization for liquids (Section 12.4). Study Question(s) assignable in OWL: 21, 22, 34.

For additional preparation for an examination on this chapter see the *Let's Review* section on pages 656–669.

KEY EQUATION

Equation 12.2 (page 576) The Clausius–Clapeyron equation relates the equilibrium vapor pressure, P, of a volatile liquid to the molar enthalpy of vaporization ($\Delta_{vap}H°$) at a given temperature, T. (R is the universal constant, 8.314472 J/K · mol.) Equation 12.2 allows you to calculate $\Delta_{vap}H°$ if you know the vapor pressures at two different temperatures. Alternatively, you may plot ln P versus $1/T$; the slope of the line is $-\Delta_{vap}H°/R$.

$$\ln\frac{P_2}{P_1} = -\frac{\Delta_{vap}H°}{R}\left[\frac{1}{T_2} - \frac{1}{T_1}\right]$$

STUDY QUESTIONS

OWL Online homework for this chapter may be assigned in OWL.

▲ denotes challenging questions.

■ denotes questions assignable in OWL.

Blue-numbered questions have answers in Appendix O and fully-worked solutions in the *Student Solutions Manual*.

Practicing Skills

Intermolecular Forces
(See Examples 12.1–12.4 and ChemistryNow Screens 12.3–12.7.)

1. What intermolecular force(s) must be overcome to
   (a) melt ice
   (b) sublime solid I_2
   (c) convert liquid NH_3 to NH_3 vapor

2. ■ What type of forces must be overcome within solid I_2 when I_2 dissolves in methanol, CH_3OH? What type of forces must be disrupted between CH_3OH molecules when I_2 dissolves? What type of forces exist between I_2 and CH_3OH molecules in solution?

3. What type of intermolecular forces must be overcome in converting each of the following from a liquid to a gas?
   (a) liquid O_2
   (b) mercury
   (c) CH_3I (methyl iodide)
   (d) CH_3CH_2OH (ethanol)

4. ■ What type of intermolecular forces must be overcome in converting each of the following from a liquid to a gas?
   (a) CO_2
   (b) NH_3
   (c) $CHCl_3$
   (d) CCl_4

5. Rank the following atoms or molecules in order of increasing strength of intermolecular forces in the pure substance. Which exists as a gas at 25 °C and 1 atm?
   (a) Ne
   (b) CH_4
   (c) CO
   (d) CCl_4

6. ■ Rank the following in order of increasing strength of intermolecular forces in the pure substances. Which exists as a gas at 25 °C and 1 atm?
   (a) $CH_3CH_2CH_2CH_3$ (butane)
   (b) CH_3OH (methanol)
   (c) He

7. ■ Which of the following compounds would be expected to form intermolecular hydrogen bonds in the liquid state?
   (a) CH_3OCH_3 (dimethyl ether)
   (b) CH_4
   (c) HF
   (d) CH_3CO_2H (acetic acid)
   (e) Br_2
   (f) CH_3OH (methanol)

8. ■ Which of the following compounds would be expected to form intermolecular hydrogen bonds in the liquid state?
   (a) H_2Se
   (b) HCO_2H (formic acid)
   (c) HI
   (d) acetone (see structure below)

$$H_3C - \overset{\overset{\textstyle O}{\|}}{C} - CH_3$$

9. ■ In each pair of ionic compounds, which is more likely to have the more negative enthalpy of hydration? Briefly explain your reasoning in each case.
   (a) LiCl or CsCl
   (b) $NaNO_3$ or $Mg(NO_3)_2$
   (c) RbCl or $NiCl_2$

10. ■ When salts of Mg^{2+}, Na^+, and Cs^+ are placed in water, the positive ion is hydrated (as is the negative ion). Which of these three cations is most strongly hydrated? Which one is least strongly hydrated?

Liquids
(See Examples 12.5 and 12.6 and ChemistryNow Screens 12.8–12.11.)

11. ■ Ethanol, CH_3CH_2OH, has a vapor pressure of 59 mm Hg at 25 °C. What quantity of energy as heat is required to evaporate 125 mL of the alcohol at 25 °C? The enthalpy of vaporization of the alcohol at 25 °C is 42.32 kJ/mol. The density of the liquid is 0.7849 g/mL.

12. ■ The enthalpy of vaporization of liquid mercury is 59.11 kJ/mol. What quantity of energy as heat is required to vaporize 0.500 mL of mercury at 357 °C, its normal boiling point? The density of mercury is 13.6 g/mL.

13. Answer the following questions using Figure 12.17:
   (a) What is the approximate equilibrium vapor pressure of water at 60 °C? Compare your answer with the data in Appendix G.
   (b) At what temperature does water have an equilibrium vapor pressure of 600 mm Hg?
   (c) Compare the equilibrium vapor pressures of water and ethanol at 70 °C. Which is higher?

14. ■ Answer the following questions using Figure 12.17:
   (a) What is the equilibrium vapor pressure of diethyl ether at room temperature (approximately 20 °C)?
   (b) Place the three compounds in Figure 12.17 in order of increasing intermolecular forces.
   (c) If the pressure in a flask is 400 mm Hg and if the temperature is 40 °C, which of the three compounds (diethyl ether, ethanol, and water) are liquids, and which are gases?

15. ■ Assume you seal 1.0 g of diethyl ether (see Figure 12.17) in an evacuated 100.-mL flask. If the flask is held at 30 °C, what is the approximate gas pressure in the flask? If the flask is placed in an ice bath, does additional liquid ether evaporate, or does some ether condense to a liquid?

16. Refer to Figure 12.17 as an aid in answering these questions:
   (a) You put some water at 60 °C in a plastic milk carton and seal the top very tightly so gas cannot enter or leave the carton. What happens when the water cools?
   (b) If you put a few drops of liquid diethyl ether on your hand, does it evaporate completely or remain a liquid?

17. ■ Which member of each of the following pairs of compounds has the higher boiling point?
   (a) O_2 or N_2 (c) HF or HI
   (b) SO_2 or CO_2 (d) SiH_4 or GeH_4

18. ■ Place the following four compounds in order of increasing boiling point:
   (a) SCl_2 (c) C_2H_6
   (b) NH_3 (d) Ne

19. ■ Vapor pressure curves for CS_2 (carbon disulfide) and CH_3NO_2 (nitromethane) are drawn here.
   (a) What are the approximate vapor pressures of CS_2 and CH_3NO_2 at 40 °C?
   (b) What type of intermolecular forces exist in the liquid phase of each compound?
   (c) What is the normal boiling point of CS_2? Of CH_3NO_2?
   (d) At what temperature does CS_2 have a vapor pressure of 600 mm Hg?
   (e) At what temperature does CH_3NO_2 have a vapor pressure of 60 mm Hg?

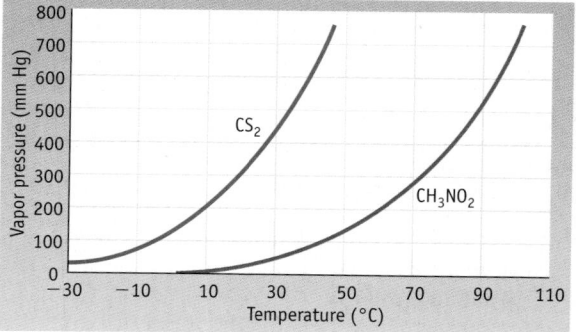

▲ more challenging   ■ in OWL   Blue-numbered questions answered in Appendix O

20. ■ Answer each of the following questions with *increases, decreases,* or *does not change.*

(a) If the intermolecular forces in a liquid increase, the normal boiling point of the liquid _____.

(b) If the intermolecular forces in a liquid decrease, the vapor pressure of the liquid _____.

(c) If the surface area of a liquid decreases, the vapor pressure _____.

(d) If the temperature of a liquid increases, the equilibrium vapor pressure _____.

21. ■ The following data are the equilibrium vapor pressure of benzene, C_6H_6, at various temperatures.

Temperature (°C)	Vapor Pressure (mm Hg)
7.6	40.
26.1	100.
60.6	400.
80.1	760.

(a) What is the normal boiling point of benzene?

(b) Plot these data so that you have a plot resembling the one in Figure 12.17. At what temperature does the liquid have an equilibrium vapor pressure of 250 mm Hg? At what temperature is it 650 mm Hg?

(c) Calculate the molar enthalpy of vaporization for benzene using the the Clausius–Clapeyron equation (Equation 12.2, page 576).

22. ■ Vapor pressure data are given here for octane, C_8H_{18}.

Temperature (°C)	Vapor Pressure (mm Hg)
25	13.6
50.	45.3
75	127.2
100.	310.8

Use the Clausius–Clapeyron equation (Equation 12.2, page 576) to calculate the molar enthalpy of vaporization of octane and its normal boiling point.

23. ■ Can carbon monoxide (T_c = 132.9 K; P_c = 34.5 atm) be liquefied at or above room temperature? Explain briefly.

24. Methane (CH_4) cannot be liquefied at room temperature, no matter how high the pressure. Propane (C_3H_8), another simple hydrocarbon, has a critical pressure of 42 atm and a critical temperature of 96.7 °C. Can this compound be liquefied at room temperature?

General Questions

These questions are not designated as to type or location in the chapter. They may combine several concepts.

25. ■ Rank the following substances in order of increasing strength of intermolecular forces: (a) Ar, (b) CH_3OH, and (c) CO_2.

26. ■ What types of intermolecular forces are important in the liquid phase of (a) C_2H_6 and (b) $(CH_3)_2CHOH$.

27. ■ Which of the following salts, Li_2SO_4 or Cs_2SO_4, is expected to have the more exothermic enthalpy of hydration?

28. ■ Select the substance in each of the following pairs that should have the higher boiling point:

(a) Br_2 or ICl

(b) neon or krypton

(c) CH_3CH_2OH (ethanol) or C_2H_4O (ethylene oxide, structure below)

$$H_2C - CH_2$$
$$\diagdown \diagup$$
$$O$$

29. ■ Use the vapor pressure curves illustrated here to answer the questions that follow.

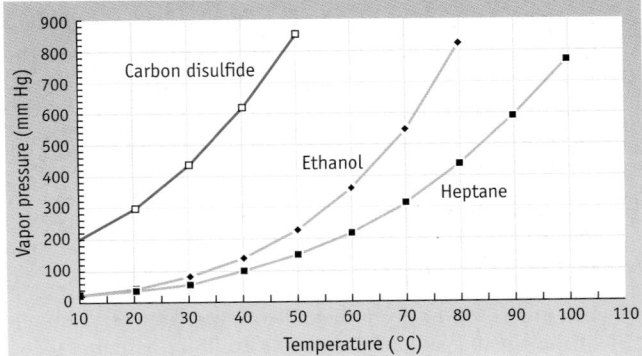

(a) What is the vapor pressure of ethanol, C_2H_5OH, at 60 °C?

(b) Considering only carbon disulfide (CS_2) and ethanol, which has the stronger intermolecular forces in the liquid state?

(c) At what temperature does heptane (C_7H_{16}) have a vapor pressure of 500 mm Hg?

(d) What are the approximate normal boiling points of each of the three substances?

(e) At a pressure of 400 mm Hg and a temperature of 70 °C, is each substance a liquid, a gas, or a mixture of liquid and gas?

30. ■ Which of the following salts will you most likely find as hydrated solids? Explain your reasoning.

(a) $Fe(NO_3)_3$ (c) NaCl

(b) $CoCl_2$ (d) $Al(NO_3)_3$

31. ■ Rank the following compounds in order of increasing molar enthalpy of vaporization: CH_3OH, C_2H_6, HCl.

32. ■ Rank the following molecules in order of increasing intermolecular forces: CH_3Cl, HCO_2H (formic acid), and CO_2.

33. Mercury and many of its compounds are dangerous poisons if breathed, swallowed, or even absorbed through the skin. The liquid metal has a vapor pressure of 0.00169 mm Hg at 24 °C. If the air in a small room is saturated with mercury vapor, how many atoms of mercury vapor occur per cubic meter?

34. ▲ ■ The following data are the equilibrium vapor pressure of limonene, $C_{10}H_{16}$, at various temperatures. (Limonene is used as a scent in commercial products.)

Temperature (°C)	Vapor Pressure (mm Hg)
14.0	1.0
53.8	10.
84.3	40.
108.3	100.
151.4	400.

(a) Plot these data as ln P versus $1/T$ so that you have plot resembling the one in Figure 12.18.
(b) At what temperature does the liquid have an equilibrium vapor pressure of 250 mm Hg? At what temperature is it 650 mm Hg?
(c) What is the normal boiling point of limonene?
(d) Calculate the molar enthalpy of vaporization for limonene using the the Clausius–Clapeyron equation (Equation 12.2).

In the Laboratory

35. You are going to prepare a silicone polymer, and one of the starting materials is dichlorodimethylsilane, $SiCl_2(CH_3)_2$. You need its normal boiling point and so measure equilibrium vapor pressures at various temperatures.

Temperature (°C)	Vapor Pressure (mm Hg)
−0.4	40.
+17.5	100.
51.9	400.
70.3	760.

(a) What is the normal boiling point of dichlorodimethylsilane?
(b) Plot these data as ln P versus $1/T$ so that you have a plot resembling the one in Figure 12.18. At what temperature does the liquid have an equilibrium vapor pressure of 250 mm Hg? At what temperature is it 650 mm Hg?
(c) Calculate the molar enthalpy of vaporization for dichlorodimethylsilane using the the Clausius–Clapeyron equation (Equation 12.2).

36. A "hand boiler" can be purchased in toy stores or at science supply companies. If you cup your hand around the bottom bulb, the volatile liquid in the boiler boils, and the liquid moves to the upper chamber. Using your knowledge of kinetic molecular theory and intermolecular forces, explain how the hand boiler works.

Charles D. Winters

37. ▲ The photos below illustrate an experiment you can do yourself. Place 10 mL of water in an empty soda can, and heat the water to boiling. Using tongs or pliers, turn the can over in a pan of cold water, making sure the opening in the can is below the water level in the pan.
(a) Describe what happens, and explain it in terms of the subject of this chapter.

(a) (b)

Charles D. Winters

(b) Prepare a molecular level sketch of the situation inside the can before heating and after heating (but prior to inverting the can).

38. ■ If you place 1.0 L of ethanol (C_2H_5OH) in a room that is 3.0 m long, 2.5 m wide, and 2.5 m high, will all the alcohol evaporate? If some liquid remains, how much will there be? The vapor pressure of ethyl alcohol at 25 °C is 59 mm Hg, and the density of the liquid at this temperature is 0.785 g/cm³.

▲ more challenging ■ in OWL Blue-numbered questions answered in Appendix O

Summary and Conceptual Questions

The following questions may use concepts from this and previous chapters.

39. ■ Acetone, CH_3COCH_3, is a common laboratory solvent. It is usually contaminated with water, however. Why does acetone absorb water so readily? Draw molecular structures showing how water and acetone can interact. What intermolecular force(s) is (are) involved in the interaction?

$$H_3C—\overset{\overset{\textstyle O}{\|}}{C}—CH_3$$

40. Cooking oil floats on top of water. From this observation, what conclusions can you draw regarding the polarity or hydrogen-bonding ability of molecules found in cooking oil?

41. ■ Liquid ethylene glycol, $HOCH_2CH_2OH$, is one of the main ingredients in commercial antifreeze. Do you predict its viscosity to be greater or less than that of ethanol, CH_3CH_2OH?

42. Liquid methanol, CH_3OH, is placed in a glass tube. Is the meniscus of the liquid concave or convex? Explain briefly.

43. Account for these facts:
    (a) Although ethanol (C_2H_5OH) (bp, 80 °C) has a higher molar mass than water (bp, 100 °C), the alcohol has a lower boiling point.
    (b) Mixing 50 mL of ethanol with 50 mL of water produces a solution with a volume slightly less than 100 mL.

44. Rationalize the observation that $CH_3CH_2CH_2OH$, 1-propanol, has a boiling point of 97.2 °C, whereas a compound with the same empirical formula, methyl ethyl ether ($CH_3CH_2OCH_3$), boils at 7.4 °C.

45. Cite two pieces of evidence to support the statement that water molecules in the liquid state exert considerable attractive force on one another.

46. During thunderstorms in the Midwest, very large hailstones can fall from the sky. (Some are the size of golf balls!) To preserve some of these stones, we put them in the freezer compartment of a frost-free refrigerator. Our friend, who is a chemistry student, tells us to use an older model that is not frost-free. Why?

47. Refer to Figure 12.12 to answer the following questions:
    (a) Of the three hydrogen halides (HX), which has the largest total intermolecular force?
    (b) Why are the dispersion forces greater for HI than for HCl?
    (c) Why are the dipole–dipole forces greater for HCl than for HI?
    (d) Of the seven molecules in Figure 12.12, which involves the largest dispersion forces? Explain why this is reasonable.

48. ▲ What quantity of energy is evolved (in joules) when 1.00 mol of liquid ammonia cools from −33.3 °C (its boiling point) to −43.3 °C? (The specific heat capacity of liquid NH_3 is 4.70 J/g · K.) Compare this with the quantity of heat evolved by 1.00 mol of liquid water cooling by exactly 10 °C. Which evolves more heat per mole on cooling 10 °C, liquid water or liquid ammonia? (*The underlying reason for the difference in heat evolved is scientifically illuminating and interesting. You can learn more by searching the Internet for specific heat capacity and its dependence on molecular properties.*)

49. A fluorocarbon, CF_4, has a critical temperature of −45.7 °C and a critical pressure of 37 atm. Are there any conditions under which this compound can be a liquid at room temperature? Explain briefly.

50. ▲ ■ The figure below is a plot of vapor pressure versus temperature for dichlorodifluoromethane, CCl_2F_2. The enthalpy of vaporization of the liquid is 165 kJ/g, and the specific heat capacity of the liquid is about 1.0 J/g · K.

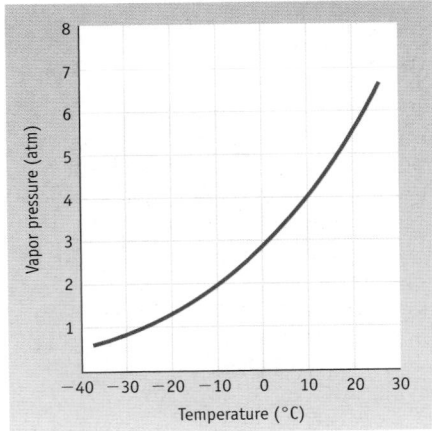

(a) What is the approximate normal boiling point of CCl_2F_2?
(b) A steel cylinder containing 25 kg of CCl_2F_2 in the form of liquid and vapor is set outdoors on a warm day (25 °C). What is the approximate pressure of the vapor in the cylinder?
(c) The cylinder valve is opened, and CCl_2F_2 vapor gushes out of the cylinder in a rapid flow. Soon, however, the flow becomes much slower, and the outside of the cylinder is coated with ice frost. When the valve is closed and the cylinder is reweighed, it is found that 20 kg of CCl_2F_2 is still in the cylinder. Why is the flow fast at first? Why does it slow down long before the cylinder is empty? Why does the outside become icy?
(d) Which of the following procedures would be effective in emptying the cylinder rapidly (and safely)? (1) Turn the cylinder upside down, and open the valve. (2) Cool the cylinder to −78 °C in dry ice, and open the valve. (3) Knock off the top of the cylinder, valve and all, with a sledge hammer.

51. Acetaminophen is used in analgesics. A model of the molecule is shown here with its electrostatic potential surface. Where are the most likely sites for hydrogen bonding?

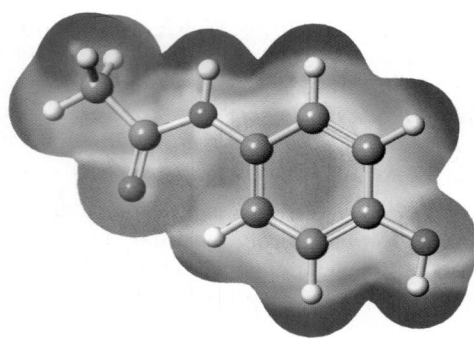

52. Shown here are models of two bases in DNA with the electrostatic potential surfaces: cytosine and guanine. What sites in these molecules are involved in hydrogen bonding with each other? Draw molecular structures showing how cytosine can hydrogen bond with guanine.

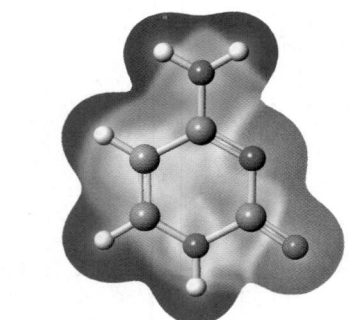

Cytosine

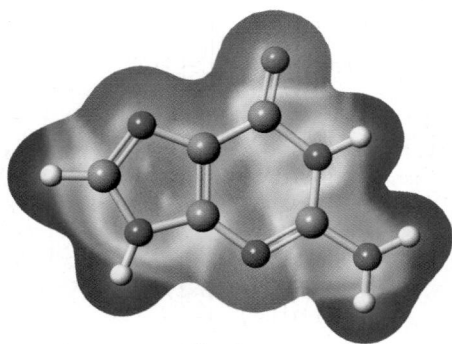

Guanine

53. List four properties of liquids that are directly determined by intermolecular forces.

54. List the following ions in order of hydration energies: Na^+, K^+, Mg^{2+}, Ca^{2+}. Explain how you determined this order.

55. Compare the boiling points of the various isomeric hydrocarbons shown in the table below. Notice the relationship between boiling point and structure; branched-chain hydrocarbons have lower boiling points than the unbranched isomer. Speculate on possible reasons for this trend. Why might the intermolecular forces be slightly different in these compounds?

Compound	Boiling point (°C)
Hexane	68.9
3-methylpentane	63.2
2-methylpentane	60.3
2,3-dimethylbutane	58.0
2,2-dimethylbutane	49.7

56. A 8.82 g sample of Br_2 is placed in an evacuated 1.00 L flask and heated to 58.8 °C, the normal boiling point of bromine. Describe the contents of the flask under these conditions.

57. Polarizability is defined as the extent to which the electron cloud surrounding an atom or molecule can be distorted by an external charge. Rank the halogens (F_2, Cl_2, Br_2, I_2) and the noble gases (He, Ne, Ar, Kr, Xe) in order of polarizability (from least polarizable to most polarizable). What properties of these substances could be used to determine this ranked order?

58. In which of the following organic molecules might we expect hydrogen bonding to occur?
 (a) methyl acetate, $CH_3CO_2CH_3$
 (b) acetaldehyde (ethanal), CH_3CHO
 (c) acetone (2-propanone) (see Question 8)
 (d) benzoic acid ($C_6H_5CO_2H$)
 (e) acetamide (CH_3CONH_2 an amide formed from acetic acid and ammonia)
 (f) N,N-dimethylacetamide [$CH_3CON(CH_3)_2$, an amide formed from acetic acid and dimethylamine]

59. A pressure cooker (a kitchen appliance) is a pot on which the top seals tightly, allowing pressure to build up inside. You put water in the pot and heat it to boiling. At the higher pressure, water boils at a higher temperature and this allows food to cook at a faster rate. Most pressure cookers have a setting of 15 psi, which means that the pressure in the pot is 15 psi above atmospheric pressure (1 atm = 14.70 psi). Use the Clausius-Clapeyron equation to calculate the temperature at which water boils in the pressure cooker.

▲ more challenging ■ in OWL   Blue-numbered questions answered in Appendix O

60. Vapor pressures of $NH_3(\ell)$ at several temperatures are given in the table below. Use this information to calculate the enthalpy of vaporization of ammonia.

Temperature (°C)	Vapor Pressure (atm)
−68.4	0.132
−45.4	0.526
−33.6	1.000
−18.7	2.00
4.7	5.00
25.7	10.00
50.1	20.00

61. Chemists sometimes carry out reactions in liquid ammonia as a solvent. With adequate safety protection these reactions can be done above ammonia's boiling point in a sealed, thick-walled glass tube. If the reaction is being carried out at 20 °C, what is the pressure of ammonia inside the tube? (Use data from the previous question to answer this question.)

62. The data in the following table was used to create the graph shown below (vp = vapor pressure of ethanol (CH_3CH_2OH) expressed in mm Hg, T = kelvin temperature)

ln(vp)	1/T (K^{-1})
2.30	0.00369
3.69	0.00342
4.61	0.00325
5.99	0.00297
6.63	0.00285

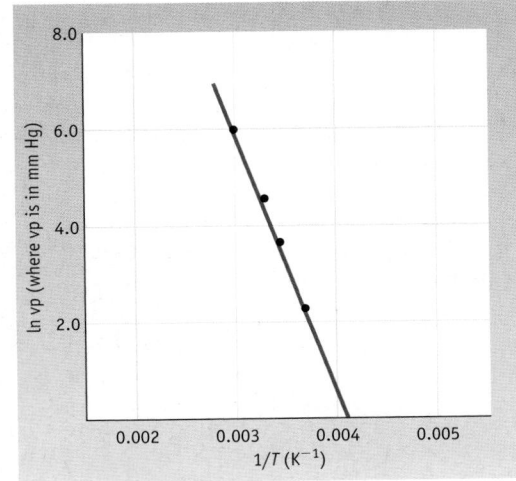

(a) Derive an equation for the straight line in this graph.
(b) Describe in words how to use the graph to determine the enthalpy of vaporization of ethanol.
(c) Calculate the vapor pressure of ethanol at 0.00 °C and at 100 °C.

13 | The Chemistry of Solids

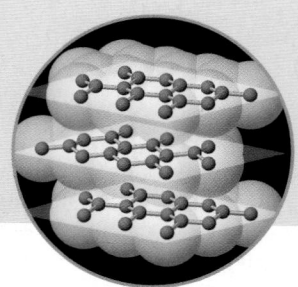

Graphite is composed of sheets of carbon atoms in six-member rings.

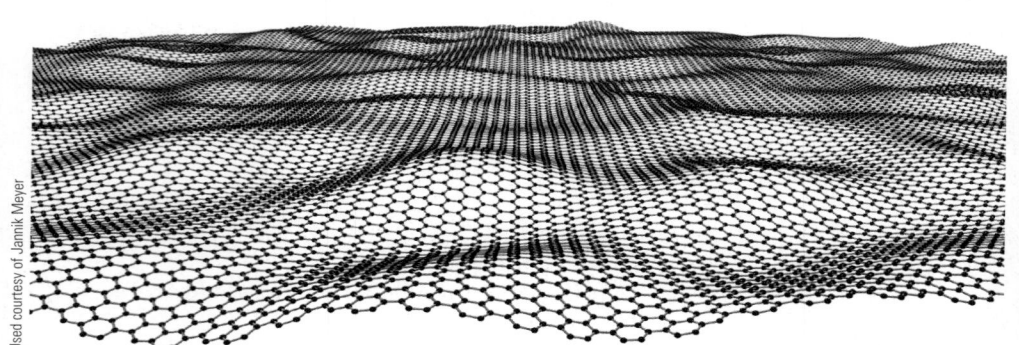

Graphene is a single sheet of six-member carbon rings. This latest material in the world of carbon chemistry has unusual electrical properties.

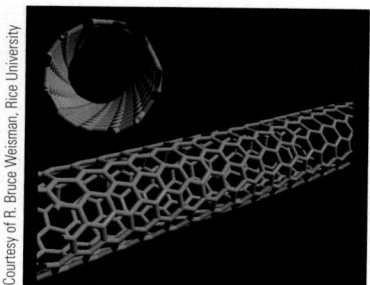

Carbon nanotubes are composed of six-member carbon rings.

Graphite to Graphene

One of the most interesting developments in chemistry in the last 20 years has been the discovery of new forms of carbon. First, there were buckyballs and then single-wall and multi-wall carbon nanotubes.

Common graphite, from which your pencil lead is made, consists of six-member rings of carbon atoms connected in sheets, and the sheets stack one on top of another like cards in a deck. But if carbon compounds are heated under the right conditions, the carbon atoms assemble into sheets, and the sheets close on themselves to form tubes. These are called **nanotubes** because the tubes are only a few nanometers in diameter. Sometimes they are single tubes, and other times there are tubes within tubes. Carbon nanotubes are at least 100 times stronger than steel but only one sixth as dense, and they conduct heat and electricity far better than copper. There has been enormous interest in their commercial applications, but there has also been difficulty in making them with consistent properties.

Now there is **graphene**, a single sheet of six-member carbon atoms. Researchers in England discovered them in a simple way: put a flake of graphite on Scotch tape, fold the tape over, and then pull it apart. The graphite layers come apart, and, if you do it enough times, only one layer—one C atom thick!—is left on the tape. This is clearly not the way to make graphene commercially, but methods have since been developed to make it in larger amounts. And now researchers are looking at ways to make graphene sheets in specific shapes, and to use them as transistors and other electronic devices.

Questions:

1. Based on a C—C distance of 139 pm, what is the side-to-side dimension of a planar, C_6 ring?

2. If a graphene sheet has a width of 1.0 micrometer, how many C_6 rings are joined across the sheet?

3. Estimate the thickness of a sheet of graphene (in pm). How did you determine this value?

Answers to these questions are in Appendix Q.

Chapter Goals

OWL *See Chapter Goals Revisited (page 610) for Study Questions keyed to these goals and assignable in OWL.*

- Understand cubic unit cells.
- Relate unit cells for ionic compounds to formulas.
- Describe the properties of solids.
- Understand the nature of phase diagrams.

Chapter Outline

13.1 Crystal Lattices and Unit Cells
13.2 Structures and Formulas of Ionic Solids
13.3 Bonding in Ionic Compounds: Lattice Energy
13.4 The Solid State: Other Kinds of Solid Materials
13.5 Phase Changes Involving Solids
13.6 Phase Diagrams

Chemistry.Now™

Throughout the text this icon introduces an opportunity for self-study or to explore interactive tutorials by signing in at **www.cengage.com/login**.

Many kinds of solids exist in the world around us (Figure 13.1 and Table 13.1). As the description of graphene shows, solid-state chemistry is one of the booming areas of science, especially because it relates to the development of interesting new materials. As we describe various kinds of solids, we hope to provide a glimpse of the reasons this area is exciting.

13.1 Crystal Lattices and Unit Cells

 Module 18

In both gases and liquids, molecules move continually and randomly, and they rotate and vibrate as well. Because of this movement, an orderly arrangement of molecules in the gaseous or liquid state is not possible. In solids, however, the molecules, atoms, or ions cannot change their relative positions (although they vibrate and occasionally rotate). Thus, a regular, repeating pattern of atoms or molecules within the structure—a long-range order—is a characteristic of most solids. The beautiful, external (macroscopic) regularity of a crystal of salt (Figure 13.1) suggests it has an internal symmetry.

TABLE 13.1 **Structures and Properties of Various Types of Solid Substances**

Type	Examples	Structural Units	Forces Holding Units Together	Typical Properties
Ionic	$NaCl$, K_2SO_4, $CaCl_2$, $(NH_4)_3PO_4$	Positive and negative ions; no discrete molecules	Ionic; attractions among charges on positive and negative ions	Hard; brittle; high melting point; poor electric conductivity as solid, good as liquid; often water-soluble
Metallic	Iron, silver, copper, other metals and alloys	Metal atoms (positive metal ions with delocalized electrons)	Metallic; electrostatic attraction among metal ions and electrons	Malleable; ductile; good electric conductivity in solid and liquid; good heat conductivity; wide range of hardness and melting points
Molecular	H_2, O_2, I_2, H_2O, CO_2, CH_4, CH_3OH, CH_3CO_2H	Molecules	Dispersion forces, dipole–dipole forces, hydrogen bonds	Low to moderate melting points and boiling points; soft; poor electric conductivity in solid and liquid
Network	Graphite, diamond, quartz, feldspars, mica	Atoms held in an infinite two- or three-dimensional network	Covalent; directional electron-pair bonds	Wide range of hardness and melting points (three-dimensional bonding > two-dimensional bonding); poor electric conductivity, with some exceptions
Amorphous	Glass, polyethylene, nylon	Covalently bonded networks with no long-range regularity	Covalent; directional electron-pair bonds	Noncrystalline; wide temperature range for melting; poor electric conductivity, with some exceptions

FIGURE 13.1
Some common solids.

Polyethylene, an
amorphous solid

Silicon,
a network solid

Aluminum,
a metallic solid

NaCl, a crystalline
ionic solid

Fisherbrand

Wash Bottle
Polyethylene
03-169-22B   250mL
Fisher Scientific

Photo: Charles D. Winters

Structures of solids can be described as three-dimensional lattices of atoms, ions, or molecules. For a crystalline solid, we can identify the **unit cell**, the smallest repeating unit that has all of the symmetry characteristic of the way the atoms, ions, or molecules are arranged in the solid.

To understand unit cells, consider first a two-dimensional lattice model, the repeating pattern of circles shown in Figure 13.2. The yellow square at the left is a unit cell because the overall pattern can be created from a group of these cells by joining them edge to edge. It is also a requirement that unit cells reflect the stoichiometry of the solid. Here, the square unit cell at the left contains one smaller sphere and one fourth of each of the four larger circles, giving a total of one small and one large circle per two-dimensional unit cell.

You may recognize that it is possible to draw other unit cells for this two-dimensional lattice. One option is the square in the middle of Figure 13.2 that fully encloses a single large circle and parts of small circles that add up to one net small circle. Yet another possible unit cell is the parallelogram at the right. Other unit

FIGURE 13.2 Unit cells for a flat, two-dimensional solid made from circular "atoms." A lattice can be represented as being built from repeating unit cells. This two-dimensional lattice can be built by translating the unit cells throughout the plane of the figure. Each cell must move by the length of one side of the unit cell. In this figure, all unit cells contain a net of one large circle and one small circle. Be sure to notice that several unit cells are possible, with two of the most obvious being squares.

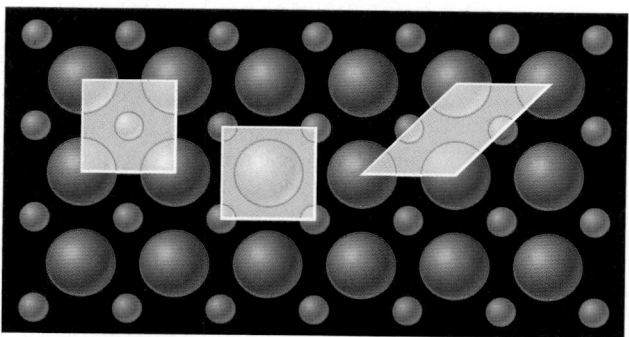

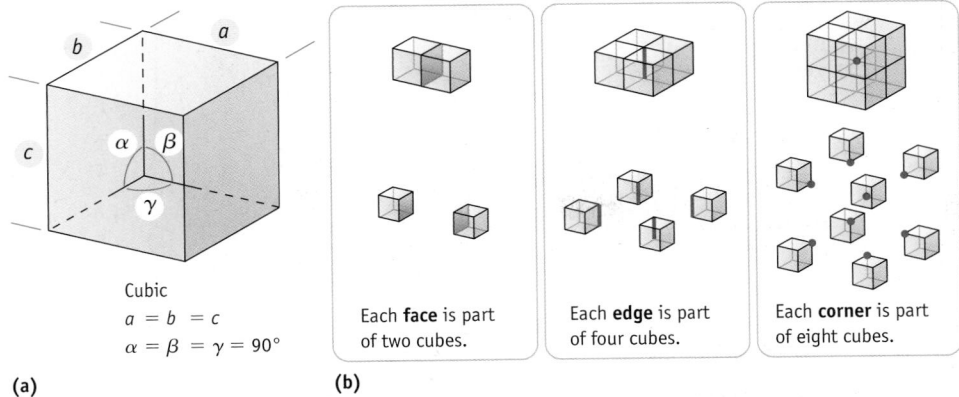

(a)
Cubic
$a = b = c$
$\alpha = \beta = \gamma = 90°$

(b)

Each **face** is part of two cubes.

Each **edge** is part of four cubes.

Each **corner** is part of eight cubes.

FIGURE 13.3 Cubic unit cells. (a) The cube is one of the seven basic unit cells that describe crystal systems. In a cube, all sides are of equal length, and all angles are 90°. In noncubic unit cells, the angles are not necessarily 90°, and the sides are not equal in length. (b) Stacking cubes to build a crystal lattice. Each crystal face is part of two cubes; each edge is part of four cubes; and each corner is part of eight cubes.

cells are possible, but it is conventional to draw unit cells in which atoms or ions are placed at the **lattice points;** that is, at the corners of the cube or other geometric object that constitutes the unit cell.

The three-dimensional lattices of solids can be built by assembling three-dimensional unit cells much like building blocks (Figure 13.3). The assemblage of these three-dimensional unit cells defines the **crystal lattice.**

To construct crystal lattices, nature uses seven three-dimensional unit cells. They differ from one another in that their sides have different relative lengths and their edges meet at different angles. The simplest of the seven crystal lattices is the **cubic unit cell,** a cell with edges of equal length that meet at 90° angles. We shall look in detail at just this structure, not only because cubic unit cells are easily visualized but also because they are commonly encountered.

Within the cubic class, three cell symmetries occur: **primitive cubic (pc), body-centered cubic (bcc),** and **face-centered cubic (fcc)** (Figure 13.4). All three have

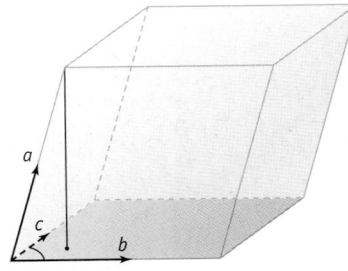

Unit cells. Of the possible unit cells, all are parallelepipeds (except for the hexagonal cell), figures in which opposite sides are parallel. In a cube, all angles (a-o-c, a-o-b, and c-o-b; where o is the origin) are 90°, and all sides are equal. In other cells, the angles and sides may be the same or different. For example, in a tetragonal cell, the angles are 90°, but $a = b \neq c$. In a triclinic cell, the sides have different lengths, the angles are different, and none equals 90°.

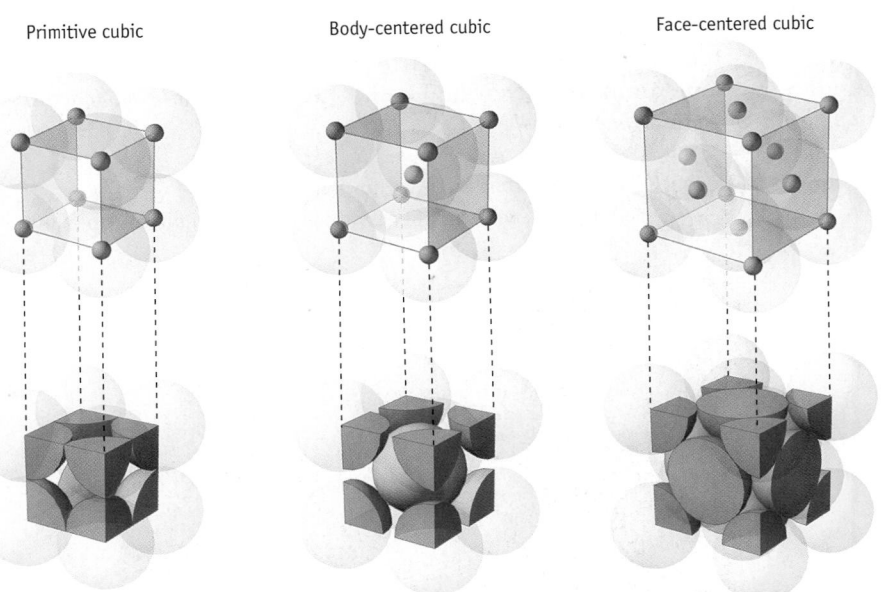

Primitive cubic

Body-centered cubic

Face-centered cubic

FIGURE 13.4 The three cubic unit cells. The top row shows the lattice points of the three cells, and the bottom row shows the same cells using space-filling spheres. The spheres in each figure represent identical atoms (or ions) centered on the lattice points. Because eight unit cells share a corner atom, only $\frac{1}{8}$ of each corner atom lies within a given unit cell; the remaining $\frac{7}{8}$ lies in seven other unit cells. Because each face of a fcc unit cell is shared with another unit cell, one half of each atom in the face of a face-centered cube lies in a given unit cell, and the other half lies in the adjoining cell.

FIGURE 13.5 Metals use four different unit cells. Three are based on the cube, and the fourth is the hexagonal unit cell (see page 595). (Many metals can crystallize in more than one structure.)

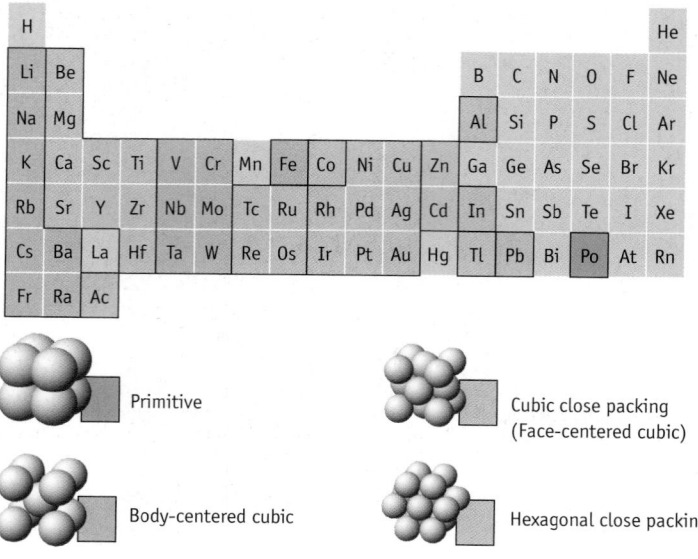

Primitive

Cubic close packing
(Face-centered cubic)

Body-centered cubic

Hexagonal close packing

identical atoms, molecules, or ions at the corners of the cubic unit cell. The bcc and fcc arrangements, however, differ from the primitive cube in that they have additional particles at other locations. The bcc structure is called "body-centered" because it has an additional particle, of the same type as those at the corners, at the center of the cube. The fcc arrangement is called "face-centered" because it has a particle, of the same type as the corner atoms, in the center of each of the six faces of the cube. Examples of each structure are found among the crystal lattices of the metals (Figure 13.5). The alkali metals, for example, are body-centered cubic, whereas nickel, copper, and aluminum are face-centered cubic. Notice that only one metal, polonium, has a primitive cubic lattice.

When the cubes pack together to make a three-dimensional crystal of a metal, the atom at each corner is shared among eight cubes (Figures 13.3, 13.4, and 13.6a). Because of this, only one eighth of each corner atom is actually within a given unit cell. Furthermore, because a cube has eight corners, and because one eighth of the atom at each corner "belongs to" a particular unit cell, the corner atoms contribute a net of one atom to a given unit cell. Thus, *the primitive cubic arrangement has one net atom within the unit cell.*

(8 corners of a cube)($\frac{1}{8}$ of each corner atom within a unit cell) =

1 net atom per unit cell for the primitive cubic unit cell

FIGURE 13.6 Atom sharing at cube corners and faces. (a) In any cubic lattice, each corner particle is shared equally among eight cubes, so one eighth of the particle is within a particular cubic unit cell. (b) In a face-centered lattice, each particle on a cube face is shared equally between two unit cells. One half of each particle of this type is within a given unit cell.

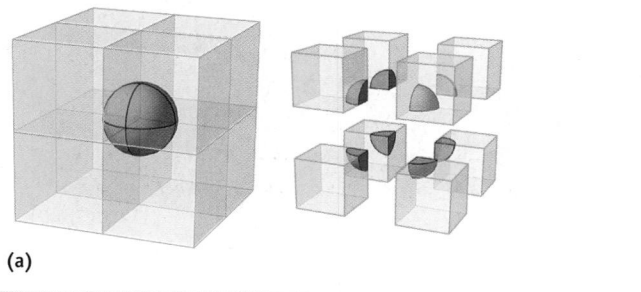

(a)

(b)

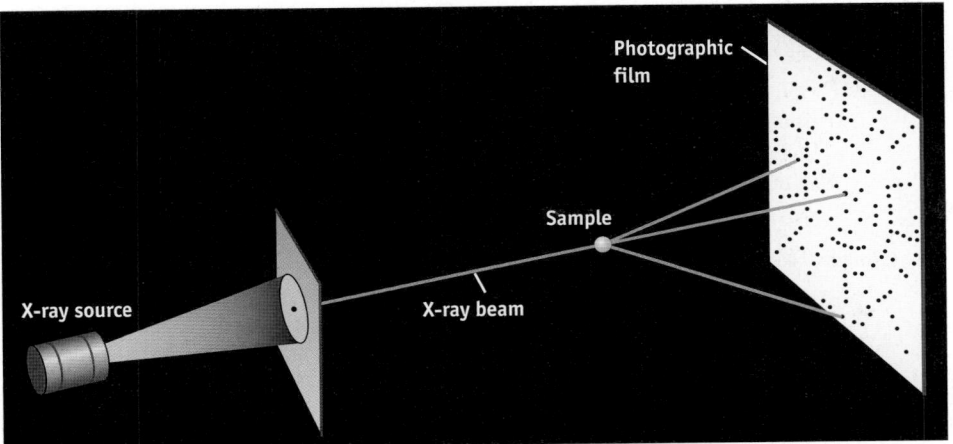

FIGURE 13.7 X-ray crystallography. In the x-ray diffraction experiment, a beam of x-rays is directed at a crystalline solid. The photons of the x-ray beam are scattered by the atoms of the solid. The scattered x-rays are detected by a photo-graphic film or an electronic detector, and the pattern of scattered x-rays is related to the locations of the atoms or ions in the crystal.

In contrast to the primitive cubic lattice, a body-centered cube has an additional atom wholly within the unit cell at the cube's center. The center particle is present in addition to those at the cube corners, so *the body-centered cubic arrangement has a net of two atoms within the unit cell.*

In a face-centered cubic arrangement, there is an atom on each of the six faces of the cube in addition to those at the cube corners. One half of each atom on a face belongs to a given unit cell (Figure 13.6b). Three net particles are therefore contributed by the particles on the faces of the cube:

(6 faces of a cube)(½ of an atom within a unit cell) =
3 net face-centered atoms within a face-centered cubic unit cell

Thus, *the face-centered cubic arrangement has a net of four atoms within the unit cell,* one contributed by the corner atoms and another three contributed by the atoms centered in the six faces.

An experimental technique, x-ray crystallography, can be used to determine the structure of a crystalline substance (Figure 13.7). Once the structure is known, the information can be combined with other experimental information to calculate such useful parameters as the radius of an atom (Study Questions 13.7–13.10).

Chemistry ⚛ Now™

Sign in at **www.cengage.com/login** and go to Chapter 13 Contents to see Screen 13.2 for a self-study module on **crystal lattices.**

■ **EXAMPLE 13.1 Determining an Atom Radius from Lattice Dimensions**

Problem Aluminum has a density of 2.699 g/cm³, and the atoms are packed in a face-centered cubic crystal lattice. What is the radius of an aluminum atom?

Strategy Our strategy for solving this problem is as follows:

1. Find the mass of a unit cell from the knowledge that it is face-centered cubic.
2. Combine the density of aluminum with the mass of the unit cell to find the cell volume.
3. Find the length of a side of the unit cell from its volume.
4. Calculate the atom radius from the edge dimension.

Charles D. Winters

Aluminum metal. The metal has a face-centered cubic unit cell with a net of four Al atoms in each unit cell.

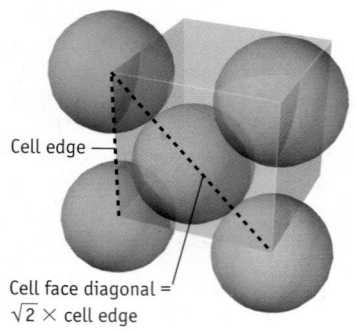

Cell edge

Cell face diagonal = $\sqrt{2}$ × cell edge

One face of a face-centered cubic unit cell. This shows the cell face diagonal, $\sqrt{2}$ × edge, is equal to four times the radius of the atoms in the lattice.

Solution

1. *Calculate the mass of the unit cell.*

$$\text{Mass of 1 Al atom} = \left(\frac{26.98 \text{ g}}{1 \text{ mol}}\right)\left(\frac{1 \text{ mol}}{6.022 \times 10^{23} \text{ atoms}}\right) = 4.480 \times 10^{-23} \text{ g/atom}$$

$$\text{Mass of unit cell} = \left(\frac{4.480 \times 10^{-23} \text{ g}}{1 \text{ Al atom}}\right)\left(\frac{4 \text{ Al atoms}}{1 \text{ unit cell}}\right) = 1.792 \times 10^{-22} \text{ g/unit cell}$$

2. *Calculate the volume of the unit cell.*

$$\text{Volume of unit cell} = \left(\frac{1.792 \times 10^{-22} \text{ g}}{\text{unit cell}}\right)\left(\frac{1 \text{ cm}^3}{2.699 \text{ g}}\right) = 6.640 \times 10^{-23} \text{ cm}^3/\text{unit cell}$$

3. *Calculate the length of a unit cell edge.* The length of the unit cell edge is the cube root of the cell volume.

$$\text{Length of unit cell edge} = \sqrt[3]{6.640 \times 10^{-23} \text{ cm}^3} = 4.049 \times 10^{-8} \text{ cm}$$

4. *Calculate the atom radius.* Notice in the model of aluminum in the margin (and in Figure 13.4) that the Al atoms at the cell corners do not touch each other. Rather, the four corner atoms touch the face-centered atom. Thus, the diagonal distance across the face of the cell is equal to four times the Al atom radius.

$$\text{Cell face diagonal} = 4 \times (\text{Al atom radius})$$

The cell diagonal is the hypotenuse of a right isosceles triangle, so, using the Pythagorean theorem,

$$(\text{Diagonal distance})^2 = 2 \times (\text{edge})^2$$

Taking the square root of both sides, we have

$$\text{Diagonal distance} = \sqrt{2} \times (\text{cell edge})$$
$$= \sqrt{2} \times (4.049 \times 10^{-8} \text{ cm}) = 5.727 \times 10^{-8} \text{ cm}$$

We divide the diagonal distance by 4 to obtain the Al atom radius in cm.

$$\text{Al atom radius} = \frac{5.727 \times 10^{-8} \text{ cm}}{4} = 1.432 \times 10^{-8} \text{ cm}$$

Atomic dimensions are often expressed in picometers, so we convert the radius to that unit.

$$1.432 \times 10^{-8} \text{ cm}\left(\frac{1 \text{ m}}{100 \text{ cm}}\right)\left(\frac{1 \text{ pm}}{1 \times 10^{-12} \text{ m}}\right) = \boxed{143.2 \text{ pm}}$$

This is in excellent agree with the radius in Figure 7.8.

EXERCISE 13.1 Determining an Atom Radius from Lattice Dimensions

Gold has a face-centered unit cell, and its density is 19.32 g/cm³. Calculate the radius of a gold atom.

EXERCISE 13.2 The Structure of Solid Iron

Iron has a density of 7.8740 g/cm³, and the radius of an iron atom is 126 pm. Verify that solid iron has a body-centered cubic unit cell. (Be sure to note that the atoms in a body-centered cubic unit cell touch along the diagonal across the cell. They do not touch along the edges of the cell.) (Hint: the diagonal distance across the unit cell is edge × $\sqrt{3}$.)

It is a "rule" that nature does things as efficiently as possible. You know this if you have ever tried to stack some oranges into a pile that doesn't fall over and that takes up as little space as possible. How did you do it? Clearly, the pyramid arrangement below on the right works, whereas the cubic one on the left does not.

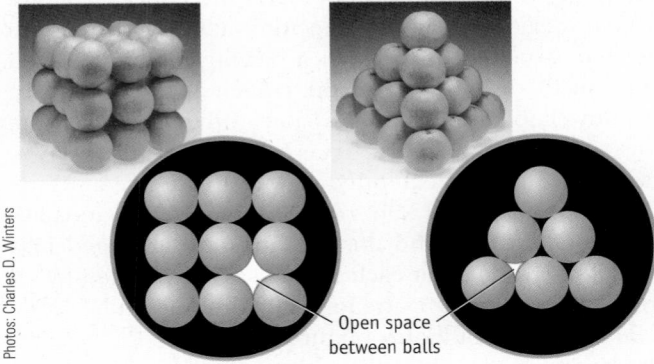

Photos: Charles D. Winters

Open space between balls

If you could look inside the pile, you would find that less open space is left in the pyramid stacking than in the cube stacking. Only 52% of the space is filled in the cubic packing arrangement. (If you could stack oranges as a body-centered cube, that would be slightly better; 68% of the space is used.) However, the best method is the pyramid stack, which is really a face-centered cubic arrangement. Oranges, atoms, or ions packed this way occupy 74% of the available space.

To fill three-dimensional space, the most efficient way to pack oranges or atoms is to begin with a hexagonal arrangement of spheres, as in this arrangement of marbles.

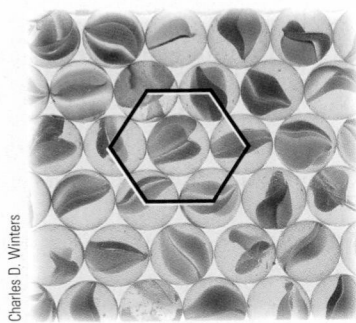

Charles D. Winters

Succeeding layers of atoms or ions are then stacked one on top of the other in two different ways. Depending on the stacking pattern (Figure 1), you will get either a **cubic close-packed (ccp)** or **hexagonal close-packed (hcp)** arrangement.

In the hcp arrangement, additional layers of particles are placed above and below a given layer, fitting into the same depressions on either side of the middle layer. In a three-dimensional crystal, the lay-

ers repeat their pattern in the manner ABABAB. . . . Atoms in each A layer are directly above the ones in another A layer; the same holds true for the B layers.

In the ccp arrangement, the atoms of the "top" layer (A) rest in depressions in the middle layer (B), and those of the "bottom" layer (C) are oriented opposite to those in the top layer. In a crystal, the pattern is repeated ABCABCABC. . . . By turning the whole crystal, you can see that the ccp arrangement is the face-centered cubic structure (Figure 2).

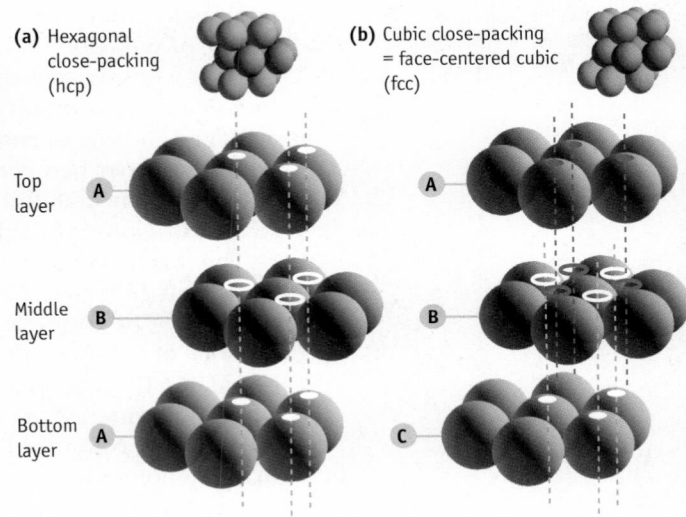

FIGURE 1 Efficient packing. The most efficient ways to pack atoms or ions in crystalline materials are hexagonal close-packing (hcp) and cubic close packing (ccp).

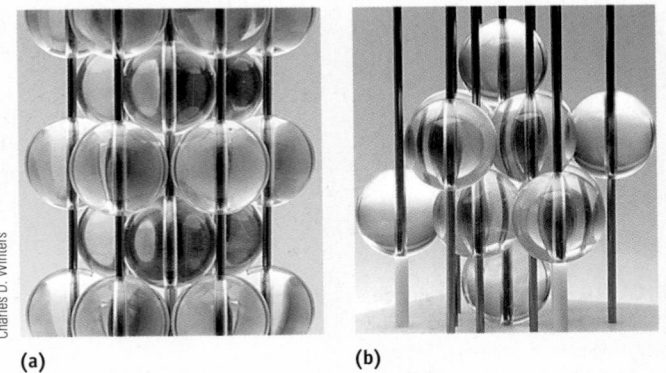

Charles D. Winters

(a)   (b)

FIGURE 2 Models of close packing. (a) A model of hexagonal close-packing, where the layers repeat in the order ABABAB. . . . (b) A face-centered unit cell (cubic close-packing), where the layers repeat in the order ABCABC. . . . (A kit from which these models can be built is available from the Institute for Chemical Education at the University of Wisconsin at Madison.)

13.2 Structures and Formulas of Ionic Solids

The lattices of many ionic compounds are built by taking a primitive cubic or face-centered cubic lattice of ions of one type and placing ions of opposite charge in the holes within the lattice. This produces a three-dimensional lattice of regularly placed ions. The smallest repeating unit in these structures is, by definition, the unit cell for the ionic compound.

The choice of the lattice and the number and location of the holes that are filled are the keys to understanding the relationship between the lattice structure and the formula of a salt. Consider, for example, the ionic compound cesium chloride, CsCl (Figure 13.8). The structure of CsCl has a primitive cubic unit cell of chloride ions. The cesium ion fits into a hole in the center of the cube. (An equivalent unit cell has a primitive cubic unit cell of Cs^+ ions with a Cl^- ion in the center of the cube.)

Next, consider the structure for NaCl. An extended view of the lattice and one unit cell are illustrated in Figures 13.9a and 13.9b, respectively. The Cl^- ions are arranged in a face-centered cubic unit cell, and the Na^+ ions are arranged in a regular manner between these ions. Notice that each Na^+ ion is surrounded by six Cl^- ions. An octahedral geometry is assumed by the ions surrounding an Na^+ ion, so the Na^+ ions are said to be in **octahedral holes** (Figure 13.9c).

The formula of an ionic compound must always be reflected in the composition of its unit cell; therefore, the formula can always be derived from the unit cell structure. The formula for NaCl can be related to this structure by counting the number of cations and anions contained in one unit cell. A face-centered cubic lattice of Cl^- ions has a net of four Cl^- ions within the unit cell. There is one Na^+ ion in the center of the unit cell, contained totally within the unit cell. In addition, there are 12 Na^+ ions along the edges of the unit cell. Each of these Na^+ ions is shared among four unit cells, so each contributes one fourth of an Na^+ ion to the unit cell, giving three additional Na^+ ions within the unit cell.

(1 Na^+ ion in the center of the unit cell) + ($\frac{1}{4}$ of Na^+ ion in each edge $\times$ 12 edges)

= net of 4 Na^+ ions in NaCl unit cell

This accounts for all of the ions contained in the unit cell: four Cl^- and four Na^+ ions. Thus, a unit cell of NaCl has a 1:1 ratio of Na^+ and Cl^- ions, as the formula requires.

Another common unit cell again has ions of one type in a face-centered cubic unit cell. Ions of the other type are located in **tetrahedral holes**, wherein each ion is surrounded by four oppositely charged ions. As illustrated in Figure 13.10, there are eight tetrahedral holes in a face-centered unit cell. In ZnS (zinc blende), the sulfide

■ **Lattice Ions and Holes** Chemists usually think of ionic lattices as being built from the larger anions with the smaller cations located in the holes that remain. For NaCl, for example, an fcc lattice is built out of the Cl^- ions (radius = 181 pm), and the smaller Na^+ cations (radius = 98 pm) are placed in appropriate holes in the lattice.

FIGURE 13.8 Cesium chloride (CsCl) unit cell. The unit cell of CsCl may be viewed in two ways. The only requirement is that the unit cell must have a net of one Cs^+ ion and one Cl^- ion. Either way, it is a simple cubic unit cell of ions of one type (Cl^- on the left or Cs^+ on the right). Generally, ionic lattices are assembled by placing the larger ions (here Cl^-) at the lattice points and placing the smaller ions (here Cs^+) in the lattice holes.

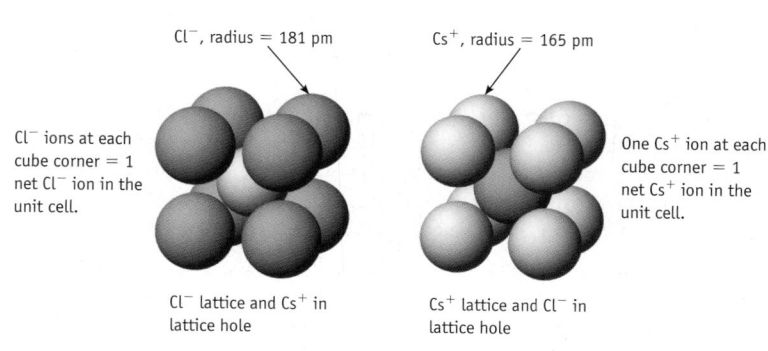

Cl^-, radius = 181 pm Cs^+, radius = 165 pm

Cl^- ions at each cube corner = 1 net Cl^- ion in the unit cell.

One Cs^+ ion at each cube corner = 1 net Cs^+ ion in the unit cell.

Cl^- lattice and Cs^+ in lattice hole

Cs^+ lattice and Cl^- in lattice hole

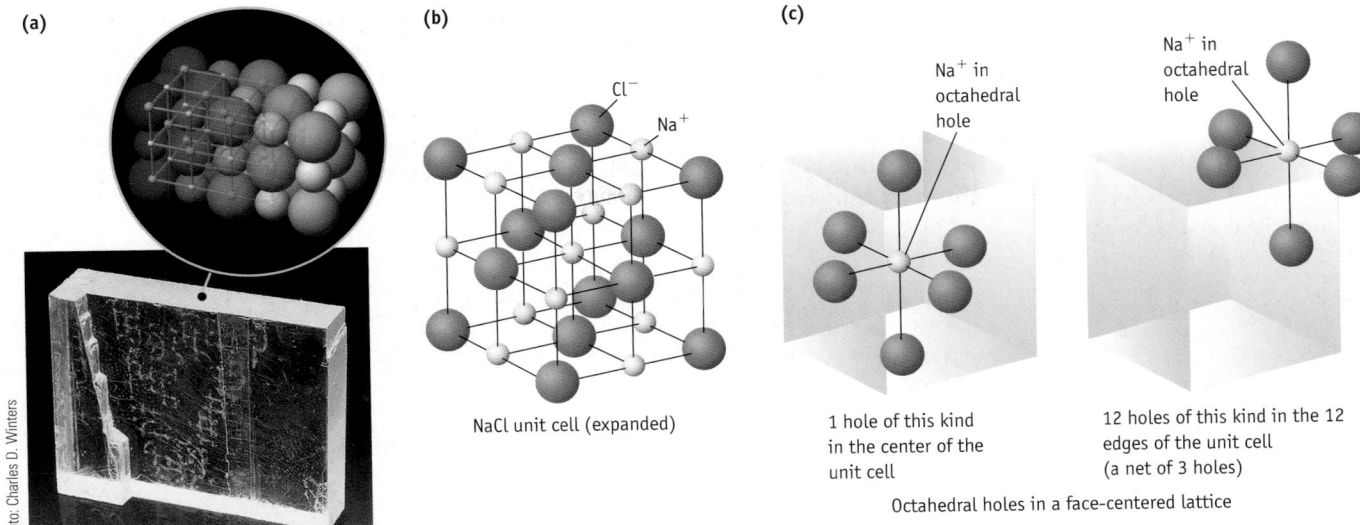

(a)

(b)

Cl⁻

Na⁺

NaCl unit cell (expanded)

(c)

Na⁺ in octahedral hole

1 hole of this kind in the center of the unit cell

Na⁺ in octahedral hole

12 holes of this kind in the 12 edges of the unit cell (a net of 3 holes)

Octahedral holes in a face-centered lattice

FIGURE 13.9 Sodium chloride. (a) Cubic NaCl is based on a face-centered cubic unit cell of Na^+ and Cl^- ions. (b) An expanded view of a sodium chloride lattice. (The lines represent the connections between lattice points.) The smaller Na^+ ions (silver) are packed into a face-centered cubic lattice of larger Cl^- ions (yellow). (c) A close-up view of the octahedral holes in the lattice.

ions (S^{2-}) form a face-centered cubic unit cell. The zinc ions (Zn^{2+}) then occupy one half of the tetrahedral holes, and each Zn^{2+} ion is surrounded by four S^{2-} ions. The unit cell consists of a net of four S^{2-} ions and four Zn^{2+} ions, which are contained wholly within the unit cell. This 1:1 ratio of the ions is reflected in the formula.

In summary, compounds with the formula MX commonly form one of three possible crystal structures:

1. M^{n+} ions occupying all the cubic holes of a primitive cubic X^{n-} lattice. Example, CsCl
2. M^{n+} ions in all the octahedral holes in a face-centered cubic X^{n-} lattice. Example, NaCl
3. M^{n+} ions occupying half of the tetrahedral holes in a face-centered cube lattice of X^{n-} ions. Example, ZnS

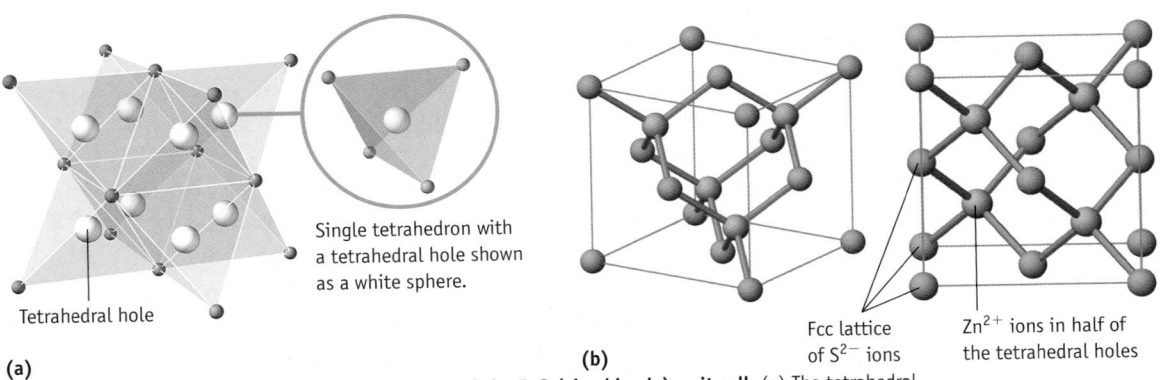

Tetrahedral hole

Single tetrahedron with a tetrahedral hole shown as a white sphere.

Fcc lattice of S^{2-} ions

Zn^{2+} ions in half of the tetrahedral holes

(a)

(b)

FIGURE 13.10 Tetrahedral holes and two views of the ZnS (zinc blende) unit cell. (a) The tetrahedral holes in a face-centered cubic lattice. (b) This unit cell is an example of a face-centered cubic lattice of ions of one type with ions of the opposite type in one half of the tetrahedral holes.

Chemists and geologists in particular have observed that the sodium chloride or "rock salt" structure is adopted by many ionic compounds, most especially by all the alkali metal halides (except CsCl, CsBr, and CsI), all the oxides and sulfides of the alkaline earth metals, and all the oxides of formula MO of the transition metals of the fourth period. Finally, the formulas of compounds must be reflected in the structures of their unit cells; therefore, the formula can always be derived from the unit cell structure.

Chemistry. ⚛. Now™

Sign in at **www.cengage.com/login** and go to Chapter 13 Contents to see Screen 13.3 to view an animation of **ionic unit cells**.

■ EXAMPLE 13.2 Ionic Structure and Formula

Problem One unit cell of the mineral perovskite is illustrated here. This compound is composed of calcium and titanium cations and oxide anions. Based on the unit cell, what is the formula of perovskite?

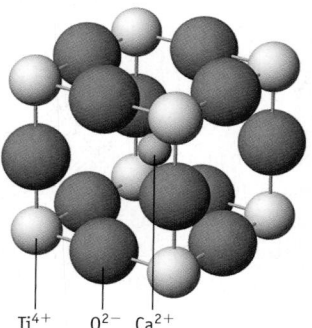

Ti^{4+} O^{2-} Ca^{2+}

Strategy Identify the ions present in the unit cell and their locations within the unit cell. Decide on the net number of ions of each kind in the cell.

Solution The unit cell has Ti^{4+} ions at the corners of the cubic unit cell, a calcium ion in the center of the cell, and oxide ions along the edges.

Number of Ti^{4+} ions:

(8 Ti^{4+} ions at cube corners) $\times$ (⅛ of each ion inside unit cell) = 1 net Ti^{4+} ion

Number of Ca^{2+} ions:

One ion is in the cube center = 1 net Ca^{2+} ion

Number of O^{2-} ions:

(12 O^{2-} ions in cube edges) $\times$ (¼ of each ion inside cell) = 3 net O^{2-} ions

Thus, the formula of perovskite is $CaTiO_3$.

Comment This is a reasonable formula. A Ca^{2+} ion and three O^{2-} ions would require a titanium ion with a 4+ charge, a reasonable value because titanium is in Group 4B of the periodic table.

■ EXAMPLE 13.3 The Relation of the Density of an Ionic Compound and its Unit Cell Dimensions

Problem Magnesium oxide has a face-centered cubic unit cell of oxide ions with magnesium ions in octahedral holes. If the radius of Mg^{2+} is 79 pm and the density of MgO is 3.56 g/cm³, what is the radius of the oxide ion?

Strategy The unit cell contains 4 MgO units, so we can calculate the mass of the unit cell. Combining the unit cell mass and the density of the solid gives us the unit cell volume, from which we can find the length of one edge of the unit cell. The edge of the unit cell is twice the radius of a Mg^{2+} ion (2 times 79 pm) plus twice the radius of an O^{2-} ion (the unknown).

Solution

1. *Calculate the mass of the unit cell.* An ionic compound of formula MX and based on a face-centered cubic lattice of X^- ions with M^+ ions in the octahedral holes has 4 MX unit per unit cell.

$$\text{Unit cell mass} = \left(\frac{40.31 \text{ g}}{1 \text{ mol MgO}}\right)\left(\frac{1 \text{ mol MgO}}{6.022 \times 10^{23} \text{ units of MgO}}\right)\left(\frac{4 \text{ MgO units}}{1 \text{ unit cell}}\right)$$
$$= 2.677 \times 10^{-22} \text{ g/unit cell}$$

2. *Calculate the volume of the unit cell from the mass and density.*

$$\text{Unit cell volume} = \left(\frac{2.667 \times 10^{-22} \text{ g}}{\text{unit cell}}\right)\left(\frac{1 \text{ cm}^3}{3.56 \text{ g}}\right) = 7.49 \times 10^{-23} \text{ cm}^3/\text{unit cell}$$

3. *Calculate the edge dimension of the unit cell in pm.*

$$\text{Unit cell edge} = (7.49 \times 10^{-23} \text{ cm}^3)^{\frac{1}{3}} = 4.22 \times 10^{-8} \text{ cm}$$

$$\text{Unit cell edge} = 4.22 \times 10^{-8} \text{ cm}\left(\frac{1 \text{ m}}{100 \text{ cm}}\right)\left(\frac{1 \times 10^{12} \text{ pm}}{1 \text{ m}}\right) = 422 \text{ pm}$$

4. *Calculate the oxide ion radius.*

One face of the MgO unit cell is shown in the margin. The O^{2-} ions define the lattice, and the Mg^{2+} and O^{2-} ions along the cell edge just touch one another. This means that one edge of the cell is equal to one O^{2-} radius (x) plus twice the Mg^{2+} radius plus one more O^{2-} radius.

$$\text{MgO unit cell edge} = x \text{ pm} + 2(79 \text{ pm}) + x \text{ pm} = 422 \text{ pm}$$

$$x = \text{oxide ion radius} = 132 \text{ pm}$$

EXERCISE 13.3 Structure and Formula

If an ionic solid has an fcc lattice of anions (X) and all of the tetrahedral holes are occupied by metal cations (M), is the formula of the compound MX, MX_2, or M_2X?

EXERCISE 13.4 Density from Cell Dimensions

Potassium chloride has the same unit cell as NaCl. Using the ion sizes in Figure 7.12, calculate the density of KCl.

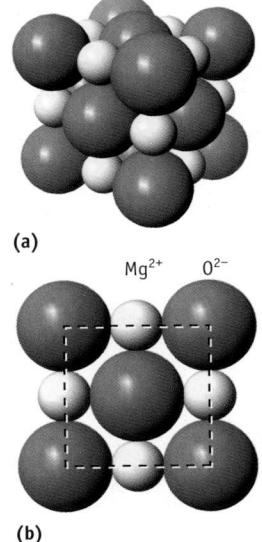

(a)

Mg^{2+} O^{2-}

(b)

Magnesium oxide. (a) A unit cell showing oxide ions in a face-centered cubic lattice with magnesium ions in the octahedral holes. (b) One face of the cell.

13.3 Bonding in Ionic Compounds: Lattice Energy

Ionic compounds typically have high melting points, an indication of the strength of the bonding in the ionic crystal lattice. A measure of that is the lattice energy, the main topic of this section.

Lattice Energy

Ionic compounds exist as solids under normal conditions. Their structures contain positive and negative ions arranged in a three-dimensional lattice (Figure 13.9). In an ionic crystal lattice, there are extensive attractions between ions of opposite charge and repulsions between ions of like charge. Each of these interactions is governed by an equation related to Coulomb's law (◀ page 78). For

TABLE 13.2 Lattice Energies of Some Ionic Compounds

Compound	$\Delta_{lattice}U$ (kJ/mol)
LiF	−1037
LiCl	−852
LiBr	−815
LiI	−761
NaF	−926
NaCl	−786
NaBr	−752
NaI	−702
KF	−821
KCl	−717
KBr	−689
KI	−649

Source: D. Cubicciotti: Lattice energies of the alkali halides and electron affinities of the halogens. *Journal of Chemical Physics*, Vol. 31, p. 1646, 1959.

example, $U_{ion\ pair}$, the energy of attractive interactions between 1 mol of ion pairs is given by

$$U_{ion\ pair} = C(N_A)\left(\frac{(n^+e)(n^-e)}{d}\right)$$

The symbol C represents a constant; d is the distance between the ion centers; n^+ is the number of positive charges on the cation; n^- is the number of negative charges on the anion; and e is the charge on an electron; n^+e is assigned a positive value, and n^-e is assigned a negative value due to the respective charges of the ions. Including Avogadro's number, N_A, allows us to calculate the energy change for 1 mol of ion pairs. Be sure to notice that the energy depends directly on the charges on the ions and inversely on the distance between them.

In an extended ionic lattice, there are multiple cation–anion interactions. Let us take NaCl as an example (Figure 13.9). If we focus on an Na^+ ion in the center of the unit cell, we see it is surrounded by, and attracted to, six Cl^- ions. Just a bit farther away from this Na^+ ion, however, there are 12 other Na^+ ions, and there is a force of repulsion between the center Na^+ and these ions. (These are 12 Na^+ ions in the edges of the cube.) And if we still focus on the "center" Na^+ ion, we see there are eight more Cl^- ions, and these are attracted to the "center" Na^+ ion. If we were to take into account *all* of the interactions between the ions in a lattice, it would be possible to calculate the **lattice energy, $\Delta_{lattice}U$**, the energy of formation of one mole of a solid crystalline ionic compound when ions in the gas phase combine (see Table 13.2). For sodium chloride, this reaction would correspond to

$$Na^+(g) + Cl^-(g) \longrightarrow NaCl(s)$$

Lattice energy is a measure of the strength of ionic bonding. Often, however, chemists use **lattice enthalpy, $\Delta_{lattice}H$** rather than lattice energy because of the difficulty of estimating some energy quantities. The same trends are seen in both, though, and, because we are dealing with a condensed phase, the numerical values are nearly identical.

We shall focus here on the dependence of lattice enthalpy on ion charges and sizes. As given by Coulomb's law, the higher the ion charges, the greater the attraction between oppositely charged ions, and so $\Delta_{lattice}H$ has a larger negative value for more highly charged ions. This is illustrated by the lattice enthalpies of MgO and NaF. The value of $\Delta_{lattice}H$ for MgO (−4050 kJ/mol) is about four times more negative than the value for NaF (−926 kJ/mol) because the charges on the Mg^{2+} and O^{2-} ions [(2+) × (2−)] are twice as large as those on Na^+ and F^- ions.

Because the attraction between ions is inversely proportional to the distance between them, the effect of ion size on lattice enthalpy is also predictable: A lattice built from smaller ions generally leads to a more negative value for the lattice enthalpy (Table 13.2 and Figure 13.11). For alkali metal halides, for example, the lattice enthalpy for lithium compounds is generally more negative than that for potassium compounds because the Li^+ ion is much smaller than the K^+ cation. Similarly, fluorides are more strongly bonded than are iodides with the same cation.

Calculating a Lattice Enthalpy from Thermodynamic Data

Lattice enthalpies can be calculated using a thermodynamic relationship known as a **Born–Haber cycle.** This calculation is an application of Hess's law (◄ page 233). Such a cycle is illustrated in Figure 13.12 for solid sodium chloride.

■ **Born–Haber Cycles** Calculation of lattice energies by this procedure is named for Max Born (1882–1970) and Fritz Haber (1868–1934), German scientists who played prominent roles in thermodynamic research.

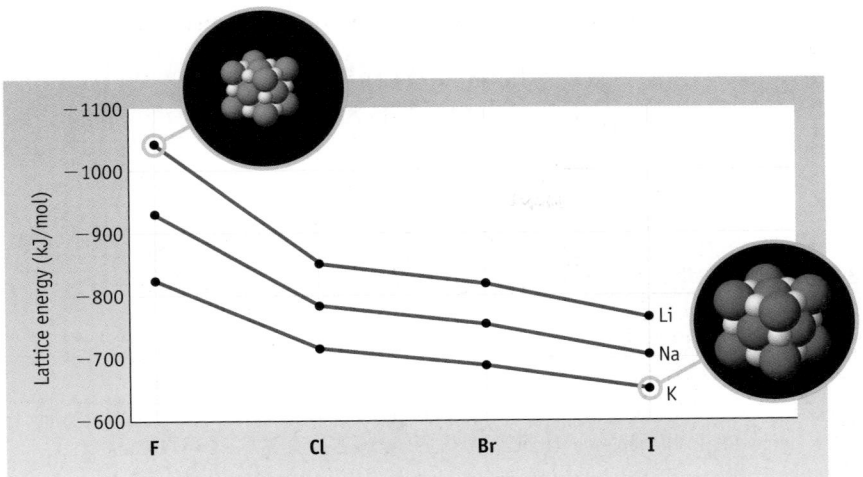

FIGURE 13.11 Lattice energy.
$\Delta_{lattice}U$ is illustrated for the formation of the alkali metal halides, MX(s), from the ions $M^+(g) + X^-(g)$.

Steps 1 and 2 in Figure 13.12 involve formation of $Na^+(g)$ and $Cl^-(g)$ ions from the elements; the enthalpy change for each of these steps is known (Appendices F and L). Step 3 in Figure 13.12 gives the lattice enthalpy, $\Delta_{lattice}H$. $\Delta_f H°$ is the standard molar enthalpy of formation of NaCl(s) (Appendix L). The enthalpy values for each step are related by the following equation:

$$\Delta_f H° \,[NaCl(s)] = \Delta H_{Step\ 1a} + \Delta H_{Step\ 1b} + \Delta H_{Step\ 2a} + \Delta H_{Step\ 2b} + \Delta H_{Step\ 3}$$

Because the values for all of these quantities are known except for $\Delta H_{Step\ 3}$ $(\Delta_{lattice}H)$, the value for this step can be calculated.

Step 1a. Enthalpy of formation of Cl(g)   = +121.3 kJ/mol (Appendix L)
Step 1b. ΔH for $Cl(g) + e^- \rightarrow Cl^-(g)$ = −349 kJ/mol (Appendix F)
Step 2a. Enthalpy of formation of Na(g)   = +107.3 kJ/mol (Appendix L)
Step 2b. ΔH for $Na(g) \rightarrow Na^+(g) + e^-$ = +496 kJ/mol (Appendix F)

The standard enthalpy of formation of NaCl(s), $\Delta_f H°$, is −411.12 kJ/mol. Combining this with the known values of Steps 1 and 2, we can calculate ΔH_{step3}, which is the lattice enthalpy, $\Delta_{lattice}H$.

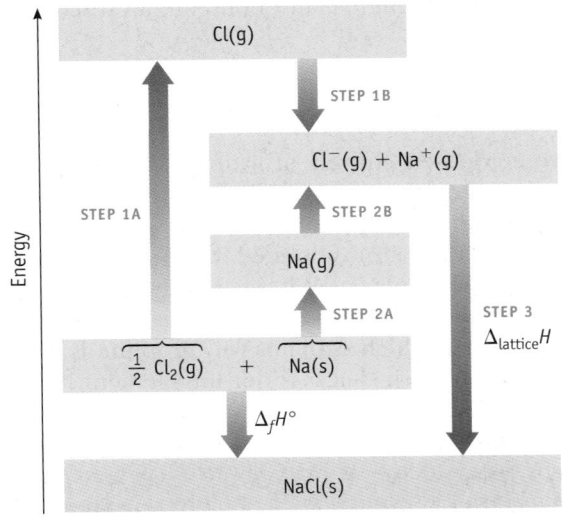

FIGURE 13.12 Born–Haber cycle for the formation of NaCl(s) from the elements. The calculation in the text uses enthalpy values, and the value obtained is the lattice enthalpy, $\Delta_{lattice}H$. The difference between $\Delta_{lattice}U$ and $\Delta_{lattice}H$ is generally not significant and can be corrected for, if desired. (Note that the energy diagram is not to scale.)

Step 3. Formation of NaCl(s) from the ions in the gas phase $= \Delta H_{step3}$

$$\Delta H_{step3} = \Delta_f H° \,[NaCl(s)] - \Delta H_{Step\ 1a} - \Delta H_{Step\ 1b} - \Delta H_{Step\ 2a} - \Delta H_{Step\ 2b}$$
$$= -411.12\ kJ/mol - 121.3\ kJ/mol - (-349\ kJ/mol) - 107.3\ kJ/mol - 496\ kJ/mol$$
$$= -787\ kJ/mol$$

Chemistry Now™

Sign in at **www.cengage.com/login** and go to Chapter 13 Contents to see Screen 13.4 for an illustration of **lattice and lattice energy.**

EXERCISE 13.5 Using Lattice Enthalpies

Calculate the molar enthalpy of formation, $\Delta_f H°$, of solid sodium iodide using the approach outlined in Figure 13.12. The required data can be found in Appendices F and L and in Table 13.2.

13.4 The Solid State: Other Kinds of Solid Materials

So far, we have described the structures of metals and simple ionic solids. Now we will look briefly at the other categories of solids: molecular solids, network solids, and amorphous solids (Table 13.1).

Molecular Solids

Compounds such as H_2O and CO_2 exist as solids under appropriate conditions. In these cases, it is molecules, rather than atoms or ions, that pack in a regular fashion in a three-dimensional lattice. You have already seen one such structure, that of ice (Figure 12.8).

The way molecules are arranged in a crystalline lattice depends on the shape of the molecules and the types of intermolecular forces. Molecules tend to pack in the most efficient manner and to align in ways that maximize intermolecular forces of attraction. Thus, the water structure was established to gain the maximum intermolecular attraction through hydrogen bonding.

It is from structural studies on molecular solids that most of the information on molecular geometries, bond lengths, and bond angles discussed in Chapter 8 was assembled.

Charles D. Winters

FIGURE 13.13 A diamond and the diamond lattice. The colors of diamonds may range from colorless to yellow, brown, or black. Poorer-quality diamonds are used extensively in industry, mainly for cutting or grinding tools. Industrial-quality diamonds are produced synthetically at present by heating graphite, along with a metal catalyst, to 1200–1500 °C and a pressure of 65–90 kilobars.

Network Solids

Network solids are composed entirely of a three-dimensional array of covalently bonded atoms. Common examples include two allotropes of carbon: graphite and diamond. Elemental silicon is also a network solid with a diamond-like structure.

Graphite consists of carbon atoms bonded together in flat sheets that cling only weakly to one another (Figure 2.7). Within the layers, each carbon atom is surrounded by three other carbon atoms in a trigonal planar arrangement. The layers can slip easily over another, which explains why graphite is soft, a good lubricant, and used in pencil lead. (Pencil "lead" is not the element lead, but rather a composite of clay and graphite.)

Diamonds have a low density ($d = 3.51\ g/cm^3$), but they are also the hardest material and the best conductor of heat known. They are transparent to visible light, as well as to infrared and ultraviolet radiation. Diamonds are electrically in-

sulating but behave as semiconductors with some advantages over silicon. In addition to their use in jewelry, many diamonds are used as abrasives and in diamond-coated cutting tools. In the structure of diamond (Figure 13.13), each carbon atom is bonded to four other carbon atoms at the corners of a tetrahedron, and this pattern extends throughout the solid.

Silicates, compounds composed of silicon and oxygen, represent an enormous class of chemical compounds. You know them in the form of sand, quartz, talc, and mica, or as a major constituent of rocks such as granite. The structure of quartz is illustrated in Figure 13.14. It consists of tetrahedral silicon atoms covalently bonded to oxygen atoms in a giant three-dimensional lattice.

Most network solids are hard and rigid and are characterized by high melting and boiling points. These characteristics reflect the fact that a great deal of energy must be provided to break the covalent bonds in the lattice. For example, silicon dioxide melts at temperatures higher than 1600 °C.

Photo: Charles D. Winters

FIGURE 13.14 Silicon dioxide.
Common quartz, SiO_2, is a network solid consisting of silicon and oxygen atoms.

Amorphous Solids

A characteristic property of pure crystalline solids—whether metals, ionic solids, or molecular solids—is that they melt at a specific temperature. For example, water melts at 0 °C, aspirin at 135 °C, lead at 327.5 °C, and NaCl at 801 °C. Because they are specific and reproducible values, melting points are often used as a means of identifying chemical compounds.

Another property of crystalline solids is that they form well-defined crystals, with smooth, flat faces. When a sharp force is applied to a crystal, it will most often cleave to give smooth, flat faces. The resulting solid particles are smaller versions of the original crystal (Figure 13.15a).

Many common solids, including ones that we encounter every day, do not have these properties, however. Glass is a good example. When glass is heated, it softens over a wide temperature range, a property useful for artisans and craftsmen who can create beautiful and functional products for our enjoyment and use. Glass also possesses a property that we would rather it not have: When glass breaks, it leaves randomly shaped pieces. Other materials that behave similarly include common polymers such as polyethylene, nylon, and other plastics.

Charles D. Winters

(a) A salt crystal can be cleaved cleanly into smaller and smaller crystals that are duplicates of the larger crystal.

(b) Glass is an amorphous solid composed of silicon and oxygen atoms. It has, however, no long-range order as in crystalline quartz.

(c) Glass can be molded and shaped into beautiful forms and, by adding metal oxides, can take on wonderful colors.

FIGURE 13.15 Crystalline and amorphous solids.

The characteristics of these amorphous solids relate to their molecular structure. At the particulate level, amorphous solids do not have a regular structure. In fact, in many ways these substances look a lot like liquids. Unlike liquids, however, the forces of attraction are strong enough that movement of the molecules or ions is restricted.

Chemistry.Now™

Sign in at **www.cengage.com/login** and go to Chapter 13 Contents to see:
- Screen 13.5 for an exercise on **molecular solids**
- Screen 13.6 for a self-study module on **network solids**
- Screen 13.7 for a self-study module on **silicate minerals**

13.5 Phase Changes Involving Solids

The shape of a crystalline solid is a reflection of its internal structure. But what about physical properties of solids, such as the temperatures at which they melt? This and many other physical properties of solids are of interest to chemists, geologists, and engineers, among others.

Melting: Conversion of Solid into Liquid

The melting point of a solid is the temperature at which the lattice collapses and the solid is converted into a liquid. Like the liquid-to-vapor transformation, melting requires energy, called the enthalpy of fusion (given in kilojoules per mole) (◄ Chapter 5).

Energy absorbed as heat on melting = enthalpy of fusion = $\Delta_{fusion}H$ (kJ/mol)
Energy evolved as heat on freezing = enthalpy of crystallization = $-\Delta_{fusion}H$ (kJ/mol)

■ **Uncle Tungsten** *Uncle Tungsten* is the title of a book by Oliver Sacks (Alfred Knopf, New York, 2001). In it, he describes growing up with an uncle who had a light bulb factory and used tungsten. He also describes other "chemical adventures."

Enthalpies of fusion can range from just a few thousand joules per mole to many thousands of joules per mole (Table 13.3). A low melting temperature will certainly mean a low value for the enthalpy of fusion, whereas high melting points are associated with high enthalpies of fusion. Figure 13.16 shows the enthalpies of fusion for the metals of the fourth through the sixth periods. Based on this figure, we see that transition metals have high enthalpies of fusion, with many of those in the sixth period being extraordinarily high. This trend parallels the trend seen with the melting points for these elements. Tungsten, which has the highest melting point of all the known elements except for carbon, also has the highest enthalpy of fusion among the transition metals. For this reason, tungsten is used for the filaments in light bulbs; no other material has been found to work better since the invention of the light bulb in 1908.

Table 13.3 presents some data for several basic types of substances: metals, polar and nonpolar molecules, and ionic solids. In general, nonpolar substances that form molecular solids have low melting points. Melting points increase within a series of related molecules, however, as the size and molar mass increase. This happens because London dispersion forces are generally larger when the molar mass is larger. Thus, increasing amounts of energy are required to break down the intermolecular forces in the solid, a principle that is reflected in an increasing enthalpy of fusion.

The ionic compounds in Table 13.3 have higher melting points and higher enthalpies of fusion than the molecular solids. This trend is due to the strong ion–ion forces present in ionic solids, forces that are reflected in high lattice energies (page 599). Because ion–ion forces depend on ion size (as well as ion charge), there is a good correlation between lattice energy and the position of the metal or

TABLE 13.3 Melting Points and Enthalpies of Fusion of Some Elements and Compounds

Compound	Melting Point (°C)	Enthalpy of Fusion (kJ/mol)	Type of Interparticle Forces
Metals			
Hg	−39	2.29	Metal bonding; see pages 657–663.
Na	98	2.60	
Al	660	10.7	
Ti	1668	20.9	
W	3422	35.2	
Molecular Solids: Nonpolar Molecules			
O_2	−219	0.440	Dispersion forces only.
F_2	−220	0.510	
Cl_2	−102	6.41	
Br_2	−7.2	10.8	
Molecular Solids: Polar Molecules			
HCl	−114	1.99	All three HX molecules have dipole–dipole
HBr	−87	2.41	forces. Dispersion forces increase with size
HI	−51	2.87	and molar mass.
H_2O	0	6.01	Hydrogen bonding and dispersion forces
Ionic Solids			
NaF	996	33.4	All ionic solids have extended ion–ion inter-
NaCl	801	28.2	actions. Note the general trend is the same
NaBr	747	26.1	as for lattice energies (see Section 13.3 and
NaI	660	23.6	Figure 13.11).

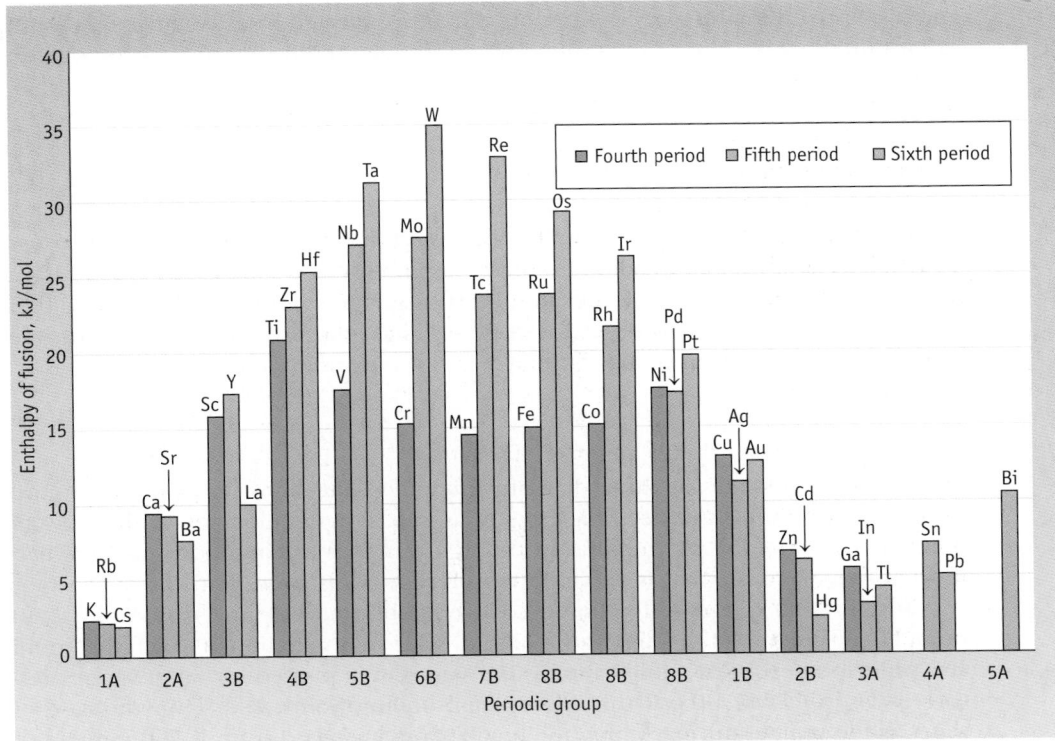

FIGURE 13.16 Enthalpy of fusion of fourth-, fifth-, and sixth-period metals. Enthalpies of fusion range from 2–5 kJ/mol for Group 1A elements to 35.2 kJ/mol for tungsten. Notice that enthalpies of fusion generally increase for group 4B–8B metals on descending the periodic table.

FIGURE 13.17 Sublimation.

Sublimation entails the conversion of a solid directly to its vapor. Here, iodine (I₂) sublimes when warmed. If an ice-filled test tube is inserted into the flask, the vapor deposits on the cold surface.

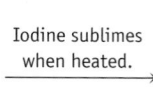

Iodine sublimes when heated.

Charles D. Winters

halogen in the periodic table. For example, the data in Table 13.3 show a decrease in melting point and enthalpy of fusion for sodium salts as the halide ion increases in size. This parallels the decrease in lattice energy seen with increasing ion size.

Sublimation: Conversion of Solid into Vapor

Molecules can escape directly from the solid to the gas phase by sublimation (Figure 13.17).

$$\text{Solid} \rightarrow \text{Gas} \qquad \text{Energy required as heat} = \Delta_{\text{sublimation}}H$$

Sublimation, like fusion and evaporation, is an endothermic process. The energy required as heat is called the **enthalpy of sublimation.** Water, which has a molar enthalpy of sublimation of 51 kJ/mol, can be converted from solid ice to water vapor quite readily. A good example of this phenomenon is the sublimation of frost from grass and trees as night turns to day on a cold morning in the winter.

13.6 Phase Diagrams

Depending on the conditions of temperature and pressure, a substance can exist as a gas, a liquid, or a solid. In addition, under certain specific conditions, two (or even three) states can coexist in equilibrium. It is possible to summarize this information in the form of a graph called a **phase diagram.** Phase diagrams are used to illustrate the relationship between phases of matter and the pressure and temperature.

Water

Figure 13.18 illustrates a phase diagram for water. The lines in a phase diagram identify the conditions under which two phases exist at equilibrium. Conversely, all points that do not fall on the lines in the figure represent conditions under which there is only one state that is stable. Line A–B represents conditions for solid–vapor equilibrium, and line A–C for liquid–solid equilibrium. The line from point A to point D, representing the temperature and pressure combination at which the liquid and vapor phases are in equilibrium, is the same curve plotted for water vapor pressure in Figure 12.17. Recall that the normal boiling point, 100 °C in the case of water, is the temperature at which the equilibrium vapor pressure is 760 mm Hg.

Point A, appropriately called the **triple point**, indicates the conditions under which all three phases coexist in equilibrium. For water, the triple point is at $P = 4.6$ mm Hg and $T = 0.01$ °C.

The line A–C shows the conditions of pressure and temperature at which solid–liquid equilibrium exists. (Because no vapor pressure is involved here, the pressure referred to is the external pressure on the liquid.) For water, this line has a negative slope; the change for water is approximately -0.01 °C for each one-atmosphere increase in pressure. That is, the higher the external pressure, the lower the melting point.

The negative slope of the water solid–liquid equilibrium line can be explained from our knowledge of the structure of water and ice. When the pressure on an object increases, common sense tells us that the volume of the object will become

Case Study

The World's Lightest Solid

The *Guinness Book of Records* calls it the "world's lightest solid" and the "best thermal insulator." Even though it is 99.8% air and has a density of only about 1 mg/cm^3, it is a light blue solid that, to the touch, feels much like Styrofoam chips that are used in packaging. It is also strong structurally, able to hold over 2000 times its weight (Figure A).

"It" is a silica aerogel, a low-density substance derived from a gel in which the liquid has been replaced by air (▶ page 666). There are aerogels based silicon and carbon as well as aluminum and other metals, but the silicon-based aerogel is the most thoroughly studied. This aerogel is made by polymerizing a compound like $Si(OC_2H_5)_4$ in alcohol. The resulting long-chain molecules form a gel that is

FIGURE A Silica aerogel. A 2.5-kg brick is supported by a piece of silica aerogel weighing about 2 g. (http://stardust.jpl.nasa.gov/photo/aerogel.html)

bathed in the alcohol. This substance is then placed in supercritical CO_2 (▶ page 609), which causes the alcohol in the nanopores in the gel to be replaced by CO_2. When the CO_2 is vented off as a gas, what remains is a highly porous aerogel with an incredibly low density.

Aerogels have been known for decades but have only recently received a lot of study. They do have amazing properties! Chief among them is their insulating ability, as illustrated in Figure B. Aerogels do not allow heat to be conducted through the lattice, and convective heat transfer is also poor because air cannot circulate throughout the lattice. One practical use for these aerogels is in insulating glass. However, before it can be truly useful for this purpose, researchers need to find a way to make completely transparent aerogel. (Silica aerogel is very light blue owing to Rayleigh scattering, the same process that makes the sky blue.) Aerogels are also biocompatible and have been studied as possible drug delivery systems.

Aerogel has been in the news in the past few years because it was used to catch comet dust in Project Stardust. A spacecraft was sent to intercept a comet in 2004 and returned to Earth in January 2006. On the spacecraft was an array holding blocks of aerogel. As the craft flew through the comet's tail, dust particles impacted the aerogel blocks and were "brought to a standstill as they tunneled through it without much heating or alteration, leaving carrot-shaped tracks." When the spacecraft was returned to Earth, scientists analyzed the particles and found that there were silicate minerals that seemed to have been formed in the inner regions of the solar

FIGURE B Aerogel as an insulator. http://stardust.jpl.nasa.gov/images/gallery/aerogelmatches.jpg

system. (See *Science*, Vol. 314, 15 December 2006.)

Questions:

1. Assume the repeating unit in the aerogel polymer is $OSi(OC_2H_5)_2$. If the polymer is 99.8% air, how many silicon atoms are there in 1.0 cm^3 of aerogel?

2. Suppose you wish to make a superinsulating window and so fill the gap between two sheets of glass with aerogel. What mass of aerogel is needed for a 180 cm × 150 cm window with a gap of 2.0 mm between the glass sheets?

Answers to these questions are in Appendix Q.

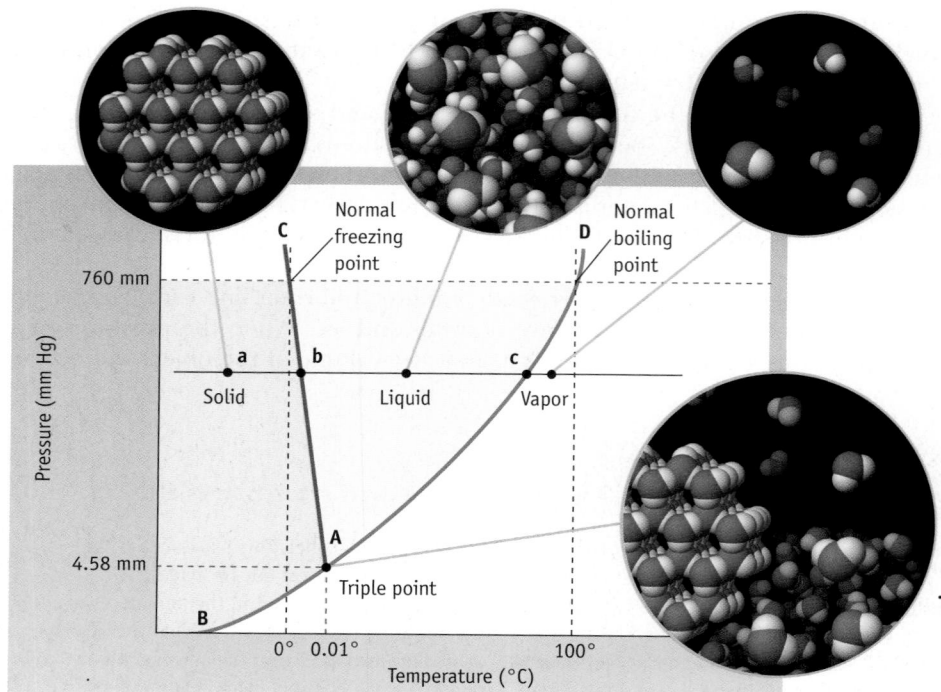

Active Figure 13.18 Phase diagram for water. The scale is intentionally exaggerated to be able to show the triple point and the negative slope of the line representing the liquid–solid equilibrium.

Chemistry Now™ Sign in at www.cengage.com/login and go to the Chapter Contents menu to explore an interactive version of this figure accompanied by an exercise.

smaller, giving the substance a higher density. Because ice is less dense than liquid water (due to the open lattice structure of ice, Figure 12.8), ice and water in equilibrium respond to increased pressure (at constant T) by melting ice to form more water because the same mass of water requires less volume.

Phase Diagrams and Thermodynamics

Let us explore the water phase diagram further by correlating phase changes with thermodynamic data. Suppose we begin with ice at −10 °C and under a pressure of 500 mm Hg (point a on Figure 13.18). As ice is heated (at constant P), it absorbs about 2.1 J/g · K in warming from point a to point b at a temperature between 0 °C and 0.01 °C. At this point, the solid is in equilibrium with liquid water. Solid–liquid equilibrium is maintained until 333 J/g has been transferred to the sample and it has become liquid water at this temperature. If the liquid, still under a pressure of 500 mm Hg, now absorbs 4.184 J/g · K, it warms to point c. The temperature at point c is about 89 °C, and equilibrium is established between liquid water and water vapor. The equilibrium vapor pressure of the liquid water is 500 mm Hg. If 2260 J/g is transferred to the liquid–vapor sample, the equilibrium vapor pressure remains 500 mm Hg until the liquid is completely converted to vapor at 89 °C.

Carbon Dioxide

The features of the phase diagram for CO_2 (Figure 13.19) are generally the same as those for water but with some important differences.

In contrast to water, the CO_2 solid–liquid equilibrium line has a positive slope. Once again, increasing pressure on the solid in equilibrium with the liquid will shift the equilibrium to the more dense phase, but for CO_2 this will be the solid. Because solid CO_2 is denser than the liquid, the newly formed solid CO_2 sinks to the bottom in a container of liquid CO_2.

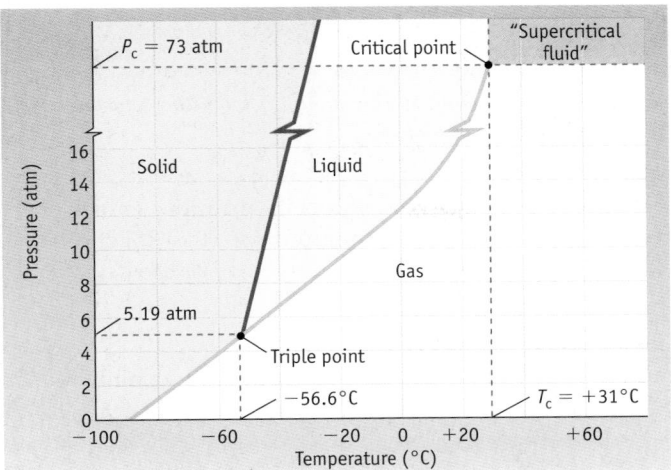

FIGURE 13.19 The phase diagram of CO₂. Notice in particular the positive slope of the solid–liquid equilibrium line. (For more on the critical point, see page 577.)

Another feature of the CO_2 phase diagram is the triple point that occurs at a pressure of 5.19 atm (3940 mm Hg) and 216.6 K (-56.6 °C). Carbon dioxide cannot be a liquid at pressures lower than this.

At pressures around normal atmospheric pressure, CO_2 will be either a solid or a gas, depending on the temperature. [At a pressure of 1 atm, solid CO_2 is in equilibrium with the gas at a temperature of 197.5 K (-78.7 °C).] As a result, as solid CO_2 warms above this temperature, it sublimes rather than melts. Carbon dioxide is called *dry ice* for this reason; it looks like water ice, but it does not melt.

From the CO_2 phase diagram, we can also learn that CO_2 gas can be converted to a liquid at room temperature (20–25 °C) by exerting a moderate pressure on the gas. In fact, CO_2 is regularly shipped in tanks as a liquid to laboratories and industrial companies.

Finally, the critical pressure and temperature for CO_2 are 73 atm and 31 °C, respectively. Because the critical temperature and pressure are easily attained in the laboratory, it is possible to observe the transformation to supercritical CO_2 (Figure 13.20).

Chemistry ⚛ Now™

Sign in at **www.cengage.com/login** and go to Chapter 13 Contents to see Screen 13.8 to view animations of **phase changes** and to do an exercise on **phase diagrams**.

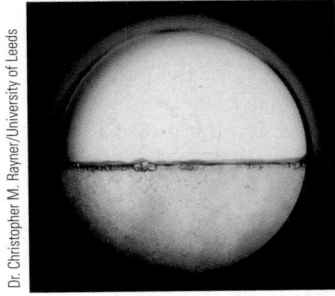 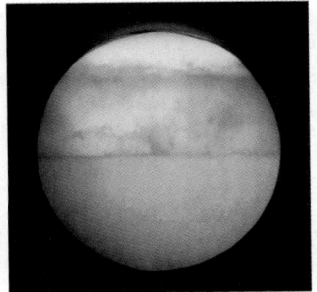 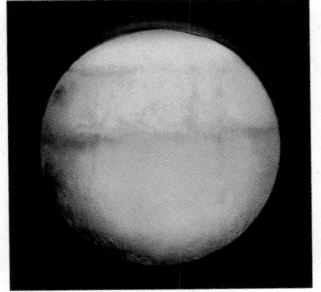 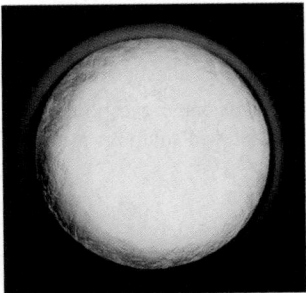

The separate phases of CO₂ are seen through the window in a high-pressure vessel.

As the sample warms and the pressure increases, the meniscus becomes less distinct.

As the temperature continues to increase, it is more difficult to distinguish the liquid and vapor phases.

Once the critical *T* and *P* are reached, distinct liquid and vapor phases are no longer in evidence. This homogeneous phase is "supercritical CO₂."

FIGURE 13.20 Transformation to supercritical CO₂.

Chapter Goals Revisited

Now that you have studied this chapter, you should ask whether you have met the chapter goals. In particular, you should be able to:

Understand cubic unit cells

a. Describe the three types of cubic unit cells: primitive cubic (pc), body-centered cubic (bcc), and face-centered cubic (fcc) (Section 13.1).

b. Relate atom size and unit cell dimensions. Study Question(s) assignable in OWL: 7, 8, 10, 26, 29, 32, 34, 36, 43; Go Chemistry Module 18.

Relate unit cells for ionic compounds to formulas

a. Understand the relation of unit cell structure and formula for ionic compounds. (Section 13.2) Study Question(s) assignable in OWL: 4, 5, 6, 8; Go Chemistry Module 18.

Describe the properties of solids

a. Understand lattice energy and how it is calculated (Section 13.3). Study Question(s) assignable in OWL: 11, 13, 14, 16, 38.

b. Characterize different types of solids: metallic (e.g., copper), ionic (e.g., NaCl and CaF_2), molecular (e.g., water and I_2), network (e.g., diamond), and amorphous (e.g., glass and many synthetic polymers) (Table 13.1). Study Question(s) assignable in OWL: 17.

c. Define the processes of melting, freezing, and sublimation and their enthalpies (Sections 13.4 and 13.5). Study Question(s) assignable in OWL: 20.

Understand the nature of phase diagrams

a. Identify the different points (triple point, normal boiling point, freezing point) and regions (solid, liquid, vapor) of a phase diagram, and use the diagram to evaluate the vapor pressure of a liquid and the relative densities of a liquid and a solid (Section 13.5). Study Question(s) assignable in OWL: 21, 22, 23, 24.

STUDY QUESTIONS

OWL Online homework for this chapter may be assigned in OWL.

▲ denotes challenging questions.

■ denotes questions assignable in OWL.

Blue-numbered questions have answers in Appendix O and fully-worked solutions in the *Student Solutions Manual*.

Practicing Skills

Metallic and Ionic Solids

(See Examples 13.1–13.3 and ChemistryNow Screens 13.2 and 13.3.)

1. Outline a two-dimensional unit cell for the pattern shown here. If the black squares are labeled A and the white squares are B, what is the simplest formula for a "compound" based on this pattern?

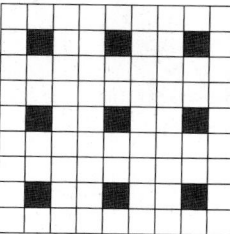

2. Outline a two-dimensional unit cell for the pattern shown here. If the black squares are labeled A and the white squares are B, what is the simplest formula for a "compound" based on this pattern?

3. One way of viewing the unit cell of perovskite was illustrated in Example 13.2. Another way is shown here. Prove that this view also leads to a formula of $CaTiO_3$.

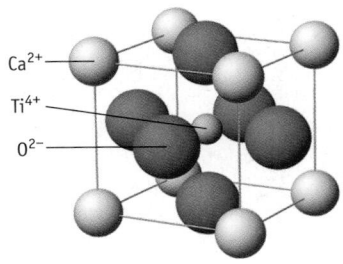

4. ■ Rutile, TiO_2, crystallizes in a structure characteristic of many other ionic compounds. How many formula units of TiO_2 are in the unit cell illustrated here? (The oxide ions marked by an x are wholly within the cell; the others are in the cell faces.)

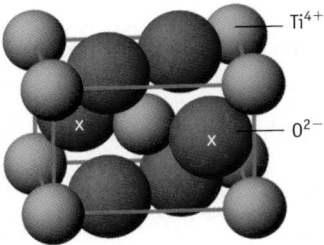

5. ■ Cuprite is a semiconductor. Oxide ions are at the cube corners and in the cube center. Copper ions are wholly within the unit cell.
   (a) What is the formula of cuprite?
   (b) What is the oxidation number of copper?

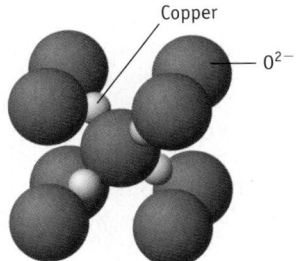

6. ■ The mineral fluorite, which is composed of calcium ions and fluoride ions, has the unit cell shown here.
   (a) What type of unit cell is described by the Ca^{2+} ions?
   (b) Where are the F^- ions located, in octahedral holes or tetrahedral holes?
   (c) Based on this unit cell, what is the formula of fluorite?

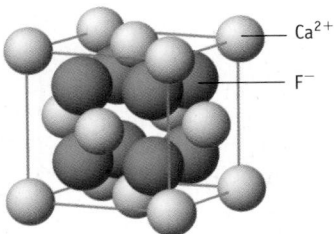

7. ■ Calcium metal crystallizes in a face-centered cubic unit cell. The density of the solid is 1.54 g/cm³. What is the radius of a calcium atom?

8. ■ The density of copper metal is 8.95 g/cm³. If the radius of a copper atom is 127.8 pm, is the copper unit cell primitive, body-centered cubic, or face-centered cubic?

9. Potassium iodide has a face-centered cubic unit cell of iodide ions with potassium ions in octahedral holes. The density of KI is 3.12 g/cm³. What is the length of one side of the unit cell? (Ion sizes are found in Table 7.12.)

10. ▲ ■ A unit cell of cesium chloride is shown on page 596. The density of the solid is 3.99 g/cm³, and the radius of the Cl^- ion is 181 pm. What is the radius of the Cs^+ ion in the center of the cell? (Assume that the Cs^+ ion touches all of the corner Cl^- ions.)

Ionic Bonding and Lattice Energy
(See ChemistryNow Screen 13.4.)

11. ■ List the following compounds in order of increasing lattice energy (from least negative to most negative): LiI, LiF, CaO, RbI.

12. Examine the trends in lattice energy in Table 13.2. The value of the lattice energy becomes somewhat more negative on going from NaI to NaBr to NaCl, and all are in the range of −700 to −800 kJ/mol. Suggest a reason for the observation that the lattice energy of NaF ($\Delta_{lattice}U = -926$ kJ/mol) is much more negative than those of the other sodium halides.

13. ■ To melt an ionic solid, energy must be supplied to disrupt the forces between ions so the regular array of ions collapses. If the distance between the anion and the cation in a crystalline solid decreases (but ion charges remain the same), should the melting point decrease or increase? Explain.

14. ■ Which compound in each of the following pairs should require the higher temperature to melt? (See Study Question 13.)
(a) NaCl or RbCl
(b) BaO or MgO
(c) NaCl or MgS

15. Calculate the molar enthalpy of formation, $\Delta_f H°$, of solid lithium fluoride using the approach outlined on pages 599-602. $\Delta_f H°$ [Li(g)] = 159.37 kJ/mol, and other required data can be found in Appendices F and L. (See also Exercise 13.5.)

16. ■ Calculate the lattice enthalpy for RbCl. In addition to data in Appendices F and L, you will need the following information:

$\Delta_f H°$ [Rb(g)] = 80.9 kJ/mol

$\Delta_f H°$ [RbCl(s)] = −435.4 kJ/mol

Other Types of Solids
(See ChemistryNow Screens 13.6 and 13.7.)

17. ■ A diamond unit cell is shown here.
(a) How many carbon atoms are in one unit cell?
(b) The unit cell can be considered as a cubic unit cell of C atoms with other C atoms in holes in the lattice. What type of unit cell is this (pc, bcc, fcc)? In what holes are other C atoms located, octahedral or tetrahedral holes?

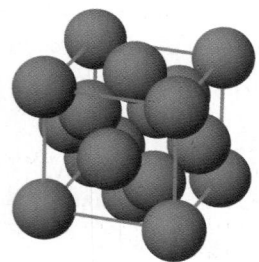

18. The structure of graphite is given in Figure 2.7.
(a) What type of intermolecular bonding forces exist between the layers of six-member carbon rings?
(b) Account for the lubricating ability of graphite. That is, why does graphite feel slippery? Why does pencil lead (which is really graphite in clay) leave black marks on paper?

Physical Properties of Solids

19. Benzene, C_6H_6, is an organic liquid that freezes at 5.5 °C (see Figure 12.1) to form beautiful, feather-like crystals. How much energy as heat is evolved when 15.5 g of benzene freezes at 5.5 °C? (The enthalpy of fusion of benzene is 9.95 kJ/mol.) If the 15.5-g sample is remelted, again at 5.5 °C, what quantity of energy as heat is required to convert it to a liquid?

20. ■ The specific heat capacity of silver is 0.235 J/g · K. Its melting point is 962 °C, and its enthalpy of fusion is 11.3 kJ/mol. What quantity of energy as heat, in joules, is required to change 5.00 g of silver from a solid at 25 °C to a liquid at 962 °C?

Phase Diagrams and Phase Changes
(See ChemistryNow Screen 13.8.)

21. ■ Consider the phase diagram of CO_2 in Figure 13.19.
(a) Is the density of liquid CO_2 greater or less than that of solid CO_2?
(b) In what phase do you find CO_2 at 5 atm and 0 °C?
(c) Can CO_2 be liquefied at 45 °C?

22. ■ Use the phase diagram given here to answer the following questions:

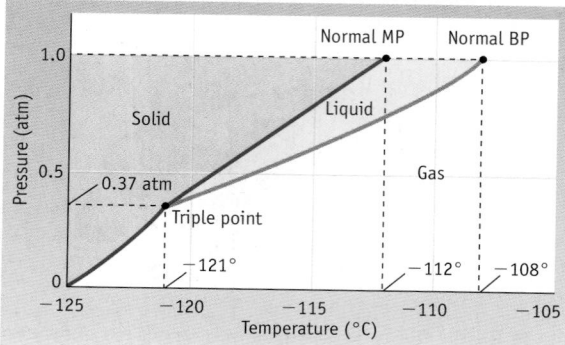

(a) In what phase is the substance found at room temperature and 1.0 atm pressure?
(b) If the pressure exerted on a sample is 0.75 atm and the temperature is −114 °C, in what phase does the substance exist?
(c) If you measure the vapor pressure of a liquid sample and find it to be 380 mm Hg, what is the temperature of the liquid phase?
(d) What is the vapor pressure of the solid at −122 °C?
(e) Which is the denser phase—solid or liquid? Explain briefly.

23. ■ Liquid ammonia, $NH_3(\ell)$, was once used in home refrigerators as the heat transfer fluid. The specific heat capacity of the liquid is 4.7 J/g · K and that of the vapor is 2.2 J/g · K. The enthalpy of vaporization is 23.33 kJ/mol at the boiling point. If you heat 12 kg of liquid ammonia from −50.0 °C to its boiling point of −33.3 °C, allow it to evaporate, and then continue warming to 0.0 °C, how much energy must you supply?

24. ■ If your air conditioner is more than several years old, it may use the chlorofluorocarbon CCl_2F_2 as the heat transfer fluid. The normal boiling point of CCl_2F_2 is −29.8 °C, and the enthalpy of vaporization is 20.11 kJ/mol. The gas and the liquid have specific heat capacities of 117.2 J/mol · K and 72.3 J/mol · K, respectively. How much energy as heat is evolved when 20.0 g of CCl_2F_2 is cooled from +40 °C to −40 °C?

▲ more challenging   ■ in OWL   Blue-numbered questions answered in Appendix O

General Questions

These questions are not designated as to type or location in the chapter. They may combine several concepts.

25. Construct a phase diagram for O_2 from the following information: normal boiling point, 90.18 K; normal melting point, 54.8 K; and triple point, 54.34 K at a pressure of 2 mm Hg. Very roughly estimate the vapor pressure of liquid O_2 at −196 °C, the lowest temperature easily reached in the laboratory. Is the density of liquid O_2 greater or less than that of solid O_2?

26. ▲ ■ Tungsten crystallizes in the unit cell shown here.

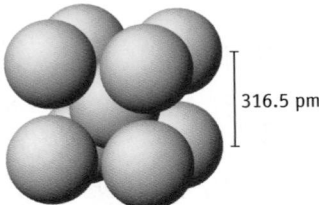

316.5 pm

    (a) What type of unit cell is this?
    (b) How many tungsten atoms occur per unit cell?
    (c) If the edge of the unit cell is 316.5 pm, what is the radius of a tungsten atom? (*Hint:* The W atoms touch each other along the diagonal line from one corner of the unit cell to the opposite corner of the unit cell.)

27. Silver crystallizes in a face-centered cubic unit cell. Each side of the unit cell has a length of 409 pm. What is the radius of a silver atom?

28. ▲ ■ The unit cell shown here is for calcium carbide. How many calcium atoms and how many carbon atoms are in each unit cell? What is the formula of calcium carbide? (Calcium ions are silver in color and carbon atoms are gray.)

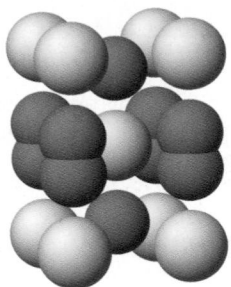

29. ■ The very dense metal iridium has a face-centered cubic unit cell and a density of 22.56 g/cm³. Use this information to calculate the radius of an atom of the element.

30. Vanadium metal has a density of 6.11 g/cm³. Assuming the vanadium atomic radius is 132 pm, is the vanadium unit cell primitive cubic, body-centered cubic, or face-centered cubic?

31. ▲ Calcium fluoride is the well-known mineral fluorite. It is known that each unit cell contains four Ca^{2+} ions and eight F^- ions and that the Ca^{2+} ions are arranged in an fcc lattice. The F^- ions fill all the tetrahedral holes in a face-centered cubic lattice of Ca^{2+} ions. The edge of the CaF_2 unit cell is 5.46295×10^{-8} cm in length. The density of the solid is 3.1805 g/cm³. Use this information to calculate Avogadro's number.

32. ▲ ■ Iron has a body-centered cubic unit cell with a cell dimension of 286.65 pm. The density of iron is 7.874 g/cm³. Use this information to calculate Avogadro's number.

33. ▲ You can get some idea of how efficiently spherical atoms or ions are packed in a three-dimensional solid by seeing how well circular atoms pack in two dimensions. Using the drawings shown here, prove that B is a more efficient way to pack circular atoms than A. A unit cell of A contains portions of four circles and one hole. In B, packing coverage can be calculated by looking at a triangle that contains portions of three circles and one hole. Show that A fills about 80% of the available space, whereas B fills closer to 90% of the available space.

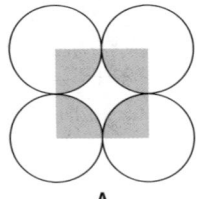 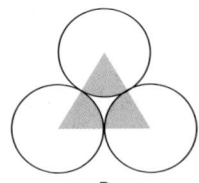

A   B

34. ▲ ■ Assuming that in a primitive cubic unit cell the spherical atoms or ions just touch along the cube's edges, calculate the percentage of empty space within the unit cell. (Recall that the volume of a sphere is $(4/3)\pi r^3$, where r is the radius of the sphere.)

35. ▲ The solid state structure of silicon is

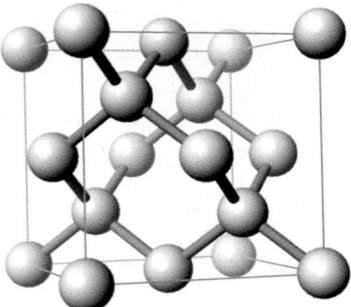

    (a) Describe this crystal as pc, bcc, or fcc. What type of holes are occupied in the lattice?
    (b) Calculate the density of silicon in g/cm³ (given that the cube edge has a length of 543.1 pm), and estimate the radius of the silicon atom. (Note: the Si atoms on the edges do not touch one another.)

36. ▲ ■ The solid state structure of silicon carbide, SiC, is shown below. Knowing that the Si—C bond length is 188.8 pm (and the Si—C—Si bond angle is 109.5°), calculate the density of SiC.

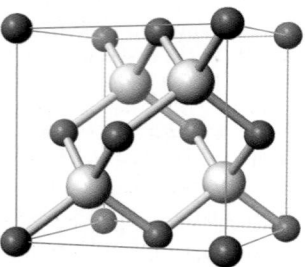

Unit cell of SiC.

Sample of silicon carbide.

37. Spinels are solids with the general formula AB_2O_4 (where A^{2+} and B^{3+} are metal cations of the same or different metals. The best-known example is common magnetite, Fe_3O_4 [which you can formulate as $(Fe^{2+})(Fe^{3+})_2O_4$]. Another example is the mineral often referred to as spinel, $MgAl_2O_4$.

A crystal of the spinel $MgAl_2O_4$ on a marble chip.

The oxide ions of spinels form a face-centered cubic lattice. In a *normal spinel,* cations occupy ⅛ of the tetrahedral sites and ½ of the octahedral sites.

(a) In $MgAl_2O_4$, in what type of holes are the magnesium and aluminum ions found?

(b) The mineral chromite has the formula $FeCr_2O_4$. What ions are involved, and in what type of holes are they found?

38. ■ Using the thermochemical data below, and an estimated value of -2481 kJ/mol for the lattice energy for Na_2O, calculate the value for the *second* electron affinity of oxygen $[O^-(g) + e^- \rightarrow O^{2-}(g)]$.

Quantity	Numerical Value (kJ/mol)
Enthalpy of atomization of Na	107.3
Ionization Energy of Na	495.9
Enthalpy of formation of solid Na_2O	−418.0
Enthalpy of formation of $O(g)$ from O_2	249.1
First electron affinity of O	−141.0

In the Laboratory

39. Lead sulfide, PbS (commonly called galena), has the same formula as ZnS.

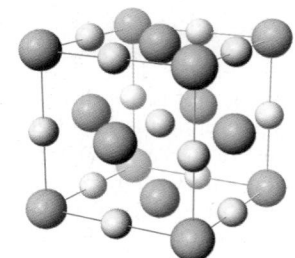

Unit cell of PbS.

Sample of galena.

Does PbS have the same solid structure as ZnS? If different, how are they different? How is the unit cell of PbS related to its formula?

▲ more challenging ■ in OWL   Blue-numbered questions answered in Appendix O

40. $CaTiO_3$, a perovskite, has the structure below.
   (a) If the density of the solid is 4.10 g/cm³, what is the length of a side of the unit cell?
   (b) Calculate the radius of the Ti^{4+} ion in the center of the unit cell. How well does your calculation agree with a literature value of 75 pm?

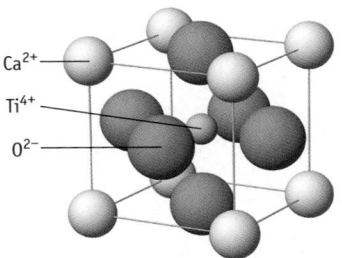

Ca²⁺
Ti⁴⁺
O²⁻

Unit cell of the perovskite CaTiO₃.

©DEA/C. Bevilacqua/Getty Images

A sample of perovskite CaTiO₃.

Summary and Conceptual Questions

The following questions may use concepts from this and previous chapters.

41. ▲ Boron phosphide, BP, is a semiconductor and a hard, abrasion-resistant material. It is made by reacting boron tribromide and phosphorus tribromide in a hydrogen atmosphere at high temperature (> 750 °C).
   (a) Write a balanced chemical equation for the synthesis of BP. *(Hint: Hydrogen is a reducing agent.)*
   (b) Boron phosphide crystallizes in a zinc blende structure, formed from boron atoms in a face-centered cubic lattice and phosphorus atoms in tetrahedral holes. How many tetrahedral holes are filled with P atoms in each unit cell?
   (c) The length of a unit cell of BP is 478 pm. What is the density of the solid in g/cm³.
   (d) Calculate the closest distance between a B and a P atom in the unit cell. (Assume the B atoms do not touch along the cell edge. The B atoms in the faces touch the B atoms at the corners of the unit cell. See page 594.)

42. ▲ Why is it not possible for a salt with the formula M_3X (Na_3PO_4, for example) to have a face-centered cubic lattice of X anions with M cations in octahedral holes?

43. ▲ ■ Two identical swimming pools are filled with uniform spheres of ice packed as closely as possible. The spheres in the first pool are the size of grains of sand; those in the second pool are the size of oranges. The ice in both pools melts. In which pool, if either, will the water level be higher? (Ignore any differences in filling space at the planes next to the walls and bottom.)

44. Spinels are described in Study Question 37. Consider two normal spinels, $CoAl_2O_4$ and $SnCo_2O_4$. What metal ions are involved in each? What are their electron configurations? Are the metal ions paramagnetic, and if so how many unpaired electrons are involved?

14 | Solutions and Their Behavior

© David Raboin, 2007

Safe Flying

You are sitting in an airport in the winter. Outside the weather is bad, with blowing snow and ice. You want to get on the plane home, but first the plane has to be de-iced. Ice and snow on the wings severely impairs the ability of wings to provide lift, so it is unsafe to try to take off unless the plane is de-iced. The fluid that is sprayed on the plane is a mixture of ethylene or propylene glycol and other substances. These are the same chemicals used in the antifreeze in your car's radiator.

Questions:

1. Why does ethylene glycol ($HOCH_2CH_2OH$) dissolve so well in water?
2. Why use a solution of ethylene glycol and water as an anti-freeze?
3. If you mix 100. g of ethylene glycol with 500. g of water, what is the freezing point of the mixture?

Answers to these questions are in Appendix Q.

Chapter Goals

See Chapter Goals Revisited (page 646) for Study Questions
keyed to these goals and assignable in OWL.

- Calculate and use the solution concentration units molality, mole frac-
tions, and weight percent.
- Understand the solution process.
- Understand and use the colligative properties of solutions.

We come into contact with solutions every day: aqueous solutions of ionic salts, gasoline with additives to improve its properties, and household cleaners such as ammonia in water. We purposely make solutions. Adding sugar, flavoring, and sometimes CO_2 to water produces a palatable soft drink. Athletes drink commercial beverages with dissolved salts to match salt concentrations in body fluids precisely, thus allowing the fluid to be taken into the body more rapidly. In medicine, saline solutions (aqueous solutions containing NaCl and other soluble salts) are infused into the body to replace lost fluids.

A **solution** is a homogeneous mixture of two or more substances in a single phase. By convention, the component present in largest amount is identified as the solvent and the other component(s) as the solute(s) (Figure 14.1). Although other types of solutions exist (such as alloys, solid solution of metals), the objective in this chapter is to develop an understanding of gases, liquids, and solids dissolved in liquid solvents.

Experience tells you that adding a solute to a pure liquid will change the proper-ties of the liquid. Indeed, that is the reason some solutions are made. For instance, adding antifreeze to the water in your car's radiator prevents the coolant from boil-ing in the summer and freezing in the winter. The changes that occur in the freezing and boiling points when a substance is dissolved in a pure liquid are two observations we shall examine in detail. These properties, as well as the osmotic pressure of a solution and changes in vapor pressure, are examples of colligative properties.

Chemistry.Now™

Throughout the text this icon introduces an opportunity for self-study or to explore interactive tutorials by signing in at **www.cengage.com/login**.

(a) Copper(II) chloride, the solute, is added to water, the solvent.

(b) Interactions between water molecules and Cu^{2+} and Cl^- ions allow the solid to dissolve. The ions are now sheathed with water molecules.

FIGURE 14.1 Making a solution of copper(II) chloride (the solute) in water (the solvent). When ionic com-pounds dissolve in water, each ion is sur-rounded by water molecules. The number of water molecules is usually six, but fewer are possible.

Photos: Charles D. Winters

$V_{soln} > 1.00$ L $V_{soln} = 1.00$ L
V_{H_2O} added $= 1.00$ L V_{H_2O} added < 1.00 L
0.100 molal solution   0.100 molar solution

FIGURE 14.2 Preparing 0.100 molal and 0.100 molar solutions. In the flask on the right, 0.100 mol (19.4 g) of K_2CrO_4 was mixed with enough water to make 1.000 L of solution. (The volumetric flask was filled to the mark on its neck, indicating that the volume is 1.000 L. Slightly less than 1.00 L of water was added.) If 1.00 kg of water was added to 0.100 mol of K_2CrO_4 in the flask on the left, the volume of solution is greater than 1.000 L. (The small pile of yellow solid in front of the flasks is 0.100 mol of K_2CrO_4.)

■ **Molarity and Molality** The use of the terms "molar" (symbol M) and "molal" (symbol *m*) is common practice among chemists. Recently, however, NIST suggested that use of these terms and symbols to represent concentrations should be discontinued and replaced with the formal units of concentration (mol/L and mol/kg).

Colligative properties are properties of solutions that depend only on the number of solute particles per solvent molecule and not on the identity of the solute.

14.1 Units of Concentration

To analyze the colligative properties of solutions, we need ways of measuring solute concentrations that reflect the number of molecules or ions of solute per molecule of solvent.

Molarity, a concentration unit useful in stoichiometry calculations, is not useful when dealing with most colligative properties. Recall that molarity (M) is defined as the number of moles of solute per liter of solution (◄ page 174), so using molarity does not allow us to identify the exact amount of solvent used to make the solution. This fact is illustrated in Figure 14.2. The flask on the right contains a 0.100 M aqueous solution of potassium chromate. It was made by adding enough water to 0.100 mol of K_2CrO_4 to make 1.000 L of solution. There is no way to identify the amount of solvent (water) that was actually added. If 1.000 L of water had been added to 0.100 mol of K_2CrO_4, as illustrated with the flask on the left in Figure 14.2, the volume of solution would be greater than 1.000 L.

Three concentration units are described here that reflect the number of molecules or ions of solute per solvent molecule: molality, mole fraction, and weight percent.

The **molality**, *m*, of a solution is defined as the amount of solute (mol) per kilogram of solvent.

$$\text{Concentration } (c, \text{ mol/kg}) = \text{molality of solute} = \frac{\text{amount of solute (mol)}}{\text{mass of solvent (kg)}} \quad (14.1)$$

The molality of K_2CrO_4 in the flask on the left side of Figure 14.2 is 0.100 mol/kg. It was prepared from 0.100 mol (19.4 g) of K_2CrO_4 and 1.00 kg (1.000 L × 1.00 kg/L) of water.

Notice that different quantities of water were used to make the 0.100 M (0.100 molar) and 0.100 *m* (0.100 molal) solutions of K_2CrO_4. This means the *molarity and the molality of a given solution cannot be the same* (although the difference may be negligibly small when the solution is quite dilute).

The **mole fraction**, *X*, of a solution component is defined as the amount of that component (n_A) divided by the total amount of all of the components of the mixture ($n_A + n_B + n_C + ...$). Mathematically it is represented as

$$\text{Mole fraction of A } (X_A) = \frac{n_A}{n_A + n_B + n_C + ...} \quad (14.2)$$

Consider a solution that contains 1.00 mol (46.1 g) of ethanol, C_2H_5OH, in 9.00 mol (162 g) of water. The mole fraction of alcohol is 0.100, and that of water is 0.900.

$$X_{ethanol} = \frac{1.00 \text{ mol ethanol}}{1.00 \text{ mol ethanol} + 9.00 \text{ mol water}} = 0.100$$

$$X_{water} = \frac{9.00 \text{ mol water}}{1.00 \text{ mol ethanol} + 9.00 \text{ mol water}} = 0.900$$

Notice that the sum of the mole fractions of the components in the solution equals 1.000, a relationship that is true for all solutions.

Weight percent is the mass of one component divided by the total mass of the mixture, multiplied by 100%:

$$\text{Weight \% A} = \frac{\text{mass of A}}{\text{mass of A + mass of B + mass of C + ...}} \times 100\% \qquad (14.3)$$

The alcohol–water mixture has 46.1 g of ethanol and 162 g of water, so the total mass of solution is 208 g, and the weight % of alcohol is

$$\text{Weight \% ethanol} = \frac{46.1 \text{ g ethanol}}{46.1 \text{ g ethanol} + 162 \text{ g water}} \times 100\% = 22.2\%$$

Weight percent is a common unit in consumer products (Figure 14.3). Vinegar, for example, is an aqueous solution containing approximately 5% acetic acid and 95% water. The label on a common household bleach lists its active ingredient as 6.00% sodium hypochlorite (NaOCl) and 94.00% inert ingredients.

Naturally occurring solutions are often very dilute. Environmental chemists, biologists, geologists, oceanographers, and others frequently use **parts per million (ppm)** to express their concentrations. The unit ppm refers to relative quantities by mass; 1.0 ppm represents 1.0 g of a substance in a sample with a total mass of 1.0 million g. Because water at 25 °C has a density of 1.0 g/mL, a concentration of 1.0 mg/L is equivalent to 1.0 mg of solute in 1000 g of water or to 1.0 g of solute in 1,000,000 g of water; that is, units of ppm and mg/L are approximately equivalent.

FIGURE 14.3 Weight percent. The composition of many common products is often given in terms of weight percent. Here, the label on the cat spray indicates it contains 1.15% active ingredients.

Chemistry ⚛ Now™

Sign in at **www.cengage.com/login** and go to Chapter 14 Contents to see Screen 14.2 for an exercise on calculating solution concentrations in various units.

■ **EXAMPLE 14.1 Calculating Mole Fractions, Molality, and Weight Percent**

Problem Assume you add 1.2 kg of ethylene glycol, $HOCH_2CH_2OH$, as an antifreeze to 4.0 kg of water in the radiator of your car. What are the mole fraction, molality, and weight percent of the ethylene glycol?

Strategy Calculate the amount of ethylene glycol and water, and then use Equations 14.1–14.3.

Solution The 1.2 kg of ethylene glycol (molar mass = 62.1 g/mol) is equivalent to 19 mol, and 4.0 kg of water represents 220 mol.

Mole fraction:

$$X_{\text{glycol}} = \frac{19 \text{ mol ethylene glycol}}{19 \text{ mol ethylene glycol} + 220 \text{ mol water}} = \boxed{0.080}$$

Molality:

$$c_{\text{glycol}} = \frac{19 \text{ mol ethylene glycol}}{4.0 \text{ kg water}} = 4.8 \text{ mol/kg} = \boxed{4.8 \text{ } m}$$

Weight percent:

$$\text{Weight \%} = \frac{1.2 \times 10^3 \text{ g ethylene glycol}}{1.2 \times 10^3 \text{g ethylene glycol} + 4.0 \times 10^3 \text{ g water}} \times 100\% = \boxed{23\%}$$

Commercial antifreeze. This solution contains ethylene glycol, $HOCH_2CH_2OH$, an organic alcohol that is readily soluble in water. Regulations specify that the weight percent of ethylene glycol in ethylene glycol–based antifreeze must be at least 75%. (The remainder of the solution can be other glycols and water.)

14.2 The Solution Process

■ **Unsaturated** The term unsaturated is used when referring to solutions with concentrations of solute that are less than that of a saturated solution.

If solid $CuCl_2$ is added to a beaker of water, the salt will begin to dissolve (see Figure 14.1). The amount of solid diminishes, and the concentrations of $Cu^{2+}(aq)$ and $Cl^-(aq)$ in the solution increase. If we continue to add $CuCl_2$, however, we will eventually reach a point when no additional $CuCl_2$ seems to dissolve. The concentrations of $Cu^{2+}(aq)$ and $Cl^-(aq)$ will not increase further, and any additional solid $CuCl_2$ added after this point will remain as a solid at the bottom of the beaker. We say that such a solution is **saturated**.

Although no change is observed on the macroscopic level, it is a different matter on the particulate level. The process of dissolving continues, with Cu^{2+} and Cl^- ions leaving the solid state and entering solution. Concurrently, a second process is occurring: the formation of solid $CuCl_2(s)$ from $Cu^{2+}(aq)$ and $Cl^-(aq)$. The rates at which $CuCl_2$ is dissolving and reprecipitating are equal in a saturated solution, so that no net change is observed on the macroscopic level.

A Closer Look

Supersaturated Solutions

Although at first glance it may seem a contradiction, it is possible for a solution to hold more dissolved solute than the amount in a saturated solution. Such solutions are referred to as **supersaturated** solutions. Supersaturated solutions are unstable, and the excess solid eventually crystallizes from the solution until the equilibrium concentration of the solute is reached.

The solubility of substances often decreases if the temperature is lowered. Supersaturated solutions are usually made by preparing a saturated solution at a given temperature and then carefully cooling it. If the rate of crystallization is slow, the solid may not precipitate when the solubility is exceeded. Going to still lower temperatures results in a solution that has more solute than the amount defined by equilibrium conditions; it is supersaturated.

When disturbed in some manner, a supersaturated solution moves toward equilibrium by precipitating solute. This change can occur rapidly, often with the evolution of thermal energy. In fact, supersaturated solutions are used in "heat packs" to apply heat to injured

Supersaturated solutions. When a supersaturated solution is disturbed, the dissolved salt (here sodium acetate, $NaCH_3CO_2$) rapidly crystallizes. (See ChemistryNow Screen 14.2 to watch a video of this process.)

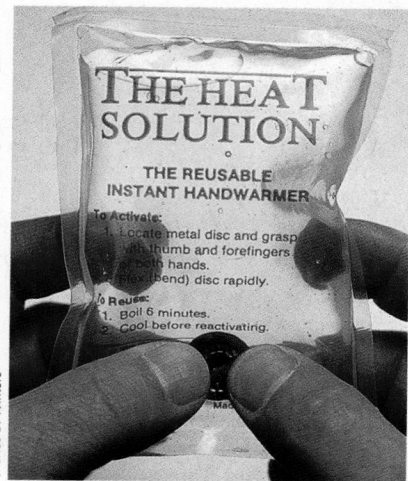

Heat of crystallization. A heat pack relies on the heat evolved by the crystallization of sodium acetate. (See ChemistryNow Screen 14.6 to watch a video of a heat pack.)

muscles. When crystallization of sodium acetate ($NaCH_3CO_2$) from a supersaturated solution in a heat pack is initiated, the tempera-

ture of the heat pack rises to about 50 °C, and crystals of solid sodium acetate are detectable inside the bag.

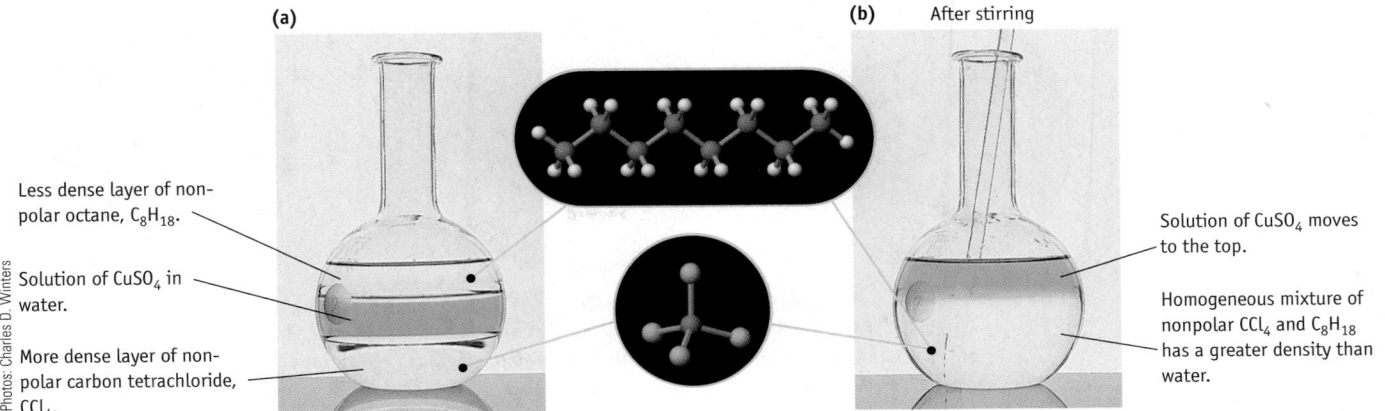

Less dense layer of non-polar octane, C_8H_{18}.

Solution of $CuSO_4$ in water.

More dense layer of non-polar carbon tetrachloride, CCl_4.

Photos: Charles D. Winters

Solution of $CuSO_4$ moves to the top.

Homogeneous mixture of nonpolar CCl_4 and C_8H_{18} has a greater density than water.

FIGURE 14.4 Miscibility. (a) The colorless, denser bottom layer is nonpolar carbon tetrachloride, CCl_4. The blue middle layer is a solution of $CuSO_4$ in water, and the colorless, less dense top layer is nonpolar octane, C_8H_{18}. This mixture was prepared by carefully layering one liquid on top of another, without mixing. (b) After stirring the mixture, the two nonpolar liquids form a homogeneous mixture. This layer of mixed liquids is under the water layer because the mixture of CCl_4 and C_8H_{18} has a greater density than water.

This process is another example of a dynamic equilibrium (◄ page 119), and we can describe the situation in terms of an equation with substances linked by a set of double arrows ($\rightleftharpoons$):

$$CuCl_2(s) \rightleftharpoons Cu^{2+}(aq) + 2\,Cl^-(aq)$$

A saturated solution gives us a way to define precisely the solubility of a solid in a liquid. **Solubility** is the concentration of solute in equilibrium with undissolved solute in a saturated solution. The solubility of $CuCl_2$, for example, is 70.6 g in 100 mL of water at 0 °C. If we add 100.0 g of $CuCl_2$ to 100 mL of water at 0 °C, we can expect 70.6 g to dissolve, and 29.4 g of solid to remain.

Liquids Dissolving in Liquids

If two liquids mix to an appreciable extent to form a solution, they are said to be **miscible**. In contrast, **immiscible** liquids do not mix to form a solution; they exist in contact with each other as separate layers (see Figures 12.5 and 14.4).

The polar compounds ethanol (C_2H_5OH) and water are miscible in all proportions as are the nonpolar liquids octane (C_8H_{18}) and carbon tetrachloride (CCl_4). On the other hand, neither C_8H_{18} nor CCl_4 is miscible with water. Observations like these have led to a familiar rule of thumb: *Like dissolves like.* That is, two or more nonpolar liquids frequently are miscible, just as are two or more polar liquids.

What is the molecular basis for the "like dissolves like" guideline? In pure water and pure ethanol, the major force between molecules is hydrogen bonding involving O—H groups. When the two liquids are mixed, hydrogen bonding between ethanol and water molecules also occurs and assists in the solution process. In contrast, molecules of pure octane or pure CCl_4, both of which are nonpolar, are held together in the liquid phase by dispersion forces (◄ Section 12.3). The energy associated with these forces of attraction is similar in value to the energy due to the forces of attraction between octane and CCl_4 molecules when these nonpolar liquids are mixed. Thus, little or no energy change occurs when octane–octane and CCl_4–CCl_4 attractive forces are replaced with octane–CCl_4 forces. The solution

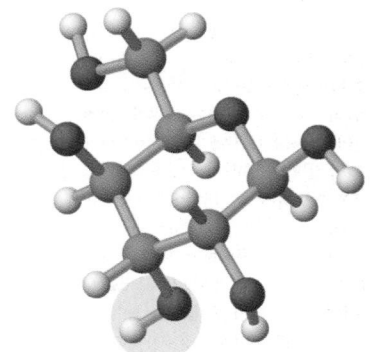

OH group

Like dissolves like. Glucose has five —OH groups on each molecule, groups that allow it to form hydrogen bonds with water molecules. As a result, glucose dissolves readily in water.

H₂O   Separate liquids   CH₃OH   Mixture

FIGURE 14.5 Driving the solution process—entropy. When two similar liquids—here water and methanol—are mixed, the molecules intermingle, and the energy of the system is more dispersed than in the two, separate pure liquids. A measure of this energy dispersal is entropy, a thermodynamic function described in more detail in Chapter 19.

process is expected to be nearly energy neutral. So, why do the liquids mix? The answer lies deeper in thermodynamics. As you shall see in Chapter 19, spontaneous changes, such as the mixing of liquids, are accompanied by an increase in entropy, a thermodynamic function that is a measure of the dispersal of the energy of the particles in the mixture relative to the pure liquids (Figure 14.5).

In contrast, polar and nonpolar liquids usually do not mix to an appreciable degree; when placed together in a container, they separate into two distinct layers (Figure 14.4). The explanation is complex and involves the interplay of the enthalpy of mixing and entropy. The enthalpy of mixing is zero or nearly so, but mixing dissimilar liquids leads to a decrease in entropy. As explained in Chapter 19, this means that mixing dissimilar liquids is not thermodynamically favorable.

Solids Dissolving in Water

The "like dissolves like" guideline also holds for molecular solids dissolving in liquids. Nonpolar solids such as naphthalene, $C_{10}H_8$, dissolve readily in nonpolar solvents such as benzene, C_6H_6, and hexane, C_6H_{14}. Iodine, I_2, a nonpolar inorganic solid, dissolves in water to some extent, but, given a choice, it dissolves to a larger extent in a nonpolar liquid such as CCl_4 (Figure 14.6). Sucrose (sugar), a polar molecular solid, is not very soluble in nonpolar solvents but is readily soluble in water, a fact that we know well because of its use to sweeten beverages. The presence of O—H groups in the structure of sugar and other substances such as glucose allows these molecules to interact with polar water molecules through hydrogen bonding.

"Like dissolves like" is a somewhat less effective but still useful guideline when considering the solubility of ionic solids. Thus, we can reasonably predict that ionic compounds, which can be considered extreme examples of polar compounds, will

■ **Entropy and the Solution Process** Although the energetics of solution formation are important, it is generally accepted that entropy is a more important contributor to the solution process. See Chapter 19 and T. P. Silverstein: "The real reason why oil and water don't mix." *Journal of Chemical Education*, Vol. 75, pp. 116–118, 1998.

Active Figure 14.6 Solubility of nonpolar iodine in polar water and nonpolar carbon tetrachloride. When a solution of nonpolar I_2 in water (the brown layer on top in the left test tube) is shaken with nonpolar CCl_4 (the colorless bottom layer in the left test tube), the I_2 transfers preferentially to the nonpolar solvent. Evidence for this is the purple color of the bottom CCl_4 layer in the test tube on the right.

Chemistry . Now™ Sign in at www.cengage.com/login and go to the Chapter Contents menu to explore an interactive version of this figure accompanied by an exercise.

Nonpolar I_2
Polar H_2O

Nonpolar CCl_4

Shake the test tube

Polar H_2O

Nonpolar CCl_4 and I_2

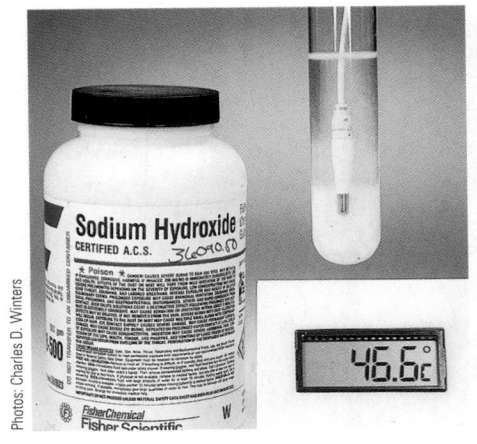
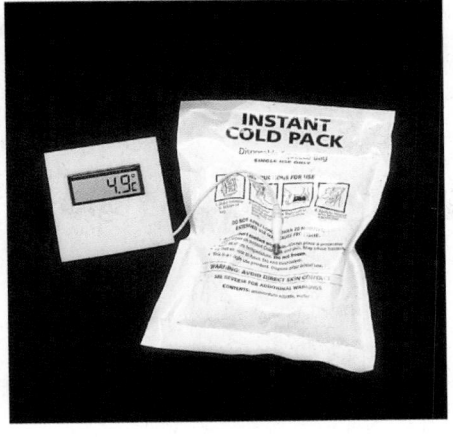

(a)   (b)

FIGURE 14.7 Dissolving ionic solids and enthalpy of solution.
(a) Dissolving NaOH in water is a strongly exothermic process. (b) A "cold pack" contains solid ammonium nitrate, NH_4NO_3, and a package of water. When the water and NH_4NO_3 are mixed and the salt dissolves, the temperature of the system drops, owing to the endothermic enthalpy of solution of ammonium nitrate ($\Delta_{soln}H° = +25.7$ kJ/mol).

not dissolve in nonpolar solvents. This fact is amply borne out by observation. Sodium chloride, for example, will not dissolve in liquids such as hexane or CCl_4, but the salt does have a significant solubility in water. Many ionic compounds are soluble in water, but, according to the solubility guidelines on page 126, there are many other ionic solids that are not.

Predicting the solubility of ionic compounds in water is complicated. As mentioned earlier, two factors—enthalpy and entropy—together determine the extent to which one substance dissolves in another. For ionic compounds dissolving in water, entropy usually (but not always) favors solution. A favorable enthalpy factor (negative ΔH) generally leads to a compound being soluble. For example, when sodium hydroxide dissolves in water, the solution warms up (Figure 14.7a), and sodium hydroxide dissolves readily in water. An unfavorable enthalpy factor, however, does not guarantee that an ionic compound will not be soluble. When ammonium nitrate dissolves in water, the solution becomes colder (Figure 14.7b), but ammonium nitrate is still very soluble in water.

Network solids, including graphite, diamond, and quartz sand (SiO_2), do not dissolve in water. Indeed, where would all the beaches be if sand dissolved in water? The covalent chemical bonding in network solids is simply too strong to be broken; the lattice remains intact when in contact with water.

Enthalpy of Solution

To understand the energetics of the solution process, let us view this process at the molecular level. We will use the process of dissolving potassium fluoride, KF, in water to illustrate what occurs, and the energy-level diagram in Figure 14.8 will assist us in following the changes.

Solid potassium fluoride has an ionic crystal lattice with alternating K^+ and F^- ions held in place by attractive forces due to their opposite charges. In water, these ions are separated from each other and *hydrated*; that is, they are surrounded by water molecules (Figure 14.1). Ion–dipole forces of attraction bind water molecules strongly to each ion. The energy change to go from the reactant, KF(s), to the products, K^+(aq) and F^-(aq), can be considered to take place in two stages:

1. Energy must be supplied to separate the ions in the lattice against their attractive forces. This is the reverse of the process defining the lattice enthalpy of an ionic compound with an enthalpy equal to $-\Delta_{lattice}H$ (◀ page 600).

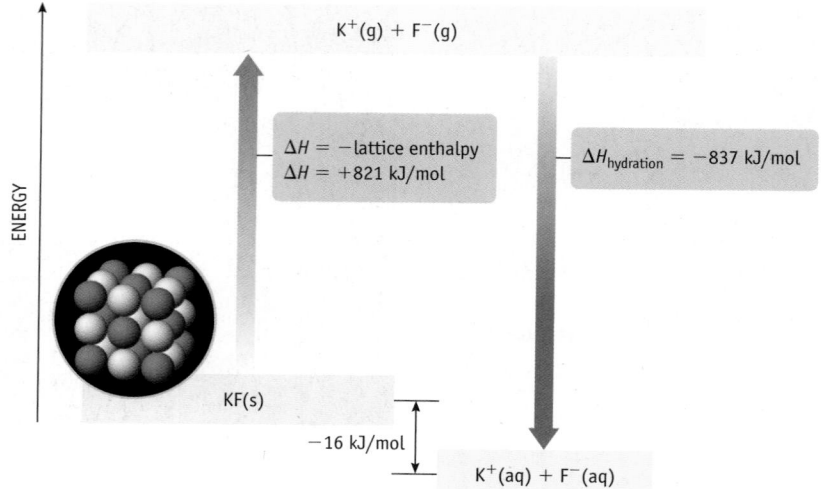

FIGURE 14.8 Model for energy changes on dissolving KF. An estimate of the magnitude of the energy change on dissolving an ionic compound in water is achieved by imagining it as occurring in two steps at the particulate level. Here, KF is first separated into cations and anions in the gas phase with an expenditure of 821 kJ per mol of KF. These ions are then hydrated, with $\Delta_{hydration}H$ estimated to be −837 kJ. Thus, the net energy change is −16 kJ, a slightly exothermic enthalpy of solution.

(See ChemistryNow Screen 14.4 for exercises on the energetics of solution formation.)

Separating the ions from one another is highly endothermic because the attractive forces between ions are strong.

2. Energy is evolved when the individual ions are transferred into water, where each ion becomes surrounded by water molecules. Again, strong forces of attraction (ion–dipole forces) are involved. This process, referred to as **hydration** when water is the solvent, is strongly exothermic.

We can therefore represent the process of dissolving KF in terms of these chemical equations:

Step 1 $KF(s) \longrightarrow K^+(g) + F^-(g)$ $-\Delta_{lattice}H$
Step 2 $K^+(g) + F^-(g) \longrightarrow K^+(aq) + F^-(aq)$ $\Delta_{hydration}H$

The overall reaction is the sum of these two steps. The enthalpy of the overall reaction, called the **enthalpy of solution** ($\Delta_{soln}H$), is the sum of the two enthalpies.

Overall $KF(s) \longrightarrow K^+(aq) + F^-(aq)$ $\Delta_{soln}H = -\Delta_{lattice}H + \Delta_{hydration}H$

We can use this to estimate the value of $\Delta_{hydration}H$. For example, we estimate the lattice energy for KF to be −821 kJ/mol using a Born-Haber cycle calculation (◄ page 600), and we measure the value of $\Delta_{soln}H$ in a calorimetry experiment to be −16.4 kJ/mol. From these two values, we can determine $\Delta_{hydration}H$ to be −837 kJ/mol.

As a general rule, to be soluble, a salt will have an enthalpy of solution that is exothermic or only slightly endothermic (Figure 14.9). In the latter instance, it is assumed that the enthalpy-disfavored solution process will be balanced by a favorable entropy of solution. If the enthalpy of solution is very endothermic—because of a low hydration energy, for example—then the compound is unlikely to be soluble. We can reasonably speculate that nonpolar solvents would not solvate ions strongly, and that solution formation would thus be energetically unfavorable. We therefore predict that an ionic compound, such as copper(II) sulfate, is not very soluble in nonpolar solvents such as carbon tetrachloride and octane (Figure 14.4).

It is also useful to recognize that the enthalpy of solution is the difference between two very large numbers. Small variations in either lattice energy or hydration enthalpies can determine whether a salt dissolves endothermically or exothermically.

Finally, notice that the two energy quantities, $\Delta_{lattice}H$ and $\Delta_{hydration}H$, are both affected by ion sizes and ion charges (◄ pages 557 and 600). A salt composed of smaller ions is expected to have a greater (more negative) lattice enthalpy because the ions can be closer together and experience higher attractive forces. However, the small

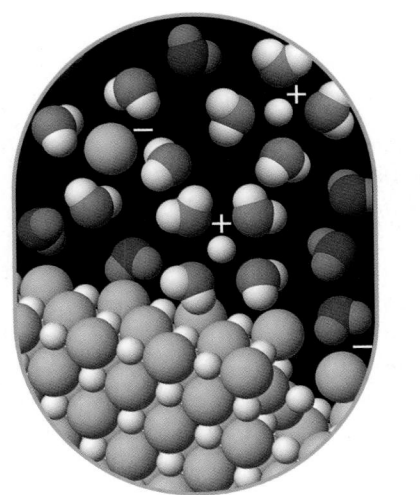

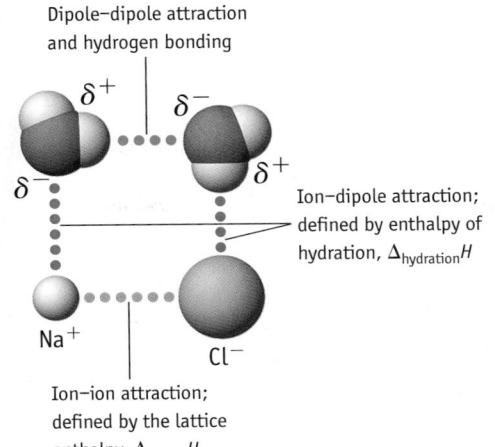

Dipole–dipole attraction
and hydrogen bonding

δ^+ δ^-

δ^- δ^+

Ion–dipole attraction;
defined by enthalpy of
hydration, $\Delta_{hydration}H$

Na^+ Cl^-

Ion–ion attraction;
defined by the lattice
enthalpy, $\Delta_{lattice}H$

size will also allow a closer approach of solvent molecules and a greater solvation enthalpy. The net result is that simple correlations of solubility with structure (ionic radii) or thermodynamic parameters ($\Delta_{lattice}H$) are generally not successful.

Enthalpy of Solution: Thermodynamic Data

As mentioned earlier, the enthalpy of solution for a salt can be measured using a calorimeter. This is usually done in an open system such as the coffee-cup calorimeter described in Section 5.6. For an experiment run under standard conditions, the resulting measurement produces a value for the standard enthalpy of solution, $\Delta_{soln}H°$, where standard conditions refer to a concentration of 1 molal.

Tables of thermodynamic values often include values for the enthalpies of formation of aqueous solutions of salts. For example, a value of $\Delta_f H°$ for NaCl(aq) of -407.3 kJ/mol is listed in Table 14.1 and Appendix L. This value refers to the formation of a 1 m solution of NaCl from the elements. It may be considered to involve the enthalpies of two steps: (1) the formation of NaCl(s) from the elements Na(s) and Cl$_2$(g) in their standard states, and (2) the formation of a 1 m solution by dissolving solid NaCl in water:

Formation of NaCl(s):   Na(s) + ½ Cl$_2$(g) $\longrightarrow$ NaCl(s) $\Delta_f H° = -411.1$ kJ/mol

Dissolving NaCl: NaCl(s) $\longrightarrow$ NaCl(aq, 1 m) $\Delta_{soln}H° = +3.9$ kJ/mol

Net process: Na(s) + ½ Cl$_2$(g) $\longrightarrow$ NaCl(aq, 1 m) $\Delta_f H° = -407.3$ kJ/mol

TABLE 14.1 **Data for Calculating Enthalpy of Solution**

Compound	$\Delta_f H°$ (s) (kJ/mol)	$\Delta_f H°$ (aq, 1 m) (kJ/mol)
LiF	−616.9	−611.1
NaF	−573.6	−572.8
KF	−568.6	−585.0
RbF	−557.7	−583.8
LiCl	−408.7	−445.6
NaCl	−411.1	−407.3
KCl	−436.7	−419.5
RbCl	−435.4	−418.3
NaOH	−425.9	−469.2
NH$_4$NO$_3$	−365.6	−339.9

Chemistry.Now™

EXAMPLE 14.2 **Calculating an Enthalpy of Solution**

Problem Use the data given in Table 14.1 to determine the enthalpy of solution for NH$_4$NO$_3$, the compound used in cold packs.

Strategy Use Equation 5.6 and data from Table 14.1 for reactants and products.

TABLE 14.2 Henry's Law
Constants (25 °C)*

Gas	k_H (mol/kg · bar)
N_2	6.0×10^{-4}
O_2	1.3×10^{-3}
CO_2	0.034

*From http://webbook.nist.gov/
chemistry/. Note: 1 bar = 0.9869 atm.

Solution The solution process for NH_4NO_3 is represented by the equation

$$NH_4NO_3(s) \longrightarrow NH_4NO_3(aq)$$

The enthalpy change for this process is calculated using enthalpies of formation given in Table 14.1:

$$\Delta_{soln}H° = \Sigma[\Delta_fH°(product)] - \Sigma[\Delta_fH°(reactant)]$$
$$= \Delta_fH°[NH_4NO_3(aq)] - \Delta_fH°[NH_4NO_3(s)]$$
$$= -339.9 \text{ kJ/mol} - (-365.6 \text{ kJ/mol}) = +25.7 \text{ kJ/mol}$$

The process is endothermic, as indicated by the fact that $\Delta_{soln}H°$ has a positive value and as verified by the experiment in Figure 14.7b.

EXERCISE 14.2 Calculating an Enthalpy of Solution

Use the data in Table 14.1 to calculate the enthalpy of solution for NaOH.

14.3 Factors Affecting Solubility: Pressure and Temperature

Pressure and temperature are two external factors that influence solubility. Both affect the solubility of gases in liquids, whereas only temperature is an important factor in the solubility of solids in liquids.

Dissolving Gases in Liquids: Henry's Law

The solubility of a gas in a liquid is directly proportional to the gas pressure. This is a statement of **Henry's law,**

$$S_g = k_HP_g \qquad (14.4)$$

where S_g is the gas solubility, P_g is the partial pressure of the gaseous solute, and k_H is Henry's law constant (Table 14.2), a constant characteristic of the solute and solvent.

Carbonated soft drinks illustrate how Henry's law works. These beverages are packed under pressure in a chamber filled with carbon dioxide gas, some of which dissolves in the beverage. When the can or bottle is opened, the partial pressure of CO_2 above the solution drops, which causes the solubility of CO_2 to drop. Gas bubbles out of the solution (Figure 14.10).

Henry's law has important consequences in SCUBA diving. When you dive, the pressure of the air you breathe must be balanced against the external pressure of the water. In deeper dives, the pressure of the gases in the SCUBA gear must be several atmospheres and, as a result, more gas dissolves in the blood. This can lead to a problem. If you ascend too rapidly, you can experience a painful and potentially lethal condition referred to as "the bends," in which nitrogen gas bubbles form in the blood as the solubility of nitrogen decreases with decreasing pressure. In an effort to prevent the bends, divers may use a helium–oxygen mixture (rather than nitrogen–oxygen) because helium is not as soluble in blood as nitrogen.

We can better understand the effect of pressure on solubility by examining the system at the particulate level. The solubility of a gas is defined as the concentration of the dissolved gas in equilibrium with the substance in the gaseous state. At equilibrium, the rate at which solute gas molecules escape the solution and enter the gaseous state equals the rate at which gas molecules reenter the solution. An increase in pressure results in more molecules of gas striking the surface of the liquid and entering solution in a given time. The solution eventually reaches a new equilibrium when the concentration of gas dissolved in the solvent is high enough

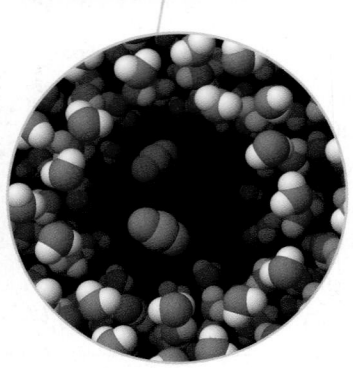

FIGURE 14.10 Gas solubility and pressure. Carbonated beverages are bottled under CO_2 pressure. When the bottle is opened, the pressure is released, and bubbles of CO_2 form within the liquid and rise to the surface. After some time, an equilibrium between dissolved CO_2 and atmospheric CO_2 is reached. Because CO_2 provides some of the taste in the beverage, the beverage tastes flat when most of its dissolved CO_2 is lost.

Photo: Charles D. Winters

that the rate of gas molecules escaping the solution again equals the rate of gas molecules entering the solution.

Chemistry ⚛ Now™

Sign in at **www.cengage.com/login** and go to Chapter 14 Contents to see Screen 14.5 for an exercise and tutorial on **Henry's law.**

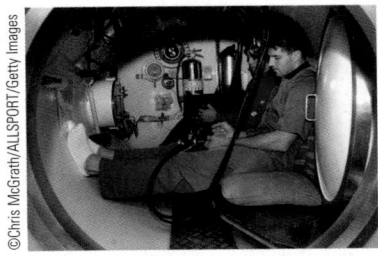

Hyperbaric chamber, an illustration of Henry's law. A person is placed inside the chamber, and the partial pressure of oxygen is raised to several times the normal, atmospheric level. This raises the amount of oxygen dissolved in blood and tissues. This technique is used to treat, among other things, decompression sickness, carbon monoxide poisoning, severe anemia, and certain nonhealing wounds.

■ **EXAMPLE 14.3 Using Henry's Law**

Problem What is the concentration of O_2 in a fresh water stream in equilibrium with air at 25 °C and 1.0 bar? Express the answer in grams of O_2 per kg of solvent.

Strategy To use Henry's law to calculate the molar solubility of oxygen, the partial pressure of O_2 in air must first be calculated.

Solution The mole fraction of O_2 in air is 0.21, and, assuming the total pressure is 1.0 bar, the partial pressure of O_2 is 0.21 bar. Using this pressure for P_g in Henry's law, we have:

$$\text{Solubility of } O_2 = k_H P_g = \left(\frac{1.3 \times 10^{-3} \text{ mol}}{\text{kg} \cdot \text{bar}} \right)(0.21 \text{ bar}) = 2.7 \times 10^{-4} \text{ mol/l}$$

This concentration, in grams per liter, can then be calculated using the molar mass of O_2:

$$\text{Solubility of } O_2 = \left(\frac{2.7 \times 10^{-4} \text{ mol}}{\text{kg}} \right)\left(\frac{32.0 \text{ g}}{\text{mol}} \right) = \boxed{0.0087 \text{ g/kg}}$$

This concentration of O_2 (8.7 mg/kg) is quite low, but it is sufficient to provide the oxygen required by aquatic life.

■ **Limitations of Henry's Law** Henry's law holds quantitatively only for gases that do not interact chemically with the solvent. It does not accurately predict the solubility of NH_3 in water, for example, because this compound gives small concentrations of NH_4^+ and OH^- in water.

EXERCISE 14.3 Using Henry's Law

What is the concentration of CO_2 in water at 25 °C when the partial pressure is 0.33 bar? (Although CO_2 reacts with water to give traces of H^+ and HCO_3^-, the reaction occurs to such a small extent that Henry's law is obeyed at low CO_2 partial pressures.)

Temperature Effects on Solubility: Le Chatelier's Principle

The solubility of all gases in water decreases with increasing temperature. You may realize this from everyday observations such as the appearance of bubbles of air as water is heated below the boiling point.

To understand the effect of temperature on the solubility of gases, let us reexamine the enthalpy of solution. Gases that dissolve to an appreciable extent in water usually do so in an exothermic process

$$\text{Gas + liquid solvent} \xrightleftharpoons{\Delta_{\text{soln}}H < 0} \text{saturated solution + energy}$$

The reverse process, loss of dissolved gas molecules from a solution, requires energy as heat. These two processes can reach equilibrium eventually.

To understand how temperature affects solubility, we turn to **Le Chatelier's principle**, which states that a change in any of the factors determining an equilibrium causes the system to adjust by shifting in the direction that reduces or counteracts the effect of the change. If a solution of a gas in a liquid is heated, for example, the equilibrium will shift to absorb some of the added energy. That is, the reaction

$$\text{Gas + liquid solvent} \xrightleftharpoons[\text{Exothermic process} \atop \Delta_{\text{soln}}H \text{ is negative.}]{} \text{saturated solution + energy}$$

Add energy. Equilibrium shifts left.

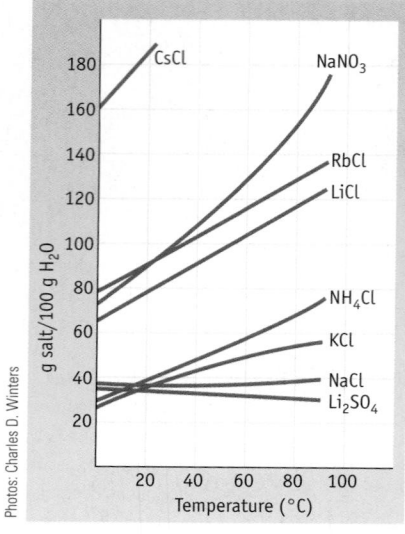

(a) Temperature dependence of the solubility of some ionic compounds.

(b) NH_4Cl dissolved in water.

(c) NH_4Cl precipitates when the solution is cooled in ice.

FIGURE 14.11 The temperature dependence of the solubility of some ionic compounds in water. Most compounds, such as NH_4Cl, increase in solubility with increasing temperature.

FIGURE 14.12 Giant crystals of potassium dihydrogen phosphate. The crystal being measured by this researcher at Lawrence Livermore Laboratory in California weighs 318 kg and measures 66 × 53 × 58 cm. The crystals were grown by suspending a thumbnail-sized seed crystal in a 6-foot tank of saturated KH_2PO_4. The temperature of the solution was gradually reduced from 65 °C over a period of about 50 days. The crystals are sliced into thin plates, which are used to convert light from a giant laser from infrared to ultraviolet.

Module 19

shifts to the left if the temperature is raised because energy is absorbed in the process that produces free gas molecules and pure solvent. This shift corresponds to less gas dissolved and a lower solubility at higher temperature—the observed result.

The solubility of solids in water is also affected by temperature, but, unlike the situation involving solutions of gases, no general pattern of behavior is observed. In Figure 14.11, the solubilities of several salts are plotted versus temperature. The solubility of many salts increases with increasing temperature, but there are notable exceptions. Predictions based on whether the enthalpy of solution is positive or negative work most of the time, but exceptions do occur.

Chemists take advantage of the variation of solubility with temperature to purify compounds. If a compound is more soluble in a given solvent at higher temperatures, an impure sample of the compound is dissolved in the solvent at a high temperature. The solution is cooled to decrease the solubility (Figure 14.11c). When the limit of solubility is reached at the lower temperature, crystals of the pure compound form. If the process is done slowly and carefully, it is sometimes possible to obtain very large crystals (Figure 14.12).

Chemistry Now™

Sign in at **www.cengage.com/login** and go to Chapter 14 Contents to see Screen 14.6 for a tutorial on **temperature and Le Chatelier's principle**.

14.4 Colligative Properties

If you dissolve some salt in water, the vapor pressure of the water over the solution will decrease, and the water will evaporate less rapidly under the same conditions. In addition, the solution will freeze below 0 °C and boil above 100 °C. These observations refer to the colligative properties of the solution, properties that depend

Sign in at **www.cengage.com/login** to download the Go Chemistry module for this section or go to **www.ichapters.com** to purchase modules.

on the relative numbers of solute and solvent particles in a solution and not on their identity.

Changes in Vapor Pressure: Raoult's Law

The equilibrium vapor pressure at a particular temperature is the pressure of the vapor when the liquid and the vapor are in equilibrium (◀ page 573). When the vapor pressure of the solvent over a solution is measured at a given temperature, it is experimentally observed that

- The vapor pressure of the solvent over the solution is lower than the vapor pressure of the pure solvent.
- The vapor pressure of the solvent, $P_{solvent}$, is proportional to the relative number of solvent molecules in the solution; that is, the solvent vapor pressure is proportional to the solvent mole fraction, $P_{solvent} \propto X_{solvent}$.

Because solvent vapor pressure is proportional to the relative number of solvent molecules, we can write the following equation for the equilibrium vapor pressure of the solvent over a solution:

$$P_{solvent} = X_{solvent}\, P°_{solvent} \qquad\qquad (14.5)$$

This equation, called **Raoult's law**, tells us that the vapor pressure of solvent over a solution ($P_{solvent}$) is some fraction of the pure solvent equilibrium vapor pressure ($P°_{solvent}$). For example, if 95% of the molecules in a solution are solvent molecules ($X_{solvent} = 0.95$), then the vapor pressure of the solvent ($P_{solvent}$) is 95% of $P°_{solvent}$.

Like the ideal gas law, Raoult's law describes a simplified model of a solution. We say that *an ideal solution is one that obeys Raoult's law*. No solution is ideal, however, just as no gas is truly ideal. Nevertheless, Raoult's law is a good approximation of solution behavior in many instances, especially at low solute concentration.

For Raoult's law to hold, the forces of attraction between solute and solvent molecules must be the same as those between solvent molecules in the pure solvent. This is frequently the case when molecules with similar structures are involved. Solutions of one hydrocarbon in another (hexane, C_6H_{14}, dissolved in octane, C_8H_{18}, for example) follow Raoult's law quite closely. If solvent–solute interactions are stronger than solvent–solvent interactions, the actual vapor pressure will be lower than calculated by Raoult's law. If the solvent–solute interactions are weaker than solvent–solvent interactions, the vapor pressure will be higher.

■ **Raoult's Law** Raoult's law is named for Francois M. Raoult (1830–1901), a professor of chemistry at the University of Grenoble in France, who did the pioneering studies in this area.

Chemistry ⚛ Now™

Sign in at **www.cengage.com/login** and go to Chapter 14 Contents to see Screen 14.7 for an exercise and a tutorial on **Raoult's law.**

■ **EXAMPLE 14.4 Using Raoult's Law**

Problem Suppose 651 g of ethylene glycol, $HOCH_2CH_2OH$, is dissolved in 1.50 kg of water. What is the vapor pressure of the water over the solution at 90 °C? Assume ideal behavior for the solution.

Strategy To use Raoult's law (Equation 14.5), we first must calculate the mole fraction of the solvent (water). We also need the vapor pressure of pure water at 90 °C (= 525.8 mm Hg, Appendix G).

It was evening on Thursday, August 21, 1986. Suddenly, people and animals around Lake Nyos in Cameroon, a small nation on the west coast of Africa, collapsed and died. By the next morning, 1700 people and hundreds of animals were dead. The calamity had no apparent cause—no fire, no earthquake, no storm. What had brought on this disaster?

Some weeks later, the mystery was solved. Lake Nyos and nearby Lake Monoun are crater lakes, which formed when cooled volcanic craters filled with water. Lake Nyos is lethal because it contains an enormous amount of dissolved carbon dioxide. The CO_2 in the lake was generated as a result of volcanic activity deep in the earth. Under the high pressures found at the bottom of the lake, a very large amount of CO_2 dissolved in the water.

On that fateful evening in 1986, something happened to disturb the lake. The CO_2-saturated water at the bottom of the lake was carried to the surface, where, under lower pressure, the gas was much less soluble. Approximately one cubic kilometer of carbon dioxide was released into the atmosphere, much like the explosive release of CO_2 from a can of carbonated beverage that has been shaken. The CO_2 shot up about 260 feet; then, because this gas is more dense than air, it hugged the ground and began to move with the prevailing breeze at about 45 miles per hour. When it reached the villages 12 miles away, vital oxygen was displaced. The result was that both people and animals were asphyxiated.

In most lakes, this situation would not occur because lake water "turns over" as the seasons change. In the autumn, the top layer of water in a lake cools; its density increases; and the water sinks. This process continues, with warmer water coming to the surface and cooler water sinking. Dissolved CO_2 at the bottom of a lake would normally be expelled in this turnover process, but geologists found that the lakes in Cameroon are different. The chemocline, the boundary between deep water, rich in gas and minerals, and the upper

Thierry Orban/Corbis, Sygma

Lake Nyos in Cameroon (western Africa), the site of a natural disaster. In 1986, a huge bubble of CO_2 escaped from the lake and asphyxiated more than 1700 people.

layer, full of fresh water, stays intact. As carbon dioxide continues to enter the lake through vents in the bottom of the lake, the water becomes saturated with this gas. It is presumed that a minor disturbance—perhaps a small earthquake, a strong wind, or an underwater landslide—caused the lake water to turn over and led to the explosive and deadly release of CO_2.

Lake Nyos remains potentially deadly. Geologists estimate that the lake contains 10.6 to 14.1 billion cubic feet (300–400 million cubic meters) of carbon dioxide. This is about 16,000 times the amount found in an average lake that size.

A team of geologists from France and the United States has been working to resolve this potential threat. In early 2001, scientists lowered a pipe, about 200 meters long, into the lake. Now the pressure of escaping carbon dioxide causes a jet of water to rise as high as 165 feet in the air. Over the course of a year, about 20 million cubic meters of gas will be released. While this has been a successful first step, more gas must be removed to make the lake entirely safe, so additional vents are planned.

Solution We first calculate the amounts of water and ethylene glycol and, from these, the mole fraction of water.

$$\text{Amount of water} = 1.50 \times 10^3 \text{ g} \left(\frac{1 \text{ mol}}{18.02 \text{ g}}\right) = 83.2 \text{ mol water}$$

$$\text{Amount of ethylene glycol} = 651 \text{ g} \left(\frac{1 \text{ mol}}{62.07 \text{ g}}\right) = 10.5 \text{ mol glycol}$$

$$X_{water} = \frac{83.2 \text{ mol water}}{83.2 \text{ mol water} + 10.5 \text{ mol glycol}} = 0.888$$

Next, we apply Raoult's law, calculating the vapor pressure from the mole fraction of water and the vapor pressure of pure water:

$$P_{water} = X_{water}P^\circ{}_{water} = (0.888)(525.8 \text{ mm Hg}) = \boxed{467 \text{ mm Hg}}$$

The dissolved solute decreases the vapor pressure by 59 mm Hg, or about 11%:

$$\Delta P_{water} = P_{water} - P^\circ{}_{water} = 467 \text{ mm Hg} - 525.8 \text{ mm Hg} = -59 \text{ mm Hg}$$

Comment Ethylene glycol dissolves easily in water, is noncorrosive, and is relatively inexpensive. Because of its high boiling point, it will not evaporate readily. These features make it ideal for use as antifreeze. It is, however, toxic to animals, so it is being replaced by less toxic propylene glycol for this application.

EXERCISE 14.4 Using Raoult's Law

Assume you dissolve 10.0 g of sucrose ($C_{12}H_{22}O_{11}$) in 225 mL (225 g) of water and warm the water to 60 °C. What is the vapor pressure of the water over this solution? (Appendix G lists $P^\circ(H_2O)$ at various temperatures.)

Adding a nonvolatile solute to a solvent lowers the vapor pressure of the solvent (Example 14.4). Raoult's law can be modified to calculate directly the lowering of the vapor pressure, $\Delta P_{solvent}$, as a function of the mole fraction of the solute.

$$\Delta P_{solvent} = P_{solvent} - P^\circ{}_{solvent}$$

Substituting Raoult's law for $P_{solvent}$, we have

$$\Delta P_{solvent} = (X_{solvent} P^\circ{}_{solvent}) - P^\circ{}_{solvent} = -(1 - X_{solvent})P^\circ{}_{solvent}$$

In a solution that has only the volatile solvent and one nonvolatile solute, the sum of the mole fraction of solvent and solute must be 1:

$$X_{solvent} + X_{solute} = 1$$

Therefore, $1 - X_{solvent} = X_{solute}$, and the equation for $\Delta P_{solvent}$ can be rewritten as

$$\Delta P_{solvent} = -X_{solute} P^\circ{}_{solvent} \qquad \textbf{(14.6)}$$

Thus, the change in the vapor pressure of the solvent is proportional to the mole fraction (the relative number of particles) of solute.

Boiling Point Elevation

Suppose you have a solution of a nonvolatile solute in the volatile solvent benzene. If the solute concentration is 0.200 mol in 100. g of benzene (C_6H_6) (= 2.00 mol/kg), this means that $X_{benzene}$ = 0.865. Using $X_{benzene}$ and applying Raoult's law, we can calculate that the vapor pressure of the solvent at 60 °C will drop from 400. mm Hg for the pure solvent to 346 mm Hg for the solution:

$$P_{benzene} = X_{benzene} \, P^{\circ}_{benzene} = (0.865)(400. \text{ mm Hg}) = 346 \text{ mm Hg}$$

This point is marked on the vapor pressure graph in Figure 14.13. Now, what is the vapor pressure when the temperature of the solution is raised another 10 °C? The vapor pressure of pure benzene, $P^{\circ}_{benzene}$, becomes larger with increasing temperature, so $P_{benzene}$ for the solution must also become larger. This new point, and additional ones calculated in the same way for other temperatures, define the vapor pressure curve for the solution (the lower curve in Figure 14.13).

An important observation we can make in Figure 14.13 is that the vapor pressure lowering caused by the nonvolatile solute leads to an increase in the boiling point. The normal boiling point of a liquid is the temperature at which its vapor pressure is equal to 1 atm or 760 mm Hg (◄ page 576). In Figure 14.13, we see that the normal boiling point of pure benzene (at 760 mm Hg) is about 80 °C. Tracing the vapor pressure curve for the solution, we also see that the vapor pressure reaches 760 mm Hg at a temperature about 5 °C higher than this value.

The vapor pressure curve and increase in the boiling point shown in Figure 14.13 refer specifically to a 2.00 m solution. We might wonder how the boiling point of the solution would vary with solute concentration. In fact, a simple relationship exists

FIGURE 14.13 Lowering the vapor pressure of benzene by addition of a nonvolatile solute. The curve drawn in red represents the vapor pressure of pure benzene, and the curve in blue represents the vapor pressure of a solution containing 0.200 mol of a solute dissolved in 0.100 kg of solvent (2.00 m). This graph was created using a series of calculations such as those shown in the text. As an alternative, the graph could be created by measuring various vapor pressures for the solution in a laboratory experiment.

(See ChemistryNow Screen 14.8 Colligative Properties, to view an animation of this vapor pressure lowering.)

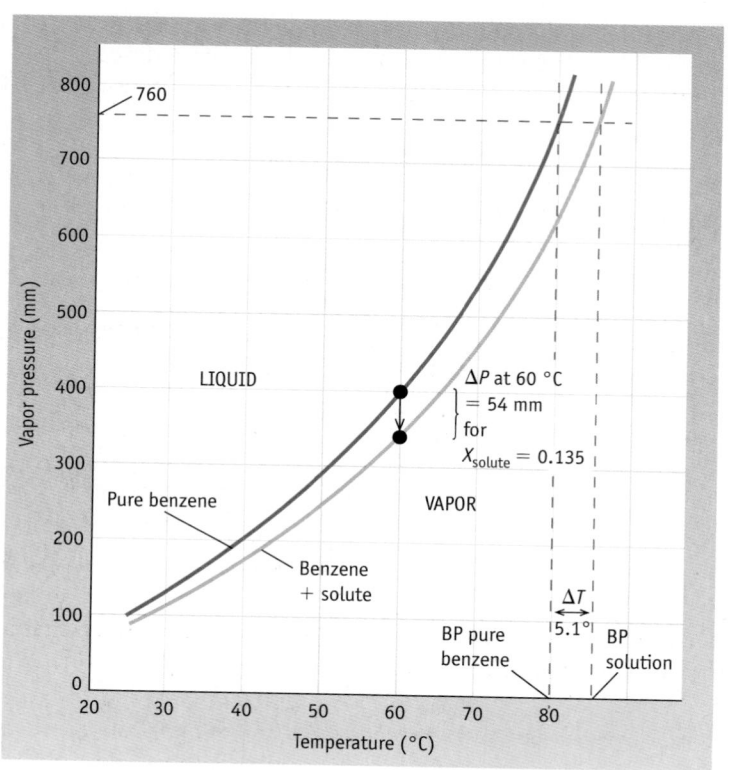

TABLE 14.3 Some Boiling Point Elevation and Freezing Point Depression Constants

Solvent	Normal Boiling Point (°C) Pure Solvent	K_{bp} (°C/m)	Normal Freezing Point (°C) Pure Solvent	K_{fp} (°C/m)
Water	100.00	+0.5121	0.0	−1.86
Benzene	80.10	+2.53	5.50	−5.12
Camphor	207.4	+5.611	179.75	−39.7
Chloroform ($CHCl_3$)	61.70	+3.63	—	—

between boiling point elevation and molal concentration: The boiling point elevation, ΔT_{bp}, is directly proportional to the molality of the solute.

$$\text{Elevation in boiling point} = \Delta T_{bp} = K_{bp}m_{solute} \qquad (14.6)$$

In this equation, K_{bp} is a proportionality constant called the **molal boiling point elevation constant**. It has the units of degrees/molal (°C/m). Values for K_{bp} are determined experimentally, and different solvents have different values (Table 14.3). Formally, the value corresponds to the elevation in boiling point for a 1 m solution.

Chemistry⚛Now™

Sign in at **www.cengage.com/login** and go to Chapter 14 Contents to see Screen 14.8 for an exercise and a tutorial on the **effect of a solute on the solution freezing point.**

■ EXAMPLE 14.5 Boiling Point Elevation

Problem Eugenol, the active ingredient in cloves, has the formula $C_{10}H_{12}O_2$. What is the boiling point of a solution containing 0.144 g of this compound dissolved in 10.0 g of benzene?

Strategy We can use Equation 14.6 to calculate the change in boiling point. This value is then added to the boiling point of pure benzene to provide the answer. To use Equation 14.6, you need a value of K_{bp} and the molality of the solution. The K_{bp} value for benzene is given in Table 14.3, but you need to calculate the molality, m.

Solution

$$0.144 \text{ g eugenol}\left(\frac{1 \text{ mol eugenol}}{164.2 \text{ g}}\right) = 8.77 \times 10^{-4} \text{ mol eugenol}$$

$$C_{eugenol} = \frac{8.77 \times 10^{-4} \text{ mol eugenol}}{0.0100 \text{ kg benzene}} = 8.77 \times 10^{-2} \text{ m}$$

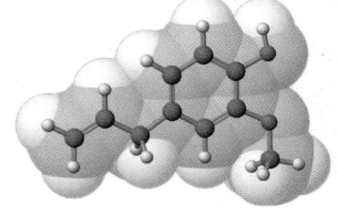

Eugenol, $C_{10}H_{12}O_2$, is an important component in oil of cloves.

Use the value for the molality to calculate the boiling point elevation and then the boiling point:

$$\Delta T_{bp} = (2.53 \text{ °C/m})(0.0877 \text{ m}) = 0.222 \text{ °C}$$

Because the boiling point rises relative to that of the pure solvent, the boiling point of the solution is

$$80.10 \text{ °C} + 0.222 \text{ °C} = \boxed{80.32 \text{ °C}}$$

EXERCISE 14.5 Boiling Point Elevation

What quantity of ethylene glycol, $HOCH_2CH_2OH$, must be added to 125 g of water to raise the boiling point by 1.0 °C? Express the answer in grams.

The elevation of the boiling point of a solvent on adding a solute has many practical consequences. One of them is the summer protection your car's engine receives from "all-season" antifreeze. The main ingredient of commercial antifreeze is ethylene glycol, $HOCH_2CH_2OH$. The car's radiator and cooling system are sealed to keep the coolant under pressure, ensuring that it will not vaporize at normal engine temperatures. When the air temperature is high in the summer, however, the radiator could "boil over" if it were not protected with "antifreeze." By adding this nonvolatile liquid, the solution in the radiator has a higher boiling point than that of pure water.

Freezing Point Depression

Another consequence of dissolving a solute in a solvent is that the freezing point of the solution is lower than that of the pure solvent (Figure 14.14). For an ideal solution, the depression of the freezing point is given by an equation similar to that for the elevation of the boiling point:

$$\text{Freezing point depression} = \Delta T_{fp} = K_{fp}m_{solute} \tag{14.7}$$

where K_{fp} is the **freezing point depression constant** in degrees per molal ($°C/m$). Values of K_{fp} for a few common solvents are given in Table 14.3. The values are negative quantities, so the result of the calculation is a negative value for ΔT_{fp}, signifying a decrease in temperature.

The practical aspects of freezing point changes from pure solvent to solution are similar to those for boiling point elevation. The very name of the liquid you add to the radiator in your car, antifreeze, indicates its purpose (see Figure 14.14a). The label on the container of antifreeze tells you, for example, to add 6 qt (5.7 L) of antifreeze to a 12-qt (11.4-L) cooling system to lower the freezing point to $-34\ °C$ and to raise the boiling point to $+109\ °C$.

EXAMPLE 14.6 Freezing Point Depression

Problem What mass of ethylene glycol, $HOCH_2CH_2OH$, must be added to 5.50 kg of water to lower the freezing point of the water from 0.0 °C to -10.0 °C?

Strategy To use Equation 14.7, you need K_{fp} (Table 14.3). You can then calculate the molality of the solution and, from this value, the amount and quantity of ethylene glycol required.

FIGURE 14.14 Freezing a solution.
(a) Adding antifreeze to water prevents the water from freezing. Here, a jar of pure water (left) and a jar of water to which automobile antifreeze had been added (right) were kept overnight in the freezing compartment of a home refrigerator. (b) When a solution freezes, it is pure solvent that solidifies. To take this photo, a purple dye was dissolved in water, and the solution was frozen slowly. Pure ice formed along the walls of the tube, and the dye stayed in solution. The concentration of the solute increased as more and more solvent was frozen out, and the resulting solution had a lower and lower freezing point. Eventually, the system contains pure, colorless ice that formed along the walls of the tube and a concentrated solution of dye in the center of the tube.

Photos: Charles D. Winters

(a)

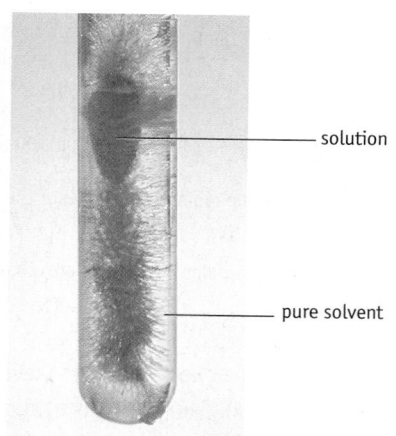

solution

pure solvent

(b)

Solution The solute concentration (molality) in a solution with a freezing point depression of $-10.0\ °C$ is

$$\text{Solute concentration } (m) = \frac{\Delta T_{fp}}{K_{fp}} = \frac{-10.0\ °C}{-1.86\ °C/m} = 5.38\ m$$

Because the solution contains 5.50 kg of water, we need 29.6 mol of ethylene glycol:

$$\left(\frac{5.38\ \text{mol glycol}}{1.00\ \text{kg water}}\right)(5.50\ \text{kg water}) = \boxed{29.6\ \text{mol glycol}}$$

The molar mass of ethylene glycol is 62.07 g/mol, so the mass required is 1840 g.

$$29.6\ \text{mol glycol}\left(\frac{62.07\ \text{g}}{1\ \text{mol}}\right) = \boxed{1840\ \text{g glycol}}$$

Comment The density of ethylene glycol is 1.11 kg/L, so the volume of glycol to be added is 1.84 kg (1 L/1.11 kg) = 1.66 L.

EXERCISE 14.6 Freezing Point Depression

In the northern United States, summer cottages are usually closed up for the winter. When doing so, the owners "winterize" the plumbing by putting antifreeze in the toilet tanks, for example. Will adding 525 g of $HOCH_2CH_2OH$ to 3.00 kg of water ensure that the water will not freeze at $-25\ °C$?

Osmotic Pressure

Osmosis is the movement of solvent molecules through a semipermeable membrane from a region of lower solute concentration to a region of higher solute concentration. This movement can be demonstrated with a simple experiment. The beaker in Figure 14.15 contains pure water, and the bag and tube hold a concentrated sugar solution. The liquids are separated by a semipermeable membrane, a thin sheet of material (such as a vegetable tissue or cellophane) through

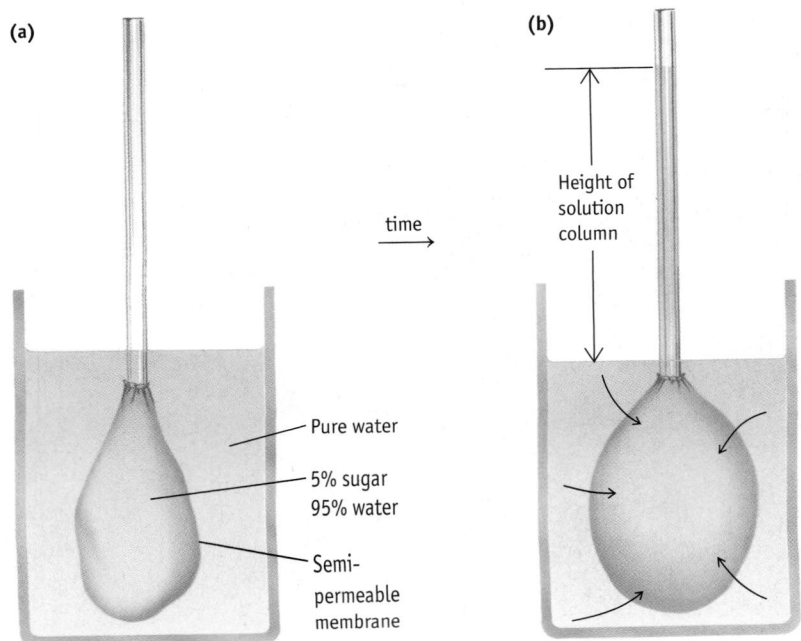

(a)

(b)

time

Height of solution column

Pure water

5% sugar
95% water

Semi-
permeable
membrane

FIGURE 14.15 The process of osmosis. (a) The bag attached to the tube contains a solution that is 5% sugar and 95% water. The beaker contains pure water. The bag is made of a material that is semipermeable, meaning that it allows water, but not sugar molecules, to pass through. (b) Over time, water flows from the region of low solute concentration (pure water) to the region of higher solute concentration (the sugar solution). Flow continues until the pressure exerted by the column of solution in the tube above the water level in the beaker is great enough to result in equal rates of passage of water molecules in both directions. The height of the column of solution (b) is a measure of the osmotic pressure.

(See ChemistryNow Screen 14.9 Colligative Properties, for an animation of **osmosis**.)

which only certain types of molecules can pass. Here, water molecules can pass through the membrane, but larger sugar molecules (or hydrated ions) cannot (Figure 14.16). When the experiment is begun, the liquid levels in the beaker and the tube are the same. Over time, however, the level of the sugar solution inside the tube rises, the level of pure water in the beaker falls, and the sugar solution becomes more dilute. Eventually, no further net change occurs; equilibrium is reached.

From a molecular point of view, the semipermeable membrane does not present a barrier to the movement of water molecules, so they move through the membrane in both directions. Over time, more water molecules pass through the membrane from the pure water side to the solution side than in the opposite direction. In effect, water molecules tend to move from regions of low solute concentration to regions of high solute concentration. The same is true for any solvent, as long as the membrane allows solvent molecules but not solute molecules or ions to pass through.

Why does the system eventually reach equilibrium? Clearly, the solution in the tube in Figure 14.15 can never reach zero sugar or salt concentration, which would be required to equalize the number of water molecules moving through the membrane in each direction in a given time. The answer lies in the fact that the solution moves higher and higher in the tube as osmosis continues and water moves into the sugar solution. Eventually, the pressure exerted by this column of solution counterbalances the pressure exerted by the water moving through the membrane from the pure water side, and no further net movement of water occurs. An equilibrium of forces is achieved. The pressure created by the column of solution for the system at equilibrium is called the **osmotic pressure**, Π. A measure of this pressure is the difference between the height of the solution in the tube and the level of pure water in the beaker.

FIGURE 14.16 Osmosis at the particulate level. Osmotic flow through a membrane that is selectively permeable (semipermeable) to water. Dissolved substances such as hydrated ions or large sugar molecules cannot diffuse.

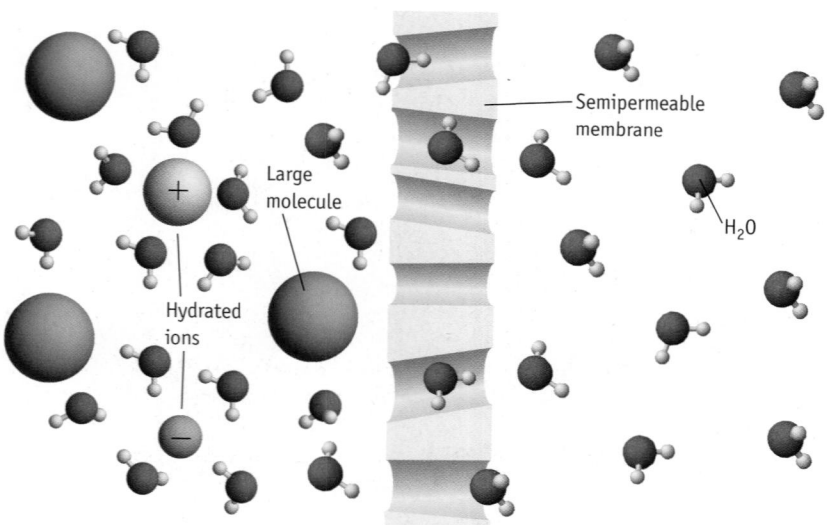

Osmotic pressure is a colligative property. From experimental measurements on dilute solutions, it is known that osmotic pressure and concentration (c) are related by the equation

$$\Pi = cRT \qquad \text{(14.8)}$$

In this equation, c is the molar concentration (in moles per liter); R is the gas constant; and T is the absolute temperature (in kelvins). Using a value for the gas law constant of $0.082057 \ \text{L} \cdot \text{atm/K} \cdot \text{mol}$ allows calculation of the osmotic pressure Π in atmospheres. This equation is analogous to the ideal gas law ($PV = nRT$), with Π taking the place of P and c being equivalent to n/V.

Because pressures on the order of 10^{-3} atm are easily measured, concentrations of very dilute solutions (as low as about 10^{-4} M) can be determined through measurements of osmotic pressure.

Other examples of osmosis are shown in Figure 14.17. In this case, the egg's membrane serves as the semipermeable membrane. Osmosis occurs in one direction if the concentration of solute is greater inside the egg than in the exterior solution and occurs in the other direction if the concentration solution is less inside the egg than it is in the exterior solution. In both cases, solvent flows from the region of low solute concentration to the region of high solute concentration.

Colligative Properties and Molar Mass Determination

Early in this book, you learned how to calculate a molecular formula from an empirical formula when given the molar mass. But how do you know the molar mass of an unknown compound? An experiment must be carried out to find this crucial piece of information, and one way to do so is to use a colligative property of a

(a) A fresh egg is placed in dilute acetic acid. The acid reacts with the $CaCO_3$ of the shell but leaves the egg membrane intact.

(b) If the egg, with its shell removed, is placed in pure water, the egg swells.

(c) If the egg, with its shell removed, is placed in a concentrated sugar solution, the egg shrivels.

FIGURE 14.17 An experiment to observe osmosis. You can try this experiment in your kitchen. In the first step, use vinegar as a source of acetic acid.

(See ChemistryNow Screen 14.1, Puzzler, and Screen 14.9, Colligative Properties, for a video of this experiment.)

Photos: Charles D. Winters

solution of the compound. The same basic logic is used for each of the colligative properties studied:

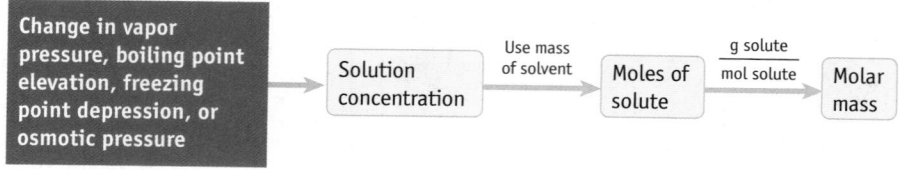

EXAMPLE 14.7 Determining Molar Mass from Boiling Point Elevation

Problem A solution prepared from 1.25 g of oil of wintergreen (methyl salicylate) in 99.0 g of benzene has a boiling point of 80.31 °C. Determine the molar mass of this compound.

Strategy Calculations using colligative properties to determine a molar mass always follow the pattern outlined in the text.

Solution We first use the boiling point elevation to calculate the solution concentration:

$$\text{Boiling point elevation } (\Delta T_{bp}) = 80.31 \text{ °C} - 80.10 \text{ °C} = 0.21 \text{ °C}$$

$$c_{\text{solute}} = \frac{\Delta T_{bp}}{K_{bp}} = \frac{0.21 \text{ °C}}{2.53 \text{ °C/}m} = 0.083 \ m$$

The amount of solute in the solution is calculated from the solution concentration:

$$\text{Amount of solute} = \left(\frac{0.083 \text{ mol}}{1.00 \text{ kg}}\right)(0.099 \text{ kg solvent}) = 0.0082 \text{ mol solute}$$

Now we can combine the amount of solute with its mass to obtain its molar mass:

$$\frac{1.25 \text{ g}}{0.0082 \text{ mol}} = \boxed{150 \text{ g/mol}}$$

Comment Methyl salicylate has the formula $C_8H_8O_3$ and a molar mass of 152.14 g/mol.

EXAMPLE 14.8 Osmotic Pressure and Molar Mass

Problem Beta-carotene is the most important of the A vitamins. Its molar mass can be determined by measuring the osmotic pressure generated by a given mass of β-carotene dissolved in the solvent chloroform. Calculate the molar mass of β-carotene if 10.0 mL of a solution containing 7.68 mg of β-carotene has an osmotic pressure of 26.57 mm Hg at 25.0 °C.

Strategy First, use Equation 14.8 to calculate the solution concentration from the osmotic pressure. Then, use the volume and concentration of the solution to calculate the amount of solute. Finally, find the molar mass of the solute from its mass and amount.

Solution The osmotic pressure can be used to calculate the concentration of β-carotene:

$$\text{Concentration (mol/L)} = \frac{\Pi}{RT} = \frac{(26.57 \text{ mm Hg})\left(\dfrac{1 \text{ atm}}{760 \text{ mm Hg}}\right)}{(0.082057 \text{ L} \cdot \text{atm/K} \cdot \text{mol})(298.2 \text{ K})}$$
$$= 1.429 \times 10^{-3} \text{ mol/L}$$

Now the amount of β-carotene dissolved in 10.0 mL of solvent can be calculated:

$$(1.429 \times 10^{-3} \text{ mol/L})(0.0100 \text{ L}) = 1.43 \times 10^{-5} \text{ mol}$$

We can combine the amount of solute with its mass to calculate its molar mass:

$$\frac{7.68 \times 10^{-3} \text{ g}}{1.43 \times 10^{-5} \text{ mol}} = \boxed{538 \text{ g/mol}}$$

Comment Beta-carotene is a hydrocarbon with the formula $C_{40}H_{56}$ (molar mass = 536.9 g/mol).

Charles D. Winters

EXERCISE 14.7 Osmotic Pressure and Molar Mass

A 1.40-g sample of polyethylene, a common plastic, is dissolved in enough benzene to give exactly 100 mL of solution. The measured osmotic pressure of the solution is 1.86 mm Hg at 25 °C. Calculate the average molar mass of the polymer.

Putting salt on ice assists in melting the ice.

Colligative Properties of Solutions Containing Ions

In the northern United States, it is common practice to scatter salt on snowy or icy roads or sidewalks. When the sun shines on the snow or patch of ice, a small amount melts, and some salt dissolves in the water. As a result of the dissolved solute, the freezing point of the solution is lower than 0 °C. The solution "eats" its way through the ice, breaking it up, and the icy patch is no longer dangerous for drivers or for people walking.

Salt (NaCl) is the most common substance used on roads because it is inexpensive and dissolves readily in water. Its relatively low molar mass means that the effect

---

A Closer Look

Osmosis and Medicine

Osmosis is of practical significance for people in the health professions. Patients who become dehydrated through illness often need to be given water and nutrients intravenously. Water cannot simply be dripped into a patient's vein, however. Rather, the intravenous solution must have the same overall solute concentration as the patient's blood: the solution must be isoosmotic or **isotonic** (Figures A and B, part a). If pure water was used, the inside of a blood cell would have a higher solute concentration

(lower water concentration), and water would flow into the cell. This hypotonic situation would cause the red blood cells to burst (lyse) (Figure B, part c). The opposite situation, hypertonicity, occurs if the intravenous solution is more concentrated than the contents of the

blood cell (Figure B, part b). In this case, the cell would lose water and shrivel up (crenate). To combat this, a dehydrated patient is rehydrated in the hospital with a sterile saline solution that is 0.16 M NaCl, a solution that is isotonic with the cells of the body.

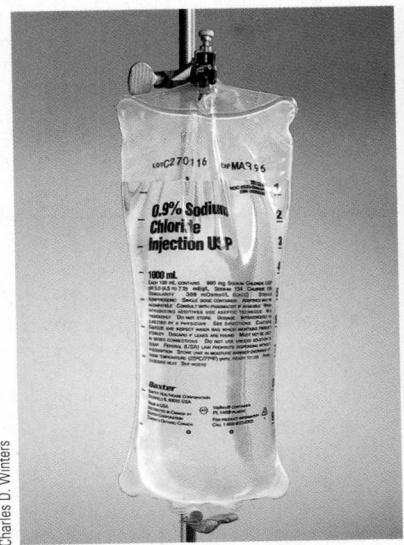

Charles D. Winters

FIGURE A An isotonic saline solution. This solution has the same molality as body fluids.

David Phillips/Science Source/Photo Researchers, Inc.

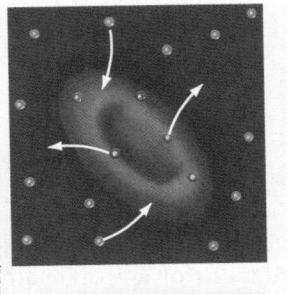
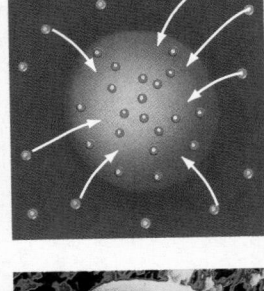

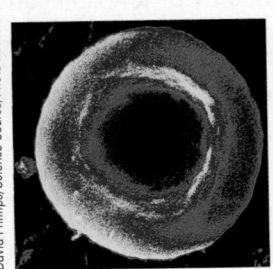
(a) Isotonic solution

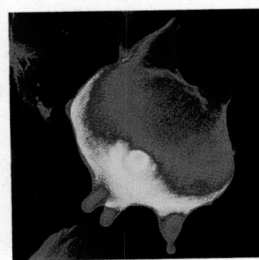
(b) Hypertonic solution

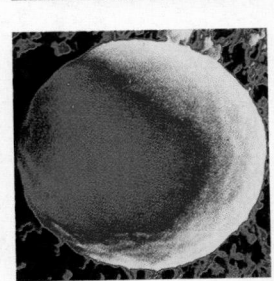
(c) Hypotonic solution

FIGURE B Osmosis and living cells. (a) A cell placed in an isotonic solution. The net movement of water into and out of the cell is zero because the concentration of solutes inside and outside the cell is the same. (b) In a hypertonic solution, the concentration of solutes outside the cell is greater than that inside. There is a net flow of water out of the cell, causing the cell to dehydrate, shrink, and perhaps die. (c) In a hypotonic solution, the concentration of solutes outside the cell is less than that inside. There is a net flow of water into the cell, causing the cell to swell and perhaps to burst (or lyse).

per gram is large. In addition, salt is especially effective because it is an electrolyte. That is, it dissolves to give ions in solution:

$$NaCl(s) \rightarrow Na^+(aq) + Cl^-(aq)$$

Recall that colligative properties depend not on what is dissolved but *only on the number of particles of solute per solvent particle*. When 1 mol of NaCl dissolves, 2 mol of ions form, which means that the effect on the freezing point of water should be twice as large as that expected for a mole of sugar. A 0.100 *m* solution of NaCl really contains two solutes, 0.100 *m* Na$^+$ and 0.100 *m* Cl$^-$. What we should use to estimate the freezing point depression is the *total* molality of solute particles:

$$m_{total} = m(Na^+) + m(Cl^-) = (0.100 + 0.100) \text{ mol/kg} = 0.200 \text{ mol/kg}$$

$$\Delta T_{fp} = (-1.86 \text{ °C/}m)(0.200 \text{ }m) = -0.372 \text{ °C}$$

To estimate the freezing point depression for an ionic compound, first find the molality of solute from the mass and molar mass of the compound and the mass of the solvent. Then, multiply the molality by the number of ions in the formula: two for NaCl, three for Na$_2$SO$_4$, four for LaCl$_3$, five for Al$_2$(SO$_4$)$_3$, and so on.

Table 14.4 shows that as the concentration of NaCl decreases, ΔT_{fp} for NaCl approaches but does not quite reach a value that is two times larger than the value determined assuming no dissociation. Likewise, ΔT_{fp} for Na$_2$SO$_4$ approaches but does not reach a value that is three times larger. The ratio of the experimentally observed value of ΔT_{fp} to the value calculated, assuming no dissociation, is called the **van't Hoff factor** after Jacobus Henrikus van't Hoff (1852–1911), who was involved in studying this phenomenon. The van't Hoff factor is represented by *i*.

$$i = \frac{\Delta T_{fp}, \text{ measured}}{\Delta T_{fp}, \text{ calculated}} = \frac{\Delta T_{fp}, \text{ measured}}{K_{fp} \ m}$$

or

$$\Delta T_{fp} \text{ measured} = K_{fp} \times m \times i \tag{14.9}$$

The numbers in the last column of Table 14.4 are van't Hoff factors. These values can be used in calculations of any colligative property. Vapor pressure lowering,

TABLE 14.4   Freezing Point Depressions of Some Ionic Solutions

Mass %	m (mol/kg)	ΔT_{fp} (measured, °C)	ΔT_{fp} (calculated, °C)	$\dfrac{\Delta T_{fp}, \text{ measured}}{\Delta T_{fp}, \text{ calculated}}$
NaCl				
0.00700	0.0120	−0.0433	−0.0223	1.94
0.500	0.0860	−0.299	−0.160	1.87
1.00	0.173	−0.593	−0.322	1.84
2.00	0.349	−1.186	−0.649	1.83
Na$_2$SO$_4$				
0.00700	0.00493	−0.0257	−0.00917	2.80
0.500	0.0354	−0.165	−0.0658	2.51
1.00	0.0711	−0.320	−0.132	2.42
2.00	0.144	−0.606	−0.268	2.26

By now, everyone has seen it on YouTube or has tried it. Drop a Mentos™ into a bottle of soda (preferably diet soda), and a geyser of soda erupts from the bottle.

A Mentos was dropped into a large bottle of Diet Coke. For more information, see J. E. Baur and M. B. Baur, *Journal of Chemical Education*, Vol. 83, pages 577–580, 2006.

It turns out this chapter, as well as the chapters on gases (Chapter 11), kinetics (Chapter 15), and equilibrium (Chapter 16) can help us explain what is happening.

Carbonated sodas are bottled under a high pressure of CO_2. Some of the gas dissolves in the soda, but some also remains in the small space above the liquid (called the "headspace"). The pressure of the CO_2 in the headspace is between 2 and 4 atm.

When the bottle cap is removed, the CO_2 in the headspace escapes rapidly. Some of the dissolved CO_2 also comes out of solution, and you observe this as bubbles of gas rising to the surface (Figure 14.10). If the bottle remains open, this continues until equilibrium is established with CO_2 in the atmosphere (where the partial pressure of CO_2 is 3.75×10^{-4} atm),

$$CO_2(\text{solution}) \rightleftharpoons CO_2(g)$$

and the soda goes "flat." If the newly opened soda bottle is undisturbed, however, the loss of CO_2 from solution is rather slow because bubble formation is not rapid, and your soda keeps its fizz.

But why is bubble formation slow? The reason for this is explained by the physics of bubble formation. For a bubble to form, nucleation sites must be available. These can be impurities in the water or the rough surface of an ice cube or bottle or drinking glass. The more nucleation sites there are available, the more rapid the bubble formation. The surface of a Mentos apparently has many such sites and promotes very rapid bubble formation.

Questions:

1. *If the headspace of a soda is 25 mL and the pressure of CO_2 in the space is 4.0 atm ($\approx$ 4.0 bar) at 25 °C, what amount of CO_2 is contained in the headspace?*

2. *If the CO_2 in the headspace escapes into the atmosphere where the partial pressure of CO_2 is 3.7×10^{-4} atm, what volume would the CO_2 occupy (at 25 °C)? By what amount did the CO_2 expand when it was released?*

3. *CO_2 obeys Henry's law to about 5 bar. What is the solubility of CO_2 in water at 25 °C when the pressure of the gas is 4.0 bar ($\approx$ 4.0 atm)? What amount of CO_2 is dissolved in 710 g of diet soda?*

4. *What is the solubility of CO_2 in water at 25 °C when the pressure of the gas is 3.7×10^{-4} bar?*

Answers to these questions are in Appendix Q.

boiling point elevation, freezing point depression, and osmotic pressure are all larger for electrolytes than for nonelectrolytes of the same molality.

The van't Hoff factor approaches a whole number (2, 3, and so on) only with very dilute solutions. In more concentrated solutions, the experimental freezing point depressions indicate that there are fewer ions in solution than expected. This behavior, which is typical of all ionic compounds, is a consequence of the strong attractions between ions. The result is as if some of the positive and negative ions are paired, decreasing the total molality of particles. Indeed, in more concentrated solutions, and especially in solvents less polar than water, ions are extensively associated in ion pairs and in even larger clusters.

EXAMPLE 14.9 Freezing Point and Ionic Solutions

Problem A 0.00200 *m* aqueous solution of an ionic compound, $Co(NH_3)_5(NO_2)Cl$, freezes at −0.00732 °C. How many moles of ions does 1.0 mol of the salt produce on being dissolved in water?

Strategy First, calculate ΔT_{fp} of the solution assuming no ions are produced. Compare this value with the actual value of ΔT_{fp}. The ratio will reflect the number of ions produced.

Solution The freezing-point depression expected for a 0.00200 *m* solution assuming that the salt does not dissociate into ions is

$$\Delta T_{\text{fp}} \text{ calculated} = K_{\text{fp}}m = (-1.86 \text{ °C})(0.0200 \text{ } m) = -3.72 \times 10^{-3} \text{ °C}$$

Now compare the calculated freezing point depression with the measured depression. This gives us the van't Hoff factor:

$$i = \frac{\Delta T_{\text{fp}}, \text{ measured}}{\Delta T_{\text{fp}}, \text{ calculated}} = \frac{-7.32 \times 10^{-3} \text{ °C}}{-3.72 \times 10^{-3} \text{ °C}} = 1.97 \approx \boxed{2}$$

It appears that 1 mol of this compound gives 2 mol of ions. In this case, the ions are $[Co(NH_3)_5(NO_2)]^+$ and Cl^-.

EXERCISE 14.8 Freezing Point and Ionic Compounds

Calculate the freezing point of 525 g of water that contains 25.0 g of NaCl. Assume *i*, the van't Hoff factor, is 1.85 for NaCl.

14.5 Colloids

Earlier in this chapter, we defined a solution broadly as a homogeneous mixture of two or more substances in a single phase (page 617). To this definition we should add that, in a true solution, no settling of the solute should be observed and the solute particles should be in the form of ions or relatively small molecules. Thus, NaCl and sugar form true solutions in water. You are also familiar with suspensions, which result, for example, if a handful of fine sand is added to water and shaken vigorously. Sand particles are still visible and gradually settle to the bottom of the beaker or bottle. **Colloidal dispersions**, also called **colloids**, represent a state intermediate between a solution and a suspension. Colloids include many of the foods you eat and the materials around you; among them are JELL-O®, milk, fog, and porcelain (see Table 14.5).

Around 1860, the British chemist Thomas Graham (1805–1869) found that substances such as starch, gelatin, glue, and albumin from eggs diffused only very slowly when placed in water, compared with sugar or salt. In addition, the former substances differ significantly in their ability to diffuse through a thin membrane: Sugar molecules can diffuse through many membranes, but the very large molecules that make up starch, gelatin, glue, and albumin do not. Moreover, Graham found that

Gold colloid. A water-soluble salt of $[AuCl_4]^-$ is reduced to give colloidal gold metal. The colloidal gold gives the dispersion its red color. (Similarly, colloidal gold is used to give a beautiful red color to glass.) Since the days of alchemy, some have claimed that drinking a colloidal gold solution "cleared the mind, increased intelligence and will power, and balanced the emotions."

TABLE 14.5 Types of Colloids

Type	Dispersing Medium	Dispersed Phase	Examples
Aerosol	Gas	Liquid	Fog, clouds, aerosol sprays
Aerosol	Gas	Solid	Smoke, airborne viruses, automobile exhaust
Foam	Liquid	Gas	Shaving cream, whipped cream
Foam	Solid	Gas	Styrofoam, marshmallow
Emulsion	Liquid	Liquid	Mayonnaise, milk, face cream
Gel	Solid	Liquid	Jelly, JELL-O®, cheese, butter
Sol	Liquid	Solid	Gold in water, milk of magnesia, mud
Solid sol	Solid	Solid	Milkglass

(a)

(b)

FIGURE 14.18 The Tyndall effect.
Colloidal dispersions scatter light, a phenomenon known as the Tyndall effect. (a) Dust in the air scatters the light coming through the trees in a forest along the Oregon coast. (b) A narrow beam of light from a laser is passed through an NaCl solution (left) and then a colloidal mixture of gelatin and water (right).

he could not crystallize these substances, whereas he could crystallize sugar, salt, and other materials that form true solutions. Graham coined the word "colloid" (from the Greek, meaning "glue") to describe this class of substances that are distinctly different from true solutions and suspensions.

We now know that it is possible to crystallize some colloidal substances, albeit with difficulty, so there really is no sharp dividing line between these classes based on this property. Colloids do, however, have two distinguishing characteristics. First, colloids generally have high molar masses; this is true of proteins such as hemoglobin that have molar masses in the thousands. Second, the particles of a colloid are relatively large (say, 1000 nm in diameter). As a consequence, they exhibit the **Tyndall effect**; they scatter visible light when dispersed in a solvent, making the mixture appear cloudy (Figure 14.18). Third, even though colloidal particles are large, they are not so large that they settle out.

Graham also gave us the words **sol** for a colloidal dispersion of a solid substance in a fluid medium and **gel** for a colloidal dispersion that has a structure that prevents it from being mobile. JELL-O® is a sol when the solid is first mixed with boiling water, but it becomes a gel when cooled. Other examples of gels are the gelatinous precipitates of $Al(OH)_3$, $Fe(OH)_3$, and $Cu(OH)_2$ (Figure 14.19).

Colloidal dispersions consist of finely divided particles that, as a result, have a very high surface area. For example, if you have one millionth of a mole of colloidal particles, each assumed to be a sphere with a diameter of 200 nm, the total surface area of the particles would be on the order of 200 million cm^2, or the size of several football fields. It is not surprising, therefore, that many of the properties of colloids depend on the properties of surfaces.

FIGURE 14.19 Gelatinous precipitates. (left) $Al(OH)_3$, (center) $Fe(OH)_3$, and (right) $Cu(OH)_2$.

Types of Colloids

Colloids are classified according to the state of the dispersed phase and the dispersing medium. Table 14.5 lists several types of colloids and gives examples of each.

Colloids with water as the dispersing medium can be classified as **hydrophobic** (from the Greek, meaning "water-fearing") or **hydrophilic** ("water-loving"). A hydrophobic colloid is one in which only weak attractive forces exist between the water and the surfaces of the colloidal particles. Examples include dispersions of metals and of nearly insoluble salts in water. When compounds like AgCl precipitate, the result is often a colloidal dispersion. The precipitation reaction occurs too rapidly for ions to gather from long distances and make large crystals, so the ions aggregate to form small particles that remain suspended in the liquid.

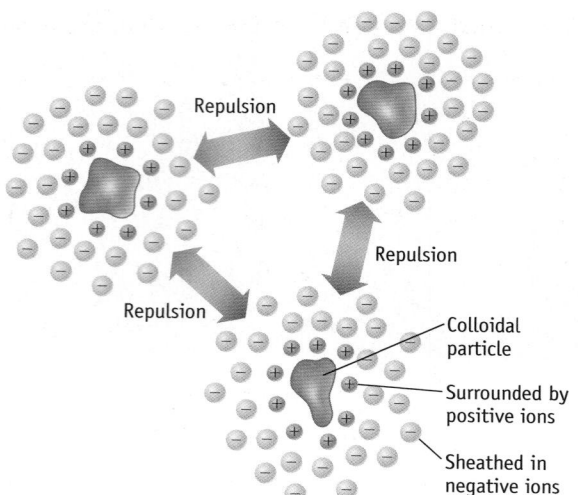

Repulsion

Repulsion

Repulsion

Colloidal particle

Surrounded by positive ions

Sheathed in negative ions

Why don't the particles come together (coagulate) and form larger particles? The answer is that the colloidal particles carry electric charges. An AgCl particle, for example, will absorb Ag^+ ions if the ions are present in substantial concentration; an attraction occurs between Ag^+ ions in solution and Cl^- ions on the surface of the particle. In this way, the colloidal particles become positively charged, allowing them to attract a secondary layer of anions. The particles, now surrounded by layers of ions, repel one another and are prevented from coming together to form a precipitate (Figure 14.20).

A stable hydrophobic colloid can be made to coagulate by introducing ions into the dispersing medium. Milk contains a colloidal suspension of protein-rich casein micelles with a hydrophobic core. When milk ferments, lactose (milk sugar) is converted to lactic acid, which forms lactate ions and hydrogen ions. The protective charges on the surfaces of the colloidal particles are overcome, and the milk coagulates; the milk solids come together in clumps called "curds."

Soil particles are often carried by water in rivers and streams as hydrophobic colloids. When river water carrying large amounts of colloidal particles meets sea water with its high concentration of salts, the particles coagulate to form the silt seen at the mouth of the river (Figure 14.21). Municipal water treatment plants often add salts such as $Al_2(SO_4)_3$ to clarify water. In aqueous solution, aluminum ions exist as $[Al(H_2O)_6]^{3+}$ cations, which neutralize the charge on the hydrophobic colloidal soil particles, causing these particles to aggregate and settle out.

Hydrophilic colloids are strongly attracted to water molecules. They often have groups such as —OH and —NH_2 on their surfaces. These groups form strong hydrogen bonds to water, thereby stabilizing the colloid. Proteins and starch are important examples of hydrophilic colloids, and homogenized milk is the most familiar example.

Emulsions are colloidal dispersions of one liquid in another, such as oil or fat in water. Familiar examples include salad dressing, mayonnaise, and milk. If vegetable oil and vinegar are mixed to make a salad dressing, the mixture quickly separates into two layers because the nonpolar oil molecules do not interact with the polar water and acetic acid (CH_3CO_2H) molecules. So why are milk and mayonnaise apparently homogeneous mixtures that do not separate into layers? The answer is that they contain an **emulsifying agent** such as soap or a protein. Lecithin is a phospholipid found in egg yolks, so mixing egg yolks with oil and vinegar stabilizes the colloidal dispersion known as mayonnaise. To understand this process

FIGURE 14.21 Formation of silt. Silt forms at a river delta as colloidal soil particles come in contact with salt water in the ocean. Here, the Ashley and Cooper Rivers empty into the Atlantic Ocean at Charleston, South Carolina. The high concentration of ions in sea water causes the colloidal soil particles to coagulate.

NASA/Peter Arnold, Inc.

further, let us look into the functioning of soaps and detergents, substances known as surfactants.

Surfactants

Soaps and detergents are emulsifying agents. Soap is made by heating a fat with sodium or potassium hydroxide (◄ page 476), which produces the anion of a fatty acid.

$$H_3C(CH_2)_{16} - \overset{\overset{O}{\|}}{C} - O^- \ Na^+$$

Hydrocarbon tail   Polar head
Soluble in oil   Soluble in water

sodium stearate, a soap

The fatty acid anion has a split personality: It has a nonpolar, hydrophobic hydrocarbon tail that is soluble in other similar hydrocarbons and a polar, hydrophilic head that is soluble in water.

Oil cannot be readily washed away from dishes or clothing with water because oil is nonpolar and thus insoluble in water. Instead, we add soap to the water to clean away the oil. The nonpolar molecules of the oil interact with the nonpolar hydrocarbon tails of the soap molecules, leaving the polar heads of the soap to interact with surrounding water molecules. The oil and water then mix (Figure 14.22). If the oily material on a piece of clothing or a dish also contains some dirt particles, that dirt can now be washed away.

Substances such as soaps that affect the properties of surfaces, and therefore affect the interaction between two phases, are called surface-active agents, or **surfactants**, for short. A surfactant used for cleaning is called a **detergent**. One function of a surfactant is to lower the surface tension of water, which enhances the cleansing action of the detergent (Figure 14.23).

Many detergents used in the home and industry are synthetic. One example is sodium laurylbenzenesulfonate, a biodegradable compound.

$$CH_3CH_2CH_2CH_2CH_2CH_2CH_2CH_2CH_2CH_2CH_2CH_2 - \bigcirc - SO_3^- \ Na^+$$

sodium laurylbenzenesulfonate

■ **Soaps and Surfactants** A sodium soap is a solid at room temperature, whereas potassium soaps are usually liquids. About 30 million tons of household and toilet soap, and synthetic and soap-based laundry detergents, are produced annually worldwide.

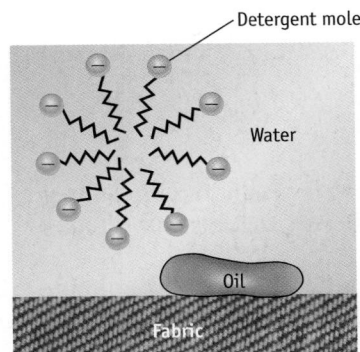
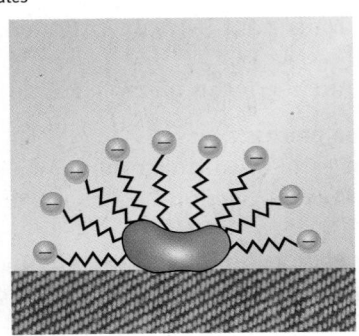
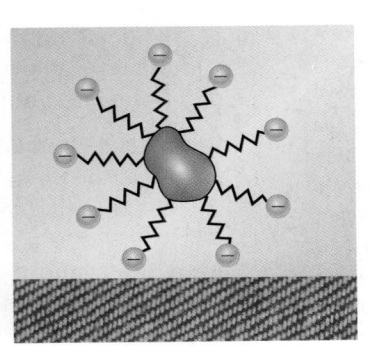
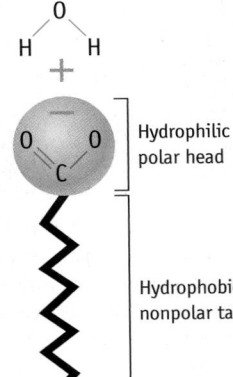

Detergent molecules

Water

Oil

Fabric

Hydrophilic polar head

Hydrophobic nonpolar tail

FIGURE 14.22 The cleaning action of soap. Soap molecules interact with water through the charged, hydrophilic end of the molecule. The long, hydrocarbon end of the molecule is hydrophobic, but it can bind through dispersion forces with hydrocarbons and other nonpolar substances.

FIGURE 14.23 Effect of a detergent on the surface tension of water. Sulfur (density = 2.1 g/cm³) is carefully placed on the surface of water (density, 1.0 g/cm³) (left). The surface tension of the water keeps the denser sulfur afloat. Several drops of detergent are then placed on the surface of the water (right). The surface tension of the water is reduced, and the sulfur sinks to the bottom of the beaker.

Photos: Charles D. Winters

add surfactant →

In general, synthetic detergents use the sulfonate group, —SO_3^-, as the polar head instead of the carboxylate group, —CO_2^-. The carboxylate anions form an insoluble precipitate with any Ca^{2+} or Mg^{2+} ions present in water. Because hard water is characterized by high concentrations of these ions, using soaps containing carboxylates produces bathtub rings and tell-tale gray clothing. The synthetic sulfonate detergents have the advantage that they do not form such precipitates because their calcium salts are more soluble in water.

Chapter Goals Revisited

Now that you have studied this chapter, you should ask whether you have met the chapter goals. In particular, you should be able to:

Calculate and use the solution concentration units molality, mole fraction, and weight percent

a. Define the terms solution, solvent, solute, and colligative properties (Section 14.1).

b. Use the following concentration units: molality, mole fraction, and weight percent. (Section 14.1). Study Question(s) assignable in OWL: 6, 9, 10, 12, 56.

c. Understand the distinctions between saturated, unsaturated, and supersaturated solutions (Section 14.2).

d. Define and illustrate the terms miscible and immiscible (Section 14.2).

Understand the solution process

a. Describe the process of dissolving a solute in a solvent, including the energy changes that may occur (Section 14.2). Study Question(s) assignable in OWL: 13, 16, 88, 93.

b. Understand the relationship of lattice enthalpy and enthalpy of hydration to the enthalpy of solution for an ionic solute (Section 14.2). Study Question(s) assignable in OWL: 77, 88.

c. Describe the effect of pressure and temperature on the solubility of a solute (Section 14.2).

d. Use Henry's law to calculate the solubility of a gas in a solvent (Section 14.2). Study Question(s) assignable in OWL: 21, 22, 67.

e. Apply Le Chatelier's principle to the change in solubility of gases with temperature changes (Section 14.2).

Understand and use the colligative properties of solutions

a. Calculate the mole fraction of a solvent ($X_{solvent}$) and the effect of a solute on solvent vapor pressure ($P_{solvent}$) using Raoult's law (Section 14.4). Study Question(s) assignable in OWL: 24, 74, 96.

b. Calculate the boiling point elevation or freezing point depression caused by a solute in a solvent (Section 14.4). Study Question(s) assignable in OWL: 28, 30, 32, 45, 53, 60; Go Chemistry Module 19.

c. Calculate the osmotic pressure (Π) for solutions (Section 14.4). Study Question(s) assignable in OWL: 47, 78, 84, 97.

d. Use colligative properties to determine the molar mass of a solute (Section 14.4). Study Question(s) assignable in OWL: 35, 39, 61, 64, 84, 85.

e. Characterize the effect of ionic solutes on colligative properties (Section 14.4). Study Question(s) assignable in OWL: 43.

f. Use the van't Hoff factor, i, in calculations involving colligative properties (Section 14.4). Study Question(s) assignable in OWL: 41, 79, 80.

KEY EQUATIONS

Equation 14.1 (page 618) Molality is defined as the amount of solute per kilogram of solvent.

$$\text{Concentration } (c, \text{ mol/kg}) = \text{molality of solute} = \frac{\text{amount of solute (mol)}}{\text{mass of solvent (kg)}}$$

Equation 14.2 (page 618) The mole fraction, X, of a solution component is defined as the number of moles of a given component of a mixture (n_A, mol) divided by the total number of moles of all of the components of the mixture.

$$\text{Mole fraction of A } (X_A) = \frac{n_A}{n_A + n_B + n_C + \ldots}$$

Equation 14.3 (page 619) Weight percent is the mass of one component divided by the total mass of the mixture (multiplied by 100%).

$$\text{Weight \% A} = \frac{\text{mass of A}}{\text{mass of A} + \text{mass of B} + \text{mass of C} + \ldots} \times 100\%$$

Equation 14.4 (page 626) Henry's law: the solubility of a gas, S_g, is equal to the product of the partial pressure of the gaseous solute (P_g) and a constant (k_H) characteristic of the solute and solvent.

$$S_g = k_H P_g$$

Equation 14.5 (page 629) Raoult's law: the equilibrium vapor pressure of a solvent over a solution at a given temperature, $P_{solvent}$, is the product of the mole fraction of the solvent ($X_{solvent}$) and the vapor pressure of the pure solvent ($P^\circ_{solvent}$).

$$P_{solvent} = X_{solvent} P^\circ_{solvent}$$

Equation 14.6 (page 631)   The elevation in boiling point of the solvent in a solution, ΔT_{bp}, is the product of the molality of the solute, m_{solute}, and a constant characteristic of the solvent, K_{bp}.

$$\text{Elevation in boiling point} = \Delta T_{bp} = K_{bp}m_{solute}$$

Equation 14.7 (page 634)   The depression of the freezing point of the solvent in a solution, ΔT_{fp}, is the product of the molality of the solute, m_{solute}, and a constant characteristic of the solvent, K_{fp}.

$$\text{Freezing point depression} = \Delta T_{fp} = K_{fp}m_{solute}$$

Equation 14.8 (page 637)   The osmotic pressure, Π, is the product of the solute concentration c (in mol/L), the universal gas constant R (0.082057 L · atm/K · mol), and the temperature T (in kelvins).

$$\Pi = cRT$$

Equation 14.9 (page 639)   This modified equation for freezing point depression accounts for the possible dissociation of a solute. The van't Hoff factor, i, the ratio of the measured freezing point depression and the freezing point depression calculated assuming no solute dissociation, is related to the relative number of particles produced by a dissolved solute.

$$\Delta T_{fp} \text{ measured} = K_{fp} \times m \times i$$

STUDY QUESTIONS

OWL Online homework for this chapter may be assigned in OWL.

▲ denotes challenging questions.

■ denotes questions assignable in OWL.

Blue-numbered questions have answers in Appendix O and fully-worked solutions in the *Student Solutions Manual*.

Practicing Skills

Concentration
(See Examples 14.1 and 14.2 and ChemistryNow Screen 14.2.)

1. Suppose you dissolve 2.56 g of succinic acid, $C_2H_4(CO_2H)_2$, in 500. mL of water. Assuming that the density of water is 1.00 g/cm³, calculate the molality, mole fraction, and weight percentage of acid in the solution.

2. ■ Assume you dissolve 45.0 g of camphor, $C_{10}H_{16}O$, in 425 mL of ethanol, C_2H_5OH. Calculate the molality, mole fraction, and weight percent of camphor in this solution. (The density of ethanol is 0.785 g/mL.)

3. Fill in the blanks in the table. Aqueous solutions are assumed.

Compound	Molality	Weight Percent	Mole Fraction
NaI	0.15	___	___
C_2H_5OH	___	5.0	___
$C_{12}H_{22}O_{11}$	0.15	___	___

4. Fill in the blanks in the table. Aqueous solutions are assumed.

Compound	Molality	Weight Percent	Mole Fraction
KNO_3	___	10.0	___
CH_3CO_2H	0.0183	___	___
$HOCH_2CH_2OH$	___	18.0	___

5. What mass of Na_2CO_3 must you add to 125 g of water to prepare 0.200 m Na_2CO_3? What is the mole fraction of Na_2CO_3 in the resulting solution?

6. ■ You want to prepare a solution that is 0.0512 m in $NaNO_3$. What mass of $NaNO_3$ must be added to 500. g of water? What is the mole fraction of $NaNO_3$ in the solution?

7. You wish to prepare an aqueous solution of glycerol, $C_3H_5(OH)_3$, in which the mole fraction of the solute is 0.093. What mass of glycerol must you add to 425 g of water to make this solution? What is the molality of the solution?

8. You want to prepare an aqueous solution of ethylene glycol, $HOCH_2CH_2OH$, in which the mole fraction of solute is 0.125. What mass of ethylene glycol, in grams, should you combine with 955 g of water? What is the molality of the solution?

9. ■ Hydrochloric acid is sold as a concentrated aqueous solution. If the molarity of commercial HCl is 12.0 and its density is 1.18 g/cm^3, calculate the following:
   (a) the molality of the solution
   (b) the weight percent of HCl in the solution

10. ■ Concentrated sulfuric acid has a density of 1.84 g/cm^3 and is 95.0% by weight H_2SO_4. What is the molality of this acid? What is its molarity?

11. The average lithium ion concentration in sea water is 0.18 ppm. What is the molality of Li^+ in sea water?

12. ■ Silver ion has an average concentration of 28 ppb (parts per billion) in U.S. water supplies.
   (a) What is the molality of the silver ion?
   (b) If you wanted 1.0×10^2 g of silver and could recover it chemically from water supplies, what volume of water in liters, would you have to treat? (Assume the density of water is 1.0 g/cm^3.)

The Solution Process
(See Example 14.3 and ChemistryNow Screens 14.3 and 14.4.)

13. ■ Which pairs of liquids will be miscible?
   (a) H_2O and $CH_3CH_2CH_2CH_3$
   (b) C_6H_6 (benzene) and CCl_4
   (c) H_2O and CH_3CO_2H

14. Acetone, CH_3COCH_3, is quite soluble in water. Explain why this should be so.

15. Use the data of Table 14.1 to calculate the enthalpy of solution of LiCl.

16. ■ Use the following data to calculate the enthalpy of solution of sodium perchlorate, $NaClO_4$:

   $\Delta_fH°(s) = -382.9$ kJ/mol   and
   $\Delta_fH°(aq, 1\ m) = -369.5$ kJ/mol

17. You make a saturated solution of NaCl at 25 °C. No solid is present in the beaker holding the solution. What can be done to increase the amount of dissolved NaCl in this solution? (See Figure 14.11.)
   (a) Add more solid NaCl.
   (b) Raise the temperature of the solution.

(c) Raise the temperature of the solution, and add some NaCl.
(d) Lower the temperature of the solution, and add some NaCl.

18. Some lithium chloride, LiCl, is dissolved in 100 mL of water in one beaker, and some Li_2SO_4 is dissolved in 100 mL of water in another beaker. Both are at 10 °C, and both are saturated solutions; some solid remains undissolved in each beaker. Describe what you would observe as the temperature is raised. The following data are available to you from a handbook of chemistry:

	Solubility (g/100 mL)	
Compound	10 °C	40 °C
Li_2SO_4	35.5	33.7
LiCl	74.5	89.8

Henry's Law
(See Example 14.4 and ChemistryNow Screen 14.5.)

19. The partial pressure of O_2 in your lungs varies from 25 mm Hg to 40 mm Hg. What mass of O_2 can dissolve in 1.0 L of water at 25 °C if the partial pressure of O_2 is 40 mm Hg?

20. ■ The Henry's law constant for O_2 in water at 25 °C is given in Table 14.2. Which of the following is a reasonable constant when the temperature is 50 °C? Explain the reason for your choice.
   (a) 6.7×10^{-4} mol/kg · bar   (c) 1.3×10^{-3} mol/kg · bar
   (b) 2.6×10^{-3} mol/kg · bar   (d) 6.4×10^{-2} mol/kg · bar

21. An unopened soda can has an aqueous CO_2 concentration of 0.0506 m at 25 °C. What is the pressure of CO_2 gas in the can?

22. ■ Hydrogen gas has a Henry's law constant of 7.8×10^{-4} mol/kg · bar at 25 °C when dissolving in water. If the total pressure of gas (H_2 gas plus water vapor) over water is 1.0 bar, what is the concentration of H_2 in the water in grams per milliliter? (See Appendix G for the vapor pressure of water.)

Raoult's Law
(See Example 14.5 and ChemistryNow Screen 14.7.)

23. A 35.0-g sample of ethylene glycol, $HOCH_2CH_2OH$, is dissolved in 500.0 g of water. The vapor pressure of water at 32 °C is 35.7 mm Hg. What is the vapor pressure of the water–ethylene glycol solution at 32 °C? (Ethylene glycol is nonvolatile.)

24. ■ Urea, $(NH_2)_2CO$, which is widely used in fertilizers and plastics, is quite soluble in water. If you dissolve 9.00 g of urea in 10.0 mL of water, what is the vapor pressure of the solution at 24 °C? Assume the density of water is 1.00 g/mL.

25. Pure ethylene glycol, HOCH$_2$CH$_2$OH, is added to 2.00 kg of water in the cooling system of a car. The vapor pressure of the water in the system when the temperature is 90 °C is 457 mm Hg. What mass of glycol was added? (Assume the solution is ideal. See Appendix G for the vapor pressure of water.)

26. Pure iodine (105 g) is dissolved in 325 g of CCl$_4$ at 65 °C. Given that the vapor pressure of CCl$_4$ at this temperature is 531 mm Hg, what is the vapor pressure of the CCl$_4$–I$_2$ solution at 65 °C? (Assume that I$_2$ does not contribute to the vapor pressure.)

Boiling Point Elevation
(See Example 14.6 and ChemistryNow Screen 14.8.)

27. Verify that 0.200 mol of a nonvolatile solute in 125 g of benzene (C$_6$H$_6$) produces a solution whose boiling point is 84.2 °C.

28. ■ What is the boiling point of a solution composed of 15.0 g of urea, (NH$_2$)$_2$CO, in 0.500 kg of water?

29. What is the boiling point of a solution composed of 15.0 g of CHCl$_3$ and 0.515 g of the nonvolatile solute acenaphthene, C$_{12}$H$_{10}$, a component of coal tar?

30. ■ A solution of glycerol, C$_3$H$_5$(OH)$_3$, in 735 g of water has a boiling point of 104.4 °C at a pressure of 760 mm Hg. What is the mass of glycerol in the solution? What is the mole fraction of the solute?

Freezing Point Depression
(See Example 14.7 and ChemistryNow Screen 14.8.)

31. A mixture of ethanol, C$_2$H$_5$OH, and water has a freezing point of −16.0 °C.
    (a) What is the molality of the alcohol?
    (b) What is the weight percent of alcohol in the solution?

32. ■ Some ethylene glycol, HOCH$_2$CH$_2$OH, is added to your car's cooling system along with 5.0 kg of water. If the freezing point of the water–glycol solution is −15.0 °C, what mass of HOCH$_2$CH$_2$OH must have been added?

33. You dissolve 15.0 g of sucrose, C$_{12}$H$_{22}$O$_{11}$, in a cup of water (225 g). What is the freezing point of the solution?

34. Assume a bottle of wine consists of an 11 weight percent solution of ethanol (C$_2$H$_5$OH) in water. If the bottle of wine is chilled to −20 °C, will the solution begin to freeze?

Colligative Properties and Molar Mass Determination
(See Example 14.8.)

35. ■ You add 0.255 g of an orange, crystalline compound whose empirical formula is C$_{10}$H$_8$Fe to 11.12 g of benzene. The boiling point of the benzene rises from 80.10 °C to 80.26 °C. What are the molar mass and molecular formula of the compound?

36. Butylated hydroxyanisole (BHA) is used as an antioxidant in margarine and other fats and oils. (It prevents oxidation and prolongs the shelf-life of the food.) What is the molar mass of BHA if 0.640 g of the compound, dissolved in 25.0 g of chloroform, produces a solution whose boiling point is 62.22 °C?

37. Benzyl acetate is one of the active components of oil of jasmine. If 0.125 g of the compound is added to 25.0 g of chloroform (CHCl$_3$), the boiling point of the solution is 61.82 °C. What is the molar mass of benzyl acetate?

38. Anthracene, a hydrocarbon obtained from coal, has an empirical formula of C$_7$H$_5$. To find its molecular formula, you dissolve 0.500 g in 30.0 g of benzene. The boiling point of pure benzene is 80.10 °C, whereas the solution has a boiling point of 80.34 °C. What is the molecular formula of anthracene?

39. ■ An aqueous solution contains 0.180 g of an unknown, nonionic solute in 50.0 g of water. The solution freezes at −0.040 °C. What is the molar mass of the solute?

40. The organic compound called aluminon is used as a reagent to test for the presence of the aluminum ion in aqueous solution. A solution of 2.50 g of aluminon in 50.0 g of water freezes at −0.197 °C. What is the molar mass of aluminon?

Colligative Properties of Ionic Compounds
(See Example 14.9 and ChemistryNow Screen 14.8.)

41. ■ If 52.5 g of LiF is dissolved in 306 g of water, what is the expected freezing point of the solution? (Assume the van't Hoff factor, *i*, for LiF is 2.)

42. To make homemade ice cream, you cool the milk and cream by immersing the container in ice and a concentrated solution of rock salt (NaCl) in water. If you want to have a water–salt solution that freezes at −10. °C, what mass of NaCl must you add to 3.0 kg of water? (Assume the van't Hoff factor, *i*, for NaCl is 1.85.)

43. ■ List the following aqueous solutions in order of increasing melting point. (The last three are all assumed to dissociate completely into ions in water.)
    (a) 0.1 *m* sugar   (c) 0.08 *m* CaCl$_2$
    (b) 0.1 *m* NaCl   (d) 0.04 *m* Na$_2$SO$_4$

44. Arrange the following aqueous solutions in order of decreasing freezing point. (The last three are all assumed to dissociate completely into ions in water.)
    (a) 0.20 *m* ethylene glycol (nonvolatile, nonelectrolyte)
    (b) 0.12 *m* K$_2$SO$_4$
    (c) 0.10 *m* MgCl$_2$
    (d) 0.12 *m* KBr

▲ more challenging   ■ in OWL   Blue-numbered questions answered in Appendix O

Osmosis
(See Example 14.10 and ChemistryNow Screen 14.9.)

45. ■ An aqueous solution contains 3.00% phenylalanine ($C_9H_{11}NO_2$) by mass. Assume the phenylalanine is nonionic and nonvolatile. Find the following:
    (a) the freezing point of the solution
    (b) the boiling point of the solution
    (c) the osmotic pressure of the solution at 25 °C

    In your view, which of these values is most easily measurable in the laboratory?

46. Estimate the osmotic pressure of human blood at 37 °C. Assume blood is isotonic with a 0.154 M NaCl solution, and assume the van't Hoff factor, i, is 1.90 for NaCl.

47. ■ An aqueous solution containing 1.00 g of bovine insulin (a protein, not ionized) per liter has an osmotic pressure of 3.1 mm Hg at 25 °C. Calculate the molar mass of bovine insulin.

48. Calculate the osmotic pressure of a 0.0120 M solution of NaCl in water at 0 °C. Assume the van't Hoff factor, i, is 1.94 for this solution.

Colloids
(See Section 14.5 and ChemistryNow Screen 14.10.)

49. When solutions of $BaCl_2$ and Na_2SO_4 are mixed, the mixture becomes cloudy. After a few days, a white solid is observed on the bottom of the beaker with a clear liquid above it.
    (a) Write a balanced equation for the reaction that occurs.
    (b) Why is the solution cloudy at first?
    (c) What happens during the few days of waiting?

50. ■ The dispersed phase of a certain colloidal dispersion consists of spheres of diameter 1.0×10^2 nm.
    (a) What are the volume ($V = \frac{4}{3}\pi r^3$) and surface area ($A = 4\pi r^2$) of each sphere?
    (b) How many spheres are required to give a total volume of 1.0 cm³? What is the total surface area of these spheres in square meters?

General Questions
These questions are not designated as to type or location in the chapter. They may combine several concepts.

51. Phenylcarbinol is used in nasal sprays as a preservative. A solution of 0.52 g of the compound in 25.0 g of water has a melting point of −0.36 °C. What is the molar mass of phenylcarbinol?

52. (a) Which aqueous solution is expected to have the higher boiling point: 0.10 m Na_2SO_4 or 0.15 m sugar?
    (b) For which aqueous solution is the vapor pressure of water higher: 0.30 m NH_4NO_3 or 0.15 m Na_2SO_4?

53. ■ Arrange the following aqueous solutions in order of (i) increasing vapor pressure of water and (ii) increasing boiling point.
    (a) 0.35 m $HOCH_2CH_2OH$ (a nonvolatile solute)
    (b) 0.50 m sugar
    (c) 0.20 m KBr (a strong electrolyte)
    (d) 0.20 m Na_2SO_4 (a strong electrolyte)

54. Making homemade ice cream is one of life's great pleasures. Fresh milk and cream, sugar, and flavorings are churned in a bucket suspended in an ice–water mixture, the freezing point of which has been lowered by adding rock salt. One manufacturer of home ice cream freezers recommends adding 2.50 lb (1130 g) of rock salt (NaCl) to 16.0 lb of ice (7250 g) in a 4-qt freezer. For the solution when this mixture melts, calculate the following:
    (a) the weight percent of NaCl
    (b) the mole fraction of NaCl
    (c) the molality of the solution

55. Dimethylglyoxime [DMG, $(CH_3CNOH)_2$] is used as a reagent to precipitate nickel ion. Assume that 53.0 g of DMG has been dissolved in 525 g of ethanol (C_2H_5OH).

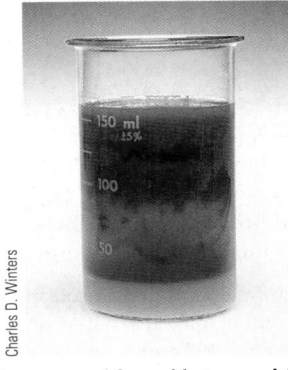

Charles D. Winters

The red, insoluble compound formed between nickel(II) ion and dimethylglyoxime (DMG) is precipitated when DMG is added to a basic solution of Ni^{2+}(aq).

    (a) What is the mole fraction of DMG?
    (b) What is the molality of the solution?
    (c) What is the vapor pressure of the ethanol over the solution at ethanol's normal boiling point of 78.4 °C?
    (d) What is the boiling point of the solution? (DMG does not produce ions in solution.) (K_{bp} for ethanol = +1.22 °C/m)

56. ■ A 10.7 m solution of NaOH has a density of 1.33 g/cm³ at 20 °C. Calculate the following:
    (a) the mole fraction of NaOH
    (b) the weight percent of NaOH
    (c) the molarity of the solution

57. Concentrated aqueous ammonia has a molarity of 14.8 mol/L and a density of 0.90 g/cm³. What is the molality of the solution? Calculate the mole fraction and weight percent of NH_3.

58. ■ If you dissolve 2.00 g of $Ca(NO_3)_2$ in 750 g of water, what is the molality of $Ca(NO_3)_2$? What is the total molality of ions in solution? (Assume total dissociation of the ionic solid.)

59. If you want a solution that is 0.100 m in ions, what mass of Na_2SO_4 must you dissolve in 125 g of water? (Assume total dissociation of the ionic solid.)

60. ■ Consider the following aqueous solutions: (i) 0.20 m $HOCH_2CH_2OH$ (nonvolatile, nonelectrolyte); (ii) 0.10 m $CaCl_2$; (iii) 0.12 m KBr; and (iv) 0.12 m Na_2SO_4.
  (a) Which solution has the highest boiling point?
  (b) Which solution has the lowest freezing point?
  (c) Which solution has the highest water vapor pressure?

61. ■ (a) Which solution is expected to have the higher boiling point: 0.20 m KBr or 0.30 m sugar?
  (b) Which aqueous solution has the lower freezing point: 0.12 m NH_4NO_3 or 0.10 m Na_2CO_3?

62. The solubility of NaCl in water at 100 °C is 39.1 g/100. g of water. Calculate the boiling point of this solution. (Assume $i = 1.85$ for NaCl.)

63. Instead of using NaCl to melt the ice on your sidewalk, you decide to use $CaCl_2$. If you add 35.0 g of $CaCl_2$ to 150. g of water, what is the freezing point of the solution? (Assume $i = 2.7$ for $CaCl_2$.)

64. ■ The smell of ripe raspberries is due to 4-(p-hydroxyphenyl)-2-butanone, which has the empirical formula C_5H_6O. To find its molecular formula, you dissolve 0.135 g in 25.0 g of chloroform, $CHCl_3$. The boiling point of the solution is 61.82 °C. What is the molecular formula of the solute?

65. Hexachlorophene has been used in germicidal soap. What is its molar mass if 0.640 g of the compound, dissolved in 25.0 g of chloroform, produces a solution whose boiling point is 61.93 °C?

66. The solubility of ammonium formate, NH_4CHO_2, in 100 g of water is 102 g at 0 °C and 546 g at 80 °C. A solution is prepared by dissolving NH_4CHO_2 in 200 g of water until no more will dissolve at 80 °C. The solution is then cooled to 0 °C. What mass of NH_4CHO_2 precipitates? (Assume that no water evaporates and that the solution is not supersaturated.)

67. ■ How much N_2 can dissolve in water at 25 °C if the N_2 partial pressure is 585 mm Hg?

68. Cigars are best stored in a "humidor" at 18 °C and 55% relative humidity. This means the pressure of water vapor should be 55% of the vapor pressure of pure water at the same temperature. The proper humidity can be maintained by placing a solution of glycerol [$C_3H_5(OH)_3$] and water in the humidor. Calculate the percent by mass of glycerol that will lower the vapor pressure of water to the desired value. (The vapor pressure of glycerol is negligible.)

69. An aqueous solution containing 10.0 g of starch per liter has an osmotic pressure of 3.8 mm Hg at 25 °C.
  (a) What is the average molar mass of starch? (Because not all starch molecules are identical, the result will be an average.)
  (b) What is the freezing point of the solution? Would it be easy to determine the molecular weight of starch by measuring the freezing point depression? (Assume that the molarity and molality are the same for this solution.)

70. Vinegar is a 5% solution (by weight) of acetic acid in water. Determine the mole fraction and molality of acetic acid. What is the concentration of acetic acid in parts per million (ppm)? Explain why it is not possible to calculate the molarity of this solution from the information provided.

71. ■ Calculate the enthalpies of solution for Li_2SO_4 and K_2SO_4. Are the solution processes exothermic or endothermic? Compare them with LiCl and KCl. What similarities or differences do you find?

Compound	$\Delta_f H°(s)$ (kJ/mol)	$\Delta_f H°(aq, 1\ m)$ (kJ/mol)
Li_2SO_4	−1436.4	−1464.4
K_2SO_4	−1437.7	−1414.0

72. ▲ Water at 25 °C has a density of 0.997 g/cm³. Calculate the molality and molarity of pure water at this temperature.

73. ▲ If a volatile solute is added to a volatile solvent, both substances contribute to the vapor pressure over the solution. Assuming an ideal solution, the vapor pressure of each is given by Raoult's law, and the total vapor pressure is the sum of the vapor pressures for each component. A solution, assumed to be ideal, is made from 1.0 mol of toluene ($C_6H_5CH_3$) and 2.0 mol of benzene (C_6H_6). The vapor pressures of the pure solvents are 22 mm Hg and 75 mm Hg, respectively, at 20 °C. What is the total vapor pressure of the mixture? What is the mole fraction of each component in the liquid and in the vapor?

74. ■ A solution is made by adding 50.0 mL of ethanol (C_2H_5OH, $d = 0.789$ g/ml) to 50.0 mL of water ($d = 0.998$ g/mL). What is the total vapor pressure over the solution at 20 °C? (See Study Question 73.) The vapor pressure of ethanol at 20 °C is 43.6 mm Hg.

75. A 2.0% (by mass) aqueous solution of novocainium chloride ($C_{13}H_{21}ClN_2O_2$) freezes at −0.237 °C. Calculate the van't Hoff factor, i. How many moles of ions are in the solution per mole of compound?

76. A solution is 4.00% (by mass) maltose and 96.00% water. It freezes at −0.229 °C.
  (a) Calculate the molar mass of maltose (which is not an ionic compound).
  (b) The density of the solution is 1.014 g/mL. Calculate the osmotic pressure of the solution.

77. ▲ The following table lists the concentrations of the principal ions in sea water:

Concentration

Ion	(ppm)
Cl^-	1.95×10^4
Na^+	1.08×10^4
Mg^{2+}	1.29×10^3
SO_4^{2-}	9.05×10^2
Ca^{2+}	4.12×10^2
K^+	3.80×10^2
Br^-	67

(a) Calculate the freezing point of water.
(b) Calculate the osmotic pressure of sea water at 25 °C. What is the minimum pressure needed to purify sea water by reverse osmosis?

78. ■ ▲ A tree is exactly 10 m tall.
(a) What must be the total molarity of the solutes if sap rises to the top of the tree by osmotic pressure at 20 °C? Assume the groundwater outside the tree is pure water and that the density of the sap is 1.0 g/mL. (1 mm Hg = 13.6 mm H_2O.)
(b) If the only solute in the sap is sucrose, $C_{12}H_{22}O_{11}$, what is its percent by mass?

79. ■ A 2.00% solution of H_2SO_4 in water freezes at −0.796 °C.
(a) Calculate the van't Hoff factor, i.
(b) Which of the following best represents sulfuric acid in a dilute aqueous solution: H_2SO_4, $H_3O^+ + HSO_4^-$, or $2 H_3O^+ + SO_4^{2-}$?

80. ■ A compound is known to be a potassium halide, KX. If 4.00 g of the salt is dissolved in exactly 100 g of water, the solution freezes at −1.28 °C. Identify the halide ion in this formula.

In the Laboratory

81. ▲ A solution of benzoic acid in benzene has a freezing point of 3.1 °C and a boiling point of 82.6 °C. (The freezing point of pure benzene is 5.50 °C, and its boiling point is 80.1 °C.) The structure of benzoic acid is

What can you conclude about the state of the benzoic acid molecules at the two different temperatures? Recall the discussion of hydrogen bonding in Section 12.2, and see Figure 12.7.

82. ▲ ■ You dissolve 5.0 mg of iodine, I_2, in 25 mL of water. You then add 10.0 mL of CCl_4 and shake the mixture. If I_2 is 85 times more soluble in CCl_4 than in H_2O (on a volume basis), what are the masses of I_2 in the water and CCl_4 layers after shaking? (See Figure 14.6.)

83. ▲ A solution of 5.00 g of acetic acid in 100. g of benzene freezes at 3.37 °C. A solution of 5.00 g of acetic acid in 100. g of water freezes at −1.49 °C. Find the molar mass of acetic acid from each of these experiments. What can you conclude about the state of the acetic acid molecules dissolved in each of these solvents? Recall the discussion of hydrogen bonding in Section 12.2 (and see Figure 12.7), and propose a structure for the species in benzene solution.

84. ▲ ■ In a police forensics lab, you examine a package that may contain heroin. However, you find the white powder is not pure heroin but a mixture of heroin ($C_{21}H_{23}O_5N$) and lactose ($C_{12}H_{22}O_{11}$). To determine the amount of heroin in the mixture, you dissolve 1.00 g of the white powdery mixture in water in a 100.0-mL volumetric flask. You find that the solution has an osmotic pressure of 539 mm Hg at 25 °C. What is the composition of the mixture?

85. ■ A newly synthesized compound containing boron and fluorine is 22.1% boron. Dissolving 0.146 g of the compound in 10.0 g of benzene gives a solution with a vapor pressure of 94.16 mm Hg at 25 °C. (The vapor pressure of pure benzene at this temperature is 95.26 mm Hg.) In a separate experiment, it is found that the compound does not have a dipole moment.
(a) What is the molecular formula for the compound?
(b) Draw a Lewis structure for the molecule, and suggest a possible molecular structure. Give the bond angles in the molecule and the hybridization of the boron atom.

86. In chemical research we often send newly synthesized compounds to commercial laboratories for analysis. These laboratories determine the weight percent of C and H by burning the compound and collecting the evolved CO_2 and H_2O. They determine the molar mass by measuring the osmotic pressure of a solution of the compound. Calculate the empirical and molecular formulas of a compound, C_xH_yCr, given the following information:
(a) The compound contains 73.94% C and 8.27% H; the remainder is chromium.
(b) At 25 °C, the osmotic pressure of a solution containing 5.00 mg of the unknown dissolved in exactly 100 mL of chloroform solution is 3.17 mm Hg.

Summary and Conceptual Questions

The following questions may use concepts from this and previous chapters.

87. In each pair of ionic compounds, which is more likely to have the more negative enthalpy of hydration? Briefly explain your reasoning in each case.
    (a) LiF or RbF
    (b) KNO_3 or $Ca(NO_3)_2$
    (c) CsBr or $CuBr_2$

88. ■ When salts of Mg^{2+}, Ca^{2+}, and Be^{2+} are placed in water, the positive ion is hydrated (as is the negative ion). Which of these three cations is most strongly hydrated? Which one is least strongly hydrated?

89. Which salt, Li_2SO_4 or Cs_2SO_4, is expected to have the more exothermic enthalpy of hydration? Explain briefly.

90. Explain why a cucumber shrivels up when it is placed in a concentrated solution of salt.

91. If you dissolve equal molar amounts of NaCl and $CaCl_2$ in water, the $CaCl_2$ lowers the freezing point of the water almost 1.5 times as much as the NaCl. Why?

92. A 100.-gram sample of sodium chloride (NaCl) is added to 100. mL of water at 0 °C. After equilibrium is reached, about 64 g of solid remains undissolved. Describe the equilibrium that exists in this system at the particulate level.

93. ■ Which of the following substances is/are likely to dissolve in water, and which is/are likely to dissolve in benzene (C_6H_6)?
    (a) $NaNO_3$
    (b) diethyl ether, $CH_3CH_2OCH_2CH_3$
    (c) naphthalene, $C_{10}H_8$ (see page 458 for structure)
    (d) NH_4Cl

94. Account for the fact that alcohols such as methanol (CH_3OH) and ethanol (C_2H_5OH) are quite miscible with water, whereas an alcohol with a long-carbon chain, such as octanol ($C_8H_{17}OH$), is poorly soluble in water.

95. Starch contains C—C, C—H, C—O, and O—H bonds. Hydrocarbons have only C—C and C—H bonds. Both starch and hydrocarbons can form colloidal dispersions in water. Which dispersion is classified as hydrophobic? Which is hydrophilic? Explain briefly.

96. ■ Which substance would have the greater influence on the vapor pressure of water when added to 1000. g of the liquid: 10.0 g of sucrose ($C_{12}H_{22}O_{11}$) or 10.0 g of ethylene glycol [$HOCH_2CH_2OH$]?

97. ■ Suppose you have two aqueous solutions separated by a semipermeable membrane. One contains 5.85 g of NaCl dissolved in 100. mL of solution, and the other contains 8.88 g of KNO_3 dissolved in 100. mL of solution. In which direction will solvent flow: from the NaCl solution to the KNO_3 solution, or from KNO_3 to NaCl? Explain briefly.

98. A protozoan (single-celled animal) that normally lives in the ocean is placed in fresh water. Will it shrivel or burst? Explain briefly.

99. In the process of distillation, a mixture of two (or more) volatile liquids is first heated to convert the volatile materials to the vapor state. Then the vapor is condensed, reforming the liquid. The net result of this liquid→ vapor→ liquid conversion is to enrich the fraction of a more volatile component in the mixture in the condensate. We can describe how this occurs using Raoult's law. Imagine that you have a mixture of 12% (by weight) ethanol and water (as formed, for example, by fermentation of grapes.)
    (a) What are the mole fractions of ethanol and water in this mixture?
    (b) This mixture is heated to 78.5 °C (the normal boiling point of ethanol). What are the equilibrium vapor pressures of ethanol and water at this temperature, assuming Raoult's Law (ideal) behavior? (You will need to derive the equilibrium vapor pressure of water at 78.5 °C from data in Appendix G.)
    (c) What are the mole fractions of ethanol and water in the vapor?
    (d) After this vapor is condensed to a liquid, to what extent has the mole fraction of ethanol been enriched? What is the mass fraction of ethanol in the condensate?

100. Sodium chloride (NaCl) is commonly used to melt ice on roads during the winter. Calcium chloride ($CaCl_2$) is sometimes used for this purpose too. Let us compare the effectiveness of equal masses of these two compounds in lowering the freezing point of water, by calculating the freezing point lowering of solutions containing 200 g of each salt in 1.00 kg of water. (An advantage of $CaCl_2$ is that it acts more quickly because it is hygroscopic, that is, it absorbs moisture from the air to give a solution and begin the process. A disadvantage is that this compound is more costly).

101. Review the trend in values of the van't Hoff factor i as a function of concentration (Table 14.4). Use the following data to calculate the van't Hoff factor for a NaCl concentration of 5.0 mass % (for which $\Delta T = -3.05$ °C) and a Na_2SO_4 concentration of 5.0 mass % (for which $\Delta T = -1.36$ °C). Are these values in line with your expectations based on the trend in the values given in Table 14.4? Speculate on why this trend is seen.

▲ more challenging   ■ in OWL   Blue-numbered questions answered in Appendix O

102. The table below give experimentally determined values for freezing points of 1.00% solutions (mass %) of a series of acids.

(a) Calculate the molality of each solution, determine the calculated freezing points, and then calculate the values of the van't Hoff factor i. Fill these values into the table.

Acid, (1.00 mass %)	molality (mol/kg H_2O)	$T_{measured}$ (°C)	$T_{calculated}$ (°C)	i
HNO_3		0.56		
CH_3CO_2H		0.32		
H_2SO_4		0.42		
$H_2C_2O_4$		0.30		
HCO_2H		0.42		
CCl_3CO_2H		0.21		

(b) Analyze the results, comparing the values of i for the various acids. How does this data relate to acid strengths? (The discussion of strong and weak acids on pages 132 and 133 will assist you to answer this question.)

103. It is interesting how the Fahrenheit temperature scale was established. One report, given by Fahrenheit in a paper in 1724, stated that the value of 0 °F was established as the freezing temperature of saturated solutions of sea salt. From the literature we find that the freezing point of a 20% by mass solution of NaCl is −16.46 °C (This is the lowest freezing temperature reported for solutions of NaCl). Does this value lend credence to this story of the establishment of the Fahrenheit scale?

104. The osmotic pressure exerted by seawater at 25 °C is about 27 atm. Calculate the concentration of ions dissolved in seawater that is needed to give an osmotic pressure of this magnitude. (Desalinization of sea water is accomplished by reverse osmosis. In this process an applied pressure forces water through a membrane against a concentration gradient. The minimum external force needed for this process will be 27 atm. Actually, to accomplish the process at a reasonable rate, the applied pressure needs to be about twice this value.)

Let's Review | Chapters 11–14

Many of us love the beach, and of course there are things of interest in chemistry there. The sand on the beach consists of many different substances, among them pulverized corals and sea shells. Another ingredient is quartz sand. A tiny portion of the structure of quartz is shown in the inset in the photograph. The water washing onto the sand is a most peculiar substance. One of its properties is that it can dissolve substances of many kinds—ionic salts and gases, among others. Water does not dissolve the sand itself, although the sand does become wet, and wet sand makes wonderful sand castles. And the ocean itself is a solution of sodium chloride plus many other dissolved salts.

THE PURPOSE OF *LET'S REVIEW*

- *Let's Review* provides additional questions for Chapters 11 through 14. Routine questions covering the concepts in a chapter are in the Study Questions at the end of that chapter and are usually identified by topic. In contrast, *Let's Review* questions combine several concepts from one or more chapters. Many come from the examinations given by the authors and others are based on actual experiments or processes in chemical research or in the chemical industries.

- *Let's Review* provides guidance for Chapters 11 through 14 as you prepare for an exam on these chapters. Although this is designated for Chapters 11 through 14 you may choose only material appropriate to the exam in your course.

- To direct your review, **Comprehensive Questions** are correlated with relevant chapter sections and with the OWL online homework system to which you may have purchased access. Some questions may include a screen shot from one of these tools so you see what resources are available to help you review.

PREPARING FOR AN EXAMINATION ON CHAPTERS 11–14

1. Review **Go Chemistry** modules for these chapters. Go Chemistry modules are available at **www.cengage.com/chemistry/kotz** or **www.ichapters.com.**

2. Take the ChemistryNow **Pre-Test** and work through your **Personalized Learning Plan.** Work through ChemistryNow **Exercises, Guided Simulations,** and **Intelligent Tutors.**

3. ☁WL If you subscribe to OWL, use the **Tutorials** in that system.

4. Work on the questions below that are relevant to a particular chapter or chapters. See the solutions to those questions at the end of this section.

5. For background and help answering a question, use the Go Chemistry and OWL questions correlated with it.

KEY POINTS TO KNOW FOR CHAPTERS 11–14

Here are some of the key points you must know to be successful in Chapters 11–14.

- The gas laws: Boyle's and Charles's laws and Avogadro's hypothesis.
- The ideal gas law, $PV = nRT$.
- Reaction stoichiometry and the gas laws.
- Kinetic-molecular theory and its connection to the gas laws and gas behavior.
- The non-ideal behavior of gases.
- Intermolecular forces and their effects.
- The importance of hydrogen bonding and the circumstances under which it occurs.
- The properties of liquids (such as melting and boiling point, vapor pressure, critical temperature and pressure).
- Unit cells of solids, especially cubic unit cells.
- Lattice energy and physical properties of solids.
- Interpretation of phase diagrams.
- Solution concentration.
- Solubility and the process of dissolving.
- Colligative properties of solutions (melting point depression, boiling point elevation, osmotic pressure).

EXAMINATION PREPARATION QUESTIONS

▲ denotes more challenging questions.

Important information about the questions that follow:

- See the Study Questions in each chapter for questions on basic concepts.
- Some of these questions arise from recent research in chemistry and the other sciences. They often involve concepts from more than one chapter and may be more challenging than those in earlier chapters. Not all chapter goals or concepts are necessarily addressed in these questions.
- **Assessing Key Points** are short-answer questions covering the Key Points to Know on this page.
- **Comprehensive Questions** bring together concepts from multiple chapters and are correlated with text sections covering that topic, with Go Chemistry modules, and with questions in OWL that may provide additional background.
- The screens shots are largely taken from Go Chemistry modules available at **www.cengage.com/chemistry/kotz** or **www.ichapters.com.**

Assessing Key Points

1. (Chapter 11) You have a 5.0 L flask filled with N_2 at a pressure of 735 mm Hg at 21 °C.
   (a) How many N_2 molecules are in the flask?
   (b) If the N_2 originally in the 5.0-L flask is placed in a 2.5-L flask and cooled to 0.0 °C, what is the pressure under the new conditions?

2. (Chapter 11) Consider the following gases: He, SO_2, CO_2, and Cl_2.
   (a) Which has the largest density (assuming that all gases are at the same T and P)?
   (b) Which gas will effuse fastest through a porous plate?

3. (Chapter 11) What volume (in liters) of O_2, measured at standard temperature and pressure, is required to oxidize 0.400 mol of phosphorus (P_4)?

$$P_4(s) + 5\ O_2(g) \rightarrow P_4O_{10}(s)$$

4. (Chapter 11) Several small molecules (besides water) are important in biochemical systems: O_2, CO, CO_2, and NO. You have isolated one of these, and to identify it you determine its molar mass. You release 0.37 g of the gas into an evacuated flask with a volume of 732 mL at 21 °C. The gas pressure in the flask is 209 mm Hg. What is the unknown gas?

5. (Chapter 11) Under which set of conditions will CO_2 deviate most from ideal gas behavior?
   (a) 1 atm, 0 °C   (c) 10 atm, 0 °C
   (b) 0.1 atm, 100 °C   (d) 1 atm, 100 °C

6. (Chapter 11) A 10.0-L flask contains the following mixture of gases at 25 °C: 16 g of O_2, 28 g of N_2, 2.0 g of He, and 4.0 g of H_2.
   (a) What is the total pressure in the flask?
   (b) Which gas exerts the largest partial pressure?

7. (Chapter 11) Air contains 21 mol % O_2. If the pressure of air in a room is 745 mm Hg, what is the partial pressure of O_2?

8. (Chapter 11) Two flasks, each with a volume of 1.00 L, contain O_2 with a pressure of 380 mm Hg. Flask A is inside the Chemistry Building where the temperature is 25 °C. Flask B is outside in the cold winter air at 0 °C.
   (a) Which flask contains the greater number of O_2 molecules?
   (b) Which flask contains O_2 molecules with greater average speed? With greater average kinetic energy?

9. (Chapter 11) Rank the following gases in order of increasing average molecular speed at a given temperature: CO, CO_2, O_2, and NH_3. (The relation between molar mass and molecular speed can be explored using Go Chemistry module 16 on the Gas Laws and the Kinetic-Molecular Theory.)

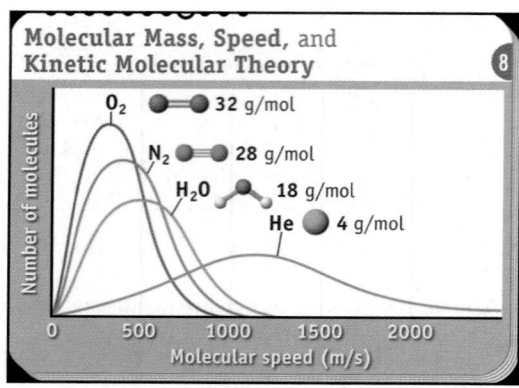

Molecular Mass, Speed, and Kinetic Molecular Theory 8

O_2 ⬤=⬤ 32 g/mol
N_2 ⬤=⬤ 28 g/mol
H_2O 🔵 18 g/mol
He ⬤ 4 g/mol

Number of molecules
Molecular speed (m/s)
0   500   1000   1500   2000

Screen from Go Chemistry module 16 on
the gas laws and kinetic-molecular theory

10. (Chapter 11) Propane reacts with O_2 according to the equation

$$C_3H_8(g) + 5\,O_2(g) \rightarrow 3\,CO_2(g) + 4\,H_2O(g)$$

You mix C_3H_8 with O_2 in the correct stoichiometric ratio, and the total pressure of the mixture is 120 mm Hg at some temperature.
(a) What are the partial pressures of C_3H_8 and O_2?
(b) What will be the partial pressure of water vapor, at the same temperature, after complete reaction?

11. (Chapter 12) In samples of which of the following pure substances will there be hydrogen bonding between molecules: H_2O, CH_3OCH_3, CH_3OH, CH_4, H_2, HNO_3?

12. (Chapter 12) Which of the following compounds would be expected to form intermolecular hydrogen bonds with water?
(a) CH_3OCH_3 (dimethyl ether)

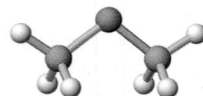

(b) C_3H_8 (propane)

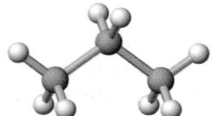

(c) CH_3CO_2H (acetic acid)

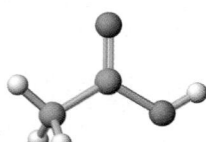

(d) Aspirin $C_6H_4(CO_2H)(CO_2CH_3)$

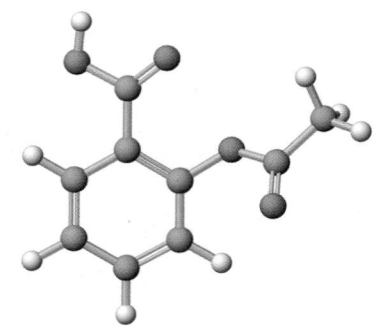

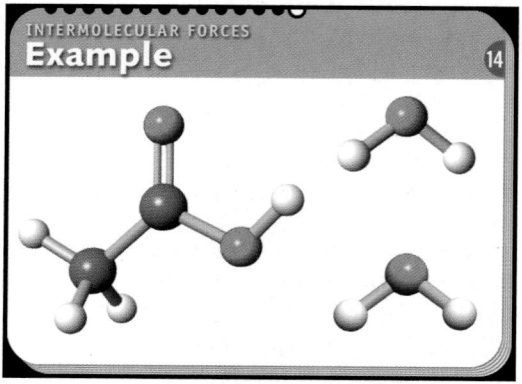

INTERMOLECULAR FORCES
Example 14

Screen from Go Chemistry module 17
on intermolecular forces.

13. (Chapter 12) Rank the following compounds in terms of increasing strength of intermolecular forces in the pure substance: Ar, CH_3OH, CO_2, NH_3

14. (Chapter 12) The following types of intermolecular forces are generally found to be important:

(i)   ion-dipole
(ii) dipole-induced dipole
(iii) dipole-dipole
(iv) induced dipole-induced dipole
(v)   hydrogen bonds

Decide which type of intermolecular force is most important for each of the following systems.
(a) Between methane (CH_4) molecules in liquid methane.
(b) Between H_2O and CH_3OH molecules in a mixture of the liquids.
(c) Between Li^+ and Cl^- ions and water in aqueous lithium chloride.
(d) Between O_2 and H_2O molecules when O_2 is dissolved in water.

15. (Chapter 12) Rank the following substances in order of increasing boiling point: (a) Ne, (b) CH_3OH, and (c) SO_2.

16. (Chapter 12) Use the vapor pressure curves for carbon disulfide (CS_2), ethanol (CH_3CH_2OH), and heptane (C_7H_{16}) below to answer the following questions:

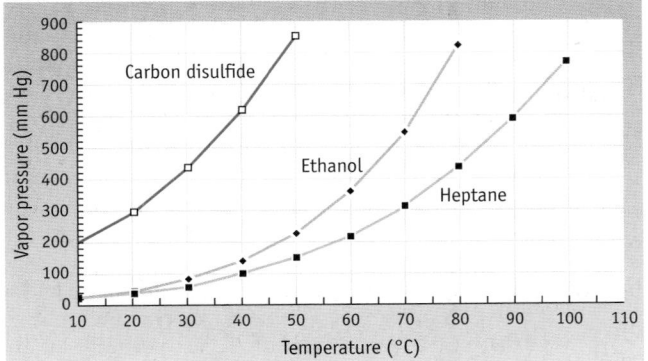

Vapor pressure curves for carbon disulfide (CS_2), ethanol (CH_3CH_2OH), and heptane (C_7H_{16})

(a) What is the vapor pressure of heptane at 70 °C?
(b) What is the normal boiling point of ethanol?
(c) What types of intermolecular forces exist
  (i) between two CS_2 molecules?
  (ii) between two heptane molecules?
  (iii) between two ethanol molecules?
(d) Decide if each substance is a liquid or vapor when the pressure is 600 mm Hg and the temperature is 50 °C.
(e) Which of these molecules is expected to dissolve readily in water?
(f) Which has the higher normal boiling point, ethanol or CS_2? Explain.
(g) Which has the higher normal boiling point, heptane or CS_2? Explain.

17. (Chapter 13) Types of solids include molecular solids, metallic solids, network solids, amorphous solids, and ionic solids. Classify each of the following solids:
(a) $CaCO_3$ (c) tungsten
(b) polyethylene   (d) solid CO_2 (dry ice)

18. (Chapter 13) Magnesium oxide has a NaCl-like crystal structure.

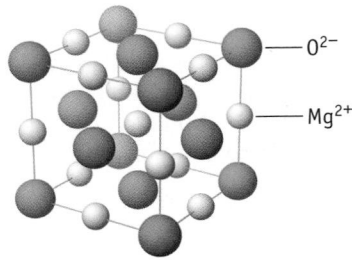

Unit cell of MgO

(a) In which type of unit cell are the O^{2-} ions arranged?
(b) How many Mg^{2+} ions are there per unit cell?

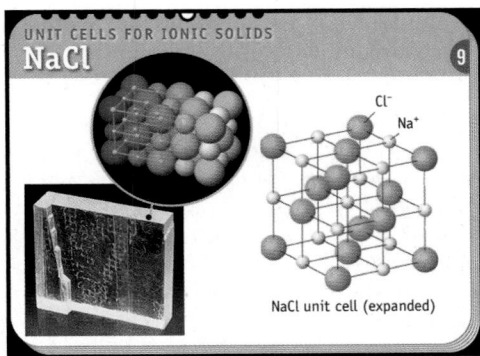

Screen from Go Chemistry module 18 on unit cells

19. (Chapter 12) List the compounds in each set in order of increasing boiling point, then explain your choice in terms of intermolecular forces.
(a) CH_3CO_2H, CH_3OCH_3, CH_3CH_2OH
(b) hexane (C_6H_{14}), octane (C_8H_{18}), propane (C_3H_8)

20. (Chapter 13) The following data are available for methane at the NIST website (National Institutes for Standards and Technology, http://webbook.nist.gov/chemistry/):

Triple point = 90.67 K at 0.117 bar
Normal melting point = 90.69 K
Normal boiling point = 111.2 K
Critical T = 190.6 K at critical P = 46.1 bar

(a) Is solid methane more or less dense than liquid methane?
(b) Can methane be liquefied at 0 °C?

21. (Chapter 14) At 20 °C you dissolve 45.0 g of dimethylglyoxime (DMG) ($C_4H_8N_2O_2$) in 500. mL of ethanol, C_2H_5OH (density of ethanol at 20 °C = 0.790 g/mL). Calculate the molality and weight percent of DMG.

22. (Chapter 14) Which of the following aqueous solutions has the highest boiling point? The lowest freezing point? The highest vapor pressure? The highest osmotic pressure?
(a) 0.20 m $C_2H_4(OH)_2$ (nonvolatile, nonelectrolyte)
(b) 0.10 m $MgCl_2$
(c) 0.12 m KBr
(d) 0.12 m K_2SO_4

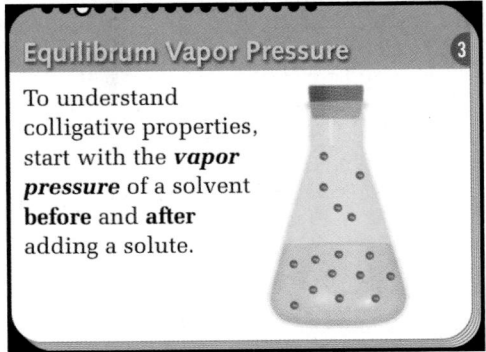

Screen from Go Chemistry module 19 on colligative properties

23. (Chapter 14) Which of the following ions should have the most negative enthalpy of hydration: Rb^+, Mg^{2+}, Na^+, or Ba^{2+}?

24. (Chapter 14) Concentrated salt solutions have boiling points lower than those calculated using the equation $\Delta T_{bp} = K_{bp} \cdot m$. Which of the following is a reasonable explanation of this observation?
(a) Positive ions repel each other more at high concentration.
(b) In solutions of higher concentration there is ion pairing.
(c) The water molecules will have a greater attraction for each other.
(d) Concentrated solutions contain small particles of nondissolved salt, thus lowering the molality.

25. (Chapter 14) You dissolve 29.3 g of NaCl in 500. g water. What is the freezing point of this solution?

26. (Chapter 14) Erythritol is a compound that occurs naturally in algae and fungi. It is about twice as sweet as sucrose. A solution of 2.50 g of erythritol in 50.0 g of water freezes at $-0.762\ °C$. What is the molar mass of the compound?

27. (Chapter 12) Below you see the OWL Simulation (12.4c) on vapor pressures. Here you can observe the behavior of the vapor pressure of pentane (C_5H_{12}) and hexane (C_6H_{14}) at various temperatures.
(a) Which has the higher vapor pressure at all temperatures and why?
(b) Vapor pressure data for hexane at two temperatures are given below. Use these to calculate the molar enthalpy of vaporization of hexane.

Temperature (K)	Vapor Pressure (mm Hg)
273	48.3
323	399.2

(c) Use the calculated $\Delta_{vap}H°$ from part (b) to estimate the normal boiling point of hexane.

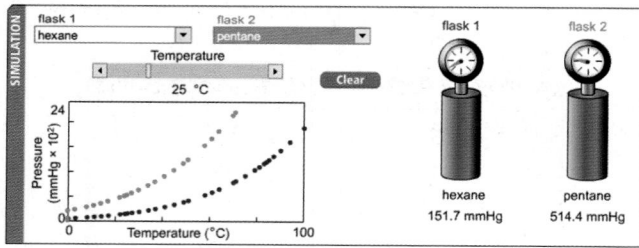

OWL Simulation 12.4c: Vapor Pressure

Comprehensive Questions

28. (Chapters 11 and 12) Researchers at the Fred Hutchison Cancer Research Center in Seattle discovered that mice can be put into a state of suspended animation by applying a low dose of hydrogen sulfide, H_2S. The breathing rate of the mice fell from 120 to 10 breaths a minute and their temperature fell to just 2 °C above ambient temperature. Six hours later the mice were revived and seemed to show no negative effects.
(a) Hydrogen sulfide is a gas at room temperature and normal atmospheric pressure whereas water is a liquid with a low vapor pressure under the same conditions. Explain this difference.
(b) The H_2S gas in the mixture of H_2S and air delivered to the mice had a concentration of 80. ppm. (A concentration of 1 ppm is 1 part per million, or one molecule in every 1 million molecules.) If you deliver 1.0 L of gas (a mixture of O_2, N_2, and H_2S) at a total pressure of 725 mm Hg at a temperature of 22 °C, what is the partial pressure of the H_2S gas?
(c) Hydrogen sulfide can be converted to sulfuric acid. If 5.2 L of H_2S gas at 130 mm Hg pressure and 25 °C is allowed to react with O_2 gas, how many liters of O_2 gas, also at 130 mm Hg pressure and 25 °C, are required for complete reaction? Assume the following reaction occurs.

$$H_2S(g) + 2\ O_2(g) \rightarrow H_2SO_4(\ell)$$

Text Sections: 11.2–11.5 and 12.2–12.4
OWL Questions: 11.4b, 11.5, 12.2-3c, 12.2–3e

29. (Chapter 11) A common industrial chemical, butyl acrylate, is made by combining acetylene (C_2H_2), butanol (C_4H_9OH), and CO in the presence of a catalyst. If you release 25.7 mg of the volatile liquid product of the reaction into a flask with a volume of 732 mL at 25 °C, the pressure is 5.10 mm Hg. What is the molar mass of the gas? Based on the reactants in the reaction, what is its formula?
Text Section: 11.3
OWL Question: 11.3f

30. (Chapters 4 and 12) Jacques Charles used 225 kg of H_2SO_4 and 450. kg of Fe to prepare H_2 gas for one of his earliest lighter-than-air balloon flights (August 1783; see text page 533). Assume that the atmospheric pressure that day was 735 mm Hg, and the temperature was 18 °C. What was the volume of the balloon (that is, the volume needed to contain this gas)? The hydrogen-forming reaction is

$$Fe(s) + H_2SO_4(aq) \rightarrow FeSO_4(s) + H_2(g)$$

Text Sections: 4.2 and 11.3
OWL Questions: 4.2f, 11.3b

31. (Chapter 11) Mercury has been poured into the U-tube, shown below, trapping air in the right side. What is the pressure of the trapped air? The (external) atmospheric pressure is 743 mm Hg.

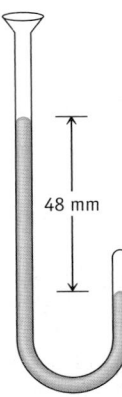

48 mm

Text Section: 11.1
OWL Question: 11.1

32. (Chapter 11) Unlike balloons made of rubber, balloons made of Mylar do not stretch. If you add gas to a Mylar balloon, the volume increases and, while filling, the pressure inside equals the pressure outside. This persists until the balloon is filled. After that, addition of gas will cause the pressure inside the balloon to increase above that of the outside atmosphere, and the volume won't change. At some point, you will exceed the tensile strength of the plastic film and the balloon will break.

(a) You place 4.8 g of dry ice [$CO_2(s)$] in a Mylar balloon whose volume when filled is 2.33 L. The dry ice sublimes and the gaseous CO_2 warms to room temperature, 18 °C. Atmospheric pressure that day is 0.98 atm. Assume there is no air inside the balloon at the start of this experiment. First, determine if the balloon is underfilled and the pressure inside is 0.98 atm or if the balloon is overfilled and the pressure inside is greater than 0.98 atm. Then, determine the actual pressure of gas inside the balloon.

(b) Compare the number of molecules of CO_2 used to fill the balloon in part (a) with the number of atoms of helium needed to fill the same balloon to the pressure calculated in (a).

(c) In which balloon (the one with He or the one with CO_2) are the gas molecules or atoms traveling at a greater average speed? Compare their relative average kinetic energies at 18 °C?

Text Sections: 11.2, 11.3, and 11.6
OWL Questions: 11.3b, 11.6e

33. (Chapter 11) Carbon dioxide, CO_2, was determined to effuse through a porous plate at the rate of 0.0330 mol/min. The same amount of an unknown gas, 0.0330 moles, is found to effuse through the same porous barrier in 104 seconds. Calculate the molar mass of the unknown gas.

Text Section: 11.7
OWL Question: 11.7c

34. (Chapters 8, 9, and 12) Bonding, structure, and properties of formamide, $HCONH_2$.

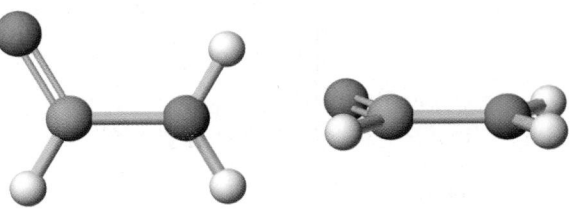

Front and side views of formamide, $HCONH_2$

(a) Draw an electron dot structure for formamide, Include all resonance structures.
(b) What is the C atom hybridization?
(c) Is the molecule polar?
(d) Can two formamide molecules interact by hydrogen bonding? Can formamide interact with water by hydrogen bonding?
(e) As indicated in the molecular model, the molecule is flat. Suggest a reason for the planar structure of the molecule.
(f) The enthalpy of vaporization of formamide at 25 °C is 60.15 kJ/mol. What is the enthalpy change for the vaporization of 10.0 g of the compound at 25 °C?

Text Sections: 8.2, 8.4, 8.8, 9.2, 12.2, and 12.4
OWL Questions: 8.4b, 8.5d, 8.8b, 9.2f, 9.2h, 12.2–3c, 12.4b

35. (Chapters 11 and 12) Acetone is a common solvent.

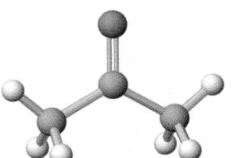

Acetone, $(CH_3)_2CO$

(a) Allyl alcohol, $CH_2{=}CH{-}CH_2OH$, is an isomer of acetone. Acetone has a vapor pressure of 100 mm Hg at +7.7 °C. Predict whether the vapor pressure of allyl alcohol is higher or lower than 100 mm Hg at this temperature. Explain.

(b) Use the Clausius-Clapeyron equation to calculate the enthalpy of vaporization of acetone from the following data.

Temperature (°C)	Vapor Pressure (mm Hg)
−9.4	40.
+7.7	100.
39.5	400.
56.5	760.

(c) Fluorination of acetone, C_3H_6O, by substituting fluorine atoms for some or all of the H atoms, produces a gaseous compound with the formula $C_3H_{6-x}F_xO$. To identify this compound its molar mass was determined by measuring gas density. The following data were obtained: Mass of gas, 1.53 g;

volume of flask = 264 mL; pressure exerted by gas, 722 mm Hg; temperature, 22 °C. Calculate the molar mass, then identify the molecular formula.

Text Sections: 11.3, 12.2, and 12.4
OWL Questions: 11.3b, 11.3f, 12.2–3c, 12.4g

36. (Chapter 13) Butane, the fuel in lighters and camping stoves, has the following physical properties:

Normal melting point = 136 K
Normal boiling point = 273 K
Triple point = 134.6 K at 7×10^{-6} bar

Construct a phase diagram for butane based on this information. Be sure to label the axes. Use S, L, and G to represent conditions for the three states of matter. Finally, use this drawing to answer the following questions:

(a) Is butane is a gas, liquid or solid at 0 °C and 400 mm Hg?

(b) Will an increase in pressure result in an increase, a decrease, or no change in the melting point of butane from its normal melting point?

(c) Between what temperatures is butane a liquid at 1.0 atm pressure?

Text Section: 13.6
OWL Question: 13.6c

37. (Chapter 13) The unit cell of one of several known molybdenum fluorides is pictured here.

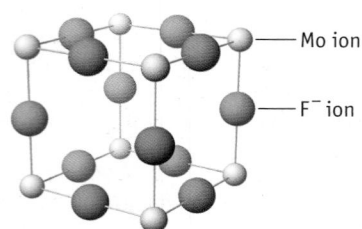

A unit cell of a molybdenum fluoride

How many molybdenum ions and how many fluoride ions are in each unit cell? What is the formula and name of this molybdenum fluoride?

Text Section: 13.2
OWL Question: 13.2c

38. (Chapter 13) The unit cell of sodium chloride is pictured below. The length of each side of the unit cell is 562.8 pm.

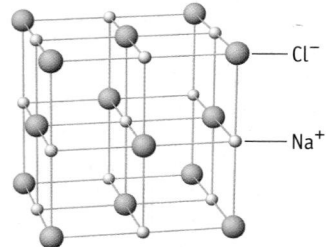

NaCl unit cell (expanded)

(a) What is the mass of one unit cell?

(b) What is the volume of one unit cell?

(c) What is the density of NaCl based on the mass and volume of the unit cell? (Compare the calculated value with a literature density of 2.17 g/cm³.)

Text Sections: 13.1 and 13.2
OWL Question: 13.2c

39. (Chapter 13) The unit cell of silver iodide is illustrated below.

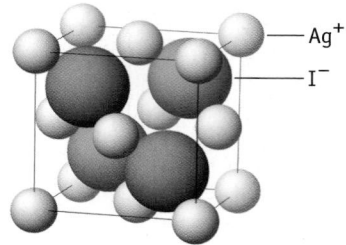

Silver iodide unit cell

(a) How many silver ions and how many iodide ions are there per unit cell?

(b) Sides of the unit cell are 649.6 pm. The density is 5.68 g/cm³. What is the mass of one unit cell?

(c) Based on the unit cell mass, what is the mass of one silver iodide formula unit and what is its molar mass? Compare this with the molar mass of silver iodide calculated from atomic weights.

Text Sections: 13.1 and 13.2
OWL Question: 13.2c

40. ▲ (Chapter 13) Units cells and close packing. Prove that the atoms packed in an idealized face-centered cubic unit cell occupy about 74% of the available space.

Text Section: 13.1
OWL Question: 13.1b

41. (Chapters 12 and 13) See the structure of quartz on page 656.

(a) What are some interesting structural features of quartz? What kind of solid does it represent?

(b) How does water interact with ordinary salt and oxygen gas so that they dissolve?

(c) Why does water have such peculiar properties? For example, for such a small molecule it has very high melting and boiling points.

(d) The quartz structure on page 656 shows the interior of the crystal. However, there are OH groups on the surface of the crystal that are attached to only one Si atom. Knowing this, explain why water can interact with sand—the sand gets wet—but it does not dissolve the sand.

Text Sections: 12.2, 12.3, 13.4, and 14.2
OWL Questions: 12.2–3c, 12.2–3e

42. (Chapters 12 and 14) Arrange the following aqueous solutions in order of (a) increasing boiling point and (b) increasing vapor pressure at 25 °C:

(i) 0.30 m C$_2$H$_4$(OH)$_2$ (ethylene glycol, nonvolatile solute)
(ii) 0.20 m CH$_3$CO$_2$H (acetic acid)
(iii) 0.20 m HNO$_3$
(iv) 0.20 m Na$_2$SO$_4$

Text Section: 14.4
OWL Questions: 14.4c, 14.4l

43. (Chapter 14) You have isolated a nonionic unknown compound from treated wastewater, and to help identify the compound you determine its molar mass. A solution of 0.238 g of the compound in 25.0 g of benzene freezes at 5.11 °C. What is the molar mass of the compound?

Text Sections: 14.4
OWL Questions: 14.4l

44. (Chapters 11 and 12) Naphthalene, C$_{10}$H$_8$, is a white solid that sublimes readily at room temperature and above.

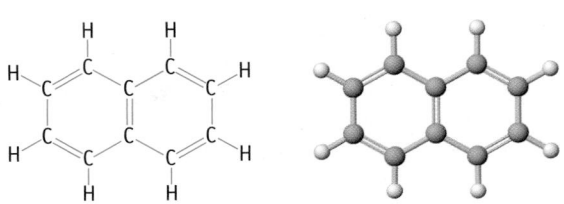

Naphthalene, C$_{10}$H$_8$

(a) If you place 1.05 g of napthalene in a 112 mL flask at 100 °C, where the vapor pressure is 18.8 mm Hg, how many molecules of the compound are in the vapor phase.
(b) Using data below, calculate the enthalpy of sublimation of the compound using the Clausius-Clapeyron equation.

Temperature (K)	Vapor Pressure (bar)
360.3	0.0142
392.7	0.0554

Text Sections: 11.3 and 12.4
OWL Questions: 11.3b, 12.4g

45. ▲ (Chapters 11 and 14) You have 2.25 g of a mixture of the organic liquids benzene and toluene in a 125 mL flask at 25 °C. Both are volatile liquids. Pure benzene has a vapor pressure of 95 mm Hg (at 25 °C), whereas that of toluene is 28 mm Hg (at 25 °C). This particular mixture of the two, however, has a total vapor pressure of 63 mm Hg.
(a) What is the mole fraction of each substance in the vapor phase?
(b) What is the mass of each substance in the vapor phase in this flask at 25 °C?

Benzene   Toluene

Text Sections: 11.5 and 14.4
OWL Questions: 11.5c, 14.4c

46. (Chapter 13) Titanium crystallizes in a face-centered cubic lattice. The metal reacts with hydrogen and carbon by allowing these elements to occupy holes in the lattice. Hydrogen atoms occupy tetrahedral holes, whereas carbon atoms occupy octahedral holes. What are the formulas of titanium hydride and titanium carbide, assuming that hydrogen atoms or carbon atoms, respectively, fill all of the appropriate holes in the lattice?

Text Section: 13.2
OWL Question: 13.2c

47. ▲ (Chapter 13) The structures of ionic solids can often be predicted by knowing the relative number of ions and their relative sizes. We begin by assuming cations are smaller than anions, and so lattices are built of anions with cations in the holes or interstices. (This is not always the case, of course, in compounds such as CsF where the cation is the larger of the two ions.) Nonetheless, the following *radius ratio rules* give reasonable predictions; that is, for a given range of cation to anion sizes, a particular coordination geometry is predicted for the cation.

Value of r_+/r_-	Coordination Geometry of the Cation
0.22–0.41	tetrahedral (Zn^{2+} in ZnS)
0.41–0.73	octahedral (Na$^+$ in NaCl)
>0.73	cubic (Cs$^+$ in CsCl)

Let us take an ionic compound MX as an example. Assume that the X anions form a primative cubic lattice and that they just touch along the edges of the lattice. Also assume the M cation in the center of the lattice touches all eight of the surrounding anions. What is the radius ratio r_+/r_- for this structure? (See Figure 13.8, but note that we assume X$^-$ ions at cube corners touch along the cube edges.)

Text Section: 13.2
OWL Question: 13.2c

Answers to Assessing Key Points Questions

1. (a) Number of N_2 molecules

    Amount of $N_2 = n = PV/RT$

    $$= \frac{735 \text{ mm Hg} \left(\dfrac{1 \text{ atm}}{760 \text{ mm Hg}} \right)(5.0 \text{ L})}{(0.08206 \dfrac{\text{L} \cdot \text{atm}}{\text{K} \cdot \text{mol}})(294 \text{ K})}$$

    $= 0.20 \text{ mol}$

    Number of molecules $=$

    $= (0.20 \text{ mol}) \left(\dfrac{6.022 \times 10^{23} \text{ molecules}}{\text{mol}} \right)$

    $= 1.2 \times 10^{23} \text{ molecules}$

    (b) Pressure under new conditions. Use the general gas law, Equation 11.3, on page 521.

    $$P_{\text{new}} = 735 \text{ mm Hg} \left(\frac{5.0 \text{ L}}{2.5 \text{ L}} \right)\left(\frac{273 \text{ K}}{294 \text{ K}} \right) = 1400 \text{ mm Hg}$$

2. (a) Equation 11.5 (page 525) states that the density of a gas is proportional to the molar mass at a given P and T. The masses are in the order He $<$ CO_2 $<$ SO_2 $<$ Cl_2. Therefore, Cl_2 has the greatest density.

    (b) The rate of effusion is inversely proportional to the square root of the molar mass (page 538). Therefore, He will diffuse most rapidly.

3. Amount of O_2 required

    $0.400 \text{ mol P}_4 \left(\dfrac{5 \text{ mol O}_2}{1 \text{ mol P}_4} \right) = 2.00 \text{ mol O}_2$

    Volume of O_2 required.

    $V = nRT/P$

    $$= \frac{(2.00 \text{ mol O}_2)\left(0.08206 \dfrac{\text{L} \cdot \text{atm}}{\text{K} \cdot \text{mol}} \right)(273 \text{ K})}{1.00 \text{ atm}}$$

    $= 44.8 \text{ L}$

    This could also have been solved using the molar volume of an ideal gas: 22.4 L/mol at STP. Thus, 2.00 mol O_2 at STP occupy twice the molar volume or 44.8 L.

4. Calculate the molar mass.

    Amount of gas $= n = \dfrac{PV}{RT}$

    $$= \frac{\left(209 \text{ mm Hg} \right)\left(\dfrac{1 \text{ atm}}{760 \text{ mm Hg}} \right)(0.732 \text{ L})}{\left(0.08206 \dfrac{\text{L} \cdot \text{atm}}{\text{K} \cdot \text{mol}} \right)(294 \text{ K})}$$

    $= 0.00834 \text{ mol}$

    Molar mass $= \dfrac{0.37 \text{ g}}{0.00834 \text{ mol}} = 44 \text{ g/mol}$

    The gas is CO_2.

5. (c) Gases at higher pressures and lower temperatures deviate most from ideality.

6. (a) The total pressure depends on the total number of molecules (moles) of gas in the flask (and T and V).

    $n(O_2) = 0.50 \text{ mol}$
    $n(N_2) = 1.0 \text{ mol}$
    $n(\text{He}) = 0.50 \text{ mol}$
    $n(H_2) = 2.0 \text{ mol}$

    Total amount $= n_{\text{total}} = 4.0 \text{ mol}$

    $$P = \frac{n_{\text{total}}RT}{V} = \frac{(4.0 \text{ mol})\left(0.08206 \dfrac{\text{L} \cdot \text{atm}}{\text{K} \cdot \text{mol}} \right)(298 \text{ K})}{10.0 \text{ L}}$$

    $= 9.8 \text{ atm}$

    See Equation 11.7 on page 531.

    (b) The gas with the highest partial pressure is that present in the largest amount, here H_2.

7. The partial pressure of a gas depends on its mole fraction, here 0.21 for O_2. (See Equation 11.8 on page 531.) Thus, the O_2 partial pressure is 160 mm Hg ($= 0.21 \times 745 \text{ mm Hg}$).

8. (a) Both flasks have the same P and same V, but B has a lower T. Therefore, B must have more molecules because more molecules are needed to produce the same P at a lower T. That is, given that $n = PV/RT$, when P, V, and R are constant, n must be greater for a lower T.

    (b) Flask A contains molecules with a greater average speed and greater average kinetic energy.

9. Molecules in order of decreasing molar mass and increasing speed: CO_2 ($M = 44$ g/mol), O_2 ($M = 32$ g/mol), CO ($M = 28$ g/mol), NH_3 ($M = 17$ g/mol).

10. (a) C_3H_8 and O_2 are mixed in a ratio of 1 mol to 5 mol.
    $X_{\text{propane}} = 1 \text{ mol}/(1 \text{ mol} + 5 \text{ mol}) = 1/6$
    $P_{\text{propane}} = X_{\text{propane}}P_{\text{total}} = (1/6)(120 \text{ mm Hg}) = 20. \text{ mm Hg}$
    $P_{\text{oxygen}} = (120 - 20.) \text{ mm Hg} = 100 \text{ mm Hg}$
    The pressure of O_2 is 5 times that of C_3H_8 as required by stoichiometry.

    (b) Pressure of water vapor

    $$P_{H_2O} = P_{\text{propane}} \left(\frac{4 \text{ mol H}_2\text{O}}{1 \text{ mol propane}} \right) = 80. \text{ mm Hg}$$

11. H_2O, CH_3OH, and HNO_3. Note that HNO_3 has an OH bond and can H-bond to neighboring nitric acid molecules.

12. A H-bond could form between H_2O and the O atom of the polar molecule CH_3OCH_3. Both acetic acid and aspirin, with OH bonds, can H-bond to water.

13. Intermolecular forces: Atoms of Ar $<$ nonpolar CO_2 $<$ polar NH_3 (with weak H-bonding) $<$ polar CH_3OH (with significant H-bonding). See pages 561–563.

14. (a) induced dipole-induced dipole forces between nonpolar CH_4 molecules.

(b) dipole-dipole and hydrogen bonding between H_2O and CH_3OH (along with induced dipole-induced dipole forces).
(c) ion-dipole forces between Li^+ and Cl^- ions and water.
(d) dipole-induced dipole forces between nonpolar O_2 and polar water.

15. Ne $(-246\ °C) <$ SO_2 $(-10.05\ °C) <$ CH_3OH $(+64.6\ °C)$
Neon atoms attract only by induced dipole-induced dipole forces, whereas SO_2 is weakly polar. Methanol molecules interact largely by dipole-dipole forces and hydrogen bonding (although induced dipole-induced dipole forces are also present).

16. (a) 300 mm Hg
(b) About 75 °C (literature value, 78.3 °C)
(c) Nonpolar CS_2 and heptane molecules interact by induced dipole-induced dipole forces. Ethanol molecules interact through dipole-dipole forces and hydrogen bonds. (Induced dipole-induced dipole forces are also present.)
(d) CS_2 is a vapor whereas both ethanol and heptane are liquids.
(e) Ethanol can interact strongly with water through both dipole-dipole forces and hydrogen bonding, so it dissolves readily in water. Neither of the nonpolar molecules, CS_2 or heptane, is miscible with water.
(f) The vapor pressure curve indicates CS_2 has a normal boiling point of about 45 °C, whereas that of ethanol is 78 °C. This makes sense because we predict that ethanol molecules interact through dipole-dipole forces and extensive hydrogen bonding, whereas CS_2 molecules interact through much weaker induced dipole-induced dipole forces.
(g) Both CS_2 and heptane are nonpolar, but heptane molecules are significantly heavier than CS_2 molecules (100.2 u versus 76.1 u) so its boiling point is predicted to be much higher. This is confirmed by the vapor pressure curves, which indicate that heptane has a normal boiling point of about 100 °C while the CS_2 normal boiling point is only about 45 °C.

17. (a) $CaCO_3$ is an ionic solid.
(b) Polyethylene is an amorphous solid (although partially crystalline polyethylene does exist).
(c) Tungsten is a metallic solid.
(d) Solid CO_2 is a molecular solid.

18. (a) The oxide ions are arranged in a face-centered cubic unit cell.
(b) There are four Mg^{2+} (and four O^{2-} ions) per unit cell.

19. (a) $CH_3OCH_3 < CH_3CH_2OH < CH_3CO_2H$
All three molecules are polar but only CH_3CH_2OH and CH_3CO_2H can interact through hydrogen

bonds. Hydrogen bonding is especially strong in CH_3CO_2H (acetic acid), which has not only an OH group but also a polar C=O group. (See Figure 12.7 on page 562.)
(b) propane $(C_3H_8) <$ hexane $(C_6H_{14}) <$ octane (C_8H_{18})
The boiling points of the nonpolar alkanes (a class of hydrocarbons with the general formula C_nH_{2n+2}) increase with increasing molar mass.

20. Phase diagram for methane, CH_4.

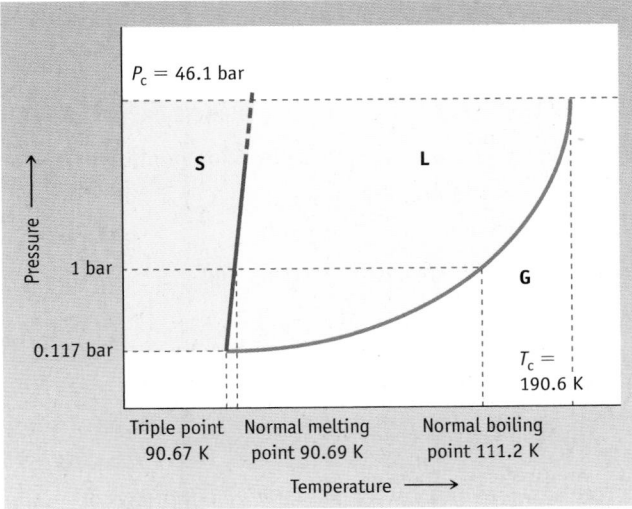

(a) Solid methane is more dense than liquid methane.
(b) No, this is above the critical temperature.

21. Molality and weight percent of dimethylglyoxime (DMG)

$$\text{Amount of DMG} = 45.0\ \text{g DMG} \left(\frac{1\ \text{mol DMG}}{116.1\ \text{g DMG}}\right)$$
$$= 0.388\ \text{mol DMG}$$
$$\text{Mass of ethanol} = 500.\ \text{mL} \left(\frac{0.790\ \text{g ethanol}}{1\ \text{mL ethanol}}\right)$$
$$= 395\ \text{g ethanol}$$

$$\text{Molality}\ (m) = \frac{0.388\ \text{mol DMG}}{0.395\ \text{kg ethanol}} = 0.982\ m$$
$$\text{Weight percent} = \left(\frac{45.0\ \text{g DMG}}{45.0\ \text{g} + 395\ \text{g}}\right)100\% = 10.2\%$$

22. The solution with the largest concentration of solute particles, $0.12\ m$ K_2SO_4, has the highest boiling point, the lowest freezing point, and the highest osmotic pressure. The solution with the smallest concentration of solute particles, $0.20\ m$ $C_2H_4(OH)_2$, has the highest vapor pressure.

23. The answer is Mg^{2+}. The enthalpy of hydration depends directly on the charge on the ion and inversely on its size. Thus, the smallest, most highly charged ion

will interact most strongly with water. Ion sizes are in the order $Rb^+ > Ba^{2+} > Na^+ > Mg^{2+}$ (Figure 7.12). (See pages 557–558 and 623–625.)

24. (b). See pages 640–641.

25. Freezing point depression. See Example 14.9.

$$\text{Mass \% NaCl} = \left(\frac{29.5 \text{ g}}{500 + 29.5 \text{ g}}\right)100\%$$
$$= 5.6\%$$

Estimate $i = 1.8$ (Table 14.4)

$$\Delta T_{fp} = K_{fp} \cdot m \cdot i = (-1.86 \text{ °C}/m)(1.00 \ m)(1.8) = -3.3 \text{ °C}$$

The van't Hoff factor, i, is 1.84 (Table 14.4, page 640).

26. Calculating molar mass using freezing point depression:

$$\Delta T_{fp} = -0.762 \text{ °C} = (-1.86 \text{ °C}/m)(c_m)$$
$$\text{Concentration} = c_m = 0.410 \ m$$
$$\left(0.410 \ \frac{\text{mol}}{\text{kg}}\right)0.0500 \text{ kg} = 0.0205 \text{ mol}$$
$$\text{Molar mass} = \frac{2.50 \text{ g}}{0.0205 \text{ mol}} = 122 \text{ g/mol}$$

Erythritol is $C_4H_{10}O_4$

27. (a) Pentane has the higher vapor pressure because it has the smaller molar mass.
    (b) At $T_1 = 0$ °C or 273 K, $P_1 = 48.3$ mm Hg
    At $T_2 = 50$ °C or 323 K, $P_2 = 399.20$ mm Hg

$$\ln \frac{P_2}{P_1} = -\frac{\Delta_{vap}H°}{R}\left[\frac{1}{T_2} - \frac{1}{T_1}\right]$$

$$\ln \frac{399.2}{48.3} = -\frac{\Delta_{vap}H°}{8.314 \text{ J/K}\cdot\text{mol}}\left[\frac{1}{323 \text{ K}} - \frac{1}{273 \text{ K}}\right]$$

$$\ln 8.265 = -\frac{\Delta_{vap}H°}{8.314 \text{ J/K}\cdot\text{mol}}\left[-5.67 \times 10^{-4}\right]1/\text{K}$$

$$\Delta_{vap}H° = 3.10 \times 10^4 \text{ J/mol or } 31.0 \text{ kJ/mol}$$

(c) Use the Clausius-Clapeyron equation with
$T_1 = 323$ K and $P_1 = 399.2$ mm Hg
$T_2 = $ boiling point of hexane and $P_2 = 760.$ mm Hg

$$\ln \frac{760}{399.2} = -\frac{3.10 \times 10^4 \text{ J/mol}}{8.314 \text{ J/K}\cdot\text{mol}}\left[\frac{1}{T_2} - \frac{1}{323 \text{ K}}\right]$$

Solving, we find $T_2 = 342$ K or 69 °C.

Solutions to Comprehensive Questions

28. (a) Water exhibits significant hydrogen bonding. Hydrogen sulfide, H_2S, does not.
    (b) Partial pressure of H_2S depends on the mole fraction of H_2S in the mixture (Equation 11.8). Here the mole fraction is the amount (moles) of H_2S divided by total amount (moles) of all gases, which is

the same as the ratio of H_2S molecules relative to the total number of molecules.

$$P_{H_2S} = (\text{mole fraction } H_2S)(P_{total})$$
$$= \left(\frac{80. \text{ molecules}}{1.0 \times 10^6 \text{ molecules}}\right)(725 \text{ mm Hg})$$
$$= 0.058 \text{ mm Hg}$$

(c) For gases at the same T and P, their volumes are directly proportional to the amount of gas. (This is Avogadro's Hypothesis; page 522. See also Example 11.5.)

$$5.2 \text{ L } H_2S\left(\frac{2 \text{ L } O_2}{1 \text{ L } H_2S}\right) = 10. \text{ L } O_2 \text{ required}$$

29. This is similar to Example 11.8, page 526.

$$n = \frac{PV}{RT} = \frac{5.10 \text{ mm Hg}\left(\frac{1 \text{ atm}}{760 \text{ mm Hg}}\right)(0.732 \text{ L})}{\left(0.08206 \ \frac{\text{L}\cdot\text{atm}}{\text{K}\cdot\text{mol}}\right)298 \text{ K}}$$

$$n = 2.01 \times 10^{-4} \text{ mol}$$

$$\text{Molar mass} = \frac{0.0257 \text{ g}}{2.01 \times 10^4 \text{ mol}} = 128 \text{ g/mol}$$

The product of the reaction, butyl acrylate, has a formula of $C_7H_{12}O_2$, formed by combining the reactants in a 1:1:1 ratio.

30. The volume of H_2 depends on its amount, and that in turn depends on which is the limiting reactant, Fe or H_2SO_4.

$$450. \times 10^3 \text{ g Fe}\left(\frac{1 \text{ mol Fe}}{55.85 \text{ g Fe}}\right) = 8.06 \times 10^3 \text{ mol Fe}$$

$$225 \times 10^3 \text{ g } H_2SO_4\left(\frac{1 \text{ mol } H_2SO_4}{98.08 \text{ g } H_2SO_4}\right)$$
$$= 2.29 \times 10^3 \text{ mol } H_2SO_4$$

The limiting reactant is H_2SO_4, which produces 2.29×10^3 mol H_2.

$$V = \frac{nRT}{P}$$

$$= \frac{(2.29 \times 10^3 \text{ mol } H_2)\left(0.08206 \ \frac{\text{L}\cdot\text{atm}}{\text{K}\cdot\text{mol}}\right)(291 \text{ K})}{735 \text{ mm Hg}\left(\frac{1 \text{ atm}}{760 \text{ mm Hg}}\right)}$$

$$V = 5.65 \times 10^4 \text{ L}$$

31. Pressure = 743 mm Hg + 48 mm Hg = 791 mm Hg

32. (a) Amount of CO_2 in the balloon:

$$\text{Amount of } CO_2 = 4.8 \text{ g } CO_2\left(\frac{1 \text{ mol } CO_2}{44.0 \text{ g } CO_2}\right)$$
$$= 0.11 \text{ mol}$$

Pressure in the balloon with $n = 0.11$ mol, $T = 291$ K, and $V = 2.33$ L.

$$P = \frac{(0.11 \text{ mol})\left(0.08206 \dfrac{\text{L} \cdot \text{atm}}{\text{K} \cdot \text{mol}}\right)(291 \text{ K})}{2.33 \text{ L}} = 1.1 \text{ atm}$$

The balloon is overfilled because the pressure generated by 0.11 mol of gas under these conditions is greater than the atmospheric pressure. The actual pressure in the balloon is 1.1 atm.

(b) The number of molecules is the same. The pressure of a gas (at a given T and V) depends only on the number of particles, not their identity.

(c) He atoms travel faster at a given T than CO_2 molecules (see Figure 11.15 and Screen 8 in Go Chemistry module 16) but their average kinetic energies are identical.

33. This problem on gas effusion uses Graham's law, Equation 11.10, page 538.

$$\frac{\text{Rate of effusion of } CO_2}{\text{Rate of effusion of unknown}} = \sqrt{\frac{\text{Molar mass unknown}}{\text{Molar mass } CO_2}}$$

$$\frac{0.0330 \text{ mol/min}}{0.0330 \text{ mol/1.73 min}} = \sqrt{\frac{\text{Unknown}}{44.0 \text{ g/mol}}}$$

$$1.73 = \sqrt{\frac{\text{Unknown}}{44.0 \text{ g/mol}}}$$

$$2.99 = \frac{\text{Unknown}}{44.0 \text{ g/mol}}$$

Unknown $= 132$ g/mol

34. (a) Electron dot structure

$$\text{:O:} \qquad \text{:O:}^-$$
$$H-C-N-H \longleftrightarrow H-C=N-H$$
$$\quad\;\; | \qquad\qquad\qquad\quad | $$
$$\quad\;\; H \qquad\qquad\qquad\quad H$$

(b) The C atom is sp^2 hybridized.

(c) The molecule is polar.

(d) Yes, the N—H of one molecule could interact with an N atom or O atom on a neighboring molecule. The formamide molecule can also hydrogen bond to water.

(e) The molecule is flat due to the resonance structure with a N=C double bond.

(f) Vaporizing 10.0 g of formamide:

Energy required as heat =

$$10.0 \text{ g HCONH}_2\left(\frac{1 \text{ mol HCONH}_2}{45.04 \text{ g HCONH}_2}\right)\left(\frac{60.15 \text{ kJ}}{1 \text{ mol HCONH}_2}\right)$$
$$= 13.4 \text{ kJ}$$

35. (a) Allyl alcohol is an alcohol (like ethanol) and has an OH group capable of hydrogen bonding. This should lower its vapor pressure at a given tempera-

ture relative to that of acetone, which, while polar, is not capable of hydrogen bonding to another acetone molecule.

(b) One can choose any two sets of temperature and pressures and use Equation 12.2. Alternatively, it is better to plot the data (as in Figure 12.18, page 575) and derive the heat of vaporization from the slope of the line. A plot of ln P versus $1/T$ gives a slope of -3875.3.

$$\text{Slope} = -3875.3 = -\Delta_{vap}H^\circ/R$$

Using $R = 8.314 \times 10^{-3}$ kJ/K·mol, and converting to kilojoules, we obtain $\Delta_{vap}H^\circ = 32.2$ kJ/mol. (A similar result is obtained using Equation 12.2, page 576.)

(c) Calculate the molar mass of the fluorination product.

$$n = \frac{PV}{RT} = \frac{722 \text{ mm Hg}\left(\dfrac{1 \text{ atm}}{760 \text{ mm Hg}}\right)(0.264 \text{ L})}{\left(0.08206 \dfrac{\text{L} \cdot \text{atm}}{\text{K} \cdot \text{mol}}\right)295 \text{ K}}$$

$$n = 0.0104 \text{ mol}$$

$$\text{Molar mass} = \frac{1.53 \text{ g}}{0.0104 \text{ mol}} = 148 \text{ g/mol}$$

The formula of the product must be C_3HF_5O. (The 3 C atoms and 1 O atom account for a mass of 52 g/mol of the 148 g/mol. The difference, 96, must be due to five F atoms and one H atom.)

36. The approximate phase diagram for butane is illustrated here. Also note that the triple point is at a very low pressure.

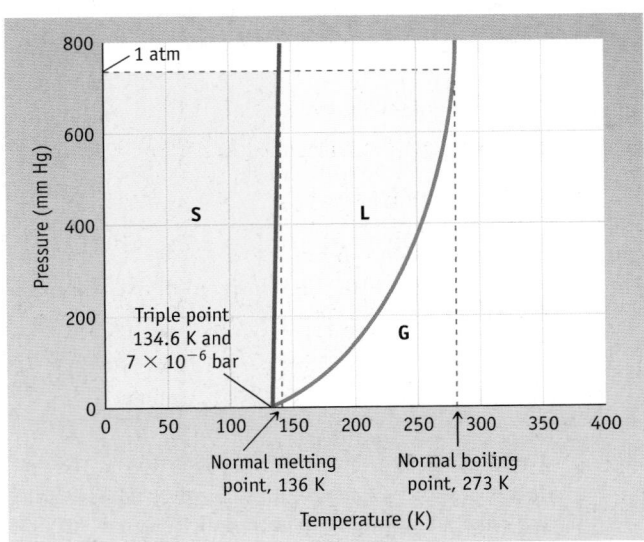

(a) At 0 °C and 400 mm Hg butane is a gas.

(b) An increase in pressure will result in an increase in melting point.

(c) Between the melting point (136 K) and the boiling point (273 K).

37. Fluoride ions occupy each of 12 edges and contribute ¼ of each ion to the unit cell for a total of three F^- ions. Mo ions are located at each corner and contribute a net of one Mo ion to the unit cell. Therefore, the formula is MoF_3 and its name is molybdenum(III) fluoride.

38. Sodium chloride unit cell.
(a) Mass of one unit cell (which contains 4 NaCl units).

$$\left(\frac{58.44 \text{ g NaCl}}{1 \text{ mol NaCl}}\right)\left(\frac{1 \text{ mol NaCl}}{6.022 \times 10^{23} \text{ formula units}}\right)$$
$$\left(\frac{4 \text{ NaCl formula units}}{1 \text{ unit cell}}\right)$$
$$= 3.882 \times 10^{-22} \text{ g NaCl/unit cell}$$

(b) Volume of one unit cell

Length of unit cell edge =
$$562.8 \text{ pm}\left(\frac{1 \text{ m}}{1 \times 10^{12} \text{ pm}}\right)\left(\frac{100 \text{ cm}}{1 \text{ m}}\right)$$
$$= 5.628 \times 10^{-8} \text{ cm}$$
$$\text{Volume} = \left(5.628 \times 10^{-8} \text{ cm}\right)^3 = 1.783 \times 10^{-22} \text{ cm}^3$$

(c) Density of NaCl

$$\text{Density} = \frac{3.882 \times 10^{-22} \text{ g NaCl}}{1.783 \times 10^{-22} \text{ cm}^3} = 2.178 \text{ g/cm}^3$$

This calculated value agrees with the literature value.

39. (a) There are 4 Ag^+ ions (as a face-centered cube) in the unit cell. There are 4 I^- ions in tetrahedral holes.
(b) First find the volume of the unit cell.

Length of unit cell edge =
$$\left(649.6 \text{ pm}\right)\left(\frac{1 \text{ m}}{1 \times 10^{12} \text{ pm}}\right)\left(\frac{100 \text{ cm}}{1 \text{ m}}\right)$$
$$= 6.496 \times 10^{-8} \text{ cm}$$
$$\text{Volume} = \left(6.496 \times 10^{-8} \text{ cm}\right)^3 = 2.741 \times 10^{-22} \text{ cm}^3$$

Use this volume with the density to derive the mass of the unit cell.

$$\left(\frac{2.741 \times 10^{-22} \text{ cm}^3}{1 \text{ unit cell}}\right)\left(\frac{5.68 \text{ g}}{1 \text{ cm}^3}\right) = \frac{1.557 \times 10^{-21} \text{ g}}{\text{unit cell}}$$

(c) There are 4 AgI units per unit cell, so the mass of 1 AgI is ¼ of 1.557×10^{-21} g or 3.893×10^{-22} g. Multiplying by Avogadro's number gives 234.4 g/mol, very close to the value from atomic weights (234.8 g/mol).

40. The key assumption here is that the atoms in a face-centered cube just touch along the diagonal dimension in each face.

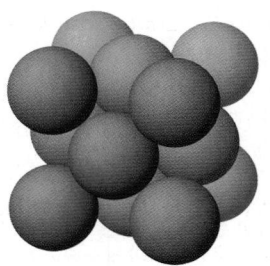

Atoms of a face-centered unit cell just touch along the face diagonal.

Let us assume the cell has an edge dimension of e, so the volume of the unit cell is e^3

Now solve for the volume of an individual atom.

Length of face diagonal = $\sqrt{2}\, e$
Face diagonal = $4 \times$ radius of an atom

Radius of an atom = $\dfrac{\sqrt{2}}{4}\, e$

Volume of an atom = $\dfrac{4}{3}\pi\left(\dfrac{\sqrt{2}}{4}\, e\right)^3$

$= 0.1851\, e^3$

There are four atoms in each unit cell, so the total volume of the atoms is $4 \times 0.1851\ e^3 = 0.7405\ e^3$. This is equivalent to 74% of the volume of the unit cell.

41. (a) The quartz structure consists of tetrahedral sp^3 hybridized Si atoms bridged by O atoms. Also notice that Si and O form six-member rings. Quartz is a covalent, network solid.
(b) The significant polarity of water molecules allows them to interact with the cations and anions of salts and bring the ions into solution. (See pages 557–558 and Figures 12.3 and 14.9.) Water molecules can also induce a dipole in nonpolar molecules such as O_2 and N_2, allowing them to dissolve to a small extent in water. (See pages 565–566.)
(c) For such a small molecule, water has unusual properties (such as its high boiling point, low vapor pressure, and high specific heat capacity). Also, it is one of only two or three substances known to have a solid phase of lower density than the liquid phase. Much of this can be explained by the hydrogen bonding capability of the molecule (see pages 561–564.)
(d) Polar water molecules interact with the OH groups on the surface of sand particles and wet the sand. However, the interaction is not strong enough to break down Si—O covalent bonds, and so the quartz sand does not dissolve in water.

42. Boiling points increase in order of increasing concentration of particles in the solution: $CH_3CO_2H <$ $C_2H_4(OH)_2 < HNO_3 < Na_2SO_4$. The vapor pressure increase is the opposite order. That is, the most concentrated solution will have the lowest vapor pressure (and thus the highest boiling point).

43. Freezing point depression. Use Equation 14.7

$$\Delta T_{fp} = (5.11 \,°C - 5.50 \,°C) = -0.39 \,°C$$

Solute concentration $(m) =$
$\Delta T_{fp}/K_{fp} = -0.39 \,°C/(-5.12 \,°C/m) = 0.076 \,m$

Amount of solute $= (0.076 \text{ mol}/1.00 \text{ kg})(0.0250 \text{ kg})$
$= 1.9 \times 10^{-3} \text{ mol}$

Molar mass $= 0.238 \text{ g}/1.9 \times 10^{-3} \text{ mol} = 1.2 \times 10^2 \text{ g/mol}$

44. (a) $n =$ amount of $C_{10}H_8$ in gas phase $= PV/RT$
When $P = 0.0247$ atm, $T = 373$, and $V = 0.112$ L,
$n = 9.05 \times 10^{-5}$ mol. So, number of molecules is
5.45×10^{19}

(b)

$$\ln \frac{P_2}{P_1} = -\frac{\Delta_{subl}H°}{R}\left[\frac{1}{T_2} - \frac{1}{T_1}\right]$$

$$\ln \frac{0.0554}{0.0142} = -\frac{\Delta_{subl}H°}{8.314 \text{ J/K}\cdot\text{mol}}\left[\frac{1}{392.7 \text{ K}} - \frac{1}{360.3 \text{ K}}\right]$$

$$\ln 3.90 = -\frac{\Delta_{subl}H°}{8.314 \text{ J/K}\cdot\text{mol}}\left[-2.290 \times 10^{-4}\right]1/K$$

$$\Delta_{subl}H° = 4.94 \times 10^4 \text{ J/mol or } 49.4 \text{ kJ/mol}$$

45. (a) P_{total} in gas phase $= 63$ mm Hg
$= X_{toluene}(28 \text{ mm Hg}) + X_{benzene}(95 \text{ mm Hg})$

Because $X_{benzene} + X_{toluene} = 1$, we have
63 mm Hg
$= (1 - X_{benzene})(28 \text{ mm Hg}) + X_{benzene}(95 \text{ mm Hg})$

Solving, we find $X_{benzene} = 0.52$. Therefore, $X_{toluene} = 0.48$.

(b) $P = 0.0829$ atm, $V = 0.125$ L, $T = 298$ K
$n = PV/RT = 4.24 \times 10^{-4}$ mol

Composition of the vapor:
$(0.52)(4.24 \times 10^{-4} \text{ mol}) = 2.2 \times 10^{-4} \text{ mol benzene}$
$(0.48)(4.24 \times 10^{-4} \text{ mol}) = 2.0 \times 10^{-4} \text{ mol toluene}$

Mass of benzene
$= (2.2 \times 10^{-4} \text{ mol})(78.1 \text{ g/mol}) = 0.017 \text{ g}$

Mass of toluene
$= (2.0 \times 10^{-4} \text{ mol})(92.1 \text{ g/mol}) = 0.019 \text{ g}$

46. A fcc lattice has a net of four Ti atoms. If all eight tetrahedral holes are filled with H atoms, this leads to a formula of TiH_2. There are only four octahedral holes in a fcc lattice, so titanium carbide is TiC.

47. In the diagram below, focus on the X^- ion in red. The distance along the cube edge, where X^- ions just touch, is $2r_-$. An X^- ions lies diagonally across the cube face at a distance of $2(2^{1/2})r_-$. (This is derived from the fact that the distance along all cube edges is $2r_-$, so the diagonal distance across a cube face must be $2(2^{1/2})r_-$.)

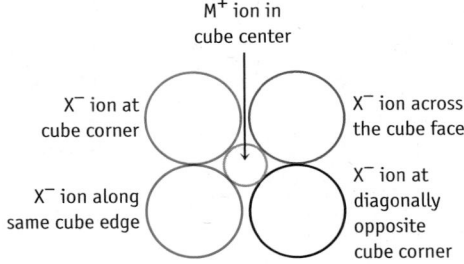

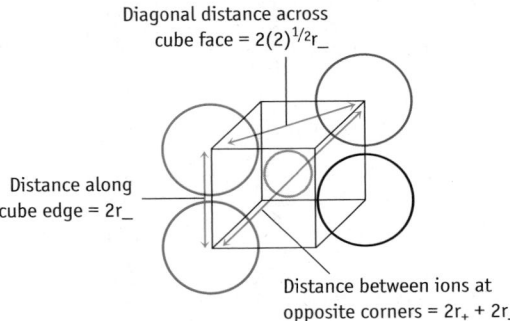

Using the Pythagorean theorem, the diagonal distance across the cube (from the X^- ion in one corner to the X^- ion in the opposite corner) is $(12)^{1/2}r_-$.

(Diagonal across the cube)$^2 = (2r_-)^2 + [2(2^{1/2})r_-]^2$
$$= 4r_-^2 + 8r_-^2 = 12r_-^2$$

This distance is also $2r_+ + 2r_-$:

$(12)^{1/2}r_- = 2r_+ + 2r_-$

$3.464r_- = 2r_+ + 2r_-$

$1.464r_- = 2r_+$

Therefore, $r_+/r_- = 0.732$

The radius ratio indicates that the coordination geometry of the cation is cubic.

15 | Chemical Kinetics: The Rates of Chemical Reactions

Charles D. Winters

Fading of the color of phenolphthalein with time

(elapsed time about 3 minutes)

Where Did the Indicator Go?

The indicator phenolphthalein is often used for the titration of a weak acid using a strong base. A change from colorless to pale pink indicates that the equivalence point in the reaction has been reached (◄ page 184). If more base is added to the solution, the color of the indicator intensifies to a bright red color.

If the solution containing phenolphthalein has a pH higher than about 12, another phenomenon is observed. Slowly, the red color fades, and the solution becomes colorless. This is due to a chemical reaction of the anion of phenolphthalein with hydroxide ion, as shown in the equation. The reaction is slow, and it is easy to measure the rate of this reaction by monitoring the intensity of color of the solution.

This chapter is about one of the fundamental areas of chemistry: the rate of reactions and how they occur. In Study Question 71, you will see some data that will allow you to discover how the rate of the phenolphthalein reaction depends on the hydroxide ion concentration, and you will derive an equation that will allow you to predict the results under other conditions.

The reaction of phenolphthalein and hydroxide ion.

Chapter Goals

OWL *See Chapter Goals Revisited (page 710) for Study Questions keyed to these goals and assignable in OWL.*

- Understand rates of reaction and the conditions affecting rates.
- Derive a rate equation, rate constant, and reaction order from experimental data.
- Use integrated rate laws.
- Understand the collision theory of reaction rates and the role of activation energy.
- Relate reaction mechanisms and rate laws.

Chapter Outline

15.1 Rates of Chemical Reactions

15.2 Reaction Conditions and Rate

15.3 Effect of Concentration on Reaction Rate

15.4 Concentration–Time Relationships: Integrated Rate Laws

15.5 A Microscopic View of Reaction Rates

15.6 Reaction Mechanisms

Chemistry‧Now™

Throughout the text this icon introduces an opportunity for self-study or to explore interactive tutorials by signing in at **www.cengage.com/login**.

■ **Macroscopic–Particulate Connections** Recall the statement from page 10 that "Chemists carry out experiments on the macroscopic level, but they think about chemistry at the particulate level."

When carrying out a chemical reaction, chemists are concerned with two issues: the *rate* at which the reaction proceeds and the *extent* to which the reaction is product-favored. Chapter 5 began to address the second question, and Chapters 16 and 19 will develop that topic further. In this chapter, we turn to the other part of our question, **chemical kinetics,** a study of the rates of chemical reactions.

The study of kinetics is divided into two parts. The first part is at the *macroscopic level,* which addresses rates of reactions: what reaction rate means, how to determine a reaction rate experimentally, and how factors such as temperature and the concentrations of reactants influence rates. The second part of this subject considers chemical reactions at the *particulate level.* Here, the concern is with the **reaction mechanism,** the detailed pathway taken by atoms and molecules as a reaction proceeds. The goal is to reconcile data in the macroscopic world of chemistry with an understanding of how and why chemical reactions occur at the particulate level—and then to apply this information to control important reactions.

15.1 Rates of Chemical Reactions

The concept of rate is encountered in many nonchemical circumstances. Common examples are the speed of an automobile, given in terms of the distance traveled per unit time (for example, kilometers per hour) and the rate of flow of water from a faucet, given as volume per unit time (perhaps liters per minute). In each case, a change is measured over an interval of time. Similarly, the rate of a chemical reaction refers to the change in concentration of a reactant or product per unit of time.

$$\text{Rate of reaction} = \frac{\text{change in concentration}}{\text{change in time}}$$

Two measurements are made to determine the average speed of an automobile: distance traveled and time elapsed. Average speed is the distance traveled divided by the time elapsed, or $\Delta(\text{distance})/\Delta(\text{time})$. If an automobile travels 3.9 km in 4.5 min (0.075 h), its average speed is (3.9 km/0.075 h), or 52 kph (or 32 mph).

Average rates of chemical reactions can be determined similarly. Two quantities, concentration and time, are measured. Concentrations can be determined in a variety of ways, sometimes directly (using a pH meter for example), sometimes by measuring a property such as absorbance of light that can be related to concentration (Figure 15.1). The average rate of the reaction is the change in the concentration per unit time—that is, $\Delta(\text{concentration})/\Delta(\text{time})$.

(a)

(b)

(c)

FIGURE 15.1 An experiment to measure rate of reaction. (a) A few drops of blue food dye were added to water, followed by a solution of bleach. Initially, the concentration of dye was about 3.4×10^{-5} M, and the bleach (NaOCl) concentration was about 0.034 M. (b and c) The dye faded as it reacted with the bleach. The absorbance of the solution can be measured at various times using a spectrophotometer, and these values can be used to determine the concentration of the dye.

Let's consider an example, the decomposition of N_2O_5 in a solvent. This reaction occurs according to the following equation:

$$N_2O_5 \rightarrow 2\ NO_2 + \tfrac{1}{2}\ O_2$$

Concentrations and time elapsed for a typical experiment done at 30.0 °C are presented as a graph in Figure 15.2.

Active Figure 15.2 A plot of reactant concentration versus time for the decomposition of N_2O_5. The average rate for a 15-min interval from 45 min to 1 h is 0.0080 mol/L · min. The instantaneous rate calculated when $[N_2O_5]$ = 0.34 M is 0.0014 mol/L · min.

Chemistry ❂ Now™ Sign in at www.cengage.com/login and go to the Chapter Contents menu to explore an interactive version of this figure accompanied by an exercise.

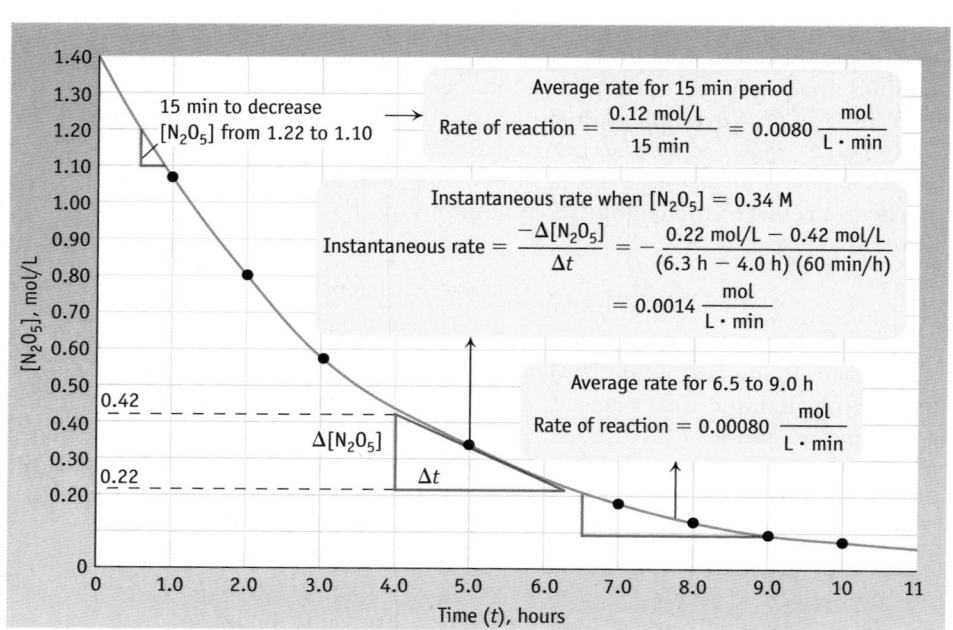

The rate of this reaction for any interval of time can be expressed as the change in concentration of N_2O_5 divided by the change in time:

■ **Representing Concentration** Recall that square brackets around a formula indicate its concentrations in mol/L (Section 4.5).

$$\text{Rate of reaction} = \frac{\text{change in } [N_2O_5]}{\text{change in time}} = -\frac{\Delta[N_2O_5]}{\Delta t}$$

The minus sign is required because the concentration of N_2O_5 decreases with time (that is, $\Delta[N_2O_5] = [N_2O_5](\text{final}) - [N_2O_5](\text{initial})$ is negative), and rate is always expressed as a positive quantity. Using data from Figure 15.2, the rate of disappearance of N_2O_5 between 40 min and 55 min is given by

■ **Calculating Changes** Recall that when we calculate a change in a quantity, we always do so by subtracting the initial quantity from the final quantity: $\Delta c = c_{final} - c_{initial}$.

$$\text{Rate} = -\frac{\Delta[N_2O_5]}{\Delta t} = -\frac{(1.10 \text{ mol/L}) - (1.22 \text{ mol/L})}{55 \text{ min} - 40 \text{ min}} = +\frac{0.12 \text{ mol/L}}{15 \text{ min}}$$

$$\text{Rate} = 0.0080 \frac{\text{mol } N_2O_5 \text{ consumed}}{L \cdot \text{min}}$$

Note the units for reaction rates; if concentration is expressed in mol/L, the units for rate will be mol/L · time.

During a chemical reaction, amounts of reactants decrease with time, and amounts of products increase. For the decomposition of N_2O_5, we could also express the rate either as $\Delta[NO_2]/\Delta t$ or as $\Delta[O_2]/\Delta t$. Rates based on changes in concentrations of products will have a positive sign because the concentration is increasing. Furthermore, the numerical values of rates defined in these ways will be different from value of $\Delta[N_2O_5]/\Delta t$. Note that the rate of decomposition of N_2O_5 is one half the rate of formation of NO_2 and twice the rate of formation of O_2. The relationship between these rate expressions is determined from the coefficients in the chemical equation.

$$\text{Rate of reaction} = -\frac{\Delta[N_2O_5]}{\Delta t} = +\frac{1}{2}\frac{\Delta[NO_2]}{\Delta t} = +2\frac{\Delta[O_2]}{\Delta t}$$

For the 15-minute interval between 40 and 55 minutes, the rates for the formation of NO_2 and O_2 are

$$\text{Rate} = \frac{\Delta[NO_2]}{\Delta t} = \frac{0.0080 \text{ mol } N_2O_5 \text{ consumed}}{L \cdot \text{min}} \times \frac{2 \text{ mol } NO_2 \text{ formed}}{1 \text{ mol } N_2O_5 \text{ consumed}}$$

$$= 0.016 \frac{\text{mol } NO_2 \text{ formed}}{L \cdot \text{min}}$$

$$\text{Rate} = \frac{\Delta[O_2]}{\Delta t} = \frac{0.0080 \text{ mol } N_2O_5 \text{ consumed}}{L \cdot \text{min}} \times \frac{\frac{1}{2} \text{ mol } O_2 \text{ formed}}{1 \text{ mol } N_2O_5 \text{ consumed}}$$

$$= 0.0040 \frac{\text{mol } O_2 \text{ formed}}{L \cdot \text{min}}$$

The graph of $[N_2O_5]$ versus time in Figure 15.2 does not give a straight line because the rate of the reaction changes during the course of the reaction. The concentration of N_2O_5 decreases rapidly at the beginning of the reaction but more slowly near the end. We can verify this by comparing the rate of disappearance of N_2O_5 calculated previously (the concentration decreased by 0.12 mol/L in 15 min) to the rate of reaction calculated for the time interval from 6.5 h to 9.0 h (when the concentration drops by 0.12 mol/L in 150 min). The rate in this later stage of this reaction is only one tenth of the previous value.

$$-\frac{\Delta[N_2O_5]}{\Delta t} = -\frac{(0.10 \text{ mol/L}) - (0.22 \text{ mol/L})}{540 \text{ min} - 390 \text{ min}} = +\frac{0.12 \text{ mol/L}}{150 \text{ min}}$$

$$= 0.00080 \frac{\text{mol}}{\text{L} \cdot \text{min}}$$

The procedure we have used to calculate the reaction rate gives the average rate over the chosen time interval.

We might also ask what the instantaneous rate is at a single point in time. In an automobile, the instantaneous rate can be read from the speedometer. For a chemical reaction, we can extract the instantaneous rate from the concentration–time graph by drawing a line tangent to the concentration–time curve at a particular time (see Figure 15.2). The instantaneous rate is obtained from the slope of this line. For example, when $[N_2O_5] = 0.34$ mol/L and $t = 5.0$ h, the rate is

■ **The Slope of a Line** The instantaneous rate in Figure 15.2 can be determined from an analysis of the slope of the line. See pages 39–41 for more on finding the slope of a line.

$$\text{Rate when } [N_2O_5] \text{ is } 0.34 \text{ M} = -\frac{\Delta[N_2O_5]}{\Delta t} = +\frac{0.20 \text{ mol/L}}{140 \text{ min}}$$

$$= 1.4 \times 10^{-3} \frac{\text{mol}}{\text{L} \cdot \text{min}}$$

At that particular moment in time, ($t = 5.0$ h), N_2O_5 is being consumed at a rate of 0.0014 mol/L · min.

Chemistry.⚛.Now™

Sign in at **www.cengage.com/login** and go to Chapter 15 Contents to see Screen 15.2 for a visualization of ways to express reaction rates.

■ **Reaction Rates and Stoichiometry**
For the general reaction $a A + b B \rightarrow c C + d D$, the international convention defines the reaction rate as

$$\text{Rate} = -\frac{1}{a}\frac{\Delta[A]}{\Delta t} = -\frac{1}{b}\frac{\Delta[B]}{\Delta t}$$

$$= +\frac{1}{c}\frac{\Delta[C]}{\Delta t} = +\frac{1}{d}\frac{\Delta[D]}{\Delta t}$$

■ **EXAMPLE 15.1 Relative Rates and Stoichiometry**

Problem Relate the rates for the disappearance of reactants and formation of products for the following reaction:

$$4 \text{ PH}_3(g) \rightarrow \text{P}_4(g) + 6 \text{ H}_2(g)$$

Strategy In this reaction, PH_3 disappears, and P_4 and H_2 are formed. Consequently, the value of $\Delta[PH_3]/\Delta t$ will be negative, whereas $\Delta[P_4]/\Delta t$ and $\Delta[H_2]/\Delta t$ will be positive. To relate the rates to each other, we divide $\Delta[\text{reagent}]/\Delta t$ by its stoichiometric coefficient in the balanced equation.

Solution Because four moles of PH_3 disappear for every one mole of P_4 formed, the numerical value of the rate of formation of P_4 is one fourth of the rate of disappearance of PH_3. Similarly, P_4 is formed at only one sixth of the rate that H_2 is formed.

$$-\frac{1}{4}\left(\frac{\Delta[PH_3]}{\Delta t}\right) = +\frac{\Delta[P_4]}{\Delta t} = +\frac{1}{6}\left(\frac{\Delta[H_2]}{\Delta t}\right)$$

■ **EXAMPLE 15.2 Rate of Reaction**

Problem Data collected on the concentration of dye as a function of time (see Figure 15.1) are given in the graph below. What is the average rate of change of the dye concentration over the first 2 min? What is the average rate of change during the fifth minute (from $t = 4$ min to $t = 5$ min)? Estimate the instantaneous rate at 4 min.

Strategy To find the average rate, calculate the difference in concentration at the beginning and end of a time period ($\Delta c = c_{final} - c_{initial}$) and divide by the elapsed time. To find the instantaneous rate at 4 minutes, draw a line tangent to the graph at the specified time. The negative of the slope of the line is the instantaneous rate.

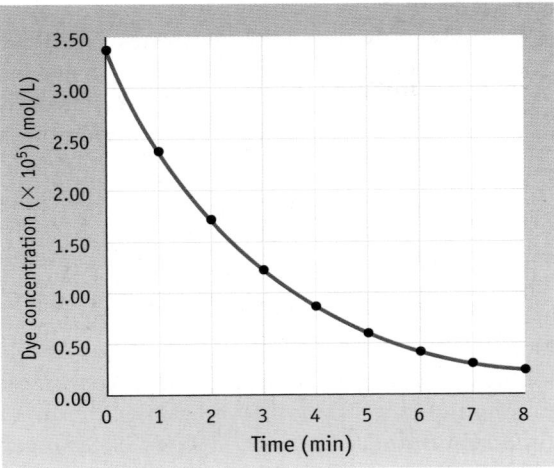

Solution The concentration of dye decreases from 3.4×10^{-5} mol/L at $t = 0$ min to 1.7×10^{-5} mol/L at $t = 2.0$ min. The average rate of the reaction in this interval of time is

$$\text{Average rate} = -\frac{\Delta[\text{Dye}]}{\Delta t} = -\frac{(1.7 \times 10^{-5} \text{ mol/L}) - (3.4 \times 10^{-5} \text{ mol/L})}{2.0 \text{ mol}}$$

$$\text{Average rate} = +\frac{8.5 \times 10^{-6} \text{ mol}}{\text{L} \cdot \text{min}}$$

The concentration of dye decreases from 0.90×10^{-5} mol/L at $t = 4.0$ min to 0.60×10^{-5} mol/L at $t = 5.0$ min. The average rate of the reaction in this interval of time is

$$\text{Average rate} = -\frac{\Delta[\text{Dye}]}{\Delta t} = -\frac{(0.60 \times 10^{-5} \text{ mol/L}) - (0.90 \times 10^{-5} \text{ mol/L})}{1.0 \text{ mol}}$$

$$\text{Average rate} = +\frac{3.0 \times 10^{-6} \text{ mol}}{\text{L} \cdot \text{min}}$$

From the slope of the line tangent to the curve, the instantaneous rate at 4 min is found to be $+3.5 \times 10^{-6}$ mol/L · min.

EXERCISE 15.1 Reaction Rates and Stoichiometry

What are the relative rates of appearance or disappearance of each product and reactant, respectively, in the decomposition of nitrosyl chloride, NOCl?

$$2 \text{ NOCl(g)} \rightarrow 2 \text{ NO(g)} + \text{Cl}_2\text{(g)}$$

EXERCISE 15.2 Rate of Reaction

Sucrose decomposes to fructose and glucose in acid solution. A plot of the concentration of sucrose as a function of time is given here. What is the rate of change of the sucrose concentration over the first 2 h? What is the rate of change over the last 2 h? Estimate the instantaneous rate at 4 h.

Chemistry.○.Now™

Sign in at **www.cengage.com/login** and go to Chapter 15 Contents to see Screen 15.2 for a self-study module on **rate of reaction**.

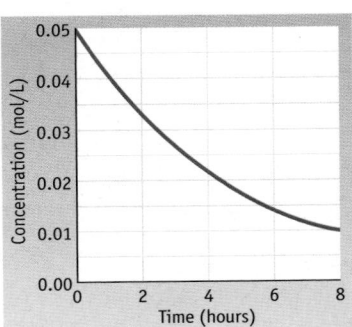

Concentration versus time for the decomposition of sucrose. (See Exercise 15.2.)

15.2 Reaction Conditions and Rate

Several factors—reactant concentrations, temperature, and presence of catalysts—affect the rate of a reaction. If the reactant is a solid, the surface area available for reaction is also a factor.

The "iodine clock reaction" (Figure 15.3) illustrates the effect of concentration and temperature. The reaction mixture contains hydrogen peroxide (H_2O_2), iodide ion (I^-), vitamin C (ascorbic acid), and starch (which is an indicator of the presence of iodine, I_2). A sequence of reactions begins with the slow oxidation of iodide ion to I_2 by H_2O_2.

$$H_2O_2(aq) + 2\ I^-(aq) + 2\ H_3O^+(aq) \rightarrow 4\ H_2O(\ell) + I_2(aq)$$

As soon as I_2 is formed in the solution, vitamin C rapidly reduces it to I^-.

$$2\ H_2O(\ell) + I_2(aq) + C_6H_8O_6(aq) \rightarrow C_6H_6O_6(aq) + 2\ H_3O^+(aq) + 2\ I^-(aq)$$

When all of the vitamin C has been consumed, I_2 remains in solution and forms a blue–black complex with starch. The time measured represents how long it has taken for the given amount of iodide ion to react. For the first experiment (A in Figure 15.3) the time required is 51 seconds. When the concentration of iodide ion is smaller (B), the time required for the vitamin C to be consumed is longer, 1 minute and 33 seconds. Finally, when the concentrations are again the same as in experiment B but the reaction mixture is heated, the reaction occurs more rapidly (56 seconds).

■ **Effect of Temperature on Reaction Rate** Cooking involves chemical reactions, and a higher temperature results in foods cooking faster. In the laboratory, reaction mixtures are often heated to make reactions occur faster.

(a) Initial Experiment. The blue color of the starch–iodine complex develops in 51 seconds.

(b) Change Concentration. The blue color of starch–iodine complex develops in 1 minute, 33 seconds when the solution is less concentrated than A.

(c) Change Temperature. The blue color of the starch–iodine complex develops in 56 seconds when the solution is the same concentration as in B but at a higher temperature.

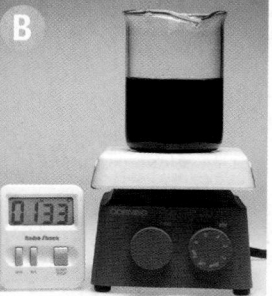

Hot bath

Solutions containing vitamin C, H_2O_2, I^-, and starch are mixed.

Smaller concentration of I^- than in Experiment A.

Same concentrations as in Experiment B, but at a higher temperature.

FIGURE 15.3 The iodine clock reaction. This reaction illustrates the effects of concentration and temperature on reaction rate. (You can do these experiments yourself with reagents available in the supermarket. For details, see S. W. Wright: "The vitamin C clock reaction," *Journal of Chemical Education*, Vol. 79, p. 41, 2002.) See ChemistryNow Screen 15.11 for a video of the iodine clock reaction.

(a)   (b)   (c)

FIGURE 15.4 Catalyzed decomposition of H_2O_2. (a) The rate of decomposition of hydrogen peroxide is increased by the catalyst MnO_2. Here, H_2O_2 (as a 30% aqueous solution) is poured onto the black solid MnO_2 and rapidly decomposes to O_2 and H_2O. Steam forms because of the high heat of reaction. (b) A bombardier beetle uses the catalyzed decomposition of H_2O_2 as a defense mechanism. The heat of the reaction lets the insect eject hot water and other irritating chemicals with explosive force. (c) A naturally occurring catalyst, called an enzyme, decomposes hydrogen peroxide. Here, the enzyme found in a potato is used to catalyze H_2O_2 decomposition, and bubbles of O_2 gas are seen rising in the solution.

Catalysts are substances that accelerate chemical reactions but are not themselves consumed. Consider the effect of a catalyst on the decomposition of hydrogen peroxide, H_2O_2, to form water and oxygen.

$$2\ H_2O_2(aq) \rightarrow O_2(g) + 2\ H_2O(\ell)$$

This decomposition is very slow; a solution of H_2O_2 can be stored for many months with only minimal change in concentration. Adding a manganese salt, an iodide-containing salt, or a biological substance called an *enzyme* causes this reaction to occur rapidly, as shown by vigorous bubbling as gaseous oxygen escapes from the solution (Figure 15.4).

The surface area of a solid reactant can also affect the reaction rate. Only molecules at the surface of a solid can come in contact with other reactants. The smaller the particles of a solid, the more molecules are found on the solid's surface. With very small particles, the effect of surface area on rate can be quite dramatic (Figure 15.5). Farmers know that explosions of fine dust particles (suspended in the air in an enclosed silo or at a feed mill) represent a major hazard.

(a)

(b)

FIGURE 15.5 The combustion of lycopodium powder. (a) The spores of this common fern burn only with difficulty when piled in a dish. (b) If the spores are ground to a fine powder and sprayed into a flame, combustion is rapid.

Chemistry ⚛ Now™

Sign in at **www.cengage.com/login** and go to Chapter 15 Contents to see:
- Screen 15.3 for a visualization of **the factors controlling rates**
- Screen 15.4 for a simulation of the **effect of concentration on rate**

15.3 Effect of Concentration on Reaction Rate

One important goal in studying the kinetics of a reaction is to determine its mechanism; that is, how the reaction occurs at the molecular level. The place to begin is to learn how concentrations of reactants affect the reaction rate.

The effect of concentration can be determined by evaluating the rate of a reaction using different concentrations of each reactant (with the temperature held constant).

Consider, for example, the decomposition of N_2O_5 to NO_2 and O_2. Figure 15.2 presented data on the concentration of N_2O_5 as a function of time. We previously calculated that, when $[N_2O_5] = 0.34$ mol/L, the instantaneous rate of disappearance of N_2O_5 is 0.0014 mol/L · min. An evaluation of the instantaneous rate of the reaction when $[N_2O_5] = 0.68$ mol/L reveals a rate of 0.0028 mol/L · min. That is, doubling the concentration of N_2O_5 doubles the reaction rate. A similar exercise shows that if $[N_2O_5]$ is 0.17 mol/L (half of 0.34 mol/L), the reaction rate is also halved. From these results, we know that the reaction rate must be directly proportional to the reactant concentration for this reaction:

$$N_2O_5 \rightarrow 2\ NO_2 + \tfrac{1}{2}\ O_2$$

$$\text{Rate of reaction} \propto [N_2O_5]$$

where the symbol $\propto$ means "proportional to."

Different relationships between reaction rate and reactant concentration are encountered in other reactions. For example, the reaction rate could be independent of concentration, or it may depend on the reactant concentration raised to some power (that is, $[\text{reactant}]^n$). If the reaction involves several reactants, the reaction rate may depend on the concentrations of each of them or on only one of them. Finally, if a catalyst is involved, its concentration may also affect the rate, as can the concentrations of products.

Rate Equations

The relationship between reactant concentration and reaction rate is expressed by an equation called a **rate equation**, or **rate law**. For the decomposition of N_2O_5 the rate equation is

$$N_2O_5(g) \rightarrow 2\ NO_2(g) + \tfrac{1}{2}\ O_2$$

$$\text{Rate of reaction} = k[N_2O_5]$$

where the proportionality constant, k, is called the **rate constant**. This rate equation tells us that this reaction rate is proportional to the concentration of the reactant. Based on this equation, we can determine that when $[N_2O_5]$ is doubled, the reaction rate doubles.

Generally, for a reaction such as

$$a\ A + b\ B \rightarrow x\ X$$

■ **Exponents on Reactant Concentrations and Reaction Stoichiometry** It is important to recognize that the exponents m and n are not necessarily the stoichiometric coefficients (a and b) for the balanced chemical equation.

the rate equation has the form

$$\text{Rate of reaction} = k[A]^m[B]^n$$

The rate equation expresses the fact that the rate of reaction is proportional to the reactant concentrations, each concentration being raised to some power. The exponents in this equation are often positive whole numbers, but they can also be negative numbers, fractions, or zero and they are determined by experiment.

If a homogeneous catalyst is present, its concentration might also be included in the rate equation, even though the catalytic species in not a product or reactant in the equation for the reaction. Consider, for example, the decomposition of hydrogen peroxide in the presence of a catalyst such as iodide ion.

$$H_2O_2(aq) \xrightarrow{\ I^-(aq)\ } H_2O(\ell) + \tfrac{1}{2}\ O_2(g)$$

Experiments show that this reaction has the following rate equation:

$$\text{Reaction rate} = k[H_2O_2][I^-]$$

Here, the concentration of I^- appears in the rate law, even though it is not involved in the balanced equation.

The Order of a Reaction

The **order** of a reaction with respect to a particular reactant is the exponent of its concentration term in the rate expression, and the **overall reaction order** is the sum of the exponents on all concentration terms. Consider, for example, the reaction of NO and Cl_2:

$$2\ NO(g) + Cl_2(g) \rightarrow 2\ NOCl(g)$$

The experimentally determined rate equation for this reaction is

$$Rate = k[NO]^2[Cl_2]$$

This reaction is second order in NO, first order in Cl_2, and third order overall. How is this related to the experimental data for the rate of disappearance of NO?

■ **The Nature of Catalysts** A catalyst does not appear as a reactant in the balanced, overall equation for the reaction, but it may appear in the rate expression. A common practice is to identify catalysts by name or symbol above the reaction arrow, as shown in the example. A homogeneous catalyst is one in the same phase as the reactants. For example, both H_2O_2 and I^- are dissolved in water.

■ **Overall Reaction Order** The overall reaction order is the sum of the reaction orders of the different reactants.

Experiment	[NO] mol/L	[Cl₂] mol/L	Rate mol/L · s
1	0.250	0.250	1.43×10^{-6}
	$\downarrow \times 2$	$\downarrow$ no change	$\downarrow \times 4$
2	0.500	0.250	5.72×10^{-6}
3	0.250	0.500	2.86×10^{-6}
4	0.500	0.500	11.4×10^{-6}

- *Compare Experiments 1 and 2:* Here, $[Cl_2]$ is held constant, and $[NO]$ is doubled. The change in $[NO]$ leads to a reaction rate increase by a factor of 4; that is, the rate is proportional to the *square* of the NO concentration.
- *Compare Experiments 1 and 3:* In experiments 1 and 3, $[NO]$ is held constant, and $[Cl_2]$ is doubled, causing the rate to double. That is, the rate is proportional to $[Cl_2]$.
- *Compare Experiments 1 and 4:* Both $[NO]$ and $[Cl_2]$ are doubled from 0.250 M to 0.500 M. From previous experiments, we know that doubling $[NO]$ should cause a four-fold increase, and doubling $[Cl_2]$ causes a two-fold increase. Therefore, doubling both concentrations should cause an eight-fold increase, as is observed ($1.43 \times 10^{-6} \times 8 = 11.4 \times 10^{-6}$ mol/L · s).

The decomposition of ammonia on a platinum surface at 856 °C is a zero order reaction.

$$NH_3(g) \rightarrow \tfrac{1}{2}\ N_2(g) + \tfrac{3}{2}\ H_2(g)$$

This means that the reaction rate is independent of NH_3 concentration.

$$Rate = k[NH_3]^0 = k$$

Reaction order is important because it gives some insight into the most interesting question of all—how the reaction occurs. This is described further in Section 15.6.

The Rate Constant, k

The rate constant, k, is a proportionality constant that relates rate and concentration at a given temperature. It is an important quantity because it enables you to find the reaction rate for a new set of concentrations. To see how to use k, consider the substitution of Cl^- ion by water in the cancer chemotherapy agent cisplatin, $Pt(NH_3)_2Cl_2$.

$$Pt(NH_3)_2Cl_2(aq) \quad + \quad H_2O(\ell) \quad \longrightarrow \quad [Pt(NH_3)_2(H_2O)Cl]^+(aq) \quad + \quad Cl^-(aq)$$

The rate law for this reaction is

$$Rate = k[Pt(NH_3)_2Cl_2]$$

and the rate constant, k, is 0.27/h at 25 °C. Knowing k allows you to calculate the rate at a particular reactant concentration—for example, when $[Pt(NH_3)_2Cl_2] = 0.018$ mol/L:

$$Rate = (0.27/h)(0.018 \text{ mol/L}) = 0.0049 \text{ mol/L} \cdot h$$

As noted, earlier, reaction rates have units of mol/L · time when concentrations are given as moles per liter. Rate constants must have units consistent with the units for the other terms in the rate equation.

- First-order reactions: the units of k are 1/time.
- Second-order reactions: the units of k are L/mol · time.
- Zero-order reaction: the units of k are mol/L · time.

■ **Some Rate Constants**

First Order	$k(1/s)$
$2 N_2O_5(g)$ $\rightarrow 4 NO_2(g) + O_2(g)$	3.38×10^{-5} at 25 °C
$C_2H_6(g) \rightarrow 2 CH_3(g)$	5.36×10^{-4} at 700 °C
Sucrose(aq, H_3O^+) $\rightarrow$ fructose(aq) + glucose(aq)	6.0×10^{-5} at 25 °C

Second Order	$k(L/mol \cdot s)$
$2 NOBr(g)$ $\rightarrow 2 NO(g) + Br_2(g)$	0.80 at 10 °C
$H_2(g) + I_2(g)$ $\rightarrow 2 HI(g)$	0.0242 at 400 °C

Determining a Rate Equation

One way to determine a rate equation is by using the "method of initial rates." The initial rate is the instantaneous reaction rate at the start of the reaction (the rate at $t = 0$). An approximate value of the initial rate can be obtained by mixing the reactants and determining $\Delta[\text{product}]/\Delta t$ or $-\Delta[\text{reactant}]/\Delta t$ after 1% to 2% of the limiting reactant has been consumed. Measuring the rate during the initial stage of a reaction is convenient because initial concentrations are known.

As an example of the determination of a reaction rate by the method of initial rates, let us consider the reaction of sodium hydroxide with methyl acetate to produce acetate ion and methanol.

$$CH_3CO_2CH_3(aq) \quad + \quad OH^-(aq) \quad \longrightarrow \quad CH_3CO_2^-(aq) \quad + \quad CH_3OH(aq)$$

Reactant concentrations and initial rates for this reaction for several experiments at 25 °C are collected in the table below.

| Experiment | Initial Concentrations (mol/L) | | Initial Reaction Rate |
	[CH₃CO₂CH₃]	[OH⁻]	(mol/L · s) at 25 °C
1	0.050 ↓ no change	0.050 ↓ × 2	0.00034 ↓ × 2
2	0.050 ↓ × 2	0.10 ↓ no change	0.00069 ↓ × 2
3	0.10	0.10	0.00137

As noted in the table, when the initial concentration of one reactant (either $CH_3CO_2CH_3$ or OH^-) is doubled while the concentration of the other reactant is held constant, the initial reaction rate doubles. This rate doubling shows that the reaction rate is directly proportional to the concentrations of both $CH_3CO_2CH_3$ and OH^-; thus, the reaction is first order in each of these reactants and second order overall. The rate law that reflects these experimental observations is

$$Rate = k[CH_3CO_2CH_3][OH^-]$$

Using this equation, we can predict that doubling both concentrations at the same time should cause the rate to go up by a factor of 4. What happens, however, if one concentration is doubled and the other is halved? The rate equation tells us the rate should not change!

If the rate equation is known, the value of k, the rate constant, can be found by substituting values for the rate and concentration into the rate equation. Using the data for the methyl acetate/hydroxide ion reaction from the first experiment, we have

$$Rate = 0.00034 \text{ mol/L} \cdot s = k(0.050 \text{ mol/L})(0.050 \text{ mol/L})$$

$$k = \frac{0.00034 \text{ mol/L} \cdot s}{(0.050 \text{ mol/L})(0.050 \text{ mol/L})} = 0.14 \text{ L/mol} \cdot s$$

Chemistry ⚛ Now™

Sign in at **www.cengage.com/login** and go to Chapter 15 Contents to see:
- Screen 15.4 for a self-study module on **control of reaction rates**
- Screen 15.5 for a simulation, a tutorial, and an exercise on **determining rate equations from a study of the effect of concentration on reaction rate**

■ EXAMPLE 15.3 Determining a Rate Equation

Problem The rate of the reaction between CO and NO_2 at 540 K

$$CO(g) + NO_2(g) \rightarrow CO_2(g) + NO(g)$$

was measured starting with various concentrations of CO and NO_2. Determine the rate equation and the value of the rate constant.

| Experiment | Initial Concentrations | | Initial Rate |
	[CO], mol/L	[NO₂], mol/L	(mol/L · h)
1	5.10×10^{-4}	0.350×10^{-4}	3.4×10^{-8}
2	5.10×10^{-4}	0.700×10^{-4}	6.8×10^{-8}
3	5.10×10^{-4}	0.175×10^{-4}	1.7×10^{-8}
4	1.02×10^{-3}	0.350×10^{-4}	6.8×10^{-8}
5	1.53×10^{-3}	0.350×10^{-4}	10.2×10^{-8}

Strategy For a reaction involving several reactants, the general approach is to keep the concentration of one reactant constant and then decide how the rate of reaction changes as the concentration of the other reagent is varied. Because the rate is proportional to the concentration of a reactant, say A, raised to some power n (the reaction order)

$$Rate \propto [A]^n$$

we can write the general equation

$$\frac{\text{Rate in experiment 2}}{\text{Rate in experiment 1}} = \frac{[A_2]^n}{[A_1]^n} = \left(\frac{[A_2]}{[A_1]}\right)^n$$

If [A] is doubled and the rate doubles from experiment 1 to experiment 2, then $n = 1$. If [A] doubles and the rate goes up by 4, then $n = 2$.

Solution In the first three experiments, the concentration of CO is held constant. In the second experiment, the NO_2 concentration has been doubled relative to Experiment 1, leading to a twofold increase in the rate. Thus, $n = 1$ and the reaction is first order in NO_2.

$$\frac{\text{Rate in experiment 2}}{\text{Rate in experiment 1}} = \frac{6.8 \times 10^{-8} \text{ mol/L} \cdot h}{3.4 \times 10^{-8} \text{ mol/L} \cdot h} = \left(\frac{0.700 \times 10^{-4}}{0.350 \times 10^{-4}}\right)^n$$
$$2 = (2)^n$$

and so $n = 1$.

This finding is confirmed by experiment 3. Decreasing $[NO_2]$ to half its original value in experiment 3 causes the rate to decrease by half.

The data in experiments 1 and 4 (with constant $[NO_2]$) show that doubling [CO] doubles the rate, and the data from experiments 1 and 5 show that tripling the concentration of CO triples the rate. These results mean that the reaction is first order in [CO]. We now know the rate equation is

$$Rate = k[CO][NO_2]$$

The rate constant, k, can be found by inserting data for one of the experiments into the rate equation. Using data from experiment 1, for example,

$$Rate = 3.4 \times 10^{-8} \text{ mol/L} \cdot h = k(5.10 \times 10^{-4} \text{ mol/L})(0.350 \times 10^{-4} \text{ mol/L})$$
$$k = 1.9 \text{ L/mol} \cdot h$$

■ EXAMPLE 15.4 Using a Rate Equation to Determine Rates

Problem Using the rate equation and rate constant determined for the reaction of CO and NO_2 at 540 K in Example 15.3, determine the initial rate of the reaction when [CO] = 3.8×10^{-4} mol/L and $[NO_2] = 0.650 \times 10^{-4}$ mol/L.

Strategy A rate equation consists of three parts: a rate, a rate constant (k), and the concentration terms. If two of these parts are known (here k and the concentrations), the third can be calculated.

Solution Substitute k (= 1.9 L/mol · h) and the concentration of each reactant into the rate law determined in Example 15.3.

$$Rate = k[CO][NO_2] = (1.9 \text{ L/mol} \cdot h)(3.8 \times 10^{-4} \text{ mol/L})(0.650 \times 10^{-4} \text{ mol/L})$$
$$Rate = 4.7 \times 10^{-8} \text{ mol/L} \cdot h$$

Comment As a check on the calculated result, it is sometimes useful to make an educated guess at the answer before carrying out the mathematical solution. We know that the reaction here is first order in both reactants. Comparing the concentration values given in this problem with the concentration values in found experiment 1 in Example 15.3, we notice that [CO] is about three fourths of the concentration value, whereas $[NO_2]$ is almost twice the value. The effects do not precisely offset each other, but we might predict that the difference in rates between this experiment and experiment 1 will be fairly small, with the rate of this experiment being just a little greater. The calculated value bears this out.

EXERCISE 15.3 Determining a Rate Equation

The initial rate of the reaction of nitrogen monoxide and oxygen

$$2\ NO(g) + O_2(g) \rightarrow 2\ NO_2(g)$$

was measured at 25 °C for various initial concentrations of NO and O_2. Determine the rate equation from these data. What is the value of the rate constant, *k*, and what are its units?

	Initial Concentrations (mol/L)		Initial Rate
Experiment	[NO]	$[O_2]$	(mol/L · s)
1	0.020	0.010	0.028
2	0.020	0.020	0.057
3	0.020	0.040	0.114
4	0.040	0.020	0.227
5	0.010	0.020	0.014

EXERCISE 15.4 Using Rate Laws

The rate constant, *k*, at 25 °C is 0.27/h for the reaction

$$Pt(NH_3)_2Cl_2(aq) + H_2O(\ell) \rightarrow [Pt(NH_3)_2(H_2O)Cl]^+(aq) + Cl^-(aq)$$

and the rate equation is

$$\text{Rate} = k[Pt(NH_3)_2Cl_2]$$

Calculate the rate of reaction when the concentration of $Pt(NH_3)_2Cl_2$ is 0.020 M.

15.4 Concentration–Time Relationships: Integrated Rate Laws

Module 20

It is often important for a chemist to know how long a reaction must proceed to reach a predetermined concentration of some reactant or product, or what the reactant and product concentrations will be after some time has elapsed. A mathematical equation that relates time and concentration—that is, an equation that describes concentration–time curves like the one shown in Figure 15.2—can be used to determine this information. With such an equation, we could calculate the concentration at any given time or the length of time needed for a given amount of reactant to react.

First-Order Reactions

Suppose the reaction "R → products" is first order. This means the reaction rate is directly proportional to the concentration of R raised to the first power, or, mathematically,

$$-\frac{\Delta[R]}{\Delta t} = k[R]$$

Using calculus, this relationship can be transformed into a very useful equation called an **integrated rate equation** (because integral calculus is used in its derivation).

$$\ln\frac{[R]_t}{[R]_0} = -kt \qquad (15.1)$$

Qualitatively, the rate of a reaction is easy to understand: it represents the change in concentration of the reactants and products. When we deal with rates of reaction quantitatively, however, we need to be specific about the reaction stoichiometry.

Consider the first order decomposition of N_2O_5, a reaction that we mentioned earlier

$$2\ N_2O_5 \rightarrow 4\ NO_2 + O_2(g)$$

The rate of the reaction can be expressed (and measured in lab) as the change in concentration of either reactants or products as a function of time. The numerical values of the rates of formation of reactants and products are related, but they are different because of the reaction stoichiometry. If we equate the rate of reaction to the rate of appearance of O_2, we would write

$$\text{Rate} = \frac{\Delta\left[O_2\right]}{\Delta t} = -\frac{1}{2}\frac{\Delta\left[N_2O_5\right]}{\Delta t} = +\frac{1}{4}\frac{\Delta\left[NO_2\right]}{\Delta t}$$

This relation is written by dividing each rate by its stoichiometric coefficient (◀ page 674).

There are two different pieces of information in the equation above. First, it gives the relationship between the rates of change of concentrations of reactants and products. Based on the reaction stoichiometry, we know that the rate of appearance of O_2 is one half the rate of disappearance of N_2O_5 and one fourth the rate of NO_2 appearance.

Second, this equation specifically defines what we mean by rate; it provides a single, numerical values for this parameter; and it tells us how to calculate the value of reaction rate from experimental data. If we were to follow the disappearance of N_2O_5 as a measure of reaction rate and base our definition of rate on the stoichiometry above, we should write the following differential form of the rate law.

$$\text{Rate} = -\frac{1}{2}\frac{\Delta\left[N_2O_5\right]}{\Delta t} = k\left[N_2O_5\right]$$

From this definition, it follows that the differential rate equation is

$$\text{Rate} = -\frac{\Delta\left[N_2O_5\right]}{\Delta t} = 2k\left[N_2O_5\right]$$

the integrated rate equation is (see page 683),

$$\ln\frac{\left[N_2O_5\right]_t}{\left[N_2O_5\right]_0} = -2kt$$

and the half-life equation is

$$t_{1/2} = 0.693/2k$$

We can also write the equation for N_2O_5 decomposition as follows:

$$N_2O_5 \rightarrow 2\ NO_2 + \tfrac{1}{2}\ O_2(g)$$

Following the reasoning above, the rate laws for the reaction written this way would be:

Differential rate equation:

$$-\frac{\Delta\left[N_2O_5\right]}{\Delta t} = k'\left[N_2O_5\right]$$

Integrated rate equation:

$$\ln\frac{\left[N_2O_5\right]_t}{\left[N_2O_5\right]_0} = -k't$$

Half-life equation:

$$t_{1/2} = 0.693/k'$$

Note that the differential and integrated rate laws derived based on the two different chemical equations have the same form, but k and k' do not have the same values. In this case, $2k = k'$.

For more on this issue, see K. T. Quisenberry and J. Tellinghuisen, *Journal of Chemical Education*, Vol. 83, pp. 510–512, 2006.

■ **Initial and Final Time, t** The time $t = 0$ does not need to correspond to the actual beginning of the experiment. It can be the time when instrument readings were started, for example, even though the reaction may have already begun.

Here, $[R]_0$ and $[R]_t$ are concentrations of the reactant at time $t = 0$ and at a later time, t, respectively. The ratio of concentrations, $[R]_t/[R]_0$, is the fraction of reactant that remains after a given time has elapsed. In words, the equation says

$$\text{Natural logarithm}\left(\frac{\text{concentration of R after some time}}{\text{concentration of R at start of experiment}}\right)$$
$$= \ln(\text{fraction of R remaining at time, } t)$$
$$= -(\text{rate constant})(\text{elapsed time})$$

Notice the negative sign in the equation. The ratio $[R]_t/[R]_0$ is less than 1 because $[R]_t$ is always less than $[R]_0$; the reactant R is consumed during the reaction. This means the logarithm of $[R]_t/[R]_0$ is negative, so the other side of the equation must also bear a negative sign.

Equation 15.1 can be used to carry out the following calculations:

- If $[R]_t/[R]_0$ is measured in the laboratory after some amount of time has elapsed, then k can be calculated.
- If $[R]_0$ and k are known, then the concentration of material remaining after a given amount of time ($[R]_t$) can be calculated.
- If k is known, then the time elapsed until a specific fraction ($[R]_t/[R]_0$) remains can be calculated.

Finally, notice that k for a first-order reaction is independent of concentration; k has units of time^{-1} (y^{-1} or s^{-1}, for example). This means we can choose any convenient unit for $[R]_t$ and $[R]_0$: moles per liter, moles, grams, number of atoms, number of molecules, or gas pressure.

Chemistry ⚛ Now™

Sign in at **www.cengage.com/login** and go to Chapter 15 Contents to see Screen 15.6 for a tutorial on **the use of the integrated first-order rate equation.**

■ **EXAMPLE 15.5 The First-Order Rate Equation**

Problem In the past, cyclopropane, C_3H_6, was used in a mixture with oxygen as an anesthetic. (This practice has almost ceased today, because the compound is flammable.) When heated, cyclopropane rearranges to propene in a first-order process.

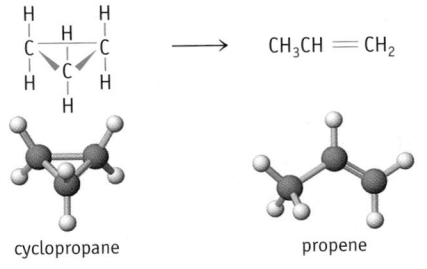

cyclopropane   propene

Rate = k[cyclopropane] k = 2.42 h^{-1} at 500 °C

If the initial concentration of cyclopropane is 0.050 mol/L, how much time (in hours) must elapse for its concentration to drop to 0.010 mol/L?

Strategy The reaction is first order in cyclopropane. You know the rate constant, k, and the initial and final concentrations. Use Equation 15.1 to calculate the time (t) elapsed to reach a concentration of 0.010 mol/L.

Solution Values for [cyclopropane]$_t$, [cyclopropane]$_0$, and k are substituted into Equation 15.1; t (time) is the unknown:

$$\ln\dfrac{\left[0.010\right]}{\left[0.050\right]} = (2.42\ \text{h}^{-1})t$$

$$t = \dfrac{-\ln(0.20)}{2.42\ \text{h}^{-1}} = \dfrac{-(-1.61)}{2.42\ \text{h}^{-1}} = \boxed{0.665\ \text{h}}$$

Comment Cycloalkanes with fewer than five carbon atoms are strained because the C—C—C bond angles cannot match the preferred 109.5°. Because of ring strain, the cyclopropane ring opens readily to form propene.

■ **EXAMPLE 15.6 Using the First-Order Rate Equation**

Problem Hydrogen peroxide decomposes in a dilute sodium hydroxide solution at 20 °C in a first-order reaction:

$H_2O_2(aq) \rightarrow H_2O(\ell) + \frac{1}{2} O_2(g)$

Rate = $k[H_2O_2]$ with k = 1.06 × 10^{-3} min^{-1}

What is the fraction remaining after 100. min if the initial concentration of H_2O_2 is 0.020 mol/L? What is the concentration of the peroxide after 100. min?

Strategy Because the reaction is first order in H_2O_2, we use Equation 15.1. Here, $[H_2O_2]_0$, k, and t are known, and we are asked to find the value of $[H_2O_2]_t$ and the fraction remaining. Recall that

$$\dfrac{\left[R\right]_t}{\left[R\right]_0} = \text{fraction remaining}$$

Once this value is known, and knowing $[H_2O_2]_0$, we can calculate $[H_2O_2]_t$.

Solution Substitute the known values into Equation 15.1.

$$\ln \frac{[H_2O_2]_t}{[H_2O_2]_0} = -kt = -(1.06 \times 10^{-3} \text{ min}^{-1})(100. \text{ min})$$

$$\ln \frac{[H_2O_2]_t}{[H_2O_2]_0} = -0.106$$

Taking the antilogarithm of -0.106 [i.e., the inverse of $\ln(-0.106)$ or $e^{-0.106}$], we find the fraction remaining to be 0.90.

$$\text{Fraction remaining} = \frac{[H_2O_2]_t}{[H_2O_2]_0} = \boxed{0.90}$$

Because $[H_2O_2]_0 = 0.020$ mol/L, this gives $\boxed{[H_2O_2]_t = 0.018 \text{ mol/L.}}$

EXERCISE 15.5 Using the First-Order Rate Equation

Sucrose, a sugar, decomposes in acid solution to give glucose and fructose. The reaction is first order in sucrose, and the rate constant at 25 °C is $k = 0.21$ h^{-1}. If the initial concentration of sucrose is 0.010 mol/L, what is its concentration after 5.0 h?

EXERCISE 15.6 Using the First-Order Rate Equation

Gaseous azomethane ($CH_3N_2CH_3$) decomposes to ethane and nitrogen when heated:

$$CH_3N_2CH_3(g) \rightarrow CH_3CH_3(g) + N_2(g)$$

The disappearance of azomethane is a first-order reaction with $k = 3.6 \times 10^{-4}$ s^{-1} at 600 K.

(a) A sample of gaseous $CH_3N_2CH_3$ is placed in a flask and heated at 600 K for 150 s. What fraction of the initial sample remains after this time?

(b) How long must a sample be heated so that 99% of the sample has decomposed?

Chemistry.Now™

Sign in at **www.cengage.com/login** and go to Chapter 15 Contents to see Screen 15.6 for a self-study module on the **first-order rate equation.**

Second-Order Reactions

Suppose the reaction "R → products" is second order. The rate equation is

$$-\frac{\Delta[R]}{\Delta t} = k[R]^2$$

Using calculus, this relationship can be transformed into the following equation that relates reactant concentration and time:

$$\frac{1}{[R]_t} - \frac{1}{[R]_0} = kt \tag{15.2}$$

The same symbolism used with first-order reactions applies: $[R]_0$ is the concentration of reactant at the time $t = 0$; $[R]_t$ is the concentration at a later time; and k is the second-order rate constant which has the units of L/mol · time.

EXAMPLE 15.7 **Using the Second-Order Integrated Rate Equation**

Problem The gas-phase decomposition of HI

$$HI(g) \rightarrow \tfrac{1}{2} H_2(g) + \tfrac{1}{2} I_2(g)$$

has the rate equation

$$-\frac{\Delta[HI]}{\Delta t} = k[HI]^2$$

where $k = 30.$ L/mol $\cdot$ min at 443 °C. How much time does it take for the concentration of HI to drop from 0.010 mol/L to 0.0050 mol/L at 443 °C?

Strategy Substitute the values of $[HI]_0$, $[HI]_t$, and k into Equation 15.2, and solve for the unknown, t.

Solution Here, $[HI]_0 = 0.010$ mol/L and $[HI]_t = 0.0050$ mol/L. Using Equation 15.2, we have

$$\frac{1}{0.0050 \text{ mol/L}} - \frac{1}{0.010 \text{ mol/L}} = (30. \text{ L/mol} \cdot \text{min})t$$

$$(2.0 \times 10^2 \text{ L/mol}) - (1.0 \times 10^2 \text{ L/mol}) = (30. \text{ L/mol} \cdot \text{min})t$$

$$t = \boxed{3.3 \text{ min}}$$

EXERCISE 15.7 **Using the Second-Order Integrated Rate Law Equation**

Using the rate constant for HI decomposition given in Example 15.7, calculate the concentration of HI after 12 min if $[HI]_0 = 0.010$ mol/L.

Zero-Order Reactions

If a reaction (R → products) is zero order, the rate equation is

$$-\frac{\Delta[R]}{\Delta t} = k[R]^0$$

This equation leads to the integrated rate equation

$$[R]_0 - [R]_t = kt \qquad \textbf{(15.3)}$$

where the units of k are mol/L $\cdot$ s.

Graphical Methods for Determining Reaction Order and the Rate Constant

We can derive a convenient way to determine the order of a reaction and its rate constant using graphical methods. Equations 15.1, 15.2, and 15.3, if rearranged slightly, have the form $y = mx + b$. This is the equation for a straight line, where m is the slope of the line and b is the y-intercept. In these equations, $x = t$ in each case.

Zero order	First order	Second order
$[R]_t = -kt + [R]_0$	$\ln [R]_t = -kt + \ln [R]_0$	$\dfrac{1}{[R]_t} = +kt + \dfrac{1}{[R]_0}$
$y \quad mx \quad b$	$y \quad mx \quad b$	$y \quad mx \quad b$

■ **Finding the Slope of a Line** See pages 39-41 for a description of methods for finding the slope of a line.

t(s)	$P \times 10^2$ atm	ln P
0	8.20	−2.50
1000	5.72	−2.86
2000	3.99	−3.22
3000	2.78	−3.58
4000	1.94	−3.94

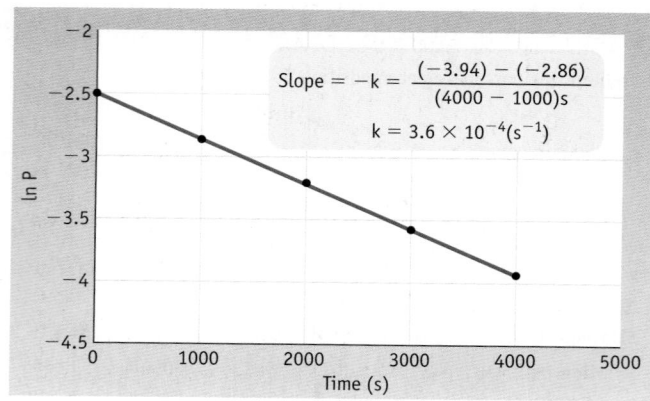

As an example of the graphical method for determining reaction order, consider the decomposition of azomethane.

$$CH_3N_2CH_3(g) \rightarrow CH_3CH_3(g) + N_2(g)$$

The decomposition of azomethane was followed at 600 K by observing the decrease in its partial pressure with time (Figure 15.6). (Recall from Chapter 11 that pressure is proportional to concentration at a given temperature and volume.) The third column lists values of ln $P(CH_3N_2CH_3)$. A plot of pressure vs. time for a first-order reaction is a curved line (see Figure 15.2). As shown in Figure 15.6, however, a graph of ln $P(CH_3N_2CH_3)$ versus time produces a straight line, showing that the reaction is first order in $CH_3N_2CH_3$. The slope of the line can be measured, and the negative of the slope equals the rate constant for the reaction, 3.6×10^{-4} s^{-1}.

The decomposition of NO_2 is a second-order process.

$$NO_2(g) \rightarrow NO(g) + \tfrac{1}{2} O_2(g)$$

$$\text{Rate} = k[NO_2]^2$$

This fact can be verified by showing that a plot of $1/[NO_2]$ versus time is a straight line (Figure 15.7). Here, the slope of the line is equal to k.

For a zero-order reaction (Figure 15.8), a plot of concentration vs. time gives a straight line with a slope equal to the negative of the rate constant.

FIGURE 15.7 A second-order reaction. A plot of $1/[NO_2]$ versus time for the decomposition of NO_2,

$$NO_2(g) \rightarrow NO(g) + \tfrac{1}{2} O_2(g)$$

results in a straight line. This confirms that this is a second-order reaction. The slope of the line equals the rate constant for this reaction.

Time (min)	$[NO_2]$ (mol/L)	$1/[NO_2]$ (L/mol)
0	0.020	50
0.50	0.015	67
1.0	0.012	83
1.5	0.010	100
2.0	0.0087	115

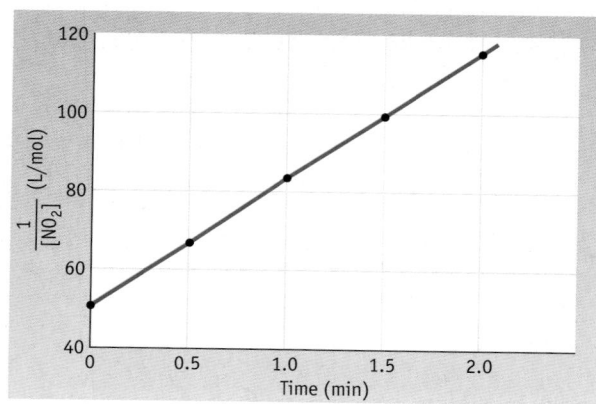

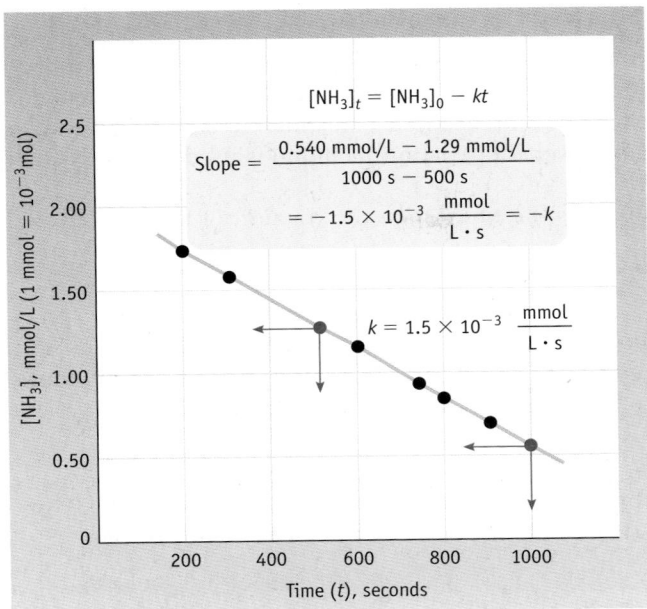

FIGURE 15.8 **Plot of a zero-order reaction.** A graph of the concentration of ammonia, $[NH_3]_t$, against time for the decomposition of NH_3.

$$2\,NH_3(g) \rightarrow N_2(g) + 3\,H_2(g)$$

on a metal surface at 856 °C is a straight line, indicating that this is a zero-order reaction. The rate constant, k, for this reaction is found from the slope of the line; $k = -\text{slope}$. (The points chosen to calculate the slope are given in red.)

Table 15.1 summarizes the relationships between concentration and time for first-, second-, and zero-order processes.

Chemistry.❁.Now™

Sign in at **www.cengage.com/login** and go to Chapter 15 Contents to see Screen 15.7 for a tutorial on **graphical methods.**

EXERCISE 15.8 Using Graphical Methods

Data for the decomposition of N_2O_5 in a particular solvent at 45 °C are as follows:

$[N_2O_5]$, mol/L	t, min
2.08	3.07
1.67	8.77
1.36	14.45
0.72	31.28

Plot $[N_2O_5]$, ln $[N_2O_5]$, and $1/[N_2O_5]$ versus time, t. What is the order of the reaction? What is the rate constant for the reaction?

TABLE 15.1 Characteristic Properties of Reactions of the Type "R $\longrightarrow$ Products"

Order	Rate Equation	Integrated Rate Equation	Straight-Line Plot	Slope	k Units
0	$-\Delta[R]/\Delta t = k[R]^0$	$[R]_0 - [R]_t = kt$	$[R]_t$ vs. t	$-k$	mol/L · time
1	$-\Delta[R]/\Delta t = k[R]^1$	$\ln([R]_t/[R]_0) = -kt$	$\ln[R]_t$ vs. t	$-k$	time^{-1}
2	$-\Delta[R]/\Delta t = k[R]^2$	$(1/[R]_t) - (1/[R]_0) = kt$	$1/[R]_t$ vs. t	k	L/mol · time

Half-Life and First-Order Reactions

The **half-life**, $t_{1/2}$, of a reaction is the time required for the concentration of a reactant to decrease to one half its initial value. Half-life is a convenient way to describe the rate at which a reactant is consumed in a chemical reaction: The longer the half-life, the slower the reaction. Half-life is used primarily when dealing with first-order processes.

The half-life, $t_{1/2}$, is the time when the fraction of the reactant R remaining is

$$[R]_t = \tfrac{1}{2}[R]_0 \quad \text{or} \quad \frac{[R]_t}{[R]_0} = \tfrac{1}{2}$$

Here, $[R]_0$ is the initial concentration, and $[R]_t$ is the concentration after the reaction is half completed. To evaluate $t_{1/2}$ for a first-order reaction, we substitute $[R]_t/[R]_0 = \tfrac{1}{2}$ and $t = t_{1/2}$ into the integrated first-order rate equation (Equation 15.1),

$$\ln\left(\tfrac{1}{2}\right) = -kt_{1/2} \quad \text{or} \quad \ln 2 = kt_{1/2}$$

Rearranging this equation (and calculating that $\ln 2 = 0.693$) provides a useful equation that relates half-life and the first-order rate constant:

$$t_{1/2} = \frac{0.693}{k} \tag{15.4}$$

This equation identifies an important feature of first-order reactions: $t_{1/2}$ *is independent of concentration.*

To illustrate the concept of half-life, consider again the first-order decomposition of azomethane, $CH_3N_2CH_3$.

$$CH_3N_2CH_3(g) \rightarrow CH_3CH_3(g) + N_2(g)$$

$$\text{Rate} = k[CH_3N_2CH_3] \text{ with } k = 3.6 \times 10^{-4}\ s^{-1} \text{ at 600 K}$$

Given a rate constant of $3.6 \times 10^{-4}\ s^{-1}$, we calculate a half-life of 1.9×10^3 s or 32 min.

$$t_{1/2} = \frac{0.693}{3.6 \times 10^{-4}\ s^{-1}} = 1.9 \times 10^3\ s$$

The partial pressure of azomethane has been plotted as a function of time in Figure 15.9, and this graph shows that P(azomethane) decreases by half every 32 minutes. The initial pressure was 820 mm Hg, but it dropped to 410 mm Hg in 32 minutes, and then dropped to 205 mm Hg in another 32 minutes. That is, after two half-lives (64 min), the pressure is $(\tfrac{1}{2}) \times (\tfrac{1}{2}) = (\tfrac{1}{2})^2 = \tfrac{1}{4}$ or 25% of the initial pressure. After three half-lives, the pressure has dropped further to 102 mm Hg or 12.5% of the initial value and equal to $(\tfrac{1}{2}) \times (\tfrac{1}{2}) \times (\tfrac{1}{2}) = (\tfrac{1}{2})^3 = \tfrac{1}{8}$ of the initial value.

It can be hard to visualize whether a reaction is fast or slow from the rate constant value. Can you tell from the rate constant, $k = 3.6 \times 10^{-4}\ s^{-1}$, whether the azomethane decomposition will take seconds, hours, or days to reach completion? Probably not, but this is easily assessed from the value of the half-life for the reaction (32 min). Now we know that we would only have to wait a few hours for the reactant to be essentially consumed.

Chemistry ·○· Now™

Sign in at **www.cengage.com/login** and go to Chapter 15 Contents to see Screen 15.8 for tutorials on **using half-life.**

■ **Half-Life and Radioactivity** Hâlf-life is a term often encountered when dealing with radioactive elements. Radioactive decay is a first-order process, and half-life is commonly used to describe how rapidly a radioactive element decays. See Chapter 23 and Example 15.9.

■ **Half-Life Equations for Other Reaction Orders**
For a zero-order reaction, R → products

$$t_{1/2} = \frac{[R]_0}{2k}$$

For a second-order reaction, R → products

$$t_{1/2} = \frac{1}{k[R]_0}$$

Note that in both cases the half-life depends on the initial concentration.

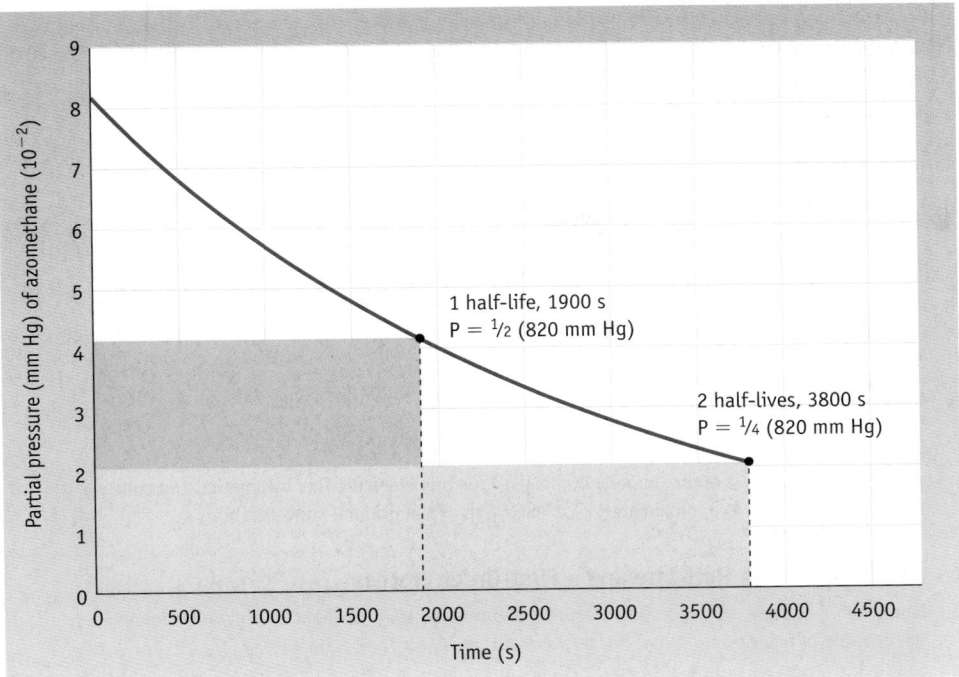

Active Figure 15.9 **Half-life of a first-order reaction.** The curve is a plot of the pressure of $CH_3N_2CH_3$ as a function of time. (The compound decomposes to CH_3CH_3 and N_2 with $k = 3.6 \times 10^{-4}$ s^{-1}). The pressure of $CH_3N_2CH_3$ is halved every 1900 s (32 min). (This plot of pressure versus time is similar in shape to plots of concentration versus time for all other first-order reactions.)

Chemistry .Ọ. Now™ Sign in at www. cengage.com/login and go to the Chapter Contents menu to explore an interactive version of this figure accompanied by an exercise.

EXAMPLE 15.8 Half-Life and a First-Order Process

Problem Sucrose, $C_{12}H_{22}O_{11}$, decomposes to fructose and glucose in acid solution with the rate law

Rate $= k[C_{12}H_{22}O_{11}]$ $k = 0.216$ h^{-1} at 25 °C

(a) What is the half-life of $C_{12}H_{22}O_{11}$ at this temperature?

(b) What amount of time is required for 87.5% of the initial concentration of $C_{12}H_{22}O_{11}$ to decompose?

Strategy (a) The decomposition of $C_{12}H_{22}O_{11}$ is first order in this compound, so Equation 15.4 can be used to calculate the half-life. (b) After 87.5% of the $C_{12}H_{22}O_{11}$ has decomposed, 12.5% (or one-eighth of the sample) remains. To reach this point, three half-lives are required.

Half-Life	Fraction Remaining
1	0.5
2	0.25
3	0.125

Therefore, we calculate the half-life from Equation 15.4 and then multiply by 3.

Solution

(a) The half-life for the reaction is

$$t_{1/2} = 0.693/k = 0.693/(0.216 \text{ h}^{-1}) = 3.21 \text{ h}$$

(b) Three half-lives must elapse before the fraction remaining is 0.125, so

Time elapsed $= 3 \times 3.21$ h $=$ **9.63 h**

EXAMPLE 15.9 Half-Life and First-Order Processes

Problem Radioactive radon-222 gas (^{222}Rn) from natural sources can seep into the basement of a home. The half-life of ^{222}Rn is 3.8 days. Assume that the radon gas is trapped in the basement and cannot escape. If a basement has 4.0×10^{13} atoms of ^{222}Rn per liter of air initially, how many atoms of ^{222}Rn per liter will remain after one month (30 days)?

Strategy Using Equation 15.1, and knowing the number of atoms at the beginning ($[R]_0$), the elapsed time (30 days), and the rate constant, we can calculate the number of atoms remaining ($[R]_t$). First, the rate constant, k, must be found from the half-life using Equation 15.4.

Solution The rate constant, k, is

$$k = \frac{0.693}{t_{1/2}} = \frac{0.693}{3.8 \text{ d}} = 0.18 \text{ d}^{-1}$$

Now use Equation 15.1 to calculate the number of atoms remaining after 30. days.

$$\ln \frac{[Rn]_t}{4.0 \times 10^{13} \text{ atom/L}} = -(0.18 \text{ d}^{-1})(30. \text{ d}) = -5.5$$

$$\frac{[Rn]_t}{4.0 \times 10^{13} \text{ atom/L}} = e^{-5.5} = 0.0042$$

$$[Rn]_t = 1.7 \times 10^{11} \text{ atom/L}$$

Comment Thirty days is approximately 8 half-lives for this element. This means that the concentration at the end of the month is approximately $(1/2)^8$ or $1/256$th of the original concentration.

EXERCISE 15.9 Half-Life and a First-Order Process

Americium is used in smoke detectors and in medicine for the treatment of certain malignancies. One isotope of americium, ^{241}Am, has a rate constant, k, for radioactive decay of 0.0016 y^{-1}. In contrast, radioactive iodine-125, which is used for studies of thyroid functioning, has a rate constant for decay of 0.011 d^{-1}.

(a) What are the half-lives of these isotopes?

(b) Which isotope decays faster?

(c) If you are given a dose of iodine-125 containing 1.6×10^{15} atoms, how many atoms remain after 2.0 days?

15.5 A Microscopic View of Reaction Rates

Throughout this book, we have turned to the particulate level of chemistry to understand chemical phenomena. Rates of reaction are no exception. Looking at the way reactions occur at the atomic and molecular levels can provide some insight into the various influences on rates of reactions.

Let us review the macroscopic observations we have made so far concerning reaction rates. We know that there are wide differences in rates of reactions—from very fast reactions like the explosion that occurs when hydrogen and oxygen are exposed to a spark or flame (Figure 1.18), to slow reactions like the formation of rust that occur over days, weeks, or years. For a specific reaction, factors that influence reaction rate include the concentrations of the reactants, the temperature of the reaction system, and the presence of catalysts. Let us look at each of these influences in more depth.

Concentration, Reaction Rate, and Collision Theory

Consider the gas-phase reaction of nitric oxide and ozone:

$$NO(g) + O_3(g) \rightarrow NO_2(g) + O_2(g)$$

The rate law for this product-favored reaction is first order in each reactant: Rate = $k[NO][O_3]$. How can this reaction have this rate law?

Let us consider the reaction at the particulate level and imagine a flask containing a mixture of NO and O_3 molecules in the gas phase. Both kinds of molecules are in rapid and random motion within the flask. They strike the walls of the vessel and collide with other molecules. For this or any other reaction to occur, the **collision theory of reaction rates** states that three conditions must be met:

1. The reacting molecules must collide with one another.
2. The reacting molecules must collide with sufficient energy to initiate the process of breaking and forming bonds.
3. The molecules must collide in an orientation that can lead to rearrangement of the atoms and the formation of products.

We shall discuss each of these conditions within the context of the effects of concentration and temperature on reaction rate.

To react, molecules must collide with one another. It is reasonable to propose that the rate of their reaction be related to the number of collisions, which is in turn related to their concentrations (Figure 15.10). Doubling the concentration of one reagent in the NO + O_3 reaction, say NO, will lead to twice the number of molecular collisions. Figure 15.10a shows a single molecule of one of the reactants (NO) moving randomly among sixteen O_3 molecules. In a given time period, it might collide with two O_3 molecules. The number of NO—O_3 collisions will double, however, if the concentration of NO molecules is doubled (to 2, as shown in Figure 15.10b) or if the number of O_3 molecules is doubled (to 32, as in Figure 15.10c). Thus, we can explain the dependence of reaction rate on concentration: The number of collisions between the two reactant molecules is directly proportional to the concentration of each reactant, and the rate of the reaction shows a first-order dependence on each reactant.

Chemistry ·Ọ· Now™

Sign in at **www.cengage.com/login** and go to Chapter 15 Contents to see Screen 15.9 for a visualization of **collision theory** and for tutorials on **using half-life.**

Temperature, Reaction Rate, and Activation Energy

In a laboratory or in the chemical industry, a chemical reaction is often carried out at elevated temperature because this allows the reaction to occur more rapidly. Conversely, it is sometimes desirable to lower the temperature to slow down a chemical reaction (to avoid an uncontrollable reaction or a potentially dangerous explosion). Chemists are very aware of the effect of temperature on the rate of a reaction.

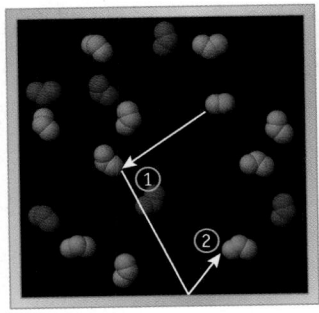

(a) 1 NO : 16 O_3 — *2 hits/second*

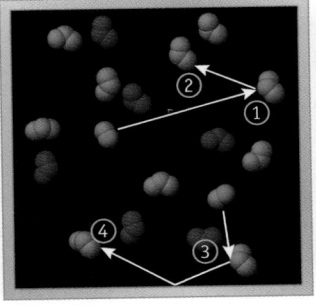

(b) 2 NO : 16 O_3 — *4 hits/second*

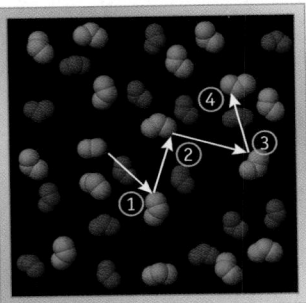

(c) 1 NO : 32 O_3 — *4 hits/second*

FIGURE 15.10 The effect of concentration on the frequency of molecular collisions. (a) A single NO molecule, moving among sixteen O_3 molecules, is shown colliding with two of them per second. (b) If two NO molecules move among 16 O_3 molecules, we would predict that four NO—O_3 collisions would occur per second. (c) If the number of O_3 molecules is doubled (to 32), the frequency of NO—O_3 collisions is also doubled, to four per second.

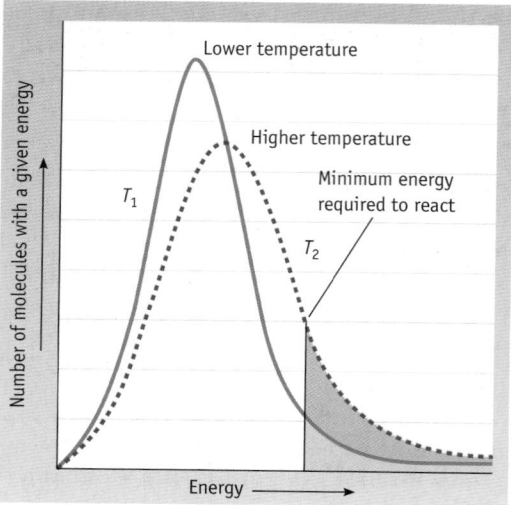

FIGURE 15.11 Energy distribution curve. The vertical axis gives the relative number of molecules possessing the energy indicated on the horizontal axis. The graph indicates the minimum energy required for an arbitrary reaction. At a higher temperature, a larger fraction of the molecules have sufficient energy to react. (Recall Figure 11.14, the Boltzmann distribution function, for a collection of gas molecules.)

A discussion of the effect of temperature on reaction rate begins with reference to distribution of energies for molecules in a sample of a gas or liquid. Recall from studying gases and liquids that the molecules in a sample have a wide range of energies, described earlier as a Boltzmann distribution of energies (◀ Figure 11.14). In any sample of a gas or liquid, some molecules have very low energies; others have very high energies; but most have some intermediate energy. As the temperature increases, the average energy of the molecules in the sample increases, as does the fraction having higher energies (Figure 15.11).

Activation Energy

Molecules require some minimum energy to react. Chemists visualize this as an energy barrier that must be surmounted by the reactants for a reaction to occur (Figure 15.12). The energy required to surmount the barrier is called the **activation energy, E_a.** If the barrier is low, the energy required is low, and a high proportion of the molecules in a sample may have sufficient energy to react. In such a case, the reaction will be fast. If the barrier is high, the activation energy is high, and only a few reactant molecules in a sample may have sufficient energy. In this case, the reaction will be slow.

To illustrate an activation energy barrier, consider the conversion of NO_2 and CO to NO and CO_2 or the reverse reaction (Figure 15.13). At the molecular level, we imagine that the reaction involves the transfer of an O atom from an NO_2 molecule to a CO molecule (or, in the reverse reaction, the transfer of an O atom from CO_2 to NO).

$$NO_2(g) + CO(g) \rightleftharpoons NO(g) + CO_2(g)$$

We can describe this process by using an energy diagram or **reaction coordinate** diagram. The horizontal axis describes the reaction progress as the reaction proceeds, and the vertical axis represents the potential energy of the system during the reaction. When NO_2 and CO approach and O atom transfer begins, an N—O bond is being broken, and a C=O bond is forming. Energy input (the activation energy) is required for this to occur. The energy of the system reaches a maximum at the **transition state**. At the transition state, sufficient energy has been concentrated in the appropriate bonds; bonds in the reactants can now break, and new bonds can form

FIGURE 15.12 An analogy to chemical activation energy. For the volleyball to go over the net, the player must give it sufficient energy.

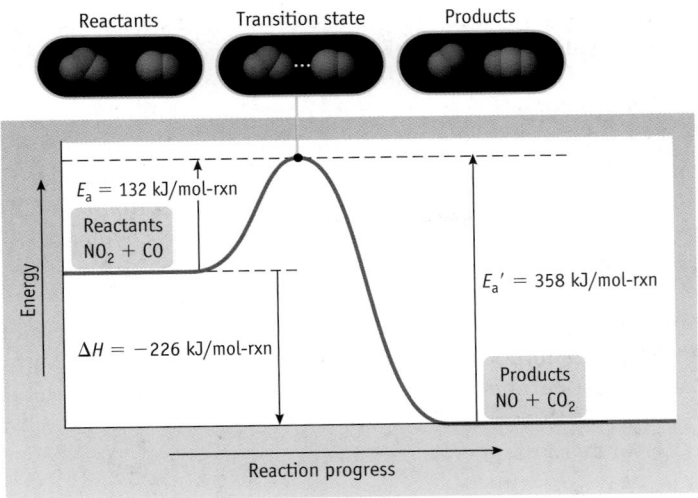

Active Figure 15.13 **Activation Energy.** The reaction of NO_2 and CO (to give NO and CO_2) has an activation energy barrier of 132 kJ/mol-rxn. The reverse reaction ($NO + CO_2 \rightarrow NO_2 + CO$) requires 358 kJ/mol-rxn. The net energy change for the reaction of NO_2 and CO is -226 kJ/mol-rxn.

Chemistry $\dot{\circ}$ Now™ Sign in at www.cengage.com/login and go to the Chapter Contents menu to explore an interactive version of this figure accompanied by an exercise.

to give products. The system is poised to go on to products. Alternatively, it can return to the reactants. Because the transition state is at a maximum in potential energy, it cannot be isolated. Using computer molecular modeling techniques, however, chemists can describe what the transition state must look like.

In the $NO_2 + CO$ reaction, 132 kJ/mol is required to reach the transition state; that is, the top of the energy barrier. As the reaction continues toward the products—as the N—O bond is finally broken and a C=O bond forms—the reaction evolves energy, 358 kJ/mol-rxn. The net energy change involved in this exothermic reaction is -226 kJ/mol-rxn.

$$\Delta U = +132 \text{ kJ/mol-rxn} + (-358 \text{ kJ/mol-rxn}) = -226 \text{ kJ/mol-rxn}$$

What happens if NO and CO_2 are mixed to form NO_2 and CO? Now the reaction requires 358 kJ/mol-rxn to reach the transition state, and 132 kJ/mol-rxn is evolved on proceeding to the product, NO_2 and CO. The reaction in this direction is endothermic, requiring an input of $+226$ kJ/mol-rxn.

Chemistry $\dot{\circ}$ Now™

Sign in at **www.cengage.com/login** and go to Chapter 15 Contents to see Screen 15.10 for a simulation of reaction coordinate diagrams.

Effect of a Temperature Increase

The conversion of NO_2 and CO to products at room temperature is slow because only a small fraction of the molecules have enough energy to reach the transition state. The rate can be increased by heating the sample. Raising the temperature increases the reaction rate by increasing the fraction of molecules with enough energy to surmount the activation energy barrier (Figure 15.11).

Effect of Molecular Orientation on Reaction Rate

Having a sufficiently high energy is necessary, but it is not sufficient to ensure that reactants will form products. The reactant molecules must also come together in the correct orientation. For the reaction of NO_2 and CO, we can imagine that the transition state structure has one of the O atoms of NO_2 beginning to bind to the

C atom of CO in preparation for O atom transfer (Figure 15.13). The lower the probability of achieving the proper alignment, the smaller the value of k, and the slower the reaction.

Imagine what happens when two or more complicated molecules collide. In only a small fraction of the collisions will the molecules come together in exactly the right orientation. Thus, only a tiny fraction of the collisions can be effective. No wonder some reactions are slow. Conversely, it is amazing that so many are fast!

The Arrhenius Equation

The observation that reaction rates depend on the energy and frequency of collisions between reacting molecules, on the temperature, and on whether the collisions have the correct geometry is summarized by the **Arrhenius equation**:

$$k = \text{rate constant} = Ae^{-E_a/RT}$$

Frequency factor

Fraction of molecules with minimum energy for reaction

(15.5)

In this equation, k is the rate constant, where R is the gas constant with a value of 8.314510×10^{-3} kJ/K · mol, and T is the kelvin temperature. The parameter A is called the **frequency factor**, and it has units of L/mol · s. It is related to the number of collisions and to the fraction of collisions that have the correct geometry; A is specific to each reaction and is temperature dependent. The factor $e^{-E_a/RT}$ represents *the fraction of molecules having the minimum energy required for reaction*; its value is always less than 1. As the table in the margin shows, this fraction changes significantly with temperature.

The Arrhenius equation has significant uses.

- It can be used to calculate E_a from the temperature, dependence of the rate constant.
- It can be used to calculate the rate constant for a given temperature, if E_a and A are known.

If rate constants of a given reaction are measured at several temperatures then one can apply graphical techniques to determine the activation energy of a reaction. Taking the natural logarithm of each side of Equation 15.5, we have

$$\ln k = \ln A + \left(-\frac{E_a}{RT}\right)$$

Rearranging this expression slightly shows that $\ln k$ and $1/T$ are related linearly.

$$\ln k = -\frac{E_a}{R}\left(\frac{1}{T}\right) + \ln A \qquad \leftarrow \text{Arrhenius equation}$$

$$\downarrow \qquad \downarrow \qquad \downarrow$$

$$y \quad = \quad mx \quad + b \qquad \leftarrow \text{Equation for straight line}$$

(15.6)

This means that, if the natural logarithm of k ($\ln k$) is plotted versus $1/T$, the result is a downward-sloping straight line with a slope of $(-E_a/R)$. The activation energy, E_a, can be obtained from the slope of this line.

■ Interpreting the Arrhenius Equation
(a) The exponential term. This gives the fraction of molecules having sufficient energy for reaction and is a function of T.

Temperature (K)	Value of $e^{-E_a/RT}$ for $E_a = $ 40 kJ/mol-rxn
298	9.7×10^{-8}
400	5.9×10^{-6}
600	3.3×10^{-4}

(b) Significance of A. Although a complete understanding of A goes beyond the level of this text, it can be noted that A becomes smaller as the reactants become larger. It reflects the fact that reacting molecules must come together in the appropriate geometry.

Chemistry Now™

Sign in at **www.cengage.com/login** and go to Chapter 15 Contents to see Screen 15.11 for a simulation and tutorials on **the temperature dependence of reaction rates** and the **Arrhenius equation.**

A Closer Look

Reaction Coordinate Diagrams

Reaction coordinate diagrams (Figure 15.13) convey a great deal of information. A reaction that would have an energy diagram like that in Figure 15.13 is the substitution of a halogen atom of CH_3Cl by an ion such as F^-. Here, the F^- ion attacks the molecule from the side opposite the Cl substituent. As F^- begins to form a bond to carbon, the C—Cl bond weakens, and the CH_3 portion of the molecule changes shape. As time progresses, the products CH_3F and Cl^- are formed.

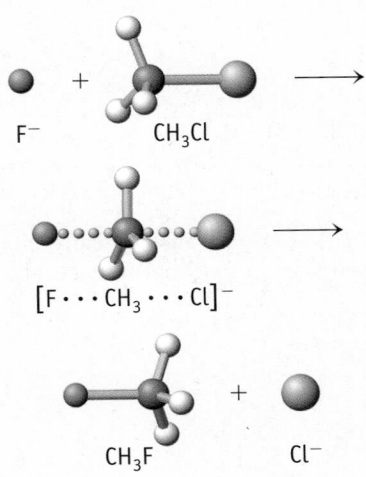

F^- + CH_3Cl →

$[F \cdots CH_3 \cdots Cl]^-$ →

CH_3F + Cl^-

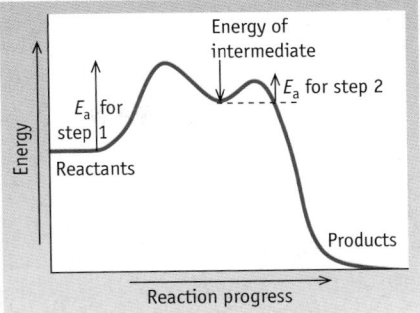

FIGURE A A reaction coordinate diagram for a two-step reaction, a process involving an intermediate.

The diagram in Figure A describes a reaction that occurs in two steps. An example of such a reaction is the substitution of the —OH group on methanol by a halide ion in the presence of acid. In the first step, an H^+ ion attaches to the O of the C—O—H group in a rapid, reversible reaction. The energy of this protonated species, $CH_3OH_2^+$, a reaction intermediate, is higher than the energies of the reactants and is represented by the dip in the curve shown in Figure A. In the second step, a halide ion, say Br^-, attacks the intermediate to produce methyl bromide, CH_3Br, and water. There is an activation energy barrier in both the first step and second step.

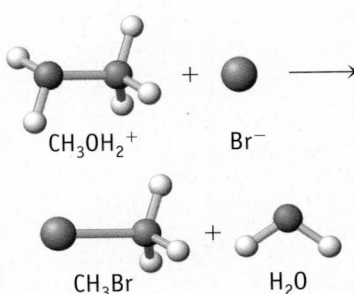

CH_3OH + H_3O^+ ⇌

$CH_3OH_2^+$ + H_2O

$CH_3OH_2^+$ + Br^- →

CH_3Br + H_2O

Notice in Figure A, as in Figure 15.13, that the energy of the products is lower than the energy of the reactants. The reaction is exothermic.

■ **EXAMPLE 15.10 Determination of E_a from the Arrhenius Equation**

Problem Using the experimental data shown in the table, calculate the activation energy E_a for the reaction

$$2\ N_2O(g) \rightarrow 2\ N_2(g) + O_2(g)$$

Experiment	Temperature (K)	k (L/mol · s)
1	1125	11.59
2	1053	1.67
3	1001	0.380
4	838	0.0011

15.5 | A Microscopic View of Reaction Rates **697**

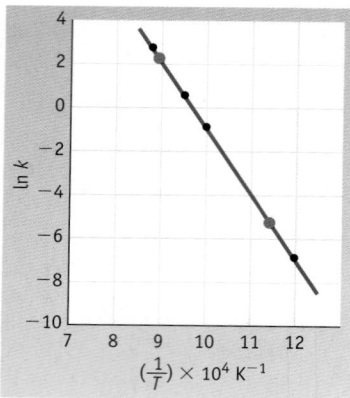

FIGURE 15.14 Arrhenius plot.
A plot of ln k versus $1/T$ for the reaction $2 N_2O(g) \rightarrow 2 N_2(g) + O_2(g)$. The slope of the line gives E_a. See Example 15.10.

Strategy To solve this problem graphically, we first need to calculate ln k and $1/T$ for each data point. These data are then plotted, and E_a is calculated from the resulting straight line (slope $= -E_a/R$).

Solution First, calculate $1/T$ and ln k.

Experiment	$1/T$ (K^{-1})	ln k
1	8.889×10^{-4}	2.4501
2	9.497×10^{-4}	0.513
3	9.990×10^{-4}	−0.968
4	11.9×10^{-4}	−6.81

Plotting these data gives the graph shown in Figure 15.14. Choosing the large blue points on the graph, the slope is found to be

$$\text{Slope} = \frac{\Delta \ln k}{\Delta(1/T)} = \frac{2.0 - (-5.6)}{(9.0 - 11.5)(10^{-4})K^{-1}} = -3.0 \times 10^4 \text{ K}$$

The activation energy is evaluated from the slope.

$$\text{Slope} = -\frac{E_a}{R} = -3.0 \times 10^4 \text{ K} = -\frac{E_a}{8.31 \times 10^{-3} \text{ kJ/K} \cdot \text{mol}}$$

$$E_a = 250 \text{ kJ/mol-rxn}$$

The activation energy, E_a, for a reaction can be obtained algebraically if k is known at two different temperatures. We can write an equation for each set of these conditions:

$$\ln k_1 = -\left(\frac{E_a}{RT_1}\right) + \ln A \quad \text{or} \quad \ln k_2 = -\left(\frac{E_a}{RT_2}\right) + \ln A$$

If one of these equations is subtracted from the other, we have

$$\ln k_2 - \ln k_1 = \ln \frac{k_2}{k_1} = -\frac{E_a}{R}\left[\frac{1}{T_2} - \frac{1}{T_1}\right] \qquad \text{(15.7)}$$

Example 15.11 demonstrates the use of this equation.

EXAMPLE 15.11 Calculating E_a Numerically

Problem Use values of k determined at two different temperatures to calculate the value of E_a for the decomposition of HI:

$$2 HI(g) \rightarrow H_2(g) + I_2(g)$$

$$k_1 = 2.15 \times 10^{-8} \text{ L/(mol} \cdot \text{s) at } 6.50 \times 10^2 \text{ K (T}_1)$$

$$k_2 = 2.39 \times 10^{-7} \text{ L/(mol} \cdot \text{s) at } 7.00 \times 10^2 \text{ K (T}_2)$$

Strategy Use Equation 15.7.

Solution

$$\ln \frac{2.39 \times 10^{-7} \text{ L/(mol} \cdot \text{s)}}{2.15 \times 10^{-8} \text{ L/(mol} \cdot \text{s)}} = -\frac{E_a}{8.315 \times 10^{-3} \text{ kJ/K} \cdot \text{mol}} \times \left[\frac{1}{7.00 \times 10^2 \text{ K}} - \frac{1}{6.50 \times 10^2 \text{ K}}\right]$$

Solving this equation gives $E_a = 180$ kJ/mol-rxn.

Comment Another way to write the difference in fractions in brackets is

$$\left[\frac{1}{T_2} - \frac{1}{T_1}\right] = \frac{T_1 - T_2}{T_1 T_2}$$

This expression is often easier to use.

■ **E_a, Reaction Rates, and Temperature**
A often-used rule of thumb is that reaction rates double for every 10 °C rise in temperature in the vicinity of room temperature.

Effect of Catalysts on Reaction Rate

Catalysts are substances that speed up the rate of a chemical reaction. We have seen several examples of catalysts in earlier discussions in this chapter: MnO_2, iodide ion, an enzyme in a potato, and hydroxide ion all catalyze the decomposition of hydrogen peroxide (Figure 15.4). In biological systems, catalysts called enzymes influence the rates of most reactions (page 702).

Catalysts are not consumed in a chemical reaction. They are, however, intimately involved in the details of the reaction at the particulate level. Their function is to provide a different pathway with a lower activation energy for the reaction. To illustrate how a catalyst participates in a reaction, let us consider the isomerization of *cis*-2-butene, to the slightly more stable isomer, *trans*-2-butene.

cis-2-butene   Transition state   trans-2-butene

End rotates

π bond breaks

The activation energy for the uncatalyzed conversion is relatively large— 264 kJ/mol-rxn—because the π bond must be broken to allow one end of the molecule to rotate into a new position. Because of the high activation energy, this is a slow reaction, and rather high temperatures are required for it to occur at a reasonable rate.

The *cis*- to *trans*-2-butene reaction is greatly accelerated by a catalyst, iodine. In the presence of iodine, this reaction can be carried out at a temperature several hundred degrees lower than for the uncatalyzed reaction. Iodine is not consumed (nor is it a product), and it does not appear in the overall balanced equation. It does appear in the reaction rate law, however; the rate of the reaction depends on the square root of the iodine concentration:

$$\text{Rate} = k[\textit{cis-}2\text{-butene}][I_2]^{1/2}$$

The presence of I_2 changes the way the reaction occurs; that is, it changes the mechanism of the reaction (Figure 15.15). The best hypothesis is that iodine molecules first dissociate to form iodine atoms (Step 1). An iodine atom then adds to one of the C atoms of the C=C double bond (Step 2). This converts the double bond between the carbon atoms to a single bond (the π bond is broken) and allows the ends of the molecule to twist freely relative to each other (Step 3). If the iodine atom then dissociates from the intermediate, the double bond can re-form

■ **Enzymes: Biological Catalysts** Catalase is an enzyme whose function is to speed up the decomposition of hydrogen peroxide. This enzyme ensures that hydrogen peroxide, which is highly toxic, does not build up in the body.

■ **Catalysts and the Economy** "One third of [the] material gross national product in the U.S. involves a catalytic process somewhere in the production chain." (Quoted in A. Bell, *Science*, Vol. 299, page 1688, 2003.)

■ **Butene Isomerization** Isomerization of *cis*-2-butene is a first order process with the rate law "Rate = k[*cis*-2-butene]." It is suggested to occur by rotation around the carbon–carbon double bond. The rate at which a molecule will isomerize is related to the fraction of molecules that have a high enough energy. (See ChemistryNow Screen 15.8 to view an animation of the interconversion of butene isomers and the energy barrier for the process.)

FIGURE 15.15 The mechanism of the iodine-catalyzed isomerization of *cis*-2-butene. *Cis*-2-butene is converted to *trans*-2-butene in the presence of a catalytic amount of iodine. Catalyzed reactions are often pictured in such diagrams to emphasize what chemists refer to as a "catalytic cycle."

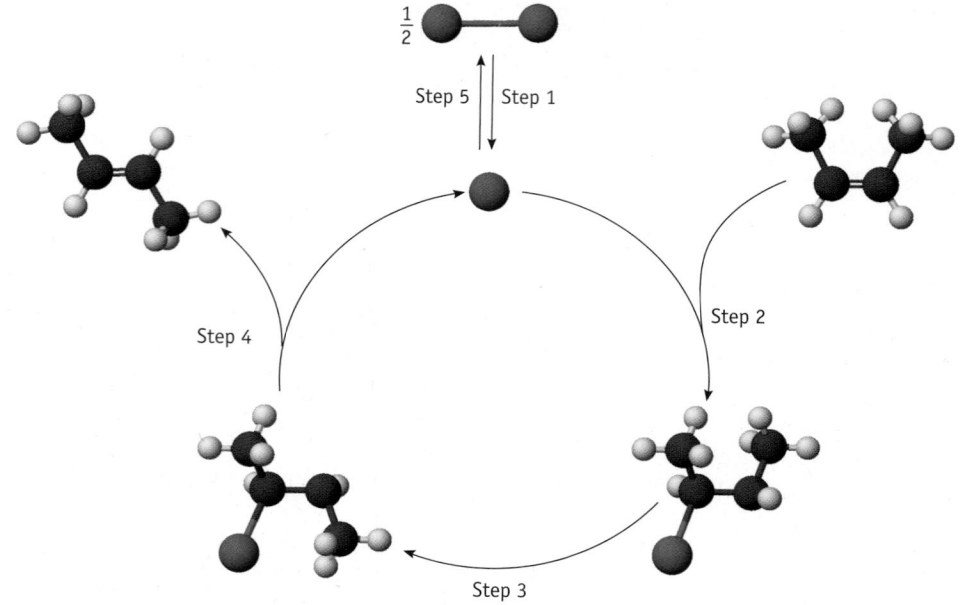

in the *trans* configuration (Step 4). The iodine atom catalyzing the rotation is now free to add to another molecule of *cis*-2-butene. The result is a kind of chain reaction, as one molecule of *cis*-2-butene after another is converted to the *trans* isomer. The chain is broken if the iodine atom recombines with another iodine atom to re-form molecular iodine.

An energy profile for the catalyzed reaction (Figure 15.16) shows that the overall energy barrier is much lower than for the uncatalyzed reaction. Five separate steps are identified for the mechanism in the energy profile. This proposed mechanism also includes a series of chemical species called **reaction intermediates,** species formed in one step of the reaction and consumed in a later step. Iodine atoms are intermediates, as are the free radical species formed when an iodine atom adds to *cis*-2-butene.

FIGURE 15.16 Energy profile for the iodine-catalyzed reaction of *cis*-2-butene. A catalyst accelerates a reaction by altering the mechanism so that the activation energy is lowered. With a smaller barrier to overcome, more reacting molecules have sufficient energy to surmount the barrier, and the reaction occurs more rapidly. The energy profile for the uncatalyzed conversion of *cis*-2-butene to *trans*-2-butene is shown by the black curve, and that for the iodine-catalyzed reaction is represented by the red curve. Notice that the shape of the barrier has changed because the mechanism has changed.

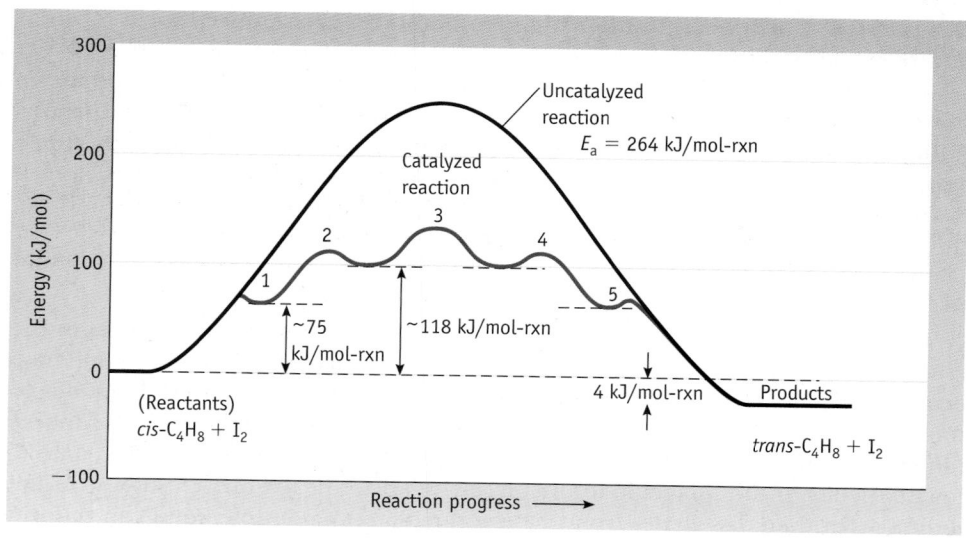

Five important points are associated with this mechanism:

- Iodine molecules, I_2, dissociate to atoms and then re-form. On the macroscopic level, the concentration of I_2 is unchanged. Iodine does not appear in the balanced, stoichiometric equation even though it appears in the rate equation. This is generally true of catalysts.
- Both the catalyst I_2 and the reactant *cis*-2-butene are in the gas phase. If a catalyst is present in the same phase as the reacting substance, it is called a *homogeneous catalyst*.
- Iodine atoms and the radical species formed by addition of an iodine atom to a 2-butene molecule are intermediates.
- The activation energy barrier to reaction is significantly lower because the mechanism changed. Dropping the activation energy from 264 kJ/mol-rxn for the uncatalyzed reaction to about 150 kJ/mol-rxn for the catalyzed process makes the catalyzed reaction 10^{15} times faster!
- The diagram of energy-versus-reaction progress has five energy barriers (five humps appear in the curve). This feature in the diagram means that the reaction occurs in a series of five steps.

What we have described here are reaction mechanisms. The uncatalyzed isomerization reaction of *cis*-2-butene is a one-step reaction mechanism, whereas the catalyzed mechanism involves a series of steps. We shall discuss reaction mechanisms in more detail in the next section.

Chemistry .Ö.Now™

Sign in at **www.cengage.com/login** and go to Chapter 15 Contents to see Screen 15.14 for tutorials on **using half-life various catalysts**, a visualization of **the effect of a catalyst on activation energy**, an interview of a scientist describing **catalyst use in industry**, two exercises on **reaction mechanisms and the effect of catalysts**, and a video exercise on **catalysis**.

15.6 Reaction Mechanisms

Rate laws help us understand **reaction mechanisms**, the sequence of bond-making and bond-breaking steps that occurs during the conversion of reactants to products. We want to analyze the changes that molecules undergo when they react. We then want to relate this description back to the macroscopic world, to the experimental observations of reaction rates.

Based on the rate equation for a reaction, and by applying chemical intuition, chemists can often make an educated guess about the mechanism for a reaction. In some reactions, the conversion of reactants to products in a single step is envisioned as the logical mechanism. For example, the uncatalyzed isomerization of *cis*-2-butene to *trans*-2-butene is best described as a single-step reaction (Figure 15.16).

Most chemical reactions occur in a sequence of steps, however. A multiple-step mechanism was proposed for the iodine-catalyzed 2-butene isomerization reaction. Another example of a reaction that occurs in several steps is the reaction of bromine and NO:

$$Br_2(g) + 2\ NO \rightarrow 2\ BrNO(g)$$

A single-step reaction would require that three reactant molecules collide simultaneously in just the right orientation. The probability of this occurring is small; thus, it would be reasonable to look for a mechanism that occurs in a series of steps, with each step involving only one or two molecules. In one possible mechanism, Br_2 and NO might combine in an initial step to produce an intermediate species,

■ **Rate Laws and Mechanisms** Rate laws are derived by experiment; they are macroscopic observations. Mechanisms are schemes we propose that speculate on how reactions occur at the particulate level.

Within any living organism, there are untold numbers of chemical reactions occurring, many of them extremely rapidly. In many cases, enzymes, natural catalysts, speed up reactions that would normally move at a snail's pace from reactants to products. Typically, enzymes give reaction rates 10^7 to 10^{14} times faster than the uncatalyzed rate.

Enzymes are typically large proteins, often containing metal ions such as Zn^{2+}. They are thought to function by bringing the reactants together in just the right orientation in a site where specific bonds can be broken and/or made.

Carbonic anhydrase is one of many enzymes important in biological processes (Figure A). Carbon dioxide dissolves in water to a small extent to produce carbonic acid, which ionizes to give H_3O^+ and HCO_3^- ions.

$$CO_2(g) \rightleftharpoons CO_2(aq) \qquad \textbf{(1)}$$

$$CO_2(aq) + H_2O(\ell) \rightleftharpoons H_2CO_3(aq) \qquad \textbf{(2)}$$

$$H_2CO_3(aq) + H_2O(\ell)$$
$$\rightleftharpoons H_3O^+(aq) + HCO_3^-(aq) \qquad \textbf{(3)}$$

Carbonic anhydrase speeds up reactions 1 and 2. Many of the H_3O^+ ions produced by ionization of H_2CO_3 (reaction 3) are picked up by hemoglobin in the blood as hemoglobin loses O_2. The resulting HCO_3^- ions are transported back to the lungs. When hemoglobin again takes on O_2, it releases H_3O^+ ions. These ions and HCO_3^- re-form H_2CO_3, from which CO_2 is liberated and exhaled.

You can do an experiment that illustrates the effect of carbonic anhydrase. First, add a small amount of NaOH to a cold, aqueous solution of CO_2. The solution becomes basic immediately because there is not enough H_2CO_3 in the solution to use up the NaOH. After some seconds, however, dissolved CO_2 slowly produces more H_2CO_3, which consumes NaOH, and the solution is again acidic.

Now try the experiment again, this time adding a few drops of blood to the solution (Figure A). Carbonic anhydrase in blood speeds up reactions 1 and 2 by a factor of about 10^7, as evidenced by the more rapid reaction under these conditions.

In 1913, Leonor Michaelis and Maud L. Menten proposed a general theory of enzyme action based on kinetic observations. They assumed that the substrate, S (the reactant), and the enzyme, E, form a complex, ES. This complex then breaks down, releasing the enzyme and the product, P.

$$E + S \rightleftharpoons ES$$

$$ES \rightarrow P$$

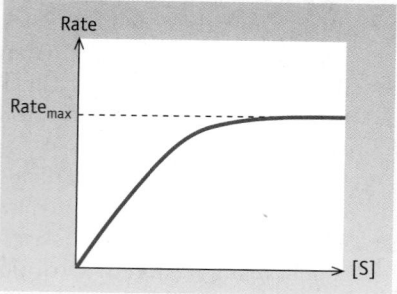

FIGURE B Rate of enzyme catalyzed reaction. This plot of substrate concentration [S] versus reaction velocity is typical of reactions catalyzed by enzymes and following the Michaelis–Menten model.

When the substrate concentration is low, the rate of the reaction is first order in S (Figure B). As [S] increases, however, the active sites in the enzyme become saturated with substrate, and the rate reaches its maximum value. Now the kinetics are zero order in substrate.

Questions:

1. Catalase can decompose hydrogen peroxide to O_2 and water about 10^7 times faster than the uncatalyzed reaction. If the latter requires one year, how much time is required by the enzyme-catalyzed reaction?

2. According to the Michaelis–Menten model, if 1/Rate is plotted versus 1/[S], the intercept of the plot (when 1/[S] = 0) is $1/Rate_{max}$. Find $Rate_{max}$ for a reaction involving carbonic anhydrase.

[S], mol/L	Rate (millimoles/min)
2.500	0.588
1.00	0.500
0.714	0.417
0.526	0.370
0.250	0.256

Answers to these questions are in Appendix Q.

(a) $t = 0$ (b) $t = 3$ sec (c) $t = 15$ sec (d) $t = 17$ sec (e) $t = 21$ sec

Photos: Charles D. Winters

FIGURE A CO_2 in water. (a) A few drops of blood are added to a cold solution of CO_2 in water. (b) A few drops of a dye (bromthymol blue) are added to the solution, the yellow color indicating an acidic solution. (c and d) A less-than-stoichiometric amount of sodium hydroxide is added, converting the H_2CO_3 to HCO_3^- (and CO_3^{2-}). The blue color of the dye indicates a basic solution. (e) The blue color begins to fade after some seconds as CO_2 forms more H_2CO_3. The amount of H_2CO_3 formed is finally sufficient to consume the added NaOH, and the solution is again acidic. Blood is a source of the enzyme carbonic anhydrase, so the last steps are noticeably more rapid than the reaction in the absence of blood.

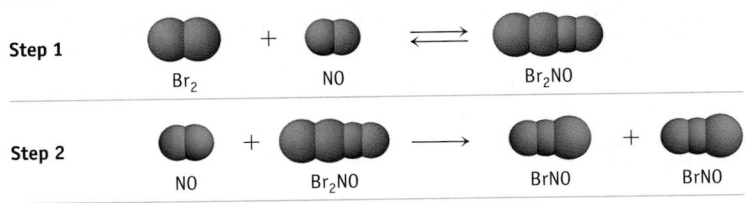

Br_2NO (Figure 15.17). This intermediate would then react with another NO molecule to give the reaction products. The equation for the overall reaction is obtained by adding the equations for these two steps:

Step 1.	$Br_2(g) + NO(g) \rightleftharpoons Br_2NO(g)$
Step 2.	$Br_2NO(g) + NO(g) \rightarrow 2\ BrNO(g)$
Overall Reaction:	$Br_2(g) + 2\ NO(g) \rightarrow 2\ BrNO(g)$

Each step in a multistep reaction sequence is an **elementary step**, defined by a chemical equation that describes a single molecular event such as the formation or rupture of a chemical bond resulting from a molecular collision. Each step has its own activation energy, E_a, and rate constant, k. Adding the equations for each step must give the balanced equation for the overall reaction, and the time required to complete all of the steps defines the overall reaction rate. The series of steps constitutes a possible reaction mechanism.

Mechanisms of reactions are usually postulated starting with experimental data. To see how this is done, we first describe three types of elementary steps in terms of the concept of *molecularity*.

Molecularity of Elementary Steps

Elementary steps are classified by the number of reactant molecules (or ions, atoms, or free radicals) that come together. This whole, positive number is called the **molecularity** of the elementary step. When one molecule is the only reactant in an elementary step, the reaction is a **unimolecular** process. A **bimolecular** elementary process involves two molecules, which may be identical (A + A → products) or different (A + B → products). The mechanism proposed for the decomposition of ozone in the stratosphere illustrates the use of these terms.

Step 1.	Unimolecular	$O_3(g) \rightarrow O_2(g) + O(g)$
Step 2.	Bimolecular	$O_3(g) + O(g) \rightarrow 2\ O_2(g)$
Overall Reaction:		$2\ O_3(g) \rightarrow 3\ O_2(g)$

A **termolecular** elementary step involves three molecules, which could be the same or different (3 A → products; 2 A + B → products; or A + B + C → products). Be aware, however, the simultaneous collision of three molecules has a low probability, unless one of the molecules involved is in high concentration, such as a solvent molecule. In fact, most termolecular processes involve the collision of two reactant molecules and a third, inert molecule. The function of the inert molecule is to absorb the excess energy produced when a new chemical bond is formed by the first two molecules. For example, N_2 is unchanged in a termolecular reaction between oxygen molecules and oxygen atoms that produces ozone in the upper atmosphere:

$$O(g) + O_2(g) + N_2(g) \rightarrow O_3(g) + \text{energetic } N_2(g)$$

The probability that four or more molecules will simultaneously collide with sufficient kinetic energy and proper orientation to react is so small that reaction molecularities greater than three are never proposed.

Rate Equations for Elementary Steps

The experimentally determined rate equation for a reaction cannot be predicted from its overall stoichiometry. In contrast, the rate equation for any elementary step is defined by the reaction stoichiometry. The rate equation of an elementary step is given by the product of the rate constant and the concentrations of the reactants in that step. We can therefore write the rate equation for any elementary step, as shown by examples in the following table:

Elementary Step	Molecularity	Rate Equation
A → product	unimolecular	Rate = $k[A]$
A + B → product	bimolecular	Rate = $k[A][B]$
A + A → product	bimolecular	Rate = $k[A]^2$
2 A + B → product	termolecular	Rate = $k[A]^2[B]$

For example, the rate laws for each of the two steps in the decomposition of ozone are

$$\text{Rate for (unimolecular) Step 1} = k[O_3]$$

$$\text{Rate for (bimolecular) Step 2} = k'[O_3][O]$$

When a reaction mechanism consists of two elementary steps, the two steps will likely occur at different rates. The two rate constants (k and k' in this example) are not expected to have the same value (nor the same units, if the two steps have different molecularities).

Molecularity and Reaction Order

A unimolecular elementary step must be first order; a bimolecular elementary step must be second order; and a termolecular elementary step must be third order. Such a direct relation between molecularity and order is emphatically not true for a multistep reaction. If you learn from an experiment that a reaction is first order, you cannot conclude that it occurs in a single, unimolecular elementary step. Similarly, a second-order rate equation does not imply that the reaction occurs in a single, bimolecular elementary step. An illustration of this is the decomposition of N_2O_5:

$$2\ N_2O_5(g) \rightarrow 4\ NO_2(g) + O_2(g)$$

Here, the rate law is "Rate = $k[N_2O_5]$," but chemists are fairly certain the mechanism involves a series of unimolecular and bimolecular steps.

To see how the experimentally observed rate equation for the overall reaction is connected with a possible mechanism or sequence of elementary steps requires some chemical intuition. We will provide only a glimpse of the subject in the next section.

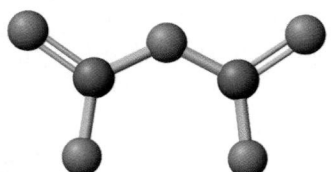

N_2O_5 Decomposition. The first step in the decomposition of N_2O_5 is thought to be the cleavage of one of the N—O bonds in the N—O—N link to give the odd-electron molecules NO_2 and NO_3. These react further to give the final products.

Chemistry Now™

Sign in at **www.cengage.com/login** and go to Chapter 15 Contents to see:
• Screen 15.12 for exercises on **reaction mechanisms**
• Screen 15.13 for exercises on **reaction mechanisms**

Problem The hypochlorite ion undergoes self-oxidation–reduction to give chlorate, ClO_3^-, and chloride ions.

$$3\ ClO^-(aq) \rightarrow ClO_3^-(aq) + 2\ Cl^-(aq)$$

This reaction is thought to occur in two steps:

Step 1: $\quad ClO^-(aq) + ClO^-(aq) \rightarrow ClO_2^-(aq) + Cl^-(aq)$

Step 2: $\quad ClO_2^-(aq) + ClO^-(aq) \rightarrow ClO_3^-(aq) + Cl^-(aq)$

What is the molecularity of each step? Write the rate equation for each reaction step. Show that the sum of these reactions gives the equation for the net reaction.

Strategy The molecularity is the number of ions or molecules involved in a reaction step. The rate equation involves the concentration of each ion or molecule in an elementary step, raised to the power of its stoichiometric coefficient.

Solution Because two ions are involved in each elementary step, each step is bimolecular. The rate equation for any elementary step involves the product of the concentrations of the reactants. Thus, in this case, the rate equations are

Step 1: $\quad$ Rate $= k[ClO^-]^2$

Step 2: $\quad$ Rate $= k'[ClO_2^-][ClO^-]$

From the equations for the two elementary steps, we see that the ClO_2^- ion is an intermediate, a product of the first step and a reactant in the second step. It therefore cancels out, and we are left with the stoichiometric equation for the overall reaction:

Step 1: $\quad ClO^-(aq) + ClO^-(aq) \rightarrow ClO_2^-(aq) + Cl^-(aq)$

Step 2: $\quad ClO_2^-(aq) + ClO^-(aq) \rightarrow ClO_3^-(aq) + Cl^-(aq)$

Sum of steps: $\quad 3\ ClO^-(aq) \rightarrow ClO_3^-(aq) + 2\ Cl^-(aq)$

EXERCISE 15.11 **Elementary Steps**

Nitrogen monoxide is reduced by hydrogen to give nitrogen and water:

$$2\ NO(g) + 2\ H_2(g) \rightarrow N_2(g) + 2\ H_2O(g)$$

One possible mechanism for this reaction is

$$2\ NO(g) \rightarrow N_2O_2(g)$$

$$N_2O_2(g) + H_2(g) \rightarrow N_2O(g) + H_2O(g)$$

$$N_2O(g) + H_2(g) \rightarrow N_2(g) + H_2O(g)$$

What is the molecularity of each of the three steps? What is the rate equation for the third step? Identify the intermediates in this reaction; how many different intermediates are there? Show that the sum of these elementary steps gives the equation for the overall reaction.

Reaction Mechanisms and Rate Equations

The dependence of rate on concentration is an experimental fact. Mechanisms, by contrast, are constructs of our imagination, intuition, and good "chemical sense." To describe a mechanism, we need to make a guess (a good guess, we hope) about how the reaction occurs at the particulate level. Several mechanisms can always be proposed that correspond to the observed rate equation, and a postulated mechanism is often wrong. A good mechanism is a worthy goal because it allows us to understand the chemistry better. A practical consequence of a good mechanism is that it allows us to predict, for example, how to control a reaction better and how to design new experiments.

One of the important guidelines of kinetics is that *products of a reaction can never be produced at a rate faster than the rate of the slowest step.* If one step in a multistep reaction is slower than the others, then *the rate of the overall reaction is limited by the combined rates of all elementary steps up through the slowest step in the mechanism.* Often the overall reaction rate and the rate of the slow step are nearly the same. If the slow step determines the rate of the reaction, it is called the **rate-determining step,** or rate-limiting step.

Imagine that a reaction takes place with a mechanism involving two sequential steps, and assume that we know the rates of both steps. The first step is slow and the second is fast:

Elementary Step 1 $A + B \xrightarrow[\text{Slow, } E_a \text{ large}]{k_1} X + M$

Elementary Step 2 $M + A \xrightarrow[\text{Fast, } E_a \text{ small}]{k_2} Y$

Overall Reaction $2A + B \longrightarrow X + Y$

In the first step, A and B come together and slowly react to form one of the products (X) plus another reactive species, M. Almost as soon as M is formed, however, it is rapidly consumed by reacting with another molecule of A to form the second product Y. The rate-determining elementary step in this example is the first step. That is, the rate of the first step is equal to the rate of the overall reaction. This step is bimolecular and so has the rate equation

$$\text{Rate} = k_1[A][B]$$

where k_1 is the rate constant for that step. The overall reaction is expected to have this same second-order rate equation.

Let us apply these ideas to the mechanism of a real reaction. Consider the reaction of nitrogen dioxide with fluorine which has a second-order rate equation:

Overall Reaction $2\,NO_2(g) + F_2(g) \rightarrow 2\,FNO_2(g)$

$$\text{Rate} = k[NO_2][F_2]$$

The rate equation immediately rules out the possibility that the reaction occurs in a single step. If the equation for the reaction represented an elementary step, the rate law would have a second-order dependence on $[NO_2]$. Because a single-step reaction is ruled out, the mechanism must include at least two steps. We can also conclude from the rate law that the rate-determining elementary step must involve NO_2 and F_2 in a 1:1 ratio. One possible mechanism proposes that molecules of NO_2 and F_2 first react to produce one molecule of the product (FNO_2) plus one F atom. In a second step, the fluorine atom produced in the first step reacts with additional NO_2 to give a second molecule of product. If the first, bimolecular step is rate determining, the rate equation would be "Rate = $k_1[NO_2][F_2]$," the same as the experimentally observed rate equation. The experimental rate constant would be the same as k_1.

Elementary Step 1   Slow $NO_2(g) + F_2(g) \xrightarrow{k_1} FNO_2(g) + F(g)$

Elementary Step 2   Fast $NO_2(g) + F(g) \xrightarrow{k_2} FNO_2(g)$

Overall Reaction $2\,NO_2(g) + F_2(g) \longrightarrow 2\,FNO_2(g)$

The fluorine atom formed in the first step of the NO_2/F_2 reaction is a reaction intermediate. It does not appear in the equation describing the overall reaction. Reaction intermediates usually have only a fleeting existence, but occasionally they have long enough lifetimes to be observed. The detection and identification of an intermediate are strong evidence for the proposed mechanism.

■ **EXAMPLE 15.13 Elementary Steps and Reaction Mechanisms**

Problem Oxygen atom transfer from NO_2 to CO produces nitrogen monoxide and carbon dioxide (Figure 15.13):

$$NO_2(g) + CO(g) \rightarrow NO(g) + CO_2(g)$$

The rate equation for this reaction at temperatures less than 500 K is:

$$Rate = k[NO_2]^2$$

Can this reaction occur in one bimolecular step?

Strategy Write the rate law based on the equation for the $NO_2 + CO$ reaction occurring as if it were an elementary step. If this rate law corresponds to the observed rate law, then a one-step mechanism is possible.

Solution If the reaction occurs by the collision of one NO_2 molecule with one CO molecule, the rate equation would be

$$Rate = k[NO_2][CO]$$

This does not agree with experiment, so the mechanism must involve more than a single step. In one possible mechanism, the reaction occurs in two, bimolecular steps, the first one slow and the second one fast:

Elementary Step 1 Slow, rate-determining

$$2\ NO_2(g) \longrightarrow NO_3(g) + NO(g)$$

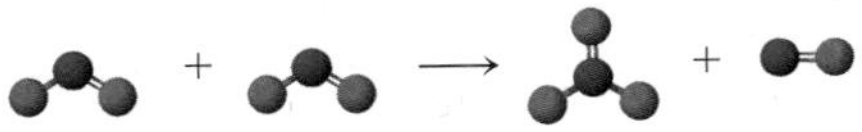

Elementary Step 2 Fast

$$NO_3(g) + CO(g) \longrightarrow NO_2(g) + CO_2(g)$$

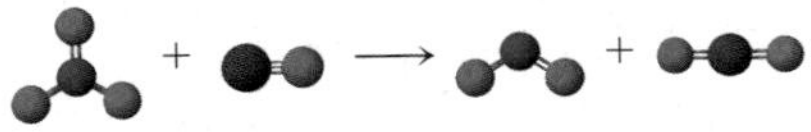

Overall Reaction

$$NO_2(g) + CO(g) \longrightarrow NO(g) + CO_2(g)$$

The first (rate-determining) step has a rate equation that agrees with experiment, so this is a possible mechanism.

EXERCISE 15.12 Elementary Steps and Reaction Mechanisms

The Raschig reaction produces hydrazine, N_2H_4, an industrially important reducing agent, from NH_3 and OCl^- in basic, aqueous solution. A proposed mechanism is

Step 1 Fast $NH_3(aq) + OCl^-(aq) \rightarrow NH_2Cl(aq) + OH^-(aq)$

Step 2 Slow $NH_2Cl(aq) + NH_3(aq) \rightarrow N_2H_5^+(aq) + Cl^-(aq)$

Step 3 Fast $N_2H_5^+(aq) + OH^-(aq) \rightarrow N_2H_4(aq) + H_2O(\ell)$

(a) What is the overall stoichiometric equation?

(b) Which step of the three is rate determining?

(c) Write the rate equation for the rate-determining elementary step.

(d) What reaction intermediates are involved?

A common two-step reaction mechanism involves an initial fast reaction that produces an intermediate, followed by a slower second step in which the intermediate is converted to the final product. The rate of the reaction is determined by the second step, for which a rate law can be written. The rate of that step, however, depends on the concentration of the intermediate. Remember, though, that the rate law must be written with respect to the reactants only. An intermediate, whose concentration will probably not be measurable, cannot appear as a term in the overall rate equation.

The reaction of nitrogen monoxide and oxygen is an example of a two-step reaction where the first step is fast and the second step is rate determining.

$$2\ NO(g) + O_2(g) \rightarrow 2\ NO_2(g)$$

$$\text{Rate} = k[NO]^2[O_2]$$

The experimentally determined rate law shows second-order dependence on NO and first-order dependence on O_2. Although this rate law would be correct for a termolecular reaction, experimental evidence indicates that an intermediate is formed in this reaction. A possible two-step mechanism that proceeds through an intermediate is

Elementary Step 1:   Fast, Equilibrium

$$NO(g) + O_2(g) \underset{k_{-1}}{\overset{k_1}{\rightleftharpoons}} OONO(g) \quad \text{intermediate}$$

Elementary Step 2:   Slow, Rate-determining

$$NO(g) + OONO(g) \overset{k_2}{\rightarrow} 2\ NO_2(g)$$

Overall Reaction

$$2\ NO(g) + O_2(g) \rightarrow 2\ NO_2(g)$$

The second step of this reaction is the slow step, and the overall rate depends on it. We can write a rate law for the second step:

$$\text{Rate} = k_2[NO][OONO]$$

This rate law cannot be compared directly with the experimental rate law because it contains the concentration of an intermediate, OONO. To eliminate the intermediate from this rate expression, we look at the rapid first step in this reaction sequence that involves an equilibrium between the intermediate species and the reactants.

At the beginning of the reaction, NO and O_2 react rapidly and produce the intermediate OONO. The rate of formation can be defined by a rate law with a rate constant k_1:

$$\text{Rate of production of OONO} = k_1[NO][O_2]$$

Because the intermediate is consumed only very slowly in the second step, it is possible for the OONO to revert to NO and O_2 before it reacts further:

$$\text{Rate of reverse reaction (OONO} \rightarrow NO + O_2) = k_{-1}[OONO]$$

As NO and O_2 form OONO, their concentrations drop, so the rate of the forward reaction decreases. At the same time, the concentration of OONO builds up, so the rate of the reverse reaction increases. At equilibrium, the rates of the forward and reverse reactions become the same.

$$\text{Rate of forward reaction} = \text{rate of reverse reaction}$$

$$k_1[NO][O_2] = k_{-1}[OONO]$$

Rearranging this equation, we find

$$\frac{k_1}{k_{-1}} = \frac{[N_2O_2]}{[NO][O_2]} = K$$

The connection between an experimental rate equation and the proposed reaction mechanism is important in chemistry.

1. Experiments must first be performed to determine the experimental rate equation.
2. A mechanism for the reaction is proposed on the basis of the experimental rate equation, the principles of stoichiometry

and molecular structure and bonding, general chemical experience, and intuition.
3. The proposed reaction mechanism is used to derive a rate equation. This rate equation can contain only those species present in the overall chemical reaction. If the derived and experimental rate equations

are the same, the postulated mechanism *may* be a reasonable hypothesis of the reaction sequence.
4. If more than one mechanism can be proposed, and they all predict derived rate equations in agreement with experiment, then more experiments must be done.

Both k_1 and k_{-1} are constants (they will change only if the temperature changes). We can define a new constant K equal to the ratio of these two constants and called the **equilibrium constant**, which is equal to the quotient $[OONO]/[NO][O_2]$. From this, we can derive an expression for the concentration of OONO:

$$[OONO] = K[NO][O_2]$$

If $K[NO][O_2]$ is substituted for $[OONO]$ in the rate law for the rate-determining elementary step, we have

$$\text{Rate} = k_2[NO][OONO] = k_2[NO]\{K[NO][O_2]\}$$

$$= k_2 K[NO]^2[O_2]$$

Because both k_2 and K are constants, their product is another constant k', and we have

$$\text{Rate} = k'[NO]^2[O_2]$$

This is exactly the rate law derived from experiment. Thus, the sequence of reactions on which the rate law is based may be a reasonable mechanism for this reaction. It is not the only possible mechanism, however. This rate equation is also consistent with the reaction occurring in a single termolecular step. Another possible mechanism is illustrated in Example 15.14.

■ **Equilibrium Constant** The important concept of chemical equilibrium was introduced in Chapter 3 and will be described in more detail in Chapters 16–19.

■ **Mechanisms with an Initial Equilibrium** In this mechanism, the forward and reverse reactions in the first elementary step are so much faster than the second elementary step that equilibrium is established before any significant amount of OONO is consumed by NO to give NO_2. The state of equilibrium for the first step remains throughout the lifetime of the overall reaction.

■ EXAMPLE 15.14 Reaction Mechanism Involving an Equilibrium Step

Problem The NO + O_2 reaction described in the text could also occur by the following mechanism:

Elementary Step 1: Fast, equilibrium

$$NO(g) + NO(g) \underset{k_{-1}}{\overset{k_1}{\rightleftharpoons}} N_2O_2(g) \text{ intermediate}$$

Elementary Step 2: Slow, rate-determining

$$N_2O_2(g) + O_2(g) \overset{k_2}{\rightarrow} 2\,NO_2(g)$$

Overall Reaction: $2\,NO(g) + O_2(g) \longrightarrow 2\,NO_2(g)$

Show that this mechanism leads to the following experimental rate law: Rate = $k[NO]^2[O_2]$.

Strategy The rate law for the rate-determining elementary step is

$$\text{Rate} = k_2[N_2O_2][O_2]$$

The intermediate N_2O_2 cannot appear in the final derived rate law. To obtain the rate law, we use the equilibrium constant expression for the first step.

Solution [N_2O_2] and [NO] are related by the equilibrium constant.

$$\frac{k_1}{k_{-1}} = \frac{[N_2O_2]}{[NO]^2} = K$$

Solving this equation for [N_2O_2] gives [N_2O_2] = $K[NO]^2$. When this is substituted into the derived rate law

$$\text{Rate} = k_2\{K[NO_2]^2\}[O_2]$$

the resulting equation is identical with the experimental rate law where $k_2K = k$.

Comment Three mechanisms have been proposed for the $NO + O_2$ reaction. The challenge for chemists is to decide which is correct. In this case, further experimentation detected the species OONO as a short-lived intermediate, confirming the mechanism involving this intermediate.

EXERCISE 15.13 Reaction Mechanism Involving a Fast Initial Step

One possible mechanism for the decomposition of nitryl chloride, NO_2Cl, is

Elementary Step 1: Fast, Equilibrium $NO_2Cl(g) \underset{k_{-1}}{\overset{k_1}{\rightleftarrows}} NO_2(g) + Cl(g)$

Elementary Step 2: Slow $NO_2Cl(g) + Cl(g) \overset{k_2}{\rightarrow} NO_2(g) + Cl_2(g)$

What is the overall reaction? What rate law would be derived from this mechanism? What effect does increasing the concentration of the product NO_2 have on the reaction rate?

Chapter Goals Revisited

Now that you have studied this chapter, you should ask whether you have met the chapter goals. In particular, you should be able to:

Understand rates of reaction and the conditions affecting rates

a. Explain the concept of reaction rate (Section 15.1).

b. Derive the average and instantaneous rates of a reaction from concentration–time data (Section 15.1). Study Question(s) assignable in OWL: 5.

c. Describe factors that affect reaction rate (i.e., reactant concentrations, temperature, presence of a catalyst, and the state of the reactants) (Section 15.2). Study Question(s) assignable in OWL: 8, 10, 62, 76, 77, 81.

Derive the rate equation, rate constant, and reaction order from experimental data

a. Define the various parts of a rate equation (the rate constant and order of reaction), and understand their significance (Section 15.3). Study Question(s) assignable in OWL: 12, 14, 68.

b. Derive a rate equation from experimental information (Section 15.3). Study Question(s) assignable in OWL: 12, 14, 48, 56, 58, 71.

Use integrated rate laws

a. Describe and use the relationships between reactant concentration and time for zero-order, first-order, and second-order reactions (Section 15.4 and Table 15.1). Study Question(s) assignable in OWL: 16, 18, 19, 20, 24; Go Chemistry Module 20.

b. Apply graphical methods for determining reaction order and the rate constant from experimental data (Section 15.4 and Table 15.1). Study Question(s) assignable in OWL: 28, 30.

c. Use the concept of half-life ($t_{1/2}$), especially for first-order reactions (Section 15.4). Study Question(s) assignable in OWL: 22, 24, 26, 60, 71.

Understand the collision theory of reaction rates and the role of activation energy

a. Describe the collision theory of reaction rates (Section 15.5).

b. Relate activation energy (E_a) to the rate and thermodynamics of a reaction (Section 15.5). Study Question(s) assignable in OWL: 36, 69, 83.

c. Use collision theory to describe the effect of reactant concentration on reaction rate (Section 15.5).

d. Understand the effect of molecular orientation on reaction rate (Section 15.5).

e. Describe the effect of temperature on reaction rate using the collision theory of reaction rates and the Arrhenius equation (Equation 15.7 and Section 15.5).

f. Use Equations 15.5, 15.6, and 15.7 to calculate the activation energy from rate constants at different temperatures (Section 15.5).

Relate reaction mechanisms and rate laws

a. Describe the functioning of a catalyst and its effect on the activation energy and mechanism of a reaction (Section 15.5).

b. Understand reaction coordinate diagrams (Section 15.5).

c. Understand the concept of a reaction mechanism (a proposed sequence of bond-making and bond-breaking steps that occurs during the conversion of reactants to products) and the relation of the mechanism to the overall, stoichiometric equation for a reaction (Section 15.6).

d. Describe the elementary steps of a mechanism, and give their molecularity (Section 15.6). Study Question(s) assignable in OWL: 40, 42, 44, 74.

e. Define the rate-determining step in a mechanism, and identify any reaction intermediates (Section 15.6). Study Question(s) assignable in OWL: 44, 69, 70, 78, 80.

KEY EQUATIONS

Equation 15.1 (page 683) Integrated rate equation for a first-order reaction (in which $-\Delta[R]/\Delta t = k[R]$).

$$\ln \frac{[R]_t}{[R]_0} = -kt$$

Here, $[R]_0$ and $[R]_t$ are concentrations of the reactant at time $t = 0$ and at a later time, t. The ratio of concentrations, $[R]_t/[R]_0$, is the fraction of reactant that remains after a given time has elapsed.

Equation 15.2 (page 686) Integrated rate equation for a second-order reaction (in which $-\Delta[R]/\Delta t = k[R]^2$).

$$\frac{1}{[R]_t} - \frac{1}{[R]_0} = kt$$

Equation 15.3 (page 687) Integrated rate equation for a zero-order reaction (in which $-\Delta[R]/\Delta t = k[R]^0$).

$$[R]_0 - [R]_t = kt$$

Equation 15.4 (page 690) The relation between the half-life ($t_{1/2}$) and the rate constant (k) for a first-order reaction.

$$t_{1/2} = \frac{0.693}{k}$$

Equation 15.5 (page 696) Arrhenius equation in exponential form

$$k = \text{rate constant} = Ae^{-E_a/RT}$$

Frequency factor

Fraction of molecules with minimum energy for reaction

A is the frequency factor; E_a is the activation energy; T is the temperature (in kelvins); and R is the gas constant ($= 8.314510 \times 10^{-3}$ kJ/K · mol).

Equation 15.6 (page 696) Expanded Arrhenius equation in logarithmic form.

$$\ln k = -\frac{E_a}{R}\left(\frac{1}{T}\right) + \ln A \quad \longleftarrow \text{Arrhenius equation}$$

$$\downarrow \qquad \downarrow \qquad \downarrow$$

$$y \quad = \quad mx \quad + b \quad \longleftarrow \text{Equation for straight line}$$

Equation 15.7 (page 698) A version of the Arrhenius equation used to calculate the activation energy for a reaction when you know the values of the rate constant at two temperatures (in kelvins).

$$\ln k_2 - \ln k_1 = \ln \frac{k_2}{k_1} = -\frac{E_a}{R}\left[\frac{1}{T_2} - \frac{1}{T_1}\right]$$

STUDY QUESTIONS

OWL Online homework for this chapter may be assigned in OWL.

▲ denotes challenging questions.

■ denotes questions assignable in OWL.

Blue-numbered questions have answers in Appendix O and fully-worked solutions in the *Student Solutions Manual*.

Practicing Skills

Reaction Rates
(See Examples 15.1–15.2, Exercises 15.1–15.2, and ChemistryNow Screen 15.2.)

1. Give the relative rates of disappearance of reactants and formation of products for each of the following reactions.
   (a) $2 O_3(g) \longrightarrow 3 O_2(g)$
   (b) $2 HOF(g) \longrightarrow 2 HF(g) + O_2(g)$

2. Give the relative rates of disappearance of reactants and formation of products for each of the following reactions.
   (a) $2 NO(g) + Br_2(g) \longrightarrow 2 NOBr(g)$
   (b) $N_2(g) + 3 H_2(g) \longrightarrow 2 NH_3(g)$

3. In the reaction $2 O_3(g) \longrightarrow 3 O_2(g)$, the rate of formation of O_2 is 1.5×10^{-3} mol/L · s. What is the rate of decomposition of O_3?

4. In the synthesis of ammonia, if $-\Delta[H_2]/\Delta t = 4.5 \times 10^{-4}$ mol/L·min, what is $\Delta[NH_3]/\Delta t$?

$$N_2(g) + 3 H_2(g) \rightarrow 2 NH_3(g)$$

5. ■ Experimental data are listed here for the reaction A $\longrightarrow$ 2 B.

Time (s)	[B] (mol/L)
0.00	0.000
10.0	0.326
20.0	0.572
30.0	0.750
40.0	0.890

(a) Prepare a graph from these data; connect the points with a smooth line; and calculate the rate of change of [B] for each 10-s interval from 0.0 to 40.0 s. Does the rate of change decrease from one time interval to the next? Suggest a reason for this result.

(b) How is the rate of change of [A] related to the rate of change of [B] in each time interval? Calculate the rate of change of [A] for the time interval from 10.0 to 20.0 s.

(c) What is the instantaneous rate, $\Delta[B]/\Delta t$, when [B] = 0.750 mol/L?

6. Phenyl acetate, an ester, reacts with water according to the equation

$$CH_3COC_6H_5 + H_2O \longrightarrow CH_3COH + C_6H_5OH$$

phenyl acetate   acetic acid   phenol

The data in the table were collected for this reaction at 5 °C.

Time (s)	[Phenyl acetate] (mol/L)
0	0.55
15.0	0.42
30.0	0.31
45.0	0.23
60.0	0.17
75.0	0.12
90.0	0.085

(a) Plot the phenyl acetate concentration versus time, and describe the shape of the curve observed.
(b) Calculate the rate of change of the phenyl acetate concentration during the period 15.0 s to 30.0 s and also during the period 75.0 s to 90.0 s. Why is one value smaller than the other?
(c) What is the rate of change of the phenol concentration during the time period 60.0 s to 75.0 s?
(d) What is the instantaneous rate at 15.0 s?

Concentration and Rate Equations
(See Examples 15.3–15.4, Exercises 15.3–15.4, and ChemistryNow Screens 15.4 and 15.5.)

7. Using the rate equation "Rate $= k[A]^2[B]$," define the order of the reaction with respect to A and B. What is the total order of the reaction?

8. ■ A reaction has the experimental rate equation Rate $= k[A]^2$. How will the rate change if the concentration of A is tripled? If the concentration of A is halved?

9. The reaction between ozone and nitrogen dioxide at 231 K is first order in both $[NO_2]$ and $[O_3]$.

$$2 NO_2(g) + O_3(g) \rightarrow N_2O_5(s) + O_2(g)$$

(a) Write the rate equation for the reaction.
(b) If the concentration of NO_2 is tripled (and $[O_3]$ is not changed), what is the change in the reaction rate?
(c) What is the effect on reaction rate if the concentration of O_3 is halved (no change in $[NO_2]$)?

10. ■ Nitrosyl bromide, NOBr, is formed from NO and Br_2:

$$2 NO(g) + Br_2(g) \rightarrow 2 NOBr(g)$$

Experiments show that this reaction is second order in NO and first order in Br_2.
(a) Write the rate equation for the reaction.
(b) How does the initial reaction rate change if the concentration of Br_2 is changed from 0.0022 mol/L to 0.0066 mol/L?
(c) What is the change in the initial rate if the concentration of NO is changed from 0.0024 mol/L to 0.0012 mol/L?

11. The data in the table are for the reaction of NO and O_2 at 660 K.

$$2 NO(g) + O_2(g) \rightarrow 2 NO_2(g)$$

Reactant Concentration (mol/L)		Rate of Disappearance of NO (mol/L · s)
[NO]	[O₂]	
0.010	0.010	2.5×10^{-5}
0.020	0.010	1.0×10^{-4}
0.010	0.020	5.0×10^{-5}

(a) Determine the order of the reaction for each reactant.
(b) Write the rate equation for the reaction.
(c) Calculate the rate constant.
(d) Calculate the rate (in mol/L · s) at the instant when $[NO] = 0.015$ mol/L and $[O_2] = 0.0050$ mol/L.
(e) At the instant when NO is reacting at the rate 1.0×10^{-4} mol/L · s, what is the rate at which O_2 is reacting and NO_2 is forming?

12. ■ The reaction

$$2 NO(g) + 2 H_2(g) \rightarrow N_2(g) + 2 H_2O(g)$$

was studied at 904 °C, and the data in the table were collected.

Reactant Concentration (mol/L)		Rate of Appearance of N₂ (mol/L · s)
[NO]	[H₂]	
0.420	0.122	0.136
0.210	0.122	0.0339
0.210	0.244	0.0678
0.105	0.488	0.0339

(a) Determine the order of the reaction for each reactant.
(b) Write the rate equation for the reaction.
(c) Calculate the rate constant for the reaction.
(d) Find the rate of appearance of N_2 at the instant when $[NO] = 0.350$ mol/L and $[H_2] = 0.205$ mol/L.

13. Data for the reaction $2 NO(g) + O_2(g) \rightarrow 2 NO_2(g)$ are given in the table.

	Concentration (mol/L)		Initial Rate
Experiment	[NO]	[O₂]	(mol/L · h)
1	3.6×10^{-4}	5.2×10^{-3}	3.4×10^{-8}
2	3.6×10^{-4}	1.04×10^{-2}	6.8×10^{-8}
3	1.8×10^{-4}	1.04×10^{-2}	1.7×10^{-8}
4	1.8×10^{-4}	5.2×10^{-3}	?

(a) What is the rate law for this reaction?
(b) What is the rate constant for the reaction?
(c) What is the initial rate of the reaction in experiment 4?

14. ■ Data for the following reaction are given in the table below.

$$CO(g) + NO_2(g) \rightarrow CO_2(g) + NO(g)$$

	Concentration (mol/L)		Initial Rate
Experiment	[CO]	[NO₂]	(mol/L · h)
1	5.0×10^{-4}	0.36×10^{-4}	3.4×10^{-8}
2	5.0×10^{-4}	0.18×10^{-4}	1.7×10^{-8}
3	1.0×10^{-3}	0.36×10^{-4}	6.8×10^{-8}
4	1.5×10^{-3}	0.72×10^{-4}	?

(a) What is the rate law for this reaction?
(b) What is the rate constant for the reaction?
(c) What is the initial rate of the reaction in experiment 4?

Concentration–Time Relationships
(See Examples 15.5–15.7, Exercises 15.5–15.7, and ChemistryNow Screen 15.6.)

15. The rate equation for the hydrolysis of sucrose to fructose and glucose

$$C_{12}H_{22}O_{11}(aq) + H_2O(\ell) \rightarrow 2 C_6H_{12}O_6(aq)$$

is $-\Delta[\text{sucrose}]/\Delta t = k[C_{12}H_{22}O_{11}]$. After 27 min at 27 °C, the sucrose concentration decreased from 0.0146 M to 0.0132 M. Find the rate constant, k.

16. ■ The decomposition of N_2O_5 in CCl_4 is a first-order reaction. If 2.56 mg of N_2O_5 is present initially, and 2.50 mg is present after 4.26 min at 55 °C, what is the value of the rate constant, k?

17. The decomposition of SO_2Cl_2 is a first-order reaction:

$$SO_2Cl_2(g) \rightarrow SO_2(g) + Cl_2(g)$$

The rate constant for the reaction is 2.8×10^{-3} min⁻¹ at 600 K. If the initial concentration of SO_2Cl_2 is 1.24×10^{-3} mol/L, how long will it take for the concentration to drop to 0.31×10^{-3} mol/L?

18. ■ The conversion of cyclopropane to propene (see Example 15.5) occurs with a first-order rate constant of 2.42×10^{-2} h⁻¹. How long will it take for the concentration of cyclopropane to decrease from an initial concentration 0.080 mol/L to 0.020 mol/L?

19. ■ Hydrogen peroxide, H_2O_2(aq), decomposes to $H_2O(\ell)$ and $O_2(g)$ in a reaction that is first order in H_2O_2 and has a rate constant $k = 1.06 \times 10^{-3}$ min⁻¹ at a given temperature.
(a) How long will it take for 15% of a sample of H_2O_2 to decompose?
(b) How long will it take for 85% of the sample to decompose?

20. ■ The decomposition of nitrogen dioxide at a high temperature

$$NO_2(g) \rightarrow NO(g) + ½ O_2(g)$$

is second order in this reactant. The rate constant for this reaction is 3.40 L/mol · min. Determine the time needed for the concentration of NO_2 to decrease from 2.00 mol/L to 1.50 mol/L.

Half-Life
(See Examples 15.8 and 15.9, Exercise 15.9, and ChemistryNow Screen 15.8.)

21. The rate equation for the decomposition of N_2O_5 (giving NO_2 and O_2) is Rate = $k[N_2O_5]$. The value of k is 6.7×10^{-5} s⁻¹ for the reaction at a particular temperature.
(a) Calculate the half-life of N_2O_5.
(b) How long does it take for the N_2O_5 concentration to drop to one tenth of its original value?

22. ■ The decomposition of SO_2Cl_2

$$SO_2Cl_2(g) \rightarrow SO_2(g) + Cl_2(g)$$

is first order in SO_2Cl_2, and the reaction has a half-life of 245 min at 600 K. If you begin with 3.6×10^{-3} mol of SO_2Cl_2 in a 1.0-L flask, how long will it take for the amount of SO_2Cl_2 to decrease to 2.00×10^{-4} mol?

23. Gaseous azomethane, $CH_3N{=}NCH_3$, decomposes in a first-order reaction when heated:

$$CH_3N{=}NCH_3(g) \rightarrow N_2(g) + C_2H_6(g)$$

The rate constant for this reaction at 600 K is 0.0216 min⁻¹. If the initial quantity of azomethane in the flask is 2.00 g, how much remains after 0.0500 h? What quantity of N_2 is formed in this time?

24. ■ The compound $Xe(CF_3)_2$ decomposes in a first-order reaction to elemental Xe with a half-life of 30. min. If you place 7.50 mg of $Xe(CF_3)_2$ in a flask, how long must you wait until only 0.25 mg of $Xe(CF_3)_2$ remains?

25. The radioactive isotope ^{64}Cu is used in the form of copper(II) acetate to study Wilson's disease. The isotope has a half-life of 12.70 h. What fraction of radioactive copper(II) acetate remains after 64 h?

26. ■ Radioactive gold-198 is used in the diagnosis of liver problems. The half-life of this isotope is 2.7 days. If you begin with a 5.6-mg sample of the isotope, how much of this sample remains after 1.0 day?

▲ more challenging ■ in OWL Blue-numbered questions answered in Appendix O

Graphical Analysis: Rate Equations and *k*
(See Exercise 15.8 and ChemistryNow Screen 15.7.)

27. Data for the decomposition of dinitrogen oxide

$$2\ N_2O(g) \rightarrow 2\ N_2(g) + O_2(g)$$

on a gold surface at 900 °C are given below. Verify that the reaction is first order by preparing a graph of ln [N_2O] versus time. Derive the rate constant from the slope of the line in this graph. Using the rate law and value of *k*, determine the decomposition rate at 900 °C when [N_2O] = 0.035 mol/L.

Time (min)	[N_2O] (mol/L)
15.0	0.0835
30.0	0.0680
80.0	0.0350
120.0	0.0220

28. ■ Ammonia decomposes when heated according to the equation

$$NH_3(g) \rightarrow NH_2(g) + H(g)$$

The data in the table for this reaction were collected at a high temperature.

Time (h)	[NH_3] (mol/L)
0	8.00×10^{-7}
25	6.75×10^{-7}
50	5.84×10^{-7}
75	5.15×10^{-7}

Plot ln [NH_3] versus time and 1/[NH_3] versus time. What is the order of this reaction with respect to NH_3? Find the rate constant for the reaction from the slope.

29. Gaseous NO_2 decomposes at 573 K.

$$2\ NO_2(g) \rightarrow 2\ NO(g) + O_2(g)$$

The concentration of NO_2 was measured as a function of time. A graph of 1/[NO_2] versus time gives a straight line with a slope of 1.1 L/mol · s. What is the rate law for this reaction? What is the rate constant?

30. ■ The decomposition of HOF occurs at 25 °C.

$$2\ HOF(g) \rightarrow 2\ HF(g) + O_2(g)$$

Using the data in the table below, determine the rate law, and then calculate the rate constant.

[HOF] (mol/L)	Time (min)
0.850	0
0.810	2.00
0.754	5.00
0.526	20.0
0.243	50.0

31. For the reaction $2\ C_2F_4 \rightarrow C_4F_8$, a graph of 1/[$C_2F_4$] versus time gives a straight line with a slope of +0.04 L/mol · s. What is the rate law for this reaction?

32. Butadiene, $C_4H_6(g)$, dimerizes when heated, forming 1,5-cyclooctadiene, C_8H_{12}. The data in the table were collected.

$$2\ H_2C=CHCH=CH_2 \longrightarrow$$

1,3-butadiene

1,5-cyclooctadiene

[C_4H_6] (mol/L)	Time (s)
1.0×10^{-2}	0
8.7×10^{-3}	200.
7.7×10^{-3}	500.
6.9×10^{-3}	800.
5.8×10^{-3}	1200.

(a) Use a graphical method to verify that this is a second-order reaction.
(b) Calculate the rate constant for the reaction.

Kinetics and Energy
(See Examples 15.10 and 15.11, and ChemistryNow Screens 15.9 and 15.10.)

33. Calculate the activation energy, E_a, for the reaction

$$2\ N_2O_5(g) \rightarrow 4\ NO_2(g) + O_2(g)$$

from the observed rate constants: *k* at 25 °C = 3.46×10^{-5} s^{-1} and *k* at 55 °C = 1.5×10^{-3} s^{-1}.

34. If the rate constant for a reaction triples when the temperature rises from 3.00×10^2 K to 3.10×10^2 K, what is the activation energy of the reaction?

35. When heated to a high temperature, cyclobutane, C_4H_8, decomposes to ethylene:

$$C_4H_8(g) \rightarrow 2\ C_2H_4(g)$$

The activation energy, E_a, for this reaction is 260 kJ/mol-rxn. At 800 K, the rate constant *k* = 0.0315 s^{-1}. Determine the value of *k* at 850 K.

36. ■ When heated, cyclopropane is converted to propene (see Example 15.5). Rate constants for this reaction at 470 °C and 510 °C are *k* = 1.10×10^{-4} s^{-1} and *k* = 1.02×10^{-3} s^{-1}, respectively. Determine the activation energy, E_a, from these data.

37. The reaction of H_2 molecules with F atoms

$$H_2(g) + F(g) \rightarrow HF(g) + H(g)$$

has an activation energy of 8 kJ/mol-rxn and an energy change of -133 kJ/mol-rxn. Draw a diagram similar to Figure 15.13 for this process. Indicate the activation energy and enthalpy change on this diagram.

38. Answer the following questions based on the diagram below.
(a) Is the reaction exothermic or endothermic?
(b) Does the reaction occur in more than one step? If so, how many?

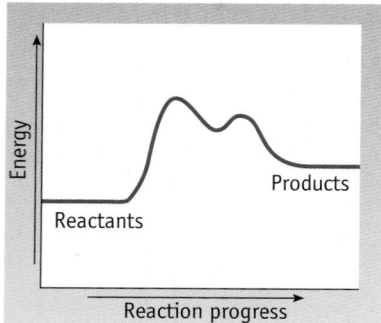

Reaction Mechanisms
(See Examples 15.12–15.14, Exercises 15.11–15.13, and ChemistryNow Screens 15.12 and 15.13.)

39. What is the rate law for each of the following elementary reactions?
(a) $NO(g) + NO_3(g) \rightarrow 2\ NO_2(g)$
(b) $Cl(g) + H_2(g) \rightarrow HCl(g) + H(g)$
(c) $(CH_3)_3CBr(aq) \rightarrow (CH_3)_3C^+(aq) + Br^-(aq)$

40. ■ What is the rate law for each of the following elementary reactions?
(a) $Cl(g) + ICl(g) \rightarrow I(g) + Cl_2(g)$
(b) $O(g) + O_3(g) \rightarrow 2\ O_2(g)$
(c) $2\ NO_2(g) \rightarrow N_2O_4(g)$

41. Ozone, O_3, in the earth's upper atmosphere decomposes according to the equation

$$2\ O_3(g) \rightarrow 3\ O_2(g)$$

The mechanism of the reaction is thought to proceed through an initial fast, reversible step followed by a slow, second step.

Step 1 Fast, reversible $\quad O_3(g) \rightleftharpoons O_2(g) + O(g)$

Step 2 Slow $\quad\quad\quad\quad O_3(g) + O(g) \rightarrow 2\ O_2(g)$

(a) Which of the steps is rate-determining?
(b) Write the rate equation for the rate determining step.

42. ■ The reaction of $NO_2(g)$ and $CO(g)$ is thought to occur in two steps:

Step 1 Slow $\quad NO_2(g) + NO_2(g) \rightarrow NO(g) + NO_3(g)$

Step 2 Fast $\quad NO_3(g) + CO(g) \rightarrow NO_2(g) + CO_2(g)$

(a) Show that the elementary steps add up to give the overall, stoichiometric equation.
(b) What is the molecularity of each step?
(c) For this mechanism to be consistent with kinetic data, what must be the experimental rate equation?
(d) Identify any intermediates in this reaction.

43. A proposed mechanism for the reaction of NO_2 and CO is

Step 1 Slow, endothermic
$$2\ NO_2(g) \rightarrow NO(g) + NO_3(g)$$

Step 2 Fast, exothermic
$$NO_3(g) + CO(g) \rightarrow NO_2(g) + CO_2(g)$$

Overall Reaction Exothermic
$$NO_2(g) + CO(g) \rightarrow NO(g) + CO_2(g)$$

(a) Identify each of the following as a reactant, product, or intermediate: $NO_2(g)$, $CO(g)$, $NO_3(g)$, $CO_2(g)$, $NO(g)$.
(b) Draw a reaction coordinate diagram for this reaction. Indicate on this drawing the activation energy for each step and the overall enthalpy change.

44. ■ The mechanism for the reaction of CH_3OH and HBr is believed to involve two steps. The overall reaction is exothermic.

Step 1 Fast, endothermic
$$CH_3OH + H^+ \rightleftharpoons CH_3OH_2^+$$

Step 2 Slow
$$CH_3OH_2^+ + Br^- \rightarrow CH_3Br + H_2O$$

(a) Write an equation for the overall reaction.
(b) Draw a reaction coordinate diagram for this reaction.
(c) Show that the rate law for this reaction is Rate $= k[CH_3OH][H^+][Br^-]$.

General Questions
These questions are not designated as to type or location in the chapter. They may combine several concepts from this and other chapters.

45. A reaction has the following experimental rate equation: Rate $= k[A]^2[B]$. If the concentration of A is doubled and the concentration of B is halved, what happens to the reaction rate?

46. For a first-order reaction, what fraction of reactant remains after five half-lives have elapsed?

▲ more challenging ■ in OWL Blue-numbered questions answered in Appendix O

47. To determine the concentration dependence of the rate of the reaction

$$H_2PO_3^-(aq) + OH^-(aq) \rightarrow HPO_3^{2-}(aq) + H_2O(\ell)$$

you might measure $[OH^-]$ as a function of time using a pH meter. (To do so, you would set up conditions under which $[H_2PO_3^-]$ remains constant by using a large excess of this reactant.) How would you prove a second-order rate dependence for $[OH^-]$?

48. ■ Data for the following reaction are given in the table.

$$2\,NO(g) + Br_2(g) \rightarrow 2\,NOBr(g)$$

Experiment	[NO] (M)	[Br₂] (M)	Initial Rate (mol/L · s)
1	1.0×10^{-2}	2.0×10^{-2}	2.4×10^{-2}
2	4.0×10^{-2}	2.0×10^{-2}	0.384
3	1.0×10^{-2}	5.0×10^{-2}	6.0×10^{-2}

What is the order of the reaction with respect to [NO] and [Br₂], and what is the overall order of the reaction?

49. Formic acid decomposes at 550 °C according to the equation

$$HCO_2H(g) \rightarrow CO_2(g) + H_2(g)$$

The reaction follows first-order kinetics. In an experiment, it is determined that 75% of a sample of HCO_2H has decomposed in 72 seconds. Determine $t_{1/2}$ for this reaction.

50. Isomerization of CH_3NC occurs slowly when CH_3NC is heated.

$$CH_3NC(g) \rightarrow CH_3CN(g)$$

To study the rate of this reaction at 488 K, data on $[CH_3NC]$ were collected at various times. Analysis led to the graph below.
(a) What is the rate law for this reaction?
(b) What is the equation for the straight line in this graph?
(c) Calculate the rate constant for this reaction.
(d) How long does it take for half of the sample to isomerize?
(e) What is the concentration of CH_3NC after 1.0×10^4 s?

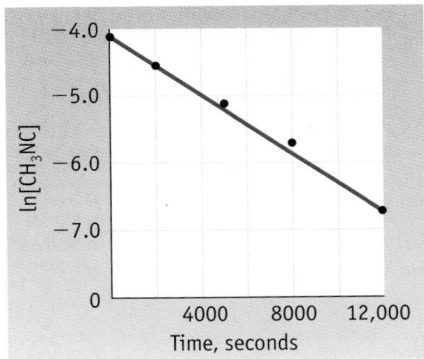

51. When heated, tetrafluoroethylene dimerizes to form octafluorocyclobutane.

$$2\,C_2F_4(g) \rightarrow C_4F_8(g)$$

To determine the rate of this reaction at 488 K, the data in the table were collected. Analysis was done graphically, as shown below:

[C₂F₄] (M)	Time (s)
0.100	0
0.080	56
0.060	150.
0.040	335
0.030	520.

(a) What is the rate law for this reaction?
(b) What is the value of the rate constant?
(c) What is the concentration of C_2F_4 after 600 s?
(d) How long will it take until the reaction is 90% complete?

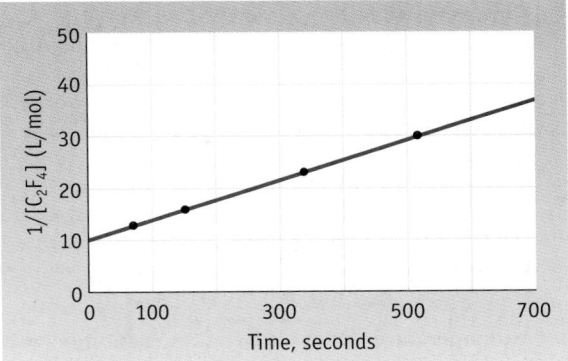

52. Data in the table were collected at 540 K for the following reaction:

$$CO(g) + NO_2(g) \rightarrow CO_2(g) + NO(g)$$

(a) Derive the rate equation.
(b) Determine the reaction order with respect to each reactant.
(c) Calculate the rate constant, giving the correct units for k.

Initial Concentration (mol/L)		Initial Rate (mol/L · h)
[CO]	[NO₂]	
5.1×10^{-4}	0.35×10^{-4}	3.4×10^{-8}
5.1×10^{-4}	0.70×10^{-4}	6.8×10^{-8}
5.1×10^{-4}	0.18×10^{-4}	1.7×10^{-8}
1.0×10^{-3}	0.35×10^{-4}	6.8×10^{-8}
1.5×10^{-3}	0.35×10^{-4}	10.2×10^{-8}

53. Ammonium cyanate, NH_4NCO, rearranges in water to give urea, $(NH_2)_2CO$.

$$NH_4NCO(aq) \rightarrow (NH_2)_2CO(aq)$$

Time (min)	[NH₄NCO] (mol/L)
0	0.458
4.50×10^1	0.370
1.07×10^2	0.292
2.30×10^2	0.212
6.00×10^2	0.114

Using the data in the table:
(a) Decide whether the reaction is first order or second order.
(b) Calculate k for this reaction.
(c) Calculate the half-life of ammonium cyanate under these conditions.
(d) Calculate the concentration of NH_4NCO after 12.0 h.

54. Nitrogen oxides, NO_x (a mixture of NO and NO_2 collectively designated as NO_x), play an essential role in the production of pollutants found in photochemical smog. The NO_x in the atmosphere is slowly broken down to N_2 and O_2 in a first-order reaction. The average half-life of NO_x in the smokestack emissions in a large city during daylight is 3.9 h.
(a) Starting with 1.50 mg in an experiment, what quantity of NO_x remains after 5.25 h?
(b) How many hours of daylight must have elapsed to decrease 1.50 mg of NO_x to 2.50×10^{-6} mg?

55. At temperatures below 500 K, the reaction between carbon monoxide and nitrogen dioxide

$$CO(g) + NO_2(g) \rightarrow CO_2(g) + NO(g)$$

has the following rate equation: Rate $= k[NO_2]^2$. Which of the three mechanisms suggested here best agrees with the experimentally observed rate equation?

Mechanism 1 Single, elementary step

$$NO_2 + CO \rightarrow CO_2 + NO$$

Mechanism 2 Two steps

Slow $NO_2 + NO_2 \rightarrow NO_3 + NO$

Fast $NO_3 + CO \rightarrow NO_2 + CO_2$

Mechanism 3 Two steps

Slow $NO_2 \rightarrow NO + O$

Fast $CO + O \rightarrow CO_2$

56. ■ ▲ Nitryl fluoride can be made by treating nitrogen dioxide with fluorine:

$$2\ NO_2(g) + F_2(g) \rightarrow 2\ NO_2F(g)$$

Use the rate data in the table to do the following:
(a) Write the rate equation for the reaction.
(b) Indicate the order of reaction with respect to each component of the reaction.
(c) Find the numerical value of the rate constant, k.

Experiment	Initial Concentrations (mol/L) [NO₂]	[F₂]	[NO₂F]	Initial Rate (mol/L · s)
1	0.001	0.005	0.001	2.0×10^{-4}
2	0.002	0.005	0.001	4.0×10^{-4}
3	0.006	0.002	0.001	4.8×10^{-4}
4	0.006	0.004	0.001	9.6×10^{-4}
5	0.001	0.001	0.001	4.0×10^{-5}
6	0.001	0.001	0.002	4.0×10^{-5}

57. The decomposition of dinitrogen pentaoxide

$$2\ N_2O_5(g) \rightarrow 4\ NO_2(g) + O_2(g)$$

has the following rate equation: Rate $= k[N_2O_5]$. It has been found experimentally that the decomposition is 20.5 % complete in 13.0 h at 298 K. Calculate the rate constant and the half-life at 298 K.

58. ■ The data in the table give the temperature dependence of the rate constant for the reaction $N_2O_5(g) \rightarrow 2\ NO_2(g) + \frac{1}{2}\ O_2(g)$. Plot these data in the appropriate way to derive the activation energy for the reaction.

$T(K)$	k (s⁻¹)
338	4.87×10^{-3}
328	1.50×10^{-3}
318	4.98×10^{-4}
308	1.35×10^{-4}
298	3.46×10^{-5}
273	7.87×10^{-7}

59. The decomposition of gaseous dimethyl ether at ordinary pressures is first order. Its half-life is 25.0 min at 500 °C:

$$CH_3OCH_3(g) \rightarrow CH_4(g) + CO(g) + H_2(g)$$

(a) Starting with 8.00 g of dimethyl ether, what mass remains (in grams) after 125 min and after 145 min?
(b) Calculate the time in minutes required to decrease 7.60 ng (nanograms) to 2.25 ng.
(c) What fraction of the original dimethyl ether remains after 150 min?

60. ■ The decomposition of phosphine, PH_3, proceeds according to the equation

$$4\ PH_3(g) \longrightarrow P_4(g) + 6\ H_2(g)$$

It is found that the reaction has the following rate equation: Rate = $k[PH_3]$. The half-life of PH_3 is 37.9 s at 120 °C.
(a) How much time is required for three-fourths of the PH_3 to decompose?
(b) What fraction of the original sample of PH_3 remains after 1.00 min?

61. The ozone in the earth's ozone layer decomposes according to the equation

$$2\ O_3(g) \longrightarrow 3\ O_2(g)$$

The mechanism of the reaction is thought to proceed through an initial fast equilibrium and a slow step:

Step 1   Fast, reversible $O_3(g) \rightleftharpoons O_2(g) + O(g)$

Step 2   Slow $O_3(g) + O(g) \longrightarrow 2\ O_2(g)$

Show that the mechanism agrees with this experimental rate law:

$$-\Delta[O_3]/\Delta t = k\ [O_3]^2/[O_2].$$

62. ■ Hundreds of different reactions can occur in the stratosphere, among them reactions that destroy the earth's ozone layer. The table below lists several (second-order) reactions of Cl atoms with ozone and organic compounds; each is given with its rate constant.

Reaction	Rate Constant (298 K, cm³/molecule · s)
(a) $Cl + O_3 \rightarrow ClO + O_2$	1.2×10^{-11}
(b) $Cl + CH_4 \rightarrow HCl + CH_3$	1.0×10^{-13}
(c) $Cl + C_3H_8 \rightarrow HCl + C_3H_7$	1.4×10^{-10}
(d) $Cl + CH_2FCl \rightarrow HCl + CHFCl$	3.0×10^{-18}

For equal concentrations of Cl and the other reactant, which is the slowest reaction? Which is the fastest reaction?

63. Data for the reaction

$$[Mn(CO)_5(CH_3CN)]^+ + NC_5H_5$$
$$\longrightarrow [Mn(CO)_5(NC_5H_5)]^+ + CH_3CN$$

are given in the table. Calculate E_a from a plot of ln k versus $1/T$.

T(K)	k(min⁻¹)
298	0.0409
308	0.0818
318	0.157

64. ■ The gas-phase reaction

$$2\ N_2O_5(g) \longrightarrow 4\ NO_2(g) + O_2(g)$$

has an activation energy of 103 kJ/mol-rxn, and the rate constant is 0.0900 min⁻¹ at 328.0 K. Find the rate constant at 318.0 K.

65. ■ ▲ Egg protein albumin is precipitated when an egg is cooked in boiling (100 °C) water. E_a for this first-order reaction is 52.0 kJ/mol. Estimate the time to prepare a 3-min egg at an altitude at which water boils at 90 °C.

66. ■ ▲ Two molecules of 1,3-butadiene (C_4H_6) form 1,5-cyclooctadiene, C_8H_{12} at higher temperatures.

$$2\ C_4H_6(g) \longrightarrow C_8H_{12}(g)$$

Use the following data to determine the order of the reaction and the rate constant, k. (Note that the total pressure is the pressure of the unreacted C_4H_6 at any time and the pressure of the C_8H_{12}.)

Time (min)	Total Pressure (mm Hg)
0	436
3.5	428
11.5	413
18.3	401
25.0	391
32.0	382
41.2	371

67. ■ ▲ Hypofluorous acid, HOF, is very unstable, decomposing in a first-order reaction to give HF and O_2, with a half-life of 30. min at room temperature:

$$HOF(g) \longrightarrow HF(g) + \tfrac{1}{2}\ O_2(g)$$

If the partial pressure of HOF in a 1.00-L flask is initially 1.00×10^2 mm Hg at 25 °C, what are the total pressure in the flask and the partial pressure of HOF after exactly 30 min? After 45 min?

68. ■ ▲ We know that the decomposition of SO_2Cl_2 is first order in SO_2Cl_2,

$$SO_2Cl_2(g) \longrightarrow SO_2(g) + Cl_2(g)$$

with a half-life of 245 min at 600 K. If you begin with a partial pressure of SO_2Cl_2 of 25 mm Hg in a 1.0-L flask, what is the partial pressure of each reactant and product after 245 min? What is the partial pressure of each reactant after 12 h?

69. ■ ▲ Nitramide, NO_2NH_2, decomposes slowly in aqueous solution according to the following reaction:

$$NO_2NH_2(aq) \rightarrow N_2O(g) + H_2O(\ell)$$

The reaction follows the experimental rate law

$$Rate = \frac{k[NO_2NH_2]}{[H_3O^+]}$$

(a) What is the apparent order of the reaction in a buffered solution?

(b) Which of the following mechanisms is the most appropriate for the interpretation of this rate law? Explain.

Mechanism 1

$$NO_2NH_2 \xrightarrow{k_1} N_2O + H_2O$$

Mechanism 2

$$NO_2NH_2 + H_3O^+ \underset{k_2'}{\overset{k_2}{\rightleftharpoons}} NO_2NH_3^+ + H_2O$$
(rapid equilibrium)

$$NO_2NH_3^+ \xrightarrow{k_3} N_2O + H_3O^+ \quad \text{(rate limiting step)}$$

Mechanism 3

$$NO_2NH_2 + H_2O \underset{k_4'}{\overset{k_4}{\rightleftharpoons}} NO_2NH^- + H_3O^+$$
(rapid equilibrium)

$$NO_2NH^- \xrightarrow{k_5} N_2O + OH^- \quad \text{(rate limiting step)}$$

$$H_3O^+ + OH^- \xrightarrow{k_6} 2\,H_2O \quad \text{(very fast reaction)}$$

(c) Show the relationship between the experimentally observed rate constant, k, and the rate constants in the selected mechanism.

(d) Show that hydroxyl ions catalyze the decomposition of nitramide.

70. ■ Many biochemical reactions are catalyzed by acids. A typical mechanism consistent with the experimental results (in which HA is the acid and X is the reactant) is

Step 1 **Fast, reversible** $HA \rightleftharpoons H^+ + A^-$

Step 2 **Fast, reversible** $X + H^+ \rightleftharpoons XH^+$

Step 3 **Slow** $XH^+ \rightarrow$ products

What rate law is derived from this mechanism? What is the order of the reaction with respect to HA? How would doubling the concentration of HA affect the reaction?

In the Laboratory

71. ■ The color change accompanying the reaction of phenolphthalein with strong base is illustrated on page 670. The change in concentration of the dye can be followed by spectrophotometry (page 190), and some data collected by that approach are given below. The initial concentrations were [phenolphthalein] = 0.0050 mol/L and [OH⁻] = 0.61 mol/L. (Data are taken from review materials for kinetics at chemed.chem.purdue.edu.)

(For more details on this reaction see L. Nicholson, *Journal of Chemical Education*, Vol. 66, page 725, 1989.)

Concentration of Phenolphthalein (mol/L)	Time (s)
0.0050	0.00
0.0045	10.5
0.0040	22.3
0.0035	35.7
0.0030	51.1
0.0025	69.3
0.0020	91.6
0.0015	120.4
0.0010	160.9
0.00050	230.3
0.00025	299.6

(a) Plot the data above as [phenolphthalein] versus time, and determine the average rate from $t = 0$ to $t = 15$ s and from $t = 100$ s to $t = 125$ s. Does the rate change? If so, why?

(b) What is the instantaneous rate at 50 s?

(c) Use a graphical method to determine the order of the reaction with respect to phenolphthalein. Write the rate law, and determine the rate constant.

(d) What is the half-life for the reaction?

72. ▲ We want to study the hydrolysis of the beautiful green, cobalt-based complex called *trans*-dichloro-bis(ethylenediamine)cobalt(III) ion,

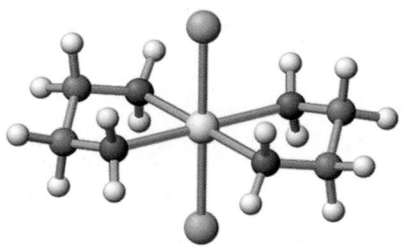

In this hydrolysis reaction, the green complex ion *trans*-$[Co(en)_2Cl_2]^+$ forms the red complex ion $[Co(en)_2(H_2O)Cl]^{2+}$ as a Cl^- ion is replaced with a water molecule on the Co^{3+} ion (en = $H_2NCH_2CH_2NH_2$).

$$\begin{array}{l} trans\text{-}[Co(en)_2Cl_2]^+(aq) + H_2O(\ell) \rightarrow \\ \textbf{green} \\ \qquad\qquad [Co(en)_2(H_2O)Cl]^{2+}(aq) + Cl^-(aq) \\ \qquad\qquad \textbf{red} \end{array}$$

▲ more challenging ■ in OWL Blue-numbered questions answered in Appendix O

The reaction progress is followed by observing the color of the solution. The original solution is green, and the final solution is red, but at some intermediate stage when both the reactant and product are present, the solution is gray.

Original solution

Intermediate solution

Final solution

Photos: Charles D. Winters

Reactions such as this have been studied extensively, and experiments suggest that the initial, slow step in the reaction is the breaking of the Co—Cl bond to give a five-coordinate intermediate. The intermediate is then attacked rapidly by water.

Slow: $trans$-$[Co(en)_2Cl_2]^+(aq) \rightarrow$
$$[Co(en)_2Cl]^{2+}(aq) + Cl^-(aq)$$

Fast: $[Co(en)_2Cl]^{2+}(aq) + H_2O(aq) \rightarrow$
$$[Co(en)_2(H_2O)Cl]^{2+}(aq)$$

(a) Based on the reaction mechanism, what is the predicted rate law?
(b) As the reaction proceeds, the color changes from green to red with an intermediate stage where the color is gray. The gray color is reached at the same time, no matter what the concentration of the green starting material (at the same temperature). How does this show the reaction is first order in the green form? Explain.

(c) The activation energy for a reaction can be found by plotting ln k versus $1/T$. However, here we do not need to measure k directly. Instead, because $k = -(1/t)\ln([R]/[R]_0)$, the time needed to achieve the gray color is a measure of k. Use the data below to find the activation energy.

Temperature °C	Time Needed to Achieve Gray Colors (for the same initial concentration)
56	156 s
60	114 s
65	88 s
75	47 s

73. The enzyme chymotrypsin catalyzes the hydrolysis of a peptide containing phenylalanine. Using the data below at a given temperature, calculate the maximum rate of the reaction, Rate$_{max}$. (For more information on enzyme catalysis and the Michaelis–Menten model, see page 702.)

Peptide Concentration (mol/L)	Reaction Rate (mol/L · min)
2.5×10^{-4}	2.2×10^{-6}
5.0×10^{-4}	3.8×10^{-6}
10.0×10^{-4}	5.9×10^{-6}
15.0×10^{-4}	7.1×10^{-6}

74. ■ The substitution of CO in $Ni(CO)_4$ by another molecule L [where L is an electron-pair donor such as $P(CH_3)_3$] was studied some years ago and led to an understanding of some of the general principles that govern the chemistry of compounds having metal–CO bonds. (See J. P. Day, F. Basolo, and R. G. Pearson: *Journal of the American Chemical Society*, Vol. 90, p. 6927, 1968.) A detailed study of the kinetics of the reaction led to the following mechanism:

Slow $\quad\quad Ni(CO)_4 \rightarrow Ni(CO)_3 + CO$

Fast $\quad\quad Ni(CO)_3 + L \rightarrow Ni(CO)_3L$

(a) What is the molecularity of each of the elementary reactions?
(b) Doubling the concentration of $Ni(CO)_4$ increased the reaction rate by a factor of 2. Doubling the concentration of L had no effect on the reaction rate. Based on this information, write the rate equation for the reaction. Does this agree with the mechanism described?
(c) The experimental rate constant for the reaction, when L = $P(C_6H_5)_3$, is 9.3×10^{-3} s^{-1} at 20 °C. If the initial concentration of $Ni(CO)_4$ is 0.025 M, what is the concentration of the product after 5.0 min?

Summary and Conceptual Questions
The following questions may use concepts from this and previous chapters.

75. Hydrogenation reactions, processes wherein H_2 is added to a molecule, are usually catalyzed. An excellent catalyst is a very finely divided metal suspended in the reaction solvent. Tell why finely divided rhodium, for example, is a much more efficient catalyst than a small block of the metal.

76. ■ ▲ Suppose you have 1000 blocks, each of which is 1.0 cm on a side. If all 1000 of these blocks are stacked to give a cube that is 10. cm on a side, what fraction of the 1000 blocks have at least one surface on the outside surface of the cube? Next, divide the 1000 blocks into eight equal piles of blocks and form them into eight cubes, 5.0 cm on a side. What fraction of the blocks now have at least one surface on the outside of the cubes? How does this mathematical model pertain to Study Question 75?

77. ■ The following statements relate to the reaction for the formation of HI:

$$H_2(g) + I_2(g) \rightarrow 2\ HI(g) \qquad Rate = k[H_2][I_2]$$

Determine which of the following statements are true. If a statement is false, indicate why it is incorrect.
(a) The reaction must occur in a single step.
(b) This is a second-order reaction overall.
(c) Raising the temperature will cause the value of k to decrease.
(d) Raising the temperature lowers the activation energy for this reaction.
(e) If the concentrations of both reactants are doubled, the rate will double.
(f) Adding a catalyst in the reaction will cause the initial rate to increase.

78. ■ Chlorine atoms contribute to the destruction of the earth's ozone layer by the following sequence of reactions:

$$Cl + O_3 \rightarrow ClO + O_2$$
$$ClO + O \rightarrow Cl + O_2$$

where the O atoms in the second step come from the decomposition of ozone by sunlight:

$$O_3(g) \rightarrow O(g) + O_2(g)$$

What is the net equation on summing these three equations? Why does this lead to ozone loss in the stratosphere? What is the role played by Cl in this sequence of reactions? What name is given to species such as ClO?

79. Describe each of the following statements as true or false. If false, rewrite the sentence to make it correct.
(a) The rate-determining elementary step in a reaction is the slowest step in a mechanism.
(b) It is possible to change the rate constant by changing the temperature.
(c) As a reaction proceeds at constant temperature, the rate remains constant.
(d) A reaction that is third order overall must involve more than one step.

80. ■ Identify which of the following statements are incorrect. If the statement is incorrect, rewrite it to be correct.
(a) Reactions are faster at a higher temperature because activation energies are lower.
(b) Rates increase with increasing concentration of reactants because there are more collisions between reactant molecules.
(c) At higher temperatures, a larger fraction of molecules have enough energy to get over the activation energy barrier.
(d) Catalyzed and uncatalyzed reactions have identical mechanisms.

81. ■ The reaction cyclopropane → propene occurs on a platinum metal surface at 200 °C. (The platinum is a catalyst.) The reaction is first order in cyclopropane. Indicate how the following quantities change (increase, decrease, or no change) as this reaction progresses, assuming constant temperature.
(a) [cyclopropane]
(b) [propene]
(c) [catalyst]
(d) the rate constant, k
(e) the order of the reaction
(f) the half-life of cyclopropane

82. Isotopes are often used as "tracers" to follow an atom through a chemical reaction, and the following is an example. Acetic acid reacts with methanol (Chapter 11).

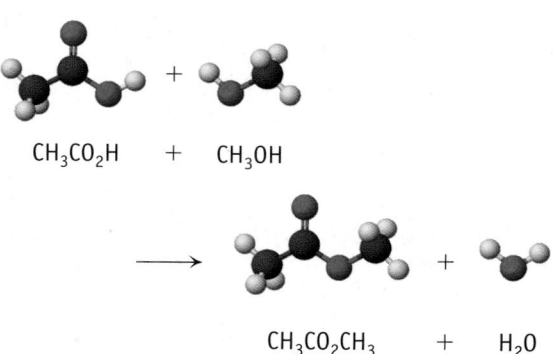

$$CH_3CO_2H \quad + \quad CH_3OH$$

$$\longrightarrow$$

$$CH_3CO_2CH_3 \quad + \quad H_2O$$

Explain how you could use the isotope ^{18}O to show whether the oxygen atom in the water comes from the —OH of the acid or the —OH of the alcohol.

83. ■ Examine the reaction coordinate diagram given here.

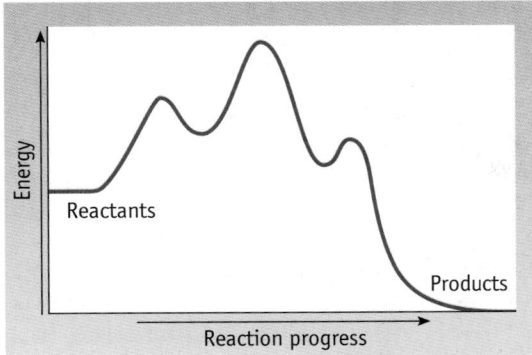

(a) How many steps are in the mechanism for the reaction described by this diagram?
(b) Is the reaction overall exothermic or endothermic?

84. Draw a reaction coordinate diagram for an exothermic reaction that occurs in a single step. Identify the activation energy and the net energy change for the reaction on this diagram. Draw a second diagram that represents the same reaction in the presence of a catalyst, assuming a single step reaction is involved here also. Identify the activation energy of this reaction and the energy change. Is the activation energy in the two drawings different? Does the energy evolved in the two reactions differ?

85. Screen 15.2 in ChemistryNow illustrates the rate at which a blue dye is bleached.
(a) What is the difference between an instantaneous rate and an average rate?
(b) Observe the graph of food dye concentration versus time on this screen. (Click the "tool" icon on this screen.) The plot shows the concentration of dye as the reaction progresses. What does the steepness of the plot at any particular time tell you about the rate of the reaction at that time?
(c) As the reaction progresses, the concentration of dye decreases as it is consumed. What happens to the reaction rate as this occurs? What is the relationship between reaction rate and dye concentration?

86. ■ Watch the video on Screen 15.4 in ChemistryNow (Control of Reaction Rates—Concentration Dependence).
(a) How does an increase in HCl concentration affect the rate of the reaction of the acid with magnesium metal?
(b) On the second portion of this screen are data for the rate of decomposition of N_2O_5 (click "More"). The initial reaction rate is given for three separate experiments, each beginning with a different concentration of N_2O_5. How is the initial reaction rate related to $[N_2O_5]$?

87. The "Microscopic View of Reactions" is described on Screen 15.9 in ChemistryNow.
(a) According to collision theory, what three conditions must be met for two molecules to react?
(b) Examine the animations that play when numbers 1 and 2 are selected. One of these occurs at a higher temperature than the other. Which one? Explain briefly.
(c) Examine the animations that play when numbers 2 and 3 are selected. Would you expect the reaction of O_3 with N_2 to be more or less sensitive to proper orientation for reaction than the reaction displayed on this screen? Explain briefly.

88. "Reaction Mechanisms and Rate Equations" are described on Screen 15.13 in ChemistryNow.
(a) What is the relationship between the stoichiometric coefficients of the reactants in an elementary step and the rate law for that step?
(b) What is the rate law for Step 2 of mechanism 2?
(c) Examine the "Isotopic Labeling" sidebar to this screen. If the transfer of an oxygen atom from NO_2 to CO occurred in a single step, would any $N^{16}O^{18}O$ be found if the reaction is started using a mixture of $N^{16}O_2$ and $N^{18}O_2$? Why or why not?

89. The mechanism for the iodide ion–catalyzed decomposition of H_2O_2 is described on Screen 15.14 (Catalysis and Reaction Rate) in ChemistryNow.
(a) Examine the mechanism for the iodide ion–catalyzed decomposition of H_2O_2. Explain how the mechanism shows that I^- is a catalyst.
(b) How does the reaction coordinate diagram show that the catalyzed reaction is expected to be faster than the uncatalyzed reaction?

16 | Principles of Reactivity: Chemical Equilibria

Solution of cobalt(II) chloride in dilute hydrochloric acid.

Dynamic and Reversible!

Chemical reactions are dynamic, as proved by experiments in which reactants and products can be interconverted by making small changes in the conditions of the reaction. Dissolving cobalt(II) chloride in dilute hydrochloric acid demonstrates this very well.

Solution in an ice bath.

Solution in a boiling water bath.

Solution after adding excess hydrochloric acid.

Solution after adding excess water.

Reactions and equilibria involving cobalt (II) ions in aqueous solution.

$$[Co(H_2O)_6]^{2+}(aq) + 4\ Cl^-(aq) \rightleftharpoons [CoCl_4]^{2-}(aq) + 6\ H_2O(\ell)$$
red   blue

The solution in the top photo shows the system is a mixture of the red cation, $[Co(H_2O)_6]^{2+}$, and the blue anion, $[CoCl_4]^{2-}$. When the solution is placed in ice, the color changes to red, and when it is put in boiling water, the color is blue. Adding excess hydrochloric acid again changes the color as does adding water.

Questions:
1. Is the conversion of the red cation to the blue anion by changing the temperature exo- or endothermic?
2. Account for the effect of adding hydrochloric acid and excess water.
3. How do these observations prove the reaction is reversible?

Answers to these questions are in Appendix Q.

724

Chapter Goals

OWL *See Chapter Goals Revisited (page 750) for Study Questions keyed to these goals and assignable in OWL.*

- Understand the nature and characteristics of chemical equilibria.
- Understand the significance of the equilibrium constant, K, and the reaction quotient, Q.
- Understand how to use K in quantitative studies of chemical equilibria.

Chapter Outline

The concept of equilibrium is fundamental in chemistry. The general concept was introduced in Chapter 3, and you have already encountered its importance in explaining such phenomena as solubility, acid–base behavior, and changes of state. These preliminary discussions of equilibrium emphasized the following concepts: that chemical reactions are reversible, that in a closed system a state of equilibrium is achieved eventually between reactants and products, and that outside forces can affect the equilibrium. A major result of our further exploration of chemical equilibria in this and the next two chapters will be an ability to describe chemical reactions in more quantitative terms.

Chemistry.Now™

Throughout the text this icon introduces an opportunity for self-study or to explore interactive tutorials by signing in at **www.cengage.com/login**.

16.1 Chemical Equilibrium: A Review

If you mix solutions of $CaCl_2$ and $NaHCO_3$, a chemical reaction is immediately detected: a gas (CO_2) bubbles from the mixture, and white solid (insoluble) $CaCO_3$ forms (Figure 16.1a). The reaction occurring is:

$$Ca^{2+}(aq) + 2\ HCO_3^-(aq) \rightarrow CaCO_3(s) + CO_2(g) + H_2O(\ell)$$

If you next add pieces of dry ice to the suspension of $CaCO_3$ (or if you bubble gaseous CO_2 into the mixture), you will observe that the solid $CaCO_3$ dissolves (Figure 16.1b). This happens because a reaction occurs that is the reverse of the reaction that led to precipitation of $CaCO_3$; that is:

$$CaCO_3(s) + CO_2(aq) + H_2O(\ell) \rightarrow Ca^{2+}(aq) + 2\ HCO_3^-(aq)$$

Now imagine what will happen if the solution of Ca^{2+} and HCO_3^- ions is in a *closed* container (unlike the reaction in Figure 16.1, which was done in an open container). As the reaction begins, Ca^{2+} and HCO_3^- react to give products at some rate. As the reactants are used up, the rate of this reaction slows. At the same time, however, the reaction products ($CaCO_3$, CO_2, and H_2O) begin to combine to reform Ca^{2+} and HCO_3^-, at a rate that increases as the amounts of $CaCO_3$ and CO_2 increase. Eventually, the rate of the forward reaction, the formation of $CaCO_3$, and the rate of the reverse reaction, the redissolving of $CaCO_3$, become equal. With $CaCO_3$ being formed and redissolving at the same rate, no further macroscopic change is observed. We have reached equilibrium, and no further *net* change is observed.

■ **Cave Chemistry** This same chemistry accounts for stalactites and stalagmites in caves. See page 119.

We describe an equilibrium system with an equation that connects reactants and products with double arrows. The double arrows, $\rightleftharpoons$, indicate that the reaction

(a)

(b)

(c)

Photos: Charles D. Winters

FIGURE 16.1 Equilibria in the $CO_2/Ca^{2+}/H_2O$ system. (a) Combining solution of $NaHCO_3$ and $CaCl_2$ produces solid $CaCO_3$. (b) If excess dry ice (the white solid) is added to the $CaCO_3$ precipitated in (a), the calcium carbonate dissolves to give $Ca^{2+}(aq)$ and $HCO_3^-(aq)$ (c). (See also Figure 3.6.)

■ **Reversibility of Reactions** All chemical reactions are reversible, in theory. You may see some of these in your laboratory. A few examples include

$NH_3(g) + HCl(g) \rightleftharpoons NH_4Cl(s)$

$CuSO_4 \cdot 5H_2O(s) \rightleftharpoons$

$\qquad CuSO_4(s) + 5\ H_2O(g)$

$(NH_4)_2CO_3(s) \rightleftharpoons$

$\qquad 2\ NH_3(g) + H_2O(g) + CO_2(g)$

Practically speaking, some reactions cannot be reversed. Frying an egg, for example, is not a reversible process in practical terms.

is reversible and that the reaction will be studied using the concepts of chemical equilibria.

$$Ca^{2+}(aq) + 2\ HCO_3^-(aq) \rightleftharpoons CaCO_3(s) + CO_2(g) + H_2O(\ell)$$

These experiments illustrate an important feature of chemical reactions: *All chemical reactions are reversible, at least in principle.* This was a key point in our earlier discussion of equilibrium (Chapter 3).

Our next step will be to move from a qualitative to a quantitative assessment of equilibrium systems. Among other things, this will lead us to the subject of product- and reactant-favored reactions (◄ page 121). Recall that a reaction that has a greater concentration of products than reactants once it has reached equilibrium is said to be *product-favored.* Similarly, a reaction that has a greater concentration of reactants than products at equilibrium is said to be *reactant-favored.*

Chemistry｡Now™

Sign in at **www.cengage.com/login** and go to Chapter 16 Contents to see:
• Screen 16.2 to watch a video of **a reversible reaction**
• Screen 16.3 for a simulation of **a chemical equilibrium**

16.2 The Equilibrium Constant and Reaction Quotient

Chemical equilibria can also be described in a quantitative fashion. The concentrations of reactants and products when a reaction has reached equilibrium are related. For the reaction of hydrogen and iodine to produce hydrogen iodide, for example, a very large number of experiments have shown that at equilibrium the ratio of the square of the HI concentration to the product of the H_2 and I_2 concentrations is a constant.

$$H_2(g) + I_2(g) \rightleftharpoons 2\ HI(g)$$

$$\frac{[HI]^2}{[H_2][I_2]} = \text{constant}\ (K)\ \text{at equilibrium}$$

This constant is always the same within experimental error for all experiments done at a given temperature. Suppose, for example, the concentrations of H_2 and I_2 in a

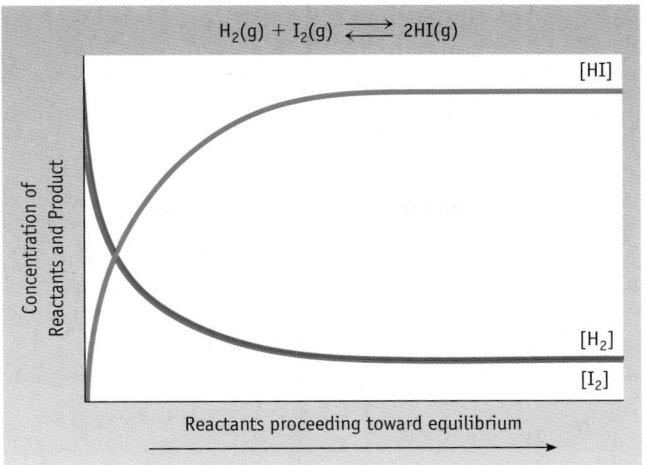

$$H_2(g) + I_2(g) \rightleftharpoons 2HI(g)$$

Concentration of Reactants and Product

[HI]

[H₂]

[I₂]

Reactants proceeding toward equilibrium

Active Figure 16.2 The reaction of H₂ and I₂ reaches equilibrium. The final concentrations of H₂, I₂, and HI depend on the initial concentrations of H₂ and I₂. If one begins with a different set of initial concentrations, the equilibrium concentrations will be different, but the quotient $[HI]^2/[H_2][I_2]$ will always be the same at a given temperature.

Chemistry ⚛ Now™ Sign in at www. cengage.com/login and go to the Chapter Contents menu to explore an interactive version of this figure accompanied by an exercise.

flask are each initially 0.0175 mol/L at 425 °C and that no HI is present. Over time, the concentrations of H_2 and I_2 will decrease, and the concentration of HI will increase until a state of equilibrium is reached (Figure 16.2). If the gases in the flask are then analyzed, the observed concentrations would be $[H_2] = [I_2] = 0.0037$ mol/L and $[HI] = 0.0276$ mol/L. The following table—which we call an **ICE table** for *initial, change*, and *equilibrium* concentrations—summarizes these results:

Equation	$H_2(g)$	+	$I_2(g)$	$\rightleftharpoons$	2 HI(g)
I = *Initial* concentration (M)	0.0175		0.0175		0
C = *Change* in concentration as reaction proceeds to equilibrium	−0.0138		−0.0138		+0.0276
E = *Equilibrium* concentration (M)	0.0037		0.0037		0.0276

■ **ICE Table: Initial, Change, and Equilibrium** Throughout our discussions of chemical equilibria, we shall express the quantitative information for reactions in an amounts table or ICE table (see Chapter 4, page 159). These tables show what the initial (*I*) concentrations are, how those concentrations change (*C*) on proceeding to equilibrium, and what the concentrations are at equilibrium (*E*).

The second line in the table gives the change in concentration of reactants and products on proceeding to equilibrium. Changes are always equal to the difference between the experimentally observed equilibrium and initial concentrations.

Change in concentration = Equilibrium concentration − Initial concentration

Putting the equilibrium concentration values from the ICE table into the expression for the constant (K) gives a value of 56 (to two significant figures).

$$\frac{[HI]^2}{[H_2][I_2]} = \frac{(0.0276)^2}{(0.0037)(0.0037)} = 56$$

Other experiments can be done on the H_2/I_2 reaction with different concentrations of reactants, or done using mixtures of reactants and products. Regardless of the initial amounts, when equilibrium is achieved, the ratio $[HI]^2/[H_2][I_2]$ is always the same (at the same temperature).

The observation that the product and reactant concentrations for the H_2 and I_2 reaction are always in the same ratio can be generalized to other reactions. For the general chemical reaction

$$a A + b B \rightleftharpoons c C + d D$$

we can define the equilibrium constant, K.

When reaction is at equilibrium

$$\text{Equilibrium constant} = K = \frac{[C]^c[D]^d}{[A]^a[B]^b}$$

(16.1)

Equation 16.1 is called the **equilibrium constant expression**. If the ratio of products to reactants as defined by Equation 16.1 matches the equilibrium constant value, the system is known to be at equilibrium. Conversely, if the ratio has a different value, the system is not at equilibrium, and we can predict in which direction the reaction will proceed to reach equilibrium.

In an equilibrium constant expression,

- All concentrations are equilibrium values.
- Product concentrations appear in the numerator, and reactant concentrations appear in the denominator.
- Each concentration is raised to the power of its stoichiometric coefficient in the balanced chemical equation.
- The value of the constant K depends on the particular reaction and on the temperature.
- Units are never given with K.

Chemistry.Now™

Sign in at **www.cengage.com/login** and go to Chapter 16 Contents to see Screen 16.4 for a simulation of **equilibrium and determination of the constant.**

Writing Equilibrium Constant Expressions

Reactions Involving Solids

The oxidation of solid, yellow sulfur produces colorless sulfur dioxide gas in a product-favored reaction (Figure 16.3).

$$S(s) + O_2(g) \rightleftharpoons SO_2(g)$$

The general principle when writing an equilibrium constant expression is to place product concentrations in the numerator and reactant concentrations in the denominator. In reactions involving solids, however, experiments show that the equilibrium concentrations of other reactants or products—here, O_2 and SO_2—do not depend on the amount of solid present (as long as some solid is present at equilibrium). The concentration of a solid such as sulfur is determined by its density, and the density is a fixed value. Therefore, the concentration of sulfur is essentially constant and is not included in the equilibrium constant expression.

$$K = \frac{[SO_2]}{[O_2]}$$

In general, *the concentrations of any solid reactants and products are not included in the equilibrium constant expression.*

Reactions in Aqueous Solutions

There are also special considerations for reactions occurring in aqueous solution in which water is either a reactant or a product. Consider ammonia, which is a weak base owing to its reaction with water.

$$NH_3(aq) + H_2O(\ell) \rightleftharpoons NH_4^+(aq) + OH^-(aq)$$

Because the water concentration is very high in a dilute ammonia solution, the concentration of water is essentially unchanged by the reaction. The general rule for such reactions in aqueous solution is that *the molar concentration of water is not included in the equilibrium constant expression.* Thus, for aqueous ammonia we write

$$K = \frac{[NH_4^+][OH^-]}{[NH_3]}$$

FIGURE 16.3 Burning sulfur.
Elemental sulfur burns in oxygen with a beautiful blue flame to give SO_2 gas.

(left margin) Charles D. Winters

Reactions Involving Gases: K_c and K_p

Concentration data can be used to calculate equilibrium constants for both aqueous and gaseous systems. In these cases, the symbol K is sometimes given the subscript "c" for "concentration," as in K_c. For gases, however, equilibrium constant expressions can be written in another way—in terms of partial pressures of reactants and products. If you rearrange the ideal gas law, $[PV = nRT]$, and recognize that the "gas concentration," (n/V), is equivalent to P/RT, you see that the partial pressure of a gas is proportional to its concentration $[P = (n/V)RT]$. If reactant and product quantities are given in partial pressures (in atmospheres or, more properly, in bars), then K is given the subscript "p," as in K_p.

$$H_2(g) + I_2(g) \rightleftharpoons 2\ HI(g)$$

$$K_p = \frac{P_{HI}^2}{P_{H_2} P_{I_2}}$$

Notice that the basic form of the equilibrium constant expression is the same as for K_c. In some cases, the numerical values of K_c and K_p are the same, but they are different when the numbers of moles of gaseous reactants and products are different. *A Closer Look: Equilibrium Constant Expressions for Gases—K_c and K_p* shows how K_c and K_p are related and how to convert from one to the other.

■ K_c **and** K_p The subscript "c" (K_c) indicates that the numerical values of concentrations in the equilibrium constant expression have units of mol/L. A subscript "p" (K_p) indicates values in units of pressure. In this chapter, we will sometimes write simply K for K_c but will always write K_p to indicate that equilibrium values are in units of pressure.

Chemistry.☼.Now™

Sign in at **www.cengage.com/login** and go to Chapter 16 Contents to see Screen 16.5 for a simulation and a tutorial on **writing equilibrium expressions.**

■ **EXAMPLE 16.1** **Writing Equilibrium Constant Expressions**

Problem Write the equilibrium constant expressions for the following reactions.

(a) $N_2(g) + 3\ H_2(g) \rightleftharpoons 2\ NH_3(g)$

(b) $H_2CO_3(aq) + H_2O(\ell) \rightleftharpoons HCO_3^-(aq) + H_3O^+(aq)$

Strategy Remember that product concentrations always appear in the numerator and reactant concentrations appear in the denominator. Each concentration should be raised to a power equal to the stoichiometric coefficient in the balanced equation. In reaction (b), the water concentration does not appear in the equilibrium constant expression.

Solution

(a) $\quad K = \dfrac{[NH_3]^2}{[N_2][H_2]^3}$ $\qquad\qquad$ (b) $\quad K = \dfrac{[HCO_3^-][H_3O^+]}{[H_2CO_3]}$

EXERCISE 16.1 **Writing Equilibrium Constant Expressions**

Write the equilibrium constant expression for each of the following reactions in terms of concentrations.

(a) $CO_2(g) + C(s) \rightleftharpoons 2\ CO(g)$

(b) $[Cu(NH_3)_4]^+(aq) \rightleftharpoons Cu^{2+}(aq) + 4\ NH_3(aq)$

(c) $CH_3CO_2H(aq) + H_2O(\ell) \rightleftharpoons CH_3CO_2^-(aq) + H_3O^+(aq)$

Many metal carbonates, such as limestone, decompose on heating to give the metal oxide and CO_2 gas.

$$CaCO_3(s) \rightleftharpoons CaO(s) + CO_2(g)$$

The equilibrium condition for this reaction can be expressed either in terms of the number of moles per liter of CO_2, $K_c = [CO_2]$ or in terms of the pressure of CO_2, $K_p = P_{CO_2}$. From the ideal gas law, you know that

$$P = (n/V)RT =$$
$$\text{(concentration in mol/L)} \times RT$$

For this reaction, we can therefore say that $P_{CO_2} = [CO_2]RT = K_p$. Because $K_c = [CO_2]$, we find that $K_p = K_c(RT)$. That is, the values of K_p and K_c are not the same; for the decomposition of calcium carbonate, K_p is the product of K_c and the factor RT.

Consider the equilibrium constant for the reaction of N_2 and H_2 to produce ammonia in terms of partial pressures, K_p.

$$N_2(g) + 3 H_2(g) \rightleftharpoons 2 NH_3(g)$$

$$K_p = \frac{(P_{NH_3})^2}{(P_{N_2})(P_{H_2})^3} = 5.8 \times 10^5$$

Does K_c, the equilibrium constant in terms of concentrations, have the same value as or a different value than K_p? We can answer this question by substituting for each pressure in K_p the equivalent expression $[C](RT)$. That is,

$$K_p = \frac{\{[NH_3](RT)\}^2}{\{[N_2](RT)\}\{[H_2](RT)\}^3} =$$
$$\frac{[NH_3]^2}{[N_2][H_2]^3} \times \frac{1}{(RT)^2} = \frac{K_c}{(RT)^2}$$

Solving for K_c we find

$$K_c = K_p(RT)^2$$
$$K_c = 5.8 \times 10^5 [(0.08206)(298)]^2 = 3.5 \times 10^8$$

Once again, you see that K_p and K_c are not the same but are related by some function of RT.

Looking carefully at these examples, we find that

$$K_p = K_c(RT)^{\Delta n}$$

where Δn is the change in the number of moles of gas on going from reactants to products.

Δn = total moles of gaseous products − total moles of gaseous reactants

For the decomposition of $CaCO_3$,

$$\Delta n = 1 - 0 = 1$$

whereas the value of Δn for the ammonia synthesis is

$$\Delta n = 2 - 4 = -2$$

The Meaning of the Equilibrium Constant, K

Table 16.1 lists a few equilibrium constants for different kinds of reactants. A large value of K means that the concentration of the products is higher than the concentrations of the reactants at equilibrium. That is, the products are favored over the reactants at equilibrium.

$K > 1$: Reaction is product-favored at equilibrium. The concentrations of products are greater than the concentrations of the reactants at equilibrium.

An example is the reaction of nitrogen monoxide and ozone.

$$NO(g) + O_3(g) \rightleftharpoons NO_2(g) + O_2(g)$$

$$K = \frac{[NO_2][O_2]}{[NO][O_3]} = 6 \times 10^{34} \text{ at } 25\ °C$$

The very large value of K indicates that, at equilibrium, $[NO_2][O_2] >> [NO][O_3]$. If stoichiometric amounts of NO and O_3 are mixed and allowed to come to equilibrium, virtually none of the reactants will be found (Figure 16.4a). Essentially, all will have been converted to NO_2 and O_2. A chemist would say that "the reaction has gone to completion."

Conversely, a small value of K means that very little of the products exist when equilibrium has been achieved (Figure 16.4b). That is, the reactants are favored over the products at equilibrium.

$K < 1$: Reaction is reactant-favored at equilibrium. Concentrations of reactants are greater than concentrations of products at equilibrium.

This is true for the formation of ozone from oxygen.

$$3/2\ O_2(g) \rightleftharpoons O_3(g)$$

$$K = \frac{[O_3]}{[O_2]^{3/2}} = 2.5 \times 10^{-29} \text{ at } 25\ °C$$

TABLE 16.1 Selected Equilibrium Constant Values

Reaction	Equilibrium Constant, K (at 25 °C)	Product- or Reactant-Favored
Combination Reaction of Nonmetals		
$S(s) + O_2(g) \rightleftharpoons SO_2(g)$	4.2×10^{52}	$K > 1$; product-favored
$2\ H_2(g) + O_2(g) \rightleftharpoons 2\ H_2O(g)$	3.2×10^{81}	$K > 1$; product-favored
$N_2(g) + 3\ H_2(g) \rightleftharpoons 2\ NH_3(g)$	3.5×10^{8}	$K > 1$; product-favored
$N_2(g) + O_2(g) \rightleftharpoons 2\ NO(g)$	1.7×10^{-3} (at 2300 K)	$K < 1$; reactant-favored
Ionization of Weak Acids and Bases		
$HCO_2H(aq) + H_2O(\ell) \rightleftharpoons HCO_2^-(aq) + H_3O^+(aq)$ formic acid	1.8×10^{-4}	$K < 1$; reactant-favored
$CH_3CO_2H(aq) + H_2O(\ell) \rightleftharpoons CH_3CO_2^-(aq) + H_3O^+(aq)$ acetic acid	1.8×10^{-5}	$K < 1$; reactant-favored
$H_2CO_3(aq) + H_2O(\ell) \rightleftharpoons HCO_3^-(aq) + H_3O^+(aq)$ carbonic acid	4.2×10^{-7}	$K < 1$; reactant-favored
$NH_3(aq) + H_2O(\ell) \rightleftharpoons NH_4^+(aq) + OH^-(aq)$ ammonia	1.8×10^{-5}	$K < 1$; reactant-favored
Dissolution of "Insoluble" Solids		
$CaCO_3(s) \rightleftharpoons Ca^{2+}(aq) + CO_3^{2-}(aq)$	3.8×10^{-9}	$K < 1$; reactant-favored
$AgCl(s) \rightleftharpoons Ag^+(aq) + Cl^-(aq)$	1.8×10^{-10}	$K < 1$; reactant-favored

The very small value of K indicates that, at equilibrium, $[O_3] << [O_2]^{3/2}$. If O_2 is placed in a flask, very little O_2 will have been converted to O_3 when equilibrium has been achieved.

When K is close to 1, it may not be immediately clear whether the reactant concentrations are larger than the product concentrations, or *vice versa*. It will depend on the form of K and thus on the reaction stoichiometry. Calculations of the concentrations will have to be done.

Chemistry ⚛ Now™

Sign in at **www.cengage.com/login** and go to Chapter 16 Contents to see Screen 16.6 for a simulation of **an equilibrium.**

(a)

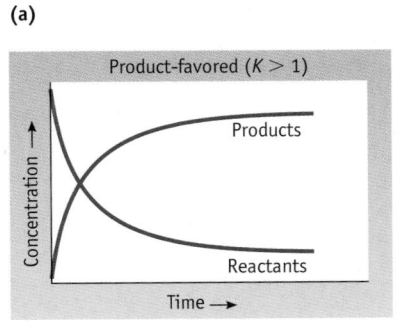

(b)

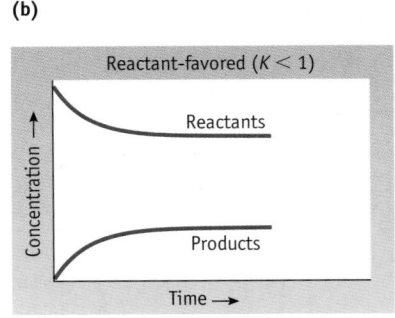

FIGURE 16.4 The difference between product- and reactant-favored reactions. In (a) the concentration of products exceeds the concentration of reactants, and the reaction is product-favored. In (b), the reactant concentrations exceed the product concentration, and the reaction is reactant-favored.

EXERCISE 16.2 The Equilibrium Constant and Extent of Reaction

Are the following reactions product- or reactant-favored at equilibrium?

(a) $[Cu(NH_3)_4]^{2+} \rightleftharpoons Cu^{2+}(aq) + 4\ NH_3(aq)$ $\quad K = 1.5 \times 10^{-13}$

(b) $[Cd(NH_3)_4]^{2+} \rightleftharpoons Cd^{2+}(aq) + 4\ NH_3(aq)$ $\quad K = 1.0 \times 10^{-7}$

If each reaction has a reactant concentration of 0.10 M, in which solution is the NH_3 concentration greater?

The Reaction Quotient, *Q*

The equilibrium constant, *K*, for a reaction has a particular numerical value when the reactants and products are at equilibrium. When the reactants and products in a reaction are not at equilibrium, however, it is convenient to calculate the reaction quotient, *Q*. For the general reaction of *A* and *B* to give *C* and *D*,

$$a\,A + b\,B \rightleftharpoons c\,C + d\,D$$

the reaction quotient is defined as

$$\text{Reaction quotient} = Q = \frac{[C]^c[D]^d}{[A]^a[B]^b} \tag{16.2}$$

■ **Comparing *Q* and *K***

Relative Magnitude	Direction of Reaction
$Q < K$	Reactants → Products
$Q = K$	Reaction at equilibrium
$Q > K$	Reactants ← Products

This expression *appears* to be just like Equation 16.1, but it is not. The concentrations of reactants and products in the expression for *Q* are those that occur *at any point* as the reaction proceeds from reactants to an equilibrium mixture. *Only when the system is at equilibrium does* $Q = K$. For the reaction of H_2 and I_2 to give HI (Figure 16.2), any combination of reactant and product concentrations before equilibrium is achieved will give a value of *Q* different than *K*.

Determining a reaction quotient is useful for two reasons. First, it will tell you whether a system is at equilibrium (when $Q = K$) or is not at equilibrium (when $Q \neq K$). Second, by comparing *Q* and *K*, we can predict what changes will occur in reactant and product concentrations as the reaction proceeds to equilibrium.

- $\boldsymbol{Q < K}$ If *Q* is less than *K*, some reactants must be converted to products for the reaction to reach equilibrium. This will decrease the reactant concentrations and increase the product concentrations. (This is the case for the system in Figure 16.5a.)
- $\boldsymbol{Q > K}$ If *Q* is greater than *K*, some products must be converted to reactants for the reaction to reach equilibrium. This will increase the reactant concentrations and decrease the product concentrations. (See Figure 16.5c)

To illustrate these points, let us consider a reaction such as the transformation of butane to isobutane (2-methylpropane).

Butane $\rightleftharpoons$ Isobutane

$CH_3CH_2CH_2CH_3 \rightleftharpoons CH_3CH(CH_3)CH_3$

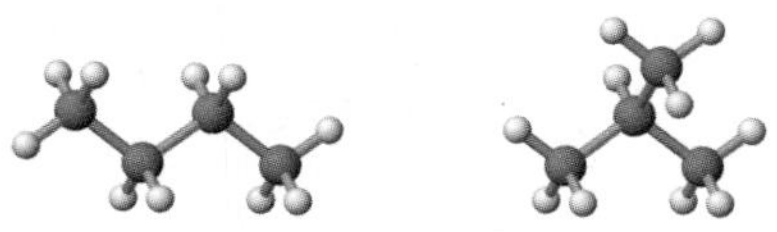

$$K_c = \frac{[\text{isobutane}]}{[\text{butane}]} = 2.50 \text{ at } 298\text{ K}$$

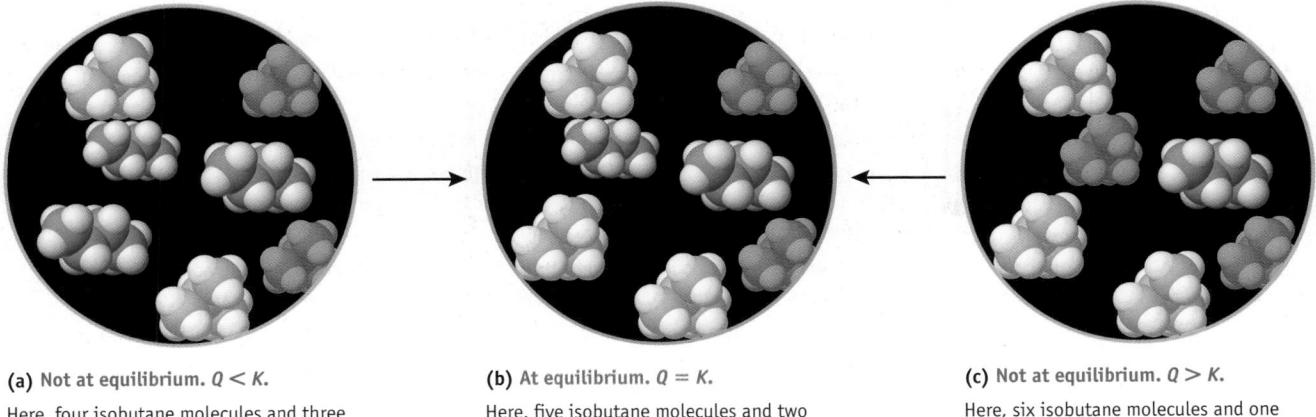

(a) Not at equilibrium. $Q < K$.

Here, four isobutane molecules and three butane molecules are present. Reaction will proceed to convert butane into isobutane to reach equilibrium.

(b) At equilibrium. $Q = K$.

Here, five isobutane molecules and two butane molecules are present. Reaction is at equilibrium.

(c) Not at equilibrium. $Q > K$.

Here, six isobutane molecules and one butane molecule are present. Reaction will proceed to convert isobutane into butane to reach equilibrium.

FIGURE 16.5 The interconversion of isobutane and butane. Only when the concentrations of isobutane and butane are in the ratio [isobutane/butane] = 2.5 is the system at equilibrium (b). With any other ratio of concentrations, there will be a net conversion of one compound into the other until equilibrium is achieved.

If the concentration of one of the compounds is known, then only one value of the other concentration will satisfy the equation for the equilibrium constant. For example, if [butane] is 1.0 mol/L, then the equilibrium concentration of isobutane, [isobutane], must be 2.5 mol/L. If [butane] is 0.63 mol/L at equilibrium, then [isobutane] is 1.6 mol/L.

$$[\text{isobutane}] = K[\text{butane}] = (2.50)(0.63 \text{ mol/L}) = 1.6 \text{ mol/L}$$

Any mixture of butane and isobutane, whether at equilibrium or not, can be represented by the reaction quotient Q ($=$[isobutane]/[butane]). Suppose you have a mixture composed of 3 mol/L of butane and 4 mol/L of isobutane (at 298 K) (Figure 16.5a). This means that the reaction quotient, Q, is

$$Q = \frac{\left[\text{isobutane}\right]}{\left[\text{butane}\right]} = \frac{4.0}{3.0} = 1.3$$

This set of concentrations clearly does not represent an equilibrium system because $Q < K$. To reach equilibrium, some butane molecules must be transformed into molecules of isobutane, thereby lowering [butane] and raising [isobutane]. This transformation will continue until the ratio [isobutane]/[butane] = 2.5; that is, until $Q = K$ (Figure 16.5b).

What happens when there is too much isobutane in the system relative to the amount of butane? Suppose [isobutane] = 6.0 mol/L but [butane] is only 1.0 mol/L (Figure 16.5c). Now the reaction quotient Q is greater than K ($Q > K$), and the system is again not at equilibrium. It will proceed to equilibrium by converting isobutane molecules to butane molecules.

Chemistry · Now™

Sign in at **www.cengage.com/login** and go to Chapter 16 Contents to see Screen 16.9 for a simulation and tutorial on **Q, the reaction quotient.**

Problem The brown gas nitrogen dioxide, NO_2, can exist in equilibrium with the colorless gas N_2O_4. $K = 170$ at 298 K for the reaction

$$2 \, NO_2(g) \rightleftharpoons N_2O_4(g) \quad K = 170$$

Suppose that, at a specific time, the concentration of NO_2 is 0.015 M and the concentration of N_2O_4 is 0.025 M. Is Q larger than, smaller than, or equal to K? If the system is not at equilibrium, in which direction will the reaction proceed to achieve equilibrium?

Strategy Write the expression for Q, and substitute the numerical values into the equation. Decide whether Q is less than, equal to, or greater than K.

Solution When the reactant and product concentrations are substituted into the reaction quotient expression, we have

$$Q = \frac{[N_2O_4]}{[NO_2]^2} = \frac{(0.025)}{(0.015)^2} = 110$$

The value of Q is less than the value of K ($Q < K$), so the reaction is not at equilibrium. The system proceeds to equilibrium by converting NO_2 to N_2O_4, increasing $[N_2O_4]$, and decreasing $[NO_2]$ until $Q = K$.

Comment When calculating Q, make sure that you raise each concentration to the power of the stoichiometric coefficient.

EXERCISE 16.3 The Reaction Quotient

Answer the following questions regarding the butane $\rightleftharpoons$ isobutane equilibrium ($K = 2.50$ at 298 K).

(a) Is the system at equilibrium when [butane] = 0.97 M and [isobutane] = 2.18 M? If it is not at equilibrium, in which direction will the reaction proceed to achieve equilibrium?

(b) Is the system at equilibrium when [butane] = 0.75 M and [isobutane] = 2.60 M? If it is not at equilibrium, in which direction will the reaction proceed to achieve equilibrium?

EXERCISE 16.4 The Reaction Quotient

At 2000 K the equilibrium constant for the formation of NO(g) is 4.0×10^{-4}.

$$N_2(g) + O_2(g) \rightleftharpoons 2 \, NO(g)$$

You have a flask in which, at 2000 K, the concentration of N_2 is 0.50 mol/L, that of O_2 is 0.25 mol/L, and that of NO is 4.2×10^{-3} mol/L. Is the system at equilibrium? If not, predict which way the reaction will proceed to achieve equilibrium.

16.3 Determining an Equilibrium Constant

When the experimental values of the concentrations of all of the reactants and products are known at equilibrium, an equilibrium constant can be calculated by substituting the data into the equilibrium constant expression. Consider this concept as it applies to the oxidation of sulfur dioxide.

$$2 \, SO_2(g) + O_2(g) \rightleftharpoons 2 \, SO_3(g)$$

In an experiment done at 852 K, the equilibrium concentrations are found to be $[SO_2] = 3.61 \times 10^{-3}$ mol/L, $[O_2] = 6.11 \times 10^{-4}$ mol/L, and $[SO_3] = 1.01 \times 10^{-2}$ mol/L. Substituting these data into the equilibrium constant expression, we can determine the value of K.

$$K = \frac{[SO_3]^2}{[SO_2]^2[O_2]} = \frac{(1.01 \times 10^{-2})^2}{(3.61 \times 10^{-3})^2(6.11 \times 10^{-4})} = 1.28 \times 10^4 \text{ at 852 K}$$

(Notice that K has a large value; at equilibrium, the oxidation of sulfur dioxide is product-favored at 852 K.)

More commonly, an experiment will provide information on the initial quantities of reactants and the concentration at equilibrium of only one of the reactants or of one of the products. The equilibrium concentrations of the rest of the reactants and products must then be inferred from the balanced chemical equation. As an example, consider again the oxidation of sulfur dioxide to sulfur trioxide. Suppose that 1.00 mol of SO_2 and 1.00 mol of O_2 are placed in a 1.00-L flask, this time at 1000 K. When equilibrium has been achieved, 0.925 mol of SO_3 has been formed. Let us use this information to calculate the equilibrium constant for the reaction. After writing the equilibrium constant expression in terms of concentrations, we set up an ICE table (page 727) showing the initial concentrations, the changes in those concentrations on proceeding to equilibrium, and the concentrations at equilibrium.

Equation	2 SO_2(g)	+	O_2(g)	⇌	2 SO_3(g)
Initial (M)	1.00		1.00		0
Change (M)	−0.925		−0.925/2		+0.925
Equilibrium (M)	1.00 − 0.925 = 0.075		1.00 − 0.925/2 = 0.54		0.925

The quantities in the ICE table result from the following analysis:

- The amount of SO_2 consumed on proceeding to equilibrium is equal to the amount of SO_3 produced (= 0.925 mol because the stoichiometric factor is [2 mol SO_2 consumed/2 mol SO_3 produced]). Because SO_2 is consumed, the change in SO_2 concentration is −0.925 M.
- The amount of O_2 consumed is half of the amount of SO_3 produced (= 0.463 mol because the stoichiometric factor is [1 mol O_2 consumed/2 mol SO_3 produced]). The amount of O_2 remaining is 0.54 M.
- The equilibrium concentration of a reactant is always the initial concentration minus the quantity consumed on proceeding to equilibrium. The equilibrium concentration of a product is always the initial concentration plus the quantity produced on proceeding to equilibrium.

With the equilibrium concentrations now known, it is possible to calculate K.

$$K = \frac{[SO_3]^2}{[SO_2]^2[O_2]} = \frac{(0.925)^2}{(0.075)^2(0.54)} = 2.8 \times 10^2 \text{ at 1000 K}$$

Chemistry ⚛ Now™

Sign in at **www.cengage.com/login** and go to Chapter 16 Contents to see:
- Screen 16.8 for a simulation and a tutorial on **determining an equilibrium constant**
- Screen 16.9 for a simulation and a tutorial on **systems at equilibrium**

■ **EXAMPLE 16.3 Calculating an Equilibrium Constant**

Problem An aqueous solution of ethanol and acetic acid, each with an initial concentration of 0.810 M, is heated to 100 °C. At equilibrium, the acetic acid concentration is 0.748 M. Calculate K for the reaction

$C_2H_5OH(aq) + CH_3CO_2H(aq) \rightleftharpoons CH_3CO_2C_2H_5(aq) + H_2O(\ell)$

ethanol   acetic acid   ethyl acetate

Strategy Always focus on defining equilibrium concentrations. The amount of acetic acid remaining is known, so the amount consumed is given by [initial concentration of reactant − concentration of reactant remaining]. Because the balanced chemical equation tells us 1 mol of ethanol reacts per mol of acetic acid, the concentration of ethanol is also known at equilibrium. Finally, the concentration of the product formed upon reaching equilibrium is calculated from the amount of reactant consumed.

Ester Preparation and Equilibrium

Esters are a common and important class of organic molecules (◀ page 729). The equilibrium constant for the reaction of an acid and an alcohol is not large, so chemists know that to achieve maximum yield of the ester they remove the water formed in the reaction. As explained in Section 16.6, this means that a larger concentration of ester can exist at equilibrium.

Solution The amount of acetic acid consumed is 0.810 M − 0.748 M = 0.062 M. This is the same as the amount of ethanol consumed and the same as the amount of ethyl acetate produced. The ICE table for this reaction is therefore

Equation	C_2H_5OH	+	CH_3CO_2H	⇌	$CH_3CO_2C_2H_5$	+	H_2O
Initial (M)	0.810		0.810		0		
Change (M)	−0.062		−0.062		+0.062		
Equilibrium (M)	0.748		0.748		0.062		

The concentration of each substance at equilibrium is now known, and K can be calculated.

$$K = \frac{[CH_3CO_2C_2H_5]}{[C_2H_5OH][CH_3CO_2H]} = \frac{0.062}{(0.748)(0.748)} = \boxed{0.11}$$

Comment Notice that water does not appear in the equilibrium expression.

EXAMPLE 16.4 Calculating an Equilibrium Constant (K_p) Using Partial Pressures

Problem Suppose a tank initially contains H_2S at a pressure of 10.00 atm and a temperature of 800 K. When the reaction

$$2\ H_2S(g) \rightleftharpoons 2\ H_2(g) + S_2(g)$$

has come to equilibrium, the partial pressure of S_2 vapor is 0.020 atm. Calculate K_p.

Strategy Recall from page 729 that the equilibrium constant expression can be written in terms of gas partial pressures or concentrations; here, the data are given in terms of partial pressures. In determining the value of an equilibrium constant, we again focus on defining equilibrium amounts. The partial pressure of $S_2(g)$ at equilibrium is known, so the amount produced in proceeding to equilibrium is given by [equilibrium partial pressure − initial partial pressure]. The balanced chemical equation tells us that 2 mol of $H_2(g)$ are produced per mole of $S_2(g)$ produced, so we can determine the partial pressure of $H_2(g)$ produced and then the partial pressure of $H_2(g)$ at equilibrium. Finally, the balanced equation also tells us that the partial pressure of $H_2S(g)$ consumed is twice the partial pressure of $S_2(g)$ produced. The equilibrium pressure of the $H_2S(g)$ is then given by $P_{initial} - P_{gas\ consumed}$.

Solution The equilibrium constant expression that we want to evaluate is

$$K_p = \frac{(P_{H_2})^2 P_{S_2}}{(P_{H_2S})^2}$$

We know that $P(H_2S)_{initial} = 10.00$ atm and that $P(S_2)_{equilibrium} = 0.020$ atm, so we can set up an ICE table that expresses the equilibrium partial pressures of each gas.

Equation	$2\ H_2S(g)$	⇌	$2\ H_2(g)$	+	$S_2(g)$
Initial (atm)	10.00		0		0
Change (atm)	−2(0.020)		+2(0.020)		+0.020
Equilibrium (atm)	9.96		0.040		0.020

Now that the partial pressures of all of the reactants and products are known, K_p can be calculated.

$$K_p = \frac{(P_{H_2})^2 P_{S_2}}{(P_{H_2S})^2} = \frac{(0.040)^2(0.020)}{(9.96)^2} = \boxed{3.2 \times 10^{-7}}$$

Comment The value of K_p will be the same as the value of K_c only when the number of moles of gaseous reactants is the same as the number of moles of gaseous products. This is not true here, so $K_p \neq K_c$. See *A Closer Look* (page 730).

EXERCISE 16.5 Calculating an Equilibrium Constant, K

A solution is prepared by dissolving 0.050 mol of diiodocyclohexane, $C_6H_{10}I_2$, in the solvent CCl_4. The total solution volume is 1.00 L. When the reaction

$$C_6H_{10}I_2 \rightleftharpoons C_6H_{10} + I_2$$

has come to equilibrium at 35 °C, the concentration of I_2 is 0.035 mol/L.

(a) What are the concentrations of $C_6H_{10}I_2$ and C_6H_{10} at equilibrium?

(b) Calculate K_c, the equilibrium constant.

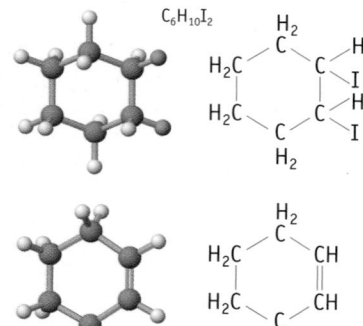

$C_6H_{10}I_2$

C_6H_{10}

16.4 Using Equilibrium Constants in Calculations

In many cases, the value of K and the initial amounts of reactants are known, and you want to know the amounts present at equilibrium. As we look at several examples of this situation, we will again use ICE tables that summarize initial conditions, final conditions, and changes on proceeding to equilibrium.

Chemistry.Now™

Sign in at **www.cengage.com/login** and go to Chapter 16 Contents to see Screen 16.10 for a tutorial on **determining equilibrium concentrations.**

■ **EXAMPLE 16.5** **Calculating Equilibrium Concentrations**

Problem The equilibrium constant K_c ($= 55.64$) for

$$H_2(g) + I_2(g) \rightleftharpoons 2\ HI(g)$$

has been determined at 425 °C. If 1.00 mol each of H_2 and I_2 are placed in a 0.500-L flask at 425 °C, what are the concentrations of H_2, I_2, and HI when equilibrium has been achieved?

Strategy Because we know the value of K_c and the initial concentrations, we can set up the equilibrium constant expression and an ICE table. We will use the equilibrium constant expression to solve for the unknown values in the table.

Solution The first step is to write the equilibrium constant expression.

$$K = \frac{[HI]^2}{[H_2][I_2]} = 55.64$$

Next, set up an ICE table to express the concentrations of H_2, I_2, and HI before reaction and upon reaching equilibrium. Here, however, we do not know the numerical values of the changes in the H_2 and I_2 concentrations on proceeding to equilibrium. Because the change in $[H_2]$ is the same as the change in $[I_2]$ and because their coefficients in the balanced equation are each 1, we express these changes as the unknown quantity x. It follows that $2x$ is the quantity of HI produced (because the stoichiometric factor is [2 mol HI produced/1 mol H_2 consumed]).

Equation	$H_2(g)$	+	$I_2(g)$	$\rightleftharpoons$	$2\ HI(g)$
Initial (M)	1.00 mol/0.500 L = 2.00 M		1.00 mol/0.500 L = 2.00 M		0 0
Change (M)	$-x$		$-x$		$+2x$
Equilibrium (M)	$2.00 - x$		$2.00 - x$		$2x$

Now the expressions for the equilibrium concentrations can be substituted into the equilibrium constant expression.

$$55.64 = \frac{(2x)^2}{(2.00 - x)(2.00 - x)} = \frac{(2x)^2}{(2.00 - x)^2}$$

In this case, the unknown quantity x can be found by taking the square root of both sides of the equation,

$$\sqrt{K} = 7.459 = \frac{2x}{2.00 - x}$$
$$7.459\ (2.00 - x) = 14.9 - 7.459x = 2x$$
$$14.9 = 9.459x$$
$$x = 1.58$$

With x known, we can solve for the equilibrium concentrations of the reactants and products.

$$[H_2] = [I_2] = 2.00 - x = 0.42\ M$$
$$[HI] = 2x = 3.16\ M$$

Comment It is always wise to verify the answer by substituting the values back into the equilibrium expression to see if your calculated K agrees with the one given in the problem. In this case, $(3.16)^2/(0.42)^2 = 57$. The slight discrepancy with the given value, $K = 55.64$, occurs because we know $[H_2]$ and $[I_2]$ to only two significant figures.

EXERCISE 16.6 Calculating Equilibrium Concentrations

At some temperature, $K_c = 33$ for the reaction

$$H_2(g) + I_2(g) \rightleftharpoons 2\,HI(g)$$

Assume the initial concentrations of both H_2 and I_2 are 6.00×10^{-3} mol/L. Find the concentration of each reactant and product at equilibrium.

Calculations Where the Solution Involves a Quadratic Expression

Suppose you are studying the decomposition of PCl_5 to form PCl_3 and Cl_2. You know that $K = 1.20$ at a given temperature.

$$PCl_5(g) \rightleftharpoons PCl_3(g) + Cl_2(g)$$

If the initial concentration of PCl_5 is 1.60 M, what will be the concentrations of reactant and products when the system reaches equilibrium? Following the procedures outlined in Example 16.5, you would set up an ICE table to define the equilibrium concentrations of reactants and products.

Reaction	$PCl_5(g)$	$\rightleftharpoons$	$PCl_3(g)$	+	$Cl_2(g)$
Initial (M)	1.60		0		0
Change (M)	$-x$		$+x$		$+x$
Equilibrium (M)	$1.60 - x$		x		x

Substituting into the equilibrium constant expression, we have

$$K = 1.20 = \frac{[PCl_3][Cl_2]}{[PCl_5]} = \frac{(x)(x)}{1.60 - x}$$

Expanding the algebraic expression results in a quadratic equation,

$$x^2 + 1.20x - 1.92 = 0$$

Using the quadratic formula (Appendix A; $a = 1$, $b = 1.20$, and $c = -1.92$), we find two roots to the equation: $x = 0.91$ and -2.11. Because a negative value of x (which represents a negative concentration) is not chemically meaningful, the answer is $x = 0.91$. Therefore, we have, at equilibrium,

$$[PCl_5] = 1.60 - 0.91 = 0.69 \text{ M}$$

$$[PCl_3] = [Cl_2] = 0.91 \text{ M}$$

Although a solution to a quadratic equation can always be obtained using the quadratic formula, in many instances an acceptable answer can be obtained by using a realistic approximation to simplify the equation. To illustrate this, let us consider another equilibrium, the dissociation of I_2 molecules to form I atoms, for which $K = 5.6 \times 10^{-12}$ at 500 K.

$$I_2(g) \rightleftharpoons 2\,I(g)$$

$$K = \frac{[I]^2}{[I_2]} = 5.6 \times 10^{-12}$$

Assuming the initial I_2 concentration is 0.45 M, and setting up the ICE table in the usual manner, we have

Reaction	$I_2(g)$	$\rightleftharpoons$	2 I(g)
Initial (M)	0.45		0
Change (M)	$-x$		$+2x$
Equilibrium (M)	$0.45 - x$		$2x$

For the equilibrium constant expression, we again arrive at a quadratic equation.

$$K = 5.6 \times 10^{-12} = \frac{(2x)^2}{(0.45 - x)}$$

Although we could solve this equation using the quadratic formula, there is a simpler way to reach an answer. Notice that the value of K is very small, indicating that the amount of I_2 that will be dissociated ($= x$) is very small. In fact, K is so small that subtracting x from the original reactant concentration (0.45 mol/L) in the denominator of the equilibrium constant expression will leave the denominator essentially unchanged. That is, $(0.45 - x)$ is essentially equal to 0.45. Thus, we drop x in the denominator and have a simpler equation to solve.

$$K = 5.6 \times 10^{-12} = \frac{(2x)^2}{(0.45)}$$

The solution to this equation gives $x = 7.9 \times 10^{-7}$. From this value, we can determine that $[I_2] = 0.45 - x \approx 0.45$ mol/L and $[I] = 2x = 1.6 \times 10^{-6}$ mol/L. Notice that the answer to the I_2 dissociation problem confirms the assumption the dissociation of I_2 is so small that $[I_2]$ at equilibrium is essentially equal to the initial concentration.

When is it possible to simplify a quadratic equation? The decision depends on both the value of the initial concentration of the reactant and the value of x, which is in turn related to the value of K. Consider the general reaction

$$A \rightleftharpoons B + C$$

where $K = [B][C]/[A]$. Assume we know K and the initial concentration of A ($= [A]_0$) and wish to find the equilibrium concentrations of B and C ($= x$). The equilibrium constant expression now is

$$K = \frac{[B][C]}{[A]} = \frac{(x)(x)}{[A]_0 - x}$$

When K is very small, the value of x will be much less than $[A]_0$, so $[A]_0 - x \approx [A]_0$. Therefore, we can write the following expression.

$$K = \frac{[B][C]}{[A]} \approx \frac{(x)(x)}{[A]_0} \tag{16.3}$$

If 100 × K < [A]₀, the approximate expression, Equation 16.3, will give acceptable values of equilibrium concentrations (to two significant figures). For more about this useful guideline, see Problem Solving Tip 16.1.

■ **Solving Quadratic Equations**
Quadratic equations are usually solved using the quadratic formula (Appendix A). An alternative is the *method of successive approximations*, also outlined in Appendix A. Most equilibrium expressions can be solved quickly by this method, and you are urged to try it. This will remove the uncertainty of whether K expressions need to be solved exactly. (There are, however, rare cases in which this does not work.)

Problem Solving Tip 16.1
When Do You Need to Use the Quadratic Formula?

In most equilibrium calculations, the quantity x may be neglected in the denominator of the equation $K = x^2/([A]_0 - x)$ if x is less than 10% of the quantity of reactant initially present. The guideline presented in the text for making the approximation that $[A]_0 - x \approx [A]_0$ when $100 \times K < [A]_0$ reflects this fact.

In general, when K is about 1 or greater, the approximation cannot be made. If K is much less than 1 and $100 \times K < [A]_0$ (you will see many such cases in Chapter 17), the approximate expression ($K = x^2/[A]_0$) gives an acceptable answer. If you are not certain, then first make the assumption that the

unknown (x) is small, and solve the approximate expression (Equation 16.3). Next, compare the "approximate" value of x with $[A]_0$. If x has a value equal to or less than 10% of $[A]_0$, then there is no need to solve the full equation using the quadratic formula.

EXAMPLE 16.6 Calculating Equilibrium Concentrations Using an Equilibrium Constant

Problem The reaction

$$N_2(g) + O_2(g) \rightleftharpoons 2 \, NO(g)$$

contributes to air pollution whenever a fuel is burned in air at a high temperature, as in a gasoline engine. At 1500 K, $K = 1.0 \times 10^{-5}$. Suppose a sample of air has $[N_2] = 0.80$ mol/L and $[O_2] = 0.20$ mol/L before any reaction occurs. Calculate the equilibrium concentrations of reactants and products after the mixture has been heated to 1500 K.

Strategy Set up an ICE table of equilibrium concentrations, and then substitute these concentrations into the equilibrium constant expression. The result will be a quadratic equation. This expression can be solved using the methods outlined in Appendix A or by using the guideline in the text to derive an acceptable, approximate answer.

Solution We first set up an ICE table of equilibrium concentrations.

Equation	$N_2(g)$	+	$O_2(g)$	$\rightleftharpoons$	$2 \, NO(g)$
Initial (M)	0.80		0.20		0
Change (M)	$-x$		$-x$		$+2x$
Equilibrium (M)	$0.80 - x$		$0.20 - x$		$2x$

Next, the equilibrium concentrations are substituted into the equilibrium constant expression.

$$K = 1.0 \times 10^{-5} = \frac{[NO]^2}{[N_2][O_2]} = \frac{[2x]^2}{(0.80 - x)(0.20 - x)}$$

We refer to the guideline (Equation 16.3) to decide whether an approximate solution is possible. Here, $100 \times K \,(= 1.0 \times 10^{-3})$ is smaller than either of the initial reactant concentrations (0.80 and 0.20). This means we can use the approximate expression

$$K = 1.0 \times 10^{-5} = \frac{[NO]^2}{[N_2][O_2]} = \frac{(2x)^2}{(0.80)(0.20)}$$

Solving this expression, we find

$$1.6 \times 10^{-6} = 4x^2$$

$$x = 6.3 \times 10^{-4}$$

Therefore, the reactant and product concentrations at equilibrium are

$$[N_2] = 0.80 - 6.3 \times 10^{-4} \approx 0.80 \text{ M}$$

$$[O_2] = 0.20 - 6.3 \times 10^{-4} \approx 0.20 \text{ M}$$

$$[NO] = 2x = 1.26 \times 10^{-3} \text{ M}$$

Comment The value of x obtained using the approximation is the same as that obtained from the quadratic formula. If the full equilibrium constant expression is expanded, we have

$$(1.0 \times 10^{-5})(0.80 - x)(0.20 - x) = 4x^2$$

$$(1.0 \times 10^{-5})(0.16 - 1.00x + x^2) = 4x^2$$

$$\underbrace{(4 - 1.0 \times 10^{-5})x^2}_{ax^2} + \underbrace{(1.0 \times 10^{-5})x}_{bx} \underbrace{- 0.16 \times 10^{-5}}_{c} = 0$$

The two roots to this equation are:

$$x = 6.3 \times 10^{-4} \text{ or } x = -6.3 \times 10^{-4}$$

The only meaningful root is identical to the approximate answer obtained above. The approximation is indeed valid in this case.

EXERCISE 16.7 Calculating an Equilibrium Concentration Using an Equilibrium Constant

Graphite and carbon dioxide are kept at constant volume at 1000 K until the reaction

$$C(\text{graphite}) + CO_2(g) \rightleftharpoons 2\, CO(g)$$

has come to equilibrium. At this temperature, $K = 0.021$. The initial concentration of CO_2 is 0.012 mol/L. Calculate the equilibrium concentration of CO.

16.5 More About Balanced Equations and Equilibrium Constants

Chemical equations can be balanced using different sets of stoichiometric coefficients. For example, the equation for the oxidation of carbon to give carbon monoxide can be written

$$C(s) + \tfrac{1}{2}\, O_2(g) \rightleftharpoons CO(g)$$

In this case, the equilibrium constant expression would be

$$K_1 = \frac{[CO]}{[O_2]^{1/2}} = 4.6 \times 10^{23} \text{ at } 25\ ^\circ C$$

You can write the chemical equation equally well, however, as

$$2\, C(s) + O_2(g) \rightleftharpoons 2\, CO(g)$$

and the equilibrium constant expression would now be

$$K_2 = \frac{[CO]^2}{[O_2]} = 2.1 \times 10^{47} \text{ at } 25\ ^\circ C$$

When you compare the two equilibrium constant expressions you find that $K_2 = (K_1)^2$; that is,

$$K_2 = \frac{[CO]^2}{[O_2]} = \left\{\frac{[CO]}{[O_2]^{1/2}}\right\}^2 = K_1^2$$

When the stoichiometric coefficients of a balanced equation are multiplied by some factor, the equilibrium constant for the new equation (K_{new}) is the old equilibrium constant (K_{old}) raised to the power of the multiplication factor.

In the case of the oxidation of carbon, the second equation was obtained by multiplying the first equation by two. Therefore, K_2 is the *square* of K_1 ($K_2 = K_1^2$).

Let us consider what happens if a chemical equation is reversed. Here, we will compare the value of K for formic acid transferring an H^+ ion to water

$$HCO_2H(aq) + H_2O(\ell) \rightleftharpoons HCO_2^-(aq) + H_3O^+(aq)$$

$$K_1 = \frac{[HCO_2^-][H_3O^+]}{[HCO_2H]} = 1.8 \times 10^{-4} \text{ at } 25\ ^\circ C$$

with the opposite reaction, the gain of an H^+ ion by the formate ion, HCO_2^-.

$$HCO_2^-(aq) + H_3O^+(aq) \rightleftharpoons HCO_2H(aq) + H_2O(\ell)$$

$$K_2 = \frac{[HCO_2H]}{[HCO_2^-][H_3O^+]} = 5.6 \times 10^3 \text{ at } 25\ ^\circ C$$

Here, $K_2 = 1/K_1$.

The equilibrium constants for a reaction and its reverse are the reciprocals of one another.

It is often useful to add two equations to obtain the equation for a net process. As an example, consider the reactions that take place when silver chloride dissolves in water (to a *very* small extent) and ammonia is added to the solution. The ammonia reacts with the silver ion to form a water-soluble compound, $Ag(NH_3)_2Cl$ (Figure 16.6). Adding the equation for dissolving solid AgCl to the equation for the reaction of Ag^+ ion with ammonia gives the equation for net reaction, dissolving solid AgCl in aqueous ammonia. (All equilibrium constants are given at 25 °C.)

$AgCl(s) \rightleftharpoons Ag^+(aq) + Cl^-(aq)$ $\qquad\qquad K_1 = [Ag^+][Cl^-] = 1.8 \times 10^{-10}$

$Ag^+(aq) + 2\ NH_3(aq) \rightleftharpoons [Ag(NH_3)_2]^+(aq)$ $\qquad K_2 = \dfrac{[Ag(NH_3)_2^+]}{[Ag^+][NH_3]^2} = 1.6 \times 10^7$

Net reaction:

$AgCl(s) + 2\ NH_3(aq) \rightleftharpoons [Ag(NH_3)_2]^+(aq) + Cl^-(aq)$

To obtain the equilibrium constant for the net reaction, K_{net}, we *multiply* the equilibrium constants for the two reactions, K_1 by K_2.

$$K_{net} = K_1 \times K_2 = [Ag^+][Cl^-] \times \frac{[Ag(NH_3)_2^+]}{[Ag^+][NH_3]^2} = \frac{[Ag(NH_3)_2^+][Cl^-]}{[NH_3]^2}$$

$$K_{net} = K_1 \times K_2 = 2.9 \times 10^{-3}$$

FIGURE 16.6 Dissolving silver chloride in aqueous ammonia. (left) A precipitate of AgCl(s) is suspended in water. (right) When aqueous ammonia is added, the ammonia reacts with the trace of silver ion in solution, the equilibrium shifts, and the silver chloride dissolves.

When two or more chemical equations are added to produce a net equation, the equilibrium constant for the net equation is the product of the equilibrium constants for the added equations.

■ **Complex Ions** This compound, [Ag(NH₃)₂]Cl, is made up of a cation (called a complex ion), $[Ag(NH_3)_2]^+$, and an anion, Cl^-. Square brackets are often used to indicate the cation is a single entity. We will discuss complex ions further in Chapters 18 and 22.

EXAMPLE 16.7 Balanced Equations and Equilibrium Constants

Problem A mixture of nitrogen, hydrogen, and ammonia is brought to equilibrium. When the equation is written using whole-number coefficients, as follows, the value of K is 3.5×10^8 at 25 °C.

Equation 1: $N_2(g) + 3 H_2(g) \rightleftharpoons 2 NH_3(g)$ $K_1 = 3.5 \times 10^8$

However, the equation can also be written as given in *Equation 2*. What is the value of K_2?

Equation 2: $\frac{1}{2} N_2(g) + \frac{3}{2} H_2(g) \rightleftharpoons NH_3(g)$ $K_2 = ?$

The decomposition of ammonia to the elements *(Equation 3)* is the reverse of its formation *(Equation 1)*. What is the value of K_3?

Equation 3: $2 NH_3(g) \rightleftharpoons N_2(g) + 3 H_2(g)$ $K_3 = ?$

Strategy Review what happens to the value of K when the stoichiometric coefficients are changed or the reaction is reversed. (See Problem Solving Tip 16.2.)

Solution To see the relation between K_1 and K_2, first write the equilibrium constant expressions for these two balanced equations.

$$K_1 = \frac{[NH_3]^2}{[N_2][H_2]^3} \qquad K_2 = \frac{[NH_3]}{[N_2]^{\frac{1}{2}}[H_2]^{\frac{3}{2}}}$$

Writing these expressions makes it clear that K_2 is the square root of K_1.

$$K_2 = (K_1)^{\frac{1}{2}} = \sqrt{K_1} = \sqrt{3.5 \times 10^8} = \boxed{1.9 \times 10^4}$$

Equation 3 is the reverse of *Equation 1*, and its equilibrium constant expression is

$$K_3 = \frac{[N_2][H_2]^3}{[NH_3]^2}$$

In this case, K_3 is the reciprocal of K_1. That is, $K_3 = 1/K_1$.

$$K_3 = \frac{1}{K_1} = \frac{1}{3.5 \times 10^8} = \boxed{2.9 \times 10^{-9}}$$

Comment As a final comment, notice that the production of ammonia from the elements has a large equilibrium constant and is product-favored (see Section 16.2). As expected, the reverse reaction, the decomposition of ammonia to its elements, has a small equilibrium constant and is reactant-favored.

EXERCISE 16.8 Manipulating Equilibrium Constant Expressions

The conversion of oxygen to ozone has a very small equilibrium constant.

$3/2 \, O_2(g) \rightleftharpoons O_3(g)$ $K = 2.5 \times 10^{-29}$

(a) What is the value of K when the equation is written using whole-number coefficients?

$3 \, O_2(g) \rightleftharpoons 2 \, O_3(g)$

(b) What is the value of K for the conversion of ozone to oxygen?

$2 \, O_3(g) \rightleftharpoons 3 \, O_2(g)$

EXERCISE 16.9 Manipulating Equilibrium Constant Expressions

The following equilibrium constants are given at 500 K:

$H_2(g) + Br_2(g) \rightleftharpoons 2 HBr(g)$ $K_p = 7.9 \times 10^{11}$

$H_2(g) \rightleftharpoons 2 H(g)$ $K_p = 4.8 \times 10^{-41}$

$Br_2(g) \rightleftharpoons 2 Br$ $K_p = 2.2 \times 10^{-15}$

Calculate K_p for the reaction of H and Br atoms to give HBr.

$H(g) + Br(g) \rightleftharpoons HBr(g)$ $K_p = ?$

16.6 Disturbing a Chemical Equilibrium

The equilibrium between reactants and products may be disturbed in three ways: (1) by changing the temperature, (2) by changing the concentration of a reactant or product, or (3) by changing the volume (for systems involving gases) (Table 16.2). *A change in any of the factors that determine the equilibrium conditions of a system will cause the system to change in such a manner as to reduce or counteract the effect of the change.* This statement is often referred to as *Le Chatelier's principle* (◄ page 627). It is a shorthand way of saying how a reaction will adjust the quantities of reactants and products so that equilibrium is restored, that is, so that the reaction quotient is once again equal to the equilibrium constant.

Chemistry ☼ Now™

Sign in at **www.cengage.com/login** and go to Chapter 16 Contents to see Screen 16.11 to view an animation of **Le Chatelier's principle.**

TABLE 16.2   Effects of Disturbances on Equilibrium Composition

Disturbance	Change as Mixture Returns to Equilibrium	Effect on Equilibrium	Effect on K
Reactions Involving Solids, Liquids, or Gases			
Rise in temperature	Heat energy is consumed by system	Shift in endothermic direction	Change
Drop in temperature	Heat energy is generated by system	Shift in exothermic direction	Change
Addition of reactant*	Some of added reactant is consumed	Product concentration increases	No change
Addition of product*	Some of added product is consumed	Reactant concentration increases	No change
Reactions Involving Gases			
Decrease in volume, increase in pressure	Pressure decreases	Composition changes to reduce total number of gas molecules	No change
Increase in volume, decrease in pressure	Pressure increases	Composition changes to increase total number of gas molecules	No change

* Does not apply when an insoluble solid reactant or product is added. Recall that their "concentrations" do not appear in the reaction quotient.

Effect of the Addition or Removal of a Reactant or Product

If the concentration of a reactant or product is changed from its equilibrium value *at a given temperature*, equilibrium will be reestablished eventually. The new equilibrium concentrations of reactants and products will be different, but the value of the equilibrium constant expression will still equal K (Table 16.1). To illustrate this, let us return to the butane/isobutane equilibrium (with $K = 2.5$).

$$CH_3CH_2CH_2CH_3 \rightleftharpoons CH_3CHCH_3 \quad\quad K = 2.5$$

with the CH_3 group shown above the central carbon.

butane   isobutane

Suppose the equilibrium mixture consists of two molecules of butane and five molecules of isobutane (Figure 16.7). The reaction quotient, Q, is 5/2 (or 2.5/1), the value of the equilibrium constant for the reaction. Now we add seven more molecules of isobutane to the mixture to give a ratio of 12 isobutane molecules to two butane molecules. The reaction quotient is now 6/1. Q is greater than K, so the system will change to reestablish equilibrium. To do so, some molecules of isobutane must be changed into butane molecules, a process that continues until the ratio [isobutane]/[butane] is once again 2.5/1. In this particular case, if two of the 12 isobutane molecules change to butane, the ratio of isobutane to butane is again equal to K (= 10/4 = 2.5/1), and equilibrium is reestablished.

Chemistry ⊙ Now™

Sign in at **www.cengage.com/login** and go to Chapter 16 Contents to see Screen 16.13 for a simulation and a tutorial on **the effect of concentration changes on an equilibrium.**

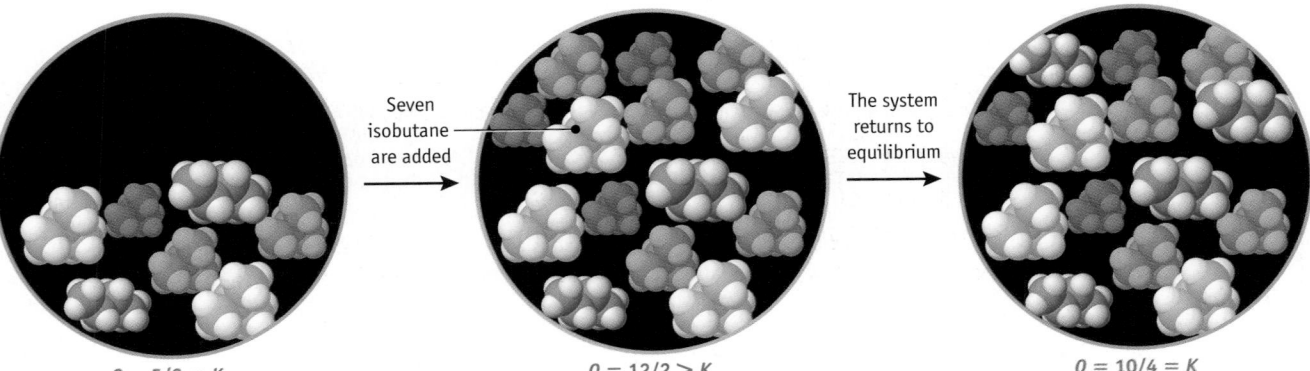

$Q = 5/2 = K$

An equilibrium mixture of five isobutane molecules and two butane molecules.

Seven isobutane are added

$Q = 12/2 > K$

Seven isobutane molecules are added, so the system is no longer at equilibrium.

The system returns to equilibrium

$Q = 10/4 = K$

A net of two isobutane molecules has changed to butane molecules, to once again give an equilibrium mixture where the ratio of isobutane to butane is 5 to 2 (or 2.5/1).

Active Figure 16.7   Addition of more reactant or product to an equilibrium system.

Chemistry ⊙ Now™ Sign in at www.cengage.com/login and go to the Chapter Contents menu to explore an interactive version of this figure accompanied by an exercise.

Problem Assume equilibrium has been established in a 1.00-L flask with [butane] = 0.500 mol/L and [isobutane] = 1.25 mol/L.

$$\text{Butane} \rightleftharpoons \text{Isobutane} \quad K = 2.50$$

Then 1.50 mol of butane is added. What are the concentrations of butane and isobutane when equilibrium is reestablished?

Strategy After adding excess butane, $Q < K$. To reestablish equilibrium, the concentration of butane must decrease, and that of isobutane must increase. Use an ICE table to track the changes. The decrease in butane concentration and the increase in isobutane concentration are both designated as x.

Solution First organize the information in a modified ICE table.

Equation	Butane	$\rightleftharpoons$	Isobutane
Initial (M)	0.500		1.25
Concentration immediately on adding butane (M)	0.500 + 1.50		1.25
Change in concentration to reestablish equilibrium (M)	−x		+x
Equilibrium (M)	0.500 + 1.50 − x		1.25 + x

The entries in this table were arrived at as follows:

(a) The concentration of butane when equilibrium is reestablished will be the original equilibrium concentration plus what was added (1.50 mol/L) minus the concentration of butane that is converted to isobutane to reestablish equilibrium. The quantity of butane converted to isobutane is unknown and so is designated as x.

(b) The concentration of isobutane when equilibrium is reestablished is the concentration that was already present (1.25 mol/L) plus the concentration formed (x mol/L) on reestablishing equilibrium.

Having defined [butane] and [isobutane] when equilibrium is reestablished and remembering that K is a constant (=2.50), we can write

$$K = 2.50 = \frac{[\text{isobutane}]}{[\text{butane}]}$$

We now calculate the new equilibrium composition:

$$2.50 = \frac{1.25 + x}{0.500 + 1.50 - x} = \frac{1.25 + x}{2.00 - x}$$

$$2.50\,(2.00 - x) = 1.25 + x$$

$$x = 1.07 \text{ mol/L}$$

[butane] = 0.500 + 1.50 − x = 0.93 M and [isobutane] = 1.25 + x = 2.32 M

Comment Check your answer to verify that [isobutane]/[butane] = 2.32/0.93 = 2.5.

EXERCISE 16.10 **Effect of Concentration Changes on Equilibrium**

Equilibrium exists between butane and isobutane when [butane] = 0.20 M and [isobutane] = 0.50 M. An additional 2.00 mol/L of isobutane is added to the mixture. What are the concentrations of butane and isobutane after equilibrium has again been attained?

Effect of Volume Changes on Gas-Phase Equilibria

For a reaction that involves gases, what happens to equilibrium concentrations or pressures if the size of the container is changed? (Such a change occurs, for example, when fuel and air are compressed in an automobile engine.) To answer this question, recall that concentrations are in moles per liter. If the volume of a gas changes, its concentration therefore must also change, and the equilibrium composition can change. As an example, consider the following equilibrium:

$$2 \, NO_2(g) \rightleftharpoons N_2O_4(g)$$

brown gas   colorless gas

$$K = \frac{[N_2O_4]}{[NO_2]^2} = 170 \text{ at } 298 \, K$$

What happens to this equilibrium if the volume of the flask holding the gases is suddenly halved? The immediate result is that the concentrations of both gases will double. For example, assume equilibrium is established when $[N_2O_4]$ is 0.0280 mol/L and $[NO_2]$ is 0.0128 mol/L. When the volume is halved, $[N_2O_4]$ becomes 0.0560 mol/L, and $[NO_2]$ is 0.0256 mol/L. The reaction quotient, Q, under these circumstances is $(0.0560)/(0.0256)^2 = 85.5$, a value less than K. Because Q is less than K, the quantity of product must increase at the expense of the reactants to return to equilibrium, and the new equilibrium composition will have a higher concentration of N_2O_4 than immediately after the volume change.

$$2 \, NO_2(g) \rightleftharpoons N_2O_4(g)$$

$\xrightarrow{\text{decrease volume of container}}$
new equilibrium favors product

The concentration of NO_2 decreases twice as much as the concentration of N_2O_4 increases because one molecule of N_2O_4 is formed by consuming two molecules of NO_2. This occurs until the reaction quotient, $Q = [N_2O_4]/[NO_2]^2$, is once again equal to K. The net effect of the volume decrease is to decrease the number of molecules in the gas phase.

The conclusions for the NO_2/N_2O_4 equilibrium can be generalized:

- For reactions involving gases, the stress of a volume decrease (a pressure increase) will be counterbalanced by a change in the equilibrium composition to one having a smaller number of gas molecules.
- For a volume increase (a pressure decrease), the equilibrium composition will favor the side of the reaction with the larger number of gas molecules.
- For a reaction in which there is no change in the number of gas molecules, such as in the reaction of H_2 and I_2 to produce HI [$H_2(g) + I_2(g) \rightleftharpoons 2 \, HI(g)$], a volume change will have no effect.

Chemistry.❍.Now™

EXERCISE 16.11 Effect of Concentration and Volume Changes on Equilibria

The formation of ammonia from its elements is an important industrial process.

$$3 \, H_2(g) + N_2(g) \rightleftharpoons 2 \, NH_3(g)$$

(a) How does the equilibrium composition change when extra H_2 is added? When extra NH_3 is added?

(b) What is the effect on the equilibrium when the volume of the system is increased?

Effect of Temperature Changes on Equilibrium Composition

The value of the equilibrium constant for a given reaction varies with temperature. Changing the temperature of a system at equilibrium is therefore different in some ways from the other means we have studied of disturbing a chemical equilibrium because the equilibrium constant itself will be different at the new temperature from what it was at the previous temperature. Predicting the exact changes in equilibrium compositions with temperature is beyond the scope of this text, but you can make a qualitative prediction about the effect if you know whether the reaction is exothermic or endothermic. As an example, consider the endothermic reaction of N_2 with O_2 to give NO.

$$N_2(g) + O_2(g) \rightleftharpoons 2\ NO(g) \qquad \Delta_r H° = +180.6\ kJ/mol\text{-}rxn$$

$$K = \frac{[NO]^2}{[N_2][O_2]}$$

■ *K for the N_2/O_2 Reaction* We are surrounded by N_2 and O_2, but you know that they do not react appreciably at room temperature. However, if a mixture of N_2 and O_2 is heated above 700 °C, as in an automobile engine, the equilibrium mixture will contain appreciable amounts of NO.

Le Chatelier's principle allows us to predict how the value of K will vary with temperature. The formation of NO from N_2 and O_2 is endothermic; that is, energy must be provided as heat for the reaction to occur. We might imagine that heat is a "reactant." If the system is at equilibrium and the temperature then increases, the system will adjust to alleviate this "stress." The way to counteract the energy input is to use up some of the energy added as heat by consuming N_2 and O_2 and producing more NO as the system returns to equilibrium. This raises the value of the numerator ($[NO]^2$) and lowers the value of the denominator ($[N_2][O_2]$) in the reaction quotient, Q, resulting in a higher value of K.

This prediction is borne out. The following table lists the equilibrium constant for this reaction at various temperatures. As predicted, the equilibrium constant and thus the proportion of NO in the equilibrium mixture increase with temperature.

Equilibrium Constant, K	Temperature (K)
4.5×10^{-31}	298
6.7×10^{-10}	900
1.7×10^{-3}	2300

As another example, consider the combination of molecules of the brown gas NO_2 to form colorless N_2O_4. An equilibrium between these compounds is readily achieved in a closed system (Figure 16.8).

$$2\ NO_2(g) \rightleftharpoons N_2O_4(g) \qquad \Delta_r H° = -57.1\ kJ/mol\text{-}rxn$$

$$K = \frac{[N_2O_4]}{[NO_2]^2}$$

Equilibrium Constant, K	Temperature (K)
1300	273
170	298

Here, the reaction is exothermic, so we might imagine heat as being a reaction "product." By lowering the temperature of the system, as in Figure 16.8, some energy is removed as heat. The removal of energy can be counteracted if the reaction produces energy as heat by the combination of NO_2 molecules to give more N_2O_4. Thus, the equilibrium concentration of NO_2 decreases; the concentration of N_2O_4 increases; and the value of K is larger at lower temperatures.

Nitrogen-containing substances are used around the world to stimulate the growth of field crops. Farmers from Portugal to Tibet have used animal waste for centuries as a "natural" fertilizer. In the 19th century, industrialized countries imported nitrogen-rich marine bird manure from Peru, Bolivia, and Chile, but the supply of this material was clearly limited. In 1898, William Ramsay (the discoverer of the noble gases) pointed out that the amount of "fixed nitrogen" in the world was being depleted and predicted that world food shortages would occur by the mid-20th century as a result. That Ramsay's prediction failed to materialize was due in part to the work of Fritz Haber (1868–1934). In about 1908, Haber developed a method making ammonia directly from the elements,

$$N_2(g) + 3\ H_2(g) \rightleftharpoons 2\ NH_3(g)$$

and, a few years later, Carl Bosch (1874–1940) perfected the industrial scale synthesis. Ammonia is now made for pennies per kilogram and is consistently ranked in the top five chemicals produced in the United States with 15–20 billion kilograms produced annually. Not only is ammonia used directly as a fertilizer, but it is also a starting material for making nitric acid and ammonium nitrate, among other things.

The manufacture of ammonia (Figure A) is a good example of the role that kinetics and chemical equilibria play in practical chemistry.

The $N_2 + H_2$ reaction is exothermic and product-favored ($K > 1$ at 25 °C).

At 25 °C, K (calc'd value) = 3.5×10^8
and $\Delta_r H° = -92.2$ kJ/mol-rxn

Unfortunately, the reaction at 25 °C is slow, so it is carried out at a higher temperature to increase the reaction rate. The problem with this, however, is that the equilibrium constant declines with temperature, as predicted by Le Chatelier's Principle.

At 450 °C, K (experimental value) = 0.16
and $\Delta_r H° = -111.3$ kJ/mol-rxn

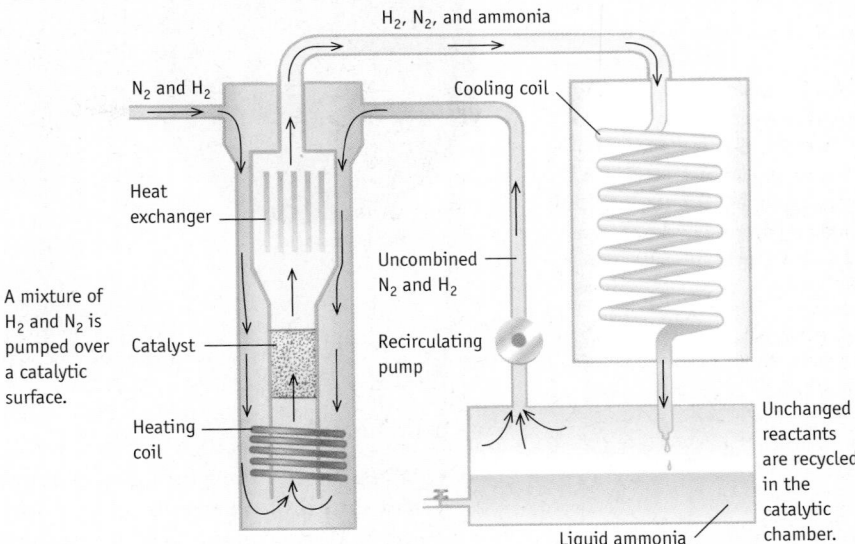

FIGURE A The Haber process for ammonia synthesis. A mixture of H_2 and N_2 is pumped over a catalytic surface. The NH_3 is collected as a liquid (at -33 °C), and unchanged reactants are recycled in the catalytic chamber.

Thus, the yield declines with increasing temperature.

There are two things that can be done. The first is to raise the pressure. This does not change the value of K, but an increase in pressure can be compensated by converting 4 mol of reactants to 2 mol of product.

In an industrial ammonia plant, it is necessary to balance reaction rate (improved at higher temperature) with product yield (K is smaller at higher temperatures). Therefore, catalysts are often used to accelerate reactions. An effective catalyst for the Haber process is Fe_3O_4 mixed with KOH, SiO_2, and Al_2O_3 (all inexpensive chemicals). Because the catalyst is not effective below 400 °C, the process is carried out at 450–500 °C and 250 atm pressure.

Questions:

1. *Anhydrous ammonia is used directly as a fertilizer, but much of it is also converted to other fertilizers, ammonium nitrate and urea.*

 (a) *How is NH_3 converted to ammonium nitrate?*
 (b) *Urea is formed in the reaction of ammonia and CO_2.*

$$2\ NH_3(g) + CO_2(g) \rightleftharpoons (NH_2)_2CO(s) + H_2O(g)$$

 Which would favor urea production, high temperature or high pressure? ($\Delta_f H°$ for solid urea = -333.1 kJ/mol-rxn)

2. *One important aspect of the Haber process is the source of the hydrogen. This is made from natural gas in a process called steam reforming.*

$$CH_4(g) + H_2O(g) \rightarrow CO(g) + 3\ H_2(g)$$
$$CO(g) + H_2O(g) \rightarrow CO_2(g) + H_2(g)$$

 (a) *Are the two reactions above endo- or exothermic?*
 (b) *To manufacture 15 billion kilograms of NH_3, how much CH_4 is required, and what mass of CO_2 is produced as a by-product?*

Answers to these questions are in Appendix Q.

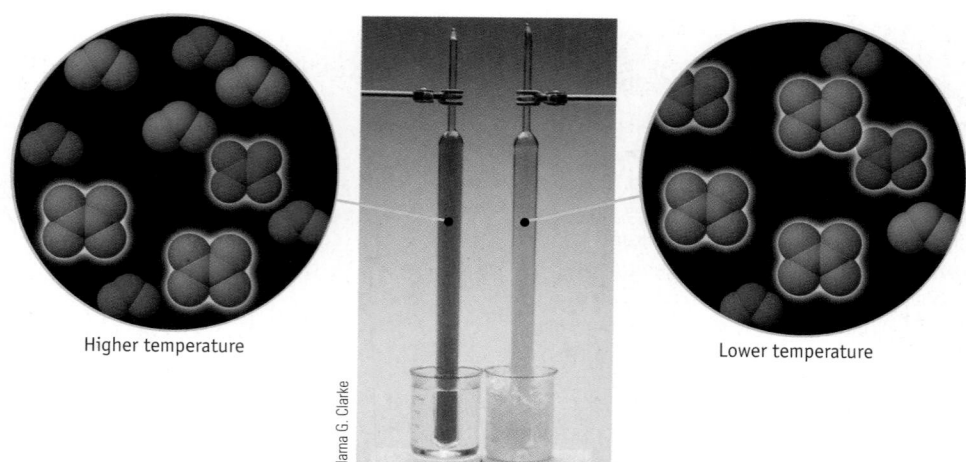

FIGURE 16.8 Effect of temperature on an equilibrium. The tubes in the photograph both contain gaseous NO_2 (brown) and N_2O_4 (colorless) at equilibrium. K is larger at the lower temperature because the equilibrium favors colorless N_2O_4. This is clearly seen in the tube at the right, where the gas in the ice bath at 0 °C is only slightly brown, which indicates a smaller concentration of the brown gas NO_2. At 50 °C (the tube at the left), the equilibrium is shifted toward NO_2, as indicated by the darker brown color.

Higher temperature

Lower temperature

Marna G. Clarke

In summary,

- When the temperature of a system at equilibrium increases, the equilibrium will shift in the direction that absorbs energy as heat (Table 16.2)—that is, in the endothermic direction.
- If the temperature decreases, the equilibrium will shift in the direction that releases energy as heat—that is, in the exothermic direction.
- Changing the temperature changes the value of K.

Chemistry ☼ Now™

Sign in at **www.cengage.com/login** and go to Chapter 16 Contents to see Screen 16.12 for a tutorial on **the effect of temperature changes.**

EXERCISE 16.12 Disturbing a Chemical Equilibrium

Does the equilibrium concentration of NOCl increase or decrease as the temperature of the system is increased?

$$2 \ NOCl(g) \rightleftharpoons 2 \ NO(g) + Cl_2(g) \quad \Delta_r H° = +77.1 \ kJ$$

Chapter Goals Revisited

Now that you have studied this chapter, you should ask whether you have met the chapter goals. In particular, you should be able to:

Understand the nature and characteristics of chemical equilibria

a. Chemical reactions are reversible and equilibria are dynamic (Section 16.1).

Understand the significance of the equilibrium constant, K, and reaction quotient, Q.

a. Write the reaction quotient, Q, for a chemical reaction (Section 16.2). When the system is at equilibrium, the reaction quotient is called the equilibrium constant expression and has a constant value called the equilibrium constant, which is symbolized by K (Equation 16.2). Study Question(s) assignable in OWL: 2,4.

b. Recognize that the concentrations of solids, pure liquids, and solvents (e.g., water) are not included in the equilibrium constant expression (Equation 16.1, Section 16.2).

c. Recognize that a large value of K ($K > 1$) means the reaction is product-favored, and the product concentrations are greater than the reactant concentrations at equilibrium. A small value of K ($K < 1$) indicates a reactant-favored reaction in which the product concentrations are smaller than the reactant concentrations at equilibrium (Section 16.2). Study Question(s) assignable in OWL: 66, 68, 70.

d. Appreciate the fact that equilibrium concentrations may be expressed in terms of reactant and product concentrations (in moles per liter) and that K is then sometimes designated as K_c. Alternatively, concentrations of gases may be represented by partial pressures, and K for such cases is designated K_p (Section 16.2).

Understand how to use K in quantitative studies of chemical equilibria

a. Use the reaction quotient (Q) to decide whether a reaction is at equilibrium ($Q = K$), or if there will be a net conversion of reactants to products ($Q < K$) or products to reactants ($Q > K$) to attain equilibrium (Section 16.2).

b. Calculate an equilibrium constant given the reactant and product concentrations at equilibrium (Section 16.3). Study Question(s) assignable in OWL: 8, 11, 29, 33, 34, 44, 61a.

c. Use equilibrium constants to calculate the concentration (or pressure) of a reactant or a product at equilibrium (Section 16.4). Study Question(s) assignable in OWL: 16, 17, 32, 36, 42, 46, 47, 50–54, 56, 58–62; Go Chemistry Module 21.

d. Know how K changes as different stoichiometric coefficients are used in a balanced equation, if the equation is reversed, or if several equations are added to give a new net equation (Section 16.5). Study Question(s) assignable in OWL: 21, 31, 37.

e. Know how to predict, using Le Chatelier's principle, the effect of a disturbance on a chemical equilibrium—a change in temperature, a change in concentrations, or a change in volume or pressure for a reaction involving gases (Section 16.6 and Table 16.2). Study Question(s) assignable in OWL: 25, 26, 28, 39, 41, 54, 62.

Chemistry ⚛ Now™ Sign in at **www.cengage.com/login** to:

- Assess your understanding with Study Questions in OWL keyed to each goal in the Goals and Homework menu for this chapter
- For quick review, download Go Chemistry mini-lecture flashcard modules (or purchase them at **www.ichapters.com**)
- Check your readiness for an exam by taking the Pre-Test and exploring the modules recommended in your Personalized Study plan.

❓ Access **How Do I Solve It?** tutorials on how to approach problem solving using concepts in this chapter.

For additional preparation for an examination on this chapter see the *Let's Review* section on pages 948–961.

KEY EQUATIONS

Equation 16.1 (page 727)   The equilibrium constant expression. At equilibrium, the ratio of products to reactants has a constant value, K (at a particular temperature). For the general reaction $aA + bB \rightleftharpoons cC + dD$,

$$\text{Equilibrium constant} = K = \frac{[C]^c[D]^d}{[A]^a[B]^b}$$

Equation 16.2 (page 732)   For the general reaction $aA + bB \rightleftharpoons cC + dD$, the ratio of product to reactant concentrations at any point in the reaction is the reaction quotient.

$$\text{Reaction quotient} = Q = \frac{[C]^c[D]^d}{[A]^a[B]^b}$$

STUDY QUESTIONS

OWL Online homework for this chapter may be assigned in OWL.

▲ denotes challenging questions.

■ denotes questions assignable in OWL.

Blue-numbered questions have answers in Appendix O and fully-worked solutions in the *Student Solutions Manual*.

Practicing Skills

Writing Equilibrium Constant Expressions
(See Example 16.1 and ChemistryNow Screens 16.3, 16.4, and 16.5.)

1. Write equilibrium constant expressions for the following reactions. For gases, use either pressures or concentrations.
(a) $2 H_2O_2(g) \rightleftharpoons 2 H_2O(g) + O_2(g)$
(b) $CO(g) + \frac{1}{2} O_2(g) \rightleftharpoons CO_2(g)$
(c) $C(s) + CO_2(g) \rightleftharpoons 2 CO(g)$
(d) $NiO(s) + CO(g) \rightleftharpoons Ni(s) + CO_2(g)$

2. ■ Write equilibrium constant expressions for the following reactions. For gases, use either pressures or concentrations.
(a) $3 O_2(g) \rightleftharpoons 2 O_3(g)$
(b) $Fe(s) + 5 CO(g) \rightleftharpoons Fe(CO)_5(g)$
(c) $(NH_4)_2CO_3(s) \rightleftharpoons 2 NH_3(g) + CO_2(g) + H_2O(g)$
(d) $Ag_2SO_4(s) \rightleftharpoons 2 Ag^+(aq) + SO_4^{2-}(aq)$

The Equilibrium Constant and Reaction Quotient
(See Example 16.2 and ChemistryNow Screen 16.9.)

3. $K = 5.6 \times 10^{-12}$ at 500 K for the dissociation of iodine molecules to iodine atoms.

$$I_2(g) \rightleftharpoons 2 I(g)$$

A mixture has $[I_2] = 0.020$ mol/L and $[I] = 2.0 \times 10^{-8}$ mol/L. Is the reaction at equilibrium (at 500 K)? If not, which way must the reaction proceed to reach equilibrium?

4. ■ The reaction

$$2 NO_2(g) \rightleftharpoons N_2O_4(g)$$

has an equilibrium constant, K_c, of 170 at 25 °C. If 2.0×10^{-3} mol of NO_2 is present in a 10.-L flask along with 1.5×10^{-3} mol of N_2O_4, is the system at equilibrium? If it is not at equilibrium, does the concentration of NO_2 increase or decrease as the system proceeds to equilibrium?

5. A mixture of SO_2, O_2, and SO_3 at 1000 K contains the gases at the following concentrations: $[SO_2] = 5.0 \times 10^{-3}$ mol/L, $[O_2] = 1.9 \times 10^{-3}$ mol/L, and $[SO_3] = 6.9 \times 10^{-3}$ mol/L. Is the reaction at equilibrium? If not, which way will the reaction proceed to reach equilibrium?

$$2 SO_2(g) + O_2(g) \rightleftharpoons 2 SO_3(g) \quad K = 279$$

6. The equilibrium constant, K_c, for the reaction

$$2 NOCl(g) \rightleftharpoons 2 NO(g) + Cl_2(g)$$

is 3.9×10^{-3} at 300 °C. A mixture contains the gases at the following concentrations: $[NOCl] = 5.0 \times 10^{-3}$ mol/L, $[NO] = 2.5 \times 10^{-3}$ mol/L, and $[Cl_2] = 2.0 \times 10^{-3}$ mol/L. Is the reaction at equilibrium at 300 °C? If not, in which direction does the reaction proceed to come to equilibrium?

Calculating an Equilibrium Constant
(See Examples 16.3 and 16.4 and ChemistryNow Screens 16.4 and 16.8.)

7. The reaction

$$PCl_5(g) \rightleftharpoons PCl_3(g) + Cl_2(g)$$

was examined at 250 °C. At equilibrium, $[PCl_5] = 4.2 \times 10^{-5}$ mol/L, $[PCl_3] = 1.3 \times 10^{-2}$ mol/L, and $[Cl_2] = 3.9 \times 10^{-3}$ mol/L. Calculate K for the reaction.

8. ■ An equilibrium mixture of SO_2, O_2, and SO_3 at a high temperature contains the gases at the following concentrations: $[SO_2] = 3.77 \times 10^{-3}$ mol/L, $[O_2] = 4.30 \times 10^{-3}$ mol/L, and $[SO_3] = 4.13 \times 10^{-3}$ mol/L. Calculate the equilibrium constant, K, for the reaction.

$$2 SO_2(g) + O_2(g) \rightleftharpoons 2 SO_3(g)$$

9. The reaction

$$C(s) + CO_2(g) \rightleftharpoons 2 CO(g)$$

occurs at high temperatures. At 700 °C, a 2.0-L flask contains 0.10 mol of CO, 0.20 mol of CO_2, and 0.40 mol of C at equilibrium.
(a) Calculate K for the reaction at 700 °C.
(b) Calculate K for the reaction, also at 700 °C, if the amounts at equilibrium in the 2.0-L flask are 0.10 mol of CO, 0.20 mol of CO_2, and 0.80 mol of C.
(c) Compare the results of (a) and (b). Does the quantity of carbon affect the value of K? Explain.

10. Hydrogen and carbon dioxide react at a high temperature to give water and carbon monoxide.

$$H_2(g) + CO_2(g) \rightleftharpoons H_2O(g) + CO(g)$$

(a) Laboratory measurements at 986 °C show that there are 0.11 mol each of CO and H_2O vapor and 0.087 mol each of H_2 and CO_2 at equilibrium in a 1.0-L container. Calculate the equilibrium constant for the reaction at 986 °C.
(b) Suppose 0.050 mol each of H_2 and CO_2 are placed in a 2.0-L container. When equilibrium is achieved at 986 °C, what amounts of CO(g) and $H_2O(g)$, in moles, would be present? [Use the value of K from part (a).]

11. ■ A mixture of CO and Cl_2 is placed in a reaction flask: [CO] = 0.0102 mol/L and [Cl_2] = 0.00609 mol/L. When the reaction

$$CO(g) + Cl_2(g) \rightleftharpoons COCl_2(g)$$

has come to equilibrium at 600 K, [Cl_2] = 0.00301 mol/L.
   (a) Calculate the concentrations of CO and $COCl_2$ at equilibrium.
   (b) Calculate K_c.

12. You place 3.00 mol of pure SO_3 in an 8.00-L flask at 1150 K. At equilibrium, 0.58 mol of O_2 has been formed. Calculate K for the reaction at 1150 K.

$$2 SO_3(g) \rightleftharpoons 2 SO_2(g) + O_2(g)$$

Using Equilibrium Constants
(See Examples 16.5 and 16.6 and ChemistryNow Screen 16.10.)

13. The value of K_c for the interconversion of butane and isobutane is 2.5 at 25 °C.

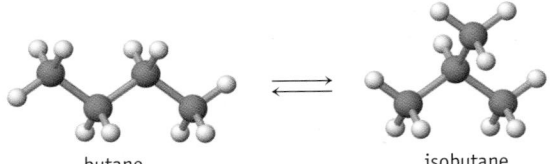

butane   isobutane

If you place 0.017 mol of butane in a 0.50-L flask at 25 °C and allow equilibrium to be established, what will be the equilibrium concentrations of the two forms of butane?

14. Cyclohexane, C_6H_{12}, a hydrocarbon, can isomerize or change into methylcyclopentane, a compound of the same formula ($C_5H_9CH_3$) but with a different molecular structure.

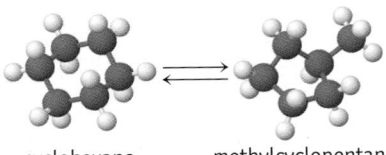

cyclohexane   methylcyclopentane

The equilibrium constant has been estimated to be 0.12 at 25 °C. If you had originally placed 0.045 mol of cyclohexane in a 2.8-L flask, what would be the concentrations of cyclohexane and methylcyclopentane when equilibrium is established?

15. The equilibrium constant for the dissociation of iodine molecules to iodine atoms

$$I_2(g) \rightleftharpoons 2 I(g)$$

is 3.76×10^{-3} at 1000 K. Suppose 0.105 mol of I_2 is placed in a 12.3-L flask at 1000 K. What are the concentrations of I_2 and I when the system comes to equilibrium?

16. ■ The equilibrium constant for the reaction

$$N_2O_4(g) \rightleftharpoons 2 NO_2(g)$$

at 25 °C is 5.88×10^{-3}. Suppose 15.6 g of N_2O_4 is placed in a 5.00-L flask at 25 °C. Calculate the following:
   (a) the amount of NO_2 (mol) present at equilibrium;
   (b) the percentage of the original N_2O_4 that is dissociated.

17. ■ Carbonyl bromide decomposes to carbon monoxide and bromine.

$$COBr_2(g) \rightleftharpoons CO(g) + Br_2(g)$$

K_c is 0.190 at 73 °C. If you place 0.500 mol of $COBr_2$ in a 2.00-L flask and heat it to 73 °C, what are the equilibrium concentrations of $COBr_2$, CO, and Br_2? What percentage of the original $COBr_2$ decomposed at this temperature?

18. Iodine dissolves in water, but its solubility in a nonpolar solvent such as CCl_4 is greater.

Nonpolar I_2
Polar H_2O

Nonpolar CCl_4

Shake the test tube →

Polar H_2O

Nonpolar CCl_4 and I_2

Extracting iodine (I_2) from water with the nonpolar solvent CCl_4. I_2 is more soluble in CCl_4 and, after shaking a mixture of water and CCl_4, the I_2 has accumulated in the more dense CCl_4 layer.

The equilibrium constant is 85.0 for the reaction

$$I_2(aq) \rightleftharpoons I_2(CCl_4)$$

You place 0.0340 g of I_2 in 100.0 mL of water. After shaking it with 10.0 mL of CCl_4, how much I_2 remains in the water layer?

Manipulating Equilibrium Constant Expressions
(See Example 16.7 and ChemistryNow Screen 16.7.)

19. Which of the following correctly relates the equilibrium constants for the two reactions shown?

$$A + B \rightleftharpoons 2 C \quad K_1$$

$$2 A + 2 B \rightleftharpoons 4 C \quad K_2$$

(a) $K_2 = 2K_1$ (c) $K_2 = 1/K_1$
(b) $K_2 = K_1^2$ (d) $K_2 = 1/K_1^2$

Photos: Charles D. Winters

20. Which of the following correctly relates the equilibrium constants for the two reactions shown?

$$A + B \rightleftharpoons 2\,C \quad K_1$$
$$C \rightleftharpoons \tfrac{1}{2}\,A + \tfrac{1}{2}\,B \quad K_2$$

(a) $K_2 = 1/(K_1)^{\frac{1}{2}}$ (c) $K_2 = K_1^2$
(b) $K_2 = 1/K_1$ (d) $K_2 = -K_1^{\frac{1}{2}}$

21. ■ Consider the following equilibria involving $SO_2(g)$ and their corresponding equilibrium constants.

$$SO_2(g) + \tfrac{1}{2}\,O_2(g) \rightleftharpoons SO_3(g) \quad K_1$$
$$2\,SO_3(g) \rightleftharpoons 2\,SO_2(g) + O_2(g) \quad K_2$$

Which of the following expressions relates K_1 to K_2?
(a) $K_2 = K_1^2$ (d) $K_2 = 1/K_1$
(b) $K_2^2 = K_1$ (e) $K_2 = 1/K_1^2$
(c) $K_2 = K_1$

22. The equilibrium constant K for the reaction

$$CO_2(g) \rightleftharpoons CO(g) + \tfrac{1}{2}\,O_2(g)$$

is 6.66×10^{-12} at 1000 K. Calculate K for the reaction

$$2\,CO(g) + O_2(g) \rightleftharpoons 2\,CO_2(g)$$

23. Calculate K for the reaction

$$SnO_2(s) + 2\,CO(g) \rightleftharpoons Sn(s) + 2\,CO_2(g)$$

given the following information:

$$SnO_2(s) + 2\,H_2(g) \rightleftharpoons Sn(s) + 2\,H_2O(g) \quad K = 8.12$$
$$H_2(g) + CO_2(g) \rightleftharpoons H_2O(g) + CO(g) \quad K = 0.771$$

24. Calculate K for the reaction

$$Fe(s) + H_2O(g) \rightleftharpoons FeO(s) + H_2(g)$$

given the following information:

$$H_2O(g) + CO(g) \rightleftharpoons H_2(g) + CO_2(g) \quad K = 1.6$$
$$FeO(s) + CO(g) \rightleftharpoons Fe(s) + CO_2(g) \quad K = 0.67$$

Disturbing a Chemical Equilibrium
(See Example 16.8 and ChemistryNow Screens 16.11–16.14.)

25. ■ Dinitrogen trioxide decomposes to NO and NO_2 in an endothermic process ($\Delta_r H = 40.5$ kJ/mol-rxn).

$$N_2O_3(g) \rightleftharpoons \text{`}NO(g) + NO_2(g)$$

Predict the effect of the following changes on the position of the equilibrium; that is, state which way the equilibrium will shift (left, right, or no change) when each of the following changes is made.
(a) adding more $N_2O_3(g)$
(b) adding more $NO_2(g)$
(c) increasing the volume of the reaction flask
(d) lowering the temperature

26. ■ K_p for the following reaction is 0.16 at 25 °C:

$$2\,NOBr(g) \rightleftharpoons 2\,NO(g) + Br_2(g)$$

The enthalpy change for the reaction at standard conditions is +16.3 k/mol-rxn. Predict the effect of the following changes on the position of the equilibrium; that is, state which way the equilibrium will shift (left, right, or no change) when each of the following changes is made.
(a) adding more $Br_2(g)$
(b) removing some $NOBr(g)$
(c) decreasing the temperature
(d) increasing the container volume

27. Consider the isomerization of butane with an equilibrium constant of $K = 2.5$. (See Study Question 13.) The system is originally at equilibrium with [butane] = 1.0 M and [isobutane] = 2.5 M.
(a) If 0.50 mol/L of isobutane is suddenly added and the system shifts to a new equilibrium position, what is the equilibrium concentration of each gas?
(b) If 0.50 mol/L of butane is added and the system shifts to a new equilibrium position, what is the equilibrium concentration of each gas?

28. ■ The decomposition of NH_4HS

$$NH_4HS(s) \rightleftharpoons NH_3(g) + H_2S(g)$$

is an endothermic process. Using Le Chatelier's principle, explain how increasing the temperature would affect the equilibrium. If more NH_4HS is added to a flask in which this equilibrium exists, how is the equilibrium affected? What if some additional NH_3 is placed in the flask? What will happen to the pressure of NH_3 if some H_2S is removed from the flask?

General Questions
These questions are not designated as to type or location in the chapter. They may combine several concepts from this and other chapters.

29. ■ Suppose 0.086 mol of Br_2 is placed in a 1.26-L flask and heated to 1756 K, a temperature at which the halogen dissociates to atoms

$$Br_2(g) \rightleftharpoons 2\,Br(g)$$

If Br_2 is 3.7% dissociated at this temperature, calculate K_c.

30. The equilibrium constant for the reaction

$$N_2(g) + O_2(g) \rightleftharpoons 2\,NO(g)$$

is 1.7×10^{-3} at 2300 K.
(a) What is K for the reaction when written as follows?

$$\tfrac{1}{2}\,N_2(g) + \tfrac{1}{2}\,O_2(g) \rightleftharpoons NO\ (g)$$

(b) What is K for the following reaction?

$$2\,NO(g) \rightleftharpoons N_2(g) + O_2(g)$$

31. ■ K_p for the formation of phosgene, $COCl_2$, is 6.5×10^{11} at 25 °C.

$$CO(g) + Cl_2(g) \rightleftharpoons COCl_2(g)$$

What is the value of K_p for the dissociation of phosgene?

$$COCl_2(g) \rightleftharpoons CO(g) + Cl_2(g)$$

32. ■ The equilibrium constant, K_c, for the following reaction is 1.05 at 350 K.

$$2\, CH_2Cl_2(g) \rightleftharpoons CH_4(g) + CCl_4(g)$$

If an equilibrium mixture of the three gases at 350 K contains 0.0206 M $CH_2Cl_2(g)$ and 0.0163 M CH_4, what is the equilibrium concentration of CCl_4?

33. ■ Carbon tetrachloride can be produced by the following reaction:

$$CS_2(g) + 3\, Cl_2(g) \rightleftharpoons S_2Cl_2(g) + CCl_4(g)$$

Suppose 1.2 mol of CS_2 and 3.6 mol of Cl_2 are placed in a 1.00-L flask. After equilibrium has been achieved, the mixture contains 0.90 mol CCl_4. Calculate K_c.

34. ■ Equal numbers of moles of H_2 gas and I_2 vapor are mixed in a flask and heated to 700 °C. The initial concentration of each gas is 0.0088 mol/L, and 78.6% of the I_2 is consumed when equilibrium is achieved according to the equation

$$H_2(g) + I_2(g) \rightleftharpoons 2\, HI(g)$$

Calculate K_c for this reaction.

35. The equilibrium constant for the butane $\rightleftharpoons$ isobutane isomerization reaction is 2.5 at 25 °C. If 1.75 mol of butane and 1.25 mol of isobutane are mixed, is the system at equilibrium? If not, when it proceeds to equilibrium, which reagent increases in concentration? Calculate the concentrations of the two compounds when the system reaches equilibrium.

36. ■ At 2300 K the equilibrium constant for the formation of $NO(g)$ is 1.7×10^{-3}.

$$N_2(g) + O_2(g) \rightleftharpoons 2\, NO(g)$$

(a) Analysis shows that the concentrations of N_2 and O_2 are both 0.25 M, and that of NO is 0.0042 M under certain conditions. Is the system at equilibrium?
(b) If the system is not at equilibrium, in which direction does the reaction proceed?
(c) When the system is at equilibrium, what are the equilibrium concentrations?

37. ■ Which of the following correctly relates the two equilibrium constants for the two reactions shown?

$$NOCl(g) \rightleftharpoons NO(g) + \tfrac{1}{2}\, Cl_2(g) \qquad K_1$$
$$2\, NO(g) + Cl_2(g) \rightleftharpoons 2\, NOCl(g) \qquad K_2$$

(a) $K_2 = -K_1{}^2$ (c) $K_2 = 1/K_1{}^2$
(b) $K_2 = 1/(K_1)^{1/2}$ (d) $K_2 = 2K_1$

38. Sulfur dioxide is readily oxidized to sulfur trioxide.

$$2\, SO_2(g) + O_2(g) \rightleftharpoons 2\, SO_3(g) \qquad K_c = 279$$

If we add 3.00 g of SO_2 and 5.00 g of O_2 to a 1.0-L flask, approximately what quantity of SO_3 will be in the flask once the reactants and the product reach equilibrium?
(a) 2.21 g (c) 3.61 g
(b) 4.56 g (d) 8.00 g

(Note: The full solution to this problem results in a cubic equation. Do not try to solve it exactly. Decide only which of the answers is most reasonable.)

39. ■ Heating a metal carbonate leads to decomposition.

$$BaCO_3(s) \rightleftharpoons BaO(s) + CO_2(g)$$

Predict the effect on the equilibrium of each change listed below. Answer by choosing (i) no change, (ii) shifts left, or (iii) shifts right.
(a) add $BaCO_3$ (c) add BaO
(b) add CO_2 (d) raise the temperature
(e) increase the volume of the flask containing the reaction

40. Carbonyl bromide decomposes to carbon monoxide and bromine.

$$COBr_2(g) \rightleftharpoons CO(g) + Br_2(g)$$

K_c is 0.190 at 73 °C. Suppose you place 0.500 mol of $COBr_2$ in a 2.00-L flask and heat it to 73 °C (Study Question 17). After equilibrium has been achieved, you add an additional 2.00 mol of CO.
(a) How is the equilibrium mixture affected by adding more CO?
(b) When equilibrium *is* reestablished, what are the new equilibrium concentrations of $COBr_2$, CO, and Br_2?
(c) How has the addition of CO affected the percentage of $COBr_2$ that decomposed?

41. ■ Phosphorus pentachloride decomposes at higher temperatures.

$$PCl_5(g) \rightleftharpoons PCl_3(g) + Cl_2(g)$$

An equilibrium mixture at some temperature consists of 3.120 g of PCl_5, 3.845 g of PCl_3, and 1.787 g of Cl_2 in a 1.00-L flask. If you add 1.418 g of Cl_2, how will the equilibrium be affected? What will the concentrations of PCl_5, PCl_3, and Cl_2 be when equilibrium is reestablished?

42. ■ Ammonium hydrogen sulfide decomposes on heating.

$$NH_4HS(s) \rightleftharpoons NH_3(g) + H_2S(g)$$

If K_p for this reaction is 0.11 at 25 °C (when the partial pressures are measured in atmospheres), what is the total pressure in the flask at equilibrium?

43. ■ Ammonium iodide dissociates reversibly to ammonia and hydrogen iodide if the salt is heated to a sufficiently high temperature.

$$NH_4I(s) \rightleftharpoons NH_3(g) + HI(g)$$

Some ammonium iodide is placed in a flask, which is then heated to 400 °C. If the total pressure in the flask when equilibrium has been achieved is 705 mm Hg, what is the value of K_p (when partial pressures are in atmospheres)?

44. ■ When solid ammonium carbamate sublimes, it dissociates completely into ammonia and carbon dioxide according to the following equation:

$$(NH_4)(H_2NCO_2)(s) \rightleftharpoons 2 NH_3(g) + CO_2(g)$$

At 25 °C, experiment shows that the total pressure of the gases in equilibrium with the solid is 0.116 atm. What is the equilibrium constant, K_p?

45. The equilibrium reaction $N_2O_4(g) \rightleftharpoons 2 NO_2(g)$ has been thoroughly studied (see Figure 16.8).
(a) If the total pressure in a flask containing NO_2 and N_2O_4 gas at 25 °C is 1.50 atm and the value of K_p at this temperature is 0.148, what fraction of the N_2O_4 has dissociated to NO_2?
(b) What happens to the fraction dissociated if the volume of the container is increased so that the total equilibrium pressure falls to 1.00 atm?

46. ■ In the gas phase, acetic acid exists as an equilibrium of monomer and dimer molecules. (The dimer consists of two molecules linked through hydrogen bonds.)

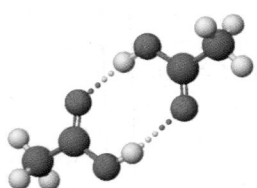

The equilibrium constant, K_c, at 25 °C for the monomer–dimer equilibrium

$$2 CH_3CO_2H \rightleftharpoons (CH_3CO_2H)_2$$

has been determined to be 3.2×10^4. Assume that acetic acid is present initially at a concentration of 5.4×10^{-4} mol/L at 25 °C and that no dimer is present initially.
(a) What percentage of the acetic acid is converted to dimer?
(b) As the temperature increases, in which direction does the equilibrium shift? (Recall that hydrogen-bond formation is an exothermic process.)

47. ■ Assume 3.60 mol of ammonia is placed in a 2.00-L vessel and allowed to decompose to the elements.

$$2 NH_3(g) \rightleftharpoons N_2(g) + 3 H_2(g)$$

If the experimental value of K is 6.3 for this reaction at the temperature in the reactor, calculate the equilibrium concentration of each reagent. What is the total pressure in the flask?

48. ■ The total pressure for a mixture of N_2O_4 and NO_2 is 1.5 atm. If $K_p = 6.75$ (at 25 °C), calculate the partial pressure of each gas in the mixture.

$$2 NO_2(g) \rightleftharpoons N_2O_4(g)$$

49. K_c for the decomposition of ammonium hydrogen sulfide is 1.8×10^{-4} at 25 °C.

$$NH_4HS(s) \rightleftharpoons NH_3(g) + H_2S(g)$$

(a) When the pure salt decomposes in a flask, what are the equilibrium concentrations of NH_3 and H_2S?
(b) If NH_4HS is placed in a flask already containing 0.020 mol/L of NH_3 and then the system is allowed to come to equilibrium, what are the equilibrium concentrations of NH_3 and H_2S?

50. ■ The equilibrium constant, K_p, is 0.15 at 25 °C for the following reaction:

$$N_2O_4(g) \rightleftharpoons 2 NO_2(g)$$

If the total pressure of the gas mixture is 2.5 atm at equilibrium, what is the partial pressure of each gas?

51. ■ ▲ A 15-L flask at 300 K contains 64.4 g of a mixture of NO_2 and N_2O_4 in equilibrium. What is the total pressure in the flask? (K_p for $2 NO_2(g) \rightleftharpoons N_2O_4(g)$ is 6.67.)

52. ■ ▲ Lanthanum oxalate decomposes when heated to lanthanum oxide, CO, and CO_2.

$$La_2(C_2O_4)_3(s) \rightleftharpoons La_2O_3(s) + 3 CO(g) + 3 CO_2(g)$$

(a) If, at equilibrium, the total pressure in a 10.0-L flask is 0.200 atm, what is the value of K_p?
(b) Suppose 0.100 mol of $La_2(C_2O_4)_3$ was originally placed in the 10.0-L flask. What quantity of $La_2(C_2O_4)_3$ remains unreacted at equilibrium at 373 K?

53. ■ ▲ The reaction of hydrogen and iodine to give hydrogen iodide has an equilibrium constant, K_c, of 56 at 435 °C.
(a) What is the value of K_p?
(b) Suppose you mix 0.45 mol of H_2 and 0.45 mol of I_2 in a 10.0-L flask at 425 °C. What is the total pressure of the mixture before and after equilibrium is achieved?
(c) What is the partial pressure of each gas at equilibrium?

▲ more challenging ■ in OWL Blue-numbered questions answered in Appendix O

54. ■ Sulfuryl chloride, SO_2Cl_2, is a compound with very irritating vapors; it is used as a reagent in the synthesis of organic compounds. When heated to a sufficiently high temperature, it decomposes to SO_2 and Cl_2.

$$SO_2Cl_2(g) \rightleftharpoons SO_2(g) + Cl_2(g) \qquad K_c = 0.045 \text{ at } 375\ °C$$

(a) A 1.00-L flask containing 6.70 g of SO_2Cl_2 is heated to 375 °C. What is the concentration of each of the compounds in the system when equilibrium is achieved? What fraction of SO_2Cl_2 has dissociated?

(b) What are the concentrations of SO_2Cl_2, SO_2, and Cl_2 at equilibrium in the 1.00-L flask at 375 °C if you begin with a mixture of SO_2Cl_2 (6.70 g) and Cl_2 (1.00 atm)? What fraction of SO_2Cl_2 has dissociated?

(c) Compare the fractions of SO_2Cl_2 in parts (a) and (b). Do they agree with your expectations based on Le Chatelier's principle?

55. ▲ Hemoglobin (Hb) can form a complex with both O_2 and CO. For the reaction

$$HbO_2(aq) + CO(g) \rightleftharpoons HbCO(aq) + O_2(g)$$

at body temperature, K is about 200. If the ratio $[HbCO]/[HbO_2]$ comes close to 1, death is probable. What partial pressure of CO in the air is likely to be fatal? Assume the partial pressure of O_2 is 0.20 atm.

56. ■ ▲ Limestone decomposes at high temperatures.

$$CaCO_3(s) \rightleftharpoons CaO(s) + CO_2(g)$$

At 1000 °C, $K_p = 3.87$. If pure $CaCO_3$ is placed in a 5.00-L flask and heated to 1000 °C, what quantity of $CaCO_3$ must decompose to achieve the equilibrium pressure of CO_2?

57. At 1800 K, oxygen dissociates very slightly into its atoms.

$$O_2(g) \rightleftharpoons 2\ O(g) \qquad K_p = 1.2 \times 10^{-10}$$

If you place 1.0 mol of O_2 in a 10.-L vessel and heat it to 1800 K, how many O atoms are present in the flask?

58. ■ ▲ Nitrosyl bromide, NOBr, is prepared by the direct reaction of NO and Br_2.

$$2\ NO(g) + Br_2(g) \rightarrow 2\ NOBr(g)$$

The compound dissociates readily at room temperature, however.

$$NOBr(g) \rightleftharpoons NO(g) + \tfrac{1}{2}\ Br_2(g)$$

Some NOBr is placed in a flask at 25 °C and allowed to dissociate. The total pressure at equilibrium is 190 mm Hg and the compound is found to be 34% dissociated. What is the value of K_p?

59. ■ ▲ Boric acid and glycerin form a complex

$$B(OH)_3(aq) + glycerin(aq) \rightleftharpoons B(OH)_3 \cdot glycerin(aq)$$

with an equilibrium constant of 0.90. If the concentration of boric acid is 0.10 M, how much glycerin should be added, per liter, so that 60.% of the boric acid is in the form of the complex?

60. ■ ▲ The dissociation of calcium carbonate has an equilibrium constant of $K_p = 1.16$ at 800 °C.

$$CaCO_3(s) \rightleftharpoons CaO(s) + CO_2(g)$$

(a) What is K_c for the reaction?

(b) If you place 22.5 g of $CaCO_3$ in a 9.56-L container at 800 °C, what is the pressure of CO_2 in the container?

(c) What percentage of the original 22.5-g sample of $CaCO_3$ remains undecomposed at equilibrium?

61. ▲ A sample of N_2O_4 gas with a pressure of 1.00 atm is placed in a flask. When equilibrium is achieved, 20.0% of the N_2O_4 has been converted to NO_2 gas.

(a) ■ Calculate K_p.

(b) If the original pressure of N_2O_4 is 0.10 atm, what is the percent dissociation of the gas? Is the result in agreement with Le Chatelier's principle?

62. ■ ▲ A reaction important in smog formation is

$$O_3(g) + NO(g) \rightleftharpoons O_2(g) + NO_2(g) \qquad K = 6.0 \times 10^{34}$$

(a) If the initial concentrations are $[O_3] = 1.0 \times 10^{-6}$ M, $[NO] = 1.0 \times 10^{-5}$ M, $[NO_2] = 2.5 \times 10^{-4}$ M, and $[O_2] = 8.2 \times 10^{-3}$ M, is the system at equilibrium? If not, in which direction does the reaction proceed?

(b) If the temperature is increased, as on a very warm day, will the concentrations of the products increase or decrease? (*Hint:* You may have to calculate the enthalpy change for the reaction to find out if it is exothermic or endothermic.)

In the Laboratory

63. ▲ The ammonia complex of trimethylborane, $(NH_3)B(CH_3)_3$, dissociates at 100 °C to its components with $K_p = 4.62$ (when the pressures are in atmospheres).

$$(NH_3)B(CH_3)_3(g) \rightleftharpoons B(CH_3)_3(g) + NH_3(g)$$

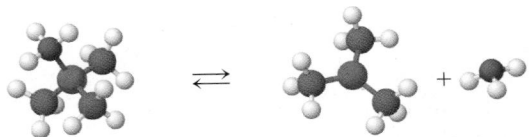

If NH_3 is changed to some other molecule, the equilibrium constant is different.

For $[(CH_3)_3P]B(CH_3)_3$ $K_p = 0.128$

For $[(CH_3)_3N]B(CH_3)_3$ $K_p = 0.472$

(a) If you begin an experiment by placing 0.010 mol of each complex in a flask, which would have the largest partial pressure of $B(CH_3)_3$ at 100 °C?

(b) If 0.73 g (0.010 mol) of $(NH_3)B(CH_3)_3$ is placed in a 100.-mL flask and heated to 100 °C, what is the partial pressure of each gas in the equilibrium mixture, and what is the total pressure? What is the percent dissociation of $(NH_3)B(CH_3)_3$?

64. The photographs below show what occurs when a solution of potassium chromate is treated with a few drops of concentrated hydrochloric acid. Some of the bright yellow chromate ion is converted to the orange dichromate ion.

$$2 CrO_4^{2-}(aq) + 2 H_3O^+(aq) \rightleftharpoons Cr_2O_7^{2-}(aq) + 3 H_2O(\ell)$$

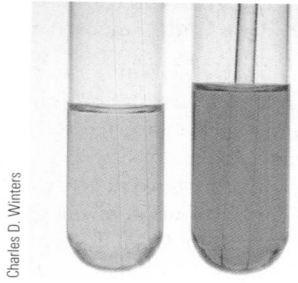

Charles D. Winters

(a) Explain this experimental observation in terms of Le Chatelier's principle.
(b) What would you observe if you treated the orange solution with sodium hydroxide? Explain your observation.

65. The photographs in (a) show what occurs when a solution of iron(III) nitrate is treated with a few drops of aqueous potassium thiocyanate. (See ChemistryNow, Screen 16.4.) The nearly colorless iron(III) ion is converted to a red $[Fe(H_2O)_5SCN]^{2+}$ ion. (This is a classic test for the presence of iron(III) ions in solution.)

$$[Fe(H_2O)_6]^{3+}(aq) + SCN^-(aq) \rightleftharpoons$$
$$[Fe(H_2O)_5SCN]^{2+}(aq) + H_2O(\ell)$$

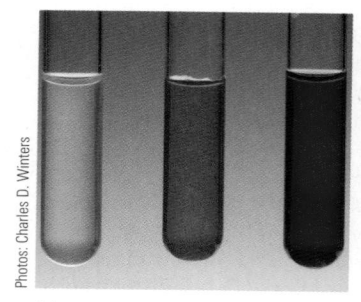
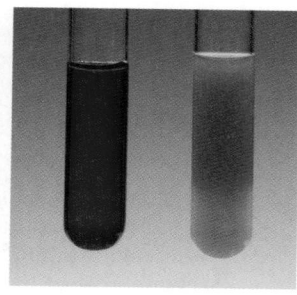

Photos: Charles D. Winters

(a) Adding KSCN   **(b) Adding Ag⁺**

(a) As more KSCN is added to the solution, the color becomes even more red. Explain this observation.
(b) Silver ions form a white precipitate with SCN⁻ ions. What would you observe on adding a few drops of aqueous silver nitrate to a red solution of $[Fe(H_2O)_5SCN]^+$ ions? Explain your observation.

66. ■ ▲ The photographs at the bottom of the page show what occurs when you add ammonia to aqueous nickel(II) nitrate and then add ethylenediamine ($NH_2CH_2CH_2NH_2$) to the intermediate blue-purple solution.

$$[Ni(H_2O)_6]^{2+}(aq) + 6 NH_3(aq)$$
green
$$\rightleftharpoons [Ni(NH_3)_6]^{2+}(aq) + 6 H_2O(\ell) \qquad K_1$$
blue-purple

$$[Ni(NH_3)_6]^{2+}(aq) + 3 NH_2CH_2CH_2NH_2(aq)$$
blue-purple
$$\rightleftharpoons [Ni(NH_2CH_2CH_2NH_2)_3]^{2+}(aq) + 6 NH_3(aq) \quad K_2$$
violet

Which equilibrium constant is greater, K_1 or K_2? Explain.

Photos: Charles D. Winters

$[Ni(H_2O)_6]^{2+}$ $\xrightarrow{NH_3}$ $[Ni(NH_3)_6]^{2+}$ Add ethylenediamine $NH_2CH_2CH_2NH_2$ $[Ni(NH_2CH_2CH_2NH_2)_3]^{2+}$

▲ more challenging   ■ in OWL   Blue-numbered questions answered in Appendix O

Summary and Conceptual Questions

The following questions may use concepts from this and previous chapters.

67. Decide whether each of the following statements is true or false. If false, change the wording to make it true.
    (a) The magnitude of the equilibrium constant is always independent of temperature.
    (b) When two chemical equations are added to give a net equation, the equilibrium constant for the net equation is the product of the equilibrium constants of the summed equations.
    (c) The equilibrium constant for a reaction has the same value as K for the reverse reaction.
    (d) Only the concentration of CO_2 appears in the equilibrium constant expression for the reaction $CaCO_3(s) \rightleftharpoons CaO(s) + CO_2(g)$.
    (e) For the reaction $CaCO_3(s) \rightleftharpoons CaO(s) + CO_2(g)$, the value of K is numerically the same, whether the amount of CO_2 is expressed as moles/liter or as gas pressure.

68. ■ Neither $PbCl_2$ nor PbF_2 is appreciably soluble in water. If solid $PbCl_2$ and solid PbF_2 are placed in equal amounts of water in separate beakers, in which beaker is the concentration of Pb^{2+} greater? Equilibrium constants for these solids dissolving in water are as follows:

    $PbCl_2(s) \rightleftharpoons Pb^{2+}(aq) + 2\ Cl^-(aq) \quad K = 1.7 \times 10^{-5}$

    $PbF_2(s) \rightleftharpoons Pb^{2+}(aq) + 2\ F^-(aq) \quad K = 3.7 \times 10^{-8}$

69. Characterize each of the following as product- or reactant-favored.
    (a) $CO(g) + \tfrac{1}{2} O_2(g) \rightleftharpoons CO_2(g)$ $K_p = 1.2 \times 10^{45}$
    (b) $H_2O(g) \rightleftharpoons H_2(g) + \tfrac{1}{2} O_2(g)$ $K_p = 9.1 \times 10^{-41}$
    (c) $CO(g) + Cl_2(g) \rightleftharpoons COCl_2(g)$ $K_p = 6.5 \times 10^{11}$

70. ■ Consider a gas-phase reaction where a colorless compound C produces a blue compound B.

    $$2\ C(g) \rightleftharpoons B(g)$$

    After reaching equilibrium, the size of the flask is halved.
    (a) What color change (if any) is observed immediately upon halving the flask size?
    (b) What color change (if any) is observed after equilibrium has been reestablished in the flask?

71. An ice cube is placed in a beaker of water at 20 °C. The ice cube partially melts, and the temperature of the water is lowered to 0 °C. At this point, both ice and water are at 0 °C, and no further change is apparent. Is the system at equilibrium? Is this a dynamic equilibrium? That is, are events still occurring at the molecular level? Suggest an experiment to test whether this is so. (*Hint:* Consider using D_2O.)

72. See the simulation on ChemistryNow, Screen 16.4.
    (a) Set the concentration of Fe^{3+} at 0.0050 M and that of SCN^- at 0.0070 M. Click the "React" button. Does the concentration of Fe^{3+} go to zero? When equilibrium is reached, what are the concentrations of the reactants and the products? What is the equilibrium constant?
    (b) Begin with $[Fe^{3+}] = [SCN^-] = 0.0$ M and $[FeSCN^{2+}] = 0.0080$ M. When equilibrium is reached, which ion has the largest concentration in solution?
    (c) Begin with $[Fe^{3+}] = 0.0010$ M, $[SCN^-] = 0.0020$ M, and $[FeSCN^{2+}] = 0.0030$ M. Describe the result of allowing this system to come to equilibrium.

17 | The Chemistry of Acids and Bases

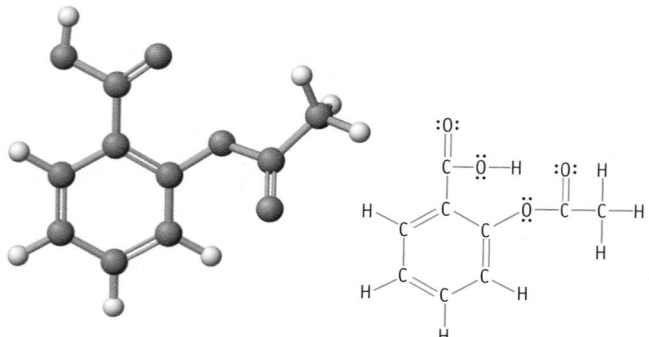

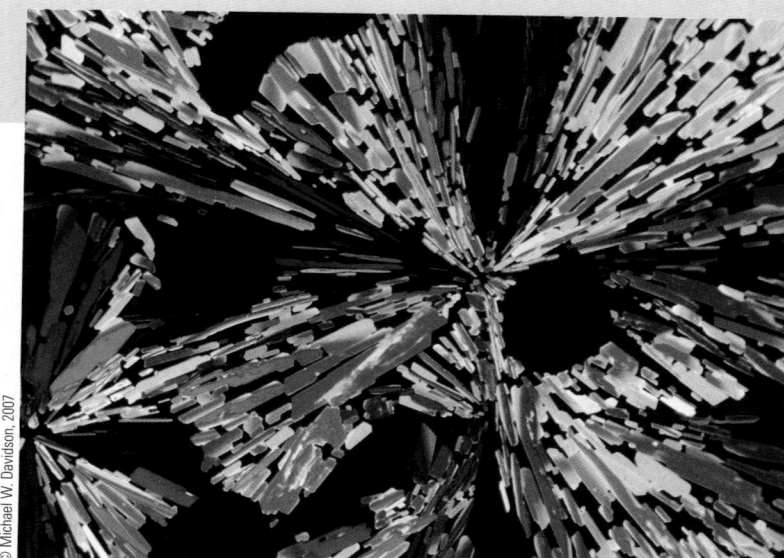

© Michael W. Davidson, 2007

Photo of crystals of aspirin taken using a microscope and polarized light.

Aspirin Is Over 100 Years Old!

Aspirin is one of the most successful non-prescription drugs ever made. Americans swallow more than 50 million aspirin tablets a day, mostly for the pain-relieving (analgesic) effects of the drug. Aspirin also wards off heart disease and thrombosis (blood clots), and it has even been suggested as a possible treatment for certain cancers and for senile dementia.

Hippocrates (460–370 BC), the ancient Greek physician, recommended an infusion of willow bark to ease the pain of childbirth. It was not until the 19th century that an Italian chemist, Raffaele Piria, isolated salicylic acid, the active compound in the bark. Soon thereafter, it was found that the acid could be extracted from a wild flower, *Spiraea ulmaria*. It is from the name of this plant that the name "aspirin" (a + spiraea) is derived.

Hippocrates's willow bark extract, salicylic acid, is an analgesic, but it is also very irritating to the stomach lining. It was therefore an important advance when chemists at Bayer Chemicals in Germany found, in 1897, that a derivative of salicylic acid, acetylsalicylic acid,

was also a useful drug and had fewer side effects. This is the compound we now call "aspirin."

Acetylsalicylic acid slowly reverts to salicylic acid, $C_6H_4(CO_2H)$ (OH), and acetic acid in the presence of moisture; therefore, if you smell the characteristic odor of acetic acid in an old bottle of aspirin tablets, they are too old and should be discarded.

Aspirin is a component of various over-the-counter medicines, such as Anacin, Ecotrin, Excedrin, and Alka-Seltzer. The latter is a combination of aspirin with citric acid and sodium bicarbonate. Sodium bicarbonate is a base and reacts with the acid to produce the sodium salt of acetylsalicylic acid, a form of aspirin that is water-soluble and quicker acting.

Questions:

1. Aspirin has a pK_a of 3.49, and that of acetic acid is 4.74. Which is the stronger acid?
2. Identify the acidic H atom in aspirin.
3. Write an equation for the ionization of aspirin.

Answers to these questions are in Appendix Q.

Acids and bases are among the most common substances in nature. Amino acids are the building blocks of proteins. The pH of the lakes, rivers, and oceans is affected by dissolved acids and bases, and your bodily functions depend on acids and bases. You were introduced to the definitions of acids and bases and to some of their chemistry in Chapter 3, but this chapter and the next take up the detailed chemistry of this important class of substances.

Chemistry.⚬.Now™

Throughout the text this icon introduces an opportunity for self-study or to explore interactive tutorials by signing in at **www.cengage.com/login**.

17.1 Acids and Bases: A Review

In Chapter 3, you were introduced to two definitions of acids and bases: the Arrhenius definition and the Brønsted–Lowry definition. According to the Arrhenius definition, an acid is any substance that, when dissolved in water, increases the concentration of hydrogen ions, H^+ (◄ page 132). An Arrhenius base is any substance that increases the concentration of hydroxide ions, OH^-, when dissolved in water. Based on the Arrhenius definition, hydrochloric acid was therefore classified as an acid, and sodium hydroxide was classified as a base.

$$HCl(aq) \rightarrow H^+(aq) + Cl^-(aq)$$

$$NaOH(aq) \rightarrow Na^+(aq) + OH^-(aq)$$

Using this definition, reactions between acids and bases involve the combination of H^+ and OH^- ions to form water (and a salt).

$$NaOH(aq) + HCl(aq) \rightarrow H_2O(\ell) + NaCl(aq)$$

The Brønsted–Lowry definition of acids and bases is more general and views acid–base behavior in terms of proton transfer from one substance to another. A Brønsted–Lowry acid is a proton (H^+) donor, and a Brønsted–Lowry base is a proton acceptor. The reaction between an acid and a base is viewed as involving an equilibrium in which a new acid and base (the conjugate base of the acid and the conjugate acid of the base) are formed. This definition extends the list of bases and the scope of acid–base reactions. In the following reaction, HCl acts as a

Brønsted–Lowry acid, and water acts as a Brønsted–Lowry base because HCl transfers a H^+ ion to H_2O to form the hydronium ion, H_3O^+.

$$HCl(aq) + H_2O(\ell) \rightleftharpoons H_3O^+(aq) + Cl^-(aq)$$

This equilibrium strongly favors formation of $H_3O^+(aq)$ and $Cl^-(aq)$; that is, HCl is a stronger acid than H_3O^+.

We will begin this chapter by looking at Brønsted–Lowry acid–base chemistry in more detail.

17.2 The Brønsted–Lowry Concept of Acids and Bases Extended

A wide variety of Brønsted–Lowry acids is known. These include some molecular compounds such as nitric acid,

$$HNO_3(aq) + H_2O(\ell) \rightleftharpoons NO_3^-(aq) + H_3O^+(aq)$$
Acid

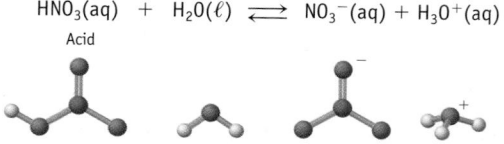

cations such as NH_4^+,

$$NH_4^+(aq) + H_2O(\ell) \rightleftharpoons NH_3(aq) + H_3O^+(aq)$$
Acid

and anions.

$$H_2PO_4^-(aq) + H_2O(\ell) \rightleftharpoons HPO_4^{2-}(aq) + H_3O^+(aq)$$

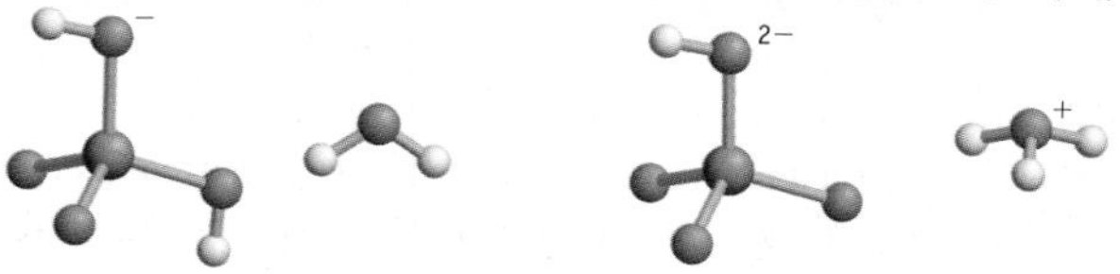

Similarly, many different types of species can act as Brønsted bases in their reactions with water. These include some molecular compounds,

$$NH_3(aq) + H_2O(\ell) \rightleftharpoons NH_4^+(aq) + OH^-(aq)$$
Base

anions,

$$CO_3^{2-}(aq) + H_2O(\ell) \rightleftharpoons HCO_3^-(aq) + OH^-(aq)$$

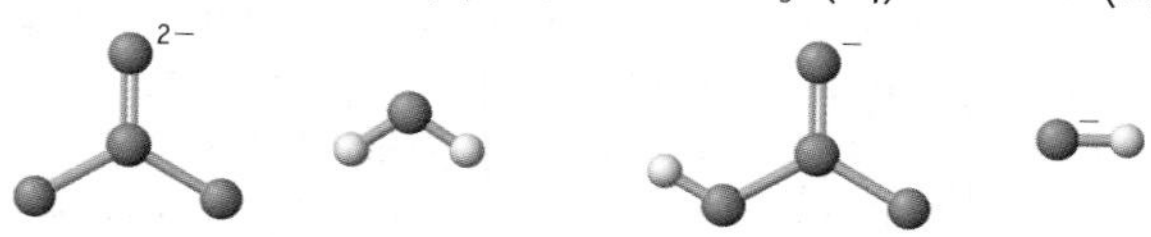

and hydrated metal cations. These cations can act as acids and bases.

$$[Fe(H_2O)_6]^{3+}(aq) + H_2O(\ell) \rightleftharpoons [Fe(H_2O)_6(OH)]^{2+}(aq) + H_3O^+(aq)$$

$$[Al(H_2O)_5(OH)]^{2+}(aq) + H_2O(\ell) \rightleftharpoons [Al(H_2O)_6]^{3+}(aq) + OH^-(aq)$$

Acids such as HF, HCl, HNO_3, and CH_3CO_2H (acetic acid) are all capable of donating one proton and so are called **monoprotic acids.** Other acids, called **polyprotic acids** (Table 17.1), are capable of donating two or more protons. A familiar example of a polyprotic acid is sulfuric acid.

$$H_2SO_4(aq) + H_2O(\ell) \rightleftharpoons HSO_4^-(aq) + H_3O^+(aq)$$

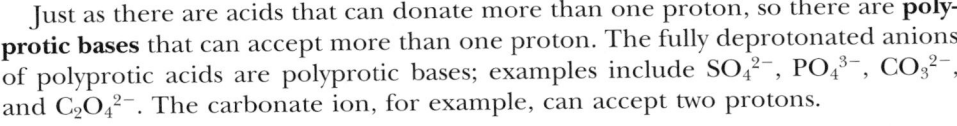

$$HSO_4^-(aq) + H_2O(\ell) \rightleftharpoons SO_4^{2-}(aq) + H_3O^+(aq)$$

Charles D. Winters

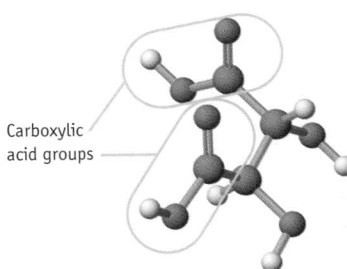

Carboxylic acid groups

Tartaric acid, $H_2C_4H_4O_6$, is a naturally occurring diprotic acid. Tartaric acid and its potassium salt are found in many fruits. The acidic protons are the H atoms of the $-CO_2H$ or carboxylic acid groups.

Just as there are acids that can donate more than one proton, so there are **polyprotic bases** that can accept more than one proton. The fully deprotonated anions of polyprotic acids are polyprotic bases; examples include SO_4^{2-}, PO_4^{3-}, CO_3^{2-}, and $C_2O_4^{2-}$. The carbonate ion, for example, can accept two protons.

$$CO_3^{2-}(aq) + H_2O(\ell) \rightleftharpoons HCO_3^-(aq) + OH^-(aq)$$

Base

$$HCO_3^-(aq) + H_2O(\ell) \rightleftharpoons H_2CO_3(aq) + OH^-(aq)$$

Base

Some molecules (such as water) and ions can behave either as Brønsted acids or bases and are referred to as being **amphiprotic** (◀ page 136). An example of an

TABLE 17.1 Polyprotic Acids and Bases

Acid Form	Amphiprotic Form	Base Form
H_2S (hydrosulfuric acid or hydrogen sulfide)	HS^- (hydrogen sulfide ion)	S^{2-} (sulfide ion)
H_3PO_4 (phosphoric acid)	$H_2PO_4^-$ (dihydrogen phosphate ion) HPO_4^{2-} (hydrogen phosphate ion)	PO_4^{3-} (phosphate ion)
H_2CO_3 (carbonic acid)	HCO_3^- (hydrogen carbonate ion or bicarbonate ion)	CO_3^{2-} (carbonate ion)
$H_2C_2O_4$ (oxalic acid)	$HC_2O_4^-$ (hydrogen oxalate ion)	$C_2O_4^{2-}$ (oxalate ion)

amphiprotic anion that is particularly important in biochemical systems is the di-hydrogen phosphate anion (Table 17.1).

$$H_2PO_4^-(aq) + H_2O(\ell) \rightleftharpoons H_3O^+(aq) + HPO_4^{2-}(aq)$$

Acid

$$H_2PO_4^{2-}(aq) + H_2O(\ell) \rightleftharpoons H_3PO_4(aq) + OH^-(aq)$$

Base

EXERCISE 17.1 Brønsted Acids and Bases

(a) Write a balanced equation for the reaction that occurs when H_3PO_4, phosphoric acid, donates a proton to water to form the dihydrogen phosphate ion. Is the dihydrogen phosphate ion an acid, a base, or amphiprotic?

(b) Write a balanced equation for the reaction that occurs when the cyanide ion, CN^-, accepts a proton from water to form HCN. Is CN^- a Brønsted acid or base?

Conjugate Acid–Base Pairs

A reaction important in the control of acidity in biological systems involves the hydrogen carbonate ion, which can act as a Brønsted base or acid in water. The equation for HCO_3^- functioning as an base exemplifies a feature of all reactions involving Brønsted acids and bases.

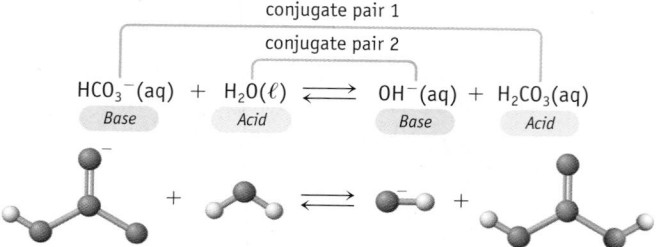

conjugate pair 1

conjugate pair 2

$$HCO_3^-(aq) + H_2O(\ell) \rightleftharpoons OH^-(aq) + H_2CO_3(aq)$$

Base   Acid   Base   Acid

In the forward direction, HCO_3^- is the Brønsted base because it captures H^+ from the Brønsted acid, H_2O. The reverse reaction, however, is also an acid–base reaction. In this case, the H_2CO_3 is the acid, and OH^- is the base.

A **conjugate acid–base pair** consists of two species that differ from each other by the presence of one hydrogen ion. Thus, H_2CO_3 and HCO_3^- comprise a conjugate acid–base pair. In this pair, HCO_3^- is the conjugate base of the acid H_2CO_3, and H_2CO_3 is the conjugate acid of the base HCO_3^-. There is a second conjugate acid–base pair in this reaction: H_2O and H_3O^+. In fact, *every reaction between a Brønsted acid and a Brønsted base involves two conjugate acid–base pairs* (Table 17.2).

Chemistry Now™

Sign in at **www.cengage.com/login** and go to Chapter 17 Contents to see Screen 17.2 for an exercise and tutorial on **acids, bases, and their conjugates.**

EXERCISE 17.2 Conjugate Acids and Bases

In the following reaction, identify the acid on the left and its conjugate base on the right. Similarly, identify the base on the left and its conjugate acid on the right.

$$HNO_3(aq) + NH_3(aq) \rightleftharpoons NH_4^+(aq) + NO_3^-(aq)$$

TABLE 17.2 Acid–Base Reactions and Conjugate Acid–Base Pairs*

Name	Acid 1		Base 2			Base 1		Acid 2
Hydrochloric acid	HCl	+	H_2O	⇌		Cl^-	+	H_3O^+
Nitric acid	HNO_3	+	H_2O	⇌		NO_3^-	+	H_3O^+
Carbonic acid	H_2CO_3	+	H_2O	⇌		HCO_3^-	+	H_3O^+
Acetic acid	CH_3CO_2H	+	H_2O	⇌		$CH_3CO_2^-$	+	H_3O^+
Hydrocyanic acid	HCN	+	H_2O	⇌		CN^-	+	H_3O^+
Hydrogen sulfide	H_2S	+	H_2O	⇌		HS^-	+	H_3O^+
Ammonia	H_2O	+	NH_3	⇌		OH^-	+	NH_4^+
Carbonate ion	H_2O	+	CO_3^{2-}	⇌		OH^-	+	HCO_3^-
Water	H_2O	+	H_2O	⇌		OH^-	+	H_3O^+

*Acid 1 and base 1 are a conjugate pair, as are base 2 and acid 2.

17.3 Water and the pH Scale

Because we generally use aqueous solutions of acids and bases, and because the acid–base reactions in your body occur in your aqueous interior, we want to consider the behavior of water in terms of chemical equilibria.

Water Autoionization and the Water Ionization Constant, K_w

An acid such as HCl does not need to be present for the hydronium ion to exist in water. In fact, two water molecules can interact with each other to produce a hydronium ion and a hydroxide ion by proton transfer from one water molecule to the other.

$$2\,H_2O(\ell) \rightleftharpoons H_3O^+(aq) + OH^-(aq)$$

This **autoionization** reaction of water was demonstrated many years ago by Friedrich Kohlrausch (1840–1910). He found that, even after water is painstakingly purified, it still conducts electricity to a very small extent because autoionization produces very low concentrations of H_3O^+ and OH^- ions. Water autoionization is the cornerstone of our concepts of aqueous acid–base behavior.

When water autoionizes, the equilibrium lies far to the left side. In fact, in pure water at 25 °C, only about two out of a billion (10^9) water molecules are ionized at any instant. To express this idea more quantitatively, we can write the equilibrium constant expression for autoionization.

$$K_w = [H_3O^+][OH^-] = 1.0 \times 10^{-14} \text{ at 25 °C} \qquad \text{(17.1)}$$

■ **K_w and Temperature** The equation $K_w = [H_3O^+][OH^-]$ is valid for pure water and for any aqueous solution. K_w is temperature dependent. Because the autoionization reaction is endothermic, K_w increases with temperature.

T (°C)	K_w
10	0.29×10^{-14}
15	0.45×10^{-14}
20	0.68×10^{-14}
25	1.01×10^{-14}
30	1.47×10^{-14}
50	5.48×10^{-14}

There are several important aspects of this equation.

- Based on the rules we have given for writing equilibrium constants, we would not include the concentration of water.
- The equilibrium constant is given a special symbol, K_w, and is known as the **autoionization constant for water.**
- Because the autoionization of water is the only source of hydronium and hydroxide ions in pure water, we know that $[H_3O^+]$ must equal $[OH^-]$ in pure water. Electrical conductivity measurements of pure water show that $[H_3O^+] = [OH^-] = 1.0 \times 10^{-7}$ M at 25 °C, so K_w has a value of 1.0×10^{-14} at 25 °C.

In pure water, the hydronium ion and hydroxide ion concentrations are equal, and the water is said to be neutral. If some acid or base is added to pure water, however, the equilibrium

$$2\ H_2O(\ell) \rightleftharpoons H_3O^+(aq) + OH^-(aq)$$

is disturbed. Adding acid raises the concentration of the H_3O^+ ions, so the solution is acidic. To oppose this increase, Le Chatelier's principle (◄ Section 16.6) predicts that a small fraction of the H_3O^+ ions will react with OH^- ions from water auto-ionization to form water. This lowers $[OH^-]$ until the product of $[H_3O^+]$ and $[OH^-]$ is again equal to 1.0×10^{-14} at 25 °C. Similarly, adding a base to pure water gives a basic solution because the OH^- ion concentration has increased. Le Chatelier's principle predicts that some of the added OH^- ions will react with H_3O^+ ions present in the solution from water autoionization, thereby lowering $[H_3O^+]$ until the value of the product $[H_3O^+]$ and $[OH^-]$ equals 1.0×10^{-14} at 25 °C.

Thus, for aqueous solutions at 25 °C, we can say that

- In a neutral solution, $[H_3O^+] = [OH^-]$. Both are equal to 1.0×10^{-7} M.
- In an acidic solution, $[H_3O^+] > [OH^-]$. $[H_3O^+] > 1.0 \times 10^{-7}$ M and $[OH^-] < 1.0 \times 10^{-7}$ M.
- In a basic solution, $[H_3O^+] < [OH^-]$. $[H_3O^+] < 1.0 \times 10^{-7}$ M and $[OH^-] > 1.0 \times 10^{-7}$ M.

Chemistry Now™

Sign in at **www.cengage.com/login** and go to Chapter 17 Contents to see Screen 17.3 for a simulation of the effect of temperature on K_w.

EXAMPLE 17.1 Ion Concentrations in a Solution of a Strong Base

Problem What are the hydroxide and hydronium ion concentrations in a 0.0012 M solution of NaOH at 25 °C?

Strategy NaOH, a strong base, is 100% dissociated into ions in water, so we assume that the OH^- ion concentration is the same as the NaOH concentration. The H_3O^+ ion concentration can then be calculated using Equation 17.1.

Solution The initial concentration of OH^- is 0.0012 M.

$$0.0012 \text{ mol NaOH per liter} \rightarrow 0.0012 \text{ M Na}^+(aq) + 0.0012 \text{ M OH}^-(aq)$$

Substituting the OH^- concentration into Equation 17.1, we have

$$K_w = 1.0 \times 10^{-14} = [H_3O^+][OH^-] = [H_3O^+](0.0012)$$

and so

$$[H_3O^+] = \frac{1.0 \times 10^{-14}}{0.0012} = 8.3 \times 10^{-12} \text{ M}$$

Comment Why didn't we take into account the ions produced by water autoionization when we calculated the concentration of hydroxide ions? It should add OH^- and H_3O^+ ions to the solution. If x is equal to the concentration of OH^- ions generated by the autoionization of water, then, when equilibrium is achieved,

$[OH^-] = (0.0012 \text{ M} + OH^- \text{ from water autoionization})$

$[OH^-] = (0.0012 \text{ M} + x)$

In pure water, the concentration of OH^- ion generated is 1.0×10^{-7} M. Le Chatelier's principle (◄ Section 16.6) suggests that the concentration should be even smaller when OH^- ions are already present in solution from NaOH; that is, x should be $<< 1.0 \times 10^{-7}$ M. This means x in the term $(0.0012 + x)$ is insignificant compared with 0.0012. (Following the rules for significant figures, the sum of 0.0012 and a number even smaller than 1.0×10^{-7} is 0.0012.) Thus, the equilibrium concentration of OH^- is equivalent to the concentration of NaOH in the solution.

Lastly, what about the Na^+ ion? As described later (page 774), alkali metal ions have no effect on the acidity or basicity of a solution.

EXERCISE 17.3 Hydronium Ion Concentration in a Solution of a Strong Acid

A solution of the strong acid HCl has $[HCl] = 4.0 \times 10^{-3}$ M. What are the concentrations of H_3O^+ and OH^- in this solution at 25 °C? (Recall that because HCl is a strong acid, it is 100% ionized in water.)

The pH Scale

The **pH** of a solution is defined as the negative of the base-10 logarithm (log) of the hydronium ion concentration (◄ Section 4.6, page 179).

$$pH = -\log[H_3O^+] \qquad \text{(4.3 and 17.2)}$$

In a similar way, we can define the pOH of a solution as the negative of the base-10 logarithm of the hydroxide ion concentration.

$$pOH = -\log[OH^-] \qquad \text{(17.3)}$$

In pure water, the hydronium and hydroxide ion concentrations are both 1.0×10^{-7} M. Therefore, for pure water at 25 °C

$$pH = -\log (1.0 \times 10^{-7}) = 7.00$$

In the same way, you can show that the pOH of pure water is also 7.00 at 25 °C.

If we take the negative logarithms of both sides of the expression $K_w = [H_3O^+][OH^-]$, we obtain another useful equation.

$$
\begin{aligned}
K_w &= 1.0 \times 10^{-14} = [H_3O^+][OH^-] \\
-\log K_w &= -\log (1.0 \times 10^{-14}) = -\log([H_3O^+][OH^-]) \\
pK_w &= 14.00 = -\log ([H_3O^+]) + (-\log[OH^-]) \\
pK_w &= 14.00 = pH + pOH
\end{aligned}
\qquad \text{(17.4)}
$$

■ **The pX Scale**
In general, $-\log X = pX$,
so $-\log K = pK$
$-\log[H_3O^+] = pH$
$-\log[OH^-] = pOH$

The sum of the pH and pOH of a solution must be equal to 14.00 at 25 °C.

As illustrated in Figures 4.11 and 17.1, solutions with pH less than 7.00 (at 25 °C) are acidic, whereas solutions with pH greater than 7.00 are basic. Solutions with pH = 7.00 at 25 °C are neutral.

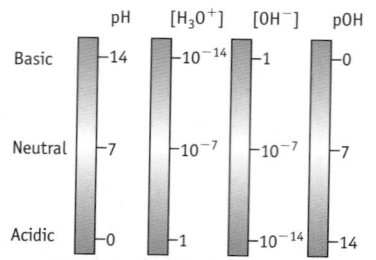

pH	$[H_3O^+]$	$[OH^-]$	pOH
Basic	14	10^{-14}	1	0
Neutral	7	10^{-7}	10^{-7}	7
Acidic	0	1	10^{-14}	14

Active Figure 17.1 pH and pOH. This figure illustrates the relationship of hydronium ion and hydroxide ion concentrations and of pH and pOH.

Chemistry ⚛ Now™ Sign in at www. cengage.com/login and go to the Chapter Contents menu to explore an interactive version of this figure accompanied by an exercise.

Calculating pH

The calculation of pH from the hydronium ion concentration, or the concentration of hydronium ion concentration from pH, was introduced in Chapter 4 (◄ page 179). Exercise 17.4 reviews those calculations.

Chemistry ⚛ Now™

Sign in at **www.cengage.com/login** and go to Chapter 17 Contents to see Screen 17.4 for a simulation and tutorial on **using pH and pOH**.

EXERCISE 17.4 Reviewing pH Calculations

(a) What is the pH of a 0.0012 M NaOH solution at 25 °C?

(b) The pH of a diet soda is 4.32 at 25 °C. What are the hydronium and hydroxide ion concentrations in the soda?

(c) If the pH of a solution containing the strong base $Sr(OH)_2$ is 10.46 at 25 °C, what is the concentration of $Sr(OH)_2$?

17.4 Equilibrium Constants for Acids and Bases

In Chapter 3, it was stated that acids and bases can be divided roughly into those that are strong electrolytes (such as HCl, HNO_3, and NaOH) and those that are weak electrolytes (such as CH_3CO_2H and NH_3) (Figure 17.2) (◄ Table 3.2, Common Acids and Bases, page 132). Hydrochloric acid is a strong acid, so 100% of the acid ionizes to produce hydronium and chloride ions. In contrast, acetic acid and ammonia are weak electrolytes. They ionize to only a very small extent in water. For example, for acetic acid, the acid, its anion, and the hydronium ion are all present at equilibrium in solution, but the ions are present in very low concentration relative to the acid concentration.

One way to define the relative strengths of a series of acids would be to measure the pH of solutions of acids of equal concentration: The lower the pH, the greater the concentration of hydronium ion, the stronger the acid. Similarly, for a series

Strong Acid

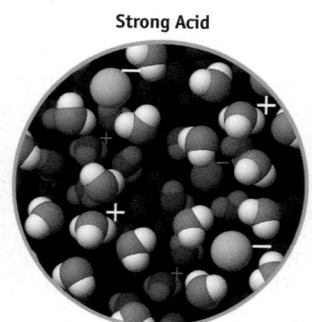

(a) HCl completely ionizes in aqueous solution.

Weak Acid

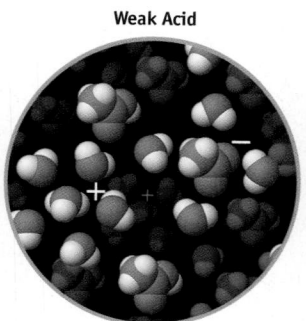

(b) Acetic acid, CH_3CO_2H, ionizes only slightly in water.

Weak Base

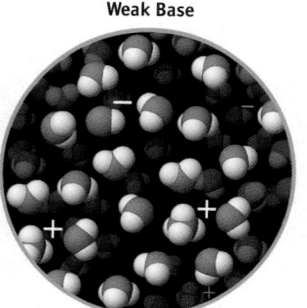

(c) The weak base ammonia reacts to a small extent with water to give a weakly basic solution.

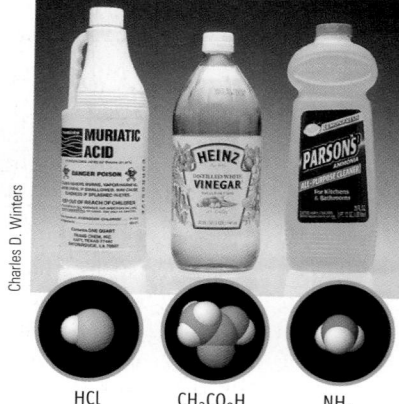

HCl CH_3CO_2H NH_3

FIGURE 17.2 Strong and weak acids and bases. (a) Hydrochloric acid, a strong acid, is sold for household use as "muriatic acid." The acid completely ionizes in water. (b) Vinegar is a solution of acetic acid, a weak acid that ionizes only to a small extent in water. (c) Ammonia is a weak base, ionizing to a small extent in water.

of weak bases, [OH$^-$] will increase, and the pH will increase as the bases become stronger.

- For a strong monoprotic acid, [H$_3$O$^+$] in solution is equal to the original acid concentration. Similarly, for a strong monoprotic base, [OH$^-$] will be equal to the original base concentration.
- For a weak acid, [H$_3$O$^+$] will be much less than the original acid concentration. That is, [H$_3$O$^+$] will be smaller than if the acid were a strong acid of the same concentration. Similarly, a weak base will give a smaller [OH$^-$] than if the base were a strong base of the same concentration.
- For a series of weak monoprotic acids (of the type HA) of the same concentration, [H$_3$O$^+$] will increase (and the pH will decline) as the acids become stronger. Similarly, for a series of weak bases, [OH$^-$] will increase (and the pH will increase) as the bases become stronger.

The relative strength of an acid or base can also be expressed quantitatively with an equilibrium constant, often called an **ionization constant.** For the general acid HA, we can write

$$HA(aq) + H_2O(\ell) \rightleftharpoons H_3O^+(aq) + A^-(aq)$$

$$K_a = \frac{[H_3O^+][A^-]}{[HA]} \qquad (17.5)$$

where the equilibrium constant, K, has a subscript "a" to indicate that it is an equilibrium constant for an acid in water. For weak acids, the value of K_a is less than 1 because the product [H$_3$O$^+$][A$^-$] is less than the equilibrium concentration of the weak acid [HA]. For a series of acids, the acid strength increases as the value of K_a increases.

Similarly, we can write the equilibrium expression for a weak base B in water. Here, we label K with a subscript "b." Its value is less than 1 for weak bases.

$$B(aq) + H_2O(\ell) \rightleftharpoons BH^+(aq) + OH^-(aq)$$

$$K_b = \frac{[BH^+][OH^-]}{[B]} \qquad (17.6)$$

Some acids and bases are listed in Table 17.3, each with its value of K_a or K_b. The following are important ideas concerning this table.

- Acids are listed in Table 17.3 at the left, and their conjugate bases are on the right.
- A large value of K indicates that ionization products are strongly favored, whereas a small value of K indicates that reactants are favored.
- The strongest acids are at the upper left. They have the largest K_a values. K_a values become smaller on descending the chart as the acid strength declines.
- The strongest bases are at the lower right. They have the largest K_b values. K_b values become larger on descending the chart as base strength increases.
- *The weaker the acid, the stronger its conjugate base.* That is, the smaller the value of K_a, the larger the value of K_b.
- Some acids or bases are listed as having K_a or K_b values that are large or very small. Acids that are stronger than H$_3$O$^+$ are completely ionized (HNO$_3$, for example), so their K_a values are "large." Their conjugate bases (such as NO$_3$$^-$) do not produce meaningful concentrations of OH$^-$ ions, so their K_b values are "very small." Similar arguments follow for strong bases and their conjugate acids.

Acid Name	Acid	K_a	Base	K_b	Base Name
Perchloric acid	$HClO_4$	large	ClO_4^-	very small	perchlorate ion
Sulfuric acid	H_2SO_4	large	HSO_4^-	very small	hydrogen sulfate ion
Hydrochloric acid	HCl	large	Cl^-	very small	chloride ion
Nitric acid	HNO_3	large	NO_3^-	very small	nitrate ion
Hydronium ion	H_3O^+	1.0	H_2O	1.0×10^{-14}	water
Sulfurous acid	H_2SO_3	1.2×10^{-2}	HSO_3^-	8.3×10^{-13}	hydrogen sulfite ion
Hydrogen sulfate ion	HSO_4^-	1.2×10^{-2}	SO_4^{2-}	8.3×10^{-13}	sulfate ion
Phosphoric acid	H_3PO_4	7.5×10^{-3}	$H_2PO_4^-$	1.3×10^{-12}	dihydrogen phosphate ion
Hexaaquairon(III) ion	$[Fe(H_2O)_6]^{3+}$	6.3×10^{-3}	$[Fe(H_2O)_5OH]^{2+}$	1.6×10^{-12}	pentaaquahydroxoiron(III) ion
Hydrofluoric acid	HF	7.2×10^{-4}	F^-	1.4×10^{-11}	fluoride ion
Nitrous acid	HNO_2	4.5×10^{-4}	NO_2^-	2.2×10^{-11}	nitrite ion
Formic acid	HCO_2H	1.8×10^{-4}	HCO_2^-	5.6×10^{-11}	formate ion
Benzoic acid	$C_6H_5CO_2H$	6.3×10^{-5}	$C_6H_5CO_2^-$	1.6×10^{-10}	benzoate ion
Acetic acid	CH_3CO_2H	1.8×10^{-5}	$CH_3CO_2^-$	5.6×10^{-10}	acetate ion
Propanoic acid	$CH_3CH_2CO_2H$	1.3×10^{-5}	$CH_3CH_2CO_2^-$	7.7×10^{-10}	propanoate ion
Hexaaquaaluminum ion	$[Al(H_2O)_6]^{3+}$	7.9×10^{-6}	$[Al(H_2O)_5OH]^{2+}$	1.3×10^{-9}	pentaaquahydroxoaluminum ion
Carbonic acid	H_2CO_3	4.2×10^{-7}	HCO_3^-	2.4×10^{-8}	hydrogen carbonate ion
Hexaaquacopper(II) ion	$[Cu(H_2O)_6]^{2+}$	1.6×10^{-7}	$[Cu(H_2O)_5OH]^+$	6.3×10^{-8}	pentaaquahydroxocopper(II) ion
Hydrogen sulfide	H_2S	1×10^{-7}	HS^-	1×10^{-7}	hydrogen sulfide ion
Dihydrogen phosphate ion	$H_2PO_4^-$	6.2×10^{-8}	HPO_4^{2-}	1.6×10^{-7}	hydrogen phosphate ion
Hydrogen sulfite ion	HSO_3^-	6.2×10^{-8}	SO_3^{2-}	1.6×10^{-7}	sulfite ion
Hypochlorous acid	$HClO$	3.5×10^{-8}	ClO^-	2.9×10^{-7}	hypochlorite ion
Hexaaqualead(II) ion	$[Pb(H_2O)_6]^{2+}$	1.5×10^{-8}	$[Pb(H_2O)_5OH]^+$	6.7×10^{-7}	pentaaquahydroxolead(II) ion
Hexaaquacobalt(II) ion	$[Co(H_2O)_6]^{2+}$	1.3×10^{-9}	$[Co(H_2O)_5OH]^+$	7.7×10^{-6}	pentaaquahydroxocobalt(II) ion
Boric acid	$B(OH)_3(H_2O)$	7.3×10^{-10}	$B(OH)_4^-$	1.4×10^{-5}	tetrahydroxoborate ion
Ammonium ion	NH_4^+	5.6×10^{-10}	NH_3	1.8×10^{-5}	ammonia
Hydrocyanic acid	HCN	4.0×10^{-10}	CN^-	2.5×10^{-5}	cyanide ion
Hexaaquairon(II) ion	$[Fe(H_2O)_6]^{2+}$	3.2×10^{-10}	$[Fe(H_2O)_5OH]^+$	3.1×10^{-5}	pentaaquahydroxoiron(II) ion
Hydrogen carbonate ion	HCO_3^-	4.8×10^{-11}	CO_3^{2-}	2.1×10^{-4}	carbonate ion
Hexaaquanickel(II) ion	$[Ni(H_2O)_6]^{2+}$	2.5×10^{-11}	$[Ni(H_2O)_5OH]^+$	4.0×10^{-4}	pentaaquahydroxonickel(II) ion
Hydrogen phosphate ion	HPO_4^{2-}	3.6×10^{-13}	PO_4^{3-}	2.8×10^{-2}	phosphate ion
Water	H_2O	1.0×10^{-14}	OH^-	1.0	hydroxide ion
Hydrogen sulfide ion*	HS^-	1×10^{-19}	S^{2-}	1×10^5	sulfide ion
Ethanol	C_2H_5OH	very small	$C_2H_5O^-$	large	ethoxide ion
Ammonia	NH_3	very small	NH_2^-	large	amide ion
Hydrogen	H_2	very small	H^-	large	hydride ion

*The values of K_a for HS^- and K_b for S^{2-} are estimates.

Increasing Acid Strength

Increasing Base Strength

To illustrate some of these ideas, let us compare some common acids and bases. For example, HF is a stronger acid than HClO, which is in turn stronger than HCO_3^-,

Decreasing acid strength →

HF	HClO	HCO_3^-
$K_a = 7.2 \times 10^{-4}$	$K_a = 3.5 \times 10^{-8}$	$K_a = 4.8 \times 10^{-11}$

and their conjugate bases become stronger from F^- to ClO^- to CO_3^{2-}.

Increasing base strength →

F^-	ClO^-	CO_3^{2-}
$K_b = 1.4 \times 10^{-11}$	$K_b = 2.9 \times 10^{-7}$	$K_b = 2.1 \times 10^{-4}$

Nature abounds in acids and bases (Figure 17.3). Many naturally occurring acids are based on the carboxyl group ($-CO_2H$), and a few are illustrated here. Notice that the organic portion of the *molecule* has an effect on its relative strength (as described further in Section 17.10).

K_a increases; acid strength increases →

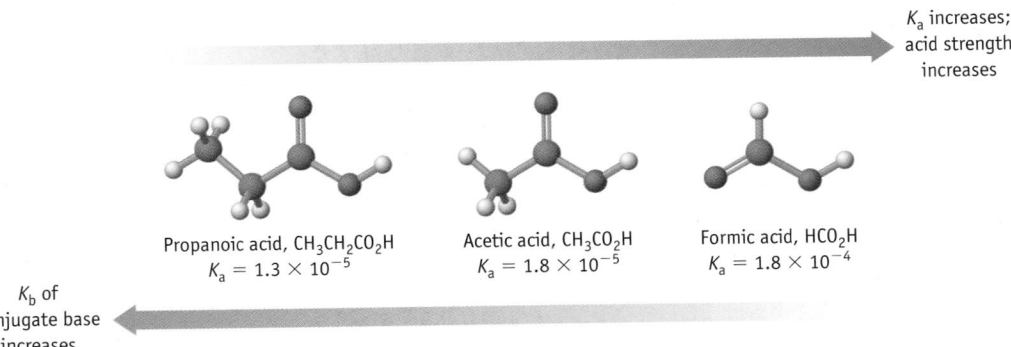

Propanoic acid, $CH_3CH_2CO_2H$
$K_a = 1.3 \times 10^{-5}$

Acetic acid, CH_3CO_2H
$K_a = 1.8 \times 10^{-5}$

Formic acid, HCO_2H
$K_a = 1.8 \times 10^{-4}$

← K_b of conjugate base increases

There are many naturally occurring weak bases as well as weak acids (Figure 17.3). Ammonia and its conjugate acid, the ammonium ion, are part of the nitrogen cycle in the environment (▶ page 951). Biological systems reduce nitrate ion to NH_3 and NH_4^+ and incorporate nitrogen into amino acids and proteins. Many bases are derived from NH_3 by replacement of the H atoms with organic groups.

Ammonia
$K_b = 1.8 \times 10^{-5}$

Methylamine
$K_b = 5.0 \times 10^{-4}$

Aniline
$K_b = 4.0 \times 10^{-10}$

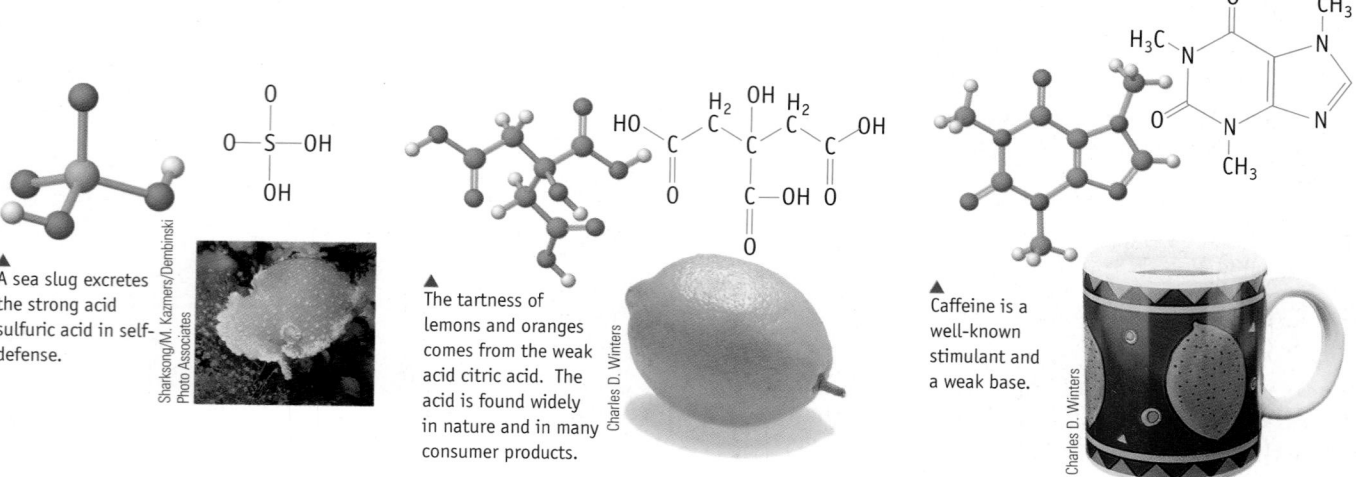

A sea slug excretes the strong acid sulfuric acid in self-defense.

The tartness of lemons and oranges comes from the weak acid citric acid. The acid is found widely in nature and in many consumer products.

Caffeine is a well-known stimulant and a weak base.

FIGURE 17.3 Natural acids and bases. Hundreds of acids and bases occur in nature. Our foods contain a wide variety, and biochemically important molecules are often acids and bases.

Ammonia is a weaker base than methylamine (K_b for NH_3 < K_b for CH_3NH_2). This means that the conjugate acid of ammonia, NH_4^+ ($K_a = 5.6 \times 10^{-10}$) is stronger than the conjugate acid of methylamine ($CH_3NH_3^+$, $K_a = 2.0 \times 10^{-11}$).

Chemistry⚛Now™

Sign in at **www.cengage.com/login** and go to Chapter 17 Contents to see:
• Screen 17.5 for tutorials on **the pH of solutions of acids and bases**
• Screen 17.6 for a table of K_a and K_b **values**

EXERCISE 17.5 Strengths of Acids and Bases

Use Table 17.2 to answer the following questions.

(a) Which is the stronger acid, H_2SO_4 or H_2SO_3?

(b) Is benzoic acid, $C_6H_5CO_2H$, stronger or weaker than acetic acid?

(c) Which has the stronger conjugate base, acetic acid or boric acid?

(d) Which is the stronger base, ammonia or the acetate ion?

(e) Which has the stronger conjugate acid, ammonia or the acetate ion?

K_a Values for Polyprotic Acids

Like all polyprotic acids, phosphoric acid ionizes in a series of steps, three in this case.

First ionization step: $K_{a1} = 7.5 \times 10^{-3}$

$$H_3PO_4(aq) + H_2O(\ell) \rightleftharpoons H_2PO_4^-(aq) + H_3O^+(aq)$$

Second ionization step: $K_{a2} = 6.2 \times 10^{-8}$

$$H_2PO_4^-(aq) + H_2O(\ell) \rightleftharpoons HPO_4^{2-}(aq) + H_3O^+(aq)$$

Third ionization step: $K_{a3} = 3.6 \times 10^{-13}$

$$HPO_4^{2-}(aq) + H_2O(\ell) \rightleftharpoons PO_4^{3-}(aq) + H_3O^+(aq)$$

Notice that the K_a value for each successive step becomes smaller and smaller because it is more difficult to remove H^+ from a negatively charged ion, such as $H_2PO_4^-$, than from a neutral molecule, such as H_3PO_4. Similarly, the larger the negative charge of the anionic acid, the more difficult it is to remove H^+. Finally, also notice that for many inorganic polyprotic acids, K_a values become smaller by about 10^{-5} for each proton removed.

Aqueous Solutions of Salts

A number of the acids and bases listed in Table 17.2 are cations or anions. As described earlier, anions can act as Brønsted bases because they can accept a proton from an acid to form the conjugate acid of the base.

$$CO_3^{2-}(aq) + H_2O(\ell) \rightleftharpoons HCO_3^-(aq) + OH^-(aq)$$

$$K_b = 2.1 \times 10^{-4}$$

You should also notice that many metal cations in water are Brønsted acids.

$$[Al(H_2O)_6]^{3+}(aq) + H_2O(\ell) \rightleftharpoons [Al(H_2O)_5(OH)]^{2+}(aq) + H_3O^+(aq)$$

$$K_a = 7.9 \times 10^{-6}$$

Table 17.4 summarizes the acid–base properties of some of the common cations and anions. As you look over this table, notice the following points:

- Anions that are conjugate bases of strong acids (for example, Cl^- and NO_3^-) are such weak bases that they have no effect on solution pH.
- There are numerous basic anions (such as CO_3^{2-}). All are the conjugate bases of weak acids.
- The acid–base behavior of anions of polyprotic acids depends on the extent of deprotonation. For example, a fully deprotonated anion (such as CO_3^{2-}) will be basic. A partially deprotonated anion (such as HCO_3^-) is amphiprotic. Its behavior will depend on the other species in the reaction.
- Alkali metal and alkaline earth cations have no measurable effect on solution pH.
- Basic cations are conjugate bases of acidic cations such as $[Al(H_2O)_6]^{3+}$.
- Acidic cations are limited to metal cations with $2+$ and $3+$ charges and to ammonium ions (and their organic derivatives).
- All metal cations are hydrated in water. That is, they form ions such as $[M(H_2O)_6]^{n+}$. However, only when M is a $2+$ or $3+$ ion, particularly a transition metal ion, does the ion act as an acid.

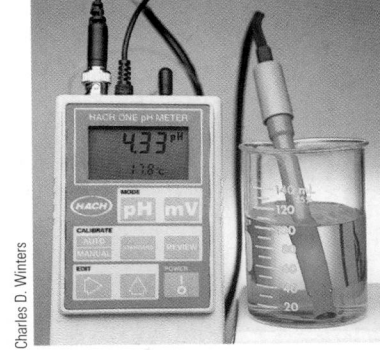

Many aqueous metal cations are Brønsted acids. A pH measurement of a dilute solution of copper(II) sulfate shows that the solution is clearly acidic. Among the common cations, Al^{3+} and transition metal ions form acidic solutions in water.

Charles D. Winters

Chemistry ♦ Now™

Sign in at **www.cengage.com/login** and go to Chapter 17 Contents to see Screen 17.11 for a simulation showing **the pH of a number of cation/anion combinations.**

■ **Hydrolysis Reactions** Chemists often say that, when ions interact with water to produce acidic or basic solutions, the ions "hydrolyze" in water, or they undergo "hydrolysis." Thus, some books refer to the K_a and K_b values of ions as "hydrolysis constants," K_h.

TABLE 17.4   Acid and Base Properties of Some Ions in Aqueous Solution

Neutral		Basic			Acidic
Anions	Cl^- NO_3^-	$CH_3CO_2^-$	CN^-	SO_4^{2-}	HSO_4^-
	Br^- ClO_4^-	HCO_2^-	PO_4^{3-}	HPO_4^{2-}	$H_2PO_4^-$
	I^-	CO_3^{2-}	HCO_3^-	SO_3^{2-}	HSO_3^-
		S^{2-}	HS^-	OCl^-	
		F^-	NO_2^-		
Cations	Li^+	$[Al(H_2O)_5(OH)]^{2+}$ (for example)			$[Al(H_2O)_6]^{3+}$ and hydrated
	Na^+ Ca^{2+}				transition metal cations
	K^+ Ba^{2+}				(such as $[Fe(H_2O)_6]^{3+}$)
					NH_4^+

■ **EXAMPLE 17.2 Acid–Base Properties of Salts**

Problem Decide whether each of the following will give rise to an acidic, basic, or neutral solution in water.

(a) $NaNO_3$ (d) $NaHCO_3$

(b) K_3PO_4 (e) NH_4F

(c) $FeCl_2$

Strategy First, decide on the cation and anion in each salt. Next, use Tables 17.3 and 17.4 to describe the properties of each ion.

Solution

(a) **$NaNO_3$:** This salt gives a neutral, aqueous solution (pH = 7). Neither the sodium ion, Na^+, nor the nitrate ion, NO_3^- (the very weak conjugate base of a strong acid), affects the solution pH.

(b) **K_3PO_4:** An aqueous solution of K_3PO_4 should be basic (pH > 7) because PO_4^{3-} is the conjugate base of the weak acid HPO_4^{2-}. The K^+ ion, like the Na^+ ion, does not affect the solution pH.

(c) **$FeCl_2$:** An aqueous solution of $FeCl_2$ should be weakly acidic (pH < 7). The Fe^{2+} ion in water, $[Fe(H_2O)_6]^{2+}$, is a Brønsted acid. In contrast, Cl^- is the very weak conjugate base of the strong acid HCl, so it does not contribute excess OH^- ions to the solution.

(d) **$NaHCO_3$:** Some additional information is needed concerning salts of amphiprotic anions such as HCO_3^-. Because they have an ionizable hydrogen, they can act as acids.

$$HCO_3^-(aq) + H_2O(\ell) \rightleftharpoons CO_3^{2-}(aq) + H_3O^+(aq) \qquad K_a = 4.8 \times 10^{-11}$$

They are also the conjugate bases of weak acids.

$$HCO_3^-(aq) + H_2O(\ell) \rightleftharpoons H_2CO_3(aq) + OH^-(aq) \qquad K_b = 2.4 \times 10^{-8}$$

Whether the solution is acidic or basic will depend on the relative magnitude of K_a and K_b. In the case of the hydrogen carbonate anion, K_b is larger than K_a, so $[OH^-]$ is larger than $[H_3O^+]$, and an aqueous solution of $NaHCO_3$ will be slightly basic.

(e) **NH_4F:** What happens if you have a salt based on an acidic cation and a basic anion? One example is ammonium fluoride. Here, the ammonium ion would decrease the pH, and the fluoride ion would increase the pH.

$$NH_4^+(aq) + H_2O(\ell) \rightleftharpoons H_3O^+(aq) + NH_3(aq) \qquad K_a(NH_4^+) = 5.6 \times 10^{-10}$$

$$F^-(aq) + H_2O(\ell) \rightleftharpoons HF(aq) + OH^-(aq) \qquad K_b (F^-) = 1.4 \times 10^{-11}$$

Because $K_a (NH_4^+) > K_b (F^-)$, the ammonium ion is a stronger acid than the fluoride ion is a base. The resulting solution should be slightly acidic.

Comment There are two important points to notice here:

• Anions that are conjugate bases of strong acids—such as Cl^- and NO_3^-—have no effect on solution pH.

• For a salt that has an acidic cation and a basic anion, the pH of the solution will be determined by the ion that is the stronger acid or base of the two.

Problem Solving Tip 17.2 Aqueous Solutions of Salts

Because aqueous solutions of salts are found in our bodies and throughout our economy and environment, it is important to know how to predict their acid and base properties. Information on the pH of an aqueous solution of a salt is summarized in Table 17.4. Consider also the following examples:

Cation	Anion	pH of the Solution
From strong base (Na^+)	From strong acid (Cl^-)	= 7 (neutral)
From strong base (K^+)	From weak acid ($CH_3CO_2^-$)	> 7 (basic)
From weak base (NH_4^+)	From strong acid (Cl^-)	< 7 (acidic)
From any weak base (BH^+)	From any weak acid (A^-)	Depends on relative strengths of BH^+ and A^-

EXERCISE 17.6 Acid–Base Properties of Salts in Aqueous Solution

For each of the following salts in water, predict whether the pH will be greater than, less than, or equal to 7.

(a) KBr **(b)** NH_4NO_3 **(c)** $AlCl_3$ **(d)** Na_2HPO_4

A Logarithmic Scale of Relative Acid Strength, pK_a

Many chemists and biochemists use a logarithmic scale to report and compare relative acid strengths.

$$pK_a = -\log K_a \tag{17.7}$$

The pK_a of an acid is the negative log of the K_a value (just as pH is the negative log of the hydronium ion concentration). For example, acetic acid has a pK_a value of 4.74.

$$pK_a = -\log (1.8 \times 10^{-5}) = 4.74$$

The pK_a value becomes smaller as the acid strength increases.

—— Acid strength increases ⟶

Propanoic acid	Acetic acid	Formic acid
$CH_3CH_2CO_2H$	CH_3CO_2H	HCO_2H
$K_a = 1.3 \times 10^{-5}$	$K_a = 1.8 \times 10^{-5}$	$K_a = 1.8 \times 10^{-4}$
$pK_a = 4.89$	$pK_a = 4.74$	$pK_a = 3.74$

⟵ pK_a increases ——

EXERCISE 17.7 A Logarithmic Scale for Acid Strength, pK_a

(a) What is the pK_a value for benzoic acid, $C_6H_5CO_2H$?

(b) Is chloroacetic acid ($ClCH_2CO_2H$), $pK_a = 2.87$, a stronger or weaker acid than benzoic acid?

(c) What is the pK_a for the conjugate acid of ammonia? Is this acid stronger or weaker than acetic acid?

Relating the Ionization Constants for an Acid and Its Conjugate Base

Let us look again at Table 17.3. From the top of the table to the bottom, the strengths of the acids decline (K_a becomes smaller), and the strengths of their conjugate bases increase (the values of K_b increase). Examining a few cases shows

■ **A Relation Among pK Values** A useful relationship for an acid–conjugate base pair can be derived from Equation 17.8.

$$pK_w = pK_a + pK_b$$

that the product of K_a for an acid and K_b for its conjugate base is equal to a constant, specifically K_w.

$$K_a \times K_b = K_w \qquad (17.8)$$

Consider the specific case of the ionization of a weak acid, say HCN, and the interaction of its conjugate base, CN^-, with H_2O.

Weak acid:	$HCN(aq) + H_2O(\ell) \rightleftharpoons H_3O^+(aq) + CN^-(aq)$	$K_a = 4.0 \times 10^{-10}$
Conjugate base:	$CN^-(aq) + H_2O(\ell) \rightleftharpoons HCN(aq) + OH^-(aq)$	$K_b = 2.5 \times 10^{-5}$
	$2\,H_2O(\ell) \rightleftharpoons H_3O^+(aq) + OH^-(aq)$	$K_w = 1.0 \times 10^{-14}$

Adding the equations gives the chemical equation for the autoionization of water, and the numerical value is indeed 1.0×10^{-14}. That is,

$$K_a \times K_b = \left(\frac{[H_3O^+][\cancel{CN^-}]}{[\cancel{HCN}]}\right)\left(\frac{[\cancel{HCN}][OH^-]}{[\cancel{CN^-}]}\right) = [H_3O^+][OH^-] = K_w$$

Equation 17.8 is useful because K_b can be calculated from K_a. The value of K_b for the cyanide ion, for example, is

$$K_b \text{ for } CN^- = \frac{K_w}{K_a \text{ for } HCN} = \frac{1.0 \times 10^{-14}}{4.0 \times 10^{-10}} = 2.5 \times 10^{-5}$$

EXERCISE 17.8 Using the Equation $K_a \times K_b = K_w$

K_a for lactic acid, $CH_3CHOHCO_2H$, is 1.4×10^{-4}. What is K_b for the conjugate base of this acid, $CH_3CHOHCO_2^-$? Where does this base fit in Table 17.3?

17.5 Predicting the Direction of Acid–Base Reactions

According to the Brønsted–Lowry theory, all acid–base reactions can be written as equilibria involving the acid and base and their conjugates.

$$\text{Acid} + \text{Base} \rightleftharpoons \text{Conjugate base of the acid} + \text{Conjugate acid of the base}$$

In Section 17.4, we used equilibrium constants to provide quantitative information about the relative strengths of acids and bases. Now we want to show how the constants can be used to decide whether a particular acid–base reaction is product- or reactant–favored at equilibrium.

Hydrochloric acid is a strong acid. Its equilibrium constant for reaction with water is very large, with the equilibrium effectively lying completely to the right.

■ ***K*** **and Product- and Reactant-Favored Reactions** Reactions with an equilibrium constant greater than 1 are said to be product-favored at equilibrium. Those with $K < 1$ are reactant-favored at equilibrium.

$$HCl(aq) + H_2O(\ell) \rightleftharpoons H_3O^+(aq) + Cl^-(aq)$$
Strong acid ($\approx$ 100% ionized), $K \gg 1$
$[H_3O^+] \approx$ initial concentration of the acid

Of the two acids here, HCl is stronger than H_3O^+. Of the two bases, H_2O and Cl^-, water is the stronger base and wins out in the competition for the proton. Thus, the equilibrium lies to the side of the chemical equation having the weaker acid and base.

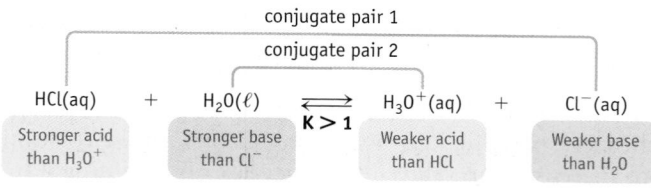

In contrast to HCl and other strong acids, acetic acid, a *weak* acid, ionizes to only a very small extent (Table 17.3).

$$CH_3CO_2H(aq) + H_2O(\ell) \rightleftharpoons H_3O^+(aq) + CH_3CO_2^-(aq)$$

Weak acid ($< 100\%$ ionized), $K = 1.8 \times 10^{-5}$

$[H_3O^+] \ll$ initial concentration of the acid

When equilibrium is achieved in a 0.1 M aqueous solution of CH_3CO_2H, the concentrations of $H_3O^+(aq)$ and $CH_3CO_2^-(aq)$ are each only about 0.001 M. Approximately 99% of the acetic acid is not ionized.

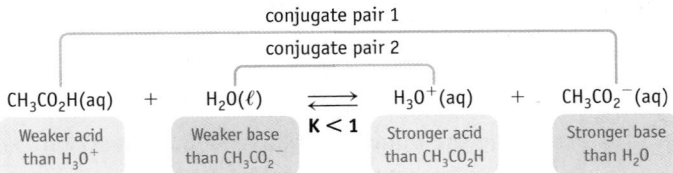

Again, the equilibrium lies toward the side of the reaction having the weaker acid and base.

These two examples of the relative extent of acid–base reactions illustrate a general principle: *All proton transfer reactions proceed from the stronger acid and base to the weaker acid and base.* Using this principle and Table 17.3, you can predict which reactions are product-favored and which are reactant-favored. Consider the possible reaction of phosphoric acid and acetate ion to give acetic acid and the dihydrogen phosphate ion. Table 17.3 informs us that H_3PO_4 is a stronger acid ($K_a = 7.5 \times 10^{-3}$) than acetic acid ($K_a = 1.8 \times 10^{-5}$), and the acetate ion ($K_b = 5.6 \times 10^{-10}$) is a stronger base than the dihydrogen phosphate ion ($K_b = 1.3 \times 10^{-12}$).

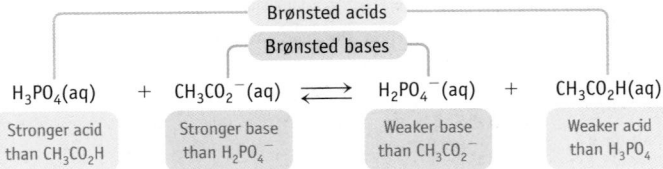

Thus, mixing phosphoric acid with sodium acetate would produce a significant amount of dihydrogen phosphate ion and acetic acid. That is, the equilibrium is predicted to lie to the right because the reaction proceeds from the stronger acid–base combination to the weaker acid–base combination.

Chemistry ⚛ Now™

Sign in at **www.cengage.com/login** and go to Chapter 17 Contents to see Screen 17.7 for a simulation on predicting the direction of acid–base reactions.

■ **EXAMPLE 17.3 Reactions of Acids and Bases**

Problem Write a balanced, net ionic equation for the reaction that occurs between acetic acid and sodium bicarbonate. Decide whether the equilibrium lies predominantly to the left or to the right.

Strategy First, identify the products of the acid–base reaction (which arise by H^+ transfer from the acid to the base). Next, identify the two acids (or the two bases) in the reaction. Finally, use Table 17.3 to decide which is the weaker of the two acids (or the weaker of the two bases). The reaction will proceed from the stronger acid (or base) to the weaker acid (or base).

Reaction of vinegar and baking soda. This reaction involves the weak acid acetic acid and the weak base HCO_3^- from sodium hydrogen carbonate. Based on the values of the equilibrium constants, the reaction is predicted to proceed to the right to produce acetate ion, CO_2, and water.

Solution Acetic acid is clearly one acid involved (and its conjugate base is the acetate ion, $CH_3CO_2^-$). The other reactant, $NaHCO_3$, is a water-soluble salt that forms Na^+ and HCO_3^- ions in water. Because acetic acid can function only as an acid, the HCO_3^- ion in this case must be the Brønsted base. Thus, hydrogen ion transfer from the acid to the base (HCO_3^- ion) could lead to the following net ionic equation:

$$CH_3CO_2H(aq) + HCO_3^-(aq) \rightleftharpoons CH_3CO_2^-(aq) + H_2CO_3(aq)$$

According to Table 17.3, H_2CO_3 is a weaker acid ($K_a = 4.2 \times 10^{-7}$) than CH_3CO_2H ($K_a = 1.8 \times 10^{-5}$), and $CH_3CO_2^-$ is a weaker base ($K_b = 5.6 \times 10^{-10}$) than HCO_3^- ($K_b = 2.4 \times 10^{-8}$). The reaction favors the side having the weaker acid and base—that is, the right side.

Comment The reaction of acetic acid and $NaHCO_3$ favors the weaker acid (H_2CO_3) and base ($CH_3CO_2^-$). In the photograph in the margin, you see that the product, H_2CO_3, also dissociates into CO_2 and H_2O because the CO_2 bubbles out of the solution: the equilibrium lies far to the right.

$$H_2CO_3(aq) \rightleftharpoons CO_2(g) + H_2O(\ell)$$

See the discussion of gas-forming reactions in Chapter 3 and of Le Chatelier's principle in Section 14.3.

EXERCISE 17.9 Predicting the Direction of an Acid–Base Reaction

(a) Which is the stronger Brønsted acid, HCO_3^- or NH_4^+? Which has the stronger conjugate base?

(b) Is a reaction between HCO_3^- ions and NH_3 product- or reactant-favored?

$$HCO_3^-(aq) + NH_3(aq) \rightleftharpoons CO_3^{2-}(aq) + NH_4^+(aq)$$

(c) You mix solutions of sodium hydrogen phosphate and ammonia. The net ionic equation for a possible reaction is

$$HPO_4^{2-}(aq) + NH_3(aq) \rightleftharpoons PO_4^{3-}(aq) + NH_4^+(aq)$$

Does the equilibrium lie to the left or to the right in this reaction?

17.6 Types of Acid–Base Reactions

The reaction of hydrochloric acid and sodium hydroxide is the classic example of a strong acid–strong base reaction, whereas the reaction of citric acid and bicarbonate ion represents the reaction of a weak acid and weak base (Figure 17.4). There are four general types of acid–base reactions.

Type of Acid–Base Reaction	Example
Strong acid + strong base	HCl and NaOH
Strong acid + weak base	HCl and NH_3
Weak acid + strong base	CH_3CO_2H and NaOH
Weak acid + weak base	Citric acid and HCO_3^-

Because acid–base reactions are among the most important classes of chemical reactions, it is useful for you to know the outcome of the various types of these reactions (Table 17.5).

TABLE 17.5 Characteristics of Acid–Base Reactions

Type	Example	Net Ionic Equation	Species Present after Equal Molar Amounts Are Mixed; pH
Strong acid + strong base	HCl + NaOH	$H_3O^+(aq) + OH^-(aq) \rightleftharpoons 2\,H_2O(\ell)$	Cl^-, Na^+, pH = 7
Strong acid + weak base	HCl + NH_3	$H_3O^+(aq) + NH_3(aq) \rightleftharpoons NH_4^+(aq) + H_2O(\ell)$	Cl^-, NH_4^+, pH < 7
Weak acid + strong base	HCO_2H + NaOH	$HCO_2H(aq) + OH^-(aq) \rightleftharpoons HCO_2^-(aq) + H_2O(\ell)$	HCO_2^-, Na^+, pH > 7
Weak acid + weak base	HCO_2H + NH_3	$HCO_2H(aq) + NH_3(aq) \rightleftharpoons HCO_2^-(aq) + NH_4^+(aq)$	HCO_2^-, NH_4^+, pH dependent on K_a and K_b of conjugate acid and base

The Reaction of a Strong Acid with a Strong Base

Strong acids and bases are effectively 100% ionized in solution. Therefore, the total ionic equation for the reaction of HCl (strong acid) and NaOH (strong base) is

$$H_3O^+(aq) + Cl^-(aq) + Na^+(aq) + OH^-(aq) \rightleftharpoons 2 H_2O(\ell) + Na^+(aq) + Cl^-(aq)$$

which leads to the following net ionic equation

$$H_3O^+(aq) + OH^-(aq) \rightleftharpoons 2 H_2O(\ell) \qquad K = 1/K_w = 1.0 \times 10^{14}$$

The net ionic equation for the reaction of any strong acid with any strong base is always simply the union of hydronium ion and hydroxide ion to give water (◄ Section 3.7). Because this reaction is the reverse of the autoionization of water, it has an equilibrium constant of $1/K_w$. This very large value of K shows that, for all practical purposes, the reactants are completely consumed to form products. Thus, if equal numbers of moles of NaOH and HCl are mixed, the result is just a solution of NaCl in water. The constituents of NaCl, Na^+ and Cl^- ions, which arise from a strong base and a strong acid, respectively, produce a neutral aqueous solution. For this reason, reactions of strong acids and bases are often called "neutralizations."

FIGURE 17.4 Reaction of a weak acid with a weak base. The bubbles coming from the tablet are carbon dioxide. This arises from the reaction of a weak Brønsted acid (citric acid) with a weak Brønsted base (HCO_3^-). The reaction is driven to completion by gas evolution.

Charles D. Winters

> Mixing equal amounts (moles) of a strong base with a strong acid produces a neutral solution (pH = 7.00 at 25 °C).

The Reaction of a Weak Acid with a Strong Base

Consider the reaction of the naturally occurring weak acid formic acid, HCO_2H, with sodium hydroxide. The net ionic equation is

$$HCO_2H(aq) + OH^-(aq) \rightleftharpoons H_2O(\ell) + HCO_2^-(aq)$$

In the reaction of formic acid with NaOH, OH^- is a much stronger base than HCO_2^- ($K_b = 5.6 \times 10^{-11}$), and the reaction is predicted to proceed to the right. If equal amounts of weak acid and base are mixed, the final solution will contain sodium formate ($NaHCO_2$), a salt that is 100% dissociated in water. The Na^+ ion is the cation of a strong base and so gives a neutral solution. The formate ion, however, is the conjugate base of a weak acid (Table 17.3), so the solution is basic. This example leads to a useful general conclusion:

■ **Formic Acid + NaOH** The equilibrium constant for the reaction of formic acid and sodium hydroxide is 1.8×10^{10}. Can you confirm this? (See Study Question 17.97.)

> Mixing equal amounts (moles) of a strong base with a weak acid produces a salt whose anion is the conjugate base of the weak acid. The solution is basic, with the pH depending on K_b for the anion.

The Reaction of a Strong Acid with a Weak Base

The net ionic equation for the reaction of the strong acid HCl and the weak base NH_3 is

$$H_3O^+(aq) + NH_3(aq) \rightleftharpoons H_2O(\ell) + NH_4^+(aq)$$

The hydronium ion, H_3O^+, is a much stronger acid than NH_4^+ ($K_a = 5.6 \times 10^{-10}$), and NH_3 is a stronger base ($K_b = 1.8 \times 10^{-5}$) than H_2O. Therefore, reaction is predicted to proceed to the right and essentially to completion. Thus, after mixing equal amounts of HCl and NH_3, the solution contains the salt ammonium chloride, NH_4Cl. The Cl^- ion has no effect on the solution pH (Tables 17.3 and 17.4). However, the NH_4^+ ion is the conjugate acid of the weak base NH_3, so the solution at the conclusion of the reaction is acidic. In general, we can conclude that

■ **Ammonia + HCl** The equilibrium constant for the reaction of a strong acid with aqueous ammonia is 1.8×10^9. Can you confirm this? (See Study Question 17.96.)

> Mixing equal amounts (moles) of a strong acid and a weak base produces a salt whose cation is the conjugate acid of the weak base. The solution is acidic, with the pH depending on K_a for the cation.

A weak acid reacting with a weak base. Baking powder contains the weak acid calcium dihydrogen phosphate, $Ca(H_2PO_4)_2$. This can react with the basic HCO_3^- ion in baking soda to give HPO_4^{2-}, CO_2 gas, and water.

■ **K for Reaction of Weak Acid and Weak Base** The equilibrium constant for the reaction between a weak acid and a weak base is $K_{net} = (K_a \cdot K_b)/K_w$. Can you confirm this? (See Study Question 17.121.)

 Module 22

The Reaction of a Weak Acid with a Weak Base

If acetic acid, a weak acid, is mixed with ammonia, a weak base, the following reaction occurs.

$$CH_3CO_2H(aq) + NH_3(aq) \rightleftharpoons NH_4^+(aq) + CH_3CO_2^-(aq)$$

You know that the reaction is product-favored because CH_3CO_2H is a stronger acid than NH_4^+ and NH_3 is a stronger base than $CH_3CO_2^-$ (Table 17.3). Thus, if equal amounts of the acid and base are mixed, the resulting solution contains ammonium acetate, $NH_4CH_3CO_2$. Is this solution acidic or basic? On page 775 you learned that this depends on the relative values of K_a for the conjugate acid (here, NH_4^+; $K_a = 5.6 \times 10^{-10}$) and K_b for the conjugate base (here, $CH_3CO_2^-$; $K_b = 5.6 \times 10^{-10}$). In this case, the values of K_a and K_b are the same, so the solution is predicted to be neutral.

> Mixing equal amounts (moles) of a weak acid and a weak base produces a salt whose cation is the conjugate acid of the weak base and whose anion is the conjugate base of the weak acid. The solution pH depends on the relative K_a and K_b values.

EXERCISE 17.10 Acid–Base Reactions

(a) Equal amounts (moles) of HCl(aq) and NaCN(aq) are mixed. Is the resulting solution acidic, basic, or neutral?

(b) Equal amounts (moles) of acetic acid and sodium sulfite, Na_2SO_3, are mixed. Is the resulting solution acidic, basic, or neutral?

17.7 Calculations with Equilibrium Constants

Determining K from Initial Concentrations and Measured pH

The K_a and K_b values found in Table 17.3 and in the more extensive tables in Appendices H and I were all determined by experiment. There are several experimental methods available, but one approach, illustrated by the following example, is to determine the pH of the solution.

Chemistry ⚛ Now™

> Sign in at **www.cengage.com/login** and go to Chapter 17 Contents to see Screen 17.8 for a tutorial on **determining K_a and K_b values.**

■ **EXAMPLE 17.4 Calculating a K_a Value from a Measured pH**

Problem A 0.10 M aqueous solution of lactic acid, $CH_3CHOHCO_2H$, has a pH of 2.43. What is the value of K_a for lactic acid?

Strategy To calculate K_a, we must know the equilibrium concentration of each species. The pH of the solution directly tells us the equilibrium concentration of H_3O^+, and we can derive the other equilibrium concentrations from this. These are used to calculate K_a.

Solution The equation for the equilibrium interaction of lactic acid with water is

$$CH_3CHOHCO_2H(aq) + H_2O(\ell) \rightleftharpoons CH_3CHOHCO_2^-(aq) + H_3O^+(aq)$$

Lactic acid   Lactate ion

and the equilibrium constant expression is

$$K_a \text{ (lactic acid)} = \frac{[H_3O^+][CH_3CHOHCO_2^-]}{[CH_3CHOHCO_2H]}$$

We begin by converting the pH to $[H_3O^+]$.

$$[H_3O^+] = 10^{-pH} = 10^{-2.43} = 3.7 \times 10^{-3} \text{ M}$$

Next, prepare an ICE table of the concentrations in the solution before equilibrium is established, the change that occurs as the reaction proceeds to equilibrium, and the concentrations when equilibrium has been achieved. (See Examples 16.2–16.5.)

Equilibrium	$CH_3CHOHCO_2H + H_2O \rightleftharpoons CH_3CHOHCO_2^- + H_3O^+$		
Initial (M)	0.10	0	0
Change (M)	$-x$	$+x$	$+x$
Equilibrium (M)	$(0.10 - x)$	x	x

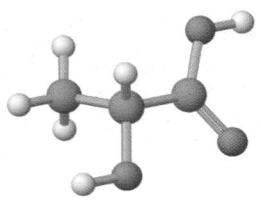

Lactic acid, $CH_3CHOHCO_2H$

Lactic acid, $CH_3CHOHCO_2H$. Lactic acid is a weak monoprotic acid that occurs naturally in sour milk and arises from metabolism in the human body.

The following points can be made concerning the ICE table.

- The quantity x represents the equilibrium concentrations of hydronium ion and lactate ion.

That is, at equilibrium $x = [H_3O^+] = [CH_3CHOHCO_2^-] = 3.7 \times 10^{-3}$ M.

- By stoichiometry, x is also the quantity of acid that ionized on proceeding to equilibrium. With these points in mind, we can calculate K_a for lactic acid.

$$K_a \text{ (lactic acid)} = \frac{[H_3O^+][CH_3CHOHCO_2^-]}{[CH_3CHOHCO_2H]}$$

$$= \frac{(3.7 \times 10^{-3})(3.7 \times 10^{-3})}{0.10 - 0.0037} = \boxed{1.4 \times 10^{-4}}$$

Comparing this value of K_a with others in Table 17.3, we see it is similar to formic acid in its strength.

Comment Hydronium ion, H_3O^+, is present in solution from lactic acid ionization and from water autoionization. Le Chatelier's principle informs us that the H_3O^+ added to the water by lactic acid will suppress the H_3O^+ coming from the water autoionization. However, because $[H_3O^+]$ from water must be less than 10^{-7} M, the pH is almost completely a reflection of H_3O^+ from lactic acid. (See Example 17.1.)

EXERCISE 17.11 Calculating a K_a Value from a Measured pH

A solution prepared from 0.055 mol of butanoic acid dissolved in sufficient water to give 1.0 L of solution has a pH of 2.72. Determine K_a for butanoic acid. The acid ionizes according to the balanced equation

$$CH_3CH_2CH_2CO_2H(aq) + H_2O(\ell) \rightleftharpoons H_3O^+(aq) + CH_3CH_2CH_2CO_2^-(aq)$$

There is an important point to notice in Example 17.4. The lactic acid concentration at equilibrium was given by $(0.10 - x)$ where x was found to be 3.7×10^{-3} M. By the usual rules governing significant figures $(0.10 - 0.0037)$ is equal to 0.10. The acid is weak, so very little of it ionizes (approximately 4%), and the equilibrium concentration of lactic acid is essentially equal to the initial acid concentration. Neglecting to subtract 0.0037 from 0.10 has no effect on the answer to two significant figures.

Like lactic acid, most weak acids (HA) are so weak that the equilibrium concentration of the acid, [HA], is effectively its initial concentration $(= [HA]_0)$. This leads to the useful conclusion that the denominator in the equilibrium constant expression for dilute solutions of most weak acids is simply $[HA]_0$, the original or initial concentration of the weak acid.

$$HA(aq) + H_2O(\ell) \rightleftharpoons H_3O^+(aq) + A^-(aq)$$

$$K_a = \frac{[H_3O^+][A^-]}{[HA]_0 - [H_3O^+]} \approx \frac{[H_3O^+][A^-]}{[HA]_0}$$

Analysis shows that

The approximation that $[HA]_{equilibrium}$ is effectively equal to $[HA]_0$
($[HA]_{equilibrium} = [HA]_0 - [H_3O^+] \approx [HA]_0$)
is valid whenever $[HA]_0$ is greater than or equal to $100 \cdot K_a$.

This is the same approximation we derived in Chapter 16 when deciding whether we needed to solve quadratic equations exactly (◄ Problem Solving Tip 16.1).

What Is the pH of an Aqueous Solution of a Weak Acid or Base?

Knowing values of the equilibrium constants for weak acids and bases enables us to calculate the pH of a solution of a weak acid or base.

Chemistry.☽.Now™

Sign in at **www.cengage.com/login** and go to Chapter 17 Contents to see Screen 17.9 for a tutorial on **estimating the pH of weak acid solutions.**

■ **EXAMPLE 17.5** **Calculating Equilibrium Concentrations and pH from K_a**

Problem Calculate the pH of a 0.020 M solution of benzoic acid ($C_6H_5CO_2H$) if $K_a = 6.3 \times 10^{-5}$ for the acid.

$$C_6H_5CO_2H(aq) + H_2O(\ell) \rightleftharpoons H_3O^+(aq) + C_6H_5CO_2^-(aq)$$

Strategy This is similar to Examples 16.5 and 16.6, where we wanted to find the concentration of a reaction product. The strategy is the same: designate the quantity of product (here $[H_3O^+]$) by x, and derive the other concentrations from that starting point.

Solution Organize the information in an ICE table

Equilibrium	$C_6H_5CO_2H + H_2O \rightleftharpoons C_6H_5CO_2^- + H_3O^+$		
Initial (M)	0.020	0	0
Change (M)	$-x$	$+x$	$+x$
Equilibrium (M)	$(0.020 - x)$	x	x

According to reaction stoichiometry,

$$[H_3O^+] = [C_6H_5CO_2^-] = x \text{ at equilibrium}$$

Stoichiometry also tells us that the quantity of acid ionized is x. Thus, the benzoic acid concentration at equilibrium is

$$[C_6H_5CO_2H] = \text{initial acid quantity} - \text{quantity of acid that ionized}$$
$$[C_6H_5CO_2H] = [C_6H_5CO_2H]_0 - x$$
$$[C_6H_5CO_2H] = 0.020 - x$$

Substituting these equilibrium concentrations into the K_a expression, we have

$$K_a = \frac{[H_3O^+][C_6H_5CO_2^-]}{[C_6H_5CO_2H]}$$

$$6.3 \times 10^{-5} = \frac{(x)(x)}{0.020 - x}$$

The value of x is small compared with 0.020 (because $[HA]_0 > 100 \cdot K_a$; 0.020 M > 6.3×10^{-3}). Therefore,

$$K_a = 6.3 \times 10^{-5} = \frac{x^2}{0.020}$$

Solving for x, we have

$$x = \sqrt{K_a \times (0.020)} = 0.0011 \text{ M}$$

and we find that

$$[H_3O^+] = [C_6H_5CO_2^-] = 0.0011 \text{ M}$$

and

$$[C_6H_5CO_2H] = (0.020 - x) = 0.019 \text{ M}$$

Finally, the pH of the solution is found to be

$$pH = -\log (1.1 \times 10^{-3}) = \boxed{2.96}$$

Comment Let us think again about the result. Because benzoic acid is weak, we made the approximation that $(0.020 - x) \approx 0.020$. If we do not make the approximation and instead solve the exact expression, $x = [H_3O^+] = 1.1 \times 10^{-3}$ M. This is the same answer to two significant figures that we obtained from the "approximate" expression. Finally, notice that we again ignored any H_3O^+ that arises from water ionization.

EXAMPLE 17.6 **Calculating Equilibrium Concentrations and pH from K_a and Using the Method of Successive Approximations**

Problem What is the pH of a 0.0010 M solution of formic acid? What is the concentration of formic acid at equilibrium? The acid is moderately weak, with $K_a = 1.8 \times 10^{-4}$.

$$HCO_2H(aq) + H_2O(\ell) \rightleftharpoons HCO_2^-(aq) + H_3O^+(aq)$$

Strategy This is similar to Example 17.5, except that an approximate solution will not be possible.

Solution The ICE table is shown here.

Equilibrium	$HCO_2H + H_2O \rightleftharpoons HCO_2^- + H_3O^+$		
Initial (M)	0.0010	0	0
Change (M)	$-x$	$+x$	$+x$
Equilibrium (M)	$(0.0010 - x)$	x	x

Substituting the values in the table into the K_a expression we have

$$K_a = \frac{[H_3O^+][HCO_2^-]}{[HCO_2H]} = 1.8 \times 10^{-4} = \frac{(x)(x)}{0.0010 - x}$$

Formic acid is a weak acid because it has a value of K_a much less than 1. In this example, however, $[HA]_0$ ($= 0.0010$ M) is *not* greater than $100 \cdot K_a$ ($= 1.8 \times 10^{-2}$), so the usual approximation is not reasonable. Thus, we have to find the equilibrium concentrations by solving the "exact" expression. This can be solved with the quadratic formula (page 740) or by successive approximations (Appendix A). Let us use the successive approximation method here.

To use the successive approximations approach, begin by solving the approximate expression for x.

$$1.8 \times 10^{-4} = \frac{(x)(x)}{0.0010}$$

Solving this, we find $x = 4.2 \times 10^{-4}$. Put this value into the expression for x in the denominator of the exact expression.

$$1.8 \times 10^{-4} = \frac{(x)(x)}{0.0010 - x} = \frac{(x)(x)}{0.0010 - 4.2 \times 10^{-4}}$$

Solving this equation for x, we now find $x = 3.2 \times 10^{-4}$. Again, put this value into the denominator, and solve for x.

$$1.8 \times 10^{-4} = \frac{(x)(x)}{0.0010 - x} = \frac{(x)(x)}{0.0010 - 3.2 \times 10^{-4}}$$

Continue this procedure until the value of x does not change from one cycle to the next. In this case, two more steps give us the result that

$$x = [H_3O^+] = [HCO_2^-] = 3.4 \times 10^{-4} \text{ M}$$

Thus,

$$[HCO_2H] = 0.0010 - x \approx 0.0007 \text{ M}$$

and the pH of the formic acid solution is

$$pH = -\log (3.4 \times 10^{-4}) = \boxed{3.47}$$

Comment If we would have used the approximate expression to find the H_3O^+ concentration, we would have obtained a value of $[H_3O^+] = 4.2 \times 10^{-4}$ M. A simplifying assumption led to a large error, about 24%. The approximate solution fails in this case because (a) the acid concentration is small and (b) the acid is not all that weak. These made invalid the approximation that $[HA]_{equilibrium} \approx [HA]_0$.

EXERCISE 17.12 Calculating Equilibrium Concentrations and pH from K_a

What are the equilibrium concentrations of acetic acid, the acetate ion, and H_3O^+ for a 0.10 M solution of acetic acid ($K_a = 1.8 \times 10^{-5}$)? What is the pH of the solution?

EXERCISE 17.13 Calculating Equilibrium Concentrations and pH from K_a

What are the equilibrium concentrations of HF, F^- ion, and H_3O^+ ion in a 0.015 M solution of HF? What is the pH of the solution?

Just as acids can be molecular species or ions, so too can bases be molecular or ionic (Figures 17.3–17.5). Many molecular bases are based on nitrogen, with ammonia being the simplest. Many other nitrogen-containing bases occur naturally; caffeine and nicotine are two that are well known. The anionic conjugate bases of weak acids make up another group of bases. The following example describes the calculation of the pH for a solution of sodium acetate.

Chemistry ☼ Now™

Sign in at **www.cengage.com/login** and go to Chapter 17 Contents to see:
- Screen 17.7 for a simulation of **the prediction of the direction of a number of acid–base reactions**
- Screen 17.11 for a simulation **of acid–base properties of salts**

FIGURE 17.5 Examples of weak bases. Weak bases in water include molecules having one or more N atoms capable of accepting an H^+ ion. Anionic bases such as benzoate and phosphate are conjugate bases of weak acids.

Benzoate ion, $C_6H_5CO_2^-$
$K_b = 1.6 \times 10^{-10}$

Phosphate ion, PO_4^{3-}
$K_b = 2.8 \times 10^{-2}$

Ammonia, NH_3
$K_b = 1.8 \times 10^{-5}$

Caffeine, $C_8H_{10}N_4O_2$
$K_b = 2.5 \times 10^{-4}$

Charles D. Winters

EXAMPLE 17.7 The pH of a Solution of a Weakly Basic Salt, Sodium Acetate

Problem What is the pH of a 0.015 M solution of sodium acetate, $NaCH_3CO_2$?

Strategy Sodium acetate will be basic in water because the acetate ion, the conjugate base of a weak acid, acetic acid, reacts with water to form OH^- (Tables 17.3 and 17.4). (Note that the sodium ion of sodium acetate does not affect the solution pH.) We shall calculate the hydroxide ion concentration in manner parallel with that in Example 17.5.

Solution The value of K_b for the acetate ion is 5.6×10^{-10} (Table 17.3).

$$CH_3CO_2^-(aq) + H_2O(\ell) \rightleftharpoons CH_3CO_2H(aq) + OH^-(aq)$$

Set up an ICE table to summarize the initial and equilibrium concentrations of the species in solution.

Equilibrium	$CH_3CO_2^-$ + H_2O	$\rightleftharpoons$	CH_3CO_2H	+	OH^-
Initial (M)	0.015		0		0
Change (M)	$-x$		$+x$		$+x$
Equilibrium (M)	$(0.015 - x)$		x		x

Next, substitute the values in the table into the K_b expression.

$$K_b = 5.6 \times 10^{-10} = \frac{[CH_3CO_2H][OH^-]}{[CH_3CO_2^-]} = \frac{x^2}{0.015 - x}$$

The acetate ion is a weak base, as reflected by the very small value of K_b. Therefore, we assume that x, the concentration of hydroxide ion generated by reaction of acetate ion with water, is very small, and we use the approximate expression to solve for x.

$$K_b = 5.6 \times 10^{-10} = \frac{x^2}{0.015}$$

$$x = [OH^-] = [CH_3CO_2H] = \sqrt{(5.6 \times 10^{-10})(0.015)} = 2.9 \times 10^{-6} \text{ M}$$

To calculate the pH of the solution, we need the hydronium ion concentration. In aqueous solutions, it is always true that, at 25 °C,

$$K_w = 1.0 \times 10^{-14} = [H_3O^+][OH^-]$$

Therefore,

$$[H_3O^+] = \frac{K_w}{[OH^-]} = \frac{1.0 \times 10^{-14}}{2.9 \times 10^{-6}} = 3.5 \times 10^{-9} \text{ M}$$

$$pH = -\log(3.5 \times 10^{-9}) = \boxed{8.46}$$

The acetate ion gives rise to a weakly basic solution.

Comment The hydroxide ion concentration (x) is indeed quite small relative to the initial acetate ion concentration. (We would have predicted this from our "rule of thumb": that $100 \cdot K_b$ should be less than the initial base concentration if we wish to use the approximate expression.)

EXERCISE 17.14 The pH of the Solution of the Conjugate Base of a Weak Acid

Sodium hypochlorite, NaClO, is used as a disinfectant in swimming pools and water treatment plants. What are the concentrations of HClO and OH^- and the pH of a 0.015 M solution of NaClO?

Chemistry ⚛ **Now™**

Sign in at **www.cengage.com/login** and go to Chapter 17 Contents to see Screen 17.10 for a tutorial on **estimating the pH following an acid–base reaction.**

Problem What is the pH of the solution that results from mixing 25 mL of 0.016 M NH_3 and 25 mL of 0.016 M HCl?

Strategy This question involves three problems in one:

(a) *Writing a Balanced Equation:* We first have to write a balanced equation for the reaction that occurs and then decide whether the reaction products are acids or bases. Here, NH_4^+ is the product of interest, and it is a weak acid.

(b) *Stoichiometry Problem:* To find the "initial" NH_4^+ concentration is a stoichiometry problem: What amount of NH_4^+ (in moles) is produced in the HCl + NH_3 reaction, and in what volume of solution is the NH_4^+ ion found?

(c) *Equilibrium Problem:* Calculating the pH involves solving an equilibrium problem. The crucial piece of information needed here is the "initial" concentration of NH_4^+ from part (b).

Solution If equal amounts (moles) of base (NH_3) and acid (HCl) are mixed, the result should be an acidic solution because the significant species remaining in solution upon completion of the reaction is NH_4^+, the conjugate acid of the weak base ammonia (see Tables 17.3 and 17.5). The chemistry can be summarized by the following net ionic equations.

(a) *Writing Balanced Equations*

Reaction of HCl (the supplier of hydronium ion) with NH_3 to give NH_4^+:

$$NH_3(aq) + H_3O^+(aq) \rightarrow NH_4^+(aq) + H_2O(\ell)$$

The reaction of NH_4^+, the product, with water:

$$NH_4^+(aq) + H_2O(\ell) \rightleftharpoons H_3O^+(aq) + NH_3(aq)$$

(b) *Stoichiometry Problem*

Amount of HCl and NH_3 consumed:

$$(0.025 \text{ L HCl})(0.016 \text{ mol/L}) = 4.0 \times 10^{-4} \text{ mol HCl}$$
$$(0.025 \text{ L } NH_3)(0.016 \text{ mol/L}) = 4.0 \times 10^{-4} \text{ mol } NH_3$$

Amount of NH_4^+ produced upon completion of the reaction:

$$4.0 \times 10^{-4} \text{ mol } NH_3 \left(\frac{1 \text{ mol } NH_4^+}{1 \text{ mol } NH_3} \right) = 4.0 \times 10^{-4} \text{ mol } NH_4^+$$

Concentration of NH_4^+: Combining 25 mL each of HCl and NH_3 gives a total solution volume of 50. mL. Therefore, the concentration of NH_4^+ is

$$[NH_4^+] = \frac{4.0 \times 10^{-4} \text{ mol}}{0.050 \text{ L}} = 8.0 \times 10^{-3} \text{ M}$$

(c) *Acid–Base Equilibrium Problem*

With the initial concentration of ammonium ion known, set up an ICE table to find the equilibrium concentration of hydronium ion.

Equilibrium	$NH_4^+ + H_2O$	$\rightleftharpoons$	NH_3	+	H_3O^+
Initial (M)	0.0080		0		0
Change	$-x$		$+x$		$+x$
Equilibrium (M)	$(0.0080 - x)$		x		x

Next, substitute the values in the table into the K_a expression for the ammonium ion. Thus, we have

$$K_a = 5.6 \times 10^{-10} = \frac{[H_3O^+][NH_3]}{[NH_4^+]} = \frac{(x)(x)}{0.0080 - x}$$

What Is the pH After Mixing Equal Molar Amounts of an Acid and a Base?

Table 17.5 summarizes the outcome of mixing various types of acids and bases. But how do you calculate a numerical value for the pH, particularly in the case of mixing a weak acid with a strong base or a weak base with a strong acid? The strategy (Example 17.8) is to recognize that this involves two related calculations: a stoichiometry calculation and an equilibrium calculation. The key to this is that

you need to know the concentration of the weak acid or weak base produced when the acid and base are mixed. You should ask yourself the following questions:

(a) What amounts of acid and base are used (in moles)? (This is a stoichiometry problem.)
(b) What is the total volume of the solution after mixing the acid and base solutions?

(c) What is the concentration of the weak acid or base produced on mixing the acid and base solutions?
(d) Using the concentration found in Step (c), what is the hydronium ion concentration in the solution? (This is an equilibrium problem.)
(e) Calculate the pH of the solution from $[H_3O^+]$.

The ammonium ion is a very weak acid, as reflected by the very small value of K_a. Therefore, x, the concentration of hydronium ion generated by reaction of ammonium ion with water, is assumed to be very small, and the approximate expression is used to solve for x. (Here $100 \cdot K_a$ is much less than the original acid concentration.)

$$K_a = 5.6 \times 10^{-10} \approx \frac{x^2}{0.0080}$$

$$x = \sqrt{(5.6 \times 10^{-10})(0.0080)}$$

$$= [H_3O^+] = [NH_3] = 2.1 \times 10^{-6} \text{ M}$$

$$pH = -\log(2.1 \times 10^{-6}) = 5.67$$

Comment As predicted (Table 17.5), the solution after mixing equal amounts of a strong acid and weak base is weakly acidic.

EXERCISE 17.15 What is the pH After the Reaction of a Weak Acid and Strong Base?

Calculate the pH after mixing 15 mL of 0.12 M acetic acid with 15 mL of 0.12 M NaOH. What are the major species in solution at equilibrium (besides water), and what are their concentrations?

17.8 Polyprotic Acids and Bases

Because polyprotic acids are capable of donating more than one proton (Table 17.1), they present us with additional problems when predicting the pH of their solutions. For many inorganic polyprotic acids, such as phosphoric acid, carbonic acid, and hydrogen sulfide, each successive loss of a proton is about 10^4 to 10^6 more difficult than the previous ionization step. This means that the first ionization step of a polyprotic acid produces up to about a million times more H_3O^+ ions than the second step. For this reason, *the pH of many inorganic polyprotic acids depends primarily on the hydronium ion generated in the first ionization step; the hydronium ion produced in the second step can be neglected.* The same principle applies to the conjugate bases of polyprotic acids. This is illustrated by the calculation of the pH of a solution of carbonate ion, an important base in our environment (Example 17.9).

Charles D. Winters

A polyprotic acid. Malic acid is a diprotic acid occurring in apples. It is also classified as an alpha-hydroxy acid because it has an OH group on the C atom next to the CO_2H (in the alpha position). It is one of a larger group of natural acids such as lactic acid, citric acid, and ascorbic acid. Alpha-hydroxy acids have been touted as an ingredient in "anti-aging" skin creams. They work by accelerating the natural process by which skin replaces the outer layer of cells with new cells.

EXAMPLE 17.9 Calculating the pH of the Solution of a Polyprotic Base

Problem The carbonate ion, CO_3^{2-}, is a base in water, forming the hydrogen carbonate ion, which in turn can form carbonic acid.

$$CO_3^{2-}(aq) + H_2O(\ell) \rightleftharpoons HCO_3^-(aq) + OH^-(aq) \qquad K_{b1} = 2.1 \times 10^{-4}$$

$$HCO_3^-(aq) + H_2O(\ell) \rightleftharpoons H_2CO_3(aq) + OH^-(aq) \qquad K_{b2} = 2.4 \times 10^{-8}$$

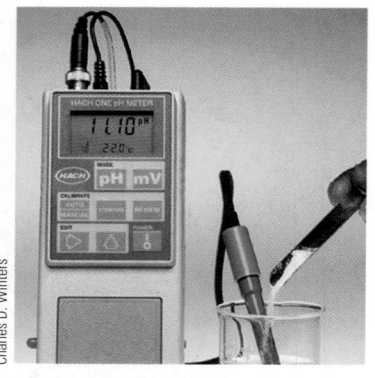

Sodium carbonate, a polyprotic base. This common substance is a base in aqueous solution. Its primary use is in the glass industry. Although it used to be manufactured, it is now mined as the mineral trona, $Na_2CO_3 \cdot NaHCO_3 \cdot 2\,H_2O$.

What is the pH of a 0.10 M solution of Na_2CO_3?

Strategy The second ionization constant, K_{b2}, is much smaller than the first, K_{b1}, so the hydroxide ion concentration in the solution results almost entirely from the first step. Therefore, let us calculate the OH^- concentration produced in the first ionization step but test the conclusion that OH^- produced in the second step is negligible.

Solution Set up an ICE table for the reaction of the carbonate ion (Equilibrium Table 1).

Equilibrium Table 1—Reaction of CO_3^{2-} Ion

Equilibrium	CO_3^{2-}	+	H_2O	$\rightleftharpoons$	HCO_3^-	+	OH^-
Initial (M)	0.10				0		0
Change	$-x$				$+x$		$+x$
Equilibrium (M)	$(0.10 - x)$				x		x

Based on this table, the equilibrium concentration of OH^- $(= x)$ can then be calculated.

$$K_{b1} = 2.1 \times 10^{-4} = \frac{[HCO_3^-][OH^-]}{[CO_3^{2-}]} = \frac{x^2}{0.10 - x}$$

Because K_{b1} is relatively small, it is reasonable to make the approximation that $(0.10 - x) \approx 0.10$. Therefore,

$$x = [HCO_3^-] = [OH^-] = \sqrt{(2.1 \times 10^{-4})(0.10)} = 4.6 \times 10^{-3}\ M$$

Using this value of $[OH^-]$, we first calculate the pOH of the solution,

$$pOH = -\log (4.6 \times 10^{-3}) = 2.34$$

and then use the relationship $pH + pOH = 14$ to calculate the pH.

$$pH = 14 - pOH = \boxed{11.66}$$

Finally, we see that the concentration of the carbonate ion is, to a good approximation, 0.10 M.

$$[CO_3^{2-}] = 0.10 - 0.0046 \approx 0.10\ M$$

Comment It is instructive to ask what the concentration of H_2CO_3 in the solution might be. If HCO_3^- were to react significantly with water to produce H_2CO_3, the pH of the solution would be affected. Let us set up a second ICE Table.

Equilibrium Table 2—Reaction of HCO_3^- Ion

Equilibrium	HCO_3^-	+	H_2O	$\rightleftharpoons$	H_2CO_3	+	OH^-
Initial (M)	4.6×10^{-3}				0		4.6×10^{-3}
Change	$-y$				$+y$		$+y$
Equilibrium (M)	$(4.6 \times 10^{-3} - y)$				y		$(4.6 \times 10^{-3} + y)$

Because K_{b2} is so small, the second step occurs to a much smaller extent than the first step. This means the amount of H_2CO_3 and OH^- produced in the second step $(= y)$ is much smaller than 10^{-3} M. Therefore, it is reasonable that both $[HCO_3^-]$ and $[OH^-]$ are very close to 4.6×10^{-3} M.

$$K_{b2} = 2.4 \times 10^{-8} = \frac{[H_2CO_3][OH^-]}{[HCO_3^-]} = \frac{(y)(4.6 \times 10^{-3})}{4.6 \times 10^{-3}}$$

Because $[HCO_3^-]$ and $[OH^-]$ have nearly identical values, they cancel from the expression, and we find that $[H_2CO_3]$ is simply equal to K_{b2}.

$$y = [H_2CO_3] = K_{b2} = 2.4 \times 10^{-8}\ M$$

For the carbonate ion, where K_1 and K_2 differ by about 10^4, the hydroxide ion is essentially all produced in the first equilibrium process.

EXERCISE 17.16 Calculating the pH of the Solution of a Polyprotic Acid

What is the pH of a 0.10 M solution of oxalic acid, $H_2C_2O_4$? What are the concentrations of H_3O^+, $HC_2O_4^-$, and the oxalate ion, $C_2O_4^{2-}$? (See Appendix H for K_a values.)

Charles D. Winters

17.9 The Lewis Concept of Acids and Bases

The concept of acid–base behavior advanced by Brønsted and Lowry in the 1920s works well for reactions involving proton transfer. A more general acid–base concept, however, was developed by Gilbert N. Lewis in the 1930s (◀ page 352). This concept is based on the sharing of electrons pairs between an acid and a base. A **Lewis acid** is a substance that can accept a pair of electrons from another atom to form a new bond, and a **Lewis base** is a substance that can donate a pair of electrons to another atom to form a new bond. This means that an acid–base reaction in the Lewis sense occurs when a molecule (or ion) donates a pair of electrons to another molecule (or ion).

$$\text{A} \quad + \quad \text{B:} \quad \rightarrow \quad \text{B}{\rightarrow}\text{A}$$
$$\text{Acid} \qquad \text{Base} \qquad \text{Adduct}$$

The product is often called an **acid–base adduct.** In Section 8.3, this type of chemical bond was called a *coordinate covalent bond.*

Case Study — Uric Acid, Gout, and Bird Droppings

All living creatures metabolize food and dispose of the waste products, many of which contain nitrogen. Ammonia is the end product of this metabolic chain for fish and marine invertebrates, for example. And fish sometimes produce the Lewis and Brønsted base trimethylamine, $N(CH_3)_3$, a water-soluble compound and the source of the characteristic "fish odor."

Unlike fish, most terrestrial animals do not have an "infinite" supply of water. Mammals have a bladder and usually live in conditions where adequate water is available. Their mechanism of disposal for most toxins is to prepare a water-soluble compound and then excrete it through the urine. Thus, urea, NH_2CONH_2, is a major by-product of nitrogen metabolism in mammals. Reptiles and desert animals do not usually have much water available, and birds cannot afford the luxury of the weight of a bladder. These animals do not make urea; rather, they convert all of their nitrogen waste to uric acid, the concentrated white solid so familiar in bird droppings.

Uric acid in bird droppings. Birds excrete uric acid, which you see as the white solid in their feces. The acidic material can cause severe environmental damage.

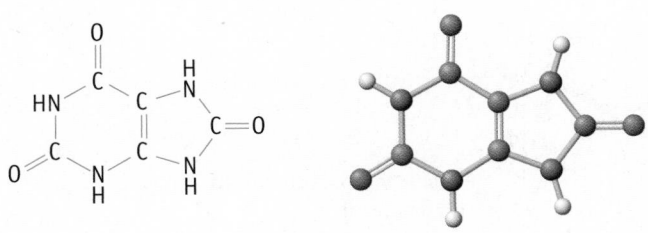

Uric acid

Uric acid can cause problems in primates because of its low water solubility. Deposits of uric acid in the joints and extremities can cause a very painful condition called *gout* or gouty arthritis. Chronic gout can also lead to lumps of uric acid around and in joints, to decreased kidney function, and to kidney stones.

You know you have gout if you experience excruciating and sudden pain with swelling and redness in a joint. Often, the first attack occurs in a big toe, but other joints such as those in the ankle, knee, wrist, fingers, and elbow can be affected as well.

Although gout may be a hereditary disease, you can help avoid the problem by eating smaller amounts of foods with high levels of the purines, which are metabolized to uric acid. These include meat, fish, dry beans, mushrooms, spinach, and asparagus. On the other hand, eating fresh fruit (especially cherries and strawberries) and most fresh vegetables can help lower uric acid levels.

Finally, gout is one of the most frequently recorded medical conditions throughout history. People such as Henry VIII, Isaac Newton, Thomas Jefferson, Benjamin Franklin, John Hancock, and Karl Marx have suffered from the condition.

Questions:

1. *A diagnosis of hyperuricemia will be made when the uric acid blood level is greater than 420 μmol/L. What is this level in milligrams of uric acid per liter?*
2. *Uric acid is a polyprotic acid with one pK_a of 5.40 and a second pK_a of 5.53. Considering only the loss of the first proton, what acid in Table 17.3 has a similar acid strength?*

Answers to these questions are in Appendix Q.

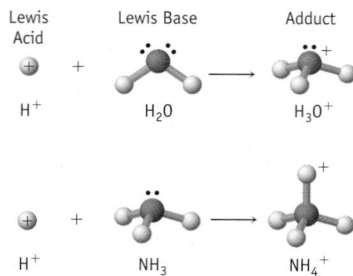

H^+ H_2O H_3O^+

H^+ NH_3 NH_4^+

FIGURE 17.6 Protonation of water and ammonia are examples of Lewis acid–base reactions.

Formation of a hydronium ion from H^+ and water is a good example of a Lewis acid–base reaction (Figure 17.6). The H^+ ion has no electrons in its valence ($1s$) shell, and the water molecule has two unshared pairs of electrons (located in sp^3 hybrid orbitals). One of the O atom lone pairs of a water molecule can be shared with an H^+ ion, thus forming an O—H bond in an H_3O^+ ion. A similar interaction occurs between H^+ and the Lewis base ammonia to form the ammonium ion. Such reactions are very common. In general, they involve Lewis acids that are cations or neutral molecules with an available, empty valence orbital and bases that are anions or neutral molecules with a lone electron pair.

Cationic Lewis Acids

Just as H^+ and water form a Lewis acid–base adduct, metal cations interact with water molecules to form hydrated cations (Figure 17.7 and page 557). In these species, coordinate covalent bonds form between the metal cation and a lone pair of electrons on the O atom of each water. For example, an iron(II) ion, Fe^{2+}, forms six coordinate covalent bonds to water.

$$Fe^{2+}(aq) + 6\ H_2O(\ell) \rightarrow [Fe(H_2O)_6]^{2+}(aq)$$

Similar structures formed by transition metal cations are generally very colorful (Figures 17.7 and 17.8 and Section 22.3). Chemists call these **complex ions** or, because of the coordinate covalent bond, **coordination complexes.** Several are listed in Table 17.3 as acids, and their behavior is described further in Section 17.10 and Chapter 22.

Like water, ammonia is an excellent Lewis base and combines with metal cations to give adducts (complex ions), which are often very colorful. For example, copper(II) ions, light blue in aqueous solution (Figure 17.7), react with ammonia to give a deep blue adduct with four ammonia molecules surrounding each Cu^{2+} ion.

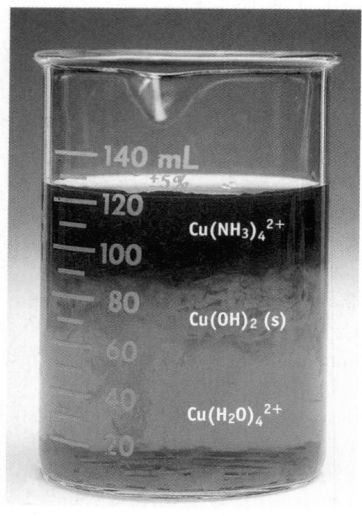

FIGURE 17.7 The Lewis acid–base complex ion $[Cu(NH_3)_4]^{2+}$. Here, aqueous ammonia was added to aqueous $CuSO_4$ (the light blue solution at the bottom of the beaker). The small concentration of OH^- in $NH_3(aq)$ first formed insoluble blue-white $Cu(OH)_2$ (the solid in the middle of the beaker). With additional NH_3, however, the deep blue, soluble complex ion formed (the solution at the top of the beaker). The model in the text shows the copper(II)–ammonia complex ion.

$$Cu^{2+}(aq) + 4\ NH_3(aq) \longrightarrow [Cu(NH_3)_4]^{2+}(aq)$$
light blue   deep blue

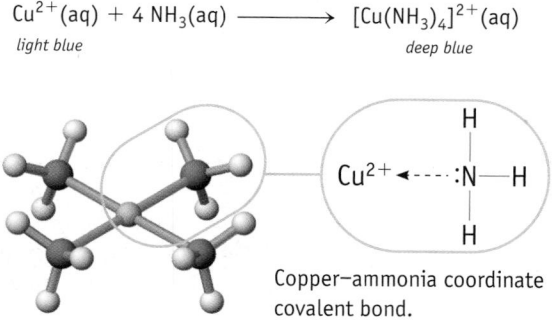

Copper–ammonia coordinate covalent bond.

Hydroxide ion, OH^-, is an excellent Lewis base and binds readily to metal cations to give metal hydroxides. An important feature of the chemistry of some metal hydroxides is that they are **amphoteric.** An amphoteric metal hydroxide can behave as an acid or a base (Table 17.6). One of the best examples of this behavior is provided by aluminum hydroxide, $Al(OH)_3$ (Figure 17.9). Adding OH^- to a precipitate of $Al(OH)_3$ produces the water-soluble $[Al(OH)_4]^-$ ion.

$$Al(OH)_3(s) + OH^-(aq) \rightarrow [Al(OH)_4]^-(aq)$$
Acid   Base

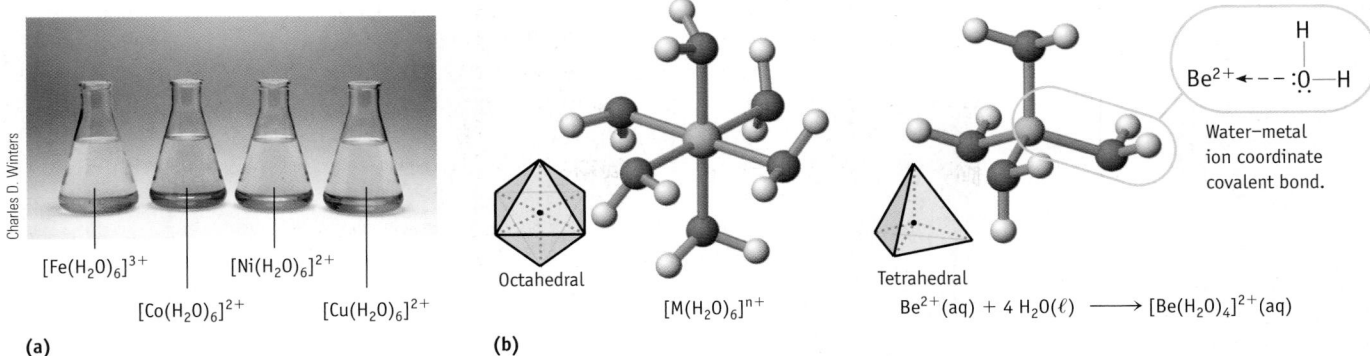

FIGURE 17.8 Metal cations in water. (a) Solutions of the nitrate salts of iron(III), cobalt(II), nickel(II), and copper(II) all have characteristic colors. (b) Models of complex ions (Lewis acid–base adducts) formed between a metal cation and water molecules. Such complexes often have six water molecules arranged octahedrally around the metal cation.

If acid is added to the $Al(OH)_3$ precipitate, it again dissolves. This time, however, aluminum hydroxide is acting as a base.

$$Al(OH)_3(s) + 3\ H_3O^+(aq) \rightarrow Al^{3+}(aq) + 6\ H_2O(\ell)$$

Base   Acid

Molecular Lewis Acids

Lewis's acid–base concept also accounts for the fact that oxides of nonmetals such as CO_2 and SO_2 behave as acids (◄ Section 3.7). Because oxygen is more electronegative than C, the C—O bonding electrons in CO_2 are polarized away from carbon and toward oxygen. This causes the carbon atom to be slightly positive, and it is this atom that the negatively charged Lewis base OH^- can attack to give, ultimately, the bicarbonate ion.

■ **CO₂ in Basic Solution** This reaction of CO_2 with OH^- is the first step in the precipitation of $CaCO_3$ when CO_2 is bubbled into a solution of $Ca(OH)_2$ (Figure 3.6, page 120).

Similarly, SO_2 reacts with aqueous OH^- to form the HSO_3^- ion.

Compounds based on the Group 3A elements boron and aluminum are among the most-studied Lewis acids. One example is a reaction in organic chemistry that is catalyzed by the Lewis acid $AlCl_3$. The mechanism of this important reaction—called the Friedel–Crafts reaction—is illustrated here. In the first step, a Lewis base,

TABLE 17.6 Some Common Amphoteric Metal Hydroxides*

Hydroxide	Reaction as a Base	Reaction as an Acid
$Al(OH)_3$	$Al(OH)_3(s) + 3\ H_3O^+(aq) \rightleftharpoons Al^{3+}(aq) + 6\ H_2O(\ell)$	$Al(OH)_3(s) + OH^-(aq) \rightleftharpoons [Al(OH)_4]^-(aq)$
$Zn(OH)_2$	$Zn(OH)_2(s) + 2\ H_3O^+(aq) \rightleftharpoons Zn^{2+}(aq) + 4\ H_2O(\ell)$	$Zn(OH)_2(s) + 2\ OH^-(aq) \rightleftharpoons [Zn(OH)_4]^{2-}(aq)$
$Sn(OH)_4$	$Sn(OH)_4(s) + 4\ H_3O^+(aq) \rightleftharpoons Sn^{4+}(aq) + 8\ H_2O(\ell)$	$Sn(OH)_4(s) + 2\ OH^-(aq) \rightleftharpoons [Sn(OH)_6]^{2-}(aq)$
$Cr(OH)_3$	$Cr(OH)_3(s) + 3\ H_3O^+(aq) \rightleftharpoons Cr^{3+}(aq) + 6\ H_2O(\ell)$	$Cr(OH)_3(s) + OH^-(aq) \rightleftharpoons [Cr(OH)_4]^-(aq)$

* The aqueous metal cations are best described as $[M(H_2O)_6]^{n+}$.

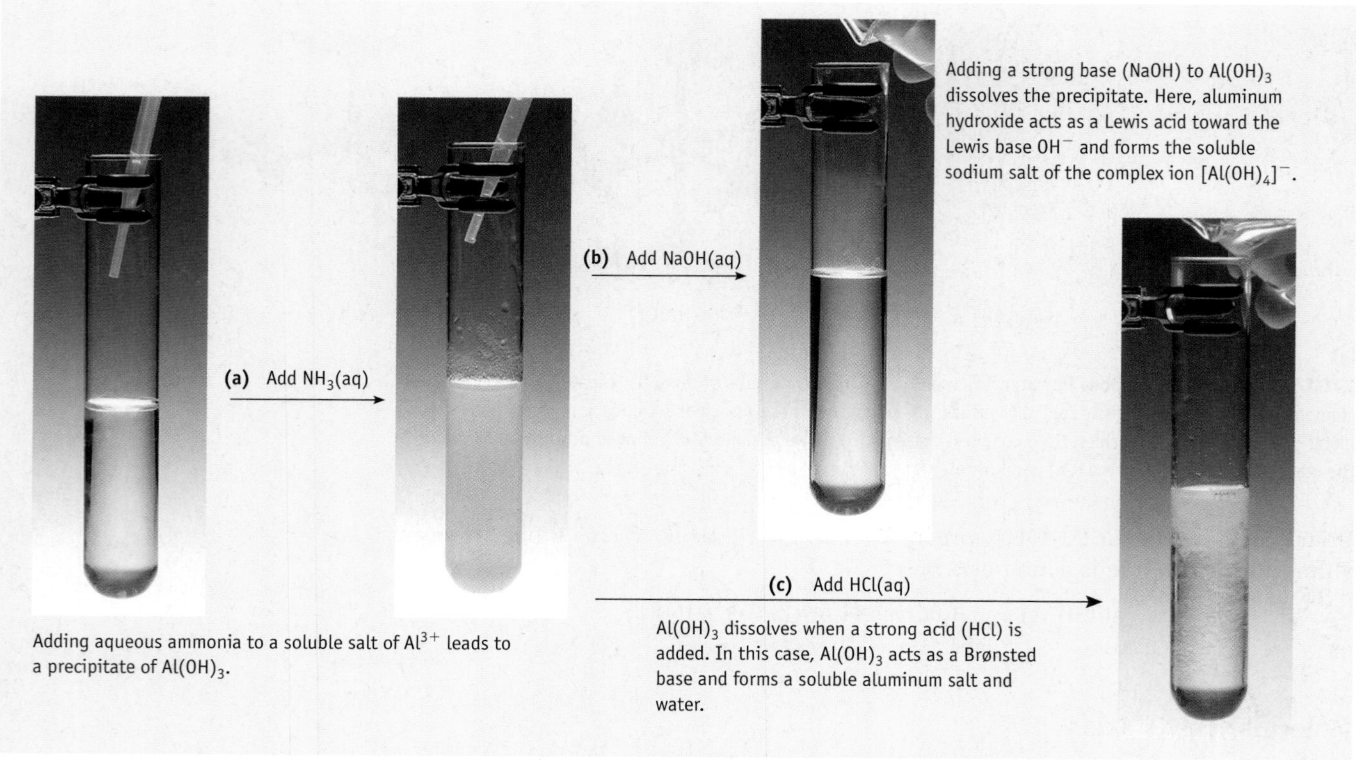

(a) Add NH₃(aq)

(b) Add NaOH(aq)

Adding a strong base (NaOH) to Al(OH)₃ dissolves the precipitate. Here, aluminum hydroxide acts as a Lewis acid toward the Lewis base OH⁻ and forms the soluble sodium salt of the complex ion [Al(OH)₄]⁻.

(c) Add HCl(aq)

Adding aqueous ammonia to a soluble salt of Al³⁺ leads to a precipitate of Al(OH)₃.

Al(OH)₃ dissolves when a strong acid (HCl) is added. In this case, Al(OH)₃ acts as a Brønsted base and forms a soluble aluminum salt and water.

Charles D. Winters

FIGURE 17.9 The amphoteric nature of Al(OH)₃. Aluminum hydroxide is formed by the reaction of aqueous Al³⁺ and ammonia.

$$Al^{3+}(aq) + 3\,NH_3(aq) + 3\,H_2O(\ell) \rightleftharpoons Al(OH)_3(s) + 3\,NH_4^+(aq)$$

Reactions of solid Al(OH)₃ with aqueous NaOH and HCl demonstrate that aluminum hydroxide is amphoteric.

the Cl⁻ ion, transfers from the reactant, here CH₃COCl, to the Lewis acid to give [AlCl₄]⁻ and an organic cation (that is stabilized by resonance). The organic cation attacks a benzene molecule to give a cationic intermediate, and this then interacts with [AlCl₄]⁻ to produce HCl and the final organic product.

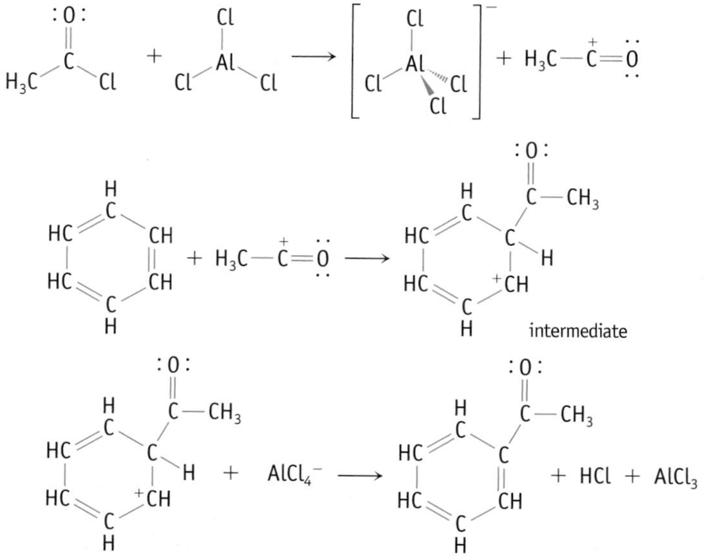

intermediate

Molecular Lewis Bases

Ammonia is widely distributed in nature and is involved as a Lewis base in numerous reactions. One example where this is important is in the conversion of ammonia to urea (NH_2CONH_2) in natural systems. The process begins with the reaction of bicarbonate ion with ATP (adenosine triphosphate), and a subsequent step in the mechanism is the following:

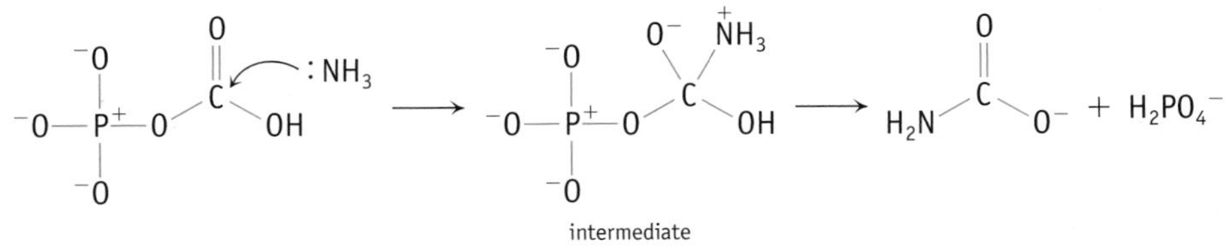

intermediate

Here, the Lewis base ammonia attacks a carbon atom with a partial positive charge. The dihydrogen phosphate ion is then released, yielding the $NH_2CO_2^-$ ion, which eventually forms urea in another step in this reaction mechanism.

Chemistry ⚛ Now™

Sign in at **www.cengage.com/login** and go to Chapter 17 Contents to see:
- Screen 17.12 for a tutorial on **Lewis acids and bases**
- Screen 17.13 for a description of **cationic Lewis acids**
- Screen 17.14 for a tutorial on **neutral Lewis acids**

EXERCISE 17.17 Lewis Acids and Bases

Describe each of the following as a Lewis acid or a Lewis base.

(a) PH_3 (c) H_2S

(b) BCl_3 (d) HS^-

Hint: In each case, draw the Lewis electron dot structure of the molecule or ion. Are there lone pairs of electrons on the central atom? If so, it can be a Lewis base. Does the central atom lack an electron pair? If so, it can behave as a Lewis acid.

17.10 Molecular Structure, Bonding, and Acid–Base Behavior

One of the most interesting aspects of chemistry is the correlation between a molecule's structure and bonding and its chemical properties. Because so many compounds are acids and bases, and play such a key role in chemistry, it is especially useful to see if there are some general principles governing acid–base behavior.

Chemistry ⚛ Now™

Sign in at **www.cengage.com/login** and go to Chapter 17 Contents to see Screen 17.15 for a self-study module on **molecular interpretation of acid–base behavior.**

Acid Strength of the Hydrogen Halides, HX

Aqueous HF is a weak Brønsted acid in water, whereas the other hydrohalic acids—aqueous HCl, HBr, and HI—are all strong acids. Experiments show that the acid strength increases in the order HF << HCl < HBr < HI. A detailed analysis of

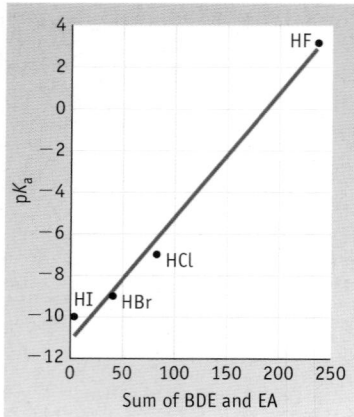

FIGURE 17.10 The effect of H—X bond energy and X electron affinity on acid strength. Stronger acids have weaker H—X bonds and more electronegative A atoms. (BDE is the bond dissociation enthalpy of the H—X bond, and EA is the electron affinity of the halogen atom.) See M. Moran, *Journal of Chemical Education*, Vol, 83, pages 800–803, 2006.

the factors that lead to these differences in acid strength in this group is complex (see *A Closer Look, Acid and Base Strength*). However, predictions about relative acid strength can be made based on the sum of two energy quantities, the energy required to break the H—X bond and the electron affinity of the halogen. That is, when a hydrohalic acid HX ionizes in water,

$$HX(aq) + H_2O(\ell) \rightarrow H_3O^+(aq) + X^-(aq)$$

the sum of the two energy terms

$$\Delta U \propto HX \text{ bond breaking enthalpy} + \text{electron affinity of X}$$

correlates with acid strength. Specifically, the more easily the H—X bond is broken and the more negative the electron affinity of X, the greater the relative strength of the acid.

The bond enthalpy and electron affinity effects can work together (a weak H—X bond and a large electron affinity of the X group) to produce a strong acid, but they can also work in opposite directions. The balance of the two effects is thus important. Let us examine some data for the Group 7A binary acids, HX.

		Increasing acid strength		
	HF	HCl	HBr	HI
pK_a	+3.14	−7	−9	−10
H—X bond strength (kJ/mol)	.565	432	366	299
Electron affinity of X (kJ/mol)	−328	−349	−325	−295
Sum (kJ/mol)	237	83	41	4

In this series of acids, the bond enthalpy factor dominates, the weakest acid, HF, has the strongest H—X bond, and the strongest acid, HI, has the weakest H—X bond. However, the electron affinity of X becomes less negative from F to I. A low electron affinity should lead to a weaker acid, but it is the *sum* of the two effects that leads to the observation that HI is the strongest acid. In Figure 17.10, you see there is a good correlation between an acid's pK_a and the *sum* of the bond breaking enthalpy and electron affinity.

TABLE 17.7 Oxoacids

Acid	pK_a
Cl-Based Oxoacids	
HOCl	7.46
HOClO ($HClO_2$)	∼ 2
HOClO_2 ($HClO_3$)	∼ −3
HOClO_3 ($HClO_4$)	∼ −8
S-Based Oxoacids	
$(HO)_2SO$ [H_2SO_3]	1.92, 7.21
$(HO)_2SO_2$ [H_2SO_4]	∼ −3, 1.92

According to Linus Pauling, for oxoacids with the general formula $(HO)_nE(O)_m$, the value of pK_a is about 8–5*m*. When *n* > 1, the pK_a increases by about 5 for each successive loss of a proton.

Comparing Oxoacids: HNO₂ and HNO₃

Nitrous acid (HNO_2) and nitric acid (HNO_3) are representative of several series of **oxoacids.** Oxoacids contain an atom (usually a nonmetal atom) bonded to one or more oxygen atoms, some with hydrogen atoms attached. Besides those based on N, you are familiar with the sulfur- and chlorine-based oxoacids (Table 17.7). In all these series of related compounds, the acid strength increases as the number of oxygen atoms bonded to the central element increases. Thus, nitric acid (HNO_3) is a stronger acid than nitrous acid (HNO_2).

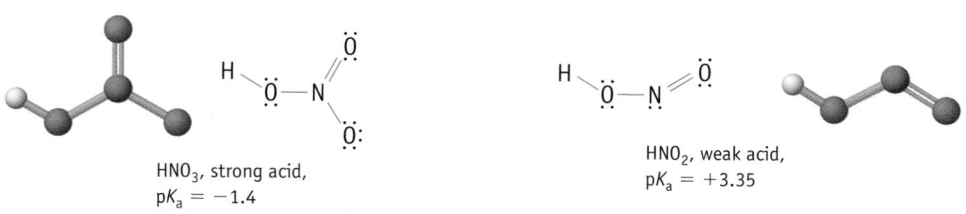

HNO_3, strong acid, $pK_a = -1.4$

HNO_2, weak acid, $pK_a = +3.35$

Although predictions about acid strength in aqueous solution are fairly simple to make, explanations are in fact quite complicated.

Acid strength is sometimes correlated with the strength and the polarity of the H—X bond, readily identifiable characteristics derived from the structure of the acid, the reactant in the ionization process. We need to point out, however, that when one is assessing any chemical reaction, it is necessary to consider both reactants and products. Looking only at the reactant when dealing with acid dissociation only takes you halfway.

When evaluating the strength of an acid HX(aq), we are looking at the following reaction

$$HX(aq) + H_2O(\ell) \rightleftharpoons H_3O^+(aq) + X^-(aq)$$

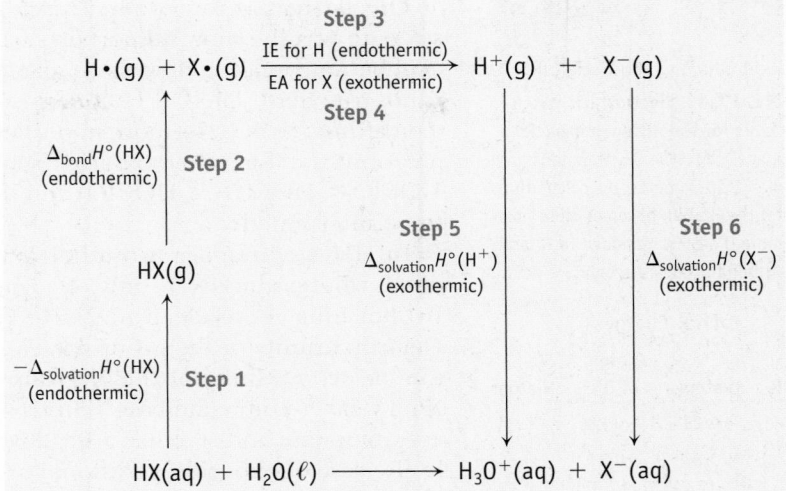

An energy diagram for the ionization of an acid HX in aqueous solution.

To fully explain the extent of ionization, we must consider characteristics of both the acid and the anion. The ability of the anion to spread out the negative charge across the ion, for example, and the solvation of the anion by the solvent are among the issues that must have some relevance in an explanation of the strength of the acid.

How enthalpy changes contribute to acid strength can be assessed using a thermochemical cycle (such as the one used to evaluate a lattice enthalpy, page 599). Consider the relative acid strengths of the hydrogen halides. The enthalpy change for the ionization of an acid in water can be related to other enthalpy changes as shown in the diagram. The solvation of H^+ (Step 5) and the ionization energy of H(g) (Step 3) are common to all of the hydrogen halides and do not contribute to the differences among hydrogen halides, but the four remaining terms are different. For the hydrogen halides, the bond dissociation enthalpy (Step 2) of HF is much larger than the dissociation enthalpies of the other hydrogen halides. However, it is compensated for significantly by the enthalpy of solvation of the anion (Step 6), which for the fluoride ion is much more exothermic than solvation energies of the other halide ions. The electron affinity is also a contributor to the differences in overall enthalpy changes. Electron affinity values vary among the halogens, but to a smaller extent than the variation in bond energy and the enthalpy of solvation of the halide ion. Differences in solvation energy for the molecular species (Step 1) are minimal.

A complete analysis of strengths of acids in aqueous solution will include consideration of both enthalpies and entropies. Entropy has yet to be discussed in this text in detail (▶ Chapter 19) but we have noted earlier (◀ page 621) that entropy plays an important role in solution chemistry, specifically in determining solubilities. It is not surprising that entropy has a role in determining acid strength, too. Indeed, differences in entropy changes are significant in accounting for the differences in acid strength of the hydrogen halides.

Although all of these terms contribute to acid strength, acid strength can often be correlated with a subset of this information, as can be seen by the examples presented in this section. We point out, however, that correlations, while highly useful to a chemist because they can be used to make important predictions, are at best only partial explanations.

Let's apply the bond enthalpy/electron affinity analysis to HNO_3 and HNO_2.

	Increasing acid strength ⟶	
	HNO₂	**HNO₃**
pK_a	+3.35	−1.4
H—O bond strength (kJ/mol)	328	423
Electron affinity of X (kJ/mol)	−219	−377
Sum (kJ/mol)	109	46

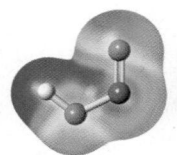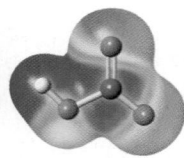

Nitrous acid, HNO_2 Nitric acid, HNO_3

FIGURE 17.11 Electrostatic potential surfaces for the nitrogen oxoacids. Both surfaces show the O—H bond is quite polar. More importantly, calculations show that the H atom becomes more positive as more O atoms are added to N, and the O—H bond becomes even more polar.

Partial Charges

Molecule	H atom	O atom of OH	N atom
HNO_2	+0.23	−0.28	+0.34
HNO_3	+0.27	−0.37	+0.66

TABLE 17.8 Correlation of Atom Formal Charge and pK_a

Central atom formal charge	pK_a
+2	−3
+1	1.92
+1	2
0	7.46

As in the case of the Group 7A acids, we again see that acid strength correlates with the sum of the bond breaking energy and X group (NO_2 or NO_3) electron affinity.

Our analysis of the Group 7A acids showed that, in this series, the H—X bond strength was the more important factor; as the H—X bond became stronger, the acid became weaker. However, a glance at the data for HNO_3 and HNO_2 shows this is not true here. The O—H bond is stronger in the stronger acid HNO_3. The electron affinity term is the more important term in this correlation. These same effects are observed for other oxyacids such as the chlorine-based oxoacids HOCl < HOClO < $HOClO_2$ < $HOClO_3$ and the S-based oxoacids (Table 17.7). How is this to be interpreted?

In HNO_3, there are two other oxygen atoms bonded to the central nitrogen atom, whereas in HNO_2 only one other oxygen is bonded to the nitrogen atom. By attaching more electronegative O atoms to nitrogen, we are increasing the electron affinity of the group attached to hydrogen, and anything that increases the electron affinity of the X group should also make HX a stronger acid and X^- a weaker conjugate base. This is another way of saying that if X^- has a way to accommodate and stabilize a negative charge, it will be a weaker conjugate base. In the case of oxoacids, additional oxygen atoms have the effect of stabilizing the anion because the negative charge on the anion can be dispersed over more atoms. In the nitrate ion, for example, the negative charge is shared equally over the three oxygen atoms. This is represented symbolically in the three resonance structures for this ion.

In nitrite ion, only two atoms share the negative charge. Therefore, NO_2^- is a stronger conjugate base than NO_3^-. In general, greater stabilization of the products formed by ionizing the acid contributes to increased acidity.

A glance at Table 17.7 and Figure 17.11 shows that another empirical correlation can be made between the structure of an acid and its acidity: In a series of related acids, the larger the formal charge on the central atom, the stronger the acid (Table 17.8). For example, the N atom formal charge in the weak acid HNO_2 is 0, whereas it is +1 in the strong acid HNO_3, and these are reflected by the results of theoretical calculations cited in Figure 17.11.

In summary, molecules such as the oxoacids can behave as stronger Brønsted acids when the anion created by loss of H^+ is stable and able to accommodate the negative charge. These conditions are promoted by

- the presence of electronegative atoms attached to the central atom.
- the possibility of resonance structures for the anion, which lead to delocalization of the negative charge over the anion and thus to a stable ion.

Why Are Carboxylic Acids Brønsted Acids?

There is a large class of organic acids, typified by acetic acid (CH_3CO_2H) (Figure 17.12), called carboxylic acids because all have the carboxylic acid group, $-CO_2H$. The arguments used to explain the acidity of oxoacids can also be applied to carboxylic acids. The O—H bond in these compounds is polar, a prerequisite for ionization.

C—H bonds not broken in water

Polar O—H bond broken by interaction of positively charged H atom with hydrogen-bonded H_2O

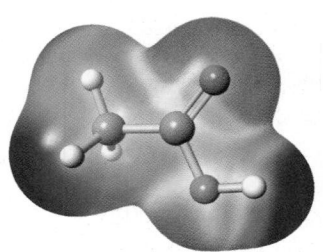

In addition, carboxylate anions are stabilized by delocalizing the negative charge over the two oxygen atoms.

FIGURE 17.12 Electrostatic potential surface and partial charges for acetic acid. The H atoms of the molecule are all positively charged, but the H atom of the OH is much more highly charged. As expected, both of the electronegative O atoms have a partial negative charge. The table below gives the computer-calculated partial charges on the acid.

Atom or Group	Calc'd Partial Charge
H of OH	+0.24
O of OH	−0.32
H of CH_3	+0.12

The simple carboxylic acids, RCO_2H in which R is a hydrocarbon group (◄ Section 10.4), do not differ markedly in acid strength (compare acetic acid, $pK_a = 4.74$, and propanoic acid, $pK_a = 4.89$, Table 17.3). The acidity of carboxylic acids is enhanced, however, if electronegative substituents replace the hydrogens in the alkyl group. Compare, for example, the pK_a values of a series of acetic acids in which hydrogen is replaced sequentially by the more electronegative element chlorine.

Acid		pK_a Value	
CH_3CO_2H	Acetic acid	4.74	
$ClCH_2CO_2H$	Chloroacetic acid	2.85	*increasing acid*
Cl_2CHCO_2H	Dichloroacetic acid	1.49	*strength*
Cl_3CCO_2H	Trichloroacetic acid	0.7	

As in the nitrogen oxoacids, increasingly electronegative substituents lead to an increase in acid strength. Indeed, recent research has found that a key role of electronegative substituents is to stabilize the negative charge of the anion. That is, compared with $CH_3CO_2^-$, the $Cl_3CCO_2^-$ anion is stabilized by the presence of the three Cl atoms, and $Cl_3CCO_2^-$ is a weaker base than $CH_3CO_2^-$.

Finally, why are the C—H hydrogens of carboxylic acids not dissociated as H^+ instead of (or in addition to) the O—H hydrogen atom? The calculated partial positive charges listed in Figure 17.12 show that the H atoms of the CH_3 group have a much smaller positive partial charge than the O—H hydrogen atom. Furthermore, in carboxylic acids, the C atom of the CH_3 group is not sufficiently electronegative to accommodate the negative charge left if the bond breaks as $C—H \rightarrow C:^- + H^+$, and the product anion is not well stabilized.

Why Are Hydrated Metal Cations Brønsted Acids?

When a coordinate covalent bond is formed between a metal cation (a Lewis acid) and a water molecule (a Lewis base), the positive charge of the metal ion and its small size means that the electrons of the $H_2O—M^{n+}$ bond are very strongly at-

■ **Polarization of O—H Bonds** Water molecules attached to a metal cation have strongly polarized O—H bonds.

$$(H_2O)_5M^{n+} \longleftarrow :O-H^{\delta+} \atop H^{\delta+}$$

tracted to the metal. As a result, the O—H bonds of the bound water molecules are polarized, just as in oxoacids and carboxylic acids. The net effect is that a H atom of a coordinated water molecule is removed as H^+ more readily than in an uncoordinated water molecule. Thus, a hydrated metal cation functions as a Brønsted acid or proton donor (Figure 17.8).

$$[Cu(H_2O)_6]^{2+} + H_2O(\ell) \rightleftharpoons [Cu(H_2O)_5(OH)]^+(aq) + H_3O^+(aq)$$

The effect of the metal ion increases with increasing charge. Consulting Table 17.3, you see that the Brønsted acidity of $+3$ ions (for example Al^{3+} and Fe^{3+}) is greater than for $+2$ cations (Cu^{2+}, Pb^{2+}, Co^{2+}, Fe^{2+}, Ni^{2+}). Ions with a single positive charge such as Na^+ and K^+ are not acidic. (This is similar to the effect of central atom formal charge in a series of related acids. See Table 17.8.)

TABLE 17.9 Basic Oxoanions

Anion	pK_b
PO_4^{3-}	1.55
HPO_4^{2-}	6.80
$H_2PO_4^-$	11.89
CO_3^{2-}	3.68
HCO_3^-	7.62
SO_3^{2-}	6.80
HSO_3^-	12.08

Why Are Anions Brønsted Bases?

Anions, particularly oxoanions such as PO_4^{3-}, are Brønsted bases. The negatively charged anion interacts with the positively charged H atom of a polar water molecule, and an H^+ ion is transferred to the anion.

The data in Table 17.9 show that, in a series of related anions, the basicity of an anionic base increases as the negative charge of the anion increases.

Why Are Ammonia and Its Derivatives Brønsted and Lewis Bases?

Ammonia is the parent compound of an enormous number of compounds that behave as Brønsted and Lewis bases (Figure 17.13). These molecules all have an electronegative N atom with a partial negative charge surrounded by three bonds and a lone pair of electrons. Owing to this negatively charged N atom, they can extract a proton from water.

FIGURE 17.13 Nitrogen-based Lewis and Brønsted bases. All have an N atom surrounded by three bonds and a lone pair of electrons.

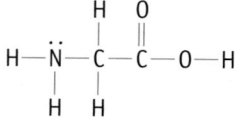

Trimethylamine   Pyridine   Nicotine   Glycine, an amino acid

In addition, the lone pair can be used to form a coordinate covalent bond to Lewis acids such as a metal cation (◄ page 790).

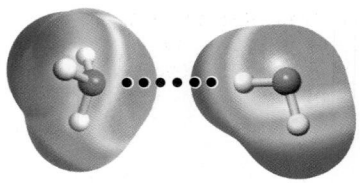

EXERCISE 17.18 Molecular Structure, Acids, and Bases

(a) Which should be the stronger acid, H_2SeO_4 or H_2SeO_3?

(b) Which should be the stronger acid, $[Fe(H_2O)_6]^{2+}$ or $[Fe(H_2O)_6]^{3+}$?

(c) Which should be the stronger acid, HOCl or HOBr?

(d) The molecule whose structure is illustrated here is amphetamine, a stimulant. Is the compound a Brønsted acid, a Lewis acid, a Brønsted base, a Lewis base, or some combination of these?

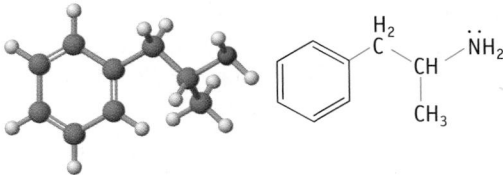

Electrostatic potential surfaces for NH_3 and H_2O. The red or negative region of these surfaces corresponds to the lone pair of electrons on N or the two pairs on O. The N atom of NH_3 has a calculated partial charge of -0.40, and the H atoms have a charge of $+0.13$. The N atom lone pair of NH_3 is involved in forming a hydrogen bond with the polar O—H bond of water. The NH_3 is both a Lewis and a Brønsted base and can remove the proton from water to form NH_4^+ and OH^-.

Chapter Goals Revisited

Now that you have studied this chapter, you should ask whether you have met the chapter goals. In particular, you should be able to:

Use the Brønsted–Lowry and Lewis theories of acids and bases
a. Define and use the Brønsted concept of acids and bases (Sections 17.1 and 17.2).

b. Recognize common monoprotic and polyprotic acids and bases, and write balanced equations for their ionization in water (Section 17.2).

c. Appreciate when a substance can be amphiprotic (Section 17.2).

d. Recognize the Brønsted acid and base in a reaction, and identify the conjugate partner of each (Section 17.2). Study Question(s) assignable in OWL: 2, 4, 8.

e. Understand the concept of water autoionization and its role in Brønsted acid–base chemistry. Use the water ionization constant, K_w (Section 17.3).

f. Use the pH concept (Section 17.3). Study Question(s) assignable in OWL: 10, 12.

g. Identify common strong acids and bases (Tables 3.2 and 17.3).

h. Recognize some common weak acids and understand that they can be neutral molecules (such as acetic acid), cations (NH_4^+ or hydrated metal ions such as $[Fe(H_2O)_6]^{2+}$, or anions (such as HCO_3^-) (Table 17.3).

Apply the principles of chemical equilibrium to acids and bases in aqueous solution
a. Write equilibrium constant expressions for weak acids and bases (Section 17.4).

b. Calculate pK_a from K_a (or K_a from pK_a), and understand how pK_a is correlated with acid strength (Section 17.4). Study Question(s) assignable in OWL: 26, 28, 30, 104, 106.

c. Understand the relationship between K_a for a weak acid and K_b for its conjugate base (Section 17.4). Study Question(s) assignable in OWL: 15, 18.

d. Write equations for acid–base reactions, and decide whether they are product- or reactant-favored at equilibrium (Section 17.5 and Table 17.5). Study Question(s) assignable in OWL: 36, 38.

Chemistry ⚛ Now™ Sign in at **www.cengage.com/login** to:
- Assess your understanding with Study Questions in OWL keyed to each goal in the Goals and Homework menu for this chapter
- For quick review, download Go Chemistry mini-lecture flashcard modules (or purchase them at **www.ichapters.com**)
- Check your readiness for an exam by taking the Pre-Test and exploring the modules recommended in your Personalized Study plan.

❓ Access **How Do I Solve It?** tutorials on how to approach problem solving using concepts in this chapter.

For additional preparation for an examination on this chapter see the *Let's Review* section on pages 948–961.

e. Calculate the equilibrium constant for a weak acid (K_a) or a weak base (K_b) from experimental information (such as pH, [H_3O^+], or [OH^-]) (Section 17.7 and Example 17.4). Study Question(s) assignable in OWL: 42, 44, 85, 107.

f. Use the equilibrium constant and other information to calculate the pH of a solution of a weak acid or weak base (Section 17.7 and Examples 17.5 and 13.7). Study Question(s) assignable in OWL: 48, 52, 56, 65, 66, 89, 91, 99; Go Chemistry Module 22.

g. Describe the acid–base properties of salts, and calculate the pH of a solution of a salt of a weak acid or of a weak base (Section 17.7 and Example 17.7). Study Question(s) assignable in OWL: 84, 92, 93, 103, 121.

Predict the outcome of reactions of acids and bases

a. Recognize the type of acid–base reaction, and describe its result (Section 17.6).

b. Calculate the pH after an acid–base reaction (Section 17.7 and Example 17.8). Study Question(s) assignable in OWL: 62, 98, 101, 102.

Understand the influence of structure and bonding on acid–base properties

a. Characterize a compound as a Lewis base (an electron-pair donor) or a Lewis acid (an electron-pair acceptor) (Section 17.9). Study Question(s) assignable in OWL: 70, 72, 108.

b. Appreciate the connection between the structure of a compound and its acidity or basicity (Section 17.10). Study Question(s) assignable in OWL: 74.

KEY EQUATIONS

Equation 17.1 (page 765): Water ionization constant.

$$K_w = [H_3O^+][OH^-] = 1.0 \times 10^{-14} \text{ at } 25 \text{ °C}$$

Equation 17.2 (page 767): Definition of pH (see also Equation 4.3).

$$pH = -\log[H_3O^+]$$

Equation 17.3 (page 767): Definition of pOH

$$pOH = -\log[OH^-]$$

Equation 17.4 (page 767): Definition of pK_w = pH + pOH (= 14.00 at 25 °C)

$$pK_w = 14.00 = pH + pOH$$

Equation 17.5 (page 769): Equilibrium expression for a general acid, HA, in water.

$$K_a = \frac{[H_3O^+][A^-]}{[HA]}$$

Equation 17.6 (page 769): Equilibrium expression for a general base, B, in water.

$$K_b = \frac{[BH^+][OH^-]}{[B]}$$

Equation 17.7 (page 775): Definition of pK_a.

$$pK_a = -\log K_a$$

Equation 17.8 (page 776): Relationship of K_a, K_b, and K_w, where K_a and K_b are for a conjugate acid–base pair.

$$K_a \times K_b = K_w$$

STUDY QUESTIONS

OWL Online homework for this chapter may be assigned in OWL.

▲ denotes challenging questions.

■ denotes questions assignable in OWL.

Blue-numbered questions have answers in Appendix O and fully-worked solutions in the *Student Solutions Manual*.

Practicing Skills

The Brønsted Concept
(See Exercises 17.1 and 17.2 and ChemistryNow Screen 17.2.)

1. Write the formula and give the name of the conjugate base of each of the following acids.
   (a) HCN   (b) HSO_4^- (c) HF

2. ■ Write the formula and give the name of the conjugate acid of each of the following bases.
   (a) NH_3 (b) HCO_3^- (c) Br^-

3. What are the products of each of the following acid–base reactions? Indicate the acid and its conjugate base and the base and its conjugate acid.
   (a) $HNO_3 + H_2O \rightarrow$
   (b) $HSO_4^- + H_2O \rightarrow$
   (c) $H_3O^+ + F^- \rightarrow$

4. ■ What are the products of each of the following acid–base reactions? Indicate the acid and its conjugate base and the base and its conjugate acid.
   (a) $HClO_4 + H_2O \rightarrow$
   (b) $NH_4^+ + H_2O \rightarrow$
   (c) $HCO_3^- + OH^- \rightarrow$

5. Write balanced equations showing how the hydrogen oxalate ion, $HC_2O_4^-$, can be both a Brønsted acid and a Brønsted base.

6. Write balanced equations showing how the HPO_4^{2-} ion of sodium hydrogen phosphate, Na_2HPO_4, can be a Brønsted acid or a Brønsted base.

7. In each of the following acid–base reactions, identify the Brønsted acid and base on the left and their conjugate partners on the right.
   (a) $HCO_2H(aq) + H_2O(\ell) \rightleftharpoons HCO_2^-(aq) + H_3O^+(aq)$
   (b) $NH_3(aq) + H_2S(aq) \rightleftharpoons NH_4^+(aq) + HS^-(aq)$
   (c) $HSO_4^-(aq) + OH^-(aq) \rightleftharpoons SO_4^{2-}(aq) + H_2O(\ell)$

8. ■ In each of the following acid–base reactions, identify the Brønsted acid and base on the left and their conjugate partners on the right.
   (a) $C_5H_5N(aq) + CH_3CO_2H(aq) \rightleftharpoons$
   $\qquad\qquad C_5H_5NH^+(aq) + CH_3CO_2^-(aq)$
   (b) $N_2H_4(aq) + HSO_4^-(aq) \rightleftharpoons$
   $\qquad\qquad N_2H_5^+(aq) + SO_4^{2-}(aq)$
   (c) $[Al(H_2O)_6]^{3+}(aq) + OH^-(aq) \rightleftharpoons$
   $\qquad\qquad [Al(H_2O)_5OH]^{2+}(aq) + H_2O(\ell)$

pH Calculations
(See Examples 4.7 and 17.1, Exercise 17.4, and ChemistryNow Screens 4.11 and 17.3–17.4.)

9. An aqueous solution has a pH of 3.75. What is the hydronium ion concentration of the solution? Is it acidic or basic?

10. ■ A saturated solution of milk of magnesia, $Mg(OH)_2$, has a pH of 10.52. What is the hydronium ion concentration of the solution? What is the hydroxide ion concentration? Is the solution acidic or basic?

11. What is the pH of a 0.0075 M solution of HCl? What is the hydroxide ion concentration of the solution?

12. ■ What is the pH of a 1.2×10^{-4} M solution of KOH? What is the hydronium ion concentration of the solution?

13. What is the pH of a 0.0015 M solution of $Ba(OH)_2$?

14. The pH of a solution of $Ba(OH)_2$ is 10.66 at 25 °C. What is the hydroxide ion concentration in the solution? If the solution volume is 125 mL, what mass of $Ba(OH)_2$ must have been dissolved?

Equilibrium Constants for Acids and Bases
(See Example 17.2, Exercise 17.5, and ChemistryNow Screen 17.6.)

15. ■ Several acids are listed here with their respective equilibrium constants:

$$C_6H_5OH(aq) + H_2O(\ell) \rightleftharpoons H_3O^+(aq) + C_6H_5O^-(aq)$$
$$K_a = 1.3 \times 10^{-10}$$

$$HCO_2H(aq) + H_2O(\ell) \rightleftharpoons H_3O^+(aq) + HCO_2^-(aq)$$
$$K_a = 1.8 \times 10^{-4}$$

$$HC_2O_4^-(aq) + H_2O(\ell) \rightleftharpoons H_3O^+(aq) + C_2O_4^{2-}(aq)$$
$$K_a = 6.4 \times 10^{-5}$$

   (a) Which is the strongest acid? Which is the weakest acid?
   (b) Which acid has the weakest conjugate base?
   (c) Which acid has the strongest conjugate base?

16. Several acids are listed here with their respective equilibrium constants.

$$HF(aq) + H_2O(\ell) \rightleftharpoons H_3O^+(aq) + F^-(aq)$$
$$K_a = 7.2 \times 10^{-4}$$

$$HPO_4^-(aq) + H_2O(\ell) \rightleftharpoons H_3O^+(aq) + PO_4^{3-}(aq)$$
$$K_a = 3.6 \times 10^{-13}$$

$$CH_3CO_2H(aq) + H_2O(\ell) \rightleftharpoons H_3O^+(aq) + CH_3CO_2^-(aq)$$
$$K_a = 1.8 \times 10^{-5}$$

   (a) Which is the strongest acid? Which is the weakest acid?
   (b) What is the conjugate base of the acid HF?
   (c) Which acid has the weakest conjugate base?
   (d) Which acid has the strongest conjugate base?

17. State which of the following ions or compounds has the strongest conjugate base, and briefly explain your choice.
    (a) HSO_4^- (b) CH_3CO_2H (c) $HOCl$

18. ■ Which of the following compounds or ions has the strongest conjugate acid? Briefly explain your choice.
    (a) CN^- (b) NH_3 (c) SO_4^{2-}

19. Dissolving K_2CO_3 in water gives a basic solution. Write a balanced equation showing how this salt can produce a basic solution.

20. Dissolving ammonium bromide in water gives an acidic solution. Write a balanced equation showing how this can occur.

21. If each of the salts listed here were dissolved in water to give a 0.10 M solution, which solution would have the highest pH? Which would have the lowest pH?
    (a) Na_2S (d) NaF
    (b) Na_3PO_4 (e) $NaCH_3CO_2$
    (c) NaH_2PO_4 (f) $AlCl_3$

22. Which of the following common food additives would give a basic solution when dissolved in water?
    (a) $NaNO_3$ (used as a meat preservative)
    (b) $NaC_6H_5CO_2$ (sodium benzoate; used as a soft-drink preservative)
    (c) Na_2HPO_4 (used as an emulsifier in the manufacture of pasteurized cheese)

pK_a: A Logarithmic Scale of Acid Strength

(See Exercise 17.7 and ChemistryNow Screen 17.6.)

23. A weak acid has a K_a of 6.5×10^{-5}. What is the value of pK_a for the acid?

24. If K_a for a weak acid is 2.4×10^{-11}, what is the value of pK_a?

25. Epinephrine hydrochloride has a pK_a value of 9.53. What is the value of K_a? Where does the acid fit in Table 17.3?

26. ■ An organic acid has $pK_a = 8.95$. What is its K_a value? Where does the acid fit in Table 17.3?

27. Which is the stronger of the following two acids?
    (a) benzoic acid, $C_6H_5CO_2H$, $pK_a = 4.20$
    (b) 2-chlorobenzoic acid, $ClC_6H_4CO_2H$, $pK_a = 2.88$

28. ■ Which is the stronger of the following two acids?
    (a) acetic acid, CH_3CO_2H, $K_a = 1.8 \times 10^{-5}$
    (b) chloroacetic acid, $ClCH_2CO_2H$, $pK_a = 2.87$

Ionization Constants for Weak Acids and Their Conjugate Bases
(See Exercise 17.8 and ChemistryNow Screen 17.6.)

29. Chloroacetic acid ($ClCH_2CO_2H$) has $K_a = 1.41 \times 10^{-3}$. What is the value of K_b for the chloroacetate ion ($ClCH_2CO_2^-$)?

30. ■ A weak base has $K_b = 1.5 \times 10^{-9}$. What is the value of K_a for the conjugate acid?

31. The trimethylammonium ion, $(CH_3)_3NH^+$, is the conjugate acid of the weak base trimethylamine, $(CH_3)_3N$. A chemical handbook gives 9.80 as the pK_a value for $(CH_3)_3NH^+$. What is the value of K_b for $(CH_3)_3N$?

32. The chromium(III) ion in water, $[Cr(H_2O)_6]^{3+}$, is a weak acid with $pK_a = 3.95$. What is the value of K_b for its conjugate base, $[Cr(H_2O)_5OH]^{2+}$?

Predicting the Direction of Acid–Base Reactions
(See Example 17.3 and ChemistryNow Screen 17.7.)

33. Acetic acid and sodium hydrogen carbonate, $NaHCO_3$, are mixed in water. Write a balanced equation for the acid–base reaction that could, in principle, occur. Using Table 17.3, decide whether the equilibrium lies predominantly to the right or to the left.

34. Ammonium chloride and sodium dihydrogen phosphate, NaH_2PO_4, are mixed in water. Write a balanced equation for the acid–base reaction that could, in principle, occur. Using Table 17.3, decide whether the equilibrium lies predominantly to the right or to the left.

35. For each of the following reactions, predict whether the equilibrium lies predominantly to the left or to the right. Explain your predictions briefly.
    (a) $NH_4^+(aq) + Br^-(aq) \rightleftharpoons NH_3(aq) + HBr(aq)$
    (b) $HPO_4^{2-}(aq) + CH_3CO_2^-(aq) \rightleftharpoons$
    $$PO_4^{3-}(aq) + CH_3CO_2H(aq)$$
    (c) $[Fe(H_2O)_6]^{3+}(aq) + HCO_3^-(aq) \rightleftharpoons$
    $$[Fe(H_2O)_5(OH)]^{2+}(aq) + H_2CO_3(aq)$$

36. ■ For each of the following reactions, predict whether the equilibrium lies predominantly to the left or to the right. Explain your predictions briefly.
    (a) $H_2S(aq) + CO_3^{2-}(aq) \rightleftharpoons HS^-(aq) + HCO_3^-(aq)$
    (b) $HCN(aq) + SO_4^{2-}(aq) \rightleftharpoons CN^-(aq) + HSO_4^-(aq)$
    (c) $SO_4^{2-}(aq) + CH_3CO_2H(aq) \rightleftharpoons$
    $$HSO_4^-(aq) + CH_3CO_2^-(aq)$$

Types of Acid–Base Reactions
(See Exercise 17.10 and ChemistryNow Screen 17.7.)

37. Equal molar quantities of sodium hydroxide and sodium hydrogen phosphate (Na_2HPO_4) are mixed.
    (a) Write the balanced, net ionic equation for the acid–base reaction that can, in principle, occur.
    (b) Does the equilibrium lie to the right or left?

38. ■ Equal molar quantities of hydrochloric acid and sodium hypochlorite ($NaClO$) are mixed.
    (a) Write the balanced, net ionic equation for the acid–base reaction that can, in principle, occur.
    (b) Does the equilibrium lie to the right or left?

39. Equal molar quantities of acetic acid and sodium hydrogen phosphate (Na_2HPO_4) are mixed.
    (a) Write a balanced, net ionic equation for the acid–base reaction that can, in principle, occur.
    (b) Does the equilibrium lie to the right or left?

40. Equal molar quantities of ammonia and sodium dihydrogen phosphate (NaH_2PO_4) are mixed.
   (a) Write a balanced, net ionic equation for the acid–base reaction that can, in principle, occur.
   (b) Does the equilibrium lie to the right or left?

Using pH to Calculate Ionization Constants
(See Example 17.4 and ChemistryNow Screen 17.8.)

41. A 0.015 M solution of hydrogen cyanate, HOCN, has a pH of 2.67.
   (a) What is the hydronium ion concentration in the solution?
   (b) What is the ionization constant, K_a, for the acid?

42. ■ A 0.10 M solution of chloroacetic acid, $ClCH_2CO_2H$, has a pH of 1.95. Calculate K_a for the acid.

43. A 0.025 M solution of hydroxylamine has a pH of 9.11. What is the value of K_b for this weak base?

$$H_2NOH(aq) + H_2O(\ell) \rightleftharpoons H_3NOH^+(aq) + OH^-(aq)$$

44. ■ Methylamine, CH_3NH_2, is a weak base.

$$CH_3NH_2(aq) + H_2O(\ell) \rightleftharpoons CH_3NH_3^+(aq) + OH^-(aq)$$

If the pH of a 0.065 M solution of the amine is 11.70, what is the value of K_b?

45. A 2.5×10^{-3} M solution of an unknown acid has a pH of 3.80 at 25 °C.
   (a) What is the hydronium ion concentration of the solution?
   (b) Is the acid a strong acid, a moderately weak acid (K_a of about 10^{-5}), or a very weak acid (K_a of about 10^{-10})?

46. A 0.015 M solution of a base has a pH of 10.09.
   (a) What are the hydronium and hydroxide ion concentrations of this solution?
   (b) Is the base a strong base, a moderately weak base (K_b of about 10^{-5}), or a very weak base (K_b of about 10^{-10})?

Using Ionization Constants
(See Examples 17.5–17.7 and ChemistryNow Screens 17.9–17.11.)

47. What are the equilibrium concentrations of hydronium ion, acetate ion, and acetic acid in a 0.20 M aqueous solution of acetic acid?

48. ■ The ionization constant of a very weak acid, HA, is 4.0×10^{-9}. Calculate the equilibrium concentrations of H_3O^+, A^-, and HA in a 0.040 M solution of the acid.

49. What are the equilibrium concentrations of H_3O^+, CN^-, and HCN in a 0.025 M solution of HCN? What is the pH of the solution?

50. Phenol (C_6H_5OH), commonly called carbolic acid, is a weak organic acid.

$$C_6H_5OH(aq) + H_2O(\ell) \rightleftharpoons C_6H_5O^-(aq) + H_3O^+(aq)$$
$$K_a = 1.3 \times 10^{-10}$$

If you dissolve 0.195 g of the acid in enough water to make 125 mL of solution, what is the equilibrium hydronium ion concentration? What is the pH of the solution?

51. What are the equilibrium concentrations of NH_3, NH_4^+, and OH^- in a 0.15 M solution of ammonia? What is the pH of the solution?

52. ■ A hypothetical weak base has $K_b = 5.0 \times 10^{-4}$. Calculate the equilibrium concentrations of the base, its conjugate acid, and OH^- in a 0.15 M solution of the base.

53. The weak base methylamine, CH_3NH_2, has $K_b = 4.2 \times 10^{-4}$. It reacts with water according to the equation

$$CH_3NH_2(aq) + H_2O(\ell) \rightleftharpoons CH_3NH_3^+(aq) + OH^-(aq)$$

Calculate the equilibrium hydroxide ion concentration in a 0.25 M solution of the base. What are the pH and pOH of the solution?

54. Calculate the pH of a 0.12 M aqueous solution of the base aniline, $C_6H_5NH_2$ ($K_b = 4.0 \times 10^{-10}$).

$$C_6H_5NH_2(aq) + H_2O(\ell) \rightleftharpoons C_6H_5NH_3^+(aq) + OH^-(aq)$$

55. Calculate the pH of a 0.0010 M aqueous solution of HF.

56. ■ A solution of hydrofluoric acid, HF, has a pH of 2.30. Calculate the equilibrium concentrations of HF, F^-, and H_3O^+, and calculate the amount of HF originally dissolved per liter.

Acid–Base Properties of Salts
(See Example 17.7 and ChemistryNow Screen 17.11.)

57. Calculate the hydronium ion concentration and pH in a 0.20 M solution of ammonium chloride, NH_4Cl.

58. ▲ Calculate the hydronium ion concentration and pH for a 0.015 M solution of sodium formate, $NaHCO_2$.

59. Sodium cyanide is the salt of the weak acid HCN. Calculate the concentrations of H_3O^+, OH^-, HCN, and Na^+ in a solution prepared by dissolving 10.8 g of NaCN in enough water to make 5.00×10^2 mL of solution at 25 °C.

60. The sodium salt of propanoic acid, $NaCH_3CH_2CO_2$, is used as an antifungal agent by veterinarians. Calculate the equilibrium concentrations of H_3O^+ and OH^-, and the pH, for a solution of 0.10 M $NaCH_3CH_2CO_2$.

pH after an Acid–Base Reaction
(See Example 17.8 and ChemistryNow Screens 17.7 and 17.10.)

61. Calculate the hydronium ion concentration and pH of the solution that results when 22.0 mL of 0.15 M acetic acid, CH_3CO_2H, is mixed with 22.0 mL of 0.15 M NaOH.

62. ■ Calculate the hydronium ion concentration and the pH when 50.0 mL of 0.40 M NH_3 is mixed with 50.0 mL of 0.40 M HCl.

▲ more challenging   ■ in OWL   Blue-numbered questions answered in Appendix O

63. For each of the following cases, decide whether the pH is less than 7, equal to 7, or greater than 7.
    (a) Equal volumes of 0.10 M acetic acid, CH_3CO_2H, and 0.10 M KOH are mixed.
    (b) 25 mL of 0.015 M NH_3 is mixed with 25 mL of 0.015 M HCl.
    (c) 150 mL of 0.20 M HNO_3 is mixed with 75 mL of 0.40 M NaOH.

64. For each of the following cases, decide whether the pH is less than 7, equal to 7, or greater than 7.
    (a) 25 mL of 0.45 M H_2SO_4 is mixed with 25 mL of 0.90 M NaOH.
    (b) 15 mL of 0.050 M formic acid, HCO_2H, is mixed with 15 mL of 0.050 M NaOH.
    (c) 25 mL of 0.15 M $H_2C_2O_4$ (oxalic acid) is mixed with 25 mL of 0.30 M NaOH. (Both H^+ ions of oxalic acid are removed with NaOH.)

Polyprotic Acids and Bases
(See Example 17.9.)

65. ■ Sulfurous acid, H_2SO_3, is a weak acid capable of providing two H^+ ions.
    (a) What is the pH of a 0.45 M solution of H_2SO_3?
    (b) What is the equilibrium concentration of the sulfite ion, SO_3^{2-}, in the 0.45 M solution of H_2SO_3?

66. ■ Ascorbic acid (vitamin C, $C_6H_8O_6$) is a diprotic acid ($K_{a1} = 6.8 \times 10^{-5}$ and $K_{a2} = 2.7 \times 10^{-12}$). What is the pH of a solution that contains 5.0 mg of acid per milliliter of solution?

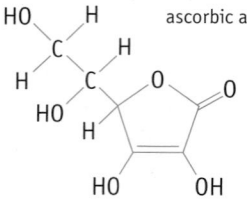
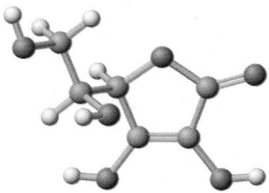

ascorbic acid

67. Hydrazine, N_2H_4, can interact with water in two steps.

$$N_2H_4(aq) + H_2O(\ell) \rightleftharpoons N_2H_5^+(aq) + OH^-(aq)$$
$$K_{b1} = 8.5 \times 10^{-7}$$

$$N_2H_5^+(aq) + H_2O(\ell) \rightleftharpoons N_2H_6^{2+}(aq) + OH^-(aq)$$
$$K_{b2} = 8.9 \times 10^{-16}$$

    (a) What is the concentration of OH^-, $N_2H_5^+$, and $N_2H_6^{2+}$ in a 0.010 M aqueous solution of hydrazine?
    (b) What is the pH of the 0.010 M solution of hydrazine?

68. Ethylenediamine, $H_2NCH_2CH_2NH_2$, can interact with water in two steps, forming OH^- in each step (see Appendix I). If you have a 0.15 M aqueous solution of the amine, calculate the concentrations of $[H_3NCH_2CH_2NH_3]^{2+}$ and OH^-.

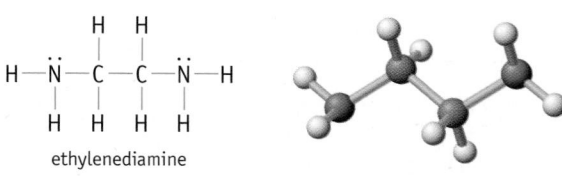

ethylenediamine

Lewis Acids and Bases
(See Exercise 17.17 and ChemistryNow Screens 17.12–17.14.)

69. Decide whether each of the following substances should be classified as a Lewis acid or a Lewis base.
    (a) H_2NOH in the reaction

    $$H_2NOH(aq) + HCl(aq) \longrightarrow [H_3NOH]Cl(aq)$$

    (b) Fe^{2+}
    (c) CH_3NH_2 (Hint: Draw the electron dot structure.)

70. ■ Decide whether each of the following substances should be classified as a Lewis acid or a Lewis base.
    (a) BCl_3 (Hint: Draw the electron dot structure.)
    (b) H_2NNH_2, hydrazine (Hint: Draw the electron dot structure.)
    (c) the reactants in the reaction

    $$Ag^+(aq) + 2NH_3(aq) \rightleftharpoons [Ag(NH_3)_2]^+(aq)$$

71. Carbon monoxide forms complexes with low-valent metals. For example, $Ni(CO)_4$ and $Fe(CO)_5$ are well known. CO also forms complexes with the iron(II) ion in hemoglobin, which prevents the hemoglobin from acting in its normal way. Is CO a Lewis acid or a Lewis base?

72. ■ Trimethylamine, $(CH_3)_3N$, is a common reagent. It interacts readily with diborane gas, B_2H_6. The latter dissociates to BH_3, and this forms a complex with the amine, $(CH_3)_3N \rightarrow BH_3$. Is the BH_3 fragment a Lewis acid or a Lewis base?

Molecular Structure, Bonding, and Acid–Base Behavior
(See Section 17.10 and Exercise 17.18.)

73. Which should be the stronger acid, HOCN or HCN? Explain briefly. (In HOCN, the H^+ ion is attached to the O atom of the OCN^- ion.)

74. ■ Which should be the stronger Brønsted acid, $[V(H_2O)_6]^{2+}$ or $[V(H_2O)_6]^{3+}$?

75. Explain why benzenesulfonic acid is a Brønsted acid.

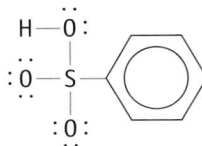

benzenesulfonic acid

76. The structure of ethylenediamine is illustrated in Study Question 68. Is this compound a Brønsted acid, a Brønsted base, a Lewis acid, or a Lewis base, or some combination of these?

General Questions on Acids and Bases

These questions are not designated as to type or location in the chapter. They may combine several concepts.

77. About this time, you may be wishing you had an aspirin. Aspirin is an organic acid (page 760) with a K_a of 3.27×10^{-4} for the reaction

$$HC_9H_7O_4(aq) + H_2O(\ell) \rightleftharpoons C_9H_7O_4^-(aq) + H_3O^+(aq)$$

If you have two tablets, each containing 0.325 g of aspirin (mixed with a neutral "binder" to hold the tablet together), and you dissolve them in a glass of water to give 225 mL of solution, what is the pH of the solution?

78. Consider the following ions: NH_4^+, CO_3^{2-}, Br^-, S^{2-}, and ClO_4^-.
(a) Which of these ions might lead to an acidic solution, and which might lead to a basic solution?
(b) Which of these anions will have no effect on the pH of an aqueous solution?
(c) Which ion is the strongest base?
(d) Write a chemical equation for the reaction of each basic anion with water.

79. A 2.50-g sample of a solid that could be $Ba(OH)_2$ or $Sr(OH)_2$ was dissolved in enough water to make 1.00 L of solution. If the pH of the solution is 12.61, what is the identity of the solid?

80. ▲ In a particular solution, acetic acid is 11% ionized at 25 °C. Calculate the pH of the solution and the mass of acetic acid dissolved to yield 1.00 L of solution.

81. Hydrogen sulfide, H_2S, and sodium acetate, $NaCH_3CO_2$, are mixed in water. Using Table 17.3, write a balanced equation for the acid–base reaction that could, in principle, occur. Does the equilibrium lie toward the products or the reactants?

82. For each of the following reactions, predict whether the equilibrium lies predominantly to the left or to the right. Explain your prediction briefly.
(a) $HCO_3^-(aq) + SO_4^{2-}(aq) \rightleftharpoons$
$$CO_3^{2-}(aq) + HSO_4^-(aq)$$
(b) $HSO_4^-(aq) + CH_3CO_2^-(aq) \rightleftharpoons$
$$SO_4^{2-}(aq) + CH_3CO_2H(aq)$$
(c) $[Co(H_2O)_6]^{2+}(aq) + CH_3CO_2^-(aq) \rightleftharpoons$
$$[Co(H_2O)_5(OH)]^+(aq) + CH_3CO_2H(aq)$$

83. A monoprotic acid HX has $K_a = 1.3 \times 10^{-3}$. Calculate the equilibrium concentrations of HX and H_3O^+ and the pH for a 0.010 M solution of the acid.

84. ■ Arrange the following 0.10 M solutions in order of increasing pH.
(a) NaCl   (d) $NaCH_3CO_2$
(b) NH_4Cl (e) KOH
(c) HCl

85. ■ *m*-Nitrophenol, a weak acid, can be used as a pH indicator because it is yellow at a pH above 8.6 and colorless at a pH below 6.8. If the pH of a 0.010 M solution of the compound is 3.44, calculate its pK_a.

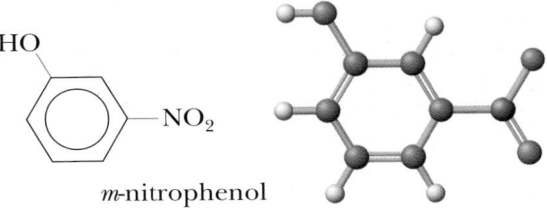

HO

NO_2

m-nitrophenol

86. The butylammonium ion, $C_4H_9NH_3^+$, has a K_a of 2.3×10^{-11}.

$$C_4H_9NH_3^+(aq) + H_2O(\ell) \rightleftharpoons H_3O^+(aq) + C_4H_9NH_2(aq)$$

(a) Calculate K_b for the conjugate base, $C_4H_9NH_2$ (butylamine).
(b) Place the butylammonium ion and its conjugate base in Table 17.3. Name an acid weaker than $C_4H_9NH_3^+$ and a base stronger than $C_4H_9NH_2$.
(c) What is the pH of a 0.015 M solution of the butylammonium chloride?

87. The local anesthetic novocaine is the hydrogen chloride salt of an organic base, procaine.

$$C_{13}H_{20}N_2O_2(aq) + HCl(aq) \longrightarrow [HC_{13}H_{20}N_2O_2]^+Cl^-(aq)$$
procaine   novocaine

The pK_a for novocaine is 8.85. What is the pH of a 0.0015 M solution of novocaine?

88. Pyridine is a weak organic base and readily forms a salt with hydrochloric acid.

$$C_5H_5N(aq) + HCl(aq) \longrightarrow C_5H_5NH^+(aq) + Cl^-(aq)$$
$$\text{pyridine} \qquad\qquad\qquad \text{pyridinium ion}$$

What is the pH of a 0.025 M solution of pyridinium hydrochloride, $[C_5H_5NH^+]Cl^-$?

89. ■ The base ethylamine ($CH_3CH_2NH_2$) has a K_b of 4.3×10^{-4}. A closely related base, ethanolamine ($HOCH_2CH_2NH_2$), has a K_b of 3.2×10^{-5}.
(a) Which of the two bases is stronger?
(b) Calculate the pH of a 0.10 M solution of the stronger base.

90. Chloroacetic acid, $ClCH_2CO_2H$, is a moderately weak acid ($K_a = 1.40 \times 10^{-3}$). If you dissolve 94.5 mg of the acid in water to give 125 mL of solution, what is the pH of the solution?

91. ■ Saccharin ($HC_7H_4NO_3S$) is a weak acid with $pK_a = 2.32$ at 25 °C. It is used in the form of sodium saccharide, $NaC_7H_4NO_3S$. What is the pH of a 0.10 M solution of sodium saccharide at 25 °C?

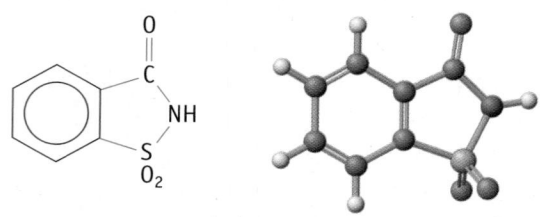

saccharin

92. ■ Given the following solutions:
(a) 0.1 M NH_3 (e) 0.1 M NH_4Cl
(b) 0.1 M Na_2CO_3 (f) 0.1 M $NaCH_3CO_2$
(c) 0.1 M $NaCl$ (g) 0.1 M $NH_4CH_3CO_2$
(d) 0.1 M CH_3CO_2H
(i) Which of the solutions are acidic?
(ii) Which of the solutions are basic?
(iii) Which of the solutions is most acidic?

93. ■ For each of the following salts, predict whether a 0.10 M solution has a pH less than, equal to, or greater than 7.
(a) $NaHSO_4$ (f) $NaNO_3$
(b) NH_4Br (g) Na_2HPO_4
(c) $KClO_4$ (h) $LiBr$
(d) Na_2CO_3 (i) $FeCl_3$
(e) $(NH_4)_2S$
Which solution has the highest pH? The lowest pH?

94. Nicotine, $C_{10}H_{14}N_2$, has two basic nitrogen atoms (page 798), and both can react with water.

$$Nic(aq) + H_2O(\ell) \rightleftharpoons NicH^+(aq) + OH^-(aq)$$

$$NicH^+(aq) + H_2O(\ell) \rightleftharpoons NicH_2^{2+}(aq) + OH^-(aq)$$

K_{b1} is 7.0×10^{-7} and K_{b2} is 1.1×10^{-10}. Calculate the approximate pH of a 0.020 M solution.

95. ■ Oxalic acid is a relatively weak diprotic acid. Calculate the equilibrium constant for the reaction shown below from K_{a1} and K_{a2}. (See Appendix H for the required K_a values.)

$$H_2C_2O_4(aq) + 2\,H_2O(\ell) \rightleftharpoons C_2O_4^{2-}(aq) + 2\,H_3O^+(aq)$$

96. ▲ The equilibrium constant for the reaction of hydrochloric acid and ammonia is 1.8×10^9 (page 779). Confirm this value.

97. ▲ The equilibrium constant for the reaction of formic acid and sodium hydroxide is 1.8×10^{10} (page 779). Confirm this value.

98. ■ ▲ Calculate the pH of the solution that results from mixing 25.0 mL of 0.14 M formic acid and 50.0 mL of 0.070 M sodium hydroxide.

99. ■ ▲ To what volume should 1.00×10^2 mL of any weak acid, HA, with a concentration 0.20 M be diluted to double the percentage ionization?

100. ▲ The hydrogen phthalate ion, $C_8H_5O_4^-$, is a weak acid with $K_a = 3.91 \times 10^{-6}$.

$$C_8H_5O_4^-(aq) + H_2O(\ell) \rightleftharpoons C_8H_4O_4^{2-}(aq) + H_3O^+(aq)$$

What is the pH of a 0.050 M solution of potassium hydrogen phthalate, $KC_8H_5O_4$? *Note:* To find the pH for a solution of the anion, we must take into account that the ion is amphiprotic. It can be shown that, for most cases of amphiprotic ions, the H_3O^+ concentration is

$$[H_3O^+] = \sqrt{K_1 \times K_2}$$

For phthalic acid, $C_8H_6O_4$, K_1 is 1.12×10^{-3}, and K_2 is 3.91×10^{-6}.

101. ■ ▲ You prepare a 0.10 M solution of oxalic acid, $H_2C_2O_4$. What molecules and ions exist in this solution? List them in order of decreasing concentration.

102. ■ ▲ You mix 30.0 mL of 0.15 M NaOH with 30.0 mL of 0.15 M acetic acid. What molecules and ions exist in this solution? List them in order of decreasing concentration.

In the Laboratory

103. ■ Describe an experiment that will allow you to place the following three bases in order of increasing base strength: NaCN, CH_3NH_2, Na_2CO_3.

104. ■ The data below compare the strength of acetic acid with a related series of acids, where the H atoms of the CH_3 group in acetic acid are successively replaced by Br.

Acid	pK_a
CH_3CO_2H	4.74
$BrCH_2CO_2H$	2.90
Br_2CHCO_2H	1.39
Br_3CCO_2H	−0.147

(a) What trend in acid strength do you observe as H is successively replaced by Br? Can you suggest a reason for this trend?

(b) Suppose each of the acids above were present as a 0.10 M aqueous solution. Which would have the highest pH? The lowest pH?

105. ▲ You have three solutions labeled A, B, and C. You know only that each contains a different cation—Na^+, NH_4^+, or H^+. Each has an anion that does not contribute to the solution pH (e.g., Cl^-). You also have two other solutions, Y and Z, each containing a different anion, Cl^- or OH^-, with a cation that does not influence solution pH (e.g., K^+). If equal amounts of B and Y are mixed, the result is an acidic solution. Mixing A and Z gives a neutral solution, whereas B and Z give a basic solution. Identify the five unknown solutions. (Adapted from D. H. Barouch: *Voyages in Conceptual Chemistry*, Boston, Jones and Bartlett, 1997.)

	Y	Z
A		neutral
B	acidic	basic
C		

106. ■ A hydrogen atom in the organic base pyridine, C_5H_5N, can be substituted by various atoms or groups to give XC_5H_4N, where X is an atom such as Cl or a group such as CH_3. The following table gives K_a values for the conjugate acids of a variety of substituted pyridines.

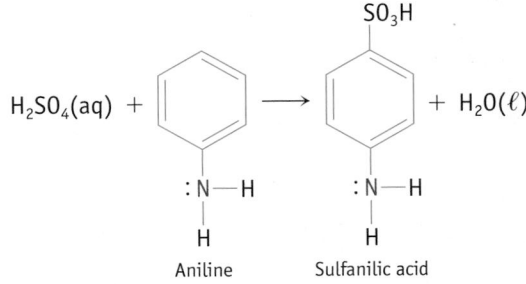

substituted pyridine   conjugate acid

Atom or Group X	K_a of Conjugate Acid
NO_2	5.9×10^{-2}
Cl	1.5×10^{-4}
H	6.8×10^{-6}
CH_3	1.0×10^{-6}

(a) Suppose each conjugate acid is dissolved in sufficient water to give a 0.050 M solution. Which solution would have the highest pH? The lowest pH?

(b) Which of the substituted pyridines is the strongest Brønsted base? Which is the weakest Brønsted base?

107. ■ Nicotinic acid, $C_6H_5NO_2$, is found in minute amounts in all living cells, but appreciable amounts occur in liver, yeast, milk, adrenal glands, white meat, and corn. Whole-wheat flour contains about 60. μg per 1g of flour. One gram (1.00 g) of the acid dissolves in water to give 60. mL of solution having a pH of 2.70. What is the approximate value of K_a for the acid?

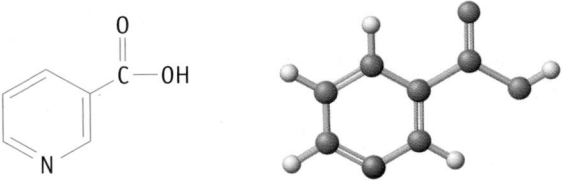

nicotinic acid

108. ■ ▲ Equilibrium constants can be measured for the dissociation of Lewis acid–base complexes such as the dimethyl ether complex of BF_3, $(CH_3)_2O{\rightarrow}BF_3$. The value of K (here K_p) for the reaction is 0.17.

$$(CH_3)_2O{\rightarrow}BF_3(g) \rightleftharpoons BF_3(g) + (CH_3)_2O(g)$$

(a) Describe each product as a Lewis acid or a Lewis base.

(b) If you place 1.00 g of the complex in a 565-mL flask at 25 °C, what is the total pressure in the flask? What are the partial pressures of the Lewis acid, the Lewis base, and the complex?

109. ▲ Sulfanilic acid, which is used in making dyes, is made by reacting aniline with sulfuric acid.

$$H_2SO_4(aq) + \text{[benzene ring with :N—H / H]} \longrightarrow \text{[benzene ring with SO}_3\text{H and :N—H / H]} + H_2O(\ell)$$

Aniline   Sulfanilic acid

(a) Is aniline a Brønsted base, a Lewis base, or both? Explain, using its possible reactions with HCl, BF_3, or other acid.

(b) Sulfanilic acid has a pK_a value of 3.23. The sodium salt of the acid, $Na(H_2NC_6H_4SO_3)$, is quite soluble in water. If you dissolve 1.25 g of the salt in water to give 125 mL of solution, what is the pH of the solution?

110. Amino acids are an important group of compounds (see page 498). At low pH, both the carboxylic acid group ($-CO_2H$) and the amine group ($-NHR$) are protonated. However, as the pH of the solution increases (say by adding base), the carboxylic acid proton is removed, usually at a pH between 2 and 3. In a middle range of pHs, the amine group is protonated, but the carboxylic acid group has lost the proton. (This is called a *zwitterion*.) At more basic pH values, the amine proton is dissociated.

$$H_3\overset{+}{N}-\underset{\underset{CH_3}{|}}{CH}-\overset{\overset{O}{||}}{C}-OH \underset{\longleftarrow}{\overset{pK_a = 2.4}{\rightleftharpoons}} H_3\overset{+}{N}-\underset{\underset{CH_3}{|}}{CH}-\overset{\overset{O}{||}}{C}-O^-$$

Alanine
Cationic form

Zwitterionic form

$$\underset{\longleftarrow}{\overset{pK_a = 9.7}{\rightleftharpoons}} H_2N-\underset{\underset{CH_3}{|}}{CH}-\overset{\overset{O}{||}}{C}-O^-$$

Anionic form

What is the pH of a 0.20 M solution of alanine hydrochloride, $[NH_3CHCH_3CO_2H]Cl$?

Summary and Conceptual Questions
The following questions may use concepts from this and previous chapters.

111. How can water be both a Brønsted base and a Lewis base? Can water be a Brønsted acid? A Lewis acid?

112. The nickel(II) ion exists as $[Ni(H_2O)_6]^{2+}$ in aqueous solution. Why is such a solution acidic? As part of your answer, include a balanced equation depicting what happens when $[Ni(H_2O)_6]^{2+}$ interacts with water.

113. The halogens form three stable, weak acids HOX.

Acid	pK_a
HOCl	7.46
HOBr	8.7
HOI	10.6

(a) Which is the strongest of these acids?

(b) Explain why the acid strength changes as the halogen atom is changed.

114. The acidity of the oxoacids was described on page 794, and a larger number of acids are listed in the table below.

E(OH)$_m$	pK_a	EO(OH)$_m$	pK_a	EO$_2$(OH)$_m$	pK_a	EO$_3$(OH)$_m$	pK_a
Very weak		Weak		Strong		Very strong	
Cl(OH)	7.5	ClO(OH)	2	ClO$_2$(OH)	−3	ClO$_3$(OH)	−10
Br(OH)	8.7	NO(OH)	3.4	NO$_2$(OH)	−1.4		
I(OH)	10.6	IO(OH)	1.6	IO$_2$(OH)	0.8		
Si(OH)$_4$	9.7	SO(OH)$_2$	1.8	SO$_2$(OH)$_2$	−3		
Sb(OH)$_4$	11.0	SeO(OH)$_2$	2.5	SeO$_2$(OH)$_2$	−3		
As(OH)$_3$	9.2	AsO(OH)$_3$	2.3				
		PO(OH)$_3$	2.1				
		HPO(OH)$_2$	1.8				
		H$_2$PO(OH)	2.0				

(a) What general trends do you see in these data?

(b) What has a greater effect on acidity, the number of O atoms bonded directly to the central atom E or the number of OH groups?

(c) Look at the acids based on Cl, N, and S. Is there a correlation of acidity with the formal charge on the central atom, E?

(d) The acid H_3PO_3 has a pK_a of 1.8, and this led to some insight into its structure. If the structure of the acid were $P(OH)_3$, what would be its predicted pK_a value? Given that this is a diprotic acid, which H atoms are lost as H^+ ions?

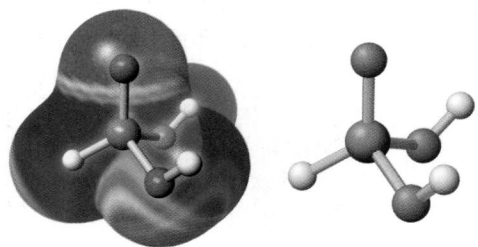

115. Perchloric acid behaves as an acid, even when it is dissolved in sulfuric acid.

(a) Write a balanced equation showing how perchloric acid can transfer a proton to sulfuric acid.

(b) Draw a Lewis electron dot structure for sulfuric acid. How can sulfuric acid function as a base?

116. You purchase a bottle of water. On checking its pH, you find that it is not neutral, as you might have expected. Instead, it is slightly acidic. Why?

117. Iodine, I_2, is much more soluble in a water solution of potassium iodide, KI, than it is in pure water. The anion found in solution is I_3^-.

(a) Draw an electron dot structure for I_3^-.

(b) Write an equation for this reaction, indicating the Lewis acid and the Lewis base.

▲ more challenging ■ in OWL Blue-numbered questions answered in Appendix O

118. ▲ Uracil is a base found in RNA (see page 504). Indicate sites in the molecule where hydrogen bonding is possible or that are sites of Lewis basicity. The electrostatic potential surface shows that one of the four C atoms in uracil has a partial negative charge. Designate that carbon atom.

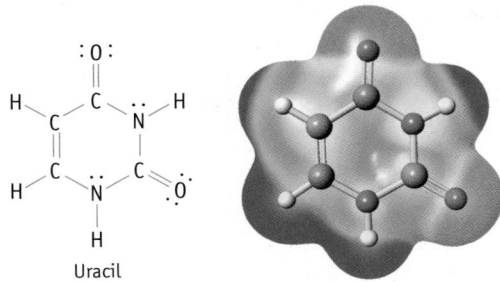

Uracil

119. Chemists often refer to the *degree of ionization* of a weak acid or base and give it the symbol α. The equilibrium constant, in terms of α and C_o, the initial acid or base concentration, is given by the useful equation

$$K = \frac{\alpha^2 C_o}{(1 - \alpha)}$$

As an example, the degree of ionization for 0.010 M acetic acid is 0.013.
   (a) Show how we can arrive at the general equation given above.
   (b) Calculate the degree of ionization for the ammonium ion in 0.10 M NH_4Cl.

120. ▲ Exploring the degree of ionization equation in Study Question 119.
   (a) Calculate the degree of ionization, α, for formic acid at the following concentrations: 0.0100 M, 0.0200 M, 0.0400 M, 0.100 M, 0.200 M, 0.400 M, 1.00 M, 2.00 M, and 4.00 M.

   (b) Plot the results of the calculation as α versus formic acid concentration. Is there a linear relationship? If not, try plotting the logarithm of C_o versus α.
   (c) What can you conclude about the relationship of the degree of ionization and the initial acid or base concentration?

121. ■ ▲ Consider a salt of a weak base and a weak acid such as ammonium cyanide. Both the NH_4^+ and CN^- ions interact with water in aqueous solution, but the net reaction can be considered as a proton transfer from NH_4^+ to CN^-.

$$NH_4^+(aq) + CN^-(aq) \rightleftharpoons NH_3(aq) + HCN(aq)$$

   (a) Show that the equilibrium constant for this reaction, K_{net}, is

$$K_{net} = \frac{K_w}{K_a K_b}$$

   where K_a is the ionization constant for the weak acid HCN and K_b is the constant for the weak base NH_3.
   (b) Calculate K_{net} for NH_4CN, $NH_4CH_3CO_2$, and NH_4F. Which salt has the largest K_{net} and why?

18 | Principles of Reactivity: Other Aspects of Aqueous Equilibria

Minerals and Gems—The Importance of Solubility

Minerals and gems are among nature's most beautiful creations. Many, such as rubies, are metal oxides, and the various types of quartz are based on silicon dioxide. Another large class of gemstones consists largely of metal silicates. These include emerald, topaz, aquamarine, and tourmaline.

Yet another large class of minerals and of a few gemstones is carbonates. Rhodochrosite, one of the most beautiful red stones, is manganese(II) carbonate. And one of the most abundant minerals on earth is limestone, calcium carbonate, which also largely composes sea shells and corals.

Mineral samples (clockwise from the top center): red rhodochrosite, yellow orpiment, golden iron pyrite, green-blue turquoise, black stibnite, purple fluorite, and blue azurite. Formulas are in the text.

Hydroxides are represented by azurite, which is a mixed carbonate/hydroxide with the formula $Cu_3(OH)_2(CO_3)_2$. Turquoise is a mixed hydroxide/phosphate based on copper(II), the source of the blue color of turquoise.

Among the most common minerals are sulfides such as golden iron pyrite (FeS_2), black stibnite (Sb_2S_3), red cinnabar (HgS), and yellow orpiment (As_2S_3).

Other smaller classes of minerals exist; one of the smallest is the class based on the halides, and the best example is fluorite. Fluorite, CaF_2, exhibits a wide range of colors from purple to green to yellow.

What do all of these minerals and gems have in common? They are all insoluble or poorly soluble in water. If they were more soluble, they would be dissolved in the world's lakes and oceans.

Questions:
1. Which is more soluble in water, $CaCO_3$ or $MnCO_3$?
2. Which is more soluble in water, HgS or PbS?
3. What is the calculated solubility of fluorite (in g/L)?

Answers to these questions are in Appendix Q.

Chapter Goals

OWL *See Chapter Goals Revisited (page 849) for Study Questions keyed to these goals and assignable in OWL.*

- Understand the common ion effect.
- Understand the control of pH in aqueous solution with buffers.
- Evaluate the pH in the course of acid–base titrations.
- Apply chemical equilibrium concepts to the solubility of ionic compounds.

Chapter Outline

In Chapter 3, we described four fundamental types of chemical reactions: acid–base reactions, precipitation reactions, gas-forming reactions, and oxidation-reduction reactions. In the present chapter, we want to apply the principles of chemical equilibria to an understanding of the first two of these kinds of reactions.

With regard to acid–base reactions, we are looking for answers to the following questions:

- How can we control the pH in a solution?
- What happens when an acid and base are mixed in any amount?

Precipitation reactions can also be understood in terms of chemical equilibria. The following questions are discussed in this chapter:

- If aqueous solutions of two ionic compounds are mixed, will precipitation occur?
- To what extent does an insoluble substance actually dissolve?
- What chemical reactions can be used to redissolve a precipitate?

Chemistry.Now™

Throughout the text this icon introduces an opportunity for self-study or to explore interactive tutorials by signing in at **www.cengage.com/login**.

18.1 The Common Ion Effect

In the previous chapter, we examined the behavior of weak acids and bases in aqueous solution. There are many cases, however, where the weak acid solution also contains a significant concentration of its conjugate base or where a weak base solution has a significant concentration of conjugate acid. The pH of such solutions will be different than those of solutions of a weak acid or base with very small amounts of conjugate bases or acids produced by ionization. The effect of a significant concentration of conjugate base on the pH of a weak acid solution, for example, is called the **common ion effect**, and it is particularly important in buffer solutions, as we shall see in Section 18.2.

Let us see how the common ion effect works. If 1.0 L of a 0.25 M acetic acid solution has a pH of 2.67, what is the pH after adding 0.10 mol of sodium acetate? Sodium acetate, $NaCH_3CO_2$, is 100% dissociated into its ions, Na^+ and $CH_3CO_2^-$, in water. Sodium ion has no effect on the pH of a solution (◀ Table 17.4 and Example 17.2). Thus, the important components of the solution are a weak acid (CH_3CO_2H) and its conjugate base ($CH_3CO_2^-$); the added acetate ion is "common" to the ionization equilibrium reaction of acetic acid.

$$CH_3CO_2H(aq) + H_2O(\ell) \rightleftharpoons H_3O^+(aq) + CH_3CO_2^-(aq)$$

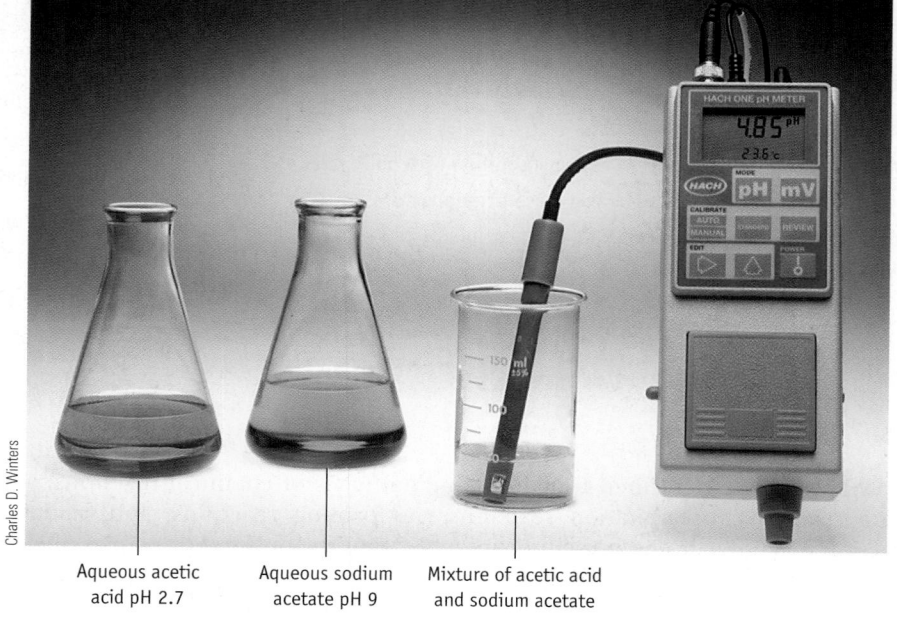

Aqueous acetic acid pH 2.7

Aqueous sodium acetate pH 9

Mixture of acetic acid and sodium acetate

Charles D. Winters

■ **The Common Ion Effect** In this ICE table, the first row (Initial) reflects the assumption that no ionization (or hydrolysis of the conjugate base) has yet occurred. Ionization of the acid in the presence of the conjugate base then produces x mol/L of hydronium ion and x mol/L more of the conjugate base.

Assume the acid ionizes to give H_3O^+ and $CH_3CO_2^-$, both in the amount x. This means that, relative to their initial concentrations, CH_3CO_2H decreases in concentration slightly (by an amount x) and $CH_3CO_2^-$ increases slightly (by an amount x).

Equation	CH_3CO_2H	+	H_2O ⇌	H_3O^+	+	$CH_3CO_2^-$
Initial (M)	0.25			0		0.10
Change (M)	$-x$			$+x$		$+x$
Equilibrium (M)	$(0.25 - x)$			x		$0.10 + x$

Because we have been able to define the equilibrium concentrations of acid and conjugate base and we know K_a, the hydronium ion concentration ($= x$) can be calculated from the usual equilibrium constant expression.

$$K_a = 1.8 \times 10^{-5} = \frac{[H_3O^+][CH_3CO_2^-]}{[CH_3CO_2H]} = \frac{(x)(0.10 + x)}{0.25 - x}$$

Now, because acetic acid is a weak acid and because it is ionizing in the presence of a significant concentration of its conjugate base, let us assume x is quite small. That is, it is reasonable to assume that $(0.10 + x)M \approx 0.10$ M and that $(0.25 - x)M \approx 0.25$ M. This leads to the "approximate" expression.

$$K_a = 1.8 \times 10^{-5} = \frac{[H_3O^+][CH_3CO_2^-]}{[CH_3CO_2H]} = \frac{(x)(0.10)}{0.25}$$

■ **Equilibrium Constants and Temperature** Unless specified otherwise, all equilibrium constants and all calculations in this chapter are at 25 °C.

Solving this, we find that $x = [H_3O^+] = 4.5 \times 10^{-5}$ M and the pH is 4.35.

Without added $NaCH_3CO_2$, which provides the "common ion" $CH_3CO_2^-$, ionization of 0.25 M acetic acid will produce H_3O^+ and $CH_3CO_2^-$ ions in a concentration of 0.0021 M (to give a pH of 2.68). Le Chatelier's principle, however, predicts that the added common ion causes the reaction to proceed less far to the right. Hence, as we have found, $x = [H_3O^+]$ is less than 0.0021 M in the presence of added acetate ion.

Sign in at **www.cengage.com/login** and go to Chapter 18 Contents to see Screen 18.2 for a simulation of the **common ion effect**.

■ **EXAMPLE 18.1 Reaction of Lactic Acid with a Deficiency of Sodium Hydroxide**

Problem What is the pH of the solution that results from adding 25.0 mL of 0.0500 M NaOH to 25.0 mL of 0.100 M lactic acid? (K_a for lactic acid = 1.4×10^{-4})

lactic acid ($HC_3H_5O_3$)
$K_a = 1.4 \times 10^{-4}$

lactate ion ($C_3H_5O_3^-$)

Strategy There are two parts to this problem: a stoichiometry problem followed by an equilibrium problem. We first calculate the concentrations of lactic acid and lactate ion that are present following the reaction of lactic acid with NaOH. Then, with the acid and conjugate base concentrations known, we follow the strategy in the text above to determine the pH.

Solution

Part 1: Stoichiometry Problem

First, consider what species remain in solution after the acid–base reaction and what the concentrations of those species are.

(a) Amounts of NaOH and lactic acid used in the reaction

$$(0.0250 \text{ L NaOH})(0.0500 \text{ mol/L}) = 1.25 \times 10^{-3} \text{ mol NaOH}$$

$$(0.0250 \text{ L lactic acid})(0.100 \text{ mol/L}) = 2.50 \times 10^{-3} \text{ mol lactic acid}$$

(b) Amount of lactate ion produced by the acid-base reaction
Recognizing that NaOH is the limiting reactant, we have

$$(1.25 \times 10^{-3} \text{ mol NaOH})\left(\frac{1 \text{ mol lactate ion}}{1 \text{ mol NaOH}}\right) = 1.25 \times 10^{-3} \text{ mol lactate ion produced}$$

(c) Amount of lactic acid consumed

$$(1.25 \times 10^{-3} \text{ mol NaOH})\left(\frac{1 \text{ mol lactic acid}}{1 \text{ mol NaOH}}\right) = 1.25 \times 10^{-3} \text{ mol lactic acid consumed}$$

(d) Amount of lactic acid remaining when reaction is complete.

2.50×10^{-3} mol lactic acid available $- 1.25 \times 10^{-3}$ mol lactic acid consumed

$$= 1.25 \times 10^{-3} \text{ mol lactic acid remaining}$$

(e) Concentrations of lactic acid and lactate ion after reaction. Note that the total solution volume after reaction is 50.0 mL or 0.050 L.

$$[\text{lactic acid}] = \frac{1.25 \times 10^{-3} \text{ mol lactic acid}}{0.0500 \text{ L}} = 2.50 \times 10^{-2} \text{ M}$$

Because the amount of lactic acid remaining is the same as the amount of lactate ion produced, we have

$$[\text{lactic acid}] = [\text{lactate ion}] = 2.50 \times 10^{-2} \text{ M}$$

Part 2: *Equilibrium Calculation*

With the "initial" concentrations known, construct a table summarizing the equilibrium concentrations.

Equilibrium	$HC_3H_5O_3 + H_2O \rightleftharpoons$	$H_3O^+ +$	$C_3H_5O_3^-$
Initial (M)	0.0250	0	0.0250
Change (M)	$-x$	$+x$	$+x$
Equilibrium (M)	$(0.0250 - x)$	x	$(0.0250 + x)$

Substituting the concentrations into the equilibrium expression, we have

$$K_a \text{ (lactic acid)} = 1.4 \times 10^{-4} = \frac{[H_3O^+][C_3H_5O_2^-]}{[HC_3H_5O_2]} = \frac{(x)(0.0250 + x)}{0.0250 - x}$$

Making the assumption that x is small with respect to 0.0250 M, we see that

$$x = [H_3O^+] = K_a = 1.4 \times 10^{-4} \text{ M}$$

which gives a pH of 3.85.

Comment There are two final points to be made:

- Our assumption that $x \ll 0.0250$ is valid.
- The pH of a solution containing only 0.100 M lactic acid solution is 2.43. Adding a base (lactate ion) increases the pH.

EXERCISE 18.1 Common Ion Effect

Assume you have a 0.30 M solution of formic acid (HCO_2H) and have added enough sodium formate ($NaHCO_2$) to make the solution 0.10 M in the salt. Calculate the pH of the formic acid solution before and after adding solid sodium formate.

EXERCISE 18.2 Mixing an Acid and a Base

What is the pH of the solution that results from adding 30.0 mL of 0.100 M NaOH to 45.0 mL of 0.100 M acetic acid?

Module 23

18.2 Controlling pH: Buffer Solutions

The normal pH of human blood is 7.4. However, the addition of a small quantity of strong acid or base, say 0.010 mol, to a liter of blood leads to a change in pH of only about 0.1 pH units. In comparison, if you add 0.010 mol of HCl to 1.0 L of pure water, the pH drops from 7 to 2. Addition of 0.010 mol of NaOH to pure water increases the pH from 7 to 12. Blood, and many other body fluids, are said to be buffered. A **buffer** causes solutions to be resistant to a change in pH when a strong acid or base is added (Figure 18.2).

There are two requirements for a buffer:

- Two substances are needed: an acid capable of reacting with added OH^- ions and a base that can consume added H_3O^+ ions.
- The acid and base must not react with each another.

These requirements mean a buffer is usually prepared from a conjugate acid–base pair: (1) a weak acid and its conjugate base (acetic and acetate ion, for example), or (2) a weak base and its conjugate acid (ammonia and ammonium ion, for example). Some buffers commonly used in the laboratory are given in Table 18.1.

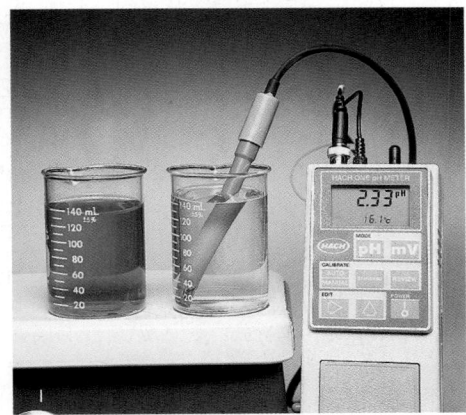

Before	After adding 0.10 M HCl

Buffered Not buffered

(a) The pH electrode is indicating the pH of water that contains a trace of acid (and bromphenol blue acid–base indicator). The solution at the left is a buffer solution with a pH of about 7. (It also contains bromphenol blue dye.)

(b) When 5 mL of 0.10 M HCl is added to each solution, the pH of the water drops several units, whereas the pH of the buffer stays constant, as implied by the fact that the indicator color did not change.

Active Figure 18.2
Buffer solutions.

Chemistry⚛Now™ Sign in at www.cengage.com/login and go to the Chapter Contents menu to explore an interactive version of this figure accompanied by an exercise.

To see how a buffer works, let us consider an acetic acid/acetate ion buffer. Acetic acid, a weak acid, is needed to consume any added hydroxide ions.

$$CH_3CO_2H(aq) + OH^-(aq) \rightleftharpoons CH_3CO_2^-(aq) + H_2O(\ell) \qquad K = 1.8 \times 10^9$$

The equilibrium constant for the reaction is very large because OH^- is a much stronger base than acetate ion, $CH_3CO_2^-$ (see Section 17.6 and Table 17.3). This means that any OH^- entering the solution from an outside source is consumed completely. In a similar way, any hydronium ion added to the solution reacts with the acetate ion present in the buffer.

$$H_3O^+(aq) + CH_3CO_2^-(aq) \rightleftharpoons H_2O(\ell) + CH_3CO_2H(aq) \qquad K = 5.6 \times 10^4$$

The equilibrium constant for this reaction is also quite large because H_3O^+ is a much stronger acid than CH_3CO_2H.

The next several examples illustrate how to calculate the pH of a buffer solution, how to prepare a buffer, and how a buffer can control the pH of a solution.

■ **Buffers and the Common Ion Effect** The common ion effect is observed for an acid (or base) ionizing in the presence of its conjugate base (or acid). A buffer is a solution of an acid, for example, and its conjugate base.

Chemistry⚛Now™

Sign in at **www.cengage.com/login** and go to Chapter 18 Contents to see:
• Screen 18.3 for a simulation and tutorials on **buffer solutions**
• Screen 18.4 for a simulation and tutorials on **pH of buffer solutions**

TABLE 18.1 Some Commonly Used Buffer Systems

Weak Acid	Conjugate Base	Acid K_a (pK_a)	Useful pH Range
Phthalic acid, $C_6H_4(CO_2H)_2$	Hydrogen phthalate ion, $C_6H_4(CO_2H)(CO_2)^-$	1.3×10^{-3} (2.89)	1.9–3.9
Acetic acid, CH_3CO_2H	Acetate ion, $CH_3CO_2^-$	1.8×10^{-5} (4.74)	3.7–5.8
Dihydrogen phosphate ion, $H_2PO_4^-$	Hydrogen phosphate ion, HPO_4^{2-}	6.2×10^{-8} (7.21)	6.2–8.2
Hydrogen phosphate ion, HPO_4^{2-}	Phosphate ion, PO_4^{3-}	3.6×10^{-13} (12.44)	11.3–13.3

Problem What is the pH of an acetic acid/sodium acetate buffer with $[CH_3CO_2H] = 0.700$ M and $[CH_3CO_2^-] = 0.600$ M?

Strategy The concentrations of the weak acid, its conjugate base, and K_a are all known, so we can use the usual equilibrium expression to calculate the hydronium ion concentration.

Solution Write a balanced equation for the ionization of acetic acid and set up an ICE table.

Equilibrium	$CH_3CO_2H + H_2O \rightleftharpoons$	H_3O^+	$+$	$CH_3CO_2^-$
Initial (M)	0.700	0		0.600
Change (M)	$-x$	$+x$		$+x$
Equilibrium (M)	$0.700 - x$	x		$0.600 + x$

The appropriate equilibrium constant expression is

$$K_a = 1.8 \times 10^{-5} = \frac{[H_3O^+][CH_3CO_2^-]}{[CH_3CO_2H]} = \frac{(x)(0.600 + x)}{0.700 - x}$$

As explained on page 814, the value of x will be very small with respect to 0.700 or 0.600, so we can use the "approximate expression" to find x, the hydronium ion concentration.

$$K_a = 1.8 \times 10^{-5} = \frac{[H_3O^+][CH_3CO_2^-]}{[CH_3CO_2H]} = \frac{(x)(0.600)}{0.700}$$

$$x = 2.1 \times 10^{-5} \text{ M}$$

$$pH = -\log (2.1 \times 10^{-5}) = \boxed{4.68}$$

Comment The pH of the buffer has a value between the pH of 0.700 M acetic acid (2.45) and 0.600 M sodium acetate (9.26).

EXERCISE 18.3 pH of a Buffer Solution

What is the pH of a buffer solution composed of 0.50 M formic acid (HCO_2H) and 0.70 M sodium formate ($NaHCO_2$)?

General Expressions for Buffer Solutions

In Example 18.2, we found the hydronium ion concentration of the acetic acid/acetate ion buffer solution by solving for x in the equation

$$K_a = 1.8 \times 10^{-5} = \frac{[H_3O^+][CH_3CO_2^-]}{[CH_3CO_2H]} = \frac{(x)(0.600)}{0.700}$$

If this equation is rearranged, we have a very useful equation that can help you better understand how a buffer works.

$$[H_3O^+] = \frac{[CH_3CO_2H]}{[CH_3CO_2^-]} \times K_a$$

That is, the hydrogen ion concentration in the acetic acid/acetate ion buffer is given by the ratio of the acid and conjugate base concentrations times the acid ionization constant. Indeed, this is true for all solutions of *a weak acid and its conjugate base.*

■ **Buffer Solutions** You will find it generally useful to consider all buffer solutions as composed of a weak acid and its conjugate base. Suppose, for example, a buffer is composed of the weak base ammonia and its conjugate acid ammonium ion. The hydronium ion concentration can be found from Equation 18.1 by assuming the buffer is composed of the weak acid NH_4^+ and its conjugate base, NH_3.

$$[H_3O^+] = \frac{[\text{acid}]}{[\text{conjugate base}]} \times K_a \qquad \text{(18.1)}$$

It is often convenient to use Equation 18.1 in a different form. If we take the negative logarithm of each side of the equation, we have

$$-\log[H_3O^+] = \left\{ -\log \frac{[\text{acid}]}{[\text{conjugate base}]} \right\} + (-\log K_a)$$

You know that $-\log[H_3O^+]$ is defined as pH, and $-\log K_a$ is defined as pK_a (◄ Sections 17.3 and 17.4). Furthermore, because

$$-\log\frac{[\text{acid}]}{[\text{conjugate base}]} = +\log\frac{[\text{conjugate base}]}{[\text{acid}]}$$

the preceding equation can be rewritten as

$$pH = pK_a + \log\frac{[\text{conjugate base}]}{[\text{acid}]} \qquad \textbf{(18.2)}$$

This equation is known as the **Henderson–Hasselbalch equation.**

Both Equations 18.1 and 18.2 show that the pH of a buffer solution is controlled by two factors: the strength of the acid (as expressed by K_a or pK_a) and the relative amounts of acid and conjugate base. The solution pH is established primarily by the value of K_a or pK_a, and the pH is fine-tuned by adjusting the acid-to-conjugate base ratio.

When the concentrations of conjugate base and acid are the same in a solution, the ratio [conjugate base]/[acid] is 1. The log of 1 is zero, so $pH = pK_a$ under these circumstances. If there is more of the conjugate base in the solution than acid, for example, then $pH > pK_a$. Conversely, if there is more acid than conjugate base in solution, then $pH < pK_a$.

■ **The Henderson–Hasselbalch Equation** Many handbooks of chemistry list acid ionization constants in terms of pK_a values, so the approximate pH values of possible buffer solutions are readily apparent.

Chemistry ⚛ Now™

Sign in at **www.cengage.com/login** and go to Chapter 18 Contents to see Screen 18.4 for a simulation and tutorial on **the Henderson–Hasselbalch equation.**

EXAMPLE 18.3 Using the Henderson–Hasselbalch Equation

Problem Benzoic acid ($C_6H_5CO_2H$, 2.00 g) and sodium benzoate ($NaC_6H_5CO_2$, 2.00 g) are dissolved in enough water to make 1.00 L of solution. Calculate the pH of the solution using the Henderson–Hasselbalch equation.

Strategy The Henderson–Hasselbalch equation requires the pK_a of the acid, and this is obtained from the K_a for the acid (see Table 17.3 or Appendix H). You will also need the acid and conjugate base concentrations.

Solution K_a for benzoic acid as 6.3×10^{-5}. Therefore,

$$pK_a = -\log(6.3 \times 10^{-5}) = 4.20$$

Next, we need the concentrations of the acid (benzoic acid) and its conjugate base (benzoate ion).

$$2.00 \text{ g benzoic acid} \left(\frac{1 \text{ mol}}{122.1 \text{ g}}\right) = 0.0164 \text{ mol benzoic acid}$$

$$2.00 \text{ g sodium benzoate} \left(\frac{1 \text{ mol}}{144.1 \text{ g}}\right) = 0.0139 \text{ mol sodium benzoate}$$

Because the solution volume is 1.00 L, the concentrations are [benzoic acid] = 0.0164 M and [sodium benzoate] = 0.0139 M. Therefore, using Equation 18.2, we have

$$pH = 4.20 + \log\frac{0.0139}{0.0164} = 4.20 + \log(0.848) = \boxed{4.13}$$

Comment Notice that the pH is less than the pK_a because the concentration of acid is greater than the concentration of the conjugate base (the ratio of conjugate base to acid concentration is less than 1).

EXERCISE 18.4 Using the Henderson–Hasselbalch Equation

Use the Henderson–Hasselbalch equation to calculate the pH of 1.00 L of a buffer solution containing 15.0 g of $NaHCO_3$ and 18.0 g of Na_2CO_3. (Consider this buffer as a solution of the weak acid HCO_3^- with CO_3^{2-} as its conjugate base.)

Preparing Buffer Solutions

To be useful, a buffer solution must have two characteristics:

- *pH Control:* It should control the pH at the desired value. The Henderson–Hasselbalch equation shows us how this can be done.

$$pH = pK_a + \log \frac{[\text{conjugate base}]}{[\text{acid}]}$$

First, an acid is chosen whose pK_a (or K_a) is near the intended value of pH (or $[H_3O^+]$). Second, the exact value of pH (or $[H_3O^+]$) is then achieved by adjusting the acid-to-conjugate base ratio. (Example 18.4 illustrates this approach.)

- *Buffer capacity:* The buffer should have the ability to keep the pH approximately constant after the addition of reasonable amounts of acid and base. For example, the concentration of acetic acid in an acetic acid/acetate ion buffer must be sufficient to consume all the hydroxide ion that may be added and still control the pH (see Example 18.4). Buffers are usually prepared as 0.10 M to 1.0 M solutions of reagents. However, any buffer will lose its capacity if too much strong acid or base is added.

Chemistry⚛Now™

Sign in at **www.cengage.com/login** and go to Chapter 18 Contents to see Screen 18.5 for a simulation and tutorials on **preparing buffer solutions.**

■ **EXAMPLE 18.4 Preparing a Buffer Solution**

Problem You wish to prepare 1.0 L of a buffer solution with a pH of 4.30. A list of possible acids (and their conjugate bases) follows:

Acid	Conjugate Base	K_a	pK_a
HSO_4^-	SO_4^{2-}	1.2×10^{-2}	1.92
CH_3CO_2H	$CH_3CO_2^-$	1.8×10^{-5}	4.75
HCO_3^-	CO_3^{2-}	4.8×10^{-11}	10.32

Which combination should be selected, and what should the ratio of acid to conjugate base be?

Strategy Use either the general equation for a buffer (Equation 18.1) or the Henderson–Hasselbalch equation (Equation 18.2). Equation 18.1 informs you that $[H_3O^+]$ should be close to the acid K_a value, and Equation 18.2 tells you that pH should be close to the acid pK_a value. This will establish which acid you will use.

Having decided which acid to use, convert pH to $[H_3O^+]$ to use Equation 18.1. If you use Equation 18.2, use the pK_a value in the table. Finally, calculate the ratio of acid to conjugate base.

Solution The hydronium ion concentration for the buffer is found from the targeted pH.

$$pH = 4.30, \text{ so } [H_3O^+] = 10^{-pH} = 10^{-4.30} = 5.0 \times 10^{-5} \text{ M}$$

Of the acids given, only acetic acid (CH_3CO_2H) has a K_a value close to that of the desired $[H_3O^+]$ (or a pK_a close to a pH of 4.30). Now you need only to adjust the ratio $[CH_3CO_2H]/[CH_3CO_2^-]$ to achieve the desired hydronium ion concentration.

$$[H_3O^+] = 5.0 \times 10^{-5} \text{ M} = \frac{[CH_3CO_2H]}{[CH_3CO_2^-]}(1.8 \times 10^{-5})$$

Rearrange this equation to find the ratio $[CH_3CO_2H]/[CH_3CO_2^-]$.

$$\frac{[CH_3CO_2H]}{[CH_3CO_2^-]} = \frac{K_a}{[H_3O^+]} = \frac{5.0 \times 10^{-5}}{1.8 \times 10^{-5}} = \frac{2.8 \text{ mol/L}}{1.0 \text{ mol/L}}$$

Therefore, if you add 0.28 mol of acetic acid and 0.10 mol of sodium acetate (or any other pair of molar quantities in the ratio 2.8/1) to enough water to make 1.0 L of solution, the buffer solution will have a pH of 4.30.

Comment If you prefer to use the Henderson–Hasselbalch equation, you would have

$$pH = 4.30 = 4.74 + \log\frac{[CH_3CO_2^-]}{[CH_3CO_2H]}$$

$$\log\frac{[CH_3CO_2^-]}{[CH_3CO_2H]} = 4.30 - 4.74 = -0.44$$

$$\frac{[CH_3CO_2^-]}{[CH_3CO_2H]} = 10^{-0.44} = 0.36$$

The ratio of conjugate base to acid, $[CH_3CO_2^-]/[CH_3CO_2H]$, is 0.36. The reciprocal of this ratio $\{= [CH_3CO_2H]/[CH_3CO_2^-] = 1/0.36)\}$ is 2.8/1. This is the same result obtained previously using Equation 18.1.

EXERCISE 18.5 Preparing a Buffer Solution

Using an acetic acid/sodium acetate buffer solution, what ratio of acid to conjugate base will you need to maintain the pH at 5.00? Describe how you would make up such a solution.

Example 18.4 illustrates several important points concerning buffer solutions. The hydronium ion concentration depends not only on the K_a value of the acid but also on the ratio of acid and conjugate base concentrations. However, even though we write these ratios in terms of reagent concentrations, it is *the relative number of moles of acid and conjugate base that is important in determining the pH of a buffer solution.* Because both reagents are dissolved in the same solution, their concentrations depend on the same solution volume. In Example 18.4, the ratio 2.8/1 for acetic acid and sodium acetate implies that 2.8 times as many moles of acid were dissolved per liter as moles of sodium acetate.

$$\frac{[CH_3CO_2H]}{[CH_3CO_2^-]} = \frac{2.8 \text{ mol } CH_3CO_2H/L}{1.0 \text{ mol } CH_3CO_2^-/L} = \frac{2.8 \text{ mol } CH_3CO_2H}{1.0 \text{ mol } CH_3CO_2^-}$$

Notice that on dividing one concentration by the other, the volumes "cancel." This means that we only need to ensure that the ratio of moles of acid to moles of conjugate base is 2.8 to 1 in this example. The acid and its conjugate base could have been dissolved in any reasonable amount of water. This also means that *diluting a buffer solution will not change its pH.* Commercially available buffer solutions are often sold as premixed, dry ingredients. To use them, you only need to mix the ingredients in some volume of pure water (Figure 18.3).

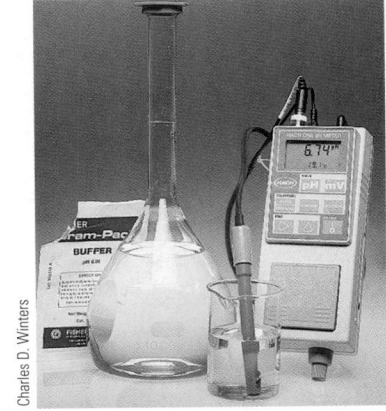

FIGURE 18.3 A commercial buffer solution. The solid acid and conjugate base in the packet are mixed with water to give a solution with the indicated pH. The quantity of water used does not matter because the ratio [acid]/[conjugate base] does not depend on the solution volume. (However, if too much water is added, the acid and conjugate base concentrations will be too low, and the buffer capacity could be exceeded. Again, buffer solutions usually have solute concentrations around 0.1 M to 1.0 M.)

Buffer Solutions

The following is a summary of important aspects of buffer solutions.

- A buffer resists changes in pH on adding small quantities of strong acid or base.
- A buffer contains a weak acid and its conjugate base.
- The hydronium ion concentration of a buffer solution can be calculated from Equation 18.1,

$$[H_3O^+] = \frac{[acid]}{[conjugate\ base]} \times K_a$$

or the pH can be calculated from the Henderson–Hasselbalch equation (Equation 18.2).

$$pH = pK_a + \log \frac{[conjugate\ base]}{[acid]}$$

- The pH depends primarily on the K_a of the weak acid and secondarily on the relative amounts of acid and conjugate base.
- The function of the weak acid of a buffer is to consume added base, and the conjugate base consumes added acid. Such reactions affect the relative quantities of weak acid and its conjugate base. Because this ratio of acid to its conjugate base has only a secondary effect on the pH, the pH can be maintained relatively constant.
- The buffer must have sufficient capacity to react with reasonable quantities of added acid or base.

How Does a Buffer Maintain pH?

Now let us explore quantitatively how a given buffer solution can maintain the pH of a solution on adding a small amount of strong acid.

Chemistry ☉ Now™

Sign in at **www.cengage.com/login** and go to Chapter 18 Contents to see Screen 18.6 for a tutorial on **adding reagents to a buffer solution**.

■ EXAMPLE 18.5 How Does a Buffer Maintain a Constant pH?

Problem What is the change in pH when 1.00 mL of 1.00 M HCl is added to (1) 1.000 L of pure water and to (2) 1.000 L of acetic acid/sodium acetate buffer with $[CH_3CO_2H] = 0.700$ M and $[CH_3CO_2^-] = 0.600$ M? (See Example 18.2, where the pH of this acetic acid/acetate ion buffer was found to be 4.68.)

Strategy HCl is a strong acid and therefore ionizes completely to supply H_3O^+ ions. Part 1 involves two steps: (a) Find the H_3O^+ concentration when diluting 1.00 mL of acid to 1.00 L. (b) Convert the value of $[H_3O^+]$ for the dilute solution to pH.

Part 2 involves three steps: (a) A stoichiometry calculation to find how the concentrations of acid and conjugate base change on adding H_3O^+. (b) An equilibrium calculation to find $[H_3O^+]$ for a buffer solution where the concentrations of CH_3CO_2H and $CH_3CO_2^-$ are slightly altered owing to the reaction of $CH_3CO_2^-$ with added H_3O^+. (c) Conversion of $[H_3O^+]$ to pH.

Solution

Part 1: *Adding Acid to Pure Water*

1.00 mL of 1.00 M HCl represents 0.00100 mol of acid. If this is added to 1.000 L of pure water, the H_3O^+ concentration of the water changes from 10^{-7} to 10^{-3},

$$c_1 \times V_1 = c_2 \times V_2$$

$$(1.00\ M)(0.00100\ L) = c_2 \times (1.001\ L)$$

$$c_2 = [H_3O^+] \text{ in diluted solution} = 1.00 \times 10^{-3}\ M$$

and so the pH falls from 7.00 to 3.00.

Part 2: *Adding Acid to an Acetic Acid/Acetate Buffer Solution*

HCl is a strong acid that is 100% ionized in water and supplies H_3O^+, which reacts completely with the base (acetate ion) in the buffer solution according to the following equation:

$$H_3O^+(aq) + CH_3CO_2^-(aq) \rightleftharpoons H_2O(\ell) + CH_3CO_2H(aq)$$

	[H₃O⁺] from Added HCl	[CH₃CO₂⁻] from Buffer	[CH₃CO₂H] from Buffer
Initial amount of acid or base (mol = $c \times V$)	0.00100	0.600	0.700
Change (mol)	−0.00100	−0.00100	+0.00100
Equilibrium (mol)	0	0.599	0.700
Concentrations after reaction (c = mol/V)	0	0.598	0.700

Because the added HCl reacts completely with acetate ion to produce acetic acid, the solution after this reaction (with $V = 1.001$ L) is once again a buffer containing only the weak acid and its salt. Now we only need to use Equation 18.1 (or the Henderson–Hasselbalch equation) to find [H₃O⁺] and the pH in the buffer solution as in Examples 18.2 and 18.3.

Equilibrium	CH_3CO_2H + H_2O ⇌	H_3O^+ +	$CH_3CO_2^-$
Initial (M)	0.700	0	0.598
Change (M)	−x	+x	+x
Equilibrium (M)	0.700 − x	x	0.598 + x

As usual, we make the approximation that x, the amount of H₃O⁺ formed by ionizing acetic acid in the presence of acetate ion, is very small compared with 0.700 M or 0.598 M. Using Equation 18.1, we calculate a pH of 4.68.

$$[H_3O^+] = x = \frac{[CH_3CO_2H]}{[CH_3CO_2^-]} \times K_a = \left(\frac{0.700 \text{ mol}}{0.598 \text{ mol}}\right)(1.8 \times 10^{-5}) = 2.1 \times 10^{-5} \text{ M}$$

$-\log(2.1 \times 10^{-5})$

$$\boxed{pH = 4.68}$$

Comment Within the number of significant figures allowed, the pH of the buffer solution does not change after adding HCl. The buffer solution contains the conjugate base of the weak acid, and the base consumed the added HCl. In contrast, pH changed by 4 units when 1 mL of 1.0 M HCl was added to 1.0 L of pure water.

EXERCISE 18.6 Buffer Solutions

Calculate the pH of 0.500 L of a buffer solution composed of 0.50 M formic acid (HCO₂H) and 0.70 M sodium formate (NaHCO₂) before and after adding 10.0 mL of 1.0 M HCl.

18.3 Acid–Base Titrations

A titration is one of the most important ways of determining accurately the quantity of an acid, a base, or some other substance in a mixture or of ascertaining the purity of a substance. You learned how to perform the stoichiometry calculations involved in titrations in Chapter 4 (◄ Section 4.7). In Chapter 17, we described the following important points regarding acid–base reactions (◄ Section 17.6):

- The pH at the equivalence point of a strong acid–strong base titration is 7. The solution at the equivalence point is truly "neutral" *only* when a strong acid is titrated with a strong base and vice versa.
- If the substance being titrated is a weak acid or base, then the pH at the equivalence point is not 7 (see Table 17.5).
  - (a) A weak acid titrated with strong base leads to pH > 7 at the equivalence point due to the conjugate base of the weak acid.
  - (b) A weak base titrated with strong acid leads to pH < 7 at the equivalence point due to the conjugate acid of the weak base.

A knowledge of buffer solutions and how they work will now allow us to more fully understand how the pH changes in the course of an acid–base reaction.

■ **Equivalence Point** The equivalence point for a reaction is the point at which one reactant has been completely consumed by addition of another reactant. See page 185.

■ **Weak Acid–Weak Base Titrations** Titrations combining a weak acid and weak base are generally not done because the equivalence point often cannot be accurately judged.

Maintenance of pH is vital to the cells of all living organisms because enzyme activity is influenced by pH. The primary protection against harmful pH changes in cells is provided by buffer systems. The intracellular pH of most cells is maintained in a range between 6.9 and 7.4. Two important biological buffer systems control pH in this range: the bicarbonate/carbonic acid system (HCO_3^-/H_2CO_3) and the phosphate system ($HPO_4^{2-}/H_2PO_4^-$).

The bicarbonate/carbonic acid buffer is important in blood plasma. Three equilibria are important here.

$$CO_2(g) \rightleftharpoons CO_2(dissolved)$$

$$CO_2(dissolved) + H_2O(\ell) \rightleftharpoons H_2CO_3(aq)$$

$$H_2CO_3(aq) + H_2O(\ell) \rightleftharpoons$$
$$H_3O^+(aq) + HCO_3^-(aq)$$

The overall equilibrium constant for the second and third steps is $pK_{overall} = 6.3$ at 37 °C, the temperature of the human body. Thus,

$$7.4 = 6.3 + \log \frac{[HCO_3^-]}{[CO_2(dissolved)]}$$

Although the value of $pK_{overall}$ is about 1 pH unit away from the blood pH, the natural partial pressure of CO_2 in the alveoli of the lungs (about 40 mm Hg) is sufficient to keep [CO_2(dissolved)] at about 1.2×10^{-3} M and [HCO_3^-] at about 1.5×10^{-2} M.

If blood pH rises above about 7.45, you can suffer from a condition called *alkalosis*. *Respiratory alkalosis* can arise from hyperventilation when a person breathes quickly to expel CO_2 from the lungs. This has the effect of lowering the CO_2 concentration, which in turn leads to a lower H_3O^+ concentration and a higher pH. This same condition can also arise from severe anxiety or from an oxygen defi-

Alkalosis. If blood pH is too high, alkalosis results. Respiratory alkalosis can be reversed by breathing into a bag, an action that recycles exhaled CO_2. This affects the carbonic acid buffer system in the body, raising the blood hydronium ion concentration. The blood pH drops back to a more normal level of 7.4.

ciency at high altitude. It can ultimately lead to overexcitability of the central nervous system, muscle spasms, convulsions, and death. One way to treat acute respiratory alkalosis is to breathe into a paper bag. The CO_2 you exhale is recycled. This raises the blood CO_2 level and causes the equilibria above to shift to the right, thus raising the hydronium ion concentration and lowering the pH.

Metabolic alkalosis can occur if you take large amounts of sodium bicarbonate to treat stomach acid (which is mostly HCl at a pH of about 4). It also commonly occurs when a person vomits profusely. This depletes the body of hydrogen ions, which leads to an increase in bicarbonate ion concentration.

Athletes can use the H_2CO_3/HCO_3^- equilibrium to enhance their performance. Strenuous activity produces high levels of lactic acid, and this can lower blood pH and cause muscle cramps. To counteract this, athletes will prepare before the race by hyperventilating for

some seconds to raise blood pH, thereby helping to neutralize the acidity from the lactic acid.

Acidosis is the opposite of alkalosis. A toddler who came to the hospital with viral gastroenteritis had *metabolic acidosis*. He had severe diarrhea, was dehydrated, and had a high rate of respiration. One function of the bicarbonate ion is to neutralize stomach acid in the intestines. However, because of his diarrhea, the toddler was losing bicarbonate ions in his stool, and his blood pH was too low. To compensate, the toddler was breathing rapidly and blowing off CO_2 through the lungs (the effect of which is to lower [H_3O^+] and raise the pH).

Respiratory acidosis results from a buildup of CO_2 in the body. This can be caused by pulmonary problems, by head injuries, or by drugs such as anesthetics and sedatives. It can be reversed by breathing rapidly and deeply. Doubling the breathing rate increases the blood pH by about 0.23 units.

Questions:

Phosphate ions are abundant in cells, both as the ions themselves and as important substituents on organic molecules. Most importantly, the pK_a for the $H_2PO_4^-$ ion is 7.20, which is very close to the high end of the normal pH range in the body.

$$H_2PO_4^-(aq) + H_2O(\ell) \rightleftharpoons$$
$$H_3O^+(aq) + HPO_4^{2-}(aq)$$

1. *What should the ratio $[HPO_4^{2-}]/[H_2PO_4^-]$ be to control the pH at 7.4?*
2. *A typical total phosphate concentration in a cell, $[HPO_4^{2-}] + [H_2PO_4^-]$, is 2.0×10^{-2} M. What are the concentrations of HPO_4^{2-} and $H_2PO_4^-$?*

Answers to these questions are in Appendix Q.

Titration of a Strong Acid with a Strong Base

Figure 18.4 illustrates what happens to the pH as 0.100 M NaOH is slowly added to 50.0 mL of 0.100 M HCl.

$$HCl(aq) + NaOH(aq) \rightarrow NaCl(aq) + H_2O(\ell)$$

Net ionic equation: $H_3O^+(aq) + OH^-(aq) \rightarrow 2\,H_2O(\ell)$

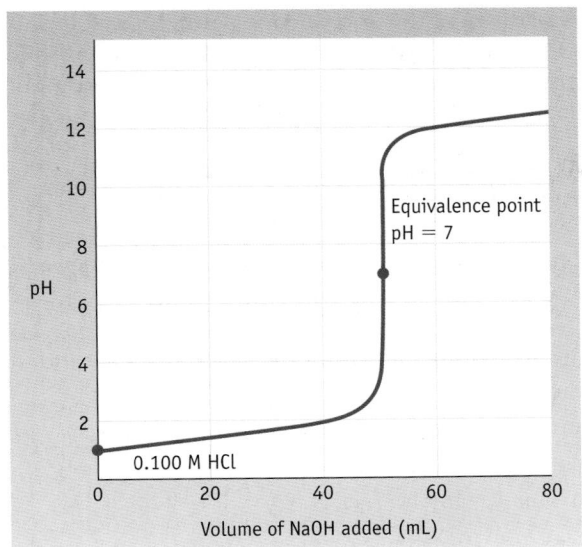

A strong acid is titrated with a strong base.

50.0 mL of 0.100 M HCl titrated
with 0.100 M NaOH

Volume of base added	pH
0.0	1.00
10.0	1.18
20.0	1.37
40.0	1.95
45.0	2.28
48.0	2.69
49.0	3.00
50.0	7.00
51.0	11.00
55.0	11.68
60.0	11.96
80.0	12.36
100.0	12.52
very large amount	13.00 (maximum)

Let us focus on four regions on this plot.

- pH of the initial solution
- pH as NaOH is added to the HCl solution before the equivalence point
- pH at the equivalence point
- pH after the equivalence point

Before beginning the titration, the 0.100 M solution of HCl has a pH of 1.00. As NaOH is added to the acid solution, the amount of HCl declines, and the acid remaining is dissolved in an ever-increasing volume of solution. Thus, $[H_3O^+]$ decreases, and the pH slowly increases. As an example, let us find the pH of the solution after 10.0 mL of 0.100 M NaOH has been added to 50.0 mL of 0.100 M HCl. Here, we set up a table to list the amounts of acid and base before reaction, the changes in those amounts, and the amounts remaining after reaction. Be sure to notice that the volume of the solution after reaction is the sum of the combined volumes of NaOH and HCl (60.0 mL or 0.0600 L in this case).

	$H_3O^+(aq)$	+	$OH^-(aq)$	$\rightarrow$	$2\ H_2O(\ell)$
Initial amount (mol = $c \times V$)	0.00500		0.00100		
Change (mol)	−0.00100		−0.00100		
After reaction (mol)	0.00400		0		
After reaction (c = mol/V)	0.00400 mol/0.0600 L = 0.0667 M		0		

After addition of 10.0 mL of NaOH, the final solution has a hydronium ion concentration of 0.0667 M, and so the pH is

$$pH = -\log[H_3O^+] = -\log(0.0667) = 1.176$$

After 49.5 mL of base has been added—that is, just before the equivalence point—we can use the same approach to show that the pH is 3.3. The solution being titrated is still quite acidic, even very close to the equivalence point.

The pH of the equivalence point in an acid–base titration is taken as the midpoint in the vertical portion of the pH versus volume of titrant curve. (The **titrant** is the substance being added during the titration.) In the HCl/NaOH titration illustrated in Figure 18.4, you see that the pH increases very rapidly near the equivalence point. In fact, in this case the pH rises 7 units (the H_3O^+ concentration increases by a factor of 10 million!) when only a drop or two of the NaOH solution is added, and the midpoint of the vertical portion of the curve is a pH of 7.00.

> The pH of the solution at the equivalence point in a strong acid–strong base reaction is always 7.00 (at 25 °C) because the solution contains a neutral salt.

After all of the HCl has been consumed and the slightest excess of NaOH has been added, the solution will be basic, and the pH will continue to increase as more NaOH is added (and the solution volume increases). For example, if we calculate the pH of the solution after 55.0 mL of 0.100 M NaOH has been added to 50.0 mL of 0.100 M HCl, we find

	$H_3O^+(aq)$	+	$OH^-(aq)$	$\rightarrow$	$2 H_2O(\ell)$
Initial amount (mol = $c \times V$)	0.00500		0.00550		
Change (mol)	−0.00500		−0.00500		
After reaction (mol)	0		0.00050		
After reaction (c = mol/V)	0		0.00050 mol/0.1050 L = 0.0048 M		

At this point, the solution has a hydroxide ion concentration of 0.0048 M. Calculate the pOH from this value, then use this to calculate pH.

$$pOH = -\log[OH^-] = -\log(0.0048) = 2.32$$

$$pH = 14.00 - pOH = 11.68$$

EXERCISE 18.7 Titration of a Strong Acid with a Strong Base

What is the pH after 25.0 mL of 0.100 M NaOH has been added to 50.0 mL of 0.100 M HCl? What is the pH after 50.50 mL of NaOH has been added?

Titration of a Weak Acid with a Strong Base

The titration of a weak acid with a strong base is somewhat different from the strong acid–strong base titration. Look carefully at the curve for the titration of 100.0 mL of 0.100 M acetic acid with 0.100 M NaOH (Figure 18.5).

$$CH_3CO_2H(aq) + NaOH(aq) \rightarrow NaCH_3CO_2(aq) + H_2O(\ell)$$

Let us focus on three important points on this curve:

- *The pH before titration begins.* The pH before any base is added can be calculated from the weak acid K_a value and the acid concentration (◀ Example 17.5).
- *The pH at the equivalence point.* At the equivalence point, the solution contains only sodium acetate, the CH_3CO_2H and NaOH having been consumed. The pH is controlled by the acetate ion, the conjugate base of acetic acid (◀ Table 17.5, page 728).
- *The pH at the halfway point (half-equivalence point) of the titration.* Here, the pH is equal to the pK_a of the weak acid, a conclusion that is discussed in more detail below.

As NaOH is added to acetic acid the base is consumed and sodium acetate is produced. Thus, at every point between the beginning of the titration (when only acetic acid is present) and the equivalence point (when only sodium acetate is present), the solution contains both acetic acid and its salt, sodium acetate. These

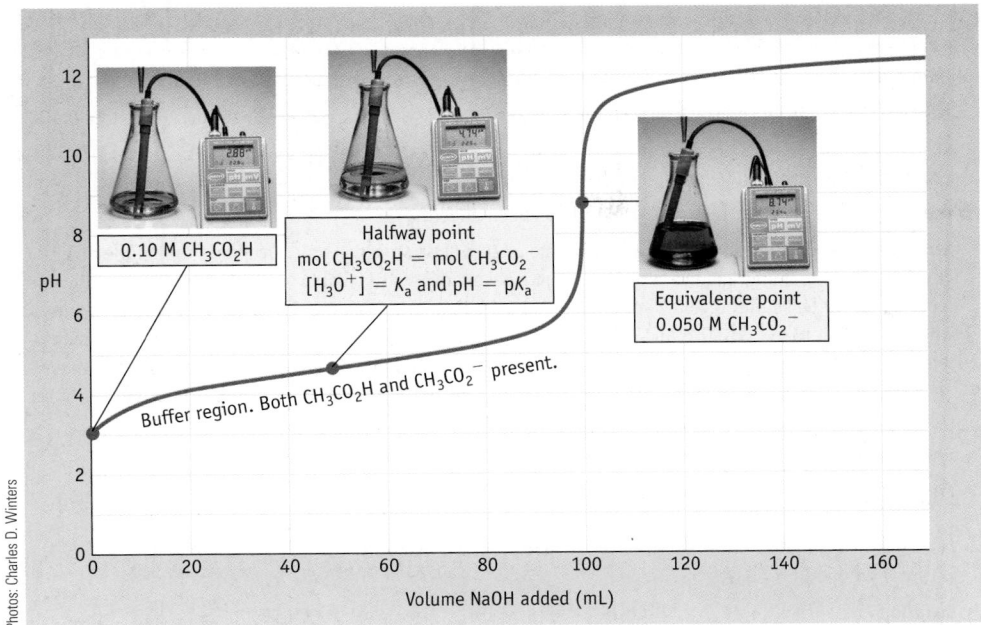

Active Figure 18.5 **The change in pH during the titration of a weak acid with a strong base.** Here, 100.0 mL of 0.100 M acetic acid is titrated with 0.100 M NaOH. Note especially the following: (a) Acetic acid is a weak acid, so the pH of the original solution is 2.87. (b) The pH at the point at which half the acid has reacted with base is equal to the pK_a for the acid ($pH = pK_a = 4.74$). (c) At the equivalence point, the solution contains the acetate ion, a weak base. Therefore, the solution is basic, with a pH of 8.72.

Chemistry.⊙.Now™ Sign in at **www.cengage.com/login** and go to the Chapter Contents menu to explore an interactive version of this figure accompanied by an exercise.

are the components of a *buffer solution*, and the hydronium ion concentration can be calculated from Equation 18.3 or 18.4.

$$[H_3O^+] = \frac{[\text{weak acid remaining}]}{[\text{conjugate base produced}]} \times K_a \qquad \textbf{(18.3)}$$

or

$$pH = pK_a + \log\frac{[\text{conjugate base produced}]}{[\text{weak acid remaining}]} \qquad \textbf{(18.4)}$$

The fact that a buffer is present at any point between the beginning of the titration and the equivalence point is the reason that the pH of the solution only rises slowly after a few milliliters of titrant has been added.

What happens when *exactly* half of the acid has been consumed by base? Half of the acid (CH_3CO_2H) has been converted to the conjugate base ($CH_3CO_2^-$), and half remains. Therefore, the concentration of weak acid remaining is equal to the concentration of conjugate base produced ($[CH_3CO_2H] = [CH_3CO_2^-]$). Using Equations 18.3 or 18.4, we see that

$$[H_3O^+] = (1) \times K_a \qquad \text{or} \qquad pH = pK_a + \log(1)$$

Because $\log(1) = 0$, we come to the following general conclusion:

> At the halfway point in the titration of a weak acid with a strong base
>
> $$[H_3O^+] = K_a \text{ and } pH = pK_a \qquad \textbf{(18.5)}$$

In the particular case of the titration of acetic acid with a strong base, $[H_3O^+] = 1.8 \times 10^{-5}$ M at the halfway point, and so the pH is 4.74. This is equal to the pK_a of acetic acid.

Chemistry.⊙.Now™

Sign in at **www.cengage.com/login** and go to Chapter 18 Contents to see Screen 18.7 for a simulation and tutorial on **titration curves**.

EXAMPLE 18.6 Titration of Acetic Acid with Sodium Hydroxide

Problem Consider the titration of 100.0 mL of 0.100 M acetic acid with 0.100 M NaOH (see Figure 18.5).

(a) What is the pH of the solution when 90.0 mL of 0.100 M NaOH has been added to 100.0 mL of 0.100 M acetic acid?

(b) What is the pH at the equivalence point?

(c) What is the pH after 110.0 mL of NaOH has been added?

Strategy The problem generally involves two major steps: (1) A stoichiometry calculation to find the quantity of acid remaining, if any, and quantity of conjugate base formed after adding NaOH. (2) Before the equivalence point, in the "buffer region," you will do an equilibrium calculation to find $[H_3O^+]$ for a buffer solution where the quantities of CH_3CO_2H and $CH_3CO_2^-$ are known from the first part of the calculation. At the equivalence point, only the conjugate base will remain, so the calculation resembles Example 17.7. After the equivalence point, the solution contains both the conjugate base of the weak acid and excess NaOH, but the latter controls the pH.

Solution

Part a: pH before the equivalence point. Let us first calculate the amounts of reactants before reaction (= concentration × volume) and then use the principles of stoichiometry to calculate the amounts of reactants and products after reaction. The limiting reactant is NaOH, so some CH_3CO_2H remains along with the product, $CH_3CO_2^-$.

Equation	CH_3CO_2H	+	OH^-	$\rightleftharpoons$	$CH_3CO_2^-$	+	H_2O
Initial (mol)	0.0100		0.00900		0		
Change (mol)	−0.00900		−0.00900		+0.00900		
After reaction (mol)	0.0010		0		0.00900		

The ratio of amounts (moles) of acid to conjugate base is the same as the ratio of their concentrations. Therefore, we can use the amounts of weak acid remaining and conjugate base formed to find the pH from Equation 18.3 (where we use amounts and not concentrations).

$$[H_3O^+] = \frac{\text{mol } CH_3CO_2H}{\text{mol } CH_3CO_2^-} \times K_a = \left(\frac{0.0010 \text{ mol}}{0.0090 \text{ mol}}\right)(1.8 \times 10^{-5}) = 2.0 \times 10^{-6} \text{ M}$$

$$pH = -\log(2.0 \times 10^{-6}) = \boxed{5.70}$$

The pH is 5.70, in agreement with Figure 18.5. Notice that this pH is appropriate for a point after the halfway point (4.74) but before the equivalence point (8.72).

Part b: pH at the equivalence point. To reach the equivalence point, 0.0100 mol of NaOH has been added to 0.0100 mol of CH_3CO_2H and 0.0100 mol of $CH_3CO_2^-$ has been formed.

Equation	CH_3CO_2H	+	OH^-	$\rightleftharpoons$	$CH_3CO_2^-$	+	H_2O
Initial (mol)	0.0100		0.0100		0		
Change (mol)	−0.0100		−0.0100		+0.0100		
After reaction (mol)	0		0		0.0100		

Because two solutions, each with a volume of 100.0 mL, have been combined, the concentration of $CH_3CO_2^-$ at the equivalence point is (0.0100 mol/0.200 L) = 0.0050 M. Next, we set up an ICE table for the hydrolysis of this weak base,

Equation	$CH_3CO_2^-$	+	H_2O	$\rightleftharpoons$	CH_3CO_2H	+	OH^-
Initial (M)	0.00500				0		0
Change (M)	−x				+x		+x
After reaction (M)	0.00500 − x				x		x

and calculate the concentration of OH^- ion using K_b for the weak base.

$$K_b \text{ for } CH_3CO_2^- = 5.6 \times 10^{-10} = \frac{[CH_3CO_2H][OH^-]}{[CH_3CO_2^-]} = \frac{(x)(x)}{0.00500 - x}$$

Making the usual assumption that x is small with respect to 0.00500 M,

$$x = [OH^-] = 1.7 \times 10^{-6} \text{ M (pOH} = 5.78)$$

$$pH = 14.00 - 5.78 = 8.22$$

Part c: *pH after the equivalence point.* Now the limiting reactant is the CH_3CO_2H, and the solution contains excess OH^- ion from the unused NaOH as well as from the hydrolysis of $CH_3CO_2^-$.

Equation	CH_3CO_2H	$+$	OH^-	$\rightleftharpoons$	$CH_3CO_2^-$	$+$	H_2O
Initial (mol)	0.0100		0.0110		0		
Change (mol)	-0.0100		-0.0100		$+0.0100$		
After reaction (mol)	0		0.0010		0.0100		

The amount of OH^- produced by $CH_3CO_2^-$ hydrolysis is very small (see part b), so the pH of the solution after the equivalence point is determined by the excess NaOH (in 210 mL of solution).

$$[OH^-] = 0.0010 \text{ mol}/0.210 \text{ L} = 4.8 \times 10^{-3} \text{ M (pOH} = 2.32)$$

$$pH = 14.00 - 2.32 = 11.68$$

EXERCISE 18.8 Titration of a Weak Acid with a Strong Base

The titration of 0.100 acetic acid with 0.100 M NaOH is described in the text. What is the pH of the solution when 35.0 mL of the base has been added to 100.0 mL of 0.100 M acetic acid?

Titration of Weak Polyprotic Acids

The titrations illustrated thus far have been for the reaction of a monoprotic acid (HA) with a base such as NaOH. It is possible to extend the discussion of titrations to polyprotic acids such as oxalic acid, $H_2C_2O_4$.

$$H_2C_2O_4(aq) + H_2O(\ell) \rightleftharpoons HC_2O_4^-(aq) + H_3O^+(aq) \qquad K_{a1} = 5.9 \times 10^{-2}$$

$$HC_2O_4^-(aq) + H_2O(\ell) \rightleftharpoons C_2O_4^-(aq) + H_3O^+(aq) \qquad K_{a2} = 6.4 \times 10^{-5}$$

Figure 18.6 illustrates the curve for the titration of 100 mL of 0.100 M oxalic acid with 0.100 M NaOH. The first significant rise in pH is experienced after 100 mL of base has been added, indicating that the first proton of the acid has been titrated.

$$H_2C_2O_4(aq) + OH^-(aq) \rightleftharpoons HC_2O_4^-(aq) + H_2O(aq)$$

When the second proton of oxalic acid is titrated, the pH again rises significantly.

$$HC_2O_4^-(aq) + OH^-(aq) \rightleftharpoons C_2O_4^{2-}(aq) + H_2O(\ell)$$

The pH at this second equivalence point is controlled by the oxalate ion, $C_2O_4^{2-}$.

$$C_2O_4^{2-}(aq) + H_2O(\ell) \rightleftharpoons HC_2O_4^-(aq) + OH^-(aq)$$

$$K_b = K_w/K_{a2} = 1.6 \times 10^{-10}$$

Calculation of the pH at the equivalence point indicates that it should be about 8.4, as observed.

Chemistry ⚛ Now™

Sign in at **www.cengage.com/login** and go to Chapter 18 Contents to see Screen 18.8 for a simulation on **titration of a weak polyprotic acid.**

FIGURE 18.6 Titration curve for a diprotic acid. The curve for the titration of 100.0 mL of 0.100 M oxalic acid ($H_2C_2O_4$, a weak diprotic acid) with 0.100 M NaOH. The first equivalence point (at 100 mL) occurs when the first hydrogen ion of $H_2C_2O_4$ is titrated, and the second (at 200 mL) occurs at the completion of the reaction. The curve for pH versus volume of NaOH added shows an initial rise at the first equivalence point and then another rise at the second equivalence point.

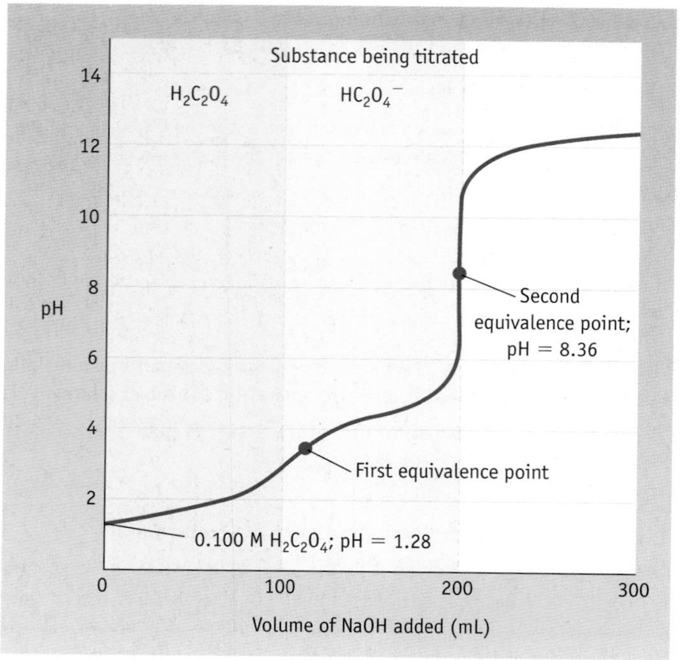

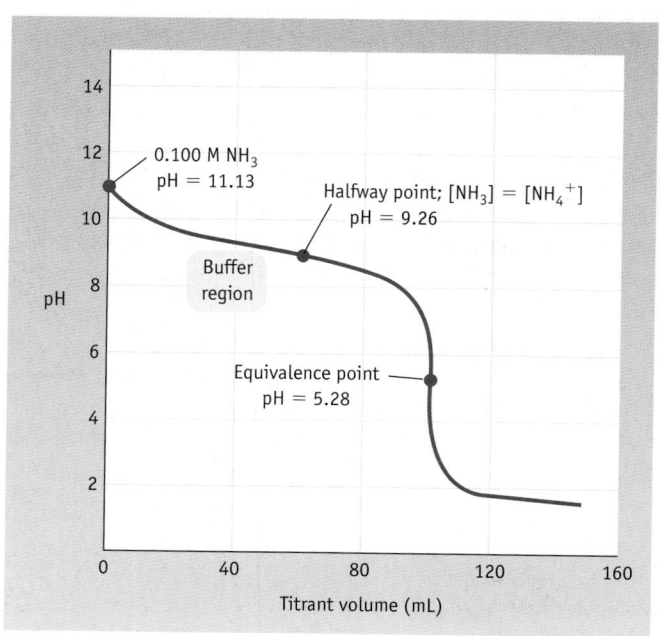

(Figure 18.6 — Substance being titrated: $H_2C_2O_4$, $HC_2O_4^-$. Second equivalence point; pH = 8.36. First equivalence point. 0.100 M $H_2C_2O_4$; pH = 1.28. Axes: pH vs Volume of NaOH added (mL))

Titration of a Weak Base with a Strong Acid

Finally, it is useful to consider the titration of a weak base with a strong acid. Figure 18.7 illustrates the pH curve for the titration of 100.0 mL of 0.100 M NH_3 with 0.100 M HCl.

$$NH_3(aq) + H_3O^+(aq) \rightleftharpoons NH_4^+(aq) + H_2O(\ell)$$

The initial pH for a 0.100 M NH_3 solution is 11.12. As the titration progresses, the important species in solution are the weak acid NH_4^+ and its conjugate base, NH_3.

$$NH_4^+(aq) + H_2O(\ell) \rightleftharpoons NH_3(aq) + H_3O^+(aq) \qquad K_a = 5.6 \times 10^{-10}$$

FIGURE 18.7 Titration of a weak base with a strong acid. The change in pH during the titration of a weak base (100.0 mL of 0.100 M NH_3) with a strong acid (0.100 M HCl). The pH at the half-neutralization point is equal to the pK_a for the conjugate acid (NH_4^+) of the weak base (NH_3) (pH = pK_a = 9.26). At the equivalence point, the solution contains the NH_4^+ ion, a weak acid, so the pH is about 5.

(Figure 18.7 — 0.100 M NH_3 pH = 11.13; Halfway point; $[NH_3] = [NH_4^+]$ pH = 9.26; Buffer region; Equivalence point pH = 5.28. Axes: pH vs Titrant volume (mL))

Calculating the pH at Various Stages of an Acid–Base Reaction

Finding the pH at or before the equivalence point for an acid–base reaction always involves several calculation steps. There are no shortcuts. Consider the *titration of a weak base, B, with a strong acid* as in Example 18.7. (The same principles apply to other acid–base reactions.)

$$H_3O^+(aq) + B(aq) \rightleftharpoons BH^+(aq) + H_2O(\ell)$$

Step 1. *Solve the stoichiometry problem.* Up to the equivalence point, acid is consumed completely to leave a solution containing some base (B) and its conjugate acid (BH$^+$). Use the principles of stoichiometry to calcu-

late (a) the amount of acid added, (b) the amount of base consumed, and (c) the amount of conjugate base (BH$^+$) formed.

Step 2. *Calculate the concentrations of base, [B], and conjugate acid, [BH$^+$].* Recognize that the volume of the solution at any point is the sum of the original volume of base solution plus the volume of acid solution added.

Step 3. *Calculate the pH before the equivalence point.* At any point before the equivalence point, the solution is a buffer solution because both the base and its conjugate acid are present. Calculate [H$_3$O$^+$] using the con-

centrations of Step 2 and the value of K_a for the conjugate acid of the weak base.

Step 4. *Calculate the pH at the equivalence point.* Calculate the concentration of the conjugate acid using the procedure of Steps 1 and 2. Use the value of K_a for the conjugate acid of the weak base and the procedure outlined in Example 18.7 (or in Example 18.6 for a weak acid). (For a titration of a weak acid with a strong base, use the value of K_b for the conjugate base of the acid and follow the procedure outlined in Example 18.6.)

At the halfway point, the concentrations of NH$_4^+$ and NH$_3$ are the same, so

$$[H_3O^+] = \frac{[NH_4^+]}{[NH_3]} \times K_a = 5.6 \times 10^{-10}$$

$$[H_3O^+] = K_a$$

$$pH = pK_a = -\log(5.6 \times 10^{-10}) = 9.25$$

As the addition of HCl to NH$_3$ continues, the pH declines slowly because of the buffering action of the NH$_3$/NH$_4^+$ combination. Near the equivalence point, however, the pH drops rapidly. At the equivalence point, the solution contains only ammonium chloride, a weak Brønsted acid, and the solution is weakly acidic.

Chemistry ⦿ Now™

Sign in at **www.cengage.com/login** and go to Chapter 18 Contents to see Screen 18.9 for a simulation on titration of a weak base with a strong acid.

EXAMPLE 18.7 Titration of Ammonia with HCl

Problem What is the pH of the solution at the equivalence point in the titration of 100.0 mL of 0.100 M ammonia with 0.100 M HCl (see Figure 18.7)?

Strategy This problem has two steps: (a) A stoichiometry calculation to find the concentration of NH$_4^+$ at the equivalence point. (b) An equilibrium calculation to find [H$_3$O$^+$] for a solution of the weak acid NH$_4^+$.

Solution

Part 1: Stoichiometry Problem

Here, we are titrating 0.0100 mol of NH$_3$ ($= c \times V$), so 0.0100 mol of HCl is required. Thus, 100.0 mL of 0.100 M HCl ($= 0.0100$ mol HCl) must be used in the titration.

Equation	NH$_3$	+	H$_3$O$^+$	$\rightleftharpoons$	NH$_4^+$	+	H$_2$O
Initial (mol $= c \times V$)	0.0100		0.0100		0		
Change on reaction (mol)	−0.0100		−0.0100		+0.0100		
After reaction (mol)	0		0		0.0100		
Concentration (M)	0		0		0.0100 mol (in 0.200L)		
					= 0.0500 M		

Part 2: *Equilibrium Problem*

When the equivalence point is reached, the solution consists of 0.0500 M NH_4^+. The pH is determined by the hydrolysis of the acid.

Equation	NH_4^+	+	H_2O	$\rightleftharpoons$	NH_3	+	H_3O^+
Initial (M)	0.0500				0		0
Change (M)	$-x$				$+x$		$+x$
Equilibrium (M)	$0.0500 - x$				x		x

Using K_a for the weak acid NH_4^+, we have

$$K_a = 5.6 \times 10^{-10} = \frac{[NH_3][H_3O^+]}{[NH_4^+]} = \frac{x}{0.0500 - x}$$

Simplifying, $x = [H_3O^+] = \sqrt{(5.6 \times 10^{-10})(0.0500)} = 5.3 \times 10^{-6}$ M

$$pH = 5.28$$

The pH at the equivalence point in this weak base–strong acid titration is indeed slightly acidic, as expected.

EXERCISE 18.9 Titration of a Weak Base with a Strong Acid

Calculate the pH after 75.0 mL of 0.100 M HCl has been added to 100.0 mL of 0.100 M NH_3. See Figure 18.7.

---

pH Indicators

Many organic compounds, both natural and synthetic, have a color that changes with pH (Figure 18.8). Not only does this add beauty and variety to our world, but it is also a useful property in chemistry.

FIGURE 18.8 Phenolphthalein, a common acid–base indicator. Phenolphthalein, a weak acid, is colorless. As the pH increases, the pink conjugate base form predominates, and the color of the solution changes. The change in color is most noticeable around pH 9. The dye is commonly used for strong acid + strong base or weak acid + strong base titrations because the pH changes from 3–4 to 10–12 in these cases. For other suitable indicator dyes, see Figure 18.10.

Phenolphthalein, Brønsted acid, colorless

$(aq) + 2\ H_2O(\ell) \rightleftharpoons 2\ H_3O^+(aq) +$

Conjugate base of phenolphthalein, Brønsted base, pink

CO_2^- (aq)

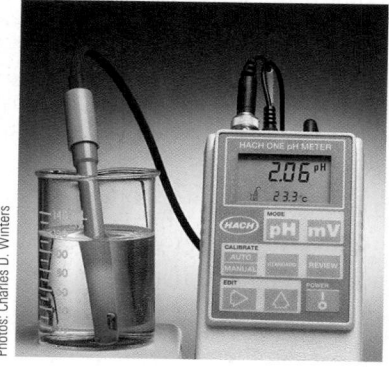
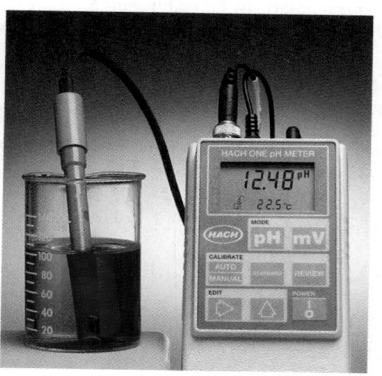

You have likely carried out an acid–base titration in the laboratory, and, before starting the titration, you would have added an **indicator**. The acid–base indicator is usually an organic compound that is itself a weak acid or weak base (similar to the compounds that give the color to flowers). In aqueous solution, the acid form is in equilibrium with its conjugate base. Abbreviating the indicator's acid formula as HInd and the formula of its conjugate base as Ind^-, we can write the equilibrium equation

$$HInd(aq) + H_2O(\ell) \rightleftharpoons H_3O^+(aq) + Ind^-(aq)$$

The important characteristic of acid–base indicators is that the acid form of the compound (HInd) has one color and the conjugate base (Ind^-) has another. To see how such compounds can be used as equivalence point indicators, let us write the usual equilibrium constant expressions for the dependence of hydronium ion concentration or pH on the indicator's ionization constant (K_a) and on the relative quantities of the acid and conjugate base.

$$[H_3O^+] = \frac{[HInd]}{[Ind^-]} \times K_a \quad or \quad pH = pK_a + \log\frac{[Ind^-]}{[HInd]} \qquad (18.6)$$

These equations inform us that

- when the hydronium ion concentration is equivalent to the value of K_a (or when pH = pK_a), then $[HInd] = [Ind^-]$
- when $[H_3O^+] > K_a$ (or pH < pK_a), then $[HInd] > [Ind^-]$
- when $[H_3O^+] < K_a$ (or pH > pK_a), then $[HInd] < [Ind^-]$

Now let us apply these conclusions to, for example, the titration of an acid with a base using an indicator whose pK_a value is nearly the same as the pH at the equivalence point (Figure 18.9). At the beginning of the titration, the pH is low and $[H_3O^+]$ is high; the acid form of the indicator (HInd) predominates. Its color is the one observed. As the titration progresses and the pH increases ($[H_3O^+]$ decreases), less of the acid HInd and more of its conjugate base exist in solution. Finally, just after we reach the equivalence point, $[Ind^-]$ is much larger than [HInd], and the color of $[Ind^-]$ is observed.

Several obvious questions remain to be answered. If you are trying to analyze for an acid and add an indicator that is a weak acid, won't this affect the analysis? Recall that you use only a tiny amount of an indicator in a titration. Although the acidic indicator molecules also react with the base as the titration progresses, so little indicator is present that the analysis is not in error.

Another question is whether you could accurately determine the pH by observing the color change of an indicator. In practice, your eyes are not quite that good. Usually, you see the color of HInd when $[HInd]/[Ind^-]$ is about 10/1, and the color of Ind^- when $[HInd]/[Ind^-]$ is about 1/10. This means the color change is observed over a hydronium ion concentration interval of about 2 pH units. However, as you can see in Figures 18.4–18.7, on passing through the equivalence point of these titrations, the pH changes by as many as 7 units.

As Figure 18.10 shows, a variety of indicators are available, each changing color in a different pH range. If you are analyzing a weak acid or base by titration, you must choose an indicator that changes color in a range that includes the pH to be observed at the equivalence point. This means that an indicator that changes color in the pH range 7 ± 2 should be used for a strong acid–strong base titration. On the other hand, the pH at the equivalence point in the titration of a weak acid with a strong base is greater than 7, and you should choose an indicator that changes color at a pH near the anticipated equivalence point.

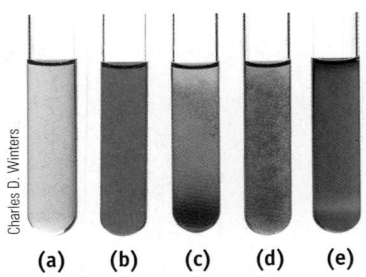

Charles D. Winters

(a) **(b)** **(c)** **(d)** **(e)**

Extract of red rose at various pH's.
(a) The pigment in red rose petals was extracted with ethanol; the extract was a faint red. (b) After adding one drop of 6 M HCl, the color changed to a vivid red. (c) Adding two drops of 6 M NH_3 produced a green color, and (d) adding 1 drop each of HCl and NH_3 (to give a buffer solution) gave a blue solution. (e) Finally, adding a few milligrams of $Al(NO_3)_3$ turned the solution deep purple. (The deep purple color with aluminum ions was so intense that the solution had to be diluted significantly to take the photo.)

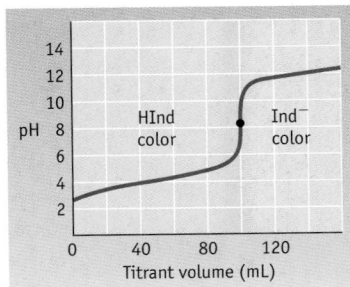

FIGURE 18.9 Indicator color changes in the course of a titration when the pK_a of the indicator HInd is about 8.

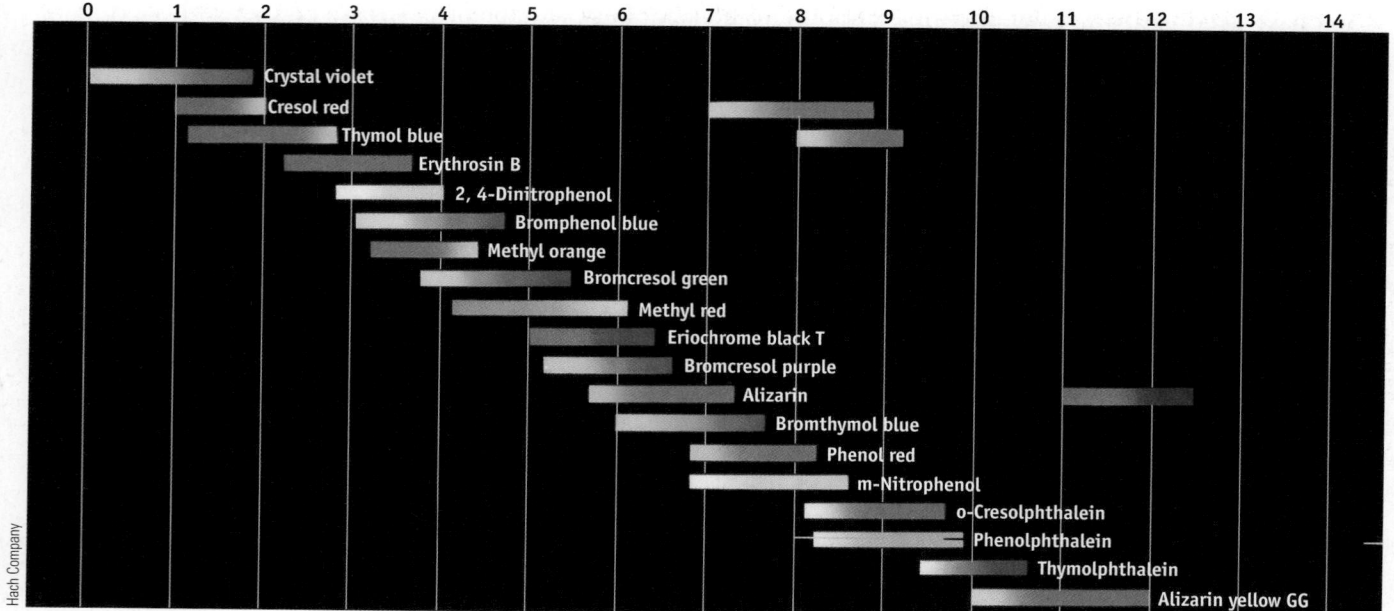

FIGURE 18.10 Common acid–base indicators. The color changes occur over a range of pH values. Notice that a few indicators have color changes over two different pH ranges.

Hach Company

Chemistry.ⓞ.Now™

Sign in at **www.cengage.com/login** and go to Chapter 18 Contents to see Screen 18.10 for a simulation on **acid–base indicators.**

EXERCISE 18.10 Indicators

Use Figure 18.10 to decide which indicator is best to use in the titration of NH_3 with HCl shown in Figure 18.7.

18.4 Solubility of Salts

Precipitation reactions (◀ Section 3.6) are exchange reactions in which one of the products is a water-insoluble compound such as $CaCO_3$,

$$CaCl_2(aq) + Na_2CO_3(aq) \rightarrow CaCO_3(s) + 2\ NaCl(aq)$$

that is, a compound having a water solubility of less than about 0.01 mole of dissolved material per liter of solution (Figure 18.11).

How do you know when to predict an insoluble compound as the product of a reaction? In Chapter 3, we listed some guidelines for predicting solubility (Figure 3.10) and mentioned a few important minerals that are insoluble in water. Now we want to make our estimates of solubility more quantitative and to explore conditions under which some compounds precipitate and others do not.

The Solubility Product Constant, K_{sp}

Silver bromide, AgBr, is used in photographic film (Figure 18.11c). If some AgBr is placed in pure water, a tiny amount of the compound dissolves, and an equilibrium is established.

$$AgBr(s) \rightleftharpoons Ag^+(aq, 7.35 \times 10^{-7}\ M) + Br^-(aq, 7.35 \times 10^{-7}\ M)$$

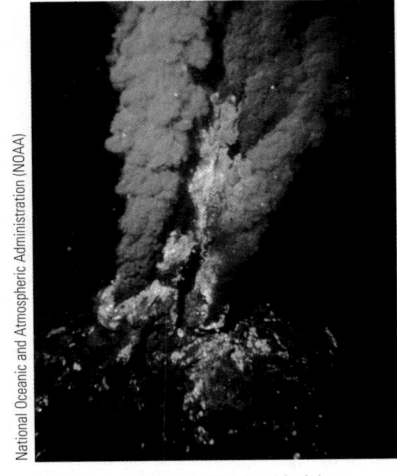

(a) Metal sulfides (and hydroxides) in a black smoker (◄ page 140).

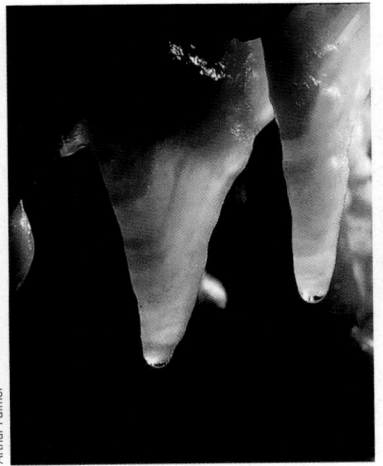

(b) CaCO₃ stalactites.

(c) Black-and-white film is coated with water-insoluble silver bromide. The image is formed by metallic silver particles.

FIGURE 18.11 Some insoluble substances.

When sufficient AgBr has dissolved and equilibrium is attained, the solution is said to be **saturated** (◄ Section 14.2), and experiments show that the concentrations of the silver and bromide ions in the solution are each about 7.35×10^{-7} M at 25 °C. The extent to which an insoluble salt dissolves can be expressed in terms of the equilibrium constant for the dissolving process. In this case, the appropriate expression is

$$K_{sp} = [Ag^+][Br^-]$$

The value of the equilibrium constant that reflects the solubility of a compound is often referred to as its **solubility product constant.** Chemists often use the notation K_{sp} for such constants, the subscript "sp" denoting a "solubility product."

The water solubility of a compound, and thus its K_{sp} value, can be estimated by determining the concentration of the cation or anion when the compound dissolves. For example, if we find that AgBr dissolves to give a silver ion concentration of 7.35×10^{-7} mol/L, we know that 7.35×10^{-7} mol of AgBr must have dissolved per liter of solution (and that the bromide ion concentration also equals 7.35×10^{-7} M). Therefore, the calculated value of the equilibrium constant for the dissolving process is

$$K_{sp} = [Ag^+][Br^-] = (7.35 \times 10^{-7})(7.35 \times 10^{-7}) = 5.40 \times 10^{-13} \text{ (at 25 °C)}$$

Equilibrium constants for the dissolving of other insoluble salts can be calculated in the same manner.

The solubility product constant, K_{sp}, for any salt always has the form

$$A_xB_y(s) \rightleftharpoons x\ A^{y+}(aq) + y\ B^{x-}(aq) \qquad K_{sp} = [A^{y+}]^x[B^{x-}]^y$$

For example,

$$CaF_2(s) \rightleftharpoons Ca^{2+}(aq) + 2\ F^-(aq) \qquad K_{sp} = [Ca^{2+}][F^-]^2 = 5.3 \times 10^{-11}$$

$$Ag_2SO_4(s) \rightleftharpoons 2\ Ag^+(aq) + SO_4{}^{2-}(aq) \qquad K_{sp} = [Ag^+]^2[SO_4{}^{2-}] = 1.2 \times 10^{-5}$$

The numerical values of K_{sp} for a few salts are given in Table 18.2, and more values are collected in Appendix J.

■ **Writing Equilibrium Constant Expressions** Solids are not included in these equations. See page 728.

TABLE 18.2 Some Common Insoluble Compounds and Their K_{sp} Values*

Formula	Name	K_{sp} (25 °C)	Common Names/Uses
$CaCO_3$	Calcium carbonate	3.4×10^{-9}	Calcite, iceland spar
$MnCO_3$	Manganese(II) carbonate	2.3×10^{-11}	Rhodochrosite (forms rose-colored crystals)
$FeCO_3$	Iron(II) carbonate	3.1×10^{-11}	Siderite
CaF_2	Calcium fluoride	5.3×10^{-11}	Fluorite (source of HF and other inorganic fluorides)
$AgCl$	Silver chloride	1.8×10^{-10}	Chlorargyrite
$AgBr$	Silver bromide	5.4×10^{-13}	Used in photographic film
$CaSO_4$	Calcium sulfate	4.9×10^{-5}	The hydrated form is commonly called gypsum
$BaSO_4$	Barium sulfate	1.1×10^{-10}	Barite (used in "drilling mud" and as a component of paints)
$SrSO_4$	Strontium sulfate	3.4×10^{-7}	Celestite
$Ca(OH)_2$	Calcium hydroxide	5.5×10^{-5}	Slaked lime

* The values in this table were taken from *Lange's Handbook of Chemistry*, 15th edition, McGraw-Hill Publishers, New York, NY (1999). Additional K_{sp} values are given in Appendix J.

Do not confuse the *solubility* of a compound with its *solubility product constant*. The *solubility* of a salt is the quantity present in some volume of a saturated solution, expressed in moles per liter, grams per 100 mL, or other units. The *solubility product constant* is an equilibrium constant. Nonetheless, there is a connection between them: If one is known, the other can be calculated.

Chemistry⚛Now™

Sign in at **www.cengage.com/login** and go to Chapter 18 Contents to see:
- Screen 18.11 for a review of **precipitation reactions**
- Screen 18.12 for a simulation on **solubility product constant**

EXERCISE 18.11 Writing K_{sp} Expressions

Write K_{sp} expressions for the following insoluble salts and look up numerical values for the constant in Appendix J.

(a) AgI   (b) BaF_2 (c) Ag_2CO_3

Relating Solubility and K_{sp}

Solubility product constants are determined by careful laboratory measurements of the concentrations of ions in solution.

Chemistry⚛Now™

Sign in at **www.cengage.com/login** and go to Chapter 18 Contents to see Screen 18.13 for a tutorial on **determining K_{sp} experimentally.**

Fluorite. The mineral fluorite is water-insoluble calcium fluoride. The mineral can vary widely in color from purple to green and to colorless. The colors are likely due to impurities.

■ EXAMPLE 18.8 K_{sp} from Solubility Measurements

Problem Calcium fluoride, the main component of the mineral fluorite, dissolves to a slight extent in water.

$$CaF_2(s) \rightleftharpoons Ca^{2+}(aq) + 2\ F^-(aq) \qquad K_{sp} = [Ca^{2+}][F^-]^2$$

Calculate the K_{sp} value for CaF_2 if the calcium ion concentration has been found to be 2.3×10^{-4} mol/L.

Strategy We first write the K_{sp} expression for CaF_2 and then substitute the numerical values for the equilibrium concentrations of the ions.

Solution When CaF_2 dissolves to a small extent in water, the balanced equation shows that the concentration of F^- ion must be twice the Ca^{2+} ion concentration.

$$\text{If } [Ca^{2+}] = 2.3 \times 10^{-4} \text{ M, then } [F^-] = 2 \times [Ca^{2+}] = 4.6 \times 10^{-4} \text{ M}$$

This means the solubility product constant is

$$K_{sp} = [Ca^{2+}][F^-]^2 = (2.3 \times 10^{-4})(4.6 \times 10^{-4})^2 = \boxed{4.9 \times 10^{-11}}$$

EXERCISE 18.12 K_{sp} from Solubility Measurements

The barium ion concentration, $[Ba^{2+}]$, in a saturated solution of barium fluoride is 7.5×10^{-3} M. Calculate the value of the K_{sp} for BaF_2.

$$BaF_2(s) \rightleftharpoons Ba^{2+}(aq) + 2\,F^-(aq)$$

K_{sp} values for insoluble salts can be used to estimate the solubility of a solid salt or to determine whether a solid will precipitate when solutions of its anion and cation are mixed. Let us first look at an example of the estimation of the solubility of a salt from its K_{sp} value.

Chemistry⊙Now™

Sign in at **www.cengage.com/login** and go to Chapter 18 Contents to see Screen 18.14 for a tutorial on **estimating salt solubility using K_{sp}**.

■ EXAMPLE 18.9 Solubility from K_{sp}

Problem The K_{sp} for $BaSO_4$ (as the mineral barite, Figure 18.12) is 1.1×10^{-10} at 25 °C. Calculate the solubility of barium sulfate in pure water in (a) moles per liter and (b) grams per liter.

Strategy When 1 mol of $BaSO_4$ dissolves, 1 mol of Ba^{2+} ions and 1 mol of SO_4^{2-} ions are produced. Thus, the solubility of $BaSO_4$ can be estimated by calculating the concentration of either Ba^{2+} or SO_4^{2-} from the solubility product constant.

Solution The equation for the solubility of $BaSO_4$ is

$$BaSO_4(s) \rightleftharpoons Ba^{2+}(aq) + SO_4^{2-}(aq) \qquad K_{sp} = [Ba^{2+}][SO_4^{2-}] = 1.1 \times 10^{-10}$$

Let us denote the solubility of $BaSO_4$ (in mol/L) by x; that is, x moles of $BaSO_4$ dissolve per liter. Therefore, both $[Ba^{2+}]$ and $[SO_4^{2-}]$ must also equal x at equilibrium.

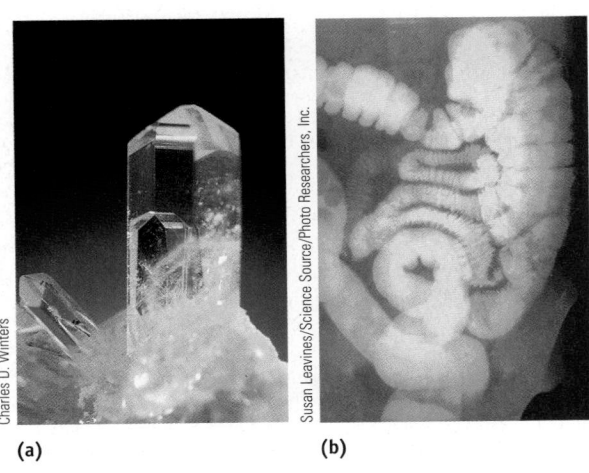

Charles D. Winters

Susan Leavines/Science Source/Photo Researchers, Inc.

(a) (b)

FIGURE 18.12 Barium sulfate. Barium sulfate, a white solid, is quite insoluble in water ($K_{sp} = 1.1 \times 10^{-10}$) (see Example 18.9). (a) A sample of the mineral barite, which is mostly barium sulfate. (b) Barium sulfate is opaque to x-rays, so it is used by physicians to examine the digestive tract. A patient drinks a "cocktail" containing $BaSO_4$, and the progress of the $BaSO_4$ through the digestive organs can be followed by x-ray analysis. This photo is an x-ray of a gastrointestinal tract after a person ingested barium sulfate. It is fortunate that $BaSO_4$ is so insoluble, because water- and acid-soluble barium salts are toxic.

Equation	BaSO$_4$(s)	$\rightleftharpoons$	Ba^{2+}(aq)	+	SO$_4{}^{2-}$(aq)
Initial (M)			0		0
Change (M)			$+x$		$+x$
Equilibrium (M)			x		x

Because K_{sp} is the product of the barium and sulfate ion concentrations, K_{sp} is the square of the solubility, x,

$$K_{sp} = [\text{Ba}^{2+}][\text{SO}_4{}^{2-}] = 1.1 \times 10^{-10} = (x)(x) = x^2$$

and so the value of x is

$$x = [\text{Ba}^{2+}] = [\text{SO}_4{}^{2-}] = \sqrt{1.1 \times 10^{-10}} = 1.0 \times 10^{-5} \text{ M}$$

The solubility of BaSO$_4$ in pure water is 1.0×10^{-5} mol/L. To find its solubility in g/L, we need only multiply by the molar mass of BaSO$_4$.

$$\text{Solubility in g/L} = (1.0 \times 10^{-5} \text{ mol/L})(233 \text{ g/mol}) = \boxed{0.0024 \text{ g/L}}$$

■ **EXAMPLE 18.10** **Solubility from K_{sp}**

Problem Knowing that the K_{sp} value for MgF$_2$ is 5.2×10^{-11}, calculate the solubility of the salt in (a) moles per liter and (b) grams per liter.

Strategy The problem is to define the salt solubility in terms that will allow us to solve the K_{sp} expression for this value. We know that, if 1 mol of MgF$_2$ dissolves, 1 mol of Mg^{2+} and 2 mol of F$^-$ appear in the solution. This means the MgF$_2$ solubility (in moles dissolved per liter) is equivalent to the concentration of Mg^{2+} ions in the solution. Thus, if the solubility of MgF$_2$ is x mol/L, then [Mg^{2+}] = x and [F$^-$] = $2x$.

Solution We begin by writing the equilibrium equation and the K_{sp} expression,

$$\text{MgF}_2(s) \rightleftharpoons \text{Mg}^{2+}(aq) + 2\text{ F}^-(aq) \qquad K_{sp} = [\text{Mg}^{2+}][\text{F}^-]^2 = 5.2 \times 10^{-11}$$

and then set up an ICE table.

Equation	MgF$_2$(s)	$\rightleftharpoons$	Mg^{2+}(aq)	+	2 F$^-$(aq)
Initial (M)			0		0
Change (M)			$+x$		$+2x$
Equilibrium (M)			x		$2x$

Substituting these values into the K_{sp} expression, we find

$$K_{sp} = [\text{Mg}^{2+}][\text{F}^-]^2 = (x)(2x)^2 = 4x^3$$

Solving the equation for x,

$$x = \sqrt[3]{\frac{K_{sp}}{4}} = \sqrt[3]{\frac{5.2 \times 10^{-11}}{4}} = 2.4 \times 10^{-4}$$

we find that 2.4×10^{-4} moles of MgF$_2$ dissolve per liter. The solubility of MgF$_2$ in grams per liter is

$$(2.4 \times 10^{-4} \text{ mol/L})(62.3 \text{ g/mol}) = \boxed{0.015 \text{ g MgF}_2/\text{L}}$$

Comment Problems like this one often provoke our students to ask such questions as, "Aren't you counting things twice when you multiply x by 2 and then square it as well?" in the expression $K_{sp} = (x)(2x)^2$. The answer is no. The 2 in the $2x$ term is based on the stoichiometry of the compound. The exponent of 2 on the F$^-$ ion concentration arises from the rules for writing equilibrium expressions.

EXERCISE 18.13 **Salt Solubility from K_{sp}**

Calculate the solubility of Ca(OH)$_2$ in mol/L and g/L using the value of K_{sp} in Appendix J.

The K_{sp} value reported for lead(II) chloride, $PbCl_2$, is 1.7×10^{-5}. If we assume the appropriate equilibrium in solution is

$$PbCl_2(s) \rightleftharpoons Pb^{2+}(aq) + 2\ Cl^-(aq)$$

the calculated solubility of $PbCl_2$ is 0.016 M. The experimental value for the solubility of the salt, however, is 0.036 M, more than twice the calculated value! What is the problem? There are several, as summarized by the diagram below.

The main problem in the lead(II) chloride case, and in many others, is that the compound dissolves but is not 100% dissociated into its constituent ions. Instead, it dissolves as the undissociated salt or forms ion pairs.

Other problems that lead to discrepancies between calculated and experimental solubilities are the reactions of ions (particularly anions) with water and complex ion formation. An example of the former effect is the reaction of sulfide ion with water, that is, hydrolysis.

$$S^{2-}(aq) + H_2O(\ell) \rightleftharpoons HS^-(aq) + OH^-(aq)$$

This means that the solubility of a metal sulfide is better described by a chemical equation such as

$$NiS(s) + H_2O(\ell) \rightleftharpoons Ni^{2+}(aq) + HS^-(aq) + OH^-(aq)$$

Complex ion formation is illustrated by the fact that lead chloride is more soluble in the presence of excess chloride ion, owing to the formation of the complex ion $PbCl_4^{2-}$.

$$PbCl_2(s) + 2\ Cl^-(aq) \rightleftharpoons PbCl_4^{2-}(aq)$$

Hydrolysis and complex ion formation are discussed further on pages 840–841 and 847–848, respectively.

For further information on these issues see:
(a) L. Meites, J. S. F. Pode, and H. C. Thomas: *Journal of Chemical Education*, Vol. 43, pp. 667–672, 1966.
(b) S. J. Hawkes: *Journal of Chemical Education*, Vol. 75, pp. 1179–1181, 1998.
(c) R. W. Clark and J. M. Bonicamp: *Journal of Chemical Education*, Vol. 75, pp. 1182–1185, 1998.
(d) R. J. Myers: *Journal of Chemical Education*, Vol. 63, pp. 687–690, 1986.

The *relative* solubilities of salts can often be deduced by comparing values of solubility product constants, but you must be careful! For example, the K_{sp} for silver chloride is

$$AgCl(s) \rightleftharpoons Ag^+(aq) + Cl^-(aq) \qquad K_{sp} = 1.8 \times 10^{-10}$$

whereas that for silver chromate is

$$Ag_2CrO_4(s) \rightleftharpoons 2\ Ag^+(aq) + CrO_4^{2-}(aq) \qquad K_{sp} = 9.0 \times 10^{-12}$$

In spite of the fact that Ag_2CrO_4 has a numerically smaller K_{sp} value than AgCl, the chromate salt is about 10 times *more* soluble than the chloride salt. If you determine solubilities from K_{sp} values as in the examples above, you would find the solubility of AgCl is 1.3×10^{-5} mol/L, whereas that of Ag_2CrO_4 is 1.3×10^{-4} mol/L. From this example and countless others, we conclude that

> Direct comparisons of the solubility of two salts on the basis of their K_{sp} values can be made only for salts having the same cation-to-anion ratio.

This means, for example, that you can directly compare solubilities of 1:1 salts such as the silver halides by comparing their K_{sp} values.

$$AgI\ (K_{sp} = 8.5 \times 10^{-17}) < AgBr\ (K_{sp} = 5.4 \times 10^{-13}) < AgCl\ (K_{sp} = 1.8 \times 10^{-10})$$

$\xrightarrow{\hspace{2cm}}$ increasing K_{sp} and increasing solubility $\longrightarrow$

■ **Comparing Solubilities** When two salts have different cation-anion ratios, you will have to do a calculation to find their solubilities. Simply comparing their K_{sp} values will not necessarily give their relative solubilities.

Similarly, you could compare 1:2 salts such as the lead halides.

$$PbI_2 (K_{sp} = 9.8 \times 10^{-9}) < PbBr_2 (K_{sp} = 6.6 \times 10^{-6}) < PbCl_2 (K_{sp} = 1.7 \times 10^{-5})$$

$\xrightarrow{\text{increasing } K_{sp} \text{ and increasing solubility}}$

but you cannot directly compare a 1:1 salt (AgCl) with a 2:1 salt (Ag_2CrO_4).

■ **Complex Ions** The solubility of a salt will increase if addition of the common ion leads to formation of a complex ion. (See Section 18.6, page 846)

EXERCISE 18.14 Comparing Solubilities

Using K_{sp} values, predict which salt in each pair is more soluble in water.

(a) AgCl or AgCN

(b) $Mg(OH)_2$ or $Ca(OH)_2$

(c) $Ca(OH)_2$ or $CaSO_4$

Solubility and the Common Ion Effect

The test tube on the left in Figure 18.13 contains a precipitate of silver acetate, $AgCH_3CO_2$, in water. The solution is saturated, and the silver ions and acetate ions in the solution are in equilibrium with solid silver acetate.

$$AgCH_3CO_2(s) \rightleftharpoons Ag^+(aq) + CH_3CO_2^-(aq)$$

But what would happen if the silver ion concentration is increased, say by adding silver nitrate? Le Chatelier's principle (◀ Section 16.6) suggests—and we observe—that more silver acetate precipitate should form because a product ion has been added, causing the equilibrium to shift to form more silver acetate.

The ionization of weak acids and bases is affected by the presence of an ion common to the equilibrium process (Section 18.1), and the effect of adding silver ions to a saturated silver acetate solution is another example of the common ion effect. Adding a common ion to a saturated solution of a salt will lower the salt solubility.

Chemistry Now™

Sign in at **www.cengage.com/login** and go to Chapter 18 Contents to see Screen 18.15 for a simulation and tutorial on the **common ion effect**.

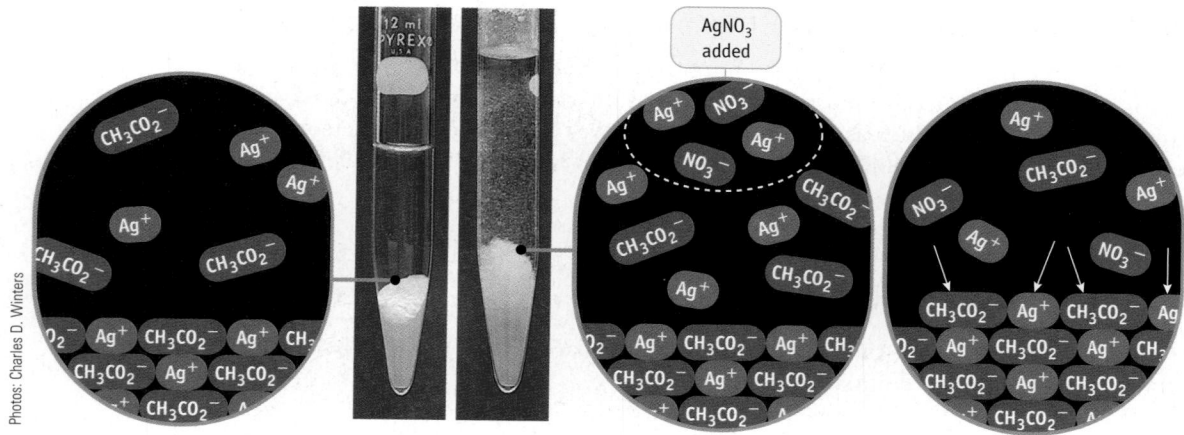

Photos: Charles D. Winters

FIGURE 18.13 The common ion effect. The tube at the left contains a saturated solution of silver acetate, $AgCH_3CO_2$. When 1.0 M $AgNO_3$ is added to the tube (right), more solid silver acetate forms.

Problem If solid AgCl is placed in 1.00 L of 0.55 M NaCl, what mass of AgCl will dissolve?

Strategy The presence of an ion common to the equilibrium suppresses the solubility of a salt. To determine the solubility of the salt under these circumstances, calculate the concentration of the ion (Ag^+ ion in this case) other than the common ion (here Cl^-).

Solution In pure water, the solubility of AgCl is equal to either $[Ag^+]$ or $[Cl^-]$.

$$AgCl(s) \rightleftharpoons Ag^+(aq) + Cl^-(aq)$$

Solubility of AgCl in pure water = $[Ag^+]$ or $[Cl^-]$ = $\sqrt{K_{sp}}$ = 1.3×10^{-5} mol/L or 0.0019 g/L

However, in water already containing a common ion, here the Cl^- ion, Le Chatelier's principle predicts that the solubility is less than 1.3×10^{-5} mol/L. In this case, the solubility of AgCl is equivalent to the concentration of Ag^+ ion in solution, so we set up an ICE table to show the concentrations of Ag^+ and Cl^- when equilibrium is attained.

Equation	AgCl(s) $\rightleftharpoons$	$Ag^+(aq)$ +	$Cl^-(aq)$
Initial (M)		0	0.55
Change (M)		$+x$	$+x$
Equilibrium (M)		x	$0.55 + x$

Some AgCl dissolves in the presence of chloride ion and produces Ag^+ and Cl^- ion concentrations of x mol/L. Because some chloride ion was already present, the total chloride ion concentration is what was already there (0.55 M) plus the amount supplied by AgCl dissociation (= x).

The equilibrium concentrations from the table are substituted into the K_{sp} expression,

$$K_{sp} = 1.8 \times 10^{-10} = [Ag^+][Cl^-] = (x)(0.55 + x)$$

and rearranged to

$$x^2 + 0.55x - K_{sp} = 0$$

This is a quadratic equation and can be solved by the methods in Appendix A. An easier approach, however, is to make the approximation that x is very small with respect to 0.55 [and so $(0.55 + x) \approx 0.55$]. This is a reasonable assumption because we know that the solubility equals 1.3×10^{-5} M without the common ion Cl^- and that it will be even smaller in the presence of added Cl^-. Therefore,

$$K_{sp} = 1.8 \times 10^{-10} = (x)(0.55)$$
$$x = [Ag^+] = 3.3 \times 10^{-10} \text{ M}$$

The solubility in grams per liter is then

$$(3.3 \times 10^{-10} \text{ mol/L})(143 \text{ g/mol}) = \boxed{4.7 \times 10^{-8} \text{ g/L}}$$

As predicted by Le Chatelier's principle, the solubility of AgCl in the presence of added Cl^- is less (3.3×10^{-10} M) than in pure water (1.3×10^{-5} M).

Comment As a final step, check the approximation by substituting the calculated value of x into the exact expression $K_{sp} = (x)(0.55 + x)$. If the product $(x)(0.55 + x)$ is the same as the given value of K_{sp}, the approximation is valid.

$$K_{sp} = (x)(0.55 + x) = (3.3 \times 10^{-10})(0.55 + 3.3 \times 10^{-10}) = 1.8 \times 10^{-10}$$

The approximation we made here is similar to the approximations we make in acid–base equilibrium problems.

Problem Calculate the solubility of silver chromate, Ag_2CrO_4, at 25 °C in the presence of 0.0050 M K_2CrO_4 solution.

$$Ag_2CrO_4(s) \rightleftharpoons 2 Ag^+(aq) + CrO_4^{2-}(aq)$$
$$K_{sp} = [Ag^+]^2[CrO_4^{2-}] = 9.0 \times 10^{-12}$$

For comparison, the solubility of Ag_2CrO_4 in pure water is 1.3×10^{-4} mol/L.

Strategy In the presence of chromate ion from the water-soluble salt K_2CrO_4, the concentration of Ag^+ ions produced by Ag_2CrO_4 will be less than in pure water. Assume the solubility of Ag_2CrO_4 is x mol/L. This means the concentration of Ag^+ ions will be $2x$ mol/L, whereas the concentration of CrO_4^{2-} ions will be x mol/L plus the amount of CrO_4^{2-} already in the solution.

Solution

Equation	$Ag_2CrO_4(s) \rightleftharpoons 2\ Ag^+(aq)$	$+$	$CrO_4^{2-}(aq)$
Initial (M)	0		0.0050
Change	$+2x$		$+x$
Equilibrium (M)	$2x$		$0.0050 + x$

Substituting the equilibrium amounts into the K_{sp} expression, we have

$$K_{sp} = 9.0 \times 10^{-12} = [Ag^+]^2[CrO_4^{2-}]$$
$$K_{sp} = (2x)^2(0.0050 + x)$$

As in Example 18.11, you can make the approximation that x is very small with respect to 0.0050, and so $(0.0050 + x) \approx 0.0050$. (This is reasonable because $[CrO_4^{2-}]$ is 0.00013 M without added chromate ion, and it is certain that x is even smaller in the presence of extra chromate ion.) Therefore, the approximate expression is

$$K_{sp} = 9.0 \times 10^{-12} = [Ag^+]^2[CrO_4^{2-}] = (2x)^2(0.0050)$$

Solving, we find x, the solubility of silver chromate in the presence of excess chromate ion, is

$$x = \text{Solubility of } Ag_2CrO_4 = \boxed{2.1 \times 10^{-5}\ M}$$

Comment The silver ion concentration in the presence of the common ion is

$$[Ag^+] = 2x = 4.2 \times 10^{-5}\ M$$

This silver ion concentration is indeed less than its value in pure water (2.6×10^{-4} M), owing to the presence of an ion "common" to the equilibrium.

EXERCISE 18.15 The Common Ion Effect and Salt Solubility

Calculate the solubility of $BaSO_4$ (a) in pure water and (b) in the presence of 0.010 M $Ba(NO_3)_2$. K_{sp} for $BaSO_4$ is 1.1×10^{-10}.

EXERCISE 18.16 The Common Ion Effect and Salt Solubility

Calculate the solubility of $Zn(CN)_2$ at 25 °C (a) in pure water and (b) in the presence of 0.10 M $Zn(NO_3)_2$. (K_{sp} for $Zn(CN)_2$ is 8.0×10^{-12}.)

Examples 18.11 and 18.12 allow us to propose two important general ideas:

- The solubility of a salt will be reduced by the presence of a common ion, in accordance with Le Chatelier's principle.
- We made the approximation that the amount of common ion added to the solution was very large in comparison with the amount of that ion coming from the insoluble salt, and this allowed us to simplify our calculations. This is almost always the case, but you should check to be sure.

The Effect of Basic Anions on Salt Solubility

The next time you are tempted to wash a supposedly insoluble salt down the kitchen or laboratory drain, stop and consider the consequences. Many metal ions such as lead, chromium, and mercury are toxic in the environment. Even if a so-called insoluble salt of one of these cations does not appear to dissolve, its solubility in water may be greater than you think, in part owing to the possibility that the anion of the salt is a weak base or the cation is a weak acid.

Lead sulfide, PbS, which is found in nature as the mineral galena (Figure 18.14), provides an example of the effect of the acid–base properties of an ion on salt solubility. When placed in water, a trace amount dissolves,

$$PbS(s) \rightleftharpoons Pb^{2+}(aq) + S^{2-}(aq)$$

and one product of the reaction is the sulfide ion. This anion is a strong base,

$$S^{2-}(aq) + H_2O(\ell) \rightleftharpoons HS^-(aq) + OH^-(aq) \qquad K_b = 1 \times 10^5$$

and it undergoes extensive hydrolysis (reaction with water) (◀ Table 17.3). The equilibrium process for dissolving PbS thus shifts to the right, and the lead ion concentration in solution is greater than expected from the simple ionization of the salt.

The lead sulfide example leads to the following general observation:

> Any salt containing an anion that is the conjugate base of a weak acid will dissolve in water to a greater extent than given by K_{sp}.

This means that salts of phosphate, acetate, carbonate, and cyanide, as well as sulfide, can be affected, because all of these anions undergo the general hydrolysis reaction

$$X^-(aq) + H_2O(\ell) \rightleftharpoons HX(aq) + OH^-(aq)$$

The observation that ions from insoluble salts can undergo hydrolysis is related to another useful, general conclusion:

> Insoluble salts in which the anion is the conjugate base of a weak acid dissolve in strong acids.

Insoluble salts containing such anions as acetate, carbonate, hydroxide, phosphate, and sulfide dissolve in strong acids. For example, you know that if a strong acid is added to a water-insoluble metal carbonate such as $CaCO_3$, the salt dissolves (◀ Section 3.4).

$$CaCO_3(s) + 2\,H_3O^+(aq) \rightarrow Ca^{2+}(aq) + 3\,H_2O(\ell) + CO_2(g)$$

You can think of this as the result of a series of reactions.

$CaCO_3(s) \rightleftharpoons Ca^{2+}(aq) + CO_3{}^{2-}(aq)$	$K_{sp} = 3.4 \times 10^{-9}$
$CO_3{}^{2-}(aq) + H_3O^+(aq) \rightleftharpoons HCO_3{}^-(aq) + H_2O(\ell)$	$1/K_{a2} = 1/4.8 \times 10^{-11} = 2.1 \times 10^{10}$
$HCO_3{}^-(aq) + H_3O^+(aq) \rightleftharpoons H_2CO_3(aq) + H_2O(\ell)$	$1/K_{a1} = 1/4.2 \times 10^{-7} = 2.4 \times 10^6$

Overall: $CaCO_3(s) + 2\,H_3O^+(aq) \rightleftharpoons Ca^{2+}(aq) + 2\,H_2O(\ell) + H_2CO_3(aq)$

$$K_{net} = (K_{sp})(1/K_{a2})(1/K_{a1}) = 1.7 \times 10^8$$

Carbonic acid, a product of this reaction, is not stable,

$$H_2CO_3(aq) \rightleftharpoons CO_2(g) + H_2O(\ell) \qquad K \approx 10^5$$

and you see CO_2 bubbling out of the solution, a process that moves the $CaCO_3 + H_3O^+$ equilibrium even further to the right. Calcium carbonate dissolves completely in strong acid!

FIGURE 18.14 Lead sulfide (galena). This and other metal sulfides dissolve in water to a greater extent than expected because the sulfide ion reacts with water to form the very stable species HS^- and OH^-.

$$PbS(s) + H_2O(\ell) \rightleftharpoons$$
$$Pb^{2+}(aq) + HS^-(aq) + OH^-(aq)$$

The model of PbS shows that the unit cell is cubic, a feature reflected by the cubic crystals of the mineral galena.

■ **Metal Sulfide Solubility** The true solubility of a metal sulfide is better represented by a modified solubility product constant, K_{spa}, which is defined as follows:

$$MS(s) \rightleftharpoons M^{2+}(aq) + S^{2-}(aq)$$
$$K_{sp} = [M^{2+}][S^{2-}]$$

$$S^{2-}(aq) + H_2O(\ell) \rightleftharpoons$$
$$HS^-(aq) + OH^-(aq)$$
$$K_b = [HS^-][OH^-]/[S^{2-}]$$

Net reaction:

$$MS(s) + H_2O(\ell) \rightleftharpoons$$
$$HS^-(aq) + M^{2+}(aq) + OH^-(aq)$$
$$K_{spa} = [M^{2+}][HS^-][OH^-] = K_{sp} \times K_b$$

Values for K_{spa} for several metal sulfides are included in Appendix J.

FIGURE 18.15 The effect of the anion on salt solubility in acid. (left) A precipitate of AgCl (white) and Ag₃PO₄ (yellow). (right) Adding a strong acid (HNO₃) dissolves Ag₃PO₄ (and leaves insoluble AgCl). The basic anion PO₄³⁻ reacts with acid to give H₃PO₄, whereas Cl⁻ is too weakly basic to form HCl.

Add strong acid →

Precipitate of
AgCl and Ag₃PO₄

Precipitate of
AgCl

Many metal sulfides are also soluble in strong acids

$$FeS(s) + 2\ H_3O^+(aq) \rightleftharpoons Fe^{2+}(aq) + H_2S(aq) + 2\ H_2O(\ell)$$

as are metal phosphates (Figure 18.15),

$$Ag_3PO_4(s) + 3\ H_3O^+(aq) \rightleftharpoons 3\ Ag^+(aq) + H_3PO_4(aq) + 3\ H_2O(\ell)$$

and metal hydroxides.

$$Mg(OH)_2(s) + 2\ H_3O^+(aq) \rightleftharpoons Mg^{2+}(aq) + 4\ H_2O(\ell)$$

In general, the solubility of a salt containing the conjugate base of a weak acid is increased by addition of a stronger acid to the solution. In contrast, salts are not soluble in strong acid if the anion is the conjugate base of a strong acid. For example, AgCl is not soluble in strong acid

$$AgCl(s) \rightleftharpoons Ag^+(aq) + Cl^-(aq) \qquad\qquad K_{sp} = 1.8 \times 10^{-10}$$

$$H_3O^+(aq) + Cl^-(aq) \rightleftharpoons HCl(aq) + H_2O(\ell) \qquad\qquad K \ll 1$$

because Cl⁻ is a very weak base (◄ Table 17.3), and so its concentration is not lowered by a reaction with the strong acid H₃O⁺ (Figure 18.15). This same conclusion would also apply to insoluble salts of Br⁻ and I⁻.

Chemistry ·ᗕ· Now™

Sign in at **www.cengage.com/login** and go to Chapter 18 Contents to see Screen 18.16 for a self-study module on **solubility and pH.**

18.5 Precipitation Reactions

FIGURE 18.16 Minerals. Minerals are insoluble salts. The minerals shown here are light purple fluorite (calcium fluoride), black hematite [iron(III) oxide], and rust brown goethite, a mixture of iron(III) oxide and iron(III) hydroxide.

Metal-bearing ores contain the metal in the form of an insoluble salt (Figure 18.16), and, to complicate matters, ores often contain several such metal salts. Many industrial methods for separating metals from their ores involve dissolving metal salts to obtain the metal ion or ions in solution. The solution is then concentrated in some manner, and a precipitating agent is added to precipitate selectively only one type of metal ion as an insoluble salt. In the case of nickel, for example, the Ni²⁺ ion can be precipitated as insoluble nickel(II) sulfide or nickel(II) carbonate.

$$Ni^{2+}(aq) + HS^-(aq) + H_2O(\ell) \rightleftharpoons NiS(s) + H_3O^+(aq) \qquad K = 1.7 \times 10^{18}$$

$$Ni^{2+}(aq) + CO_3^{2-}(aq) \rightleftharpoons NiCO_3(s) \qquad\qquad\qquad K = 3.2 \times 10^{10}$$

The final step in obtaining the metal itself is to reduce the metal cation to the metal either chemically or electrochemically (▶ Chapter 20).

Our immediate goal is to work out methods to determine whether a precipitate will form under a given set of conditions. For example, if Ag^+ and Cl^- are present at some given concentrations, will AgCl precipitate from the solution?

K_{sp} and the Reaction Quotient, Q

Silver chloride, like silver bromide, is used in photographic films. It dissolves to a very small extent in water and has a correspondingly small value of K_{sp}.

$$AgCl(s) \rightleftharpoons Ag^+(aq) + Cl^-(aq) \qquad\qquad K_{sp} = [Ag^+][Cl^-] = 1.8 \times 10^{-10}$$

But let us look at the problem from the other direction: If a solution contains Ag^+ and Cl^- ions at some concentration, will AgCl precipitate from solution? This is the same question we asked in Section 16.3 when we wanted to know if a given mixture of reactants and products was an equilibrium mixture, if the reactants continued to form products, or if products would revert to reactants. The procedure there was to calculate the reaction quotient, Q.

For silver chloride, the expression for the reaction quotient, Q, is

$$Q = [Ag^+][Cl^-]$$

Recall that *the difference between Q and K is that the concentrations in the reaction quotient expression may or may not be those at equilibrium.* For the case of a slightly soluble salt such as AgCl, we can reach the following conclusions (◀ Section 16.3).

1. If $Q = K_{sp}$, the solution is saturated.

When the product of the ion concentrations is equal to K_{sp}, the ion concentrations have reached their maximum value.

2. If $Q < K_{sp}$, the solution is not saturated.

This can mean two things: (i) If solid AgCl is present, more will dissolve until equilibrium is achieved (when $Q = K_{sp}$). (ii) If solid AgCl is not already present, more $Ag^+(aq)$ or more $Cl^-(aq)$ (or both) could be added to the solution until precipitation of solid AgCl begins (when $Q > K_{sp}$).

3. If $Q > K_{sp}$, the system is not at equilibrium; precipitation will occur.

The concentrations of Ag^+ and Cl^- in solution are too high, and AgCl will precipitate until $Q = K_{sp}$.

Chemistry ⚛ Now™

Sign in at **www.cengage.com/login** and go to Chapter 18 Contents to see Screen 18.17 for a simulation and tutorial on **when a precipitation reaction can occur.**

■ **EXAMPLE 18.13 Solubility and the Reaction Quotient**

Problem Solid AgCl has been placed in a beaker of water. After some time, the concentrations of Ag^+ and Cl^- are each 1.2×10^{-5} mol/L. Has the system reached equilibrium? If not, will more AgCl dissolve?

Strategy Use the experimental ion concentrations to calculate the reaction quotient Q. Compare Q and K_{sp} to decide if the system is at equilibrium (if $Q = K_{sp}$).

Solution For this AgCl case,

$$Q = [Ag^+][Cl^-] = (1.2 \times 10^{-5})(1.2 \times 10^{-5}) = 1.4 \times 10^{-10}$$

Here, Q is less than K_{sp} (1.8×10^{-10}). The solution is not yet saturated, and AgCl will continue to dissolve until $Q = K_{sp}$, at which point $[Ag^+] = [Cl^-] = 1.3 \times 10^{-5}$ M. That is, an additional 0.1×10^{-5} mol of AgCl (about 1.9 mg) will dissolve per liter.

EXERCISE 18.17 Solubility and the Reaction Quotient

Solid PbI_2 ($K_{sp} = 9.8 \times 10^{-9}$) is placed in a beaker of water. After a period of time, the lead(II) concentration is measured and found to be 1.1×10^{-3} M. Has the system yet reached equilibrium? That is, is the solution saturated? If not, will more PbI_2 dissolve?

K_{sp}, the Reaction Quotient, and Precipitation Reactions

With some knowledge of the reaction quotient, we can decide (1) if a precipitate will form when the ion concentrations are known or (2) what concentrations of ions are required to begin the precipitation of an insoluble salt.

Suppose the concentration of aqueous magnesium ion in a solution is 1.5×10^{-6} M. If enough NaOH is added to make the solution 1.0×10^{-4} M in hydroxide ion, OH^-, will precipitation of $Mg(OH)_2$ occur ($K_{sp} = 5.6 \times 10^{-12}$)? If not, will it occur if the concentration of OH^- is increased to 1.0×10^{-2} M?

Our strategy will be as in Example 18.13. That is, use the ion concentrations to calculate the value of Q and then compare Q with K_{sp} to decide if the system is at equilibrium. Let us begin with the equation for the dissolution of insoluble $Mg(OH)_2$.

$$Mg(OH)_2(s) \rightleftharpoons Mg^{2+}(aq) + 2\,OH^-(aq)$$

When the concentrations of magnesium and hydroxide ions are those stated above, we find that Q is less than K_{sp}.

$$Q = [Mg^{2+}][OH^-]^2 = (1.5 \times 10^{-6})(1.0 \times 10^{-4})^2 = 1.5 \times 10^{-14}$$

$$Q\,(1.5 \times 10^{-14}) < K_{sp}\,(5.6 \times 10^{-12})$$

This means the solution is not yet saturated, and precipitation does not occur.

When $[OH^-]$ is increased to 1.0×10^{-2} M, the reaction quotient is 1.5×10^{-10},

$$Q = (1.5 \times 10^{-6})(1.0 \times 10^{-2})^2$$

$$Q = 1.5 \times 10^{-10} > K_{sp}\,(5.6 \times 10^{-12})$$

The reaction quotient is now *larger* than K_{sp}. Precipitation of $Mg(OH)_2$ occurs and will continue until the Mg^{2+} and OH^- ion concentrations have declined to the point where their product is equal to K_{sp}.

EXERCISE 18.18 Deciding Whether a Precipitate Will Form

Will $SrSO_4$ precipitate from a solution containing 2.5×10^{-4} M strontium ion, Sr^{2+}, if enough of the soluble salt Na_2SO_4 is added to make the solution 2.5×10^{-4} M in SO_4^{2-}? K_{sp} for $SrSO_4$ is 3.4×10^{-7}.

Now that we know how to decide if a precipitate will form when the concentration of each ion is known, let us turn to the problem of deciding how much of the precipitating agent is required to begin the precipitation of an ion at a given concentration level.

Problem The concentration of barium ion, Ba^{2+}, in a solution is 0.010 M.

(a) What concentration of sulfate ion, $SO_4{}^{2-}$, is required once $BaSO_4$ has started to precipitate?

(b) When the concentration of sulfate ion in the solution reaches 0.015 M, what concentration of barium ion will remain in solution?

Strategy There are three variables in the K_{sp} expression: K_{sp} and the anion and cation concentrations. Here, we know K_{sp} (1.1×10^{-10}) and one of the ion concentrations. We can then calculate the other ion concentration.

Solution Let us begin by writing the balanced equation for the equilibrium that will exist when $BaSO_4$ has been precipitated.

$$BaSO_4(s) \rightleftharpoons Ba^{2+}(aq) + SO_4{}^{2-}(aq) \qquad K_{sp} = [Ba^{2+}][SO_4{}^{2-}] = 1.1 \times 10^{-10}$$

(a) When the product of the ion concentrations exceeds the K_{sp} ($= 1.1 \times 10^{-10}$)—that is, when $Q > K_{sp}$—precipitation will occur. The Ba^{2+} ion concentration is known (0.010 M), so the $SO_4{}^{2-}$ ion concentration necessary for precipitation can be calculated.

$$[SO_4{}^{2-}] = \frac{K_{sp}}{[Ba^{2+}]} = \frac{1.1 \times 10^{-10}}{0.010} = \boxed{1.1 \times 10^{-8} \text{ M}}$$

The result tells us that if the sulfate ion is just slightly greater than 1.1×10^{-8} M, $BaSO_4$ will begin to precipitate; $Q = [Ba^{2+}][SO_4{}^{2-}]$ would then be greater than K_{sp}.

(b) If the sulfate ion concentration is increased to 0.015 M, the maximum concentration of Ba^{2+} ion that can exist in solution (in equilibrium with $BaSO_4$) is

$$[Ba^{2+}] = \frac{K_{sp}}{[SO_4{}^{2-}]} = \frac{1.1 \times 10^{-10}}{0.015} = \boxed{7.3 \times 10^{-9} \text{ M}}$$

Comment The fact that the barium ion concentration is so small under these circumstances means that the Ba^{2+} ion has been essentially completely removed from solution. (It began at 0.010 M and has dropped by a factor of about 10 million.) The Ba^{2+} ion precipitation is, for all practical purposes, complete.

Problem Suppose you mix 100.0 mL of 0.0200 M $BaCl_2$ with 50.0 mL of 0.0300 M Na_2SO_4. Will $BaSO_4$ ($K_{sp} = 1.1 \times 10^{-10}$) precipitate?

Strategy Here, we mix two solutions, one containing Ba^{2+} ions and the other $SO_4{}^{2-}$ ions. First, find the concentration of each of these ions after mixing. Then, knowing the ion concentrations in the diluted solution, calculate Q and compare it with the K_{sp} value for $BaSO_4$.

Solution First, use the equation $c_1V_1 = c_2V_2$ (◀ Section 4.5) to calculate c_2, the concentration of the Ba^{2+} or $SO_4{}^{2-}$ ions after mixing, to give a new solution with a volume of 150.0 mL ($= V_2$).

$$[Ba^{2+}] \text{ after mixing} = \frac{(0.0200 \text{ mol/L})(0.1000 \text{ L})}{0.1500 \text{ L}} = 0.0133 \text{ M}$$

$$[SO_4{}^{2-}] \text{ after mixing} = \frac{(0.0300 \text{ mol/L})(0.0500 \text{ L})}{0.1500 \text{ L}} = 0.0100 \text{ M}$$

Now the reaction quotient can be calculated.

$$Q = [Ba^{2+}][SO_4{}^{2-}] = (0.0133)(0.0100) = 1.33 \times 10^{-4}$$

Q is much larger than K_{sp}, so $BaSO_4$ precipitates.

EXERCISE 18.19 **Ion Concentrations Required to Begin Precipitation**

What is the minimum concentration of I^- that can cause precipitation of PbI_2 from a 0.050 M solution of $Pb(NO_3)_2$? K_{sp} for PbI_2 is 8.7×10^{-9}. What concentration of Pb^{2+} ions remains in solution when the concentration of I^- is 0.0015 M?

Dimethylglyoximate complex of Ni²⁺ ion

[Ni(NH₃)₆]²⁺

[Ni(H₂O)₆]²⁺

FIGURE 18.17 Complex ions.
The green solution contains soluble $Ni(H_2O)_6{}^{2+}$ ions in which water molecules are bound to Ni^{2+} ions by ion–dipole forces. This complex ion gives the solution its green color. The Ni^{2+}-ammonia complex ion is purple. The red, insoluble solid is the dimethylglyoximate complex of the Ni^{2+} ion [Ni(C₄H₇O₂N₂)₂] (model at top). Formation of this beautiful red insoluble compound is the classical test for the presence of the aqueous Ni^{2+} ion.

Charles D. Winters

■ **Complex Ions** Complex ions are prevalent in chemistry and are the basis of such biologically important substances as hemoglobin and vitamin B₁₂. They are described in more detail in Chapter 22.

EXERCISE 18.20 K_{sp} and Precipitation

You have 100.0 mL of 0.0010 M silver nitrate. Will AgCl precipitate if you add 5.0 mL of 0.025 M HCl?

18.6 Equilibria Involving Complex Ions

Metal ions exist in aqueous solution as complex ions (◀ Section 17.10) (Figure 18.17). Complex ions consist of the metal ion and other molecules or ions bound into a single entity. In water, metal ions are always surrounded by water molecules, with the negative end of the polar water molecule, the oxygen atom, attracted to the positive metal ion. In the case of Ni^{2+}, the ion exists as $[Ni(H_2O)_6]^{2+}$ in water. On adding ammonia, water molecules are displaced successively, and in the presence of a high enough concentration of ammonia, the complex ion $[Ni(NH_3)_6]^{2+}$ exists. Many organic molecules also form complex ions with metal ions, one example being the complex with the dimethylglyoximate ion in Figure 18.17.

The molecules or ions that bind to metal ions are called **ligands** (▶ Chapter 22). In aqueous solution, metal ions and ligands exist in equilibrium, and the equilibrium constants for these reactions are referred to as **formation constants, K_f** (Appendix K). For example,

$$Cu^{2+}(aq) + NH_3(aq) \rightleftharpoons [Cu(NH_3)]^{2+}(aq) \qquad K_{f1} = 2.0 \times 10^4$$

$$[Cu(NH_3)]^{2+}(aq) + NH_3(aq) \rightleftharpoons [Cu(NH_3)_2]^{2+}(aq) \qquad K_{f2} = 4.7 \times 10^3$$

$$[Cu(NH_3)_2]^{2+}(aq) + NH_3(aq) \rightleftharpoons [Cu(NH_3)_3]^{2+}(aq) \qquad K_{f3} = 1.1 \times 10^3$$

$$[Cu(NH_3)_3]^{2+}(aq) + NH_3(aq) \rightleftharpoons [Cu(NH_3)_4]^{2+}(aq) \qquad K_{f4} = 2.0 \times 10^2$$

(In these reactions, Cu^{2+} begins as $[Cu(H_2O)_4]^{2+}$. Ammonia successively displaces the water molecules.) Overall, the formation of the tetraammine copper(II) complex ion has an equilibrium constant of 2.1×10^{13} ($= K_{f1} \times K_{f2} \times K_{f3} \times K_{f4}$).

$$Cu^{2+}(aq) + 4\ NH_3(aq) \rightleftharpoons [Cu(NH_3)_4]^{2+}(aq) \qquad K_f = 2.1 \times 10^{13}$$

■ **EXAMPLE 8.16 Complex Ion Equilibria**

Problem What is the concentration of Cd^{2+} ions in a solution prepared by adding 0.00100 mol of Cd(NO₃)₂ to 1.00 L of 1.50 M NH₃? K_f for complex ion $[Cd(NH_3)_4]^{2+}$ is 1.3×10^7.

Strategy The formation constant for the complex ion is very large, so we can assume nearly all of the Cd^{2+} ions are in that form. That is, the initial concentration of the complex ion, $[Cd(NH_3)_4]^{2+}$, is 0.00100 M. This then dissociates to produce Cd^{2+} ions in solution.

Solution Let us set up an ICE table for the dissociation of $[Cd(NH_3)_4]^{2+}$.

Equation	$[Cd(NH_3)_4]^{2+}(aq)$	$\rightleftharpoons$	$Cd^{2+}(aq)$	+	$4\ NH_3(aq)$
Initial (M)	0.00100		0		1.50 − 0.00400 M
Change	−x		+x		+4x
Equilibrium (M)	0.00100 − x ≈ 0.00100		x		1.50 − 0.00400 + 4x ≈ 1.50

$$K = \frac{1}{K_f} = \frac{1}{1.3 \times 10^7} = \frac{[Cd^{2+}][NH_3]^4}{\{[Cd(NH_3)_4]^{2+}\}} = \frac{(x)(1.50)}{0.000100}$$

$$x = [Cd^{2+}] = 5.1 \times 10^{-11} \text{ M}$$

18.7 Solubility and Complex Ions

Silver chloride dissolves neither in water nor in strong acid, but it does dissolve in ammonia because it forms a water-soluble complex ion, $[Ag(NH_3)_2]^+$ (Figure 18.18).

$$AgCl(s) + 2\,NH_3(aq) \rightleftharpoons [Ag(NH_3)_2]^+(aq) + Cl^-(aq)$$

We can view dissolving AgCl(s) in this way as a two-step process. First, AgCl dissolves minimally in water, giving $Ag^+(aq)$ and $Cl^-(aq)$ ion. Then, the $Ag^+(aq)$ ion combines with NH_3 to give the ammonia complex. Lowering the $Ag^+(aq)$ concentration through complexation with NH_3 shifts the solubility equilibrium to the right, and more solid AgCl dissolves.

$$AgCl(s) \rightleftharpoons Ag^+(aq) + Cl^-(aq) \qquad\qquad K_{sp} = 1.8 \times 10^{-10}$$

$$Ag^+(aq) + 2\,NH_3(aq) \rightleftharpoons [Ag(NH_3)_2]^+(aq) \qquad\qquad K_f = 1.6 \times 10^7$$

This is an example of combining or "coupling" two (or more) equilibria where one is a product-favored reaction and the other is reactant-favored.

The large value of the formation constant for $[Ag(NH_3)_2]^+$ means that the equilibrium lies well to the right, and AgCl dissolves in the presence of NH_3. If we combine K_f with K_{sp}, we obtain the net equilibrium constant for the interaction of AgCl and aqueous ammonia.

$$K_{net} = K_{sp} \times K_f = (1.8 \times 10^{-10})(1.6 \times 10^7) = 2.9 \times 10^{-3}$$

$$K_{net} = 2.9 \times 10^{-3} = \frac{\{[Ag(NH_3)_2]^+\}[Cl^-]}{[NH_3]^2}$$

Even though the value of K_{net} seems small, if we use a large concentration of NH_3, the concentration of $[Ag(NH_3)_2]^+$ in solution can be high. Silver chloride is thus much more soluble in the presence of ammonia than in pure water.

The stabilities of various complex ions involving silver(I) can be compared by comparing values of their formation constants.

Formation Equilibrium	K_f
$Ag^+(aq) + 2\,Cl^-(aq) \rightleftharpoons [AgCl_2]^-(aq)$	2.5×10^5
$Ag^+(aq) + 2\,S_2O_3{}^{2-}(aq) \rightleftharpoons [Ag(S_2O_3)_2]^{3-}(aq)$	2.0×10^{13}
$Ag^+(aq) + 2\,CN^-(aq) \rightleftharpoons [Ag(CN)_2]^-(aq)$	5.6×10^{18}

The formation of all three silver complexes is strongly product-favored. The cyanide complex ion $[Ag(CN)_2]^-$ is the most stable of the three.

Figure 18.18 shows what happens as complex ions are formed. Beginning with a precipitate of AgCl, adding aqueous ammonia dissolves the precipitate to give the soluble complex ion $[Ag(NH_3)_2]^+$. Silver bromide is even more stable than $[Ag(NH_3)_2]^+$, so AgBr ($K_{sp} = 5.4 \times 10^{-13}$) forms in preference to the complex ion on adding bromide ion. If thiosulfate ion, $S_2O_3{}^{2-}$, is then added, AgBr dissolves due to the formation of $[Ag(S_2O_3)_2]^{3-}$, a complex ion with a large formation constant (2.0×10^{13}).

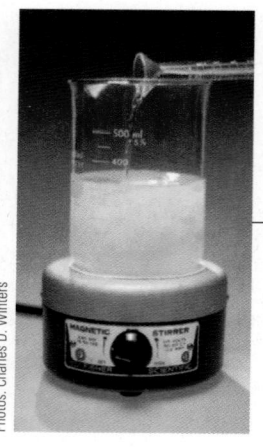

AgCl(s),
$K_{sp} = 1.8 \times 10^{-10}$

(a) AgCl precipitates on adding NaCl(aq) to AgNO$_3$(aq) (see Figure 3.7).

NH$_3$(aq) →

$[Ag(NH_3)_2]^+$(aq)

(b) The precipitate of AgCl dissolves on adding aqueous NH$_3$ to give water-soluble $[Ag(NH_3)_2]^+$.

NaBr(aq) →

AgBr(s),
$K_{sp} = 5.4 \times 10^{-13}$

(c) The silver-ammonia complex ion is changed to insoluble AgBr on adding NaBr(aq).

Na$_2$S$_2$O$_3$(aq) →

$[Ag(S_2O_3)_2]^{3-}$(aq)

(d) Solid AgBr is dissolved on adding Na$_2$S$_2$O$_3$(aq). The product is the water-soluble complex ion $[Ag(S_2O_3)_2]^{3-}$.

FIGURE 18.18 Forming and dissolving precipitates. Insoluble compounds often dissolve upon addition of a complexing agent.

Chemistry ☌ Now™

Sign in at **www.cengage.com/login** and go to Chapter 18 Contents to see:
- Screen 18.18 for more information on **combining equilibria**
- Screen 18.19 for a tutorial on **complex ion formation and solubility**

■ **EXAMPLE 18.17 Complex Ions and Solubility**

Problem What is the value of the equilibrium constant, K_{net}, for dissolving AgBr in a solution containing the thiosulfate ion, S$_2$O$_3^{2-}$ (Figure 18.18)? Explain why AgBr dissolves readily on adding aqueous sodium thiosulfate to the solid.

Strategy Summing several equilibrium processes gives the net chemical equation. K_{net} is the product of the values of K of the summed chemical equations. (See the preceding text and Section 16.10.)

Solution The overall reaction for dissolving AgBr in the presence of the thiosulfate anion is the sum of two equilibrium processes.

$$AgBr(s) \rightleftharpoons Ag^+(aq) + Br^-(aq) \qquad\qquad K_{sp} = 5.0 \times 10^{-13}$$

$$Ag^+(aq) + 2\,S_2O_3^{2-}(aq) \rightleftharpoons [Ag(S_2O_3)_2]^{3-}(aq) \qquad\qquad K_f = 2.0 \times 10^{13}$$

Net chemical equation:

$$AgBr(aq) + 2\,S_2O_3^{2-}(aq) \rightleftharpoons [Ag(S_2O_3)_2]^{3-}(aq) + Br^-(aq) \qquad K_{net} = K_{sp} \times K_f = 1.0 \times 10^1$$

The value of K_{net} is greater than 1, indicating a product-favored reaction. AgBr is predicted to dissolve readily in aqueous Na$_2$S$_2$O$_3$, as observed (Figure 18.18).

EXERCISE 18.22 Complex Ions and Solubility

Calculate the value of the equilibrium constant, K_{net}, for dissolving Cu(OH)$_2$ in aqueous ammonia (to form the complex ion $[Cu(NH_3)_4]^{2+}$) (see Figure 17.7).

Chapter Goals Revisited

Now that you have studied this chapter, you should ask whether you have met the chapter goals. In particular, you should be able to:

Understand the common ion effect

(a) Predict the effect of the addition of a "common ion" on the pH of the solution of a weak acid or base (Section 18.1). Study Question(s) assignable in OWL: 2, 4, 109.

Understand the control of pH in aqueous solutions with buffers

(a) Describe the functioning of buffer solutions. (Section 18.2) Go Chemistry Module 23.

(b) Use the Henderson–Hasselbalch equation (Equation 18.2) to calculate the pH of a buffer solution of given composition. Study Question(s) assignable in OWL: 6, 7, 14.

(c) Describe how a buffer solution of a given pH can be prepared. Study Question(s) assignable in OWL: 9, 16, 83, 90, 101, 102, 109.

(d) Calculate the pH of a buffer solution before and after adding acid or base. Study Question(s) assignable in OWL: 20, 22, 74, 76, 82.

Evaluate the pH in the course of acid–base titrations

(a) Predict the pH of an acid–base reaction at its equivalence point (Section 18.3; see also Sections 17.5 and 17.6).

Acid	Base	pH at Equivalence Point
Strong	Strong	= 7 (neutral)
Strong	Weak	< 7 (acidic)
Weak	Strong	> 7 (basic)

Study Question(s) assignable in OWL: 24, 74, 76, 98, 108.

(b) Understand the differences between the titration curves for a strong acid–strong base titration and titrations in which one of the substances is weak.

(c) Describe how an indicator functions in an acid–base titration. Study Question(s) assignable in OWL: 32, 72, 80, 96, 105.

Apply chemical equilibrium concepts to the solubility of ionic compounds

(a) Write the equilibrium constant expression—relating concentrations of ions in solutions to K_{sp}—for any insoluble salt (Section 18.4).

(b) Calculate K_{sp} values from experimental data (Section 18.4). Study Question(s) assignable in OWL: 40, 42.

(c) Estimate the solubility of a salt from the value of K_{sp} (Section 18.4). Study Question(s) assignable in OWL: 46, 48, 72, 80, 96, 105.

(d) Calculate the solubility of a salt in the presence of a common ion (Section 18.4). Study Question(s) assignable in OWL: 54.

(e) Understand how hydrolysis of basic anions affects the solubility of a salt (Section 18.4). Study Question(s) assignable in OWL: 58.

(f) Decide if a precipitate will form when the ion concentrations are known Section 18.5). Study Question(s) assignable in OWL: 36, 60, 64, 70, 88, 89.

(g) Calculate the ion concentrations that are required to begin the precipitation of an insoluble salt (Section 18.5).

(h) Understand that the formation of a complex ion can increase the solubility of an insoluble salt (Section 18.6). Study Question(s) assignable in OWL: 66, 70, 92.

Chemistry.Now™ Sign in at **www.cengage.com/login** to:

- Assess your understanding with Study Questions in OWL keyed to each goal in the Goals and Homework menu for this chapter
- For quick review, download Go Chemistry mini-lecture flashcard modules (or purchase them at **www.ichapters.com**)
- Check your readiness for an exam by taking the Pre-Test and exploring the modules recommended in your Personalized Study plan.

Access **How Do I Solve It?** tutorials on how to approach problem solving using concepts in this chapter.

For additional preparation for an examination on this chapter see the *Let's Review* section on pages 948–961.

KEY EQUATIONS

Equation 18.1 (page 816)   Hydronium ion concentration in a buffer solution composed of a weak acid and its conjugate base.

$$[H_3O^+] = \frac{[\text{acid}]}{[\text{conjugate base}]} \times K_a$$

Equation 18.2 (page 817)   Henderson–Hasselbalch equation. To calculate the pH of a buffer solution composed of a weak acid and its conjugate base.

$$pH = pK_a + \log\frac{[\text{conjugate base}]}{[\text{acid}]}$$

Equation 18.3 (page 825)   Equation to calculate the hydronium ion concentration before the equivalence point in the titration of a weak acid with a strong base. See also Equation 18.4 for the version of the equation based on the Henderson–Hasselbalch equation.

$$[H_3O^+] = \frac{[\text{weak acid remaining}]}{[\text{conjugate base produced}]} \times K_a$$

Equation 18.5 (page 825)   The relationship between the pH of the solution and the pK_a of the weak acid (or $[H_3O^+]$ and K_a) at the halfway or half-neutralization point in the titration of a weak acid with a strong base (or of a weak base with a strong acid).

$$[H_3O^+] = K_a \text{ and } pH = pK_a$$

STUDY QUESTIONS

OWL Online homework for this chapter may be assigned in OWL.

▲ denotes challenging questions.

■ denotes questions assignable in OWL.

Blue-numbered questions have answers in Appendix O and fully-worked solutions in the *Student Solutions Manual*.

Practicing Skills

The Common Ion Effect and Buffer Solutions
(*See Examples 18.1 and 18.2 and ChemistryNow Screens 18.2–18.4.*)

1. Does the pH of the solution increase, decrease, or stay the same when you
    (a) Add solid ammonium chloride to a dilute aqueous solution of NH_3?
    (b) Add solid sodium acetate to a dilute aqueous solution of acetic acid?
    (c) Add solid NaCl to a dilute aqueous solution of NaOH?

2. ■ Does the pH of the solution increase, decrease, or stay the same when you
    (a) Add solid sodium oxalate, $Na_2C_2O_4$, to 50.0 mL of 0.015 M oxalic acid, $H_2C_2O_4$?
    (b) Add solid ammonium chloride to 75 mL of 0.016 M HCl?
    (c) Add 20.0 g of NaCl to 1.0 L of 0.10 M sodium acetate, $NaCH_3CO_2$?

3. What is the pH of a solution that consists of 0.20 M ammonia, NH_3, and 0.20 M ammonium chloride, NH_4Cl?

4. ■ What is the pH of 0.15 M acetic acid to which 1.56 g of sodium acetate, $NaCH_3CO_2$, has been added?

5. What is the pH of the solution that results from adding 30.0 mL of 0.015 M KOH to 50.0 mL of 0.015 M benzoic acid?

6. ■ What is the pH of the solution that results from adding 25.0 mL of 0.12 M HCl to 25.0 mL of 0.43 M NH_3?

7. ■ What is the pH of the buffer solution that contains 2.2 g of NH_4Cl in 250 mL of 0.12 M NH_3? Is the final pH lower or higher than the pH of the 0.12 M ammonia solution?

8. Lactic acid ($CH_3CHOHCO_2H$) is found in sour milk, in sauerkraut, and in muscles after activity. (K_a for lactic acid $= 1.4 \times 10^{-4}$.)
   (a) If 2.75 g of $NaCH_3CHOHCO_2$, sodium lactate, is added to 5.00×10^2 mL of 0.100 M lactic acid, what is the pH of the resulting buffer solution?
   (b) Is the pH of the buffered solution lower or higher than the pH of the lactic acid solution?

9. ■ What mass of sodium acetate, $NaCH_3CO_2$, must be added to 1.00 L of 0.10 M acetic acid to give a solution with a pH of 4.50?

10. What mass of ammonium chloride, NH_4Cl, must be added to exactly 5.00×10^2 mL of 0.10 M NH_3 solution to give a solution with a pH of 9.00?

Using the Henderson–Hasselbalch Equation
(See Example 18.3 and ChemistryNow Screen 18.4.)

11. Calculate the pH of a solution that has an acetic acid concentration of 0.050 M and a sodium acetate concentration of 0.075 M.

12. Calculate the pH of a solution that has an ammonium chloride concentration of 0.050 M and an ammonia concentration of 0.045 M.

13. A buffer is composed of formic acid and its conjugate base, the formate ion.
    (a) What is the pH of a solution that has a formic acid concentration of 0.050 M and a sodium formate concentration of 0.035 M?
    (b) What must the ratio of acid to conjugate base be to increase the pH by 0.5 unit from the value calculated in part (a)?

14. ■ A buffer solution is composed of 1.360 g of KH_2PO_4 and 5.677 g of Na_2HPO_4.
    (a) What is the pH of the buffer solution?
    (b) What mass of KH_2PO_4 must be added to decrease the buffer solution pH by 0.5 unit from the value calculated in part (a)?

Preparing a Buffer Solution
(See Example 18.4 and ChemistryNow Screen 18.5.)

15. Which of the following combinations would be the best to buffer the pH of a solution at approximately 9?
    (a) HCl and NaCl
    (b) NH_3 and NH_4Cl
    (c) CH_3CO_2H and $NaCH_3CO_2$

16. ■ Which of the following combinations would be the best choice to buffer the pH of a solution at approximately 7?
    (a) H_3PO_4 and NaH_2PO_4
    (b) NaH_2PO_4 and Na_2HPO_4
    (c) Na_2HPO_4 and Na_3PO_4

17. Describe how to prepare a buffer solution from NaH_2PO_4 and Na_2HPO_4 to have a pH of 7.5.

18. Describe how to prepare a buffer solution from NH_3 and NH_4Cl to have a pH of 9.5.

Adding an Acid or a Base to a Buffer Solution
(See Example 18.5 and ChemistryNow Screen 18.6.)

19. A buffer solution was prepared by adding 4.95 g of sodium acetate, $NaCH_3CO_2$, to 2.50×10^2 mL of 0.150 M acetic acid, CH_3CO_2H.
    (a) What is the pH of the buffer?
    (b) What is the pH of 1.00×10^2 mL of the buffer solution if you add 82 mg of NaOH to the solution?

20. ■ You dissolve 0.425 g of NaOH in 2.00 L of a buffer solution that has $[H_2PO_4^-] = [HPO_4^{2-}] = 0.132$ M. What is the pH of the solution before adding NaOH? After adding NaOH?

21. A buffer solution is prepared by adding 0.125 mol of ammonium chloride to 5.00×10^2 mL of 0.500 M solution of ammonia.
    (a) What is the pH of the buffer?
    (b) If 0.0100 mol of HCl gas is bubbled into 5.00×10^2 mL of the buffer, what is the new pH of the solution?

22. ■ What will be the pH change when 20.0 mL of 0.100 M NaOH is added to 80.0 mL of a buffer solution consisting of 0.169 M NH_3 and 0.183 M NH_4Cl?

More about Acid–Base Reactions: Titrations
(See Examples 18.6 and 18.7 and ChemistryNow Screen 18.7.)

23. Phenol, C_6H_5OH, is a weak organic acid. Suppose 0.515 g of the compound is dissolved in exactly 125 mL of water. The resulting solution is titrated with 0.123 M NaOH.

$$C_6H_5OH(aq) + OH^-(aq) \rightleftharpoons C_6H_5O^-(aq) + H_2O(\ell)$$

   (a) What is the pH of the original solution of phenol?
   (b) What are the concentrations of all of the following ions at the equivalence point: Na^+, H_3O^+, OH^-, and $C_6H_5O^-$?
   (c) What is the pH of the solution at the equivalence point?

24. ■ Assume you dissolve 0.235 g of the weak acid benzoic acid, $C_6H_5CO_2H$, in enough water to make 1.00×10^2 mL of solution and then titrate the solution with 0.108 M NaOH.

$$C_6H_5CO_2H(aq) + OH^-(aq) \rightleftharpoons C_6H_5CO_2^-(aq) + H_2O(\ell)$$

   (a) What was the pH of the original benzoic acid solution?
   (b) What are the concentrations of all of the following ions at the equivalence point: Na^+, H_3O^+, OH^-, and $C_6H_5CO_2^-$?
   (c) What is the pH of the solution at the equivalence point?

▲ more challenging   ■ in OWL   Blue-numbered questions answered in Appendix O

25. You require 36.78 mL of 0.0105 M HCl to reach the equivalence point in the titration of 25.0 mL of aqueous ammonia.
(a) What was the concentration of NH_3 in the original ammonia solution?
(b) What are the concentrations of H_3O^+, OH^-, and NH_4^+ at the equivalence point?
(c) What is the pH of the solution at the equivalence point?

26. A solution of the weak base aniline, $C_6H_5NH_2$, in 25.0 mL of water requires 25.67 mL of 0.175 M HCl to reach the equivalence point.

$$C_6H_5NH_2(aq) + H_3O^+(aq) \rightleftharpoons C_6H_5NH_3^+(aq) + H_2O(\ell)$$

(a) What was the concentration of aniline in the original solution?
(b) What are the concentrations of H_3O^+, OH^-, and $C_6H_5NH_3^+$ at the equivalence point?
(c) What is the pH of the solution at the equivalence point?

Titration Curves and Indicators
(See Figures 18.4–18.10 and ChemistryNow Screen 18.7.)

27. Without doing detailed calculations, sketch the curve for the titration of 30.0 mL of 0.10 M NaOH with 0.10 M HCl. Indicate the approximate pH at the beginning of the titration and at the equivalence point. What is the total solution volume at the equivalence point?

28. Without doing detailed calculations, sketch the curve for the titration of 50 mL of 0.050 M pyridine, C_5H_5N (a weak base), with 0.10 M HCl. Indicate the approximate pH at the beginning of the titration and at the equivalence point. What is the total solution volume at the equivalence point?

29. You titrate 25.0 mL of 0.10 M NH_3 with 0.10 M HCl.
(a) What is the pH of the NH_3 solution before the titration begins?
(b) What is the pH at the equivalence point?
(c) What is the pH at the halfway point of the titration?
(d) What indicator in Figure 18.10 could be used to detect the equivalence point?
(e) Calculate the pH of the solution after adding 5.00, 15.0, 20.0, 22.0, and 30.0 mL of the acid. Combine this information with that in parts (a)–(c) and plot the titration curve.

30. Construct a rough plot of pH versus volume of base for the titration of 25.0 mL of 0.050 M HCN with 0.075 M NaOH.
(a) What is the pH before any NaOH is added?
(b) What is the pH at the halfway point of the titration?
(c) What is the pH when 95% of the required NaOH has been added?

(d) What volume of base, in milliliters, is required to reach the equivalence point?
(e) What is the pH at the equivalence point?
(f) What indicator would be most suitable for this titration? (See Figure 18.10.)
(g) What is the pH when 105% of the required base has been added?

31. Using Figure 18.10, suggest an indicator to use in each of the following titrations:
(a) The weak base pyridine is titrated with HCl.
(b) Formic acid is titrated with NaOH.
(c) Ethylenediamine, a weak diprotic base, is titrated with HCl.

32. ■ Using Figure 18.10, suggest an indicator to use in each of the following titrations.
(a) $NaHCO_3$ is titrated to CO_3^{2-} with NaOH.
(b) Hypochlorous acid is titrated with NaOH.
(c) Trimethylamine is titrated with HCl.

Solubility Guidelines
(Review Section 3.5, Figure 3.10, and Example 3.2; also see ChemistryNow.)

33. Name two insoluble salts of each of the following ions.
(a) Cl^-
(b) Zn^{2+}
(c) Fe^{2+}

34. Name two insoluble salts of each of the following ions.
(a) SO_4^{2-}
(b) Ni^{2+}
(c) Br^-

35. Using the solubility guidelines (Figure 3.10), predict whether each of the following is insoluble or soluble in water.
(a) $(NH_4)_2CO_3$
(b) $ZnSO_4$
(c) NiS
(d) $BaSO_4$

36. ■ Predict whether each of the following is insoluble or soluble in water.
(a) $Pb(NO_3)_2$
(b) $Fe(OH)_3$
(c) $ZnCl_2$
(d) CuS

Writing Solubility Product Constant Expressions
(See Exercise 18.11 and ChemistryNow Screen 18.9.)

37. For each of the following insoluble salts, (1) write a balanced equation showing the equilibrium occurring when the salt is added to water, and (2) write the K_{sp} expression.
(a) AgCN
(b) $NiCO_3$
(c) $AuBr_3$

38. For each of the following insoluble salts, (1) write a balanced equation showing the equilibrium occurring when the salt is added to water, and (2) write the K_{sp} expression.
   (a) $PbSO_4$
   (b) BaF_2
   (c) Ag_3PO_4

Calculating K_{sp}
(See Example 18.8 and ChemistryNow Screen 18.10.)

39. When 1.55 g of solid thallium(I) bromide is added to 1.00 L of water, the salt dissolves to a small extent.

$$TlBr(s) \rightleftharpoons Tl^+(aq) + Br^-(aq)$$

The thallium(I) and bromide ions in equilibrium with TlBr each have a concentration of 1.9×10^{-3} M. What is the value of K_{sp} for TlBr?

40. ■ At 20 °C, a saturated aqueous solution of silver acetate, $AgCH_3CO_2$, contains 1.0 g of the silver compound dissolved in 100.0 mL of solution. Calculate K_{sp} for silver acetate.

$$AgCH_3CO_2(s) \rightleftharpoons Ag^+(aq) + CH_3CO_2^-(aq)$$

41. When 250 mg of SrF_2, strontium fluoride, is added to 1.00 L of water, the salt dissolves to a very small extent.

$$SrF_2(s) \rightleftharpoons Sr^{2+}(aq) + 2 F^-(aq)$$

At equilibrium, the concentration of Sr^{2+} is found to be 1.03×10^{-3} M. What is the value of K_{sp} for SrF_2?

42. ■ Calcium hydroxide, $Ca(OH)_2$, dissolves in water to the extent of 1.3 g per liter. What is the value of K_{sp} for $Ca(OH)_2$?

$$Ca(OH)_2(s) \rightleftharpoons Ca^{2+}(aq) + 2 OH^-(aq)$$

43. You add 0.979 g of $Pb(OH)_2$ to 1.00 L of pure water at 25 °C. The pH is 9.15. Estimate the value of K_{sp} for $Pb(OH)_2$.

44. You place 1.234 g of solid $Ca(OH)_2$ in 1.00 L of pure water at 25 °C. The pH of the solution is found to be 12.68. Estimate the value of K_{sp} for $Ca(OH)_2$.

Estimating Salt Solubility from K_{sp}
(See Examples 18.9 and 18.10, Exercise 8.14, and ChemistryNow Screen 18.11.)

45. Estimate the solubility of silver iodide in pure water at 25 °C (a) in moles per liter and (b) in grams per liter.

$$AgI(s) \rightleftharpoons Ag^+(aq) + I^-(aq)$$

46. ■ What is the molar concentration of $Au^+(aq)$ in a saturated solution of AuCl in pure water at 25 °C?

$$AuCl(s) \rightleftharpoons Au^+(aq) + Cl^-(aq)$$

47. Estimate the solubility of calcium fluoride, CaF_2, (a) in moles per liter and (b) in grams per liter of pure water.

$$CaF_2(s) \rightleftharpoons Ca^{2+}(aq) + 2 F^-(aq)$$

48. ■ Estimate the solubility of lead(II) bromide (a) in moles per liter and (b) in grams per liter of pure water.

49. The K_{sp} value for radium sulfate, $RaSO_4$, is 4.2×10^{-11}. If 25 mg of radium sulfate is placed in 1.00×10^2 mL of water, does all of it dissolve? If not, how much dissolves?

50. If 55 mg of lead(II) sulfate is placed in 250 mL of pure water, does all of it dissolve? If not, how much dissolves?

51. Use K_{sp} values to decide which compound in each of the following pairs is the more soluble.
   (a) $PbCl_2$ or $PbBr_2$
   (b) HgS or FeS
   (c) $Fe(OH)_2$ or $Zn(OH)_2$

52. Use K_{sp} values to decide which compound in each of the following pairs is the more soluble.
   (a) AgBr or AgSCN
   (b) $SrCO_3$ or $SrSO_4$
   (c) AgI or PbI_2
   (d) MgF_2 or CaF_2

The Common Ion Effect and Salt Solubility
(See Examples 18.11 and 18.12 and ChemistryNow Screen 18.12.)

53. Calculate the molar solubility of silver thiocyanate, AgSCN, in pure water and in water containing 0.010 M NaSCN.

54. ■ Calculate the solubility of silver bromide, AgBr, in moles per liter, in pure water. Compare this value with the molar solubility of AgBr in 225 mL of water to which 0.15 g of NaBr has been added.

55. Compare the solubility, in milligrams per milliliter, of silver iodide, AgI, (a) in pure water and (b) in water that is 0.020 M in $AgNO_3$.

56. What is the solubility, in milligrams per milliliter, of BaF_2, (a) in pure water and (b) in water containing 5.0 mg/mL KF?

The Effect of Basic Anions on Salt Solubility
(See pages 882–883 and ChemistryNow Screen 18.13.)

57. Which insoluble compound in each pair should be more soluble in nitric acid than in pure water?
   (a) $PbCl_2$ or PbS
   (b) Ag_2CO_3 or AgI
   (c) $Al(OH)_3$ or AgCl

58. ■ Which compound in each pair is more soluble in water than is predicted by a calculation from K_{sp}?
   (a) AgI or Ag_2CO_3
   (b) $PbCO_3$ or $PbCl_2$
   (c) AgCl or AgCN

Precipitation Reactions

(See Examples 18.13–18.15 and ChemistryNow Screen 18.14.)

59. You have a solution that has a lead(II) ion concentration of 0.0012 M.

$$PbCl_2(s) \rightleftharpoons Pb^{2+}(aq) + 2\ Cl^-(aq)$$

If enough soluble chloride-containing salt is added so that the Cl^- concentration is 0.010 M, will $PbCl_2$ precipitate?

60. ■ Sodium carbonate is added to a solution in which the concentration of Ni^{2+} ion is 0.0024 M.

$$NiCO_3(s) \rightleftharpoons Ni^{2+}(aq) + CO_3{}^{2-}(aq)$$

Will precipitation of $NiCO_3$ occur (a) when the concentration of the carbonate ion is 1.0×10^{-6} M or (b) when it is 100 times greater (or 1.0×10^{-4} M)?

61. If the concentration of Zn^{2+} in 10.0 mL of water is 1.63×10^{-4} M, will zinc hydroxide, $Zn(OH)_2$, precipitate when 4.0 mg of NaOH is added?

62. You have 95 mL of a solution that has a lead(II) concentration of 0.0012 M. Will $PbCl_2$ precipitate when 1.20 g of solid NaCl is added?

63. If the concentration of Mg^{2+} ion in seawater is 1350 mg per liter, what OH^- concentration is required to precipitate $Mg(OH)_2$?

64. ■ Will a precipitate of $Mg(OH)_2$ form when 25.0 mL of 0.010 M NaOH is combined with 75.0 mL of a 0.10 M solution of magnesium chloride?

Equilibria Involving Complex Ions

(See Examples 18.16 and 18.17 and ChemistryNow Screen 18.16.)

65. Zinc hydroxide is amphoteric (page 791). Use equilibrium constants to show that, given sufficient OH^-, $Zn(OH)_2$ can dissolve in NaOH.

66. ■ Solid silver iodide, AgI, can be dissolved by adding aqueous sodium cyanide to it. Calculate K_{net} for the following reaction.

$$AgI(s) + 2\ CN^-(aq) \rightleftharpoons [Ag(CN)_2]^-(aq) + I^-(aq)$$

67. ▲ What amount of ammonia (moles) must be added to dissolve 0.050 mol of AgCl suspended in 1.0 L of water?

68. Can you dissolve 15.0 mg of AuCl in 100.0 mL of water if you add 15.0 mL of 6.00 M NaCN?

69. What is the solubility of AgCl (a) in pure water and (b) in 1.0 M NH_3?

70. ■ ▲ Suppose you mix 50.0 mL of 0.200 M NaCN with 10.0 mL of 0.100 M $AgNO_3$. Will the compound $Ag[Ag(CN)_2]$ precipitate? The equilibria involved are:

$$Ag[Ag(CN)_2](s) \rightleftharpoons Ag^+(aq) + [Ag(CN)_2]^-(aq)$$
$$K_{sp} = 5.0 \times 10^{-12}$$

$$Ag^+(aq) + 2\ CN^-(aq) \rightleftharpoons [Ag(CN)_2]^-(aq)$$
$$K_f = 5.0 \times 10^{21}$$

General Questions

These questions are not designated as to type or location in the chapter. They may combine several concepts.

71. In each of the following cases, decide whether a precipitate will form when mixing the indicated reagents, and write a balanced equation for the reaction.
(a) $NaBr(aq) + AgNO_3(aq)$
(b) $KCl(aq) + Pb(NO_3)_2(aq)$

72. ■ In each of the following cases, decide whether a precipitate will form when mixing the indicated reagents, and write a balanced equation for the reaction.
(a) $Na_2SO_4(aq) + Mg(NO_3)_2(aq)$
(b) $K_3PO_4(aq) + FeCl_3(aq)$

73. If you mix 48 mL of 0.0012 M $BaCl_2$ with 24 mL of 1.0×10^{-6} M Na_2SO_4, will a precipitate of $BaSO_4$ form?

74. ■ Calculate the hydronium ion concentration and the pH of the solution that results when 20.0 mL of 0.15 M acetic acid, CH_3CO_2H, is mixed with 5.0 mL of 0.17 M NaOH.

75. Calculate the hydronium ion concentration and the pH of the solution that results when 50.0 mL of 0.40 M NH_3 is mixed with 25.0 mL of 0.20 M HCl.

76. ■ For each of the following cases, decide whether the pH is less than 7, equal to 7, or greater than 7.
(a) Equal volumes of 0.10 M acetic acid, CH_3CO_2H, and 0.10 M KOH are mixed.
(b) 25 mL of 0.015 M NH_3 is mixed with 12 mL of 0.015 M HCl.
(c) 150 mL of 0.20 M HNO_3 is mixed with 75 mL of 0.40 M NaOH.
(d) 25 mL of 0.45 M H_2SO_4 is mixed with 25 mL of 0.90 M NaOH.

77. Rank the following compounds in order of increasing solubility in water: Na_2CO_3, $BaCO_3$, Ag_2CO_3.

78. A sample of hard water contains about 2.0×10^{-3} M Ca^{2+}. A soluble fluoride-containing salt such as NaF is added to "fluoridate" the water (to aid in the prevention of dental caries). What is the maximum concentration of F^- that can be present without precipitating CaF_2?

Dietary sources of fluoride ion. Adding fluoride ion to drinking water (or toothpaste) prevents the formation of dental caries.

79. What is the pH of a buffer solution prepared from 5.15 g of NH_4NO_3 and 0.10 L of 0.15 M NH_3? What is the new pH if the solution is diluted with pure water to a volume of 5.00×10^2 mL?

80. ■ If you place 5.0 mg of $SrSO_4$ in 1.0 L of pure water, will all of the salt dissolve before equilibrium is established, or will some salt remain undissolved?

Charles D. Winters

$SO_4{}^{2-}$

Celestite, SrSO₄
Strontium sulfate

81. Describe the effect on the pH of the following actions:
(a) Adding sodium acetate, $NaCH_3CO_2$, to 0.100 M CH_3CO_2H
(b) Adding $NaNO_3$ to 0.100 M HNO_3
(c) Explain why there is or is not an effect in each case.

82. ■ What volume of 0.120 M NaOH must be added to 100. mL of 0.100 M $NaHC_2O_4$ to reach a pH of 4.70?

83. ■ ▲ A buffer solution is prepared by dissolving 1.50 g each of benzoic acid, $C_6H_5CO_2H$, and sodium benzoate, $NaC_6H_5CO_2$, in 150.0 mL of solution.
(a) What is the pH of this buffer solution?
(b) Which buffer component must be added, and what quantity is needed to change the pH to 4.00?
(c) What quantity of 2.0 M NaOH or 2.0 M HCl must be added to the buffer to change the pH to 4.00?

84. What volume of 0.200 M HCl must be added to 500.0 mL of 0.250 M NH_3 to have a buffer with a pH of 9.00?

85. What is the equilibrium constant for the following reaction?

$$AgCl(s) + I^-(aq) \rightleftharpoons AgI(s) + Cl^-(aq)$$

Does the equilibrium lie predominantly to the left or to the right? Will AgI form if iodide ion, I^-, is added to a saturated solution of AgCl?

86. Calculate the equilibrium constant for the following reaction.

$$Zn(OH)_2(s) + 2\ CN^-(aq) \rightleftharpoons Zn(CN)_2(s) + 2\ OH^-(aq)$$

Does the equilibrium lie predominantly to the left or to the right? Can zinc hydroxide be transformed into zinc cyanide by adding a soluble salt of the cyanide ion?

87. ▲ In principle, the ions Ba^{2+} and Ca^{2+} can be separated by the difference in solubility of their fluorides, BaF_2 and CaF_2. If you have a solution that is 0.10 M in both Ba^{2+} and Ca^{2+}, CaF_2 will begin to precipitate first as fluoride ion is added slowly to the solution.
(a) What concentration of fluoride ion will precipitate the maximum amount of Ca^{2+} ion without precipitating BaF_2?
(b) What concentration of Ca^{2+} remains in solution when BaF_2 just begins to precipitate?

88. ■ ▲ A solution contains 0.10 M iodide ion, I^-, and 0.10 M carbonate ion, $CO_3{}^{2-}$.
(a) If solid $Pb(NO_3)_2$ is slowly added to the solution, which salt will precipitate first, PbI_2 or $PbCO_3$?
(b) What will be the concentration of the first ion that precipitates ($CO_3{}^{2-}$ or I^-) when the second, more soluble salt begins to precipitate?

Charles D. Winters

Lead iodide ($K_{sp} = 9.8 \times 10^{-9}$) is a bright yellow solid.

89. ■ ▲ A solution contains Ca^{2+} and Pb^{2+} ions, both at a concentration of 0.010 M. You wish to separate the two ions from each other as completely as possible by precipitating one but not the other using aqueous Na_2SO_4 as the precipitating agent.
(a) Which will precipitate first as sodium sulfate is added, $CaSO_4$ or $PbSO_4$?
(b) What will be the concentration of the first ion that precipitates (Ca^{2+} or Pb^{2+}) when the second, more soluble salt begins to precipitate?

90. ■ Buffer capacity is defined as the number of moles of a strong acid or strong base that are required to change the pH of one liter of the buffer solution by one unit. What is the buffer capacity of a solution that is 0.10 M in acetic acid and 0.10 M in sodium acetate?

91. The Ca^{2+} ion in hard water can be precipitated as $CaCO_3$ by adding soda ash, Na_2CO_3. If the calcium ion concentration in hard water is 0.010 M and if the Na_2CO_3 is added until the carbonate ion concentration is 0.050 M, what percentage of the calcium ions have been removed from the water? (You may neglect carbonate ion hydrolysis.)

This sample of calcium carbonate ($K_{sp} = 3.4 \times 10^{-9}$) was deposited in a cave formation.

92. ■ Some photographic film is coated with crystals of AgBr suspended in gelatin. Some of the silver ions are reduced to silver metal on exposure to light. Unexposed AgBr is then dissolved with sodium thiosulfate in the "fixing" step.

$$AgBr(s) + 2\ S_2O_3{}^{2-}(aq) \rightleftharpoons$$
$$[Ag(S_2O_3)_2]^{3-}(aq) + Br^-(aq)$$

(a) What is the equilibrium constant for the reaction above?
(b) What mass of $Na_2S_2O_3$ must be added to dissolve 1.00 g of AgBr suspended in 1.00 L of water?

In the Laboratory

93. Each pair of ions below is found together in aqueous solution. Using the table of solubility product constants in Appendix J, devise a way to separate these ions by precipitating one of them as an insoluble salt and leaving the other in solution.
(a) Ba^{2+} and Na^+
(b) Ni^{2+} and Pb^{2+}

94. ■ Each pair of ions below is found together in aqueous solution. Using the table of solubility product constants in Appendix J, devise a way to separate these ions by adding one reagent to precipitate one of them as an insoluble salt and leave the other in solution.
(a) Cu^{2+} and Ag^+
(b) Al^{3+} and Fe^{3+}

95. ▲ The cations Ba^{2+} and Sr^{2+} can be precipitated as very insoluble sulfates.
(a) If you add sodium sulfate to a solution containing these metal cations, each with a concentration of 0.10 M, which is precipitated first, $BaSO_4$ or $SrSO_4$?
(b) What will be the concentration of the first ion that precipitates (Ba^{2+} or Sr^{2+}) when the second, more soluble salt begins to precipitate?

96. ■ ▲ You will often work with salts of Fe^{3+}, Pb^{2+}, and Al^{3+} in the laboratory. (All are found in nature, and all are important economically.) If you have a solution containing these three ions, each at a concentration of 0.10 M, what is the order in which their hydroxides precipitate as aqueous NaOH is slowly added to the solution?

97. Aniline hydrochloride, $(C_6H_5NH_3)Cl$, is a weak acid. (Its conjugate base is the weak base aniline, $C_6H_5NH_2$.) The acid can be titrated with a strong base such as NaOH.

$$C_6H_5NH_3{}^+(aq) + OH^-(aq) \rightleftharpoons$$
$$C_6H_5NH_2(aq) + H_2O(\ell)$$

Assume 50.0 mL of 0.100 M aniline hydrochloride is titrated with 0.185 M NaOH. (K_a for aniline hydrochloride is 2.4×10^{-5}.)
(a) What is the pH of the $(C_6H_5NH_3)Cl$ solution before the titration begins?
(b) What is the pH at the equivalence point?
(c) What is the pH at the halfway point of the titration?
(d) Which indicator in Figure 18.10 could be used to detect the equivalence point?
(e) Calculate the pH of the solution after adding 10.0, 20.0, and 30.0 mL of base.
(f) Combine the information in parts (a), (b), and (e), and plot an approximate titration curve.

▲ more challenging   ■ in OWL   Blue-numbered questions answered in Appendix O

98. ■ The weak base ethanolamine, $HOCH_2CH_2NH_2$, can be titrated with HCl.

$$HOCH_2CH_2NH_2(aq) + H_3O^+(aq) \rightleftharpoons$$
$$HOCH_2CH_2NH_3^+(aq) + H_2O(\ell)$$

Assume you have 25.0 mL of a 0.010 M solution of ethanolamine and titrate it with 0.0095 M HCl. (K_b for ethanolamine is 3.2×10^{-5}.)

(a) What is the pH of the ethanolamine solution before the titration begins?

(b) What is the pH at the equivalence point?

(c) What is the pH at the halfway point of the titration?

(d) Which indicator in Figure 18.10 would be the best choice to detect the equivalence point?

(e) Calculate the pH of the solution after adding 5.00, 10.0, 20.0, and 30.0 mL of the acid.

(f) Combine the information in parts (a), (b), and (e), and plot an approximate titration curve.

99. For the titration of 50.0 mL of 0.150 M ethylamine, $C_2H_5NH_2$, with 0.100 M HCl, find the pH at each of the following points, and then use that information to sketch the titration curve and decide on an appropriate indicator.

(a) At the beginning, before HCl is added

(b) At the halfway point in the titration

(c) When 75% of the required acid has been added

(d) At the equivalence point

(e) When 10.0 mL more HCl has been added than is required

(f) Sketch the titration curve.

(g) Suggest an appropriate indicator for this titration.

100. A buffer solution with a pH of 12.00 consists of Na_3PO_4 and Na_2HPO_4. The volume of solution is 200.0 mL.

(a) Which component of the buffer is present in a larger amount?

(b) If the concentration of Na_3PO_4 is 0.400 M, what mass of Na_2HPO_4 is present?

(c) Which component of the buffer must be added to change the pH to 12.25? What mass of that component is required?

101. ■ To have a buffer with a pH of 2.50, what volume of 0.150 M NaOH must be added to 100. mL of 0.230 M H_3PO_4?

102. ■ ▲ What mass of Na_3PO_4 must be added to 80.0 mL of 0.200 M HCl to obtain a buffer with a pH of 7.75?

103. You have a solution that contains $AgNO_3$, $Pb(NO_3)_2$, and $Cu(NO_3)_2$. Devise a separation method that results in having Ag^+ in one test tube, Pb^{2+} ions in another, and Cu^{2+} in a third test tube. Use solubility guidelines and K_{sp} and K_f values.

104. Once you have separated the three salts in Study Question 103 into three test tubes, you now need to confirm their presence.

(a) For Pb^{2+} ion, one way to do this is to treat a precipitate of $PbCl_2$ with K_2CrO_4 to produce $PbCrO_4$. Using K_{sp} values, confirm that the chloride salt should be converted to the chromate salt.

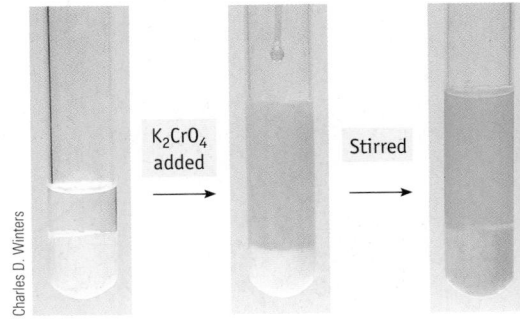

White $PbCl_2$ is converted to yellow $PbCrO_4$ on adding K_2CrO_4.

(b) Suggest a method of confirming the presence of Ag^+ and Cu^{2+} ions using complex ions.

Summary and Conceptual Questions
The following questions may use concepts from this and previous chapters.

105. ■ Suggest a method for separating a precipitate consisting of a mixture of solid CuS and solid $Cu(OH)_2$.

106. Which of the following barium salts should dissolve in a strong acid such as HCl: $Ba(OH)_2$, $BaSO_4$, or $BaCO_3$?

107. Explain why the solubility of Ag_3PO_4 can be greater in water than is calculated from the K_{sp} value of the salt.

108. ■ Two acids, each approximately 0.01 M in concentration, are titrated separately with a strong base. The acids show the following pH values at the equivalence point: HA, pH = 9.5, and HB, pH = 8.5.
(a) Which is the stronger acid, HA or HB?
(b) Which of the conjugate bases, A⁻ or B⁻, is the stronger base?

109. ■ Composition diagrams, commonly known as "alpha plots," are often used to visualize the species in a solution of an acid or base as the pH is varied. The diagram for 0.100 M acetic acid is shown here.

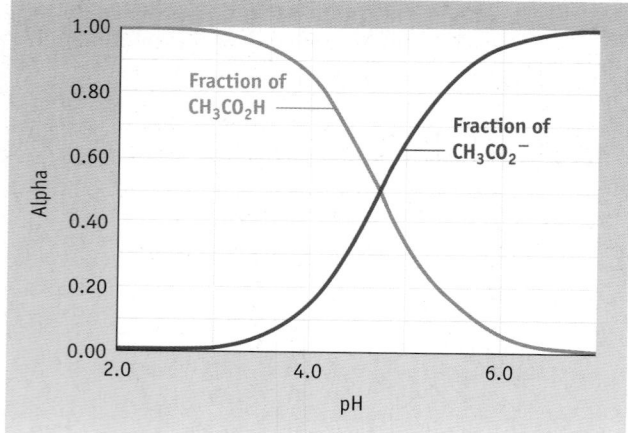

The plot shows how the fraction [= alpha (α)] of acetic acid in solution,

$$\alpha = \frac{[CH_3CO_2H]}{[CH_3CO_2H] + [CH_3CO_2^-]}$$

changes as the pH increases (blue curve). (The red curve shows how the fraction of acetate ion, $CH_3CO_2^-$, changes as the pH increases.) Alpha plots are another way of viewing the relative concentrations of acetic acid and acetate ion as a strong base is added to a solution of acetic acid in the course of a titration.
(a) Explain why the fraction of acetic acid declines and that of acetate ion increases as the pH increases.
(b) Which species predominates at a pH of 4, acetic acid or acetate ion? What is the situation at a pH of 6?
(c) Consider the point where the two lines cross. The fraction of acetic acid in the solution is 0.5, and so is that of acetate ion. That is, the solution is half acid and half conjugate base; their concentrations are equal. At this point, the graph shows the pH is 4.74. Explain why the pH at this point is 4.74.

110. The composition diagram, or alpha plot, for the important acid–base system of carbonic acid, H_2CO_3, is illustrated below. (See Study Question 109 for more information on such diagrams.)

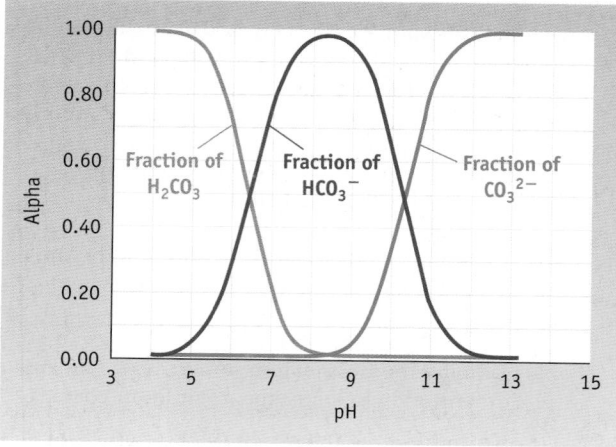

(a) Explain why the fraction of bicarbonate ion, HCO_3^-, rises and then falls as the pH increases.
(b) What is the composition of the solution when the pH is 6.0? When the pH is 10.0?
(c) If you wanted to buffer a solution at a pH of 11.0, what should be the ratio of HCO_3^- to CO_3^{2-}?

111. The chemical name for aspirin is acetylsalicylic acid. It is believed that the analgesic and other desirable properties of aspirin are due not to the aspirin itself but rather to the simpler compound salicylic acid, $C_6H_4(OH)CO_2H$, that results from the breakdown of aspirin in the stomach.

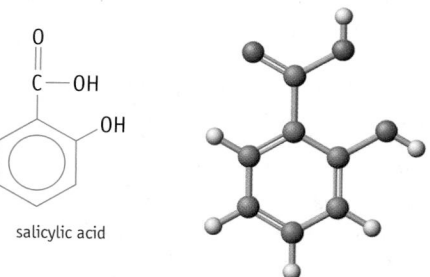

salicylic acid

(a) Give approximate values for the following bond angles in the acid: (i) C—C—C in the ring; (ii) O—C=O; (iii) either of the C—O—H angles; and (iv) C—C—H.
(b) What is the hybridization of the C atoms of the ring? Of the C atom in the —CO_2H group?
(c) Experiment shows that 1.00 g of the acid will dissolve in 460 mL of water. If the pH of this solution is 2.4, what is K_a for the acid?

(d) If you have salicylic acid in your stomach and if the pH of gastric juice is 2.0, calculate the percentage of salicylic acid that will be present in the stomach in the form of the salicylate ion, $C_6H_4(OH)CO_2^-$.

(e) Assume you have 25.0 mL of a 0.014 M solution of salicylic acid and titrate it with 0.010 M NaOH. What is the pH at the halfway point of the titration? What is the pH at the equivalence point?

112. Aluminum chloride reacts with phosphoric acid to give $AlPO_4$. The substance is used industrially as adhesives, binders, and cements.

(a) Write the balanced equation for the preparation of $AlPO_4$ from aluminum chloride and phosphoric acid.

(b) If you begin with 152 g of aluminum chloride and 3.00 L of 0.750 M phosphoric acid, what is the theoretical yield of $AlPO_4$?

(c) If you place 25.0 g of $AlPO_4$ in 1.00 L of water, what are the concentrations of Al^{3+} and PO_4^{3-} at equilibrium? (Neglect hydrolysis of aqueous Al^{3+} and PO_4^{3-} ion.) K_{sp} for $AlPO_4$ is 1.3×10^{-20}.

(d) Does the solubility of $AlPO_4$ increase or decrease on adding HCl? Explain.

Charles D. Winters

This is a sample of hydrated aluminum phosphate, a mineral known as augelite.

19 | Principles of Reactivity: Entropy and Free Energy

Can Ethanol Contribute to Energy and Environmental Goals?

About 3.4 billion gallons of ethanol were blended into gasoline in 2004. According to A. E. Farrell, et al. (*Science*, Vol. 311, pp. 506–508, 2006), this amounted to about 2% of all gasoline sold by volume and 1.3% of its energy content. This is a significant contribution to the energy used in the United States, and it promises to be larger in the future. Therefore, the use of ethanol as a substitute for gasoline has been widely discussed in the popular press and in the scientific literature.

Charles D. Winters

Thus far, the ethanol used as a fuel in the United States is largely derived from corn.

Let us focus on two points at the beginning of this chapter: the energetics of ethanol combustion and the production of the greenhouse gas, CO_2. Let us compare the energy and amount of CO_2 released by burning 1.00 kg of liquid ethanol (C_2H_5OH) and, to represent gasoline, 1.00 kg of liquid octane (C_8H_{18}).

Questions:

1. Calculate $\Delta_r H°$ and $\Delta_r G°$ for the combustion of 1.00 kg each of liquid ethanol and liquid octane. Which fuel releases more energy per kilogram? [Values for $\Delta_f H°$ and $S°$ are located in Appendix L. In addition, for liquid octane at 298 K, $\Delta_f H° = -250.0$ kJ/mol and $S° = 361.2$ J/K · mol.]

2. Compare the two fuels on the basis of the release of CO_2, a common greenhouse gas. Which fuel produces more CO_2 per kilogram?

3. On the basis of this simple comparison and neglecting the energy costs involved in producing 1.00 kg each of ethanol and octane, which is the better fuel in terms of energy production and greenhouse gases?

Answers to these questions are in Appendix Q.

Change is central to chemistry, so it is important to understand the factors that determine whether a change will occur. In chemistry, we encounter many examples of chemical change (chemical reactions) and physical change (the formation of mixtures, expansion of gases, and changes of state, to name a few). Chemists use the term **spontaneous** to represent a change that occurs without outside intervention. *Spontaneous changes occur only in the direction that leads to equilibrium.* Whether or not the process is spontaneous does not tell us anything about the rate of the change or the extent to which a process will occur before equilibrium is reached. It says only that the change will occur in a specific direction (toward equilibrium) and will occur naturally and unaided.

If a piece of hot metal is placed in a beaker of cold water, energy is transferred spontaneously as heat from the hot metal to the cooler water (Figure 19.1), and energy transfer will continue until the two objects are at the same temperature and thermal equilibrium is attained. Similarly, chemical reactions proceed spontaneously until equilibrium is reached, regardless of whether the position of the equilibrium favors products or reactants. We readily recognize that, starting with pure reactants, all product-favored reactions must be spontaneous, such as the formation of water from gaseous hydrogen and oxygen and the neutralization of $H_3O^+(aq)$ and $OH^-(aq)$ (◄ Chapter 3). Notice, however, that reactant-favored reactions are also spontaneous until equilibrium is achieved. Even though the dissolution of $CaCO_3$ is reactant-favored at equilibrium, if you place a handful of $CaCO_3$ in water, the process of dissolving will proceed spontaneously until equilibrium is reached.

All physical and chemical changes occur in a direction toward achieving equilibrium. Systems never change spontaneously in a direction that takes them farther from equilibrium. Given two objects at the same temperature, in contact but thermally isolated from their surroundings, it will never happen that one will heat up while the other becomes colder. Gas molecules will never spontaneously congregate at one end of a flask. Similarly, once equilibrium is established, the small amount of dissolved $CaCO_3$ in equilibrium with solid $CaCO_3$ will not spontaneously precipitate from solution.

The factors that determine the directionality and extent of change are among the topics of this chapter.

Chemistry ⦿ Now™

Throughout the text this icon introduces an opportunity for self-study or to explore interactive tutorials by signing in at **www.cengage.com/login**.

Charles D. Winters

FIGURE 19.1 A spontaneous process. The heated metal cylinder is placed in water. Energy transfers as heat spontaneously from the metal to water, that is, from the hotter object to the cooler object.

A Review of Concepts of Thermodynamics

To understand the thermodynamic concepts introduced in this chapter, be sure to review the ideas of Chapter 5.

System: The part of the universe under study.

Surroundings: The rest of the universe exclusive of the system, capable of exchanging energy and/or matter with the system.

Exothermic: Energy transfers as heat from the system to the surroundings.

Endothermic: Energy transfers as heat from the surroundings to the system.

First law of thermodynamics: The law of conservation of energy, $\Delta U = q + w$. The change in internal energy of a system is the sum of energy transferred as heat to or from the system and the work done on or by the system. The first law states that energy cannot be created or destroyed.

Enthalpy change: The energy transferred as heat at constant pressure.

State function: A quantity whose value depends only on the state of the system; changes in a state function can be calculated by taking into account the initial and final states of a system.

Standard conditions: Pressure of 1 bar (1 bar = 0.98692 atm) and solution concentration of 1 *m*.

Standard enthalpy of formation, $\Delta_f H°$: The enthalpy change occurring when a compound is formed from its elements in their standard states.

19.1 Spontaneity and Energy Transfer as Heat

■ **Spontaneous Processes** A spontaneous physical or chemical change proceeds to equilibrium without outside intervention. Such a process may or may not be product-favored at equilibrium.

We can readily recognize many chemical reactions that are spontaneous, such as hydrogen and oxygen combining to form water, methane burning to give CO_2 and H_2O, Na and Cl_2 reacting to form NaCl, HCl(aq), and NaOH(aq), reacting to form H_2O and NaCl(aq). A common feature of these reactions is that they are exothermic, so it would be tempting to conclude that evolution of energy as heat is the criterion that determines whether a reaction or process is spontaneous. Further inspection, however, reveals significant flaws in this reasoning. This is especially evident with the inclusion of some common spontaneous changes that are endothermic or energy neutral:

- *Dissolving NH_4NO_3.* The ionic compound NH_4NO_3 dissolves spontaneously in water. The process is endothermic ($\Delta_r H° = +25.7$ kJ/mol).
- *Expansion of a gas into a vacuum.* A system is set up with two flasks connected by a valve (Figure 19.2). One flask is filled with a gas, and the other is evacuated. When the valve is opened, the gas will flow spontaneously from one flask to the other until the pressure is the same throughout. The expansion of an ideal gas is energy neutral (although expansion of most real gases is endothermic).
- *Phase changes.* Melting of ice is an endothermic process. Above 0 °C, the melting of ice is spontaneous. Below 0 °C, melting of ice is not spontaneous. At 0 °C, no net change will occur; liquid water and ice coexist at equilibrium. This example illustrates that temperature can have a role in determining spontaneity and that equilibrium is somehow an important aspect of the problem.
- *Energy transfer as heat.* The temperature of a cold soft drink sitting in a warm environment will rise until the beverage reaches the ambient temperature. The energy required for this process comes from the surroundings. Energy transfer as heat from a hotter object (the surroundings) to a cooler object (the soft drink) is spontaneous.
- The reaction of H_2 and I_2 to form HI is endothermic, and the reverse reaction, the decomposition of HI to form H_2 and I_2, is exothermic. If $H_2(g)$ and $I_2(g)$ are mixed, a reaction forming HI will occur [$H_2(g) + I_2(g) \rightleftharpoons 2\,HI(g)$] until equilibrium is reached. Furthermore, if HI(g) is placed in a container, there will also be a reaction, but in the reverse direction, until equilibrium is achieved. Notice that approach to equilibrium occurs spontaneously from either direction.

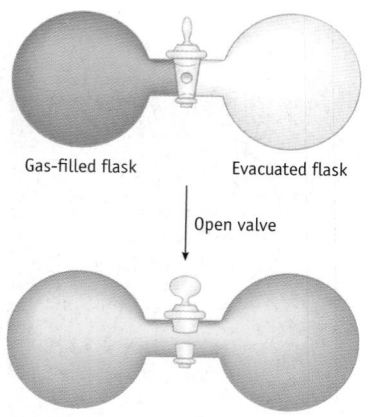

Gas-filled flask   Evacuated flask

Open valve

When the valve is opened the gas expands irreversibly to fill both flasks.

FIGURE 19.2 Spontaneous expansion of a gas. (See ChemistryNow Screen 19.3 to view an animation of this figure.)

On further reflection, it is logical to conclude that evolution of heat cannot be a sufficient criterion in determining spontaneity. The first law of thermodynamics tells us that in any process energy must be conserved. If energy is transferred out of a system, then the same amount of energy must be transferred to the surroundings. Exothermicity of the system is always accompanied by an endothermic change in the surroundings. If energy evolution were the only factor determining whether a change is spontaneous, then for every spontaneous process there would be a corresponding nonspontaneous change in the surroundings. We must search further than the first law of thermodynamics to determine whether a change is spontaneous.

19.2 Dispersal of Energy: Entropy

We have shown that we cannot use energy itself as an indicator of spontaneity because energy is conserved in any process; we always end up with the same amount of energy as we had at the beginning. Imagine dropping this book on the floor. (But don't actually do it!) It would fall spontaneously. The initial potential energy it has from being a certain distance above the floor is converted to kinetic energy. When the book hits the floor, the kinetic energy of the book is converted into other forms of kinetic energy: acoustic energy and thermal energy of the book, floor, and air, since these are all heated up somewhat. Through all of these processes, the total energy is conserved. There is a directionality to this process, however. The book will spontaneously fall to the ground, but we will not observe a book on its own jump spontaneously from the floor up to a desk. Is there a way to predict this directionality?

Let us consider the initial and final states for this process. Initially, the energy is concentrated in the book—the book has a certain potential energy as it is held above the floor. At the end of the process, the energy has been dispersed to the air, floor, and book. The energy has gone from being concentrated to being more dispersed. This is the indicator for which we have been searching. *In a spontaneous process, energy goes from being more concentrated to being more dispersed.*

There is a state function (◀ Section 5.4) called **entropy (S)** that allows us to quantify this. The **second law of thermodynamics** states that *a spontaneous process is one that results in an increase of the entropy of the universe.* In a spontaneous process, therefore, ΔS(universe) is greater than zero; this corresponds to energy being dispersed in the process.

Because thermal energy is caused by the random motion of particles, potential energy is dispersed when it is converted to thermal energy. This conversion occurs when energy is transferred as heat, q. It is therefore not surprising that q is a part of the mathematical definition of ΔS. This is not the whole picture, however, in part because q is not a state function. In addition, the effect of a given quantity of energy transferred as heat on energy dispersal is different at different temperatures. It turns out that a given q has a greater effect at a lower temperature than at a higher temperature; that is, the extent of energy dispersal is inversely proportional to the temperature.

Our proposed definition for ΔS is thus q/T, but this is still not quite correct. We must be a little more specific about q. The value of q used in the calculation of an entropy change must be the energy transferred as heat under what are called *reversible conditions*, q_{rev} (see *A Closer Look: Reversible and Irreversible Processes*). Adding energy by heating an object slowly (adding energy in very small increments) approximates a reversible process. Our mathematical definition of ΔS is therefore q_{rev} divided by the absolute (Kelvin) temperature:

$$\Delta S = \frac{q_{rev}}{T}$$

(19.1)

As this equation predicts, the units for entropy are J/K.

■ **Entropy** For a more complete discussion of entropy, see the papers by F. L. Lambert, such as "Entropy Is Simple, Qualitatively," *Journal of Chemical Education*, Vol. 79, pp. 1241–1246, 2002, and references therein. See also Lambert's site: **www.entropysite.com.** Finally, see A. H. Jungermann, "Entropy and the Shelf Model," *Journal of Chemical Education*, Vol. 83, pp. 1686–1694, 2006.

To determine entropy changes experimentally, the energy transferred by heating and cooling must be measured for a reversible process. But what is a reversible process?

The test for reversibility is that after carrying out a change along a given path (for example, energy added as heat), it must be possible to return to the starting point by the same path (energy taken away as heat) without altering the surroundings. Melting of ice and freezing of water at 0 °C are examples of reversible processes. Given a mixture of ice and water at equilibrium, adding energy as heat in small increments will convert ice to water; removing energy as heat in small increments will convert water back to ice.

Reversibility is closely associated with equilibrium. Assume that we have a system at equilibrium. Reversible changes can then be made by very slightly perturbing the equilibrium and letting the system readjust.

Spontaneous processes are often not reversible. Suppose a gas is allowed to expand into a vacuum. No work is done in this process because there is no force to resist expansion. To return the system to its original state, it is necessary to compress the gas. Doing so means doing work on the system, however, because the system will not return to its original state on its own. In this process, the energy content of the surroundings decreases by the amount of work expended by

the surroundings. The system can be restored to its original state, but the surroundings will be altered in the process.

In summary, there are two important points concerning reversibility:

- At every step along a reversible pathway between two states, the system remains at equilibrium.
- Spontaneous processes often follow irreversible pathways and involve nonequilibrium conditions.

To determine the entropy change for a process, it is necessary to identify a reversible pathway. Only then can an entropy change for the process be calculated from q_{rev} and the Kelvin temperature.

19.3 Entropy: A Microscopic Understanding

We have stated that entropy is a measure of the extent of energy dispersal. In all spontaneous physical and chemical changes, energy changes from being localized or concentrated in a system to becoming dispersed or spread out in the system and its surroundings. In a spontaneous process, the change in entropy, ΔS, of the universe indicates the extent to which energy is dispersed in a process carried out at a temperature T. So far, however, we have not explained why dispersal of energy occurs, nor have we given an equation for entropy itself. In order to do this, we will need to consider energy in its quantized form and matter on the atomic level.

Dispersal of Energy

We can explore the dispersal of energy using a simple example: energy being transferred as heat between hot and cold gaseous atoms. Consider an experiment involving two containers, one holding hot atoms and the other with cold atoms (Figure 19.3). Because they have translational energy, the atoms move randomly in each container and collide with the walls. When the containers are in contact, energy is transferred through the container walls. Eventually, both containers will be at the same temperature; the energy originally localized in the hotter atoms is distributed over a greater number of atoms; and the atoms in each container will have the same distribution of energies.

For further insight, let us look at a statistical explanation to show why energy is dispersed in a system. With statistical arguments, systems must include large numbers of particles for the arguments to be accurate. It will be easiest, however, if we look first at simple examples to understand the underlying concept and then extrapolate our conclusions to larger systems.

Consider a simple system in which, initially, there is one atom (1) with two discrete packets, or quanta, of energy and three other atoms (2, 3, and 4) with no energy (Figure 19.4). When these four atoms are brought together, the total energy in the system is 2 quanta. Collisions among the atoms allow energy to be transferred so that,

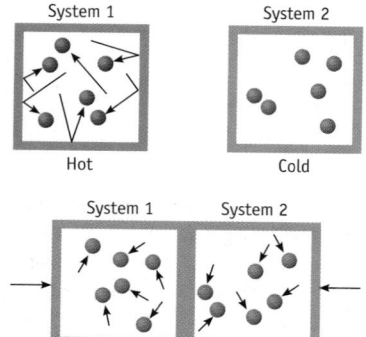

FIGURE 19.3 Energy transfer between molecules in the gas phase.

Possible distribution of energy packets

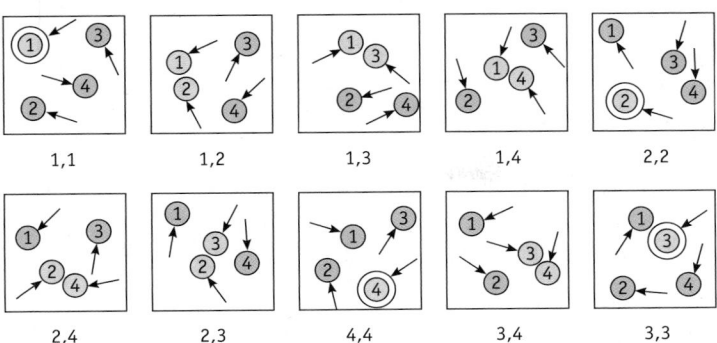

1,1   1,2   1,3   1,4   2,2

2,4   2,3   4,4   3,4   3,3

FIGURE 19.4 Energy dispersal.
Possible ways of distributing two packets of energy among four atoms. To keep our analysis simple, we assume that initially there is one atom with two quanta of energy and three atoms (2, 3 and 4) with no energy. The figure shows that there are 10 different ways to distribute the two quanta of energy over four atoms.

over time, all distributions of the two packets of energy over the four atoms are seen. There are 10 different ways to distribute these 2 quanta of energy over the four atoms. Each of these 10 different ways to distribute the energy is called a **microstate.** In only one of the microstates do the 2 quanta remain on atom 1. In fact, only in 4 of the 10 microstates [1, 1; 2, 2; 3, 3; and 4, 4] is the energy concentrated on a single atom. In the majority of cases, 6 out of 10, the energy is distributed to two different atoms. Even in a small sample (four atoms) with only two packets of energy, it is more likely that at any given time the energy will be distributed to two atoms rather than concentrated on a single atom. There is a distinct preference that the energy will be dispersed over a greater number of atoms.

Let us now add more atoms to our system. We again consider one atom (1) with 2 quanta of energy present but now have five other atoms (2, 3, 4, 5, and 6) with no energy initially. Collisions let the energy be transferred between the atoms, and we now find there are 21 possible microstates (Figure 19.5). There are six microstates in which the energy is concentrated on one atom, including one in which the energy is still on atom 1, but there are now 15 microstates in which the energy is present on two atoms. As the number of particles increases, the number of microstates available increases dramatically, and the fraction of microstates in which the energy is concentrated rather than dispersed goes down dramatically. It is much more likely that the energy will be dispersed than concentrated.

Now let us return to an example using a total of four atoms, but in which we have increased the quantity of energy from 2 quanta to 6 quanta. Assume that we start with two atoms having 3 quanta of energy each. The other two atoms initially have zero energy (Figure 19.6). Through collisions, energy can be transferred to achieve different distributions of energy among the four atoms. In all, there are 84 microstates, falling into nine basic patterns. For example, one possible arrangement has one atom with 3 quanta of energy, and three atoms with 1 quantum each. There are four microstates in which this is true (Figure 19.6c). Increasing the number of quanta from 2 to 6 with the same number of atoms increased the num-

Number of Microstates	Distribution of 2 Quanta of Energy Among Six Atoms					
6	1:1	2:2	3:3	4:4	5:5	6:6
5	1:2	2:3	3:4	4:5	5:6	
4	1:3	2:4	3:5	4:6		
3	1:4	2:5	3:6			
2	1:5	2:6				
1	1:6					

FIGURE 19.5 Distributing 2 quanta of energy among six atoms. The result is a total of 21 ways—21 microstates—of distributing 2 quanta of energy among six atoms.

FIGURE 19.6 Energy dispersal.

Possible ways of distributing 6 quanta of energy among four atoms. A total of 84 microstates is possible.

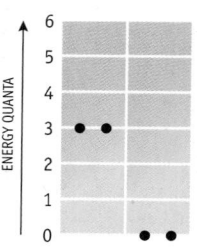

(a) Initially, four particles are separated from each other. Two particles each have 3 quanta of energy, and the other two have none. A total of 6 quanta of energy will be distributed once the particles interact.

Number of different ways to achieve this arrangement

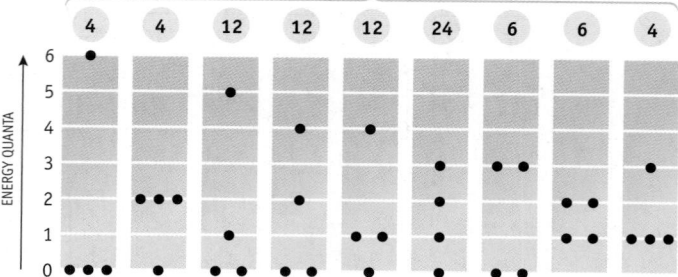

(b) Once the particles begin to interact, there are nine ways to distribute the 6 available quanta. Each of these arrangements will have multiple ways of distributing the energy among the four atoms. Part (c) shows how the arrangement on the right can be achieved four ways.

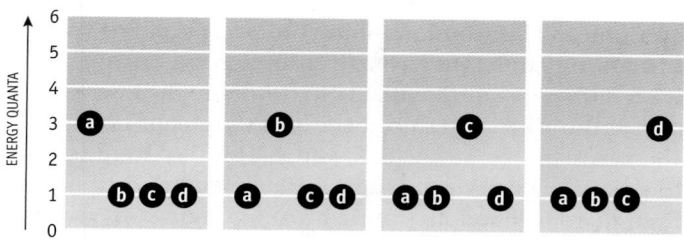

(c) There are four different ways to have four particles (a, b, c, and d) such that one particle has 3 quanta of energy and the other three each have 1 quantum of energy.

Ludwig Boltzmann (1844–1906).
Engraved on his tombstone in Vienna, Austria, is his equation defining entropy. The constant k is now known as Boltzmann's constant.

Oesper Collection in the History of Chemistry, University of Cincinnati

■ **How Many Microstates?** To give you a sense of the number of microstates available to a substance, consider a mole of ice at 273 K, where $S° = 41.3$ J/K · mol. Using Boltzmann's equation, we find that $W = 10^{1,299,000,000,000,000,000,000,000}$. That is, there are many, many more microstates for 1 mol of ice than there are atoms in the universe (about 10^{80}).

ber of possible microstates from 10 to 84. In this case, the amount of energy that is dispersed resulted in an increase in the number of microstates.

A statistical analysis for larger aggregates of atoms and energy quanta is increasingly complex, but the conclusions are even more compelling. As the number of particles and/or quanta increases, the number of energy microstates grows rapidly. These allow the extent over which the energy is dispersed and/or the amount of the energy dispersed to increase. Ludwig Boltzmann proposed that the entropy of a system (the dispersal of energy at a given temperature) results from the number of microstates available. *As the number of microstates increases, so does the entropy of the system.* He enunciated this idea over 100 years ago in the equation

$$S = k \ln W \qquad (19.2)$$

which states that the entropy of a system, S, is proportional to the natural logarithm of the number of accessible microstates, W, that belong to a given energy of a system or substance. (The proportionality constant, k, is now known as the **Boltzmann's constant**.) Within these microstates, it turns out that those states that disperse energy over the largest number of atoms are vastly more probable than the others.

Dispersal of Matter: Dispersal of Energy Revisited

In many processes, it appears that the dispersal of matter also contributes to spontaneity. We shall see, however, that these effects can also be explained in terms of energy dispersal. Let us examine a specific case. Matter dispersal was illustrated in

Figure 19.2 by the expansion of a gas into a vacuum. How is this spontaneous expansion of a gas related to energy dispersal and entropy?

We begin with the premise that all energy is quantized and that this applies to any system, including gas molecules in a room or in a reaction flask. You know from the previous discussion of kinetic molecular theory that the molecules in a gas sample have a distribution of energies (◄ Figure 11.14) (often referred to as a Boltzmann distribution). The molecules are assigned to (or "occupy") quantized microstates, most of them in states near the average energy of the system, but fewer of them in states of high or low energy. (For a gas in a laboratory-sized container, the energy levels are so closely spaced that, for most purposes, there is a continuum of energy states.)

When the gas expands to fill a larger container, the average energy of the sample and the energy for the particles in a given energy range are constant. However, quantum mechanics shows (for now, you will have to take our word for it) that as a consequence of having a larger volume in which the molecules can move in the expanded state, there is an increase in the number of microstates and that those microstates are even more closely spaced than before (Figure 19.7). The result of this greater density of microstates is that the number of microstates available to the gas particles increases when the gas expands. Gas expansion, a dispersal of matter, leads to the dispersal of energy over a larger number of more closely spaced microstates and thus to an increase in entropy.

The logic applied to the expansion of a gas into a vacuum can be used to rationalize the mixing of two gases, the mixing of two liquids, or the dissolution of a solid in a liquid (Figure 19.8). For example, if flasks containing O_2 and N_2 are connected (in an experimental setup like that in Figure 19.2), the two gases diffuse together, eventually leading to a mixture in which O_2 and N_2 molecules are evenly distributed throughout the total volume. A mixture of O_2 and N_2 will never separate into samples of each component of its own accord. The gases spontaneously move toward a situation in which each gas and its energy are maximally dispersed. The energy of the system is dispersed over a larger number of microstates, and the entropy of the system increases. Indeed, this is a large part of the explanation for the fact that similar liquids (such as oil and gasoline or water and ethanol) will readily form homogeneous solutions. Recall the rule of thumb that "like dissolves like" (◄ Chapter 14).

■ **Statistical Thermodynamics** The arguments presented here come from a branch of chemistry called statistical thermodynamics. For an accessible treatment see H. Jungermann, *Journal of Chemical Education*, Vol. 83, pp. 1686–1694, 2006.

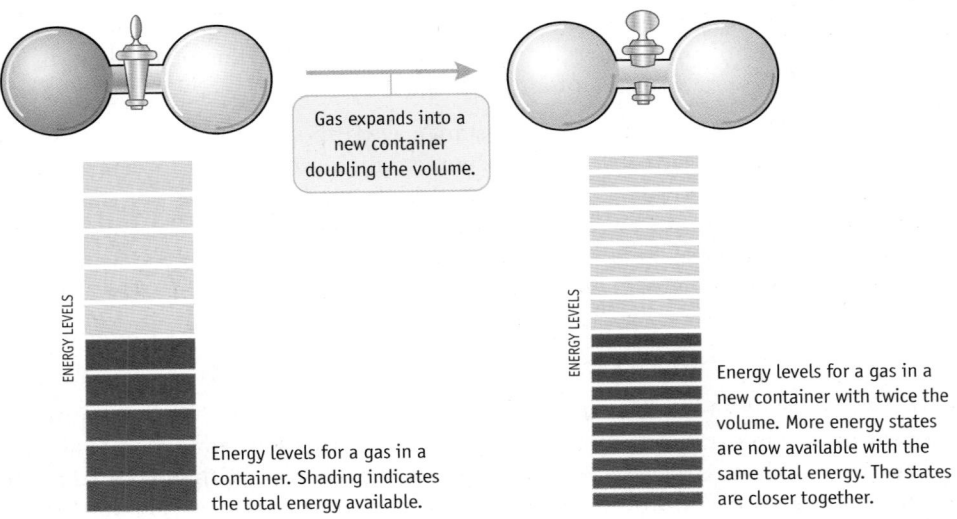

Energy levels for a gas in a container. Shading indicates the total energy available.

Gas expands into a new container doubling the volume.

Energy levels for a gas in a new container with twice the volume. More energy states are now available with the same total energy. The states are closer together.

FIGURE 19.7 Energy (and matter) dispersal. As the size of the container for the chemical or physical change increases, the number of microstates accessible to the atoms or molecules of the system increases, and the density of states increases. A consequence of the distribution of molecules over a greater number of microstates is an increase in entropy.

Note that for a gas in a container of the size likely to be found in a laboratory, the energy levels are so closely spaced that we do not need to think in terms of quantization of energy levels. For most purposes, the system can be regarded as having a continuum of energy levels.

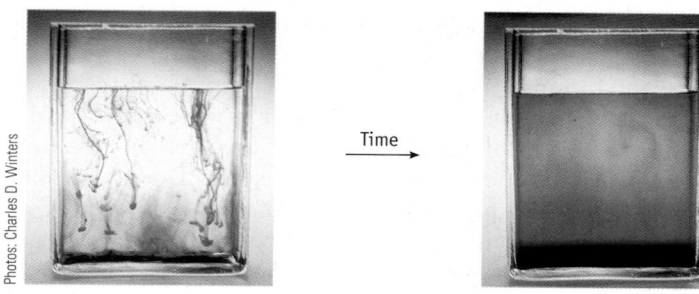

FIGURE 19.8 **Dissolving KMnO₄ in water.** A small quantity of solid, purple KMnO₄ is added to water (left). With time, the solid dissolves, and the highly colored MnO_4^- ions (and the K^+ ions) become dispersed throughout the solution. Entropy makes a large contribution to the mixing of liquids and solutions.

Time

■ **Entropy Change on Gas Expansion** The entropy change for a gas expansion can be calculated from

$$\Delta S = nR\ln(V_{final}/V_{initial})$$

At a given temperature, V is proportional to the number of microstates, so the equation is related to $k \ln(W_{final}/W_{initial})$.

A Summary: Entropy, Entropy Change, and Energy Dispersal

According to Boltzmann's equation for entropy, entropy is proportional to the number of ways that energy can be dispersed in a substance, that is, to the number of microstates available to the system (W). Thus, there will be a change in entropy, ΔS, if there is a change in the number of microstates over which energy can be dispersed.

$$\Delta S = S_{final} - S_{initial} = k\,(\ln W_{final} - \ln W_{initial}) = k\ln(W_{final}/W_{initial})$$

Our focus as chemists is on ΔS, and we shall be mainly concerned with the dispersion of energy in systems and surroundings during a physical or chemical change.

19.4 Entropy Measurement and Values

For any substance under a given set of conditions, a numerical value for entropy can be determined. The greater the dispersal of energy, the greater the entropy and the larger the value of S. The point of reference for entropy values is established by the **third law of thermodynamics.** Defined by Ludwig Boltzmann, the third law states that *a perfect crystal at 0 K has zero entropy; that is, S = 0.* The entropy of an element or compound under any other set of conditions is the entropy gained by converting the substance from 0 K to those conditions.

To determine the value of S, it is necessary to measure the energy transferred as heat under reversible conditions for the conversion from 0 K to the defined conditions and then to use Equation 19.1 ($\Delta S = q_{rev}/T$). Because it is necessary to add energy as heat to raise the temperature, all substances have positive entropy values at temperatures above 0 K. Negative values of entropy cannot occur. Recognizing that entropy is directly related to energy added as heat allows us to predict several general features of entropy values:

■ **Negative Entropy Values** A glance at thermodynamic tables indicates that ions in aqueous solution can and do have negative entropy values listed. However, these are not absolute entropies. For ions, the entropy of $H^+(aq)$ is arbitrarily assigned a standard entropy of zero.

- Raising the temperature of a substance corresponds to adding energy as heat. Thus, the entropy of a substance will increase with an increase in temperature.
- Conversions from solid to liquid and from liquid to gas typically require large inputs of energy as heat. Consequently, there is a large increase in entropy in conversions involving changes of state (Figure 19.9).

Standard Entropy Values, $S°$

The standard state of a substance is its state under a pressure of 1 bar (approximately 1 atmosphere) and at the temperature under consideration. We introduced the concept of standard states into the earlier discussion of enthalpy (◄ Chapter 5), and we can similarly define the entropy of any substance in its standard state.

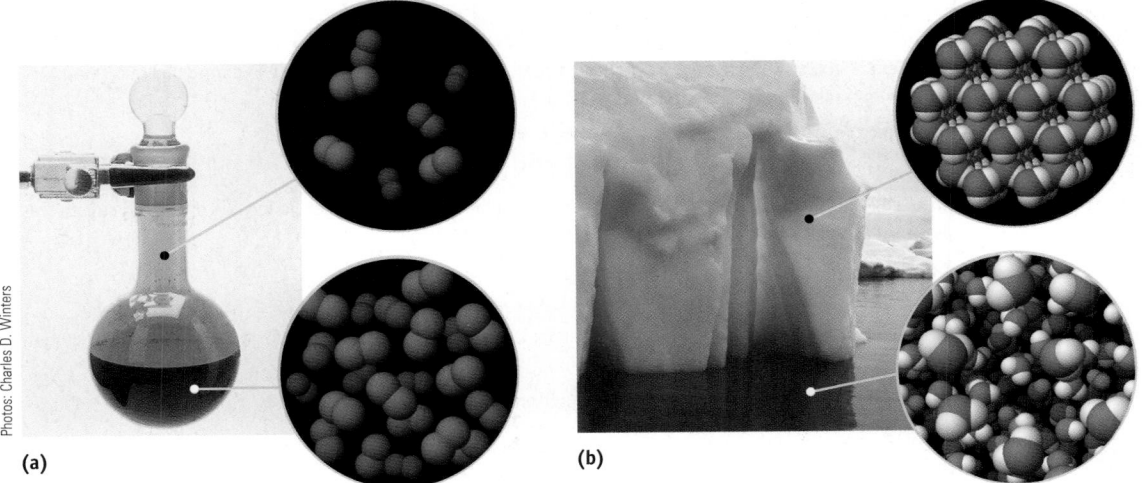

FIGURE 19.9 **Entropy and states of matter.** (a) The entropy of liquid bromine, $Br_2(\ell)$, is 152.2 J/K · mol, and that for bromine vapor is 245.47 J/K · mol. (b) The entropy of ice, which has a highly ordered molecular arrangement, is smaller than the entropy of liquid water. (Sign in at **www.cengage.com/login** and go to Chapter 19 Contents to see Screen 19.4 for a self-study module on entropy.)

The standard entropy, $S°$, of a substance is the entropy gained by converting it from a perfect crystal at 0 K to standard state conditions (1 bar, 1 molal for a solution). The units for standard entropy values are J/K · mol. Generally, values of $S°$ found in tables of data refer to a temperature of 298 K. Standard entropies at 298 K for a few substances are given in Table 19.1, and many more are available in Appendix L. More extensive lists of $S°$ values can be found in standard reference sources such as the NIST tables (**webbook.nist.gov**).

Scanning a list of standard entropies (such as those in Appendix L) will show that *large molecules generally have larger entropies than small molecules.* This seems reasonable; with a larger molecule, there are more ways for the molecule to rotate and vibrate, which provides a larger number of energy microstates over which energy can be distributed. As an example, consider the standard entropies for methane (CH_4), ethane (C_2H_6), and propane (C_3H_8), whose values are 186.3, 229.2, and 270.3 J/K · mol, respectively. Also, *molecules with more complex structures have larger entropies than molecules with simpler structures.* The effect of molecular structure can also be seen when comparing atoms or molecules of similar molar mass: Gaseous argon, CO_2, and C_3H_8 have entropies of 154.9, 213.7, and 270.3 J/K · mol, respectively.

Tables of entropy values also confirm the hypothesis that *entropies of gases are larger than those for liquids, and entropies of liquids are larger than those for solids.* In a solid, the particles have fixed positions in the solid lattice. When a solid melts, these particles have more freedom to assume different positions, resulting in an increase in the number of microstates available and an increase in entropy. When a liquid evaporates, constraints due to forces between the particles nearly disappear; the volume increases greatly; and a large entropy increase occurs. For example, the standard entropies of $I_2(s)$, $Br_2(\ell)$, and $Cl_2(g)$ are 116.1, 152.2, and 223.1 J/K · mol, respectively.

Finally, as illustrated in Figure 19.9, *for a given substance, a large increase in entropy accompanies changes of state,* reflecting the relatively large energy transfer as heat required to carry out these processes (as well as the dispersion of energy over a larger number of available microstates). For example, the entropies of liquid and gaseous water are 65.95 and 188.84 J/K · mol.

TABLE 19.1 Standard Molar Entropy Values at 298 K

Substance	Entropy, $S°$ (J/K · mol)
C(graphite)	5.6
C(diamond)	2.377
C(vapor)	158.1
$H_2(g)$	130.7
$O_2(g)$	205.1
$H_2O(g)$	188.84
$H_2O(\ell)$	69.95

$S°$ (J/K · mol)

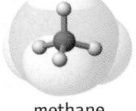

186.3

methane

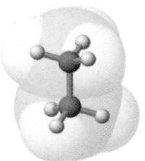

229.2

ethane

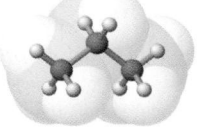

270.3

propane

Problem Which substance has the higher entropy under standard conditions? Explain your reasoning. Check your answer against data in Appendix L.

(a) $NO_2(g)$ or $N_2O_4(g)$

(b) $I_2(g)$ or $I_2(s)$

Strategy Entropy decreases in the order gas > liquid > solid, and larger molecules of related substances have greater entropy than smaller molecules.

Solution

(a) Both NO_2 and N_2O_4 are gases. N_2O_4 is a larger molecule than NO_2 and so is expected to have the higher standard entropy. $S°$ values in Appendix L confirm this prediction: $S°$ for $NO_2(g)$ is 240.04 J/K · mol, and $S°$ for $N_2O_4(g)$ is 304.38 J/K · mol.

(b) For a given substance, gases have higher entropies than solids. $S°$ for $I_2(g)$ is 260.69 J/K · mol; $S°$ for $I_2(s)$ is 116.135 J/K · mol.

EXERCISE 19.1 **Entropy Comparisons**

Predict which substance has the higher entropy and explain your reasoning.

(a) $O_2(g)$ or $O_3(g)$

(b) $SnCl_4(\ell)$ or $SnCl_4(g)$

Determining Entropy Changes in Physical and Chemical Processes

It is also possible to use standard entropy values quantitatively to calculate the change in entropy that occurs in various processes under standard conditions. The standard entropy change is the sum of the standard entropies of the products minus the sum of the standard entropies of the reactants.

$$\Delta_r S° = \Sigma S°(\text{products}) - \Sigma S°(\text{reactants}) \quad \text{(19.3)}$$

This equation allows us to calculate entropy changes for a *system* in which reactants are completely converted to products, under standard conditions. To illustrate, let us calculate $\Delta_r S°$ for the oxidation of NO with O_2.

$$2\ NO(g) + O_2(g) \rightarrow 2\ NO_2(g)$$

Here, we subtract the entropies of the reactants (2 mol NO and 1 mol O_2) from the entropy of the products (2 mol NO_2).

$$\Delta_r S° = (2\ \text{mol}\ NO_2/\text{mol-rxn})(240.0\ \text{J/K} \cdot \text{mol}) -$$
$$[(2\ \text{mol}\ NO(g)/\text{mol-rxn})(210.8\ \text{J/K} \cdot \text{mol}) + (1\ \text{mol}\ O_2/\text{mol-rxn})(205.1\ \text{J/K} \cdot \text{mol})]$$
$$= -146.7\ \text{J/K} \cdot \text{mol-rxn}$$

The entropy of the system decreases, as is generally observed when some number of gaseous reactants has been converted to fewer molecules of gaseous products.

Problem Calculate the standard entropy changes for the following processes. Do the calculations match predictions?

(a) Evaporation of 1.00 mol of liquid ethanol to ethanol vapor

$$C_2H_5OH(\ell) \rightarrow C_2H_5OH(g)$$

(b) Formation of ammonia from hydrogen and nitrogen.

$$N_2(g) + 3\ H_2(g) \rightarrow 2\ NH_3(g)$$

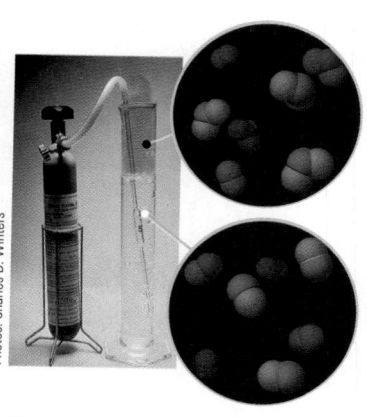

The reaction of NO with O_2. The entropy of the system decreases when two molecules of gas are produced from three molecules of gaseous reactants.

Photos: Charles D. Winters

The discussion to this point, along with the examples and exercises, allows the listing of several general principles involving entropy changes:

- The entropy of a substance will increase in going from a solid to a liquid to a gas.
- The entropy of any substance increases as the temperature is raised. Energy must be added to a system to increase its temperature (that is, $q > 0$), so q_{rev}/T is necessarily positive.
- The entropy of a gas increases with an increase in volume. A larger volume provides a larger number of energy states over which to disperse energy.
- Reactions that increase the number of moles of gases in a system are accompanied by an increase in entropy.

Strategy Entropy changes for each system can be calculated from values of standard entropies (Appendix L) using Equation 19.3. Predictions are made using the guidelines given in the text: An entropy increase is predicted going from solid to liquid to gas and if there is an increase in the number of moles of gas.

Solution

(a) Evaporation of ethanol

$\Delta_r S° = \Sigma S°(\text{products}) - \Sigma S°(\text{reactants})$

$= (1 \text{ mol } C_2H_5OH(g)/\text{mol-rxn})\{S°[C_2H_5OH(g)]\} - (1 \text{ mol } C_2H_5OH(\ell)/\text{mol-rxn})\{S°[C_2H_5OH(\ell)]\}$

$= (1 \text{ mol } C_2H_5OH(g)/\text{mol-rxn})(282.70 \text{ J/K} \cdot \text{mol}) - (1 \text{ mol } C_2H_5OH(\ell)/\text{mol-rxn})(160.7 \text{ J/K} \cdot \text{mol})$

$= +122.0 \text{ J/K} \cdot \text{mol-rxn}$

A large positive value for the entropy change is expected because the process converts ethanol from a liquid to a vapor.

(b) Formation of ammonia

$\Delta_r S° = \Sigma S°(\text{products}) - \Sigma S°(\text{reactants})$

$= (2 \text{ mol } NH_3(g)/\text{mol-rxn})\{S°[NH_3(g)]\} -$
$\quad\quad [(1 \text{ mol } N_2(g)/\text{mol-rxn})\{S°[N_2(g)]\} + (3 \text{ mol } H_2(g)/\text{mol-rxn})\{S°[H_2(g)]\}]$

$= (2 \text{ mol } NH_3(g)/\text{mol-rxn})(192.77 \text{ J/K} \cdot \text{mol}) -$
$\quad\quad [(1 \text{ mol } N_2(g)/\text{mol-rxn})(191.56 \text{ J/K} \cdot \text{mol}) + (3 \text{ mol } H_2(g)/\text{mol-rxn})(130.7 \text{ J/K} \cdot \text{mol})]$

$= -198.12 \text{ J/K} \cdot \text{mol-rxn}$

A decrease in entropy is predicted for this reaction because the number of moles of gases decreases from four to two.

Comment Values of entropies in tables are based on 1 mol of the compound. In part (b), the number of moles of reactants and products per mole of reaction is defined by the stoichiometric coefficients in the balanced chemical equation.

■ **Amount of Substance and Thermodynamic Calculations** In the calculation here and in all others in this chapter, when we write, for example,

282.70 J/K · mol

for the standard entropy of ethanol at 298 K, we mean

282.70 J/K · mol $C_2H_5OH(\ell)$

The identifying formula has been left off for the sake of simplicity.

EXERCISE 19.2 Calculating the Entropy Change for a Reaction, $\Delta_r S°$

Calculate the standard entropy changes for the following processes using the entropy values in Appendix L. Is the sign of the calculated values of $\Delta_r S°$ in accord with predictions?

(a) Dissolving 1 mol of $NH_4Cl(s)$ in water: $NH_4Cl(s) \rightarrow NH_4Cl(aq)$

(b) Oxidation of ethanol: $C_2H_5OH(g) + 3 O_2(g) \rightarrow 2 CO_2(g) + 3 H_2O(g)$

19.5 Entropy Changes and Spontaneity

As illustrated by Example 19.2, the standard entropy change *for the system* in a physical or chemical change can be either positive (evaporation of ethanol) or negative (synthesis of ammonia from nitrogen and hydrogen). How does this information contribute to determining the spontaneity of the process?

■ **Spontaneity and the Second Law**
Spontaneous change is accompanied by an increase in entropy in the universe. This is in contrast to enthalpy and internal energy. According to the first law, the energy contained in the universe is constant.

As discussed previously (page 863), spontaneity is determined by the *second law of thermodynamics*, which states that *a spontaneous process is one that results in an increase of entropy in the universe.* The universe has two parts: the system and its surroundings (◄ Section 5.1), and it makes sense that the entropy change for the universe is the sum of the entropy changes for the system and the surroundings. Under standard conditions, the entropy change for the universe, $\Delta S°$(universe) is

$$\Delta S°\text{(universe)} = \Delta S°\text{(system)} + \Delta S°\text{(surroundings)} \qquad \text{(19.4)}$$

The calculation in Example 19.2 gave us the entropy change under standard conditions for a system, only half of the information needed. Now we will have to determine how the change being studied affects the entropy of the surroundings so that we can then find the entropy change for the universe.

The value of $\Delta S°$(universe) calculated from Equation 19.4 is the entropy change when reactants are converted *completely* to products, with all species at standard conditions. *A process is spontaneous under standard conditions if $\Delta S°$(universe) is greater than zero.* As an example of the determination of reaction spontaneity, let us calculate $\Delta S°$(universe) for the reaction currently used to manufacture methanol, CH_3OH.

$$CO(g) + 2\ H_2(g) \rightarrow CH_3OH(\ell)$$

If $\Delta S°$(universe) is positive, the conversion of 1 mol of CO(g) and 2 mol of H_2(g) to 1 mol of $CH_3OH(\ell)$ will be spontaneous under standard conditions.

■ **Using $\Delta S°$(universe)** For a process that is spontaneous under standard conditions:

$\Delta S°$(universe) > 0

For a process at equilibrium under standard conditions:

$\Delta S°$(universe) = 0

For a process that is not spontaneous under standard conditions:

$\Delta S°$(universe) < 0

Note that these conclusions refer to the complete conversion of reactants to products.

Calculating $\Delta S°$(system) To calculate $\Delta S°$(system), we start by defining the system to include the reactants and products. This means that $\Delta S°$(system) corresponds to the entropy change for the reaction, $\Delta_r S°$. Calculation of this entropy change follows the procedure given in Example 19.2.

$\Delta S°\text{(system)} = \Delta_r S° = \Sigma\Delta S°\text{(products)} - \Sigma\Delta S°\text{(reactants)}$

$= (1\ \text{mol } CH_3OH(\ell)/\text{mol-rxn})\{S°[CH_3OH(\ell)]\} -$
$\qquad [(1\ \text{mol } CO(g)/\text{mol-rxn})\{S°[CO(g)]\} + (2\ \text{mol } H_2(g)/\text{mol-rxn})\{S°[H_2(g)]\}]$

$= (1\ \text{mol } CH_3OH(\ell)/\text{mol-rxn})(127.2\ \text{J/K} \cdot \text{mol}) -$
$\qquad [(1\ \text{mol } CO(g)/\text{mol-rxn})(197.7\ \text{J/K} \cdot \text{mol}) + (2\ \text{mol } H_2(g)/\text{mol-rxn})(130.7\ \text{J/K} \cdot \text{mol})]$

$= -331.9\ \text{J/K} \cdot \text{mol-rxn}$

A decrease in entropy for the system is expected because three moles of gaseous reactants are converted to one mole of a liquid product.

Calculating $\Delta S°$(surroundings) We now need to calculate the entropy change for the surroundings. Recall from Equation 19.1 that for a reversible change, ΔS is equal to q_{rev}/T. Under constant pressure conditions and assuming a reversible process, the entropy change in the surroundings results from the fact that the enthalpy change for the reaction ($q_p = \Delta H$) affects the surroundings. That is, the energy associated with an exothermic chemical reaction is dispersed into the surroundings. Recognizing that $\Delta H°$(surroundings) $= -\Delta_r H°$(system), the entropy change for the surroundings can be calculated by the equation

$$\Delta S°\text{(surroundings)} = \Delta H°\text{(surroundings)}/T = -\Delta_r H°\text{(system)}/T$$

For the synthesis of methanol by the reaction given, the enthalpy change is -127.9 kJ/mol-rxn, calculated from enthalpy of formation data.

$$\Delta H°(\text{system}) = \Sigma \Delta_f H°(\text{products}) - \Sigma \Delta_f H°(\text{reactants})$$

$$= (1 \text{ mol } CH_3OH(\ell)/\text{mol-rxn})\{\Delta_f H°[CH_3OH(\ell)]\} - $$
$$[(1 \text{ mol } CO(g)/\text{mol-rxn})\{\Delta_f H°[CO(g)]\} + $$
$$(2 \text{ mol } H_2(g)/\text{mol-rxn})\{\Delta_f H°[H_2(g)]\}]$$

$$= (1 \text{ mol } CH_3OH(\ell)/\text{mol-rxn})(-238.4 \text{ kJ/mol}) - $$
$$[(1 \text{ mol } CO(g)/\text{mol-rxn})(-110.5 \text{ kJ/mol}) + $$
$$(2 \text{ mol } H_2(g)/\text{mol-rxn})(0 \text{ kJ/mol})]$$

$$= -127.9 \text{ kJ/mol-rxn}$$

Assuming that the process is reversible and occurs at a constant temperature and pressure, the entropy change for the surroundings in the methanol synthesis is $+429.2$ J/K · mol-rxn, calculated as follows.

$$\Delta S°(\text{surroundings}) = -\Delta_r H°(\text{system})/T$$

$$= -[(-127.9 \text{ kJ/mol-rxn})/298 \text{ K}](1000 \text{ J/kJ})$$

$$= +429.2 \text{ J/K} \cdot \text{mol-rxn}$$

Calculating $\Delta S°$(universe), the Entropy Change for the System and Surroundings

The pieces are now in place to calculate the entropy change in the universe. For the formation of $CH_3OH(\ell)$ from $CO(g)$ and $H_2(g)$, $\Delta S°$(universe), is

$$\Delta S°(\text{universe}) = \Delta S°(\text{system}) + \Delta S°(\text{surroundings})$$

$$= -331.9 \text{ J/K} \cdot \text{mol-rxn} + 429.2 \text{ J/K} \cdot \text{mol-rxn}$$

$$= +97.3 \text{ J/K} \cdot \text{mol-rxn}$$

The positive value indicates an increase in the entropy of the universe. It follows from the second law of thermodynamics that this reaction is spontaneous.

Chemistry‿Now™

Sign in at **www.cengage.com/login** and go to Chapter 19 Contents to see:
- Screen 19.5 for a simulation and tutorial on **calculating ΔS for a reaction**
- Screen 19.6 for a simulation and tutorial on **the second law of thermodynamics**

■ **EXAMPLE 19.3 Determining Whether a Process Is Spontaneous**

Problem Show that $\Delta S°$(universe) is positive for the process of dissolving NaCl in water at 298 K.

Strategy The process occurring is NaCl(s) → NaCl(aq). The entropy change for the system, $\Delta S°$(system), can be calculated from values of $S°$ for the two species using Equation 19.3. $\Delta S°$(surroundings) is determined by dividing $-\Delta_r H°$ for the process by the Kelvin temperature. The sum of these two entropy changes is $\Delta S°$(universe). Values of $\Delta_f H°$ and $S°$ for NaCl(s) and NaCl(aq) are obtained from Appendix L.

Solution

Calculate $\Delta S°$(system)

$$\Delta S°(\text{system}) = \Sigma S°(\text{products}) - \Sigma S°(\text{reactants})$$

$$= (1 \text{ mol } NaCl(aq)/\text{mol-rxn})\{S°[NaCl(aq)]\} - (1 \text{ mol } NaCl(s)/\text{mol-rxn})\{S°[NaCl(s)]\}$$

$$= (1 \text{ mol } NaCl(aq)/\text{mol-rxn})(115.5 \text{ J/K} \cdot \text{mol}) - (1 \text{ mol } NaCl(s)/\text{mol-rxn})(72.11 \text{ J/K} \cdot \text{mol})$$

$$= +43.4 \text{ J/K} \cdot \text{mol-rxn}$$

It is important to
reiterate that when we calculate $\Delta H°$ or
$\Delta S°$ for a reaction, this is the value for
the complete conversion of reactants to
products under standard conditions. If
$\Delta S°$(universe) is > 0, the reaction as
written is spontaneous *under standard
conditions*. However, one can calculate
values for ΔS(universe) (without the superscript zero) for *nonstandard* conditions. If ΔS(universe) > 0, the reaction
is spontaneous under those conditions.
However, it is possible that this same reaction under standard conditions is not
spontaneous [$\Delta S°$(universe) < 0]. We
will return to this point in Sections 19.6
and 19.7.

Calculate $\Delta S°$(surroundings)

$$\Delta_r H°(\text{system}) = \Sigma \Delta_f H°(\text{products}) - \Sigma \Delta_f H°(\text{reactants})$$

$$= (1 \text{ mol NaCl(aq)/mol-rxn})\{\Delta_f H°[\text{NaCl(aq)}]\} - (1 \text{ mol NaCl(s)/mol-rxn})\{\Delta_f H°[\text{NaCl(s)}]\}$$

$$= (1 \text{ mol NaCl(aq)/mol-rxn})(-407.27 \text{ kJ/mol}) - (1 \text{ mol NaCl(s)/mol-rxn})(-411.12 \text{ kJ/mol})$$

$$= +3.85 \text{ kJ/mol-rxn}$$

The entropy change of the surroundings is determined by dividing $-\Delta_r H°$(system) by the Kelvin temperature.

$$\Delta S°(\text{surroundings}) = -\Delta_r H°(\text{system})/T$$

$$= [(-3.85 \text{ kJ/mol-rxn}/298 \text{ K})](1000 \text{ J/1 kJ})$$

$$= -12.9 \text{ J/K} \cdot \text{mol-rxn}$$

Calculate $\Delta S°$(universe)

The overall entropy change—the change of entropy in the universe—is the sum of the values for the system and the surroundings.

$$\Delta S°(\text{universe}) = \Delta S°(\text{system}) + \Delta S°(\text{surroundings})$$

$$= +43.4 \text{ J/K} \cdot \text{mol-rxn} - 12.9 \text{ J/K} \cdot \text{mol-rxn}$$

$$= +30.5 \text{ J/K} \cdot \text{mol-rxn}$$

Comment The sum of the two entropy quantities is positive, indicating that the entropy in the universe increases; thus, the process is spontaneous under standard conditions. Notice, however, that the spontaneity of the process results from $\Delta S°$(system) and not from $\Delta S°$(surroundings).

In Summary: Spontaneous or Not?

In the preceding examples, predictions about the spontaneity of a process under standard conditions were made using values of $\Delta S°$(system) and $\Delta H°$(system) calculated from tables of thermodynamic data. It will be useful to look at all possibilities that result from the interplay of these two quantities. There are four possible outcomes when these two quantities are paired (Table 19.2). In two, $\Delta H°$(system) and $\Delta S°$(system) work in concert (Types 1 and 4 in Table 19.2). In the other two, the two quantities are opposed (Types 2 and 3).

Processes in which both the standard enthalpy and entropy changes favor energy dispersal (Type 1) are always spontaneous under standard conditions. Processes disfavored by both their standard enthalpy and entropy changes in the system (Type 4) can *never* be spontaneous under standard conditions. Let us consider examples that illustrate each situation.

Combustion reactions are always exothermic and often produce a larger number of product molecules from a few reactant molecules. They are Type 1 reactions. The equation for the combustion of butane is an example.

$$2 \text{ C}_4\text{H}_{10}(g) + 13 \text{ O}_2(g) \rightarrow 8 \text{ CO}_2(g) + 10 \text{ H}_2\text{O}(g)$$

TABLE 19.2 Predicting Whether a Reaction Will Be Spontaneous Under Standard Conditions

Reaction Type	$\Delta H°$(system)	$\Delta S°$(system)	Spontaneous Process (Standard Conditions)
1	Exothermic, < 0	Positive, > 0	Spontaneous at all temperatures. $\Delta S°$(universe) > 0.
2	Exothermic, < 0	Negative, < 0	Depends on relative magnitudes of $\Delta H°$ and $\Delta S°$. Spontaneous at lower temperatures.
3	Endothermic, > 0	Positive, > 0	Depends on relative magnitudes of $\Delta H°$ and $\Delta S°$. Spontaneous at higher temperatures.
4	Endothermic, > 0	Negative, < 0	Not spontaneous at any temperature. $\Delta S°$(universe) < 0.

For this reaction, $\Delta_r H° = -5315.1$ kJ, and $\Delta_r S° = 312.4$ J/K. Both contribute to this reaction's being spontaneous under standard conditions.

Hydrazine, N_2H_4, is used as a high-energy rocket fuel. Synthesis of N_2H_4 from gaseous N_2 and H_2 would be attractive because these reactants are inexpensive.

$$N_2(g) + 2\ H_2(g) \rightarrow N_2H_4(\ell)$$

However, this reaction fits into the Type 4 category. The reaction is endothermic ($\Delta_r H° = +50.63$ kJ/mol-rxn), and the entropy change is negative ($\Delta_r S° = -331.4$ J/K·mol-rxn) (1 mol of liquid is produced from 3 mol of gases), so the reaction is not spontaneous under standard conditions, and complete conversion of reactants to products will not occur without outside intervention.

In the two other possible outcomes, entropy and enthalpy changes oppose each other. A process could be favored by the enthalpy change but disfavored by the entropy change (Type 2), or vice versa (Type 3). In either instance, whether a process is spontaneous depends on which factor is more important.

Temperature also influences the value of $\Delta S°$(universe). Because the enthalpy change for the surroundings is divided by the temperature to obtain $\Delta S°$(surroundings), the numerical value of $\Delta S°$(surroundings) will be smaller (either less positive or less negative) at higher temperatures. In contrast, $\Delta S°$(system) and $\Delta H°$(system) do not vary much with temperature. Thus, the effect of $\Delta S°$(surroundings) relative to $\Delta S°$(system) is diminished at higher temperature. Stated another way, at higher temperature, the enthalpy change becomes a less important factor in determining the overall entropy change. Consider the two cases where $\Delta H°$(system) and $\Delta S°$(system) are in opposition (Table 19.2):

- Type 2: Exothermic processes with $\Delta S°$(system) < 0. Such processes become less favorable with an increase in temperature.
- Type 3: Endothermic processes with $\Delta S°$(system) > 0. These processes become more favorable as the temperature increases.

The effect of temperature is illustrated by two examples. The first is the reaction of N_2 and H_2 to form NH_3. The reaction is exothermic, and thus it is favored by energy dispersal to the surroundings. The entropy change for the system is unfavorable, however, because the reaction, $N_2(g) + 3\ H_2(g) \rightarrow 2\ NH_3(g)$, converts four moles of gaseous reactants to two moles of gaseous products. The favorable enthalpy effect $[\Delta_r S°(\text{surroundings}) = -\Delta_r H°(\text{system})/T]$ becomes less important at higher temperatures. Furthermore, it is reasonable to expect that the reaction will not be spontaneous if the temperature is high enough.

The second example considers the thermal decomposition of NH_4Cl (Figure 19.10). At room temperature, NH_4Cl is a stable, white, crystalline salt. When heated strongly, it decomposes to $NH_3(g)$ and $HCl(g)$. The reaction is endothermic (enthalpy-disfavored) but entropy-favored because of the formation of two moles of gas from one mole of a solid reactant. The reaction is increasingly favored at higher temperatures.

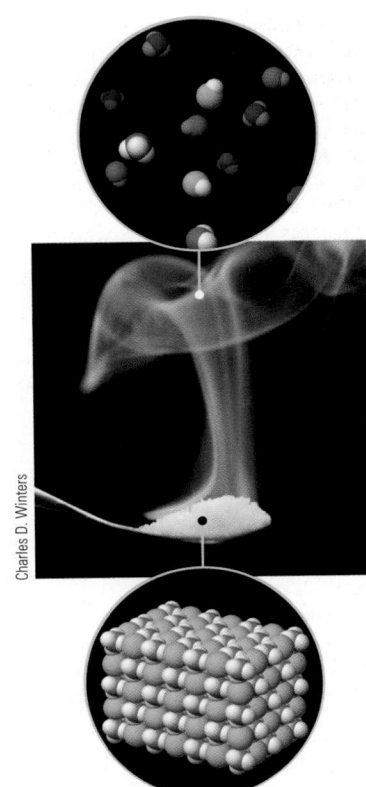

Charles D. Winters

FIGURE 19.10 Thermal decomposition of $NH_4Cl(s)$. White, solid ammonium chloride, $NH_4Cl(s)$, is heated in a spoon. At high temperatures, decomposition to form $NH_3(g)$ and $HCl(g)$ is spontaneous. At lower temperatures, the reverse reaction, forming $NH_4Cl(s)$, is spontaneous. As gaseous $HCl(g)$ and $NH_3(g)$ cool, they recombine to form solid NH_4Cl, the white "smoke" seen in this photo.

EXERCISE 19.3 Is a Reaction Spontaneous?

Classify the following reactions as one of the four types of reactions summarized in Table 19.2.

Reaction	$\Delta_r H°$ (at 298 K) (kJ/mol-rxn)	$\Delta_r S°$ (at 298 K) (J/K · mol-rxn)
(a) $CH_4(g) + 2\ O_2(g) \rightarrow 2\ H_2O(\ell) + CO_2(g)$	−890.6	−242.8
(b) $2\ Fe_2O_3(s) + 3\ C(\text{graphite}) \rightarrow 4\ Fe(s) + 3\ CO_2(g)$	+467.9	+560.7
(c) $C(\text{graphite}) + O_2(g) \rightarrow CO_2(g)$	−393.5	+3.1
(d) $N_2(g) + 3\ F_2(g) \rightarrow 2\ NF_3(g)$	−264.2	−277.8

 **Module 24**

■ **J. Willard Gibbs (1839–1903)** Gibbs received a Ph.D. from Yale University in 1863. His was the first Ph.D. in science awarded from an American university.

Burndy Library/Courtesy Emilio Segre Visual Archives

19.6 Gibbs Free Energy

The method used so far to determine whether a process is spontaneous required evaluation of two quantities, $\Delta S°(system)$ and $\Delta S°(surroundings)$. Wouldn't it be convenient to have a single thermodynamic function that serves the same purpose? A function associated with the system only—one that does not require assessment of the surroundings—would be even better. Such a function exists. It is called the **Gibbs free energy**, with the name honoring J. Willard Gibbs (1839–1903). Gibbs free energy, G, often referred to simply as "free energy," is defined mathematically as

$$G = H - TS$$

where H is enthalpy, T is the Kelvin temperature, and S is entropy. In this equation, G, H, and S all refer to the system. Because enthalpy and entropy are state functions (◄ Section 5.4), free energy is also a state function.

Every substance possesses free energy, but the actual quantity is seldom known. Instead, just as with enthalpy (H) and internal energy (U), we are concerned with *changes* in free energy, ΔG, that occur in chemical and physical processes.

Let us first see how to use free energy as a way to determine whether a reaction is spontaneous. We can then ask further questions about the meaning of the term "free energy" and its use in deciding whether a reaction is product- or reactant-favored.

The Change in the Gibbs Free Energy, ΔG

Recall the equation defining the entropy change for the universe:

$$\Delta S(universe) = \Delta S(surroundings) + \Delta S(system)$$

The entropy change of the surroundings equals the negative of the change in enthalpy of the system divided by T. Thus,

$$\Delta S(universe) = -\Delta H(system)/T + \Delta S(system)$$

Multiplying through this equation by $-T$, gives the equation

$$-T\Delta S(universe) = \Delta H(system) - T\Delta S(system)$$

Gibbs defined the free energy function so that $\Delta G(system) = -T\Delta S(universe)$. Combining terms and simplifying give the general expression relating changes in free energy to the enthalpy and entropy changes in the system.

$$\Delta G = \Delta H - T\Delta S$$

876

Sign in at **www.cengage.com/login** to download the Go Chemistry module for this section or go to **www.ichapters.com** to purchase modules.

Under standard conditions, we can rewrite the Gibbs free energy equation as

$$\Delta G° = \Delta H° - T\Delta S° \qquad (19.5)$$

Gibbs Free Energy, Spontaneity, and Chemical Equilibrium

Because $\Delta_r G°$ is related directly to $\Delta S°$(universe), the Gibbs free energy can be used as a criterion of spontaneity for physical and chemical changes. As shown earlier, the signs of $\Delta_r G°$ and $\Delta S°$(universe) will be opposites [$\Delta_r G°$ (system) = $-T\Delta S°$(universe)]. Therefore, we find the following relationships:

$\Delta_r G° < 0$ The process is spontaneous in the direction written under standard conditions.

$\Delta_r G° = 0$ The process is at equilibrium under standard conditions.

$\Delta_r G° > 0$ The process is not spontaneous in the direction written under standard conditions.

To better understand the Gibbs function, let us examine the diagrams in Figure 19.11. The free energy of pure reactants is plotted on the left, and the free energy of the pure products on the right. The extent of reaction, plotted on the *x*-axis, goes from zero (pure reactants) to one (pure products). In both cases in Figure 19.11, the free energy initially declines as reactants begin to form products; it reaches a minimum at equilibrium and then increases again as we move from the equilibrium position to pure products. *The free energy at equilibrium, where there is a mixture of reactants and products, is always lower than the free energy of the pure reactants and of the pure products. A reaction proceeds spontaneously toward the minimum in free energy, which corresponds to equilibrium.*

$\Delta_r G°$ is the change in free energy accompanying the chemical reaction in which the reactants are converted completely to the products under standard

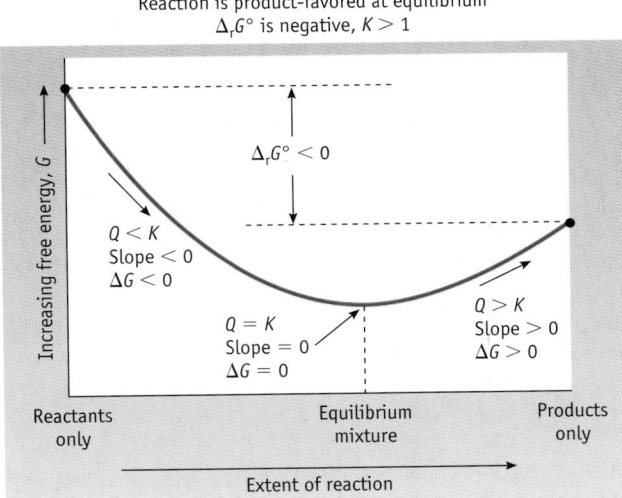
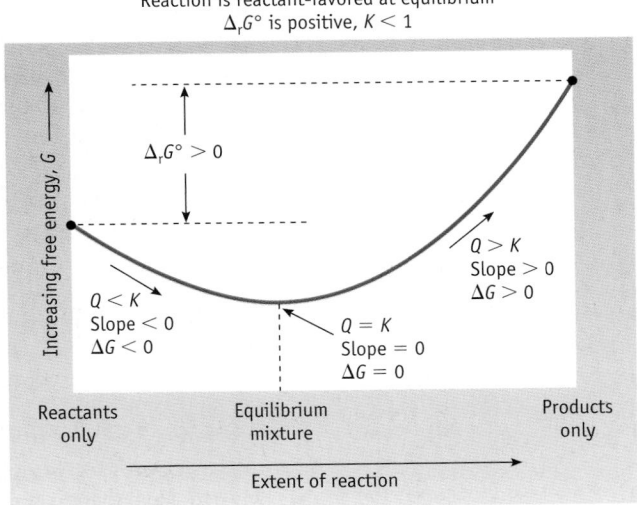

(a)   (b)

FIGURE 19.11 Free energy changes in the course of a reaction. The difference in free energy between the pure reactants in their standard states and the pure products in their standard states is $\Delta_r G°$. Here, Q is the reaction quotient, and K is the equilibrium constant.

conditions. Mathematically, it is the difference in free energy between the products and the reactants under standard conditions. If the free energy of the products is less than that of the reactants, then $\Delta_r G° < 0$, and the reaction is spontaneous under standard conditions (Figure 19.11a). Conversely, if the free energy of the products is greater than that of the reactants, then $\Delta_r G°$ is positive ($\Delta_r G° > 0$), and the reaction is not spontaneous under standard conditions (Figure 19.11b).

Finally, notice that in Figure 19.11a, the equilibrium position occurs closer to the product side than to the reactant side. This is a product-favored reaction at equilibrium. In Figure 19.11b, we find the opposite. The reaction is reactant-favored at equilibrium. It is no accident that the reaction with a negative $\Delta_r G°$ is product-favored, whereas the one with the positive $\Delta_r G°$ is reactant-favored at equilibrium. It turns out that this is always true as the discussion below will show.

Now let us now consider what happens to the instantaneous slope of the curve in Figure 19.11 as the reaction proceeds. Initially, this slope is negative, corresponding to a negative ΔG in moving from point to point. Eventually, however, the free energy reaches a minimum. At this point, the instantaneous slope of the graph is zero ($\Delta G = 0$) and the reaction has reached equilibrium. If we move past the equilibrium point, the instantaneous slope is positive ($\Delta G > 0$); proceeding further to products is not spontaneous. In fact, the reverse reaction will occur spontaneously; the reaction will once again proceed toward equilibrium.

The relationship of $\Delta_r G°$ (the value of $\Delta_r G$ under standard conditions) and the value of $\Delta_r G$ under nonstandard conditions is given by Equation 19.6

$$\Delta_r G = \Delta_r G° + RT \ln Q \qquad \text{(19.6)}$$

where R is the universal gas constant, T is the temperature in kelvins, and Q is the reaction quotient (◀ Section 16.2).

$$Q = \frac{[C]^c[D]^d}{[A]^a[B]^b} \text{ for } aA + bB \rightarrow cC + dD$$

Equation 19.6 informs us that, at a given temperature, $\Delta_r G$ is determined by the values of $\Delta_r G°$ and Q. Further, as long as the reaction is "descending" from the free energy of the pure reactants to the equilibrium position, $\Delta_r G$ is negative, and the reaction is spontaneous in the forward direction (and $Q < K$).

When the system reaches equilibrium, no further net change in concentration of reactants and products will occur, and $\Delta_r G = 0$ and $Q = K$. Substituting these values into Equation 19.6 gives

$$0 = \Delta_r G° + RT \ln K \text{ (at equilibrium)}$$

Rearranging this equation leads to a useful relationship between the standard free energy change for a reaction and the equilibrium constant, K, Equation 19.7:

$$\Delta_r G° = -RT \ln K \qquad \text{(19.7)}$$

From this equation, we learn that, when $\Delta_r G°$ is negative, K is greater than 1, and we say the reaction is *product-favored*. The more negative the value of $\Delta_r G°$, the larger the equilibrium constant. This makes sense because, as described in Chapter 16, large equilibrium constants are associated with product-favored reactions. The converse is also true: For *reactant-favored* reactions, $\Delta_r G°$ is positive, and K is less than 1. Finally, if $K = 1$ (a special set of conditions), then $\Delta_r G° = 0$.

A Summary: Gibbs Free Energy ($\Delta_r G$ and $\Delta_r G°$), the Reaction Quotient (Q) and Equilibrium Constant (K), and Reaction Favorability

Let us now summarize the relationships among $\Delta_r G°$, $\Delta_r G$, Q, and K.

- In Figure 19.11, you see that free energy decreases to a minimum as a system approaches equilibrium. The free energy of the mixture of reactants and products at equilibrium is always lower than the free energy of the pure reactants or of the pure products.
- When $\Delta_r G < 0$, the reaction is proceeding spontaneously toward equilibrium and $Q < K$.
- When $\Delta_r G > 0$, the reaction is beyond the equilibrium point and is not spontaneous in the forward direction. It will be spontaneous in the reverse direction; $Q > K$.
- When $\Delta_r G = 0$, the reaction is at equilibrium; $Q = K$.
- When $\Delta_r G° < 0$, the reaction is *spontaneous under standard conditions*. The system will proceed to an equilibrium position at which point the products will dominate in the reaction mixture because $K > 1$. That is, the reaction is product-favored at equilibrium.
- When $\Delta_r G° > 0$, the reaction is *not spontaneous under standard conditions*. The system will proceed to the equilibrium position at which the reactants will dominate in the equilibrium mixture because $K < 1$. That is, the reaction is *reactant-favored*.
- For the special condition where $\Delta_r G° = 0$, the reaction is at equilibrium at standard conditions, with $K = 1$.

A reactant-favored process. If a sample of yellow lead iodide is placed in pure water, a small amount of the compound will dissolve spontaneously ($\Delta_r G < 0$ and $Q < K$) until equilibrium is reached. Because PbI_2 is quite insoluble ($K_{sp} = 9.8 \times 10^{-9}$), however, the process of dissolving the compound is reactant-favored. We may conclude, therefore, that the value of $\Delta_r G°$ is positive.

What Is "Free" Energy?

The term "free energy" was not arbitrarily chosen. In any given process, the free energy represents the maximum energy available to do useful work (mathematically, $\Delta G = w_{max}$). In this context, the word "free" means "available."

To illustrate the reasoning behind this relationship, consider a reaction carried out under standard conditions and in which energy is evolved as heat ($\Delta_r H° < 0$) and entropy decreases ($\Delta_r S° < 0$).

$$2 H_2(g) + O_2(g) \rightarrow 2 H_2O(g)$$

$\Delta_r H° = -483.6$ kJ/mol-rxn and $\Delta_r S° = -88.8$ J/K · mol-rxn

$\Delta_r G° = -483.6$ kJ/mol-rxn $- (298 \text{ K})(-0.0888 \text{ kJ/mol-rxn}) = -457.2$ kJ/mol-rxn

At first glance, it might seem reasonable that all the energy released as heat (-483.6 kJ/mol-rxn) would be available. This energy could be transferred to the surroundings and would thus be available to do work. This is not the case, however. A negative entropy change in this reaction means that energy is less dispersed in the products than in the reactants. A portion of the energy released as heat from the reaction must be used to reverse energy dispersal in the system; that is, to concentrate energy in the product. The energy left over is "free," or available to perform work. Here, the free energy change amounts to -457.2 kJ/mol-rxn.

19.7 Calculating and Using Free Energy

Standard Free Energy of Formation

The standard free energy of formation of a compound, $\Delta_f G°$, is the free energy change that occurs to form one mole of the compound from the component elements, with products and reactants in their standard states. By defining $\Delta_f G°$ in this way, *the free energy of formation of an element in its standard state is zero.*

Just as the standard enthalpy or entropy change for a reaction can be calculated using values of $\Delta_f H°$ (Equation 5.6) or $S°$ (Equation 19.3), the standard free energy change for a reaction can be calculated from values of $\Delta_f G°$:

$$\Delta_r G° = \Sigma \Delta_f G°(\text{products}) - \Sigma \Delta_f G°(\text{reactants})$$ (19.8)

Calculating $\Delta_r G°$, the Free Energy Change for a Reaction Under Standard Conditions

The free energy change for a reaction under standard conditions can be calculated from thermodynamic data in two ways, either from standard enthalpy and entropy changes using values of $\Delta_f H°$ and $S°$ (as we did for the formation of H_2O just above) or directly from values of $\Delta_f G°$ found in tables. These calculations are illustrated in the following two examples.

Chemistry. Now™

Sign in at **www.cengage.com/login** and go to Chapter 19 Contents to see Screen 19.7 for an exercise and tutorials on **Gibbs free energy**.

EXAMPLE 19.4 **Calculating $\Delta_r G°$ from $\Delta_r H°$ and $\Delta_r S°$**

Problem Calculate the standard free energy change, $\Delta_r G°$, for the formation of methane from carbon and hydrogen at 298 K, using tabulated values of $\Delta_f H°$ and $\Delta S°$. Is the reaction spontaneous under standard conditions? Is it product-favored or reactant-favored at equilibrium?

$$C(\text{graphite}) + 2\ H_2(g) \rightarrow CH_4(g)$$

Strategy The values of $\Delta_f H°$ and $S°$ needed in this problem are found in Appendix L. These are first combined to find $\Delta_r H°$ and $\Delta_r S°$. With these values known, $\Delta_r G°$ can be calculated using Equation 19.5. When doing the calculation, remember that $S°$ values are given in units of J/K · mol, whereas $\Delta_f H°$ values are given in units of kJ/mol.

Solution

	C(graphite)	H_2(g)	CH_4(g)
$\Delta_f H°$ (kJ/mol)	0	0	−74.9
$S°$ (J/K·mol)	+5.6	+130.7	+186.3

From these values, we can find both $\Delta_r H°$ and $\Delta_r S°$ for the reaction:

$\Delta_r H° = \Sigma \Delta_f H°(\text{products}) - \Sigma \Delta_f H°(\text{reactants})$

   = (1 mol CH_4(g)/mol-rxn){$\Delta_f H°[CH_4(g)]$} −[(1 mol C(graphite)/mol-rxn){$\Delta_f H°[C(\text{graphite})]$} + (2 mol H_2(g)/mol-rxn){$\Delta_f H°[H_2(g)]$}]

   = (1 mol CH_4(g)/mol-rxn)(−74.9 kJ/mol) − [(1 mol C(graphite)/mol-rxn)(0 kJ/mol) + (2 mol H_2(g)/mol-rxn)(0 kJ/mol)]

   = −74.9 kJ/mol-rxn

$\Delta_r S° = \Sigma \Delta S°(\text{products}) - \Sigma \Delta S°(\text{reactants})$

   = (1 mol CH_4(g)/mol-rxn){$S°[CH_4(g)]$} − [(1 mol C(graphite)/mol-rxn){$S°[C(\text{graphite})]$} + (2 mol H_2(g)/mol-rxn){$S°[H_2(g)]$}]

   = (1 mol CH_4(g)/mol-rxn)(186.3 J/K · mol) − [1 mol C(graphite)/mol-rxn](5.6 J/K · mol) + (2 mol H_2(g)/mol-rxn)(130.7 J/K · mol)]

   = −80.7 J/K · mol-rxn

Combining the values of $\Delta_rH°$ and $\Delta_rS°$ using Equation 19.5 gives $\Delta_rG°$.

$$\Delta_rG° = \Delta_rH° - T\Delta_rS°$$
$$= -74.9 \text{ kJ/mol-rxn} - [(298 \text{ K})(-80.7 \text{ J/K} \cdot \text{mol-rxn})](1 \text{ kJ}/1000 \text{ J})$$
$$= -50.9 \text{ kJ/mol-rxn}$$

$\Delta_rG°$ is negative at 298 K, so the reaction is predicted to be spontaneous under standard conditions at this temperature. It is also predicted to be product-favored at equilibrium.

■ **Enthalpy- and Entropy-Driven Reactions** In Example 19.4, the product $T\Delta_rS°$ is negative (-24.0 J/mol-rxn) and disfavors the reaction. However, the entropy change is relatively small, and $\Delta_rH° = -74.9$ kJ/mol-rxn) is the dominant term. Chemists call this an "enthalpy-driven reaction."

■ **EXAMPLE 19.5** Calculating $\Delta_rG°$ Using Free Energies of Formation

Problem Calculate the standard free energy change for the combustion of one mole of methane using values for standard free energies of formation of the products and reactants. Is the reaction spontaneous under standard conditions? Is it product-favored or reactant-favored at equilibrium?

Strategy Write a balanced equation for the reaction. Then, use Equation 19.8 with values of $\Delta_fG°$ obtained from Appendix L.

Solution The balanced equation and values of $\Delta_fG°$ for each reactant and product are:

$$CH_4(g) + 2 O_2(g) \rightarrow 2 H_2O(g) + CO_2(g)$$

$\Delta_fG°$(kJ/mol)	-50.8	0	-228.6	-394.4

Because $\Delta_fG°$ values are given for 1 mol of each substance (the units are kJ/mol), each value of $\Delta_fG°$ must be multiplied by the number of moles defined by the stoichiometric coefficient in the balanced chemical equation.

$$\Delta_rG°(\text{system}) = \Sigma\Delta_fG°(\text{products}) - \Sigma\Delta_fG°(\text{reactants})$$
$$= [(2 \text{ mol } H_2O(g)/\text{mol-rxn})\{\Delta_fG°[H_2O(g)]\} + (1 \text{ mol } CO_2(g)/\text{mol-rxn})\{\Delta_fG°[CO_2(g)]\}]$$
$$- [(1 \text{ mol } CH_4(g)/\text{mol-rxn})\{\Delta_fG°[CH_4(g)]\} + (2 \text{ mol } O_2(g)/\text{mol-rxn})\{\Delta_fG°[O_2(g)]\}]$$
$$= [(2 \text{ mol } H_2O(g)/\text{mol-rxn})(-228.6 \text{ kJ/mol}) + (1 \text{ mol } CO_2(g)/\text{mol-rxn})(-394.4 \text{ kJ/mol})\}$$
$$- [(1 \text{ mol } CH_4(g)/\text{mol-rxn})(-50.8 \text{ kJ/mol}) - (2 \text{ mol } O_2(g)/\text{mol-rxn})(0 \text{ kJ/mol})]$$
$$= -800.8 \text{ kJ/mol-rxn}$$

The large negative value of $\Delta_rG°$ indicates that the reaction is spontaneous under standard conditions and that it is product-favored at equilibrium.

Comment Common errors made by students in this calculation are (1) overlooking the stoichiometric coefficients in the equation and (2) confusing the signs for the terms when using Equation 19.8.

EXERCISE 19.6 Calculating $\Delta_rG°$ from $\Delta_rH°$ and $\Delta_rS°$

Using values of $\Delta_fH°$ and $S°$ to find $\Delta_rH°$ and $\Delta_rS°$, calculate the free energy change, $\Delta_rG°$, for the formation of 2 mol of $NH_3(g)$ from the elements at standard conditions and 25 °C. $N_2(g) + 3 H_2(g) \rightarrow 2 NH_3(g)$.

EXERCISE 19.7 Calculating $\Delta_rG°$ from $\Delta_fG°$

Calculate the standard free energy change for the oxidation of 1.00 mol of $SO_2(g)$ to form $SO_3(g)$ using values of $\Delta_fG°$.

Free Energy and Temperature

The definition for free energy, $G = H - TS$, informs us that free energy is a function of temperature, so $\Delta_rG°$ will change as the temperature changes (Figure 19.12). A consequence of this dependence on temperature is that, in certain instances, reactions can be product-favored at equilibrium at one temperature

■ **Entropy- or Enthalpy-Favored** Table 19.2 describes the balance of $\Delta H°$ and $\Delta S°$ and the effect of temperature on reaction spontaneity.

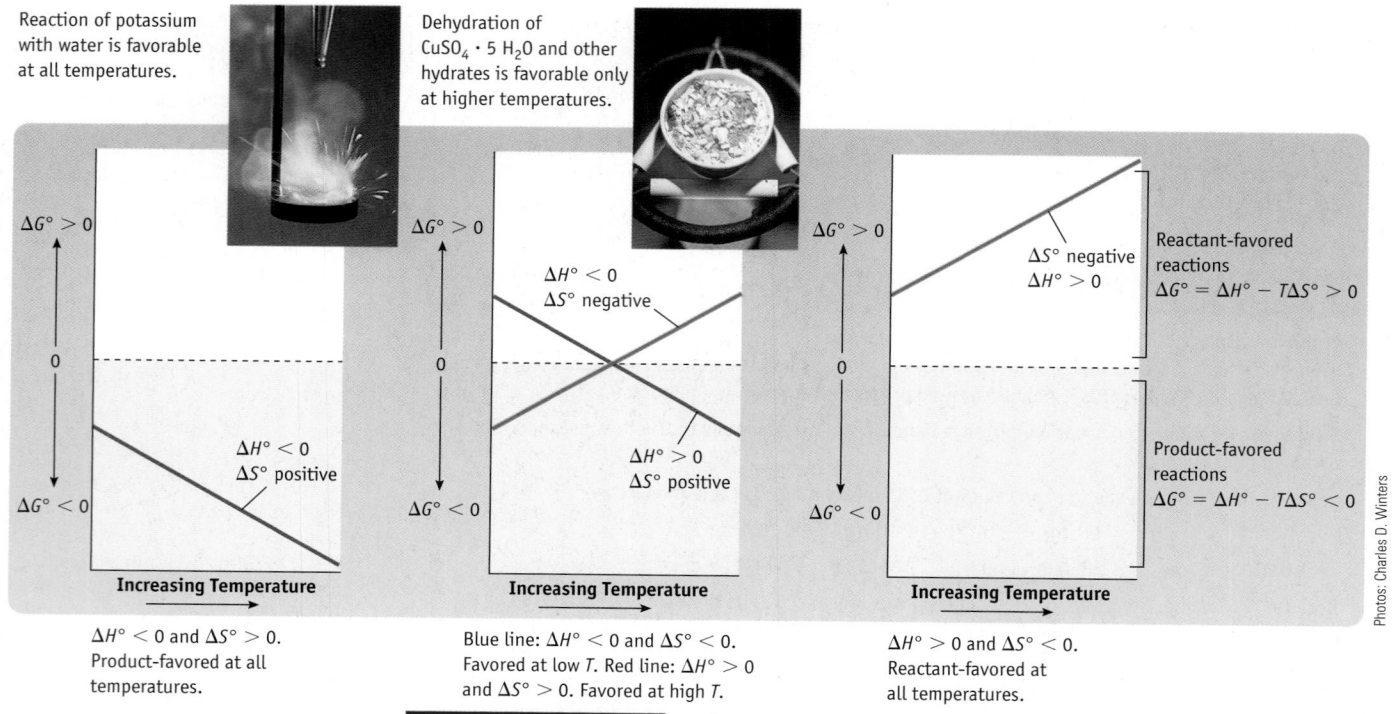

Reaction of potassium with water is favorable at all temperatures.

Dehydration of $CuSO_4 \cdot 5 H_2O$ and other hydrates is favorable only at higher temperatures.

$\Delta G° > 0$

0

$\Delta G° < 0$

$\Delta H° < 0$
$\Delta S°$ positive

Increasing Temperature

$\Delta H° < 0$ and $\Delta S° > 0$.
Product-favored at all temperatures.

$\Delta G° > 0$

0

$\Delta G° < 0$

$\Delta H° < 0$
$\Delta S°$ negative

$\Delta H° > 0$
$\Delta S°$ positive

Increasing Temperature

Blue line: $\Delta H° < 0$ and $\Delta S° < 0$.
Favored at low T. Red line: $\Delta H° > 0$
and $\Delta S° > 0$. Favored at high T.

$\Delta G° > 0$

0

$\Delta G° < 0$

$\Delta S°$ negative
$\Delta H° > 0$

Reactant-favored reactions
$\Delta G° = \Delta H° - T\Delta S° > 0$

Product-favored reactions
$\Delta G° = \Delta H° - T\Delta S° < 0$

Increasing Temperature

$\Delta H° > 0$ and $\Delta S° < 0$.
Reactant-favored at all temperatures.

Photos: Charles D. Winters

Active Figure 19.12 The variation in $\Delta_r G°$ with temperature.

Chemistry⚬Now™ Sign in at www.cengage.com/login and go to the Chapter Contents menu to explore an interactive version of this figure accompanied by an exercise.

and reactant-favored at another. Those instances arise when the $\Delta_r H°$ and $T\Delta_r S°$ terms work in opposite directions:

- Processes that are entropy-favored ($\Delta_r S° > 0$) and enthalpy-disfavored ($\Delta_r H° > 0$)
- Processes that are enthalpy-favored ($\Delta_r H° < 0$) and entropy-disfavored ($\Delta_r S° < 0$)

Let us explore the relationship of $\Delta G°$ and T further and illustrate how it can be used to advantage.

Calcium carbonate is the primary component of limestone, marble, and seashells. Heating $CaCO_3$ produces lime, CaO, an important chemical, along with gaseous CO_2. The data below from Appendix L are at 298 K (25 °C).

	$CaCO_3(s)$	→	$CaO(s)$	+	$CO_2(g)$
$\Delta_f G°$ (kJ/mol)	−1129.16		−603.42		−394.36
$\Delta_f H°$ (kJ/mol)	−1207.6		−635.09		−393.51
$S°$ (J/K · mol)	91.7		38.2		213.74

For the conversion of 1 mol of $CaCO_3(s)$ to 1 mol of CaO(s) under standard conditions, $\Delta_r G° = +131.38$ kJ, $\Delta_r H° = +179.0$ kJ, and $\Delta_r S° = +160.2$ J/K. Although the reaction is entropy-favored, the large positive and unfavorable enthalpy change dominates at 298 K. Thus, the standard free energy change is positive at 298 K and 1 bar, indicating that the reaction is reactant-favored at equilibrium under the given conditions.

The temperature dependence of $\Delta_r G°$ provides a means to turn the $CaCO_3$ decomposition into a product-favored reaction. Notice that the entropy change in the reaction is positive as a result of the formation of CO_2 gas in the reaction. Thus, raising the temperature results in the value of $T\Delta_r S°$ becoming increasingly large. At a high enough temperature, $T\Delta_r S°$ will outweigh the enthalpy effect, and the process will become product-favored at equilibrium.

How high must the temperature be for this reaction to become product-favored? An estimate of the temperature can be obtained using Equation 19.5, by calculating the temperature at which $\Delta_r G° = 0$. Above that temperature, $\Delta_r G°$ will have a negative value.

$$\Delta_r G° = \Delta_r H° - T\Delta_r S°$$

$$0 = (179.0 \text{ kJ/mol-rxn})(1000 \text{ J/kJ}) - T(160.2 \text{ J/K} \cdot \text{mol-rxn})$$

$$T = 1117 \text{ K (or 844 °C)}$$

How accurate is this result? As noted earlier, we can obtain only an approximate answer from this calculation. One source of error is the assumption that $\Delta_r H°$ and $\Delta S°$ do not vary with temperature, which is not strictly true. There is always a small variation in these values when the temperature changes—not large enough to be important if the temperature range is narrow, but potentially a problem over wider temperature ranges such as seen in this example. As an estimate, however, a temperature in the range of 850 °C for this reaction is reasonable.

■ **$CaCO_3$ Decomposition** Experiments show that the pressure of CO_2 in an equilibrium system [$CaCO_3(s) \rightleftharpoons CaO(s) + CO_2(g)$; $\Delta G° = 0$] is 1 bar at about 900 °C, close to our estimated temperature.

Chemistry .Now™

Sign in at **www.cengage.com/login** and go to Chapter 19 Contents to see Screen 19.8 for a simulation and tutorial on **the relationship of $\Delta H°$, $\Delta S°$, and T.**

■ **EXAMPLE 19.6 Effect of Temperature on $\Delta_r G°$**

Problem The decomposition of liquid $Ni(CO)_4$ to produce nickel metal and carbon monoxide has a $\Delta_r G°$ value of 40 kJ/mol-rxn at 25 °C.

$$Ni(CO)_4(\ell) \rightarrow Ni(s) + 4 CO(g)$$

Use values of $\Delta_f H°$ and $S°$ for the reactant and products to estimate the temperature at which the reaction becomes product-favored at equilibrium.

Strategy The reaction is reactant-favored at equilibrium at 298 K. However, if the entropy change is positive for the reaction and the reaction is endothermic (with a positive value of $\Delta_r H°$), then a higher temperature may allow the reaction to become product-favored at equilibrium. Therefore, we first find $\Delta_r H°$ and $\Delta_r S°$ to see if their values meet our criteria for spontaneity at a higher temperature, and then we calculate the temperature at which the following condition is met: $0 = \Delta_r H° - T\Delta_r S°$.

Solution Values for $\Delta_f H°$ and $S°$ are obtained from the chemical literature for the substances involved.

	$Ni(CO)_4(\ell)$	→	$Ni(s)$	+	$4 CO(g)$
$\Delta_f H°$(kJ/mol)	−632.0		0		−110.525
$S°$(J/K · mol)	320.1		29.87		197.67

For a process in which 1 mol of liquid $Ni(CO)_4$ is converted to 1 mol of $Ni(s)$ and 4 mol of $CO(g)$, we find

$$\Delta_r H° = +189.9 \text{ kJ/mol-rxn}$$

$$\Delta_r S° = +500.5 \text{ J/K mol-rxn}$$

At 298 K, the reaction is reactant-favored at equilibrium largely because it is quite endothermic. However, a positive entropy change should allow the reaction to be product-favored at equilibrium at a higher temperature. Therefore, we use the values of $\Delta_r H°$ and $\Delta_r S°$ to find the temperature at which $\Delta_r G° = 0$.

$$\Delta_r G° = \Delta_r H° - T\Delta_r S°$$

$$0 = (189.9 \text{ kJ/mol-rxn})(1000 \text{ J/kJ}) - T(500.5 \text{ J/K·mol-rxn})$$

$$T = \boxed{379.4 \text{ K (or } 106.2 \text{ °C)}}$$

Case Study

Thermodynamics and Living Things

The laws of thermodynamics apply to all chemical reactions. It should come as no surprise, therefore, that issues of spontaneity and ΔG arise in studies of biochemical reactions. For biochemical processes, however, a different standard state is often used. Most of the usual definition is retained: 1 bar pressure for gases and 1 m concentration for aqueous solutes with the exception of one very important solute. Rather than using a standard state of 1 molal for hydronium ions (corresponding to a pH of about 0), biochemists use a hydronium concentration of 1×10^{-7} M, corresponding to a pH of 7. This pH is much more useful for biochemical reactions. When biochemists use this as the standard state, they write the symbol ′ next to the thermodynamic function. For example, they would write $\Delta G°′$ (pronounced *delta G zero prime*).

Living things require energy to perform their many functions. One of the main reactions involved in providing this energy is the reaction of adenosine triphosphate (ATP) with water, a reaction for which $\Delta_r G°′ = -30.5$ kJ/mol–rxn (◄ *The Chemistry of Life: Biochemistry*).

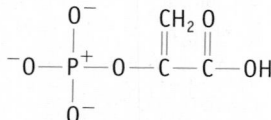

ATP, adenosine triphosphate

One of the key functions of the process of respiration is to produce molecules of ATP for our bodies to use. ATP is produced in the reaction of adenosine diphosphate (ADP) with hydrogen phosphate ($HP_i = HPO_4^{2-}$),

$$ADP + HP_i + H^+ \rightarrow ATP + H_2O$$
$$\Delta_r G°′ = +30.5 \text{ kJ/mol}$$

a reaction that is reactant-favored at equilibrium. How then do our bodies get this reaction to occur? The answer is to couple the production of ATP with another reaction that is even more product-favored than ATP production is reactant-favored. For example, organisms carry out the oxidation of carbohydrates in a multistep process, producing energy. One of the compounds produced in the process called *glycolysis* is phosphoenolpyruvate (PEP).

PEP, phosphoenolpyruvate

Its reaction with water is product-favored at equilibrium

$$PEP + H_2O \rightarrow Pyruvate + HP_i$$
$$\Delta_r G°′ = -61.9 \text{ kJ/mol}$$

This reaction and the ATP formation are linked through the HP_i that is produced in the PEP reaction. If both reactions are carried out, we obtain the following

$$PEP + H_2O \rightarrow Pyruvate + HP_i$$
$$\Delta_r G°′ = -61.9 \text{ kJ/mol}$$
$$ADP + HP_i + H^+ \rightarrow ATP + H_2O$$
$$\Delta_r G°′ = +30.5 \text{ kJ/mol}$$

$$PEP + ADP + H^+ \rightarrow Pyruvate + ATP$$
$$\Delta_r G°′ = -31.4 \text{ kJ/mol}$$

The overall reaction has a negative value for $\Delta_r G°′$ and thus is product-favored at equilibrium. ATP is formed in this process.

The coupling of reactions to produce a system that is product-favored is used in a multitude of reactions that occur in our bodies.

John Katz

Living things use ATP to produce energy.

Questions:

1. *Consider the hydrolysis reactions of creatine phosphate and adenosine-5′-monophosphate.*

   Creatine Phosphate + H_2O
   $$\rightarrow Creatine + HP_i$$
   $$\Delta_r G°′ = -43.3 \text{ kJ/mol}$$

   Adenosine-5′-Monophosphate + H_2O
   $$\rightarrow adenosine + HP_i + H^+$$
   $$\Delta_r G°′ = -9.2 \text{ kJ/mol}$$

   In which direction does a reaction that is product-favored at equilibrium result: for creatine phosphate to transfer phosphate to adenosine or for adenosine-5′-monophosphate to transfer phosphate to creatine?

2. *Assume the reaction A(aq) + B(aq) → C(aq) + H_3O^+(aq) produces one hydronium ion. What is the mathematical relationship between $\Delta G°′$ and $\Delta G°$ at 25° C? (Hint: Use the equation $\Delta G = \Delta G° + RT \ln Q$ and substitute $\Delta G°′$ for ΔG.)*

Answers to these questions are in Appendix Q.

EXERCISE 19.8 Effect of Temperature on $\Delta_rG°$

Oxygen was first prepared by Joseph Priestley (1733–1804) by heating HgO. Use data in Appendix L to estimate the temperature required to decompose HgO(s) into Hg(ℓ) and O_2(g).

Using the Relationship Between $\Delta_rG°$ and K

Equation 19.7 provides a direct route to determine the standard free energy change from experimentally determined equilibrium constants. Alternatively, it allows calculation of an equilibrium constant from thermochemical data contained in tables or obtained from an experiment.

Chemistry ⚛ Now™

Sign in at **www.cengage.com/login** and go to Chapter 19 Contents to see Screen 19.9 for a simulation and tutorial on **$\Delta G°$ and K.**

EXAMPLE 19.7 Calculating K_p from $\Delta_rG°$

Problem Determine the standard free energy change, $\Delta_rG°$, for the formation of 1.00 mol of NH_3(g) from nitrogen and hydrogen, and use this value to calculate the equilibrium constant for this reaction at 25 °C.

Strategy The free energy of formation of ammonia represents the free energy change to form 1.00 mol of NH_3(g) from the elements. The equilibrium constant for this reaction is calculated from $\Delta_rG°$ using Equation 19.7. Because the reactants and products are gases, the calculated value will be K_p.

Solution Begin by specifying a balanced equation for the chemical reaction under investigation.

$$\tfrac{1}{2} N_2(g) + \tfrac{3}{2} H_2(g) \rightleftharpoons NH_3(g)$$

The free energy change for this reaction is -16.37 kJ/mol-rxn ($\Delta_rG° = \Delta_fG°$ for NH_3(g); Appendix L). In a calculation of K_p using Equation 19.7, we will need consistent units. The gas constant, R, is 8.3145 J/K·mol, so the value of $\Delta_rG°$ must be in J/mol-rxn (and not kJ/mol-rxn). The temperature is 298 K.

$$\Delta_rG° = -RT \ln K$$
$$-16{,}370 \text{ J/mol-rxn} = (-8.3145 \text{ J/K·mol-rxn})(298.15 \text{ K}) \ln K_p$$
$$\ln K_p = 6.604$$
$$K_p = 7.38 \times 10^2$$

Comment This example illustrates how to calculate equilibrium constants from thermodynamic data. In fact, many equilibrium constants you find in the chemical literature are not experimentally determined but are instead calculated from thermodynamic data in this way.

EXAMPLE 19.8 Calculating $\Delta_rG°$ from K_{sp} for an Insoluble Solid

Problem The value of K_{sp} for AgCl(s) at 25 °C is 1.8×10^{-10}. Use this value in Equation 19.7 to determine $\Delta_rG°$ for the process Ag^+(aq) + Cl^-(aq) $\rightleftharpoons$ AgCl(s) at 25 °C.

Strategy The chemical equation given is the opposite of the equation used to define K_{sp}; therefore, the equilibrium constant for this reaction is $1/K_{sp}$. This value is used to calculate $\Delta_rG°$.

Solution For Ag^+(aq) + Cl^-(aq) $\rightleftharpoons$ AgCl(s),
$$K = 1/K_{sp} = 1/ 1.8 \times 10^{-10} = 5.6 \times 10^9$$
$$\Delta_rG° = -RT \ln K = -(8.3145 \text{ J/K·mol-rxn})(298.15 \text{ K}) \ln(5.6 \times 10^9)$$
$$= -56 \text{ kJ/mol-rxn}$$

Comment The negative value of $\Delta_rG°$ indicates that the precipitation of AgCl from Ag^+(aq) and Cl^-(aq) is product-favored at equilibrium.

Chapter Goals Revisited

Now that you have studied this chapter, you should ask whether you have met the chapter goals. In particular, you should be able to:

Understand the concept of entropy and its relationship to reaction spontaneity

a. Understand that entropy is a measure of energy dispersal (Section 19.2). Study Question(s) assignable in OWL: 2.

b. Recognize that an entropy change can be determined experimentally as the energy transferred as heat for a reversible process divided by the Kelvin temperature. (*A Closer Look*, Section 19.3.) Study Question(s) assignable in OWL: 40.

c. Identify common processes that are entropy favored (Section 19.4).

Calculate the change in entropy for system, surroundings, and the universe to determine whether a process is spontaneous

a. Calculate entropy changes from tables of standard entropy values for compounds (Section 19.4). Study Question(s) assignable in OWL: 4, 6, 11.

b. Use standard entropy and enthalpy changes to predict whether a reaction will be spontaneous under standard conditions (Section 19.5 and Table 19.2). Study Question(s) assignable in OWL: 10, 12, 33, 35, 47, 55, 67, 72.

c. Recognize how temperature influences whether a reaction is spontaneous (Section 19.5). Study Question(s) assignable in OWL: 14, 25, 26.

Understand and use the Gibbs free energy

a. Understand the connection between enthalpy and entropy changes and the Gibbs free energy change for a process (Section 19.6).

b. Understand the relationship of $\Delta_r G$, $\Delta_r G°$, Q, K, reaction spontaneity, and product- or reactant-favorability (Section 19.6).

Q	ΔG	Spontaneous?
$Q < K$	$\Delta G < 0$	Spontaneous to the right as the equation is written
$Q = K$	$\Delta G = 0$	Reaction is at equilibrium
$Q > K$	$\Delta G > 0$	Not spontaneous to the right; spontaneous to the left

K	$\Delta G°$	Reactant-Favored or Product-Favored at Equilibrium?	Spontaneous Under Standard Conditions?
$K \gg 1$	$\Delta G° < 0$	Product-favored	Spontaneous under standard conditions
$K = 1$	$\Delta G° = 0$	$[C]^c[D]^d = [A]^a[B]^b$ at equilibrium	At equilibrium under standard conditions
$K \ll 1$	$\Delta G° > 0$	Reactant-favored	Not spontaneous under standard conditions

c. Describe and use the relationship between the free energy change under standard conditions and equilibrium constants, and calculate K from $\Delta_r G°$ (Sections 19.6 and 19.7). Study Question(s) assignable in OWL: 28, 30, 44, 48, 50, 61; Go Chemistry Module 24.

d. Calculate the change in free energy at standard conditions for a reaction from the enthalpy and entropy changes under standard conditions or from the standard free energy of formation of reactants and products ($\Delta_f G°$) (Section 19.7). Study Question(s) assignable in OWL: 16, 18, 20, 22, 46, 56, 75, 79.

e. Know how free energy changes with temperature (Section 19.7). Study Question(s) assignable in OWL: 24, 57, 59, 60, 63, 65, 70.

KEY EQUATIONS

Equation 19.1 (page 863): Calculate the entropy change from the energy transferred as heat for a reversible process and the temperature at which it occurs.

$$\Delta S = \frac{q_{rev}}{T}$$

Equation 19.2 (page 866) The Boltzmann equation: The entropy of a system, S, is proportional to the number of accessible microstates, W, belonging to a given energy of a system or substance.

$$S = k \ln W$$

Equation 19.3 (page 870): Calculate the standard entropy change under standard conditions for a process from the tabulated entropies of the products and reactants.

$$\Delta_r S^\circ = \Sigma S^\circ(\text{products}) - \Sigma S^\circ(\text{reactants})$$

Equation 19.4 (page 872): Calculate the total entropy change for a system and its surroundings, to determine whether a process is spontaneous under standard conditions.

$$\Delta S^\circ(\text{universe}) = \Delta S^\circ(\text{system}) + \Delta S^\circ(\text{surroundings})$$

Equation 19.5 (page 877): Calculate the free energy change for a process from enthalpy and entropy changes.

$$\Delta_r G^\circ = \Delta_r H^\circ - T\Delta_r S^\circ$$

Equation 19.6 (page 878): Relates the free energy change under nonstandard conditions ($\Delta_r G$) to the standard free energy change ($\Delta_r G^\circ$) and the reaction quotient Q.

$$\Delta_r G = \Delta_r G^\circ + RT \ln Q$$

Equation 19.7 (page 878): Relates the standard free energy change for a reaction and its equilibrium constant.

$$\Delta_r G^\circ = -RT \ln K$$

Equation 19.8 (page 880): Calculate the standard free energy change for a reaction using tabulated values of $\Delta_f G^\circ$.

$$\Delta_r G^\circ = \Sigma \Delta_f G^\circ(\text{products}) - \Sigma \Delta_f G^\circ(\text{reactants})$$

STUDY QUESTIONS

OWL Online homework for this chapter may be assigned in OWL.

▲ denotes challenging questions.

■ denotes questions assignable in OWL.

Blue-numbered questions have answers in Appendix O and fully-worked solutions in the *Student Solutions Manual*.

Practicing Skills

Entropy
(See Examples 19.1 and 19.2 and ChemistryNow Screens 19.4 and 19.5.)

1. Which substance has the higher entropy?
   (a) dry ice (solid CO_2) at -78 °C or $CO_2(g)$ at 0 °C
   (b) liquid water at 25 °C or liquid water at 50 °C
   (c) pure alumina, $Al_2O_3(s)$, or ruby (Ruby is Al_2O_3 in which some Al^{3+} ions in the crystalline lattice are replaced with Cr^{3+} ions.)
   (d) one mole of $N_2(g)$ at 1 bar pressure or one mole of $N_2(g)$ at 10 bar pressure (both at 298 K)

2. ■ Which substance has the higher entropy?
  (a) a sample of pure silicon (to be used in a computer chip) or a piece of silicon containing a trace of another element such as boron or phosphorus
  (b) $O_2(g)$ at 0 °C or $O_2(g)$ at −50 °C
  (c) $I_2(s)$ or $I_2(g)$, both at room temperature
  (d) one mole of $O_2(g)$ at 1 bar pressure or one mole of $O_2(g)$ at 0.01 bar pressure (both at 298 K)

3. Use $S°$ values to calculate the standard entropy change, $\Delta_r S°$, for each of the following processes and comment on the sign of the change.
  (a) $KOH(s) \rightarrow KOH(aq)$
  (b) $Na(g) \rightarrow Na(s)$
  (c) $Br_2(\ell) \rightarrow Br_2(g)$
  (d) $HCl(g) \rightarrow HCl(aq)$

4. ■ Use $S°$ values to calculate the standard entropy change, $\Delta_r S°$, for each of the following changes, and comment on the sign of the change.
  (a) $NH_4Cl(s) \rightarrow NH_4Cl(aq)$
  (b) $CH_3OH(\ell) \rightarrow CH_3OH(g)$
  (c) $CCl_4(g) \rightarrow CCl_4(\ell)$
  (d) $NaCl(s) \rightarrow NaCl(g)$

5. Calculate the standard entropy change for the formation of 1.0 mol of the following compounds from the elements at 25 °C.
  (a) $HCl(g)$ (b) $Ca(OH)_2(s)$

6. ■ Calculate the standard entropy change for the formation of 1.0 mol of the following compounds from the elements at 25 °C.
  (a) $H_2S(g)$ (b) $MgCO_3(s)$

7. ■ Calculate the standard entropy change for each of the following reactions at 25 °C. Comment on the sign of $\Delta_r S°$.
  (a) $2 Al(s) + 3 Cl_2(g) \rightarrow 2 AlCl_3(s)$
  (b) $2 CH_3OH(\ell) + 3 O_2(g) \rightarrow 2 CO_2(g) + 4 H_2O(g)$

8. Calculate the standard entropy change for each of the following reactions at 25 °C. Comment on the sign of $\Delta_r S°$.
  (a) $2 Na(s) + 2 H_2O(\ell) \rightarrow 2 NaOH(aq) + H_2(g)$
  (b) $Na_2CO_3(s) + 2 HCl(aq) \rightarrow 2 NaCl(aq) + H_2O(\ell) + CO_2(g)$

$\Delta_r S°$(universe) and Spontaneity
(See Example 19.3 and ChemistryNow Screen 19.6.)

9. Is the reaction $Si(s) + 2 Cl_2(g) \rightarrow SiCl_4(g)$ spontaneous under standard conditions at 298 K? Answer this question by calculating $\Delta S°$(system), $\Delta S°$(surroundings), and $\Delta S°$(universe). (Define reactants and products as the system.)

10. ■ Is the reaction $Si(s) + 2 H_2(g) \rightarrow SiH_4(g)$ spontaneous under standard conditions at 298 K? Answer this question by calculating calculating $\Delta S°$(system), $\Delta S°$(surroundings), and $\Delta S°$(universe). (Define reactants and products as the system.)

11. Calculate $\Delta S°$(universe) for the decomposition of 1 mol of liquid water to form gaseous hydrogen and oxygen. Is this reaction spontaneous under these conditions at 25 °C? Explain your answer briefly.

12. ■ Calculate $\Delta S°$(universe) for the formation of 1 mol $HCl(g)$ from gaseous hydrogen and chlorine. Is this reaction spontaneous under these conditions at 25 °C? Explain your answer briefly.

13. Classify each of the reactions according to one of the four reaction types summarized in Table 19.2.
  (a) $Fe_2O_3(s) + 2 Al(s) \rightarrow 2 Fe(s) + Al_2O_3(s)$

  $\Delta_r H° = -851.5$ kJ/mol-rxn
  $\Delta_r S° = -375.2$ J/K · mol-rxn

  (b) $N_2(g) + 2 O_2(g) \rightarrow 2 NO_2(g)$

  $\Delta_r H° = 66.2$ kJ/mol-rxn
  $\Delta_r S° = -121.6$ J/K · mol-rxn

14. ■ Classify each of the reactions according to one of the four reaction types summarized in Table 19.2.
  (a) $C_6H_{12}O_6(s) + 6 O_2(g) \rightarrow 6 CO_2(g) + 6 H_2O(\ell)$

  $\Delta_r H° = -673$ kJ/mol-rxn
  $\Delta_r S° = 60.4$ J/K · mol-rxn

  (b) $MgO(s) + C(graphite) \rightarrow Mg(s) + CO(g)$

  $\Delta_r H° = 490.7$ kJ/mol-rxn
  $\Delta_r S° = 197.9$ J/K · mol-rxn

Gibbs Free Energy
(See Example 19.4; see ChemistryNow Screen 19.7.)

15. Using values of $\Delta_f H°$ and $S°$, calculate $\Delta_r G°$ for each of the following reactions at 25 °C.
  (a) $2 Pb(s) + O_2(g) \rightarrow 2 PbO(s)$
  (b) $NH_3(g) + HNO_3(aq) \rightarrow NH_4NO_3(aq)$

  Which of these reactions is (are) predicted to be product-favored at equilibrium? Are the reactions enthalpy- or entropy-driven?

16. ■ Using values of $\Delta_f H°$ and $S°$, calculate $\Delta_r G°$ for each of the following reactions at 25 °C.
  (a) $2 Na(s) + 2 H_2O(\ell) \rightarrow 2 NaOH(aq) + H_2(g)$
  (b) $6 C(graphite) + 3 H_2(g) \rightarrow C_6H_6(\ell)$

  Which of these reactions is (are) predicted to be product-favored at equilibrium? Are the reactions enthalpy- or entropy-driven?

17. Using values of $\Delta_f H°$ and $S°$, calculate the standard molar free energy of formation, $\Delta_f G°$, for each of the following compounds:
  (a) $CS_2(g)$
  (b) $NaOH(s)$
  (c) $ICl(g)$

  Compare your calculated values of $\Delta_f G°$ with those listed in Appendix L. Which of these formation reactions are predicted to be spontaneous under standard conditions at 25 °C?

▲ more challenging   ■ in OWL   Blue-numbered questions answered in Appendix O

18. ■ Using values of $\Delta_f H°$ and $S°$, calculate the standard molar free energy of formation, $\Delta_f G°$, for each of the following:
(a) $Ca(OH)_2(s)$
(b) $Cl(g)$
(c) $Na_2CO_3(s)$

Compare your calculated values of $\Delta_f G°$ with those listed in Appendix L. Which of these formation reactions are predicted to be spontaneous under standard conditions at 25 °C?

Free Energy of Formation
(See Example 19.5; see ChemistryNow Screen 19.7.)

19. Using values of $\Delta_f G°$, calculate $\Delta_r G°$ for each of the following reactions at 25 °C. Which are product-favored at equilibrium?
(a) $2\,K(s) + Cl_2(g) \rightarrow 2\,KCl(s)$
(b) $2\,CuO(s) \rightarrow 2\,Cu(s) + O_2(g)$
(c) $4\,NH_3(g) + 7\,O_2(g) \rightarrow 4\,NO_2(g) + 6\,H_2O(g)$

20. ■ Using values of $\Delta_f G°$, calculate $\Delta_r G°$ for each of the following reactions at 25 °C. Which are product-favored at equilibrium?
(a) $HgS(s) + O_2(g) \rightarrow Hg(\ell) + SO_2(g)$
(b) $2\,H_2S(g) + 3\,O_2(g) \rightarrow 2\,H_2O(g) + 2\,SO_2(g)$
(c) $SiCl_4(g) + 2\,Mg(s) \rightarrow 2\,MgCl_2(s) + Si(s)$

21. For the reaction $BaCO_3(s) \rightarrow BaO(s) + CO_2(g)$, $\Delta_r G° = +219.7$ kJ. Using this value and other data available in Appendix L, calculate the value of $\Delta_f G°$ for $BaCO_3(s)$.

22. ■ For the reaction $TiCl_2(s) + Cl_2(g) \rightarrow TiCl_4(\ell)$, $\Delta_r G° = -272.8$ kJ. Using this value and other data available in Appendix L, calculate the value of $\Delta_f G°$ for $TiCl_2(s)$.

Effect of Temperature on ΔG
(See Example 19.6 and ChemistryNow Screen 19.8.)

23. Determine whether the reactions listed below are entropy-favored or disfavored under standard conditions. Predict how an increase in temperature will affect the value of $\Delta_r G°$.
(a) $N_2(g) + 2\,O_2(g) \rightarrow 2\,NO_2(g)$
(b) $2\,C(s) + O_2(g) \rightarrow 2\,CO(g)$
(c) $CaO(s) + CO_2(g) \rightarrow CaCO_3(s)$
(d) $2\,NaCl(s) \rightarrow 2\,Na(s) + Cl_2(g)$

24. ■ Determine whether the reactions listed below are entropy-favored or disfavored under standard conditions. Predict how an increase in temperature will affect the value of $\Delta_r G°$.
(a) $I_2(g) \rightarrow 2\,I(g)$
(b) $2\,SO_2(g) + O_2(g) \rightarrow 2\,SO_3(g)$
(c) $SiCl_4(g) + 2\,H_2O(\ell) \rightarrow SiO_2(s) + 4\,HCl(g)$
(d) $P_4(s, white) + 6\,H_2(g) \rightarrow 4\,PH_3(g)$

25. ■ Heating some metal carbonates, among them magnesium carbonate, leads to their decomposition.

$$MgCO_3(s) \rightarrow MgO(s) + CO_2(g)$$

(a) Calculate $\Delta_r H°$ and $\Delta_r S°$ for the reaction.
(b) Is the reaction spontaneous under standard conditions at 298 K?
(c) Is the reaction predicted to be spontaneous at higher temperatures?

26. ■ Calculate $\Delta_r H°$ and $\Delta_r S°$ for the reaction of tin(IV) oxide with carbon.

$$SnO_2(s) + C(s) \rightarrow Sn(s) + CO_2(g)$$

(a) Is the reaction spontaneous under standard conditions at 298 K?
(b) Is the reaction predicted to be spontaneous at higher temperatures?

Free Energy and Equilibrium Constants
(See Example 19.7; use $\Delta G° = -RT \ln K$; see ChemistryNow Screen 19.9.)

27. The standard free energy change, $\Delta_r G°$, for the formation of $NO(g)$ from its elements is $+86.58$ kJ/mol at 25 °C. Calculate K_p at this temperature for the equilibrium

$$\tfrac{1}{2}\,N_2(g) + \tfrac{1}{2}\,O_2(g) \rightleftharpoons NO(g)$$

Comment on the sign of $\Delta G°$ and the magnitude of K_p.

28. ■ The standard free energy change, $\Delta_r G°$, for the formation of $O_3(g)$ from $O_2(g)$ is $+163.2$ kJ/mol at 25 °C. Calculate K_p at this temperature for the equilibrium

$$3\,O_2(g) \rightleftharpoons 2\,O_3(g)$$

Comment on the sign of $\Delta G°$ and the magnitude of K_p.

29. Calculate $\Delta_r G°$ at 25 °C for the formation of one mol of $C_2H_6(g)$ from $C_2H_4(g)$ and $H_2(g)$. Use this value to calculate K_p for the equilibrium.

$$C_2H_4(g) + H_2(g) \rightleftharpoons C_2H_6(g)$$

Comment on the sign of $\Delta_r G°$ and the magnitude of K_p.

30. ■ Calculate $\Delta_r G°$ at 25 °C for the formation of 1 mol of $C_2H_5OH(g)$ from $C_2H_4(g)$ and $H_2O(g)$. Use this value to calculate K_p for the equilibrium.

$$C_2H_4(g) + H_2O(g) \rightleftharpoons C_2H_5OH(g)$$

Comment on the sign of $\Delta_r G°$ and the magnitude of K_p.

General Questions

These questions are not designated as to type or location in the chapter. They may combine several concepts.

31. Compare the formulas in each set of compounds, and decide which is expected to have the higher entropy. Assume all are at the same temperature. Check your answers using data in Appendix L.
    (a) HF(g), HCl(g), or HBr(g)
    (b) $NH_4Cl(s)$ or $NH_4Cl(aq)$
    (c) $C_2H_4(g)$ or $N_2(g)$ (two substances with the same molar mass)
    (a) NaCl(s) or NaCl(g)

32. Using standard entropy values, calculate $\Delta_rS°$ for the formation of 1.0 mol of $NH_3(g)$ from $N_2(g)$ and $H_2(g)$ at 25 °C.

33. ■ About 5 billion kilograms of benzene, C_6H_6, are made each year. Benzene is used as a starting material for many other compounds and as a solvent (although it is also a carcinogen, and its use is restricted). One compound that can be made from benzene is cyclohexane, C_6H_{12}.

$$C_6H_6(\ell) + 3\ H_2(g) \rightarrow C_6H_{12}(\ell)$$

$$\Delta_rH° = -206.7\ kJ;\ \Delta_rS° = -361.5\ J/K$$

Is this reaction predicted to be product-favored at equilibrium at 25 °C? Is the reaction enthalpy- or entropy-driven?

34. Hydrogenation, the addition of hydrogen to an organic compound, is an industrially important reaction. Calculate $\Delta_rH°$, $\Delta_rS°$, and $\Delta_rG°$ for the hydrogenation of octene, C_8H_{16}, to give octane, C_8H_{18}, at 25 °C. Is the reaction product- or reactant-favored at equilibrium?

$$C_8H_{16}(g) + H_2(g) \rightarrow C_8H_{18}(g)$$

Along with data in Appendix L, the following information is needed for this calculation.

Compound	$\Delta_fH°$ (kJ/mol)	$S°$ (J/K · mol)
Octene	−82.93	462.8
Octane	−208.45	463.639

35. ■ Is the combustion of ethane, C_2H_6, product-favored at equilibrium at 25 °C?

$$C_2H_6(g) + \tfrac{7}{2}O_2(g) \rightarrow 2CO_2(g) + 3\ H_2O(g)$$

Answer the question by calculating the value of $\Delta S°$ (universe) at 298 K, using values of $\Delta_fH°$ and $S°$ in Appendix L. Does the answer agree with your preconceived idea of this reaction?

36. Write a balanced equation that depicts the formation of 1 mol of $Fe_2O_3(s)$ from its elements. What is the standard free energy of formation of 1.00 mol of $Fe_2O_3(s)$? What is the value of $\Delta G°$ when 454 g (1 lb) of $Fe_2O_3(s)$ is formed from the elements?

37. When vapors from hydrochloric acid and aqueous ammonia come in contact, they react, producing a white "cloud" of solid NH_4Cl (Figure 19.10).

$$HCl(g) + NH_3(g) \rightleftharpoons NH_4Cl(s)$$

Defining the reactants and products as the system under study:
    (a) Predict whether $\Delta S°$(system), $\Delta S°$(surroundings), $\Delta S°$(universe), $\Delta_rH°$, and $\Delta_rG°$ (at 298 K) are greater than zero, equal to zero, or less than zero; and explain your prediction. Verify your predictions by calculating values for each of these quantities.
    (b) Calculate the value of K_p for this reaction at 298 K.

38. Calculate $\Delta S°$(system), $\Delta S°$(surroundings), $\Delta S°$(universe) for each of the following processes at 298 K, and comment on how these systems differ.
    (a) $HNO_3(g) \rightarrow HNO_3(aq)$
    (b) $NaOH(s) \rightarrow NaOH(aq)$

39. Methanol is now widely used as a fuel in race cars. Consider the following reaction as a possible synthetic route to methanol.

$$C(graphite) + \tfrac{1}{2}O_2(g) + 2\ H_2(g) \rightleftharpoons CH_3OH(\ell)$$

Calculate K_p for the formation of methanol at 298 K using this reaction. Would a different temperature be better suited to this reaction?

40. ■ The enthalpy of vaporization of liquid diethyl ether, $(C_2H_5)_2O$, is 26.0 kJ/mol at the boiling point of 35.0 °C. Calculate $\Delta S°$ for a vapor-to-liquid transformation at 35.0 °C.

41. Calculate the entropy change, $\Delta S°$, for the vaporization of ethanol, C_2H_5OH, at its normal boiling point, 78.0 °C. The enthalpy of vaporization of ethanol is 39.3 kJ/mol.

42. Using thermodynamic data, estimate the normal boiling point of ethanol. (Recall that liquid and vapor are in equilibrium at 1.0 atm pressure at the normal boiling point.) The actual normal boiling point is 78 °C. How well does your calculated result agree with the actual value?

43. The following reaction is reactant-favored at equilibrium at room temperature.

$$COCl_2(g) \rightarrow CO(g) + Cl_2(g)$$

Will raising or lowering the temperature make it product-favored?

44. ■ When calcium carbonate is heated strongly, CO_2 gas is evolved. The equilibrium pressure of CO_2 is 1.00 bar at 897 °C, and $\Delta_rH°$ at 298 K is 179.0 kJ.

$$CaCO_3(s) \rightarrow CaO(s) + CO_2(g)$$

Estimate the value of $\Delta_rS°$ at 897 °C for the reaction.

▲ more challenging ■ in OWL Blue-numbered questions answered in Appendix O

45. Sodium reacts violently with water according to the equation

$$Na(s) + H_2O(\ell) \rightarrow NaOH(aq) + \frac{1}{2} H_2(g)$$

Without doing calculations, predict the signs of $\Delta_r H°$ and $\Delta_r S°$ for the reaction. Verify your prediction with a calculation.

46. ■ Yeast can produce ethanol by the fermentation of glucose $(C_6H_{12}O_6)$, which is the basis for the production of most alcoholic beverages.

$$C_6H_{12}O_6(aq) \rightarrow 2\ C_2H_5OH(\ell) + 2\ CO_2(g)$$

Calculate $\Delta_r H°$, $\Delta_r S°$, and $\Delta_r G°$ for the reaction at 25 °C. Is the reaction product- or reactant-favored? In addition to the thermodynamic values in Appendix L, you will need the following data for $C_6H_{12}O_6(aq)$:

$\Delta_f H° = -1260.0$ kJ/mol; $S° = 289$ J/K · mol; and $\Delta_f G° = -918.8$ kJ/mol.

47. ■ Elemental boron, in the form of thin fibers, can be made by reducing a boron halide with H_2.

$$BCl_3(g) + \frac{3}{2} H_2(g) \rightarrow B(s) + 3HCl(g)$$

Calculate $\Delta_r H°$, $\Delta_r S°$, and $\Delta_r G°$ at 25 °C for this reaction. Is the reaction predicted to be product-favored at equilibrium at 25 °C? If so, is it enthalpy- or entropy-driven? [$S°$ for B(s) is 5.86 J/K · mol.]

48. ■ ▲ Estimate the vapor pressure of ethanol at 37 °C using thermodynamic data. Express the result in mm of mercury.

49. The equilibrium constant, K_p, for $N_2O_4(g) \rightleftharpoons$ $2\ NO_2(g)$ is 0.14 at 25 °C. Calculate $\Delta_r G°$ for the conversion of $N_2O_4(g)$ to $NO_2(g)$ from this constant, and compare this value with that determined from the $\Delta_f G°$ values in Appendix L.

50. ■ ▲ Estimate the boiling point of water in Denver, Colorado (where the altitude is 1.60 km and the atmospheric pressure is 630 mm Hg or 0.840 bar).

51. The equilibrium constant for the butane $\rightleftharpoons$ isobutane equilibrium at 25 °C is 2.50. Calculate $\Delta_r G°$ at this temperature in units of kJ/mol.

butane $\rightleftharpoons$ isobutane

$$CH_3CH_2CH_2CH_3 \quad \rightleftharpoons \quad \underset{\underset{CH_3}{|}}{CH_3CHCH_3}$$

$$K_c = \frac{[isobutane]}{[butane]} = 2.50 \text{ at } 298 \text{ K}$$

52. ■ A crucial reaction for the production of synthetic fuels is the conversion of coal to H_2 with steam. The chemical reaction is

$$C(s) + H_2O(g) \rightarrow CO(g) + H_2(g)$$

(a) Calculate $\Delta_r G°$ for this reaction at 25 °C, assuming C(s) is graphite.
(b) Calculate K_p for the reaction at 25 °C.
(c) Is the reaction predicted to be product-favored at equilibrium at 25 °C? If not, at what temperature will it become so?

53. Calculate $\Delta_r G°$ for the decomposition of sulfur trioxide to sulfur dioxide and oxygen.

$$2\ SO_3(g) \rightleftharpoons 2\ SO_2(g) + O_2(g)$$

(a) Is the reaction product-favored at equilibrium at 25 °C?
(b) If the reaction is not product-favored at 25 °C, is there a temperature at which it will become so? Estimate this temperature.
(c) What is the equilibrium constant for the reaction at 1500 °C?

54. Methanol can be made by partial oxidation of methane by $O_2(g)$.

$$CH_4(g) + \frac{1}{2} O_2(g) \rightleftharpoons CH_3OH(\ell)$$

(a) Determine $\Delta S°$(system), $\Delta S°$(surroundings), and $\Delta S°$(universe) for this process.
(b) Is this reaction product-favored at equilibrium at 25 °C?

55. ■ A cave in Mexico was recently discovered to have some interesting chemistry. Hydrogen sulfide, H_2S, reacts with oxygen in the cave to give sulfuric acid, which drips from the ceiling in droplets with a pH less than 1. The reaction occurring is

$$H_2S(g) + 2\ O_2(g) \rightarrow H_2SO_4(\ell)$$

Calculate $\Delta_r H°$, $\Delta_r S°$, and $\Delta_r G°$. Is the reaction product-favored at equilibrium at 25 °C? Is it enthalpy- or entropy-driven?

56. ■ Wet limestone is used to scrub SO_2 gas from the exhaust gases of power plants. One possible reaction gives hydrated calcium sulfite:

$$CaCO_3(s) + SO_2(g) + \frac{1}{2} H_2O(\ell) \rightleftharpoons$$
$$CaSO_3 \cdot \frac{1}{2} H_2O(s) + CO_2(g)$$

Another reaction gives hydrated calcium sulfate:

$$CaCO_3(s) + SO_2(g) + \frac{1}{2} H_2O(\ell) + \frac{1}{2} O_2(g) \rightleftharpoons$$
$$CaSO_4 \cdot \frac{1}{2} H_2O(s) + CO_2(g)$$

(a) Which is the more product-favored reaction? Use the data in the table on the next page and any other information needed in Appendix L to calculate $\Delta_r G°$ for each reaction at 25 °C.

▲ more challenging   ■ in OWL   Blue-numbered questions answered in Appendix O

	CaSO$_3$ · ½ H$_2$O(s)	CaSO$_4$ · ½ H$_2$O(s)
$\Delta_fH°$ (kJ/mol)	−1311.7	−1574.65
$S°$ (J/K · mol)	121.3	134.8

(b) Calculate $\Delta_rG°$ for the reaction

CaSO$_3$ · ½ H$_2$O(s) + ½ O$_2$(g) $\rightleftharpoons$ CaSO$_4$ · ½ H$_2$O(s)

Is this reaction product- or reactant-favored at equilibrium?

57. ■ Sulfur undergoes a phase transition between 80 and 100 °C.

$$S_8(\text{rhombic}) \rightarrow S_8(\text{monoclinic})$$

$\Delta_rH° = 3.213$ kJ/mol-rxn $\Delta_rS° = 8.7$ J/K · mol-rxn

(a) Estimate $\Delta_rG°$ for the transition at 80.0 °C and 110.0 °C. What do these results tell you about the stability of the two forms of sulfur at each of these temperatures?
(b) Calculate the temperature at which $\Delta_rG° = 0$. What is the significance of this temperature?

58. Calculate the entropy change for dissolving HCl gas in water at 25 °C. Is the sign of $\Delta S°$ what you expected? Why or why not?

In the Laboratory

59. ■ Some metal oxides can be decomposed to the metal and oxygen under reasonable conditions. Is the decomposition of silver(I) oxide product-favored at 25 °C?

$$2 \text{ Ag}_2\text{O}(s) \rightarrow 4 \text{ Ag}(s) + \text{O}_2(g)$$

If not, can it become so if the temperature is raised? At what temperature does the reaction become product-favored?

60. ■ Copper(II) oxide, CuO, can be reduced to copper metal with hydrogen at higher temperatures.

$$\text{CuO}(s) + \text{H}_2(g) \rightarrow \text{Cu}(s) + \text{H}_2\text{O}(g)$$

Is this reaction product- or reactant-favored at equilibrium at 298 K?

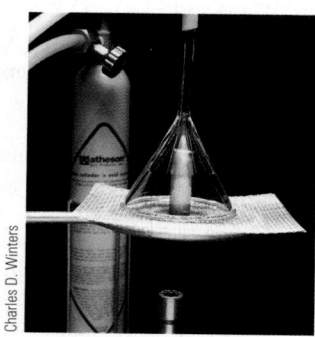

If copper metal is heated in air, a black film of CuO forms on the surface. In this photo, the heated bar, covered with a black CuO film, has been bathed in hydrogen gas. Black, solid CuO is reduced rapidly to copper at higher temperatures.

Charles D. Winters

61. ■ Calculate $\Delta_fG°$ for HI(g) at 350 °C, given the following equilibrium partial pressures: $P(\text{H}_2) = 0.132$ bar, $P(\text{I}_2) = 0.295$ bar, and $P(\text{HI}) = 1.61$ bar. At 350 °C and 1 bar, I$_2$ is a gas.

$$\frac{1}{2} \text{ H}_2(g) + \frac{1}{2} \text{ I}_2(g) \rightleftharpoons \text{HI}(g)$$

62. ■ Calculate the equilibrium constant for the formation of NiO at 1627 °C. Can the reaction proceed in the forward direction if the initial pressure of O$_2$ is below 1.00 mm Hg? {$\Delta_fG°$ [NiO(s)] = −72.1 kJ/mol at 1627 °C}

$$\text{Ni}(s) + \frac{1}{2} \text{ O}_2(g) \rightleftharpoons \text{NiO}(s)$$

63. ■ Titanium(IV) oxide is converted to titanium carbide with carbon at a high temperature.

$$\text{TiO}_2(s) + 3 \text{ C}(s) \rightarrow 2 \text{ CO}(g) + \text{TiC}(s)$$

Compound	Free Energies of Formation at 727 °C, kJ/mol
TiO$_2$(s)	−757.8
TiC(s)	−162.6
CO(g)	−200.2

(a) Calculate $\Delta_rG°$ and K at 727 °C
(b) Is the reaction product-favored at equilibrium at this temperature?
(c) How can the reactant or product concentrations be adjusted for the reaction to be product-favored at 727 °C?

64. Cisplatin [*cis*-diamminedichloroplatinum(II)] is a potent treatment for certain types of cancers, but the *trans* isomer is not effective. (They are called *isomers* because the two compounds have the same formula but a different arrangement of atoms.) What is the equilibrium constant at 298 K for the transformation of the *cis* to the *trans* isomer? Which is more thermodynamically stable, the *cis* or the *trans* isomer?

Compound	$\Delta_fH°$ (kJ/mol, 298 K)	$\Delta_fG°$ (kJ/mol, 298 K)
Cis-Pt(NH$_3$)$_2$Cl$_2$	−467.4	−228.7
Trans-Pt(NH$_3$)$_2$Cl$_2$	−480.3	−222.8

cis isomer   trans isomer

▲ more challenging   ■ in OWL   Blue-numbered questions answered in Appendix O

Summary and Conceptual Questions

The following questions may use concepts from this and previous chapters.

65. ■ ▲ Mercury vapor is dangerous because it can be breathed into the lungs. We wish to estimate the vapor pressure of mercury at two different temperatures from the following data:

	$\Delta_f H°$ (kJ/mol)	$S°$ (J/K · mol)	$\Delta_f G°$ (kJ/mol)
Hg(ℓ)	0	76.02	0
Hg(g)	61.38	174.97	31.88

Estimate the temperature at which K_p for the process Hg(ℓ) $\rightleftharpoons$ Hg(g) is equal to (a) 1.00 and (b) 1/760. What is the vapor pressure at each of these temperatures? (Experimental vapor pressures are 1.00 mm Hg at 126.2 °C and 1.00 bar at 356.6 °C.) (Note: The temperature at which $P = 1.00$ bar can be calculated from thermodynamic data. To find the other temperature, you will need to use the temperature for $P = 1.00$ bar and the Clausius–Clapeyron equation on page 576.)

66. Explain why each of the following statements is incorrect.
    (a) Entropy increases in all spontaneous reactions.
    (b) Reactions with a negative free energy change ($\Delta_r G° < 0$) are product-favored and occur with rapid transformation of reactants to products.
    (c) All spontaneous processes are exothermic.
    (d) Endothermic processes are never spontaneous.

67. ■ Decide whether each of the following statements is true or false. If false, rewrite it to make it true.
    (a) The entropy of a substance increases on going from the liquid to the vapor state at any temperature.
    (b) An exothermic reaction will always be spontaneous.
    (c) Reactions with a positive $\Delta_r H°$ and a positive $\Delta_r S°$ can never be product-favored.
    (d) If $\Delta_r G°$ for a reaction is negative, the reaction will have an equilibrium constant greater than 1.

68. Under what conditions is the entropy of a pure substance 0 J/K · mol? Could a substance at standard conditions have a value of 0 J/K · mol? A negative entropy value? Are there any conditions under which a substance will have negative entropy? Explain your answer.

69. In Chapter 14, you learned that entropy, as well as enthalpy, plays a role in the solution process. If $\Delta H°$ for the solution process is zero, explain how the process can be driven by entropy.

70. ■ ▲ Consider the formation of NO(g) from its elements.

$$N_2(g) + O_2(g) \rightleftharpoons 2 NO(g)$$

(a) Calculate K_p at 25 °C. Is the reaction product-favored at this temperature?
(b) Assuming $\Delta_r H°$ and $\Delta_r S°$ are nearly constant with temperature, calculate $\Delta_r G°$ at 700 °C. Estimate K_p from the new value of $\Delta_r G°$ at 700 °C. Is the reaction product-favored at 700 °C?
(c) Using K_p at 700 °C, calculate the equilibrium partial pressures of the three gases if you mix 1.00 bar each of N_2 and O_2.

71. Write a chemical equation for the oxidation of $C_2H_6(g)$ by $O_2(g)$ to form $CO_2(g)$ and $H_2O(g)$. Defining this as the system:
    (a) Predict whether the signs of $\Delta S°$ (system), $\Delta S°$ (surroundings), and $\Delta S°$ (universe) will be greater than zero, equal to zero, or less than zero. Explain your prediction.
    (b) Predict the signs of $\Delta_r H°$ and $\Delta_r G°$. Explain how you made this prediction.
    (c) Will the value of K_p be very large, very small, or near 1? Will the equilibrium constant, K_p, for this system be larger or smaller at temperatures greater than 298 K? Explain how you made this prediction.

72. ■ The normal melting point of benzene, C_6H_6, is 5.5 °C. For the process of melting, what is the sign of each of the following?
    (a) $\Delta H°$ (c) $\Delta G°$ at 5.5 °C   (e) $\Delta G°$ at 25.0 °C
    (b) $\Delta S°$ (d) $\Delta G°$ at 0.0 °C

73. Calculate the standard molar entropy change, $\Delta_r S°$, for each of the following reactions at 25 °C:

1. $C(s) + 2 H_2(g) \rightarrow CH_4(g)$

2. $CH_4(g) + \frac{1}{2} O_2(g) \rightarrow CH_3OH(\ell)$

3. $C(s) + 2 H_2(g) + \frac{1}{2} O_2(g) \rightarrow CH_3OH(\ell)$

Verify that these values are related by the equation $\Delta_r S°_1 + \Delta_r S°_2 = \Delta_r S°_3$. What general principle is illustrated here?

74. For each of the following processes, predict the algebraic sign of $\Delta_r H°$, $\Delta_r S°$, and $\Delta_r G°$. No calculations are necessary; use your common sense.
    (a) The decomposition of liquid water to give gaseous oxygen and hydrogen, a process that requires a considerable amount of energy.
    (b) Dynamite is a mixture of nitroglycerin, $C_3H_5N_3O_9$, and diatomaceous earth. The explosive decomposition of nitroglycerin gives gaseous products such as water, CO_2, and others; much heat is evolved.
    (c) The combustion of gasoline in the engine of your car, as exemplified by the combustion of octane.

$$2 C_8H_{18}(g) + 25 O_2(g) \rightarrow 16 CO_2(g) + 18 H_2O(g)$$

75. ■ "Heater Meals" are food packages that contain their own heat source. Just pour water into the heater unit, wait a few minutes, and voilà! You have a hot meal.

$$Mg(s) + 2\,H_2O(\ell) \rightarrow Mg(OH)_2(s) + H_2(g)$$

Charles D. Winters

The heat for the heater unit is produced by the reaction of magnesium with water.

(a) Confirm that this is a spontaneous reaction under standard conditions.
(b) What mass of magnesium is required to produce sufficient energy to heat 225 mL of water (density = 0.995 g/mL) from 25 °C to the boiling point?

76. *Abba's Refrigerator* was described on page 222 is an example of the validity of the second law of thermodynamics. Explain how the second law applies to this simple but useful device.

77. Oxygen dissolved in water can cause corrosion in hot-water heating systems. To remove oxygen, hydrazine (N_2H_4) is often added. Hydrazine reacts with dissolved O_2 to form water and N_2.
(a) Write a balanced chemical equation for the reaction of hydrazine and oxygen. Identify the oxidizing and reducing agents in this redox reaction.
(b) Calculate $\Delta_rH°$, $\Delta_rS°$, and $\Delta_rG°$ for this reaction involving 1 mol of N_2H_4 at 25 °C.
(c) Because this is an exothermic reaction, energy is evolved as heat. What temperature change is expected in a heating system containing 5.5×10^4 L of water? (Assume no energy is lost to the surroundings.)
(d) The mass of a hot-water heating system is 5.5×10^4 kg. What amount of O_2 (in moles) would be present in this system if it is filled with water saturated with O_2? (The solubility of O_2 in water at 25 °C is 0.000434 g per 100 g of water.)
(e) Assume hydrazine is available as a 5.0% solution in water. What mass of this solution should be added to totally consume the dissolved O_2 [described in part (d)]?
(f) Assuming the N_2 escapes as a gas, calculate the volume of $N_2(g)$ (measured at 273 K and 1.00 bar) that will be produced.

78. The formation of diamond from graphite is a process of considerable importance.

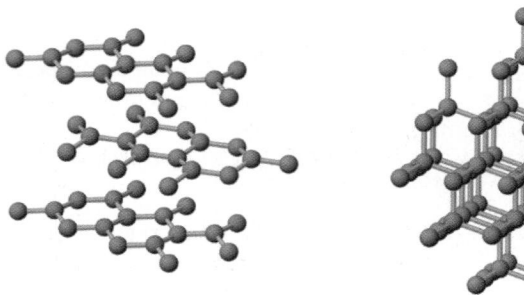

graphite   diamond

(a) Using data in Appendix L, calculate $\Delta_rS°$, $\Delta_rH°$, and $\Delta_rG°$ for this process at 25 °C.
(b) The calculations will suggest that this process is not possible at any temperature. However, the synthesis of diamonds by this reaction is a commercial process. How can this contradiction be rationalized? (Note: In the industrial synthesis, high pressure and high temperatures are used.)

79. ■ Iodine, I_2, dissolves readily in carbon tetrachloride. For this process, $\Delta H° = 0$ kJ/mol.

$$I_2(s) \rightarrow I_2 \text{ (in CCl}_4 \text{ solution)}$$

What is the sign of $\Delta_rG°$? Is the dissolving process entropy driven or enthalpy driven? Explain briefly.

80. Use the simulation on Screen 19.8 of ChemistryNow to answer the following questions.
(a) Consider the reaction of Fe_2O_3 and C. How does $\Delta_rG°$ vary with temperature? Is there a temperature at which the reaction is spontaneous?
(b) Consider the reaction of HCl and Na_2CO_3. Is there a temperature at which the reaction is no longer spontaneous?
(c) Is the spontaneity of a reaction dependent on or independent of temperature?

81. Use the simulation on Screen 19.6 of ChemistryNow to answer the following questions.
(a) Does the spontaneity of the decomposition of CH_3OH to the elements change as the temperature increases?
(b) Is there a temperature between 400 K and 1000 K at which the decomposition is spontaneous?

82. Use the simulation on Screen 19.6 of ChemistryNow to answer the following questions regarding the reaction of NO and Cl_2 to produce NOCl.
(a) What is $\Delta S°$ (system) at 400 K for this reaction?
(b) Does $\Delta S°$ (system) change with temperature?
(c) Does $\Delta S°$ (surroundings) change with temperature?

(d) Does $\Delta S°$(universe) always change with an increase in temperature?

(e) Do exothermic reactions always lead to positive values of $\Delta S°$(universe)?

(f) Is the NO + Cl_2 reaction spontaneous at 400 K? At 700 K?

83. ■ ▲ The Haber–Bosch process for the production of ammonia is one of the key processes in industrialized countries.

$$N_2(g) + 3\ H_2(g) \rightleftharpoons 2\ NH_3(g)$$

(a) Calculate $\Delta_r G°$ for the reaction at 298 K, 800 K, and 1300 K. Data at 298 K are in Appendix L. Data for the other temperatures are as follows:

Temperature	$\Delta_r H°$ (kJ/mol)	$\Delta_r S°$ (J/K · mol)
800 K	−107.4	−225.4
1300 K	−112.4	−228.0

How does the free energy change for the reaction change with temperature?

(b) Calculate the equilibrium constant for the reaction at 298 K, 800 K, and 1300 K.

(c) Calculate the mole fraction of ammonia in the equilibrium mixture at each of the temperatures. At what temperature is the mole fraction of NH_3 the largest?

84. ▲ Muscle cells need energy to contract. One biochemical pathway for energy transfer is the breakdown of glucose to pyruvate in a process called glycolysis. In the presence of sufficient oxygen in the cell, pyruvate is oxidized to CO_2 and H_2O to make further energy available. However, under extreme conditions not enough oxygen can be supplied to the cells, so muscle cells produce lactate ion according to the reaction

Pyruvate

Lactate

where $\Delta_r G°' = -25.1$ kJ/mol. In living cells, the pH value is about 7. The hydronium ion concentration is constant and is included in $\Delta G°$, which is then called $\Delta_r G°'$ (as explained on page 884). (This problem is taken from the problems for the 36th International Chemistry Olympiad for high school students held in Kiel, Germany in 2004.)

(a) Calculate $\Delta_r G°$ for the reaction at 25 °C.

(b) Calculate the equilibrium constant K'. (The hydronium ion concentration is included in the constant. That is, $K' = K \cdot [H_3O^+]$ for the reaction at 25 °C and pH = 7.0.)

(c) $\Delta_r G°'$ is the free energy change under standard conditions; that is, the concentrations of all reactants (except H_3O^+) are 1.00 mol/L. Calculate $\Delta_r G'$ at 25 °C, assuming the following concentrations in the cell: pyruvate, 380 μmol/L; NADH, 50 μmol/L; lactate ion, 3700 μmol/L; and NAD^+ ion, 540 μmol/L.

20 | Principles of Reactivity: Electron Transfer Reactions

New euro coins that use different metal alloys.

Don't Hold onto That Money!

Nickel Allergy from Coins

Shortly after the new euro coins were introduced in European countries in 2002, people showed up in hospitals with strange allergies. These allergic reactions were soon identified as arising from nickel, presumably from the coins.

The surface of the 1- and 2-euro coins consists of a white Cu-Ni alloy (75% Cu and 25% Ni) and a yellow nickel-brass (75% Cu, 20% Zn, and 5% Ni). Skin tests with these coins showed that patients did get a rash from the coins, so there was initially quite a controversy about the coins. More extensive testing, however, showed that the euro coins did not release any more nickel than other coins with a similar composition.

Nickel allergy, caused by nickel(II) ions, is one of the most common causes of contact dermatitis, a skin inflammation that results in swollen, reddened, and itchy skin. Up to 15% of women are allergic to nickel, probably from nickel in less expensive costume jewelry. Unfortunately, there is no cure. One can only prevent it by staying away from nickel-containing objects, which is not easy to do because so many articles (such as watchbands, hairpins, eyeglass frames, paper clips, keys, and tools) contain nickel.

Questions:

Experiments show that metal ions, Ni^{2+} and Cu^{2+}, are present on the surface of coins, presumably from corrosion. In one experiment, the bimetallic euro coins were put in salty "artificial sweat," and the coins showed signs of significant corrosion. Under these conditions, the yellow outer ring of the 1-euro coin had a tiny negative charge, and the white inner portion had a slight positive charge.

1. What electrochemical reactions are possible that could involve Cu^{2+} and Ni or Ni^{2+} and Cu?
2. Could either reaction produce an electric current?
3. If such a reaction occurs under standard conditions, what is the value of the electric potential, $E°_{cell}$?

Answers to these questions are in Appendix Q.

Chapter Goals

OWL *See Chapter Goals Revisited (page 939) for Study Questions keyed to these goals and assignable in OWL.*

- Balance equations for oxidation–reduction reactions in acidic or basic solutions using the half-reaction approach.
- Understand the principles underlying voltaic cells.
- Understand how to use electrochemical potentials.
- Explore electrolysis, the use of electrical energy to produce chemical change.

Chapter Outline

L et us introduce you to electrochemistry and electron transfer reactions with a simple experiment. Place a piece of copper in an aqueous solution of silver nitrate. After a short time, metallic silver deposits on the copper, and the solution takes on the blue color typical of aqueous Cu^{2+} ions (Figure 20.1). The following oxidation–reduction (redox) reaction has occurred:

$$Cu(s) + 2\ Ag^+(aq) \rightarrow Cu^{2+}(aq) + 2\ Ag(s)$$

At the particulate level, Ag^+ ions in solution come into direct contact with the copper surface where the transfer of electrons occurs. Two electrons are transferred

Chemistry Now™

Throughout the text this icon introduces an opportunity for self-study or to explore interactive tutorials by signing in at **www.cengage.com/login**.

A clean piece of copper wire will be placed in a solution of silver nitrate, $AgNO_3$.

Add $AgNO_3(aq)$

With time, the copper reduces Ag^+ ions to silver metal crystals, and the copper metal is oxidized to copper ions, Cu^{2+}.

After several days

The blue color of the solution is due to the presence of aqueous copper(II) ions.

Silver ions in solution

Surface of copper wire

Cu^{2+}

Photos: Charles D. Winters

FIGURE 20.1 The oxidation of copper by silver ions. Note that water molecules are not shown for clarity. (See ChemistryNow for photographs of this reaction sequence.)

from a Cu atom to two Ag^+ ions. Copper ions, Cu^{2+}, enter the solution, and silver atoms are deposited on the copper surface. This product-favored reaction continues until one or both of the reactants is consumed.

The reaction between copper metal and silver ions can be used to generate an electric current if the experiment is carried out in a different way. If the reactants, $Cu(s)$ and $Ag^+(aq)$, are in direct contact, electrons will be transferred directly from copper atoms to silver ions, and an increase in temperature (heating) rather than electrical work will result. Instead, the reaction has to be done in an apparatus that allows electrons to be transferred from one reactant to the other through an electrical circuit. The movement of electrons through the circuit constitutes an electric current that can be used to light a light bulb or to run a motor.

Devices that use chemical reactions to produce an electric current are called **voltaic cells** or **galvanic cells**, names honoring Count Alessandro Volta (1745–1827) and Luigi Galvani (1737–1798). All voltaic cells work in the same general way. They use product-favored redox reactions composed of an oxidation and a reduction. The cell is constructed so that electrons produced by the reducing agent are transferred through an electric circuit to the oxidizing agent.

A voltaic cell converts chemical energy to electrical energy. The opposite process, the use of electric energy to effect a chemical change, occurs in **electrolysis**. An example is the electrolysis of water (Figure 1.12), in which electrical energy is used to split water into its component elements, hydrogen and oxygen. Electrolysis is also used to electroplate one metal onto another, to obtain aluminum from its common ore (bauxite, mostly Al_2O_3), and to prepare important chemicals such as chlorine.

Electrochemistry is the field of chemistry that considers chemical reactions that produce or are caused by electrical energy. Because all electrochemical reactions are oxidation–reduction (redox) reactions, we begin our exploration of this subject by first describing electron transfer reactions in more detail.

■ **Two Types of Electrochemical Processes**
- Chemical change can produce an electric current in a voltaic cell.
- Electric energy can cause chemical change in the process of electrolysis.

 **Module 25**

■ **Oxidation Numbers** Oxidation numbers (page 144) can be used to determine whether a substance is oxidized or reduced. An element is oxidized if its oxidation number increases. The oxidation number decreases in a reduction.

20.1 Oxidation–Reduction Reactions

In an oxidation–reduction reaction, electron transfer occurs between a reducing agent and an oxidizing agent [see Section 3.9]. The essential features of all electron transfer reactions are as follows:

- One reactant is oxidized, and one is reduced.
- The extent of oxidation and reduction must balance.
- The oxidizing agent (the chemical species causing oxidation) is reduced.
- The reducing agent (the chemical species causing reduction) is oxidized.

These aspects of oxidation–reduction or redox reactions are illustrated for the reaction of copper metal and silver ion (Figure 20.1).

Cu oxidized, oxidation number increases;
Cu is the reducing agent.

$$Cu(s) + 2\,Ag^+(aq) \longrightarrow Cu^{2+}(aq) + 2\,Ag(s)$$

Ag^+ reduced, oxidation number decreases;
Ag^+ is the oxidizing agent.

Balancing Oxidation–Reduction Equations

All equations for oxidation–reduction reactions must be balanced for both mass and charge. The same number of atoms appear in the products and reactants of an equation, and the sum of electric charges of all the species on each side of the equation arrow must be the same. Charge balance guarantees that the number of electrons produced in oxidation equals the number of electrons consumed in reduction.

Balancing some redox equations can be complicated, but fortunately some systematic procedures can be used in these cases. Here, we describe the **half-reaction method**, a procedure that involves writing separate, balanced equations for the oxidation and reduction processes called half-reactions. One half-reaction describes the oxidation part of the reaction, and a second half-reaction describes the reduction part.

When a reaction has been determined to involve oxidation and reduction (by noting, for example, that oxidation state changes have occurred), the equation is separated into two half-reactions, which are then balanced for mass and charge. The equation for the overall reaction is then the sum of these two balanced half-reactions, after adjustments have been made (if necessary) in one or both half-reaction equations so that the numbers of electrons transferred from reducing agent to oxidizing agent balance. For example, the half-reactions for the reaction of copper metal with silver ions are

Reduction half-reaction: $\qquad Ag^+(aq) + e^- \rightarrow Ag(s)$

Oxidation half-reaction: $\qquad Cu(s) \rightarrow Cu^{2+}(aq) + 2\ e^-$

Notice that the equations for the half-reactions are themselves balanced for mass and charge. In the copper half-reaction, there is one Cu atom on each side of the equation (mass balance). The electric charge on the right side of the equation is 0 (the sum of +2 for the ion and −2 for two electrons), as it is on the left side (charge balance).

To produce the net chemical equation, we will add the two half-reactions. First, however, we must multiply the silver half-reaction by 2.

$$2\ Ag^+(aq) + 2\ e^- \rightarrow 2\ Ag(s)$$

Each mole of copper atoms produces two moles of electrons, and two moles of Ag^+ ions are required to consume those electrons.

Finally, adding the two half-reactions and canceling electrons from both sides leads to the net ionic equation for the reaction.

Reduction half-reaction: $\qquad 2\ [Ag^+(aq) + e^- \rightarrow Ag(s)]$

Oxidation half-reaction: $\qquad \underline{Cu(s) \rightarrow Cu^{2+}(aq) + 2\ e^-}$

Net ionic equation $\qquad Cu(s) + 2\ Ag^+(aq) \rightarrow Cu^{2+}(aq) + 2\ Ag(s)$

The resulting net ionic equation is balanced for mass and charge.

Chemistry.⚗.Now™

Sign in at **www.cengage.com/login** and go to Chapter 20 Contents to see:
- Screen 20.2 for a self-study module on various types of **oxidation–reduction reactions**
- Screen 20.3 for a self-study module on **methods of balancing redox reactions in acidic solution**

FIGURE 20.2 Reduction of Cu^{2+} by Al. (a) A ball of aluminum foil is added to a solution of $Cu(NO_3)_2$ and NaCl. (b) A coating of copper is soon seen on the surface of the aluminum, and the reaction generates a significant amount of heat. (Aluminum always has a thin coating of Al_2O_3 on the surface, which protects the metal from further reaction. However, in the presence of Cl^- ion, the coating is breached, and reaction occurs.) See Example 20.1.

Photos: Charles D. Winters

(a)

(b)

■ EXAMPLE 20.1 Balancing Oxidation–Reduction Equations

Problem Balance the following net ionic equation

$$Al(s) + Cu^{2+}(aq) \rightarrow Al^{3+}(aq) + Cu(s)$$

Identify the oxidizing agent, the reducing agent, the substance oxidized, and the substance reduced. Write balanced half-reactions and the balanced net ionic equation. See Figure 20.2 for photographs of this reaction.

Strategy First, make sure the reaction is an oxidation–reduction reaction by checking each element to see whether the oxidation numbers change. Next, separate the equation into half-reactions, identifying what has been reduced (oxidizing agent) and what has been oxidized (reducing agent). Then balance the half-reactions, first for mass and then for charge. Finally, add the two half-reactions, after ensuring that the reducing agent half-reaction involves the same number of moles of electrons as the oxidizing agent half-reaction.

Solution

Step 1. Recognize the reaction as an oxidation–reduction reaction.

Here, the oxidation number for aluminum changes from 0 to +3, and the oxidation number of copper changes from +2 to 0. Aluminum is oxidized and serves as the reducing agent. Copper(II) ions are reduced, and Cu^{2+} is the oxidizing agent.

Step 2. Separate the process into half-reactions.

Reduction: $\qquad\qquad\qquad Cu^{2+}(aq) \rightarrow Cu(s)$
(Oxidation number of Cu decreases.)

Oxidation: $\qquad\qquad\qquad Al(s) \rightarrow Al^{3+}(aq)$
(Oxidation number of Al increases.)

Step 3. Balance each half-reaction for mass.

Both half-reactions are already balanced for mass.

Step 4. Balance each half-reaction for charge.

To balance the equations for charge, add electrons to the more positive side of each half-reaction.

Reduction: $\qquad\qquad\qquad 2\ e^- + Cu^{2+}(aq) \rightarrow Cu(s)$
Each Cu^{2+} ion requires two electrons.

Oxidation: $\qquad\qquad\qquad Al(s) \rightarrow Al^{3+}(aq) + 3\ e^-$
Each Al atom releases three electrons.

Step 5. Multiply each half-reaction by an appropriate factor.

The reducing agent must donate as many electrons as the oxidizing agent acquires. Three Cu^{2+} ions are required to take on the six electrons produced by two Al atoms. Thus, we multiply the Cu^{2+}/Cu half-reaction by 3 and the Al/Al^{3+} half-reaction by 2.

Reduction: $\qquad\qquad\qquad 3[2\ e^- + Cu^{2+}(aq) \rightarrow Cu(s)]$
Oxidation: $\qquad\qquad\qquad 2[Al(s) \rightarrow Al^{3+}(aq) + 3\ e^-]$

Step 6. Add the half-reactions to produce the overall balanced equation.

Reduction:	$6\,e^- + 3\,Cu^{2+}(aq) \rightarrow 3\,Cu(s)$
Oxidation:	$2\,Al(s) \rightarrow 2\,Al^{3+}(aq) + 6\,e^-$
Net ionic equation:	$3\,Cu^{2+}(aq) + 2\,Al(s) \rightarrow 3\,Cu(s) + 2\,Al^{3+}(aq)$

Step 7. Simplify by eliminating reactants and products that appear on both sides.

This step is not required here.

Comment You should always check the overall equation to ensure there is mass and charge balance. In this case, three Cu atoms and two Al atoms appear on each side. The net electric charge on each side is $+6$. The equation is balanced.

EXERCISE 20.1 Balancing Oxidation–Reduction Equations

Aluminum reacts with nonoxidizing acids to give $Al^{3+}(aq)$ and $H_2(g)$. The (unbalanced) equation is

$$Al(s) + H^+(aq) \rightarrow Al^{3+}(aq) + H_2(g)$$

Write balanced equations for the half-reactions and the balanced net ionic equation. Identify the oxidizing agent, the reducing agent, the substance oxidized, and the substance reduced.

■ **Balancing Equations in Acid Solution** To simplify equations, we shall use H^+ instead of H_3O^+ when balancing equations in acid solution.

Balancing Equations in Acid Solution

When balancing equations for redox reactions in aqueous solution, it is sometimes necessary to add water molecules (H_2O) and either $H^+(aq)$ in acidic solution or $OH^-(aq)$ in basic solution to the equation. Equations that include oxoanions such as SO_4^{2-}, NO_3^-, ClO^-, CrO_4^{2-}, and MnO_4^- and organic compounds fall into this category. The process is outlined in Example 20.2 for the reduction of an oxocation in acid solution and in Example 20.3 for a reaction in basic solution.

■ **EXAMPLE 20.2 Balancing Equations for Oxidation–Reduction Reactions in Acid Solution**

Problem Balance the net ionic equation for the reaction of the dioxovanadium(V) ion, VO_2^+, with zinc in acid solution to form VO^{2+} (see Figure 20.3).

$$VO_2^+(aq) + Zn(s) \rightarrow VO^{2+}(aq) + Zn^{2+}(aq)$$

Strategy Follow the strategy outlined in the text and Example 20.1. Note that water and H^+ ions will appear as product and reactant, respectively, in the half-reaction for the reduction of VO_2^+ ion. (But H_2O and H^+ will never appear on the same side of the balanced half-reaction.)

Solution

Step 1. Recognize the reaction as an oxidation–reduction reaction.

The oxidation number of V changes from $+5$ in VO_2^+ to $+4$ in VO^{2+}. The oxidation number of Zn changes from 0 in the metal to $+2$ in Zn^{2+}.

Step 2. Separate the process into half-reactions.

Oxidation:	$Zn(s) \rightarrow Zn^{2+}(aq)$
	Zn(s) is oxidized and is the reducing agent.
Reduction:	$VO_2^+(aq) \rightarrow VO^{2+}(aq)$
	$VO_2^+(aq)$ is reduced and is the oxidizing agent.

Step 3. Balance the half-reactions for mass.

Begin by balancing all atoms except H and O. (These atoms are always the last to be balanced because they often appear in more than one reactant or product.)

Zinc half-reaction:	$Zn(s) \rightarrow Zn^{2+}(aq)$

This half-reaction is already balanced for mass.

Vanadium half-reaction:	$VO_2^+(aq) \rightarrow VO^{2+}(aq)$

The VO$_2^+$ ion is yellow in acid solution.

VO$_2^+$

Add Zn

Zn added. With time, the yellow VO$_2^+$ ion is reduced to blue VO^{2+} ion.

VO^{2+}

With time, the blue VO^{2+} ion is further reduced to green V^{3+} ion.

V^{3+}

Finally, green V^{3+} ion is reduced to violet V^{2+} ion.

V^{2+}

Photos: Charles D. Winters

FIGURE 20.3 Reduction of vanadium(V) with zinc. See Example 20.2 for the balanced equation for the first stage of the reaction.

The V atoms in this half-reaction are already balanced. An oxygen-containing species must be added to the right side of the equation to achieve an O atom balance, however.

$$VO_2^+(aq) \rightarrow VO^{2+}(aq) + (\text{need 1 O atom})$$

In acid solution, add H$_2$O to the side requiring O atoms, one H$_2$O molecule for each O atom required.

$$VO_2^+(aq) \rightarrow VO^{2+}(aq) + H_2O(\ell)$$

There are now two unbalanced H atoms on the right. Because the reaction occurs in an acidic solution, H$^+$ ions are present. Therefore, a mass balance for H can be achieved by adding H$^+$ to the side of the equation deficient in H atoms. Here, two H$^+$ ions are added to the left side of the equation.

$$2 H^+(aq) + VO_2^+(aq) \rightarrow VO^{2+}(aq) + H_2O(\ell)$$

Step 4. Balance the half-reactions for charge by adding electrons to the more positive side to make the charges equal on both sides.

Two electrons are added to the right side of the zinc half-reaction to bring its charge down to the same value as is present on the left side (in this case, zero).

Zinc half-reaction: $\qquad$ $Zn(s) \rightarrow Zn^{2+}(aq) + 2\ e^-$

The mass-balanced VO$_2^+$ equation has a net charge of 3+ on the left side and 2+ on the right. Therefore, 1 e^- is added to the more positive left side.

Vanadium half-reaction: $\qquad$ $e^- + 2 H^+(aq) + VO_2^+(aq) \rightarrow VO^{2+}(aq) + H_2O(\ell)$

As a check on your work, notice that the vanadium atom changes in oxidation number from +5 to +4 and so needs to acquire one electron.

Step 5. Multiply the half-reactions by appropriate factors so that the reducing agent donates as many electrons as the oxidizing agent consumes.

Here, the oxidation half-reaction supplies 2 mol of electrons per mol of Zn, and the reduction half-reaction consumes 1 mol of electrons per mol of VO$_2^+$. Therefore, the reduction half-reaction must be multiplied by 2. Now 2 mol of the oxidizing agent (VO$_2^+$) consumes the 2 mol of electrons provided per mole of the reducing agent (Zn).

$$Zn(s) \rightarrow Zn^{2+}(aq) + 2\ e^-$$
$$2[e^- + 2 H^+(aq) + VO_2^+(aq) \rightarrow VO^{2+}(aq) + H_2O(\ell)]$$

Step 6. Add the half-reactions to give the balanced, overall equation.

Oxidation half-reaction: $Zn(s) \rightarrow Zn^{2+}(aq) + 2\ e^-$

Reduction half-reaction: $2\ e^- + 4\ H^+(aq) + 2\ VO_2^+(aq) \rightarrow 2\ VO^{2+}(aq) + 2\ H_2O(\ell)$

Net ionic equation: $Zn(s) + 4\ H^+(aq) + 2\ VO_2^+(aq) \rightarrow Zn^{2+}(aq) + 2\ VO^{2+}(aq) + 2\ H_2O(\ell)$

Step 7. Simplify by eliminating reactants and products that appear on both sides.

This step is not required here.

Comment Check the overall equation to ensure that there is a mass and charge balance.

Mass balance: 1 Zn, 2 V, 4 H, and 4 O

Charge balance: Each side has a net charge of 6+.

EXERCISE 20.2 Balancing Oxidation–Reduction Equations

The yellow dioxovanadium(V) ion, $VO_2^+(aq)$, is reduced by zinc metal in three steps. The first step reduces it to blue $VO^{2+}(aq)$ (Example 20.2). This ion is further reduced to green $V^{3+}(aq)$ in the second step, and V^{3+} can be reduced to violet $V^{2+}(aq)$ in a third step. In each step, zinc is oxidized to $Zn^{2+}(aq)$. Write balanced net ionic equations for Steps 2 and 3. (This reduction sequence is shown in Figure 20.3.)

FIGURE 20.4 The reaction of purple permanganate ion (MnO_4^-) with iron(II) ions in acid solution. The products are the nearly colorless Mn^{2+} and Fe^{3+} ions.

EXERCISE 20.3 Balancing Equations for Oxidation–Reduction Reactions in Acid Solution

A common laboratory analysis for iron is to titrate aqueous iron(II) ion with a solution of potassium permanganate of precisely known concentration. Use the half-reaction method to write the balanced net ionic equation for the reaction in acid solution.

$$MnO_4^-(aq) + Fe^{2+}(aq) \rightarrow Mn^{2+}(aq) + Fe^{3+}(aq)$$

Identify the oxidizing agent, the reducing agent, the substance oxidized, and the substance reduced. See Figure 20.4.

Balancing Equations in Basic Solution

Example 20.2 and Exercises 20.2 and 20.3 illustrate the technique of balancing equations for redox reactions involving oxocations and oxoanions that occur in acid solution. Under these conditions, H^+ ion or the H^+/H_2O pair can be used to achieve a balanced equation if required. Conversely, in basic solution, only OH^- ion or the OH^-/H_2O pair can be used.

Problem Solving Tip 20.1

- Hydrogen balance can be achieved only with H^+/H_2O (in acid) or OH^-/H_2O (in base). Never add H or H_2 to balance hydrogen.
- Use H_2O or OH^- as appropriate to balance oxygen. Never add O atoms, O^{2-} ions, or O_2 for O balance.

Balancing Oxidation–Reduction Equations: A Summary

- Never include $H^+(aq)$ and $OH^-(aq)$ in the same equation. A solution can be either acidic or basic, never both.
- The number of electrons in a half-reaction reflects the change in oxidation number of the element being oxidized or reduced.
- Electrons are always a component of half-reactions but should never appear in the overall equation.

- Include charges in the formulas for ions. Omitting the charge, or writing the charge incorrectly, is one of the most common errors seen on student papers.
- The best way to become competent in balancing redox equations is to practice, practice, practice.

Problem Aluminum metal is oxidized in aqueous base, with water serving as the oxidizing agent. The products of the reaction are $[Al(OH)_4]^-(aq)$ and $H_2(g)$. Write a balanced net ionic equation for this reaction.

Strategy First, identify the oxidation and reduction half-reactions, and then balance them for mass and charge. Finally, add the balanced half-reactions to obtain the balanced net ionic equation for the reaction.

Solution

Step 1. Recognize the reaction as an oxidation–reduction reaction.

The unbalanced equation is

$$Al(s) + H_2O(\ell) \rightarrow [Al(OH)_4]^-(aq) + H_2(g)$$

Here, aluminum is oxidized, with its oxidation number changing from 0 to +3. Hydrogen is reduced, with its oxidation number decreasing from +1 to zero.

Step 2. Separate the process into half-reactions.

Oxidation half-reaction: $Al(s) \rightarrow [Al(OH)_4]^-(aq)$

(Al oxidation number increased from 0 to +3.)

Reduction half-reaction: $H_2O(\ell) \rightarrow H_2(g)$

(H oxidation number decreased from +1 to 0.)

Step 3. Balance the half-reactions for mass.

Addition of OH^- and/or H_2O is required for mass balance in both half-reactions. In the case of the aluminum half-reaction, we simply add OH^- ions to the left side.

Oxidation half-reaction: $Al(s) + 4\ OH^-(aq) \rightarrow [Al(OH)_4]^-(aq)$

To balance the half-reaction for water reduction, notice that an oxygen-containing species must appear on the right side of the equation. Because H_2O is a reactant, we use OH^-, which is present in this basic solution, as the other product.

Reduction half-reaction: $2\ H_2O(\ell) \rightarrow H_2(g) + 2\ OH^-(aq)$

Step 4. Balance the half-reactions for charge.

Electrons are added to balance charge.

Oxidation half-reaction: $Al(s) + 4\ OH^-(aq) \rightarrow [Al(OH)_4]^-(aq) + 3\ e^-$

Reduction half-reaction: $2\ H_2O(\ell) + 2\ e^- \rightarrow H_2(g) + 2\ OH^-(aq)$

Step 5. Multiply the half-reactions by appropriate factors so that the reducing agent donates as many electrons as the oxidizing agent consumes.

Here, electron balance is achieved by using 2 mol of Al to provide 6 mol of e^-, which are then acquired by 6 mol of H_2O.

Oxidation half-reaction: $2[Al(s) + 4\ OH^-(aq) \rightarrow [Al(OH)_4]^-(aq) + 3\ e^-]$

Reduction half-reaction: $3[2\ H_2O(\ell) + 2\ e^- \rightarrow H_2(g) + 2\ OH^-(aq)]$

Step 6. Add the half-reactions.

$$2\ Al(s) + 8\ OH^-(aq) \rightarrow 2\ [Al(OH)_4]^-(aq) + 6\ e^-$$
$$6\ H_2O(\ell) + 6\ e^- \rightarrow 3\ H_2(g) + 6\ OH^-(aq)]$$

Net equation: $2\ Al(s) + 8\ OH^-(aq) + 6\ H_2O(\ell) \rightarrow 2\ [Al(OH)_4]^-(aq) + 3\ H_2(g) + 6\ OH^-(aq)$

Step 7. Simplify by eliminating reactants and products that appear on both sides.

Six OH^- ions can be canceled from the two sides of the equation:

$$2\ Al(s) + 2\ OH^-(aq) + 6\ H_2O(\ell) \rightarrow 2\ [Al(OH)_4]^-(aq) + 3\ H_2(g)$$

Comment The final equation is balanced for mass and charge.

Mass balance:	2 Al, 14 H, and 8 O
Charge balance:	There is a net −2 charge on each side.

Problem Solving Tip 20.2 — An Alternative Method of Balancing Equations in Basic Solution

Balancing redox equations in basic solution, which may require you to use OH^- and H_2O, can sometimes be more challenging than doing so in acidic solution. One of the ways to balance such equations for reactions in basic solution is to first balance it as if it were in acidic solution and then add enough OH^- ions to both sides of the equation so that the H^+ ions are converted to water. Taking the half-reaction for the reduction of ClO^- ion to Cl_2, we have:

(a) Balance in acid

$$4\,H^+(aq) + 2\,ClO^-(aq) + 2\,e^- \rightarrow Cl_2(g) + 2\,H_2O(\ell)$$

(b) Add four OH^- ions to both sides

$$4\,OH^-(aq) + 4\,H^+(aq) + 2\,ClO^-(aq) + 2\,e^- \rightarrow$$
$$Cl_2(g) + 2\,H_2O(\ell) + 4\,OH^-(aq)$$

(c) Combine OH^- and H^+ to form water where appropriate

$$4\,H_2O(\ell) + 2\,ClO^-(aq) + 2\,e^- \rightarrow Cl_2(g) + 2\,H_2O(\ell) + 4\,OH^-(aq)$$

(d) Simplify

$$2\,H_2O(\ell) + 2\,ClO^-(aq) + 2\,e^- \rightarrow Cl_2(g) + 4\,OH^-(aq)$$

EXERCISE 20.4 Balancing Equations for Oxidation–Reduction Reactions in Basic Solution

Voltaic cells based on the reduction of sulfur are under development. One such cell involves the reaction of sulfur with aluminum under basic conditions.

$$Al(s) + S(s) \rightarrow Al(OH)_3(s) + HS^-(aq)$$

(a) Balance this equation, showing each balanced half-reaction.

(b) Identify the oxidizing and reducing agents, the substance oxidized, and the substance reduced.

20.2 Simple Voltaic Cells

Let us use the reaction of copper metal and silver ions (Figure 20.1) as the basis of a voltaic cell. To do so, we place the components of the two half-reactions in separate compartments (Figure 20.5). This prevents the copper metal from transferring electrons directly to silver ions. Instead, electrons will be transferred through an external circuit, and useful work can potentially be done.

The copper half-cell (on the left in Figure 20.5) holds copper metal that serves as one electrode and a solution containing copper(II) ions. The half-cell on the right uses a silver electrode and a solution containing silver(I) ions. Important features of this simple cell are as follows:

- *The two half-cells are connected with a **salt bridge** that allows cations and anions to move between the two half-cells.* The electrolyte chosen for the salt bridge should contain ions that will not react with chemical reagents in both half-cells. In the example in Figure 20.5, $NaNO_3$ is used.
- *In all electrochemical cells, the **anode** is the electrode at which oxidation occurs. The electrode at which reduction occurs is always the **cathode**.* (In Figure 20.5, the copper electrode is the anode, and the silver electrode is the cathode.)
- *A negative sign can be assigned to the anode in a voltaic cell, and the cathode is marked with a positive sign.* The chemical oxidation occurring at the anode, which produces electrons, gives it a negative charge. Electric current in the external circuit of a voltaic cell consists of electrons moving from the negative to the positive electrode.
- *In all electrochemical cells, electrons flow in the external circuit from the anode to the cathode.*

■ **Salt Bridges** A simple salt bridge can be made by adding gelatin to a solution of an electrolyte. Gelatin makes the contents semi-rigid so that the salt bridge is easier to handle. Porous glass disks and permeable membranes are alternatives to a salt bridge. These devices allow ions to traverse from one half-cell to the other while keeping the two solutions from mixing.

FIGURE 20.5 A voltaic cell using
FIGURE 20.5 A voltaic cell using
Cu(s) | Cu²⁺(aq) and Ag(s) | Ag⁺(aq)
half cells. Electrons flow through the
external circuit from the anode (the
copper electrode) to the cathode (silver
electrode). In the salt bridge, which contains aqueous NaNO₃, negative NO₃⁻(aq)
ions migrate toward the copper half-cell,
and positive Na⁺(aq) ions migrate toward
the silver half-cell. Using 1.0 M Cu²⁺(aq)
and 1.0 M Ag⁺(aq) solutions, this cell will
generate 0.46 volts.

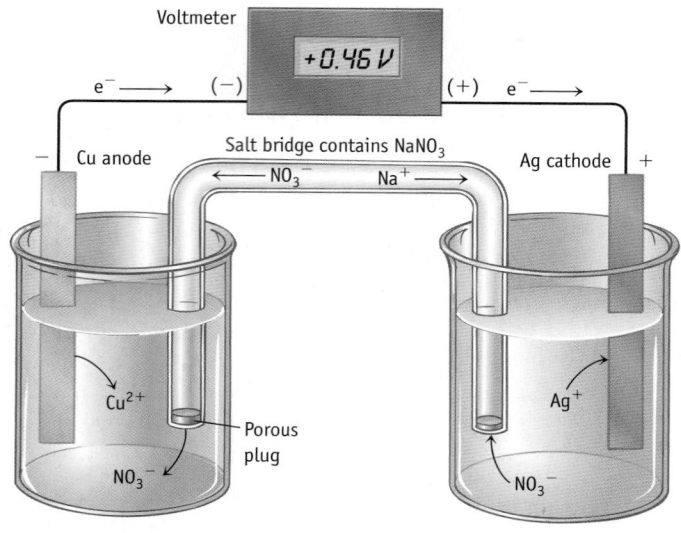

Net reaction: Cu(s) + 2 Ag⁺(aq) ⟶ Cu²⁺(aq) + 2 Ag(s)

The chemistry occurring in the cell pictured in Figure 20.5 is summarized by the
following half-reactions and net ionic equation:

Cathode (reduction):	2 Ag⁺(aq) + 2 e⁻ → 2 Ag(s)
Anode (oxidation):	Cu(s) → Cu²⁺(aq) + 2 e⁻
Net ionic equation:	Cu(s) + 2 Ag⁺(aq) → Cu²⁺(aq) + 2 Ag(s)

The salt bridge is required in a voltaic cell for the reaction to proceed. In the
Cu/Ag⁺ voltaic cell, anions move in the salt bridge toward the copper half-cell, and
cations move toward the silver half-cell (Figure 20.5). As Cu²⁺(aq) ions are formed
in the copper half-cell by oxidation of copper metal, negative ions enter that cell
from the salt bridge (and positive ions leave the cell), so that the numbers of
positive and negative charges in the half-cell compartment remain in balance.
Likewise, in the silver half-cell, negative ions move out of the half-cell into the salt
bridge, and positive ions move into the cell as Ag⁺ (aq) ions are reduced to silver
metal. A complete circuit is required for current to flow. If the salt bridge is removed, reactions at the electrodes will cease.

In Figure 20.5, the electrodes are connected by wires to a voltmeter. In an
alternative set-up, the connections might be to a light bulb or other device that
uses electricity. Electrons are produced by oxidation of copper, and Cu²⁺(aq)
ions enter the solution. The electrons traverse the external circuit to the silver
electrode, where they reduce Ag⁺(aq) ions to silver metal. To balance the extent
of oxidation and reduction, two Ag⁺(aq) ions are reduced for every Cu²⁺(aq)
ion formed. The main features of this and of all other voltaic cells are summarized
in Figure 20.6.

■ **Electron and Ion Flow** It is helpful
to notice that in an electrochemical cell
the negative electrons and negatively
charged anions make a "circle." That is,
electrons move from anode to cathode in
the external circuit, and negative anions
move from the cathode compartment,
through the salt bridge, to the anode
compartment.

Chemistry �Now™

Sign in at **www.cengage.com/login** and go to Chapter 20 Contents to see Screen 20.4 for an animation of **a
cell based on zinc and copper.**

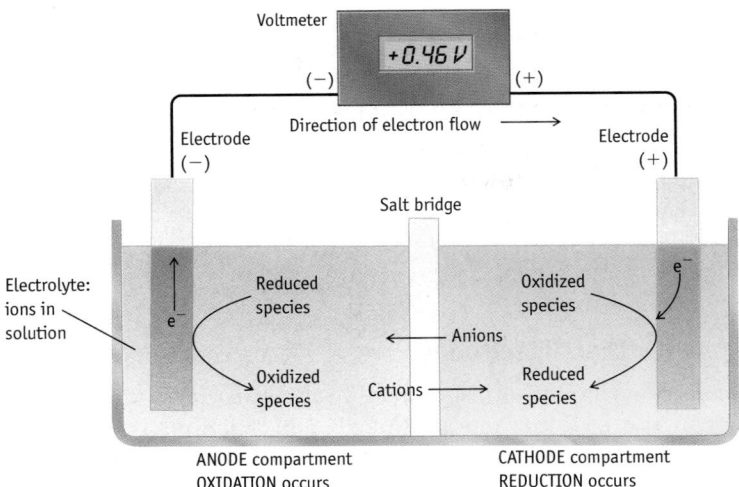

Voltmeter

+0.46 V

(−)   (+)

Direction of electron flow →

Electrode (−)   Electrode (+)

Salt bridge

Electrolyte: ions in solution

e⁻

Reduced species   Oxidized species

Oxidized species   ← Anions   Reduced species

Cations →

ANODE compartment
OXIDATION occurs

CATHODE compartment
REDUCTION occurs

FIGURE 20.6 Summary of terms used in a voltaic cell. Electrons move from the anode, the site of oxidation, through the external circuit to the cathode, the site of reduction. Charge balance in each half-cell is achieved by migration of ions through the salt bridge. Negative ions move from the reduction half-cell to the oxidation half-cell and positive ions move in the opposite direction.

EXAMPLE 20.4 Electrochemical Cells

Problem Describe how to set up a voltaic cell to generate an electric current using the reaction

$$Fe(s) + Cu^{2+}(aq) \rightarrow Cu(s) + Fe^{2+}(aq)$$

Which electrode is the anode, and which is the cathode? In which direction do electrons flow in the external circuit? In which direction do the positive and negative ions flow in the salt bridge? Write equations for the half-reactions that occur at each electrode.

Strategy First, identify the two different half-cells that make up the cell. Next, decide in which half-cell oxidation occurs and in which reduction occurs.

Solution This voltaic cell is similar to the one diagrammed in Figure 20.5. One half-cell contains an iron electrode and a solution of an iron(II) salt such as $Fe(NO_3)_2$. The other half-cell contains a copper electrode and a soluble copper(II) salt such as $Cu(NO_3)_2$. The two half-cells are linked with a salt bridge containing an electrolyte such as KNO_3. Iron is oxidized, so the iron electrode is the anode:

  Oxidation, anode: $Fe(s) \rightarrow Fe^{2+}(aq) + 2\,e^-$

Because copper(II) ions are reduced, the copper electrode is the cathode. The cathodic half-reaction is

  Reduction, cathode: $Cu^{2+}(aq) + 2\,e^- \rightarrow Cu(s)$

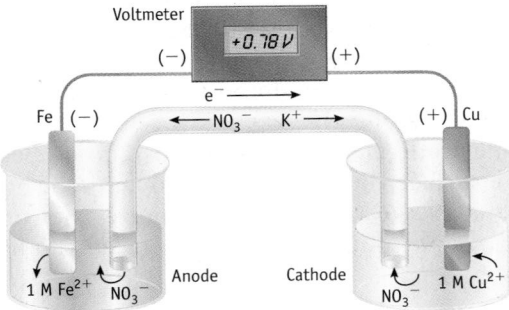

Voltmeter

+0.78 V

(−)   (+)

e⁻ →

Fe (−)   ← NO₃⁻   K⁺ →   (+) Cu

Anode   Cathode

1 M Fe²⁺   NO₃⁻   NO₃⁻   1 M Cu²⁺

In the external circuit, electrons flow from the iron electrode (anode) to the copper electrode (cathode). In the salt bridge, negative ions flow toward the $Fe \mid Fe^{2+}(aq)$ half-cell, and positive ions flow in the opposite direction.

Voltaic Cells with Inert Electrodes

In the half-cells described so far, the metal used as an electrode is also a reactant or a product in the redox reaction. Not all half-reactions involve a metal as a reactant or product, however. With the exception of carbon in the form of graphite, most nonmetals are unsuitable as electrode materials because they do not conduct electricity. It is not possible to make an electrode from a gas, a liquid (except mercury), or a solution. Ionic solids do not make satisfactory electrodes because the ions are locked tightly in a crystal lattice, and these materials do not conduct electricity.

In situations where reactants and products cannot serve as the electrode material, an inert or chemically unreactive electrode must be used. Such electrodes are made of materials that conduct an electric current but that are neither oxidized nor reduced in the cell.

Consider constructing a voltaic cell to accommodate the following product-favored reaction:

$$2\,Fe^{3+}(aq) + H_2(g) \rightarrow 2\,Fe^{2+}(aq) + 2\,H^+(aq)$$

Reduction half reaction: $Fe^{3+}(aq) + e^- \rightarrow Fe^{2+}(aq)$

Oxidation half reaction: $H_2(g) \rightarrow 2\,H^+(aq) + 2\,e^-$

Neither the reactants nor the products can be used as an electrode material. Therefore, the two half-cells are set up so that the reactants and products come in contact with an electrode such as graphite where they can accept or give up electrons. Graphite is a commonly used electrode material: It is a conductor of electricity, and it is inexpensive (essential in commercial cells) and not readily oxidized under the conditions encountered in most cells. Mercury is used in certain types of cells. Platinum and gold are also commonly used because both are chemically inert under most circumstances, but they are generally too costly for commercial cells.

The *hydrogen electrode* is particularly important in the field of electrochemistry because it is used as a reference in assigning cell voltages (see Section 20.4) (Figure 20.7). The electrode material is platinum, chosen because hydrogen adsorbs on the metal's surface. In this half-cell's operation, hydrogen is bubbled over the electrode, and a large surface area maximizes the contact of the gas and the electrode. The aqueous solution contains $H^+(aq)$. The half-reactions involving $H^+(aq)$ and $H_2(g)$

$$2\,H^+(aq) + 2\,e^- \rightarrow H_2(g) \qquad or \qquad H_2(g) \rightarrow 2\,H^+(aq) + 2\,e^-$$

take place at the electrode surface, and the electrons involved in the reaction are conducted to or from the reaction site by the metal electrode.

A half-cell using the reduction of $Fe^{3+}(aq)$ to $Fe^{2+}(aq)$ can also be set up with a platinum electrode. In this case, the solution surrounding the electrode contains

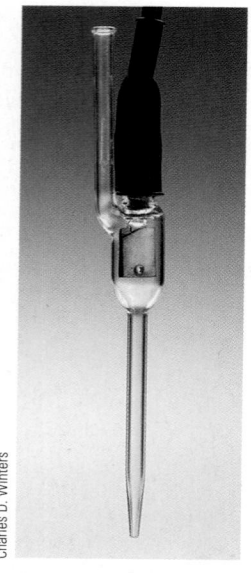

Charles D. Winters

FIGURE 20.7 Hydrogen electrode. Hydrogen gas is bubbled over a platinum electrode in a solution containing H^+ ions. Such electrodes function best if they have a large surface area. Often, platinum wires are woven into a gauze, or the metal surface is roughened either by abrasion or by chemical treatment to increase the surface area.

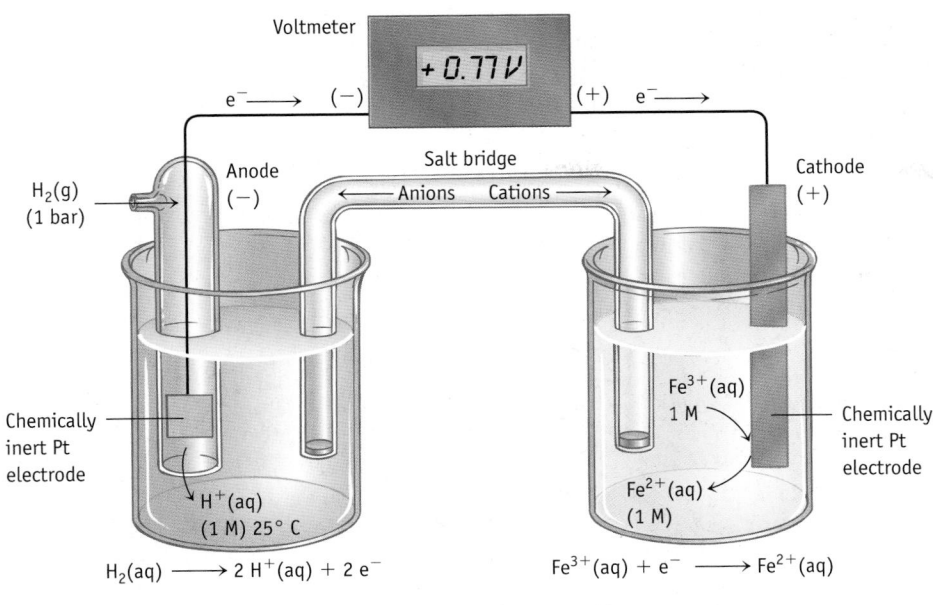

Voltmeter

+0.77 V

$e^- \longrightarrow$ (−)   (+) $e^- \longrightarrow$

Anode (−)

H_2(g) (1 bar)

Salt bridge

← Anions   Cations →

Cathode (+)

Fe^{3+}(aq) 1 M

Chemically inert Pt electrode

Chemically inert Pt electrode

H^+(aq) (1 M) 25° C

Fe^{2+}(aq) (1 M)

H_2(aq) $\longrightarrow$ 2 H^+(aq) + 2 e^-

Fe^{3+}(aq) + e^- $\longrightarrow$ Fe^{2+}(aq)

Net reaction: 2 Fe^{3+}(aq) + H_2(aq) $\longrightarrow$ 2 Fe^{2+}(aq) + 2 H^+(aq)

iron ions in two different oxidation states. Transfer of electrons to or from the reactant occurs at the electrode surface.

A voltaic cell involving the reduction of Fe^{3+}(aq, 1.0 M) to Fe^{2+}(aq, 1.0 M) with H_2 gas is illustrated in Figure 20.8. In this cell, the hydrogen electrode is the anode (H_2 is oxidized to H^+), and the iron-containing compartment is the cathode (Fe^{3+} is reduced to Fe^{2+}). The cell produces 0.77 V.

Electrochemical Cell Notations

Chemists often use a shorthand notation to simplify cell descriptions. For example, the cell involving the reduction of silver ion with copper metal is written as

$$Cu(s) | Cu^{2+}(aq, 1.0 M) || Ag^+(aq, 1.0 M) | Ag(s)$$

The cell using H_2 gas to reduce Fe^{3+} ions is written as

$$Pt | H_2(P = 1 \text{ bar}) | H^+(aq, 1.0 M) || Fe^{3+}(aq, 1.0 M), Fe^{2+}(aq, 1.0 M) | Pt$$

Anode information   Cathode information

By convention, on the left we write the anode and information with respect to the solution with which it is in contact. A single vertical line (|) indicates a phase boundary, and double vertical lines (||) indicate a salt bridge.

20.3 Commercial Voltaic Cells

The cells described so far are unlikely to have practical use. They are neither compact nor robust, high priorities for most applications. In most situations, it is also important that the cell produce a constant voltage, but a problem with the cells described so far is that the voltage produced varies as the concentrations of ions in solution change (see Section 20.5). Also, the current production is low.

Voltaic cells are also called galvanic cells after an Italian physician Luigi Galvani (1737–1798), who carried out early studies of what he called "animal electricity," studies that brought new words into our language—among them "galvanic" and "galvanize."

Around 1780, Galvani observed that the electric current from a static electricity generator caused the contraction of the muscles in a frog's leg. Investigating further, he found he could induce contractions when the muscle was in contact with two different metals. Because no external source of electricity was applied to the muscles, Galvani concluded the frog's muscles were themselves generating electricity. This was evidence, he believed, of a kind of "vital energy" or "animal electricity," which was related to but different from "natural electricity" generated by machines or lightning.

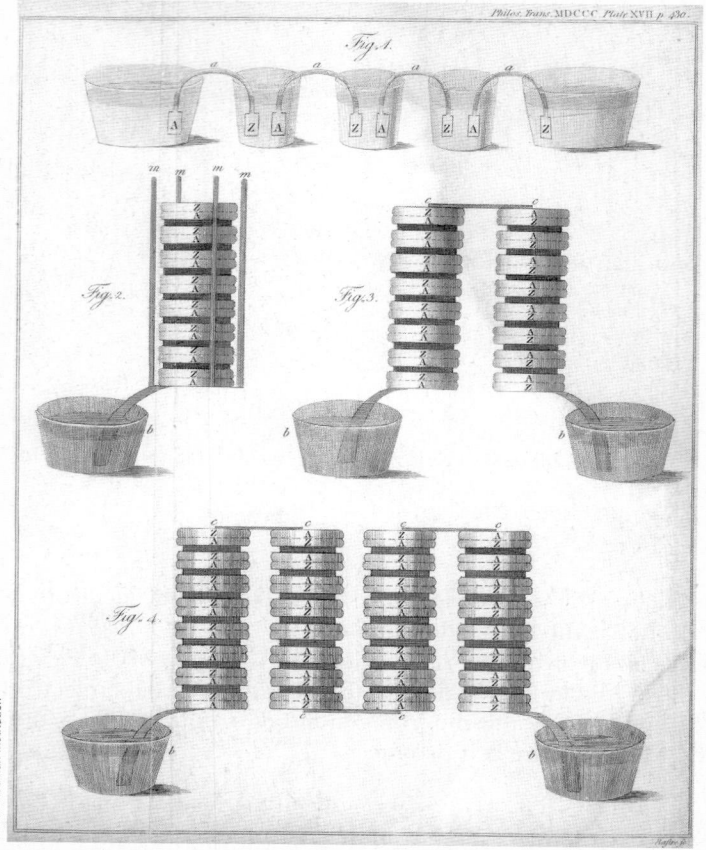

Alessandro Volta, 1745–1827.

Volta's "voltaic pile." These drawings done by Volta show the arrangement of silver and zinc disks used to generate an electric current.

Alessandro Volta repeated Galvani's experiments, with the same results, but he came to different conclusions. Volta proposed that an electric current was generated by the contact between two different metals—an explanation we now know to be correct—and that the frog muscle was simply detecting the small current generated.

To prove his hypothesis, Volta built the first "electric pile" in 1800. This was a series of metal disks of two kinds (silver and zinc), separated by paper disks soaked in acid or salt solutions. Soon after Volta announced his discovery, Carlisle and Nicholson in England used the electricity from a "pile" to decompose water into hydrogen and oxygen. Within a few years, the great English chemist Humphry Davy used a more powerful voltaic pile to isolate potassium and sodium metals by electrolysis.

Attempting to draw a large current results in a drop in voltage because the current depends on how fast ions in solution migrate to the electrode. Ion concentrations near the electrode become depleted if current is drawn rapidly, resulting in a decline in voltage.

The electrical work that can be drawn from a voltaic cell depends on the quantity of reagents consumed. A voltaic cell must have a large mass of reactants to produce current over a prolonged period. In addition, a voltaic cell that can be recharged is

■ **Cell Potentials and Reactant and Product Concentrations** Concentrations of species in a cell affect the potential, as discussed in Section 20.5.

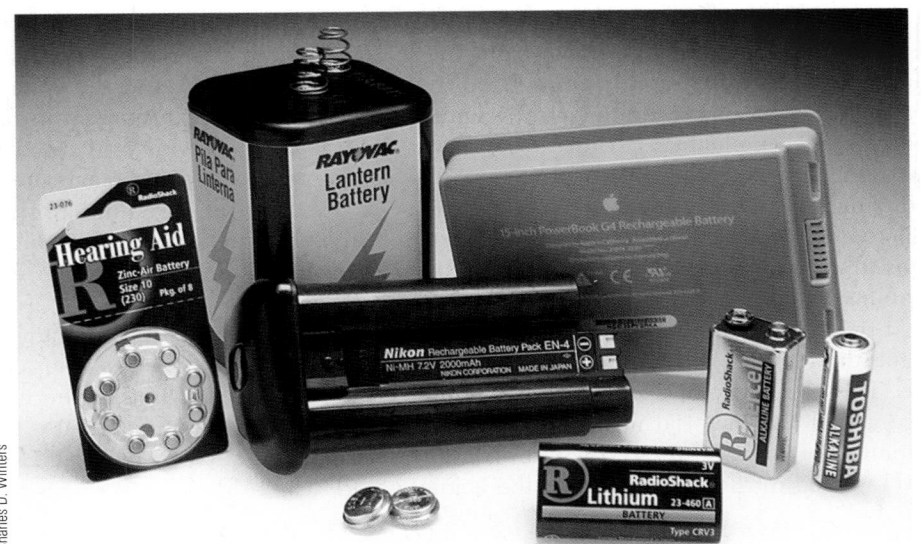

FIGURE 20.9 Some commercial voltaic cells. Commercial voltaic cells provide energy for a wide range of devices, come in a myriad of sizes and shapes, and produce different voltages. Some are rechargeable; others are discarded after use. One might think that there is nothing further to learn about batteries, but this is not true. Research on these devices is actively pursued in the chemical community.

attractive. Recharging a cell means returning the reagents to their original sites in the cell. In the cells described so far, the movement of ions in the cell mixes the reagents, and they cannot be "unmixed" after the cell has been running.

Batteries can be classified as primary and secondary. **Primary batteries** cannot be returned to their original state by recharging, so when the reactants are consumed, the battery is "dead" and must be discarded. **Secondary batteries** are often called **storage batteries** or **rechargeable batteries**. The reactions in these batteries can be reversed; thus, the batteries can be recharged.

Years of development have led to many different commercial voltaic cells to meet specific needs (Figure 20.9), and several common ones are described below. All adhere to the principles that have been developed in earlier discussions.

Primary Batteries: Dry Cells and Alkaline Batteries

If you buy an inexpensive flashlight battery or dry cell battery, it might be a modern version of a voltaic cell invented by George LeClanché in 1866 (Figure 20.10). Zinc serves as the anode, and the cathode is a graphite rod placed down the center of the device. These cells are often called "dry cells" because there is no visible liquid phase. However, water is present, so the cell contains a moist paste of NH_4Cl, $ZnCl_2$, and MnO_2. The moisture is necessary because the ions present must be in a medium in which they can migrate from one electrode to the other. The cell generates a potential of 1.5 V using the following half-reactions:

Cathode, reduction: $\quad 2\ NH_4^+(aq) + 2\ e^- \rightarrow 2\ NH_3(g) + H_2(g)$

Anode, oxidation: $\quad\quad\quad Zn(s) \rightarrow Zn^{2+}(aq) + 2\ e^-$

The two gases formed at the cathode will build up pressure and could cause the cell to rupture. This problem is avoided, however, by two other reactions that take place in the cell. Ammonia molecules bind to Zn^{2+} ions, and hydrogen gas is oxidized by MnO_2 to water.

$$Zn^{2+}(aq) + 2\ NH_3(g) + 2\ Cl^-(aq) \rightarrow Zn(NH_3)_2Cl_2(s)$$

$$2\ MnO_2(s) + H_2(g) \rightarrow Mn_2O_3(s) + H_2O(\ell)$$

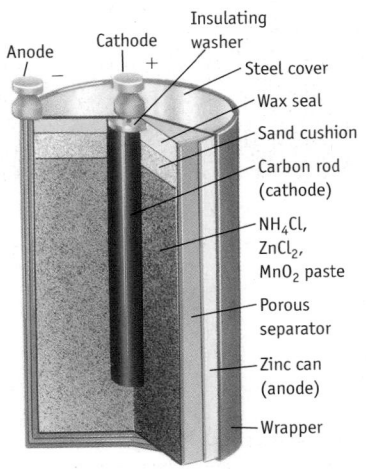

FIGURE 20.10 The common LeClanché dry cell battery.

LeClanché cells were widely used because of their low cost, but they have several disadvantages. If current is drawn from the battery rapidly, the gaseous products cannot be consumed rapidly enough, so the cell resistance rises, and the voltage drops. In addition, the zinc electrode and ammonium ions are in contact in the cell, and these chemicals react slowly. Recall that zinc reacts with acid to form hydrogen. The ammonium ion, $NH_4^+(aq)$, is a weak Brønsted acid and reacts slowly with zinc. Because of this reaction, these voltaic cells cannot be stored indefinitely, a fact you may have learned from experience. When the zinc outer shell deteriorates, the battery can leak acid and perhaps damage the appliance in which it is contained.

At the present time, you are more likely to use **alkaline batteries** in your camera or flashlight. They generate current up to 50% longer than a dry cell of the same size. The chemistry of alkaline cells is quite similar to that in a LeClanché cell, except that the material inside the cell is basic (alkaline). Alkaline cells use the oxidation of zinc and the reduction of MnO_2 to generate a current, but NaOH or KOH is used in the cell instead of the acidic salt NH_4Cl.

Cathode, reduction: $\quad 2\ MnO_2(s) + H_2O(\ell) + 2\ e^- \rightarrow Mn_2O_3(s) + 2\ OH^-(aq)$

Anode, oxidation: $\quad Zn(s) + 2\ OH^-(aq) \rightarrow ZnO(s) + H_2O(\ell) + 2\ e^-$

Alkaline cells, which produce 1.54 V (approximately the same voltage as the LeClanché cell), have the further advantage that the cell potential does not decline under high current loads because no gases are formed.

Prior to 2000, mercury-containing batteries were widely used in calculators, cameras, watches, heart pacemakers, and other devices. However, these small batteries were banned in the United States in the 1990s because of environmental problems. They have been replaced by several other types of batteries, such as silver oxide batteries and zinc-oxygen batteries. Both operate under alkaline conditions, and both have zinc anodes. In the silver oxide battery, which produces a voltage of about 1.5 V, the cell reactions are

Cathode, reduction: $\quad Ag_2O(s) + H_2O(\ell) + 2\ e^- \rightarrow 2\ Ag(s) + 2\ OH^-(aq)$

Anode, oxidation: $\quad Zn(s) + 2\ OH^-(aq) \rightarrow ZnO(s) + H_2O(\ell) + 2\ e^-$

The zinc-oxygen battery, which produces about 1.15–1.35 V, is unique in that atmospheric oxygen and not a metal oxide is the oxidizing agent.

Cathode, reduction: $\quad O_2(g) + 2\ H_2O(\ell) + 4\ e^- \rightarrow 4\ OH^-(aq)$

Anode, oxidation: $\quad Zn(s) + 2\ OH^-(aq) \rightarrow ZnO(s) + H_2O(\ell) + 2\ e^-$

These batteries have found use in hearing aids, pagers, and medical devices.

Secondary or Rechargeable Batteries

When a LeClanché cell or an alkaline cell ceases to produce a usable electric current, it is discarded. In contrast, some types of cells can be recharged, often hundreds of times. Recharging requires applying an electric current from an external source to restore the cell to its original state.

An automobile battery—the **lead storage battery**—is probably the best-known rechargeable battery (Figure 20.11). The 12-V version of this battery contains six voltaic cells, each generating about 2 V. The lead storage battery can produce a large initial current, an essential feature when starting an automobile engine.

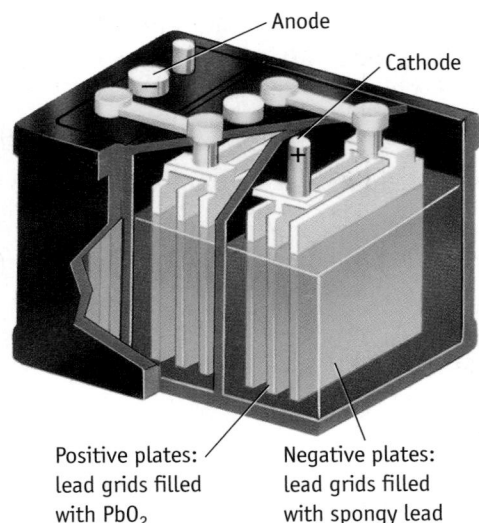

Anode
Cathode

Positive plates:
lead grids filled
with PbO_2

Negative plates:
lead grids filled
with spongy lead

FIGURE 20.11 **Lead storage battery, a secondary or rechargeable battery.** The negative plates (anode) are lead grids filled with spongy lead. The positive plates (cathode) are lead grids filled with lead(IV) oxide, PbO_2. Each cell of the battery generates 2 V.

The anode of a lead storage battery is metallic lead. The cathode is also made of lead, but it is covered with a layer of compressed, insoluble lead(IV) oxide, PbO_2. The electrodes, arranged alternately in a stack and separated by thin fiberglass sheets, are immersed in aqueous sulfuric acid. When the cell supplies electrical energy, the lead anode is oxidized to lead(II) sulfate, an insoluble substance that adheres to the electrode surface. The two electrons produced per lead atom move through the external circuit to the cathode, where PbO_2 is reduced to Pb^{2+} ions that, in the presence of H_2SO_4, also form lead(II) sulfate.

Cathode, reduction: $\quad PbO_2(s) + 4\ H^+(aq) + SO_4^{2-}(aq) + 2\ e^- \rightarrow PbSO_4(s) + 2\ H_2O(\ell)$

Anode, oxidation: $\quad Pb(s) + SO_4^{2-}(aq) \rightarrow PbSO_4(s) + 2\ e^-$

Net ionic equation: $\quad Pb(s) + PbO_2(s) + 2\ H_2SO_4(aq) \rightarrow 2\ PbSO_4(s) + 2\ H_2O(\ell)$

When current is generated, sulfuric acid is consumed and water is formed. Because water is less dense than sulfuric acid, the density of the solution decreases during this process. Therefore, one way to determine whether a lead storage battery needs to be recharged is to measure the density of the solution.

A lead storage battery is recharged by supplying electrical energy. The $PbSO_4$ coating the surfaces of the electrodes is converted back to metallic lead and PbO_2, and sulfuric acid is regenerated. Recharging this battery is possible because the reactants and products remain attached to the electrode surface. The lifetime of a lead storage battery is limited, however, because, with time, the coatings of PbO_2 and $PbSO_4$ flake off of the surface and fall to the bottom of the battery case.

Scientists and engineers would like to find an alternative to lead storage batteries, especially for use in cars. Lead storage batteries have the disadvantage of being large and heavy. In addition, lead and its compounds are toxic and their disposal adds a further complication. Nevertheless, at this time, the advantages of lead storage batteries outweigh their disadvantages.

Nickel-cadmium ("Ni-cad") batteries, used in a variety of cordless appliances such as telephones, video camcorders, and cordless power tools, are lightweight and rechargeable. The chemistry of the cell utilizes the oxidation of cadmium and the reduction of nickel(III) oxide under basic conditions. As with the lead storage battery, the reactants and products formed when producing a current are solids that adhere to the electrodes.

Cathode, reduction: $\quad\quad\quad\quad\quad NiO(OH)(s) + H_2O(\ell) + e^- \rightarrow Ni(OH)_2(s) + OH^-(aq)$

Anode, oxidation: $\quad\quad\quad\quad\quad Cd(s) + 2\ OH^-(aq) \rightarrow Cd(OH)_2(s) + 2\ e^-$

Ni-cad batteries produce a nearly constant voltage. However, their cost is relatively high, and there are restrictions on their disposal because cadmium compounds are toxic and present an environmental hazard.

Fuel Cells and Hybrid Cars

An advantage of voltaic cells is that they are small and portable, but their size is also a limitation. The amount of electric current produced is limited by the quantity of reagents contained in the cell. When one of the reactants is completely consumed, the cell will no longer generate a current. Fuel cells avoid this limitation because the reactants (fuel and oxidant) can be supplied continuously to the cell from an external reservoir.

Although the first fuel cells were constructed more than 150 years ago, little was done to develop this technology until the space program rekindled interest in these devices. Hydrogen-oxygen fuel cells have been used in NASA's Gemini, Apollo, and Space Shuttle programs. Not only are they lightweight and efficient, but they also have the added benefit that they generate drinking water for the ship's crew. The fuel cells on board the Space Shuttle deliver the same power as batteries weighing 10 times as much.

In a hydrogen-oxygen fuel cell (Figure 20.12), hydrogen is pumped onto the anode of the cell, and O_2 (or air) is directed to the cathode where the following reactions occur:

Cathode, reduction: $\quad\quad\quad\quad\quad O_2(g) + 2\ H_2O(\ell) + 4\ e^- \rightarrow 4\ OH^-(aq)$

Anode, oxidation: $\quad\quad\quad\quad\quad H_2(g) \rightarrow 2\ H^+(aq) + 2\ e^-$

■ **Energy for Automobiles** Energy available from systems that can be used to power an automobile.

Chemical System	W · h/kg* (1 W · h = 3600 J)
Lead-acid battery	18–56
Nickel-cadmium battery	33–70
Sodium-sulfur battery	80–140
Lithium polymer battery	150
Gasoline-air combustion engine	12,200

* watt-hour/kilogram

FIGURE 20.12 Fuel cell design. Hydrogen gas is oxidized to $H^+(aq)$ at the anode surface. On the other side of the proton exchange membrane (PEM), oxygen gas is reduced to $OH^-(aq)$. The $H^+(aq)$ ions travel through the PEM and combine with $OH^-(aq)$, forming water.

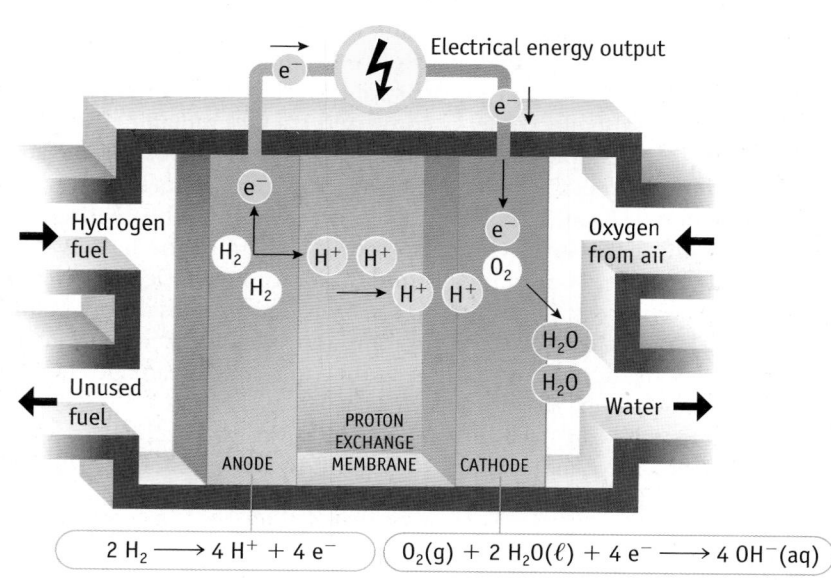

$2\ H_2 \longrightarrow 4\ H^+ + 4\ e^- \quad\quad\quad O_2(g) + 2\ H_2O(\ell) + 4\ e^- \longrightarrow 4\ OH^-(aq)$

The two halves of the cell are separated by a special material called a proton exchange membrane (PEM). Protons, $H^+(aq)$, formed at the anode traverse the PEM and react with the hydroxide ions produced at the cathode, forming water. The net reaction in the cell is thus the formation of water from H_2 and O_2. Cells currently in use run at temperatures of 70–140 °C and produce about 0.9 V.

Hydrogen-oxygen fuel cells operate at 40–60% efficiency and meet most of the requirements for use in automobiles: they operate at room temperature or slightly above, start rapidly, and develop a high current density. Cost is a serious problem, however, and it appears that a substantial shift away from the internal combustion engine remains a long way off. For this reason, several major car manufacturers have designed electric cars that use various types of batteries to provide the power to drive the car. The most commonly employed type for automotive use is the lead storage battery, but these devices are problematic, owing to their mass. To produce one mole of electrons requires 321 g of reactants in lead storage batteries. As a result, these batteries rank very low among various options in power per kilogram of battery weight. In fact, the power available from any type of battery is much less than that available from an equivalent mass of gasoline.

Hybrid cars appear to offer an interim solution. These vehicles combine a small gasoline-fueled engine with an electric motor and batteries for storage of electric energy. Currently, hybrid cars use rechargeable nickel-metal hydride batteries. Electrons are generated when H atoms interact with OH^- ions at the metal alloy anode.

$$\text{Alloy(H)} + OH^- \rightarrow \text{Alloy} + H_2O + e^-$$

The reaction at the cathode is the same as in Ni-cad batteries.

$$NiOOH + H_2O + e^- \rightarrow Ni(OH)_2 + OH^-$$

Hybrid car. This car combines a gasoline-fueled engine with an electric motor and rechargable batteries. Its fuel efficiency is about double that of the current generation of cars using only gasoline engines.

©AP Photo/Shizuo Kambayashi, File

Chemistry.Now™

Sign in at **www.cengage.com/login** and go to Chapter 20 Contents to see Screen 20.5 to view animations of **various types of batteries.**

20.4 Standard Electrochemical Potentials

Different electrochemical cells produce different voltages: 1.5 V for the LeClanché and alkaline cells, about 1.25 V for a Ni-Cd battery, and about 2.0 V for the individual cells in a lead storage battery. In this section, we want to identify the various factors affecting cell voltages and develop procedures to calculate the voltage of a cell based on the chemistry in the cell and the conditions used.

Electromotive Force

Electrons generated at the anode of an electrochemical cell move through the external circuit toward the cathode, and the force needed to move the electrons arises from a difference in the potential energy of electrons at the two electrodes. This difference in potential energy per electrical charge is called the **electromotive force** or **emf**, for which the literal meaning is "force causing electrons to move." Emf has units of volts (V); 1 volt is the potential difference needed to impart one joule of energy to an electric charge of one coulomb (1 J = 1 V × 1 C). *One coulomb is the quantity of charge that passes a point in an electric circuit when a current of 1 ampere flows for 1 second (1 C = 1 A × 1 s).*

■ **Electrochemical Units**
• The coulomb (abbreviated C) is the standard (SI) unit of electrical charge (Appendix C.3).
• 1 joule = 1 volt × 1 coulomb.
• 1 coulomb = 1 ampere × 1 second.

Measuring Standard Potentials

Imagine you planned to study cell voltages in a laboratory with two objectives: (1) to understand the factors that affect these values and (2) to be able to predict the potential of a voltaic cell. You might construct a number of different half-cells, link them together in various combinations to form voltaic cells (as in Figure 20.13), and measure the cell potentials. After a few experiments, it would become apparent that cell voltages depend on a number of factors: the half-cells used (i.e., the reaction in each half-cell and the overall or net reaction in the cell), the concentrations of reactants and products in solution, the pressure of gaseous reactants, and the temperature.

So that we can later compare the potential of one half-cell with another, let us measure all cell voltages under **standard conditions**:

- Reactants and products are present in their standard states.
- Solutes in aqueous solution have a concentration of 1.0 M.
- Gaseous reactants or products have a pressure of 1.0 bar.

A cell potential measured under these conditions is called the **standard potential** and is denoted by $E°_{cell}$. Unless otherwise specified, all values of $E°_{cell}$ refer to measurements at 298 K (25 °C).

Suppose you set up a number of standard half-cells and connect each in turn to a **standard hydrogen electrode (SHE)**. Your apparatus would look like the voltaic cell in Figure 20.13. For now, we will concentrate on three aspects of this cell:

1. *The reaction that occurs.* The reaction occurring in the cell pictured in Figure 20.13 could be *either* the reduction of Zn^{2+} ions with H_2 gas

$$Zn^{2+}(aq) + H_2(g) \rightarrow Zn(s) + 2 H^+(aq)$$

$Zn^{2+}(aq)$ is the oxidizing agent, and H_2 is the reducing agent.
Standard hydrogen electrode would be the anode (negative electrode).

or the reduction of $H^+(aq)$ ions by $Zn(s)$.

$$Zn(s) + 2 H^+(aq) \rightarrow Zn^{2+}(aq) + H_2(g)$$

Zn is the reducing agent, and $H^+(aq)$ is the oxidizing agent.
Standard hydrogen electrode would be the cathode (positive electrode).

Active Figure 20.13 A voltaic cell using $Zn\,|\,Zn^{2+}$ (aq, 1.0 M) and $H_2\,|\,H^+$ (aq, 1.0 M) half cells. (a) Zinc metal reacts readily with aqueous HCl. (b) When zinc and acid are combined in an electrochemical cell, the cell generates a potential of 0.76 V under standard conditions. The electrode in the $H_2\,|\,H^+$ (aq, 1.0 M) half-cell is the cathode, and the Zn electrode is the anode. Electrons flow in the external circuit to the hydrogen half-cell from the zinc half-cell. The positive sign of the measured voltage indicates that the hydrogen electrode is the cathode or positive electrode.

Chemistry Now™ Sign in at www.cengage.com/login and go to the Chapter Contents menu to explore an interactive version of this figure accompanied by an exercise.

Charles D. Winters

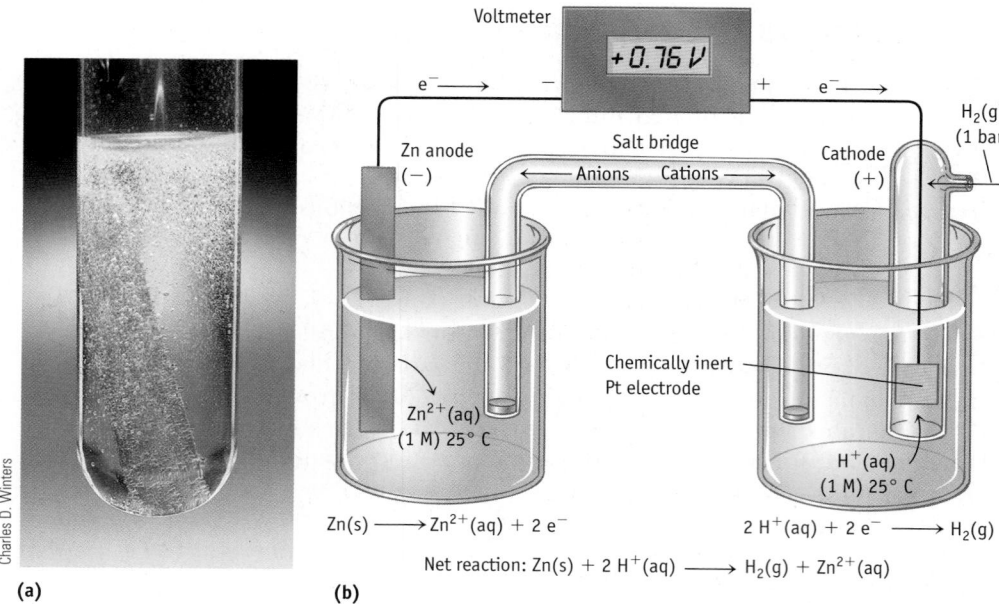

(a)

(b)

All the substances named in these equations are present in the cell. The reaction that actually occurs is the one that is product-favored. That is, the reaction occurring is the one in which the reactants are the stronger reducing and oxidizing agents.

2. *Direction of electron flow in the external circuit.* In a voltaic cell, electrons always flow from the anode (negative electrode) to the cathode (positive electrode). That is, *electrons move from the electrode of higher potential energy to the one of lower potential energy.* We can tell the direction of electron movement by placing a voltmeter in the circuit. A positive potential is observed if the voltmeter terminal with a plus sign (+) is connected to the positive electrode [and the terminal with the minus sign (−) is connected to the negative electrode]. Connected in the opposite way (plus to minus and minus to plus), the voltmeter will show a negative value on the digital readout.

3. *Cell potential.* In Figure 20.13, the voltmeter is hooked up with its positive terminal connected to the hydrogen half-cell, and a reading of +0.76 V is observed. The hydrogen electrode is thus the positive electrode or cathode, and the reactions occurring in this cell must be

Reduction, cathode:	$2\,H^+(aq) + 2\,e^- \rightarrow H_2(g)$
Oxidation, anode:	$Zn(s) \rightarrow Zn^{2+}(aq) + 2\,e^-$
Net cell reaction:	$Zn(s) + 2\,H^+(aq) \rightarrow Zn^{2+}(aq) + H_2(g)$

This result confirms that, of the two oxidizing agents present in the cell, $H^+(aq)$ is better than $Zn^{2+}(aq)$ and that Zn metal is a better reducing agent than H_2 gas.

A potential of +0.76 V is measured for the oxidation of zinc with hydrogen ion. This value reflects the difference in potential energy of an electron at each electrode. From the direction of flow of electrons in the external circuit (Zn electrode → H_2 electrode), we conclude that the potential energy of an electron at the zinc electrode is higher than the potential energy of the electron at the hydrogen electrode.

Hundreds of electrochemical cells like that shown in Figure 20.13 can be set up, allowing us to determine the relative oxidizing or reducing ability of various chemical species and to determine the electrical potential generated by the reaction under standard conditions. A few results are given in Figure 20.14, where half-reactions are listed as reductions. That is, the chemical species on the left are oxidizing agents and are listed in descending oxidizing ability.

Standard Reduction Potentials

By doing experiments such as that illustrated by Figure 20.13, we not only have a notion of the relative oxidizing and reducing abilities of various chemical species, but we can also rank them quantitatively.

If E°_{cell} is a measure of the standard potential for the cell, then $E^\circ_{cathode}$ and E°_{anode} can be taken as measures of electrode potential. Because E°_{cell} reflects the difference in electrode potentials, E°_{cell} must be the difference between $E^\circ_{cathode}$ and E°_{anode}.

$$E^\circ_{cell} = E^\circ_{cathode} - E^\circ_{anode} \tag{20.1}$$

Here, $E^\circ_{cathode}$ and E°_{anode} are the standard *reduction* potentials for the half-cell reactions that occur at the cathode and anode, respectively. Equation 20.1 is important for three reasons:

- If we have values for $E^\circ_{cathode}$ and E°_{anode}, we can calculate the standard potential, E°_{cell}, for a voltaic cell.

■ **Equation 20.1** Equation 20.1 is another example of calculating a change from $X_{final} - X_{initial}$. Electrons move to the cathode (the "final" state) from the anode (the "initial" state). Thus, Equation 20.1 resembles equations you have seen previously in this book (such as Equations 5.6 and 6.5).

Emf and cell potential (E_{cell}) are often used synonymously, but the two are subtly different. E_{cell} is a measured quantity, so its value is affected by how the measurement is made. To understand this point, consider as an analogy water in a pipe under pressure. Water pressure can be viewed as analogous to emf; it represents a force that will cause water in the pipe to move. If we open a faucet, water will flow. Opening the faucet will, however, decrease the pressure in the system.

Emf is the potential difference when no current flows. To measure E_{cell}, a voltmeter is placed in the external circuit. Although voltmeters have high internal resistance to minimize current flow, a small current flows nonetheless. As a result, the value of E_{cell} will be slightly different than the emf.

Finally, there is a difference between a potential and a voltage. The voltage of a cell has a magnitude but no sign. In contrast, the potential of a half-reaction or a cell has a sign (+ or −) and a magnitude.

• *When the calculated value of $E°_{cell}$ is positive, the reaction as written is predicted to be product-favored at equilibrium.* Conversely, if the calculated value of $E°_{cell}$ is negative, the reaction is predicted to be reactant-favored at equilibrium. Such a reaction will be product-favored at equilibrium in a direction opposite to the way it is written.

• If we measure $E°_{cell}$ and know either $E°_{cathode}$ or $E°_{anode}$, we can calculate the other value. This value would tell us how one half-cell reaction compares with others in terms of relative oxidizing or reducing ability.

But here is a dilemma. One cannot measure individual half-cell potentials. Just as values for $\Delta_f H°$ and $\Delta_f G°$ were established by choosing a reference point (the elements in their standard states), scientists have selected a reference point for half-reactions. We assign a potential of exactly 0 V to the half-reaction that occurs at a standard hydrogen electrode (SHE).

$$2 \text{ H}^+(aq, 1 \text{ M}) + 2 e^- \rightarrow \text{H}_2(g, 1 \text{ bar}) \quad E° = 0.00 \text{ V}$$

With this standard, we can now determine $E°$ values for half-cells by measuring $E°_{cell}$ in experiments such as those described in Figures 20.8 and 20.13, where one of the electrodes is the standard hydrogen electrode. We can then quantify the information with reduction potential tables such as Figure 20.14 and use these values to make predictions about $E°_{cell}$ for new voltaic cells.

Tables of Standard Reduction Potentials

The experimental approach just described leads to lists of $E°$ values such as seen in Figure 20.14, Table 20.1, and Appendix M. Let us list some important points concerning these tables and then illustrate them in the discussion and examples that follow.

1. Reactions are written as "oxidized form + electrons → reduced form." The species on the left side of the reaction arrow is an oxidizing agent, and the species on the right side of the reaction arrow is a reducing agent. Therefore, *all potentials are for reduction reactions.*

2. The more positive the value of $E°$ for the reactions in Figure 20.14, Table 20.1, and similar tables, the better the oxidizing ability of the ion or compound on the left side of the reaction. This means *$F_2(g)$ is the best oxidizing agent in the table.* Lithium ion at the lower-left corner of Table 20.1 is the poorest oxidizing agent because its $E°$ value is the most negative.

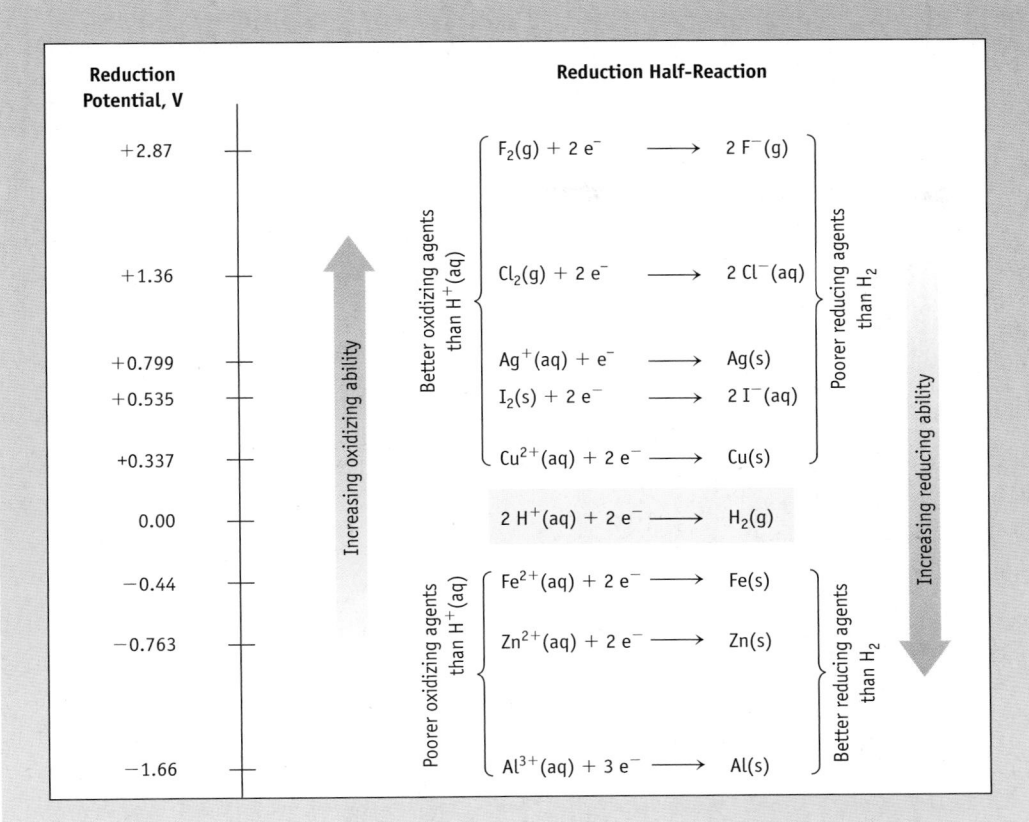

FIGURE 20.14 A potential ladder for reduction half-reactions. The relative position of a half-reaction on this potential ladder reflects the relative ability of the species at the left to act as an oxidizing agent. The higher the compound or ion is in list, the better it is as an oxidizing agent. Conversely, the atoms or ions on the right are reducing agents. The lower they are in the list, the better they are as a reducing agent. The potential for each half-reaction is given with its reduction potential, $E°_{cathode}$. (For more information see J. R. Runo and D. G. Peters, *Journal of Chemical Education*, Volume 70, page 708, 1993.)

3. The more negative the value of the reduction potential, $E°$, the less likely the half-reaction will occur as a reduction, and the more likely the reverse half-reaction will occur (as an oxidation). Thus, Li(s) is the strongest reducing agent in the table, and F^- is the weakest reducing agent. The reducing agents in the table (the ions, elements, and compounds at the right) increase in strength from the top to the bottom.

4. When a reaction is reversed (to give "reduced form → oxidized form + electrons"), the sign of $E°$ is reversed, but the magnitude of $E°$ is unaffected.

$$Fe^{3+}(aq, 1\ M) + e^- \rightarrow Fe^{2+}(aq, 1\ M) \qquad E° = +0.771\ V$$

$$Fe^{2+}(aq, 1\ M) \rightarrow Fe^{3+}(aq, 1\ M) + e^- \qquad E° = -0.771\ V$$

5. The reaction between any substance on the left in this table (an oxidizing agent) with any substance *lower* than it on the right (a reducing agent) is product-favored at equilibrium. This has been called the *northwest–southeast*

■ **$E°$ Values** An extensive listing of $E°$ values is found in Appendix M, and still larger tables of data can be found in chemistry reference books. A common convention, used in Appendix M, lists standard reduction potentials in two groups, one for acid and neutral solutions and the other for basic solutions.

TABLE 20.1 Standard Reduction Potentials in Aqueous Solution at 25 °C*

Reduction Half-Reaction		$E°$ (V)
$F_2(g) + 2\ e^-$	$\rightarrow 2\ F^-(aq)$	+2.87
$H_2O_2(aq) + 2\ H^+(aq) + 2\ e^-$	$\rightarrow 2\ H_2O(\ell)$	+1.77
$PbO_2(s) + SO_4^{2-}(aq) + 4\ H^+(aq) + 2\ e^-$	$\rightarrow PbSO_4(s) + 2\ H_2O(\ell)$	+1.685
$MnO_4^-(aq) + 8\ H^+(aq) + 5\ e^-$	$\rightarrow Mn^{2+}(aq) + 4\ H_2O(\ell)$	+1.51
$Au^{3+}(aq) + 3\ e^-$	$\rightarrow Au(s)$	+1.50
$Cl_2(g) + 2\ e^-$	$\rightarrow 2\ Cl^-(aq)$	+1.36
$Cr_2O_7^{2-}(aq) + 14\ H^+(aq) + 6\ e^-$	$\rightarrow 2\ Cr^{3+}(aq) + 7\ H_2O(\ell)$	+1.33
$O_2(g) + 4\ H^+(aq) + 4\ e^-$	$\rightarrow 2\ H_2O(\ell)$	+1.229
$Br_2(\ell) + 2\ e^-$	$\rightarrow 2\ Br^-(aq)$	+1.08
$NO_3^-(aq) + 4\ H^+(aq) + 3\ e^-$	$\rightarrow NO(g) + 2\ H_2O(\ell)$	+0.96
$OCl^-(aq) + H_2O(\ell) + 2\ e^-$	$\rightarrow Cl^-(aq) + 2\ OH^-(aq)$	+0.89
$Hg^{2+}(aq) + 2\ e^-$	$\rightarrow Hg(\ell)$	+0.855
$Ag^+(aq) + e^-$	$\rightarrow Ag(s)$	+0.799
$Hg_2^{2+}(aq) + 2\ e^-$	$\rightarrow 2\ Hg(\ell)$	+0.789
$Fe^{3+}(aq) + e^-$	$\rightarrow Fe^{2+}(aq)$	+0.771
$I_2(s) + 2\ e^-$	$\rightarrow 2\ I^-(aq)$	+0.535
$O_2(g) + 2\ H_2O(\ell) + 4\ e^-$	$\rightarrow 4\ OH^-(aq)$	+0.40
$Cu^{2+}(aq) + 2\ e^-$	$\rightarrow Cu(s)$	+0.337
$Sn^{4+}(aq) + 2\ e^-$	$\rightarrow Sn^{2+}(aq)$	+0.15
$2\ H^+(aq) + 2\ e^-$	$\rightarrow H_2(g)$	0.00
$Sn^{2+}(aq) + 2\ e^-$	$\rightarrow Sn(s)$	−0.14
$Ni^{2+}(aq) + 2\ e^-$	$\rightarrow Ni(s)$	−0.25
$V^{3+}(aq) + e^-$	$\rightarrow V^{2+}(aq)$	−0.255
$PbSO_4(s) + 2\ e^-$	$\rightarrow Pb(s) + SO_4^{2-}(aq)$	−0.356
$Cd^{2+}(aq) + 2\ e^-$	$\rightarrow Cd(s)$	−0.40
$Fe^{2+}(aq) + 2\ e^-$	$\rightarrow Fe(s)$	−0.44
$Zn^{2+}(aq) + 2\ e^-$	$\rightarrow Zn(s)$	−0.763
$2\ H_2O(\ell) + 2\ e^-$	$\rightarrow H_2(g) + 2\ OH^-(aq)$	−0.8277
$Al^{3+}(aq) + 3\ e^-$	$\rightarrow Al(s)$	−1.66
$Mg^{2+}(aq) + 2\ e^-$	$\rightarrow Mg(s)$	−2.37
$Na^+(aq) + e^-$	$\rightarrow Na(s)$	−2.714
$K^+(aq) + e^-$	$\rightarrow K(s)$	−2.925
$Li^+(aq) + e^-$	$\rightarrow Li(s)$	−3.045

Increasing strength of oxidizing agents

Increasing strength of reducing agents

* In volts (V) versus the standard hydrogen electrode.

rule. Product-favored reactions will always involve a reducing agent that is "southeast" of the proposed oxidizing agent.

■ **Northwest–Southeast Rule** This guideline is a reflection of the idea of moving down a potential energy "ladder" in a product-favored reaction.

Reduction Half-Reaction

$$I_2(s) + 2\,e^- \longrightarrow 2\,I^-(aq)$$
$$Cu^{2+}(aq) + 2\,e^- \longrightarrow Cu(s)$$
$$2\,H^+(aq) + 2\,e^- \longrightarrow H_2(g)$$
$$Fe^{2+}(aq) + 2\,e^- \longrightarrow Fe(s)$$
$$Zn^{2+}(aq) + 2\,e^- \longrightarrow Zn(s)$$

The northwest–southeast rule: The reducing agent always lies to the southeast of the oxidizing agent in a product-favored reaction.

For example, Zn can reduce Fe^{2+}, H^+, Cu^{2+}, and I_2, but, of the species on this list, Cu can reduce only I_2.

6. The algebraic sign of the half-reaction reduction potential is the sign of the electrode when it is attached to the H_2/H^+ standard cell (see Figures 20.8 and 20.13).

7. Electrochemical potentials depend on the nature of the reactants and products and their concentrations, not on the quantities of material used. Therefore, changing the stoichiometric coefficients for a half-reaction does not change the value of $E°$. For example, the reduction of Fe^{3+} has an $E°$ of +0.771 V, whether the reaction is written as

$$Fe^{3+}(aq, 1\ M) + e^- \rightarrow Fe^{2+}(aq, 1\ M) \qquad E° = +0.771\ V$$

or as

$$2\,Fe^{3+}(aq, 1\ M) + 2\,e^- \rightarrow 2\,Fe^{2+}(aq, 1\ M) \qquad E° = +0.771\ V$$

■ **Changing Stoichiometric Coefficients** The volt is defined as "energy/charge" (V = J/C). Multiplying a reaction by some number causes both the energy and the charge to be multiplied by that number. Thus, the ratio "energy/charge = volt" does not change.

Using Tables of Standard Reduction Potentials

Tables or "ladders" of standard reduction potentials are immensely useful. They allow you to predict the potential of a new voltaic cell, provide information that can be used to balance redox equations, and help predict which redox reactions are product-favored.

Calculating Standard Cell Potentials, $E°_{cell}$

The standard reduction potentials for half-reactions were obtained by measuring cell potentials. It makes sense, therefore, that these values can be combined to give the potential of some new cell.

The net reaction occurring in a voltaic cell using silver and copper half-cells is

$$2\,Ag^+(aq) + Cu(s) \rightarrow 2\,Ag(s) + Cu^{2+}(aq)$$

The silver electrode is the cathode, and the copper electrode is the anode. We know this because silver ion is reduced (to silver metal) and copper metal is oxidized (to Cu^{2+} ions). (Recall that oxidations always occur at the anode and reductions at the cathode.) Also notice that the $Cu^{2+}|Cu$ half-reaction is "southeast" of the $Ag^+|Ag$ half-reaction in the potential ladder (Figure 20.14 and Table 20.1).

$$E°_{cathode} = +0.799\ V \qquad Ag^+(aq) + e^- \longrightarrow Ag(s)$$

"Distance" from $E°_{cathode}$ to $E°_{anode}$ is 0.799 V − 0.337 V = 0.462 V.

Cu is "southeast" of Ag^+

$$E°_{anode} = +0.337\ V \qquad Cu^{2+}(aq) + 2\,e^- \longrightarrow Cu(s)$$

The potential for the voltaic cell is the difference between the standard reduction potentials for the two half-reactions.

$$E°_{cell} = E°_{cathode} - E°_{anode}$$

$$E°_{cell} = (+0.799 \text{ V}) - (+0.337 \text{ V})$$

$$E°_{cell} = +0.462 \text{ V}$$

Notice that the value of $E°_{cell}$ is related to the "distance" between the cathode and anode reactions on the potential ladder. The products have a lower potential energy than the reactants, and the cell potential, $E°_{cell}$, has a positive value.

A positive potential calculated for the Ag$^+$|Ag and Cu^{2+}|Cu cell ($E°_{cell} = +0.462$ V) confirms that the reduction of silver ions in water with copper metal is product-favored at equilibrium (Figure 20.1). We might ask, however, about the value of $E°_{cell}$ if a reactant-favored equation had been selected. For example, what is $E°_{cell}$ for the reduction of copper ions with silver metal?

Cathode, reduction:	$Cu^{2+}(aq) + 2 e^- \rightarrow Cu(s)$
Anode, oxidation:	$2 Ag(s) \rightarrow 2 Ag^+(aq) + 2 e^-$
Net ionic equation:	$2 Ag (s) + Cu^{2+}(aq) \rightarrow 2 Ag^+(aq) + Cu(s)$

Cell Voltage Calculation

$$E°_{cathode} = + 0.337 \text{ V and } E°_{anode} = + 0.799 \text{ V}$$

$$E°_{cell} = E°_{cathode} - E°_{anode} = (+0.337 \text{ V}) - (0.799 \text{ V})$$

$$E°_{cell} = - 0.462 \text{ V}$$

The negative sign for $E°_{cell}$ indicates that the reaction as written is reactant-favored at equilibrium. The products of the reaction (Ag$^+$ and Cu) have a higher potential energy than the reactants (Ag and Cu^{2+}). For the indicated reaction to occur, a potential of at least 0.462 V would have to be imposed on the system by an external source of electricity (see Section 20.7).

Chemistry ⚛ Now™

Sign in at **www.cengage.com/login** and go to Chapter 20 Contents to see:
• Screen 20.5 for demonstration of **the potentials of various cells**
• Screen 20.6 for a simulation and tutorial on **standard potentials**

EXERCISE 20.6 Calculating Standard Cell Potentials

The net reaction that occurs in a voltaic cell is

$$Zn(s) + 2 Ag^+(aq) \rightarrow Zn^{2+}(aq) + 2 Ag(s)$$

Identify the half-reactions that occur at the anode and the cathode, and calculate a potential for the cell assuming standard conditions.

Relative Strengths of Oxidizing and Reducing Agents

Five half-reactions, selected from Appendix M, are arranged from the half-reaction with the highest (most positive) $E°$ value to the one with the lowest (most negative) value.

$E°$, V		Reduction Half-Reaction
+1.36	↑ Increasing strength as oxidizing agents	$Cl_2(g) + 2\ e^- \longrightarrow 2\ Cl^-(aq)$
+0.80		$Ag^+(aq) + e^- \longrightarrow Ag(s)$
+0.00		$2\ H^+(aq) + 2\ e^- \longrightarrow H_2(g)$
−0.25		$Ni^{2+}(aq) + 2\ e^- \longrightarrow Ni(s)$
−0.76		$Zn^{2+}(aq) + 2\ e^- \longrightarrow Zn(s)$

- The list on the left is headed by Cl_2, an element that is a strong oxidizing agent and thus is easily reduced. At the bottom of the list is $Zn^{2+}(aq)$, an ion not easily reduced and thus a poor oxidizing agent.
- On the right, the list is headed by $Cl^-(aq)$, an ion that can be oxidized to Cl_2 only with difficulty. It is a very poor reducing agent. At the bottom of the list is zinc metal, which is quite easy to oxidize and a good reducing agent.

By arranging these half-reactions based on $E°$ values, we have also arranged the chemical species on the two sides of the equation in order of their strengths as oxidizing or reducing agents. In this list, from strongest to weakest, the order is

$$\text{Oxidizing agents: } Cl_2 > Ag^+ > H^+ > Ni^{2+} > Zn^{2+}$$
$$\text{strong} \longrightarrow \text{weak}$$

$$\text{Reducing agents: } Zn > Ni > H_2 > Ag > Cl^-$$
$$\text{strong} \longrightarrow \text{weak}$$

Finally, notice that the value of $E°_{cell}$ is greater the farther apart the oxidizing and reducing agents are on the potential ladder. For example,

$$Zn(s) + Cl_2(g) \rightarrow Zn^{2+}(aq) + 2\ Cl^-(aq) \qquad E° = +2.12\text{ V}$$

is more strongly product-favored than the reduction of hydrogen ions with nickel metal

$$Ni(s) + 2\ H^+(aq) \rightarrow Ni^{2+}(aq) + H_2(g) \qquad E° = +0.25\text{ V}$$

EXAMPLE 20.5 Ranking Oxidizing and Reducing Agents

Problem Use the table of standard reduction potentials (Table 20.1) to do the following:

(a) Rank the halogens in order of their strength as oxidizing agents.

(b) Decide whether hydrogen peroxide (H_2O_2) in acid solution is a stronger oxidizing agent than Cl_2.

(c) Decide which of the halogens is capable of oxidizing gold metal to $Au^{3+}(aq)$.

Strategy The ability of a species on the left side of a reduction potential table to function as an oxidizing agent declines on descending the list (see points 2 and 3, pages 918-919).

Solution

(a) Ranking halogens according to oxidizing ability. The halogens (F_2, Cl_2, Br_2, and I_2) appear in the upper-left portion of the table, with F_2 being highest, followed in order by the other three species. Their strengths as oxidizing agents are $F_2 > Cl_2 > Br_2 > I_2$. (The ability of bromine to oxidize iodide ions to molecular iodine is illustrated in Figure 20.15.)

FIGURE 20.15 The reaction of bromine and iodide ion. This experiment proves that Br_2 is a better oxidizing agent than I_2. The presence of I_2 in the bottom layer in the photo on the right indicates that the added Br_2 was able to oxidize the iodide ions originally present to molecular iodine (I_2).

The test tube contains an aqueous solution of KI (top layer) and immiscible CCl_4 (bottom layer).

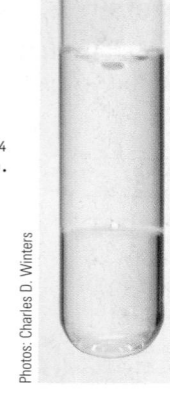

Add Br_2 to solution of KI, and shake.

After adding a few drops of Br_2 in water, the I_2 produced collects in the bottom CCl_4 layer and gives it a purple color. (The top layer contains excess Br_2 in water.)

Photos: Charles D. Winters

(b) Comparing hydrogen peroxide and chlorine. H_2O_2 lies just below F_2 but well above Cl_2 in the potential ladder (Table 20.1). Thus, H_2O_2 is a weaker oxidizing agent than F_2 but a stronger one than Cl_2. (Note that the $E°$ value for H_2O_2 refers to an acidic solution and standard conditions.)

(c) Which halogen will oxidize gold metal to gold(III) ions? The $Au^{3+} \mid Au$ half-reaction is listed below the $F_2 \mid F^-$ half-reaction and just above the $Cl_2 \mid Cl^-$ half-reaction. This tells us that, among the halogens, only F_2 is capable of oxidizing Au to Au^{3+} under standard conditions. That is, for the reaction of Au and F_2,

Oxidation, anode:	$Au(s) \rightarrow Au^{3+}(aq) + 3\ e^-$
Reduction, cathode:	$F_2(g) + 2\ e^- \rightarrow 2\ F^-(aq)$
Net ionic equation:	$3\ F_2(g) + 2\ Au(s) \rightarrow 6\ F^-(aq) + 2\ Au^{3+}(aq)$

$E°_{cell} = E°_{cathode} - E°_{anode} = +2.87\ V - (+1.50\ V) = +1.37\ V$

F_2 is a stronger oxidizing agent than Au^{3+}, so the reaction proceeds from left to right as written. (This is confirmed by a positive value of $E°_{cell}$.) For the reaction of Cl_2 and Au, Table 20.1 shows us that Cl_2 is a weaker oxidizing agent than Au^{3+}, so the reaction would be expected to proceed in the opposite direction.

Oxidation, anode:	$Au(s) \rightarrow Au^{3+}(aq) + 3\ e^-$
Reduction, cathode:	$Cl_2(aq) + 2\ e^- \rightarrow 2\ Cl^-(aq)$
Net ionic equation:	$3\ Cl_2(aq) + 2\ Au(s) \rightarrow 6\ Cl^-(aq) + 2\ Au^{3+}(aq)$

$E°_{cell} = E°_{cathode} - E°_{anode} = +1.36\ V - (+1.50\ V) = -0.14\ V$

This is confirmed by the negative value for $E°_{cell}$.

Comment In part (c), we calculated $E°_{cell}$ for two reactions. To achieve a balanced net ionic equation, we added the half-reactions, but only after multiplying the gold half-reaction by 2 and the halogen, half-reaction by 3. (This means 6 mol of electrons was transferred from 2 mol Au to 3 mol Cl_2.) Notice that this multiplication does not change the value of $E°$ for the half-reactions because cell potentials do not depend on the quantity of material.

EXERCISE 20.7 Relative Oxidizing and Reducing Ability

Which metal in the following list is easiest to oxidize: Fe, Ag, Zn, Mg, Au? Which metal is the most difficult to oxidize?

EXERCISE 20.8 Using a Table of Standard Reduction Potentials to Predict Chemical Reactions

Determine whether the following redox equations are product-favored at equilibrium.

(a) $Ni^{2+}(aq) + H_2(g) \rightarrow Ni(s) + 2\ H^+(aq)$

(b) $2\ Fe^{3+}(aq) + 2\ I^-(aq) \rightarrow 2\ Fe^{2+}(aq) + I_2(s)$

(c) $Br_2(\ell) + 2\ Cl^-(aq) \rightarrow 2\ Br^-(aq) + Cl_2(g)$

(d) $Cr_2O_7^{2-}(aq) + 6\ Fe^{2+}(aq) + 14\ H^+(aq) \rightarrow 2\ Cr^{3+}(aq) + 6\ Fe^{3+}(aq) + 7\ H_2O(\ell)$

20.5 Electrochemical Cells Under Nonstandard Conditions

Electrochemical cells seldom operate under standard conditions in the real world. Even if the cell is constructed with all dissolved species at 1 M, reactant concentra-tions decrease and product concentrations increase in the course of the reaction. Changing concentrations of reactants and products will affect the cell voltage. Thus, we need to ask what happens to cell potentials under nonstandard conditions.

The Nernst Equation

Based on both theory and experimental results, it has been determined that cell potentials are related to concentrations of reactants and products and to tempera-ture, as follows:

$$E = E° - (RT/nF) \ln Q \tag{20.2}$$

In this equation, which is known as the **Nernst equation**, R is the gas constant $(8.314472 \text{ J/K} \cdot \text{mol})$; T is the temperature (K); and n is the number of moles of electrons transferred between oxidizing and reducing agents (as determined by the balanced equation for the reaction). The symbol F represents the **Faraday constant** $(9.6485338 \times 10^4 \text{ C/mol})$. *One Faraday is the quantity of electric charge carried by one mole of electrons.* The term Q is the reaction quotient, an expression relating the concentrations of the products and reactants raised to an appropriate power as defined by the stoichiometric coefficients in the balanced, net equation [see Equation 16.2, Section 16.2]. Substituting values for the constants in Equation 20.2, and using 298 K as the temperature, gives

$$E = E° - \frac{0.0257}{n} \ln Q \quad \text{at 25 °C} \tag{20.3}$$

or, in a commonly used form using base-10 logarithms,

$$E = E° - \frac{0.0591}{n} \log Q$$

In essence, the term $(RT/nF)\ln Q$ "corrects" the standard potential $E°$ for nonstan-dard conditions or concentrations.

Chemistry ⚛ Now™

Sign in at **www.cengage.com/login** and go to Chapter 20 Contents to see Screen 20.8 for a tutorial on **the Nernst equation.**

■ **Walther Nernst (1864–1941)** Nernst was a German physicist and chemist known for his work relating to the third law of thermodynamics.

■ **Units of R and F** The gas constant R has units of J/K · mol, and F has units of coulombs per mol (C/mol). Because $1 \text{ J} = 1 \text{ C} \cdot \text{V}$, the factor RT/nF has units of volts.

Problem A voltaic cell is set up at 25 °C with the half-cells: $Al^{3+}(0.0010\ M)\,|\,Al$ and $Ni^{2+}(0.50\ M)\,|\,Ni$. Write an equation for the reaction that occurs when the cell generates an electric current, and determine the cell potential.

Strategy The first step is to determine which substance is oxidized (Al or Ni) by looking at the appropriate half-reactions in Table 20.1 and deciding which is the better reducing agent (Example 20.5). Next, add the half-reactions to determine the net ionic equation, and calculate $E°$. Finally, use the Nernst equation to calculate E, the nonstandard potential.

Solution Aluminum metal is a stronger reducing agent than Ni metal. (Conversely, Ni^{2+} is a better oxidizing agent than Al^{3+}.) Therefore, Al is oxidized, and the $Al^{3+}\,|\,Al$ compartment is the anode.

Cathode, reduction:	$Ni^{2+}(aq) + 2\ e^- \rightarrow Ni(s)$
Anode, oxidation:	$Al(s) \rightarrow Al^{3+}(aq) + 3\ e^-$
Net ionic equation:	$2\ Al(s) + 3\ Ni^{2+}(aq) \rightarrow 2\ Al^{3+}(aq) + 3\ Ni(s)$

$$E°_{cell} = E°_{cathode} - E°_{anode}$$

$$E°_{cell} = (-0.25\ V) - (-1.66\ V) = 1.41\ V$$

The expression for Q is written based on the cell reaction. In the net reaction, $Al^{3+}(aq)$ has a coefficient of 2, so this concentration is squared. Similarly, $[Ni^{2+}(aq)]$ is cubed. Solids are not included in the expression for Q (◀ Section 16.1).

$$Q = \frac{[Al^{3+}]^2}{[Ni^{2+}]^3}$$

The net equation requires transfer of six electrons from two Al atoms to three Ni^{2+} ions, so $n = 6$. Substituting for $E°$, n and Q in the Nernst equation gives

$$E_{cell} = E°_{cell} - \frac{0.0257}{n} \ln \frac{[Al^{3+}]^2}{[Ni^{2+}]^3}$$

$$= +1.41\ V - \frac{0.0257}{6} \ln \frac{[0.0010]^2}{[0.50]^3}$$

$$= +1.41\ V - 0.00428 \ln (8.0 \times 10^{-6})$$

$$= +1.41\ V - 0.00428 (-11.7)$$

$$= \boxed{1.46\ V}$$

Comment Notice that E_{cell} is larger than $E°_{cell}$ because the product concentration, $[Al^{3+}]$, is much smaller than 1.0 M. Generally, when product concentrations are smaller initially than the reactant concentrations in a product-favored reaction, the cell potential is more positive than $E°$.

EXERCISE 20.9 Variation of E_{cell} with Concentration

A voltaic cell is set up with an aluminum electrode in a 0.025 M $Al(NO_3)_3(aq)$ solution and an iron electrode in a 0.50 M $Fe(NO_3)_2(aq)$ solution. Determine the cell potential, E_{cell}, at 298 K.

Example 20.6 demonstrates the calculation of a cell potential if concentrations are known. It is also useful to apply the Nernst equation in the opposite sense, using a measured cell potential to determine an unknown concentration. A device that does just this is the pH meter (Figure 20.16). In an electrochemical cell in which $H^+(aq)$ is a reactant or product, the cell voltage will vary predictably with the hydrogen ion concentration. The cell voltage is measured and the value used to calculate pH. Example 20.7 illustrates how E_{cell} varies with the hydrogen ion concentration in a simple cell.

Problem A voltaic cell is set up with copper and hydrogen half-cells. Standard conditions are employed in the copper half-cell, Cu^{2+}(aq, 1.00 M)|Cu(s). The hydrogen gas pressure is 1.00 bar, and [H^+(aq)] in the hydrogen half-cell is the unknown. A value of 0.490 V is recorded for E_{cell} at 298 K. Determine the pH of the solution.

Strategy We first decide which is the better oxidizing and reducing agent so as to decide what net reaction is occurring in the cell. With this known, $E°_{cell}$ can be calculated. The only unknown quantity in the Nernst equation is the concentration of hydrogen ion, from which we can calculate the solution pH.

Solution Hydrogen is a better reducing agent than copper metal, so Cu(s)|Cu^{2+}(aq, 1.00 M) is the cathode, and H_2(g, 1.00 bar)|H^+(aq, ? M) is the anode.

Cathode, reduction:	Cu^{2+}(aq) + 2 e^- → Cu(s)
Anode, oxidation:	H_2(g) → 2 H^+(aq) + 2 e^-
Net ionic equation:	H_2(g) + Cu^{2+}(aq) → Cu(s) + 2 H^+(aq)

$$E°_{cell} = E°_{cathode} - E°_{anode}$$

$$E°_{cell} = (+0.337\ V) - (0.00\ V) = +0.337\ V$$

The reaction quotient, Q, is derived from the balanced net ionic equation.

$$Q = \frac{[H^+]^2}{[Cu^{2+}]P_{H_2}}$$

The net equation requires the transfer of two electrons, so $n = 2$. The value of [Cu^{2+}] is 1.00 M, but [H^+] is unknown. Substitute this information into the Nernst equation (and don't overlook the fact that [H^+] is squared in the expression for Q).

$$E = E° - \frac{0.0257}{n}\ln\frac{[H^+]^2}{[Cu^{2+}]P_{H_2}}$$

$$0.490\ V = 0.337\ V - \frac{0.0257}{2}\ln\frac{[H^+]^2}{(1.00)(1.00)}$$

$$-11.9 = \ln [H^+]^2$$

$$[H^+] = 2.6 \times 10^{-3}\ M$$

$$pH = 2.59$$

EXERCISE 20.10 **Using the Nernst Equation**

The half-cells Fe^{2+}(aq, 0.024 M)|Fe(s) and H^+(aq, 0.056 M)|H_2(1.0 bar) are linked by a salt bridge to create a voltaic cell. Determine the cell potential, E_{cell}, at 298 K.

In the real world, using a hydrogen electrode in a pH meter is not practical. The apparatus is clumsy; it is anything but robust; and platinum (for the electrode) is costly. Common pH meters use a glass electrode, so called because it contains a thin glass membrane separating the cell from the solution whose pH is to be measured (Figure 20.16). Inside the glass electrode is a silver wire coated with AgCl and a solution of HCl; outside is the solution of unknown pH to be evaluated. A Ag/AgCl or calomel electrode—a common reference electrode using a mercury(I)–mercury redox couple (Hg_2Cl_2|Hg)—serves as the second electrode of the cell. The potential across the glass membrane depends on [H^+]. Common pH meters give a direct readout of pH.

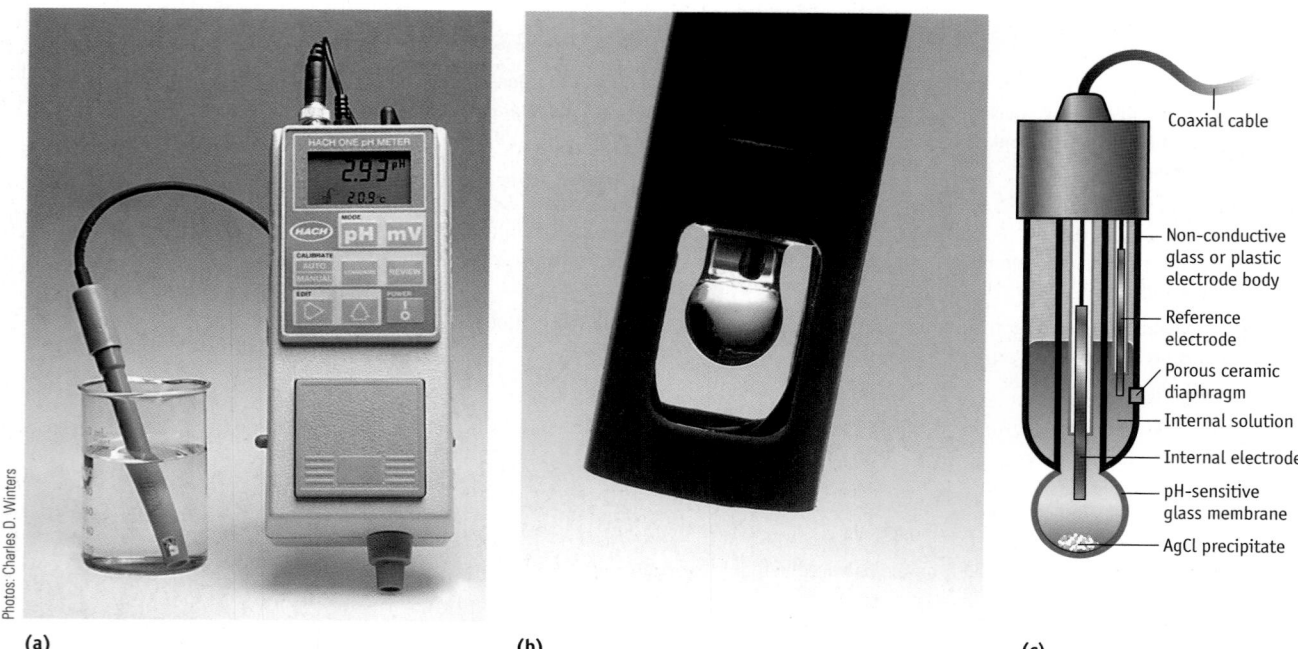

(a)　　　　　　　　　　　　　**(b)**　　　　　　　　　　　　　**(c)**

Coaxial cable

Non-conductive glass or plastic electrode body

Reference electrode

Porous ceramic diaphragm

Internal solution

Internal electrode

pH-sensitive glass membrane

AgCl precipitate

FIGURE 20.16 Measuring pH. (a) A pH portable meter that can be used in the field. (b) The tip of a glass electrode for measuring pH. (c) A schematic diagram of a glass electrode. (See ChemistryNow Screen 17.4 for an animation of the operation of a glass electrode for pH measurement.)

20.6 Electrochemistry and Thermodynamics

Work and Free Energy

The first law of thermodynamics [Section 5.4] states that the internal energy change in a system (ΔU) is related to two quantities, heat (q) and work (w): $\Delta U = q + w$. This equation also applies to chemical changes that occur in a voltaic cell. As current flows, energy is transferred from the system (the voltaic cell) to the surroundings.

In a voltaic cell, the decrease in internal energy in the system will manifest itself ideally as electrical work done on the surroundings by the system. In practice, however, some energy is usually evolved as heat by the voltaic cell. The maximum work done by an electrochemical system (ideally, assuming no heat is generated) is proportional to the potential difference (volts) and the quantity of charge (coulombs):

$$w_{max} = nFE \tag{20.4}$$

In this equation, E is the cell voltage, and nF is the quantity of electric charge transferred from anode to cathode.

The free energy change for a process is, by definition, the maximum amount of work that can be obtained [Section 19.6]. Because the maximum work and the cell potential are related, $E°$ and $\Delta_r G°$ can be related mathematically (taking care to assign signs correctly). The maximum work done on the surroundings when electricity is produced by a voltaic cell is $+nFE$, with the positive sign denoting an increase in energy in the surroundings. The energy content of the cell decreases by this amount. Thus, $\Delta_r G$ for the voltaic cell has the opposite sign.

$$\Delta_r G = -nFE \tag{20.5}$$

Under standard conditions, the appropriate equation is

$$\Delta_r G° = -nFE°$$ (20.6)

This expression shows that, the more positive the value of $E°$, the larger and more negative the value of $\Delta_r G°$ for the reaction. Also, because of the relationship between $\Delta_r G°$ and K, the farther apart the half-reactions on the potential ladder, the more strongly product-favored the reaction is at equilibrium.

■ **Units in Equation 20.6** n has units of mol e^-, and F has units of (C/mol e^-). Therefore, nF has units of coulombs (C). Because 1 J = 1 C · V, the product nFE will have units of energy (J).

■ **EXAMPLE 20.8 The Relation Between $E°$ and $\Delta_r G°$**

Problem The standard cell potential, $E°_{cell}$ for the reduction of silver ions with copper metal (Figure 20.5) is +0.462 V at 25 °C. Calculate $\Delta_r G°$ for this reaction.

Strategy We use Equation 20.6, where F is a constant and $E°_{cell}$ is given. The only problem here is to determine the value of n, the number of moles of electrons transferred between copper metal and silver ions in the balanced equation.

Solution In this cell, copper is the anode, and silver is the cathode. The overall cell reaction is

$$Cu(s) + 2\,Ag^+(aq) \rightarrow Cu^{2+}(aq) + 2\,Ag(s)$$

which means that each mole of copper transfers two moles of electrons to two moles of Ag^+ ions. That is, $n = 2$. Now use Equation 20.6.

$$\Delta_r G° = -nFE° = -(2\ mol\ e^-)(96{,}485\ C/mol\ e^-)(0.462\ V) = -89{,}200\ C \cdot V$$

Because 1 C · V = 1 J, we have

$$\Delta_r G° = -89{,}200\ J\ or\ -89.2\ kJ$$

Comment This example demonstrates a very effective method of obtaining thermodynamic values from relatively simple electrochemical experiments.

EXERCISE 20.11 The Relationship Between $E°$ and $\Delta_r G°$

The following reaction has an $E°$ value of −0.76 V:

$$H_2(g) + Zn^{2+}(aq) \rightarrow Zn(s) + 2\,H^+(aq)$$

Calculate $\Delta_r G°$ for this reaction. Is the reaction product- or reactant-favored at equilibrium?

$E°$ and the Equilibrium Constant

When a voltaic cell produces an electric current, the reactant concentrations decrease, and the product concentrations increase. The cell voltage also changes; as reactants are converted to products, the value of E_{cell} decreases. Eventually, the cell potential reaches zero; no further net reaction occurs; and equilibrium is achieved.

This situation can be analyzed using the Nernst equation. When $E_{cell} = 0$, the reactants and products are at equilibrium, and the reaction quotient, Q, is equal to the equilibrium constant, K. Substituting the appropriate symbols and values into the Nernst equation,

$$E = 0 = E° - \frac{0.0257}{n}\ln K$$

and collecting terms gives an equation that relates the cell potential and equilibrium constant:

$$\ln K = \frac{nE°}{0.0257} \quad \text{at 25 °C}$$ (20.7)

■ **K and $E°$** The farther apart half-reactions for a product-favored reaction are on the potential ladder, the larger the value of K.

Equation 20.7 can be used to determine values for equilibrium constants, as illustrated in Example 20.9 and Exercise 20.12.

EXAMPLE 20.9 $E°$ and Equilibrium Constants

Problem Calculate the equilibrium constant for the reaction

$$Fe(s) + Cd^{2+}(aq) \rightleftharpoons Fe^{2+}(aq) + Cd(s)$$

Strategy First, determine $E°_{cell}$ from $E°$ values for the two half-reactions (see Example 20.5) and from those the value of n, the other parameter required in Equation 20.7.

Solution The half-reactions and $E°$ values are

Cathode, reduction: $Cd^{2+}(aq) + 2\ e^- \rightarrow Cd(s)$

Anode, oxidation: $\underline{Fe(s) \rightarrow Fe^{2+}(aq) + 2\ e^-}$

Net ionic equation: $Fe(s) + Cd^{2+}(aq) \rightleftharpoons Fe^{2+}(aq) + Cd(s)$

$E°_{cell} = E°_{cathode} - E°_{anode}$

$E°_{cell} = (-0.40\ V) - (-0.44\ V) = +0.04\ V$

Now substitute $n = 2$ and $E°_{cell}$ into Equation 20.7.

$$\ln K = \frac{nE°}{0.0257} = \frac{(2)(0.04\ V)}{0.0257} = 3.1$$

$$K = 20$$

Comment The relatively small positive voltage (0.04 V) for the cell indicates that the cell reaction is only mildly product-favored. A value of 20 for the equilibrium constant is in accord with this observation.

EXERCISE 20.12 $E°$ and Equilibrium Constants

Calculate the equilibrium constant at 25 °C for the reaction

$$2\ Ag^+(aq) + Hg(\ell) \rightleftharpoons 2\ Ag(s) + Hg^{2+}(aq)$$

The relationships between $E°$, K, and $\Delta_r G°$, which is summarized in Table 20.2, can be used to obtain equilibrium constants for many different chemical systems. For example, let us construct an electrode in which an insoluble ionic compound (such as AgCl) is a component of the half-cell. For this purpose, a silver electrode with a surface layer of AgCl can be prepared. The reaction occurring at this electrode is then

$$AgCl(s) + e^- \rightarrow Ag(s) + Cl^-(aq)$$

The standard reduction potential for this half-cell (Appendix M) is $+0.222$ V. When this half-reaction is paired with a standard silver electrode in an electrochemical cell, the cell reactions are

Cathode, reduction: $AgCl(s) + e^- \rightarrow Ag(s) + Cl^-(aq)$

Anode, oxidation: $\underline{Ag(s) \rightarrow Ag^+(aq) + e^-}$

Net ionic equation: $AgCl(s) \rightarrow Ag^+(aq) + Cl^-(aq)$

$E°_{cell} = E°_{cathode} - E°_{anode} = (+0.222\ V) - (+0.799\ V) = -0.577\ V$

TABLE 20.2 Summary of the Relationship of K, $\Delta_r G°$, and $E°$

K	$\Delta_r G°$	$E°$	Reactant-Favored or Product-Favored at Equilibrium?	Spontaneous under Standard Conditions?
$K \gg 1$	$\Delta_r G° < 0$	$E° > 0$	Product-favored	Spontaneous under standard conditions
$K = 1$	$\Delta_r G° = 0$	$E° = 0$	$[C]^c[D]^d = [A]^a[B]^b$ at equilibrium	At equilibrium under standard conditions
$K \ll 1$	$\Delta_r G° > 0$	$E° < 0$	Reactant-favored	Not spontaneous under standard conditions.

The equation for the net reaction represents the equilibrium of solid AgCl and its ions. The cell potential is negative, indicating a reactant-favored process, as would be expected based on the low solubility of AgCl. Using Equation 20.7, the value of the equilibrium constant [K_{sp}, Section 18.4] can be obtained from $E°_{cell}$.

$$\ln K = \frac{nE°}{0.0257} = \frac{(1)(-0.577 \text{ V})}{0.0257} = -22.5$$

$$K_{sp} = e^{-22.5} = 2 \times 10^{-10}$$

EXERCISE 20.13 Determining an Equilibrium Constant

In Appendix M, the following standard reduction potential is reported:

$$[Zn(CN)_4]^{2-}(aq) + 2 e^- \rightarrow Zn(s) + 4 CN^-(aq) \qquad E° = -1.26 \text{ V}$$

Use this information, along with the data on the $Zn^{2+}(aq)|Zn$ half-cell, to calculate the equilibrium constant for the reaction

$$Zn^{2+}(aq) + 4 CN^-(aq) \rightarrow [Zn(CN)_4]^{2-}(aq)$$

The value calculated is the formation constant for this complex ion at 25 °C.

20.7 Electrolysis: Chemical Change Using Electrical Energy

Thus far, we have described electrochemical cells that use product-favored redox reactions to generate an electric current. Equally important, however, is the opposite process, **electrolysis**, the use of electrical energy to bring about chemical change.

Electrolysis of water is a classic chemistry experiment, and the electroplating of metals is another example of electrolysis (Figure 20.17). In electroplating, an electric current is passed through a solution containing a salt of the metal to be plated. The object to be plated is the cathode. When metal ions in solution are reduced, the metal deposits on the object's surface.

Electrolysis is an important procedure because it is widely used in the refining of metals such as aluminum and in the production of chemicals such as chlorine.

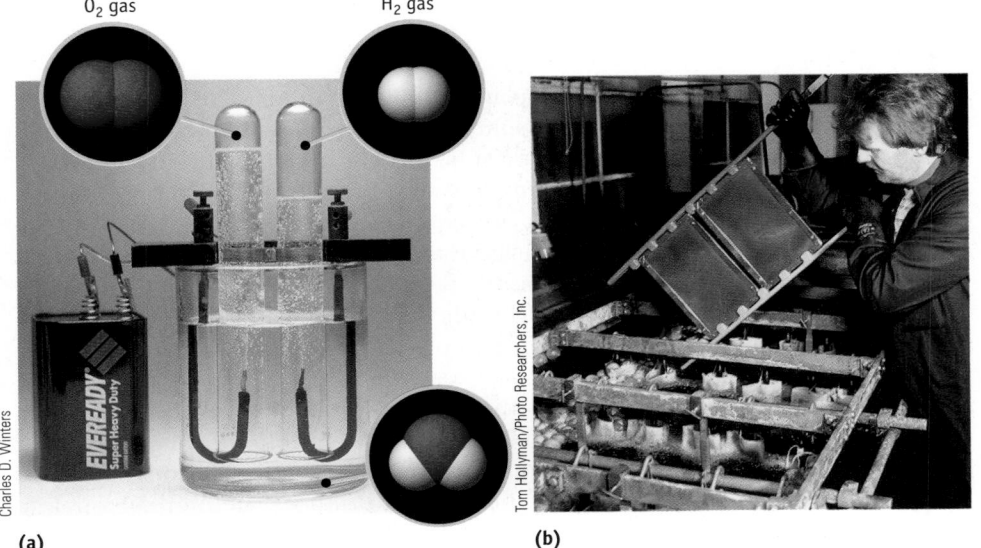

O₂ gas H₂ gas

(a) (b)

Charles D. Winters

Tom Hollyman/Photo Researchers, Inc.

FIGURE 20.17 Electrolysis.
(a) Electrolysis of water produces hydrogen and oxygen gas. (b) Electroplating adds a layer of metal to the surface of an object, either to protect the object from corrosion or to improve its physical appearance. The procedure uses an electrolysis cell, set up with the object to be plated as the cathode and a solution containing a salt of the metal to be plated.

Manganese is a key component of some oxidation–reduction cycles in the oceans. According to an article in the journal *Science*, it "can perform this role because it exists in multiple oxidation states and is recycled rapidly between these states by bacterial processes."

Figure A shows how this cycle was thought to work. Manganese(II) ions in subsurface water are oxidized to form manganese(IV) oxide, MnO_2. Particles of this insoluble solid sink toward the ocean floor. However, some encounter hydrogen sulfide, which is produced in the ocean depths, rising toward the surface. Another redox reaction occurs, producing sulfur and manganese(II) ions. The newly formed Mn^{2+} ions diffuse upward, where they are again oxidized.

The manganese cycle had been thought to involve only the +2 and +4 oxidation states of manganese, and analyses of water samples assumed the dissolved manganese existed only as Mn^{2+} ions. One reason for this is that the intermediate oxidation state, Mn^{3+}, is not predicted to be stable in water. It should disproportionate to the +2 and +4 states.

$$2\ Mn^{3+}(aq) + 2\ H_2O(\ell) \rightarrow$$
$$Mn^{2+}(aq) + MnO_2(s) + 4\ H^+(aq)$$

It is known, however, that Mn^{3+} can exist when complexed with species such as pyrophosphate ions, $P_2O_7^{4-}$.

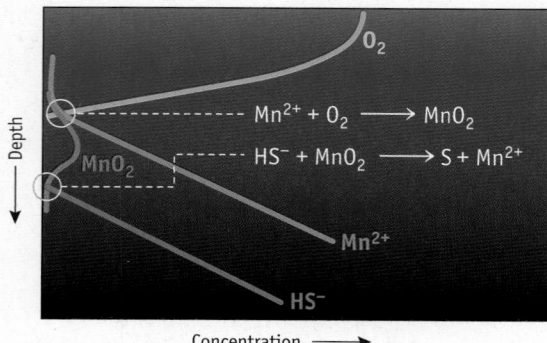

Figure A Manganese chemistry in the oceans. Relative concentrations of important species as a function of depth in the oceans. See K. S. Johnson, *Science*, Vol. 313, p. 1896, 2006 and R. E. Trouwborst, et al., *Science*, Vol. 313, pp. 1955–1957, 2006.

Several years ago, geochemists suggested that Mn^{3+} ions could exist in natural water. They could be produced by bacterial action and stabilized by phosphate from ATP or ADP. They speculated that the Mn^{3+} ion could play an important part of the natural manganese cycle.

Now, other researchers have indeed discovered that, in oxygen-poor waters, the manganese(III) ion, Mn^{3+}, can persist. These ions were found in anoxic zones (zones without dissolved oxygen) below 100 m in the Black Sea and below about 15 m in the Chesapeake Bay. It is now clear that Mn^{3+} ions, which had previously been known only in the laboratory, can exist in natural waters under the right circumstances and that the manganese cycle may have to be revised.

Questions:

1. Given the following reduction potentials, show that Mn^{3+} should disproportionate to Mn^{2+} and MnO_2 at standard conditions.
$$4\ H^+(aq) + MnO_2(s) + e^- \rightarrow$$
$$Mn^{3+}(aq) + 2\ H_2O(\ell)$$
$E° = 0.95\ V$
$$Mn^{3+}(aq) + e^- \rightarrow Mn^{2+}(aq)$$
$E° = 1.50\ V$

2. Balance the following equations in acid solution.
   (a) Reduction of MnO_2 with HS^- to Mn^{2+} and S
   (b) Oxidation of Mn^{2+} with O_2 to MnO_2

3. Calculate $E°$ for the oxidation of Mn^{2+} with O_2 to MnO_2.

Answers to these questions are in Appendix Q.

Electrolysis of Molten Salts

All electrolysis experiments are set up in a similar manner. The material to be electrolyzed, either a molten salt or a solution, is contained in an electrolysis cell. As was the case with voltaic cells, ions must be present in the liquid or solution for a current to flow. The movement of ions constitutes the electric current within the cell. The cell has two electrodes that are connected to a source of DC (direct-current) voltage. If a high enough voltage is applied, chemical reactions occur at the two electrodes. Reduction occurs at the negatively charged cathode, with electrons being transferred from that electrode to a chemical species in the cell. Oxidation occurs at the positive anode, with electrons from a chemical species being transferred to that electrode.

Let us first focus our attention on the chemical reactions that occur at each electrode in the electrolysis of a molten salt. Sodium chloride melts at about 800 °C, and in the molten state sodium ions (Na^+) and chloride ions (Cl^-) are freed from their rigid arrangement in the crystalline lattice. Therefore, if a poten-

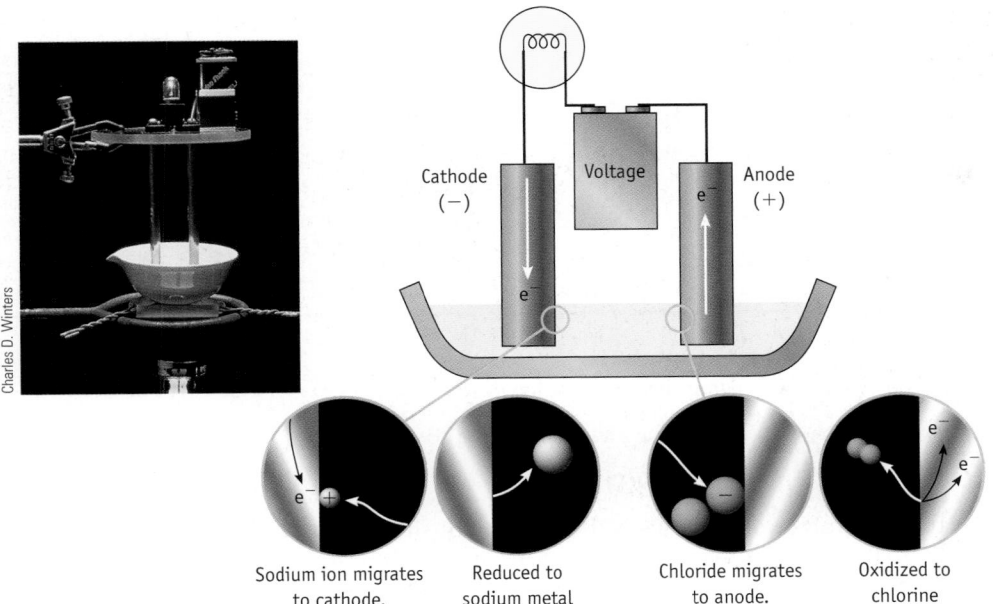

FIGURE 20.18 The preparation of sodium and chlorine by the electrolysis of molten NaCl. In the molten state, sodium ions migrate to the negative cathode, where they are reduced to sodium metal. Chloride ions migrate to the positive anode, where they are oxidized to elemental chlorine.

Cathode (−)   Voltage   Anode (+)

e^-

Sodium ion migrates to cathode.

Reduced to sodium metal

Chloride migrates to anode.

Oxidized to chlorine

Charles D. Winters

tial is applied to the electrodes, sodium ions are attracted to the negative electrode, and chloride ions are attracted to the positive electrode (Figure 20.18). If the potential is high enough, chemical reactions occur at each electrode. At the negative cathode, Na^+ ions accept electrons and are reduced to sodium metal (a liquid at this temperature). Simultaneously, at the positive anode, chloride ions give up electrons and form elemental chlorine.

Cathode (−), reduction:	$2\ Na^+ + 2\ e^- \rightarrow 2\ Na(\ell)$
Anode (+), oxidation:	$2\ Cl^- \rightarrow Cl_2(g) + 2\ e^-$
Net ionic equation:	$2\ Na^+ + 2\ Cl^- \rightarrow 2\ Na(\ell) + Cl_2(g)$

Electrons move through the external circuit under the force exerted by the applied potential, and the movement of positive and negative ions in the molten salt constitutes the current within the cell. Finally, it is important to recognize that the reaction is not spontaneous. The energy required for this reaction to occur has been provided by the electric current.

Electrolysis of Aqueous Solutions

Sodium ions (Na^+) and chloride ions (Cl^-) are the primary species present in molten NaCl. Only chloride ions can be oxidized, and only sodium ions can be reduced. Electrolyses of aqueous solutions are more complicated than electrolyses of molten salts, however, because water is now present. Water is an *electroactive* substance; that is, it can be oxidized or reduced in an electrochemical process.

Consider the electrolysis of aqueous sodium iodide (Figure 20.19). In this experiment, the electrolysis cell contains $Na^+(aq)$, $I^-(aq)$, and H_2O molecules. Possible *reduction reactions* at the *negative cathode* include

$$Na^+(aq) + e^- \rightarrow Na(s)$$

$$2\ H_2O(\ell) + 2\ e^- \rightarrow H_2(g) + 2\ OH^-(aq)$$

Whether you are describing a voltaic cell or an electrolysis cell, the terms "anode" and "cathode" always refer to the electrodes at which oxidation and reduction occur, respectively. The polarity of the electrodes is reversed, however.

Type of Cell	Electrode	Function	Polarity
Voltaic	Anode	Oxidation	−
	Cathode	Reduction	+
Electrolysis	Anode	Oxidation	+
	Cathode	Reduction	−

Possible *oxidation reactions* at the *positive anode* are

$$2\ I^-(aq) \rightarrow I_2(aq) + 2\ e^-$$

$$2\ H_2O(\ell) \rightarrow O_2(g) + 4\ H^+(aq) + 4\ e^-$$

In the electrolysis of aqueous NaI, experiment shows that $H_2(g)$ and $OH^-(aq)$ are formed by water reduction at the cathode, and iodine is formed at the anode (Figure 20.19). Thus, the overall cell process can be summarized by the following equations:

Cathode (−), reduction:	$2\ H_2O(\ell) + 2\ e^- \rightarrow H_2(g) + 2\ OH^-(aq)$
Anode (+), oxidation:	$2\ I^-(aq) \rightarrow I_2(aq) + 2\ e^-$
Net ionic equation:	$2\ H_2O(\ell) + 2\ I^-(aq) \rightarrow H_2(g) + 2\ OH^-(aq) + I_2(aq)$

where E°_{cell} has a negative value.

$$E^\circ_{cell} = E^\circ_{cathode} - E^\circ_{anode} = (-0.8277\ V) - (+0.621\ V) = -1.449\ V$$

This process is not spontaneous under standard conditions, and a potential of *at least* 1.45 V must be *applied* to the cell for these reactions to occur. If the process had involved the oxidation of water instead of iodide ion at the anode, the required potential would be −2.057 V [$E^\circ_{cathode} - E^\circ_{anode} = (-0.8277\ V) - (+1.229\ V)$], and if the reaction involving the reduction of Na^+ and the oxidation of I^- had occurred, the

FIGURE 20.19 Electrolysis of aqueous NaI. A solution of NaI(aq) is electrolyzed, a potential applied using an external source of electricity. A drop of phenolphthalein has been added to the solution in this experiment so that the formation of $OH^-(aq)$ can be detected (by the red color of the indicator in basic solution). Iodine forms at the anode, and H_2 and OH^- form at the cathode.

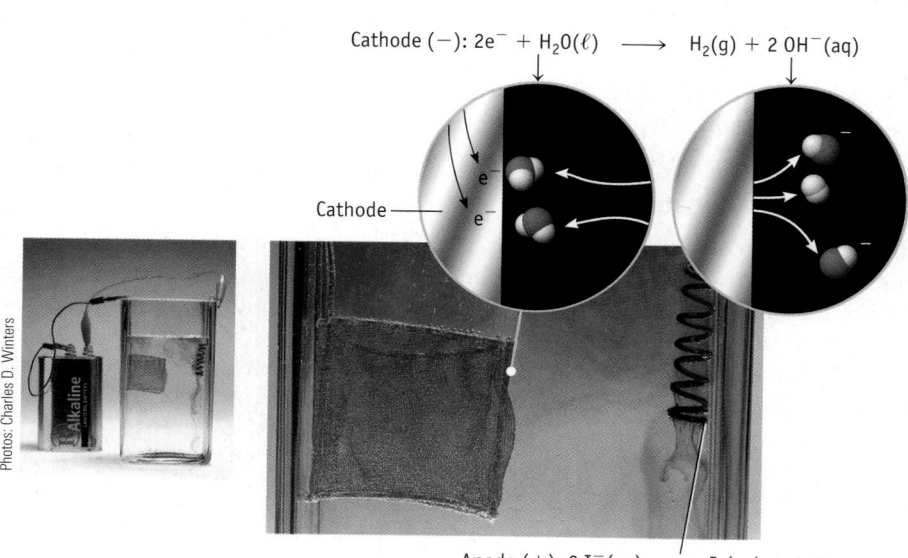

Cathode (−): $2e^- + H_2O(\ell) \longrightarrow H_2(g) + 2\ OH^-(aq)$

Cathode

Anode (+): $2\ I^-(aq) \longrightarrow I_2(aq) + 2e^-$

Photos: Charles D. Winters

required potential would be -3.335 V [$E°_{cathode} - E°_{anode} = (-2.714 V) - (+0.621 V)$]. The reaction occurring is the one requiring the smaller applied potential, so the net cell reaction in the electrolysis of NaI(aq) is the oxidation of iodide and reduction of water.

What happens if an aqueous solution of some other metal halide such as $SnCl_2$ is electrolyzed? As before, consult Appendix M, and consider all possible half-reactions. In this case, aqueous Sn^{2+} ion is much more easily reduced ($E° = -0.14$ V) than water ($E° = -0.83$ V) at the cathode, so tin metal is produced. At the anode, two oxidations are possible: Cl^-(aq) to Cl_2(g) or H_2O to O_2(g). Experiments show that chloride ion is generally oxidized in preference to water, so the reactions occurring on electrolysis of aqueous tin(II) chloride are (Figure 20.20)

■ **Overvoltage** Voltages higher than the minimum are typically used to speed up reactions that would otherwise be slow. The term overvoltage is often used when describing experiments; this refers to the voltage needed to make a reaction occur at a reasonable rate.

Cathode (−), reduction:	$Sn^{2+}(aq) + 2\ e^- \rightarrow Sn(s)$
Anode (+), oxidation:	$2\ Cl^-(aq) \rightarrow Cl_2(g) + 2\ e^-$
Net ionic equation:	$Sn^{2+}(aq) + 2\ Cl^-(aq) \rightarrow Sn(s) + Cl_2(g)$

$$E°_{cell} = E°_{cathode} - E°_{anode} = (-0.14\ V) - (+1.36\ V) = -1.50\ V$$

Formation of Cl_2 at the anode in the electrolysis of $SnCl_2$(aq) is contrary to a prediction based on $E°$ values. If the electrode reactions were

Cathode (−), reduction:	$Sn^{2+}(aq) + 2\ e^- \rightarrow Sn(s)$
Anode (+), oxidation:	$2\ H_2O(\ell) \rightarrow O_2(g) + 4\ H^+(aq) + 4\ e^-$

$$E°_{cell} = (-0.14\ V) - (+1.23\ V) = -1.37\ V$$

a smaller applied potential would seemingly be required. To explain the formation of chlorine instead of oxygen, we must take into account rates of reaction. This problem occurs in the commercially important electrolysis of aqueous NaCl, where a voltage high enough to oxidize both Cl^- and H_2O is used. However, because chloride ion is oxidized much faster than H_2O, the result is that Cl_2 is the major product in this electrolysis.

Another instance in which rates are important concerns electrode materials. Graphite, commonly used to make inert electrodes, can be oxidized. For the half-reaction $CO_2(g) + 4\ H^+(aq) + 4\ e^- \rightarrow C(s) + 2\ H_2O(\ell)$, $E°$ is $+0.20$ V, indicating that carbon is slightly easier to oxidize than copper ($E° = +0.34$ V). Based on this value, oxidation of a graphite electrode might reasonably be expected to occur during an electrolysis. And indeed it does, albeit slowly; graphite electrodes used in electrolysis cells slowly deteriorate and eventually have to be replaced.

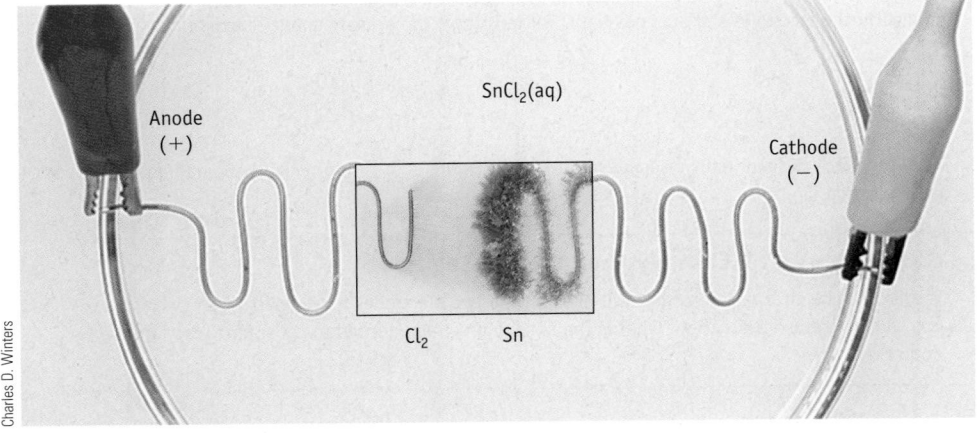

FIGURE 20.20 Electrolysis of aqueous tin(II) chloride. Tin metal collects at the negative cathode. Chlorine gas is formed at the positive anode. Elemental chlorine is formed in the cell, in spite of the fact that the potential for the oxidation of Cl^- is more negative than that for oxidation of water. (That is, chlorine should be less readily oxidized than water.) This is the result of chemical kinetics and illustrates the complexity of some aqueous electrochemistry.

Charles D. Winters

One other factor—the concentration of electroactive species in solution—must be taken into account when discussing electrolyses. As shown in Section 20.6, the potential at which a species in solution is oxidized or reduced depends on concentration. Unless standard conditions are used, predictions based on $E°$ values are merely qualitative. In addition, the rate of a half-reaction depends on the concentration of the electroactive substance at the electrode surface. At a very low concentration, the rate of the redox reaction may depend on the rate at which an ion diffuses from the solution to the electrode surface.

Chemistry‿⚛‿Now™

Sign in at **www.cengage.com/login** and go to Chapter 20 Contents to see Screen 20.11 for an illustration of **water electrolysis.**

■ **EXAMPLE 20.10 Electrolysis of Aqueous Solutions**

Problem Predict how products of electrolyses of aqueous solutions of NaF, NaCl, NaBr, and NaI are likely to be different. (The electrolysis of NaI is illustrated in Figure 20.19.)

Strategy The main criterion used to predict the chemistry in an electrolytic cell should be the ease of oxidation and reduction, an assessment based on $E°$ values.

Solution The cathode reaction in all four examples presents no problem—water is reduced to hydroxide ion and H_2 gas in preference to reduction of $Na^+(aq)$ (as in the electrolysis of aqueous NaI). Thus, the primary cathode reaction in all cases is

$$2 H_2O(\ell) + 2 e^- \rightarrow H_2(g) + 2 OH^-(aq)$$

$$E°_{cathode} = -0.83 \text{ V}$$

At the anode, we need to assess the ease of oxidation of the halide ions relative to water. Based on $E°$ values, the ease of oxidation of halide ions is $I^-(aq) > Br^-(aq) > Cl^-(aq) \gg F^-(aq)$. Fluoride ion is much more difficult to oxidize than water, and electrolysis of an aqueous solution containing this ion results exclusively in O_2 formation. The primary anode reaction for NaF(aq) is

$$2 H_2O(\ell) \rightarrow O_2(g) + 4 H^+(aq) + 4 e^-$$

Therefore, in this case,

$$E°_{cell} = (-0.83 \text{ V}) - (+1.23 \text{ V}) = -2.06 \text{ V}$$

Recall that chlorine is the primary product at the anode in the electrolysis of aqueous solutions of chloride salts. Therefore, the anode reaction is

$$2 Cl^-(aq) \rightarrow Cl_2(g) + 2 e^-$$

$$E°_{cell} = (-0.83 \text{ V}) - (+1.36 \text{ V}) = -2.19 \text{ V}$$

Bromide ions are considerably easier to oxidize than chloride ions. Br_2 may be expected as the primary product in the electrolysis of aqueous NaBr. For NaBr(aq), the primary anode reaction is

$$2 Br^-(aq) \rightarrow Br_2(\ell) + 2 e^-$$

so $E°_{cell}$ is

$$E°_{cell} = (-0.83 \text{ V}) - (+1.08 \text{ V}) = -1.91 \text{ V}$$

Thus, the electrolysis of NaBr resembles that of NaI (Figure 20.19) in producing the halogen, hydrogen, and hydroxide ion.

EXERCISE 20.14 Electrolysis of Aqueous Solutions

Predict the chemical reactions that will occur at the two electrodes in the electrolysis of an aqueous sodium hydroxide solution. What is the minimum voltage needed to cause this reaction to occur?

20.8 Counting Electrons

Metallic silver is produced at the cathode in the electrolysis of aqueous $AgNO_3$ in which one mole of electrons is required to produce one mole of silver. In contrast, two moles of electrons are required to produce one mole of tin (Figure 20.20):

$$Sn^{2+}(aq) + 2\ e^- \rightarrow Sn(s)$$

It follows that if the number of moles of electrons flowing through the electrolysis cell could be measured, the number of moles of silver or tin produced could be calculated. Conversely, if the amount of silver or tin produced is known, then the number of moles of electrons moving through the circuit could be calculated.

The number of moles of electrons consumed or produced in an electron transfer reaction is obtained by measuring the current flowing in the external electric circuit in a given time. The **current** flowing in an electrical circuit is the amount of charge (in units of coulombs, C) per unit time, and the usual unit for current is the ampere (A). (One ampere equals the passage of one coulomb of charge per second.)

$$\text{Current (amperes, A)} = \frac{\text{electric charge (coulombs, C)}}{\text{time, } t \text{ (seconds, s)}} \qquad \textbf{(20.8)}$$

The current passing through an electrochemical cell and the time for which the current flows are easily measured quantities. Therefore, the charge (in coulombs) that passes through a cell can be obtained by multiplying the current (in amperes) by the time (in seconds). Knowing the charge and using the Faraday constant as a conversion factor, we can calculate the number of moles of electrons that passed through an electrochemical cell. In turn, we can use this quantity to calculate the quantities of reactants and products. The following example illustrates this type of calculation.

Chemistry .Ö. Now™

Sign in at **www.cengage.com/login** and go to Chapter 20 Contents to see Screen 20.12 for a tutorial on **quantitative aspects of electrochemistry.**

Historical Perspectives — Electrochemistry and Michael Faraday

The terms anion, cation, electrode, and electrolyte originated with Michael Faraday (1791–1867), one of the most influential people in the history of chemistry. Faraday was apprenticed to a bookbinder in London when he was 13. This situation suited him perfectly, as he enjoyed reading the books sent to the shop for binding. By chance, one of these volumes was a small book on chemistry, which whetted his appetite for science, and he began performing experiments on electricity. In 1812, a patron of the shop invited Faraday to accompany him to the Royal Institute to attend a lecture by one of the most famous chemists of the day, Sir Humphry Davy. Faraday was so intrigued by Davy's lecture that he wrote to ask Davy for a position as an assistant. He was accepted and began work in 1813. Faraday was so talented that his work proved extraordinarily fruitful, and he was made the director of the laboratory of the Royal Institute about 12 years later.

It has been said that Faraday's contributions were so enormous that, had there been Nobel Prizes when he was alive, he would have received at least six. These prizes could have been awarded for discoveries such as the following:

- Electromagnetic induction, which led to the first transformer and electric motor
- The laws of electrolysis (the effect of electric current on chemicals)
- The magnetic properties of matter
- Benzene and other organic chemicals (which led to important chemical industries)
- The "Faraday effect" (the rotation of the plane of polarized light by a magnetic field)
- The introduction of the concept of electric and magnetic fields

In addition to making discoveries that had profound effects on science, Faraday was an educator. He wrote and spoke about his work in memorable ways, especially in lectures to the general public that helped to popularize science.

Michael Faraday (1791–1867)

Oesper Collection in the History of Chemistry, University of Cincinnati

Problem A current of 2.40 A is passed through a solution containing Cu^{2+}(aq) for 30.0 minutes, with copper metal being deposited at the cathode. What mass of copper, in grams, is deposited?

Strategy A roadmap for this calculation is as follows:

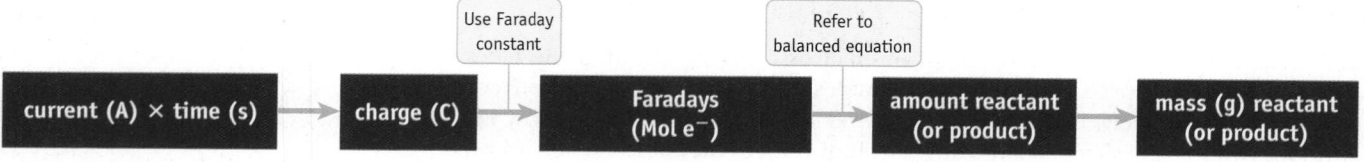

Solution

1. Calculate the charge (number of coulombs) passing through the cell in 30.0 min.

$$\text{Charge (C)} = \text{current (A)} \times \text{time (s)}$$
$$= (2.40 \text{ A})(30.0 \text{ min})(60.0 \text{ s/min})$$
$$= 4.32 \times 10^3 \text{ C}$$

2. Calculate the number of moles of electrons (i.e., the number of Faradays of electricity).

$$(4.32 \times 10^3 \text{ C})\left(\frac{1 \text{ mol } e^-}{96,485 \text{ C}}\right) = 4.48 \times 10^{-2} \text{ mol } e^-$$

3. Calculate the amount of copper and, from this, the mass of copper.

$$\text{mass of copper} = (4.48 \times 10^{-2} \text{ mol } e^-)\left(\frac{1 \text{ mol Cu}}{2 \text{ mol } e^-}\right)\left(\frac{63.55 \text{ g Cu}}{1 \text{ mol Cu}}\right) = \boxed{1.42 \text{ g}}$$

Comment The key relation in this calculation is current = charge/time. Most situations will involve knowing two of these three quantities from experiment and calculating the third.

■ **Faraday Constant** The Faraday constant is the charge carried by 1 mol of electrons:

$$9.6485338 \times 10^4 \text{ C/mol } e^-$$

EXERCISE 20.15 **Using the Faraday Constant**

Calculate the mass of O_2 produced in the electrolysis of water, using a current of 0.445 A for a period of 45 minutes.

EXERCISE 20.16 **Using the Faraday Constant**

In the commercial production of sodium by electrolysis, the cell operates at 7.0 V and a current of 25×10^3 A. What mass of sodium can be produced in one hour?

Chapter Goals Revisited

Now that you have studied this chapter, you should ask whether you have met the chapter goals. In particular, you should be able to:

Balance equations for oxidation–reduction reactions in acidic or basic solutions using the half-reaction approach Study Question(s) assignable in OWL: 2, 4-6, 16; Go Chemistry Module 25.

Understand the principles underlying voltaic cells

a. In a voltaic cell, identify the half-reactions occurring at the anode and the cathode, the polarity of the electrodes, the direction of electron flow in the external circuit, and the direction of ion flow in the salt bridge (Section 20.2). Study Question(s) assignable in OWL: 8, 10, 16, 51.

b. Appreciate the chemistry and advantages and disadvantages of dry cells, alkaline batteries, lead storage batteries, and Ni-cad batteries (Section 20.3).

c. Understand how fuel cells work, and recognize the difference between batteries and fuel cells (Section 20.3).

Understand how to use electrochemical potentials

a. Understand the process by which standard reduction potentials are determined, and identify standard conditions as applied to electrochemistry (Section 20.4).

b. Describe the standard hydrogen electrode ($E° = 0.00$ V), and explain how it is used as the standard to determine the standard potentials of half-reactions (Section 20.4).

c. Know how to use standard reduction potentials to determine cell voltages for cells under standard conditions (Equation 20.1). Study Question(s) assignable in OWL: 14, 16, 18, 56, 57.

d. Know how to use a table of standard reduction potentials (Table 20.1 and Appendix M) to rank the strengths of oxidizing and reducing agents, to predict which substances can reduce or oxidize another species, and to predict whether redox reactions will be product-favored or reactant-favored (Sections 20.4 and 20.5). Study Question(s) assignable in OWL: 20, 22, 24, 55, 56, 82.

e. Use the Nernst equation (Equations 20.2 and 20.3) to calculate the cell potential under nonstandard conditions (Section 20.5). Study Question(s) assignable in OWL: 26, 28, 30, 36.

f. Explain how cell voltage relates to ion concentration, and explain how this allows the determination of pH (Section 20.5) and other ion concentrations.

g. Use the relationships between cell voltage ($E°_{cell}$) and free energy ($\Delta_r G°$) (Equations 20.5 and 20.6) and between $E°_{cell}$ and an equilibrium constant for the cell reaction (Equation 20.7) (Section 20.6 and Table 20.2). Study Question(s) assignable in OWL: 32, 34, 60, 61, 63, 78, 86, 88.

Explore electrolysis, the use of electrical energy to produce chemical change

a. Describe the chemical processes occurring in an electrolysis. Recognize the factors that determine which substances are oxidized and reduced at the electrodes (Section 20.7). Study Question(s) assignable in OWL: 40, 41.

b. Relate the amount of a substance oxidized or reduced to the amount of current and the time the current flows (Section 20.8). Study Question(s) assignable in OWL: 44, 46, 48, 64-66, 73, 81.

Chemistry.◯.Now™ Sign in at www.cengage.com/login to:

- Assess your understanding with Study Questions in OWL keyed to each goal in the Goals and Homework menu for this chapter
- For quick review, download Go Chemistry mini-lecture flashcard modules (or purchase them at **www.ichapters.com**)
- Check your readiness for an exam by taking the Pre-Test and exploring the modules recommended in your Personalized Study plan.

Access **How Do I Solve It?** tutorials on how to approach problem solving using concepts in this chapter.

For additional preparation for an examination on this chapter see the *Let's Review* section on pages 948–961.

KEY EQUATIONS

Equation 20.1 (page 917): Calculating a standard cell potential, $E°_{cell}$, from standard half-cell potentials.

$$E°_{cell} = E°_{cathode} - E°_{anode}$$

Equation 20.3 (page 925): Nernst equation (at 298 K).

$$E = E° - \frac{0.0257}{n} \ln Q$$

E is the cell potential under nonstandard conditions; n is the number of electrons transferred from the reducing agent to the oxidizing agent (according to the balanced equation); and Q is the reaction quotient.

Equation 20.6 (page 929): Relationship between standard free energy change and the standard cell potential.

$$\Delta G° = -nFE°$$

F is the Faraday constant, 96,485 C/mol e^-.

Equation 20.7 (page 929): Relationship between the equilibrium constant and the standard cell potential for a reaction (at 298 K).

$$\ln K = \frac{nE°}{0.0257}$$

Equation 20.8 (page 937): Relationship between current, electric charge, and time.

$$\text{Current (amperes, A)} = \frac{\text{electric charge (coulombs, C)}}{\text{time, } t \text{ (seconds, s)}}$$

STUDY QUESTIONS

OWL Online homework for this chapter may be assigned in OWL.

▲ denotes challenging questions.

■ denotes questions assignable in OWL.

Blue-numbered questions have answers in Appendix O and fully-worked solutions in the *Student Solutions Manual*.

Practicing Skills

Balancing Equations for Oxidation–Reduction Reactions
(See Examples 20.1–20.3 and ChemistryNow Screen 20.3.)

When balancing the following redox equations, it may be necessary to add H^+(aq) or H^+(aq) plus H_2O for reactions in acid, and OH^-(aq) or OH^-(aq) plus H_2O for reactions in base.

1. Write balanced equations for the following half-reactions. Specify whether each is an oxidation or reduction.
   (a) $Cr(s) \rightarrow Cr^{3+}(aq)$ (in acid)
   (b) $AsH_3(g) \rightarrow As(s)$ (in acid)
   (c) $VO_3^-(aq) \rightarrow V^{2+}(aq)$ (in acid)
   (d) $Ag(s) \rightarrow Ag_2O(s)$ (in base)

2. ■ Write balanced equations for the following half-reactions. Specify whether each is an oxidation or reduction.
   (a) $H_2O_2(aq) \rightarrow O_2(g)$ (in acid)
   (b) $H_2C_2O_4(aq) \rightarrow CO_2(g)$ (in acid)
   (c) $NO_3^-(aq) \rightarrow NO(g)$ (in acid)
   (d) $MnO_4^-(aq) \rightarrow MnO_2(s)$ (in base)

3. Balance the following redox equations. All occur in acid solution.
   (a) $Ag(s) + NO_3^-(aq) \rightarrow NO_2(g) + Ag^+(aq)$
   (b) $MnO_4^-(aq) + HSO_3^-(aq) \rightarrow$
   $$Mn^{2+}(aq) + SO_4^{2-}(aq)$$
   (c) $Zn(s) + NO_3^-(aq) \rightarrow Zn^{2+}(aq) + N_2O(g)$
   (d) $Cr(s) + NO_3^-(aq) \rightarrow Cr^{3+}(aq) + NO(g)$

4. ■ Balance the following redox equations. All occur in acid solution.
   (a) $Sn(s) + H^+(aq) \rightarrow Sn^{2+}(aq) + H_2(g)$
   (b) $Cr_2O_7^{2-}(aq) + Fe^{2+}(aq) \rightarrow Cr^{3+}(aq) + Fe^{3+}(aq)$
   (c) $MnO_2(s) + Cl^-(aq) \rightarrow Mn^{2+}(aq) + Cl_2(g)$
   (d) $CH_2O(aq) + Ag^+(aq) \rightarrow HCO_2H(aq) + Ag(s)$

5. ■ Balance the following redox equations. All occur in basic solution.
   (a) $Al(s) + H_2O(\ell) \rightarrow Al(OH)_4^-(aq) + H_2(g)$
   (b) $CrO_4^{2-}(aq) + SO_3^{2-}(aq) \rightarrow Cr(OH)_3(s) + SO_4^{2-}(aq)$
   (c) $Zn(s) + Cu(OH)_2(s) \rightarrow [Zn(OH)_4]^{2-}(aq) + Cu(s)$
   (d) $HS^-(aq) + ClO_3^-(aq) \rightarrow S(s) + Cl^-(aq)$

6. ■ Balance the following redox equations. All occur in basic solution.
   (a) $Fe(OH)_3(s) + Cr(s) \rightarrow Cr(OH)_3(s) + Fe(OH)_2(s)$
   (b) $NiO_2(s) + Zn(s) \rightarrow Ni(OH)_2(s) + Zn(OH)_2(s)$
   (c) $Fe(OH)_2(s) + CrO_4^{2-}(aq) \rightarrow$
   $$Fe(OH)_3(s) + [Cr(OH)_4]^-(aq)$$
   (d) $N_2H_4(aq) + Ag_2O(s) \rightarrow N_2(g) + Ag(s)$

Constructing Voltaic Cells
(See Example 20.4 and ChemistryNow Screen 20.4.)

7. A voltaic cell is constructed using the reaction of chromium metal and iron(II) ion.
   $$2\ Cr(s) + 3\ Fe^{2+}(aq) \rightarrow 2\ Cr^{3+}(aq) + 3\ Fe(s)$$
   Complete the following sentences: Electrons in the external circuit flow from the ___ electrode to the ___ electrode. Negative ions move in the salt bridge from the ___ half-cell to the ___ half-cell. The half-reaction at the anode is ___, and that at the cathode is ___.

8. ■ A voltaic cell is constructed using the reaction
   $$Mg(s) + 2\ H^+(aq) \rightarrow Mg^{2+}(aq) + H_2(g)$$
   (a) Write equations for the oxidation and reduction half-reactions.
   (b) Which half-reaction occurs in the anode compartment, and which occurs in the cathode compartment?
   (c) Complete the following sentences: Electrons in the external circuit flow from the ___ electrode to the ___ electrode. Negative ions move in the salt bridge from the ___ half-cell to the ___ half-cell. The half-reaction at the anode is ___, and that at the cathode is ___.

9. The half-cells $Fe^{2+}(aq)\ |\ Fe(s)$ and $O_2(g)\ |\ H_2O$ (in acid solution) are linked to create a voltaic cell.
   (a) Write equations for the oxidation and reduction half-reactions and for the overall (cell) reaction.
   (b) Which half-reaction occurs in the anode compartment, and which occurs in the cathode compartment?
   (c) Complete the following sentences: Electrons in the external circuit flow from the ___ electrode to the ___ electrode. Negative ions move in the salt bridge from the ___ half-cell to the ___ half-cell.

10. ■ The half-cells $Sn^2(aq)\ |\ Sn(s)$ and $Cl_2(g)\ |\ Cl^-(aq)$ are linked to create a voltaic cell.
    (a) Write equations for the oxidation and reduction half-reactions and for the overall (cell) reaction.
    (b) Which half-reaction occurs in the anode compartment, and which occurs in the cathode compartment?

(c) Complete the following sentences: Electrons in the external circuit flow from the ___ electrode to the ___ electrode. Negative ions move in the salt bridge from the ___ half-cell to the ___ half-cell.

Commercial Cells

11. What are the similarities and differences between dry cells, alkaline batteries, and Ni-cad batteries?

12. What reactions occur when a lead storage battery is re-charged?

Standard Electrochemical Potentials
(See Example 20.5 and ChemistryNow Screens 20.6 and 20.7.)

13. Calculate the value of $E°$ for each of the following reactions. Decide whether each is product-favored in the direction written.
    (a) $2\ I^-(aq) + Zn^{2+}(aq) \rightarrow I_2(s) + Zn(s)$
    (b) $Zn^{2+}(aq) + Ni(s) \rightarrow Zn(s) + Ni^{2+}(aq)$
    (c) $2\ Cl^-(aq) + Cu^{2+}(aq) \rightarrow Cu(s) + Cl_2(g)$
    (d) $Fe^{2+}(aq) + Ag^+(aq) \rightarrow Fe^{3+}(aq) + Ag(s)$

14. ■ Calculate the value of $E°$ for each of the following reactions. Decide whether each is product-favored in the direction written. [Reaction (d) occurs in basic solution.]
    (a) $Br_2(\ell) + Mg(s) \rightarrow Mg^{2+}(aq) + 2\ Br^-(aq)$
    (b) $Zn^{2+}(aq) + Mg(s) \rightarrow Zn(s) + Mg^{2+}(aq)$
    (c) $Sn^{2+}(aq) + 2\ Ag^+(aq) \rightarrow Sn^{4+}(aq) + 2\ Ag(s)$
    (d) $2\ Zn(s) + O_2(g) + 2\ H_2O(\ell) + 4\ OH^-(aq) \rightarrow$
    $$2\ [Zn(OH)_4]^{2-}(aq)$$

15. Balance each of the following unbalanced equations; then calculate the standard potential, $E°$, and decide whether each is product-favored as written. (All reactions occur in acid solution.)
    (a) $Sn^{2+}(aq) + Ag(s) \rightarrow Sn(s) + Ag^+(aq)$
    (b) $Al(s) + Sn^{4+}(aq) \rightarrow Sn^{2+}(aq) + Al^{3+}(aq)$
    (c) $ClO_3^-(aq) + Ce^{3+}(aq) \rightarrow Cl_2(g) + Ce^{4+}(aq)$
    (d) $Cu(s) + NO_3^-(aq) \rightarrow Cu^{2+}(aq) + NO(g)$

16. ■ Balance each of the following unbalanced equations; then calculate the standard potential, $E°$, and decide whether each is product-favored as written. (All reactions occur in acid solution.)
    (a) $I_2(s) + Br^-(aq) \rightarrow I^-(aq) + Br_2(\ell)$
    (b) $Fe^{2+}(aq) + Cu^{2+}(aq) \rightarrow Cu(s) + Fe^{3+}(aq)$
    (c) $Fe^{2+}(aq) + Cr_2O_7^{2-}(aq) \rightarrow Fe^{3+}(aq) + Cr^{3+}(aq)$
    (d) $MnO_4^-(aq) + HNO_2(aq) \rightarrow Mn^{2+}(aq) + NO_3^-(aq)$

17. Consider the following half-reactions:

Half-Reaction	$E°$ (V)
$Cu^{2+}(aq) + 2\,e^- \rightarrow Cu(s)$	+0.34
$Sn^{2+}(aq) + 2\,e^- \rightarrow Sn(s)$	−0.14
$Fe^{2+}(aq) + 2\,e^- \rightarrow Fe(s)$	−0.44
$Zn^{2+}(aq) + 2\,e^- \rightarrow Zn(s)$	−0.76
$Al^{3+}(aq) + 3\,e^- \rightarrow Al(s)$	−1.66

(a) Based on $E°$ values, which metal is the most easily oxidized?

(b) Which metals on this list are capable of reducing $Fe^{2+}(aq)$ to $Fe(s)$?

(c) Write a balanced chemical equation for the reaction of $Fe^{2+}(aq)$ with $Sn(s)$. Is this reaction product-favored or reactant-favored?

(d) Write a balanced chemical equation for the reaction of $Zn^{2+}(aq)$ with $Sn(s)$. Is this reaction product-favored or reactant-favored?

18. ■ Consider the following half-reactions:

Half-Reaction	$E°$ (V)
$MnO_4^-(aq) + 8\,H^+(aq) + 5\,e^- \rightarrow Mn^{2+}(aq) + 4\,H_2O(\ell)$	+1.51
$BrO_3^-(aq) + 6\,H^+(aq) + 6\,e^- \rightarrow Br^-(aq) + 3\,H_2O(\ell)$	+1.47
$Cr_2O_7^{2-}(aq) + 14\,H^+(aq) + 6\,e^- \rightarrow 2\,Cr^{3+}(aq) + 7\,H_2O(\ell)$	+1.33
$NO_3^-(aq) + 4\,H^+(aq) + 3\,e^- \rightarrow NO(g) + 2\,H_2O(\ell)$	+0.96
$SO_4^{2-}(aq) + 4\,H^+(aq) + 2\,e^- \rightarrow SO_2(g) + 2\,H_2O(\ell)$	+0.20

(a) Choosing from among the reactants in these half-reactions, identify the strongest and weakest oxidizing agents.

(b) Which of the oxidizing agents listed is (are) capable of oxidizing $Br^-(aq)$ to $BrO_3^-(aq)$ (in acid solution)?

(c) Write a balanced chemical equation for the reaction of $Cr_2O_7^{2-}(aq)$ with $SO_2(g)$ in acid solution. Is this reaction product-favored or reactant-favored?

(d) Write a balanced chemical equation for the reaction of $Cr_2O_7^{2-}(aq)$ with $Mn^{2+}(aq)$. Is this reaction product-favored or reactant-favored?

Ranking Oxidizing and Reducing Agents

(See Example 20.5 and ChemistryNow Screen 20.7.) Use a table of standard reduction potentials (Table 20.1 or Appendix M) to answer Study Questions 19–24.

19. Which of the following elements is the best reducing agent under standard conditions?
(a) Cu   (d) Ag
(b) Zn   (e) Cr
(c) Fe

20. ■ From the following list, identify those elements that are easier to oxidize than $H_2(g)$.
(a) Cu   (d) Ag
(b) Zn   (e) Cr
(c) Fe

21. Which of the following ions is most easily reduced?
(a) $Cu^{2+}(aq)$ (d) $Ag^+(aq)$
(b) $Zn^{2+}(aq)$ (e) $Al^{3+}(aq)$
(c) $Fe^{2+}(aq)$

22. ■ From the following list, identify the ions that are more easily reduced than $H^+(aq)$.
(a) $Cu^{2+}(aq)$ (d) $Ag^+(aq)$
(b) $Zn^{2+}(aq)$ (e) $Al^{3+}(aq)$
(c) $Fe^{2+}(aq)$

23. (a) Which halogen is most easily reduced: F_2, Cl_2, Br_2, or I_2 in acidic solution?
(b) Identify the halogens that are better oxidizing agents than $MnO_2(s)$ in acidic solution.

24. ■ (a) Which ion is most easily oxidized to the elemental halogen: F^-, Cl^-, Br^-, or I^- in acidic solution?
(b) Identify the halide ions that are more easily oxidized than $H_2O(\ell)$ in acidic solution.

Electrochemical Cells Under Nonstandard Conditions
(See Examples 20.6 and 20.7 and ChemistryNow Screen 20.8.)

25. Calculate the potential delivered by a voltaic cell using the following reaction if all dissolved species are 2.5×10^{-2} M and the pressure of H_2 is 1.0 bar.

$$Zn(s) + 2\,H_2O(\ell) + 2\,OH^-(aq) \rightarrow [Zn(OH)_4]^{2-}(aq) + H_2\,(g)$$

26. ■ Calculate the potential developed by a voltaic cell using the following reaction if all dissolved species are 0.015 M.

$$2\,Fe^{2+}(aq) + H_2O_2(aq) + 2\,H^+(aq) \rightarrow 2\,Fe^{3+}(aq) + 2\,H_2O(\ell)$$

27. One half-cell in a voltaic cell is constructed from a silver wire dipped into a 0.25 M solution of $AgNO_3$. The other half-cell consists of a zinc electrode in a 0.010 M solution of $Zn(NO_3)_2$. Calculate the cell potential.

28. ■ One half-cell in a voltaic cell is constructed from a copper wire dipped into a 4.8×10^{-3} M solution of $Cu(NO_3)_2$. The other half-cell consists of a zinc electrode in a 0.40 M solution of $Zn(NO_3)_2$. Calculate the cell potential.

29. One half-cell in a voltaic cell is constructed from a silver wire dipped into a $AgNO_3$ solution of unknown concentration. The other half-cell consists of a zinc electrode in a 1.0 M solution of $Zn(NO_3)_2$. A potential of 1.48 V is measured for this cell. Use this information to calculate the concentration of $Ag^+(aq)$.

30. ■ One half-cell in a voltaic cell is constructed from an iron wire dipped into an $Fe(NO_3)_2$ solution of unknown concentration. The other half-cell is a standard hydrogen electrode. A potential of 0.49 V is measured for this cell. Use this information to calculate the concentration of $Fe^{2+}(aq)$.

▲ more challenging   ■ in OWL   Blue-numbered questions answered in Appendix O

Electrochemistry, Thermodynamics, and Equilibrium
(See Examples 20.8 and 20.9 and ChemistryNow Screen 20.9.)

31. Calculate $\Delta_r G°$ and the equilibrium constant for the following reactions.
    (a) $2\ Fe^{3+}(aq) + 2\ I^-(aq) \rightleftharpoons 2\ Fe^{2+}(aq) + I_2(aq)$
    (b) $I_2(aq) + 2\ Br^-(aq) \rightleftharpoons 2\ I^-(aq) + Br_2(aq)$

32. ■ Calculate $\Delta_r G°$ and the equilibrium constant for the following reactions.
    (a) $Zn^{2+}(aq) + Ni(s) \rightleftharpoons Zn(s) + Ni^{2+}(aq)$
    (b) $Cu(s) + 2\ Ag^+(aq) \rightleftharpoons Cu^{2+}(aq) + 2\ Ag(s)$

33. Use standard reduction potentials (Appendix M) for the half-reactions $AgBr(s) + e^- \rightarrow Ag(s) + Br^-(aq)$ and $Ag^+(aq) + e^- \rightarrow Ag(s)$ to calculate the value of K_{sp} for AgBr.

34. ■ Use the standard reduction potentials (Appendix M) for the half-reactions $Hg_2Cl_2(s) + 2\ e^- \rightarrow 2\ Hg(\ell) + 2\ Cl^-(aq)$ and $Hg_2^{2+}(aq) + 2\ e^- \rightarrow 2\ Hg(\ell)$ to calculate the value of K_{sp} for Hg_2Cl_2.

35. Use the standard reduction potentials (Appendix M) for the half-reactions $[AuCl_4]^-(aq) + 3\ e^- \rightarrow Au(s) + 4\ Cl^-(aq)$ and $Au^{3+}(aq) + 3\ e^- \rightarrow Au(s)$ to calculate the value of $K_{formation}$ for the complex ion $[AuCl_4]^-(aq)$.

36. ■ Use the standard reduction potentials (Appendix M) for the half-reactions $[Zn(OH)_4]^{2-}(aq) + 2\ e^- \rightarrow Zn(s) + 4\ OH^-(aq)$ and $Zn^{2+}(aq) + 2\ e^- \rightarrow Zn(s)$ to calculate the value of $K_{formation}$ for the complex ion $[Zn(OH)_4]^{2-}$.

Electrolysis
(See Section 20.7, Example 20.10, and ChemistryNow Screen 20.10.)

37. Diagram the apparatus used to electrolyze molten NaCl. Identify the anode and the cathode. Trace the movement of electrons through the external circuit and the movement of ions in the electrolysis cell.

38. Diagram the apparatus used to electrolyze aqueous $CuCl_2$. Identify the reaction products, the anode, and the cathode. Trace the movement of electrons through the external circuit and the movement of ions in the electrolysis cell.

39. Which product, O_2 or F_2, is more likely to form at the anode in the electrolysis of an aqueous solution of KF? Explain your reasoning.

40. ■ Which product, Ca or H_2, is more likely to form at the cathode in the electrolysis of $CaCl_2$? Explain your reasoning.

41. ■ An aqueous solution of KBr is placed in a beaker with two inert platinum electrodes. When the cell is attached to an external source of electrical energy, electrolysis occurs.
    (a) Hydrogen gas and hydroxide ion form at the cathode. Write an equation for the half-reaction that occurs at this electrode.
    (b) Bromine is the primary product at the anode. Write an equation for its formation.

42. An aqueous solution of Na_2S is placed in a beaker with two inert platinum electrodes. When the cell is attached to an external battery, electrolysis occurs.
    (a) Hydrogen gas and hydroxide ion form at the cathode. Write an equation for the half-reaction that occurs at this electrode.
    (b) Sulfur is the primary product at the anode. Write an equation for its formation.

Counting Electrons
(See Example 20.11 and ChemistryNow Screen 20.12.)

43. In the electrolysis of a solution containing $Ni^{2+}(aq)$, metallic Ni(s) deposits on the cathode. Using a current of 0.150 A for 12.2 min, what mass of nickel will form?

44. ■ In the electrolysis of a solution containing $Ag^+(aq)$, metallic Ag(s) deposits on the cathode. Using a current of 1.12 A for 2.40 h, what mass of silver forms?

45. Electrolysis of a solution of $CuSO_4(aq)$ to give copper metal is carried out using a current of 0.66 A. How long should electrolysis continue to produce 0.50 g of copper?

46. ■ Electrolysis of a solution of $Zn(NO_3)_2(aq)$ to give zinc metal is carried out using a current of 2.12 A. How long should electrolysis continue in order to prepare 2.5 g of zinc?

47. A voltaic cell can be built using the reaction between Al metal and O_2 from the air. If the Al anode of this cell consists of 84 g of aluminum, how many hours can the cell produce 1.0 A of electricity, assuming an unlimited supply of O_2?

48. ■ Assume the specifications of a Ni-Cd voltaic cell include delivery of 0.25 A of current for 1.00 h. What is the minimum mass of the cadmium that must be used to make the anode in this cell?

General Questions
These questions are not designated as to type or location in the chapter. They may combine several concepts.

49. Write balanced equations for the following half-reactions.
    (a) $UO_2^+(aq) \rightarrow U^{4+}(aq)$ (acid solution)
    (b) $ClO_3^-(aq) \rightarrow Cl^-(aq)$ (acid solution)
    (c) $N_2H_4(aq) \rightarrow N_2(g)$ (basic solution)
    (d) $ClO^-(aq) \rightarrow Cl^-(aq)$ (basic solution)

50. Balance the following equations.
(a) $Zn(s) + VO^{2+}(aq) \rightarrow$
$$Zn^{2+}(aq) + V^{3+}(aq) \quad \text{(acid solution)}$$
(b) $Zn(s) + VO_3^-(aq) \rightarrow$
$$V^{2+}(aq) + Zn^{2+}(aq) \quad \text{(acid solution)}$$
(c) $Zn(s) + ClO^-(aq) \rightarrow$
$$Zn(OH)_2(s) + Cl^-(aq) \text{ (basic solution)}$$
(d) $ClO^-(aq) + [Cr(OH)_4]^-(aq) \rightarrow$
$$Cl^-(aq) + CrO_4^{2-}(aq) \text{ (basic solution)}$$

51. ■ Magnesium metal is oxidized, and silver ions are reduced in a voltaic cell using $Mg^{2+}(aq, 1\ M)\ |\ Mg$ and $Ag^+(aq, 1\ M)\ |\ Ag$ half-cells.

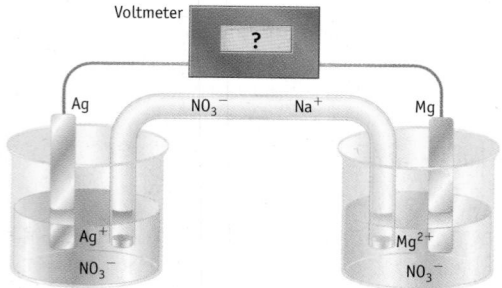

Voltmeter
?
Ag NO_3^- Na^+ Mg
Ag^+ Mg^{2+}
NO_3^- NO_3^-

(a) Label each part of the cell.
(b) Write equations for the half-reactions occurring at the anode and the cathode, and write an equation for the net reaction in the cell.
(c) Trace the movement of electrons in the external circuit. Assuming the salt bridge contains $NaNO_3$, trace the movement of the Na^+ and NO_3^- ions in the salt bridge that occurs when a voltaic cell produces current. Why is a salt bridge required in a cell?

52. You want to set up a series of voltaic cells with specific cell voltages. A $Zn^{2+}(aq, 1.0\ M)\ |\ Zn(s)$ half-cell is in one compartment. Identify several half-cells that you could use so that the cell potential will be close to (a) 1.1 V and (b) 0.50 V. Consider cells in which zinc can be either the cathode or the anode.

53. You want to set up a series of voltaic cells with specific cell potentials. The $Ag^+(aq, 1.0\ M)\ |\ Ag(s)$ half-cell is one of the compartments. Identify several half-cells that you could use so that the cell potential will be close to (a) 1.7 V and (b) 0.50 V. Consider cells in which silver can be either the cathode or the anode.

54. Which of the following reactions is (are) product-favored?
(a) $Zn(s) + I_2(s) \rightarrow Zn^{2+}(aq) + 2\ I^-(aq)$
(b) $2\ Cl^-(aq) + I_2(s) \rightarrow Cl_2(g) + 2\ I^-(aq)$
(c) $2\ Na^+(aq) + 2\ Cl^-(aq) \rightarrow 2\ Na(s) + Cl_2(g)$
(d) $2\ K(s) + H_2O(\ell) \rightarrow$
$$2\ K^+(aq) + H_2(g) + 2\ OH^-(aq)$$

55. ■ In the table of standard reduction potentials, locate the half-reactions for the reductions of the following metal ions to the metal: $Sn^{2+}(aq)$, $Au^+(aq)$, $Zn^{2+}(aq)$, $Co^{2+}(aq)$, $Ag^+(aq)$, $Cu^{2+}(aq)$. Among the metal ions and metals that make up these half-reactions:
(a) Which metal ion is the weakest oxidizing agent?
(b) Which metal ion is the strongest oxidizing agent?
(c) Which metal is the strongest reducing agent?
(d) Which metal is the weakest reducing agent?
(e) Will $Sn(s)$ reduce $Cu^{2+}(aq)$ to $Cu(s)$?
(f) Will $Ag(s)$ reduce $Co^{2+}(aq)$ to $Co(s)$?
(g) Which metal ions on the list can be reduced by $Sn(s)$?
(h) What metals can be oxidized by $Ag^+(aq)$?

56. ■ ▲ In the table of standard reduction potentials, locate the half-reactions for the reductions of the following nonmetals: F_2, Cl_2, Br_2, I_2 (reduction to halide ions), and O_2, S, Se (reduction to H_2X in aqueous acid). Among the elements, ions, and compounds that make up these half-reactions:
(a) Which element is the weakest oxidizing agent?
(b) Which element is the weakest reducing agent?
(c) Which of the elements listed is (are) capable of oxidizing H_2O to O_2?
(d) Which of these elements listed is (are) capable of oxidizing H_2S to S?
(e) Is O_2 capable of oxidizing I^- to I_2, in acid solution?
(f) Is S capable of oxidizing I^- to I_2?
(g) Is the reaction $H_2S(aq) + Se(s) \rightarrow H_2Se(aq) + S(s)$ product-favored?
(h) Is the reaction $H_2S(aq) + I_2(s) \rightarrow 2\ H^+(aq) + 2\ I^-(aq) + S(s)$ product-favored?

57. ■ Four voltaic cells are set up. In each, one half-cell contains a standard hydrogen electrode. The second half-cell is one of the following: $Cr^{3+}(aq, 1.0\ M)\ |\ Cr(s)$, $Fe^{2+}(aq, 1.0\ M)\ |\ Fe(s)$, $Cu^{2+}(aq, 1.0\ M)\ |\ Cu(s)$, or $Mg^{2+}(aq, 1.0\ M)\ |\ Mg(s)$.
(a) In which of the voltaic cells does the hydrogen electrode serve as the cathode?
(b) Which voltaic cell produces the highest voltage? Which produces the lowest voltage?

58. The following half-cells are available: $Ag^+(aq, 1.0\ M)\ |\ Ag(s)$, $Zn^{2+}(aq, 1.0\ M)\ |\ Zn(s)$, $Cu^{2+}(aq, 1.0\ M)\ |\ Cu(s)$, and $Co^{2+}(aq, 1.0\ M)\ |\ Co(s)$. Linking any two half-cells makes a voltaic cell. Given four different half-cells, six voltaic cells are possible. These are labeled, for simplicity, Ag-Zn, Ag-Cu, Ag-Co, Zn-Cu, Zn-Co, and Cu-Co.
(a) In which of the voltaic cells does the copper electrode serve as the cathode? In which of the voltaic cells does the cobalt electrode serve as the anode?
(b) Which combination of half-cells generates the highest potential? Which combination generates the lowest potential?

59. The reaction occurring in the cell in which Al_2O_3 and aluminum salts are electrolyzed is $Al^{3+}(aq) + 3\ e^- \rightarrow Al(s)$. If the electrolysis cell operates at 5.0 V and 1.0×10^5 A, what mass of aluminum metal can be produced in a 24-h day?

60. ■ ▲ A cell is constructed using the following half-reactions:

$Ag^+(aq) + e^- \rightarrow Ag(s)$

$Ag_2SO_4(s) + 2\ e^- \rightarrow$
$\qquad\qquad 2\ Ag(s) + SO_4^{2-}(aq) \quad E° = 0.653\ V$

(a) What reactions should be observed at the anode and cathode?
(b) Calculate the solubility product constant, K_{sp}, for Ag_2SO_4.

61. ■ ▲ A potential of 0.142 V is recorded (under standard conditions) for a voltaic cell constructed using the following half reactions:

Cathode: $\quad Pb^{2+}(aq) + 2\ e^- \rightarrow Pb(s)$

Anode: $\quad PbCl_2(s) + 2\ e^- \rightarrow Pb(s) + 2\ Cl^-(aq)$

Net: $\quad Pb^{2+}(aq) + 2\ Cl^-(aq) \rightarrow PbCl_2(s)$

(a) What is the standard reduction potential for the anode reaction?
(b) Estimate the solubility product, K_{sp}, for $PbCl_2$.

62. What is the value of $E°$ for the following half-reaction?

$$Ag_2CrO_4(s) + 2\ e^- \rightarrow 2\ Ag(s) + CrO_4^{2-}(aq)$$

63. ■ The standard voltage, $E°$, for the reaction of $Zn(s)$ and $Cl_2(g)$ is +2.12 V. What is the standard free energy change, $\Delta_r G°$, for the reaction?

64. ■ ▲ An electrolysis cell for aluminum production operates at 5.0 V and a current of 1.0×10^5 A. Calculate the number of kilowatt-hours of energy required to produce 1 metric ton (1.0×10^3 kg) of aluminum. (1 kWh = 3.6×10^6 J and 1 J = 1 C · V.)

65. ■ ▲ Electrolysis of molten NaCl is done in cells operating at 7.0 V and 4.0×10^4 A. What mass of $Na(s)$ and $Cl_2(g)$ can be produced in one day in such a cell? What is the energy consumption in kilowatt-hours? (1 kWh = 3.6×10^6 J and 1 J = 1 C · V.)

66. ■ ▲ A current of 0.0100 A is passed through a solution of rhodium sulfate, causing reduction of the metal ion to the metal. After 3.00 h, 0.038 g of Rh has been deposited. What is the charge on the rhodium ion, Rh^{n+}? What is the formula for rhodium sulfate?

67. ▲ A current of 0.44 A is passed through a solution of ruthenium nitrate causing reduction of the metal ion to the metal. After 25.0 min, 0.345 g of Ru has been deposited. What is the charge on the ruthenium ion, Ru^{n+}? What is the formula for ruthenium nitrate?

68. The total charge that can be delivered by a large dry cell battery before its voltage drops too low is usually about 35 amp-hours. (One amp-hour is the charge that passes through a circuit when 1 A flows for 1 h.) What mass of Zn is consumed when 35 amp-hours are drawn from the cell?

69. Chlorine gas is obtained commercially by electrolysis of brine (a concentrated aqueous solution of NaCl). If the electrolysis cells operate at 4.6 V and 3.0×10^5 A, what mass of chlorine can be produced in a 24-h day?

70. ▲ Write balanced equations for the following reduction half-reactions involving organic compounds.
(a) $HCO_2H \rightarrow CH_2O$ (acid solution)
(b) $C_6H_5CO_2H \rightarrow C_6H_5CH_3$ (acid solution)
(c) $CH_3CH_2CHO \rightarrow CH_3CH_2CH_2OH$ (acid solution)
(d) $CH_3OH \rightarrow CH_4$ (acid solution)

71. ▲ Balance the following equations involving organic compounds.
(a) $Ag^+(aq) + C_6H_5CHO(aq) \rightarrow$
$\qquad\qquad Ag(s) + C_6H_5CO_2H(aq)$ (acid solution)
(b) $CH_3CH_2OH + Cr_2O_7^{2-}(aq) \rightarrow$
$\qquad\qquad CH_3CO_2H(aq) + Cr^{3+}(aq)$ (acid solution)

72. A voltaic cell is constructed in which one half-cell consists of a silver wire in an aqueous solution of $AgNO_3$. The other half-cell consists of an inert platinum wire in an aqueous solution containing $Fe^{2+}(aq)$ and $Fe^{3+}(aq)$.
(a) Calculate the cell potential, assuming standard conditions.
(b) Write the net ionic equation for the reaction occurring in the cell.
(c) In this voltaic cell, which electrode is the anode, and which is the cathode?
(d) If $[Ag^+]$ is 0.10 M, and $[Fe^{2+}]$ and $[Fe^{3+}]$ are both 1.0 M, what is the cell potential? Is the net cell reaction still that used in part (a)? If not, what is the net reaction under the new conditions?

73. ■ An expensive but lighter alternative to the lead storage battery is the silver-zinc battery.

$$Ag_2O(s) + Zn(s) + H_2O(\ell) \rightarrow Zn(OH)_2(s) + 2\ Ag(s)$$

The electrolyte is 40% KOH, and silver–silver oxide electrodes are separated from zinc–zinc hydroxide electrodes by a plastic sheet that is permeable to hydroxide ions. Under normal operating conditions, the battery has a potential of 1.59 V.
(a) How much energy can be produced per gram of reactants in the silver-zinc battery? Assume the battery produces a current of 0.10 A.
(b) How much energy can be produced per gram of reactants in the standard lead storage battery? Assume the battery produces a current of 0.10 A at 2.0 V.
(c) Which battery (silver-zinc or lead storage) produces the greater energy per gram of reactants?

74. The specifications for a lead storage battery include delivery of a steady 1.5 A of current for 15 h.
  (a) What is the minimum mass of lead that will be used in the anode?
  (b) What mass of PbO_2 must be used in the cathode?
  (c) Assume that the volume of the battery is 0.50 L. What is the minimum molarity of H_2SO_4 necessary?

75. Manganese may play an important role in chemical cycles in the oceans (page 932). Two reactions involving manganese are the reduction of nitrate ions (to NO) with Mn^{2+} ions and the oxidation of ammonia (to N_2) with MnO_2.
  (a) Write balanced chemical equations for these reactions (in acid solution).
  (b) Calculate $E°_{cell}$ for the reactions. (One half-reaction potential you need is for reduction of N_2 to NH_4^+, $E° = -0.272$ V.)

76. ▲ You want to use electrolysis to plate a cylindrical object (radius = 2.50 and length = 20.00 cm) with a coating of nickel metal, 4.0 mm thick. You place the object in a bath containing a salt (Na_2SO_4). One electrode is impure nickel, and the other is the object to be plated. The electrolyzing potential is 2.50 V.
  (a) Which is the anode, and which is the cathode in the experiment? What half-reaction occurs at each electrode?
  (b) Calculate the number of kilowatt-hours (kWh) of energy required to carry out the electrolysis. (1 kWh = 3.6×10^6 J and 1 J = 1 C × 1 V).

77. ▲ Iron(II) ion undergoes a disproportionation reaction to give Fe(s) and the iron(III) ion. That is, iron(II) ion is both oxidized and reduced within the same reaction.

$$3\ Fe^{2+}(aq) \rightarrow Fe(s) + 2\ Fe^{3+}(aq)$$

  (a) What two half-reactions make up the disproportionation reaction?
  (b) Use the values of the standard reduction potentials for the two half-reactions in part (a) to determine whether this disproportionation reaction is product-favored.
  (c) What is the equilibrium constant for this reaction?

78. ■ ▲ Copper(I) ion disproportionates to copper metal and copper(II) ion. (See Study Question 77.)

$$2\ Cu^+(aq) \rightarrow Cu(s) + Cu^{2+}(aq)$$

  (a) What two half-reactions make up the disproportionation reaction?
  (b) Use values of the standard reduction potentials for the two half-reactions in part (a) to determine whether this disproportionation reaction is spontaneous.
  (c) What is the equilibrium constant for this reaction? If you have a solution that initially contains 0.10 mol of Cu^+ in 1.0 L of water, what are the concentrations of Cu^+ and Cu^{2+} at equilibrium?

In the Laboratory

79. Consider an electrochemical cell based on the half-reactions $Ni^{2+}(aq) + 2\ e^- \rightarrow Ni(s)$ and $Cd^{2+}(aq) + 2\ e^- \rightarrow Cd(s)$.
  (a) Diagram the cell, and label each of the components (including the anode, cathode, and salt bridge).
  (b) Use the equations for the half-reactions to write a balanced, net ionic equation for the overall cell reaction.
  (c) What is the polarity of each electrode?
  (d) What is the value of $E°_{cell}$?
  (e) In which direction do electrons flow in the external circuit?
  (f) Assume that a salt bridge containing $NaNO_3$ connects the two half-cells. In which direction do the $Na^+(aq)$ ions move? In which direction do the $NO_3^-(aq)$ ions move?
  (g) Calculate the equilibrium constant for the reaction.
  (h) If the concentration of Cd^{2+} is reduced to 0.010 M and $[Ni^{2+}] = 1.0$ M, what is the value of E_{cell}? Is the net reaction still the reaction given in part (b)?
  (i) If 0.050 A is drawn from the battery, how long can it last if you begin with 1.0 L of each of the solutions and each was initially 1.0 M in dissolved species? Each electrode weighs 50.0 g in the beginning.

80. An old method of measuring the current flowing in a circuit was to use a "silver coulometer." The current passed first through a solution of $Ag^+(aq)$ and then into another solution containing an electroactive species. The amount of silver metal deposited at the cathode was weighed. From the mass of silver, the number of atoms of silver was calculated. Since the reduction of a silver ion requires one electron, this value equalled the number of electrons passing through the circuit. If the time was noted, the average current could be calculated. If, in such an experiment, 0.052 g of Ag is deposited during 450 s, what was the current flowing in the circuit?

81. ■ A "silver coulometer" (Study Question 80) was used in the past to measure the current flowing in an electrochemical cell. Suppose you found that the current flowing through an electrolysis cell deposited 0.089 g of Ag metal at the cathode after exactly 10 min. If this same current then passed through a cell containing gold(III) ion in the form of $[AuCl_4]^-$, how much gold was deposited at the cathode in that electrolysis cell?

82. ■ ▲ Four metals, A, B, C, and D, exhibit the following properties:
  (a) Only A and C react with 1.0 M hydrochloric acid to give $H_2(g)$.
  (b) When C is added to solutions of the ions of the other metals, metallic B, D, and A are formed.
  (c) Metal D reduces B^{n+} to give metallic B and D^{n+}.

Based on this information, arrange the four metals in order of increasing ability to act as reducing agents.

83. ▲ A solution of KI is added dropwise to a pale blue solution of $Cu(NO_3)_2$. The solution changes to a brown color, and a precipitate of CuI forms. In contrast, no change is observed if solutions of KCl and KBr are added to aqueous $Cu(NO_3)_2$. Consult the table of standard reduction potentials to explain the dissimilar results seen with the different halides. Write an equation for the reaction that occurs when solutions of KI and $Cu(NO_3)_2$ are mixed.

84. ▲ The amount of oxygen, O_2, dissolved in a water sample at 25 °C can be determined by titration. The first step is to add solutions of $MnSO_4$ and NaOH to the water to convert the dissolved oxygen to MnO_2. A solution of H_2SO_4 and KI is then added to convert the MnO_2 to Mn^{2+}, and the iodide ion is converted to I_2. The I_2 is then titrated with standardized $Na_2S_2O_3$.
   (a) Balance the equation for the reaction of Mn^{2+} ions with O_2 in basic solution.
   (b) Balance the equation for the reaction of MnO_2 with I^- in acid solution.
   (c) Balance the equation for the reaction of $S_2O_3^{2-}$ with I_2.
   (d) Calculate the amount of O_2 in 25.0 mL of water if the titration requires 2.45 mL of 0.0112 M $Na_2S_2O_3$ solution.

Summary and Conceptual Questions

The following questions may use concepts from this and previous chapters.

85. Fluorinated organic compounds are important commercially, since they are used as herbicides, flame retardants, and fire-extinguishing agents, among other things. A reaction such as

$$CH_3SO_2F + 3 HF \rightarrow CF_3SO_2F + 3 H_2$$

is carried out electrochemically in liquid HF as the solvent.
   (a) If you electrolyze 150 g of CH_3SO_2F, what mass of HF is required, and what mass of each product can be isolated?
   (b) Is H_2 produced at the anode or the cathode of the electrolysis cell?
   (c) A typical electrolysis cell operates at 8.0 V and 250 A. How many kilowatt-hours of energy does one such cell consume in 24 h?

86. ■ ▲ The free energy change for a reaction, $\Delta_r G°$, is the maximum energy that can be extracted from the process, whereas $\Delta_r H°$ is the total chemical potential energy change. The efficiency of a fuel cell is the ratio of these two quantities.

$$\text{Efficiency} = \frac{\Delta_r G°}{\Delta_r H°} \times 100\%$$

Consider the hydrogen-oxygen fuel cell, where the net reaction is

$$H_2(g) + \tfrac{1}{2} O_2(g) \rightarrow H_2O(\ell)$$

   (a) Calculate the efficiency of the fuel cell under standard conditions.
   (b) Calculate the efficiency of the fuel cell if the product is water vapor instead of liquid water.
   (c) Does the efficiency depend on the state of the reaction product? Why or why not?

87. A hydrogen-oxygen fuel cell operates on the simple reaction

$$H_2(g) + \tfrac{1}{2} O_2(g) \rightarrow H_2O(\ell)$$

If the cell is designed to produce 1.5 A of current and if the hydrogen is contained in a 1.0-L tank at 200 atm pressure at 25 °C, how long can the fuel cell operate before the hydrogen runs out? (Assume there is an unlimited supply of O_2.)

88. ■ ▲ (a) Is it easier to reduce water in acid or base? To evaluate this, consider the half-reaction

$$2 H_2O(\ell) + 2 e^- \rightarrow 2 OH^-(aq) + H_2(g)$$
$$E° = -0.83 \text{ V}$$

   (b) What is the reduction potential for water for solutions at pH = 7 (neutral) and pH = 1 (acid)? Comment on the value of $E°$ at pH = 1.

89. ▲ Living organisms derive energy from the oxidation of food, typified by glucose.

$$C_6H_{12}O_6(aq) + 6 O_2(g) \rightarrow 6 CO_2(g) + 6 H_2O(\ell)$$

Electrons in this redox process are transferred from glucose to oxygen in a series of at least 25 steps. It is instructive to calculate the total daily current flow in a typical organism and the rate of energy expenditure (power). (See T. P. Chirpich: *Journal of Chemical Education*, Vol. 52, p. 99, 1975.)
   (a) The molar enthalpy of combustion of glucose is −2800 kJ/mol-rxn. If you are on a typical daily diet of 2400 Cal (kilocalories), what amount of glucose (in moles) must be consumed in a day if glucose is the only source of energy? What amount of O_2 must be consumed in the oxidation process?
   (b) How many moles of electrons must be supplied to reduce the amount of O_2 calculated in part (a)?
   (c) Based on the answer in part (b), calculate the current flowing, per second, in your body from the combustion of glucose.
   (d) If the average standard potential in the electron transport chain is 1.0 V, what is the rate of energy expenditure in watts?

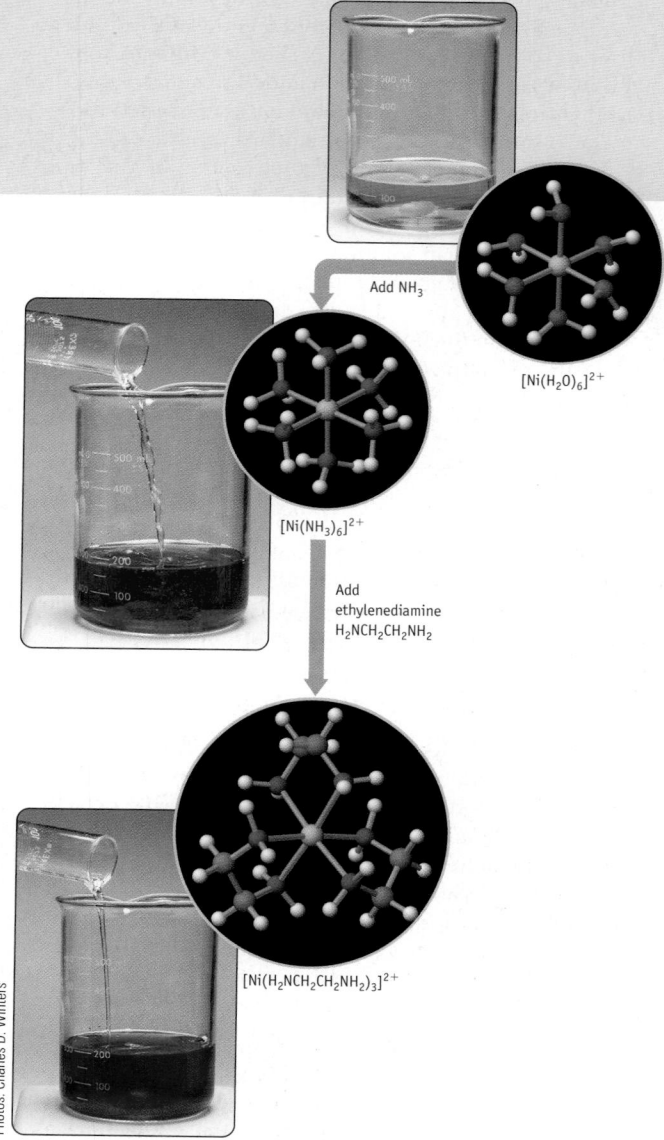

Chemists and non-chemists alike are drawn to the wonderful colors of many chemical compounds. Here you see an aqueous solution of nickel(II) chloride. When the nickel(II) salt dissolves, a green solution is obtained, owing to the presence of the complex ion $[Ni(H_2O)_6]^{2+}$ in solution.

As aqueous ammonia, NH_3(aq), is added to the green solution it turns a characteristic blue color. The color arises from another complex ion, $[Ni(NH_3)_6]^{2+}$, in which ammonia molecules have taken the place of water molecules.

Interestingly, when we add another compound—ethylenediamine, $H_2NCH_2CH_2NH_2$—the blue color of the ammonia-containing ion is replaced by the purple color of the complex ion, $[Ni(H_2NCH_2CH_2NH_2)_3]^{2+}$.

In this series of chapters you have learned more about the reactivity of molecules and how to predict when one compound can be transformed into another.

Add NH_3

$[Ni(H_2O)_6]^{2+}$

$[Ni(NH_3)_6]^{2+}$

Add ethylenediamine $H_2NCH_2CH_2NH_2$

$[Ni(H_2NCH_2CH_2NH_2)_3]^{2+}$

Photos: Charles D. Winters

THE PURPOSE OF *LET'S REVIEW*

- *Let's Review* provides additional questions for Chapters 15 through 20. Routine questions covering the concepts in a chapter are in the Study Questions at the end of that chapter and are usually identified by topic. In contrast, *Let's Review* questions combine several concepts from one or more chapters. Many come from the examinations given by the authors and others are based on actual experiments or processes in chemical research or in the chemical industries.

- *Let's Review* provides guidance for Chapters 15 through 20 as you prepare for an exam on these chapters. Although this is designated for Chapters 15 through 20 you may choose only material appropriate to the exam in your course.

- To direct your review, **Comprehensive Questions** are correlated with relevant chapter sections and with the OWL online homework

system to which you may have purchased access. Some questions may include a screen shot from one of these tools so you see what resources are available to help you review.

PREPARING FOR AN EXAMINATION ON CHAPTERS 15–20

1. Review **Go Chemistry** modules for these chapters. Go Chemistry modules are available at **www.cengage.com/chemistry/kotz** or **www.ichapters.com**.
2. Take the ChemistryNow **Pre-Test** and work through your **Personalized Learning Plan.** Work through ChemistryNow **Exercises, Guided Simulations,** and **Intelligent Tutors.**
3. **OWL** If you subscribe to OWL, use the **Tutorials** in that system.
4. Work on the questions below that are relevant to a particular chapter or chapters. See the solutions to those questions at the end of this section.
5. For background and help answering a question, use the Go Chemistry and OWL questions correlated with it.

KEY POINTS TO KNOW FOR CHAPTERS 15–20

Here are some of the key points you must know to be successful in Chapters 15–20.

- Rates of reaction and factors affecting reaction rates.
- Rate equations and integrated rate laws.
- Collision theory of reaction rates and activation energy.
- Reaction mechanisms.
- The nature of chemical equilibria.
- The reaction quotient (Q) and equilibrium constant (K).
- The Brønsted-Lowry and Lewis theories of acids and bases.
- Chemical equilibria involving acids, bases, and insoluble salts in aqueous solution, and pH calculations for acids, bases, and salts.
- Factors affecting the strengths of acids and bases.
- The nature of buffer solutions.
- The outcome of acid-base reactions (including titrations).
- Reaction spontaneity, free energy, and entropy.
- The relationship of free energy changes and equilibrium constants and whether a reaction is product- or reactant-favored.
- Balancing equations for redox reactions.
- Voltaic cells and electrochemical potentials under standard and nonstandard conditions.
- Electrolysis and electrical energy.

EXAMINATION PREPARATION QUESTIONS

▲ denotes more challenging questions.

Important information about the questions that follow:

- See the Study Questions in each chapter for questions on basic concepts.
- Some of these questions arise from recent research in chemistry and the other sciences. They often involve concepts from more than one chapter and may be more challenging than those in

earlier chapters. Not all chapter goals or concepts are necessarily addressed in these questions.
- **Assessing Key Points** are short-answer questions covering the Key Points to Know on this page.
- **Comprehensive Questions** bring together concepts from multiple chapters and are correlated with text sections covering that topic, with Go Chemistry modules, and with questions in OWL that may provide additional background.
- The screen shots are largely taken from Go Chemistry modules available at **www.cengage.com/chemistry/kotz** or **www.ichapters.com**.

Assessing Key Points

1. (Chapter 15) A few drops of blue food dye were added to water followed by a solution of bleach. (Initially, the concentration of dye was about 3.4×10^{-5} M, and the bleach (NaOCl) concentration was about 0.034 M.) The dye faded as it reacted with the bleach. The color change was followed by a spectrophotometer, and the data are plotted below. (See ChemistryNow, Screen 15.2)

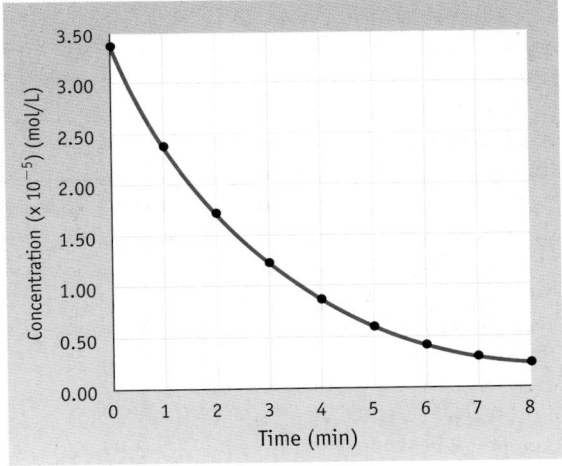

(a) What is the average rate of reaction over the first 2 minutes?
(b) What is the approximate half-life of the reaction?
(c) Does the rate of reaction decline, stay the same, or increase with time?

2. (Chapter 15) The reduction of NO with hydrogen produces nitrogen and water.

$$2\,NO(g) + 2\,H_2(g) \rightarrow N_2(g) + 2\,H_2O(g)$$

(a) The reaction is second order in NO and third order overall. What is the rate law for the reaction?
(b) If [NO] is increased by a factor of 5, how does the rate of the reaction change?
(c) If [H_2] is increased by a factor of 5, how does the rate of the reaction change?

3. (Chapter 15) Given the initial rate data for the reaction A + B → C, determine the rate expression for the reaction. (The reaction is catalyzed by molecule D.)

[A], M	[B], M	[D], M	$\Delta[C]/\Delta t$ (mol/L·s)
0.10	0.20	0.10	2.58
0.10	0.10	0.10	1.29
0.24	0.10	0.20	2.58
0.10	0.20	0.20	5.16

(a) $\Delta[C]/\Delta t = k[A][D]^2$
(b) $\Delta[C]/\Delta t = k[A][B][D]$
(c) $\Delta[C]/\Delta t = k[B][D]$
(d) $\Delta[C]/\Delta t = k[A][B]$

4. (Chapter 15) Three reactions have the rate law Rate = $k[\text{Reactant}]^m$ where m is the order of reaction. (For assistance, see the OWL Simulation 15.3c.)

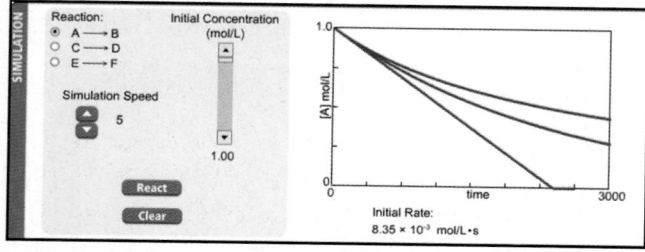

OWL Simulation 15.3c: Concentration Dependence of Rates

(a) For A → B, when [A] = 0.5 M, Rate = 4.18 × 10^{-3} mol/L·s. When [A] = 1.0 M, Rate = 8.35 × 10^{-3} mol/L·s. Is m 0, 1, or 2?
(b) For C → D, when [C] = 0.5 M Rate = 2.09 × 10^{-3} mol/L·s. When [C] = 1.0 M, Rate = 8.35 × 10^{-3} mol/L·s. Is m 0, 1, or 2?
(c) For E → F, when [E] = 0.5 M Rate = 8.35 × 10^{-3} mol/L·s. When [E] = 1.0 M, Rate = 8.35 × 10^{-3} mol/L·s. Is m 0, 1, or 2?
(d) Which of the three curves in the figure—top, middle, or bottom—corresponds to the reaction E → F?

5. (Chapter 15) A reaction that occurs in our environment is the oxidation of NO to the brown gas NO_2.

$$2\ NO(g) + O_2(g) \rightarrow 2\ NO_2(g)$$

The mechanism of the reaction is thought to be

Step 1 $2\ NO(g) \rightleftharpoons N_2O_2(g)$
                                   rapidly established equilibrium
Step 2 $N_2O_2(g) + O_2(g) \rightarrow 2\ NO_2(g)$ slow

Which is the rate determining step? Is there an intermediate in the reaction?

6. (Chapter 15) The decomposition of SO_2Cl_2 to SO_2 and Cl_2 is first order in SO_2Cl_2.

$$SO_2Cl_2(g) \rightarrow SO_2(g) + Cl_2(g)$$

$$\text{Rate} = k\,[SO_2Cl_2] \text{ where } k = 0.17/\text{hr}$$

(a) What is the rate of decomposition when $[SO_2Cl_2]$ = 0.010 M?
(b) What is the half-life of the reaction?
(c) If the initial pressure of SO_2Cl_2 in a flask is 0.050 atm, what is the pressure of all gases (i.e., the total pressure) in the flask after the reaction has proceeded for one half-life period?

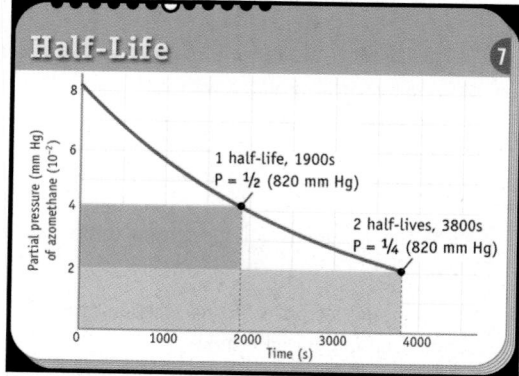

Screen from Go Chemistry module 20 on kinetics

7. (Chapter 16) A mixture of SO_2, O_2, and SO_3 at 1000 K contains the gases at the following concentrations: $[SO_2] = 5.0 \times 10^{-3}$ mol/L, $[O_2] = 1.9 \times 10^{-3}$ mol/L, and $[SO_3] = 6.9 \times 10^{-3}$ mol/L. Which way will the reaction proceed to reach equilibrium?

$$2\ SO_2(g) + O_2(g) \rightleftharpoons 2\ SO_3(g)\ \ K_c = 279$$

8. (Chapter 16) You place 0.010 mol of $N_2O_4(g)$ in a 2.0 L flask at 200 °C. After reaching equilibrium, $[N_2O_4]$ = 0.0042 M.

$$N_2O_4(g) \rightleftharpoons 2\ NO_2(g)$$

Fill in the table below and then calculate K_c for the reaction at 200 °C.

	$N_2O_4(g) \rightleftharpoons 2\ NO_2(g)$	
Initial concentration (M)	____	0
Change in concentration (M)	____	____
Equilibrium concentration (M)	0.0042	____

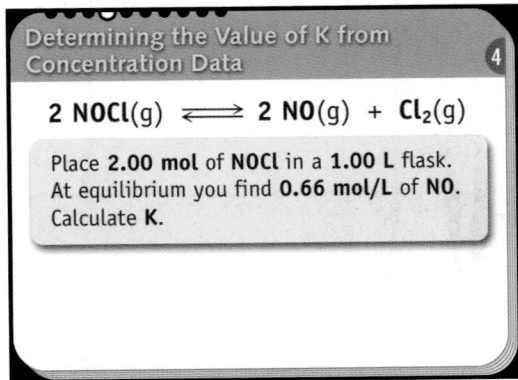

Determining the Value of K from Concentration Data 4

$$2\ NOCl(g) \rightleftharpoons 2\ NO(g) + Cl_2(g)$$

Place **2.00 mol** of **NOCl** in a **1.00 L** flask. At equilibrium you find **0.66 mol/L** of **NO**. Calculate **K**.

Screen from Go Chemistry module 21 on equilibrium

9. (Chapter 16) Nitrosyl bromide, $NOBr(g)$, decomposes according to the equation

$$NOBr(g) \rightleftharpoons NO(g) + 1/2\ Br_2(g)$$
$$K_c = 0.021 \text{ at } 350\ °C$$

If 1.5 mol of NOBr, 0.40 mol of NO, and 0.40 mol of Br_2 are mixed in a 1.0 L flask at 350 °C, will any net reaction occur? If a net reaction is observed, will NO be formed or consumed?

10. (Chapter 16) Samples of NO_2 and N_2O_4 are in equilibrium at some temperature. If $[N_2O_4] = 4.6 \times 10^{-5}$ M, what is $[NO_2]$?

$$2\ NO_2(g) \rightleftharpoons N_2O_4(g)\ \ K_c = 240$$

11. (Chapter 16) Calculate K_c for the reaction

$$SnO_2(s) + 2\ CO(g) \rightleftharpoons Sn(s) + 2\ CO_2(g)$$

given the following information:

$$SnO_2(s) + 2\ H_2(g) \rightleftharpoons Sn(s) + 2\ H_2O(g) \quad K_c = 8.12$$
$$H_2(g) + CO_2(g) \rightleftharpoons CO(g) + H_2O(g) \quad K_c = 0.771$$

12. (Chapter 16) Heating ammonium hydrogen sulfide leads to decomposition.

$$\text{heat} + NH_4HS(s) \rightleftharpoons NH_3(g) + H_2S(g)$$

Predict the effect on the equilibrium of each change listed below. Answer by choosing (1) no change, (2) shifts left, or (3) shifts right.
(a) Add solid NH_4HS
(b) Add NH_3 gas
(c) Add H_2S gas
(d) Raise the temperature
(e) Increase the volume of the flask containing the reaction

13. (Chapter 17) What is the pH of a 0.020 M NaOH solution?

14. (Chapter 17) Conjugate acids and bases:
(a) What is the conjugate base of formic acid, HCO_2H?
(b) What is the conjugate base of the $H_2PO_4^-$ ion?
(c) What is the conjugate acid of the HCO_3^- ion?

15. (Chapter 17) Which of the following is NOT an acid-base conjugate pair?
(a) HClO and Cl^- (c) HNO_2 and NO_2^-
(b) HF and F^- (d) CO_3^{2-} and HCO_3^-

16. (Chapter 17) For each solution below, decide if the pH is less than 7, equal to 7, or greater than 7 at 25 °C.
(a) 0.10 M HNO_3 (d) 0.45 M KBr
(b) 0.012 M KOH   (e) 0.25 M Na_3PO_4
(c) 0.15 M formic acid   (f) 0.095 M $AlCl_3$

17. (Chapter 17) What is the pH of a 0.020 M solution of NH_3 (at 25 °C)?

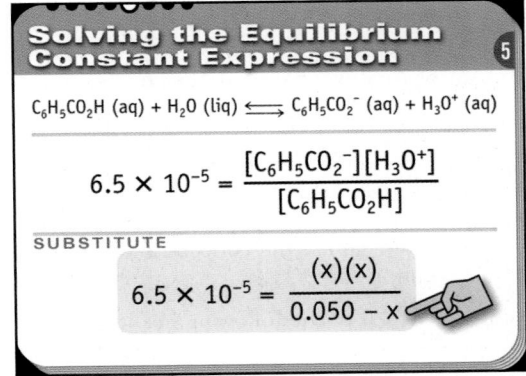

Solving the Equilibrium Constant Expression 5

$$C_6H_5CO_2H\ (aq) + H_2O\ (liq) \rightleftharpoons C_6H_5CO_2^-\ (aq) + H_3O^+\ (aq)$$

$$6.5 \times 10^{-5} = \frac{[C_6H_5CO_2^-][H_3O^+]}{[C_6H_5CO_2H]}$$

SUBSTITUTE

$$6.5 \times 10^{-5} = \frac{(x)(x)}{0.050 - x}$$

Screen from Go Chemistry module 22 on solving an acid-base problem

18. (Chapter 17) A 0.040 M solution of a weak acid has a pH of 3.02 at 25 °C. What is the value of K_a for the acid?

19. (Chapter 17) What are the concentrations of H_3O^+ and OH^- and what is the pH of a 0.15 M solution of Na_2CO_3 (at 25 °C)?

20. (Chapter 17) What is the pH of the solution obtained when 12.5 mL of 0.40 M NaOH is added to 40.0 mL of 0.125 M HCl (at 25 °C)?

21. (Chapter 17) Lewis acids and bases. The presence of iron(III) ion in aqueous solution can be detected by adding thiocyanate ion, SCN^- to give a deep red complex ion. Identify the Lewis acids and bases in the following equation.

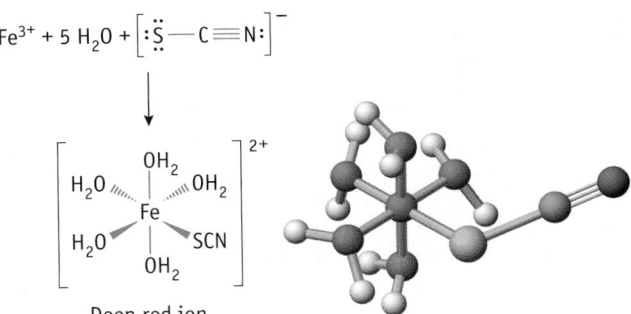

Deep red ion

22. (Chapter 18) Titrations. What is the pH at the half-neutralization point in a titration of formic acid (HCO_2H) with NaOH?

23. (Chapter 18) For each of the following cases, decide whether the pH is less than, equal to, or greater than 7 (at 25 °C).
(a) Equal volumes of 0.10 M acetic acid, CH_3CO_2H, and 0.10 M KOH are mixed.
(b) 25 mL of 0.015 M NH_3 is mixed with 25 mL of 0.015 M HCl
(c) 100. mL of 0.0020 M HNO_3 is mixed with 50. mL of 0.0040 M NaOH.

24. (Chapter 18) Decide which compound in each of the following pairs of salts is the more soluble in water.
(a) AgBr or AgSCN   (b) AgCl or Ag_2CO_3

25. (Chapter 18) Rank the following compounds in order of increasing molar solubility in water: Na_2CO_3, CaF_2, $BaCO_3$, Ag_2CO_3

26. (Chapter 18) Milk of magnesia is an aqueous suspension of $Mg(OH)_2$. What are the concentrations of H_3O^+ and OH^- in solution (at 25 °C)?

27. (Chapter 18) Which of the following insoluble compounds—MnS, $Al(OH)_3$, $Ca_3(PO_4)_2$, $MgCO_3$, AgCl, PbI_2—will not dissolve in 6 M HCl? List all correct answers.

28. (Chapter 18) You have a solution of NH_4Cl. Will the addition of NH_3 increase or decrease the pH or have no effect?

29. (Chapter 18) Suppose that in a 0.10 M $HClO_2$ solution, about 29% of the molecules have been converted to H_3O^+ and ClO_2^- ions. In this solution $[HClO_2] =$ 0.071 M, $[H_3O^+] = 0.029$ M, and $[ClO_2^-] = 0.029$ M. (OWL Simulation 18.1 explores this common ion effect.)

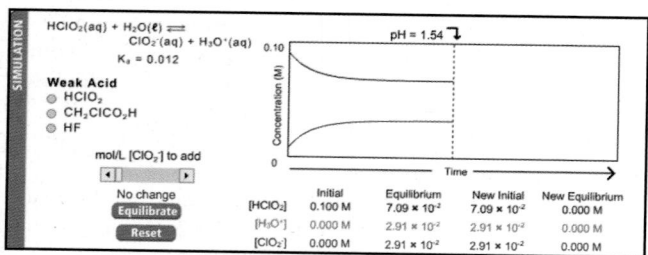

OWL Simulation 18.1: Common Ion Effect

(a) If more ClO_2^- ions are added to the solution described above (by adding $NaClO_2$), will the percentage ionization of $HClO_2$ be larger or smaller than 29% or will there be no change? Will the pH increase, decrease, or stay the same?
(b) ▲ Now take 1.00 L of the solution described above (in which $[HClO_2] = 0.071$ M, $[H_3O^+] = 0.029$ M, and $[ClO_2^-] = 0.029$ M) and add 0.010 mol of

$NaClO_2$. Determine the concentration of each species in the new solution. ($K_a = 0.012$ at 25 °C)

30. (Chapter 18) What is the pH of a buffer prepared by mixing 100. mL of 0.20 M NH_4Cl and 200. mL of 0.10 M NH_3?

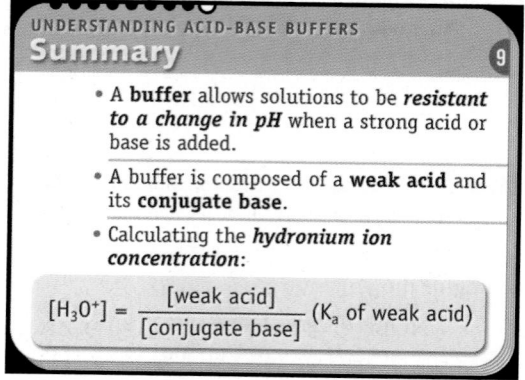

Screen from Go Chemistry module 23 on buffers

31. (Chapter 19) Calculate the standard entropy change for the following reaction using data in Appendix L.

$$F_2(g) + H_2(g) \rightarrow 2 \, HF(g)$$

32. (Chapter 19) Which of the following do you expect to have the largest molar entropy at 25 °C?
(a) $H_2O(\ell)$ (c) $O_2(g)$
(b) $H_2O(s)$ (d) $CCl_4(g)$

33. (Chapter 19) In which of the following physical or chemical changes do you expect to have an increase in entropy?
(a) $Fe(s) \rightarrow Fe(\ell)$
(b) $NH_3(g) + HCl(g) \rightarrow NH_4Cl(s)$
(c) $2 \, Fe(s) + 3/2 \, O_2(g) \rightarrow Fe_2O_3(s)$
(d) $HF(\ell) \rightarrow HF(g)$

34. (Chapter 19) Calculate $\Delta_r G°$ for the following reaction using data in Appendix L.

$$N_2(g) + 3 \, H_2O(\ell) \rightarrow 2 \, NH_3(g) + 3/2 \, O_2(g)$$

35. (Chapter 19) For the following general reaction, what can be said about the spontaneity at different temperatures?

$$A + B \rightarrow C + D; \Delta_r H° \text{ is positive and } \Delta_r S° \text{ is negative}$$

(a) Spontaneous at all temperatures
(b) Spontaneous only at high temperature
(c) Spontaneous only at low temperature
(d) Not spontaneous at any temperature

36. (Chapter 19) Given the following information, calculate $\Delta_r G°$ for the reaction below at 25 °C. Is the reaction spontaneous under standard conditions?

$$NiO(s) + 2 \, HCl(g) \rightarrow NiCl_2(s) + H_2O(g)$$

$\Delta_r H° = -122.8$ kJ/mol-rxn

and $\Delta_r S° = -123.9$ J/K·mol-rxn

37. (Chapter 19) When sodium is added to water, the following reaction takes place readily.

$$Na(s) + H_2O(\ell) \rightarrow NaOH(aq) + 1/2\ H_2(g) \quad \Delta_r H° < 0$$

What can be said about this reaction?
(a) $\Delta_r G°$ is positive.
(b) $\Delta_r S°$ is negative.
(c) $\Delta_r G°$ will become less negative with increasing temperature.
(d) $\Delta_r G°$ will become more negative with increasing temperature.

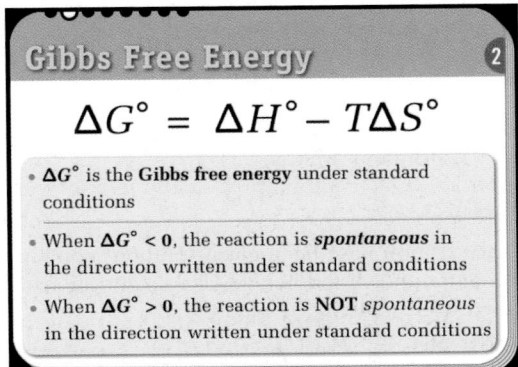

Screen from Go Chemistry module 24 on free energy

38. (Chapter 19) Acetic acid has an ionization constant of 1.8×10^{-5}. What is the predicted sign for $\Delta_r G°$ for the ionization of acetic acid at 25 °C? What is the value of $\Delta_r G°$?

39. (Chapter 19) In the reaction of two Cl atoms to give a Cl_2 molecule $[2\ Cl(g) \rightarrow Cl_2(g)]$, decide if the sign of the enthalpy and entropy changes are positive or negative.

40. (Chapter 20) Balance the following oxidation-reduction reaction in acid solution. Designate the oxidizing and reducing agents and the substances oxidized and reduced.

$$MnO_4^-(aq) + C_2O_4^{2-}(aq) \rightarrow Mn^{2+}(aq) + CO_2(g)$$

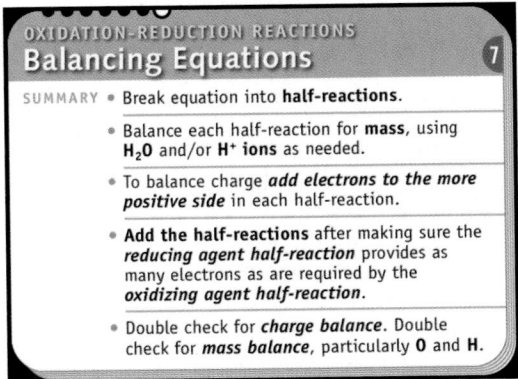

Screen from Go Chemistry module 25 on balancing equations

41. (Chapter 20) Use the small table of reduction potentials below to answer the questions that follow.

Half Reaction			E° (volts)
$Cl_2(g) + 2e^-$	$\rightarrow$	$2\ Cl^-(aq)$	+1.36
$Ag^+(aq) + e^-$	$\rightarrow$	$Ag(s)$	+0.80
$I_2(s) + 2e^-$	$\rightarrow$	$2\ I^-(aq)$	+0.535
$Cu^{2+}(aq) + 2e^-$	$\rightarrow$	$Cu(s)$	+0.34
$Pb^{2+}(aq) + 2e^-$	$\rightarrow$	$Pb(s)$	−0.126
$Ni^{2+}(aq) + 2e^-$	$\rightarrow$	$Ni(s)$	−0.25
$Zn^{2+}(aq) + 2e^-$	$\rightarrow$	$Zn(s)$	−0.76
$V^{2+}(aq) + 2e^-$	$\rightarrow$	$V(s)$	−1.18
$Al^{3+}(aq) + 3e^-$	$\rightarrow$	$Al(s)$	−1.66

(a) What is the weakest oxidizing agent in the list?
(b) What is the strongest oxidizing agent?
(c) What is the strongest reducing agent?
(d) What is the weakest reducing agent?
(e) Will $Pb(s)$ reduce $V^{2+}(aq)$ to $V(s)$?
(f) Will $I_2(s)$ oxidize Cl^- to $Cl_2(g)$?
(g) Identify the ions or compounds that can be reduced by $Pb(s)$.

42. (Chapter 20) Consider the electrochemical cell diagrammed below.

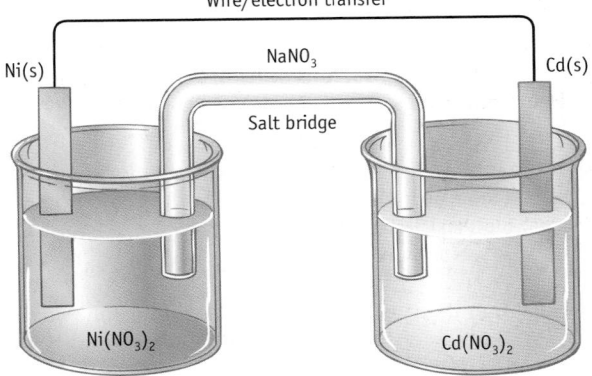

(a) Write the balanced net ionic equation for the reaction occurring in the cell.
(b) Indicate the direction of electron transfer.
(c) Which electrode is the anode and which is the cathode? Indicate the signs of the electrodes.
(d) Indicate the substance oxidized and the substance reduced.
(e) Calculate the standard cell potential, $E°$.
(f) Tell in which direction the Na^+ and NO_3^- ions flow in the salt bridge.

43. (Chapter 20) Consider the reaction

$$Cu(s) + 2\,Ag^+(aq) \rightarrow Cu^{2+}(aq) + 2\,Ag(s)$$

If $[Ag^+] = 1.0$ M and $[Cu^{2+}] = 0.020$ M, is the cell potential E (a) greater than $E°$; (b) less than $E°$; or (c) equal to $E°$?

44. (Chapter 20) If you electrolyze a solution of $Ni^{2+}(aq)$ to form $Ni(s)$ and use a current of 0.15 amps for 10. minutes, what mass of $Ni(s)$ is produced?

45. (Chapter 20) Permanganate ions and copper react in acid solution to give manganese(II) and copper(II) ions.
(a) Balance the net ionic equation for this reaction.
(b) Calculate $E°$ for the reaction.
(c) Calculate the cell potential under the following conditions: $[MnO_4^-] = 1.00$ M; $[Mn^{2+}] = 0.100$ M; $[Cu^{2+}] = 0.100$ M; and $[H_3O^+] = 0.500$ M.

Comprehensive Questions

46. (Chapter 15) Data in the table refers to the reaction

$$2\,NO(g) + H_2(g) \rightarrow N_2O(g) + H_2O(g)$$

Experiment	Initial [NO] (mol/L)	Initial [H₂] (mol/L)	Rate (mol/L · s)
1	2.16×10^{-2}	1.4×10^{-2}	1.2×10^{-2}
2	6.48×10^{-2}	1.4×10^{-2}	1.08×10^{-1}
3	4.32×10^{-2}	2.8×10^{-2}	9.6×10^{-2}

(a) What is the rate law equation for this reaction?
(b) What is the value and units of the rate constant k?
Text Section: 15.3
OWL Question: 15.3e

47. (Chapters 16 and 19) Heating ammonium chloride causes it to decompose to ammonia and hydrogen chloride. (See Figure 19.10, page 875).

$$NH_4Cl(s) \rightleftharpoons NH_3(g) + HCl(g)$$

(a) When the system has reached equilibrium, what is the effect on the equilibrium of adding more solid NH_4Cl? Of adding NH_3 gas?
(b) Predict the signs of $\Delta_rH°$ and $\Delta_rS°$ for NH_4Cl decomposition. Verify by calculating the enthalpy and entropy changes for the decomposition reaction from data in Appendix L.
(c) Is the reaction predicted to be product- or reactant-favored at 400 °C? Verify the prediction by calculating $\Delta_rG°$ and then calculate the pressure of ammonia in a flask at this temperature.
Text Sections: 16.4, 16.6, and 19.4–19.7
OWL Questions: 16.3b, 16.4b, 16.6d, 16.6m, 19.4c, 19.7c, 19.7f, 19.7i

48. (Chapter 17) A 0.44 M solution of hydroxyacetic acid, $HOCH_2CO_2H$, is 1.8% ionized. Calculate the pH of the solution and the value of the acid ionization equilibrium constant, K_a.
Text Section: 17.7
OWL Questions: 17.4a, 17.7b, 17.7d, 17.7e

49. (Chapter 17) Acid-base chemistry
(a) List the following acids in order of increasing acid strength: HF, NH_4^+, H_3PO_4, CH_3CO_2H, HNO_3.
(b) Use the ranking of relative acid strength to predict whether the equilibrium $HF(aq) + CH_3CO_2^-(aq) \rightleftharpoons F^-(aq) + CH_3CO_2H(aq)$ is product-favored or reactant-favored.
Text Sections: 17.4–17.5
OWL Questions: 17.4b, 17.4c

50. (Chapter 18) Refer to the Table of K_{sp} values in Appendix J and identify the most and least soluble silver salt, from among the following: $AgCl$, AgI, $AgCH_3CO_2$, $AgCN$, $AgBr$, and $AgSCN$.
Text Section: 18.4
OWL Question: 18.4d

51. (Chapter 18) You have been given solutions containing the compounds listed below. All concentrations are assumed to be 0.50 M.
  (i) $NH_3 + NH_4Cl$
  (ii) $Na_2HPO_4 + NaH_2PO_4$
  (iii) $HNO_3 + NaNO_3$
  (iv) $H_3PO_4 + NaH_2PO_4$
  (v) $NaF + HF$
(a) Which are buffer solutions?
(b) Which solution, among those listed, has the highest pH? The lowest pH?
(c) Assume you need a solution buffered at pH = 7.4. Select one of the solutions from the list, then describe how you would adjust its pH to achieve the desired value.
Text Section: 18.2
OWL Questions: 18.2d, 18.2j

52. (Chapter 18) Titration of chloroacetic acid in water with aqueous NaOH:
(a) Chloroacetic acid, $ClCH_2CO_2H$, has a pK_a of 2.867. What is the value of K_a?
(b) Write the net ionic equation for the reaction of chloroacetic acid with NaOH.
(c) What volume of 0.128 M NaOH solution is required to titrate 50.0 mL of 0.154 M acid to the equivalence point?
(d) Which of the following indicators: phenolphthalein, methyl red, or bromthymol blue, would be most suitable for this titration?
(e) What is the pH at the half-neutralization point?
(f) What is the pH at the equivalence point?
Text Section: 18.3
OWL Questions: 17.7i, 18.3e, 18.3f, 18.3h

53. (Chapter 20) Write balanced chemical equations for the following:

(a) $Cr_2O_7^{2-} + I^- \rightarrow Cr^{3+} + I_2$ (in acid).

(b) $MnO_4^- + HS^- \rightarrow MnO_2 + SO_4^{2-}$ (in base)

In each case identify the substance reduced, the reducing agent, and the change in oxidation state of chromium and manganese in these reactions.

Text Section: 20.1
OWL Questions: 20.1b, 20.1d, 20.1e

54. (Chapter 20) Electrochemical cells:

(a) Sketch a picture of the voltaic cell $Zn(s) \mid Zn^{2+}$ (1.0 M) $\parallel Sn^{4+}$(1.0 M) $\mid Sn^{2+}$(1.0 M) $\mid Pt(s)$. On the drawing, identify the anode, cathode, and the direction of flow of electrons in the external circuit.

(b) Assume the cell has a salt bridge containing $NaNO_3$. In what direction does each ion in the salt bridge flow?

(c) Write a balanced chemical equation for the overall cell reaction.

(d) What is $E°$ for this cell?

Text Sections: 20.2 and 20.4
OWL Questions: 20.2b, 20.4c

55. (Chapter 20) Refer to the table of standard reduction potentials to answer this question. Questions can have more than one correct answer. List all correct answers.

(a) Which of the following metals react with H^+(aq) to produce H_2: Ag, Mn, Sn, Cu, Mg?

(b) Which of the following metal ions is most easily reduced: Li^+, Mg^{2+}, Sn^{2+}, Fe^{2+}?

(c) Which of the following metal ions can be reduced to the metal by Sn: Ag^+, Ni^{2+}, Mg^{2+}, Fe^{2+}?

(d) Which of the species listed below is the strongest reducing agent: Cl^-, H_2, Mg^{2+}, Br^-?

Text Section: 20.4
OWL Questions: 20.2b, 20.4c

56. (Chapter 20) In the electrolysis of a solution containing Cr^{3+}, how long should one run a current of 2.50 amperes to obtain 5.00 g of Cr?

Text Section: 20.8
OWL Question: 20.8b

57. (Chapter 18) The curve of pH versus volume of HCl added for the titration of 50.0 mL of 0.10 M diethylamine with 0.10 M aqueous HCl is shown below.

(a) Is diethylamine, $(C_2H_5)_2NH$, a weak acid or weak base in water?

(b) Write a balanced equation for the reaction of the amine with HCl.

(c) Use the graph of pH versus added HCl to determine the approximate pH at the half-neutralization point? Use this value to estimate the value of K_b for the hydrolysis of diethylamine.

(d) What is the approximate pH of the solution at the equivalence point? Verify your observation on the graph with a calculation.

(e) Explain briefly why this solution is acidic or basic at the equivalence point.

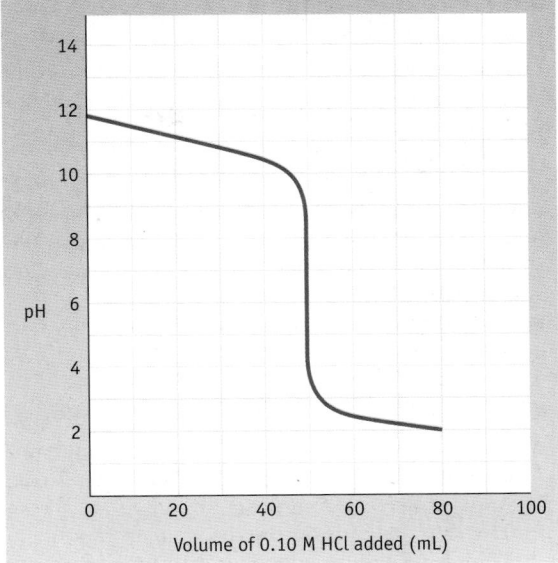

Text Section: 18.3
OWL Question: 18.3g

58. (Chapter 18) On page 948 you see photos of the reaction of aqueous nickel(II) ion with ammonia to give a complex ion,

$[Ni(H_2O)_6]^{2+}$(aq) $+ 6 NH_3$(aq)
$\rightleftharpoons [Ni(NH_3)_6]^{2+}$(aq) $+ 6 H_2O$(aq)

and then the reaction of that complex ion with the organic compound ethylenediamine to give another colorful complex ion.

$[Ni(NH_3)_6]^{2+}$(aq) $+ 3 H_2NCH_2CH_2NH_2$(aq)
$\rightleftharpoons [Ni(H_2NCH_2CH_2NH_2)_3]^{2+}$(aq) $+ 6 NH_3$(aq)

(a) What is the pH of a 0.10 M aqueous solution of nickel(II) chloride? (See Table 17.3, page 770.)

(b) What is the approximate pH of a 0.025 M aqueous solution of ethylenediamine? (See Appendix I for the K_b value.)

(c) In forming the complex ion $[Ni(NH_3)_6]^{2+}$ what is the Lewis acid and what is the Lewis base?

(d) Is the reaction of Ni^{2+}(aq) with ammonia product- or reactant-favored at equilibrium? (See the discussion of formation constants on page 846 and Appendix K.)

(e) Given the formation constants below, calculate the equilibrium constant and $\Delta_r G°$ for the reaction of $[Ni(NH_3)_6]^{2+}$(aq) with ethylenediamine at 25 °C.

Complex Ion	Formation Constant
$[Ni(NH_3)_6]^{2+}$(aq)	5.5×10^8
$[Ni(H_2NCH_2CH_2NH_2)_3]^{2+}$(aq)	1.9×10^{18}

Comment on what thermodynamic function controls the outcome of the reaction, $\Delta_r H°$ or $\Delta_r S°$.

Text Sections: 16.5, 17.3, 17.7, 17.9, and 19.7
OWL Questions: 16.5a, 16.5b, 17.3f, 17.7e, 17.7g, 17.7h, 17.9e, 18.7c, 19.7i

59. (Chapter 19) One way in which hydrogen gas is produced is to dehydrogenate ethane over a suitable catalyst at a high temperature.

$$C_2H_6(g) \rightleftharpoons C_2H_4(g) + H_2(g)$$

Assume $\Delta_r G°$ is 22.4 kJ/mol-rxn at 900 K. What is the mole percent of hydrogen at equilibrium if this process is carried out at 900 K and with an initial partial pressure of C_2H_6 of 1.00 atm?

Text Sections: 16.4 and 19.7
OWL Questions: 16.3b, 16.4b, 19.7i

Answers to Assessing Key Points Questions

1. (a) 0.85×10^{-5} mol/L·min. Divide the change in concentration by the time period over which it occurs.
   (b) Approximately 2 minutes
   (c) The rate depends on the dye concentration. Therefore, the rate declines with time because the concentration of the dye declines with time.

2. (a) Rate = $k[NO]^2[H_2]$. The sum of the exponents is 3.
   (b) The rate will increase 25-fold (5^2).
   (c) The rate increases by a factor of 5.

3. (c) $\Delta C/\Delta t = k[B][D]$. Comparing lines 1 and 2 of the data you see that the rate doubles when [B] doubles. Therefore, the reaction is 1st order in B. Comparing lines 1 and 4 you find that the rate doubles when [D] doubles, so the reaction is 1st order in D. Comparing lines 3 and 4 shows that the rate doubles with a doubling of [B], as expected, but the increase in [A] has no effect.

4. (a) $m = 1$; the rate doubles when concentration of A doubles.
   (b) $m = 2$; the rate increases by a factor of 4 when concentration of C doubles.
   (c) $m = 0$; there is no change in rate when the concentration of E changes.
   (d) Bottom. For a zero order reaction Rate = k. The concentration versus time curve is a straight line with a slope equal to $-k$.

5. Step 2 is rate determining and N_2O_2 is an intermediate.

6. (a) Rate = $(0.17/hr)(0.010$ mol/L$)$ = 0.0017 mol/L·h
   (b) $t_{1/2} = 0.693/k$ = 4.1 hr
   (c)

	SO_2Cl_2 $\rightleftharpoons$	SO_2 +	Cl_2
initial P (atm)	0.050	0	0
change in P (atm)	-0.025	$+0.025$	$+0.025$
final P (atm)	0.025	0.025	0.025

   Total final pressure = 0.075 atm

7. Calculate Q, the reaction quotient.

$$Q_c = \frac{[SO_3]^2}{[SO_2]^2[O_2]} = \frac{\left(6.9 \times 10^{-3}\right)^2}{\left(5.0 \times 10^{-3}\right)^2\left(1.9 \times 10^{-3}\right)}$$
$$Q_c = 1.0 \times 10^3$$

Because $Q > K$, the concentration of product is too large and that of the reactants is too small. The reaction will proceed to the left to attain equilibrium.

8.

	N_2O_4	$\rightleftharpoons$ 2 NO_2
Initial (M)	0.0050	0
Change (M)	-0.0008	$+2 \times 0.0008$
Equilibrium (M)	0.0042	0.0016

The additions to the table are in bold. The final concentration of NO_2 is derived from the change in N_2O_4 concentration.

$$K_c = \frac{[NO_2]^2}{[N_2O_4]} = \frac{(0.0016)^2}{0.0042} = 6.1 \times 10^{-4}$$

9. $Q = \dfrac{[NO][Br_2]^{1/2}}{[NOBr]} = \dfrac{(0.40)(0.40)^{1/2}}{1.5} = 0.17$

   $Q > K_c$. Therefore, reaction is the reverse of the equation as written. and NO is consumed.

10. $K_c = 240 = \dfrac{[N_2O_4]}{[NO_2]^2} = \dfrac{(4.6 \times 10^{-5})}{[NO_2]^2}$

    $[NO_2] = 4.4 \times 10^{-4}$ M

11. See Section 16.5 and Problem-Solving Tip 16.2.

    $$SnO_2(s) + 2 H_2(g) \rightleftharpoons Sn(s) + 2 H_2O(g)$$
    $$K_c = K_1 = 8.12$$

    $$2 [CO(g) + H_2O(g) \rightleftharpoons H_2(g) + CO_2(g)]$$
    $$K_c = (1/K_2)^2 = (1/0.771)^2$$

    Summed equations:

    $$SnO_2(s) + 2 CO(g) \rightleftharpoons Sn(s) + 2 CO_2(g)$$
    $$K_{net} = K_1 \times (1/K_2)^2 = 13.7$$

12. (a) No change   (d) Shifts right
    (b) Shifts left   (e) Shifts right
    (c) Shifts left

13. NaOH is a strong base so $[NaOH] = [OH^-]$

    pOH = $-\log [OH^-]$ = $-\log (0.020)$ = 1.70
    pH + pOH = 14.00, so pH = 12.30

    Alternatively, we first solve for $[H_3O^+]$

    $K_w = [H_3O^+][OH^-] = 1.00 \times 10^{-14}$
    $[H_3O^+] = 5.0 \times 10^{-13}$ M

    and this gives a pH of 12.30.

14. See Table 17.3 on page 770.
    (a) HCO_2^- (b) HPO_4^{2-} (c) H_2CO_3

15. (a)

16. (a) Strong acid. pH < 7.
    (b) Strong base. pH > 7
    (c) Weak acid. pH < 7
    (d) Neutral salt. pH = 7
    (e) PO_4^{3-} is a relatively strong weak base ($K_b = 2.8 \times 10^{-2}$). pH > 7. See Problem-Solving Tip 17.2, page 775.
    (f) Al^{3+} is a weak acid. pH < 7

17. Set up an ICE table for the weak base, NH_3

	$NH_3(aq)$ + $H_2O(\ell)$ $\rightleftharpoons$ $NH_4^+(aq)$ + $OH^-(aq)$		
Initial	0.020	0	0
Change	$-x$	$+x$	$+x$
Equilibrium	$0.020 - x$	x	x

$$K_b = 1.8 \times 10^{-5} = \frac{[NH_4^+][OH^-]}{[NH_3]}$$

$$1.8 \times 10^{-5} = \frac{[x]^2}{0.020 - x}$$

Assuming x is $<< 0.020$
$x = [OH^-] = 6.0 \times 10^{-4}$ M
$pOH = -\log [OH^-] = 3.22$
$pH + pOH = 14.00$
$pH = 10.78$

18. Set up an ICE table for a weak acid HA where $[H_3O^+] = 10^{-pH} = 9.5 \times 10^{-4}$ M

	$HA(aq)$ + $H_2O(\ell)$ $\rightleftharpoons$ $H_3O^+(aq)$ + $A^-(aq)$		
Initial	0.040	0	0
Change	$-x$	$+x$	$+x$
Equilibrium	$0.040 - x$	x	x

where $x = 9.5 \times 10^{-4}$ M

$$K_a = \frac{[H_3O^+][A^-]}{[HA]} = \frac{\left(9.5 \times 10^{-4}\right)^2}{0.040 - 9.5 \times 10^{-4}} = 2.3 \times 10^{-5}$$

19. Set up an ICE table for the CO_3^{2-} ion behaving as a weak, monoprotic base.

	$CO_3^{2-}(aq)$ + $H_2O(\ell)$ $\rightleftharpoons$ $HCO_3^-(aq)$ + $OH^-(aq)$		
Initial	0.15	0	0
Change	$-x$	$+x$	$+x$
Equilibrium	$0.15 - x$	x	x

$$K_b = \frac{[HCO_3^-][OH^-]}{[CO_3^{2-}]}$$

$$2.1 \times 10^{-4} = \frac{x^2}{0.15 - x}$$

Assuming $x << 0.15$ M
$x = [OH^-] = 5.6 \times 10^{-3}$ M
$pOH = 2.25$ and so $pH = 11.75$
$[H_3O^+] = 10^{-pH} = 1.8 \times 10^{-12}$

The small concentration of the product of CO_3^{2-} hydrolysis, HCO_3^-, does not affect the pH significantly.

20. Amount of NaOH used $= c \cdot V = 5.0 \times 10^{-3}$ mol
Amount of HCl used $= c \cdot V = 5.0 \times 10^{-3}$ mol
All of the NaOH and HCl are consumed in the reaction leaving only water and the neutral salt NaCl. The pH of the solution must be 7.00 (at 25 °C).

21. Fe^{3+} is a Lewis acid, an electron pair acceptor (as are all aqueous transition metal cations). Water and SCN^- ion are both electron pair donors, Lewis bases. See Section 17.9.

22. $HCO_2H(aq)$ + $OH^-(aq)$ $\rightleftharpoons$ $HCO_2^-(aq)$ + $H_2O(\ell)$
At the half-neutralization point of a titration of a weak acid with a strong base the solution contains half of the original acid and an equal amount of weak conjugate base. The solution is a buffer with $[H_3O^+] = K_a$ (and pH = pK_a). Here $[H_3O^+] = 1.8 \times 10^{-4}$ M and pH = 3.74. See Equation 18.5, page 825.

23. (a) $CH_3CO_2H(aq)$ + $OH^-(aq)$
                        $\rightleftharpoons CH_3CO_2^-(aq)$ + $H_2O(\ell)$
    This is the reaction of a weak acid with an equal amount of a strong base. The product is the weak conjugate base of the acid, so the pH is greater than 7 after reaction is complete.

    (b) $NH_3(aq)$ + $H_3O^+(aq)$ $\rightleftharpoons$ $NH_4^+(aq)$ + $H_2O(\ell)$
    This is the reaction of a weak base with an equal amount of a strong acid. The product is the weak conjugate acid of the base, so the pH is less than 7 after reaction is complete.

    (c) $H_3O^+(aq)$ + $OH^-(aq)$ $\rightleftharpoons$ $2 H_2O(\ell)$
    This is the reaction of a strong acid with an equal amount of strong base. The solution consists of a neutral salt in water; pH = 7.0.

24. See Section 18.4 and page 834 in particular.
    (a) When two salts have the same formula type (for example, both have one cation and one anion) we can directly compare K_{sp} values to judge their relative solubility.
        AgSCN (1.0×10^{-12}) > AgBr (5.4×10^{-13})
    AgSCN is more soluble.

(b) For AgCl and Ag_2CO_3 we have to calculate their solubilities.

Solubility of $AgCl = (K_{sp})^{1/2} = (1.8 \times 10^{-10})^{1/2}$
$$= 1.3 \times 10^{-5} \text{ M}$$

Solubility of Ag_2CO_3

$Ag_2CO_3(s) \rightleftharpoons 2\, Ag^+(aq) + CO_3^{2-}(aq)$

$K_{sp} = [Ag^+]^2[CO_3^{2-}] = (2x)^2(x) = 8.5 \times 10^{-12}$

where $x = [CO_3^{2-}]$ and is equivalent to the molar solubility of the salt.

$[CO_3^{2-}] = 1.3 \times 10^{-4}$ M = molar solubility of Ag_2CO_3

Even though Ag_2CO_3 has a smaller K_{sp} value than AgCl, its molar solubility is greater.

25. Na_2CO_3 is a soluble salt.
$BaCO_3$. Solubility from $K_{sp} = 5.1 \times 10^{-5}$ M
CaF_2. Solubility from $K_{sp} = 2.4 \times 10^{-4}$ M
Ag_2CO_3. Solubility from $K_{sp} = 1.3 \times 10^{-4}$ M

Order of increasing molar solubility:
$BaCO_3 < Ag_2CO_3 < CaF_2 < Na_2CO_3$

26. $Mg(OH)_2(s) \rightleftharpoons Mg^{2+}(aq) + 2\, OH^-(aq)$
$K_{sp} = 5.6 \times 10^{-12} = [Mg^{2+}][OH^-]^2 = (x)(2x)^2$
$x = 1.1 \times 10^{-4}$ M
$[OH^-] = 2x = 2.2 \times 10^{-4}$ M
$[H_3O^+] = K_w/[OH^-] = 4.5 \times 10^{-11}$ M

27. Dissolve in 6 M HCl: MnS, $Ca_3(PO_4)_2$, $Al(OH)_3$, $MgCO_3$. Only these salts contain basic anions (which are conjugate bases of weak acids). The other two salts (AgCl and PbI_2) will not dissolve in 6 M HCl.

28. $NH_4^+(aq) + H_2O(\ell) \rightleftharpoons NH_3(aq) + H_3O^+(aq)$
Ammonium ion is in equilibrium with a small amount of NH_3. Adding the weak base NH_3 shifts the equilibrium to the left and raises the pH.

29. The results of this question can be confirmed using the OWL Simulation.
(a) Adding ClO_2^- leads to a lower percent ionization. The pH increases (as expected when a weak base is added).
(b)

$HClO_2(aq) + H_2O(\ell) \rightleftharpoons H_3O^+(aq) + ClO_2^-(aq)$			
Initial	0.071	0.029	0.039
Change	$-x$	$+x$	$+x$
Equilibrium	$0.071 - x$	$0.029 + x$	$0.039 + x$

$K_a = 0.012 = \dfrac{(0.029 + x)(0.039 + x)}{0.071 - x}$

Solving this quadratic equation, we find $x = -0.0037$, which leads to $[HClO_2] = 0.075$ M, $[H_3O^+] = 0.025$ M, and $[ClO_2^-] = 0.035$ M.

30. Use Equation 18.1 to calculate the hydronium ion concentration and then calculate the pH.

$[H_3O^+] = \dfrac{[NH_4^+]}{[NH_3]} K_a$

$= \left(\dfrac{0.020 \text{ mol } NH_4^+}{0.020 \text{ mol } NH_3} \right) 5.6 \times 10^{-10} = 5.6 \times 10^{-10}$ M

pH = 9.25.

31. Equation 19.3, page 870
$\Delta_r S° = \Sigma\, S°(\text{product}) - \Sigma\, S°(\text{reactants})$
$\Delta_r S° = 2\, S°(HF) - [S°(H_2) + S°(F_2)]$
$\Delta_r S° = (2 \text{ mol } HF/1 \text{ mol-rxn})(173.78 \text{ J/K·mol})$
$\quad - [(1 \text{ mol } H_2/1 \text{ mol-rxn})(130.7 \text{ J/K·mol})$
$\quad\quad + (1 \text{ mol } F_2/1 \text{ mol-rxn})(202.8 \text{ J/K·mol})]$
$\Delta_r S° = 14.1$ J/K·mol-rxn

32. (d). CCl_4 has more atoms in the molecule than the others and is in the gas phase.

33. (a) and (d)

34. See Equation 19.8, page 880.
$\Delta_r G° = \Sigma\, \Delta_f G°(\text{products}) - \Sigma\, \Delta_f G°(\text{reactants})$
$\Delta_r G° = 2\, \Delta_f G°\, [NH_3(g)] - 3\, \Delta_f G°\, [H_2O(\ell)]$
$= (2 \text{ mol } NH_3/1 \text{ mol-rxn})(-16.37 \text{ kJ/mol})$
$\quad - (3 \text{ mol } H_2O(\ell)/1 \text{ mol-rxn})(-237.15 \text{ kJ/mol})$
$= +678.71$ kJ/mol-rxn

35. (d), not spontaneous at any temperature. See Table 19.2, page 874.

36. $\Delta_r G° = \Delta_r H° - T\Delta_r S°$
$\Delta_r G° = -122.8 \text{ kJ} - (298 \text{ K})(-0.1239 \text{ kJ/K})$
$\Delta_r G° = -85.9$ kJ

The reaction is spontaneous.

37. (d) $\Delta_r G°$ becomes more negative with increasing T because $\Delta_r S$ is positive (and $\Delta_r H°$ is negative). See the left-most panel in Figure 19.12, page 882.

38. (a) The sign of $\Delta_r G°$ is predicted to be positive for a reaction for which K is less than 1.
(b) $\Delta_r G° = -RT\ln K$
$= -(8.3145 \text{ J/K·mol})(298 \text{ K}) \ln(1.8 \times 10^{-5})$
$\Delta_r G° = 2.71 \times 10^4$ J/mol-rxn

39. Both $\Delta_r H$ and $\Delta_r S$ are predicted to be negative. The combination of two atoms to form one molecule is always an exothermic process. In addition, when two atoms combine to form one molecule, $\Delta_r S < 0$.

40. MnO_4^- is the oxidizing agent and is reduced
$MnO_4^-(aq) + 8\, H^+(aq) + 5\, e^- \rightarrow Mn^{2+}(aq) + 4\, H_2O(\ell)$
$C_2O_4^{2-}$ is the reducing agent and is oxidized
$C_2O_4^{2-}(aq) \rightarrow 2\, CO_2(g) + 2\, e^-$
Complete equation:
$2\, MnO_4^-(aq) + 16\, H^+(aq) + 5\, C_2O_4^{2-}(aq)$
$\quad\quad \rightleftharpoons 2\, Mn^{2+}(aq) + 8\, H_2O(\ell) + 10\, CO_2(g)$

41. (a) Al^{3+}
    (b) Cl_2
    (c) Al
    (d) Cl^-
    (e) No, Pb will not reduce V^{2+}
    (f) No, I_2 will not oxidize Cl^-
    (g) Cl_2, Ag^+, I_2, and Cu^{2+}

42. (a) From Table 20.1, page 920, we know that Cd will reduce Ni^{2+} to Ni. Therefore,

$$Cd(s) + Ni^{2+}(aq) \rightarrow Cd^{2+}(aq) + Ni(s)$$

   (b) Electrons transfer in the external wire from Cd to Ni.
   (c) Cd is the site of oxidation, is the anode, and is labeled negative. The Ni electrode is the cathode and is labeled positive.
   (d) Cd is oxidized to Cd^{2+} and Ni^{2+} is reduced to Ni.
   (e) $E°_{cell} = E°_{cathode} - E°_{anode} = -0.25\ V - (-0.40\ V)$
       $E°_{cell} = +0.15\ V$
   (f) Anions flow into the Cd cell (to balance the charge of the Cd^{2+} ions being generated), and the cations flow into the Ni cell.

43. Using the Nernst equation, we have

$$E = E° - \frac{0.0257}{2} \ln \frac{[Cu^{2+}]}{[Ag^+]^2}$$

$$E = +0.462\ V - 0.0129 \ln \frac{0.020}{(1.0)^2}$$

$$E = 0.512\ V$$

The electrochemical potential is more positive than $E°$.

44. The charge passed in the 10.-minute (600 second) time period is:

$$(0.15\ amp)(600\ s) = 90.\ coulombs$$

$$\text{Amount of charge} = 90.\ C \left(\frac{1\ mol\ electrons}{96500\ C} \right)$$

$$= 9.3 \times 10^{-4}\ mol\ e^-$$

$$9.3 \times 10^{-4}\ mol\ e^- \left(\frac{1\ mol\ Ni\ deposited}{2\ mol\ e^-} \right)$$

$$= 4.7 \times 10^{-4}\ mol\ Ni$$

$$4.7 \times 10^{-4}\ mol\ Ni \left(\frac{58.7\ g\ Ni}{1\ mol\ Ni} \right) = 0.027\ g\ Ni$$

45. (a) $MnO_4^-(aq) + 8\ H^+(aq) + 5\ e^- \rightarrow$
                                        $Mn^{2+}(aq) + 4\ H_2O(\ell)$
       $Cu(s) \rightarrow Cu^{2+}(aq) + 2\ e^-$
       _____
       $2\ MnO_4^-(aq) + 5\ Cu(s) + 16\ H^+(aq) \rightarrow$
                 $2\ Mn^{2+}(aq) + 5\ Cu^{2+}(aq) + 8\ H_2O(\ell)$

   (b) $E°_{cell} = E°_{cathode} - E°_{anode}$
       $E°_{cell} = +1.51\ V - (0.34\ V) = +1.17\ V$

   (c) $E = E° - \left(\frac{0.0257}{10} \right) \ln \frac{(0.100)^2(0.100)^5}{(1.00)^2(0.500)^{16}} = 1.18\ V$

Solutions to Comprehensive Questions

46. (a) Rate $= k[NO]^2[H_2]$. Compare experiments 1 and 2: tripling $[NO]$ increases the rate by a factor of 9, indicating the reaction is second order in $[NO]$. Compare experiments 1 and 3: doubling $[NO]$ and $[H_2]$ increases the rate by a factor of 8. You know that doubling $[NO]$ increases the rate by 4-fold. To achieve an increase by a factor of 8 after doubling both $[NO]$ and $[H_2]$ must mean the reaction is first-order in H_2.

   (b) Using the first set of data to calculate k:

$$k = \frac{\text{Rate}}{[NO]^2[H_2]}$$

$$= \frac{1.2 \times 10^{-2}\ mol/L}{(2.16 \times 10^{-2}\ mol/L)^2(1.4 \times 10^{-2}\ mol/L)}$$

$$= 1.8 \times 10^3\ L^2/mol^2 \cdot s$$

47. (a) Addition of solid NH_4Cl has no effect. Addition of gaseous NH_3 will cause the equilibrium to shift to the left, forming more solid NH_4Cl and consuming some of the HCl and NH_3. The final concentration of $NH_3(g)$ will be greater than the original, whereas the final concentration of $HCl(g)$ will be less than the original.

   (b) Predictions: $\Delta_r H°$: positive (heat must be added). $\Delta_r S°$: positive (conversion of 1 mole of solid to 2 moles of gases).

$$\Delta_r H° = \Delta_f H°[NH_3(g)] + \Delta_f H°[HCl(g)]$$
$$- \Delta_f H°[NH_4Cl(s)]$$
$$= (1\ mol\ NH_3/1\ mol\text{-}rxn)(-45.90\ kJ/mol)$$
$$+ (1\ mol\ HCl/1\ mol\text{-}rxn)(-92.31\ kJ/mol)$$
$$- (1\ mol\ NH_4Cl/1\ mol\text{-}rxn)(-314.55\ kJ/mol)$$
$$= 176.34\ kJ/mol\text{-}rxn$$

$$\Delta_r S° = S°[NH_3(g)] + S°[HCl(g)] - S°[NH_4Cl(s)]$$
$$= (1\ mol\ NH_3/1\ mol\text{-}rxn)(192.77\ J/mol \cdot K)$$
$$+ (1\ mol\ HCl/1\ mol\text{-}rxn)(186.2\ J/mol \cdot K)$$
$$- (1\ mol\ NH_4Cl/1\ mol\text{-}rxn)(94.85\ J/mol \cdot K)$$
$$= 284.1\ J/K \cdot mol\text{-}rxn$$

   (c) Prediction: because of the favorable entropy term, this reaction will become product-favored at equilibrium at higher temperatures. A calculation is needed to determine if 400 °C is a high enough temperature. (Note that 400 °C = 673 K. Also note that we assume $\Delta_r H°$ and $\Delta_r S°$ do not change significantly with temperature.)

$$\Delta_r G° = \Delta_r H° - T \Delta_r S°$$
$$= 176.34\ kJ/mol\text{-}rxn$$
$$- (673\ K)(0.2841\ kJ/K \cdot mol\text{-}rxn)$$
$$= -14.9\ kJ/mol\text{-}rxn$$

   The negative sign indicates that the reaction is product-favored at this temperature.

   To calculate $P(NH_3)$, first determine the equilibrium constant K_p for this reaction, then use this in an equilibrium calculation.

$$\Delta_r G^\circ = -RT \ln K$$

$$\ln K_p = -\frac{(-14900\ \text{J/mol})}{(8.3145\ \text{J/K} \cdot \text{mol})(673\ \text{K})} = 2.66$$

$K_p = 14.3$

$K_p = P_{NH_3} P_{HCl}$

If $P_{NH_3} = P_{HCl} = x$

then $K_p = 14.3 = x^2$ and $x = 3.8$

$P_{NH_3} = P_{HCl} = 3.8$ atm

48. Set up an ICE table. Here the acid is ionized to the extent of 1.8% or $(0.018)(0.44\ \text{M}) = 0.0079$ M

	$HOCH_2CO_2H \rightleftharpoons H_3O^+ +$		$HOCH_2CO_2^-$
Initial (M)	0.44	0	0
Change (M)	−0.0079	+0.0079	+0.0079
Equilib. (M)	0.43	0.0079	0.0079

Because $[H_3O^+] = 0.0079$ M, pH = 2.10

$$K_a = \frac{[H_3O^+][HOCH_2CO_2^-]}{[HOCH_2CO_2H]}$$

$$K_a = \frac{(0.0079)^2}{0.43} = 1.5 \times 10^{-4}$$

49. Refer to K_a values in Table 17.3, page 770.
(a) Acid strength:
  $NH_4^+ < CH_3CO_2H < HF < H_3PO_4 < HNO_3$
(b) Product-favored. (Brønsted acid–base reactions favor the weaker acid and weaker base.)

50. Most soluble: $AgCH_3CO_2$, least soluble: AgCN

51. (a) Combinations (i), (ii), (iv), and (v) contain a weak acid and its weak conjugate base and are buffer solutions.
(b) If the concentrations of the two species in the buffer are equal, pH = pK_a. The solution with highest pH is (i) and the solution with the lowest pH is (iii).
(c) Select the buffer system for which the pK_a is closest to 7.40. This is (ii) for which $pK_a = 7.21$. To adjust the pH to 7.40, add base (either additional Na_2HPO_4 or NaOH, which would convert some of the NaH_2PO_4 to Na_2HPO_4).

52. (a) $K_a = 10^{-pK_a} = 10^{-2.867} = 1.36 \times 10^{-3}$
(b) $ClCH_2CO_2H(aq) + OH^-(aq)$
  $\rightleftharpoons H_2O(\ell) + ClCH_2CO_2^-(aq)$
(c) moles acid ($c_{acid} \times V_{acid}$)
  = moles base ($c_{base} \times V_{base}$)
  $(0.154\ \text{mol/L})(0.0500\ \text{L}) = (0.128\ \text{mol/L})(V_{base})$
  $V_{base} = 0.0602$ L (= 60.2 mL)
(d) Phenolphthalein. Choose an indicator that changes color near the pH at the equivalence point of the titration. In this case, the pH at the equivalence point is slightly basic. (Figure 18.10, page 832, shows the ranges of color changes for indicators.)
(e) pH = pK_a = 2.867

(f) At the equivalence point, the solution contains 0.00770 moles $ClCH_2CO_2^-$ in a total volume of 0.1102 L (0.0602 + 0.0500 L). The concentration of this anion is 0.0699 M (0.0077 mol/0.1102 L). The anion is weakly basic:

$ClCH_2CO_2^-(aq) + H_2O(\ell)$
  $\rightleftharpoons ClCH_2CO_2H(aq) + OH^-(aq)$

For this equilibrium

$K_b = K_w/K_a = (1.0 \times 10^{-14})/(1.36 \times 10^{-3})$
  $= 7.4 \times 10^{-12}$

$$K_b = \frac{[ClCH_2CO_2H][OH^-]}{[ClCH_2CO_2^-]}$$

$$7.4 \times 10^{-12} = \frac{(x)(x)}{0.0699 - x}$$

$x = [OH^-] = 7.2 \times 10^{-7}$ M
pOH = 6.14
and so pH = 14.00 − 6.14 = 7.86

53. (a) $Cr_2O_7^{2-} + 14\ H^+ + 6\ e^- \rightarrow 2\ Cr^{3+} + 7\ H_2O$
  $3[2\ I^- \rightarrow I_2 + 2\ e^-]$

  $Cr_2O_7^{2-} + 14\ H^+ + 6\ I^- \rightarrow 2\ Cr^{3+} + 7\ H_2O + 3\ I_2$

  $Cr_2O_7^{2-}$ is reduced, I^- is the reducing agent, and the oxidation state of chromium changes from +6 to +3.
(b) $8[MnO_4^- + 2\ H_2O + 3\ e^- \rightarrow MnO_2 + 4\ OH^-]$
  $3[HS^- + 9\ OH^- \rightarrow SO_4^{2-} + 5\ H_2O + 8\ e^-]$

  $8\ MnO_4^- + 3\ HS^- + H_2O$
    $\rightarrow 8\ MnO_2 + 5\ OH^- + 3\ SO_4^{2-}$

  MnO_4^- is reduced, HS^- is the reducing agent, and the oxidation state of the manganese changes from +7 to +4.

54. (a) Cell using Zn as the anode and a chemically inert Pt electrode as the cathode.

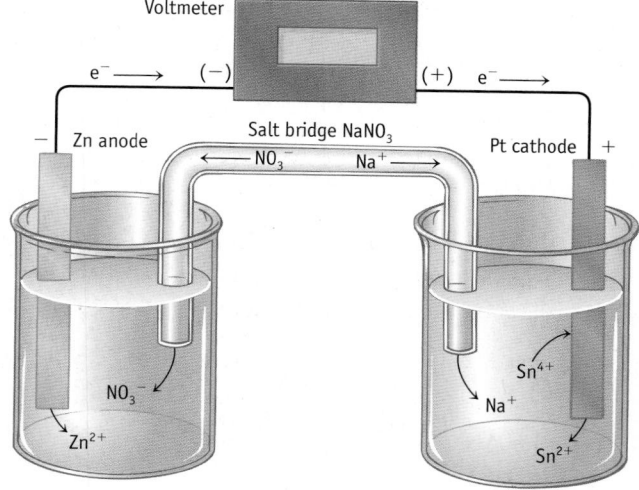

(b) The Na^+ ions move toward the $Sn^{4+} \mid Sn^{2+}$ (Pt) half-cell. The NO_3^- ions move toward the $Zn \mid Zn^{2+}$ half-cell.

(c) $Zn + Sn^{4+} \rightarrow Zn^{2+} + Sn^{2+}$

(d) $E°_{cell} = E°_{cathode} - E°_{anode}$
$= +0.15 \text{ V} - (-0.76 \text{ V}) = 0.91 \text{ V}$

55. For discussion of methodology for part (a) see "Northwest-southeast rule," page 921:

(a) Sn, Mg, and Mn

(b) Sn^{2+}

(c) Ag^+

(d) H_2

56. First, calculate moles of electrons required, next calculate the quantity of charge, and then use charge and current to calculate time required. (See Example 20.11.)

$$\text{Mol } e^- = (5.00 \text{ g Cr})\left(\frac{1 \text{ mol Cr}}{52.0 \text{ g Cr}}\right)\left(\frac{3 \text{ mol } e^-}{1 \text{ mol Cr}}\right)$$

$$= 0.288 \text{ mol } e^-$$

$$\text{Charge (C)} = (0.288 \text{ mol } e^-)\left(\frac{96,500 \text{ C}}{\text{mol } e^-}\right)$$

$$= 2.78 \times 10^4 \text{ C}$$

Charge (C) = current (A) × time (s)

time = $(2.78 \times 10^4 \text{ C}/2.50 \text{ A})$
$= 1.11 \times 10^4 \text{ s } (=186 \text{ min})$

57. (a) The pH of the original solution is almost 12, so diethylamine is a weak base. Note that $[OH^-]$ for a 0.10 M solution is a little less than 0.010 M, indicating less than 10% of the base reacts with H_2O to form OH^-.

(b) $(C_2H_5)_2NH(aq) + HCl(aq)$
$\rightleftharpoons (C_2H_5)_2NH_2{}^+(aq) + Cl^-(aq)$

(c) At the half-neutralization point (after 25 mL of 0.10 M HCl has been added), pOH = 3.0. (pOH = 14.00 − pH where the pH = 11.0). pK_b = pOH, so $K_b = 1.0 \times 10^{-3}$. (Literature value = 6.3×10^{-4})

(d) The equivalence point occurs when exactly the amount of acid required has been added. Here 50.0 mL of a 0.10 M solution of the weak base requires 50.0 mL of 0.10 M HCl, and you observe a significant drop in the pH at this volume of acid. The pH at the mid-point of the vertical portion of the curve is the pH at the equivalence point, here about 6.2. The solution should be slightly acidic, as observed. At the equivalence point the solution contains the weak acid $(C_2H_5)_2NH_2{}^+$. The calculation of the equivalence point pH is outlined as follows:

Amount of $(C_2H_5)_2NH$ titrated = 0.0050 mol
Amount of $(C_2H_5)_2NH_2{}^+$ produced = 0.0050 mol
$[(C_2H_5)_2NH_2{}^+]$ at equivalence point
$= (0.0050 \text{ mol}/0.100 \text{ L}) = 0.050 \text{ M}$
K_b for $(C_2H_5)_2NH$ (from part c) = 1.0×10^{-3} so
K_a for $(C_2H_5)_2NH_2{}^+ = K_w/K_b = 1.0 \times 10^{-11}$

$$K_a = 1.0 \times 10^{-11} = \frac{[H_3O^+][(C_2H_5)_2NH]}{[(C_2H_5)_2NH_2{}^+]} = \frac{[H_3O^+]^2}{0.050}$$

$[H_3O^+] = 7.1 \times 10^{-7}$ M so pH = 6.15

(e) The solution contains $(C_2H_5)_2NH_2{}^+(aq)$, a weak acid.

58. (a) K_a for $Ni^{2+}(aq) = 2.5 \times 10^{-11}$. Use Equation 17.5 (page 769) to calculate the hydronium ion concentration. From $[H_3O^+]$ we find pH = 5.80.

(b) K_{b1} for ethylenediamine = 8.5×10^{-5}. Use Equation 17.6 to calculate $[OH^-]$ (= 1.5×10^{-3} M). Based on this we calculate a pOH of 2.84, which leads to a pH of 11.16 (14.00 − 2.84 = 11.16). (Note that ethylenediamine can undergo a second ionization (K_{b2} = 2.7×10^{-8}), which will have only a minimal effect on pH.)

(c) Ni^{2+} is an electron-pair acceptor, a Lewis acid. NH_3, with its lone pair, is a Lewis base. (See Section 17.9.)

(d) K_f for the formation of $[Ni(NH_3)_6]^{2+}(aq)$ is 5.6×10^8. The reaction is product-favored at equilibrium.

(e) Calculating K_{net}.

$[Ni(NH_3)_6]^{2+}(aq) + 6 H_2O(\ell)$
$\rightleftharpoons [Ni(H_2O)_6]^{2+}(aq) + 6 NH_3(aq)$
$\qquad\qquad 1/K_{f1} = 1/5.5 \times 10^8$

$[Ni(H_2O)_6]^{2+}(aq) + 3 H_2NCH_2CH_2NH_2(aq)$
$\rightleftharpoons [Ni(H_2NCH_2CH_2NH_2)_3]^{2+}(aq) + 6 H_2O(\ell)$
$\qquad\qquad K_{f2} = 1.9 \times 10^{18}$

$[Ni(NH_3)_6]^{2+}(aq) + 3 H_2NCH_2CH_2NH_2(aq)$
$\rightleftharpoons [Ni(H_2NCH_2CH_2NH_2)_3]^{2+}(aq) + 6 NH_3(aq)$
$\qquad\qquad K_{net} = ?$

$K_{net} = (1/K_{f1})K_{f2} = 3.5 \times 10^9$
$\Delta_r G° = -RT \ln K = -54 \text{ kJ/mol at 298 K}$

This spontaneous (and product-favored) reaction is largely controlled by $\Delta_r S°$. $\Delta_r H°$ is probably about 0 because 6 Ni-NH$_3$ bonds are exchanged for bonds between Ni and the 6 N atoms of the three ethylenediamine molecules. $\Delta_r S°$ is expected to be large and positive because four ions or molecules are replaced by seven product ions or molecules.

59. From $\Delta_r G°$ we use Equation 19.7 (page 878) to calculate $K_p = 5.0 \times 10^{-2}$.

	$C_2H_6(g)$	$\rightleftharpoons$ $C_2H_4(g)$	+ $H_2(g)$
Initial	1.00 atm	0	0
Change	−x	+x	+x
Equilibrium	1.00 − x	x	x

$K_p = (x^2)/(1.00 - x)$

Solving this quadratic expression, we find x = 0.20 atm. Therefore, at equilibrium $P(C_2H_4) = P(H_2) = 0.20$ atm and $P(C_2H_6) = 0.80$ atm. This means $P(\text{total}) =$ 1.20 atm.

Mol % H$_2$ = $[P(H_2)/P(\text{total})]100\%$
$= [(0.20 \text{ atm})/(1.20 \text{ atm})]100\% = 17\% \text{ H}_2$

21 | The Chemistry of the Main Group Elements

Charles D. Winters

Quartz (SiO$_2$), dry ice (solid CO$_2$), and pure silicon.

Carbon and Silicon

Carbon and silicon are both highly significant elements in the earth's crust. Mendeleev placed them in the same periodic group based on the similarity in stoichiometry of their simple compounds such as their oxides (CO$_2$ and SiO$_2$). We know now that carbon is the backbone of millions of organic compounds. As we will see in this chapter, silicon, the second most abundant element in the earth's crust, is vitally important in the structures of a large number of minerals.

Probe a bit further into silicon chemistry, however, and what emerges are the surprising differences between these elements. We get a hint of this when we compare the two oxides, CO$_2$, a gas above −78 °C and 1 atm pressure, and SiO$_2$, a rock hard solid with a very high melting point. Another interesting contrast can be made between the reactions of the two simple hydrogen compounds, CH$_4$ and SiH$_4$, with water. The reaction of methane with water is reactant-favored, whereas silane will explode on contact with water.

In this chapter, we will evaluate and summarize the inorganic chemistry of the main group elements and explore the similarities and differences between elements in each periodic group.

Questions:

1. Write balanced chemical equations for the reactions of water with CH$_4$ (forming CO$_2$ and H$_2$O) and SiH$_4$ (forming SiO$_2$ and H$_2$).
2. Using enthalpy of formation data, calculate the standard enthalpy change for the reactions in Question 1.
3. Look up the electronegativities of carbon, silicon, and hydrogen. What conclusion can you draw concerning the polarity of C—H and Si—H bonds?
4. Carbon and silicon compounds with the empirical formulas (CH$_3$)$_2$CO (acetone) and (CH$_3$)$_2$SiO (a silicone polymer) also have quite different structures (Chapter 10). Draw Lewis structures for these species. This difference, along with the difference between structures of CO$_2$ and SiO$_2$, suggests a general observation about silicon compounds. Based on that observation, do you expect that a silicon compound with a structure similar to ethene (C$_2$H$_4$) exists?

Answers to these questions are in Appendix Q.

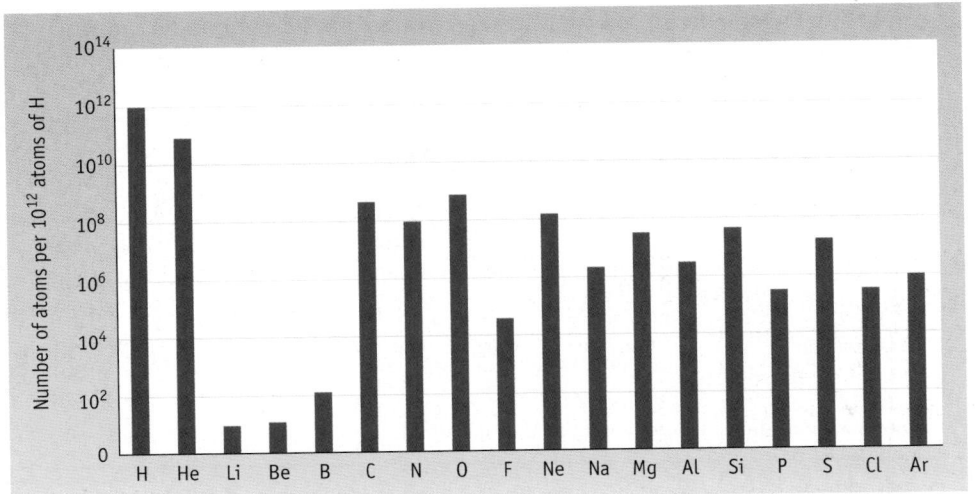
The main group or A-Group elements occupy an important place in the world of chemistry. Eight of the 10 most abundant elements on the earth are in these groups. Likewise, the top 10 chemicals produced by the U.S. chemical industry are all main group elements or their compounds.

Because main group elements and their compounds are economically important—and because they have interesting chemistries—we devote this chapter to a brief survey of these elements.

Chemistry.Now™

Throughout the text this icon introduces an opportunity for self-study or to explore interactive tutorials by signing in at **www.cengage.com/login**.

21.1 Element Abundances

The abundance of the first 18 elements in the solar system is plotted against their atomic numbers in Figure 21.1. As you can see, hydrogen and helium are the most abundant by a wide margin because most of the mass of the solar system resides in the sun, and these elements are the sun's primary components. Lithium, beryllium, and boron are low in abundance, but carbon's abundance is very high. From this point on, with the exception of iron and nickel, elemental abundances gradually decline as the atomic number increases.

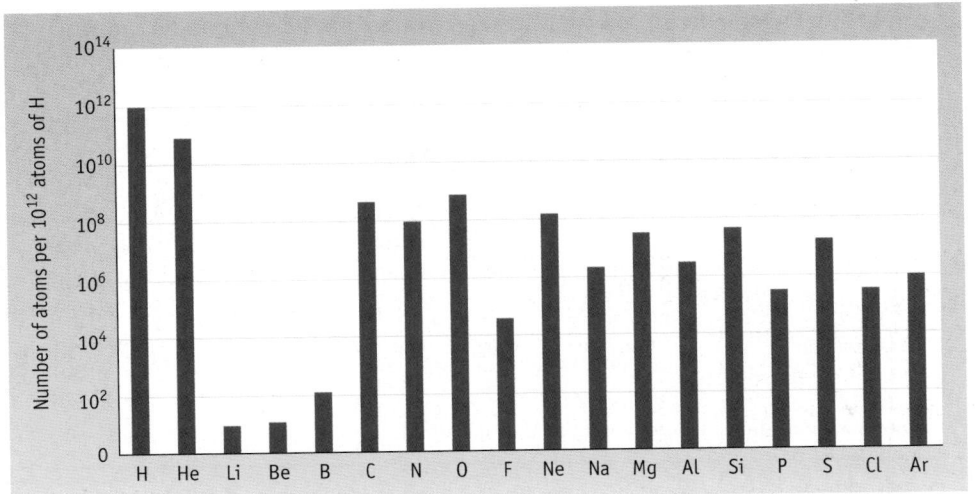

FIGURE 21.1 Abundance of elements 1–18. Li, Be, and B have relatively low abundances because they are circumvented when elements are made in stars. The common elements such as C, O, and Ne are made in stars by the accretion of alpha particles (helium nuclei). Helium has an atomic number of 2. If three He atoms combine, they produce an atom with atomic number 6 (carbon). Adding yet another He atom gives an atom with atomic number 8 (oxygen), and so on. (Notice that the vertical axis uses a logarithmic scale. This means, for example, there are 10^{12} H atoms for every 100 B atoms.)

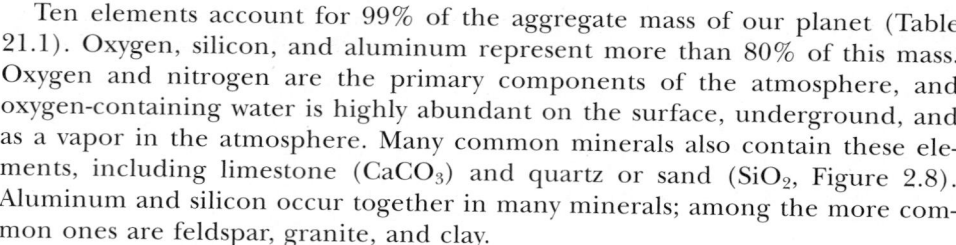

Ten elements account for 99% of the aggregate mass of our planet (Table 21.1). Oxygen, silicon, and aluminum represent more than 80% of this mass. Oxygen and nitrogen are the primary components of the atmosphere, and oxygen-containing water is highly abundant on the surface, underground, and as a vapor in the atmosphere. Many common minerals also contain these elements, including limestone ($CaCO_3$) and quartz or sand (SiO_2, Figure 2.8). Aluminum and silicon occur together in many minerals; among the more common ones are feldspar, granite, and clay.

TABLE 21.1 The 10 Most Abundant Elements in Earth's Crust

Rank	Element	Abundance (ppm)*
1	Oxygen	474,000
2	Silicon	277,000
3	Aluminum	82,000
4	Iron	56,300
5	Calcium	41,000
6	Sodium	23,600
7	Magnesium	23,300
8	Potassium	21,000
9	Titanium	5,600
10	Hydrogen	1,520

*ppm = g per 1000 kg. Most abundance data taken from J. Emsley: *The Elements*, New York, Oxford University Press, 3rd edition, 1998.

21.2 The Periodic Table: A Guide to the Elements

The similarities in the properties of certain elements guided Mendeleev when he created the first periodic table (◄ page 59). He placed elements in groups based partly on the composition of their common compounds with oxygen and hydrogen (see Table 21.2). We now understand that the elements are grouped according to the arrangements of their valence electrons.

Recall that the metallic character of the elements declines on moving from left to right in the periodic table. Elements in Group 1A, the alkali metals, are the most metallic elements in the periodic table. Elements on the far right are nonmetals, and in between are the metalloids. Metallic character also increases from the top of a group to the bottom. This is especially well illustrated by Group 4A. Carbon, at the top of the group, is a nonmetal; silicon and germanium are metalloids; and tin and lead are metals (Figure 21.2). The significance of metallic character in a discussion of the chemistry of the elements is readily apparent; metals typically form ionic compounds, whereas compounds composed only of nonmetals are covalent. Typically, ionic compounds are crystalline solids that have high melting points and conduct electricity in the molten state. Covalent compounds, on the other hand, can be gases, liquids, or solids and have low melting and boiling points.

Valence Electrons

The ns and np electrons are the valence electrons for main group elements (where n is the period in which the element is found) (◄ Section 7.4). The chemical behavior of an element is determined by the valence electrons.

When considering electronic structure, a useful reference point is the noble gases (Group 8A), elements having filled electron subshells. Helium has an electron configuration of $1s^2$; the other noble gases have ns^2np^6 valence electron configura-

FIGURE 21.2 Group 4A elements. A nonmetal, carbon (graphite crucible); a metalloid, silicon (round, lustrous bar); and metals tin (chips of metal) and lead (a bullet, a toy, and a sphere).

Charles D. Winters

TABLE 21.2 Similarities within Periodic Groups*

Group	1A	2A	3A	4A	5A	6A	7A
Common oxide	M_2O	MO	M_2O_3	EO_2	E_4O_{10}	EO_3	E_2O_7
Common hydride	MH	MH_2	MH_3	EH_4	EH_3	EH_2	EH
Highest oxidation state	+1	+2	+3	+4	+5	+6	+7
Common oxoanion			BO_3^{3-}	CO_3^{2-}	NO_3^{-}	SO_4^{2-}	ClO_4^{-}
				SiO_4^{4-}	PO_4^{3-}		

*M denotes a metal and E denotes a nonmetal or metalloid.

tions. The dominant characteristic of the noble gases is their lack of reactivity. Indeed, the first two elements in the group do not form any compounds that can be isolated. The other four elements are now known to have limited chemistry, however, and the discovery of xenon compounds in the 1960s ranks as one of the most interesting developments in modern chemistry.

Ionic Compounds of Main Group Elements

Ions of main group elements having filled s and p subshells are very common—justifying the often-seen statement that elements react in ways that achieve a "noble gas configuration." The elements in Groups 1A and 2A form 1+ and 2+ ions with electron configurations that are the same as those for the previous noble gases. All common compounds of these elements (e.g., NaCl, CaCO$_3$) are ionic. The metallic elements in Group 3A (aluminum, gallium, indium, and thallium, but not the metalloid boron) form compounds containing 3+ ions.

Elements of Groups 6A and 7A can also achieve a noble gas configuration by adding electrons. The Group 7A elements (halogens) form anions with a 1− charge (the halide ions, F$^-$, Cl$^-$, Br$^-$, I$^-$), and the Group 6A elements form anions with a 2− charge (O^{2-}, S^{2-}, Se^{2-}, Te^{2-}). In Group 5A chemistry, 3− ions with a noble gas configuration (such as the nitride ion, N^{3-}) are also known. The energy required to form highly charged anions is large, however, which means that other types of chemical behavior will usually take precedence.

■ **EXAMPLE 21.1 Reactions of Group 1A–3A Elements**

Problem Give the formula and name for the product in each of the following reactions. Write a balanced chemical equation for the reaction.

(a) Ca(s) + S$_8$(s)

(b) Rb(s) + I$_2$(s)

(c) lithium and chlorine

(d) aluminum and oxygen

Strategy Predictions are based on the assumption that ions are formed with the electron configuration of the nearest noble gas. Group 1A elements form 1+ ions; Group 2A elements form 2+ ions; and metals in Group 3A form 3+ ions. In their reactions with metals, halogen atoms typically add a single electron to give anions with a 1− charge; Group 6A elements add two electrons to form anions with a 2− charge. For names of products, refer to the nomenclature discussion on page 77.

Solution

	Balanced Equation	Product Name
(a)	8 Ca(s) + S$_8$(s) → 8 CaS(s)	Calcium sulfide
(b)	2 Rb(s) + I$_2$(s) → 2 RbI(s)	Rubidium iodide
(c)	2 Li(s) + Cl$_2$(g) → 2 LiCl(s)	Lithium chloride
(d)	4 Al(s) + 3 O$_2$(g) → 2 Al$_2$O$_3$(s)	Aluminum oxide

EXERCISE 21.1 Main Group Element Chemistry

Write a balanced chemical equation for a reaction forming the following compounds from the elements.

(a) NaBr   **(c)** PbO

(b) CaSe   **(d)** AlCl$_3$

Molecular Compounds of Main Group Elements

Many avenues of reactivity are open to nonmetallic main group elements. Reactions with metals generally result in formation of ionic compounds, whereas compounds containing only metalloids and nonmetallic elements are generally molecular in nature.

Molecular compounds are encountered with the Group 3A element boron (Figure 21.3), and the chemistry of carbon in Group 4A is dominated by molecular compounds with covalent bonds (◀ Chapters 8 and 10). Similarly, nitrogen chemistry is dominated by molecular compounds. Consider ammonia, NH_3; the various nitrogen oxides; and nitric acid, HNO_3. In each of these species, nitrogen bonds covalently to another nonmetallic element. Also in Group 5A, phosphorus reacts with chlorine to produce the molecular compounds PCl_3 and PCl_5 (◀ page 113).

The valence electron configurations of an element determine the composition of its molecular compounds. Involving all the valence electrons in the formation of a compound is a frequent occurrence in main group element chemistry. We should not be surprised to discover compounds in which the central element has the highest possible oxidation number (such as P in PF_5). The highest oxidation number is readily apparent: it equals the group number. Thus, the highest (and only) oxidation number of sodium in its compounds is $+1$; the highest oxidation number of C is $+4$; and the highest oxidation number of phosphorus is $+5$ (Tables 21.2 and 21.3).

FIGURE 21.3 Boron halides. Liquid BBr_3 (left) and solid BI_3 (right). Formed from a metalloid and a nonmetal, both are molecular compounds. Both are sealed in glass ampules to prevent these boron compounds from reacting with H_2O in the air.

TABLE 21.3 Fluorine Compounds Formed by Main Group Elements

Group	Compound	Bonding
1A	NaF	Ionic
2A	MgF_2	Ionic
3A	AlF_3	Ionic
4A	SiF_4	Covalent
5A	PF_5	Covalent
6A	SF_6	Covalent
7A	IF_7	Covalent
8A	XeF_4	Covalent

■ **EXAMPLE 21.2 Predicting Formulas for Compounds of Main Group Elements**

Problem Predict the formula for each of the following:

(a) the product of the reaction between germanium and excess oxygen

(b) the product of the reaction of arsenic and fluorine

(c) a compound formed from phosphorus and excess chlorine

(d) an anion of selenic acid

Strategy We will predict that in each reaction the element other than the halogen or oxygen in each product achieves its most positive oxidation number, a value equal to the number of its periodic group.

Solution

(a) The Group 4A element germanium should have a maximum oxidation number of $+4$. Thus, its oxide has the formula GeO_2.

(b) Arsenic, in Group 5A, reacts vigorously with fluorine to form AsF_5, in which arsenic has an oxidation number of $+5$.

(c) PCl_5 is formed when the Group 5A element phosphorus reacts with excess chlorine.

(d) The chemistries of S and Se are similar. Sulfur, in Group 6A, has a maximum oxidation number of $+6$, so it forms SO_3 and sulfuric acid, H_2SO_4. Selenium, also in Group 6A, has analogous chemistry, forming SeO_3 and selenic acid, H_2SeO_4. The anion of this acid is the selenate ion, SeO_4^{2-}.

EXERCISE 21.2 Predicting Formulas for Main Group Compounds

Write the formula for each of the following:

(a) hydrogen telluride   **(c)** selenium hexachloride

(b) sodium arsenate   **(d)** perbromic acid

There are many similarities among elements in the same periodic group. This means you can use compounds of more common elements as examples when you encounter compounds of elements with which you are not familiar. For example, water, H_2O, is the simplest hydrogen compound of oxygen. You can reasonably expect the hydrogen compounds of other Group 6A elements to be H_2S, H_2Se, and H_2Te; all are well known.

■ EXAMPLE 21.3 Predicting Formulas

Problem Predict the formula for each of the following:

(a) a compound of hydrogen and phosphorus

(b) the hypobromite ion

(c) germane (the simplest hydrogen compound of germanium)

(d) two oxides of tellurium

Strategy Recall as examples some of the compounds of lighter elements in a group, and then assume other elements in that group will form analogous compounds.

Solution

(a) Phosphine, PH_3, has a composition analogous to ammonia, NH_3.

(b) Hypobromite ion, BrO^-, is similar to the hypochlorite ion, ClO^-, the anion of hypochlorous acid ($HClO$).

(c) GeH_4 is analogous to CH_4 and SiH_4, other Group 4A hydrogen compounds.

(d) Te and S are in Group 6A. TeO_2 and TeO_3 are analogs of the oxides of sulfur, SO_2 and SO_3.

■ EXAMPLE 21.4 Recognizing Incorrect Formulas

Problem One formula is incorrect in each of the following groups. Pick out the incorrect formula, and indicate why it is incorrect.

(a) $CsSO_4$, KCl, $NaNO_3$, Li_2O

(b) MgO, CaI_2, $BaPO_4$, $CaCO_3$

(c) CO, CO_2, CO_3

(d) PF_5, PF_4^+, PF_2, PF_6^-

Strategy Look for errors such as incorrect charges on ions or an oxidation number exceeding the maximum possible for the periodic group.

Solution

(a) $CsSO_4$. Sulfate ion has a 2− charge, so this formula would require a Cs^{2+} ion. Cesium, in Group 1A, forms only 1+ ions. The formula of cesium sulfate is Cs_2SO_4.

(b) $BaPO_4$. This formula implies a Ba^{3+} ion (because the phosphate anion is PO_4^{3-}). The cation charge does not equal the group number. The formula of barium phosphate is $Ba_3(PO_4)_2$.

(c) CO_3. Given that O has an oxidation number of −2, carbon would have an oxidation number of +6. Carbon is in Group 4A, however, and can have a maximum oxidation number of +4.

(d) PF_2. This species has an odd number of electrons. Very few odd electron molecules are commonly seen. Examples include NO, NO_2, and ClO_2.

Comment To chemists, this exercise is second nature. Incorrect formulas stand out. You will find that your ability to write and recognize correct formulas will grow as you learn more chemistry.

EXERCISE 21.3 Predicting Formulas

Identify a compound or ion based on a second-period element that has a formula and Lewis structure analogous to each of the following:

(a) PH_4^+

(b) S_2^{2-}

(c) P_2H_4

(d) PF_3

A Closer Look

Hydrogen, Helium, and Balloons

In 1783, Jacques Charles first used hydrogen to fill a balloon large enough to float above the French countryside (◀ page 516). In World War I, hydrogen-filled observation balloons were used. The Graf Zeppelin, a passenger-carrying dirigible built in Germany in 1928, was also filled with hydrogen. It carried more than 13,000 people between Germany and the United States until 1937, when it was replaced by the Hindenburg. The Hindenburg was designed to be filled with helium. At that time, World War II was approaching, and the United

States, which has much of the world's supply of helium, would not sell the gas to Germany. As a consequence, the Hindenburg had to use hydrogen. The Hindenburg exploded and burned when landing in Lakehurst, New Jersey, in May 1937. Of the 62 people on board, only about half escaped uninjured. As a result of this disaster, hydrogen has acquired a reputation as being a very dangerous substance. Actually, it is as safe to handle as any other fuel, as evidenced by the large quantities used in rockets today.

Mary Evans Picture Library/Photo Researchers, Inc.

The Hindenburg. This hydrogen-filled dirigible crashed in Lakehurst, New Jersey, in May 1937. Some have speculated that the aluminum paint coating the skin of the dirigible was involved in sparking the fire.

EXERCISE 21.4 Recognizing Incorrect Formulas

Explain why compounds with the following formulas would not be expected to exist: ClO, Na_2Cl, $CaCH_3CO_2$, C_3H_7.

21.3 Hydrogen

Chemical and Physical Properties of Hydrogen

Hydrogen has three isotopes, two of them stable (protium and deuterium) and one radioactive (tritium).

Isotopes of Hydrogen

Isotope Mass (u)	Symbol	Name
1.0078	^1H (H)	Hydrogen (protium)
2.0141	^2H (D)	Deuterium
3.0160	^3H (T)	Tritium

Of the three isotopes, only H and D are found in nature in significant quantities. Tritium, which is produced by cosmic ray bombardment of nitrogen in the atmosphere, is found to the extent of 1 atom per 10^{18} atoms of ordinary hydrogen. Tritium has a half-life of 12.26 years.

Under standard conditions, hydrogen is a colorless gas. Its very low boiling point, 20.7 K, reflects its nonpolar character and low molar mass. As the least dense gas known, it is ideal for filling lighter-than-air craft.

Deuterium compounds have been the subject of much research. One important observation is that, because D has twice the mass of H, reactions involving D atom transfer are slightly slower than those involving H atoms. This knowledge led to a way to produce D_2O or "heavy water." Hydrogen can be produced, albeit expensively, by electrolysis of water (Figure 21.4).

$$2 H_2O(\ell) + \text{electrical energy} \rightarrow 2 H_2(g) + O_2(g)$$

Any sample of natural water always contains a tiny concentration of D_2O. When electrolyzed, H_2O is electrolyzed more rapidly than D_2O. Thus, as the electrolysis proceeds, the liquid remaining is enriched in D_2O. Repeating this process many times will eventually give pure D_2O, often called "heavy water." Large amounts of D_2O are now produced because this compound is used as a moderator in some nuclear reactors that are used for power generation.

Hydrogen combines chemically with virtually every other element, except the noble gases. There are three different types of binary hydrogen-containing compounds.

Ionic metal hydrides are formed in the reaction of H_2 with a Group 1A or 2A metal.

$$2 Na(s) + H_2(g) \rightarrow 2 NaH(s)$$

$$Ca(s) + H_2(g) \rightarrow CaH_2(s)$$

These compounds contain the hydride ion, H^-, in which hydrogen has a -1 oxidation number.

Molecular compounds (such as H_2O, HF, and NH_3) are generally formed by direct combination of hydrogen with nonmetallic elements (Figure 21.5). The oxidation number of the hydrogen atom in these compounds is $+1$, but covalent bonds to hydrogen are the rule.

$$N_2(g) + 3 H_2(g) \rightarrow 2 NH_3(g)$$

$$F_2(g) + H_2(g) \rightarrow 2 HF(g)$$

Hydrogen is absorbed by many metals to form *interstitial hydrides*, the third general class of hydrogen compounds. This name refers to the structures of these species, in which the hydrogen atoms reside in the spaces between the metal atoms (called *interstices*) in the crystal lattice. Palladium metal, for example, can soak up 1000 times its volume of hydrogen (at STP). Most interstitial hydrides are non-stoichiometric; that is, the ratio of metal and hydrogen is not a whole number. When interstitial metal hydrides are heated, H_2 is driven out. This phenomenon allows these materials to store H_2, just as a sponge can store water. It suggests one way to store hydrogen for use as a fuel in automobiles (◄ page 264).

Preparation of Hydrogen

About 300 billion liters (STP) of hydrogen gas are produced annually worldwide, and virtually all is used immediately in the manufacture of ammonia (► Section 21.8), methanol (◄ Section 10.3), or other chemicals.

Some hydrogen is made from coal and steam, a reaction that has been used for more than 100 years.

$$C(s) + H_2O(g) \longrightarrow \underline{H_2(g) + CO(g)}$$
$$\text{water gas or synthesis gas}$$

$$\Delta_r H° = +131 \text{ kJ/mol-rxn}$$

The reaction is carried out by injecting water into a bed of red-hot coke. The mixture of gases produced, called *water gas* or *synthesis gas*, was used until about 1950 as a fuel for cooking, heating, and lighting. However, it has serious drawbacks. It

Charles D. Winters

FIGURE 21.4 Electrolysis of water.
Electrolysis of water (containing dilute H_2SO_4 as an electrolyte) gives O_2 (left) and H_2 (right).

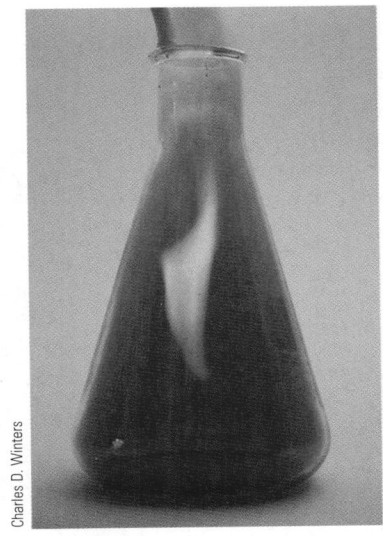

Charles D. Winters

FIGURE 21.5 The reaction of H_2 and Br_2. Hydrogen gas burns in an atmosphere of bromine vapor to give hydrogen bromide.

FIGURE 21.6 Production of water gas. Water gas, also called synthesis gas, is a mixture of CO and H_2. It is produced by treating coal, coke, or a hydrocarbon like methane with steam at high temperatures in plants such as that pictured here. Methane has the advantage that it gives more total H_2 per gram than other hydrocarbons, and the ratio of the by-product CO_2 to H_2 is lower.

produces only about half as much heat as an equal amount of methane does, and the flame is nearly invisible. Moreover, because it contains carbon monoxide, water gas is toxic.

The largest quantity of hydrogen is now produced by the *catalytic steam reformation of hydrocarbons* such as methane in natural gas (Figure 21.6). Methane reacts with steam at high temperature to give H_2 and CO.

$$CH_4(g) + H_2O(g) \rightarrow 3\ H_2(g) + CO(g) \qquad \Delta_r H° = +206\ kJ/mol\text{-}rxn$$

The reaction is rapid at 900–1000 °C and goes nearly to completion. More hydrogen can be obtained in a second step in which the CO formed in the first step reacts with more water. This so-called *water gas shift reaction* is run at 400–500 °C and is slightly exothermic.

$$H_2O(g) + CO(g) \rightarrow H_2(g) + CO_2(g) \qquad \Delta_r H° = -41\ kJ/mol\text{-}rxn$$

The CO_2 formed in the process is removed by reaction with CaO (to give solid $CaCO_3$), leaving fairly pure hydrogen.

Perhaps the cleanest way to make hydrogen on a relatively large scale is the electrolysis of water (Figure 21.4). This approach provides not only hydrogen gas but also high-purity O_2. Because electricity is quite expensive, however, this method is not generally used commercially.

Table 21.4 and Figure 21.7 give examples of reactions used to produce H_2 gas in the laboratory. The most often used method is the reaction of a metal with an acid. Alternatively, the reaction of aluminum with aqueous NaOH (Figure 21.7b) also generates hydrogen. During World War II, this reaction was used to obtain hydrogen to inflate small balloons for weather observation and to raise radio antennas. Metallic aluminum was plentiful at the time because it came from damaged aircraft.

The combination of a metal hydride and water (Figure 21.7c) is an efficient but expensive way to synthesize H_2 in the laboratory. The reaction is more commonly used in laboratories to dry organic solvents because the metal hydride reacts with traces of water present in the solvent.

EXERCISE 21.5 Hydrogen Chemistry

Use bond enthalpies (page 389) to estimate the enthalpy change for the reaction of methane and water to give hydrogen and carbon monoxide (with all compounds in the gas phase).

FIGURE 21.7
Producing hydrogen gas.

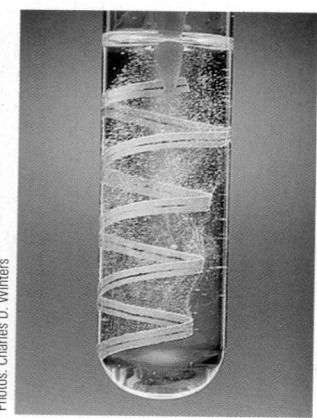

(a) The reaction of magnesium and acid. The products are hydrogen gas and a magnesium salt.

(b) The reaction of aluminum and NaOH. The products of this reaction are hydrogen gas and a solution of Na[Al(OH)$_4$].

(c) The reaction of CaH_2 and water. The products are hydrogen gas and Ca(OH)$_2$.

TABLE 21.4 Methods for Preparing H₂ in the Laboratory

1. Metal + Acid → metal salt + H₂

   $Mg(s) + 2\ HCl(aq) \rightarrow MgCl_2(aq) + H_2(g)$

2. Metal + H₂O → metal hydroxide or oxide + H₂

   $2\ Na(s) + 2\ H_2O(\ell) \rightarrow 2\ NaOH(aq) + H_2(g)$

   $2\ Fe(s) + 3\ H_2O(\ell) \rightarrow Fe_2O_3(s) + 3\ H_2(g)$

   $2\ Al(s) + 2\ KOH(aq) + 6\ H_2O(\ell) \rightarrow 2\ K[Al(OH)_4](aq) + 3\ H_2(g)$

3. Metal hydride + H₂O → metal hydroxide + H₂

   $CaH_2(s) + 2\ H_2O(\ell) \rightarrow Ca(OH)_2(s) + 2\ H_2(g)$

FIGURE 21.8 The importance of salt. All animals, including humans, need a certain amount of salt in their diet. Sodium ions are important in maintaining electrolyte balance and in regulating osmotic pressure. For an interesting account of the importance of salt in society, culture, history, and economy, see *Salt, A World History*, by M. Kurlansky, New York, Penguin Books, 2002.

21.4 The Alkali Metals, Group 1A

Sodium and potassium are, respectively, the sixth and eighth most abundant elements in the earth's crust by mass. In contrast, lithium is relatively rare, as are rubidium and cesium. Only traces of radioactive francium occur in nature. Its longest-lived isotope (^{223}Fr) has a half-life of only 22 minutes.

The Group 1A elements are metals, and all are highly reactive with oxygen, water, and other oxidizing agents (see Figure 7.13, page 329). In all cases, compounds of the Group 1A metals contain the element as a 1+ ion. The free metal is never found in nature.

Most sodium and potassium compounds are water-soluble (◄ solubility guidelines, Figure 3.10), so it is not surprising that sodium and potassium compounds are found either in the oceans or in underground deposits that are the residue of ancient seas. To a much smaller extent, these elements are also found in minerals, such as Chilean saltpeter ($NaNO_3$).

Despite the fact that sodium is only slightly more abundant than potassium on the earth, sea water contains significantly more sodium than potassium (2.8% NaCl versus 0.8% KCl). Why the great difference? Most compounds of both elements are water-soluble, so why didn't rain dissolve Na- and K-containing minerals over the centuries and carry them down to the sea, so that they appear in the same proportions in the oceans as on land? The answer lies in the fact that potassium is an important factor in plant growth. Most plants contain four to six times as much combined potassium as sodium. Thus, most of the potassium ions in groundwater from dissolved minerals are taken up preferentially by plants, whereas sodium salts continue on to the oceans. (Because plants require potassium, commercial fertilizers usually contain a significant amount of potassium salts.)

Some NaCl is essential in the diet of humans and other animals because many biological functions are controlled by the concentrations of Na^+ and Cl^- ions (Figure 21.8). The fact that salt has long been recognized as important is evident in surprising ways. For example, we are paid a "salary" for work done. This word is derived from the Latin *salarium*, which meant "salt money" because Roman soldiers were paid in salt.

Preparation of Sodium and Potassium

Sodium is produced by reducing sodium ions in sodium salts. However, common chemical reducing agents are not powerful enough to convert sodium ions to sodium metal. Because of this, the metals are usually prepared by electrolysis.

Group 1A
Alkali metals

| Lithium 3 **Li** 20 ppm |
| Sodium 11 **Na** 23,600 ppm |
| Potassium 19 **K** 21,000 ppm |
| Rubidium 37 **Rb** 90 ppm |
| Cesium 55 **Cs** 0.0003 ppm |
| Francium 87 **Fr** trace |

Element abundances are in parts per million in the earth's crust.

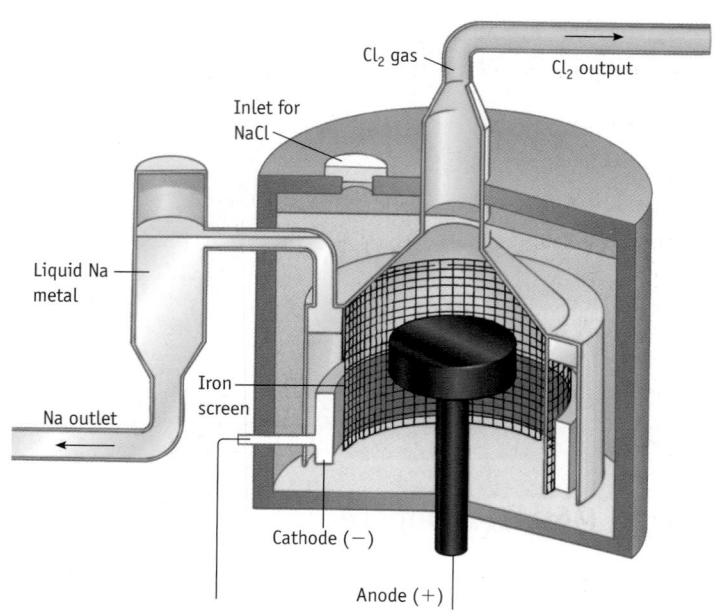

FIGURE 21.9. A Downs cell for preparing sodium. A circular iron cathode is separated from the graphite anode by an iron screen. At the temperature of the electrolysis, about 600 °C, sodium is a liquid. It floats to the top and is drawn off periodically. Chlorine gas is produced at the anode and collected inside the inverted cone in the center of the cell.

The English chemist Sir Humphry Davy first isolated sodium in 1807 by the electrolysis of molten sodium carbonate. However, the element remained a laboratory curiosity until 1824, when it was found sodium could be used to reduce aluminum chloride to aluminum metal. At that time, metallic aluminum was rare and very valuable, so this discovery inspired considerable interest in manufacturing sodium. By 1886, a practical method of sodium production had been devised (the reduction of NaOH with carbon). Unfortunately for sodium producers, in this same year Charles Hall and Paul Heroult invented the electrolytic method for aluminum production (▶ page 980), thereby eliminating this market for sodium.

Sodium is currently produced by the electrolysis of molten NaCl (◀ Section 20.7). The Downs cell for the electrolysis of molten NaCl operates at 7 to 8 V with currents of 25,000 to 40,000 amps (Figure 21.9). The cell is filled with a mixture of dry NaCl, $CaCl_2$, and $BaCl_2$. Adding other salts to NaCl lowers the melting point from that of pure NaCl (800.7 °C) to about 600 °C. [Recall that solutions have lower melting points than pure solvents (Chapter 14).] Sodium is produced at a copper or iron cathode that surrounds a circular graphite anode. Directly over the cathode is an inverted trough in which the low-density, molten sodium (melting point, 97.8 °C) collects. Chlorine, a valuable by-product, collects at the anode.

Potassium can also be made by electrolysis. Molten potassium is soluble in molten KCl, however, making separation of the metal difficult. The preferred method for preparation of potassium uses the reaction of sodium vapor with molten KCl, with potassium being continually removed from the equilibrium mixture.

$$Na(g) + KCl(\ell) \rightleftharpoons K(g) + NaCl(\ell)$$

Properties of Sodium and Potassium

Sodium and potassium are silvery metals that are soft and easily cut with a knife (see Figure 2.6). They are just a bit less dense than water. Their melting points are quite low, 97.8 °C for sodium and 63.7 °C for potassium.

All of the alkali metals are highly reactive. When exposed to moist air, the metal surface quickly becomes coated with a film of oxide or hydroxide. Consequently, the metals must be stored in a way that avoids contact with air, typically by placing them in kerosene or mineral oil.

■ **Alkali Metals React with Water—Thermodynamics and Kinetics** The alkali metals all react vigorously with water, and it is easily observed that the violence of the reaction increases with atomic number. This seems counter to the argument presented in *A Closer Look* that lithium is the best reducing agent. However, the reducing ability of a metal is a thermodynamic property, whereas the violence of the reaction is mainly a consequence of reaction rate.

The Reducing Ability of the Alkali Metals

The uses of the Group 1A metals depend on their reducing ability. The values of $E°$ reveal that Li is the best reducing agent in the group, whereas Na is the poorest; the remainder of these metals have roughly comparable reducing ability.

Reduction Potential

Element	$E°$ (V)
$Li^+ + e^- \rightarrow Li$	−3.045
$Na^+ + e^- \rightarrow Na$	−2.714
$K^+ + e^- \rightarrow K$	−2.925
$Rb^+ + e^- \rightarrow Rb$	−2.925
$Cs^+ + e^- \rightarrow Cs$	−2.92

Analysis of $E°$ is a thermodynamic problem, and to understand it better we can break the process of metal oxidation, $M(s) \rightarrow M^+(aq) + e^-$, into a series of steps. Here, we imagine that the metal sublimes to vapor, an electron is removed to form the gaseous cation, and the cation is hydrated. The first two steps require energy, but the last is exother-

$$M(g) \xrightarrow{IE \text{ (ionization energy)}} M^+(g) + e^-$$

$$\Delta_{sub}H \uparrow \qquad \qquad \downarrow \Delta_{hyd}H$$

$$M(s) \xrightarrow{\Delta_r H_{net}} M^+(aq) + e^-$$

mic. From Hess's law (page 233), we know that the overall energy change should be

$$\Delta_r H_{net} = \Delta_{sub}H + IE + \Delta_{hyd}H$$

The element that is the best reducing agent should have the most negative (or least positive) value of ΔH. That is, the best reducing agent should be the metal that has the most exothermic value for its hydration energy because this can offset the energy of the endothermic steps ($\Delta_{sub}H$ and IE). For the alkali metals, enthalpies of hydration range from −506 kJ/mol for Li^+ to −180 kJ/mol for Cs^+. The fact that $\Delta_{hyd}H$ is so much greater for Li^+ than for Cs^+ largely accounts for the difference in reducing ability.

While this analysis of the problem gives us a reasonable explanation for the great reducing ability of lithium, recall that $E°$ is directly related to $\Delta_r G°$ and not to $\Delta H°$. However, $\Delta_r G°$ is largely determined by $\Delta_r H°$, so it is possible to relate variations in $E°$ to variations in $\Delta_r H°$.

Charles D. Winters

Potassium is a very good reducing agent and reacts vigorously with water.

The high reactivity of Group 1A metals is exemplified by their reaction with water, which generates an aqueous solution of the metal hydroxide and hydrogen gas (Figure 7.13, page 329),

$$2 Na(s) + 2 H_2O(\ell) \rightarrow 2 Na^+(aq) + 2 OH^-(aq) + H_2(g)$$

and their reaction with any of the halogens to yield a metal halide (Figure 1.4),

$$2 Na(s) + Cl_2(g) \rightarrow 2 NaCl(s)$$

$$2 K(s) + Br_2(\ell) \rightarrow 2 KBr(s)$$

Chemistry often produces surprises. Group 1A metal oxides, M_2O, are known, but they are not the principal products of reactions between the Group 1A elements and oxygen. Instead, the primary product of the reaction of sodium and oxygen is sodium *peroxide*, Na_2O_2, whereas the principal product from the reaction of potassium and oxygen is KO_2, potassium *superoxide*.

$$2 Na(s) + O_2(g) \rightarrow Na_2O_2(s)$$

$$K(s) + O_2(g) \rightarrow KO_2(s)$$

Both Na_2O_2 and KO_2 are ionic compounds. The Group 1A cation is paired with either the peroxide ion (O_2^{2-}) or the superoxide ion (O_2^-). These compounds are not merely laboratory curiosities. They are used in oxygen generation devices in places where people are confined, such as submarines, aircraft, and spacecraft, or when an emergency supply is needed. When a person breathes, 0.82 L of CO_2 is exhaled for every 1 L of O_2 inhaled. Thus, a requirement of an O_2 generation system is that it should produce a larger volume of O_2 than the volume of CO_2

Courtesy of Mine Safety Appliances Company

FIGURE 21.10. A closed-circuit breathing apparatus that generates its own oxygen. One source of oxygen is potassium superoxide (KO_2). Both carbon dioxide and moisture exhaled by the wearer into the breathing tube react with the KO_2 to generate oxygen. Because the rate of the chemical reaction is determined by the quantity of moisture and carbon dioxide exhaled, the production of oxygen is regulated automatically. With each exhalation, more oxygen is produced by volume than is required by the user.

taken in. This requirement is met with superoxides (Figure 21.10). With KO_2 the reaction is

$$4\ KO_2(s) + 2\ CO_2(g) \rightarrow 2\ K_2CO_3(s) + 3\ O_2(g)$$

Important Lithium, Sodium, and Potassium Compounds

Electrolysis of aqueous sodium chloride (*brine*) is the basis of one of the largest chemical industries in the United States.

$$2\ NaCl(aq) + 2\ H_2O(\ell) \rightarrow Cl_2(g) + 2\ NaOH(aq) + H_2(g)$$

Two of the products from this process—chlorine and sodium hydroxide—give the industry its name: the *chlor-alkali industry*. More than 10 billion kilograms of Cl_2 and NaOH is produced annually in the United States.

Sodium carbonate, Na_2CO_3, is another commercially important compound of sodium. It is also known by two common names, *soda ash* and *washing soda*. In the past, it was largely manufactured by combining NaCl, ammonia, and CO_2 in the *Solvay process* (which remains the method of choice in many countries). In the United States, however, sodium carbonate is obtained from naturally occurring deposits of the mineral *trona*, $Na_2CO_3 \cdot NaHCO_3 \cdot 2\ H_2O$ (Figure 21.11).

Owing to the environmental problems associated with the chlor-alkali process, considerable interest has arisen in the possibility of manufacturing sodium hydroxide by other methods. This has led to a revival of the old "soda-lime process," which produces NaOH from inexpensive lime (CaO) and soda ash (Na_2CO_3).

$$Na_2CO_3(aq) + CaO(s) + H_2O(\ell) \rightarrow 2\ NaOH(aq) + CaCO_3(s)$$

The insoluble calcium carbonate by-product is filtered off, then heated (calcining) to convert it to lime, which is recycled into the reaction system.

$$CaCO_3(s) \rightarrow CaO(s) + CO_2(g)$$

Sodium bicarbonate, $NaHCO_3$, also known as *baking soda*, is another common compound of sodium. Not only is $NaHCO_3$ used in cooking, but it is also added in small amounts to table salt. NaCl is often contaminated with small amounts of $MgCl_2$. The magnesium salt is hygroscopic; that is, it picks water up from the air

FIGURE 21.11 Producing soda ash. Trona mined in Wyoming and California is processed into soda ash (Na_2CO_3) and other sodium-based chemicals. Soda ash is the ninth most widely used chemical in the United States. Domestically, about half of all soda ash production is used in making glass. The remainder goes to make chemicals such as sodium silicate, sodium phosphate, and sodium cyanide. Some is also used to make detergents, in the pulp and paper industry, and in water treatment.

(a) (Above) A mine in California. The mineral trona is taken from a mine 1600 feet deep.

(b) (Right) Blocks of trona are cut from the face of the mine.

and, in doing so, causes the NaCl to clump. Adding $NaHCO_3$ converts $MgCl_2$ to magnesium carbonate, a nonhygroscopic salt.

$$MgCl_2(s) + 2\ NaHCO_3(s) \rightarrow MgCO_3(s) + 2\ NaCl(s) + H_2O(\ell) + CO_2(g)$$

Large deposits of sodium nitrate, $NaNO_3$, are found in Chile, which explains its common name of "Chile saltpeter." These deposits are thought to have formed by bacterial action on organisms in shallow seas. The initial product was ammonia, which was subsequently oxidized to nitrate ion; combination with sea salt led to sodium nitrate. Because nitrates in general, and alkali metal nitrates in particular, are highly water-soluble, deposits of $NaNO_3$ are found only in areas with very little rainfall.

Sodium nitrate is important because it can be converted to potassium nitrate by an exchange reaction.

$$NaNO_3(aq) + KCl(aq) \rightleftharpoons KNO_3(aq) + NaCl(s)$$

Equilibrium favors the products here because, of the four salts involved in this reaction, NaCl is least soluble in hot water. Sodium chloride precipitates, and the KNO_3 that remains in solution can be recovered by evaporating the water.

Potassium nitrate has been used for centuries as the oxidizing agent in gunpowder. A mixture of KNO_3, charcoal, and sulfur will spontaneously react when ignited.

$$2\ KNO_3(s) + 4\ C(s) \rightarrow K_2CO_3(s) + 3\ CO(g) + N_2(g)$$

$$2\ KNO_3(s) + 2\ S(s) \rightarrow K_2SO_4(s) + SO_2(g) + N_2(g)$$

Notice that both reactions (which are doubtless more complex than those written here) produce gases. These gases propel the bullet from a gun or cause a firecracker to explode.

Lithium carbonate, Li_2CO_3, has been used for more than 40 years as a treatment for bipolar disorder, an illness that involves alternating periods of depression or overexcitement that can extend over a few weeks to a year or more. Although the alkali metal salt is efficient in controlling the symptoms of bipolar disorder, its mechanism of action is not understood.

EXERCISE 21.6 Brine Electrolysis

What current must be used in a Downs cell operating at 7.0 V to produce 1.00 metric ton (exactly 1000 kg) of sodium per day? Assume 100% efficiency.

21.5 The Alkaline Earth Elements, Group 2A

The "earth" part of the name alkaline earth dates back to the days of medieval alchemy. To alchemists, any solid that did not melt and was not changed by fire into another substance was called an "earth." Compounds of the Group 2A elements, such CaO, were alkaline according to experimental tests conducted by the alchemists: they had a bitter taste and neutralized acids. With very high melting points, these compounds were unaffected by fire.

Calcium and magnesium rank fifth and eighth, respectively, in abundance on the earth. Both elements form many commercially important compounds, and we shall focus our attention on these species.

Like the Group 1A elements, the Group 2A elements are very reactive, so they are found in nature as compounds. Unlike most of the compounds of the Group 1A metals, however, many compounds of the Group 2A elements have low water solubility, which explains their occurrence in various minerals (Figure 21.12).

Group 2A
Alkaline earths

| Beryllium |
| 4 |
| **Be** |
| 2.6 ppm |

| Magnesium |
| 12 |
| **Mg** |
| 23,300 ppm |

| Calcium |
| 20 |
| **Ca** |
| 41,000 ppm |

| Strontium |
| 38 |
| **Sr** |
| 370 ppm |

| Barium |
| 56 |
| **Ba** |
| 500 ppm |

| Radium |
| 88 |
| **Ra** |
| 6×10^{-7} ppm |

Element abundances are in parts per million in the earth's crust.

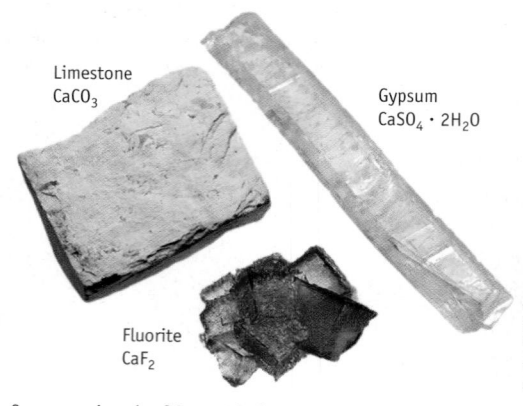

Limestone
CaCO₃

Gypsum
CaSO₄ · 2H₂O

Fluorite
CaF₂

Charles D. Winters

Common minerals of Group 2A elements.

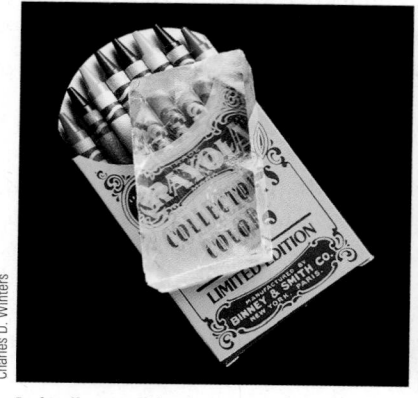

Charles D. Winters

Icelandic spar. This mineral, one of a number of crystalline forms of $CaCO_3$, displays birefringence, a property in which a double image is formed when light passes through the crystal.

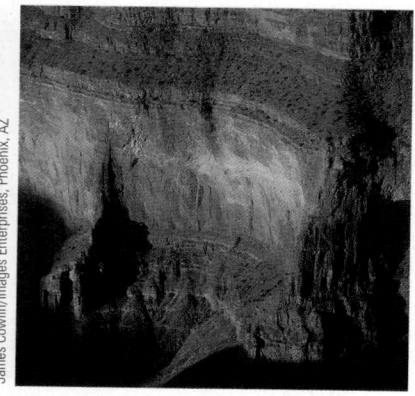

James Cowlin/Images Enterprises, Phoenix, AZ

The walls of the Grand Canyon in Arizona are largely limestone or dolomite.

FIGURE 21.12 Various minerals containing calcium and magnesium.

Calcium minerals include limestone ($CaCO_3$), gypsum ($CaSO_4 \cdot 2\,H_2O$), and fluorite (CaF_2). Magnesite ($MgCO_3$), talc or soapstone ($3\,MgO \cdot 4\,SiO_2 \cdot H_2O$), and asbestos ($3\,MgO \cdot 4\,SiO_2 \cdot 2\,H_2O$) are common magnesium-containing minerals. The mineral dolomite, $MgCa(CO_3)_2$, contains both magnesium and calcium.

Limestone, a sedimentary rock, is found widely on the earth's surface. Many of these deposits contain the fossilized remains of marine life. Other forms of calcium carbonate include marble and Icelandic spar, the latter occurring as large, clear crystals with the interesting optical property of birefringence.

Properties of Calcium and Magnesium

Calcium and magnesium are fairly high-melting, silvery metals. The chemical properties of these elements present few surprises. They are oxidized by a wide range of oxidizing agents to form ionic compounds that contain the M^{2+} ion. For example, these elements combine with halogens to form MX_2, with oxygen or sulfur to form MO or MS, and with water to form hydrogen and the metal hydroxide, $M(OH)_2$ (Figure 21.13). With acids, hydrogen is evolved (see Figure 21.6), and a salt of the metal cation and the anion of the acid results.

Metallurgy of Magnesium

Several hundred thousand tons of magnesium are produced annually, largely for use in lightweight alloys. (Magnesium has a very low density, 1.74 g/cm³.) Most aluminum used today contains about 5% magnesium to improve its mechanical properties and to make it more resistant to corrosion. Other alloys having more magnesium than aluminum are used when a high strength-to-weight ratio is needed and when corrosion resistance is important, such as in aircraft and automotive parts and in lightweight tools.

Interestingly, magnesium-containing minerals are not the source of this element. Most magnesium is obtained from sea water, in which Mg^{2+} ion is present in a concentration of about 0.05 M. To obtain magnesium metal, magnesium ions in sea water are first precipitated (Figure 21.14) as the relatively insoluble hydroxide [K_{sp} for $Mg(OH)_2 = 5.6 \times 10^{-12}$]. Calcium hydroxide, the source of OH^- in this reaction, is prepared in a sequence of reactions beginning with $CaCO_3$, which may be in the form of seashells. Heating $CaCO_3$ gives CO_2 and CaO, and addition of

Charles D. Winters

FIGURE 21.13 The reaction of calcium and warm water. Hydrogen bubbles are seen rising from the metal surface. The other reaction product is $Ca(OH)_2$. The inset is a model of hexagonal close-packed calcium metal (see page 595).

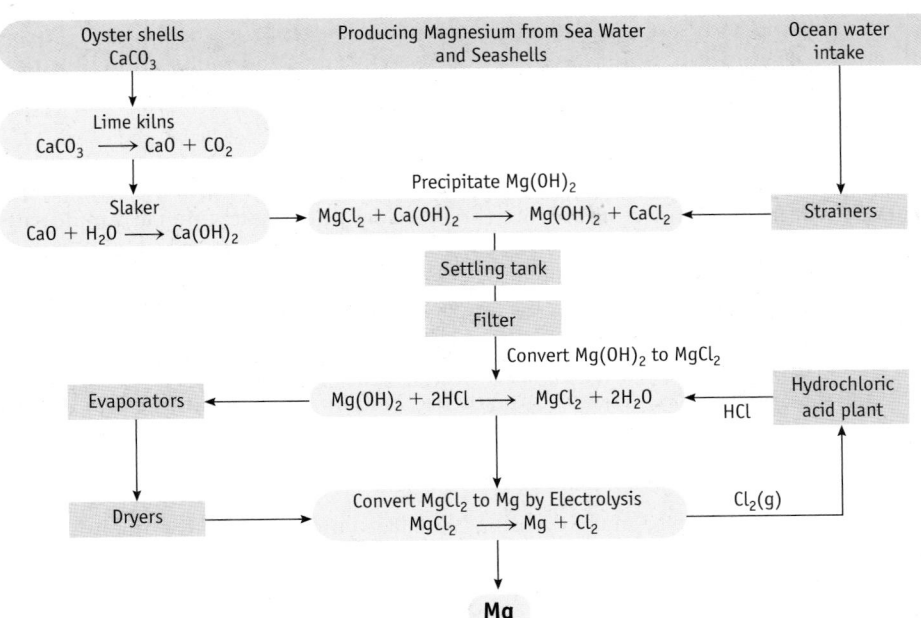

FIGURE 21.14 The process used to produce magnesium metal from the magnesium in sea water.

Producing Magnesium from Sea Water and Seashells

Oyster shells
CaCO₃

Ocean water intake

Lime kilns
$CaCO_3 \longrightarrow CaO + CO_2$

Slaker
$CaO + H_2O \longrightarrow Ca(OH)_2$

Precipitate $Mg(OH)_2$

$MgCl_2 + Ca(OH)_2 \longrightarrow Mg(OH)_2 + CaCl_2$

Strainers

Settling tank

Filter

Convert $Mg(OH)_2$ to $MgCl_2$

Evaporators

$Mg(OH)_2 + 2HCl \longrightarrow MgCl_2 + 2H_2O$

Hydrochloric acid plant

HCl

Dryers

Convert $MgCl_2$ to Mg by Electrolysis
$MgCl_2 \longrightarrow Mg + Cl_2$

$Cl_2(g)$

Mg

water to CaO gives calcium hydroxide. When $Ca(OH)_2$ is added to sea water, $Mg(OH)_2$ precipitates:

$$Mg^{2+}(aq) + Ca(OH)_2(s) \rightleftharpoons Mg(OH)_2(s) + Ca^{2+}(aq)$$

Magnesium hydroxide is isolated by filtration and then converted to magnesium chloride by reaction with hydrochloric acid.

$$Mg(OH)_2(s) + 2\ HCl(aq) \rightarrow MgCl_2(aq) + 2\ H_2O(\ell)$$

Chemical Perspectives

Alkaline Earth Metals and Biology

Plants and animals derive energy from the oxidation of a sugar, glucose, with oxygen. Plants are unique, however, in being able to synthesize glucose from CO_2 and H_2O by using sunlight as an energy source. This process is initiated by chlorophyll, a very large, magnesium-based molecule.

In your body, the metal ions Na^+, K^+, Mg^{2+}, and Ca^{2+} serve regulatory functions. Although the two alkaline earth metal ions are required by living systems, the other Group 2A elements are toxic. Beryllium compounds are carcinogenic, and soluble barium salts are poisons. You may be concerned if your physician asks you to drink a "barium cocktail" to check the condition of your digestive tract. Don't be afraid, because the "cocktail" contains very insoluble $BaSO_4$ ($K_{sp} = 1.1 \times 10^{-10}$), so it passes through your digestive tract without a significant amount being absorbed. Barium sulfate is opaque to x-rays, so its path through your organs appears on the developed x-ray.

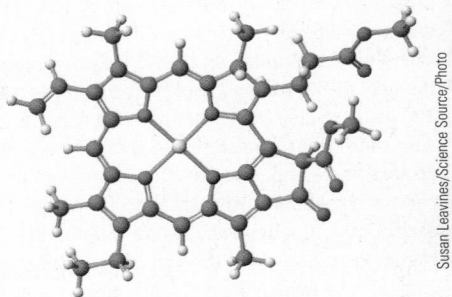

A molecule of chlorophyll. Magnesium is its central element.

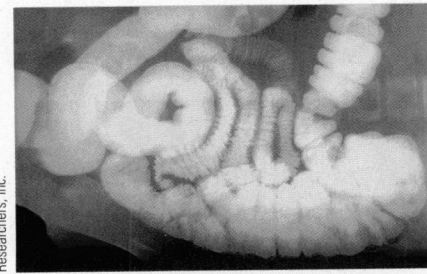

Susan Leavines/Science Source/Photo Researchers, Inc.

X-ray of a gastrointestinal tract using $BaSO_4$ to make the organs visible.

The calcium-containing compound hydroxyapatite is the main component of tooth enamel. Cavities in your teeth form when acids (such as soft drinks) decompose the weakly basic hydroxyapatite coating.

$$Ca_5(OH)(PO_4)_3(s) + 4\ H_3O^+(aq) \rightarrow$$
$$5\ Ca^{2+}(aq) + 3\ HPO_4^{2-}(aq) + 5\ H_2O(\ell)$$

This reaction can be prevented by converting hydroxyapatite to the much more acid-resistant coating of fluoroapatite.

$$Ca_5(OH)(PO_4)_3(s) + F^-(aq) \rightarrow$$
$$Ca_5F(PO_4)_3(s) + OH^-(aq)$$

The source of the fluoride ion can be sodium fluoride or sodium monofluorophosphate (Na_2FPO_3, commonly known as MFP) in your toothpaste.

After evaporating the water, anhydrous magnesium chloride remains. Solid $MgCl_2$ melts at 714 °C, and the molten salt is electrolyzed to give the metal and chlorine.

$$MgCl_2(\ell) \rightarrow Mg(s) + Cl_2(g)$$

Calcium Minerals and Their Applications

The most common calcium minerals are the fluoride, phosphate, and carbonate salts of the element. Fluorite, CaF_2, and fluoroapatite, $Ca_5F(PO_4)_3$, are important as commercial sources of fluorine. Almost half of the CaF_2 mined is used in the steel industry, where it is added to the mixture of materials that is melted to make crude iron. The CaF_2 acts to remove some impurities and improves the separation of molten metal from silicates and other by-products resulting from the reduction of iron ore to the metal (Chapter 22). A second major use of fluorite is in the manufacture of hydrofluoric acid by a reaction of the mineral with concentrated sulfuric acid.

$$CaF_2(s) + H_2SO_4(\ell) \rightarrow 2\ HF(g) + CaSO_4(s)$$

Hydrofluoric acid is used to make cryolite, Na_3AlF_6, a material needed in aluminum production (▶ Section 21.6) and in the manufacture of fluorocarbons such as tetrafluoroethylene, the precursor to Teflon (Table 10.12).

Apatites have the general formula $Ca_5X(PO_4)_3$ (X = F, Cl, OH). More than 100 million tons of apatite is mined annually, with Florida alone accounting for about one third of the world's output. Most of this material is converted to phosphoric acid by reaction with sulfuric acid. Phosphoric acid is needed in the manufacture of a multitude of products, including fertilizers and detergents, baking powder, and various food products (▶ Section 21.8.).

Chemical Perspectives

Of Romans, Limestone, and Champagne

The stones of the Appian Way in Italy, a road conceived by the Roman senate in about 310 B.C., are cemented with mortar made from limestone. The Appian Way was intended to serve as a military road linking Rome to seaports from which soldiers could embark to Greece and other Mediterranean ports. The road stretches 560 kilometers (350 miles) from Rome to Brindisi on the Adriatic Sea (at the heel of the Italian "boot"). It took almost 200 years to construct. The road had a standard width of 14 Roman feet, approximately 20 feet, large enough to allow two chariots to pass, and featured two sidewalks of 4 feet each. Every 10 miles or so, there were horse-changing stations with taverns, shops, and *latrinae*, the famous Roman restrooms.

All over the Roman Empire, buildings, temples, and aqueducts were constructed of blocks of limestone and marble, and the mortar to cement the blocks was made by heating the chips from stone cutting (to give CaO). In central France, the Romans dug chalk (also $CaCO_3$) from the ground for cementing sandstone blocks. This activity created huge caves that remain to this day and are used for aging and storing champagne.

The Appian Way in Italy.

Champagne in a limestone cave in France.

Calcium carbonate and calcium oxide (*lime*) are of special interest. The thermal decomposition of $CaCO_3$ to give lime (and CO_2) is one of the oldest chemical reactions known. Lime is one of the top 10 industrial chemicals produced today, with about 20 billion kilograms produced annually.

Limestone, which consists mostly of calcium carbonate, has been used in agriculture for centuries. It is spread on fields to neutralize acidic compounds in the soil and to supply Ca^{2+}, an essential nutrient. Because magnesium carbonate is often present in limestone, "liming" a field also supplies Mg^{2+}, another important nutrient for plants.

For several thousand years, lime has been used in *mortar* (a lime, sand, and water paste) to secure stones to one another in building houses, walls, and roads. The Chinese used it to set stones in the Great Wall. The Romans perfected its use, and the fact that many of their constructions still stand today is testament both to their skill and to the usefulness of lime. The famous Appian Way used lime mortar between several layers of its stones.

The utility of mortar depends on some simple chemistry. Mortar consists of one part lime to three parts sand, with water added to make a thick paste. The first reaction, referred to as *slaking*, occurs after the solids are mixed with water. This produces a slurry containing calcium hydroxide, which is known as *slaked lime*.

$$CaO(s) + H_2O(\ell) \rightleftharpoons Ca(OH)_2(s)$$

When the wet mortar mix is placed between bricks or stone blocks, it slowly reacts with CO_2 from the air, and the slaked lime is converted to calcium carbonate.

$$Ca(OH)_2(s) + CO_2(g) \rightleftharpoons CaCO_3(s) + H_2O(\ell)$$

The sand grains are bound together by the particles of calcium carbonate.

Charles D. Winters

Apatite. The mineral has the general formula of $Ca_5X(PO_4)_3$ (X = F, Cl, OH). (The apatite is the elongated crystal in the center of a matrix of other rock.)

■ **Dissolving Limestone** Figure 3.6 illustrates the equilibrium involving $CaCO_3$, CO_2, H_2O, Ca^{2+}, and HCO_3^-.

EXERCISE 21.7 Beryllium Chemistry

Beryllium, the lightest element in Group 2A, has some important industrial applications, but exposure (by breathing) to some of its compounds can cause berylliosis. Search the World Wide Web for the uses of the element and the causes and symptoms of berylliosis.

21.6 Boron, Aluminum, and the Group 3A Elements

With Group 3A, we see the first evidence of a change from metallic behavior of the elements at the left side of the periodic table to nonmetal behavior on the right side of the table. Boron is a metalloid, whereas all the other elements of Group 3A are metals.

The elements of Group 3A vary widely in their relative abundances on earth. Aluminum is the third most abundant element in the earth's crust (82,000 ppm), whereas the other elements of the group are relatively rare, and, except for boron, their compounds have limited commercial uses.

Chemistry of the Group 3A Elements

It is generally recognized that a chemical similarity exists between some elements diagonally situated in the periodic table. This diagonal relationship means that lithium and magnesium share some chemical properties, as do Be and Al, and B and Si. For example:

- Boric oxide, B_2O_3, and boric acid, $B(OH)_3$, are weakly acidic, as are SiO_2 and its acid, orthosilic acid (H_4SiO_4). Boron–oxygen compounds, borates, are often chemically similar to silicon–oxygen compounds, silicates.
- Both $Be(OH)_2$ and $Al(OH)_3$ are amphoteric, dissolving in a strong base such as aqueous NaOH (◄ page 791).

Group 3A

| Boron |
| 5 |
| **B** |
| 10 ppm |

| Aluminum |
| 13 |
| **Al** |
| 82,000 ppm |

| Gallium |
| 31 |
| **Ga** |
| 18 ppm |

| Indium |
| 49 |
| **In** |
| 0.05 ppm |

| Thallium |
| 81 |
| **Tl** |
| 0.6 ppm |

Element abundances are in parts per million in the earth's crust.

No, hard water doesn't refer to ice. It is the name given to water containing high concentrations of Ca^{2+}(aq) and, in some instances, Mg^{2+}(aq) and other divalent metal cations. Accompanying these cations will be various anions, including in particular the hydrogen carbonate anion, HCO_3^-(aq).

Water obtained from reservoirs that store rainwater does not usually contain high concentrations of these ions, and so is not classified as being "hard water." In many parts of the country, however, the municipal water supply is obtained from aquifers deep underground. If rainwater, containing some dissolved CO_2, has to percolate down through layers of limestone ($CaCO_3$) to get into the aquifer, a small amount of the solid will dissolve because of the following equilibrium:

$$CaCO_3(s) + CO_2(aq) + H_2O(\ell) \rightleftharpoons$$
$$Ca^{2+}(aq) + 2\,HCO_3^-(aq)$$

If hard water containing Ca^{2+}(aq) and HCO_3^-(aq) is heated, or even if it is left to stand in an open vessel, CO_2 will be expelled, and the equilibrium will shift, precipitating $CaCO_3$(s) (◀ page 120). This can be a small problem in a teakettle but a bigger problem in an industrial setting, where the solid $CaCO_3$ can clog pipes. Another consequence of hard water is the formation of a scum when soaps are added to water. Recall that soap is made by hydrolysis of fats (saponification, page 476); soap scum is a precipitate of the calcium salt of a long chain carboxylic acid.

To avoid the problems associated with hard water, chemists and engineers have devised ways to soften water, that is, to decrease the concentration of the offending cations. In a water treatment plant for a municipality or a large industrial facility, most of the water hardness will be removed chemically, mainly by treatment with calcium oxide (lime, CaO). If HCO_3^- ions are present along with Ca^{2+} and/or Mg^{2+}, the following reactions occur:

$$Ca^{2+}(aq) + 2\,HCO_3^-(aq) + CaO(s) \rightarrow$$
$$2\,CaCO_3(s) + H_2O(\ell)$$

$$Mg^{2+}(aq) + 2\,HCO_3^-(aq) + CaO(s) \rightarrow$$
$$CaCO_3(s) + MgCO_3(s) + H_2O(\ell)$$

Although it seems odd to add CaO to remove calcium ions, notice that adding one mole of CaO leads to the precipitation of two moles of Ca^{2+} as $CaCO_3$.

On a smaller scale, most home water purification systems use ion exchange to soften water (Figure). This process involves the replacement of an ion adsorbed onto a solid ion-exchange resin by an ion in solution. Zeolites (▶ page 989), naturally occurring aluminosilicate minerals, were at one time used as ion exchange materials. Now, synthetic organic polymers with negatively charged functional groups (such as carboxylate groups, $—CO_2^-$) are the most commonly used resins for this purpose. Sodium ions, Na^+, are present in the resin to balance the negative charges of the carboxylate groups. The affinity of a surface for multicharged cations is greater than for monovalent cations. Therefore, when a solution of hard water is passed over the surface of the ion exchange resin, Ca^{2+} and Mg^{2+} (and other divalent ions if present) readily replace Na^+ ions in an ion exchange column. This process can be illustrated in a general way by the equilibrium

$$2\,NaX + Ca^{2+}(aq) \rightleftharpoons CaX_2 + 2\,Na^+(aq)$$

where X represents an adsorption site on the ion exchange resin. The equilibrium favors adsorption of Ca^{2+} and release of Na^+. However, the equilibrium is reversed if Na^+(aq) ions are present in high concentration, and this allows regeneration of the ion-exchange resin. A solution containing a high concentration of Na^+ (usually from salt, NaCl) is passed through the resin to convert the resin back to its initial form.

Questions:

1. *Assume that a sample of hard water contains 50 mg/L of Mg^{2+} and 150 mg/L of Ca^{2+}, with HCO_3^- as the accompanying anion. What mass of CaO should be added to 1.0 L of this aqueous solution to cause precipitation of $CaCO_3$ and $MgCO_3$? What is the total mass of the two solids formed?*

2. *One way to remove the calcium carbonate residue in a teakettle is to add vinegar (a dilute solution of acetic acid). Write a chemical equation to explain this process. What kind of a reaction is this?*

Answers to these questions are in Appendix Q.

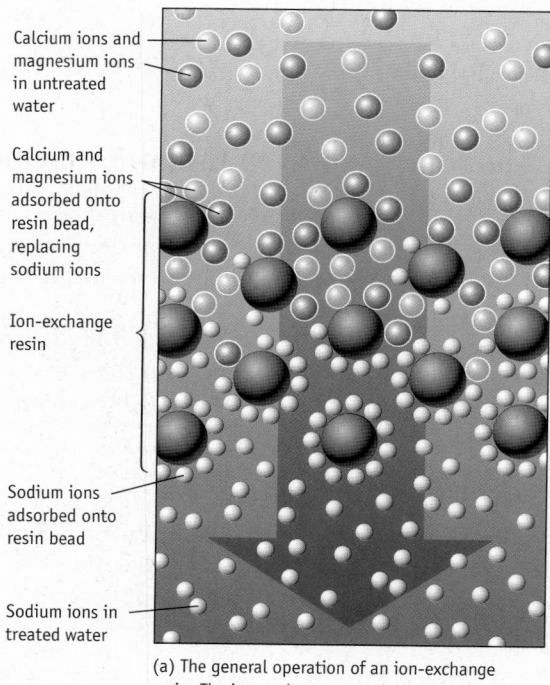

Calcium ions and magnesium ions in untreated water

Calcium and magnesium ions adsorbed onto resin bead, replacing sodium ions

Ion-exchange resin

Sodium ions adsorbed onto resin bead

Sodium ions in treated water

(a) The general operation of an ion-exchange resin. The ion-exchange material is usually a polymeric material formed into small beads.

Water softening by ion exchange in the home. The ion exchange resin is usually a polymeric material formed into small beads.

- Chlorides, bromides, and iodides of boron and silicon (such as BCl_3 and $SiCl_4$) react vigorously with water.
- The hydrides of boron and silicon are simple, molecular species; are volatile and flammable; and react readily with water.
- Beryllium hydride and aluminum hydride are colorless, nonvolatile solids that are extensively polymerized through Be—H—Be and Al—H—Al three-centered, two-electron bonds (see page 431).

Finally, the Group 3A elements are characterized by electron configurations of the type ns^2np^1. This means that each may lose three electrons to have a +3 oxidation number, although the heavier elements, especially thallium, also form compounds with an oxidation number of +1.

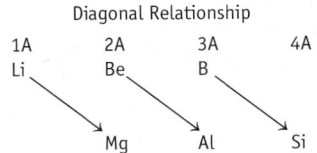

Diagonal Relationship

1A	2A	3A	4A
Li	Be	B	
	Mg	Al	Si

■ **Diagonal Relationship** The chemistries of elements diagonally situated in the periodic table are often quite similar.

Boron Minerals and Production of the Element

Although boron has a low abundance on earth, its minerals are found in concentrated deposits. Large deposits of borax, $Na_2B_4O_7 \cdot 10\ H_2O$, are currently mined in the Mojave Desert near the town of Boron, California (Figure 21.15).

Isolation of pure, elemental boron from boron-containing minerals is extremely difficult and is done in small quantities. Like most metals and metalloids, boron can be obtained by chemically or electrolytically reducing an oxide or halide. Magnesium has often been used for chemical reductions, but the product of this reaction is a noncrystalline boron of low purity.

$$B_2O_3(s) + 3\ Mg(s) \rightarrow 2\ B(s) + 3\ MgO(s)$$

Boron has several allotropes, all characterized by having an icosahedron of boron atoms as one structural element (Figure 21.15c). Partly as a result of extended covalent bonding, elemental boron is a very hard and refractory (resistant to heat) semiconductor. In this regard, it differs from the other Group 3A elements; Al, Ga, In, and Tl are all relatively low-melting, rather soft metals with high electrical conductivity.

Metallic Aluminum and Its Production

The low cost of aluminum and the excellent characteristics of its alloys with other metals (low density, strength, ease of handling in fabrication, and inertness toward corrosion, among others), have led to its widespread use. You know it best in the form of aluminum foil, aluminum cans, and parts of aircraft.

Charles D. Winters

Gallium. Gallium, with a melting point of 29.8 °C, is one of the few metals that can be a liquid at or near room temperature. (Others are Hg and Cs.)

(a)

© George Gerster/Photo Researchers, Inc.

(b)

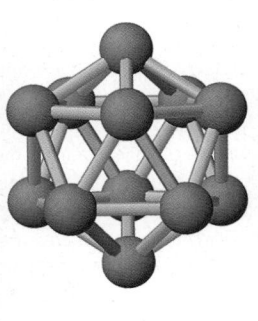

(c)

FIGURE 21.15 Boron. (a) A borax mine near the town of Boron, California. (b) Crystalline borax, $Na_2B_4O_7 \cdot 10\ H_2O$. (c) All allotropes of elemental boron have an icosahedron (a 20-sided polyhedron) of 12 covalently linked boron atoms as a structural element.

Pure aluminum is soft and weak; moreover, it loses strength rapidly at temperatures higher than 300 °C. What we call "aluminum" is actually aluminum alloyed with small amounts of other elements to strengthen the metal and improve its properties. A typical alloy may contain about 4% copper with smaller amounts of silicon, magnesium, and manganese. Softer, more corrosion-resistant alloys for window frames, furniture, highway signs, and cooking utensils may include only manganese.

The standard reduction potential of aluminum $[Al^{3+}(aq) + 3\ e^- \rightarrow Al(s)$; $E° = -1.66\ V]$ tells you that aluminum is easily oxidized. From this, we might expect aluminum to be highly susceptible to corrosion but, in fact, it is quite resistant. Aluminum's corrosion resistance is due to the formation of a thin, tough, and transparent skin of Al_2O_3 that adheres to the metal surface. An important feature of the protective oxide layer is that it rapidly self-repairs. If you penetrate the surface coating by scratching it or using some chemical agent, the exposed metal surface immediately reacts with oxygen (or another oxidizing agent) to form a new layer of oxide over the damaged area (Figure 21.16).

Aluminum was first prepared by reducing $AlCl_3$ using sodium or potassium. This was a costly process, and, in the 19th century, aluminum was a precious metal. At the 1855 Paris Exposition, in fact, a sample of aluminum was exhibited along with the crown jewels of France. In an interesting coincidence, in 1886 Frenchman Paul Heroult (1863–1914) and American Charles Hall (1863–1914) simultaneously and independently conceived of the electrochemical method used today. The Hall–Heroult method bears the names of the two discoverers.

Aluminum is found in nature as aluminosilicates, minerals such as clay that are based on aluminum, silicon, and oxygen. As these minerals weather, they break down to various forms of hydrated aluminum oxide, $Al_2O_3 \cdot n\ H_2O$, called *bauxite*. Mined in huge quantities, bauxite is the raw material from which aluminum is obtained. The first step is to purify the ore, separating Al_2O_3 from iron and silicon oxides. This is done by the *Bayer process*, which relies on the amphoteric, basic, or acidic nature of the various oxides. Silica, SiO_2, is an acidic oxide; Al_2O_3 is amphoteric; and Fe_2O_3 is a basic oxide. Silica and Al_2O_3 dissolve in a hot concentrated solution of caustic soda (NaOH), leaving insoluble Fe_2O_3 to be filtered out.

$$Al_2O_3(s) + 2\ NaOH(aq) + 3\ H_2O(\ell) \rightarrow 2\ Na[Al(OH)_4](aq)$$

$$SiO_2(s) + 2\ NaOH(aq) + 2\ H_2O(\ell) \rightarrow Na_2[Si(OH)_6](aq)$$

If a solution containing aluminate and silicate anions is treated with CO_2, Al_2O_3 precipitates, and the silicate ion remains in solution. Recall that CO_2 is an acidic

■ **Charles Martin Hall (1863–1914)**

Hall was only 22 years old when he worked out the electrolytic process for extracting aluminum from Al_2O_3 in a woodshed behind the family home in Oberlin, Ohio. He went on to found a company that eventually became ALCOA, the Aluminum Corporation of America.

Oesper Collection in the History of Chemistry/ University of Cincinnati

FIGURE 21.16 Corrosion of aluminum. (a) A ball of aluminum foil is added to a solution of copper(II) nitrate and sodium chloride. Normally, the coating of chemically inert Al_2O_3 on the surface of aluminum protects the metal from further oxidation. (b) In the presence of the Cl^- ion, the coating of Al_2O_3 is breached, and aluminum reduces copper(II) ions to copper metal. The reaction is rapid and so exothermic that the water can boil on the surface of the foil. [The blue color of aqueous copper(II) ions will fade as these ions are consumed in the reaction.]

Photos: Charles D. Winters

(a)

(b)

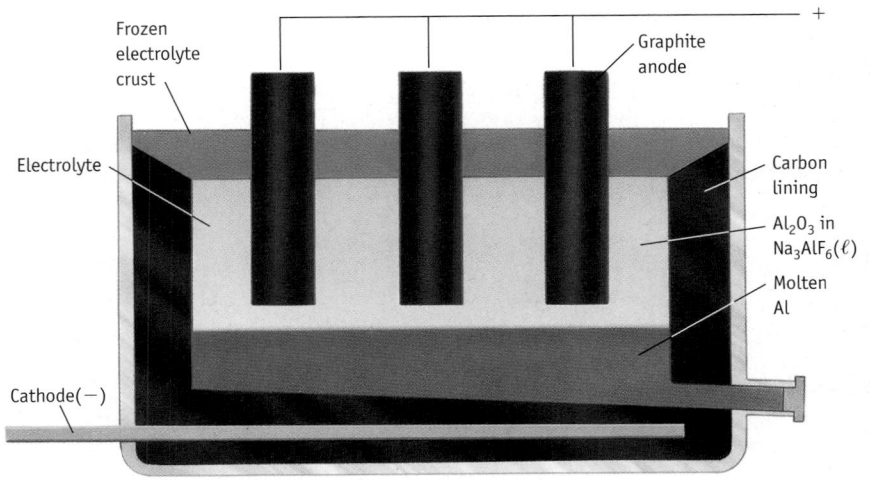

(a) Electrolysis of aluminum oxide to produce aluminum metal.

(b) Molten aluminum from recycled metal.

Active Figure 21.17 **Industrial production of aluminum.** (a) Purified aluminum-containing ore (bauxite), essentially Al_2O_3, is mixed with cryolite (Na_3AlF_6). Cryolite acts as a flux or solvent for the process, as it melts below 1173 K. The aluminum-containing substances are reduced at the graphite cathode to give molten aluminum. Oxygen is produced at the graphite anode, and the gas reacts slowly with the carbon to give CO_2, leading to eventual destruction of the electrode. (b) Molten aluminum alloy, produced from recycled metal, at 760 °C, in 1.6×10^4-kg capacity crucibles.

Chemistry.⚛.Now™ Sign in at www.cengage.com/login and go to the Chapter Contents menu to explore an interactive version of this figure accompanied by an exercise.

oxide that forms the weak acid H_2CO_3 in water, so the Al_2O_3 precipitation in this step is an acid–base reaction.

$$H_2CO_3(aq) + 2\, Na[Al(OH)_4](aq) \rightarrow Na_2CO_3(aq) + Al_2O_3(s) + 5\, H_2O(\ell)$$

Metallic aluminum is obtained from purified bauxite by electrolysis (Figure 21.17). Bauxite is first mixed with cryolite, Na_3AlF_6, to give a lower-melting mixture (melting temperature = 980 °C) that is electrolyzed in a cell with graphite electrodes. The cell operates at a relatively low voltage (4.0–5.5 V) but with an extremely high current (50,000–150,000 A). Aluminum is produced at the cathode and oxygen at the anode. To produce 1 kg of aluminum requires 13 to 16 kilowatt-hours of energy plus the energy required to maintain the high temperature.

Boron Compounds

Borax, $Na_2B_4O_7 \cdot 10\, H_2O$, is the most important boron–oxygen compound and is the form of the element most often found in nature. It has been used for centuries in metallurgy because of the ability of molten borax to dissolve other metal oxides. That is, borax is used as a *flux* that cleans the surfaces of metals to be joined and permits a good metal-to-metal contact.

The formula for borax gives little information about its structure. The anion is better described by the formula $[B_4O_5(OH)_4]^{2-}$, the structure of which illustrates two commonly observed structural features in inorganic chemistry. First, many minerals consist of MO_n groups that share O atoms. Second, the sharing of O atoms between two metals or metalloids often leads to MO rings.

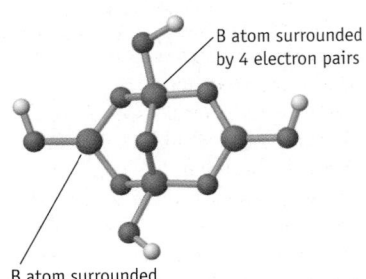

B atom surrounded by 4 electron pairs

B atom surrounded by 3 electron pairs

The borate ion of borax, $[B_4O_5(OH)_4]^{2-}$.

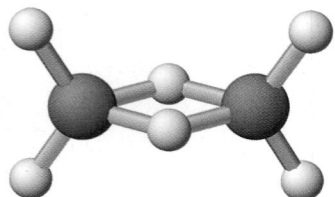

■ **Borax in Fire Retardants** The second largest use for boric acid and borates is as a flame retardant for cellulose home insulation. Such insulation is often made of scrap paper, which is inexpensive but flammable. To control the flammability, 5–10% of the weight of the insulation is boric acid.

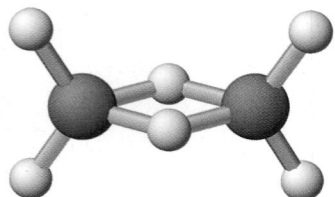

The structure of diborane, B_2H_6, the simplest member of a family of boron hydrides. See also page 431.

Sodium borohydride, $NaBH_4$, is an excellent reducing agent. Here, silver ions are reduced to finely divided silver metal.

After refinement, borax can be treated with sulfuric acid to produce boric acid, $B(OH)_3$.

$$Na_2B_4O_7 \cdot 10\ H_2O(s) + H_2SO_4(aq) \rightarrow 4\ B(OH)_3(aq) + Na_2SO_4(aq) + 5\ H_2O(\ell)$$

The chemistry of boric acid incorporates both Lewis and Brønsted acid behavior. Hydronium ions are produced by a Lewis–acid base interaction between boric acid and water.

$$K_a = 7.3 \times 10^{-10}$$

Because of its weak acid properties and slight biological activity, boric acid has been used for many years as an antiseptic. Furthermore, because boric acid is a weak acid, salts of borate ions, such as the $[B_4O_5(OH)_4]^{2-}$ ion in borax, are weak bases.

Boric acid is dehydrated to boric oxide when strongly heated.

$$2\ B(OH)_3(s) \rightarrow B_2O_3(s) + 3\ H_2O(\ell)$$

By far the largest use for the oxide is in the manufacture of borosilicate glass. This type of glass is composed of 76% SiO_2, 13% B_2O_3, and much smaller amounts of Al_2O_3 and Na_2O. The presence of boric oxide gives the glass a higher softening temperature, imparts a better resistance to attack by acids, and makes the glass expand less on heating.

Like its metalloid neighbor silicon, boron forms a series of molecular compounds with hydrogen. Because boron is slightly less electronegative than hydrogen, these compounds are described as hydrides, in which the H atoms bear a partial negative charge. More than 20 neutral boron hydrides, or boranes, with the general formula B_xH_y are known. The simplest of these is diborane, B_2H_6, where x is 2 and y is 6. This colorless, gaseous compound has a boiling point of -92.6 °C. This molecule is described as electron deficient since there are apparently not enough electrons to attach all of the atoms using two-electron bonds. Instead, the description of bonding uses 3-center 2-electron bonds in the B-H-B bridges (◀ page 431).

Diborane has an endothermic enthalpy of formation ($\Delta_f H° = +41.0$ kJ/mol), which contributes to the high exothermicity of oxidation of the compound. Diborane burns in air to give boric oxide and water vapor in an extremely exothermic reaction. It is not surprising that diborane and other boron hydrides were once considered as possible rocket fuels.

$$B_2H_6(g) + 3\ O_2(g) \rightarrow B_2O_3(s) + 3\ H_2O(g) \quad \Delta_r H° = -2038\ \text{kJ/mol-rxn}$$

Diborane can be synthesized from sodium borohydride, $NaBH_4$, the only B—H compound produced in ton quantities.

$$2\ NaBH_4(s) + I_2(s) \rightarrow B_2H_6(g) + 2\ NaI(s) + H_2(g)$$

Sodium borohydride, $NaBH_4$, a white, crystalline, water-soluble solid, is made from NaH and borate esters such as $B(OCH_3)_3$.

$$4\ NaH(s) + B(OCH_3)_3(g) \rightarrow NaBH_4(s) + 3\ NaOCH_3(s)$$

The main use of $NaBH_4$ is as a reducing agent in organic synthesis. We previously encountered its use to reduce aldehydes, carboxylic acids, and ketones in Chapter 10.

Aluminum Compounds

Aluminum is an excellent reducing agent, so it reacts readily with hydrochloric acid. In contrast, it does not react with nitric acid, a stronger oxidizing agent than hydrochloric acid. It turns out that nitric acid does rapidly oxidize the surface of aluminum, but the resulting film of Al_2O_3 that is produced protects the metal from further attack. This protection allows nitric acid to be shipped in aluminum tanks.

Various salts of aluminum dissolve in water, giving the hydrated Al^{3+}(aq) ion. These solutions are acidic (◄ Table 17.3, page 770) because the hydrated ion is a weak Brønsted acid.

$$[Al(H_2O)_6]^{3+}(aq) + H_2O(\ell) \rightleftharpoons [Al(H_2O)_5(OH)]^{2+}(aq) + H_3O^+(aq)$$

Adding acid shifts the equilibrium to the left, whereas adding base causes the equilibrium to shift to the right. Addition of sufficient hydroxide ion results ultimately in precipitation of the hydrated oxide $Al_2O_3 \cdot 3\ H_2O$.

Aluminum oxide, Al_2O_3, formed by dehydrating the hydrated oxide, is quite insoluble in water and generally resistant to chemical attack. In the crystalline form, aluminum oxide is known as *corundum*. This material is extraordinarily hard, a property that leads to its use as an abrasive in grinding wheels, "sandpaper," and toothpaste.

Some gems are impure aluminum oxide. Rubies, beautiful red crystals prized for jewelry and used in some lasers, are composed of Al_2O_3 contaminated with a small amount of Cr^{3+} (Figure 21.18). The Cr^{3+} ions replacing some of the Al^{3+} ions in the crystal lattice is the source of the red color. Synthetic rubies were first made in 1902, and the worldwide capacity is now about 200,000 kg/year; much of this production is used for jewel bearings in watches and instruments. Blue sapphires consist of Al_2O_3 with Fe^{2+} and Ti^{4+} impurities in place of Al^{3+} ions.

Boron forms halides such as gaseous BF_3 and BCl_3 that have the expected planar, trigonal molecular geometry of halogen atoms surrounding an sp^2 hybridized boron atom. In contrast, the aluminum halides are all solids and have more interesting structures. Aluminum bromide, which is made by the very exothermic reaction of aluminum metal and bromine (Figure 2.12, page 67),

$$2\ Al(s) + 3\ Br_2(\ell) \rightarrow Al_2Br_6(s)$$

is composed of two units of $AlBr_3$. That is, Al_2Br_6 is a dimer of $AlBr_3$ units. The structure resembles that of diborane in that bridging atoms appear between the two Al atoms. However, Al_2Br_6 is not electron deficient; the bridge is formed when a Br atom on one $AlBr_3$ uses a lone pair to form a coordinate covalent bond to a neighboring tetrahedral, sp^3-hybridized aluminum atom.

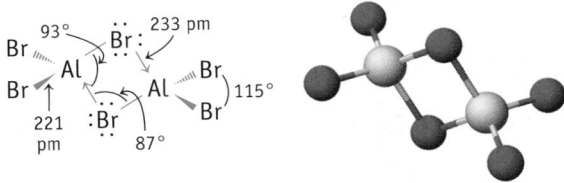

The structure of Al_2Br_6. The bonding in Al_2Br_6 is not unique to the aluminum halides. Metal–halogen–metal bridges are found in many other metal–halogen compounds.

Aluminum does not react with nitric acid. Nitric acid, a strongly oxidizing acid, reacts vigorously with copper (left), but aluminum (right) is untouched.

Charles D. Winters

Chip Clark, Smithsonian Museum of Natural History

FIGURE 21.18 Forms of corundum. Corundum is a crystalline form of aluminum oxide. Both rubies and sapphires are a form of corundum in which a few Al^{3+} ions have been replaced by ions such as Cr^{3+}, Fe^{2+} or Ti^{4+}. (*top*) The Star of Asia sapphire. (*middle*) Various sapphires. (*bottom*) Uncut corundum.

Both aluminum bromide and aluminum iodide have this structure. Aluminum chloride has a different solid state structure, but it exists as dimeric molecules in the vapor state.

Aluminum chloride can react with a chloride ion to form the anion $[AlCl_4]^-$. Aluminum fluoride, in contrast, can accommodate three additional F^- ions to form an octahedral $[AlF_6]^{3-}$ ion. This anion is found in cryolite, Na_3AlF_6, the compound added to aluminum oxide in the electrolytic production of aluminum metal. Apparently, the Al^{3+} ion can bind to six of the smaller F^- ions, whereas only four of the larger Cl^-, Br^-, or I^- ions can surround an Al^{3+} ion.

Chemistry ⚛ Now™

Sign in at **www.cengage.com/login** and go to Chapter 21 Contents to see Screen 21.5 for an exercise on **the chemistry of aluminum compounds.**

EXERCISE 21.8 Gallium Chemistry

(a) Gallium hydroxide, like aluminum hydroxide, is amphoteric. Write a balanced equation to show how this hydroxide can dissolve in both HCl(aq) and NaOH(aq).

(b) Gallium ion in water, Ga^{3+}(aq), has a K_a value of 1.2×10^{-3}. Is this ion a stronger or a weaker acid than Al^{3+}(aq)?

21.7 Silicon and the Group 4A Elements

Carbon is a nonmetal; silicon and germanium are classified as metalloids; tin and lead are metals. As a result, the elements of Group 4A have a broad range of chemical behavior.

The Group 4A elements are characterized by half-filled valence shells with two electrons in the ns orbital and two electrons in np orbitals. The bonding in carbon and silicon compounds is largely covalent and involves sharing four electron pairs with neighboring atoms. In germanium compounds, the +4 oxidation state is common (GeO_2 and $GeCl_4$), but some +2 oxidation state compounds exist (GeI_2). Oxidation numbers of both +2, and +4 are common in compounds of tin and lead (such as $SnCl_2$, $SnCl_4$, PbO, and PbO_2). Oxidation numbers two units less than the group number are often encountered for heavier elements in Groups 3A–7A.

Silicon

Silicon is second after oxygen in abundance in the earth's crust, so it is not surprising that we are surrounded by silicon-containing materials: bricks, pottery, porcelain, lubricants, sealants, computer chips, and solar cells. The computer revolution is based on the semiconducting properties of silicon.

Reasonably pure silicon can be made in large quantities by heating pure silica sand with purified coke to approximately 3000 °C in an electric furnace.

$$SiO_2(s) + 2\ C(s) \rightarrow Si(\ell) + 2\ CO(g)$$

The molten silicon is drawn off the bottom of the furnace and allowed to cool to a shiny blue-gray solid. Because extremely high-purity silicon is needed for the electronics industry, purifying raw silicon requires several steps. First, the silicon in the impure sample is allowed to react with chlorine to convert the silicon to liquid silicon tetrachloride.

$$Si(s) + 2\ Cl_2(g) \rightarrow SiCl_4(\ell)$$

Group 4A

| Carbon |
| 6 |
| **C** |
| 480 ppm |

| Silicon |
| 14 |
| **Si** |
| 277,000 ppm |

| Germanium |
| 32 |
| **Ge** |
| 1.8 ppm |

| Tin |
| 50 |
| **Sn** |
| 2.2 ppm |

| Lead |
| 82 |
| **Pb** |
| 14 ppm |

Element abundances are in parts per million in the earth's crust.

Silicon tetrachloride (boiling point of 57.6 °C) is carefully purified by distillation and then reduced to silicon using magnesium.

$$SiCl_4(g) + 2\ Mg(s) \rightarrow 2\ MgCl_2(s) + Si(s)$$

The magnesium chloride is washed out with water, and the silicon is remelted and cast into bars. A final purification is carried out by zone refining, a process in which a special heating device is used to melt a narrow segment of the silicon rod. The heater is moved slowly down the rod. Impurities contained in the silicon tend to remain in the liquid phase because the melting point of a mixture is lower than that of the pure element (Chapter 14). The silicon that crystallizes above the heated zone is therefore of a higher purity (Figure 21.19).

Silicon Dioxide

The simplest oxide of silicon is SiO_2, commonly called *silica*, a constituent of many rocks such as granite and sandstone. Quartz is a pure crystalline form of silica, but impurities in quartz produce gemstones such as amethyst (Figure 21.20).

Silica and CO_2 are oxides of two elements in the same chemical group, so similarities between them might be expected. In fact, SiO_2 is a high-melting solid (quartz melts at 1610 °C), whereas CO_2 is a gas at room temperature and 1 bar. This great disparity arises from the different structures of the two oxides. Carbon dioxide is a molecular compound, with the carbon atom linked to each oxygen atom by a double bond. In contrast, SiO_2 is a network solid, which is the preferred structure because the bond energy of two Si=O double bonds is much less than the bond energy of four Si—O single bonds. The contrast between SiO_2 and CO_2 exemplifies a more general phenomenon. Multiple bonds, often encountered between second-period elements, are rare among elements in the third and higher periods. There are many compounds with multiple bonds to carbon but very few compounds featuring multiple bonds to silicon.

Quartz crystals are used to control the frequency of radio and television transmissions. Because these and related applications use so much quartz, there is not enough natural quartz to fulfill demand, and quartz is therefore synthesized. Noncrystalline, or vitreous, quartz, made by melting pure silica sand, is placed in a steel "bomb," and dilute aqueous NaOH is added. A "seed" crystal is placed in the mixture, just as you might use a seed crystal in a hot sugar solution to grow

FIGURE 21.19 **Pure silicon.** The manufacture of very pure silicon begins with producing the volatile liquid silanes $SiCl_4$ or $SiHCl_3$. After carefully purifying these by distillation, they are reduced to elemental silicon with extremely pure Mg or Zn. The resulting spongy silicon is purified by zone refining. The end result is a cylindrical rod of ultrapure silicon such as those seen in this photograph. Thin wafers of silicon are cut from the bars and are the basis for the semiconducting chips in computers and other devices.

FIGURE 21.20 **Various forms of quartz.**

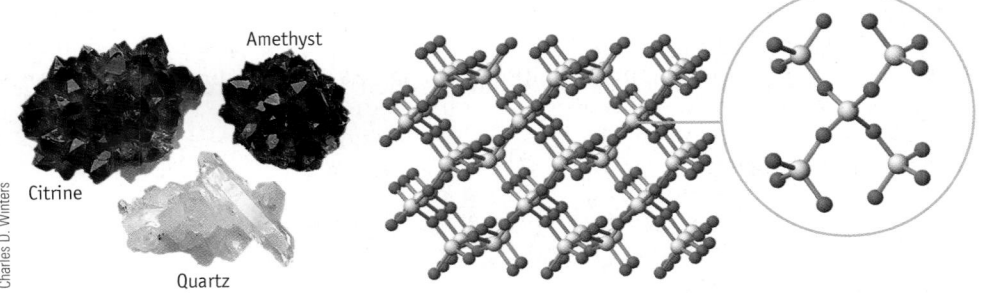

(a) Pure quartz is colorless, but the presence of small amounts of impurities adds color. Purple amethyst and brown citrine crystals are quartz with iron impurities.

(b) Quartz is a network solid in which each Si atom is bound tetrahedrally to four O atoms, each O atom linked to another Si atom. The basic structure consists of a lattice of Si and O atoms.

Synthetic quartz. These crystals were grown from silica in sodium hydroxide. The colors come from added Co^{2+} ions (blue) or Fe^{2+} ions (brown).

rock candy. When the mixture is heated above the critical temperature of water (above 400 °C and 1700 atm) over a period of days, pure quartz crystallizes.

Silicon dioxide is resistant to attack by all acids except HF, with which it reacts to give SiF_4 and H_2O.

$$SiO_2(s) + 4\ HF(\ell) \rightarrow SiF_4(g) + 2\ H_2O(\ell)$$

Silicon dioxide also dissolves slowly in hot, molten NaOH or Na_2CO_3 to give Na_4SiO_4, sodium silicate.

$$SiO_2(s) + 2\ Na_2CO_3(\ell) \rightarrow Na_4SiO_4(s) + 2\ CO_2(g)$$

After the molten mixture has cooled, hot water under pressure is added. This partially dissolves the material to give a solution of sodium silicate. After filtering off insoluble sand or glass, the solvent is evaporated to leave sodium silicate, called *water glass*. The biggest single use of this material is in household and industrial detergents, in which it is included because a sodium silicate solution maintains pH by its buffering ability. Additionally, sodium silicate is used in various adhesives and binders, especially for gluing corrugated cardboard boxes.

If sodium silicate is treated with acid, a gelatinous precipitate of SiO_2 called *silica gel* is obtained. Washed and dried, silica gel is a highly porous material with dozens of uses. It is a drying agent, readily absorbing up to 40% of its own weight of water. Small packets of silica gel are often placed in packing boxes of merchandise during storage. The material is frequently stained with $(NH_4)_2CoCl_4$, a humidity detector that is pink when hydrated and blue when dry.

Silicate Minerals with Chain and Ribbon Structures

The structure and chemistry of silicate minerals is an enormous topic in geology and chemistry. Although all silicates are built from tetrahedral SiO_4 units, they have different properties and a wide variety of structures because of the way these tetrahedral SiO_4 units link together.

The simplest silicates, *orthosilicates*, contain SiO_4^{4-} anions. The 4− charge of the anion is balanced by four M^+ ions, two M^{2+} ions, or a combination of ions. Olivine, an important mineral in the earth's mantle, contains Mg^{2+} and Fe^{2+}, with the Fe^{2+} ion giving the mineral its characteristic olive color, and gem-like zircons are $ZrSiO_4$. Calcium orthosilicate, Ca_2SiO_4, is a component of Portland cement, the most common type of cement used in many parts of the world. (It consists mostly of a mixture of CaO and SiO_2 with the remainder largely aluminum and iron oxides.)

A group of minerals called *pyroxenes* have as their basic structural unit a chain of SiO_4 tetrahedra.

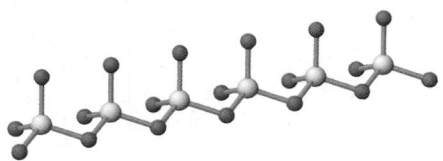

If two such chains are linked together by sharing oxygen atoms, the result is an *amphibole*, of which the asbestos minerals are one example. The molecular chain results in asbestos being a fibrous material.

Silica gel. Silica gel is solid, noncrystalline SiO_2. Packages of the material are often used to keep electronic equipment dry when stored. Silica gel is also used to clarify beer; passing beer through a bed of silica gel removes minute particles that would otherwise make the brew cloudy. Yet another use is in kitty litter.

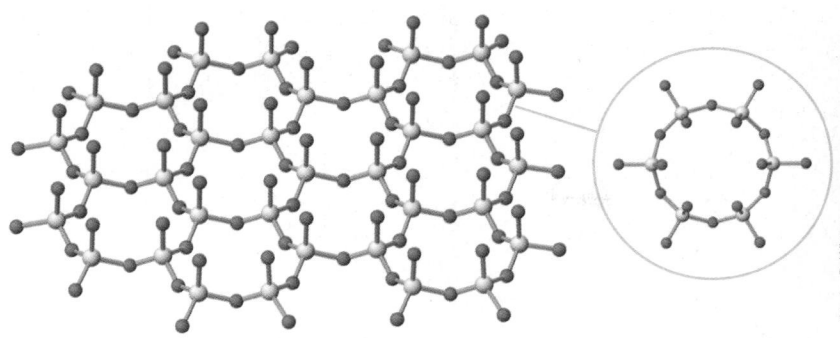

FIGURE 21.21 Mica, a sheet silicate. The sheet-like molecular structure of mica explains its physical appearance. As in the pyroxenes, each silicon is bonded to four oxygen atoms, but the Si and O atoms form a sheet of six-member rings of Si atoms with O atoms in each edge. The ratio of Si to O in this structure is 1 to 2.5. A formula of $SiO_{2.5}$ requires a positive ion, such as Na^+, to counterbalance the charge. Thus, mica and other sheet silicates, and aluminosilicates such as talc and many clays, have positive ions between the sheets. The sheet structure leads to the characteristic feature of mica, which is often found as "books" of thin, silicate sheets. Mica is used in furnace windows and as insulation, and flecks of mica give the glitter to "metallic" paints.

Silicates with Sheet Structures and Aluminosilicates

Linking many silicate chains together produces a sheet of SiO_4 tetrahedra (Figure 21.21). This sheet is the basic structural feature of some of the earth's most important minerals, particularly the clay minerals (such as china clay), mica, talc, and the chrysotile form of asbestos. However, these minerals do not contain just silicon and oxygen. Rather, they are often referred to as *aluminosilicates* because they frequently have Al^{3+} ions in place of Si^{4+} (which means that other positive ions such as Na^+, K^+, and Mg^{2+} must also be present in the lattice to balance the net negative and positive charges). In kaolinite clay, for example, the sheet of SiO_4 tetrahedra is bonded to a sheet of AlO_6 octahedra. In addition, some Si^{4+} ions can be replaced by Al^{3+} atoms. Another example is muscovite, a form of mica. Aluminum ions have replaced some Si^{4+} ions, and there are charge-balancing K^+ ions, so it is best represented by the formula $KAl_2(OH)_2(Si_3AlO_{10})$.

There are some interesting uses of clays, one being in medicine (Figure 21.22). In certain cultures, clay is eaten for medicinal purposes. Several remedies for the relief of upset stomach contain highly purified clays that absorb excess stomach acid as well as potentially harmful bacteria and their toxins by exchanging the intersheet cations in the clays for the toxins, which are often organic cations.

Other aluminosilicates include the feldspars, common minerals that make up about 60% of the earth's crust, and zeolites (Figure 21.22). Both materials are composed of SiO_4 tetrahedra in which some of the Si atoms have been replaced by Al atoms, along with alkali and alkaline earth metal ions for charge balance. The main feature of zeolite structures is their regularly shaped tunnels and cavities. Hole diameters are between 300 and 1000 pm, and small molecules such as water can fit into the cavities of the zeolite structure. As a result, zeolites can be used as drying agents to selectively absorb water from air or a solvent. Small amounts of zeolites are often sealed into multipane windows to keep the air dry between the panes.

Zeolites are also used as catalysts. ExxonMobil, for example, has patented a process in which methanol, CH_3OH, is converted to gasoline in the presence of specially tailored zeolites. In addition, zeolites are added to detergents, where they function as water-softening agents because the sodium ions of the zeolite can be exchanged for Ca^{2+} ions in hard water, effectively removing Ca^{2+} ions from the water.

Kaolinite Clay. The basic structural feature of many clays, and kaolinite in particular, is a sheet of SiO_4 tetrahedra (black and red spheres) bonded to a sheet of AlO_6 octahedra (gray and green spheres).

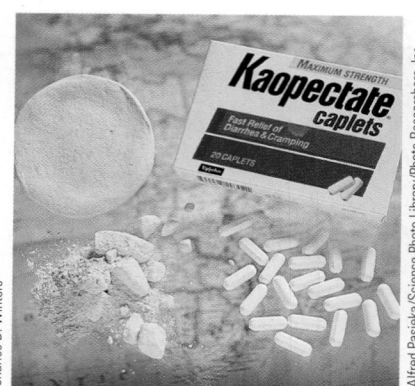

Charles D. Winters

(a) Remedies for stomach upset. One of the ingredients in Kaopectate is kaolin, one form of clay. The off-white objects are pieces of clay purchased in a market in Ghana, West Africa. This clay was made to be eaten as a remedy for stomach ailments. Eating clay is widespread among the world's different cultures.

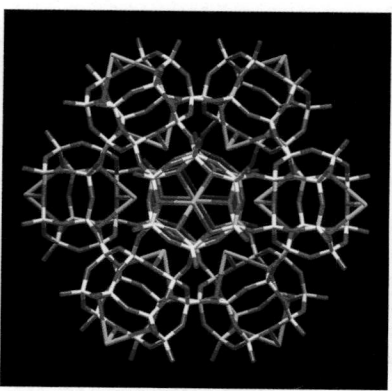

Alfred Pasieka/Science Photo Library/Photo Researchers, Inc.

(b) The stucture of a zeolite. Zeolites, which have Si, Al, and O linked in a polyhedral framework, are often portrayed in drawings like this. Each edge consists of a Si—O—Si, Al—O—Si, or Al—O—Al bond. The channels in the framework can selectively capture small molecules or ions or act as catalytic sites.

Charles D. Winters

(c) Apophyllite, a crystalline zeolite.

Charles D. Winters

(d) Consumer products that remove odor-causing molecules from the air often contain zeolites.

FIGURE 21.22. Aluminosilicates.

Chemistry ⚛ Now™

Sign in at **www.cengage.com/login** and go to Chapter 21 Contents to see Screen 21.6 for an exercise on **the structural chemistry of silicon–oxygen compounds.**

Silicone Polymers

Silicon and chloromethane (CH_3Cl) react at 300 °C in the presence of a catalyst, Cu powder. The primary product of this reaction is $(CH_3)_2SiCl_2$.

$$Si(s) + 2\ CH_3Cl(g) \rightarrow (CH_3)_2SiCl_2(\ell)$$

Halides of Group 4A elements other than carbon hydrolyze readily. Thus, the reaction of $(CH_3)_2SiCl_2$ with water initially produces $(CH_3)_2Si(OH)_2$. On standing, these molecules combine to form a condensation polymer by eliminating water. The polymer is called polydimethylsiloxane, a member of the *silicone* family of polymers.

$$(CH_3)_2SiCl_2 + 2\ H_2O \rightarrow (CH_3)_2Si(OH)_2 + 2\ HCl$$

$$n\ (CH_3)_2Si(OH)_2 \rightarrow [-(CH_3)_2SiO-]_n + n\ H_2O$$

Silicone polymers are nontoxic and have good stability to heat, light, and oxygen; they are chemically inert and have valuable antistick and antifoam properties. They can take the form of oils, greases, and resins. Some have rubber-like properties ("Silly Putty," for example, is a silicone polymer). More than 1 million tons of silicone polymers are made worldwide annually. These materials are used in a wide variety of products: lubricants, peel-off labels, lipstick, suntan lotion, car polish, and building caulk.

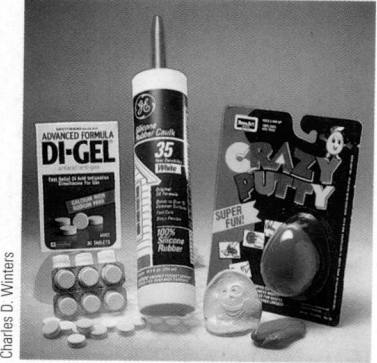

Charles D. Winters

Silicone. Some examples of products containing silicones, polymers with repeating —R_2Si—O— units.

EXERCISE 21.9 Silicon Chemistry

Silicon-oxygen rings are a common structural feature in silicate chemistry. Draw the structure for the anion $Si_3O_9^{6-}$, which is found in minerals such as benitoite. The ring has three Si atoms and three O atoms, and there are two other O atoms on each Si atom.

Lead anchors the bottom of Group 4A. One of a handful of elements known since ancient times, it has a variety of modern uses. It ranks fifth among metals in usage behind iron, copper, aluminum, and zinc. The major uses of the metal and its compounds are in storage batteries (page 913), pigments, ammunition, solders, plumbing, and bearings.

Unfortunately, lead and its compounds are cumulative poisons, particularly in children. At a blood level as low as 50 ppb (parts per billion), blood pressure is elevated; intelligence is affected at 100 ppb; and blood levels higher than 800 ppb can lead to coma and possible death. Health experts believe that more than 200,000 children become ill from lead poisoning annually, a problem caused chiefly by children eating paint containing lead-based pigments. Older homes often contain lead-based paint because white lead [$2 PbCO_3 \cdot Pb(OH)_2$] was the pigment used in white paint until about 40 years ago, when it was replaced by TiO_2. Lead salts have a sweet taste, which may contribute to the tendency of children to chew on painted objects.

The symptoms of lead poisoning are, among others, nausea, abdominal pain, irritability, headaches, and excess lethargy or hyperactivity. Indeed, these describe some of the symptoms of the illness that affected Ludwig van Beethoven. As a child, he was recognized as a musical prodigy and was thought to be the greatest pianist in Europe by the

Ludwig van Beethoven (1770–1827).

time he was 19. But then he fell ill, and, by the time he was 29, he wrote to his brother to say he was considering suicide. By the time he died in 1827 at the age of 56, his belly, arms, and legs were swollen, and he complained constantly of pain in his joints and in his big toe. It is said he wandered the streets of Vienna with long, uncombed hair, dressed in a top hat and long coat, and scribbling in a notebook.

An autopsy at the time showed he died of kidney failure. Kidney stones had destroyed his kidneys, stones that presumably came from gout, the buildup of uric acid in his body. (Gout leads to joint pain, among other things. See the Case Study, page 789.) But why did he have gout?

It was well known in the time of the Roman Empire that lead and its salts are toxic. The Romans drank wine sweetened with a very concentrated grape juice syrup that was prepared by boiling the juice in a lead kettle. The resulting syrup, called Sapa, had a very high concentration of lead, and many Romans contracted gout. So, if Beethoven enjoyed drinking wine, which was often kept in lead-glass decanters, he could have contracted gout and lead poisoning. One scientist has also noted that he may have been one of a small number of people who have a "metal metabolism disorder," a condition that prevents the excretion of toxic metals like lead.

In 2005, scientists at Argonne National Laboratory examined fragments of Beethoven's hair and skull and found both were extremely high in lead. The hair sample, for example, had 60 ppm lead, about 100 times higher than normal.

The mystery of what caused Beethoven's death has been solved. But what remains a mystery is how he contracted lead poisoning.

Questions:

1. *If blood contains 50 ppb lead, how many atoms of lead are there in 1.0 L of blood?*
2. *Research has found that port wine stored for a year in lead-glass decanters contains 2000 ppm lead. If the decanter contains 750 mL of wine (d = 1.0 g/mL), what mass of lead has been extracted into the wine?*

Answers to these question are in Appendix Q.

21.8 Nitrogen, Phosphorus, and the Group 5A Elements

Group 5A elements are characterized by the ns^2np^3 configuration with its half-filled np subshell. In compounds of the Group 5A elements, the primary oxidation numbers are +3 and +5, although common nitrogen compounds display a range of oxidation numbers from −3 to +3 and +5. Once again, as in Groups 3A and 4A, the most positive oxidation number is less common for the heavier elements. In many arsenic, antimony, and bismuth compounds, the element has an oxidation number of +3 state. Not surprisingly, compounds of these elements with oxidation numbers of +5 are powerful oxidizing agents.

This part of our tour of the main group elements will concentrate on the chemistries of nitrogen and phosphorus. Nitrogen is found primarily as N_2 in the atmosphere, where it constitutes 78.1% by volume (75.5% by weight). In contrast, phosphorus occurs in the earth's crust in solids. More than 200 different phosphorus-containing minerals are known; all contain the tetrahedral phosphate ion, PO_4^{3-}, or a derivative

Group 5A

Nitrogen
7
N
25 ppm

Phosphorus
15
P
1000 ppm

Arsenic
33
As
1.5 ppm

Antimony
51
Sb
0.2 ppm

Bismuth
83
Bi
0.048 ppm

Element abundances are in parts per million in the earth's crust.

of this ion. By far, the most abundant phosphorus-containing minerals are apatites (◄ page 978).

Nitrogen and its compounds play a key role in our economy, with ammonia making a particularly notable contribution. Phosphoric acid is an important commodity chemical, and it finds its greatest use in producing fertilizers.

Both phosphorus and nitrogen are part of every living organism. Phosphorus is contained in nucleic acids and phospholipids, and nitrogen occurs in proteins and nucleic acids (see *The Chemistry of Life: Biochemistry*, page 497).

Properties of Nitrogen and Phosphorus

Nitrogen (N_2) is a colorless gas that liquifies at 77 K (-196 °C) (Figure 12.1, page 556). Its most notable feature is its reluctance to react with other elements or compounds because the N≡N triple bond has a large bond enthalpy (945 kJ/mol) and because the molecule is nonpolar. Nitrogen does, however, react with hydrogen to give ammonia in the presence of a catalyst (◄ Case Study, page 749) and with a few metals (notably lithium and magnesium) to give metal nitrides, compounds containing the N^{3-} ion.

$$3 \text{ Mg(s)} + N_2\text{(g)} \longrightarrow \text{Mg}_3\text{N}_2\text{(s)}$$
magnesium nitride

Elemental nitrogen is a very useful material. Because of its lack of reactivity, it is used to provide a nonoxidizing atmosphere for packaged foods and wine and to pressurize electric cables and telephone wires. Liquid nitrogen is valuable as a coolant in freezing biological samples such as blood and semen, in freeze-drying food, and for other applications that require extremely low temperatures.

Elemental phosphorus was first derived from human waste (see *A Closer Look: Making Phosphorus*, page 997), but it is now produced by the reduction of phosphate minerals in an electric furnace.

$$2 \text{ Ca}_3(\text{PO}_4)_2\text{(s)} + 10 \text{ C(s)} + 6 \text{ SiO}_2\text{(s)} \rightarrow \text{P}_4\text{(g)} + 6 \text{ CaSiO}_3\text{(s)} + 10 \text{ CO(g)}$$

White phosphorus is the most stable allotrope of phosphorus. Rather than occurring as a diatomic molecule with a triple bond, like its second-period relative nitrogen (N_2), phosphorus is made up of tetrahedral P_4 molecules in which each P atom is joined to three others via single bonds. Red phosphorus is a polymer of P_4 units.

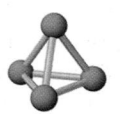

White phosphorus, P_4

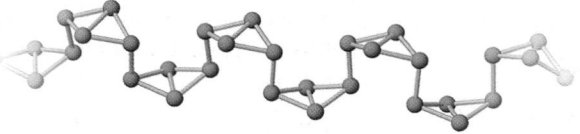

Polymeric red phosphorus

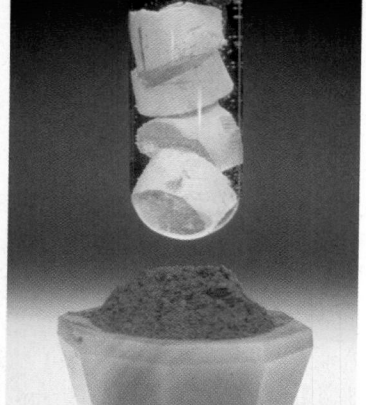

The red and white allotropes of phosphorus.

Nitrogen Compounds

A notable feature of the chemistry of nitrogen is the wide diversity of its compounds. Compounds with nitrogen in all oxidation numbers between -3 and $+5$ are known (Figure 21.23).

Hydrogen Compounds of Nitrogen: Ammonia and Hydrazine

Ammonia is a gas at room temperature and pressure. It has a very penetrating odor and condenses to a liquid at $-33\ °C$ under 1 bar of pressure. Solutions in water, often referred to as ammonium hydroxide, are basic due to the reaction of ammonia with water (◄ Section 17.5 and Figure 3.13).

$$NH_3(aq) + H_2O(\ell) \rightleftharpoons NH_4^+(aq) + OH^-(aq) \quad K_b = 1.8 \times 10^{-5} \text{ at } 25\ °C$$

Ammonia is a major industrial chemical and is prepared by the Haber process (◄ page 749), largely for use as a fertilizer.

Hydrazine, N_2H_4, is a colorless, fuming liquid with an ammonia-like odor (mp, $2.0\ °C$; bp, $113.5\ °C$). Almost 1 million kilograms of hydrazine is produced annually by the Raschig process—the oxidation of ammonia with alkaline sodium hypochlorite in the presence of gelatin (which is added to suppress metal-catalyzed side reactions that lower the yield of hydrazine).

$$2\ NH_3(aq) + NaClO(aq) \rightleftharpoons N_2H_4(aq) + NaCl(aq) + H_2O(\ell)$$

Hydrazine, like ammonia, is also a base,

$$N_2H_4(aq) + H_2O(\ell) \rightleftharpoons N_2H_5^+(aq) + OH^-(aq) \qquad K_b = 8.5 \times 10^{-7}$$

and it is a strong reducing agent, as reflected in the reduction potential for the following reaction of N_2 in basic solution:

$$N_2(g) + 4\ H_2O(\ell) + 4\ e^- \rightarrow N_2H_4(aq) + 4\ OH^-(aq) \qquad E° = -1.15\ V$$

Hydrazine's reducing ability is exploited in its use in wastewater treatment for chemical plants. It removes oxidizing ions such as CrO_4^{2-} by reducing them, thus preventing them from entering the environment. A related use is the treatment of water boilers in large electric-generating plants. Oxygen dissolved in the water presents a serious problem in these plants because the dissolved gas can oxidize (corrode) the metal of the boiler and pipes. Hydrazine reduces the amount of dissolved oxygen in water.

$$N_2H_4(aq) + O_2(g) \rightarrow N_2(g) + 2\ H_2O(\ell)$$

Oxides and Oxoacids of Nitrogen

Nitrogen is unique among all elements in the number of binary oxides it forms (Table 21.5). All are thermodynamically unstable with respect to decomposition to N_2 and O_2; that is, all have positive $\Delta_f G°$ values. Most are slow to decompose, however, and so are described as kinetically stable.

Dinitrogen monoxide, N_2O, commonly called *nitrous oxide*, is a nontoxic, odorless, and tasteless gas in which nitrogen has the lowest oxidation number ($+1$) among nitrogen oxides. It can be made by the careful decomposition of ammonium nitrate at $250\ °C$.

$$NH_4NO_3(s) \rightarrow N_2O(g) + 2\ H_2O(g)$$

It is used as an anesthetic in minor surgery and has been called "laughing gas" because of its euphoriant effects. Because it is soluble in vegetable fats, the largest commercial use of N_2O is as a propellant and aerating agent in cans of whipped cream.

Nitrogen monoxide, NO, is an odd-electron molecule. It has 11 valence electrons, giving it one unpaired electron and making it a free radical. The compound has recently been the subject of intense research because it has been found to be important in a number of biochemical processes (◄ page 367).

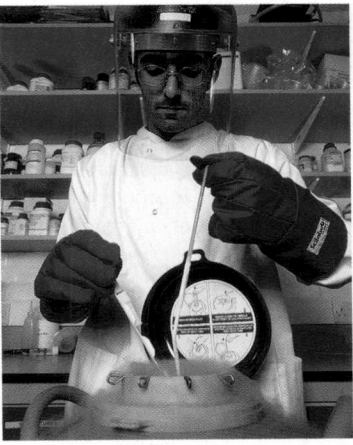

Liquid nitrogen. Biological samples—such as embryos or semen from animals or humans—can be stored in liquid nitrogen (at $-196\ °C$) for long periods of time.

	Compound & Oxidation Number of N
	Ammonia, -3
	Hydrazine, -2
	Dinitrogen, 0
	Dinitrogen oxide, $+1$
	Nitrogen monoxide, $+2$
	Nitrogen dioxide, $+4$
	Nitric acid, $+5$

Active Figure 21.23

Compounds and oxidation numbers for nitrogen. In its compounds, the N atom can have oxidation states ranging from -3 to $+5$.

Chemistry ⊙ Now™ Sign in at www.cengage.com/login and go to the Chapter 21 Contents menu to explore an interactive version of this figure accompanied by an exercise.

by Jeffrey Keaffaber, University of Florida
Large saltwater aquariums like Sea World in Florida, the Shedd Aquarium in Chicago, and the new Georgia Aquarium in Atlanta are a continual source of enjoyment. So are smaller aquariums in your home. Maintaining these facilities is not trivial, however; a healthy environment for its marine inhabitants is essential. For this, chemistry plays an important role.

A key part of aquarium maintenance involves control of the concentrations of various dissolved nitrogen-containing species, including ammonia, nitrite ion, and nitrate ion, all of which are stressful to fish at low concentrations and toxic in higher concentrations. The chemistry that relates to maintaining proper balance among these species is called the *nitrogen cycle*.

© Scripps Institution of Oceanography, UC San Diego. Used with permission.

Nitrification

The nitrogen cycle begins with the production of ammonia (and, in acid solution, its conjugate acid the ammonium ion, NH_4^+), fundamental waste products of protein metabolism in an aquarium habitat. Unless removed, the ammonia concentration will build up over time. To remove it, the aquarium water is cycled through sand filters infused with aerobic, oxygen-loving bacteria. These bacteria utilize enzymes that catalyze the oxidation of ammonia and ammonium ion by O_2 to form first nitrite ion and then nitrate ion. The overall process is called *nitrification*, and the saltwater bacteria that mediate each oxidation step are *Nitrosococcus sp.* and *Nitrococcus sp.*, respectively. Half-reactions representing this chemistry are:

Oxidation half-reactions:

$$NH_4^+(aq) + 8\ OH^-(aq) \rightarrow$$
$$NO_2^-(aq) + 6\ H_2O(\ell) + 6\ e^-$$

$$NO_2^-(aq) + 2\ OH^-(aq) \rightarrow$$
$$NO_3^-(aq) + H_2O(\ell) + 2\ e^-$$

Reduction half-reaction:

$$O_2(aq) + 2\ H_2O(\ell) + 4\ e^- \rightarrow 4\ OH^-(aq)$$

When setting up an aquarium at home, it is appropriate to monitor the concentrations of the various nitrogen species. Initially the NH_3/NH_4^+ concentration rises, but then it begins to fall as oxidation occurs. With time, the nitrite ion concentration builds up, peaks, and then decreases, with an accompanying increase in nitrate ion concentration. To reach a stable situation, as much as six weeks may be required.

Denitrification

Nitrate is much less toxic than ammonia and the nitrite ion, but its buildup must also be limited. In a small aquarium, nitrate ion concentration can be controlled by partial exchange of water. However, because of environmental restrictions this is not possible for large aquariums; they must use a closed water treatment process.

To remedy the build up the nitrate ion, another biologically catalyzed process is used that reduces the nitrate ion to nitrogen gas, N_2. A reducing agent is required, and early designs of denitrifying filters utilized methanol, CH_3OH, as the reducing agent. Among naturally occurring saltwater bacteria capable of nitrate reduction under low oxygen (anoxic) conditions, *Pseudomonas sp.*, is commonly used. The bacteria, utilizing enzymes to catalyze reaction of nitrate and methanol to form N_2 and CO_2, are introduced to sand filters where methanol is added.

A stable pH is also important to the health of aquarium fish. Therefore, the marine environment in a saltwater aquarium is maintained at a relatively constant pH of 8.0-8.2. To aid in this, the CO_2 produced by methanol oxidation remains dissolved in solution, and increases the buffer capacity of the seawater.

Questions:

1. *Write a balanced net ionic equation for the oxidation of NH_4^+ by O_2 to produce H_2O and NO_2^-.*

2. *Write half-reactions for the reduction of NO_3^- to N_2 and for the oxidation of CH_3OH to CO_2 in basic solution. Then, combine these half-reactions to obtain the balanced equation for the reduction of NO_3^- by CH_3OH.*

3. *Consider the carbon-containing species CO_2, H_2CO_3, HCO_3^-, and CO_3^{2-}. Which one is present in largest concentration at the pH conditions of the aquarium? Give a short explanation. K_a of $H_2CO_3 = 4.2 \times 10^{-7}$ and K_a of $HCO_3^- = 4.8 \times 10^{-11}$. (See Study Question 18-110.)*

4. *A large, 2.2×10^7 L, aquarium contains 1.7×10^4 kg of dissolved NO_3^-. Calculate nitrate concentrations in ppm (mg/L) N, ppm NO_3^-, and the molar concentration of NO_3^-.*

Answers to these questions are in Appendix Q.

TABLE 21.5 Some Oxides of Nitrogen

Formula	Name	Structure	Nitrogen Oxidation Number	Description
N_2O	Dinitrogen monoxide (nitrous oxide)	:N≡N—O̤: linear	+1	Colorless gas (laughing gas)
NO	Nitrogen monoxide (nitric oxide)	*	+2	Colorless gas; odd-electron molecule (paramagnetic)
N_2O_3	Dinitrogen trioxide	O̤ O̤ N—N O̤ planar	+3	Blue solid (mp, −100.7 °C); reversibly dissociates to NO and NO_2
NO_2	Nitrogen dioxide	N O̤ O̤	+4	Brown, paramagnetic gas; odd-electron molecule
N_2O_4	Dinitrogen tetraoxide	O̤ O̤ N—N O̤ O̤ planar	+4	Colorless liquid/gas; dissociates to NO_2 (see Figure 16.8)
N_2O_5	Dinitrogen pentaoxide	O̤ O O̤ N N O̤ O̤	+5	Colorless solid

*It is not possible to draw a Lewis structure that accurately represents the electronic structure of NO. See Chapter 8. Also note that only one resonance structure is shown for each structure.

Nitrogen dioxide, NO_2, is the brown gas you see when a bottle of nitric acid is allowed to stand in the sunlight.

$$2\ HNO_3(aq) \rightarrow 2\ NO_2(g) + H_2O(\ell) + \tfrac{1}{2}\ O_2(g)$$

Nitrogen dioxide is also a culprit in air pollution (◄ page 951). Nitrogen monoxide forms when atmospheric nitrogen and oxygen are heated in internal combustion engines. Released into the atmosphere, NO rapidly reacts with O_2 to form NO_2.

$$2\ NO(g) + O_2(g) \rightarrow 2\ NO_2(g)$$

Nitrogen dioxide has 17 valence electrons, so it is also an odd-electron molecule. Because the odd electron largely resides on the N atom, two NO_2 molecules can combine, forming an N—N bond and producing N_2O_4, *dinitrogen tetraoxide*.

$$2\ NO_2(g) \longrightarrow N_2O_4(g)$$

deep brown gas   colorless (mp, −11.2 °C)

Solid N_2O_4 is colorless and consists entirely of N_2O_4 molecules. However, as the solid melts and the temperature increases to the boiling point, the color darkens as N_2O_4 dissociates to form brown NO_2. At the normal boiling point (21.5 °C), the distinctly brown gas consists of 15.9% NO_2 and 84.1% N_2O_4.

Charles D. Winters

Nitrous oxide, N_2O. This oxide readily dissolves in fats, so the gas is added, under pressure, to cans of cream. When the valve is opened, the gas expands, whipping the cream. N_2O is also an anesthetic and is considered safe for medical uses. However, significant dangers arise from using it as a recreational drug. Long-term use can induce nerve damage and cause such problems as weakness and loss of feeling.

When NO_2 is bubbled into water, nitric acid and nitrous acid form.

$$2 NO_2(g) + H_2O(\ell) \rightarrow \underset{\text{nitric acid}}{HNO_3(aq)} + \underset{\text{nitrous acid}}{HNO_2(aq)}$$

Nitric acid has been known for centuries and has become an important compound in our modern economy. The oldest way to make the acid is to treat $NaNO_3$ with sulfuric acid (Figure 21.24).

$$2 NaNO_3(s) + H_2SO_4(\ell) \rightarrow 2 HNO_3(\ell) + Na_2SO_4(s)$$

Enormous quantities of nitric acid are now produced industrially by the oxidation of ammonia in the multistep *Ostwald process*. The acid has many applications, but by far the greatest amount is turned into ammonium nitrate (for use as a fertilizer) by the reaction of nitric acid and ammonia.

Nitric acid is a powerful oxidizing agent, as the large, positive $E°$ values for the following half-reactions illustrate:

$$NO_3^-(aq) + 4 H_3O^+(aq) + 3\ e^- \rightarrow NO(g) + 6 H_2O(\ell) \qquad E° = +0.96\ V$$

$$NO_3^-(aq) + 2 H_3O^+(aq) + e^- \rightarrow NO_2(g) + 3 H_2O(\ell) \qquad E° = +0.80\ V$$

Concentrated nitric acid attacks and oxidizes most metals. (Aluminum is an exception; see page 985.) In this process, the nitrate ion is reduced to one of the nitrogen oxides. Which oxide is formed depends on the metal and on reaction conditions. In the case of copper, for example, either NO or NO_2 is produced, depending on the concentration of the acid (Figure 21.24b).

In dilute acid:

$$3 Cu(s) + 8 H_3O^+(aq) + 2 NO_3^-(aq) \rightarrow 3 Cu^{2+}(aq) + 12 H_2O(\ell) + 2 NO(g)$$

In concentrated acid:

$$Cu(s) + 4 H_3O^+(aq) + 2 NO_3^-(aq) \rightarrow Cu^{2+}(aq) + 6 H_2O(\ell) + 2 NO_2(g)$$

Four metals (Au, Pt, Rh, and Ir) that are not attacked by nitric acid are often described as the "noble metals." The alchemists of the 14th century, however, knew that if they mixed HNO_3 with HCl in a ratio of about 1 : 3, this aqua regia, or "kingly water," would attack even gold, the noblest of metals.

$$10 Au(s) + 6 NO_3^-(aq) + 40 Cl^-(aq) + 36 H_3O^+(aq) \rightarrow$$
$$10 [AuCl_4]^-(aq) + 3 N_2(g) + 54 H_2O(\ell)$$

FIGURE 21.24 The preparation and properties of nitric acid. (a) Nitric acid is prepared by the reaction of sulfuric acid and sodium nitrate. Pure HNO_3 is colorless, but samples of the acid are often brown because of NO_2 formed by decomposition of the acid. This gas fills the apparatus and colors the liquid in the distillation flask. (b) When concentrated nitric acid reacts with copper, the metal is oxidized to copper(II) ions, and NO_2 gas is a reaction product.

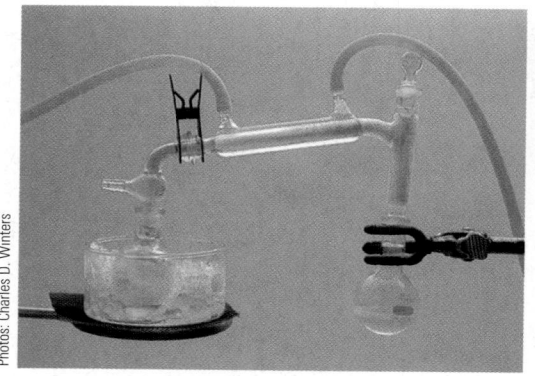

(a) Preparation of nitric acid.

(b) Reaction of HNO_3 with copper.

He stoked his small furnace with more charcoal and pumped the bellows until his retort glowed red hot. Suddenly something strange began to happen. Glowing fumes filled the vessel and from the end of the retort dripped a shining liquid that burst into flames.

J. Emsley: *The 13th Element*, p. 5.
New York, John Wiley, 2000.

John Emsley begins his story of phosphorus, its discovery, and its uses, by imagining what the German alchemist Hennig Brandt must have seen in his laboratory that day in 1669. (See page 338 for an artist's conception of the discovery of phosphorus by Brandt.) He was in search of the philosopher's stone, the magic elixir that would turn the crudest substance into gold.

Brandt was experimenting with urine, which had served as the source of useful chemicals since Roman times. It is not surprising that phosphorus could be extracted from this source. Humans consume much more phosphorus, in the form of phosphate, than they require, and the excess phosphorus (about 1.4 g per day) is excreted in the urine. It is nonetheless extraordinary that Brandt was able to isolate the element. According to an 18th-century chemistry book, about 30 g of phosphorus could be obtained from 60 gallons of urine. And the process was not simple. Another 18th-century recipe states that "50 or 60 pails full" of urine was to be used. "Let it lie steeping . . . till it putrefy and breed worms." The chemist was then to reduce the whole to a paste and finally to heat the paste very strongly in a retort. After some days, phosphorus distilled from the mixture and was collected in water. (We know now that carbon from the organic compounds in the urine would have reduced the phosphate to phosphorus.) Phosphorus was made in this manner for more than 100 years.

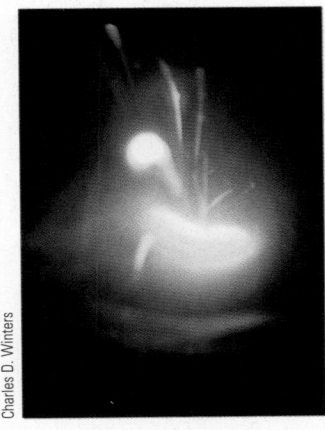

Charles D. Winters

The glow of phosphorus burning in air.

EXERCISE 21.10 Nitrogen Oxide Chemistry

Dinitrogen monoxide can be made by the decomposition of NH_4NO_3.

(a) A Lewis electron dot structure of N_2O is given in Table 21.5. Is it the only possible structure? If other structures are possible, is the one in Table 21.5 the most important?

(b) Is the decomposition of $NH_4NO_3(s)$ to give $N_2O(g)$ and $H_2O(g)$ endothermic or exothermic?

Hydrogen Compounds of Phosphorus and Other Group 5A Elements

The phosphorus analog of ammonia, phosphine (PH_3), is a poisonous, highly reactive gas with a faint garlic-like odor. Industrially, it is made by the reaction of white phosphorus and aqueous NaOH.

$$P_4(s) + 3\ KOH(aq) + 3\ H_2O(\ell) \rightarrow PH_3(g) + 3\ KH_2PO_2(aq)$$

The other hydrides of the heavier Group 5A elements are also toxic and become more unstable as the atomic number of the element increases. Nonetheless, arsine (AsH_3) is used in the semiconductor industry as a starting material in the preparation of gallium arsenide (GaAs) semiconductors.

Phosphorus Oxides and Sulfides

The most important compounds of phosphorus are those with oxygen, and there are at least six simple binary compounds containing just phosphorus and oxygen. All of them can be thought of as being derived structurally from the P_4 tetrahedron of white phosphorus. For example, if P_4 is carefully oxidized, P_4O_6 is formed; an O atom has been placed into each P—P bond in the tetrahedron (Figure 21.25).

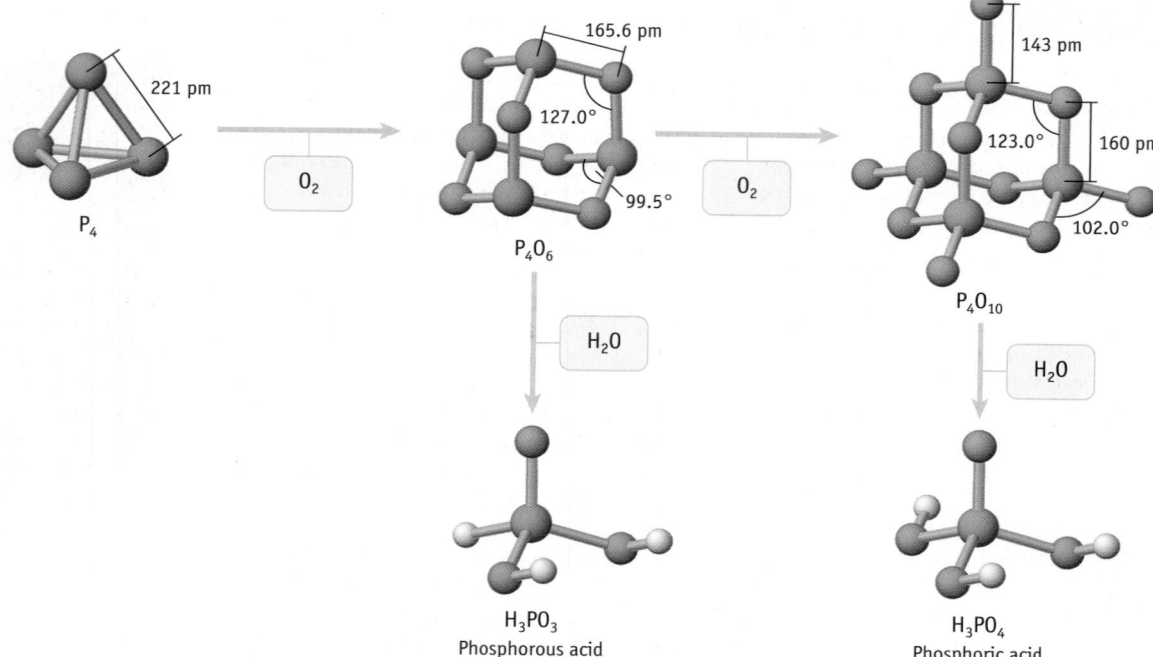

FIGURE 21.25 Phosphorus oxides. Other binary P—O compounds have formulas between P_4O_6 and P_4O_{10}. They are formed by starting with P_4O_6 and adding O atoms successively to the P atom vertices.

The most common and important phosphorus oxide is P_4O_{10}, a fine white powder commonly called "phosphorus pentaoxide" because its empirical formula is P_2O_5. In P_4O_{10}, each phosphorus atom is surrounded tetrahedrally by O atoms.

Phosphorus also forms a series of compounds with sulfur. Of these, the most important is P_4S_3.

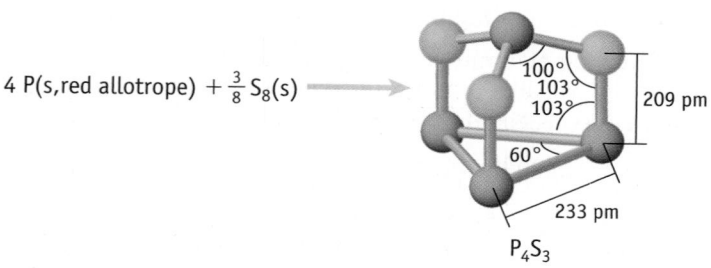

$$4\ P(s, \text{red allotrope}) + \tfrac{3}{8}\ S_8(s) \longrightarrow$$

P_4S_3

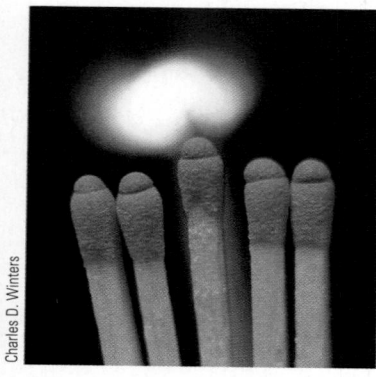

Charles D. Winters

Matches. The head of a "strike anywhere" match contains P_4S_3 and the oxidizing agent $KClO_3$. (Other components are ground glass, Fe_2O_3, ZnO, and glue.) Safety matches have sulfur (3–5%) and $KClO_3$ (45–55%) in the match head and red phosphorus in the striking strip.

In this phosphorus sulfide, S atoms are placed into only three of the P—P bonds. The principal use of P_4S_3 is in "strike anywhere" matches, the kind that light when you rub the head against a rough object. The active ingredients are P_4S_3 and the powerful oxidizing agent potassium chlorate, $KClO_3$. The "safety match" is now more common than the "strike anywhere" match. In safety matches, the head is predominantly $KClO_3$, and the material on the match book is red phosphorus (about 50%), Sb_2S_3, Fe_2O_3, and glue.

Phosphorus Oxoacids and Their Salts

A few of the many known phosphorus oxoacids are illustrated in Table 21.6. Indeed, there are so many acids and their salts in this category that structural principles have been developed to organize and understand them.

(a) All P atoms in the oxoacids and their anions (conjugate bases) are four-coordinate and tetrahedral.

(b) All the P atoms in the acids have at least one P—OH group (and this occurs often in the anions as well). In every case, the H atom is ionizable as H^+.

(c) Some oxoacids have one or more P—H bonds. This H atom is not ionizable as H^+.

(d) Polymerization can occur by P—O—P bond formation to give both linear and cyclic species. Two P atoms are never joined by more than one P—O—P bridge.

(e) When a P atom is surrounded only by O atoms (as in H_3PO_4), its oxidation number is +5. For each P—OH that is replaced by P—H, the oxidation number drops by 2 (because P is considered more electronegative than H). For example, the oxidation number of P in H_3PO_2 is +1.

FIGURE 21.26 Reaction of P_4O_{10} and water. The white solid oxide reacts vigorously with water to give orthophosphoric acid, H_3PO_4. (The heat generated vaporizes the water, so steam is visible.)

Orthophosphoric acid, H_3PO_4, and its salts are far more important commercially than other P—O acids. Millions of tons of phosphoric acid are made annually, some using white phosphorus as the starting material. The element is burned in oxygen to give P_4O_{10}, and the oxide reacts with water to produce the acid (Figure 21.26).

$$P_4O_{10}(s) + 6\ H_2O(\ell) \rightarrow 4\ H_3PO_4(aq)$$

TABLE 21.6 Phosphorus Oxoacids

Formula	Name	Structure
H_3PO_4	Orthophosphoric acid	
$H_4P_2O_7$	Pyrophosphoric acid (diphosphoric acid)	
$(HPO_3)_3$	Metaphosphoric acid	
H_3PO_3	Phosphorous acid (phosphonic acid)	
H_3PO_2	Hypophosphorous acid (phosphinic acid)	

(a) **Mining phosphate rock.** Phosphate rock is primarily $Ca_3(PO_4)_2$, and most mined in the United States comes from Florida.

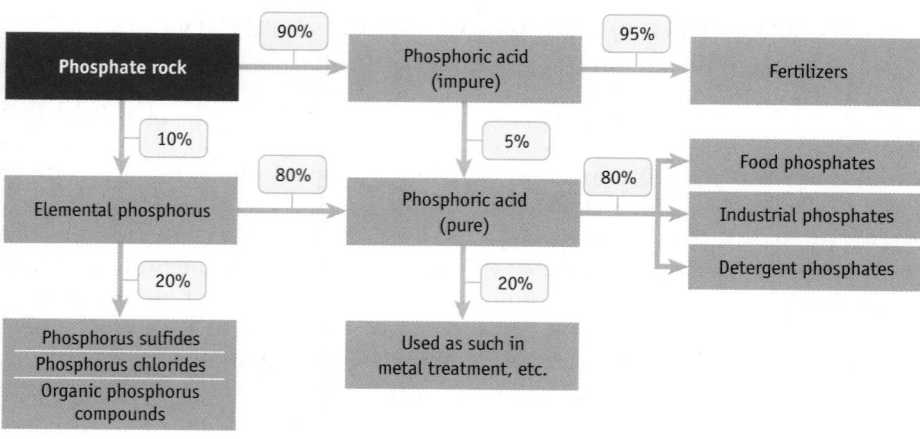

(b) **Uses of phosphorus and phosphoric acid.**

FIGURE 21.27 Uses of phosphate rock, phosphorus, and phosphoric acid.

This approach gives a pure product, so it is employed to make phosphoric acid for use in food products in particular. The acid is nontoxic, and it gives the tart or sour taste to carbonated "soft drinks," such as various colas (about 0.05% H_3PO_4) or root beer (about 0.01% H_3PO_4).

A major use for phosphoric acid is to impart corrosion resistance to metal objects such as nuts and bolts, tools, and car-engine parts by plunging the object into a hot acid bath. Car bodies are similarly treated with phosphoric acid containing metal ions such as Zn^{2+}, and aluminum trim is "polished" by treating it with the acid.

The reaction of H_3PO_4 with strong bases produces salts such as NaH_2PO_4, Na_2HPO_4, and Na_3PO_4. In industry, the monosodium and disodium salts are produced using Na_2CO_3 as the base, but an excess of the stronger (and more expensive) base NaOH is required to remove the third proton to give Na_3PO_4.

Sodium phosphate (Na_3PO_4) is used in scouring powders and paint strippers because the anion PO_4^{3-} is a relatively strong base in water ($K_b = 2.8 \times 10^{-2}$). Sodium monohydrogen phosphate, Na_2HPO_4, which has a less basic anion than PO_4^{3-}, is widely used in food products. Kraft has patented a process using the salt in the manufacture of pasteurized cheese, for example. Thousands of tons of Na_2HPO_4 are still used for this purpose, even though the function of the salt in this process is not completely understood. In addition, a small amount of Na_2HPO_4 in pudding mixes enables the mix to gel in cold water, and the basic anion raises the pH of cereals to provide "quick-cooking" breakfast cereal. (The OH^- ion from HPO_4^{2-} hydrolysis accelerates the breakdown of the cellulose material in the cereal.)

Calcium phosphates are used in a broad spectrum of products. For example, the weak acid $Ca(H_2PO_4)_2 \cdot H_2O$ is used as the acid leavening agent in baking powder. A typical baking powder contains (along with inert ingredients) 28% $NaHCO_3$, 10.7% $Ca(H_2PO_4)_2 \cdot H_2O$, and 21.4% $NaAl(SO_4)_2$ (also a weak acid). The weak acids react with sodium bicarbonate to produce CO_2 gas. For example,

$$Ca(H_2PO_4)_2 \cdot H_2O(s) + 2\ NaHCO_3(aq) \rightarrow 2\ CO_2(g) + 3\ H_2O(\ell) + Na_2HPO_4(aq) + CaHPO_4(aq)$$

Finally, calcium monohydrogen phosphate, $CaHPO_4$, is used as an abrasive and polishing agent in toothpaste.

21.9 Oxygen, Sulfur, and the Group 6A Elements

Oxygen is by far the most abundant element in the earth's crust, representing slightly less than 50% of it by weight. It is present as elemental oxygen in the atmosphere and is combined with other elements in water and in many minerals. Scientists believe that elemental oxygen did not appear on this planet until about 3.5 billion years ago, when it was formed on the planet by plants through the process of photosynthesis.

Sulfur, seventeenth in abundance in the earth's crust, is also found in its elemental form in nature, but only in certain concentrated deposits. Sulfur-containing compounds occur in natural gas and oil. In minerals, sulfur occurs as the sulfide ion (for example, in cinnabar, HgS, and galena, PbS), as the disulfide ion (in iron pyrite, FeS_2, or "fool's gold"), and as sulfate ion (e.g., in gypsum, $CaSO_4 \cdot 2\ H_2O$). Sulfur oxides (SO_2 and SO_3) also occur in nature, primarily as products of volcanic activity (Figure 21.28).

In the United States, most sulfur—about 10 million tons per year—is obtained from deposits of the element found along the Gulf of Mexico. These deposits occur typically at a depth of 150 to 750 m below the surface in layers about 30 m thick. They are thought to have been formed by anaerobic ("without elemental oxygen") bacteria acting on sedimentary sulfate deposits such as gypsum.

Preparation and Properties of the Elements

Pure oxygen is obtained by the fractional distillation of air and is among the top five industrial chemicals produced in the United States. Oxygen can be made in the laboratory by electrolysis of water (Figure 21.4) and by the catalyzed decomposition of metal chlorates such as $KClO_3$.

$$2\ KClO_3(s) \xrightarrow{\text{catalyst}} 2\ KCl(s) + 3\ O_2(g)$$

At room temperature and pressure, oxygen is a colorless gas, but it is pale blue when condensed to the liquid at $-183\ °C$ (◄ Figure 9.15). As described in Section 9.3, diatomic oxygen is paramagnetic because it has two unpaired electrons.

An allotrope of oxygen, ozone (O_3), is a blue, diamagnetic gas with an odor so strong that it can be detected in concentrations as low as 0.05 ppm. Ozone is synthesized by passing O_2 through an electric discharge or by irradiating O_2 with ultraviolet light. It is often in the news because of the realization that the earth's protective layer of ozone in the stratosphere is being disrupted by chlorofluorocarbons and other chemicals (◄ page 953).

Sulfur has numerous allotropes. The most common and most stable allotrope is the yellow, orthorhombic form, which consists of S_8 molecules with the sulfur atoms arranged in a crown-shaped ring (Figure 21.29a). Less stable allotropes are known that have rings of 6 to 20 sulfur atoms. Another form of sulfur, called plastic sulfur, has a molecular structure with chains of sulfur atoms (Figure 21.29b).

Sulfur is obtained from underground deposits by a process developed by Herman Frasch (1851–1914) about 1900. Superheated water (at 165 °C) and then air are forced into the deposit. The sulfur melts (mp, 113 °C) and is forced to the surface as a frothy, yellow stream, from which it solidifies.

Selenium and tellurium are comparatively rare on earth, having abundances about the same as those of silver and gold, respectively. Because their chemistry is similar to that of sulfur, they are often found in minerals associated with the sulfides of copper, silver, iron, and arsenic, and they are recovered as by-products of the industries devoted to those metals.

Group 6A
Oxygen 8 O 474,000 ppm
Sulfur 16 S 260 ppm
Selenium 34 Se 0.5 ppm
Tellurium 52 Te 0.005 ppm
Polonium 84 Po trace

Element abundances are in parts per million in the earth's crust.

FIGURE 21.28 Sulfur spewing from a volcano in Indonesia.

FIGURE 21.29 Sulfur allotropes.
(a) At room temperature, sulfur exists as a bright yellow solid composed of S_8 rings. (b) When heated, the rings break open, and eventually form chains of S atoms in a material described as "plastic sulfur."

(a)   (b)

Selenium has a range of uses, including in glass making. A cadmium sulfide/selenide mixture is added to glass to give it a brilliant red color (Figure 21.30a). The most familiar use of selenium is in xerography, a word meaning "dry printing" and a process at the heart of the modern copy machine. Most photocopy machines use an aluminum plate or roller coated with selenium. Light coming from the imaging lens selectively discharges a static electric charge on the selenium surface, and the black toner sticks only on the areas that remain charged. A copy is made when the toner is transferred to a sheet of plain paper.

The heaviest element of Group 6A, polonium, is radioactive and found only in trace amounts on earth. It was discovered in Paris, France, in 1898 by Marie Sklodowska Curie (1867–1934) and her husband Pierre Curie (1859-1906). The Curies painstakingly separated this element from a large quantity of pitchblende, a uranium-containing ore.

Chemistry Now™

Sign in at **www.cengage.com/login** and go to Chapter 21 Contents to see Screen 21.8 for an exercise on **sulfur chemistry.**

FIGURE 21.30 Uses of selenium.
(a) Glass takes on a brilliant red color when a mixture of cadmium sulfide/selenide (CdS, CdSe) is added to it.
(b) These sample bottles hold suspensions of quantum dots, nanometer-sized crystals of CdSe dispersed in a polymer matrix. The crystals emit light in the visible range when excited by ultraviolet light. Light emission at different wavelengths is achieved by changing the particle size. Crystals of PbS and PbSe can be made that emit light in the infrared range.

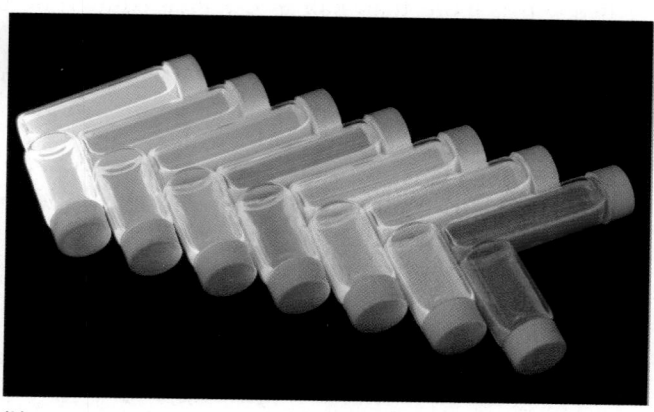

(a)   (b)

Sulfur Compounds

Hydrogen sulfide, H_2S, has a bent molecular geometry, like water. Unlike water, however, H_2S is a gas under standard conditions (mp, -85.6 °C; bp, -60.3 °C) because its intermolecular forces are weak compared with the strong hydrogen bonding in water (see Figure 12.6). Hydrogen sulfide is poisonous, comparable in toxicity to hydrogen cyanide, but fortunately it has a terrible odor and is detectable in concentrations as low as 0.02 ppm. You must be careful with H_2S, though. Because it has an anesthetic effect, your nose rapidly loses its ability to detect it. Death occurs at H_2S concentrations of 100 ppm.

Sulfur is often found as the sulfide ion in conjunction with metals because all metal sulfides (except those based on Group 1A metals) are insoluble. The recovery of metals from their sulfide ores usually begins by heating the ore in air.

$$2\ PbS(s) + 3\ O_2(g) \rightarrow 2\ PbO(s) + 2\ SO_2(g)$$

Here, lead sulfide is converted to lead(II) oxide, and this is further reduced to lead using carbon or carbon monoxide in a blast furnace.

$$PbO(s) + CO(g) \rightarrow Pb(\ell) + CO_2(g)$$

Alternatively, the oxide can be reduced to elemental lead by combining it with fresh lead sulfide.

$$2\ PbO(s) + PbS(s) \rightarrow 3\ Pb(s) + SO_2(g)$$

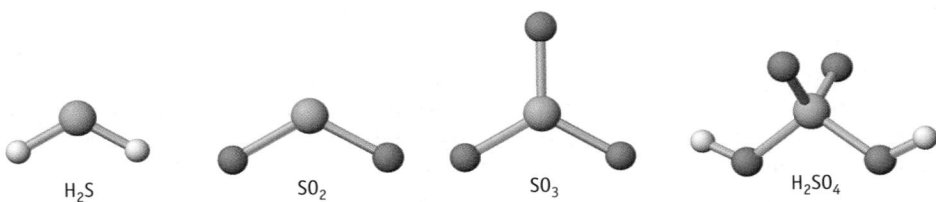

Models of some common sulfur-containing molecules: H_2S, SO_2, SO_3, and H_2SO_4.

Sulfur dioxide (SO_2), a colorless, toxic gas with a sharp odor, is produced on an enormous scale by the combustion of sulfur and by roasting sulfide ores in air. The combustion of sulfur in sulfur-containing coal and fuel oil creates particularly large environmental problems. It has been estimated that about 2.0×10^8 tons of sulfur oxides (primarily SO_2) are released into the atmosphere each year by human activities; this is more than half of the total emitted by all other natural sources of sulfur in the environment.

Sulfur dioxide readily dissolves in water. The most important reaction of this gas is its oxidation to SO_3.

$$SO_2(g) + \tfrac{1}{2}\ O_2(g) \rightarrow SO_3(g) \qquad \Delta_rH° = -98.9 \text{ kJ/mol-rxn}$$

Sulfur trioxide is almost never isolated but is converted directly to sulfuric acid by reaction with water in the "contact process."

The largest use of sulfur is the production of sulfuric acid, H_2SO_4, the compound produced in largest quantity by the chemical industry (◄ page 135). In the United States, roughly 70% of the acid is used to manufacture superphosphate fertilizer from phosphate rock. Plants need a soluble form of phosphorus for growth, but calcium phosphate and apatite [$Ca_5X(PO_4)_3$, X = F, OH, Cl] are insoluble. Treating phosphate-containing minerals with sulfuric acid produces a mixture of soluble

■ **Bad Breath** Halitosis or "bad breath" is due to three sulfur-containing compounds: H_2S, CH_3SH (methyl mercaptan), and $(CH_3)_2S$ (dimethyl sulfide). All three can be detected in very tiny concentrations. For example, your nose knows if as little as 0.2 microgram of CH_3SH is present per liter of air. The compounds result from bacteria's attack on the sulfur-containing amino acids cysteine and methionine in food particles in the mouth. A general rule: if something smells bad, it probably contains sulfur! (See Case Study, page 524.)

Charles D. Winters

Common household products containing sulfur or sulfur-based compounds.

Sulfur chemistry can be important in cave formation, as a spectacular example in the jungles of southern Mexico amply demonstrates. Toxic hydrogen sulfide gas spews from the Cueva de Villa Luz along with water that is milky white with suspended sulfur particles. The cave can be followed downward to a large underground stream and a maze of actively enlarging cave passages. Water rises into the cave from underlying sulfur-bearing strata, releasing hydrogen sulfide at concentrations up to 150 ppm. Yellow sulfur crystallizes on the cave walls around the inlets. The sulfur and sulfuric acid are produced by the following reactions:

$$2 H_2S(g) + O_2(g) \rightarrow 2 S(s) + 2 H_2O(\ell)$$

$$2 S(s) + 2 H_2O(\ell) + 3 O_2(g) \rightarrow 2 H_2SO_4(aq)$$

The cave atmosphere is poisonous to humans, so gas masks are essential for would-be explorers. But surprisingly, the cave is teeming with life. Several species of bacteria

thrive on sulfur compounds in acidic environments. The chemical energy released in their metabolism is used to obtain carbon for their bodies from calcium carbonate and carbon dioxide, both of which are abundant in the cave. One result is that bacterial filaments hang from the walls and ceilings in bundles. Because the filaments look like something coming from a runny nose, cave explorers refer to them as "snot-tites." Other microbes feed on the bacteria, and so on up the food chain—which includes spiders, gnats, and

pygmy snails—all the way to sardine-like fish that swim in the cave stream. This entire ecosystem is supported by reactions involving sulfur within the cave.

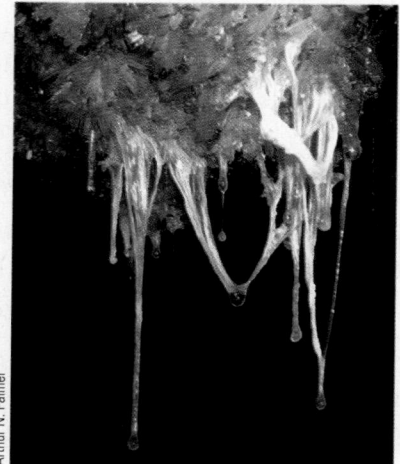

Snot-tites. Filaments of sulfur-oxidizing bacteria (dubbed "snot-tites") hang from the ceiling of a Mexican cave containing an atmosphere rich in hydrogen sulfide. The bacteria thrive on the energy released by oxidation of the hydrogen sulfide, forming the base of a complex food chain. Droplets of sulfuric acid on the filaments have an average pH of 1.4, with some as low as zero! Drops that landed on explorers in the cave burned their skin and disintegrated their clothing.

Arthur N. Palmer

phosphates. The balanced equation for the reaction of excess sulfuric acid and calcium phosphate, for example, is

$$Ca_3(PO_4)_2(s) + 3 H_2SO_4(\ell) \rightarrow 2 H_3PO_4(\ell) + 3 CaSO_4(s)$$

but it does not tell the whole story. Concentrated superphosphate fertilizer is actually mostly $CaHPO_4$ or $Ca(H_2PO_4)_2$ plus some H_3PO_4 and $CaSO_4$. (Notice that the chemical principle behind this reaction is that sulfuric acid is a stronger acid than H_3PO_4 (Table 17.3), so the PO_4^{3-} ion is protonated by sulfuric acid.)

Smaller amounts of sulfuric acid are used in the conversion of ilmenite, a titanium-bearing ore, to TiO_2, which is then used as a white pigment in paint, plastics, and paper. The acid is also used to manufacture iron and steel as well as petroleum products, synthetic polymers, and paper.

Chemistry ⚛ Now™

Sign in at **www.cengage.com/login** and go to Chapter 21 Contents to see Screen 21.9 for an exercise on **the structural chemistry of sulfur compounds.**

EXERCISE 21.11 Sulfur Chemistry

Metal sulfides roasted in air produce metal oxides.

$$2 ZnS(s) + 3 O_2(g) \rightarrow 2 ZnO(s) + 2 SO_2(g)$$

Use thermodynamics to decide if the reaction is product- or reactant-favored at equilibrium at 298 K. Will the reaction be more or less product-favored at a high temperature?

21.10 The Halogens, Group 7A

Fluorine and chlorine are the most abundant halogens in the earth's crust, with fluorine somewhat more abundant than chlorine. If their abundance in sea water is measured, however, the situation is quite different. Chlorine has an abundance in sea water of 18,000 ppm, whereas the abundance of fluorine in the same source is only 1.3 ppm. This variation is a result of the differences in the solubility of their salts and plays a role in the methods used to recover the elements themselves.

Preparation of the Elements

Fluorine

The water-insoluble mineral fluorspar (calcium fluoride, CaF_2) is one of the many sources of fluorine. Because the mineral was originally used as a flux in metalworking, its name comes from the Latin word meaning "to flow." In the 17th century, it was discovered that solid CaF_2 would emit light when heated, and the phenomenon was called *fluorescence*. In the early 1800s, when it was recognized that a new element was contained in fluorspar, A. M. Ampère (1775–1836) suggested that the element be called fluorine.

Although fluorine was recognized as an element by 1812, it was not until 1886 that it was isolated by the French chemist Henri Moisson (1852–1907) in elemental form as a very pale yellow gas by the electrolysis of KF dissolved in anhydrous HF. Indeed, because F_2 is such a powerful oxidizing agent, chemical oxidation of F^- to F_2 is not feasible, and electrolysis is the only practical way to obtain gaseous F_2 (Figure 21.31).

The preparation of F_2 is difficult because F_2 is so reactive. It oxidizes (corrodes) the equipment and reacts violently with traces of grease or other contaminants. Furthermore, the products of electrolysis, F_2 and H_2, can recombine explosively, so they must not be allowed to come into contact with each other. (Compare with the reaction of H_2 and Br_2 in Figure 21.5.) Current U.S. production of fluorine is approximately 5000 metric tons per year.

Chlorine

Chlorine is a strong oxidizing agent, and to prepare this element from chloride ion by a chemical reaction requires a stronger oxidizing agent. Permanganate or dichromate ion in acid solution will serve this purpose (Figure 21.32). Elemental chlorine was first made by the Swedish chemist Karl Wilhelm Scheele (1742–1786) in 1774, who combined sodium chloride with an oxidizing agent in an acidic solution.

Industrially, chlorine is made by electrolysis of brine (concentrated aqueous NaCl). The other product of the electrolysis, NaOH, is also a valuable industrial chemical. About 80% of the chlorine produced is made using an electrochemical cell similar to the one depicted in Figure 21.33. Oxidation of chloride ion to Cl_2 gas occurs at the anode and reduction of water occurs at the cathode.

Anode reaction (oxidation)	$2\ Cl^-(aq) \rightarrow Cl_2(g) + 2\ e^-$
Cathode reaction (reduction)	$2\ H_2O(\ell) + 2\ e^- \rightarrow H_2(g) + 2\ OH^-(aq)$

Activated titanium is used for the anode, and stainless steel or nickel is preferred for the cathode in the electrolytic cell. The anode and cathode compartments are separated by a membrane that is not permeable to water but allows Na^+ ions to pass to maintain the charge balance. Thus, the membrane functions as a "salt" bridge between the anode and cathode compartments. The energy consumption of these cells is in the range of 2000–2500 kWh per ton of NaOH produced.

Group 7A
Halogens

Fluorine 9 **F** 950 ppm	
Chlorine 17 **Cl** 130 ppm	
Bromine 35 **Br** 0.37 ppm	
Iodine 53 **I** 0.14 ppm	
Astatine 85 **At** trace	

Element abundances are in parts per million in the earth's crust.

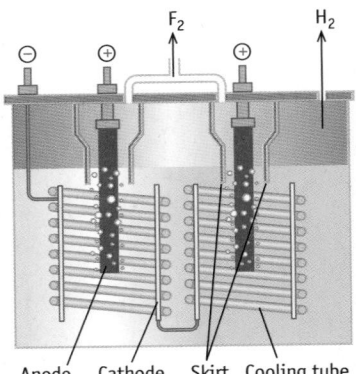

Anode   Cathode   Skirt   Cooling tube

FIGURE 21.31 Schematic of an electrolysis cell for producing fluorine.

FIGURE 21.32 Chlorine preparation. Chlorine is prepared by oxidation of chloride ion using a strong oxidizing agent. Here, oxidation of NaCl is accomplished using $K_2Cr_2O_7$ in H_2SO_4. (The Cl_2 gas is bubbled into water in a receiving flask.)

Bromine

The standard reduction potentials of the halogens indicate that their strength as oxidizing agents decreases going from F_2 to I_2.

Half-Reaction	Reduction Potential ($E°$, V)
$F_2(g) + 2\ e^- \rightarrow 2\ F^-(aq)$	2.87
$Cl_2(g) + 2\ e^- \rightarrow 2\ Cl^-(aq)$	1.36
$Br_2(\ell) + 2\ e^- \rightarrow 2\ Br^-(aq)$	1.08
$I_2(s) + 2\ e^- \rightarrow 2\ I^-(aq)$	0.535

This means that Cl_2 will oxidize Br^- ions to Br_2 in aqueous solution, for example.

$$Cl_2(aq) + 2\ Br^-(aq) \rightarrow 2\ Cl^-(aq) + Br_2(aq)$$

$$E°_{net} = E°_{cathode} - E°_{anode} = 1.36\ V - (1.08\ V) = +0.28\ V$$

In fact, this is the commercial method of preparing bromine when NaBr is obtained from natural brine wells in Arkansas and Michigan.

Iodine

Iodine is a lustrous, purple-black solid, easily sublimed at room temperature and atmospheric pressure (Figure 13.17). The element was first isolated in 1811 from seaweed and kelp, extracts of which had long been used for treatment of goiter, the enlargement of the thyroid gland. It is now known that the thyroid gland produces a growth-regulating hormone (thyroxine) that contains iodine. Consequently, most table salt in the United States has 0.01% NaI added to provide the necessary iodine in the diet.

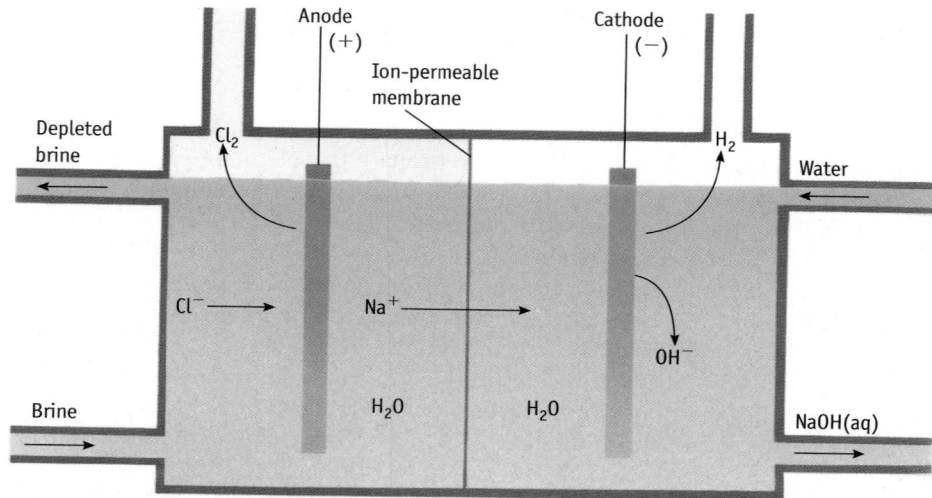

Active Figure 21.33 A membrane cell for the production of NaOH and Cl_2 gas from a saturated, aqueous solution of NaCl (brine). Here, the anode and cathode compartments are separated by a water-impermeable but ion-conducting membrane. A widely used membrane is made of Nafion, a fluorine-containing polymer that is a relative of polytetrafluoroethylene (Teflon). Brine is fed into the anode compartment and dilute sodium hydroxide or water into the cathode compartment. Overflow pipes carry the evolved gases and NaOH away from the chambers of the electrolysis cell.

Chemistry ☉ Now™ Sign in at www.cengage.com/login and go to the Chapter 21 Contents menu to explore an interactive version of this figure accompanied by an exercise.

FIGURE 21.34 The preparation of iodine. A mixture of sodium iodide and manganese(IV) oxide was placed in the flask (left). On adding concentrated sulfuric acid (right), brown iodine vapor is evolved.

$$2\ NaI(s) + 2\ H_2SO_4(aq) + MnO_2(s) \rightarrow$$
$$Na_2SO_4(aq) + MnSO_4(aq)$$
$$+ 2\ H_2O(\ell) + I_2(g)$$

A laboratory method for preparing I_2 is illustrated in Figure 21.34. The commercial preparation depends on the source of I^- and its concentration. One method is interesting because it involves some chemistry described earlier in this book. Iodide ions are first precipitated with silver ions to give insoluble AgI.

$$I^-(aq) + Ag^+(aq) \rightarrow AgI(s)$$

This is reduced by clean scrap iron to give iron(II) iodide and metallic silver.

$$2\ AgI(s) + Fe(s) \rightarrow FeI_2(aq) + 2\ Ag(s)$$

The silver is recycled by oxidizing it with nitric acid (forming silver nitrate) which is then reused. Finally, iodide ion from water-soluble FeI_2 is oxidized to iodine with chlorine [with iron(III) chloride as a by-product].

$$2\ FeI_2(aq) + 3\ Cl_2(aq) \rightarrow 2\ I_2(s) + 2\ FeCl_3(aq)$$

Fluorine Compounds

Fluorine is the most reactive of all of the elements, forming compounds with every element except He and Ne. In most cases, the elements combine directly, and some reactions can be so vigorous as to be explosive. This reactivity can be explained by at least two features of fluorine chemistry: the relatively weak F—F bond compared with chlorine and bromine, and, in particular, the relatively strong bonds formed by fluorine to other elements. This is illustrated by the table of bond dissociation enthalpies in the margin.

In addition to its oxidizing ability, another notable characteristic of fluorine is its small size. These properties lead to the formation of compounds where a number of F atoms can be bonded to a central element in a high oxidation state. Examples include PtF_6, UF_6, IF_7, and XeF_4.

Hydrogen fluoride is an important industrial chemical. More than 1 million tons of hydrogen fluoride is produced annually worldwide, almost all by the action of concentrated sulfuric acid on fluorspar.

$$CaF_2(s) + H_2SO_4(\ell) \rightarrow CaSO_4(s) + 2\ HF(g)$$

The U.S. capacity for HF production is approximately 210,000 metric tons, but currently demand is exceeding supply for this chemical. Anhydrous HF is used in

Bond Dissociation Enthalpies of Some Halogen Compounds (kJ/mol)

X	X—X	H—X	C—X (in CX_4)
F	155	565	485
Cl	242	432	339
Br	193	366	285
I	151	299	213

a broad range of industries: in the production of refrigerants, herbicides, pharmaceuticals, high-octane gasoline, aluminum, plastics, electrical components, and fluorescent lightbulbs.

The fluorspar used to produce HF must be very pure and free of SiO_2 because HF reacts readily with silicon dioxide.

$$SiO_2(s) + 4 HF(aq) \rightarrow SiF_4(g) + 2 H_2O(\ell)$$

$$SiF_4(g) + 2 HF(aq) \rightarrow H_2SiF_6(aq)$$

This series of reactions explains why HF can be used to etch or frost glass (such as the inside of fluorescent light bulbs). It also explains why HF is not shipped in glass containers (unlike HCl, for example).

The aluminum industry consumes about 10–40 kg of cryolite, Na_3AlF_6, per metric ton of aluminum produced. The reason is that cryolite is added to aluminum oxide to produce a lower-melting mixture that can be electrolyzed. Cryolite is found in only small quantities in nature, so it is made in various ways, among them the following reaction:

$$6 HF(aq) + Al(OH)_3(s) + 3 NaOH(aq) \rightarrow Na_3AlF_6(s) + 6 H_2O(\ell)$$

About 3% of the hydrofluoric acid produced is used in uranium fuel production. To separate uranium isotopes in a gas centrifuge (◄ page 523), the uranium must be in the form of a volatile compound. Naturally occurring uranium is processed to give UO_2. This oxide is treated with hydrogen fluoride to give UF_4, which is then reacted with F_2 to produce the volatile solid UF_6.

$$UO_2(s) + 4 HF(aq) \rightarrow UF_4(s) + 2 H_2O(\ell)$$

$$UF_4(s) + F_2(g) \rightarrow UF_6(s)$$

This last step consumes 70–80% of fluorine produced annually.

Chlorine Compounds

Hydrogen Chloride

Hydrochloric acid, an aqueous solution of hydrogen chloride, is a valuable industrial chemical. Hydrogen chloride gas can be prepared by the reaction of hydrogen and chlorine, but the rapid, exothermic reaction is difficult to control. The classical method of making HCl in the laboratory uses the reaction of NaCl and sulfuric acid, a procedure that takes advantage of the facts that HCl is a gas and that H_2SO_4 will not oxidize the chloride ion.

$$2 NaCl(s) + H_2SO_4(\ell) \rightarrow Na_2SO_4(s) + 2 HCl(g)$$

Hydrogen chloride gas has a sharp, irritating odor. Both gaseous and aqueous HCl react with metals and metal oxides to give metal chlorides and, depending on the reactant, hydrogen or water.

$$Mg(s) + 2 HCl(aq) \rightarrow MgCl_2(aq) + H_2(g)$$

$$ZnO(s) + 2 HCl(aq) \rightarrow ZnCl_2(aq) + H_2O(\ell)$$

Oxoacids of Chlorine

Oxoacids of chlorine range from HClO, in which chlorine has an oxidation number of +1, to $HClO_4$, in which the oxidation number is equal to the group number, +7. All are strong oxidizing agents.

Oxoacids of Chlorine

Acid	Name	Anion	Name
HClO	Hypochlorous	ClO^-	Hypochlorite
$HClO_2$	Chlorous	ClO_2^-	Chlorite
$HClO_3$	Chloric	ClO_3^-	Chlorate
$HClO_4$	Perchloric	ClO_4^-	Perchlorate

Hypochlorous acid, HClO, forms when chlorine dissolves in water. In this reaction, half of the chlorine is oxidized to hypochlorite ion and half is reduced to chloride ion in a **disproportionation reaction**.

$$Cl_2(g) + 2\ H_2O(\ell) \rightleftharpoons H_3O^+(aq) + HClO(aq) + Cl^-(aq)$$

■ **Disproportionation** A reaction in which an element or compound is simultaneously oxidized and reduced is called a disproportionation reaction. Here, Cl_2 is oxidized to ClO^- and reduced to Cl^-.

If Cl_2 is dissolved in cold aqueous NaOH instead of in pure water, hypochlorite ion and chloride ion form.

$$Cl_2(g) + 2\ OH^-(aq) \rightleftharpoons ClO^-(aq) + Cl^-(aq) + H_2O(\ell)$$

Under basic conditions, the equilibrium lies far to the right. The resulting alkaline solution is the "liquid bleach" used in home laundries. The bleaching action of this solution is a result of the oxidizing ability of ClO^-. Most dyes are colored organic compounds, and hypochlorite ion oxidizes dyes to colorless products.

When calcium hydroxide is combined with Cl_2, solid $Ca(ClO)_2$ is the product. This compound is easily handled and is the "chlorine" that is sold for swimming pool disinfection.

When a basic solution of hypochlorite ion is heated, another disproportionation occurs, forming chlorate ion and chloride ion:

$$3\ ClO^-(aq) \rightarrow ClO_3^-(aq) + 2\ Cl^-(aq)$$

Sodium and potassium chlorates are made in large quantities this way. The sodium salt can be reduced to ClO_2, a compound used for bleaching paper pulp. Some $NaClO_3$ is also converted to potassium chlorate, $KClO_3$, the preferred oxidizing agent in fireworks and a component of safety matches.

Perchlorates, salts containing ClO_4^-, are powerful oxidants. Pure perchloric acid, $HClO_4$, is a colorless liquid that explodes if shocked. It explosively oxidizes organic materials and rapidly oxidizes silver and gold. Dilute aqueous solutions of the acid are safe to handle, however.

Perchlorate salts of most metals are usually relatively stable, albeit unpredictable. Great care should be used when handling any perchlorate salt. Ammonium perchlorate, for example, bursts into flame if heated above 200 °C.

$$2\ NH_4ClO_4(s) \rightarrow N_2(g) + Cl_2(g) + 2\ O_2(g) + 4\ H_2O(g)$$

The strong oxidizing ability of the ammonium salt accounts for its use as the oxidizer in the solid booster rockets for the Space Shuttle. The solid propellant in these rockets is largely NH_4ClO_4, the remainder being the reducing agent, powdered aluminum. Each launch requires about 750 tons of ammonium perchlorate, and more than half of the sodium perchlorate currently manufactured is converted to the ammonium salt. The process for making this conversion is an exchange reaction that takes advantage of the fact that ammonium perchlorate is less soluble in water than sodium perchlorate:

$$NaClO_4(aq) + NH_4Cl(aq) \rightleftharpoons NaCl(aq) + NH_4ClO_4(s)$$

Use of a perchlorate salt. The solid-fuel booster rockets of the Space Shuttle utilize a mixture of NH_4ClO_4 (oxidizing agent) and Al powder (reducing agent).

Metals generally react with hydrogen halides to give the metal halide and hydrogen. Determine whether this is true for silver by calculating $\Delta_r G°$ for the reaction with each of the hydrogen halides.

$$Ag(s) + HX(g) \rightarrow AgX(s) + \tfrac{1}{2} H_2(g)$$

The reaction is spontaneous under standard conditions (and product-favored at equilibrium) if $\Delta_r G°$ is negative. The required free energies of formation are (in kJ/mol)

HX, $\Delta_f G°$ (kJ/mol)	AgX, $\Delta_f G°$ (kJ/mol)
HF, −273.2	AgF, −193.8
HCl, −95.09	AgCl, −109.76
HBr, −53.45	AgBr, −96.90
HI, +1.56	AgI, −66.19

Chapter Goals Revisited

Now that you have studied this chapter, you should ask whether you have met the chapter goals. In particular, you should be able to:

Relate the formulas and properties of compounds to the periodic table

a. Predict several chemical reactions of the Group A elements (Section 21.2). Study Question(s) assignable in OWL: 12.

b. Predict similarities and differences among the elements in a given group, based on the periodic properties (Section 21.2). Study Question(s) assignable in OWL: 22, 32, 34, 35.

c. Know which reactions produce ionic compounds, and predict formulas for common ions and common ionic compounds based on electron configurations (Section 21.2). Study Question(s) assignable in OWL: 14, 16, 26.

d. Recognize when a formula is incorrectly written, based on general principles governing electron configurations (Section 21.2).

Describe the chemistry of the main group or A-Group elements, particularly H; Na and K; Mg and Ca; B and Al; Si; N and P; O and S; and F and Cl

a. Identify the most abundant elements, know how they are obtained, and list some of their common chemical and physical properties.

b. Be able to summarize briefly a series of facts about the most common compounds of main group elements (ionic or covalent bonding, color, solubility, simple reaction chemistry) (Sections 21.3–21.10). Study Question(s) assignable in OWL: 86, 88.

c. Identify uses of common elements and compounds, and understand the chemistry that relates to their usage (Sections 21.3–21.10).

Apply the principles of stoichiometry, thermodynamics, and electrochemistry to the chemistry of the main group elements Study Question(s) assignable in OWL: 18, 24, 29, 32, 34, 43, 48, 50, 54, 58, 61, 75, 86, 88.

STUDY QUESTIONS

OWL Online homework for this chapter may be assigned in OWL.

▲ denotes challenging questions.

■ denotes questions assignable in OWL.

Blue-numbered questions have answers in Appendix O and fully-worked solutions in the *Student Solutions Manual*.

Practicing Skills

Properties of the Elements

1. Give examples of two basic oxides. Write equations illustrating the formation of each oxide from its component elements. Write another chemical equation that illustrates the basic character of each oxide.

2. Give examples of two acidic oxides. Write equations illustrating the formation of each oxide from its component elements. Write another chemical equation that illustrates the acidic character of each oxide.

3. Give the name and symbol of each element having the valence configuration [noble gas] ns^2np^1.

4. Give symbols and names for four monatomic ions that have the same electron configuration as argon.

5. Select one of the alkali metals, and write a balanced chemical equation for its reaction with chlorine. Is the reaction likely to be exothermic or endothermic? Is the product ionic or molecular?

6. Select one of the alkaline earth metals and write a balanced chemical equation for its reaction with oxygen. Is the reaction likely to be exothermic or endothermic? Is the product ionic or molecular?

7. For the product of the reaction you selected in Study Question 5, predict the following physical properties: color, state of matter (s, ℓ, or g), solubility in water.

8. For the product of the reaction you selected in Study Question 6, predict the following physical properties: color, state of matter (s, ℓ, or g), solubility in water.

9. Would you expect to find calcium occurring naturally in the earth's crust as a free element? Why or why not?

10. Which of the first 10 elements in the periodic table are found as free elements in the earth's crust? Which elements in this group occur in the earth's crust only as part of a chemical compound?

11. Place the following oxides in order of increasing basicity: CO_2, SiO_2, SnO_2.

12. ■ Place the following oxides in order of increasing basicity: Na_2O, Al_2O_3, SiO_2, SO_3.

13. Complete and balance the equations for the following reactions. [Assume an excess of oxygen for (d).]
    (a) $Na(s) + Br_2(\ell) \rightarrow$
    (b) $Mg(s) + O_2(g) \rightarrow$
    (c) $Al(s) + F_2(g) \rightarrow$
    (d) $C(s) + O_2(g) \rightarrow$

14. ■ Complete and balance the equations for the following reactions:
    (a) $K(s) + I_2(g) \rightarrow$
    (b) $Ba(s) + O_2(g) \rightarrow$
    (c) $Al(s) + S_8(s) \rightarrow$
    (d) $Si(s) + Cl_2(g) \rightarrow$

Hydrogen

15. Write balanced chemical equations for the reaction of hydrogen gas with oxygen, chlorine, and nitrogen.

16. ■ Write an equation for the reaction of potassium and hydrogen. Name the product. Is it ionic or covalent? Predict one physical property and one chemical property of this compound.

17. Write a balanced chemical equation for the preparation of H_2 (and CO) by the reaction of CH_4 and water. Using data in Appendix L, calculate $\Delta_r H°$, $\Delta_r G°$, and $\Delta_r S°$ for this reaction.

18. ■ Using data in Appendix L, calculate $\Delta_r H°$, $\Delta_r G°$, and $\Delta_r S°$ for the reaction of carbon and water to give CO and H_2.

19. A method recently suggested for the preparation of hydrogen (and oxygen) from water proceeds as follows:
    (a) Sulfuric acid and hydrogen iodide are formed from sulfur dioxide, water, and iodine.
    (b) The sulfuric acid from the first step is decomposed by heat to water, sulfur dioxide, and oxygen.
    (c) The hydrogen iodide from the first step is decomposed with heat to hydrogen and iodine.

    Write a balanced equation for each of these steps, and show that their sum is the decomposition of water to form hydrogen and oxygen.

20. Compare the mass of H_2 expected from the reaction of steam (H_2O) per mole of methane, petroleum, and coal. (Assume complete reaction in each case. Use CH_2 and CH as representative formulas for petroleum and coal, respectively.)

Alkali Metals

21. Write equations for the reaction of sodium with each of the halogens. Predict at least two physical properties that are common to all of the alkali metal halides.

22. ■ Write balanced equations for the reaction of lithium, sodium, and potassium with O_2. Specify which metal forms an oxide, which forms a peroxide, and which forms a superoxide.

23. The electrolysis of aqueous NaCl gives NaOH, Cl_2, and H_2.
    (a) Write a balanced equation for the process.
    (b) In the United States, 1.19×10^{10} kg of NaOH and 1.14×10^{10} kg of Cl_2 were produced in a recent year. Does the ratio of masses of NaOH and Cl_2 produced agree with the ratio of masses expected from the balanced equation? If not, what does this tell you about the way in which NaOH and Cl_2 are actually produced? Is the electrolysis of aqueous NaCl the only source of these chemicals?

24. ■ (a) Write equations for the half-reactions that occur at the cathode and the anode when an aqueous solution of KCl is electrolyzed. Which chemical species is oxidized, and which chemical species is reduced in this reaction?
    (b) Predict the products formed when an aqueous solution of CsI is electrolyzed.

Alkaline Earth Elements

25. When magnesium burns in air, it forms both an oxide and a nitride. Write balanced equations for the formation of both compounds.

26. ■ Calcium reacts with hydrogen gas at 300–400 °C to form a hydride. This compound reacts readily with water, so it is an excellent drying agent for organic solvents.
    (a) Write a balanced equation showing the formation of calcium hydride from Ca and H_2.
    (b) Write a balanced equation for the reaction of calcium hydride with water (Figure 21.7).

27. Name three uses of limestone. Write a balanced equation for the reaction of limestone with CO_2 in water.

28. Explain what is meant by "hard water." What causes hard water, and what problems are associated with it?

29. ■ Calcium oxide, CaO, is used to remove SO_2 from power plant exhaust. These two compounds react to give solid $CaSO_3$. What mass of SO_2 can be removed using 1.2×10^3 kg of CaO?

30. $Ca(OH)_2$ has a K_{sp} of 5.5×10^{-5}, whereas K_{sp} for $Mg(OH)_2$ is 5.6×10^{-12}. Calculate the equilibrium constant for the reaction

    $$Ca(OH)_2(s) + Mg^{2+}(aq) \rightleftharpoons Ca^{2+}(aq) + Mg(OH)_2(s)$$

    Explain why this reaction can be used in the commercial isolation of magnesium from sea water.

Boron and Aluminum

31. Draw a possible structure for the cyclic anion in the salt $K_3B_3O_6$ and the anion in $Ca_2B_2O_5$.

32. ■ The boron trihalides (except BF_3) hydrolyze completely to boric acid and the acid HX.
    (a) Write a balanced equation for the reaction of BCl_3 with water.
    (b) Calculate $\Delta_r H°$ for the hydrolysis of BCl_3 using data in Appendix L and the following information: $\Delta_f H°$ [$BCl_3(g)$] = −403 kJ/mol; $\Delta_f H°$ [$B(OH)_3(s)$] = −1094 kJ/mol.

33. When boron hydrides burn in air, the reaction is very exothermic.
    (a) Write a balanced equation for the combustion of $B_5H_9(g)$ in air to give $B_2O_3(s)$ and $H_2O(\ell)$.
    (b) Calculate the enthalpy of combustion for $B_5H_9(g)$ ($\Delta_f H°$ = 73.2 kJ/mol), and compare it with the enthalpy of combustion of B_2H_6 on page 984. (The enthalpy of formation of $B_2O_3(s)$ is −1271.9 kJ/mol.)
    (c) Compare the enthalpy of combustion of $C_2H_6(g)$ with that of $B_2H_6(g)$. Which transfers more energy as heat per gram?

34. ■ Diborane can be prepared by the reaction of $NaBH_4$ and I_2. Which substance is oxidized, and which is reduced?

35. ■ Write balanced equations for the reactions of aluminum with HCl(aq), Cl_2, and O_2.

36. (a) Write a balanced equation for the reaction of Al and $H_2O(\ell)$ to produce H_2 and Al_2O_3.
    (b) Using thermodynamic data in Appendix L, calculate $\Delta_r H°$, $\Delta_r S°$, and $\Delta_r G°$ for this reaction. Do these data indicate that the reaction should favor the products?
    (c) Why is aluminum metal unaffected by water?

37. Aluminum dissolves readily in hot aqueous NaOH to give the aluminate ion, $[Al(OH)_4]^-$, and H_2. Write a balanced equation for this reaction. If you begin with 13.2 g of Al, what volume (in milliliters) of H_2 gas is produced when the gas is measured at 22.5 °C and a pressure of 735 mm Hg?

38. Alumina, Al_2O_3, is amphoteric. Among examples of its amphoteric character are the reactions that occur when Al_2O_3 is heated strongly or "fused" with acidic oxides and basic oxides.
    (a) Write a balanced equation for the reaction of alumina with silica, an acidic oxide, to give aluminum metasilicate, $Al_2(SiO_3)_3$.
    (b) Write a balanced equation for the reaction of alumina with the basic oxide CaO to give calcium aluminate, $Ca(AlO_2)_2$.

39. Aluminum sulfate is the most commercially important aluminum compound, after aluminum oxide and aluminum hydroxide. It is produced from the reaction of aluminum oxide and sulfuric acid. What mass (in kilograms) of aluminum oxide and sulfuric acid must be used to manufacture 1.00 kg of aluminum sulfate?

▲ more challenging ■ in OWL Blue-numbered questions answered in Appendix O

40. "Aerated" concrete bricks are widely used building materials. They are obtained by mixing gas-forming additives with a moist mixture of lime, cement, and possibly sand. Industrially, the following reaction is important:

$$2\ Al(s) + 3\ Ca(OH)_2(s) + 6\ H_2O(\ell) \rightarrow$$
$$3\ CaO \cdot Al_2O_3 \cdot 6\ H_2O(s) + 3\ H_2(g)$$

Assume that the mixture of reactants contains 0.56 g of Al (as well as excess calcium hydroxide and water) for each brick. What volume of hydrogen gas do you expect at 26 °C and a pressure of 745 mm Hg)?

Silicon

41. Describe the structure of pyroxenes (see page 988). What is the ratio of silicon to oxygen in this type of silicate?

42. Describe how ultrapure silicon can be produced from sand.

43. ■ Silicate structures: Draw a structure, and give the charge for a silicate anion with the formula $[Si_6O_{18}]^{n-}$.

44. Silicates often have chain, ribbon, or sheet structures. One of the simpler ribbon structures is $[Si_2O_5{}^{2-}]_n$. Draw a structure for this anionic material.

Nitrogen and Phosphorus

45. Consult the data in Appendix L. Are any of the nitrogen oxides listed there stable with respect to decomposition to N_2 and O_2?

46. Use data in Appendix L to calculate the enthalpy and free energy change for the reaction

$$2\ NO_2(g) \rightarrow N_2O_4(g)$$

Is this reaction exothermic or endothermic? Is the reaction product- or reactant-favored?

47. Use data in Appendix L to calculate the enthalpy and free energy change for the reaction

$$2\ NO(g) + O_2(g) \rightarrow 2\ NO_2(g)$$

Is this reaction exothermic or endothermic? Is the reaction product- or reactant-favored?

48. ■ The overall reaction involved in the industrial synthesis of nitric acid is

$$NH_3(g) + 2\ O_2(g) \rightarrow HNO_3(aq) + H_2O(\ell)$$

Calculate $\Delta_rG°$ for this reaction and its equilibrium constant at 25 °C.

49. A major use of hydrazine, N_2H_4, is in steam boilers in power plants.
(a) The reaction of hydrazine with O_2 dissolved in water gives N_2 and water. Write a balanced equation for this reaction.

(b) O_2 dissolves in water to the extent of 0.0044 g in 100. mL of water at 20 °C. To consume all of the dissolved O_2 in 3.00×10^4 L of water (enough to fill a small swimming pool), what mass of N_2H_4 is needed?

50. ■ Before hydrazine came into use to remove dissolved oxygen in the water in steam boilers, Na_2SO_3 was commonly used for this purpose:

$$2\ Na_2SO_3(aq) + O_2(aq) \rightarrow 2\ Na_2SO_4(aq)$$

What mass of Na_2SO_3 is required to remove O_2 from 3.00×10^4 L of water as outlined in Study Question 49?

51. Review the structure of phosphorous acid in Table 21.6.
(a) What is the oxidation number of the phosphorus atom in this acid?
(b) Draw the structure of diphosphorous acid, $H_4P_2O_5$. What is the maximum number of protons this acid can dissociate in water?

52. Unlike carbon, which can form extended chains of atoms, nitrogen can form chains of very limited length. Draw the Lewis electron dot structure of the azide ion, N_3^-. Is the ion linear or bent?

Oxygen and Sulfur

53. In the "contact process" for making sulfuric acid, sulfur is first burned to SO_2. Environmental restrictions allow no more than 0.30% of this SO_2 to be vented to the atmosphere.
(a) If enough sulfur is burned in a plant to produce 1.80×10^6 kg of pure, anhydrous H_2SO_4 per day, what is the maximum amount of SO_2 that is allowed to be exhausted to the atmosphere?
(b) One way to prevent any SO_2 from reaching the atmosphere is to "scrub" the exhaust gases with slaked lime, $Ca(OH)_2$:

$$Ca(OH)_2(s) + SO_2(g) \rightarrow CaSO_3(s) + H_2O(\ell)$$
$$2\ CaSO_3(s) + O_2(g) \rightarrow 2\ CaSO_4(s)$$

What mass of $Ca(OH)_2$ (in kilograms) is needed to remove the SO_2 calculated in part (a)?

54. ■ A sulfuric acid plant produces an enormous amount of heat. To keep costs as low as possible, much of this heat is used to make steam to generate electricity. Some of the electricity is used to run the plant, and the excess is sold to the local electrical utility. Three reactions are important in sulfuric acid production: (1) burning S to SO_2; (2) oxidation of SO_2 to SO_3; and (3) reaction of SO_3 with H_2O:

$$SO_3(g) + H_2O\ (in\ 98\%\ H_2SO_4) \rightarrow H_2SO_4(\ell)$$

The enthalpy change of the third reaction is −130 kJ/mol. Estimate the enthalpy change when 1.00 mol of S is used to produce 1.00 mol of H_2SO_4. How much energy is produced per metric ton of H_2SO_4?

▲ more challenging   ■ in OWL   Blue-numbered questions answered in Appendix O

55. Sulfur forms anionic chains of S atoms called polysulfides. Draw a Lewis electron dot structure for the S_2^{2-} ion. The S_2^{2-} ion is the disulfide ion, an analogue of the peroxide ion. It occurs in iron pyrites, FeS_2.

56. Sulfur forms a range of compounds with fluorine. Draw Lewis electron dot structures for S_2F_2 (connectivity is FSSF), SF_2, SF_4, SF_6, and S_2F_{10}. What is the oxidation number of sulfur in each of these compounds?

Fluorine and Chlorine

57. The halogen oxides and oxoanions are good oxidizing agents. For example, the reduction of bromate ion has an $E°$ value of 1.44 V in acid solution:

$$2\ BrO_3^-(aq) + 12\ H^+(aq) + 10\ e^- \rightarrow$$
$$Br_2(aq) + 6\ H_2O(\ell)$$

Is it possible to oxidize aqueous 1.0 M Mn^{2+} to aqueous MnO_4^- with 1.0 M bromate ion?

58. ■ The hypohalite ions, XO^-, are the anions of weak acids. Calculate the pH of a 0.10 M solution of NaClO. What is the concentration of HClO in this solution?

59. Bromine is obtained from brine wells. The process involves treating water containing bromide ion with Cl_2 and extracting the Br_2 from the solution using an organic solvent. Write a balanced equation for the reaction of Cl_2 and Br^-. What are the oxidizing and reducing agents in this reaction? Using the table of standard reduction potentials (Appendix M), verify that this is a product-favored reaction.

60. To prepare chlorine from chloride ion a strong oxidizing agent is required. The dichromate ion, $Cr_2O_7^{2-}$, is one example (see Figure 21.32). Consult the table of standard reduction potentials (Appendix M), and identify several other oxidizing agents that may be suitable. Write balanced equations for the reactions of these substances with chloride ion.

61. ■ If an electrolytic cell for producing F_2 (Figure 21.31) operates at 5.00×10^3 A (at 10.0 V), what mass of F_2 can be produced per 24-hour day? Assume the conversion of F^- to F_2 is 100%.

62. Halogens combine with one another to produce *interhalogens* such as BrF_3. Sketch a possible molecular structure for this molecule, and decide if the F—Br—F bond angles will be less than or greater than ideal.

General Questions

The questions are not designated as to type or location in the chapter. They may combine several concepts.

63. For each of the third-period elements (Na through Ar), identify the following:
 (a) whether the element is a metal, nonmetal, or metalloid
 (b) the color and appearance of the element

(c) the state of the element (s, ℓ, or g) under standard conditions

For help in this question, consult Figure 2.4 or use the periodic table "tool" in ChemistryNow. The latter provides a picture of each element and a listing of its properties.

64. Consider the chemistries of C, Si, Ge, and Sn.
 (a) Write a balanced chemical equation to depict the reaction of each element with elemental chlorine.
 (b) Describe the bonding in each of the products of the reactions with chlorine as ionic or covalent.
 (c) Compare the reactions, if any, of some Group 4A chlorides —CCl_4, $SiCl_4$, and $SnCl_4$— with water.

65. Consider the chemistries of the elements potassium, calcium, gallium, germanium, and arsenic.
 (a) Write a balanced chemical equation depicting the reaction of each element with elemental chlorine.
 (b) Describe the bonding in each of the products of the reactions with chlorine as ionic or covalent.
 (c) Draw Lewis electron dot structures for the products of the reactions of gallium and arsenic with chlorine. What are their electron-pair and molecular geometries?

66. When BCl_3 gas is passed through an electric discharge, small amounts of the reactive molecule B_2Cl_4 are produced. (The molecule has a B—B covalent bond.)
 (a) Draw a Lewis electron dot structure for B_2Cl_4.
 (b) Describe the hybridization of the B atoms in the molecule and the geometry around each B atom.

67. Complete and balance the following equations.
 (a) $KClO_3$ + heat →
 (b) $H_2S(g) + O_2(g) \rightarrow$
 (c) $Na(s) + O_2(g) \rightarrow$
 (d) $P_4(s) + KOH(aq) + H_2O(\ell) \rightarrow$
 (e) $NH_4NO_3(s)$ + heat →
 (f) $In(s) + Br_2(\ell) \rightarrow$
 (g) $SnCl_4(\ell) + H_2O(\ell) \rightarrow$

68. (a) Heating barium oxide in pure oxygen gives barium peroxide. Write a balanced equation for this reaction.
 (b) Barium peroxide is an excellent oxidizing agent. Write a balanced equation for the reaction of iron with barium peroxide to give iron(III) oxide and barium oxide.

69. Worldwide production of silicon carbide, SiC, is several hundred thousand tons annually. If you want to produce 1.0×10^5 metric tons of SiC, what mass (metric tons) of silicon sand (SiO_2) will you use if 70% of the sand is converted to SiC?

70. To store 2.88 kg of gasoline with an energy equivalence of 1.43×10^8 J requires a volume of 4.1 L. In comparison, 1.0 kg of H_2 has the same energy equivalence. What volume is required if this quantity of H_2 is to be stored at 25 °C and 1.0 atm of pressure?

71. Using data in Appendix L, calculate $\Delta_r G^\circ$ values for the decomposition of MCO_3 to MO and CO_2 where M = Mg, Ca, Ba. What is the relative tendency of these carbonates to decompose?

72. Ammonium perchlorate is used as the oxidizer in the solid-fuel booster rockets of the Space Shuttle. Assume that one launch requires 700 tons (6.35×10^5 kg) of the salt, and the salt decomposes according to the equation on page 1009.
    (a) What mass of water is produced? What mass of O_2 is produced?
    (b) If the O_2 produced is assumed to react with the powdered aluminum present in the rocket engine, what mass of aluminum is required to use up all of the O_2?
    (c) What mass of Al_2O_3 is produced?

73. ▲ Metals react with hydrogen halides (such as HCl) to give the metal halide and hydrogen:

    $$M(s) + n\,HX(g) \rightarrow MX_n(s) + \tfrac{1}{2}n\,H_2(g)$$

    The free energy change for the reaction is $\Delta_r G^\circ = \Delta_f G^\circ(MX_n) - n\,\Delta_f G^\circ[HX(g)]$
    (a) $\Delta_f G^\circ$ for HCl(g) is -95.1 kJ/mol. What must be the value for $\Delta_f G^\circ$ for MX_n for the reaction to be product-favored?
    (b) Which of the following metals is (are) predicted to have product-favored reactions with HCl(g): Ba, Pb, Hg, Ti?

74. Halogens form polyhalide ions. Sketch Lewis electron dot structures and molecular structures for the following ions:
    (a) I_3^-
    (b) $BrCl_2^-$
    (c) ClF_2^+
    (d) An iodide ion and two iodine molecules form the I_5^- ion. Here, the ion has five I atoms in a row, but the ion is not linear. Draw the Lewis dot structure for the ion, and propose a structure for the ion.

75. ■ The standard enthalpy of formation of OF_2 gas is $+24.5$ kJ/mol. Calculate the average O—F bond enthalpy.

76. Calcium fluoride can be used in the fluoridation of municipal water supplies. If you want to achieve a fluoride ion concentration of 2.0×10^{-5} M, what mass of CaF_2 must you use for 1.0×10^6 L of water?

77. The steering rockets in the Space Shuttle use N_2O_4 and a derivative of hydrazine, 1,1-dimethylhydrazine (page 249). This mixture is called a *hypergolic fuel* because it ignites when the reactants come into contact:

    $H_2NN(CH_3)_2(\ell) + 2\,N_2O_4(\ell) \rightarrow$
    $\qquad\qquad 3\,N_2(g) + 4\,H_2O(g) + 2\,CO_2(g)$

    (a) Identify the oxidizing agent and the reducing agent in this reaction.

(b) The same propulsion system was used by the Lunar Lander on moon missions in the 1970s. If the Lander used 4100 kg of $H_2NN(CH_3)_2$, what mass (in kilograms) of N_2O_4 was required to react with it? What mass (in kilograms) of each of the reaction products was generated?

78. ▲ Liquid HCN is dangerously unstable with respect to trimer formation—that is, formation of $(HCN)_3$ with a cyclic structure.
    (a) Propose a structure for this cyclic trimer.
    (b) Estimate the energy of the trimerization reaction using bond dissociation enthalpies (Table 8.10).

79. Use $\Delta_f H^\circ$ data in Appendix L to calculate the enthalpy change of the reaction

    $$2\,N_2(g) + 5\,O_2(g) + 2\,H_2O(\ell) \rightarrow 4\,HNO_3(aq)$$

    Speculate on whether such a reaction could be used to "fix" nitrogen. Would research to find ways to accomplish this reaction be a useful endeavor?

80. ▲ Phosphorus forms an extensive series of oxoanions.
    (a) Draw a structure, and give the charge for an oxophosphate anion with the formula $[P_4O_{13}]^{n-}$. How many ionizable H atoms should the completely protonated acid have?
    (b) Draw a structure, and give the charge for an oxophosphate anion with the formula $[P_4O_{12}]^{n-}$. How many ionizable H atoms should the completely protonated acid have?

81. Boron and hydrogen form an extensive family of compounds, and the diagram below shows how they are related by reaction.

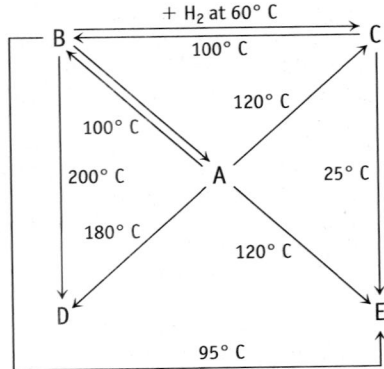

The following table gives the weight percent of boron in each of the compounds. Derive the empirical and molecular formulas of compounds A–D.

Substance	State (at STP)	Mass Percent B	Molar mass (g/mol)
A	Gas	78.3	27.7
B	Gas	81.2	53.3
C	Liquid	83.1	65.1
D	Liquid	85.7	63.1
E	Solid	88.5	122.2

82. ▲ In 1774, C. Scheele obtained a gas by reacting pyrolusite (MnO_2) with sulfuric acid. The gas, which had been obtained that same year by Joseph Priestley by a different method, was an element, **A**.

(a) What is the element isolated by Scheele and Priestley?

(b) Element **A** combines with almost all other elements. For example, with cesium it gives a compound in which the mass percent of **A** is 19.39%. The element combines with hydrogen to give a compound with a mass percent of element **A** of 94.12%. Determine the formulas of the cesium and hydrogen compounds.

(c) The compounds of cesium and hydrogen with element **A** react with one another. Write a balanced equation for the reaction.

In the Laboratory

83. One material needed to make silicones is dichlorodimethylsilane, $(CH_3)_2SiCl_2$. It is made by treating silicon powder at about 300 °C with CH_3Cl in the presence of a copper-containing catalyst.

(a) Write a balanced equation for the reaction.

(b) Assume you carry out the reaction on a small scale with 2.65 g of silicon. To measure the CH_3Cl gas, you fill a 5.60-L flask at 24.5 °C. What pressure of CH_3Cl gas must you have in the flask to have the stoichiometrically correct amount of the compound?

(c) What mass of $(CH_3)_2SiCl_2$ can be produced from 2.65 g of Si and excess CH_3Cl?

84. Sodium borohydride, $NaBH_4$, reduces many metal ions to the metal.

(a) Write a balanced equation for the reaction of $NaBH_4$ with $AgNO_3$ in water to give silver metal, H_2 gas, boric acid, and sodium nitrate (page 984).

(b) What mass of silver can be produced from 575 mL of 0.011 M $AgNO_3$ and 13.0 g of $NaBH_4$?

85. A common analytical method for hydrazine involves its oxidation with iodate ion, IO_3^-, in acid solution. In the process, hydrazine acts as a four-electron reducing agent.

$$N_2(g) + 5\ H_3O^+(aq) + 4\ e^- \rightarrow$$
$$N_2H_5^+(aq) + 5\ H_2O(\ell) \qquad E° = -0.23\ V$$

Write the balanced equation for the reaction of hydrazine in acid solution ($N_2H_5^+$) with $IO_3^-(aq)$ to give N_2 and I_2. Calculate $E°$ for this reaction.

86. ■ When 1.00 g of a white solid **A** is strongly heated, you obtain another white solid, **B**, and a gas. An experiment is carried out on the gas, showing that it exerts a pressure of 209 mm Hg in a 450-mL flask at 25 °C. Bubbling the gas into a solution of $Ca(OH)_2$ gives another white solid, **C**. If the white solid **B** is added to water, the resulting solution turns red litmus paper blue.

Addition of aqueous HCl to the solution of **B** and evaporation of the resulting solution to dryness yield 1.055 g of a white solid **D**. When **D** is placed in a Bunsen burner flame, it colors the flame green. Finally, if the aqueous solution of **B** is treated with sulfuric acid, a white precipitate, **E**, forms. Identify the lettered compounds in the reaction scheme.

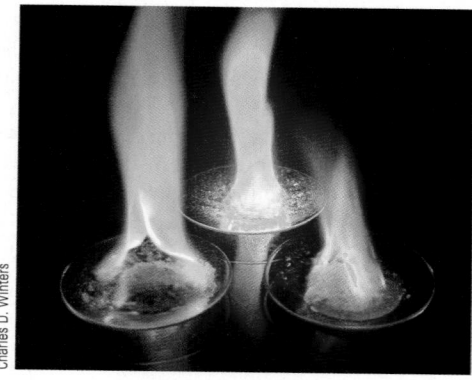

Charles D. Winters

The salts $CaCl_2$, $SrCl_2$, and $BaCl_2$ were suspended in methanol. When the methanol is set ablaze, the heat of combustion causes the salts to emit light of characteristic wavelengths: calcium salts are yellow; strontium salts are red; and barium salts are green-yellow.

87. ▲ In 1937, R. Schwartz and M. Schmiesser prepared a yellow-orange bromine oxide (BrO_2) by treating Br_2 with ozone in a fluorocarbon solvent. Many years later, J. Pascal found that, on heating, this oxide decomposed to two other oxides, a less volatile golden yellow oxide (**A**) and a more volatile deep-brown oxide (**B**). Oxide **B** was later identified as Br_2O. To determine the formula for oxide **A**, a sample was treated with iodide ion. The reaction liberated iodine, which was titrated to an equivalence point with 17.7 mL of 0.065 M sodium thiosulfate.

$$I_2(aq) + 2\ S_2O_3^{2-}(aq) \rightarrow 2\ I^-(aq) + S_4O_6^{2-}(aq)$$

Compound **A** was also treated with $AgNO_3$, and 14.4 mL of 0.020 M $AgNO_3$ was required to completely precipitate the bromine from the sample.

(a) What is the formula of the unknown bromine oxide A?

(b) Draw Lewis structures for **A** and Br_2O. Speculate on their molecular geometry.

88. ■ A mixture of PCl_5 (12.41 g) and excess NH_4Cl was heated at 145 °C for six hours. The two reacted in equimolar amounts and evolved 5.14 L of HCl (at STP). Three substances (**A**, **B**, and **C**) were isolated from the reaction mixture. The three substances had the same elemental composition but differed in their molar mass. Substance **A**, had a molar mass of 347.7 g/mol and **B** had a molar mass of 463.5 g/mol. Give the empirical and molecular formulas for **A** and **B** and draw a reasonable Lewis structure for **A**.

Summary and Conceptual Questions

The following questions may use concepts from this and previous chapters.

89. Dinitrogen trioxide, N_2O_3, has the structure shown here.

The oxide is unstable, decomposing to NO and NO_2 in the gas phase at 25 °C.

$$N_2O_3(g) \rightarrow NO(g) + NO_2(g)$$

(a) Explain why one N—O bond distance in N_2O_3 is 114.2 pm, whereas the other two bonds are longer (121 pm) and nearly equal to each other.

(b) For the decomposition reaction, $\Delta_r H° = +40.5$ kJ/mol and $\Delta_r G° = -1.59$ kJ/mol. Calculate $\Delta S°$ and K for the reaction at 298 K.

(c) Calculate $\Delta_f H°$ for $N_2O_3(g)$.

90. ▲ The density of lead is 11.350 g/cm³, and the metal crystallizes in a face-centered cubic unit cell. Estimate the radius of the lead atom.

91. You have a 1.0-L flask that contains a mixture of argon and hydrogen. The pressure inside the flask is 745 mm Hg, and the temperature is 22 °C. Describe an experiment that you could use to determine the percentage of hydrogen in this mixture.

92. The boron atom in boric acid, $B(OH)_3$, is bonded to three —OH groups. In the solid state, the —OH groups are in turn hydrogen-bonded to —OH groups in neighboring molecules.

(a) Draw the Lewis structure for boric acid.

(b) What is the hybridization of the boron atom in the acid?

(c) Sketch a picture showing how hydrogen bonding can occur between neighboring molecules.

93. How would you extinguish a sodium fire in the laboratory? What is the worst thing you could do?

94. Tin(IV) oxide, cassiterite, is the main ore of tin. It crystallizes in a rutile-like unit cell (Question 4, page 611).

(a) How many tin(IV) ions and oxide ions are there per unit cell of this oxide?

(b) Is it thermodynamically feasible to transform solid SnO_2 into liquid $SnCl_4$ by reaction of the oxide with gaseous HCl? What is the equilibrium constant for this reaction at 25 °C?

95. You are given a stoppered flask that contains hydrogen, nitrogen, or oxygen. Suggest an experiment to identify the gas.

96. The structure of nitric acid is illustrated on page 993.

(a) Why are the N—O bonds the same length, and why are both shorter than the N—OH bond length?

(b) Rationalize the bond angles in the molecule.

(c) What is the hybridization of the central N atom? Which orbitals overlap to form the N—O π bond?

97. Assume an electrolysis cell that produces chlorine from aqueous sodium chloride operates at 4.6 V (with a current of 3.0×10^5 A). Calculate the number of kilowatt-hours of energy required to produce 1.00 kg of chlorine (1 kWh = 1 kilowatt-hour = 3.6×10^6 J).

98. Sodium metal is produced by electrolysis of molten sodium chloride. The cell operates at 7.0 V with a current of 25×10^3 A.

(a) What mass of sodium can be produced in 1 h?

(b) How many kilowatt-hours of electricity are used to produce 1.00 kg of sodium metal (1 kWh = 3.6×10^6 J)?

99. The reduction potentials for the Group 3A metals, $E°$, are given below. What trend or trends do you observe in these data? What can you learn about the chemistry of the Group 3A elements from these data?

Half-Reaction	Reduction Potential ($E°$, V)
$Al^{3+}(aq) + 3 e^- \longrightarrow Al(s)$	-1.66
$Ga^{3+}(aq) + 3 e^- \longrightarrow Ga(s)$	-0.53
$In^{3+}(aq) + 3 e^- \longrightarrow In(s)$	-0.338
$Tl^{3+}(aq) + 3 e^- \longrightarrow Tl(s)$	$+0.72$

100. (a) Magnesium is obtained from sea water. If the concentration of Mg^{2+} in sea water is 0.050 M, what volume of sea water (in liters) must be treated to obtain 1.00 kg of magnesium metal? What mass of lime (CaO; in kilograms) must be used to precipitate the magnesium in this volume of sea water?

(b) When 1.2×10^3 kg of molten $MgCl_2$ is electrolyzed to produce magnesium, what mass (in kilograms) of metal is produced at the cathode? What is produced at the anode? What is the mass of this product? What is the total number of faradays of electricity used in the process?

(c) One industrial process has an energy consumption of 18.5 kWh/kg of Mg. How many joules are required per mole (1 kWh = 1 kilowatt-hour = 3.6×10^6 J)? How does this energy compare with the energy of the following process?

$$MgCl_2(s) \rightarrow Mg(s) + Cl_2(g)?$$

22 | The Chemistry of the Transition Elements

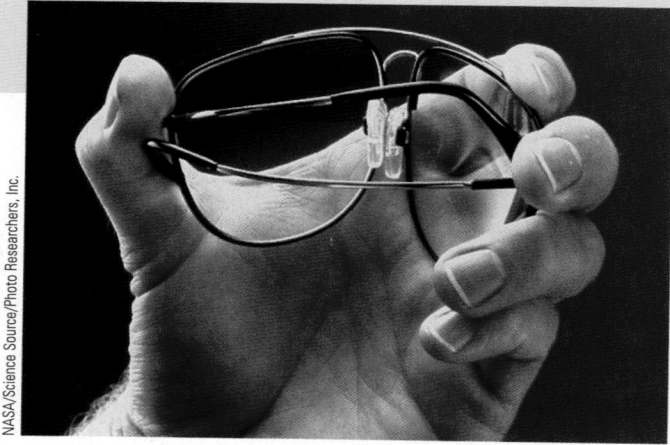

Nitinol frames for glasses. Can you do this with your eye glasses? If you can, it is likely they are made of nitinol, a nickel–titanium alloy. They snap back to the proper fit even after being twisted like a pretzel.

Memory Metal

In the 1960s, William J. Buehler, an engineer at the Naval Ordnance Laboratory in Maryland, was looking for a material for use in the nose cone of a Navy missile. It was important that the material be impact- and heat-resistant and not lose these properties when bent and shaped. He prepared long, thin strips of an alloy of nickel and titanium to demonstrate that it could be folded and unfolded many times without breaking. At a meeting to discuss this material, one of his associates held a cigarette lighter to a folded-up piece of metal and was amazed to observe that the metal strip immediately unfolded and assumed its original shape. Thus, memory metal was discovered. This unusual alloy is now called *nitinol*, a name constructed out of "nickel," "titanium," and "Naval Ordnance Laboratory."

Memory metal is an alloy with roughly the same number of Ni and Ti atoms. When the atoms are arranged in the highly symmetrical austenite phase, the alloy is relatively rigid. In this phase a specific shape is established that will be "remembered." If the alloy is cooled below its "phase transition temperature," it enters a less symmetrical but flexible phase (martensite). Below this transition temperature, the metal is fairly soft and may be bent and twisted out of shape. When warmed above the phase transition temperature, nitinol returns to its original shape. The temperature at which the change in shape occurs varies with small differences in the nickel-to-titanium ratio.

Besides eye glasses frames, nitinol is now used in stents to reinforce blood vessels and in orthodontics.

Questions:

1. What are the dimensions of the austenite unit cell? Assume the Ti and Ni atoms are just touching along the unit cell diagonal. (Atom radii: Ti = 145 pm; Ni = 125 pm.)
2. Calculate the density of nitinol based on the austenite unit cell parameters. Does the calculated density of the austenite unit cell agree with the reported density of 6.5 g/cm³?
3. Are Ti and Ni atoms paramagnetic or diamagnetic?

Answers to these questions are in Appendix Q.

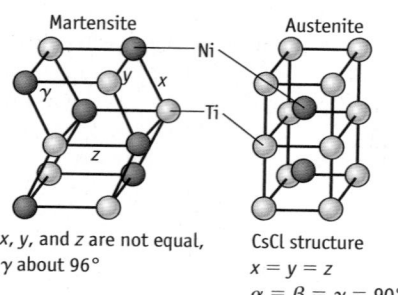

x, y, and z are not equal, γ about 96°

CsCl structure
$x = y = z$
$\alpha = \beta = \gamma = 90°$

Two phases of nitinol. The austenite form has a structure like CsCl (page 622).

Chapter Goals

⊙WL *See Chapter Goals Revisited (page 1054) for Study Questions keyed to these goals and assignable in OWL.*

- Identify and explain the chemical and physical properties of the transition elements.
- Understand the composition, structure, and bonding in coordination compounds.
- Relate ligand field theory to the magnetic and spectroscopic properties of the complexes.
- Apply the effective atomic number (EAN) rule to simple organometallic complexes of the transition metals.

Chapter Outline

22.1 Properties of the Transition Elements

22.2 Metallurgy

22.3 Coordination Compounds

22.4 Structures of Coordination Compounds

22.5 Bonding in Coordination Compounds

22.6 Colors of Coordination Compounds

22.7 Organometallic Chemistry: The Chemistry of Low-Valent Metal–Organic Complexes

Chemistry ⚛ Now™

Throughout the text this icon introduces an opportunity for self-study or to explore interactive tutorials by signing in at **www.cengage.com/login**.

The transition elements are the large block of elements in the central portion of the periodic table. All are metals and bridge the *s*-block elements at the left and the *p*-block elements on the right (Figure 22.1). The transition elements are often divided into two groups, depending on the valence electrons involved in their chemistry. The first group are the **d-block elements,** because their occurrence in the periodic table coincides with the filling of the *d* orbitals. The second group are the **f-block elements,** characterized by filling of the *f* orbitals. Contained within this group of elements are two subgroups: the *lanthanides,* elements that occur between La and Hf, and the *actinides,* elements that occur between Ac and Rf.

This chapter focuses primarily on the *d*-block elements, and within this group we concentrate mainly on the elements in the fourth period, that is, the elements of the first transition series, scandium to zinc.

22.1 Properties of the Transition Elements

The *d*-block metals include elements with a wide range of properties. They encompass the most common metal used in construction and manufacturing (iron), metals that are valued for their beauty (gold, silver, and platinum), and metals used

Fourth-period transition metals:
left to right, Ti, V, Cr, Mn, Fe, Co, Ni, Cu

FIGURE 22.1 The transition metals. The *d*-block elements (transition elements) and *f*-block elements are highlighted in a darker shade of purple.

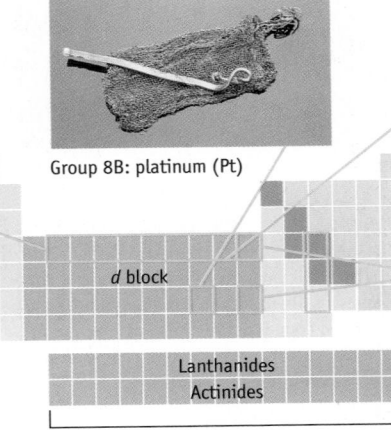

Group 8B: platinum (Pt)

d block

Lanthanides
Actinides

f block

Group 1B: copper (Cu)

Group 1B: silver (Ag)

Group 1B: gold (Au)

Group 2B: left, zinc (Zn); right, mercury (Hg)

in coins (nickel, copper, and zinc). There are metals used in modern technology (titanium) and metals known and used in early civilizations (copper, silver, gold, and iron). The *d*-block contains the densest elements (osmium, $d = 22.49$ g/cm^3, and iridium, $d = 22.41$ g/cm^3), the metals with the highest and lowest melting points (tungsten, mp = 3410 °C, and mercury, mp = -38.9 °C), and one of two radioactive elements with atomic numbers less than 83 [technetium (Tc), atomic number 43; the other is promethium (Pm), atomic number 61, in the *f*-block].

With the exception of mercury, the transition elements are solids, often with high melting and boiling points. They have a metallic sheen and conduct electricity and heat. They react with various oxidizing agents to give ionic compounds. There is considerable variation in such reactions among the elements, however. Because silver, gold, and platinum resist oxidation, for example, they are used for jewelry and decorative items.

Certain *d*-block elements are particularly important in living organisms. Cobalt is the crucial element in vitamin B$_{12}$, which is part of a catalyst essential for several biochemical reactions. Hemoglobin and myoglobin, oxygen-carrying and storage proteins, contain iron (see page 1033). Molybdenum and iron, together with sulfur, form the reactive portion of nitrogenase, a biological catalyst used by nitrogen-fixing organisms to convert atmospheric nitrogen into ammonia.

Many transition metal compounds are highly colored, which makes them useful as pigments in paints and dyes (Figure 22.2). Prussian blue, Fe$_4$[Fe(CN)$_6$]$_3 \cdot$ 14 H$_2$O is a "bluing agent" used in engineering blueprints and in the laundry to brighten yellowed white cloth. A common pigment (artist's cadmium yellow) contains cadmium sulfide (CdS), and the white in most white paints is titanium(IV) oxide, TiO$_2$.

The presence of transition metal ions in crystalline silicates or alumina transforms these common materials into gemstones. Iron(II) ions cause the yellow color in citrine, and chromium(III) ions produce the red color of a ruby. Transition metal complexes in small quantities add color to glass. Blue glass contains a small amount of a cobalt(III) oxide, and addition of chromium(III) oxide to glass gives a green color. Old window panes sometimes take on a purple color over time as a

(a) Paint pigments: yellow, CdS; green, Cr$_2$O$_3$; white, TiO$_2$ and ZnO; purple, Mn$_3$(PO$_4$)$_2$; blue, Co$_2$O$_3$ and Al$_2$O$_3$; ochre, Fe$_2$O$_3$.

(b) Small amounts of transition metal compounds are used to color glass: blue, Co$_2$O$_3$; green, copper or chromium oxides; purple, nickel or cobalt oxides; red, copper oxide; iridescent green, uranium oxide.

(c) Traces of transition metal ions are responsible for the colors of green jade (iron), red corundum (chromium), blue azurite, blue-green turquoise (copper), and purple amethyst (iron).

FIGURE 22.2 Colorful chemistry. Transition metal compounds are often colored, a property that leads to specific uses.

consequence of oxidation of traces of manganese(II) ion present in the glass to permanganate ion (MnO_4^-).

In the next few pages, we will examine the properties of the transition elements, concentrating on the underlying principles that govern these properties.

Electron Configurations

Because chemical behavior is related to electron structure, it is important to know the electron configurations of the *d*-block elements (Table 22.1) and their common ions (◄ Section 7.4). Recall that the configuration of these metals has the general form [noble gas core]$(n - 1)d^b ns^a$; that is, valence electrons for the transition elements reside in the *ns* and $(n - 1)d$ subshells.

Oxidation and Reduction

A characteristic chemical property of all metals is that they undergo oxidation by a wide range of oxidizing agents such as oxygen, the halogens, and aqueous acids. Standard reduction potentials for the elements of the first transition series can be used to predict which elements will be oxidized by a given oxidizing agent. For example, all of these metals except vanadium and copper are oxidized by aqueous HCl (Table 22.2). This feature, which dominates the chemistry of these elements, is sometimes highly undesirable (see *Chemical Perspectives: Corrosion of Iron*, page 1023.)

When a transition metal is oxidized, the outermost *s* electrons are removed, followed by one or more *d* electrons. With a few exceptions, transition metal ions have the electron configuration [noble gas core]$(n - 1)d^x$. In contrast to ions formed by main group elements, transition metal cations often possess unpaired electrons, resulting in paramagnetism (◄ page 292). They are frequently colored as well, due to the absorption of light in the visible region of the electromagnetic spectrum. Color and magnetism figure prominently in a discussion of the properties and bonding of these elements, as you shall see shortly.

In the first transition series, the most commonly encountered metal ions have oxidation numbers of +2 and +3 (Table 22.2). With iron, for example, oxidation

TABLE 22.1 Electron Configurations of the Fourth-Period Transition Elements

	spdf Configuration	Box Notation (3*d*)	Box Notation (4*s*)
Sc	[Ar]$3d^1 4s^2$	↑ ☐ ☐ ☐ ☐	↑↓
Ti	[Ar]$3d^2 4s^2$	↑ ↑ ☐ ☐ ☐	↑↓
V	[Ar]$3d^3 4s^2$	↑ ↑ ↑ ☐ ☐	↑↓
Cr	[Ar]$3d^5 4s^1$	↑ ↑ ↑ ↑ ↑	↑
Mn	[Ar]$3d^5 4s^2$	↑ ↑ ↑ ↑ ↑	↑↓
Fe	[Ar]$3d^6 4s^2$	↑↓ ↑ ↑ ↑ ↑	↑↓
Co	[Ar]$3d^7 4s^2$	↑↓ ↑↓ ↑ ↑ ↑	↑↓
Ni	[Ar]$3d^8 4s^2$	↑↓ ↑↓ ↑↓ ↑ ↑	↑↓
Cu	[Ar]$3d^{10} 4s^1$	↑↓ ↑↓ ↑↓ ↑↓ ↑↓	↑
Zn	[Ar]$3d^{10} 4s^2$	↑↓ ↑↓ ↑↓ ↑↓ ↑↓	↑↓

TABLE 22.2 Products from Reactions of the Elements in the First Transition Series with O_2, Cl_2, or Aqueous HCl

Element	Reaction with O_2*	Reaction with Cl_2	Reaction with Aqueous HCl
Scandium	Sc_2O_3	$ScCl_3$	$Sc^{3+}(aq)$
Titanium	TiO_2	$TiCl_4$	$Ti^{3+}(aq)$
Vanadium	V_2O_5	VCl_4	NR†
Chromium	Cr_2O_3	$CrCl_3$	$Cr^{2+}(aq)$
Manganese	MnO_2	$MnCl_2$	$Mn^{2+}(aq)$
Iron	Fe_2O_3	$FeCl_3$	$Fe^{2+}(aq)$
Cobalt	Co_2O_3	$CoCl_2$	$Co^{2+}(aq)$
Nickel	NiO	$NiCl_2$	$Ni^{2+}(aq)$
Copper	CuO	$CuCl_2$	NR†
Zinc	ZnO	$ZnCl_2$	$Zn^{2+}(aq)$

* Product obtained with excess oxygen.
† NR = no reaction.

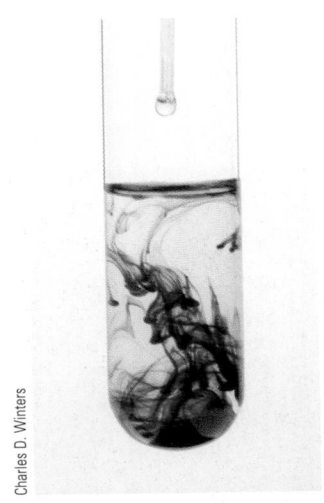

Charles D. Winters

Prussian blue. When Fe^{3+} ions are added to $[Fe(CN)_6]^{4-}$ ions in water (or Fe^{2+} ions are added to $[Fe(CN)_6]^{3-}$ ions), a deep blue compound called Prussian blue forms. The formula of the compound is $Fe_4[Fe(CN)_6]_3 \cdot 14\ H_2O$. The color arises from electron transfer between the Fe(II) and Fe(III) ions in the compound.

FIGURE 22.3 **Typical reactions of transition metals.** These metals react with oxygen, with halogens, and with acids under appropriate conditions. (a) Steel wool reacts with O_2; (b) steel wool reacts with chlorine gas, Cl_2; and (c) iron chips react with aqueous HCl.

Photos: Charles D. Winters

(a) (b) (c)

converts $Fe([Ar]3d^64s^2)$ to either $Fe^{2+}([Ar]3d^6)$ or $Fe^{3+}([Ar]3d^5)$. Iron reacts with chlorine to give $FeCl_3$, and it reacts with aqueous acids to produce $Fe^{2+}(aq)$ and H_2 (Figure 22.3). Despite the preponderance of 2+ and 3+ ions in compounds of the first transition metal series, the range of possible oxidation states for these compounds is broad (Figure 22.4). Earlier in this text, we encountered chromium with a +6 oxidation number (CrO_4^{2-}, $Cr_2O_7^{2-}$), manganese with an oxidation number of +7 (MnO_4^-), silver and copper as 1+ ions, and vanadium oxidation numbers that can range from +5 to +2 (Figure 20.3).

Higher oxidation numbers are more common in compounds of the elements in the second and third transition series. For example, the naturally occurring

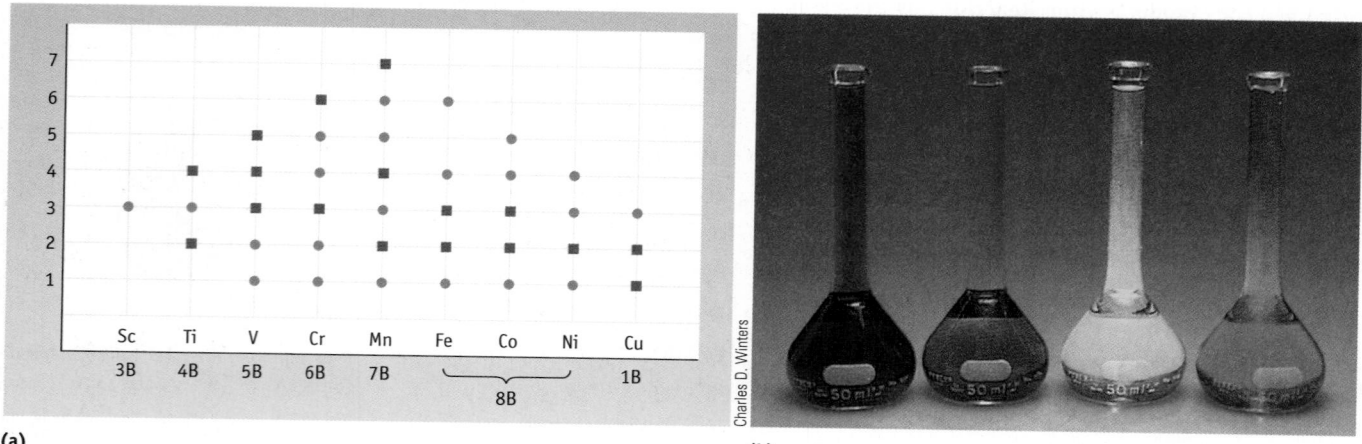

Charles D. Winters

(a) (b)

FIGURE 22.4 **Oxidation states of the transition elements in the first transition series.** (a) The most common oxidation states are indicated with red squares; less common oxidation states are indicated with blue dots. (b) Aqueous solutions of chromium compounds with two different oxidation numbers: +3 in $Cr(NO_3)_3$ (violet) and $CrCl_3$ (green), and +6 in K_2CrO_4 (yellow) and $K_2Cr_2O_7$ (orange).

It is hard not to be aware of corrosion. Those of us who live in the northern part of the United States are well aware of the problems of rust on our automobiles. It is estimated that 20% of iron production each year goes solely to replace iron that has rusted away.

Qualitatively, we describe corrosion as the deterioration of metals by a product-favored oxidation reaction. The corrosion of iron, for example, converts iron metal to red-brown rust, which is hydrated iron(III) oxide, $Fe_2O_3 \cdot H_2O$. This process requires both air and water, and it is enhanced if the water contains dissolved ions and if the metal is stressed (e.g., if it has dents, cuts, and scrapes on the surface.)

The corrosion process occurs in what is essentially a small electrochemical cell. There is an anode and a cathode, an electrical connection between the two (the metal itself), and an electrolyte in contact with both anode and cathode. When a metal corrodes, the metal is oxidized on anodic areas of the metal surface.

Anode, oxidation $M(s) \longrightarrow M^{n+} + n\,e^-$

The electrons are consumed by several possible half-reactions in cathodic areas.

Cathode, reduction

$$2\,H_3O^+(aq) + 2\,e^- \longrightarrow H_2(g) + 2\,H_2O(\ell)$$

$$2\,H_2O(\ell) + 2\,e^- \longrightarrow H_2(g) + 2\,OH^-(aq)$$

$$O_2(g) + 2\,H_2O(\ell) + 4\,e^- \longrightarrow 4\,OH^-(aq)$$

The rate of iron corrosion is controlled by the rate of the cathodic process. Of the three possible cathodic reactions, the one that is fastest is determined by acidity and the amount of oxygen present. If little or no oxygen is present—as when a piece of iron is buried in soil such as moist clay—hydrogen ion or water is reduced, and $H_2(g)$ and hydroxide ions are

the products. Iron(II) hydroxide is relatively insoluble and will precipitate on the metal surface, inhibiting the further formation of Fe^{2+}.

Anode	$Fe(s) \longrightarrow Fe^{2+}(aq) + 2\,e^-$
Cathode	$2\,H_2O(\ell) + 2\,e^- \longrightarrow H_2(g) + 2\,OH^-(aq)$
Precipitation	$Fe^{2+}(aq) + 2\,OH^-(aq) \longrightarrow Fe(OH)_2(s)$
Net reaction	$Fe(s) + 2\,H_2O(\ell) \longrightarrow H_2(g) + Fe(OH)_2(s)$

If both water and O_2 are present, the chemistry of iron corrosion is somewhat different, and the corrosion reaction is about 100 times faster than without oxygen.

Anode	$2\,Fe(s) \longrightarrow 2\,Fe^{2+}(aq) + 4\,e^-$
Cathode	$O_2(g) + 2\,H_2O(\ell) + 4\,e^- \longrightarrow 4\,OH^-(aq)$
Precipitation	$2\,Fe^{2+}(aq) + 4\,OH^-(aq) \longrightarrow 2\,Fe(OH)_2(s)$
Net reaction	$2\,Fe(s) + 2\,H_2O(\ell) + O_2(g) \longrightarrow 2\,Fe(OH)_2(s)$

If oxygen is present but not in excess, further oxidation of the iron(II) hydroxide leads to the formation of magnetic iron oxide Fe_3O_4, (which can be thought of as a mixed oxide of Fe_2O_3 and FeO).

$$6\,Fe(OH)_2(s) + O_2(g) \longrightarrow 2\,Fe_3O_4 \cdot H_2O(s) + 4\,H_2O(\ell)$$
green hydrated magnetite

$$Fe_3O_4 \cdot H_2O(s) \longrightarrow H_2O(\ell) + Fe_3O_4(s)$$
black magnetite

It is the black magnetite that you find coating an iron object that has corroded by resting in moist soil.

If the iron object has free access to oxygen and water, as in the open or in flowing water, red-brown iron(III) oxide will form.

$$4\,Fe(OH)_2(s) + O_2(g) \longrightarrow 2\,Fe_2O_3 \cdot H_2O(s) + 2\,H_2O(\ell)$$
red-brown

This is the familiar rust you see on cars and buildings, and the substance that colors the water red in some mountain streams or in your home.

The corrosion or rusting of iron results in major economic loss.

Anode and cathode reactions in iron corrosion. Two iron nails were placed in an agar gel that contains phenolphthalein and $K_3[Fe(CN)_6]$. Iron(II) ion, formed at the tip and where the nail is bent, reacts with $[Fe(CN)_6]^{3-}$ to form blue-green $Fe_4[Fe(CN)_6]_3 \cdot 14\,H_2O$ (Prussian blue). Hydrogen and $OH^-(aq)$ are formed at the other parts of the surface of the nail, the latter being detected by the red color of the 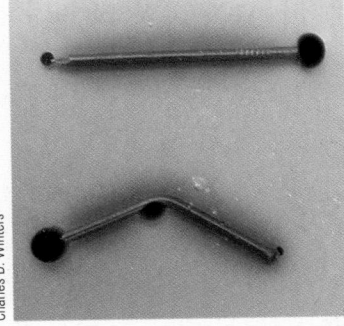 acid–base indicator. In this electrochemical cell, regions of stress—the ends and the bent region of the nail—act as anodes, and the remainder of the surface serves as the cathode.

sources of molybdenum and tungsten are the ores molybdenite (MoS_2) and wolframite (WO_3). This general trend is carried over in the *f*-block. The lanthanides form primarily 3+ ions. In contrast, actinide elements usually have higher oxidation numbers in their compounds; +4 and even +6 are typical. For example, UO_3 is a common oxide of uranium, and UF_6 is a compound important in processing uranium fuel for nuclear reactors [▶ Section 23.6].

Chemistry .ọ. Now™

Sign in at **www.cengage.com/login** and go to Chapter 22 Contents to see Screen 22.2 for an exercise on **transition metal compounds.**

Periodic Trends in the *d*-Block: Size, Density, Melting Point

The periodic table is the most useful single reference source for a chemist. Not only does it provide data that have everyday use, but it also organizes the elements with respect to their chemical and physical properties. Let us look at three physical properties of the transition elements that vary periodically: atomic radii, density and melting point.

Metal Atom Radii

The variation in atomic radii for the transition elements in the fourth, fifth, and sixth periods is illustrated in Figure 7.9. The radii of the transition elements vary over a fairly narrow range, with a small decrease to a minimum being observed around the middle of this group of elements. This similarity of radii can be understood based on electron configurations. Atom size is determined by the electrons in the outermost orbital, which for these elements is the *ns* orbital ($n = 4$, 5, or 6). Progressing from left to right in the periodic table, the size decline expected from increasing the number of protons in the nucleus is mostly canceled out by an opposing effect, repulsion from additional electrons in the $(n - 1)d$ orbitals.

The radii of the *d*-block elements in the fifth and sixth periods in each group are almost identical. The reason is that the lanthanide elements immediately precede the third series of *d*-block elements. The filling of 4*f* orbitals is accompanied by a steady contraction in size, consistent with the general trend of decreasing size from left to right in the periodic table. At the point where the 5*d* orbitals begin to fill again, the radii have decreased to a size similar to that of elements in the previous period. The decrease in size that results from the filling of the 4*f* orbitals is given a specific name, the **lanthanide contraction.**

The similar sizes of the second- and third-period *d*-block elements have significant consequences for their chemistry. For example, the "platinum group metals" (Ru, Os, Rh, Ir, Pd, and Pt) form similar compounds. Thus, it is not surprising that minerals containing these metals are found in the same geological zones on earth. Nor is it surprising that it is difficult to separate these elements from one another.

Density

The variation in metal radii causes the densities of the transition elements to first increase and then decrease across a period (Figure 22.5a). Although the overall change in radii among these elements is small, the effect is magnified because the volume is actually changing with the cube of the radius [$V = (4/3)\pi r^3$].

The lanthanide contraction explains why elements in the sixth period have the highest density. The relatively small radii of sixth-period transition metals, combined with the fact that their atomic masses are considerably larger than

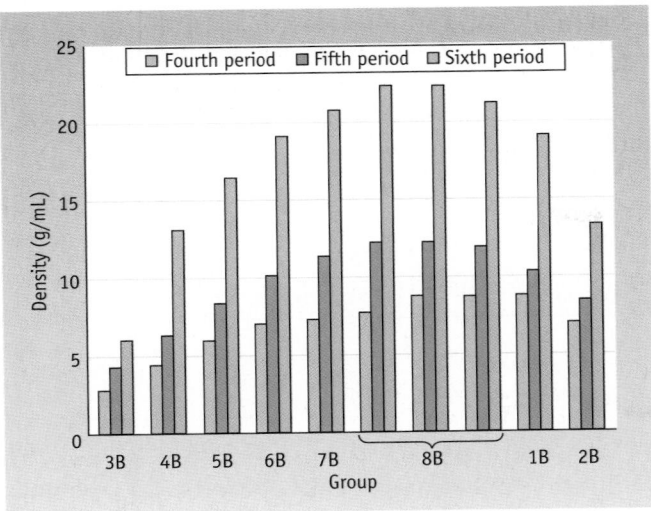

(a)

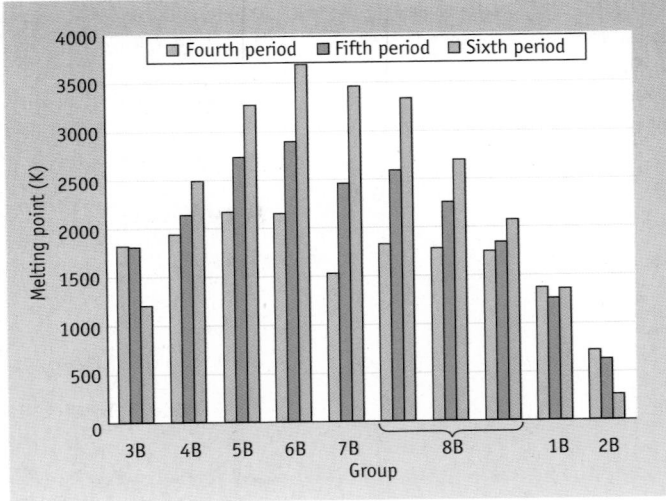

(b)

FIGURE 22.5 Periodic properties in the transition series. Density (a) and melting point (b) of the *d*-block elements.

their counterparts in the fifth period, causes sixth-period metal densities to be very large.

Melting Point

The melting point of any substance reflects the forces of attraction between the atoms, molecules, or ions that compose the solid. With transition elements, the melting points rise to a maximum around the middle of the series (Figure 22.5b), then descend. Again, these elements' electron configurations provide us with an explanation. The variation in melting point indicates that the strongest metallic bonds occur when the *d* subshell is about half filled. This is also the point at which the largest number of electrons occupy the bonding molecular orbitals in the metal. (See the discussion of bonding in metals on page 657.)

Chemistry ⚛ Now™

Sign in at **www.cengage.com/login** and go to Chapter 22 Contents to see Screen 22.3 for more on **transition metal chemistry.**

22.2 Metallurgy

A few metals occur in nature as the free elements. This group includes copper (Figure 22.6), silver, and gold. Most metals, however, are found as oxides, sulfides, halides, carbonates, or other ionic compounds (Figure 22.7). Some metal-containing mineral deposits have little economic value, either because the concentration of the metal is too low or because the metal is difficult to separate from impurities. The relatively few minerals from which elements can be obtained profitably are called *ores* (Figure 22.7). **Metallurgy** is the general name given to the process of obtaining metals from their ores.

Very few ores are chemically pure substances. Instead, the desired mineral is usually mixed with large quantities of impurities such as sand and clay, called **gangue** (pronounced "gang"). Generally, the first step in a metallurgical process is to sep-

FIGURE 22.6 Naturally occurring copper. Copper occurs as the metal (native copper) and as minerals such as blue azurite [2 $CuCO_3 \cdot Cu(OH)_2$] and malachite [$CuCO_3 \cdot Cu(OH)_2$].

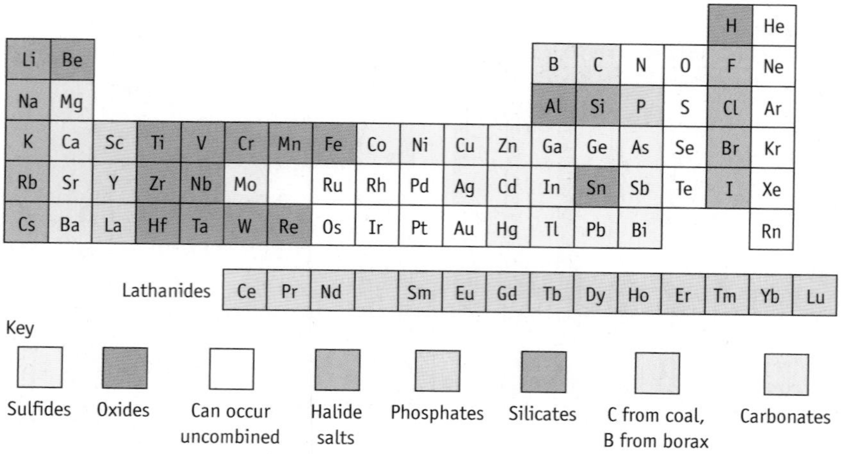

FIGURE 22.7 Major sources of the elements. A few transition metals, such as copper and gold, occur naturally as the metal. Most other elements are found naturally as oxides, sulfides, or other salts.

Key

Sulfides | Oxides | Can occur uncombined | Halide salts | Phosphates | Silicates | C from coal, B from borax | Carbonates

arate the mineral from the gangue. Then the ore is converted to the metal, a reduction process. Pyrometallurgy and hydrometallurgy are two methods of recovering metals from their ores. As the names imply, **pyrometallurgy** involves high temperatures and **hydrometallurgy** uses aqueous solutions (and thus is limited to the relatively low temperatures at which water is a liquid). Iron and copper metallurgy illustrate these two methods of metal production.

Pyrometallurgy: Iron Production

The production of iron from its ores is carried out in a blast furnace (Figure 22.8). The furnace is charged with a mixture of ore (usually hematite, Fe_2O_3), coke (which is primarily carbon), and limestone ($CaCO_3$). A blast of hot air forced in at the bottom of the furnace causes the coke to burn with such an intense heat that the temperature at the bottom is almost 1500 °C. The quantity of air input is controlled so that carbon monoxide is the primary product. Both carbon and carbon monoxide participate in the reduction of iron(III) oxide to give impure metal.

$$Fe_2O_3(s) + 3\ C(s) \longrightarrow 2\ Fe(\ell) + 3\ CO(g)$$

$$Fe_2O_3(s) + 3\ CO(g) \longrightarrow 2\ Fe(\ell) + 3\ CO_2(g)$$

■ **Coke: A Reducing Agent** Coke is made by heating coal in a tall, narrow oven that is sealed to keep out oxygen. Heating drives off volatile chemicals, including benzene and ammonia. What remains is nearly pure carbon.

Much of the carbon dioxide formed in the reduction process (and from heating the limestone) is reduced on contact with unburned coke and produces more reducing agent.

$$CO_2(g) + C(s) \longrightarrow 2\ CO(g)$$

The molten iron flows down through the furnace and collects at the bottom, where it is tapped off through an opening in the side. This impure iron is called *cast iron* or *pig iron*. Usually, the impure metal is either brittle or soft (undesirable properties for most uses) due to the presence of impurities such as elemental carbon, phosphorus, and sulfur.

Iron ores generally contain silicate minerals and silicon dioxide. Lime (CaO), formed when limestone is heated, reacts with these materials to give calcium silicate.

$$SiO_2(s) + CaO(s) \longrightarrow CaSiO_3(\ell)$$

This is an acid–base reaction because CaO is a basic oxide and SiO_2 is an acidic oxide. The calcium silicate, molten at the temperature of the blast furnace and less

Charge of ore, coke, and limestone

Flue gas

230 °C

525 °C

Hot gases used to preheat air

Reducing zone

945 °C

1510 °C

Heated air

Slag

Molten iron

dense than molten iron, floats on the iron. Other nonmetal oxides dissolve in this layer and the mixture, called *slag*, is easily removed.

Pig iron from the blast furnace may contain as much as 4.5% carbon, 0.3% phosphorus, 0.04% sulfur, 1.5% silicon, and some other elements as well. The impure iron must be purified to remove these nonmetal components. Several processes are available to accomplish this task, but the most important uses the *basic oxygen furnace* (Figure 22.9). The process in the furnace removes much of the carbon and all of the phosphorus, sulfur, and silicon. Pure oxygen is blown into the molten pig iron and oxidizes phosphorus to P_4O_{10}, sulfur to SO_2, and carbon to CO_2. These nonmetal oxides either escape as gases or react with basic oxides such as CaO that are added or are used to line the furnace. For example,

$$P_4O_{10}(g) + 6\ CaO(s) \longrightarrow 2\ Ca_3(PO_4)_2(\ell)$$

The result is ordinary *carbon steel*. Almost any degree of flexibility, hardness, strength, and malleability can be achieved in carbon steel by reheating and cooling in a process called *tempering*. The resulting material can then be used in a wide variety of applications. The major disadvantages of carbon steel are that it corrodes easily and that it loses its properties when heated strongly.

Other transition metals, such as chromium, manganese, and nickel, can be added during the steel-making process, giving *alloys* (solid solutions of two or more metals; see *The Chemistry of Modern Materials*, page 656) that have

Bethlehem Steel Corp.

FIGURE 22.9 Molten iron being poured from a basic oxygen furnace.

FIGURE 22.10 Enriching copper ore by the flotation process. The less dense particles of Cu_2S are trapped in the soap bubbles and float. The denser gangue settles to the bottom.

specific physical, chemical, and mechanical properties. One well-known alloy is stainless steel, which contains 18% to 20% Cr and 8% to 12% Ni. Stainless steel is much more resistant to corrosion than carbon steel. Another alloy of iron is Alnico V. Used in loudspeaker magnets because of its permanent magnetism, it contains five elements: Al (8%), Ni (14%), Co (24%), Cu (3%), and Fe (51%).

Hydrometallurgy: Copper Production

In contrast to iron ores, which are mostly oxides, most copper minerals are sulfides. Copper-bearing minerals include chalcopyrite ($CuFeS_2$), chalcocite (Cu_2S), and covellite (CuS). Because ores containing these minerals generally have a very low percentage of copper, enrichment is necessary. This step is carried out by a process known as *flotation*. First, the ore is finely powdered. Next, oil is added and the mixture is agitated with soapy water in a large tank (Figure 22.10). At the same time, compressed air is forced through the mixture, so that the lightweight, oil-covered copper sulfide particles are carried to the top as a frothy mixture. The heavier gangue settles to the bottom of the tank, and the copper-laden froth is skimmed off.

Hydrometallurgy can be used to obtain copper from an enriched ore. In one method, enriched chalcopyrite ore is treated with a solution of copper(II) chloride. A reaction ensues that leaves copper in the form of solid, insoluble CuCl, which is easily separated from the iron that remains in solution as aqueous $FeCl_2$.

$$CuFeS_2(s) + 3\ CuCl_2(aq) \longrightarrow 4\ CuCl(s) + FeCl_2(aq) + 2\ S(s)$$

Aqueous NaCl is then added, and CuCl dissolves because of the formation of the complex ion $[CuCl_2]^-$.

$$CuCl(s) + Cl^-(aq) \longrightarrow [CuCl_2]^-(aq)$$

Copper(I) compounds in solution are unstable with respect to Cu(0) and Cu(II). Thus, $[CuCl_2]^-$ disproportionates to the metal and $CuCl_2$, and the latter is used to treat further ore.

$$2\ [CuCl_2]^-(aq) \longrightarrow Cu(s) + Cu^{2+}(aq) + 4\ Cl^-(aq)$$

Approximately 10% of the copper produced in the United States is obtained with the aid of bacteria. Acidified water is sprayed onto copper-mining wastes that contain low levels of copper. As the water trickles down through the crushed rock, the bacterium *Thiobacillus ferrooxidans* breaks down the iron sulfides in the rock and converts iron(II) to iron(III). Iron(III) ions oxidize the sulfide ion of copper sulfide to sulfate ions, leaving copper(II) ions in solution. Then the copper(II) ion is reduced to metallic copper by reaction with iron.

$$Cu^{2+}(aq) + Fe(s) \longrightarrow Cu(s) + Fe^{2+}(aq)$$

The purity of the copper obtained via these metallurgical processes is about 99%, but this is not acceptable because even traces of impurities greatly diminish the electrical conductivity of the metal. Consequently, a further purification step is needed—one involving electrolysis (Figure 22.11). Thin sheets of pure copper metal and slabs of impure copper are immersed in a solution containing $CuSO_4$ and H_2SO_4. The pure copper sheets serve as the cathode of an electrolysis cell, and the impure slabs are the anode. Copper in the impure sample is oxidized to copper(II) ions at the anode, and copper(II) ions in solution are reduced to pure copper at the cathode.

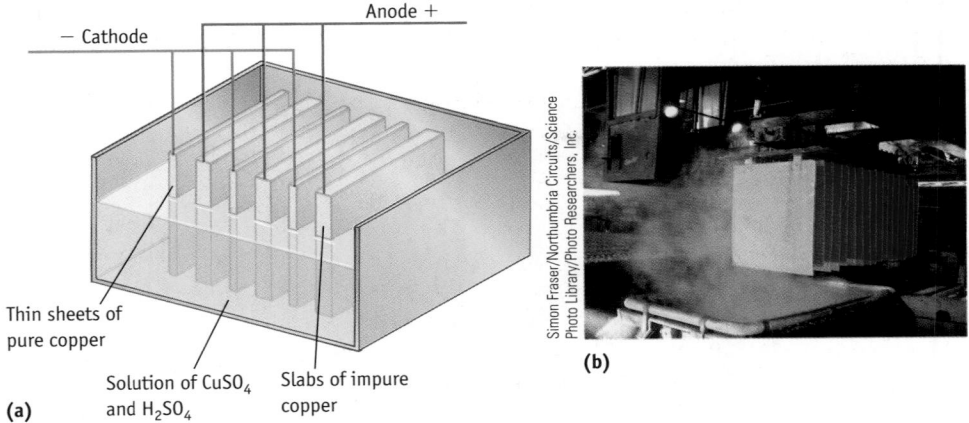

- Cathode

Anode +

Thin sheets of
pure copper

Solution of $CuSO_4$
and H_2SO_4

Slabs of impure
copper

(a)

Simon Fraser/Northumbria Circuits/Science
Photo Library/Photo Researchers, Inc.

(b)

FIGURE 22.11 Electrolytic refining of copper. (a) Slabs of impure copper, called "blister copper," form the anode, and pure copper is deposited at the cathode. (b) The electrolysis cells at a copper refinery.

22.3 Coordination Compounds

When metal salts dissolve, water molecules cluster around the ions (page 617). The negative end of each polar water molecule is attracted to the positively charged metal ion, and the positive end of the water molecule is attracted to the anion. As noted earlier (◄ Section 12.2), the energy of the ion–solvent interaction (solvation energy) is an important aspect of the solution process. But there is much more to this story.

Complexes and Ligands

A green solution formed by dissolving nickel(II) chloride in water contains Ni^{2+} (aq) and Cl^-(aq) ions (Figure 22.12). If the solvent is removed, a green crystalline solid is obtained. The formula of this solid is often written as $NiCl_2 \cdot 6\ H_2O$, and the compound is called nickel(II) chloride hexahydrate. Addition of ammonia to the aqueous nickel(II) chloride solution gives a lilac-colored solution from which another compound, $NiCl_2 \cdot 6\ NH_3$, can be isolated. This formula looks very similar to the formula for the hydrate, with ammonia substituted for water.

What are these two nickel species? The formulas identify the compositions of the compounds but fail to give information about their structures. Because properties of compounds derive from their structures, we need to evaluate the structures in more detail. Typically, metal compounds are ionic, and solid ionic compounds have structures with cations and anions arranged in a regular array. The structure of hydrated nickel chloride contains cations with the formula $[Ni(H_2O)_6]^{2+}$ and chloride anions. The structure of the ammonia-containing compound is similar to the hydrate; it is made up of $[Ni(NH_3)_6]^{2+}$ cations and chloride anions.

Ions such as $[Ni(H_2O)_6]^{2+}$ and $[Ni(NH_3)_6]^{2+}$, in which a metal ion and either water or ammonia molecules compose a single structural unit, are examples of **coordination complexes,** also known as **complex ions** (Figure 22.13). Compounds containing a coordination complex as part of the structure are called **coordination compounds,** and their chemistry is known as **coordination chemistry.** Although the older "hydrate" formulas are still used, the preferred method of writing the formula for coordination compounds places the metal atom or ion and the molecules or anions directly bonded to it within brackets to show that it is a single structural entity. Thus, the formula for the nickel(II)–ammonia compound is better written as $[Ni(NH_3)_6]Cl_2$.

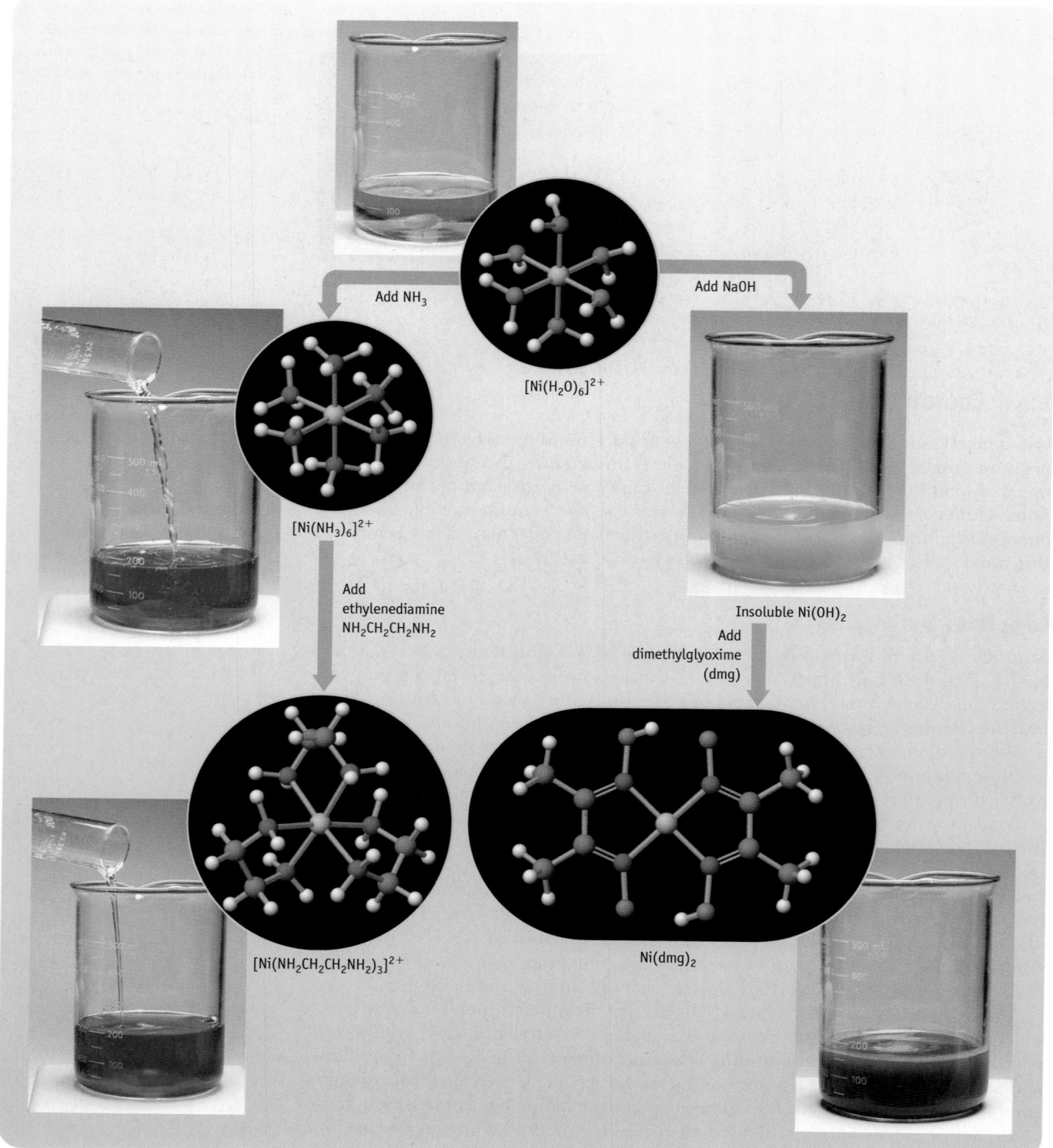

Add NH$_3$

[Ni(H$_2$O)$_6$]$^{2+}$

Add NaOH

[Ni(NH$_3$)$_6$]$^{2+}$

Add
ethylenediamine
NH$_2$CH$_2$CH$_2$NH$_2$

Insoluble Ni(OH)$_2$

Add
dimethylglyoxime
(dmg)

[Ni(NH$_2$CH$_2$CH$_2$NH$_2$)$_3$]$^{2+}$

Ni(dmg)$_2$

FIGURE 22.12 Coordination compounds of Ni^{2+} ion. The transition metals and their ions form a wide range of compounds, often with beautiful colors and interesting structures. One purpose of this chapter is to explore some commonly observed structures and explain how these compounds can be so colorful.

Photos: Charles D. Winters

All coordination complexes contain a metal atom or ion as the central part of the structure. Bonded to the metal are molecules or ions called **ligands** (from the Latin verb *ligare*, meaning "to bind"). In the preceding examples, water and ammonia are the ligands. The number of ligand atoms attached to the metal defines the **coordination number** of the metal. The geometry described by the attached ligands is called the **coordination geometry.** In the nickel complex ion $[Ni(NH_3)_6]^{2+}$ (Figure 22.12), the six ligands are arranged in a regular octahedral geometry around the central metal ion.

Ligands can be either neutral molecules or anions (or, in rare instances, cations). The characteristic feature of a ligand is that it contains a lone pair of electrons. In the classic description of bonding in a coordination complex, the lone pair of electrons on a ligand is shared with the metal ion. The attachment is a coordinate covalent bond (◄ Section 8.5), because the electron pair being shared was originally on the ligand. The name "coordination complex" derives from the name given to this kind of bonding.

The net charge on a coordination complex is the sum of the charges on the metal and its attached groups. Complexes can be cations (as in the two nickel complexes used as examples here), anions, or uncharged.

Ligands such as H_2O and NH_3, which coordinate to the metal via a single Lewis base atom, are termed **monodentate.** The word "dentate" comes from the Latin *dentis*, meaning "tooth," so NH_3 is a "one-toothed" ligand. Some ligands attach to the metal with more than one donor atom. These ligands are called **polydentate.** Ethylenediamine (1,2-diaminoethane), $H_2NCH_2CH_2NH_2$, often abbreviated as en; oxalate ion, $C_2O_4^{2-}$ (ox^{2-}); and phenanthroline, $C_{12}H_8N_2$ (phen), are examples of the wide variety of bidentate ligands (Figure 22.14). Structures and examples of some complex ions with **bidentate** ligands are shown in Figure 22.15.

Polydentate ligands are also called **chelating ligands,** or just chelates (pronounced "key-lates"). The name derives from the Greek *chele*, meaning "claw." Because two or more bonds are broken to separate the ligand from the metal, complexes with chelated ligands have greater stability than those with monodentate ligands. Chelated complexes are important in everyday life. One way to clean the rust out of water-cooled automobile engines and steam boilers is to add a solution of oxalic acid. Iron oxide reacts with oxalic acid to give a water-soluble iron oxalate complex ion:

$$3 H_2O(\ell) + Fe_2O_3(s) + 6 H_2C_2O_4(aq) \longrightarrow 2 [Fe(C_2O_4)_3]^{3-}(aq) + 6 H_3O^+(aq)$$

Ethylenediaminetetraacetate ion ($EDTA^{4-}$), a hexadentate ligand, is an excellent chelating ligand (Figure 22.16). It can wrap around a metal ion, encapsulating it. Salts of this anion are often added to commercial salad dressings to remove traces of free metal ions from solution; otherwise, these metal ions can act as catalysts for the oxidation of the oils in the dressing. Without $EDTA^{4-}$, the dressing would

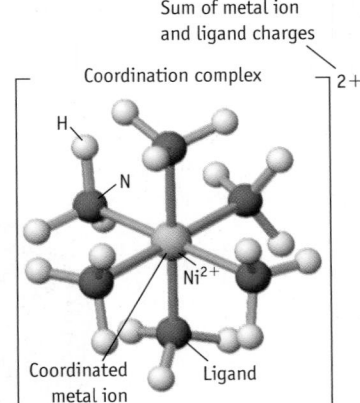

Sum of metal ion
and ligand charges

Coordination complex

Coordinated
metal ion

Ligand

$[Ni(NH_3)_6]^{2+}$

FIGURE 22.13 A coordination complex. In the $[Ni(NH_3)_6]^{2+}$ ion, the ligands are NH_3 molecules. Because the metal has a 2+ charge and the ligands have no charge, the charge on the complex ion is 2+.

■ **Ligands Are Lewis Bases** Ligands are Lewis bases because they furnish the electron pair; the metal ion is a Lewis acid because it accepts electron pairs (see Section 17.9). Thus, the coordinate covalent bond between ligand and metal can be viewed as a Lewis acid–Lewis base interaction.

■ **Bidentate Ligands** All common bidentate ligands bind to *adjacent* sites on the metal.

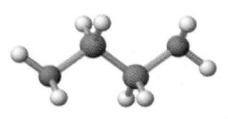
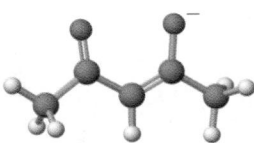
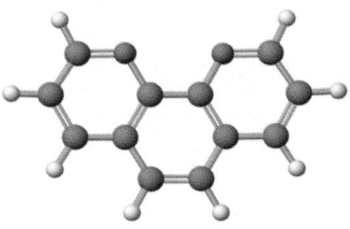

(a) $H_2NCH_2CH_2NH_2$, en   **(b)** $C_2O_4^{2-}$, ox   **(c)** $CH_3COCHCOCH_3^-$, acac$^-$ **(d)** $C_{12}H_8N_2$, phen

FIGURE 22.14 Common bidentate ligands. (a) Ethylenediamine, $H_2NCH_2CH_2NH_2$; (b) oxalate ion, $C_2O_4^{2-}$; (c) acetylacetonate ion, $CH_3COCHCOCH_3^-$; (d) phenanthroline, $C_{12}H_8N_2$. Coordination of these bidentate ligands to a transition metal ion results in five- or six-member metal-containing rings and no ring strain.

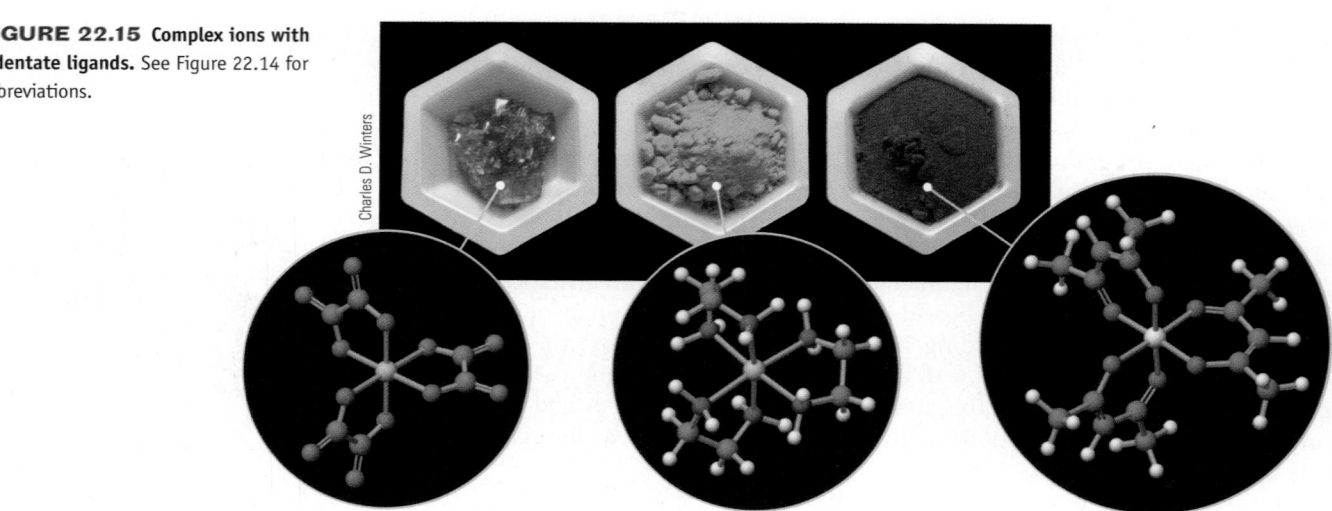

FIGURE 22.15 Complex ions with bidentate ligands. See Figure 22.14 for abbreviations.

Charles D. Winters

$[Fe(C_2O_4)_3]^{3-}$ $[Co(en)_3]^{3+}$ $Cr(acac)_3$

quickly become rancid. Another use is in bathroom cleansers. The $EDTA^{4-}$ ion removes deposits of $CaCO_3$ and $MgCO_3$ left by hard water by coordinating to Ca^{2+} or Mg^{2+} to create soluble complex ions.

Complexes with polydentate ligands play particularly important roles in biochemistry, one example of which is described in *A Closer Look: Hemoglobin.*

Formulas of Coordination Compounds

It is useful to be able to predict the formula of a coordination complex, given the metal ion and ligands, and to derive the oxidation number of the coordinated metal ion, given the formula in a coordination compound. The following examples explore these issues.

EXAMPLE 22.1 Formulas of Coordination Complexes

Problem Give the formulas of the following coordination complexes:

(a) A Ni^{2+} ion is bound to two water molecules and two bidentate oxalate ions.

(b) A Co^{3+} ion is bound to one Cl^- ion, one ammonia molecule, and two bidentate ethylenediamine (en) molecules.

Strategy The problem requires determining the net charge, which equals the sum of the charges of the various component parts of the complex ion. With that information, the metal and ligands can be assembled in the formula, which is placed in brackets, and the net charge indicated.

FIGURE 22.16 $EDTA^{4-}$, a hexadentate ligand. (a) Ethylenediaminetetraacetate, $EDTA^{4-}$. (b) $[Co(EDTA)]^-$. Notice the five- and six-member rings created when this ligand bonds to the metal.

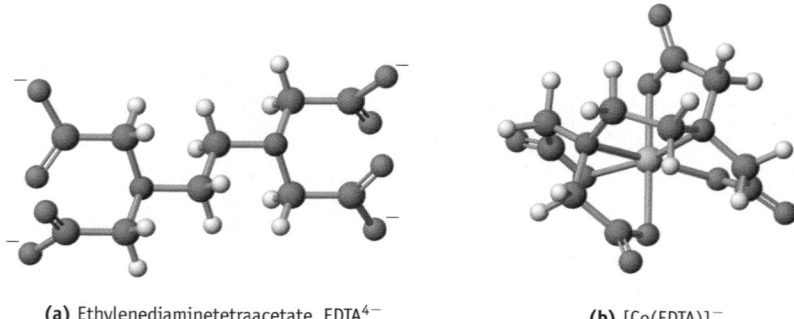

(a) Ethylenediaminetetraacetate, $EDTA^{4-}$ **(b)** $[Co(EDTA)]^-$

Hemoglobin

Metal-containing coordination compounds figure prominently in many biochemical reactions. Perhaps the best-known example is hemoglobin, the chemical in the blood responsible for O_2 transport. It is also one of the most thoroughly studied bioinorganic compounds.

As described in *The Chemistry of Life: Biochemistry* (page 496), hemoglobin (Hb) is a large iron-containing protein. It includes four polypeptide segments, each containing an iron(II) ion locked inside a porphyrin ring system and coordinated to a nitrogen atom

Porphyrin

$$\downarrow -2\,H^+$$

Porphyrin^{2-}

Porphyrin ring of the heme group. The tetradentate ligand surrounding the iron(II) ion in hemoglobin is a dianion of a substituted molecule called a porphyrin. Because of the double bonds in this structure, all of the carbon and nitrogen atoms in the dianion of the porphyrin lie in a plane. In addition, the nitrogen lone pairs are directed toward the center of the molecule, and the molecular dimensions are such that a metal ion may fit nicely into the cavity.

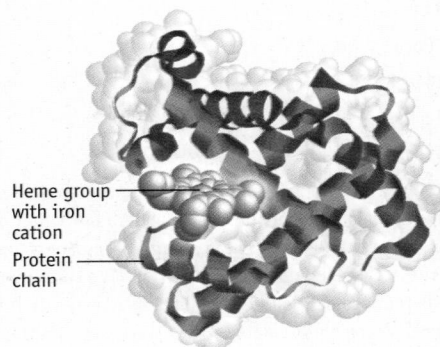

Heme group with iron cation

Protein chain

Myoglobin (Mb)

The heme group in myoglobin. This protein is a close relative of hemoglobin. The heme group with its iron ion is shown.

from another part of the protein. A sixth site is available to attach to oxygen.

One segment of the hemoglobin molecule resembles the myoglobin structure shown above. (Myoglobin, the oxygen-storage protein in muscle, has only one polypeptide chain with an enclosed heme group. It is the oxygen storage protein in muscle.) In this case, the iron-containing heme group is enclosed with a polypeptide chain. The iron ion in the porphyrin ring is shown. The first and sixth coordination positions are taken up by nitrogen atoms from amino acids of the polypeptide chain.

Hemoglobin functions by reversibly adding oxygen to the sixth coordination position of each iron, giving a complex called oxyhemoglobin.

Because hemoglobin features four iron centers, a maximum of four molecules of oxygen can bind to the molecule. The binding to oxygen is cooperative; that is, binding one molecule enhances the tendency to bind the second, third, and fourth molecules.

Formation of the oxygenated complex is favored, but not too highly, because oxygen must also be released by the molecule to body tissues. Interestingly, an increase in acidity leads to a decrease in the stability of the oxygenated complex. This phenomenon is known as the *Bohr effect*, named for Christian Bohr, Niels Bohr's father. Release of oxygen in tissues is facilitated by an increase in acidity that results from the presence of CO_2 formed by metabolism.

Among the notable properties of hemoglobin is its ability to form a complex with carbon monoxide. This complex is very stable, with the equilibrium constant for the following reaction being about 200 (where Hb is hemoglobin):

$$HbO_2(aq) + CO(g) \rightleftharpoons HbCO(aq) + O_2(g)$$

When CO complexes with iron, the oxygen-carrying capacity of hemoglobin is lost. Consequently, CO is highly toxic to humans. Exposure to even small amounts greatly reduces the capacity of the blood to transport oxygen.

Hemoglobin abnormalities are well known. One of the most common abnormalities causes sickle cell anemia and was described on page 500.

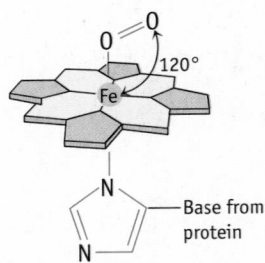

Base from protein

Oxygen binding. Oxygen binds to the iron of the heme group in oxyhemoglobin (and in myoglobin). Interestingly, the Fe—O—O angle is bent.

Solution

(a) This complex ion is constructed from two neutral H_2O molecules, two $C_2O_4^{2-}$ ions, and one Ni^{2+} ion, so the net charge on the complex is $2-$. The formula for the complex ion is

$$[Ni(C_2O_4)_2(H_2O)_2]^{2-}$$

(b) This cobalt(III) complex combines two en molecules and one NH_3 molecule, both having no charge, as well as one Cl^- ion and a Co^{3+} ion. The net charge is $2+$. The formula for this complex (writing out the entire formula for ethylenediamine) is

$$[Co(H_2NCH_2CH_2NH_2)_2(NH_3)Cl]^{2+}$$

Problem In each of the following complexes, determine the metal's oxidation number and coordination number.

(a) $[Co(en)_2(NO_2)_2]Cl$

(b) $Pt(NH_3)_2(C_2O_4)$

(c) $Pt(NH_3)_2Cl_4$

(d) $[Co(NH_3)_5Cl]SO_4$

Strategy Each formula consists of a complex ion or molecule made up of the metal ion, neutral and/or anionic ligands (the part inside the square brackets), and a counterion (outside the brackets). The oxidation number of the metal is the charge necessary to balance the sum of the negative charges associated with the anionic ligands and counterion. The coordination number is the number of donor atoms in the ligands that are bonded to the metal. Remember that the bidentate ligands in these examples (en, oxalate ion) attach to the metal at two sites and that the counterion is not part of the complex ion—that is, it is not a ligand.

Solution

(a) The chloride ion with a 1− charge, outside the brackets, shows that the charge on the complex ion must be 1+. There are two nitrite ions (NO_2^-) and two neutral bidentate ethylenediamine ligands in the complex. To give a 1+ charge on the complex ion, the cobalt ion must have a charge of 3+; that is, the sum of 2− (two nitrites), 0 (two en ligands), and 3+ (the cobalt ion) equals 1+. Each en ligand fills two coordination positions, and the two nitrite ions fill two more positions. The coordination number of the metal is 6.

(b) There is an oxalate ion ($C_2O_4^{2-}$) and two neutral ammonia ligands. To balance the charge on the oxalate ion, platinum must have a 2+ charge; that is, it has an oxidation number of +2. The coordination number is 4, with an oxalate ligand filling two coordination positions and each ammonia molecule filling one.

(c) There are four chloride ions (Cl^-) and two neutral ammonia ligands. In this complex, the oxidation number of the metal is +4, and the coordination number is 6.

(d) There is one chloride ion (Cl^-) and five neutral ammonia ligands. The counter ion is sulfate with a 2− charge, so the overall charge on the complex is 2+. The oxidation number of the metal is +3 and the coordination number is 6 (sulfate is not coordinated to the metal).

EXERCISE 22.1 Formulas of Coordination Compounds

(a) What is the formula of a complex ion composed of one Co^{3+} ion, three ammonia molecules, and three Cl^- ions?

(b) Determine the metal's oxidation number and coordination number in (i) $K_3[Co(NO_2)_6]$ and in (ii) $Mn(NH_3)_4Cl_2$.

Naming Coordination Compounds

Just as rules govern naming of inorganic and organic compounds, coordination compounds are named according to an established system. The three compounds below are named according to the rules that follow.

Compound	Systematic Name
$[Ni(H_2O)_6]SO_4$	Hexaaquanickel(II) sulfate
$[Cr(en)_2(CN)_2]Cl$	Dicyanobis(ethylenediamine)chromium(III) chloride
$K[Pt(NH_3)Cl_3]$	Potassium amminetrichloroplatinate(II)

1. In naming a coordination compound that is a salt, name the cation first and then the anion. (This is how all salts are commonly named.)
2. When giving the name of the complex ion or molecule, name the ligands first, in alphabetical order, followed by the name of the metal. (When determining alphabetical order, the prefix is not considered part of the name.)

3. Ligands and their names:
   (a) If a ligand is an anion whose name ends in *-ite* or *-ate*, the final *e* is changed to *o* (sulfate ⟶ sulfato or nitrite ⟶ nitrito).
   (b) If the ligand is an anion whose name ends in *-ide*, the ending is changed to *o* (chloride ⟶ chloro, cyanide ⟶ cyano).
   (c) If the ligand is a neutral molecule, its common name is usually used with several important exceptions: Water as a ligand is referred to as *aqua;* ammonia is called *ammine;* and CO is called *carbonyl.*
   (d) When there is more than one of a particular monodentate ligand with a simple name, the number of ligands is designated by the appropriate prefix: *di, tri, tetra, penta,* or *hexa.* If the ligand name is complicated, the prefix changes to *bis, tris, tetrakis, pentakis,* or *hexakis,* followed by the ligand name in parentheses.
4. If the coordination complex is an anion, the suffix *-ate* is added to the metal name.
5. Following the name of the metal, the oxidation number of the metal is given in Roman numerals.

EXAMPLE 22.3 Naming Coordination Compounds

Problem Name the following compounds:

(a) $[Cu(NH_3)_4]SO_4$

(b) $K_2[CoCl_4]$

(c) $Co(phen)_2Cl_2$

(d) $[Co(en)_2(H_2O)Cl]Cl_2$

Strategy Apply the rules for nomenclature given above.

Solution

(a) The complex ion (in square brackets) is composed of four NH_3 molecules (named *ammine* in a complex) and the copper ion. To balance the 2− charge on the sulfate counterion, copper must have a 2+ charge. The compound's name is

tetraamminecopper(II) sulfate

(b) The complex ion $[CoCl_4]^{2-}$ has a 2− charge. With four Cl^- ligands, the cobalt ion must have a +2 charge, so the sum of charges is 2−. The name of the compound is

potassium tetrachlorocobaltate(II)

(c) This is a neutral coordination compound. The ligands include two Cl^- ions and two neutral bidentate *phen* (phenanthroline) ligands. The metal ion must have a 2+ charge (Co^{2+}). The name, listing ligands in alphabetical order, is

dichlorobis(phenanthroline)cobalt(II)

(d) The complex ion has a 2− charge because it is paired with two uncoordinated Cl^- ions. The cobalt ion is Co^{3+} because it is bonded to two neutral en ligands, one neutral water, and one Cl^-. The name is

aquachlorobis(ethylenediamine)cobalt(III) chloride

EXERCISE 22.2 Naming Coordination Compounds

Name the following coordination compounds.

(a) $[Ni(H_2O)_6]SO_4$

(b) $[Cr(en)_2(CN)_2]Cl$

(c) $K[Pt(NH_3)Cl_3]$

(d) $K[CuCl_2]$

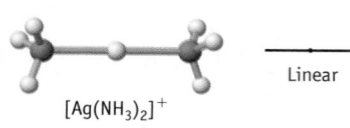

[Ag(NH₃)₂]⁺

Linear

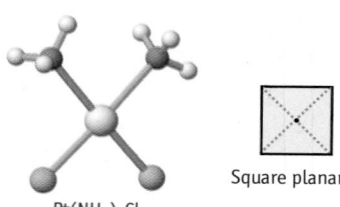

Pt(NH₃)₂Cl₂

Square planar

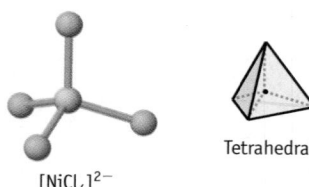

[NiCl₄]²⁻

Tetrahedral

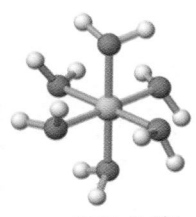

[Ni(H₂O)₆]²⁺

Octahedral

22.4 Structures of Coordination Compounds

Common Coordination Geometries

The geometry of a coordination complex is defined by the arrangement of donor atoms of the ligands around the central metal ion. Metal ions in coordination compounds can have coordination numbers ranging from 2 to 12. Only complexes with coordination numbers of 2, 4, and 6 are common, however, so we will concentrate on species such as $[ML_2]^{n\pm}$, $[ML_4]^{n\pm}$, and $[ML_6]^{n\pm}$, where M is the metal ion and L is a monodentate ligand. Within these stoichiometries, the following geometries are encountered:

- All $[ML_2]^{n\pm}$ complexes are linear. The two ligands are on opposite sides of the metal, and the L—M—L bond angle is 180°. Common examples include $[Ag(NH_3)_2]^+$ and $[CuCl_2]^-$.
- Tetrahedral geometry occurs in many $[ML_4]^{n\pm}$ complexes. Examples include $TiCl_4$, $[CoCl_4]^{2-}$, $[NiCl_4]^{2-}$, and $[Zn(NH_3)_4]^{2+}$.
- Some $[ML_4]^{n\pm}$ complexes can have square planar geometry. This geometry is most often seen with metal ions that have eight d electrons. Examples include $Pt(NH_3)_2Cl_2$, $[Ni(CN)_4]^{2-}$, and the nickel complex with the dimethylglyoximate (dmg⁻) ligand in Figure 22.12.
- Octahedral geometry is found in complexes with the stoichiometry $[ML_6]^{n\pm}$ (Figure 22.12).

Chemistry ·Now™

Sign in at **www.cengage.com/login** and go to Chapter 22 Contents to see Screen 22.5 for an exercise on **compound geometries**.

Isomerism

Isomerism is one of the most interesting aspects of molecular structure. Recall that the chemistry of organic compounds is greatly enlivened by the multitude of isomeric compounds that are known.

Isomers are classified as follows:

- *Structural isomers* have the same molecular formula but different bonding arrangements of atoms.
- *Stereoisomers* have the same atom-to-atom bonding sequence, but the atoms differ in their arrangement in space. There are two types of stereoisomers: geometric isomers (such as *cis* and *trans* alkenes, page 421) and optical isomers (non-superimposable mirror images that have the unique property that they rotate planar polarized light, page 445).

All three types of isomerism, structural, geometric, and optical, are encountered in coordination chemistry.

Structural Isomerism

The two most important types of structural isomerism in coordination chemistry are coordination isomerism and linkage isomerism. **Coordination isomerism** occurs when it is possible to exchange a coordinated ligand and the uncoordinated counterion. For example, dark violet $[Co(NH_3)_5Br]SO_4$ and red $[Co(NH_3)_5SO_4]Br$ are coordination isomers. In the first compound, bromide ion is a ligand and sulfate is a counterion; in the second, sulfate is a ligand and bromide is the counterion. A diagnostic test for this kind of isomer is often made based on chemical reactions.

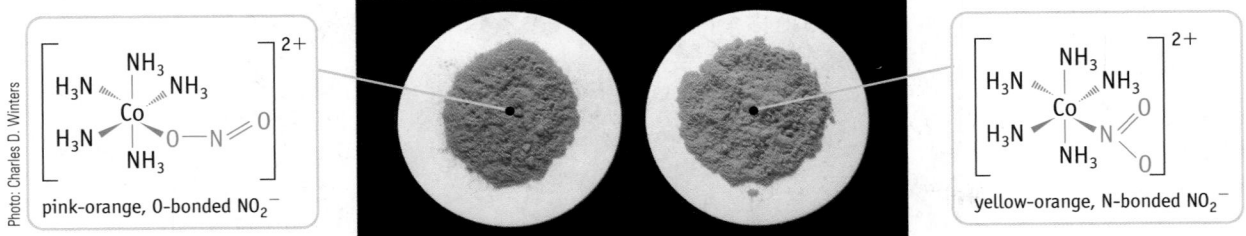

FIGURE 22.17 Linkage isomers, [Co(NH₃)₅ONO]²⁺ and [Co(NH₃)₅NO₂]²⁺. These complexes, whose systematic names are pentaamminenitritocobalt(III) and pentaamminenitrocobalt(III), were the first known examples of this type of isomerism.

For example, these two compounds can be distinguished by precipitation reactions. Addition of Ba^{2+}(aq) to a solution of $[Co(NH_3)_5Br]SO_4$ gives a precipitate of $BaSO_4$, indicating the presence of sulfate ion in solution. In contrast, no reaction occurs if Ba^{2+}(aq) is added to a solution of $[Co(NH_3)_5SO_4]Br$. In this complex, sulfate ion is attached to Co^{3+} and is not a free ion in solution.

$$[Co(NH_3)_5Br]SO_4 + Ba^{2+}(aq) \longrightarrow BaSO_4(s) + [CO(NH_3)_5Br]^{2+}(aq)$$

$$[Co(NH_3)_5SO_4]Br + Ba^{2+}(aq) \longrightarrow \text{no reaction}$$

Linkage isomerism occurs when it is possible to attach a ligand to the metal through different atoms. The two most common ligands with which linkage isomerism arises are thiocyanate, SCN^-, and nitrite, NO_2^-. The Lewis structure of the thiocyanate ion shows that there are lone pairs of electrons on sulfur and nitrogen. The ligand can attach to a metal either through sulfur (called S-bonded thiocyanate) or through nitrogen (called N-bonded thiocyanate). Nitrite ion can attach either at oxygen or at nitrogen. The former are called nitrito complexes; the latter are nitro complexes (Figure 22.17).

Ligands forming linkage isomers

Bind to metal ion using either lone pair

Bind to metal ion using either lone pair

Geometric Isomerism

Geometric isomerism results when the atoms bonded directly to the metal have a different spatial arrangement. The simplest example of geometric isomerism in coordination chemistry is *cis-trans* isomerism, which occurs in both square-planar and octahedral complexes. An example of *cis-trans* isomerism is seen in the square-planar complex $Pt(NH_3)_2Cl_2$ (Figure 22.18a). In this complex, the two Cl^- ions can be either adjacent to each other (*cis*) or on opposite sides of the metal (*trans*). The *cis* isomer is effective in the treatment of testicular, ovarian, bladder, and osteogenic sarcoma cancers, but the *trans* isomer has no effect on these diseases.

Cis-trans isomerism in an octahedral complex is illustrated by a complex ion with two bidentate ethylenediamine ligands and two chloride ligands, $[Co(H_2NCH_2CH_2NH_2)_2Cl_2]^+$. In this complex, the two Cl^- ions occupy positions that are either adjacent (the purple *cis* isomer) or opposite (the green *trans* isomer) (Figure 22.18b).

■ *Cis-Trans* **Isomerism** *Cis-trans* isomerism is not possible for tetrahedral complexes. All L—M—L angles in tetrahedral geometry are 109.5°, and all positions are equivalent in this three-dimensional structure.

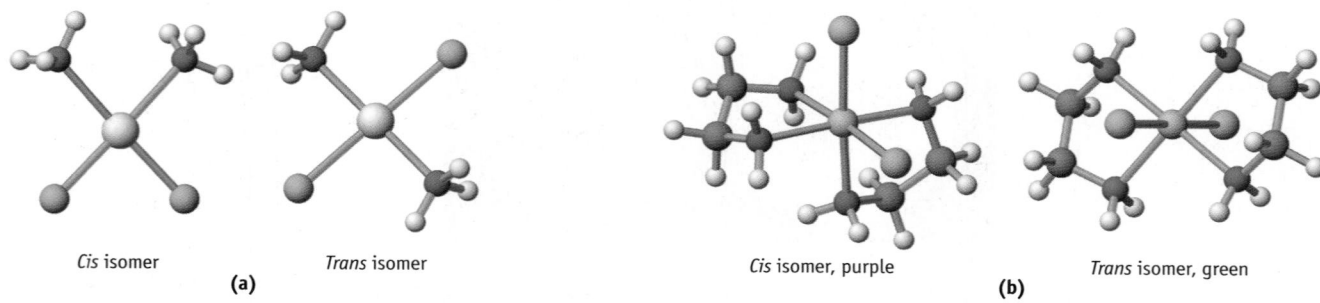

Cis isomer   *Trans* isomer   *Cis* isomer, purple   *Trans* isomer, green

(a)   **(b)**

FIGURE 22.18 *Cis-trans* isomers. (a) The square planar complex $Pt(NH_3)_2Cl_2$ can exist in two geometries, *cis* and *trans*. (b) Similarly, *cis* and *trans* octahedral isomers are possible for $[Co(en)_2Cl_2]^+$.

Another common type of geometric isomerism occurs for octahedral complexes with the general formula MX_3Y_3. A *fac* isomer has three identical ligands lying at the corners of a triangular face of an octahedron defined by the ligands (*fac* = facial), whereas the ligands follow a meridian in the *mer* isomer (*mer* = meridional). *Fac* and *mer* isomers of $Cr(NH_3)_3Cl_3$ are shown in Figure 22.19.

Optical Isomerism

■ **Optical Isomerism** Square-planar complexes are incapable of optical isomerism based at the metal center; mirror images are always superimposable. Chiral tetrahedral complexes are possible, but examples of complexes with a metal bonded tetrahedrally to four different monodentate ligands are rare.

Optical isomerism (chirality) occurs for octahedral complexes when the metal ion coordinates to three bidentate ligands or when the metal ion coordinates to two bidentate ligands and two monodentate ligands in a *cis* position. The complexes $[Co(en)_3]^{3+}$ and *cis*-$[Co(en)_2Cl_2]^+$, illustrated in Figure 22.20, are examples of chiral complexes. The diagnostic test for chirality is met with both species: Mirror images of these molecules are not superimposable (page 446). Solutions of the optical isomers rotate plane-polarized light in opposite directions.

Chemistry.⚗.Now™

Sign in at **www.cengage.com/login** and go to Chapter 22 Contents to see Screen 22.6 for an exercise on **isomerism in coordination chemistry.**

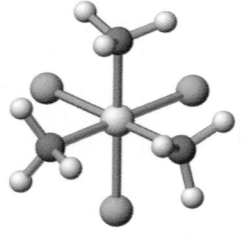

fac isomer

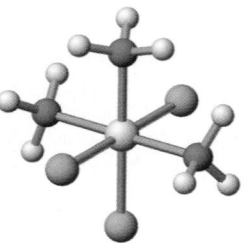

mer isomer

FIGURE 22.19 *Fac* and *mer* isomers of $Cr(NH_3)_3Cl_3$. In the *fac* isomer, the three chloride ligands (and the three ammonia ligands) are arranged at the corners of a triangular face. In the *mer* isomer, the three similar ligands follow a meridian.

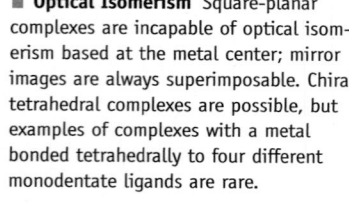

■ **EXAMPLE 22.4 Isomerism in Coordination Chemistry**

Problem For which of the following complexes do isomers exist? If isomers are possible, identify the type of isomerism (structural or geometric). Determine whether the coordination complex is capable of exhibiting optical isomerism.

(a) $[Co(NH_3)_4Cl_2]^+$ **(b)** $Pt(NH_3)_2(CN)_2$ (square planar)

(c) $Co(NH_3)_3Cl_3$ **(e)** $K_3[Fe(C_2O_4)_3]$

(d) $Zn(NH_3)_2Cl_2$ (tetrahedral)   **(f)** $[Co(NH_3)_5SCN]^{2+}$

Strategy Determine the number of ligands attached to the metal, and decide whether the ligands are monodentate or bidentate. Knowing how many donor atoms are coordinated to the metal (the coordination number) will allow you to establish the metal geometry. At that point, it is necessary to recall the possible types of isomers for each geometry. The only isomerism possible for square–planar complexes is geometric (*cis* and *trans*). Tetrahedral complexes do not have isomers. Six-coordinate metals of the formula MA_4B_2 can be either *cis* or *trans*. *Mer* and *fac* isomers are possible with a stoichiometry of MA_3B_3. Optical activity arises for metal complexes of the formula *cis*-M(bidentate)$_2X_2$ and M(bidentate)$_3$ (among others). Drawing pictures of the molecules will help you visualize the isomers.

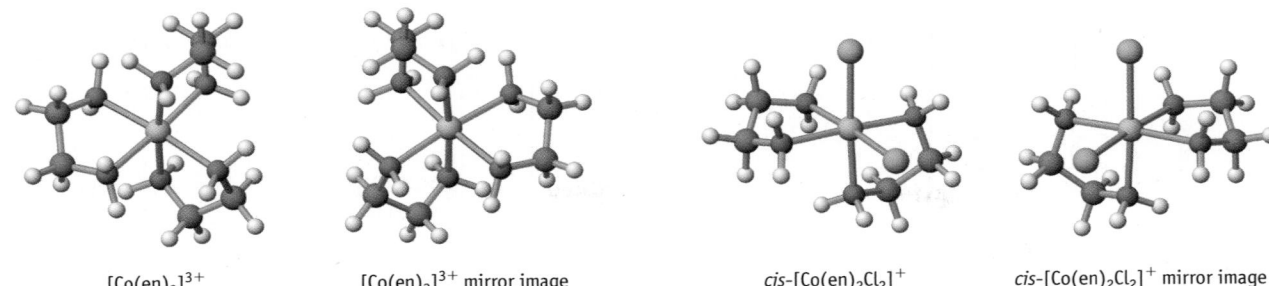

[Co(en)₃]³⁺   [Co(en)₃]³⁺ mirror image   cis-[Co(en)₂Cl₂]⁺   cis-[Co(en)₂Cl₂]⁺ mirror image

FIGURE 22.20 Chiral metal complexes. Both $[Co(en)_3]^{3+}$ and cis-$[Co(en)_2Cl_2]^+$ are chiral. Notice that the mirror images of the two compounds are not superimposable.

Solution

(a) Two geometric isomers can be drawn for octahedral complexes with a formula of MA_4B_2, such as this one. One isomer has two Cl^- ions in *cis* positions (adjacent positions, at a 90° angle), and the other isomer has the Cl^- ligands in *trans* positions (with a 180° angle between the ligands). Optical isomers are not possible.

cis isomer   *trans* isomer

(b) In this square-planar complex, the two NH_3 ligands (and the two CN^- ligands) can be either *cis* or *trans*. These are geometric isomers. Optical isomers are not possible.

cis isomer   *trans* isomer

(c) Two geometric isomers of this octahedral complex, with chloride ligands either *fac* or *mer*, are possible. In the *fac* isomer, the three Cl^- ligands are all at 90° to each other; in the *mer* isomer, two Cl^- ligands are at 180°, and the third is 90° from the other two. Optical isomers are not possible.

fac isomer   *mer* isomer

(d) Only a single structure is possible for tetrahedral complexes such as $Zn(NH_3)_2Cl_2$.

(e) Ignore the counterions, K^+. The anion is an octahedral complex—remember that the bidentate oxalate ion occupies two coordination sites of the metal, and that three oxalate ligands means that the metal has a coordination number of 6. Mirror images of complexes of the stoichiometry $M(bidentate)_3$ are not superimposable; therefore, two optical isomers are possible. (Here the ligands, $C_2O_4^{2-}$, are drawn abbreviated as O—O.)

Nonsuperimposable mirror images of $[Fe(ox)_3]^{3-}$

(f) Only linkage isomerism (structural isomerism) is possible for this octahedral cobalt complex. Either the sulfur or the nitrogen of the SCN^- anion can be attached to the cobalt(III) ion in this complex.

$$\begin{bmatrix} & NH_3 & \\ H_3N\cdots & | & \cdots NH_3 \\ & Co & \\ H_3N & | & SCN \\ & NH_3 & \end{bmatrix}^{2+} \quad \begin{bmatrix} & NH_3 & \\ H_3N\cdots & | & \cdots NH_3 \\ & Co & \\ H_3N & | & NCS \\ & NH_3 & \end{bmatrix}^{2+}$$

S-bonded SCN^- N-bonded SCN^-

EXERCISE 22.3 Isomers in Coordination Complexes

What types of isomers are possible for the following complexes?

(a) $K[Co(NH_3)_2Cl_4]$

(b) $Pt(en)Cl_2$ (square planar)

(c) $[Co(NH_3)_5Cl]^{2+}$

(d) $[Ru(phen)_3]Cl_3$

(e) $Na_2[MnCl_4]$ (tetrahedral)

(f) $[Co(NH_3)_5NO_2]^{2+}$

22.5 Bonding in Coordination Compounds

Metal–ligand bonding in a coordination complex was described earlier in this chapter as being covalent, resulting from the sharing of an electron pair between the metal and the ligand donor atom. Although frequently used, this description is not capable of explaining the color and magnetic behavior of complexes. As a consequence, the covalent bonding picture has now largely been superseded by two other bonding models: molecular orbital theory and ligand field theory.

The bonding model based on molecular orbital theory assumes that the metal and the ligand bond through the molecular orbitals formed by atomic orbital overlap between metal and ligand. The **ligand field model,** in contrast, focuses on repulsion (and destabilization) of electrons in the metal coordination sphere. The ligand field model also assumes that the positive metal ion and the negative ligand lone pair are attracted electrostatically; that is, the bond arises when a positively charged metal ion attracts a negative ion or the negative end of a polar molecule. For the most part, the molecular orbital and ligand field models predict similar, qualitative results regarding color and magnetic behavior. Here, we will focus on the ligand field approach and illustrate how it explains color and magnetism of transition metal complexes.

The *d* Orbitals: Ligand Field Theory

To understand ligand field theory, it is necessary to look at the *d* orbitals, particularly with regard to their orientation relative to the positions of ligands in a metal complex.

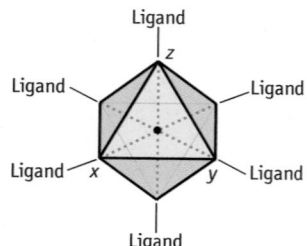

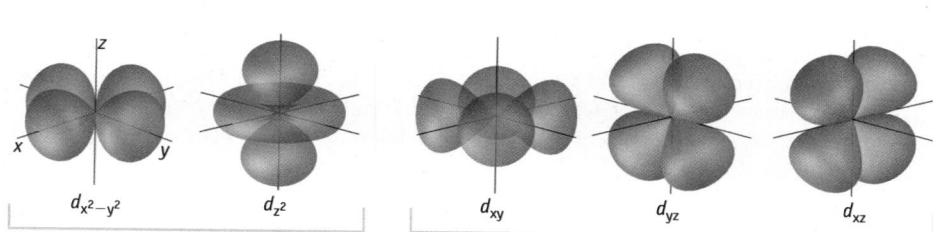

$d_{x^2-y^2}$ d_{z^2} d_{xy} d_{yz} d_{xz}

Orbitals are **along** x, y, z   Orbitals are **between** x, y, z

FIGURE 22.21 The *d* orbitals. The five *d* orbitals and their spatial relation to the ligands on the x-, y-, and z-axes.

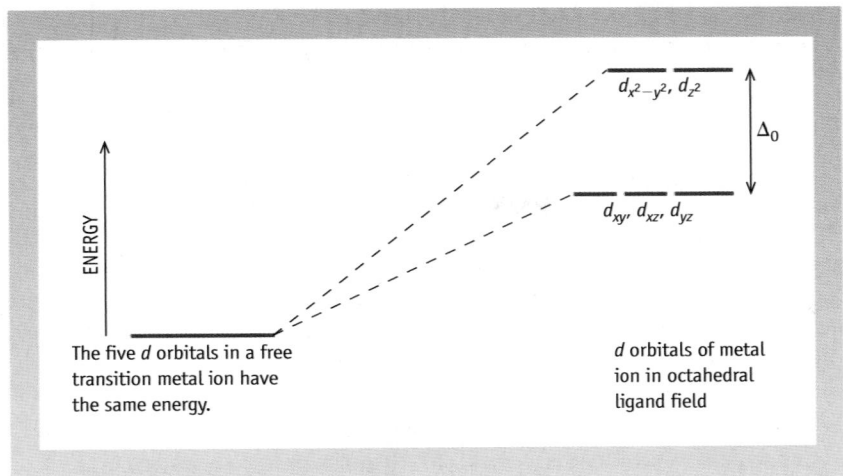

FIGURE 22.22 Ligand field splitting for an octahedral complex. The d-orbital energies increase as the ligands approach the metal along the x-, y-, and z-axes. The d_{xy}, d_{xz}, and d_{yz} orbitals, not pointed toward the ligands, are less destabilized than the $d_{x^2-y^2}$ and d_{z^2} orbitals. Thus, the d_{xy}, d_{xz}, and d_{yz} orbitals are at lower energy. (Δ_0 stands for the splitting in a octahedral ligand field.)

We look first at octahedral complexes. Assume the ligands in an octahedral complex lie along the x-, y-, and z-axes. This results in the five d orbitals (Figure 22.21) being subdivided into two sets: the $d_{x^2-y^2}$ and d_{z^2} orbitals in one set and the d_{xy}, d_{xz}, and d_{yz} orbitals in the second. The $d_{x^2-y^2}$ and d_{z^2} orbitals are directed along the x-, y-, and z-axes, whereas the orbitals of the second group are aligned between these axes.

In an isolated atom or ion, the five d orbitals have the same energy. For a metal atom or ion in a coordination complex, however, the d orbitals have different energies. According to the ligand field model, repulsion between d electrons on the metal and electron pairs of the ligands destabilizes electrons that reside in the d orbitals; that is, it causes their energy to increase. Electrons in the various d orbitals are not affected equally, however, because of their different orientations in space relative to the position of the ligand lone pairs (Figure 22.22). Electrons in the $d_{x^2-y^2}$ and d_{z^2} orbitals experience a larger repulsion because these orbitals point directly at the incoming ligand electron pairs. A smaller repulsive effect is experienced by electrons in the d_{xy}, d_{xz}, and d_{yz} orbitals. The difference in degree of repulsion means that an energy difference exists between the two sets of orbitals. This difference, called the **ligand field splitting** and denoted by the symbol Δ_0, is a function of the metal and the ligands and varies predictably from one complex to another.

A different splitting pattern is encountered with square-planar complexes (Figure 22.23). Assume that the four ligands are along the x- and y-axes. The $d_{x^2-y^2}$ orbital also points along these axes, so it has the highest energy. The d_{xy} orbital (which also lies in the xy-plane, but does not point at the ligands) is next highest in energy, followed by the d_{z^2} orbital. The d_{xz} and d_{yz} orbitals, both of which partially point in the z-direction, have the lowest energy.

The d-orbital splitting pattern for a tetrahedral complex is the reverse of the pattern observed for octahedral complexes. Three orbitals (d_{xz}, d_{xy}, d_{yz}) are higher in energy, whereas the $d_{x^2-y^2}$ and d_{z^2} orbitals are below them in energy (Figure 22.23).

Electron Configurations and Magnetic Properties

The d-orbital splitting in coordination complexes provides the means to explain both the magnetic behavior and the color of these complexes. To understand this explanation, however, we must first understand how to assign electrons to the various orbitals in each geometry.

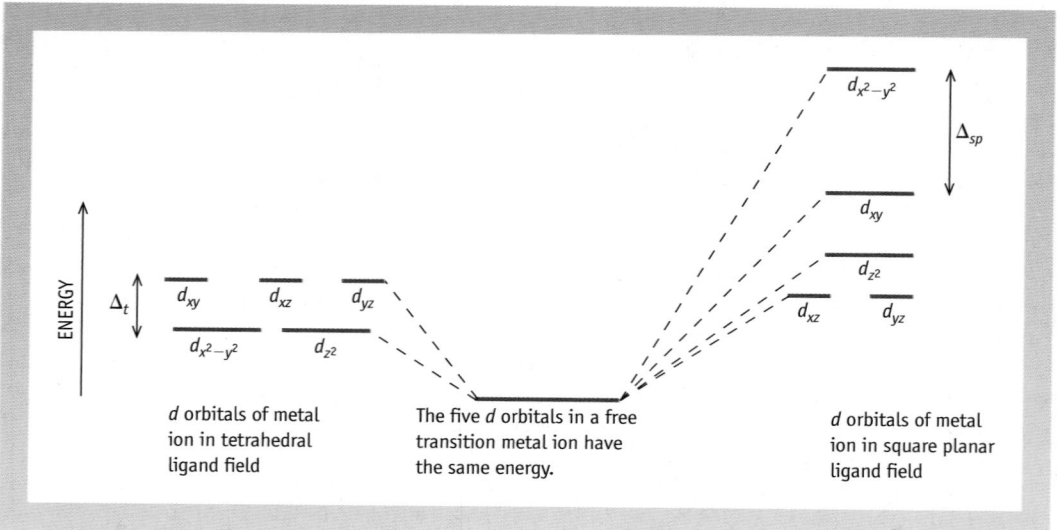

FIGURE 22.23 Splitting of the d orbitals in (*left*) tetrahedral and (*right*) square planar geometries. (Δ_t and Δ_{sp} are, respectively, the splitting in tetrahedral and square planar ligand fields.)

A gaseous Cr^{2+} ion has the electron configuration $[Ar]3d^4$. The term "gaseous" in this context is used to denote a single, isolated atom or ion with all other particles located an infinite distance away. In this situation, the five $3d$ orbitals have the same energy. The four electrons reside singly in different d orbitals, according to Hund's rule, and the Cr^{2+} ion has four unpaired electrons.

Cr(II) electron configuration

Cr^{2+} [Ar]$3d^4$ $\boxed{\uparrow|\uparrow|\uparrow|\uparrow|\,}$ $\boxed{}$

$3d$ $4s$

When the Cr^{2+} ion is part of an octahedral complex, the five d orbitals do not have identical energies. As illustrated in Figure 22.22, these orbitals divide into two sets, with the d_{xy}, d_{xz}, and d_{yz} orbitals having a lower energy than the $d_{x^2-y^2}$ and d_{z^2} orbitals. Having two sets of orbitals means that two different electron configurations are possible (Figure 22.24). Three of the four d electrons in Cr^{2+} are assigned to the lower-energy d_{xy}, d_{xz}, and d_{yz} orbitals. The fourth electron either can be assigned to an orbital in the higher-energy $d_{x^2-y^2}$ and d_{z^2} set or can pair up with an electron

FIGURE 22.24 High- and low-spin cases for an octahedral chromium(II) complex. (*left, high spin*) If the ligand field splitting (Δ_0) is smaller than the pairing energy (P), the electrons are placed in different orbitals, and the complex has four unpaired electrons. (*right, low spin*) If the splitting is larger than the pairing energy, all four electrons will be in the lower-energy orbital set. This requires pairing two electrons in one of the orbitals, so the complex will have two unpaired electrons.

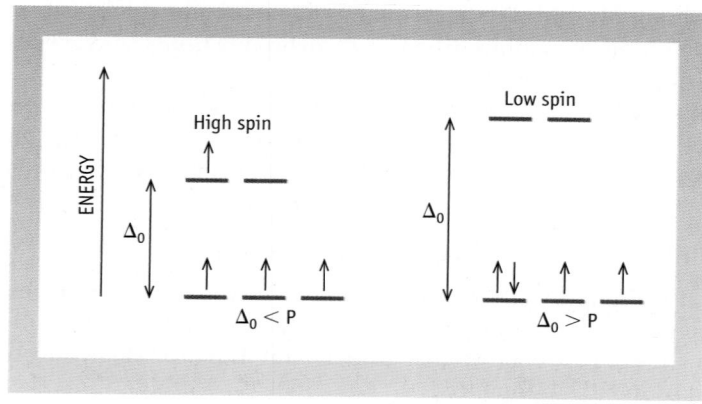

already in the lower-energy set. The first arrangement is called **high spin,** because it has the maximum number of unpaired electrons, four in the case of Cr^{2+}. The second arrangement is called **low spin,** because it has the minimum number of unpaired electrons possible.

At first glance, a high-spin configuration appears to contradict conventional thinking. It seems logical that the most stable situation would occur when electrons occupy the lowest-energy orbitals. A second factor intervenes, however. Because electrons are negatively charged, repulsion increases when they are assigned to the same orbital. This destabilizing effect bears the name **pairing energy.** The preference for an electron to be in the lowest-energy orbital and the pairing energy have opposing effects (Figure 22.24).

Low-spin complexes arise when the splitting of the d orbitals by the ligand field is large—that is, when Δ_0 has a large value. The energy gained by putting all of the electrons in the lowest-energy level is the dominant effect. In contrast, high-spin complexes occur if the value of Δ_0 is small.

For octahedral complexes, high- and low-spin complexes can occur only for configurations d^4 through d^7 (Figure 22.25). Complexes of the d^6 metal ion, Fe^{2+}, for example, can have either high spin or low spin. The complex formed when the Fe^{2+} ion is placed in water, $[Fe(H_2O)_6]^{2+}$, is high spin, whereas the $[Fe(CN)_6]^{4-}$ complex ion is low spin.

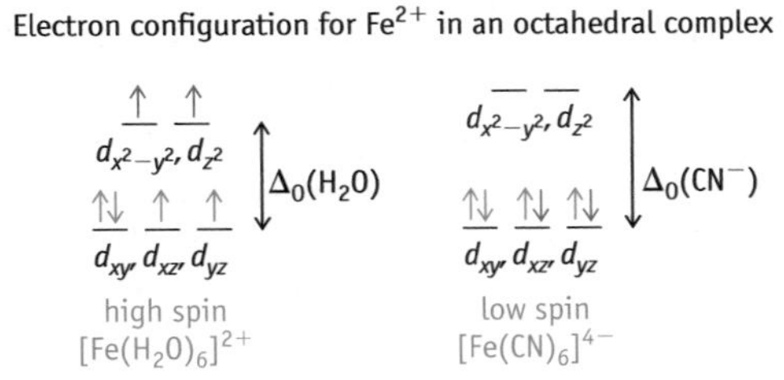

Electron configuration for Fe^{2+} in an octahedral complex

$$
\begin{array}{cc}
\text{high spin} & \text{low spin} \\
[Fe(H_2O)_6]^{2+} & [Fe(CN)_6]^{4-}
\end{array}
$$

$\Delta_0(H_2O)$ $\Delta_0(CN^-)$

It is possible to tell whether a complex is high or low spin by examining its magnetic behavior. The high-spin complex $[Fe(H_2O)_6]^{2+}$ has four unpaired electrons and is *paramagnetic* (attracted by a magnet), whereas the low-spin $[Fe(CN)_6]^{4-}$ complex has no unpaired electrons and is *diamagnetic* (repelled by a magnet) (◄ page 293).

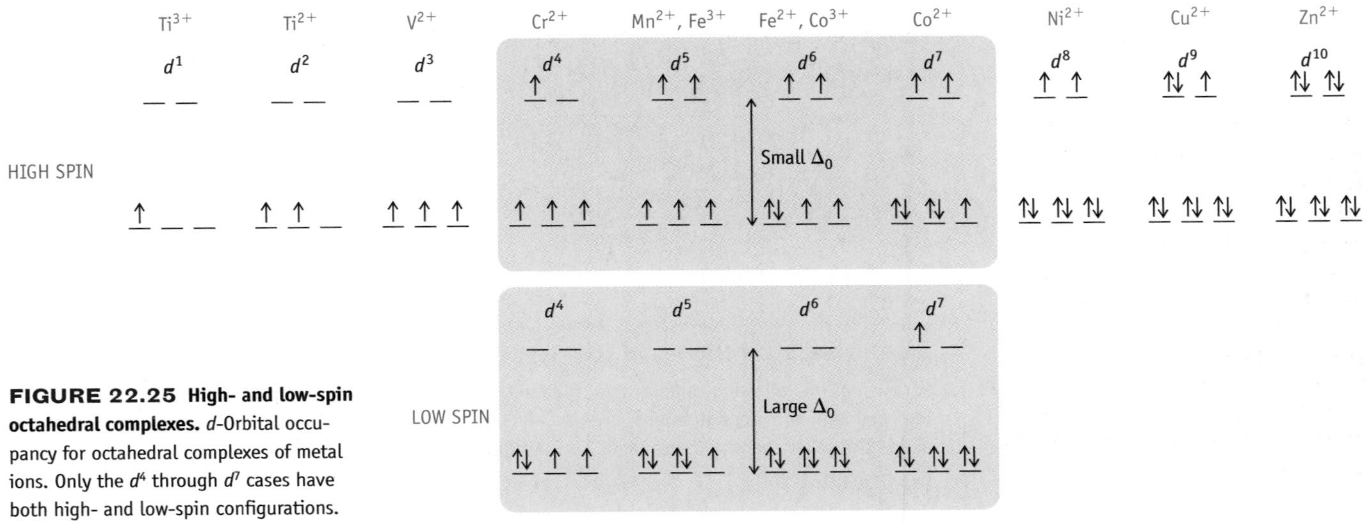

FIGURE 22.25 High- and low-spin octahedral complexes. *d*-Orbital occupancy for octahedral complexes of metal ions. Only the d^4 through d^7 cases have both high- and low-spin configurations.

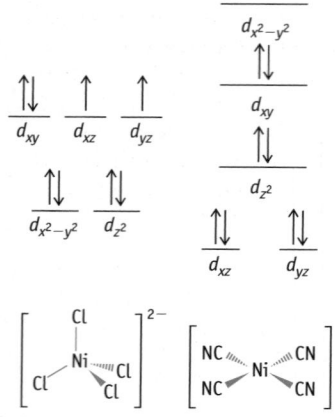

Nickel(II) complexes and magnetism. The anion $[NiCl_4]^{2-}$ is a paramagnetic tetrahedral complex. In contrast, $[Ni(CN)_4]^{2-}$ is a diamagnetic square-planar complex.

Most complexes of Pd^{2+} and Pt^{2+} ions are square planar, the electron configuration of these metals being [noble gas]$(n-1)d^8$. In a square-planar complex, there are four sets of orbitals (Figure 22.22). All except the highest-energy orbital are filled, and all electrons are paired, resulting in diamagnetic (low-spin) complexes.

Nickel, which is found above palladium in the periodic table, forms both square-planar and tetrahedral complexes. For example, the complex ion $[Ni(CN)_4]^{2-}$ is square planar, whereas the $[NiCl_4]^{2-}$ ion is tetrahedral. Magnetism allows us to differentiate between these two geometries. Based on the ligand field splitting pattern, the cyanide complex is expected to be diamagnetic, whereas the chloride complex is paramagnetic with two unpaired electrons.

Chemistry ⚗ Now™

Sign in at **www.cengage.com/login** and go to Chapter 22 Contents to see simulation of **bonding and electronic structure in transition metal complexes.**

■ **EXAMPLE 22.5 High- and Low-Spin Complexes and Magnetism**

Problem Give the electron configuration for each of the following complexes. How many unpaired electrons are present in each complex? Are the complexes paramagnetic or diamagnetic?

(a) low-spin $[Co(NH_3)_6]^{3+}$ 　　　　　　　**(b)** high-spin $[CoF_6]^{3-}$

Strategy These ions are complexes of Co^{3+}, which has a d^6 valence electron configuration. Set up an energy-level diagram for an octahedral complex. In low-spin complexes, the electrons are added preferentially to the lower-energy set of orbitals. In high-spin complexes, the first five electrons are added singly to each of the five orbitals, then additional electrons are paired with electrons in orbitals in the lower-energy set.

Solution

(a) The six electrons of the Co^{3+} ion fill the lower-energy set of orbitals entirely. This d^6 complex ion has no unpaired electrons and is diamagnetic.

(b) To obtain the electron configuration in high-spin $[CoF_6]^{3-}$, place one electron in each of the five d orbitals, and then place the sixth electron in one of the lower-energy orbitals. The complex has four unpaired electrons and is paramagnetic.

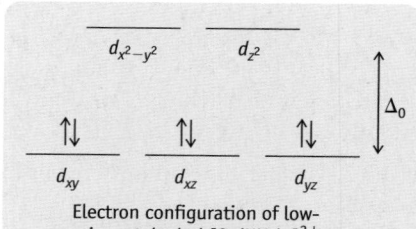

Electron configuration of low-spin, octahedral $[Co(NH_3)_6]^{3+}$

(a)

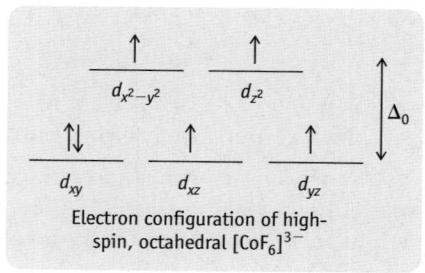

Electron configuration of high-spin, octahedral $[CoF_6]^{3-}$

(b)

EXERCISE 22.4 High- and Low-Spin Configurations and Magnetism

For each of the following complex ions, give the oxidation number of the metal, depict possible low- and high-spin configurations, give the number of unpaired electrons in each configuration, and tell whether each is paramagnetic or diamagnetic.

(a) $[Ru(H_2O)_6]^{2+}$ 　　　　　　　　　**(b)** $[Ni(NH_3)_6]^{2+}$

FIGURE 22.26 Aqueous solutions of some transition metal ions. Compounds of transition metal elements are often colored, whereas those of main group metals are usually colorless. Pictured here, from left to right, are solutions of the nitrate salts of Fe^{3+}, Co^{2+}, Ni^{2+}, Cu^{2+}, and Zn^{2+}.

22.6 Colors of Coordination Compounds

One of the most interesting features of compounds of the transition elements is their colors (Figure 22.26). In contrast, compounds of main group metals are usually colorless. The color of transition metal compounds results from *d*-orbital splitting. Before discussing how *d*-orbital splitting is involved, we need to look more closely at what we mean by color.

Color

Visible light, consisting of radiation with wavelengths from 400 to 700 nm (◄ Section 6.1), represents a very small portion of the electromagnetic spectrum. Within this region are all the colors you see when white light passes through a prism: red, orange, yellow, green, blue, indigo, and violet (ROY G BIV). Each color is identified with a portion of the wavelength range.

Isaac Newton did experiments with light and established that the mind's perception of color requires only three colors! When we see white light, we are seeing a mixture of all of the colors—in other words, the superposition of red, green, and blue. If one or more of these colors is absent, the light of the other colors that reaches your eyes is interpreted by your mind as color.

Figure 22.27 will help you in analyzing perceived colors. This color wheel shows the three primary colors—red, green, and blue—as overlapping disks arranged in a triangle. The secondary colors—cyan, magenta, and yellow—appear where two disks overlap. The overlap of all three disks in the center produces white light.

The colors we perceive are determined as follows:

- Light of a single primary color is perceived as that color: Red light is perceived as red, green light as green, blue light as blue.
- Light made up of two primary colors is perceived as the color shown where the disks in Figure 22.27 overlap: Red and green light together appear yellow; green and blue light together are perceived as cyan; and red and blue light are perceived as magenta.
- Light made up of the three primary colors is white (colorless).

In discussing the color of a substance such as a coordination complex *in solution*, these guidelines are turned around.

- Red color is the result of the absence of green and blue light from white light.
- Green color results if red and blue light are absent from white light.
- Blue color results if red and green light are absent.

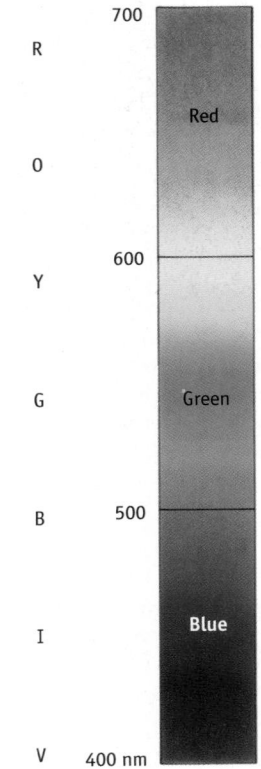

The ROY G BIV spectrum of colors of visible light. The colors used in printing this book are cyan, magenta, yellow, and black. The blue in ROY G BIV is actually cyan, according to color industry standards. Magenta doesn't have its own wavelength region. Rather, it is a mixture of blue and red.

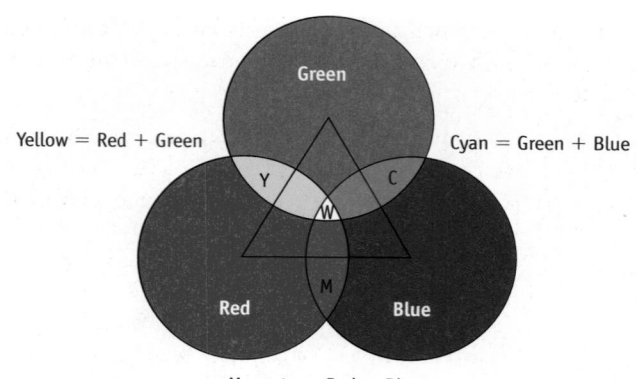

FIGURE 22.27 Using color disks to analyze colors. The three primary colors are red, green, and blue. Adding light of two primary colors gives the secondary colors yellow (= red + green), cyan (= green + blue), and magenta (= red + blue). Adding all three primary colors results in white light.

Charles D. Winters

FIGURE 22.28 Light absorption and color. The color of a solution is due to the color of the light *not* absorbed by the solution. Here, a solution of Ni^{2+} ion in water absorbs red and blue light and so appears green. See also Figures 4.15–4.19.

■ **Spectrophotometry** See Section 4.8 for a description of spectrophotometry.

The secondary colors are rationalized similarly. Absorption of blue light gives yellow (the color across from it in Figure 22.27); absorption of red light results in cyan; and absorption of green light results in magenta.

Now we can apply these ideas to explain colors in transition metal complexes. Focus on what kind of light is *absorbed*. A solution of $[Ni(H_2O)_6]^{2+}$ is green. Green light is the result of removing red and blue light from white light. As white light passes through an aqueous solution of Ni^{2+}, red and blue light are absorbed, and green light is allowed to pass (Figure 22.28). Similarly, the $[Co(NH_3)_6]^{3+}$ ion is yellow because blue light has been absorbed and red and green light pass through.

The Spectrochemical Series

Recall that atomic spectra are obtained when electrons are excited from one energy level to another (◄ Section 6.3). The energy of the light absorbed or emitted is related to the energy levels of the atom or ion under study. The concept that light is absorbed when electrons move from lower to higher energy levels applies to all substances, not just atoms. It is the basic premise for the absorption of light for transition metal coordination complexes.

In coordination complexes, the splitting between d orbitals often corresponds to the energy of visible light, so light in the visible region of the spectrum is absorbed when electrons move from a lower-energy d orbital to a higher-energy d orbital. This change, as an electron moves between two orbitals having different energies in a complex, is called a ***d*-to-*d* transition.** Qualitatively, such a transition for $[Co(NH_3)_6]^{3+}$ might be represented using an energy-level diagram such as that shown here.

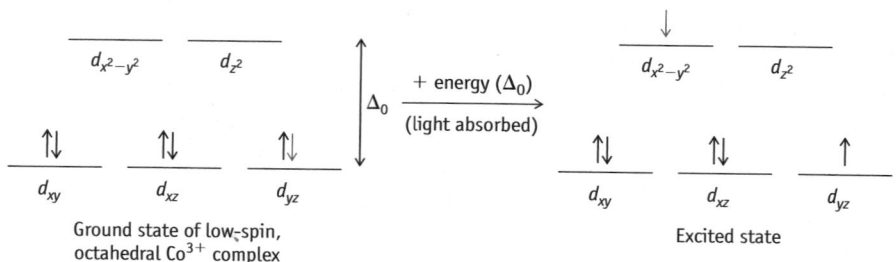

Experiments with coordination complexes reveal that, for a given metal ion, some ligands cause a small energy separation of the d orbitals, whereas others cause a large separation. In other words, some ligands create a small ligand field, and others create a large one. An example is seen in the spectroscopic data for several cobalt(III) complexes presented in Table 22.3.

- Both $[Co(NH_3)_6]^{3+}$ and $[Co(en)_3]^{3+}$ are yellow-orange, because they absorb light in the blue portion of the visible spectrum. These compounds have very similar spectra, to be expected because both have six amine-type donor atoms (H—NH_2 or R—NH_2).
- Although $[Co(CN)_6]^{3-}$ does not have an absorption band in the visible region, it is pale yellow. Light absorption occurs in the ultraviolet region, but the absorption is broad and extends minimally into the visible (blue) region.
- $[Co(C_2O_4)_3]^{3-}$ and $[Co(H_2O)_6]^{3+}$ have similar absorptions, in the yellow and violet regions. Their colors are shades of green with a small difference due to the relative amount of light of each color being absorbed.

The absorption maxima among the listed complexes range from 700 nm for $[CoF_6]^{3-}$ to 310 nm for $[Co(CN)_6]^{3-}$. The ligands change from member to member of this series, and we can conclude that the energy of the light absorbed by the complex is related to the different ligand field splittings, Δ_0, caused by the different ligands. Fluoride ion causes the smallest splitting of the d orbitals among the complexes listed in Table 22.3, whereas cyanide causes the largest splitting.

Spectra of complexes of other metals provide similar results. Based on this information, ligands can be listed in order of their ability to split the d orbitals. This list is called the **spectrochemical series** because it was determined by spectroscopy. A short list, with some of the more common ligands, follows:

$$F^-, Cl^-, Br^-, I^- < C_2O_4{}^{2-} < H_2O < NH_3 = en < phen < CN^-$$

small orbital splitting   large orbital splitting
small Δ_0 large Δ_0

The spectrochemical series is applicable to a wide range of metal complexes. Indeed, the ability of ligand field theory to explain the differences in the colors of the transition metal complexes is one of the strengths of this theory.

Based on the relative position of a ligand in the series, predictions can be made about a compound's magnetic behavior. Recall that d^4, d^5, d^6, and d^7 complexes can be high or low spin, depending on the ligand field splitting, Δ_0. Complexes

TABLE 22.3 The Colors of Some Co^{3+} Complexes*

Complex Ion	Wavelength of Light Absorbed (nm)	Color of Light Absorbed	Color of Complex
$[CoF_6]^{3-}$	700	Red	Green
$[Co(C_2O_4)_3]^{3-}$	600, 420	Yellow, violet	Dark green
$[Co(H_2O)_6]^{3+}$	600, 400	Yellow, violet	Blue-green
$[Co(NH_3)_6]^{3+}$	475, 340	Blue, ultraviolet	Yellow-orange
$[Co(en)_3]^{3+}$	470, 340	Blue, ultraviolet	Yellow-orange
$[Co(CN)_6]^{3-}$	310	Ultraviolet	Pale yellow

*The complex with fluoride ion, $[CoF_6]^{3-}$, is high spin and has one absorption band. The other complexes are low spin and have two absorption bands. In all but one case, one of these absorptions occurs in the visible region of the spectrum. The wavelengths are measured at the top of that absorption band.

formed with ligands near the left end of the spectrochemical series are expected to have small Δ_0 values and, therefore, are likely to be high spin. In contrast, complexes with ligands near the right end are expected to have large Δ_0 values and low-spin configurations. The complex $[CoF_6]^{3-}$ is high spin, whereas $[Co(NH_3)_6]^{3+}$ and the other complexes in Table 22.3 are low spin.

Chemistry⸱☌⸱Now™

Sign in at **www.cengage.com/login** and go to Chapter 22 Contents to see Screen 22.8 for a simulation on **the absorption and transmission of light by transition metal complexes.**

■ **EXAMPLE 22.6** **Spectrochemical Series**

Problem An aqueous solution of $[Fe(H_2O)_6]^{2+}$ is light blue-green. Do you expect the d^6 Fe^{2+} ion in this complex to have a high- or low-spin configuration? How would you make this determination by conducting an experiment?

Strategy Use the color wheel in Figure 22.27. The color of the complex, blue-green, tells us what kind of light is transmitted (blue and green), from which we learn what kind of light has been absorbed (red). Red light is at the low-energy end of the visible spectrum. From this fact, we can predict that the d-orbital splitting must be small. Our answer to the question derives from that conclusion.

Solution The low energy of the light absorbed suggests that $[Fe(H_2O)_6]^{2+}$ is likely to be a high-spin complex.

If the complex is high spin, it will have four unpaired electrons and be paramagnetic; if it is low spin, it will have no unpaired electrons and be diamagnetic. Identifying the presence of four unpaired electrons by measuring the compound's magnetism can be used to verify the high-spin configuration experimentally.

22.7 Organometallic Chemistry: The Chemistry of Low-Valent Metal–Organic Complexes

One of the largest and most active areas of chemistry over the past half-century has been the field of organometallic chemistry, the study of molecules having metal–carbon bonds. Thousands of such compounds have been made and characterized, and much of the activity has involved transition metals. Many have unique bonding modes and structures. In recent years, organometallic compounds have also found

There are many naturally occurring metal-based molecules such as heme, vitamin B_{12}, and the enzyme involved in fixing nitrogen (nitrogenase). Chemists have also synthesized various metal-based compounds for medical purposes. One of these, *cisplatin* [$PtCl_2(NH_3)_2$], was known for many years, but it was discovered serendipitously to be effective in treatment of certain kinds of cancers.

In 1965, Barnett Rosenberg, a biophysicist at Michigan State University, set out to study the effect of electric fields on living cells, but the results of his experiments were very different from his expectations. He and his students had placed an aqueous suspension of live *Escherichia coli* bacteria in an electric field between supposedly inert platinum electrodes. Much to their surprise, they found that cell growth was significantly affected. After careful experimentation, the effect on cell division was found to be due to a trace of the complex $PtCl_4(NH_3)_2$ formed by an electrolytic process involving the platinum electrode in the presence of ammonia in the growth medium.

To follow up on this interesting discovery, Rosenberg and his students tested the effect of *cis-* and *trans-*$PtCl_2(NH_3)_2$ on cell growth and found that only the *cis* isomer was effective. This led Rosenberg and others to study the effect of so-called *cisplatin* on cancer cell

$k = 7.6 \times 10^{-5} \text{ s}^{-1}$ $pK_a = 6.6$ $k = 2.3 \times 10^{-4} \text{ s}^{-1}$ $pK_a = 5.5$ $pK_a = 7.3$

growth, and the result is that cisplatin and similar compounds are now used to treat genitourinary tumors. In fact, testicular cancer in particular is now considered largely curable because of cisplatin chemotherapy.

The chemistry of cisplatin has now been thoroughly studied and illustrates many of the principles of transition metal coordination chemistry. It has been found that cisplatin has a half-life of 2.5 h for the replacement of a Cl^- ligand by water at 310 K (in a first order reaction) and that the replacement of a second Cl^- ligand by water is slightly faster.

The aqua species are acidic and damaging to the kidneys, so cisplatin is generally used in a saline solution to prevent the hydrolysis reactions. It has been found that, in blood plasma at pH 7.4 and with a Cl^- ion concentration of about 1.04×10^{-5} M, $PtCl_2(NH_3)_2$

and $PtCl(OH)(NH_3)_2$ are the dominant species. In the cell nucleus, however, the Cl^- ion concentration is lower, and the aqua species are present in higher concentration.

Questions:
1. If a patient is given 10.0 mg of cisplatin, what quantity remains as cisplatin at 24 hours?
2. At a pH of 7.4, what is the ratio of concentrations of $[PtCl(NH_3)_2(H_2O)]^+$ and $PtCl(NH_3)_2(OH)$?

Answers to these questions are in Appendix Q.

---

particularly widespread use as reagents in organic synthesis and as catalysts for economically important chemical reactions.

Carbon Monoxide Complexes of Metals

In the earlier discussion of hemoglobin (page 1033), you learned that the iron in this biologically important complex binds not only to O_2 but also to CO. Our understanding of metal–CO complexes, however, emerged from the solution to a problem in industrial chemistry at the end of the 19th century.

The synthesis of sodium carbonate from NaCl, CO_2, NH_3, and H_2O by the Solvay process was an important chemical industry in the late 19th century (and remains so today in some parts of the world; page 974). In the late 1800s, a Solvay plant in England had a problem: the valves used to conduct the gaseous reactants and products rapidly corroded. A German chemist, Ludwig Mond (1839–1909), traced this problem to a small quantity of CO in the gas stream. Carbon monoxide gas reacted with nickel metal in the valves to form $Ni(CO)_4$ (Figure 22.29), tetracarbonyl nickel, a volatile liquid with a low boiling point (bp 47 °C). The deterioration of the valves occurred when the gaseous $Ni(CO)_4$ that formed was carried away in the effluent gas stream.

$$Ni(s) + 4\ CO(g) \rightleftharpoons Ni(CO)_4(g)$$

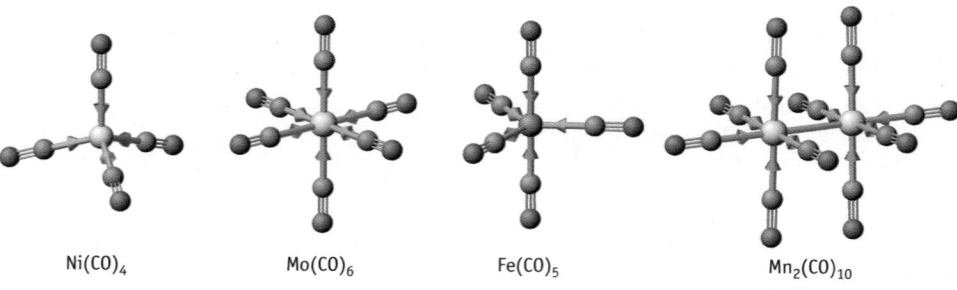

FIGURE 22.29 Metals carbonyls. $Ni(CO)_4$ is a tetrahedral molecule. Pentacarbonyliron(0) [$Fe(CO)_5$] is trigonal bipyramidal, whereas $Mo(CO)_6$ is octahedral, and the geometry around the manganese atom in $Mn_2(CO)_{10}$ is likewise octahedral (with the sixth position being an Mn—Mn bond).

$Ni(CO)_4$ $Mo(CO)_6$ $Fe(CO)_5$ $Mn_2(CO)_{10}$

■ **Terminology in Organometallic Chemistry** The standard terminology of coordination chemistry applies to metal carbonyls. In tetracarbonylnickel(0), for example, the metal is formally zerovalent, and CO molecules are ligands. The metal has a coordination number of 4 and a tetrahedral coordination geometry.

Mond determined that the reaction forming $Ni(CO)_4$ is reversible; at moderate temperatures or at low pressures, CO is liberated, and nickel metal reforms. He then exploited the formation and decomposition reactions in a process to obtain pure nickel. Nickel and cobalt are generally found together in nature. Because of this, the two metals are obtained together when ores are refined, and they are difficult to separate. However, if a mixture of the metals is exposed to CO, nickel is converted to $Ni(CO)_4$ whereas cobalt is unchanged. Volatile $Ni(CO)_4$ is easily separated from solid cobalt metal. The $Ni(CO)_4$ can then be decomposed to give pure nickel. The Mond process, as it is now known, was the preferred procedure to obtain pure nickel for the first half of the 20th century.

Nickel is unique among metals in its facile reaction with CO, but many other transition metal carbonyl compounds are now known and can be synthesized by a variety of procedures. One of the most common is reductive carbonylation, in which a metal salt is reduced in the presence of CO, usually under high pressure. In effect, reduction of the metal salt gives metal atoms. Before these very reactive atoms aggregate to form the unreactive bulk metal, however, they react with CO. Metal carbonyls of most of the transition metals can be made by this route. Simple examples include hexacarbonyls of the Group 6B metals [$Cr(CO)_6$, $Mo(CO)_6$, and $WCO)_6$,] as well as $Fe(CO)_5$ and $Mn_2(CO)_{10}$ (Figure 22.29).

The Effective Atomic Number Rule and Bonding in Organometallic Compounds

An important observation has guided researchers studying these metal–CO complexes and other organometallic compounds. The **effective atomic number (EAN) rule,** now often referred to as the **18-electron rule,** states that compounds in which the sum of the metal valence electrons plus the electrons donated by the ligand groups totals 18 are likely to be stable. Thus, the 18-electron rule predicts the stoichiometry of a number of compounds. Iron(0), for example, which has eight valence electrons, would be expected to coordinate to five CO ligands. Each CO donates two electrons for a total of 10; adding these to the eight valence electrons on the metal gives 18 electrons around the Fe atom (Figure 22.30). We now recognize that the 18-electron rule is similar to the octet rule in main group chemistry, in that it defines the likely number of bonds to an element.

The bonding in traditional coordination compounds is described as being due to attractive forces between a positively charged metal ion and a polar molecule or an anion, and the properties of these species are in accord with substantial ionic character to the metal-ligand bond. In metal carbonyls, the zerovalent metal lacks a charge, and CO is only slightly polar. Both features argue against ionic bonding. The best model for these species instead describes the bonding between

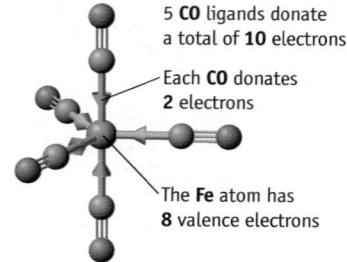

5 **CO** ligands donate a total of **10** electrons

Each **CO** donates **2** electrons

The **Fe** atom has **8** valence electrons

FIGURE 22.30 The EAN rule and $Fe(CO)_5$. The EAN or 18-electron rule states that stable organometallic compounds frequently have 18 valence electrons around the central metal. (There are also many 16-electron molecules, particularly of the heavier transition metals. See Study Question 22.34.) Here, the zerovalent Fe atom has the configuration [Ar]$3d^64s^2$, so eight valence electrons are available for bonding.

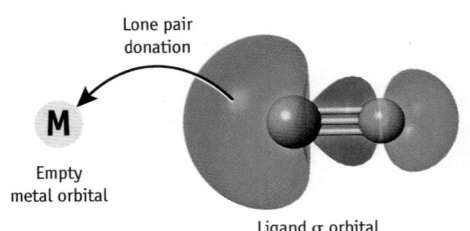

Lone pair donation

M

Empty metal orbital

Ligand σ orbital

Ligand to metal sigma bonding.
Donation of **CO** lone pair to empty orbital on **M**.

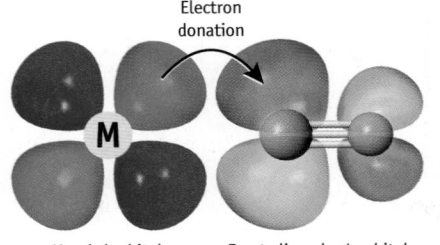

Electron donation

M

Metal *d* orbital   Empty ligand π* orbital

Metal to ligand pi bonding.
Donation of electrons from filled **M** *d* orbital to empty pi* antibonding orbital on **CO**.

FIGURE 22.31 Bonding in metal carbonyls. The current understanding is that the CO ligand donates a lone pair of electrons to the low-valent metal to form a sigma bond. The electron-rich metal then donates electrons from a *d* orbital to the antibonding π* orbital of the CO. There is a "synergistic" effect; the sigma and pi bonds complement each other.

the metal and CO as covalent. Each CO donates a C-atom lone pair to the metal atom to form a sigma bond (Figure 22.31). However, carbon monoxide is a very poor donor, and this alone would not lead to these species being stable. Rather, in conjunction with the sigma bond, the electron-rich metal donates a pair of electrons to form a π bond formed by overlap of a *d* orbital of the metal and a π* antibonding orbital of CO. The latter interaction is described as *d*π–*p*π bonding. Based on this model of bonding, carbon monoxide in these compounds is best described as a σ donor and π acceptor ligand.

Ligands in Organometallic Compounds

The bonding model for metal–CO complexes leads to important conclusions: only metals of low charge and with filled or partially filled *d* orbitals can form stable bonds to CO, and only ligands capable of forming π bonds with the metal are capable of forming low-valent metal compounds. Thus, this area is dominated by low-valent metals and special types of ligands that are capable of π bonding.

Some of the most common ligands in coordination chemistry cannot engage in π bonding and thus cannot form low-valent compounds with transition metals. For example, low-valent metal complexes with NH_3 or amines (such as $N(CH_3)_3$) do not exist, but phosphine complexes of zerovalent metals are well known. Phosphines, such as $P(CH_3)_3$, are the phosphorus analogs of amines and so have a lone pair of electrons on the P atom. Thus, phosphines can donate this lone pair to a metal to form a sigma bond. In addition, phosphorus atoms have empty 3*d* orbitals, and these can form a *d*π–*p*π bond with the filled *d*-orbitals of a low-valent metal. Ammonia, with no empty valence orbitals to overlap with a filled metal *d* orbitals, cannot form such π bonds.

Yet another class of molecules that can serve as ligands in organometallic compounds are organic species such as ethylene (C_2H_4) and benzene (C_6H_6). For example, in the anion of Zeise's salt, ethylene binds to a Pt^{2+} ion through donation of the two π electrons of the double bond (Figure 22.32). As in metal carbonyls, there is also a metal-to-ligand π bond formed by overlap of filled metal *d* orbitals with the antibonding π orbitals from the ligand. This combination of bonding modes strengthens the metal-ligand bond.

Benzene can be thought of as a tridentate ligand capable of donating three π electron pairs to a metal atom (which then donates *d* electrons back to the ligand in a π-type interaction). Such molecules also obey the 18-electron rule. For example, in dibenzenechromium (Figure 22.33), the Cr(0) atom with six valence electrons is bound to two ligands, each donating six electrons.

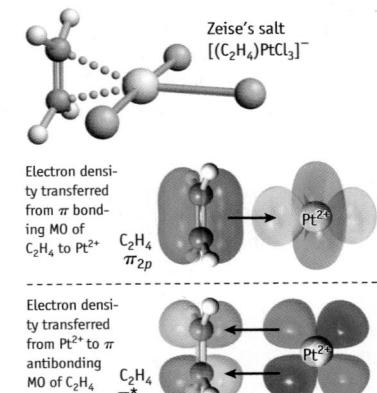

Zeise's salt [(C₂H₄)PtCl₃]⁻

Electron density transferred from π bonding MO of C_2H_4 to Pt^{2+} C_2H_4 π_{2p}

Electron density transferred from Pt^{2+} to π antibonding MO of C_2H_4 C_2H_4 π^*_{2p}

FIGURE 22.32 Bonding in the anion of Zeise's salt.

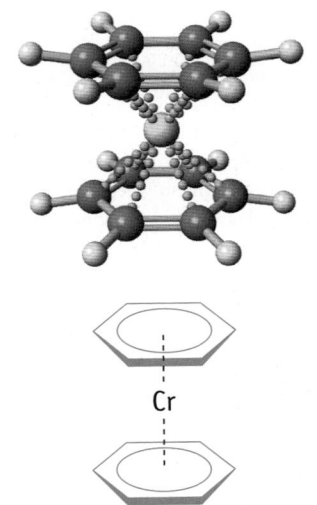

Cr

FIGURE 22.33 Dibenzenechromium. Two views of the molecule. Top: a computer-generated model. Bottom: a line drawing typically used by chemists.

Unexpected discoveries open up new areas of science. One example was the synthesis of compounds of Xe (page 405), a result that destroyed the myth that the noble gases were unreactive and led to a rich chemistry of these elements. At approximately the same time, another discovery, the synthesis of ferrocene, $Fe(C_5H_5)_2$, set the stage for the rapid and exciting growth of organometallic chemistry, the chemistry of compounds containing metal–carbon bonds. This destroyed another common myth of the time, that metal–carbon bonds are inherently unstable. Xenon compounds and ferrocene spearheaded a renaissance in inorganic chemistry that continues to this day.

The synthesis of ferrocene in two quite dissimilar research laboratories was accidental and unexpected. The first report, from an academic laboratory, described the reaction of the cyclopentadienide anion, $[C_5H_5]^-$ with $FeCl_2$. This reaction was intended to provide a precursor to an elusive organic compound fulvalene, $(C_5H_4)_2$ but a completely new substance—ferrocene—was obtained instead. The second report, from an industrial laboratory, described a high temperature process in which cyclopentadiene was passed over a liquid ammonia catalyst that contained, among other things, iron(II) oxide.

$2\ C_5H_5MgCl + FeCl_2 \rightarrow Fe(\eta^5\text{-}C_5H_5)_2 + MgCl_2$
(in diethyl ether)

$2\ C_5H_6(g) + FeO(s) \rightarrow Fe(\eta^5\text{-}C_5H_5)_2(s) + H_2O(g)$
(at high temperature)

The properties of ferrocene were unexpected. Ferrocene is a diamagnetic orange solid, has a relatively low melting (mp 173 °C), and is soluble in organic solvents but not in water. Most striking is its thermal and oxidative stability. Ferrocene is unaffected by oxygen,

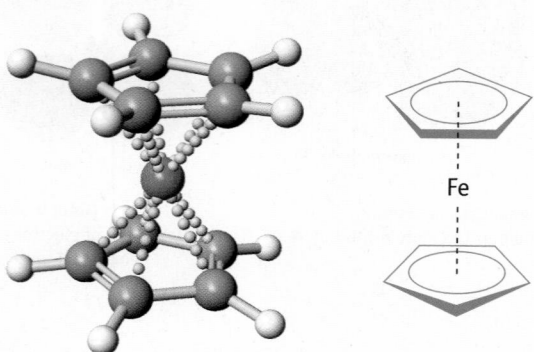

The structure of ferrocene, $Fe(\eta^5\text{-}C_5H_5)_2$

water, aqueous bases and nonoxidizing acids under ambient conditions, and can be heated to over 450 °C. These observations contradicted conventional wisdom that held that metal–carbon bonds were weak and unstable, hard to make, and reactive.

The structure of ferrocene was quickly established by x-ray crystallography. Like dibenzenechromium (Figure 22.23), ferrocene is a molecular "sandwich" compound, containing an iron atom sandwiched between two planar hydrocarbon rings (Figure). Iron(II), a d^6 metal ion, is in its low spin configuration. The cyclopentadienyl anions can be thought of as tridentate ligands with the six π electrons (three pairs) of each organic ring being donated to the metal ion.

Once the structure of ferrocene was known, the race was on to make other complexes with unsaturated hydrocarbon ligands. Synthesis of cyclopentadienyl compounds of other metals soon followed, and now hundreds are known in combination with CO, benzene, ethylene, and many other carbon-containing compounds. The discovery of ferrocene was one of the keys that unlocked the field of organometallic chemistry.

Questions:

1. Rationalize ferrocene's diamagnetism.

2. Dibenzenechromium is also a "sandwich" compound. What is the oxidation state of chromium in this compound? Is it diamagnetic or paramagnetic?

3. Do ferrocene and dibenzenechromium obey the 18-electron rule (page 1048)?

4. Ferrocene can be oxidized to form the ferrocenium cation, $[Fe(\eta\text{-}C_5H_5)_2]^+$. The standard reduction potential for the ferrocenium–ferrocene half-reaction is 0.400 V. Identify several oxidizing agents in Appendix M that are capable of oxidizing ferrocene. Is elemental chlorine, Cl_2, a sufficiently strong oxidizing agent to carry out this oxidation?

5. Write an equation for one way to synthesize nickelocene, $Ni(\eta^5\text{-}C_5H_5)_2$. Nickelocene is paramagnetic. Predict the number of unpaired electrons in this compound.

Answers to these questions are in Appendix Q.

Dibenzenechromium is one of many organometallic compounds often referred to as "sandwich" compounds. (See *Case Study: Ferrocene.*) These are molecular compounds in which a low-valent metal atom is "sandwiched" between two organic ligands. In addition, they are often referred to as π complexes because the π electrons of the ligand are involved in bonding. Modern terminology uses the Greek letter eta (η) to indicate this type of attachment, so dibenzenechromium is properly symbolized as $Cr(\eta^6\text{-}C_6H_6)_2$ (where the superscript 6 indicates the number of carbon atoms involved in bonding on each ligand).

Problem Show that each of the following molecules or ions satisfies the EAN rule.

(a) $[Fe(CO)_2](\eta^5\text{-}C_5H_5)]^-$

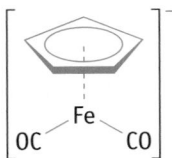

(b) $[Mn(CO)_5]^-$

(c) $Co(C_2H_4)_2(\eta^5\text{-}C_5H_5)$

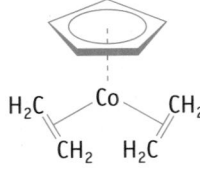

Strategy A complex obeys the EAN rule if the total number of electrons around the metal (valence electrons from the metal itself + electrons donated by the ligands) equals 18. Recognize that CO and C_2H_4 are both two-electron donors and that $C_5H_5^-$ is a six-electron donor. For the metal center, take its total number of valence electrons, and add or subtract electrons as necessary to adjust for negative or positive charges.

Solution

(a) The overall charge is $1-$, which is equal to the charge on the $C_5H_5^-$ group. Thus, the Fe atom must have no charge.

> 6 electrons for $C_5H_5^-$ + 8 electrons for Fe + 4 electrons for 2 CO groups = 18 electrons

(b) Because CO is neutral the Mn center must have a negative charge. This means the manganese center has effectively eight valence electrons. Together with the five CO groups, each donating two electrons, the total is 18 electrons.

(c) This is a neutral molecule, so the negative charge on the $C_5H_5^-$ group must be balanced by a positive charge on Co. The Co^+ ion has eight valence electrons. Each C_2H_4 molecule donates two electrons.

> 6 electrons for $C_5H_5^-$ + 8 electrons for Co^+ + 4 electrons for 2 C_2H_4 molecules = 18 electrons

---

EXERCISE 22.5 **The Effective Atomic Number Rule**

Show that the two molecules below satisfy the EAN rule.

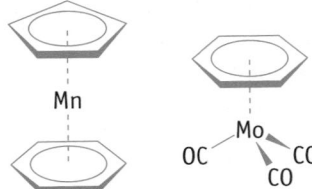

Chapter Goals Revisited

Chemistry ⊙ Now™ Sign in at **www. cengage.com/login** to:

- Assess your understanding with Study Questions in OWL keyed to each goal in the Goals and Homework menu for this chapter
- For quick review, download Go Chemistry mini-lecture flashcard modules (or purchase them at **www.ichapters.com**)
- Check your readiness for an exam by taking the Pre-Test and exploring the modules recommended in your Personalized Study plan.

❓ Access **How Do I Solve It?** tutorials on how to approach problem solving using concepts in this chapter.

Now that you have studied this chapter, you should ask whether you have met the chapter goals. In particular, you should be able to:

Identify and explain the chemical and physical properties of the transition elements
  a. Identify the general classes of transition elements (Section 22.1).
  b. Identify the transition metals from their symbols and positions in the periodic table, and recall some physical and chemical properties (Section 22.1).
  c. Understand the electrochemical nature of corrosion (Section 22.1).
  d. Describe the metallurgy of iron and copper (Section 22.2).

Understand the composition, structure, and bonding in coordination compounds
  a. Given the formula for a coordination complex, identify the metal and its oxidation state, the ligands, the coordination number and coordination geometry, and the overall charge on the complex (Section 22.3). Relate names and formulas of complexes. Study Question(s) assignable in OWL: 18, 20, 48, 57.
  b. Given the formula for a complex, be able to recognize whether isomers will exist, and draw their structures (Section 22.4). Study Question(s) assignable in OWL: 28, 40, 48, 50.
  c. Describe the bonding in coordination complexes (Section 22.5).
  d. Apply the principles of stoichiometry, thermodynamics, and equilibrium to transition metal compounds. Study Question(s) assignable in OWL: 42, 55, 59, 64, 67, 68, 70.

Relate ligand field theory to the magnetic and spectroscopic properties of complexes
  a. Understand why substances are colored (Section 22.6). Study Question(s) assignable in OWL: 32.
  b. Understand the relationship between the ligand field splitting, magnetism, and color of complexes (Section 22.6). Study Question(s) assignable in OWL: 26, 28, 59, 60, 63.

Apply the effective atomic number rule to simple organometallic compounds of the transition metals.
  a. Apply the EAN rule to molecules containing a low-valent metal and ligands such as C_6H_6, C_2H_4, and CO.

STUDY QUESTIONS

OWL Online homework for this chapter may be assigned in OWL.

▲ denotes challenging questions.

■ denotes questions assignable in OWL.

Blue-numbered questions have answers in Appendix O and fully-worked solutions in the *Student Solutions Manual*.

Practicing Skills

Properties of Transition Elements
(See Section 22.1 and Example 7.3.)

1. Give the electron configuration for each of the following ions, and tell whether each is paramagnetic or diamagnetic.
   (a) Cr^{3+} (b) V^{2+} (c) Ni^{2+} (d) Cu^+

2. Identify two transition metal cations with the following electron configurations.
   (a) $[Ar]3d^6$ (b) $[Ar]3d^{10}$ (c) $[Ar]3d^5$ (d) $[Ar]3d^8$

3. Identify a cation of a first series transition metal that is isoelectronic with each of the following.
   (a) Fe^{3+} (b) Zn^{2+} (c) Fe^{2+} (d) Cr^{3+}

4. Match up the isoelectronic ions on the following list.

   Cu^+ Mn^{2+} Fe^{2+} Co^{3+} Fe^{3+} Zn^{2+} Ti^{2+} V^{3+}

5. The following equations represent various ways of obtaining transition metals from their compounds. Balance each equation.
   (a) $Cr_2O_3(s) + Al(s) \longrightarrow Al_2O_3(s) + Cr(s)$
   (b) $TiCl_4(\ell) + Mg(s) \longrightarrow Ti(s) + MgCl_2(s)$
   (c) $[Ag(CN)_2]^-(aq) + Zn(s) \longrightarrow$
   $Ag(s) + [Zn(CN)_4]^{2-}(aq)$
   (d) $Mn_3O_4(s) + Al(s) \longrightarrow Mn(s) + Al_2O_3(s)$

6. Identify the products of each reaction, and balance the equation.
   (a) $CuSO_4(aq) + Zn(s) \longrightarrow$
   (b) $Zn(s) + HCl(aq) \longrightarrow$
   (c) $Fe(s) + Cl_2(g) \longrightarrow$
   (d) $V(s) + O_2(g) \longrightarrow$

Formulas of Coordination Compounds
(See Examples 22.1 and 22.2.)

7. Which of the following ligands is expected to be monodentate, and which might be polydentate?
   (a) CH_3NH_2
   (b) CH_3CN
   (c) N_3^-
   (d) en
   (e) Br^-
   (f) phen

8. One of the following nitrogen compounds or ions is not capable of serving as a ligand: NH_4^+, NH_3, NH_2^-. Identify this species, and explain your answer.

9. Give the oxidation number of the metal ion in each of the following compounds.
   (a) $[Mn(NH_3)_6]SO_4$
   (b) $K_3[Co(CN)_6]$
   (c) $[Co(NH_3)_4Cl_2]Cl$
   (d) $Cr(en)_2Cl_2$

10. Give the oxidation number of the metal ion in each of the following complexes.
    (a) $[Fe(NH_3)_6]^{2+}$
    (b) $[Zn(CN)_4]^{2-}$
    (c) $[Co(NH_3)_5(NO_2)]^+$
    (d) $[Cu(en)_2]^{2+}$

11. Give the formula of a complex constructed from one Ni^{2+} ion, one ethylenediamine ligand, three ammonia molecules, and one water molecule. Is the complex neutral or is it charged? If charged, give the charge.

12. Give the formula of a complex constructed from one Cr^{3+} ion, two ethylenediamine ligands, and two ammonia molecules. Is the complex neutral or is it charged? If charged, give the charge.

Naming Coordination Compounds
(See Example 22.3.)

13. Write formulas for the following ions or compounds.
    (a) dichlorobis(ethylenediamine)nickel(II)
    (b) potassium tetrachloroplatinate(II)
    (c) potassium dicyanocuprate(I)
    (d) tetraamminediaquairon(II)

14. Write formulas for the following ions or compounds.
    (a) diamminetriaquahydroxochromium(II) nitrate
    (b) hexaammineiron(III) nitrate
    (c) pentacarbonyliron(0) (where the ligand is CO)
    (d) ammonium tetrachlorocuprate(II)

15. Name the following ions or compounds.
    (a) $[Ni(C_2O_4)_2(H_2O)_2]^{2-}$
    (b) $[Co(en)_2Br_2]^+$
    (c) $[Co(en)_2(NH_3)Cl]^{2+}$
    (d) $Pt(NH_3)_2(C_2O_4)$

16. Name the following ions or compounds.
    (a) $[Co(H_2O)_4Cl_2]^+$
    (b) $Co(H_2O)_3F_3$
    (c) $[Pt(NH_3)Br_3]^-$
    (d) $[Co(en)(NH_3)_3Cl]^{2+}$

17. Give the name or formula for each ion or compound, as appropriate.
    (a) pentaaquahydroxoiron(III) ion
    (b) $K_2[Ni(CN)_4]$
    (c) $K[Cr(C_2O_4)_2(H_2O)_2]$
    (d) ammonium tetrachloroplatinate(II)

18. ■ Give the name or formula for each ion or compound, as appropriate.
    (a) tetraaquadichlorochromium(III) chloride
    (b) $[Cr(NH_3)_5SO_4]Cl$
    (c) sodium tetrachlorocobaltate(II)
    (d) $[Fe(C_2O_4)_3]^{3-}$

Isomerism
(See Example 22.4.)

19. Draw all possible geometric isomers of the following.
    (a) $Fe(NH_3)_4Cl_2$
    (b) $Pt(NH_3)_2(SCN)(Br)$ (SCN^- is bonded to Pt^{2+} through S)
    (c) $Co(NH_3)_3(NO_2)_3$ (NO_2^- is bonded to Co^{3+} through N)
    (d) $[Co(en)Cl_4]^-$

20. ■ In which of the following complexes are geometric isomers possible? If isomers are possible, draw their structures and label them as *cis* or *trans*, or as *fac* or *mer*.
    (a) $[Co(H_2O)_4Cl_2]^+$
    (b) $Co(NH_3)_3F_3$
    (c) $[Pt(NH_3)Br_3]^-$
    (d) $[Co(en)_2(NH_3)Cl]^{2+}$

21. Determine whether the following complexes have a chiral metal center.
    (a) $[Fe(en)_3]^{2+}$
    (b) trans-$[Co(en)_2Br_2]^+$
    (c) *fac*-$[Co(en)(H_2O)Cl_3]$
    (d) square-planar $Pt(NH_3)(H_2O)(Cl)(NO_2)$

22. Four geometric isomers are possible for $[Co(en)(NH_3)_2(H_2O)Cl]^+$. Draw the structures of all four. (Two of the isomers are chiral, meaning that each has a non-superimposable mirror image.)

Magnetic Properties of Complexes
(See Example 22.5.)

23. The following are low-spin complexes. Use the ligand field model to find the electron configuration of each ion. Determine which are diamagnetic. Give the number of unpaired electrons for the paramagnetic complexes.
    (a) $[Mn(CN)_6]^{4-}$
    (b) $[Co(NH_3)_6]Cl_3$
    (c) $[Fe(H_2O)_6]^{3+}$
    (d) $[Cr(en)_3]SO_4$

24. The following are high-spin complexes. Use the ligand field model to find the electron configuration of each ion, and determine the number of unpaired electrons in each.
    (a) $K_4[FeF_6]$
    (b) $[MnF_6]^{4-}$
    (c) $[Cr(H_2O)_6]^{2+}$
    (d) $(NH_4)_3[FeF_6]$

25. Determine the number of unpaired electrons in the following tetrahedral complexes. All tetrahedral complexes are high spin.
    (a) $[FeCl_4]^{2-}$
    (b) $Na_2[CoCl_4]$
    (c) $[MnCl_4]^{2-}$
    (d) $(NH_4)_2[ZnCl_4]$

26. ■ Determine the number of unpaired electrons in the following tetrahedral complexes. All tetrahedral complexes are high spin.
    (a) $[Zn(H_2O)_4]^{2+}$
    (b) $VOCl_3$
    (c) $Mn(NH_3)_2Cl_2$
    (d) $[Cu(en)_2]^{2+}$

27. For the high-spin complex $[Fe(H_2O)_6]SO_4$, identify the following:
    (a) the coordination number of iron
    (b) the coordination geometry for iron
    (c) the oxidation number of iron
    (d) the number of unpaired electrons
    (e) whether the complex is diamagnetic or paramagnetic

28. ■ For the low-spin complex $[Co(en)(NH_3)_2Cl_2]ClO_4$, identify the following:
    (a) the coordination number of cobalt
    (b) the coordination geometry for cobalt
    (c) the oxidation number of cobalt
    (d) the number of unpaired electrons
    (e) whether the complex is diamagnetic or paramagnetic
    (f) Draw any geometric isomers.

29. The anion $[NiCl_4]^{2-}$ is paramagnetic, but when CN^- ions are added, the product, $[Ni(CN)_4]^{2-}$, is diamagnetic. Explain this observation.

$$[NiCl_4]^{2-}(aq) + 4\ CN^-(aq) \longrightarrow$$
paramagnetic
$$[Ni(CN)_4]^{2-}(aq) + 4\ Cl^-(aq)$$
diamagnetic

30. An aqueous solution of iron(II) sulfate is paramagnetic. If NH_3 is added, the solution becomes diamagnetic. Why does the magnetism change?

Spectroscopy of Complexes
(See Example 22.6.)

31. In water, the titanium(III) ion, $[Ti(H_2O)_6]^{3+}$, has a broad absorption band at about 500 nm. What color light is absorbed by the ion?

32. ■ In water, the chromium(II) ion, $[Cr(H_2O)_6]^{2+}$, absorbs light with a wavelength of about 700 nm. What color is the solution?

Organometallic Compounds
(See Example 22.7.)

33. Show that the molecules and ions below satisfy the EAN rule.
    (a) $[Mn(CO)_6]^+$ (b)   (c)

(In (b) PR_3 is a phosphine such as $P(C_6H_5)_3$, a two-electron donor ligand.)

34. Many organometallic compounds of the transition metals satisfy the 18-electron rule. However, there also are many other stable molecules that have only 16-valence electrons. These often have the capability of adding more ligands and function as catalysts in chemical reactions (see Study Question 71). (In the molecules below, PR_3 is a phosphine such as $P(C_6H_5)_3$, a two-electron donor ligand. For electron counting purposes, the CH_3 or methyl group is considered an anion, $(CH_3)^-$, and also a two-electron donor ligand.) Which molecules below have 18-valence electrons and which have 16?

General Questions
These questions are not designated as to type or location in the chapter. They may contain several concepts.

35. Describe an experiment that would determine whether nickel in $K_2[NiCl_4]$ is square planar or tetrahedral.

36. Which of the following low-spin complexes has the greatest number of unpaired electrons?
    (a) $[Cr(H_2O)_6]^{3+}$
    (b) $[Mn(H_2O)_6]^{2+}$
    (c) $[Fe(H_2O)_6]^{2+}$
    (d) $[Ni(H_2O)_6]^{2+}$

37. How many unpaired electrons are expected for high-spin and low-spin complexes of Fe^{2+}?

38. Excess silver nitrate is added to a solution containing 1.0 mol of $[Co(NH_3)_4Cl_2]Cl$. What amount of AgCl (in moles) will precipitate?

39. Which of the following complexes is (are) square planar?
    (a) $[Ti(CN)_4]^{2-}$
    (b) $[Ni(CN)_4]^{2-}$
    (c) $[Zn(CN)_4]^{2-}$
    (d) $[Pt(CN)_4]^{2-}$

▲ more challenging   ■ in OWL   Blue-numbered questions answered in Appendix O

40. ■ Which of the following complexes containing the oxalate ion is (are) chiral?
    (a) $[Fe(C_2O_4)Cl_4]^{2-}$
    (b) cis-$[Fe(C_2O_4)_2Cl_2]^{2-}$
    (c) trans-$[Fe(C_2O_4)_2Cl_2]^{2-}$

41. How many geometric isomers are possible for the square-planar complex $[Pt(NH_3)(CN)Cl_2]^-$?

42. ■ For a tetrahedral complex of a metal in the first transition series, which of the following statements concerning energies of the $3d$ orbitals is correct?
    (a) The five d orbitals have the same energy.
    (b) The $d_{x^2-y^2}$ and d_{z^2} orbitals are higher in energy than the d_{xz}, d_{yz}, and d_{xy} orbitals.
    (c) The d_{xz}, d_{yz}, and d_{xy} orbitals are higher in energy than the $d_{x^2-y^2}$ and d_{z^2} orbitals.
    (d) The d orbitals all have different energies.

43. A transition metal complex absorbs 425-nm light. What is its color?
    (a) red   (c) yellow
    (b) green   (d) blue

44. ■ For the low-spin complex $[Fe(en)_2Cl_2]Cl$, identify the following.
    (a) the oxidation number of iron
    (b) the coordination number for iron
    (c) the coordination geometry for iron
    (d) the number of unpaired electrons per metal atom
    (e) whether the complex is diamagnetic or paramagnetic
    (f) the number of geometric isomers

45. For the high-spin complex $Mn(NH_3)_4Cl_2$, identify the following.
    (a) the oxidation number of manganese
    (b) the coordination number for manganese
    (c) the coordination geometry for manganese
    (d) the number of unpaired electrons per metal atom
    (e) whether the complex is diamagnetic or paramagnetic
    (f) the number of geometric isomers

46. ■ A platinum-containing compound, known as Magnus's green salt, has the formula $[Pt(NH_3)_4][PtCl_4]$ (in which both platinum ions are Pt^{2+}). Name the cation and the anion.

47. Early in the 20th century, complexes sometimes were given names based on their colors. Two compounds with the formula $CoCl_3 \cdot 4 NH_3$ were named praseocobalt chloride (praseo = green) and violio-cobalt chloride (violet color). We now know that these compounds are octahedral cobalt complexes and that they are cis and trans isomers. Draw the structures of these two compounds, and name them using systematic nomenclature.

48. ■ Give the formula and name of a square-planar complex of Pt^{2+} with one nitrite ion (NO_2^-, which binds to Pt^{2+} through N), one chloride ion, and two ammonia molecules as ligands. Are isomers possible? If so, draw the structure of each isomer, and tell what type of isomerism is observed.

49. Give the formula of the complex formed from one Co^{3+} ion, two ethylenediamine molecules, one water molecule, and one chloride ion. Is the complex neutral or charged? If charged, give the net charge on the ion.

50. ■ ▲ How many geometric isomers of the complex $[Cr(dmen)_3]^{3+}$ can exist? (dmen is the bidentate ligand 1,1-dimethylethylenediamine.)

$$(CH_3)_2\ddot{N}CH_2CH_2\ddot{N}H_2$$
1,1-Dimethylethylenediamine, dmen

51. ▲ Diethylenetriamine (dien) is capable of serving as a tridentate ligand.

$$H_2\ddot{N}CH_2CH_2—\underset{\underset{H}{|}}{N}—CH_2CH_2\ddot{N}H_2$$
Diethylenetriamine, dien

    (a) Draw the structures of fac-$Cr(dien)Cl_3$ and mer-$Cr(dien)Cl_3$.
    (b) Two different geometric isomers of mer-$Cr(dien)Cl_2Br$ are possible. Draw the structure for each.
    (c) Three different geometric isomers are possible for $[Cr(dien)_2]^{3+}$. Two have the dien ligand in a fac configuration, and one has the ligand in a mer orientation. Draw the structure of each isomer.

52. From experiment, we know that $[CoF_6]^{3-}$ is paramagnetic and $[Co(NH_3)_6]^{3+}$ is diamagnetic. Using the ligand field model, depict the electron configuration for each ion, and use this model to explain the magnetic property. What can you conclude about the effect of the ligand on the magnitude of Δ_0?

53. Three geometric isomers are possible for $[Co(en)(NH_3)_2(H_2O)_2]^{3+}$. One of the three is chiral; that is, it has a non-superimposable mirror image. Draw the structures of the three isomers. Which one is chiral?

54. The square-planar complex $Pt(en)Cl_2$ has chloride ligands in a cis configuration. No trans isomer is known. Based on the bond lengths and bond angles of carbon and nitrogen in the ethylenediamine ligand, explain why the trans compound is not possible.

55. ■ The complex $[Mn(H_2O)_6]^{2+}$ has five unpaired electrons, whereas $[Mn(CN)_6]^{4-}$ has only one. Using the ligand field model, depict the electron configuration for each ion. What can you conclude about the effects of the different ligands on the magnitude of Δ_0?

▲ more challenging   ■ in OWL   Blue-numbered questions answered in Appendix O

56. Experiments show that $K_4[Cr(CN)_6]$ is paramagnetic and has two unpaired electrons. The related complex $K_4[Cr(SCN)_6]$ is paramagnetic and has four unpaired electrons. Account for the magnetism of each compound using the ligand field model. Predict where the SCN^- ion occurs in the spectrochemical series relative to CN^-.

57. ■ Give a systematic name or the formula for the following:
(a) $(NH_4)_2[CuCl_4]$
(b) $Mo(CO)_6$
(c) tetraaquadichlorochromium(III) chloride
(d) aquabis(ethylenediamine)thiocyanatocobalt(III) nitrate

58. When $CrCl_3$ dissolves in water, three different species can be obtained.
(a) $[Cr(H_2O)_6]Cl_3$, violet
(b) $[Cr(H_2O)_5Cl]Cl_2$, pale green
(c) $[Cr(H_2O)_4Cl_2]Cl$, dark green

If diethyl ether is added, a fourth complex can be obtained: $Cr(H_2O)_3Cl_3$ (brown). Describe an experiment that will allow you to differentiate these complexes.

59. ■ ▲ The complex ion $[Co(CO_3)_3]^{3-}$, an octahedral complex with bidentate carbonate ions as ligands, has one absorption in the visible region of the spectrum at 640 nm. From this information:
(a) Predict the color of this complex, and explain your reasoning.
(b) Is the carbonate ion as weak- or strong-field ligand?
(c) Predict whether $[Co(CO_3)_3]^{3-}$ will be paramagnetic or diamagnetic.

60. ■ ▲ The glycinate ion, $H_2NCH_2CO_2^-$, formed by deprotonation of the amino acid glycine, can function as a bidentate ligand, coordinating to a metal through the nitrogen of the amino group and one of the oxygen atoms.

Glycinate ion, a bidentate ligand

Site of bonding to transition metal ion

A copper complex of this ligand has the formula $Cu(H_2NCH_2CO_2)_2(H_2O)_2$. For this complex, determine the following.
(a) the oxidation state of copper
(b) the coordination number of copper
(c) the number of unpaired electrons
(d) whether the complex is diamagnetic or paramagnetic

61. ▲ Draw structures for the five possible geometric isomers of $Cu(H_2NCH_2CO_2)_2(H_2O)_2$. Are any of these species chiral? (See the structure of the ligand in Study Question 60.)

62. Chromium forms two anionic carbonyls, $[Cr(CO)_5]^{x-}$ and $[Cr(CO)_4]^{y-}$. What are the values of x and y?

63. ■ Nickel and palladium both form complexes of the general formula $M(PR_3)_2Cl_2$ (where PR_3 is a phosphine such as $P(C_6H_5)_3$, triphenylphosphine). The nickel(II) compound is paramagnetic whereas the palladium(II) compound is diamagnetic.
(a) Explain the magnetic properties of these compounds.
(b) How many isomers of each compound are expected?

64. ■ ▲ The transition metals form a class of compounds called metal carbonyls, an example of which is the tetrahedral complex $Ni(CO)_4$. Given the following thermodynamic data (at 298 K):

	$\Delta_f H°$ (kJ/mol)	$S°$ (J/K · mol)
Ni(s)	0	29.87
CO(g)	−110.525	+197.674
Ni(CO)$_4$(g)	−602.9	+410.6

(a) Calculate the equilibrium constant for the formation of $Ni(CO)_4(g)$ from nickel metal and CO gas.
(b) Is the reaction of Ni(s) and CO(g) product- or reactant-favored?
(c) Is the reaction more or less product-favored at higher temperatures? How could this reaction be used in the purification of nickel metal?

In the Laboratory

65. Two different coordination compounds containing one cobalt(III) ion, five ammonia molecules, one bromide ion, and one sulfate ion exist. The dark violet form (A) gives a precipitate upon addition of aqueous $BaCl_2$. No reaction is seen upon addition of aqueous $BaCl_2$ to the violet-red form (B). Suggest structures for these two compounds, and write a chemical equation for the reaction of (A) with aqueous $BaCl_2$.

66. Three different compounds of chromium(III) with water and chloride ion have the same composition: 19.51% Cr, 39.92% Cl, and 40.57% H_2O. One of the compounds is violet and dissolves in water to give a complex ion with a 3+ charge and three chloride ions. All three chloride ions precipitate immediately as AgCl on adding $AgNO_3$. Draw the structure of the complex ion, and name the compound. Write a net ionic equation for the reaction of this compound with silver nitrate.

67. ■ ▲ A 0.213-g sample of uranyl(VI) nitrate, $UO_2(NO_3)_2$, is dissolved in 20.0 mL of 1.0 M H_2SO_4 and shaken with Zn. The zinc reduces the uranyl ion, UO_2^{2+}, to a uranium ion, U^{n+}. To determine the value of n, this solution is titrated with $KMnO_4$. Permanganate is reduced to Mn^{2+} and U^{n+} is oxidized back to UO_2^{2+}.

   (a) In the titration, 12.47 mL of 0.0173 M $KMnO_4$ was required to reach the equivalence point. Use this information to determine the charge on the ion U^{n+}.

   (b) With the identity of U^{n+} now established, write a balanced net ionic equation for the reduction of UO_2^{2+} by zinc (assume acidic conditions).

   (c) Write a balanced net ionic equation for the oxidation of U^{n+} to UO_2^{2+} by MnO_4^- in acid.

68. ■ ▲ You have isolated a solid organometallic compound containing manganese, some number of CO ligands, and one or more CH_3 ligands. To find the molecular formula of the compound, you burn 0.225 g of the solid in oxygen and isolate 0.283 g of CO_2 and 0.0290 g of H_2O. The molar mass of the compound is 210 g/mol. Suggest a plausible formula and structure for the molecule. (Make sure it satisfies the EAN rule. The CH_3 group can be thought of as a CH_3^- ion and is a two-electron donor ligand.)

Summary and Conceptual Questions

The following questions may use concepts from this and previous chapters.

69. The stability of analogous complexes $[ML_6]^{n+}$ (relative to ligand dissociation) is in the general order Mn^{2+}, Fe^{2+}, Co^{2+}, Ni^{2+}, Cu^{2+}, Zn^{2+}. This order of ions is called the Irving–Williams series. Look up the values of the formation constants for the ammonia complexes of Co^{2+}, Ni^{2+}, Cu^{2+}, and Zn^{2+} in Appendix K, and verify this statement.

70. ■ ▲ In this question, we explore the differences between metal coordination by monodentate and bidentate ligands. Formation constants, K_f, for $[Ni(NH_3)_6]^{2+}(aq)$ and $[Ni(en)_3]^{2+}(aq)$ are as follows:

$$Ni^{2+}(aq) + 6\,NH_3(aq) \longrightarrow [Ni(NH_3)_6]^{2+}(aq)$$
$$K_f = 10^8$$

$$Ni^{2+}(aq) + 3\,en(aq) \longrightarrow [Ni(en)_3]^{2+}(aq)$$
$$K_f = 10^{18}$$

The difference in K_f between these complexes indicates a higher thermodynamic stability for the chelated complex, caused by the *chelate effect*. Recall that K is related to the standard free energy of the reaction by $\Delta_r G° = -RT \ln K$ and $\Delta_r G° = \Delta_r H° - T\Delta S°$. We know from experiment that $\Delta_r H°$ for the NH_3 reaction is -109 kJ/mol-rxn, and $\Delta_r H°$ for the ethylenediamine reaction is -117 kJ/mol-rxn. Is the difference in $\Delta_r H°$ sufficient to account for the 10^{10} difference in K_f? Comment on the role of entropy in the second reaction.

71. As mentioned on page 1047, transition metal organometallic compounds have found use as catalysts. One example is Wilkinson's catalyst, a rhodium compound $[RhCl(PR_3)_3]$ used in the hydrogenation of alkenes. The steps involved in the catalytic process are outlined below.

Indicate whether the rhodium compounds in each step have 18- or 16-valence electrons. (See Study Question 34.)

Step 1—Addition of H_2 to the rhodium center of Wilkinson's catalyst. (For electron counting purposes H is considered a hydride ion, H^-, a two-electron donor.)

Step 2—Loss of a PR_3 ligand (a two-electron donor) to open a coordination site. (PR_3 is a phosphine such as $P(C_6H_5)_3$, triphenylphosphine.)

Step 3—Addition of the alkene to the open site.

Step 4—Rearrangement to add H to the double bond. (Here the $-CH_2CH_3$ group is a two-electron donor and can be thought of as a $[CH_2CH_3]^-$ anion for electron counting purposes.)

Step 5—Loss of the alkane

Step 6—Regeneration of the catalyst.

Net reaction: $CH_2{=}CH_2 + H_2 \longrightarrow CH_3CH_3$

23 | Nuclear Chemistry

A Primordial Nuclear Reactor

The natural nuclear reactors in West Africa have been called "one of the greatest natural phenomena that ever occurred." In 1972, a French scientist noticed that the uranium taken from a mine in Oklo, Gabon was strangely deficient in ^{235}U. Uranium exists in nature as two principal isotopes, ^{238}U (99.275% abundant) and ^{235}U (0.72% abundant). It is ^{235}U that most readily undergoes nuclear fission and is used to fuel nuclear power plants around the world. But the uranium found in the Oklo mines had an isotope ratio like that of the spent fuel that comes from modern reactors. On this and other evidence, scientists concluded that ^{235}U at the Oklo mine was once about 3% of the total and that a "natural" fission process occurred in the bed of uranium ore nearly 2 billion years ago.

But intriguing questions can be raised: why fission could occur to a significant extent in this natural deposit of uranium and why the "reactor" didn't explode. Apparently, there must have been a moderator of neutron energy and a regulation mechanism. In a modern nuclear power reactor, control rods slow down the neutrons from nuclear fission so that they can induce fission in other ^{235}U nuclei; that is, they moderate the neutron energy. Without a moderator, the neutrons just fly off. In the Oklo reactors, water seeping into the bed of uranium ore could have acted as a moderator.

The reason the Oklo reactor did not explode is that water could have also been the regulator. As the fission process heated the water, it boiled off as steam. This caused the fission to stop, but it began again when more water seeped in. Scientists now believe this natural reactor

Courtesy of Francois Gauthier-Lafaye.

The natural nuclear reactor in Oklo, Gabon (West Africa). Nearly two billion years ago, a natural formation containing uranium oxide (the yellow material) underwent fission that started and stopped over a period of a million years.

would turn on for about 30 minutes and then shut down for several hours before turning on again. There is evidence these natural reactors functioned intermittently for about 1 million years, until the concentration of uranium isotopes was too low to keep the reaction going.

Questions:

1. How many protons and neutrons are there in the ^{235}U and ^{238}U nuclei?
2. Although plutonium does not occur naturally on earth now, it is thought to have been produced in the Oklo reactor (and then decayed). Write balanced nuclear equations for:
   (a) the reaction of ^{238}U and a neutron to give ^{239}U
   (b) the decay of ^{239}Pu to ^{239}Np and then to ^{239}Pu by beta emission
   (c) the decay of ^{239}Pu to ^{235}U by alpha emission

Answers to these questions are in Appendix Q.

History of science scholars cite three pillars of modern chemistry: technology, medicine, and alchemy. The third of these pillars, alchemy, was pursued in many cultures on three continents for well over 1000 years. Simply stated, the goal of the ancient alchemists was to turn less valuable materials into gold. We now recognize the futility of these efforts, because this goal is not reachable by chemical processes. We also know that it *is* possible to transmute one element into another. This happens naturally in the decomposition of uranium and other radioactive elements, and scientists can intentionally carry out such reactions in the laboratory. The goal is no longer to make gold, however. Far more important and valuable products of nuclear reactions are possible.

Nuclear chemistry encompasses a wide range of topics that share one thing in common: they involve changes in the nucleus of an atom. While "chemistry" is a major focus in this chapter, the subject cuts across many areas of science. Radioactive isotopes are used in medicine. Nuclear power provides a sizable fraction of energy for modern society. And, then there are nuclear weapons. . . .

Chemistry⚛Now™

Throughout the text this icon introduces an opportunity for self-study or to explore interactive tutorials by signing in at **www.cengage.com/login**.

23.1 Natural Radioactivity

In the late 19th century, while studying radiation emanating from uranium and thorium, Ernest Rutherford (1871–1937) stated, "There are present at least two distinct types of radiation—one that is readily absorbed, which will be termed for convenience **α (alpha) radiation,** and the other of a more penetrative character, which will be termed **β (beta) radiation.**" Subsequently, charge-to-mass ratio measurements showed that α radiation is composed of helium nuclei (He^{2+}) and β radiation is composed of electrons (e^-) (Table 23.1).

Rutherford hedged his bet when he said at least two types of radiation existed. A third type was later discovered by the French scientist Paul Villard (1860–1934);

■ **Discovery of Radioactivity** The discovery of radioactivity by Henri Becquerel and the isolation of radium and polonium from pitchblende, a uranium ore, by Marie Curie were described in *Milestones in the Development of Chemistry*, page 338.

TABLE 23.1 Characteristics of α, β, and γ Radiation

Name	Symbols	Charge	Mass (g/particle)
Alpha	^4_2He, $^4_2\alpha$	2+	6.65×10^{-24}
Beta	$^0_{-1}e$, $^0_{-1}\beta$	1−	9.11×10^{-28}
Gamma	γ	0	0

FIGURE 23.1 The relative penetrating ability of α, β, and γ radiation.
Highly charged α particles interact strongly with matter and are stopped by a piece of paper. Beta particles, with less mass and a lower charge, interact to a lesser extent with matter and thus can penetrate farther. Gamma radiation is the most penetrating.

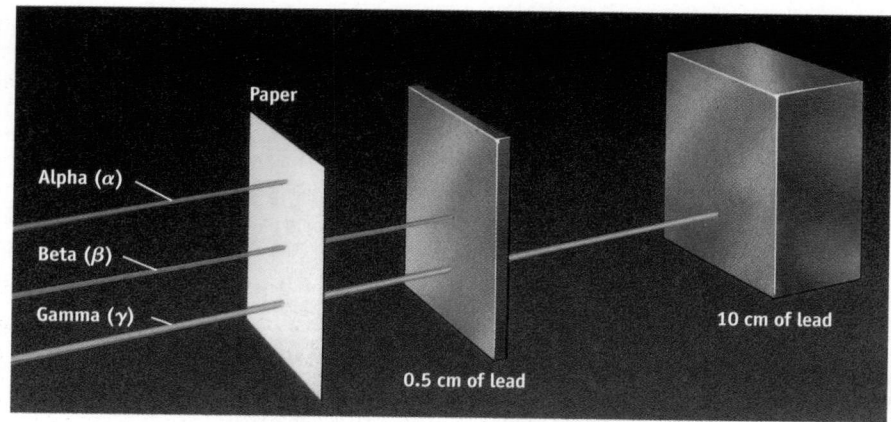

■ **Common Symbols: α and β** Symbols used to represent alpha and beta particles do not include a superscript to show that they have a charge.

he named it γ **(gamma) radiation,** using the third letter in the Greek alphabet in keeping with Rutherford's scheme. Unlike α and β radiation, γ radiation is not affected by electric and magnetic fields. Rather, it is a form of electromagnetic radiation like x-rays but even more energetic.

Early studies measured the penetrating power of the three types of radiation (Figure 23.1). Alpha radiation is the least penetrating; it can be stopped by several sheets of ordinary paper or clothing. Aluminum that is at least 0.5 cm thick is needed to stop β particles; they can penetrate several millimeters of living bone or tissue. Gamma radiation is the most penetrating. Thick layers of lead or concrete are required to shield the body from this radiation, and γ-rays can pass completely through the human body.

Alpha and β particles typically possess high kinetic energies. The energy of γ radiation is similarly very high. The energy associated with this radiation is transferred to any material used to stop the particle or absorb the radiation. This fact is important because the damage caused by radiation is related to the energy absorbed (see Section 23.8).

23.2 Nuclear Reactions and Radioactive Decay

Equations for Nuclear Reactions

In 1903, Rutherford and Frederick Soddy (1877–1956) proposed that radioactivity is the result of a natural change of an isotope of one element into an isotope of a different element. Such processes are called **nuclear reactions.**

Consider a reaction in which radium-226 (the isotope of radium with mass number 226) emits an α particle to form radon-222. The equation for this reaction is

$$^{226}_{88}\text{Ra} \rightarrow {}^{4}_{2}\alpha + {}^{222}_{86}\text{Rn}$$

■ **Symbols Used in Nuclear Equations**
The mass number is included as a superscript, and the atomic number is included as a subscript preceding the symbols for reactants and products. This is done to facilitate balancing these equations.

In a nuclear reaction, the sum of the mass numbers of reacting particles must equal the sum of the mass numbers of products. Furthermore, to maintain nuclear charge balance, the sum of the atomic numbers of the products must equal the sum of the atomic numbers of the reactants. These principles are illustrated using the preceding nuclear equation:

	$^{226}_{88}\text{Ra}$	$\rightarrow$	$^{4}_{2}\alpha$	+	$^{222}_{86}\text{Rn}$
	radium-226	$\rightarrow$	α particle	+	radon-222
Mass number: (protons + neutrons)	226	=	4	+	222
Atomic number: (protons)	88	=	2	+	86

Alpha particle emission causes a decrease of two units in atomic number and four units in the mass number.

Similarly, nuclear mass and nuclear charge balance accompany β particle emission, as illustrated by the decomposition of uranium-239:

	$^{239}_{92}U$	$\rightarrow$	$^{0}_{-1}\beta$	$+$	$^{239}_{93}Np$
	uranium-239	$\rightarrow$	β particle	$+$	neptunium-239
Mass number: (protons + neutrons)	239	=	0	+	239
Atomic number: (protons)	92	=	-1	+	93

The β particle has a charge of $1-$. Charge balance requires that the atomic number of the product be one unit greater than the atomic number of the reacting nucleus. The mass number does not change in this process.

How does a nucleus, composed of protons and neutrons, eject an electron? It is a complex process, but the net result is the conversion within the nucleus of a neutron to a proton and an electron.

$$^{1}_{0}n \longrightarrow {}^{0}_{-1}e \ + \ {}^{1}_{1}p$$

neutron   electron   proton

Notice that the mass and charge numbers balance in this equation.

What is the origin of the gamma radiation that accompanies most nuclear reactions? Recall that a photon of visible light is emitted when an atom undergoes a transition from an excited electronic state to a lower energy state ($\blacktriangleleft$ Section 6.3). Gamma radiation originates from transitions between nuclear energy levels. Nuclear reactions often result in the formation of a product nucleus in an excited nuclear state. One option is to return to the ground state by emitting the excess energy as a photon. The high energy of γ radiation is a measure of the large energy difference between the energy levels in the nucleus.

Chemistry⚛Now™

Sign in at **www.cengage.com/login** and go to Chapter 23 Contents to see:
• Screen 23.2 for a tutorial on **balancing equations for nuclear reactions**
• Screen 23.3 for a tutorial on **modes of radioactive decay**

EXERCISE 23.1 Mass and Charge Balance in Nuclear Reactions

Write equations for the following nuclear reactions, and confirm that they are balanced with respect to nuclear mass and nuclear charge.

(a) the emission of an α particle by radon-222 to form polonium-218

(b) the emission of a β particle by polonium-218 to form astatine-218

EXERCISE 23.2 Gamma Ray Energies

Calculate the energy per photon, and the energy per mole of photons, for γ radiation with a wavelength of 2.0×10^{-12} m. (*Hint:* Review similar calculations on the energy of photons of visible light, Section 6.2.)

■ **Energy Units** Gamma ray energies are often reported with the unit *MeV*, which stands for 1 million electron volts. One electron volt (1 eV) is the energy of an electron that has been accelerated by a potential of one volt. The conversion factor between electron volts and joules is $1 \text{ eV} = 1.60218 \times 10^{-19}$ J.

Radioactive Decay Series

Several naturally occurring radioactive isotopes are found to decay to form a product that is also radioactive. When this happens, the initial nuclear reaction is followed by a second nuclear reaction; if the situation is repeated, a third and a fourth nuclear reaction occur; and so on. Eventually, a nonradioactive isotope is formed to end the series. Such a sequence of nuclear reactions is called a **radioactive decay series.** In each step of this nuclear reaction sequence, the reactant nucleus is called the *parent,* and the product called the *daughter.*

Uranium-238, the most abundant of three naturally occurring uranium isotopes, heads one of four radioactive decay series. This series begins with the loss of an α particle from $^{238}_{92}$U to form radioactive $^{234}_{90}$Th. Thorium-234 then decomposes by β emission to $^{234}_{91}$Pa, which emits a β particle to give $^{234}_{92}$U. Uranium-234 is an α emitter, forming $^{230}_{90}$Th. Further α and β emissions follow, until the series ends with formation of the stable, nonradioactive isotope, $^{206}_{82}$Pb. In all, this radioactive decay series converting $^{238}_{92}$U to $^{206}_{82}$Pb is made up of 14 reactions, with eight α and six β particles being emitted. The series is portrayed graphically by plotting atomic number versus mass number (Figure 23.2). An equation can be written for each step in the sequence. Equations for the first four steps in the uranium-238 radioactive decay series are:

Step 1. $^{238}_{92}$U $\rightarrow$ $^{234}_{90}$Th $+$ $^{4}_{2}\alpha$

Step 2. $^{234}_{90}$Th $\rightarrow$ $^{234}_{91}$Pa $+$ $^{0}_{-1}\beta$

Step 3. $^{234}_{91}$Pa $\rightarrow$ $^{234}_{92}$U $+$ $^{0}_{-1}\beta$

Step 4. $^{234}_{92}$U $\rightarrow$ $^{230}_{90}$Th $+$ $^{4}_{2}\alpha$

Uranium ore contains trace quantities of the radioactive elements formed in the radioactive decay series. A significant development in nuclear chemistry was Marie Curie's discovery in 1898 of radium and polonium as trace components of pitchblende, a uranium ore. The amount of each of these elements is small because the isotopes of these elements have short half-lives. Marie Curie isolated only a single gram of radium from 7 tons of ore. It is a credit to her skills as a chemist that she

FIGURE 23.2 The uranium-238 radioactive decay series. The steps in this radioactive decay series are shown graphically in this plot of mass number versus atomic number. Each α decay step lowers the atomic number by two units and the mass number by four units. Beta particle emission does not change the mass but raises the atomic number by one unit. Half-lives of the isotopes are included on the chart.

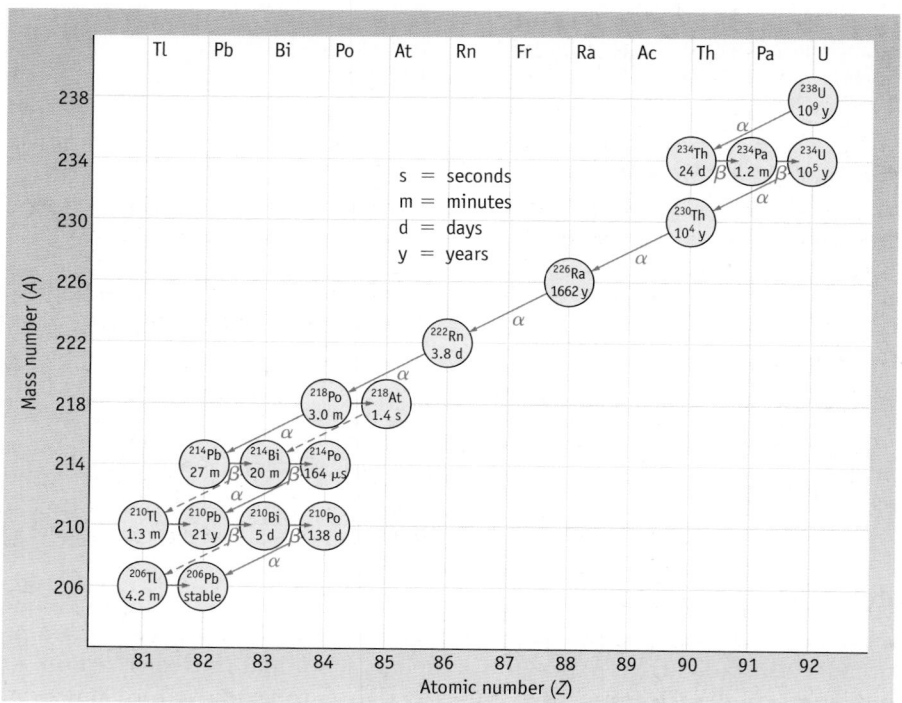

extracted sufficient amounts of radium and polonium from uranium ore to identify these elements.

The uranium-238 radioactive decay series is also the source of the environmental hazard radon. Trace quantities of uranium are often present naturally in the soil and rocks, and radon-222 is being continuously formed. Because radon is chemically inert, it is not trapped by chemical processes in soil or water and is free to seep into mines or into homes through pores in cement block walls, through cracks in the basement floor or walls, or around pipes. Because it is more dense than air, radon tends to collect in low spots, and its concentration can build up in a basement if steps are not taken to remove it.

The major health hazard from radon, when it is inhaled by humans, arises not from radon itself but from its decomposition product, polonium.

$$^{222}_{86}Rn \rightarrow {}^{218}_{84}Po + {}^{4}_{2}\alpha \qquad t_{1/2} = 3.82 \text{ days}$$

$$^{218}_{84}Po \rightarrow {}^{214}_{82}Pb + {}^{4}_{2}\alpha \qquad t_{1/2} = 3.04 \text{ minutes}$$

Radon does not undergo chemical reactions or form compounds that can be taken up in the body. Polonium, however, is not chemically inert. Polonium-218 can lodge in body tissues, where it undergoes α decay to give lead-214, another radioactive isotope. The range of an α particle in body tissue is quite small, perhaps 0.7 mm. This is approximately the thickness of the epithelial cells of the lungs, however, so α particle radiation can cause serious damage to lung tissues.

Virtually every home in the United States has some level of radon, and kits can be purchased to test for the presence of this gas. If radon gas is detected in your home, you should take corrective actions such as sealing cracks around the foundation and in the basement. It may be reassuring to know that the health risks associated with radon are low. The likelihood of getting lung cancer from exposure to radon is about the same as the likelihood of dying in an accident in your home.

Charles D. Winters

Radon detector. This kit is intended for use in the home to detect radon gas. The small device is placed in the home's basement for a given time period and is then sent to a laboratory to measure the amount of radon that might be present.

■ **EXAMPLE 23.1 Radioactive Decay Series**

Problem A second radioactive decay series begins with $^{235}_{92}U$ and ends with $^{207}_{82}Pb$.

(a) How many α and β particles are emitted in this series?

(b) The first three steps of this series are (in order) α, β, and α emission. Write an equation for each of these steps.

Strategy First, find the total change in atomic number and mass number. A combination of α and β particles is required that will decrease the total nuclear mass by 28 (235 − 207) and at the same time decrease the atomic number by 10 (92 − 82).

Each equation must give symbols for the parent and daughter nuclei and the emitted particle. In the equations, the sums of the atomic numbers and mass numbers for reactants and products must be equal.

Solution

(a) Mass declines by 28 mass units (235 − 207). Because a decrease of 4 mass units occurs with each α emission, 7 α particles must be emitted. Also, for each α emission, the atomic number decreases by 2. Emission of 7 α particles would cause the atomic number to decrease by 14, but the actual decrease in atomic number is 10 (92 − 82). This means that 4 β particles must also have been emitted because each β emission *increases* the atomic number of the product by one unit. Thus, the radioactive decay sequence involves emission of 7 α and 4 β particles.

(b) Step 1. $^{235}_{92}U \rightarrow {}^{231}_{90}Th + {}^{4}_{2}\alpha$

Step 2. $^{231}_{90}Th \rightarrow {}^{231}_{91}Pa + {}^{0}_{-1}\beta$

Step 3. $^{231}_{91}Pa \rightarrow {}^{227}_{89}Ac + {}^{4}_{2}\alpha$

Comment Notice in Figure 23.2 that all daughter nuclei for the series beginning with $^{238}_{92}U$ have mass numbers differing by four units: 238, 234, 230, . . . , 206. This series is sometimes called the *4n + 2 series* because each mass number (*M*) fits the equation $4n + 2 = M$, where *n* is an integer (*n* is 59 for the first member of this series). For the series headed by $^{235}_{92}U$, the mass numbers are 235, 231, 227, . . . , 207; this is the *4n + 3 series*.

Two other decay series are possible. One, called the *4n series* and beginning with ^{232}Th, is found in nature; the other, the *4n + 1 series*, is not. No member of this series has a very long half-life. During the 5 billion years since this planet was formed, all members of this series have completely decayed.

EXERCISE 23.3 Radioactive Decay Series

(a) Six α and four β particles are emitted in the thorium-232 radioactive decay series before a stable isotope is reached. What is the final product in this series?

(b) The first three steps in the thorium-232 decay series (in order) are α, β, and β emission. Write an equation for each step.

Other Types of Radioactive Decay

Most naturally occurring radioactive elements decay by emission of α, β, and γ radiation. Other nuclear decay processes became known, however, when new radioactive elements were synthesized by artificial means. These include **positron** ($_{+1}^{0}\beta$) **emission** and **electron capture.**

Positrons ($_{+1}^{0}\beta$) and electrons have the same mass but opposite charge. The positron is the antimatter analogue to an electron. Positron emission by polonium-207, for example, results in the formation of bismuth-207.

	$^{207}_{84}$Po	$\rightarrow$	$_{+1}^{0}\beta$	+	$^{207}_{83}$Bi
	polonium-207	$\rightarrow$	positron	+	bismuth-207
Mass number: (protons + neutrons)	207	=	0	+	207
Atomic number: (protons)	84	=	1	+	83

To retain charge balance, positron decay results in a decrease in the atomic number.

In *electron capture,* an extranuclear electron is captured by the nucleus. The mass number is unchanged, and the atomic number is reduced by 1. (In an old nomenclature, the innermost electron shell was called the K shell, and electron capture was called *K capture.*)

	$^{7}_{4}$Be	+	$_{-1}^{0}e$	$\rightarrow$	$^{7}_{3}$Li
	beryllium-7	+	electron	$\rightarrow$	lithium-7
Mass number: (protons + neutrons)	7	+	0	=	7
Atomic number: (protons)	4	+	-1	=	3

In summary, most unstable nuclei decay by one of four paths: α or β decay, positron emission, or electron capture. Gamma radiation often accompanies these processes. Section 23.6 introduces a fifth way that nuclei decompose, *fission.*

EXAMPLE 23.2 Nuclear Reactions

Problem Complete the following equations. Give the symbol, mass number, and atomic number of the product species.

(a) $^{37}_{18}Ar + _{-1}^{0}e \rightarrow$?

(b) $^{11}_{6}C \rightarrow ^{11}_{5}B +$?

(c) $^{35}_{16}S \rightarrow ^{35}_{17}Cl +$?

(d) $^{30}_{15}P \rightarrow _{+1}^{0}\beta +$?

■ **Positrons** Positrons were discovered by Carl Anderson (1905–1991) in 1932. The positron is one of a group of particles that are known as *antimatter*. If matter and antimatter particles collide, mutual annihilation occurs, with energy being emitted.

■ **Neutrinos and Antineutrinos** Beta particles having a wide range of energies are emitted. To balance the energy associated with β decay, it is necessary to postulate the concurrent emission of another particle, the *antineutrino*. Similarly, neutrino emission accompanies positron emission. Much study has gone into detecting neutrinos and antineutrinos. These massless, chargeless particles are not included when writing nuclear equations.

Strategy The missing product in each reaction can be determined by recognizing that the sums of mass numbers and atomic numbers for products and reactants must be equal. When you know the nuclear mass and nuclear charge of the product, you can identify it with the appropriate symbol.

Solution

(a) This is an electron capture reaction. The product has a mass number of $37 + 0 = 37$ and an atomic number of $18 - 1 = 17$. Therefore, the symbol for the product is $^{37}_{17}Cl$.

(b) This missing particle has a mass of zero and a charge of 1+; these are the characteristics of a positron, $^{0}_{+1}\beta$. If this particle is included in the equation, the sums of the atomic numbers ($6 = 5 + 1$) and the mass numbers (11) on either side of the equation are equal.

(c) A beta particle, $^{0}_{-1}\beta$, is required to balance the mass numbers (35) and atomic numbers ($16 = 17 - 1$) in the equation.

(d) The product nucleus has mass number 30 and atomic number 14. This identifies the unknown as $^{30}_{14}Si$.

EXERCISE 23.4 Nuclear Reactions

Indicate the symbol, the mass number, and the atomic number of the missing product in each of the following nuclear reactions.

(a) $^{13}_{7}N \rightarrow ^{13}_{6}C + ?$ **(c)** $^{90}_{38}Sr \rightarrow ^{90}_{39}Y + ?$

(b) $^{41}_{20}Ca + ^{0}_{-1}e \rightarrow ?$ **(d)** $^{22}_{11}Na \rightarrow ? + ^{0}_{-1}\beta$

23.3 Stability of Atomic Nuclei

We can learn something about nuclear stability from Figure 23.3. In this plot, the horizontal axis represents the number of protons, and the vertical axis gives the number of neutrons for known isotopes. Each circle represents an isotope identified by the number of neutrons and protons contained in its nucleus. The black circles represent stable (nonradioactive) isotopes, about 300 in number, and the red circles represent some of the known radioactive isotopes. For example, the three isotopes of hydrogen are $^{1}_{1}H$ and $^{2}_{1}H$ (neither is radioactive) and $^{3}_{1}H$ (tritium, radioactive). For lithium, the third element, isotopes with mass numbers 4, 5, 6, and 7 are known. The isotopes with masses of 6 and 7 (shown in black) are stable, whereas the other two isotopes (in red) are radioactive.

Figure 23.3 contains the following information about nuclear stability:

- Stable isotopes fall in a very narrow range called the **band of stability.** It is remarkable how few isotopes are stable.
- Only two stable isotopes ($^{1}_{1}H$ and $^{3}_{2}He$) have more protons than neutrons.
- Up to calcium ($Z = 20$), stable isotopes often have equal numbers of protons and neutrons or only one or two more neutrons than protons.
- Beyond calcium, the neutron–proton ratio is always greater than 1. As the mass increases, the band of stable isotopes deviates more and more from a line in which $N = Z$.
- Beyond bismuth (83 protons and 126 neutrons), all isotopes are unstable and radioactive. There is apparently no nuclear "superglue" strong enough to hold heavy nuclei together.
- The lifetimes of unstable nuclei are shorter for the heaviest nuclei. For example, half of a sample of $^{238}_{92}U$ disintegrates in 4.5 billion years, whereas half of a sample of $^{257}_{103}Lr$ is gone in only 0.65 second. Isotopes that fall farther from the band of stability tend to have shorter half-lives than do unstable isotopes nearer to the band of stability.
- Elements of even atomic number have more stable isotopes than do those of odd atomic number. More stable isotopes have an even number of neutrons

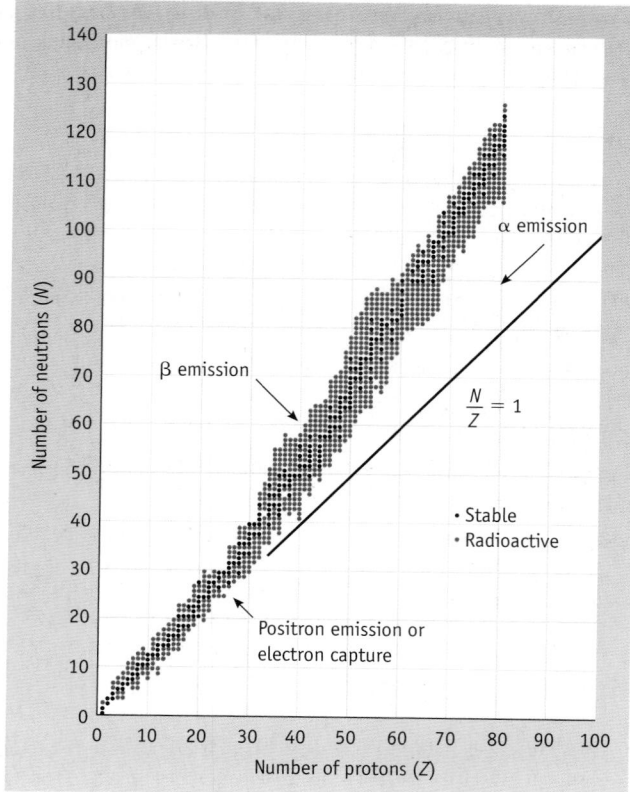

than have an odd number. Roughly 200 isotopes have an even number of neutrons and an even number of protons, whereas only about 120 isotopes have an odd number of either protons or neutrons. Only five stable isotopes (^1_1H, ^6_3Li, $^{10}_5B$, $^{14}_7N$, and $^{180}_{73}Ta$) have odd numbers of both protons and neutrons.

The Band of Stability and Radioactive Decay

Besides being a criterion for stability, the neutron–proton ratio can assist in predicting what type of radioactive decay will be observed. Unstable nuclei decay in a manner that brings them toward a stable neutron–proton ratio—that is, toward the band of stability.

- All elements beyond bismuth ($Z = 83$) are unstable. To reach the band of stability starting with these elements, a process that decreases the atomic number is needed. Alpha emission is an effective way to lower Z, the atomic number, because each emission decreases the atomic number by 2. For example, americium, the radioactive element used in smoke detectors, decays by α emission:

$$^{243}_{95}Am \rightarrow \ ^4_2\alpha + \ ^{239}_{93}Np$$

- Beta emission occurs for isotopes that have a high neutron–proton ratio—that is, isotopes above the band of stability. With β decay, the atomic number increases by 1, and the mass number remains constant, resulting in a lower n/p ratio.

$$^{60}_{27}Co \rightarrow \ ^0_{-1}\beta + \ ^{60}_{28}Ni$$

- Isotopes with a low neutron–proton ratio, below the band of stability, decay by positron emission or by electron capture. Both processes lead to product nuclei with a lower atomic number and the same mass number:

$$^{13}_{7}N \rightarrow {}^{0}_{+1}\beta + {}^{13}_{6}C$$

$$^{41}_{20}Ca + {}^{0}_{-1}e \rightarrow {}^{41}_{19}K$$

Chemistry ⚛ Now™

Sign in at **www.cengage.com/login** and go to Chapter 23 Contents to see Screen 23.3 for a tutorial on **predicting modes of radioactive decay.**

■ **EXAMPLE 23.3** **Predicting Modes of Radioactive Decay**

Problem Identify probable mode(s) of decay for each isotope and write an equation for the decay process.

(a) oxygen-15, $^{15}_{8}O$ **(b)** uranium-234, $^{234}_{92}U$ **(c)** fluorine-20, $^{20}_{9}F$ **(d)** manganese-56, $^{56}_{25}Mn$

Strategy In parts (a), (c), and (d), compare the mass number with the atomic mass. If the mass number of the isotope is higher than the atomic weight, then there are too many neutrons, and β emission is likely. If the mass number is lower than the atomic weight, then there are too few neutrons, and positron emission or electron capture is the more likely process. It is not possible to choose between the latter two modes of decay without further information. For part (b), note that isotopes with atomic number greater than 83 are likely to be α emitters.

Solution

(a) Oxygen-15 has 7 neutrons and 8 protons, so the n/p ratio is less than 1—too low for ^{15}O to be stable. Nuclei with too few neutrons are expected to decay by either positron emission or electron capture. In this instance, the process is $^{0}_{+1}\beta$ emission, and the equation is $^{15}_{8}O \rightarrow {}^{0}_{+1}\beta + {}^{15}_{7}N$.

(b) Alpha emission is a common mode of decay for isotopes of elements with atomic numbers higher than 83. The decay of uranium-234 is one example:

$$^{234}_{92}U \rightarrow {}^{230}_{90}Th + {}^{4}_{2}\alpha$$

(c) Fluorine-20 has 11 neutrons and 9 protons, a high n/p ratio. The ratio is lowered by β emission :

$$^{20}_{9}F \rightarrow {}^{0}_{-1}\beta + {}^{20}_{10}Ne$$

(d) The atomic weight of manganese is 54.85. The higher mass number, 56, suggests that this radioactive isotope has an excess of neutrons, in which case it would be expected to decay by β emission :

$$^{56}_{25}Mn \rightarrow {}^{0}_{-1}\beta + {}^{56}_{26}Fe$$

Comment Be aware that predictions made in this manner will be right much of the time, but exceptions will sometimes occur.

EXERCISE 23.5 **Predicting Modes of Radioactive Decay**

Write an equation for the probable mode of decay for each of the following unstable isotopes, and write an equation for that nuclear reaction.

(a) silicon-32, $^{32}_{14}Si$ **(c)** plutonium-239, $^{239}_{94}Pu$

(b) titanium-45, $^{45}_{22}Ti$ **(d)** potassium-42, $^{42}_{19}K$

Nuclear Binding Energy

An atomic nucleus can contain as many as 83 protons and still be stable. For stability, nuclear binding (attractive) forces must be greater than the electrostatic repulsive forces between the closely packed protons in the nucleus. **Nuclear binding energy,** E_b, is defined as the energy required to separate the nucleus of an atom into protons and neutrons. For example, the nuclear binding energy for deuterium is the energy required to convert one mole of deuterium ($^2_1$H) nuclei into one mole of protons and one mole of neutrons.

$$^2_1\text{H} \rightarrow {}^1_1\text{p} + {}^1_0\text{n} \qquad E_b = 2.15 \times 10^8 \text{ kJ/mol}$$

The positive sign for E_b indicates that energy is required for this process. A deuterium nucleus is more stable than an isolated proton and an isolated neutron, just as the H_2 molecule is more stable than two isolated H atoms. Recall, however, that the H—H bond energy is only 436 kJ/mol. The energy holding a proton and a neutron together in a deuterium nucleus, 2.15×10^8 kJ/mol, is about 500,000 times larger than the typical covalent bond energies.

To further understand nuclear binding energy, we turn to an experimental observation and a theory. The experimental observation is that the mass of a nucleus is always less than the sum of the masses of its constituent protons and neutrons. The theory is that the "missing mass," called the **mass defect,** is equated with energy that holds the nuclear particles together.

The mass defect for deuterium is the difference between the mass of a deuterium nucleus and the sum of the masses of a proton and a neutron. Mass spectrometric measurements (◀ Section 2.3) give the accurate masses of these particles to a high level of precision, providing the numbers needed to carry out calculations of mass defects.

Masses of atomic nuclei are not generally listed in reference tables, but masses of atoms are. Calculation of the mass defect can be carried out using masses of atoms instead of masses of nuclei. By using atomic masses, we are including in this calculation the masses of extranuclear electrons in the reactants and the products. Because the same number of extranuclear electrons appears in products and reactants, this does not affect the result. Thus, for one mole of deuterium nuclei, the mass defect is found as follows:

$$\begin{array}{ccccc} ^2_1\text{H} & \rightarrow & ^1_1\text{H} & + & ^1_0\text{n} \\ 2.01410 \text{ g/mol} & & 1.007825 \text{ g/mol} & & 1.008665 \text{ g/mol} \end{array}$$

$$\begin{aligned} \text{Mass defect} = \Delta m &= \text{mass of products} - \text{mass of reactants} \\ &= [1.007825 \text{ g/mol} + 1.008665 \text{ g/mol}] - 2.01410 \text{ g/mol} \\ &= 0.00239 \text{ g/mol} \end{aligned}$$

The relationship between mass and energy is contained in Albert Einstein's 1905 theory of special relativity, which holds that mass and energy are different manifestations of the same quantity. Einstein defined the energy–mass relationship: energy is equivalent to mass times the square of the speed of light; that is, $E = mc^2$. In the case of atomic nuclei, it is assumed that the missing mass (the mass defect, Δm) is equated with the binding energy holding the nucleus together.

$$E_b = (\Delta m)c^2 \tag{23.1}$$

If Δm is given in kilograms and the speed of light is given in meters per second, E_b will have units of joules (because $1 \text{ J} = 1 \text{ kg} \cdot \text{m}^2/\text{s}^2$). For the decomposition of one mole of deuterium nuclei to one mole of protons and one mole of neutrons, we have

$$E_b = (2.39 \times 10^{-6} \text{ kg/mol})(2.998 \times 10^8 \text{ m/s})^2$$

$$= 2.15 \times 10^{11} \text{ J/mol of } ^2_1\text{H nuclei} \ (= 2.15 \times 10^8 \text{ kJ/mol of } ^2_1\text{H nuclei})$$

The nuclear stabilities of different elements are compared using the **binding energy per mole of nucleons.** (**Nucleon** is the general name given to nuclear particles—that is, protons and neutrons.) A deuterium nucleus contains two nucle-

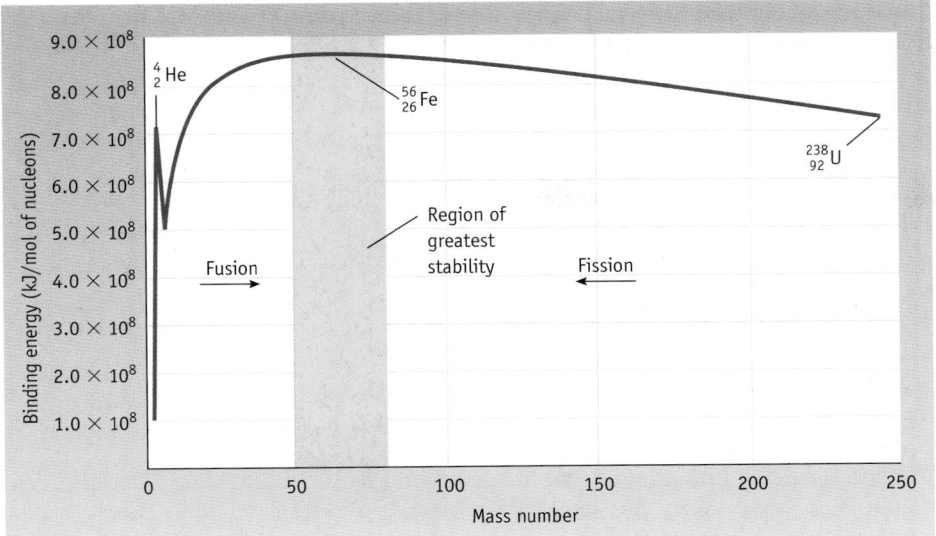

FIGURE 23.4 Relative stability of nuclei. Binding energy per nucleon for the most stable isotope of elements between hydrogen and uranium is plotted as a function of mass number. (Fission and fusion are discussed on pages 1080–1082.)

ons, so the binding energy per mole of nucleons, E_b/n, is 2.15×10^8 kJ/mol divided by 2, or 1.08×10^8 kJ/mol nucleon.

$$E_b/n = \left(\frac{2.15 \times 10^8 \text{ kJ}}{\text{mol } {}^2_1\text{H nuclei}} \right)\left(\frac{1 \text{ mol } {}^2_1\text{H nuclei}}{2 \text{ mol nucleons}} \right)$$

$$E_b/n = 1.08 \times 10^8 \text{ kJ/mol nucleons}$$

The binding energy per nucleon can be calculated for any atom whose mass is known. Then, to compare nuclear stabilities, binding energies per nucleon are plotted as a function of mass number (Figure 23.4). The greater the binding energy per nucleon, the greater the stability of the nucleus. From the graph in Figure 23.4, the point of maximum nuclear stability occurs at a mass of 56 (i.e., at iron in the periodic table).

Chemistry .ᐧ. Now™

Sign in at **www.cengage.com/login** and go to Chapter 23 Contents to see:
- Screen 23.4 for a simulation on **isotope stability**
- Screen 23.5 for a tutorial on **calculating binding energy**

EXAMPLE 23.4 Nuclear Binding Energy

Problem Calculate the binding energy, E_b (in kJ/mol), and the binding energy per nucleon, E_b/n (in kJ/mol nucleon), for carbon-12.

Strategy First, determine the mass defect, then use Equation 23.1 to determine the binding energy. There are 12 nuclear particles in carbon-12, so dividing the nuclear binding energy by 12 will give the binding energy per nucleon.

Solution The mass of ${}^1_1\text{H}$ is 1.007825 g/mol, and the mass of ${}^1_0\text{n}$ is 1.008665 g/mol. Carbon-12, ${}^{12}_6\text{C}$, is the standard for the atomic masses in the periodic table, and its mass is defined as exactly 12 g/mol

$$\Delta m = [(6 \times \text{mass } {}^1_1\text{H}) + (6 \times \text{mass } {}^1_0\text{n})] - \text{mass } {}^{12}_6\text{C}$$

$$= [(6 \times 1.007825 \text{ g/mol}) + (6 \times 1.008665 \text{ g/mol})] - 12.000000 \text{ g/mol}$$

$$= 9.8940 \times 10^{-2} \text{ g/mol nuclei}$$

The binding energy is calculated using Equation 23.1. Using the mass in kilograms and the speed of light in meters per second gives the binding energy in joules:

$$E_b = (\Delta m)c^2$$
$$= (9.8940 \times 10^{-5} \text{ kg/mol})(2.99792 \times 10^8 \text{ m/s})^2$$
$$= 8.89 \times 10^{12} \text{ J/mol nuclei } (= 8.89 \times 10^9 \text{ kJ/mol nuclei})$$

The binding energy per nucleon, E_b/n, is determined by dividing the binding energy by 12 (the number of nucleons)

$$\frac{E_b}{n} = \frac{8.89 \times 10^9 \text{ kJ/mol nuclei}}{12 \text{ mol nucleons/mol nuclei}}$$
$$= 7.41 \times 10^8 \text{ kJ/mol nucleons}$$

EXERCISE 23.6 Nuclear Binding Energy

Calculate the binding energy per nucleon, in kilojoules per mole, for lithium-6. The molar mass of $^{6}_{3}\text{Li}$ is 6.015125 g/mol.

23.4 Rates of Nuclear Decay

Half-Life

When a new radioactive isotope is identified, its *half-life* is usually measured. Half-life ($t_{1/2}$) is used in nuclear chemistry in the same way it is used when discussing the kinetics of first-order chemical reactions (◀ Section 15.4): It is the time required for half of a sample to decay to products (Figure 23.5). Recall that for first-order kinetics the half-life is independent of the amount of sample.

Half-lives for radioactive isotopes cover a wide range of values. Uranium-238 has one of the longer half-lives, 4.47×10^9 years, a length of time close to the age of the earth (estimated at 4.5–4.6 × 10^9 years). Roughly half of the uranium-238 present when the planet was formed is still around. At the other end of the range of half-lives are isotopes such as element 112, whose 277 isotope has a half-life of 240 microseconds (1 μs = 1 × 10^{-6} s).

Half-life provides an easy way to estimate the time required before a radioactive element is no longer a health hazard. Strontium-90, for example, is a β emitter

FIGURE 23.5 Decay of 20.0 mg of oxygen-15. After each half-life period of 2.0 min, the mass of oxygen-15 decreases by one half.

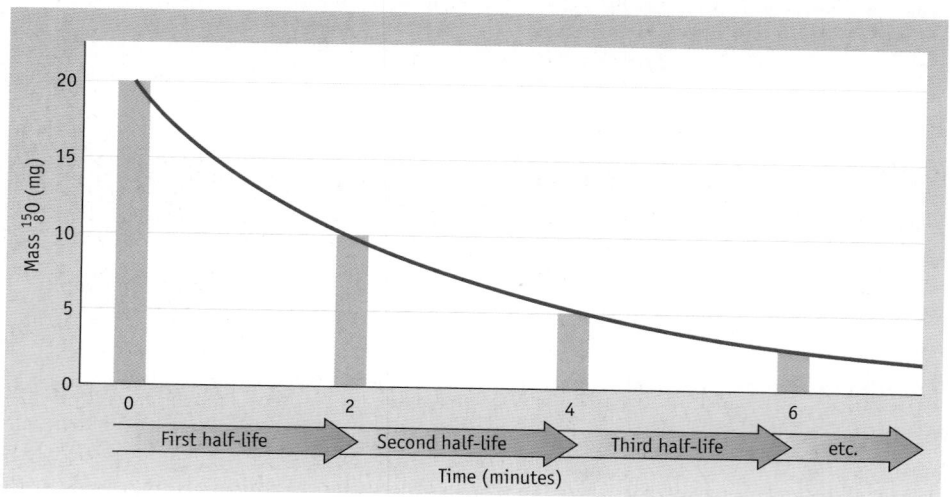

with a half-life of 29.1 years. Significant quantities of strontium-90 were dispersed into the environment in atmospheric nuclear bomb tests in the 1960s and 1970s, and from the half-life, we know that a little less than half is still around. The health problems associated with strontium-90 arise because calcium and strontium have similar chemical properties. Strontium-90 is taken into the body and deposited in bone, taking the place of calcium. Radiation damage by strontium-90 in bone has been directly linked to bone-related cancers.

■ **Half-Life and Temperature** Unlike what is observed in chemical kinetics, temperature does not affect the rate of nuclear decay.

■ **EXAMPLE 23.5 Using Half-Life**

Problem Radioactive iodine-131, used to treat hyperthyroidism, has a half-life of 8.04 days.

(a) If you have 8.8 μg (micrograms) of this isotope, what mass remains after 32.2 days?

(b) How long will it take for a sample of iodine-131 to decay to one eighth of its activity?

(c) Estimate the length of time necessary for the sample to decay to 10% of its original activity.

Strategy This problem asks you to use half-life to qualitatively assess the rate of decay. After one half-life, half of the sample remains. After another half-life, the amount of sample is again decreased by half to one fourth of its original value. (This situation is illustrated in Figure 23.5.) To answer these questions, assess the number of half-lives that have elapsed and use this information to determine the amount of sample remaining.

Solution

(a) The time elapsed, 32.2 days, is 4 half-lives (32.2/8.04 = 4). The amount of iodine-131 has decreased to 1/16 of the original amount [1/2 × 1/2 × 1/2 × 1/2 = $(1/2)^4$ = 1/16]. The amount of iodine remaining is 8.8 μg × $(1/2)^4$ or 0.55 μg .

(b) After 3 half-lives , the amount of iodine-131 remaining is 1/8 (= $1/2)^3$ of the original amount. The amount remaining is 8.8 μg × $(1/2)^3$ = 1.1 μg.

(c) After 3 half-lives, 1/8 (12.5%) of the sample remains; after 4 half-lives, 1/16 (6.25%) remains. It will take between 3 and 4 half-lives, between 24.15 and 32.2 days, to decrease the amount of sample to 10% of its original value.

Comment You will find it useful to make approximations as we have done in (c). An exact time can be calculated from the first-order rate law (pages 683 and 1074).

EXERCISE 23.7 Using Half-Life

Tritium ($^3_1$H), a radioactive isotope of hydrogen has a half-life of 12.3 years.

(a) Starting with 1.5 mg of this isotope, how many milligrams remain after 49.2 years?

(b) How long will it take for a sample of tritium to decay to one eighth of its activity?

(c) Estimate the length of time necessary for the sample to decay to 1% of its original activity.

Kinetics of Nuclear Decay

The rate of nuclear decay is determined from measurements of the **activity** (A) of a sample. Activity refers to the number of disintegrations observed per unit time, a quantity that can be measured readily with devices such as a Geiger–Müller counter (Figure 23.6). *Activity is proportional to the number of radioactive atoms present (N).*

$$A \propto N \qquad\qquad (23.2)$$

If the number of radioactive nuclei N is reduced by half, the activity of the sample will be half as large. Doubling N will double the activity. This evidence indicates that the rate of decomposition is first order with respect to N. Consequently, the equations describing rates of radioactive decay are the same as those used to de-

■ **Ways of Expressing Activity** Common units for activity are dps (disintegrations per second) and dpm (disintegrations per minute).

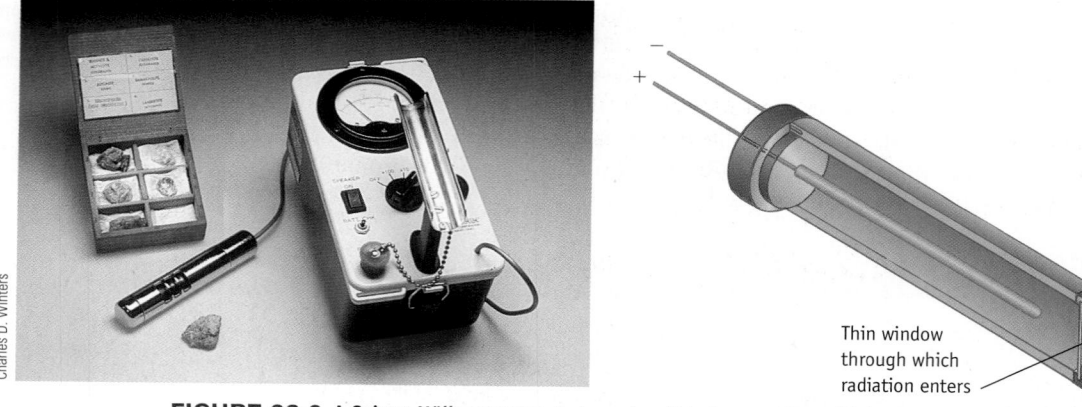

FIGURE 23.6 A Geiger–Müller counter. A charged particle (an α or β particle) enters the gas-filled tube (diagram at the right) and ionizes the gas. The gaseous ions migrate to electrically charged plates and are recorded as a pulse of electric current. The current is amplified and used to operate a counter. A sample of carnotite, a mineral containing uranium oxide, is also shown in the photograph.

Thin window through which radiation enters

scribe first-order chemical reactions; the change in the number of radioactive atoms N per unit of time is proportional to N:

$$\frac{\Delta N}{\Delta t} = -kN \tag{23.3}$$

The integrated rate equation can be written in two ways depending on the data used:

$$\ln\left(\frac{N}{N_0}\right) = -kt \tag{23.4}$$

or

$$\ln\left(\frac{A}{A_0}\right) = -kt \tag{23.5}$$

Here, N_0 and A_0 are the number of atoms and the activity of the sample initially, respectively, and N and A are the number of atoms and the activity of the sample after time t, respectively. Thus, N/N_0 is the fraction of atoms remaining after a given time (t), and A/A_0 is the fraction of the activity remaining after the same period. In these equations, k is the rate constant (decay constant) for the isotope in question. The relationship between half-life and the first-order rate constant is the same as seen with chemical kinetics (Equation 15.4, page 690):

$$t_{1/2} = \frac{0.693}{k} \tag{23.6}$$

Equations 23.3–23.6 are useful in several ways:

- If the activity (A) or the number of radioactive nuclei (N) is measured in the laboratory over some period t, then k can be calculated. The decay constant k can then be used to determine the half-life of the sample.
- If k is known, the fraction of a radioactive sample (N/N_0) still present after some time t has elapsed can be calculated.
- If k is known, the time required for that isotope to decay to a fraction of the original activity (A/A_0) can be calculated.

EXAMPLE 23.6 Determination of Half-Life

Problem A sample of radon-222 has an initial α particle activity (A_0) of 7.0×10^4 dps (disintegrations per second). After 6.6 days, its activity (A) is 2.1×10^4 dps. What is the half-life of radon-222?

Strategy Values for A, A_0, and t are given. The problem can be solved using Equation 23.5 with k as the unknown. Once k is found, the half-life can be calculated using Equation 23.6.

Solution

$$\ln(2.1 \times 10^4 \text{ dps}/7.0 \times 10^4 \text{ dps}) = -k\,(6.6 \text{ day})$$

$$\ln(0.30) = -k(6.6 \text{ day})$$

$$k = 0.18 \text{ days}^{-1}$$

From k we obtain $t_{1/2}$:

$$t_{1/2} = 0.693/0.18 \text{ days}^{-1} = \boxed{3.8 \text{ days}}$$

Comments Notice that the activity decreased to between one half and one fourth of its original value. The 6.6 days of elapsed time represents one full half-life and part of another half-life.

EXAMPLE 23.7 Time Required for a Radioactive Sample to Partially Decay

Problem Gallium citrate, containing the radioactive isotope gallium-67, is used medically as a tumor-seeking agent. It has a half-life of 78.2 h. How long will it take for a sample of gallium citrate to decay to 10.0% of its original activity?

Strategy Use Equation 23.5 to solve this problem. In this case, the unknown is the time t. The rate constant k is calculated from the half-life using Equation 23.6. Although we do not have specific values of activity, the value of A/A_0 is known. Because A is 10.0% of A_0, the value of A/A_0 is 0.100.

Solution First, determine k:

$$k = 0.693/t_{1/2} = 0.693/78.2 \text{ h}$$

$$k = 8.86 \times 10^{-3} \text{ h}^{-1}$$

Then substitute the given values of A/A_0 and k into Equation 23.5:

$$\ln(A/A_0) = -kt$$

$$\ln(0.100) = -(8.86 \times 10^{-3} \text{ h}^{-1})t$$

$$t = \boxed{2.60 \times 10^2 \text{ h}}$$

Comments The time required is between three half-lives ($3 \times 78.2 \text{ h} = 235 \text{ h}$) and four half-lives ($4 \times 78.2 \text{ h} = 313 \text{ h}$).

EXERCISE 23.8 Determination of Half-Life

A sample of $Ca_3(PO_4)_2$ containing phosphorus-32 has an activity of 3.35×10^3 dpm. Two days later, the activity is 3.18×10^3 dpm. Calculate the half-life of phosphorus-32.

EXERCISE 23.9 Time Required for a Radioactive Sample to Partially Decay

A highly radioactive sample of nuclear waste products with a half-life of 200. years is stored in an underground tank. How long will it take for the activity to diminish from an initial activity of 6.50×10^{12} dpm to a fairly harmless activity of 3.00×10^3 dpm?

Radiocarbon Dating

In certain situations, the age of a material can be determined based on the rate of decay of a radioactive isotope. The best-known example of this procedure is the use of carbon-14 to date historical artifacts.

Carbon is primarily carbon-12 and carbon-13 with isotopic abundances of 98.9% and 1.1%, respectively. In addition, traces of a third isotope, carbon-14, are present to the extent of about 1 in 10^{12} atoms in atmospheric CO_2 and in living materials.

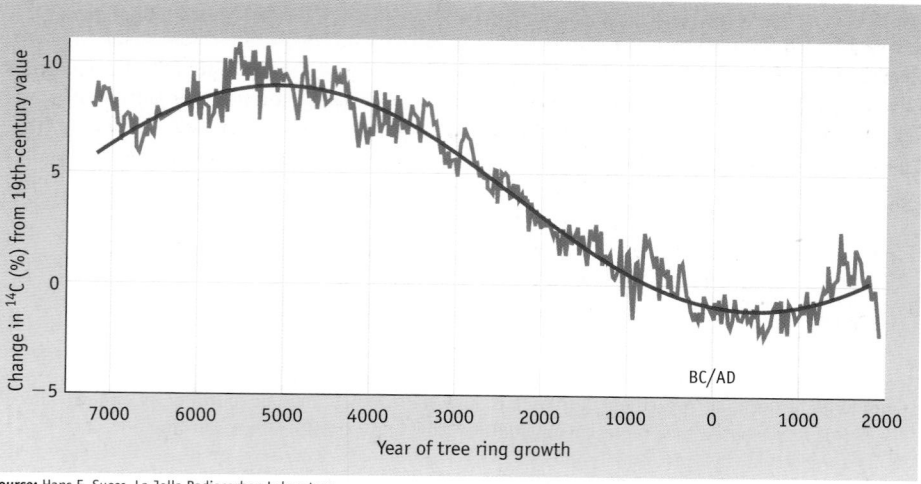

FIGURE 23.7 Variation of atmospheric carbon-14 activity. The amount of carbon-14 has varied with variation in cosmic ray activity. To obtain the data for the pre-1990 part of the curve shown in this graph, scientists carried out carbon-14 dating of artifacts for which the age was accurately known (often through written records). Similar results can be obtained using carbon-14 dating of tree rings.

Source: Hans E. Suess, La Jolla Radiocarbon Laboratory

■ **Willard Libby (1908–1980)** Libby received the 1960 Nobel Prize in chemistry for developing carbon-14 dating techniques. Carbon-14 dating is widely used in fields such as anthropology.

Oesper Collection in the History of Chemistry, University of Cincinnati

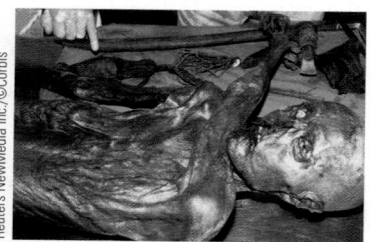

FIGURE 23.8 The Ice Man. The world's oldest preserved human remains were discovered in the ice of a glacier high in the Alps. Carbon-14 dating techniques allowed scientists to determine that he lived about 5300 years ago.

Carbon-14 is a β emitter with a half-life of 5730 years. A 1-gram sample of carbon from living material will show about 14 disintegrations per minute, not a lot of radioactivity but nevertheless detectable by modern methods.

Carbon-14 is formed in the upper atmosphere by nuclear reactions initiated by neutrons in cosmic radiation:

$$^{14}_{7}\text{N} + ^{1}_{0}\text{n} \rightarrow ^{14}_{6}\text{C} + ^{1}_{1}\text{H}$$

Once formed, carbon-14 is oxidized to $^{14}\text{CO}_2$. This product enters the carbon cycle, circulating through the atmosphere, oceans, and biosphere.

The usefulness of carbon-14 for dating comes about in the following way. Plants absorb CO_2 and convert it to organic compounds, thereby incorporating carbon-14 into living tissue. As long as a plant remains alive, this process will continue, and the percentage of carbon that is carbon-14 in the plant will equal the percentage in the atmosphere. When the plant dies, carbon-14 will no longer be taken up. Radioactive decay continues, however, with the carbon-14 activity decreasing over time. After 5730 years, the activity will be 7 dpm/g; after 11,460 years, it will be 3.5 dpm/g; and so on. By measuring the activity of a sample, and knowing the half-life of carbon-14, it is possible to calculate when a plant (or an animal that was eating plants) died.

As with all experimental procedures, carbon-14 dating has limitations. The procedure assumes that the amount of carbon-14 in the atmosphere hundreds or thousands of years ago is the same as it is now. We know that this isn't exactly true; the percentage has varied by as much as 10% (Figure 23.7). Furthermore, it is not possible to use carbon-14 to date an object that is less than about 100 years old; the radiation level from carbon-14 will not change enough in this short time period to permit accurate detection of a difference from the initial value. In most instances, the accuracy of the measurement is, in fact, only about ±100 years. Finally, it is not possible to determine ages of objects much older than about 40,000 years. By then, after nearly seven half-lives, the radioactivity will have decreased virtually to zero. But for the span of time between 100 and 40,000 years, this technique has provided important information (Figure 23.8).

Chemistry .⟨⟩. Now™

Sign in at **www.cengage.com/login** and go to Chapter 23 Contents to see:
- Screen 23.3 for an exercise on **the Geiger counter**
- Screen 23.6 for a tutorial on **half-life and radiochemical dating**

Problem To test the concept of carbon-14 dating, J. R. Arnold and W. F. Libby applied this technique to analyze samples of acacia and cyprus wood whose ages were already known. (The acacia wood, which was supplied by the Metropolitan Museum of Art in New York, came from the tomb of Zoser, the first Egyptian pharaoh to be entombed in a pyramid. The cyprus wood was from the tomb of Sneferu.) The average activity based on five determinations was 7.04 dpm per gram of carbon. Assume (as Arnold and Libby did) that the activity of carbon-14, A_0, is 12.6 dpm per gram of carbon. Calculate the approximate age of the sample.

Strategy First, determine the rate constant for the decay of carbon-14 from its half-life ($t_{1/2}$ for ^{14}C is 5.73×10^3 years). Then, use Equation 23.5.

Solution

$$k = 0.693/t_{1/2} = 0.693/5730 \text{ yr}$$

$$= 1.21 \times 10^{-4} \text{ yr}^{-1}$$

$$\ln (A/A_0) = -kt$$

$$\ln \left(\frac{7.04 \text{ dpm/g}}{12.6 \text{ dpm/g}} \right) = (-1.21 \times 10^{-4} \text{ yr}^{-1})t$$

$$t = 4.8 \times 10^3 \text{ yr}$$

The wood is about 4800 years old.

Comment This problem uses real data from an early research paper in which the carbon-14 dating method was being tested. The age of the wood was known to be 4750 ± 250 years. (See J. R. Arnold and W. F. Libby: *Science,* Vol. 110, p. 678, 1949.)

EXERCISE 23.10 Radiochemical Dating

A sample of the inner part of a redwood tree felled in 1874 was shown to have ^{14}C activity of 9.32 dpm/g. Calculate the approximate age of the tree when it was cut down. Compare this age with that obtained from tree ring data, which estimated that the tree began to grow in 979 ± 52 BC. Use 13.4 dpm/g for the value of A_0.

23.5 Artificial Nuclear Reactions

How many different isotopes are found on earth? All of the stable isotopes occur naturally. A few unstable (radioactive) isotopes that have long half-lives are found in nature; the best-known examples are uranium-235, uranium-238, and thorium-232. Trace quantities of other radioactive isotopes with short half-lives are present because they are being formed continuously by nuclear reactions. They include isotopes of radium, polonium, and radon, along with other elements produced in various radioactive decay series, and carbon-14, formed in a nuclear reaction initiated by cosmic radiation.

Naturally occurring isotopes account for only a very small fraction of the currently known radioactive isotopes, however. The rest—several thousand—have been synthesized via artificial nuclear reactions, sometimes referred to as transmutation.

The first artificial nuclear reaction was identified by Rutherford about 80 years ago. Recall the classic experiment that led to the nuclear model of the atom (See *Milestones in the Development of Chemistry,* page 338) in which gold foil was bombarded with α particles. In the years following that experiment, Rutherford and his coworkers bombarded many other elements with α particles. In 1919, one of these experiments led to an unexpected result: when nitrogen atoms were bombarded with α particles, protons were detected among the products. Rutherford correctly concluded that a nuclear reaction had occurred. Nitrogen had undergone a *transmutation* to oxygen:

$$^{4}_{2}He + ^{14}_{7}N \rightarrow ^{17}_{8}O + ^{1}_{1}H$$

During the next decade, other nuclear reactions were discovered by bombarding other elements with α particles. Progress was slow, however, because in most cases α particles are simply scattered by target nuclei. The bombarding particles cannot get close enough to the nucleus to react because of the strong repulsive forces between the positively charged α particle and the positively charged atomic nucleus.

Two advances were made in 1932 that greatly extended nuclear reaction chemistry. The first involved the use of particle accelerators to create high-energy particles as projectiles. The second was the use of neutrons as the bombarding particles.

The α particles used in the early studies on nuclear reactions came from naturally radioactive materials such as uranium and had relatively low energies, at least by today's standards. Particles with higher energy were needed, so J. D. Cockcroft (1897–1967) and E. T. S. Walton (1903–1995), working in Rutherford's laboratory in Cambridge, England, turned to protons. Protons are formed when hydrogen atoms ionize in a cathode-ray tube, and it was known that they could be accelerated to higher energy by applying a high voltage. Cockcroft and Walton found that when energetic protons struck a lithium target, the following reaction occurs:

$$\mathrm{{}^{7}_{3}Li + {}^{1}_{1}p \rightarrow 2\ {}^{4}_{2}He}$$

This was the first example of a reaction initiated by a particle that had been artificially accelerated to high energy. Since this experiment was conducted, the technique has been developed much further, and the use of particle accelerators in nuclear chemistry is now commonplace. Particle accelerators operate on the principle that a charged particle placed between charged plates will be accelerated to a high speed and high energy. Modern examples of this process are seen in the synthesis of the transuranium elements, several of which are described in more detail in *A Closer Look: The Search for New Elements.*

Experiments using neutrons as bombarding particles were first carried out in both the United States and Great Britain in 1932. Nitrogen, oxygen, fluorine, and neon were bombarded with energetic neutrons, and α particles were detected among the products. Using neutrons made sense: because neutrons have no charge, it was reasoned that these particles would not be repelled by the positively charged nucleus particles. Thus, neutrons did not need high energies to react.

In 1934, Enrico Fermi (1901–1954) and his coworkers showed that nuclear reactions using neutrons are more favorable if the neutrons have low energy. A low energy neutron is simply captured by the nucleus, giving a product in which the mass number is increased by one unit. Because of the low energy of the bombarding particle, the product nucleus does not have sufficient energy to fragment in these reactions. The new nucleus is produced in an excited state, however; when the nucleus returns to the ground state, a γ-ray is emitted. Reactions in which a neutron is captured and a γ-ray is emitted are called **(n, γ) reactions.**

The (n, γ) reactions are the source of many of the radioisotopes used in medicine and chemistry. An example is radioactive phosphorus, $\mathrm{{}^{32}_{15}P}$, which is used in chemical studies such as tracing the uptake of phosphorus in the body.

$$\mathrm{{}^{31}_{15}P + {}^{1}_{0}n \rightarrow {}^{32}_{15}P + \gamma}$$

Transuranium elements, elements with an atomic number greater than 92, were first made in a nuclear reaction sequence beginning with an (n, γ) reaction. Scientists at the University of California at Berkeley bombarded uranium-238 with neutrons. Among the products identified were neptunium-239 and plutonium-239. These new elements were formed when ^{239}U decayed by β radiation.

$$\mathrm{{}^{238}_{92}U + {}^{1}_{0}n \rightarrow {}^{239}_{92}U}$$
$$\mathrm{{}^{239}_{92}U \rightarrow {}^{239}_{93}Np + {}^{0}_{-1}\beta}$$
$$\mathrm{{}^{239}_{93}Np \rightarrow {}^{239}_{94}Pu + {}^{0}_{-1}\beta}$$

■ **Discovery of Neutrons** Neutrons had been predicted to exist for more than a decade before they were identified in 1932 by James Chadwick (1891–1974). Chadwick produced neutrons in a nuclear reaction between α particles and beryllium: $\mathrm{{}^{4}_{2}\alpha + {}^{9}_{4}Be \rightarrow {}^{12}_{6}C + {}^{1}_{0}n}$.

Lawrence Berkeley Laboratory

■ **Glenn T. Seaborg (1912–1999)** Seaborg figured out that thorium and the elements that followed it fit under the lanthanides in the periodic table. For this insight, he and Edwin McMillan shared the 1951 Nobel Prize in chemistry. Over a 21-year period, Seaborg and his colleagues synthesized 10 new transuranium elements (Pu through Lr). To honor Seaborg's scientific contributions, the name "seaborgium" was assigned to element 106. It marked the first time an element was named for a living person.

■ **Transuranium Elements in Nature** Neptunium, plutonium, and americium were unknown prior to their preparation via these nuclear reactions. Later, these elements were found to be present in trace quantities in uranium ores.

A Closer Look

The Search for New Elements

By 1936, guided first by Mendeleev's predictions and later by atomic theory, chemists had identified all but two of the elements with atomic numbers between 1 and 92. From this point onward, all new elements to be discovered came from artificial nuclear reactions. Two gaps in the periodic table were filled when radioactive technetium and promethium, the last two elements with atomic numbers less than 92, were identified in 1937 and 1942, respectively. The first success in the search for elements with atomic numbers higher than 92 came with the 1940 discovery of neptunium and plutonium.

Since 1950, laboratories in the United States (Lawrence Berkeley National Laboratory), Russia (Joint Institute for Nuclear Research at Dubna, near Moscow),

and Europe (Institute for Heavy Ion Research at Darmstadt, Germany) have competed to make new elements. Syntheses of new transuranium elements use a standard methodology. An element of fairly high atomic number is bombarded with a beam of high-energy particles. Initially, neutrons were used; later, helium nuclei and then larger nuclei such as ^{11}B and ^{12}C were employed; and, more recently, highly charged ions of elements such as calcium, chromium, cobalt, and zinc have been chosen. The bombarding particle fuses with the nucleus of the target atom, forming a new nucleus that lasts for a short time before decomposing. New elements are detected by their decomposition products, a signature of particles with specific masses and energies.

By using bigger particles and higher energies, the list of known elements reached 106 by the end of the 1970s. To further extend the search, Russian scientists employed a new idea, matching precisely the energy of the bombarding particle with the energy required to fuse the nuclei. This technique enabled the synthesis of elements 107, 108, and 109 in Darmstadt in the early 1980s, and the synthesis of elements 110, 111, and 112 in the following decade. Lifetimes of these elements were in the millisecond range; the 277 isotope of element 112, for example, mass has a half-life of 240 μs.

Yet another breakthrough was needed to extend the list further. Scientists have long known that isotopes with specific *magic numbers* of neutrons and protons are more stable. Elements with 2, 8, 20, 50, and 82 protons are members of this category, as are elements with 126 neutrons. The magic numbers correspond to filled shells in the nucleus. Their significance is analogous to the significance of filled shells for electronic structure. Theory had predicted that the next magic numbers would be 114 protons and 184 neutrons. Using this information, researchers discovered element 114 in early 1999. The Dubna group reporting this discovery found that the mass 289 isotope had an exceptionally long half-life, about 20 s.

At the time this book was written, 117 elements were known. Will research yield further new elements? It would be hard to say no, given past successes in this area of research, but the quest becomes ever more difficult as scientists venture to the very limits of nuclear stability.

Fermilab Visual Media Services, Batavia, IL

Fermilab. The tunnel housing the four-mile-long particle accelerator at Batavia, Illinois

Four years later, a similar reaction sequence was used to make americium-241. Plutonium-239 was found to add two neutrons to form plutonium-241, which decays by β emission to give americium-241.

■ **EXAMPLE 23.9 Nuclear Reactions**

Problem Write equations for the nuclear reactions described below.

(a) Fluorine-19 undergoes an (n, γ) reaction to give a radioactive product that decays by $_{-1}^{0}\beta$ emission. (Write equations for both nuclear reactions.)

(b) A common neutron source is a plutonium–beryllium alloy. Plutonium-239 is an α emitter. When beryllium-9 (the only stable isotope of beryllium) reacts with α particles emitted by plutonium, neutrons are ejected. (Write equations for both reactions.)

Strategy The equations are written so that both mass and charge are balanced.

Solution

(a) $^{19}_{9}\text{F} + ^{1}_{0}\text{n} \rightarrow ^{20}_{9}\text{F} + \gamma$

$^{20}_{9}\text{F} \rightarrow ^{20}_{10}\text{Ne} + ^{0}_{-1}\beta$

(b) $^{239}_{94}\text{Pu} \rightarrow ^{235}_{92}\text{U} + ^{4}_{2}\alpha$

$^{4}_{2}\alpha + ^{9}_{4}\text{Be} \rightarrow ^{12}_{6}\text{C} + ^{1}_{0}\text{n}$

23.6 Nuclear Fission

In 1938, two chemists, Otto Hahn (1879–1968) and Fritz Strassman (1902–1980), isolated and identified barium in a sample of uranium that had been bombarded with neutrons. How was barium formed? The answer to that question explained one of the most significant scientific discoveries of the 20th century. The uranium nucleus had split into smaller pieces in the process we now call **nuclear fission.**

The details of nuclear fission were unraveled through the work of a number of scientists. They determined that a uranium-235 nucleus initially captured a neutron to form uranium-236. This isotope underwent nuclear fission to produce two new nuclei, one with a mass number around 140 and the other with a mass around 90, along with several neutrons (Figure 23.9). The nuclear reactions that led to formation of barium when a sample of ^{235}U was bombarded with neutrons are

$$^{235}_{92}\text{U} + ^{1}_{0}\text{n} \rightarrow ^{236}_{92}\text{U}$$
$$^{236}_{92}\text{U} \rightarrow ^{141}_{56}\text{Ba} + ^{92}_{36}\text{Kr} + 3 ^{1}_{0}\text{n}$$

An important aspect of fission reactions is that they produce more neutrons than are used to initiate the process. Under the right circumstances, these neutrons then serve to continue the reaction. If one or more of these neutrons are captured by another ^{235}U nucleus, then a further reaction can occur, releasing still more neutrons. This sequence repeats over and over. Such a mechanism, in which each step generates a reactant to continue the reaction, is called a **chain reaction.**

A nuclear fission chain reaction has three general steps:

1. *Initiation.* The reaction of a single atom is needed to start the chain. Fission of ^{235}U is initiated by the absorption of a neutron.
2. *Propagation.* This part of the process repeats itself over and over, with each step yielding more product. The fission of ^{236}U releases neutrons that initiate the fission of other uranium atoms.
3. *Termination.* Eventually, the chain will end. Termination could occur if the reactant (^{235}U) is used up, or if the neutrons that continue the chain escape from the sample without being captured by ^{235}U.

To harness the energy produced in a nuclear reaction, it is necessary to control the rate at which a fission reaction occurs. This is managed by balancing the propagation and termination steps by limiting the number of neutrons available. In a nuclear reactor, this balance is accomplished by using cadmium rods to absorb neutrons. By withdrawing or inserting the rods, the number of neutrons available to propagate the chain can be changed, and the rate of the fission reaction (and the rate of energy production) can be increased or decreased.

Uranium-235 and plutonium-239 are the fissionable isotopes most commonly used in power reactors. Natural uranium contains only 0.72% of uranium-235; more than 99% of the natural element is uranium-238. The percentage of uranium-235 in natural uranium is too small to sustain a chain reaction, however, so the uranium used for nuclear fuel must be enriched in this isotope. One way to do so is by

■ **Fission Reactions** In the fission of uranium-236, a large number of different fission products (elements) are formed. Barium was the element first identified, and its identification provided the key that led to recognition that fission had occurred.

■ **Lise Meitner (1878–1968)** Meitner's greatest contribution to 20th-century science was her explanation of the process of nuclear fission. She and her nephew, Otto Frisch, also a physicist, published a paper in 1939 that was the first to use the term "nuclear fission." Element number 109 is named meitnerium to honor Meitner's contributions. The leader of the team that discovered this element said that "She should be honored as the most significant woman scientist of [the 20th] century."

AIP-Emilio Segré Visual Archives, Herzfeld Collection

■ **The Atomic Bomb** In an atomic bomb, each nuclear fission step produces 3 neutrons, which leads to about 3 more fissions and 9 more neutrons, which leads to 9 more fission steps and 27 more neutrons, and so on. The rate depends on the number of neutrons, so the nuclear reaction occurs faster and faster as more and more neutrons are formed, leading to an enormous output of energy in a short time span.

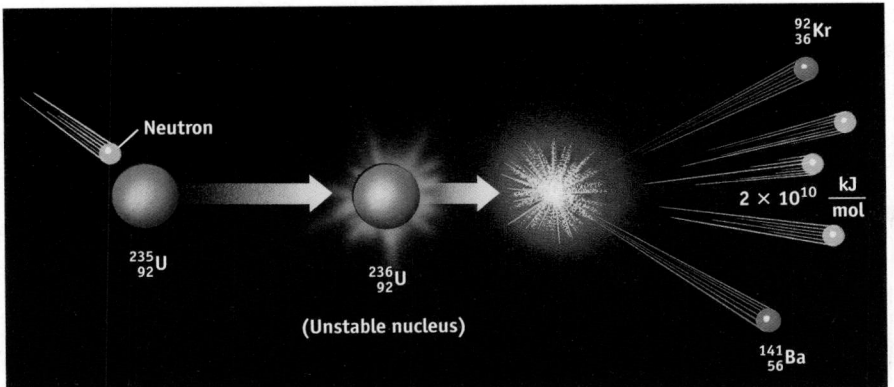

FIGURE 23.9 Nuclear fission.
Neutron capture by $^{235}_{92}U$ produces $^{236}_{92}U$. This isotope undergoes fission, which yields several fragments along with several neutrons. These neutrons initiate further nuclear reactions by adding to other $^{235}_{92}U$ nuclei. The process is highly exothermic, producing about 2×10^{10} kJ/mol.

gaseous diffusion (◄ Section 11.7). Plutonium, which occurs naturally in only trace quantities, must be made via a nuclear reaction. The raw material for this nuclear synthesis is the more abundant uranium isotope, ^{238}U. Addition of a neutron to ^{238}U gives ^{239}U, which, as noted earlier, undergoes two β emissions to form ^{239}Pu.

Currently, there are over 100 operating nuclear power plants in the United States and more than 400 worldwide. About 20% of this country's electricity (and 17% of the world's energy) comes from nuclear power (Table 23.2). Although one might imagine that nuclear energy would be called upon to meet the ever-increasing needs of society, no new nuclear power plants are under construction in the United States. Among other things, the disasters at Chernobyl (in the former Soviet Union) in 1986 and Three Mile Island (in Pennsylvania) in 1979 have sensitized the public to the issue of safety. The cost to construct a nuclear power plant (measured in terms of dollars per kilowatt-hour of power) is considerably more than the cost for a natural gas–powered facility, and the regulatory restrictions for nuclear power are burdensome. Disposal of highly radioactive nuclear waste is another thorny problem, with 20 metric tons of waste being generated per year at each reactor.

In addition to technical problems, nuclear energy production brings with it significant geopolitical security concerns. The process for enriching uranium for use in a reactor is the same process used for generating weapons-grade uranium. Also, some nuclear reactors are designed so that one by-product of their operation is the isotope plutonium-239, which can be removed and used in a nuclear weapon. Despite these problems, nuclear fission is an important part of the energy profile in a number of countries. For example, three fourths of power production in France and one third in Japan is nuclear generated.

TABLE 23.2 Percentage of Electricity Produced Using Nuclear Power Plants

Country (rank)	Total Power from Nuclear Energy (%)
1. France	75.0
2. Lithuania	73.1
3. Belgium	57.7
4. Bulgaria	47.1
5. Slovak Republic	47.0
6. Sweden	46.8
. . .	
19. United States	19.9
20. Russia	14.4
21. Canada	12.7

Source: Chemical and Engineering News, p. 42, Oct. 2, 2000.

23.7 Nuclear Fusion

In a **nuclear fusion** reaction, several small nuclei react to form a larger nucleus. Tremendous amounts of energy can be generated by such reactions. An example is the fusion of deuterium and tritium nuclei to form ^4_2He and a neutron:

$$^2_1H + ^3_1H \rightarrow ^4_2He + ^1_0n \qquad \Delta E = -1.7 \times 10^9 \text{ kJ/mol}$$

Fusion reactions provide the energy of our sun and other stars. Scientists have long dreamed of being able to harness fusion to provide power. To do so, a temperature of 10^6 to 10^7 K, like that in the interior of the sun, would be required to bring the positively charged nuclei together with enough energy to overcome nuclear repulsions. At the very high temperatures needed for a fusion reaction, mat-

■ **Radon in Your Home** You should test your home for the presence of radon gas (◄ page 1065). The activity level should be less than 4 picocuries per liter of air.

ter does not exist as atoms or molecules; instead, matter is in the form of a *plasma* made up of unbound nuclei and electrons.

Three critical requirements must be met before nuclear fusion could represent a viable energy source. First, the temperature must be high enough for fusion to occur. The fusion of deuterium and tritium, for example, requires a temperature of 10^7 K or more. Second, the plasma must be confined long enough to release a net output of energy. Third, the energy must be recovered in some usable form.

Harnessing a nuclear fusion reaction for a peaceful use has not yet been achieved. Nevertheless, many attractive features encourage continuing research in this field. The hydrogen used as "fuel" is cheap and available in almost unlimited amounts. As a further benefit, most radioisotopes produced by fusion have short half-lives, so they remain a radiation hazard for only a short time.

23.8 Radiation Health and Safety

Units for Measuring Radiation

Several units of measurement are used to describe levels and doses of radioactivity. As is the case in everyday life, the units used in the United States are not the same as the SI units of measurement.

In the United States, the degree of radioactivity is often measured in **curies** (Ci). Less commonly used in the United States is the SI unit, the **becquerel** (Bq). Both units measure the number of disintegrations per second; 1 Ci is 3.7×10^{10} dps (disintegrations per second), while 1 Bq represents 1 dps. The curie and the becquerel are used to report the amount of radioactivity when multiple kinds of unstable nuclei are decaying and to report amounts necessary for medical purposes.

By itself, the degree of radioactivity does not provide a good measure of the amount of energy in the radiation or the amount of damage that the radiation can cause to living tissue. Two additional kinds of information are necessary. The first is the amount of energy absorbed; the second is the effectiveness of the particular kind of radiation in causing tissue damage. The amount of energy absorbed by living tissue is measured in **rads.** *Rad* is an acronym for "radiation absorbed dose." One rad represents 0.01 J of energy absorbed per kilogram of tissue. Its SI equivalent is the **gray** (Gy); 1 Gy denotes the absorption of 1 J per kilogram of tissue.

Different forms of radiation cause different amounts of biological damage. The amount of damage depends on how strongly a form of radiation interacts with matter. Alpha particles cannot penetrate the body any farther than the outer layer of skin. If α particles are emitted within the body, however, they will do between 10 and 20 times the amount of damage done by γ-rays, which can go entirely through a human body without being stopped. In determining the amount of biological damage to living tissue, differences in damaging power are accounted for using a "quality factor." This quality factor has been set at 1 for β and γ radiation, 5 for low-energy protons and neutrons, and 20 for α particles or high-energy protons and neutrons.

■ **The Roentgen** The roentgen (R) is an older unit of radiation exposure. It is defined as the amount of x-rays or γ radiation that will produce 2.08×10^9 ions in 1 cm^3 of dry air. The roentgen and the rad are similar in size. Wilhelm Roentgen (1845–1923) first produced and detected x-radiation. Element 111 has been named roentgenium in his honor.

Biological damage is quantified in a unit called the **rem** (an acronym for "roentgen equivalent man"). A dose of radiation in rem is determined by multiplying the energy absorbed in rads by the quality factor for that kind of radiation. The rad and the rem are very large in comparison to normal exposures to radiation, so it is more common to express exposures in millirems (mrem). The SI equivalent of the rem is the **sievert** (Sv), determined by multiplying the dose in grays by the quality factor.

Radiation: Doses and Effects

Exposure to a small amount of radiation is unavoidable. Earth is constantly being bombarded with radioactive particles from outer space. There is also some exposure to radioactive elements that occur naturally on earth, including ^{14}C, ^{40}K (a radioactive isotope that occurs naturally in 0.0117% abundance), ^{238}U, and ^{232}Th. Radioactive elements in the environment that were created artificially (in the fallout from nuclear bomb tests, for example) also contribute to this exposure. For some people, medical procedures using radioisotopes are a major contributor.

The average dose of background radioactivity to which a person in the U.S. is exposed is about 200 mrem per year (Table 23.3). Well over half of that amount comes from natural sources over which we have no control. Of the 60–70 mrem per year exposure that comes from artificial sources, nearly 90% is delivered in medical procedures such as x-ray examinations and radiation therapy. Considering the controversy surrounding nuclear power, it is interesting to note that less than 0.5% of the total annual background dose of radiation that the average person receives can be attributed to the nuclear power industry.

Describing the biological effects of a dose of radiation precisely is not a simple matter. The amount of damage done depends not only on the kind of radiation and the amount of energy absorbed, but also on the particular tissues exposed and the rate at which the dose builds up. A great deal has been learned about the effects of radiation on the human body by studying the survivors of the bombs dropped over Japan in World War II and the workers exposed to radiation from

TABLE 23.3 Radiation Exposure of an Individual for One Year from Natural and Artificial Sources

	Millirem/Year	Percentage
Natural Sources		
Cosmic radiation	50.0	25.8
The earth	47.0	24.2
Building materials	3.0	1.5
Inhaled from the air	5.0	2.6
Elements found naturally in human tissue	21.0	10.8
Subtotal	**126.0**	**64.9**
Medical Sources		
Diagnostic x-rays	50.0	25.8
Radiotherapy	10.0	5.2
Internal diagnosis	1.0	0.5
Subtotal	**61.0**	**31.5**
Other Artificial Sources		
Nuclear power industry	0.85	0.4
Luminous watch dials, TV tubes	2.0	1.0
Fallout from nuclear tests	4.0	2.1
Subtotal	**6.9**	**3.5**
Total	**193.9**	**99.9**

What Is a Safe Exposure?

Is the exposure to natural background radiation totally without effect? Can you equate the effect of a single dose and the effect of cumulative, smaller doses that are spread out over a long period of time? The assumption generally made is that no "safe maximum dose," or level below which absolutely no damage will occur, exists. However, the accuracy of this assumption has come into question. These issues are not testable with human subjects, and tests based on animal studies are not completely reliable because of the uncertainty of species-to-species variations.

The model used by government regulators to set exposure limits assumes that the relationship between exposure to radiation and incidence of radiation-induced problems, such as cancer, anemia, and immune system problems, is linear. Under this assumption, if a dose of $2x$ rem causes damage in 20% of the population, then a dose of x rem will cause damage in 10% of the population. But is this true? Cells do possess mechanisms for repairing damage. Many scientists believe that this self-repair mechanism renders the human body less susceptible to damage from smaller doses of radiation, because the damage will be repaired as part of the normal course of events. They argue that, at extremely low doses of radiation, the self-repair response results in less damage.

The bottom line is that much still remains to be learned in this area. And the stakes are significant.

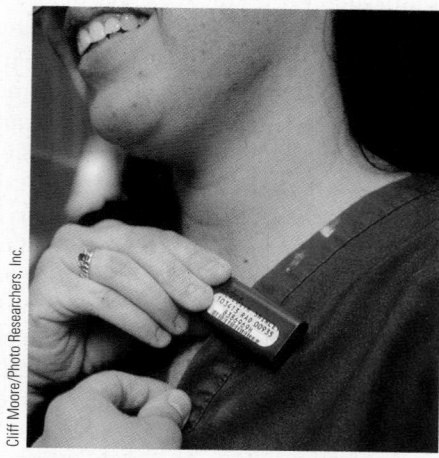

The film badge. These badges, worn by scientists using radioactive materials, are used to monitor cumulative exposure to radiation.

the reactor disaster at Chernobyl. From studies of the health of these survivors, we have learned that the effects of radiation are not generally observable below a single dose of 25 rem. At the other extreme, a single dose of >200 rem will be fatal to about half the population (Table 23.4).

Our information is more accurate when dealing with single, large doses than it is for the effects of chronic, smaller doses of radiation. One current issue of debate in the scientific community is how to judge the effects of multiple smaller doses or long-term exposure (see *A Closer Look: What Is A Safe Exposure?*).

23.9 Applications of Nuclear Chemistry

We tend to think about nuclear chemistry in terms of power plants and bombs. In truth, radioactive elements are now used in all areas of science and medicine, and they are of ever-increasing importance to our lives. Because describing all of their uses would take several books, we have selected just a few examples to illustrate the diversity of applications of radioactivity.

TABLE 23.4 Effects of a Single Dose of Radiation

Dose (rem)	Effect
0–25	No effect observed
26–50	Small decrease in white blood cell count
51–100	Significant decrease in white blood cell count, lesions
101–200	Loss of hair, nausea
201–500	Hemorrhaging, ulcers, death in 50% of population
500	Death

Nuclear Medicine: Medical Imaging

Diagnostic procedures using nuclear chemistry are essential in medical imaging, which entails the creation of images of specific parts of the body. There are three principal components to constructing a radioisotope-based image:

- A radioactive isotope, administered as the element or incorporated into a compound, that concentrates the radioactive isotope in the tissue to be imaged
- A method of detecting the type of radiation involved
- A computer to assemble the information from the detector into a meaningful image

The choice of a radioisotope and the manner in which it is administered are determined by the tissue in question. A compound containing the isotope must be absorbed more by the target tissue than by the rest of the body. Table 23.5 lists radioisotopes that are commonly used in nuclear imaging processes, their half-lives, and the tissues they are used to image. All of the isotopes in Table 23.5 are γ emitters; γ radiation is preferred for imaging because it is less damaging to the body in small doses than either α or β radiation.

Technetium-99m is used in more than 85% of the diagnostic scans done in hospitals each year (see *A Closer Look: Technetium-99m*). The "m" stands for *metastable*, a term used to identify an unstable state that exists for a finite period of time. Recall that atoms in excited electronic states emit visible, infrared, and ultraviolet radiation (◀ Chapter 6). Similarly, a nucleus in an excited state gives up its excess energy, but in this case a much higher energy is involved, and the emission occurs as γ radiation. The γ-rays given off by ^{99m}Tc are detected to produce the image (Figure 23.10).

Another medical imaging technique based on nuclear chemistry is positron emission tomography (PET). In PET, an isotope that decays by positron emission is incorporated into a carrier compound and given to the patient. When emitted, the positron travels no more than a few millimeters before undergoing matter–antimatter annihilation.

$$_{+1}^{0}\beta + {}_{-1}^{0}e \rightarrow 2\gamma$$

The two emitted γ-rays travel in opposite directions. By determining where high numbers of γ-rays are being emitted, one can construct a map showing where the positron emitter is located in the body.

An isotope often used in PET is ^{15}O. A patient is given gaseous O_2 that contains ^{15}O. This isotope travels throughout the body in the bloodstream, allowing images of the brain and bloodstream (Figure 23.11) to be obtained. Because positron emitters are typically very short-lived, PET facilities must be located near a cyclotron where the radioactive nuclei are prepared and then immediately incorporated into a carrier compound.

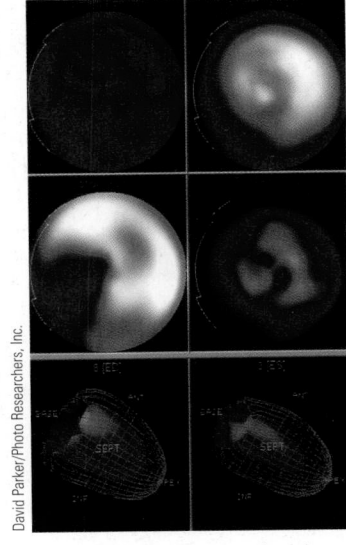

David Parker/Photo Researchers, Inc.

FIGURE 23.10 Heart imaging with technetium-99m. The radioactive element technetium-99m, a gamma emitter, is injected into a patient's vein in the form of the pertechnetate ion (TcO_4^-) or as a complex ion with an organic ligand. A series of scans of the gamma emissions of the isotope are made while the patient is resting and then again after strenuous exercise. Bright areas in the scans indicate that the isotope is binding to the tissue in that area. The scans in this figure show a normal heart function.

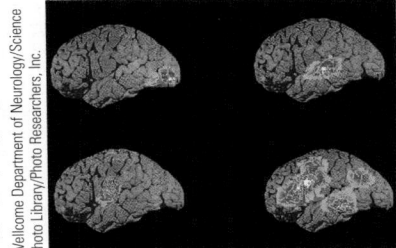

Wellcome Department of Neurology/Science Photo Library/Photo Researchers, Inc.

FIGURE 23.11 PET scans of the brain. These scans show the left side of the brain; red indicates an area of highest activity. (*upper left*) *Sight* activates the visual area in the occipital cortex at the back of the brain. (*upper right*) *Hearing* activates the auditory area in the superior temporal cortex of the brain. (*lower left*) *Speaking* activates the speech centers in the insula and motor cortex. (*lower right*) *Thinking* about verbs, and speaking them, generates high activity, including in the hearing, speaking, temporal, and parietal areas.

TABLE 23.5 Radioisotopes Used in Medical Diagnostic Procedures

Radioisotope	Half-Life (h)	Imaging
^{99m}Tc	6.0	Thyroid, brain, kidneys
^{201}Tl	73.0	Heart
^{123}I	13.2	Thyroid
^{67}Ga	78.2	Various tumors and abscesses
^{18}F	1.8	Brain, sites of metabolic activity

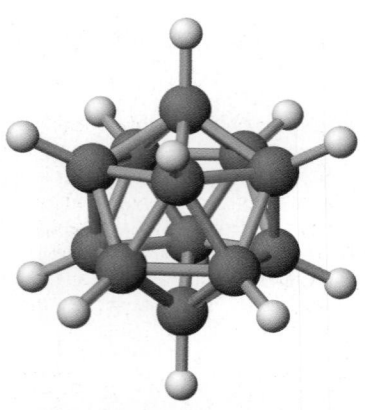

One of the compounds used in BNCT is Na$_2$[B$_{12}$H$_{12}$]. The structure of the B$_{12}$H$_{12}^{2-}$ anion is a regular polyhedron with 20 sides, called an icosahedron.

Nuclear Medicine: Radiation Therapy

To treat most cancers, it is necessary to use radiation that can penetrate the body to the location of the tumor. Gamma radiation from a cobalt-60 source is commonly used. Unfortunately, the penetrating ability of γ-rays makes it virtually impossible to destroy diseased tissue without also damaging healthy tissue in the process. Nevertheless, this technique is a regularly sanctioned procedure, and its successes are well known.

To avoid the side effects associated with more traditional forms of radiation therapy, a new form of treatment has been explored in the last 10 to 15 years, called *boron neutron capture therapy* (BNCT). BNCT is unusual in that boron-10, the isotope of boron used as part of the treatment, is not radioactive. Boron-10 is highly effective in capturing neutrons, however—2500 times better than boron-11, and eight times better than uranium-235. When the nucleus of a boron-10 atom captures a neutron, the resulting boron-11 nucleus has so much energy that it fragments to form an α particle and a lithium-7 atom. Although the α particles do a great deal of damage, because their penetrating power is so low, the damage remains confined to an area not much larger than one or two cells in diameter.

In a typical BNCT treatment, a solution of a boron compound is injected into the tumor. After a few hours, the tumor is bombarded with neutrons. The α particles are produced only at the site of the tumor, and the production stops when the neutron bombardment ends.

Analytical Methods: The Use of Radioactive Isotopes as Tracers

Radioactive isotopes can be used to help determine the fate of compounds in the body or in the environment. These studies begin with a compound that contains a radioactive isotope of one of its component elements. In biology, for example, scientists can use radioactive isotopes to measure the uptake of nutrients. Plants take up phosphorus-containing compounds from the soil through their roots. By adding a small amount of radioactive ^{32}P, a β emitter with a half-life of 14.3 days, to fertilizer and then measuring the rate at which the radioactivity appears in the leaves, plant biologists can determine the rate at which phosphorus is taken up. The outcome can assist scientists in identifying hybrid strains of plants that can absorb phosphorus quickly, resulting in faster-maturing crops, better yields per acre, and more food or fiber at less expense.

To measure pesticide levels, a pesticide can be tagged with a radioisotope and then applied to a test field. By counting the disintegrations of the radioactive tracer, information can be obtained about how much pesticide accumulates in the soil, is taken up by the plant, and is carried off in runoff surface water. After these tests are completed, the radioactive isotope decays to harmless levels in a few days or a few weeks because of the short half-lives of the isotopes used.

Analytical Methods: Isotope Dilution

Imagine, for the moment, that you wanted to estimate the volume of blood in an animal subject. How might you do this? Obviously, draining the blood and measuring its volume in volumetric glassware is not a desirable option.

One technique uses a method called isotope dilution. In this process, a small amount of radioactive isotope is injected into the bloodstream. After a period of time to allow the isotope to become distributed throughout the body, a blood sample is taken and its radioactivity measured. The calculation used to determine the total blood volume is illustrated in the next example.

STUDY QUESTIONS

⬤WL Online homework for this chapter may be assigned in OWL.

▲ denotes challenging questions.

■ denotes questions assignable in OWL.

Blue-numbered questions have answers in Appendix O and fully-worked solutions in the *Student Solutions Manual*.

Practicing Skills

Important Concepts

1. Some important discoveries in scientific history that contributed to the development of nuclear chemistry are listed below. Briefly, describe each discovery, identify prominent scientists who contributed to it, and comment on the significance of the discovery to the development of this field.
   (a) 1896, the discovery of radioactivity
   (b) 1898, the identification of radium and polonium
   (c) 1918, the first artificial nuclear reaction
   (d) 1932, (n, γ) reactions
   (e) 1939, fission reactions

2. In Chapter 3, the law of conservation of mass was introduced as an important principle in chemistry. The discovery of nuclear reactions forced scientists to modify this law. Explain why, and give an example illustrating that mass is not conserved in a nuclear reaction.

3. A graph of binding energy per nucleon is shown in Figure 23.4. Explain how the data used to construct this graph were obtained.

4. How is Figure 23.3 used to predict the type of decomposition for unstable (radioactive) isotopes?

5. Outline how nuclear reactions are carried out in the laboratory. Describe the artificial nuclear reactions used to make an element with an atomic number greater than 92.

6. What mathematical equations define the rates of decay for radioactive elements?

7. Explain how carbon-14 is used to estimate the ages of archeological artifacts. What are the limitations for use of this technique?

8. Describe how the concept of half-life for nuclear decay is used.

9. What is a radioactive decay series? Explain why radium and polonium are found in uranium ores.

10. The interaction of radiation with matter has both positive and negative consequences. Discuss briefly the hazards of radiation and the way that radiation can be used in medicine.

Nuclear Reactions
(See Examples 23.1 and 23.2.)

11. Complete the following nuclear equations. Write the mass number and atomic number for the remaining particle, as well as its symbol.
    (a) $^{54}_{26}\text{Fe} + ^{4}_{2}\text{He} \longrightarrow 2\,^{1}_{0}\text{n} + ?$
    (b) $^{27}_{13}\text{Al} + ^{4}_{2}\text{He} \longrightarrow ^{30}_{15}\text{P} + ?$
    (c) $^{32}_{16}\text{S} + ^{1}_{0}\text{n} \longrightarrow ^{1}_{1}\text{H} + ?$
    (d) $^{96}_{42}\text{Mo} + ^{2}_{1}\text{H} \longrightarrow ^{1}_{0}\text{n} + ?$
    (e) $^{98}_{42}\text{Mo} + ^{1}_{0}\text{n} \longrightarrow ^{99}_{43}\text{Tc} + ?$
    (f) $^{18}_{9}\text{F} \longrightarrow ^{18}_{8}\text{O} + ?$

12. ■ Complete the following nuclear equations. Write the mass number, atomic number, and symbol for the remaining particle.
    (a) $^{9}_{4}\text{Be} + ? \longrightarrow ^{6}_{3}\text{Li} + ^{4}_{2}\text{He}$
    (b) $? + ^{1}_{0}\text{n} \longrightarrow ^{24}_{11}\text{Na} + ^{4}_{2}\text{He}$
    (c) $^{40}_{20}\text{Ca} + ? \longrightarrow ^{40}_{19}\text{K} + ^{1}_{1}\text{H}$
    (d) $^{241}_{95}\text{Am} + ^{4}_{2}\text{He} \longrightarrow ^{243}_{97}\text{Bk} + ?$
    (e) $^{246}_{96}\text{Cm} + ^{12}_{6}\text{C} \longrightarrow 4\,^{1}_{0}\text{n} + ?$
    (f) $^{238}_{92}\text{U} + ? \longrightarrow ^{249}_{100}\text{Fm} + 5\,^{1}_{0}\text{n}$

13. Complete the following nuclear equations. Write the mass number, atomic number, and symbol for the remaining particle.
    (a) $^{111}_{47}\text{Ag} \longrightarrow ^{111}_{48}\text{Cd} + ?$
    (b) $^{87}_{36}\text{Kr} \longrightarrow ^{0}_{-1}\beta + ?$
    (c) $^{231}_{91}\text{Pa} \longrightarrow ^{227}_{89}\text{Ac} + ?$
    (d) $^{230}_{90}\text{Th} \longrightarrow ^{4}_{2}\text{He} + ?$
    (e) $^{82}_{35}\text{Br} \longrightarrow ^{82}_{36}\text{Kr} + ?$
    (f) $? \longrightarrow ^{24}_{12}\text{Mg} + ^{0}_{-1}\beta$

14. Complete the following nuclear equations. Write the mass number, atomic number, and symbol for the remaining particle.
    (a) $^{19}_{10}\text{Ne} \longrightarrow ^{0}_{+1}\beta + ?$
    (b) $^{59}_{26}\text{Fe} \longrightarrow ^{0}_{-1}\beta + ?$
    (c) $^{40}_{19}\text{K} \longrightarrow ^{0}_{-1}\beta + ?$
    (d) $^{37}_{18}\text{Ar} + ^{0}_{-1}\text{e}$ (electron capture) $\longrightarrow ?$
    (e) $^{55}_{26}\text{Fe} + ^{0}_{-1}\text{e}$ (electron capture) $\longrightarrow ?$
    (f) $^{26}_{13}\text{Al} \longrightarrow ^{25}_{12}\text{Mg} + ?$

15. The uranium-235 radioactive decay series, beginning with $^{235}_{92}\text{U}$ and ending with $^{207}_{82}\text{Pb}$, occurs in the following sequence: $\alpha, \beta, \alpha, \beta, \alpha, \alpha, \alpha, \alpha, \beta, \beta, \alpha$. Write an equation for each step in this series.

16. ■ The thorium-232 radioactive decay series, beginning with $^{232}_{90}\text{Th}$ and ending with $^{208}_{82}\text{Pb}$, occurs in the following sequence: $\alpha, \beta, \beta, \alpha, \alpha, \alpha, \alpha, \beta, \beta, \alpha$. Write an equation for each step in this series.

Nuclear Stability and Nuclear Decay
(See Examples 23.3 and 23.4.)

17. ■ What particle is emitted in the following nuclear reactions? Write an equation for each reaction.
(a) Gold-198 decays to mercury-198.
(b) Radon-222 decays to polonium-218.
(c) Cesium-137 decays to barium-137.
(d) Indium-110 decays to cadmium-110.

18. ■ What is the product of the following nuclear decay processes? Write an equation for each process.
(a) Gallium-67 decays by electron capture.
(b) Potassium-38 decays with positron emission.
(c) Technetium-99m decays with γ emission.
(d) Manganese-56 decays by β emission.

19. Predict the probable mode of decay for each of the following radioactive isotopes, and write an equation to show the products of decay.
(a) Bromine-80m   (c) Cobalt-61
(b) Californium-240   (d) Carbon-11

20. ■ Predict the probable mode of decay for each of the following radioactive isotopes, and write an equation to show the products of decay.
(a) Manganese-54   (c) Silver-110
(b) Americium-241   (d) Mercury-197m

21. (a) Which of the following nuclei decay by $_{-1}^{0}\beta$ decay?

$$^{3}\text{H} \quad ^{16}\text{O} \quad ^{20}\text{F} \quad ^{13}\text{N}$$

(b) Which of the following nuclei decays by $_{+1}^{0}\beta$ decay?

$$^{238}\text{U} \quad ^{19}\text{F} \quad ^{22}\text{Na} \quad ^{24}\text{Na}$$

22. (a) Which of the following nuclei decay by $_{-1}^{0}\beta$ decay?

$$^{1}\text{H} \quad ^{23}\text{Mg} \quad ^{32}\text{P} \quad ^{20}\text{Ne}$$

(b) Which of the following nuclei decay by $_{+1}^{0}\beta$ decay?

$$^{235}\text{U} \quad ^{35}\text{Cl} \quad ^{38}\text{K} \quad ^{24}\text{Na}$$

23. ■ Boron has two stable isotopes, ^{10}B and ^{11}B. Calculate the binding energies per nucleon of these two nuclei. The required masses (in g/mol) are $_{1}^{1}\text{H} = 1.00783$, $_{0}^{1}\text{n} = 1.00867$, $_{5}^{10}\text{B} = 10.01294$, and $_{5}^{11}\text{B} = 11.00931$.

24. Calculate the binding energy in kilojoules per mole of nucleons of P for the formation of ^{30}P and ^{31}P. The required masses (in g/mol) are $_{1}^{1}\text{H} = 1.00783$, $_{0}^{1}\text{n} = 1.00867$, $_{15}^{30}\text{P} = 29.97832$, and $_{15}^{31}\text{P} = 30.97376$.

25. Calculate the binding energy per nucleon for calcium-40, and compare your result with the value in Figure 23.4. Masses needed for this calculation are (in g/mol) $_{1}^{1}\text{H} = 1.00783$, $_{0}^{1}\text{n} = 1.00867$, and $_{20}^{40}\text{Ca} = 39.96259$.

26. Calculate the binding energy per nucleon for iron-56. Masses needed for this calculation (in g/mol) are $_{1}^{1}\text{H} = 1.00783$, $_{0}^{1}\text{n} = 1.00867$, and $_{26}^{56}\text{Fe} = 55.9349$. Compare the result of your calculation to the value for iron-56 in the graph in Figure 23.4.

27. Calculate the binding energy per mole of nucleons for $_{8}^{16}\text{O}$. Masses needed for this calculations are $_{1}^{1}\text{H} = 1.00783$, $_{0}^{1}\text{n} = 1.00867$, and $_{8}^{16}\text{O} = 15.99492$.

28. Calculate the binding energy per nucleon for nitrogen-14. The mass of nitrogen-14 is 14.003074.

Rates of Radioactive Decay
(See Examples 23.5 and 23.6.)

29. Copper acetate containing ^{64}Cu is used to study brain tumors. This isotope has a half-life of 12.7 h. If you begin with 25.0 μg of ^{64}Cu, what mass in micrograms remains after 63.5 h?

30. ■ Gold-198 is used in the diagnosis of liver problems. The half-life of ^{198}Au is 2.69 days. If you begin with 2.8 μg of this gold isotope, what mass remains after 10.8 days?

31. Iodine-131 is used to treat thyroid cancer.
(a) The isotope decays by β particle emission. Write a balanced equation for this process.
(b) Iodine-131 has a half-life of 8.04 days. If you begin with 2.4 μg of radioactive ^{131}I, what mass remains after 40.2 days?

32. ■ Phosphorus-32 is used in the form of Na_2HPO_4 in the treatment of chronic myeloid leukemia, among other things.
(a) The isotope decays by β particle emission. Write a balanced equation for this process.
(b) The half-life of ^{32}P is 14.3 days. If you begin with 4.8 μg of radioactive ^{32}P in the form of Na_2HPO_4, what mass remains after 28.6 days (about one month)?

33. Gallium-67 ($t_{1/2} = 78.25$ h) is used in the medical diagnosis of certain kinds of tumors. If you ingest a compound containing 0.015 mg of this isotope, what mass (in milligrams) remains in your body after 13 days? (Assume none is excreted.)

34. ■ Iodine-131 ($t_{1/2} = 8.04$ days), a β emitter, is used to treat thyroid cancer.
(a) Write an equation for the decomposition of ^{131}I.
(b) If you ingest a sample of NaI containing ^{131}I, how much time is required for the activity to decrease to 35.0% of its original value?

35. Radon has been the focus of much attention recently because it is often found in homes. Radon-222 emits α particles and has a half-life of 3.82 d.
(a) Write a balanced equation to show this process.
(b) How long does it take for a sample of ^{222}Rn to decrease to 20.0% of its original activity?

36. ■ Strontium-90 is a hazardous radioactive isotope that resulted from atmospheric testing of nuclear weapons. A sample of strontium carbonate containing ^{90}Sr is found to have an activity of 1.0×10^3 dpm. One year later, the activity of this sample is 975 dpm.

▲ more challenging   ■ in OWL   Blue-numbered questions answered in Appendix O

(a) Calculate the half-life of strontium-90 from this information.

(b) How long will it take for the activity of this sample to drop to 1.0% of the initial value?

37. Radioactive cobalt-60 is used extensively in nuclear medicine as a γ-ray source. It is made by a neutron capture reaction from cobalt-59 and is a β emitter; β emission is accompanied by strong γ radiation. The half-life of cobalt-60 is 5.27 years.

(a) How long will it take for a cobalt-60 source to decrease to one eighth of its original activity?

(b) What fraction of the activity of a cobalt-60 source remains after 1.0 year?

38. Scandium occurs in nature as a single isotope, scandium-45. Neutron irradiation produces scandium-46, a β emitter with a half-life of 83.8 days. If the initial activity is 7.0×10^4 dpm, draw a graph showing disintegrations per minute as a function of time during a period of one year.

Nuclear Reactions
(See Example 23.9.)

39. Americium-240 is made by bombarding plutonium-239 with α particles. In addition to ^{240}Am, the products are a proton and two neutrons. Write a balanced equation for this process.

40. There are two isotopes of americium, both with half-lives sufficiently long to allow the handling of large quantities. Americium-241, with a half-life of 432 years, is an α emitter. It is used in smoke detectors. The isotope is formed from ^{239}Pu by absorption of two neutrons followed by emission of a β particle. Write a balanced equation for this process.

41. ■ The superheavy element ^{287}Uuq was made by firing a beam of ^{48}Ca ions at ^{242}Pu. Three neutrons were ejected in the reaction. Write a balanced nuclear equation for the synthesis of ^{287}Uuq.

42. To synthesize the heavier transuranium elements, a nucleus must be bombarded with a relatively large particle. If you know the products are californium-246 and four neutrons, with what particle would you bombard uranium-238 atoms?

43. Deuterium nuclei ($^2_1$H) are particularly effective as bombarding particles to carry out nuclear reactions. Complete the following equations:

(A) $^{114}_{48}\text{Cd} + ^2_1\text{H} \longrightarrow ? + ^1_1\text{H}$

(B) $^6_3\text{Li} + ^2_1\text{H} \longrightarrow ? + ^1_0\text{n}$

(C) $^{40}_{20}\text{Ca} + ^2_1\text{H} \longrightarrow ^{38}_{19}\text{K} + ?$

(D) $? + ^2_1\text{H} \longrightarrow ^{65}_{30}\text{Zn} + \gamma$

44. Element ^{287}114 decayed by α emission with a half-life of about 5 s. Write an equation for this process.

45. Boron is an effective absorber of neutrons. When boron-10 adds a neutron, an α particle is emitted. Write an equation for this nuclear reaction.

46. Some of the reactions explored by Rutherford and others are listed below. Identify the unknown species in each reaction.

(a) $^{14}_7\text{N} + ^4_2\text{He} \longrightarrow ^{17}_8\text{O} + ?$

(b) $^9_4\text{Be} + ^4_2\text{He} \longrightarrow ? + ^1_0\text{n}$

(c) $? + ^4_2\text{He} \longrightarrow ^{30}_{15}\text{P} + ^1_0\text{n}$

(d) $^{239}_{94}\text{Pu} + ^4_2\text{He} \longrightarrow ? + ^1_0\text{n}$

General Questions
These questions are not designated as to type or location in the chapter. They may combine several concepts.

47. ■ ▲ A technique to date geological samples uses rubidium-87, a long-lived radioactive isotope of rubidium ($t_{1/2} = 4.8 \times 10^{10}$ years). Rubidium-87 decays by β emission to strontium-87. If the rubidium-87 is part of a rock or mineral, then strontium-87 will remain trapped within the crystalline structure of the rock. The age of the rock dates back to the time when the rock solidified. Chemical analysis of the rock gives the amounts of ^{87}Rb and ^{87}Sr. From these data, the fraction of ^{87}Rb that remains can be calculated.

Analysis of a stony meteorite determined that 1.8 mmol of ^{87}Rb and 1.6 mmol of ^{87}Sr were present. Estimate the age of the meteorite. (*Hint:* The amount of ^{87}Rb at t_0 is moles ^{87}Rb + moles ^{87}Sr.)

48. Tritium, $^3_1$H, is one of the nuclei used in fusion reactions. This isotope is radioactive, with a half-life of 12.3 years. Like carbon-14, tritium is formed in the upper atmosphere from cosmic radiation, and it is found in trace amounts on earth. To obtain the amounts required for a fusion reaction, however, it must be made via a nuclear reaction. The reaction of $^6_3$Li with a neutron produces tritium and an α particle. Write an equation for this nuclear reaction.

49. Phosphorus occurs in nature as a single isotope, phosphorus-31. Neutron irradiation of phosphorus-31 produces phosphorus-32, a β emitter with a half-life of 14.28 days. Assume you have a sample containing phosphorus-32 that has a rate of decay of 3.2×10^6 dpm. Draw a graph showing disintegrations per minute as a function of time during a period of one year.

50. ■ In June 1972, natural fission reactors, which operated billions of years ago, were discovered in Oklo, Gabon (page 1060). At present, natural uranium contains 0.72% ^{235}U. How many years ago did natural uranium contain 3.0% ^{235}U, the amount needed to sustain a natural reactor? ($t_{1/2}$ for ^{235}U is 7.04×10^8 years.)

51. If a shortage in worldwide supplies of fissionable uranium arose, it would be possible to use other fissionable nuclei. Plutonium, one such fuel, can be made in "breeder" reactors that manufacture more fuel than they consume. The sequence of reactions by which plutonium is made is as follows:
    (a) A ^{238}U nucleus undergoes an (n, γ) to produce ^{239}U.
    (b) ^{239}U decays by β emission ($t_{1/2}$ = 23.5 min) to give an isotope of neptunium.
    (c) This neptunium isotope decays by β emission to give a plutonium isotope.
    (d) The plutonium isotope is fissionable. On collision of one of these plutonium isotopes with a neutron, fission occurs, with at least two neutrons and two other nuclei as products.

    Write an equation for each of the nuclear reactions.

52. ■ When a neutron is captured by an atomic nucleus, energy is released as γ radiation. This energy can be calculated based on the change in mass in converting reactants to products.

    For the nuclear reaction $^6_3Li + ^1_0n \longrightarrow ^7_3Li + \gamma$:

    (a) Calculate the energy evolved in this reaction (per atom). Masses needed (in g/mol) are ^6_3Li = 6.01512, ^1_0n = 1.00867, and ^7_3Li = 7.01600.
    (b) Use the answer in part (a) to calculate the wavelength of the γ-rays emitted in the reaction.

In the Laboratory

53. A piece of charred bone found in the ruins of a Native American village has a $^{14}C : ^{12}C$ ratio that is 72% of the ratio found in living organisms. Calculate the age of the bone fragment ($t_{1/2}$ for ^{14}C is 5.73 × 103 y).

54. ■ A sample of wood from a Thracian chariot found in an excavation in Bulgaria has a ^{14}C activity of 11.2 dpm/g. Estimate the age of the chariot and the year it was made ($t_{1/2}$ for ^{14}C is 5.73 × 10³ years, and the activity of ^{14}C in living material is 14.0 dpm/g).

55. The isotope of polonium that was most likely isolated by Marie Curie in her pioneering studies is polonium-210. A sample of this element was prepared in a nuclear reaction. Initially, its activity (α emission) was 7840 dpm. Measuring radioactivity over time produced the data below. Determine the half-life of polonium-210.

Activity (dpm)	Time (days)
7840	0
7570	7
7300	14
5920	56
5470	72

56. Sodium-23 (in a sample of NaCl) is subjected to neutron bombardment in a nuclear reactor to produce ^{24}Na. When removed from the reactor, the sample is radioactive, with β activity of 2.54 × 10⁴ dpm. The decrease in radioactivity over time was studied, producing the following data:

Activity (dpm)	Time (h)
2.54 × 10⁴	0
2.42 × 10⁴	1
2.31 × 10⁴	2
2.00 × 10⁴	5
1.60 × 10⁴	10
1.01 × 10⁴	20

    (a) Write equations for the neutron capture reaction and for the reaction in which the product of this reaction decays by β emission.
    (b) Determine the half-life of sodium-24.

57. The age of minerals can sometimes be determined by measuring the amounts of ^{206}Pb and ^{238}U in a sample. This determination assumes that all of the ^{206}Pb in the sample comes from the decay of ^{238}U. The date obtained identifies when the rock solidified. Assume that the ratio of ^{206}Pb to ^{238}U in an igneous rock sample is 0.33. Calculate the age of the rock. ($t_{1/2}$ for ^{238}U is 4.5 × 10⁹ y.)

58. ■ The oldest-known fossil found in South Africa has been dated based on the decay of Rb-87.

$$^{87}Rb \longrightarrow ^{87}Sr + ^0_{-1}\beta \qquad t_{1/2} = 4.8 \times 10^{10} \text{ y}$$

    If the ratio of the present quantity of ^{87}Rb to the original quantity is 0.951, calculate the age of the fossil.

59. To measure the volume of the blood system of an animal, the following experiment was done. A 1.0-mL sample of an aqueous solution containing tritium, with an activity of 2.0 × 10⁶ dps, was injected into the animal's bloodstream. After time was allowed for complete circulatory mixing, a 1.0-mL blood sample was withdrawn and found to have an activity of 1.5 × 10⁴ dps. What was the volume of the circulatory system? (The half-life of tritium is 12.3 y, so this experiment assumes that only a negligible amount of tritium has decayed in the time of the experiment.)

60. Suppose that you hydrolyze 4.644 g of a protein to form a mixture of different amino acids. To this is added a 2.80-mg sample of ^{14}C-labeled threonine (one of the amino acids present). The activity of this small sample is 1950 dpm. A chromatographic separation of the amino acids is carried out, and a small sample of pure threonine is separated. This sample has an activity of 550 dpm. What fraction of the threonine present was separated? What is the total amount of threonine in the sample?

Summary and Conceptual Questions

The following questions may use concepts from this and previous chapters.

61. ■ The average energy output of a good grade of coal is 2.6×10^7 kJ/ton. Fission of 1 mol of ^{235}U releases 2.1×10^{10} kJ. Find the number of tons of coal needed to produce the same energy as 1 lb of ^{235}U. (See Appendix C for conversion factors.)

62. ■ Collision of an electron and a positron results in formation of two γ-rays. In the process, their masses are converted completely into energy.
    (a) Calculate the energy evolved from the annihilation of an electron and a positron, in kilojoules per mole.
    (b) Using Planck's equation (Equation 6.2), determine the frequency of the γ -rays emitted in this process.

63. The principle underlying the isotope dilution method can be applied to many kinds of problems. Suppose that you, a marine biologist, want to estimate the number of fish in a lake. You release 1000 tagged fish, and after allowing an adequate amount of time for the fish to disperse evenly in the lake, you catch 5250 fish and find that 27 of them have tags. How many fish are in the lake?

64. ▲ Radioactive isotopes are often used as "tracers" to follow an atom through a chemical reaction. The following is an example of this process: acetic acid reacts with methanol, CH_3OH, by eliminating a molecule of H_2O to form methyl acetate, $CH_3CO_2CH_3$. Explain how you would use the radioactive isotope ^{15}O to show whether the oxygen atom in the water product comes from the —OH of the acid or the —OH of the alcohol.

65. ▲ Radioactive decay series begin with a very long-lived isotope. For example, the half-life of ^{238}U is 4.5×10^9 y. Each series is identified by the name of the long-lived parent isotope of highest mass.
    (a) The uranium-238 radioactive decay series is sometimes referred to as the $4n + 2$ series because the masses of all 13 members of this series can be expressed by the equation $m = 4n + 2$, where m is the mass number and n is an integer. Explain why the masses are correlated in this way. (See the Comment in Example 23.1.)
    (b) Two other radioactive decay series identified in minerals in the earth's crust are the thorium-232 series and the uranium-235 series. Do the masses of the isotopes in these series conform to a simple mathematical equation? If so, identify the equation.
    (c) Identify the radioactive decay series to which each of the following isotopes belongs: $^{226}_{88}$Ra, $^{215}_{86}$At, $^{228}_{90}$Th, $^{210}_{83}$Bi.
    (d) Evaluation reveals that one series of elements, the $4n + 1$ series, is not present in the earth's crust. Speculate why.

66. ▲ The thorium decay series includes the isotope $^{228}_{90}$Th. Determine the sequence of nuclei on going from $^{232}_{90}$Th to $^{228}_{90}$Th.

67. ▲ The last unknown element between bismuth and uranium was discovered by Lise Meitner (1878–1968) and Otto Hahn (1879–1968) in 1918. They obtained ^{231}Pa by chemical extraction of pitchblende, in which its concentration is about 1 ppm. This isotope, an α emitter, has a half-life of 3.27×10^4 y.
    (a) Which radioactive decay series (the uranium-235, uranium-238, or thorium-232 series) contains ^{231}Pa as a member? (See the Comment in Example 23.1.)
    (b) Suggest a possible sequence of nuclear reactions starting with the long-lived isotope that eventually forms this isotope.
    (c) What quantity of ore would be required to isolate 1.0 g of ^{231}Pa, assuming 100% yield?
    (d) Write an equation for the radioactive decay process for ^{231}Pa.

68. ▲ You might wonder how it is possible to determine the half-life of long-lived radioactive isotopes such as ^{238}U. With a half-life of more than 10^9 y, the radioactivity of a sample of uranium will not measurably change in your lifetime. In fact, you can calculate the half-life using the mathematics governing first-order reactions.

    It can be shown that a 1.0-mg sample of ^{238}U decays at the rate of 12 α emissions per second. Set up a mathematical equation for the rate of decay, $\Delta N/\Delta t = -kN$, where N is the number of nuclei in the 1.0-mg sample and $\Delta N/\Delta t$ is 12 dps. Solve this equation for the rate constant for this process, and then relate the rate constant to the half-life of the reaction. Carry out this calculation, and compare your result with the literature value, 4.5×10^9 years.

69. ▲ Marie and Pierre Curie isolated radium and polonium from uranium ore (pitchblende, which contains ^{238}U and ^{235}U). Which of the following isotopes of radium and polonium can be found in the uranium ore? (Hint: consider both the isotope half lives and the decay series starting with ^{238}U and ^{235}U.)

Isotope	Half-life
^{226}Ra	1620 y
^{225}Ra	14.8 d
^{228}Ra	6.7 y
^{216}Po	0.15 s
^{210}Po	138.4 d

List of Appendices

A | Using Logarithms and the Quadratic Equation

An introductory chemistry course requires basic algebra plus a knowledge of (1) exponential (or scientific) notation, (2) logarithms, and (3) quadratic equations. The use of exponential notation was reviewed on pages 32–35, and this appendix reviews the last two topics.

A.1 Logarithms

Two types of logarithms are used in this text: (1) common logarithms (abbreviated log) whose base is 10 and (2) natural logarithms (abbreviated ln) whose base is e ($= 2.71828$):

$$\log x = n, \text{ where } x = 10^n$$
$$\ln x = m, \text{ where } x = e^m$$

Most equations in chemistry and physics were developed in natural, or base e, logarithms, and we follow this practice in this text. The relation between log and ln is

$$\ln x = 2.303 \log x$$

Despite the different bases of the two logarithms, they are used in the same manner. What follows is largely a description of the use of common logarithms.

A common logarithm is the power to which you must raise 10 to obtain the number. For example, the log of 100 is 2, since you must raise 10 to the second power to obtain 100. Other examples are

$$
\begin{aligned}
\log 1000 &= \log (10^3) = 3 \\
\log 10 &= \log (10^1) = 1 \\
\log 1 &= \log (10^0) = 0 \\
\log 0.1 &= \log (10^{-1}) = -1 \\
\log 0.0001 &= \log (10^{-4}) = -4
\end{aligned}
$$

To obtain the common logarithm of a number other than a simple power of 10, you must resort to a log table or an electronic calculator. For example,

$$
\begin{aligned}
\log 2.10 &= 0.3222, \text{ which means that } 10^{0.3222} = 2.10 \\
\log 5.16 &= 0.7126, \text{ which means that } 10^{0.7126} = 5.16 \\
\log 3.125 &= 0.49485, \text{ which means that } 10^{0.49485} = 3.125
\end{aligned}
$$

To check this on your calculator, enter the number, and then press the "log" key.

To obtain the natural logarithm ln of the numbers shown here, use a calculator having this function. Enter each number, and press "ln:"

$$\ln 2.10 = 0.7419, \text{ which means that } e^{0.7419} = 2.10$$
$$\ln 5.16 = 1.6409, \text{ which means that } e^{1.6409} = 5.16$$

To find the common logarithm of a number greater than 10 or less than 1 with a log table, first express the number in scientific notation. Then find the log of each part of the number and add the logs. For example,

$$\log 241 = \log (2.41 \times 10^2) = \log 2.41 + \log 10^2$$
$$= 0.382 + 2 = 2.382$$
$$\log 0.00573 = \log (5.73 \times 10^{-3}) = \log 5.73 + \log 10^{-3}$$
$$= 0.758 + (-3) = -2.242$$

Significant Figures and Logarithms

Notice that the mantissa has as many significant figures as the number whose log was found. (So that you could more clearly see the result obtained with a calculator or a table, this rule was not strictly followed until the last two examples.)

> ■ **Logarithms and Nomenclature**
> The number to the left of the decimal in a logarithm is called the **characteristic,** and the number to the right of the decimal is the **mantissa.**

Obtaining Antilogarithms

If you are given the logarithm of a number, and find the number from it, you have obtained the "antilogarithm," or "antilog," of the number. Two common procedures used by electronic calculators to do this are:

Procedure A	Procedure B
1. Enter the log or ln.	1. Enter the log or ln.
2. Press 2ndF.	2. Press INV.
3. Press 10^x or e^x.	3. Press log or ln x.

Test one or the other of these procedures with the following examples:
1. Find the number whose log is 5.234:
   Recall that log $x = n$, where $x = 10^n$. In this case, $n = 5.234$. Enter that number in your calculator, and find the value of 10^n, the antilog. In this case,

   $$10^{5.234} = 10^{0.234} \times 10^5 = 1.71 \times 10^5$$

   Notice that the characteristic (5) sets the decimal point; it is the power of 10 in the exponential form. The mantissa (0.234) gives the value of the number x.
2. Find the number whose log is -3.456:

   $$10^{-3.456} = 10^{0.544} \times 10^{-4} = 3.50 \times 10^{-4}$$

   Notice here that -3.456 must be expressed as the sum of -4 and $+0.544$.

Mathematical Operations Using Logarithms

Because logarithms are exponents, operations involving them follow the same rules used for exponents. Thus, multiplying two numbers can be done by adding logarithms:

$$\log xy = \log x + \log y$$

For example, we multiply 563 by 125 by adding their logarithms and finding the antilogarithm of the result:

$$\log 563 = 2.751$$
$$\log 125 = \underline{2.097}$$
$$\log xy = 4.848$$
$$xy = 10^{4.848} = 10^4 \times 10^{0.848} = 7.05 \times 10^4$$

One number (x) can be divided by another (y) by subtraction of their logarithms:

$$\log \frac{x}{y} = \log x - \log y$$

For example, to divide 125 by 742,

$$\log 125 = 2.097$$
$$-\log 742 = \underline{2.870}$$
$$\log \frac{x}{y} = -0.773$$
$$\frac{x}{y} = 10^{-0.773} = 10^{0.227} \times 10^{-1} = 1.68 \times 10^{-1}$$

Similarly, powers and roots of numbers can be found using logarithms.

$$\log x^y = y(\log x)$$
$$\log \sqrt[y]{x} = \log x^{1/y} = \frac{1}{y} \log x$$

As an example, find the fourth power of 5.23. We first find the log of 5.23 and then multiply it by 4. The result, 2.874, is the log of the answer. Therefore, we find the antilog of 2.874:

$$(5.23)^4 = ?$$
$$\log (5.23)^4 = 4 \log 5.23 = 4(0.719) = 2.874$$
$$(5.23)^4 = 10^{2.874} = 748$$

As another example, find the fifth root of 1.89×10^{-9}:

$$\sqrt[5]{1.89 \times 10^{-9}} = (1.89 \times 10^{-9})^{1/5} = ?$$
$$\log(1.89 \times 10^{-9})^{1/5} = \frac{1}{5}\log(1.89 \times 10^{-9}) = \frac{1}{5}(-8.724) = -1.745$$

The answer is the antilog of -1.745:

$$(1.89 \times 10^{-9})^{1/5} = 10^{-1.745} = 1.8 \times 10^{-2}$$

A.2 Quadratic Equations

Algebraic equations of the form $ax^2 + bx + c = 0$ are called **quadratic equations.** The coefficients a, b, and c may be either positive or negative. The two roots of the equation may be found using the *quadratic formula:*

$$x = \frac{-b \pm \sqrt{b^2 - 4ac}}{2a}$$

As an example, solve the equation $5x^2 - 3x - 2 = 0$. Here $a = 5$, $b = -3$, and $c = -2$. Therefore,

$$x = \frac{3 \pm \sqrt{(-3)^2 - 4(5)(-2)}}{2(5)}$$
$$= \frac{3 \pm [2(5) / \sqrt{9 - (-40)}]}{10} = \frac{3 \pm \sqrt{49}}{10} = \frac{3 \pm 7}{10}$$
$$= 1 \text{ and} - 0.4$$

How do you know which of the two roots is the correct answer? You have to decide in each case which root has physical significance. It is *usually* true in this course, however, that negative values are not significant.

When you have solved a quadratic expression, you should always check your values by substitution into the original equation. In the previous example, we find that $5(1)^2 - 3(1) - 2 = 0$ and that $5(-0.4)^2 - 3(-0.4) - 2 = 0$.

The most likely place you will encounter quadratic equations is in the chapters on chemical equilibria, particularly in Chapters 16 through 18. Here, you will often be faced with solving an equation such as

$$1.8 \times 10^{-4} = \frac{x^2}{0.0010 - x}$$

This equation can certainly be solved using the quadratic equation (to give $x = 3.4 \times 10^{-4}$). You may find the **method of successive approximations** to be especially convenient, however. Here we begin by making a reasonable approximation of x. This approximate value is substituted into the original equation, which is then solved to give what is hoped to be a more correct value of x. This process is repeated until the answer converges on a particular value of x—that is, until the value of x derived from two successive approximations is the same.

Step 1: First, assume that x is so small that $(0.0010 - x) \approx 0.0010$. This means that

$$x^2 = 1.8 \times 10^{-4} (0.0010)$$
$$x = 4.2 \times 10^{-4} \text{ (to 2 significant figures)}$$

Step 2: Substitute the value of x from Step 1 into the denominator of the original equation, and again solve for x:

$$x^2 = 1.8 \times 10^{-4}(0.0010 - 0.00042)$$
$$x = 3.2 \times 10^{-4}$$

Step 3: Repeat Step 2 using the value of x found in that step:

$$x = \sqrt{1.8 \times 10^{-4}(0.0010 - 0.00032)} = 3.5 \times 10^{-4}$$

Step 4: Continue repeating the calculation, using the value of x found in the previous step:

$$x = \sqrt{1.8 \times 10^{-4}(0.0010 - 0.00035)} = 3.4 \times 10^{-4}$$

Step 5: $\qquad x = \sqrt{1.8 \times 10^{-4}(0.0010 - 0.00034)} = 3.4 \times 10^{-4}$

Here, we find that iterations after the fourth step give the same value for x, indicating that we have arrived at a valid answer (and the same one obtained from the quadratic formula).

Here are several final thoughts on using the method of successive approximations. First, in some cases the method does not work. Successive steps may give answers that are random or that diverge from the correct value. In Chapters 16 through 18, you confront quadratic equations of the form $K = x^2/(C - x)$. The method of approximations works as long as $K < 4C$ (assuming one begins with $x = 0$ as the first guess, that is, $K \approx x^2/C$). This is always going to be true for weak acids and bases (the topic of Chapters 17 and 18), but it may *not* be the case for problems involving gas phase equilibria (Chapter 16), where K can be quite large.

Second, values of K in the equation $K = x^2/(C - x)$ are usually known only to two significant figures. We are therefore justified in carrying out successive steps until two answers are the same to two significant figures.

Finally, we highly recommend this method of solving quadratic equations, especially those in Chapters 17 and 18. If your calculator has a memory function, successive approximations can be carried out easily and rapidly.

B* Some Important Physical Concepts

B.1 Matter

The tendency to maintain a constant velocity is called inertia. Thus, unless acted on by an unbalanced force, a body at rest remains at rest, and a body in motion remains in motion with uniform velocity. Matter is anything that exhibits inertia; the quantity of matter is its mass.

B.2 Motion

Motion is the change of position or location in space. Objects can have the following classes of motion:

- Translation occurs when the center of mass of an object changes its location. Example: a car moving on the highway.
- Rotation occurs when each point of a moving object moves in a circle about an axis through the center of mass. Examples: a spinning top, a rotating molecule.
- Vibration is a periodic distortion of and then recovery of original shape. Examples: a struck tuning fork, a vibrating molecule.

B.3 Force and Weight

Force is that which changes the velocity of a body; it is defined as

$$\text{Force} = \text{mass} \times \text{acceleration}$$

The SI unit of force is the **newton,** N, whose dimensions are kilograms times meter per second squared ($kg \cdot m/s^2$). A newton is therefore the force needed to change the velocity of a mass of 1 kilogram by 1 meter per second in a time of 1 second.

---

*Adapted from F. Brescia, J. Arents, H. Meislich, et al.: *General Chemistry,* 5th ed. Philadelphia, Harcourt Brace, 1988.

Because the earth's gravity is not the same everywhere, the weight corresponding to a given mass is not a constant. At any given spot on earth, gravity is constant, however, and therefore weight is proportional to mass. When a balance tells us that a given sample (the "unknown") has the same weight as another sample (the "weights," as given by a scale reading or by a total of counterweights), it also tells us that the two masses are equal. The balance is therefore a valid instrument for measuring the mass of an object independently of slight variations in the force of gravity.

B.4 Pressure*

Pressure is force per unit area. The SI unit, called the pascal, Pa, is

$$1 \text{ pascal} = \frac{1 \text{ newton}}{m^2} = \frac{1 \text{ kg} \cdot m/s^2}{m^2} = \frac{1 \text{ kg}}{m \cdot s^2}$$

The International System of Units also recognizes the bar, which is 10^5 Pa and which is close to standard atmospheric pressure (Table 1).

TABLE 1   Pressure Conversions

From	To	Multiply By
atmosphere	mm Hg	760 mm Hg/atm (exactly)
atmosphere	lb/in²	14.6960 lb/(in² · atm)
atmosphere	kPa	101.325 kPa/atm
bar	Pa	10^5 Pa/bar (exactly)
bar	lb/in²	14.5038 lb/(in² · bar)
mm Hg	torr	1 torr/mm Hg (exactly)

Chemists also express pressure in terms of the heights of liquid columns, especially water and mercury. This usage is not completely satisfactory, because the pressure exerted by a given column of a given liquid is not a constant but depends on the temperature (which influences the density of the liquid) and the location (which influences gravity). Such units are therefore not part of the SI, and their use is now discouraged. The older units are still used in books and journals, however, and chemists must be familiar with them.

The pressure of a liquid or a gas depends only on the depth (or height) and is exerted equally in all directions. At sea level, the pressure exerted by the earth's atmosphere supports a column of mercury about 0.76 m (76 cm, or 760 mm) high.

One **standard atmosphere** (atm) is the pressure exerted by exactly 76 cm of mercury at 0 °C (density, 13.5951 g/cm³) and at standard gravity, 9.80665 m/s². The **bar** is equivalent to 0.9869 atm. One **torr** is the pressure exerted by exactly 1 mm of mercury at 0 °C and standard gravity.

B.5 Energy and Power

The SI unit of energy is the product of the units of force and distance, or kilograms times meter per second squared (kg · m/s²) times meters (× m), which is kg · m²/s²; this unit is called the **joule**, J. The joule is thus the work done when a force of 1 newton acts through a distance of 1 meter.

*See Section 11.1.

Work may also be done by moving an electric charge in an electric field. When the charge being moved is 1 coulomb (C), and the potential difference between its initial and final positions is 1 volt (V), the work is 1 joule. Thus,

$$1 \text{ joule} = 1 \text{ coulomb volt (CV)}$$

Another unit of electric work that is not part of the International System of Units but is still in use is the **electron volt,** eV, which is the work required to move an electron against a potential difference of 1 volt. (It is also the kinetic energy acquired by an electron when it is accelerated by a potential difference of 1 volt.) Because the charge on an electron is 1.602×10^{-19} C, we have

$$1 \text{ eV} = 1.602 \times 10^{-19} \text{ CV} \times \frac{1 \text{ J}}{1 \text{ CV}} = 1.602 \times 10^{-19} \text{ J}$$

If this value is multiplied by Avogadro's number, we obtain the energy involved in moving 1 mole of electron charges (1 faraday) in a field produced by a potential difference of 1 volt:

$$1 \frac{\text{eV}}{\text{particle}} = \frac{1.602 \times 10^{-19} \text{ J}}{\text{particle}} \times \frac{6.022 \times 10^{23} \text{particles}}{\text{mol}} \cdot \frac{1 \text{ kJ}}{1000 \text{ J}} = 96.49 \text{ kJ/mol}$$

Power is the amount of energy delivered per unit time. The SI unit is the watt, W, which is 1 joule per second. One kilowatt, kW, is 1000 W. Watt hours and kilowatt hours are therefore units of energy (Table 2). For example, 1000 watts, or 1 kilowatt, is

$$1.0 \times 10^3 \text{W} \times \frac{1 \text{ J}}{1 \text{ W} \cdot \text{s}} \cdot \frac{3.6 \times 10^3 \text{ s}}{1 \text{ h}} = 3.6 \times 10^6 \text{ J}$$

TABLE 2   Energy Conversions

From	To	Multiply By
calorie (cal)	joule	4.184 J/cal (exactly)
kilocalorie (kcal)	cal	10^3 cal/kcal (exactly)
kilocalorie	joule	4.184×10^3 J/kcal (exactly)
liter atmosphere (L · atm)	joule	101.325 J/L · atm
electron volt (eV)	joule	1.60218×10^{-19} J/eV
electron volt per particle	kilojoules per mole	96.485 kJ · particle/eV · mol
coulomb volt (CV)	joule	1 CV/J (exactly)
kilowatt hour (kWh)	kcal	860.4 kcal/kWh
kilowatt hour	joule	3.6×10^6 J/kWh (exactly)
British thermal unit (Btu)	calorie	252 cal/Btu

C Abbreviations and Useful Conversion Factors

TABLE 3 Some Common Abbreviations and Standard Symbols

Term	Abbreviation	Term	Abbreviation
Activation energy	E_a	Entropy	S
Ampere	A	Standard entropy	$S°$
Aqueous Solution	aq	Entropy change for reaction	$\Delta_r S°$
Atmosphere, unit of pressure	atm	Equilibrium constant	K
Atomic mass unit	u	Concentration basis	K_c
Avogadro's constant	N_A	Pressure basis	K_p
Bar, unit of pressure	bar	Ionization weak acid	K_a
Body-centered cubic	bcc	Ionization weak base	K_b
Bohr radius	a_0	Solubility product	K_{sp}
Boiling point	bp	Formation constant	K_{form}
Celsius temperature, °C	T	Ethylenediamine	en
Charge number of an ion	z	Face-centered cubic	fcc
Coulomb, electric charge	C	Faraday constant	F
Curie, radioactivity	Ci	Gas constant	R
Cycles per second, hertz	Hz	Gibbs free energy	G
Debye, unit of electric dipole	D	Standard free energy	$G°$
Electron	e^-	Standard free energy of formation	$\Delta_f G°$
Electron volt	eV	Free energy change for reaction	$\Delta_r G°$
Electronegativity	χ	Half-life	$t_{1/2}$
Energy	E	Heat	q
Enthalpy	H	Hertz	Hz
Standard enthalpy	$H°$	Hour	h
Standard enthalpy of formation	$\Delta_f H°$	Joule	J
Standard enthalpy of reaction	$\Delta_r H°$	Kelvin	K

TABLE 3 Some Common Abbreviations and Standard Symbols (continued)

Term	Abbreviation	Term	Abbreviation
Kilocalorie	kcal	Pressure	
Liquid	ℓ	Pascal, unit of pressure	Pa
Logarithm, base 10	log	In atmospheres	atm
Logarithm, base *e* ·	ln	In millimeters of mercury	mm Hg
Minute	min	Proton number	Z
Molar	M	Rate constant	k
Molar mass	*M*	Primitive cubic (unit cell)	pc
Mole	mol	Standard temperature and pressure	STP
Osmotic pressure	Π	Volt	V
Planck's constant	*h*	Watt	W
Pound	lb	Wavelength	λ

C.1 Fundamental Units of the SI System

The metric system was begun by the French National Assembly in 1790 and has undergone many modifications. The International System of Units or *Système International* (SI), which represents an extension of the metric system, was adopted by the 11th General Conference of Weights and Measures in 1960. It is constructed from seven base units, each of which represents a particular physical quantity (Table 4).

TABLE 4 SI Fundamental Units

Physical Quantity	Name of Unit	Symbol
Length	meter	m
Mass	kilogram	kg
Time	second	s
Temperature	kelvin	K
Amount of substance	mole	mol
Electric current	ampere	A
Luminous intensity	candela	cd

The first five units listed in Table 4 are particularly useful in general chemistry and are defined as follows:

1. The *meter* was redefined in 1960 to be equal to 1,650,763.73 wavelengths of a certain line in the emission spectrum of krypton-86.
2. The *kilogram* represents the mass of a platinum–iridium block kept at the International Bureau of Weights and Measures at Sèvres, France.
3. The *second* was redefined in 1967 as the duration of 9,192,631,770 periods of a certain line in the microwave spectrum of cesium-133.

4. The *kelvin* is 1/273.15 of the temperature interval between absolute zero and the triple point of water.
5. The *mole* is the amount of substance that contains as many entities as there are atoms in exactly 0.012 kg of carbon-12 (12 g of ^{12}C atoms).

C.2 Prefixes Used with Traditional Metric Units and SI Units

Decimal fractions and multiples of metric and SI units are designated by using the prefixes listed in Table 5. Those most commonly used in general chemistry appear in italics.

C.3 Derived SI Units

In the International System of Units, all physical quantities are represented by appropriate combinations of the base units listed in Table 4. A list of the derived units frequently used in general chemistry is given in Table 6.

TABLE 5 Traditional Metric and SI Prefixes

Factor	Prefix	Symbol	Factor	Prefix	Symbol
10^{12}	tera	T	10^{-1}	*deci*	d
10^{9}	giga	G	10^{-2}	*centi*	c
10^{6}	mega	M	10^{-3}	*milli*	m
10^{3}	*kilo*	k	10^{-6}	micro	μ
10^{2}	hecto	h	10^{-9}	*nano*	n
10^{1}	deka	da	10^{-12}	*pico*	p
			10^{-15}	femto	f
			10^{-18}	atto	a

TABLE 6 Derived SI Units

Physical Quantity	Name of Unit	Symbol	Definition
Area	square meter	m^2	
Volume	cubic meter	m^3	
Density	kilogram per cubic meter	kg/m^3	
Force	newton	N	$kg \cdot m/s^2$
Pressure	pascal	Pa	N/m^2
Energy	joule	J	$kg \cdot m^2/s^2$
Electric charge	coulomb	C	$A \cdot s$
Electric potential difference	volt	V	$J/(A \cdot s)$

TABLE 7 Common Units of Mass and Weight

1 Pound = 453.39 Grams

1 kilogram = 1000 grams = 2.205 pounds

1 gram = 1000 milligrams

1 gram = 6.022×10^{23} atomic mass units

1 atomic mass unit = 1.6605×10^{-24} gram

1 short ton = 2000 pounds = 907.2 kilograms

1 long ton = 2240 pounds

1 metric tonne = 1000 kilograms = 2205 pounds

TABLE 8 Common Units of Length

1 inch = 2.54 centimeters (Exactly)

1 mile = 5280 feet = 1.609 kilometers

1 yard = 36 inches = 0.9144 meter

1 meter = 100 centimeters = 39.37 inches = 3.281 feet = 1.094 yards

1 kilometer = 1000 meters = 1094 yards = 0.6215 mile

1 Ångstrom = 1.0×10^{-8} centimeter = 0.10 nanometer = 100 picometers

   = 1.0×10^{-10} meter = 3.937×10^{-9} inch

TABLE 9 Common Units of Volume

1 quart = 0.9463 liter
1 liter = 1.0567 quarts

1 liter = 1 cubic decimeter = 1000 cubic centimeters = 0.001 cubic meter

1 milliliter = 1 cubic centimeter = 0.001 liter = 1.056×10^{-3} quart

1 cubic foot = 28.316 liters = 29.924 quarts = 7.481 gallons

D | Physical Constants

TABLE 10

Quantity	Symbol	Traditional Units	SI Units
Acceleration of gravity	g	980.6 cm/s	9.806 m/s
Atomic mass unit (1/12 the mass of ^{12}C atom)	u	1.6605×10^{-24} g	1.6605×10^{-27} kg
Avogadro's number	N	$6.02214179 \times 10^{23}$ particles/mol	$6.02214179 \times 10^{23}$ particles/mol
Bohr radius	a_0	0.052918 nm	5.2918×10^{-11} m
		5.2918×10^{-9} cm	
Boltzmann constant	k	1.3807×10^{-16} erg/K	1.3807×10^{-23} J/K
Charge-to-mass ratio of electron	e/m	1.7588×10^{8} C/g	1.7588×10^{11} C/kg
Electronic charge	e	1.6022×10^{-19} C	1.6022×10^{-19} C
		4.8033×10^{-10} esu	
Electron rest mass	m_e	9.1094×10^{-28} g	9.1094×10^{-31} kg
		0.00054858 amu	
Faraday constant	F	96,485 C/mol e$^-$	96,485 C/mol e$^-$
		23.06 kcal/V · mol e$^-$	96,485 J/V · mol e$^-$
Gas constant	R	$0.082057 \dfrac{L \cdot atm}{mol \cdot K}$	$8.3145 \dfrac{Pa \cdot dm^3}{mol \cdot K}$
		$1.987 \dfrac{cal}{mol \cdot K}$	8.3145 J/mol · K
Molar volume (STP)	V_m	22.414 L/mol	22.414×10^{-3} m^3/mol
			22.414 dm^3/mol
Neutron rest mass	m_n	1.67493×10^{-24} g	1.67493×10^{-27} kg
		1.008665 amu	
Planck's constant	h	6.6261×10^{-27} erg · s	$6.6260693 \times 10^{-34}$ J · s

TABLE 10 (continued)

Quantity	Symbol	Traditional Units	SI Units
Proton rest mass	m_p	1.6726×10^{-24} g	1.6726×10^{-27} kg
		1.007276 amu	
Rydberg constant	R_a	3.289×10^{15} cycles/s	1.0974×10^7 m^{-1}
	Rhc		2.1799×10^{-18} J
Velocity of light (in a vacuum)	c	2.9979×10^{10} cm/s	2.9979×10^8 m/s
		(186,282 miles/s)	

$\pi = 3.1416$

$e = 2.7183$

$\ln X = 2.303 \log X$

TABLE 11 Specific Heats and Heat Capacities for Some Common Substances at 25 °C

Substance	Specific Heat (J/g · K)	Molar Heat Capacity (J/mol · K)
Al(s)	0.897	24.2
Ca(s)	0.646	25.9
Cu(s)	0.385	24.5
Fe(s)	0.449	25.1
Hg(ℓ)	0.140	28.0
H_2O(s), ice	2.06	37.1
H_2O(ℓ), water	4.184	75.4
H_2O(g), steam	1.86	33.6
C_6H_6(ℓ), benzene	1.74	136
C_6H_6(g), benzene	1.06	82.4
C_2H_5OH(ℓ), ethanol	2.44	112.3
C_2H_5OH(g), ethanol	1.41	65.4
$(C_2H_5)_2O$(ℓ), diethyl ether	2.33	172.6
$(C_2H_5)_2O$(g), diethyl ether	1.61	119.5

TABLE 12 Heats of Transformation and Transformation Temperatures of Several Substances

Substance	MP (°C)	Heat of Fusion		BP (°C)	Heat of Vaporization	
		J/g	kJ/mol		J/g	kJ/mol
*Elements**						
Al	660	395	10.7	2518	12083	294
Ca	842	212	8.5	1484	3767	155
Cu	1085	209	13.3	2567	4720	300
Fe	1535	267	13.8	2861	6088	340
Hg	−38.8	11	2.29	357	295	59.1
Compounds						
H_2O	0.00	333	6.01	100.0	2260	40.7
CH_4	−182.5	58.6	0.94	−161.5	511	8.2
C_2H_5OH	−114	109	5.02	78.3	838	38.6
C_6H_6	5.48	127.4	9.95	80.0	393	30.7
$(C_2H_5)_2O$	−116.3	98.1	7.27	34.6	357	26.5

*Data for the elements are taken from J. A. Dean: *Lange's Handbook of Chemistry*, 15th Edition. New York, McGraw-Hill Publishers, 1999.

E | A Brief Guide to Naming Organic Compounds

It seems a daunting task—to devise a systematic procedure that gives each organic compound a unique name—but that is what has been done. A set of rules was developed to name organic compounds by the International Union of Pure and Applied Chemistry (IUPAC). The IUPAC nomenclature allows chemists to write a name for any compound based on its structure or to identify the formula and structure for a compound from its name. In this book, we have generally used the IUPAC nomenclature scheme when naming compounds.

In addition to the systematic names, many compounds have common names. The common names came into existence before the nomenclature rules were developed, and they have continued in use. For some compounds, these names are so well entrenched that they are used most of the time. One such compound is acetic acid, which is almost always referred to by that name and not by its systematic name, ethanoic acid.

The general procedure for systematic naming of organic compounds begins with the nomenclature for hydrocarbons. Other organic compounds are then named as derivatives of hydrocarbons. Nomenclature rules for simple organic compounds are given in the following section.

E.1 Hydrocarbons

Alkanes

The names of alkanes end in "-ane." When naming a specific alkane, the root of the name identifies the longest carbon chain in a compound. Specific substituent groups attached to this carbon chain are identified by name and position.

Alkanes with chains of from one to ten carbon atoms are given in Table 10.2. After the first four compounds, the names derive from Latin numbers—pentane, hexane, heptane, octane, nonane, decane—and this regular naming continues for higher alkanes. For substituted alkanes, the substituent groups on a hydrocarbon chain must be identified both by a name and by the position of substitution; this information precedes the root of the name. The position is indicated by a number that refers to the carbon atom to which the substituent is attached. (Numbering of the carbon atoms in a chain should begin at the end of the carbon chain that allows the substituent groups to have the lowest numbers.)

Names of hydrocarbon substituents are derived from the name of the hydrocarbon. The group —CH_3, derived by taking a hydrogen from methane, is called the methyl group; the C_2H_5 group is the ethyl group. The nomenclature scheme is easily extended to derivatives of hydrocarbons with other substituent groups such as —Cl (chloro), —NO_2 (nitro), —CN (cyano), —D (deuterio), and so on (Table 13). If two or more of the same substituent groups occur, the prefixes "di-," "tri-," and "tetra-" are added. When different substituent groups are present, they are generally listed in alphabetical order.

TABLE 13   Names of Common Substituent Groups

Formula	Name	Formula	Name
—CH_3	methyl	—D	deuterio
—C_2H_5	ethyl	—Cl	chloro
—$CH_2CH_2CH_3$	1-propyl (*n*-propyl)	—Br	bromo
—$CH(CH_3)_2$	2-propyl (isopropyl)	—F	fluoro
—$CH{=}CH_2$	ethenyl (vinyl)	—CN	cyano
—C_6H_5	phenyl	—NO_2	nitro
—OH	hydroxo		
—NH_2	amino		

Example:

$$\underset{\text{CH}_3\text{CH}_2\overset{\displaystyle|}{\underset{\displaystyle\text{CH}_3}{\text{C}}}\text{HCH}_2\overset{\displaystyle|}{\underset{\displaystyle\text{C}_2\text{H}_5}{\text{C}}}\text{HCH}_2\text{CH}_3}{}$$

Step	Information to include	Contribution to name
1.	An alkane	name will end in "-ane"
2.	Longest chain is 7 carbons	name as a *heptane*
3.	—CH_3 group at carbon 3	3-*methyl*
4.	—C_2H_5 group at carbon 5	5-*ethyl*
Name:		5-ethyl-3-methylheptane

Cycloalkanes are named based on the ring size and by adding the prefix "cyclo"; for example, the cycloalkane with a six-member ring of carbons is called cyclohexane.

Alkenes

Alkenes have names ending in "-ene." The name of an alkene must specify the length of the carbon chain and the position of the double bond (and when appropriate, the configuration, either *cis* or *trans*). As with alkanes, both identity and position of substituent groups must be given. The carbon chain is numbered from the end that gives the double bond the lowest number.

Compounds with two double bonds are called dienes, and they are named similarly—specifying the positions of the double bonds and the name and position of any substituent groups.

For example, the compound $H_2C{=}C(CH_3)CH(CH_3)CH_2CH_3$ has a five-carbon chain with a double bond between carbon atoms 1 and 2 and methyl groups on carbon atoms 2 and 3. Its name using IUPAC nomenclature is **2,3-dimethyl-1-pentene**. The compound $CH_3CH{=}CHCCl_3$ with a *cis* configuration around the double bond is named **1,1,1-trichloro-*cis*-2-butene**. The compound $H_2C{=}C(Cl)CH{=}CH_2$ is **2-chloro-1,3-butadiene**.

Alkynes

The naming of alkynes is similar to the naming of alkenes, except that *cis–trans* isomerism isn't a factor. The ending "-yne" on a name identifies a compound as an alkyne.

Benzene Derivatives

The carbon atoms in the six-member ring are numbered 1 through 6, and the name and position of substituent groups are given. The two examples shown here are **1-ethyl-3-methylbenzene** and **1,4-diaminobenzene**.

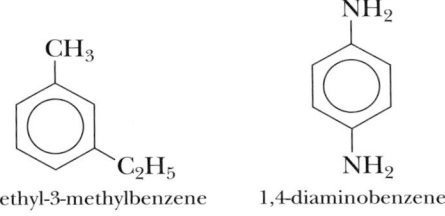

1-ethyl-3-methylbenzene   1,4-diaminobenzene

E.2 Derivatives of Hydrocarbons

The names for alcohols, aldehydes, ketones, and acids are based on the name of the hydrocarbon with an appropriate suffix to denote the class of compound, as follows:

- **Alcohols:** Substitute "-ol" for the final "-e" in the name of the hydrocarbon, and designate the position of the —OH group by the number of the carbon atom. For example, $CH_3CH_2CHOHCH_3$ is named as a derivative of the 4-carbon hydrocarbon butane. The —OH group is attached to the second carbon, so the name is 2-butanol.
- **Aldehydes:** Substitute "-al" for the final "-e" in the name of the hydrocarbon. The carbon atom of an aldehyde is, by definition, carbon-1 in the hydrocarbon chain. For example, the compound $CH_3CH(CH_3)CH_2CH_2CHO$ contains a 5-carbon chain with the aldehyde functional group being carbon-1 and the —CH_3 group at position 4; thus, the name is **4-methylpentanal.**
- **Ketones:** Substitute "-one" for the final "-e" in the name of the hydrocarbon. The position of the ketone functional group (the carbonyl group) is indicated by the number of the carbon atom. For example, the compound $CH_3COCH_2CH(C_2H_5)CH_2CH_3$ has the carbonyl group at the 2 position and an ethyl group at the 4 position of a 6-carbon chain; its name is **4-ethyl-2-hexanone.**
- **Carboxylic acids (organic acids):** Substitute "-oic" for the final "-e" in the name of the hydrocarbon. The carbon atoms in the longest chain are counted beginning with the carboxylic carbon atom. For example, *trans-*

$CH_3CH=CHCH_2CO_2H$ is named as a derivative of *trans*-3-pentene—that is, **trans-3-pentenoic acid.**

An **ester** is named as a derivative of the alcohol and acid from which it is made. The name of an ester is obtained by splitting the formula RCO_2R' into two parts, the RCO_2— portion and the —R' portion. The —R' portion comes from the alcohol and is identified by the hydrocarbon group name; derivatives of ethanol, for example, are called *ethyl* esters. The acid part of the compound is named by dropping the "-oic" ending for the acid and replacing it by "-oate." The compound $CH_3CH_2CO_2CH_3$ is named **methyl propanoate.**

Notice that an anion derived from a carboxylic acid by loss of the acidic proton is named the same way. Thus, $CH_3CH_2CO_2^-$ is the **propanoate anion,** and the sodium salt of this anion, $Na(CH_3CH_2CO_2)$, is **sodium propanoate.**

F | Values for the Ionization Energies and Electron Affinities of the Elements

1A (1)	2A (2)	3B (3)	4B (4)	5B (5)	6B (6)	7B (7)	8B (8,9,10)			1B (11)	2B (12)	3A (13)	4A (14)	5A (15)	6A (16)	7A (17)	8 (18)
H 1312																	He 2371
Li 520	Be 899											B 801	C 1086	N 1402	O 1314	F 1681	Ne 2081
Na 496	Mg 738											Al 578	Si 786	P 1012	S 1000	Cl 1251	Ar 1521
K 419	Ca 599	Sc 631	Ti 658	V 650	Cr 652	Mn 717	Fe 759	Co 758	Ni 757	Cu 745	Zn 906	Ga 579	Ge 762	As 947	Se 941	Br 1140	Kr 1351
Rb 403	Sr 550	Y 617	Zr 661	Nb 664	Mo 685	Tc 702	Ru 711	Rh 720	Pd 804	Ag 731	Cd 868	In 558	Sn 709	Sb 834	Te 869	I 1008	Xe 1170
Cs 377	Ba 503	La 538	Hf 681	Ta 761	W 770	Re 760	Os 840	Ir 880	Pt 870	Au 890	Hg 1007	Tl 589	Pb 715	Bi 703	Po 812	At 890	Rn 1037

TABLE 14   Electron Affinity Values for Some Elements (kJ/mol)*

H							
−72.77							
Li	Be	B	C	N		O	F
−59.63	0†	−26.7	−121.85	0		−140.98	−328.0
Na	Mg	Al	Si	P		S	Cl
−52.87	0	−42.6	−133.6	−72.07		−200.41	−349.0
K	Ca	Ga	Ge	As		Se	Br
−48.39	0	−30	−120	−78		−194.97	−324.7
Rb	Sr	In	Sn	Sb		Te	I
−46.89	0	−30	−120	−103		−190.16	−295.16
Cs	Ba	Tl	Pb	Bi		Po	At
−45.51	0	−20	−35.1	−91.3		−180	−270

*Data taken from H. Hotop and W. C. Lineberger: *Journal of Physical Chemistry, Reference Data*, Vol. 14, p. 731, 1985. (This paper also includes data for the transition metals.) Some values are known to more than two decimal places.
†Elements with an electron affinity of zero indicate that a stable anion A⁻ of the element does not exist in the gas phase.

G Vapor Pressure of Water at Various Temperatures

TABLE 15 Vapor Pressure of Water at Various Temperatures

Temperature (°C)	Vapor Pressure (torr)	Temperature (°C)	Vapor Pressure (torr)	Temperature (°C)	Vapor Pressure (torr)	Temperature (°C)	Vapor Pressure (torr)
−10	2.1	21	18.7	51	97.2	81	369.7
−9	2.3	22	19.8	52	102.1	82	384.9
−8	2.5	23	21.1	53	107.2	83	400.6
−7	2.7	24	22.4	54	112.5	84	416.8
−6	2.9	25	23.8	55	118.0	85	433.6
−5	3.2	26	25.2	56	123.8	86	450.9
−4	3.4	27	26.7	57	129.8	87	468.7
−3	3.7	28	28.3	58	136.1	88	487.1
−2	4.0	29	30.0	59	142.6	89	506.1
−1	4.3	30	31.8	60	149.4	90	525.8
0	4.6	31	33.7	61	156.4	91	546.1
1	4.9	32	35.7	62	163.8	92	567.0
2	5.3	33	37.7	63	171.4	93	588.6
3	5.7	34	39.9	64	179.3	94	610.9
4	6.1	35	42.2	65	187.5	95	633.9
5	6.5	36	44.6	66	196.1	96	657.6
6	7.0	37	47.1	67	205.0	97	682.1
7	7.5	38	49.7	68	214.2	98	707.3
8	8.0	39	52.4	69	223.7	99	733.2
9	8.6	40	55.3	70	233.7	100	760.0
10	9.2	41	58.3	71	243.9	101	787.6
11	9.8	42	61.5	72	254.6	102	815.9
12	10.5	43	64.8	73	265.7	103	845.1
13	11.2	44	68.3	74	277.2	104	875.1
14	12.0	45	71.9	75	289.1	105	906.1
15	12.8	46	75.7	76	301.4	106	937.9
16	13.6	47	79.6	77	314.1	107	970.6
17	14.5	48	83.7	78	327.3	108	1004.4
18	15.5	49	88.0	79	341.0	109	1038.9
19	16.5	50	92.5	80	355.1	110	1074.6
20	17.5						

H | Ionization Constants for Weak Acids at 25 °C

TABLE 16 Ionization Constants for Weak Acids at 25 °C

Acid	Formula and Ionization Equation	K_a
Ascetic	$CH_3CO_2H \rightleftarrows H^+ + CH_3CO_2^-$	1.8×10^{-5}
Arsenic	$H_3AsO_4 \rightleftarrows H^+ + H_2AsO_4^-$	$K_1 = 2.5 \times 10^{-4}$
	$H_2AsO_4^- \rightleftarrows H^+ + HAsO_4^{2-}$	$K_2 = 5.6 \times 10^{-3}$
	$HAsO_4^{2-} \rightleftarrows H^+ + AsO_4^{3-}$	$K_3 = 3.0 \times 10^{-13}$
Arsenous	$H_3AsO_3 \rightleftarrows H^+ + H_2AsO_3^-$	$K_1 = 6.0 \times 10^{-10}$
	$H_2AsO_3^- \rightleftarrows H^+ + HAsO_3^{2-}$	$K_2 = 3.0 \times 10^{-14}$
Benzoic	$C_6H_5CO_2H \rightleftarrows H^+ + C_6H_5CO_2^-$	6.3×10^{-5}
Boric	$H_3BO_3 \rightleftarrows H^+ + H_2BO_3^-$	$K_1 = 7.3 \times 10^{-10}$
	$H_2BO_3 \rightleftarrows H^+ + HBO_3^{2-}$	$K_2 = 1.8 \times 10^{-13}$
	$HBO_3^{2-} \rightleftarrows H^+ + BO_3^{3-}$	$K_3 = 1.6 \times 10^{-14}$
Carbonic	$H_2CO_3 \rightleftarrows H^+ + HCO_3^-$	$K_1 = 4.2 \times 10^{-7}$
	$HCO_3^- \rightleftarrows H^+ + CO_3^{2-}$	$K_2 = 4.8 \times 10^{-11}$
Citric	$H_3C_6H_5O_7 \rightleftarrows H^+ + H_2C_6H_5O_7^-$	$K_1 = 7.4 \times 10^{-3}$
	$H_2C_6H_5O_7^- \rightleftarrows H^+ + HC_6H_5O_7^{2-}$	$K_2 = 1.7 \times 10^{-5}$
	$HC_6H_5O_7^{2-} \rightleftarrows H^+ + C_6H_5O_7^{3-}$	$K_3 = 4.0 \times 10^{-7}$
Cyanic	$HOCN \rightleftarrows H^+ + OCN^-$	3.5×10^{-4}
Formic	$HCO_2H \rightleftarrows H^+ + HCO_2^-$	1.8×10^{-4}
Hydrazoic	$HN_3 \rightleftarrows H^+ + N_3^-$	1.9×10^{-5}
Hydrocyanic	$HCN \rightleftarrows H^+ + CN^-$	4.0×10^{-10}
Hydrofluoric	$HF \rightleftarrows H^+ + F^-$	7.2×10^{-4}
Hydrogen peroxide	$H_2O_2 \rightleftarrows H^+ + HO_2^-$	2.4×10^{-12}
Hydrosulfuric	$H_2S \rightleftarrows H^+ + HS^-$	$K_1 = 1 \times 10^{-7}$
	$HS^- \rightleftarrows H^+ + S^{2-}$	$K_2 = 1 \times 10^{-19}$
Hypobromous	$HOBr \rightleftarrows H^+ + OBr^-$	2.5×10^{-9}

(continued)

TABLE 16   Ionization Constants for Weak Acids at 25 °C *(continued)*

Acid	Formula and Ionization Equation	K_a
Hypochlorous	$HOCl \rightleftharpoons H^+ + OCl^-$	3.5×10^{-8}
Nitrous	$HNO_2 \rightleftharpoons H^+ + NO_2^-$	4.5×10^{-4}
Oxalic	$H_2C_2O_4 \rightleftharpoons H^+ + HC_2O_4^-$	$K_1 = 5.9 \times 10^{-2}$
	$HC_2O_4^- \rightleftharpoons H^+ + C_2O_4^{2-}$	$K_2 = 6.4 \times 10^{-5}$
Phenol	$C_6H_5OH \rightleftharpoons H^+ + C_6H_5O^-$	1.3×10^{-10}
Phosphoric	$H_3PO_4 \rightleftharpoons H^+ + H_2PO_4^-$	$K_1 = 7.5 \times 10^{-3}$
	$H_2PO_4^- \rightleftharpoons H^+ + HPO_4^{2-}$	$K_2 = 6.2 \times 10^{-8}$
	$HPO_4^{2-} \rightleftharpoons H^+ + PO_4^{3-}$	$K_3 = 3.6 \times 10^{-13}$
Phosphorous	$H_3PO_3 \rightleftharpoons H^+ + H_2PO_3^-$	$K_1 = 1.6 \times 10^{-2}$
	$H_2PO_3 \rightleftharpoons H^+ + HPO_3^{2-}$	$K_2 = 7.0 \times 10^{-7}$
Selenic	$H_2SeO_4 \rightleftharpoons H^+ + HSeO_4^-$	$K_1 = $ very large
	$HSeO_4^- \rightleftharpoons H^+ + SeO_4^{2-}$	$K_2 = 1.2 \times 10^{-2}$
Selenous	$HSeO_3 \rightleftharpoons H^+ + HSeO_3^-$	$K_1 = 2.7 \times 10^{-3}$
	$HSeO_3^- \rightleftharpoons H^+ + SeO_3^{2-}$	$K_2 = 2.5 \times 10^{-7}$
Sulfuric	$H_2SO_4 \rightleftharpoons H^+ + HSO_4^-$	$K_1 = $ very large
	$HSO_4^- \rightleftharpoons H^+ + SO_4^{2-}$	$K_2 = 1.2 \times 10^{-2}$
Sulfurous	$H_2SO_3 \rightleftharpoons H^+ + HSO_3^-$	$K_1 = 1.2 \times 10^{-2}$
	$HSO_3^- \rightleftharpoons H^+ + SO_3^{2-}$	$K_2 = 6.2 \times 10^{-8}$
Tellurous	$H_2TeO_3 \rightleftharpoons H^+ + HTeO_3^-$	$K_1 = 2 \times 10^{-3}$
	$HTeO_3^- \rightleftharpoons H^+ + TeO_3^{2-}$	$K_2 = 1 \times 10^{-8}$

Ionization Constants for Weak Bases at 25 °C

TABLE 17   Ionization Constants for Weak Bases at 25 °C

Base	Formula and Ionization Equation	K_b
Ammonia	$NH_3 + H_2O \rightleftharpoons NH_4^+ + OH^-$	1.8×10^{-5}
Aniline	$C_6H_5NH_2 + H_2O \rightleftharpoons C_6H_5NH_3^+ + OH^-$	4.0×10^{-10}
Dimethylamine	$(CH_3)_2NH + H_2O \rightleftharpoons (CH_3)_2NH_2^+ + OH^-$	7.4×10^{-4}
Ethylenediamine	$H_2NCH_2CH_2NH_2 + H_2O \rightleftharpoons H_2NCH_2CH_2NH_3^+ \ OH^-$	$K_1 = 8.5 \times 10^{-5}$
	$H_2NCH_2CH_2NH_3^+ + H_2O \rightleftharpoons H_3NCH_2CH_2NH_3^{2+} \ OH^-$	$K_2 = 2.7 \times 10^{-8}$
Hydrazine	$N_2H_4 + H_2O \rightleftharpoons N_2H_5^+ + OH^-$	$K_1 = 8.5 \times 10^{-7}$
	$N_2H_5^+ + H_2O \rightleftharpoons N_2H_6^{2+} + OH^-$	$K_2 = 8.9 \times 10^{-16}$
Hydroxylamine	$NH_2OH + H_2O \rightleftharpoons NH_3OH^+ + OH^-$	6.6×10^{-9}
Methylamine	$CH_3NH_2 + H_2O \rightleftharpoons CH_3NH_3^+ + OH^-$	5.0×10^{-4}
Pyridine	$C_5H_5N + H_2O \rightleftharpoons C_5H_5NH^+ + OH^-$	1.5×10^{-9}
Trimethylamine	$(CH_3)_3N + H_2O \rightleftharpoons (CH_3)_3NH^+ + OH^-$	7.4×10^{-5}
Ethylamine	$C_2H_5NH_2 + H_2O \rightleftharpoons C_2H_5NH_3^+ + OH^-$	4.3×10^{-4}

J | Solubility Product Constants for Some Inorganic Compounds at 25 °C

TABLE 18A   Solubility Produce Constants (25 °C)

Cation	Compound	K_{sp}	Cation	Compound	K_{sp}
Ba^{2+}	*$BaCrO_4$	1.2×10^{-10}	Mg^{2+}	$MgCO_3$	6.8×10^{-6}
	$BaCO_3$	2.6×10^{-9}		MgF_2	5.2×10^{-11}
	BaF_2	1.8×10^{-7}		$Mg(OH)_2$	5.6×10^{-12}
	*$BaSO_4$	1.1×10^{-10}	Mn^{2+}	$MnCO_3$	2.3×10^{-11}
Ca^{2+}	$CaCO_3$ (calcite)	3.4×10^{-9}		*$Mn(OH)_2$	1.9×10^{-13}
	*CaF_2	5.3×10^{-11}	Hg_2^{2+}	*Hg_2Br_2	6.4×10^{-23}
	*$Ca(OH)_2$	5.5×10^{-5}		Hg_2Cl_2	1.4×10^{-18}
	$CaSO_4$	4.9×10^{-5}		*Hg_2I_2	2.9×10^{-29}
$Cu^{+,2+}$	$CuBr$	6.3×10^{-9}		Hg_2SO_4	6.5×10^{-7}
	CuI	1.3×10^{-12}	Ni^{2+}	$NiCO_3$	1.4×10^{-7}
	$Cu(OH)_2$	2.2×10^{-20}		$Ni(OH)_2$	5.5×10^{-16}
	$CuSCN$	1.8×10^{-13}	Ag^+	*$AgBr$	5.4×10^{-13}
Au^+	$AuCl$	2.0×10^{-13}		*$AgBrO_3$	5.4×10^{-5}
Fe^{2+}	$FeCO_3$	3.1×10^{-11}		$AgCH_3CO_2$	1.9×10^{-3}
	$Fe(OH)_2$	4.9×10^{-17}		$AgCN$	6.0×10^{-17}
Pb^{2+}	$PbBr_2$	6.6×10^{-6}		Ag_2CO_3	8.5×10^{-12}
	$PbCO_3$	7.4×10^{-14}		*$Ag_2C_2O_4$	5.4×10^{-12}
	$PbCl_2$	1.7×10^{-5}		*$AgCl$	1.8×10^{-10}
	$PbCrO_4$	2.8×10^{-13}		Ag_2CrO_4	1.1×10^{-12}
	PbF_2	3.3×10^{-8}		*AgI	8.5×10^{-17}
	PbI_2	9.8×10^{-9}		$AgSCN$	1.0×10^{-12}
	$Pb(OH)_2$	1.4×10^{-15}		*Ag_2SO_4	1.2×10^{-5}
	$PbSO_4$	2.5×10^{-8}			

(continued)

Cation	Compound	K_{sp}	Cation	Compound	K_{sp}
Sr^{2+}	$SrCO_3$	5.6×10^{-10}	Zn^{2+}	$Zn(OH)_2$	3×10^{-17}
	SrF_2	4.3×10^{-9}		$Zn(CN)_2$	8.0×10^{-12}
	$SrSO_4$	3.4×10^{-7}			
Tl^+	$TlBr$	3.7×10^{-6}			
	$TlCl$	1.9×10^{-4}			
	TlI	5.5×10^{-8}			

The values reported in this table were taken from J. A. Dean: *Lange's Handbook of Chemistry,* 15th Edition. New York, McGraw-Hill Publishers, 1999. Values have been rounded off to two significant figures.
*Calculated solubility from these K_{sp} values will match experimental solubility for this compound within a factor of 2. Experimental values for solubilities are given in R. W. Clark and J. M. Bonicamp: *Journal of Chemical Education,* Vol. 75, p. 1182, 1998.

TABLE 18B K_{spa} Values* for Some Metal Sulfides (25 °C)

Substance	K_{spa}
HgS (red)	4×10^{-54}
HgS (black)	2×10^{-53}
Ag_2S	6×10^{-51}
CuS	6×10^{-37}
PbS	3×10^{-28}
CdS	8×10^{-28}
SnS	1×10^{-26}
FeS	6×10^{-19}

*The equilibrium constant value K_{spa} for metal sulfides refers to the equilibrium $MS(s) + H_2O(\ell) \rightleftharpoons M^{2+}(aq) + OH^-(aq) + HS^-(aq)$; see R. J. Myers, *Journal of Chemical Education,* Vol. 63, p. 687, 1986.

K Formation Constants for Some Complex Ions in Aqueous Solution

TABLE 19 Formation Constants for Some Complex Ions in Aqueous Solution*

Formation Equilibrium	K
$Ag^+ + 2\ Br^- \rightleftharpoons [AgBr_2]^-$	2.1×10^7
$Ag^+ + 2\ Cl^- \rightleftharpoons [AgCl_2]^-$	1.1×10^5
$Ag^+ + 2\ CN^- \rightleftharpoons [Ag(CN)_2]^-$	1.3×10^{21}
$Ag^+ + 2\ S_2O_3^{2-} \rightleftharpoons [Ag(S_2O_3)_2]^{3-}$	2.9×10^{13}
$Ag^+ + 2\ NH_3 \rightleftharpoons [Ag(NH_3)_2]^+$	1.1×10^7
$Al^{3+} + 6\ F^- \rightleftharpoons [AlF_6]^{3-}$	6.9×10^{19}
$Al^{3+} + 4\ OH^- \rightleftharpoons [Al(OH)_4]^-$	1.1×10^{33}
$Au^+ + 2\ CN^- \rightleftharpoons [Au(CN)_2]^-$	2.0×10^{38}
$Cd^{2+} + 4\ CN^- \rightleftharpoons [Cd(CN)_4]^{2-}$	6.0×10^{18}
$Cd^{2+} + 4\ NH_3 \rightleftharpoons [Cd(NH_3)_4]^{2+}$	1.3×10^7
$Co^{2+} + 6\ NH_3 \rightleftharpoons [Co(NH_3)_6]^{2+}$	1.3×10^5
$Cu^+ + 2\ CN^- \rightleftharpoons [Cu(CN)_2]^-$	1.0×10^{24}
$Cu^+ + 2\ Cl^- \rightleftharpoons [Cu(Cl)_2]^-$	3.2×10^5
$Cu^{2+} + 4\ NH_3 \rightleftharpoons [Cu(NH_3)_4]^{2+}$	2.1×10^{13}
$Fe^{2+} + 6\ CN^- \rightleftharpoons [Fe(CN)_6]^{4-}$	1.0×10^{35}
$Hg^{2+} + 4\ Cl^- \rightleftharpoons [HgCl_4]^{2-}$	1.2×10^{15}
$Ni^{2+} + 4\ CN^- \rightleftharpoons [Ni(CN)_4]^{2-}$	2.0×10^{31}
$Ni^{2+} + 6\ NH_3 \rightleftharpoons [Ni(NH_3)_6]^{2+}$	5.5×10^8
$Zn^{2+} + 4\ OH^- \rightleftharpoons [Zn(OH)_4]^{2-}$	4.6×10^{17}
$Zn^{2+} + 4\ NH_3 \rightleftharpoons [Zn(NH_3)_4]^{2+}$	2.9×10^9

*Data reported in this table are taken from J. A. Dean: *Lange's Handbook of Chemistry,* 15th Edition. New York, McGraw-Hill Publishers, 1999.

Selected Thermodynamic Values

TABLE 20 **Selected Thermodynamic Values***

Species	ΔH_f° (298.15 K) (kJ/mol)	S° (298.15 K) (J/K · mol)	ΔG_f° (298.15 K) (kJ/mol)
Aluminum			
Al(s)	0	28.3	0
$AlCl_3$(s)	−705.63	109.29	−630.0
Al_2O_3(s)	−1675.7	50.92	−1582.3
Barium			
$BaCl_2$(s)	−858.6	123.68	−810.4
$BaCO_3$(s)	−1213	112.1	−1134.41
BaO(s)	−548.1	72.05	−520.38
$BaSO_4$(s)	−1473.2	132.2	−1362.2
Beryllium			
Be(s)	0	9.5	0
$Be(OH)_2$(s)	−902.5	51.9	−815.0
Boron			
BCl_3(g)	−402.96	290.17	−387.95
Bromine			
Br(g)	111.884	175.022	82.396
$Br_2(\ell)$	0	152.2	0
Br_2(g)	30.91	245.47	3.12
BrF_3(g)	−255.60	292.53	−229.43
HBr(g)	−36.29	198.70	−53.45
			(continued)

*Most thermodynamic data are taken from the NIST Webbook at **http://webbook.nist.gov**.

TABLE 20 Selected Thermodynamic Values* *(continued)*

Species	ΔH_f° (298.15 K) (kJ/mol)	S° (298.15 K) (J/K · mol)	ΔG_f° (298.15 K) (kJ/mol)
Calcium			
Ca(s)	0	41.59	0
Ca(g)	178.2	158.884	144.3
Ca^{2+}(g)	1925.90	—	—
CaC_2(s)	−59.8	70.	−64.93
$CaCO_3$(s, calcite)	−1207.6	91.7	−1129.16
$CaCl_2$(s)	−795.8	104.6	−748.1
CaF_2(s)	−1219.6	68.87	−1167.3
CaH_2(s)	−186.2	42	−147.2
CaO(s)	−635.09	38.2	−603.42
CaS(s)	−482.4	56.5	−477.4
$Ca(OH)_2$(s)	−986.09	83.39	−898.43
$Ca(OH)_2$(aq)	−1002.82		−868.07
$CaSO_4$(s)	−1434.52	106.5	−1322.02
Carbon			
C(s, graphite)	0	5.6	0
C(s, diamond)	1.8	2.377	2.900
C(g)	716.67	158.1	671.2
CCl_4(ℓ)	−128.4	214.39	−57.63
CCl_4(g)	−95.98	309.65	−53.61
$CHCl_3$(ℓ)	−134.47	201.7	−73.66
$CHCl_3$(g)	−103.18	295.61	−70.4
CH_4(g, methane)	−74.87	186.26	−50.8
C_2H_2(g, ethyne)	226.73	200.94	209.20
C_2H_4(g, ethene)	52.47	219.36	68.35
C_2H_6(g, ethane)	−83.85	229.2	−31.89
C_3H_8(g, propane)	−104.7	270.3	−24.4
C_6H_6(ℓ, benzene)	48.95	173.26	124.21
CH_3OH(ℓ, methanol)	−238.4	127.19	−166.14
CH_3OH(g, methanol)	−201.0	239.7	−162.5
C_2H_5OH(ℓ, ethanol)	−277.0	160.7	−174.7
C_2H_5OH(g, ethanol)	−235.3	282.70	−168.49
CO(g)	−110.525	197.674	−137.168
CO_2(g)	−393.509	213.74	−394.359
CS_2(ℓ)	89.41	151	65.2
CS_2(g)	116.7	237.8	66.61
$COCl_2$(g)	−218.8	283.53	−204.6

(continued)

TABLE 20 Selected Thermodynamic Values* *(continued)*

Species	ΔH_f° (298.15 K) (kJ/mol)	S° (298.15 K) (J/K · mol)	ΔG_f° (298.15 K) (kJ/mol)
Cesium			
Cs(s)	0	85.23	0
Cs$^+$(g)	457.964	—	—
CsCl(s)	−443.04	101.17	−414.53
Chlorine			
Cl(g)	121.3	165.19	105.3
Cl$^-$(g)	−233.13	—	—
Cl$_2$(g)	0	223.08	0
HCl(g)	−92.31	186.2	−95.09
HCl(aq)	−167.159	56.5	−131.26
Chromium			
Cr(s)	0	23.62	0
Cr$_2$O$_3$(s)	−1134.7	80.65	−1052.95
CrCl$_3$(s)	−556.5	123.0	−486.1
Copper			
Cu(s)	0	33.17	0
CuO(s)	−156.06	42.59	−128.3
CuCl$_2$(s)	−220.1	108.07	−175.7
CuSO$_4$(s)	−769.98	109.05	−660.75
Fluorine			
F$_2$(g)	0	202.8	0
F(g)	78.99	158.754	61.91
F$^-$(g)	−255.39	—	—
F$^-$(aq)	−332.63		−278.79
HF(g)	−273.3	173.779	−273.2
HF(aq)	−332.63	88.7	−278.79
Hydrogen			
H$_2$(g)	0	130.7	0
H(g)	217.965	114.713	203.247
H$^+$(g)	1536.202	—	—
H$_2$O(ℓ)	−285.83	69.95	−237.15
H$_2$O(g)	−241.83	188.84	−228.59
H$_2$O$_2$(ℓ)	−187.78	109.6	−120.35
Iodine			
I$_2$(s)	0	116.135	0
I$_2$(g)	62.438	260.69	19.327
I(g)	106.838	180.791	70.250

(continued)

TABLE 20 Selected Thermodynamic Values* *(continued)*

Species	ΔH_f° (298.15 K) (kJ/mol)	S° (298.15 K) (J/K · mol)	ΔG_f° (298.15 K) (kJ/mol)
I⁻(g)	−197	—	—
ICl(g)	17.51	247.56	−5.73
Iron			
Fe(s)	0	27.78	0
FeO(s)	−272	—	—
Fe₂O₃(s, hematite)	−825.5	87.40	−742.2
Fe₃O₄(s, magnetite)	−1118.4	146.4	−1015.4
FeCl₂(s)	−341.79	117.95	−302.30
FeCl₃(s)	−399.49	142.3	−344.00
FeS₂(s, pyrite)	−178.2	52.93	−166.9
Fe(CO)₅(ℓ)	−774.0	338.1	−705.3
Lead			
Pb(s)	0	64.81	0
PbCl₂(s)	−359.41	136.0	−314.10
PbO(s, yellow)	−219	66.5	−196
PbO₂(s)	−277.4	68.6	−217.39
PbS(s)	−100.4	91.2	−98.7
Lithium			
Li(s)	0	29.12	0
Li⁺(g)	685.783	—	—
LiOH(s)	−484.93	42.81	−438.96
LiOH(aq)	−508.48	2.80	−450.58
LiCl(s)	−408.701	59.33	−384.37
Magnesium			
Mg(s)	0	32.67	0
MgCl₂(s)	−641.62	89.62	−592.09
MgCO₃(s)	−1111.69	65.84	−1028.2
MgO(s)	−601.24	26.85	−568.93
Mg(OH)₂(s)	−924.54	63.18	−833.51
MgS(s)	−346.0	50.33	−341.8
Mercury			
Hg(ℓ)	0	76.02	0
HgCl₂(s)	−224.3	146.0	−178.6
HgO(s, red)	−90.83	70.29	−58.539
HgS(s, red)	−58.2	82.4	−50.6

(continued)

TABLE 20   Selected Thermodynamic Values* *(continued)*

Species	ΔH_f° (298.15 K) (kJ/mol)	S° (298.15 K) (J/K · mol)	ΔG_f° (298.15 K) (kJ/mol)
Nickel			
Ni(s)	0	29.87	0
NiO(s)	−239.7	37.99	−211.7
NiCl$_2$(s)	−305.332	97.65	−259.032
Nitrogen			
N$_2$(g)	0	191.56	0
N(g)	472.704	153.298	455.563
NH$_3$(g)	−45.90	192.77	−16.37
N$_2$H$_4$(ℓ)	50.63	121.52	149.45
NH$_4$Cl(s)	−314.55	94.85	−203.08
NH$_4$Cl(aq)	−299.66	169.9	−210.57
NH$_4$NO$_3$(s)	−365.56	151.08	−183.84
NH$_4$NO$_3$(aq)	−339.87	259.8	−190.57
NO(g)	90.29	210.76	86.58
NO$_2$(g)	33.1	240.04	51.23
N$_2$O(g)	82.05	219.85	104.20
N$_2$O$_4$(g)	9.08	304.38	97.73
NOCl(g)	51.71	261.8	66.08
HNO$_3$(ℓ)	−174.10	155.60	−80.71
HNO$_3$(g)	−135.06	266.38	−74.72
HNO$_3$(aq)	−207.36	146.4	−111.25
Oxygen			
O$_2$(g)	0	205.07	0
O(g)	249.170	161.055	231.731
O$_3$(g)	142.67	238.92	163.2
Phosphorus			
P$_4$(s, white)	0	41.1	0
P$_4$(s, red)	−17.6	22.80	−12.1
P(g)	314.64	163.193	278.25
PH$_3$(g)	22.89	210.24	30.91
PCl$_3$(g)	−287.0	311.78	−267.8
P$_4$O$_{10}$(s)	−2984.0	228.86	−2697.7
H$_3$PO$_4$(ℓ)	−1279.0	110.5	−1119.1
Potassium			
K(s)	0	64.63	0
KCl(s)	−436.68	82.56	−408.77
KClO$_3$(s)	−397.73	143.1	−296.25
KI(s)	−327.90	106.32	−324.892

(continued)

TABLE 20 Selected Thermodynamic Values* *(continued)*

Species	ΔH_f° (298.15 K) (kJ/mol)	S° (298.15 K) (J/K · mol)	ΔG_f° (298.15 K) (kJ/mol)
KOH(s)	−424.72	78.9	−378.92
KOH(aq)	−482.37	91.6	−440.50
Silicon			
Si(s)	0	18.82	0
SiBr$_4$(ℓ)	−457.3	277.8	−443.9
SiC(s)	−65.3	16.61	−62.8
SiCL$_4$(g)	−662.75	330.86	−622.76
SiH$_4$(g)	34.31	204.65	56.84
SiF$_4$(g)	−1614.94	282.49	−1572.65
SiO$_2$(s, quartz)	−910.86	41.46	−856.97
Silver			
Ag(s)	0	42.55	0
Ag$_2$O(s)	−31.1	121.3	−11.32
AgCl(s)	−127.01	96.25	−109.76
AgNO$_3$(s)	−124.39	140.92	−33.41
Sodium			
Na(s)	0	51.21	0
Na(g)	107.3	153.765	76.83
Na$^+$(g)	609.358	—	—
NaBr(s)	−361.02	86.82	−348.983
NaCl(s)	−411.12	72.11	−384.04
NaCl(g)	−181.42	229.79	−201.33
NaCl(aq)	−407.27	115.5	−393.133
NaOH(s)	−425.93	64.46	−379.75
NaOH(aq)	−469.15	48.1	−418.09
Na$_2$CO$_3$(s)	−1130.77	134.79	−1048.08
Sulfur			
S(s, rhombic)	0	32.1	0
S(g)	278.98	167.83	236.51
S$_2$Cl$_2$(g)	−18.4	331.5	−31.8
SF$_6$(g)	−1209	291.82	−1105.3
H$_2$S(g)	−20.63	205.79	−33.56
SO$_2$(g)	−296.84	248.21	−300.13
SO$_3$(g)	−395.77	256.77	−371.04
SOCl$_2$(g)	−212.5	309.77	−198.3
H$_2$SO$_4$(ℓ)	−814	156.9	−689.96
H$_2$SO$_4$(aq)	−909.27	20.1	−744.53

(continued)

TABLE 20 Selected Thermodynamic Values* *(continued)*

Species	ΔH_f° (298.15 K) (kJ/mol)	S° (298.15 K) (J/K · mol)	ΔG_f° (298.15 K) (kJ/mol)
Tin			
Sn(s, white)	0	51.08	0
Sn(s, gray)	−2.09	44.14	0.13
$SnCl_4(\ell)$	−511.3	258.6	−440.15
$SnCl_4(g)$	−471.5	365.8	−432.31
$SnO_2(s)$	−577.63	49.04	−515.88
Titanium			
Ti(s)	0	30.72	0
$TiCl_4(\ell)$	−804.2	252.34	−737.2
$TiCl_4(g)$	−763.16	354.84	−726.7
$TiO_2(s)$	−939.7	49.92	−884.5
Zinc			
Zn(s)	0	41.63	0
$ZnCl_2(s)$	−415.05	111.46	−369.398
ZnO(s)	−348.28	43.64	−318.30
ZnS(s, sphalerite)	−205.98	57.7	−201.29

M | Standard Reduction Potentials in Aqueous Solution at 25 °C

TABLE 21 Standard Reduction Potentials in Aqueous Solution at 25 °C

Acidic Solution	Standard Reduction Potential $E°$ (volts)
$F_2(g) + 2 e^- \longrightarrow 2 F^-(aq)$	2.87
$Co^{3+}(aq) + e^- \longrightarrow Co^{2+}(aq)$	1.82
$Pb^{4+}(aq) + 2 e^- \longrightarrow Pb^{2+}(aq)$	1.8
$H_2O_2(aq) + 2 H^+(aq) + 2 e^- \longrightarrow 2 H_2O$	1.77
$NiO_2(s) + 4 H^+(aq) + 2 e^- \longrightarrow Ni^{2+}(aq) + 2 H_2O$	1.7
$PbO_2(s) + SO_4^{2-}(aq) + 4 H^+(aq) + 2 e^- \longrightarrow PbSO_4(s) + 2 H_2O$	1.685
$Au^+(aq) + e^- \longrightarrow Au(s)$	1.68
$2 HClO(aq) + 2 H^+(aq) + 2 e^- \longrightarrow Cl_2(g) + 2 H_2O$	1.63
$Ce^{4+}(aq) + e^- \longrightarrow Ce^{3+}(aq)$	1.61
$NaBiO_3(s) + 6 H^+(aq) + 2 e^- \longrightarrow Bi^{3+}(aq) + Na^+(aq) + 3 H_2O$	≈ 1.6
$MnO_4^-(aq) + 8 H^+(aq) + 5 e^- \longrightarrow Mn^{2+}(aq) + 4 H_2O$	1.51
$Au^{3+}(aq) + 3 e^- \longrightarrow Au(s)$	1.50
$ClO_3^-(aq) + 6 H^+(aq) + 5 e^- \longrightarrow \frac{1}{2} Cl_2(g) + 3 H_2O$	1.47
$BrO_3^-(aq) + 6 H^+(aq) + 6 e^- \longrightarrow Br^-(aq) + 3 H_2O$	1.44
$Cl_2(g) + 2 e^- \longrightarrow 2 Cl^-(aq)$	1.36
$Cr_2O_7^{2-}(aq) + 14 H^+(aq) + 6 e^- \longrightarrow 2 Cr^{3+}(aq) + 7 H_2O$	1.33
$N_2H_5^+(aq) + 3 H^+(aq) + 2 e^- \longrightarrow 2 NH_4^+(aq)$	1.24
$MnO_2(s) + 4 H^+(aq) + 2 e^- \longrightarrow Mn^{2+}(aq) + 2 H_2O$	1.23
$O_2(g) + 4 H^+(aq) + 4 e^- \longrightarrow 2 H_2O$	1.229
$Pt^{2+}(aq) + 2 e^- \longrightarrow Pt(s)$	1.2
$IO_3^-(aq) + 6 H^+(aq) + 5 e^- \longrightarrow \frac{1}{2} I_2(aq) + 3 H_2O$	1.195

(continued)

Acidic Solution	Standard Reduction Potential $E°$ (volts)
$ClO_4^-(aq) + 2\ H^+(aq) + 2\ e^- \longrightarrow ClO_3^-(aq) + H_2O$	1.19
$Br_2(\ell) + 2\ e^- \longrightarrow 2\ Br^-(aq)$	1.08
$AuCl_4^-(aq) + 3\ e^- \longrightarrow Au(s) + 4\ Cl^-(aq)$	1.00
$Pd^{2+}(aq) + 2\ e^- \longrightarrow Pd(s)$	0.987
$NO_3^-(aq) + 4\ H^+(aq) + 3\ e^- \longrightarrow NO(g) + 2\ H_2O$	0.96
$NO_3^-(aq) + 3\ H^+(aq) + 2\ e^- \longrightarrow HNO_2(aq) + H_2O$	0.94
$2\ Hg^+(aq) + 2\ e^- \longrightarrow Hg_2^{2+}(aq)$	0.920
$Hg^{2+}(aq) + 2\ e^- \longrightarrow Hg(\ell)$	0.855
$Ag^+(aq) + e^- \longrightarrow Ag(s)$	0.7994
$Hg_2^{2+}(aq) + 2\ e^- \longrightarrow 2\ Hg(\ell)$	0.789
$Fe^{3+}(aq) + e^- \longrightarrow Fe^{2+}(aq)$	0.771
$SbCl_6^-(aq) + 2\ e^- \longrightarrow SbCl_4^-(aq) + 2\ Cl^-(aq)$	0.75
$[PtCl_4]^{2+}(aq) + 2\ e^- \longrightarrow Pt(s) + 4\ Cl^-(aq)$	0.73
$O_2(g) + 2\ H^+(aq) + 2\ e^- \longrightarrow H_2O_2(aq)$	0.682
$[PtCl_6]^{2-}(aq) + 2\ e^- \longrightarrow [PtCl_4]^{2-}(aq) + 2\ Cl^-(aq)$	0.68
$I_2(aq) + 2\ e^- \longrightarrow 2\ I^-(aq)$	0.621
$H_3AsO_4(aq) + 2\ H^+(aq) + 2\ e^- \longrightarrow H_3AsO_3(aq) + H_2O$	0.58
$I_2(s) + 2\ e^- \longrightarrow 2\ I^-(aq)$	0.535
$TeO_2(s) + 4\ H^+(aq) + 4\ e^- \longrightarrow Te(s) + 2\ H_2O$	0.529
$Cu^+(aq) + e^- \longrightarrow Cu(s)$	0.521
$[RhCl_6]^{3-}(aq) + 3\ e^- \longrightarrow Rh(s) + 6\ Cl^-(aq)$	0.44
$Cu^{2+}(aq) + 2\ e^- \longrightarrow Cu(s)$	0.337
$Hg_2Cl_2(s) + 2\ e^- \longrightarrow 2\ Hg(\ell) + 2\ Cl^-(aq)$	0.27
$AgCl(s) + e^- \longrightarrow Ag(s) + Cl^-(aq)$	0.222
$SO_4^{2-}(aq) + 4\ H^+(aq) + 2\ e^- \longrightarrow SO_2(g) + 2\ H_2O$	0.20
$SO_4^{2-}(aq) + 4\ H^+(aq) + 2\ e^- \longrightarrow H_2SO_3(aq) + H_2O$	0.17
$Cu^{2+}(aq) + e^- \longrightarrow Cu^+(aq)$	0.153
$Sn^{4+}(aq) + 2\ e^- \longrightarrow Sn^{2+}(aq)$	0.15
$S(s) + 2\ H^+ + 2\ e^- \longrightarrow H_2S(aq)$	0.14
$AgBr(s) + e^- \longrightarrow Ag(s) + Br^-(aq)$	0.0713
$2\ H^+(aq) + 2\ e^- \longrightarrow H_2(g)\ (reference\ electrode)$	0.0000
$N_2O(g) + 6\ H^+(aq) + H_2O + 4\ e^- \longrightarrow 2\ NH_3OH^+(aq)$	−0.05
$Pb^{2+}(aq) + 2\ e^- \longrightarrow Pb(s)$	−0.126
$Sn^{2+}(aq) + 2\ e^- \longrightarrow Sn(s)$	−0.14
$AgI(s) + e^- \longrightarrow Ag(s) + I^-(aq)$	−0.15
$[SnF_6]^{2-}(aq) + 4\ e^- \longrightarrow Sn(s) + 6\ F^-(aq)$	−0.25
$Ni^{2+}(aq) + 2\ e^- \longrightarrow Ni(s)$	−0.25
$Co^{2+}(aq) + 2\ e^- \longrightarrow Co(s)$	−0.28

(continued)

TABLE 21 Standard Reduction Potentials in Aqueous Solution at 25 °C *(continued)*

Acidic Solution	Standard Reduction Potential $E°$ (volts)
$Tl^+(aq) + e^- \longrightarrow Tl(s)$	-0.34
$PbSO_4(s) + 2\ e^- \longrightarrow Pb(s) + SO_4^{2-}(aq)$	-0.356
$Se(s) + 2\ H^+(aq) + 2\ e^- \longrightarrow H_2Se(aq)$	-0.40
$Cd^{2+}(aq) + 2\ e^- \longrightarrow Cd(s)$	-0.403
$Cr^{3+}(aq) + e^- \longrightarrow Cr^{2+}(aq)$	-0.41
$Fe^{2+}(aq) + 2\ e^- \longrightarrow Fe(s)$	-0.44
$2\ CO_2(g) + 2\ H^+(aq) + 2\ e^- \longrightarrow H_2C_2O_4(aq)$	-0.49
$Ga^{3+}(aq) + 3\ e^- \longrightarrow Ga(s)$	-0.53
$HgS(s) + 2\ H^+(aq) + 2\ e^- \longrightarrow Hg(\ell) + H_2S(g)$	-0.72
$Cr^{3+}(aq) + 3\ e^- \longrightarrow Cr(s)$	-0.74
$Zn^{2+}(aq) + 2\ e^- \longrightarrow Zn(s)$	-0.763
$Cr^{2+}(aq) + 2\ e^- \longrightarrow Cr(s)$	-0.91
$FeS(s) + 2\ e^- \longrightarrow Fe(s) + S^{2-}(aq)$	-1.01
$Mn^{2+}(aq) + 2\ e^- \longrightarrow Mn(s)$	-1.18
$V^{2+}(aq) + 2\ e^- \longrightarrow V(s)$	-1.18
$CdS(s) + 2\ e^- \longrightarrow Cd(s) + S^{2-}(aq)$	-1.21
$ZnS(s) + 2\ e^- \longrightarrow Zn(s) + S^{2-}(aq)$	-1.44
$Zr^{4+}(aq) + 4\ e^- \longrightarrow Zr(s)$	-1.53
$Al^{3+}(aq) + 3\ e^- \longrightarrow Al(s)$	-1.66
$Mg^{2+}(aq) + 2\ e^- \longrightarrow Mg(s)$	-2.37
$Na^+(aq) + e^- \longrightarrow Na(s)$	-2.714
$Ca^{2+}(aq) + 2\ e^- \longrightarrow Ca(s)$	-2.87
$Sr^{2+}(aq) + 2\ e^- \longrightarrow Sr(s)$	-2.89
$Ba^{2+}(aq) + 2\ e^- \longrightarrow Ba(s)$	-2.90
$Rb^+(aq) + e^- \longrightarrow Rb(s)$	-2.925
$K^+(aq) + e^- \longrightarrow K(s)$	-2.925
$Li^+(aq) + e^- \longrightarrow Li(s)$	-3.045

Basic Solution

$ClO^-(aq) + H_2O + 2\ e^- \longrightarrow Cl^-(aq) + 2\ OH^-(aq)$	0.89
$OOH^-(aq) + H_2O + 2\ e^- \longrightarrow 3\ OH^-(aq)$	0.88
$2\ NH_2OH(aq) + 2\ e^- \longrightarrow N_2H_4(aq) + 2\ OH^-(aq)$	0.74
$ClO_3^-(aq) + 3\ H_2O + 6\ e^- \longrightarrow Cl^-(aq) + 6\ OH^-(aq)$	0.62
$MnO_4^-(aq) + 2\ H_2O + 3\ e^- \longrightarrow MnO_2(s) + 4\ OH^-(aq)$	0.588
$MnO_4^-(aq) + e^- \longrightarrow MnO_4^{2-}(aq)$	0.564
$NiO_2(s) + 2\ H_2O + 2\ e^- \longrightarrow Ni(OH)_2(s) + 2\ OH^-(aq)$	0.49
$Ag_2CrO_4(s) + 2\ e^- \longrightarrow 2\ Ag(s) + CrO_4^{2-}(aq)$	0.446
$O_2(g) + 2\ H_2O + 4\ e^- \longrightarrow 4\ OH^-(aq)$	0.40

(continued)

TABLE 21 Standard Reduction Potentials in Aqueous Solution at 25 °C *(continued)*

Acidic Solution	Standard Reduction Potential $E°$ (volts)
$ClO_4^-(aq) + H_2O + 2\ e^- \longrightarrow ClO_3^-(aq) + 2\ OH^-(aq)$	0.36
$Ag_2O(s) + H_2O + 2\ e^- \longrightarrow 2\ Ag(s) + 2\ OH^-(aq)$	0.34
$2\ NO_2^-(aq) + 3\ H_2O + 4\ e^- \longrightarrow N_2O(g) + 6\ OH^-(aq)$	0.15
$N_2H_4(aq) + 2\ H_2O + 2\ e^- \longrightarrow 2\ NH_3(aq) + 2\ OH^-(aq)$	0.10
$[Co(NH_3)_6]^{3+}(aq) + e^- \longrightarrow [Co(NH_3)_6]^{2+}(aq)$	0.10
$HgO(s) + H_2O + 2\ e^- \longrightarrow Hg(\ell) + 2\ OH^-(aq)$	0.0984
$O_2(g) + H_2O + 2\ e^- \longrightarrow OOH^-(aq) + OH^-(aq)$	0.076
$NO_3^-(aq) + H_2O + 2\ e^- \longrightarrow NO_2^-(aq) + 2\ OH^-(aq)$	0.01
$MnO_2(s) + 2\ H_2O + 2\ e^- \longrightarrow Mn(OH)_2(s) + 2\ OH^-(aq)$	−0.05
$CrO_4^{2-}(aq) + 4\ H_2O + 3\ e^- \longrightarrow Cr(OH)_3(s) + 5\ OH^-(aq)$	−0.12
$Cu(OH)_2(s) + 2\ e^- \longrightarrow Cu(s) + 2\ OH^-(aq)$	−0.36
$S(s) + 2\ e^- \longrightarrow S^{2-}(aq)$	−0.48
$Fe(OH)_3(s) + e^- \longrightarrow Fe(OH)_2(s) + OH^-(aq)$	−0.56
$2\ H_2O + 2\ e^- \longrightarrow H_2(g) + 2\ OH^-(aq)$	−0.8277
$2\ NO_3^-(aq) + 2\ H_2O + 2\ e^- \longrightarrow N_2O_4(g) + 4\ OH^-(aq)$	−0.85
$Fe(OH)_2(s) + 2\ e^- \longrightarrow Fe(s) + 2\ OH^-(aq)$	−0.877
$SO_4^{2-}(aq) + H_2O + 2\ e^- \longrightarrow SO_3^{2-}(aq) + 2\ OH^-(aq)$	−0.93
$N_2(g) + 4\ H_2O + 4\ e^- \longrightarrow N_2H_4(aq) + 4\ OH^-(aq)$	−1.15
$[Zn(OH)_4]^{2-}(aq) + 2\ e^- \longrightarrow Zn(s) + 4\ OH^-(aq)$	−1.22
$Zn(OH)_2(s) + 2\ e^- \longrightarrow Zn(s) + 2\ OH^-(aq)$	−1.245
$[Zn(CN)_4]^{2-}(aq) + 2\ e^- \longrightarrow Zn(s) + 4\ CN^-(aq)$	−1.26
$Cr(OH)_3(s) + 3\ e^- \longrightarrow Cr(s) + 3\ OH^-(aq)$	−1.30
$SiO_3^{2-}(aq) + 3\ H_2O + 4\ e^- \longrightarrow Si(s) + 6\ OH^-(aq)$	−1.70

N | Answers to Exercises

Chapter 1

1.1 (a) Na = sodium; Cl = chlorine; Cr = chromium
(b) Zinc = Zn; nickel = Ni; potassium = K

1.2 (a) Iron: lustrous solid, metallic, good conductor of heat and electricity, malleable, ductile, attracted to a magnet
(b) Water: colorless liquid (at room temperature); melting point is 0 °C, and boiling point is 100 °C, density ~ 1 g/cm^2
(c) Table salt: solid, white crystals, soluble in water
(d) Oxygen: colorless gas (at room temperature), low solubility in water

1.3 Chemical changes: the fuel in the campfire burns in air (combustion). Physical changes: water boils. Energy evolved in combustion is transferred to the water, to the water container, and to the surrounding air.

Let's Review

LR 1 [77 K − 273.15 K] (1 °C/K) = −196 °C

LR 2 Convert thickness to cm: 0.25 mm(1 cm/10 mm) = 0.025 cm
Volume = length × width × thickness
V = (2.50 cm)(2.50 cm)(0.025 cm) = 0.16 cm^3 (answer has 2 significant figures.)

LR 3 (a) (750 mL)(1 L/1000 mL) = 0.75 L
(0.75 L)(10 dL/L) = 7.5 dL
(b) 2.0 qt = 0.50 gal
(0.50 gal)(3.786 L/gal) = 1.9 L
(1.9 L)(1 dm^3/1 L) = 1.9 dm^3

LR 4 (a) Mass in kilograms = (5.59 g)(1 kg/1000 g) = 0.00559 kg
Mass in milligrams = 5.59 g (10^3 mg/g) = 5.59 × 10^3 mg
(b) (0.02 μg/L)(1 g/10^6 μg) = 2 × 10^{-8} g/L

LR 5 Student A: average = −0.1 °C; average deviation = 0.2 °C; error = −0.1 °C. Student B: average = +0.01 °C; average deviation = 0.02 °C; error = +0.01 °C. Student B's values are more accurate and less precise.

LR 6 (a) 2.33 × 10^7 has three significant figures; 50.5 has three significant figures; 200 has one significant figure. (200. or 2.00 × 10^2 would express this number with three significant figures.)
(b) The product of 10.26 and 0.063 is 0.65, a number with two significant figures. (10.26 has four significant figures, whereas 0.063 has two.)
The sum of 10.26 and 0.063 is 10.32. The number 10.26 has only two numbers to the right of the decimal, so the sum must also have two numbers after the decimal.
(c) x = 3.9 × 10^6. The difference between 110.7 and 64 is 47. Dividing 47 by 0.056 and 0.00216 gives an answer with two significant figures.

LR 7 (a) (198 cm)(1 m/100 cm) = 1.98 m;
(198 cm)(1 ft/30.48 cm) = 6.50 ft
(b) (2.33 × 10^7 m^2)(1 km^2/10^6 m^2) = 23.3 km^2
(c) (19,320 kg/m^3)(10^3 g/1 kg)(1 m^3/10^6 cm^3) = 19.32 g/cm^3
(d) (9.0 × 10^3 pc)(206,265 AU/1 pc)(1.496 × 10^8 km/1 AU) = 2.8 × 10^{17} km

LR 8 Read from the graph, the mass of 50 beans is about 123 g.

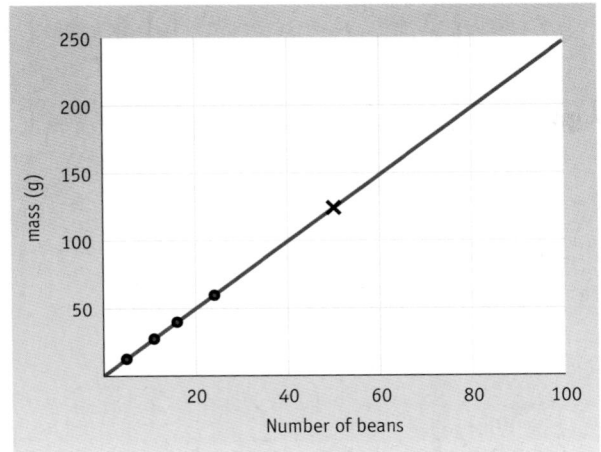

LR 9 Change all dimensions to centimeters: 7.6 m = 760 cm; 2.74 m = 274 cm; 0.13 mm = 0.013 cm.

Volume of paint = (760 cm)(274 cm)(0.013 cm) = 2.7×10^3 cm^3

Volume (L) = $(2.7 \times 10^3$ cm$^3)(1$ L$/10^3$ cm$^3) = 2.7$ L

Mass = $(2.7 \times 10^3$ cm$^3)(0.914$ g/cm$^3) = 2.5 \times 10^3$ g

Chapter 2

2.1 (a) Mass number with 26 protons and 30 neutrons is 56
(b) $(59.930788$ u$)(1.661 \times 10^{-24}$ g/u$) = 9.955 \times 10^{-23}$ g
(c) ^{64}Zn has 30 protons, 30 electrons, and $(64 - 30)$ = 34 neutrons.
(d) The mass of a ^{64}Zn atom is 63.929/12.0... . or 5.3274 times the mass of a ^{12}C atom. (Note that mass of ^{12}C is defined as an exact value.)

2.2 The mass number of the second silver isotope is 109 (62 + 47). Symbol: ^{109}Ag, abundance = 48.161%.

2.3 Use Equation 2.2 for the calculation.
Atomic mass = $(34.96885)(75.77/100) + (36.96590)(24.23/100) = 35.45$. (Accuracy is limited by the value of the percent abundance to 4 significant figures.)

2.4 There are eight elements in the third period. Sodium (Na), magnesium (Mg), and aluminum (Al) are metals. Silicon (Si) is a metalloid. Phosphorus (P), sulfur (S), chlorine (Cl), and argon (Ar) are nonmetals.

2.5 The molecular formula is $C_3H_7NO_2S$. You will often see its formula written as $HSCH_2CH(N^+H_3)CO_2^-$ to better identify the molecule's structure.

2.6 (a) K^+ is formed if K loses one electron. K^+ has the same number of electrons as Ar.
(b) Se^{2-} is formed by adding two electrons to an atom of Se. It has the same number of electrons as Kr.

(c) Ba^{2+} is formed if Ba loses two electrons; Ba^{2+} has the same number of electrons as Xe.
(d) Cs^+ is formed if Cs loses one electron. It has the same number of electrons as Xe.

2.7 (a) (1) NaF: 1 Na^+ and 1 F^- ion. (2) $Cu(NO_3)_2$: 1 Cu^{2+} and 2 NO_3^- ions. (3) $NaCH_3CO_2$: 1 Na^+ and 1 $CH_3CO_2^-$ ion.
(b) $FeCl_2$, $FeCl_3$
(c) Na_2S, Na_3PO_4, BaS, $Ba_3(PO_4)_2$

2.8 (1) (a) NH_4NO_3; (b) $CoSO_4$; (c) $Ni(CN)_2$; (d) V_2O_3; (e) $Ba(CH_3CO_2)_2$; (f) $Ca(ClO)_2$
(2) (a) magnesium bromide; (b) lithium carbonate; (c) potassium hydrogen sulfite; (d) potassium permanganate; (e) ammonium sulfide; (f) copper(I) chloride and copper(II) chloride

2.9 The force of attraction between ions is proportional to the product of the ion charges (Coulomb's law). The force of attraction between Mg^{2+} and O^{2-} ions in MgO is approximately four times greater than the force of attraction between Na^+ and Cl^- ions in NaCl, so a much higher temperature is required to disrupt the orderly array of ions in crystalline MgO.

2.10 (1) (a) CO_2; (b) PI_3; (c) SCl_2; (d) BF_3; (e) O_2F_2; (f) XeO_3
(2) (a) dinitrogen tetrafluoride; (b) hydrogen bromide; (c) sulfur tetrafluoride; (d) boron trichloride; (e) tetraphosphorus decaoxide; (f) chlorine trifluoride

2.11 (a) $(1.5$ mol Si$)(28.1$ g/mol$) = 42$ g Si
(b) $(454$ g S$)(1.00$ mol S/32.07 g$) = 14.2$ mol S
$(14.2$ mol S$)(6.022 \times 10^{23}$ atoms/mol$) = 8.53 \times 10^{24}$ atoms S

2.12 $(2.6 \times 10^{24}$ atoms$)(1.000$ mol/6.022×10^{23} atoms$)(197.0$ g Au/1.000 mol$) = 850$ g Au
Volume = $(850$ g Au$)(1.00$ cm$^3/19.32$ g$) = 44$ cm^3
Volume = 44 cm^3 = (thickness)(area) = (0.10 cm)(area)
Area = 440 cm^2
Length = width = $\sqrt{440 \text{ cm}^2} = 21$ cm

2.13 (a) Citric acid: 192.1 g/mol; magnesium carbonate: 84.3 g/mol
(b) 454 g citric acid $(1.000$ mol/192.1 g$) = 2.36$ mol citric acid
(c) 0.125 mol $MgCO_3$ $(84.3$ g/mol$) = 10.5$ g $MgCO_3$

2.14 (a) 1.00 mol $(NH_4)_2CO_3$ (molar mass 96.09 g/mol) has 28.0 g of N (29.2%), 8.06 g of H (8.39%), 12.0 g of C (12.5%), and 48.0 g of O (50.0%)
(b) 454 g C_8H_{18} (1 mol C_8H_{18}/114.2 g)(8 mol C/1 mol C_8H_{18})(12.01 g C/1 mol C) = 382 g C

2.15 (a) C_5H_4 (b) $C_2H_4O_2$

2.16 $(88.17$ g C$)(1$ mol C/12.011 g C$) = 7.341$ mol C

$(11.83 \text{ g H})(1 \text{ mol H}/1.008 \text{ g H}) = 11.74 \text{ mol H}$

$11.74 \text{ mol H}/7.341 \text{ mol C} = 1.6 \text{ mol H}/1 \text{ mol C}$
$= (8/5); (\text{mol H}/1 \text{ mol C}) = 8 \text{ mol H}/5 \text{ mol C}$

The empirical formula is C_5H_8. The molar mass, 68.11 g/mol, closely matches this formula, so C_5H_8 is also the molecular formula.

2.17 $(78.90 \text{ g C})(1 \text{ mol C}/12.011 \text{ g C}) = 6.569 \text{ mol C}$
$(10.59 \text{ g H})(1 \text{ mol H}/1.008 \text{ g H}) = 10.51 \text{ mol H}$
$(10.51 \text{ g O})(1 \text{ mol O}/16.00 \text{ g O}) = 0.6569 \text{ mol O}$

$10.51 \text{ mol H}/0.6569 \text{ mol O} = 16 \text{ mol H}/1 \text{ mol O}$

$6.569 \text{ mol C}/0.6569 \text{ mol O} = 10 \text{ mol C}/1 \text{ mol O}$

The empirical formula is $C_{10}H_{16}O$.

2.18 $(0.586 \text{ g K})(1 \text{ mol K}/39.10 \text{ g K}) = 0.0150 \text{ mol K}$
$(0.480 \text{ g O})(1 \text{ mol O}/16.00 \text{ g O}) = 0.0300 \text{ mol O}$

The ratio of moles K to moles O atoms is 1 to 2; the empirical formula is KO_2.

2.19 Mass of water lost on heating is $0.235 \text{ g} - 0.128 \text{ g}$ $= 0.107 \text{ g}; 0.128 \text{ g NiCl}_2$ remain

$(0.107 \text{ g H}_2O)(1 \text{ mol H}_2O/18.016 \text{ g H}_2O)$ $= 0.00594 \text{ mol H}_2O$

$(0.128 \text{ g NiCl}_2)(1 \text{ mol NiCl}_2/129.6 \text{ g NiCl}_2)$ $= 0.000988 \text{ mol NiCl}_2$

Mole ratio $= 0.00594 \text{ mol H}_2O/0.000988 \text{ mol}$ $\text{NiCl}_2 = 6.01$: Therefore $x = 6$

The formula for the hydrate is $\text{NiCl}_2 \cdot 6 \text{ H}_2O$.

Chapter 3

3.1 (a) Stoichiometric coefficients: 2 for Al, 3 for Br_2, and 1 for Al_2Br_6
(b) 8000 atoms of Al requires $(3/2)8000 = 12{,}000$ molecules of Br_2

3.2 (a) $2 \text{ C}_4\text{H}_{10}(g) + 13 \text{ O}_2(g) \longrightarrow$
$8 \text{ CO}_2(g) + 10 \text{ H}_2\text{O}(\ell)$
(b) $2 \text{ Pb}(\text{C}_2\text{H}_5)_4(\ell) + 27 \text{ O}_2(g) \longrightarrow$
$2 \text{ PbO}(s) + 16 \text{ CO}_2(g) + 20 \text{ H}_2\text{O}(\ell)$

3.3 Epsom salt is an electrolyte, and methanol is a non-electrolyte.

3.4 (a) $LiNO_3$ is soluble and gives $Li^+(aq)$ and $NO_3^-(aq)$ ions.
(b) $CaCl_2$ is soluble and gives $Ca^{2+}(aq)$ and $Cl^-(aq)$ ions.
(c) CuO is not water-soluble.
(d) $NaCH_3CO_2$ is soluble and gives $Na^+(aq)$ and $CH_3CO_2^-(aq)$ ions.

3.5 (a) $\text{Na}_2\text{CO}_3(aq) + \text{CuCl}_2(aq) \longrightarrow$
$2 \text{ NaCl}(aq) + \text{CuCO}_3(s)$
(b) No reaction; no insoluble compound is produced.

(c) $\text{NiCl}_2(aq) + 2 \text{ KOH}(aq) \longrightarrow$
$\text{Ni(OH)}_2(s) + 2 \text{ KCl}(aq)$

3.6 (a) $\text{AlCl}_3(aq) + \text{Na}_3\text{PO}_4(aq) \longrightarrow$
$\text{AlPO}_4(s) + 3 \text{ NaCl}(aq)$
$\text{Al}^{3+}(aq) + \text{PO}_4^{3-}(aq) \longrightarrow \text{AlPO}_4(s)$
(b) $\text{FeCl}_3(aq) + 3 \text{ KOH}(aq) \longrightarrow$
$\text{Fe(OH)}_3(s) + 3 \text{ KCl}(aq)$
$\text{Fe}^{3+}(aq) + 3 \text{ OH}^-(aq) \longrightarrow \text{Fe(OH)}_3(s)$
(c) $\text{Pb(NO}_3)_2(aq) + 2 \text{ KCl}(aq) \longrightarrow$
$\text{PbCl}_2(s) + 2 \text{ KNO}_3(aq)$
$\text{Pb}^{2+}(aq) + 2 \text{ Cl}^-(aq) \rightleftarrows \text{PbCl}_2(s)$

3.7 (a) $\text{H}_3\text{O}(aq)$ and $\text{NO}_3^-(aq)$
(b) $\text{Ba}^{2+}(aq)$ and $2 \text{ OH}^-(aq)$

3.8 (a) $\text{H}_3\text{PO}_4(aq) + \text{H}_2\text{O}(\ell) \rightleftarrows$
$\text{H}_3\text{O}^+(aq) + \text{H}_2\text{PO}_4^-(aq)$
(b) Acting as a base:
$\text{H}_2\text{PO}_4^-(aq) + \text{H}_2\text{O}(\ell) \rightleftarrows$
$\text{H}_3\text{PO}_4(aq) + \text{OH}^-(aq)$

Acting as an acid:
$\text{H}_2\text{PO}_4^-(aq) + \text{H}_2\text{O}(\ell) \rightleftarrows$
$\text{HPO}_4^{2-}(aq) + \text{H}_3\text{O}^+(\ell)$

Because $\text{H}_2\text{PO}_4^-(aq)$ can react as a Brønsted acid and as a base, it is said to be amphiprotic.
(c) $\text{CN}^-(aq) + \text{H}_2\text{O}(\ell) \rightleftarrows \text{HCN}(aq) + \text{OH}^-(aq)$; cyanide ion is a Brønsted base.

3.9 $\text{Mg(OH)}_2(s) + 2 \text{ HCl}(aq) \longrightarrow$
$\text{MgCl}_2(aq) + 2 \text{ H}_2\text{O}(\ell)$

Net ionic equation: $\text{Mg(OH)}_2(s) + 2 \text{ H}^+(aq) \longrightarrow$
$\text{Mg}^{2+}(aq) + 2 \text{ H}_2\text{O}(\ell)$

3.10 Metals form basic oxides; nonmetals form acidic oxides.
(a) SeO_2 is an acidic oxide; (b) MgO is a basic oxide; and (c) P_4O_{10} is an acidic oxide.

3.11 (a) $\text{BaCO}_3(s) + 2 \text{ HNO}_3(aq) \longrightarrow$
$\text{Ba(NO}_3)_2(aq) + \text{CO}_2(g) + \text{H}_2\text{O}(\ell)$
Barium carbonate and nitric acid produce barium nitrate, carbon dioxide, and water.
(b) $(\text{NH}_4)_2\text{SO}_4(aq) + 2 \text{ NaOH}(aq) \longrightarrow$
$2 \text{ NH}_3(g) + \text{Na}_2\text{SO}_4(aq) + 2 \text{ H}_2\text{O}(\ell)$

3.12 (a) Fe in Fe_2O_3, +3; (b) S in H_2SO_4, +6;
(c) C in CO_3^{2-}, +4; (d) N in NO_2^+, +5

3.13 Dichromate ion is the oxidizing agent and is reduced. (Cr with a +6 oxidation number is reduced to Cr^{3+} with a +3 oxidation number.) Ethanol is the reducing agent and is oxidized. (The C atoms in ethanol have an oxidation number of -2. The oxidation number is 0 in acetic acid.)

3.14 (b) Cu is the reducing agent and Cl_2 is the oxidizing agent.
(d) $S_2O_3^{2-}$ is the reducing agent and I_2 is the oxidizing agent.

3.15 (a) Gas-forming reaction:
$$CuCO_3(s) + H_2SO_4(aq) \longrightarrow$$
$$CuSO_4(aq) + H_2O(\ell) + CO_2(g)$$

Net ionic equation:
$$CuCO_3(s) + 2 H_3O(aq) \longrightarrow$$
$$Cu^{2+}(aq) + 3 H_2O(\ell) + CO_2(g)$$

(b) Oxidation-reduction: $Ga(s) + O_2(g) \longrightarrow$
$$Ga_2O_3(s)$$

(c) Acid–base reaction:
$$Ba(OH)_2(s) + 2 HNO_3(aq) \longrightarrow$$
$$Ba(NO_3)_2(aq) + 2 H_2O(\ell)$$

Net ionic equation:
$$Ba(OH)_2(s) + 2 H_3O(aq) \longrightarrow$$
$$Ba^{2+}(aq) + 4 H_2O(\ell)$$

(d) Precipitation reaction:
$$CuCl_2(aq) + (NH_4)_2S(aq) \longrightarrow$$
$$CuS(s) + 2 NH_4Cl(aq)$$

Net ionic equation:
$$Cu^{2+}(aq) + S^{2-}(aq) \longrightarrow CuS(s)$$

Chapter 4

4.1 $(454 \text{ g } C_3H_8)(1 \text{ mol } C_3H_8/44.10 \text{ g } C_3H_8)$
$= 10.3 \text{ mol } C_3H_8$

$10.3 \text{ mol } C_3H_8 (5 \text{ mol } O_2/1 \text{ mol } C_3H_8)$
$(32.00 \text{ g } O_2/1 \text{ mol } O_2) = 1650 \text{ g } O_2$

$(10.3 \text{ mol } C_3H_8)(3 \text{ mol } CO_2/1 \text{ mol } C_3H_8)$
$(44.01 \text{ g } CO_2/1 \text{ mol } CO_2) = 1360 \text{ g } CO_2$

$(10.3 \text{ mol } C_3H_8)(4 \text{ mol } H_2O/1 \text{ mol } C_3H_8)$
$(18.02 \text{ g } H_2O/1 \text{ mol } H_2O) = 742 \text{ g } H_2O$

4.2 (a) Amount Al $= (50.0 \text{ g Al})(1 \text{ mol Al}/26.98 \text{ g Al})$
$= 1.85 \text{ mol Al}$

Amount $Fe_2O_3 = (50.0 \text{ g } Fe_2O_3)(1 \text{ mol}$
$Fe_2O_3/159.7 \text{ g } Fe_2O_3) = 0.313 \text{ mol } Fe_2O_3$

Mol Al/mol $Fe_2O_3 = 1.853/0.3131 = 5.92$

This is more than the 2:1 ratio required, so the limiting reactant is Fe_2O_3.

(b) Mass Fe $= (0.313 \text{ mol } Fe_2O_3)(2 \text{ mol Fe}/1 \text{ mol}$
$Fe_2O_3)(55.85 \text{ g Fe}/1 \text{ mol Fe}) = 35.0 \text{ g Fe}$

4.3 Theoretical yield $= 125 \text{ g } Al_4C_3(1 \text{ mol } Al_4C_3/143.95 \text{ g}$
$Al_4C_3)(3 \text{ mol } CH_4/1 \text{ mol } Al_4C_3)(16.04 \text{ g } CH_4/1 \text{ mol}$
$CH_4) = 41.8 \text{ g } CH_4$

Percent yield $= (13.6 \text{ g}/41.8 \text{ g})(100\%) = 33.0\%$

4.4 $(0.143 \text{ g } O_2)(1 \text{ mol } O_2/32.00 \text{ g } O_2)(3 \text{ mol } TiO_2/$
$3 \text{ mol } O_2)(79.88 \text{ g } TiO_2/1 \text{ mol } TiO_2) = 0.357 \text{ g } TiO_2$

Percent TiO_2 in sample $= (0.357 \text{ g}/2.367 \text{ g})(100\%)$
$= 15.1\%$

4.5 $(1.612 \text{ g } CO_2)(1 \text{ mol } CO_2/44.01 \text{ g } CO_2)(1 \text{ mol C}/$
$1 \text{ mol } CO_2) = 0.03663 \text{ mol C}$

$(0.7425 \text{ g } H_2O)(1 \text{ mol } H_2O/18.01 \text{ g } H_2O)(2 \text{ mol H}/$
$1 \text{ mol } H_2O) = 0.08243 \text{ mol H}$

$0.08243 \text{ mol H}/0.03663 \text{ mol} = 2.250 \text{ H}/1 \text{ C} = 9 \text{ H}/4 \text{ C}$

The empirical formula is C_4H_9, which has a molar mass of 57 g/mol. This is one half of the measured value of molar mass, so the molecular formula is C_8H_{18}.

4.6 $(0.240 \text{ g } CO_2)(1 \text{ mol } CO_2/44.01 \text{ g } CO_2)(1 \text{ mol C}/1$
$\text{mol } CO_2)(12.01 \text{ g C}/1 \text{ mol C}) = 0.06549 \text{ g C}$

$(0.0982 \text{ g } H_2O)(1 \text{ mol } H_2O/18.02 \text{ g } H_2O)(2 \text{ mol H}/1$
$\text{mol } H_2O)(1.008 \text{ g H}/1 \text{ mol H}) = 0.01099 \text{ g H}$

Mass O (by difference) $= 0.1342 \text{ g} - 0.06549 \text{ g} -$
$0.01099 \text{ g} = 0.05772 \text{ g}$

Amount C $= 0.06549 \text{ g}(1 \text{ mol C}/12.01 \text{ g C}) =$
0.00545 mol C

Amount H $= 0.01099 \text{ g H}(1 \text{ mol H}/1.008 \text{ g H}) =$
0.01090 mol H

Amount O $= 0.05772 \text{ g O}(1 \text{ mol O}/16.00 \text{ g O}) =$
0.00361 mol O

To find a whole-number ratio, divide each value by 0.00361; this gives 1.51 mol C : 3.02 mol H : 1 mol O. Multiply each value by 2, and round off to 3 mol C : 6 mol H : 2 mol O. The empirical formula is $C_3H_6O_2$; given the molar mass of 74.1, this is also the molecular formula.

4.7 $(26.3 \text{ g})(1 \text{ mol } NaHCO_3/84.01 \text{ g } NaHCO_3) = 0.313$
$\text{mol } NaHCO_3$

$0.313 \text{ mol } NaHCO_3/0.200 \text{ L} = 1.57 \text{ M}$

Ion concentrations: $[Na^+] = [HCO_3^-] = 1.57 \text{ M}$

4.8 First, determine the mass of $AgNO_3$ required.

Amount of $AgNO_3$ required $= (0.0200 \text{ M})(0.250 \text{ L})$
$= 5.00 \times 10^{-3} \text{ mol}$

Mass of $AgNO_3 = (5.00 \times 10^{-3} \text{ mol})(169.9 \text{ g/mol})$
$= 0.850 \text{ g } AgNO_3$

Weigh out 0.850 g $AgNO_3$. Then, dissolve it in a small amount of water in the volumetric flask. After the solid is dissolved, fill the flask to the mark.

4.9 $(2.00 \text{ M})(V_{conc}) = (1.00 \text{ M})(0.250 \text{ L}); V_{conc} = 0.125 \text{ L}$

To prepare the solution, measure accurately 125 mL of 2.00 M NaOH into a 250-mL volumetric flask, and add water to give a total volume of 250 mL.

4.10 (a) pH $= -\log(2.6 \times 10^{-2}) = 1.59$
(b) $-\log[H^+] = 3.80$; $[H^+] = 1.5 \times 10^{-4} \text{ M}$

4.11 HCl is the limiting reagent.

$(0.350 \text{ mol HCl}/1 \text{ L})(0.0750 \text{ L})(1 \text{ mol } CO_2/$
$2 \text{ mol HCl})(44.01 \text{ g } CO_2/1 \text{ mol } CO_2) = 0.578 \text{ g } CO_2$

4.12 $(0.953 \text{ mol NaOH}/1 \text{ L})(0.02833 \text{ L NaOH}) =$
0.0270 mol NaOH

$(0.0270 \text{ mol NaOH})(1 \text{ mol } CH_3CO_2H/1 \text{ mol NaOH})$
$= 0.0270 \text{ mol } CH_3CO_2H$

$(0.0270 \text{ mol } CH_3CO_2H)(60.05 \text{ g/mol}) = 1.62 \text{ g}$
CH_3CO_2H

$0.0270 \text{ mol } CH_3CO_2H/0.0250 \text{ L} = 1.08 \text{ M}$

4.13 $(0.100 \text{ mol HCl}/1 \text{ L})(0.02967 \text{ L}) = 0.00297 \text{ mol HCl}$

$(0.00297 \text{ mol HCl})(1 \text{ mol NaOH}/1 \text{ mol HCl}) = 0.00297 \text{ mol NaOH}$

$0.00297 \text{ mol NaOH}/0.0250 \text{ L} = 0.119 \text{ M NaOH}$

4.14 Mol acid = mol base = $(0.323 \text{ mol/L})(0.03008 \text{ L}) = 9.716 \times 10^{-3} \text{ mol}$

Molar mass = $0.856 \text{ g acid}/9.716 \times 10^{-3} \text{ mol}$
acid = 88.1 g/mol

4.15 $(0.196 \text{ mol Na}_2\text{S}_2\text{O}_3/1 \text{ L})(0.02030 \text{ L}) = 0.00398 \text{ mol Na}_2\text{S}_2\text{O}_3$

$(0.00398 \text{ mol Na}_2\text{S}_2\text{O}_3)(1 \text{ mol I}_2/2 \text{ mol Na}_2\text{S}_2\text{O}_3) = 0.00199 \text{ mol I}_2$

0.00199 mol I_2 is in excess, and was not used in the reaction with ascorbic acid.

I_2 originally added = $(0.0520 \text{ mol I}_2/1 \text{ L})(0.05000 \text{ L}) = 0.00260 \text{ mol I}_2$

I_2 used in reaction with ascorbic acid = $0.00260 \text{ mol} - 0.00199 \text{ mol} = 6.1 \times 10^{-4} \text{ mol I}_2$

$(6.1 \times 10^{-4} \text{ mol I}_2)(1 \text{ mol C}_6\text{H}_8\text{O}_6/1 \text{ mol I}_2)(176.1 \text{ g}/1 \text{ mol}) = 0.11 \text{ g C}_6\text{H}_8\text{O}_6$

Chapter 5

5.1 (a) $(3800 \text{ calories})(4.184 \text{ J/calorie}) = 1.6 \times 10^4 \text{ J}$
(b) $(250 \text{ calories})(1000 \text{ calories/calorie})(4.184 \text{ J/calorie})(1 \text{ kJ}/1000 \text{ J}) = 1.0 \times 10^3 \text{ kJ}$

5.2 $C = 59.8 \text{ J}/[(25.0 \text{ g})(1.00 \text{ K})] = 2.39 \text{ J/g} \cdot \text{K}$

5.3 $(15.5 \text{ g})(C_{\text{metal}})(18.9 \text{ °C} - 100.0 \text{ °C}) + (55.5 \text{ g})(4.184 \text{ J/g} \cdot \text{K})(18.9 \text{ °C} - 16.5 \text{ °C}) = 0$

$C_{\text{metal}} = 0.44 \text{ J/g} \cdot \text{K}$

5.4 Energy transferred as heat from tea + energy as heat expended to melt ice = 0

$(250 \text{ g})(4.2 \text{ J/g} \cdot \text{K})(273.2 \text{ K} - 291.4 \text{ K}) + x \text{ g }(333 \text{ J/g}) = 0$

$x = 57 \text{ g}$

57 g of ice melts with energy as heat supplied by cooling 250 g of tea from 18.2 °C (291.4 K) to 0 °C (273.2 K)

Mass of ice remaining = mass of ice initially − mass of ice melted

Mass of ice remaining = 75 g − 57 g = 18 g

5.5 $(15.0 \text{ g C}_2\text{H}_6)(1 \text{ mol C}_2\text{H}_6/30.07 \text{ g C}_2\text{H}_6) = 0.4988 \text{ mol C}_2\text{H}_6$

$\Delta_r H = 0.4988 \text{ mol C}_2\text{H}_6(1 \text{ mol-rxn}/2 \text{ mol C}_2\text{H}_6)(-2857.3 \text{ kJ/mol-rxn})$

$= -713 \text{ kJ}$

5.6 Mass of final solution = 400. g

$\Delta T = 27.78 \text{ °C} - 25.10 \text{ °C} = 2.68 \text{ °C} = 2.68 \text{ K}$

Amount of HCl used = amount of NaOH used = $C \times V = (0.400 \text{ mol/L}) \times 0.200 \text{ L} = 0.0800 \text{ mol}$

Energy transferred as heat by acid–base reaction + energy gained as heat to warm solution = 0

$q_{\text{rxn}} + (4.20 \text{ J/g} \cdot \text{K})(400. \text{ g})(2.68 \text{ K}) = 0$

$q_{\text{rxn}} = -4.50 \times 10^3 \text{ J}$

This represents the energy transferred as heat in the reaction of 0.0800 mol HCl.

Energy transferred as heat per mole = $\Delta_r H = -4.50 \text{ kJ}/0.0800 \text{ mol HCl} = -56.3 \text{ kJ/mol HCl}$

5.7 (a) Energy evolved as heat in reaction + energy as heat absorbed by H_2O + energy as heat absorbed by bomb = 0

$q_{\text{rxn}} + (1.50 \times 10^3 \text{ g})(4.20 \text{ J/g} \cdot \text{K})(27.32 \text{ °C} - 25.00 \text{ °C}) + (837 \text{ J/K})(27.32 \text{ K} - 25.00 \text{ K}) = 0$

$q_{\text{rxn}} = -16,600 \text{ J}$ (energy as heat evolved in burning 1.0 g sucrose)

(b) Energy evolved as heat per mole = $(-16.6 \text{ kJ/g sucrose})(342.2 \text{ g sucrose}/1 \text{ mol sucrose}) = -5650 \text{ kJ/mol sucrose}$

5.8 $\text{C(s)} + \text{O}_2\text{(g)} \longrightarrow \text{CO}_2\text{(g)} \qquad \Delta_r H_1^\circ = -393.5 \text{ kJ}$
$2 [\text{S(s)} + \text{O}_2\text{(g)} \longrightarrow \text{SO}_2\text{(g)}]$
$\qquad\qquad\qquad \Delta_r H_2^\circ = 2(-296.8) = -593.6 \text{ kJ}$
$\text{CO}_2\text{(g)} + 2 \text{ SO}_2\text{(g)} \longrightarrow \text{CS}_2\text{(g)} + 3 \text{ O}_2\text{(g)}$
$\qquad\qquad\qquad \Delta_r H_3^\circ = +1103.9 \text{ kJ}$

Net: $\text{C(s)} + 2 \text{ S(s)} \longrightarrow \text{CS}_2\text{(g)}$
$\Delta_r H^\circ_{\text{net}} = \Delta_r H_1^\circ + \Delta_r H_2^\circ + \Delta_r H_3^\circ = +116.8 \text{ kJ}$

5.9 $\text{Fe(s)} + \tfrac{3}{2} \text{ Cl}_2\text{(g)} \longrightarrow \text{FeCl}_3\text{(s)}$
$12 \text{ C(s, graphite)} + 11 \text{ H}_2\text{(g)} + 11\tfrac{1}{2} \text{ O}_2\text{(g)} \longrightarrow \text{C}_{12}\text{H}_{22}\text{O}_{11}\text{(s)}$

5.10 $\Delta_r H^\circ = (6 \text{ mol/mol-rxn})\Delta_f H^\circ [\text{CO}_2\text{(g)}] + (3 \text{ mol/mol-rxn})\Delta_f H^\circ[\text{H}_2\text{O}(\ell)] - \{(1 \text{ mol}/1 \text{ mol-rxn})\Delta_f H^\circ [\text{C}_6\text{H}_6(\ell)] + (\tfrac{15}{2} \text{ mol/mol-rxn}) \Delta_f H^\circ [\text{O}_2\text{(g)}]\} = (6 \text{ mol/mol-rxn})(-393.5 \text{ kJ/mol}) + (3 \text{ mol/mol-rxn})(-285.8 \text{ J/mol}) - (1 \text{ mol/mol-rxn})(+49.0 \text{ kJ/mol}) - 0$

$= -3267.4 \text{ kJ/mol-rxn}$

Chapter 6

6.1 (a) Highest frequency, violet; lowest frequency, red
(b) The FM radio frequency, 91.7 MHz, is lower than the frequency of a microwave oven, 2.45 GHz.
(c) The wavelength of x-rays is shorter than the wavelength of ultraviolet light.

6.2 Orange light: 6.25×10^2 nm $= 6.25 \times 10^{-7}$ m

$\nu = (2.998 \times 10^8 \text{ m/s})/6.25 \times 10^{-7}$ m
$= 4.80 \times 10^{14} \text{ s}^{-1}$

$E = (6.626 \times 10^{-34} \text{ J} \cdot \text{s/photon})(4.80 \times 10^{14} \text{ s}^{-1})$
$\qquad (6.022 \times 10^{23} \text{ photons/mol})$

$\qquad = 1.92 \times 10^5 \text{ J/mol}$

Microwave: $E = (6.626 \times 10^{-34} \text{ J} \cdot \text{s/photon})$
$\qquad (2.45 \times 10^9 \text{ s}^{-1})(6.022 \times$
$\qquad 10^{23} \text{ photons/mol})$

$\qquad = 0.978 \text{ J/mol}$

Orange (625-nm) light is about 200,000 times more energetic than 2.45-GHz microwaves.

6.3 (a) E (per atom) $= -Rhc/n^2$
$\qquad = (-2.179 \times 10^{-18})/(3^2) \text{ J/atom}$
$\qquad = -2.421 \times 10^{-19} \text{ J/atom}$

(b) E (per mol) $= (-2.421 \times 10^{-19} \text{ J/atom})$
$\qquad (6.022 \times 10^{23} \text{ atoms/mol})$
$\qquad (1 \text{ kJ}/10^3 \text{ J})$

$\qquad = -145.8 \text{ kJ/mol}$

6.4 The least energetic line is from the electron transition from $n = 2$ to $n = 1$.

$\Delta E = -Rhc[1/1^2 - 1/2^2]$
$\qquad = -(2.179 \times 10^{-18} \text{ J/atom})(3/4)$
$\qquad = -1.634 \times 10^{-18} \text{ J/atom}$

$\nu = \Delta E/h$
$\qquad = (-1.634 \times 10^{-18} \text{ J/atom})/(6.626 \times 10^{-34} \text{ J} \cdot \text{s})$
$\qquad = 2.466 \times 10^{15} \text{ s}^{-1}$

$\lambda = c/\nu = (2.998 \times 10^8 \text{ m/s}^{-1})/(2.466 \times 10^{15} \text{ s}^{-1})$
$\qquad = 1.216 \times 10^{-7} \text{ m (or 121.6 nm)}$

6.5 Energy per atom $= \Delta E = -Rhc[1/\infty^2 - 1/1^2]$
$\qquad = 2.179 \times 10^{-18} \text{ J/atom}$

Energy per mole $= (2.179 \times 10^{-18} \text{ J/atom})(6.022 \times 10^{23} \text{ atoms/mol})$
$\qquad = 1.312 \times 10^6 \text{ J/mol} (= 1312 \text{ kJ/mol})$

6.6 First, calculate the velocity of the neutron:

$v = [2E/m]^{1/2} = [2(6.21 \times 10^{-21} \text{ kg} \cdot \text{m}^2 \text{ s}^{-2})/(1.675 \times 10^{-27} \text{ kg})]^{1/2}$
$\qquad = 2720 \text{ m} \cdot \text{s}^{-1}$

Use this value in the de Broglie equation:

$\lambda = h/mv = (6.626 \times 10^{-34} \text{ kg} \cdot \text{m}^2 \text{ s}^{-2})/$
$\qquad (1.675 \times 10^{-31} \text{ kg})(2720 \text{ m s}^{-1})$
$\qquad = 1.45 \times 10^{-6} \text{ m}$

6.7 (a) $\ell = 0$ or 1; (b) $m_\ell = -1$, 0, or $+1$, p subshell; (c) d subshell; (d) $\ell = 0$ and $m_\ell = 0$; (e) 3 orbitals in the p subshell; (f) 7 values of m_ℓ and 7 orbitals

6.8 (a)

Orbital	n	ℓ
6s	6	0
4p	4	1
5d	5	2
4f	4	3

(b) A $4p$ orbital has one nodal plane; a $6d$ orbital has two nodal planes.

Chapter 7

7.1 (a) $4s$ ($n + \ell = 4$) filled before $4p$ ($n + \ell = 5$)
(b) $6s$ ($n + \ell = 6$) filled before $5d$ ($n + \ell = 7$)
(c) $5s$ ($n + \ell = 5$) filled before $4f$ ($n + \ell = 7$)

7.2 (a) chlorine (Cl)
(b) $1s^2 2s^2 2p^6 3s^2 3p^3$

(c) Calcium has two valence electrons in the 4s subshell. Quantum numbers for these two electrons are $n = 4$, $\ell = 0$, $m_\ell = 0$, and $m_s = \pm 1/2$

7.3 Obtain the answers from Table 7.3.

7.4

All three ions are paramagnetic with three, two, and four unpaired electrons, respectively.

7.5 Increasing atomic radius: C < Si < Al

7.6 (a) Increasing atomic radius: C < B < Al
(b) Increasing ionization energy: Al < B < C
(c) Carbon is predicted to have the most negative electron affinity.

7.7 Trend in ionic radii: $S^{2-} > Cl^- > K^+$. These ions are isoelectronic (they all have the Ar configuration). The size decreases with increased nuclear charge, the higher nuclear charge resulting in a greater force of attraction of the electrons by the nucleus.

7.8 $MgCl_3$, if it existed, would presumably contain one Mg^{3+} ion (and three Cl^- ions). The formation of Mg^{3+} is energetically unfavorable, with a huge input of energy being required to remove the third electron (a core electron).

Chapter 8

8.1

$$\left[\begin{array}{c} H \\ | \\ H-N-H \\ | \\ H \end{array} \right]^+ \quad :C\equiv O: \quad [:N\equiv O:]^+ \quad \left[\begin{array}{c} :O: \\ || \\ :O-S-O: \\ || \\ :O: \end{array} \right]^{2-}$$

8.2

$$\begin{array}{c} H \\ | \\ H-C-O-H \\ | \\ H \end{array} \qquad \begin{array}{c} \ddot{O} \\ H-N-O-H \\ | \\ H \end{array}$$

methanol   hydroxylamine

8.3

$$\left[\begin{array}{c} :O: \\ || \\ H-O-P-O-H \\ | \\ :O: \end{array} \right]^-$$

8.4 (a) The acetylide ion, C_2^{2-}, and the N_2 molecule have the same number of valence electrons (10) and identical electronic structures; that is, they are isoelectronic.
(b) Ozone, O_3, is isoelectronic with NO_2^-; hydroxide ion, OH^-, is isoelectronic with HF.

8.5 (a) CN^- : formal charge on C is -1; formal charge on N is 0.
(b) SO_3^{2-}: formal charge on S is $+2$; formal charge on each O is -1.

8.6 Resonance structures for the HCO_3^- ion:

$$\left[\begin{array}{c} \ddot{O}=C-\ddot{O}: \\ | \\ :O-H \end{array} \right]^- \longleftrightarrow \left[\begin{array}{c} :\ddot{O}-C=\ddot{O} \\ | \\ :O-H \end{array} \right]^-$$

(a) No. Three resonance structures are needed in the description of CO_3^{2-}; only two are needed to describe HCO_3^-.
(b) In each resonance structure, Carbon's formal charge is 0. The oxygen of the $-OH$ group and the double-bonded oxygen have a formal charge of zero; the singly bonded oxygen has a formal charge of -1. The average formal charge on the latter two oxygen atoms is $-\frac{1}{2}$. In the carbonate ion, the three oxygen atoms have an average formal charge of $-\frac{2}{3}$.
(c) H^+ would be expected to add to one of the oxygens with a negative formal charge; that is, one of the oxygens with formal charge of $-\frac{1}{2}$ in this structure.

8.7 $\left[:\ddot{F}-\ddot{Cl}-\ddot{F}: \right]^+$ ClF_2^+, 2 bond pairs and 2 lone pairs.

$\left[:\ddot{F}-\ddot{Cl}-\ddot{F}: \right]^-$ ClF_2^-, 2 bond pairs and 3 lone pairs.

8.8 Tetrahedral geometry around carbon. The Cl—C—Cl bond angle will be close to $109.5°$.

8.9 For each species, the electron-pair geometry and the molecular shape are the same. BF_3: trigonal planar; BF_4^-: tetrahedral. Adding F^- to BF_3 adds an electron pair to the central atom and changes the shape.

8.10 The electron-pair geometry around I is trigonal bipyramidal. The molecular geometry of the ion is linear.

$$\left[\begin{array}{c} :\ddot{Cl}: \\ | \\ :-I \\ | \\ :\ddot{Cl}: \end{array} \right]^-$$

8.11 (a) In PO_4^{3-}, there is tetrahedral electron-pair geometry. The molecular geometry is also tetrahedral.

$$\left[\begin{array}{c} :O: \\ || \\ :\ddot{O}-P-\ddot{O}: \\ | \\ :O: \end{array} \right]^{3-}$$

(b) In SO_3^{2-}, there is tetrahedral electron-pair geometry. The molecular geometry is trigonal pyramidal.

$$\left[\begin{array}{c} :\ddot{O}-S-\ddot{O}: \\ | \\ :O: \end{array} \right]^{2-}$$

(c) In IF_5, there is octahedral electron-pair geometry. The molecular geometry is square pyramidal.

$$\begin{array}{c} F \\ F \cdots | \cdots F \\ I \\ F \diagup | \diagdown F \end{array}$$

8.12 (a) The H atom is positive in each case. H—F ($\Delta\chi = 1.8$) is more polar than H—I ($\Delta\chi = 0.5$).
(b) B—F ($\Delta\chi = 2.0$) is more polar than B—C ($\Delta\chi = 0.5$). In B—F, F is the negative pole, and B is the positive pole. In B—C, C is the negative pole, and B is the positive pole.
(c) C—Si ($\Delta\chi = 0.6$) is more polar than C—S ($\Delta\chi = 0.1$). In C—Si, C is the negative pole, and Si is the positive pole. In C—S, S is the negative pole, and C the positive pole.

8.13

$$\overset{-1 \quad +1 \quad 0}{:\!\overset{..}{\underset{..}{O}}\!-\!\overset{..}{\underset{..}{S}}\!=\!\overset{..}{O}} \longleftrightarrow \overset{0 \quad +1 \quad -1}{\overset{..}{O}\!=\!\overset{..}{\underset{..}{S}}\!-\!\overset{..}{\underset{..}{O}}\!:}$$

The S—O bonds are polar, with the negative end being the O atom. (The O atom is more electronegative than the S atom.) Formal charges show that these bonds are, in fact, polar, with the O atom being the more negative atom.

8.14 (a) $BFCl_2$, polar, negative side is the F atom because F is the most electronegative atom in the molecule.

(b) NH_2Cl, polar, negative side is the Cl atom.

(c) SCl_2, polar, Cl atoms are on the negative side.

8.15 (a)

Formal charges: S = +1, O = −1, Cl = 0

(Lewis structure of $SOCl_2$ with formal charges indicated)

(b) Geometry: trigonal pyramidal

(c) The molecule is polar. The positive charge is on sulfur, the negative charge on oxygen.

8.16 (a) C—N: bond order 1; C=N: bond order 2; C ≡ N: bond order 3. Bond length: C—N > C=N > C ≡ N

(b) $$\left[:\!\overset{..}{\underset{..}{O}}\!-\!\overset{..}{N}\!=\!\overset{..}{O}\right]^{-} \longleftrightarrow \left[\overset{..}{O}\!=\!\overset{..}{N}\!-\!\overset{..}{\underset{..}{O}}\!:\right]^{-}$$

The N-O bond order in NO_2^- is 1.5. Therefore, the NO bond length (124 pm) should be between the length of a N—O single bond (136 pm) and a N=O double bond (115 pm).

8.17 $CH_4(g) + 2 O_2(g) \longrightarrow CO_2(g) + 2 H_2O(g)$

Break 4 C—H bonds and 2 O=O bonds:
(4 mol)(413 kJ/mol) + (2 mol)(498 kJ/mol) = 2648 kJ

Make 2 C=O bonds and 4 H—O bonds:
(2 mol)(745 kJ/mol) + (4 mol)(463 kJ/mol) = 3342 kJ

$\Delta_r H° = 2648$ kJ − 3342 kJ = −694 kJ/mol-rxn
(value calculated using enthalpies of formation = −797 kJ/mol-rxn)

Chapter 9

9.1 The oxygen atom in H_3O^+ is sp^3 hybridized. The three O—H bonds are formed by overlap of oxygen sp^3 and hydrogen $1s$ orbitals. The fourth sp^3 orbital contains a lone pair of electrons.

The carbon and nitrogen atoms in CH_3NH_2 are sp^3 hybridized. The C—H bonds arise from overlap of carbon sp^3 orbitals and hydrogen $1s$ orbitals. The bond between C and N is formed by overlap of sp^3 orbitals from these atoms. Overlap of nitrogen sp^3 and hydrogen $1s$ orbitals gives the two N—H bonds, and there is a lone pair in the remaining sp^3 orbital on nitrogen.

9.2 (a) BH_4^-, tetrahedral electron-pair geometry, sp^3
(b) SF_5^-, octahedral electron-pair geometry, sp^3d^2
(c) SOF_4, trigonal-bipyramidal electron-pair geometry, sp^3d
(d) ClF_3, trigonal-bipyramidal electron-pair geometry, sp^3d
(e) BCl_3, trigonal-planar electron-pair geometry, sp^2
(f) XeO_6^{4-}, octahedral electron-pair geometry, sp^3d^2

9.3 The two CH_3 carbon atoms are sp^3 hybridized, and the center carbon atom is sp^2 hybridized. For each of the carbon atoms in the methyl groups, the sp^3 orbitals overlap with hydrogen $1s$ orbitals to form the three C—H bonds, and the fourth sp^3 orbital overlaps with an sp^2 orbital on the central carbon atom, forming a carbon–carbon sigma bond. Overlap of an sp^2 orbital on the central carbon and an oxygen sp^2 orbital gives the sigma bond between these elements. The pi bond between carbon and oxygen arises by overlap of a p orbital from each element.

9.4 A triple bond links the two nitrogen atoms, each of which also has one lone pair. Each nitrogen is sp hybridized. One sp orbital contains the lone pair; the other is used to form the sigma bond between the two atoms. Two pi bonds arise by overlap of p orbitals on the two atoms, perpendicular to the molecular axis.

9.5 Bond angles: H—C—H = 109.5°, H—C—C = 109.5°, C—C—N = 180°. Carbon in the CH_3 group is sp^3 hybridized; the central C and the N are sp hybridized. The three C—H bonds form by overlap of an H $1s$ orbital with one of the sp^3 orbitals of the CH_3 group; the fourth sp^3 orbital overlaps with an sp orbital on the central C to form a sigma bond. The triple bond between C and N is a combination of a sigma bond (the sp orbital on C overlaps with the sp orbital on N) and two pi bonds (overlap of two sets of p orbitals on these elements). The remaining sp orbital on N contains a lone pair.

9.6 H_2^+: $(\sigma_1 s)^1$ The ion has a bond order of ½ and is expected to exist. A bond order of ½ is predicted for He_2^+ and H_2^-, both of which are predicted to have electron configurations $(\sigma_1 s)^2 (\sigma^*_1 s)^1$.

9.7 Li_2^- is predicted to have an electron configuration $(\sigma_1 s)^2$ $(\sigma^*_1 s)^2$ $(\sigma_2 s)^2$ $(\sigma^*_2 s)^1$ and a bond order of ½, the positive value implying that the ion might exist.

9.8 O_2^+: [core electrons] $(\sigma_2 s)^2$ $(\sigma^*_2 s)^2$ $(\pi_2 p)^4$ $(\sigma_2 p)^2$ $(\pi^*_2 p)^1$. The bond order is 2.5. The ion is paramagnetic with one unpaired electron.

Chapter 10

10.1 (a) Isomers of C_7H_{16}

$CH_3CH_2CH_2CH_2CH_2CH_2CH_3$ heptane

$$CH_3CH_2CH_2CH_2\underset{\underset{CH_3}{|}}{C}HCH_3$$ 2-methylhexane

$$CH_3CH_2CH_2\underset{\underset{CH_3}{|}}{C}HCH_2CH_3$$ 3-methylhexane

$$CH_3CH_2\underset{\underset{CH_3}{|}}{C}H\underset{\overset{CH_3}{|}}{C}HCH_3$$ 2,3-dimethylpentane

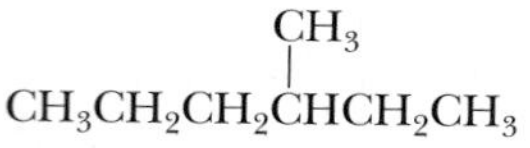

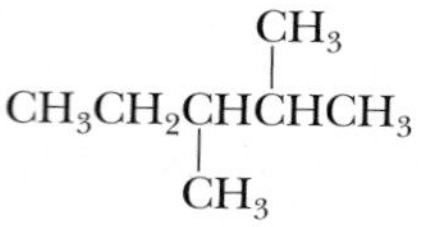

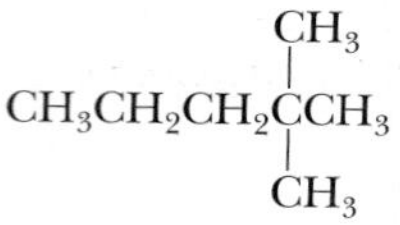

$$CH_3CH_2CH_2\underset{\underset{CH_3}{|}}{\overset{\overset{CH_3}{|}}{C}}CH_3$$ 2,2-dimethylpentane

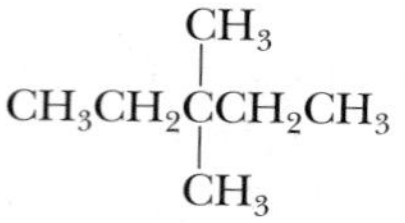

$$CH_3CH_2\underset{\underset{CH_3}{|}}{\overset{\overset{CH_3}{|}}{C}}CH_2CH_3$$ 3,3-dimethylpentane

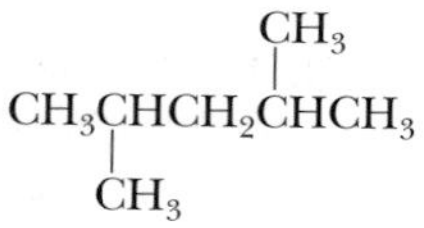

$$CH_3\underset{\underset{CH_3}{|}}{C}HCH_2\underset{\overset{CH_3}{|}}{C}HCH_3$$ 2,4-dimethylpentane

2-Ethylpentane is pictured on page 450.

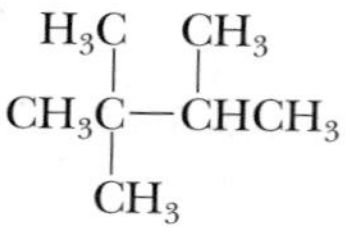

$$\underset{\underset{CH_3}{|}}{\overset{\overset{H_3C}{|}}{CH_3C}}-\overset{\overset{CH_3}{|}}{C}HCH_3$$ 2,2,3-trimethylbutane

(b) Two isomers, 3-methylhexane, and 2,3-dimethylpentane, are chiral.

10.2 The names accompany the structures in the answer to Exercise 10.1.

10.3 Isomers of C_6H_{12} in which the longest chain has six C atoms:

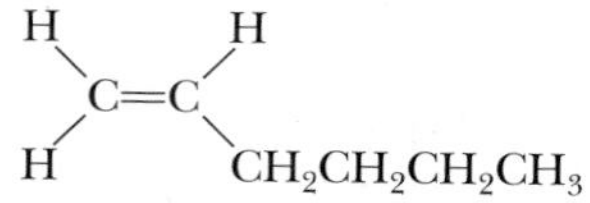

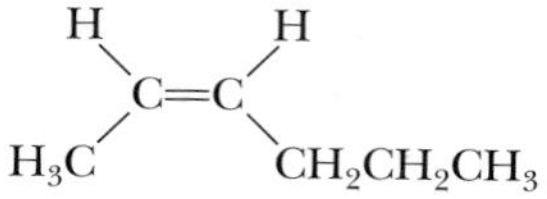

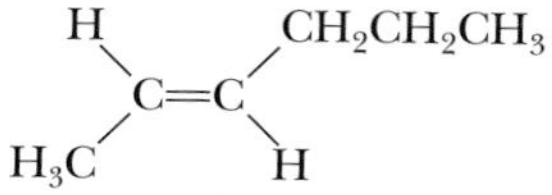

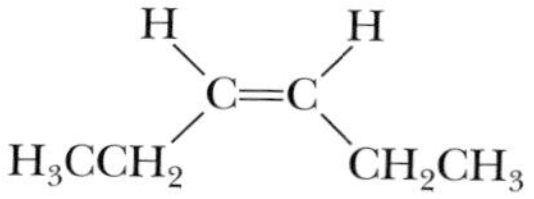

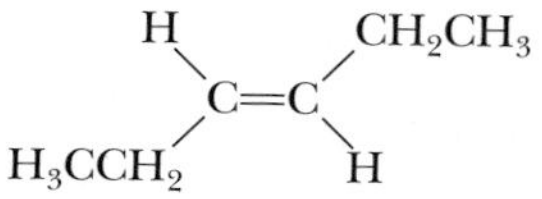

Names (in order, top to bottom): 1-hexene, *cis*-2-hexene, *trans*-2-hexene, *cis*-3-hexene, *trans*-3-hexene. None of these isomers is chiral.

10.4 (a)   (b)

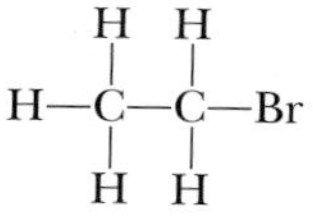

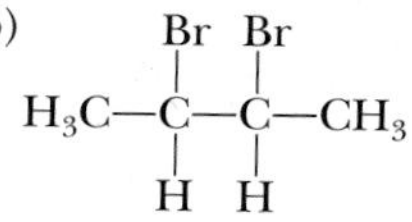

bromoethane   2,3-dibromobutane

10.5 1,4-diaminobenzene

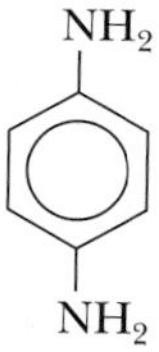

10.6 $CH_3CH_2CH_2CH_2OH$ 1-butanol

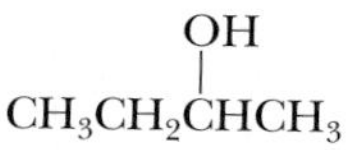

$$CH_3CH_2\underset{\overset{OH}{|}}{C}HCH_3$$ 2-butanol

$$CH_3\underset{\underset{CH_3}{|}}{C}HCH_2OH$$ 2-methyl-1-propanol

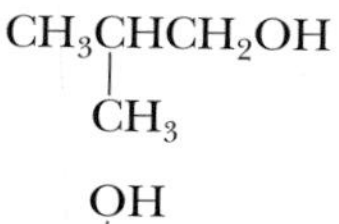

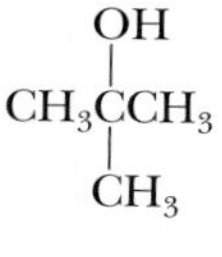

$$CH_3\underset{\underset{CH_3}{|}}{\overset{\overset{OH}{|}}{C}}CH_3$$ 2-methyl-2-propanol

10.7 (a)

$CH_3CH_2CH_2\overset{\overset{\displaystyle O}{\|}}{C}CH_3$ 2-pentanone

$CH_3CH_2\overset{\overset{\displaystyle O}{\|}}{C}CH_2CH_3$ 3-pentanone

$CH_3CH_2CH_2CH_2\overset{\overset{\displaystyle O}{\|}}{C}H$ pentanal

$CH_3\underset{\underset{\displaystyle CH_3}{|}}{C}HCH_2\overset{\overset{\displaystyle O}{\|}}{C}H$ 3-methylbutanal

(b) $CH_3\underset{\underset{\displaystyle OH}{|}}{C}HCH_2CH_2CH_3$,   2-pentanol

10.8 (a) 1-butanol gives butanal $CH_3CH_2CH_2\overset{\overset{\displaystyle O}{\|}}{C}H$

(b) 2-butanol gives butanone $CH_3CH_2\overset{\overset{\displaystyle O}{\|}}{C}CH_3$

(c) 2-methyl-1-propanol gives 2-methylpropanal

$CH_3\underset{\underset{\displaystyle CH_3}{|}}{\overset{\overset{\displaystyle H}{|}}{C}}-\overset{\overset{\displaystyle O}{\|}}{C}H$

The oxidation products from these three reactions are structural isomers.

10.9 (a)

$CH_3CH_2\overset{\overset{\displaystyle O}{\|}}{C}OCH_3$ methyl propanoate

(b)

$CH_3CH_2CH_2\overset{\overset{\displaystyle O}{\|}}{C}OCH_2CH_2CH_2CH_3$

               butyl butanoate

(c)

$CH_3CH_2CH_2CH_2CH_2\overset{\overset{\displaystyle O}{\|}}{C}OCH_2CH_3$

               ethyl hexanoate

10.10 (a) Propyl acetate is formed from acetic acid and propanol:

$CH_3\overset{\overset{\displaystyle O}{\|}}{C}OH + CH_3CH_2CH_2OH$

(b) 3-Methylpentyl benzoate is formed from benzoic acid and 3-methylpentanol:

$-\overset{\overset{\displaystyle O}{\|}}{C}-OH + CH_3CH_2\underset{\underset{\displaystyle CH_3}{|}}{C}HCH_2CH_2OH$

(c) Ethyl salicylate is formed from salicylic acid and ethanol:

$-\overset{\overset{\displaystyle O}{\|}}{C}-OH + CH_3CH_2OH$

10.11 (a) $CH_3CH_2CH_2OH$: 1-propanol, has an alcohol (—OH) group

CH_3CO_2H: ethanoic acid (acetic acid), has a carboxylic acid (—CO_2H) group

$CH_3CH_2NH_2$: ethylamine, has an amino (—NH_2) group

(b) 1-propyl ethanoate (propyl acetate)

(c) Oxidation of this primary alcohol first gives propanal, CH_3CH_2CHO. Further oxidation gives propanoic acid, $CH_3CH_2CO_2H$.

(d) *N*-ethylacetamide, $CH_3CONHCH_2CH_3$

(e) The amine is protonated by hydrochloric acid, forming ethylammonium chloride, $[CH_3CH_2NH_3]Cl$.

10.12 Kevlar is a polyamide polymer, prepared by the reaction of terephthalic acid and 1,4-diaminobenzene.

$n\ H_2NC_6H_4NH_2 + n\ HO_2CC_6H_4CO_2H \longrightarrow$
$\ \ \ \ \ \ \ \ \ \ \ \ -(-HNC_6H_4NHCOC_6H_4CO-)_n- + 2n\ H_2O$

Chapter 11

11.1 0.83 bar (0.82 atm) > 75 kPa (0.74 atm) > 0.63 atm > 250 mm Hg (0.33 atm)

11.2 $P_1 = 55$ mm Hg and $V_1 = 125$ mL; $P_2 = 78$ mm Hg and $V_2 = ?$

$V_2 = V_1(P_1/P_2) = (125$ mL$)(55$ mm Hg$/78$ mm Hg$)$
$= 88$ mL

11.3 $V_1 = 45$ L and $T_1 = 298$ K; $V_2 = ?$ and $T_2 = 263$ K

$V_2 = V_1(T_2/T_1) = (45$ L$)(263$ K$/298$ K$) = 40.$ L

11.4 $V_2 = V_1(P_1/P_2)(T_2/T_1)$

$= (22$ L$)(150$ atm$/0.993$ atm$)(295$ K$/304$ K$)$

$= 3200$ L

At 5.0 L per balloon, there is sufficient He to fill 640 balloons.

11.5 44.8 L of O_2 is required; 44.8 L of $H_2O(g)$ and 22.4 L $CO_2(g)$ are produced.

11.6 $PV = nRT$

$(750/760$ atm$)(V) =$
$(1300$ mol$)(0.08206$ L $\cdot$ atm$/$mol $\cdot$ K$)(296$ K$)$

$V = 3.2 \times 10^4$ L

11.7 $d = PM/RT$; $M = dRT/P$

$M = (5.02 \text{ g/L})(0.082057 \text{ L} \cdot \text{atm/mol} \cdot \text{K})$
$(288.2 \text{ K})/(745/760 \text{ atm}) = 121 \text{ g/mol}$

11.8 $PV = (m/M)RT$; $M = mRT/PV$

$M = (0.105 \text{ g})(0.082057 \text{ L} \cdot \text{atm/mol} \cdot \text{K})$
$(296.2 \text{ K})/[(561/760) \text{ atm } 0.125 \text{ L})] = 27.7 \text{ g/mol}$

11.9 $n(H_2) = PV/RT$

$= (542/760 \text{ atm})(355 \text{ L})/(0.08206 \text{ L} \cdot \text{atm/mol} \cdot \text{K})$
(298.2 K)

$n(H_2) = 10.3 \text{ mol}$

$n(NH_3) = (10.3 \text{ mol } H_2)(2 \text{ mol } NH_3/3 \text{ mol } H_2)$
$= 6.87 \text{ mol } NH_3$

$P(125 \text{ L}) = (6.87 \text{ mol})(0.082057 \text{ L} \cdot \text{atm/mol} \cdot \text{K})$
(298.2 K)

$P(NH_3) = 1.35 \text{ atm}$

11.10 $P_{\text{halothane}} (5.00 \text{ L})$
$= (0.0760 \text{ mol})(0.08206 \text{ L} \cdot \text{atm/mol} \cdot \text{K}) (298.2 \text{ K})$

$P_{\text{halothane}} = 0.372 \text{ atm (or 283 mm Hg)}$

$P_{\text{oxygen}} (5.00 \text{ L})$
$= (0.734 \text{ mol})(0.08206 \text{ L} \cdot \text{atm/mol} \cdot \text{K})(298.2 \text{ K})$

$P_{\text{oxygen}} = 3.59 \text{ atm (or 2730 mm Hg)}$

$P_{\text{total}} = P_{\text{halothane}} + P_{\text{oxygen}}$
$= 283 \text{ mm Hg} + 2730 \text{ mm Hg} = 3010 \text{ mm Hg}$

11.11 For He: Use Equation 11.9, with $M = 4.00 \times 10^{-3}$ kg/mol, $T = 298$ K, and $R = 8.314$ J/mol · K to calculate the rms speed of 1360 m/s. A similar calculation for N_2, with $M = 28.01 \times 10^{-3}$ kg/mol, gives an rms speed of 515 m/s.

11.12 The molar mass of CH_4 is 16.0 g/mol.

$$\frac{\text{Rate for } CH_4}{\text{Rate for unknown}} = \frac{n \text{ molecules/1.50 min}}{n \text{ molecules/4.73 min}} = \sqrt{\frac{M_{\text{unknown}}}{16.0}}$$

$M_{\text{unknown}} = 159 \text{ g/mol}$

11.13 $P(1.00 \text{ L})$
$= (10.0 \text{ mol})(0.082057 \text{ L} \cdot \text{atm/mol} \cdot \text{K}) (298 \text{ K})$

$P = 245 \text{ atm (calculated by } PV = nRT)$

$P = 320 \text{ atm (calculated by van der Waals equation)}$

Chapter 12

12.1 Because F^- is the smaller ion, water molecules can approach most closely and interact more strongly. Thus, F^- should have the more negative enthalpy of hydration.

12.2

$$H_3C-O \overset{H}{\underset{\underset{CH_3}{H-O}}{\diagup}}$$

Hydrogen bonding in methanol entails the attraction of the hydrogen atom bearing a partial positive charge (δ^+) on one molecule to the oxygen atom bearing a partial negative charge (δ^-) on a second molecule. The strong attractive force of hydrogen bonding will cause the boiling point and the enthalpy of vaporization of methanol to be quite high.

12.3 Water is a polar solvent, while hexane and CCl_4 are nonpolar. London dispersion forces are the primary forces of attraction between all pairs of dissimilar solvents. For mixtures of water with the other solvents, dipole–induced dipole forces will also be important.

12.4 (a) O_2: induced dipole–induced dipole forces only.
(b) CH_3OH: strong hydrogen bonding (dipole–dipole forces) as well as induced dipole–induced dipole forces.
(c) Forces between water molecules: strong hydrogen bonding and induced dipole–induced dipole forces. Between N_2 and H_2O: dipole–induced dipole forces and induced dipole–induced dipole forces.

Relative strengths: a < forces between N_2 and H_2O in c < b < forces between water molecules in c.

12.5 $(1.00 \times 10^3 \text{ g})(1 \text{ mol}/32.04 \text{ g})(35.2 \text{ kJ/mol})$
$= 1.10 \times 10^3 \text{ kJ}$

12.6 (a) At 40 °C, the vapor pressure of ethanol is about 120 mm Hg.
(b) The equilibrium vapor pressure of ethanol at 60 °C is about 320 mm Hg. At 60 °C and 600 mm Hg, ethanol is a liquid. If vapor is present, it will condense to a liquid.

12.7 $PV = nRT$

$P = 0.50 \text{ g } (1 \text{ mol}/18.02 \text{ g})(0.0821 \text{ L} \cdot \text{atm/mol} \cdot \text{K})$
$(333 \text{ K})/5.0 \text{ L}$

$P = 0.15 \text{ atm.}$

Convert to mm Hg: $P = (0.15 \text{ atm})(760 \text{ mm Hg}/1 \text{ atm}) = 120 \text{ mm Hg}$. The vapor pressure of water at 60 °C is 149.4 mm Hg (Appendix G). The calculated pressure is lower than this, so all the water (0.50 g) evaporates. If 2.0 g of water is used, the calculated pressure, 460 mm Hg, exceeds the vapor pressure. In this case, only part of the water will evaporate.

12.8 Use the Clausius–Clapeyron equation, with $P_1 = 57.0$ mm Hg, $T_1 = 250.4$ K, $P_2 = 534$ mm Hg, and $T_2 = 298.2$ K.

$\ln [P_2/P_1] = \Delta_{\text{vap}}H/R [1/T_1 - 1/T_2]$
$= [\Delta_{\text{vap}}H/R][(T_2 - T_1)/T_1T_2]$

$\ln [534/57.0] = \Delta_{\text{vap}}H/(0.0083145 \text{ kJ/K} \cdot \text{mol})$
$[47.8/(250.4)(298.2)]$

$\Delta_{\text{vap}}H = 29.1 \text{ kJ/mol}$

12.9 Glycerol is predicted to have a higher viscosity than ethanol. It is a larger molecule than ethanol, and there are higher forces of attraction between molecules because each molecule has three OH groups that hydrogen-bond to other molecules.

Chapter 13

13.1 The strategy to solve this problem is given in Example 13.1.

Step 1. Mass of the unit cell

= (197.0 g/mol)(1 mol/6.022 × 10²³ atom/mol)(4 atoms/unit cell)

= 1.309×10^{-21} g/unit cell

Step 2. Volume of unit cell

= (1.309×10^{-21} g/unit cell)(1 cm³/19.32 g)

= 6.773×10^{-23} cm³/unit cell

Step 3. Length of side of unit cell

= [6.773×10^{-23} cm³/unit cell]$^{1/3}$ = 4.076×10^{-8} cm

Step 4. Calculate the radius from the edge dimension.

Diagonal distance = 4.076×10^{-8} cm (2½) = 4 (r_{Au})

r_{Au} = 1.441×10^{-8} cm (= 144.1 pm)

13.2 To verify a body centered cubic structure, calculate the mass contained in the unit cell. If the structure is bcc, then the mass will be the mass of 2 Fe atoms. (Other possibilities: fcc − mass of 4 Fe; primitive cubic − mass of 1 Fe atom). This calculation uses the four steps from the previous exercise in reverse order.

Step 1. Use radius of Fe to calculate cell dimensions. In a body-centered cube, atoms touch across the diagonal of the cube.

Diagonal distance = side dimension ($\sqrt{3}$) = 4 r_{Fe}

Side dimension of cube = 4 (1.26×10^{-8} cm)/($\sqrt{3}$) = 2.910×10^{-8} cm

Step 2. Calculate unit cell volume

Unit cell volume = (2.910×10^{-8} cm)³ = 2.464×10^{-23} cm³

Step 3. Combine unit cell volume and density to find the mass of the unit cell.

Mass of unit cell = 2.464×10^{-23} cm³ (7.8740 g/cm³) = 1.940×10^{-22} g

Step 4. Calculate the mass of 2 Fe atoms, and compare this to the answer from step 3.

Mass of 2 Fe atoms

= 55.85 g/mol (1 mol/6.022 × 10²³ atoms)(2 atoms)

= 1.85×10^{-22} g).

This is a fairly good match, and clearly much better than the two other possibilities, primitive and fcc.

13.3 M₂X; In a face-centered cubic unit cell, there are four anions and eight tetrahedral holes in which to place metal ions. All of the tetrahedral holes are inside the unit cell, so the ratio of atoms in the unit cell is 2 : 1.

13.4 We need to calculate the mass and volume of the unit cell from the information given. The density of KCl will then be mass/volume. Select units so the density is calculated as g/cm³

Step 1. Mass: the unit cell contains 4 K⁺ ions and 4 Cl⁻ ions

Unit cell mass = (39.10 g/mol)(1 mol/6.022 × 10²³ K⁺ ions)(4 K⁺ ions) + (35.45 g/mol)(1 mol/6.022 × 10²³ Cl⁻ ions)(4 Cl⁻ ions)

= 2.355×10^{-22} g + 2.597×10^{-22} g = 4.952×10^{-22} g

Step 2. Volume: assuming K⁺ and Cl⁻ ions touch along one edge of the cube, the side dimension = 2 r_{K^+} + 2 r_{Cl^-}. The volume of the cube is the cube of this value. (Convert the ionic radius from pm to cm.)

V = [2(1.33×10^{-8} cm) + 2(1.81×10^{-8} cm)]³ = 2.477×10^{-22} cm³

Step 3: density = mass/volume = 4.952×10^{-22} g/2.477×10^{-22} cm³) = 2.00 g/cm³

13.5 Use the Born–Haber cycle equation shown on pages 600–602. The unknown in this problem is the enthalpy of formation of NaI(s).

$\Delta_f H°$ [NaI(s)] = $\Delta H_{Step\,1a}$ + $\Delta H_{Step\,1b}$ + $\Delta H_{Step\,2a}$ + $\Delta H_{Step\,2b}$ + $\Delta_{lattice} H$

Step 1a. Enthalpy of formation of I(g) = +106.8 kJ/mol (Appendix L)

Step 1b. ΔH for I(g) + e⁻ → I⁻(g) = −295 kJ/mol (Appendix F)

Step 2a. Enthalpy of formation of Na(g) = +107.3 kJ/mol (Appendix L)

Step 2b. ΔH for Na(g) → Na⁺(g) + e⁻ = +496 kJ/mol (Appendix F)

Step 3 = $\Delta_{lattice} H$ = −702 kJ/mol (Table 13.2)

$\Delta_f H°$ [NaI(s)] = −287 kJ/mol

Chapter 14

14.1 (a) 10.0 g sucrose = 0.0292 mol; 250 g H₂O = 13.9 mol

$X_{sucrose}$ = (0.0292 mol)/(0.0292 mol + 13.9 mol) = 0.00210

$c_{sucrose}$ = (0.0292 mol sucrose)/(0.250 kg solvent) = 0.117 m

Weight % sucrose = (10.0 g sucrose/260 g soln)(100%) = 3.85%

(b) 1.08×10^4 ppm = 1.08×10^4 mg NaCl per 1000 g soln

$$= (1.08 \times 10^4 \text{ mg Na}/1000 \text{ g soln})$$
$$(1050 \text{ g soln}/1 \text{ L})$$
$$= 1.13 \times 10^4 \text{ mg Na/L}$$
$$= 11.3 \text{ g Na/L}$$

$(11.3 \text{ g Na/L})(58.44 \text{ g NaCl}/23.0 \text{ g Na}) =$
28.7 g NaCl/L

14.2 $\Delta_{soln}H° = \Delta_f H° [NaOH(aq)] - \Delta_f H° [NaOH(s)]$
$= -469.2 \text{ kJ/mol} - (-425.9 \text{ kJ/mol})$
$= -43.3 \text{ kJ/mol}$

14.3 Solubility of $CO_2 = k_H P_g = 0.034 \text{ mol/kg} \cdot \text{bar} \times$
$0.33 \text{ bar} = 1.1 \times 10^{-2}$ M

14.4 The solution contains sucrose $[(10.0 \text{ g})(1 \text{ mol}/342.3 \text{ g})$
$= 0.0292 \text{ mol}]$ in water $[(225 \text{ g})(1 \text{ mol}/18.02 \text{ g})$
$= 12.5 \text{ mol}]$.

$X_{water} = (12.5 \text{ mol } H_2O)/(12.5 \text{ mol} + 0.0292 \text{ mol})$
$= 0.998$

$P_{water} = x_{water}P°_{water} = 0.998(149.4 \text{ mm Hg})$
$= 149 \text{ mm Hg}$

14.5 $c_{glycol} = \Delta T_{bp}/K_{bp} = 1.0 \text{ °C}/(0.512 \text{ °C}/m) =$
$1.95 \ m = 1.95 \text{ mol/kg}$

$mass_{glycol} = (1.95 \text{ mol/kg})(0.125 \text{ kg})(62.02 \text{ g/mol})$
$= 15 \text{ g}$

14.6 $c_{glycol} = (525 \text{ g})(1 \text{ mol}/62.07 \text{ g})/(3.00 \text{ kg}) = 2.82 \ m$

$\Delta T_{fp} = K_{fp} \times m = (-1.86 \text{ °C}/m)(2.82 \ m) = -5.24 \text{ °C}$

You will be protected only to about -5 °C and not to -25 °C.

14.7 $c \text{ (mol/L)} = \Pi/RT = [(1.86 \text{ mm Hg})(1 \text{ atm}/$
$760 \text{ mm Hg})]/[(0.08206 \text{ L} \cdot \text{atm/mol} \cdot \text{K})(298 \text{ K})]$
$= 1.00 \times 10^{-4}$ M

$(1.00 \times 10^{-4} \text{ mol/L})(0.100 \text{ L}) = 1.0 \times 10^{-5} \text{ mol}$

Molar mass $= 1.40 \text{ g}/1.00 \times 10^{-5} \text{ mol}$
$= 1.4 \times 10^5 \text{ g/mol}$

(Assuming the polymer is composed of CH_2 units, the polymer is about 10,000 units long.)

14.8 $c_{NaCl} = (25.0 \text{ g NaCl})(1 \text{ mol}/58.44 \text{ g})/(0.525 \text{ kg})$
$= 0.815 \ m$

$\Delta T_{fp} = K_{fp} \times m \times i = (-1.86 \text{ °C}/m)(0.815 \ m)(1.85)$
$= -2.80 \text{ °C}$

Chapter 15

15.1 $-\frac{1}{2} (\Delta[NOCl]/\Delta t) = \frac{1}{2}(\Delta[NO]/\Delta t) = \Delta[Cl_2]/\Delta t$

15.2 For the first two hours:
$-\Delta[sucrose]/\Delta t = [(0.033 - 0.050) \text{ mol/L}]/(2.0 \text{ h})$
$= 0.0080 \text{ mol/L} \cdot \text{h}$

For the last two hours:
$\Delta[sucrose]/\Delta t = -[(0.010 - 0.015) \text{ mol/L}]/(2.0 \text{ h})$
$= 0.0025 \text{ mol/L} \cdot \text{h}$

Instantaneous rate at 4 h = 0.0045 mol/L · h. (Calculated from the slope of a line tangent to the curve at the defined concentration.)

15.3 Compare experiments 1 and 2: Doubling $[O_2]$ causes the rate to double, so the rate is first order in $[O_2]$. Compare experiments 2 and 4: Doubling $[NO]$ causes the rate to increase by a factor of 4, so the rate is second order in $[NO]$. Thus, the rate law is

Rate = $k[NO]^2[O_2]$

Using the data in experiment 1 to determine k:
$0.028 \text{ mol/L} \cdot \text{s} = k[0.020 \text{ mol/L}]^2[0.010 \text{ mol/L}]$
$k = 7.0 \times 10^3 \text{ L}^2/\text{mol}^2 \cdot \text{s}$

15.4 Rate = $k[Pt(NH_3)_2Cl_2] = (0.27 \text{ h}^{-1})(0.020 \text{ mol/L})$
$= 0.0054 \text{ mol/L} \cdot \text{h}$

15.5 $\ln ([sucrose]/[sucrose]_o) = -kt$
$\ln ([sucrose]/[0.010]) = -(0.21 \text{ h}^{-1})(5.0 \text{ h})$
$[sucrose] = 0.0035 \text{ mol/L}$

15.6 (a) The fraction remaining is
$[CH_3N_2CH_3]/[CH_3N_2CH_3]_o$.

$\ln ([CH_3N_2CH_3]/[CH_3N_2CH_3]_o)$
$= -(3.6 \times 10^{-4} \text{ s}^{-1})(150 \text{ s})$
$[CH_3N_2CH_3]/[CH_3N_2CH_3]_o = 0.95$

(b) After the reaction is 99% complete
$[CH_3N_2CH_3]/[CH_3N_2CH_3]_o = 0.010$.
$\ln (0.010) = -(3.6 \times 10^{-4} \text{ s}^{-1})(t)$
$t = 1.3 \times 10^4 \text{ s} (220 \text{ min})$

15.7 $1/[HI] - 1/[HI]_o = kt$
$1/[HI] - 1/[0.010 \text{ M}] = (30. \text{ L/mol} \cdot \text{min})(12 \text{ min})$
$[HI] = 0.0022 \text{ M}$

15.8

Concentration versus time

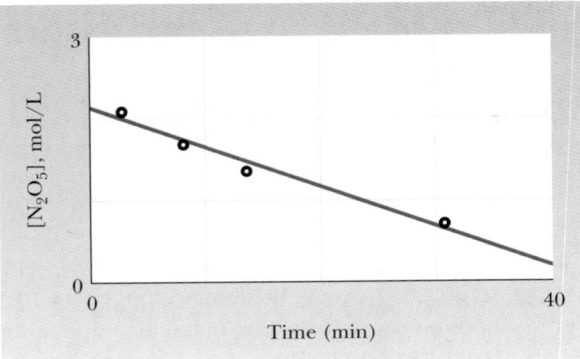

ln [N₂O₅] versus time

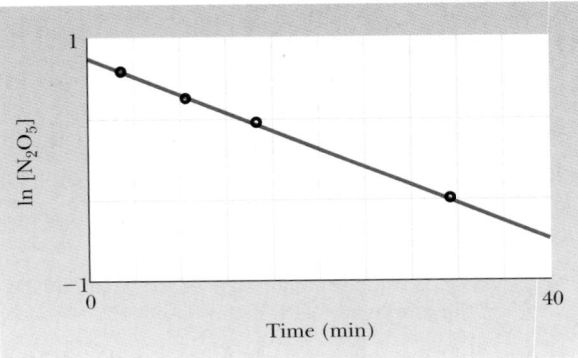

1/[N₂O₅] versus time

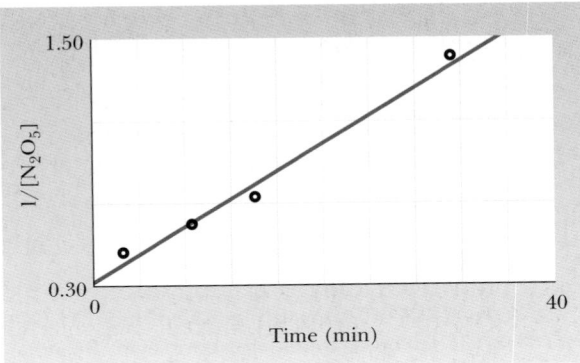

The plot of ln [N₂O₅] versus time has the best linear fit, indicating that this is a first-order reaction. The rate constant is determined from the slope:
$k = -\text{slope} = 0.038 \text{ min}^{-1}$.

15.9 (a) For ^{241}Am, $t_{1/2} = 0.693/k = 0.693/(0.0016 \text{ y}^{-1})$
$= 430 \text{ y}$

For ^{125}I, $t_{1/2} = 0.693/(0.011 \text{ d}^{-1}) = 63 \text{ d}$

(b) ^{125}I decays much faster.
(c) $\ln [(n)/(1.6 \times 10^{15} \text{ atoms})] = -(0.011 \text{ d}^{-1})$
(2.0 d)

$n/1.6 \times 10^{15} \text{ atoms} = 0.978; \ n = 1.57 \times 10^{15} \text{ atoms}$

Since the answer should have two significant figures, we should round this off to 1.6×10^{15} atoms. The approximately 2% that has decayed is not discernable within the limits of accuracy of the data presented.

15.10 $\ln (k_2/k_1) = (-E_a/R)(1/T_2 - 1/T_1)$

$\ln [(1.00 \times 10^4)/(4.5 \times 10^3)] = -(E_a/8.315 \times 10^{-3} \text{ kJ/mol} \cdot \text{K})(1/283 \text{ K} - 1/274 \text{ K})$

$E_a = 57 \text{ kJ/mol}$

15.11 All three steps are bimolecular.

For step 3: Rate $= k[\text{N}_2\text{O}][\text{H}_2]$.

There are two intermediates, $\text{N}_2\text{O}_2(g)$ and $\text{N}_2\text{O}(g)$.

When the three equations are added, N_2O_2 (a product in the first step and a reactant in the second step) and N_2O (a product in the second step and a reactant in the third step) cancel, leaving the net equation: 2 NO(g) + 2 H₂(g) $\longrightarrow$
$\text{N}_2(g) + 2 \text{H}_2\text{O}(g)$.

15.12 (a) 2 NH₃(aq) + OCl⁻(aq) $\longrightarrow$ N₂H₄(aq) + Cl⁻(aq) + H₂O(ℓ)
(b) The second step is the rate-determining step.
(c) Rate $= k[\text{NH}_2\text{Cl}][\text{NH}_3]$
(d) NH₂Cl, N₂H₅⁺, and OH⁻ are intermediates.

15.13 Overall reaction: 2 NO₂Cl(g) $\longrightarrow$
2 NO₂(g) + Cl₂(g)

Rate $= k'[\text{NO}_2\text{Cl}]^2/[\text{NO}_2]$ (where $k' = k_1 k_2/k_1$)

Increasing [NO₂] causes the reaction rate to decrease.

Chapter 16

16.1 (a) $K = [\text{CO}]^2/[\text{CO}_2]$
(b) $K = [\text{Cu}^{2+}][\text{NH}_3]^4/[\text{Cu(NH}_3)_4^{2+}]$
(c) $K = [\text{H}_3\text{O}^+][\text{CH}_3\text{CO}_2^-]/[\text{CH}_3\text{CO}_2\text{H}]$

16.2 (a) Both reactions are reactant-favored ($K < 1$).
(b) [NH₃] in the second solution is greater. K for this reaction is larger, so the reactant, Cd(NH₃)₄²⁺, dissociates to a greater extent.

16.3 (a) $Q = [2.18]/[0.97] = 2.3$. The system is not at equilibrium; $Q < K$. To reach equilibrium, [isobutane] will increase and [butane] will decrease.
(b) $Q = [2.60]/[0.75] = 3.5$. The system is not at equilibrium; $Q > K$. To reach equilibrium, [butane] will increase and [isobutane] will decrease.

16.4 $Q = [NO]^2/[N_2][O_2] = [4.2 \times 10^{-3}]^2/[0.50][0.25]$
$= 1.4 \times 10^{-4}$

$Q < K$, so the reaction is not at equilibrium. To reach equilibrium, [NO] will increase and [N$_2$] and [O$_2$] will decrease.

16.5 (a)

Equation	$C_6H_{10}I_2$	$\rightleftharpoons$	C_6H_{10} +	I_2
Initial (M)	0.050		0	0
Change (M)	−0.035		+0.035	+0.035
Equilibrium (M)	0.015		0.035	0.035

(b) $K = (0.035)(0.035)/(0.015) = 0.082$

16.6

Equation	H_2	+	I_2	$\rightleftharpoons$	2 HI
Initial (M)	6.00×10^{-3}		6.00×10^{-3}		0
Change (M)	−x		−x		+2x
Equilibrium (M)	$0.00600 - x$		$0.00600 - x$		+2x

$$K_c = 33 = \frac{(2x)^2}{(0.00600 - x)^2}$$

$x = 0.0045$ M, so [H$_2$] = [I$_2$] = 0.0015 M and [HI] = 0.0090 M.

16.7

Equation	C(s) + CO_2 (g)	$\rightleftharpoons$	2 CO(g)
Initial (M)	0.012		0
Change (M)	−x		+2x
Equilibrium (M)	$0.012 - x$		2x

$$K_c = 0.021 = \frac{(2x)^2}{(0.012 - x)}$$

$x = $ [CO$_2$] = 0.0057 M and 2x = [CO] = 0.011 M

16.8 (a) $K' = K^2 = (2.5 \times 10^{-29})^2 = 6.3 \times 10^{-58}$
(b) $K'' = 1/K^2 = 1/(6.3 \times 10^{-58}) = 1.6 \times 10^{57}$

16.9 Manipulate the equations and equilibrium constants as follows:

½ H$_2$(g) + ½ Br$_2$(g) $\rightleftharpoons$ HBr(g)
$\qquad\qquad K_1' = (K_1)^{1/2} = 8.9 \times 10^5$

H(g) $\rightleftharpoons$ ½ H$_2$(g) $\quad K_2' = 1/(K_2)^{1/2} = 1.4 \times 10^{20}$

Br(g) $\rightleftharpoons$ ½ Br$_2$(g) $\quad K_3' = 1/(K_3)^{1/2} = 2.1 \times 10^7$

Net: H(g) + Br(g) $\rightleftharpoons$ HBr(g
$\qquad\qquad K_{net} = K_1'K_2'K_3' = 2.6 \times 10^{33}$

16.10

Equation	butane	$\rightleftharpoons$	isobutane
Initial (M)	0.20		0.50
After adding 2.0 M more isobutene	0.20		2.0 + 0.50
Change (M)	+x		−x
Equilibrium (M)	0.20 + x		2.50 − x

$$K = \frac{[\text{isobutane}]}{[\text{butane}]} = \frac{(2.50 - x)}{(0.20 + x)} = 2.50$$

Solving for x gives $x = 0.57$ M. Therefore, [isobutene] = 2.50 − 0.55 = 1.93 M and [butane] = 0.20 + 0.57 = 0.77 M.

16.11 (a) Adding H$_2$ shifts the equilibrium to the right, increasing [NH$_3$]. Adding NH$_3$ shifts the equilibrium to the left, increasing [N$_2$] and [H$_2$].
(b) An increase in volume shifts the equilibrium to the left.

16.12 With an increase in temperature, the value of K will become larger. To adjust and attain equilibrium, [NOCl] will decrease.

Chapter 17

17.1 (a) H$_3$PO$_4$(aq) + H$_2$O(ℓ) $\rightleftharpoons$
$\qquad\qquad\qquad$ H$_3$O$^+$(aq) + H$_2$PO$_4^-$(aq)
H$_2$PO$_4^-$ can either donate or accept a proton; therefore, it is amphiprotic.
(b) CN$^-$(aq) + H$_2$O(ℓ) $\rightleftharpoons$ HCN(aq) + OH$^-$(aq)
CN$^-$ is a Brønsted base; it is capable of accepting a proton.

17.2 NO$_3^-$ is the conjugate base of the acid HNO$_3$; NH$_4^+$ is the conjugate acid of the base NH$_3$.

17.3 [H$_3$O$^+$] = 4.0×10^{-3} M; [OH$^-$] = K_w/[H$_3$O$^+$] = 2.5×10^{-12} M

17.4 (a) pOH = −log [0.0012] = 2.92; pH = 14.00 − pOH = 11.08
(b) [H$_3$O$^+$] = 4.8×10^{-5} mol/L; [OH$^-$] = 2.1×10^{-10} mol/L
(c) pOH = 14.00 − 10.46 = 3.54; [OH$^-$] = 2.9×10^{-4} mol/L. The solubility of Sr(OH)$_2$ is half of this value (because 1 mol Sr(OH)$_2$ gives two mol OH$^-$ when dissolved), or 1.4×10^{-4} mol/L.

17.5 Answer this question by comparing values of K_a and K_b from Table 17.3.
(a) H$_2$SO$_4$ is stronger than H$_2$SO$_3$.
(b) C$_6$H$_5$CO$_2$H is a stronger acid than CH$_3$CO$_2$H.
(c) The conjugate base of boric acid, B(OH)$_4^-$, is a stronger base than the conjugate base of acetic acid, CH$_3$CO$_2^-$.
(d) Ammonia is a stronger base than acetate ion.
(e) The conjugate acid of acetate ion, CH$_3$CO$_2$H, is a stronger acid than the conjugate acid of ammonia, NH$_4^+$.

17.6 (a) pH = 7
(b) pH < 7 (NH$_4^+$ is an acid)
(c) pH < 7 [Al(H$_2$O)$_6$]$^{3+}$ is an acid
(d) pH > 7 (HPO$_4^{2-}$ is a stronger base than it is an acid)

17.7 (a) $pK_a = -\log [6.3 \times 10^{-5}] = 4.20$

(b) $ClCH_2CO_2H$ is stronger (the pK_a of 2.87 is less than a pK_a of 4.20)

(c) pK_a for NH_4^+, the conjugate acid of NH_3, is $-\log [5.6 \times 10^{-10}] = 9.26$. It is a weaker acid than acetic acid, for which $K_a = 1.8 \times 10^{-5}$.

17.8 K_b for the lactate ion $= K_w/K_a = 7.1 \times 10^{-11}$. It is a slightly stronger base than the formate, nitrite, and fluoride ions, and a weaker base than the benzoate ion.

17.9 (a) NH_4^+ is a stronger acid than HCO_3^-. CO_3^{2-}, the conjugate base of HCO_3^-, is a stronger base than NH_3, the conjugate base of NH_4^+.

(b) Reactant-favored; the reactants are the weaker acid and base.

(c) Reactant-favored; the reactants are the weaker acid and base.

17.10 (a) The two compounds react and form a solution containing HCN and NaCl. The solution is acidic (HCN is an acid).

(b) $CH_3CO_2H(aq) + SO_3^{2-}(aq) \rightleftharpoons$
$\qquad\qquad HSO_3^-(aq) + CH_3CO_2^-(aq)$

The solution is acidic, because HSO_3^- is a stronger acid than $CH_3CO_2^-$ is a base.

17.11 From the pH, we can calculate $[H_3O^+] = 1.9 \times 10^{-3}$ M. Also, $[\text{butanoate}^-] = [H_3O^+] = 1.9 \times 10^{-3}$ M. Use these values along with [butanoic acid] to calculate K_a.

$K_a = [1.9 \times 10^{-3}][1.9 \times 10^{-3}]/(0.055 - 1.9 \times 10^{-3})$
$= 6.8 \times 10^{-5}$

17.12 $K_a = 1.8 \times 10^{-5} = [x][x]/(0.10 - x)$

$x = [H_3O^+] = [CH_3CO_2^-] = 1.3 \times 10^{-3}$ M;
$[CH_3CO_2H] = 0.099$ M; pH $= 2.89$

17.13 $K_a = 7.2 \times 10^{-4} = [x][x]/(0.015 - x)$

The x in the denominator cannot be dropped. This equation must be solved with the quadratic formula or by successive approximations.

$x = [H_3O^+] = [F^-] = 2.9 \times 10^{-3}$ M

$[HF] = 0.015 - 2.9 \times 10^{-3} = 0.012$ M

pH $= 2.54$

17.14 $OCl^-(aq) + H_2O(\ell) \rightleftharpoons HOCl(aq) + OH^-(aq)$

$K_b = 2.9 \times 10^{-7} = [x][x]/(0.015 - x)$

$x = [OH^-] = [HOCl] = 6.6 \times 10^{-5}$ M

pOH $= 4.18$; pH $= 9.82$

17.15 Equivalent amounts of acid and base react to form water, $CH_3CO_2^-$ and Na^+. Acetate ion hydrolyzes to a small extent, giving CH_3CO_2H and OH^-. We need to determine $[CH_3CO_2^-]$ and then solve a weak base equilibrium problem to determine $[OH^-]$.

Amount $CH_3CO_2^- = $ mol base $= 0.12$ mol/L $\times 0.015$ L

$= 1.8 \times 10^{-3}$ mol

Total volume $= 0.030$ L, so $[CH_3CO_2^-] =$
$(1.8 \times 10^{-3}$ mol$)/0.030$ L $= 0.060$ M

$CH_3CO_2^-(aq) + H_2O(\ell) \rightleftharpoons$
$\qquad\qquad CH_3CO_2H(aq) + OH^-(aq)$

$K_b = 5.6 \times 10^{-10} = [x][x]/(0.060 - x)$

$x = [OH^-] = [CH_3CO_2H] = 5.8 \times 10^{-6}$ M

pOH $= 5.24$; pH $= 8.76$

17.16 $H_2C_2O_4(aq) + H_2O(\ell) \rightleftharpoons$
$\qquad\qquad H_3O^+(aq) + HC_2O_4^-(aq)$

$K_{a1} = 5.9 \times 10^{-2} = [x][x]/(0.10 - x)$

The x in the denominator cannot be dropped. This equation must be solved with the quadratic formula or by successive approximations.

$x = [H_3O^+] = [HC_2O_4^-] = 5.3 \times 10^{-2}$ M

pH $= 1.28$

$K_{b2} = [H_3O^+][C_2O_4^{2-}]/[HC_2O_4^-]$; because
$[H_3O^+] = [HC_2O_4^-]$

$[C_2O_4^{2-}] = K_{a2} = 6.4 \times 10^{-5}$ M

17.17 (a) Lewis base (electron-pair donor)

(b) Lewis acid (electron-pair acceptor)

(c) Lewis base (electron-pair donor)

(d) Lewis base (electron-pair donor)

17.18 (a) H_2SeO_4

(b) $Fe(H_2O)_6^{3+}$

(c) HOCl

(d) Amphetamine is a primary amine and a (weak) base. It is both a Brønsted base and a Lewis base.

Chapter 18

18.1 pH of 0.30 M HCO_2H:

$K_a = [H_3O^+][HCO_2^-]/[HCO_2H]$

$1.8 \times 10^{-4} = [x][x]/[0.30 - x]$

$x = 7.3 \times 10^{-3}$ M; pH $= 2.14$

pH of 0.30 M formic acid $+$ 0.10 M $NaHCO_2$

$K_a = [H_3O^+][HCO_2^-]/[HCO_2H]$

$1.8 \times 10^{-4} = [x][0.10 + x]/(0.30 - x)$

$x = 5.4 \times 10^{-4}$ M; pH $= 3.27$

18.2 NaOH: $(0.100$ mol/L$)(0.0300$ L$) = 3.00 \times 10^{-3}$ mol

CH_3CO_2H: $(0.100$ mol/L$)(0.0450$ L$) =$
4.50×10^{-3} mol

3.00×10^{-3} mol NaOH reacts with 3.00×10^{-3} mol CH_3CO_2H, forming 3.00×10^{-3} mol $CH_3CO_2^-$; 1.50×10^{-3} mol unreacted CH_3CO_2H remains in solution. The total volume is 75.0 mL. Use these values to calculate $[CH_3CO_2H]$ and $[CH_3CO_2^-]$, and use these concentrations in a weak acid equilibrium calculation to obtain $[H_3O^+]$ and pH.

$[CH_3CO_2H] = 1.5 \times 10^{-3}$ mol/0.075 L = 0.0200 M

$[CH_3CO_2^-] = 3.0 \times 10^{-3}$ mol/0.075 L = 0.0400 M

$K_a = [H_3O^+][CH_3CO_2^-]/[CH_3CO_2H]$

$1.8 \times 10^{-5} = [x][0.0400 + x]/(0.0200 - x)$

$x = [H_3O^+] = 9.0 \times 10^{-6}$ M; pH = 5.05

18.3 pH = pK_a + log {[base]/[acid]}

pH = $-\log (1.8 \times 10^{-4})$ + log {[0.70]/[0.50]}

pH = 3.74 + 0.15 = 3.89

18.4 (15.0 g NaHCO$_3$)(1 mol/84.01 g) = 0.179 mol NaHCO$_3$, and (18.0 g Na$_2$CO$_3$)(1 mol/106.0 g) = 0.170 mol Na$_2$CO$_3$

pH = pK_a + log {[base]/[acid]}

pH = $-\log (4.8 \times 10^{-11})$ + log {[0.170]/[0.179]}

pH = 10.32 − 0.02 = 10.30

18.5 pH = pK_a + log {[base]/[acid]}

$5.00 = -\log (1.8 \times 10^{-5})$ + log {[base]/[acid]}

$5.00 = 4.74$ + log {[base]/[acid]}

[base]/[acid] = 1.8

To prepare this buffer solution, the ratio [base]/[acid] must equal 1.8. For example, you can dissolve 1.8 mol (148 g) of NaCH$_3$CO$_2$ and 1.0 mol (60.05 g) of CH$_3$CO$_2$H in enough water to make 1.0 L of solution.

18.6 Initial pH (before adding acid):

pH = pK_a + log {[base]/[acid]}

  = $-\log (1.8 \times 10^{-4})$ + log {[0.70]/[0.50]}

  = 3.74 + 0.15 = 3.89

After adding acid, the added HCl will react with the weak base (formate ion) and form more formic acid. The net effect is to change the ratio of [base]/[acid] in the buffer solution.

Initial amount HCO$_2$H = 0.50 mol/L × 0.500 L = 0.250 mol

Initial amount HCO$_2^-$ = 0.70 mol/L × 0.50 L = 0.350 mol

Amount HCl added = 1.0 mol/L × 0.010 L = 0.010 mol

Amount HCO$_2$H after HCl addition = 0.250 mol + 0.010 mol = 0.26 mol

Initial amount HCO$_2^-$ after HCl addition = 0.350 mol − 0.010 mol = 0.34 mol

pH = pK_a + log {[base]/[acid]}

pH = $-\log (1.8 \times 10^{-4})$ + log {[0.340]/[0.260]}

pH = 3.74 + 0.12 = 3.86

18.7 After addition of 25.0 mL base, half of the acid has been neutralized.

Initial amount HCl = 0.100 mol/L × 0.0500 L = 0.00500 mol

Amount NaOH added = 0.100 mol/L × 0.0250 L = 0.00250 mol

Amount HCl after reaction: 0.00500 − 0.00250 = 0.00250 mol HCl

[HCl] after reaction = 0.00250 mol/0.0750 L = 0.0333 M

This is a strong acid and completely ionized, so $[H_3O^+]$ = 0.0333 M and pH = 1.48.

After 50.50 mL base is added, a small excess of base is present in the 100.5 mL (0.1005 L) of solution. (Volume of excess base added is 0.50 mL = 5.0×10^{-4} L.)

Amount excess base = 0.100 mol/L × 5.0×10^{-4} L = 5.0×10^{-5} mol

$[OH^-] = 5.0 \times 10^{-5}$ mol/0.1005 L = 4.9×10^{-4} M

pOH = $-\log (4.9 \times 10^{-4})$ = 3.31; pH = 14.00 − pOH = 10.69

18.8 35.0 mL base will partially neutralize the acid.

Initial amount CH$_3$CO$_2$H = (0.100 mol/L)(0.1000 L) = 0.0100 mol

Amount NaOH added = (0.10 mol/L)(0.035 L) = 0.0035 mol

Amount CH$_3$CO$_2$H after reaction = 0.0100 − 0.0035 = 0.0065 mol

Amount CH$_3$CO$_2^-$ after reaction = 0.0035 mol

[CH$_3$CO$_2$H] after reaction = 0.0065 mol/0.135 L = 0.0481 M

[CH$_3$CO$_2^-$] after reaction = 0.00350 mol/0.135 L = 0.0259 M

$K_a = [H_3O^+][CH_3CO_2^-]/[CH_3CO_2H]$

$1.8 \times 10^{-5} = [x][0.0259 + x]/[0.0481 - x]$

$x = [H_3O^+] = 3.34 \times 10^{-5}$ M; pH = 4.48

18.9 75.0 mL acid will partially neutralize the base.

Initial amount NH$_3$ = (0.100 mol/L)(0.1000 L) = 0.0100 mol

Amount HCl added = (0.100 mol/L)(0.0750 L) = 0.00750 mol

Amount NH$_3$ after reaction = 0.0100 − 0.00750 = 0.0025 mol

Amount NH$_4^+$ after reaction = 0.00750 mol

Solve using the Henderson–Hasselbach equation; use K_a for the weak acid NH$_4^+$:

pH = pK_a + log {[base]/[acid]}

pH = $-\log (5.6 \times 10^{-10})$ + log {[0.0025]/[0.00750]}

pH = 9.25 − 0.48 = 8.77

18.10 An indicator that changes color near the pH at the equivalence point is required. Possible indicators include methyl red, bromcresol green, and Eriochrome black T; all change color in the pH range of 5–6.

18.11 (a) $AgI(s) \rightleftharpoons Ag^+(aq) + I^-(aq)$

$K_{sp} = [Ag^+][I^-]$; $K_{sp} = 8.5 \times 10^{-17}$

(b) $BaF_2(s) \rightleftharpoons Ba^{2+}(aq) + 2\,F^-(aq)$

$K_{sp} = [Ba^{2+}][F^-]^2$; $K_{sp} = 1.8 \times 10^{-7}$

(c) $Ag_2CO_3(s) \rightleftharpoons 2\,Ag^+(aq) + CO_3{}^{2-}(aq)$

$K_{sp} = [Ag^+]^2[CO_3{}^{2-}]$; $K_{sp} = 8.5 \times 10^{-12}$

18.12 $[Ba^{2+}] = 3.6 \times 10^{-3}$ M; $[F^-] = 7.2 \times 10^{-3}$ M

$K_{sp} = [Ba^{2+}][F^-]^2$

$K_{sp} = [3.6 \times 10^{-3}][7.2 \times 10^{-3}]^2 = 1.9 \times 10^{-7}$

18.13 $Ca(OH)_2(s) \rightleftharpoons Ca^{2+}(aq) + 2\,OH^-(aq)$

$K_{sp} = [Ca^{2+}][OH^-]^2$; $K_{sp} = 5.5 \times 10^{-5}$

$5.5 \times 10^{-5} = [x][2x]^2$ (where $x =$ solubility in mol/L)

$x = 2.4 \times 10^{-2}$ mol/L

Solubility in g/L = $(2.4 \times 10^{-2}$ mol/L$)$

$(74.1$ g/mol$) = 1.8$ g/L

18.14 (a) AgCl

(b) $Ca(OH)_2$

(c) Because these compounds have different stoichiometries, the most soluble cannot be identified without doing a calculation. The solubility of $Ca(OH)_2$ is 2.4×10^{-2} M (from Exercise 18.13); $Ca(OH)_2$ is more soluble than $CaSO_4$, whose solubility is 7.0×10^{-3} M $\{K_{sp} = [Ca^{2+}][SO_4{}^{2-}]; 4.9 \times 10^{-5} = [x][x]; x = 7.0 \times 10^{-3}$ M$\}$.

18.15 (a) In pure water:

$K_{sp} = [Ba^{2+}][SO_4{}^{2-}]$; $1.1 \times 10^{-10} = [x][x]$;

$x = 1.0 \times 10^{-5}$ mol/L

(b) In 0.010 M $Ba(NO_3)_2$, which furnishes 0.010 M Ba^{2+} in solution:

$K_{sp} = [Ba^{2+}][SO_4{}^{2-}]$; $1.1 \times 10^{-10} =$ $[0.010 + x][x]$; $x = 1.1 \times 10^{-8}$ mol/L

18.16 (a) In pure water:

$K_{sp} = [Zn^{2+}][CN^-]^2$; $8.0 \times 10^{-12} = [x][2x]^2 = 4x^3$

Solubility = $x = 1.3 \times 10^{-4}$ mol/L

(b) In 0.10 M $Zn(NO_3)_2$, which furnishes 0.10 M Zn^{2+} in solution:

$K_{sp} = [Zn^{2+}][CN^-]^2$; $8.0 \times 10^{-12} = [0.10 + x][2x]^2$

Solubility = $x = 4.5 \times 10^{-6}$ mol/L

18.17 When $[Pb^{2+}] = 1.1 \times 10^{-3}$ M, $[I^-] = 2.2 \times 10^{-3}$ M.

$Q = [Pb^{2+}][I^-]^2 = [1.1 \times 10^{-3}][2.2 \times 10^{-3}]^2 = 5.3 \times 10^{-9}$

This value is less than K_{sp}, which means that the system has not yet reached equilibrium and more PbI_2 will dissolve.

18.18 $Q = [Sr^{2+}][SO_4{}^{2-}] = [2.5 \times 10^{-4}][2.5 \times 10^{-4}] = 6.3 \times 10^{-8}$

This value is less than K_{sp}, which means that the system has not yet reached equilibrium. Precipitation will not occur.

18.19 $K_{sp} = [Pb^{2+}][I^-]^2$. Let x be the concentration of I^- required at equilibrium.

$9.8 \times 10^{-9} = [0.050][x]^2$

$x = [I^-] = 4.4 \times 10^{-5}$ mol/L. A concentration greater than this value will result in precipitation of PbI_2.

Let x be the concentration of Pb^{2+} in solution, in equilibrium with 0.0015 M I^-.

$9.8 \times 10^{-9} = [x][1.5 \times 10^{-3}]^2$

$x = [Pb^{2+}] = 4.4 \times 10^{-3}$ M

18.20 First, determine the concentrations of Ag^+ and Cl^-; then calculate Q, and see whether it is greater than or less than K_{sp}. Concentrations are calculated using the final volume, 105 mL, in the equation $C_{dil} \times V_{dil} = C_{conc} \times V_{conc}$.

$[Ag^+](0.105$ L$) = (0.0010$ mol/L$)(0.100$ L$)$

$[Ag^+] = 9.5 \times 10^{-4}$ M

$[Cl^-](0.105$ L$) = (0.025$ M$)(0.005$ L$)$

$[Cl^-] = 1.2 \times 10^{-3}$ M

$Q = [Ag^+][Cl^-] = [9.5 \times 10^{-4}][1.2 \times 10^{-3}] = 1.1 \times 10^{-6}$

Because $Q > K_{sp}$, precipitation occurs.

18.21 The logic for the solution of this exercise is outlined in Example 8.16.

Equation	$Ag(NH_3)_2{}^+ \rightleftharpoons$	$Ag^+ +$	$2\,NH_3$
Initial (M)	0.005		$1.0 - 2(0.005)$
Change	$-x$	$+x$	$+2x$
Equilibrium (M)	$0.005 - x$	x	0.99

$K = 1/K_f = 1/1.1 \times 10^7 = [x][0.99]^2/0.005$

$x = [Ag^+] = 4.6 \times 10^{-10}$ mol/L

18.22 $Cu(OH)_2(s) \rightleftharpoons Cu^{2+}(aq) + 2\,OH^-(aq)$

$K_{sp} = [Cu^{2+}][OH^-]^2$

$Cu^{2+}(aq) + 4\,NH_3(aq) \rightleftharpoons Cu(NH_3)_4{}^{2+}(aq)$

$K_{form} = [Cu(NH_3)_4{}^{2+}]/[Cu^{2+}][NH_3]^4$

Net: $Cu(OH)_2(s) + 4\,NH_3(aq) \rightleftharpoons$ $Cu(NH_3)_4{}^{2+}(aq) + 2\,OH^-(aq)$

$K_{net} = K_{sp} \times K_{form} = (2.2 \times 10^{-20})(6.8 \times 10^{12}) = 1.5 \times 10^{-7}$

Chapter 19

19.1 (a) O_3; larger molecules generally have higher entropies than smaller molecules.

(b) $SnCl_4(g)$; gases have higher entropies than liquids.

19.2 (a) $\Delta_r S^\circ = \Sigma S^\circ(\text{products}) - \Sigma S^\circ(\text{reactants})$

$\Delta_r S^\circ = S^\circ[NH_4Cl(aq)]) - S^\circ[NH_4Cl(s)]$

$\Delta_r S° = (1 \text{ mol/mol-rxn})(169.9 \text{ J/mol} \cdot \text{K})$
$\qquad - (1 \text{ mol/mol-rxn})(94.85 \text{ J/mol} \cdot \text{K})$
$\qquad = 75.1 \text{ J/K} \cdot \text{mol-rxn}$

A gain in entropy for the formation of a mixture (solution) is expected.

(b) $\Delta_r S° = 2\ S°(CO_2) + 3\ S°(H_2O) -$
$[S°(C_2H_5OH) + 3\ S°(O_2)]$

$\Delta_r S° = (2 \text{ mol/mol-rxn})(213.74 \text{ J/mol} \cdot \text{K})$
$\qquad + (3 \text{ mol/mol-rxn})(188.84 \text{ J/mol} \cdot \text{K})$
$\qquad - [(1 \text{ mol/mol-rxn})(282.70 \text{ J/mol} \cdot \text{K})$
$\qquad + (3 \text{ mol/mol-rxn})(205.07 \text{ J/mol} \cdot \text{K})]$

$\Delta_r S° = +96.09 \text{ J/K} \cdot \text{mol-rxn}$

An increase in entropy is expected because there is a increase in the number of moles of gases.

19.3   (a) Type 2
     (b) Type 3
     (c) Type 1
     (d) Type 2

19.4 $\Delta S°(\text{system}) = 2\ S°(HCl) - [S°(H_2) + S°(Cl_2)]$

$\Delta S°(\text{system}) = (2 \text{ mol/mol-rxn})(186.2 \text{ J/mol} \cdot \text{K})$
$\qquad - [(1 \text{ mol/mol-rxn})(130.7 \text{ J/mol} \cdot \text{K})$
$\qquad + (1 \text{ mol/mol-rxn})(223.08 \text{ J/mol} \cdot \text{K})]$
$\qquad = 18.6 \text{ J/K} \cdot \text{mol-rxn}$

$\Delta S°(\text{surroundings}) = -\Delta H°(\text{system})/T =$
$-(-184,620 \text{ J/mol-rxn}/298 \text{ K}) = 619.5 \text{ J/K} \cdot \text{mol-rxn}$

$\Delta S°(\text{universe}) = \Delta S°(\text{system}) + \Delta S°(\text{surroundings})$
$= 18.6 \text{ J/K} \cdot \text{mol-rxn} + 619.5 \text{ J/K} \cdot \text{mol-rxn} =$
$638.1 \text{ J/K} \cdot \text{mol-rxn}$

19.5 $\Delta S°(\text{system}) = \Delta_r S° = 560.7 \text{ J/K} \cdot \text{mol-rxn}$

At 298 K, $\Delta S°(\text{surroundings}) =$
$\qquad\qquad\qquad -(467,900 \text{ J/mol-rxn})/298 \text{ K}$
$\qquad\qquad\qquad = -1570 \text{ J/K} \cdot \text{mol-rxn}$

$\Delta S°_{\text{univ}} = \Delta S°(\text{system}) + \Delta S°(\text{surroundings})$
$\qquad = 560.7 \text{ J/K} \cdot \text{mol-rxn} - 1570 \text{ J/K} \cdot \text{mol-rxn}$
$\qquad = -1010 \text{ J/K} \cdot \text{mol-rxn}$

The negative sign indicates that the process is not spontaneous. At higher temperature, the value of $-\Delta H°(\text{system})/T$ will be less negative. At a high enough temperature, $\Delta S°(\text{surroundings})$ will outweigh $\Delta S°(\text{system})$ and the reaction will be spontaneous.

19.6   For the reaction $N_2(g) + 3\ H_2(g) \longrightarrow 2\ NH_3(g)$:

$\Delta_r H° = 2\ \Delta_f H°$ for $NH_3(g) = (2 \text{ mol/mol-rxn})$
$(-45.90 \text{ kJ/mol}) = -91.80 \text{ kJ/mol-rxn}$

$\Delta_r S° = 2\ S°(NH_3) - [S°(N_2) + 3\ S°(H_2)]$

$\Delta_r S° = (2 \text{ mol/mol-rxn})(192.77 \text{ J/ mol} \cdot \text{K}) - [(1$
$\text{mol/mol-rxn})(191.56 \text{ J/mol} \cdot \text{K}) + (3 \text{ mol/mol-}$
$\text{rxn})(130.7 \text{ J/mol} \cdot \text{K})]$

$\Delta_r S° = -198.1 \text{ J/K} \cdot \text{mol-rxn} \ (= 0.198 \text{ kJ/K} \cdot \text{mol-rxn})$

$\Delta_r G° = \Delta_r H° - T\Delta_r S° =$
$-91.80 \text{ kJ/mol-rxn} - (298 \text{ K})(-0.198 \text{ kJ/K} \cdot \text{mol-rxn})$

$\Delta_r G° = -32.8 \text{ kJ/mol-rxn}$

19.7 $SO_2(g) + \frac{1}{2}\ O_2(g) \longrightarrow SO_3(g)$

$\Delta_r G° = \Sigma\ \Delta_f G°(\text{products}) - \Sigma\ \Delta_f G°(\text{reactants})$

$\Delta_r G° = (1 \text{ mol/mol-rxn})\Delta G°[SO_3(g)] - \{(1 \text{ mol/}$
$\text{mol-rxn})\Delta G°[SO_2(g)] + 0.5 \text{ mol/mol-rxn})$
$\Delta G°[O_2(g)]\}$

$\Delta_r G° = -371.04 \text{ kJ/mol-rxn} - (-300.13 \text{ kJ/mol-}$
$\text{rxn} + 0)$

$\qquad = -70.91 \text{ kJ/mol-rxn}$

19.8 $HgO(s) \longrightarrow Hg(\ell) + \frac{1}{2}\ O_2(g)$; determine the temperature at which $\Delta_r G° = \Delta_r H° - T\Delta_r S° = 0$. T is the unknown in this problem.

$\Delta_r H° = [-\Delta_f H°$ for $HgO(s)] = 90.83 \text{ kJ/mol-rxn}$

$\Delta_r S° = S°[Hg(\ell)] + \frac{1}{2}\ S°(O_2) - S°[HgO(s)]$

$\Delta_r S° = (1 \text{ mol/mol-rxn})(76.02 \text{ J/mol} \cdot \text{K})$
$\qquad + [(0.5 \text{ mol/mol-rxn})(205.07 \text{ J/mol} \cdot \text{K})$
$\qquad - (1 \text{ mol/mol-rxn})(70.29 \text{ J/mol} \cdot \text{K})]$
$\qquad = 108.26 \text{ J/K} \cdot \text{mol-rxn}$

$\Delta_r H° - T(\Delta_r S°) = 90,830 \text{ J/mol-rxn} -$
$T(108.27 \text{ J/mol-rxn})/\text{K}) = 0$

$T = 839 \text{ K } (566 \text{ °C})$

19.9 $C(s) + CO_2(g) \rightleftharpoons 2\ CO(g)$

$\Delta_r G° = \Sigma\ \Delta_f G°(\text{products}) - \Sigma\ \Delta_f G°(\text{reactants})$

$\Delta_r G° = 2\ \Delta_f G°(CO) - \Delta_f G°(CO_2)$

$\Delta_r G° = (2 \text{ mol/mol-rxn})(-137.17 \text{ kJ/mol}) -$
$(1 \text{ mol/mol-rxn})(-394.36 \text{ kJ/mol})$

$\Delta_r G° = 120.02 \text{ kJ/mol-rxn}$

$\Delta_r G° = -RT \ln K$

$120,020 \text{ J/mol-rxn}$
$\qquad\qquad = -(8.3145 \text{ J/mol-rxn} \cdot \text{K})(298 \text{ K})(\ln K)$

$K = 8.94 \times 10^{-22}$

Chapter 20

20.1   Oxidation half-reaction: $Al(s) \longrightarrow Al^{3+}(aq) + 3\ e^-$

Reduction half-reaction: $2\ H^+(aq) + 2\ e^- \longrightarrow$
$\qquad\qquad\qquad\qquad\qquad\qquad\qquad H_2(g)$

Overall reaction: $2\ Al(s) + 6\ H^+(aq) \longrightarrow$
$\qquad\qquad\qquad\qquad\qquad 2\ Al^{3+}(aq) + 3\ H_2(g)$

Al is the reducing agent and is oxidized; $H^+(aq)$ is the oxidizing agent and is reduced.

20.2 $2\ VO^{2+}(aq) + Zn(s) + 4\ H^+(aq) \longrightarrow$
$\qquad\qquad\qquad Zn^{2+}(aq) + 2\ V^{3+}(aq) + 2\ H_2O(\ell)$

$2\ V^{3+}(aq) + Zn(s) \longrightarrow 2\ V^{2+}(aq) + Zn^{2+}(aq)$

20.3   Oxidation (Fe^{2+}, the reducing agent, is oxidized):
$Fe^{2+}(aq) \longrightarrow Fe^{3+}(aq) + e^-$

Reduction (MnO_4^-, the oxidizing agent, is reduced)

$$MnO_4^-(aq) + 8\ H^+(aq) + 5\ e^- \longrightarrow Mn^{2+}(aq) + 4\ H_2O(\ell)$$

Overall reaction:

$$MnO_4^-(aq) + 8\ H^+(aq) + 5\ Fe^{2+}(aq) \longrightarrow Mn^{2+}(aq) + 5\ Fe^{3+}(aq) + 4\ H_2O(\ell)$$

20.4 (a) Oxidation half-reaction:

$$Al(s) + 3\ OH^-(aq) \longrightarrow Al(OH)_3(s) + 3\ e^-$$

Reduction half-reaction:

$$S(s) + H_2O(\ell) + 2\ e^- \longrightarrow HS^-(aq) + OH^-(aq)$$

Overall reaction:

$$2\ Al(s) + 3\ S(s) + 3\ H_2O(\ell) + 3\ OH^-(aq) \longrightarrow 2\ Al(OH)_3(s) + 3\ HS^-(aq)$$

(b) Aluminum is the reducing agent and is oxidized; sulfur is the oxidizing agent and is reduced.

20.5 Construct two half-cells, the first with a silver electrode and a solution containing $Ag^+(aq)$, and the second with a nickel electrode and a solution containing $Ni^{2+}(aq)$. Connect the two half-cells with a salt bridge. When the electrodes are connected through an external circuit, electrons will flow from the anode (the nickel electrode) to the cathode (the silver electrode). The overall cell reaction is $Ni(s) + 2\ Ag^+(aq) \longrightarrow Ni^{2+}(aq) + 2\ Ag(s)$. To maintain electrical neutrality in the two half-cells, negative ions will flow from the $Ag\ |\ Ag^+$ half-cell to the $Ni\ |\ Ni^{2+}$ half-cell, and positive ions will flow in the opposite direction.

20.6 Anode reaction: $Zn(s) \longrightarrow Zn^{2+}(aq) + 2\ e^-$

Cathode reaction: $2\ Ag^+(aq) + 2\ e^- \longrightarrow 2\ Ag(s)$

$E^\circ_{cell} = E^\circ_{cathode} - E^\circ_{anode} = 0.80\ V - (-0.76\ V)$
$= 1.56\ V$

20.7 Mg is easiest to oxidize, and Au is the most difficult. (See Table 20.1.)

20.8 Use the "northwest–southeast rule" or calculate the cell voltage to determine whether a reaction is product-favored. Reactions (a) and (c) are reactant-favored; reactions (b) and (d) are product-favored.

20.9 Overall reaction: $2\ Al(s) + 3\ Fe^{2+}(aq) \longrightarrow 2\ Al^{3+}(aq) + 3\ Fe(s)$

($E^\circ_{cell} = 1.22\ V$, $n = 6$)

$E_{cell} = E^\circ_{cell} - (0.0257/n)\ \ln\ \{[Al^{3+}]^2/[Fe^{2+}]^3\}$
$= 1.22 - (0.0257/6)\ \ln\ \{[0.025]^2/[0.50]^3\}$
$= 1.22\ V - (-0.023)\ V = 1.24\ V$

20.10 Overall reaction: $Fe(s) + 2\ H^+(aq) \longrightarrow Fe^{2+}(aq) + H_2(g)$

($E^\circ_{cell} = 0.44\ V$, $n = 2$)

$E_{cell} = E^\circ_{cell} - (0.0257/n)\ \ln\ \{[Fe^{2+}]P_{H_2}/[H^+]^2\}$

$= 0.44 - (0.0257/2)\ \ln\ \{[0.024]1.0/[0.056]^2\}$
$= 0.44\ V - 0.026\ V = 0.41\ V$

20.11 $\Delta_rG^\circ = -nFE^\circ = -(2\ mol\ e^-)(96,500\ C/mol\ e^-)$
$(-0.76\ V)(1\ J/1\ C \cdot V)$
$= 146,680\ J\ (= 150\ kJ)$

The negative value of E° and the positive value of ΔG° both indicate a reactant-favored reaction.

20.12 $E^\circ_{cell} = E^\circ_{cathode} - E^\circ_{anode} = 0.80\ V - 0.855\ V$
$= -0.055\ V$; $n = 2$

$E^\circ = (0.0257/n)\ \ln\ K$

$-0.055 = (0.0257/2)\ \ln\ K$

$K = 0.014$

20.13 Cathode: $Zn^{2+}(aq) + 2\ e^- \longrightarrow Zn(s)\ E^\circ_{cathode} = -0.76\ V$

Anode: $Zn(s) + 4\ CN^-(aq) \longrightarrow [Zn(CN)_4^{2-}] + 2\ e^-\ E^\circ_{anode} = -1.26\ V$

Overall: $Zn^{2+}(aq) + 4\ CN^-(aq) \longrightarrow [Zn(CN)_4^{2-}]\ E^\circ_{cell} = 0.50\ V$

$E^\circ = (0.0257/n)\ \ln\ K$

$0.50 = (0.0257/2)\ \ln\ K$

$K = 7.9 \times 10^{16}$

20.14 Cathode: $2\ H_2O(\ell) + 2\ e^- \longrightarrow 2\ OH^-(aq) + H_2(g)$

$E^\circ_{cathode} = -0.83\ V$

Anode: $4\ OH^-(aq) \longrightarrow O_2(g) + 2\ H_2O(\ell) + 4\ e^-$

$E^\circ_{anode} = 0.40\ V$

Overall: $2\ H_2O(\ell) \longrightarrow 2\ H_2(g) + O_2(g)$

$E^\circ_{cell} = E^\circ_{cathode} - E^\circ_{anode} = -0.83\ V - 0.40\ V$
$= -1.23\ V$

This is the minimum voltage needed to cause this reaction to occur.

20.15 O_2 is formed at the anode, by the reaction

$2\ H_2O(\ell) \longrightarrow 4\ H^+(aq) + O_2(g) + 4\ e^-$.

$(0.445\ A)(45\ min)(60\ s/min)(1\ C/1\ A \cdot s)(1\ mol\ e^-/96,500\ C)(1\ mol\ O_2/4\ mol\ e^-)(32\ g\ O_2/1\ mol\ O_2) = 0.10\ g\ O_2$

20.16 The cathode reaction (electrolysis of molten NaCl) is $Na^+(melt) + e^- \longrightarrow Na(\ell)$.

$(25 \times 10^3\ A)(60\ min)(60\ s/min)(1\ C/1\ A \cdot s)$
$(1\ mol\ e^-/96,500\ C)(1\ mol\ Na/mol\ e^-)$
$(23\ g\ Na/1\ mol\ Na)$
$= 21,450\ g\ Na = 21\ kg$

Chapter 21

21.1 (a) $2\ Na(s) + Br_2(\ell) \longrightarrow 2\ NaBr(s)$
(b) $Ca(s) + Se(s) \longrightarrow CaSe(s)$
(c) $2\ Pb(s) + O_2(g) \longrightarrow 2\ PbO(s)$

Lead(II) oxide, a red compound commonly called litharge, is the most widely used inorganic lead compound. Maroon-colored lead(IV) oxide is the product of lead oxidation in lead-acid storage batteries (Chapter 21). Other oxides such as Pb_3O_4 also exist.

(d) $2\ Al(s) + 3\ Cl_2(g) \longrightarrow 2\ AlCl_3(s)$

21.2 (a) H_2Te
(b) Na_3AsO_4
(c) $SeCl_6$
(d) $HBrO_4$

21.3 (a) NH_4^+ (ammonium ion)
(b) O_2^{2-} (peroxide ion)
(c) N_2H_4 (hydrazine)
(d) NF_3 (nitrogen trifluoride)

21.4 (a) ClO is an odd-electron molecule, and Cl has the unlikely oxidation number of +2.
(b) In Na_2Cl, chlorine would have the unlikely charge of 2− (to balance the two positive charges of the two Na^+ ions).
(c) This compound would require either the calcium ion to have the formula Ca^+ or the acetate ion to have the formula $CH_3CO_2^{2-}$. In all of its compounds, calcium occurs as the Ca^{2+} ion. The acetate ion, formed from acetic acid by loss of H^+, has a 1− charge.
(d) No octet structure for C_3H_7 can be drawn. This species has an odd number of electrons.

21.5 $CH_4(g) + H_2O(g) \longrightarrow 3\ H_2(g) + CO(g)$
Bonds broken: 4 C—H and 2 O—H (sum = 2578 kJ)
$4\ \Delta H(C{-}H) = 4(413\text{ kJ}) = 1652$ kJ
$2\ \Delta H(O{-}H) = 4(463\text{ kJ}) = 926$ kJ
Bonds formed: 3 H—H and 1 C≡O (sum = 2354 kJ)
$3\ \Delta H(H{-}H) = 3(436\text{ kJ}) = 1308$ kJ
$\Delta H(CO) = 1046$ kJ
Estimated energy of reaction = 2578 kJ − 2354 kJ
$= +224$ kJ

21.6 Cathode reaction: $Na^+ + e^- \longrightarrow Na(\ell)$; 1 F, or 96,500 C, is required to form 1 mol of Na. There are (24 h) (60 min/h) (60 s/min) = 86,400 s in 1 day. 1000 kg = 1.000×10^6 g, so
$(1.000 \times 10^6$ g Na$)(1$ mol Na/23.00 g Na$)(96{,}500$ C/mol Na$)(1$ A · s/1 C$)(1/86{,}400$ s$) = 4.855 \times 10^4$ A

21.7 Some interesting topics: gemstones of the mineral beryl; uses of Be in the aerospace industry and in nuclear reactors; beryllium–copper alloys; severe health hazards when beryllium or its compounds get into the lungs.

21.8 (a) $Ga(OH)_3(s) + 3\ H^+(aq) \longrightarrow Ga^{3+}(aq) + 3\ H_2O(\ell)$
$Ga(OH)_3(s) + OH^-(aq) \longrightarrow Ga(OH)_4^-(aq)$
(b) $Ga^{3+}(aq)$ $(K_a = 1.2 \times 10^{-3})$ is stronger acid than $Al^{3+}(aq)$ $(K_a = 7.9 \times 10^{-6})$

21.9

21.10 (a) $:N{\equiv}N{-}\ddot{\underset{..}{O}}: \longleftrightarrow \ddot{N}{=}N{=}\ddot{O} \longleftrightarrow :\ddot{\underset{..}{N}}{-}N{\equiv}O:$
A   B   C
Resonance structure A has formal charges of N = 0, N = +1, O = −1 (from left to right) and is the most favorable structure. For B, N = −1, N = +1, O = 0, and for C, N = −2, N = +1, O = +1. Structure C is clearly unfavorable. B is not as favorable as A because the more electronegative atom (O) has a 0 charge whereas N is −1.
(b) $NH_4NO_3(s) \longrightarrow N_2O(g) + 2\ H_2O(g)$
$\Delta_r H° = \Sigma\Delta_f H°(\text{products}) - \Sigma\Delta_f H°(\text{reactants})$
$\Delta_r H° = \Delta_f H°(N_2O) + 2\ \Delta_f H°(H_2O) - \Delta_f H°(NH_4NO_3)$
$= 82.05$ kJ $+ 2(-241.83$ kJ$) - (-365.56$ kJ$) = -36.05$ kJ
The reaction is exothermic.

21.11 First, calculate $\Delta_r G°$, $\Delta_r H°$, and $\Delta_r S°$ for this reaction, using data from Appendix L.
$\Delta_r G° = \Sigma\Delta_f G°(\text{products}) - \Sigma\Delta_f G°(\text{reactants})$
$\Delta_r G° = 2\ \Delta_f G°(ZnO) + 2\ \Delta_f G°(SO_2) - 2\ \Delta_f G°(ZnS) - 3\ \Delta_f G°(O_2)$
$= 2(-318.30$ kJ$) + 2(-300.13$ kJ$) - 2(-201.29$ kJ$) - 0$
$= -834.28$ kJ. The reaction is product-favored at 298 K.
$\Delta_r H° = 2\ \Delta_f H°(ZnO) + 2\ \Delta_f H°(SO_2) - 2\ \Delta_f H°(ZnS) - 3\ \Delta_f H°(O_2)$
$= 2(-348.28$ kJ$) + 2(-296.84$ kJ$) - [2(-205.98$ kJ$) + 0] = -878.28$ kJ
$\Delta_r S° = 2\ S°(ZnO) + 2\ S°(SO_2) - 2\ S°(ZnS) - 3\ S°(O_2)$
$= 2(43.64$ J/K$) + 2(248.21$ J/K$) - [2(57.7$ J/K$) + 3(205.07$ J/K$)]$
$= -146.9$ J/K

This reaction is enthalpy favored and entropy disfavored. The reaction will become less favored at higher temperatures. See Table 19.2.

21.12 For the reaction $HX + Ag \longrightarrow AgX + \frac{1}{2}\ H_2$:
$\Delta_r G° = \Sigma\Delta_f G°(\text{products}) - \Sigma\Delta_f G°(\text{reactants})$
$\Delta_r G° = \Delta_f G°(AgX) - \Delta_f G°(HX)$
For HF: $\Delta_r G° = +79.4$ kJ; reactant favored
For HCl: $\Delta_r G° = -14.67$ kJ; product favored
For HBr: $\Delta G° = -43.45$ kJ; product favored
For HI: $\Delta_r G° = -67.75$ kJ; product favored

Chapter 22

22.1 (a) $Co(NH_3)_3Cl_3$
(b) (i) $K_3[Co(NO_2)_6]$: a complex of cobalt(III) with a coordination number of 6
(ii) $Mn(NH_3)_4Cl_2$: a complex of manganese(II) with a coordination number of 6

22.2 (a) hexaaquanickel(II) sulfate
(b) dicyanobis(ethylenediamine)chromium(III) chloride
(c) potassium amminetrichloroplatinate(II)
(d) potassium dichlorocuprate(I)

22.3 (a) Geometric isomers are possible (with the NH_3 ligands in *cis* and *trans* positions).
(b) Only a single structure is possible.
(c) Only a single structure is possible.
(d) This compound is chiral; there are two optical isomers.
(e) Only a single structure is possible.
(f) Two structural isomers are possible based on coordination of the NO_2^- ligand through oxygen or nitrogen.

22.4 (a) $[Ru(H_2O)_6]^{2+}$: An octahedral complex of ruthenium(II) (d^6). A low-spin complex has no unpaired electrons and is diamagnetic. A high-spin complex has four unpaired electrons and is paramagnetic.

$$\frac{\uparrow}{d_{x^2-y^2}} \quad \frac{\uparrow}{d_{z^2}} \qquad \frac{\quad}{d_{x^2-y^2}} \quad \frac{\quad}{d_{z^2}}$$

$$\frac{\uparrow\downarrow}{d_{xy}} \quad \frac{\uparrow}{d_{xz}} \quad \frac{\uparrow}{d_{yz}} \qquad \frac{\uparrow\downarrow}{d_{xy}} \quad \frac{\uparrow\downarrow}{d_{xz}} \quad \frac{\uparrow\downarrow}{d_{yz}}$$

high-spin Ru^{2+} low-spin Ru^{2+}

(b) $[Ni(NH_3)_6]^{2+}$: An octahedral complex of nickel(II) (d^8). Only one electron configuration is possible; it has two unpaired electrons and is paramagnetic.

$$\frac{\uparrow}{d_{x^2-y^2}} \quad \frac{\uparrow}{d_{z^2}}$$

$$\frac{\uparrow\downarrow}{d_{xy}} \quad \frac{\uparrow\downarrow}{d_{xz}} \quad \frac{\uparrow\downarrow}{d_{yz}}$$

Ni^{2+} ion (d^8)

22.5 (a) The $C_5H_5^-$ ligand is an anion (6 electrons), C_6H_6 is a neutral ligand (6 electrons), so Mn must be $+1$ (6 valence electrons). There is a total of 18 valence electrons.
(b) The ligands in this complex are all neutral, so the Mo atom must have no charge. The C_6H_6 ligand contributes six electrons, each Co contributes two electrons for a total of six, and Mo has six valence electrons. The total is 18 electrons.

Chapter 23

23.1 (a) $^{222}_{86}Rn \longrightarrow {}^{218}_{84}Po + {}^4_2\alpha$
(b) $^{218}_{84}Po \longrightarrow {}^{218}_{85}At + {}^0_{-1}\beta$

23.2 (a) E (per photon) $= h\upsilon = hc/\lambda$
$E = [(6.626 \times 10^{-34}\,J \cdot s/photon)$
$\qquad (3.00 \times 10^8\,m/s)]/(2.0 \times 10^{-12})$
$E = 9.94 \times 10^{-14}\,J/photon$
E (per mole) $= (9.94 \times 10^{-14}\,J/photon)$
$\qquad (6.022 \times 10^{23}\,photons/mol)$
E (per mole) $= 5.99 \times 10^{10}\,J/mol$

23.3 (a) Emission of six α particles leads to a decrease of 24 in the mass number and a decrease of 12 in the atomic number. Emission of four β particles increases the atomic number by 4, but doesn't affect the mass. The final product of this process has a mass number of $232 - 24 = 208$ and an atomic number of $90 - 12 + 4 = 82$, identifying it as $^{208}_{82}Pb$.
(b) Step 1: $^{232}_{90}Th \longrightarrow {}^{228}_{88}Ra + {}^4_2\alpha$
Step 2: $^{228}_{88}Ra \longrightarrow {}^{228}_{89}Ac + {}^0_{-1}\beta$
Step 3: $^{228}_{89}Ac \longrightarrow {}^{228}_{90}Th + {}^0_{-1}\beta$

23.4 (a) $^0_{+1}\beta$ (b) $^{41}_{19}K$ (c) $^0_{-1}\beta$ (d) $^{22}_{12}Mg$

23.5 (a) $^{32}_{14}Si \longrightarrow {}^{32}_{15}P + {}^0_{-1}\beta$
(b) $^{45}_{22}Ti \longrightarrow {}^{45}_{21}Sc + {}^0_{+1}\beta$ or ${}^{45}_{22}Ti + {}^0_{-1}e \longrightarrow$
$^{45}_{21}Sc$

(c) $^{239}_{94}Pu \longrightarrow \alpha + {}^{45}_{22}U$
(d) $^{42}_{19}K \longrightarrow {}^{42}_{20}Ca + {}^0_{-1}\beta$

23.6 $\Delta m = 0.03438\,g/mol$
$\Delta E = (3.438 \times 10^{-5}\,kg/mol)(2.998 \times 10^8)^2$
$\qquad = 3.090 \times 10^{12}\,J/mol\ (= 3.090 \times 10^9\,kJ/mol)$
$E_b = 5.150 \times 10^8\,kJ/mol\ nucleons$

23.7 (a) 49.2 years is exactly 4 half-lives; quantity remaining $= 1.5\,mg(1/2)^4 = 0.094\,mg$
(b) 3 half-lives, 36.9 years
(c) 1% is between 6 half-lives, 73.8 years (1/64 remains), and 7 half-lives, 86.1 years (1/128 remains)

23.8 $\ln([A]/[A_o]) = -kt$
$\ln([3.18 \times 10^3]/[3.35 \times 10^3]) = -k(2.00\,d)$
$k = 0.0260\,d^{-1}$
$t_{1/2} = 0.693/k = 0.693/(0.0260\,d^{-1}) = 26.7\,d$

23.9 $k = 0.693/t_{1/2} = 0.693/200\,y = 3.47 \times 10^{-3}\,y^{-1}$
$\ln([A]/[A_o]) = -kt$
$\ln([3.00 \times 10^3]/[6.50 \times 10^{12}]) = -(3.47 \times 10^{-3}\,y^{-1})t$
$\ln(4.62 \times 10^{-10}) = -(3.47 \times 10^{-3}\,y^{-1})t$
$t = 6190\,y$

23.10 $\ln([A]/[A_o]) = -kt$
$\ln([9.32]/[13.4]) = -(1.21 \times 10^{-4}\,y^{-1})t$
$t = 3.00 \times 10^3\,y$

23.11 3000 dpm/x = 1200 dpm/ 60.0 mg
$x = 150\,mg$

Answers to Selected Study Questions

CHAPTER 1

1.1 (a) C, carbon
(b) K, potassium
(c) Cl, chlorine
(d) P, phosphorus
(e) Mg, magnesium
(f) Ni, nickel

1.3 (a) Ba, barium
(b) Ti, titanium
(c) Cr, chromium
(d) Pb, lead
(e) As, arsenic
(f) Zn, zinc

1.5 (a) Na (element) and NaCl (compound)
(b) Sugar (compound) and carbon (element)
(c) Gold (element) and gold chloride (compound)

1.7 (a) Physical property
(b) Chemical property
(c) Chemical property
(d) Physical property
(e) Physical property
(f) Physical property

1.9 (a) Physical (colorless liquid) and chemical (burns in air)
(b) Physical (shiny metal, orange liquid) and chemical (reacts with bromine)

1.11 (a) Qualitative: blue-green color, solid physical state
Quantitative: density = 2.65 g/cm^3 and mass = 2.5 g
(b) Density, physical state, and color are intensive properties, whereas mass is an extensive property.
(c) Volume = 0.94 cm^3

1.13 Observations c, e, and f are chemical properties

1.15 calcium, Ca; fluorine, F

The crystals are cubic in shape because the atoms are arranged in cubic structures.

1.17 The macroscopic view is the photograph of NaCl, and the particulate view is the drawing of the ions in a cubic arrangement. The structure of the compound at the particulate level determines the properties that are observed at the macroscopic level.

1.19 The density of the plastic is less than that of CCl$_4$, so the plastic will float on the liquid CCl$_4$. Aluminum is more dense than CCl$_4$, so aluminum will sink when placed in CCl$_4$.

1.21 The three liquids will form three separate layers with hexane on the top, water in the middle, and perfluorohexane on the bottom. The HDPE will float at the interface of the hexane and water layers. The PVC will float at the interface of the water and perfluorohexane layers. The Teflon will sink to the bottom of the cylinder.

1.23 HDPE will float in ethylene glycol, water, acetic acid, and glycerol.

1.25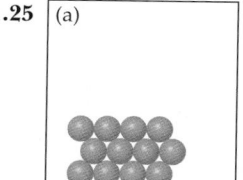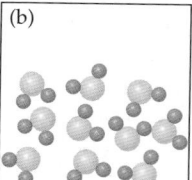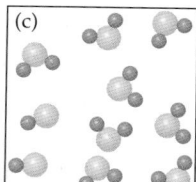

1.27 The sample's density and melting point could be compared to those of pure silver.

1.29 If too much sugar is excreted, the density of the urine would be higher than normal. If too much water is excreted, the density would be lower than normal.

1.31 (a) Solid potassium metal reacts with liquid water to produce gaseous hydrogen and a homogeneous mixture (solution) of potassium hydroxide in liquid water.

(b) The reaction is a chemical change.

(c) The reactants are potassium and water. The products are hydrogen gas and a water (aqueous) solution of potassium hydroxide. Heat and light are also evolved.

(d) Among the qualitative observations are (i) the reaction is violent, and (ii) heat and light (a purple flame) are produced.

1.33 (a) The water could be evaporated by heating the solution, leaving the salt behind.

(b) Use a magnet to attract the iron away from lead, which is not magnetic.

(c) Mixing the solids with water will dissolve only the sugar. Filtration would separate the solid sulfur from the sugar solution. Finally, the sugar could be separated from the water by evaporating the water.

1.35 Separate the iron from a weighed sample of cereal by passing a magnet through a mixture of the cereal and water after the flakes have become a gooey paste. Remove the iron flakes from the magnet and weigh them to determine the mass of iron in this mass of cereal.

1.37 Physical change

LET'S REVIEW: THE TOOLS OF QUANTITATIVE CHEMISTRY

1 298 K

3 (a) 289 K
(b) 97 °C
(c) 310 K (3.1×10^2 K)

5 42,195 m; 26.219 miles

7 5.3 cm²; 5.3×10^{-4} m²

9 250. cm³; 0.250 L, 2.50×10^{-4} m³; 0.250 dm³

11 2.52×10^3 g

13 555 g

15 Choice (c), zinc

17 (a) Method A with all data included:
average = 2.4 g/cm³

Method B with all data included:
average = 3.480 g/cm³

For B, the 5.811 g/cm³ data point can be excluded because it is more than twice as large as all other points for case Method B. Using only the first three points, average = 2.703 g/cm³

(b) Method A: error = 0.3 g/cm³ or about 10%

Method B: error = 0.001 g/cm³ or about 0.04%

(c) Method A: standard deviation = 0.2 g/cm³

Method B (including all data points):
st. dev. = 1.554 g/cm³

Method B (excluding the 5.811 g/cm³ data point):
st. dev. = 0.002 g/cm³

(d) Method B's average value is both more precise and more accurate so long as the 5.811 g/cm³ data point is excluded.

19 (a) 5.4×10^{-2} g, two significant figures
(b) 5.462×10^3 g, four significant figures
(c) 7.92×10^{-4} g, three significant figures
(d) 1.6×10^3 mL, two significant figures

21 (a) 9.44×10^{-3}
(b) 5694
(c) 11.9
(d) 0.122

23

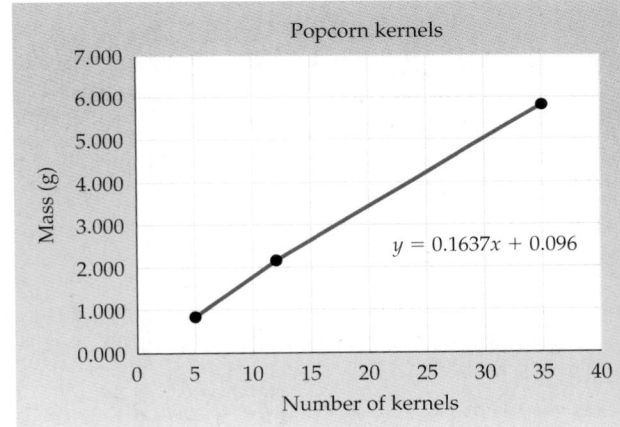

Slope: 0.1637 g/kernel

The slope represents the average mass of a popcorn kernel.

Mass of 20 popcorn kernels = 3.370 g

There are 127 kernels in a sample with a mass of 20.88 g.

25 (a) $y = -4.00x + 20.00$
(b) $y = -4.00$

27 $C = 0.0823$

29 $T = 295$

31 0.197 nm; 197 pm

33 (a) 7.5×10^{-6} m; (b) 7.5×10^3 nm; (c) 7.5×10^6 pm

35 50. mg procaine hydrochloride

37 The volume of the marbles is 99 mL − 61 mL = 38 mL. This yields a density of 2.5 g/cm³.

39 (a) 0.178 nm^3; $1.78 \times 10^{-22} \text{ cm}^3$
(b) $3.86 \times 10^{-22} \text{ g}$
(c) $9.68 \times 10^{-23} \text{ g}$

41 Your normal body temperature (about 98.6 °F) is 37 °C. As this is higher than gallium's melting point, the metal will melt in your hand.

43 (a) 15%
(b) 3.63×10^3 kernels

45 $8.0 \times 10^4 \text{ kg}$ of sodium fluoride per year

47 245 g sulfuric acid

49 (a) 272 mL ice
(b) The ice cannot be contained in the can.

51 7.99 g/cm^3

53 (a) 8.7 g/cm^3
(b) The metal is probably cadmium, but the calculated density is close to that of cobalt, nickel, and copper. Further testing should be done on the metal.

55 0.0927 cm

57 (a) 1.143×10^{21} atoms; 54.9% of the lattic is filled with atoms; 24% of the lattice is open space.

Atoms are spheres. When spheres are packed together, they touch only at certain points, therefore leaving spaces in the structure.

(b) Four atoms

59 Al, aluminum

61

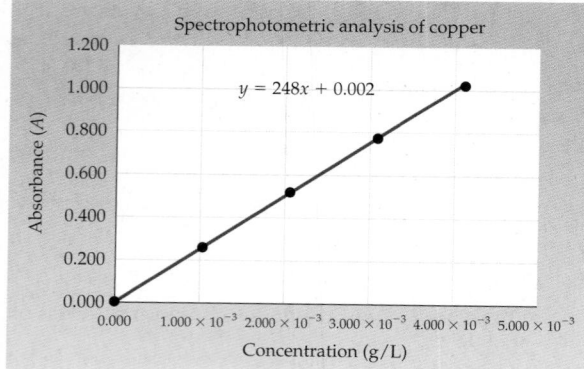

When absorbance = 0.635, concentration = $2.55 \times 10^{-3} \text{ g/L} = 2.55 \times 10^{-3} \text{ mg/mL}$

63

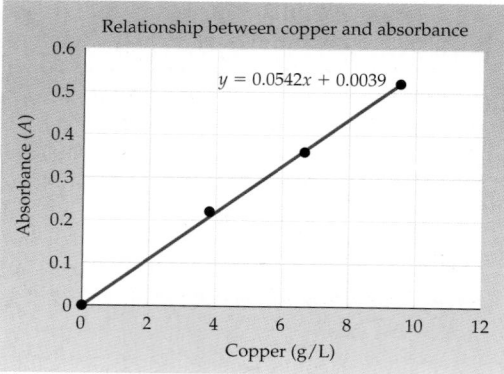

Slope = 0.054; y-intercept = 0.004; the absorbance for 5.00 g/L of copper is 0.27

CHAPTER 2

2.1 Atoms contain the following fundamental particles: protons (+1 charge), neutrons (zero charge), and electrons (−1 charge). Protons and neutrons are in the nucleus of an atom. Electrons are the least massive of the three particles.

2.3 (a) $^{27}_{12}\text{Mg}$
(b) $^{48}_{22}\text{Ti}$
(c) $^{62}_{30}\text{Zn}$

2.5

Element	Electrons	Protons	Neutrons
^{24}Mg	12	12	12
^{119}Sn	50	50	69
^{232}Th	90	90	142
^{13}C	6	6	7
^{63}Cu	29	29	34
^{205}Bi	83	83	122

2.7 $^{57}_{27}\text{Co}$, $^{58}_{27}\text{Co}$, $^{60}_{27}\text{Co}$

2.9 ^{205}Tl is more abundant than ^{203}Tl. The atomic mass of thallium is closer to 205 than to 203.

2.11 $(0.0750)(6.015121) + (0.9250)(7.016003) = 6.94$

2.13 (c), About 50%. Actual percent $^{107}\text{Ag} = 51.839\%$

2.15 ^{69}Ga, 60.12%; ^{71}Ga, 39.88%

2.17

	Symbol	Atomic No.	Atomic Mass	Group	Period	
Titanium	Ti	22	47.867	4B(IUPAC 4)	4	Metal
Thallium	Tl	81	204.3833	3A(IUPAC 13)	6	Metal

2.19 Eight elements: periods 2 and 3. 18 elements: periods 4 and 5. 32 elements: period 6.

2.21 (a) Nonmetals: C, Cl
(b) Main group elements: C, Ca, Cl, Cs
(c) Lanthanides: Ce
(d) Transition elements: Cr, Co, Cd, Ce, Cm, Cu, Cf
(e) Actinides: Cm, Cf
(f) Gases: Cl

2.23 Metals: Na, Ni, Np
Metalloids: None in this list
Nonmetals: N, Ne

2.25 Molecular Formula: H_2SO_4.
Structural Formula:

$$\begin{array}{c} O \\ \| \\ O-S-O-H \\ | \\ O-H \end{array}$$

The structure is not flat. The O atoms are arranged around the sulfur at the corners of a tetrahedron. The hydrogen atoms are connected to two of the oxygen atoms.

2.27 (a) Mg^{2+}
(b) Zn^{2+}
(c) Ni^{2+}
(d) Ga^{3+}

2.29 (a) Ba^{2+}
(b) Ti^{4+}
(c) $PO_4{}^{3-}$
(d) $HCO_3{}^{-}$
(e) S^{2-}
(f) $ClO_4{}^{-}$
(g) Co^{2+}
(h) $SO_4{}^{2-}$

2.31 K loses one electron per atom to form a K^+ ion. It has the same number of electrons as an Ar atom.

2.33 Ba^{2+} and Br^- ions. The compound's formula is $BaBr_2$.

2.35 (a) Two K^+ ions and one S^{2-} ion
(b) One Co^{2+} ion and one $SO_4{}^{2-}$ ion
(c) One K^+ ion and one $MnO_4{}^-$ ion
(d) Three $NH_4{}^+$ ions and one $PO_4{}^{3-}$ ion
(e) One Ca^{2+} ion and two ClO^- ions
(f) One Na^+ ion and one $CH_3CO_2{}^-$ ion

2.37 Co^{2+} gives CoO and Co^{3+} gives Co_2O_3

2.39 (a) $AlCl_2$ should be $AlCl_3$ (based on an Al^{3+} ion and three Cl^- ions).
(b) KF_2 should be KF (based on a K^+ ion and an F^- ion).
(c) Ga_2O_3 is correct.
(d) MgS is correct.

2.41 (a) potassium sulfide
(b) cobalt(II) sulfate
(c) ammonium phosphate
(d) calcium hypochlorite

2.43 (a) $(NH_4)_2CO_3$
(b) CaI_2
(c) $CuBr_2$
(d) $AlPO_4$
(e) $AgCH_3CO_2$

2.45 Compounds with Na^+: Na_2CO_3 (sodium carbonate) and NaI (sodium iodide). Compounds with Ba^{2+}: $BaCO_3$ (barium carbonate) and BaI_2 (barium iodide).

2.47 The force of attraction is stronger in NaF than in NaI because the distance between ion centers is smaller in NaF (235 pm) than in NaI (322 pm).

2.49 (a) nitrogen trifluoride
(b) hydrogen iodide
(c) boron triiodide
(d) phosphorus pentafluoride

2.51 (a) SCl_2
(b) N_2O_5
(c) $SiCl_4$
(d) B_2O_3

2.53 (a) 67 g Al
(b) 0.0698 g Fe
(c) 0.60 g Ca
(d) 1.32×10^4 g Ne

2.55 (a) 1.9998 mol Cu
(b) 0.0017 mol Li
(c) 2.1×10^{-5} mol Am
(d) 0.250 mol Al

2.57 Of these elements, He has the smallest molar mass, and Fe has the largest molar mass. Therefore, 1.0 g of He has the largest number of atoms in these samples, and 1.0 g of Fe has the smallest number of atoms.

2.59 (a) 159.7 g/mol
(b) 117.2 g/mol
(c) 176.1 g/mol

2.61 (a) 290.8 g/mol
(b) 249.7 g/mol

2.63 (a) 1.53 g
(b) 4.60 g
(c) 4.60 g
(d) 1.48 g

2.65 Amount of SO_3 = 12.5 mol
Number of molecules = 7.52×10^{24} molecules
Number of S atoms = 7.52×10^{24} atoms
Number of O atoms = 2.26×10^{25} atoms

2.67 (a) 86.60% Pb and 13.40% S
(b) 81.71% C and 18.29% H
(c) 79.96% C, 9.394% H, and 10.65% O

2.69 66.46% copper in CuS. 15.0 g of CuS is needed to obtain 10.0 g of Cu.

2.71 $C_4H_6O_4$

2.73 (a) CH, 26.0 g/mol; C_2H_2
(b) CHO, 116.1 g/mol; $C_4H_4O_4$
(c) CH_2, 112.2 g/mol, C_8H_{16}

2.75 Empirical formula, CH; molecular formula, C_2H_2

2.77 Empirical formula, C_3H_4; molecular formula, C_9H_{12}

2.79 Empirical and molecular formulas are both $C_8H_8O_3$

2.81 XeF_2

2.83 ZnI_2

2.85

Symbol	^{58}Ni	^{33}S	^{20}Ne	^{55}Mn
Protons	28	16	10	25
Neutrons	30	17	10	30
Electrons	28	16	10	25
Name	nickel	sulfur	neon	manganese

2.87

S	N
B	I

2.89 (a) 1.0552×10^{-22} g for 1 Cu atom
(b) 6.286×10^{-22} dollars for 1 Cu atom

2.91 (a) strontium
(b) zirconium
(c) carbon
(d) arsenic
(e) iodine
(f) magnesium
(g) krypton
(h) sulfur
(i) germanium or arsenic

2.93 (a) 0.25 mol U
(b) 0.50 mol Na
(c) 10 atoms of Fe

2.95 40.2 g H_2 (b) < 103 g C   (c) < 182 g Al
(f) < 210 g Si   (d) < 212 g Na   (e) < 351 g Fe
(a) < 650 g $Cl_2(g)$

2.97 (a) Atomic mass of O = 15.873 u; Avogadro's
number = 5.9802×10^{23} particles per mole
(b) Atomic mass of H = 1.00798 u; Avogadro's number = 6.0279×10^{23} particles per mole

2.99 $(NH_4)_2CO_3$, $(NH_4)_2SO_4$, $NiCO_3$, $NiSO_4$

2.101 All of these compounds have one atom of some element plus three Cl atoms. The highest mass percent of chlorine will occur in the compound having the lightest central element. Here, that element is B, so BCl_3 should have the highest mass percent of Cl (90.77%).

2.103 The molar mass of adenine ($C_5H_5N_5$) is 135.13 g/mol. 3.0×10^{23} molecules represents 67 g. Thus, 3.0×10^{23} molecules of adenine has a larger mass than 40.0 g of the compound.

2.105 1.7×10^{21} molecules of water

2.107 245.75 g/mol. Mass percent: 25.86% Cu, 22.80% N, 5.742% H, 13.05% S, and 32.55% O. In 10.5 g of compound there are 2.72 g Cu and 0.770 g H_2O.

2.109 Empirical formula of malic acid: $C_4H_6O_5$

2.111 $Fe_2(CO)_9$

2.113 (a) $C_7H_5NO_3S$

(b) 6.82×10^{-4} mol saccarin
(c) 21.9 mg S

2.115 (a) NaClO, ionic
(b) BI_3
(c) $Al(ClO_4)_3$, ionic
(d) $Ca(CH_3CO_2)_2$, ionic
(e) $KMnO_4$, ionic
(f) $(NH_4)_2SO_3$, ionic
(g) KH_2PO_4, ionic
(h) S_2Cl_2
(i) ClF_3
(j) PF_3

2.117 (a) Empirical formula = molecular formula = CF_2O_2
(b) Empirical formula = C_5H_4; molecular formula = $C_{10}H_8$

2.119 Empirical formula and molecular formula = $C_5H_{14}N_2$

2.121 $C_9H_7MnO_3$

2.123 68.42% Cr; 1.2×10^3 kg Cr_2O_3

2.125 Empirical formula = ICl_3; molecular formula = I_2Cl_6

2.127 7.35 kg of iron

2.129 (d) Na_2MoO_4

2.131 5.52×10^{-4} mol $C_{21}H_{15}Bi_3O_{12}$; 0.346 g Bi

2.133 The molar mass of the compound is 154 g/mol. The unknown element is carbon.

2.135 $n = 19$.

2.137 (a) 2.3×10^{14} g/cm³
(b) 3.34×10^{-3} g/cm³
(c) The nucleus is much more dense than the space occupied by the electrons.

2.139 (a) 0.0130 mol Ni
(b) NiF_2
(c) nickel(II) fluoride

2.141 Formula is $MgSO_4 \cdot 7\ H_2O$

2.143 Volume = 3.0 cm^3; length of side = 1.4 cm

2.145 1.0028×10^{23} atoms C. If the accuracy is ± 0.0001 g, the maximum mass could be 2.0001 g, which also represents 1.0028×10^{23} atoms C.

2.147 Choice c. The calculated mole ratio is 0.78 mol H_2O per mol $CaCl_2$. The student should heat the crucible again and then reweigh it. More water might be driven off.

2.149 Required data: density of iron, molar mass of iron, Avogadro's number.

$$1.00\ cm^3 \left(\frac{7.87\ g}{1\ cm^3}\right)\left(\frac{1\ mol}{55.85\ g}\right)\left(\frac{6.02 \times 10^{23}\ atoms}{1\ mol}\right) =$$
$$8.49 \times 10^{22}\ atoms\ Fe$$

2.151 Barium would be more reactive than calcium, so a more vigorous evolution of hydrogen should occur. Reactivity increases on descending the periodic table, at least for Groups 1A and 2A.

2.153 When words are written with the pink, hydrated compound, the words are not visible. However, when heated, the hydrated salt loses water to form anhydrous $CoCl_2$, which is deep blue. The words are then visible.

CHAPTER 3

3.1 $C_5H_{12}(\ell) + 8\ O_2(g) \rightarrow 5\ CO_2(g) + 6\ H_2O(g)$

3.3 (a) $4\ Cr(s) + 3\ O_2(g) \rightarrow 2\ Cr_2O_3(s)$
(b) $Cu_2S(s) + O_2(g) \rightarrow 2\ Cu(s) + SO_2(g)$
(c) $C_6H_5CH_3(\ell) + 9\ O_2(g) \rightarrow 4\ H_2O(\ell) + 7\ CO_2(g)$

3.5 (a) $Fe_2O_3(s) + 3\ Mg(s) \rightarrow 3\ MgO(s) + 2\ Fe(s)$
Reactants = iron(III) oxide, magnesium
Products = magnesium oxide, iron
(b) $AlCl_3(s) + 3\ NaOH(aq) \rightarrow$
$Al(OH)_3(s) + 3\ NaCl(aq)$
Reactants = aluminum chloride, sodium hydroxide
Products = aluminum hydroxide, sodium chloride
(c) $2\ NaNO_3(s) + H_2SO_4(\ell) \rightarrow$
$Na_2SO_4(s) + 2\ HNO_3(\ell)$
Reactants = sodium nitrate, sulfuric acid
Products = sodium sulfate, nitric acid
(d) $NiCO_3(s) + 2\ HNO_3(aq) \rightarrow$
$Ni(NO_3)_2(aq) + CO_2(g) + H_2O(\ell)$
Reactants = nickel(II) carbonate, nitric acid
Products = nickel(II) nitrate, carbon dioxide, water

3.7 The reaction involving HCl is more product-favored at equilibrium.

3.9 Electrolytes are compounds whose aqueous solutions conduct electricity. Given an aqueous solution containing a strong electrolyte and another aqueous solution containing a weak electrolyte at the same concentration, the solution containing the strong electrolyte (such as NaCl) will conduct electricity much better than will be the one containing the weak electrolyte (such as acetic acid).

3.11 (a) $CuCl_2$
(b) $AgNO_3$
(c) All are water-soluble

3.13 (a) K^+ and OH^- ions
(b) K^+ and SO_4^{2-} ions
(c) Li^+ and NO_3^- ions
(d) NH_4^+ and SO_4^{2-} ions

3.15 (a) Soluble, Na^+ and CO_3^{2-} ions
(b) Soluble, Cu^{2+} and SO_4^{2-} ions
(c) Insoluble
(d) Soluble, Ba^{2+} and Br^- ions

3.17 $CdCl_2(aq) + 2\ NaOH(aq) \rightarrow$
$Cd(OH)_2(s) + 2\ NaCl(aq)$

$Cd^{2+}(aq) + 2\ OH^-(aq) \rightarrow Cd(OH)_2(s)$

3.19 (a) $NiCl_2(aq) + (NH_4)_2S(aq) \rightarrow NiS(s) + 2\ NH_4Cl(aq)$

$Ni^{2+}(aq) + S^{2-}(aq) \rightarrow NiS(s)$

(b) $3\ Mn(NO_3)_2(aq) + 2\ Na_3PO_4(aq) \rightarrow$
$Mn_3(PO_4)_2(s) + 6\ NaNO_3(aq)$

$3\ Mn^{2+}(aq) + 2\ PO_4^{3-}(aq) \rightarrow Mn_3(PO_4)_2(s)$

3.21 $HNO_3(aq) + H_2O(\ell) \rightarrow H_3O^+(aq) + NO_3^-(aq)$

3.23 $H_2C_2O_4(aq) + H_2O(\ell) \rightarrow H_3O^+(aq) + HC_2O_4^-(aq)$

$HC_2O_4^-(aq) + H_2O(\ell) \rightarrow H_3O^+(aq) + C_2O_4^{2-}(aq)$

3.25 $MgO(s) + H_2O(\ell) \rightarrow Mg(OH)_2(s)$

3.27 (a) Acetic acid reacts with magnesium hydroxide to give magnesium acetate and water.

$2\ CH_3CO_2H(aq) + Mg(OH)_2(s) \rightarrow$
$Mg(CH_3CO_2)_2(aq) + 2\ H_2O(\ell)$

Brønsted acid: acetic acid; Brønsted base: magnesium hydroxide
(b) Perchloric acid reacts with ammonia to give ammonium perchlorate

$HClO_4(aq) + NH_3(aq) \rightarrow NH_4ClO_4(aq)$

Brønsted acid: perchloric acid; Brønsted base: ammonia

3.29 $Ba(OH)_2(aq) + 2\ HNO_3(aq) \rightarrow$
$Ba(NO_3)_2(aq) + 2\ H_2O(\ell)$

3.31 Strong Brønsted acid examples: hydrochloric acid, nitric acid

Strong Brønsted base example: sodium hydroxide

3.33 (a) $(NH_4)_2CO_3(aq) + Cu(NO_3)_2(aq) \rightarrow$
$$CuCO_3(s) + 2\ NH_4NO_3(aq)$$

$$CO_3^{2-}(aq) + Cu^{2+}(aq) \rightarrow CuCO_3(s)$$

(b) $Pb(OH)_2(s) + 2\ HCl(aq) \rightarrow PbCl_2(s) + 2\ H_2O(\ell)$

$Pb(OH)_2(s) + 2\ H_3O^+(aq) + 2\ Cl^-(aq) \rightarrow$
$$PbCl_2(s) + 4\ H_2O(\ell)$$

(c) $BaCO_3(s) + 2\ HCl(aq) \rightarrow$
$$BaCl_2(aq) + H_2O(\ell) + CO_2(g)$$

$BaCO_3(s) + 2\ H_3O^+(aq) \rightarrow$
$$Ba^{2+}(aq) + 3\ H_2O(\ell) + CO_2(g)$$

(d) $2\ CH_3CO_2H(aq) + Ni(OH)_2(s) \rightarrow$
$$Ni(CH_3CO_2)_2(aq) + 2\ H_2O(\ell)$$

$2\ CH_3CO_2H(aq) + Ni(OH)_2(s) \rightarrow$
$$Ni^{2+}(aq) + 2\ CH_3CO_2^-(aq) + 2\ H_2O(\ell)$$

3.35 (a) $AgNO_3(aq) + KI(aq) \rightarrow AgI(s) + KNO_3(aq)$

$$Ag^+(aq) + I^-(aq) \rightarrow AgI(s)$$

(b) $Ba(OH)_2(aq) + 2\ HNO_3(aq) \rightarrow$
$$Ba(NO_3)_2(aq) + 2\ H_2O(\ell)$$

$$OH^-(aq) + H_3O^+(aq) \rightarrow 2\ H_2O(\ell)$$

(c) $2\ Na_3PO_4(aq) + 3\ Ni(NO_3)_2(aq) \rightarrow$
$$Ni_3(PO_4)_2(s) + 6\ NaNO_3(aq)$$

$$2\ PO_4^{3-}(aq) + 3\ Ni^{2+}(aq) \rightarrow Ni_3(PO_4)_2(s)$$

3.37 $FeCO_3(s) + 2\ HNO_3(aq) \rightarrow$
$$Fe(NO_3)_2(aq) + CO_2(g) + H_2O(\ell)$$

Iron(II) carbonate reacts with nitric acid to give iron(II) nitrate, carbon dioxide, and water.

3.39 $(NH_4)_2S(aq) + 2\ HBr(aq) \rightarrow 2\ NH_4Br(aq) + H_2S(g)$

Ammonium sulfide reacts with hydrobromic acid to give ammonium bromide and hydrogen sulfide.

3.41 (a) $Br = +5$ and $O = -2$
(b) $C = +3$ each and $O = -2$
(c) $F = -1$
(d) $Ca = +2$ and $H = -1$
(e) $H = +1$, $Si = +4$, and $O = -2$
(f) $H = +1$, $S = +6$, and $O = -2$

3.43 (a) Oxidation–reduction
Zn is oxidized from 0 to +2, and N in NO_3^- is reduced from +5 to +4 in NO_2.
(b) Acid–base reaction
(c) Oxidation–reduction

Calcium is oxidized from 0 to +2 in $Ca(OH)_2$, and H is reduced from +1 in H_2O to 0 in H_2.

3.45 (a) O_2 is the oxidizing agent (as it always is) and so C_2H_4 is the reducing agent. In this process, C_2H_4 is oxidized, and O_2 is reduced.

(b) Si is oxidized from 0 in Si to +4 in $SiCl_4$. Cl_2 is reduced from 0 in Cl_2 to -1 in Cl^-. Si is the reducing agent, and Cl_2 is the oxidizing agent.

3.47 (a) Acid–base
$Ba(OH)_2(aq) + 2\ HCl(aq) \rightarrow$
$$BaCl_2(aq) + 2\ H_2O(\ell)$$
(b) Gas-forming
$2\ HNO_3(aq) + CoCO_3(s) \rightarrow$
$$Co(NO_3)_2(aq) + H_2O(\ell) + CO_2(g)$$
(c) Precipitation
$2\ Na_3PO_4(aq) + 3\ Cu(NO_3)_2(aq) \rightarrow$
$$Cu_3(PO_4)_2(s) + 6\ NaNO_3(aq)$$

3.49 a) Precipitation
$$MnCl_2(aq) + Na_2S(aq) \rightarrow MnS(s) + 2\ NaCl(aq)$$
$$Mn^{2+}(aq) + S^{2-}(aq) \rightarrow MnS(s)$$
(b) Precipitation
$$K_2CO_3(aq) + ZnCl_2(aq) \rightarrow ZnCO_3(s) + 2\ KCl(aq)$$
$$CO_3^{2-}(aq) + Zn^{2+}(aq) \rightarrow ZnCO_3(s)$$

3.51 (a) $CuCl_2(aq) + H_2S(aq) \rightarrow CuS(s) + 2\ HCl(aq)$
precipitation
(b) $H_3PO_4(aq) + 3\ KOH(aq) \rightarrow$
$$3\ H_2O(\ell) + K_3PO_4(aq)$$
acid–base
(c) $Ca(s) + 2\ HBr(aq) \rightarrow H_2(g) + CaBr_2(aq)$
oxidation–reduction and gas-forming
(d) $MgCl_2(aq) + 2\ H_2O(\ell) \rightarrow$
$$Mg(OH)_2(s) + 2\ HCl(aq)$$
precipitation

3.53 (a) $CO_2(g) + 2\ NH_3(g) \rightarrow NH_2CONH_2(s) + H_2O(\ell)$
(b) $UO_2(s) + 4\ HF(aq) \rightarrow UF_4(s) + 2\ H_2O(\ell)$
$$UF_4(s) + F_2(g) \rightarrow UF_6(s)$$
(c) $TiO_2(s) + 2\ Cl_2(g) + 2\ C(s) \rightarrow$
$$TiCl_4(\ell) + 2\ CO(g)$$
$$TiCl_4(\ell) + 2\ Mg(s) \rightarrow Ti(s) + 2\ MgCl_2(s)$$

3.55 (a) NaBr, KBr, or other alkali metal bromides; Group 2A bromides; other metal bromides except AgBr, Hg_2Br_2, and $PbBr_2$
(b) $Al(OH)_3$ and transition metal hydroxides
(c) Alkaline earth carbonates ($CaCO_3$) or transition metal carbonates ($NiCO_3$)
(d) Metal nitrates are generally water-soluble [e.g., $NaNO_3$, $Ni(NO_3)_2$].
(e) CH_3CO_2H, other acids containing the $-CO_2H$ group

3.57 Water soluble: $Cu(NO_3)_2$, $CuCl_2$. Water-insoluble: $CuCO_3$, $Cu_3(PO_4)_2$

3.59 Spectator ion, NO_3^-. Acid–base reaction.

$$2 H_3O^+(aq) + Mg(OH)_2(s) \rightarrow 4 H_2O(\ell) + Mg^{2+}(aq)$$

3.61 (a) Cl_2 is reduced (to Cl^-) and Br^- is oxidized (to Br_2).

(b) Cl_2 is the oxidizing agent and Br^- is the reducing agent.

3.63 (a) $MgCO_3(s) + 2 H_3O^+(aq) \rightarrow$
$$CO_2(g) + Mg^{2+}(aq) + 3 H_2O(\ell)$$

Chloride ion (Cl^-) is the spectator ion.

(b) Gas-forming reaction

3.65 (a) H_2O, NH_3, NH_4^+, and OH^- (and a trace of H_3O^+)

weak Brønsted base

(b) H_2O, CH_3CO_2H, $CH_3CO_2^-$, and H_3O^+ (and a trace of OH^-)

weak Brønsted acid

(c) H_2O, Na^+, and OH^- (and a trace of H_3O^+)

strong Brønsted base

(d) H_2O, H_3O^+, and Br^- (and a trace of OH^-)

strong Brønsted acid

3.67 (a) $K_2CO_3(aq) + 2 HClO_4(aq) \rightarrow$
$$2 KClO_4(aq) + CO_2(g) + H_2O(\ell)$$
gas-forming

Potassium carbonate and perchloric acid react to form potassium perchlorate, carbon dioxide, and water

$$CO_3^{2-}(aq) + 2 H_3O^+(aq) \rightarrow CO_2(g) + 3 H_2O(\ell)$$

(b) $FeCl_2(aq) + (NH_4)_2S(aq) \rightarrow$
$$FeS(s) + 2 NH_4Cl(aq)$$
precipitation

Iron(II) chloride and ammonium sulfide react to form iron(II) sulfide and ammonium chloride

$$Fe^{2+}(aq) + S^{2-}(aq) \rightarrow FeS(s)$$

(c) $Fe(NO_3)_2(aq) + Na_2CO_3(aq) \rightarrow$
$$FeCO_3(s) + 2 NaNO_3(aq)$$
precipitation

Iron(II) nitrate and sodium carbonate react to form iron(II) carbonate and sodium nitrate

$$Fe^{2+}(aq) + CO_3^{2-}(aq) \rightarrow FeCO_3(s)$$

(d) $3 NaOH(aq) + FeCl_3(aq) \rightarrow$
$$3 NaCl(aq) + Fe(OH)_3(s)$$
precipitation

Sodium hydroxide and iron(III) chloride react to form sodium chloride and iron(III) hydroxide

$$3 OH^-(aq) + Fe^{3+}(aq) \rightarrow Fe(OH)_3(s)$$

3.69 (a) Reactants: $Na(+1)$, $I(-1)$, $H(+1)$, $S(+6)$, $O(-2)$, $Mn(+4)$

Products: $Na(+1)$, $S(+6)$, $O(-2)$, $Mn(+2)$, $I(0)$, $H(+1)$

(b) The oxidizing agent is MnO_2, and NaI is oxidized. The reducing agent is NaI, and MnO_2 is reduced.

(c) Based on the picture, the reaction is product-favored.

(d) Sodium iodide, sulfuric acid, and manganese(IV) oxide react to form sodium sulfate, manganese(II) sulfate, and water.

3.71 Among the reactions that could be used are the following:

$$MgCO_3(s) + 2 HCl(aq) \rightarrow$$
$$MgCl_2(aq) + CO_2(g) + H_2O(\ell)$$

$$MgS(s) + 2 HCl(aq) \rightarrow MgCl_2(aq) + H_2S(g)$$

$$MgSO_3(s) + 2 HCl(aq) \rightarrow$$
$$MgCl_2(aq) + SO_2(g) + H_2O(\ell)$$

In each case, the resulting solution could be evaporated to obtain the desired magnesium chloride.

3.73 The Ag^+ was reduced (to silver metal), and the glucose was oxidized (to $C_6H_{12}O_7$). The Ag^+ is the oxidizing agent, and the glucose is the reducing agent.

3.75 Weak electrolyte test: Compare the conductivity of a solution of lactic acid and that of an equal concentration of a strong acid. The conductivity of the lactic acid solution should be significantly less.

Reversible reaction: The fact that lactic acid is an electrolyte indicates that the reaction proceeds in the forward direction. To test whether the ionization is reversible, one could prepare a solution containing as much lactic acid as it will hold and then add a strong acid (to provide H_3O^+). If the reaction proceeds in the reverse direction, this will cause some lactic acid to precipitate.

3.77 (a) Several precipitation reactions are possible:

i. $BaCl_2(aq) + H_2SO_4(aq) \rightarrow$
$$BaSO_4(s) + 2 HCl(aq)$$

ii. $BaCl_2(aq) + Na_2SO_4(aq) \rightarrow$
$$BaSO_4(s) + 2 NaCl(aq)$$

iii. $Ba(OH)_2(aq) + H_2SO_4(aq) \rightarrow$
$$BaSO_4(s) + 2 H_2O(\ell)$$

(b) Gas-forming reaction:

$$BaCO_3(s) + H_2SO_4(aq) \rightarrow$$
$$BaSO_4(s) + CO_2(g) + H_2O(\ell)$$

4.1 4.5 mol O_2; 310 g Al_2O_3

4.3 22.7 g Br_2; 25.3 g Al_2Br_6

4.5 (a) CO_2, carbon dioxide, and H_2O, water
(b) $CH_4(g) + 2\,O_2(g) \rightarrow CO_2(g) + 2\,H_2O(\ell)$
(c) 102 g O_2
(d) 128 g products

4.7

Equation	$2\,PbS(s)$	$+\;3\,O_2(g)$	$\rightarrow\;2\,PbO(s)$	$+\;2\,SO_2(g)$
Initial (mol)	2.5	3.8	0	0
Change (mol)	-2.5	$-\frac{3}{2}(2.5)$ $= -3.8$	$+\frac{2}{2}(2.5)$ $= +2.5$	$+\frac{2}{2}(2.5)$ $= +2.5$
Final (mol)	0	0	2.5	2.5

The amounts table shows that 2.5 mol of PbS requires $\frac{3}{2}(2.5) = 3.8$ mol of O_2 and produces 2.5 mol of PbO and 2.5 mol of SO_2.

4.9 (a) Balanced equation: $4\,Cr(s) + 3\,O_2(g) \rightarrow 2\,Cr_2O_3(s)$
(b) 0.175 g of Cr is equivalent to 0.00337 mol

Equation	$4\,Cr(s)$	$+\;3\,O_2(g)$	$\rightarrow$	$2\,Cr_2O_3(s)$
Initial (mol)	0.00337	0.00252 mol		0
Change (mol)	-0.00337	$-\frac{3}{4}(0.00337)$ $= -0.00252$		$\frac{2}{4}(0.00337)$ $= +0.00168$
Final (mol)	0	0		0.00168

The 0.00168 mol Cr_2O_3 produced corresponds to 0.256 g Cr_2O_3.
(c) 0.081 g O_2

4.11 0.11 mol of Na_2SO_4 and 0.62 mol of C are mixed. Sodium sulfate is the limiting reactant. Therefore, 0.11 mol of Na_2S is formed, or 8.2 g.

4.13 F_2 is the limiting reactant.

4.15 (a) CH_4 is the limiting reactant.
(b) 375 g H_2
(c) Excess $H_2O = 1390$ g

4.17 (a) $2\,C_6H_{14}(\ell) + 19\,O_2(g) \rightarrow 12\,CO_2(g) + 14\,H_2O(g)$
(b) O_2 is the limiting reactant. Products are 187 g of CO_2 and 89.2 g of H_2O.
(c) 154 g of hexane remains
(d)

Equation	$2\,C_6H_{14}(\ell)$	$+\;19\,O_2(g)$	$\rightarrow\;12\,CO_2(g)$	$+\;14\,H_2O(g)$
Initial (mol)	2.49	6.72	0	0
Change (mol)	-0.707	-6.72	$+4.24$	$+4.95$
Final (mol)	1.78	0	4.24	4.95

4.19 $(332\ \text{g}/407\ \text{g})100\% = 81.6\%$

4.21 (a) 14.3 g $Cu(NH_3)_4SO_4$
(b) 88.3% yield

4.23 91.9% hydrate

4.25 84.3% $CaCO_3$

4.27 1.467% Tl_2SO_4

4.29 Empirical formula = CH

4.31 Empirical formula = CH_2; molecular formula = C_5H_{10}

4.33 Empirical formula = CH_3O; molecular formula = $C_2H_6O_2$

4.35 $Ni(CO)_4$

4.37 $[Na_2CO_3] = 0.254$ M; $[Na^+] = 0.508$ M; $[CO_3^{2-}] = 0.254$ M

4.39 0.494 g $KMnO_4$

4.41 5.08×10^3 mL

4.43 (a) 0.50 M NH_4^+ and 0.25 M SO_4^{2-}
(b) 0.246 M Na^+ and 0.123 M CO_3^{2-}
(c) 0.056 M H^+ and 0.056 M NO_3^-

4.45 A mass of 1.06 g of Na_2CO_3 is required. After weighing out this quantity of Na_2CO_3, transfer it to a 500.-mL volumetric flask. Rinse any solid from the neck of the flask while filling the flask with distilled water. Dissolve the solute in water. Add water until the bottom of the meniscus of the water is at the top of the scribed mark on the neck of the flask. Thoroughly mix the solution.

4.47 0.0750 M

4.49 Method (a) is correct. Method (b) gives an acid concentration of 0.15 M.

4.51 0.00340 M

4.53 $[H_3O^+] = 10^{-pH} = 4.0 \times 10^{-4}$ M; the solution is acidic.

4.55 HNO_3 is a strong acid, so $[H_3O^+] = 0.0013$ M. pH = 2.89.

4.57

	pH	$[H_3O^+]$	Acidic/Basic
(a)	1.00	0.10 M	Acidic
(b)	10.50	3.2×10^{-11} M	Basic
(c)	4.89	1.3×10^{-5} M	Acidic
(d)	7.64	2.3×10^{-8} M	Basic

4.59 268 mL

4.61 210 g NaOH and 190 g Cl_2

4.63 174 mL of $Na_2S_2O_3$

4.65 1.50×10^3 mL of $Pb(NO_3)_2$

4.67 44.6 mL

4.69 1.052 M HCl

4.71 104 g/mol

4.73 12.8% Fe

4.75

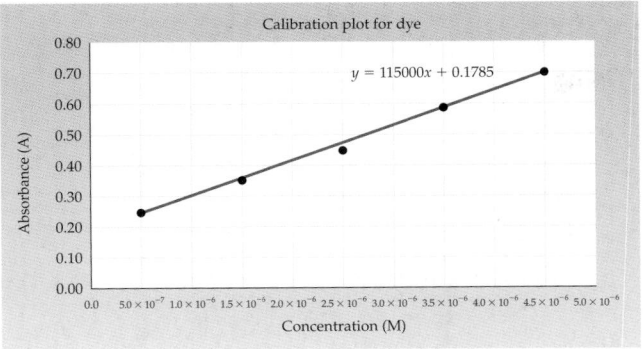

(a) slope = 1.2×10^5 M^{-1}; y-intercept = 0.18 M
(b) 3.0×10^{-6} M

4.77 (a) Products = $CO_2(g)$ and $H_2O(g)$
(b) $2\,C_6H_6(\ell) + 15\,O_2(g) \rightarrow 12\,CO_2(g) + 6\,H_2O(g)$
(c) 49.28 g O_2
(d) 65.32 g products (= sum of C_6H_6 mass and O_2 mass)

4.79 0.28 g arginine, 0.21 g ornithine

4.81 (a) titanium(IV) chloride, water, titanium(IV) oxide, hydrogen chloride
(b) 4.60 g H_2O
(c) 10.2 TiO_2, 18.6 g HCl

4.83 8.33 g NaN_3

4.85 Mass percent saccharin = 75.92%

4.87 SiH_4

4.89 C_3H_2O

4.91 1.85 kg H_2SO_4

4.93 The calculated molar mass of the metal is 1.2×10^2 g/mol. The metal is probably tin (118.67 g/mol).

4.95 479 kg Cl_2

4.97 66.5 kg CaO

4.99 1.29 g C_4H_8 (45.1%) and 1.57 g C_4H_{10} (54.9%)

4.101 62.2% Cu_2S and 26.8% CuS

4.103 (a) $MgCO_3(s) + 2\,H_3O^+(aq) \rightarrow$
$CO_2(g) + Mg^{2+}(aq) + 2\,H_2O(\ell)$
(b) Gas-forming reaction
(c) 0.15 g

4.105 15.0 g of $NaHCO_3$ require 1190 mL of 0.15 M acetic acid. Therefore, acetic acid is the limiting reactant. (Conversely, 125 mL of 0.15 M acetic acid requires only 1.58 g of $NaHCO_3$.) 1.54 g of $NaCH_3CO_2$ produced.

4.107 3.13 g $Na_2S_2O_3$, 96.8%

4.109 (a) pH = 0.979
(b) $[H_3O^+]$ = 0.0028 M; the solution is acidic.
(c) $[H_3O^+]$ = 2.1×10^{-10} M; the solution is basic.
(d) The new solution's concentration is 0.102 M HCl; the pH = 0.990

4.111 The concentration of hydrochloric acid is 2.92 M; the pH is −0.465

4.113 1.56 g of $CaCO_3$ required; 1.00 g $CaCO_3$ remain; 1.73 g $CaCl_2$ produced.

4.115 Volume of water in the pool = 7.6×10^4 L

4.117 (a) Au, gold, has been oxidized and is the reducing agent.

O$_2$, oxygen, has been reduced and is the oxidizing agent.

(b) 26 L NaCN solution

4.119 The concentration of Na_2CO_3 in the first solution prepared is 0.0275 M, in the second solution prepared the concentration of Na_2CO_3 is 0.00110 M.

4.121 (a) First reaction: oxidizing agent = Cu^{2+} and reducing agent = I^-

Second reaction: oxidizing agent = I_3^- and reducing agent = $S_2O_3^{2-}$

(b) 67.3% copper

4.123 $x = 6$; $Co(NH_3)_6Cl_3$.

4.125 11.48% 2,4-D

4.127 3.3 mol H_2O/mol $CaCl_2$

4.129 (a) Slope = 2.06×10^5; 0.024
(b) 1.20×10^{-4} g/L
(c) 0.413 mg PO_4^{3-}

4.131 The total mass of the beakers and products after reaction is equal to the total mass before the reaction (161.170 g) because no gases were produced in the reaction and there is conservation of mass in chemical reactions.

4.133 The balanced chemical equation indicates that the stoichiometric ratio of HCl to Zn is 2 mol HCl/1 mol Zn. In each reaction, there is 0.100 mol of HCl present. In reaction 1, there is 0.107 mol of Zn present. This gives a 0.93 mole HCl/mol Zn ratio, indicating that HCl is the limiting reactant. In reaction 2, there is 0.050 mol of Zn, giving a 2.0 mol HCl/mol Zn ratio. This indicates that the two reactants are present in exactly the correct stoichiometric ratio. In reaction 3, there is 0.020 mol of Zn, giving a 5.0 mol HCl/mol Zn ratio. This indicates that the HCl is present in excess and that the zinc is the limiting reactant.

4.135 If both students base their calculations on the amount of HCl solution pipeted into the flask (20 mL), then the second student's result will be (e), the same as the first student's. However, if the HCl concentration is calculated using the diluted solution volume, student 1 will use a volume of 40 mL, and student 2 will use a volume of 80 mL in the calculation. The second student's result will be (c), half that of the first student's.

4.137 150 mg/dL. Person is intoxicated.

CHAPTER 5

5.1 Mechanical energy is used to move the lever, which in turn moves gears. The device produces electrical energy and radiant energy.

5.3 5.0×10^6 J

5.5 170 kcal is equivalent to 710 kJ, considerably greater than 280 kJ.

5.7 0.140 J/g · K

5.9 2.44 kJ

5.11 32.8 °C

5.13 20.7 °C

5.15 47.8 °C

5.17 0.40 J/g · K

5.19 330 kJ

5.21 49.3 kJ

5.23 273 J

5.25 9.97×10^5 J

5.27 Reaction is exothermic because $\Delta_r H°$ is negative. The heat evolved is 2.38 kJ.

5.29 3.3×10^4 kJ

5.31 $\Delta H = -56$ kJ/mol CsOH

5.33 0.52 J/g · K

5.35 $\Delta_r H = +23$ kJ/mol-rxn

5.37 297 kJ/mol SO_2

5.39 3.09×10^3 kJ/mol $C_6H_5CO_2H$

5.41 0.236 J/g · K

5.43 (a) $\Delta_r H° = -126$ kJ/mol-rxn
(b)

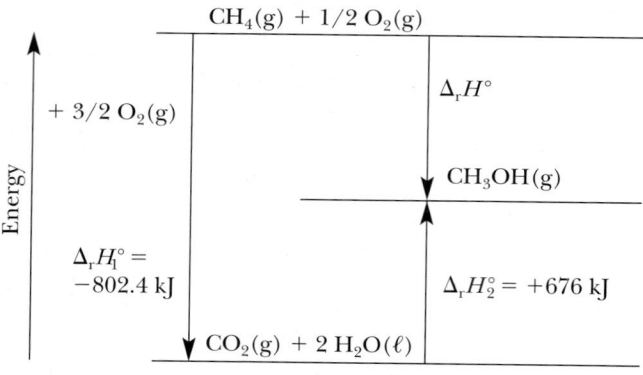

5.45 $\Delta_r H° = +90.3$ kJ/mol-rxn

5.47 $C(s) + 2 H_2(g) + 1/2 O_2(g) \rightarrow CH_3OH(\ell)$

$\Delta_f H° = -238.4$ kJ/mol

5.49 (a) $2 Cr(s) + 3/2 O_2(g) \rightarrow Cr_2O_3(s)$

$\Delta_f H° = -1134.7$ kJ/mol

(b) 2.4 g is equivalent to 0.046 mol of Cr. This will produce 26 kJ of energy transferred as heat.

5.51 (a) $\Delta H° = -24$ kJ for 1.0 g of phosphorus
(b) $\Delta H° = -18$ kJ for 0.2 mol NO
(c) $\Delta H° = -16.9$ kJ for the formation of 2.40 g of NaCl(s)
(d) $\Delta H° = -1.8 \times 10^3$ kJ for the oxidation of 250 g of iron

5.53 (a) $\Delta_r H° = -906.2$ kJ
(b) The heat evolved is 133 kJ for the oxidation of 10.0 g of NH_3

5.55 (a) $\Delta_r H° = +161.6$ kJ/mol-rxn; the reaction is endothermic.
(b)

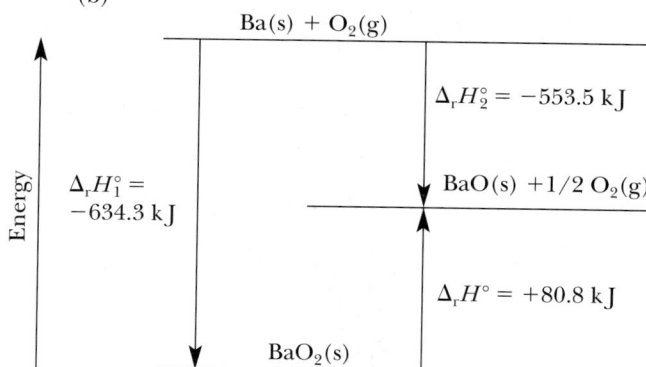

5.57 $\Delta_f H° = +77.7$ kJ/mol for naphthalene

5.59 (a) Exothermic: a process in which energy is transferred as heat from a system to its surroundings. (The combustion of methane is exothermic.)

Endothermic: a process in which energy is transferred as heat from the surroundings to the system. (Ice melting is endothermic.)

(b) System: the object or collection of objects being studied. (A chemical reaction—the system—taking place inside a calorimeter—the surroundings.)

Surroundings: everything outside the system that can exchange mass or energy with the system. (The calorimeter and everything outside the calorimeter comprise the surroundings.)

(c) Specific heat capacity: the quantity of energy that must be transferred as heat to raise the temperature of 1 gram of a substance 1 kelvin. (The specific heat capacity of water is 4.184 J/g · K.)

(d) State function: a quantity that is characterized by changes that do not depend on the path chosen to go from the initial state to the final state. (Enthalpy and internal energy are state functions.)

(e) Standard state: the most stable form of a substance in the physical state that exists at a pressure of 1 bar and at a specified temperature. (The standard state of carbon at 25 °C is graphite.)

(f) Enthalpy change, ΔH: the energy transferred as heat at constant pressure. (The enthalpy change for melting ice at 0 °C is 6.00 kJ/mol.)

(g) Standard enthalpy of formation: the enthalpy change for the formation of 1 mol of a compound in its standard state directly from the component elements in their standard states. ($\Delta_f H°$ for liquid water is −285.83 kJ/mol)

5.61 (a) System: reaction between methane and oxygen

Surroundings: the furnace and the rest of the universe. Energy is transferred as heat from the system to the surroundings.

(b) System: water drops

Surroundings: skin and the rest of the universe

Energy is transferred as heat from the surroundings to the system

(c) System: water

Surroundings: freezer and the rest of the universe

Energy is transferred as heat from the system to the surroundings

(d) System: reaction of aluminum and iron(III) oxide

Surroundings: flask, laboratory bench, and rest of the universe

Energy is transferred as heat from the system to the surroundings.

5.63 Standard state of oxygen is gas, $O_2(g)$.

$$O_2(g) \rightarrow 2\ O(g),\ \Delta_r H° = +498.34\ \text{kJ, endothermic}$$

$$3/2\ O_2(g) \rightarrow O_3(g),\ \Delta_r H° = +142.67\ \text{kJ}$$

5.65

$SnBr_2(s) + TiCl_2(s) \rightarrow SnCl_2(s) + TiBr_2(s)$	$\Delta_r H° = -4.2$ kJ	
$SnCl_2(s) + Cl_2(g) \rightarrow SnCl_4(\ell)$	$\Delta_r H° = -195$ kJ	
$TiCl_4(\ell) \rightarrow TiCl_2(s) + Cl_2(g)$	$\Delta_r H° = +273$ kJ	
$SnBr_2(s) + TiCl_4(\ell) \rightarrow SnCl_4(\ell) + TiBr_2(s)$	$\Delta_r H° = +74$ kJ	

5.67 $C_{Ag} = 0.24$ J/g · K

5.69 Mass of ice melted = 75.4 g

5.71 Final temperature = 278 K (4.8 °C)

5.73 (a) When summed, the following equations give the balanced equation for the formation of $B_2H_6(g)$ from the elements.

$2\ B(s) + 3/2\ O_2(g) \rightarrow B_2O_3(s)$	$\Delta_r H° = -1271.9$ kJ
$3\ H_2(g) + 3/2\ O_2(g) \rightarrow 3\ H_2O(g)$	$\Delta_r H° = -725.4$ kJ
$B_2O_3(s) + 3\ H_2O(g) \rightarrow B_2H_6(g) + 3\ O_2(g)$	$\Delta_r H° = +2032.9$ kJ
$2\ B(s) + 3\ H_2(g) \rightarrow B_2H_6(g)$	$\Delta_r H° = +35.6$ kJ

(b) The enthalpy of formation of $B_2H_6(g)$ is +35.6 kJ/mol

(c)

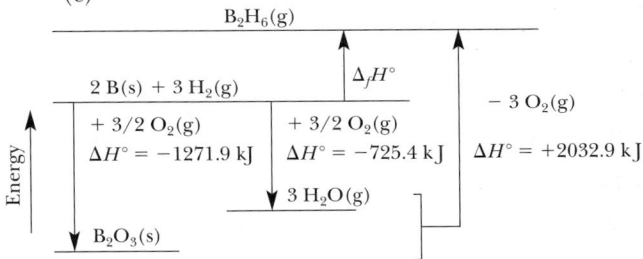

(d) The formation of $B_2H_6(g)$ is reactant-favored.

5.75 (a) $\Delta_r H° = +131.31$ kJ
(b) Reactant-favored
(c) 1.0932×10^7 kJ

5.77 Assuming $CO_2(g)$ and $H_2O(\ell)$ are the products of combustion:

$\Delta_r H°$ for isooctane is −5461.3 kJ/mol or −47.81 kJ per gram

$\Delta_r H°$ for liquid methanol is −726.77 kJ/mol or −22.682 kJ per gram

5.79 (a) Adding the equations as they are given in the question results in the desired equation for the formation of $SrCO_3(s)$. The calculated $\Delta_r H° = -1220.$ kJ/mol.

(b)

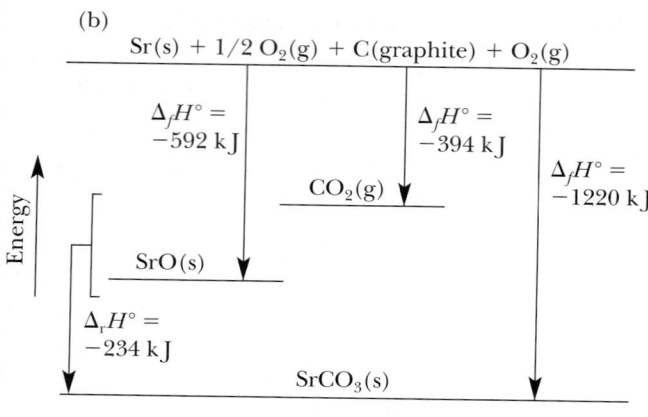

5.81 $\Delta_r H° = -305.3$ kJ

5.83 $C_{Pb} = 0.121$ J/g · K

5.85 $\Delta_r H = -69$ kJ/mol AgCl

5.87 36.0 kJ evolved per mol of NH_4NO_3

5.89 The standard enthalpy change, $\Delta_r H°$, is -352.88 kJ. The quantity of magnesium needed is 0.43 g.

5.91 (a) product-favored
(b) reactant-favored

5.93 The enthalpy change for each of the three reactions below is known or can be measured by calorimetry. The three equations sum to give the enthalpy of formation of $CaSO_4(s)$.

$$Ca(s) + 1/2\ O_2(g) \rightarrow CaO(s) \qquad \Delta_r H° = \Delta_f H°$$
$$= -635.09\ kJ$$

$$1/8\ S_8(s) + 3/2\ O_2(g) \rightarrow SO_3(g) \qquad \Delta_r H° = \Delta_f H°$$
$$= -395.77\ kJ$$

$$CaO(s) + SO_3(g) \rightarrow CaSO_4(s) \qquad \Delta_r H° = -402.7\ kJ$$

$$Ca(s) + 1/8\ S_8(s) + 2\ O_2(g) \rightarrow CaSO_4(s) \qquad \Delta_r H° = \Delta_f H°$$
$$= -1433.6\ kJ$$

5.95

Metal	Molar Heat Capacity (J/mol · K)
Al	24.2
Fe	25.1
Cu	24.5
Au	25.4

All the metals have a molar heat capacity of 24.8 J/mol · K plus or minus 0.6 J/mol · K. Therefore, assuming the molar heat capacity of Ag is 24.8 J/mol · K, its specific heat capacity is 0.230 J/g · K. This is very close to the experimental value of 0.236 J/g · K.

5.97 120 g of CH_4 required (assuming $H_2O(g)$ as product)

5.99 1.6×10^{11} kJ released to the surroundings. This is equivalent to 3.8×10^4 tons of dynamite.

5.101 (a)

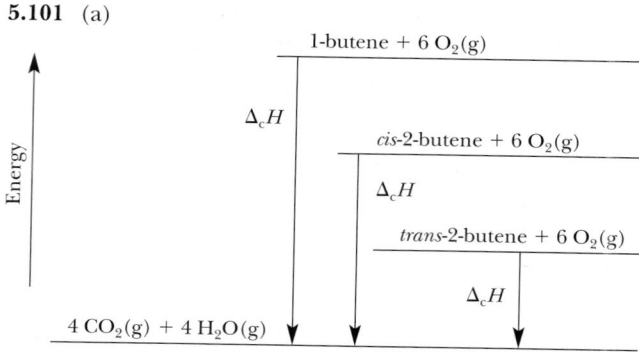

(b) *cis*-2-butene: $\Delta_f H° = 146.1$ kJ/mol

trans-2-butene: $\Delta_f H° = 142.8$ kJ/mol

1-butene: $\Delta_f H° = 155.3$ kJ/mol

(c)

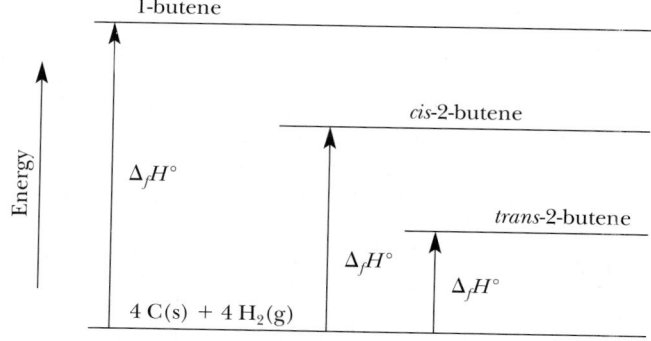

(d) -3.3 kJ/mol-rxn

5.103 (a) -726 kJ/mol Mg
(b) 25.0 °C

5.105 (a) Methane
(b) Methane
(c) -279 kJ
(d) $CH_4(g) + 2\ O_2(g) \rightarrow CH_3OH(\ell)$

5.107 (a) Metal Heated = 100.0 g of Al; Metal Cooled = 50.0 g of Au; Final Temperature = 26 °C
(b) Metal Heated = 50.0 g of Zn; Metal Cooled = 50.0 g of Al; Final Temperature = 21 °C

CHAPTER 6

6.1 (a) microwaves
(b) red light
(c) infrared

6.3 (a) Green light has a higher frequency than amber light
(b) 5.04×10^{14} s^{-1}

6.5 Frequency = 6.0×10^{14} s^{-1}; energy per photon = 4.0×10^{-19} J; energy per mol of photons = 2.4×10^5 J

6.7 Frequency $= 7.5676 \times 10^{14}$ s^{-1}; energy per photon $= 5.0144 \times 10^{-19}$ J; 302 kJ/mol of photons

6.9 In order of increasing energy: FM station < microwaves < yellow light < x-rays

6.11 Light with a wavelength as long as 600 nm would be sufficient. This is in the visible region.

6.13 (a) The light of shortest wavelength has a wavelength of 253.652 nm.
(b) Frequency $= 1.18190 \times 10^{15}$ s^{-1}. Energy per photon $= 7.83139 \times 10^{-19}$ J/photon.
(c) The lines at 404 (violet) and 436 nm (blue) are in the visible region of the spectrum.

6.15 The color is violet. $n_{initial} = 6$ and $n_{final} = 2$

6.17 (a) 10 lines possible
(b) Highest frequency (highest energy), $n = 5$ to $n = 1$
(c) Longest wavelength (lowest energy), $n = 5$ to $n = 4$

6.19 (a) $n = 3$ to $n = 2$
(b) $n = 4$ to $n = 1$; The energy levels are progressively closer at higher levels, so the energy difference from $n = 4$ to $n = 1$ is greater than from $n = 5$ to $n = 2$.

6.21 Wavelength $= 102.6$ nm and frequency $= 2.923 \times 10^{15}$ s^{-1}. Light with these properties is in the ultraviolet region.

6.23 Wavelength $= 0.29$ nm

6.25 The wavelength is 2.2×10^{-25} nm. (Calculated from $\lambda = h/m \cdot v$, where m is the ball's mass in kg and v is the velocity.) To have a wavelength of 5.6×10^{-3} nm, the ball would have to travel at 1.2×10^{-21} m/s.

6.27 (a) $n = 4$, $\ell = 0, 1, 2, 3$
(b) When $\ell = 2$, $m_\ell = -2, -1, 0, 1, 2$
(c) For a 4s orbital, $n = 4$, $\ell = 0$, and $m_\ell = 0$
(d) For a 4f orbital, $n = 4$, $\ell = 3$, and $m_\ell = -3, -2, -1, 0, 1, 2, 3$

6.29 Set 1: $n = 4$, $\ell = 1$, and $m_\ell = -1$

Set 2: $n = 4$, $\ell = 1$, and $m_\ell = 0$

Set 3: $n = 4$, $\ell = 1$, and $m_\ell = +1$

6.31 Four subshells. (The number of subshells in a shell is always equal to n.)

6.33 (a) ℓ must have a value no greater than $n - 1$.
(b) When $\ell = 0$, m_ℓ can only equal 0.
(c) When $\ell = 0$, m_ℓ can only equal 0.

6.35 (a) None. The quantum number set is not possible. When $\ell = 0$, m_ℓ can only equal 0.
(b) 3 orbitals
(c) 11 orbitals
(d) 1 orbital

6.37 (a) $m_s = 0$ is not possible. m_s may only have values of $\pm 1/2$.

One possible set of quantum numbers: $n = 4$, $\ell = 2$, $m_\ell = 0$, $m_s = +1/2$

(b) m_ℓ cannot equal -3 in this case. If $\ell = 1$, m_ℓ can only be -1, 0, or 1.

One possible set of quantum numbers: $n = 3$, $\ell = 1$, $m_\ell = -1$, $m_s = -1/2$

(c) $\ell = 3$ is not possible in this case. The maximum value of ℓ is $n - 1$.

One possible set of quantum numbers: $n = 3$, $\ell = 2$, $m_\ell = -1$, $m_s = +1/2$

6.39 2d and 3f orbitals cannot exist. The $n = 2$ shell consists only of s and p subshells. The $n = 3$ shell consists only of s, p, and d subshells.

6.41 (a) For 2p: $n = 2$, $\ell = 1$, and $m_\ell = -1$, 0, or $+1$
(b) For 3d: $n = 3$, $\ell = 2$, and $m_\ell = -2, -1, 0, +1$, or $+2$
(c) For 4f: $n = 4$, $\ell = 3$, and $m_\ell = -3, -2, -1, 0, +1, +2$, or $+3$

6.43 4d

6.45 (a) 2s has 0 nodal surfaces that pass through the nucleus ($\ell = 0$).
(b) 5d has 2 nodal surfaces that pass through the nucleus ($\ell = 2$).
(c) 5f has three nodal surfaces that pass through the nucleus ($\ell = 3$).

6.47 (a) Correct
(b) Incorrect. The intensity of a light beam is independent of frequency and is related to the number of photons of light with a certain energy.
(c) Correct

6.49 Considering only angular nodes (nodal surfaces that pass through the nucleus):

s orbital	0 nodal surfaces
p orbitals	1 nodal surface or plane passing through the nucleus
d orbitals	2 nodal surfaces or planes passing through the nucleus
f orbitals	3 nodal surfaces or planes passing through the nucleus

6.51

ℓ value	Orbital Type
3	f
0	s
1	p
2	d

6.53 Considering only angular nodes (nodal surfaces that pass through the nucleus):

Orbital Type	Number of Orbitals in a Given Subshell	Number of Nodal Surfaces
s	1	0
p	3	1
d	5	2
f	7	3

6.55 (a) Green light
(b) Red light has a wavelength of 680 nm, and green light has a wavelength of 500 nm.
(c) Green light has a higher frequency than red light.

6.57 (a) Wavelength = 0.35 m
(b) Energy = 0.34 J/mol
(c) Blue light (with λ = 420 nm) has an energy of 280 kJ/mol of photons.
(d) Blue light has an energy (per mol of photons) that is 840,000 times greater than a mole of photons from a cell phone.

6.59 The ionization energy for He^+ is 5248 kJ/mol. This is four times the ionization energy for the H atom.

6.61 $1s < 2s = 2p < 3s = 3p = 3d < 4s$

In the H atom orbitals in the same shell (e.g., $2s$ and $2p$) have the same energy.

6.63 Frequency = 2.836×10^{20} s^{-1} and wavelength = 1.057×10^{-12} m

6.65 260 s or 4.3 min

6.67 (a) size and energy
(b) ℓ
(c) more
(d) 7 (when ℓ = 3 these are f orbitals)
(e) one orbital
(f) (left to right) d, s, and p
(g) ℓ = 0, 1, 2, 3, 4
(h) 16 orbitals ($1s$, $3p$, $5d$, and $7f$) ($= n^2$)
(i) paramagnetic

6.69 (a) Drawing (a) is a ferromagnetic solid, (b) is a diamagnetic solid, and (c) is a paramagnetic solid.
(b) Substance (a) would be most strongly attracted to a magnet, whereas (b) would be least strongly attracted.

6.71 The pickle glows because it was made by soaking a cucumber in brine, a concentrated solution of NaCl. The sodium atoms in the pickle are excited by the electric current and release energy as yellow light as they return to the ground state. Excited sodium atoms are the source of the yellow light you see in fireworks and in certain kinds of street lighting.

6.73 (a) λ = 0.0005 cm = 5 μm
(b) The left side is the higher energy side, and the right side is the lower energy side.
(c) The interaction with O—H requires more energy.

6.75 (c)

6.77 An experiment can be done that shows that the electron can behave as a particle, and another experiment can be done to show that it has wave properties. (However, no single experiment shows both properties of the electron.) The modern view of atomic structure is based on the wave properties of the electron.

6.79 (a) and (b)

6.81 Radiation with a wavelength of 93.8 nm is sufficient to raise the electron to the n = 6 quantum level (see Figure 6.10). There should be 15 emission lines involving transitions from n = 6 to lower energy levels. (There are five lines for transitions from n = 6 to lower levels, four lines for n = 5 to lower levels, three for n = 4 to lower levels, two lines for n = 3 to lower levels, and one line for n = 2 to n = 1.) Wavelengths for many of the lines are given in Figure 6.10. For example, there will be an emission involving an electron moving from n = 6 to n = 2 with a wavelength of 410.2 nm.

6.83 (a) Group 7B (IUPAC Group 7); Period 5
(b) n = 5, ℓ = 0, m_ℓ = 0, m_s = +1/2
(c) λ = 8.79×10^{-12} m; ν = 3.41×10^{19} s^{-1}
(d) (i) $HTcO_4(aq) + NaOH(aq) \rightarrow$
$H_2O(\ell) + NaTcO_4(aq)$
(ii) 8.5×10^{-3} g $NaTcO_4$ produced;
1.8×10^{-3} g NaOH needed
(e) 0.28 mg $NaTcO_4$; 0.00015 M

6.85 Six emission lines are observed. More than one line is observed because the following changes in energy levels are possible: from n = 4 to n = 3, n = 2, and n = 1 (three lines), from n = 3 to n = 2 and n = 1 (2 lines), and from n = 2 to n = 1 (one line).

CHAPTER 7

7.1 (a) Phosphorus: $1s^2 2s^2 2p^6 3s^2 3p^3$

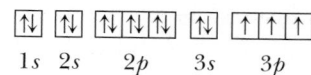
1s 2s 2p 3s 3p

The element is in the third period in Group 5A. Therefore, it has five electrons in the third shell.
(b) Chlorine: $1s^2 2s^2 2p^6 3s^2 3p^5$

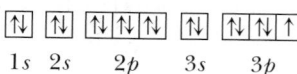
1s 2s 2p 3s 3p

The element is in the third period and in Group 7A. Therefore, it has seven electrons in the third shell.

7.3 (a) Chromium: $1s^2 2s^2 2p^6 3s^2 3p^6 3d^5 4s^1$
(b) Iron: $1s^2 2s^2 2p^6 3s^2 3p^6 3d^6 4s^2$

7.5 (a) Arsenic: $1s^2 2s^2 2p^6 3s^2 3p^6 3d^{10} 4s^2 4p^3$;
$[Ar]3d^{10}4s^2 4p^3$
(b) Krypton: $1s^2 2s^2 2p^6 3s^2 3p^6 3d^{10} 4s^2 4p^6$;
$[Ar]3d^{10}4s^2 4p^6 = [Kr]$

7.7 (a) Tantalum: This is the third element in the transition series in the sixth period. Therefore, it has a core equivalent to Xe plus two 6s electrons, 14 4f electrons, and three electrons in 5d:
$[Xe]4f^{14}5d^3 6s^2$
(b) Platinum: This is the eighth element in the transition series in the sixth period. Therefore, it is predicted to have a core equivalent to Xe plus two 6s electrons, 14 4f electrons, and eight electrons in 5d: $[Xe]4f^{14}5d^8 6s^2$. In reality, its actual configuration (Table 7.3) is $[Xe]4f^{14}5d^9 6s^1$.

7.9 Americium: $[Rn]5f^7 7s^2$ (see Table 7.3)

7.11 (a) 2
(b) 1
(c) none (because ℓ cannot equal n)

7.13 Magnesium: $1s^2 2s^2 2p^6 3s^2$

[Ne] ⇅
3s

Quantum numbers for the two electrons in the 3s orbital:

$n = 3$, $\ell = 0$, $m_\ell = 0$, and $m_s = +1/2$

$n = 3$, $\ell = 0$, $m_\ell = 0$, and $m_s = -1/2$

7.15 Gallium: $1s^2 2s^2 2p^6 3s^2 3p^6 3d^{10} 4s^2 4p^1$

[Ar] ⇅⇅⇅⇅⇅ ⇅ ↑
       3d   4s 4p

Quantum numbers for the 4p electron:

$n = 4$, $\ell = 1$, $m_\ell = -1, 0,$ or $+1$, and $m_s = +\frac{1}{2}$ or $-\frac{1}{2}$

7.17 (a) Mg^{2+} ion

⇅ ⇅ ⇅⇅⇅
1s 2s 2p

(b) K^+ ion

⇅ ⇅ ⇅⇅⇅ ⇅ ⇅⇅⇅
1s 2s 2p   3s 3p

(c) Cl^- ion (Note that both Cl^- and K^+ have the same configuration; both are equivalent to Ar.)

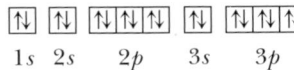

⇅ ⇅ ⇅⇅⇅ ⇅ ⇅⇅⇅
1s 2s 2p   3s 3p

(d) O^{2-} ion

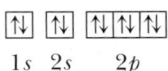

⇅ ⇅ ⇅⇅⇅
1s 2s 2p

7.19 (a) V (paramagnetic; three unpaired electrons)

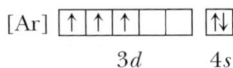

[Ar] ↑ ↑ ↑ □ □   ⇅
        3d   4s

(b) V^{2+} ion (paramagnetic, three unpaired electrons)

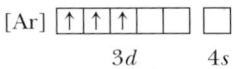

[Ar] ↑ ↑ ↑ □ □   □
        3d   4s

(c) V^{5+} ion. This ion has an electron configuration equivalent to argon, [Ar]. It is diamagnetic with no unpaired electrons.

7.21 (a) Manganese

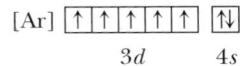

[Ar] ↑ ↑ ↑ ↑ ↑   ⇅
        3d   4s

(b) Mn^{4+}

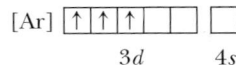

[Ar] ↑ ↑ ↑ □ □   □
        3d   4s

(c) The 4^+ ion is paramagnetic to the extent of three unpaired electrons.
(d) 3

7.23 Increasing size: C < B < Al < Na < K

7.25 (a) Cl^-
(b) Al
(c) In

7.27 (c)

7.29 (a) Largest radius, Na
(b) Most negative electron affinity: O
(c) Ionization energy: Na < Mg < P < O

7.31 (a) Increasing ionization energy: S < O < F. S is less than O because the IE decreases down a group. F is greater than O because IE generally increases across a period.
(b) Largest IE: O. IE decreases down a group.
(c) Most negative electron affinity: Cl. Electron affinity becomes more negative across the periodic table and on ascending a group.
(d) Largest Size: O^{2-}. Negative ions are larger than their corresponding neutral atoms. F^- is thus larger than F. O^{2-} and F^- are isoelectronic, but the O^{2-} ion has only eight protons in its nucleus to attract the 10 electrons, whereas the F^- has nine protons, making the O^{2-} ion larger.

7.33 Uranium configuration: $[Rn]5f^36d^17s^2$

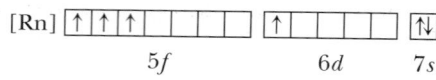

Uranium(IV) ion, U^{4+}: $[Rn]5f^2$

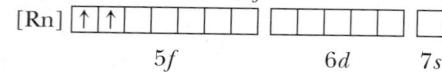

Both U and U^{4+} are paramagnetic.

7.35 (a) Atomic number = 20
(b) Total number of s electrons = 8
(c) Total number of p electrons = 12
(d) Total number of d electrons = 0
(e) The element is Ca, calcium, a metal.

7.37 (a) Valid. Possible elements are Li and Be.
(b) Not valid. The maximum value of ℓ is $(n - 1)$.
(c) Valid. Possible elements are B through Ne.
(d) Valid. Possible elements are Y through Cd.

7.39 (a) Neodymium, Nd: $[Xe]4f^46s^2$ (Table 7.3)

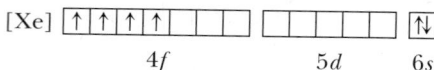

Iron, Fe: $[Ar]3d^64s^2$

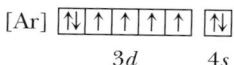

Boron, B: $[He]2s^22p^1$

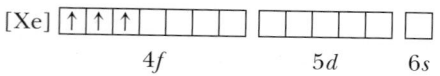

(b) All three elements have unpaired electrons and so should be paramagnetic.
(c) Neodymium(III) ion, Nd^{3+}: $[Xe]4f^3$

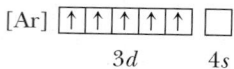

Iron(III) ion, Fe^{3+}: $[Ar]3d^5$

Both neodymium(III) and iron(III) have unpaired electrons and are paramagnetic.

7.41 K < Ca < Si < P

7.43 (a) metal
(b) B
(c) A
(d) A
(e) Rb_2Se

7.45 In^{4+}: Indium has three outer shell electrons and so is unlikely to form a 4^+ ion.

Fe^{6+}: Although iron has eight electrons in its $3d$ and $4s$ orbitals, ions with a 6^+ charge are highly unlikely. The ionization energy is too large.

Sn^{5+}: Tin has four outer shell electrons and so is unlikely to form a 5^+ ion.

7.47 (a) Se
(b) Br^-
(c) Na
(d) N
(e) N^{3-}

7.49 (a) Na
(b) C
(c) Na < Al < B < C

7.51 (a) Cobalt
(b) Paramagnetic
(c) Four unpaired electrons

7.53 (a) 0.421 g
(b) paramagnetic; 2 unpaired electrons
(c) 99.8 mg; the nickel powder will stick to a magnet.

7.55 Li has three electrons ($1s^22s^1$) and Li^+ has only two electrons ($1s^2$). The ion is smaller than the atom because there are only two electrons to be held by three protons in the ion. Also, an electron in a larger orbital has been removed. Fluorine atoms have nine electrons and nine protons ($1s^22s^22p^5$). The anion, F^-, has one additional electron, which means that 10 electrons must be held by only nine protons, and the ion is larger than the atom.

7.57 Element 1 comes from Group 4A (IUPAC Group 14). The first two IEs correspond to removing electrons from a p subshell. With the third IE, there is a fairly large jump in IE corresponding to removing an electron from an s subshell. The fourth electron removed comes from the same s subshell and therefore does not increase the IE by as much. None of the IEs are large enough to correspond to removing an electron from a lower energy level.

Element 2 comes from Group 3A (IUPAC Group 13). There is a large change in IE between the third and fourth IEs. The first three IEs correspond to removing electrons from the same energy level. The large jump at the fourth IE corresponds to having to remove the electron from a lower energy level.

7.59 Most stable: (d) The two electrons are in separate orbitals, following Hund's rule, and are of the same spin.

Least stable: (a) In this case the electrons violate both Hund's rule and the Pauli exclusion principle.

7.61 K $(1s^22s^22p^63s^23p^64s^1) \rightarrow$ K$^+$ $(1s^22s^22p^63s^23p^6)$

K$^+$ $(1s^22s^22p^63s^23p^6) \rightarrow$ K^{2+} $(1s^22s^22p^63s^23p^5)$

The first ionization is for the removal of an electron from the valence shell of electrons. The second electron, however, is removed from the $3p$ subshell. This subshell is significantly lower in energy than the $4s$ subshell, and considerably more energy is required to remove this second electron.

7.63 (a) In going from one element to the next across the period, the effective nuclear charge increases slightly and the attraction between the nucleus and the electrons increases.

(b) The size of fourth period transition elements, for example, is a reflection of the size of the $4s$ orbital. As d electrons are added across the series, protons are added to the nucleus. Adding protons should lead to a decreased atom size, but the effect of the protons is balanced by repulsions of the $3d$ electrons and $4s$ electrons, and the atom size is changed little.

7.65 Among the arguments for a compound composed of Mg^{2+} and O^{2-} are:

(a) Chemical experience suggests that all Group 2A elements form 2^+ cations, and that oxygen is typically the O^{2-} ion in its compounds.

(b) Other alkaline earth elements form oxides such as BeO, CaO, and BaO.

A possible experiment is to measure the melting point of the compound. An ionic compound such as NaF (with ions having 1^+ and 1^- charges) melts at 990 °C, whereas a compound analogous to MgO, CaO, melts at a much higher temperature (2580 °C).

7.67 (a) The effective nuclear charge increases, causing the valence orbital energies to become more negative on moving across the period.

(b) As the valence orbital energies become more negative, it is increasingly difficult to remove an electron from the atom, and the IE increases. Toward the end of the period, the orbital energies have become so negative that removing an electron requires significant energy. Instead, the effective nuclear charge has reached the point that it is energetically more favorable for the atom to gain an electron, corresponding to a more negative electron affinity.

(c) The valence orbital energies are in the order:

Li $(-520.7$ kJ$)$ < Be $(-899.3$ kJ$)$ > B $(-800.8$ kJ$)$ < C $(-1029$ kJ$)$

This means it is more difficult to remove an electron from Be than from either Li or B. The energy is more negative for C than for B, so it is more difficult to remove an electron from C than from B.

7.69 The size declines across this series of elements while their mass increases. Thus, the mass per volume, the density, increases.

7.71 (a) Element 113: [Rn]$5f^{14}6d^{10}7s^27p^1$
Element 115: [Rn]$5f^{14}6d^{10}7s^27p^3$

(b) Element 113 is in Group 3A (with elements such as boron and aluminum), and element 115 is in Group 5A (with elements such as nitrogen and phosphorus).

(c) Americium $(Z = 95)$ + argon $(Z = 18)$ = element 113

7.73 (a) Sulfur electron configuration

↑↓	↑↓	↑↓ ↑↓ ↑↓	↑↓	↑↓ ↑ ↑
$1s$	$2s$	$2p$	$3s$	$3p$

(b) $n = 3$, $\ell = 1$, $m_\ell = 1$, and $m_s = +1/2$

(c) S has the smallest ionization energy and O has the smallest radius.

(d) S is smaller than S^{2-} ion

(e) 584 g SCl$_2$

(f) 10.0 g of SCl$_2$ is the limiting reactant, and 11.6 g of SOCl$_2$ can be produced.

(g) $\Delta_f H°[\text{SCl}_2(\text{g})] = -17.6$ kJ/mol

7.75 (a) Z* for F is 5.2; Z* for Ne is 5.85. The effective nuclear charge increases from O to F to Ne. As the effective nuclear charge increases, the atomic radius decreases, and the first ionization energy increases.

(b) Z* for a $3d$ electron in Mn is 13.7; for a $4s$ electron it is only 3.1. The effective nuclear charge experienced by a $4s$ electron is much smaller than that experienced by a $3d$ electron. A $4s$ electron in Mn is thus more easily removed.

CHAPTER 8

8.1. (a) Group 6A, six valence electrons
(b) Group 3A, three valence electrons
(c) Group 1A, one valence electron
(d) Group 2A, two valence electrons
(e) Group 7A, seven valence electrons
(f) Group 6A, six valence electrons

8.3 Group 3A, three bonds
Group 4A, four bonds
Group 5A, three bonds (for a neutral compound)
Group 6A, two bonds (for a neutral compound)
Group 7A, one (for a neutral compound)

8.5 (a) NF$_3$, 26 valence electrons

$$\ddot{\text{F}}-\ddot{\text{N}}-\ddot{\text{F}}$$
$$|$$
$$\ddot{\text{F}}$$

(b) ClO₃⁻, 26 valence electrons

$$\left[\ddot{\text{O}}\text{—}\overset{..}{\underset{\underset{\ddot{\text{O}}:}{|}}{\text{Cl}}}\text{—}\ddot{\text{O}}: \right]^{-}$$

(c) HOBr, 14 valence electrons

$$\text{H}\text{—}\ddot{\text{O}}\text{—}\ddot{\text{Br}}:$$

(d) SO₃²⁻, 26 valence electrons

$$\left[:\ddot{\text{O}}\text{—}\overset{..}{\underset{\underset{\ddot{\text{O}}:}{|}}{\text{S}}}\text{—}\ddot{\text{O}}: \right]^{2-}$$

8.7 (a) CHClF₂, 26 valence electrons

$$:\ddot{\text{Cl}}\text{—}\overset{\text{H}}{\underset{\underset{:\ddot{\text{F}}:}{|}}{\text{C}}}\text{—}\ddot{\text{F}}:$$

(b) CH₃CO₂H, 24 valence electrons

$$\text{H}\text{—}\overset{\text{H}}{\underset{\underset{\text{H}}{|}}{\text{C}}}\text{—}\overset{:\ddot{\text{O}}:}{\underset{}{\text{C}}}\text{—}\ddot{\text{O}}\text{—}\text{H}$$

(c) CH₃CN, 16 valence electrons

$$\text{H}\text{—}\overset{\text{H}}{\underset{\underset{\text{H}}{|}}{\text{C}}}\text{—}\text{C}\equiv\text{N}:$$

(d) H₂CCCH₂, 16 valence electrons

$$\text{H}\text{—}\overset{\text{H}}{\underset{}{\text{C}}}\text{=}\text{C}\text{=}\overset{\text{H}}{\underset{}{\text{C}}}\text{—}\text{H}$$

8.9 (a) SO₂, 18 valence electrons

$$:\ddot{\text{O}}\text{—}\text{S}\text{=}\ddot{\text{O}} \longleftrightarrow \ddot{\text{O}}\text{=}\text{S}\text{—}\ddot{\text{O}}:$$

(b) HNO₂, 18 valence electrons

$$\text{H}\text{—}\ddot{\text{O}}\text{—}\ddot{\text{N}}\text{=}\ddot{\text{O}}$$

(c) SCN⁻, 16 valence electrons

$$\left[\ddot{\text{S}}\text{=}\text{C}\text{=}\ddot{\text{N}}\right]^{-} \longleftrightarrow \left[:\text{S}\equiv\text{C}\text{—}\ddot{\text{N}}:\right]^{-} \longleftrightarrow \left[:\ddot{\text{S}}\text{—}\text{C}\equiv\text{N}\right]^{-}$$

8.11 (a) BrF₃, 28 valence electrons

$$:\overset{\ddot{\text{F}}:}{\underset{\underset{:\ddot{\text{F}}:}{|}}{\ddot{\text{Br}}}}\text{—}\ddot{\text{F}}:$$

(b) I₃⁻, 22 valence electrons

$$\left[\overset{:\ddot{\text{I}}:}{\underset{\underset{:\ddot{\text{I}}:}{|}}{\ddot{\text{I}}}} \right]^{-}$$

(c) XeO₂F₂, 34 valence electrons

$$:\ddot{\text{O}}\text{—}\overset{:\ddot{\text{F}}:}{\underset{\underset{:\ddot{\text{F}}:}{|}}{\text{Xe}}}\text{—}\ddot{\text{O}}:$$

(d) XeF₃⁺, 28 valence electrons

$$:\overset{:\ddot{\text{F}}:}{\underset{\underset{:\ddot{\text{F}}:}{|}}{\text{Xe}}}\text{—}\ddot{\text{F}}:$$

8.13 (a) N = 0; H = 0
(b) P = +1; O = −1
(c) B = −1; H = 0
(d) All are zero.

8.15 (a) N = +1; O = 0
(b) The central N is 0. The singly bonded O atom is −1, and the doubly bonded O atom is 0.

$$\left[:\ddot{\text{O}}\text{—}\ddot{\text{N}}\text{=}\ddot{\text{O}}\right]^{-} \longleftrightarrow \left[\ddot{\text{O}}\text{=}\ddot{\text{N}}\text{—}\ddot{\text{O}}:\right]^{-}$$

(c) N and F are both 0.
(d) The central N atom is +1, one of the O atoms is −1, and the other two O atoms are both 0.

$$\text{H}\text{—}\overset{0}{\ddot{\text{O}}}\text{—}\overset{+1}{\underset{\underset{\underset{-1}{:\ddot{\text{O}}:}}{|}}{\text{N}}}\text{=}\overset{0}{\ddot{\text{O}}}$$

8.17 (a) Electron-pair geometry around N is tetrahedral. Molecular geometry is trigonal pyramidal.

$$:\ddot{\text{Cl}}\text{—}\overset{..}{\underset{\underset{\text{H}}{|}}{\text{N}}}\text{—}\text{H}$$

(b) Electron-pair geometry around O is tetrahedral. Molecular geometry is bent.

$$:\ddot{\text{Cl}}\text{—}\ddot{\text{O}}\text{—}\ddot{\text{Cl}}:$$

(c) Electron-pair geometry around C is linear. Molecular geometry is linear.

$$\left[\ddot{\text{S}}\text{=}\text{C}\text{=}\ddot{\text{N}}\right]^{-}$$

(d) Electron-pair geometry around O is tetrahedral. The molecular geometry is bent.

$$\text{H}\text{—}\ddot{\text{O}}\text{—}\ddot{\text{F}}:$$

8.19 (a) Electron-pair geometry around C is linear. Molecular geometry is linear.

$$\ddot{O}=C=\ddot{O}$$

(b) Electron-pair geometry around N is trigonal planar. Molecular geometry is bent.

$$\left[:\ddot{O}-\ddot{N}=\ddot{O}\right]^{-}$$

(c) Electron-pair geometry around O is trigonal planar. Molecular geometry is bent.

$$\ddot{O}=\ddot{O}-\ddot{O}:$$

(d) Electron-pair geometry around Cl atom is tetrahedral. Molecular geometry is bent.

$$\left[:\ddot{O}-\ddot{Cl}-\ddot{O}:\right]^{-}$$

All have two atoms attached to the central atom. As the bond and lone pairs vary, the electron-pair geometries vary from linear to tetrahedral, and the molecular geometries vary from linear to bent.

8.21 (a) Electron-pair geometry around Cl is trigonal bipyramidal. Molecular geometry is linear.

$$\left[:\ddot{F}-\ddot{Cl}-\ddot{F}:\right]^{-}$$

(b) Electron-pair geometry around Cl is trigonal bipyramidal. Molecular geometry is T-shaped.

$$:\ddot{F}-\ddot{Cl}-\ddot{F}:$$
$$|$$
$$:\ddot{F}:$$

(c) Electron-pair geometry around Cl is octahedral. Molecular geometry is square planar.

$$\left[\begin{array}{c}:\ddot{F}:\\ |\\ :\ddot{F}-\ddot{Cl}-\ddot{F}:\\ |\\ :\ddot{F}:\end{array}\right]^{-}$$

(d) Electron-pair geometry around Cl is octahedral. Molecular geometry is a square pyramid.

$$:\ddot{F}:$$
$$:F\text{''''}|\quad \ddot{F}:$$
$$\quad Cl$$
$$:\ddot{F} \quad \ddot{F}:$$

8.23 (a) Ideal O—S—O angle = 120°
(b) 120°
(c) 120°
(d) H—C—H = 109° and C—C—N angle = 180°

8.25 1 = 120°; 2 = 109°; 3 = 120°; 4 = 109°; 5 = 109°

The chain cannot be linear because the first two carbon atoms in the chain have bond angles of 109° and the final one has a bond angle of 120°. These bond angles do not lead to a linear chain.

8.27

$$\overset{\longrightarrow}{C-O}$$
$$+\delta \quad -\delta$$

$$\overset{\longrightarrow}{C-N}$$
$$+\delta \quad -\delta$$

CO is more polar

$$\overset{\longrightarrow}{P-Cl}$$
$$+\delta \quad -\delta$$

$$\overset{\longrightarrow}{P-Br}$$
$$+\delta \quad -\delta$$

PCl is more polar

$$\overset{\longrightarrow}{B-O}$$
$$+\delta \quad -\delta$$

$$\overset{\longrightarrow}{B-S}$$
$$+\delta \quad -\delta$$

BO is more polar

$$\overset{\longrightarrow}{B-F}$$
$$+\delta \quad -\delta$$

$$\overset{\longrightarrow}{B-I}$$
$$+\delta \quad -\delta$$

BF is more polar

8.29 (a) CH and CO bonds are polar.
(b) The CO bond is most polar, and O is the most negative atom.

8.31 (a) OH⁻: The formal charge on O is −1 and on H it is 0.
(b) BH₄⁻: Even though the formal charge on B is −1 and on H is 0, H is slightly more electronegative than B. The four H atoms are therefore more likely to bear the −1 charge of the ion. The BH bonds are polar with the H atom the negative end.
(c) The CH and CO bonds are all polar (but the C—C bond is not). The negative charge in the CO bonds lies on the O atoms.

8.33 Structure C is most reasonable. The charges are as small as possible and the negative charge resides on the more electronegative atom.

$$\overset{-2\ +1\ +1}{:\ddot{N}-N\equiv O:} \longleftrightarrow \overset{-1\ +1\ 0}{\ddot{N}=N=\ddot{O}} \longleftrightarrow \overset{0\ +1\ -1}{:N\equiv N-\ddot{O}:}$$
$$\qquad A \qquad\qquad\qquad B \qquad\qquad\qquad C$$

8.35 (a)

$$\left[:\overset{-1}{\ddot{O}}-\overset{0}{N}=\overset{0}{\ddot{O}}\right]^{-} \longleftrightarrow \left[\overset{0}{\ddot{O}}=\overset{0}{N}-\overset{-1}{\ddot{O}:}\right]^{-}$$

(b) If an H⁺ ion were to attack NO₂⁻, it would attach to an O atom because the O atoms bear the negative charge in this ion.

(c)

$$H-\ddot{O}-N=\ddot{O}: \longleftrightarrow :\ddot{O}-N=\ddot{O}-H$$

The structure on the left is strongly favored because all of the atoms have zero formal charge, whereas the structure on the right has a −1 formal charge on one oxygen and a +1 formal charge on the other.

8.37 (i) The most polar bonds are in H_2O (because O and H have the largest difference in electronegativity).
(ii) Not polar: CO_2 and CCl_4
(iii) The F atom is more negatively charged.

8.39 (a) $BeCl_2$, nonpolar linear molecule
(b) HBF_2, polar trigonal planar molecule with F atoms the negative end of the dipole and the H atom the positive end.
(c) CH_3Cl, polar tetrahedral molecule. The Cl atom is the negative end of the dipole and the three H atoms are on the positive side of the molecule.
(d) SO_3, a nonpolar trigonal planar molecule

8.41 (a) Two C—H bonds, bond order is 1; 1 C=O bond, bond order is 2.
(b) Three S—O single bonds, bond order is 1.
(c) Two nitrogen–oxygen double bonds, bond order is 2.
(d) One N=O double bond, bond order is 2; one N—Cl bond, bond order is 1.

8.43 (a) B—Cl
(b) C—O
(c) P—O
(d) C=O

8.45 NO bond orders: 2 in NO_2^+, 1.5 in NO_2^-; 1.33 in NO_3^-. The NO bond is longest in NO_3^- and shortest in NO_2^+.

8.47 The CO bond in carbon monoxide is a triple bond, so it is both shorter and stronger than the CO double bond in H_2CO.

8.49 $\Delta_r H = -126$ kJ

8.51 O—F bond dissociation energy = 192 kJ/mol

8.53

Element	Valence Electrons
Li	1
Ti	4
Zn	2
Si	4
Cl	7

8.55 SeF_4, BrF_4^-, XeF_4

8.57

$$\left[\overset{\overset{\displaystyle :O:}{\parallel}}{H-C-\ddot{O}:} \right]^- \longleftrightarrow \left[\overset{\displaystyle :\ddot{O}:}{H-C=\ddot{O}} \right]^-$$

Bond order = 3/2

8.59 To estimate the enthalpy change, we need energies for the following bonds: O=O, H—H, and H—O.

Energy to break bonds = 498 kJ (for O=O) + 2 × 436 kJ (for H—H) = +1370 kJ.

Energy evolved when bonds are made = 4 × 463 kJ (for O—H) = −1852 kJ

Total energy = −482 kJ

8.61 All the species in the series have 16 valence electrons and all are linear.

(a) $\ddot{O}=C=\ddot{O} \longleftrightarrow :\ddot{O}-C\equiv O: \longleftrightarrow :O\equiv C-\ddot{O}:$

(b)

$$\left[\ddot{N}=N=\ddot{N} \right]^- \longleftrightarrow \left[:\ddot{N}-N\equiv N: \right]^- \longleftrightarrow \left[:N\equiv N-\ddot{N}: \right]^-$$

(c)

$$\left[\ddot{O}=C=\ddot{N} \right]^- \longleftrightarrow \left[:\ddot{O}-C\equiv N: \right]^- \longleftrightarrow \left[:O\equiv C-\ddot{N}: \right]^-$$

8.63 The N—O bonds in NO_2^- have a bond order of 1.5, whereas in NO_2^+ the bond order is 2. The shorter bonds (110 pm) are the NO bonds with the higher bond order (in NO_2^+), whereas the longer bonds (124 pm) in NO_2^- have a lower bond order.

8.65 The F—Cl—F bond angle in ClF_2^+, which has a tetrahedral electron-pair geometry, is approximately 109°.

$$\left[:\ddot{F}-\ddot{Cl}-\ddot{F}: \right]^+$$

The ClF_2^- ion has a trigonal-bipyramidal electron-pair geometry with F atoms in the axial positions and the lone pairs in the equatorial positions. Therefore, the F—C—F angle is 180°.

$$\left[:\ddot{F}-\ddot{Cl}-\ddot{F}: \right]^-$$

8.67 An H^+ ion will attach to an O atom of SO_3^{2-} and not to the S atom. The O atoms each have a formal charge of −1, whereas the S atom formal charge is +1.

$$\left[:\ddot{O}-\overset{\overset{\displaystyle |}{S}}{\underset{\underset{\displaystyle :\ddot{O}:}{|}}{}}-\ddot{O}: \right]^{2-}$$

8.69 (a) Calculation from bond energies: $\Delta_r H° = -1070$ kJ/mol-rxn; $\Delta H° = -535$ kJ/mol CH_3OH
(b) Calculation from thermochemical data: $\Delta_r H° = -1352.3$ kJ/mol-rxn; $\Delta H° = -676$ kJ/mol CH_3OH

8.71 (a)

$$\underset{-1 \quad +1 \quad -1}{\left[:C\equiv N-\ddot{O}: \right]^-} \longleftrightarrow \underset{-2 \quad +1 \quad 0}{\left[\ddot{C}=N=\ddot{O} \right]^-} \longleftrightarrow \underset{-3 \quad +1 \quad +1}{\left[:\ddot{C}-N\equiv O: \right]^-}$$

(b) The first resonance structure is the most reasonable because oxygen, the most electronegative atom, has a negative formal charge, and the unfavorable negative charge on the least electronegative atom, carbon, is smallest.

(c) This species is so unstable because carbon, the least electronegative element in the ion, has a negative formal charge. In addition, all three resonance structures have an unfavorable charge distribution.

8.73

(a) XeF_2 has three lone pairs around the Xe atom. The electron-pair geometry is trigonal bipyramidal. Because lone pairs require more space than bond pairs, it is better to place the lone pairs in the equator of the bipyramid where the angles between them are 120°.
(b) Like XeF_2, ClF_3 has a trigonal bipyramidal electron-pair geometry, but with only two lone pairs around the Cl. These are again placed in the equatorial plane where the angle between them is 120°.

8.75 (a) Angle 1 = 109°; angle 2 = 120°; angle 3 = 109°; angle 4 = 109°; and angle 5 = 109°.
(b) The O—H bond is the most polar bond.

8.77 $\Delta_rH = +146$ kJ $= 2 (\Delta H_{C-N}) + \Delta H_{C=O} - [\Delta H_{N-N} + \Delta H_{C\equiv O}]$

8.79 (a) Two C—H bonds and one O=O are broken and two O—C bonds and two H—O bonds are made in the reaction. $\Delta_rH = -318$ kJ. The reaction is exothermic.
(b) Acetone is polar.
(c) The O—H hydrogen atoms are the most positive in dihydroxyacetone.

8.81 (a) The C=C bond is stronger than the C—C bond.
(b) The C—C single bond is longer than the C=C double bond.
(c) Ethylene is nonpolar, whereas acrolein is polar.
(d) The reaction is exothermic ($\Delta_rH = -45$ kJ).

8.83 $\Delta_rH = -211$ kJ

8.85 Methanol is a polar solvent. Methanol contains two bonds of significant polarity, the C—O bond and the O—H bond. The C—O—H atoms are in a bent configuration, leading to a polar molecule. Toluene contains only carbon and hydrogen atoms, which have similar electronegativites and which are arranged in tetrahedral or trigonal planar geometries, leading to a molecule that is largely nonpolar.

8.87 (a)

The bond angles are all approximately 109°.

(b) The sulfur atom should have a slight partial negative charge, and the carbons should have slight partial positive charges. The molecule has a bent shape and is polar.
(c) 1.6×10^{18} molecules

8.89 (a) Odd electron molecules: BrO (13 electrons)
(b) $Br_2(g) \rightarrow 2\ Br(g)$ $\Delta_rH = +193$ kJ
$2\ Br(g) + O_2(g) \rightarrow 2\ BrO(g)$ $\Delta_rH = +96$ kJ
$BrO(g) + H_2O(g) \rightarrow HOBr(g) + OH(g)$ $\Delta_rH = 0$ kJ
(c) ΔH of formation [HOBr(g)] $= -101$ kJ/mol
(d) The reactions in part (b) are endothermic (or thermal-neutral for the third reaction), and the enthalpy of formation in part (c) is exothermic.

8.91 (a) BF_3 is a nonpolar molecule, but replacing one or two F atoms with an H atom (HBF_2 and H_2BF) gives polar molecules.
(b) $BeCl_2$ is not polar, whereas replacing a Cl atom with a Br atom gives a polar molecule ($BeClBr$).

CHAPTER 9

9.1 The electron-pair and molecular geometry of $CHCl_3$ are both tetrahedral. Each C—Cl bond is formed by the overlap of an sp^3 hybrid orbital on the C atom with a $3p$ orbital on a Cl atom to form a sigma bond. A C—H sigma bond is formed by the overlap of an sp^3 hybrid orbital on the C atom with an H atom $1s$ orbital.

9.3

	Electron-Pair Geometry	Molecular Geometry	Hybrid Orbital Set
(a)	trigonal planar	trigonal planar	sp^2
(b)	linear	linear	sp
(c)	tetrahedral	tetrahedral	sp^3
(d)	trigonal planar	trigonal planar	sp^2

9.5 (a) C, sp^3; O, sp^3
(b) CH_3, sp^3; middle C, sp^2; CH_2, sp^2
(c) CH_2, sp^3; CO_2H, sp^2; N, sp^3

9.7 (a) Electron-pair geometry is octahedral. Molecular geometry is octahedral. S: sp^3d^2

(b) Electron-pair geometry is trigonal-bipyramidal. Molecular geometry is seesaw. Se: sp^3d

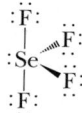

(c) Electron-pair geometry is trigonal-bipyramidal. Molecular geometry is linear. I: sp^3d

$$\left[\begin{array}{c} :\ddot{C}l: \\ | \\ :I: \\ | \\ :\ddot{C}l: \end{array} \right]^{-}$$

(d) Electron-pair geometry is octahedral. Molecular geometry is square-planar. Xe: sp^3d^2

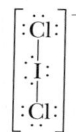

9.9 There are 32 valence electrons in both HPO_2F_2 and its anion. Both have a tetrahedral molecular geometry, and so the P atom in both is sp^3 hybridized.

$$H-\ddot{O}-\overset{:\ddot{O}:}{\underset{:\ddot{F}:}{P}}-\ddot{F}: \qquad \left[:\ddot{O}-\overset{:\ddot{O}:}{\underset{:\ddot{F}:}{P}}-\ddot{F}: \right]^{-}$$

9.11 The C atom is sp^2-hybridized. Two of the sp^2 hybrid orbitals are used to form C—Cl sigma bonds, and the third is used to form the C—O sigma bond. The p orbital not used in the C atom hybrid orbitals is used to form the CO pi bond.

9.13

H₃C   CH₃   H   CH₃
   C=C   C=C
H   H   Cl   H

cis isomer   *trans* isomer

9.15 H_2^+ ion: $(\sigma_{1s})^1$. Bond order is 0.5. The bond in H_2^+ is weaker than in H_2 (bond order =1).

9.17 MO diagram for C_2^{2-} ion

——— σ^*_{2p}

——— ——— π^*_{2p}

⇅ σ_{2p}

⇅   ⇅ π_{2p}

⇅ σ^*_{2s}

⇅ σ_{2s}

The ion has 10 valence electrons (isoelectronic with N_2). There are one net sigma bond and two net pi bonds, for a bond order of 3. The bond order increases by 1 on going from C_2 to C_2^{2-}. The ion is not paramagnetic.

9.19 (a) CO has 10 valence electrons

$$[core](\sigma_{2s})^2(\sigma^*_{2s})^2(\pi_{2p})^4(\sigma_{2p})^2$$

(b) σ_{2p}
(c) Diamagnetic
(d) There are net 1 σ bond and 2 π bonds; bond order is 3.

9.21

$$\left[:\ddot{F}-\overset{:\ddot{F}:}{\underset{:\ddot{F}:}{Al}}-\ddot{F}: \right]^{-}$$

The electron pair and molecular geometries are both tetrahedral. The Al atom is sp^3 hybridized, and so the Al—F bonds are formed by overlap of an Al sp^3 orbital with a p orbital on each F atom. The formal charge on each of the fluorines is zero, and that on the Al is −1. This is not a reasonable charge distribution because the less electronegative atom, aluminum, has the negative charge.

9.23

Molecule/Ion	O—S—O Angle	Hybrid Orbitals
SO_2	120°	sp^2
SO_3	120°	sp^2
SO_3^{2-}	109°	sp^3
SO_4^{2-}	109°	sp^3

9.25

$$\left[:\ddot{O}-\ddot{N}=\ddot{O} \right]^{-} \longleftrightarrow \left[\ddot{O}=\ddot{N}-\ddot{O}: \right]^{-}$$

The electron-pair geometry is trigonal planar. The molecular geometry is bent (or angular). The O—N—O angle will be about 120°, the average N—O bond order is 3/2, and the N atom is sp^2 hybridized.

9.27 The resonance structures of N_2O, with formal charges, are shown here.

$$\overset{-2}{:\ddot{N}}-\overset{+1}{N}\equiv\overset{+1}{O}: \longleftrightarrow \overset{-1}{\ddot{N}}=\overset{+1}{N}=\overset{0}{\ddot{O}} \longleftrightarrow :\overset{0}{N}\equiv\overset{+1}{N}-\overset{-1}{\ddot{O}}:$$

A   B   C

The central N atom is sp hybridized in all structures. The two sp hybrid orbitals on the central N atom are used to form N—N and N—O σ bonds. The two p orbitals not used in the N atom hybridization are used to form the required π bonds.

9.29 (a) All three have the formula C_2H_4O. They are usually referred to as structural isomers.
(b) *Ethylene oxide:* Both C atoms are sp^3 hybridized.
Acetaldehyde: The CH_3 carbon atom has sp^3 hybridization, and the other C atom is sp^2 hybridized.
Vinyl alcohol: Both C atoms are sp^2 hybridized.

(c) *Ethylene oxide:* 109°.
   Acetaldehyde: 109°
   Vinyl alcohol: 120°.
(d) All are polar.
(e) Acetaldehyde has the strongest CO bond, and vinyl alcohol has the strongest C—C bond.

9.31 (a) CH_3 carbon atom: sp^3
   C=N carbon atom: sp^2
   N atom: sp^2
(b) C—N—O bond angle = 120°

9.33 (a) $C(1) = sp^2$; $O(2) = sp^3$; $N(3) = sp^3$; $C(4) = sp^3$;
   $P(5) = sp^3$
(b) Angle A = 120°; angle B = 109°; angle C = 109°;
   angle D = 109°
(c) The P—O and O—H bonds are most polar
   ($\Delta\chi = 1.3$).

9.35 (a) C=O bond is most polar.
(b) 18 sigma bonds and five pi bonds
(c)

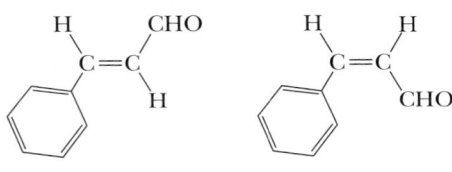

trans isomer   *cis* isomer

(d) All C atoms are sp^2 hybridized.
(e) All bond angles are 120°.

9.37 (a) The Sb in SbF_5 is sp^3d hybridized; whereas it is
   sp^3d^2 hybridized in SbF_6^-.
(b) The molecular geometry of the H_2F^+ ion is bent
   or angular, and the F atom is sp^3 hybridized.

$$\left[\begin{array}{c} \ddot{F} \cdots \text{H} \\ \text{H} \end{array} \right]^-$$

9.39 (a) The peroxide ion has a bond order of 1.

$$\left[:\ddot{O}—\ddot{O}: \right]^{2-}$$

(b) [core electrons] $(\sigma_{2s})^2(\sigma^*_{2s})^2(\sigma_{2p})^2(\pi_{2p})^4(\pi^*_{2p})^4$

This configuration also leads to a bond order of 1.

(c) Both theories lead to a diamagnetic ion with a
   bond order of 1.

9.41 Paramagnetic diatomic molecules: B_2 and O_2

Bond order of 1: Li_2, B_2, F_2; Bond order of 2: C_2 and
O_2; Highest bond order: N_2

9.43 CN has nine valence electrons
   [core electrons] $(\sigma_{2s})^2(\sigma^*_{2s})^2(\pi_{2p})^4(\sigma_{2p})^1$
(a) HOMO, σ_{2p}
(b, c) Bond order = 2.5 (0.5 σ bond and 2 π bonds)
(d) Paramagnetic

9.45 (a) All C atoms are sp^3 hybridized
(b) About 109°
(c) Polar
(d) The six-membered ring cannot be planar, owing
   to the tetrahedral C atoms of the ring. The bond
   angles are all 109°.

9.47 (a) The geometry about the boron atom is trigonal
   planar in BF_3, but tetrahedral in H_3N—BF_3.
(b) Boron is sp^2 hybridized in BF_3 but sp^3 hybridized
   in H_3N—BF_3.
(c) Yes
(d) The ammonia molecule is polar with the N atom
   partially negative. While the BF_3 molecule is nonpolar overall, each of the B—F bonds is polarized
   such that the B has a partial positive charge. The
   partially negative N in NH_3 is attracted to the partially positive B in BF_3.
(e) One of the lone pairs on the oxygen of H_2O can
   form a coordinate covalent bond with the B in
   BF_3. The resulting compound would be (the lone
   pairs on the F's not shown):

$$\begin{array}{ccc} & \text{H} & \text{F} \\ \text{H}—\text{O}—\text{B}—\text{F} \\ & & \text{F} \end{array}$$

9.49 (a) NH_2^-: electron-pair geometry = tetrahedral, molecular geometry = bent, hybridization of N = sp^3

SO_3: electron-pair geometry = molecular geometry = trigonal planar, hybridization of S = sp^2

(b)

$$\left[\begin{array}{c} :\ddot{O}: \\ \text{H} \quad \| \\ \text{H}\text{—N}\text{—S}\text{—}\ddot{O}: \\ \quad \| \\ \ddot{O}: \end{array} \right]^-$$

The bond angles around the N and the S are all
approximately 109°.
(c) The N does not undergo any change in its hybrid-
   ication; the S changes from sp^2 to sp^3.
(d) The SO_3 is the acceptor of an electron pair in this
   reaction. The electrostatic potential map confirms
   this to be reasonable because the sulfur has a partial positive charge.

9.51 A C atom may form, at most, four hybrid orbitals
   (sp^3). The minimum number is two, for example, the
   sp hybrid orbitals used by carbon in CO. Carbon has
   only four valence orbitals, so it cannot form more
   than four hybrid orbitals.

9.53 (a) C, sp^2; N, sp^3

(b) The amide or peptide link has two resonance structures (shown here with formal charges on the O and N atoms). Structure B is less favorable, owing to the separation of charge.

(c) The fact that the amide link is planar indicates that structure B has some importance.

The principal sites of positive charge are the nitrogen in the amide linkage, and the hydrogen of the —O—H group. The principal regions of negative charge are oxygen atoms and the nitrogen of the free —NH_2 group.

9.55 MO theory is better to use when explaining or understanding the effect of adding energy to molecules. A molecule can absorb energy and an electron can thus be promoted to a higher level. Using MO theory, one can see how this can occur. Additionally, MO theory is a better model to use to predict whether a molecule is paramagnetic.

9.57 Lowest Energy = Orbital C < Orbital B < Orbital A = Highest Energy

9.59 (a) The attractive forces must be greater than the repulsive forces if a covalent bond is to form.

(b) As the atoms approach each other, the energy drops as the electron clouds overlap and electron density increases between the two nuclei. If the atoms approach still more closely, electrostatic repulsion of the nuclei for each other and of the electrons for each other increases dramatically.

(c) In neon, all of the orbitals in the $2s$ and $2p$ sublevels are filled with paired electrons; there is no orbital available that can overlap with another orbital on another atom. In the case of fluorine, there is an orbital on each atom that is not completely filled that can overlap with another orbital to form a bond.

9.61 (a) The molecule with the double bond requires a great deal more energy because the π bond must be broken in order for the ends of the molecules to rotate relative to each other.

(b) No. The carbon–carbon double bonds in the molecule prevent the CH_2 fragments from rotating.

CHAPTER 10

10.1 Heptane

10.3 $C_{14}H_{30}$ is an alkane and C_5H_{10} could be a cycloalkane.

10.5 2,3-dimethylbutane

10.7 (a) 2,3-Dimethylhexane

(b) 2,3-Dimethyloctane

(c) 3-Ethylheptane

(d) 3-Ethyl-2-methylhexane

10.9

2-methylheptane

4-methylheptane

3-methylheptane. The C atom with an asterisk is chiral.

10.11

4-ethylheptane. The compound is not chiral.

3-ethylheptane. Not chiral.

10.13 C_4H_{10}, butane: a low-molecular–weight fuel gas at room temperature and pressure. Slightly soluble in water.

$C_{12}H_{26}$, dodecane: a colorless liquid at room temperature. Expected to be insoluble in water but quite soluble in nonpolar solvents.

10.15

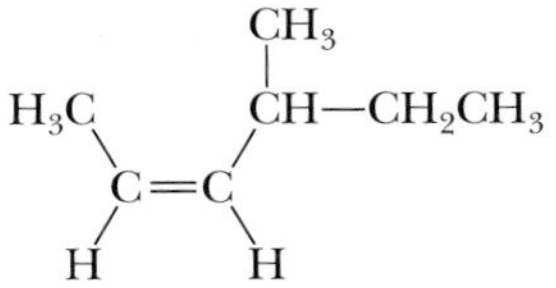

cis-4-methyl-2-hexene

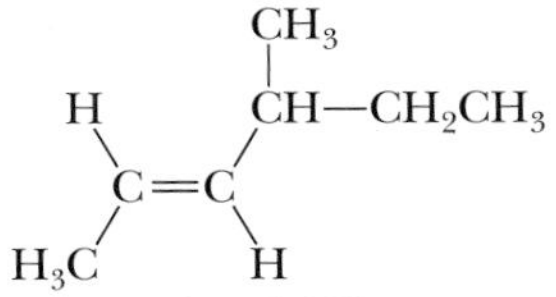

trans-4-methyl-2-hexene

10.17 (a)

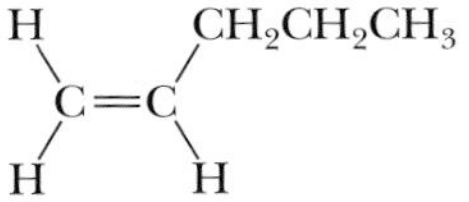

1-pentene

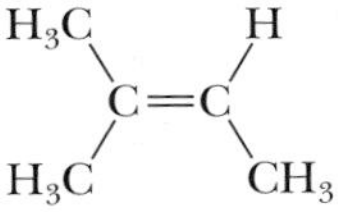

2-methyl-2-butene

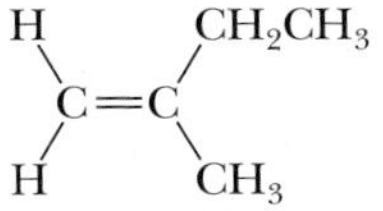

2-methyl-1-butene

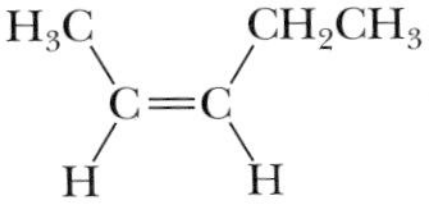

cis-2-pentene

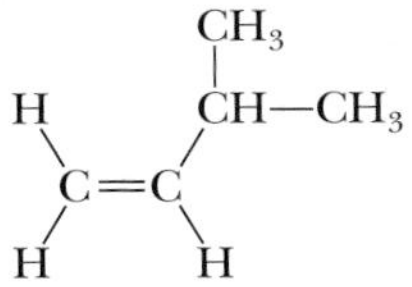

3-methyl-1-butene

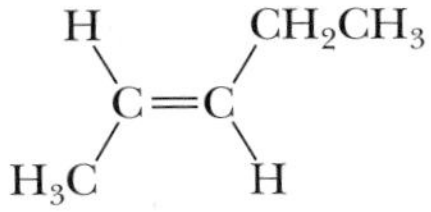

trans-2-pentene

(b)

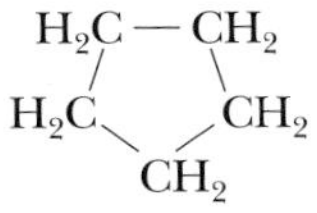

cyclopentane

10.19 (a) 1,2-Dibromopropane, $CH_3CHBrCH_2Br$
(b) Pentane, C_5H_{12}

10.21 1-Butene, $CH_3CH_2CH=CH_2$, or 1-butene

10.23 Four isomers are possible.

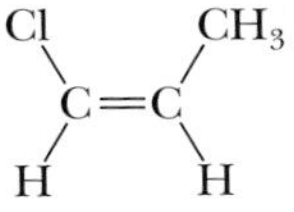

cis-1-chloropropene

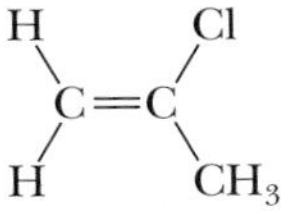

2-chloropropene

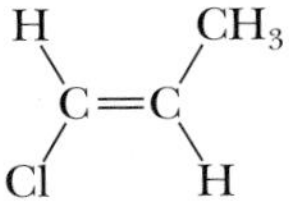

trans-1-chloropropene

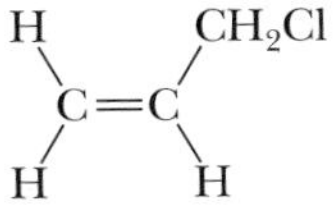

3-chloro-1-propene

10.25

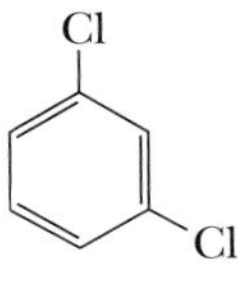

m-dichlorobenzene

o-bromotoluene

10.27

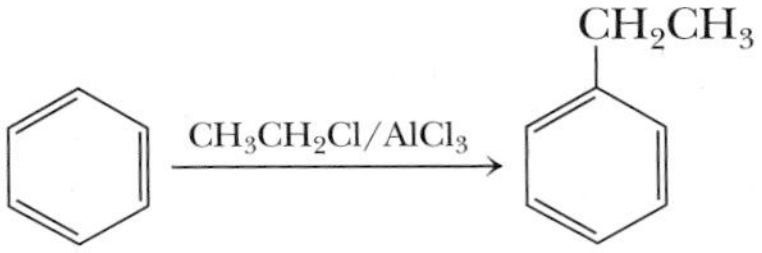

ethylbenzene

10.29

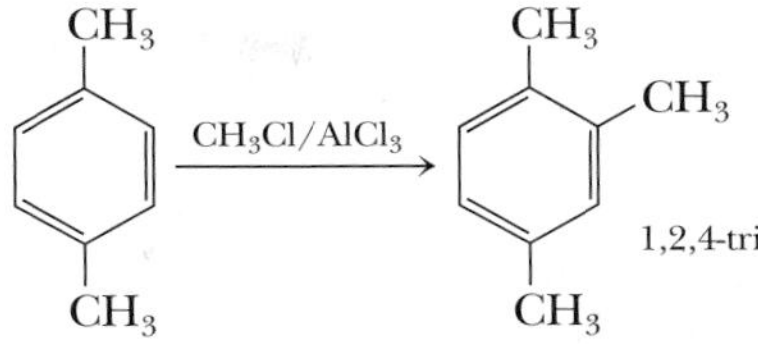

1,2,4-trimethylbenzene

10.31 (a) 1-Propanol, primary
(b) 1-Butanol, primary
(c) 2-Methyl-2-propanol, tertiary
(d) 2-Methyl-2-butanol, tertiary

10.33 (a) Ethylamine, $CH_3CH_2NH_2$
(b) Dipropylamine, $(CH_3CH_2CH_2)_2NH$

(c) Butyldimethylamine

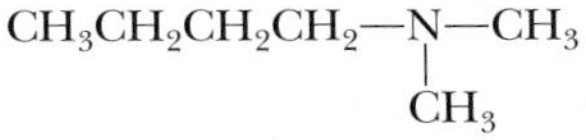

(d) triethylamine

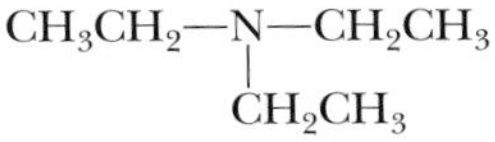

10.33 (a) 1-butanol, $CH_3CH_2CH_2CH_2OH$
(b) 2-butanol

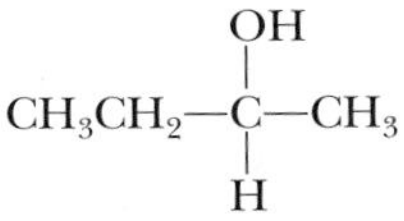

(c) 2-methyl-1-propanol

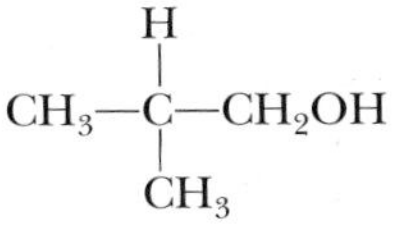

(d) 2-methyl-2-propanol

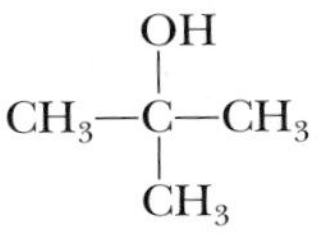

10.37 (a) $C_6H_5NH_2(aq) + HCl(aq) \rightarrow (C_6H_5NH_3)Cl(aq)$
(b) $(CH_3)_3N(aq) + H_2SO_4(aq) \rightarrow$
$[(CH_3)_3NH]HSO_4(aq)$

10.39

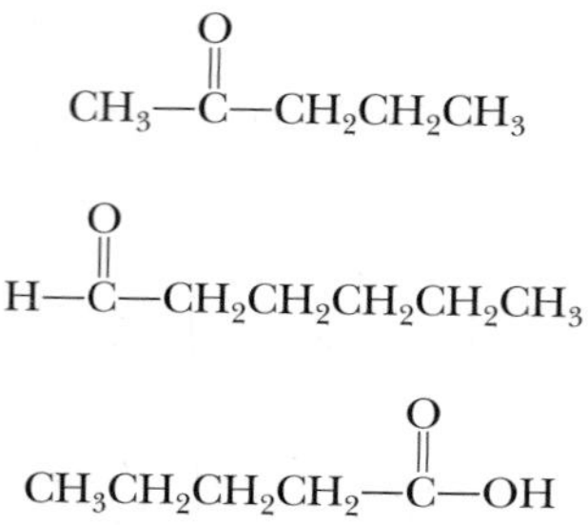

$$CH_3-\overset{\overset{\displaystyle O}{\|}}{C}-CH_2CH_2CH_3$$

$$H-\overset{\overset{\displaystyle O}{\|}}{C}-CH_2CH_2CH_2CH_2CH_3$$

$$CH_3CH_2CH_2CH_2-\overset{\overset{\displaystyle O}{\|}}{C}-OH$$

10.41 (a) Acid, 3-methylpentanoic acid
(b) Ester, methyl propanoate
(c) Ester, butyl acetate (or butyl ethanoate)
(d) Acid, *p*-bromobenzoic acid

10.43 (a) Pentanoic acid (see Question 39c)
(b) 1-Pentanol, $CH_3CH_2CH_2CH_2CH_2OH$

(c) $$H_3C-\overset{\overset{\displaystyle OH}{|}}{\underset{\underset{\displaystyle H}{|}}{C}}-CH_2CH_2CH_2CH_2CH_2CH_3$$

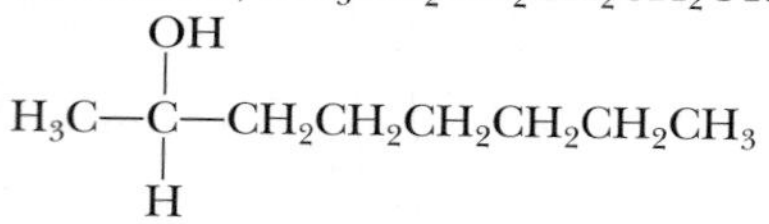

(d) No reaction. A ketone is not oxidized by $KMnO_4$.

10.45 Step 1: Oxidize 1-propanol to propanoic acid.

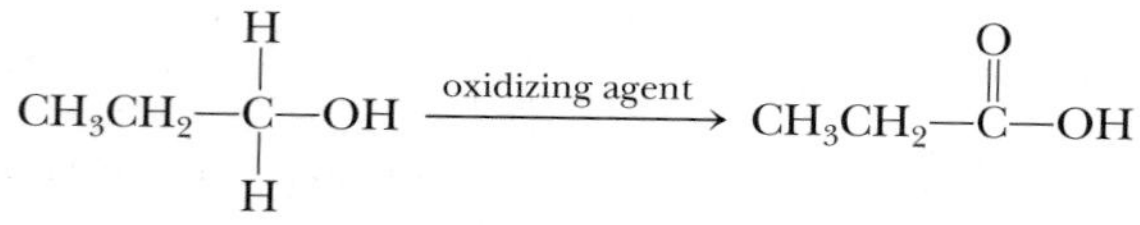

$$CH_3CH_2-\overset{\overset{\displaystyle H}{|}}{\underset{\underset{\displaystyle H}{|}}{C}}-OH \xrightarrow{\text{oxidizing agent}} CH_3CH_2-\overset{\overset{\displaystyle O}{\|}}{C}-OH$$

Step 2: Combine propanoic acid and 1-propanol.

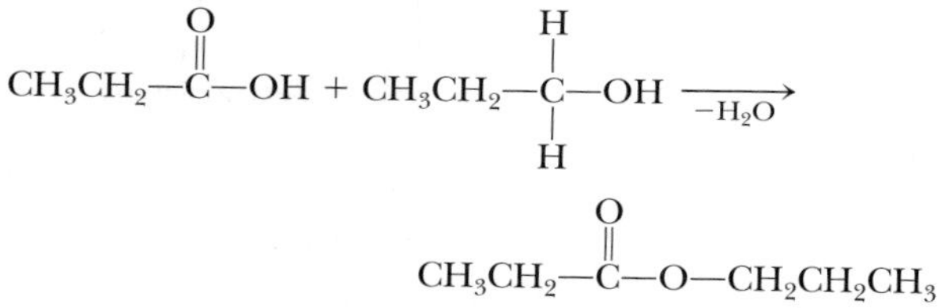

$$CH_3CH_2-\overset{\overset{\displaystyle O}{\|}}{C}-OH + CH_3CH_2-\overset{\overset{\displaystyle H}{|}}{\underset{\underset{\displaystyle H}{|}}{C}}-OH \xrightarrow{-H_2O}$$

$$CH_3CH_2-\overset{\overset{\displaystyle O}{\|}}{C}-O-CH_2CH_2CH_3$$

10.47 Sodium acetate, $NaCH_3CO_2$, and 1-butanol, $CH_3CH_2CH_2CH_2OH$

10.49 (a) Trigonal planar
(b) 120°
(c) The molecule is chiral. There are four different groups around the carbon atom marked 2.
(d) The acidic H atom is the H attached to the CO_2H (carboxyl) group.

10.51 (a) Alcohol   (c) Acid
(b) Amide   (d) Ester

10.53 (a) Prepare polyvinyl acetate (PVA) from vinylacetate.

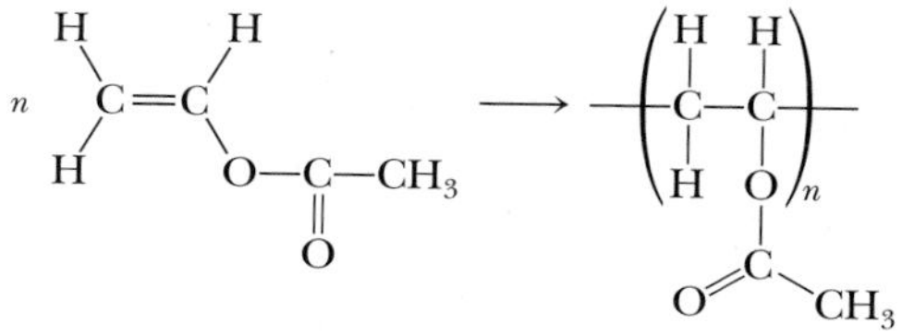

(b) The three units of PVA:

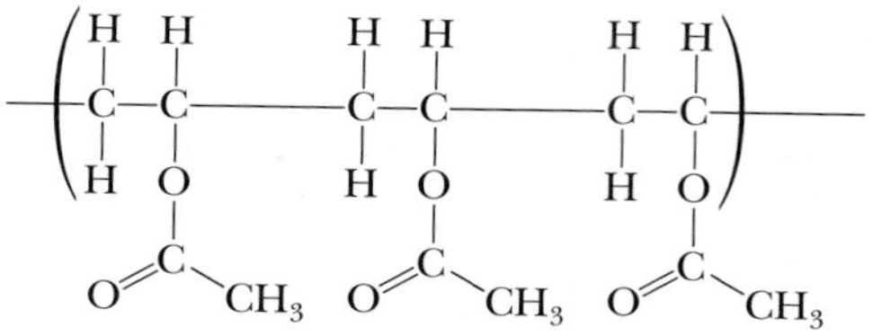

(c) Hydrolysis of polyvinyl alcohol

10.55 Illustrated here is a segment of a copolymer composed of two units of 1,1–dichloroethylene and two units of chloroethylene.

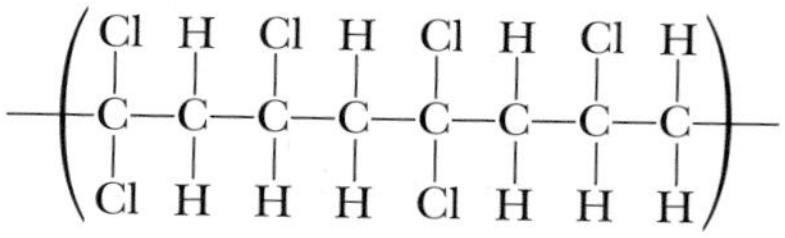

10.57 (a)

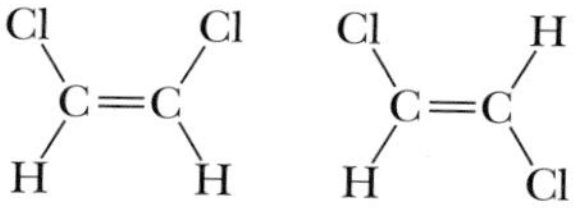

cis isomer   *trans* isomer

(b)

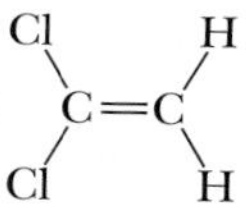

10.59

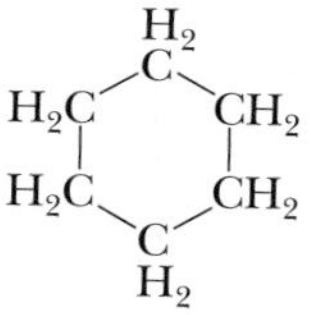

cyclohexane 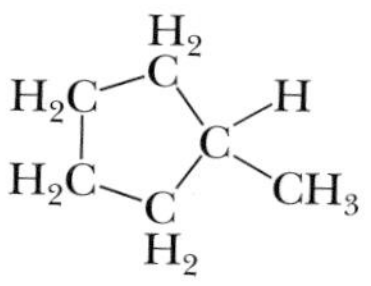   methylcyclopentane

$$CH_3CH=CHCH_2CH_2CH_3$$
2-hexene
Other isomers are possible by moving the double bond and with a branched chain.

10.61

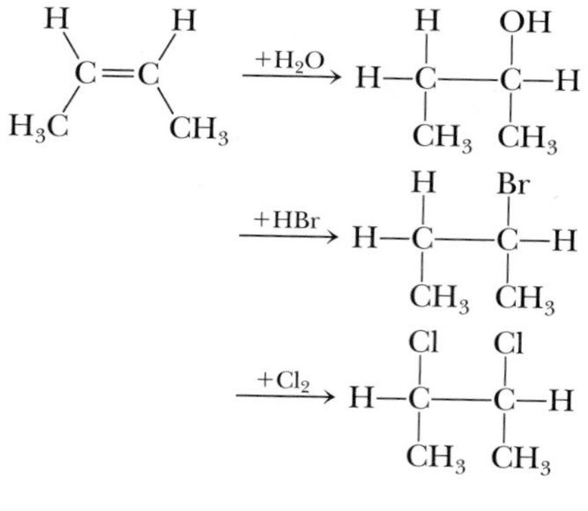

10.63 (a)

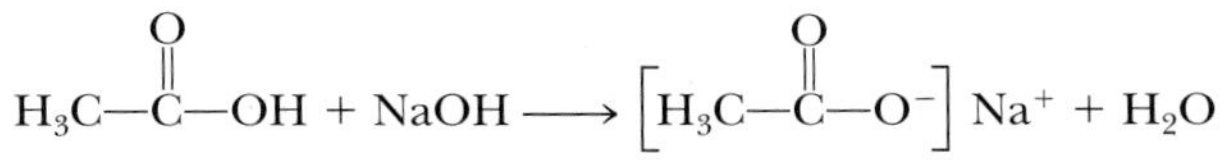

$$H_3C-\overset{\overset{\displaystyle O}{\|}}{C}-OH + NaOH \longrightarrow \left[H_3C-\overset{\overset{\displaystyle O}{\|}}{C}-O^-\right] Na^+ + H_2O$$

(b)

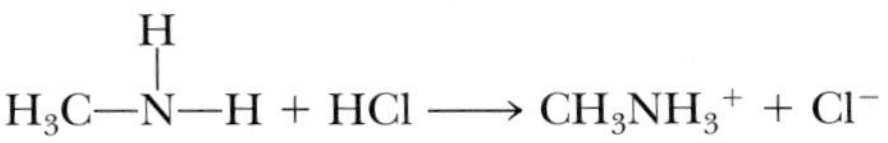

$$H_3C-\overset{\overset{\displaystyle H}{|}}{N}-H + HCl \longrightarrow CH_3NH_3{}^+ + Cl^-$$

10.65

$$n\ HOCH_2CH_2OH + n\ HO-\overset{\overset{\displaystyle O}{\|}}{C}-\underset{}{\bigcirc}-\overset{\overset{\displaystyle O}{\|}}{C}-OH \longrightarrow$$

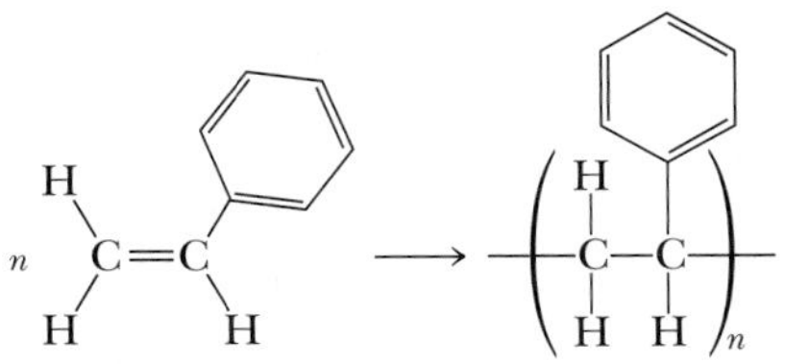

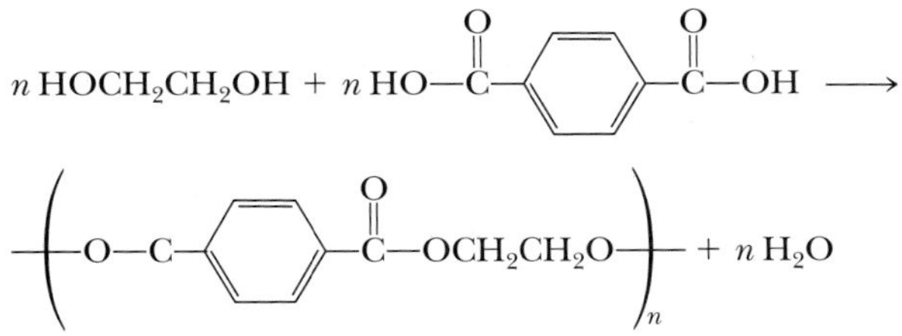

10.67 (a) 2, 3-Dimethylpentane

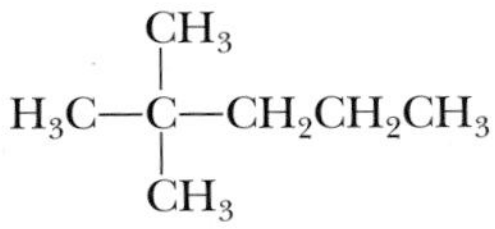

$$H_3C-\overset{\overset{\displaystyle CH_3}{|}}{\underset{\underset{\displaystyle CH_3}{|}}{C}}-CH_2CH_2CH_3$$

(b) 3, 3-Dimethylpentane

$$CH_3CH_2-\overset{\overset{\displaystyle CH_2CH_3}{|}}{\underset{\underset{\displaystyle CH_2CH_3}{|}}{C}}-CH_2CH_3$$

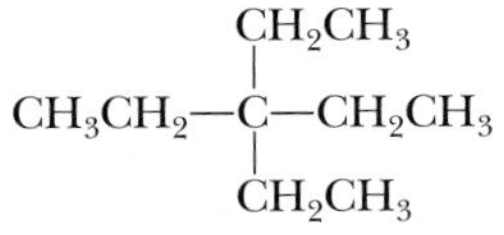

(c) 3-Ethyl-2-methylpentane

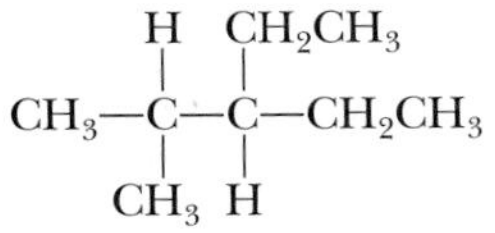

$$CH_3-\overset{\overset{\displaystyle H}{|}}{\underset{\underset{\displaystyle CH_3}{|}}{C}}-\overset{\overset{\displaystyle CH_2CH_3}{|}}{\underset{\underset{\displaystyle H}{|}}{C}}-CH_2CH_3$$

(d) 3-Ethylhexane

$$CH_3CH_2-\overset{\overset{\displaystyle CH_2CH_3}{|}}{\underset{\underset{\displaystyle H}{|}}{C}}-CH_2CH_2CH_3$$

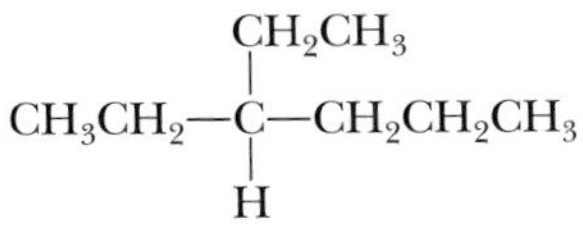

10.69

1,1-Dichloropropane

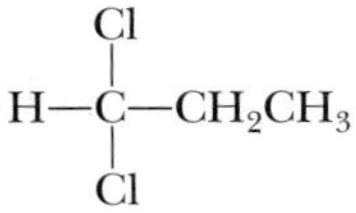

$$H-\overset{\overset{\displaystyle Cl}{|}}{\underset{\underset{\displaystyle Cl}{|}}{C}}-CH_2CH_3$$

1,2-Dichloropropane

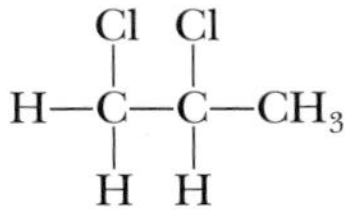

$$H-\overset{\overset{\displaystyle Cl}{|}}{\underset{\underset{\displaystyle H}{|}}{C}}-\overset{\overset{\displaystyle Cl}{|}}{\underset{\underset{\displaystyle H}{|}}{C}}-CH_3$$

1,3-Dichloropropane

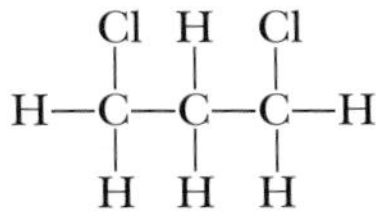

$$H-\overset{\overset{\displaystyle Cl}{|}}{\underset{\underset{\displaystyle H}{|}}{C}}-\overset{\overset{\displaystyle H}{|}}{\underset{\underset{\displaystyle H}{|}}{C}}-\overset{\overset{\displaystyle Cl}{|}}{\underset{\underset{\displaystyle H}{|}}{C}}-H$$

2,2-Dichloropropane

$$H-\overset{\overset{\displaystyle H}{|}}{\underset{\underset{\displaystyle H}{|}}{C}}-\overset{\overset{\displaystyle Cl}{|}}{\underset{\underset{\displaystyle Cl}{|}}{C}}-\overset{\overset{\displaystyle H}{|}}{\underset{\underset{\displaystyle H}{|}}{C}}-H$$

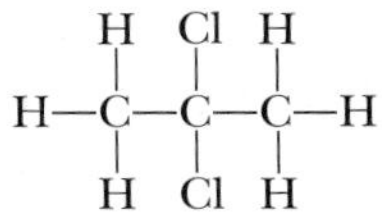

10.71

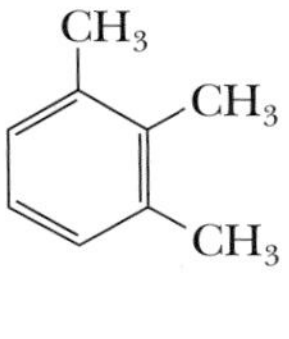

1,2,3-trimethylbenzene 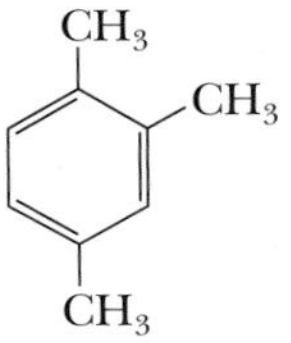   1,2,4-trimethylbenzene 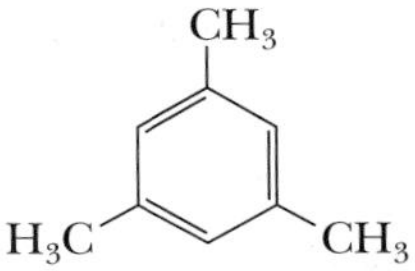   1,3,5-trimethylbenzene

10.73 Replace the carboxylic acid group with an H atom.

10.75

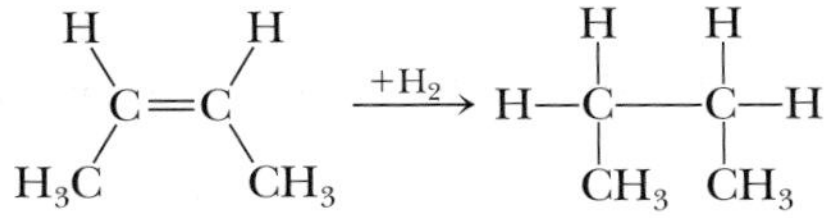

butane (not chiral)

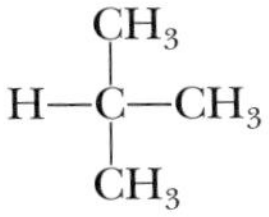

$$H-\overset{\overset{\displaystyle CH_3}{|}}{\underset{\underset{\displaystyle CH_3}{|}}{C}}-CH_3$$

10.77

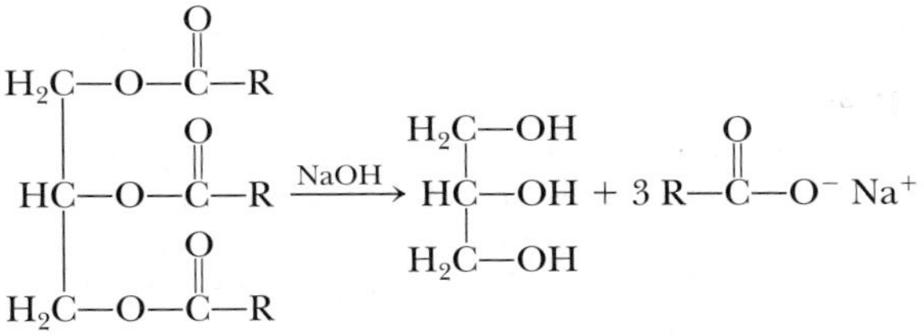

glyceryl trilaurate   glycerol   sodium laurate

10.79

add H₂ →

$H-\overset{\overset{H}{|}}{\underset{\underset{H}{|}}{C}}-\overset{\overset{CH_2OH}{|}}{\underset{\underset{H}{|}}{C}}-H$

oxidize →

allyl/acrylic structure: $\overset{H}{\underset{H}{C}}=\overset{CO_2H}{\underset{H}{C}}$

polymerize →

$\left(-\overset{H}{\underset{H}{C}}-\overset{CH_2OH}{\underset{H}{C}}-\overset{H}{\underset{H}{C}}-\overset{CH_2OH}{\underset{H}{C}}-\right)_n$

CH_3CO_2H →

$H_3C-\overset{O}{\overset{||}{C}}-O-CH_2CH=CH_2$

(starting material: $\overset{H}{\underset{H}{C}}=\overset{CH_2OH}{\underset{H}{C}}$)

10.81 (a)

$H-\overset{H}{\underset{H}{C}}-\overset{H}{C}=\overset{H}{C}-H \xrightarrow{+HBr} H-\overset{H}{\underset{H}{C}}-\overset{Br}{\underset{H}{C}}-\overset{H}{\underset{H}{C}}-H$

2-bromopropane

(b)

$H_3C-\overset{H}{\underset{H}{C}}-\overset{CH_3}{C}=\overset{H}{C}-H \xrightarrow{+H_2O} H_3C-\overset{H}{\underset{H}{C}}-\overset{CH_3}{\underset{OH}{C}}-\overset{H}{\underset{H}{C}}-H$

2-methyl-2-butanol

(c)

$H_3C-\overset{H}{C}=\overset{CH_3}{C}-\overset{H}{\underset{H}{C}}-H \xrightarrow{+H_2O} H_3C-\overset{H}{\underset{H}{C}}-\overset{CH_3}{\underset{OH}{C}}-\overset{H}{\underset{H}{C}}-H$

10.83 Compound (b), acetaldehyde, and (c), ethanol, produce acetic acid when oxidized.

10.85 Cyclohexene, a cyclic alkene, will add Br_2 readily (to give $C_6H_{12}Br_2$). Benzene, however, needs much more stringent conditions to react with bromine; then Br_2 will substitute for H atoms on benzene and not add to the ring.

10.87 (a) The compound is either propanone, a ketone, or propanal, an aldehyde.

$H-\overset{H}{\underset{H}{C}}-\overset{O}{\overset{||}{C}}-\overset{H}{\underset{H}{C}}-H$ $H-\overset{H}{\underset{H}{C}}-\overset{H}{\underset{H}{C}}-\overset{O}{\overset{||}{C}}-H$

propanone (a ketone)   propanal (an aldehyde)

(b) The ketone will not undergo oxidation, but the aldehyde will be oxidized to the acid, $CH_3CH_2CO_2H$. Thus, the unknown is likely propanal.

(c) Propanoic acid

10.89 2-Propanol will react with an oxidizing agent such as $KMnO_4$ (to give the ketone), whereas methyl ethyl ether ($CH_3OC_2H_5$) will not react. In addition, the alcohol should be more soluble in water than the ether.

10.91

$H_2C=\overset{H}{\underset{H}{C}}-\overset{CH_3}{\underset{CH_3}{C}}-\overset{H}{\underset{H}{C}}-CH_3$

X = 3,3-dimethyl-1-pentene

$\downarrow +H_2O$

$H_3C-\overset{OH}{\underset{H}{C}}-\overset{CH_3}{\underset{CH_3}{C}}-\overset{H}{\underset{H}{C}}-CH_3 \xrightarrow{\text{oxidizing agent}} H_3C-\overset{O}{\overset{||}{C}}-\overset{CH_3}{\underset{CH_3}{C}}-\overset{H}{\underset{H}{C}}-CH_3$

Y = 3,3-dimethyl-2-pentanol   3,3-dimethyl-2-pentanone

10.93

$H-\overset{H}{\underset{H}{C}}-H$ methane   four single bonds

$\overset{O}{\overset{||}{\underset{H\quad H}{C}}}$ formaldehyde   one double bond and two single bonds

$\overset{H}{\underset{H}{C}}=C=\overset{H}{\underset{H}{C}}$ allene   two double bonds

$H-C\equiv C-H$ acetylene   one single bond and one triple bond

10.95 (a) Cross-linking makes the material very rigid and inflexible.

(b) The OH groups give the polymer a high affinity for water.

(c) Hydrogen bonding allows the chains to form coils and sheets with high tensile strength.

10.97 (a) Ethane heat of combustion = -47.51 kJ/g
Ethanol heat of combustion = -26.82 kJ/g

(b) The heat obtained from the combustion of ethanol is less negative than for ethane, so partially oxidizing ethane to form ethanol decreases the amount of energy per mole available from the combustion of the substance.

10.99 (a) Empirical formula, CHO

(b) Molecular formula, $C_4H_4O_4$

(c)

$HO-\overset{O}{\overset{||}{C}}-\overset{H}{C}=\overset{H}{C}-\overset{O}{\overset{||}{C}}-OH$

(d) All four C atoms are sp^2 hybridized.

(e) 120°

11.1 (a) 0.58 atm
(b) 0.59 bar
(c) 59 kPa

11.3 (a) 0.754 bar
(b) 650 kPa
(c) 934 kPa

11.5 2.70×10^2 mm Hg

11.7 3.7 L

11.9 250 mm Hg

11.11 3.2×10^2 mm Hg

11.13 9.72 atm

11.15 (a) 75 mL O_2
(b) 150 mL NO_2

11.17 0.919 atm

11.19 $V = 2.9$ L

11.21 1.9×10^6 g He

11.23 3.7×10^{-4} g/L

11.25 34.0 g/mol

11.27 57.5 g/mol

11.29 Molar mass = 74.9 g/mol; B_6H_{10}

11.31 0.039 mol H_2; 0.096 atm; 73 mm Hg

11.33 170 g NaN_3

11.35 1.7 atm O_2

11.37 4.1 atm H_2; 1.6 atm Ar; total pressure = 5.7 atm

11.39 (a) 0.30 mol halothane/1 mol O_2
(b) 3.0×10^2 g halothane

11.41 (a) CO_2 has the higher kinetic energy.
(b) The average speed of the H_2 molecules is greater than the average speed of the CO_2 molecules.
(c) The number of CO_2 molecules is greater than the number of H_2 molecules $[n(CO_2) = 1.8n(H_2)]$.
(d) The mass of CO_2 is greater than the mass of H_2.

11.43 Average speed of CO_2 molecule = 3.65×10^4 cm/s

11.45 Average speed increases (and molar mass decreases) in the order $CH_2F_2 < Ar < N_2 < CH_4$.

11.47 (a) F_2 (38 g/mol) effuses faster than CO_2 (44 g/mol).
(b) N_2 (28 g/mol) effuses faster than O_2 (32 g/mol).
(c) C_2H_4 (28.1 g/mol) effuses faster than C_2H_6 (30.1 g/mol).
(d) $CFCl_3$ (137 g/mol) effuses faster than $C_2Cl_2F_4$ (171 g/mol).

11.49 36 g/mol

11.51 P from the van der Waals equation = 26.0 atm

P from the ideal gas law = 30.6 atm

11.53 (a) Standard atmosphere: 1 atm; 760 mm Hg; 101.325 kPa; 1.013 bar.
(b) N_2 partial pressure: 0.780 atm; 593 mm Hg; 79.1 kPa; 0.791 bar
(c) H_2 pressure: 131 atm; 9.98×10^4 mm Hg; 1.33×10^4 kPa; 133 bar
(d) Air: 0.333 atm; 253 mm Hg; 33.7 kPa; 0.337 bar

11.55 $T = 290.$ K or 17 °C

11.57 $2 \, C_4H_9SH(g) + 15 \, O_2(g) \rightarrow$
$8 \, CO_2(g) + 10 \, H_2O(g) + 2 \, SO_2(g)$

Total pressure = 37.3 mm Hg. Partial pressures: CO_2 = 14.9 mm Hg, H_2O = 18.6 mm Hg, and SO_2 = 3.73 mm Hg.

11.59 4 mol

11.61 Ni is the limiting reactant; 1.31 g $Ni(CO)_4$

11.63 (a, b) Sample 4 (He) has the largest number of molecules and sample 3 (H_2 at 27 °C and 760 mm Hg) has the fewest number of molecules.
(c) Sample 2 (Ar)

11.65 8.54 g $Fe(CO)_5$

11.67 S_2F_{10}

11.69 (a) 28.7 g/mol $\simeq$ 29 g/mol
(b) X of O_2 = 0.17 and X of N_2 = 0.83

11.71 Molar mass = 86.4 g/mol. The gas is probably ClO_2F.

11.73 $n(He)$ = 0.0128 mol

11.75 Weight percent $KClO_3$ = 69.1%

11.77 (a) $NO_2 < O_2 < NO$
(b) $P(O_2) = 75$ mm Hg
(c) $P(NO_2) = 150$ mm Hg

11.79 $P(NH_3) = 69$ mm Hg and $P(F_2) = 51$ mm Hg

Pressure after reaction = 17 mm Hg

11.81 At 20 °C, there is 7.8×10^{-3} g H_2O/L. At 0 °C, there is 4.6×10^{-3} g H_2O/L.

11.83 The mixture contains 0.22 g CO_2 and 0.77 g CO.

$P(CO_2) = 0.22$ atm; $P(O_2) = 0.12$ atm; $P(CO) = 1.22$ atm

11.85 The formula of the iron compound is $Fe(CO)_5$.

11.87 (a) $P(B_2H_6) = 0.0160$ atm
(b) $P(H_2) = 0.0320$ atm, so $P_{total} = 0.0480$ atm

11.89 Amount of Na_2CO_3 = 0.00424 mol
Amount of $NaHCO_3$ = 0.00951 mol
Amount of CO_2 produced = 0.0138 mol
Volume of CO_2 produced = 0.343 L

11.91 Decomposition of 1 mol of $Cu(NO_3)_2$ should give 2 mol NO_2 and ½ mol of O_2. Total actual amount = 4.72×10^{-3} mol of gas.
(a) Average molar mass = 41.3 g/mol.
(b) Mole fractions: $X(NO_2) = 0.666$ and $X(O_2) = 0.334$
(c) Amount of each gas: 3.13×10^{-3} mol NO_2 and 1.57×10^{-3} mol O_2
(d) If some NO_2 molecules combine to form N_2O_4, the apparent mole fraction of NO_2 would be smaller than expected (= 0.8). As this is the case, it is apparent that some N_2O_4 has been formed (as is observed in the experiment).

11.93 (a) 10.0 g of O_2 represents more molecules than 10.0 g of CO_2. Therefore, O_2 has the greater partial pressure.
(b) The average speed of the O_2 molecules is greater than the average speed of the CO_2 molecules.
(c) The gases are at the same temperature and so have the same average kinetic energy.

11.95 (a) $P(C_2H_2) > P(CO)$
(b) There are more molecules in the C_2H_2 container than in the CO container.

11.97 (a) Not a gas. A gas would expand to an infinite volume.
(b) Not a gas. A density of 8.2 g/mL is typical of a solid.
(c) Insufficient information
(d) Gas

11.99 (a) There are more molecules of H_2 than atoms of He.
(b) The mass of He is greater than the mass of H_2.

11.101 The speed of gas molecules is related to the square root of the absolute temperature, so a doubling of the temperature will lead to an increase of about $(2)^{1/2}$ or 1.4.

CHAPTER 12

12.1 (a) Dipole–dipole interactions (and hydrogen bonds)
(b) Induced dipole–induced dipole forces
(c) Dipole–dipole interactions (and hydrogen bonds)

12.3 (a) Induced dipole–induced dipole forces
(b) Induced dipole–induced dipole forces
(c) Dipole–dipole forces
(d) Dipole–dipole forces (and hydrogen bonding)

12.5 The predicted order of increasing strength is $Ne < CH_4 < CO < CCl_4$. In this case, prediction does not quite agree with reality. The boiling points are Ne (−246 °C) < CO (−192 °C) < CH_4 (−162 °C) < CCl_4 (77 °C).

12.7 (c) HF; (d) acetic acid; (f) CH_3OH

12.9 (a) LiCl. The Li^+ ion is smaller than Cs^+ (Figure 7.12), which makes the ion–ion forces of attraction stronger in LiCl.
(b) $Mg(NO_3)_2$. The Mg^{2+} ion is smaller than the Na^+ ion (Figure 7.12), and the magnesium ion has a 2+ charge (as opposed to 1+ for sodium). Both of these effects lead to stronger ion–ion forces of attraction in magnesium nitrate.
(c) $NiCl_2$. The nickel(II) ion has a larger charge than Rb^+ and is considerably smaller. Both effects mean that there are stronger ion–ion forces of attraction in nickel(II) chloride.

12.11 $q = +90.1$ kJ

12.13 (a) Water vapor pressure is about 150 mm Hg at 60 °C. (Appendix G gives a value of 149.4 mm Hg at 60 °C.)
(b) 600 mm Hg at about 93 °C
(c) At 70 °C, ethanol has a vapor pressure of about 520 mm Hg, whereas that of water is about 225 mm Hg.

12.15 At 30 °C, the vapor pressure of ether is about 590 mm Hg. (This pressure requires 0.23 g of ether in the vapor phase at the given conditions, so there is sufficient ether in the flask.) At 0 °C, the vapor pressure is about 160 mm Hg, so some ether condenses when the temperature declines.

12.17 (a) O_2 (−183 °C) (bp of N_2 = −196 °C)
(b) SO_2 (−10 °C) (CO_2 sublimes at −78 °C)
(c) HF (+19.7 °C) (HI, −35.6 °C)
(d) GeH_4 (−90.0 °C) (SiH_4, −111.8 °C)

12.19 (a) CS_2, about 620 mm Hg; CH_3NO_2, about 80 mm Hg
(b) CS_2, induced dipole–induced dipole forces; CH_3NO_2, dipole–dipole forces
(c) CS_2, about 46 °C; CH_3NO_2, about 100 °C
(d) About 39 °C
(e) About 34 °C

12.21 (a) 80.1 °C
(b) At about 48 °C, the liquid has a vapor pressure of 250 mm Hg.

The vapor pressure is 650 mm Hg at 75 °C.

(c) 33.5 kJ/mol (from slope of plot)

12.23 No, CO cannot be liquefied at room temperature because the critical temperature is lower than room temperature.

12.25 $Ar < CO_2 < CH_3OH$

12.27 Li^+ ions are smaller than Cs^+ ions (78 pm and 165 pm, respectively; see Figure 7.12). Thus, there will be a stronger attractive force between Li^+ ion and water molecules than between Cs^+ ions and water molecules.

12.29 (a) 350 mm Hg
(b) Ethanol (lower vapor pressure at every temperature)
(c) 84 °C
(d) CS_2, 46 °C; C_2H_5OH, 78 °C; C_7H_{16}, 99 °C
(e) CS_2, gas; C_2H_5OH, gas; C_7H_{16}, liquid

12.31 Molar enthalpy of vaporization increases with increasing intermolecular forces: C_2H_6 (14.69 kJ/mol; induced dipole) < HCl (16.15 kJ/mol; dipole) < CH_3OH (35.21 kJ/mol, hydrogen bonds). (The molar enthalpies of vaporization here are given at the boiling point of the liquid.)

12.33 5.49×10^{19} atoms/m^3

12.35 (a) 70.3 °C
(b)

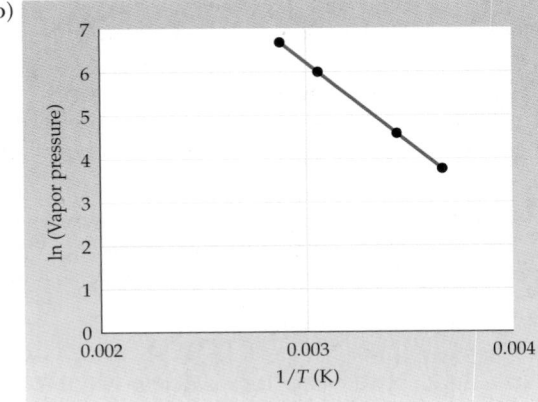

Using the equation for the straight line in the plot

$$\ln P = -3885\ (1/T) + 17.949$$

we calculate that $T = 312.6$ K (39.5 °C) when $P = 250$ mm Hg. When $P = 650$ mm Hg, $T = 338.7$ K (65.5 °C).
(c) Calculated $\Delta_{vap}H = 32.3$ kJ/mol

12.37 When the can is inverted in cold water, the water vapor pressure in the can, which was approximately 760 mm Hg, drops rapidly—say, to 9 mm Hg at 10 °C. This creates a partial vacuum in the can, and the can is crushed because of the difference in pressure inside the can and the pressure of the atmosphere pressing down on the outside of the can.

12.39 Acetone and water can interact by hydrogen bonding.

12.41 Glycol's viscosity will be greater than ethanol's, owing to the greater hydrogen-bonding capacity of glycol.

12.43 (a) Water has two OH bonds and two lone pairs, whereas the O atom of ethanol has only one OH bond (and two lone pairs). More extensive hydrogen bonding is likely for water.
(b) Water and ethanol interact extensively through hydrogen bonding, so the volume is expected to be slightly smaller than the sum of the two volumes.

12.45 Two pieces of evidence for $H_2O(\ell)$ having considerable intermolecular attractive forces:
(a) Based on the boiling points of the Group 6A hydrides (Figure 12.6), the boiling point of water should be approximately −80 °C. The actual boiling point of 100 °C reflects the significant hydrogen bonding that occurs.
(b) Liquid water has a specific heat capacity that is higher than almost any other liquid. This reflects the fact that a relatively larger amount of energy is necessary to overcome intermolecular forces and raise the temperature of the liquid.

12.47 (a) HI, hydrogen iodide
(b) The large iodine atom in HI leads to a significant polarizability for the molecule and thus to a large dispersion force.
(c) The dipole moment of HCl (1.07 D, Table 9.8) is larger than for HI (0.38 D).
(d) HI. See part (b).

12.49 A gas can be liquefied at or below its critical temperature. The critical temperature for CF_4 ($-45.7\ °C$) is below room temperature ($25\ °C$), so it cannot be liquefied at room temperature.

12.51 Hydrogen bonding is most likely at the O—H group at the "right" end of the molecule, and at the C=O and N—H groups in the amide group (—NH—CO—).

CHAPTER 13

13.1 Two possible unit cells are illustrated here. The simplest formula is AB_8.

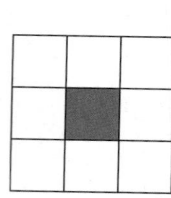 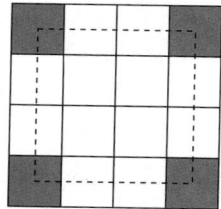

13.3 Ca^{2+} ions at eight corners = 1 net Ca^{2+} ion

O^{2-} ions in six faces = 3 net O^{2-} ions

Ti^{4+} ion in center of unit cell = 1 net Ti^{4+} ion

Formula = $CaTiO_3$

13.5 (a) There are eight O^{2-} ions at the corners and one in the center for a net of two O^{2-} ions per unit cell. There are four Cu ions in the interior in tetrahedral holes. The ratio of ions is Cu_2O.
(b) The oxidation number of copper must be +1.

13.7 Calcium atom radius = 197 pm

13.9 There are three ways the edge dimensions can be calculated:
(a) Calculate mass of unit cell ($= 1.103 \times 10^{-21}$ g/uc)

Calculate volume of unit cell from mass ($= 3.53 \times 10^{-22}$ cm^3/uc)

Calculate edge length from volume ($= 707$ pm)

(b) Assume I^- ions touch along the cell diagonal (see Exercise 13.2) and use I^- radius to find the edge length. Radius $I^- = 220$ pm

Edge $= 4(220\ \text{pm})/2^{1/2} = 622$ pm

(c) Assume the I^- and K^+ ions touch along the cell edge (page 599)

Edge $= 2 \times I^-$ radius $+ 2 \times K^+$ radius $= 706$ pm

Methods (a) and (c) agree. It is apparent that the sizes of the ions are such that the I^- ions cannot touch along the cell diagonal.

13.11 Increasing lattice energy: RbI < LiI < LiF < CaO

13.13 As the ion–ion distance decreases, the force of attraction between ions increases. This should make the lattice more stable, and more energy should be required to melt the compound.

13.15 $\Delta_f H° = -607$ kJ/mol

13.17 (a) Eight C atoms per unit cell. There are eight corners (= 1 net C atom), six faces (= 3 net C atoms), and four internal C atoms.
(b) Face-centered cubic (fcc) with C atoms in the tetrahedral holes.

13.19 q (for fusion) $= -1.97$ kJ; q (for melting) $= +1.97$ kJ

13.21 (a) The density of liquid CO_2 is less than that of solid CO_2.
(b) CO_2 is a gas at 5 atm and 0 °C.
(c) Critical temperature = 31 °C, so CO_2 cannot be liquefied at 45 °C.

13.23 q (to heat the liquid) $= 9.4 \times 10^2$ kJ

q (to vaporize NH_3) $= 1.6 \times 10^4$ kJ

q (to heat the vapor) $= 8.8 \times 10^2$ kJ

$q_{total} = 1.83 \times 10^4$ kJ

13.25 O_2 phase diagram. (i) Note the slight positive slope of the solid–liquid equilibrium line. It indicates that the density of solid O_2 is greater than that of liquid O_2. (ii) Using the diagram here, the vapor pressure of O_2 at 77 K is between 150 mm Hg and 200 mm Hg.

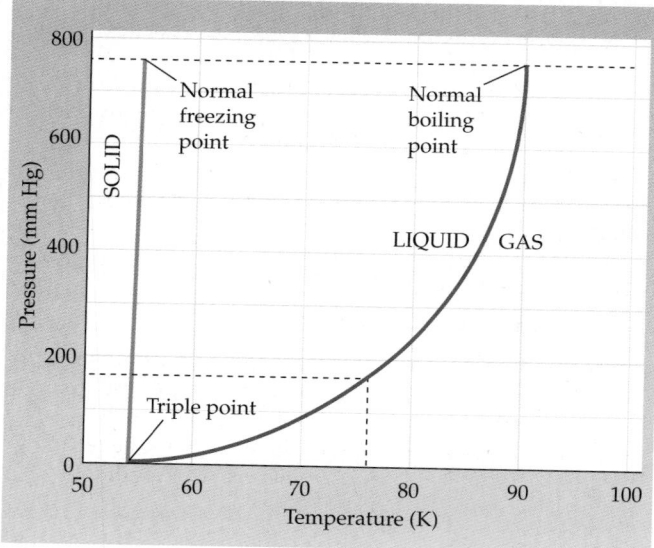

13.27 Radius of silver = 145 pm

13.29 1.356×10^{-8} cm (literature value is 1.357×10^{-8} cm)

13.31 Mass of 1 CaF_2 unit calculated from crystal data = 1.2963×10^{-22} g. Divide molar mass of CaF_2 (78.077 g/mol) by mass of 1 CaF_2 to obtain Avogadro's number. Calculated value = 6.0230×10^{23} CaF_2/mol.

13.33 Diagram A leads to a surface coverage of 78.5%. Diagram B leads to 90.7% coverage.

13.35 (a) The lattice can be described as an fcc lattice of Si atoms with Si atoms in one half of the tetrahedral holes.
  (b) There are eight Si atoms in the unit cell.

  Mass of unit cell = 3.731×10^{-22} g

  Volume of unit cell = 1.602×10^{-22} cm^3

  Density = 2.329 g/cm^3 (which is the same as the literature value)

  In the Si unit cell we cannot assume the atoms touch along the edge or along the face diagonal. Instead, we know that the Si atoms in the tetrahedral holes are bonded to the Si atoms at the corner.

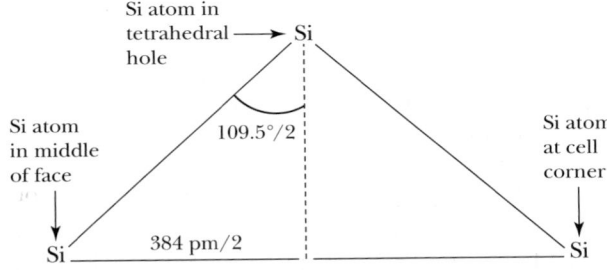

  Distance = 1/2 (cell diagonal) = 384 pm

  Distance across cell face diagonal = 768 pm

  Sin (109.5°/2) = 0.817 = (768 pm/2)/(Si-Si distance)

  Distance from Si in tetrahedral hole to face or corner Si = 235 pm

  Si radius = 118 pm

  Table 7.8 gives Si radius as 117 pm

13.37 (a) Mg^{2+} ions are in $\frac{1}{8}$ of the eight possible tetrahedral holes, and Al^{3+} ions are in $\frac{1}{2}$ of the four available octahedral holes.
  (b) Fe^{2+} ions are in $\frac{1}{8}$ of the eight possible tetrahedral holes, and Cr^{3+} ions are in $\frac{1}{2}$ of the four available octahedral holes.

13.39 Lead sulfide has the same structure as sodium chloride, not the same structure as ZnS. There are four Pb^{2+} ions and four S^{2-} ions per unit cell, a 1:1 ratio that matches the compound formula.

13.41 (a) $BBr_3(g) + PBr_3(g) + 3\ H_2(g) \rightarrow$
  $$BP(s) + 6\ HBr(g)$$

(b) If B atoms are in an fcc lattice, then the P atoms must be in $\frac{1}{2}$ of the tetrahedral holes. (In this way it resembles Si in Question 13.35.)

(c) Unit cell volume = 1.092×10^{-22} cm^3
  Unit cell mass = 2.775×10^{-22} g
  Density = 2.54 g/cm^3

(d) The solution to this problem is identical to Question 13.35. In the BP lattice, the cell face diagonal is 676 pm. Therefore, the calculated BP distance is 207 pm.

13.43 Assuming the spheres are packed in an identical way, the water levels are the same. A face-centered cubic lattice, for example, uses 74% of the available space, regardless of the sphere size.

CHAPTER 14

14.1 (a) Concentration (m) = 0.0434 m
  (b) Mole fraction of acid = 0.000781
  (c) Weight percent of acid = 0.509%

14.3 NaI: 0.15 m; 2.2%; $X = 2.7 \times 10^{-3}$

  CH_3CH_2OH: 1.1 m; 5.0%; $X = 0.020$

  $C_{12}H_{22}O_{11}$: 0.15 m; 4.9%; $X = 2.7 \times 10^{-3}$

14.5 2.65 g Na_2CO_3; $X(Na_2CO_3) = 3.59 \times 10^{-3}$

14.7 220 g glycerol; 5.7 m

14.9 16.2 m; 37.1%

14.11 Molality = 2.6×10^{-5} m (assuming that 1 kg of seawater is equivalent to 1 kg of solvent)

14.13 (b) and (c)

14.15 $\Delta_{soln}H°$ for LiCl = −36.9 kJ/mol. This is an exothermic enthalpy of solution, as compared with the very slightly endothermic value for NaCl.

14.17 Above about 40 °C the solubility increases with temperature; therefore, add more NaCl and raise the temperature.

14.19 2×10^{-3} g O_2

14.21 1130 mm Hg or 1.49 bar

14.23 35.0 mm Hg

14.25 $X(H_2O) = 0.869$; 16.7 mol glycol; 1040 g glycol

14.27 Calculated boiling point = 84.2 °C

14.29 $\Delta T_{bp} = 0.808$ °C; solution boiling point = 62.51 °C

14.31 Molality = 8.60 m; 28.4%

14.33 Molality = 0.195 m; $\Delta T_{fp} = −0.362$ °C

14.35 Molar mass = 360 g/mol; $C_{20}H_{16}Fe_2$

14.37 Molar mass = 150 g/mol

14.39 Molar mass = 170 g/mol

14.41 Freezing point = -24.6 °C

14.43 0.080 m $CaCl_2$ < 0.10 m NaCl < 0.040 m Na_2SO_4 < 0.10 sugar

14.45 (a) $\Delta T_{fp} = -0.348$ °C; fp = -0.348 °C
(b) $\Delta T_{bp} = +0.0959$ °C; bp = 100.0959 °C
(c) $\Pi = 4.58$ atm

The osmotic pressure is large and can be measured with a small experimental error.

14.47 Molar mass = 6.0×10^3 g/mol

14.49 (a) $BaCl_2(aq) + Na_2SO_4(aq) \rightarrow$
$$BaSO_4(s) + 2\,NaCl(aq)$$
(b) Initially, the $BaSO_4$ particles form a colloidal suspension.
(c) Over time, the particles of $BaSO_4(s)$ grow and precipitate.

14.51 Molar mass = 110 g/mol

14.53 (a) Increase in vapor pressure of water

0.20 m Na_2SO_4 < 0.50 m sugar < 0.20 m KBr < 0.35 m ethylene glycol

(b) Increase in boiling point

0.35 m ethylene glycol < 0.20 m KBr < 0.50 m sugar < 0.20 m Na_2SO_4

14.55 (a) 0.456 mol DMG and 11.4 mol ethanol; $X(DMG) = 0.0385$
(b) 0.869 m
(c) VP ethanol over the solution at 78.4 °C = 730.7 mm Hg
(d) bp = 79.5 °C

14.57 For ammonia: 23 m; 28%; $X(NH_3) = 0.29$

14.59 0.592 g Na_2SO_4

14.61 (a) 0.20 m KBr; (b) 0.10 m Na_2CO_3

14.63 Freezing point = -11 °C

14.65 4.0×10^2 g/mol

14.67 4.7×10^{-4} mol/kg

14.69 (a) Molar mass = 4.9×10^4 g/mol
(b) $\Delta T_{fp} = -3.8 \times 10^{-4}$ °C

14.71 $\Delta_{soln}H°$ [Li_2SO_4] = -28.0 kJ/mol

$\Delta_{soln}H°$ [LiCl] = -36.9 kJ/mol

$\Delta_{soln}H°$ [K_2SO_4] = $+23.7$ kJ/mol

$\Delta_{soln}H°$ [KCl] = $+17.2$ kJ/mol

Both lithium compounds have exothermic enthalpies of solution, whereas both potassium compounds have endothermic values. Consistent with this is the fact that lithium salts (LiCl) are often more water-soluble than potassium salts (KCl) (see Figure 14.11).

14.73 X(benzene in solution) = 0.67 and X(toluene in solution) = 0.33

$$P_{total} = P_{toluene} + P_{benzene} = 7.3 \text{ mm Hg} + 50. \text{ mm Hg}$$
$$= 57 \text{ mm Hg}$$

$$X(\text{toluene in vapor}) = \frac{7.3 \text{ mm Hg}}{57 \text{ mm Hg}} = 0.13$$

$$X(\text{benzene in vapor}) = \frac{50. \text{ mm Hg}}{57 \text{ mm Hg}} = 0.87$$

14.75 $i = 1.7$. That is, there is 1.7 mol of ions in solution per mole of compound.

14.77 (a) Calculate the number of moles of ions in 10^6 g H_2O: 550. mol Cl^-; 470. mol Na^+; 53.1 mol Mg^{2+}; 9.42 mol $SO_4{}^{2-}$; 10.3 mol Ca^{2+}; 9.72 mol K^+; 0.84 mol Br^-. Total moles of ions = 1.103×10^3 per 10^6 g water. This gives ΔT_{fp} of -2.05 °C.
(b) $\Pi = 27.0$ atm. This means that a minimum pressure of 27 atm would have to be used in a reverse osmosis device.

14.79 (a) $i = 2.06$
(b) There are approximately two particles in solution, so $H^+ + HSO_4{}^-$ best represents H_2SO_4 in aqueous solution.

14.81 The calculated molality at the freezing point of benzene is 0.47 m, whereas it is 0.99 m at the boiling point. A higher molality at the higher temperature indicates more molecules are dissolved. Therefore, assuming benzoic acid forms dimers like acetic acid (Figure 12.7), dimer formation is more prevalent at the lower temperature. In this process two molecules become one entity, lowering the number of separate species in solution and lowering the molality.

14.83 Molar mass in benzene = 1.20×10^2 g/mol; molar mass in water = 62.4 g/mol. The actual molar mass of acetic acid is 60.1 g/mol. In benzene, the molecules of acetic acid form "dimers." That is, two molecules form a single unit through hydrogen bonding. See Figure 12.7 on page 562.

14.85 (a) Molar mass = 97.6 g/mol; empirical formula, BF_2, and molecular formula, B_2F_4
(b)

14.87 See the discussion and data on page 558.
(a) The enthalpy of hydration of LiF is more negative than that for RbF because the Li^+ ion is much smaller than the Rb^+ ion.

(b) The enthalpy of hydration for $Ca(NO_3)_2$ is larger than that for KNO_3 owing to the +2 charge on the Ca^{2+} ion (and its smaller size).

(c) The enthalpy of hydration is greater for $CuBr_2$ than for $CsBr$ because Cu^{2+} has a larger charge than Cs^+, and the Cu^{2+} ion is smaller than the Cs^+ ion.

14.89 Li_2SO_4 should have a more negative enthalpy of hydration than Cs_2SO_4 because the Li^+ ion is smaller than the Cs^+ ion.

14.91 Colligative properties depend on the number of ions or molecules in solution. Each mole of $CaCl_2$ provides 1.5 times as many ions as each mole of $NaCl$.

14.93 Benzene is a nonpolar solvent. Thus, ionic substances such as $NaNO_3$ and NH_4Cl will certainly not dissolve. However, naphthalene is also nonpolar and resembles benzene in its structure; it should dissolve very well. (A chemical handbook gives a solubility of 33 g naphthalene per 100 g benzene.) Diethyl ether is weakly polar and will also be miscible to some extent with benzene.

14.95 The C—C and C—H bonds in hydrocarbons are nonpolar or weakly polar and tend to make such dispersions hydrophobic (water-hating). The C—O and O—H bonds in starch present opportunities for hydrogen bonding with water. Hence, starch is expected to be more hydrophilic.

14.97 $[NaCl] = 1.0$ M and $[KNO_3] = 0.88$ M. The KNO_3 solution has a higher solvent concentration, so solvent will flow from the KNO_3 solution to the $NaCl$ solution.

CHAPTER 15

15.1 (a) $-\dfrac{1}{2}\dfrac{\Delta[O_3]}{\Delta t} = \dfrac{1}{3}\dfrac{\Delta[O_2]}{\Delta t}$

(b) $-\dfrac{1}{2}\dfrac{\Delta[HOF]}{\Delta t} = \dfrac{1}{2}\dfrac{\Delta[HF]}{\Delta t} = \dfrac{\Delta[O_2]}{\Delta t}$

15.3 $\dfrac{1}{3}\dfrac{\Delta[O_2]}{\Delta t} = -\dfrac{1}{2}\dfrac{\Delta[O_3]}{\Delta t}$ or $\dfrac{\Delta[O_2]}{\Delta t} = -\dfrac{2}{3}\dfrac{\Delta[O_2]}{\Delta t}$

so $\Delta[O_3]/\Delta t = -1.0 \times 10^{-3}$ mol/L · s.

15.5 (a) The graph of [B] (product concentration) versus time shows [B] increasing from zero. The line is curved, indicating the rate changes with time; thus the rate depends on concentration. Rates for the four 10–s intervals are as follows: 0–10 s, 0.0326 mol/L · s; from 10–20 s,

0.0246 mol/L · s; 20–30 s, 0.0178 mol/L · s; 30–40 s, 0.0140 mol/L · s.

(b) $-\dfrac{\Delta[A]}{\Delta t} = \dfrac{1}{2}\dfrac{\Delta[B]}{\Delta t}$ throughout the reaction

In the interval 10–20 s, $\dfrac{\Delta[A]}{\Delta t} = -0.0123 \dfrac{\text{mol}}{\text{L} \cdot \text{s}}$

(c) Instantaneous rate when $[B] = 0.750$ mol/L

$$= \dfrac{\Delta[B]}{\Delta t} = 0.0163 \dfrac{\text{mol}}{\text{L} \cdot \text{s}}$$

15.7 The reaction is second order in A, first order in B, and third order overall.

15.9 (a) Rate $= k[NO_2][O_3]$
(b) If $[NO_2]$ is tripled, the rate triples.
(c) If $[O_3]$ is halved, the rate is halved.

15.11 (a) The reaction is second order in [NO] and first order in $[O_2]$.

(b) $\dfrac{-\Delta[NO]}{\Delta t} = k[NO]^2[O_2]$

(c) $k = 13$ L²/mol² · s

(d) $\dfrac{-\Delta[NO]}{\Delta t} = -1.4 \times 10^{-5}$ mol/L · s

(e) When $-\Delta[NO]/\Delta t = 1.0 \times 10^{-4}$ mol/L · s, $\Delta[O_2]/\Delta t = 5.0 \times 10^{-5}$ mol/L · s and $\Delta[NO_2]/\Delta t = 1.0 \times 10^{-4}$ mol/L · s.

15.13 (a) Rate $= k[NO]^2[O_2]$
(b) $k = 50.$ L²/mol² · h
(c) Rate $= 8.5 \times 10^{-9}$ mol/L · h

15.15 $k = 3.73 \times 10^{-3}$ min⁻¹

15.17 5.0×10^2 min

15.19 (a) 153 min
(b) 1790 min

15.21 (a) $t_{1/2} = 10,000$ s (b) 34,000 s

15.23 0.1.87 g azomethane remains; 0.063 g N_2 formed

15.25 Fraction of ^{64}Cu remaining $= 0.030$

15.27 The straight line obtained in a graph of $\ln[N_2O]$ versus time indicates a first-order reaction.

$k = (\text{−slope}) = 0.0127$ min⁻¹

The rate when $[N_2O] = 0.035$ mol/L is 4.4×10^{-4} mol/L · min.

15.29 The graph of $1/[NO_2]$ versus time gives a straight line, indicating the reaction is second order with respect to $[NO_2]$ (see Table 15.1 on page 689). The slope of the line is k, so $k = 1.1$ L/mol · s.

15.31 $-\Delta[C_2F_4]/\Delta t = k[C_2F_4]^2 = (0.04$ L/mol · s$)[C_2F_4]^2$

15.33 Activation energy $= 102$ kJ/mol

15.35 $k = 0.3 \text{ s}^{-1}$

15.37

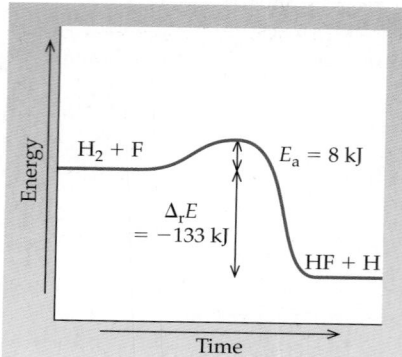

15.39 (a) Rate $= k[NO_3][NO]$
(b) Rate $= k[Cl][H_2]$
(c) Rate $= k[(CH_3)_3CBr]$

15.41 (a) The Second step   (b) Rate $= k[O_3][O]$

15.43 (a) NO_2 is a reactant in the first step and a product in the second step. CO is a reactant in the second step. NO_3 is an intermediate, and CO_2 is a product. NO is a product.
(b) Reaction coordinate diagram

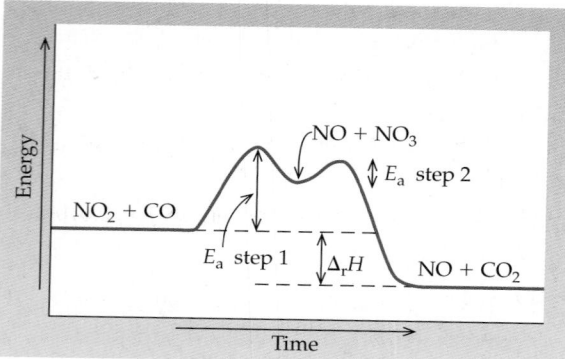

15.45 Doubling the concentration of A will increase the rate by a factor of 4 because the concentration of A appears in the rate law as $[A]^2$. Halving the concentration of B will halve the rate The net result is that the rate of the reaction will double.

15.47 After measuring pH as a function of time, one could then calculate pOH and then $[OH^-]$. Finally, a plot of $1/[OH^-]$ versus time would give a straight line with a slope equal to k.

15.49 72 s represents two half-lives, so $t_{1/2} = 36$ s.

15.51 (a) A plot of $1/[C_2F_4]$ versus time indicates the reaction is second order with respect to $[C_2F_4]$. The rate law is Rate $= k[C_2F_4]^2$.
(b) The rate constant ($=$ slope of the line) is about 0.045 L/mol · s. (The graph does not allow a very accurate calculation.)

(c) Using $k = 0.045$ L/mol · s, the concentration after 600 s is 0.03 M (to 1 significant figure).
(d) Time $= 2000$ s (using k from part a).

15.53 (a) A plot of $1/[NH_4NCO]$ versus time is linear, so the reaction is second order with respect to NH_4NCO.
(b) Slope $= k = 0.0109$ L/mol · min.
(c) $t_{1/2} = 200.$ min
(d) $[NH_4NCO] = 0.0997$ mol/L

15.55 Mechanism 2

15.57 $k = 0.018 \text{ h}^{-1}$ and $t_{1/2} = 39$ h

15.59 (a) After 125 min, 0.251 g remains. After 145, 0.144 g remains.
(b) Time $= 43.9$ min
(c) Fraction remaining $= 0.016$

15.61 The rate equation for the slow step is Rate $= k[O_3][O]$. The equilibrium constant, K, for step 1 is $K = [O_2][O]/[O_3]$. Solving this for $[O]$, we have $[O] = K[O_3]/[O_2]$. Substituting the expression for $[O]$ into the rate equation we find

Rate $= k[O_3]\{K[O_3]/[O_2]\} = kK[O_3]^2/[O_2]$

15.63 The slope of the ln k versus $1/T$ plot is -6370. From slope $= -E_a/R$, we derive $E_a = 53.0$ kJ/mol.

15.65 Estimated time at 90 °C $= 4.76$ min

15.67 After 30 min (one half-life), $P_{HOF} = 50.0$ mm Hg and $P_{total} = 125.0$ mm Hg. After 45 min, $P_{HOF} = 35.4$ mm Hg and $P_{total} = 132$ mm Hg.

15.69 (a) Reaction is first-order in NO_2NH_2 and -1 for H_3O^+.

(b, c) Mechanism 3.

In step 1, $K = k_4/k_4'$
$= [NO_2NH^-][H_3O^+]/[NO_2NH_2]$

Rearrange this and substitute into the rate law for the slow step.

Rate $= k_5[NO_2NH^-] = k_5K[NO_2NH_2]/[H_3O^+]$

This is the same as the experimental rate law, where the overall rate constant $k = k_5K$.

(d) Addition of OH^- ions will shift the equilibrium in step 1 to produce a larger concentration of NO_2NH^-, the reactant in the rate-determining step.

15.71 (a) Average rate for $t = 0$ to $t = 15$ is about 4.7×10^{-5} M/s. For $t = 100$ s to 125 s, the average rate is about 1.6×10^{-5} M/s. The rate slows because the rate of the reaction is dependent on the concentration of reactant and this concentration is declining with time.
(b) Instantaneous rate at 50 s is about 2.7×10^{-5} M/s.

(c) A plot of ln (concentration) versus time is a straight line with an equation of $y = -0.010\,x - 5.2984$. The slope, which is equal to $-k$, is -0.010, so $k = 0.010\ s^{-1}$.

(d) From the data the half-life is 69.3 s, and the same value comes from the relation $t_{1/2} = \ln 2/k$.

15.73 A plot of 1/Rate versus 1/[S] gives the equation

$$1/\text{Rate} = 94\,(1/[S]) + 7.5 \times 10^4$$

and so $\text{Rate}_{\text{max}} = 1/(7.5 \times 10^4) = 1.3 \times 10^{-5}\ M\ min^{-1}$.

15.75 The finely divided rhodium metal will have a significantly greater surface area than the small block of metal. This leads to a large increase in the number of reaction sites and vastly increases the reaction rate.

15.77 (a) False. The reaction may occur in a single step but this does not have to be true.
(b) True
(c) False. Raising the temperature increases the value of k.
(d) False. Temperature has no effect on the value of E_a.
(e) False. If the concentrations of both reactants are doubled, the rate will increase by a factor of 4.
(f) True

15.79 (a) True
(b) True
(c) False. As a reaction proceeds, the reactant concentration decreases and the rate decreases.
(d) False. It is possible to have a one-step mechanism for a third-order reaction if the slow, rate-determining step is termolecular.

15.81 (a) Decrease   (d) No change
(b) Increase   (e) No change
(c) No change   (f) No change

15.83 (a) There are three mechanistic steps.
(b) The overall reaction is exothermic.

15.85 (a) The average rate is calculated over a period of time, whereas the instantaneous rate is the rate of reaction at some instant in time.
(b) The reaction rate decreases with time as the dye concentration decreases.
(c) See part (b).

15.87 (a) Molecules must collide with enough energy to overcome the activation energy, and they must be in the correct orientation.
(b) In animation 2 the molecules are moving faster, so they are at a higher temperature.
(c) Less sensitive. The O_3 must collide with NO in the correct orientation for a reaction to occur. The O_3 and N_2 collisions do not depend to the same extent on orientation because N_2 is a symmetrical, diatomic molecule.

15.89 (a) I^- is regenerated during the second step in the mechanism.
(b) The activation energy is smaller for the catalyzed reaction.

CHAPTER 16

16.1 (a) $K = \dfrac{[H_2O]^2[O_2]}{[H_2O_2]^2}$

(b) $K = \dfrac{[CO_2]}{[CO][O_2]^{1/2}}$

(c) $K = \dfrac{[CO]}{[CO_2]}$

(d) $K = \dfrac{[CO_2]}{[CO]}$

16.3 $Q = (2.0 \times 10^{-8})^2/(0.020) = 2.0 \times 10^{-14}$
$Q < K$ so the reaction proceeds to the right.

16.5 $Q = 1.0 \times 10^3$, so $Q > K$ and the reaction is not at equilibrium. It proceeds to the left to convert products to reactants.

16.7 $K = 1.2$

16.9 (a) $K = 0.025$
(b) $K = 0.025$
(c) The amount of solid does not affect the equilibrium.

16.11 (a) $[COCl_2] = 0.00308\ M$; $[CO] = 0.00712\ M$
(b) $K = 144$

16.13 [isobutane] $= 0.024\ M$; [butane] $= 0.010\ M$

16.15 $[I_2] = 6.14 \times 10^{-3}\ M$; $[I] = 4.79 \times 10^{-3}\ M$

16.17 $[COBr_2] = 0.107\ M$; $[CO] = [Br_2] = 0.143\ M$
57.1% of the $COBr_2$ has decomposed.

16.19 (b)

16.21 (e) $K_2 = 1/(K_1)^2$

16.23 $K = 13.7$

16.25 (a) Equilibrium shifts to the right
(b) Equilibrium shifts to the left
(c) Equilibrium shifts to the right
(d) Equilibrium shifts to the left

16.27 Equilibrium concentrations are the same under both circumstances: [butane] $= 1.1\ M$ and [isobutane] $= 2.9\ M$.

16.29 $K = 3.9 \times 10^{-4}$

16.31 For decomposition of $COCl_2$, $K = 1/(K$ for $COCl_2$ formation$) = 1/(6.5 \times 10^{11}) = 1.5 \times 10^{-12}$

16.33 $K = 4$

16.35 Q is less than K, so the system shifts to form more isobutane.

At equilibrium, [butane] = 0.86 M and [isobutane] = 2.14 M.

16.37 The second equation has been reversed and multiplied by 2.
(c) $K_2 = 1/K_1^2$

16.39 (a) No change (d) Shifts right
(b) Shifts left (e) Shifts right
(c) No change

16.41 (a) The equilibrium will shift to the left on adding more Cl_2.
(b) K is calculated (from the quantities of reactants and products at equilibrium) to be 0.0470. After Cl_2 is added, the concentrations are: $[PCl_5]$ = 0.0199 M, $[PCl_3]$ = 0.0231 M, and $[Cl_2]$ = 0.0403 M.

16.43 $K_p = 0.215$

16.45 (a) Fraction dissociated = 0.15
(b) Fraction dissociated = 0.189. If the pressure decreases, the equilibrium shifts to the right, increasing the fraction of N_2O_4 dissociated.

16.47 $[NH_3]$ = 0.67 M; $[N_2]$ = 0.57 M; $[H_2]$ = 1.7 M; P_{total} = 180 atm

16.49 (a) $[NH_3]$ = $[H_2S]$ = 0.013 M
(b) $[NH_3]$ = 0.027 M and $[H_2S]$ = 0.0067 M

16.51 $P(NO_2)$ = 0.379 atm and $P(N_2O_4)$ = 0.960 atm; $P(total)$ = 1.339 atm

16.53 (a) $K_p = K_c$ = 56. Because 2 mol of reactants gives 2 mol of product, Δn does not change and $K_p = K_c$ (see page 730).

(b, c) Initial $P(H_2)$ = $P(I_2)$ = 2.6 atm and P_{total} = 5.2 atm

At equilibrium, $P(H_2)$ = $P(I_2)$ = 0.54 atm and $P(HI)$ = 4.1 atm. Therefore, P_{total} = 5.2 atm. The initial total pressure and the equilibrium total pressure are the same owing to the reaction stoichiometry. Percent dissociation = 69%

16.55 $P(CO)$ = 0.0010 atm

16.57 1.7×10^{18} O atoms

16.59 Glycerin concentration should be 1.7 M

16.61 (a) $K_p = 0.20$
(b) When initial $[N_2O_4]$ = 1.00 atm, the equilibrium pressures are $[N_2O_4]$ = 0.80 atm and $[NO_2]$ = 0.40 atm. When initial $[N_2O_4]$ = 0.10 atm, the equilibrium pressures are $[N_2O_4]$ = 0.050 atm and $[NO_2]$ = 0.10 atm. The percent dissociation is now 50.%. This is in accord with Le Chatelier's principle: If the initial pressure of the reactant

decreases, the equilibrium shifts to the right, increasing the fraction of the reactant dissociated. See also Question 16.45.

16.63 (a) The flask containing $(H_3N)B(CH_3)_3$ will have the largest partial pressure of $B(CH_3)_3$.
(b) $P[B(CH_3)_3]$ = $P(NH_3)$ = 2.1 and $P[(H_3N)B(CH_3)_3]$ = 1.0 atm

P_{total} = 5.2 atm

Percent dissociation = 69%

16.65 (a) As more KSCN is added, Le Chatelier's principle predicts more of the red complex ion $[Fe(H_2O)_5(SCN)]^+$ will form.
(b) Adding Ag^+ ions leads to a precipitate of AgSCN, thus removing SCN^- ions from solution. The equilibrium shifts left, dropping the concentration of the red complex ion.

16.67 (a) False. The magnitude of K is always dependent on temperature.
(b) True
(c) False. The equilibrium constant for a reaction is the reciprocal of the value of K for its reverse.
(d) True
(e) False. Δn = 1 so $K_p = K_c(RT)$

16.69 (a) Product-favored, $K \gg 1$
(b) Reactant-favored, $K \ll 1$
(c) Product-favored, $K \gg 1$

16.71 The system is not at equilibrium because it continues to gain energy from the surroundings. The temperature of the water/ice mixture will remain at 0 °C until all the ice is melted, then the temperature will rise as more energy is gained. Only if the beaker of water/ice were moved to a perfectly insulated compartment, also at 0 °C, would it attain equilibrium at 0 °C. In this case, it would be a dynamic equilibrium with water molecules moving from the solid to the liquid phase and from the liquid to the solid phase. The quantity of ice would not change. If a D_2O ice cube was added to some $H_2O(\ell)$, an equilibrium would be obtained. The amount of D_2O in the liquid phase would increase due to the continuing molecular exchange. The water could then be sampled for the presence of D_2O.

CHAPTER 17

17.1 (a) CN^-, cyanide ion
(b) SO_4^{2-}, sulfate ion
(c) F^-, fluoride ion

17.3 (a) $H_3O^+(aq) + NO_3^-(aq)$; $H_3O^+(aq)$ is the conjugate acid of H_2O, and $NO_3^-(aq)$ is the conjugate base of HNO_3.
(b) $H_3O^+(aq) + SO_4^{2-}(aq)$; $H_3O^+(aq)$ is the conjugate acid of H_2O, and $SO_4^{2-}(aq)$ is the conjugate base of HSO_4^-.
(c) $H_2O + HF$; H_2O is the conjugate base of H_3O^+, and HF is the conjugate acid of F^-.

17.5 Brønsted acid: $HC_2O_4^-(aq) + H_2O(\ell) \rightleftharpoons$
$$H_3O^+(aq) + C_2O_4^{2-}(aq)$$

Brønsted base: $HC_2O_4^-(aq) + H_2O(\ell) \rightleftharpoons$
$$H_2C_2O_4(aq) + OH^-(aq)$$

17.7

	Acid (A)	Base (B)	Conjugate Base of A	Conjugate Acid of B
(a)	HCO_2H	H_2O	HCO_2^-	H_3O^+
(b)	H_2S	NH_3	HS^-	NH_4^+
(c)	HSO_4^-	OH^-	SO_4^{2-}	H_2O

17.9 $[H_3O^+] = 1.8 \times 10^{-4}$ M; acidic

17.11 HCl is a strong acid, so $[H_3O^+] = $ concentration of the acid. $[H_3O^+] = 0.0075$ M and $[OH^-] = 1.3 \times 10^{-12}$ M. pH = 2.12.

17.13 $Ba(OH)_2$ is a strong base, so $[OH^-] = 2 \times$ concentration of the base.

$[OH^-] = 3.0 \times 10^{-3}$ M; pOH = 2.52; and pH = 11.48

17.15 (a) The strongest acid is HCO_2H (largest K_a) and the weakest acid is C_6H_5OH (smallest K_a).
(b) The strongest acid (HCO_2H) has the weakest conjugate base.
(c) The weakest acid (C_6H_5OH) has the strongest conjugate base.

17.17 (c) HClO, the weakest acid in this list (Table 17.3), has the strongest conjugate base.

17.19 $CO_3^{2-}(aq) + H_2O(\ell) \rightarrow HCO_3^-(aq) + OH^-(aq)$

17.21 Highest pH, Na_2S; lowest pH, $AlCl_3$ (which gives the weak acid $[Al(H_2O)_6]^{3+}$ in solution)

17.23 $pK_a = 4.19$

17.25 $K_a = 3.0 \times 10^{-10}$

17.27 2-Chlorobenzoic acid has the smaller pK_a value.

17.29 $K_b = 7.09 \times 10^{-12}$

17.31 $K_b = 6.3 \times 10^{-5}$

17.33 $CH_3CO_2H(aq) + HCO_3^-(aq) \rightleftharpoons$
$$CH_3CO_2^-(aq) + H_2CO_3(aq)$$

Equilibrium lies predominantly to the right because CH_3CO_2H is a stronger acid than H_2CO_3.

17.35 (a) Left; NH_3 and HBr are the stronger base and acid, respectively.
(b) Left; PO_4^{3-} and CH_3CO_2H are the stronger base and acid, respectively.
(c) Right; $[Fe(H_2O)_6]^{3+}$ and HCO_3^- are the stronger acid and base, respectively.

17.37 (a) $OH^-(aq) + HPO_4^{2-}(aq) \rightleftharpoons$
$$H_2O(\ell) + PO_4^{3-}(aq)$$
(b) OH^- is a stronger base than PO_4^{3-}, so the equilibrium will lie to the right. (The predominant species in solution is PO_4^{3-}, so the solution is likely to be basic because PO_4^{3-} is the conjugate base of a weak acid.)

17.39 (a) $CH_3CO_2H(aq) + HPO_4^{2-}(aq) \rightleftharpoons$
$$CH_3CO_2^-(aq) + H_2PO_4^-(aq)$$
(b) CH_3CO_2H is a stronger acid than $H_2PO_4^-$, so the equilibrium will lie to the right.

17.41 (a) 2.1×10^{-3} M; (b) $K_a = 3.5 \times 10^{-4}$

17.43 $K_b = 6.6 \times 10^{-9}$

17.45 (a) $[H_3O^+] = 1.6 \times 10^{-4}$ M
(b) Moderately weak; $K_a = 1.1 \times 10^{-5}$

17.47 $[CH_3CO_2^-] = [H_3O^+] = 1.9 \times 10^{-3}$ M and $[CH_3CO_2H] = 0.20$ M

17.49 $[H_3O^+] = [CN^-] = 3.2 \times 10^{-6}$ M; $[HCN] = 0.025$ M; pH = 5.50

17.51 $[NH_4^+] = [OH^-] = 1.64 \times 10^{-3}$ M; $[NH_3] = 0.15$ M; pH = 11.22

17.53 $[OH^-] = 0.0102$ M; pH = 12.01; pOH = 1.99

17.55 pH = 3.25

17.57 $[H_3O^+] = 1.1 \times 10^{-5}$ M; pH = 4.98

17.59 $[HCN] = [OH^-] = 3.3 \times 10^{-3}$ M; $[H_3O^+] = 3.0 \times 10^{-12}$ M; $[Na^+] = 0.441$ M

17.61 $[H_3O^+] = 1.5 \times 10^{-9}$ M; pH = 8.81

17.63 (a) The reaction produces acetate ion, the conjugate base of acetic acid. The solution is weakly basic. pH is greater than 7.
(b) The reaction produces NH_4^+, the conjugate acid of NH_3. The solution is weakly acidic. pH is less than 7.
(c) The reaction mixes equal molar amounts of strong base and strong acid. The solution will be neutral. pH will be 7.

17.65 (a) pH = 1.17; (b) $[SO_3^{2-}] = 6.2 \times 10^{-8}$ M

17.67 (a) $[OH^-] = [N_2H_5^+] = 9.2 \times 10^{-5}$ M; $[N_2H_6^{2+}] = 8.9 \times 10^{-16}$ M
(b) pH = 9.96

17.69 (a) Lewis base
(b) Lewis acid

(c) Lewis base (owing to lone pair of electrons on the N atom)

17.71 CO is a Lewis base in its reactions with transition metal atoms. It donates a lone pair of electrons on the C atom.

17.73 HOCN should be a stronger acid than HCN because the H atom in HOCN is attached to a highly electronegative O atom. This induces a positive charge on the H atom, making it more readily removed by an interaction with water.

17.75 The S atom is surrounded by four highly electronegative O atoms. The inductive effect of these atoms induces a positive charge on the H atom, making it susceptible to removal by water.

17.77 pH = 2.671

17.79 Both $Ba(OH)_2$ and $Sr(OH)_2$ dissolve completely in water to provide M^{2+} and OH^- ions. 2.50 g $Sr(OH)_2$ in 1.00 L of water gives $[Sr^{2+}] = 0.021$ M and $[OH^-] = 0.041$ M. The concentration of OH^- is reflected in a pH of 12.61.

17.81 $H_2S(aq) + CH_3CO_2^-(aq) \rightleftharpoons$
$$CH_3CO_2H(aq) + HS^-(aq)$$

The equilibrium lies to the left and favors the reactants.

17.83 $[X^-] = [H_3O^+] = 3.0 \times 10^{-3}$ M; $[HX] = 0.007$ M; pH = 2.52

17.85 $K_a = 1.4 \times 10^{-5}$; $pK_a = 4.86$

17.87 pH = 5.84

17.89 (a) Ethylamine is a stronger base than ethanolamine.
(b) For ethylamine, the pH of the solution is 11.82.

17.91 pH = 7.66

17.93 Acidic: $NaHSO_4$, NH_4Br, $FeCl_3$
Neutral: $KClO_4$, $NaNO_3$, LiBr
Basic: Na_2CO_3, $(NH_4)_2S$, Na_2HPO_4
$(NH_4)_2S$, highest pH. $NaHSO_4$, lowest pH.

17.95 $K_{net} = K_{a1} \times K_{a2} = 3.8 \times 10^{-6}$

17.97 For the reaction $HCO_2H(aq) + OH^-(aq) \rightarrow H_2O(\ell) + HCO_2^-(aq)$, $K_{net} = K_a$ (for HCO_2H) $\times [1/K_w] = 1.8 \times 10^{10}$

17.99 To double the percent ionization, you must dilute 100 mL of solution to 400 mL.

17.101 $H_2O > H_2C_2O_4 > HC_2O_4^- = H_3O^+ > C_2O_4^{2-} > OH^-$

17.103 Measure the pH of the 0.1 M solutions of the three bases. The solution containing the strongest base will have the highest pH. The solution having the weakest base will have the lowest pH.

17.105 The possible cation–anion combinations are NaCl (neutral), NaOH (basic), NH_4Cl (acidic), NH_4OH (basic), HCl (acidic), and H_2O (neutral).

A = H^+ solution; B = NH_4^+ solution; C = Na^+ solution; Y = Cl^- solution; Z = OH^- solution

17.107 $K_a = 3.0 \times 10^{-5}$

17.109 (a) Aniline is both a Brønsted and a Lewis base. As a proton acceptor it gives $C_6H_5NH_3^+$. The N atom can also donate an electron pair to give a Lewis acid–base adduct, $F_3B \leftarrow NH_2C_6H_5$.
(b) pH = 7.97

17.111 Water can both accept a proton (a Brønsted base) and donate a lone pair (a Lewis base). Water can also donate a proton (Brønsted acid), but it cannot accept a pair of electrons (and act as a Lewis acid).

17.113 (a) HOCl is the strongest acid (smallest pK_a and largest K_a), and HOI is the weakest acid.
(b) Cl is more electronegative than I, so the OCl^- anion is more stable than the OI^- anion.

17.115 (a) $HClO_4 + H_2SO_4 \rightleftharpoons ClO_4^- + H_3SO_4^+$
(b) The O atoms on sulfuric acid have lone pairs of electrons that can be used to bind to an H^+ ion.

17.117 (a) $\left[:\!\ddot{I}\!-\!\ddot{I}\!-\!\ddot{I}\!: \right]^-$
(b) $I^-(aq)$ [Lewis base] + $I_2(aq)$ [Lewis acid] $\rightarrow$ $I_3^-(aq)$

17.119 (a) For the weak acid HA, the concentrations at equilibrium are $[HA] = C_0 - \alpha C_0$, $[H_3O^+] = [A^-] = \alpha C_0$. Putting these into the usual expression for K_a we have $K_a = \alpha^2 C_0/(1-\alpha)$.
(b) For 0.10 M NH_4^+, $\alpha = 7.5 \times 10^{-5}$ (reflecting the fact that NH_4^+ is a much weaker acid than acetic acid).

17.121 (a) Add the three equations.

$NH_4^+(aq) + H_2O(\ell) \rightleftharpoons NH_3(aq) + H_3O^+(aq)$

$K_1 = K_w/K_b$

$CN^-(aq) + H_2O(\ell) \rightleftharpoons HCN(aq) + OH^-(aq)$

$K_2 = K_w/K_a$

$H_3O^+(aq) + OH^-(aq) \rightleftharpoons 2\,H_2O(\ell)$ $K_3 = 1/K_w$

$NH_4^+(aq) + CN^-(aq) \rightleftharpoons NH_3(aq) + HCN(aq)$

$K_{net} = K_1 K_2 K_3 = K_w/K_a K_b$

(b) The salts NH_4CN, $NH_4CH_3CO_2$, and NH_4F have K_{net} values of 1.4, 3.1×10^{-5}, and 7.7×10^{-7}, respectively. Only in the case of NH_4CN is the base (the cyanide ion) strong enough to remove a proton from the ammonium ion and produce a significant concentration of products.

(c) The pH of a solution will depend on the relative strengths of the anionic base and the cationic acid. In part (d) the anion and cation were equal in strength, so the solution was neutral. For NH_4CN, the CN^- ion is a stronger base ($K_b = 2.5 \times 10^{-5}$) than NH_4^+ is an acid ($K_a = 5.6 \times 10^{-10}$), so the solution is predicted to be basic.

CHAPTER 18

18.1 (a) Decrease pH; (b) increase pH; (c) no change in pH

18.3 pH = 9.25

18.5 pH = 4.38

18.7 pH = 9.12; pH of buffer is lower than the pH of the original solution of NH_3(pH = 11.17).

18.9 4.7 g

18.11 pH = 4.92

18.13 (a) pH = 3.59; (b) $[HCO_2H]/[HCO_2^-]$ = 0.45

18.15 (b) NH_3 + NH_4Cl

18.17 The buffer must have a ratio of 0.51 mol NaH_2PO_4 to 1 mol Na_2HPO_4. For example, dissolve 0.51 mol NaH_2PO_4 (61 g) and 1.0 mol Na_2HPO_4 (140 g) in some amount of water.

18.19 (a) pH = 4.95; (b) pH = 5.05

18.21 (a) pH = 9.55; (b) pH = 9.50

18.23 (a) Original pH = 5.62
(b) $[Na^+]$ = 0.0323 M, $[OH^-]$ = 1.5×10^{-3} M, $[H_3O^+]$ = 6.5×10^{-12} M, and $[C_6H_5O^-]$ = 0.0308 M
(c) pH = 11.19

18.25 (a) Original NH_3 concentration = 0.0154 M
(b) At the equivalence point $[H_3O^+]$ = 1.9×10^{-6} M, $[OH^-]$ = 5.3×10^{-9} M, $[NH_4^+]$ = 6.25×10^{-3} M.
(c) pH at equivalence point = 5.73

18.27 The titration curve begins at pH = 13.00 and drops slowly as HCl is added. Just before the equivalence point (when 30.0 mL of acid has been added), the curve falls steeply. The pH at the equivalence point is exactly 7. Just after the equivalence point, the curve flattens again and begins to approach the final pH of just over 1.0. The total volume at the equivalence point is 60.0 mL.

18.29 (a) Starting pH = 11.12
(b) pH at equivalence point = 5.28
(c) pH at midpoint (half-neutralization point) = 9.25
(d) Methyl red, bromcresol green
(e)

Acid (mL)	Added pH
5.00	9.85
15.0	9.08
20.0	8.65
22.0	8.39
30.0	2.04

18.31 See Figure 18.10 on page 832.
(a) Thymol blue or bromphenol blue
(b) Phenolphthalein
(c) Methyl red; thymol blue

18.33 (a) Silver chloride, AgCl; lead chloride, $PbCl_2$
(b) Zinc carbonate, $ZnCO_3$; zinc sulfide, ZnS
(c) Iron(II) carbonate, $FeCO_3$; iron(II) oxalate, FeC_2O_4

18.35 (a) and (b) are soluble, (c) and (d) are insoluble.

18.37 (a) $AgCN(s) \rightarrow Ag^+(aq) + CN^-(aq)$,
$K_{sp} = [Ag^+][CN^-]$
(b) $NiCO_3(s) \rightarrow Ni^{2+}(aq) + CO_3^{2-}(aq)$,
$K_{sp} = [Ni^{2+}][CO_3^{2-}]$
(c) $AuBr_3(s) \rightarrow Au^{3+}(aq) + 3\ Br^-(aq)$,
$K_{sp} = [Au^{3+}][Br^-]^3$

18.39 $K_{sp} = (1.9 \times 10^{-3})^2 = 3.6 \times 10^{-6}$

18.41 $K_{sp} = 4.37 \times 10^{-9}$

18.43 $K_{sp} = 1.4 \times 10^{-15}$

18.45 (a) 9.2×10^{-9} M; (b) 2.2×10^{-6} g/L

18.47 (a) 2.4×10^{-4} M; (b) 0.018 g/L

18.49 Only 2.1×10^{-4} g dissolves.

18.51 (a) $PbCl_2$; (b) FeS; (c) $Fe(OH)_2$

18.53 Solubility in pure water = 1.0×10^{-6} mol/L; solubility in 0.010 M SCN^- = 1.0×10^{-10} mol/L

18.55 (a) Solubility in pure water = 2.2×10^{-6} mg/mL
(b) Solubility in 0.020 M $AgNO_3$ = 1.0×10^{-12} mg/mL

18.57 (a) PbS
(b) Ag_2CO_3
(c) $Al(OH)_3$

18.59 $Q < K_{sp}$, so no precipitate forms.

18.61 $Q > K_{sp}$; $Zn(OH)_2$ will precipitate.

18.63 $[OH^-]$ must exceed 1.0×10^{-5} M.

18.65 Using K_{sp} for $Zn(OH)_2$ and K_{form} for $Zn(OH)_4^{2-}$, K_{net} for

$$Zn(OH)_2(s) + 2\,OH^-(aq) \rightleftarrows Zn(OH)_4^{2-}(aq)$$

is 13.8. This indicates that the reaction is definitely product-favored.

18.67 K_{net} for $AgCl(s) + 2\,NH_3(aq) \rightleftarrows Ag(NH_3)_2^+(aq) + Cl^-(aq)$ is 2.0×10^{-3}. When all the AgCl dissolves, $[Ag(NH_3)_2^+] = [Cl^-] = 0.050$ M. To achieve these concentrations, $[NH_3]$ must be 1.12 M. Therefore, the amount of NH_3 added must be 2×0.050 mol/L (to react with the AgCl) plus 1.25 mol/L (to achieve the proper equilibrium concentration). The total is 1.22 mol/L NH_3.

18.69 (a) Solubility in pure water $= 1.3 \times 10^{-5}$ mol/L or 0.0019 g/L.
(b) K_{net} for $AgCl(s) + 2\,NH_3(aq) \rightleftarrows Ag(NH_3)_2^+(aq) + Cl^-(aq)$ is 2.0×10^{-3}. When using 1.0 M NH_3, the concentrations of species in solution are $[Ag(NH_3)_2^+] = [Cl^-] = 0.041$ M and so $[NH_3] = 1.0 - 2(0.041)$ M or about 0.9 M. The amount of AgCl dissolved is 0.041 mol/L or 5.88 g/L.

18.71 (a) $NaBr(aq) + AgNO_3(aq) \rightarrow$
$$NaNO_3(aq) + AgBr(s)$$
(b) $2\,KCl(aq) + Pb(NO_3)_2(aq) \rightarrow$
$$2\,KNO_3(aq) + PbCl_2(s)$$

18.73 $Q > K_{sp}$, so $BaSO_4$ precipitates.

18.75 $[H_3O^+] = 1.9 \times 10^{-10}$ M; pH = 9.73

18.77 $BaCO_3 < Ag_2CO_3 < Na_2CO_3$

18.79 Original pH = 8.62; dilution will not affect the pH.

18.81 (a) 0.100 M acetic acid has a pH of 2.87. Adding sodium acetate slowly raises the pH.
(b) Adding $NaNO_3$ to 0.100 M HNO_3 has no effect on the pH.
(c) In part (a), adding the conjugate base of a weak acid creates a buffer solution. In part (b), HNO_3 is a strong acid, and its conjugate base (NO_3^-) is so weak that the base has no effect on the complete ionization of the acid.

18.83 (a) pH = 4.13
(b) 0.6 g of $C_6H_5CO_2H$
(c) 8.2 mL of 2.0 M HCl should be added

18.85 $K = 2.1 \times 10^6$; yes, AgI forms

18.87 (a) $[F^-] = 1.3 \times 10^{-3}$ M; (b) $[Ca^{2+}] = 2.9 \times 10^{-5}$ M

18.89 (a) $PbSO_4$ will precipitate first.
(b) $[Pb^{2+}] = 5.1 \times 10^{-6}$ M

18.91 When $[CO_3^{2-}] = 0.050$ M, $[Ca^{2+}] = 6.8 \times 10^{-8}$ M. This means only 6.8×10^{-4} % of the ions remain, or that essentially all of the calcium ions have been removed.

18.93 (a) Add H_2SO_4, precipitating $BaSO_4$ and leaving $Na^+(aq)$ in solution.
(b) Add HCl or another source of chloride ion. $PbCl_2$ will precipitate, but $NiCl_2$ is water-soluble.

18.95 (a) $BaSO_4$ will precipitate first.
(b) $[Ba^{2+}] = 1.8 \times 10^{-7}$ M

18.97 (a) pH = 2.81
(b) pH at equivalence point = 8.72
(c) pH at the midpoint = pK_a = 4.62
(d) Phenolphthalein
(e) After 10.0 mL, pH = 4.39.
After 20.0 mL, pH = 5.07.
After 30.0 mL, pH = 11.84.
(f) A plot of pH versus volume of NaOH added would begin at a pH of 2.81, rise slightly to the midpoint at pH = 4.62, and then begin to rise more steeply as the equivalence point is approached (when the volume of NaOH added is 27.0 mL). The pH rises vertically through the equivalence point, and then begins to level off above a pH of about 11.0.

18.99 The K_b value for ethylamine (4.27×10^{-4}) is found in Appendix I.
(a) pH = 11.89
(b) Midpoint pH = 10.63
(c) pH = 10.15
(d) pH = 5.93 at the equivalence point
(e) pH = 2.13
(f) Titration curve

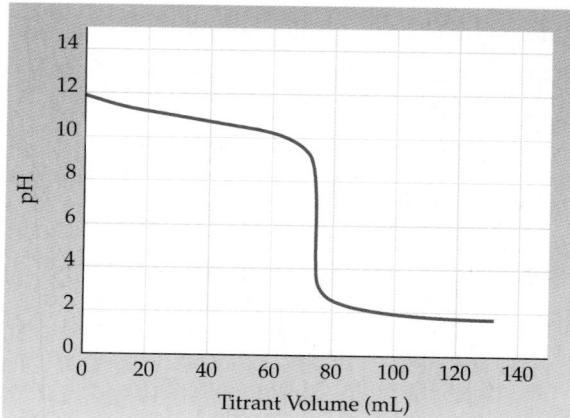

(g) Alizarin or bromcresol purple (see Figure 18.10)

18.101 110 mL NaOH

18.103 Add dilute HCl, say 1 M HCl, to a solution of the salts. Both AgCl and $PbCl_2$ will precipitate, but Cu^{2+} ions will stay in solution (as $CuCl_2$ is water-soluble). Decant off the copper-containing solution to leave a precipitate of white AgCl and $PbCl_2$. Lead(II) chloride ($K_{sp} = 1.7 \times 10^{-5}$) is much more soluble than AgCl ($K_{sp} = 1.8 \times 10^{-10}$). Warming the precipitates in water will dissolve the $PbCl_2$ and leave the AgCl as a white solid.

18.105 $Cu(OH)_2$ will dissolve in a nonoxidizing acid such as HCl, whereas CuS will not.

18.107 When Ag_3PO_4 dissolves slightly, it produces a small concentration of the phosphate ion, PO_4^{3-}. This ion is a strong base and hydrolyzes to HPO_4^{2-}. As this reaction removes the PO_4^{3-} ion from equilibrium with Ag_3PO_4, the equilibrium shifts to the right, producing more PO_4^{3-} and Ag^+ ions. Thus, Ag_3PO_4 dissolves to a greater extent than might be calculated from a K_{sp} value (unless the K_{sp} value was actually determined experimentally).

18.109 (a) Base is added to increase the pH. The added base reacts with acetic acid to form more acetate ions in the mixture. Thus, the fraction of acid declines and the fraction of conjugate base rises (i.e., the ratio $[CH_3CO_2H]/[CH_3CO_2^-]$ decreases) as the pH rises.
(b) At pH = 4, acid predominates (85% acid and 15% acetate ions). At pH = 6, acetate ions predominate (95% acetate ions and 5% acid).
(c) At the point the lines cross, $[CH_3CO_2H] = [CH_3CO_2^-]$. At this point pH = pK_a, so pK_a for acetic acid is 4.75.

18.111 (a) C—C—C angle, 120°; O—C=O, 120°; C—O—H, 109°; C—C—H, 120°
(b) Both the ring C atoms and the C in CO_2H are sp^2 hybridized.
(c) $K_a = 1 \times 10^{-3}$
(d) 10%
(e) pH at half-way point = pK_a = 3.0; pH at equivalence point = 7.3

CHAPTER 19

19.1 (a) For a given substance at a given temperature, a gas always has a greater entropy than the liquid. Matter and energy are more dispersed.
(b) Liquid water at 50 °C
(c) Ruby
(d) One mole of N_2 at 1 bar

19.3 (a) $\Delta_r S° = +12.7$ J/K · mol-rxn. Entropy increases.
(b) $\Delta_r S° = -102.55$ J/K · mol-rxn. Significant decrease in entropy.

(c) $\Delta_r S° = +93.2$ J/K · mol-rxn. Entropy increases.
(d) $\Delta_r S° = -129.7$ J/K · mol-rxn. The solution has a smaller entropy (with H^+ forming H_3O^+ and hydrogen bonding occurring) than HCl in the gaseous state.

19.5 (a) $\Delta_r S° = +9.3$ J/K · mol-rxn; (b) $\Delta_r S° = -293.97$ J/K · mol-rxn

19.7 (a) $\Delta_r S° = -507.3$ J/K · mol-rxn; entropy declines as a gaseous reactant is incorporated in a solid compound.
(b) $\Delta_r S° = +313.25$ J/K · mol-rxn; entropy increases as five molecules (two of them in the gas phase) form six molecules of products (all gases).

19.9 $\Delta_{sys}S° = -134.18$ J/K · mol-rxn; $\Delta_{sys}H° = -662.75$ kJ/mol-rxn; $\Delta_{surr}S° = +2222.9$ J/K · mol-rxn; $\Delta_{univ}S° = +2088.7$ J/K · mol-rxn

19.11 $\Delta_{sys}S° = +163.3$ J/K · mol-rxn; $\Delta_{sys}H° = +285.83$ kJ/mol-rxn; $\Delta_{surr}S° = -958.68$ J/K · mol-rxn; $\Delta_{univ}S° = -795.4$ J/K

The reaction is not spontaneous, because the overall entropy change in the universe is negative. The reaction is disfavored by energy dispersal.

19.13 (a) Type 2. The reaction is enthalpy-favored but entropy-disfavored. It is more favorable at low temperatures.
(b) Type 4. This endothermic reaction is not favored by the enthalpy change nor is it favored by the entropy change. It is not spontaneous under any conditions.

19.15 (a) $\Delta_r H° = -438$ kJ/mol-rxn; $\Delta_r S° = -201.7$ J/K · mol-rxn; $\Delta_r G° = -378$ kJ/mol-rxn. The reaction is product-favored and is enthalpy-driven.
(b) $\Delta_r H° = -86.61$ kJ/mol-rxn; $\Delta_r S° = -79.4$ J/K · mol-rxn; $\Delta_r G° = -62.9$ kJ/mol-rxn

The reaction is product-favored. The enthalpy change favors the reaction.

19.17 (a) $\Delta_r H° = +116.7$ kJ/mol-rxn; $\Delta_r S° = +168.0$ J/K mol-rxn; $\Delta_f G° = +66.6$ kJ/mol
(b) $\Delta_r H° = -425.93$ kJ/mol-rxn; $\Delta_r S° = -154.6$ J/K · mol-rxn; $\Delta_f G° = -379.82$ kJ/mol
(c) $\Delta_r H° = +17.51$ kJ/mol-rxn; $\Delta_r S° = +77.95$ J/K mol-rxn; $\Delta_f G° = -5.73$ kJ/mol

19.19 (a) $\Delta_r G° = -817.54$ kJ/mol-rxn; spontaneous
(b) $\Delta_r G° = +256.6$ kJ/mol-rxn; not spontaneous
(c) $\Delta_r G° = -1101.14$ kJ/mol-rxn; spontaneous

19.21 $\Delta_f G°$ [$BaCO_3(s)$] = -1134.4 kJ/mol

19.23 (a) $\Delta_r H° = +66.2$ kJ/mol-rxn; $\Delta_r S° = -121.62$ J/K · mol-rxn; $\Delta_r G° = +102.5$ kJ/mol-rxn

Both the enthalpy and the entropy changes indicate the reaction is not spontaneous. There is no temperature to which it will become spontaneous. This is a case like that in the right panel in Figure 19.12 and is a Type 4 reaction (Table 19.2).

(b) $\Delta_r H° = -221.05$ kJ/mol-rxn; $\Delta_r S° = +179.1$ J/K · mol-rxn; $\Delta_r G° = -283.99$ kJ/mol-rxn

The reaction is favored by both enthalpy and entropy and is product-favored at all temperatures. This is a case like that in the left panel in Figure 19.12 and is a Type 1 reaction.

(c) $\Delta_r H° = -179.0$ kJ/mol-rxn; $\Delta_r S° = -160.2$ J/K · mol-rxn; $\Delta_r G° = -131.4$ kJ/mol-rxn

The reaction is favored by the enthalpy change but disfavored by the entropy change. The reaction becomes less product-favored as the temperature increases; it is a case like the upper line in the middle panel of Figure 19.12.

(d) $\Delta_r H° = +822.2$ kJ/mol-rxn; $\Delta_r S° = +181.28$ J/K · mol-rxn; $\Delta_r G° = +768.08$ kJ/mol-rxn

The reaction is not favored by the enthalpy change but favored by the entropy change. The reaction becomes more product-favored as the temperature increases; it is a case like the lower line in the middle panel of Figure 19.12.

19.25 (a) $\Delta_r S° = +174.75$ J/K · mol-rxn; $\Delta_r H° = +116.94$ kJ/mol-rxn
(b) $\Delta_r G° = +64.87$ kJ/mol-rxn. The reaction is not spontaneous at 298 K.
(c) As the temperature increases, $\Delta_r S°$ becomes more important, so $\Delta_r G°$ can become negative at a sufficiently high temperature.

19.27 $K = 6.8 \times 10^{-16}$. Note that K is very small and that $\Delta G°$ is positive. Both indicate a reactant-favored process.

19.29 $\Delta_r G° = -100.24$ kJ/mol-rxn and $K_p = 3.64 \times 10^{17}$. Both the free energy change and K indicate a product-favored process.

19.31 (a) HBr
(b) $NH_4Cl(aq)$
(c) $C_2H_4(g)$
(d) $NaCl(g)$

19.33 $\Delta_r G° = -98.9$ kJ/mol-rxn. The reaction is spontaneous under standard conditions and is enthalpy-driven.

19.35 $\Delta_r H° = -1428.66$ kJ/mol-rxn; $\Delta_r S° = +47.1$ J/K · mol-rxn; $\Delta_{univ} S° = +4840$ J/K · mol-rxn. Combustion reactions are spontaneous, and this is confirmed by the sign of $\Delta_{univ} S°$.

19.37 (a) The reaction occurs spontaneously and is product-favored. Therefore, $\Delta_{univ} S°$ is positive and $\Delta_r G°$ is negative. The reaction is likely to be exothermic, so $\Delta_r H°$ is negative, and $\Delta_{surr} S°$ is positive. $\Delta_{sys} S°$ is

expected to be negative because two moles of gas form one mole of solid. The calculated values are as follows:

$\Delta_{sys} S° = -284.2$ J/K · mol-rxn

$\Delta_r H° = -176.34$ kJ/mol-rxn

$\Delta_{surr} S° = +591.45$ J/K · mol-rxn

$\Delta_{univ} S° = +307.3$ J/K · mol-rxn

$\Delta_r G° = -91.64$ kJ/mol-rxn

(b) $K_p = 1.13 \times 10^{16}$

19.39 $K_p = 1.3 \times 10^{29}$ at 298 K ($\Delta G° = -166.1$ kJ/mol-rxn). The reaction is already extremely product-favored at 298 K. A higher temperature, however, would make the reaction less product-favored because $\Delta_r S°$ has a negative value (-242.3 J/K · mol-rxn).

19.41 At the boiling point, $\Delta G° = 0 = \Delta H° - T\Delta S°$.

Here $\Delta S° = \Delta H°/T = 112$ J/K · mol-rxn at 351.15 K.

19.43 $\Delta_r S°$ is $+137.2$ J/K · mol-rxn. A positive entropy change means that raising the temperature will increase the product favorability of the reaction (because $T\Delta S°$ will become more negative).

19.45 The reaction is exothermic, so $\Delta_r H°$ should be negative. Also, a gas and an aqueous solution are formed, so $\Delta_r S°$ should be positive. The calculated values are $\Delta_r H° = -183.32$ kJ/mol-rxn (with a negative sign as expected) and $\Delta_r S° = -7.7$ J/K · mol-rxn

The entropy change is slightly negative, not positive as predicted. The reason for this is the negative entropy change upon dissolving NaOH. Apparently the OH^- ions in water hydrogen-bond with water molecules, an effect that also leads to a small, negative entropy change.

19.47 $\Delta_r H° = +126.03$ kJ/mol-rxn; $\Delta_r S° = +78.2$ J/K · mol-rxn; and $\Delta_r G° = +103$ kJ/mol-rxn. The reaction is not predicted to be spontaneous under standard conditions.

19.49 $\Delta_r G°$ from K value = 4.87 kJ/mol-rxn

$\Delta_r G°$ from free energies of formation = 4.73 kJ/mol-rxn

19.51 $\Delta_r G° = -2.27$ kJ/mol-rxn

19.53 (a) $\Delta_r G° = +141.82$ kJ/mol-rxn, so the reaction is not spontaneous.

(b) $\Delta_r H° = +197.86$ kJ/mol-rxn; $\Delta_r S° = +187.95$ J/K · mol-rxn

$T = \Delta_r H°/ \Delta_r S° = 1052.7$ K or 779.6 °C

(c) $\Delta_r G°$ at 1500 °C (1773 K) = -135.4 kJ/mol-rxn

K_p at 1500 °C = 1×10^4

19.55 $\Delta_r S° = -459.0$ J/K · mol-rxn; $\Delta_r H° = -793$ kJ/mol-rxn;

$\Delta_r G° = -657$ kJ/mol-rxn

The reaction is spontaneous and enthalpy-driven.

19.57 (a) $\Delta_r G°$ at 80.0 °C = +0.14 kJ/mol-rxn

$\Delta_r G°$ at 110.0 °C = -0.12 kJ/mol-rxn

Rhombic sulfur is more stable than monoclinic sulfur at 80 °C, but the reverse is true at 110 °C.

(b) T = 370 K or about 96 °C

19.59 $\Delta_r G°$ at 298 K = 22.64 kJ/mol; reaction is not product-favored.

It does become product-favored above 469 K (196 °C).

19.61 $\Delta_f G°$ [HI(g)] = -10.9 kJ/mol

19.63 (a) $\Delta_r G°$ = +194.8 kJ/mol-rxn and K = 6.68 × 10^{-11}
(b) The reaction is not spontaneous at 727 °C.
(c) Keep the pressure of CO as low as possible (by removing it during the course of the reciton).

19.65 $K_p = P_{Hg(g)}$ at any temperature.

K_p = 1 at 620.3 K or 347.2 °C when $P_{Hg(g)}$ = 1.000 bar.

T when $P_{Hg(g)}$ = (1/760) bar is 393.3 K or 125.2 °C.

19.67 (a) True
(b) False. Whether an exothermic system is spontaneous also depends on the entropy change for the system.
(c) False. Reactions with + $\Delta_r H°$ and + $\Delta_r S°$ are spontaneous at higher temperatures.
(d) True

19.69 Dissolving a solid such as NaCl in water is a spontaneous process. Thus, $\Delta G°$ < 0. If $\Delta H°$ = 0, then the only way the free energy change can be negative is if $\Delta S°$ is positive. Generally the entropy change is the important factor in forming a solution.

19.71 2 C_2H_6(g) + 7 O_2(g) → 4 CO_2(g) + 6 H_2O(g)
(a) Not only is this an exothermic combustion reaction, but there is also an increase in the number of molecules from reactants to products. Therefore, we would predict an increase in $\Delta S°$ for both the system and the surroundings and thus for the universe as well.
(b) The exothermic reaction has $\Delta_r H°$ < 0. Combined with a positive $\Delta_{sys} S°$, the value of $\Delta_r G°$ is negative.
(c) The value of K_p is likely to be much greater than 1. Further, because $\Delta_{sys} S°$ is positive, the value of K_p will be even larger at a higher temperature. (See the left panel of Figure 19.12.)

19.73 Reaction 1: $\Delta_r S_1° = -80.7$ J/K · mol-rxn

Reaction 2: $\Delta_r S_2° = -161.60$ J/K · mol-rxn

Reaction 3: $\Delta_r S_3° = -242.3$ J/K · mol-rxn

$\Delta_r S_1° + \Delta_r S_2° = \Delta_r S_3°$

19.75 (a) $\Delta_r H°$ = -352.88 kJ/mol-rxn and $\Delta_r S°$ = +21.31 J/K · mol-rxn. Therefore, at 298 K, $\Delta_r G°$ = -359.23 kJ/mol-rxn.
(b) 4.84 g of Mg is required.

19.77 (a) N_2H_4(ℓ) + O_2(g) → 2 H_2O(ℓ) + N_2(g)

O_2 is the oxidizing agent and N_2H_4 is the reducing agent.

(b) $\Delta_r H°$ = -622.29 kJ/mol-rxn and $\Delta_r S°$ = +4.87 J/K · mol-rxn. Therefore, at 298 K, $\Delta_r G°$ = -623.77 kJ/mol-rxn.
(c) 0.0027 K
(d) 7.5 mol O_2
(e) 4.8 × 10^3 g solution
(f) 7.5 mol N_2(g) occupies 170 L at 273 K and 1.0 atm of pressure.

19.79 Iodine dissolves readily, so the process is spontaneous and $\Delta G°$ must be less than zero. Because $\Delta H°$ = 0, the process is entropy-driven.

19.81 (a) The spontaneity decreases as temperature increases.
(b) There is no temperature between 400 K and 1000 K at which the decomposition is spontaneous.

19.83 (a, b)

Temperature (K)	$\Delta_r G°$ (kJ)	kJ/mol
298 K	-32.74 K	5.48 × 10^5
800 K	+72.92 K	1.73 × 10^{-5}
1300 K	+184.0 K	4.05 × 10^{-8}

(c) The largest mole fraction of NH_3 in an equilibrium mixture will be at 298 K.

CHAPTER 20

20.1 (a) Cr(s) → Cr^{3+}(aq) + 3 e$^-$

Cr is a reducing agent; this is an oxidation reaction.

(b) AsH_3(g) → As(s) + 3 H$^+$(aq) + 3 e$^-$

AsH_3 is a reducing agent; this is an oxidation reaction.

(c) $VO_3^-(aq) + 6\ H^+(aq) + 3\ e^- \rightarrow$
$$V^{2+}(aq) + 3\ H_2O(\ell)$$

$VO_3^-(aq)$ is an oxidizing agent; this is a reduction reaction.

(d) $2\ Ag(s) + 2\ OH^-(aq) \rightarrow$
$$Ag_2O(s) + H_2O(\ell) + 2e^-$$

Silver is a reducing agent; this is an oxidation reaction.

20.3 (a) $Ag(s) \rightarrow Ag^+(aq) + e^-$

$e^- + NO_3^-(aq) + 2\ H^+(aq) \rightarrow NO_2(g) + H_2O(\ell)$

$\overline{Ag(s) + NO_3^-(aq) + 2\ H^+(aq) \rightarrow}$
$$Ag^+(aq) + NO_2(g) + H_2O(\ell)$$

(b) $2[MnO_4^-(aq) + 8\ H^+(aq) + 5\ e^- \rightarrow$
$$Mn^{2+}(aq) + 4\ H_2O(\ell)]$$

$5[HSO_3^-(aq) + H_2O(\ell) \rightarrow$
$$SO_4^{2-}(aq) + 3\ H^+(aq) + 2\ e^-]$$

$\overline{2\ MnO_4^-(aq) + H^+(aq) + 5\ HSO_3^-(aq) \rightarrow}$
$$2\ Mn^{2+}(aq) + 3\ H_2O(\ell) + 5\ SO_4^{2-}(aq)$$

(c) $4[Zn(s) \rightarrow Zn^{2+}(aq) + 2\ e^-]$

$2\ NO_3^-(aq) + 10\ H^+(aq) + 8\ e^- \rightarrow$
$$N_2O(g) + 5\ H_2O(\ell)$$

$\overline{4\ Zn(s) + 2\ NO_3^-(aq) + 10\ H^+(aq) \rightarrow}$
$$4\ Zn^{2+}(aq) + N_2O(g) + 5\ H_2O(\ell)$$

(d) $Cr(s) \rightarrow Cr^{3+}(aq) + 3\ e^-$

$3\ e^- + NO_3^-(aq) + 4\ H^+(aq) \rightarrow$
$$NO(g) + 2\ H_2O(\ell)$$

$\overline{Cr(s) + NO_3^-(aq) + 4\ H^+(aq) \rightarrow}$
$$Cr^{3+}(aq) + NO(g) + 2\ H_2O(\ell)$$

20.5 (a) $2[Al(s) + 4\ OH^-(aq) \rightarrow$
$$Al(OH)_4^-(aq) + 3\ e^-]$$

$3[2\ H_2O(\ell) + 2\ e^- \rightarrow H_2(g) + 2\ OH^-(aq)]$

$\overline{2\ Al(s) + 2\ OH^-(aq) + 6\ H_2O(\ell) \rightarrow}$
$$2\ Al(OH)_4^-(aq) + 3\ H_2(g)$$

(b) $2[CrO_4^{2-}(aq) + 4\ H_2O(\ell) + 3\ e^- \rightarrow$
$$Cr(OH)_3(s) + 5\ OH^-(aq)]$$

$3[SO_3^{2-}(aq) + 2\ OH^-(aq) \rightarrow$
$$SO_4^{2-}(aq) + H_2O(\ell) + 2\ e^-]$$

$\overline{2\ CrO_4^{2-}(aq) + 3\ SO_3^{2-}(aq) + 5\ H_2O(\ell) \rightarrow}$
$$2\ Cr(OH)_3(s) + 3\ SO_4^{2-}(aq) + 4\ OH^-(aq)$$

(c) $Zn(s) + 4\ OH^-(aq) \rightarrow Zn(OH)_4^{2-}(aq) + 2\ e^-$

$Cu(OH)_2(s) + 2\ e^- \rightarrow Cu(s) + 2\ OH^-(aq)$

$\overline{Zn(s) + 2\ OH^-(aq) + Cu(OH)_2(s) \rightarrow}$
$$Zn(OH)_4^{2-}(aq) + Cu(s)$$

(d) $3[HS^-(aq) + OH^-(aq) \rightarrow$
$$S(s) + H_2O(\ell) + 2\ e^-]$$

$ClO_3^-(aq) + 3\ H_2O(\ell) + 6\ e^- \rightarrow$
$$Cl^-(aq) + 6\ OH^-(aq)$$

$\overline{3\ HS^-(aq) + ClO_3^-(aq) \rightarrow}$
$$3\ S(s) + Cl^-(aq) + 3\ OH^-(aq)$$

20.7 Electrons flow from the Cr electrode to the Fe electrode. Negative ions move via the salt bridge from the Fe/Fe^{2+} half-cell to the Cr/Cr^{3+} half-cell (and positive ions move in the opposite direction).

Anode (oxidation): $Cr(s) \rightarrow Cr^{3+}(aq) + 3\ e^-$

Cathode (reduction): $Fe^{2+}(aq) + 2\ e^- \rightarrow Fe(s)$

20.9 (a) Oxidation: $Fe(s) \rightarrow Fe^{2+}(aq) + 2\ e^-$
Reduction: $O_2(g) + 4\ H^+(aq) + 4\ e^- \rightarrow 2\ H_2O(\ell)$
Overall: $2\ Fe(s) + O_2(g) + 4\ H^+(aq) \rightarrow$
$$2\ Fe^{2+}(aq) + 2\ H_2O(\ell)$$

(b) Anode, oxidation: $Fe(s) \rightarrow Fe^{2+}(aq) + 2\ e^-$
Cathode, reduction: $O_2(g) + 4\ H^+(aq) + 4\ e^- \rightarrow$
$$2\ H_2O(\ell)$$

(c) Electrons flow from the negative anode (Fe) to the positive cathode (site of the O_2 half-reaction). Negative ions move through the salt bridge from the cathode compartment in which the O_2 reduction occurs to the anode compartment in which Fe oxidation occurs (and positive ions move in the opposite direction).

20.11 (a) All are primary batteries, not rechargeable.
(b) Dry cells and alkaline batteries have Zn anodes. Ni-Cd batteries have a cadmium anode.
(c) Dry cells have an acidic environment, whereas the environment is alkaline for alkaline and Ni-Cd cells.

20.13 (a) $E°_{cell} = -1.298$ V; not product-favored
(b) $E°_{cell} = -0.51$ V; not product-favored
(c) $E°_{cell} = -1.023$ V; not product-favored
(d) $E°_{cell} = +0.029$ V; product-favored

20.15 (a) $Sn^{2+}(aq) + 2\ Ag(s) \rightarrow Sn(s) + 2\ Ag^+(aq)$

$E°_{cell} = -0.94$ V; not product-favored

(b) $3\ Sn^{4+}(aq) + 2\ Al(s) \rightarrow 3\ Sn^{2+}(aq) + 2\ Al^{3+}(aq)$

$E°_{cell} = +1.81$ V; product-favored

(c) $2\ ClO_3^-(aq) + 10\ Ce^{3+}(aq) + 12\ H^+(aq) \rightarrow$
$$Cl_2(aq) + 10\ Ce^{4+}(aq) + 6\ H_2O(\ell)$$

$E°_{cell} = -0.14$ V; not product-favored

(d) $3\ Cu(s) + 2\ NO_3^-(aq) + 8\ H^+(aq) \rightarrow$
$$3\ Cu^{2+}(aq) + 2\ NO(g) + 4\ H_2O(\ell)$$

$E°_{cell} = +0.62$ V; product-favored

20.17 (a) Al
 (b) Zn and Al
 (c) $Fe^{2+}(aq) + Sn(s) \rightarrow Fe(s) + Sn^{2+}(aq)$; reactant-favored
 (d) $Zn^{2+}(aq) + Sn(s) \rightarrow Zn(s) + Sn^{2+}(aq)$; reactant-favored

20.19 Best reducing agent, Cr(s). (Use Appendix M)

20.21 Ag^+

20.23 See Example 20.5
 (a) F_2, most readily reduced
 (b) F_2 and Cl_2

20.25 $E°_{cell} = +0.3923$ V. When $[Zn(OH)_4{}^{2-}] = [OH^-] = 0.025$ M and $P(H_2) = 1.0$ bar, $E_{cell} = 0.345$ V.

20.27 $E°_{cell} = +1.563$ V and $E_{cell} = +1.58$ V.

20.29 When $E°_{cell} = +1.563$ V, $E_{cell} = 1.48$ V, $n = 2$, and $[Zn^{2+}] = 1.0$ M, the concentration of $Ag^+ = 0.040$ M.

20.31 (a) $\Delta_r G° = -29.0$ kJ; $K = 1 \times 10^5$
 (b) $\Delta_r G° = +88.6$ kJ; $K = 3 \times 10^{-16}$

20.33 $E°_{cell}$ for $AgBr(s) \rightarrow Ag^+(aq) + Br^-(aq)$ is -0.7281.
 $K_{sp} = 4.9 \times 10^{-13}$

20.35 $K_{formation} = 2 \times 10^{25}$

20.37 See Figure 20.18. Electrons from the battery or other source enter the cathode where they are transferred to Na^+ ions, reducing the ions to Na metal. Chloride ions move toward the positively charged anode where an electron is transferred from each Cl^- ion, and Cl_2 gas is formed.

20.39 O_2 from the oxidation of water is more likely than F_2. See Example 20.10.

20.41 See Example 20.10.
 (a) Cathode: $2 H_2O(\ell) + 2 e^- \rightarrow H_2(g) + 2 OH^-(aq)$
 (b) Anode: $2 Br^-(aq) \rightarrow Br_2(\ell) + 2 e^-$

20.43 Mass of Ni = 0.0334 g

20.45 Time = 2300 s or 38 min

20.47 Time = 250 h

20.49 (a) $UO_2{}^+(aq) + 4 H^+(aq) + e^- \rightarrow U^{4+}(aq) + 2 H_2O(\ell)$
 (b) $ClO_3{}^-(aq) + 6 H^+(aq) + 6 e^- \rightarrow Cl^-(aq) + 3 H_2O(\ell)$
 (c) $N_2H_4(aq) + 4 OH^-(aq) \rightarrow N_2(g) + 4 H_2O(\ell) + 4 e^-$
 (d) $ClO^-(aq) + H_2O(\ell) + 2 e^- \rightarrow Cl^-(aq) + 2 OH^-(aq)$

20.51 (a,c) The electrode at the right is a magnesium anode. (Magnesium metal supplies electrons and is oxidized to Mg^{2+} ions.) Electrons pass through the wire to the silver cathode, where Ag^+ ions are reduced to silver metal. Nitrate ions move via the salt bridge from the $AgNO_3$ solution to the $Mg(NO_3)_2$ solution (and Na^+ ions move in the opposite direction).
 (b) Anode: $Mg(s) \rightarrow Mg^{2+}(aq) + 2 e^-$
 Cathode: $Ag^+(aq) + e^- \rightarrow Ag(s)$
 Net reaction: $Mg(s) + 2 Ag^+(aq) \rightarrow Mg^{2+}(aq) + 2 Ag(s)$

20.53 (a) For 1.7 V:
 Use chromium as the anode to reduce $Ag^+(aq)$ to Ag(s) at the cathode. The cell potential is +1.71 V.
 (b) For 0.5 V:
 (i) Use copper as the anode to reduce silver ions to silver metal at the cathode. The cell potential is +0.46 V.
 (ii) Use silver as the anode to reduce chlorine to chloride ions. The cell potential would be +0.56 V. (In practice, this setup is not likely to work well because the product would be insoluble silver chloride.)

20.55 (a) $Zn^{2+}(aq)$ (c) Zn(s)
 (b) $Au^+(aq)$ (d) Au(s)
 (e) Yes, Sn(s) will reduce Cu^{2+} (as well as Ag^+ and Au^+).
 (f) No, Ag(s) can only reduce $Au^+(aq)$.
 (g) See part (e).
 (h) $Ag^+(aq)$ can oxidize Cu, Sn, Co, and Zn.

20.57 (a) The cathode is the site of reduction, so the half-reaction must be $2 H^+(aq) + 2 e^- \rightarrow H_2(g)$. This is the case with the following half-reactions: $Cr^{3+}(aq)|Cr(s)$, $Fe^{2+}(aq)|Fe(s)$, and $Mg^{2+}(aq)|Mg(s)$.
 (b) Choosing from the half-cells in part (a), the reaction of Mg(s) and $H^+(aq)$ would produce the most positive potential (2.37 V), and the reaction of H_2 with Cu^{2+} would produce the least positive potential (+0.337 V).

20.59 8.1×10^5 g Al

20.61 (a) $E°_{anode} = -0.268$ V
 (b) $K_{sp} = 2 \times 10^{-5}$

20.63 $\Delta_r G° = -409$ kJ

20.65 6700 kWh; 820 kg Na; 1300 kg Cl_2

20.67 Ru^{2+}, $Ru(NO_3)_2$

20.69 9.5×10^6 g Cl_2 per day

20.71 (a) $2[Ag^+(aq) + e^+ \rightarrow Ag(s)]$

$C_6H_5CHO(aq) + H_2O(\ell) \rightarrow$
$ C_6H_5CO_2H(aq) + 2\,H^+(aq) + 2\,e^-$
$\overline{}$
$2Ag^+(aq) + C_6H_5CHO(aq) + H_2O(\ell) \rightarrow$
$ C_6H_5CO_2H(aq) + 2\,H^+(aq) + 2\,Ag(s)$

(b) $3[CH_3CH_2OH(aq) + H_2O(\ell) \rightarrow$
$ CH_3CO_2H(aq) + 4\,H^+(aq) + 4\,e^-]$
$2[Cr_2O_7{}^{2-}(aq) + 14\,H^+(aq) + 6\,e^- \rightarrow$
$ 2\,Cr^{3+}(aq) + 7\,H_2O(\ell)]$
$\overline{}$
$3\,CH_3CH_2OH(aq) +$
$ 2\,Cr_2O_7{}^{2-}(aq) + 16\,H^+(aq) \rightarrow$
$ 3\,CH_3CO_2H(aq) + 4\,Cr^{3+}(aq) + 11\,H_2O(\ell)$

20.73 (a) 0.974 kJ/g
(b) 0.60 kJ/g
(c) The silver-zinc battery produces more energy per gram of reactants.

20.75 (a) $2\,NO_3{}^-(aq) + 3\,Mn^{2+}(aq) + 2\,H_2O(\ell) \rightarrow$
$ 2\,NO(g) + 3\,MnO_2(s) + 4\,H^+(aq)$

$3\,MnO_2(s) + 4\,H^+(aq) + 2\,NH_4{}^+(aq) \rightarrow$
$ N_2(g) + 3\,Mn^{2+}(aq) + 6\,H_2O(\ell)$

(b) $E°$ for the reduction of $NO_3{}^-$ to NO is -0.27 V.
$E°$ for the oxidation of $NH_4{}^+$ to N_2 is $+1.50$ V.

20.77 (a) $Fe^{2+}(aq) + 2\,e^- \rightarrow Fe(s)$
$2[Fe^{2+}(aq) \rightarrow Fe^{3+}(aq) + e^-]$
$3\,Fe^{2+}(aq) \rightarrow Fe(s) + 2\,Fe^{3+}(aq)$
(b) $E°_{cell} = -1.21$ V; not product-favored
(c) $K = 1 \times 10^{-41}$

20.79 (a)

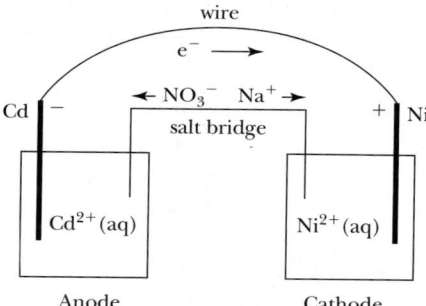

Anode   Cathode

(b) Anode: $Cd(s) \rightarrow Cd^{2+}(aq) + 2\,e^-$
Cathode: $Ni^{2+}(aq) + 2\,e^- \rightarrow Ni(s)$
Net: $Cd(s) + Ni^{2+}(aq) \rightarrow Cd^{2+}(aq) + Ni(s)$
(c) The anode is negative and the cathode is positive.
(d) $E°_{cell} = E°_{cathode} - E°_{anode} =$
$(-0.25$ V$) - (-0.40$ V$) = +0.15$ V
(e) Electrons flow from anode (Cd) to cathode (Ni).
(f) Na^+ ions move from the anode compartment to the cathode compartment. Anions move in the opposite direction.
(g) $K = 1 \times 10^5$
(h) $E_{cell} = 0.21$ V
(i) 480 h

20.81 0.054 g Au

20.83 I^- is the strongest reducing agent of the three halide ions. Iodide ion reduces Cu^{2+} to Cu^+, forming insoluble $CuI(s)$.

$2\,Cu^{2+}(aq) + 4\,I^-(aq) \rightarrow 2\,CuI(s) + I_2(aq)$

20.85 (a) 92 g HF required; 230 g CF_3SO_2F and 9.3 g H_2 isolated
(b) H_2 is produced at the cathode.
(c) 48 kWh

20.87 290 h

20.89 (a) 3.6 mol glucose and 22 mol O_2
(b) 86 mole electrons
(c) 96 amps
(d) 96 watts

CHAPTER 21

21.1 $4\,Li(s) + O_2(g) \rightarrow 2\,Li_2O(s)$

$Li_2O(s) + H_2O(\ell) \rightarrow 2\,LiOH(aq)$

$2\,Ca(s) + O_2(g) \rightarrow 2\,CaO(s)$

$CaO(s) + H_2O(\ell) \rightarrow Ca(OH)_2(s)$

21.3 These are the elements of Group 3A: boron, B; aluminum, Al; gallium, Ga; indium, In; and thallium, Tl.

21.5 $2\,Na(s) + Cl_2(g) \rightarrow 2\,NaCl(s)$

The reaction is exothermic and the product is ionic. See Figure 1.4.

21.7 The product, NaCl, is a colorless solid and is soluble in water. Other alkali metal chlorides have similar properties.

21.9 Calcium will not exist in the earth's crust because the metal reacts with water.

21.11 Increasing basicity: $CO_2 < SiO_2 < SnO_2$

21.13 (a) $2\,Na(s) + Br_2(\ell) \rightarrow 2\,NaBr(s)$
(b) $2\,Mg(s) + O_2(g) \rightarrow 2\,MgO(s)$
(c) $2\,Al(s) + 3\,F_2(g) \rightarrow 2\,AlF_3(s)$
(d) $C(s) + O_2(g) \rightarrow CO_2(g)$

21.15 $2\,H_2(g) + O_2(g) \rightarrow 2\,H_2O(g)$
$H_2(g) + Cl_2(g) \rightarrow 2\,HCl(g)$
$3\,H_2(g) + N_2(g) \rightarrow 2\,NH_3(g)$

21.17 $CH_4(g) + H_2O(g) \rightarrow CO(g) + 3\,H_2(g)$

$\Delta_r H° = +206.2$ kJ; $\Delta_r S° = +214.7$ J/K; $\Delta_r G° = +142.2$ kJ (at 298.15 K).

21.19 Step 1: $2\,SO_2(g) + 4\,H_2O(\ell) + 2\,I_2(s) \rightarrow$
$ 2\,H_2SO_4(\ell) + 4\,HI(g)$

Step 2: $2\,H_2SO_4(\ell) \rightarrow$
$ 2\,H_2O(\ell) + 2\,SO_2(g) + O_2(g)$

Step 3: $4 HI(g) \rightarrow 2 H_2(g) + 2 I_2(g)$

Net: $2 H_2O(\ell) \rightarrow 2 H_2(g) + O_2(g)$

21.21 $2 Na(s) + F_2(g) \rightarrow 2 NaF(s)$

$2 Na(s) + Cl_2(g) \rightarrow 2 NaCl(s)$

$2 Na(s) + Br_2(\ell) \rightarrow 2 NaBr(s)$

$2 Na(s) + I_2(s) \rightarrow 2 NaI(s)$

The alkali metal halides are white, crystalline solids. They have high melting and boiling points, and are soluble in water.

21.23 (a) $2 Cl^-(aq) + 2 H_2O(\ell) \rightarrow$
$$Cl_2(g) + H_2(g) + 2 OH^-(aq)$$
(b) If this were the only process used to produce chlorine, the mass of Cl_2 reported for industrial production would be 0.88 times the mass of NaOH produced (2 mol NaCl, 117 g, would yield 2 mol NaOH, 80 g, and 1 mol Cl_2, 70 g). The amounts quoted indicate a Cl_2-to-NaOH mass ratio 0.96. Chlorine is presumably also prepared by other routes than this one.

21.25 $2 Mg(s) + O_2(g) \rightarrow 2 MgO(s)$

$3 Mg(s) + N_2(g) \rightarrow Mg_3N_2(s)$

21.27 $CaCO_3$ is used in agriculture to neutralize acidic soil, to prepare CaO for use in mortar, and in steel production.

$CaCO_3(s) + H_2O(\ell) + CO_2(g) \rightarrow$
$$Ca^{2+}(aq) + 2 HCO_3^-(aq)$$

21.29 1.4×10^6 g SO_2

21.31

$B_3O_6^{3-}$

$B_2O_5^{4-}$

21.33 (a) $2 B_5H_9(g) + 12 O_2(g) \rightarrow 5 B_2O_3(s) + 9 H_2O(g)$
(b) Enthalpy of combustion of B_5H_9 = -4341.2 kJ/mol. This is more than double the enthalpy of combustion of B_2H_6.
(c) Enthalpy of combustion of $C_2H_6(g)$ [to give $CO_2(g)$ and $H_2O(g)$] = -1428.7 kJ/mol. C_2H_6 produces 47.5 kJ/g, whereas diborane produces much more (73.7 kJ/g).

21.35 $2 Al(s) + 6 HCl(aq) \rightarrow$
$$2 Al^{3+}(aq) + 6 Cl^-(aq) + 3 H_2(g)$$

$2 Al(s) + 3 Cl_2(g) \rightarrow 2 AlCl_3(s)$

$4 Al(s) + 3 O_2(g) \rightarrow 2 Al_2O_3(s)$

21.37 $2 Al(s) + 2 OH^-(aq) + 6 H_2O(\ell) \rightarrow$
$$2 Al(OH)_4^-(aq) + 3 H_2(g)$$

Volume of H_2 obtained from 13.2 g Al = 18.4 L

21.39 $Al_2O_3(s) + 3 H_2SO_4(aq) \rightarrow Al_2(SO_4)_3(s) + 3 H_2O(\ell)$

Mass of H_2SO_4 required = 860 g and mass of Al_2O_3 required = 298 g.

21.41 Pyroxenes have as their basic structural unit an extended chain of linked SiO_4 tetrahedra. The ratio of Si to O is 1 to 3.

21.43 This structure has a six-member ring of Si atoms with O atom bridges. Each Si also has two O atoms attached. The basic unit is SiO_3^{2-}, and the overall charge is -12 in $[(SiO_3)_6]^{-12}$. (Electron lone pairs are omitted in the following structure.)

21.45 Consider the general decomposition reaction:

$$N_xO_y \rightarrow {}^x/_2 N_2 + {}^y/_2 O_2$$

The value of $\Delta G°$ can be obtained for all N_xO_y molecules because $\Delta_r G° = -\Delta_f G°$. These data show that the decomposition reaction is spontaneous for all of the nitrogen oxides. All are unstable with respect to decomposition to the elements.

Compound	$-\Delta_f G°$ (kJ/mol)
NO(g)	-86.58
NO_2	-51.23
N_2O	-104.20
N_2O_4	-97.73

21.47 $\Delta_r H° = -114.4$ kJ; exothermic $\Delta_r G° = -70.7$ kJ, product-favored at equilibrium

21.49 (a) $N_2H_4(aq) + O_2(g) \rightarrow N_2(g) + 2 H_2O(\ell)$
(b) 1.32×10^3 g

21.51 (a) Oxidation number = $+3$
(b) Diphosphonic acid ($H_4P_2O_5$) should be a diprotic acid (losing the two H atoms attached to O atoms).

21.53 (a) 3.5×10^3 kg SO_2
(b) 4.1×10^3 kg $Ca(OH)_2$

21.55

$$\left[:\!\overset{..}{\underset{..}{S}}\!-\!\overset{..}{\underset{..}{S}}\!: \right]^{2-}$$

disulfide ion

21.57 $E°_{cell} = E°_{cathode} - E°_{anode} = +1.44 \text{ V} - (+1.51 \text{ V}) = -0.07 \text{ V}$

The reaction is not product-favored under standard conditions.

21.59 $Cl_2(aq) + 2\, Br^-(aq) \rightarrow 2\, Cl^-(aq) + Br_2(aq)$

Cl_2 is the oxidizing agent, Br^- is the reducing agent; $E°_{cell} = 0.28$ V.

21.61 The reaction consumes 4.32×10^8 C to produce 8.51×10^4 g F_2.

21.63

Element	Appearance	State
Na, Mg, Al	Silvery metal	Solids
Si	black, shiny metalloid	Solid
P	White, red, and black allotropes; nonmetal	Solid
S	Yellow nonmetal	Solid
Cl	Pale green nonmetal	Gas
Ar	Colorless nonmetal	Gas

21.65 (a) $2\, K(s) + Cl_2(g) \rightarrow 2\, KCl(s)$

$Ca(s) + Cl_2(g) \rightarrow CaCl_2(s)$

$2\, Ga(s) + 3\, Cl_2(g) \rightarrow 2\, GaCl_3(s)$

$Ge(s) + 2\, Cl_2(g) \rightarrow GeCl_4(\ell)$

$2\, As(s) + 3\, Cl_2(g) \rightarrow 2\, AsCl_3(\ell)$

($AsCl_5$ has been prepared but is not stable.)

(b) KCl and $CaCl_2$ are ionic; the other products are covalent.
(c) $GaCl_3$ is planar trigonal; $AsCl_3$ is pyramidal.

21.67 (a) $2\, KClO_3(s) \rightarrow 2\, KCl(s) + 3\, O_2(g)$
(b) $2\, H_2S(g) + 3\, O_2(g) \rightarrow 2\, H_2O(g) + 2\, SO_2(g)$
(c) $2\, Na(s) + O_2(g) \rightarrow Na_2O_2(s)$
(d) $P_4(s) + 3\, KOH(aq) + 3\, H_2O(\ell) \rightarrow$
$PH_3(g) + 3\, KH_2PO_4(aq)$
(e) $NH_4NO_3(s) \rightarrow N_2O(g) + 2\, H_2O(g)$
(f) $2\, In(s) + 3\, Br_2(\ell) \rightarrow 2\, InBr_3(s)$
(g) $SnCl_4(\ell) + 2\, H_2O(\ell) \rightarrow SnO_2(s) + 4\, HCl(aq)$

21.69 1.4×10^5 metric tons

21.71 Mg: $\Delta_r G° = +64.9$ kJ

Ca: $\Delta_r G° = +131.40$ kJ

Ba: $\Delta_r G° = +219.4$ kJ

Relative tendency to decompose:
$MgCO_3 > CaCO_3 > BaCO_3$

21.73 (a) $\Delta_f G°$ should be more negative than $(-95.1 \text{ kJ}) \times n$.
(b) Ba, Pb, Ti

21.75 O—F bond energy = 190 kJ/mol

21.77 (a) N_2O_4 is the oxidizing agent (N is reduced from $+4$ to 0 in N_2), and $H_2NN(CH_3)_2$ is the reducing agent.
(b) 1.3×10^4 kg N_2O_4 is required. Product masses: 5.7×10^3 kg N_2; 4.9×10^3 kg H_2O; 6.0×10^3 kg CO_2.

21.79 $\Delta_r H° = -257.78$ kJ. This reaction is entropy-disfavored, however, with $\Delta_r S° = -963$ J/K because of the decrease in the number of moles of gases. Combining these values gives $\Delta_r G° = +29.19$ kJ, indicating that under standard conditions at 298 K the reaction is not spontaneous. (The reaction has a favorable $\Delta_r G°$ at temperatures less than 268 K, indicating that further research on this system might be worthwhile. Note that at that temperature water is a solid.)

21.81 $A = B_2H_6$; $B = B_4H_{10}$; $C = B_5H_{11}$; $D = B_5H_9$; $E = B_{10}H_{14}$

21.83 (a) $2\, CH_3Cl(g) + Si(s) \rightarrow (CH_3)_2SiCl_2(\ell)$
(b) 0.823 atm
(c) 12.2 g

21.85 $5\, N_2H_5^+(aq) + 4\, IO_3^-(aq) \rightarrow$
$5\, N_2(g) + 2\, I_2(aq) + H^+(aq) + 12\, H_2O(\ell)$

$E°_{net} = 1.43$ V

21.87 (a) Br_2O_3
(b) The structure of Br_2O is reasonably well known. Several possible structures for Br_2O_3 can be imagined, but experiment confirms the structure below.

21.89 (a) The NO bond with a length of 114.2 pm is a double bond. The other two NO bonds (with a length of 121 pm) have a bond order of 1.5 (as there are two resonance structures involving these bonds).

(b) $K = 1.90$; $\Delta_r S° = 141$ J/K · mol-rxn
(c) $\Delta_f H° = 82.9$ kJ/mol

21.91 The flask contains a fixed number of moles of gas at the given pressure and temperature. One could burn the mixture because only the H_2 will combust; the argon is untouched. Cooling the gases from combustion would remove water (the combustion product of H_2) and leave only Ar in the gas phase. Measuring its pressure in a calibrated volume at a known temperature would allow one to calculate the amount of Ar that was in the original mixture.

21.93 Generally, a sodium fire can be extinguished by smothering it with sand. The worst choice is to use water (which reacts violently with sodium to give H_2 gas and NaOH).

21.95 Nitrogen is a relatively unreactive gas, so it will not participate in any reaction typical of hydrogen or oxygen. The most obvious property of H_2 is that it burns, so attempting to burn a small sample of the gas would immediately confirm or deny the presence of H_2. If O_2 is present, it can be detected by allowing it to react as an oxidizing agent. There are many reactions known with low-valent metals, especially transition metal ions in solution, that can be detected by color changes.

21.97 3.5 kWh

21.99 The reducing ability of the Group 3A metals declines considerably on descending the group, with the largest drop occurring on going from Al to Ga. The reducing ability of gallium and indium are similar, but another large change is observed on going to thallium. In fact, thallium is most stable in the +1 oxidation state. This same tendency for elements to be more stable with lower oxidation numbers is seen in Groups 4A (Ge and Pb) and 5A (Bi).

CHAPTER 22

22.1 (a) Cr^{3+}: $[Ar]3d^3$, paramagnetic
(b) V^{2+}: $[Ar]3d^3$, paramagnetic
(c) Ni^{2+}: $[Ar]3d^8$, paramagnetic
(d) Cu^+: $[Ar]3d^{10}$, diamagnetic

22.3 (a) Fe^{3+}: $[Ar]3d^5$, isoelectronic with Mn^{2+}
(b) Zn^{2+}: $[Ar]3d^{10}$, isoelectronic with Cu^+
(c) Fe^{2+}: $[Ar]3d^6$, isoelectronic with Co^{3+}
(d) Cr^{3+}: $[Ar]3d^3$, isoelectronic with V^{2+}

22.5 (a) $Cr_2O_3(s) + 2\ Al(s) \rightarrow Al_2O_3(s) + 2\ Cr(s)$
(b) $TiCl_4(\ell) + 2\ Mg(s) \rightarrow Ti(s) + 2\ MgCl_2(s)$
(c) $2\ [Ag(CN)_2]^-(aq) + Zn(s) \rightarrow$
$\qquad 2\ Ag(s) + [Zn(CN)_4]^{2-}(aq)$
(d) $3\ Mn_3O_4(s) + 8\ Al(s) \rightarrow 9\ Mn(s) + 4\ Al_2O_3(s)$

22.7 Monodentate: CH_3NH_2, CH_3CN, N_3^-, Br^-

Bidentate: en, phen (see Figure 22.14)

22.9 (a) Mn^{2+} (c) Co^{3+}
(b) Co^{3+} (d) Cr^{2+}

22.11 $[Ni(en)(NH_3)_3(H_2O)]^{2+}$

22.13 (a) $Ni(en)_2Cl_2$ (en = $H_2NCH_2CH_2NH_2$)
(b) $K_2[PtCl_4]$
(c) $K[Cu(CN)_2]$
(d) $[Fe(NH_3)_4(H_2O)_2]^{2+}$

22.15 (a) Diaquabis(oxalato)nickelate(II) ion
(b) Dibromobis(ethylenediamine)cobalt(III) ion
(c) Amminechlorobis(ethylenediamine)cobalt(III) ion
(d) Diammineoxalatoplatinum(II)

22.17 (a) $[Fe(H_2O)_5OH]^{2+}$
(b) Potassium tetracyanonickelate(II)
(c) Potassium diaquabis(oxalato)chromate(III)
(d) $(NH_4)_2[PtCl_4]$

22.19

22.21 For a discussion of chirality, see Chapter 10, page 446).
(a) Fe^{2+} is a chiral center.
(b) Co^{3+} is not a chiral center.
(c) Neither of the two possible isomers is chiral.
(d) No. Square-planar complexes are never chiral.

22.23 (a) $[Mn(CN)_6]^{4-}$: d^5, low-spin Mn^{2+} complex is paramagnetic.

$$\underline{\uparrow\downarrow} \quad \underline{\uparrow\downarrow} \quad \underline{\uparrow}$$

(b) $[Co(NH_3)_6]^{3+}$: d^6, low-spin Co^{3+} complex is diamagnetic.

$$\underline{\uparrow\downarrow} \quad \underline{\uparrow\downarrow} \quad \underline{\uparrow\downarrow}$$

(c) $[Fe(H_2O)_6]^{3+}$: d^5, low-spin Fe^{3+} complex is paramagnetic (1 unpaired electron; same as part a).
(d) $[Cr(en)_3]^{2+}$: d^4, Cr^{3+} complex is paramagnetic (2 unpaired electrons).

$$\underline{\uparrow\downarrow} \quad \underline{\uparrow} \quad \underline{\uparrow}$$

22.25 (a) Fe^{2+}, d^6, paramagnetic, four unpaired electrons
(b) Co^{2+}, d^7, paramagnetic, three unpaired electrons
(c) Mn^{2+}, d^5, paramagnetic, five unpaired electrons
(d) Zn^{2+}, d^{10}, diamagnetic, zero unpaired electrons

22.27 (a) 6
(b) octahedral
(c) +2
(d) four unpaired electrons (high spin)
(e) paramagnetic

22.29 With four ligands, complexes of the d^8 Ni^{2+} ion can be either tetrahedral or square planar. The CN^- ligand is at one end of the spectrochemical series and leads to a large ligand field splitting, whereas Cl^- is at the opposite end and often leads to complexes with small orbital splitting. With ligands such as CN^- the complex will be square planar (and for a d^8 ion it will be diamagnetic). With a weak field ligand (Cl^-) the complex will be tetrahedral and, for the d^8 ion, two electrons will be unpaired, giving a paramagnetic complex.

22.31 The light absorbed is in the blue region of the spectrum (page 271). Therefore, the light transmitted—which is the color of the solution—is yellow.

22.33 (a) The Mn^+ ion in this complex has six d electrons. Each CO contributes two electrons, giving a total of 18 for the complex ion.
(b) The $C_5H_5^-$ ligand contributes six electrons, CO and PR_3 each contribute two electrons, for a total of 10 electrons for the ligands. The cobalt is effectively a Co^+ ion and contributes eight d electrons. The total is 18 electrons.
(c) The $C_5H_5^-$ ligand contributes six electrons, each CO contributes two electrons, for a total of 12 electrons for the ligands. The manganese is effectively a Mn^+ ion and contributes six d electrons. The total is 18 electrons.

22.35 Determine the magnetic properties of the complex. Square-planar Ni^{2+} (d^8) complexes are diamagnetic, whereas tetrahedral complexes are paramagnetic.

22.37 Fe^{2+} has a d^6 configuration. Low-spin octahedral complexes are diamagnetic, whereas high-spin octahedral complexes of this ion have four unpaired electrons and are paramagnetic.

22.39 Square-planar complexes most often arise from d^8 transition metal ions. Therefore, it is likely that $[Ni(CN)_4]^{2-}$ (Ni^{2+}) and $[Pt(CN)_4]^{2-}$ (Pt^{2+}) are square planar. (See also Study Questions 22.29 and 22.65.)

22.41 Two geometric isomers are possible.

22.43 Absorbing at 425 nm means the complex is absorbing light in the blue-violet end of the spectrum. Therefore, red and green light are transmitted, and the complex appears yellow (see Figure 22.27).

22.45 (a) Mn^{2+}; (b) 6; (c) octahedral; (d) 5; (e) paramagnetic; (f) *cis* and *trans* isomers exist.

22.47 Name: tetraamminedichlorocobalt(III) ion

cis   *trans*

22.49 $[Co(en)_2(H_2O)Cl]^{2+}$

22.51

mer   *fac*

trans chlorides   *cis* chlorides

22.53

$[...]^{3+}$ complex with N N (chelate), Co center, NH$_3$, H$_2$O, OH$_2$, NH$_3$

H$_2$O and NH$_3$
cis, chiral

$[...]^{3+}$ complex with N N (chelate), Co center, NH$_3$, H$_3$N, OH$_2$, OH$_2$

H$_2$O *cis* and
NH$_3$ *trans*,
not chiral

$[...]^{3+}$ complex with N N (chelate), Co center, OH$_2$, H$_2$O, NH$_3$, NH$_3$

H$_2$O *trans* and
NH$_3$ *cis*, not
chiral

22.55 In $[Mn(H_2O)_6]^{2+}$ and $[Mn(CN)_6]^{4-}$, Mn has an oxidation number of $+2$ (Mn is a d^5 ion).

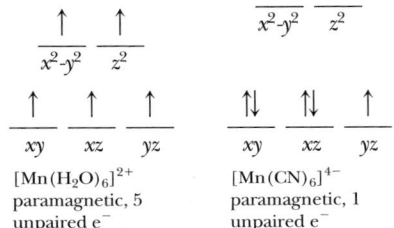

$[Mn(H_2O)_6]^{2+}$
paramagnetic, 5
unpaired e^-

$[Mn(CN)_6]^{4-}$
paramagnetic, 1
unpaired e^-

This shows that Δ_o for CN^- is greater than for H_2O.

22.57 (a) ammonium tetrachlorocuprate(II)
(b) hexacarbonylmolybdenum(0)
(c) $[Cr(H_2O)_4Cl_2]Cl$
(d) $[Co(H_2O)(NH_2CH_2CH_2NH_2)_2(SCN)](NO_3)_2$

22.59 (a) The light absorbed is in the orange region of the spectrum (page 1043). Therefore, the light transmitted (the color of the solution) is blue or cyan.
(b) Using the cobalt(III) complexes in Table 22.3 as a guide, we might place CO_3^{2-} between F^- and the oxalato ion, $C_2O_4^{2-}$.
(c) Δ_o is small, so the complex should be high spin and paramagnetic.

22.61

N O = H_2N—CH_2—CO_2^-

[Eight $[...]^{2-}$ Cu complexes shown, arranged in pairs labeled "enantiometric pair"]

enantiometric pair

enantiometric pair

enantiometric pair

22.63 (a) In complexes such as $M(PR_3)Cl_2$ the metal is Ni^{2+} or Pd^{2+}, both of which are d^8 metal ions. If an Ni^{2+} complex is paramagnetic it must be tetrahedral, whereas the Pd^{2+} must be square planar. (A d^8 metal complex cannot be diamagnetic if it has a tetrahedral structure.)

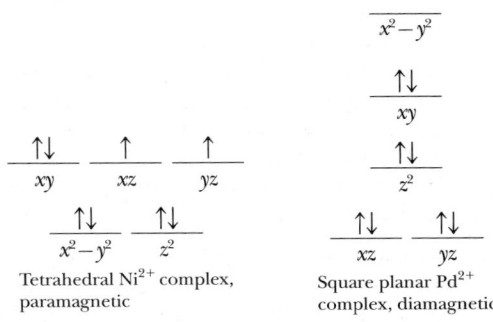

Tetrahedral Ni^{2+} complex,
paramagnetic

Square planar Pd^{2+}
complex, diamagnetic

(b) A tetrahedral Ni^{2+} complex cannot have isomers, whereas a square planar complex of the type $M(PR_3)_2Cl_2$ can have *cis* and *trans* isomers. See page 1036.

22.65 A, dark violet isomer: $[Co(NH_3)_5Br]SO_4$

B, violet-red isomer: $[Co(NH_3)_5(SO_4)]Br$

$[Co(NH_3)_5Br]SO_4(aq) + BaCl_2(aq) \rightarrow$
$[Co(NH_3)_5Br]Cl_2(aq) + BaSO_4(s)$

22.67 (a) There is 5.41×10^{-4} mol of $UO_2(NO_3)_2$, and this provides 5.41×10^{-4} mol of U^{n+} ions on reduction by Zn. The 5.41×10^{-4} mol U^{n+} requires 2.16×10^{-4} mol MnO_4^- to reach the equivalence point. This is a ratio of 5 mol of U^{n+} ions to 2 mol MnO_4^- ions. The 2 mol MnO_4^- ions require 10 mol of e^- (to go to Mn^{2+} ions), so 5 mol of U^{n+} ions provide 10 mol e^- (on going to UO_2^{2+} ions, with a uranium oxidation number of +6). This means the U^{n+} ion must be U^{4+}.

(b) $Zn(s) \rightarrow Zn^{2+}(aq) + 2\ e^-$

$$UO_2^{2+}(aq) + 4\ H^+(aq) + 2\ e^- \rightarrow$$
$$U^{4+}(aq) + 2\ H_2O(\ell)$$
$$\overline{}$$
$$UO_2^{2+}(aq) + 4\ H^+(aq) + Zn(s) \rightarrow$$
$$U^{4+}(aq) + 2\ H_2O(\ell) + Zn^{2+}(aq)$$

(c) $5[U^{4+}(aq) + 2\ H_2O(\ell) \rightarrow$
$ UO_2^{2+}(aq) + 4\ H^+(aq) + 2\ e^-]$

$2[MnO_4^-(aq) + 8\ H^+(aq) + 5\ e^- \rightarrow$
$ Mn^{2+}(aq) + 4\ H_2O(\ell)]$
$$\overline{}$$
$5\ U^{4+}(aq) + 2\ MnO_4^-(aq) + 2\ H_2O(\ell) \rightarrow$
$ 5\ UO_2^{2+}(aq) + 4\ H^+(aq) + 2\ Mn^{2+}(aq)$

22.69

Ion	$K_{formation}$ (ammine complexes)
Co^{2+}	1.3×10^5
Ni^{2+}	5.5×10^8
Cu^{2+}	2.1×10^{13}
Zn^{2+}	2.9×10^9

The data for these hexammine complexes do indeed, verify the Irving-Williams series. In the book *Chemistry of the Elements* (N. N. Greenwood and A. Earnshaw: 2nd edition, p. 908, Oxford, England, Butterworth-Heinemann, 1997), it is stated: "the stabilities of corresponding complexes of the bivalent ions of the first transition series, irrespective of the particular ligand involved, usually vary in the Irving-Williams order, . . . , which is the reverse of the order for the cation radii. These observations are consistent with the view that, at least for metals in oxidation states +2 and +3, the coordinate bond is largely electrostatic. This was a major factor in the acceptance of the crystal field theory."

22.71 Wilkinson's catalyst and the EAN rule.

Step 1: Rhodium-containing reactant: Each PR_3 ligand donates two electrons as does the Cl^- ligand. The Rh^+ ion has 8 d electrons. Total electrons = 16.

Step 1: Rhodium-containing product. Assuming that the H ligand is H^-, each donates two electrons, as do Cl^- and the two PR_3 ligands. The metal center is Rh^{3+}, a d^6 metal ion. Total electrons = 18.

Step 2: The product has 16 electrons because one PR_3 ligand has been dissociated.

Step 3: The product has 18 electrons. The two-electron donor ligand CH_2CH_2 has replaced the dissociated PR_3 ligand.

Step 4: The product has 16 electrons. There are three anionic, two-electron donor ligands (Cl^-, H^-, and $CH_3CH_2^-$), two two-electron donor PR_3 ligands, and an Rh^{3+} ion (d^6).

Step 5: The product has 14 electrons. It is an Rh^+ complex (d^8) with two PR_3 ligands (two electrons each) and one Cl^- (two electrons). (It is likely a solvent molecule fills the vacant site here to give a transient, 16-electron complex.)

Step 6: The product is once again the active, 16-electron catalyst.

CHAPTER 23

23.11 (a) $^{56}_{28}Ni$; (b) ^1_0n; (c) $^{32}_{15}P$; (d) $^{97}_{43}Tc$; (e) $^0_{-1}\beta$; (f) ^0_1e (positron)

23.13 (a) $^0_{-1}\beta$; (b) $^{87}_{37}Rb$; (c) $^4_2\alpha$; (d) $^{226}_{88}Ra$; (e) $^0_{-1}\beta$; (f) $^{24}_{11}Na$

23.15 $^{235}_{92}U \rightarrow ^{231}_{90}Th + ^4_2\alpha$

$^{231}_{90}Th \rightarrow ^{231}_{91}Pa + ^0_{-1}\beta$

$^{231}_{91}Pa \rightarrow ^{227}_{89}Ac + ^4_2\alpha$

$^{227}_{89}Ac \rightarrow ^{227}_{90}Th + ^0_{-1}\beta$

$^{227}_{90}Th \rightarrow ^{223}_{88}Ra + ^4_2\alpha$

$^{223}_{88}Ra \rightarrow ^{219}_{86}Rn + ^4_2\alpha$

$^{219}_{86}Rn \rightarrow ^{215}_{84}Po + ^4_2\alpha$

$^{215}_{84}Po \rightarrow ^{211}_{82}Pb + ^4_2\alpha$

$^{211}_{82}Pb \rightarrow ^{211}_{83}Bi + ^0_{-1}\beta$

$^{211}_{83}Bi \rightarrow ^{211}_{84}Po + ^0_{-1}\beta$

$^{211}_{84}Po \rightarrow ^{207}_{82}Pb + ^4_2\alpha$

23.17 (a) $^{198}_{79}Au \rightarrow ^{198}_{80}Hg + ^0_{-1}\beta$
(b) $^{222}_{86}Rn \rightarrow ^{218}_{84}Po + ^4_2\alpha$
(c) $^{137}_{55}Cs \rightarrow ^{137}_{56}Ba + ^0_{-1}\beta$
(d) $^{110}_{49}In \rightarrow ^{110}_{48}Cd + ^0_1e$

23.19 (a) $^{80}_{35}Br$ has a high neutron/proton ratio of 45/35. Beta decay will allow the ratio to decrease: $^{80}_{35}Br \rightarrow ^{80}_{36}Kr + ^0_{-1}\beta$. Some ^{80m}Br decays by gamma emission.
(b) Alpha decay is likely: $^{240}_{98}Cf \rightarrow ^{236}_{96}Cm + ^4_2\alpha$
(c) Cobalt-61 has a high n/p ratio so beta decay is likely:

$^{61}_{27}Co \rightarrow ^{61}_{28}Kr + ^0_{-1}\beta$

(d) Carbon-11 has only 5 neutrons so K-capture or positron emission may occur:

$$^{11}_{6}C + ^{0}_{-1}e \rightarrow ^{11}_{5}B$$

$$^{11}_{6}C \rightarrow ^{11}_{5}B + ^{0}_{1}e$$

23.21 Generally beta decay will occur when the n/p ratio is high, whereas positron emission will occur when the n/p ratio is low.
(a) Beta decay: $^{20}_{9}F \rightarrow ^{20}_{10}Ne + ^{0}_{-1}\beta$

$$^{3}_{1}H \rightarrow ^{3}_{2}He + ^{0}_{-1}\beta$$

(b) Positron emission

$$^{22}_{11}Na \rightarrow ^{22}_{10}Ne + ^{0}_{1}\beta$$

23.23 Binding energy per nucleon for $^{11}B = 6.70 \times 10^8$ kJ

Binding energy per nucleon for $^{10}B = 6.26 \times 10^8$ kJ

23.25 8.256×10^8 kJ/nucleon

23.27 7.700×10^8 kJ/nucleon

23.29 0.781 micrograms

23.31 (a) $^{131}_{53}I \rightarrow ^{131}_{54}Xe + ^{0}_{-1}\beta$
(b) 0.075 micrograms

23.33 9.5×10^{-4} mg

23.35 (a) $^{222}_{86}Rn \rightarrow ^{218}_{84}Po + ^{4}_{2}\alpha$
(b) Time = 8.87 d

23.37 (a) 15.8 y; (b) 88%

23.39 $^{239}_{94}Pu + + ^{4}_{2}\alpha \rightarrow ^{240}_{95}Am + ^{1}_{1}H + 2 ^{1}_{0}n$

23.41 $^{48}_{20}Ca + ^{242}_{94}Pu \rightarrow ^{287}_{114}Uuq + 3 ^{1}_{0}n$

23.43 (a) $^{115}_{48}Cd$ (b) $^{7}_{4}Be$ (c) $^{4}_{2}\alpha$ (d) $^{63}_{29}Cu$

23.45 $^{10}_{5}B + ^{1}_{0}n \rightarrow ^{7}_{3}Li + ^{4}_{2}\alpha$

23.47 Time = 4.4×10^{10} y

23.49 If $t_{1/2} = 14.28$ d, then $k = 4.854 \times 10^{-2}$ d^{-1}. If the original disintegration rate is 3.2×10^6 dpm, then (from the integrated first order rate equation), the rate after 365 d is 0.065 dpm. The plot will resemble Figure 23.5.

23.51 (a) $^{238}_{92}U + ^{1}_{0}n \rightarrow ^{239}_{92}U$
(b) $^{239}_{92}U \rightarrow ^{239}_{93}Np + ^{0}_{-1}\beta$
(c) $^{239}_{93}Np \rightarrow ^{239}_{94}Pu + ^{0}_{-1}\beta$
(d) $^{239}_{94}Pu + ^{1}_{0}n \rightarrow 2 ^{1}_{0}n + energy + other nuclei$

23.53 About 2700 years old

23.55 Plot ln(activity) versus time. The slope of the plot is $-k$, the rate constant for decay. Here, $k = 0.0050$ d^{-1}, so $t_{1/2} = 140$ d.

23.57 Time = 1.9×10^9 y

23.59 130 mL

23.61 Energy obtained from 1.000 lb (452.6 g) of $^{235}U = 4.05 \times 10^{-10}$ kJ

Mass of coal required = 1.6×10^3 ton (or about 3 million pounds of coal)

23.63 27 fish tagged fish out of 5250 fish caught represents 0.51% of the fish in the lake. Therefore, 1000 fish put into the lake represent 0.51% of the fish in the lake, or 0.51% of 190,000 fish.

23.65 (a) The mass decreases by 4 units (with an $^{4}_{2}\alpha$ emission) or is unchanged (with a $^{0}_{-1}\beta$ emission) so the only masses possible are 4 units apart.
(b) ^{232}Th series, $m = 4n$; ^{235}U series $m = 4n + 3$
(c) ^{226}Ra and ^{210}Bi, $4n + 2$ series; ^{215}At, $4n + 3$ series; ^{228}Th, $4n$ series)
(d) Each series is headed by a long-lived isotope (in the order of 10^9 years, the age of the Earth.) The $4n + 1$ series is missing because there is no long-lived isotope in this series. Over geologic time, all the members of this series have decayed completely.

23.67 (a) ^{231}Pa isotope belongs to the ^{235}U decay series (see Question 23.65b).
(b) $^{235}_{92}U \rightarrow ^{231}_{90}Th + ^{4}_{2}\alpha$

$$^{231}_{90}Th \rightarrow ^{231}_{91}Pa + ^{0}_{-1}\beta$$

(c) Pa-231 is present to the extent of 1 part per million. Therefore, 1 million grams of pitchblende need to be used to obtain 1 g of Pa-231.
(d) $^{231}_{91}Pa \rightarrow ^{227}_{89}Ac + ^{4}_{2}\alpha$

23.69 Pitchblende contains $^{238}_{92}U$ and $^{235}_{92}U$. Thus, both radium and polonium isotopes must belong to either the $4n + 2$ or $4n + 3$ decay series. Furthermore, the isotopes must have sufficiently long half-lives in order to survive the separation and isolation process. These criteria are satisfied by ^{226}Ra and ^{210}Po.

P | Answers to Selected Interchapter Study Questions

The Interchapters are available as electronic files at www.cengage. com/chemistry/kotz

THE CHEMISTRY OF FUELS AND ENERGY SOURCES

1. (a) From methane: $H_2O(g) + CH_4(g) \rightarrow 3\,H_2(g) + CO(g)$

100. g CH_4(1 mol CH_4/16.043 g) (3 mol H_2/mol CH_4) (2.016 g H_2/1 mol H_2) = 37.7 g of H_2 produced

(b) From petroleum: $H_2O(g) + CH_2(\ell) \rightarrow 2\,H_2(g) + CO\ (g)$

100. g CH_2(1 mol CH_2/14.026 g CH_2) (2 mol H_2/1 mol CH_2) (2.016 g H_2/ 1 mol H_2) = 28.7 g H_2 produced

(c) From coal: $H_2O(g) + C(s) \rightarrow H_2(g) + CO(g)$

100. g C(1 mol C/12.011 g C) (1 mol H_2/mole C) (2.016 g H_2/ 1 mol H_2) = 16.8 g H_2 produced.

3. 70. lb(453.6 g/lb) (33 kJ/g) = 1.0×10^6 kJ

5. Assume burning oil produces 43 kJ/g (the value for crude petroleum in Table 2)

7.0 gal(3.785 L/gal) (1000 cm³/L) (0.8 g/cm³) (43 kJ/g) = 0.9×10^6 kJ. Uncertainty in the numbers is one significant figure. This value is close to the value for the energy obtained by burning from 70 kg of coal (calculated in Q.3.)

7. Per gram: (5.45×10^3 kJ/mol) (1 mol/114.26 g) = 47.7 kJ/g

Per liter: (47.7 kJ/g) (688 g/L) = 3.28×10^4 kJ/L

9. The factor for converting kW-h to kJ is 1 kW-h = 3600 kJ

(940 kW-h/yr) (3600 kJ/kW-h) = 3.4×10^6 kJ/yr

11. First, calculate $\Delta_r H°$ for the reaction $CH_3OH(\ell) + 1.5\ O_2(g) \rightarrow CO_2(g) + 2\,H_2O(\ell)$, using enthalpies of formation ($\Delta_r H° = 726.7$ kJ/mol-rxn). Use molar mass and density to calculate energy per L [−726.7 kJ/mol-rxn (1 mol-rxn/32.04 g) (787 g/ L) = 17.9×10^3 kJ/L]. Then use the kW-h to kJ conversion factor from Q. 9 to obtain the answer [(17.9×10^3 kJ/L) (1 kW-h/3600 kJ) = 4.96 kW-h/L].

13. Area of parking lot = 325 m × 50.0 m = 1.63×10^4 m²

2.6×10^7 J/m²(1.63×10^4 m²) = 4.3×10^{11} J

15. Amount of Pd = 1.0 cm³(12.0 g/cm³) (1 mol/106.4 g) = 0.113 mol

amount of H = 0.084 g(1 mol/1.008 g) = 0.0833 mol

mol H per mol Pd = 0.083/0.113 = 0.74: Simplest formula for this compound is $PdH_{0.74}$ (Because the compound is nonstoichiometric, we will not write a formula with a whole number ratio. For these compounds, it is common practice to set the amount of metal [Pd] to be an integer and H as a non-integer.)

17. Energy per gal. of gas = (48.0 kJ/g)
$(0.737 \text{ g/cm}^3)(1000 \text{ cm}^3/\text{L})(3.785 \text{ L/gal})$ = 1.34×10^5 kJ/gal

Energy to travel 1 mile = (1.00 mile/ 55.0 gal/mile)$(1.34 \times 10^5$ kJ/gal$)$ = 2440 kJ

MILESTONES IN THE DEVELOPMENT OF CHEMISTRY AND THE MODERN VIEW OF ATOMS AND MOLECULES

1. Atoms are not solid, hard, or impenetrable. They have mass (an important aspect of Dalton's hypothesis), and we now know that atoms are in rapid motion at all temperatures above absolute zero (the kinetic-molecular theory).

3. mass e/mass $p = 9.109383 \times 10^{-28}$ g/1.672622 $\times 10^{-24}$ g $= 5.446170 \times 10^{-4}$. (Mass of p and e obtained from Table 2.1, page 52.) The proton is 1,834 times more massive than an electron. Dalton's estimate was off by a factor of about 2.

THE CHEMISTRY OF LIFE: BIOCHEMISTRY

1. (a)

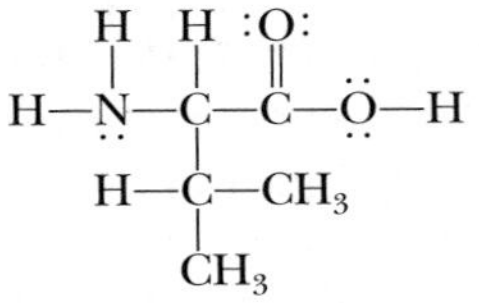

(b)

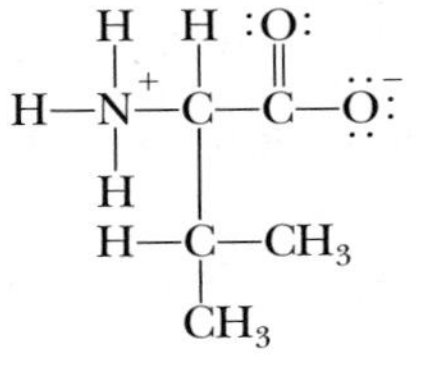

(c) The zwitterionic form is the predominant form at physiological pH.

3.

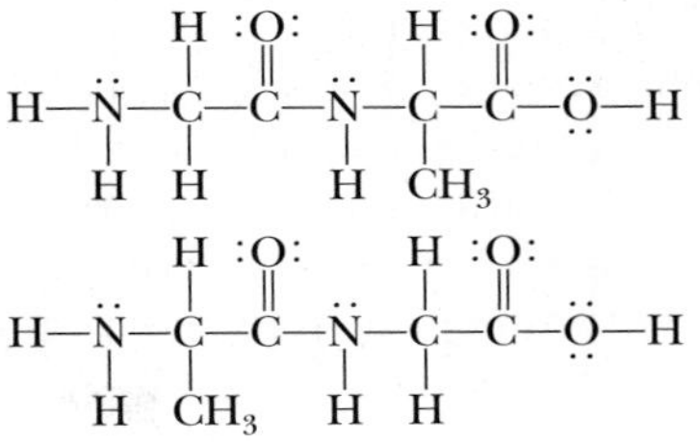

5.

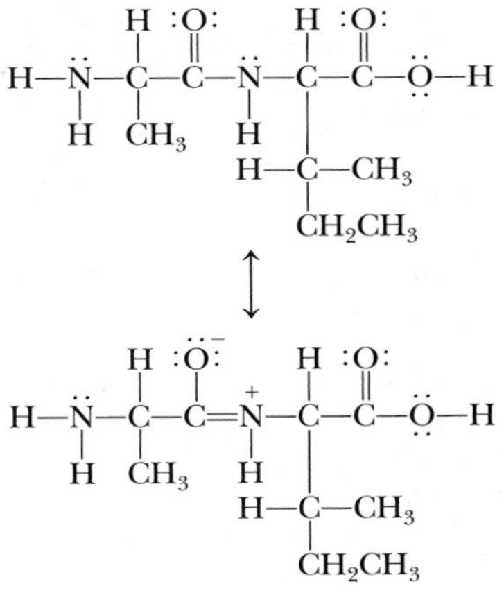

7. (a) The structure of ribose is given in Figure 13.

(b) Adenosine

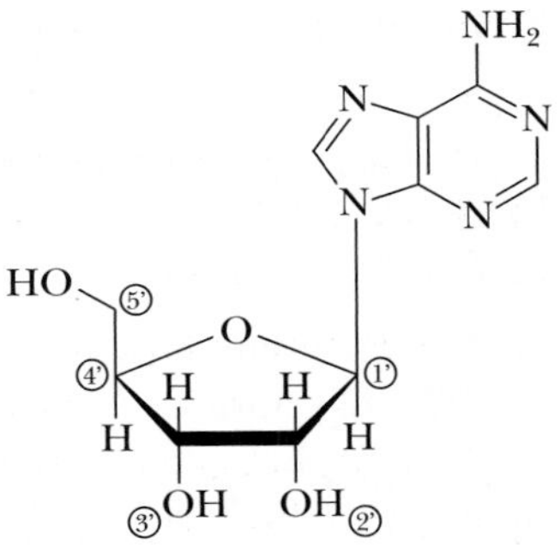

(c) Adenosine-5'-monophosphate

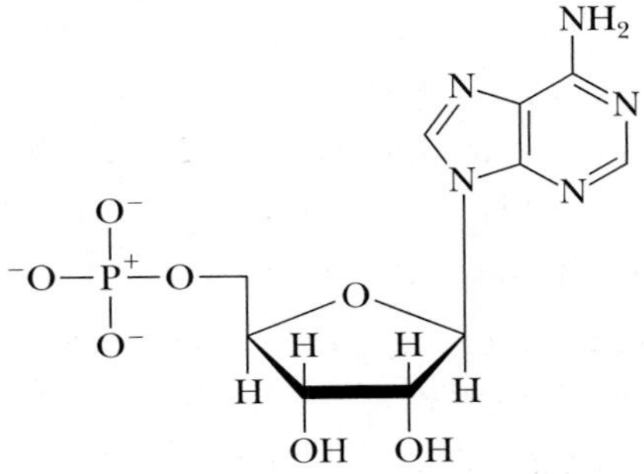

9. The sequences differ in the positions of attachments of the phosphate to deoxyribose on adjacent units. Consider the A-T attachments. In ATGC, the attachment is from the 5′ position on A to the 3′ position on T. In CGTA, the attachment is from the 3′ position on A to the 5′ position on T.

11. (a) 5′-GAATCGCGT-3′

    (b) 5′-GAAUCGCGU-3′

    (c) 5′-UUC-3′, 5′-CGA-3′, and 5′-ACG-3′

    (d) glutamic acid, serine, and arginine

13. (a) In transcription, a strand of RNA complementary to the segment of DNA is constructed.

    (b) In translation, an amino acid sequence is constructed based on the information in a mRNA sequence.

15. The 4-ring structure present in all steroids is given in Figure 18a.

17. (a) False (b) True (c) True (d) True

19. (a) $6 \, CO_2(g) + 6 \, H_2O(\ell) \rightarrow$
    $$C_6H_{12}O_6(s) + 6 \, O_2(g)$$

    $\Delta_rH° = \Delta_fH°(\text{products}) - \Delta_fH°(\text{reactants})$

    $\Delta_rH° = (1 \text{ mol } C_6H_{12}O_6/\text{mol-rxn})$
    $[\Delta_fH°(C_6H_{12}O_6)] - (6 \text{ mol } H_2O/\text{mol-rxn})$
    $[\Delta_fH°(H_2O)] - (6 \text{ mol } CO_2/\text{mol-rxn})$
    $[\Delta_fH°(CO_2)]$

    $\Delta_rH° = (1 \text{ mol } C_6H_{12}O_6/\text{mol-rxn})$
    $(-1273.3 \text{ kJ/mol } C_6H_{12}O_6) - (6 \text{ mol }$
    $H_2O/\text{mol-rxn})(-285.8 \text{ kJ/mol } H_2O) -$
    $(6 \text{ mol } CO_2/\text{mol-rxn})(-393.5 \text{ kJ/mol } CO_2)$

    $\Delta_rH° = +2{,}803 \text{ kJ/mol-rxn}$

    (b) $(2803 \text{ kJ/mol})(1 \text{ mol}/6.022 \times 10^{23}$ molecules)$(1000 \text{ J}/1 \text{ kJ}) = 4.655 \times 10^{-18} \text{ J/molecule}$

    (c) $\lambda = 650 \text{ nm}(1 \text{ m}/10^9 \text{ nm}) = 6.50 \times 10^{-7} \text{ m}$

    $E = hc/\lambda = (6.626 \times 10^{-34} \text{ J} \cdot \text{s})$
    $(3.00 \times 10^8 \text{ m} \cdot \text{s}^{-1})/(6.50 \times 10^{-7} \text{ m}) =$
    $3.06 \times 10^{-19} \text{ J}$

    (d) The amount of energy per photon is less than the amount of required per molecule of glucose, therefore multiple photons must be absorbed.

THE CHEMISTRY OF MODERN MATERIALS

1. The GaAs band gap is 140 kJ/mol. Use the equations $E = h\nu$ and $\lambda \times \nu = c$ to calculate a wavelength of 854 nm corresponding to this energy. Radiation of this wavelength is in the infrared portion of the spectrum.

3. The amount of light falling on a single solar cell = 925 W/m² $[(1 \text{ m}^2/10^4 \text{ cm}^2)$ $(1.0 \text{ cm}^2/\text{cell}) = 0.0925 \text{ W/cell.}]$ Using the conversion factor 1 W = 1 J/s, the energy incident on the cell is (0.0925 W/cell) $(1 \text{J/W} \cdot \text{s})(60 \text{ sec/min}) = 5.55 \text{ J/(min} \cdot \text{cell)}$. At 25% efficiency, the energy absorbed for each cell is 1.39 J/min.

5. The density of dry air at 25 °C and 1.0 atm. is 1.2 g/L (see page 526), so the mass of air in aerogel is $0.99(1.2 \times 10^{-3} \text{ g}) = 1.2 \times 10^{-3}$ g. Add to this 0.023 g, the mass of 0.010 cm³ of SiO_2 (density of SiO_2, from web, is 2.3 g/cm³, mass of 0.010 cm³ is 0.023 g). Thus, the total mass is 0.0012 g + 0.023 g = 0.024 g, and the density of aerogel is 0.024 g/cm³.

ENVIRONMENTAL CHEMISTRY

1. $[Na^+] = 0.460 \text{ mol/L}$, $[Cl^-] = 0.550 \text{ mol/L}$; a larger amount of chloride than sodium ion is present in a sample of seawater.

3. The amount of NaCl is limited by the amount of sodium present. From 1.0 L sample of seawater, a maximum of 0.460 mol NaCl could be obtained. The mass of this amount of NaCl is 26.9 g $[(0.460 \text{ mol/L})(1.00 \text{ L})(58.43 \text{ g NaCl}/1 \text{ mol NaCl}) = 26.9 \text{ g}]$.

5. For gases, ppm refers to numbers of particles, and hence to mole fractions (see footnote to Table 1). Gas pressure exerted is directly proportional to mole fraction. Thus, 40,000 ppm water vapor would exert a pressure of 40,000/1,000,000[th] of one atmosphere, or 30.4 mm Hg (0.040 × 760 mm Hg). This would be the case at a little over 29 °C, at 100% humidity.

7. The concentration of Mg^{2+} in seawater is 52 mmol/L (Table 2). Assuming that all this is converted to Mg metal, one would expect to obtain 1.26 g from 1.0 L of seawater [0.052 mol(24.31 g/mol) = 1.26 g]. To obtain 100 kg of Mg, 79,000 L of seawater [100. kg(1000 g/kg)(1 L/1.26 g) = 7.9×10^4 L] would be needed.

9. (a) The volume occupied by 25 g of ice is 33 cm³ [25 g(1 cm³/0.92 g) = 33 cm³]. However, only 92% of the ice is submerged and the water displaced by ice (the volume of ice under the surface of water) is 25 cm³ (0.92 × 33 cm³ = 25 cm³). Thus, the liquid level in the graduated cylinder will be 125 mL.

(b) Melting 25 g of ice will produce 25 mL of liquid water. The water level will be 125 mL (the same as in (a), that is the water level won't rise as the ice melts).

Q | Answers to Chapter Opening Puzzler and Case Study Questions

CHAPTER 1

Puzzler:

1. Sports drinks: colored, liquid, homogeneous, slightly more dense than pure water. (Dissolved salts raise the density of a solution: e.g., seawater is more dense than pure water.)

2. These drinks are often sold in 500-mL bottles. This is equivalent to 0.50 L or 5.0 dL.

Case Study: Ancient and Modern Hair Coloring

1. Lead (Pb); calcium (Ca)

2. $d = 11.35$ g/cm^3

3. S

4. Calcium hydroxide, known as slaked lime, is made by adding water (slaking) to lime, CaO

5. Sulfide ions (S^{2-}) are on the corners and faces of a cube; lead ions Pb^{2+} lie along each edge.

6. The overall structures are identical. The yellow spheres (S^{2-} in PbS, and Cl^- in NaCl) are at the corners and on the faces of a cube; the spheres representing Pb^{2+} and Na^+ lie along the cube's edges. The small difference in appearance is due to the relative sizes of the spheres.

LET'S REVIEW

Case Study: Out of Gas!

1. Fuel density in kg/L: (1.77 lb/L) (0.4536 kg/lb) = 0.803 kg/L

2. Mass of fuel already in tank: 7682 L (0.803 kg/L) = 6170 kg

   Mass of fuel needed: 22,300 kg − 6,170 kg = 16,100 kg (Answer has three significant figures.)

   Volume of fuel needed: 16,130 kg (1 L/0.803 kg) = 20,100 L

CHAPTER 2

Puzzler:

1. Eka-silicon is germanium. Its atomic weight is 72.61 (predicted 72), and its density is 5.32 g/cm^3 (predicted value 5.5 g/cm^3).

2. Other elements missing from Mendeleev's periodic table include Sc, Ga, the noble gases (He, Ne, Ar, Kr, Xe), and all of the radioactive elements except Th and U.

Case Study: Catching Cheaters with Isotopes

1. 7 neutrons

2. 8 neutrons

3. ^{14}C is formed in the upper atmosphere by a nuclear reaction initiated by cosmic radiation. The equation for its formation is $^{14}_{7}N + ^{1}_{0}n \rightarrow$ $^{14}_{6}C + ^{1}_{1}H$. (See discussion in Chapter 23 on equations for nuclear reactions.)

Case Study: What's in Those French Fries?

1. Acrylamide: C_3H_5NO, molar mass = 71.08; % N = (14.00/71.07)(100%) = 19.70 %.

Asparagine, $C_4H_8O_3N_2$, molar mass = 132.12; % N = (28.00/132.12)(100%) = 21.20 %. Asparagine has the higher percent nitrogen.

2. Body mass in kg = 150 lb(0.4536 kg/1 lb) = 68.0 kg

Total mass ingested = (0.0002 mg/kg body wt) (68.0 kg body wt) = 1.4×10^{-2} mg

Number of molecules = 1.4×10^{-2} mg (1 g/1000 mg)(1 mol/71.08 g)(6.022×10^{23} molecules/mol) = 1×10^{17} molecules (1 significant figure)

CHAPTER 3

Puzzler:

$Fe^{2+}(aq) + H_2S(aq) \rightarrow FeS(s) + 2 H^+(aq)$
$2 Bi^{3+}(aq) + 3 H_2S(aq) \rightarrow Bi_2S_3(s) + 6 H^+(aq)$
$Ca^{2+}(aq) + SO_4{}^{2-}(aq) \rightarrow CaSO_4(s)$

Case Study: Killing Bacteria with Silver

1. 100×10^{15} Ag^+ ions(1 mol/6.022 x 10^{23} ions) = 2×10^{-7} mol Ag^+

2. 2×10^{-7} mol Ag^+(107.9 g Ag^+/1 mol Ag^+) = 2×10^{-5} g Ag^+ ions

CHAPTER 4

Puzzler:

1. Oxidation-reduction reactions.

2. Oxidation of Fe gives Fe_2O_3; oxidation of Al gives Al_2O_3.

3. The mass of Al_2O_3 formed by oxidation of 1.0 g Al = 1.0 g Al (1 mol Al/26.98 g Al) (1 mol Al_2O_3/2 mol Al)(102.0 g Al_2O_3/1 mol Al_2O_3) = 1.9 g Al_2O_3.

Case Study: How Much Salt Is There in Seawater?

1. Step 1: Calculate the amount of Cl^- in the diluted solution from titration data.

Mol Cl^- in 50 mL of dilute solution = mol Ag^+ = (0.100 mol/L)(0.02625 L) = 2.63×10^{-3} mol Cl^-

Step 2: Calculate the concentration of Cl^- in the dilute solution.

Concentration of Cl^- in dilute solution = 2.63×10^{-3} mol/0.0500 L = 5.26×10^{-2} M

Step 3: Calculate the concentration of Cl^- in seawater.

Seawater was initially diluted to one hundredth its original concentration. Thus, the concentration of Cl^- in seawater (undiluted) = 5.25 M

Case Study: Forensic Chemistry: Titrations and Food Tampering

1. Step 1: Calculate the amount of I_2 in solution from titration data:

Amount I_2 = (0.0425 mol $S_2O_3{}^{2-}$/L)(0.0253 L) (1 mol I_2/2 mol $S_2O_3{}^{2-}$) = 5.38×10^{-4} mol I_2

Step 2: Calculate the amount of NaClO present based on the amount of I_2 formed, and from that value calculate the mass of NaClO.

Mass NaClO = 5.38×10^{-4} mol I_2(1 mol HClO/1 mol I_2)(1 mol NaClO/1 mol HClO) (74.44 g NaClO/1 mol NaClO) = 0.0400 g NaClO

CHAPTER 5

Puzzler:

Step 1: Calculate mass of air in the balloon

Mass air = 1100 m^3(1,200 g/m^3) = 1.3×10^6 g

Step 2: Calculate energy as heat needed to raise the temperature of air in the balloon.

Energy as heat = $C \times m \times \Delta T$ = (1.01 J/g · K) $(1.3 \times 10^6$ g$)(383$ K − 295 K$) = 1.2 \times 10^8$ J $(= 1.2 \times 10^5$ kJ$)$

Step 3: Calculate enthalpy change for the oxidation of 1.00 g propane from enthalpy of formation data. Assume formation of water vapor, $H_2O(g)$, in this reaction.

$C_3H_8(g) + 5\ O_2(g) \rightarrow 3\ CO_2(g) + 4\ H_2O(g)$

$\Delta_rH° = \Delta_fH°(\text{products}) - \Delta_fH°(\text{reactants})$ = (3 mol CO_2/mol-rxn)$[\Delta_fH°(CO_2)]$ + (4 mol H_2O/mol-rxn) $[\Delta_fH°(H_2O)]$ − (1 mol C_3H_8/mol-rxn)$[\Delta_fH°(C_3H_8)]$

$\Delta_rH°$ = (3 mol CO_2/mol-rxn)$[-393.5$ kJ/mol $CO_2]$ + (4 mol H_2O/mol-rxn)$[-241.8$ kJ/mol $H_2O]$ − (1 mol C_3H_8/mol-rxn)$[-104.7$ kJ/mol $C_3H_8)]$ = −2043 kJ/mol-rxn

q = −2043 kJ/mol-rxn(1 mol C_3H_8/mol-rxn) (1 mol C_3H_8/44.09 g C_3H_8) = −46.33 kJ/g C_3H_8

Step 4: Use answers from Steps 2 and 3 to calculate mass of propane needed to produce energy as heat needed.)

mass $C_3H_8 = 1.2 \times 10^5$ kJ(1 g C_3H_8/46.33 kJ) = 2.5×10^3 g C_3H_8

(Answer has two significant figures.)

Case Study: Abba's Refrigerator

1. To evaporate 95 g H_2O: q = 44.0 kJ/mol (1 mol/18.02 g)(95 g) = 232 kJ (= 232,000 J)

   Temperature change if 750 g H_2O gives up 232 kJ of energy as heat:

   $Q = C \times m \times \Delta T$

   −232,000 J = (4.184 J/ g · K)(750 g)(ΔT); ΔT = −74 K

Case Study: The Fuel Controversy: Alcohol and Gasoline

In the following, we assume water vapor, $H_2O(g)$, is formed upon oxidation.

1. Burning ethanol: $C_2H_5OH(\ell) + 3\ O_2(g) \rightarrow$ $2\ CO_2(g) + 3\ H_2O(g)$

   $\Delta_rH°$ = (2 mol CO_2/mol-rxn)$[\Delta_fH°(CO_2)]$ + (3 mol H_2O/mol-rxn)$[\Delta_fH°(H_2O)]$ − (1 mol C_2H_5OH/mol-rxn)$[\Delta_fH°(C_2H_5OH)]$

$\Delta_rH°$ = (2 mol CO_2/mol-rxn)$[-393.5$ kJ/mol $CO_2]$ + (3 mol H_2O/mol-rxn)$[-241.8$ kJ/mol $H_2O]$ − (1 mol C_2H_5OH/mol-rxn)$[-277.0$ kJ/mol $C_2H_5OH)]$ = −1235.4 kJ/mol-rxn

1 mol ethanol per 1 mol-rxn; therefore, q per mol is −1235.4 kJ/mol

q per gram: −1235.4 kJ/mol(1mol C_2H_5OH/ 46.07 g C_2H_5OH) = −26.80 kJ/g C_2H_5OH

Burning octane: $C_8H_{18}(\ell) + 12.5\ O_2(g) \rightarrow$ $8\ CO_2(g) + 9\ H_2O(g)$

$\Delta_rH°$ = (8 mol CO_2/mol-rxn)$[\Delta_fH°(CO_2)]$ + (9 mol H_2O/mol-rxn)$[\Delta_fH°(H_2O)]$ − (1 mol C_8H_{18}/mol-rxn)$[\Delta_fH°(C_8H_{18})]$

$\Delta_rH°$ = (8 mol CO_2/mol-rxn)$[-393.5$ kJ/mol $CO_2]$ + (9 mol H_2O/mol-rxn)$[-241.8$ kJ/mol $H_2O]$ − (1 mol C_8H_{18}/mol-rxn)$[-250.1$ kJ/mol $C_8H_{18})]$ = −5070.1 kJ/mol-rxn

1 mol octane per mol-rxn; therefore, q per mol is −5070.1 kJ/mol

q per gram: −5070.1 kJ/1 mol C_8H_{18} (1 mol C_8H_{18}/114.2 g C_8H_{18}) = −44.40 kJ/g C_8H_{18}

2. For ethanol, per liter: q = −26.80 kJ/g (785 g/L) = −2.10 × 10^4 kJ/L

   For octane, per liter: q = −44.40 kJ/g (699 g/L) = 3.10 × 10^4 kJ/L

   Octane produces almost 50% more energy per liter of fuel.

3. Mass of CO_2 per liter of ethanol: = 1.000 L (785 g C_2H_5OH/L)(1 mol C_2H_5OH /46.07 g C_2H_5OH)(2 mol CO_2/1 mol C_2H_5OH)(44.01 g CO_2/1 mol CO_2) = 1.50 × 10^3 g CO_2

   Mass of CO_2 per liter of octane: = 1.000 L (699 g C_8H_{18}/L)(1 mol C_8H_{18} /114.2 g C_8H_{18})(8 mol CO_2/1 mol C_8H_{18})(44.01 g CO_2/1 mol CO_2) = 2.15 × 10^3 g CO_2

4. Volume of ethanol needed to obtain 3.10 × 10^4 kJ of energy from oxidation: 2.10 × 10^4 kJ/L C_2H_5OH)(x) = 3.10 × 10^4 kJ (x is volume of ethanol)

   Volume of ethanol = x = 1.48 L

   Mass of CO_2 produced by burning 1.48 L of ethanol = (1.50 × 10^3 g CO_2/L C_2H_5OH) (1.48 L C_2H_5OH) = 2.22 × 10^3 g CO_2

   To obtain the same amount of energy, slightly more CO_2 is produced by burning ethanol than for octane.

5. Your car will travel about 50% farther on a liter of octane, and it will produce slightly less CO_2 emissions, than if you burned 1.0 L of ethanol.

CHAPTER 6
Puzzler:

1. Red light has the longer wavelength.

2. Green light has the higher energy.

3. The energy of light emitted by atoms is determined by the energy levels of the electrons in an atom. See discussion in the text, page 275.

Case Study: What Makes the Colors in Fireworks?

1. Yellow light is from 589 and 590 nm emissions.

2. Primary emission for Sr is red: this has a longer wavelength than yellow light.

3. $4 Mg(s) + KClO_4(s) \rightarrow KCl(s) + 4 MgO(s)$

CHAPTER 7
Puzzler:

1. Cr: $[Ar]3d^5 4s^1$; Cr^{3+}: $[Ar]3d^3$; CrO_4^{2-} (chromium(VI)): $[Ar]$

2. Cr^{3+} is paramagnetic with three unpaired electrons.

3. Pb in $PbCrO_4$ is present as Pb^{2+}: $[Xe]4f^{14}5d^{10}6s^2$

Case Study: Metals in Biochemistry and Medicine

1. Fe^{2+}: $[Ar]3d^6$; Fe^{3+}: $[Ar]3d^5$

2. Both iron ions are paramagnetic.

3. Cu^+: $[Ar]3d^{10}$; Cu^{2+}: $[Ar]3d^9$; Cu^{2+} is paramagnetic; Cu^+ is diamagnetic.

4. The slightly larger size of Cu compared to Fe is related to greater electron–electron repulsions.

5. Fe^{2+} is larger than Fe^{3+} and will fit less well into the structure. As a result, some distortion of the ring structure from planarity occurs.

CHAPTER 8
Puzzler:

1. Carbon and phosphorus (in phosphate) achieve the noble gas configuration by forming four bonds.

2. In each instance, there are four bonds to the element; VSEPR predicts that these atoms will have tetrahedral geometry with 109.5° angles.

3. Bond angles in these rings are 120°. To achieve this preferred bond angle, the rings must be planar.

4. Thymine and cytosine are polar molecules.

Case Study: The Importance of an Odd Electron Molecule, NO

1. $\left[\ddot{O} = \ddot{N} - \ddot{O} - \ddot{O} : \right]^{-}$

2. There is a double bond between N and the terminal O.

3. Resonance structures are not needed to describe the bonding in this ion.

CHAPTER 9
Puzzler:

1. XeF_2 is linear. The electron pair geometry is trigonal bipyramidal. Three lone pairs are located in the equatorial plane, and the two F atoms are located in the axial positions. This symmetrical structure will not have a dipole.

2. The Xe atom is sp^3d hybridized. Xe-F bonds: overlap of Xe sp^3d orbitals with F 2p orbital. 3 lone pairs in Xe sp^3d orbitals.

3. This 36-electron molecule has a bent molecular structure.

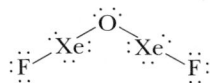

Case Study: Two Chemical Bonding Mysteries

1. Eight two-electron bonds, which would require 16 electrons, four more than the 12 available.

2. The compound has sp^3 hybridized B and N atoms and is polar. The B atom has a -1 formal charge and N has a $+1$ form charge. All bond angles are about $109°$.

3. $(54.3 \times 10^{-3}$ g $AgBF_4)(1$ mol$/194.7$ g$) = 2.79 \times 10^{-4}$ mol

The amount of $Ag(C_2H_4)_xBF_4$ that must have decomposed is 2.79×10^{-4} mol.

Molar mass of unknown $= (62.1 \times 10^{-3}$ g$)/$ $(2.79 \times 10^{-4}$ mol$) = 223$ g/mol

The compound $Ag(C_2H_4)BF_4$ where $x = 1$ has a molar mass of 223 g/mol.

CHAPTER 10

Puzzler:

1. (a) Trigonal planar, sp^2 hybridized. The other carbon atoms in this molecule have tetrahedral geometry and sp^3 hybridization.

(b) The non-planarity allows all of the atoms in the molecule to assume an unstrained geometry.

(c) Actually, there are two chiral centers, labeled with an asterisk (*) in the drawing below.

2. Camphor is a ketone.

Case Study: Biodiesel, a Fuel for the Future

1. $C_{12}H_{25}CO_2CH_3(\ell) + 20\ O_2(g) \rightarrow 14\ CO_2(g) + 14\ H_2O(g)$

2. $\Delta_rH° = (14$ mol CO_2/mol-rxn$)[\Delta_fH°(CO_2)] + (14$ mol H_2O/mol-rxn$)[\Delta_fH°(H_2O)] - (1$ mol $C_{12}H_{25}CO_2CH_3$/mol-rxn$)[\Delta_fH°(C_{12}H_{25}CO_2CH_3)]$

$\Delta_rH° = (14$ mol CO_2/mol-rxn$)[-393.5$ kJ/mol $CO_2] + (14$ mol H_2O/mol-rxn$)[-241.8$ kJ/mol $H_2O] - (1$ mol $C_{12}H_{25}CO_2CH_3$/mol-rxn$)[-771.0$ kJ/mol $C_{12}H_{25}CO_2CH_3)] = -8123.2$ kJ/mol-rxn

1 mol methyl myristate per mol-rxn, so q per mol $= -8123.2$ kJ/mol

3. Burning hexadecane: $C_{16}H_{34}(\ell) + 24.5\ O_2(g) \rightarrow 16\ CO_2(g) + 17\ H_2O(g)$

$\Delta_rH° = (16$ mol CO_2/mol-rxn$)[\Delta_fH°(CO_2)] + (17$ mol H_2O/mol-rxn$)[\Delta_fH°(H_2O)] - (1$ mol $C_{16}H_{34}$/mol-rxn$)[\Delta_fH°(C_{16}H_{34})]$

$\Delta_rH° = (16$ mol CO_2/mol-rxn$)[-393.5$ kJ/mol $CO_2] + (17$ mol H_2O/mol-rxn$)[-241.8$ kJ/mol $H_2O] - (1$ mol $C_{16}H_{34}$/mol-rxn$)[-456.1$ kJ/mol $C_{16}H_{34})] = -9950.5$ kJ/mol-rxn

1 mole hexadecane per mol-rxn, so q per mol: -9950.5 kJ/mol

For methyl myristate, q per liter $= (-8123.2$ kJ/mol$)(1$ mol$/228.4$ g$)(0.86$ g/L$) = -30.6$ kJ/L

For hexadecane, q per liter $= (-9950.5$ kJ/mol$)(1$ mol$/226.43$ g$)(0.77$ g/1 L$) = -33.8$ kJ/L

CHAPTER 11

Puzzler:

1. $P(O_2)$ at 3000 m is 70% of 0.21 atm, the value $P(O_2)$ at sea level, thus $P(O_2)$ at 3000 m $= 0.21$ atm $\times 0.70 = 0.15$ atm (110 mm Hg). At the top of Everest, $P(O_2) = 0.21$ atm $\times 0.29 = 0.061$ atm (46 mm Hg).

2. Blood saturation levels (estimated from table): at 3000 m, $>95\%$; at top of Everest, 75%.

Case Study: You Stink

1. To calculate $P(CH_3SH)$, use the ideal gas law:
   $V = 1.00$ m^3(10^6 cm^3/m^3)(1 L/10^3 cm^3) = 1.00×10^3 L;

   $n = 1.5 \times 10^{-3}$ g(1 mol/48.11 g) = 3.1×10^{-5} mol

   $P = nRT/V = [3.1 \times 10^{-5}$ mol(0.08205 L atm/mol · K)(298 K)]/1.0×10^3 L = 7.6×10^{-7} atm. (5.8×10^{-4} mm Hg)

   Molecules per m^3 = 3.1×10^{-5} mol (6.022×10^{23} molecules/mol) = 1.9×10^{19} molecules

2. Bond angles: H—C—H and H—C—S, 109.5°; C—S—H somewhat less than 109°.

3. Polar

4. It should behave as an ideal gas at moderate pressures and temperatures well above its boiling point.

5. H$_2$S (with the lowest molar mass) will diffuse fastest.

CHAPTER 12

Puzzler:

1. In ice, water molecules are not packed as closely as they are in liquid water. This structure results so that hydrogen bonding interactions between water molecules are maximized.

   A piece of ice floats at a level where it will displace its weight of seawater. Most of the volume of an iceberg is below the water line.

2. A 1000 cm^3 piece of ice (mass = 917 g) would float with [0.917/1.026](100%) = 89.4% below the surface or 10.6% above the surface.

Case Study: The Mystery of the Disappearing Fingerprints

1. The chemical compounds in a child's fingerprints are more volatile because they have lower molecular weights than compounds in adults' fingerprints.

CHAPTER 13

Puzzler:

1. This geometry problem is solved using the numbers shown on the drawing.

   $x^2 + (69.5)^2 = (139)^2$

   Solving, $x = 120$ pm.

   The side-to-side distance is twice this value or 240. pm

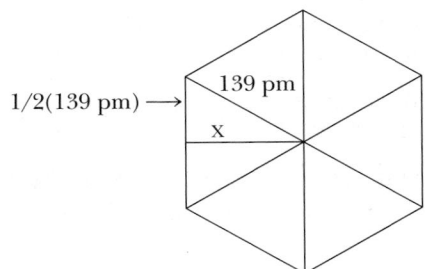

2. 1.00 μm = 1.00×10^{-4} cm and 240 pm = 2.4×10^{-8} cm.

   The number of C$_6$ rings spanning 1 μm is 1.00×10^{-4} cm/2.40×10^{-8} cm = 4.17×10^3 rings

3. Graphene is described as being one carbon atom thick so the thickness is twice the radius of a carbon atom or 154 pm.

Case Study: The World's Lightest Solid

1. The mass of 1.00 cm^3 of aerogel is 1.00 mg (1.00×10^{-3} g) and 0.2% of this, 2.00×10^{-6} g, is the mass of the polymer. The number of silicon atoms in 1.00 cm^3 = 2.00×10^{-6} g (1 mol (C$_2$H$_5$O)$_2$SiO/134.2 g)(1 mol Si/1 mol (C$_2$H$_5$O)$_2$SiO)(6.022×10^{23} atoms Si/mol Si) = 9.0×10^{15} atoms Si.

2. Volume between glass panes = 150 cm × 180 cm × 0.2 cm = 5,400 cm^3

   Density of aerogel = 1.00×10^{-3} g/cm^3, so the mass of aerogel needed = 5400 cm^3(1.00×10^{-3} g/cm^3) = 5.4 g.

CHAPTER 14

Puzzler:

1. "Like dissolves like." Both liquids are polar, and both are capable of strong hydrogen bonding.

2. Ethylene glycol, a nonvolatile solute, lowers the freezing point. It is not corrosive. The liquids are miscible in all proportions.

3. $c_{glycol} = 100.$ g$(1 \text{ mol}/62.07 \text{ g})/0.500 \text{ kg} = 3.22 \text{ m}$

   $\Delta T_{fp} = -k_{fp} m_{solute} = -1.86 \text{ °C}/m \times 3.22 \ m = -6.0 \text{ °C}; \ T_{fp} = -6.0 \text{ °C}$

Case Study: Henry's Law in a Soda Bottle

1. $PV = nRT$

   $4.0 \text{ atm}(0.025 \text{ L}) = n(0.08205 \text{ L} \cdot \text{atm/mol} \cdot \text{K})$ 298 K; $n = 4.1 \times 10^{-3}$ mol

2. $P_1 V_1 = P_2 V_2$

   $4.0 \text{ atm}(0.025 \text{ L}) = 3.7 \times 10^{-4} \text{ atm } (V_2)$; $V_2 = 270 \text{ L}$

3. Solubility of $CO_2 = k_H P_g = 0.034 \text{ mol/kg} \cdot \text{bar}$ (4.0 bar) = 0.14 mol/kg

   Amount dissolved in 710 mL of diet cola (assume density is 1.0 g/cm^3) = 0.14 × 0.71 kg = 0.099 mol

4. Solubility of $CO_2 = k_H P_g = 0.034 \text{ mol/kg} \cdot \text{bar}$ (3.7×10^{-4} bar) = 1.3×10^{-5} mol/kg

CHAPTER 15

Puzzler:

See the answer to Study Question 71 for this chapter in Appendix O.

Case Study: Enzymes: Nature's Catalysts

1. To decompose an equivalent amount of H_2O_2 catalytically would take 1.0×10^{-7} years; this is equivalent to 3.2 s.

2.

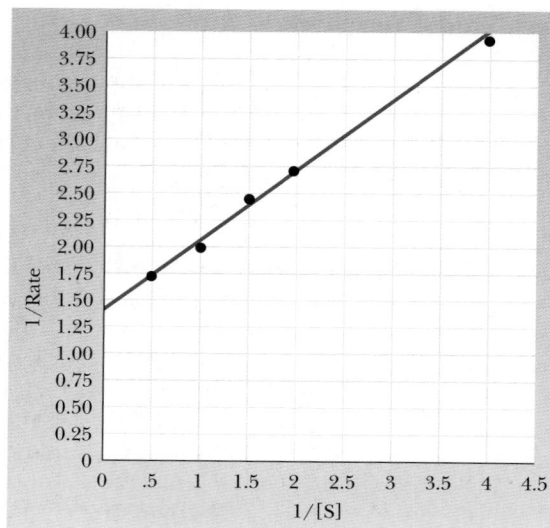

[S]	1/[S]	Rate	1/Rate
2.50	0.400	0.588	1.70
1.00	1.00	0.500	2.00
0.714	1.40	0.417	2.40
0.526	1.90	0.370	2.70
0.250	4.00	0.256	3.91

From the graph, we obtain a value of 1/Rate = 1.47 when 1/[S] = 0. From this, $R_{max} = 0.68$ mmol/min.

CHAPTER 16

Puzzler:

1. Endothermic. Raising the temperature (adding energy as heat) leads to conversion of reactants to products.

2. Apply LeChatelier's Principle: the system adjusts to addition of Cl^- by forming more $[CoCl_4]^{2-}$ and to addition of water by forming more $[Co(H_2O)_6]^{2+}$.

3. The various stresses applied have caused the system to adjust in either direction. (Better evidence: show that when heating and cooling the system is *repeated several times* the system cycles back and forth between the two colors.)

Case Study: Applying Equilibrium Concepts— The Haber-Bosch Process

1. (a) Oxidize part of the NH_3 to HNO_3, then react NH_3 and HNO_3 (an acid–base reaction) to form NH_4NO_3.

    $$4 NH_3 + 5O_2 \rightarrow 4 NO_2 + 6 H_2O$$

    $$2 NO_2 + H_2O \rightarrow HNO_3 + HNO_2$$

    $$HNO_3 + NH_3 \rightarrow NH_4NO_3$$

    (b) $\Delta_r H° = $ (1 mol $[(NH_2)_2CO]$ /mol-rxn) $[\Delta_f H°\{(NH_2)_2CO\}] + $ (1 mol H_2O/mol-rxn) $[\Delta_f H°(H_2O)] - $ (2 mol NH_3/mol-rxn) $[\Delta_f H°(NH_3)] - $ (1 mol CO_2/mol-rxn) $[\Delta_f H°(CO_2)]$

    $\Delta_r H° = $ (1 mol $[(NH_2)_2CO]$ /mol-rxn) (-333.1 kJ/mol) + (1 mol H_2O/mol-rxn) (-241.8 kJ/mol) $-$ (2 mol NH_3/mol-rxn) (-45.90 kJ/mol) $-$ (1 mol CO_2/mol-rxn) (-393.5 kJ/mol)

    $\Delta_r H° = -89.6$ kJ/mol-rxn.

    The reaction as written is exothermic so the equilibrium will be more favorable for product formation at a low temperature. The reaction converts three moles of gaseous reactants to one mole of gaseous products; thus, high pressure will be more favorable to product formation.

2. (a) For $CH_4(g) + H_2O(g) \rightarrow CO(g) + 3 H_2(g)$

    $\Delta_r H° = $ (1 mol CO/mol-rxn)$[\Delta_f H°(CO)] - $ (1 mol CH_4/mol-rxn)$[\Delta_f H°(CH_4)] - $ (1 mol H_2O/mol-rxn)$[\Delta_f H°(H_2O)]$

    $\Delta_r H° = $ (1 mol CO/mol-rxn)(-110.5 kJ/mol) $-$ (1 mol CH_4/mol-rxn)(-74.87 kJ/mol)] $-$ (1 mol H_2O/mol-rxn)(-241.8 kJ/mol)] $= 206.2$ kJ/mol-rxn (endothermic)

    For $CO(g) + H_2O(g) \rightarrow CO_2(g) + H_2(g)$

    $\Delta_r H° = $ (1 mol CO_2/mol-rxn)$[\Delta_f H°(CO_2)] - $ (1 mol CO/mol-rxn)$[\Delta_f H°(CO)] - $ (1 mol H_2O/mol-rxn)$[\Delta_f H°(H_2O)]$

    $\Delta_r H° = $ (1 mol CO_2/mol-rxn)(-393.5 kJ/mol) $-$ (1 mol CO/mol-rxn)(-110.5 kJ/mol)] $-$ (1 mol H_2O/mol-rxn)(-241.8 kJ/mol)] $= -41.2$ kJ/mol-rxn (exothermic)

(b) (15 billion kg $= 1.5 \times 10^{13}$ g)

    Add the two equations:
    $$CH_4(g) + 2 H_2O(g) \rightarrow CO_2(g) + 4 H_2(g)$$

    CH_4 required $= (1.5 \times 10^{13}$ g $NH_3)$ (1 mole NH_3/17.03 g NH_3) (3 moles H_2/2 moles NH_3) (1 mole CH_4/4 moles H_2) (16.04 g CH_4/1 mole CH_4) $= 5.3 \times 10^{12}$ g CH_4

    CO_2 formed $= (1.5 \times 10^{13}$ g $NH_3)$ (1 mole NH_3/17.03 g NH_3) (3 moles H_2/2 moles NH_3) (1 mole CO_2/4 moles H_2) (44.01 g CO_2/1 mole CO_2) $= 1.5 \times 10^{13}$ g CO_2

CHAPTER 17

Puzzler:

1. Aspirin, with a larger pK_a, is a stronger acid than acetic acid.

2. The acid hydrogen is the H on the $-CO_2H$ (carboxylic acid) functional group.

3. $C_6H_4(OCOCH_3)CO_2H + H_2O \rightarrow$ $C_6H_4(OH)CO_2H + CH_3CO_2H$

Case Study: Uric Acid, Gout, and Bird Droppings

1. $(420\ \mu mol/L) (10^{-6}$ mol/$\mu mol)$ $(168.12$ g/mol$)$ $(10^3$ mg/g$) = 71$ mg/L

2. The closest match to this pK_a is for $[Al(H_2O)_6]^{3+}$, $pK_a = 5.10$

CHAPTER 18

Puzzler:

1. $CaCO_3$ (K_{sp} for $CaCO_3 = 3.4 \times 10^{-9} > K_{sp}$ for $MnCO_3 = 2.3 \times 10^{-11}$)

2. PbS

3. $CaF_2(s) \rightleftharpoons Ca^{2+}(aq) + 2 F^-(aq)$ ($K_{sp} = 5.3 \times 10^{-11}$)

    Define solubility (mol/L) as x; then $[Ca^{2+}] = x$ and $[F^-] = 2x$

    $5.3 \times 10^{-11} = [Ca^{2+}][F^-]^2 = [x][2x]^2$

    $x = 2.4 \times 10^{-4}$; solubility $= 2.4 \times 10^{-4}$ mol/L

Case Study: Take a Deep Breath!

1. $pH = pK_a + log[HPO_4^{2-}]/[H_2PO_4^-]$

   $7.4 = 7.20 + log[HPO_4^{2-}]/[H_2PO_4^-]$

   $[HPO_4^{2-}]/[H_2PO_4^-] = 1.6$

2. Assign $x = [HPO_4^{2-}]$, then
   $[H_2PO_4^-] = (0.020 - x)$

   $1.6 = x/(0.020 - x)$; $x = 0.012$

   $[HPO_4^{2-}] = x = 0.012$ mol/L

   $[H_2PO_4^-] = 0.20 - x = 0.0080$ mol/L

CHAPTER 19

Puzzler:

1. Ethanol oxidation: $C_2H_5OH(\ell) + 3\ O_2(g) \rightarrow 2\ CO_2(g) + 3\ H_2O(g)$

   The enthalpy change per gram, -26.80 kJ/g, was calculated for the Case Study in Chapter 5 (see page A-124). From this, the enthalpy change per kg is -2.680×10^4 kJ/kg.

   C_8H_{18} oxidation: $C_8H_{18}(\lambda) + 12.5\ O_2(g) \rightarrow 8\ CO_2(g) + 9\ H_2O(g)$

   The enthalpy change per gram, -44.4 kJ/g, was calculated for the Case Study in Chapter 5 (see page A-124). From this, the enthalpy change per kg is 4.44×10^4 kJ/kg.

2. Ethanol oxidation, free energy change:

   $\Delta_r G^\circ = (2\text{ mol }CO_2/\text{mol-rxn})[\Delta_f G^\circ(CO_2)] + (3\text{ mol }H_2O/\text{mol-rxn})[\Delta_f G^\circ(H_2O)] - (1\text{ mol }C_2H_5OH/\text{mol-rxn})[\Delta_f G^\circ(C_2H_5OH)]$

   $\Delta_r G^\circ = (2\text{ mol }CO_2/\text{mol-rxn})[-394.4\text{ kJ/mol }CO_2] + (3\text{ mol }H_2O/\text{mol-rxn})[-228.6\text{ kJ/mol }H_2O] - (1\text{ mol }C_2H_5OH/\text{mol-rxn})[-174.7\text{ kJ/mol }C_2H_5OH] = -1300.\text{ kJ/mol-rxn}$

   1 mol ethanol per 1 mol-rxn; therefore $\Delta_r G^\circ$ per mol: $-1300.$ kJ/mol

   $\Delta_r G^\circ$ per kg: $-1300.$ kJ/mol(1 mol C_2H_5OH/46.07 g C_2H_5OH)(1000 g/kg) $= -2.822 \times 10^4$ kJ/kg C_2H_5OH

C_8H_{18} oxidation, free energy change:
$\Delta_r G^\circ = \Delta_r H^\circ - T\ \Delta_r S^\circ$. ($\Delta_r H^\circ$ from above. We need to calculate $\Delta_r S^\circ$ for this reaction.)

$\Delta_r S^\circ = (8\text{ mol }CO_2/\text{mol-rxn})S^\circ(CO_2)] + (9\text{ mol }H_2O/\text{mol})[S^\circ(H_2O)] - (1\text{ mol }C_8H_{18}/\text{mol})[S^\circ(C_8H_{18})] - (12.5\text{ mol }O_2)[S^\circ(O_2)]$

$\Delta_r S^\circ = (8\text{ mol }CO_2/\text{mol-rxn})[213.74\text{ J/K}\cdot\text{mol }CO_2] + (9\text{ mol }H_2O/\text{mol-rxn})[188.84\text{ J/K}\cdot\text{mol }H_2O] - (1\text{ mol }C_8H_{18}/\text{mol-rxn})[361.2\text{ kJ/K}\cdot\text{mol }C_8H_{18}] - (12.5\text{ mol }O_2/\text{mol-rxn})[205.07\text{ J/K}\cdot\text{mol }O_2] = 587.5\text{ J/K}\cdot\text{mol-rxn}$ (= 0.5875 kJ/K $\cdot$ mol-rxn)

$\Delta_r G^\circ = \Delta_r H^\circ - T\ \Delta_r S^\circ = -5.070$ kJ/mol $- 298.2$ K(0.5875 kJ/K $\cdot$ mol-rxn) $= -5,245$ kJ/mol-rxn

$\Delta_r G^\circ$ per kg $= (-5,275\text{ kJ/mol-rxn})(1\text{ mol-rxn/mol }C_8H_{18})(1\text{ mol}/114.3\text{ g})(1\text{ kg}/1000\text{ g}) = -4.59 \times 10^4$ kJ/kg

3. For the oxidation of ethanol, entropy changes increase the energy available to do useful work. For oxidation of hydrogen, the opposite is true.

4. The difference in values of $\Delta_r H^\circ$ and $\Delta_r G^\circ$ result because energy is expended or acquired to achieve a higher dispersion of energy in the universe (system and surroundings).

Case Study: Thermodynamics and Living Things

1. Creatine phosphate + $H_2O \rightarrow$ Creatine + HP_i + H^+ $\quad\Delta G^\circ = -43.3$ kJ/mol

   Adenosine + $HP_i \rightarrow$ Adenosine monophosphate + H_2O $\quad\Delta G^\circ = +9.2$ kJ/mol

   Net reaction (sum of the two reactions):

   Creatine phosphate + Adenosine $\rightarrow$ Creatine + Adenosine monophosphate

   For this $\Delta G^\circ = -43.3$ kJ/mol $+ 9.2$ kJ/mol $= -34.1$ kJ/mol; the negative value indicates that the transfer of phosphate from creatine phosphate to adenosine is product-favored.

2. $\Delta G^{\circ'} = \Delta G^\circ + RT\ ln[C][H_3O^+]/[A][B] = \Delta G^\circ + (8.31 \times 10^{-3})(298)\ ln[1][1 \times 10^{-7}]/[1][1]$

   $\Delta G^{\circ'} = \Delta G^\circ - 34.2$ kJ/mol

CHAPTER 20

Puzzler:

Possible reactions are:

1) $Cu^{2+}(aq) + Ni(s) \rightarrow Cu(s) + Ni^{2+}(aq)$

2) $Cu(s) + Ni^{2+}(aq) \rightarrow Cu^{2+}(aq) + Ni(s)$.

A reaction given by equation (1) would produce an electric current of 0.59 volts. [$E°_{cell} = E°$(cathode) $- E°$(anode) $= 0.34$ V $- (-0.25$ V)]

Case Study: Manganese in the Oceans

1. Cathode reaction: $Mn^{3+} + e^- \rightarrow Mn^{2+}$

   Anode reaction: $Mn^{3+} + 2\,H_2O \rightarrow MnO_2 + 4\,H^+ + e^-$

   Net reaction: $2\,Mn^{3+} + 2\,H_2O \rightarrow MnO_2 + Mn^{2+} + 4\,H^+$

   $E°_{cell} = E°$(cathode) $- E°$(anode) $= 1.50$ V $- 0.95$ V] $= 0.55$ V

   The positive value associated with disproportionation (the net reaction) is positive, indicating a product-favored reaction.

2. (a) $MnO_2 + H_2S + 2\,H^+ \rightarrow Mn^{2+} + S + 2\,H_2O$

   (b) $2\,Mn^{2+} + O_2 + 2\,H_2O \rightarrow 2\,MnO_2 + 4\,H^+$

3. Cathode reaction: $O_2 + 4\,H^+ + 4\,e^- \rightarrow 2\,H_2O$ ($E° = 1.229$ V)

   Anode reaction: $Mn^{2+} + 2\,H_2O \rightarrow MnO_2 + 4\,H^+ + 2\,e^-$ ($E° = 1.23$ V, from Appendix M)

   $E°_{cell} = E°$(cathode) $- E°$(anode) $= 1.229$ V $- 1.23$ V $= 0$ V.

CHAPTER 21

Puzzler:

1. $CH_4(g) + 2\,H_2O(\ell) \rightarrow CO_2(g) + 4\,H_2(g)$

   $SiH_4(g) + 2\,H_2O(\ell) \rightarrow SiO_2(s) + 4\,H_2(g)$

2. For CH_4: assumes $H_2O(\ell)$ is the reactant

   $\Delta_r H° = (1$ mol CO_2/mol-rxn)$[\Delta_f H°(CO_2)] - (1$ mol CH_4/mol-rxn)$[\Delta_f H°(CH_4)] - (2$ mol H_2O/mol-rxn)$[\Delta_f H°(H_2O)]$

   $\Delta_r H° = (1$ mol CO_2/mol-rxn)$(-393.5$ kJ/mol) $- (1$ mol CH_4/mol-rxn)$(-74.87$ kJ/mol)] $- (2$ mol H_2O/mol-rxn)$(-285.8$ kJ/mol)] $= 252.4$ kJ/mol-rxn

   For SiH_4: assumes $H_2O(\ell)$ is the reactant

   $\Delta_r H° = (1$ mol SiO_2/mol-rxn)$[\Delta_f H°(SiO_2)] - (1$ mol SiH_4/mol-rxn)$[\Delta_f H°(SiH_4)] - (2$ mol H_2O/mol-rxn)$[\Delta_f H°(H_2O)]$

   $\Delta_r H° = (1$ mol SiO_2)/mol-rxn)$(-910.86$ kJ/mol) $- (1$ mol SiH_4/mol-rxn)$(34.31$ kJ/mol)] $- (2$ mol H_2O/mol-rxn)$(-285.8$ kJ/mol)] $= -373.6$ kJ/mol-rxn

3. Electronegativities: C 2.5, Si, 1.9, H 2.2. From this we conclude that polarities of C—H and Si—H bonds are in the opposite directions: in SiH_4, the H has a slight negative charge (it is hydridic) and in CH_4 the H has a slight positive charge.

4. General observation from these examples: Carbon often bonds to other atoms via double bonds, whereas Si does not. We would not expect $H_2Si{=}SiH_2$ to exist as a molecular species; instead a polymeric structure $[-SiH_2SiH_2^-]_x$ is predicted.

Case Study: Hard Water

1. For Mg^{2+}: (50 mg)(1 mmol Mg^{2+}/24.31 mg)(1 mmol CaO/mmol Mg^{2+})(56.07 mg CaO/1 mmol CaO) $= 115.3$ mg CaO

   For Ca^{2+}: (50 mg)(1 mmol Ca^{2+}/40.08 mg)(1 mmol CaO/mmol Ca^{2+})(56.07 mg CaO/1 mmol CaO) $= 209.8$ mg CaO

   Total CaO $= 115.3$ mg $+ 209.9$ mg $= 330$ mg (2 significant figures)

   We get 2 mol $CaCO_3$ per mole Ca^{2+} and 1 mol each of $CaCO_3$ and $MgCO_3$ per mol Mg^{2+}

   $CaCO_3$ from Ca^{2+} reaction: (0.150 g Ca^{2+})(1 mol/40.08 g Ca^{2+})(2 mol $CaCO_3$/1 mol Ca^{2+})(100.1 g $CaCO_3$/1 mol $CaCO_3$) $= 0.749$ g

$CaCO_3$ from Mg^{2+} reaction: $(0.050 \text{ g } Mg^{2+})$ $(1 \text{ mol}/24.31 \text{ g } Mg^{2+})(1 \text{ mol } CaCO_3/1 \text{ mol } Mg^{2+})(100.1 \text{ g } CaCO_3/1 \text{ mol } CaCO_3) =$ 0.0.206 g

$MgCO_3$ from Mg^{2+} reaction: $(0.050 \text{ g } Mg^{2+})$ $(1 \text{ mol}/24.31 \text{ g } Mg^{2+})(1 \text{ mol } MgCO_3/1 \text{ mol } Mg^{2+})(84.31 \text{ g } CaCO_3/1 \text{ mol } CaCO_3) =$ 0.173 g

Total mass of solids = 0.747 g + 0.206 g + 0.173 g = 1.1 g (2 significant figures)

Case Study: Lead, a Mystery Solved

1. 50 ppb is 50 g in 1×10^9 g of blood. Assume the density of blood is 1.0 g/mL. In 1.0×10^3 mL (i.e., 1.0 L) of blood, there will be 50×10^{-6} g of Pb. From this:

50×10^{-6} g (1 mol Pb/207.2 g Pb) $(6.022 \times 10^{23}$ atoms Pb/mol Pb) = 1.5×10^{17} atoms Pb

Case Study: A Healthy Aquarium and the Nitrogen Cycle

1. $2 NH_4^+(aq) + 4 OH^-(aq) + 3 O_2(aq) \rightarrow 2 NO_2^-(aq) + 6 H_2O(\ell)$

2. Reduction half-reaction: $2 NO_3^-(aq) + 6 H_2O(\ell) + 10 e^- \rightarrow N_2(g) + 12 OH^-(aq)$

Oxidation half-reaction: $CH_3OH(aq) + 6 OH^-(aq) \rightarrow CO_2(aq) + 5 H_2O(\ell) + 6 e^-$

Net: $6 NO_3^-(aq) + 5 CH_3OH \rightarrow 3 N_2(g) + 5 CO_2(aq) + 6 OH^-(aq) + 7 H_2O(\ell)$

3. HCO_3^- is the predominant species. Recall that when acid and base concentrations are equal, pH = pK_a. If H_2CO_3 and HCO_3^- are present in equal concentrations, the pH would be about 6.4. If HCO_3^- and CO_3^{2-} are present in equal concentrations, the pH would be 10.2. For the pH to be about 8 (in a salt water aquarium), $[HCO_3^-]$ would have to be higher than either of the other carbonate species.

4. Conc. of N in ppm (mg N/L) = $[(1.7 \times 10^4 \text{ kg } NO_3^-)(10^6 \text{ mg } NO_3^-/\text{kg } NO_3^-)(14.0 \text{ mg N}/62.0 \text{ mg } NO_3^-)]/(2.2 \times 10^7 \text{ L}) =$ 1.7×10^2 mg/L = 1.7×10^2 ppm

Conc. of NO_3^- in ppm (mg/L) = $(1.7 \times 10^4$ kg$)$ $(10^6$ mg/kg$)/(2.2 \times 10^7$ L$) = 770$ mg/L

Conc. of NO_3^- in mol/L = $[(1.7 \times 10^4 \text{ kg})$ $(10^3 \text{ g/kg})(1 \text{ mol}/62.0 \text{ g})]/(2.2 \times 10^7 \text{ L}) =$ 0.012 mol/L

CHAPTER 22

Puzzler:

1. Define length of the side of the cube as x, then the length of the diagonal across the cube is $x\sqrt{3}$. This is set equal to $2 r_{Ti} + 2 r_{Ni}$, i.e., $x\sqrt{3} = 2 r_{Ti} + 2 r_{Ni} = 540$ pm; $x = 312$ pm ($a = b = c = 3.12 \times 10^{-8}$ cm)

2. Calculated density:

Mass of one unit cell is the mass of one Ti and one Ni atom = $(47.87 \text{ g/mol})(1 \text{ mol}/6.022 \times 10^{23} \text{ atoms Ti}) + (58.69 \text{ g/mol})(1 \text{ mol}/6.022 \times 10^{23} \text{ atoms Ti}) = 1.77 \times 10^{-22}$ g

Volume of the unit cell is $x^3 =$ $(3.12 \times 10^{-8} \text{ cm})^3 = 3.04 \times 10^{-23}$ cm^3

Calculated density = 1.77×10^{-22} g/3.04×10^{-23} cm^3 = 5.82 g/cm^3

The agreement is not very good, probably because atoms don't pack together as tightly as is assumed.

3. As free atoms, both Ti and Ni are paramagnetic.

Case Study: Accidental Discoveries

1. First order kinetics: $\ln[x/x_o] = - kt$

$\ln[x/10 \text{ mg}] = - 7.6 \times 10^{-5} s^{-1}$ [24 h $\times$ 3600 s/h]

$x/10$ mg $= 1.4 \times 10^{-3}$; $x = 1.4 \times 10^{-2}$ mg remain

2. Use Henderson-Hasselbalch equation for this acid dissociation equilibrium.

$pH = pK_a + \log[\text{base/acid}]$

$7.4 = 6.6 + \log\{[PtCl(NH_3)_2OH]/[PtCl(NH_3)_2(H_2O)]\}$

$[PtCl(NH_3)_2OH]/[PtCl(NH_3)_2(H_2O)] = 6.3$

Case Study: Ferrocene

1. Fe^{2+} in ferrocene has an electron configuration [Ar] $3d^6$ and is present in the low spin state.

2. Cr (0). Cr(0) in this compound is assumed to have an electron configuration [Ar] $3d^6$ and is present in the low spin state.

3. Both are in accord the 18 electron rule.

4. Select oxidizing agents from Table 20.1 (page 920) based on the northeast-southwest rule (above $E° = 0.400$ v). Common oxidizing agents include the halogens, H_2O_2 and MnO_4^-.

5. $NiCl_2 + 2 Na[C_5H_5] \rightarrow Ni(\eta\text{-}C_5H_5)_2 + 2 NaCl$. Nickelocene is predicted to have 2 unpaired electrons (Ni^{2+}, with a d^8 configuration, in an octahedral environment.)

CHAPTER 23

Puzzler:

1. ^{235}U: 92 protons, $235 - 92 = 143$ neutrons

   ^{238}U: 92 protons, 146 neutrons

2. (a) $^{238}U + {}^1_0n \rightarrow {}^{239}U$

   (b) $^{239}U \rightarrow {}^{239}Np + {}^{\ 0}_{-1}\beta$

   $^{239}Np \rightarrow {}^{239}Pu + {}^{\ 0}_{-1}\beta$

   (c) $^{239}Pu \rightarrow {}^{235}U + {}^4_2\alpha$

Case Study: Nuclear Medicine and Hypothyroidism:

1. $^{131}I \rightarrow {}^{131}Xe + {}^{\ 0}_{-1}\beta$

2. Calculate the fraction ($= f$) of each remaining after 7 days

   For ^{123}I: $k = 0.693/t_{1/2} = 0.693/13.3$ h $= 0.0521$ h^{-1}

   $\ln(f) = -0.0521$ $h^{-1}[7\ d(24\ h/d)]$

   $f = 1.6 \times 10^{-4}$

   For ^{131}I: $k = 0.693/t_{1/2} = 0.693/8.04$ d $= 0.0862$ d^{-1}

   $\ln(f) = -0.0862$ $d^{-1}(7\ d)$

   $f = 0.55$

   Ratio of amounts remaining, $[^{131}I]/[^{123}I] = 0.55/(1.6 \times 10^{-4}) = 3400$

   The amount of the ^{131}I isotope is 3400 times greater than the amount of ^{123}I.

Index/Glossary

Italicized page numbers indicate pages containing illustrations, and those followed by "t" indicate tables. Glossary terms, printed in boldface, are defined here as well as in the text.

air bags, 515, 522, *523*
alanine, 498
  zwitterionic form, 808
albite, dissolved by rain
    water, 186
albumin, precipitation of, 719
alchemy, 339, 1061
alcohol(s) Any of a class of
    organic compounds charac-
    terized by the presence of a
    hydroxyl group bonded to a
    saturated carbon atom,
    461–465
  energy content of, 215
  naming of, A-19
  oxidation to carbonyl com-
    pounds, 468
  solubility in water, 465
aldehyde(s) Any of a class of
    organic compounds charac-
    terized by the presence of a
    carbonyl group, in which the
    carbon atom is bonded to at
    least one hydrogen atom,
    468–470
aldehydes, naming of, A-19
alkali metal(s) The metals in
    Group 1A of the periodic
    table, 62
  electron configuration of,
    311
  ions, enthalpy of hydra-
    tion, 557, 558t
  reaction with oxygen, 973
  reaction with water, 62, *63,*
    971, 973
  reduction potentials of,
    973
alkaline battery, 912
alkaline earth metal(s) The
    elements in Group 2A of the
    periodic table, 62, 975–979
  biological uses of, 977
  electron configuration of,
    311
alkalosis, 822
alkane(s) Any of a class of
    hydrocarbons in which each
    carbon atom is bonded to
    four other atoms, 448–452
  derivatives of, 462t
  general formula of, 447t
  naming of, A-17
  properties of, 452
  reaction with chlorine, 452
  reaction with oxygen, 452
  standard enthalpies of
    vaporization of, 572t
AlkA-Seltzer®, *149,* 760
  composition of, 104

alkene(s) Any of a class of
    hydrocarbons in which there
    is at least one carbon–car-
    bon double bond, 453–457
  general formula of, 447t
  hydrogenation of, 457
  naming of, A-18
alkyl groups Hydrocarbon sub-
    stituents, 451
alkylation, of benzene, 461
alkyne(s) Any of a class of
    hydrocarbons in which there
    is at least one carbon–car-
    bon triple bond, 456
  general formula of, 447t
  naming of, A-19
allene, structure of, 440, 444
allergy, to nickel, 896
allicin, 541
allotrope(s) Different forms of
    the same element that exist
    in the same physical state
    under the same conditions of
    temperature and pressure, 63
  boron, 981
  carbon, 63
  oxygen, 1001. *See also* ozone.
  phosphorus, 65, 992
  sulfur, 65, 1001
alloy(s),
  iron, 1027
  magnesium in, 976
  memory metal, 1018
alnico V, 1028
  ferromagnetism of, 292
alpha particle(s), 1061
  bombardment with, 1077
  predicting emission of,
    1068
alpha plot(s), 857
alpha radiation Radiation that
    is readily absorbed, 343
alpha-hydroxy acid(s), *787*
altitude sickness, 514
alum, formula of, 110
alumina, amphoterism of,
    1012
aluminosilicates, 989
  separation of, 982
aluminum, abundance of,
    63
  chemistry of, 985
  density of, 44
  production of, 981–982
  reaction with bromine, 67,
    207
  reaction with copper ions,
    900
  reaction with iron(III)
    oxide, 147

reaction with potassium
    hydroxide, 199
  reaction with sodium
    hydroxide, 970
  reaction with water, 904
  reduction by sodium, 972
aluminum bromide, dimer-
    ization of, 985
aluminum carbide, reaction
    with water, 169
aluminum chloride, prepa-
    ration of, 197
aluminum hydroxide,
    amphoterism of, 790,
    792
aluminum oxide, 982
  amphoterism of, 982
aluminum sulfate, 1012
amalgam, 925
americium, 1079
amide link, 486
amide(s) Any of a class of
    organic compounds charac-
    terized by the presence of an
    amino group, 468, 475–478
amine(s) A derivative of
    ammonia in which one or
    more of the hydrogen atoms
    are replaced by organic
    groups, 466
  as acids and bases, 798
α-amino acid(s) An amino acid
    in which the amine group
    and the carboxyl group are
    both attached to the same
    carbon atom.
  chirality of, 498
  zwitterionic form, 808
amino group A functional
    group related to ammonia,
    in which some or all of the
    hydrogen atoms are replaced
    by organic groups, 468,
    475
2-aminobenzoic acid, 494
ammonia, aqueous, equilib-
    rium constant expres-
    sion for, 728
  bond angles in, 370, *371*
  combustion of, balanced
    equation for, 118
  decomposition of, 679,
    689, 715
  as Lewis base, 793
  as ligand, 1031
  molecular polarity of, 383
  orbital hybridization in,
    411
  oxidation of, 163, *164*
  percent composition of, 89

pH of, 179
  production of, as equilib-
    rium process, 119
  by Haber process, 749
  equilibrium constant for,
    743
  spontaneity of, 875
  stoichiometry of, 527
  reaction with acetic acid,
    780
  reaction with boron trifluo-
    oride, 364, 438
  reaction with copper sul-
    fate, 197
  reaction with hydrochloric
    acid, 779
  reaction with hydrogen
    chloride, 138, 533, 890
  reaction with nickel(II)
    nitrate and ethylenedi-
    amine, 758
  reaction with sodium hypo-
    chlorite, 993
  reaction with water, 136
  relation to amines, 466
  synthesis of, equilibrium
    constant, 885
  titration with hydrogen
    chloride, 828–830
  waste product of fish
    metabolism, 994
  as weak base, 771
ammonium carbamate, dis-
    sociation of, 756
ammonium chloride,
    decomposition of, 875
  in dry cell battery, 911
  reaction with calcium
    oxide, 196
ammonium cyanate, conver-
    sion to urea, 718
ammonium dichromate,
    decomposition of, 155,
    550
ammonium formate, solubil-
    ity of, 652
ammonium hydrogen sul-
    fide, decomposition of,
    754, 755
ammonium iodide, dissocia-
    tion of, 756
ammonium ion, 73
  in Lewis adduct, 790
ammonium nitrate, decom-
    position of, 250
  dissolution of, 862
  enthalpy of solution, 623
  in cold pack, 245
ammonium perchlorate, in
    rocket fuel, 1009, 1015

amorphous solid(s) A solid that lacks long-range regular structure and displays a melting range instead of a specific melting point, 603

amount, of pure substance, 82

amounts table, 159

ampere (A) The unit of electric current, 937

Ampère, André Marie, 1005

amphetamine, structure of, 437, 799

amphibole, 988

amphiprotic substance A substance that can behave as either a Brønsted acid or a Brønsted base, 136, 763, 790, 791t

amphoteric substance, aluminum oxide, 982

amplitude The maximum height of a wave, as measured from the axis of propagation, 270

analysis, chemical. *See* chemical analysis.
 spectrophotometric, 192

Anderson, Carl, 1066

angstrom unit, *28*

angular (azimuthal) momentum quantum number, 285
 number of nodal surfaces and, 291

anhydrous compound The substance remaining after the water has been removed (usually by heating) from a hydrated compound, 97

aniline, as weak base, 771
 reaction with sulfuric acid, 467
 structure of, 459, 808

aniline hydrochloride, reaction with sodium hydroxide, 856

anilinium sulfate, 467

anion(s) An ion with a negative electric charge, 71
 as Brønsted acids and bases, 762
 as Brønsted bases, 798
 effect on salt solubility, 840
 as Lewis bases, 790
 in living cells and sea water, 122t
 naming, 76
 noble gas electron configuration in, 330
 sizes of, 326

anode rays, 343

anode The electrode of an electrochemical cell at which oxidation occurs, 905
 in corrosion, 1023

anthracene, 650

antibonding molecular orbital A molecular orbital in which the energy of the electrons is higher than that of the parent orbital electrons, 423

anticodon A three-nucleotide sequence in tRNA, 505

antifreeze, 616, 634
 ethylene glycol in, 619

antilogarithms, A-3

antimatter, 1066

antimony, isotopic abundance of, 57

antimony pentafluoride, reaction with hydrogen fluoride, 436

antineutrino, 1066

apatite(s), 977, 978

Appian Way, mortar in, 978

approximations, successive, method of, 739, A-5

aqua regia, 339, 996

aquarium, nitrogen cycle in, 994

aquation reaction, 720

aqueous solution A solution in which the solvent is water, 121
 balancing redox equations in, 901–905
 electrolysis in, 933
 equilibrium constant expression for, 728

arginine, 201

argon, density of, 23

argyria, 148

Arnold, James R., 1077

aromatic compound(s) Any of a class of hydrocarbons characterized by the presence of a benzene ring or related structure, 421, 442, 458–461
 general formula of, 447t
 naming of, A-19

Arrhenius, Svante, 131

Arrhenius equation A mathematical expression that relates reaction rate to activation energy, collision frequency, molecular orientation, and temperature, 696

arsine, 997

asbestos, 976, 988

ascorbic acid, reaction with iodine, 676
 structure of, 107, 491, 804
 titration of, 189, 200

asparagine, structure of, 96

aspirin, absorption spectrum of, 302
 history of, 760
 melting point of, *17*, 44
 molar mass of, 86
 preparation of, 197
 structure of, *350*, 436, 459
 synthesis of, 168

astronomical unit, *33*

atmosphere. *See also* air.
 composition of, 534
 pressure–temperature profile of, 533
 standard. *See* standard atmosphere (atm).

atom(s) The smallest particle of an element that retains the characteristic chemical properties of that element, 13
 ancient Greek ideas of, 339
 Bohr model of, 276–278
 composition of, 53
 electron configurations. *See* electron configuration(s).
 mass of, 52
 quantization of energy in, 276, 284
 size of, 52, 319. *See also* atomic radius.
 structure of, 51

atomic bomb, 1080

atomic mass The average mass of an atom in a natural sample of the element, 55
 Dalton and, 341

atomic mass unit (*u*) The unit of a scale of relative atomic masses of the elements; 1 u = 1/12 of the mass of a carbon atom with six protons and six neutrons, 52
 equivalent in grams, 52

atomic number (*Z*) The number of protons in the nucleus of an atom of an element, 52, 344
 chemical periodicity and, 60
 even versus odd, and nuclear stability, 1067
 in nuclear symbol, 1062

atomic orbital(s) The matter wave for an allowed energy state of an electron in an atom, 285–287
 assignment of electrons to, 306–316
 energies of, and electron assignments, 306–316, 336t
 number of electrons in, 306t
 order of energies in, 307
 orientations of, 290
 overlapping of, in valence bond theory, 406
 quantum numbers of, 285
 shapes of, 287–291

atomic radius, bond length and, 388
 effective nuclear charge and, 320
 periodicity, 319
 transition elements, 1024

atomic reactor, 1080

atomic theory of matter A theory that describes the structure and behavior of substances in terms of ultimate chemical particles called atoms and molecules, 51

atomic weight. *See* atomic mass.

aurora borealis, 268

austenite, 1018

autoionization of water Interaction of two water molecules to produce a hydronium ion and a hydroxide ion by proton transfer, 765

automobile, hybrid gasoline-electric, 915

average reaction rate, 674

Avogadro, Amedeo, 83, 522

Avogadro's hypothesis Equal volumes of gases under the same conditions of temperature and pressure have equal numbers of particles, 522

Avogadro's law, kinetic-molecular theory and, 537

Avogadro's number The number of particles in one mole of any substance (6.022 × 10^{23}), 83

axial position, in cyclohexane structure, 453
 in trigonal-bipyramidal molecular geometry, 372

azimuthal quantum number, 285

azomethane, decomposition of, 688, 690, 714
azurite, *21, 1025*

background radiation, 1083
back-titration, 204
bacteria, copper production by, 1028
thermophilic, 16
bain-Marie, 339
baking powder, *780*, 1000
baking soda, 140, 974
reaction with vinegar, 777
balance, laboratory, precision of, *35*
balanced chemical equation A chemical equation showing the relative amounts of reactants and products, 116–118
enthalpy and, 227
equilibrium constant and, 741–744
ball-and-stick model(s) A diagram in which spheres represent atoms, and sticks represent the bonds holding them together, 70, 445
balloon, hot air, 208, *525*
hydrogen and helium, 968
models of electron pair geometries, 368
weather, *521*
Balmer, Johann, 276
Balmer series A series of spectral lines that have energies in the visible region, 276, 279
band of stability, nuclear, 1067
bar A unit of pressure; 1 bar = 100 kPa, 516, A-8
barium carbonate, decomposition of, 755
barium chloride, as strong electrolyte, 124
precipitation of, 845
reaction with sodium sulfate, 130
barium nitrate, in fireworks, 281
barium sulfate, as x-ray contrast agent, 977
precipitation of, 845
solubility of, 835
barometer An apparatus used to measure atmospheric pressure, 516
base(s) A substance that, when dissolved in pure water, increases the concentration of hydroxide ions,

131–139. *See also* Brønsted base(s), Lewis base(s).
acids and, 760–809. *See also* acid–base reaction(s).
Arrhenius definition of, 132
Brønsted definition, 761
Brønsted-Lowry definition, 133–136
common, 132t
Lewis definition of, 789–793
of logarithms, A-2
reaction with acids, 136–138
strengths of, 769. *See also* strong base, weak base.
direction of reaction and, 776
base ionization constant (K_b) The equilibrium constant for the ionization of a base in aqueous solution, 769, 770t
relation to conjugate acid ionization constant, 775
base units, SI, 25t, A-11
basic oxide(s) An oxide of a metal that acts as a base, 139
basic oxygen furnace, 1027
basic solution A solution in which the concentration of hydronium ions is less than the concentration of hydroxide ion, 766
battery A device consisting of two or more electrochemical cells, 911
energy per kilogram, 914t
bauxite, 982
Bayer process, 982
becquerel The SI unit of radioactivity, 1 decomposition per second, 1082
Becquerel, Henri, 342
Beer-Lambert law The absorbance of a sample is proportional to the path length and the concentration, 191
Beethoven, Ludwig van, 991
bends, 626
benzaldehyde, structure of, 469
benzene, boiling point elevation and freezing point depression constants for, 633t
bonding in, resonance structures in, 361, 421

derivatives of, 459, A-19
liquid and solid volumes, *556*
molecular orbital configuration of, 432
in organometallic compounds, 1051
reactions of, 461
structure of, 342, 459
vapor pressure of, 583, 632
benzenesulfonic acid, structure of, 805
benzoic acid, 471t
buffer solution of, 817
structure of, 245, 459, 653
benzonitrile, structure of, 444
benzyl acetate, 475
benzyl butanoate, 474t
beryllium dichloride, orbital hybridization in, 414
beta particle(s) An electron ejected at high speed from certain radioactive substances, 1061
predicting emission of, 1068
beta radiation Radiation of a penetrative character, 343
bicarbonate ion. *See also* hydrogen carbonate ion.
in biological buffer system, 822
bidentate ligands, 1031
bimolecular process A process that involves two molecules, 703
binary compound(s) A compound formed from two elements, 81
binding energy The energy required to separate a nucleus into individual protons and neutrons, 1069–1072
per nucleon, 1070
biochemistry, thermodynamics and, 884
biodiesel, 479
birefringence, *976*
bismuth subsalicylate, formula of, 109
in Pepto-Bismol, *128*
black powder, 281
black smokers, metal sulfides from, 112
black tongue, Pepto-Bismol and, *128*

blackbody radiation, 272
blast furnace, 1026
entropy and, 876
bleach, detection in food tampering, 188
hypochlorite ion in, 1009
sodium hypochlorite in, 619
blood, buffers in, 814, 822
oxygen saturation of, 514
pH of, 179, 822
blood alcohol level (BAL), 207
blue vitriol, 97
boat form, 453
body-centered cubic (bcc) unit cell, 591
Bohanan, Art, 579
Bohr, Christian, 1033
Bohr, Niels, 276, 346
Bohr effect, in hemoglobin, 1033
boiling point The temperature at which the vapor pressure of a liquid is equal to the external pressure on the liquid, 576
of common compounds, 572t
hydrogen bonding and, 561
intermolecular forces and, 560t
boiling point elevation, 632
boiling point elevation constant (K_{bp}), 633
Boltzmann, Ludwig, 536, 866
Boltzmann distribution curves. *See* Maxwell-Boltzmann distribution curves.
bomb calorimeter, 231, *232*
bombardier beetle, *677*
bond(s) An interaction between two or more atoms that holds them together by reducing the potential energy of their electrons, 349. *See also* bonding.
coordinate covalent, 364, 789, 1031
covalent, 349
formation of, 349
ionic, 349
multiple, 354
molecular geometry and, 373
polar, 375–379
properties of, 386–391

ferent substances, 18. *See also* reaction(s).

chemical compound(s). *See* compound(s).

chemical equation(s) A written representation of a chemical reaction, showing the reactants and products, their physical states, and the direction in which the reaction proceeds, 19, 113
  balancing, 116–118, 899–905
  manipulating, equilibrium constant and, 741–744

chemical equilibrium A condition in which the forward and reverse reaction rates in a chemical system are equal, 118–121, 724–759
  factors affecting, 744–750

chemical formula. *See* formula(s).

chemical kinetics The study of the rates of chemical reactions under various conditions and of reaction mechanisms, 670–723

chemical potential energy, 210

chemical property An indication of whether and how readily a material undergoes a chemical change, 19

chemical reaction(s). *See* reaction(s).

chemistry, history of, 338–347

chemocline, 630

china clay, 989

chiral compound A molecule that is not superimposable on its mirror image, 445, 1038. *See also* enantiomers.
  optical activity of, 342, 445

chlor-alkali industry, 974

chloramine, 958

chlorate ion, formal charges in, 360
  Lewis structure of, 354

chlorine,
  formation by aqueous electrolysis, 935
  from sodium chloride electrolysis, 972
  oxoacids of, 1008
  production of, 1005
  reaction with alkanes, 452
  reaction with iron, 115
  reaction with phosphorus, 113, 159

reaction with sodium, *4*, 146, 349, *350*

chlorine dioxide, as disinfectant, 553

chlorine oxide, in chlorine catalytic cycle, 722

chlorine trifluoride, reaction with nickel(II) oxide, 551

chlorobenzene, structure of, 459

chloroform, 452
  boiling point elevation and freezing point depression constants of, 633t
  enthalpy of formation, 250

chloromethane, 244
  enthalpy of formation, 249

chlorophyll, magnesium in, 977

cholesterol, 1

chromate ion, water pollution by, 304

chromium(III) picolinate, 304

chymotrypsin, 721

cinnabar, 3, 810, 1001

cinnamaldehyde, structure of, 436, 469

cisplatin, atomic distances in, 45
  discovery of, 1049
  isomerization of, 892, 1037
  preparation of, 204
  rate of substitution reaction, 680
  structure of, 102

cis-trans isomers, 420, 445, 699
  cisplatin, 1049
  in coordination compounds, 1037

citric acid, 471t
  reaction with sodium hydrogen carbonate, 149
  structure of, *772*

Clapeyron, Émile, 575

clathrate, 567

Clausius, Rudolf, 575

Clausius-Clapeyron equation, 575

clay(s), 989

cleavage, of crystalline solids, 603

clock reaction, iodine, 676

close packing, in crystal lattice, 595

coagulation, of colloids, 644

coal tar, aromatic compounds from, 458t

cobalt, colors of complexes of, 1047t

cobalt-60, gamma rays from, 300

cobalt(II) chloride, reaction with hydrochloric acid, 724

cobalt(II) chloride hexahydrate, 97, *559*

Cockcroft, J. D., 1078

coefficient(s), stoichiometric, 115, 728

coffee, decaffeination with supercritical carbon dioxide, 577

coffee-cup calorimeter, 230

cohesive force A force of attraction between molecules of a single substance, 579

coins, nickel in, 896

coke, in iron production, 1026
  water gas from, 969

cold pack, 245

colligative properties The properties of a solution that depend only on the number of solute particles per solvent molecule and not on the nature of the solute or solvent, 617, 628–642
  of solutions of ionic compounds, 639

collision theory A theory of reaction rates that assumes that molecules must collide in order to react, 692

colloid(s) A state of matter intermediate between a solution and a suspension, in which solute particles are large enough to scatter light but too small to settle out, 642–646
  types of, 642t

color(s), fireworks, 281
  of acid–base indicators, *832*
  of coordination compounds, 1045–1048
  neon signs, 303
  of transition metal compounds, 1020
  visible light, 270, 1045

combined gas law. *See* general gas law.

combustion analysis, determining empirical formula by, 171–173

combustion calorimeter, 231

combustion reaction The reaction of a compound with molecular oxygen to form products in which all elements are combined with oxygen; also called burning, 116, 117

common ion effect The limiting of acid (or base) ionization caused by addition of its conjugate base (or conjugate acid), 811–814
  solubility and, 838

common logarithms, A-2

common names, 451
  of binary compounds, 82

compact disc player, light energy in, 273

completion, reaction going to, 730

complex(es), 790. *See also* coordination compound(s).
  formation constants of, 846, A-26t
  in enzyme-catalyzed reaction, 702
  solubility and, 846–848

composition diagram(s), 857

compound(s) Matter that is composed of two or more kinds of atoms chemically combined in definite proportions, 13
  binary, naming, 81
  coordination. *See* coordination compound(s).
  covalent, 350
  determining formulas of, 88–95
  hydrated, 96, 1029
  ionic, 70–80
  ionization energies and, 330
  molecular, 80–82
  naming, 77
  odd-electron, 366, 429
  specific heat capacity of, 216t
  standard molar enthalpy of formation of, 236

compressibility The change in volume with change in pressure, 517

cyclohexane, isomerization of, 753
  spontaneity of synthesis from benzene, 890
  structure of, 452
cyclohexene, structure of, 455
1,5-cyclooctadiene, 715, 719
cyclopentadienyl ion, in ferrocene, 1052
cyclopentane, structure of, 444, 452
cyclopropane, conversion to propene, 685, 714
  structure of, 453
cysteine, 498
  molecular geometry of, 374
  structure of, 69
cytosine, 348, 392
  electrostatic potential surface of, 586
  hydrogen bonding to guanine, 565

d-block elements Transition elements whose occurrence in the periodic table coincides with the filling of the d orbitals, 1019
d orbital(s), 1040. *See also* atomic orbital(s).
d-to-d transition The change that occurs when an electron moves between two orbitals having different energies in a complex, 1046
Dacron, 485
Dalton, John, 52, 340, 530
Dalton's law of partial pressures The total pressure of a mixture of gases is the sum of the pressures of the components of the mixture, 530
data, graphing of, 40
dating, radiochemical, 1075
Davisson, C. J., 282
Davy, Humphry, 910, 937, 972
DDT, 7
de Broglie, Louis Victor, 282
Debye, Peter, *381*
debye unit, 380
decay constant, for radioactivity, 1074
decay series, radioactive, 1063–1066
deciliter, 29
decomposition, determining formula by, 93
decompression sickness, 626

deep-sea diving, gas laws and, 540–542
DEET, structure of, 104
defined quantity, significant figures in, 36
de-icing fluid, 616
delta (Δ), symbol for change, 215
Democritus, 339
denitrification, by bacteria, 994
density The ratio of the mass of an object to its volume, 15
  of air, 526
  balloons and, *525*
  of gas, calculation from ideal gas law, 525
  periodicity of, 336
  of sulfuric acid in lead storage battery, 913
  of transition elements, 1024
  units of, 15
dental amalgam, 925
deoxyribonucleic acid (DNA) The genetic material in cells.
  bonding in, 348
  hydrogen bonding in, 565
  molecular geometry of, 392
  structure of, *28*
deoxyribose, 473
  structure of, 348, *393*
derivative, 3
derived units, SI, A-12
dermatitis, contact, 896
detergent A surfactant used for cleaning, 645
deuterium, 54
  binding energy of, 1070
  fusion of, 1082
  preparation of, 528, 969
Dewar, Michael, 430
diabetes, acetone in, 201
diagonal relationship, in periodic table, 979
diamagnetism The physical property of being repelled by a magnetic field, resulting from having all electrons paired, 295, 428, 1044
diamminedichloroplatinum (II), isomers of, 1037
diamond,
  density of, 46
  structure of, *46*, 64
  synthesis of, 602, 894
  unit cell of, 612
diapers, synthetic polymers in, 487

diatomic molecules, heteronuclear, 429
  homonuclear, 427
  of elements, *65*
dibenzenechromium, *1051*
diberyllium cation, 426
diborane, 984
  enthalpy of formation, 248
  hybridization in, 430
  reaction with oxygen, 549
  synthesis of, 155, 551
dichlorine oxide, production of, 548
trans-dichlorobis(ethylenediamine)cobalt(III) ion, 720–721
dichlorodifluoromethane, vapor pressure of, 585
dichlorodimethylsilane, 1016
  vapor pressure of, 584
dichlorodiphenyltrichloroethane (DDT), 7
1,2-dichloroethylene, isomers of, 421
  molecular polarity of, 385
2,4-dichlorophenoxyacetic acid (2,4-D), 205
dichromate ion, as oxidizing agent, 146t
  reaction with ethanol, 148
diene(s) A hydrocarbon containing two double bonds, 455
dienes, naming of, A-19
dietary Calorie, 214
diethyl ether, 465
  enthalpy of vaporization, 890
  vapor pressure curves for, *574*
diethyl ketone, 470t
diethylenetriamine, 1057
diffraction, of electrons, 282
  of x-rays by crystals, 593
diffusion The gradual mixing of the molecules of two or more substances by random molecular motion, 538
  probability and, 866–868
dihelium, molecular orbital energy level diagram of, 424
dihydrogen phosphate ion, buffer solution of, 815t
dihydroxyacetone, structure of, 107, 401

diiodocyclohexane, 736
dilithium, molecular orbital energy level diagram of, 425
dilution, buffer pH and, 819
  preparation of solutions by, 177
  serial, 180
dimensional analysis A general problem-solving approach that uses the dimensions or units of each value to guide you through calculations, 38
dimethyl ether, decomposition of, 718
  structure of, *68*, 444
2,3-dimethylbutane, structure of, *173*, 450
dimethyldichlorosilane, 549
1,1-dimethylethylenediamine, 1057
dimethylglyoximate ion, *846*
dimethylglyoxime (DMG), 651
  reaction with nickel(II) ion, 170
  structure of, 104
1,1-dimethylhydrazine, as fuel, 249, 1015
dimethylsulfide, 541
  as greenhouse gas, 402
dinitrogen, bonding in, 352
dinitrogen monoxide, dissociation of, 399
dinitrogen oxide, 993, 995t
  decomposition of, 715
dinitrogen pentaoxide, 995t
  decomposition of, 672, 718
    mechanism, 704
    rate equation, 678, 684
dinitrogen tetraoxide, 995t
  decomposition of, 747, 748
dinitrogen trioxide, 995t
  decomposition of, 754
  structure of, 1017
dioxovanadium(V) ion, reaction with zinc, 901–902
dioxygen. *See* oxygen.
dipolar bond. *See* polar covalent bond.
dipole(s), induced, 566
dipole–dipole attraction The electrostatic force between two neutral molecules that have permanent dipole moments, 558

hydrogen bonding Attraction between a hydrogen atom and a very electronegative atom to produce an unusually strong dipole–dipole attraction, 465, 561–565
in DNA, 393
in polyamides, 486
hydrogen bromide, reaction with methanol, 716
hydrogen chloride, as strong electrolyte, 125
emitted by volcanoes, 186
production of, 1008
reaction with ammonia, 138, 533, 890
reaction with magnesium, 230
reaction with 2-methylpropene, 457
reaction with sodium hydroxide, 136
titration with ammonia, 828–830
titration with sodium hydroxide, 823
hydrogen electrode, 908
as pH meter, 926–928
standard, 916, 918
hydrogen fluoride, electrostatic potential map of, 382
production of, 1007–1008
reaction with antimony pentafluoride, 436
reaction with silica, 988
reaction with silicon dioxide, 1008
sigma bond in, 407
hydrogen halides, acidity and structure of, 793
standard enthalpies of formation of, 236t
standard enthalpies of vaporization of, 572t
hydrogen iodide, decomposition of, 687
equilibrium with hydrogen and iodine, 862
hydrogen ion. See hydronium ion.
hydrogen peroxide, catalyzed decomposition of, 677
decomposition of, 685, 714
hydrogen phosphate ion, amphiprotic nature of, 764
buffer solution of, 815t

hydrogen phthalate ion, buffer solution of, 815t
hydrogen sulfide, as polyprotic acid, 763t
dissociation of, 736
odor of, 541
properties of, 1003
reaction with oxygen, 891
sulfur-oxidizing bacteria and, 1004
hydrogenation An addition reaction in which the reagent is molecular hydrogen, 390, 457
of oils in foods, 476
thermodynamics of, 890
hydrolysis reaction A reaction with water in which a bond to oxygen is broken, 473
of anions of insoluble salts, 841
of esters, 479
of fats, 476
of ions in water, 774
hydrometallurgy Recovery of metals from their ores by reactions in aqueous solution, 1026, 1028
hydronium ion, H_3O^+(aq), 134
as Lewis adduct, 790
concentration expressed as pH, 179
hydrophilic and hydrophobic colloids, 643
hydroxide(s), precipitation of, 128
solubility in strong acids, 841
hydroxide ion, OH^- (aq), 133
formal charges in, 360
in minerals, 810
hydroxyapatite, 977
p-hydroxyphenyl-2-butanone, 469
hydroxyproline, structure of, 400
hygroscopic salt, 974
hyperbaric chamber, 627
hypergolic fuel, 1015
hyperthyroidism, 1089
hypertonic solution, 639
hyperuricemia, 789
hypochlorite ion, formal charges in, 359
self oxidation-reduction, 705
hypochlorous acid, 1009

hypofluorous acid, decomposition of, 719
hypothesis A tentative explanation or prediction based on experimental observations, 4
hypothyroidism, 1089
hypotonic solution, 639
hypoxia, 514

ice, density of, 15
hydrogen bonding in, 563
melting of, 220–221
slipperiness of, 608
structure of, 69, 563
ice calorimeter, 246
Ice Man, radiochemical dating of, 1076
ICE table A table that indicates initial, change, and equilibrium concentrations, 727, 735
icebergs, density of, 554
Icelandic spar, 976
ideal gas A simplification of real gases in which it is assumed that there are no forces between the molecules and that the molecules occupy no volume, 524
ideal gas law A law that relates pressure, volume, number of moles, and temperature for an ideal gas, 524–527
departures from, 542, 555
osmotic pressure equation and, 637
stoichiometry and, 527–530
ideal solution A solution that obeys Raoult's law, 629
ilmenite, 1004
imaging, medical, 1085
immiscible liquids Liquids that do not mix to form a solution but exist in contact with each other, forming layers, 621, 924
indicator(s) A substance used to signal the equivalence point of a titration by a change in some physical property such as color, 184
acid–base, 181, 670, 830–832
induced dipole(s) Separation of charge in a normally nonpolar molecule, caused by the approach of a polar molecule, 566
induced dipole/ induced dipole attraction The electrostatic force between two

neutral molecules, both having induced dipoles, 566
inert gas(es). See noble gas(es).
infrared (IR) radiation, 270, 274
initial rate The instantaneous reaction rate at the start of the reaction, 680
ink, invisible, 111
inner transition elements. See actinide(s), lanthanide(s).
insoluble compound(s), 832
solubility product constants of, 834t
instantaneous reaction rate, 674
insulin, 499
integrated rate equation, 683–692
for nuclear decay, 1074
integrity, in science, 6
intensive properties Physical properties that do not depend on the amount of matter present, 16
intercept, of straight-line graph, 40, 687
interhalogens, 1014
intermediate. See reaction intermediate.
intermolecular forces Interactions between molecules, between ions, or between molecules and ions, 465, 543, 554–587
determining types of, 568
energies of, 556, 569t
internal energy The sum of the potential and kinetic energies of the particles in the system, 224
internal energy change, measurement of, 231
relation to enthalpy change, 225
International Union of Pure and Applied Chemistry (IUPAC), 451
interstitial hydrides, 969
intravenous solution(s), tonicity of, 639
iodine, as catalyst, 699
clock reaction, 676
dissociation of, 738
production of, 156, 1006–1007
reaction with hydrogen, 737

reaction with sodium thiosulfate, 188
solubility in carbon tetrachloride, 753
solubility in liquids, 568
solubility in polar and nonpolar solvents, 622
iodine-131, radioactive halflife, 1073
treatment of hyperthyroidism, 1089
2-iodobenzoic acid, 494
ion(s) An atom or group of atoms that has lost or gained one or more electrons so that it is not electrically neutral, 14, 70. *See also* anion(s); cation(s).
acid–base properties of, 774t
in aqueous solution, 121
balancing charges of, 74, 75
complex. *See* coordination compound(s).
concentrations of, 176
direction of flow in voltaic cells, 906
electrical attraction to water, 123
electron configurations of, 316–318
formation by metals and nonmetals, 71
hydration of, 557
in living cells and sea water, 122t
monatomic, 72
noble gas electron configuration in, 330
polyatomic, 73
predicting charge of, 73
sizes of, 326
spectator, 129
ion–dipole attraction The electrostatic force between an ion and a neutral molecule that has a permanent dipole moment, 557
ion exchange, in water softener, 980
ionic bond(s) The attraction between a positive and a negative ion resulting from the complete (or nearly complete) transfer of one or more electrons from one atom to another, 349
ionic compound(s) A compound formed by the combi-

nation of positive and negative ions, 70–80
bonding in, 599–602
colligative properties of solutions of, 639
crystal cleavage, 79, *80*
formulas of, 74
lattice energy of, 599–602
of main group elements, 965
melting point of, 604, 605t
naming, 77
properties of, 78
solubility in water, 125, 622, *625*
temperature and, *628*
ionic radius, lattice energy and, 604
periodicity of, 326–328
solubility and, 624
ionic solid(s) A solid formed by the condensation of anions and cations, 596–599
ionization, degree of, 809
ionization constant(s) The equilibrium constant for an ionization reaction, 766
acid and base, 769, 770t, A-23t, A-25t
water, 766
ionization energy The energy required to remove an electron from an atom or ion in the gas phase, 280, 321
periodicity of, 321–323
values of, A-21t
iridium, density of, 1020
iron, biochemistry of, 327
in breakfast cereal, 23
combustion of, *239*
corrosion of, 1023
in hemoglobin, 499, 1033
most stable isotope, 1071
production of, 1026
reaction with carbon monoxide, 549
reaction with chlorine, 115
reaction with copper ions, 907
reaction with hydrochloric acid, 547
reaction with oxygen, 116
iron carbonyl, production of, 549
iron(II) gluconate, 103
iron(III) hydroxide, formation by precipitation, 128

iron(II) ion, disproportionation reaction, 946
oxidation–reduction titration of, 188-189
reaction with permanganate ion, 147
iron(III) ion, paramagnetism of, 317, *318*
iron(II) nitrate, reaction with potassium thiocyanate, 758
iron(III) oxide, formation by corrosion, 1023
reaction with aluminum, 147
reaction with carbon monoxide, 141
reduction of, 1026
iron pyrite, 13, *14*, 810, 1001
density of, 49
structure of, 615
irreversible process A process that involves nonequilibrium conditions, 864
isobutane, conversion to butane, 732, *733*
isoelectronic species Molecules or ions that have the same number of valence electrons and comparable Lewis structures, 358
isoleucine, 498
isomerization, *cis-trans*, 699
in petroleum refining, 461
isomers Two or more compounds with the same molecular formula but different arrangements of atoms, 421
cis-trans. *See cis-trans* isomers.
mer-fac, 1038
number of, 448
of organic compounds, 444–446
structural. *See* structural isomers.
isooctane, as fuel, 249
combustion of, 244
in gasoline, 461
isoprene, in rubber, 483
isopropyl alcohol, 463t
isostructural species, 358
isotonic solution, 639
isotope(s) Atoms with the same atomic number but different mass numbers, because of a difference in the number of neutrons, 53–55, 344
hydrogen, 968
in mass spectra, 95

metastable, 1085
percent abundance of, 54, 56t
radioactive, as tracers, 722, 1086
separation by effusion, 540
stable and unstable, 1067
isotope dilution, volume measurement by, 1086
isotope labeling, 473
isotope ratio mass spectrometry, 58

jasmine, oil of, 475
JELL-O®, 643
joule (J) The SI unit of energy, 214, A-8
Joule, James P., 213, 214

K capture. *See* electron capture.
kaolin, 989
Kekulé, August, 341, 421, 459
kelvin (K), 27, 520, A-12
in heat calculations, 218
Kelvin, Lord (William Thomson), *27*, 520
Kelvin temperature scale A scale in which the unit is the same size as the Celsius degree but the zero point is the lowest possible temperature, 27. *See also* absolute zero.
ketone(s) Any of a class of organic compounds characterized by the presence of a carbonyl group, in which the carbon atom is bonded to two other carbon atoms, 468–470
ketones, naming of, A-19
Kevlar, structure of, 487
kilocalorie (kcal) A unit of energy equivalent to 1002 calories, 214, A-9
kilogram (kg) The SI base unit of mass, 29, A-11
kilojoule (kJ) A unit of energy equivalent to 1000 joules, 214
kilopascal (kPa), 516
kinetic energy The energy of a moving object, dependent on its mass and velocity, 8, 210
distribution in gas, 694
of alpha and beta particles, 1062
of gas molecules, temperature and, 533

methanol (Continued)
reaction with hydrogen bromide, 716
spontaneity of formation reaction, 872
synthesis of, 165, 890
methionine, 541
methyl acetate, reaction with sodium hydroxide, 680
methyl chloride, 452
mass spectrum of, 110
reaction with halide ions, 697
reaction with silicon, 549
methyl ethyl ketone, 470t
methyl mercaptan, 541
methyl salicylate, 474, 638
N-methylacetamide, structure of, 402, 475
methylamine, as weak base, 771
electrostatic potential map of, 382
methylamines, 466
2-methyl-1,3-butadiene. See isoprene.
3-methylbutyl acetate, 474t
methylcyclopentane, isomerization of, 753
methylene blue, 204
methylene chloride, 452
2-methylpentane, structure of, 449
2-methylpropene, reaction with hydrogen chloride, 457
structure of, 444, 453
metric system A decimal system for recording and reporting scientific measurements, in which all units are expressed as powers of 10 times some basic unit, 25
mica, structure of, 989
Michaelis, Leonor, 702
microstates, 865
microwave radiation, 270
milk, coagulation of, 644
freezing of, 22
millerite, 170
Millikan, Robert, 344
milliliter (mL) A unit of volume equivalent to one thousandth of a liter; 1 mL = 1 cm3, 29
millimeter of mercury (mm Hg) A common unit of pressure, defined as the pressure that can support a 1-millimeter

column of mercury; 760 mm Hg = 1 atm, 516, A-8
mineral oil, density of, 42
minerals, analysis of, 169
clay, 989
silicate, 988
solubility of, 810
miscible liquids Liquids that mix to an appreciable extent to form a solution, 621
mixture(s) A combination of two or more substances in which each substance retains its identity, 10–11, 14
analysis of, 169–173
gaseous, partial pressures in, 530–532
models, molecular, 69
moderator, nuclear, 1060
Mohr method, 186
Moisson, Henri, 1005
molal boiling point elevation constant (K_{bp}), 633
molality (m) The number of moles of solute per kilogram of solvent, 618
molar absorptivity, 192
molar enthalpy of vaporization ($\Delta_{vap}H°$), relation to molar enthalpy of condensation, 571
molar heat capacity, 216, A-15t
molar mass (M) The mass in grams of one mole of particles of any substance, 83
from colligative properties, 637–638
determination by titration, 187
effusion rate and, 538
from ideal gas law, 526
molecular speed and, 536
polarizability and, 566
molar volume, standard, 524
molarity (M) The number of moles of solute per liter of solution, 174, 618
mole (mol) The SI base unit for amount of substance, 82, A-12
conversion to mass units, 83
of reaction, 167, 227
mole fraction (X) The ratio of the number of moles of one substance to the total number of moles in a mixture of substances, 531, 618

molecular compound(s) A compound formed by the combination of atoms without significant ionic character, 80–82. See also covalent compound(s).
as Brønsted acids and bases, 762
as Lewis acids, 791
of main group elements, 966
as nonelectrolytes, 124
molecular formula A written formula that expresses the number of atoms of each type within one molecule of a compound, 68
determining, 88–95
empirical formula and, 90
relation to empirical formula, 91
molecular geometry The arrangement in space of the central atom and the atoms directly attached to it, 370
hybrid orbitals and, 410
molecular polarity and, 380–386, 394t
multiple bonds and, 373
molecular models, 69
molecular orbital(s), bonding and antibonding, 423
from atomic p orbitals, 426
molecular orbital (MO) theory A model of bonding in which pure atomic orbitals combine to produce molecular orbitals that are delocalized over two or more atoms, 405, 422–432, 1040
molecular orbital theory, for metals and semiconductors, 657
resonance and, 431
molecular polarity, 380–386, 394t
intermolecular forces and, 557
of lipids, 508
miscibility and, 621
of surfactants, 645
molecular solid(s) A solid formed by the condensation of covalently bonded molecules, 602
solubilities of, 622

molecular structure, acid-base properties and, 793–799
bonding and, 348–403
entropy and, 869
VSEPR model of, 367–375
molecular weight. See molar mass.
molecularity The number of particles colliding in an elementary step, 703
reaction order and, 704
molecule(s) The smallest unit of a compound that retains the composition and properties of that compound, 14
calculating mass of, 87
collisions of, reaction rate and, 692
early definition of, 341
nonpolar, interactions of, 565–568
polar, interactions of, 560
shapes of, 367–375
speeds in gases, 533
molybdenite, 1024
molybdenum, generation of technetium from, 1087
monatomic ion(s) An ion consisting of one atom bearing an electric charge, 72
naming, 76
Mond, Ludwig, 1049
Mond process, 1050
monodentate ligand(s) A ligand that coordinates to the metal via a single Lewis base atom, 1031
monomer(s) The small units from which a polymer is constructed, 478
monoprotic acid A Brønsted acid that can donate one proton, 763
monosaccharides, 473
monounsaturated fatty acid, 476
moon, rock samples analyzed, 1088
moral issues in science, 7
mortar, lime in, 978, 979
Moseley, Henry G. J., 60, 344
mosquitos, DDT for killing, 7
Mulliken, Robert S., 404
multiple bonding, valence bond theory of, 416–421

multiple bonds, 354
  molecular geometry and, 373
  in resonance structures, 361
mutation, of retroviruses, 507
Mylar, 485
myoglobin, 1033
myristic acid, 579

naming, of alcohols, 463t, A-19
  of aldehydes and ketones, 470t, A-19
  of alkanes, 448t, 450, A-17
  of alkenes, 454, A-18
  of alkynes, 456t, A-19
  of anions and cations, 76
  of aromatic compounds, A-19
  of benzene derivatives, A-19
  of binary nonmetal compounds, 81
  of carboxylic acids, 471, A-19
  of coordination compounds, 1034
  of esters, 473, 474t, A-20
  of ionic compounds, 77
nanometer, 27
nanotubes, carbon, 588
naphthalene, enthalpy of formation, 247
  melting point, *17*
  solubility in benzene, 622
  structure of, 458
National Institute of Standards and Technology (NIST), 30, 175, 236
natural gas, 258
natural logarithms, A-2
neon, density of, 23
  line emission spectrum of, *276*
  mass spectrum of, *55*
neptunium, 1078
Nernst, Walther, 925
Nernst equation A mathematical expression that relates the potential of an electrochemical cell to the concentrations of the cell reactants and products, 925
net ionic equation(s) A chemical equation involving only those substances undergoing chemical changes in the

course of the reaction, 129–131
  of strong acid–strong base reactions, 137
network solid(s) A solid composed of a network of covalently bonded atoms, 602
  silicon dioxide, 987
  solubilities of, 623
neutral solution A solution in which the concentrations of hydronium ion and hydroxide ion are equal, 766
neutralization reaction(s) An acid–base reaction that produces a neutral solution of a salt and water, 137, 779
neutrino(s) A massless, chargeless particle emitted by some nuclear reactions, 1066
neutron(s) An electrically neutral subatomic particle found in the nucleus, 51
  bombardment with, 1078
  conversion to electron and proton, 1063
  demonstration of, 347
  in nuclear reactor, 1060
  nuclear stability and, 1067
neutron activation analysis, 1088
neutron capture reactions, 1078
newton (N) The SI unit of force, $1 \text{ N} = 1 \text{ kg} \cdot \text{m/s}^2$, A-7
Newton, Isaac, 340
Nicholson, William, 910
nickel, allergy to, 896
  in alnico V, 292
  coordination complex with ammonia, 1031
  density of, 44
  in memory metal, 1018
  reaction with oxygen, 892
nickel(II) carbonate, reaction with sulfuric acid, 141
nickel carbonyl, 1049
  decomposition of, temperature and spontaneity, 883
nickel(II) chloride hexahydrate, 98, 1029, *1030*
nickel(II) complexes, solubility of, *846*
nickel(II) formate, 335
nickel(II) ions, light absorption by, 190

nickel(II) nitrate, reaction with ammonia and ethylenediamine, 758
nickel(II) oxide, reaction with chlorine trifluoride, 551
nickel sulfide, quantitative analysis of, 170
nickel tetracarbonyl, substitution of, 721
nickel-cadmium (ni-cad) battery, 913
nicotine, structure of, 468, 798
nicotinic acid, structure of, 807
nitinol, 1018
nitramid, decomposition of, 720
nitrate ion, concentration in aquarium, 994
  molecular geometry of, 374
  resonance structures of, 362
  structure of, 357
nitration, of benzene, 461
nitric acid, 996
  as oxidizing agent, 146t
  pH of, 181
  production by Ostwald process, 996
  production from ammonia, 163
  reaction with copper, 146
  strength of, 794
  structure of, 357
nitric oxide. *See* nitrogen monoxide.
nitride(s), 992
nitrification, by bacteria, 994
nitrite ion, concentration in aquarium, 994
  linkage isomers containing, 1037
  molecular geometry of, 374
  resonance structures of, 363
nitrito complex, 1037
nitro complex, 1037
nitrogen, abundance of, 991
  bond order in, 386
  chemistry of, 991–996
  compounds of, hydrogen bonding in, 561
  compounds with hydrogen, 993

dissociation energy of triple bond, 992
  fixation of, 64, 951
  Henry's law constant, 626t
  liquid and gas volumes, *556*
  liquid, *519*, 992
  molecular orbital configuration of, 428
  oxidation states of, 992
  oxides of, 993, 995t
  reaction with hydrogen, 527
  reaction with oxygen, 740, 748
  transmutation to oxygen, 1077
nitrogen dioxide, 995t
  decomposition of, 714
  dimerization of, 367, *368*, 734, 748, 995
  free radical, 366
  reaction with carbon monoxide, 681, 707
  reaction with fluorine, 706
  reaction with water, 139
nitrogen fixation The process by which nitrogen gas is converted to useful nitrogen-containing compounds, such as ammonia, 64
nitrogen metabolism, urea and uric acid from, 789
nitrogen monoxide, 993, 995t
  biological roles of, 367
  free radical, 366
  molecular orbital configuration of, 429
  oxidation of, 244
  reaction with bromine, 701, 713
  reaction with oxygen, mechanism of, 708–710
nitrogen narcosis, 542
nitrogen oxide, enthalpy of formation, 246
nitrogen trifluoride, molecular polarity of, 384
  structure of, 356
nitrogenous base(s), pairing of, 565
nitroglycerin, *464*
  decomposition of, 238
nitromethane, vapor pressure of, 582
nitronium ion, Lewis structure of, 354
m-nitrophenol, structure of, 805

petroleum, 259
    chemistry of, 461
    energy of combustion, 257t
pH The negative of the base-10 logarithm of the hydrogen ion concentration; a measure of acidity, 179–182, 767
    in aquarium, 994
    in buffer solutions, 814–821
    of blood, 822
    calculating equilibrium constant from, 780
    calculating from equilibrium constant, 782–787
    change in, during acid–base titration, 821
    common ion effect and, 811–814
pH meter, *181*, 927, *928*
phase change, as spontaneous process, 862
    condensation, 571
    heat transfer in, 220
    vaporization, 571
phase diagram A graph showing which phases of a substance exist at various temperatures and pressures, 606–609
phase transition temperature, 1018
phenanthroline, as ligand, 1031
phenol, structure of, 459
phenolphthalein, *830*
    structure of, 670
phenyl acetate, hydrolysis of, 713
phenylalanine, structure of, 397, 491
Philosopher's Stone, 340
phosgene, 398
    molecular polarity of, 381, *382*
phosphate ion, buffer solution of, 815t
    in biological buffer system, 822
    spectrophotometric analysis of, 205
phosphates, solubility in strong acids, 841
phosphine, 997
    decomposition of, 719
phosphines, in organometallic compounds, 1051
phosphoenolpyruvate (PEP), 884

phosphoric acid, 1000
    as polyprotic acid, 763t, 773
    structure of, 808
phosphorus, allotropes of, 65, 992
    chemistry of, 997–1000
    coordinate covalent bonds to, 365
    discovery of, 340, 997
    oxides of, 997
    reaction with chlorine, 113, 159
    reaction with oxygen, 116
    sulfides of, 998
phosphorus oxoacids, 999
phosphorus pentachloride, decomposition of, 738, 752, 755
phosphorus pentafluoride, orbital hybridization in, 414–415
phosphorus trichloride, enthalpy of formation, 246
phosphoserine, structure of, 436
photocell, *274*
photoelectric effect The ejection of electrons from a metal bombarded with light of at least a minimum frequency, 273
photon(s) A "particle" of electromagnetic radiation having zero mass and an energy given by Planck's law, 273
photosynthesis The process by which plants make sugar, 511
phthalic acid, buffer solution of, 815t
physical change(s) A change that involves only physical properties, 17
physical properties Properties of a substance that can be observed and measured without changing the composition of the substance, 14–16
    temperature dependence of, 15
pi (π) bond(s) The second (and third, if present) bond in a multiple bond; results from sideways overlap of p atomic orbitals, 417, 419
    in ozone and benzene, 431
    molecular orbital view of, 427

pickle, light from, 301
picometer, 27
pie filling, specific heat capacity of, 216
pig iron, 1026
pigment(s), 18
pile, voltaic, 910
Piria, Raffaele, 760
pitchblende, 342
pKa The negative of the base-10 logarithm of the acid ionization constant, 775
    at midpoint of acid–base titration, 825
    pH of buffer solution and, 817
planar node. See atomic orbital(s) and nodal surface.
Planck, Max, 272, 346
Planck's constant (h) The proportionality constant that relates the frequency of radiation to its energy, 272
Planck's equation, 271–273
plasma A gas-like phase of matter that consists of charged particles, 1082
plaster of Paris, 97
plastic(s), recycling symbols, 494
plastic sulfur, 1001
plating, by electrolysis, 931
platinum, in cisplatin, 1049
    in oxidation of ammonia, 163, *164*
    in Zeise's salt, 430
platinum electrode, 908
platinum group metals, 1024
Plexiglas, 481t
plotting. See graph(s).
plutonium, 1078
plutonium-239, fission of, 1080
pOH The negative of the base-10 logarithm of the hydroxide ion concentration; a measure of basicity, 767
poisoning, carbon monoxide, 1033
    lead, 991
polar covalent bond A covalent bond in which there is unequal sharing of the bonding electron pair, 375
polarity, bond, 375–379
    molecular, 380–386, 394t
    intermolecular forces and, 557

solubility of alcohols and, 465
solubility of carboxylic acids and, 471
polarizability The extent to which the electron cloud of an atom or molecule can be distorted by an external electric charge, 566
polarized light, rotation by optically active compounds, 445, *446*
polonium, 65, 342, 1002
    from decay of uranium, 1064, 1065
polyacrylate polymer, in disposable diapers, 487
polyacrylonitrile, 481t
polyamide(s) A condensation polymer formed by elimination of water between two types of monomers, one with two carboxylic acid groups and the other with two amine groups, 485
polyatomic ion(s) An ion consisting of more than one atom, 73
    names and formulas of, 74t, 76
    oxidation numbers in, 145
polydentate ligand(s) A ligand that attaches to a metal with more than one donor atom, 1031
polydimethylsiloxane, 990
polyester(s) A condensation polymer formed by elimination of water between two types of monomers, one with two carboxylic acid groups and the other with two alcohol groups, 485
polyethylene, 480, 481t
    high density (HDPE), density of, 22
    in disposable diapers, 487
polyethylene terephthalate (PET), 485, 493
polyisoprene, 483
polymer(s) A large molecule composed of many smaller repeating units, usually arranged in a chain, 478–487
    addition, 480–484
    classification of, 480
    condensation, 480, 484–487
    silicone, 990

polymethyl methacrylate, 481t

polypropylene, 481t
in disposable diapers, 487

polyprotic acid(s) A Brønsted acid that can donate more than one proton, 763, 773
pH of, 787
titration of, 827

polyprotic base(s) A Brønsted base that can accept more than one proton, 763
pH of, 787

polystyrene, 481t, 482
empirical formula of, 109

polytetrafluoroethylene, 481t

polyunsaturated fatty acid, 476

polyvinyl acetate (PVA), 481t

polyvinyl alcohol, 482

polyvinyl chloride (PVC), 481t
density of, 22

popcorn, percent yield of, 168

porphyrin, 1033

Portland cement, 988

positron(s) A nuclear particle having the same mass as an electron but a positive charge, 1066
emitters of, 1085
predicting emission of, 1069

positron emission tomography (PET), 1085

potassium, preparation of, 972
reaction with water, 23

potassium chlorate, decomposition of, 1001
in fireworks, 281

potassium chromate, reaction with hydrochloric acid, 758

potassium dichromate, 177
in alcohol test, 469

potassium dihydrogen phosphate, crystallization of, 628

potassium fluoride, dissolution of, 623

potassium hydrogen phthalate, as primary standard, 199

potassium hydroxide, reaction with aluminum, 199

potassium iodide, reaction with lead nitrate, 206

potassium ions, pumping in cells, 511

potassium nitrate, 975
in fireworks, 281

potassium perchlorate, in fireworks, 281
preparation of, 202

potassium permanganate, 175
absorption spectrum of, 192
dissolution of, 868
reaction with iron(II) ion, 903
in redox titration, 189

potassium salts, density of, 46

potassium superoxide, 973
reaction with carbon dioxide, 548

potassium thiocyanate, reaction with iron(II) nitrate, 758

potassium uranyl sulfate, 342

potential, of electrochemical cell, 915–924

potential energy The energy that results from an object's position, 210
bond formation and, 406
of electron in hydrogen atom, 276

potential ladder, 919

pounds per square inch (psi), 517

power The amount of energy delivered per unit time, A-9

powers, calculating with logarithms, A-4
on calculator, 34

precipitate A water-insoluble solid product of a reaction, usually of water-soluble reactants, 127

precipitation reaction(s) An exchange reaction that produces an insoluble salt, or precipitate, from soluble reactants, 127–131, 149, 832–842
solubility product constant and, 842–845

precision The agreement of repeated measurements of a quantity with one another, 30

prefixes, for ligands, 1035
for SI units, 26t, A-11

pressure The force exerted on an object divided by the area over which the force is exerted, 516, A-8
atmospheric, altitude and, 514
critical, 577
effect on solubility, 626
gas, volume and, 518
partial. *See* partial pressure.
relation to boiling point, 576
standard, 524
units of, 516, A-8
vapor. *See* vapor pressure.

pressure–volume work, 224–225

Priestley, Joseph, 114

primary alcohols, 468

primary battery A battery that cannot be returned to its original state by recharging, 911

primary standard A pure, solid acid or base that can be accurately weighed for preparation of a titrating reagent, 186

primitive cubic (pc) unit cell, 591

principal quantum number, 277, 285

probability, diffusion and, 866–868
in quantum mechanics, 284

Problem Solving Tip, aqueous solutions of salts, 775
balanced equations and equilibrium constants, 744
balancing equations in basic solution, 905
balancing oxidation–reduction equations, 903
buffer solutions, 820
common entropy-favored processes, 871
concepts of thermodynamics, 862
determining ionic compounds, 80
determining strong and weak acids, 771
drawing Lewis electron dot structures, 355
drawing structural formulas, 451

electrochemical conventions for voltaic cells and electrolysis cells, 934
finding empirical and molecular formulas, 91
formulas for ions and ionic compounds, 78
ligand field theory, 1048
pH during acid–base reaction, 829
pH of equal molar amounts of acid and base, 787
preparing a solution by dilution, 179
reactions with a limiting reactant, 167
relating rate equations and reaction mechanisms, 709
resonance structures, 362
stoichiometry calculations involving solutions, 183
stoichiometry calculations, 160
units for temperature and specific heat capacity, 218
using calculator, 34
using Hess's law, 236
using the quadratic formula, 740
writing net ionic equations, 130

problem-solving strategies, 42

procaine, 805

procaine hydrochloride, 46

product(s) A substance formed in a chemical reaction, 18, 114
effect of adding or removing, 745
heat as, 748
in equilibrium constant expression, 728
rate of concentration change, 673

product-favored reaction(s) A system in which, when a reaction appears to stop, products predominate over reactants, 121
equilibrium constant for, 730
predicting, 874, 878

Friedel–Crafts, 791–792
gas laws and, 527–530
gas-forming, 139–141, 150
hydrogenation, 390
hydrolysis, 473
moles of, 167, 227
neutralization, 137, 779
neutron capture, 1078
nuclear, 1062–1067
  artificial, 1077–1080
  rates of, 1072–1077
order of. *See* reaction order.
oxidation–reduction, 141–148, 150, 896–947. *See also* oxidation–reduction reaction(s).
precipitation, 127–131, 149, 832–842
  solubility product constant and, 842–845
product-favored vs. reactant-favored, 121, 239, 730, 861
  predicting, 874, 878
rate of. *See* reaction rate(s).
reductive carbonylation, 1050
reverse, equilibrium constant expression for, 742
reversibility of, 118, 726
standard enthalpy of, 227
standard reduction potentials of, 917, 920t
substitution, 461
trans-esterification, 479
water gas, 263, 969
reaction coordinate diagram, 694, 697
reaction intermediate A species that is produced in one step of a reaction mechanism and completely consumed in a later step, 700
in rate law, 708
reaction mechanism(s) The sequence of events at the molecular level that control the speed and outcome of a reaction, 671, 701–710
effect of catalyst on, 700
rate equation and, 705–710
reaction order The exponent of a concentration term in the reaction's rate equation, 679
determining, 681
molecularity and, 704

reaction quotient (Q) The product of concentrations of products divided by the product of concentrations of reactants, each raised to the power of its stoichiometric coefficient in the chemical equation, 732–734. *See also* equilibrium constant.
Gibbs free energy change and, 878–879
relation to cell potential, 925
solubility product constant and, 843
reaction rate(s) The change in concentration of a reagent per unit time, 671–675
Arrhenius equation and, 696
average vs. instantaneous, 674
catalysts and, 699–701
collision theory of, 692
conditions affecting, 676
effect of temperature, 693
expression for. *See* rate equation(s).
initial, 680
radioactive disintegration, 1072–1077
redox reactions, 935
stoichiometry and, 673, 674
receptor proteins, 509
rechargeable battery, 911
redox reaction(s). *See* oxidation–reduction reaction(s).
reducing agent(s) The substance that donates electrons and is oxidized in an oxidation–reduction reaction, 141, 898
relative strengths of, 917, 923
reduction The gain of electrons by an atom, ion, or molecule, 141
of transition metals, 1021
reduction potential(s), standard, 917, 920t
reduction reaction(s), of aldehydes and ketones, 469
reductive carbonylation reaction, 1050
reference dose (RfD), 96

reformation, in petroleum refining, 461
refrigerator, pot-in-pot, 222
rem A unit of radiation dosage to biological tissue, 1082
replication, of DNA, 504
resin, in ion exchanger, 980
resonance, in amides, 477
molecular orbital theory and, 431
resonance stabilization, 460
resonance structure(s) The possible structures of a molecule for which more than one Lewis structure can be written, differing by the number of bond pairs between a given pair of atoms, 361–363
benzene, 361, 421
carbonate ion, 362
effect on acid strength, 796
nitrate ion, 362
nitrite ion, 363
ozone, 361
respiration, 511
production of ATP by, 884
reverse osmosis, 957
reversibility, equilibrium and, 725
of chemical reactions, 118
reversible process A process for which it is possible to return to the starting conditions along the same path without altering the surroundings, 864
Rhazes (Abu Bakr Mohammad ibn Zakariyya al-Razi), 339
rhodochrosite, 154, 810
ring structure, in benzene, 421
RNA. *See* ribonucleic acid.
Roberts, Ainé, *533*
rock salt structure, 598
roentgen A unit of radiation dosage, 1082
root-mean-square (rms) speed The square root of the average of the squares of the speeds of the molecules in a sample, 536
roots, calculating with logarithms, A-4
on calculator, 34
Rosenberg, Barnett, 1049
rotation, A-7
around bonds in alkanes, 449

around sigma and pi bonds, 420
of polarized light, 445
rounding off, 37
ROY G BIV, 1045
rubber, isoprene in, 483
natural and synthetic, 483
styrene-butadiene, 484
vulcanized, 483
rubidium, radiochemical dating with, 1093
ruby, ion charges in, 75
synthetic, 985
Rush, Benjamin, 442
rust, 1023. *See also* iron(III) oxide.
Rutherford, Ernest, 51, 341, 343, 1061, 1077
rutile, unit cell of, 611
Rydberg, Johannes, 276
Rydberg constant, 276
Rydberg equation, 276

s-block elements Elements with the valence electron configuration of ns1 or ns2, 312
s orbital(s). *See* atomic orbital(s).
saccharin, 202
structure of, 108, 458, 806
safety match, 998
salad dressing, as emulsion, 644
salicylic acid, 168, 474, 760
structure of, 858
salt(s) An ionic compound whose cation comes from a base and whose anion comes from an acid, 136–138
acid–base properties of, 773
calculating pH of aqueous solution, 785
concentration in sea water, 186
electrolysis of, 932
hydrated, 559
insoluble, precipitation of, 842–845
solubility of, 832–842
solubility product constants of, 834t
salt bridge A device for maintaining the balance of ion charges in the compartments of an electrochemical cell, 905

standard molar enthalpy of formation ($\Delta_f H°$), enthalpy of solution from, 625
  values of, A-29t
standard molar enthalpy of vaporization ($\Delta_{vap} H°$) The energy required to convert one mole of a substance from a liquid to a gas, 570, 572t
standard molar entropy ($S°$) The entropy of a substance in its most stable form at a pressure of 1 bar, 868, 869t
  values of, A-29t
standard molar free energy of formation ($\Delta_f G°$) The free energy change for the formation of one mole of a compound from its elements, all in their standard states, 879
  values of, A-29t
standard molar volume The volume occupied by one mole of gas at standard temperature and pressure; 22.414 L, 524
standard potential ($E°$cell) The potential of an electrochemical cell measured under standard conditions, 916
  of alkali metals, 973
  calculation of, 917, 921
  equilibrium constant calculated from, 929
standard reaction enthalpy ($\Delta_r H°$) The enthalpy change of a reaction that occurs with all reactants and products in their standard states, 227
  product-favored vs. reactant-favored reactions and, 239
standard reduction potential(s), 917, 920t
  of halogens, 1006t
  values of, A-36t
standard state The most stable form of an element or compound in the physical state in which it exists at 1 bar and the specified temperature, 227, 862

standard temperature and pressure (STP) A temperature of 0 °C and a pressure of exactly 1 atm, 524
standardization The accurate determination of the concentration of an acid, base, or other reagent for use in a titration, 186
standing wave A single-frequency wave having fixed points of zero amplitude, 284
starch, 473
starch-iodide paper, 188
stars, elements formed in, 51
state(s), ground and excited, 277
  physical, changes of, 219
  of matter, 7, 555
  reaction enthalpy and, 228
  standard. *See* standard state.
state function A quantity whose value is determined only by the state of the system, 226, 862
stearic acid, 471t
steel, production of, 1027
stem cell scandal, 6
stereoisomers Two or more compounds with the same molecular formula and the same atom-to-atom bonding, but with different arrangements of the atoms in space, 445
sterilization, by irradiation, 1088
steroids, 1
stibnite, 109, 810
stoichiometric coefficients The multiplying numbers assigned to the species in a chemical equation in order to balance the equation, 115
  electrochemical cell potential and, 921
  exponents in rate equation vs., 678
  fractional, 227
  in equilibrium constant expression, 728
stoichiometric factor(s) A conversion factor relating moles of one species in a reaction to

moles of another species in the same reaction, 160, 528
  in solution stoichiometry, 182
  in titrations, 185
stoichiometry The study of the quantitative relations between amounts of reactants and products, 115
  ICE table and, 727
  ideal gas law and, 527–530
  integrated rate equation and, 684
  mass relationships in, 159–162
  of reactions in aqueous solution, 182–189
  reaction rates and, 673, 674
storage battery, 911
STP. *See* standard temperature and pressure.
strained hydrocarbons Compounds in which an unfavorable geometry is imposed around carbon, 453
Strassman, Fritz, 1080
strategies, problem-solving, 42
strong acid(s) An acid that ionizes completely in aqueous solution, 133, 768
  reaction with strong base, 778
  reaction with weak base, 779
  titration of, 822–824
strong base(s) A base that ionizes completely in aqueous solution, 133, 768
strong electrolyte A substance that dissolves in water to form a good conductor of electricity, 124
strontium, in fireworks, 281
  isotopes of, 101
strontium-90, radioactive half-life, 1072
strontium carbonate, enthalpy of formation, 249
structural formula A variation of a molecular formula that expresses how the atoms in a compound are connected, 68, 445
structural isomers Two or more compounds with the same molecular formula but with

different atoms bonded to each other, 444, 1036
  of alcohols, 464
  of alkanes, 448
  of alkenes, 453
styrene, enthalpy of formation, 247
  structure of, 459
styrene-butadiene rubber (SBR), 484
Styrofoam, 481t
Styron, 481t
subatomic particles A collective term for protons, neutrons, and electrons, 51
  properties of, 52t
sublimation The direct conversion of a solid to a gas, 223, 606
submicroscopic level Representations of chemical phenomena in terms of atoms and molecules; also called particulate level, 9
subshells, labels for, 285
  number of electrons in, 306t
  order of energies of, 307
substance(s), pure A form of matter that cannot be separated into two different species by any physical technique, and that has a unique set of properties, 10
substance(s), pure, amount of, 82
substituent groups, common, A-18t
substitution reaction(s), of aromatic compounds, 461
substrate, in enzyme-catalyzed reaction, 702
successive approximations, method of, 739, 783–784
successive equilibria, 846
sucrose, as nonelectrolyte, 125
  enthalpy of combustion, 229
  half-life of, 691
  hydrolysis of, 714
  rate of decomposition of, 675
  structure of, 473
sugar, dietary Calories in, 229
  reaction with silver ion, 157

thyroid gland, imaging of, 1087
  treatment of hyperthyroidism, 1089
thyroxine, 1006, 1089
tin, density of, 44
tin(II) chloride, aqueous, electrolysis of, 935
tin iodide, formula of, 93
tin(IV) oxide, 1017
titanium, density of, 44
  in memory metal, 1018
titanium(IV) chloride, reaction with water, 201
  synthesis of, 155
titanium(IV) oxide, 1004
  as pigment, 1020
  quantitative analysis of, 171
  reaction with carbon, 892
titrant The substance being added during a titration, 823
titration A procedure for quantitative analysis of a substance by an essentially complete reaction in solution with a measured quantity of a reagent of known concentration, 183–185
  acid–base, 183, 821–832
  curves for, 823, 825
  oxidation–reduction, 188-189
Tollen's test, 157
toluene, structure of, 458
tonicity, 639
torr A unit of pressure equivalent to one millimeter of mercury, 516, A-8
Torricelli, Evangelista, 516
tracer, radioactive, 1086
trans-esterification reaction, 479
trans-fats, 476
transition, d-to-d, 1046
transition elements Some elements that lie in rows 4 to 7 of the periodic table, comprising scandium through zinc, yttrium through cadmium, and lanthanum through mercury, 66, 1018–1059
  atomic radii, 320, *321*
  cations formed by, 72
  commercial production of, 1025–1028
  electron configuration of, 315, 317, 1021

naming in ionic compounds, 77
  oxidation numbers of, 1021
  properties of, 1019–1025
transition state The arrangement of reacting molecules and atoms at the point of maximum potential energy, 694
translation, A-7
  of RNA, 506
transmittance (T) The ratio of the amount of light passing through the sample to the amount of light that initially fell on the sample, 190
transmutation, 1077. *See also* nuclear reaction(s).
transport proteins, 509
transuranium elements Elements with atomic numbers greater than 92, 1078
travertine, 16
trenbolone, 3
trichlorobenzene, isomers of, 460
trigonal-bipyramidal electron-pair geometry, orbital hybridization and, *410*, 414
trigonal-bipyramidal molecular geometry, 369
  axial and equatorial positions in, 372
trigonal-planar electron-pair geometry, orbital hybridization and, *410*, 413
trigonal-planar molecular geometry, 369
  in carbon compounds, 443
trigonal-pyramidal molecular geometry, 370
triiodide ion, orbital hybridization in, 416
trimethylamine, 789
  structure of, 798
trimethylborane, dissociation of, 757
triple bond A bond formed by sharing three pairs of electrons, one pair in a sigma bond and the other two in pi bonds, 354
  valence bond theory of, 419
triple point The temperature and pressure at which the

solid, liquid, and vapor phases of a substance are in equilibrium, 607
tritium, 54, 968, 1093
  fusion of, 1082
trona, 974
T-shaped molecular geometry, 372
tungsten, enthalpy of fusion of, 604
  melting point of, 1020
  unit cell of, 613
tungsten(IV) oxide, reaction with hydrogen, 155
turquoise, 810
  density of, 21
Tyndall effect The scattering of visible light caused by particles of a colloid that are relatively large and dispersed in a solvent, 643

U.S. Anti-Doping Agency (USADA), 1, 58
U.S. Environmental Protection Agency (EPA), 96
U.S. Food and Drug Administration (FDA), 188, 215
ultraviolet catastrophe, 272
ultraviolet radiation, 270
  skin damage and, *275*
uncertainty principle. *See* Heisenberg's uncertainty principle.
unimolecular process A process that involves one molecule, 703
unit cell(s) The smallest repeating unit in a crystal lattice, 590
  number of atoms in, 592
  shapes of, *591*
unit(s), of measurement, 25–29, 516
  SI, 25, A-11
universe, entropy change for, 872
  total energy of, 211
unpaired electrons, paramagnetism of, 292
unsaturated compound(s) A hydrocarbon containing double or triple carbon–carbon bonds, 456
unsaturated solution(s), reaction quotient in, 844
uracil, structure of, 402, 809

uranium(VI) fluoride, synthesis of, 155
uranium, fission reaction of, 1080
  isotopes of, 1060
  isotopic enrichment, 1080
  isotopic separation of, 540, 1008
  radioactive series from, 1064
uranium-235, fission of, 1080
uranium-238, radioactive half-life, 1072
uranium hexafluoride, 540, 1008, 1024
uranium(IV) oxide, 110
uranyl(IV) nitrate, 1059
urea, 789
  conversion to ammonium cyanate, 718
  production of, 201
  structure of, 397
  synthesis of, 155
uric acid, 789
urine, phosphorus distilled from, 997

valence bond (VB) theory A model of bonding in which a bond arises from the overlap of atomic orbitals on two atoms to give a bonding orbital with electrons localized between the atoms, 405–422
valence electron(s) The outermost and most reactive electrons of an atom, 311, 349–351
  Lewis symbols and, 351
  of main group elements, 964
valence shell electron pair repulsion (VSEPR) model A model for predicting the shapes of molecules in which structural electron pairs are arranged around each atom to maximize the angles between them, 368
valency, 341
valeric acid, 472t
van der Waals, Johannes, 543
van der Waals equation A mathematical expression that describes the behavior of nonideal gases, 543

yield, of product in a chemical reaction, 168

Zeise's salt, 430, 1051
zeolite(s), 989
  in ion exchanger, 980
zeroes, as significant figures, 36

zero-order reaction, 679
  half-life of, 690
  integrated rate equation, 687
zinc, density of, 44
  reaction with dioxovanadium(V) ion, 901–902

reaction with hydrochloric acid, *132*, 206
zinc blende, structure of, 597
zinc chloride, in dry cell battery, 911
zinc sulfide, 596, *597*
zinc-oxygen battery, 912

zone refining, 987
Zosimos, 339
zwitterion An amino acid in which both the amine group and the carboxyl group are ionized, 808

PHYSICAL AND CHEMICAL CONSTANTS

Avogadro's number	$N = 6.0221415 \times 10^{23}/\text{mol}$
Electronic charge	$e = 1.60217653 \times 10^{-19}$ C
Faraday's constant	$F = 9.6485338 \times 10^4$ C/mol electrons
Gas constant	$R = 8.314472$ J/K $\cdot$ mol
	$= 0.082057$ L $\cdot$ atm/K $\cdot$ mol

π	$\pi = 3.1415926536$
Planck's constant	$h = 6.6260693 \times 10^{-34}$ J $\cdot$ sec
Speed of light (in a vacuum)	$c = 2.99792458 \times 10^8$ m/sec

USEFUL CONVERSION FACTORS AND RELATIONSHIPS

Length
SI unit: Meter (m)
- 1 kilometer = 1000 meters
  - = 0.62137 mile
- 1 meter = 100 centimeters
- 1 centimeter = 10 millimeters
- 1 nanometer = 1.00×10^{-9} meter
- 1 picometer = 1.00×10^{-12} meter
- 1 inch = 2.54 centimeter (exactly)
- 1 Ångstrom = 1.00×10^{-10} meter

Mass
SI unit: Kilogram (kg)
- 1 kilogram = 1000 grams
- 1 gram = 1000 milligrams
- 1 pound = 453.59237 grams = 16 ounces
- 1 ton = 2000 pounds

Volume
SI unit: Cubic meter (m³)
- 1 liter (L) = 1.00×10^{-3} m^3
  - = 1000 cm^3
  - = 1.056710 quarts
- 1 gallon = 4.00 quarts

Energy
SI unit: Joule (J)
- 1 joule = 1 kg $\cdot$ m^2/s^2
  - = 0.23901 calorie
  - = 1 C $\times$ 1 V
- 1 calorie = 4.184 joules

Pressure
SI unit: Pascal (Pa)
- 1 pascal = 1 N/m^2
  - = 1 kg/m $\cdot$ s^2
- 1 atmosphere = 101.325 kilopascals
  - = 760 mm Hg = 760 torr
  - = 14.70 lb/in^2
  - = 1.01325 bar
- 1 bar = 10^5 Pa (exactly)

Temperature
SI unit: kelvin (K)
- 0 K = -273.15 °C
- K = °C + 273.15°C
- ? °C = (5 °C/9 °F)(°F $-$ 32 °F)
- ? °F = (9 °F/5 °C)(°C) + 32 °F

LOCATION OF USEFUL TABLES AND FIGURES

Atomic and Molecular Properties

Atomic electron configurations	Table 7.3
Atomic radii	Figures 7.8, 7.9
Bond dissociation enthalpies	Table 8.9
Bond lengths	Table 8.8
Electron affinity	Figure 7.11, Appendix F
Electronegativity	Figure 8.11
Elements and their unit cells	Figure 13.5
Hybrid orbitals	Figure 9.5
Ionic radii	Figure 7.12
Ionization energies	Figure 7.10, Table 7.5

Thermodynamic Properties

Enthalpy, free energy, entropy	Appendix L
Lattice energies	Table 13.2
Specific heat capacities	Appendix D

Acids, Bases and Salts

Common acids and bases	Table 3.2
Formation constants	Appendix K
Ionization constants for weak acids and bases	Table 17.3, Appendix H, I
Names and composition of polyatomic ions	Table 2.4
Solubility guidelines	Figure 3.10
Solubility constants	Appendix J

Miscellaneous

Charges on common monatomic cations and anions	Figure 2.18
Common polymers	Table 10.12
Oxidizing and reducing agents	Table 3.4
Selected alkanes	Table 10.2
Standard reduction potentials	Table 20.1, Appendix M